Harper's Book of Facts; a Classified Encyclopaedia of the History of the World, a Record of History From 4004 B.C. to 1906 A.D., With More Than One Hundred Thousand References to Subjects in the Realms of Science, Literature, Art, and Government;

HARPER'S
BOOK OF FACTS

A CLASSIFIED ENCYCLOPÆDIA OF THE

HISTORY OF THE WORLD

A RECORD OF HISTORY

FROM 4004 B.C. TO 1906 A.D.

WITH MORE THAN ONE HUNDRED THOUSAND REFERENCES
TO SUBJECTS IN THE REALMS OF

SCIENCE, LITERATURE, ART, AND GOVERNMENT

COMPILED BY A STAFF OF SCHOLARS AND
STATISTICIANS UNDER THE EDITORSHIP OF

CHARLTON T. LEWIS, Ph.D.
FORMERLY PROFESSOR AT THE STATE NORMAL UNIVERSITY OF ILLINOIS
AND AT TROY UNIVERSITY, AND LECTURER AT YALE, HARVARD, CORNELL UNIVERSITIES, ETC. ETC.

SIXTY CENTURIES OF PROGRESS AND
KNOWLEDGE IN ONE VOLUME

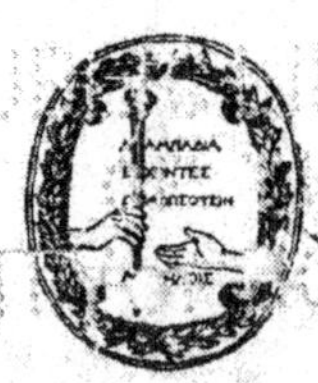

NEW YORK AND LONDON
HARPER & BROTHERS, PUBLISHERS
MCMVI

A TABLE OF
CONTEMPORARY EUROPEAN SOVEREIGNS
FROM A.D. 1066 TO A.D. 1906

A TABLE OF THE
COUNTRIES, POPULATION, AND RULERS
OF THE WORLD

TABLE OF CONTEMPORARY

Great Britain.		France.	Peninsula.			Germany.	Hungary.
ENGLAND.	SCOTLAND.		CASTILE AND LEON.	ARRAGON.	PORTUGAL.		
1066. Will. I. 1087. Will. II.	1057. Malc. 3. 1093. Donald 1094. Dunc. 1094. Donald again. 1098. Edgar.	1060. Philip I.	1066. Sancho II. 1072. Alfonso VI.	1065. Sancho. 1094. Peter.	1065. Sancho of Castile. 1072. Alfonso VI. 1093. Henry, *count*.	1056. Hen. 4, *emperor*.	1064. Solom. 1075. Geisa. 1076. Lad. 1. 1098. Coloman.
1100. Hen. 1. 1135. Steph. 1154. Hen. 2. 1172. (*Ireld. annexed.*) 1189. Rich. 1. 1199. John.	1107. Alex. I. 1124. Dav. I. 1153. Mal. IV. 1165. Will.	1108. Louis VI. 1137. Louis VII. 1180. Philip II.	1109. Urraca and Alfonso VII. 1126. Alfon. VII. 1157. Sancho III. 1158. Alfon. VIII. 1188. Alfon. IX. (Leon.)	1104. Alfonso I. 1134. Ramiro. 1137. Petronella and Raymond. 1163. Alfonso II. 1196. Peter II.	1112. Alfonso, as *count*. 1139. Alfonso I., as *king*. 1185. Sancho I.	1106. Hen. 5. 1125. Loth. 2. 1138. Conr. 3. 1152. Fred. 1. 1190. Hen. 6. 1198. Philip.	1114. Step. 2. 1131. Bela 2. 1141. Geisa 3. 1161. Step. 3. 1173. Bela 3. 1196. Emeric
1216. Hen. 3. 1272. Ed. 1. 1282. (*Wales annexed.*)	1214. Alex. 2. 1249. Alex. 3. *Interregnum.* 1292. John Baliol.	1223. Louis VIII. 1226. Louis IX. 1270. Philip III. 1285. Philip IV.	1214. Henry 1. 1217. Ferdin. III. (Castile.) 1230. (Leon.) 1252. Alfonso X. 1284. Sancho IV. 1295. Ferdin. IV.	1213. James I. 1276. Peter III. 1285. Alfons. III. 1291. James II.	1212. Alfonso II. 1223. Sancho II. 1248. Alfon. III. 1279. Dionysius or Denis.	1208. Otho 4. 1215. Fred. 2. 1250. Con. 4. 1[illegible]. Will. 1257. Rich. [illegible]. Rodolph. 1292. Adolp. 1298. Alb. 1.	1204. Ladislas II. 1205. Andrew II. 1235. Bela 4. 1270. Ste. 4. 1272. Lad. 3. 1290. And. 3.
1307. Ed. II. 1327. Ed III. 1377. Rich. 2. 1399. Hen. 4.	1306. Robert (Bruce) I. 1329. Dav. II. 1332. Ed. Bal. 1342. Dav. II. again. 1371. Rob. II. (Stuart) 1390. Rob. 3.	1314. Louis X. 1316. John I. Phil. V. 1321. Chas. IV. 1328. Phil. VI. 1350. John II. 1364. Chas. V. 1380. Chas. VI.	1312. Alfonso XI. 1350. Peter. 1369. Henry. 1379. John I. 1390. Henry II.	1327. Alfonso IV. 1336. Peter IV. 1387. John I. 1395 Martin.	1325. Alfonso IV. 1357. Peter. 1367. Ferdinand. 1383. John I.	1308. Hen. 7. 1314. Lou. 5 1347. Chas. 4. 1378. Wenceslas. 1400. Rupert.	1301. Charobert. 1342. Louis. 1382. Mary. 1387. Mary & Sigismund.
1413. Hen. 5. 1422. Hen. 6. 1461. Ed. IV. 1483. Ed. V. Rich. 3. 1485. Hen. 7.	1406. Jas. I. 1437. Jas. II. 1460. Jas. III. 1488. Jas. IV.	1422. Chas. VII. 1461. Louis XI. 1483. Chas. VIII. 1498. Louis XII.	1406. John II. 1454 Henry IV. 1474. Isabella.	1410. *Interregnum.* 1412. Ferdinand of Sicily. 1416. Alfonso V. 1458. John II. 1479. Ferdin. II.	1433. Edward. 1438. Alfonso V. 1481. John II. 1495. Emanuel.	1410. Sigismund. 1438. Albert. 1440. Fred. 3. 1493. Max. 1. 1499. *Switz. independ.*	1440. Lad. 4. 1445. Lad. 5. 1458. Matthias. 1490. Lad. 6.
			Spain. 1479. Ferdinand and Isabella.				

PREFACE

Perhaps the most useful of all books of reference for the general reader and the family circle is the Dictionary of Dates, first prepared by Joseph Haydn in 1841. His design was "to attempt the compression of the greatest body of general information that has ever appeared in a single volume, and to produce a book of reference whose extensive usefulness may render its possession material to every individual." It has passed through twenty large editions, each new one carefully corrected as to the past and brought down by additions to its date, until it is esteemed by those to whom London is the world's centre as the model repertory of facts in history, science, art, and literature. It has also had a large sale in the United States.

But the usefulness of the work in America has been limited by its comparative neglect of the Western Hemisphere. The insular mind of the mother-country has never yet fully awakened to the change in the centre of civilization which has resulted from the growth of the New World. To residents of this continent it is surprising that Europe and its dependencies still seem to so many intelligent minds of the older nations substantially to comprise humanity in its present interests and hopes, as well as in its memorable past. Multitudes who have long made the Dictionary of Dates a constant companion, illustrating their reading and satisfying curiosity on the thousand and one questions which conversation and study hourly suggest, have felt this limitation of its field of view as a defect. They have wished for the ideal Book of Facts, which should represent the greater civilization of both hemispheres as fully as the earlier work represents that of Europe and the East. It has been the ambition of the compilers of the present work, to make such a book.

Taking from the magnificent compilation of Haydn and his successors every fac which has more than a narrow and local interest, they have added, in a form so minutely classified as to be accessible in all detail at a glance, the events worth notice in the entir history of the Western Hemisphere and of each of its political divisions. The United States, for example, and every State singly, are represented by chronological tables in which the origin, foundation, political changes, and economic activities of each may b ret. Each of the principal cities is similarly treated. Events of national importanc are themselves independently recorded. Inasmuch as the curiosity of the American reader is commonly much more varied than that of his British cousin, it has been found expedient to extend the field of view, especially in literature, science, and art, by inserting in each of these departments of knowledge whole classes of facts, more recondite or more detailed than had seemed necessary in the London work. No attempt, of course, is made to embody the systematic elements of any branch of study, such as are presented in educational treatises; but apart from this it has been the aim of the compiler to make a hand-book of universal knowledge, which will furnish ready and accurate answers to the questions of fact which are likely to arise in active inquiring minds. If this ideal is too high to be attainable, it will still be found, as the editors and the publishers confidently believe, that the BOOK OF FACTS contains by far the largest amount of precise and accurate information on subjects of general interest that has ever been condensed into a single volume.

N.B.—In a work of this character endless repetition can be avoided only by cross references. These are made in this book by printing in SMALL CAPITALS the article referred to. Whenever a word appears in SMALL CAPITALS it is a title to be consulted for further information.

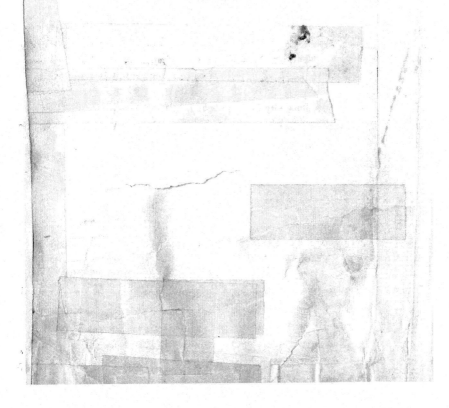

EUROPEAN SOVEREIGNS.

Scandinavia.			Poland.	Eastern Empire.	Italy.		
SWEDEN.	NORWAY.	DENMARK.			POPES.	NAPLES AND SICILY.	
1066. Halstan. 1090. Ingo.	1069. Olaf. 1093. Magnus.	1047. Sweyn II. 1076. Harold. 1080. Canute IV. 1086. Olaus IV. 1095. Eric I.	1058. Boleslas. 1082. Ladislas.	1068. Rom. 4 1071. Mich. 7. 1078. Nicep. 3 1081. Alexius	1061. Alex. II. 1073. Greg. VII. 1086. Victor III. 1088. Urban II. 1099. Pascal II.		
1112. Philip. 1118. Ingo II. 1129. Swerker. 1155. Eric I. 1161. Char. VII. 1167. Canute. 1199. Swerk. II.	1103. Sigurd I., and others. 1122. Sigurd I. 1130. Magnus IV. and others. *Civil war and anarchy.* 1186. Swerro.	1105. Eric II. 1137. Eric III. 1147. Sweyn III. Canute V. 1157. Waldemar. 1182. Canute VI.	1102. Boles. 3 1138. Lad. 2. 1145. Boles. 4 1173. Miecislas III. 1178. Casimir II. 1194. Lesk. 5.	1118. John Comnenus. 1143. Manuel Comnenus. 1180. Alex. 2. 1183. Andronicus C. 1185. Isaac 2. 1195. Alex. 3.	1118. Gelas. II. 1119. Calixt. II. 1124. Honor. II. 1130. Innoc. II. 1143. Celest. II. 1144. Lucius II. 1145. Eugen. III. 1153. Anasta. IV. 1154. Adrian IV. 1159. Alex. III. 1181. Lucius III. 1185. Urban III. 1187. Greg. VIII. Clem. III. 1191. Celest. III. 1198. Innoc. III.	1131. Roger Guiscard II. 1154. William I. 1166. William I. 1189. Tancred. 1194. William III. 1197. Fred. II. of Germany.	
1210. Eric II. 1216. John I. 1222. Eric III. 1250. Birger Jarl 1266. Waldemar. 1275. Magnus I. 1290. Birger II.	1202. Hako III. and others. 1207. Hako IV. 1263. Magnus VI. 1280. Eric. 1299. Hako V.	1202. Walde. II. 1241. Eric IV. 1250. Abel. 1252. Christoph. 1259. Eric V.	1200. Miec. 3. 1202. Lad. 3. 1227. Boles. 5. 1279. Lesk. 6. 1289. *Anarch.* 1290. Premislas. 1296. Ladis. 4	1204. Theodo. 1222. John Ducas. 1255. Theo. 2. 1258. John Lascaris. 1259. Mich. 8. 1282. Andronicus II.	1216. Honor. III. 1227. Greg. IX. 1241. Celest. IV. 1243. Innoc. IV. 1254. Alex. IV. 1261. Urban IV. 1265. Clem. IV. 1268-9. *Vacant.* 1271. Gregory X. 1276. Innoc. V. Adrian V. 1276. John XXI. 1277. Nichol. III. 1281. Martin IV. 1285. Honor. IV. 1288. Nich. IV. 1292-3. *Vacant.* 1294. Celest. V. Bonif. VIII.	1250. Conrad. 1254. Conradin. 1258. Manfred. 1266. Charles of Anjou. 1285. Chas. 2.	**Sicily.** 1282. Peter of Arragon. 1285. James. 1295. Fred. 2.
1319. Magn. II. 1350. Eric IV. 1359. Magnus II. 1363. Albert. 1389. Margaret.	1319. *United to Sweden.* 1389. *United to Denmark.*	1320. Christopher II. 1334. *Interregnm.* 1340. Wald. III. 1375. *Interregnm.* 1376. Olaus V. 1387. Margaret.	1300. Winceslas. 1333. Cas. 3. 1370. Louis. 1382. Mary. 1384. Hedw. 1396. Lad. 5.	1332. And. 3. 1341. John 5. 1391. Manuel VI.	1303. Bened. XI. 1305. Clement V. (*Avignon*). 1314-15. *Vacant.* 1316. John XXII. 1334. Bene. XII. 1342. Clem. VI. 1352. Innoc. VI. 1362. Urban V. (*Rome*). 1370. Greg. XI. 1378. Urban VI. 1389. Bonif. IX.	1309. Robt. 1343. Joan & Andrew of Hung. 1349. Louis. 1381. Chas. 3. 1385. Ladislas.	1337. Peter 2. 1342. Louis. 1355. Fred. 3. 1376. Maria & Martin.
1412. Eric XIII. 1440. Christopher III. 1448. Chas. VIII. 1457. Christian I. 1483. John of Denmark.		1448. Christian I. 1481. John.	1434. Lad. 6. 1445. Casi. 4. 1492. Albert	1425. John 6. 1448. Constant. 13. **Turkey.** 1433. Mahomet II. 1481. Bajaz. 2	1404. Innoc. VII. 1406. Greg. XII. 1409. Alex. V. 1410. John XXIII 1417. Martin V. 1431. Eugen. IV. 1447. Nicholas V. 1455. Calix. III. 1458. Pius II. 1464. Paul II. 1471. Sixtus IV. 1484. Inno. VIII. 1492. Alex. VI.	1414. Joan 2. 1435. Alfonso I. 1458. Ferd. 1. 1494. Alfo. 2. 1495. Ferd. 2. 1496. Fred. 2.	1402. Mart. 1. 1409. Mart. 2. (*United to Arragon.*) 1410. Ferd. 1. 1416. Alfo. 1. 1458. John. 1479. Ferd.

TABLE OF CONTEMPORARY

Great Britain.		France.	Peninsula.			Germany.	Hungary.
England.	Scotland.		Castile and Leon.	Arragon.	Portugal.		
1509. Hen. 8.	1513. Jas. V.	1515. Francis I.	1504. Joanna & Philip I.	Ferdinand II.	1521. John III.	1519. Chas. V. (I. of Sp.)	1516. Lou. II. 1526. Jn. Zapolski and Ferdin. II.
			Spain.				
			1512. Ferd. V. (Cast.) *II.* (Arragon). 1516. Charles I. (V. of Germ. 1519).			(Emperors—Kings of Hungary.)	
1547. Ed. VI. 1553. Mary. 1558. Eliz.	1542. Mary. 1567. Jas. VI.	1547. Henry II. 1559. Francis II. 1560. Charles IX. 1574. Henry III. 1589. Henry IV.	1556. Philip II. 1598. Philip III.	**Holland.** 1579. William of Orange, *stadtholder.* 1587. Maurice.	1557. Sebastian. 1578. Henry. 1580. *Annexed to Spain.*	1558. Ferdinand. 1564. Maximilian II. 1576. Rodolph II.	
1603. Jas. I. (VI. of Scot.) rles I. mmonwealth. rles II. nes II. liam and Mary. liam III.		1610. Louis XIII. 1643. Louis XIV.	1621. Philip IV. 1665. Charles II. 1700. Philip V.	1625. Fred. Hen. 1647. William II. 1650-72. *No stadtholder.* 1672. Will. Hen. (Will. III. *of England.*)	*Kingdom restored* 1640. John of Braganza. 1656. Alfonso VI. 1667. Peter, *regent.* 1683. Peter II.	1612. Mathias. 1619. Ferdinand II. 1637. Ferdinand III. 1658. Leopold I.	
ne. orge I. orge II. orge III. nited States independent.]		1715. Louis XV. 1774. Louis XVI. 1793. Lou. XVII. *Republic* I.	1724. (*abdicated*). " Louis. Philip V. again. 1746. Ferd. VI. 1759. Chas. III. 1788. Chas. IV. (*abdicated*).	1702-47. *No stadtholder.* 1747. Will. Hen. 1757. Will. IV. 1795. *Annexed to France.*	1706. John V. 1750. Joseph. 1777. Maria and Peter III. 1786. Maria, alone. 1791. John, *regent*	1705. Joseph 1711. Chas. 6. 1742. Chas. 7. 1745. Francis 1765. Jos. 2. 1790. Leop. 2. 1792. Fran. 2.	**Prussia.** 1701. Fred. 1. 1713. Fred. William 1. 1740. Fred. 2. 1786. Fred.-William 2. 1797. Fred.-William 3.
eorge, Prince of Wales, *regent.*) eorge IV. William IV. ictoria. Edward VII.		1802. Consulate. 1804. Napoleon I. 1814. Lou. XVIII. 1824. Charles X. 1830. Lou. Philip. 1848. *Republic* II. 1852. Napol. III. 1870. *Repub.* III. 1871. L. A. Thiers president. 1873 Marshal MacMahon. 1879. Jules Grévy. 1887. Sadi Carnot. 1894. Casimir-Périer. 18[illegible]. Felix Faure. 1899. Emile Loubet.	1808. Ferd. VII. (*dethroned*). Jos. Bonap. 1814. Ferd. VII. (*restored*). 1833. Isabella II. 1868. (*dethroned*). 1870. Amadeus. (*abdicated*) 1873. 1873. *Republic.* 1874. Alfons. XII. died 25 Nov. 1885. 18[illegible]. Alfons. XIII.	1806. Louis, *king.* **Netherlands.** 1814. Will. Fred. *king.** 1840. William II. 1849. Will. III. 1890. Wilhelmina.	1816. John VI. 1826. Peter IV. Maria II. 1828. Miguel. 1833. Maria II. 1853. Peter V. 1861. Luis I. 1889. Carlos I.	**Austria.** 1806. Fran. I. 1835. Ferd. 2. 1848. Francis Joseph.	1840. Fred.-William 4. 1869. Will. 1. 1871. German *emperor.* 1888. Fred. III. 1888 William II.

* **Belgium.**—1831. Leopold I.
1865. Leopold II.

EUROPEAN SOVEREIGNS, *continued.*

Scandinavia.			Poland.	Turkish Empire.	Italy.		
SWEDEN.	NORWAY.	DENMARK.			POPES.	NAPLES AND SICILY.	
1520. Christian II. 1523. Gustavus Vasa. 1560. Eric XIV. 1563. John III. 1592. Sigismund	**Russia.*** 1533. Ivan IV. 1584. Feodor I. 1598. Boris.	1513. Christn. II. 1523. Fredrick I. *and Norway.* 1534. Christ. III. 1559. Fred. II. 1588. Christn. IV.	1501. Alex. 1506. Sig. I. 1548. Sig. II. 1573. Henry. 1575. Steph. 1587. Sig. 3.	1512. Selim. 1520. Solyman II. 1566. Sel. 2. 1574. Amurath III. 1595. Mah. 3.	1503. Pius III. Julius II. 1513. Leo X. 1522. Adrian VI. 1523. Clem. VII. 1534. Paul III. 1550. Julius III. 1555. Marcel. II. Paul IV. 1559. Pius IV. 1566. Pius V. 1572. Greg. XIII. 1585. Sixtus V. 1590. Urban VII. Greg. XIV. 1591. Innoc. IX. 1592. Clem. VIII.	1501. *United to Spain.*	
1604. Chas. IX. 1611. Gustavus Adolphus. 1633. Christina. 1654. Chas. X. 1660. Chas. XI. 1697. Chas. XII.	1606. Basil. 1613. Michael (Romanoff). 1645. Alexis. 1676. Feodor. 1682. Ivan V. & Peter I. 1689. Peter I.	1648. Fred. III. 1670. Christn. V. 1699. Fred. IV.	1632. Lad. 7. 1648. John C. 1669. Mich. 1674. John Sobieski. 1697. Fredk. August. 1.	1603. Ach. 1. 1617. Mus. 1. 1618. Osm. 2. 1622. Mustapha, again. 1623. Am. 4. 1640. Ibrah. 1648. Mah. 4. 1687. Sol. 3. 1691. Ach. 2. 1695. Mus. 2.	1605. Leo. XI. Paul V. 1621. Greg. XV. 1623. Urban VIII. 1644. Innocent X. 1655. Alex. VII. 1667. Clem. IX. 1670. Clem. X. 1676. Innoc. XI. 1689. Alex. VIII. 1691. Innoc. XII.		
1719. Ulrica and Frederick I. 1741. Fred. I. 1751. Adolphus Frederick. 1771. Gustav. III. 1792. Gustav. IV.	1725. Cather. I. 1727. Peter II. 1730. Anne. 1740. Ivan VI. 1741. Elizabeth. 1762. Peter III. Cather. II. 1796. Paul I.	1730. Christn. VI. 1746. Fred. V. 1766. Christ. VII. 1784. Prince Fred. *regent.*	1704. Stan. 1. 1709. Fredk. Augustus, *restored.* 1733. Fredk. August. 2. 1764. Stan. 2. 1795. *Partition.*	1703. Ach. 3. 1730. Mah. 5. 1754. Osm. 3. 1757. Mus. 3. 1774. Abdul-Hamid I. or Ach. 4. 1789. Selm. 3.	1700. Clem. XI. 1721. Inno. XIII. 1724. Bene. XIII. 1730. Clem. XII. 1740. Bene. XIV. 1758. Clem. XIII. 1769. Clem. XIV. 1775. Pius VI. 1800. Pius VII.	**Naples and Sicily.** 1713. Chas. 3. *Naples.* Victor-Am. of Savoy, *Sicily.* 1720 *Annexed to Germany.* 1738. Chas. 4. *Naples.* [illegible] Fred. 4 *Sicily.*	**Sardinia.†** 1720. Victor-Amadeus. 1730. Charles Emman. 1. 1773. Victor-Amadeus 2. 1796. Charles Emman. 2.
1809. Chas. XIII. 1814. *Norway annexed.* 1818. Chas. XIV. 1844. Oscar I. 1859. Chas. XV. 1872. Oscar II. **Norway.** Union dissolved 1905. Haakon VII.	1801. Alexand. I. 1828. Nicholas. 1855. Alex. II. 1881. Alex. III. 1894. Nicholas II.	1808. Fred. VI. 1814. *Norway taken away.* 1839. Chris. VIII. 1848. Fred. VII. 1863. Chrisn. IX.	**Greece.** 1832. Otho I. 1863. Geo. I.	1807. Mus. 4. 1808. Mahmud 6. 1839. Abdul Medjid. 1861. Abdul Aziz. 1876. Amurath V. *May* 1876. Abdul-Hamid II. *Aug.*	1823. Leo XII. 1829. Pius VIII. 1831. Greg. XVI. 1846. Pius IX. 1878. Leo XIII. 1903. Pius X.	**Naples.** 1806. Joseph Bonaparte 1808. Joach. Murat. **Naples and Sicily.** 1815. Ferd. 1. 1825. Fran. 1. 1830. Ferd. 2. 1859. Fran. 2. 1860 *Annexed to Italy.* **Italy.** 1861. Victor-Emmanuel. 1878. Humbert. 1900. Victor-Emmanuel III.	1802. Victor-Emman. 1. 1805 *Annexed to kingdom of Italy.* 1814. Victor-Emman. 1. 1821. Charles Felix. 1831. Charles Albert. 1849. Victor-Emman. 2.

* See Article RUSSIA for preceding Rulers.
† See Article SAVOY.

POPULATION AND GOVERNMENTS OF THE WORLD.

(According to the Almanach de Gotha; see articles POPULATION, *and the countries throughout the book.)*

COUNTRIES—RELIGIONS.	POPULATION	RULERS.	BIRTH.	ACCESSION.
Anhalt, *E.* *Population in* Dec. 1900	316,027	Frederick, *duke*	19 Aug. 1856	1904
Argentine Confederation, *R.C.* Dec. 1900	4,794,149	Gen. Roca, *president*	1843	12 Oct. 1898.
Austrian Emp. *R.C.* (after cession 1866) Dec. 1900	45,310,835	Francis-Joseph, *emperor*	18 Aug. 1 30	2 Dec. 1848.
Baden, *R.C.* Dec. 1900	1,866,584	Frederick, *grand-duke*	9 Sept. 1826	5 Sept. 1856.
Bavaria, *R.C.* (after cessions 1866) 1900	6,175,153	Otho, *king*	27 April, 1848	13 June, 1886.
Belgium, *R.C.* Dec. 1900	6,815,054	Leopold II., *king*	9 April, 1835	10 Dec. 1865.
Bolivia, *R.C.* 1897	2,000,000	Gen. José M. Pando, *pres.*	25 Dec. 1849	25 Oct. 1899.
Brazil, *R.C.* 1891	17,000,000	Dr. F. de P. R. Alves	. . .	15 Nov. 1902.
Brunswick, *L.* 1900	464,333	Prince Albert of Prussia, *regt.*	8 May, 1837	21 Oct. 1885.
Bulgaria 1900	3,733,189	Ferdinand, *prince*	26 Feb. 1861	7 July, 1887.
Chili, *R.C.* (estimated) 1899	3,110,085	Sen. German Riesco	. . .	18 Sept. 1901.
Chinese Empire (estimated), *B.* 1897	302,241,669	Kwang Hsu, *emperor*	15 Aug. 1871	12 Jan. 1875.
Colombia, state, *R.C.* 1895	5,000,000	J. M. Marroquin, *president*	7 Aug. 1827	Jan. 1900.
Costa Rica, *R.C.* (estimated) 1899	310,000	Asencion Esquivel, *pres.*	. . .	8 May, 1902.
Denmark & colonies, *L.* (estm.) 1901	2,578,699	Christian IX., *king*	8 April, 1818	15 Nov. 1863.
Egypt, &c., *M.* 1897	9,700,000	Abbas Hilmi, *khedive*	14 July, 1874	7 Jan. 1892.
Equater (Ecuador), *R.C.* 1897	1,270,000	Gen. L. Plaza, *president*	. . .	17 Sept. 1901.
France alone, *R.C.* 1896	38,517,975	Emile Loubet, *president*	31 Dec. 1838	18 Feb. 1899.
Germany, *R.C.*, *L.* and *E.* Dec. 1900	56,356,246	William II., *emperor*	27 Jan. 1859	15 June, 1888.
Great Britain and colonies, *P.* (estimated) 1901	394,064,800	Edward VII., *king*	9 Nov. 1841	22 Jan. 1901.
Greece & Ion. Is. *G.C.* (estim.) 1896	2,430,807	George I., *king*	24 Dec. 1845	5 June, 1863.
Guatemala, *R.C.* 1900	1,574,338	Manuel E. Cabrera, *pres.*	. . .	2 Oct. 1898.
Hayti (estimated) 1894	1,000,000	Gen. Nord Alexis, *pres.*	. . .	1902.
Hesse-Darmstadt, *L.* 1900	1,119,893	Ernest Louis, *grand-duke*	25 Nov. 1868	13 March, 1892.
Holland, not colonies, *C.* Dec. 1900	5,179,138	Wilhelmina, *queen*	31 Aug. 1880	23 Nov. 1890.
Honduras, *R.C.* 1900	587,500	Gen. M. Bonilla, *president*	1849	1 Feb. 1903.
Italy, *R.C.* 1901	32,449,754	Victor Emmanuel, III., *king*	11 Nov. 1869	20 July, 1900.
Japan (estimated) 1899	46,456,911	Mutsuhito, *mikado*	3 Nov. 1852	13 Feb. 1867.
Liberia, *P.* 1897	1,500,000	*president*	. . .	May, 1903.
Liechtenstein, *R.C.* 1891	9,434	John II., *prince*	5 Oct. 1840	12 Nov. 1858.
Lippe, *C.* Dec. 1900	139,238	Alexander, *prince*	16 Jan. 1831	20 March, 1895.
Luxemburg, *R.C.* 1900	236,543	Adolphus, *grand-duke*	24 July, 1817	23 Nov. 1890.
Mecklenburg-Schwerin, *L.* Dec. 1900	607,835	Frederic Francis IV. *gd.-duke*	9 April, 1882	10 April, 1897.
Mecklenburg-Strelitz, *L.* 1900	102,628	Frederic William, *grnd-duke*	17 Oct. 1819	6 Sept. 1860.
Mexico, *R.C.* (estimated) 1900	13,545,462	Porfirio Diaz, *president*	. . .	1 Dec. 1884.
Monaco, *R.C.* 1901	15,180	Albert Honoré Charles, *prince*	13 Nov. 1848	10 Sept. 1889.
Montenegro, *G.C.* (estimated) 1891	200,000	Nicholas I., *prince*	7 Oct. 1841	14 Aug. 1860.
Morocco, *M.* about	8,000,000	Muley Abdul Aziz, *sultan*	. . .	11 June, 1894.
Nicaragua, *R.C.* 1897	310,000	Gen. Zelaya, *president*	1852	June, 1901.
Oldenburg, *P.* (estimated) 1900	399,183	Frederick Augustus, *gd. duke*	16 Nov. 1852	13 June, 1900.
Panama, *R.C.* 1896	311,000			
Papal States *annexed to Italy* 1870				
Paraguay, *R.C.* [illegible]	635,571	Sen. Escurra, *president*	. . .	28 Sept. 1902.
Persia, *M.* (estimated)	7,500,000	Muzaffer-ed-Deen, *shah*	25 March, 1853	1 May, 1896.
Peru, *R.C.* (estimated) 1890	4,559,550	Sen. Manuel Candamo, *pres.*	. . .	8 Sept. 1903.
Portugal, *R.C.* Dec. 1900	5,428,800	Carlos, *king*	28 Sept. 1863	19 Oct. 1889.
Prussia, *E.* Dec. 1900	34,468,730	William II., *king*	27 Jan. 1859	15 June, 1888.
Reuss, *L.* 1900	138,993	Henry XXIV., *prince*	20 March, 1878	10 April, 1902.
Roumania 1899	5,912,520	Chs. of Hohenzollern, *king*	20 April, 1839	20 April, 1866.
Russia, *G.C.*, Poland, &c. (est.) 1897	129,211,113	Nicholas II., *czar*	18 May, 1868	1 Nov. 1894.
San Marino, *R.C.* (estimated) 1901	9,535	*Capitani reggenti*		
San Salvador *R.C.* Jan. 1901	915,512	Sen. Escalon, *president*	24 March, 1857	1 March, 1903.
Saxe-Altenburg, *P.* 1900	194,914	Ernest, *duke*	16 Sept. 1826	3 Aug. 1853.
Saxe-Coburg-Gotha, *L.* 1900	229,550	Charles Edward	19 July, 1884	30 July, 1900.
Saxe-Meiningen, *L.* 1900	250,683	George II., *duke*	2 April, 1826	20 Sept. 1866.
Saxe-Weimar-Eisenach, *L.* 1900	362,873	William Ernest, *grand-duke*	10 June, 1876	5 Jan. 1901.
Saxony, *P.* 1900	4,199,758	George, *king*	8 Aug. 1832	19 June, 1902.
Schaumburg-Lippe, *L.* 1900	43,132	George, *prince*	10 Oct. 1846	8 May, 1893.
Schwartzburg-Rudolstadt, *L.* 1900	93,059	Gonthier, *prince*	21 Aug. 1852	19 Jan. 1890.
Schwartzburg-Sondershaus, *L.* 1900	80,898	Charles, *prince*	7 Aug. 1830	17 July, 1880.
Servia, *G.C.* 1900	2,493,770	Peter I., *king*	1844	15 June, 1903.
Spain, *R.C.* Dec. 1897	18,089,500	Alfonso XIII., *king*	17 May, 1886	17 May, 188[illegible]
St. Domingo, *R.C.* (estimated) 1887	350,000	A. Woss, *president*	. . .	1903.
Sweden, Norway, *L.* (estmtd.) 1900	7,376,321	Oscar II., *king*	21 Jan. 1829	18 Sept. 1872.
Switzerland, *R.C.* and *P.* Dec. 1900	3,313,817	B. Comtesse, *president*	. . .	1 Jan. 1904.
Transvaal, *C.* (estimated) 1895	325,000	Lord Milner, *governor*	. . .	21 June, 1902.
Turkish Empire, *M.* (estimtd.) 1897	39,500,000	Abdul-Hamid II., *sultan*	22 Sept. 1842	31 Aug. 1876.
Uruguay, *R.C.* Dec. 1900	930,680	Sen. Batele, *president*	. . .	1 March, 1903.
Venezuela, *R.C.* 1891	2,323,527	Gen. Castro, *president*	12 Oct. 1860	28 Oct. 1901.
Würtemberg, *L.* 1900	2,169,434	William II., *king*	25 Feb. 1848	6 Oct. 1891.
United States of N. America, *P.* 1900	76,356,000	Theodore Roosevelt, *pres.*	27 Oct. 1858	14 Sept. 1901.

PREDOMINANT RELIGIONS.—*R.C.*, Roman Catholic; *G.C.*, Greek Church; *P.*, Protestant; *L.*, Lutheran; *E.*, Evangelical Church—a combination of Calvinists and Lutherans; *C.*, Calvinist or Reformed; *M.*, Mahometan; *B.*, Buddhist.

HARPER'S BOOK OF FACTS

A CLASSIFIED HISTORY OF THE WORLD

A. *Etre marqué à l'A*, to be of first-class quality A is the distinctive mark of money minted in Paris, which is purer and freer from alloy than any other in France

Aa (from Latin *aqua*, water), the name of about 40 small rivers in Europe

A 1. Symbol used in the Record of American and Foreign Shipping and in Lloyd's Register of British and Foreign Shipping, in rating vessels for insurance A 1 is the highest Hence A 1 is used of the highest mercantile credit and, colloquially, A 1 or A No 1 is equivalent to first-class—first-rate "An A number one cook, and no mistake"—*Mrs Stowe*

Aaron's Breastplate, described Exod xxviii 15-29 (1491 B C., *Usher*), contained precious stones emblematic of the several tribes of Israel, thus.

First row	ZEBULON. *Carbuncle*	ISSACHAR. *Topaz.*	JUDAH *Sardius.*
Second "	GAD. *Diamond*	SIMEON *Sapphire.*	REUBEN *Emerald.*
Third "	BENJAMIN *Amethyst*	MANASSEH *Agate*	EPHRAIM *Ligure*
Fourth "	NAPHTALI *Jasper*	ASHER. *Onyx*	DAN *Beryl*

"As the Hebrew is written from right to left, the stones with their inscribed names would probably appear as above This is the order of the tribes as they were arranged in their camp and on the march"—"*The Tabernacle,*" *Henry W Soltau*, p 206

A. B. Plot. Ninian Edwards, ex-United States senator from Ill, attacks William H Crawford, sec of the Treasury, candidate for president, in letters signed A B., reflecting on his integrity Edwards is sent on a public mission to Mexico and while on his way, Apr 1824, avers the authorship and makes new accusations Recalled for investigation, he fails to sustain the charges. UNITED STATES, *Apr* 1824.

abacus, the uppermost part of the capital of a column, usually a slab or tile, just under the architrave That on the Corinthian column is ascribed to Callimachus, about 540 B C (2) A frame traversed by stiff wires, on which beads are strung Used by the Greeks, Romans, and Chinese

Abæ, N. Greece, early celebrated for its oracle of Apollo, of greater antiquity than that at Delphi

abattoirs (*a-bat-wor'*), slaughter-houses for cattle First erected near Paris in 1818, at Edinburgh, 1851, London, 1855, and in the United States, 1866

Abbassides, descendants of Mahomet's uncle, Abbas-Ben-Abdul-Motalleb. Merwan II, the last of the Ommiades, was defeated and slain by Abul Abbas in 750, who became caliph 37 Abbasside caliphs (including Haroun al-Raschid, 786-809) reigned from 750 to 1258. They settled at Bagdad, built by Al-Mansour about 762 Their color was black, that of the Fatimites green, that of the Ommiades white

Abbaye (*ab-bay'-ee*), a military prison in Paris, where 164 prisoners were murdered by republicans led by Maillard. At this time, 2-5 Sept. 1792, 1200 persons in all were murdered, among them the princess de Lamballe FRANCE, *Sept* 1792

Abbe, Cleveland WEATHER BUREAU

abbess, the head of a convent or abbey for women In England they attended ecclesiastical councils as early as 694, when they took precedence of presbyters in signing the acts

Abbeville (*abb-veel'*) N France, an ancient city famous for the Gothic church of St Wolfram Here Henry III, of England met Louis IX of France and made peace, renouncing Normandy and other provinces, 20 May, 1259

abbeys, monasteries for men or women MONACHISM and CONVENTS The first abbey founded in England was at Bangor in 560, in France, at Poitiers, about 360, in Ireland in the 5th century in Scotland in the 6th century 110 alien priories were suppressed in England 2 Henry V 1414—*Salmon* The disorders in these establishments led to their destruction in Britain After visitations of inquiry, king Henry VIII began to suppress small monasteries to raise revenues for Wolsey's colleges at Oxford and Ipswich 3 June, 1525, many were suppressed in 1536, and all religious houses by parliament, 1539-40 Many abbeys were suppressed in France in 1790, in Spain in 1837 and 1868, and in Italy in 1866 73 After Henry VIII suppressed the English monasteries many of the buildings were made private dwellings, still called abbeys—for example, "Newstead Abbey," the home of lord Byron

abbot (from *ab*, father) the head of an abbey In England mitred abbots were lords of parliament, 27 abbots and 2 priors thus distinguished, 1329 the number reduced to 25 in 1396 — *Coke* The abbots of Reading Glastonbury, and St John's Colchester were executed as traitors for denying the king's supremacy probably for not surrendering their abbeys, 1539 GLASTONBURY In the reign of Henry VIII 26 abbots sat in the House of Lords

Abbotsford, the residence of sir Walter Scott on the Tweed, begun in 1817 and finished in 1824 Sir Walter devised the name fancying that the abbots of Melrose, in ancient times, forded the Tweed here He had resided here but one year when his reverse came, his publishers failing The property was, however, wholly disencumbered in 1847 Here sir Walter died, 1832, and his son-in-law, J G Lockhart 1854.

A B C Club, a name adopted by certain republican enthusiasts in Paris professing to relieve the *abaissés*, or depressed. Their insurrection 5 June, 1832, suppressed with bloodshed, 6 June, is described by Victor Hugo in "*Les Misérables*" (1862).

Abd-el-Kader, general of the Algerians [illegible] French invasion, born near Mascara, 1807, [illegible] Mascara 1831, defeated and captured by the Fren[illegible] 1847, released by Napoleon III, 1852, d at Dam[illegible] ALGIERS

Abde'ra, a city in Thrace, where was born, about 490 B C., Democritus, known as the "laughing philosopher," but in truth of the materialistic school and a theorizer in the direction of the modern doctrine of Atomism ATOMS.

abdications of sovereigns, voluntary or compulsory, have been numerous; the chief are those of

Sulla, Roman dictator, voluntary....................B.C. 79
Diocletian, Roman emperor, voluntary....................A.D. 305
Stephen II. of Hungary, voluntary, from a bed of sickness; assumes the habit of a monk, and dies the same year........ 1131
Albert the Bear, of Brandenburg, voluntary.................... 1168
John Balliol of Scotland, compelled by Edward I. of England.. 1296
Eric VII. of Denmark, and XIII. of Sweden, virtually deposed. 1439
Charles V. as emperor, voluntary.................... 1555
" " as ruler of the Netherlands, in favor of his son Philip....................25 Oct. 1555
Charles V., as king of Spain, in favor of his son Philip..16 Jan. 1556
Christina of Sweden, voluntary....................6 June, 1654
John Casimer of Poland, voluntary; retires to a cloister...... 1668
James II. of England, fled....................11 Dec. 1688
His flight declared an abdication by lords and commons.
Frederick Augustus II. of Poland, compelled by Charles XII. of Sweden.................... 1706
Philip V. of Spain, voluntary, in favor of his son, who, after a reign of eight months, dies; Philip resumes.................... 1724
Victor Amadeus II. of Sardinia, voluntary, in favor of his son, Charles Emmanuel.................... 1730
Amadeus [illegible] to marry the countess of San Sebastian. Afterwards [illegible] and attempting to regain power, he dies in prison.................... 1732
Charles of the Two Sicilies, voluntary, on accession to the throne of Spain as Charles III.................... 1759
Stanislaus II. of Poland, compelled by the partition of the kingdom.................... 1795
Charles Emmanuel IV. of Sardinia, in favor of his brother, Victor Emmanuel....................4 June, 1802
Francis II., emperor of Germany; [illegible] emperor of Austria....................11 Aug. 1804
Charles IV. of Spain, compelled by the people, in favor of his son....................19 Mch. 1808
Restored by Napoleon, then abdicates in favor of Napoleon....................11 May, 1808
Joseph Bonaparte, of Naples (for Spain), at request of Napoleon....................1 June, 1808
Gustavus IV. of Sweden, compelled....................29 Mch. 1809
Louis of Holland, brother of Napoleon, at his order, Holland annexed to France....................1 July, 1810
Napoleon I. of France, compelled....................5 Apr. 1814
Napoleon I. of France, compelled....................22 June, 1815
Victor Emmanuel, of Sardinia, compelled, in favor of his brother, Charles Felix....................13 Mch. 1821
Pedro IV. of Portugal (Pedro I. of Brazil), in favor of his daughter....................2 May, 1826
Charles X. of France, compelled, in favor of his grandson, Henry, duke of Bordeaux, later count of Chambord (Henry V.), who is not accepted by the French....................2 Aug. 1830
Pedro I. of Brazil (IV. of Portugal), in favor of his son, Pedro II....................7 Apr. 1831
William I. of Holland, in favor of his son, William II....8 Oct. 1840
Louis Philippe of France, compelled by the people, in favor of his grandson, the count of Paris; not accepted......24 Feb. 1848
Ferdinand of Austria, compelled, in favor of his nephew, Francis Joseph I....................2 Dec. 1848
Charles Albert of Sardinia, in favor of his son, Victor Emmanuel II....................23 Mch. 1849
Isabella II. of Spain, fled to France....................25 June, 1870
Amadeus of Spain (second son of Victor Emmanuel II.), voluntary....................11 Feb. 1873
Milan I. of Servia, voluntary, in favor of his son.......6 Mch. 1889
Pedro II. of Brazil, compelled by the people..........15 Nov. 1889
Brazil declares a republic.

Abecedarians, followers of Nicholas Storch, an Anabaptist in the 16th century, named from rejecting worldly knowledge, even of the alphabet, lest it impede the soul in apprehension of divine truth.

abecedarium, a logical machine, constructed by Mr. William Stanley Jevons, and described in his "Principles of Science," 1874; designed, by symbolic terms, to perform all the processes of analytic reasoning with infallible accuracy.

A Becket, Thomas. BECKET.

Abelard, a teacher of theology and logic, in 1118 fell in love with Heloïse, niece of Fulbert, a canon of Paris, became her tutor, and seduced her. After compulsory marriage, he placed her temporarily in a convent. Having been cruelly mutilated at the instigation of her relatives, he entered the abbey of St. Denis, whence he was driven, accused of heresy, for censuring the dissoluteness of monks. He then built and lectured at the oratory of the Paraclete (or Comforter) which eventually he made a convent, with Heloïse for the abbess. He died under charge of heresy, 21 Apr., 1142, and was buried in the Paraclete, where also Heloïse was laid, 17 May, 1164. Their ashes were removed to the garden of the Muséum Français in 1800, and to the cemetery of Père la Chaise in 1817. Their epistles, etc., were published in 1616. PHILOSOPHY.

Abenakis or **Abnakis,** a tribe of Indians of the Algonquin class, inhabiting at the time of the first English settlements lands now in Maine. The river Penobscot bears the name of one tribe, Androscoggin of another. INDIANS.

Abencerra'ges, a powerful Moorish tribe of Granada, opposed to the Zegris. From [illegible] to [illegible] their quarrels deluged Granada with blood and hastened the fall of the kingdom. They were exterminated by Boabdil (Abu Abdallah), the last king, who was dethroned by Ferdinand and Isabella in 1492; his dominions were annexed to Castile.

Abensberg, Bavaria. The Austrians were here defeated by Napoleon I., 20 Apr., 1809.

Abercrombie, James, 1706–81. FORT TICONDEROGA.

Aberdeen, N. Scotland, said to have been founded in the 3d century, and made a city about 893. Old Aberdeen was made a royal burgh in 1154; it was burned by the English in 1336; and soon after New Aberdeen was built.

The university was founded by bishop William Elphinstone, who had a bull from pope Alexander VI. in 1494. King's college was erected in 1500–6. Marischal college was founded by George Keith, earl marischal of Scotland, in 1593; rebuilt in 1837. In 1858 the university and colleges were united.

Aber Edw, S. Radnorshire. Near here Llewelyn, the last independent prince of Wales, was surprised, defeated, and slain by the lords marchers, 11 Dec. 1282.

aberration of light; discovered by James Bradley, observing an apparent motion of the fixed stars, 1727.

Abhorrers, a name given in 1679 (reign of Charles II.) to the court party in England, the opponents of those (afterwards Whigs) who addressed the king for the immediate assembly of parliament, which was delayed because it was adverse to the court. The court party (afterwards Tories) expressed abhorrence of men who would encroach on the royal prerogative, 1680.—*Hume.* The commons expelled several Abhorrers, among them sir Francis Withens, whom they sent to the Tower, and prayed the king to remove others from places of trust. They resolved, "that it is the undoubted right of the subject to petition for the calling of a parliament, and that to traduce such petitions as tumultuous and seditious is to contribute to the design of altering the constitution." Oct. 1680.

Abingdon Law. In 1644–45, lord Essex and Waller held Abingdon, an ancient abbey town in Berks, against Charles I. It was unsuccessfully attacked by sir Stephen Hawkins in 1644, and by prince Rupert in 1645; when the defenders put every Irish prisoner to death without trial; hence the term "Abingdon law"—"first hang the offender, then try him."

abiogenesis (*a*, not, *βίος*, life, *γένεσις*, origin), the production of living from non-living matter, proposed by professor Huxley in his British Association address, 1870, instead of the less accurate phrase "spontaneous generation."

abjuration of the pope was enjoined by statutes of Henry VIII., Elizabeth, and James I., that of certain doctrines of the church of Rome by Charles II. 1673. The oath of abjuration of the house of Stuart was enjoined by stat. Will. III. 1702; the form was changed in after-reigns. By 21 & 22 Vict. c. 48 (1858) one oath was substituted for the three oaths of abjuration, allegiance, and supremacy. OATHS.

Abner, cousin of Saul, first king of Israel; after Saul died, 1055 B.C., supports his son Ishbosheth against David; alienated from Ishbosheth, he arranges secretly with David to bring Israel over to him, but is treacherously slain, 1048 B.C., by Joab, almost immediately after. The celebrated dirge over his grave by David has been thus translated:

"Should Abner die as a villain dies?—
Thy hands—not bound,
Thy feet—not brought into fetters;
As one falls before the sons of wickedness, fellest thou."

Abo (*ä'boo* or *o'-boo*), a port of Russia, founded before 1157, was till 1809 capital of Swedish Finland, but then ceded to Russia. The university, erected by Gustavus Adolphus and Christina, 1640 et seq., was removed to Helsingfors, 1827. By the *peace of Abo* Sweden ceded part of Finland to Russia, 18 Aug. 1743.

abolition of slavery in the United States. SLAVERY.

Abolitionists, a term applied to those desiring the immediate abolition of slavery in the United States. Most of the northern states passed laws before 1800 for gradual emancipation, and the disposition of the whole country then, and some time after, towards slavery was mere toleration with hope of its ultimate extinction. But the more southern states, under climatic, productive, and territorial influences, gradually came to regard slavery as not only right, but a blessing. The slavery agitation had two periods: during the first, 1780–1819, it was general and spiritless; during the second, 1820–65, it became sectional and aggressive. During the latter period the term *Abolitionists* was first applied to the agitators for emancipation. The Abolitionists, in the preamble to the Constitution of the American Anti-Slavery Society, organized at Philadelphia, Dec. 1833, advocate "The immediate emancipation of the slaves; elevation of the race, recognition of their equality in civil and religious privileges"—all to be accomplished without physical force. Immediate abolition being their supreme aim, both Church and State were subordinate to this idea. Restive under delay, they often tried the patience of their more conservative but no less humane coadjutors. SLAVERY.

aborig'ines (without origin), a name given to the earliest known inhabitants of Italy (whence the Latini); now applied to the original inhabitants of any country. INDIANS.

Aboukir (*ä-boo-keer'*), Egypt, the ancient Canopus. In the bay Nelson defeated the French fleet, 1 Aug. 1798. NILE. A Turkish army of 15,000 was defeated here by 5000 French under Bonaparte, 25 July, 1799. A British expedition to Egypt, under general sir Ralph Abercromby, landed, and Aboukir surrendered after a sanguinary conflict with the French, 8 Mch. 1801. ALEXANDRIA.

Abracadăb'ra, a magical word once used as a charm against ague and fevers. Its meaning and origin are disputed. As a charm it was written so as to form an inverted triangle by dropping the last letter at each successive repetition.

Abraham or **Abram,** father of the Israelites, first-born son of Terah, a Shemite, who left Ur of the Chaldees, in northeast Mesopotamia, with Abram and Lot, and moved westward, entering Canaan 1921 B.C. (*Usher*). Sojourned in Egypt one year, 1920 B.C.; died in Canaan, 1821 B.C. The era of Abraham, used by Eusebius, began 1 Oct. 2016 B.C.

Abraham, Heights or Plains of, near Quebec, named "from Abraham Martin, a pilot known as Maître Abraham, who owned a piece of land here in the early times of the colony."—*F. Parkman* ("Montcalm and Wolfe," vol. ii., p. 289.) On this plateau was fought a battle between French and English, 13 Sept. 1759, gaining Canada for the English. Both commanders, Montcalm and Wolfe, were killed, the latter at the moment of victory.

Abrahamites, a sect holding the errors of Paulus, suppressed by Cyriacus, the patriarch of Antioch, early in the 9th century. (2) A sect in Bohemia professing the faith of Abraham, and accepting from the Scriptures only the Ten Commandments and the Lord's Prayer. Being required to unite with some one of the religions tolerated in the empire, and refusing, they were banished by emperor Joseph II. in 1783.

Abrantes, Portugal. By a treaty between France and Portugal, signed here 29 Sept. 1801, the war was ended, and the French army withdrew; money compensation was fixed, and territories in Guiana ceded to France. At the convention of Cintra, 22 Aug. 1808, it was surrendered to the English by the French. Junot, one of Napoleon's marshals, derived his title of "duke of Abrantes" from this town.

Absalom, one of the sons of David, king of Israel, rebels, is defeated and slain by Joab (1024–23 B.C.). 2 Sam. xv.–xix.

absinthe, a strong liquor made by steeping flowers and leaves of wormwood in alcohol, chiefly at Neufchatel in Switzerland, but also in many places in France. It became popular in France during the war with Algiers (1844–47), when the French soldiers mixed it with wine to keep off fever. It is the most dangerous of the favorite *liqueurs*, and the French government has forbidden its use in the army and navy.

absolution. Till the 3d century the consent of the congregation was necessary to absolution; but soon after the power was reserved to the bishop; and in the 13th century the form "I absolve thee" was general, though it remained for the Council of Trent, in the 16th century, to decree this form, instead of "The Lord absolve thee." HOLY CROSS.

abstinence. It is said that St. Anthony lived to the age of 105 on 12 ounces of bread and water daily, and James the hermit to the age of 104; that St. Epiphanius lived to 115; Simeon the Stylite to 112; and Kentigern, commonly called St. Mungo, to 185 years of age.—*Spottiswood.*

Cicely de Ridgway, said to have fasted 40 days rather than plead when charged with the murder of her husband, John; discharged as miraculously saved, 1347.

Ann Moore, the "Fasting Woman of Tutbury," Staffordshire, said to have lived 20 months without food; her imposture was detected by Dr. A. Henderson, Nov. 1808.

An impostor named Cavanagh, at Newry in Ireland, reported to have lived 2 years without meat or drink, Aug. 1840; was exposed in England, and imprisoned, Nov. 1841.

Sarah Jacobs, the Welsh fasting girl, aged 13, said by her father to have lived more than a year without food; after close watch for a week, died from exhaustion, 17 Dec. 1869. Her parents were sentenced at Carmarthen to imprisonment for fraud, 15 July, 1870.

Dr. Tanner, at New York, fasted 40 days, drinking a little water; losing 36 lbs. from 157½ lbs.; noon 28 June to noon 7 Aug. 1880.

Louise Lateau, Belgian fanatic, at Bois d'Haine, said to have lived 12 years without food; died, aged 33, Aug. 1883. She had wounds resembling the stigmata of the crucifix.

The members of the Arctic Expedition of 1881–84, lieut. Greely commanding (NORTHEAST AND NORTHWEST PASSAGE), passed the winter of 1883–84 at lat. 78° 45′ N., long. 74° 15′ W. From 1 Nov. to 1 Mch. the daily allowance for each man was 14.88 ounces of solid food, the army ration being 46 ounces. From 1 Mch. to 12 May the daily ration was 10 ounces of bread and meat, with 1 to 3 ounces of shrimps. From 12 May to 22 June, when the survivors were rescued, there was no food to serve: only a few shrimps, reindeer moss, and black lichen scraped from the rocks were found. There was water, but brackish. But 7 were alive when found, out of 25, and 1 died soon after. Average loss in weight, about 48 lbs. each. Average atmospheric temperature, 5 to 10° Fahrenheit.

Giovanni Succi, an Italian, ended a fast of 40 days at the Westminster Aquarium, London, Eng., 26 Apr. 1890. He was permitted to drink water and to smoke. His loss of weight averaged ½ lb. a day.

Succi began a 45 days' fast in city of New York, 5 Nov. 1890, ended successfully 20 Dec. 1890. His weight fell from 147¾ lbs. to 104¾ lbs. He drank 21 qts. of mineral water and 9½ qts. of Croton water.

At the Westminster Aquarium, London, he engaged to fast 52 days, but stopped on the 44th day, 29 Jan. 1892.

Other recent cases of still longer abstinence are not sufficiently attested.

Abu, a famous mountain in W. India, with ancient JAIN temples, attracting pilgrims for Buddhist worship.

Abu Klea Wells, about 120 miles from Khartoum. Here gen. sir Herbert Stewart defeated the Mahdi's troops, 17 Jan. 1885. SOUDAN.

Aby'dos, an ancient city of Upper Egypt, now Arabat-el-Matfoon. Here are the ruins of the temple of Osiris in which Mr. Bankes discovered in 1818 the "Tablet of Abydos," dedicated to his ancestors by Pharaoh Rameses II. (1311–1245 B.C.), bought for the British Museum, 1837. A second tablet, the "New Tablet of Abydos," more complete, was discovered here (1864–65), by M. Auguste Mariette (Mariette Bey), bearing names or partial records of 76 Pharaohs prior to Rameses II. EGYPT; HELLESPONT.

Abyssinia, a country of Eastern Africa, having Nubia on the north and northwest, the Danakils on the east-southeast, the Gallas on the south, and on the west the region of the Upper Nile. Its one seaport, Massowah, on the Red sea, is controlled by Italy. It contains about 158,000 square miles and a population between 3,000,000 and 4,000,000. The name Abyssinia is derived from the Arabic word *Habesch*, signifying mixture or confusion; changed by the Portuguese into Abassia, and so into Abyssinia. The chief ruler is styled Negus, and the governors of the three chief provinces—Tigré, in the north; Amhara, central; and Shoa, in the south—are termed Ras. Abyssinia was included in the ancient kingdom of Ethiopia. The Hebrews had intercourse with the Ethiopians, and after the destruction of Jerusalem by the Romans many Jews settled here, bringing the Jewish religion. The kingdom of Auxumite (its chief town Auxume) flourished in the 1st and 2d centuries. The religion of the Abyssinians is a corrupt Christianity, introduced about 329 by Frumentius, and during the 5th century the monastic system spread largely. About 527, instigated by the Greek emperor Justinian, Abyssinia conquered Yemen, Arabia, and held it 67 years. Judith, a Jewish princess, about 960, murdered part of the royal family and reigned 40 years. The young king, however, escaped, and the royal house was restored in 1268 in his descendant, Icon Amlac. A belief long prevailed in Europe of a Christian kingdom in the Far East whose monarch was "Prester John," and the Portuguese who arrived here in 1490 identified it with Abyssinia, and presented the emperor a letter from the king of Portugal. The Portuguese missions commenced soon afterwards, and after much opposition were expelled in 1633. The encroachment of the Gallas and intestine disorders soon broke the empire into petty governments, and kept Europeans away, until the visits of James Bruce, 1768-73; Henry Salt, 1809-10; Dr. Edward Rüppell, 1831-34; major Harris, 1841; Mansfield Parkyns, 1844-47.

Treaty of commerce with king of Shoa concluded by capt. Harris....16 Nov. 1841

Mr. Plowden (made British consul at Massowah, 1848) concludes treaty with Ras Ali, ruler of Amhara.........2 Nov. 1849

Ras Ali deposed by his son-in-law Theodore, who is crowned as *negus*, or king of kings.....11 Feb. 1855

Protestant missionaries received, replacing Roman Catholics, "

Mr. Plowden (who had joined the party of Theodore) killed by rebels, Feb.; Theodore overcomes the rebels.......... 1860

Capt. C. D. Cameron succeeds consul Plowden..........Nov. 1861

Received by Theodore, 7 Oct.; is sent with a letter for the queen, desiring alliance against the Turks, which arrived 12 Feb. 1863

This letter is not answered; Cameron, ordered by earl Russell to remain at Massowah, returns to Abyssinia........June, "

Rev. H. Stern, missionary, beaten and imprisoned for alleged intrusion upon Theodore..........Oct. "

Cameron, and all British subjects and missionaries, imprisoned for pretended insults, 3 Jan.; report of imprisonment reached London. 7 May; prisoners sent to Magdala, and chained like criminals..........Nov. 1864

Mr. Hermuzd Rassam, a Chaldee Christian, first assistant British political resident at Aden, sent to Abyssinia; arrives at Massowah, 24 July; lieut. Prideaux and Dr. Blanc appointed to accompany him.......... "

Mr. Rassam having negotiated without effect for a year, Mr. Gifford Palgrave appointed by ea[illegible] Abyssinia, July; but stopped learning [illegible] Theodore has invited [illegible], 12 Aug. 1865

Mr. Rassam, lieut. Prideaux, and Dr. Blanc at Matemma from Massowah, 21 Nov. 1865; well received by Theodore..28 Jan. 1866

Prisoners released 12 March; seized and imprisoned about 13 Apr. "

Mr. Flad sent to England by Theodore for British workmen, April; arrives, July; introduced to queen; receives from her autograph letter dated..........4 Oct. "

Mr. Flad returned with workmen to Massowah, 29 Oct.; Theodore received the queen's letter....about 19 Dec. "

Lord Stanley's ultimatum to Theodore, demanding release of captives in three months (not received), sent......16 Apr. 1867

Mr. Flad received by king, sent to his family in prison..May, "

Preparations for war; sir Robert Napier appointed commander; force sails from Bombay..........14 Sept. "

Formal letter from British government to Theodore (never arrived)..........9 Sept. "

Advanced brigade (3500) sail from Bombay, 7, 8 Oct.; land at Zulla..........21 Oct. "

Napier's proclamation issued in Abyssinia..........26 Oct. "

British parliament meets; queen's speech announces war, 19 Nov.; 2,000,000*l.* voted..........26, 27 Nov. "

Third ultimatum sent by sir R. Napier; intercepted by a rebel chief and given to Mr. Rassam, who suppressed it as likely to endanger the lives of the captives.......... 1868

Arrival of sir R. Napier at Annesley bay..........4 Jan. "

Battle of Arogee; Theodore's troops attack British first brigade; defeated with much slaughter (Good Friday)..10 Apr. "

Mutiny of Abyssinian troops; Magdala bombarded and stormed; Theodore kills himself..........13 Apr. "

Magdala burned to the ground (MAGDALA)..........17 Apr. "

Returned troops arrive at Plymouth..........21 June, "

[Cattle employed in the expedition: 45 elephants, 7417 camels, 12,920 mules and ponies, 7083 bullocks, 827 donkeys. Many natives in transport service.]

Theodore's son Alamayoú, aged 7, arrives at Plymouth..14 July, "

Pension of 350*l.* to col. Cameron [died 30 May, 1870]; 5000*l.* given to Mr. Rassam; 2000*l.* to Dr. Blanc; 2000*l.* to lieut. Prideaux; announced..........23 Dec. "

Prince Alamayoú sailed to India for education (returned to England end of 1871)..........26 Jan. 1869

Expenses of the war: 5,000,000*l.* voted 18 Dec. 1868; 3,300,000*l.* more voted..........4 Mch. "

[Total: 8,977,500*l.*, Feb. 1880.]

Kassa, king of Tigré, proposes to be crowned emperor and negus of all Abyssinia, 21 Nov.; punishes Catholic missionaries for partisanship; forms alliance with Egypt..........July, 1871

Kassa crowned at Axum as Johanni II..........12 Jan. 1872

War with Egypt; Khedive's troops enter Abyssinia; natives retire, but surprise and defeat Egyptians at Kherad Iska (a massacre) and at Gonda Gouddi (desperate fight)....16 Oct. 1875

Abyssinians defeated in three days' conflict.......17-19 Feb. 1876

Johanni defeats Menelek, king of Shoa..........June, 1877

Prince Alamayoú dies at Leeds, 14 Nov.; buried at Windsor.. 1879

Johanni receives admiral Hewitt from Suakim and signs treaty with English..........about 26 May, 1884

Abyssinian envoys arrive at Plymouth, Eng..........Aug. 1884

Italians occupy Massowah and hoist their flag..........5 Feb. 1885

The Mahdists invade Abyssinia.......... 1885-86

Detachment of 540 Italian troops near Dogali destroyed by 20,000 Abyssinians under Ras Aloula..........Jan. 1887

Italian government determines on war.......... "

British government appealed to by Johanni; ineffectual negotiation.......... "

Italian army at Massowah consists of 238 officers, 4772 men, and 160 pieces of artillery.......... 1888

Further re-enforced by 13,000 officers and men.......... "

Overtures of peace by Johanni, who rejects conditions offered by Italian government..........31 Mch. "

France, Greece, and Turkey protest against occupation of Massowah by Italians.......... "

Italian government annexes Zulla..........Aug. "

Johanni repulsed and mortally wounded in attack on dervishes' stronghold at Metumneh on the frontier of Soudan, 10 Mch. 1889

The king's camp taken and his army routed..........12 " "

The Italians take formal possession of Keren..........2 June, "

King Menelek of Shoa crowned as negus at Adira, the sacred city of Abyssinia..........Sept. "

The Italians treat with Menelek, who accepts Italian protectorate over Ethiopia; ratified by king of Italy......25 Sept. "

Italian government assumes protectorate of Abyssinia..13 Oct. 1889

Under treaty of 1889 and a convention ratified..........25 Feb. 1890

Abyssinia is wholly under Italian influence.

Abyssinian Era is reckoned from the creation, 5493 B.C., 29 Aug. old style. To reduce Abyssinian time to the JULIAN YEAR, subtract 5492 years, 125 days.

Aca'cians, followers of Acacius, bishop of Cæsarea, in the 4th century, in peculiar doctrines of Christ's person. (2) Partisans of Acacius, patriarch of Constantinople, promoter of the HENOTICON, 482-484.

academies. *Academia* was a shady grove without the walls of Athens (bequeathed by Academus for gymnastic exercises), where Plato first taught philosophy, and his followers took the title of Academics, 378 B.C.—*Stanley.* This school of philosophy lasted till Cicero's time, gradually branching, however, into several schools. Ptolemy Soter, Greek conqueror of Egypt, established at Alexandria an academy about 314 B.C.—the origin of the library at Alexandria, the most famous of the ancient world. The Saracens, after the conquest of Spain, established academies at Granada, Cordova, and as far east as Samarcand. Charlemagne founded an academy at the instigation of Alcuin, and Alfred one that grew into the university of Oxford. The modern academy is not always a school, but often an association of learned men for the advancement of science, literature, and the arts, sometimes aided, if not endowed, by the State. There are many such organizations known as societies, associations, lyceums, institutes, museums, etc., but this list contains only those known as academies.

PRINCIPAL ACADEMIES ARRANGED BY DATE.

Paris, *Sorbonne* (suppressed 1790; on the reorganization of the university of France in 1808, it became the seat of the academy of France).......... 1255

Florence, Belles-lettres.......... 1272

Toulouse, Floral Games (*Jeaux Floraux*); still bears the name. 1323

Milan, Architecture.......... 1380

Paris, Painting.......... 1391

Basel.......... 1460

Naples, *Rossana*.......... 1540

Paris, Music.......... 1543

Verona, Music.......... 1543

Parma, *Innominati*.......... 1553

Naples, Mathematics.......... 1560

Perosa, *Insensati*.......... 1561

" *Filigirti*.......... 1574

Florence, *Della Crusca*, now united with the *Fiorentina* (established by Cosmo I. 1549) under that name.......... 1582

Rome, *Lincei*.......... 1600

Faenza, *Philoponi*.......... 1611

Padua, Poetry.......... 1612

Rome, *Umoristi*.......... 1613

" *Fantascici*.......... 1625

Brescia, *Erranti*.......... 1626

Paris, the French, established by Richelieu.......... 1635

Ancona, *Caglinosi*.......... 1642

Palermo, Medical.......... 164[illegible]

Paris, Fine Arts.......... 1648

Vienna, *Academia Naturæ Curiosorum*.......... 1652

Rome, *Infecondi*.......... 1653

Florence, *Del Cimento* (by Cardinal de' Medici).......... 1657

Germany, *Naturæ Curiosi*, now Leopoldine	1662
Paris, *Inscriptions et Belles-lettres*, established by Colbert	1663
Rome, Painting	1665
Paris, Sciences, established by Colbert	1666
Paris, Architecture	1671
" Music	1672
Soissons	1675
Nîmes, Royal	1682
Angers, Belles-lettres	1685
Bologna, Ecclesiastical	1687
Rome, *Arcadi*	1690
Bologna, Mathematics	1690
Naples, Science	1695
Dresden, Fine Arts	1697
Berlin, Royal, Leibnitz first President	1700
Venice, Medical	1701
Berlin, Princes	1703
Bordeaux, Arts, Science, and Belles-lettres	1703
Mantua, *Vigilanti*, Science	1704
Vienna, Sculpture and the Arts	1705
Caen, Science and Belles-lettres	1705
Montpellier, Royal Academy of Sciences	1706
Lyons, Science, Belles-lettres, and Art	1710
Bologna, Science and Art	1712
Bordeaux, Ethnology and Science (suppressed 1793, restored 1816)	1712
Madrid, Royal	1713
Geneva, Medical	1715
Milan, Science	1719
Upsala, Sweden, Science	1720
St. Petersburg, Science, established by Catherine I	1725
Marseilles, Belles-lettres (suppressed 1793, reorganized 1802)	1726
Cortona, Italy, Etruscan Antiquities	1726
Madrid, History	1730
London, Music	1734
Göttingen	1734
Rouen, Science and Art	1737
Stockholm, Fine Arts, etc	1739
Dijon, Science, Belles-lettres, and Arts (suppressed 1793, restored 1800)	1740
Stockholm, Science	1741
Dublin, Arts	1742
Copenhagen, Science, established by Count Holstein	1743
Montauban, France, Archæology	1744
Amiens, France	1750
Genoa, Painting	1751
Rome, English	1752
Madrid, Painting and Arts	1753
Valladolid, Spain, History and Geography	1753
Stockholm, Belles-lettres	1753
Warsaw, Language and History	1753
Erfurt, Germany, Science	1754
Vienna, Oriental Language	1754
Mannheim, Baden, Science, founded by elector Chas. Theodore	1755
Naples, *Herculaneum*, Archæology and History	1755
Turin, Italy, Science	1759
Munich, Arts and Science	1759
Haerlem, Science	1760
St. Petersburg, Arts	1764
London, Royal, Fine Arts (reorganized 1865)	1768
Brussels, Belles-lettres, Science, and Fine Arts (reorganized 1845)	1773
Mannheim, Sculpture	1775
Turin, Fine Arts, "The Albertine" (see above, 1759)	1778
Naples, Science and Belles-lettres	1779
Munich, Science	1779
Lisbon, Science	1779
Boston, U. S., Arts and Science	1780
Verona, Science	1780
Stockholm, Agriculture	1781
Toulouse, Science, Inscriptions, Belles-lettres	1782
Dublin, Royal, Science	1782
Genoa, Science	1783
Stockholm, Royal, 1753; reorganized, History and Antiquities added	1786
Padua, Science, Letters, and Arts	1792
Paris, Natural Philosophy	1796
Berlin, Architecture	1799
Connecticut, New Haven, U. S., Arts and Science	1799
Pennsylvania, Phila., U. S., Fine Arts	1807
Florence, Antiquities, Tuscan	1807
Philadelphia, Pa., U. S., Natural Science	1818
Dublin, Sculpture	1823
New York, National, of Design	1828
Paris, of Morals and Politics. (The "Institute of France," established by Louis XVI., at first consisted of 4 Academies.) This was added	1832
Rome, *Nuovi Lincei* (see above, 1600)	1847
Washington, D. C., U. S., National, incorporated by Congress	1863
New York, Science (formerly Lyceum of Natural History, 1817)	1876
Philadelphia, American, of Political and Social Science	1889

SOCIETIES AND INSTITUTIONS OF ART AND SCIENCE.

academy, an educational institution, in grade between a school and a college. EDUCATIONAL INSTITUTIONS.

academy, military. ANNAPOLIS and WEST POINT.

Aca'dia, the British provinces now known as Nova Scotia and New Brunswick, especially the former, so called by the French who planted a colony at Port Royal, now Annapolis, under Poutrincourt, 1605; the English make an easy conquest of it, 1654; Acadia restored to France by the treaty of Breda, 1667; Massachusetts fits out a small fleet under sir William Phipps, which retakes Acadia, 1690; retaken by the French under Villabon, 1692; restored to the English by the treaty of Utrecht, 1713. Under these changes the French inhabitants remained undisturbed (settled along the bay of Fundy from Annapolis to the basin of Minas) up to 1755. New England, apprehensive of the French from this quarter —they having established forts at the isthmus connecting Nova Scotia with New Brunswick, and also at the mouth of the St. John's river, N. B.—sent an expedition under John Winslow, of 3000 troops from Boston, and seized the forts, with little resistance, 16 June, 1755. The French inhabitants of Acadia were then between 14,000 and 15,000. By the terms granted them when the British authorities took possession of the province, 1713, they were excused from any obligation to bear arms against France, and were thence known as "French Neutrals." New England insisted that they were not really neutral, but dangerous neighbors, being French and Roman Catholics. It was argued that these people could not remain, and if ordered to quit the country would retire to Canada and strengthen the enemy there. A pitiless scheme was therefore devised, whereby the inhabitants could be captured, or rather kidnapped, without being able to resist, and transported to the English colonies along the Atlantic. Assembled, under various pretences, at their parish church, they were surrounded by troops, made prisoners, and hurried on board the ships. In the intentional hurry and confusion wives were separated from husbands, children from parents, and thus carried away, never again to be united. Their lands, crops, cattle, and money—everything except the scantiest wardrobe—were declared forfeit to the crown; and to impoverish those who escaped capture, the growing crops, houses, barns, and cattle, as far as possible, were destroyed. More than a thousand of these exiles were carried to Massachusetts, and others scattered from Massachusetts to Georgia. From these uncongenial localities survivors wandered—some in search of lost relatives, others of their native tongue—to France, to St. Domingo, to Canada, to Louisiana. To such as reached Louisiana, lands were assigned in the district west of New Orleans, bordering on the "Bayou Teche," still known as the "Acadian Land," and the inhabitants as "Cajuns." These, from a few thousands, now number over 200,000. The "Evangeline" of Longfellow is founded on this event.

Acale'phæ (Gr. ἀκαλήφη, nettle), the scientific name for jelly-fish, sea-nettles, etc.

Acanthus, a genus of plants of the natural order *Acanthaceæ*, whose foliage is supposed to have suggested the decoration of the Corinthian capital ascribed to Callimachus, about 540 B.C.

Acapul'co, Mexico, a city on the Pacific coast almost directly south of the city of Mexico. During the 18th century it traded largely with Manilla, capital of the Philippine islands. Com. George Anson, in the British ship *Centurion*, captured a Spanish galleon, from Acapulco to Manilla, laden with gold and precious wares, estimated at $5,000,000, June, 1743. He returned to Spithead, Eng., having circumnavigated the globe, 15 June, 1744.

Acarna'nia, N. Greece. The people were prominent in the Peloponnesian war, and had asked help from Athens against the Ambracians, 432 B.C. They were subdued by Sparta in 390; took part in 200 with Macedon against the Romans, by whom they were defeated in 197 and subjugated in 145.

Acca'dians, the primitive inhabitants of Babylonia. The city "Accad" was grouped with Babel, Erech, and Calneh in the land of Shinar (Gen. x. 10). They are believed to have been of Turanian origin, and to have come from the north of Europe and Asia, their language antedating the proper Assyrian cuneiform inscriptions. Such scholars as Rev. A. H. Sayce, Prof. Paul Haupt, M. François Lenormant, and Geo. Smith, of the department of oriental antiquities of the British museum, and other distinguished philologists and antiquarians, have thrown much light on the history of those primitive times, by deciphering the cuneiform writing of the brick-legends of their earliest kings These people are now considered the earliest civilizers of eastern Asia, the source of the philosophy and arts of the Assyrians and the Phœnicians, and hence of Greece "Whole sciences that have dominated the thought of men and changed the face of the world are found to have had their beginnings and an astonishing development among this gifted and reflective people." —*Amer Journal of Philology*, vol III p 469, 1882 ASSYRIA and TURANIAN

accents were first introduced in Greek by Aristophanes of Byzantium, a grammarian and critic who taught at Alexandria about 264 B C Accents were first used by the French in the reign of Louis XIII (about 1610)

Accession, The, i e that of the House of Hanover to the throne of Great Britain, in the person of George I elector of Hanover son of Sophia, daughter of Elizabeth, daughter of James I He succeeded, 1 Aug 1714, by the act of settlement passed under William III 12 June, 1702, which limited the succession to his mother (as a Protestant) if queen Anne should die without issue

ac'cessory is one who participates in a crime, not as principal, but by aid, counsel, or concealment. In treason and in misdemeanors, the law regards all guilty as principals

Ac'cius, a tragic poet of Rome born about 190 B C Cicero, when a boy, knew him Few fragments of his writings remain

acclimatization, the adaptation to changed climate of any organic life That of men has been most fully tested by immigration into America Dr W H Thomson reported to the surgeon-general in 1862, after examining 9000 men, a far higher average of physical strength and endurance in native Americans than in any class of immigrants

accordion, a small free-reed wind instrument with keys, invented at Vienna by Damian about 1828, and now made chiefly in Paris

accusers. Occult writers, such as Agrippa, make accusers the eighth order of devils, whose chief is called Asteroth or Spy In Rev XII 10, the devil is called "the accuser of the brethren" *False accusers* were to be hanged by 24 Henry VI 1446, and burned in the face with an F by 37 Henry VIII 1545 —*Stow*

Accel'dama, a field said to have been bought with thirty pieces of silver given to Judas for betraying Christ, is shown to travellers Matt. xxvii 8, Acts i. 19 —This name was given to an estate purchased by judge Jeffreys after the "bloody assizes" in 1685

ace'tylene, a luminous hydrocarbon gas resembling coal gas, discovered by Berthelot, and made known in 1862

Achaia (*a-ka'-ya*). N. Peloponnesus, Greece, said to have been settled by Achæus, the son of Xuthus, about 1330 B C (?) The kingdom was united with Sicyon or subject to the Ætolians, until about 281 B C. The Achæi, descendants of Achæus, originally inhabited the neighborhood of Argos, but when the Heraclidæ drove them thence, they retired among the Ionians, expelled the natives, and seized their thirteen cities, viz Pellene, Ægira, Ægium, Bura, Tritæa, Leontium, Rhypes, Cerynea, Olenos, Helice, Patræ, Dyme, and Pharæ, forming the Achæan League

	B C
Achaia invaded by Epaminondas	366
The Achæan League revived by 4 cities about 280, and by others	275, 274
Aratus made prætor	245
The league joined by Corinth (captured 243), Megara, etc	242-228
Supported by Athens and Antigonus Doson	229
The Achæans defeated at Ladocea by the Spartans, under Cleomenes III, 226, defeat them at Sellasia	221
Social war begun, battle of Caphyæ in Arcadia, Aratus defeated,	220
The Peloponnesus ravaged by the Ætolians	219
Peace of Naupactus	217
Aratus poisoned at Ægium	213
Philopœmen head of the league, defeats the Spartan tyrant Machanidas.	[illegible]
Alliance of the league with the Romans	[illegible]
Philopœmen defeated by Nabis in a naval battle	[illegible]
All the Peloponnesus joins the league	[illegible]
War with Messenia Philopœmen made prisoner and slain	183
The Achæans overrun Messenia with fire and sword	[illegible]
The Romans enter Achaia and carry off numbers, including Polybius the historian	[illegible]
War with Rome, 150, Metellus enters Greece	147
The Achæans defeated by Mummius at Leucopetra, 147, the league dissolved, Corinth taken Greece subjected to Rome, and named the province of Achaia	146
	A D
Achaia made a Latin principality by William of Champlitte	1205
Obtained by Geoffrey Villehardouin 1210, by Geoffrey II	1218
By his brother William, 1246, who conquers the Moors, 1248, makes war with the emperor Michael, 1259, and gains three fortresses	1262
Succeeded by Isabella, 1277, who marries Florenz of Hainault.	1291
Their daughter Maud, princess, 1311, thrice married, forcibly married to John de Gravina, and dies in prison	1324
Achaia, a fief of Naples	1246-1430
Conquered by the Turks	about 1540

Acheen', Atcheen', or Achin', a kingdom in the north of the island of Sumatra Visited by the Portuguese, 1506. The Dutch established factories, 1599, the English, 1602 The French sought a foothold here in 1621, but failed By a formal understanding between the English and the Dutch in 1824, the latter agreed not to begin hostilities against the Acheenese This understanding was abandoned, 2 Nov 1871 The Dutch land a force at Acheen, Apr 1873

Capture the capital	24 Jan 1874
Acheen reported subdued by the Dutch	1881
War breaks out afresh	1882
Ship *Nisero* stranded on the territory of the chief of Pangab, a Malay dependant of Tuku Imam Muda, the rajah of Tenom, subject to the sultan of Acheen	16 Nov 1883
18 British and 6 other sailors made prisoners, the captain released to negotiate, efforts to secure release fail, Dutch storm Tenom, the prisoners carried away	7 Jan 1884
Rajah demands free trade and subjection to Great Britain, British government counsels conciliation	May, "
Prisoners released 11 Sept., Dutch pay 100,000 guilders and raise the blockade as ransom, 20 prisoners released, the others having died of hardship and ill treatment, arrived in Thames	24 Oct "
The officers of the *Nisero* set free were tried in Holland for culpable negligence, and were convicted but sentence was suspended on account of suffering	1885
Coast blockaded by the Dutch	"
Great Britain urged to interfere to protect the pepper trade	1886
Tuku Omar, an Acheenese captures a steamship killing all but captain's wife and engineer, the Dutch pay $25,000 for ransom	"
The Dutch government plans a railroad to the coal fields on the Umbile river to be completed in six years, coal beds supposed to contain 200 000 000 tons	1887
The strongest foe to the Dutch, the berri berri disease	1888
Reverses to the Dutch army during	1889
The Dutch government after great sacrifice of life, and expenditure of 200 000,000 guilders has not subdued Acheen	1890
The Dutch gain some successes, and blockade the entire north coast	"
War continues.	1891

Ach'onry, Sligo, N Ireland a bishopric founded by St Finian, who built the church of Achad or Achonry, about 520, for his disciple Nathy (Dathy, or David) first bishop The see, held with Killala since 1612, was united with Tuam in 1834

achromat'ic telescopes, in which different kinds of glass are so combined as to correct one another's irregularities of refraction, and transmit pure, uncolored light were invented by John Dollond, and described in *Phil Trans.* of the Royal Society, London, 1753–58.

acids (now defined as salts of hydrogen) are generally soluble in water, redden organic blues, decompose carbonates and destroy alkalies, forming alkaline salts. The number of acids was increased by the Arabs, Geber (8th century) knew nitric and sulphuric acid Theories of acids were put forth by Becher (1669), Lemery (1675), and Stahl (1723) After the discovery of oxygen by Priestley, 1 Aug 1774, Lavoisier (1778) concluded that oxygen was a constituent of all acids, but about 1810, Davy, Gay-Lussac, and others proved acids to exist without oxygen In 1816 Dulong proposed the binary or hydrogen theory of acids, and in 1837 Liebig applied the theories of Davy and Dulong to explain the constitution of several organic acids. In 1852 oxygen acids were termed anhydrides by Gerhardt Many acids have been discovered in the advance of organic chemistry.—*Watts* Scheele (1742–86) discovered most of the vegetable acids, or suggested methods for their discrimination.

ac'olytes (Gr. ἀκόλουθος, attendant), an inferior order of clergy in the Latin church, unknown to the Greek church for [illegible] years after Christ

acoustics (from the Greek *ἀκούω*, I hear), the science of sound, was so named by Sauveur in the 17th century To Pythagoras, about 500 B.C, is ascribed the doctrine of different sounds produced by vibrating strings of varied length, and the communication of sound to the ear by the vibrating atmosphere It was mentioned by Aristotle, 300 B.C, explained by Galileo, 1600 A D, and investigated by Newton in 1700 Biot, Savart, Wheatstone, Lissajous Helmholtz, Henry, Tyndall, and others in the present century have promoted the science

A speaking trumpet or horn by which Alexander called soldiers ten miles away, is alluded to in an old manuscript found in the Vatican Library quoted by Kircher in 1652
Velocity of sound first measured by P Mersenne in 1657, and by the Academicians of Florence 1660
Robert Hooke experiments before the Royal Society making musical sounds by the teeth of a rapidly revolving wheel striking the edge of a card 27 July, 1681
Velocity of sound measured by Walker in England 1698
Sauveur pronounces the lowest sound to be that produced in a pipe of 40 ft., corresponding to 25 vibrations per second 1700
Modes of vibration corresponding to higher tones of strings, discovered by Noble and Pigot in Oxford 1676, and independently by Sauveur 1701
Experiment illustrating the absence of sound in a vacuum by a bell struck in the receiver of an air pump shown the Royal Society by a philosopher named Hawksbee 1705
Galileo's theorem of the harmonic curve demonstrated by Brook Taylor 1714
Resultant tones in music discovered in 1745 by the German organist Sorge, and independently by the Italian violinist Tartini 1754
First exact experiments on the velocity of sound in air by La Caille, Maraldi Cassini de Thury, and others, a commission of the Academy of Sciences at the Paris Observatory, the Pyramid of Montmartre, the Mill of Fontenay aux Roses and the Chateau de Lay at Montlhéry result 1093 ft per second at 0° cent 1758
Sounds produced by combustion of hydrogen in tubes, by Dr Higgins 1777
Successful experiments on imitating vowel sounds mechanically, by Von Kempelen of Vienna and by Kratzenstein, before Academy of St Petersburg 1779
Ernest Florens Frederic Chladni discovers the formation of nodal lines in symmetrical figures on glass plates vibrated by a violin bow across the edge 1785
Sounds of hydrogen gas burning in tubes investigated by Chladni and G De la Rive 1802
Velocity of sound made between Montlhery and Villejuif, about 61 007 ft, measured at request of Laplace by the Bureau des Longitudes, result, 1086 ft per second at zero 1822
Velocity of sound in water 4708 ft per second determined by Messrs Colladon and Sturm in lake Geneva between Rolle and Thonon about 8 miles (Previous experiments by Beudant at Marseilles) 1826
Prof Robison producing musical sounds by quick succession of puffs of air invents the first form of the SIREN, improved by Cagniard de la Tour in 1827
Arthur Trevelyan discovers cause of production of sound by contact of two metals unequally heated, noted by M Schwartz of Saxony in 1805, and constructs his so called "rocker" about 1829
Savart estimates the range of perception of the human ear at from 7 vibrations to 24 000 per second 1830
Experiments on propagation of sound in water, off the coast of the United States by Mr Bonnycastle 1838
CHRONOSCOPE invented by sir Charles Wheatstone 1840
Demonstration of rising pitch in the sound of an approaching locomotive whistle and the corresponding fall after the train passes, made by M Buys Ballot on the Dutch railway between Utrecht and Maarsen 1845
Count Schaffgotsch of Berlin shows that a gas flame surmounted by a short tube may be extinguished by a voice pitched to the note of the tube 1856-57
Action of sound upon a naked fish tail flame first observed by Dr Leconte at a musical party in the United States. 1858
Léon Scott devises the *Phonautograph* an instrument for regulating the vibrations of a sounding body—the first form of the PHONOGRAPH about 1858
Paper by prof Joseph Henry, on causes of aberration of sound, especially in FOG SIGNALS, before the Washington Philosophical Society 11 Dec 1872
Prof Tyndall begins investigations on transmission of sound, and aberration, especially in fog signals, under the auspices of Trinity House England 19 May, 1873
Experiments on diffraction of sound and production of *sound shadows* in water, by prof John Leconte and his son in San Francisco bay, show that the exposed ends of thick glass tubes, placed horizontally in the water between two piles, the nearest one 40 ft from a dynamite cartridge used in blasting a reef, were shattered by the explosion, while the portion in the sound shadow of the piles remained intact 1874
Experiments on aberrations of sound in fog signals described to Philosophical Society of Washington by Arnold B Johnson 22 Oct 1881
Captain Journee of the French army proves by projectiles that when air is displaced at a greater velocity than that of ordinary vibration, an explosive report results 23 Jan 1888
J Violle and Theodore Vautier describe before the Paris Academy experiments showing that the velocity of sound diminishes with intensity, and that pitch has no influence on velocity 3 Apr 1888

acre, the principal land measure in Great Britain and the United States The English imperial or standard acre by statute (Geo IV 1824) contains 4840 square yards, and is used in the United States The French *hectare*, the measure in France, Germany Italy, and Spain = 2 acres, 1 rood, and 35.38 perches The old Roman *jugerum* was about $\frac{5}{8}$ of an acre.

Acre or **Acca,** anciently Ptolemais in Syria, 80 miles north-northwest from Jerusalem, was taken by Saracens in 638, by the crusaders under Baldwin I in 1104, by Saladin in 1187; and again by Richard I and other crusaders, 12 July, 1191, after a siege of 2 years, with a loss of 6 archbishops, 12 bishops, 40 earls, 500 barons, and 300,000 soldiers. It was then named *St Jean d'Acre* It was retaken by Saracens, 1291, when 60,000 Christians perished, and the nuns, who had mangled their faces to preserve chastity, were put to death Acre was gallantly defended by Djezzar Pacha against Bonaparte, till relieved by sir Sidney Smith, who resisted twelve attempts by the French, between 16 March and 20 May, 1799, when Bonaparte retreated. Acre, as a Turkish pachalic, was seized 27 May, 1832, by Ibrahim Pacha, who had revolted On 3 Nov 1840, it was stormed by the allied fleet under sir Robert Stopford, and taken after a bombardment of a few hours, the Egyptians losing upwards of 2000 in killed and wounded and 3000 prisoners, while the British had but 12 killed and 42 wounded SYRIA and TURKEY

acropolis, a citadel usually on the summit of a rock or hill The most celebrated was at Athens Its principal entrance, a splendid structure, bore the name of *Propylaea* Besides other temples it contained the PARTHENON, or temple of Minerva

acrostic, a poem in which the first or last letters of each line, read downwards form a word, is said to have been invented by Porphyrius Optalianus in the fourth century Double acrostics became very popular in 1867 Edgar Allan Poe worked the name of Frances Sargent Osgood in the poem "A Valentine," and that of Sarah Anna Lewis in another, "An Enigma," so that the name was found by reading the first letter of the first line, the second letter of the second, the third letter of the third, and so on

Acs or **Acz** (*atch*), Hungary The Hungarians under Gorgey were defeated here by Austrians and Russians on 2 and 10 July, 1849

Act of Settlement, etc. ACCESSION, SUCCESSION, SUPREMACY, and UNIFORMITY ACTS

Acta Diurna, a kind of Roman gazette containing an authorized account of daily transactions Its origin is attributed to Julius Cæsar, by some to Servius Tullius, 550 B.C

Acta Sanctorum ("acts of the saints"), a publication of the Jesuits, begun in 1643, interrupted in 1794, when 54 volumes, bringing the work down to 15 Oct, had been published, it was resumed in 1837, and 6 more volumes had been published in 1867 The writers have been named *Bollandists* from John Bolland, who published the first two volumes.

actinometer, an instrument to measure the heating power of solar rays, invented by sir John F Herschel, and described by him in 1825 SUN.

Actium, a promontory of Acarnania, W Greece, near which, 2 Sept 31 B.C, the fleet of Octavianus Cæsar and that of Marc Antony and Cleopatra fought and decided the fate of Antony, 300 of his galleys going over to Cæsar This victory made Octavianus master of the world, and the Roman empire is commonly dated 1 Jan 30 B C. (the *Actian Era*) The conqueror built Nicopolis (the city of victory), and instituted the Actian games

actresses appear to have been unknown to the ancients, men or eunuchs performing the female parts. Charles II is said to have first encouraged the appearance of women on the stage in England in 1662, but Anne, queen of James I had previously performed in a theatre at court.—*Theat Biog* Mrs Davenport as *Roxalana* and Mrs Saunderson (afterwards Mrs Betterton) as *Ianthe*, in Davenant's "Siege of Rhodes," in 1661, were the first English public actresses, although Mrs Coleman enacted *Ianthe* in the same play to a select audience in 1656. THEATRES.

acts, in dramatic poetry, first employed by the Romans. *Five* acts are mentioned by Horace ("Art of Poetry") as the rule (about 8 B.C.).

Acts of the Apostles, Luke's continuation of his Gospel, ending 68 A.D.

acts of the British Parliament. PARLIAMENT. The following are celebrated early statutes:

Provisions of Merton, 1235-36.
Statute of Marlborough, 1267.
" of Bigamy, 1275-76.
" of Gloucester, the earliest statute of record, 6 Edw. I. 1278.
" of Mortmain, 1279.
Quo Warranto, Oct. 1280.
Statute of Merchants or Acton-Burnel, 1283.
Statutes of Wales, 1284.
" of Winchester, Oct. 1284.
" of Westminster, 1275, 1285, 1290.
Statute forbidding taxes without consent of parliament, 1297.
" of Præmunire, 1306.
Statutes first printed in the reign of Richard III., 1483.
" of the Realm, from Magna Charta to George I., printed from original records and MSS. in 12 vols. folio, under direction of commissioners appointed in 1801, 1811-28.
Publication of the revised edition of the Statutes (1325-1878), 18 volumes, published, 1870-85.

Adamites, a sect said to have existed about 130 A.D., and to have been naked in their religious assemblies, asserting that if Adam had not sinned there would have been no marriages. Their chief was named Prodicus; they deified the elements, rejected prayer, and said it was not necessary to confess Christ.—*Eusebius.* A sect of this name arose at Antwerp in the 12th century, under Tandemus or Tanchelin, whose followers, 3000 soldiers and others, committed many crimes. It became extinct soon after his death; but a similar sect, named Turlupins, appeared soon after in Savoy and Dauphiny. Picard, a Fleming, revived it in Bohemia, about 1415; it was suppressed by Ziska, 1420.

Adams, Fort, one of the three chief fortresses of the United States, mounting 500 guns; built 1824-39 at the entrance of Newport harbor, R. I. FORTS.

Adams, John, administration of. UNITED STATES, 1797.

Adams, John Quincy, administration of. UNITED STATES, 1825.

Adamses, The Three. John Adams (1735-1826), second president of the United States; his son, John Quincy Adams (1767-1848), sixth president of the United States; and his son, Charles Francis Adams (1807-86), distinguished diplomatist, minister to England, 1861-68.

Adelaide, capital of South Australia, founded in 1836. It contained 14,000 inhabitants in 1850, and 18,259 in 1855; about 30,000 in 1875; 133,220 in 1891. It was made a bishopric in 1847. University founded, 1876.

Aden, a free port on the southern coast of Arabia, near the entrance to the Red sea, where in Dec. 1836 a British ship was wrecked and plundered. The sultan promised compensation and agreed to cede the place to the English. His son repudiating this agreement, a British force, under capt. H. Smith, of the *Volage*, seized Aden, 19 Jan. 1839. It is now a garrison and coal depot for Indian steamers, etc.

Adige (*ä'-de-je*), a river of the Austrian Tyrol and N. Italy, near which the Austrians defeated the French on 26, 30 Mch. and 5 Apr. 1799.

Adirondack Mountains, in the N. of the state of New York. Mount Marcy, the highest, is 5344 ft. high. Extensive deposits of magnetic iron ore were discovered, 1835. A topographical survey by the state, under Verplanck Colvin, was begun, 1872. NEW YORK, 1885.

administrations of England and of Great Britain. Until the Restoration, 1660, there was no cabinet in the modern sense. The sovereign was aided by privy-councillors, varying in number, the men and offices being frequently changed. The cabinet as distinct from the privy council became prominent under William III., and the control of the chief, now termed the *premier*, began in the reign of Anne. "The era of ministries may most properly be reckoned from the day of the meeting of the parliament after the general election of 1698."—*Macaulay.* Till 1850 the cabinet council usually consisted of 12 members. In 1850 the number was 15. In 1868 the Gladstone cabinet consisted of the same number; that of Disraeli, in Feb. 1874, of 12; that of Gladstone, 1892, 17, as follows:

1. *First lord of the treasury and lord of privy seal.* ***William E. Gladstone, premier.***
2. *Lord high chancellor.*
3. *Lord president of the council and secretary of state for India.*
4. *Home secretary.*
5. *Foreign "*
6. *Colonial "*
7. *War "*
8. *First lord of the admiralty.*
9. *Chancellor of the exchequer.*
10. *Chief secretary for Ireland.*
11. *Secretary for Scotland.*
12. *President of the board of trade.*
13. *President of the local government board.*
14. *First commissioner of works.*
15. *Chancellor of duchy of Lancaster.*
16. *Postmaster-general.*
17. *Vice-president of the committee of council on education.*

The *average duration* of a ministry has been set down at four, five, and six years; but some ministries have lasted much longer: sir Robert Walpole was minister from 1721 to 1742 (21 years); Mr. Pitt, 1783 to 1801 (18 years); and lord Liverpool, 1812 to 1827 (15 years). Several ministries have not lasted beyond a few months, as the *Coalition Ministry* in 1783, and the "*Talents*" Ministry in 1806. The "*Short-lived*" Administration lasted 10 to 12 Feb. 1746.

Henry VIII.—Archbishop Warham; bishops Fisher and Fox; earl of Surrey, etc. 1509
Cardinal Thomas Wolsey, etc. 1514
Earl of Surrey; Tunstall, bishop of London, etc. 1523
Sir Thomas More; bishops Tunstall and Gardiner, and Cranmer (afterwards archbishop of Canterbury) 1529
Archbishop Cranmer; lord Cromwell, afterwards earl of Essex; Thomas Boleyn, earl of Wiltshire, etc. 1532
Thomas, duke of Norfolk; Henry, earl of Surrey; Thomas, lord Audley; bishop Gardiner; sir Ralph Sadler, etc. 1540
Lord Wriothesley; Thomas, duke of Norfolk; lord Lisle; sir William Petre; sir William Paget, etc. 1544
Edward VI.—Lord Wriothesley, earl of Southampton, lord chancellor (expelled); Edward, earl of Hertford, lord protector, created duke of Somerset; John, lord Russell; Henry, earl of Arundel; Thomas, lord Seymour; sir William Paget; sir William Petre, etc. 1547
John Dudley, late lord Lisle and earl of Warwick, created duke of Northumberland; John, earl of Bedford; bishop Goodrich, sir William Cecil, etc. 1551
Mary.—Stephen Gardiner, bishop of Winchester; Edmund Bonner, bishop of London; William, marquess of Winchester; sir Edward Hastings, etc. 1554
Elizabeth.—Sir Nicholas Bacon; Edward, lord Clinton; sir Robert Dudley, afterwards earl of Leicester; sir William Cecil, afterwards lord Burleigh 1558
William, lord Burleigh (minister during nearly all the reign); sir Nicholas Bacon, etc. 1572
Lord Burleigh; sir Thomas Bromley; Robert Devereux, earl of Essex (a favorite); earl of Leicester; earl of Lincoln; sir Walter Mildmay; sir Francis Walsingham, etc. 1579
Lord Burleigh; Robert, earl of Essex; sir Christopher Hatton, etc. 1587
Thomas Sackville, lord Buckhurst, afterwards earl of Dorset; sir Thomas Egerton, afterwards lord Ellesmere and viscount Brackley; sir Robert Cecil, etc. 1599
James I.—Thomas, earl of Dorset; Thomas, lord Ellesmere; Charles, earl of Nottingham; Thomas, earl of Suffolk; Edward, earl of Worcester; Robert Cecil, afterwards earl of Salisbury, etc. 1603
Robert Cecil, earl of Salisbury; Thomas, lord Ellesmere; Henry, earl of Northampton; Charles, earl of Nottingham; Thomas, earl of Suffolk, etc. 1609
Henry, earl of Northampton; Thomas, lord Ellesmere; Edward, earl of Worcester; sir Ralph Winwood; Charles, earl of Nottingham; Robert, viscount Rochester, afterwards earl of Somerset, etc. 1612
Thomas, lord Ellesmere; Thomas, earl of Suffolk; Charles, earl of Nottingham; sir George Villiers (a favorite), afterwards viscount Villiers, and successively earl, marquess, and duke of Buckingham 1615
Sir Henry Montagu, afterwards viscount Mandeville and earl of Manchester 1620
Lionel, lord Cranfield, afterwards earl of Middlesex; Edward, earl of Worcester; John, earl of Bristol; John Williams, dean of Westminster; George Villiers, marquess of Buckingham; sir Edward Conway, etc. 1621
Charles I.—Richard, lord Weston, afterwards earl of Portland; sir Thomas Coventry, afterwards lord Coventry; Henry, earl of Manchester (succeeded by James, earl of Marlborough, who gave place to Edward, lord, afterwards viscount, Conway); William Laud, bishop of London; sir Robert Merton, etc. 1628
William Laud, archbishop of Canterbury; Francis, lord Cotting-

ton; James, marquess of Hamilton; Edward, earl of Dorset; sir John Coke; sir Francis Windebank, etc. … 1635

William Juxon, bishop of London; sir John Finch, afterwards lord Finch; Francis, lord Cottington; Wentworth, earl of Strafford; Algernon, earl of Northumberland; James, marquess of Hamilton; Laud, archbishop of Canterbury; sir Francis Windebank; sir Henry Vane, etc. … 1640

[The king beheaded, 30 Jan. 1649.]

Commonwealth.—Oliver Cromwell, protector, named a council, not to exceed 21 members, or be less than 13. … 1653

Richard Cromwell, his son, succeeded on Oliver's death. A council of officers ruled at Wallingford house. … 1658

Charles II.—Sir Edward Hyde, afterwards earl of Clarendon; George Monk, created duke of Albemarle; Edward Moutagu, created earl of Sandwich; lord Saye and Sele; earl of Manchester; lord Seymour; sir Robert Long, etc. … 1660

George Monk, duke of Albemarle, first commissioner of the treasury, etc. … 1667

"*Cabal*" Ministry: Clifford, Ashley, Buckingham, Arlington, Lauderdale (CABAL). … 1670

Thomas, lord Clifford; Anthony, earl of Shaftesbury; Henry, earl of Arlington; Arthur, earl of Anglesey; sir Thomas Osborne, created viscount Latimer; Henry Coventry; sir George Carteret; Edward Seymour, etc. … 1672

Thomas, viscount Latimer, afterwards earl of Danby, lord high treasurer. … 26 June, 1673

Arthur, earl of Essex (succeeded by Lawrence Hyde, afterwards earl of Rochester); Robert, earl of Sunderland, etc. … 1679

[The king nominated a new council on 21 Apr. 1679, of 30 members only, chiefly the great officers of state and of the household.]

Sidney, lord Godolphin; Lawrence, earl of Rochester; Daniel, earl of Nottingham; Robert, earl of Sunderland; sir Thomas Chicheley; George, lord Dartmouth; Henry, earl of Clarendon; earls of Bath and Radnor. … 1684

James II.—Lawrence, earl of Rochester; George, marquess of Halifax; sir George Jeffreys, afterwards lord Jeffreys; Henry, earl of Clarendon; sir John Ernley; viscount Preston, etc. … 1685

The earl of Rochester displaced, John, lord Belasyse, made first commissioner of the treasury in his room, 4 Jan.; earl of Sunderland president of the council; viscount Preston, secretary of state, etc. … 1687–88

[King left Whitehall by night 11 Dec. 1688; fled from Rochester 18 Dec., and landed at Ambleteuse, in France, 20 Dec.]

William III. and Mary.—Charles, viscount Mordaunt; Thomas Osborne, earl of Danby, created marquess of Carmarthen, afterwards duke of Leeds; George, marquess of Halifax; Arthur Herbert, afterwards lord Torrington; earls of Shrewsbury, Nottingham, and Sunderland; earl of Dorset and Middlesex; William, earl (afterwards duke) of Devonshire; lord Godolphin; lord Montagu; lord De la Mere, etc. … 1689

Sidney, lord Godolphin; Thomas, earl of Danby; Richard Hampden; Thomas, earl of Pembroke; Henry, viscount Sydney; Daniel, earl of Nottingham, etc. … 1690

Sir John Somers became lord Somers in 1697, and lord chancellor; Charles Montagu, afterwards lord Halifax, made first commissioner of the treasury, 1 May, 1698, succeeded by Ford, earl of Tankerville. … 1699

PREMIERS OF ENGLAND FROM 1700, AND LENGTH OF ADMINISTRATIONS.

Anne.—Sidney, earl of Godolphin … 8 May, 1702
Robert Harley, earl of Oxford … 29 May, 1711
Charles, duke of Shrewsbury (made premier three days before the queen's death) … 29 July, 1714
George I.—Charles, earl of Halifax (dies 19 May, 1715; succeeded by the earl of Carlisle) … 5 Oct. "
Robert Walpole … Oct. 1715
James, earl Stanhope … 15 Apr. 1717
Charles, earl of Sunderland … Mch. 1718
Robert Walpole, earl of Orford … 1721
George II.—Robert Walpole, earl of Orford … 1727
Earl of Wilmington (dies 26 July, 1743) … Feb. 1742
Henry Pelham … 25 Aug. 1743
Henry Pelham, *Broad-bottom* administration … Nov. 1744
Earl of Bath, *Short-lived* administration … 10-12 Feb. 1746
Henry Pelham (again) … 12 Feb. "
Thomas H. Pelham, duke of Newcastle … Apr. 1754
Duke of Devonshire (William Pitt virtually premier) … 16 Nov. 1756
Duke of Newcastle (and William Pitt) … June, 1757
George III.—Duke of Newcastle (and William Pitt) … 1760
John, earl of Bute … May, 1762
George Grenville … 8 Apr. 1763
Charles, marquess of Rockingham … 13 July, 1765
William Pitt, earl of Chatham … Aug. 1766
Augustus Henry, duke of Grafton … Dec. 1767
Frederick, lord North. (Lord North was minister during the whole of the American war) … Jan. 1770
Marquess of Rockingham (dies 1 July, 1782. Charles James Fox and Edmund Burke were members of this cabinet), Mch. 1782
William Petty, earl of Shelburne … July, "
William Henry Cavendish, duke of Portland (called the "Coalition Ministry") … 5 Apr. 1783
William Pitt (second son of the earl of Chatham) … 18 Dec. "
Henry Addington … Mch. 1801
William Pitt (dies 23 Jan. 1806) … 12 May, 1804
George, lord Grenville … Feb. 1806
Duke of Portland (dies 30 Oct. 1809) … 25 Mch 1807
Spencer Perceval … Nov. 1809
Regency.—Spencer Perceval (shot by Bellingham in the lobby of the House of Commons, 11 May, 1812) … 5 Feb. 1811
Robert, earl of Liverpool … May, 1812
George IV.—Robert, earl of Liverpool … 29 Jan. 1820
George Canning (dies 8 Aug. 1827) … 24 Apr. 1827
Viscount Goderich … 8 Aug. "
Duke of Wellington … Jan. 1828
William IV.—Duke of Wellington (resigns 16 Nov. 1830), 26 June, 1830
Charles, earl Grey … Nov. "
William Lamb, viscount Melbourne (administration dissolved, Nov. 1834; seals of office in the hands of the duke of Wellington) … July, 1834
Sir Robert Peel … Dec. "
Viscount Melbourne … Apr. 1835
Victoria.—Viscount Melbourne … 20 June, 1837
Viscount Melbourne resigns, 8 May, 1839, but returns to power, 10 May, 1839
Sir Robert Peel (resigns 29 June, 1846) … Sept. 1841
Lord John Russell … July, 1846
Lord John Russell resigns, 21 Feb. 1851, but is induced (after the failure of lord Stanley's party to form an administration) to return to power … 3 Mch. 1851
Edward, earl of Derby … 27 Feb. 1852
Earl of Aberdeen … 28 Dec. "
Henry, viscount Palmerston … 7 Feb. 1855
Edward, earl of Derby … 25 Feb. 1858
Viscount Palmerston (d. 18 Oct. 1865. Lord Palmerston was premier during the American civil war) … 18 June, 1859
John, earl Russell … Oct. 1865
Edward, earl of Derby … 6 July, 1866
Benjamin Disraeli … 29 Feb. 1868
William Ewart Gladstone … 9 Dec. "
Benjamin Disraeli (earl of Beaconsfield, 16 Aug. 1876) … 21 Feb. 1874
William E. Gladstone … 28 Apr. 1880
Robert, marquis of Salisbury (resigned in consequence of a minority on the amendment to the address [329–250], 27 Jan. 1886) … 24 June, 1885
William E. Gladstone (resigned in consequence of a majority against his Irish Home Rule bill [343-313], 20 July, 1886), 26 Feb. 1886
Robert, marquis of Salisbury (resigned in consequence of want of confidence voted by the Commons [350-310], 11 Aug. 1892), 26 July. "
William E. Gladstone (resigns, 3 Mch. 1894) … 18 Aug. 1892
Archibald Philip Primrose, lord Rosebery … 3 Mch. 1894

administrations of the U. S. UNITED STATES.

admiral. The title first appears in England about 1300, but earlier in France.—*Sir Harris Nicolas.* The name is doubtless of Asiatic origin, as it appears to have been unknown in Europe before the crusades. Before the word admiral the title of *custos maris* was in use.—*Encycl. Brit.* 9th ed. Alfred, Athelstan, Edgar, Harold, and other kings were commanders of their own fleets. The first French admiral is said to have been appointed 1284. The rank of *admiral of the English seas* was first given to William de Leybourne by Edward I. in 1297.—*Spelman; Rymer.* The first Lord High Admiral in England was created by Richard II. in 1385; there had been previously high admirals of *districts*—the north, west, and south. The duties have generally been executed by lords commissioners. ADMIRALTY. A similar dignity existed in Scotland from the reign of Robert III. In 1673, Charles II. bestowed it on his natural son Charles Lennox, an infant, afterwards duke of Richmond, who resigned the office to the crown in 1703; after the union it was discontinued. The dignity of lord high admiral of Ireland (of brief existence) was conferred upon James Butler by Henry VIII. in May, 1534. *Admiral of the Fleet* is the highest rank in the royal navy, corresponding to field-marshal in the army. NAVY, of Great Britain.

admiral, United States. NAVY, U. S., 1864–66–91, etc.

Ad'miralty, Court of (English), a court for the trial of causes relating to maritime affairs, said to have been erected by Edward III. in 1357. The United States navy is controlled by the secretary of the navy, and admiralty jurisdiction is exercised by the circuit and district courts.

adoption controversy in Spain towards the close of the 8th century. The archbishop of Toledo, [illegible] dus, and the bishop of Urgel, Felix, maintained that [illegible] human nature was the son of God only by adoption. [illegible] recanted before a synod called by Charlemagne at Ratisbon, 792. The archbishop, however, secure in his see at Toledo, retained his views.

Ad'riano'ple, in Turkey, named for its restorer, emperor Hadrian (who died 10 July, 138). Near here Constant[illegible] defeated Licinius and gained the empire, 3 July, 323; and the emperor Valens was defeated and slain by the Goths, 9 Aug. 378. Adrianople was taken by the Turks, under Amurath, in 1361, and was their capital till the capture of Constantinople in 1453. It was taken by the Russians on 20 Aug. 1829, and restored 14 Sept. same year; occupied by the Russians, without resistance, 20 Jan. 1878. Pop. 1890, 150,000. TURKEY.

Adriatic. The annual ceremony of the doge of Venice wedding the Adriatic sea (instituted about 1173; first omitted, 1797) took place on Ascension day. The doge dropped a ring into the sea from his Bucentaur, or state barge, attended by his nobility and foreign ambassadors.

Adullam, a cave to which David fled from the persecution of Saul about 1062 B.C. (1 Sam. xxii. 1, 2). As a gathering place for "every one that was in distress," or "in debt," or "discontented," it has often been humorously alluded to, as by the baron of Bradwardine in "Waverley," chap. 57.

adultery was punished with death by the law of Moses (1490 B.C.; Lev. xx. 10), and by Lycurgus (884 B.C.). The early Saxons burned the adulteress and erected a gibbet over her ashes, whereon they hanged the adulterer. The ears and nose were cut off under Canute, 1031. Adultery was made capital by parliament, 14 May, 1650, but there is no record of this law taking effect, and it was repealed at the Restoration. In New England adultery was made capital to both parties, and several suffered for it, 1662.—*Hardie.* Till 1857 in Great Britain the legal redress against the man was by civil action for money compensation, the woman was liable to divorce. By 20 and 21 Vict. c. 85 (1857), the "action for criminal conversation" was abolished, and the Court for Divorce and Matrimonial Causes established with power to grant divorce for adultery and ill-usage. DIVORCE. An act was passed, 1869, permitting parties to give evidence. In the United States adultery is variously punished under state laws, usually by fine or imprisonment or both. It is also a cause for absolute divorce in nearly all the states.

Advent (*adventus*, arrival). The period of the approach of the Nativity. The season includes four Sundays, previous to Christmas, the first the nearest Sunday to St. Andrew's day (Nov. 30), before or after. Homilies respecting Advent are mentioned prior to 378, and it has been recognized since the 6th century as the commencement of the ecclesiastical year.

Adventists. An American sect who look for the early second coming of Christ, which is spoken of in the New Testament. It arose from the preaching of William Miller from 1833 to 18[illegible], when he predicted the coming. MILLERITES.

advertisements in newspapers were not general in England till the beginning of the 18th century. A penalty of 50*l.* was inflicted on persons advertising a reward for stolen goods with "No questions asked," and on the printer, 1754. The *advertisement duty* (first enacted 1712), formerly charged by lines, was afterwards fixed in England at 3*s.* 6*d.* and in Ireland at 2*s.* 6*d.* each advertisement. The duty (further reduced, in England to 1*s.* 6*d.* and in Ireland to [illegible] each; in 1833) was abolished in 1853.

Early advertisements are found in *Perfect Occurences of every Date*, 26 Mch. to 2 Apr. 1647, and *Mercurius Elencticus*, 4 Oct. 1648

The American system of advertising agencies was originated by Orlando Bourne in 1828, and was followed in 1840 by V. B. Palmer, who established agencies in Philadelphia, New York, and Boston. The system was vastly extended about 1860.

Æ'diles. Roman city officers of three degrees, named from their charge of the *ædes*, or temple, of Ceres. (1) Two plebeian ædiles were appointed with the tribunes to look after buildings, weights and measures, the supply of provisions and water, etc., 494 B.C. (2) The *ædiles curules*, at first patricians, were appointed 365 B.C. (3) Julius Cæsar appointed *ædiles cereales* for watching over the supply of corn. The ædiles became a police under the emperors.

Ædui or **Hedui,** a Celtic people, N. E. France, who were delivered from subjection to the Romans by Julius Cæsar, 58 B.C.; but afterwards, opposing him, were subjugated by him, 52. Their insurrection, headed by Julius Sacrovir, 21 A.D., was quelled by C. Silius.

Æga'tes Isles, west of Sicily; near these, during the first Punic war, the Roman consul C. Lutatius Catulus gained a decisive victory over the Carthaginian fleet under Hanno, 10 Mch. 241 B.C. Peace ensued, the Romans obtaining Sicily and a tribute of 3200 talents.

Ægi'na, a Greek island, rival of Athens, was humbled by Themistocles, 485 B.C., and its works destroyed, 455. Its inhabitants expelled, 431, were restored by Sparta, 404; they renewed war with Athens, 388, and made peace, 387.

Æne'id, the great Latin epic poem on the adventures of Æneas, written about 24 B.C. by Virgil (*Publius Vergilius Maro*), who died 22 Sept. 19 B.C., aged 51, leaving it unfinished. Was first printed in 1469 at Rome.

ænigma. Samson's riddle (about 1141 B.C.; Judg. xiv. 12) is the earliest on record. Gale attributes ænigmatical speeches to the Egyptians. The ancient oracles occasionally gave responses admitting of contrary interpretations. In Nero's time the Romans had recourse to this method of concealing truth. The following epitaph on Fair Rosamond (mistress of Henry II. of England, about 1173) is a mediæval specimen: "Hic jacet in tombâ Rosa mundi, non Rosa munda; Non redolet, sed olet, quæ redolere solet."

Æo'lia, in Asia Minor, was colonized by a principal branch of the Hellenic race about 1124 B.C. The Æolians built several large cities, both on the mainland and the neighboring islands; Mitylene, in Lesbos, was considered the capital.

Æolian Harp (from *Æolus*, god of the wind). A stringed instrument, upon which the wind produces musical sounds, first described by Kircher, about 1650.

æoli'na, a free-reed wind-instrument, invented by Wheatstone in 1829.

æol'opile, a hollow ball with an orifice in which a tube might be screwed, used in 17th century as a boiler for experimental steam-engines; a similar apparatus is described by Vitruvius, 1st century A.D.

Æqui, an ancient Italian race, inhabiting the upper valley of the Anio (now Teverone), a branch of the Tiber, were finally subdued by the Romans and their lands annexed, 302 B.C.

A'erated Waters. Apparatus for combining gases with water were patented by Thomson in 1807, F. C. Bakewell in 1832 and 1847, Tylor in 1840, and by others. BREAD.

Ae'rians, followers of Aerius, a presbyter in the 4th century, who held bishop and presbyter the same; that there was no Pasch to be observed by Christians; that Lent and other fasts should not be observed; and that no prayers be offered for the dead.—*Epiphanius.*

a'ërolites. METEORS.

a'ëronautics and **a'ërostatics.** BALLOONS and FLYING.

a'ërophore, an apparatus invented by M. Denayrouze to furnish pure air in the midst of smoke and fire. It comprises an air-pump, lamp, and flexible tubing. It was tried at Chatham, Eng., 12–14 Jan. 1875, and reported successful. A gold medal was awarded to the inventor at the Vienna Exhibition, 1873.

Æscula'pius, god of medicine; his worship introduced at Rome about 291 B.C.

Æsop's Fables. FABLES.

æsthet'ics (from Gr. αἴσθησις, perception), the science of the beautiful and sublime (especially in art); a term invented by Baumgarten, a German philosopher, whose work "Æsthetica" was published in 1750.

Æto'lia, in Greece, named for Ætolus of Elis, who is said to have accidentally killed a son of Phoroneus, king of Argos, left the Peloponnesus, and settled here. After the ruin of Athens and Sparta, the Ætolians became the rivals of the Achæans, and were alternately allies and enemies of Rome.

	B.C.
Ætolians join Sparta against Athens	455
Ætolian [illegible] tribes opposes Macedon	323
Invaded by Antipater during the Lamian war	322
Aid in [illegible] of the Gauls	279
Invade the Peloponnesus, ravage Messenia (Social war), and defeat the Achæans at Caphyæ	220

Philip V. of Macedon invades Ætolia, and takes Thermum; peace of Naupactus concluded........ 217
Alliance with Rome........ 211
Deserted by the Romans, the Ætolians make peace with Philip. 205
War with Philip, 200; he is defeated at Cynoscephalæ........ 197
Ætolians invite the kings of Macedon, Syria, and Sparta to coalesce against the Romans........ 193–92
Defeat of the allies near Thermopylæ........ 191
Conquered by the Romans under Fulvius........ 189
Leading patriots massacred by the Roman party........ 167
Ætolia made a province of Rome........ 146
Theodorus Angelus, a noble Grecian, seizes Ætolia and Epirus. He leaves Ætolia to his son Michael, who maintains it against Michael Palæologus, first emperor of the Greeks after the expulsion of the Latins from Constantinople........ A.D. 1260
Seized by the Turks........ 1432
Turks driven out by George Castriot (Scanderbeg), who with a small army withstands the whole Ottoman power...... 1450–67
[The Venetians in possession at his death.]
Turks again in possession........ 1478
[Now included in the Kingdom of Greece.]

affinity. Marriage within certain degrees of kindred has been prohibited almost universally, but has often taken place. The Jewish law is given in Lev. xviii. (1490 B.C.). In the English prayer-book the table restricting marriage within certain degrees was set forth by authority, 1563. Prohibited marriages were made incestuous and unlawful by the 99th canon in 1603. All marriages within forbidden degrees are declared void by 5 and 6 Will. IV. c. 54, 1835. MARRIAGE (of Wife's Sister). These degrees were set forth in 25 Henry VIII. c. 22, 1533–34.

affirmation. QUAKERS. The affirmation was altered in 1702, 1721, 1837, and in Apr. 1859.—The indulgence was granted to persons formerly Quakers, who had seceded from that sect, 2 Vict. 1838; and extended to other dissenters by 9 Geo. IV. c. 32, 1828, and 18 and 19 Vict. c. 2, 1855. For Mr. Bradlaugh's case, see PARLIAMENT, 1880–81.

Afghanistan′, a mountainous country in Central Asia reaching from Beloochistan northward to the Oxus; and from the frontier of Persia on the west to the Punjab on the east; in each direction about 500 miles; with a population of about ,000,000. The chief cities are Cabool, *the capital, to the east*, Herat in the west, Kandahar in the south, and Balkh in the north. There is no unity or permanence in the government. The several districts, although nominally under one head, "the ameer," have their petty rulers, called "sirdars," each governing in his own fashion.

Early Afghan conquests in India........ 1200–90
Conquests *by Genghis Khan about 1221, and by Tamerlane*.... 1398
Baber conquered Cabool........ 1525
[On his death Afghanistan divided between Persia and Hindostan.]
Afghans revolt in 1720; invade Persia and take Ispahan; repulsed by Nadir Shah in 1728, who subdues the whole of the country........ 1738
On his assassination, one of his officers, Ahmed Shah, an Afghan, made Afghanistan independent........ 1747
Timur Shah succeeds, 1773; dies........ 1793
Zeman becomes ameer; dethroned........ 1800
Mahmud Shah, son, ameer, 1800; deposed by his brother, 1803; restored, 1809; flees from Cabool and becomes ruler at Herat. 1816
Dost Mahomed Khan becomes ameer........ 1826
Is dethroned by the British and sent to Calcutta; Suja Shah restored........ 1838
British occupation of Cabool; insurrection; sir Alexander Burnes and 23 others killed........2 Nov. 1841
Akbar Khan, son of Dost Mahomed, head of rebels; invites sir Wm. Macnaghten to meet, and assassinates him and others. 23 Dec. "
British army leaving Cabool is massacred by Ghilzais in Khyber pass; of 3849 soldiers and about 12,000 camp-followers only Dr. Brydone and four or five natives escape...6–13 Jan. 1842
Sir George Pollock forces Khyber pass; defeats Akbar Khan at Tezeen; captures Cabool and releases lady Sale and others, 16 Sept.; retires........12 Oct. "
Dost Mahomed ameer........ "
He dies, appointing Shere Ali, his third son, to succeed..9 June, 1863
Shere Ali honorably received at Umballah by viceroy of India, earl of Mayo, and receives a subsidy........27 Mch. *et seq.* 1869
Limits of his territory defined........June, 1870
Shere Ali agrees to new boundaries and receives another British subsidy........Oct. 1873
Shere Ali rejects a British resident; subsidy withheld; he raises an army........ 1877–78
The ameer signs a treaty with Russia, accepting Russian protectorate........Aug. 1878
Intercourse with the British declined........Sept. "
Mission with military escort under sir Neville B. Chamberlain, commander of Madras army, starts from Peshawur..21 Sept. "
Forced to retire in the Khyber pass........24 Sept. "
British send an ultimatum (answer required before Nov. 20), 28 Oct. "

British army formed in three divisions: at Quettah, ..., and Kuram (34,730 natives; 12,740 Europeans)..about 6 Nov. 1878
British army advances, 21 Nov.; gen. Roberts victorious at Peiwar pass, 2 Dec; and occupies Jellalabad........20 Dec. "
Shere Ali flees from Cabool to Balkh, 13 Dec.; Yakoob Khan, son of the ameer, assumes command; Russian mission withdraws........Dec. "
Gen. Roberts proclaims annexation of Kuram........26 Dec. "
Candahar abandoned 6 Jan.; entered by gen. Stewart unopposed........7 Jan. 1879
Death of Shere Ali........20 Feb. "
Yakoob Khan, son of late ameer, arrives at Gandamak to negotiate 8 May; recognized as ameer........9 May, "
Peace signed at Gandamak (British to occupy Khyber pass and Kuram and Pisheen valleys; to have resident at Cabool; and pay annual subsidy of 60,000*l.* to ameer), 26 May; ratified 30 May; British troops retire........8 June, "
Sir Louis Cavagnari and escort honorably received at Cabool, 24 July, "
Several regiments of Afghan soldiers arrive in Cabool from Herat about 13 Aug., aided by populace, they besiege British residents, who, after brave resistance, are massacred (including sir L. Cavagnari........3, 4 Sept.
Gen. Roberts marches towards Cabool........6 Sept. *et seq.*
Gen. Baker reaches Kushi, 24 Sept.; receives ameer Yakoob with son, gen. Daoud, and suite........27 Sept.
Gen. Roberts arrives at Cabool, 28 Sept.; occupies Dakka, 29 Sept.
Battle of Charasiab with Afghans before Cabool; about 7 killed and wounded........6 Oct.
Enemy decamps; about 98 guns abandoned........8, 9 Oct.
Gen. Roberts visits the abandoned Bala Hissar, 11 Oct.; enters Cabool, 12 Oct.; Jellalabad occupied by Gough........14
Gen. Roberts's proclamation; heavy fine; martial law; Hills to be military governor, with Gholam Hussein K. 14
Proclamation of gen. Roberts announcing British occupation of Cabool, etc........30 Oct. "
Gen. Roberts concentrates forces in Sherpur cantonments, 14 Dec. "
Afghans (25,000) defeated with great loss near Sherpur cantonments, by gens. Roberts and Gough........23 Dec. "
Cabool left by the enemy, 24 Dec.; the city and Bala Hissar reoccupied by the British........26 Dec. "
Enemy dispersed........28 Dec. "
Gen. Roberts proclaims amnesty with few exceptions; hill tribes generally subdued........about 6 Jan. 1880
Sir D. Stewart takes chief command at Cabool........2 May, "
Gen. Burrows (with about 2400 men) sent from Bombay towards Candahar........1 July, "
Abdur-Rahman, cousin of Ayoob Khan, recognized as ameer at Cabool by the British, and proclaimed........22 July, "
Ayoob Khan (son of the late ameer Shere Ali), governor of Herat, marches upon Candahar with about 12,000 men and 20 guns; repulses gen. Burrows with heavy loss on both sides; many officers of 66th regiment killed........27 July, "
Candahar citadel held by about 4000 British........28 July, "
Ayoob encamped at Kokaran........9 Aug. "
Gen. sir F. Roberts with about 10,000 men, etc., marches from Cabool to relieve Candahar........9 Aug. "
Sir D. Stewart, after interview with ameer Abdur-Rahman, withdraws troops from Cabool........11 Aug. "
Ineffectual sortie from Candahar, under gen. Primrose, against Deh Kwajee village; heavy loss on both sides; several officers, among them gen. Brooke, and 180 men killed..16 Aug. "
Ayoob Khan's army (strengthened by Ghilzais) 20,000 about 25 Aug.; retires from Candahar........about 30 Aug. "
Gen. Roberts arrives at Candahar, 31 Aug.; declines Ayoob's terms; disperses his army at Mazra near the Argundab; captures camp at Baba Wali Kotal........1 Sept. "
Alleged expenses of the war, 1878–80, 16,605,000*l.*........Jan. 1881
Russian correspondence with ameer Shere Ali in 1878 published; explained by Russia as relating to probable war in the East........9, 10 Feb. "
Thanks of parliament to gen. Roberts and army........5 May, "
Prospect of war between Ayoob Khan of Herat and Abdur-Rahman of Cabool........May, June, "
Ayoob Khan defeats ameer's army under Gholam-Hyder at Karez-i-atta, 26 July; enters Candahar........30 July, "
Ameer Abdur-Rahman defeats Ayoob Khan and drives him into Persia........4 Oct. "
Abdur-Rahman virtual ruler of all Afghanistan........Oct. "
Ameer accepts subsidy from British Indian government, 21 July, 1883
Ameer accepts proposal of a frontier commission........Aug. 1884
Ameer meets lord Dufferin, viceroy of India, at Rawul Pindi, 2 Apr.; declares at a grand durbar that England and Afghanistan will stand side by side, 8 Apr.; leaves.....12 Apr. 1885
Ayoob Khan again advances from Persia; is defeated; surrenders to the English and is removed to India........ 1887
Ameer suppresses a revolt of the Ghilzai........ "
Another insurrection under Ishak Khan suppressed........ 1888
Ameer, a vigorous ruler, supported by the government of India "
Joint Anglo-Russian Boundary Commissioners determine boundary between Russian territory and Afghanistan.4 Feb. "
Central Asia railroad finished to Samarcand, and opened by the Russian government........July, "
[Total cost of the line, 43,000,000 rubles; *distance from* the Caspian sea to Samarcand, 900 miles.]
Great Britain disputes with Russia respecting the PAMIR frontier........Sept.–Oct. 1891

Afric[illegible] [illegible]**e Greeks) is the vast southwestern peninsula of the Old World, connected with Asia by the narrow isthmus of Suez. It is triangular in form, with its base to the north. The Mediterranean lies on the north, the Red sea and Indian ocean on the east, and the Atlantic on the west. From Ras-el-Kerun, its most northerly point, to cape Agulhas, its most southerly point, is about 5000 miles, and from cape Guardafui on the east to cape Verde on the west it is 4600. Area about 12,000,000 square miles; said to have been first peopled by Ham. For its history, see ABYSSINIA, ALGIERS, ASHANTEE, CAPE OF GOOD HOPE, CARTHAGE, CYRENE, CONGO FREE STATE, EGYPT, LIBERIA, MOROCCO, SAHARA, [illegible]N, SOUTH AFRICA, ZAMBESIA, GERMAN EAST and WEST AFRICA, etc.**

[illegible] ope discovered by Diaz, 148[illegible].
[illegible] doubles the cape and explores the c[illegible] [illegible].
[illegible] ements begun, 1450.
[illegible] nts visit Guinea, 1550; Elizabeth grants a patent to [illegible] mpany, 1588.
[illegible] the cape founded, 1650.
[illegible] led up the Gambia, 1723.
[illegible] ed his travels in 1768. NILE.
[illegible] settled by the English, 1787.
[illegible] ed to Africa, 22 May, 1795; again, 30 Jan. 1804, and [illegible]. PARK.
[illegible] Salt, 1805 and 1809; Burckhardt, 1812; Campbell, [illegible]ann, 1816; Denham, Clapperton, and Dr. Oudray, [illegible] cross the Great Desert south to lake TCHAD.
[illegible] by American philanthropists, 1822 (LIBERIA), [illegible]ions, 1826; the brothers Lander, 1830.
[illegible] to colonize central Africa (for which the English [illegible] ed 60,000*l.*), consisting of the *Albert*, *Wilberforce*, [illegible] steamships, began ascent of the Niger, 20 Aug. 1841. [illegible] was abandoned owing to disease, heat, and hard[illegible] the vessels returned and cast anchor at Clarence [illegible] Po, 17 Oct. 1841.
[illegible] explored the SAHARA in 1845-46, and in 1849 (by direction of Foreign Office) he left England to explore central Africa with Drs. Barth and Overweg. He died 4 Mch. 1851; Overweg died 27 Sept. 1852.
Dr. Vogel sent out with reinforcements to Dr. Barth, 20 Feb. 1853; in Apr. 1857, said to have been assassinated.
Dr. Barth returning to England, received Royal Geographical Society's medal, [illegible] May, 1856. His travels were published in 5 vols. [illegible].
Dr. David Livingstone, a missionary, returned to England in Dec. 1856, after 16 years of travel, mostly on foot, in the heart of south Africa. He walked about 11,000 miles, principally over country hitherto unexplored. His book was published in Nov. 1857. In Feb. 1858, he was appointed British consul for Portuguese possessions in Africa, and left England soon after.
Du Chaillu's travels in central Africa, 1856-59, excited much controversy, 1861.
Second expedition of Dr. Livingstone, Mch. 1858.
Capt. John H. Speke, [illegible] 1858.
Capts. Speke and Grant announce the discovery of a source of the Nile in lake Victoria Nyanza, 23 Feb. 1863. They also discover Albert Nyanza, 140 miles long and 40 broad.
Du Chaillu starts on a fresh expedition, 6 Aug. 1863; returned to London late in 1865. He described his journey to the Royal Geographical Society, 8 Jan. 1866.
Livingstone returns 23 July, 1864.
Death of Dr. W. B. Baikie, at Sierra Leone, 30 Nov. 1864. [As special envoy to negro tribes near the Niger from the Foreign Office, about 1854, he opened commercial relations with central Africa.]
Sir Samuel Baker visits the lake discovered by Speke, and called it lake Albert Nyanza, 14 Mch. 1864.
Livingstone British consul for inner Africa, 24 Mch. 1865.
Narrative of Livingstone's Zambesi expedition, 1858-64, published 1866.
Livingstone left Zanzibar to continue his search for the sources of the Nile, Mch. 1866.
Expedition of E. D. Young in search of Livingstone, sailed 9 July, 1867; returning, reported to Royal Geographical Society belief that Livingstone was alive, 27 Jan. 1868.
Letter from Dr. Livingstone dated Bembo, 2 Mch. 1867; heard of down to Dec. 1867.
His despatch to lord Clarendon dated 7 July, 1868; read to Royal Geographical Society, 8 Nov. 1869.
Letter dated 30 May, 1869, published Dec. 1869.
Expedition of sir Samuel Baker to suppress slave-trade on the Upper Nile (Kover), Jan. 1870.
Expedition to seek Livingstone, under lieut. Dawson, organized by Royal Geographical Society; started 9 Feb. 1872.
[Returned hearing that Stanley had found Livingstone.]
Dutch Guinea settlements purchased and transferred (ELMINA), 6 Apr. 1872.
Expedition to seek Livingstone sent by James Gordon Bennett of the *New York Herald*, at a cost of 8000*l.*
Henry M. Stanley, chief of expedition, left Zanzibar, found Livingstone at Ujiji, near Unyanyembe, 10 Nov. 1871, remained with him till 14 Mch. 1872, and brought away his diary and other documents. Stanley reported Livingstone at Ujiji.
Reports that Livingstone is alive, May, June, 1872.
Controversy between Stanley, members of lieut. Dawson's expedition, Dr. Livingstone, Dr. Kirk, the Royal Geographical Society, and others, Aug.-Oct. 1872.
Letter from Dr. Livingstone at Ujiji, dated Nov. 1871, to Mr. Bennett (*New York Herald*, 26 July, reprinted in *Times*, 27 July, 1872), describes his explorations and painful journey to Ujiji; meeting Stanley; he speaks of the Nile springs as about 600 miles south of south end of lake Victoria Nyanza; and of about 700 miles of water-shed in central Africa, of which he had explored about 600; and of waters gathered into four, and then into two, mighty rivers in the great Nile valley (?) between 10° and 12° S. lat. Second letter (dated Feb. 1872) describes horrors of slave-trade in east Africa, printed in *Times* 29 July, 1872.
Livingstone's despatches of 1 and 15 Nov. 1871, received by Foreign Office, 1 Aug. 1872; letter of 1 July, 1871, received 2 Oct. 1872.
Stanley described discovery of Livingstone to British Association at Brighton before ex-emperor and ex-empress of the French, 16 Aug.; received a gold snuff-box from queen about 30 Aug. 1872.
New expedition, under sir Bartle Frere, to Zanzibar, to suppress east African slave-trade; lieut. Verney Lovett Cameron's offer to aid Livingstone's expedition was accepted; sailed 20 Nov. 1872. ZANZIBAR.
Expedition to explore upper part of Congo (Mr. Young of Kelly to subscribe 2000*l.*, Royal Geographical Society to aid) proposed Nov. 1872.
Lieut. Verney Cameron, after the finding of Livingstone, continued his explorations, 1872-73.
Livingstone died of dysentery in Ilala, central Africa (his pupil Jacob Wainwright, a young negro missionary, present), 1 May, 1873, aged 60; remains interred in Westminster Abbey, 18 Apr. 1874; last journals published Dec. 1874.
Leaving Ujiji, 14 May, 1874, Cameron followed Livingstone's route; explored 1200 miles of fertile country, arriving at Portuguese settlements, 4 Nov. 1875.
He was received by Royal Geographical Society, and gave account of his journey, 11 Apr. 1876.
Stanley (supported by *Daily Telegraph* and *New York Herald*) surveyed lake Victoria Nyanza (about 300 miles by 180), 1875.
Stanley reports survey of lake Tanganyika; he left Ujiji, crossed Africa from east to west, identified the Lualaba with Congo river, which has an uninterrupted course of over 1400 miles, 24 Aug. 1876-6 Aug. 1877.
Arrives at Cape Town, 21 Oct. 1877; in London, 22 Jan. 1878; published "Through the Dark Continent," May, 1878.
Italian expedition of marchese Antinori well received by king of Scioa; announced 2 Dec. 1876; his death reported, Nov. 1877.
Portuguese government grants 20,000*l.* for expedition into the interior, announced Dec. 1876.
Dr. Güssfeld, a German, entered southwest central Africa, 1873; declared difficulties insuperable, 1875.
Portuguese government send major Serpa Pinto through Africa; discovers affluents of the Zambesi, 1877.
Stanley, with an international Belgian expedition, explored the Congo, 1879-80.
Royal Geographical Society's expedition into east Africa, under Mr. A. Keith Johnston, leaves England 14 Nov. 1878; starts from Zanzibar about 14 May, 1879. Mr. Johnston dies 28 June; succeeded by Joseph Thomson, who returns to England, Aug. 1880.
Trade route with 4 stations on the Congo reported established by Stanley, 14 Aug. 1882.
Royal Geographical Society grants 2500*l.* for an expedition to Africa; Joseph Thomson starts 13 Dec. 1882; after successful exploration arrives at Zanzibar in June, 1884; describes his travels to the Royal Geographical Society, 3 Nov. 1884.
Death of Dr. Moffat, missionary and traveller, aged 87, 9 Aug. 1883.
H. H. Johnston arrives at Kilimanjaro, June, 1884; builds village at height of 11,000 feet, Oct.; ascends to 16,200 feet from summit of Kibō, Nov. 1884.
Stanley's "Explorations of the Congo and Founding of its Free State" published by Harper & Bros., 1885.
Emin Pasha, associate of gen. Gordon, holds Wadelai as governor of equatorial Africa since 1878 with black troops; news brought by Dr. Junker, who reports to Royal Geographical Society his travels in central Africa in 1885-86, 9 May, 1887.
Expedition of Stanley on behalf of the Emin Pasha Committee starts from London, 21 Jan. 1887.

[They embarked with natives at Zanzibar for the west coast, 25 Feb., and sailed up the Congo. After danger and suffering through famine, disease, and native opposition, Stanley met Emin Pasha on lake Nyanza, 29 Apr. 1888; and with him and remains of his party arrived at the German station Bogamoya, 5 Dec. 1889. During this expedition Stanley makes important discoveries—locating the "Mountains of the Moon," the race of pigmies, and discovers lake Albert Edward Nyanza, 16 June, 1889. He and his officers (except maj. Barttelot, killed by one of his carriers, 19 July, 1888) arrived at Cairo, 14 Jan. 1890; at Rome, 11 Apr.; at Brussels, 19 Apr.; in London, 26 Apr.; dined with the queen, 6 May; with his companions, lieut. Stairs, surgeon Thomas H. Parke, capt. Nelson, A. M. Jephson, and Bonny, received gold medals of the Royal Geographical Society, from the prince of Wales, 5 May. He received the freedom of the city of London, 13 May; of Edinburgh, 11 June; and of Glasgow, Dundee, Aberdeen, Newcastle-on-Tyne, and Manchester, in June. His book, entitled "In Darkest Africa; or, the Quest, Rescue, and Retreat of Emin, governor of Equatoria," was published 28 June. He married Miss Dorothy Tennant at Westminster Abbey, 12 July, 1890.]

Emin Pasha, after a long illness occasioned by a fall from a veranda at Bogamoya, 5 Dec. 1889, arrives at Zanzibar, 2 Mch. 1890. Enters the German service, and proceeds with a military expedition to Victoria Nyanza, 31 Mch. 1890.
Maj. Gaetani Casati, born in 1838; left Italy for Africa, Dec. 1879; at

Khartoum, May, 1880, with Emin Pasha 1883–89, received by the khedive at Cairo, 4 May, 1890, by the king of Italy 17 July His book, "Ten Years in Equatoria—the return with Emin Pasha," published Mch. 1891

The principal nations of Europe claim enormous possessions in Africa, which may be said to be divided among them British Africa comprises British Guinea, British South Africa, British East Africa with an area of 2,570,926 square miles, and a population of over 40,000,000 French Africa comprises most of the Mediterranean coast, Sahara, western Soudan, French Congo, island of Madagascar, with an area of 2,902,621 square miles, and a population of 24,000,000 Portuguese Africa, East and West Africa and islands, area, 850,000 square miles Spanish Africa, northwestern coast, area, 204,000 square miles. German Africa, East and Southwest Africa, area, 822,000 square miles Italian Africa, Abyssinia, Somal, Galla, etc, area, 602,000 square miles Turkish Africa, Egypt and Tripoli, area, 866,000 square miles ANGLO-FRENCH AGREEMENTS, SOUTH AFRICAN WAR, etc.

Agamen'ticus, now York county, Maine, settled by the English, 1636 MAINE

agapæ (*ag'-a-pē*, Gr ἀγάπη, love charity), "feasts of charity," referred to Jude 12, and described by Tertullian, held by early Christians of all ranks as one family Disorders creeping in, these feasts were forbidden in churches by the councils of Laodicea (366) and Carthage (390) They are still recognized by the Greek church and are held weekly by the Glasites or Sandemanians, and in a modified form by Moravians, Wesleyans, Methodists and others

Agapemone (*ag-a-pem'-ō-ne*, Greek, the abode of love), an establishment at Charlinch, near Bridgewater, Somersetshire, founded in 1845, where Henry James Prince and his deluded followers formerly persons of property, lived in common, professing to seek innocent recreation and to maintain spiritual marriage It is described by Mr Hepworth Dixon in his "Spiritual Wives," published in Jan 1868 Meetings of the sect were held at Hamp near Bridgewater, Dec 1872

Ag'awam, Indian name of Ipswich, Mass, settled by colonists from Boston, 1633 Incorporated as Ipswich, 1634

Age. Annalists have divided the time between the creation and the birth of Christ into ages. Hesiod (about 850 B.C.) described the Golden, Silver, Brazen, and Iron ages. DARK AGES

	B C
FIRST AGE (from the Creation to the Deluge)	4004–2349
SECOND AGE (to Abraham's entrance into Canaan)	2348–1922
THIRD AGE (to the Exodus from Egypt)	1921–1491
FOURTH AGE (to the founding of Solomon's Temple)	1490–1015
FIFTH AGE (to the capture of Jerusalem)	1014–588
SIXTH AGE (to the birth of Christ)	586–4
SEVENTH AGE, to the present time	

age. In Greece and Rome 25 was full age for both sexes, but a greater age was requisite for holding certain offices—*e.g* 30 for tribunes, 43 for consuls In England the minority of a male terminates at 21, and of a female in some cases, as that of a queen, at 18 In 1547, the majority of Edward VI was, by the will of his father, fixed at 18 years, his father, Henry VIII, had assumed the reins of government in 1509, when still younger. A *male* at 12 may take the oath of allegiance, at 14 may consent to marriage or choose a guardian, at 17 may be an executor, and at 21 is of age, but according to the statute of wills, 7 Will IV and 1 Vict c 26, 1837, no will made under the age of 21 is valid A *female* at 12 may consent to marriage, at 14 may choose a guardian, and at 21 is of age In the United States the legal age of majority is 21 years, but in some states 18 is the legal age for women Men of 18 and women of 16 may devise property by will, and at 14 and 12, respectively, in some states, may contract marriage The president and vice president of the United States must be 35 years of age, senators 30, and members of the House of Representatives 25

"Age of Reason," by Thomas Paine (b England, 1737, d. New York, 1809), written while in France, 1792–94, a work at that time celebrated for freedom of thought "CRISIS" and "COMMON SENSE"

Aghrim (*awg-rim'*), a small village in Galway, Ireland, where the forces of William III, under gen Ginkell, defeated those of James II, under St Ruth, numbering 25,000, 12 July, 1691, and broke the power of James in Ireland St Ruth was killed Gen Ginkell was created earl of Athlone

Agincourt (*a-zhang-koor'*) or **Azincour,** N France, a village where Henry V of England, with about 9000 men, defeated about 60,000 French on St Crispin's day, 25 Oct 1415 Of the French there were, according to some accounts, 10,000 killed, including the dukes of Alençon, Brabant and Bar, the archbishop of Sens, 1 marshal, 13 earls, 92 barons, and 1500 knights, and 14,000 prisoners were taken among whom were the dukes of Orleans and Bourbon, and 7000 barons, knights, and gentlemen The English lost the duke of York, the earl of Suffolk, and about 20 others St Remy asserts, with more probability, that the English lost 1600 men Henry V soon after obtained the kingdom of France

Agnadello (*an-ya-del'-lo*), N E Italy Here Louis XII of France routed the Venetians some of whom were accused of cowardice and treachery, 14 May, 1509 This is also termed the battle of the Rivolta

agnoi'tæ (Gr ἀγνοία, ignorance), a sect founded by Theophronius of Cappadocia about 370, said to have doubted the omniscience of God (2) Followers of Themistius of Alexandria, about 530, who held peculiar views of Christ's body and doubted his divinity

agnostics, philosophers who deny all knowledge but that acquired by the senses COMTE, PHILOSOPHY

agonis'tici (Gr ἀγών, a conflict) were African ascetics, a branch of the DONATISTS in the 4th century They preached with boldness and incurred persecution

A'gra, N W India, founded by Akbar in 1566 was the capital of the great Mogul MAUSOLEUMS In 1658 Aurungzebe removed to Delhi The fortress of Agra, "the key of Hindostan," in the war with the Mahrattas surrendered to the British, under gen Lake, 17 Oct 1803, after one day's siege 162 pieces of ordnance and 240,000*l* were captured 11 June, 1857, the city was abandoned to mutineers by the Europeans, who took refuge in the fort, whence they were rescued by maj Montgomery and col Greathed Allahabad was made capital of the northwest provinces of India, instead of Agra, in 1861

A'gram. ZAGRAB

agrarian law (*Agraria lex*) decreed an equal division among the Roman people of all lands acquired by conquest, limiting the possessions of each person It was first proposed by the consul Spurius Cassius, 486 B C, and occasioned his judicial murder when he went out of office in 485 An agrarian law was passed by the tribune Licinius Stolo, 370, and for demanding extensions Tiberius Gracchus in 133, and his brother Caius [illegible] Livius Drusus, a tribune, was murdered for a like cause 91 Julius Cæsar propitiated the plebeians by an agrarian law in 59 In modern times the term has been applied to a division of the lands of the rich among the poor, frequently proposed by demagogues, such as *Gracchus* Babeuf, editor of the *Tribun du Peuple*, in 1794. BABEUF CONSPIRACY.

agriculture. Cain and Noah were agriculturists, Gen iv 2, ix 21 The Egyptians were from the first an agricultural people The Babylonians, Romans, and Israelites were also great agricultural nations of antiquity

Cato the censor (died 149 B C) and Varro (died 28 B C) were eminent Roman writers on agriculture.

Virgil's "Georgics" 30 B C Agriculture in England improved by the Romans after 44 A D

Fitzherbert's "Book of Husbandry," printed 1524

Tusser's "Five Hundred Points of Husbandry," 1562

Googe's "Whole Art of Husbandry," 1578

Blythe's "Improver," 1649

Hartlib's "Legacy" 1650

Mortimer's "Whole Art of Husbandry," 1706

Jethro Tull's "Horse hoeing Husbandry," 1731

Arthur Young's "Agricultural Works," 1783–86

Dickson's "Practical Agriculture or Complete System of Modern Husbandry," 1805

Neither Indian corn, potatoes, squash, carrots, cabbage nor turnips were known in England until after the beginning of the 16th century

About the end of the 18th century fallowing was gradually superseded by turnips and green crops

"History of Agriculture and Prices in England (1259–1400)," by James T Rogers, pub 1866

AGRICULTURAL SOCIETIES —The first mentioned in Great Britain was the Society of Improvers of Agriculture in Scotland instituted in 1723 A Dublin agricultural society (1749) stimulated agriculture in Ireland, its origin is attributed to Mr Prior of Rathdowney, Queen's county in 1731 The Bath and West of England Society established 1777, and the Highland Society of Scotland, 1793. County agricultural societies are now numerous

London Board of Agriculture established by parliament, 1793.

Royal Agricultural Society of England established in 1838 by the chief landed proprietors; incorporated by royal charter, 26 Mch. 1840; holds two meetings annually—one in London, the other in the country; awards prizes, and publishes a valuable journal.

Royal Agricultural Society of Ireland instituted, 1841.

"Chambers of Agriculture" were established in France in 1851. In Great Britain, 1868, they had increased from 36 to 70. A journal commenced early in 1868.

Royal Agricultural College at Cirencester chartered, 1845.

Suffolk Agricultural College at Bury St. Edmunds opened, 1874. Other colleges opened.

Royal Agricultural Benevolent Institution.—It relieves farmers and their widows and orphans; founded chiefly by Mr. Mechi, 1860.

Agricultural returns of Great Britain were issued for the first time by the newly constituted Agricultural Department, 1883. Second return presented 27 Oct. 1884, and continued annually.

Board of agriculture established at Paris, 1889; at Vienna, 2 Sept. 1890; and at The Hague, 7 Sept. 1891.

AGRICULTURAL STATISTICS OF FOREIGN COUNTRIES.—CROPS.

	Wheat (bu.).	Barley (bu.).	Oats (bu.).	Rye (bu.).	Maize (bu.).	Potatoes.	Hay (tons).
Austria, 1890	42,701,285	52,766,395	101,009,177		18,628,940	162,042,311 cwt.	11,357,953
Belgium "	18,969,500	3,978,018	29,639,219	19,087,750		54,687,470 cwt.	5,830,223
Denmark "	3,910,302	22,980,283	35,665,185	16,207,205		11,956,274 bu.	649,300
France "	321,518,670	47,182,492	257,497,070	66,468,372	23,080,788	217,247,479 cwt.	20,823,768
Germany "	55,710,252	44,984,680	96,691,527	115,472,499		458,923,630 bu.	24,561,252
Holland, 1887	6,677,421	5,076,833	11,750,183	13,349,911		74,393,368 bu.	
Hungary, 1890	143,453,475	51,278,549	51,635,589	48,632,463	87,132,554	81,826,253 bu.	6,578,040
Italy, 1890	127,380,000	10,623,250	18,425,000	4,200,000	72,649,500	11,877,943 cwt.	17,144,660
Sweden, 1890	3,834,050	15,599,100	70,840,275	21,579,525		33,914,375 bu.	1,805,500
Russia in Europe, 1890	206,329,430	158,077,228	523,996,203	652,389,089	23,476,399	320,565,621 bu.	
Great Britain and Ireland, 1891	72,127,263	72,129,095	112,386,261			6,090,047 tons	12,671,447

AGRICULTURAL STATISTICS OF FOREIGN COUNTRIES.—LIVE-STOCK.

	Horses.	Milch Cows.	Other Cattle.	Sheep.	Swine.
Austria, 1890	1,548,197	4,254,303	4,389,633	3,186,787	3,549,700
Belgium, 1880	271,974	796,178	586,637	365,400	646,375
Denmark, 1888	375,533	954,250	505,277	1,225,196	770,785
France, 1890	2,862,273	6,509,325	7,053,360	21,658,416	6,017,238
Germany, 1883	3,522,545	9,087,293	6,699,471	19,189,715	9,206,195
Holland, 1887	274,300	907,200	618,400	804,300	490,254
Hungary, 1884	1,748,859	1,752,406	3,126,632	10,594,831	4,803,639
Italy, 1890	720,000	1,864,827	2,918,400	6,900,000	1,800,000
Sweden, 1889	479,992	1,542,281	789,152	1,338,193	621,635
		Cattle.			
Russia in Europe, 1888	19,663,336	24,609,264		44,465,454	9,242,997
Great Britain and Ireland, 1891	2,026,170	11,343,686		33,533,988	4,272,764

In 1890 there were in Italy 800,000 mules and 1,000,000 asses.

Agriculture in the United States.

Cattle first brought to America by Columbus in his second voyage, 1493.

Swine brought into the territory of southern U. S. by De Soto, 1538.

First slave-labor in this territory at the founding of St. Augustine, 1565.

Tobacco carried to England from America by Raleigh, 1586. Potatoes introduced into England from America, 1586, by Raleigh.

Wheat, barley, rye, and oats introduced into the United States by the earliest settlers, 1607–20; buckwheat by Swedes and Dutch.

First cattle and swine brought to Massachusetts, 1624.

Hops first introduced about 1628.

First horses in Massachusetts, 1629–30.

First apples picked in the colonies in Boston, 1639.

Jared Eliot, a clergyman of Connecticut, published valuable essays on agriculture, 1747.

New Jersey first in wheat production of the colonies, 1750.

Sugar-cane brought into Louisiana, 1751.

First improved cattle brought to the United States, 1783.

South Carolina and Philadelphia agricultural societies founded, 1784.

New York State Agricultural Society founded, 26 Feb. 1791. Robert R. Livingston, first president. Incorporated, 1798.

Massachusetts Agricultural Society established, 1792.

[Most states have them now, and issue annual reports.]

First cotton (8 bales) sent from United States to England, and seized by custom-house on the ground that the United States cannot have produced so much, 1784.

First recorded United States thresher patent, 1791.

Whitney's cotton-gin invented, 1793.

First cast-iron plough patent to Newbold of New Jersey, 1797.

Jefferson investigates scientifically the mould-board question, 1798.

First agricultural exhibition in the United States at Georgetown, D.C., 10 May, 1810.

Plough patent to Jethro Wood of Scipio, N. Y., issued, 1810–19.

The American Farmer, oldest agricultural paper in the United States, pub. Baltimore, 1819.

The State Board of Agriculture for New York established at Albany, 1819.

American Institute of Agriculture, New York, incorporated, 1829.

First useful mowing-machine (Manning's) patented in the United States, 1831.

First useful reaper patents in the United States (Schnebley's and Hussey's, both of Maryland) granted, 1833.

E. C. Bellinger of South Carolina obtains a patent for a steam plough, 1833.

Guano begins to come into use about 1840.

The American Agriculturist, Geo. Peter, publisher, New York, first issue. Apr. 1842.

Pennsylvania the first state in the production of wheat; yield, 15,000,000 bushels, 1850.

Yale College Agricultural Department established, 1852.

World's Fair, New York, promotes use of agricultural machinery, 1853.

Sorghum introduced into France from China, 1851, and from France into the United States, 1854.

Trial of threshing, reaping, and mowing machines in France—American machines preëminent, 1855.

Ohio first state in the production of wheat, 1855.

First agricultural college established in the United States at Cleveland, Ohio, 1855.

One at Lansing, Mich., 1857.

Illinois first state in the production of wheat, 1860.

Agricultural college established at Bellefonte, Centre county, Pa., 1862.

Agricultural college act passed by congress; granting to the several states 30,000 acres of land for each senator and representative in congress under the apportionment of 1860, to endow at least one college, 1862. EDUCATION.

Department of Agriculture established by congress, 15 May, 1862, under a commissioner of agriculture.

Organization of the Grangers (an association of farmers to protect their interests), 1867.

Farmer's Bulletin, published to notify farmers of weather changes, 1872.

Poultry World, first published, 1873.

Great sale of short-horned *neat cattle* at New York Mills, 1873.

[Cow sold for $4600; a five-months calf for $2700; and 109 animals for $382,000, or $3587 each.]

Connecticut establishes the first agricultural experiment station at Sheffield Scientific School; first report published, 1877.

[Most of the states now have them.]

First great cotton fair at Atlanta, Ga., 1881.

Department of Agriculture created an executive department, 21 May, 1888; approved, 11 Feb. 1889.

[The secretary of this department a member of the cabinet.]

North and South Dakota the first states in the production of wheat, 1890.

United States Weather Bureau transferred from the War Department to the Department of Agriculture, and Mark W. Harrington appointed chief, 30 June, 1891.

R. G. Dyrenforth and his staff experiment in artificial rain production by dynamite bombs, etc., near Midland, Tex., and other places, Aug. 1891.

TABLE SHOWING PRODUCTION OF CEREALS IN THE UNITED STATES.

	1840.	1850.	1860.	1870.	1880.	1891.
Corn (bu.)	377,531,875	592,071,104	838,792,740	1,094,255,000	1,717,434,543	2,060,154,000
Wheat "	84,823,272	100,485,944	173,104,924	235,884,700	498,549,868	611,780,000
Oats "	123,071,341	146,584,179	172,643,185	247,277,400	417,885,380	738,394,000
Barley "	4,161,504	5,167,015	15,825,898	26,295,400	45,165,346	75,000,000
Rye "	18,645,567	14,188,813	21,101,380	15,473,600	24,540,829	33,000,000

TABLE SHOWING PRODUCTION OF COTTON, HAY, ETC., IN THE UNITED STATES.

	1840.	1850.	1860.	1870.	1880.	1890.
Cotton (bales)	1,976,198	2,469,093	5,387,052	3,011,996	5,757,397	7,313,726
Hay (tons)	10,248,108	13,838,642	19,083,896	24,525,000	31,925,233	1893 65,766,158
Tobacco (lbs.)	219,163,319	199,752,655	434,209,461	262,735,341	449,880,014	1889. 565,795,000
Potatoes (bu.)	108,298,060	65,797,896	111,148,867	114,775,000	167,659,570	1888. 201,984,140

TABLE SHOWING NUMBER OF HORSES, CATTLE, ETC., IN THE UNITED STATES.

	1840.	1850.	1860.	1870.	1880.	1894.
Iorses }		4,336,719	6,249,174	8,248,800	11,201,800	16,081,139
	4,335,699					
Iules }		559,331	1,151,148	1,179,500	1,729,500	2,352,231
Iilch Cows }		6,385,094	8,581,735	10,095,600	12,027,000	15,487,400
	14,971,586					
'attle }		11,993,813	17,034,284	15,388,500	21,231,000	36,608,168
heep	19,311,374	21,723,220	22,471,275	40,853,000	40,765,900	45,048,017
wine	26,301,293	30,354,213	33,512,867	26,751,400	34,034,100	45,206,498

See, also, the various staples separately—viz.: COTTON, SUGAR, 'OBACCO, etc.

Agrigentum (now Girgenti), a city of Sicily, built about 82 B.C. It was governed by tyrants from 566 to 470; among hese were Phalaris (BRAZEN BULL); Alcamanes; Theron, who, vith his stepfather Gelon, defeated the Carthaginians at Himera, 480; and Thrasydæus, his son, expelled in 470, when a epublic was established. It was taken by the Carthaginians n 405 B.C., and held, except during short intervals, till gained y the Romans in 262 B.C. From 825 till 1086 it was held by he Saracens.

Ahith'ophel, counsellor of king David, and afterwards f Absalom. His wise counsel being slighted in the pursuit f the king (2 Sam. xvii. 14), he retires to his home and hangs imself, 1023 B.C. (2 Sam. xvii. 23). The only deliberate suicide n the Old Testament.

air or **atmosphere.** Anaximenes of Miletus (530 B.C.) declared air a self-existent deity, the first cause of everything. PHILOSOPHY. Posidonius (about 79 B.C.) estimated the eight of the atmosphere at 800 stadia. The pressure of air, bout 15 lbs. to the square inch, was discovered by Galileo, 1564; lemonstrated by Torricelli (who invented the barometer) about 643 A.D.; and was found by Pascal, in 1647, to vary with the eight. Halley, Newton, and others have illustrated the agency nd influences of the air by various experiments, and numerous nventions have followed—among others, the *Air-gun* of Guter f Nuremberg about 1656; the *Air-pump*, invented by Otto on Guericke of Magdeburg about 1650; improved by Robert Boyle in 1657, by Robert Hooke about 1659 (Sprengel's air-pump, invented 1863, converts the space to be occupied into Torricelian vacuum); and the *Air-pipe*, invented by Suton, a brewer of London, about 1756. The density and elasticity of air were determined by Boyle; and its relation to light nd sound by Hooke, Newton, and Derham. The atmosphere s supposed to extend above the earth about 45 miles. Its omposition, about 77 parts of nitrogen, 21 of oxygen, and 2 f other matters (such as carbonic acid, watery vapor, a trace f ammonia, etc.), was ascertained by Priestley (who discovered oxygen gas in 1774), Scheele (1775), Lavoisier, and Cavendish. Under the investigations of Dr. R. Angus Smith, F.R.S., it is found that the percentage of oxygen in seahore air and in the Scotch moors and highlands is 20.999; vhile in the free air of towns it may sink to 20.92, sitting-room vhich feels close 20.89, lighted by petroleum lamp 20.83, gallery of theatre 20.36, when candles go out 18.5, scarcely mainaining life 17.2. The laws of refraction were investigated by Dr. Bradley, 1737. The researches of Dr. Schönbein, a German chemist of Basel, between 1840 and 1859, discovered two tates of the oxygen in the air, which he calls *ozone* and *antozone.* Dr. Stenhouse's *Air-filters* (in which powdered charcoal s used) were first set up at the Mansion-house, London, in 1854. In 1858 Dr. R. Angus Smith made known a chemical nethod of ascertaining the amount of organic matter in the ir, and published his "Air and Rain" in 1872. Raoul Pictet of Geneva and Cailletet of Paris, by means of great pressure nd intense cold, compressed air into the liquid state, Dec. 1877; Jan. 1878. At the Royal Institution, London, prof. James Dewar exhibited liquid air obtained at the temperature of −192° Cent., 5 June, 1885. ACOUSTICS, ATMOSPHERIC RAILWAY, BALLOONS, NITROGEN, OXYGEN, OZONE, and PNEUMATIC DESPATCH.

The *Aero-steam Engine*, the invention of George Warsop, a mechanic of Nottingham, who, by employing compressed air united with steam, was said to save 47 per cent. of fuel. The plan was reported to the British Association at Exeter in Aug. 1869, and was said to act successfully in a tug steamer (for China) in the Thames, 26 Mch. 1870.
Col. Beaumont's *air-engine* for propelling railway-carriages, tried at Woolwich, reported successful (a little steam is used), 6 Oct. 1880.
Victor Popp applies compressed air as a motive power to clocks, 1881.
An *Air-telegraph*, employing waves of air in a tube instead of electricity, invented by sig. Guattari, was exhibited in London in 1870.
Isaac Wilkinson patented a method of compressing air by column of water in 1757, and William Mann patented stage-pumping by compressed air in 1829. Compressed air was employed in boring the Cenis tunnel, and is now in general use in mining, etc.
Tram-cars driven by compressed air in London, June, 1883.
The *Aerograph*, an air-brush, an application of compressed air, invented by mr. C. L. Burdick (1893).
Prof. Dewar gave six well-illustrated lectures on "Air, gaseous and liquid," at the Royal Institution, London, 28 Dec. 1893 to 9 Jan. 1894. (Some of the air of the room was liquefied in the presence of the audience.) Again, 1 Apr. 1898.
Argon, helium, neon, kryphon and xenon discovered, 1895–1900.

Aix-la-Chapelle (Ger. Aachen), a Roman city, now in Rhenish Prussia. Several ecclesiastical councils held here (799–1165). Here Charlemagne was born, 742, and died, 814, having built the minster (796–804) and conferred many privileges on the city, in which 55 emperors have since been crowned. The city was taken by the French in Dec. 1792; retaken by the Austrians, Mch. 1793; by the French, Sept. 1794; ceded to Prussia, 1814.

First treaty of peace signed here was between France and Spain, when France yielded Franche-Comté, but retained her conquests in the Netherlands, 2 May, 1668.
Second celebrated treaty between Great Britain, France, Holland, Germany, Spain, and Genoa, 7 Oct. 1748. AUSTRIAN SUCCESSION.
Congress of sovereigns of Austria, Russia, and Prussia, with ministers from England and France, here signed a convention, 9 Oct. 1818, for withdrawal of army of occupation from France.

Ajaccio (*ä-yät'-cho*), chief town in Corsica, noted as the birthplace of Napoleon Bonaparte, born (5 Feb. 1768, baptismal register; doubtful), 15 Aug. 1769.

Ajnadin' or **Aiznadin',** Syria. Here the Mahometans defeated the army of the emperor Heraclius, 13 July, 633. They took Damascus in 634.

Akerman, Bessarabia. After being several times taken, it was ceded to Russia in 1812. Here a treaty between Russia and Turkey was concluded, 4 Sept. 1826, which secured the former navigation of the Black Sea, recognized the Danubian principalities, etc.

Akhalzikh (*ä-kal-zeek'*), Armenia. Near here prince Paskiewitch and the Russians defeated the Turks, 24 Aug., and gained the city, 28 Aug. 1828.

Alabama (an Indian word, meaning "Here we rest"), a southern state of the Union, the 22d in order of admission.

It lies between lat. 30° 15′ and 35° N., and between lon. 84° 56′ and 88° 48′ W. from Greenwich. Its length north to south is 336 miles; its greatest breadth, 200 miles; area, 52,230 square miles. Pop. 1900, 1,828,697. Number of counties, 66. Capital, Montgomery.

A.D.

De Soto leads about 1000 men from Florida to the Mississippi ... 1540
France claims all the Mississippi valley (LOUISIANA) ... 1697
De Bienville (LOUISIANA) builds fort St. Louis on the west side of Mobile Bay ... 1702
Colony removed to present site of Mobile ... 1711
Fort Toulouse built by French at the confluence of the Coosa and Tallapoosa rivers ... 1714
All the territory now Alabama north of 31° and west to the Mississippi ceded to England by France ... 1763
[West Florida from 1764 to 1781 included much of the present territory of Alabama and Mississippi. The British province of west Florida was bounded by 32° 28′ N., while all Alabama north of 32° 28′ was in the British province of Illinois.]
Spain declares war against Great Britain ... 8 May, 1779
Don Bernardo de Galvez Spanish governor of Louisiana. Captures Mobile ... 14 Mch. 1780
Great Britain cedes to the United States all territory east of the Mississippi except Florida, the boundary of west Florida

being again fixed at 31° N, and cedes Florida back to Spain by treaties of 1783

A treaty between the Federal government and the Choctaw Indians confirming the cession of the territory obtained by the British from that tribe 3 Jan 1786

Georgia claims to include by royal charter what is now Alabama and Mississippi and creates Houstoun county out of part of Alabama north of the Tennessee river 1785

Spain claims west Florida 32° 28' N, and occupies the territory, but relinquishes her claims north of 31° after tedious negotiations Mch 1798

This region from 31° to 32° 28' N lat, between the Mississippi and the Chattahoochee, is formed by congress into the Mississippi territory "

Winthrop Sargent of Massachusetts appointed by president Adams first governor "

[Seat of government, Natchez on the Mississippi]

Spanish garrison at Fort St Stephen relieved by Federal troops, May, 1799

Washington county, comprising all east of the Pearl river to the Chattahoochee formed by gov Sargent June, 1800

First census of Washington county, showing 733 whites, 494 negro slaves, and 23 free negroes "

[Mobile not included being under Spanish rule]

Congress provides a legislature for the territory "

President Jefferson appoints William C C Claiborne of Tennessee governor 1801

Georgia cedes to the U S all between the 31st and the 35th parallels for $1 250 000 24 Apr 1802

Congress extends the Mississippi territory to 35° N 1804

Robert Williams of North Carolina governor 1805

Madison county created 1808

David Holmes of Virginia governor 1809

Baldwin county created "

The three counties in what is now Alabama have 6422 whites and 2624 negroes 1810

Madison Gazette started at Huntsville 1812

Spanish garrison at fort Charlotte (Mobile) surrenders to the U S forces under gen Wilkinson 13 Apr 1813

U S. forces occupy Spanish west Florida and the district E of Pearl river and S of 31° N is added to the Mississippi territory 1812-13

First engagement in the war with the Creek (so called by the whites because of the numerous creeks within their territory) or Muscogee Indians on Burnt Corn creek 27 July, 1813

[The whites under col Caller repulsed]

Fort Mimms a stockade near the E bank of the Alabama river (now Baldwin county), is surprised at midday by 1000 Creek warriors led by Weatherford and the prophet Francis There were in the fort 245 men with arms, and 308 women and children After a stubborn resistance till 5 P M they are overpowered—about 50 escape 30 Aug "

Battle of Tallasahatchee (now in Calhoun county) The Indians defeated by gen Coffee 3 Nov "

Battle of Talladega. Gen Jackson defeats the Indians, 9 Nov "

Capt. Sam Dale's "Canoe fight" with Indians. 12 Nov "

Hillabee Town Massacre of Indians by gen White This attack was made without the knowledge of Jackson 18 Nov "

Auttose towns Indians defeated by gen Floyd and towns destroyed 29 Nov "

Econochoca or "Holy Ground" Indians defeated by gen Claiborne 23 Dec "

Battles of Emuckfau and Enotochopco (now in Tallapoosa county) The Indians attack and are repulsed 22 24 Jan 1814

Calebee river Indian attack repulsed by gen Floyd 27 Jan "

Gen Jackson re enforced, attacks Indians fortified at Great Horse shoe Bend (Tohopeka) of Tallapoosa river 27 Mch "

[By this, the bloodiest battle of the war, the power of the Indians was destroyed]

Indians by treaty cede to the U S. nearly half the present state of Alabama. 9 Aug "

Gen. Jackson captures Pensacola, Fla 7 Nov "

Chickasaw Indians, by treaty, relinquish all claim to the country south of the Tennessee for $65 000 14 Sept 1816

Territory east of what is now Mississippi organized as the territory of Alabama 3 Mch 1817

William Wyatt Bibb appointed governor by Monroe "

Territorial legislature first meets at St Stephens 19 Jan 1818

Congress authorizes Alabama to form a state constitution, 2 Mch 1819

Convention at Huntsville to frame a constitution, conclude their labors 2 Aug "

First general assembly at Huntsville, 45 representatives and 22 senators 25 Oct. "

William W Bibb chosen governor 9 Nov "

Joint resolution of congress admitting Alabama into the Union approved by president Monroe 14 Dec. "

The seat of government removed to Cahaba 1820

Pop of the state (whites, 85,451, negroes, 42,450) 127,901 "

Rank as to pop 19 "

Pop per sq mile 2 4 "

Act to establish a state university at Tuscaloosa passed. 18 Dec "

[It was not opened until 18 Apr 1831]

State bank established and located at Cahaba. "

The principal towns in Alabama were Huntsville, Claiborne, Mobile, Cahaba, St Stephens, Florence, and Montgomery in "

Gen Lafayette received at the capital 1824

Seat of government removed to Tuscaloosa 1826

William Weatherford, the Indian warrior and chief at the fort Mimms massacre, dies in Monroe county "

Spring Hill college (R C.) at Mobile opened 1826

University of Alabama (non-sec) at Tuscaloosa opened 1831

First cotton factory erected in Madison 1832

Creeks cede to the U S all their lands east of the Mississippi for $210,000 by treaty "

First railroad completed from Tuscumbia to Decatur, 44 miles 1834

Cherokees cede their lands to the state by treaty 29 Dec 1835

[They receive $5,000,000 and 7 000 000 acres beyond the Mississippi—to remove within 2 years.]

Great financial convulsion in 1837

Howard College (Baptist) at Birmingham opened 1842

Seat of government removed to Montgomery 1847

Medical college of Ala founded at Mobile 1859

Pop of the state about the time of its secession (whites, 526,431, negro slaves, 435,080, free negroes, 2690) 964,201 1860

Rank as to pop 13 "

Pop to the sq mile 18 7 "

Per cent of increase 24 9 "

The general assembly by resolution requires the governor if a BLACK REPUBLICAN be elected president of the U S in November to order elections of delegates to a constitutional convention 24 Feb "

Alabama passes an ordinance of secession by 61 to 39, the fourth state to secede 11 Jan 1861

Alabama seizes U S arsenal and arms at Mobile, and occupies forts Morgan and Gaines at entrance of Mobile bay Jan "

Provisional congress of delegates from 6 seceded states meet at Montgomery 4 Feb "

Adopt a provisional constitution 8 Feb "

Jefferson Davis inaugurated president of the Confederacy at Montgomery 18 Feb "

Seat of confederate government removed from Montgomery to Richmond, Va July, "

There were liberated by the Emancipation Proclamation 435 132 slaves in Alabama 1 Jan 1863

Confederate fleet defeated in Mobile bay by admiral Farragut 5 Aug 1864

[State furnishes to the confederate service 65 regiments of infantry, 12 regiments of cavalry, and 22 batteries of artillery Brewer's "History of Alabama."]

Mobile evacuated by confederate forces 12 Apr 1865

State convention meets and annuls ordinance of secession, 25 Sept. "

New constitution adopted 5 Nov "

[This constitution was not ratified until Nov 1875]

State was admitted to a representation in congress by act passed over president's veto 25 June, 1868

Under proclamation of gov elect W H Smith, 26 June, the legislature assembles and ratifies the 14th Amendment to the Constitution of the U S 13 July, "

State turned over to civil authorities by gen Meade 14 July, "

Immigration convention meets at Montgomery 2 June 1869

Gov Smith, claiming majority in state election of 8 Nov, files injunction restraining president of senate from counting votes for governor 25 Nov 1870

Votes for lieut governor being counted, E H Moren is declared elected and is inaugurated, as ex officio president of the senate he then counts the votes for governor—R. B Lindsay, 77,721, W H Smith, 76,292. 26 Nov "

An amicable settlement of dispute after suit to recover books, papers, etc., of the governor's office begun by gov Lindsay, 7 Dec. "

Birmingham founded (chief iron centre of Ala.) 1871

University of Alabama reorganized and opened 4 Oct. "

George Goldthwaite, dem, elected U S senator, 7 Dec 1870, qualifies 15 Jan 1872

Legislature passes a new election law, provides for an agricultural college, and adjourns 26 Feb "

State Agricultural and Mechanical College at Auburn chartered and opened "

Election returns of 5 Nov disputed Republican members of legislature organize at U S court house in Montgomery, democratic members at state capitol, each claiming a constitutional quorum Gov Lindsay recognizes the latter 18 Nov "

David P Lewis, rep, declared elected governor, 23 Nov, and assumes the office, recognizing the court house legislature, 25 Nov "

Legislative dispute referred to attorney general of the U S., who proposes a compromise to take effect 18 Dec when the senate organizes at the capitol, the court-house assembly continuing its sessions 18 Dec "

Pursuant to adjournment, 21 Dec, both houses meet 13 Jan. 1873, to examine contested seats and transact business independently until a joint resolution passed by the lower house is agreed to informing the governor of the organization of the general assembly 1 Feb. 1873

State normal college at Florence opened "

State normal and industrial school opened at Huntsville "

Colored labor state convention meets at Montgomery 18 Nov "

Constitutional convention meets at Montgomery 6 Sept. 1875

New state constitution ratified by 95 672 to 30,004. 16 Nov "

Act to fund state debt in new bonds at reduced interest and surrender certain securities held by the state, approved 23 Feb. 1876

First biennial session of legislature under new constitution, begins 15 Nov "

Act to establish a public school system, a superintendent of education to be elected every two years, etc. 1876-77

John T Morgan, dem, senator, presents credentials in the U S senate 27 Feb. 1877

Act granting $75 to any resident of the state who lost an arm or leg in the confederate army 1879

George S. Houston qualifies as U. S. senator..........18 Mch. 1879

U. S. senator George S. Houston dies..................31 Dec. "

Luke Pryor, dem., qualifies as U. S. senator under executive appointment to fill vacancy..........................15 Jan. 1880

James L. Pugh, U. S. senator-elect, qualifies...........6 Dec. "

State normal and industrial school opened at Tuskegee....... 1881

State treasurer I. H. Vincent absconds, leaving a deficit of about $212,000..Jan. 1883

State agricultural department goes into operation with E. C. Betts of Madison county as commissioner...........1 Sept. "

Alabama normal college for girls at Livingston opened........ "

State normal school at Jackson opened...................... "

Congress grants the state 46,080 acres of land for the benefit of the university...................................23 Apr. 1884

Foundation of a monument to the confederate soldiers of the state laid on the grounds of the capitol in Montgomery by Jefferson Davis....................................29 Apr. 1886

State agricultural and mechanical college burned; loss $100,000, 24 June, 1887

State normal school at Troy opened........................ "

Lease of convicts in state penitentiary awarded to the East Tennessee Coal, Iron, and Railroad company, the convicts to be employed in the Pratt coal mines near Birmingham..... 1888

Alabama academy for the blind opened at Talladega.......... "

Southern interstate immigration convention, nearly 600 delegates from all the southern states meet at Montgomery, 12 Dec. 1888

ALA

Mardi Gras, Good Friday, and 26 Apr. added to the legal holidays, and $50,000 appropriated for relief of disabled confederate soldiers or their widows by the legislature of...... 1888-89

Southern interstate farmers' association meets in Montgomery, 21 Aug. 1889

Rube Burrows, a notorious criminal and murderer, breaks jail and is shot and killed at Birmingham................8 Oct. 1890

Ex-gov. E. A. O'Neil dies at Florence..................7 Nov. "

Eleventh annual convention of American federation of labor at Birmingham, meets..................................14 Dec. 1891

4955 disabled confederate soldiers apply for pensions, each received $26.50 from a fund of $131,362.02 raised by special tax.. 1892

[38 blind applicants received each $38.57.]

Conference of colored people at Tuskegee, in the "black belt," to consider the condition of the race; regretting the poverty of the South, and lack of means for education, inability to build school-houses or furnish teachers, etc., it admitted the friendliness and fairness of the whites, etc............. "

Two state tickets in the field—gov. Thomas G. Jones heading Conservatives, and ex-commissioner of agriculture R. F. Kolb, the "Jeffersonian Democrats." Two platforms issued; Kolb defeated, charges frauds at the polls............Aug. "

GOVERNORS OF THE MISSISSIPPI TERRITORY.

Including the present States of Alabama and Mississippi.

Names.	Term of Office.	Remarks.
Winthrop Sargent..........................	1799 to 1801	Appointed by president Adams from Massachusetts.
Wm. C. C. Claiborne.......................	1801 " 1805	" " " Jefferson " Tennessee.
Robt. Williams............................	1805 " 1809	" " North Carolina.
David Holmes..............................	1809 " 1817	" " Virginia.

GOVERNOR OF THE TERRITORY OF ALABAMA.

Wm. Wyatt Bibb............................	Mch. 1817 to Nov. 1819	

GOVERNORS OF THE STATE OF ALABAMA.

Wm. Wyatt Bibb............................	Nov. 1819 to July, 1820	Died in office.
Thomas Bibb...............................	July, 1820 " Nov. 1821	
Isreal Pickens............................	Nov. 1821 " " 1825	
John Murphy...............................	" 1825 " " 1829	
Gabriel Moore.............................	" 1829 " Mch. 1831	Elected U. S. senator.
Saml. B. Moore............................	Mch. 1831 " Nov. 1831	
John Gayle................................	Nov. 1831 " " 1835	
Clement C. Clay...........................	" 1835 " July, 1837	Elected U. S. senator.
Hugh McVay................................	July, 1837 " Nov. 1837	
Arthur P. Bagby...........................	Nov. 1837 " " 1841	Elected U. S. senator, 1841.
Benj. Fitzpatrick.........................	" 1841 " " 1845	Elected U. S. senator, 1853.
Joshua L. Martin..........................	" 1845 " " 1847	
Reuben Chapman............................	" 1847 " " 1849	
Henry Watkins Collier.....................	" 1849 " " 1853	
John A. Winston...........................	" 1853 " " 1857	
Andrew B. Moore...........................	" 1857 " " 1861	
John Gill Shorter.........................	" 1861 " " 1863	Confederate government.
Thomas H. Watts...........................	" 1863 " Apr. 1865	" "
	Interregnum of two months.	
Lewis E. Parsons..........................	June, 1865 to Dec. 1865	Appointed provisional governor by president Johnson.
Robt. M. Patton...........................	Dec. 1865 " July, 1868	
Wm. H. Smith..............................	July, 1868 " Nov. 1870	Appointed by an act of congress.
Robt. B. Lindsay..........................	Nov. 1870 " " 1872	
David B. Lewis............................	" 1872 " " 1874	
Geo. S. Houston...........................	" 1874 " " 1876	
"	" 1876 " " 1878	
Rufus W. Cobb.............................	" 1878 " " 1880	No republican ticket placed in nomination.
"	" 1880 " " 1882	
Edward N. O'Neal..........................	" 1882 " " 1884	
"	" 1884 " " 1886	
Thomas Seay...............................	" 1886 " " 1888	
"	" 1888 " " 1890	
Thomas G. Jones...........................	" 1890 " " 1892	
"	" 1892 " " 1894	
William C. Oates..........................	" 1894 " " 1896	

UNITED STATES SENATORS FROM THE STATE OF ALABAMA.

Names.	No. of Congress.	Date.	Remarks.
William R. King...........	16th to 28th	1819 to 1844	Elected president *pro tem.* 1 July, 1836, 28 Jan. 1837, 2 July, 1838, and 25 Feb. 1839. Resigned 15 Apr. 1844.
John W. Walker............	16th " 17th	1819 " 1822	Resigned.
William Kelley............	17th " 19th	1823 " 1825	Elected in place of Walker.
Henry Chambers............	19th	1825 " 1826	Died 25 Jan. 1826.
Israel Pickens............	19th to 20th	1826	Appointed in place of Chambers.
John McKinley.............	19th " 22d	1826 to 1831	Elected " "
Gabriel Moore.............	22d " 25th	1831 " 1837	
Clement C. Clay...........	25th " 27th	1837 " 1841	Resigned 1841.
Arthur P. Bagby...........	27th " 30th	1841 " 1848	Elected in place of Clay. Seated 27 Dec. 1841. Resigned 16 June, 1848.
Dixon H. Lewis............	28th " 30th	1844 " 1848	Appointed in place of King. Seated 7 May, 1844. Died 25 Oct. 1848.
William R. King...........	30th " 32d	1848 " 1852	Appointed in place of Bagby. Seated 13 July, 1848. Elected by legislature. President *pro tem.* 6 May, 1850. Resigned 1852. Elected vice-president of the U. S. Died 18 Apr. 1853.
Benj. Fitzpatrick.........	30th " 36th	1848 " 1861	Appointed in place of Lewis. Seated 11 Dec. 1848. Afterwards elected in place of King. President *pro tem.* 9 Mch. 1859. Retires from the Senate 21 Jan. 1861. Died 25 Nov. 1869.
Jeremiah Clemens..........	31st " 33d	1849 " 1853	
Clement C. Clay, jun......	33d " 36th	1853 " 1861	Retires from the Senate 21 Jan. 1861. Died 9 Sept. 1866.

37th, 38th, and 39th Congress vacant.

UNITED STATES SENATORS FROM THE STATE OF ALABAMA.—(*Continued.*)

Names.	No. of Congress.	Date.	Remarks.
George E. Spencer..........	40th to 46th	1868 to 1879	Seated 25 July, 1868.
Williard Warner..........	40th " 42d	1868 " 1871	" 21 " "
George Goldthwaite........	42d " 45th	1872 " 1877	" 15 June, 1872.
John T. Morgan............	45th " ——	1877 " ——	" 27 Feb. 1877. Term expires 1901.
——	——	——	For Houston and Pryor, see State Record, 1879.
James L. Pugh............	47th to ——	1880 to ——	Seated 6 Dec. 1880. Term expires 1897.

Alabama, a steam-vessel of 1040 tons, with 2 engines of 300 horse-power, built by the Lairds at Birkenhead, Eng., and launched 15 May, 1862, for the confederate service. She was first known as "290," her number on the list built by the Lairds. She carried 8 guns—1 Blakely 100-pound rifled, 1 8-inch solid shot, and 6 32-pounders—and a crew of 144 men under capt. Semmes. She did great damage to the American mercantile shipping. On 19 June, 1864, off Cherbourg, France, she encountered the federal war-ship *Kearsarge*, capt. Winslow, carrying 7 guns—2 11-inch pivot smooth-bores, 1 28-pound rifled, 4 32-pounders—with a crew of 163. After an engagement of one hour the *Alabama* surrendered, and soon after sank. Her loss was 9 men killed and 21 wounded; the *Kearsarge* lost 3 wounded, 1 mortally.

Alabama Claims and **Award.** Claims against Great Britain for losses sustained by the U. S. through depredations on her commerce by confederate vessels fitted out or supplied in English ports. As finally presented they were as follows:

	No. of vessels destroyed.	Loss.
Alabama......................	58	$6,547,609.86
Boston......................	1	400.00
Chickamauga......................	3	95,654.85
Florida......................	38	3,698,609.34
Georgia......................	5	383,976.50
Nashville......................	1	69,536.70
Retribution......................	2	20,334.52
Sallie......................	1	5,540.00
Shenandoah......................	40	6,488,320.31
Sumter......................	3	10,695.83
Tallahassee......................	17	579,955.55
For losses from increased war premiums............		1,120,795.15
		$19,021,428.61

Discussion between the two governments respecting claims for damage by the *Alabama* and other confederate cruisers. 1865
A fruitless convention for their settlement by a commission signed at London................................10 Nov. 1868
Second convention, signed by earl of Clarendon and Mr. Reverdy Johnson, 14 Jan.; rejected by U. S. senate.....13 Apr. 1869
Joint commission (*British*, earl de Grey, sir Stafford Northcote, and others; *American*, sec. Fish, gen. Schenck, and others) to settle fishery disputes, Alabama claims, etc. Announced, 9 Feb.; met at Washington, 27 Feb.; signs a treaty at Washington..8 May, 1871
Commission for Anglo-American claims met at Washington, 25 Sept. "
Formal meeting of the arbitration commission at Geneva (adjourns to 15 June)..................................18 Dec. "
British and American cases presented 20 Dec. Excitement in England at introduction of claims for indirect losses into the American case; loss by transfer of trade from American to British ships, increased rates of marine insurance, and losses by prolongation of war.......................Jan. 1872
Correspondence between the governments; British despatch, 3 Feb.; reply, 1 Mch.; continued; counter-cases presented at Geneva..15 Apr. "
Continued correspondence, supplementary treaty, both nations agree to abstain from claims for indirect losses, presented to American senate; approved.......................25 May, "
British government object to certain modifications; further correspondence; excitement in Parliament; proposed adjournment of meeting of arbitration commission; differences about mode of procedure; Congress adjourns, leaving affair unsettled......................................10 June, "
Arbitration tribunal, consisting of count Frederic Sclopis for Italy, president; baron Staempfli for Switzerland; vicomte d'Itajuba for Brazil; Mr. C. F. Adams for United States; and sir Alexander E. Cockburn for Great Britain, meet at Geneva. The British government presents a note of existing differences; the conference adjourns.......................15 June, "
Further adjournment, 17 June; the arbitrators declare indirect claims contrary to international law, 19 June; president Grant consents to their withdrawal...............25 June, "
British government withdraw application for adjournment of conference......................................27 June, "
Tribunal records decision against indirect claims and long adjournment, and adjourns to 15 July................28 June, "
Final meeting; all the arbitrators agree to award damages for injuries done by the *Alabama;* four for those done by the *Florida;* and three for those done by the *Shenandoah.* The judgment not signed by sir A. Cockburn, whose reasons were published; the damages awarded (including interest), about 3,229,166*l.* 13*s.* 4*d.*; those claimed, 9,476,166*l.* 13*s.* 4*d.* (Decision based on admission of a *new ex-post-facto* international law, by Great Britain by treaty of Washington).....14 Sept. 1872
Judgment of sir A. Cockburn admitting award for the *Alabama*, opposing other awards, yet counselling submission to the judgment, signed 14 Sept., and published in *London Gazette* with other documents.......................20 Sept. "
3,200,000*l.* were voted; the receipt of 3,196,874*l.* ($15,500,000) acknowledged by sec. Fish..........................Sept. 1873
All awards made; about $8,000,000 surplus.................. 1876
Increased by interest to $9,500,000.......................... 1885

Alabama Letter, The. Henry Clay, whig candidate for president in 1844, had a fair prospect for election when his letter to a friend in Alabama on the annexation of Texas appeared in the *North Alabamian* on 16 Aug., in which he said he would be glad to see it annexed "without dishonor, without war, with the common consent of the Union, and upon fair terms." It was represented by his adversaries as a complete change of policy on his part. The whig campaign became "defensive" from this time and resulted in defeat. UNITED STATES.

alabas'ter, a variety of gypsum or sulphate of lime which is used in the manufacture of various ornamental articles, as vases, statuettes, clock-cases, etc. The word is said to be derived from the Arabic, *albatstraton*, "the whitish stone." When pure it is of a brilliant pearly white lustre, so soft as to be easily scratched with the finger-nail, and slightly soluble in water. Florence, in Italy, is the centre of the alabaster trade in that country. Oriental alabaster, the name applied to the stalagmitic variety of carbonate of lime (harder than the sulphate), found on the floors of limestone caves, is an entirely different material from the sulphate. It is usually clouded, and hence is sometimes known as onyx marble. The alabaster procured from quarries known to the ancients, and now worked in the province of Oran, Algeria, is of the latter kind. This is the kind referred to in the Bible, and the *ἀλαβαστρίτης* of the Greeks, and was held in high esteem by the civilized nations of antiquity. In the Sloanean Museum there is an Egyptian sarcophagus in Oriental alabaster, covered with hieroglyphics, which was purchased by sir John Sloane for 2000 guineas.

Alad'din and his Wonderful Lamp, one of the tales of the "Arabian Nights." Aladdin was the son of a poor widow. He became possessor of a magic ring and lamp, the rubbing of which brought to him and subjected to his service two jinns, the jinn of the lamp the most powerful. By his aid he succeeded in marrying the sultan's daughter and in building a magnificent palace, whose—

> "Broad-based flights of marble stairs
> Ran up with golden balustrade . . .
> The fourscore windows all alight
> As with the quintessence of flame,
> A million tapers flaring bright
> From twisted silvers look'd to shame
> The hollow-vaulted dark, and stream'd
> Upon the mooned domes aloof . . ."
> —*Tennyson*, "Recollections of the Arabian Nights."

After the death of the sultan Aladdin succeeded him. "To most general readers the charming tale of Aladdin and his lamp, as related in our common English version of the 'Arabian Nights,' which was made early in the 18th century from Galland's selections rendered into French, is doubtless a typical Eastern fiction. It does not, however, occur in any known Arabian text of 'The Thousand and One Nights' (Elf Layla wa Layla). This story and three others, viz.: 'Ali Baba,' 'Prince Ahmed,' and 'The two Envious Sisters' were, on the first publication of Galland's '*Mille et une Nuits*,' generally considered as his own invention; but it is probable that Galland heard them in the East, where he sojourned many years, as they all occur in Asiatic collections."—*W. A. Clouston*, "Popular Tales and Fictions, their Migrations and Transformations."

Aladja Dagh (*a-la'ja dag*), near Kars, Armenia.

ALA

Iere the Turks, under Ahmed Mukhtar, after severe conflicts, vere defeated by Russians, under grand-duke Michael and ens. Loris Melikoff, Lazareff, and Heimann, 14, 15 Oct 1877
'he Turkish army was divided and broken up, the strong camp taken, with many prisoners including 7 pashas, and 38 guns The Russian strategy was highly commended This disaster which led to the investment of Kars was attributed to Mukhtar's maintaining too extended lines, which were turned (20 miles with only 40,000 men, when 200,000 were required)

Alais (*a-lā'*), a town in southern France in the department of Gard, also, the name of a treaty of peace (1629) terminating the religious wars in France

Al'amance, Battle of NORTH CAROLINA, 1771

Alam'bagh, a fort near Lucknow, India, held by gen Outram against the Sepoys from Nov 1857 until Mch 1858

A'lamo, a fort, originally a Spanish mission, in Texas, ear San Antonio Here occurred the massacre of the Alamo, Mch 1836, when a Mexican force of 1500 or 2000 men, under Santa Aña, after having besieged and bombarded its garrison f 140 Texans, under col Travis, from 23 Feb, stormed the lace and took it, after being twice repulsed Col David Crockett was killed here But 6 Texans were left alive after he assault, and these were murdered in cold blood in Santa Aña's presence, by his order after surrender on promise of rotection Mexican loss, 500 TEXAS

Ala'ni, a Tartar race, invaded Parthia, 75 A D They oined the Huns in invading the Roman empire, and were efeated by Theodosius, 379-382 They were subdued by the Visigoths, 452, and eventually incorporated with them

Al Aa'raaf, the Mohammedan Limbo, also, the subect of an unfinished poem by Edgar A Poe

Alarcon' or **Alarcos',** a small town and fort in cenral Spain. Here the Spaniards, under Alfonso IX, king of Castile, were totally defeated by the Moors, 19 July, 1195

Al'aric, Alric, i e "all rich," a chief, and aftervards king of the VISIGOTHS, a member of the noble race of he Balti (Baltha) In the service of Theodosius the Great, Alaric, bold and artful, acquired that knowledge and art of var which he afterwards so fatally exerted for the destruction of Rome On the death of Theodosius, 395 A D, the Goths, under the leadership of Alaric, withdrew their allegiance to he Eastern or Greek emperor, and invaded Greece No attempt was made to defend that country, and it was soon ravaged from Thrace to Sparta Athens secured safety by paying heavily for it At last Stilicho, the able general of the emperor Honorius, met him, and compelled him to retreat. After this Arcadius, emperor of the Eastern Empire, either hrough fear or as a bribe, appointed him master-general of Eastern Illyricum, 398 A D. This position he occupied until his invasion of Italy, 400-403, in the latter year he was signally defeated by Stilicho at POLLENTIA, 29 Mch 403, after which he ultimately retired to the banks of the Danube, where he recuperated his losses through his several defeats by added allies, etc., and was again ready to march to the capture of Rome in 409 A D. It was, according to Gibbon, 619 years after Hannibal's approach to the walls of Rome with his Numidian cavalry that Alaric the Goth not only approached but besieged it. This first siege was discontinued on the payment of 5000 lbs. of gold and 30,000 lbs of silver, besides other articles of great value Whether, if there were a treaty, it was violated by the Romans nothing is definitely known, but the same year, 409, Alaric was again before its walls Other treaties followed which could not or would not be fulfilled, and Alaric for the third and last time was before its walls, its gates being opened to him on 24 Mch 410, 1163 years after its foundation Alaric, after giving the city up to sack and pillage for 6 days, withdrew. Some historians attempt to show that Alaric treated Rome with leniency, it certainly can be said that he left most of it standing. Alaric after this proceeded southward, ravaging the country as far as the river Busentinus, where, near Consentia, he died, 410 A D To conceal the place of his burial the water of this small river was turned from its bed in which he was buried, and then was returned to its original course to further conceal his burial-place. With barbaric cruelty the prisoners or slaves who did the work were all killed

Alas'ka, formerly Russian America, is bounded on the north by the Arctic ocean on the east by the British possessions, on the south by the Pacific ocean, and on the west by the Behring sea and straits From the main portion of the territory a narrow strip with a breadth of about 30 miles extends southeast along the Pacific coast, and terminates at the confines of British Columbia in 54° 40′ N lat From north to south the extreme length is 1100 miles, and greatest breadth, 800 miles It contains about 577,390 sq miles The distance between Portland channel, 52° n lat 130° w lon separating the lower part of Alaska from British America and Atoo, the westernmost island of the Aleutian chain, is 2100 miles If Atoo be accepted as the western extremity of the United States, San Francisco is nearly its geographical centre of longitude Capital, Sitka

This territory was first discovered by a Russian expedition under command of Behring 1741
Territory granted to a Russian American fur company by emperor Paul 1799
This charter renewed 1839
[New Archangel now Sitka, on the island of Sitka, was and is the principal settlement and capital]
Privileges of the fur company expired 1863
Ceded by Russia to the United States for $7,200,000, by treaty signed 30 Mch and ratified 20 June, 1867
Formal possession taken by the United States 9 Oct "
Alaska made by congress a military and collection district 1870
Congress provided a civil government 17 May, 1884
Rev Sheldon Jackson appointed general agent of education for the territory Apr 1885
A P Swineford arrives at Sitka as governor 15 Sept. "
Gold first discovered at Silver Bay, near Sitka in 1887
Expedition sent by the U S Coast and Geodetic Survey, under J E McGrath, to determine the exact boundary between Alaska and the British possessions June, 1889
The North American Commercial company secures the Alaskan fur seal rights for 20 years 28 Feb 1890
Population reported by the census agent, 31,000, consisting of 900 Aleuts 5000 Indians 18,000 Esquimaux, 2300 Chinese, and 4800 whites 29 Aug 1891
Mt St Elias, 18 000 ft, successfully climbed by the duke of the Abruzzi and 9 others. .. 1897
Convention respecting the boundary signed at Washington, 30 Jan "
Gold discovered in the Hay, Buffalo, and other rivers that run into the Great Slave lake Jan 1898
New government mining regulations in the Yukon district, issued by Canada 17 Jan "
Avalanche in the Chilkoot pass, nearly 200 persons killed, 3 Apr "
Steamer from Klondike, with 35 miners and $200 000 of gold, arrives at Victoria, B C, 29 Aug [nearly $1,000,000 in value arrived there] . 15 July, "
Lord Herschell, sir Wilfrid Laurier, sir R Cartwright, and sir L H Davies (Canada) appointed British high commissioners for the international commission between United States and Canada, 29 June, mr Chas Fairbanks and four others appointed U S commissioners 16 July, meet at Quebec, 23 Aug *et seq* "
Serious fires at Dawson city, 14 Oct. (again 25 Apr and 3 July, 1899) "
Gold discovered in the N W, in the Yukon district and (on the Klondike by Geo McCormack, 17 Aug 1896), about 250,000 square miles rapid development, new government mining regulations, July, great rush to the Klondike gold fields, much suffering at Dawson city, site belonging to Joseph Ladue provisions scarce miners leaving, Aug, starvation averted (maj Walsh appointed governor, early 1898) Dec. "
Postage rate reduced from 3 to 2 cents to U S N A and all parts of Canada . . Dec "
International commission (U S and Canada) adjourns, disputed questions, Alaskan boundary, etc, remitted to the two governments, 20 Feb, lord Herschell, the president, dies suddenly 1 Mch 1899
Sir Charles Tupper's motion for a judicial inquiry into the administration of the Yukon, defeated, majority of 50, 30 June, "
Dominion day (32d) kept from the Atlantic to the Pacific, 1 July, "
The Yukon and White Pass railway, connecting at Lake Bennett with boats for the Dawson and Yukon valley, opened July, "
Temporary boundary-line of Alaska agreed upon with England 12 Oct "
Provisional boundary between Canada and Alaska, proposed by U S N A, accepted by Great Britain 20 Oct. "
Alaska Geographical Society, organized 1898, 1200 members, incorporated 1900
Investigation ordered by pres Roosevelt in consequence of numerous complaints and scandals connected with the administration of justice . "
Great fire in Dawson city, Klondike, estimated damage $400,000 , 10 Jan "
Civil government for the "District of Alaska," enacted 6 June, "
Relief for Cape Nome miners authorized by Congress, 31 Aug "
Estimated value of gold produced in Alaska over $25,000,000, 1897-1902
Treaty for a boundary commission, 3 British and 3 Americans, ratified . . . 11 Feb 1903

First meeting of the commissioners (U. S., Great Britain, and Canada) at the foreign office..........3 Sept. 1903
Award signed..........20 Oct. "
The U. S. and Canada joint survey to mark the boundary-lines, begins work.......... 1904
Judge Melville C. Brown's resignation demanded, Frank H. Richards, U. S. marshal, removed from office by the president, and Royal A. Gunnison appointed to succeed judge Brown.......... "
Alaska created a see of the orthodox Greek Church, bish. Innocent appointed.......... "
Wireless telegraphy introduced between Cape Nome and St. Michaels, 107 miles..........Aug. "
Great fire in Dawson, loss $250,000..........24 Sept. "
U. S. Supreme Court decides that the right to trial by common law exists in Alaska..........10 Apr. 1905
Population, 1890, 30,329; 1900, 63,592..........

MILITARY GOVERNOR.

Gen. Lovell H. Rousseau.......... 1867

CIVIL GOVERNORS.

John H.. Kinkead.......... 1884–85
Alfred P. Swineford.......... 1885–89
Lyman E. Knapp.......... 1889–93
James Sheakley.......... 1893–97
John G. Brady.......... 1897–

Alaska boundary award. Secretary Hay and sir Michael Herbert, the British ambassador, on 24 Jan. 1903, signed a treaty at Washington providing for the settlement of the Alaskan boundary question. Efforts in that direction had been put forth for a long time, the Canadian miners being anxious to get through the Klondike to the sea without passing through American territory and the Americans insisting upon their right to the coast-line and the control of the ports. The treaty provided for the reference of all these boundary questions to a mixed tribunal, three on each side, to determine the interpretation to be placed on the treaty of 1825 between Great Britain and Russia, which defined the boundaries between British America and Alaska. The commissioners appointed by the president were sec. of war Elihu Root, sen. Henry Cabot Lodge, and sen. George Turner. The commissioners on the part of Great Britain were lord chief jus. Alverstone, sir Louis A. Jetté, and A. B. Aylesworth. The last two are Canadians. The commission sat in London and announced its decision 20 Oct. The two Canadian members of the commission declined to sign it.

THE AWARD.

The official digest of the decision is as follows. It is in the form of answers to seven questions contained in the Hay-Herbert treaty of 1903.

Q.—What is intended as the point of commencement of the line?
A.—The line commences at cape Muzon.
Q.—What channel is the Portland channel?
A.—The Portland channel passes north of Pearse and Wales islands, and enters the ocean through Tongas passage, between Wales and Sitklan islands.
Q.—What course should the line take from the point of commencement to the entrance to Portland channel?
A.—A straight line to the middle of the entrance of Tongas passage.
Q.—What point on the 56th par. is the line to be drawn from the head of the Portland channel, and what course should it follow between these points?
A.—A straight line between Salmon and Bear rivers direct to the 56th par. of lat.
Q.—In extending the line of demarcation northward from said point on 56° of n. lat. following the crest of the mountains situated parallel to the coast until its intersection with 141° of lon. w. of Greenwich, subject to the condition that if such line should anywhere exceed the distance of 10 marine leagues from the ocean, then the boundary between the British and the Russian territory should be formed by a line parallel to the sinuosities of the coast, and distant therefrom not more than 10 marine leagues, was it the intention and meaning of said convention of 1825 that there should remain in the exclusive possession of Russia a continuous fringe or strip of coast on the mainland not exceeding 10 marine leagues in width, separating the British possessions from the bays, ports, inlets, havens, and waters of the ocean, and extending from the said point on 56° of lat. n. to a point intersecting 141° of lon. w. of the meridian of Greenwich?
A.—Answered in the affirmative.

The sixth question was based on the possibility that this question would be answered in the negative, and therefore did not call for a decision.

Q.—What, if any exist, are the mountains referred to as situated parallel to the coast, which mountains, when within 10 marine leagues from the coast are declared to form the eastern boundary?
A.—The majority of the tribunal have selected the line of peaks starting at the head of Portland channel, and running along the high mountains on the outer edge of the mountains, shown on the maps of survey made in 1893, extending to mount Whipple, and thence along what is known as the Hunter line of 1878, crossing the Stikine river about 24 miles from its mouth, thence northerly along the high peaks of Kate's Needle, from Kate's Needle to the Devil's Thumb. The tribunal stated that there was not sufficient evidence, owing to the absence of a complete survey, to identify the mountains which correspond to those intended by the treaty. This contemplates a further survey of that portion by the two governments.

From the vicinity of the Devil's Thumb the line runs to the continental watershed, thence through White and Taiya or Chilkoot passes, westerly to a mountain indicated on the map attached to the treaty as 6850 ft., thence to another mountain 5800 ft., and from that point in a somewhat curved line across the head of the glaciers to mount Fairweather. This places the Canadian outpost on the upper water of Chilkat river in British territory, and the mining camps of Porcupine and Glacier creek in American territory. From mount Fairweather the line passes north on high peaks along the mountains indicated on the map by mounts Pinta, Ruhama, and Vancouver to mount St. Elias.

STATEMENT BY PRESIDENT ROOSEVELT.

The president, in his annual message, 7 Dec. 1903, made the following references to the settlement of the Alaska boundary question:

By this award the right of the United States to the control of a continuous strip or border of the mainland shore, skirting all the tidewater inlets and sinuosities of the coast, is confirmed; the entrance to Portland canal (concerning which legitimate doubt appeared) is defined as passing by Tongas inlet, and to the northwestward of Wales and Pearse islands; a line is drawn from the head of Portland canal to 56° of n. lat.; and the interior border line of the strip is fixed by lines connecting certain mountain summits lying between Portland canal and mount St. Elias, and running along the crest of the divide separating the coast slope from the inland watershed at the only part of the frontier where the drainage ridge approaches the coast within the distance of 10 marine leagues stipulated by the treaty as the extreme width of the strip around the heads of Lynn canal and its branches.

While the line so traced follows the provisional demarcation of 1878 at the crossing of the Stikine river, and that of 1899 at the summits of the White and Chilkoot passes, it runs much farther inland from the Klehini than the temporary line of the later *modus vivendi*, and leaves the entire mining district of the Porcupine river and Glacier creek within the jurisdiction of the United States.

The result is satisfactory in every way. It is of great material advantage to our people in the far Northwest. It has removed from the field of discussion and possible danger a question liable to become more acutely accentuated with each passing year.

Alba Longa, an ancient city of Italy, said to have been founded by Ascanius, son of Æneas, 1152 B.C. Its history is mythical.

Ascanius, son of Æneas, 1152 B.C.; Sylvius Posthumus, 1143; Æneas Sylvius..........B.C. 1114
Reign of Latinus, 1048; Alba, 1038; Atys, or Capetus, 1002; Capys, 976; Capetus.......... 916
Reign of Tiberinus, 903; being defeated in battle near the river Albula, he throws himself into the stream, is drowned, and hence this river is called the Tiber.......... 895
Agrippa, 891; Romulus Silvius, 864; Aventinus, 845; Procas, 808; Numitor.......... 795
Amulius, brother of Numitor, seizes the throne, 794; killed by Romulus, who restores his grandfather Numitor.......... 754
Romulus builds and fortifies Rome.......... 753
Alba conquered by Tullus Hostilius, and incorporated with Rome.......... 665

Alba'nia, a province of European Turkey, part of ancient Epirus. The Albanians became independent during the decline of the Greek empire. They were successfully attacked by the Turks in 1388. From 1443, under George Castriot (Scanderbeg), they baffled the efforts of Amurath II. to subdue them till the siege of Scutari in 1478, when they submitted to his successor, Mahomet II., Ali Pacha of Janina, in 1812, defeated the Turkish pachas, and governed Albania ably, but cruelly and despotically, till Feb. 1822, when he and two sons were slain, after surrendering under promise of safety. A revolt in Albania was suppressed in 1843. Area, about 18,944 sq. miles; pop. about 1,300,000.

An Albanian league (favored by the Turks) formed to resist cession of any part of the country to Austria and Montenegro in April, said to have caused the death of Mehemet Ali..7 Sept. 1878
Country semi-independent..........Apr. 1879
Army formed rebel against Turkey..........Apr. 1880
League forces defeated in attack on Dervish Pacha in Uskub between Pristma and Prisend, 19 Apr.; he reported the country settled, but asked reinforcements; more fighting; Albanians said to be defeated, struggle almost over..........12 May, 1881
Revolt of chiefs, severe fights, 2, 3 June, 1883. Turks defeated with loss; reported dispersion of chiefs about 8 June. Continued fighting 12 June et seq. Turks successful in fight; Albanians submit, announced 21 June. Unsettled 25 June. Insurrection subsiding about 19 July. Albanians appeal to the powers for annexation to Greece, about 3 Nov. General disorder and much brigandage reported, Aug. 1884. Continued disturbance.......... 1890–92

Albans, St., Hertfordshire, England, near the Roman Verulam, named for Alban, the British protomartyr, said to have been beheaded during the persecution by Diocletian, 23 June, 286. A stately monastery to his memory was erected bout 795, by Offa, king of Mercia, who granted it many privileges Its superior sat as premier abbot in parliament till the dissolution in 1539 Francis Bacon made baron Verulam July, 1618, and viscount St Albans Jan 1621 A meeting was held 22 June, 1871, to raise funds to restore the abbey, the earl of Verulam chairman The results were favorable, and the work was confided to Mr G Gilbert Scott, who issued a report in June, 1872 Verulam was built on the site of the capital of Cassivelaunus taken by Julius Cæsar, 54 B.C It was retaken, after much slaughter, by Boadicea or Boudicea, queen of the Iceni 61 A D

First battle of St Albans Lancastrians defeated their leader, Edmund duke of Somerset, slain, and king Henry VI taken by duke of York and partisans 22 or 23 May 1455

Second battle queen Margaret totally defeated Yorkists under earl of Warwick, and rescued the king Shrove-Tuesday, 17 Feb 1461

St Albans incorporated by Edward VI 1553.

Disfranchised for bribery, 17 June, 1852

Albans, St., raid (VERMONT), Oct 1864

Albany or **Albainn,** ancient name of the Scottish Highlands. Robert Stewart, brother of king Robert III, was created first duke of Albany in 1398, and the title has since belonged to the crown of Scotland

Albany, capital of the state of New York Pop 1890, 94,923 STATE OF NEW YORK throughout

Albemarle, the confederate iron-clad ram, was built by John L Porter in the Roanoke river in 1863 She was 152 ft long, 45 ft wide, with a draught of 8 ft 2 engines of 200 horse-power each, and armed with 2 rifled Brooke's guns, each worked through 3 port-holes as occasion required In Apr 1864, the ram sank the U S vessel *Northfield*, and on 5 May engaged 7 U S war vessels in Albemarle sound, among them the *Sassacus*, which attempted to sink her by ramming, but failed, the fight continued until dark, when both retired, the *Albemarle* returning to Plymouth badly damaged, where on the night of 27 Oct 1864, she was sunk by lieut W B Cushing of the U S navy by a torpedo Subsequently raised and towed to the Norfolk navy yard, where, stripped of her armament, machinery, etc, she was sold 15 Oct. 1867, for $3200

Albigen'ses, a name given to persons who opposed the church of Rome, living at Albi in Languedoc, and at Toulouse, in the 12th century They were persecuted as Manichæans 1163, and a crusade (proclaimed by pope Innocent III) against them began in 1207 Simon de Montfort commanded 500 000 men, and at Bezieres, 1209, he and the pope's legate put friends and foes to the sword, saying, "God will find his own" At Minerba he burned 150 of the Albigenses alive, and at La Vaur he hanged the governor and beheaded the chief people, drowning the governor's wife and murdering other women He defeated Raymond, count of Toulouse, but was himself killed in 1218 Louis VIII and IX, kings of France, supported the crusade, count Raymond was subdued, and abdicated in 1229, and the heretics were given up to the Inquisition They had little in common with the WALDENSES

Albion. Britain is so called by Aristotle Julius Cæsar and others are said to have named it (from *albus*, white) from its chalky cliffs.

Albion, New, name given to California by sir Francis Drake when he took possession in 1577

Albue'ra or **Albuhe'ra,** Estremadura, Spain Here the French, under marshal Soult, were defeated by the British and Anglo-Spanish army, under marshal (afterwards lord) Beresford, 16 May, 1811

Albufera, E. Central Spain, a lagoon near which the French marshal Suchet (afterwards duke of Albufera) defeated the Spaniards under Blake, 4 Jan 1812, this led to his capture of Valencia on 9 Jan

Alcala', Spain, near the Roman Complutum. At the university here was printed the Complutensian Polyglot Bible, at the expense of cardinal Ximenes, 1502-15 Cervantes was born here, 1547

Alcan'tara, a town on the Tagus, W. Spain A fine bridge was built here by Trajan about 104 The duke of Alva acquired Portugal for Spain by defeating the Portuguese army here, 24 June, 1580. The Spanish military order of knighthood of Alcantara was established in 1156 The sovereign of Spain has been grand master since 1495

Alcaz'ar-Kebeer' (the great palace) near Fez, N W Africa, where the Moors totally defeated the Portuguese, whose gallant king Sebastian was slain, 4 Aug 1578 The Portuguese disbelieved his death and long expected his return—this led to the appearance of five impostors

al'chemy, the forerunner of chemistry, its chief objects being the discovery of the philosopher's stone (which was to effect the transmutation of metals into gold) an alkahest, or universal menstruum, and the elixir of life M Martin Ziegler patented a method of producing a "vital fluid" by combining nitrogen and carbon in a porous cell containing ammonia, immersed in a vessel filled with molasses. The current was to flow through silk threads attached to the vessel, about 1868 The alchemists asserted that their founder was Hermes *Trismegistus* (thrice greatest), an ancient Egyptian king Pliny says the emperor Caligula was the first who prepared natural arsenic, to make gold of it, but desisted, because the charge exceeded the profit Modern science dates from three discoveries First that of Copernicus in astronomy, which served to destroy astrology, second, the weight of the atmosphere by Torricelli and Pascal, and third, oxygen

Zosimus wrote on the subject about 410

The Arabians cultivated alchemy and were followed (in the 13th century) by Roger Bacon Albert Groot commonly known as Albertus Magnus Aquinas Raymond Lullius, Basil Valentine (born 1394), Paracelsus (died 1541) and others

In 1404 the craft of multiplying gold and silver was made felony by 5 Henry IV c 4, repealed in 1689

A license to practise alchemy with all metals and minerals was granted one Richard Carter 1476.—*Rymer's Fœdera*

Dr Price of Guildford England, in 1782, published his experiments, and brought specimens of gold to the king affirming that they were made by means of a red and white powder Being a fellow of the Royal Society he was required, under pain of expulsion to repeat his experiments before members of the society, but after much equivocation he took poison and died, Aug, 1783

alcohol. Pure spirit of wine or hydrated alcohol is said to have been obtained by the distillation of fermented liquors by Abucasis in the 12th century, and made anhydrous by Raymond Lullius in the 13th century by carbonate of potassium Alcohol has never been solidified, but becomes viscid at very low temperatures In 1820, Faraday and Hennell obtained traces of alcohol by passing olefiant gas (bicarburetted hydrogen) through sulphuric acid, and in 1862 this process was examined and confirmed by Berthelot BRANDY, DISTILLATION GIN, RUM, and SPIRITS About 250 medical men including the president of the Royal College of Physicians and many hospital officials, issued a caution concerning the use of alcohol in medicine, Dec 1871. TEMPERANCE

Alden, John, one of the first passengers in the *Mayflower*, 1620 Marries Priscilla Mullens, "The Puritan Maiden" Characters in Longfellow's "Miles Standish" MASSACHUSETTS

alderman. The Saxon *ealdorman* was next to the king and frequently a viceroy, but after the Danes came the title was gradually displaced by *earl*. Aldermen in corporations are next in dignity to the mayor They were appointed in London (where there are 26) in 1242, and in Dublin (where there are 24) in 1323 Aldermen chosen for life instead of annually, 17 Rich II 1394 Present mode of election established, 11 Geo I 1725 Aldermen made justices of the peace, 15 Geo II 1741 London aldermen are elected by wards The corresponding term in Scotland is *baillie* In most cities of the U S the aldermen are elected by wards and form a legislative common council

Al'derney, an island in the English Channel, with Jersey, etc, was acquired by William the Conqueror, 1066. The strait called 'The Race' is celebrated for two fatal occurrences William of Normandy, son of Henry I of England, and many young nobles (140 youths of the principal families of France and Britain), were overtaken by a storm and lost, 25 Nov 1120 The British man-of-war *Victory*, of 100 guns and 1100 men, was wrecked here, 5 Oct 1744, the admiral, sir John Balchen, and all his crew, perished Through it the French escaped when defeated at La Hogue by admirals Russell and Rooke, 19 May, 1692 The construction of a breakwater, to make Alderney a naval station, was begun in 1852, but was suspended by parliament in 1871 In 1874 the control of the harbor and lands was transferred from the board of trade to the admiralty and the war department. The island is about 8 miles in circumference, and is noted for its breed of cows.

Aldershot Camp, on a moor near Farnham, about 35 miles from London. In Apr. 1854, the war-office, with a grant of 1,000,000*l.*, purchased 4000 acres of land for a permanent camp for 20,000 men.

Additional land purchased in 1856.
Barracks since erected for 4000 infantry, 1500 cavalry, and several batteries of artillery.

Aldine Press, that of Aldo Manuzio (Aldus Manutius) at Venice, produced many first editions of Greek, Latin, and Italian classics, beginning in 1494 with Musæus.

ale, beer, and **wine,** according to fable, invented by Bacchus. Ale was known in 404 B.C. Herodotus ascribes the art of brewing barley-wine to Isis, the wife of Osiris, and such a beverage is mentioned by Xenophon, 401 B.C. The Romans learned from the Egyptians to prepare fermented liquor from corn.—*Tacitus.* Ale-houses are mentioned in the laws of Ina, king of Wessex. Booths were set up in England, 728, and laws passed for their regulation. None but freemen were allowed to keep ale-houses in London, 13 Edw. I. 1285. They were further regulated by 5 and 6 Edw. VI. c. 25, 1551. By 1 James I. c. 9, 1603, one full quart of the best, or two quarts of small ale, were to be sold for one penny. Excise duty on ale and beer was imposed by parliament in 1643, and continued by Charles II., 1660; repealed, 1 Will. IV. c. 51, 1830. PORTER, VICTUALLERS, and WINE.

Alemanni or **All Men** (*i. e.* men of all nations), hence *Allemand,* German. A body of Suevi, who took this name, were defeated by Caracalla, 214. After several repulses they invaded the empire, but Aurelian subdued them in three battles, 271. They were again vanquished by Julian, 356, 357; by Jovinus, 368; and were subjugated by Clovis at Tolbiac (or Zulpich), 496. The Suabians are their descendants.

Aleppo, N. Syria, a large town named Berœa by Seleucus Nicator, about 299 B.C. The pachalic of Aleppo is one of the five governments of Syria. It was taken by the Saracens, 638 A.D., who restored its ancient name Haleb or Chaleb; by Saladin, 1193; and sacked by Timour, Nov. 1400. Its depopulation by plague has been frequent: 60,000 persons were said to have perished by it in 1797; many in 1827. The cholera raged here in 1832. Aleppo suffered from terrible earthquakes in 1822 and 1830, and has been the scene of fanatical massacres. On 16 Oct. 1850, Mahometans attacked the Christians, burning everything. 3 churches were destroyed, 5 plundered, and thousands of persons slain. The loss of property amounted to about a million sterling; no interference was attempted by the pacha.

"In Aleppo once,
Where a malignant and a turban'd Turk
Beat a Venetian, and traduc'd the state."
Shakespeare, "Othello," act v. sc. ii.

Alesia, a strongly fortified city of the Mandubii, a tribe of ancient Gaul near the head-waters of the Seine (central France), where the final struggle between the Romans, under Cæsar, and the united Gauls, under Vercingetorix, took place, 52 B.C., ending in the complete overthrow of the Gauls. Cæsar destroyed the city. It was rebuilt, but again destroyed by the Normans in the 9th century.

Alessandria, a city of Piedmont, built in 1168 under the name of Cæsar by the Milanese and Cremonese, to defend the Tanaro against Frederick Barbarossa, emperor of Germany, and afterwards named after pope Alexander III. It has often been besieged. The French took it in 1796, were driven out by Suwarrow, 21 July, 1799, recovered it after Marengo, 14 June, 1800, and held it till 1814, when the fortifications erected by Napoleon were destroyed. These have been restored since June, 1856.

Aleutian Isles, in the N. Pacific ocean, discovered by Behring, 1741; visited by Cook, 1778; settled by Russians, 1785; included in cession of ALASKA to U. S. 1867.

Alexander, Era of, dated from the death of Alexander the Great, 12 Nov. 323 B.C. In computing it the Creation was dated 5502 years before Christ, our year 1 A.D. being reckoned 5503, and our year 284 A.D. was called 5786. But after this 10 years were omitted, and the next was called 5777. This is still the ABYSSINIAN ERA. The date is reduced to the Christian era by subtracting 5502 before 5786, and by subtracting 5492 thereafter.

Alexandria, Egypt, with walls 15 miles in circuit, founded by Alexander the Great, 332 B.C.; buried here, 322; later, the residence of Greek sovereigns of EGYPT, the Ptolemies, 323. 17 councils were held here, 231–633 A.D.

	B.C.
Ptolemy Soter erects the Museum, Serapeum, Pharos, and other edifices, and begins the library about	298
These works completed by his son, P. Philadelphus, and grandson, P. Euergetes	283–222
Alexandria taken by Julius Cæsar; when a library fabled to contain 700,000 vols., including every known literary work, whether Egyptian, Jewish, Greek, Latin, Phœnician, Chaldee, Syriac, or Persian, is burned	48
Which Antony replaces by one brought from Pergamus	36
	A.D.
City restored by Hadrian	122
Massacre of the youth by Caracalla in revenge for an insult	215
Alexandria, supporting the usurper Achilleus, is taken by Diocletian after a long siege	297
Disturbed by feuds between Athanasians and Arians	321
George of Cappadocia killed, 362, Athanasius finally restored	363
50,000 persons perish by an earthquake	365
Paganism suppressed by Theodosius; a second library burned (the SERAPEUM)	390
Alexandria captured by Chosroes II. of Persia	616
And by Amrou, general of the caliph Omar, who ordered the library burned, supplying the baths with fuel for six months 22 Dec.	640
[The saying ascribed to Omar—"That if the books agreed with the book of God, they were useless; if they disagreed, they were pernicious"—is denied by Mahometans. It is also attributed to Theophilus, archbishop of Alexandria (390), and to cardinal Ximenes (1500).]	
Recovered by the Greeks; retaken by Amrou	644
Cairo founded by Saracens; hastening decay of Alexandria	969
Alexandria plundered by the crusaders	1365
French capture Alexandria July,	1798
Battle of Alexandria, or Canopus: the British under gen. sir Ralph Abercromby defeat the French under Menou 21 Mch.	1801
Abercromby dies of his wounds, 28 Mch.; Menou surrenders it with 10,000 French to the British 2 Sept.	"
Alexandria taken by British under Fraser, 20 Mch.; evacuated by them 23 Sept.	1807
By the convention of Alexandria, Egypt was guaranteed to Mehemet Ali and his successors	1841
Railway to Cairo built	1851
New port, first stone laid by the khedive 15 May,	1871
The fellow of the obelisk of London (reared at Heliopolis about 1500 B.C. by Thothmes III. and removed to Alexandria about 25 B.C.) was offered to the U. S. in	1877
Offer confirmed May,	1879
Steamer bearing the obelisk sailed from Alexandria 12 June,	1880
Arrives at NEW YORK 20 July,	"

Alexandria, a city of Virginia on the Potomac, 7 miles below Washington. Here on 24 May, 1861, E. E. Ellsworth, col. of the New York Fire Zouaves, was shot, after taking down a confederate flag from the roof of the Marshall house, by Jackson, the proprietor. Jackson was immediately after shot by a soldier of the regiment. VIRGINIA, 1861.

Alexandrian Codex, a MS. of the Septuagint said to have been written by a lady named Thecla in the 6th century, and to have belonged to the patriarch of Alexandria in 1098; was presented to Charles I. of England in 1628 by Cyrillus Lascaris, patriarch of Constantinople; placed in the British museum in 1753, and printed in facsimile, 1786–1821.

Alexandrian Era. MUNDANE.

Alexandrian Library. ALEXANDRIA and LIBRARIES.

Alexandrian Schools of Philosophy. The first school arose soon after the foundation of Alexandria, 332 B.C.; flourished under the Ptolemies till about 100 B.C.; including Euclid (300), Archimedes (287–212), Apollonius (250), Hipparchus (150), and Hero (150). The second school arose about 140 A.D., and lasted till about 400. Its most eminent members were Ptolemy, the author of the Ptolemaic system (150), Diophantus the arithmetician, and Pappus the geometer (350). PHILOSOPHY.

Alexandrines, verses of 12 syllables, forming six iambic feet, named from Alexander of Paris, who introduced it into French literature about 1164. It corresponds with the iambric trimeter, the principal metre of dramatic dialogue in Greek and Latin, and is the heroic verse of French classic writers, but is not suited to German or English poetry, exɔt in bringing to an end a sonorous stanza or system of verses. ɪe last line of the Spenserian stanza is an Alexandrine. In pe's "Essay on Criticism" it is thus exemplified:

> "A needless Alexandrine ends the song,
> That, like a wounded snake, drags its slow length along."

ɪe longest English poem wholly in Alexandrine verse is ayton's "Polyolbion," pub. 1612–22.

Alfalfa, a species of Chilian grass or clover well fitted m its long "tap root" to live and grow where other grass-would wither through excessive droughts. Grown exten-ely in the western United States, especially in California, lorado, Washington, Arizona, etc. Excellent forage for cat-, of rapid growth, yielding under favorable circumstances 3 ɔps a year and from 6 to 10 tons per acre.

Alford, N. Scotland, Battle of. Gen. Baillie, with a large dy of covenanters, was defeated by the marquess of Montrose, July, 1645.

Al'gebar, an Arabic and poetical name of the constella-n Orion.

> "Begirt with many a blazing star
> Stood the great giant Algebar,
> Orion, hunter of the beast!"
> —*Longfellow*, "Occult of Orion."

al'gebra, the generalized method of computation, called Newton "universal arithmetic," in which signs represent erations and symbols stand for quantities; Diophantus, the ɔuted inventor, wrote about 350 A.D. The Arabs, who ɔught algebra to Spain, ascribe the invention to Mohammed Buzia̦ıa, about 850 A.D. Leonardo Bonaccio of Pisa intro-ced Indian algebra into Italy in 1220. In 1494 Luca Paccioli blished the first printed book on algebra in Europe.—*Serret.* me algebraic signs were introduced either by Christophe ıdolph (1522–26) or Michael Stifelius of Nuremberg, 1544, d others by Francis Vieta, in 1590, when algebra came into neral use.—*Moréri.* Jerome Cardan published his "Ars agna," containing his rule, 1545. The first treatise in the ıglish language on algebra was written by Robert Recorde, ıcher of mathematics, Cambridge, about 1557; here, for the st time, the modern sign for equality was used. Thos. Har-ɪt's important discoveries appeared in his "Artis Analyticæ axis," 1631. Descartes applied algebra to geometry about 37. The binomial theorem of Newton, the basis of the doc-ne of fluxions, and the new analysis, 1666. "The Greek ȝebra was as nothing compared with the Greek geometry; d the Hindu geometry was as little worthy of comparison ıth the Hindu algebra."—*Calcutta Review* (1846), p. 540.

Important writers on algebra:

ophantus	350	Harriot	1631
ınacci	1220	Descartes	1637
cciolì or D. ɔurgo	1494	Pascal	1654
ıdolph	1522	Isaac Newton (binomial theorem)	1666
ifelius	1544	Leibnitz	1677
ɪrdan	1545	Lagrange	1767
ɪrrari (first to resolve biquadratic equations)	1545	Euler	1770
stalea	1546	Budan	1807
ɪcorde	1557	Horner	1819
eta	1590	Sturm	1835
rard	1629	Bourdon	1840

[But the most wonderful development of algebraic analysis has taken place in recent years; the works of Whitworth, Salmon, Todhunter, and others in England; of Barnard, Bartlett, and others in America, and of scores of great investigators in Germany and France, form a library of problems successfully solved by algebraic methods in all branches of science.]

Algesiras or **Old Gibraltar,** S. Spain. Here ɪe Moors entered Spain in 711, and held it till taken by Al-nso XI., Mch. 1344.

Algiers, now **Algeria,** N.W. Africa, part of the an-ent Mauritania; conquered by Romans, 46 B.C.; by Van-als, 439 A.D.; recovered for the empire by Belisarius, 534; ıd subdued by Arabs about 690. Pop. of Algeria in 1866, 921,146; in 1886, 3,817,465. Sq. miles, 122,867.

ɔwn of Algiers founded by Arabs near site of Icosium...about 935
ecoming seat of Barbary pirates, captured by Ferdinand of Spain, 1509; retaken by Horuc and Haydreddin Barbarossa, and made capital of a state; governed by a dey, nominally subject to Turkey...1516–20
mperor Charles V. loses a fine fleet and an army in an expedition against Algiers...1541
lgiers terrified into pacific measures by Blake, 1655; by Du Quesne...1683–84
Treaty with the U. S...1795
War declared against the U. S...1815
Commodore Decatur enters the bay of Algiers with a U. S. fleet and dictates a peace...28 June, "
British fleet, under lord Exmouth, bombards the pirate city, 27 Aug. 1816
A new treaty; Christian slavery abolished... "
Treaty of peace with the U. S...22 Dec. "
French armament under Bourmont and Duperré captures Algiers; dey deposed, barbarian government overthrown, 5 July, 1830
Arab chief Abd-el-Kader preaches a holy war, and attacks the French, at first successfully...1833
He is recognized as emir of Mascara by the French...1834
France announces intention to retain Algiers...20 May, "
War renewed...1835–36
Abd-el-Kader submits to French supremacy...30 May, "
War renewed; French defeated...Dec. 1839
Algeria annexed to France, the emir declared a rebel....Feb. 1842
He is defeated by Bugeaud at Isly...14 Aug. 1844
500 Arabs in a cave at Karthani refuse to surrender; suffocated by smoke; said to have been ordered by gen. Pelissier .18 June, 1845
Abd-el-Kader surrenders to Lamoricière...23 Dec. 1847

[He, with suite, embarked at Oran, landed at Toulon 28 Dec. following; was removed to castle of Amboise, near Tours, 2 Nov. 1848, and released by Louis Napoleon, 16 Oct. 1852, after swearing on the Koran never to disturb Africa again. He was to reside at Broussa, in Asia Minor; but in consequence of the earthquake at that place, 28 Feb. 1855, removed to Constantinople. In July, 1860, Abd-el-Kader held the citadel of Damascus, and protected Christians whom he had rescued from massacre by the Turks. He received honors from the English, French, and Sardinian sovereigns. He visited Paris and London in Aug. 1865. He offered to serve in the French army in July, 1870. Died at Damascus, 26 May, 1883, aged 75 years.]

Arab tribes attack French; defeated...31 Oct. and 6 Nov. 1859
Algiers visited by Napoleon III...Sept. 1860
Marshal Pelissier, duke of Malakhoff, appointed governor-general of Algeria...Nov. "
Death of marshal Pelissier, 22 May; MacMahon, duke of Magenta, succeeds him...8 Sept. 1864
Fresh revolts; insurgents defeated by Jolivet...2 Oct. "
10,500 refugees from Alsace-Lorraine emigrate to Algeria...1871
Gen. Chanzy gov.; replaced by Albert Grévy...1878
Dispute with Tunis; outrages by savage tribes, Kroumirs, etc. (TUNIS)...Apr. 1881
Troops sent from France in anticipation of insurrection...Aug. "
Resignation of gov. A. Grévy...6 Nov. "
M. Louis Tirman appointed...Dec. "
Annexation of the province Mazab to Algeria...Dec. 1882

Algonquins. INDIANS.

Alhambra, a Moorish palace and fortress near Granada, S. Spain, founded by Mohammed I. of Granada about 1253, surrendered to the Christians about Nov. 1491. The ruins are described in a magnificent work by Owen Jones and Jules Goury, pub. 1842–45. Washington Irving wrote of the palace and its surroundings a pleasing work, entitled "The Alhambra," pub. 1832.

Ali, sect of (Shiites, or Fatimites). Ali (a son of Abu Talib, uncle of Mahomet), one of the prophet's earliest supporters, becoming his vizier, 613, when quite young, and marrying his daughter, Fatima, about 632; caliph, 655; assassinated, 23 Jan. 661. He was called by the prophet, As'ad Allah Al-ghalib, "the lion of God, always victorious." Ali's right to succeed to the caliphate divided the Mahometan world into two great sects, the SONNITES and the SHIITES, the former denying and the latter affirming it. The Turks belong to the former, the Persians to the latter sect.

The first four successors of Mahomet—Abubeker, Omar, Othman, and Ali, his chief agents in establishing his religion and extirpating unbelievers, and whom he styled the "cutting swords of God"—all died violent deaths; and his family was extirpated within thirty years after his decease.

Alien and Sedition Laws. In 1798, when war between France and the United States was threatened, there were in the United States, by estimate, 30,000 Frenchmen organized in clubs, and 50,000 sympathizers with France who had been British subjects. In apprehension of danger, congress, 25 June, authorized the president to banish alien enemies at his discretion during the ensuing two years. Another act authorizing the president to apprehend and remove alien enemies was passed 6 July. These alien laws were never actively enforced. The sedition act of 14 July, 1798, defined sedition and affixed severe penalties to it. These laws were very unpopular, and helped to drive the federal party from power. RESOLUTIONS OF 1798.

aliens or **foreigners** were banished from England in 1155, being thought too numerous. In 1343 they were excluded from ecclesiastical benefices. By 2 Rich. II. st. 1, 1378, they were much relieved In 1353, under Edward III, half of each jury empanelled to try an alien must consist of foreigners — "The Encyclopædic Dict," *Jury* They were restrained from exercising any trade or handicraft by retail, 1483, a prohibition relaxed in 1663

Alien priories (cells and estates belonging to foreign persons) suppressed in England 1414
The alien act passed Jan 1793
Act to register aliens 1795
Baron Geramb a fashionable foreigner, known at court, ordered out of England 6 Apr 1812
Bill to abolish naturalization by holding stock in the banks of Scotland June 1820
New registration act, 7 Geo IV 1826 This last act was repealed and another statute passed, 6 Will IV 1836
The rigor of alien laws mitigated in 1844 and 1847
"Foreigners have reclaimed our marshes drained our fens fished our seas and built our bridges and harbors"—*Smiles*, 1861
Their status defined by naturalization act 12 May, 1870

An act of congress relieving from alienage children of citizens of the United States, born elsewhere was passed 1855 In 1857 the attorney-general held that a citizen of the United States may renounce his citizenship Aliens are readily naturalized in the United States NATURALIZATION In the United States aliens may sue and be sued, but cannot serve a process, vote or hold office Some states restrict the power of aliens to hold real estate, others do not The inheritance of property of aliens has been the subject of several treaties between the United States and foreign nations UNITED STATES, 1855, etc

Aliwal, *a village of N W India, site of an obstinate* battle, 28 Jan 1846, between the Sikh army under sirdar Runjoor Singh Majeethea, 19,000 strong, with 68 guns, and British under sir Harry Smith, 12,000 men with 32 guns. The Sikhs were defeated with nearly 6000 killed or drowned

alizar'ine, a crystalline body, the coloring principle of madder, discovered by Robiquet and Colin in 1831 Schunck showed that the finest madder colors contained only alizarine combined with alkalies and fatty acids Graebe and Liebermann obtained anthracene from alizarine in 1868, and alizarine from anthracene in 1869 The crystalline body anthracene was discovered in coal oils by Dumas and Laurent in 1832 MADDER

Aljubarrota, Portugal *Here John I of Portugal* defeated John I of Castile, and secured his country's independence, 14 Aug 1385.

al'kalies (from *kali*, Arabic name for the plant from which an alkaline substance was first procured) are ammonia, potash, soda, and lithia. Black explained the difference between caustic and mild alkalies in 1736

Fixed alkalies potash and soda, decomposed, and the metals potassium and sodium freed by Humphry Davy at the Royal Institution, London, 1807
Dr Ure invented an alkalimeter, 1816
Alkalies are extensively manufactured in Lancashire and Cheshire, by decomposing common salt (chloride of sodium) by a process invented by a Frenchman Le Blanc, about 1792
Losh obtained crystals of soda from brine about 1814 Various modifications of these processes are now in use.
"Alkali works" are works for manufacturing alkali, sulphates of soda sulphate of potash and in which muriatic gas is evolved
William Gossage's process for condensing muriatic acid gas patented in 1836
"Ammonia process" of making soda invented by Dyer and Hemming in 1838, patents respecting it taken out by Solvay, 1863, 1867 1872, Gossage, 1854, Schloesing, 1854, 1858, Young, 1871, 1872, Weldon, 1872, 1873, and by others.
Walter Weldon received French Lavoisier medal for important improvements in the alkali manufacture, July 1877
To stop injury to vegetation by alkali works in Lancashire and Cheshire the alkali works act "for the more effectual condensation [of 95 per cent] of muriatic acid gas" (or hydrochloric acid) was passed 28 July, 1863, came into operation 1 Jan. 1864, proved successful was re enacted 1868, and amended 1874
James Greenwood produced caustic soda and chlorine from common salt by electrolytic process, Jan 1892

Allahabad' (city of God), N.W. Hindostan, the "holy city" of the Indian Mahometans, at the junction of the rivers Jumna and Ganges The province of Allahabad was successively subject to the sovereigns of Delhi and Oude, but in 1801 was partly and in 1803 wholly incorporated with the British possessions. By treaty here, Bengal, etc., was ceded to the English in 1765 During the Indian mutiny several sepoy regiments rebelled and massacred their officers, 4 June, 1857, col. Neil marched promptly from Benares and suppressed the insurrection In Nov 1861, lord Canning made this city the capital of the N W provinces

Allatoo'na Pass (Ga), battle of, fought 6 Oct 1864. After his evacuation of Atlanta, Hood covered the road to Macon Soon, however, he shifted southward to the West Point road, and then boldly pushed northward against Sherman's communications Sherman followed him with the bulk of his army, but on 6 Oct had only reached Kenesaw. Hood, farther north that day attacked Allatoona Pass, the most important station on the road, stored with one and a half million of rations, defended by 1944 men Gen Corse conducted the defence successfully until Sherman arrived, when Hood was compelled to withdraw Corse was severely wounded Union loss, 707

allegiance. In the United States the paramount allegiance of a citizen is due to the general government and not to the particular state in which he was born or is domiciled OATH.

allegory abounds in the Bible and in Homer see Jacob's blessing upon his sons Gen xlix (1689 B C), Ps lxxx., and all the prophets. Spenser's "Faerie Queene" (1590) and Bunyan's "Pilgrim's Progress" (1678) are allegories throughout The *Spectator* (1711), by Addison, Steele, and others, abounds in allegories The allegorical interpretation of Scripture is said to have begun with Origen in the 3d century "But he who was of the bondwoman was born after the flesh, but he of the freewoman was by promise Which things are an *allegory*"—Gal iv 23, 24

Allen, Ethan FORT TICONDEROGA and VERMONT

Allia, Italy, a small river flowing into the Tiber, where Brennus and the Gauls defeated the Romans, 16 July, 390 B C. The Gauls sacked Rome, and the day was thereafter held to be unlucky (*nefastus*), and no public business was permitted to be done thereon

alliance, treaties of, between the high European powers. The following are the principal

Of Leipsic	9 Apr 1631
Of Vienna	27 May, 1657
The Triple	28 Jan 1668
Of Warsaw	31 Mch 1683
The Grand	12 May, 1689
The Hague	4 Jan 1717
The Quadruple	2 Aug. 1718
Of Vienna	16 Mch. 1731
Of Versailles	1 May, 1756
Germanic	23 July, 1785
Of Paris	16 May, 1795
Of St Petersburg	8 Apr 1805
Austrian	14 Mch 1812
Of Sweden	24 Mch "
Of Töplitz	9 Sept. 1813
Holy Alliance	26 Sept. 1815
Of England, France, and Turkey (at Constantinople)	12 Mch 1854
Of England and France ratified	3 Apr "
Of Sardinia with the western powers (at Turin)	26 Jan. 1855
Of Sweden with the western powers	19 Dec "
Of Prussia and Italy	June, 1866
Of Germany, Austria, and Italy	13 Mch 1987

COALITIONS, CONVENTIONS, TREATIES, UNITED KINGDOM.

Alliance, Farmers' POLITICAL PARTIES

Allob'roges, Gauls, defeated by Q Fabius Maximus, near the confluence of the Rhone and the Saone, 121 B.C

All-saints' Day (1 Nov) or **All-Hallows,** a festival common to the Roman Catholic, English, and Lutheran churches, said to have been begun by pope Boniface IV. about 607, celebrated in the Pantheon at Rome, and established by pope Gregory IV (about 830) for commemoration of saints and martyrs in whose honor no particular day is assigned The reformers of the English church, 1549, struck out of their calendar many anniversaries, leaving only those at their time connected with popular feeling or tradition. HALLOWEEN

All-souls' Day (2 Nov), a festival of the Roman Catholic church to commemorate the souls of the faithful, instituted, it is said, at Cluny about 993 or 1000

Allsman, Andrew, The case of A confederate, col. Porter, during a raid upon Palmyra, Mo., in Sept. 1862, captured, among others, an old and respected citizen of that place, Andrew Allsman, who was not paroled as the others were, but carried off and it was believed would be put to death by his captors Gen. John McNeil, then in command of the district of N.E. Missouri, hearing of this, circulated widely a notice, 8 Oct. 1862 (even leaving a copy with the wife of col. Porter), that if Allsman was not returned unharmed within ten days, ten prisoners of col. Porter's band would be shot. As Allsman was not returned, ten men were selected to pay the penalty, and were shot at Palmyra, 18 Oct. A vindictive retaliatory order was issued by president Davis, 17 Nov. 1862, but was never carried out.

Alma, a river in the Crimea, near which was fought a battle on 20 Sept. 1854. The allied armies—English, French, and Turkish (about 57,000 men)—crossed the Alma and attacked 40,000 Russians, driving them back with a loss of about 5000. Total loss of the allies, 3400.

almanac (borrowed from the Arabic *al manakh'*), a calendar; a word of unknown origin, which appeared in Arabic in the 16th century. The Egyptians computed time by instruments. An almanac was published by the Greeks at Alexandria about the 2d century. In the British museum and universities are specimens of early almanacs. Michael Nostradamus, the astrologer, wrote an almanac in the style of Merlin, 1556.—*Dufresnoy.* Prof. Augustus de Morgan's valuable "Book of Almanacs, with an index of reference, by which the almanac may be found for every year," was published in March, 1851. Among the earlier and more remarkable almanacs were

Solomon Jarchus.................................... 1150
John Somer's Calendar, written in Oxford.................... 1380
Purbach.................................... 1450–61
One in Lambeth palace, written in.................... 1460
First printed one, published at Buda.................... 1472
Shepheard's Kalendar (first printed in England) by Richard Pynson.................................... 1497
Regiomontanus.................................... 1475–1506
Tybalt's Prognostications.................................... 1533
Almanac Liégeois.................................... 1636
Lilly's Ephemeris.................................... 1644
Poor Robin's Almanac.................................... 1652
British Merlin.................................... 1658
Connaissance des Temps (by Picard).................... 1679
Edinburgh Almanac.................................... 1683
Almanach de France.................................... 1699
Moore's Almanac.................................... 1698 or 1713
Lady's Diary.................................... 1705
Season on the Seasons.................................... 1735
Gentleman's Diary.................................... 1741
Almanach de Gotha.................................... 1764
Nautical Almanac, begun by Dr. Neville Maskelyne (materially improved, 1834).................................... 1767
British Imperial Kalendar.................................... 1809
Hone's Every-day Book.................................... 1826
British Almanac and Companion.................................... 1828
Anniversary Calendar, published by W. Kidd.................... 1832
Chambers's Book of Days.................................... 1862–63
Whitaker's Almanack.................................... 1869

[The Stationers' company claimed the exclusive right of publishing almanacs by letters-patent from James I. to them and the two universities; but the monopoly was broken by the court of Common Pleas in 1775. A bill to renew the privilege was lost in 1779. The *Stamp Duty* on English almanacs, first imposed in 1710, was abolished in Aug. 1834; since when almanacs are innumerable, being issued by tradesmen with their goods.]

almanacs, American. No copy is known to exist of the almanac of 1639, the first published in America, calculated for New England by William Pierce, mariner; another, the "Boston Almanac," by John Foster, 1676. William Bradford at Philadelphia published an almanac of 20 pages, 1685, commonly received as the first almanac published in the colonies (PENNSYLVANIA); a copy from the Brinley library sold in New York, Mch. 1882, for $555.00.

First in New York, by J. Clap.................................... 1697
" " Boston, " Samuel Clough.................................... 1700
New England Almanac, B. Green & J. Allen.................... 1703
Nathaniel Ames's (father of Fisher Ames) Astronomical Diary and Almanac, for 50 years from.................................... 1725
Leeds's American Almanac, Philadelphia.................... 1726
First almanac in Rhode Island, Newport, James Franklin..... 1728
" " " Virginia, Warne's, Williamsburg.................... 1731
Poor Richard's Almanac, Philadelphia, Benj. Franklin..... 1732–86
Father Abraham's Almanac, Philadelphia.................... 1759–99
Low's Almanac, Boston.................................... 1762–1827
First almanac in Providence, R. I., Benj. West.................... 1763
" " " Md., Annapolis.................................... 1763
Webster's Calender or the Albany Almanac (the oldest family almanac still published in the U. S.).................... 1784
Thomas Farmer's Almanac, Boston, still continues.................... 1793
Family Christian Almanac.................................... 1821
First church almanac (Prot. Epis.).................................... 1830
Catholic Almanac and Directory.................................... 1833
First comic almanac.................................... about 1834
" Methodist almanac.................................... 1834
" Baptist almanac.................................... 1842
Nautical almanac.................................... 1855
First Presbyterian almanac.................................... 1858
American Almanac and Repository of Useful Knowledge, pub. Cambridge, Mass. 1830–61. Continued as Spofford's American Almanac, pub. Washington, D. C.................... 1878–90
Whig Almanac, 1838, Horace Greeley. Continued as the Tribune Almanac from.................................... 1855
Evening Journal Almanac, Albany (discontinued 1893)..... 1830–92
New York World Almanac.................................... 1868
Daily News Almanac, Chicago.................................... 1885

[Many daily journals in the United States publish almanacs containing elaborate political and industrial statistics.]

Almanza, S.E. Spain. Here on 25 Apr. 1707, English, Dutch, and Portuguese forces under the earl of Galway were defeated by French and Spanish commanded by James Fitzjames, duke of Berwick (illegitimate son of James II.). Most of the English were killed or made prisoners, the Portuguese fleeing at the first charge.

Almeida (*ăl-mā'e-da*), Portugal, a frontier town, captured by Massena, 27 Aug. 1810. The French entered Spain, leaving a garrison at Almeida; blockaded by the English, 6 Apr. 1811; retaken by Wellington, 11 May, and Massena retired from Portugal.

Almena'ra, a village, N.E. Spain, where, on 28 July, 1710, an English and German army defeated the Spanish army supporting Philip V. Stanhope, the English general, killed the Spanish general, Amezaga, in single conflict—an event unparalleled in modern warfare.

Al'mohades, a faction of Mahometans in Africa, followers of Mohammed ben Abdalla, surnamed El-Mehedi, about 1120; subdued Morocco, 1145; entered Spain and took Seville, Cordova, and Granada, 1146–56; founded a dynasty and ruled Spain till 1232, and Africa till 1278.

al'moner, anciently a clergyman who gave the poor the first dish from the royal table or alms in money. By an ancient canon all bishops were required to keep almoners. In France the grand-almoner was the highest ecclesiastical dignitary before the revolution, 1789. Queen Victoria's almoner (rev. dr. Wellesley, dean of Windsor, appointed 28 May, 1870), or the sub-almoner, distributes the queen's gifts on MAUNDY-THURSDAY.

Almo'ravides, Mahometan partisans in Africa, rose about 1050; entered Spain by invitation, 1086; were overcome by the Almohades in 1147.

almshouses for aged and infirm persons have been founded in large numbers in England since the abolition of religious houses at the reformation in the 16th century. A list of those in London will be found in Low's "Charities of London." POOR.

Alnwick (*an'nick;* Saxon *Ealnwic*), on the river Alne in Northumberland, England, was given at the Conquest to Ivo de Vesci. It has long belonged to the Percies. Malcolm, king of Scotland, besieged Alnwick, and he and his sons were killed 13 Nov. 1093. It was taken by David I. in 1136, and attempted in July, 1174, by William the Lion, who was defeated and taken prisoner. It was burned by king John in 1215, and by the Scots in 1448. Since 1854 the castle has been splendidly repaired and enlarged.

alpa'ca or **paco,** a species of the llama; its soft hairy wool is largely used in cloths. It was introduced into England, about 1836, by the earl of Derby. An alpaca factory (covering eleven acres), with a town, park, almshouses, etc., for the work-people, was erected at Saltaire, near Shipley, Yorkshire, by Titus Salt in 1852. A statue of him at Bradford was unveiled 1 Aug. 1874. He died 29 Dec. 1876. Factories erected in several parts of the United States.

alphabet, from ἄλφα (alpha) and βῆτα (beta), the first two of the Greek letters; Hebrew, *aleph* and *beth.* Our alphabet has a history which may be traced as follows:

Characters.	Time.	Peoples.
Egyptian (Hieroglyphic).	4000 B.C.	Hamitic.
" Hieratic.	1900 B.C.	"
Old Semitic (written from right to left, without true vowels, and invariably 22 letters).	Adopted from the Egyptian.	Semitic.
Phœnician (written from right to left, without true vowels, and invariably 22 letters).	About 1100 B.C.	Semitic.
Old Greek.	Close of 9th century B.C.	Aryan.
Latin.	About 600 A.D.	"
English.	——	"

About 1500 B.C. a Semitic people, probably the Israelites in Egypt, adopted the Egyptian symbols, using them for what is known as old Semitic, as seen in the Siloam inscription at Jerusalem and the Moabite stone now in the Louvre at Paris. Though no writings in the Phoenician language have descended to our time we have sufficient authority for the number and form of their letters. The opinion of De Rougé and others, that the Phoenicians adopted the old Semitic symbols, is generally accepted. It is interesting to see what truth there is in the old Greek legend of Cadmus, son of Agenor, of Egypt, [illegible] introducing [illegible] from Phoenicia or Egypt an alphabet of 16 letters, viz. A ἄλφα, B βῆτα, Γ γάμμα, Δ δέλτα, E ἔψιλον, I ἰῶτα, K κάππα, Λ λάμβδα, M μῦ, N νῦ, O ὄ μικρόν, Π πῖ, P ῥῶ, Σ σίγμα, T ταῦ. Additions were made to these later by the Greeks themselves, until about 400 B.C. they had 24 letters. "That the Greek alphabet is derived from the Phoenician, the analogy of the two proves beyond dispute."—Grote, "History of Greece," vol. iii. p. 340. The Greek alphabet thus acquired was carried by the Chalcidians of Euboea at the end of the 8th century B.C., to Cumae in Campania, Italy, where, teaching the early Romans, it was transmitted by them to Latin Christendom, and so became the literary alphabet of Europe and America. It is now, except the Arabic, the only alphabet with any claim to cosmopolitan extension. Of nearly 200 alphabets known, about 50 are now in use, mostly derived from those named above. The alphabets of the principal nations contain the following number of letters:

English	26	Hebrew	22
French	25	Arabic	28
Italian	20	Persian	32
Spanish	27	Turkish	33
German	26	Sanscrit	48
Slavonic	42	Chinese radical characters	214
Russian	36	Chinese alphabet said to be invented by bishop [illegible]	
Latin	22	Gen of Canton (1850).	
Greek	24		

Dr. Taylor's learned work, "The Alphabet," was published May, 1883. EGYPT; HIEROGLYPHICS.

Alphonsine Tables, astronomical [illegible] posed by Spanish and Arab astronomers, and [illegible] 1252 under Alphonso X. of Castile (the Wise), [illegible] to have expended 400,000 ducats upon the [illegible] the preface. The Spanish government began [illegible] 1863.

Alps, European mountains. [illegible] Italy were passed by Hannibal, [illegible] [illegible] and by Napoleon I., May, 1800. [illegible] [illegible] Simplon, connecting France and [illegible] [illegible] order of Napoleon, between 1800 [illegible] [illegible] club of British travellers in the [illegible] and published, in two works, "Peaks [illegible] 1859; and a journal since. [illegible]

They are named:

Maritime,
Cottian (Mt. Cenis [illegible]),
Dauphine,
Graian,
Pennine { Great St. Bernard, Mt. Rosa and [illegible], Matterhorn, Simplon Pass.
Bernese,
North Swiss,

Alsace or **Elsass**, [illegible] Austrasia, afterwards the [illegible] Lower Rhine, was incorporated [illegible] 17th century. A portion [illegible] whole, including Strasburg, [illegible] by the Germans, Aug.–Sept. [illegible] [illegible] to choose their nationality [illegible] emigrated into France. The [illegible] [illegible] was introduced [illegible] as a province of the German [illegible] having been ceded by France [illegible] 10 May, 1871. DELFHT. [illegible] to the German parliament.

Alsatia, a name given to the [illegible] Whitefriars, is described in Scott's "Fortunes [illegible] rights of sanctuary were abolished in 1697.

Alsen, Denmark, besieged by the Prussians, and heroically defended, 26 June; taken, 29 June, 1864.

altar. One was built by Noah, 2348 B.C. (Gen. viii. 20); others by Abraham, 1921 (Gen. xii. 8). Directions for making altars are given, Exod. xx. 24 (1491 B.C.). Altars were raised to Zeus in Greece, by Cecrops, 1556 B.C. He introduced among the Greeks the worship of the deities of Egypt.

Scripture. The Lord's table was called "altar" for 300 years after Christ (Heb. xiii. 10). Christian altars in churches were instituted by pope Sixtus I., 135 A.D., and were first consecrated by pope Sylvester. The Church of England terms the table on which the elements are placed an altar. Since the time of Elizabeth there has been much controversy on the subject, and the Puritans in the civil war destroyed many ancient stone altars, substituting wooden tables. In Jan. 1845, it was decided, in the Arches court, that stone altars were not to be erected in English churches.

Altenkirchen, Prussia. Here the French defeated the Austrians, 4 June, 1796; but were defeated, and their general Marceau killed, 19 Sept. following.

alter ego (another or second I), applied to Spanish viceroys when exercising regal power; used at Naples when the hereditary prince was appointed vicar-general during an insurrection in July, 1820.

Alton riot. Rev. Elijah P. Lovejoy established the St. Louis Observer in the city of St. Louis, Mo., 22 Nov. 1833. Taking decided grounds against slavery, Apr. 1835, he is obliged to remove his paper, going to Alton, Ill., 8 Sept. 1836. His press is destroyed on the night of 21 Aug. 1837; another press destroyed by a body of disguised men 21 Sept., as it was landed. A third press arrives 7 Nov., and is stored for safekeeping in a stone building guarded by citizens, who are attacked by an armed mob the same night. During the riot, which lasted several hours, Mr. Lovejoy is shot and instantly killed, and the press destroyed. The leaders of the mob are tried but acquitted. ILLINOIS and UNITED STATES, [illegible]

Altona, Holstein, N. Germany, acquired by the Danes, [illegible] and made a city, [illegible]; was occupied first by the [illegible] federal troops, 24 [illegible] 1863, and then by the Prussians; the federal diet [illegible], 12 Feb. 1864.

Alt-Ranstadt, [illegible] where the treaty of peace [illegible] by Charles XII. [illegible] to Frederick Augustus [illegible] was signed [illegible]

alum, a salt, [illegible] been first discovered at [illegible] in Syria, [illegible] in Tuscany about 1470; [illegible] by sir T. Chaloner, in [illegible] 1608; discovered in [illegible] [illegible] is used as a mordant in [illegible] bread, and in the paper [illegible]

[illegible] other buildings near [illegible] [illegible] rebels, 23 Sept. 18[illegible] [illegible] under sir James [illegible] [illegible] sepoys on 12 [illegible] [illegible] by sir C[illegible]

[illegible]

was published in 1859. An aluminium manufactory was established at Newcastle, Eng., in 1860, by Messrs. Bell. They obtain the metal from a French mineral, bauxite. Their aluminium bronze, an alloy of 10 per cent. of aluminium and 90 per cent. of copper, invented by dr. John Percy, F.R.S., was made into watch-cases, etc., by Messrs. Reid of Newcastle, in 1862. Other important works are established in England. One at Birmingham produces the metal on a large scale. The principal works in the United States are the Cowles Electric Smelting and Aluminium Works at Cleveland, O., and another at Lockport, N. Y.,—the latter running 7 dynamos of 312 horse-power. The alloys of aluminium are numerous and useful. Aluminium brass has been selected by the United States government for propeller blades of the war-vessels now in course of construction. The cost of the production of the metal is constantly lessening.

Amadis of Gaul, a Spanish or Portuguese romance, stated to have been written about 1342 by Vasco de Lobeira. It was enlarged by De Montalvo about 1465; and first printed (in Spanish), 1519; in French, 1540-56. LITERATURE, Spanish.

Am'alekites (descendants of Amalek, grandson of Esau, the brother of Jacob) attacked the Israelites, 1491 B.C., when perpetual war was denounced against them. They were subdued by Saul about 1079; by David, 1058 and 1056; and by the Simeonites about 715 B.C.

Amal'fi, a city on the gulf of Salerno, Naples, in the 8th century became the seat of a republic and of flourishing commerce till 1075, when it was taken by Roger Guiscard and eventually incorporated with Naples. The Pisans, in their sack of the town in 1135, are said to have found the Pandects of Justinian, and thus revived the study of Roman law; the story is now doubted. Flavio Gioia, a native of Amalfi, is the reputed discoverer of the mariner's compass, about 1302.

Am'ana Inspirationists, A Pietist community which came from Germany in 1842, under Christian Metz, and settled at Ebenezer, near Buffalo, N. Y. In 1856, "commanded by inspiration," they removed to Iowa and settled at Amana, on the Iowa river, about 75 miles from Davenport. They are one of the largest and richest communities in the United States.

Am'azon, a river in S. America, discovered by Vicente Yañez Pinzon in 1500, explored by Francisco Orellana in 1540. Coming from Peru, he sailed down the Amazon to the Atlantic, and, observing armed women on its banks, he called the country Amazonia, and the river, previously called Marañon, the Amazon.

Amazons, fabled tribes or warlike communities of women in Scythia, Asia, and Africa. They were said to be descendants of Scythians of Cappadocia, where their husbands, having made incursions, were all slain in ambuscades. The widows formed a feminine state, declaring matrimony a shameful servitude.—*Quintus Curtius.* They were said to have been [illegible] by Theseus, about 1251 B.C. According to Homer [illegible] allies of the Trojans in the siege of Troy, where [illegible] Penthesilea was slain by Achilles. Theseus and [illegible], queen of the Amazons, are characters in Shakespeare's [illegible] Midsummer-Night's Dream," in which Theseus alludes to his defeat of Hippolyta in battle:

> "Hippolyta, I woo'd thee with my sword,
> And won thy love doing thee injuries;
> But I will wed thee in another key,
> With pomp, with triumph, and with revelling."
>
> —*Act I. sc. 1.*

[illegible]ns were constantly at war; and, for ease in hand[illegible]ns, their right breasts were destroyed, whence their [illegible] the Greek—*ἀ*, without, *μαζός*, breast. Others de[illegible]ne from *maza*, the moon, which they are supposed [illegible]shipped. About 330 B.C. their queen Thalestris [illegible] under the Great, in Asia, with 300 women in her [illegible]*us Curtius.*

[illegible]adors, Accredited agents and representatives [illegible] are referred to in early ages. In most [illegible] great privileges, and in England they are [illegible] secured against arrest. England has now [illegible] 27 ministers, and about 50 chief consuls [illegible] besides inferior agents. The dip[illegible] the different governments rank thus: (1)

ambassadors; (2) envoys and ministers plenipotentiary; (3) ministers resident; (4) chargés d'affaires. The United States sent no[t a] higher rank than envoys extraordinary and ministers plenipotentiary until 1893, [illegible] Great Britain being the first ambassador. [illegible]

[illegible]

Plen[illegible] of the United States, in the principal powers of Europe.

[illegible]

amber, a carbonaceous mineral, of great repute from the earliest time, principally found in northern Europe, also in [illegible], in the United States, and in Asia; anciently [illegible] medicine. Theophrastus wrote upon it, 300 B.C. 150 tonnes found in one year on the sands of the shore near Pillau [illegible]. The origin of amber is much disputed. It is considered by Berzelius to have been a resin dissolved in [illegible]. It often contains perfect insects. Sir D. Brewster regards it as indurated vegetable juice. When rubbed it evolves electricity, and from its Greek name, *ēlectron*, the word electricity is derived.

ambergris, a solid fatty inflammable substance of a dull grey or blackish color, variegated like marble, and of a sweet earthy odor. It is a morbid secretion formed in the intestines of the spermaceti whale, as was first satisfactorily established by Dr. Swediaur in a communication to the Royal Society (*Philosophical Transactions,* vol. lxxiii.).

Amblef, near Cologne, Germany. Here Charles Martel defeated Chilperic II. and Ragenfrid, mayor of the Neustrians, 716.

Amboise (*om-bwoz'*), C. France. Here a conspiracy of the Huguenots (here first so called) against Francis II., Catherine de' Medicis, and the Guises, was suppressed in Jan. 1560; 1200 massacred. On 19 March, 1563, the Pacification of Amboise was published, granting toleration to the Huguenots. The civil war was, however, soon renewed.

Amboy'na, chief of the Molucca isles, discovered about 1512 by the Portuguese, but not wholly occupied by them till 1580; taken by the Dutch, 1605. The English factors were cruelly tortured and put to death, 17 Feb. 1624, by the Dutch, on an accusation of a conspiracy to expel them from the island, when the two nations shared in the pepper trade of Java. Cromwell compelled the Dutch to give 4300*l.* to the descendants of the sufferers. Amboyna was seized by the English, 16 Feb. 1796, but was restored by the treaty of Amiens in 1802. It was again seized by the British, 17-19 Feb. 1810, and again restored at the peace of May, 1814.

ambulances. Wheeled ambulances for the rapid

About 1900 B.C. a Semitic people, probably the Israelites in Egypt, adopted the Egyptian symbols, using them for what is known as old Semitic, as seen in the Siloam inscription at Jerusalem and the Moabite stone now in the Louvre at Paris. Though no writings in the Phœnician language have descended to our time, we have sufficient authority for the number and form of their letters. The opinion of De Rouge and others, that the Phœnicians adopted the old Semitic symbols, is generally accepted. It is instructive to see what truth there is in the old Greek legend of Cadmus, son of Agenor, of Egyptian descent, introducing into Greece from Phœnicia or Egypt an alphabet of 16 letters: viz., A, *ἄλφα*; B, *βῆτα*; Γ, *γάμμα*; Δ, *δέλτα*; E, *ἒ ψιλόν*; F, *Ϝαῦ*; I, *ἰῶτα*; K, *κάππα*; Λ, *λάμβδα*; M, *μῦ*; N, *νῦ*; O, *ὂ μικρόν*; Π, *πῖ*; P, *ρῶ*; Σ, *σίγμα*, T, *ταῦ*. Additions were made to these later by the Greeks themselves, until about 400 B.C. they had 24 letters. "That the Greek alphabet is derived from the Phœnician, the analogy of the two proves beyond dispute."—*Grote*, "History of Greece," vol. iii. p. 340. The Greek alphabet thus acquired was carried by the Chalcidians of Eubœa, at the end of the 9th century B.C., to Cumae in Campania, Italy, where, reaching the early Romans, it was transmitted by them to Latin Christendom, and so became the literary alphabet of Europe and America. It is now, except the Arabic, the only alphabet with any claim to cosmopolitan extension. Of nearly 200 alphabets known, about 50 are now in use, mostly derived from those named above. The alphabets of the principal nations contain the following number of letters:

English	26	Hebrew	22
French	25	Arabic	28
Italian	22	Persian	32
Spanish	27	Turkish	28
German	26	Sanscrit	44
Slavonic	42	Chinese radical characters	214
Russian	35	Chinese alphabet said to be invented by bishop Eligius Cosi of Canton (1880)	33
Latin	22		
Greek	24		

Dr. Taylor's learned work, "The Alphabet," was published May, 1883. EGYPT; HIEROGLYPHICS.

Alphonsine Tables, astronomical tables, composed by Spanish and Arab astronomers, and collected in 1253 under Alphonso X. of Castile (the Wise), who is said to have expended 400,000 crowns upon the work, and wrote the preface. The Spanish government began a republication, 1863.

Alps, European mountains. Those between France and Italy were passed by Hannibal, 218 B.C.; by the Romans, 154 B.C.; and by Napoleon I., May, 1800. Roads over Mont Cenis and the Simplon, connecting France and Italy, were constructed by order of Napoleon, between 1801–6. SIMPLON. The Alpine club of British travellers in the Alps was founded in 1858, and published its first work, "Peaks, Passes, and Glaciers," 1859; and a journal since. MATTERHORN; MONT BLANC.

They are named,

Maritime,
Cottian (MT. CENIS TUNNEL),
Dauphine,
Graian,
Pennine { Great St. Bernard, Mt. Blanc and Rosa, Matterhorn, Simplon Pass,
Bernese,
North Swiss,
Lepontine (ST. GOTHARD TUNNEL),
Rhoetian,
Lombard,
Vindelician,
Northern Noric,
Central Tyrol,
Styrian,
South Tyrol,
Venetian, and
South Eastern.

Alsace′ or **Elsass,** formerly part of the kingdom of Austrasia, afterwards the French departments of the Upper and Lower Rhine, was incorporated with the German empire in the 10th century. A portion was restored to France, 1648, and the whole, including Strasburg, in 1697. Alsace was reconquered by the Germans, Aug.–Sept. 1870. The Alsatians were permitted to choose their nationality, before 30 Sept. 1872. 45,000 emigrated into France. The German system of compulsory education was introduced. Alsace-Lorraine was constituted a province of the German empire by law of 9 June, 1871, having been ceded by France by the treaty of peace concluded 10 May, 1871. BELFORT. The province sends 15 members to the German parliament.

Alsa′tia, a name given to the precinct of Whitefriars, London, is described in Scott's "Fortunes of Nigel." Its privilege of sanctuary was abolished in 1697.

Alsen, Denmark, besieged by the Prussians, and heroically defended, 26 June; taken, 29 June, 1864.

altar. One was built by Noah, 2348 B.C. (Gen. viii. 20); others by Abraham, 1921 (Gen. xii. 8). Directions for making an altar are given, Exod. xx. 24 (1491 B.C.). Altars were raised to Zeus, in Greece, by Cecrops, 1556 B.C. He introduced among the Greeks the worship of the deities of Egypt. —*Herodotus.* The Lord's table was called "altar" for 300 years after Christ (Heb. xiii. 10). Christian altars in churches were instituted by pope Sixtus I., 135 A.D.; and were first consecrated by pope Sylvester. The Church of England terms the table on which the elements are placed an *altar.* Since the time of Elizabeth there has been much controversy on the subject, and the Puritans in the civil war destroyed many ancient stone altars, substituting wooden tables. In Jan. 1845, it was decided, in the Arches court, that *stone altars* were not to be erected in English churches.

Altenkirchen, Prussia. Here the French defeated the Austrians, 4 June, 1796; but were defeated, and their general, Marceau, killed, 19 Sept. following.

alter ego (*another* or *second I*), applied to Spanish viceroys when exercising regal power; used at Naples when the crown-prince was appointed vicar-general during an insurrection in July, 1820.

Alton riot. Rev. Elijah P. Lovejoy established the *St. Louis Observer* in the city of St. Louis, Mo., 22 Nov. 1833. Taking decided grounds against slavery, Apr. 1835, he is obliged to remove his paper, going to Alton, Ill., 8 Sept. 1836. Here his press is destroyed on the night of 21 Aug. 1837; another press destroyed by a body of disguised men 21 Sept., as soon as landed. A third press arrives 7 Nov., and is stored for safe keeping in a stone building guarded by citizens, who are attacked by an armed mob the same night. During the siege, which lasted several hours, Mr. Lovejoy is shot and instantly killed, and the press destroyed. The leaders of the mob were tried but acquitted. ILLINOIS and UNITED STATES, 1837.

Alto′na, Holstein, N. Germany, acquired by the Danes, 1660, and made a city, 1664. It was occupied first by the German federal troops, 24 Dec. 1863, and then by the Prussians (the federal diet protesting), 12 Feb. 1864.

Alt-Ranstadt, Prussia, where the treaty of peace dictated by Charles XII. of Sweden to Frederick Augustus of Poland was signed 24 Sept. 1706, o. s.

alum, a salt, is said to have been first discovered at Roccha, in Syria, about 1300; found in Tuscany about 1470; its manufacture perfected in England by sir T. Challoner, in large alum works near Whitby in 1608; discovered in Ireland, 1757; in Anglesey, 1790. Alum is used as a mordant in dyeing, to harden tallow, to whiten bread, and in the paper manufacture.

Alumbagh, a palace with other buildings near Lucknow, Oude, India, taken from the rebels, 23 Sept. 1857, and heroically defended by the British under sir James Outram. He defeated an attack of 30,000 sepoys on 12 Jan. 1858, and of 20,000 on 21 Feb. and was relieved by sir Colin Campbell in March.

alumin′ium, a metal, the base of the earth alumina, which is combined with silica in clay, and which was distinguished from lime by Marggraff in 1754. Oerstedt in 1826 obtained the chloride of aluminium; in 1827 the metal was obtained from it by F. Wöhler, but was long a scientific curiosity, the process being expensive. It is never found in a metallic state, but always with oxygen in the form of Al_2O_3. The production was afterwards simplified by Bunsen and others, especially by H. Ste.-Claire Deville, who in 1856 succeeded in procuring considerable quantities. First bar exhibited at Palais de l'Industrie, 1855. It is very light (sp. g. 2.25), malleable, and sonorous; its atomic weight 27.4 to 27.5; density 2.5 to 2.67 when hammered; electrical conductivity 4 times that of iron; when pure does not rust, and is not acted on by sulphur or any acid except hydrochloric. The eagles of the French colors have been made of it, and many other ornamental and useful articles. Helmet made for the king of Denmark, 1856. Deville's work, "De l'Aluminium," was published in 1859 An aluminium manufactory was established at Newcastle, Eng, in 1860, by Messrs. Bell They obtain the metal from a French mineral, bauxite Their aluminium bronze, an alloy of 10 per cent of aluminium and 90 per cent of copper, invented by dr John Percy, F R S, was made into watch-cases, etc, by Messrs. Reid of Newcastle, in 1862 Other important works are established in England One at Birmingham produces the metal on a large scale The principal works in the United States are the Cowles Electric Smelting and Aluminium Works at Cleveland, O, and another at Lockport, N Y —the latter running 2 dynamos of 217 horse-power The alloys of aluminium are numerous and useful Aluminium brass has been selected by the United States government for propeller blades of the war-vessels now in course of construction The cost of the production of the metal is constantly lessening

Amadis of Gaul, a Spanish or Portuguese romance stated to have been written about 1342 by Vasco de Lobeira It was enlarged by De Montalvo about 1485, and first printed (in Spanish), 1519, in French, 1540-56 LITERATURE, Spanish

Am'alekites (descendants of Amalek, grandson of Esau, the brother of Jacob) attacked the Israelites, 1491 B C, when perpetual war was denounced against them They were subdued by Saul about 1079 by David, 1058 and 1056 and by the Simeonites about 715 B C

Amal'fi, a city on the gulf of Salerno, Naples, in the 8th century became the seat of a republic and of flourishing commerce till 1075 when it was taken by Roger Guiscard and eventually incorporated with Naples The Pisans, in their sack of the town in 1135, are said to have found the Pandects of Justinian, and thus revived the study of Roman law, the story is now doubted Flavio Gioia, a native of Amalfi, is the reputed discoverer of the mariner s compass, about 1302

Am'ana Inspirationists. A Pietist community which came from Germany in 1842, under Christian Metz, and settled at Ebenezer, near Buffalo, N Y In 1855, commanded by inspiration," they removed to Iowa and settled at Amana, on the Iowa river, about 75 miles from Davenport They are one of the largest and richest communities in the United States

Am'azon, a river in S America, discovered by Vicente Yañez Pinzon in 1500, explored by Francisco Orellana in 1540 Coming from Peru, he sailed down the Amazon to the Atlantic, and observing armed women on its banks, he called the country Amazonia, and the river, previously called Marañon, the Amazon

Amazons, fabled tribes or warlike communities of women in Scythia, Asia, and Africa They were said to be descendants of Scythians of Cappadocia, where their husbands, having made incursions, were all slain in ambuscades The widows formed a feminine state, declaring matrimony a shameful servitude —*Quintus Curtius* They were said to have been conquered by Theseus, about 1231 B C According to Homer they were allies of the Trojans in the siege of Troy, where their queen Penthesilea was slain by Achilles Theseus and Hippolyta, queen of the Amazons, are characters in Shakespeare's "Midsummer-Night's Dream," in which Theseus alludes to his defeat of Hippolyta in battle

"Hippolyta, I woo'd thee with my sword,
And won thy love doing thee injuries,
But I will wed thee in another key
With pomp, with triumph, and with revelling"
—Act I sc. i

The Amazons were constantly at war, and, for ease in handling weapons, their right breasts were destroyed whence their name from the Greek—*ἀ*, without, *μαζός*, breast. Others derive the name from *maza*, the moon, which they are supposed to have worshipped About 330 B.C their queen Thalestris visited Alexander the Great, in Asia, with 300 women in her train.—*Quintus Curtius*

ambassadors. Accredited agents and representatives between monarchs are referred to in early ages. In most countries they have great privileges, and in England they and their servants are secured against arrest. England has now (1893) 8 ambassadors, 27 ministers, and about 36 chief consuls, resident at foreign courts, besides inferior agents. The diplomatic agents of the different governments rank thus (1) ambassadors, (2) envoys and ministers plenipotentiary, (3) ministers resident, (4) chargés d'affaires The United States sent none of higher rank than envoys extraordinary and ministers plenipotentiary, until 1893, Thomas F Bayard of Delaware, to Great Britain being the first ambassador UNITED STATES, 1893

The Russian ambassador s imprisonment for debt to a lace merchant 27 July, 1708 led to the statute of 7 Anne for the protection of ambassadors 1708

Two men convicted of arresting the servant of an ambassador were sentenced to be conducted to the house of the ambassador with a label on their breasts, to ask his pardon, one of them was also imprisoned for three months and the other fined 12 May, 1780

The first ministers of the United States to France were Dr Franklin Silas Deane, and Arthur Lee 1778 Deane and Lee were soon recalled and Franklin made sole envoy

The first minister plenipotentiary from the United States to England, John Adams presented to the king 1 June 1785, the first from Great Britain to America was Mr Hammond in 1791

First ministers, under the constitution, to the principal powers of Europe

Gouverneur Morris N Y commissioner, Great Britain	13 Oct	1789
William Short, Va, chargé d affaires, France (first commission signed by Washington)	6 Apr	1790
William Carmichael Md, chargé d affaires, Spain	11 Apr	"
David Humphrey, Conn, minister resident Portugal	21 Feb.	1791
Thomas Pinckney, S C, minister plenipotentiary, Great Britain	12 Jan	1792
Gouverneur Morris, N Y, minister plenipotentiary, France,	12 Jan	"
William Short, Va, minister resident Netherlands	16 Jan	"
John Jay N Y, envoy extraordinary Great Britain	19 Apr	1794
John Q Adams Mass, minister plenipotentiary, Prussia,	1 June,	1797
John Q Adams minister plenipotentiary Russia	27 June,	1809
Jonathan Russell, R I minister plenipotentiary, Norway and Sweden	18 Jan	1814
Henry Wheaton, N Y, chargé d'affaires, Denmark	3 Mch	1827
David Porter (admiral) chargé d'affaires Turkey		1831
John Nelson Md, chargé d affaires, Roman States and kingdom Two Sicilies		"
Henry A Muhlenberg Pa, minister plenipotentiary, Austria		1838
George P Marsh, Vt, minister plenipotentiary Italy		1861
George Bancroft, N Y, minister plenipotentiary, German Empire		1871
Thomas F Bayard Del ambassador (the first) to Great Britain		1893
James B. Eustis, La, ambassador (the first) to France		1893

amber, a carbonaceous mineral, of great repute from the earliest time, principally found in northern Europe, also in southern Europe, in the United States, and in Asia, anciently esteemed as medicine Theophrastus wrote upon it, 300 B C 150 tons were found in one year on the sands of the shore near Pillau —*Phillips* The origin of amber is much disputed It is considered by Berzelius to have been a resin dissolved in volatile oil It often contains perfect insects Sir D Brewster regards it as indurated vegetable juice. When rubbed it evolves electricity, and from its Greek name, *ἤλεκτρον*, the word *electricity* is derived

ambergris, a solid fatty inflammable substance of a dull gray or blackish color, variegated like marble, and of a sweet earthy odor It is a morbid secretion formed in the intestines of the spermaceti whale, as was first satisfactorily established by Dr Swediaur in a communication to the Royal Society (*Philosophical Transactions*, vol lxxiii)

Amblef, near Cologne, Germany. Here Charles Martel defeated Chilperic II and Ragenfroi, mayor of the Neustrians, 716.

Amboise (*am-bwaz'*), C. France. Here a conspiracy of the Huguenots (here first so called) against Francis II, Catherine de' Medicis, and the Guises, was suppressed in Jan 1560, 1200 massacred On 19 March, 1563, the Pacification of Amboise was published granting toleration to the Huguenots The civil war was, however, soon renewed

Amboy'na, chief of the Molucca isles, discovered about 1512 by the Portuguese, but not wholly occupied by them till 1580, taken by the Dutch, 1605. The English factors were cruelly tortured and put to death, 17 Feb 1624, by the Dutch, on an accusation of a conspiracy to expel them from the island, where the two nations shared in the pepper trade of Java. Cromwell compelled the Dutch to give £300,000 to the descendants of the sufferers Amboyna was seized by the English, 16 Feb. 1796, but was restored by the treaty of Amiens in 1802. It was again seized by the British, 17-19 Feb. 1810; and again restored at the peace of May, 1814

ambulances. Wheeled ambulances for the rapid

transportation of wounded soldiers from the battle-field are due to the French surgeon, Larrey, who employed them in the army of the Rhine in 1792 Ambulance wagons did not exist in the British army even during the Crimean war, they were introduced into the service, however, by lord Hubert's commission in 1857-58

Congress establishes a uniform system of ambulances in the United States 11 Mch 1864

Bellevue hospital ambulance service established in New York, at the suggestion of the commissioners of public charities, by M T S Brennan 1869

St John's Ambulance Association established in England by the duke of Manchester for the purpose of disseminating general information as to first aid to the sick and injured 1877

Street ambulance branch of the London hospital association established with 55 stations 1880

amen, an ancient Hebrew word meaning *true, faithful, certain,* used in Jewish and Christian assemblies at the end of prayer see 1 Cor xiv 16 (59 A D). It is translated "*verily,*" in the Gospels

amende honorable, in France, in the 9th century, a punishment for traitors and sacrilegious persons the offender was delivered to the hangman, stripped of his shirt, a rope round his neck, and a taper in his hand, he was led into court to beg pardon of God and the country Death or banishment sometimes followed The term is often applied to a recantation or an apology to an injured person

Amendments of the Constitution of the United States. CONSTITUTION

Amer'ica, the western continent comprising North, Central, and South America. From its northern point, Point Barrow, 71° 21′ n lat, to its southern, Cape Horn, 55° 58′ s lat., it extends 127° 22′ of latitude, while from Cape Prince of Wales, 167° 30′ w. lon, its western limit, to Cape St Roque, 35° 20′ w lon, its eastern, it extends 132° 10′ of longitude, with an area of 17,598,220 sq miles, North America being 9,537,154, Central 30[illegible],531, and South, 7,755,535, including the islands Pop 1890 N America, including Central, about 88,500,000, S America, 33,300,000 Its name is derived from Amerigo Vespucci, a Florentine merchant, who, born in 1451, died in 1512 He accompanied Ojeda in his voyage on the eastern coast in 1498, and described the country in letters to friends in Italy He is charged with presumptuously inserting "Tierra de Amerigo" in his maps Irving discusses the question in the Appendix to the "Life of Columbus," but comes to no conclusion Humboldt asserts that the name was given to the continent in the popular works of W[illegible], a German geographer, without the knowledge of Vespucci America is the native place of maize, the turkey, the potato, Peruvian bark, tobacco, and the tomato Of its history prior to Columbus little is known The Spaniards found in Mexico and Peru a people far more civilized than elsewhere on the continent, but whether their civilization was advancing or receding is conjectural Ruins of cities in Central America and Mexico seem to be relics of still higher civilization

CONJECTURAL HISTORY

B.C

(1) The Pre Toltec period, semi mythic traditions of the earliest civilization, to about 500 A D (2) The Toltec period, to the 11th century A D (3) The Chichimic period to the establishment of the Aztec power (4) The Aztec period, ending in 1523 by the Spanish conquest.

Civilization of aborigines of Mexico and Central America begun by the advent of Votan about 955

Zamna introduces the Maya civilization and founds Mayapan, capital of what is now Yucatan . . about 800

Pirua dynasty probably begins in Peru 476

[The Toltecs arrive in Mexico and Central America about the Christian era, and displace the previous government]

[The lunar calendar introduced] A.D.

Mexican history begins according to Ixtlilxochitl 503

Toltecs established throughout Mexico 600

Pirua dynasty declines in Peru ... 830

End of the Toltec power in Mexico . . 1050

Incas rule begins in Peru 1240

Rise of Aztec power and founding of city of Mexico . 1325

Overthrow of Aztec power by Spaniards under Cortez 1523

Hieroglyphic documents containing traditions of the Pre-Toltec or Votan period said to have been publicly destroyed by Francisco Nuñez de la Vega, bishop of Chiapas 1691

[The best connected account of the histories of the ancient peoples of Central America and Mexico is by abbé Brasseur de Bourbourg, 4 tomes, 8vo, 1857-59]

THE NORSEMEN IN ICELAND, GREENLAND, AND AMERICA

Iceland discovered by Nadodd, a Norse rover 861

First settlement by Norsemen 875

Grumbiorn sights a western land 876

Land discovered by Eric the Red, and named Greenland 982

Second voyage from Iceland to Greenland by Eric 985

Bjarni sails from Iceland for Greenland, but is driven south by a storm and sights land at Cape Cod or Nantucket, also at Newfoundland, and returns to Greenland 985

Voyage of Leif, son of Eric the Red He sails in 1 ship with 35 men in search of the land seen by Bjarni 1000

Touching the Labrador coast, stops near Boston, Mass, or farther south, for the winter He loads his vessel with timber, he returns to Greenland in the spring of 1001

[He calls the land Vinland, from its grapes]

[Thorwald, Leif's brother, visits Vinland in 1002, and winters near Mt Hope bay, R I In the spring of 1003 he sent a party of his men to explore the coast, perhaps as far south as Cape May]

Thorwald explores the coast eastward, and is killed in a skirmish with the natives (skraelings) somewhere near Boston . 1004

His companions return to Greenland 1005

[Thorfinn Karlsefne sails with 3 ships and 160 persons (5 of them young married women) from Greenland to establish a colony about 1007-8 Landing in Rhode Island, he remains in Vinland three years where he has a son, ancestor of Albert Thorwaldsen the Danish sculptor]

Icelandic manuscripts mention a bishop in Vinland in 1121, and other voyages there in 1125, 1135 and 1147

[The fullest relation of these discoveries is the "Codex Flatöiensis," written 1387-95 now preserved in the Royal Library at Copenhagen, found in a monastery on the island of Flato, on the western coast of Iceland]

[Nicolo Zeno, a Venetian, in Greenland about 1390, met fishermen who had visited the coast of America]

Latest tidings of Vinland 1347

Esquimaux appear in Greenland . 1349

Communication with Greenland ceases about . 1400

ERA OF PERMANENT DISCOVERY

Pizigani's map of the Atlantic 1367-73

Bethancourt settles the Canary islands 1402

Madeira islands re discovered by the Portuguese 1418-20

These islands previously discovered by Machan, an Englishman, 1327-78 MADEIRA

The "Claudius Clavus" map giving the earliest delineation of any part of America (Greenland) . 1427

"Narrative and Critical Hist of America," vol [illegible] p 117

Columbus born 1435-36 (?) 1445

Visits England and Iceland prior to 1470

Columbus in Portugal 1470-84

Marco Polo's travels first printed . 1477

Columbus in Spain Announces his views to Ferdinand and Isabella. 1485-86

The views of Columbus referred to a junto of ecclesiastics which declares them vain and impracticable SALAMANCA 1487-90

Columbus leaves Spain for France Jan. 1492

[But is recalled while on his journey]

Ferdinand and Isabella arrange with Columbus 17 Apr

Columbus sailed on his *first* expedition from Palos in Andalusia on Friday, with 3 vessels supplied by the sovereigns of Spain—the *Santa Maria*, a decked vessel with a crew of 50 men, with Columbus in command, and 2 caravels—the *Pinta* with 30 men, under Martin Alonso Pinzon, and the *Niña* with 24 men, under Vicente Yañez Pinzon, brother of Martin 3 Aug.

[The cost of outfit was about $9000]

Leaves the Canary islands 6 Sept.

Influenced by Pinzon, he changes his course from due west to southwest . 7 Oct.

[The original course would have struck the coast of Florida]

Rodrigo de Triana, a sailor on the *Niña*, discovers land at 2 A M. Friday 12 Oct

Columbus lands on Guanahani one of the Bahamas, takes possession in the name of Ferdinand and Isabella of Castile and names it San Salvador, Friday . 12 Oct.

He discovers Cuba, 28 Oct, and Hispaniola (now Hayti) where he builds a fort, La Navidad 6 Dec.

Columbus sails for Spain in the *Niña*, the *Santa Maria* having been abandoned 4 Jan 1493

Reaches Palos 15 Mch

Received with distinguished honors by the Spanish court at Barcelona Apr,

Bull of demarcation between Spain and Portugal issued by pope Alexander VI . 3-4 May

The letter of Columbus to Ferdinand and Isabella describing his voyage first printed in Latin .

He sails from Cadiz on his *second* expedition 25 Sept

His fleet consisted of 3 galleons and 14 caravels, with 1500 men besides animals and material for colonization, discovers the Caribbee isles—Dominica, 3 Nov, Guadaloupe, 4 Nov, Antigua, 10 Nov, finding his previous settlement destroyed and colony dispersed, he founds Isabella in Hispaniola the first Christian city in the New World Dec

He discovers Jamaica, 3 May, and Evangelista (now Isle of Pines), 13 June, war with the natives of Hispaniola . . 1494

Visits various isles and explores their coasts . 1495-96

Returns to Spain to meet charges, reaches Cadiz 11 June, 1496

Patent from Henry VII. of Eng to John Cabot and his 3 sons 5 Mch 1495-96

John Cabot discovers the North American continent 24 June, 1497

Columbus sails with 6 ships on his *third* voyage, 30 May 1498

covers Trinidad, 31 July, lands on *terra firma* without knowing it to be a new continent, naming it Isla Santa 1 Aug 1498
Discovers the mouth of the Orinoco Aug "
Alonso de Ojeda discovers Surinam, June, and the gulf of Venezuela Amerigo Vespucci *accompanies him on this voyage*, 1499
Amerigo Vespucci's first voyage "
Vicente Yañez Pinzon discovers Brazil, 20 Jan, and the river Amazon 26 Jan 1500
Pedro Alvarez de Cabral of Portugal, discovers Brazil 22 Apr, and takes possession of for the king of Portugal 3 May,
Gasper Cortereal in the service of Portugal, discovers Labrador,
Francisco de Bobadilla appointed governor of Hispaniola and leaves Spain July "
Bobadilla arrests Columbus on his arrival at Hispaniola and sends him to Spain in irons He is received with honor at court and the charges dismissed without inquiry 17 Dec.
The first map to show "America" is Las Casas's "
Columbus sails on his *fourth* and last voyage with 4 caravels and 150 men from Cadiz 9 May, 1502
Discovers the island of Martinique 13 June,
Discovers various islands on the coast of Honduras and explores the coast of the Isthmus July "
Amerigo Vespucci on the South American coast 1501-3
Columbus finally leaves the New World for Spain 12 Sept 1504
Queen Isabella of Spain dies 26 Nov "
Columbus dies at Valladolid 20 May, 1506

[He was buried at Valladolid, but his remains were soon after transferred to Seville where his son Diego was buried In 1536 the remains of both were carried to San Domingo and reburied in the cathedral On the cession of that island to the French in 1795-96 they were (as was supposed) taken to the cathedral in Havana. But many believe they still rest in San Domingo The success of Columbus as a discoverer was "a conquest of reflection" (Humboldt)]

Juan Diaz de Solis and Vicente Yañez Pinzon are on the southeast coast of Yucatan .

[De Cordova 1517, Grijalva 1518, Cortez, 1519]

Waldseemüller's or the "Admiral's" map probably 1507
Cuba found to be an island 1508
First English publication to mention America 1509
Francisco Pizarro reaches Darien "
Alonso de Ojeda founds San Sebastian, the first colony in South America 1510
Diego Velasquez subjugates Cuba and founds Havana 1511
Juan Ponce de Leon discovers Florida 27 Mch 1512
Lands near St. Augustine 8 Apr "
Vespucci dies at Seville Spain aged 61 years "
Vasco Nuñez Balboa, crossing the isthmus of Darien, discovers the Pacific and takes possession of it for the king of Spain calling it the "South Sea" 25 Sept. 1513
Juan Diaz de Solis discovers the La Plata Jan 1516

[He is killed by natives in an attempt to land This river named in 1527 from silver plate possessed by natives]

Spaniards at Darien hear of the empire of the Incas 1512-17
Ferdinand of Spain dies 23 Jan 1516
Las Casas made "Universal Protector of the Indians" "
Francisco Fernandez de Cordova discovers Mexico 1517
Vasco Nuñez Balboa executed at Darien "
Ancient ruins in Cozumel observed by the Spaniards "
Grijalva at Cozumel and Vera Cruz, penetrates Yucatan and names it New Spain 1518
Hernando Cortez sails from Cuba to conquer Mexico 18 Feb 1519
First letter of Cortez on the conquest of Mexico to Charles V of Spain 10 July, "
Panama founded by Pedrarias "
Montezuma, emperor of the Mexicans, dies 30 June, 1520
Magellan discovers the straits which bear his name, and passes into the Pacific ocean 21 Oct 27 Nov "
Cortez accomplishes the conquest of Mexico 1521
Pizarro sails from Panama for Peru, but returns for supplies and repairs 14 Nov 1524
Francis de Hoces, in command of one of the ships of Loyasa, discovers cape Horn 1525
Narvaez's expedition to the upper gulf of California 1527
Pizarro enters Peru and destroys the government (PERU) 1531-33
Jacques Cartier enters the gulf of St. Lawrence and sails to the present site of Montreal FRENCH IN AMERICA 1534-5
Ferdinand de Grijalva's expedition, equipped by Cortez, discovers CALIFORNIA, Lower 1534
Antonio de Mendoza appointed viceroy of Mexico, the first in the New World 1535-50
Francisco Orellana explores eastward from Peru, down the Amazon reaching the ocean (voyage of seven months) Aug 1541
Don Pedro de Valdivia invades and conquers Chili "
Cortez returns to Spain, 1540, and dies there aged 62 1547
Las Casas returns to Spain "
Davis discovers the strait that bears his name 1585
Falkland islands discovered by Davis 1592

[For the further settlement and history of America, see the countries of North and South America, the United States, and the several states]

PRINCIPAL PERSONS CONNECTED WITH THE DISCOVERY OF AMERICA, AND WHY KNOWN.

ALMAGRO, DIEGO DE, Spanish adventurer, b. Spain, 1463 (?), with Pizarro in Peru, put to death by Pizarro July, 1538
AYLLON, LUCAS VASQUEZ DE, Spanish explorer, d. Virginia, 18 Oct 1526

[Sailing, with 3 vessels and 600 persons, with supplies for a colony, along the coast, he enters Chesapeake bay and attempts a settlement near Jamestown where he died His colonists returned to San Domingo in the spring of 1527]

BALBOA, VASCO NUÑEZ, Spanish adventurer b Spain 1475, executed at Darien on a charge of treason, 1517, the discoverer of the Pacific ocean 25 Sept. 1513
BOBADILLA, FRANCISCO b Spain sent to San Domingo to relieve Columbus sent Columbus and his brother Diego back to Spain in chains He loses his life by shipwreck on his return voyage 29 June, 1502
CABOT JOHN, Venetian date of birth and death unknown In the service of Henry VII of Eng, discovers the mainland of North America (supposed coast of Labrador) 24 June, 1497
CABOT SEBASTIAN, son of John, b Venice 1475 (?) d London about 1557, the discoverer of Newfoundland and explorer of the North American coast 1498-1517
CABRAL, PEDRO ALVAREZ DE Portuguese navigator, d about 1526, the discoverer of Brazil 22 Apr 1500
CARTIER JACQUES b St Malo France 1494, d about 1555, the discoverer of the river St Lawrence 1534-35
COLUMBUS, CHRISTOPHER, b Genoa, 1435-45 (?), died at Valladolid Spain 20 May 1506 The discoverer of the New World (AMERICA) 1492-98
CORDOVA, FRANCISCO FERNANDEZ DE d Cuba, 1518, discovers Mexico and explores the coast of Yucatan 1517
CORONADO, FRANCESCO VASQUEZ DE, d 1542, explorer of the territory north of Mexico, now New Mexico, Arizona, and Colorado 1540-42
CORTEREAL, GASPER Portuguese navigator, b Lisbon d 1501

[Sails along the coast of North America and names Labrador, returns to Lisbon and sails on his second voyage 1501, but never returns]

CORTEZ, HERNANDO, Spanish adventurer b Spain, 1485 d Spain 2 Dec 1547, conqueror of Mexico 1519.
DAVIS, JOHN b Eng 1550 d coast of Malacca 1605 discoverer of Davis's strait, 1585, of the Falkland islands 15
DE SOTO, FERNANDO, b Spain 1495 (?), d on the banks of the Mississippi, June 1542, explorer of the southern U S, discoverer of the Mississippi 1540-42
DRAKE SIR FRANCIS, b Eng 1537 (?), d Puerto Bello 27 Dec 1595, explores the coast of California 1578-79, first Englishman to sail around the globe, reaching England 1580
FROBISHER, SIR MARTIN, b Eng 1536, d Plymouth, Eng 7 Nov 1594, discovers Frobisher's strait 21 July 1576
GOMEZ ESTEBAN Spanish navigator, b. Spain, 1478 (?), d at sea, 1530 (?), explores the eastern coast 1525

[Perhaps as far north as Conn]

GRIJALVA JUAN DE, b Spain, d Nicaragua, 21 Jan 1527 Explores Yucatan and hears of Mexico and Montezuma 1518
HUDSON HENRY, b Eng, discoverer and explorer of the Hudson river in the interests of the Dutch, Sept 1609 and Hudson bay, 1611 Sent adrift in an open boat by his crew and never heard of afterwards 1611
LAS CASAS, BARTHOLOMEW, b Seville, Spain 1474, d Spain, July, 1566 Accompanies Columbus to America, 1493, and during the next 50 years crosses the Atlantic 14 times in the interest of the natives Made "Universal Protector of the Indians" by the Spanish government 1516

[His whole life was spent in trying to assuage the suffering of the Indians and free them from the cruelty of the Spaniards]

MAGELLAN, FERNANDO Portuguese navigator b 1470 Discovers the strait of [illegible] which he enters 21 Oct 1520, and names passing through into the ocean, 27 Nov 1520, to which he gave the name Pacific He was killed at one of the Philippine islands, by the natives, 17 Apr 1521 Only one of his ships under Sebastian del Cano, reached Seville (the first ship to circumnavigate the globe) 8 Sept. 1522
OJEDA, ALONSO DE Spanish adventurer, b Spain 1465, d Hispaniola 1515 Accompanies Columbus on his second voyage With Amerigo Vespucci he explores the northern coast of South America, 1499, and established a settlement at San Sebastian 1510
PINZON MARTIN ALONSO, Spanish navigator, b Spain, 1441, d. Spain 1493

[Commander of the *Pinta* in the first voyage of Columbus. Attempts to deprive Columbus of the discovery, is baffled and disgraced]

PINZON, VICENTE YAÑEZ, brother of Alonso b Spain 1460, d Spain 1524 Commands the *Niña* in Columbus's first voyage Discovers cape St. Augustine, Brazil, 20 Jan 1500, and the mouth of the Amazon, 26 Jan Explores the east coast of Yucatan 1506
PIZARRO, FRANCISCO, Spanish adventurer, b Spain about 1471, assassinated at Lima Peru, 26 June, 1541 The destroyer of the Peruvian government 1531-33
PONCE DE LEON, JUAN Spanish soldier b 1460 (?), d Cuba, 1521 The discoverer of Florida, 27 Mch 1512, landing at St Augustine 2 Apr 1512

[Sailing south he discovers the Tortugas and explores the western shores of Florida]

SOLIS, JUAN DIAZ DE, Spanish navigator, b Spain, 1471, d South America, 1516 Reputed the most experienced navigator of his time Discovers the river La Plata, S A, Jan 1516

[Killed by Indians on that river]

VERAZZANO GIOVANNI DE, Florentine navigator, b near Florence, 1470, d either at Newfoundland or Puerto del Rico, 1527 Explores for France the North American coast as far north as New York and Narragansett bays 1524
VESPUCCI AMERICO, b. Florence, 1451? d Spain, 12 Feb 1512. Explorer of the South American coast 1499-1504

[The western continent is named for him, as is believed, unjustly AMERICA.]

America, Central, that part of America which lies between the isthmuses of Tehuantepec and Panama originally one state under Spain, the kingdom of Guatemala, now divided into the republics of Guatemala, San Salvador, Honduras, Nicaragua, Costa Rica, and the territory of Balize or British Honduras The total area of these States is 175,865 sq miles, with a pop of about 3,000 000 The States declared their independence 21 Sept 1821, and seceded from the Mexican confederation, 21 July, 1823 They made a treaty of union, 21 March, 1847 There has been among them since much anarchy and bloodshed In Jan 1863, a war began between Guatemala (afterwards joined by Nicaragua) and San Salvador (afterwards supported by Honduras) The latter were defeated at Santa Rosa, 16 June, and San Salvador was taken 26 Oct, the president of San Salvador, Barrios, fled, and Carrera, the dictator of Guatemala, became master of the confederacy In Feb 1885, gen Barrios, president of Guatemala, attempts the union of the five states with himself as dictator He is, however, opposed by all except Honduras He is defeated and killed in an engagement at Chalchuapas, 2 Apr 1885 and a peace is concluded the 16th of same month DARIEN, PANAMA, and the States separately

America, South, the western continent south of the isthmus of Darien It lies mostly in the torrid zone, but extends to 56° s lat It contains 6 900,000 sq miles, with about 26,400,000 people Its extreme length is 4800 miles, and its greatest width 3760 It includes the Argentine Republic Bolivia, Brazil, Chili, Colombia, Ecuador, Guiana, Paraguay Peru, Uruguay, Venezuela For its history see each state

American Association for the Advancement of Science, resembling the British association, held its first meeting at Philadelphia, 1848, and annually since, as follows

1	Philadelphia Pa,		W C Redfield	pres	Sept	1848
2	Cambridge Mass,	prof	Jos Henry,	"	Aug	1849
3	Charleston, S C,	"	A D Bache,	"	Mar	1850
4	New Haven, Conn,	"	"	"	Aug	"
[illegible]	Cincinnati, O,	"	"	"	May,	1851
[illegible]	Albany, N Y,	"	L Agassiz,	"	Aug	"
	Cleveland, O,	"	Benj Peirce,	"	July,	1853
	Washington, D C,	"	J D Dana,	"	Apr	1854
	Providence, R I,	"	John Torrey,	"	Aug	1855
10	Albany N Y,	"	Jas Hall	"		1856
11	Montreal, Quebec,	"	J W Bailey,	"	"	1857
12	Baltimore, Md,	"	A Caswell,	"	Apr	1858
13	Springfield Mass,	"	S Alexander,	"	Aug	1859
14	Newport, R I,	"	Isaac Lea, LL D	"	"	1860
15	Buffalo, N Y,	"	F A P Barnard,	"	"	1866
16	Burlington Vt,	"	J S Newberry,	"	"	1867
17	Chicago, Ill,	"	B A Gould	"	"	1868
18	Salem Mass	"	J W Foster	"	"	1869
19	Troy, N Y,	"	William Chauvenet	"	"	1870
20	Indianapolis, Ind,	"	Asa Gray,	"	"	1871
21	Dubuque, Iowa,	"	J Lawrence Smith,	"	"	1872
22.	Portland, Me	"	Joseph Lovering,	"	"	1873
23	Hartford Conn,	"	J L Le Conte,	"	"	1874
24	Detroit, Mich,	"	J E Hilgard,	"	"	1875
25	Buffalo, N Y,	"	W B Rogers,		"	1876
26	Nashville Tenn,	"	Simon Newcomb,	"	"	1877
27	St Louis, Mo	"	O C Marsh	"	"	1878
28.	Saratoga N Y,	"	G F Barker,	"	"	1879
29	Boston Mass,	"	L H Morgan,	"	"	1880
30	Cincinnati, O	"	G J Brush,	"	"	1881
31	Montreal, Quebec,	"	J W Dawson,	"	"	1882
32	Minneapolis, Minn	"	C A Young,	"	"	1883
33	Philadelphia Pa,	"	J P Lesley,	"	Sept	1884
34	Ann Arbor, Mich,	"	H A Newton,	"	Aug	1885
35	Buffalo, N Y,	"	E S. Morse,	"	"	1886
36	New York, N Y	"	S P Langley,	"	"	1887
37	Cleveland O,	"	J W Powell	"	"	1888
38	Toronto, Ont,	"	T C Mendenhall,	"	"	1889
39	Indianapolis Ind,	"	G L Goodale,	"	"	1890
40	Washington D C,	"	Joseph Le Conte,	"	"	1891
41	Rochester, N Y,	"	William Harkness,	"	"	1892
42.	Madison, Wis,				"	1893

American Institute of Instruction, incorporated in Massachusetts, 1831 Meets annually in various cities for educational discussion Francis Wayland, first president.

American organ, a free-reed keyed wind instrument, somewhat like the harmonium as a principle, discovered about 1835 by a workman of Alexandre of Paris The invention was taken to America, where instruments were made by Mason & Hamlin of Boston about 1860

American Party. POLITICAL PARTIES

American System. TARIFF.

Americanisms explained in a dictionary by John R. Bartlett, first published in 1848, reprinted, 1859, revised ed 1878

amethyst, the ninth stone upon the breastplate of the Jewish high-priest, 1491 B C AARON'S BREASTPLATE It is of a rich violet color One worth 200 rix-dollars, rendered colorless equalled a diamond in lustre, valued at 18,000 gold crowns.—*De Boot* Amethysts discovered at Kerry, in Ireland, in 1775

Amiens (*am'e-enz*), a city of Picardy, N France, the cathedral was built in 1220 Taken by the Spanish, 11 Mch, retaken by the French, 25 Sept 1597 The formal "Peace of Amiens" between Great Britain, Holland, France, and Spain was signed here 27 Mch 1802, by the marquis of Cornwallis for England, Joseph Bonaparte for France, Azara for Spain, and Schimmelpenninck for Holland After a conflict, in which the French were defeated 27 Nov 1870, the German general, Von Goeben, entered Amiens, 28 Nov Here Peter the Hermit was born about 1050 Pop 1886, 80,288

Amistad, Case of the. A Portuguese slaver landed a cargo of kidnapped Africans near Havana, a few days afterwards they were placed on board the *Amistad* to be taken to Principe On the voyage the negroes, led by Cinque, captured the vessel but killed only the captain and the cook They then ordered the white crew to take the ship to Africa, but the sailors brought her into American waters, where she was seized by lieut Geding, of the U S brig *Washington*, and brought into New London, Conn, 29 Aug 1839 A committee, consisting of S S Jocelyn, Joshua Leavitt, and Lewis Tappan, was appointed in New York to solicit funds and employ counsel to protect the rights of the negroes. After a great struggle the court, through justice Story, pronounced them free Their return to Africa founded the Mendi mission UNITED STATES and CONNECTICUT, 1839

ammonia, a volatile alkali, mainly produced by organic decomposition, named by reputed production from heated camels' dung near the temple of Jupiter Ammon in Libya Shown to be a compound of nitrogen and hydrogen by Joseph Priestley, 1774. By the recent labors of chemists both the oxide of the hypothetical metal ammonium, and ammonium amalgam, have been formed, and specimens of each were shown at the Royal Institution in 1856 by Dr A W Hofmann An apparatus to improve the voice and lungs by inhaling combinations of ammonia, hydrogen, etc, called the *ammoniaphone*, was invented by Dr Carter Moffat of Edinburgh, 1883

Ammonites, descended from Ben-Ammi, the son of Lot (1897 B C), invaded Canaan and made the Israelites tributaries, but were defeated by Jephthah, 1143 B.C On a second invasion, with threats to put out the right eyes of all they subdued, Saul overthrew them, 1095 B.C. They were afterwards many times vanquished, and Antiochus the Great took Rabbah, their capital, and destroyed the walls, 198 B.C.—*Josephus.* In natural history, ammonites are a large genus of extinct cuttle-fish, so called from fancied resemblance to the horns of Jupiter Ammon, the Egyptian sun-god

"Huge ammonites and the first bones of time"—*Tennyson*

amnesty (a general pardon) was granted by Thrasybulus, the Athenian patriot, after expelling the thirty tyrants, 403 B.C Acts of amnesty were passed after the civil war in 1651 and after the two rebellions in England in 1715 and 1745 —After his victorious campaign in Italy Napoleon III of France granted an amnesty to all political offenders, 17 Aug, 1859 —President Lincoln issued a proclamation of conditional amnesty to former rebels, 8 Dec. 1863 President Johnson issued amnesty proclamations on 29 May, 1865, 7 Sept 1867, 4 July, 1868, and 25 Dec 1868. This last offered complete amnesty to all who had been in rebellion, its validity was contested An amnesty was granted by act of congress, 10 Apr 1871, and another, 22 May, 1872, which restored the political privileges of all participants in the rebellion, excepting only about 600 persons.—An amnesty for political offences was granted by the emperor of Austria at his coronation as king of Hungary, 8 June, 1867.—An amnesty association on behalf of the Fenians was active in Great Britain, Oct. 1873 —2245 French communists pardoned by decree, published 17

Jan 1879, many others during the year A general amnesty for political offences passed by the chamber (333 140) 21 June, 1880

amœba (*a-mē'bä*) PROTOPLASM

Amphictyon'ic Council, according to tradition founded 1498 [1113, *Clinton*] B C at Thermopylæ, by Amphictyon, for the general interests of Greece, and composed of 12 of the wisest and most virtuous men of various cities, still existed 31 B.C Its special office was to attend to the temples and oracles of Delphi It required the Greek states to punish the Phocians for plundering Delphi, and thus caused the sacred wars, 595-586 and 356-346 B C

Amphip'olis, Macedon, N Greece Founded by the Athenians, 437 B.C , seized by Brasidas the Spartan 424, both he and the Athenian general Cleon were killed in Cleon's fruitless attempt to capture the city, 422

amphithe'atres, round or oval buildings said to have been first constructed by Curio, 76 B C, and by Julius Cæsar, 46 B C , to exhibit combats of gladiators with wild beasts, etc They were generally built of wood, but Statilius Taurus made one of stone, under Augustus Cæsar, the Flavian amphitheatre (capable of holding 87,000 persons) was built between 70 A D and 80 COLISEUM The amphitheatre at Verona was next in size, and then that of Nismes

Amphitrite (*am-fi-tri'tē*), in Greek mythology the supreme goddess of the sea, wife of Poseidon (Neptune)

amputation, in surgery, was greatly improved by the invention of the tourniquet by Morel, a French surgeon in 1674, and of the flap-method by Lowdham of Exeter, in 1679 SURGERY and MEDICAL SCIENCE

Am'sterdam, Holland The castle of Amstel was commenced in 1100, the building of the city in 1203 Its commerce grew at the expense of Antwerp after 1609 The exchange was built in 1634, the stadthouse, in 1648, cost 3,000,000 guilders, it stood on 13,659 piles, 282 ft long, 255 wide, and 116 high Amsterdam surrendered to the king of Prussia, who invaded Holland in favor of the stadtholder, in 1787 The French were admitted without resistance, 18 Jan 1795 The Dutch government was restored in Dec 1813 A crystal palace for an industrial exhibition was opened by prince Frederick of the Netherlands, 16 Aug 1864 The canal, from Amsterdam to the North sea, opened by the king, 1 Nov 1876 A new university opened, Dec 1877 Pop 1890, 417,539

amyl (*am'il*), a chemical alcohol radical (first isolated by professor Edward Frankland in 1849)

amylene (*am'-i-leen*), a hydrocarbon, a colorless mobile liquid, first procured by M Balard of Paris, in 1844, by distilling fusel oil (potato-spirit) with chloride of zinc The vapor was first used as an anæsthetic by Dr Snow, in 1856, and has since been tried in many hospitals, but is more unpleasant than chloroform, and very dangerous to life

anabaptists, opponents of baptism, usually applied to those who reject infant baptism BAPTISTS The name was first given to Thomas Munzer, Storck, and other fanatics who preached in Saxony in 1521, and excited a rebellion of the lower classes in Germany The allied princes of the empire, led by Philip, landgrave of Hesse, put down the rebellion, and Munzer was defeated, captured, put to the torture, and ultimately beheaded in 1525. A similar insurrection took place in Westphalia, headed by Matthias, 1533 , and, after his assassination, by John Boccoldt of Leyden, who was crowned "king of Sion" in Münster, 24 June, 1534 Münster was taken in June, 1535, and John was put to death in the most cruel manner that could be devised, 13 Feb. 1536. It was in the year 1534, when Boccoldt was in the height of his glory in Munster, that Ignatius Loyola took the first steps towards founding the order of the Jesuits, and the extension and rapid success of that celebrated fraternity are to be attributed in a very large measure to the reaction against Protestantism produced by the share which the anabaptists took in the peasants' war and the character of the spiritual sovereignty which they set up at Munster while it was in their hands Several anabaptists were executed in England in 1535, 1538, and 1540. On 6 Jan 1661, about 80 anabaptists in London appeared in arms, headed by their preacher, Thomas Venner, a wine-cooper. They fought desperately, and killed many soldiers brought against them. Their leader and 16 others were executed 19 and 21 Jan

Anab'asis (Gr *ἀνάβασις*, a march into the interior), the title of Xenophon's narrative of the expedition of Cyrus the Younger against his brother, 401 B C RETREAT OF THE TEN THOUSAND GREEKS

Anacreontic verse, of the bacchanalian strain, named after Anacreon of Teos, the Greek lyric poet died about 559 B C His odes have been frequently translated, Thomas Moore's version was published in 1800 "We sang the songs of Anacreon—the songs of the son of Teos"—*Poe* LITERATURE

anæsthetics. AMYLENE, CHLOROFORM, COCAINE, ETHER, KEROSOLENE NITROUS ACID, OPIUM Intense cold has been employed in deadening pain

anagrams, formed by the transposition of the letters of a word or sentence (as *army* from *Mary*), are said to have been made by ancient Jews, Greeks, etc On the question put by Pilate to our Saviour, "*Quid est veritas?*" (What is truth?) we have the anagram, "*Est vir qui adest*" (The man who is here), from "*Horatio Nelson*" is "*Honor est a Nilo*" (Honor is from the Nile), William Noy, attorney-general to Charles I, *I moyl in law* Such trifles began to be popular in Europe in the 16th century

Anam' or **Annam',** an empire of Asia, to the east of India, comprising Tonquin, Cochin China, part of Cambodia, and various islands in the Chinese sea , said to have been conquered by the Chinese, 234 B.C , and held by them till 263 A D In 1406 they reconquered it, but abandoned it in 1428 After much anarchy, bishop Adran, a French missionary, obtained the friendship of Louis XVI for his pupil Gia-long, son of the nominally reigning monarch, and with a few of his countrymen established Gia-long on the throne, who reigned till his death, in 1821, when his son became king In consequence of the persecution of Christians, war broke out with the French, who defeated the army of Anam, 10,000 strong, about 22 Apr 1859, when 500 were killed On 3 June, 1862, peace was made, 3 provinces were ceded to the French, and persecution ceased An insurrection in these provinces against the French, begun about 17 Dec 1862, was suppressed in Feb. 1863 Ambassadors from Anam to regain the ceded provinces reached Paris, Sept 1863, had no success These provinces were annexed to the French empire by proclamation, 25 June, 1867 Several native Christians were massacred by order of a bonze, Lay, 1868

Hoang Nam succeeded his father, Thieutri as king	1847
By treaty at Saigon, France recognized the independence of the king of Anam his ports were opened to commerce, and toleration of Christians was secured	15 Mch 1874
Tu Duc emperor 34 years resists the French in TONQUIN, 1883, dies aged 54, 17 July 1883, Hephinea succeeds	
French protectorate recognized by treaty at Hué	25 Aug 1883
King assassinated by enemies of the French, succeeded by You Duc	about 14 Dec "
A prince who promoted massacre of Christians in Dec and Jan executed	about 26 May 1884
King dies, succeeded by his brother Kieupbuo , announced	2 Aug "
The French repulse an attack on their camp at Hué, and capture the regent Thu Hong	5-6 July, 1885
Chanl Mong proclaimed king	14 Sept "
The king dies, his son, 10 years old, called Thau-thai, proclaimed	31 Jan 1889
Taken by the French to Algeria as a prisoner	June, 1892

anath'ema (Gr *ἀνάθημα*, a votive offering), the sentence of excommunication (1 Cor xvi 22) used by the early churches, 365 EXCOMMUNICATION Pope Pius IX propounded a series of anathemas, Feb 1870

Anato'lia, Asia Minor, comprises the ancient Lycia, Caria, Lydia, Mysia, Bithynia, Paphlagonia, and Phrygia

anat'omy (Gr *ἀνατομή*, a cutting up) The structure of the human body became a branch of medical education under the second Hippocrates, who was born 460 B C and died about 377 Aristotle made his chief anatomical investigations between 334 and 327 B.C Herophilus and Erasistratus of Alexandria first applied dissection to men, previously confined to animals, 300 and 293 B.C., followed by Celsus early in the 1st, and by Galen in the 2d century A D Pope Boniface VIII forbade human dissection, 1297 In modern times the revival of anatomical study began in Italy with Mondini of

Bologna, flourished about 1315, and Eustachi, about 1495-1500, after whom are named a tube in the ear and a valvular membrane in the heart Fallopio or Fallopius, 1523-62, gave name to the Fallopian tubes of the uterus The first anatomical plates designed by Titian were employed by Vesalius about 1538 Leonardo da Vinci, Raphael, and Michael Angelo studied anatomy Of the early English anatomists the most illustrious was Harvey, born 1578 He discovered the circulation of the blood, 1616 and published his great work 1628, died 1657 William and John Hunter, 1718-83 and 1728-93 Quain's and Wilson's large anatomical plates, pub 1842, and Bourgery's work by Jacob, 1830-55 *Comparative anatomy* has been treated systematically in the present century by Cuvier, Owen, Muller, Huxley, and others In England the schools were long supplied with bodies unlawfully exhumed from graves, and, until 1832, the bodies of executed murderers were surrendered for dissection In the reign of Henry VIII of England surgeons were granted four bodies of executed malefactors for "*anathomyes*," and the privilege was extended in following reigns, but crimes committed by resurrection-men to supply surgical schools (robbing churchyards and even murder—BURKING) led to a statute in 1832 which abated the ignominy of dissection by prohibiting that of executed murderers, and provided for the wants of surgeons by permitting, under certain regulations, the dissection of persons dying in workhouses, etc. The act also appointed inspectors of anatomy, regulated the schools, and required persons practising anatomy to obtain a license MEDICAL SCIENCE, SURGERY

anchorets and **anchorites.** MONACHISM

anchors were invented by the Tuscans.—*Pliny* The second tooth, or fluke, was added by Anacharsis the Scythian (592 B C) —*Strabo* Anchors are said to have been forged in England 578 A D The admiralty anchor was introduced about 1841 Anchors improved by Pering and Rodgers about 1828, by Porter, 1838, by Costell, 1818, by Trotman, 1853, and by others Trotman's is attached to the queen's yacht *Fairy* Acts for the proving and sale of chain cables and anchors were passed in 1864 and 1871

ancient buildings of England A society for their protection from injudicious restoration, etc, was established in 1877, lord Houghton, prof S Colvin Thomas Carlyle, and many eminent artists, members

ancient history beginning in the Scriptures 4004 B.C., and with Herodotus about 1687 B.C. is considered to end with the fall of the Eastern empire, 476 A D

ancient monuments in Britain Bills to preserve these (especially the prehistoric ones) have been long delayed in parliament One by sir John Lubbock, read second time, 7 March, 1877, was withdrawn, again read second time, 19 Feb 1878, read second time in the lords, 11 Mch 1880 Such bills became laws at last, 1882 and 1892

Ancient Order of United Workmen. UNITED WORKMEN, ANCIENT ORDER OF

ancients. COUNCILS, FRENCH

Anco'na, an ancient Roman port on the Adriatic The mole was built by Trajan, 107. After many changes of rulers (Lombards, Saracens, Greeks, and Germans), Ancona was annexed to the papal states in 1532, taken by the French, 1797, retaken by the Austrians, 1799, reoccupied by the French, 1801, restored to the pope, 1802, occupied by the French in 1832, evacuated in 1838, and, after an insurrection was bombarded and captured by the Austrians, 18 June, 1849 The Marches (comprising this city) rebelled against the papal government in Sept 1860 Lamoriciere, the papal general, fled to Ancona after his defeat at Castelfidardo, but surrendered with the city and garrison, 29 Sept The king of Sardinia entered soon after

Andalu'sia, a province of S Spain, once part of ancient Lusitania and Bætica The name is corrupted from Vandalitia it having been held by the Vandals from 419 to 429, when it was acquired by the Visigoths, whom the moors expelled in 711, establishing the kingdom of Cordova, which stood till 1236

An'daman Islands, bay of Bengal, inhabited by dwarfs in lowest barbarism At Port Blair, on South island, made a penal settlement for Sepoy rebels in 1858, the earl of Mayo, viceroy of India, was assassinated by Shere Alee, a convict, 8 Feb 1872, when going on board the *Glasgow*

Andernach, Rhenish Prussia, once an imperial city Near here, the emperor Charles I, while attempting to deprive his nephews of their inheritance, was defeated by one of them, Louis of Saxony, 8 Oct 876

Anderson, Major Robert FORT SUMTER.

Andersonville prison. An open pen on a hill-side held 1540 by 750 feet, surrounded by a stockade, near Andersonville, Ga, in which prisoners of war were first lodged by the Confederates, 15 Feb 1864 In one year 44,882 prisoners were received, of whom 12 926 died of starvation and want of proper care Henry Wirz, one of the prison officers, was hanged 10 Nov 1865 for his cruelty to prisoners under his charge There is a national cemetery here which contains 13,714 graves CEMETERIES

Andes, Cordillera de los, the great mountain system of South America, forms a continuous line of mountainous highlands along its western coast, and under different names traverses the North American continent, terminating at Point Barrow VOLCANOES

Chimborazo Ecuador, 21 420 ft, perpetually snowclad, was ascended by Alexander von Humboldt to the height of 19 286 ft., 23 June 1802 by Boussingault and Hall, 19 695 ft, 16 Dec. 1831, by Edward Whymper, 20 545 ft, 3 Jan, and 20,499 ft, 3 July, 1880

Cotopaxi, Ecuador, volcanic, ascended by Ed Whymper, 19,600 ft., 18 Feb 1880

He also first ascended Antisana, Ecuador 19,260 ft, 10 Mch; and Cayambe Ecuador, 19 200 ft, 4 Apr 1880

In Bolivia the volcano of Sahama is 23 000 ft. in elevation, the peak of Illimani 21,300, and Sorata 24 800

The culminating peak of the Andes in Chili is Aconcagua (22 427 ft), the other principal summits are the Cuna del Mercedario (22,302 ft), the volcanoes of Tupungato (20,269 ft), and San José (20,000 ft), several others range from 16,000 to 19 000 ft

Andorra, a small republic in the Pyrenees, with the title "the valleys and sovereignties of Andorra," made independent by Charlemagne about 778, reserving certain rights to the bishop of Urgel The feudal sovereignty, long belonging to the counts of Foix, reverted to the French king, Henry IV, in 1589, but was given up in 1790 On 27 Mar 1806, an imperial decree restored old relations between Andorra and France The republic is governed by a council elected for four years, but magistrates are appointed alternately by the French government and the Spanish bishop of Urgel, to both of whom tribute is paid The population is about 10,000. Andorra, though neutral, was attacked by Carlists in Sept. 1874

André, Major John, born London, 1751 Execution of, 1780 NEW YORK

Andrew, St., said to have been martyred by crucifixion, 30 Nov 69, at Patræ, in Achaia His festival was instituted about 359 The Royal Society's anniversary is kept on St Andrew's day. The Russian order of St Andrew was instituted in 1698 by Peter I For the British order, see THISTLE.

Andrew's, St., E Scotland, made a royal burgh in 1140 Here Robert Bruce held his first parliament in 1309, and here Wishart was burned by archbishop Beaton, 1545, who was murdered here, 1546 The university was founded, 1411, by bishop Wardlaw The cathedral (built 1159-1318) was destroyed by a mob, excited by a sermon of John Knox, June, 1559 Sir R Sibbald's list of bishops commences with Killach, 872 The see became archiepiscopal in 1470, but ceased in 1688. BISHOPS

Andros, sir Edmund CONNECTICUT, 1687; MASSACHUSETTS, 1686, NEW YORK, 1674, etc

Andrussov, Peace of (30 Jan 1667), between Russia and Poland, for 13 years, with mutual concessions, although the latter had been generally victorious.

anemom'eter (Gr ἄνεμος, the wind), to measure the velocity of wind, was invented by Wolfius in 1709 The extreme velocity was thought by Dr. Lind to be 93 miles per hour Osler's and Whewell's anemometers were highly approved of in 1844 "Robinson's anemometer is the simplest and best."—*Buchan*, 1867.

aneroid. BAROMETER.

angel, a gold coin, impressed with an angel, weighing four pennyweights, valued at 6s 8d in the reign of Henry VI, and at 10s in the reign of Elizabeth, 1562 The *angelot*, a gold coin, value half an angel, was struck at Paris when held by the English 1431 —*Wood* COIN

Angers, W Central France, the Roman Juliomagus, possessing an amphitheatre, afterwards Andegavum, the capital of Anjou It was frequently besieged, and many councils were held in it between 453 and 1448, for ecclesiastical discipline

> 'You men of Angers open wide your gates
> And let young Arthur duke of Bretagne in'
> —*Shakespeare*, "King John," act ii sc i

Angevin or **Angevine,** pertaining to Anjou, especially applied to the family of Plantagenets, descended from Geoffrey Plantagenet, count of Anjou, and Maud or Matilda, daughter of Henry I of England They reigned in England from Henry II's accession, 1154, to Richard III's death, 1485 ANJOU

Anglesey, a small island containing 193,511 acres, called by the Romans Mona, separated from N Wales by the Menai strait, seat of Druids, who were massacred in great numbers when Suetonius Paulinus ravaged the isle, 61 A D It was conquered by Agricola in 78, occupied by Normans, 1090, and, with all Wales, annexed by Edward I in 1281 He built the fortress of Beaumaris in 1295 The Menai suspension bridge was erected 1818-25 and the Britannia tubular bridge 1849-50

Anglican Church. CHURCH OF ENGLAND

angling. Allusion is made to it in the Bible, Amos iv 2 (787 B.C.)

Oppian wrote his "Halieutics," a Greek epic poem on fishes and fishing about 198 A D

In the book on "Hawkynge and Huntynge," by Juliana Berners, or Barnes, prioress of Sopwith, near St Albans, reimprinted at Westmestre by Wynkyn de Worde' in 1496 is 'The treatise of fysshyng with an Angle"

Izaak Walton's "Compleat Angler" was first published in 1653

Anglo-French agreements, etc, with Great Britain respecting Africa

ANGLO FRENCH AGREEMENT signed by marquis of Salisbury and M Waddington French ambassador in London 5 Aug 1890, recognizing British protectorate over Zanzibar and French over Madagascar The delimitation of territories in Africa subject to the influence of France to be settled by two commissioners at Paris

ANGLO GERMAN AGREEMENT of 1890 determined the boundaries of British and German territories in E Africa, the protectorate of Zanzibar, Witu, Somaliland of Vitu, was given to Great Britain Heligoland ceded to Germany, signed at Berlin by sir Edward Malet and sir Henry Percy Anderson for England by gen von Caprivi and Dr Krauel for Germany, 1 July, ratified by act of parliament approved 4 Aug 1890

ANGLO ITALIAN AGREEMENT respecting Africa Sir Evelyn Baring and gen sir Francis Grenfell received at Rome by sig Crispi, 24 Sept. 1890 Conference at Naples lord Dufferin and sig Crispi present, no result, 4-10 Oct 1890 Treaty for the delimitation of British and Italian spheres of influence in E Africa, signed at Rome 15 Apr 1891

ANGLO PORTUGUESE AGREEMENT delimiting territories subject to the influence of Great Britain and Portugal in E Africa, text of agreement settled in London, 20 Aug and published in *The Times* Free navigation of the Zambesi, and uninterrupted communication between British territories insured, 20 Aug 1890 Portugal gives up claim to Zambesi and Nyassaland Agreement annulled, and a *modus vivendi* agreed to, 14 Nov 1890 New modified treaty, signed at Lisbon, 11 June, 1891, and afterwards ratified

Anglo-Saxons or **Angles,** named from a village near Sleswick, called *Anglen*, whose population (called *Angli* by Tacitus) joined the first Saxon freebooters East Anglia was a kingdom of the heptarchy founded by the Angles, one of whose chiefs, Uffa, assumed the title of king, 571, the kingdom ceased in 792 BRITAIN Cædmon paraphrased part of the Bible in Anglo-Saxon about 680, a translation of the gospels was made by abbot Egbert, of Iona, 721, of Boethius, Orosius, etc., by Alfred, 888 The Anglo-Saxon laws were printed by government in 1840 The Anglo-Saxon language was spoken in England from about 450 to 1066 A D

A professorship of Anglo Saxon was founded at Oxford by Dr Richard Rawlinson in 1795, one at Cambridge by Dr Joseph Bosworth in 1867

Ango'la, S W Africa, settled by the Portuguese soon after the discovery by Diego Cam, about 1484. Loanda, their capital, was built 1578. These possessions of the Portuguese in west Africa extend from the mouth of the Congo, 6° S lat., to the mouth of the Cunene, lat 18° 30′ S, and consist of the smaller districts of Ambriz, Benguela, and Mossamedes Area about 600,000 sq miles, pop 10,000,000

Ango'ra, a city and province of Turkey in Asia As the ancient city Ancyra it belonged to Phrygia, and afterwards became the chief town in Galatia It was the seat of one of the earliest Christian churches, and councils were held here, 314, 358, 375 Near it on the 28 July, 1402, Tamerlane defeated and captured the Turkish sultan Bajazet In 1415 it was recovered by Mahomet I, and since has belonged to the Turkish empire The province is famous for its Angora goats, which produce the mohair of commerce

Angoulême, the Roman Iculisma, capital of the province of Angoumois, Central France, W was a bishopric in 260 Angoulême became an independent country about 866, was united to the French crown in 1308, was held by the English, 1360 to 1372, in the reign of Edward III The count of Angoulême became king of France as Francis I in 1515

Anguilla, Snake island, West Indies, settled by the British, 1666 Valuable deposits of phosphate of lime were found here in 1859

Anhalt, House of in Germany, deduces its origin from Berenthobaldus, who made war upon the Thuringians in the 6th century In 1606 the principality was divided among the four sons of Joachim Ernest by the eldest, John-George Thus began the four branches—Anhalt Dessau (descended from John-George), Zerbst extinct, 1793, Plotzgau, or Coethen, extinct, 1847, and Bernburg, extinct, 1863 (the last duke died without issue, 22 Aug 1863) The princes of Anhalt became dukes in 1809 Anhalt, though a duchy of the German empire, is internally an hereditary constitutional monarchy (by law 19 Feb 1872), area, 870 sq miles, pop in 1871, 203,437; in 1875, 213,565, 1886, 230,000 Anhalt joined the North German Confederation, 18 Aug 1866

Anholt, Island of, Denmark, occupied by England, 18 May, 1809, in the French war, because Danish cruisers injured British commerce The Danes made a fruitless attempt to regain it, 27 March, 1811

an'iline, an oily alkaline body, discovered in 1826 by Unverdorben among the products of distillation of indigo From benzole Bechamp, in 1856, obtained it by treatment with concentrated nitric acid and reducing agents The scientific relations of aniline have been carefully examined by several chemists, especially by Dr A W Hofmann It was long known to yield colored compounds, but it was not till 1856 that W. H Perkin showed how a violet oxidation-product (mauve) could be applied in dyeing Aniline is now manufactured on a large scale for the commercial production of "mauve' and 'magenta" (rosaniline), and other coloring matters—aniline blue, 1861, violet, 1863, "night" green, etc

animal magnetism (to cure diseases by *sympathetic affection*) was introduced by father Hehl, a Jesuit, at Vienna, about 1774, and had its dupes in France and England about 1788-89 Hehl for a short time associated with Mesmer, but they soon quarrelled Mr Perkins (died 1799) invented "metallic tractors for collecting, condensing, and applying animal magnetism,' for the cure of rheumatism, etc, but drs Falconer and Haygarth put an end to his pretensions by performing the same cures with a pair of *wooden* tractors. —*Brande* MESMERISM Animal magnetism exposed by commissions of the French Academy of Sciences, 1837-38, investigation closed as of a "dead letter," 1840

animal'cules. Leeuwenhoek's microscopical discoveries were published in the Philosophical Transactions of the Royal Society for 1677, in his "Arcana Naturæ," at Leyden, 1696 The works of Ehrenberg, of Berlin, on the "Infusorial Animalculæ," etc, were issued 1838-57 Pritchard's 'Infusoria," ed 1861, and W. Savile Kent's 'Manual of Infusoria," 3 vols 1880-82 are valuable The Rev W H Dallinger and Dr Drysdale have made microscopical observations of bacteria and other low forms of life, 1873-89

animals, cruelty to Mr Martin, M P, zealously labored to repress it, and in 1824 the *Royal Society for the Prevention of Cruelty to Animals* was instituted Its new house in Jermyn street, London, was founded 4 May, 1869. It opposed vivisection in 1860 in unison with a French society, and in Oct. 1873, offered premiums for improved trucks for conveying cattle. A jubilee congress of this and similar societies met in London, 17 June, 1874. Convictions obtained by the society, 1835 to June, 1876, 28,209. VIVISECTION. Martin's act was passed 1822, and similar acts in 1827, 1835, 1837, 1849, and 1854. Dogs were forbidden to be used for draught in 1839.

Fellowship of Animals' Friends, organized about 10 July, 1879; earl of Shaftesbury, president.

The American Society for the Prevention of Cruelty to Animals (Henry Bergh, president) was organized in New York city, 1865. It has branches and auxiliary societies in many cities of the Union, and nearly all the states have passed laws punishing cruelty to animals with fine and imprisonment.

Sheltering Home of Animals, established at Brighton, Mass., by Ellen M. Gifford, where homeless and maimed dogs and cats are taken to be cured and protected.

animism, the doctrine that the soul is the only cause of life, and that the functions of animals and plants depend upon vitality and not on mere chemical and mechanical action, was opposed by Descartes and others. MATERIALISM, PHILOSOPHY.

Anjou (*an-zhoo'*), a province, W. France, was taken by Henry II. of England from his brother Geoffrey, in 1156; their father Geoffrey Plantagenet, count of Anjou, having married the empress Matilda in 1127. ANGEVIN. It was taken by king John from Philip of France in 1205; reconquered by Edward III.; relinquished by him at the peace of Brétigny in 1360, and given by Charles V. to his brother Louis with the title of duke. The university was formed in 1349.

1360. Louis I., duke, invested by the pope with the dominions of Joanna of Naples, 1381; his invading army destroyed by the plague, 1383; he dies, 1384.

1384. Louis II., his son, receives the same grant, but is also unsuccessful.

Louis III., adopted by Joanna, dies 1434.

1434. Regnier or René le bon (a prisoner) declared king of Naples, 1435; his daughter, Margaret, married Henry VI. of England, 1415; he was expelled from Anjou by Louis XI., 1474, and his estates confiscated.

Francis, duke of Alençon, brother to Henry III. of France, became duke of Anjou; at one time he favored the Protestants, and vainly offered marriage to Elizabeth of England, 1581-82; died 1584.

Anjou or **Beaugé,** Battle of, between the English and French; the latter commanded by the dauphin of France, 2[illegible] Mch. 1421. The English were defeated; the duke of Clarence was slain by sir Allan Swinton, a Scotch knight, and [illegible]0 men fell; the earls of Somerset, Dorset, and Huntington were taken. This battle turned the [illegible] of success against the English.

annals (*annales*, from *annus*, a year). A record of historical events arranged year by year. The annual record of the Roman state for its first 6 centuries said to have been kept by the Pontifex Maximus. Many modern books bear the title of annals, as Grotius's "Annales," in imitation of Tacitus, 1557; Baronius, "Annales Ecclesiastici," for the first 12 centuries of the Christian era; Hailes's "Annals of Scotland from the Accession of Malcolm III. to the Accession of the House of Stuart"; "Annals of the Congress of the United States," 1789-1824; changed to *Congressional Register*, 1825-36; to *Congressional Globe*, 1837.

Annap'olis, capital of Maryland. The United States Naval Academy was founded here in 1845 by George Bancroft, then sec. of the navy. It was removed to Newport, R. I., in May, 1861, owing to the civil war, but re-established at Annapolis in Sept. 1865. MARYLAND, 1696, NAVY, U. S., etc.

annexation, United States. The area of the United States at the close of the revolution, 1783, was 827,844 sq. miles. Since that time have been added:

		Sq. miles.	Cost.
Louisiana, purchased of France	1803	1,171,931	$15,000,000
Florida, " " Spain	1819	59,268	5,000,000
Texas, by asking for admission	1845	376,133	
Mexican Cession	1848	545,783	*28,250,000
Gadsden Purchase, from Mexico	1853	45,535	10,000,000
Alaska, purchased of Russia	1867	577,390	7,200,000

* Paid to Mexico, $18,250,000; to Texas, $10,000,000.

Anno Domini, A.D., the year of our Lord, of Grace, of the Incarnation, of the Circumcision, and of the Crucifixion (*Trabeationis*). The Christian era begins Jan. 1 in the middle of the 4th year of the 194th Olympiad, the 753d year of the building of Rome, and in 4714 of the Julian period. This era was invented by a monk, Dionysius Exiguus, or Denys le Petit, about 532. It was introduced into Italy in the 6th century, and ordered to be used by bishops by the council of Chelsea, in 816; but was not generally employed for several centuries. Charles III. of Germany was the first who added "in the year of our Lord" to his reign, in 879. Some believe that Christ was born Friday, 5 Apr. 4 B.C.

Annual Register, a summary of the history of England for each year (beginning with 1758, and continued to the present time), commenced by R. & J. Dodsley. (Edmund Burke at first wrote the whole work, but afterwards became only an occasional contributor.—*Prior.*) A similar work, "Annuaire des Deux Mondes," begun in Paris, 1850.

annuities. The annual payment of a fixed sum, for a term of years, or for one or more lives. In England in 1512, 20*l.* a year were given to a lady of the court for services; and 6*l.* 13*s.* 4*d.* for the maintenance of a gentleman, 1536. 13*l.* 6*s.* 8*d.* deemed competent to support a gentleman in the study of the law, 1554. An act empowered that government to borrow one million sterling upon an annuity of 14 per cent., 4-6 Will. and Mary, 1691-93. This mode of borrowing soon became general among governments. An annuity of 1*l.* 2*s.* 11*d.*, accumulating at 10 per cent. compound interest, amounts in 100 years to 20,000*l.* The Government (English) Annuities and Life Assurances Act, passed in 1864 for the benefit of the working classes, enables that government to grant deferred annuities for small instalments. Works on annuities were published by De Witt, 1671; De Moivre, 1724; Simpson, 1742; Tables by Price, 1792; Milne, 1815; Jones, 1843; Farre, 1864; Institute of Actuaries, 1872. PENSIONS.

annunciation of the Virgin Mary, 25 Mch., LADY-DAY, a festival commemorating the tidings brought to Mary by the angel Gabriel (Luke i. 26); its origin is referred to the 4th or 5th century. The *religious order* of the Annunciation was instituted 1232, and the *military order*, in Savoy, by Amadeus, count of Savoy, about 1362, in memory of Amadeus I., who bravely defended Rhodes against the Turks, 1355. New statutes, 1869.

anointing, an ancient ceremony at the inauguration of priests, kings, and bishops. Aaron was anointed as high-priest, 1491 B.C.; and Saul as king, 1095 B.C. Alfred the Great is said to have been the first king anointed in England, 871 A.D.; and Edgar in Scotland, 1098. The *religious* rite is derived from the epistle of James v. 14. about 60 A.D. It is said that in 550, persons in expectation of death were anointed with consecrated oil, and that this was the origin of extreme unction as a sacrament of the church.

anorth'oscope, a new optical apparatus, described by Dr. Carpenter in 1868. In it distorted figures lose their distortion in rapid motion.

ant, a small insect of many genera and hundreds of species, found in all parts of the world except the polar regions. They are the most intelligent of all creatures except men, and naturalists report proofs of industry, strength, and associated effort in their communities which seem like fairy tales. Huber's "Traité des Mœurs des Fourmis" has been translated. Sir John Lubbock in England ("Ants, Bees, and Wasps"), and the Rev. H. McCook in this country ("The Ants of Texas") have described the latest and best observations on them.

antagonism as a *beneficial universal principle* in nature was discussed by sir W. R. Grove in a discourse at the Royal Institution, London, 20 Apr. 1888.

Antal'cidas, Peace of. In 387 B.C. Antalcidas the Lacedæmonian made peace with Artaxerxes of Persia, on behalf of Greece, especially of Sparta, giving up the cities of Ionia to the king.

Antarctic Continent. SOUTHERN CONTINENT.

antediluvian history. This is entirely Biblical (Gen. iv. v. vi.), the deluge occurring 2348 B.C., or in the year of the world 1656 (*Usher*). According to Whiston, the population of the world was then 549,755,000,000!

anthems. Originally hymns sung in alternate parts; now applied to sacred music adapted to psalms or other scriptural words. Hilary, bishop of Poicti [illegible] mbrose composed them about the middle of th [illegible] —*Lenglet* Introduced into the church service in 386.—[illegible] Ignatius is said to have introduced them into the Greek, and St Ambrose into the Western, church Introduced into the Reformed churches under Elizabeth about 1560 MUSIC.

ENGLISH ANTHEM WRITERS 1520-1625, Tye, Tallis, Byrd Gibbons, 1650-1720 Humphrey, Blow, Purcell Croft, Clarke, 1720-1845, Greene, Boyce, Hayes, Kent, Battishill, Attwood, Walmisley

anthology (Gr ανθολογια =(1) a flower-gathering, (2) a collection of poems) The Greek anthology was a collection of popular epigrams and small poems written by Archilochus, Sappho, Simonides, Meleager, Plato, and others, between 680 and 95 B.C, collected by Meleager, Philippus, Agathias, and others, especially by Maximus Planudes, a monk in the 14th century, A D A MS collection by Constantine Cephalas was found at Heidelberg by Salmasius in 1606, and published by Brunck, 1772-76 Translations have been made by Bland, Merivale, and others

anthropology (Gr ἄνθρωπος, man), science of the natural history of man "In the general classification of knowledge it is the highest section of zoology, or the science of animals, itself the highest section of biology, or the science of life" First anthropological society held its first meeting, London, 24 Feb 1863 The *Anthropological Review* first came out in May, 1863 The anthropological and ethnological societies were amalgamated 17 Jan 1871, and styled 'The Anthropological Institute" An anthropological congress at Paris was opened 16 Aug 1878, others since, at Moscow, 13 Aug 1892 For the races of mankind, see ETHNOLOGY

anthropomorphism (Gr ἀνθρωπομορφος, of human form), the ascription to divine beings of human form or attributes, the conception by man of divinities in his own likeness This tendency of the human mind is regarded by Feuerbach and other atheistic philosophers as the source of all religions

antichrist (opponent of Christ), 1 John ii 18, termed the "man of sin," 2 Thess. ii 3, of these passages many interpretations have been given, and many myths were current in the middle ages respecting the incarnation of the devil, etc Roman Catholic and Protestant writers have applied the term to one another. It has also been ascribed to many false Messiahs.

Antietam Creek (*an-tee'tam*), battle of MARYLAND CAMPAIGN On this battle-field a national cemetery was dedicated, 17 Sept 1867

Anti-Federal party. POLITICAL PARTIES.

Antilles. ISLANDS, IMAGINARY, WEST INDIES

Anti-Masonic party. POLITICAL PARTIES

an'timony, a white, brittle metal, compounds of which were early known, used to blacken eyes in the East (2 Kings ix. 30, and Jer iv. 30) Mixed with lead it forms printing-type metal. Basil Valentine wrote of antimony about 1410 —*Priestley* Antimony also enters into Britannia metal, and is an active principle in tartar-emetic and in James's powder, both extensively used as medicines Antimonial wine is a solution of tartar-emetic in sherry

Anti-Nebraska. POLITICAL PARTIES, UNITED STATES, 1854, etc

Antinomian (Gr ἀντί, against, and νομος, law). John Agricola so called by Luther (in 1538), as holding "that it mattered not how wicked a man was if he had but faith" (Opposed to Rom. iii 28, and v 1, 2) He retracted these doctrines in 1540. The Antinomians of England, who followed Dr Tobias Crisp (d 1642) in teaching that the sins of the elect were assumed by Christ so as not to be charged to them, were condemned by the British parliament, 1648.

Antioch, now **Antakieh,** Syria, built by Seleucus, 300 B.C. (after the battle of Ipsus, 301), called "Queen of the East." Here the disciples were first called Christians, 42 A D (Acts xi. 26). Antioch was taken by Persians, 540, by Saracens about 638, recovered for the Eastern empire, 966, lost again in 1086, retaken by Crusaders in June, 1098, made capital of a principality, 1099, and held by them till captured by the sultan of Egypt, June, 1268 It was taken from the Turks in the Syrian war, 1 Aug 1832, by Ibrahim Pasha, but restored at the peace Antioch suffered by an earthquake, and about 1600 persons were killed, 3 Apr. 1872 —The Era of Antioch, used by early Christian writers of Antioch and Alexandria, placed Creation 5492 years B C 31 councils were held at Antioch, 252-1161 SYRIA

Anti-Pedobaptists. PEDOBAPTISTS

antip'odes (Gr ἀντί, *opposite*, and πόδες, *feet*), inhabitants of the opposite side of our globe Plato is said to be the first who thought antipodes possible (about 388 B.C.) Boniface, archbishop of Mentz, legate of pope Zachary, is said to have denounced a bishop as a heretic for believing in them, 741 A D The antipodes of England are southeast of New Zealand, near Antipodes island

anti-pope, a claimant of the papal chair, in opposition to the regularly elected pope About thirty such were set up, usually by French and Italian factions, from 1305 to 1439. (In the list of POPES, anti-popes are in italics.)

antiquaries. A college of antiquaries is said to have existed in Ireland, 700 B C The annual International Congress of Prehistoric Archæology originated at La Spezzia in 1865, meetings have been held since at Paris, Norwich, etc

A society was founded by archbishop Parker, Camden, Stow, and others in 1572 —*Spelman.*

Application was made to Elizabeth for a charter, her death ensued, and her successor, James I, was far from favoring the design

The "Antiquaries' Feast," mentioned by Ashmole, 2 July 1659

The Society of Antiquaries revived, 1707, received its charter of incorporation from George II, 2 Nov 1751, met in Chancery Lane 1753, apartments in Somerset House (granted 1776), occupied, 15 Feb. 1781, removed to Burlington House 1874 first meeting, 14 Jan 1875 Memoirs entitled "Archæologia," first published in 1770, president, earl Stanhope, elected 1846, d 24 Dec 1875, succeeded by Frederic Ouvry, by the earl of Carnarvon, 1878.

British Archæological Association founded Dec. 1843

Archæological Institute of Great Britain formed by a seceding part of the association, 1845

Society of Antiquaries of Edinburgh founded in 1780.

Since 1845 many county archæological societies have been formed in the United Kingdom

The Society of Antiquaries of France (1814) began in 1805 as the Celtic Academy

The *Antiquary*, a magazine began 1880

The American Antiquarian Society, incorporated at Worcester, Mass, 12 Oct. 1812

United States National Museum, organized at Washington, D C 1846 It possesses among other valuable material a collection of casts from PALENQUE, and other places in Yucatan and Mexico, procured by Mr Charney and purchased by Pierre Lorillard The government grants it $75 000 per annum

Numismatic and Antiquarian Society, instituted at Philadelphia, Pa., 1 Jan 1858

Peabody Museum, founded at Cambridge, Mass, 8 Oct. 1866 Connected with Harvard university This is the leading archæological institution in the U S

Archæological Institute of America organized at Boston, Mass 17 May, 1879 Object, the promotion and direction of archæological investigations, both American and foreign The *American Journal of Archæology and History of the Fine Arts* is the official organ of this institute established 1885 pub quarterly

American School of Classical Study at Athens, Greece, founded by the Archæological Institute of America 2 Oct 1882 Supported by a number of the principal colleges in the U S It co operates with the Archæological Institute in conducting explorations and excavations of classic sites, etc. EGYPT

anti-rentism. The first settled territory in the state of New York along the Hudson was granted by the Dutch government to settlers termed "patroons" in fee, especially in Albany, Rensselaer, Delaware, Greene, and Columbia counties The largest manors were that about Albany, granted in 1630 to the Van Rensselaers, and confirmed by James II, and at first covering over 300,000, acres, lying mostly in Albany and Rensselaer counties, and the Livingston manor, in Columbia county, granted in 1686, covering 160,240 acres The original Dutch settlers were satisfied with the conditions offered by the patroons. But difficulties began soon after the Revolution, and on 7 Jan. 1795, the Livingston manor tenantry called on the legislature to examine the patroon's title, claiming that the grant was fraudulently enlarged The trouble subsided until the death of Stephen Van Rensselaer, in 1839, when the rents had fallen into arrears and the attempt to collect for his successor was resisted. "Anti renters" became an organized body in state politics, supported by the "Seward wing" of the Whigs and the "Barnburners" of the Democracy, and secs 12, 13, 14, and 15 of art. I of the state constitution of 1846 were introduced by their efforts In a suit brought by the attorney-gen. against Harmon Livingston to try his title the state was beaten. Troops were sent to Rensselaersville from Albany in 1839 to enforce the law, but there was no foe to subdue. In Aug. 1845, an officer named Steele was shot while trying to collect rent in Delaware county. Gov. Wright proclaimed the county in a state of insurrection. In this act the disturbance culminated. Two persons were convicted and sentenced to death for this murder, but gov. Wright, commuted the sentence to imprisonment for life, and his successor gov. Young, pardoned them in 1847. These vast manorial estates have now been broken up among small proprietors.

anti-slavery party. FREE-SOIL PARTY, POLITICAL PARTIES, SLAVERY IN THE U. S.

anti-slavery societies. SLAVERY, UNITED STATES.

Anti-Trinitarians. Theodotus of Byzantium, about 200 A.D., is supposed to have been the first theologian to assert the simple humanity of Jesus. This doctrine, advocated by Arius about 318, spread widely after the Reformation, when it was adopted by Lælius and Faustus Socinus. ARIANS, SOCINIANS, UNITARIANS.

Antium, maritime city of Latium, now Porto d'Anzio, near Rome; struggled long for independence, but became a Roman colony after the Latin war, 340–338 B.C. It is mentioned by Horace, and was a favorite retreat of emperors and wealthy Romans, who erected villas in its vicinity. The treasures in the temple of Fortune here were taken by Octavius Cæsar in his war with Antony, 41 B.C.

Antwerp (Fr. *Anvers*), the principal port of Belgium, mentioned in history, 517. It was a small republic in the 11th century, and was the first commercial city in Europe till the wars of the 16th century. Pop. 1891, 227,225.

Its fine exchange built....................1531
[It was taken by the Spaniards and given up to a three days' pillage, 4 Nov. 1576, termed the "Spanish Fury."]
Taken after 14 months' siege by the prince of Parma, 17 Aug. 1585
Truce of Antwerp (between Spain and United Provinces) for 12 years concluded....................29 Mch. 1609
Peter Paul Rubens (b. Siegen, Westphalia, 29 June, 1577) dies....................30 May, 1640
Much injured by tolls on the Scheldt levied by the treaty of Münster....................1648
After Marlborough's victory at Ramillies, Antwerp surrenders at once....................6 June, 1706
The Barrier treaty concluded here....................16 Nov. 1715
Taken by marshal Saxe....................9 May, 1746
Occupied by the French....................1792–93, 1794–1814
Great Napoleon wharves built....................1803–10
Civil war between the Belgians and the House of Orange. BELGIUM....................1830–31
Belgian troops, entering Antwerp, were opposed by a Dutch garrison, who, after a hard fight, being driven into the citadel, cannonaded the town with red-hot balls....................27 Oct. 1830
The citadel bombarded by the French, 4 Dec.; surrendered by gen. Chassé....................23 Dec. 1832
Exchange burned; archives, etc., destroyed....................2 Aug. 1858
A fine-art fête held....................17–20 " 1861
Great Napoleon wharf destroyed by fire; loss, 25 lives and about 400,000*l.*....................2 Dec. "
Great fête at the opening of the port by the abolition of the Scheldt dues....................3 Aug. 1863
Fortifications constructed....................1860–70
Statue of Leopold I. uncovered....................2 Aug. 1868
Plantin-Moretus Museum, containing collections of about 300 years—viz., 12,000 old letters, printing-types, portraits, etc., made by the Plantins (descendants of Charles de Tiercelin, seigneur de la Roche du Maine), who were printers to the kings of Spain—opened about....................20 Aug. 1877

Anvar-i-Suhaili, or the Lights of Canopus, the ancient Persian version of the ancient fables of Pilpay, Bidpai, or Vishnu Sarma, made by Husain Vaiz, at the order of Nushirvan, king of Persia. The English translation by E. B. Eastwick published 1854. FABLES.

Apaches. INDIANS.

ap'atite, mineral phosphate of lime, about 1856, began to be largely employed as a fertilizer. It abounds in Norway, and in Sombrero, a small West India island.

Apoc'alypse or Revelation, written by St. John in the isle of Patmos about 95 A.D.; others ascribe it to Cerinthus, the heretic, or John, the presbyter, of Ephesus. In the first centuries many churches disowned it; and in the fourth century it was excluded from the sacred canon by the council of Laodicea, but received by other councils, and confirmed by [illegible] held in 1545 *et seq.* Although the book had [illegible] by Luther, Michaelis, and others, and its author[illegible] ages, from the time of Justin Martyr [illegible] his first "Apology for Christians" in 139 A.D.), its [illegible] authority is generally accepted.

[illegible] (Gr. ἀπόκρυφα, concealed writings), the [illegible] early church to books or treatises claimed [illegible]ed, but not admitted to the canon of Scripture, [illegible]o 14 books added to the Hebrew Bible in the [illegible]ek and Latin versions. The preface to the Apoc[illegible] "These books are neyther found in the Hebrue [illegible] Chalde."—*Bible*, 1539. Their history ends 135 B.C. [illegible]ot in the Jewish canon, were rejected at the council [illegible] about 366 A.D., but were received as canonical by [illegible]ic council of Trent, 8 Apr. 1546. Parts of them [illegible]as lessons of the church of England, by the 6th [illegible]3, but many of these were omitted by the act passed [illegible]

	B.C.
[illegible]	from about 623–445
[illegible]	" * *
[illegible]	" 734–678
[illegible]	" 656
[illegible]	" 510
[illegible] Solomon	* *
[illegible]us	300 or 180
[illegible]	* *
[illegible] Three Children	* *
[illegible] Susannah	* *
[illegible] Dragon	* *
Prayer of Manasses	676
1 Maccabees	about 323–135
2 Maccabees	from about 187–161

The Apocryphal New Testament consists of forged gospels and epistles, never received by the churches.

Apollinarists, followers of Apollinaris, a reader in the church of Laodicea, who taught (366) that the divinity of Christ was instead of a soul to him; that his flesh was pre-existent, was sent down from heaven, and conveyed through the Virgin, that there were two sons, one born of God, the other of the Virgin, etc. These opinions were condemned by the council of Constantinople, 381.

Apollo, son of Zeus and Leto, god of the fine arts, medicine, music, poetry, and eloquence, in many nations of antiquity identified with the sun, had many temples and statues. His most splendid temple, at Delphi, was built 1263 B.C. DELPHI. His temple at Daphne, built 434 B.C., during a pestilence, was burned 362 A.D., and the Christians were accused of the crime. —*Lenglet.* The statue of Apollo Belvedere, discovered at Antium in 1503, was purchased by pope Julius II. and placed in the Vatican. SCULPTURE.

apologies for Christianity were addressed by Justin Martyr to the emperor Antoninus Pius about 139, and to the Roman senate about 164. Apologies were written by Quadratus, Aristides, and other early fathers of the church.

Apostles (Gr. ἀπόστολος, one sent forth). 12 were appointed by Christ, 31 A.D.—viz., Simon Peter and Andrew (brothers), James and John (sons of Zebedee), Philip, Nathanael (or Bartholomew), Matthew (or Levi), Thomas, James the Less (son of Alphæus), Simon the Canaanite and Jude or Thaddeus (brothers), and Judas Iscariot. Matthias was elected in the room of Judas Iscariot, 33 A.D. (Acts i.); and Paul and Barnabas were appointed by the Holy Spirit, 45 A.D. (Acts xiii. 2). "The Teaching of the Twelve Apostles," a small vellum volume in Greek, dated about 1056, discovered by Philotheos Bryennios, metropolitan of Nicomedea, in the library of the Holy Sepulchre monastery at Constantinople in 1873; and published by him in 1875. The composition is ascribed to the 1st century. The text, with English translation and introduction, was published by R. D. Hitchcock and Francis Brown in 1884; improved edition, spring, 1885. In law, "the apostles" are a summary of a case sent by any court to an appellate court for review.

Apostles' Creed, erroneously so called, is mentioned as the Roman creed by Rufinus (d. about 410). Irenæus, bishop of Lyons (d. 202), gives a creed resembling it. Its repetition in public worship was ordained in the Greek church at Antioch, and in the Roman church in the 11th century, whence it passed to the church of England.

Apostolic Succession is claimed to be the transmission through the laying on of hands of the power and authority committed by Christ to his apostles for the guidance and government of the church Those who hold the doctrine of apostolic succession claim that Christ as the head of the church established through his apostles a hierarchical order which has continued unbroken from its establishment to the present This excludes all from the ministry who cannot show proper ordination This doctrine is held by the Roman Catholic church and most Episcopalians The rev John H Blunt, M A F S A, in his dictionary of "Doctrinal and Historical Theology," says, "The doctrine of the 'apostolic succession' has been held by the most learned writers of the church of England, as Andrews, Bramhall, Hammond Hall, Taylor, Wilson, and many others, and is the only foundation on which episcopacy can rest as a divine institution" All Episcopalians do not so believe Dean Alford declares, "It is a fiction of which I find in the New Testament no trace", and archbishop Whately says, "There is not a minister in Christendom who is able to trace up with any degree of certainty his own spiritual pedigree" Opponents say that Paul never received apostolic ordination, that there is no historical evidence of an unbroken line of succession, that ministers are a divine order only in the sense that it is the divine will that there should be an office of the ministry in the Christian church for divinely appointed work

Apostolical. CANONS and FATHERS

Apostol'ici, a sect, at the end of the 2d century, which renounced marriage, wine, flesh, etc Another sect, founded by Sagarelli about 1261, wandered about, clothed in white, with long beards, dishevelled hair, and bare heads, accompanied by women called spiritual sisters preaching against the corruptions of the church of Rome, and predicting its downfall They renounced baptism, the mass, purgatory, etc, and by their enemies were accused of licentiousness Sagarelli was burned alive at Parma in 1300, his followers were dispersed in 1307, and extirpated about 1404

apoth'ecary (literally, a keeper of a storehouse) On 10 Oct 1345, Edward III settled sixpence per diem for life on Coursus de Gangeland, *apothecarius London'*, for taking care of him during his severe illness in Scotland —*Rymer's Fœdera* In 1518 the physicians of London were incorporated, and the barber surgeons in 1540 But independently of the physicians and the surgeons there were irregular practitioners who were molested by their rivals, and an act was passed in 1543 for their protection. As many of these practitioners kept shops for the sale of medicines, the term "apothecary" was applied to their calling PHARMACY and MEDICAL SCIENCE

Apothecaries incorporated with grocers. 1606
London Apothecaries' company separated from the Grocers' and incorporated 1617, hall built 1670
Their practice regulated and their authority extended through England by the Apothecaries act, 1815, amended, 1825, they are authorized to license practitioners of medicine in 1874
[In the U S an apothecary is simply a seller of drugs, under such restrictions as to competency and license as are imposed by the law of each state]

apotheo'sis (Gr. ἀποθέωσις, deification), the elevation of a king or hero to the rank of a god Julius Cæsar was deified by order of Augustus, 13 B.C "Sixty persons altogether are recorded as having been raised to divine honors from the time of Cæsar to that of Constantine The establishment of Christianity put an end to apotheosis as an avowed belief and a public ceremony, although the principle on which it rested is still conspicuous in the adoration and invocation of saints by the Latin, Greek, and African churches."—*Encyc. Brit* 9th ed

Appala'chian Mountains, the general name of a vast system of elevation near the eastern or Atlantic coast of the United States The name is taken from a tribe of Indians, the Appalachees, living in middle Florida, or near the Appalachicola river The range extend from northern Alabama to northern Maine, 1400 miles, known in New Hampshire as the WHITE MOUNTAINS, in Vermont as the Green, in New York as the ADIRONDACK and CATSKILL, in Pennsylvania as the Alleghany, in Virginia as the Blue Ridge, in North Carolina as the Smoky, in Tennessee and Alabama as the Cumberland, and in Georgia as the Sand, Lookout, etc Mt. Mitchell, in North Carolina, is the highest peak, 6711 ft.; Balsam Cone, in the same range (Smoky) and state is second, 6671 ft

appeal or assize of battle. By the old law of England a prosecutor, when dissatisfied with the acquittal or the pardon of the accused, might institute an action, within a year, for the penalty, when the accused must either accept a new trial by jury or demand a "wager of battle," that is, a duel with the prosecutor, to determine his guilt or innocence In 1817 a young maid Mary Ashford, was believed to have been violated and murdered by Abraham Thornton who, on trial was acquitted On appeal, he claimed his right by wager of battle, which the court allowed, but the appellant (the brother of the maid) refused the challenge, and the accused was discharged, 16 Apr 1818 This law was repealed by 59 Geo III c 46, 1819

In 1631 lord Rea impeached David Ramsey of treason, and offered battle in proof, a commission was appointed, but the duel was prohibited by king James I

appeals. In the time of Alfred (869-901), appeals lay from courts of justice to the king in council, but being soon overwhelmed with appeals from all parts of England, he framed a body of laws which long served as the basis of English jurisprudence The house of lords is the highest court of appeal in civil causes. Courts of appeal at the exchequer chamber, in error from the judgments of the superior and criminal courts, were regulated by statutes in 1830 and 1848 Appeals from English tribunals to the pope were first introduced about 1151, were long vainly opposed, and were abolished by Henry VIII 1534, restored by Mary, 1554, again abolished by Elizabeth, 1559 A proposition for establishing an imperial court of appeal submitted to the house of lords by the lord chancellor Hatherly, 15 Apr, was referred to a select committee 30 Apr 1872 A similar proposition by lord chancellor Selborne, 13 Feb 1873 PRIVY COUNCIL, and JUSTICES, LORD.

The jurisdiction of the house of lords as a court of appeal was abolished by the Judicature act, 1873 The abolition was suspended in 1875, and a provisional court established which first sat 8 Nov 1875 present the lord chancellor, lord Coleridge, baron Bramwell and justice Brett
The house of lords was reconstructed as a court of final appeal by the Appellate Jurisdiction act introduced by lord Cairns, 11 Feb, and passed 11 Aug 1876
Two lords of appeal are appointed, to be peers for life Appeals may be heard during prorogation or dissolution of parliament
The new Supreme Court of Appeal first sat 21 Nov 1876 COURTS OF THE UNITED STATES.

Appenzell, a Swiss canton, threw off the supremacy of the abbots of St Gall early in the 15th century, and became the 13th member of the Swiss confederation 1513 Furnished soldiers to the Catholic party of France against Henry IV in the battle of Ivry, 1590

"With all its priest led citizens and all its rebel peers,
And Appenzell's stout infantry and Egmont's Flemish spears"
—*Macaulay*

Appian Way (*appia via*) ROADS.

apples (*Pyrus Malus*) Several kinds are indigenous to England, but those in general use have come from the continent. Richard Harris, fruiterer to Henry VIII, is said to have planted orchards in Kent, and lord Scudamore, ambassador to France in the reign of Charles I, planted many in Herefordshire Ray reckons 78 varieties of apples in his day (1688) The Romans had 22 varieties (*Pliny*) No country in the world excels the northern United States in this fruit, either in quality, quantity, or variety. FLOWERS AND PLANTS

apportionment of members of congress REPRESENTATIVES

apprentices. Those of London were obliged to wear blue cloaks in summer and blue gowns in winter in the reign of Elizabeth, 1558 10 pounds was then a great apprentice fee. From 20 to 100 pounds were given in the reign of James I —*Stow's Survey* The apprentice tax enacted 43 Geo III 1802 The term of 7 years, not to expire till the apprentice was 24 years old, required by the statute of Elizabeth (1563), was abolished in 1814 Adam Smith strongly disapproved of apprenticeship. An act for the protection of apprentices, etc, was passed in 1851 The apprentices of London have been, at times, very riotous, they rose in insurrection against foreigners on Evil May-day, 1 May, 1517. LONDON

appropriations of church property began in the

time of William I. The parochial clergy, commonly Saxons, were impoverished by bishops and higher clergy (generally Normans), to enrich monasteries possessed by the conqueror's friends. Where the tithes were so appropriated the vicar had only such a competency as the bishop or superior thought fit to allow. Pope Alexander IV. complained of this as the bane of religion, the destruction of the church, and a poison that infected the nation. Lay appropriations began after the dissolution of the monasteries, 1536.

appropriations by Congress. The Congress of the United States makes appropriations for the expenses of the government for each fiscal year ending June 30. The following is a list of the different objects for which the appropriations are made:

Deficiencies.	Forts and fortifications.
Legislative, executive, and judicial.	Military academy.
Sundry civil.	Post-office department.
Army.	Pensions.
Navy.	Consular and diplomatic.
Indian.	Agricultural department.
River and harbor.	District of Columbia.
	Miscellaneous.

The total appropriations for the year 1893 were $304,710,198; 1894, $319,011,847; 1895, $301,788,820; 1896, $293,057,105; 1897, $302,786,386; 1898, $311,179,557; 1899, $673,050,293; 1900, $462,509,750; 1901, $457,152,149; 1902, $479,365,657; 1903, $486,439,306; 1904, $464,846,770; 1905, $467,159,517.

a'pricot, *Prunus Armeniaca*, from Asia Minor, said to have been first planted in England about 1540 by the gardener of Henry VIII.

April, the fourth month of our year, the second of the ancient Romans. In many countries, as England, France, Germany, and the United States, the custom has long prevailed of seeking victims on the 1st of April for practical jokes. Its origin is unknown. In Scotland the subject of the trick is called a "gowk," in the United States an "April fool," and in France "*poisson d'Avril*," "April fish."

ap'teryx (wingless), a bird of New Zealand, first brought to England in 1813, and in the collection of the earl of Derby. Fossil specimens of a gigantic species (named *Dinornis*) were discovered in New Zealand by Walter Mantell in 1843 and since.

Apu'lia, a province in S. E. Italy. The people favored Hannibal, and were severely punished by the Romans at his retreat, 207 B.C. Apulia was conquered by the Normans, whose leader Guiscard received the title of duke of Apulia from pope Nicholas II. in 1059. After many changes of masters it was absorbed into the kingdom of Naples in 1435.

Aqua'rians. A branch of the Encratites, followers of Tatian, about 170 A.D., who denounced marriage, used water instead of wine in the Lord's supper, and met secretly at night during persecution; also certain Christians in Africa, in the 3d century, who took water instead of wine in the eucharist, and were censured by Cyprian (martyred 258).

aqua'rium or **aquaviva'rium,** a vessel containing water (marine or fresh) in which animals and plants may coexist, mutually supporting each other; snails being introduced as scavengers. In 1849 N. B. Ward succeeded in growing seaweeds in artificial sea-water; in 1850 R. Warington demonstrated the conditions necessary for the growth of animals and plants in jars of water; and in 1853 the glass tanks in the Zoölogical Gardens, Regent's Park, London, were set up by D. Mitchell. In 1854 Mr. Gosse published "The Aquarium." W. Alford Lloyd, late of Portland Road, London, by his enterprise in collecting specimens, did much to increase the value and interest of aquaria and erected several. The great aquarium (50 yards long and 12 wide) at the Jardin d'Acclimatation at Paris, was constructed under his direction in 1860. He also constructed the aquarium at Hamburg and others. That at Brighton was inaugurated by prince Arthur, 30 Mch., and publicly opened by the mayor, 10 Aug. 1872. That at the Crystal Palace was opened Jan. 1872.

a'queducts, artificial channels or conduits for conveying water, especially for supplying large cities. The structures of masonry or iron by which such channels cross rivers or valleys are properly called aqueduct bridges. An aqueduct built by Eupalinus, an architect of Megara, to supply the city of Samos with water is described by Herodotus (b. 484 B.C.). Its southern entrance was accidentally discovered in 1883. Among the finest and best preserved of the ancient Grecian aqueducts, still in use at Syracuse, are one 12 miles long, feeding the fountain of Arethusa from the Anapus, and one from the springs of Mt. Crimiti. Of the ancient Roman aqueducts and more modern structures the following examples are noteworthy:

B.C.

Aqua Appia at Rome, about 10 miles in length, begun by Appius Claudius 312

Aqua Marcia, at Rome, length 60 miles, about 7 miles built on arches and high enough to supply water to the summit of the Capitoline mount; built by Q. Marcius Rex.......... 144

Aqua Julia, at Rome; total length about 15 miles, 7 of which were above ground, partly on arches. Part of the distance it was carried above and on the same foundation with Aqua Tepula and Aqua Marcia; built.......... 33

Aqueduct at Nismes, or Pont du Gard, to carry water from the Eure and the Airan to Nismes, a distance of about 25 miles. It crosses the river Gardon at a height of over 150 ft. on a bridge 885 ft. long, with 3 tiers of arches. Supposed to have been built about 27

A.D.

Aqua Claudia, about 46, and Anio Novus, about 59 miles long, over 9 miles built on arches, some 109 ft. in height, united near Rome, and were carried on the same foundation one above the other. Built.......... 38-52

Aqueduct bridge of Spoleto; length, 810 ft.; height, 420 ft.; composed of 2 tiers of gothic arches, 10 below and 30 above, built by Theodoric, king of the Goths, over the river De la Morgia 741

Aqueduct to supply water of the Belgrade valley to Constantinople includes the Crooked aqueduct, the aqueduct of Justinian, 840 ft. long and 112 high, probably erected in the time of Constantine, and the Long aqueduct, 85 ft. in height, 2229 in length, and composed of 2 tiers of arches, 50 in the upper and 48 in the lower. The latter structure was erected by Suleiman the Magnificent.......... 1550

Acqua Paola, supplying the Vatican at Rome, composed of the ancient Aqua Trajana, built 110 A.D., and restored by Belisarius, 537 A.D., and the Alsictina, united and restored by Paul V.......... 1611

Aqueduct bridge of Maintenon, to convey the waters of the Eure to Versailles, 4400 ft. in length, 200 ft. high; work begun 1684, and after costing 22,000,000 francs, abandoned... 1688

Aqueduct bridge at Lisbon, crosses a valley 2400 ft. in width by several arches, the largest 250 ft. in height and 115 ft. span, completed in.......... 1738

Aqueduct of Arcueil, ten miles long, built to supply Paris, passes over the valley of Arcueil by a bridge, 1200 ft. long and 72 ft. high, consisting of 25 arches. It was originally built by Julian, 360 A.D.; was repaired in 1613 by order of Mary de Medici to supply the Luxembourg; rebuilt in 1634, and again in.......... 1777

Aqueduct bridge carrying the Ellesmere canal over the river Ceiriog, in Wales; length, 710 ft.; height, 70 ft. The first in which iron plates forming the bottom were used; work begun, 17 June, 1796; completed.......... 1801

Aqueduct bridge on Ellesmere canal, over the Dee, 1007 ft. long, 126 ft. high; completed by T. Telford and opened....26 Dec. 1805

Canal de l'Ourcq, 60 miles in length, built to supply Paris...1801-22

Roquefavour aqueduct bridge over the Arc, France, 1289 ft. long; built on 3 stages of arches a total height of 271 ft.; cost, $750,000; is a part of the Marseilles conduit to supply waters of the Durance river, built..........1841-47

High bridge, carries the old Croton aqueduct, N.Y., over the Harlem river. Conduit consists of 2 3-foot cast-iron and 1 7-foot wrought-iron pipe on a granite bridge of 15 spans 100 ft. above high-water. Length of aqueduct, 38¼ miles; built 1837-42

Aqueduct bridge carrying the Ganges canal over the river Solani, is 920 ft. in length, and consists of 15 arches. The canal crosses the valley, which is 2 to 3 miles wide, on a raised embankment averaging 17 ft. in height. Canal opened 1854

Washington aqueduct, supplying Washington, D.C., with water from the Potomac, crosses Cabin John creek on a single arch of masonry, with a span of 220 ft. On the same line is the Georgetown creek bridge, 200 ft. span, with 2 arches of iron pipe 4 ft. in diameter, used as water conduits. Aqueduct built..........1852-59

Loch Katrine aqueduct of the Glasgow water-works, is 35 miles in length, about 26 of which is aqueduct proper. 8 valleys are crossed by iron siphon-pipes, and on the line is the Drymen bridge, and one 70 ft. in height at Ballewan. Aqueduct built..........1855-Oct. 1859

Vanne aqueduct, 83 miles in length, supplies Paris with water from the Dhuys and Vanne. 37 miles are constructed of Béton Aggloméré. There are 8 or 10 bridges, 2½ to 3 miles of arches, and 11 miles of tunnels. Aqueduct completed..... 1869

Aqueduct from Kaiserbrunn springs to Rosenhugel, 2 miles from Vienna; total length, 56½ miles. There are 16 miles of tunnels and 9½ miles of masonry bridges, the finest of which is the Mödling, crossing a narrow gorge from tunnel to tunnel. Aqueduct begun, 1869, and completed, at a cost of nearly $11,000,000 ....Sept. 1873

Conduit supplying Boston from Sudbury river, crosses the Charles by a granite aqueduct bridge 475 ft. long and 75 ft. high; length of aqueduct, 16 miles. Aqueduct built.....1875-78

Aqueduct to supply Baltimore with water from Gunpowder river a continuous tunnel 7 miles long begun 1875, opening celebrated Oct 1881
Aqueduct 16 miles long to supply Venice with water, begun in 1880, completed and inaugurated 23d July 1885
Aqueduct to supply Liverpool with water from the Vyrnwy valley, North Wales, 68 miles in length, authorized 1880, water let into the distributing reservoir at Prescott, 19 June, 1891
CROTON AQUEDUCT, TUNNELS

Aquid'aban, Paraguay Here the war with Brazil ended with the defeat and death of president Lopez, 1 Mch 1870

Aq'uila, S Italy Near here the Arragonese under the condottiere Braccio Forte-Braccio were defeated by the allied papal, Neapolitan, and Milanese army under Jacob Caldora, 2 June, 1424 Braccio, a wounded prisoner, refused to take food, and died, 5 June

Aquile'ia, Istria, made a Roman colony about 180 B.C and fortified 168 A D Constantine II was slain in a battle with Constans, fought at Aquileia towards the close of Mch 340 Maximus defeated and slain by Theodosius, near Aquileia, 28 July, 388 Theodosius defeated Eugenius and Arbogastes, the Gaul, near Aquileia, and remained sole emperor, 6 Sept 394 Eugenius was put to death, and Arbogastes died by his own hand St Ambrose held a synod here in 381 In 452 Aquileia was almost totally destroyed by Attila the Hun, and near it in 489 Theodoric and the Ostrogoths totally defeated Odoacer, the king of Italy

Aquitaine', the Roman province Aquitania (S.W. France), so called from its inhabitants, the Aquitani, conquered by the Romans, 28 B C, by the Visigoths, 418 A D, taken from them by Clovis in 507 Henry II of England obtained it with his wife Eleanor, 1152 It was made a principality for Edward the Black Prince in 1362, but annexed to France in 1370 The title, duke of Aquitaine, was assumed by Henry V of England, by right of conquest, in 1418. The province was lost in the reign of Henry VI

Ara'bia, W Asia The terms *Petræa* (stony), *Felix* (happy), and *Deserta* are said to have been applied to its divisions by Ptolemy, about 110 A D The Arabs claim descent from Ishmael, the eldest son of Abraham, born 1910 B.C (Gen xvi) Arabia was unsuccessfully invaded by Gallus, Roman governor of Egypt, 24 B.C In 622 A D, Arabians under the name of Saracens, followers of Mahomet (b at Mecca, 570), their general and prophet, commenced their conquests MAHOMETANISM Arabia was conquered by Ottomans, 1518-39 The Arabs fostered literature and science, especially mathematics, astronomy, and chemistry The Koran was written in Arabic (622-632) The Bible was printed in Arabic in 1671 WAHABEES The aggression of the Turks on the South Arabs excited jealousy in England, and was checked by the sultan Nov 1873 An Egyptian commission for the preservation of Arab monuments was appointed Jan 1882. Area, 173,700 sq miles, pop estimated, 6,000,000

Arabian Nights' Entertainments (or 1001 Nights) are the "Contes Arabes" collected by Antoine Galland, a French Orientalist who travelled under the patronage of Colbert. They were published in Paris in 12 vols. in 1704-8, but their authenticity was doubted for many years It is now admitted that they were composed in substantially their present form not long after 1500 A D, but scholars have found in various languages much older originals for many of the best of them. The best English translation is that of E W Lane, published 1839, with notes and illustrations Sir Richard Burton in 1887 found two of these tales in Arabic in a Persian library ALADDIN.

Arabic figures (1, 2, 3, etc) ARITHMETIC.

Ar'agon, part of the Roman Tarraconensis, a kingdom, N. E Spain, was conquered by the Carthaginians, who were expelled by the Romans about 200 B.C It became an independent monarchy in 1035 A D. SPAIN

Aram, Aramæa, from the Hebrew Aram ("high land," as distinguished from Canaan, "low land"), a name given to the country N E of Palestine, including Syria Babylonia, and Mesopotamia The people used two dialects in the west, Syriac, in the east, Aramaic (improperly termed Chaldee), called Hebrew at the time of Christ

Aranjuez (*a-ran-hweth'*), C Spain, contains a fine royal palace, at which several important treaties were concluded On 17 Mch 1808 an insurrection against Charles IV and his favorite, Godoy, the prince of peace, compelled Charles to abdicate in favor of his son, Ferdinand VII, 19 Mch

Arap'ahoes. INDIANS

Ar'arat, a mountain in Armenia (about 17,112 feet above the sea-level), on which Noah's ark is supposed to have rested, 2319 B C The Persians call it Koh-i-Nuh (Noah's mountain) the Armenians Masis, the Turks, Agri-Dagh

It was ascended by Dr Parrot 27 Sept 1829, by major Stuart, 1856, and by others since Mr James Bryce who ascended 11, 12 Sept 1876 describes the summit as a little plain of snow silent and desolate with a bright green sky above, the view, stern, green, and monotonous.

Arauca'nia, a district on the Pacific coast of South America, extending northward about 190 miles from the parallel of 40 S lat Its inhabitants waged intermittent war with the Spaniards from 1537 to 1773 when their independence was recognized They are now nominally subject to Chili

Arau'sio, now **Orange,** S E France Through the jealousy of the Roman proconsul, Q Servilius Cæpio, who would not wait for the army of the consul C Manlius, both were routed here by the Cimbri, 105 B C

Arbe'la. The third and decisive battle between Alexander the Great and Darius Codomannus decided the fate of Persia, 1 Oct 331 B C, on a plain in Assyria, between Arbela and Gaugamela The army of Darius consisted of 1,000,000 foot and 10,000 horse, the Macedonian army amounted to only 40 000 foot and 7000 horse —*Arrian* The gold and silver found in Susa, Persepolis and Babylon, which fell to Alexander from this victory, amounted to thirty millions sterling, and the jewels and other precious spoil belonging to Darius, sufficed to load 20,000 mules and 5000 camels.—*Plutarch*

arbitration (in law) Submission to arbitration was authorized and made equivalent to the decision of a jury by 9 and 10 Will III (1698) Submissions to arbitration may be made rules of any court, and arbitrators may compel attendance of witnesses, 3 and 4 Will IV c 42 (1833) The Common Law Procedure act (1854) authorizes judges of superior courts to order compulsory arbitration, and, by an act of 1859, railway companies may settle disputes with each other by arbitration The Arbitration (Masters and Workmen) act was passed 6 Aug 1872 In New York and some other states, arbitrations and references are provided for by law, and the awards may have the force of judgments of courts of record ALABAMA CLAIMS, FISHERIES.

Arbitration treaties. Nov 1, 1904, the secretary of state and the French ambassador signed a treaty, providing for the settlement by arbitration of disputes between the United States and France Differences which may arise of a legal nature or relating to the interpretation of treaties existing between the two contracting parties, and which it may not have been possible to settle by diplomacy, shall be referred to the Permanent Court of Arbitration established at the Hague by the convention of the 29th of July, 1899, provided, nevertheless, that they do not affect the vital interests, the independence, or the honor of the two contracting states, and do not concern the interests of third parties In each individual case the high contracting parties, before appealing to the Permanent Court of Arbitration, shall conclude a special arrangement defining clearly the matter in dispute, the scope of the power of the arbitrators, and the period to be fixed for the formation of the arbitral tribunal and the several stages of the proceedings The present agreement is concluded for a period of five years from the day of signature of this treaty The treaty with France was followed by treaties of the same tenor with Germany, Switzerland, Portugal, and Great Britain. Italy, Russia, and Mexico were ready to negotiate like treaties PEACE CONFERENCE

Arbor Day, for restoring forest trees, devised and recommended by gov Morton of Nebraska, especially to raise a barrier of trees to protect the land from the fierce winds of the west and south The day became exceedingly popular, and most of the states have legalized it

Texas legalized.	22 Feb. 1889
Vermont, not legalized, but observed	1855
Wisconsin, legalized	30 Apr 1880

Arbuthnot and Ambrister, Case of. Alexander Arbuthnot, a Scotchman, then nearly 70 years of age, came to Florida from New Providence in his own schooner in 1817, to trade with the Indians. Ambrister, born in London in 1785, was a lieutenant in the English marine service, and was present at the battle of Waterloo. For fighting a duel with a brother officer he was suspended for one year. While with his uncle, the governor of New Providence, he met Arbuthnot, with whom he visited Florida. Here it was alleged they became implicated in Indian difficulties that gen Jackson was sent to quell in 1818. By order of gen. Jackson, Arbuthnot and Ambrister were seized and tried by a military court convened 26 Apr 1818, at Fort St Marks, Fla, gen Ed P Gaines president, for inciting the Creek Indians to war against the United States. Ambrister made no defence, but threw himself on the mercy of the court. Arbuthnot was sentenced to be hanged. Ambrister was first sentenced to be shot, but his sentence was commuted to fifty stripes on the bare back, and confinement at hard labor, with ball and chain, for one year. Gen Jackson disapproved the commutation, and ordered the original sentence in both cases to be carried out, which was done, 30 Apr 1818. This arbitrary act of Jackson created great excitement at the time, and the attention of Congress was called to it. UNITED STATES, 1819

ar'butus. The *Arbutus Andrachne*, Oriental strawberry tree, was brought to England from the Levant about 1724. FLOWERS and PLANTS

Arca'dia, a country in the centre of the Peloponnesus, Greece. The Arcadians regarded their nation as the most ancient of Greece, and older than the moon (*προσέληνος, antelunar*), though Doderlein thinks it may mean pre-Hellenic). Pelasgus is said, in their mythology, to have taught them to feed on acorns, as more nutritious than herbs, their former food, for which they honored him as a god, 1521 B C. Arcas afterwards taught them agriculture and the art of weaving. From this second benefactor the people and their country were respectively called Arcades and Arcadia. Here Pan, their tutelary deity, invented the flute.

> "And round us all the thicket rang
> To many a flute of Arcady."
> —*Tennyson*, "In Memoriam," xxiii

The early history of Arcadia is that of the separate towns, which had no common political interests till the time of Epaminondas. All dates and events earlier than the 7th century B C are mythical.

	B.C
Aristocrates I (of Orchomenus) put to death for offering violence to the priestess of Artemis.	715
Aristocrates II stoned, a republic founded	681
Arcadians fight under Sparta in the Persian wars.	490–475
Supremacy of Sparta (acknowledged 560) abolished by the Thebans, Megalopolis founded by Epaminondas	371
Arcadians allied with Athens, defeated by Archidamus.	367
Arcadia, having joined the Achæan league, on its suppression is annexed by Rome	146

arch. It appears in early Egyptian and Assyrian architecture. The oldest arch in Europe is probably in the CLOACA MAXIMA, at Rome, constructed under the early kings, about 588 B.C. The ancient Chinese bridges are of great magnitude, and are built with stone arches much like those of the Romans. Triumphal arches were a leading feature of Roman architecture, especially those of Titus (80 A D.), of Trajan (114), and of Constantine (312). The arches in London parks were erected about 1828. The Marble arch, formerly before Buckingham palace (whence it was removed to Cumberland gate, Hyde park, in 1851) was modelled from the arch of Constantine. BRIDGES.

archæology, the science of antiquities. ANTIQUARIES.

archæop'teryx (ancient bird), the earliest known bird, found in the lithographic slate of Solenhofen, by Herman von Meyer and dr Haberlein in 1861, closely resembling a reptile. It was described by Owen in 1863.

Archangel, N Russia, a city, named from a monastery founded here, and dedicated to St Michael in 1584. The passage to Archangel was discovered by the English navigator Richard Chancellor in 1553, it was the only seaport of Russia till the formation of the docks at Cronstadt, and foundation of St Petersburg in 1703. A fire destroyed the cathedral and upwards of 3000 houses in June, 1793. Pop 1890, 20,000.

archbishop (Gr. ἀρχιεπίσκοπος), a title given in the 4th and 5th centuries to bishops of chief cities such as Rome, Alexandria, Antioch, and Constantinople, who presided over other metropolitans and bishops in surrounding districts. The word is first found in the Apology against the Arians, by Athanasius, who died 373. The Eastern archbishops have since been styled *patriarchs.—Riddle*

Before the Saxons came to England there were 3 archbishops, London, York and Caerleon upon Usk, but soon after St Augustin settled the metropolitan see at Canterbury, 602. CANTERBURY
York continued archiepiscopal, but London and Caerleon lost the dignity. ST DAVID'S
The bishoprics in Scotland were under the jurisdiction of the archbishop of York until the archbishoprics of St. Andrew's and Glasgow were created in 1470 and 1491, these last were discontinued at the Revolution of 1688. GLASGOW, ST ANDREW'S
The bishop of Moray, etc., is now styled *Primus*
The rank of archbishop was early in Ireland
4 archbishops were constituted Armagh, Cashel, Dublin, and Tuam (until then the archbishop of Canterbury had jurisdiction over Irish as well as English bishops, as the archbishop of York had over those of Scotland), 1151
Of these 4 archbishoprics 2 were reduced to bishoprics (Cashel and Tuam) under the stat 3 and 4 Will IV (leaving Armagh and Dublin), which also reduced the 22 sees in Ireland to 12, 1833

archdeacon, originally the first or eldest deacon, who attended the bishop without power, but since the council of Nice his function has become a dignity above a priest's. The appointment in Great Britain is referred to the 8th century. There are 75 archdeacons in England (1878), 2 or more to assist each bishop in the inspection and management of his diocese. The archdeacon's court is the lowest in ecclesiastical polity, an appeal lies from it to the consistorial court, by 24 Henry VIII (1532). A few dioceses of the Protestant Episcopal church in the United States have introduced the title of archdeacon.

archery, the art of using the bow and arrow, especially the long bow, as distinguished from the cross-bow or arbalist, is ascribed to Apollo, who communicated it to the Cretans.

	B C
Ishmael "became an archer" (Gen xxi 20)	1892
Philistine archers overcame Saul (1 Sam xxxi 3)	1056
David commanded the use of the bow to be taught (2 Sam i 18).	1055
Aster of Amphipolis, slighted by Philip, king of Macedon, at the siege of Methone shot an arrow inscribed, "Aimed at Philip's right eye," which it put out, Philip drew out the arrow with these words, "If Philip take the town, Aster shall be hanged," and kept his word	353
	A D
Archery introduced into England previous to	440
Harold and his two brothers were killed by arrows from cross bows of Norman soldiers at battle of Hastings	1066
Richard I revived archery in England in 1190, himself killed by an arrow while besieging the castle of a vassal in Normandy	1199
[The victories of Crecy (1346), Poitiers (1356), and Agincourt (1415), were won chiefly by archers]	
4000 archers of the king surrounded the houses of parliament ready to shoot, pacified by the king 21 Richard II.—*Stow*	1397
Citizens of London formed companies of archers in the reign of Edward III, and a corporate body called "The Fraternity of St. George" 29 Henry VIII	1538
Roger Ascham's "Toxophilus, the School of Shooting" pub	1571
Scorton Annual Arrow Meetings—a silver arrow shot for, articles agreed to	14 May, 1673
Royal company of archers instituted by the marquess of Athol, as the king's body guard for Scotland	1676
The long bow was 6 ft long, the arrow 3 ft., usual range from 300 to 500 yards. Robin Hood is said to have shot from 600 to 800 yards. The cross bow was fixed to a stock, and discharged with a trigger	
The use of the long bow was taught in Kenyon College, Ohio, as early as 1833. The archery revival in America dates from the year 1877, when the first club was organized in Oakland, Cal	

ARTILLERY COMPANY, TOXOPHILITES

architecture (Lat. *architectura*, from Gr. ἀρχιτέκτων, chief artificer). The five great orders are, the Doric, Ionic, and Corinthian (*Greek*), the Tuscan and Composite (*Roman*). Gothic as well as Saracenic or Arabian arose about the 9th century. ORDERS and GOTHIC. The architecture of a people is an index of their mental and moral qualities, and of the state of civilization which they have reached. It may be considered more trustworthy than language in settling the question of race.—*Encyclopædic Dictionary*. The five great orders of architecture do not include all known styles. The Chinese have one in eastern Asia, and in India are several

nd there existed more or less remote a Phœnician, a Jewish, n Assyrian, a Babylonian, a Persepolitan, and a Sassanian, nd in America the Mexican and Peruvian, while Europe has he Cyclopean, Etruscan, and Druidical The following are he leading styles or phases of English architecture, arranged n chronological order

I	Norman	1066–1154
II	Transitional from Norman to Pointed	1154–1189
III	Early English, First Pointed or Lancet	1189–1272
IV	Transition from Early Pointed to Complete	1272–1307
V	Decorated	1307–1377
VI	Transitional from Decorated to Perpendicular	1377–1399
VII	Perpendicular	1399–1547
III	Tudor	1550–1600
IX	Jacobean	1603–1641

REPRESENTATIVE STRUCTURES

GYPTIAN —Pyramids of Cheops or Suphis, Chephren and Mycerinus at Gizeh EGYPT iv dynasty
Great Sphinx and Temple EGYPT, iv dynasty
Obelisk of Osortasen at Heliopolis, cir 2400 B C EGYPT, xii dynasty
Temples of Karnac Luxor, Isamboul and the Colossi or vocal Memnon, cir 2000–1500 B C EGYPT, xviii dynasty
NDIAN —Rock hewn temple or Chaitya cave at Karli 86 B C
Dravidian temple at Seringham 17th century
Temple at Chillambaram 17th–18th "
Perumal pagoda at Madura 18th "
NCIENT GRECIAN —*Cyclopean* or *Pelasgic* —Walls of Tiryns and Mycenæ, Gate of the Lions, "The Treasury" or tomb of Atreus 1200–1000
Doric —Temple of Pallas (Minerva) at Corinth . 655–581
Temple of Zeus (Jupiter) at Ægina 508–499
" of Theseus at Athens, built 469
" at Agrigentum begun 480
" of Poseidon (Neptune) at Pæstum . cir 450
" of Apollo Epicurus in Arcadia cir 450
Parthenon of Athens, finished 438
Ionic —Temple of Here (Juno) at Samos cir 700
Temple of Artemis (Diana) at Ephesus 544
" on the river at Ilyssus 484
" of Erectheus at Athens 420
Corinthian. —Temple of Zeus (Jupiter) Olympius at Athens, 6th–2d century B C
Tower of the Winds at Athens cir 350
Monument of Lysicrates at Athens 335
Combination of Orders —Temple of Athene (Minerva) at Tegea cir 300
NCIENT ROMAN —Temple of Capitoline Jupiter, dedicated 507
Pantheon at Rome 27
Temple of Vesta at Tivoli cir 27
" the Sun at Palmyra, rebuilt by Romans A.D
Colosseum at Rome, dedicated 80
Roman temple at Nismes, France (Maison Carrée), 2d century A D
Temple of Jupiter at Baalbec . 150
" the Sun at Baalbec 200
ARLY CHRISTIAN —Basilica of San Paolo fuori le Mura at Rome 388–395
Basilica of St Clement's at Rome, 4th century, rebuilt, 1099–1118
BYZANTINE —Church of St. Sophia at Constantinople, commenced 532
Church of St. Mark's at Venice . 977–1085
" St. Antonio at Padua 1237–1307
ROMANESQUE —Baptistery and church of San Miniato at Florence. cir 1013
Church of Holy Apostles at Cologne, apse erected 1035
" St Saturnin at Toulouse, dedicated. 1096
Cathedral of Pisa, Italy 1067–1118
Church of San Zenone at Verona, Lombardy, 12th century
Cathedral of Parma Italy, 12th century
Church of San Michele at Lucca, Italy 1188
" St Stephen at Caen, France 1066–1077
" St. Trinité at Caen, France, commenced 1083
ANGLO NORMAN —Winchester cathedral 1070–1493
Norwich cathedral 1096–1135
Chapter house at Bristol . 1155–1170
Canterbury cathedral rebuilt . .. 1175
SARACENIC.—Mosque at Cordova Spain 786–796
Mosque of Ibn Touloun, Cairo 876
" the sultan Barkook and tombs of the Mamelukes, Cairo 1149
Mosque at Old Delhi India commenced about 1190
Alhambra at Granada, Spain . . 1273–1333
Mosque of the sultan Hassan, Egypt 1356
" at Futtepore Sikri, India. cir 1560–1600
Palace at Delhi, India cir 1628–1658
Taj Mahal at Agra, India cir 1628–1658
GOTHIC —Cathedral of St Denis, France, consecrated 1144
Convent church at Alcobaça, Portugal 1148–1222
Cathedral of Paris, (Notre Dame), France 1163–1214
" Chartres, France, completed 1260
" Rheims, France, 1211, dedicated 1241
" Amiens " 1220–1257
Church of San Francisco at Assisi 1228–1253
Cathedral of Strasburg Germany, nave finished . 1275
" Toledo Spain, begun 1227
" Siena, Italy, begun 1243
" Cologne, Germany, 1248, choir completed . 1322
Cathedral of Burgos, Spain western façade 1442
Sta Maria del Fiore of Florence, Italy 1294–1444
Church at Batalha, Portugal 1385
Cathedral of Milan, Italy 1385–1440
Convent of Certosa at Pavia Italy 1396, façade built 1473
" church at Belem Portugal, commenced 1500
RENAISSANCE —*Florentine* —Church of San Lorenzo at Florence, completed, 15th century
Church of San Spirito, Florence, Brunelleschi, arch 1377–1444
Church of San Andrea at Mantua, Alberti, arch 1470–1472
Riccardi palace, Florence begun 1430
Pitti palace, " 1435
Rucellai palace, " " 1460
Strozzi palace, " " 1489
Venetian —Palazzo Vendramini Calergi, begun 1481
Library of St Mark's 1536
Grimani palace cir 1540–1550
Church of San Giorgio Maggiore, Palladio, arch 1518–1580
" Santa Maria della Salute 1632
" " " Zobenico 1680
Dogana at Venice, architect unknown (?) 1682
Roman —Vatican, reconstruction begun 1447
St Peter's church, 1450, dedicated 1626
Cancellaria palace begun cir 1495
Court of the Loggie Vatican, Bramante, arch 1444–1540
Belvedere court, Vatican, begun 1506
Farnese palace, begun 1530
Borghese palace 1590
Barberini palace 1624–1630
Terra Cotta —Façade of the Certosa at Pavia, Italy, begun 1473
French —Louvre Paris begun 1204
Chateau of Chambord, begun 1526
Church of St. Eustache, Paris 1532
Luxembourg palace begun cir 1611
New palace at Versailles begun 1661
Dome of the Invalides, Paris 1680–1706
Church of St Genevieve or Pantheon of Paris 1755–1781
Spanish —Cathedral of Granada begun 1529
Escurial, near Madrid 1563–1593
Cathedral of Valladolid begun cir 1560–90
" Zaragoza (del Pilar) begun 1677
English —Banqueting house, Whitehall 1619–1621
St Paul's church Covent Garden 1631
St. Stephen's church, Walbrook, completed 1679
ST PAUL'S cathedral 1675–1710
MEXICAN, AMERICAN and MODERN —Cathedral of Mexico, 1573–1657
Cathedral of Arequipa Peru 1621–1656, rebuilt 1844
Theatre at Bordeaux France 1773–1780
Capitol at Washington, D C 1793–1867
Glyptothek at Munich, completed 1830
Theatre and museum at Berlin 1825–1835
Windsor castle, restoration begun 1826
Walhalla near Ratisbon Bavaria, completed 1839
St Isaac's church St Petersburg 1818–1858
Houses of parliament at London or palace of Westminster, begun 1840
New opera house at Paris, opened 6 Jan 1875

EMINENT ARCHITECTS.

Agamedes, Greek, fl 1450 B C	[illegible] Trophonius built the temples of Apollo at Delphos, Poseidon near Mantinea, and Apollo near Tebadea.
Daedalus, Greek, fl 1250 B.C.	Built the Cretan labyrinth
Theodorus Greek, fl 700 B C	Built labyrinth of Lemnos and the temple of Here at Samos
Hermogenes, Greek, fl 650 B C	Built temple of Artemis in Magnesia, and temple of Bacchus at Trois.
Ctesiphon Greek, fl 600 B C	Designed and commenced the temple of Artemis (Diana) at Ephesus, carried on by his son Metagenes.
Antistates Antimachides, Calleschros, and Porinus, fl 555 B C	Architects of the marble temple to Zeus (Jupiter) Olympius at Athens
Callimachus, Greek, fl. 540 B.C	Invented the Corinthian capital and established the proportions of the Corinthian order
Daphnis, Greek, fl 500 B C	Erected the marble temple of Apollo at Miletus in concert with Peonius and Demetrius, and completed the temple of Artemis (Diana) at Ephesus
Mycon, Greek, fl 500 B C	Built the temple of Theseus
Agaptos, Greek, fl 450 B C	Inventor of porticos around the square attached to the Greek Stadii built the portico at Elis
Callicrates, Greek, fl 450 B C	Built the Parthenon at Athens in company with Ictinus.
Ictinus Greek, fl 450 B C	Architect of the Parthenon at Athens, built the temple of Apollo Epicurus.
Libon Greek, fl 450 B C	Built temple of Zeus near Olympia
Andronicus, Greek, fl 350 B C	Built the Tower of the Winds at Athens
Dinocrates, Greek, fl 330 B.C.	Builder of Alexandria.
Sostratus the Cnidian, fl 300 B C	Built the lighthouse on the isle of Pharos
Cossutius, Roman, fl. 200 B C.	One of the first Romans to adopt the Grecian orders, finished the temple of Zeus Olympius at Athens.

Vitruvius Pollio, Roman, fl. 30 B.C.	Writer on architecture; built temple of Justice at Fano.
Severus and Celer, Roman, fl. 50 A.D.	Architects to Nero, who employed them in construction of the "Golden House."
C. Julius Lacer, Roman, fl. 80 A.D.	Built temple of San Giuliano at Alcantara, Spain; 6-arch bridge over the Tagus.
Apollodorus, Greek, fl. 100	Architect to Trajan; built a stone bridge over *the Danube in Lower Hungary*, the Great square of Trajan, Basilica Nepia, baths of Trajan, etc.
Detrianus, Greek, fl. 120	Architect to Adrian; restored the Pantheon, the forum of Augustus, etc.; built the mausoleum of Adrian, and the bridge of St. Angelo.
Anthemius of Lydia, and Isidorus of Miletus, fl. 525	Built church of St. Sophia at Constantinople.
Romualdus, French, fl. 840	Built cathedral of Rheims; destroyed by fire in 1215.
Buschetto da Dulichio, Italian, fl. 1016	Architect of the cathedral of Pisa.
Pietro de Ustamber, Spanish, fl. 1020	Built cathedral of Chartres.
Guglielmo, or Wilhelm, German, fl. 1170	Built the leaning tower of Pisa, begun in 1174.
Robert de Lusarche, French, fl. 1220	Designed cathedral of Amiens.
Arnolfo, Florentine, 1250–1310	Built abbey and church of Santa Croce, Florence.
Andrea da Pisa, Italian, 1270–1345	Designed the castle of Scarperia, arsenal at Venice, and church of San Giovanni, begun at Pistoja in 1337.
Robert de Couci, French, fl. 1300	Rebuilt cathedral of Rheims
William de Wykeham, English, 1324–1405	Built new college, Oxford, rebuilt the greater part of Winchester cathedral, and planned part of Windsor castle.
Filippo Brunelleschi, Italian, 1377–1444	Completed cathedral of S. Maria del Fiore at Florence as far as the lantern; built Pitti palace at Florence to second story; built church of San Spirito.
Leon Battista Alberti, Italian, 1398–1472	Built church of St. Francis at Rimini, tribune of the church della Nunziata at Florence, church of S. Andrea at Mantua, and was one of the principal restorers of ancient architecture.
Michelozzo Michelozzi, Florentine, 1402–1470	Built palazzo Riccardi at Florence.
Donato Lazzari, called Bramante d' Urbino, Italian, 1444–1540	The first architect of St. Peter's church at Rome.
Michael Angelo Buonarotti, Italian, 1474–1563	Built cupola of St. Peter's.
Jacopo Tatti, called Sansovino, Italian, 1479–1570	Built library of St. Mark's at Venice, 1536; and Palazzo Corner, begun in 1532.
Baldassare da Siena Peruzzi, Italian, 1481–1536	Employed as architect of St. Peter's. Designed palazzo Massimo at Rome, palace of La Farnesina at Longara, and gate of S. Michele in Bosco. Made plans and model for cathedral of Carpi.
Antonio da San Gallo, Italian, 1482–1546	Architect on St. Peter's; commenced the Farnese palace.
Michele San Micheli, Italian, 1484–1559	Built palazzo Grimani at Venice, cathedral of Monte Fiascone, and church of S. Domenico at Orvieto. Introduced triangular and pentangular bastions on fortresses.
Giovanni Battista di Toledo, Spanish, –1567	Assisted in planning the Strada di Toledo in Naples. Built the church of S. Iago, near Cuença. Commenced the Escurial.
Galeazzo Alessi, Italian, 1500–1572	Built the church of the Madonna at Genoa; completed the fortress of Perugia.
Bartolomeo Ammanati, Italian, 1511–1589	Built new bridge of the Trinity over the Arno at Florence; completed Pitti palace at Florence; continued palazzo Rucellai at Florence.
Andrea Palladio, Italian, 1518–1580	Wrote a treatise on architecture, 1570. Built villa Capra, or Rotonda, near Vicenza, church of S. Giorgio Maggiore, Venice; church of Il Redentore, Venice, and palazzo Barbaro at Maser in the Trevigiano.
Giovanni d' Herrera, Spanish—d. 1597	Completed the Escurial begun by Giovanni Battista di Toledo; built palace of Aranjuez, and bridge of Segovia.
Giacomo da Vignola Barozzi, Italian, 1507–1573	Architect of St. Peter's; built Caparola palace, 30 miles from Rome.
Domenico Fontana, Italian, 1543–1607	Built chapel of the Persepio in S. Maria Maggiore, and the little palace Della Villa at Rome. Raised obelisks and built parts of the Vatican and Quirinal palaces.
Vincenzio Scamozzi, Italian, 1552–1616	Built fortress of Palma near Friuli, Procuratie Nuove, and palazzo Cornaro, Venice.

ARC

Carlo Maderno, Italian, 1556–1629	Completed St. Peter's, and the palace at Monte Cavallo; built palazzo Mattei. Partly completed the Barberini palace of Urban VIII.
Inigo Jones, English, 1572–1652	Built the Banqueting-house at Whitehall; Covent Garden, London, etc.
Giovanni Lorenzo Bernini, Italian, 1589–1680	Built portico of St. Peter's, chapel in church of Sta. Maria della Vittoria, Rome, part *of Barberini palace, the Chigi palace*, and Collegio Urbano di Propaganda Fide.
Alessandro Algardi, Italian, 1598–1654	Built villa Pamfili at Rome.
François Mansard, French, 1598–1666	Restored the Hôtel Toulouse; built for president de Longueil the château de Maisons near St. Germain en Laie. Inventor of the Mansard roof.
Francesco Borromini, Italian, 1599–1667	Built the church of S. Carlino, and the façade of the church of St. Agnes in the *piazza Navona*, Rome.
Alonso Cano, Spanish, 1601–1667	Called the Michael Angelo of Spain, being at once painter, sculptor, and architect.
Claudius Perrault, French, 1613–1688	Designed the east façade and colonnades of the Louvre, and a triumphal arch at entrance of Faubourg St. Antoine.
Sir Christopher Wren, English, 1632–1723	Built St. Paul's cathedral (first stone laid 21 June, 1675). Built "The Monument," London, St. Stephen's church, Walbrook, and more than 50 others.
Jules Hardouin Mansard, French, 1645–1708	Built the dome *of the* Hôtel des Invalides, la galerie du Palais Royal, Château de Clagny, mansion of St. Cyr, etc.
Johann Bernard Fischers, German, 1650–1738	Built the palace of Schönbrunn, 1696, and church of St. Charles Borromeo, at Vienna, 1716.
Augustin Charles d'Aviler, French, 1653–1700	Built the archiepiscopal palace at Toulouse, and the gate at Montpellier called La Porte Perou, designed by D'Orbay.
Robert de Cotte, French, 1657–1735	Built Ionic colonnade of palace of Trianon *gallery of Toulouse, chapel of Louis XIII.* in cathedral at Paris. First to introduce ornamenting of rooms by means of mirrors.
Germain Boffrand, French, 1667–1754	Published a book on architecture at Paris, 1745. Built hospital of the Enfants Trouvés at Paris.
Abate Filippo Ivara, Italian, 1685–1735	Façades of church of Carmelites at Turin, and cathedral of Milan. Finished cupola of S. Andrea, Mantua, and of cathedral at Como.
Ferdinando Fuga, Italian, 1699	Designed the Triclinio in the piazza of St. John Lateran and Corsini palace, Rome. Erected Reclusorio hospital.
Luigi Vanvitelli, Italian, 1700–1773	An architect of St. Peter's. Built convent of S. Agostino at Rome, royal palace of Charles III. at Caserta, Italy, and churches of S. Marcellino, Della Rotonda, and La Nunziata at Naples.
M. Louis, French	Built theatre at Bordeaux.
James Wyatt, English, 1743–1813	Built *Oxford* street Pantheon, London; finished in 1772, afterwards destroyed by fire. Built Fonthill abbey, Huntworth church, etc.
Sir John Soane, English, 1752–1837	Architect of Bank of England.
B. H. Latrobe, American, 1764–1820	Succeeded Dr. William Thornton as architect of the Capitol at Washington. Designed the original columns in the Capitol (purely American) representing cornstalks *bound together*.
Karl Friedrich Schinkel, German, 1781–1841	Built theatre, museum, and new guard-house at Berlin.
Leon von Klenze, German, 1784–1864	Built Walhalla near Ratisbon, and Glyptothek at Munich.
Alfonzo Ricard de Montferrand	Built church of St. Isaac at St. Petersburg, Russia.
Sir Charles Barry, English, 1795–1860	Architect of houses of Parliament.
Henry H. Richardson, American, 1838–1886.	Built Trinity Church, Boston; State Capitol, Albany, N. Y.

An architectural club was formed in 1791. An architectural society existed in London in 1806. The Royal Institute of British Architects was founded in 1834—Earl de Grey, president, 1835–61. The Architectural Society, established in 1831, was united to the Institute in 1842. The Architectural Association began about 1846. The Architectural Museum, Westminster, opened 21 July, 1869.

Mr. James Fergusson's "History of Architecture" (the best), 2d ed. 1874–76.

American Institute of Architects, organized and incorporated in New York in 1857. *Holds annual conventions at different places* and publishes proceedings. Various cities have independent organizations, but are enrolled as chapters of the institute and their members become associate members of that body.

archons. When royalty was abolished at Athens, in memory of king Codrus, killed in battle, 1044 or 1068 B.C., the executive government was vested in magistrates called archons, elected for life. Medon, eldest son of Codrus, was the first. The office was limited to 10 years, 752 B.C., and was conferred on 9 persons for 1 year, 683 B.C.—In the eastern empire the title was given to certain high officers of the court.

Arco'le, Lombardy, where battles between the French under Bonaparte and the Austrians under field-marshal Alvinzi were fought 14-17 Nov 1796 The Austrians lost 18,000 men in killed, wounded, and prisoners, 4 flags, and 18 guns The French lost about 15,000, and became masters of Italy In one contest Bonaparte was rescued from imminent danger by his troops.

Ar'cot (East Indies) This city (founded 1716) was taken by col Clive, 31 Aug 1751, was retaken, 1758 but again surrendered to col Coote, 10 Feb 1760, besieged and taken by Hyder Ali, who defeated the British under col Baillie, 31 Oct 1780 Arcot has been subject to Great Britain since 1801 INDIA

Arctic expeditions. NORTHWEST PASSAGE and FRANKLIN'S EXPEDITION The German Arctic society applying to the German government, a committee of 13 professors was appointed, who reported that no more expeditions should be sent out, but stations established for scientific observations, 1876

Arctic Ocean. OCEAN

Arctu'rus (Gr Ἀρκτοῦρος = Bear-ward), a fixed star of the first magnitude in the constellation Bootes It is one of the brightest stars in the northern heavens According to Humboldt it has moved in latitude 5' in 752 years, and in 20 centuries has moved 2½ times the apparent diameter of the moon As this star stands in solitary grandeur in the sky, it is probably not the star mentioned in Job ix. 9, xxxviii 32 STARS, FIXED

Arden, Forest of Formerly a densely wooded tract in England lying between the Avon and the Severn river, and extending indefinitely northward, the scene of one of Shakespeare's loveliest dramas

> " *Oliver* Where will the old duke live?
> "*Charles* They say he is already in the forest of Arden, and a many merry men with him, and there they live like the old Robin Hood of England, they say many young gentlemen flock to him every day, and fleet the time carelessly as they did in the golden world " —"As You Like It," act i sc. i

Ardennes, an extensive hilly forest in the southeast corner of Belgium, also a frontier department of France bordering on Belgium near the field of Waterloo, the wood of Soignies being a remnant of this forest

> "And Ardennes waves above them her green leaves "
> —*Byron*, "Childe Harold's Pilgrimage "

Areiop'agus or **Areop'agus,** the supreme tribunal or council of elders in Athens, which sat upon the hill called Ἄρειος πάγος, the hill of Mars, from the legend that Mars was there tried for the murder of Halirrhotius, who had violated his daughter Alcippe This court was of immemorial antiquity, and preserved its dignity and influence, in spite of political changes, for many centuries Its powers were enlarged by Solon about 594 B C, and diminished by Pericles, 461 B.C Paul preached on Mars' hill 52 A D (Acts xvii)

areom'eter or **aræom'eter** (from Gr ἀραιός, thin), an instrument for measuring the density and specific gravity of fluids Baume described his areometer in 1768 Others have been made by Nicholson and Mohr

Arequi'pa, Peru, founded by Pizarro, 1539, was destroyed by an earthquake, 13 Aug 1868, surrendered to the Chilians, 25 Oct. 1883

Arethu'sa (Gr Ἀρέθουσα), a famous fountain in the island of Ortygia in Syracuse, fabled to have been an Arcadian nymph turned into a perennial spring by Artemis, to save her from the pursuit of the river-god Alpheus, and then to have flowed under the land and sea, and reappeared in Syracuse; hence Shelley's poem of Arethusa

Arezzo (*a-ret'zo*), near the ancient Arretium or Aretinum, an Etrurian city, which made peace with Rome for 30 years, 308 B C, was besieged by the Galli Senones about 283 B.C., who defeated the Roman army Metellus sent to its relief—a disgrace avenged signally by Dolabella Arezzo was an ancient bishopric, the cathedral founded in 1277. It is renowned as the birthplace of Mæcenas, Petrarch, Vasari, and other eminent men Michael Angelo was born in the vicinity.

Argenta'ria, now **Colmar,** Alsace, N E France, where the Roman emperor Gratian totally defeated the Alemanni and secured the peace of Gaul, May, 378

Argentine, or **La Plata, Confederation,** S America 14 provinces (Buenos Ayres, one) This country was discovered by the Spaniards in 1515, settled by them in 1553, and formed part of the viceroyalty of Peru till 1778 when it became that of Rio de la Plata It joined the insurrection in 1811, and became independent in 1816 It was at war with Brazil from 1826 to 1828 for the possession of Uruguay, which became independent as Montevideo, and at war with France 1838-40 Pop in 1869 1,877,490 BUENOS AYRES

Buenos Ayres seceded in 1853, reunited		1859
J Urquiza elected president, 20 Nov 1853, was succeeded by Dr S Derqui	8 Feb	1860
An insurrection in San Juan in Nov 1860, suppressed in Jan		1862
Gen Bartholomew Mitre, elected for 6 years, assumed the president's office	12 Oct	"
Lopez, president of Paraguay declared war against Mitre and invaded the Argentine territories, May Mitre declared war against Paraguay, 16 Apr, and made alliance with Brazil and Uruguay	4 May	1865
[See BUENOS AYRES for the disputes with that state, and BRAZIL for the war with PARAGUAY]		
Col Dominique F Sarmiento elected president for 6 years,	12 Oct.	1868
He suppresses the insurrection of Corrientes	Nov	"
Urquiza murdered	12 Apr	1870
Treaty with Brazil	Jan	1873
Defeat of Lopez Jourdan rebel, announced	Dec	"
Dr N Avellaneda inaugurated president for 6 years	12 Oct	1874
Insurrection of Mitre at Buenos Ayres, Sept-Nov, suppressed, he submits	2 Dec	"
National bank stops, suspension of specie payments by government	16 May,	1876
End of rebellion, capture of Jourdan, announced	12 Dec	"
Disputes with Buenos Ayres, settled	June-July,	1880
Gen Roca (opposed to supremacy of Buenos Ayres) nominated for president opposed by Dr Tejedor	June-July,	"
Gen Roca becomes president	Oct	"
Tranquillity restored, Buenos Ayres to be definitive capital of the republic	7 Dec	"
Political disturbances frequent, insurrections, etc		1880-90
Great financial disturbance		1890-92

Arginu'sæ, isles between Lesbos and Asia Minor, near these Conon and the Athenian fleet defeated the Spartan admiral Callicratidas, 406 B C

Ar'gonauts, in Greek legend, a band 50 in number including many famous heroes of legendary Greece, under Jason, sailed in the ship *Argo* from Iolcos in Thessaly, to Æa in Colchis, on the eastern shore of the Black Sea, to fetch the GOLDEN FLEECE, then in the possession of Æetes, king of Colchis, and guarded by a dragon in a grove sacred to Mars Only through the aid of Medea daughter of king Æetes, was the expedition successful "One of the most celebrated and widely diffused among the ancient tales of Greece Not only are we unable to assign the date or identify the crew or decipher the log-book of the *Argo*, but we have no means of settling even the preliminary question whether the voyage was actual or legendary from the beginning —*Grote*, "Hist of Greece," vol i p 237 The Argonauts and their voyage have been a theme for poets ancient and modern

> " I swear to Jove that only in my hand,
> The fleece shall be when I again take land
> To see my father's hall "
> —*Wm Morris*, "Jason "

Argos, the most ancient city of Greece, said to have been founded either by Inachus, 1856 B C., or his son Phoroneus, 1807, received its name from Argus, the fourth of the Inachidæ, 1711 B C But its history is wholly mythical until the 8th century B.C.

		B C
Pheidon's prosperous rule		770-730
Argives fine Sicyon and Ægina for helping Cleomenes of Sparta		514
Sparta becomes superior to Argos		495-490
Themistocles an exile at Argos		471
Argives destroy Mycenæ and regain superiority		468
Peloponnesian war—Argos, long neutral, joins Athens		420
Aristocratical party makes peace with Sparta, and overthrows democracy		417
A reaction—alliance with Athens resumed		395
War with Sparta, combat of 300 on each side		347
Pyrrhus of Epirus, besieging Argos, slain		272
Argos governed by tyrants supported by Macedon, freed, joins Achæan league		229
Subjugated by Romans		146
		A D
Argos taken from Venetians		1686
Taken by Turks 1716, who held it until		1826
United to GREECE under king Otho	25 Jan	1833

Arians, followers of Arius of Alexandria (d. 336), who preached that the Son of God was a secondary God created by the Father, who raised him above all men, but not equal with the Father. A violent controversy arose, which was taken up by Constantine, who presided at the first great œcumenical council of Nice, June to Aug. 325, and the Arians were condemned; but their doctrine long prevailed. It was favored by *Constantius II.* 341; *carried into Africa by* Vandals in the 5th century; into Asia by Goths. Servetus published his treatise against the Trinity, 1531, and was burned, 1553. Leggatt, an Arian, was burned at Smithfield in 1614. ATHANASIAN CREED, SOCINIANS, UNITARIANS.

Arica, Peru, destroyed by an earthquake, and inundated by waves of the sea, 13 Aug. 1868.

Aristotelian philosophy. PHILOSOPHY and LIBRARIES.

Aristotle, works of, etc.

Barthélemy St. Hilaire's complete translation of Aristotle, 35 vols., published early in.......... 1891

A papyrus containing the lost treatise of Aristotle on the "Constitution of Athens," discovered in Egypt and conveyed to the British museum, was published *by the trustees*, with a preface and notes by F. G. Kenyon, Jan.; and photographs of the MS. were published Mch 1891. The work was previously known only by extracts in ancient writers. The MS. was considered genuine by Barthélemy St. Hilaire..Mch. 1891

A family tomb, discovered at Eretria, in the island of Eubœa, by Dr. Charles Waldstein, early in 1891, was considered by *him to be probably that of Aristotle's family.*

arithmetic said to have been introduced from Egypt into Greece by Thales about 600 B.C. The Chinese used the abacus, or *swanpan*, at an early period. The ancient Hindus are said to have had a decimal system.

The oldest treatise upon arithmetic is by Euclid (7th, 8th, and 9th books of his "Elements") about..........B.C. 300

A.D.

The sexagesimal arithmetic of Ptolemy used.......... 130

Diophantus of Alexandria author of 13 books of arithmetical questions (6 are extant) about.......... 156

Notation by 9 digits and zero (Arabic figures) known in the 6th century in Hindostan; introduced thence into Arabia, about 900; into Spain, about 980; into France, by Gerbert, 991; into England, probably in the 14th century.

Maximus Planudes.......... 1350

Date in Caxton's "Mirrour of the World," Arabic characters, is, 1480

Arithmetic of decimals invented.......... 1482

John Sherwood's (bishop of Durham) "Ludus Arithmo-Machinæ," printed at Rome.......... "

Luca Paccioli's (Di Borgo) "Summa de Arithmetica" was one of the earliest works on arithmetic.......... 1494

First arithmetic printed in England ("De Arte Supputandi") by Tonstall, bishop of Durham.......... 1522

Robert Recorde's "Grounde of Artes" and "Whetstone of Witte" were arithmetical works of great value.......... 1558

Nicolò Tartaglia, Italian mathematician, died.......... 1559

Michael Stéfelius, "Arithmetica Integra," 1544, said to have been the inventor of the signs of + and −..........1486–1567

Peter Ramus, "Arithmetices Libri Duo, et Algebra Totidem" 1515–72

Theory of decimal fractions perfected by Napier in his "Rhabdologia".......... 1617

James Hodder's "Arithmetic," London.......... 1661

Cocker's "Arithmetic" appeared in.......... 1677

John Marsh, "Decimal Arithmetic Made Perfect".......... 1742

Nystrom's "Tonal System," with 16 as a basis, pub.......... 1862

Sawyer's "Automatic System," pub.......... 1878

arithmetic in the United States. One of the earliest American arithmetics was a work called "Arithmetic—Vulgar and Decimal," published at Boston, 1724; author unknown. Up *to the time of the revolution*, the English and foreign works mentioned above were in use in the colonies. Since 1800, arithmetics for school use have been very numerous. In 1846, at New Haven, Conn., James B. Thompson published his "Mental Arithmetic," which reached its 125th ed. in 1858. Other popular writers have been David Adams, Joseph Ray, Charles Davies, Pliny E. Chase, Benjamin Greenleaf, Dana P. Colburn, Horatio Robinson. The principal works published in the U. S. from 1780 to 1800 are as follows:

School-master's Assistant; Thomas Dilworth, London, 1781, and Hartford, Conn. (23d ed.).......... 1786

New and Complete System of Arithmetic, Nicholas Pike, Newburyport, 1788; Worcester.......... 1797

Treatise on Arithmetic in Theory and Practice, John Gough, Boston.......... 1789

Preceptor's Assistant or Student's Guide, John Vinall, Boston, 1792

The Federal Arithmetician, Thomas Sarjeant, Philadelphia..... 1793

Introduction to Arithmetic, Erastus Root, Norwich, Conn..... 1795

The American Accountant, William Milns, New York.......... 1797

The American Tutor's Assistant, *John Todd and others*, Philadelphia, Pa. (3d ed.).......... "

The American Arithmetic, David Cook, New Haven, Conn..... 1800

The School-master's Assistant, Nathan Daboll, New London, Conn.......... "

[Used almost universally in the U. S. until 1840.]

Arizona, a territory of the United States between 31° and 37° *n. lat.*, and between 109° and 114° 40′ w. lon. Utah and Nevada lie on the north, on the east is New Mexico, Mexico on the south, California and Nevada on the west. It contains about 113,916 sq. miles. It has 11 counties—Apache, Cochiso, Coconimo, Gila, Graham, Maricopa, Mohave, Pima, Pinal, Yavapai, and Yuma. Pop. 1880, 40,440; 1890, 59,620; 1900, 122,931. Capital, Phœnix.

First explorations made by Vasquez Coronado sent from Mexico by viceroy Mendozo.......... 1540

Spaniards again enter and establish a military post where Tucson now stands.......... 1580

Jesuit missionaries on Santa Cruz river, about.......... 1600

Spaniards from Mexico form settlements from Tucson to the Mexican line, and partly occupy the country for nearly 150 years. They are finally driven out by the Indians before 1821

First hunters and trappers from the U. S. probably visited Arizona in.......... 1824

All Arizona north of the river Gila is included in cession by Mexico to U. S. by treaty of Guadalupe Hidalgo.......2 Feb. 1848

First American settlers were persons on their way to California, who stopped on the Gila to engage in stock-raising.......... 1849

GADSDEN PURCHASE brought to the U. S. all of Arizona south of the Gila..........30 Dec. 1853

Act *of Congress organizing the territory*..........24 Feb. 1863

Gov. John N. Goodwin, in camp at Navajo springs, formally organizes the territorial government and fixes its temporary seat near fort Whipple..........29 Dec. "

First territorial legislature adopts a mining law and the so-called Howell code of general laws; sits....26 Sept.–10 Nov. 1864

Tucson made the capital by a majority of 1 vote.......... 1867

Arizona a military district by order of gen. Halleck......Oct. "

Act to establish public schools in the territory and a board of education and levying a tax of 10 cts. on each $100.......... 1868

Maj. J. W. Powell, for the Smithsonian Institution, with a party of 10, in 4 boats, descends the canyon of the Colorado from Green river to rio Virgin..........May–Aug. 1869

Arizona and southern California made a military department, headquarters at fort Whipple.......... "

40 citizens and 100 Pápagos from Tucson and vicinity massacre 85 Indian prisoners of war (77 of them women and children) at camp Grant, and capture 30, who are sold to the Pápagos as slaves. (108 persons were *afterwards tried for murder* and acquitted.)..........Apr. 1871

"Arizona Diamond Swindle." Excitement over supposed diamond fields in Arizona; the San Francisco and New York Mining and Commercial Co., with a capital of $10,000,000, formed; Clarence King, U. S. geologist, finds the field "salted" with rough diamonds from Africa, Brazil, etc.......... 1872

A long war waged by gen. Crook with hostile Apaches in Arizona ends by surrender of the Tontos, Hualapais, and Yavapais in 1873, and other bands in.......... 1874

Mormon colonists from Utah settle in Apache co..........Mch. 1876

Prescott chosen as permanent capital.......... 1877

New public-school law enacted.......... 1883

Raid of Loco's band of Chiricahua Indians in the valley of the Gila begins..........19 Apr. "

Acts to establish an insane asylum at Phœnix, a normal school at Tempe, and the university of Arizona at Tucson, Jan.–Mch. 1885

Act providing that no polygamist or bigamist shall vote or hold office..........Jan.–Mch "

Congress appropriates $2000 to repair the ruin of Casa Grande, near Florence, Pinal co., reserving from settlement the entire site of the ancient city..........2d Mch. 1889

State capital removed from Prescott to Phœnix........4 Feb. 1890

40 lives lost by broken mining-dam on the Hassayampa river, 23 Feb. "

Yuma *nearly destroyed by flood*..........27 Feb. 1891

Friday after 1 Feb. each year made a legal holiday as Labor day..........19 Jan.–19 Mch. "

11 bills submitted to gov. Zulick for approval, 22 Mch. 1889; as 60 consecutive days had passed since the organization of the legislature, he left them unsigned, assuming that the session had expired by limitation. The territorial supreme court declared the session legal for 60 days of actual legislative work, and the bills became laws without the governor's approval. "

Discovery of a lake forming in Salton Sink from the overflow of the Colorado river..........29 June "

Constitutional convention meets at Phœnix, 7 Sept., and adopts a complete constitution..........2 Oct. "

Ex-gov. A. P. K. Safford dies at Tarpon springs, Fla...16 Dec. "

Land reclaimed by irrigation, 348,000 acres up to.......... 1892

[Capable of being reclaimed under the present water development, 1,730,000 acres. Supposed amount that can be reclaimed with the water available in the territory, 24,000,000 acres.]

GOVERNORS OF THE TERRITORY.

R. C. McCormick	1867–69	Frederick Tuttle	1882–85
A. P. K. Safford	1870–77	C. Meyer Zulick	1885–89
John P. Hoyt	1878	Lewis Wolfley	1889–91
John C. Fremont	1879–82	Nathan O. Murphy	1892–96

Ark. God commanded Noah to preach repentance and to build an ark; see Gen. vi., vii. After the deluge the ark rested (2348 B.C.) "upon the mountains of ARARAT," Gen. viii. 4. Some assert Apamea, in Phrygia, 300 miles west of Ararat, to be the spot; and medals have been struck there with a chest on the waters, and the letters NOE, and 2 doves. The Ark of the Covenant, made by Moses to contain the 2 tables of the law, 1491 B.C. (Exod. xxv.), was placed in Solomon's temple, 1004 B.C. (1 Kings viii.).

Arkan'sas (formerly Arkansaw'), a southwestern state between 33° and 36° 30′ n. lat., and 89° 40′ and 94° 42′ w. lon. from Greenwich. The state of Missouri bounds it on the north, and the Mississippi river and the southeast corner of Missouri on the east, Louisiana on the south, and the Indian territory mostly on the west. It contains 75 counties; area, 53,045 sq miles. Pop. 1890, 1,128,179; 1900, 1,211,564. Capital, Little Rock.

This state probably visited by De Soto.............. 1541
La Salle passes down the Mississippi to its mouth.............. 1682
Louis XV. of France grants to John Law, originator of the "Mississippi scheme," a tract of land on the Arkansas river (Law however neglects it). (LAW'S BUBBLE)................ 1720
Transfer by France to Spain of Louisiana includes the present state of Arkansas..................................3 Nov 1762
First settlement at Arkansas Post.................................. 1785
Spain cedes Louisiana to France by treaty of Ildefonso........ 1800
Province of Louisiana ceded by France to the U. S., who pay $11,250,000 and assume the "French spoliation claims"... 1803
Missouri territory established, including Arkansas and all north of the state of Louisiana and west of the Mississippi......... 1812
Arkansas territory, including all north of the state of Louisiana, and south of 36° 30′, and west from the Mississippi river to the 100° meridian, formed..............................2 Mch. 1819
Arkansas Gazette, first newspaper in the territory, published at Little Rock, Wm. E. Woodruff, editor..................20 Nov. "
Western boundary fixed, reducing its area to the present limits of the state... 1828
Admitted into the Union, the 25th state. Pop. 52,240..15 June, 1836
U. S. arsenal at Little Rock seized by the state authorities, 8 Feb. 1861
Arkansas convention met..........................about 1 Mch. "
Was visited by William S. Oldham of the confederate congress and a commissioner from Jefferson Davis; but voted against secession (vote 39 to 35)..................................16 Mch. "
Arsenals seized at Napoleon and fort Smith ....23-24 Apr. "
Act of secession adopted by the legislature—yeas, 69; nay, 1, 6 May, "

[The negative vote was cast by Dr. Isaac Murphy, afterwards (1864–1868) governor.]

Battle of Pea Ridge between union and confederate forces. 6–7 Mch. 1862

[Union gen. Samuel R. Curtis had about 10,250 men. The Confederates under gens. Earl Van Dorn, Sterling Price, and Ben. McCulloch, numbering 14,000, were forced to retire with severe loss; gen. McCulloch was killed. Pea Ridge is in the northwestern corner of the state, in Benton county.]

Union troops under gen. Washburne occupy Helena...11 July, "
Battle of Prairie Grove. U. S. gens. Francis J. Herron and James G. Blunt; confederate gen. Thomas C. Hindman. Confederates retire during the night with a loss of 1317. Federal loss, 1148...................................7 Dec. "
Arkansas Post captured with 5000 men by the U. S. forces under McClernand, Sherman, and admiral Porter..........11 Jan. 1863
Confederate gens. T. H. Holmes and Sterling Price with about 8000 men attempt to retake Helena. Gen. B. M. Prentiss with about 4000 men repulses them with heavy loss..4 July, 1863
Union forces occupy Little Rock.......................10 Sept. "
Union state convention assembles to form a new constitution, 8 Jan. 1864
Dr. Isaac Murphy provisional governor; inaugurated...22 Jan. "
Constitution ratified by vote of the people..............14 Mch. "

[The legislature under this constitution is not recognized by congress.]

Arkansas and Mississippi formed into the 4th military district under gen. Edward O. C. Ord.................................. 1867
New constitution reported.......................................4 Feb. 1868
" " adopted and ratified.................13 Mch. "
State readmitted to the Union over Johnson's veto...22 June, "
Military commander gen. A. C. Gillem turns over the state to the civil authorities...................................22 June, "
Gen. Thomas C. Hindman assassinated at Helena by one of his former soldiers.. "
Powell Clayton elected governor.. "
Gov. Clayton places 10 counties under martial law......9 Nov. "
Elisha Baxter nominated for governor by the Rep. party, and Joseph Brooks by the Liberal Rep. party...................... 1872
Disturbance occasioned by frauds charged against both parties in the election continues throughout.........................1873–74
Convention called to revise the constitution meets....14 July, 1874

[The fifth convened in the state, the other years being 1836, 1861, 1864, 1868.]

New constitution ratified by a majority of 53,860.......13 Oct. "
" " proclaimed...............................30 Oct. "

[Governor's term reduced from 4 to 2 years. Office of lieut.-gov. abolished, president of the senate substituted.]

Election frauds and outrages occur.................................. 1888
C. R. Breckenridge, Dem., and John M. Clayton, Rep., vigorously contest the 2d congressional district.......................... "
John M. Clayton assassinated at Plummersville..........29 Jan. 1889

[He claimed to have been elected, and was collecting evidence to contest the election at this time.]

State treasurer Woodruff short in his accounts about $138,800, 13 Jan. 1891

[1st trial, Oct. 1891, of ex state treasurer Wm. E. Woodruff, jury disagree; 2d trial, Apr. 1892, verdict, not guilty, released.]

Legislature passes Australian ballot law........................ "
U. S. senate confirms the president's appointment of congressman C. R. Breckonridge to be minister to Russia....20 July, 1894

TERRITORIAL GOVERNORS OF ARKANSAS.

Names.	Term of office.	Remarks.
James Miller...........	1819 to 1825	
George Izard...........	1825 " 1829	
John Pope..............	1829 " 1835	
William S. Fulton......	1835 " 1836	

STATE GOVERNORS OF ARKANSAS.

Names.	Term of office.	Remarks.
James S. Conway........	1836 to 1840	
Archibald Yell.........	1840 " 1844	
Samuel Adams...........	1844 " 1844	Acting.
Thomas S. Drew.........	1844 " 1848	
John S. Roane..........	1848 " 1852	
Elias N. Conway........	[illegible] " 1860	
Henry M. Rector........	1860 " 1862	
Harris Flanagin........	1862 " 1864	
Isaac Murphy...........	1864 " 1868	
Powell Clayton.........	1868 " 1871	Elected to the U. S. Senate.
Orzo H. Hadley.........	1871 " 1872	Acting.
Elisha Baxter..........	1872 " 1874	
Augustus H. Garland....	1874 " 1876	Elected U. S. Senator.
Wm. R. Miller..........	1877 " 1881	
Thos. J. Churchill.....	1881 " 1883	
Jas. H. Berry..........	1883 " 1885	
Simon P. Hughes........	1885 " 1889	
James P. Eagle.........	1889 " 1893	
Wm. M. Fishback........	1893 " 1895	
James P. Clarke........	1895 " 1897	

UNITED STATES SENATORS FROM THE STATE OF ARKANSAS.

Names.	No. of Congress.	Date.	Remarks.
William S. Fulton..........	24th to 28th	1836 to 1844	Seated 5 Dec. 1836. Died 15 Aug. 1844.
Ambrose H. Sevier..........	24th " 30th	1836 " 1848	Resigned 15 Mch. 1848.
Chester Ashley.............	28th " 30th	1844 " 1848	Elected in place of Fulton. Died 29 Apr. 1848.
Solon Borland..............	30th " 33d	1848 " 1853	Elected in place of Sevier.
Wm. K. Sebastian...........	30th " 36th	1848 " 1861	Appointed in place of Ashley. Seated 31 May, 1848.
Robert W. Johnson..........	33d " 36th	1853 " 1861	Elected in place of Borland.
		37th, 38th, and 39th Congress vacant.	
Alexander McDonald.........	40th to 42d	1868 to 1871	Seated 23 June, 1868.
Benj. F. Rice..............	40th " 43d	1868 " 1873	" 24 " "
Powell Clayton.............	42d " 45th	1871 " 1877	
Stephen W. Dorsey..........	44th " 46th	1873 " 1879	
Augustus H. Garland........	45th " 49th	1877 " 1885	Resigned. Appointed attorney-gen. of U. S.
James D. Walker............	46th " 49th	1879 " 1885	
James K. Jones.............	49th " ——	1885 " ——	Term expires 1897.
James H. Berry.............	49th " ——	1885 " ——	Elected in place of Garland. Term expires 1901.

Arkan'sas, a powerful iron-clad ram, built by the confederates for the protection of Vicksburg at their navy-yard on the Yazoo river several miles above its mouth. The *Arkansas* was a formidable vessel with flat top, from which rose a single smoke-stack, and heavily armored sides set at an angle of 45°. She left the navy-yard on the morning of 15 July, 1862, in pursuit of the federal gunboat *Tyler* and steam-ram *Queen of the West*, which had been sent up the Yazoo to watch proceedings, and retreated under fire from the bow guns of the *Arkansas*, which was vigorously returned from the stern guns of the *Tyler* and *Queen of the West.* The rest of the federal fleet was lying at anchor above the mouth of the Yazoo, fires banked and no steam on The booming of cannon was the first intimation they had of the approaching ram, and, taken by surprise, they could do nothing but open fire upon the *Arkansas*, which successfully withstood the terrible broadsides from the federal fleet, and, steaming past them, took up her position under the bluffs of Vicksburg where she was perfectly sheltered by the batteries Two unsuccessful attempts were made to destroy the *Arkansas*, one by bombardment the evening of 15 July, and one by use of rams 22 July She was finally destroyed while disabled, 6 Aug 1862, in the Mississippi above Baton Rouge An incendiary shell, the invention of com Porter, entering the indentation made previously by a solid shot fired from the *Essex*, set fire to the condensed cotton packing and wood-work, and, fire reaching the magazine, the *Arkansas* blew up with a terrific explosion BATON ROUGE, VICKSBURG

Arkansas Post. ARKANSAS, 1785 1863

Arkansas river. MISSISSIPPI RIVER

Ark'low, a maritime town and parish in county Wicklow, Ireland, famous as the site of the "Wicklow Gold Mines," opened in 1796, and soon abandoned, which long afforded a theme for burlesque and jest Four miles southwest of the town is the Croghan-Kinshela, a mountain rising 2064 ft above the sea level, in and about which 11 different metals have been found, including gold, which was discovered in one of the mountain streams in 1775 The discovery was kept secret for 20 years, but in 1796 became public, and thousands hurried to the spot, and in a few weeks had secured $50,000 worth of the precious metal The government then took possession of the mines and began operations, but the works were destroyed in the insurrection of 1798 Mining was afterwards resumed, the products failing to cover expenses, however, after renewed search and critical investigation in 1801, the mines were finally abandoned A battle between the Irish rebels and English under gen Needham, in which the former were defeated, was fought here 10 June, 1798

Ark of the Covenant, described in Exodus, chapter xxv, was the only piece of furniture in the inner or "most holy" apartment of the ancient Jewish tabernacle It was a chest of shittim wood, 2½ cubits in length and 1½ cubits in breadth and height, covered with gold within and without. The lid, of solid gold, was called the "mercy seat," and was overshadowed by 2 cherubim of gold facing the centre The ark at one time contained, besides the 2 tables of stone containing the ten commandments, a pot of manna, and Aaron's rod that budded The Ark of the Covenant was the appointed symbol to the Israelites of the presence of God and of his covenant with his chosen people It was carried through the wilderness during the 40 years' wanderings by Levites, supported on 2 poles of shittim wood, plated with gold, which were passed through 2 rings of gold on each side of the body of the ark. It was placed in Solomon's temple about 1004 B.C., and was probably destroyed during the siege of Jerusalem by Nebuchadnezzar and the burning of the temple, 587 B.C

Arl'berg, a branch of the Rhaetian Alps in the Tyrol and Vorarlberg, between the sources of the Lech and Ill rivers Before the completion of the tunnel from Langen to St Anton, in 1884, traffic between Venice, Trieste, and Switzerland was mainly by the road across this mountain-chain, made by emperor Joseph II. in 1786, and greatly improved since 1835 TUNNELS

Arles (*arl*, Lat *Arelatum*, from the Celtic *Ar-lait*, near the waters), S France (said to have been founded 2000 B.C), a powerful Roman city, made capital of Provence by Boson in 879 A.D, and of the kingdom of Arles or Transjurane Burgundy by Rodolph II in 933 He was succeeded by Conrad I 937, and by Rodolph III 993, who at his death, 1032, transmitted his kingdom to the emperor Conrad II After various changes, it was annexed to France in 1486 Many councils (314-1275) were held at Arles, the most celebrated in 314, when British bishops were present.

Arma'da, the Invincible, collected and equipped by Philip II, king of Spain, for the subjugation of England. The following particulars are taken from Morant's account (accompanying Pine's engravings of the tapestries formerly in the House of Lords), printed 1739 Described in Kingsley's "Westward Ho!" and Froude's "History of England"

It consisted of 132 ships (besides caravels), 3165 cannon, 8766 sailors 2088 galley slaves 21 855 soldiers 1355 volunteers (noblemen, gentlemen and their attendants) and 150 monks, with Martin Alarco vicar of the Inquisition—commanded by the duke of Medina Sidonia		1587
English fleet under lord Charles Howard, sir Francis Drake and sir John Hawkins, ready for sea, and three armies on land,	Dec	"
Armada sailed from Lisbon, soon dispersed by a storm,	19 May,	1588
Re collected entered the Channel off Cornwall	19 July,	"
Suffered in engagements (sharpest on 25 July)	21-27 July,	"
Dispersed by fire ships sent into their midst	28 July,	"
Many vessels sunk or taken by the English	29 July,	"
The remainder retreat under adverse winds, around Scotland and Ireland, to Spain, suffering from severe storms.	Aug and Sept	"
[Computed Spanish loss 35 ships 13,000 men]		
Queen attended a thanksgiving at St Paul's, and a medal was struck inscribed "*Deus flavit et dissipati sunt*"	24 Nov	"
Annual thanksgiving sermon endowed by Mr Chapman, who died		1616
National memorial founded	19 July,	1888
"Spanish Story of the Armada," by Froude, pub		1892

Armagh (*ar ma'*), metropolis of N Ireland from the 5th to the 9th century, seat of the first ecclesiastical dignity in Ireland, founded by St Patrick, first bishop, about 444, said to have built the first cathedral, 450 6 saints of the Roman calendar have been bishops of this see The see was reconstituted (PALLIUM) in 1151 —*Beatson* Armagh was ravaged by the Danes on Easter day, 852, and by O'Neil in 1564 ARCHBISHOP

Armagnacs (*ar-man'yac*) a faction in France, followers of the duke of Orleans, murdered by the Burgundians, 23 Nov 1407, derived their name from his father in law, the count of Armagnac About 3500 of them were massacred at Paris in June, 1418, by their opponents, followers of the duke of Burgundy The quarrel divided France from 1390 until the treaty of Arras was made, 1435, between the duke of Burgundy and Charles VII During this period Henry V of England entered France, assisted largely by the Burgundian faction

armed neutrality, the confederacy against England, formed by Russia, Sweden, and Denmark, 1780, ended, 1781, renewed, and a treaty ratified to cause their flags to be respected by the belligerent powers, 16 Dec. 1800 Great Britain rejecting principle that neutral flags protect neutral bottoms, war ensued, and Nelson and Parker destroyed the fleet of Denmark before Copenhagen, 2 Apr 1801 This event and the murder of the emperor Paul of Russia, led to the dissolution of the armed neutrality

Arme'nia, formerly a vast country in Asia extending from the Caspian sea to Asia Minor and northward to the Caucassus, now shared by Russia, Persia, and Turkey Here Noah is said to have resided when he left the ark, 2348 B.C. Armenia belonged successively to the Assyrian, Median, and Persian empires, and after the defeat of Antiochus the Great, 190 B.C, to the Greek kings of Syria. The Romans formed kingdoms of Armenia Major and Minor, disturbed by frequent aggressions of Parthians In all political troubles the Armenians have maintained Christianity and a church governed by patriarchs not subject to Rome All Christendom has been agitated by the oppression and cruelty of the Turks towards Armenian Christians, 1894 and 1895 Since 1715 an Armenian convent has existed at Venice, where books are printed in the Armenian language

	B.C.
City of Artaxarta built	186
Antiochus Epiphanes invades Armenia	165
Tigranes the Great reigns in Armenia Major	95
Becomes king of Syria, and assumes the title of "king of kings"	83
Defeated by Lucullus, 69, he yields his crown to Pompey	66
His son, Artavasdes, reigns, 54, assists Pompey against Julius Cæsar, 48, and the Parthians against Mark Antony	36
Antony subdues and sends him in silver chains to Egypt	34
Artaxias, his son made king by the Parthians	33
Deposed by the Romans, who enthrone Tigranes II	20
	A.D
Armenia subjected to Parthia	15
Reconquered by Germanicus, grandson of Augustus	18
Tiridates made king by the Romans	58
Parthian conquerors of Armenia are expelled by Trajan	115
Severus makes Volagarses king of part of Armenia	199
Christianity introduced	between 100-300
Armenia added to the Persian empire	232
Tiridates obtains the throne through Diocletian, 286, is expelled by Narses, 294, restored by Galerius	298

On his death, Armenia becomes subject to Persia, 342; is made neutral by Rome and Persia........ 384
Rome and Persia divide Armenia by treaty........ 443
Armenian version of the Bible begun by Miesrob........ 410
Armenia conquered and reconquered by Greek and Persian sovereigns........ 577–687
And by the Greek emperors and Mahometans........ 693–1065
Armenian church reconciled to Rome........ about 1330
Leon VI., last king of Armenia, taken prisoner by the Saracens, 1375; released, he dies at Paris........ 1393
Overrun by the Mongols, 1235; by Timour, 1383; by the Turks, 1516; by the Persians, 1534; by the Turks........ 1583
Shah Abbas of Persia yielding Armenia to the Turks, transports 22,000 Armenian families to Persia........ 1604
Armenia overrun by the Russians........ 1828
Surrender of Erzeroum........ 9 July, 1829
By the Berlin treaty, Kars, Ardahan, and Batoum were ceded to Russia, with other changes........ July, 1878
SYRIA and RUSSO-TURKISH WARS, I. and II.

ar'millary sphere, an astronomical instrument fitted with brass circles to show the greater and lesser circles of the sphere in their natural position and motion. It is said to have been invented by Eratosthenes about 255 B.C., and was employed by Tycho Brahe and others.

Arminians or **Remonstrants,** from James Arminius (or Harmensen), a Protestant divine of Leyden, Holland (b. 1560; d. 19 Oct. 1609), whose followers presented a Remonstrance to the states-general in 1610. They separated from the Calvinists, rejecting predestination, etc. Their doctrines were condemned in 1619 at the synod of Dort; they were exiled till 1625. The Calvinists were sometimes styled Gomarists, from Gomar, opponent of Arminius. James I. and Charles I. favored Arminian doctrine.

armor. That of Goliath is described (about 1063 B.C.), 1 Sam. xvii. 5. Skins and padded hides were early used, and brass and iron armor, in plates or scales, followed. The body armor of the Britons was skins of wild beasts, exchanged, after the Roman conquest, for the well-tanned leathern cuirass.—*Tacitus.* Hengist is said to have had scale armor, 449 A.D. The earliest historical collections of arms and armor date back no further than 1500 A.D. The oldest is that of Louis XII. at Amboise in 1520. That at Dresden was begun about 1553, and the Ambras collection at Vienna in 1570. Other collections are scattered throughout Europe. Among the principal are those at St. Petersburg and at Madrid. The collection at the Tower of London contains about 6000 examples from the early middle ages downwards.

Norman armor formed breeches and jacket........ 1066
The hauberk had its hood of the same piece........ 1100
John wore a surtout over a hauberk of rings set edgeways........ 1199
Heavy cavalry covered with a coat of mail. Some horsemen had vizors and skull-caps........ about 1216
Armor exceedingly splendid........ about 1350
Black armor, used not only for battle, but for mourning, Henry V........ 1413
Armor of Henry VII. consisted of a cuirass of steel, in the form of a pair of stays........ about 1500
Armor ceased to reach below the knees, Charles I........ 1625

[In the reign of Charles II. officers wore no other armor than a large gorget, which is commemorated in the diminutive ornament known at the present day.—*Meyrick.*]

armorial bearings became hereditary at the close of the 12th century. They were employed by the crusaders, 1100. The lines to denote colors in arms, by their direction or intersection, were invented by Columbière in 1639. The armorial bearings of the English sovereigns are given under ENGLAND. Armorial bearings were taxed in 1798, and again in 1808. The tax produced 64,515*l.* in the year ending 31 March, 1868; 1878, 83,104*l.*; 1884, 78,766*l.* The tax is now 2*l.* 2*s.*; if not on carriages, it is 1*l.* 1*s.* annually (1889). Sir Bernard Burke's "General Armory," 1883, contains the arms of above 60,000 British families.

Armorica, now **Brittany,** N. France, was conquered by Julius Cæsar, 56 B.C. Many Gauls are said to have retired thither and preserved the Celtic tongue, 584 A.D. BRITTANY.

arms. The club was the first offensive weapon; then followed the mace, battle-axe, pike, spear, javelin, sword and dagger, bows and arrows. Pliny ascribes the invention of the sling to the Phœnicians. See article on each weapon.

army. Egypt was the first country to have a military organization. Trained by his father, Sesostris or Rameses III. seems to have been the first military organizer of Egypt, about 1620 B.C. The first guards and regular troops of a standing army were formed by Saul, 1093.—*Eusebius.* Cyrus, founder of the Persian empire, devised the military organization which established his power, 557 B.C. Xerxes was three years preparing to invade Greece, and his army is represented to have numbered 1,700,000 foot and 80,000 horse. The Greeks originated the "phalanx," which became the basis of all their tactics, and was perfected in the Macedonian phalanx by Philip of Macedon, about 360 B.C. This phalanx, as finally formed by Alexander, numbered 16,384 heavy-armed infantry. It was formed 16 deep. The principal weapon was the pike, 24 ft. long. The nucleus of the Roman army was the legion, ascribed to Romulus, but reorganized by Servius Tullius and lasting until the disruption of the Roman Empire. It consisted of 10 cohorts, each of 6 centuries. At first the legion contained 3000 infantry and 300 cavalry, but it was gradually increased to 4500 and finally to 6000. The number of the legions varied. Under Augustus there were 45. They were usually designated by numerals in the order in which they were levied.—The history of armies (European) since the overthrow of the Roman empire may be divided into four periods: (1) The barbarous stage, when the armies were national and denominated hordes, being without tactics or organization; (2) the feudal period, when the army was made up of well-equipped knights and men-at-arms, followed by peasants or slaves; (3) the standing-army period, the army forming a distinct class, tactics and organization becoming a science (1400 to 1800); (4) armies once more national under conscription embracing the whole male population between certain ages, trained and organized with science and skill. (See Table.) The first modern standing army was maintained by Charles VII. of France, 1445. The British army mainly arose in the reign of Charles II. in 1661, in consequence of the extinction of feudal tenures. The first five regiments of British infantry were established between 1633 and 1680. James II. established several regiments of dragoon guards (1685–88). In 1685 the army consisted of 7000 foot and 1700 horse. Standing armies were introduced by Charles I. in 1638; were declared illegal in England, 31 Car. II. 1679; but one was then gradually forming, which was maintained by William III., 1689, when the mutiny act was passed. Grose's "History of the British Army" was published in 1801.

ESTIMATED NUMBER OF SOLDIERS IN THE CHIEF EUROPEAN ARMIES, 1892.

Nation.	Peace-footing. All branches.	Active Army and Field Reserve.	Possible War-footing. All branches.	Remarks.
Austria.....	309,187	1,554,479	4,000,000	Military service is obligatory on all men who have completed their 20th year. Only certain family conditions and physical and mental incapacity cause exemption. No substitutes are allowed.
Gt. Britain..	140,968	204,626	1,179,626	The distinction between the British army and that of almost every other state of Europe is that the service is *voluntary.* Enlistments are by free choice for a definite term.
British Col..	....	225,000		
France......	570,000	2,376,588	3,240,000	The active army is composed of all the young men not exempt who have reached the age of 20, and the reserve of those who have passed through the active army. In 1887 all exemptions were abolished.
Germany....	513,983	2,471,925	2,977,629	No substitution is allowed. Every German capable of bearing arms must serve in the standing army for 7 years from the 20th of his age, 3 in active service and 4 in the reserve.
Italy........	241,722	1,053,934	2,586,437	Universal liability to arms forms the basis of the military organization. The time of service in the standing army for the first category of recruits is 5 years in infantry, 4 in cavalry, and 3 in other arms. Period of service in standing army and reserve 19 years.

ESTIMATED NUMBER OF SOLDIERS IN THE CHIEF EUROPEAN ARMIES, 1892.—(*Continued.*)

Nation.	Peace-footing. All branches.	Active Army and Field Reserve.	Possible War-footing. All branches.	Remarks.
Spain.......	89,908	154,388	1,135,196	All Spaniards past 20 are liable to be drawn for the permanent army, in which they serve 3 years; they then serve 3 years in the first or active reserve, and 6 years in the second reserve. By a payment of 1500 pesetas any one can purchase exemption.
Turkey.....	185,000	479,864	960,464	By a law of 1869 the military service is compulsory for all Turks, and is carried out either by recruiting or by ballot. The length of service is 20 years, 4 in the active army, 2 in the first reserve, 6 in the second reserve, and 8 in the Landsturm.
Russia......	840,500	2,606,592	7,812,792	All men must serve from the 21st year, 4 years in the active army, 13 years in the reserve, and 5 years in the Zapas or second reserve. In the European armies the troops are divided into field, fortress, local, reserve, second reserve, and auxiliary.

army, United States, the Continental, or army of the revolution, was organized by the continental congress, 15 June, 1775. George Washington commander-in-chief with the rank of maj.-gen.

This congress at the same time chose 4 maj-gens. and 8 brig.-gens., and appointed 1 adj.-gen., 1 quartermaster-gen., 1 commissary-gen., 1 paymaster-gen., and 1 chief-engineer.

Congress established a board of war and ordnance consisting of 5 members, 12 June, 1776. UNITED STATES.

During the continuation of this board from 1776 to 1781 there were 6 secretaries. In Feb. 1781, congress created the office of sec. of war, with gen. Benjamin Lincoln as secretary, from 30 Oct. 1781.

Continental army was disbanded, 5 Nov. 1783.

1000 men were however retained until the peace establishment could be organized. UNITED STATES, 1775–89.

TROOPS (CONTINENTAL AND MILITIA) FURNISHED BY THE THIRTEEN STATES DURING THE REVOLUTION, 1775 TO 1783 INCLUSIVE.

State.	1775	1776		1777		1778		1779		1780		1781		1782	1783	Total.	Total.
	Cont'ls.	Cont'ls.	Militia.	Cont'ls.	Militia.	Cont'ls.	Militia.	Cont'ls.	Militia.	Cont'ls.	Militia.	Cont'ls.	Militia.	Cont'ls.	Cont'ls.	Cont'ls.	Militia.
N. H....	2,824	3,019	....	1,172	1,111	1,283	....	1,004	222	1,017	760	700	....	744	733	12,496	2,093
Mass....	16,444	13,372	4,000	7,816	2,775	7,010	1,927	6,287	1,451	4,553	3,436	3,732	1,566	4,423	4,370	68,007	15,155
R. I.....	1,193	798	1,102	548	....	630	2,426	507	756	915	....	464	....	481	372	5,908	4,284
Conn....	4,507	6,390	5,737	4,563	....	4,010	....	3,544	....	3,133	554	2,420	1,501	1,732	1,740	32,039	7,792
N. Y....	2,075	3,629	1,715	1,903	921	2,194	....	2,256	....	2,179	668	1,728	....	1,198	1,169	18,331	3,304
N. J.....	....	3,193	5,893	1,408	....	1,586	....	1,276	....	1,105	162	823	....	660	675	10,726	6,055
Penn....	400	5,519	4,876	4,983	2,481	3,684	....	3,476	....	3,337	....	1,346	....	1,265	1,598	25,608	7,357
Del......	....	609	145	229	....	349	....	317	....	325	231	89	....	162	235	2,317	376
Md.....	....	637	2,592	2,030	1,535	3,307	....	2,849	....	2,065	....	770	....	1,280	974	13,912	4,127
Va......	....	6,181	....	5,744	1,289	5,236	....	3,973	....	2,486	....	1,215	4,331	1,204	629	26,668	5,620
N. C.....	....	1,134	....	1,281	....	1,287	....	1,214	2,706	....	....	545	....	1,105	697	7,263	2,706
S. C.....	....	2,069	....	1,650	....	1,650	....	....	....	....	....	....	....	....	139	5,508	....
Ga......	....	351	....	1,423	....	673	....	87	....	....	....	....	....	....	145	2,079	....
Total...	27,443	46,901	26,060	34,750	10,112	32,899	4,353	26,790	5,135	21,115	5,811	13,832	7,398	14,256	13,476	231,462	58,869

Conjectural estimate of militia employed from the different states in addition to the above.

1775....from 3 to 9 months......	10,180
1776.... " 4 " 8 "	16,700
1777.... " 2 " 8 "	23,800
1778.... " 2 " 6 "	13,800
1779.... " 2 " 9 "	12,350
1780.... " 2 " 12 "	16,000
1781......	8,750
1782......	3,750
Additional militia....	105,330
Militia proper....	58,869
Continentals....	231,462
Total....	395,661

Army under the Constitution. The constitution of the United States, art. 1, sec. 2, empowers congress "to raise and support armies," and art. 2, sec. 2, designates the president as commander-in-chief of the army and navy, and of the militia when called into the service of the United States.

The War dept. was established by act of..............7 Aug. 1789

The standing army was first organized under the code of the continental congress of 1776, the basis of the present articles of war, though greatly modified in 1806. Congress fixes the rank and file at 1216, comprising 1 regiment of infantry (12 companies) and 1 regiment of artillery (4 companies)..3 Sept. 1790

An *additional* regiment of 900 men was authorized 1791

The army consisted of 4 regiments of infantry, of 8 companies each, 2 companies of light dragoons, and a corps of artillerists and engineers, with 1 maj.-gen. and 1 brig.-gen. 1796

The maj.-gen. was discharged as unnecessary............... 1797

A provisional force of 10,000 men raised owing to the threatening attitude of France.................................. 1798

[Washington made commander-in-chief, with rank of lieut.-gen. As the danger passed, the army was reduced to its former size.]

Office and title of lieut.-gen. abolished by congress.....3 Mch. 1799

A provisional volunteer force of 25,000 authorized by congress for the war with England, besides volunteers and militia.... 1812

[This did not affect the regular army.]

Force disbanded 1815

1 regiment of dragoons, the first, authorized................. 1833

2 regiments of dragoons authorized............................ 1836

The whole number of troops of the line was 7244 men at the breaking out of the Mexican war.............................. 1846

The regular army was increased to 20,000 by enlistments aside from volunteers; 9 new regiments of infantry, 1 of dragoons, 1 of mounted rifles, were added during the war, but discharged except the mounted rifles....................... 1849

2 regiments of infantry and 2 of cavalry added to the army... 1855

Total number of line troops, 12,931 in 1860

The grade of lieut.-gen. was revived in "brevet," and held by gen. Winfield Scott from 15 Feb. 1855, until his retirement ..Nov. 1861

[The rank was revived in 1864, and conferred upon gen. Grant.]

The president by proclamation added to the regular army 11 regiments, viz., 1 of cavalry, 1189 officers and men; 1 of artillery of 12 batteries, 6 pieces each, 1909 men; and 9 of infantry of 3 battalions of 8 companies each, 22,068 officers and men..4 May, 1861

Flogging abolished in the army ....5 Aug. 1861

TROOPS FURNISHED THE GOVERNMENT DURING THE CIVIL WAR FROM 1861 TO 1865.

Under call of 15 Apr. 1861, for 75,000 men for 3 mos.......	91,816
Under call of 3 May, 1861, for 500,000 men for 6 mos., 1 yr., 2 yrs., 3 yrs..........	700,680
Under call of 2 July, 1862, for 300,000 men for 3 years.....	421,465
Under call of 4 Aug. 1862, for 300,000 men for 9 mos.......	87,588
Under proclamation, 15 June, 1863, men for 6 mos..........	16,361
Under call of 17 Oct. 1863 (including drafted men of 1863), and call of 1 Feb. 1864, for 500,000 for 3 yrs..........	317,092
Under call of 14 Mch. 1864, for 200,000 for 3 yrs..........	259,515
Militia for 100 days, mustered in between Apr. 23 and July 18, 1864..........	83,612
Under call of 18 July, 1864, for 500,000 (reduced by excess credits of previous calls) for 1 yr., 2 yrs., 3 yrs., and 4 yrs..	385,163
Under call of 19 Dec. 1864, for 300,000 men for 1 yr., 2 yrs., 3 yrs., 4 yrs..........	211,752
Other troops furnished by states and territories which, after first call, had not been called upon for quotas when general call for troops was made..........	182,357
By special authority granted May and June, 1862, New York, Illinois, and Indiana furnished for 3 mos..........	15,007
Total..........	2,772,408
Number of men who paid commutation..........	86,724
Grand total..........	2,859,132
Aggregate reduced to a 3 yrs.' standard	2,320,272

ACTUAL STRENGTH OF THE ARMY BETWEEN 1 JAN. 1860, AND 1 MAY, 1865.

Date.	Regulars.	Volunteers.	Total.
1 Jan. 1860	16,435	—	16,43
1 " 1861	16,367	—	16,367
1 July, "	16,422	170,329	186,75
1 Jan. 1862	22,425	553,492	575,91
31 Mch. "	23,308	613,818	637,12
1 Jan. 1863	25,463	892,728	918,19
1 " 1864	24,636	836,101	860,73
1 " 1865	22,019	937,441	959,46
31 Mch. "	21,669	958,417	980,08
1 May, "			1,000,51

here were absent from the army, volunteers and regulars, 338,536, or about one third of the total force..........1 Jan. 1865

he regular army reached its maximum strength, 56,815, Oct. 1867

[aximum strength fixed by congress at 25,000 enlisted men, 15 Aug. 1876

TRENGTH OF THE REGULAR ARMY OF THE UNITED STATES, 1 JAN. 1893.

[aj.-generals		3
rig.-generals		6
taff department		2,467
avalry, 10 regiments,	Commissioned	432
	Enlisted	6,050
rtillery, 5 "	Commissioned	280
	Enlisted	3,675
afantry, 25 "	Commissioned	877
	Enlisted	12,125
[ilitary academy,	Professors	7
	Cadets	347
arious others unattached, etc.		2,233
	Total	28,502
etired officers		607
" enlisted men		735

TRENGTH OF THE MILITIA FORCE OF THE UNITED STATES, 1892–93.

State.	Organized Aggregate.	Unorganized but Available.
labama	2,958	160,000
rkansas	1,094	116,620
alifornia	4,218	153,389
olorado	825	86,000
onnecticut	2,687	91,766
elaware	501	38,000
lorida	1,021	47,705
eorgia	4,577	264,021
daho	308	10,000
llinois	4,389	550,000
ndiana	2,459	468,608
owa	2,443	243,299
ansas	1,738	250,000
entucky	1,319	395,000
ouisiana	1,152	138,439
laine	1,114	96,937
laryland	2,094	125,000
lassachusetts	5,511	339,691
lichigan	2,515	400,000
linnesota	1,838	154,000
lississippi	1,712	233,480
lissouri	2,387	350,000
lontana	570	34,350
ebraska	1,073	125,000
evada	575	10,540
ew Hampshire	1,229	34,000
ew Jersey	4,233	284,887
ew York	13,539	650,000
orth Carolina	1,586	235,000
orth Dakota	513	36,178
hio	5,373	600,000
regon	1,506	40,796
ennsylvania	8,469	735,622
hode Island	1,434	47,000
outh Carolina	5,616	116,000
outh Dakota	526	60,000
ennessee	1,357	290,246
exas	3,368	300,000
ermont	786	44,164
irginia	2,844	220,000
Vashington	1,145	59,600
Vest Virginia	728	90,000
Visconsin	2,737	308,717
Vyoming	309	13.000
erritories	2,297	74,203
Total	110,673	9,121,258

STAFF-DEPARTMENT OF THE UNITED STATES ARMY.

With the exception of the quartermaster-general's department he highest rank in the staff-department of the Army prior to 1861 was colonel. From that date the rank of the heads of the different departments has been gradually changed to that of brig.-gen., until now they all bear that rank. The following is a list of the names of those who first ranked as brig.-gen. in the different departments.

Thomas S. Jessup,	q.m.-gen.,	as brig.-gen. from	8 May, 1818
Lorenzo Thomas,	adjt.-gen.,	" "	3 Aug. 1861
Jas. W. Ripley,	chief of ord.,	" "	3 Aug. "
Wm. A. Hammond,	surg.-gen.,	" "	25 Apr. 1862
Joseph P. Taylor,	commissary-gen.,	" "	9 Feb. 1863
Joseph G. Totten,	chief of engineers,	" "	3 Mch. "
Joseph Holt,	judge-advocate gen.,	" "	22 June, 1864
Benj. W. Brice,	paymaster-gen.,	" "	28 July, 1866
Randolph B. Marcy,	inspector-gen.,	" "	12 Dec. 1878
Albert J. Myer,	chief sig. off.,	" "	16 June, 1880

SALARIES PAID COMMISSIONED OFFICERS OF THE U. S. ARMY.

Rank.	Amount per year.	Remarks.
Maj.-gen.	$7,500	
Brig.-gen.	5,500	
Colonel	3,500	Increase of 10 per cent. every 5 years of service up to $4,500, the limit.
Lt. Col.	3,000	Increase of 10 per cent. every 5 years of service up to $4,000, the limit.
Major	2,500	Increase of 10 per cent. every 5 years of service for 20 years.
Capt. m't'd.	2,000	" " "
" not "	1,800	" " "
Regt. adjt.	1,800	" " "
" q.m.	1,800	" " "
1st Lt. m't'd.	1,600	" " "
" not "	1,500	" " "
2d Lt. m't'd.	1,500	" " "
" not "	1,400	" " "
Chaplain	1,500	" " "

Retired officers receive 75 per cent. of pay (salary and increase) of their rank (act July 15, 1870, sec. 24) with the exception of the chaplain, who receives 90 per cent.

The pay of privates to sergeants inclusive ranges from $13 to $45 per month the first year, and from $16 to $48 per month the next four years, and after that from $18 to $50 a month.

PRINCIPAL DEPARTMENT ARMIES OF THE CIVIL WAR.

ARMY OF THE CUMBERLAND organized 30 Oct. 1862. First commander, maj.-gen. Wm. S. Rosecrans—3 corps, 14th, 20th, 21st. Battle of Stone river or Murfreesboro, 31 Dec. 1862–2 Jan. 1863, victorious. Battle of Chickamauga, defeated, 19–20 Sept. 1863. 20th and 21st corps consolidated, forming the 4th corps, Oct. 1863; maj.-gen. George H. Thomas 2d commander, relieving gen. Rosecrans, Oct. 1863. 11th and 12th corps of the army of the Potomac united with the army of the Cumberland, Oct. 1863. Defeats confederates in a series of battles around Chattanooga, Nov. 1863–11th and 12th corps consolidated, Jan. 1864, forming the 20th. Participates in the Atlanta campaign, 1864. The 14th and 20th corps accompany gen. Sherman on his "march to the sea." The 4th corps, returning to Nashville, engages in the battle of Franklin, 30 Nov. 1864, and of Nashville, 15–16 Dec. 1864.

ARMY OF THE GULF organized 1863, including the troops within the dept. of the Gulf. Mostly comprised of the 19th corps, maj.-gen. N. P. Banks commander. Engaged in the siege of PORT HUDSON and in the RED RIVER CAMPAIGN, Mch., Apr. 1864.

ARMY OF THE JAMES (i. e. the James river) comprised the 10th and 18th corps, and cavalry under command of maj.-gen. Benj. F. Butler; and acting in conjunction with the army of the Potomac, operated south of Richmond around Petersburg, 1864.

ARMY OF THE MIDDLE MILITARY DIV., organized Aug. 1864, comprised the 6th, 8th, and 19th corps, with 2 divs. of cavalry under command of maj.-gen. Philip H. Sheridan. Battle of Winchester, 19 Sept. 1864; battle of Fisher's Hill, 25 Sept. 1864; and battle of Cedar Creek, 19 Oct 1[illegible]; all victorious.

ARMY OF THE OHIO organized 9 Nov. 1861, maj.-gen. Don Carlos Buell 1st commander. Aids in securing victory at the battle of Shiloh or PITTSBURG LANDING, 6–7 Apr. 1862; Perrysville, 8 Oct. 1862. Gen. Buell relieved, 30 Oct. 1862, Wm. S. Rosecrans in command. Changed to ARMY OF THE CUMBERLAND. Reorganized, maj.-gen. H. G. Wright in command, 1862; maj. gen. Ambrose E. Burnside, 1863, operating in east Tenn.; maj.-gen. John G. Foster, 1864; maj.-gen. John M. Schofield, 28 Jan. 1864. Atlanta campaign. Battles of Franklin and Nashville, 1864; Fort Fisher, 1865.

ARMY OF THE POTOMAC organized July, 1861, maj.-gen. George B. McClellan 1st commander. 7 days' battles before Richmond, June and July, 1862. Battle of Antietam, 17 Sept. 1862; victorious. Maj.-gen. Ambrose E. Burnside 2d commander, 5 Nov. 1862. Battle of Fredericksburg, 10 Dec. 1862; defeated. Gen. Burnside relieved, 25 Jan. 1863; maj.-gen. Joseph Hooker 3d commander. Battle of Chancellorsville, 2, 3, and 4 May, 1863; defeated. Gen. Hooker relieved, 27 June, 1863; maj.-gen. George G. Meade 4th commander. Battle of Gettysburg, 1–3 July, 1863; victorious. Under gen. Grant, general-in-chief, fought the battles of the Wilderness, 5–6 May, 1864; Spottsylvania, 11 May, 1864; Cold Harbor, 3 June, 1864. Siege of Richmond, 1864–65.

ARMY OF THE TENNESSEE organized Apr. 1862, maj.-gen. H. W. Halleck commander; maj.-gen. U. S. Grant in command, 17 July, 1862. It comprised the 13th, 15th, 16th, and 17th corps, 18 Dec. 1862. Vicksburg campaign and capture of Vicksburg, 4 July, 1863. Maj.-gen. William T. Sherman in command, 27 Oct. 1863. Participates in the battles around Chattanooga, Nov. 1863. Maj.-gen. J. B. McPherson in command, 12 Mch. 1864. Atlanta campaign. Maj.-gen. O. O. Howard appointed to the command on the death of gen. McPherson, killed 22 July, 1864. With Sherman on the march through Ga. John A. Logan in command, 19 May, 1865.

ARMY OF VIRGINIA organized 26 June, 1862, maj.-gen. John Pope commander. It comprised 3 corps and about 5000 cavalry. With the army of the Potomac it fought the battles of Groveton and second Bull Run, 29 and 30 Aug. 1862; defeated. Gen. Pope relieved at his own request, and the army merged in that of the Potomac.

GENERAL OFFICERS OF THE CONTINENTAL ARMY OF THE REVOLUTION, WITH THEIR RANK AND DATE OF COMMISSIONS, FROM WHAT STATES APPOINTED, TOGETHER WITH DATE AND PLACE OF BIRTH AND DEATH.

Names.	Rank and Date of Commission.		Born, where and when.	Died, where and when.	App. from	Remarks.
Washington, George	Maj.-Gen'l. and Commander-in-chief,	15 June, 1775	Virginia ....22 Feb. 1732	Virginia..........14 Dec. 1799	Va.	First president of the U. S., 1789–97.
	BRIG.-GEN'L.	MAJ.-GEN'L.				
Alexander, Wm. (lord Stirling)	1 Mch. 1776	19 Feb. 1777	New York City 1726	Albany, N. Y......15 Jan. 1783	N. J.	STIRLING.
Armstrong, John	1 Mch. 1776	....	Ireland.......... 1725	Carlisle, Pa........9 Mch. 1795	Pa.	Resigned, 4 Apr. 1777.
Arnold, Benedict	10 Jan. 1776	17 Feb. 1777	Norwich, Conn.....3 Jan. 1741	London, Eng.....14 June, 1801	Conn.	Deserted to the British army, 25 Sept. 1780.
Cadwalader, John	21 Feb. 1777	....	Philadelphia, Pa...10 Jan. 1742	Pennsylvania.....11 Feb. 1786	Pa.	Fights a duel with and severely wounds gen. Conway, 1778.
Clinton, George	25 Mch. 1777	....	Ulster Co., N. Y...26 July, 1739	Washington, D. C..30 Apr. 1812	N. Y.	First gov. of the state of New York, 20 Apr. 1777.
Clinton, James	9 Aug. 1776	....	Ulster Co., N. Y....9 Aug. 1736	Orange Co., N. Y...22 Dec. 1812	N. Y.	
Conway, Thomas	13 May, 1777	13 Dec. 1777	Ireland..........27 Feb. 1733	..........about 1800	France	One of the secret enemies of Washington. Resigned, 1778.
Dayton, Elias	7 Jan. 1783	....	New Jersey..........July, 1737	New Jersey.......17 July, 1807	N. J.	
De Borre, Prud'Homme	1 Dec. 1776	....	France..........	....	France	Resigned, 14 Dec. 1777.
Du Coudray, Philip	....	11 Aug. 1777	France..........	Pennsylvania.....17 Sept. 1777	....	Inspector-gen. of ordnance. Drowned in the Schuylkill, 1777.
De Fermoy, Mathias, A. R	5 Nov. 1776	....	France..........	....	....	Resigned, Jan. 1778.
De Haas, John P	21 Feb. 1777	....	Holland.......... 1735	Philadelphia, Pa...3 June, 1786	Pa.	
De Kalb, John (baron)	....	15 Sept. 1777	Bavaria.......... 1721	South Carolina....19 Aug. 1780	....	Killed at the battle of Camden, S. C.
De Rouarie, Armand T	26 Mch. 1783	....	France..........14 Apr. 1756	France.......... 1792	....	Returned to France at the close of the revolution.
De Woedtke, Frederick William	16 Mch. 1776	....	Prussia.......... 1740	New York.......31 July, 1776	....	
Duportail, Louis L. B	17 Nov. 1777	16 Nov. 1781	France..........about 1750	At sea.......... 1802	France	Directing engineer at siege of Yorktown. Revisited U.S. to escape "reign of terror," 1794. Died on return voyage to France.
Frye, Joseph	10 Jan. 1776	....	Massachusetts.......Apr. 1711	Maine.......... 1794	Mass.	Resigned, 22 Apr. 1776, on account of infirmities.
Gadsden, Christopher	16 Sept. 1776	....	Charleston, S. C.......... 1724	Charleston, S. C...28 Aug. 1805	S. C.	Resigned, 1779.
Gates, Horatio	17 June, 1775	16 May, 1776	England.......... 1728	New York City....10 Apr. 1806	Va.	First adjt.-gen. of the continental army. Defeats Burgoyne at Saratoga. Is defeated at Camden, S. C.
Gist, Mordecai	9 Jan. 1779	....	Baltimore, Md.......... 1743	Charleston.......... 1792	Md.	
Glover, John	21 Feb. 1777	....	Salem, Mass.......5 Nov. 1732	Massachusetts.....30 Jan. 1797	Mass.	He commanded one of the best regiments in the continental army.
Greaton, John	7 Jan. 1783	....	Massachusetts... 10 Mch. 1741	Massachusetts.....16 Dec. 1783	Mass.	
Greene, Nathaniel	22 June, 1775	9 Aug. 1776	Rhode Island......6 June, 1742	Georgia..........12 June, 1786	R. I.	One of the most distinguished officers in the revolution.
Hand, Edward	1 Apr. 1777	....	Ireland..........31 Dec. 1744	Pennsylvania......3 Sept. 1802	Pa.	Served throughout the revolution.
Heath, William	22 June, 1775	9 Aug. 1776	Massachusetts.....2 Mch. 1737	Massachusetts.....24 Jan. 1814	Mass.	Rendered great service throughout the war.
Hogan, James	9 Jan. 1779	....	....		N. C.	
Howe, Robert	1 Mch. 1776	20 Oct. 1777	North Carolina.......... 1732	North Carolina.......... 1785	N. C.	
Huger, Isaac	9 Jan. 1779	....	South Carolina....19 Mch. 1742	Charleston, S. C....17 Oct. 1797	S. C.	
Huntington, Jedediah	12 May, 1777	....	Connecticut........4 Aug. 1743	Connecticut......25 Sept. 1818	Conn.	At the close of the war, brevet major-gen.
Irvine, William	12 May, 1779	....	Ireland..........3 Nov. 1741	Philadelphia, Pa..29 July, 1804	Pa.	Came to the U. S. from Ireland, 1763.
Knox, Henry	27 Dec. 1776	22 Mch. 1782	Boston..........25 July, 1750	Thomaston, Me....25 Nov. 1806	Mass.	Commanded the artillery of the main army during the whole war.
Lafayette, de, M.J.P.R.Y.G.M. (marquis)	....	31 July, 1777	France..........6 Sept. 1757	Paris..........20 May, 1834	....	Invited by congress, visited the U. S. 1824.
Learned, Ebenezer	2 Apr. 1777	....	Massachusetts..........	Massachusetts. 1801	Mass.	Resigned on account of infirmities, 1778.
Lee, Charles	....	17 June, 1775	England.......... 1731	Philadelphia, Pa....2 Oct. 1782	Va.	Suspended from command for 1 year, 12 Aug. 1778, for conduct at battle of Monmouth; dismissed, 10 Jan. 1780.
Lewis, Andrew	1 Mch. 1776	....	Ireland.......... 1720	Virginia..........26 Sept. 1780	Va.	Distinguished in Indian warfare. Resigned, 15 Apr. 1777.
Lincoln, Benjamin	....	19 Feb. 1777	Massachusetts.....24 Jan. 1733	Massachusetts.....9 May, 1810	Mass.	Sec. of war from 1781 to 1784.

	BRIG.-GEN'L.	MAJ.-GEN'L.				
Maxwell, William	23 Oct. 1776	....	Ireland	New Jersey......12 Nov. 1798	N. J.	Resigned, June 22, 1780.
McDougall, Alexander	9 Aug. 1776	20 Oct. 1777	Scotland......1731	New York......8 June, 1786	N. Y.	
McIntosh, Lachlan	16 Sept. 1776	....	Scotland......1725	Savannah, Ga......1806	Ga.	Kills Button Gwinnett in a duel, 15 May, 1777.
Mercer, Hugh	5 June, 1776	....	Scotland......1721	Princeton......12 Jan. 1777	Va.	Died of wounds received at battle of Princeton.
Mifflin, Thomas	16 May, 1776	19 Feb. 1777	Philadelphia, Pa......1744	Lancaster, Pa......20 Jan. 1800	Pa.	Resigned, 25 Feb. 1779.
Montgomery, Richard	22 June, 1775	9 Dec. 1775	Ireland......2 Dec. 1736	Quebec......31 Dec. 1775	N. Y.	Killed in the assault on Quebec.
Moore, James	1 Mch. 1776	....	North Carolina......1737	......15 Jan. 1777	N. C.	
Morgan, Daniel	13 Oct. 1780	....	New Jersey......1736	Virginia......6 July, 1802	Va.	Congress voted him a gold medal for his victory at Cowpens.
Moultrie, William	16 Sept. 1776	15 Oct. 1782	England......1731	South Carolina...27 Sept. 1805	S. C.	The gallant defence of fort Moultrie was due to him.
Muhlenberg, John Peter G	21 Feb. 1777	....	Pennsylvania......1 Oct. 1746	Pennsylvania......1 Oct. 1807	Va.	Ordained and officiated as a clergyman until the revolution.
Nash, Francis	5 Feb. 1777	....	Virginia......10 May, 1720	Pennsylvania......7 Oct. 1777	N. C.	Died of wounds received at the battle of Germantown.
Nixon, John	9 Aug. 1776	....	Massachusetts......4 Mch. 1725	Vermont......24 Mch. 1815	Mass.	Resigned on account of poor health, 1780.
Parsons, Samuel H	9 Aug. 1776	23 Oct. 1780	Connecticut......14 May, 1737	Pennsylvania......17 Nov. 1789	Conn.	Drowned in Big Beaver river, Pa
Paterson, John	21 Feb. 1777	....	Connecticut......1744	New York......19 July, 1808	Mass.	
Pomeroy, Seth	22 June, 1775	....	Massachusetts....20 May, 1706	New York......19 Feb. 1777	Mass.	Fought as a private at battle of Bunker Hill. Resigned, July, 1775.
Poor, Enoch	21 Feb. 1777	....	Massachusetts....21 June, 1736	New Jersey......8 Sept. 1780	N. H.	Killed in a duel with a French officer near Hackensack, N. J.
Pulaski, Casimir (count)	15 Sept. 1777	....	Poland......4 Mch. 1748	Georgia......Oct. 11, 1777	....	Died of wounds received at siege of Savannah, Ga.
Putnam, Israel	....	19 June, 1775	Massachusetts......7 Jan. 1718	Connecticut......19 May, 1790	Conn.	
Putnam, Rufus	7 Jan. 1783	....	Massachusetts......9 Apr. 1738	Ohio......1 May, 1824	Mass.	Cousin of Israel Putnam. One of the first settlers of Marietta, Ohio, 1788.
Reed, James	9 Aug. 1776	....	Massachusetts......1724	Massachusetts....13 Feb. 1807	N. H.	Retired on account of sickness, 1776.
Schuyler, Philip	....	19 June, 1775	New York......22 Nov. 1733	Albany, N. Y......18 Nov. 1804	N. Y.	Resigned, 19 Apr. 1779.
Scott, Charles	1 Apr. 1777	....	Virginia......1733	Kentucky......22 Oct. 1813	Va.	
Smallwood, William	23 Oct. 1776	15 Sept. 1780	Maryland......1732	Maryland......14 Feb. 1792	Md.	
Spencer, Joseph	22 June, 1775	9 Aug. 1776	Connecticut......1714	Connecticut......13 Jan. 1789	Conn.	Resigned, 14 June, 1778.
Stark, John	5 Oct. 1777	....	New Hampshire...28 Aug. 1728	New Hampshire...8 May, 1822	N. H.	
Steuben, Frederick W. A. (baron)	....	20 Mch. 1778	Prussia......15 Nov. 1730	New York......28 Nov. 1794	....	He contributed largely to the success of the war.
St. Clair, Arthur	9 Aug. 1776	19 Feb. 1777	Scotland......1734	Pennsylvania......31 Aug. 1818	Pa.	
Stephens, Adam	4 Sept. 1776	19 Feb. 1777	Virginia......1730	Virginia......1791	Va.	Brave and able, but dismissed, 1778, for habitual intoxication.
Sullivan, John	22 June, 1775	9 Aug. 1776	Maine......17 Feb. 1740	New Hampshire...23 Jan. 1795	N. H.	Resigned on account of shattered health, 30 Nov. 1779, receiving a vote of thanks from congress.
Sumner, Jethro	9 Jan. 1779	....	Virginia......1730	North Carolina......1790	N. C.	
Thomas, John	22 June, 1775	6 Mch. 1776	Massachusetts......1725	Canada......30 May, 1776	Mass.	Died of the small-pox on the retreat from Canada.
Thompson, William	1 Mch. 1776	....	Ireland......1725	Pennsylvania......4 Sept. 1781	Pa.	
Varnum, James M	21 Feb. 1777	....	Massachusetts....17 Dec. 1748	Ohio......10 Jan. 1789	R. I.	Resigned, 5 Mch. 1779. One of the first settlers of Marietta, Ohio, 1788.
Ward, Artemas	....	17 June, 1775	Massachusetts......1727	Massachusetts......28 Oct. 1800	Mass.	First maj.-gen. appointed by congress. Resigned, 21 Apr. 1776.
Wayne, Anthony	21 Feb. 1777	....	Pennsylvania......1 Jan. 1745	Pennsylvania......15 Dec. 1796	Pa.	Distinguished, but especially noted for his storming and capture of Stony Point on the Hudson, 15 July, 1779.
Weedon, George	21 Feb. 1777	....	Virginia......1730	Virginia......1790	Va.	
Whitcomb, John	5 June, 1776	....	Massachusetts......1720	Massachusetts......1812	Mass.	In the service but a short time. Resigned because of old age.
Williams, Otho H	9 May, 1782	....	Maryland......1749	Maryland......1794	Md.	
Woodford, William	21 Feb. 1777	....	Virginia......1735	New York City...13 Nov. 1780	Va.	
Wooster, David	22 June, 1775	....	Connecticut......2 Mch. 1710	Connecticut......2 May, 1777	Conn.	Died of wounds received at battle of Ridgefield.
Marion, Francis	....	....	South Carolina......1732	South Carolina...27 Feb. 1795	S. C.	Famous partisan; brig.-gen. state troops, Aug. 1780.
Pickens, Andrew	....	....	Pennsylvania....19 Sept. 1739	South Carolina...17 Aug. 1817	S. C.	" " "
Sumter, Thomas	....	....	Virginia......1734	South Carolina...1 June, 1832	S. C.	" " " July, 1780.

GENERAL OFFICERS COMMISSIONED IN THE REGULAR ARMY OF THE UNITED STATES SINCE THE INAUGURATION OF THE FIRST PRESIDENT, INCLUDING THOSE OF THE STAFF DEPARTMENTS, BUT NOT THOSE OF BREVET RANK. (m. acad.—military academy.)

Names.	Brig.-gen.	Maj.-gen.	Lieut.-gen.	General.	Born, where and when.	Died, where and when.	App. from	Remarks.
Alvord, Benjamin......	22 July, 1876	....	....	....	Vermont.......18 Aug. 1813	........16 Oct. 1884	Vt. m. acad.	Paymaster-gen. Retired, 8 June, 1880.
Anderson, Robert......	15 May, 1861	....	....	....	Kentucky.....14 June, 1805	France..........26 Oct. 1871	Ky. m. acad.	Distinguished for his defence of fort Sumter, 1861.
Armstrong, John.......	6 July, 1812	....	....	....	Pennsylvania...25 Nov. 1758	New York.....1 Apr. 1843	N. Y.	Resigned, 13 Jan. 1813. Sec. of war, 1813–14.
Atkinson, Henry.......	13 May, 1820	....	....	....	North Carolina........ 1782	Missouri......14 June, 1842	N. C.	Commanded at the battle of Bad Axe.
Augur, Christopher C...	4 Mch. 1869	....	....	....	New York............ 1821	....	Mich. m. acad.	Retired, 10 July, 1885.
Baird, Absalom........	22 Sept. 1885	....	....	....	Pennsylvania..20 Aug. 1824	....	Pa. m. acad.	Inspector-gen. Retired, 20 Aug. 1888.
Barnes, Joseph K......	22 Aug. 1864	....	....	....	Pennsylvania..27 July, 1817	Wash., D. C.....5 Apr. 1883	Pa.	Surgeon-gen.
Batchelder, Richard N..	9 July, 1890	....	....	....	New Hampshire.......	....	N. H.	Quartermaster-gen.
Benet, Stephen V.......	23 June, 1874	....	....	....	Florida........22 Jan. 1827	....	Fla. m. acad.	Chief of ordnance. Retired, 22 Jan. 1891.
Bissell, Daniel........	9 Mch. 1814	....	....	....	....	Missouri........14 Dec. 1833	Conn.	Retained in the re-organization of the army as col. 1st infantry, 17 May, 1815.
Bloomfield, Joseph.....	27 Mch. 1812	....	....	....	New Jersey......	New Jersey......3 Oct. 1823	N. J.	Service terminated upon the reduction of the army, 1815.
Boyd, John Parker......	26 Aug. 1812	....	....	....	Massachusetts..21 Dec. 1764	Massachusetts....4 Oct. 1830	Mass.	" " " " "
Breckenridge, Joseph C.	12 Feb. 1889	....	....	....	Maryland......14 Jan. 1842	....	Ky.	Inspector-gen., 26 Jan. 1889.
Brice, Benjamin W......	28 July, 1866	....	....	....	Virginia.......... 1809	Wash., D. C.....4 Dec. 1892	Ohio m. acad.	Paymaster-gen. Retired, 1 Jan. 1872.
Brooke, John R........	6 Apr. 1888	....	....	....	Pennsylvania..21 July, 1838	....	Pa.	
Brown, Jacob..........	19 July, 1813	24 Jan. 1814	....	....	Pennsylvania...9 May, 1775	Wash., D. C.....24 Feb. 1828	N. Y.	Commanding northern division of the army, 1815–21. Gen.-in-chief, 1821–28.
Brown, Nathan W.......	8 June, 1880	....	....	....	New York.......... 1819	....	N. Y.	Paymaster-gen. Retired, 6 Feb. 1882.
Cadwalader, George.....	3 Mch. 1847	....	....	....	Pennsylvania........ 1804	Pennsylvania....3 Feb. 1879	Pa.	Service terminated upon the reduction of the army, 1848. Maj.-gen. vols. 1862.
Canby, Edward R. S.....	28 July, 1866	....	....	....	Kentucky......... 1819	Oregon.........11 Apr. 1873	Ind. m. acad.	Killed by the Modoc Indians.
Carlin, William P.......	17 May, 1893	....	....	....	Illinois........24 Nov. 1829	....	Ill. m. acad.	Retired, 24 Nov. 1893.
Carr, Eugene A.........	19 July, 1892	....	....	....	New York, Erie Co.... 1830	....	N. Y. m. acad.	Retired, 15 Feb. 1893.
Carroll, Samuel S.......	....	9 June, 1869	....	....	Wash., D. C....21 Sept. 1832	Wash., D. C.....28 Jan. 1893	D. C. m. acad.	Retired, 9 June, 1869, as maj.-gen.
Casey, Thomas L........	6 July, 1888	....	....	....	New York.....10 May, 1831	....	At large "	Chief of engineers.
Cass, Lewis............	12 Mch. 1813	....	....	....	New Hampshire..9 Oct. 1782	Michigan......17 June, 1866	Ohio.	Resigned, 1 May, 1814.
Chandler, John.........	8 July, 1812	....	....	....	New Hampshire....... 1760	Maine.........25 Sept. 1841	Me.	Service terminated upon the reduction of the army, 1815.
Cooke, Philip St. George.	12 Nov. 1861	....	....	....	Virginia......13 June, 1809	....	Va. m. acad.	Retired, 29 Oct. 1873.
Covington, Leonard.....	1 Aug. 1813	....	....	....	Maryland.......30 Oct. 1768	Upper Canada. 14 Nov. 1813	Md.	Died of wounds received in battle of Chrysler's Fields, U.C., 1813.
Crane, Charles H.......	3 July, 1882	....	....	....	Rhode Island..19 July, 1825	Wash., D. C.....10 Oct. 1883	Mass.	Surgeon-gen.
Crawford, Samuel W....	19 Feb. 1873	....	....	....	Pennsylvania...8 Nov. 1829	Phila., Pa.......3 Nov. 1892	Pa.	Retired, 3 Mch. 1875.
Crook, George.........	29 Oct. 1873	6 Apr. 1888	....	....	Ohio..........8 Sept. 1828	Chicago.......20 Mch. 1890	Ohio m. acad.	
Cushing, Thomas H.....	6 July, 1812	....	....	....	Massachusetts........ 1755	Connecticut....19 Oct. 1822	Mass.	Service terminated upon the reduction of the army, 1815.
Davie, Wm. R..........	19 July, 1798	....	....	....	England.......20 June, 1756	South Carolina..8 Nov. 1820	N. C.	Provisional army. Disbanded, 15 June, 1800.
Davis, Nelson H........	11 Mch. 1885	....	....	....	Massachusetts, 20 Sept. 1821	....	Mass. m. acad.	Inspector-gen. Retired, 20 Sept. 1885.
Dearborn, Henry.......	....	27 Jan. 1812	....	....	New Hampshire, 23 Feb. 1751	Massachusetts...6 June, 1829	Mass.	Gen.-in-chief, 1812–15.
Delafield, Richard......	22 Apr. 1864	....	....	....	New York......1 Sept. 1798	Wash., D. C......5 Nov. 1873	N. Y. m. acad.	Chief of engineers. Retired, 8 Aug. 1866.
Drum, Richard C.......	15 June, 1880	....	....	....	Pennsylvania..28 May, 1825	....	Pa.	Adjt.-gen. Retired, 28 May, 1889.
Duane, James C........	11 Oct. 1886	....	....	....	New York....30 June, 1824	....	N. Y. m. acad.	Chief of engineers. Retired, 30 June, 1888.
Du Barry, Beekman....	10 July, 1890	....	....	....	New Jersey........ 1828	....	D. C. m. acad.	Commissary-gen. Retired, 4 Dec. 1892.
Dunn, Wm. McK.......	1 Dec. 1875	....	....	....	Indiana........12 Dec. 1814	Virginia.......24 July, 1887	Ind.	Judge-advocate-gen. Retired, 22 Jan. 1881.
Dyer, Alexander B.....	12 Sept. 1864	....	....	....	Virginia........10 Jan. 1815	Wash., D. C....20 May, 1874	Mo. m. acad.	Chief of ordnance.
Eaton, Amos B.........	29 June, 1864	....	....	....	New York.....12 May, 1806	Connecticut....21 Feb. 1877	N. Y. m. acad.	Commissary-gen. Retired, 1 May, 1874.
Emory, Wm. H.........	1 July, 1876	....	....	....	Maryland.......9 Sept. 1811	....	Md. m. acad.	Retired, 1 July, 1876.
Fessenden, Francis.....	1 Nov. 1866	...	....	....	Maine........18 Mch. 1839	....	Me.	" 1 Nov. 1866.
Flagler, Daniel W......	23 Jan. 1891	...	....	....	New York........	....	N. Y. m. acad.	Chief of ordnance.

GENERAL OFFICERS COMMISSIONED IN THE REGULAR ARMY OF THE UNITED STATES.—*Continued.*

Names.	Brig.-gen.	Maj.-gen.	Lieut.-gen.	General.	Born, where and when.	Died, where and when.	App. from	Remarks.
Flournoy, Thomas......	18 June, 1812	....	....	....	....	....	N. C.	Resigned, 13 Sept. 1813.
Forsyth, James W......	8 Nov. 1894	....	....	....	Ohio.................. 1835	....	Ohio m. acad.	
Frémont, John C.......	....	14 May, 1861	....	....	Georgia ....21 Jan. 1813	New York.....13 July, 1890	Cal.	Resigned, 4 June, 1864.
Gaines, Edmund P.....	9 Mch 1814	....	....	....	Virginia........20 Mch. 1777	Louisiana......6 June, 1849	Tenn.	
Gansevoort, Peter......	15 Feb. 1809	....	....	....	New York......17 July, 1749	Albany, N. Y....2 July, 1812	N. Y.	Served with distinction throughout war of revolution.
Gibbon, John	10 July, 1885	....	....	....	Pennsylvania...20 Apr. 1826		N. C. m. acad.	Retired, 20 Apr. 1891.
Grant, Ulysses S........	....	4 July, 1863	2 Mch. 1864	25 July, 1866	Ohio...........27 Apr. 1822	New York......23 July, 1885	Ill. m. acad.	Gen.-in-chief, 1864–69. President of the U. S. 1869–77. Retired, with pay and rank of gen. 3 Mch. 1885.
Greely, Adolphus W....	3 Mch. 1887	....	....	....	Massachusetts..27 Mch. 1844	....	La.	Chief signal officer.
Grierson, Benj. H.......	5 Apr. 1890	....	....	....	Pennsylvania...8 July, 1826	....	Pa.	Retired, July 8, 1890. Distinguished cavalry officer, 1862–64.
Halleck, Henry W......	....	19 Aug. 1861	....	....	New York......16 Jan. 1815	Louisville, Ky....9 Jan. 1872	N. Y. m. acad.	Gen.-in-chief, 1862–64.
Hamilton, Alexander....	....	19 July, 1798	....	....	Nevis, W. I......11 Jan. 1757	New York.....12 July, 1804	N. Y.	Provisional army. Disbanded, 15 June, 1800.
Hammond, Wm. A......	25 Apr. 1862	....	....	....	Maryland......28 Aug. 1828	....	Md.	Sur.-gen. Dismissed, 21 Aug. 1864. Restored to the army and placed on retired list, 27 Aug. 1879.
Hampton, Wade........	15 Feb. 1809	2 Mch. 1813	....	....	South Carolina......... 1754	South Carolina...4 Feb. 1835	S. C.	Resigned, 6 Apr. 1814.
Hancock, Winfield S....	12 Aug. 1864	26 July, 1866	....	....	Pennsylvania...14 Feb. 1824	New York...... 9 Feb. 1886	Pa. m. acad.	Nominated by democratic party for president of the U. S., 24 June, 1880.
Hand, Edward..........	....	19 July, 1798	....	....	Ireland.........31 Dec. 1744	Pennsylvania....3 Sept. 1802	Pa.	Provisional army. Disbanded, 15 June, 1800.
Hardin, Martin D.......	15 Dec. 1870	....	....	....	Illinois................. 1808	....	At large "	Retired, 15 Dec. 1870.
Harney, Wm. S.........	14 June, 1858	....	....	....	Tennessee......27 Aug. 1800	Florida.........9 May, 1889	La.	" 1 Aug. 1863.
Harrison, Wm. Henry...	22 Aug. 1812	2 Mch. 1813	....	....	Virginia.........9 Feb. 1773	Wash., D. C......4 Apr. 1841	Ind.	Resigned, 31 May, 1814. Elected by whig party 9th president of the U. S.
Hawkins, John P.......	22 Dec. 1892	....	....	....	Indiana................ 1830	....	Ind. m. acad.	Commissary-gen. Retired 29 Sept. 1894.
Hazen, Wm. B..........	8 Dec. 1880	....	....	....	Vermont.......27 Sept. 1830	Wash., D. C.....16 Jan. 1887	Ohio m. acad.	Chief signal officer.
Holabird, Samuel B.....	2 July, 1883	....	....	....	Connecticut...16 June, 1826	....	Conn. m. acad.	Quartermaster-gen. Retired, 16 June, 1890.
Holt, Joseph............	22 June, 1864	....	....	....	Kentucky.......6 Jan. 1807	....	D. C.	Judge advocate-gen. Retired, 1 Dec. 1875.
Hooker, Joseph	20 Sept. 1862	15 Oct. 1868	....	....	Massachusetts....Nov. 1814	New York......31 Oct. 1879	Mass. m. acad.	Retired, 15 Oct. 1868.
Howard, Benjamin.....	12 Mch. 1813	....	....	....	Virginia............... 1760	Missouri.......18 Sept. 1814	La.	
Howard, Oliver O.......	21 Dec. 1864	19 Mch. 1886	....	....	Maine...........8 Nov. 1830	....	Me. m. acad.	Retired, 8 Nov. 1894.
Hull, William..........	8 Apr. 1812	....	....	....	Connecticut...24 June, 1753	Massachusetts..25 Nov 1825	Mich. ter.	Cashiered (now considered unjustly), 25 Apr. 1814, for surrendering Detroit, 15 Aug. 1812.
Humphreys, Andrew A..	8 Aug. 1866	....	....	....	Pennsylvania...2 Nov. 1810	Wash., D. C.....27 Dec. 1883	Pa. m. acad.	Chief of engineers. Retired, 30 June, 1879.
Huntington, Ebenezer..	19 July, 1798	....	....	....	Connecticut....26 Dec. 1754	Connecticut....17 June, 1834	Conn.	Provisional army. Disbanded, 15 June, 1800.
Ingalls, Rufus..........	23 Feb. 1882	....	....	....	Maine.........23 Aug. 1820	....	Me. m. acad.	Retired, 1 July, 1883.
Izard, George	12 Mch. 1813	....	....	....	South Carolina......... 1777	Arkansas ......22 Nov. 1828	S. C.	Service terminated upon the reduction of the army, 1815.
Jackson, Andrew.......	19 Apr. 1814	1 May, 1814	....	....	South Carolina, 15 Mch. 1767	Tennessee......8 June, 1845	Tenn.	Resigned, Mch. 1821. President of the U. S., 1829–37.
Jessup, Thomas S.......	8 May, 1818	....	....	....	Virginia................ 1788	Wash., D. C....10 June, 1860	Ohio	Quartermaster-gen.
Johnson, Richard W....	3 Mch. 1875	....	....	....	Kentucky.......7 Feb. 1827	....	Ky. m. acad.	Retired, 3 Mch. 1875.
Johnston, Joseph E.....	28 June, 1860	....	....	....	Virginia..........Feb. 1807	Wash., D. C....21 Mch. 1891	Va. m. acad.	Quartermaster-gen. Resigned, 22 Apr. 1861, to enter the confederate service.
Jones, Roger...........	20 Aug. 1838	....	....	....	District of Columbia...	Virginia.........26 Jan. 1889	D. C.	Inspector-gen.
Kautz, August V.......	20 Apr. 1891	....	....	....	Germany........5 Jan. 1828		Ohio m. acad.	Retired, 5 Jan. 1892.
Kearney, Stephen W....	30 June, 1846	....	....	....	New Jersey.....30 Aug. 1794	Missouri........31 Oct. 1848	N. Y.	
Kelton, John C.........	7 June, 1889	....	....	....	Pennsylvania..24 June, 1828	Wash., D. C....15 July, 1893	Pa. m. acad.	Adjt.-gen. Retired, 24 June, 1892.
Lee, Henry	....	19 July, 1798	....	....	Virginia........29 Jan. 1756	Georgia........25 Mch. 1818	Va.	Provisional army. Disbanded, 15 June, 1800.
Lewis, Morgan.........	3 Apr. 1812	2 Mch. 1813	....	....	New York......16 Oct. 1754	New York.......7 Apr. 1844	N. Y.	Service terminated upon the reduction of the army, 1815.
Long, Eli..............	3 Mch. 1875	....	....	....	Kentucky.....27 June, 1836	....	Ky.	Retired, 3 Mch. 1875.

McArthur, Duncan ...	12 Mch. 1813	.	..	....	New York	14 June, 1772	Ohio.	28 Apr 1839	Ohio	Service terminated upon the reduction of the army, 1815
McClellan, George B .	.	14 May, 1861	....	..	Pennsylvania	3 Dec 1826	Orange, N J	29 Oct. 1885	Ohio m acad	Gen in chief, 1 Nov 1861, to 11 Mch 1862 Resigned 8 Nov 1864 Nominated for the presidency by the democratic party, 1 Sept. 1864
McCook, Alexander McD	11 July, 1890	8 Nov 1894	....		Ohio	1831			Ohio m acad	
McDowell, Irvin	14 May, 1861	25 Nov 1872	.	.	Ohio	15 Oct 1818	California	4 May, 1885	Ohio m acad	Retired 15 Oct. 1882
Macfeely, Robert	14 Apr 1875		.		Pennsylvania	1828			Pa m acad	Commissary gen Retired, 1 July, 1890
Mackenzie, Ranald S	26 Oct. 1882		.		New York	27 July, 1840	Staten I, N Y	19 Jan 1889	At large	Retired, 24 Mch 1884
McIntosh, John B	30 July, 1870				Florida	6 June, 1829	New Jersey	29 June, 1888	At large	" 30 July, 1870
Macomb, Alexander	24 Jan 1814	24 May, 1828			Michigan	3 Apr 1782	Wash D C	25 June, 1841	N Y	Gen. in chief, 24 May, 1828, to 25 June, 1841
McPherson, James B	1 Aug 1863		.		Ohio.	14 Nov 1828	Georgia.	22 July, 1864	Ohio m acad	Killed near Atlanta, Ga.
Mansfield, Joseph K. F	14 May, 1851			..	Connecticut	22 Dec 1803	Maryland	18 Sept 1862	Conn m acad	Died of wounds received at battle of Antietam
Marcy, Randolph B	12 Dec. 1878				Massachusetts	9 Apr 1812	New Jersey	22 Nov 1887	Mass m acad	Inspector gen
Meade, George G	3 July, 1863	18 Aug 1864	..	.	Spain.	31 Dec 1815	Pennsylvania	6 Nov 1872	Pa m acad	Commanded army of Potomac, 28 June, 1863 to 1 July 1865
Meigs, Montgomery C.	15 May, 1861		...		Georgia	3 May, 1816	Wash , D C	2 Jan 1892	Pa. m acad	Quartermaster gen Retired, 6 Feb 1882
Merritt Wesley	16 Apr 1887		..		New York	16 June, 1836			Ill m acad	
Miles, Nelson A	15 Dec 1880	5 Apr 1890	...		Massachusetts	8 Aug 1839			Mass	
Moore, John.	18 Nov 1886	...			Indiana	16 Aug 1826	..		Ind	Surgeon gen Retired, 1890.
Murray, Robert . .	23 Nov 1883	....	..	.	Maryland	6 Aug 1822			Md.	" " " 6 Aug 1886.
Myer, Albert J .	16 June, 1880	..		.	New York	20 Sept 1827	Buffalo, N Y	24 Aug 1880	N Y	Chief signal officer
Newton, John	6 Mch 1884	.			Virginia	24 Aug 1820			Va. m acad	Chief of engineers Retired 26 Aug 1886.
North, William . .	19 July, 1798	.		.	Maine	1755	New York	4 Jan 1836	N Y	Provisional army Disbanded, 15 June, 1800.
Ord, Edward O. C .	26 July, 1866	...	.		Maryland	18 Oct 1818	Havana, Cuba	27 July, 1883	D C m acad	Retired, 6 Dec 1880
Otis, Elwell S. ..	28 Nov 1893	....	..	.	Maryland	25 Mch 1838			N Y	
Parker, Daniel	22 Nov 1814	.	..	..	Massachusetts.	29 Jan. 1782	Wash , D C	5 Apr 1846	Mass	Inspector gen , paymaster gen 1 June, 1821 Superseded, 8 May, 1822
Parker, Thomas	12 Mch 1813	.	....	..	Virginia	1753	Virginia	22 Jan 1820	Va.	Resigned, 1 Nov 1814
Paul, Gabriel R.	28 July, 1866		..	.	Missouri .	22 Mch 1813	Wash , D C	5 May, 1886	Mo m acad.	Retired, 28 July, 1866
Pierce, Franklin .	3 Mch. 1847	....	.	.	New Hampshire	23 Nov 1804	New Hampshire	8 Oct 1869	N H	Resigned 20 Mch 1848 President of the U S. 1853-57
Pike, Zebulon M.	12 Mch 1813				New Jersey	5 Jan 1779	Upper Canada	27 Apr 1813	N J	Killed in the attack on York (now Toronto), Upper Canada
Pillow, Gideon J. .	1 July, 1846	13 Apr 1847	.		Tennessee .	8 June, 1806	Arkansas.	8 Oct. 1878	Tenn	Service terminated upon the reduction of the army, 1848 In the confederate service
Pinckney, Charles C ..	...	1 July, 1798			South Carolina	25 Feb 1746	South Carolina	16 Aug 1825	S C.	Provisional army Disbanded 15 June, 1800
Pinckney, Thomas.		27 Mch 1812			South Carolina.	23 Oct. 1750	South Carolina	2 Nov 1828	S C	Service terminated upon the reduction of the army 1815
Pope, John	14 July, 1862	26 Oct. 1882			Illinois	12 Mch 1823	Sandusky, O	23 Sept. 1892	Ill m acad	Retired, 16 Mch 1886
Posey, Thomas	14 Feb. 1793	..			Virginia	9 July, 1750	Illinois	19 Mch 1818	Va	Resigned, 28 Feb 1794
Potter, Joseph H. .	1 Apr 1886	.	..		New Hampshire	12 Oct 1822	Columbus, O	1 Dec. 1892	N H m acad	Retired, 12 Oct 1886
Putnam, Rufus . ..	4 May, 1792	.	....		Massachusetts	9 Apr 1738	Ohio	4 May, 1824	N W ter	Resigned, 14 Feb 1793.
Quitman, John A.	1 July, 1846	14 Apr. 1847	..		New York	1 Sept. 1799	Mississippi	17 July, 1858	Miss	Service terminated upon the reduction of the army, 1848
Ramsey, George D .	15 Sept 1863				Virginia	21 Feb 1802	Wash , D C	23 May, 1882	D C. m acad	Chief of ordnance Retired, 12 Sept 1864
Rawlins, John A ..	3 Mch 1865		.		Illinois	13 Feb 1831	Wash , D C	6 Sept 1869	Ill	Chief of staff to gen Grant
Ricketts, James B	...	3 Jan. 1867	..		New York	21 June, 1817	Wash D C	22 Sept. 1887	N Y m acad	Retired, 3 Jan 1867
Ripley, Eleazer W .	15 Apr 1814		..		New Hampshire.	15 Apr 1782	Louisiana	2 Mch. 1839	Mass	Resigned 1 Feb 1820
Ripley, James W ..	3 Aug 1861	.	.		Connecticut.	10 Dec 1794	Connecticut	16 Mch. 1870	Conn m acad	Chief of ordnance Retired, 15 Sept 1863
Robinson, John C. ...	..	6 May, 1869	.		New York	10 Apr 1817	.		N Y	Retired 6 May, 1869
Rochester, William B .	17 Feb 1882		..	.	New York	15 Feb 1826	.		N Y	Paymaster gen Retired, 1890
Rosecrans, William S	16 May, 1861	.	...	....	Ohio . ..	6 Dec 1819	. .		Ohio m acad	Commanded army of Cumberland, Oct 1862 to Oct 1863 Resigned, 28 Mch 1867 Appointed brig -gen 27 Feb. 1889 (act 27 Feb. 1889) Retired, 2 Mch 1889
Rousseau, Lovell H ..	28 Mch. 1867	...	....	....	Kentucky ..	4 Aug 1818	Louisiana .	8 Jan. 1869	Ky	

Names.	Brig.-gen.	Maj.-gen.	Lieut.-gen.	General.	Born, where and when.	Died, where and when.	App. from	Remarks.
Rucker, Daniel H.	13 Feb. 1882	....	....	....	New Jersey.....28 Apr. 1812	....	Mich.	Quartermaster-gen. Retired, 23 Feb. 1882.
Ruger, Thomas H.	19 Mch. 1886	8 Feb. 1895	....	....	New York.......2 Apr. 1833	....	Wis.	
Ruggles, George D.	6 Nov. 1893	....	....	....	New York......11 Sept. 1833	....	N. Y. m. acad.	Adjt.-gen.
Sacket, Delos B.	10 Jan. 1881	....	....	....	New York......14 Apr. 1822	Wash., D. C......8 Mch. 1885	N. Y. m. acad.	Inspector-gen.
St. Clair, Arthur.	....	4 Mch. 1791	....	....	Scotland.............. 1734	Pennsylvania...31 Aug. 1818	Pa.	Gen.-in-chief, 4 Mch. 1791, to 5 Mch. 1792. Resigned, 1792.
Schofield, John M.	30 Nov. 1864	4 Mch. 1869	6 Feb. 1895	....	New York......29 Sept. 1831	....	Ill. m. acad.	Gen.-in-chief, 6 Aug. 1888.
Scott, Win eld.	9 Mch. 1814	25 June, 1841	....	....	Virginia.......13 June, 1786	W. Point, N. Y..29 May, 1866	Va.	Gen.-in-chief, 1841–61. Rank of lieut.-gen. in brevet bestowed upon him, 1855.
Sevier, John.	19 July, 1798	....	....	....	Virginia.............. 1745	Georgia.........24 Sept. 1815	Tenn.	Provisional army. Disbanded, 15 June, 1800.
Sheridan, Philip H.	20 Sept. 1864	8 Nov. 1864	4 Mch. 1869	29 May, 1888	Albany, N. Y....6 Mch. 1831	Nonquitt, Mass...5 Aug. 1888	Ohio m. acad.	Gen.-in-chief, 1883–88. Special act of Congress restored the grade of general in his case.
Sherman, William T.	4 July, 1863	12 Aug. 1864	25 July, 1866	4 Mch. 1869	Ohio............8 Feb. 1820	New York......14 Feb. 1891	Ohio m. acad.	Gen.-in-chief, 1869–83.
Shiras, Alexander E.	23 June, 1874	....	....	....	Pennsylvania...10 Aug. 1812	Wash., D. C.....14 Apr. 1875	N. J. m. acad.	Commissary-gen.
Sickles, Daniel E.	....	14 Apr. 1869	....	....	New York city..20 Oct. 1823	....	N. Y.	Retired, 14 Apr. 1869.
Smith, Persifer F.	30 Dec. 1856	....	....	....	Pennsylvania......Nov. 1798	Kansas.........17 May, 1858	La.	
Smith, Thomas A.	24 Jan. 1814	....	....	....	....	 1818	Ga.	In reorganized army, 1815, retained as col. of rifle regiment.
Smith, William.	10 Mch. 1890	....	....	....	Vermont..............	....	Minn.	Paymaster-gen.
Stanley, David S.	24 Mch. 1884	....	....	....	Ohio............1 June, 1828	....	Ohio m. acad.	Retired, 1 June, 1892.
Stearnberg, George M.	3 June, 1893	....	....	....	New York......8 June, 1838	....	N. Y.	Surgeon-gen.
Sumner, Edwin V.	16 Mch. 1861	....	....	....	Massachusetts......Jan. 1796	New York......21 Mch. 1863	N. Y.	
Sutherland, Charles.	23 Dec. 1890	....	....	....	Pennsylvania.......... 1829	....	Pa.	Surgeon-gen. Retired, 29 May, 1893.
Swaim, David G.	18 Feb. 1881	....	....	....	Ohio..........22 July, 1834	....	Ohio.	Judge-adv.-gen. Court-mart., suspended 12 yrs., 1885. Reinstated 1 Dec., retired 22 Dec. 1894.
Swartwout, Robert.	21 Mch. 1813	....	....	....	New York............ 1778	New York......19 July, 1848	N. Y.	Quartermaster-gen. Service terminated, Apr. 1816.
Sweeney, Thomas W.	11 May, 1870	....	....	....	Ireland.........25 Dec. 1820	Astoria, N. Y....10 Apr. 1892	N. Y.	Retired, 11 May, 1870.
Taylor, Joseph P.	9 Feb. 1863	....	....	....	Kentucky.......4 May, 1796	Wash., D. C....29 June, 1864	Ky.	Commissary-gen.
Taylor, Zachary.	....	29 June, 1846	....	....	Virginia........24 Sept. 1784	Wash., D. C......9 July, 1850	Ky.	Resigned, 31 Jan. 1849. President of the U. S., 1849–50.
Terry, Alfred H.	15 Jan. 1865	3 Mch. 1886	....	....	Connecticut.....10 Nov. 1827	....	Conn.	Retired, 5 Apr. 1888.
Thomas, George H.	27 Oct. 1863	15 Dec. 1864	....	....	Virginia........31 July, 1816	California......28 Mch. 1870	Va. m. acad.	Commanded army of Cumberland from Oct. 1863.
Thomas, Lorenzo.	3 Aug. 1861	....	....	....	Delaware.......26 Oct. 1804	Wash., D. C......2 Mch. 1875	Del. m. acad.	Adjt.-gen. Retired, 22 Feb. 1869.
Totten, Joseph G.	3 Mch. 1863	....	....	....	Connecticut.....23 Aug. 1788	Wash., D. C.....22 Apr. 1864	Conn. m. acad.	Chief of engineers.
Townsend, Edward D.	22 Feb. 1869	....	....	....	Massachusetts..12 Aug. 1817	Wash., D. C....11 May, 1893	Mass. m. acad.	Adjt.-gen. Retired, 15 June, 1880.
Twiggs, David E.	30 June, 1846	....	....	....	Georgia............... 1790	Georgia.........15 Sept. 1862	Ga.	Dismissed the service, 1 Mch. 1861.
Washington, George.	....	....	3 July, 1798	....	Virginia........22 Feb. 1732	Virginia........14 Dec. 1799	Va.	First president of the U. S., 1789–97. Gen.-in-chief, 3 July, 1798, to 14 Dec. 1799. Although congress created the office of general of the armies of the U. S., 3 Mch. 1799, the commission was never issued. "Washington died in office under his lieut.-gen.'s commission, the proposed new appointment not being conferred upon him."—Am. St. Rep. Mil. Aff., vol. i. p. 147.
Washington, William A.	19 July, 1798	....	....	....	V ginia........28 Feb. 1752	South Carolina...6 Mch. 1810	S. C.	Provisional army. Disbanded, 15 June, 1800.
Wayne, Anthony.	....	5 Mch. 1792	....	....	Pcnnsylvania....1 Jan. 1745	Pennsylvania...15 Dec. 1796	Pa.	Gen.-in-chief, 1792–96. Defeats the Indians at Fallen Timbers, Ohio.
Wheaton, Frank.	16 Apr. 1892	....	....	....	Rhode Island....8 May, 1833	....	R. I.	
White, Anthony W.	11 July, 1798	....	....	....	Virginia.........7 July, 1750	New Jersey.....10 Feb. 1803	Va.	Provisional army. Disbanded, 15 June, 1800.
Wilkinson, James.	5 Mch. 1792	2 Mch. 1813	....	....	Maryland..............1757	City of Mexico..28 Dec. 1825	Md.	Gen.-in-chief, 1800–1812. Service terminated upon the reduction of the army, 1815.
Willcox, Orlando B.	13 Oct. 1886	....	....	....	Michigan.......16 Apr. 1823	....	Mich. m. acad.	Retired, 16 Apr. 1887.
Williams, David R.	9 July, 1813	....	....	....	South Carolina..10 Mch. 1776	South Carolina..15 Nov. 1830	S. C.	Resigned, 6 Apr. 1814.
Williams, Robert.	5 July, 1892	....	....	....	Virginia.........5 Nov. 1829	....	Va. m. acad.	Adjt.-gen. Retired, 5 Nov. 1893.
Winchester, James.	27 Mch. 1812	....	....	....	Maryland.......6 Feb. 1752	Tennessee......27 July, 1826	Tenn.	Resigned, 21 Mch. 1815.
Winder, William H.	12 Mch. 1813	....	....	....	Maryland.......18 Feb. 1775	Maryland......24 May, 1824	Md.	Service terminated upon the reduction of the army, 1815.
Wood, Thomas J.	3 Mch. 1875	....	....	....	Kentucky......25 Sept. 1823	....	Ky. m. acad.	Retired, 3 Mch. 1875.
Wool, John E.	25 June, 1841	16 May, 1862	....	....	New York......20 Feb. 1784	New York......10 Nov. 1869	N. Y.	Retired, 1 Aug. 1863.
Wright, Horatio G.	30 June, 1879	....	....	....	Connecticut.....6 Mch. 1820	....	Conn. m. acad.	Chief of engineers. Retired, 22 Mch. 1884.

NUMBER OF TROOPS EMPLOYED (REGULAR AND MILITIA) IN THE SERVICE OF THE UNITED STATES IN ITS SEVERAL WARS.

Name.	Length of war.	Number of troops employed.		Total.
		Regulars.	Militia.	
Revolution	19 Apr. 1775 to 11 Apr. 1783	231,462	58,869—proper. 105,332—conjectural. 164,201	395,663
Northwestern Indians	19 Sept. 1790 to 3 Aug. 1795	....	....	8,983
France	9 July, 1798 " 30 Sept. 1800	....	....	4,593
Tripoli	10 June, 1801 " 4 June, 1805	....	....	3,330
Creek Indian	27 July, 1813 " 9 Aug. 1814	600	13,181	13,781
England	18 June, 1812 " 17 Feb. 1815	85,000	471,622	556,622
Seminole	20 Nov. 1817 " 21 Oct. 1818	1,000	6,911	7,911
Black Hawk	21 Apr. 1831 " 31 Sept. 1832	1,339	5,126	6,465
Cherokee	1836 " 1837	935	12,483	13,418
Florida Indian	23 Dec. 1835 " 14 Aug. 1843	11,169	29,953	41,122
Aroostook disturbance	1838 " 1839	....	1,500	1,500
Mexican	24 Apr. 1846 " 4 July, 1848	30,954	73,776	104,730
Civil War	12 Apr. 1861 " 9 Apr. 1865	....	.....	2,772,408

GENERALS-IN-CHIEF OF THE ARMIES OF THE UNITED STATES UNDER THE CONSTITUTION.

Names.	Term of Service.	Rank.
Josiah Harmar	Sept. 1789 to Mch. 1791	Lt.-col.
Arthur St. Clair	4 Mch. 1791 " 5 Mch. 1792	Maj.-gen.
Anthony Wayne	5 Mch. 1792 " 15 Dec. 1796	"
James Wilkinson	15 Dec. 1796 " 3 July, 1798	Brig.-gen.
George Washington	3 July, 1798 " 14 Dec. 1799	Lt.-gen.
James Wilkinson	15 June, 1800 " 27 Jan. 1812	Brig.-gen.
Henry Dearborn	27 Jan. 1812 " 15 June, 1815	Maj.-gen.
Jacob Brown	15 June, 1815 " 24 Feb. 1828	"
Alexander Macomb	24 May, 1828 " 25 June, 1841	"
Winfield Scott	25 June, 1841 " 1 Nov. 1861	Maj.-gen. & brev. lt.-gen.
George B. McClellan	1 Nov. 1861 " 11 Mch. 1862	Maj.-gen.
Henry W. Halleck	11 July, 1862 " 12 Mch. 1864	"
Ulysses S. Grant	12 Mch. 1864 " 25 July, 1866	Lt.-gen.
"	25 July, 1866 " 4 Mch. 1869	General.
William T. Sherman	4 Mch. 1869 " 1 Nov. 1883	"
Philip H. Sheridan	1 Nov. 1883 " 5 Aug. 1888	Lt.-gen. & gen.
John M. Schofield	14 Aug. 1888	Maj.-gen.

Arnold, Benedict, treason of. UNITED STATES and NEW YORK, 1780.

aromatics. Acron of Agrigentum is said first to have made great fires and burned aromatics in them, to purify the air; thus stopping the plague at Athens, 429 B.C.

Aroo'stook disturbance. In 1837–39 the unsettled boundary between Maine and New Brunswick nearly led to active hostilities on the Aroostook river. Maine sent armed men to erect fortifications, and congress authorized the president to resist the encroachments of the British. Gen. Scott arranged a truce and joint occupation. The boundaries were finally adjusted by treaty, Aug. 9, 1842. ASHBURTON TREATY and U. S. RECORD, 1839.

Arpi'num, now **Arpi'no,** S. Italy. Originally a Volscian town; it passed into the hands of the Samnites, and thence under the dominion of Rome. Its inhabitants became Roman citizens in 302 B.C., and received the right of voting, 188 B.C. Here Caius Marius was born, about 157 B.C., and Cicero, 3 Jan. 106 B.C.

Arques (*Arc*), N. France. Near here the league army, commanded by the duc de Mayenne, was defeated by Henry IV., 21 Sept. 1589.

arraignment consists in reading the indictment and calling upon the prisoner to plead to it. In England, formerly, persons who refused to plead in cases of felony were pressed to death by weights on the breast. A person standing mute was declared convicted by an act passed 1772; but in 1827 the court was directed to enter a plea of "not guilty" in such cases. MUTE.

Arras, N. E. France, the country of the ancient Atrebates, the seat of a bishop since 390. Here a treaty was concluded between the king of France and duke of Burgundy, the latter abandoning his alliance with England, 21 Sept. 1435. By another treaty of Maximilian of Austria with Louis XI. of France, Burgundy and Artois were given to the dauphin as a marriage portion, 23 Dec. 1482.—*Velly.* Arras was held by the Austrians from 1493 till 1640, when it was taken by Louis XIII.

arrest for debt practically abolished in England, 1869. For the United States, DEBTORS.

Arsac'idæ, a Parthian dynasty, from Arsaces, about 250 B.C. to Artabanus, killed in battle with Artaxerxes, founder of the Sassanidæ, 226 A.D.

arsenal, a military or naval repository. The principal one in England is at WOOLWICH. Nearly every state in the United States has at least one arsenal or armory for its militia. New York has 14. The Rock Island arsenal, Ill., is the most completely equipped arsenal of the U. S. Most of the U. S. arsenals are designed for construction and repairs as well as supply; but not the state or city arsenals. The national arsenals are at:

Name.	Place.	Estab.
Allegheny	Pittsburg, Pa.	1814
Augusta	Augusta, Ga.	1826
Benicia	Benicia, Cal.	1851
Columbia	Columbia, Tenn.	1889
Frankford	Philadelphia, Pa.	1816
Indianapolis	Indianapolis, Ind.	1863
Kennebec	Augusta, Me.	1827
Monroe	Old Point Comfort, Va.	1838
New York	Governor's Island	1836
Rock Island	Rock Island, Ill.	1863
San Antonio	San Antonio, Tex.	1855
Watervliet	West Troy, N. Y.	1814
Watertown	Watertown, Mass.	1816

Arsenians, partisans of Arsenius, patriarch of Constantinople, who excommunicated the emperor Michael Palæologus for blinding his colleague, young John Lascaris, 1261, and was deposed 1264.

arsenic, a steel-gray colored brittle metal, used with lead in making small shot. The name is popularly applied to *arsenious acid*, a compound of the metal with oxygen, which is highly poisonous. It was known in early times, being mentioned by Theophrastus, a Greek philosopher, b. 382 B.C. Brandt, in 1733, made the first accurate experiments on its chemical nature. Arsenic acid, prepared from the white arsenic or arsenious acid of commerce, is largely used in making aniline dyes. Brilliant greens on wall-papers often contain this acid, but the popular notion that such colors can poison the air has no foundation.

arson, punished with death by the Saxons, remained a capital crime on the consolidation of the laws in 1827 and 1837. It is punishable in England by penal servitude for life and minor degrees of imprisonment. In some states the law remains as in England; others punish firing an inhabited house by imprisonment for life. There are various degrees of arson, with minor punishments for minor degrees.

Arsouf, Syria. At a battle here Richard I. of England, commanding the Christian forces, reduced to 30,000, defeated Saladin's army of 300,000 Saracens and other infidels, on 6 Sept. 1191. Ascalon surrendered and Richard marched towards Jerusalem, 1192.

Ar'temis, a Greek goddess; called by the Romans DIANA.—An asteroid, the 105th. It was discovered by J. C. Watson, 16 Sept. 1868.

Artemis'ium, a promontory in Eubœa, near which indecisive conflicts took place between the Greek and Persian fleets for three days, 480 B.C. The former retired on hearing of the battle of Thermopylæ.

artesian wells (from *Artesia*, now Artois, in France, where there are many) are formed by boring through upper soil to strata containing water which has percolated from a higher level, and which rises to that level through the boring-tube. The following are some of the deepest wells in the world:

EUROPE.

Location.	Depth.	Bored.	Remarks.
Passy, France	2000 ft.	1855-61	5,582,000 gals. daily; rises 54 ft.
La Chapelle, Paris	2950 "	1866-69	
Grenelle, "	1798 "	1833-41	Warm, 82° Fahr.; 743,040 gals. daily; rises 32 ft.
Neusalwerk, near Minden	2288 "	1858	
Kissingen, Bavaria	1878½ "	1850-78	1,077,000 gals. daily. Mineral; rises 58 ft.
Sperenberg, near Berlin	4194 "	....	Salt. Salt-bed reached at 280 ft. and not passed. The deepest well in the world.
Pesth, Hungary	3182 "	1868-79	Hot, 165° Fahr.

UNITED STATES.

Location.	Depth.	Bored.	Remarks.
St. Louis, Mo.	2197 ft.	1849-52	108,000 gals. daily. Salty.
" "	3843 "	1866-70	Does not rise to the surface. Salty.
Louisville, Ky.	2086 "	1856-57	330,000 gals. daily. Mineral.
Columbus, O.	2775¼ "	....	Water saline, 91° Fahr.; no force.
Continental Hotel, Phila.	206 "	....	72,000 gals. daily.
Charleston, S. C.	1250 "	1848	28,800 gals. daily. Saline.

South Dakota, sometimes called the "Artesian state," has many powerful artesian wells in the valley of the James river, from 800 to 1600 ft. deep, affording a bountiful supply of pure water. The water from great depths is always warmer than at the surface.

Arthur, king of Britain, said, mythically, to have lived 502–532 A.D.

The events of his life and the conflicts of the knights of his ROUND TABLE, as sung by the Welsh poets Taliesin, Llywarch Hên, and Aneurin, were incorporated into a Latin history by Geoffrey of Monmouth, about 1115, who died 1154; put into French verse by Geoffrey Gaisnar, and by Wace soon after; and into an English poem called Brut by Layamon....about 1205
Walter Map, by incorporating in his version the legend of the HOLY GRAIL, introduced the religious element ....about 1171
Sir Thomas Malory's "Morte d'Arthur," printed 1485
Lord Lytton's "King Arthur," pub. 1848
Tennyson's "Idyls of the King".........................1859-69

Arthur's, Chester A., administration. UNITED STATES, 1881.

artichokes are said to have been introduced from the East into western Europe in the 15th century, and to have reached England in the 16th.

articles of confederation for the American Colonies. CONFEDERATION, ARTICLES OF, and UNITED STATES, 1778.

articles of religion. On 8 June, 1536, after long disputes, the English clergy in convocation published "Articles decreed by the king's highness," Henry VIII., who in 1539, by the "Statute of Six Articles," proclaimed the acknowledgment of transubstantiation, communion in one kind, vows of chastity, private masses, celibacy of the clergy, and auricular confession. Offenders were punishable as heretics. In 1551 42 were prepared, and published in 1553. These were modified by the convocation, and reduced to 39 in Jan. 1563; which received the royal authority (queen Elizabeth's) and the authority of parliament in 1571. These articles may be classified thus: (1) articles i.-v., the doctrine of the Trinity; (2) vi.-viii., the rule of faith; (3) ix.-xviii., doctrines concerning sin, redemption, and their cognate notions; (4) xix.-xxxix., the general theory of the church and the doctrine of the sacraments. They also give prominence to the tenets which distinguish the church of England from that of Rome. The supremacy of the pope is denied in art. xxxvii.; the infallibility of the church of Rome and of the general councils, xix., xxi.; the enforced celibacy of the clergy, xxxii.; the denial of the cup to the laity, xxx.; transubstantiation, xxviii.; 5 out of 7 of the alleged 7 sacraments, xxv.; purgatory, relics, and the worship of images, xxii.; and works of supererogation, xiv. The *Lambeth Articles*, of a more Calvinistic character, proposed by archbishop Whitgift, were withdrawn because of the displeasure of queen Elizabeth, 1595. 104 articles were drawn up for Ireland by archbishop Usher in 1614; but in 1635 the Irish church adopted the English articles. PERTH ARTICLES. The 39 articles were excluded from the studies at Oxford in Nov. 1871.

articles of war were decreed by Richard I. and John. Those made by Richard II. in 1385 appear in "Grose's Military Antiquities." The British articles now in force are based upon an act, passed by William III. in 1689, to regulate the army about to engage in his continental warfare. In the United States, congress only can make articles of war. These have been based on the English articles and mutiny act. They were first adopted by the continental congress, July 30, 1775, and extended Mch. 20, 1776; enacted again, with little alteration, Apr. 10, 1806. Some additions were made from 1861–65, and in 1874 they were codified as section 1342 of the Revised Statutes of the U. S.

artificers and manufacturers. Their affairs were severely regulated by the statutes of laborers in England, 1349, 1350, 1360, 1549, and especially 1562. They were prohibited from leaving the country, and those abroad were outlawed if they did not return within 6 months after notice. A fine of 100*l.* and imprisonment for 3 months were penalties for seducing them from the realm, by 9 Geo. II. 1736, and other statutes. The law was modified in 1824.

artillery, a term once including all heavy military engines for projectiles now restricted to cannon. A small piece was contrived by Schwartz, a German cordelier, soon after the invention of gunpowder, in 1330. Artillery is said to have been used by the Moors of Algesiras, in Spain, in 1343; and at the battle of Crecy, in 1346, when Edward III. had 4 pieces of cannon. The English had artillery at the siege of Calais, 1347, and the Venetians against the Genoese at sea, 1377.—*Voltaire.* Said to have been cast, with mortars for bombshells, by Flemish artists, in Sussex, 1543.—*Rymer's* "Foedora." Made of brass, 1635; improvements by Browne, 1728. BOMBS, CANNON, CARRONADES (under CARRON), FIRE-ARMS, HOWITZERS, MORTARS, PETARD, ROCKETS. The royal artillery regiment was established in the reign of Anne.

Honorable Artillery Company of London, instituted in 1585, having ceased, was revived in 1610. It met for military exercise at the Artillery ground, Finsbury, where the London archers had met since 1498 (ARCHERY). In the civil war, 1642–48, the company sustained parliament with great effect. It numbered 1200 in 1803, and 800 in 1861. Since 1842 officers are appointed by the queen.
The Ancient and Honorable Artillery Company, of Boston, Mass., the oldest military organization in the U. S., organized 1638
Its printed series of annual sermons begins with the discourse of Urian Oakes 1672

Artois (*Ar-twa'*), N. France, a province once held by the Atrebates, conquered by the Franks in the 5th century, given by Charles the Bold, with Flanders, as a dowry to his daughter Judith, on her marriage with Baldwin Bras-de-fer in 863. Louis XV. created his grandson, Charles Philippe, count of Artois, who became king as Charles X., 16 Sept. 1824.

Reunited to the crown by Philip Augustus 1180
Formed into a county for his brother Robert, by Louis IX.... 1237
Acquired, with Flanders, through marriage, by the duke of Burgundy 1384
Passed, by marriage of Mary of Burgundy to Maximilian, to the house of Austria 1477
Restored to France 1482
Reverted to Austria.. 1493
Conquered for France 1640
Finally confirmed to it by the treaty of Nimeguen...10 Aug. 1678

arts. In the 8th century, the circle of sciences was composed of 7 liberal arts—the *trivium* (grammar, rhetoric, logic), the *quadrivium* (arithmetic, music, geometry, and astronomy) —*Harris* Aside from the arts of the races of Egypt and the East, the history of the manual arts of architecture, sculpture, and painting falls naturally into 4 periods (1) the Greek and Roman period, from about 700 B.C to 400 A D, (2) the Christian period, from 400 to 1260 in Italy, and about 1460 in northern Europe, (3) the Renaissance period, till about 1620, (4) the modern period —"Fine Arts," *Encyc Brit*, 9th ed

The Royal Society of England obtained its charter 2 Apr 1663
First public exhibition by the artists of the British metropolis took place at the rooms of the Society of Arts 1760
Repeated there for several years, till the Royal Academy was founded 1768
Society of British Artists was instituted 21 May, 1823
Their first exhibition opened 19 April, 1824
Art Union of London, 444 West Strand, was founded 14 Feb 1837, and chartered 1 Dec 1846 The Art Union Indemnity act was passed 3 Aug 1844
Arundel Society for the promotion of the knowledge of art, established in England 1848
Pre Raphaelites became prominent about 1850
Society for the Encouragement of the Fine Arts founded in Dec 1858
Art unions began in France and Germany early in the present century (First in Britain was established at Edinburgh)
Burlington Fine Arts Club, for exhibition of works of art, etc, founded 1868
A memorial of a convention for promoting reproductions of works of art for museums of all countries signed by prince of Wales crown princes of Prussia Russia, Denmark, Sweden, Italy, Saxony, and others, sent to the duke of Marlborough 12 Mch 1868
National Association for the advancement of art, first meeting in Liverpool (meets annually) 3-7 Dec 1888
Arts and Crafts Society, begun "
Society of Portrait Painters, founded 1891

In the United States

Pennsylvania Academy of Fine Arts, Phil, organized Dec 1805, incorporated 28 Mch 1806
[Two or more exhibitions held every year The oldest institution of its kind in the U S]
National Academy of Design, N Y, instituted 1826, incorporated 1828
[Academicians limited to 100, associates to 100]
Philadelphia School of Design for Women, founded 1847, incorporated 1853
[Object, instruction of women in decorative art]
Cooper Union N Y, for the advancement of science and art, founded by Peter Cooper 1857
[Aim, to afford instruction in the art of design to women]
American Water Color Society, N Y, organized 1868
Museum of Fine Arts, Boston, incorporated 1870
[Object, preservation and exhibition of works of art]
Metropolitan Museum of Art, N Y, chartered 13 Apr "
[To encourage the study of the fine arts]
Corcoran's Gallery of Art Washington, D C, chartered 24 May, 1870, opened 1874
[With an endowment of $900 000]
Pennsylvania Museum and School of Industrial Art, Phil, incorporated 26 Feb 1876
[Similar in plan to the South Kensington museum and school in LONDON, Eng]
Society of American Artists, N Y, organized 1878
[Object, the advancement of the fine arts]
Art Institute of Chicago, organized 24 May, 1879
Cincinnati Museum Association, incorporated 15 Feb 1881
[General plan similar to that of SOUTH KENSINGTON Eng]
American Art Union, N Y, incorporated 11 May, 1883
[Object, to promote interest in the fine arts by establishing galleries for the exhibition and sale of works of art, holding art exhibitions in different parts of the country, publishing engravings and other artistic works, and an art journal, establishing an artists benevolent fund, and promoting social intercourse among members]
National Academy of Art, established in the District of Columbia by an act of the 52d congress 1892

ACADEMIES, ARCHITECTURE, NATIONAL GALLERY, PAINTING, ROYAL ACADEMY, SCULPTURE, etc

Arundel Castle, Sussex, built by the Saxons about 800 The duke of Norfolk enjoys the earldom of Arundel, as a feudal honor, by inheritance and possession of the castle, without other creation Philip Howard, son of the attainted duke of Norfolk, was made earl of Arundel, by summons, as possessor of this castle, 1580 It was thoroughly repaired by a late duke

Arundelian Marbles, one containing the chronology of ancient history from 1582 to 355 B.C., and said to have been sculptured 264 B C They consist of 37 statues, 128 busts, and 250 inscriptions, found in the isle of PAROS about 1610. They were collected by W. Petty, purchased by lord Arundel, and given by his grandson, Henry Howard, afterwards duke of Norfolk, to the university of Oxford in 1667, and are therefore called also Oxford Marbles The inscriptions are Greek A variorum edition of the inscriptions, by Maittaire, appeared, 1732, a fine one by Chandler, 1763, and translations by Selden, 1628, by Prideaux, 1676

Ar'yan, in Sanscrit signifying (1) a tribe or nation, (2) noble A family of nations sometimes inaccurately called *Japhetic*, more commonly Indo-European or Indo-Germanic "The ancestors of most modern Europeans lived together as one people, speaking the primeval Aryan tongue, in central Asia and apparently near the Pamir steppe Their separation took place at so remote a period that while they seem to have known gold, silver, and copper, they were unacquainted with iron"—*Max Muller*, "Science of Language," vol ii. p 258 The Aryan race invaded India in remote antiquity, possibly 1700 B C, and still remain the dominant race there. The Aryan stock not Asiatic but European This view is supported by canon Isaac Taylor, A H Sayce, by the Germans, O Schrader, Karl Penka, Posche, Geiger, and in France by M de Lapouge "The conclusion may be accepted that the Aryan people originated in western Europe and migrated eastward"—*Brinton's* "Races and Peoples," p 147. LANGUAGE

as, a Roman weight, a pound, also a coin of varying weight. Originally about 400 B C, it was nominally 12 ounces of copper, but gradually fell to 2 ounces, and at last, in 80 B.C, to ½ ounce, worth about 1½ cents.

Asaph, St., N Wales, a bishopric said to have been founded by Kentigern, bishop of Glasgow. On returning into Scotland, about 560, he left St. Asaph his successor, from whom the see is named It is valued in the king's books at 187*l* 11*s* 6*d*. The present cathedral was erected by bishop Redman, 1472-95 By an order in council, 1838, the sees of St. Asaph and Bangor were to be united on the next vacancy in either, and the bishopric of Manchester created. This order was annulled in 1846 Present income 4200*l* MANCHESTER. The cathedral, restored by sir Gilbert Scott, reopened 2 Sept 1875.

asbestos, a native fossil stone regarded as a variety of hornblende, which may be split into threads and filaments, and is unconsumed by fire Cloth was made of it by the Egyptians (*Herodotus*), and napkins in the time of Pliny, 74 A D., and also paper The spinning of asbestos known at Venice about 1500. —*Porta* The finest asbestos was discovered in Canada in 1874, but it is found in all parts of the globe It is mined in Virginia, North and South Carolina, Maryland, Delaware, and Staten Island in N Y It is steadily increasing in usefulness.

As'calon, Syria, a city of the Philistines, shared the fate of Phœnicia and Judea The Egyptian army was defeated here by the crusaders under Godfrey of Bouillon, 12 Aug 1099 Ascalon was besieged by the latter in 1148, taken in 1153, and again in 1191 Its fortifications were destroyed for fear of the crusaders by the sultan, 1270

Ascension, an island in the Atlantic ocean, 800 miles northwest of St Helena, discovered by the Portuguese on Ascension day, 20 May, 1501, and seized by the English, Oct. 1815.

Ascension Day or **Holy Thursday,** when the church celebrates the ascension of Jesus, the fortieth day after his resurrection, 14 May, 33, first commemorated, it is said, 68

Aschaffenburg, on the Maine, Bavaria, S W. Germany Here, on 14 July, 1866, the Prussians defeated the German Federal army, captured the town, and took 2000 prisoners.

As'culum, now **As'coli,** Apulia, S. Italy Near it Pyrrhus of Epirus defeated the Romans, 279 B.C. Asculum, a city of the Piceni, with all their country, was conquered by the consul Sempronius, 268 B.C. Here Andrea, general of the emperor Henry VI, endeavoring to wrest Naples from Tancred, was defeated and slain, 1190 A D.

Ashan'tees, a warlike negro people inhabiting the country above the Gold Coast, W. Africa. Trouble arising between the English of the Gold Coast and the Ashantees, sir Garnet Wolseley, sent by the English government with troops into their country, 4 Oct 1873, took and destroyed their chief town, Coomassie, 6 Feb. 1874 Treaty of peace—terms. perpetual peace, indemnity of 50,000 oz of gold, supremacy over other tribes renounced, free trade guaranteed, and human

:rifices prohibited—signed, 13 Feb. 1874. Expedition cost ,500,000.

Ashburton Treaty, so called from lord Ashburton lexander Baring, head of the house of Baring brothers), nmissioner for Great Britain, who with Daniel Webster, :retary of state under president Tyler, framed the treaty; :ned at Washington, 9 Aug. 1842; ratified, 20th same mouth; d proclaimed 10 Nov. Besides providing for the extradition criminals, etc., it settled the boundary line between Canada d Maine. AROOSTOOK.

Ashdod or **Azo'tus,** seat of the worship of the Phœ-:ian god Dagon, which fell before the ark of the Lord, capt-:d by the Philistines from the Israelites, about 1141 B.C. (1 m. v.). Ashdod was taken by the Egyptians after 29 years' ge, the longest recorded.

Ashdown or **Assendune,** now thought to be As-ı, Berks, where Ethelred and his brother Alfred defeated the ınes in 871. At Ashdown, near Saffron-Walden, Essex, Ca-te defeated Edmund Ironside with great slaughter, 1016.

ıdition says that the day after the battle in 871 Alfred caused his ırmy to carve the figure of a white horse, the standard of Hengist,)y cutting out the sod from the face of the chalk rocks, at the side of the valley. Thomas Hughes ("Tom Brown"), in his book, 'The Scouring of the White Horse" (1859), describes the work ınd festival on 17 and 18 Sept. 1857, a ceremony performed at in-ervals from time immemorial. Records are found of the "scour-ng" 27 May, 1755; 15 May, 1776; 1780, 1785, 1803, 1812 or 1813, .9, 20 Sept., 1825; Sept. 1843.

Ashmolean Museum (books, manuscripts, coins, :.), presented to the university of Oxford by Elias Ashmole, rald and antiquary, was opened 1682. It included the col-:tions of the Tradescants, to whom he was executor. He :d at Lambeth in 1692. The Ashmolean Society, Oxford :ientific), was established in 1828.

Ash'taroth, a Phœnician goddess, occasionally wor-ipped by the Israelites (see Judg. ii. 13), about 1406 B.C.; Solomon, about 984 B.C. (1 Kings, xi. 5).

Ash-Wednesday, the first day of Lent, which in rly times began on the Sunday now called the first in Lent. is said that pope Felix III., in 487, added the four days pre-ling the old Lent Sunday to make number of fasting days ; that Gregory the Great (pope, 590) introduced the sprink-g of ashes on the first additional day, and hence the name *ies Cinerum,* or Ash-Wednesday. The Reformers rejected is practice "as being a mere shadow, or vain show."

Asia, the largest division of the globe, so called by the :eeks from the nymph Asia, daughter of Oceanus and Tethys, d wife of Japhet. Asia was the first quarter of the world opled—here the law of God was first promulgated; here any of the greatest monarchies had their rise; and hence ost of the arts and sciences have been derived. Its early story is found in the Bible and in Herodotus, who relates e wars of Crœsus, Cyrus, and others. Its enormous area 7,300,000 sq. miles), nearly five times that of Europe, is third of the land of the earth's surface. It is 5300 miles om the southern point of the Malay peninsula to the most rthern cape, and from the isthmus of Suez to the East cape is 6700 miles. Two great progressive European powers, ıssia and Great Britain, now hold sway over more than two ths of Asia, and the principal political changes in Asia for :o centuries have had their origin in the steady growth of ese powers. The British have extended their empire tow-ds Burmah and inner China, and northwestward to Afghan-:an. The Russians have passed southward through the ıucasus and have occupied the region about Mero and Sa-arcand. A belt of about 200 miles separates these two Eu-pean powers from each other. AFGHANISTAN, CHINA, INDIA, :ws, PERSIA, SIBERIA, TURKEY, etc.

Asia Minor, now **Anato'lia,** comprised the Ionian lonies on the coast, the early seats of Greek civilization, and :e countries of Cappadocia, Caria, Bithynia, Galatia, Lycia, ydia, Mysia, and Phrygia, with the cities of Ephesus, Smyr-ı, and Troy. From the rise of the Assyrian monarchy, about 900 B.C., to that of the Turks under Osman, Asia Minor might : called the battle-field of the East.

	B.C.
rst settlement of the Ionian Greeks....about	1043
sia Minor subdued by the Medes.... "	711
Conquered by Cyrus....about	546
Contest between the Greeks and Persians....begins	544
Asia Minor conquered by Alexander....	332
Contended for by his successors; separate kingdoms established,	321-278
	A.D.
Gradually acquired by the Romans....188 B.C. to	15
Possessed by the Persians....	609
Partially recovered by the emperor Basil....	874
Invaded by Timour....	1402
Taken from the Greek emperor by the Turks under Mahomet I.,	1413

TURKEY.

Asiatic societies. The Asiatic Society of Bengal, at Calcutta, was established by sir William Jones in 1784, the bounds of its investigation to be the geographical limits of Asia. The Royal Asiatic Society, which has several branches in India, was founded in 1823. It established the Oriental Translation Fund in 1828, which had published 83 volumes of Eastern literature in 1865; the Literary Society of Madras, 1845.

Asmonæans, the proper name of the family termed MACCABEES.

Asperne, Great, a town, and Essling, a village near the Danube and Vienna, the scene of desperate conflicts be-tween the Austrians under the archduke Charles and the French under Napoleon, Massena, etc., on 21-22 May, 1809, ending in the retreat of Napoleon. The Austrian loss exceeded 20,000 men, and the French 30,000. Marshal Lannes mortally wounded, 22 May; died, 31 May. The bridge of the Danube was destroyed, and Napoleon's retreat endangered; but the success of the Austrians was fruitless.

asphalt, a solid bituminous substance, probably derived from decayed vegetable matter; used as building material in ancient Babylon. Its application for this purpose was revived by Eyrini d'Eyrinis, a Swiss physician of Greek origin, who discovered beds of it near Neufchatel in 1712. Asphalt stone was found at Seyssel, near Geneva, in 1802; and, after several failures, count Sassenay brought it into use for pavement about 1832. The artificial asphalt from gas-works began to be used as pavement about 1838. Claridge's patent asphalt was laid down in Trafalgar square, Jan. 1864. Various kinds of asphalt pavement have been since laid in London and New York. The most celebrated deposit of natural bitumen is on the island of TRINIDAD, whence the United States obtains its chief supply. Extensively used in paving cities throughout the U. S.

Aspromon'te, Naples. Here Garibaldi was defeated, wounded, and taken prisoner, 29 Aug. 1862, having risen against the French occupation of Rome.

As'sam', N. E. India, acquired by the British in 1825, and surrendered by the king of Ava in 1826. The tea-plant was discovered here by Mr. Bruce in 1823. A superintendent of tea-forests was appointed in 1836, cultivation of tea having been recommended by lord William Bentinck in 1834. The Assam tea company, which imported Chinese laborers and coolies, was established in 1839. In later years the planta-tions declined through over-speculation and neglect of the la-borers; as a remedy, a labor act was passed at Calcutta about July, 1867.

assassins or **assassinians,** fanatical Mahometans, following Hassan-ben-Sabah, settled in Persia about 1090. In Syria they possessed a large tract of land among the moun-tains of Lebanon. They murdered the marquess of Montfer-rat in 1192, Lewis of Bavaria in 1213, and the khan of Tar-tary in 1254. They were extirpated in Persia about 1258 and in Syria about 1272. The chief of the corps was named "An-cient of the Mountain" and "Old Man of the Mountain." They trained up young people to assassinate persons designated by their chief.—*Hénault.* From them came the word *assassin.*

REMARKABLE ASSASSINATIONS AND ATTEMPTS, ARRANGED BY DATES.

	B.C.
Artaxerxes III. of Persia, by Bagoas....about	338
Philip II. of Macedon, by Pausanias....	336
Darius III. of Persia, by Bessus....July,	330
Julius Cæsar, by Brutus and others....15 Mch.	44
	A.D.
Edmund the Elder of England....26 Mch.	946
Edward the Martyr of England....18 "	979
Thomas à Becket, archbishop of Canterbury....29 Dec.	1170
Albert I., emperor of Germany, by his nephew John...1 May,	1308
Edward II. of England....27 Sept.	1327

Louis Valois, duke of Orleans, by Burgundians 23 Nov 1407
John the Fearless duke of Burgundy, by Orleanists 10 Sept 1419
James I of Scotland, by nobles 21 Feb 1437
Edward V of England, by order of Richard, duke of Gloucester, July, 1483
James III of Scotland, by nobles 11 June 1488
David Beaton cardinal by Reformers 29 May, 1546
James Murray, earl regent of Scotland, by Hamilton of Bothwellhaugh at Linlithgow 21 Jan 1570
William, prince of Orange, by Balthasar Gerard (TORTURE) 10 July, 1584
Henry, duke of Guise by order of Henry III of France 23 Dec 1588
Louis of Guise, cardinal of Lorraine, by order of Henry III of France 24 Dec "
Henry III of France, by Jacques Clément 2 Aug 1589
Henry IV of France, attempt by Jean Châtel 27 Dec 1594
" " " " killed by Ravaillac (TORTURE) 14 May 1610
George Villiers duke of Buckingham, by John Felton 28 Aug 1628
William III of England, *plot* to assassinate 14 Feb 1696
Louis XV of France, *attempt*, by Damiens (TORTURE) 5 Jan 1757
Gustavus III of Sweden, Ankarström 16 Mch , d 29 Mch 1792
Marat, by Charlotte Corday 13 July, 1793
George III of England, *mad attempt* by Margaret Nicholson, 2 Aug 1786, again, by James Hatfield 15 May, 1800
Napoleon I, *attempt* by an infernal machine 24 Dec. "
Paul, czar of Russia, by nobles 24 Mch 1801
Spencer Perceval premier of England, by Bellingham 11 May, 1812
George IV (when regent) *attempt* 28 Jan 1817
August Kotzebue German dramatist, for political motives, by Karl Sand 23 Mch. 1819
Charles, duc de Berri (father of the comte de Chambord), 13 Feb 1820
Capo d Istria, count, Greek statesman (TORTURE) 9 Oct 1831
Andrew Jackson president U S, *attempt*. 30 Jan 1835
Louis Philippe of France, many *attempts* by Fieschi, 28 July, 1835, by Alibaud, 25 June, 1836, by Meunier, 27 Dec 1836, by Darmes, 15 Oct 1840, by Lecomte 14 Apr 1846, by Henry, 29 July, 1846
Denis Affre, archbishop of Paris 27 June, 1848
Rossi conte Pellegrino, Roman statesman 15 Nov "
Frederick William IV of Prussia, *attempt*, by Sefelage 22 May, 1850
Francis Joseph of Austria *attempt*, by Libenyi 18 Feb 1853
Ferdinand Charles III, duke of Parma 27 Mch 1854
Isabella II of Spain, *attempts*, by La Riva, 4 May, 1847, by Merino, 2 Feb 1852, by Raymond Fuentes 28 May, 1856
Napoleon III, *attempts* by Pianori 28 Apr 1855, by Bellemarre 8 Sept 1855, by Orsini and others (FRANCE) 14 Jan 1858
Daniel, prince of Montenegro 13 Aug 1860
Abraham Lincoln, president of the U S, at Ford s theatre Washington, by John Wilkes Booth, on the evening of 14 Apr d 15 Apr 1865
Michael, prince of Servia 10 June, 1868
Prim, marshal of Spain, 28 Dec , d 30 Dec. 1870
Georges Darboy, archbishop of Paris, by communists 24 May, 1871
Richard, earl of Mayo gov gen of India, by Shere Ali, a convict, in Andaman islands 8 Feb. 1872
Amadeus, duke of Aosta, when king of Spain, *attempt* 19 July, "
Bismarck, prince, *attempt*, by Blind, 7 May, 1866, by Kullman, 13 July, 1874
Abdul Aziz, sultan of Turkey 4 June, 1876
Hussein Avni and other Turkish ministers, by Hassan a Circassian officer 15 June, "
William I of Prussia and Germany, *attempts*, by Oscar Becker, 14 July, 1861, by Hödel, 11 May, 1878, by Dr Nobiling 2 June, 1878
Mehemet Ali, pacha, by Albanians 7 Sept "
Humbert I, king of Italy, *attempt* by John Passanante 17 Nov "
Lytton, lord, viceroy of India, *attempt*, by Busa. 12 Dec. "
Alfonso XII of Spain, *attempts*, by J O Moncasi, 25 Oct 1878, by Francisco Otero Gonzalez 30 Dec 1879
Loris Melikoff, Russian gen *attempt* 4 Mch 1880
Bratiano, premier of Roumania, *attempt*, by J Pietraro 14 Dec "
Alexander II of Russia, *attempts*, by Karakozow at St Petersburg 16 Apr 1866, by Berezowski at Paris 6 June, 1867, by Alexander Solovieff, 14 Apr 1879, by undermining a railway train 1 Dec. 1879, by explosion of Winter palace St Petersburg 17 Feb. 1880, killed by explosion of a bomb thrown by a man who is himself killed, St. Petersburg 2 p m 13 Mch 1881
Garfield, James A, president of the U S, shot by Charles Jules Guiteau, Washington, 2 July, 1881, d from his wounds, 19 Sept. 1881, Guiteau convicted of murder in the first degree, 26 Jan 1882, sentenced 2 Feb, hanged on 30 June, 1882
Marie François Sadi Carnot, president of France, stabbed mortally at Lyons by Cesare Santo, an anarchist, Sunday, 24 June, 1894

assay of gold and silver originated with the bishop of Salisbury, a royal treasurer in the reign of Henry I.—*Du Cange* But some kind of assay was practised as early as the Roman conquest Assay, early established in England, was regulated by statutes, 1238, 1700, and 1705 The alloy of gold is silver and copper, that of silver is copper British standard gold is 2 carats of alloy to 22 of fine gold Standard silver is 18 dwts of copper to 11 oz 2 dwts of fine silver PYX. The U S assay office, New York city, receives from $20,000,000 to $100,000,000 in crude bullion of gold and silver to be assayed every year. There are also offices at Boise City, Idaho, Helena, Mont.; and St Louis Mo. COINAGE.

Assaye (*as-sā'*), E Indies The British army, under gen. Arthur Wellesley (afterwards duke of Wellington), entered the Mahratta states on the south, took the fort of Ahmednuggur, 12 Aug, and defeated Scindiah and the rajah of Berar at Assaye, 23 Sept 1803 This was Wellesley's first great battle, with only 4500 men against 50,000 The enemy fled, leaving artillery, etc

assessed taxes. By some the date is referred to Ethelbert, in 991, to Henry VIII 1522, and to William III 1689, when a land-tax was imposed in England LAND-TAX, TAXES

assien'to, a contract of the king of Spain with other powers to supply negro slaves to Spanish America, began with the Flemings By treaty of Utrecht, 13 July 1713, Great Britain engaged to furnish 4800 negroes annually for 30 years The contract was renewed in 1748, but given up in 1750. GUINEA.

assignats (*as-seen-yah'*), a forced paper currency, first issued by the revolutionary assembly of France, Apr 1790 At one period 8 000,000,000 francs, or nearly $1 600,000,000 of this paper were in circulation.—*Alison.* Assignats were superseded by mandats in 1796

Assin'iboines. INDIANS

assize courts (from *assideo*, I sit), ancient in England, in old law-books defined as an assembly of knights and other substantial men, with the justice, to meet at a certain time and place regulated by Magna Charta, 1215 The present justices of assize and *nisi prius* are derived from the statute of Westminster, 13 Edw I 1284 —*Coke, Blackstone* "The king doth will that no lord, or other of the country, shall sit upon the bench with the justices to take assize in their sessions in the counties of England, upon great forfeiture to the king" 20 Rich II 1396 —*Statutes, Brough act* Assizes are general or special, general when the judges go their circuits, and special when a commission is issued for one or more causes. BLOODY ASSIZES

assize of Jerusalem, a code of laws compiled under Godfrey of Bouillon, king of Jerusalem, in 1100

associations. BRITISH NATIONAL ASSOCIATIONS, CHRISTIAN SOCIETIES, etc.

Assumption, Feast of the, 15 Aug, observed by the church of Rome in honor of the Virgin Mary, said to have been taken up to heaven, body and spirit, on this day, 45 A D, in her 75th year It was instituted in the 7th century, and enjoined by the council of Mentz, 813

Assyria, originally **Assur,** an Asiatic country between Mesopotamia and Media, the seat of the earliest recorded monarchy Till recently its history was mainly derived from Greek historians, Ctesias, Herodotus, and Diodorus Siculus, Berosus, a Græco-Chaldean priest, and the Holy Scriptures The discovery by sir Austin Layard of the Ninevite antiquities, now in the British museum, and the deciphering of cuneiform inscriptions by Grotefend, sir H Rawlinson, and other scholars, have thrown much light upon Assyrian history The chronologers, Blair, Usher, Hales, and Clinton, differ much in the dates The results of recent investigations are given in the rev G Rawlinson's "Five Great Monarchies of the Ancient World," prof A. H Sayce's "Assyria its Princes, Priests, and People," 1885, and W Boscawen's article "Assyria," in "Chambers's Encyclopædia," 1888.

B C.
Nimrod or Belus reigns [2554 *H* 2235 *C*] 2245
"Asshur builded Nineveh" (Gen x 11) about 2218
Ninus son of Belus, reigns in Assyria, and names his capital Nineveh [2182 *C*] 2069
Babylon taken by Ninus, who, having subdued the Armenians, Persians, Bactrians, and all Asia Minor, establishes the Assyrian monarchy, with Nineveh as seat of empire —*Blair* [2233 *C*] 2059
Ninyas, an infant, succeeds Ninus 2017
Semiramis, mother of Ninyas, usurps the government, enlarges and embellishes Babylon [2130 *C*] 2007
She invades Libya, Ethiopia, and India.—*Lenglet* 1975
She is put to death by her son Ninyas 1965
Ninyas put to death, and Arius reigns 1927
Reign of Aralius 1897
Belochus, the last king of the race of Ninus 1446
He makes his daughter Atossa, surnamed Semiramis II, his associate on the throne 1433
Atossa procures the death of her father, and marries Belatores (or Belaperes), who reigns 1421

Sardanapalus, luxurious and effeminate when attacked by Arbaces, satrap of Media, suddenly becomes energetic and warlike, defends Nineveh for 2 years; when overcome, burns himself in his palace, with his wives and treasures, ending the first Assyrian empire.—*Ctesias*........ 876

[All given above is mythical. The following is based upon the records in the ancient Assyrian tablets and the Bible.]

Assyria, a province of Babylonia, becomes independent; first king, Bel-kapkapi; under his successors the kingdom is greatly enlarged; Rimmon-nirari I. becomes powerful about 1320

His son, Shalmaneser I., founds Calah, and his grandson, Tiglath Adar I., captures Babylon........ 1280

His descendant, Tiglath-pileser I., a great conqueror and the real founder of the Assyrian empire........ 1140

His son, Assur-bel-Kala, a weak prince........ 1110

Empire falls into decay for nearly 2 centuries.

Empire revives under Assur-dân II., and is fully restored by his successors, Rimmon-nirari II........911-889

And Assur-natsir-pal........883-888

His son, Shalmaneser II., makes large conquests in W. Asia 858 et seq.

At Karkar he defeats Benhadad, king of Damascus, Ahab, king of Israel, and Irkhuleni, king of Hamath........ 854

Empire enlarged by his son, Samas-Rimmon II........823-810

Assyrian eponym canon records a solar eclipse, and is thereby the basis of Assyrian chronology........ 763

Assur-nirari king; many revolts........753 et seq.

Pulu, or Pul, usurps the throne and styles himself Tiglath-Pileser. He consolidated the empire, reformed government, quelled revolts, and enlarged his dominions by conquest of Babylon, etc........745-727

His weak son, Shalmaneser IV., king, 727; died or was murdered by Sargon the Tartan, who continues the war in Assyria, captures Samaria, and replaces the inhabitants by colonists (2 Kings xvii.)........ 720

At the battle of Raphia he checks the advances of Egypt, and captures the rich Hittite capital, Carchemish........ 717

Merodach-baladan III. raises a revolt against Sargon, who, after a severe campaign, captures Babylon and is proclaimed king 710

Sargon is killed in his new palace........July, 705

His son Sennacherib, succeeds him.

Babylonia revolts; Merodach-baladan returns, but is defeated at Kisu; Sennacherib conquers Phœnicia, and, offended by Hezekiah, ravages Judæa and besieges Jerusalem, which is saved by the sudden destruction of his army (Isa. xxxvii. 36-38); he is killed by his sons........Dec. 681

His son Esar-haddon defeats his brothers, reigns at Nineveh, and reorganizes the empire........680 et seq.

He invades Judæa, makes Manasseh prisoner.

He invades Egypt, captures Memphis, and after a long campaign subdues and becomes ruler of nearly all the ancient world........675 et seq.

Disturbed by a rising in Egypt and conspiracies at home, he makes his son Assur-bani-pal king at Nineveh, Apr. 669, and dies during a campaign, Oct. 667. Assur-bani-pal, weak but ambitious, continues war in Egypt, captures Thebes, invades Phœnicia, and takes Tyre.

He appoints his brother, Samas-sum-yukin, viceroy of Babylon, who heads a revolt, which lasts five years; Babylon is taken, and the rebel burns himself in his palace with many followers........ 647

Gradual fall of the empire; new revolts; Egypt independent; Kandanalu, viceroy of Babylon, and his successor, father of Nebuchadnezzar, independent; Assur-bani-pal succeeded by his son Assur-etil-iliyukinni........ 640

Essar-haddon II. (the Sarakos of Ctesias) the last king; the N.E. provinces invaded by a vast confederation under the command of Kazaril (Cyaxares the Mede).

Disruption and anarchy closed by siege and destruction of Nineveh........about 606

Assyria becomes a Median province.

Assyria subdued by Alexander the Great........ 332

Afterwards part of the kingdoms of Syria, Parthia, and Persia. A.D.

Conquered by the Turks........ 1637

Explored by col. Chesney and the Euphrates exploring expedition........1835-37

Layard's "Discoveries," publ........1848-53

Mr. George Smith, of British Museum, began to study inscriptions, 1866 (received aid from *Daily Telegraph*), and started to explore Assyrian remains, 20 June, 1873; worked in 1873-74; publ. "Assyrian Discoveries"........Mch. 1875

Classes for the study of Assyrian language formed; A. H. Sayce publishes Assyrian grammar........ "

Smith started to renew explorations, Oct. 1875; died at Aleppo, 19 Aug. 1876

Explorations resumed by Hormusd Rassam. NINEVEH.

asteroids. PLANETS.

Astor Library, New York. John Jacob Astor (b. at Waldorf, near Heidelberg, 17 July, 1763; d. in New York, 29 Mch. 1848) left by will $400,000 to establish "a public library in the city of New York." It was opened 9 Jan. 1854, with about 80,000 volumes. In Jan. 1856, William B. Astor, son of the founder, gave land to double the building. In 1879 John Jacob Astor (the second) gave land and an additional building; also built a central vestibule, frescoed, and ornamented with 24 classic busts in marble. The cost of these improvements was about $250,000. The number of books in the library is 300,000, very few of them duplicates, while fiction, except of the highest order, is excluded. The library is rich in books of value to scholars, and it is maintained as a scholar's, not a popular, library.

AST

Astor-place riots, made by friends of Edwin Forrest to interrupt Mr. Macready's acting at the Astor-place Opera-house in New York, 10 May, 1849. NEW YORK.

Astorga, N.W. Spain, the ancient Asturica Augusta, was taken by the French, 22 Apr. 1810, and treated with great severity.

Astoria, Oregon, at the mouth of the Columbia river, founded in 1810 by John Jacob Astor as a station for his fur trade. It is the subject of a picturesque descriptive work, entitled "Astoria," by Washington Irving, 1836. Irving never visited the station, but wrote from documents furnished by Astor, and from recollections of another northwestern fur-trading post. OREGON.

Astracan, S.E. Russia, a province acquired from the Mogul's empire in 1554; visited and settled by Peter the Great in 1722.

astrolabe, an instrument for observing stars, said to have been employed by Hipparchus about 130 B.C., and by Ptolemy about 140 A.D. The modern astrolabe was described by Fabricius in 1513.

astrology. Judicial astrology was cultivated by the Chaldæans, and transmitted to the Egyptians, Greeks, and Romans. It was much in vogue in Italy and France in the time of Catherine de' Medicis (married to Francis I. of France, 1533).—*Hénault*. It is said that Bede, 673-735, was addicted to it; and Roger Bacon, 1214-92. Lord Burleigh is said to have calculated the nativity of Elizabeth, who, like other contemporary princes, was a dupe of Dee the astrologer. At the birth of Louis XIV. of France (1638) a certain Morin de Villefranche was placed behind a curtain to cast the nativity of the future king. It is said that Lilly was consulted by Charles I. of England respecting his projected escape from Carisbrook castle in 1647.—*Ferguson*. In England Swift may be said to have given the death-blow to astrology by his famous squib entitled "Predictions for the Year 1708," by Isaac Bickerstaff, Esq. Astrological almanacs still published in London, 1892.

astronomer-royal. GREENWICH.

astronomy. The earliest astronomical observations were made at Babylon, it is said, about 2234 B.C. The study was much advanced in Chaldæa under Nabonassar; was known to the Chinese about 1100 B.C.; some say many centuries before. COMETS, ECLIPSES, MOON, OBSERVATORIES, PLANETS, STARS, SUN, TELESCOPES.

B.C.

Lunar eclipses observed at Babylon, and recorded by Ptolemy, about 720

Spherical form of the earth, and the true cause of lunar eclipses, taught by Thales........about 600

Anaximander erects the first sun-dial at Sparta........ 545

Phamenides of Elea said to have discovered the identity of morning and evening star........520-460

Further discoveries by Pythagoras, who taught the doctrine of celestial motions, and believed in the plurality of habitable worlds; died........about 470

Diogenes of Apollonia states that the inclination of the earth's axis causes the seasons........ 450

Meton erects the first sun-dial at Athens........ 433

Meton introduces the luni-solar cycle of 19 years........ 432

Eudoxus introduces into Greece the year of 365¼ days........ 370

Treatises of Aristotle "concerning the heavens," and of Autolycus "on the motions of the sphere" (earliest extant works on astronomy)........about 350

Aratus writes a poem on astronomy........ 281

Archimedes observes solstices, etc........ 212

Hipparchus, the "Newton of Greece," determines mean motion of sun and moon; discovers precession of equinoxes, etc...160-125

The precession of the equinoxes confirmed, and the places and distances of the planets discovered, by Ptolemy........139-161 A.D.

Omar Khayyám, a Persian astronomer, proposed to reform the calendar by interpolating 1 day every 4th year, postponing to the 33d year the interpolation belonging to the 32d year. This would have produced an error of only 1 day in 5000 years; the error of the Gregorian calendar is 1 day in 3325 years........ 1052

Astronomy and geography cultivated by the Arabs about 760; brought into Europe........about 1200

ALPHONSINE TABLES composed........about 1253

Clocks first used in astronomy........about 1500

True doctrine of the solar system revived by Copernicus, founder of modern astronomy; his "Revolution of the Heavenly Bodies" publ........ 1543

Astronomy advanced by Tycho Brahe, who adheres to the Ptolemaic system about 1582
Galileo constructs a telescope, 1609, and discovers Jupiter's satellites, etc 8 Jan 1610
True laws of the planetary motions announced by Kepler, 1st and 2d, 1609, 3d 1618
Various forms of telescopes and other instruments used in astronomy invented 1608–40
Gassendi observes the first recorded transit of Mercury over the sun, and measures the diameter of the planet 1631
Cartesian system published by Descartes 1637
Transit of Venus first observed by Horrox 24 Nov 1639
Huyghens completes the discovery of Saturn's ring 1654
Cassini draws his meridian line, after Dante (Bologna) 1655
Huyghens discovers the first satellite (Titan) of Saturn "
Aberration of light discovered by Horrebow 1659
Gregory invents a reflecting telescope 1663
Discoveries of Picard 1669
Charts of the moon constructed by Scheiner, Langrenus, Hevelius, Riccioli, etc about 1670
Discoveries of Römer on the velocity of light, and his observation of Jupiter's satellites 1675
Greenwich observatory founded "
Motion of the sun round its own axis proved by Halley 1676
Four satellites of Saturn discovered by Cassini 1671–84
Newton's "Principia" published, and the system, as now taught, demonstrated 1687
Catalogue of the stars made by Flamsteed 1688
Cassini's chart of the full moon executed 1692
Halley predicts the return of the comet (of 1758) 1705
Flamsteed's "Historia Cœlestis" publ 1725
Aberration of the light of the stars discovered and explained by Dr Bradley 1727
John Harrison produces chronometers for determining the longitude, 1735 et seq, and obtains the reward (Harrison's Timepiece) 1764
"Nautical Almanac" first publ 1767
Sir Wm Herschel's first observation of the nebula in Orion 1774
Wilson proves sun spots to be depressed "
The earth's mean density ascertained by Maskelyne "
Celestial inequalities found by Lagrange 1780
Uranus discovered by Herschel (Georgium Sidus) 13 Mch 1781
Herschel's first catalogue of double stars "
He investigates the earth's motion in space 1783
Herschel's first catalogue of nebulæ 1786
He discovers two moons of Uranus 11 Jan 1787
Acceleration of the moon's mean motion explained by Laplace, 19 Nov "
Herschel's second catalogue of nebulæ 1789
His 40 foot reflector finished "
Two inner moons of Saturn seen by it "
Atmospheric refraction in Venus by Schröter 1792
Saturn's rotation 10 h 16 min, shown by Herschel 1794
"Nebular Hypothesis," by Laplace publ 1796
Herschel first measures comparative brightness of stars "
Olbers's method of computing comets' orbits 1797
"Mécanique Céleste," Laplace, 2 vols publ 1799
Meteoric shower at Cumanea, seen by Humboldt "
Ceres discovered by Piazzi 1 Jan 1801
Pallas " Olbers. 28 Mch 1802
Binary stars discovered by Herschel "
Juno discovered by Harding 2 Sept 1804
Vesta " " Olbers 29 Mch 1807
Perihelion passage of great comet 12 Sept 1811
Fraunhofer maps 324 dark lines in the sun's spectrum 1815
The earth passes through a comet's tail 26 June, 1819
First calculated return of a comet (Encke's) 24 May, 1822
Sir Wm Herschel dies 25 Aug "
Correction for "personal equation" introduced by Bessel 1823
Spectra of fixed stars examined by Fraunhofer "
Sun's distance determined by Encke 95,250,000 miles 1824
Schwabe's observations of sun spots begun 1826
Biela discovers "Biela's comet" 27 Feb. "
Observatory at Cape of Good Hope finished 1829
First magnetic observatory at Gottingen 1833
Star shower in N America 12, 13 Nov "
Sir John Herschel lands at Cape of Good Hope 16 June, 1834
Halley's comet passes perihelion 16 Nov 1835
Annular eclipse of sun, "Baily's beads" seen 15 May, 1836
Eta Argus bursts out into brilliancy, seen by Herschel Dec. 1837
Parallax of 61 Cygni measured by Bessel, the first fixed star 1838
" of Alpha Centauri announced by Henderson 9 Jan 1839
J W Draper attempts to photograph the moon 1840
Change in light waves by motion proved by Doppler 1842
Baily completes experiments on weight of the earth "
Total eclipse of sun, corona observed by Baily, Struve, and others 8 July, "
Great comet seen at noon by the naked eye 28 Feb. 1843
Spiral nebulæ discovered by the earl of Rosse's Parsonstown reflector Apr 1845
Sun daguerreotyped by Foucault and Fizeau 2 Apr "
Neptune's place assigned by calculations by Adams Dec "
Duplicate division of Biela's comet seen at Yale college 29 Dec "
Heat found in moon's rays by Melloni 1846
Neptune discovered by Galle at Leverrier's direction 23 Sept. "
Satellite of Neptune discovered by Lassell 10 Oct "
Third satellite of Uranus discovered by Lassell 14 Sept. 1847
Fourth discovered by O Struve 8 Oct. "
Sir J Herschel's cyclone theory of sun spots "
Displacement of Fraunhofer's lines by motion, noted by Fizeau, 1848
New star in Ophiuchus seen by Hind 27 Apr "
Hyperion (a satellite [illegible] covered by Bond and Lassell, 29 Sept. 1848
Speed of light first [illegible] experiment by Fizeau 1849
Vega photographed [illegible] llege 17 July, 1850
Saturn's dusky ring disc[illegible] by Bond 15 Nov "
Periodicity of sun spots ascertained by Schwabe 1851
Magnetic period of sun spots proved by Sabine 6 May, 1852
Variable nebula in Taurus discovered by Hind 11 Oct. "
Estimated distance of sun reduced by Hansen 1854
Saturn's rings shown to be meteoric by Clerk Maxwell 1857
Double star photography begun at Harvard college 27 Apr "
Photography of the sun begun at Kew 1858
Spectrum analysis taught by Kirchhoff and Bunsen 1859
Kirchhoff describes the chemical constitution of the sun 15 Dec "
New star found in Scorpio by Auwers 21 May, 1860
The earth in the tail of a great comet 30 June, 1861
Kirchhoff's map of the sun's spectrum 1861–62
Hydrogen discovered in the sun by Ångström 1862
Companion of Sirius discovered by Alvan Clark, jr 31 Jan "
Sun's distance determined by velocity of light, Foucault "
Rotation period of Mars ascertained by Kaiser 5 Mch 1864
Spectra of Betelgeux and Aldebaran examined by Huggins "
" of Tempel's comet examined by Donati 5 Aug "
Gaseous nebulæ discovered by Huggins 29 Aug "
Comet of 1862 proved to have identical orbit with August meteors by Schiaparelli 1866
Lunar crater Linné disappears, announced by Schmidt Oct. "
Meteoric shower in Europe, as predicted by H A Newton, 13 Nov "
Period of November meteors determined by Adams 1867
Velocity of Sirius from the earth determined by Huggins 1868
Death of sir John Herschel 11 May, 1871
Line displacements by sun's rotation proved by Vogel "
Lord Rosse's investigations of the moon's heat published 1872
Cornu's experiments on velocity of light "
Meteoric shower ascribed to Biela's comet 27 Nov "
Earth's mean density ascertained by Cornu and Baille 1873
Transit of Venus 8 Dec. 1874
New star in Cygnus discovered by Schmidt 24 Nov 1876
Spectrum of Vega photographed by Huggins "
Oxygen lines in the sun's spectrum found by H. Draper 1877
Two satellites of Mars discovered by Hall at Washington, 16, 17 Aug. "
Canals of Mars discovered by Schiaparelli "
Changes in Trifid nebula announced by Holden "
Spectra of sun spots observed at South Kensington 1879
Early history of the moon by G H Darwin "
Great southern comet seen at Cordoba 31 Jan 1880
Draper photographs the nebula in Orion 30 Sept. "
Tidal retardation investigated by G H Darwin 1881
Spectrum of Tebbutt's comet photographed by Huggins, 24 June, "
Saturn's ring system measured by Struve 1882
Sodium rays found in spectrum of comet at Dunecht 27 May, "
Great comet disappears at perihelion, Cape of Good Hope, 17 Sept. "
Iron lines in sun's spectrum seen by Copeland and Lohse, 18 Sept. "
Doubling of canals in Mars discovered by Schiaparelli "
Tidal observations prove the earth rigid G H Darwin "
Great comet of 1882 seen from Cordoba, 470,000,000 miles away, 1 June, 1883
Sirius found to be returning towards the earth, Greenwich, 16 Nov "
Parallaxes of 9 southern stars found by Gill and Elken "
Pickering's photometric catalogue of 4260 stars 1884
Moon's heat spectrum measured by Langley Feb 1885
Orbit of 61 Cygni computed by Peters "
Paul and Henry discover nebula in the Pleiades by photography, 16 Nov "
Meteoric shower from Biela's comet 27 Nov "
New variable star in Orion found by Gore 13 Dec "
Rotation period of Mars determined by Bakhuysen "
Pleiades (40) photographed together at Harvard 26 Jan 1886
" photographed with large nebula around, three hours' exposure, by Roberts 24 Oct "
Great comet found by Struve to have same orbit with those of 1843 1880, and 1882 18 Jan 1887
G F Chambers's "Handbook of Astronomy," new edition 1889–90
C H F Peters, of Hamilton College observatory, N Y, b. Schleswig 19 Sept 1813, d 19 July, 1890
Norman Lockyer announces his theory of the constitution of the heavenly bodies (Meteors) 17 Nov 1891
Fifth satellite of Jupiter discovered by E E Barnard, of the Lick observatory 9 Sept 1892

Astu'rias (Ovie'do since 1833), N W Spain, an ancient principality Here Pelayo collected the Gothic fugitives, about 713, founded a new kingdom, and checked Moorish conquest For his successors, Spain The heir-apparent has borne the title "prince of Asturias" since 1388, when it was assumed by Henry, son of John I, king of Leon, on his marriage with a descendant of Peter of Castile In 1808 the junta of Asturias began organized resistance to French usurpation

asylums or **privileged places,** at first, were places of refuge for those who by accident or necessity had violated the law. God commanded the Jews to build cities of refuge, 1451 B.C (Numb. xxv) The Heraclidæ are said to have built one at Athens to protect themselves against their enemies and Cadmus one at Thebes, 1490 B.C., and Romulus one at Mount Palatine, 751 B.C. SANCTUARIES.

ateliers nationaux (*at le-ā nas'yo-nō*, national workshops) were established by the French provisional government in Feb. 1848. They interfered with private trade, about 100,000 workmen throwing themselves upon the government for labor and payment. The breaking-up of the system led to fearful conflicts in June following, and it was abolished in July.

Athanasian Creed. Athanasius of Alexandria, was elected bishop, 326. He opposed the doctrines of Arius (who denied Christ's divinity), was several times exiled and died in 373.

Lumby in "History of the Creeds" (1874) asserts that this creed, beginning "*Quicunque vult*," was not composed by Athanasius; that it is made up of two distinct parts, and was originally written in Latin and put into its present shape between 814 and 850; not connected with Athanasius's name by any trustworthy authority before 809, set forth first in Gaul about 870, gradually extended into Italy, Britain, etc., accepted by the Greek church about 1200.

This creed asserts the procession of the Holy Ghost from the Father and the Son. FILIOQUE.

Dr. Waterland's "Critical History" of this creed publ. 1723. He ascribes it to Hilary, bishop of Arles, from 430 to 449 A.D.

Much agitation against the general use of this creed has arisen in the church of England among both clergy and laity, 1870-73.

Modifications approved by several bishops were negatived by the lower house in convocation (62-7) early in May, 1872. The vote was rejected by the bishops, and the agitation continued.

In a letter to the earl of Shaftesbury, 22 July, 1872, the archbishops of Canterbury and York expressed their hope of devising a way for rendering the reading of the creed during public worship not compulsory.

Great meeting of laity at St. James's Hall in defence of the creed, 31 Jan. 1873.

atheism (from the Greek *a*, without, *θεος*, God.—Psa. xiv. 1). The writings of Epicurus, Lucretius, and many modern philosophers deny the existence of a personal deity. PHILOSOPHY.

Athenæ'a were great festivals celebrated at Athens in honor of Pallas-Athene. One was called Panathenæa, the other Chalcea; they are said to have been instituted by Erichthonius about 1495 B.C., and revived by Theseus, who caused them to be observed by all the Athenians, the first every fifth year, 1234 B.C.—*Plutarch.*

Athenæ'um, a place at Athens, sacred to Pallas-Athene, where the poets and philosophers recited their compositions. That of Rome, of great beauty, was erected by the emperor Hadrian, 125.—The Athenæum club of London was formed in 1823. The club-house was erected in 1829-30 on the site of the late Carlton palace; it is of Grecian architecture, and the frieze is an exact copy of the Panathenaic procession which formed the frieze of the Parthenon.—The Boston Athenæum, Boston, Mass., originated in the Anthology club, and dates from 1804. It was incorporated 1807. It is an association of private persons, but its art gallery and its library, among the finest in the United States, are practically open to scholars and students not members of the society. First public exhibition in 1826.—The *Athenæum*, an English weekly literary and scientific journal, first appeared in 1828.

Athens, the capital of ancient Attica and of modern Greece. The first mythical sovereign is Ogyges, who reigned in Bœotia, and was master of Attica, then called Ionia. In his reign (about 1764 B.C.) a deluge laid waste the country, which so remained till the arrival of the Egyptian Cecrops and a colony, by whom the land was re-peopled and 12 cities founded, 1556 B.C. The chief city, first called Cecropia, was afterwards named Athens in honor of Pallas-Athene, her worship having been introduced by Erichthonius, 1495 B.C. Athens was ruled by 17 successive kings (487 years), by 13 *perpetual* archons (316 years), 7 *decennial* archons (70 years), and lastly, by *annual* archons (760 years). It attained great power, and the number of its illustrious citizens has never been equalled by any other city in the same time. The ancients called Athens *Astu*, the *city*, by eminence, and one of the eyes of Greece. GREECE.

B.C.
Arrival of Cecrops [1558 *Hales*, 1433 *Clinton*].—*Usher* 1556
Areopagus established 1507
Deucalion arrives in Attica 1502
Reign of Amphictyon [1499 *H.*] 1497
Panathenæan games [1481 *H.*] 1495
Erichthonius reigns 1487
Erechtheus teaches husbandry 1485
Eleusinian mysteries introduced by Eumolpus 1356
Erechtheus killed in battle with the Eleusinians 1347
Ægeus invades Attica and ascends the throne 1283
He throws himself into the sea and is drowned; hence the name of the Ægean sea.—*Eusebius* 1235
Theseus, his son, succeeds and reigns 30 years
He collects his subjects into one city and names it Athens 1234
Reign of Mnestheus, 1205; of Demophoon 1182
Court of Ephetæ established 1179
Prytaneum instituted 1178
Melanthus conquers Xuthus in single combat and is chosen king 1128
Reign of Codrus his son, the last king 1092
In a battle with the Heraclidæ Codrus is killed. He had resolved to perish, the oracle having declared that the victory should be with the side whose leader was killed 1070
Royalty abolished; Athens governed by archons; Medon the first [1070 *H.*] 1044
Alcmeon, last perpetual archon, dies 753
Charops, 1st decennial archon 748
[Perhaps the first trustworthy date in Athenian history.]
Hippomenes deposed for his cruelty 714
Eryxias, 7th and last decennial archon, dies 684
Creon, 1st annual archon 683
Draco, 12th annual archon, publishes his laws, said to have been written in blood 621
Revolution of Cylon 612
SACRED WAR (the first), Cirrha in Phocis near Delphi destroyed 595
Solon supersedes Draco's laws by his excellent code 594
Pisistratus, the "tyrant," seizes the supreme power 560; flight of Solon 559. Pisistratus establishes his government 537; collects a public library 531; dies 527
First tragedy acted at Athens on a wagon by Thespis 535
Hipparchus assassinated by Harmodius and Aristogeiton 514
Law of ostracism adopted; Hippias and the Pisistratidæ banished 510
Lemnos taken by Miltiades 504
Persian invaders defeated at Marathon 490
Death of Miltiades 489
Aristides, surnamed the *Just*, banished 483
Athens taken by Xerxes 480
Burned to the ground by Mardonius 479
Rebuilt and fortified by Themistocles; Piræus built 478
Themistocles banished 471
Cimon, son of Miltiades, overruns all Thrace 469
Pericles takes part in public affairs 469; he and Cimon adorn Athens 464; the latter banished 461
Athens begins to tyrannize over Greece 459
Long wall built 457
SACRED WAR (the second) 448
Tolmidas conducts an expedition into Bœotia and is defeated and killed near Coronea 447
30 years' truce between Athenians and Lacedæmonians 445
Herodotus said to have read his history in the council at Athens.
Pericles obtains the government 444
" subdues Samos 440
Satirical comedies prohibited at Athens
Alliance between Athens and Corcyra, then at war with Corinth 433, leads to the Peloponnesian war (lasted 27 years); it began 431
A dreadful plague, which had ravaged Ethiopia, Libya, Egypt and Persia, extends to Athens and continues for 5 years 430
Death of Pericles of the plague 429
Disastrous expedition against Sicily; death of commanders Demosthenes and Nicias; Athenian fleet destroyed by Gylippus 415–413
Government of the "400" 411
Alcibiades defeats the Lacedæmonians at Cyzicus 410
Alcibiades, accused of aspiring to sovereign power, banished 407
Athens victorious in a sea fight at Arginusæ 406
Athenian fleet destroyed by Lysander at Ægospotami 405
He besieges Athens by land and sea; its walls are destroyed and it capitulates, and the Peloponnesian war terminates 404
Rule of the 30 tyrants, who are overthrown by Thrasybulus 403
Socrates (aged 70) put to death 399
Corinthian war begins 395
Conon rebuilds the long walls and fortifies the Piræus 393
Plato founds the Academy 388
War against Sparta 378
Lacedæmonian fleet defeated at Naxos by Chabrias 376
General peace 371
Philip, king of Macedon, opposes the Athenians (MACEDON) 359
SACRED WAR (the third) 357-55
First Philippic of Demosthenes 352
Peace with Macedon 346
Battle of Cheronæa; Athenians and Thebans defeated by Philip 7 Aug. 338
Philip assassinated by Pausanias 336
Athens submits to Alexander, who spares the orators 335
Death of Alexander 323
Lamian war, the Athenians and others rise against Macedon, 323; defeated at Cranon; Demosthenes poisons himself 322
Athens surrenders to Cassander, who governs well, 318; execution of Phocion 317
Demetrius Poliorcetes expels Demetrius Phalereus and restores the Athenian democracy, 307; the latter takes the chair of philosophy 296
League between Athens, Sparta and Egypt 277
Athens taken by Antigonus Gonatas, king of Macedon 268; restored by Aratus 256

Athenians join the Achæan league.............................. 229
They join the Ætolians against Macedon, and send for assistance to Rome.. 215
Roman fleet arrives at Athens................................. 211
Romans proclaim liberty at Athens............................. 196
Subjugation of Greece... 144
Athenians implore assistance against the Romans from Mithridates, king of Pontus, whose general, Archelaus, makes himself master of Piræus.............................about 87
Athens besieged by Sylla, the Roman general; it is reduced to surrender by famine.................................... " 86
Cicero studies at Athens, 79; and Horace...................... 42
Athenians desert Pompey, to follow the interests of Cæsar.... 47

A. D.

Athens visited by the apostle Paul............................ 52
Many temples, etc., erected by Hadrian....................... 122–35
Athens taken by Alaric, and spared from slaughter........... 396
Acquired by Otho de la Roche, and afterwards made a duchy.. 1205
Subjected by the Turks.. 1444
" " Mahomet II.. 1456
" " the Venetians... 1466
Restored to the Turks... 1479
Athens suffers much during the war of independence, 1821–27.
Taken by the Turks (Greece)........................17 May, 1827
Becomes the capital of the kingdom of modern Greece......... 1833
Pop. 41,298, 1861; 44,510, 1871; 68,677, 1879; 107,251........ 1889

Atherton gag. To prevent discussion of slavery in the House of Representatives, C. G. Atherton, of New Hampshire, introduced a resolution, passed 11 Dec. 1838, that all petitions and papers relating to that subject should be "laid on the table without being debated, printed, or referred." It was rescinded in 1845. Petitions, United States.

Athlone, Roscommon, Ireland, was burned during the civil war in 1641. After the battle of the Boyne, col. R. Grace held Athlone for James II. against a besieging army, but fell when it was taken by assault by Ginkell, 30 June, 1691. Aghrim.

Atlanta Campaign (6 May–2 Sept. 1864), in which gens. Sherman and Johnston were antagonists, until the latter was relieved by Hood, is one of the most interesting of the American civil war. Gen. Sherman, at the instance of gen. Grant, succeeded him in command of the military division of the Mississippi, 14 Mch. 1864. This division embraced 4 departments—the Cumberland, Ohio, Tennessee, and Arkansas. The objective point of the campaign was Atlanta, Ga. The forces under gen. Sherman comprised

	Infantry.	Cavalry.	Artillery.	Total.
The army of the Cumberland, under maj.-gen. George H. Thomas.	54,568	3828	2377	60,773
Of the Tenn., maj.-gen. Jas. B. McPherson.	22,437	624	1404	24,465
Of the Ohio, maj.-gen. John M. Schofield.	11,183	1697	679	13,559
Total	[illegible]	6149	4460	98,797

with 254 guns. Estimated strength of the confederate forces, 60,000, under gen. Joseph E. Johnston. The confederate position was at Dalton, about 90 miles from Atlanta, its front covered by a ridge or mountain known as "Rocky Face." The following are the important events of the campaign, during which the opposing forces constantly confronted each other, the one falling back, the other advancing, but with no general engagement.

Gen. Sherman advances on Dalton, 4 May, with the army of the Cumberland in the centre; that of the Tennessee on the right; that of the Ohio on the left. The army of the Cumberland demonstrates in front of the confederate position at Rocky Face ridge, while McPherson is sent with the army of the Tennessee to turn the confederate left and seize Resaca or some other point in the rear of the confederates. McPherson thinking his force not strong enough to occupy Resaca, fortifies himself at Snake Creek Gap. Sherman reinforces him with gen. Schofield's command and a portion of the army of the Cumberland. This compels Johnston to evacuate Dalton and fall back on Resaca..........................6–14 May, 1864
Battle of Resaca, partial engagement of the troops under Howard, Hooker, and Schofield, beginning about 3 P.M...15 May, "
This engagement, coupled with the continued flanking movement of McPherson, compels the confederates to fall back from Resaca to Cassville..........................16–19 May, "
Jeff. C. Davis with a division of the army of the Cumberland occupies Rome, destroying the mills and founderies...17 May, "
Johnston retreats across the Etowah on the night of 19 May, " and occupies a fortified position covering the Allatoona pass.
Sherman crosses the Etowah and moves on Dallas....23 May, "
Gen. Hooker, moving from Burnt Hickory towards Dallas with the 20th corps, meets the confederates at Pumpkinvine creek in a severe but indecisive engagement..............25 May, "
Confederates occupy a strongly intrenched position from Dallas to Marietta, including Kenesaw, Lost, and Pine mountains, 26 May, "
Confederates attack McPherson at Dallas; repulsed...28 May, "
Gen. Sherman, moving his army to the left, envelopes Allatoona pass and compels the confederates to evacuate it as well as their intrenched positions at Ackworth and New Hope church, 1–6 June, 1864
[Allatoona pass made a depot of supplies by gen. Sherman.]
Gen. Frank Blair joins Sherman with 2 divisions of the 17th corps and a brigade of cavalry, raising his effective force to quite its original strength..........................8 June, "
Gen. Sherman moves his troops to Big Shanty and close up to Kenesaw...11 June, "
During an artillery duel the confederate general Leonidas Polk is killed on Pine mountain..........................14 June, "
Confederates retire from Pine mountain, 15 June, and Lost mountain...17 June, "
Confederates attempt to break Sherman's line at the intersection of Thomas's right and Schofield's left near what is known as "the Kulp house." The attack falls on Williams's division of the 20th corps and Haskell's of the 23d; repulsed with severe loss to the confederates..........................22 June, "
Sherman's unsuccessful assault on Kenesaw (battle of Kenesaw mountain) with loss of 3000, including gens. Harker and Dan. McCook, killed Confederate loss, 442..............27 June, "
Gen. Sherman again orders McPherson forward on the confederates' left flank, threatening to cross the Chattahoochee at Turner's ferry. The confederates abandon Kenesaw and fall back to the Chattahoochee..........................2 July, "
Gen. Sherman shifts his troops from the right to the left—the army of the Tennessee being now on the extreme left—and crossing the Chattahoochee at three points, compels Johnston to abandon the Chattahoochee and establish a new line covering Atlanta..............................4–17 July, "
Confederate gen. Johnston relieved, and gen. J. B. Hood of Texas appointed in his place..........................17 July, "
Battle of Peach tree Creek. Newton's division of the 4th corps, the 20th corps, and Johnson's division of the 14th corps, on crossing Peach tree creek are attacked in force by confederates about 2 P.M..................................20 July, "
[The confederates are repulsed with a loss of not less than 2000, while the union loss is 1500.]
Rousseau starts from Decatur, Ala., with 2000 cavalry upon his raid against the West Point railroad (10 July); crosses the Coosa, and defeats Clanton (13 July); strikes the railroad, destroys a portion of it, and joins Sherman...........22 July, "
Battle of Decatur or Atlanta. This is the severest battle of the campaign and results in the loss to the union army of 3722 and the death of gen. McPherson..............22 July, "
[Hood surprises the extreme left of the army of the Tennessee about noon on the 22d, and for several hours prospects vary, but as the union troops consolidate, he is repulsed. Gen. McPherson falling, gen. John A. Logan assumes temporary command of the army of the Tennessee.]
Maj.-gen. O. O. Howard appointed to the command of the army of the Tennessee..................................27 July, "
[Maj.-gen. Joseph Hooker of the 20th corps, feeling slighted at the appointment of gen. Howard, is relieved at his own request, maj.-gen. Henry W. Slocum succeeding.]
Army of the Tennessee moves from the extreme left to the extreme right, with the general aim of driving Hood out of Atlanta by flanking him..........................26–27 July, "
Gen. Hood, taking advantage of this movement, attacks the extreme right of the army of the Tennessee, 15th corps, Logan's—well supported, however, by Blair's and Dodge's corps, at Ezra's church..............................28 July, "
[This battle commences in earnest about noon and continues until 4 P.M., when the confederates retire with a loss of 2000. The union loss 600.]
Gen. Sherman sends gen. Stoneman on a raid towards Macon, Ga., with about 5000 cavalry..........................28 July, "
[Stoneman is captured with part of his command.]
Siege of Atlanta..1–26 Aug. "
Gen. Kilpatrick raids around Atlanta, destroying the West Point and Macon railroad..........................18–22 Aug. "
Gen. Sherman discontinues the direct siege of Atlanta, withdrawing the 20th corps (Slocum's) to an intrenched position on the Chattahoochee, and moves the rest of the army south of Atlanta...25–28 Aug. "
Army of the Tennessee, attacked by the confederate gen. Hardee at Jonesboro, about 20 miles south of Atlanta, repulses him. A counter attack is made by the 14th corps under gen. Jeff. C. Davis late in the afternoon, but owing to the lack of support and the lateness of the hour it fails to take the confederates' position..........................31 Aug. "
Confederates retire to Lovejoy during the night of....31 Aug. "
Gen. Hood, blowing up his magazines and destroying his stores, evacuates Atlanta..................................1–2 Sept. "
Atlanta occupied by gen. Slocum with 20th corps......3 Sept. "
Gen. Sherman returns to Atlanta from Lovejoy with his army, 5–7 Sept. "
A truce of 10 days between Hood and Sherman to remove the remaining inhabitants from Atlanta, 446 families, 2035 persons, being sent south, fully accomplished by.......21 Sept. "
Allatoona Pass, Sherman's Great March.

Atlantic Ocean. Deep-sea sounding, Oceans.

Atlantic telegraph. Electric telegraph, under Electricity.

atmol'ysis, a method of separating the constituent gases of a compound (such as atmospheric air) by passing it through a vessel of porous material (such as graphite); made known in Aug 1863, by the discoverer, the late prof T Graham, F R S, master of the mint

atmospheric railways. The idea of atmospheric pressure as a motor was conceived by Papin, the French engineer, about 1680 Experiments were made on a line of rail across Wormwood Scrubs, London, between Shepherd's Bush and the Great Western railroad, to test atmospheric tubes, the working of the air-pump, and speed of carriages upon this principle in June, 1840, and then on a line between Croydon and London, 1845 Atmospheric pressure was tried and abandoned in 1848, on the South Devon line An atmospheric railway was *commenced between Dalkey and Killiney*, in the vicinity of Dublin, in Sept 1843, opened 29 Mch 1844, discontinued in 1855 A similar railway was proposed in the streets of London by T W Rammell in 1857 Mr Rammell's pneumatic railway was put in action successfully at the Crystal Palace on 27 Aug 1864, and following days An act for a pneumatic railway between the Waterloo railway station and Whitehall was passed in July, 1865 Atmospheric pressure was proposed for a submarine railway from Dover to Calais in 1869 PNEUMATIC DESPATCH

atomic theory, in chemistry, deals with the indivisible particles of all substances The results of fragmentary investigations by his predecessors (such as Wenzel, in 1777) were collected by John Dalton in four laws of combining proportion, which have received the name of "atomic theory" His "Chemical Philosophy" containing his views appeared in 1808 Dr C Daubeny's work on the atomic theory was published in 1850 In his standard of atomic weights Dalton takes hydrogen as 1 Berzelius, who began elaborate researches on the subject in 1818, adopts oxygen as 100 The former standard is used in England, the latter on the continent The theory assumes widely varying forms in the speculations of recent chemists In 1855 Hinrichs propounded a new hypothetical science, *Atomechanics*, in which *pantogen*, composed of panatoms, is regarded as the primary chemical principle

atoms. Democritus (ABDERA) held that all things consist of innumerable indestructible atoms, varying in form, and combined in obedience to mechanical laws, that the soul consists of free, smooth, round atoms, like those of fire, and that nothing happens by chance His philosophy was adopted by Epicurus (about 306 B C), whose doctrines are poetically expounded by Lucretius in his "De Rerum Natura" ("On the Nature of Things"), 57 B C A modified atomic philosophy was adopted by Gassendi, who died 1655 A D

Atrebates, a Belgic people, subdued by Cæsar, 57 B.C ARTOIS

attainder, acts of, punishing a person by declaring his "blood attainted," and involving forfeiture of property, have been numerous. Two witnesses in cases of high-treason are necessary where corruption of blood is incurred, unless the party accused shall confess or stand mute, 7 and 8 Will III 1694-95 —*Blackstone.* The attainder of lord Russell, who was beheaded in Lincoln's-inn-fields, 21 July, 1683, was reversed under William, in 1689 The rolls and records of the acts of attainder passed in the reign of James II were cancelled and publicly burned, 2 Oct 1695 Among the last acts reversed was the attaint of the children of lord Edward Fitzgerald (who was implicated in the rebellion in Ireland of 1798), 1 July, 1819 In 1814 and 1833 the severity of attainders was mitigated Several attainders reversed about 1827, and one in 1853 (the earl of Perth). In the United States the constitution says "No bill of attainder shall be passed, and no attainder of treason, in consequence of a judicial sentence, shall work corruption of blood or forfeiture, except during the life of the person attainted"

Attica. ATHENS.

At'tila, surnamed the "Scourge of God," and thus distinguished for his conquests and his crimes, having ravaged the Eastern empire from 445 to 450, when he made peace with Theodosius. He invaded the Western empire, 450, and was defeated by Aetius at Chalons, 451 (one of the most desperate contests recorded in history), he then retired into Pannonia, where tradition says he died by bursting a blood-vessel on his nuptials with Ildico, a beautiful virgin, 453

attorney (from *tour*, turn), a person appointed or deputed by another to act in his behalf An attorney-in-fact, is one authorized, usually by written document, under seal, to contract for and bind his principal, to execute transfers of stock, deeds, etc An attorney-at-law is one whose business it is to represent others before courts of law and throughout the processes of litigation The number in England in the reign of Edward III was under 100 In the 32d of Henry VI, 1454, a law reduced the practitioners in Norfolk, Norwich, and Suffolk from 80 to 14, and restricted their increase The number of attorneys practising in the United Kingdom in 1872 was said to be 13,821 The qualifications and practice of attorneys and solicitors are regulated by acts passed in 1843, 1860 1870, and 1874 By the Supreme Judicature act attorneys are styled solicitors since Nov 1875 SOLICITORS In the United States the term attorney is commonly applied to every member of the legal profession, including advocates, counsel, and solicitors The conditions of admission to practice as attorneys in the courts are prescribed in each state by law and differ widely

attorney-general. In England a law officer of the crown, appointed by letters-patent He exhibits informations and prosecutes for the sovereign in matters criminal, and files bills in exchequer for claims concerning the crown in inheritance or profit Others may bring bills against the sovereign's attorney The first English attorney-general was William Bonneville, 1277 The attorney-general is not a member of the cabinet, but he goes out with the ministry from which he receives his appointment

attorney-general, United States CABINET

attraction, described by Copernicus, about 1520, as an appetence or appetite which the Creator impressed upon all parts of matter, by Kepler, 1605, as a corporeal affection tending to union In 1687, sir Isaac Newton published his "Principia" expounding as a law of nature the key to all movements of the solar system, the attraction of every portion of matter for every other, in direct proportion to its mass and in inverse proportion to the square of the distance Dr C William Siemens exhibited and described his attraction-meter at the Royal Society, 1876 ELECTRICITY GRAVITATION, MAGNETISM

Attu, one of the Aleutian islands, the most westerly point of the United States It lies 400 miles from Kamchatka Calling Attu the western extremity of the U S, the city of San Francisco, Cal, is near the middle of its geographical extent east and west, the territories of the U S stretching through 120° of longitude

Atwood's machine, for proving the laws of accelerated motion by the falling of weights, invented by George Atwood, described 1784 He died 11 July, 1807

aubaine, a right of the French kings, from the beginning of the monarchy, whereby they claimed the property of every unnaturalized stranger who died in the country, was abolished by the National Assembly in 1790-91, re-established by Napoleon in 1804, and finally annulled, 14 July, 1819

Auberoche, Guienne, S France The earl of Derby defeated the French, besieging this place, 19 Aug 1344

Auckland, capital of New Zealand (north island), was founded Sept 1840 The population of the district in 1857 was estimated at 15,000 Europeans and 35,000 natives The seat of government was removed to Wellington, on Cook's strait, Dec. 1864

auction, a method of sale known to the Romans, mentioned by Petronius Arbiter (about 66 A.D). The first in England was about 1700, by Elihu Yale (founder of YALE COLLEGE) a governor of fort George now Madras, in the East Indies, who thus sold the goods he had brought home Auction and sales tax began 1779 Various acts of parliament have regulated auctions and imposed duties, in some cases as high as 5 per cent By 8 Vict c 15, 1845, the duties were repealed, and a charge imposed "on the license to be taken out by all auctioneers in the United Kingdom of 10*l*." In 1858 there were 4358 licenses granted, producing 43,580*l*. The abuses at auctions, termed "knock-outs," caused by combinations of brokers and others excited attention in Sept 1866 An act regulating sales of land by auction was passed 15 July, 1867. Certain auctions are now permitted without license to the auctioneer, as of goods and chattels under distress for rent, and sales under the small debts acts for Scotland and Ireland.—Abuses at auctions in the United States have led to various statutory regulations in the several states. In New York, auctioneers must give bonds in $100,000 for faithful conduct of business, must make semi-annual accounts of sales, and pay to the state a percentage on sales of goods, with some exemptions.

Audiani, followers of Audæus of Mesopotamia, expelled from the Syrian church about 338 A.D. for reproving the vices of the clergy. He was banished to Scythia, where he is said to have made many converts. His followers celebrate Easter at the time of the Jewish Passover, and attribute a human figure to the Deity.

audiometer (from *audio*, I hear), an instrument to measure the keenness of the sense of hearing, invented by prof. Hughes. It consists of a battery of two Leclanché's cells, with a simple microphone and telephone; described to the Royal Society, 15 May, 1879.

audiphone, an instrument to assist dulness of hearing, invented by R. G. Rhodes of Chicago, and modified by M. Colladon of Geneva, in 1880. It consists of a thin sheet of hard ebonite rubber or card-board, to be placed against the teeth, through which and other bones vibrations are conveyed to the auditory nerve.

auditor (Lat., a hearer), a person authorized to investigate and settle accounts. The treasury of the United States has 6 auditors for different branches of its accounts. Most of the states and corporations in extended business have auditors for similar work.

Auerstädt, Prussia. Here, on 14 Oct. 1806, the French, under Davoust, signally defeated the Prussians, under Blucher. JENA.

Aughrim. AGHRIM.

Augsburg, Bavaria, originally a colony settled by Augustus, about 12 B.C.; became a free city, and flourished during the middle ages. Here many important diets of the empire have been held. In 952 A.D. a council confirmed the order for the celibacy of the priesthood. Augsburg has suffered much by war, having been taken by siege—in 788, 1703, 1704, and, last, by the French, 10 Oct. 1805, who restored it to Bavaria in March, 1806.

Augsburg Diet, summoned by the emperor Charles V. to settle the religious disputes of Germany, met 20 June, and separated ....Nov. 1530
Confession of Augsburg, compiled by Melanchthon, Luther, and others, signed by the Protestant princes, presented to the emperor Charles V., and read to the diet ....25 June, "
Interim of Augsburg, a document issued by Charles V.: an attempt to reconcile the Catholics and Protestants (it was fruitless, and was withdrawn)....read 15 May, 1548
"Peace of Religion," signed at Augsburg.............25 Sept. 1555
League of Augsburg, for maintenance of the treaties of Münster, Nimeguen: a treaty between Holland and other powers against France....signed 9 July, 1686

augur, an officer of ancient Rome charged with the interpretation of auspices or natural signs foreboding future events. Thunder and lightning, the flight of birds, and many other sights and sounds in nature, were regarded as divine warnings or encouragements. Tradition ascribes the foundation of the college of augurs, 3 in number, to Numa, 710 B.C. The number was gradually increased, and was 15 at the time of Sulla, 81 B.C. The college of augurs was abolished by Theodosius about 390 A.D.—The superstition which connects the flight of birds with supernatural guidance in husbandry and other enterprises is very ancient, being mentioned by Hesiod; and it still survives in many countries.

August, the 8th month of the Roman year (previously called *Sextilis*, or the 6th from March), by a decree of the senate received its present name in honor of Augustus Cæsar, in the year 8 B.C., because in this month he was created consul, had thrice triumphed in Rome, added Egypt to the Roman empire, and made an end of the civil wars. He added one day to the month, making it 31 days.—Shooting-stars on the 10th of Aug. were observed in the middle ages, and termed "St. Lawrence's tears." Their periodicity was noticed by Mr. Forster early in the present century.

Augusta, Siege of. Augusta, Ga., was held by a force under a loyalist named Brown in the spring of 1781. While gen. Greene besieged FORT NINETY-SIX, Lee, Pickens, Clarke, and other Southern partisan leaders laid siege to Augusta, beginning 23 May, and on 5 June Brown surrendered. The Americans lost 51 men killed and wounded; the British lost 52 killed, and 334, including the wounded, were taken prisoners

Augustan Age, the years during which Caius Octavius (Cæsar Augustus), nephew of Julius Cæsar, was emperor of Rome, 27 B.C.–14 A.D., distinguished for its splendid attainments in arts, arms, and especially in literature—the days of Horace, Virgil, Ovid, and Livy. The reign of Louis XIV. is called the Augustan age of France; the reign of Anne, the Augustan age of England.

Augustan Era began 14 Feb. 27 B.C., or 727 years after the foundation of Rome.

Augustin (or Austin) Friars, a religious order, its origin ascribed to St. Augustin, bishop of Hippo, who died 430. They first appeared about the 11th century as the Austin of Black Canons, and the order was constituted by pope Alexander IV., 1256. The rule requires poverty, humility, and chastity. Martin Luther was an Augustin monk. The Augustins held the doctrine of free grace, and were rivals of the Dominicans. The order appeared in England soon after the conquest, and had 32 houses at the suppression, 1536. One of their churches, at Austin Friars, London, erected 1354, and since the Reformation used by Dutch Protestants, was partly destroyed by fire, 22 Nov. 1862. It was restored, and reopened 1 Oct. 1865. A religious house of the order, dedicated to St. Monica, mother of Augustin, was founded in Hoxton square, London, 1864.

Aulic Council, one of the two highest courts of the German empire, established by Maximilian I. The Imperial Chamber, civil and criminal, was instituted at Worms, 1495, and afterwards held at Spires and Wetzler; and the Aulic Council at Vienna, 1506. These courts, of concurrent jurisdiction, heard appeals in particular cases from the courts of the Germanic states.

Auray, N.W. France. Here, on 29 Sept. 1364, the English, under John Chandos, defeated the French and captured their leader Du Guesclin. Charles of Blois, made duke of Brittany by the king of France, was slain, and a peace was made in April, 1365.

auricular confession. Confession at the ear (Lat. *auris*) of the priest was an early practice, said to have been forbidden in the 4th century by Nectarius, archbishop of Constantinople. It was enjoined by the council of Lateran in 1215, and by the council of Trent in 1551. It was one of the 6 articles of faith enacted by Henry VIII. in 1539, but was abolished in England at the Reformation. Its revival has been attempted by the party in the church of England called Puseyites, Tractarians, or Ritualists. PUSEYISM.

Rev. Alfred Poole, curate of St. Barnabas, Knightsbridge, was suspended by his bishop for practising auricular confession in June, 1858, and the suspension was confirmed in Jan. 1859. A similar attempt by the rev. Temple West at Boyne Hill, in Sept. 1858, excited public discussion.
In May, 1873, 483 clergymen of the church of England petitioned convocation for the education, selection, and licensing of duly qualified confessors under the canon law. Disapproved by the bishops.
Letter from the bishop of London directing confession to God; that to the minister optional, 21 July, 1873.
Archdeacon Denison (in a letter) denounces all opposing auricular confession, 22 Aug. 1873.
Address of 96 peers against auricular confession to archbishop of Canterbury about 9 Aug. 1877. HOLY CROSS.

au'riflamma or oriflamme, the national banner in French history, belonging to the abbey of St. Denis, and suspended over his tomb. Louis le Gros was the first king who took it from the abbey to battle, 1124.—*Hénault.* It appeared for the last time at Agincourt, 25 Oct. 1415.—*Tillet.* Others say at Montlhéry, 16 July, 1465.

auro'ra boreā'lis and auro'ra austrā'lis (northern and southern polar light), rarely seen in central Europe, frequent in the arctic and antarctic regions. The first described appearance was seen in London, 1560; the next in 1564, 7 Oct. In Brabant, Cornelius Gemm describes two seen in the year 1575; compares them to spears, fortified cities, and armies fighting in the air. In 1621, in Sept., one was observed in France, and described by Gassendi, who gave it the name of *Aurora borealis*. No English writer mentions its appearance from 1574 until 1707, when a small one was noted in Nov. From 1621 to 1707 there is no mention made of an aurora borealis at any place. In Mch. 1716, an aurora extended from the west of Ireland to the confines of Russia, mentioned by Dr. Halley, which from its brilliancy attracted universal attention. The whole horizon lat. 57° N. was overspread with continuous haze of a dismal red during a whole night, Nov. 1765.—Mr. Foster, the companion of capt. Cook, saw the aurora in lat. 58° S. The aurora is now attributed to the passage of electric light through rarefied air in the polar regions. In Aug. and Sept. 1859, brilliant auroras were very frequent, telegraph-wires were seriously affected, and communications interrupted.

Brilliant display throughout Canada, the northern U. S. and Europe, 15 Apr. 1869. The Western Union Tel. worked their lines without the aid of a battery through the Middle and Eastern states. From Philadelphia to Pittsburg a battery was not needed. This display extended as far south as Richmond, Va. Another noticeable display 24 Oct. 1870, visible in northern and western U. S., Canada, England, France, Germany, and most of Europe; lasted from 11 P.M. until 3 A.M. Telegraph wires were again affected. Another display 4 Feb. 1872; also 18 Apr. 1873; and during the year 1882 on 16–17 Apr., 14 and 18 May, 4 Aug., 2 Oct., 13 Nov.—all very marked. During this year, at the Finnish station at Sodankyla, Herr Sophus Tromholt, experimenting with electricity on a large scale, placing the batteries along a range of hills, produced an artificial aurora differing in no respect from the real aurora. Prof. C. Piazzi-Smith sums up the final mean result of a vast number of observations by the members of the Scottish Meteorological Society, showing what months the auroral displays are the most frequent. These observations show that Feb. and Oct. stand first, while Mch. and Sept. follow. Prof. Elias Loomis notes that the aurora is periodic, the grandest displays being at intervals of about 60 years, and less marked at intervals of 10 to 11 years; and that the maximum and minimum displays tend to correspond with the increase and decrease of the solar spots.

auscultation. STETHOSCOPE.

Austerlitz, a town in Moravia, where a battle was fought between the French and the allied Austrian and Russian armies, 2 Dec. 1805. As Alexander of Russia, Francis of Austria, and Napoleon of France, commanded, it is sometimes called the "battle of the 3 emperors." The killed and wounded exceeded 30,000 of the allies, who lost 40 standards, 150 pieces of cannon, and thousands of prisoners. The decisive victory of the French led to the treaty of Presburg, signed 26 Dec. 1805. PRESBURG.

Australa'sia, the 5th great division of the world. This name, given by De Brosses, includes Australia, Van Diemen's Land, New Guinea, New Zealand, New Britain, New Caledonia, etc., mostly discovered within two centuries. Accidental discoveries were made by Spaniards as early as 1526; but the first accurate knowledge of these lands is due to the Dutch, who in 1606 explored part of the coast of Papua, or New Guinea. Torres, a Spaniard, passed through the strait which now bears his name, between that island and Australia, and gave the first correct report of the latter, 1606. The Dutch continued their discoveries. Grant in 1800, and Flinders again (1801-5), completed the survey.—*M'Culloch.*

Austra'lia (formerly **New Holland**), the largest island or smallest continent; including five provinces—NEW SOUTH WALES, QUEENSLAND, SOUTH AUSTRALIA, VICTORIA (formerly Port Phillip), and WEST AUSTRALIA (or Swan River). Area, 2,957,000 sq. miles. Pop. 1888, 3,546,725.

R. H. Major, in 1872, alleged that Australia was known to the French prior to ... 1531
Alleged discovery by Manoel Godinho de Eredia, a Portuguese. 1601
The Dutch also discover Australia ... Mch. 1606
Coast surveyed by Dutch navigators; north, by Zeachen, 1618; west, by Edels, 1619; south, by Nuyts, 1627; north, by Carpenter ... 1627
Tasman coasts S. Australia and Van Diemen's Land ... 1642-44
Terra Australis (western Australia) named New Holland by order of the states-general ... 1665
William Dampier lands in Australia ... Jan. 1686
William Dampier explores the west and northwest coasts ... 1684-90
Explorations of Willis and Carteret ... 1763-66
Capt. Cook, sir Joseph Banks, and others land at Botany Bay, and name the country "New South Wales" ... 28 Apr. 1770
Exploration of Furneaux ... 1773
Governor Phillip founds Sydney near Port Jackson, with 1030 persons ... 26 Jan. 1788
[The 82d anniversary of this event was kept with much festivity, 26 Jan. 1870.]

AUS

Great distress in consequence of the loss of the store-ship *Guardian*, capt. Riou ... 1790
Voyages of Bligh ... 1789-92
First church erected ... Aug. 1793
Government gazette first printed ... 1795
Bass's strait discovered by Bass and Flinders ... 1798
First brick church built ... 1802
Colony of Van Diemen's Land (now Tasmania) established ... 1803
Grant, 1800, and Flinders survey the coasts of Australia ... 1801-5
Insurrection of Irish convicts quelled ... 1804
Gov. Bligh, for his tyranny, deposed and sent home ... 1808
Superseded by gov. Macquarie ... 1809
Population, 29,783 (three fourths convicts) ... 1821
Expeditions into the interior by Wentworth, Lawson, Blox-land, 1813; Oxley, etc. ... 1817-23
West Australia formed into a province ... 1829
Legislative council established ... "
Sturt's expeditions into S. Australia ... 1828-31
South Australia erected into a province ... Aug. 1834
First Roman Catholic bishop (Polding) arrives ... Sept. 1835
Port Phillip (now Victoria) colonized ... Nov. "
First church of England bishop of Australia (Broughton) arrives ... June, 1836
Sir T. Mitchell's expeditions into E. Australia ... 1831-36
Colony of South Australia founded ... Dec. "
Eyre's expedition overland from Adelaide to King George's sound ... 1836-37
Melbourne founded ... Nov. 1837
Capt. Grey explores N. W. Australia ... 1837-39
Count Strzelecki explores New South Wales and Tasmania, 1838-43; discovers gold-fields in Bathurst, Wellington, etc. (kept secret by sir George Gipps) ... 1839
Suspension of transportation ... "
Strzelecki explores the Australian Alps; discovers Gipps's Land; Eyre explores W. Australia ... 1840
Census—87,200 males; 43,700 females ... 1841
Incorporation of city of Sydney ... 1842
Leichhardt's expedition (never returns) ... 1844
Sturt proceeds from S. Australia to the middle of the continent ... 1845
Great exertions of Mrs. Chisholm; establishment of "Home for Female Emigrants" ... 1841-46
Census (including Port Phillip)—114,700 males; 74,800 females. 1846
Kennedy's expedition, 1847; killed ... 1848
Agitation against revival of transportation by earl Grey ... 1849
Port Phillip erected into a separate province as Victoria ... 1850
Gold discovered by Mr. Hargraves, etc. ... 1851
Census—males, 106,000; females, 81,000 (exclusive of Victoria, 80,000) ... "
Mints established ... March, 1853
Transportation ceases ... "
Gregory's explorations of interior ... 1848, 1855-58
Death of archdeacon Cowper (aged 80), after about fifty years' residence ... July, 1858
Queensland made a province ... 4 Dec. 1859
Expedition into the interior under Mr. Landells organized, Aug. 1860
Robert O'Hara Burke, William John Wills, and others start from Melbourne ... 20 Aug. "
Burke, Wills, and two others cross Australia to gulf of Carpentaria; all perish on their return except John King, who arrives at Melbourne ... Nov. 1861
J. McDonall Stuart's expeditions ... 1858-62
Stuart, McKinlay, and Landsborough cross Australia from sea to sea ... 1861-62
Remains of Burke and Wills recovered; public funeral . . 21 Jan. 1863
General resistance throughout Australia to the reception of British convicts in W. Australia ... about June, 1864
Cessation of transportation to Australia in 3 years announced amid much rejoicing ... 26 Jan. 1865
Total population of Australia, exclusive of natives, 1,298,667, Jan. 1866
Capt. Cadell discovers mouth of the river Roper on the west coast of the gulf of Carpentaria, and fine pastoral country, lat. 14° 45′ S ... Nov. 1867
Great drought, 1,000,000 animals perish ... 1868
Ernest Morrison walks across the continent from the gulf of Carpentaria to Melbourne in 120 days, starting about 18 Dec. 1882
Gradual formation of a defensive Australian fleet and army ... 1883
Intercolonial conference of delegates on proposed annexation of New Guinea at Sydney recommended ... 6 Dec. "
Formation of Australasian federal commission ... 7-8 Dec. "
Charles Winnicke's exploring party map 40,000 miles of unknown country; announced ... Jan. 1884
Victoria, Tasmania, and Queensland accept the scheme of federation ... Aug. "
Opposed by New South Wales ... about 1 Nov. "
Several states protest against the German annexations in New Guinea, etc ... Dec. "
British flag hoisted on Woodlark and other islands ... Jan. 1885
Australian colonies proffer military contingents for the Soudan; thanked by the queen ... Feb. "
Government of Victoria introduces irrigation bill to borrow 4,000,000*l.* for supplying water to 3,242,000 acres of arid land. 1886
Rabbit pest continues, although the government has expended over 100,000*l.* Government offers a prize of 25,000*l.* for a satisfactory specific; without definite results ... 1887
Exploring expedition sent into British New Guinea from Queensland; discoveries valuable ... "
M. Pasteur sends three delegates from Paris with a supply of microbes du choléra des poules, with which he hopes to win the 25,000*l.* prize for the extermination of rabbits ... 1888

Workingmen of Australia remit to England 50,000*l.* to aid the London dock-strikers.......... 1889
[No definite account ever rendered of it.]

Great financial depression; many bank failures throughout the different provinces..........Jan.-May, 1893

Austra'sia, *Oesterreich* (Eastern Kingdom), also called Metz, a French kingdom from the 6th to the 8th century. It began with the division of the realm of Clovis by his sons, 511, and ended when Carloman became a monk, yielding the throne to his brother Pepin, as sole king of France, 747.

Austria, *Oesterreich* (Eastern Kingdom), anciently Noricum and part of Pannonia, was annexed to the Roman empire about 33 A.D.; overrun by the Huns, Avars, etc., during the 5th and 6th centuries, and taken from them by Charlemagne, 791-96. He divided the government, establishing margraves of eastern Bavaria and Austria. Louis the German, son of Louis le Débonnaire, about 817, subjugated Radbod, margrave of Austria; but in 883 the descendants of the latter rose in Bavaria against the emperor Charles the Fat, and eventually the margraves of Austria were declared immediate princes of the empire. In 1156 the margraviate was made an hereditary duchy by the emperor Frederic I.; and in 1453 it was raised to an archduchy by the emperor Frederic III. Rudolph, count of Hapsburg, elected emperor of Germany in 1273, acquired Austria in 1278; and from 1493 to 1804 his descendants were emperors of Germany. On 11 Aug. 1804, the emperor Francis II. renounced the title of emperor of Germany, and became hereditary emperor of Austria as Francis I. The political constitution of the empire is based upon (1) the pragmatic sanction of Charles VI., 1734, which declares the indivisibility of the empire and regulates the succession; (2) the pragmatic sanction of Francis I., 1 Aug. 1804, when he became emperor of Austria only; (3) the diploma of Francis Joseph, 20 Oct. 1860, granting legislative power to the provincial states and the council of the empire (Reichsrath); (4) the law of 26 Feb. 1861, on national representation. Self-government was granted to Hungary, 17 Feb. 1867. The empire was named the Austro-Hungarian monarchy, by decree, 14 Nov. 1868. The empire is now divided into two parts, separated by the river Leithe. The Cis-Leithan section comprises 14 provincial diets: Galicia, Bohemia, Silesia, Moravia, lower and upper Austria, Styria, Tyrol and Voralburg, Salzburg, Carinthia, Carniola, Trieste, and Istria, Dalmatia, and the Bukovina. The Trans-Leithan section comprises Hungary, Transylvania, Croatia, Slavonia, and the city of Fiume. Area, 241,000 sq. miles, with a pop. 1900, Austria, 26,150,708; Hungary, 19,254,559.

Frederic II., the last male of the h[illegible] of Bamberg, killed in battle with the Hungarians..........15 June, 1246

Disputed succession; the emperor Frederic II. sequesters the provinces, appointing Otto, count of Eberstein, governor for the emperor; they are seized by Ladislaus, margrave of Moravia, in right of his wife, Frederic's niece, Gertrude; he dies childless.......... 1247

Herman, margrave of Baden, marries Gertrude, and holds the provinces till his death.......... 1250

Premislas Ottocar of Bohemia acquires the provinces.......... 1254

Compelled to cede Styria to Hungary, he makes war and recovers it, in consequence of a great victory.......... 1260

He inherits Carinthia, 1263; refuses title of emperor of Germany, 1272; and does homage to Rudolph of Hapsburg, elected emperor.......... 1273

War against Ottocar as a rebel; he is compelled to cede Austria, Carinthia, and Styria to Rudolph.......... 1274

War renewed; Ottocar perishes in battle of Marchfeld..26 Aug. 1278

Albert I. assassinated by his nephew while attempting to enslave the Swiss..........1 May, 1308

Successful revolt of the Swiss.......... 1307-9

They totally defeat the Austrians under duke Leopold at Morgarten..........16 Nov. 1315

Tyrol acquired.......... 1363

Duke Leopold imposes toll on the Swiss; they resist; he makes war, and is defeated and slain at Sempach..........July, 1386

Duke Albert V. obtains Bohemia and Hungary, and is elected emperor of Germany.......... 1437

Emperor Frederick III., head of house of Hapsburg, creates the archduchy of Austria with sovereign power..........6 Jan. 1453

Austria divided between him and his relatives, 1457; war ensues between them till.......... 1463

Low Countries accrue to Austria by marriage of Maximilian with the heiress of Burgundy.......... 1477

Also Spain, by marriage of Philip I. of Austria with the heiress of Aragon and Castile.......... 1496

Bohemia and Hungary united to Austria under Ferdinand I... 1526

Austria harassed by Turkish invasions..........1529-45

Charles V., reigning over Germany, Austria, Bohemia, Hungary, Spain, the Netherlands, and their dependencies; abdicates (SPAIN).......... 1556

THIRTY YEARS' WAR..........1618-48

War of the SPANISH SUCCESSION..........1701-14

Mantua ceded to the emperor..........3 Jan. 1708

By treaty of Utrecht he obtains part of duchy of Milan..11 Apr. 1713

" Rastadt he acquires the Netherlands.......... 1714

Naples, etc., added to his dominions..........15 Nov. 1715

Further additions on the east (Temeswar, etc.) by peace of Passarowitz.......... 1718

Naples and Sicily given up to Spain.......... 1735

Death of Charles VI., last sovereign of the male line of house of Hapsburg; his daughter, Maria Theresa, becomes queen of Hungary..........20 Oct. 1740

Maria Theresa attacked by Prussia, France, Bavaria, and Saxony; supported by Great Britain (AUSTRIAN SUCCESSION, war of).......... 1741

Francis, duke of Lorraine, who had married Maria Theresa in 1736, elected emperor of Germany, as Francis I.......... 1745

Peace of Aix-la-Chapelle, Parma, Milan, etc., ceded to Spain... 1748

SEVEN YEARS' WAR; part of Silesia ceded to Prussia..........1756-63

Galicia, etc., acquired from Poland.......... 1772

War with France (BATTLES)..........1792-97

By treaty of Campo Formio, the emperor gives up Lombardy and obtains Venice..........15 Oct. 1797

Treaty of Luneville (more losses).......... 1801

Francis II., emperor of Germany, becomes Francis I., hereditary emperor of Austria..........11 Aug. 1804

His declaration of war against France..........5 Aug. 1805

Capitulation of his army at Ulm..........20 Oct. "

Napoleon enters Vienna..........14 Nov. "

Austrians and Russians defeated at AUSTERLITZ..........2 Dec. "

Treaty of PRESBURG, Austria loses Venice and Tyrol.....1 Jan. 1806

Vienna evacuated by the French..........12 Jan. "

Dissolution of the German empire, and formal abdication of the emperor..........6 Aug. "

French again take Vienna..........13 May, 1809

Restore it at peace..........24 Oct. "

Napoleon marries archduchess Maria Louisa, daughter of the emperor..........1 Apr. 1810

Congress at Vienna..........2 Oct. 1814

Treaty of Vienna..........25 Feb. 1815
[Italian provinces restored with additions—Lombardo-Venetian kingdom established, 7 Apr.]

Francis I. dies; Ferdinand I. succeeds..........2 Mch. 1835

Insurrection at Vienna; flight of Metternich..........13 Mch. 1848

" in Italy (MILAN, SARDINIA, VENICE)..........18 Mch. "

" at Vienna; emperor flies to Innspruck, 15-17 May, "

Revolution in HUNGARY..........11 Sept. "

Insurrection at Vienna; murder of count Latour..........6 Oct. "

Emperor abdicates in favor of his nephew, Francis Joseph, 2 Dec. "

Attempted assassination of emperor by Libenyi, 18 Feb.; who was executed..........28 Feb. 1853

Austrians enter Danubian principalities..........Aug. 1854

Alliance with England and France on Eastern question..2 Dec. "

Concordat grants the pope great power in the empire..18 Aug. 1855

Amnesty for political offenders of 1848-49..........12 July, 1856

Austrians quit the Danube principalities..........Mch. 1857

Diplomatic relations between Austria and Sardinia broken off in consequence..........28-30 Mch. "

Excitement throughout Europe, caused by the address of the emperor Napoleon III. to the Austrian ambassador...1 Jan. 1859

Emperor of Austria replies in a similar tone..........4 Jan. "

Austria enlarges her armies in Italy, and fortifies the line of the Ticino between her provinces and Sardinia...Feb. and Mch. "

Intervention of Russia; proposal for a congress; disputes on admission of Sardinia; Sardinia and France prepare for war, Mch. and Apr. "

Austria demands disarmament of Sardinia and dismissal of volunteers from other states within three days..........23 Apr. "

This demand rejected..........26 Apr. "

Austrians cross the Ticino..........26 Apr. "

French troops enter Piedmont..........27 Apr. "

France declares war (to expel Austrians from Italy)....3 May, "

Austrians defeated at Montebello, 20 May; at Palestro, 30-31 May; at Magenta, 4 June; at Malegnano (Marignano), 8 June, "

Prince Metternich dies, aged 86 (he had been active in wars and negotiations of Napoleon I.)..........11 June, "

Austrians defeated at Solferino (near the Mincio); emperors of Austria and France and king of Sardinia present. 24 June, "

Armistice agreed upon, 6 July; emperors meet, 11 July; preliminaries of peace signed at Villafranca (Lombardy given to Sardinia; an Italian confederation proposed).....12 July, "

Manifesto justifying the peace issued to the army, 12 July; to the people..........15 July, "

Patent issued, granting greatly increased privileges to the Protestants; announced..........Sept. "

Treaty of Zurich, confirming the preliminaries of Villafranca, signed..........10 Nov. "

Decrees removing Jewish disabilities.......6, 10 Jan., 18 Feb. 1860

Patent issued for summoning imperial council (Reichsrath) of representatives elected by provincial diets..........5 Mch. "

Austria protests against annexation of Tuscany, etc., by Sardinia..........Mch. "

Proscribed Hungarian count Teleki, at Dresden, given up to Austria about 20 Dec.; released on parole..........31 Dec. "

Amnesty for political offences in Hungary, Croatia, etc..7 Jan. 1861

New constitution for Austrian monarchy publ..........26 Feb. "

Civil and political rights granted to Protestants throughout empire, except Hungary and Venice..........8 Apr. "

Meeting of Reichsrath—no deputies from Hungary, Croatia, Transylvania, Venetia, or Istria..........29 Apr. "

Amnesty to political offenders in Hungary..........18 Nov. 186[illegible]

Reduction in the army assented to, and a personal liberty law passed Dec 1862
Insurrection in Russian Poland Jan , Austria joins in the intercession of England and France Apr 1863
Transylvanian deputies accept constitution and take seats in Reichsrath 20 Oct "
Austria joins Prussia in war with DENMARK Jan 1864
Galicia and Cracow declared in state of siege 29 Feb
Archduke Maximilian emperor of MEXICO Apr "
Peace with Denmark signed at Vienna 30 Oct
Emperor opens Reichsrath 14 Nov , free debate, state of siege in Galicia censured Dec "
Convention of GASTEIN signed 14 Aug 1865
Emperor's rescript suppressing the constitution with the view of giving autonomy to HUNGARY 20 Sept "
Rejoicings in Hungary, dissatisfaction in Austria Croatia etc Nov Dec "
Amnesty for Italy issued 1 Jan 1866
Disputes with Prussia on Holstein Jan , Mch
Preparations for war begin Mch "
Archduke Albrecht commander of southern army, 6 May , Benedek of northern 12 May "
War declared by Prussia 18 June, by ITALY 20 June, "
Austrians enter Silesia, 18 June , and Prussians Bohemia, 23 June, "
Italians defeated by archduke Albrecht at Custozza 24 June, "
Prussian victories at Nachod etc 27-29 June, "
Benedek defeated at Königgratz and Sadowa 3 July, "

[For details of the war ITALY PRUSSIA]

Emperor cedes Venetia to Napoleon, and requests intervention 4 July, "
Preliminaries of peace signed at Nikolsburg 26 July, "
Treaty of peace with Prussia at Prague 23 Aug "
" " Italy at Vienna, ceding Venetia, 3 Oct , the iron crown given up 11 Oct "
Quadrilateral and Venice surrendered to the Italians 11-19 Oct "
Baron Ferdinand von Beust late Saxon minister of foreign affairs, made Austrian foreign minister 30 Oct "
Extraordinary diet convoked (for 25 Feb) 3 Jan 1867
Autonomy for Hungary announced, resignation of Belcredi, 4 Feb , Von Beust president of council 7 Feb "
Rescript restoring a separate ministry for Hungary count Andrassy president 17 Feb "
Reichsrath opened at Vienna 20 May, "
Czechs (of Bohemia and Moravia) Croats Slavonians, Serbs, Roumans (of Transylvania), and Poles (of Galicia) protest against absorption, and demand national legislative powers, May and July, "
Emperor and empress crowned king and queen of Hungary at Buda 8 June, "
Von Beust chancellor of the empire 23 June, "
Arrangements for dividing the financial affairs of Austria and Hungary, signed 13 Sept "
Changes (respecting marriage and education) in the concordat proposed Sept "
28 bishops demand maintenance of concordat 28 Sept "
Letter from emperor to cardinal Rauscher, for liberty of conscience in opposition to the concordat, concordat almost annulled by lower house Oct "
Dualism accepted by the Reichsrath at Vienna Nov "
Civil-marriages bill (annulling clerical jurisdiction over them) passed by upper house, after sharp resistance 21-23 Mch , received emperor's assent 25 May 1868
Continued opposition of clergy to government Jan 1869
Neutrality in the Franco Prussian war announced 18 July 1870
Concordat with Rome suspended because of promulgation of doctrine of papal infallibility 30 July "
Ministry support Great Britain in opposing the Russian repudiation of treaty of Paris (RUSSIA) Nov "
Austrian army, 864,869 regulars, 187,527 landwehr (militia), Dec "
New German empire recognized by the emperor Jan 1871
Resignation of count Beust, arch chancellor, much excitement 6 Nov "
Count Andrassy appointed minister of imperial household and of foreign affairs, Von Beust ambassador at London, Lonyay, premier of Hungary 13-14 Nov "
Reichsrath opened by the emperor with speech announcing political and educational reforms 28 Dec "
New constitutional law promulgated giving the emperor power to order new elections of the chambers 13 Mch 1872
Reform bill passed changing the Reichsrath into a national representative assembly 10 Mch 1873
Elections for Reichsrath 228 constitutionalists, 125 federals, 30 Oct , Reichsrath opened by the emperor, 5 Nov , 25th anniversary of the emperor's accession celebrated, amnesty for political offenders 2 Dec "
Encyclical letter from the pope condemning the new ecclesiastical laws, dated 7 Mch 1874
Protest of Austrian bishops, both parties adopt Cavour's cry, "A free church in a free state" Apr "
New bed of Danube inaugurated by emperor 30 May, 1875
Death of ex emperor Ferdinand 29 June, "
Declaration of neutrality in Russo Turkish war by Austria and Hungary, foreign policy to be for "the interest of the monarchy, to the exclusion of all antipathies and sympathies," M de Tisza (Hungarian) 26 June, 1877
Count Andrassy at the Berlin conference 13 June-13 July, 1878
Austria to occupy and administer Bosnia and Herzegovina, by treaty of Berlin 13 July, "
Austrians enter, and war ensues (BOSNIA) 29 July, "
Bosnia occupied (except Novi Bazar) Oct 1878
Andrassy resigns, baron Haymerle made foreign minister and president of council 8 Oct 1879
Marriage of archduke Rudolph and princess Stephanie of Belgium 10 May 1881
Sudden death of baron Haymerle 10 Oct "
Insurrection in Herzegovina etc , skirmishes with Austrians, 18-31 Jan , insurgents defeated 1882
Provisional government said to have been formed by insurgents about 9 Feb "
Mahometans sympathize with Christian insurgents Feb "
Successful advance of the Austrians, capture of Dreglia announced 14 Mch "
Insurgents adopting guerilla warfare about 12 May "
"New German People's party" formed, manifesto published, about 29 May, "
Execution of Oberdank a soldier, for attempted assassination of emperor 20 Dec "
600th anniversary of establishment of house of Hapsburg celebrated 27 Dec "
Slavonic agitation against Germans and Magyars and taxation (CROATIA), Aug -Sept , conciliatory policy of government Sept 1883
Birth of princess to archduke Rudolph and the princess Stephanie 2 Sept "
Much social disaffection at Vienna, 2 detective policemen assassinated, Hlubek Bloch Jan 1884
Corpl Hermann Stellmacher, assassin of Bloch captured 25 Jan a great conspiracy suspected, law decreed by count Taaffe repressing public meetings the press, trials by jury etc , 30 Jan , many arrested or expelled Jan "
Government measures pass the chambers 1 Feb "
Hugo Schenk and Schlossarek executed for murder of several servant-girls 22 Apr "
Stellmacher executed 8 Aug "
Reichsrath dissolves Apr 1885
Czar of Russia meets the emperor at Kremsier in Moldavia 25 Aug "
A bill for creating a Landsturm introduced in the Reichsrath and passed 16 Apr 1886

[Giving the nation a war footing of 1,500,000]

Death of count F von Beust, great liberal statesman, ex chancellor 24 Oct "
Treaty of alliance with Germany and Italy signed 13 Mch 1887
Defensive treaty with Germany against Russian or other aggression, 7 Oct 1879, first published 3 Feb 1888
The crown prince Franz Karl Joseph Rudolph d at Meyerling, 30 Jan 1889

[Supposed suicide in consequence of a love affair with the young baroness Vetsera—physicians report mental alienation]

New army bill as amended by the Hungarian diet adopted by the upper house 8 Apr "
Catholic congress of nobles and clergy meets at Vienna 29 Apr "
Death of count Alfred Potocki (aged 72) 20 May, "
Temporary reconciliation of the Czechs and Germans in Bohemia, by the intervention of the emperor 17-19 Jan 1890
Count Julius Andrassy d in Istria 18 Feb "
Resignation of the prime-minister Koloman Tisza 7 Mch "

[Succeeded by count Julius Szapary]

Riot of about 1000 workmen — —, on the Galician frontier, suppressed by military 24 Apr "
Labor agitation strikes with rioting in different provinces, Apr , gradually subsides May, "
Marriage of the emperor's youngest daughter, archduchess Marie Valerie, to the archduke Francis Salvator 31 July, "
Austrian fleet under archduke Stephen reviewed by queen Victoria off Cowes, Isle of Wight 11 Aug "
Great loss of life and property through floods 12-14 Aug "
The compromise between the Germans and the Czechs in Bohemia not effected 30 Nov "
Result of elections German Liberals, 110, Poles 57, Young Czechs 36, Old Czechs 10, Clericals, 31 Bohemian Conservatives, 18, miscellaneous, 93 total, 353 15 Mch 1891
The German Liberals and Poles support count Taaffe's ministry about 26 Mch "
New treaty of commerce between Austria Hungary and Germany signed at Vienna 3 May, "
The triple alliance renewed 28 June, "
New commercial treaty with Germany, Italy, Belgium, and Switzerland . 25 Jan 1892
Currency reform bill passed 27 May, "
The new bourse tax passed, 18 Sept 1892, goes into operation, 1 Jan 1893
Meeting of Christian socialists at Vienna 13 Mch "
Heavy rains and destructive inundations in Bukowina and in Galicia, reported 7 June, "
Strike of 8000 miners at Kladno, reported 12 June, "
The Reichsrath reopened, count Taaffe introduces a bill for electoral reform, leading to universal suffrage 10 Oct "
Ministerial crisis, conference of heads of parties 4 Nov "
Count Taaffe succeeded by Windischgrätz 12 Nov "
Opening of the Reichsrath, statement of prince Windischgrätz . 23 Nov "
Trial of anarchists (14), 8 sentenced to various terms of imprisonment, 6 acquitted 19-23 Feb 1894
Commercial treaty between Austria Hungary and Russia, ratified . 6 July, "
Death of the archduke Albrecht, eminent in the army, liberal, and popular (b 1817), son of archduke Charles 18 Feb 1895
Death of prince Richard Metternich, diplomatist 1 Mch "

26 students tried at Tarnopol, Galicia, for high treason and conspiring for the independence of Poland, 4 Mch , all acquitted 13 Mch 1895
Resignation of count Kalnoky, foreign minister, on account of differences with Hungary respecting the action of the papal nuncio, mgr Agliardi, 16 May, succeeded by count Agenor Goluchowski, conservative and clerical 17 May "
Resignation of the Windischgrätz (coalition) ministry, through the withdrawal of the German liberals 19 June, "
Provisional cabinet count Kielmansegg, premier 20 June, "
Death of the archduke Ladislaus by an accident Sept. "
New ministry, count Badeni, premier 2 Oct "
Opening of the Reichsrath, count Badeni declares a neutral policy 22 Oct. "
Financial crisis at Vienna and Budapest 9 Nov "
Death of count Taaffe, ex premier (aged 63) 29 Nov "
Anti Semitic movement 1895-1896
Death of the archduke Karl Ludwig, heir presumptive 19 May, "
Electoral reform bill passed by the Reichsrath 28 May, "
Differences between Austria and Hungary settled by compromise at a meeting of the ministers in Vienna 19 July, "
The archduchess Maria Dorothea, niece of the emperor, married to the duke of Orleans at Vienna. 5 Nov "
The railway laborers' association dissolved by government order 21 Mch 1897
The Badeni cabinet resigns, 2 Apr , resignation not accepted by the emperor 4 Apr "
Impeachment of the ministry, disorderly scenes in the Reichsrath, 6 7, 24 May, deadlock, the session closed, 2 June, reassembled 23 Sept "
Duel between count Badeni and herr Wolf 25 Sept "
Nearly 24 hours debate in the Reichsrath on the renewal of the *Ausgleich* with Hungary, violent scenes, socialists expelled, Badeni resigns 28 Nov , Gautsch forms a new ministry, 30 Nov , deadlock, 12 Dec , the Reichsrath closed by decree 29 Dec. "
Count Kalnoky (b 29 Dec 1832), foreign minister from 1881-95, d 13 Feb 1898
The language ordinances (modified) published 5 Mch "
Baron Gautsch resigns, 5 Mch , new cabinet formed by count Thun 7 Mch "
Bills for the renewal of the *Ausgleich* introduced 20 Apr "
Jubilee of the emperor's reign celebrated. 8 May, "
Reichsrath reassembled (deadlock), 1 June, *et seq* , prorogued, 13 June, "
Assassination of the empress Elizabeth at Geneva by Luigi Lucchem (aged 25), an Italian anarchist 10 Sept. "
Lucchem sentenced to life imprisonment 10 Nov "
Impeachment of count Badeni carried by a majority of 8 in the Reichsrath 26 Apr , rejected in the lower house 17 Nov "
Jubilee amnesty to army and navy, issued 20 Nov "
Increasing agrarian revolt against clerical interference in secular affairs 21 Nov "
Count Thun protests against the expulsion of Austrians from Prussia 29 Nov "
The Austro Hungarian *Ausgleich* renewed for 1899 by imperial rescript 31 Dec. "
Disorderly scenes in the Reichsrath 15 Dec 1898-17 Jan 1899
Reichsrath prorogued 1 Feb "
Mass meetings of social democrats in Vienna, 6 Feb , manifesto against the Germans by the Young Czechs, issued 11 Feb "
Conference of R C bishops of Vienna, at Austria, on the "emancipation from Rome" movement 12 Apr "
Johann Strauss, "Walzerkönig" popular composer, d (aged 73), 3 June, public funeral at Vienna 6 June, "
Negotiations respecting the Austro Hungarian *Ausgleich*, 24 May, a bill passed second reading 4 July, "
Count Thun's ministry promulgates the outstanding portions of the *Ausgleich* and resigns, 23 Sept. , count Clary forms a cabinet 1 Oct. "
Jewish meeting at Vienna to protest against the charge of ritual murder revived against their creed 7 Oct "
Language ordinances repealed, announced 17 Oct "
Reichsrath meets, premier states neutral policy, 18 Oct., stormy scene, sitting closed 24 Oct. "
Fatal Czech riots in Moravia, German and Jewish houses looted, troops called out 22-24 Oct. "
Anti Semitism and agitation against the use of German as the official language, rioting in Bohemia and Moravia Nov "
Disorder in the Reichsrath provoked by the Czechs and Anti Semites, 9, 10 Nov , crisis averted by the emperor, 20, 21 Nov "
Count Clary's cabinet resigns. 21 Dec. "
Dr von Wittek forms a "provisional ministry" 22 Dec "
The emperor intimates firmly to dr Stransky, a Czech leader, that the language of the army must remain German 13 Jan 1900
Coal miners' strike, 91,000 men involved, commission of inquiry appointed, reported 23 Jan "
Nationality conference (Czechs and Germans) on the language question, 5 Feb , sub committee appointed 22 Mch "
New language bills for Bohemia and Moravia introduced, noisy scene in the Reichsrath 8 May, "
Deadlock continues, session closed by the emperor 9 June, "
The emperor attends the army manœuvres in Galicia, receives a Polish parliamentary deputation, threatens the suspension of the constitution if obstruction continues 13 Sept "
Elections, 3 Jan , defeat of Clericals and Anti Semites, reported, 15 Jan , the Reichsrath opened 31 Jan. 1901
Violent scenes in the Reichsrath. 20 Feb. "
Pan Germanic union, advocating emancipation from Rome, meets in Vienna 5 May, "
Dr Lueger and the Anti Semitic party beaten at the polls in lower Austria 2 July, 1901
Reichsrath meets, the premier protests against the nationality strife 17 Oct. "
Manifesto against obstruction issued by the Germans in the Reichsrath 19 Nov "
Anti clerical association founded, first meeting held in Vienna, 18 Dec. "
Reichsrath Pan Germanic demonstration, 18 Mch , uproar over the language question 9 Apr 1902
Conference of Austrian and Hungarian premiers on the *Ausgleich* and tariff questions May, "
The triple alliance renewed 28 June, "
Riots in Agram Sept "
Reichsrath meets, 15 Oct , deadlock on the *Ausgleich* negotiations 17 Oct "
Violent scenes between Czechs and Germans 11, 13 Nov "
Renewal of *Ausgleich* for 10 years, agreed to 31 Dec "
Act of economic union with Hungary, signed, 11 Jan , new customs tariff, etc 15, 17 Jan 1903
Sugar convention ratified 31 Jan "
Debt conversion bill passed 16 Feb "
Army bills passed 20 Feb "
Dispute between Austrian and Hungarian parliaments respecting the sugar allotment system 29 July, "
Inter parliamentary conference at Vienna adopt resolution in favor of a new international congress to consider the disarmament schemes formulated by Russia in 1898 9 Sept "
Austro Hungarian army bill virtually repealed by the adoption of a Polish amendment to a German urgency motion sanctioning the enrolment of the ordinary Austrian contingent of 54,924 recruits 26 Sept "
Czar visits the emperor at Vienna, 30 Sept., imperial conference on Macedonian affairs 2 Oct "
Austro Russian instructions for the execution of the reforms in Macedonia presented to the sultan of Turkey, 22 Oct , reform scheme accepted by the porte 25 Nov "
Troops revolt in Hungary 4 Jan 1904
Mobs stone the palace of the emperor at Buda Pesth 16 Mch "
New Hungarian emigration law causes dissatisfaction 1 Apr "
Riots at Grosswardein, Hungary 24 Apr "
A Dvorak, composer, d at Prague 1 May, "
Maurus Jokai author, d at Buda Pesth 6 May, "
Dr Herzl, Zionist d at Vienna . 3 July, "
Mormonism prohibited in Hungary 22 Sept. "
Rioting in Hungarian parliament Nov 1904-Jan 1905
Hungarian parliament dissolved 4 Jan "
The liberal government defeated at the polls (the first time since 1867) . 27 Jan "
Kossuth party demands use of Hungarian language 21 Mch "

MARGRAVES OF AUSTRIA.

Leopold I 928, Albert I, 1018, Ernest 1056, Leopold II, 1075, Leopold III, 1096, Albert II, 1136, Leopold IV, 1136, Henry II, 1142 (made a duke, 1156)

DUKES

1150 Henry II
1177 Leopold V He captured Richard I of England when returning *incognito from the crusade*, and was compelled to surrender him to the emperor Henry VI
1194 Frederic I, the Catholic
1198 Leopold VI, the Glorious. Killed in battle
1230 Frederic II, the Warlike Killed in a battle with Hungarians, 15 June, 1246.
Interregnum
1276 Rudolph I
1282 Albert I and his brother, Rudolph II. **Albert, emperor of** Germany, 1298
1308 Frederic I and Leopold I
1326 Frederic I
1330 Albert II and Otho, his brother
1339 Albert II
1358 Rudolph IV
1365 Albert III and Leopold II or III (killed at Sempach)
1395 William I and brothers and their cousin Albert IV
1411 The same. The provinces divided into duchies of Austria and Carinthia, and county of Tyrol
1411 Albert V, duke of Austria, obtains Bohemia and Moravia, elected king of Hungary and emperor, 1437, dies, 1439, succeeded by his posthumous son
1439 Ladislaus, who dies childless, 1457
1457 The emperor Frederic III and Albert VI
1493 Maximilian I, son of Frederic III. (archduke), emperor, GERMANY, 1493-1804

EMPERORS.

1804 Francis I, b 1768 (late Francis II of Germany), styled emperor of Austria only, 11 Aug 1804, resigned empire of Germany, 6 Aug 1806, d 2 Mch 1835
1835 Ferdinand, his son, 2 Mch , abdicated in favor of his nephew (his brother Francis Charles having renounced his rights), 2 Dec 1848, b 1793, d 29 June, 1875.
1848. Francis Joseph (son of Francis Charles), b 18 Aug. 1830, succeeded, 2 Dec 1848, married 24 Apr 1854, to Elizabeth of Bavaria, crowned king of Hungary, 8 June, 1867
Heir presumptive archduke Franz Ferdinand, b. 18 Dec. 1863, nephew of the emperor and son of archduke Karl Ludwig

Austrian Succession, War of (1740-1748) Charles IV, emperor of Germany without male heirs, desirous of securing the succession to his daughter, Maria Theresa, queen of Hungary and Bohemia, in 1731 framed the pragmatic sanction. England and most powers of Europe, except France, Spain, and Sardinia, acceded. The emperor died 20 Oct. 1740, when Maria Theresa assumed the title. Immediately counter-claims to the succession were advanced by the electors of Bavaria and Saxony and the kings of Poland and Spain, while Sardinia claimed a portion of the empire, and Frederick II. of Prussia wanted Silesia. France espoused the cause of Bavaria, while England alone offered assistance to the queen. The war that ensued is termed that of the Austrian succession, in which nearly all Europe took part. The succession was confirmed to the queen by the peace of Aix-la-Chapelle, 1748.

authors. LITERATURE.

auto-da-fé ("act of faith"), the term given to the punishment of a heretic (generally burning alive), inflicted by the INQUISITION. The first auto-da-fé was held by Torquemada at Seville, in 1481. The last was probably that mentioned by Llorente, the historian of the Inquisition, as solemnized in Mexico in 1815.

automaton figures or **androides,** made to imitate the actions of living beings, are of early invention. Archytas's flying dove was formed about 400 B.C. Friar Bacon is said to have made a brazen head which spoke, 1264 A.D. Albertus Magnus spent 30 years in making another. A coach and 2 horses, with a footman, a page, a lady inside, were made by Camus for Louis XIV. when a child, 1649; the horses and figures moved naturally, variously, and perfectly. Vaucanson, in 1738, made an artificial duck, which performed many functions of a real one—eating, drinking, and quacking; and he also made a flute-player. The writing automaton, exhibited in 1769, was a pentagraph worked by a hidden confederate. An automaton chess-player, invented by baron Kempelen, of Presburg, Hungary, 1769, and known as "Maelzel's chess-player," excited intense curiosity wherever exhibited for many years; this was also worked by a concealed person; so was the "invisible girl," 1800. Maelzel made a trumpeter about 1809. Early in this century an automaton was exhibited in London which pronounced several sentences with tolerable distinctness. The "anthropoglossus," an alleged talking-machine, exhibited at St. James's hall, London, July, 1864, was proved to be a gross imposition. The exhibition of the talking-machine of prof. Faber, of Vienna, in London, began 27 Aug. 1870, at the Palais Royal, Argyll street, W. The automatic chess-player at the Crystal Palace, 1873. Psycho, an automaton card-player, invented by J. N. Maskelyne and John Algernon Clarke, exhibited in London, Jan. 1875. An automaton hare was hunted at Hendon, near London, 9 Sept. 1876.

automobile. The industry having been established in the United States within the last 10 years, statistics are difficult to gather, and, as a result, a large amount of misinformation has been scattered broadcast regarding the growth and present status of the industry. With the formation of the National Association of Automobile Manufacturers, which is composed of 60 makers of motor cars, besides 50 associate members who make accessories and parts, and the formation during 1904 of the Motor and Accessories Manufacturers' Association, statistics are more readily gathered. 30 members of the National Association of Automobile Manufacturers are also members of the Association of Licensed Automobile Manufacturers, and 7 concerns who handle imported cars only have formed a Licensed Importers' Association and pay a royalty to the owners of the Selden patent. During 1904 about 600 complete automobiles were imported, which, with the duty of 45 per cent. and the cost of transportation added, average in cost about $6000 each, making a total gross valuation of imported cars of $3,600,000—from France, Germany, Italy, England, Belgium, and Switzerland, leading in value and numbers in the order named. The unlicensed makers made about 5000 cars, costing on an average $900 apiece, a gross total of $4,500,000. The licensed makers produced about 20,000 cars, of an average value of $1200 apiece, a total gross valuation of $24,000,000. For the Jan. show in New York (1905) space was taken by 95 makers of complete cars, also by 111 makers of accessories and parts. For the Chicago show in Feb. 1905, space was taken by 72 makers of complete cars and by 84 makers of accessories and parts. These makers and figures show the real strength and status of the industry. The West is still the seat of the manufacturing industry, over 50 per cent. of the total output of the United States being made in the state of Michigan, in or about the city of Detroit. The other states follow in the order of their production—Ohio, Wisconsin, Massachusetts, New York, Indiana, Pennsylvania, Connecticut, Illinois, and Missouri. A large export business has been built up on low-priced runabout cars, in which the United States lead the world on account of their low price, durability, and simplicity. The use of electric vehicles has not materially increased during 1904, excepting in the large cities, where they are largely used for commercial purposes and public cab service, notably so in New York city, where 500 are in daily use. The production of steam automobiles has largely decreased, and, as a type, may be said to be extinct, except for their production in touring cars in Cleveland, O., under the steam generator flash system. The old-style tubular-boiler steam wagon is, however, sold in a limited way in the New England states, where 3 of their manufacturers are located. The demand and the production of automobiles of the gasolene type, viz., cylinder fired, was the leading feature of the industry during 1904. It was confidently expected at the beginning of 1904 that the sale of automobiles would have reached a larger figure during the year than they actually did. The demand was present, but during the selling season the manufacturers were unable to secure a proper amount of the right material, and hence the supply fell short of the demand. 21 states in the United States have license laws regulating the use of automobiles, and, as showing that this indicates their large use in these states, the states are named herewith: Alabama, Connecticut, Delaware, District of Columbia, Illinois, Iowa, Kansas, Kentucky, Maine, Maryland, Massachusetts, Minnesota, Mississippi, New Jersey, New York, Ohio, Pennsylvania, Rhode Island, Tennessee, Vermont, Virginia. Taking the registered licensed figures from these states, it is estimated that there were about 50,000 automobiles in use at the close of 1904 throughout the United States. New York state leads

BEST AMERICAN TRACK RECORDS. (Corrected to January 1, 1905.

Distance.	Time. m. s.	Record Holder.	Power.	H. P.	Weight of Machine.	Place and Date. All in 1904.
1 mile.......	51 1-5	Barney Oldfield	Gasolene	60	1432 to 2204 lbs.	Denver, Col., 4 Nov.
2 miles......	1.47 1-5	" "	"	"	" "	" "
3 miles......	2.43 1-5	" "	"	"	" "	" "
4 miles......	3.36 2-5	" "	"	"	" "	" "
5 miles......	4.30	" "	"	"	" "	" "
6 miles......	5.25	" "	"	"	" "	" 6 Nov.
7 miles......	6.10	" "	"	"	" "	" 4 Nov.
8 miles......	7.14	" "	"	"	" "	" "
9 miles......	8.17	Charles Basle	"	90	" "	Providence, R. I., 10 Sept.
10 miles......	9.12 3-5	Barney Oldfield	"	60	" "	Empire, N. Y. city, 29 Oct.

During the record-breaking trial of Oldfield 5 Nov. 1904, he also made new world's records from 11 to 20 miles inclusive, as follows: 11 miles, 10.18 1-5; 12 miles, 11.15, 13 miles, 12.12 1-5; 14 miles, 13.00; 15 miles, 14.05; 16 miles, 15.01; 17 miles, 15.57; 18 miles, 16.53; 19 miles, 17.49 2-5; 20 miles, 18.45 2-5.

Earl Kiser, with 80 H. P. machine, at Cleveland, 19 Oct. 1904, made world's records from 21 to 25 miles, as follows: 21 miles, 20.04 2-5; 22 miles, 21.01 2-5; 23 miles, 21.59 3-5; 24 miles, 22.58; 25 miles, 23.59.

Charles Gorndt, with a 40 H. P. machine, at Cleveland, 19 Oct. 1904, made world's records from 30 to 50 miles inclusive, as follows: 30 miles, 33.20 4-5; 35 miles, 38.46 3-5; 40 miles, 44.30 2.5; 45 miles, 49.55 3-5; 50 miles, 55.42.

Harry S. Harkness, with 60 H. P. machine, at Elkwood, N. J., 18 Aug. 1904, made the following records; 55 miles, 1.07.04 2-5; 60 miles, 1.12.40 3-5.

Emil Voig holds the best authenticated American record of 2 hours 52 minutes for 100 miles, made on Long Island, 26 Apr. 1902.

with 15,500; Massachusetts, 6600. As an evidence of the growth of the industry in New York state, the records show that at the end of 1901, 950 automobiles were registered; at the end of 1902, 2000; at the end of 1903, 8835; at the end of 1904, 15,550. Prices range from $425 to $8000, with an average price of about $1200, the makers preferring to maintain the price and make a better product for the money rather than to reduce the price and to reduce the quality. There are 16 makers of motor cycles in the United States. The motor cycle has not as yet caught on with the American public, owing to some mechanical details and our bad roads. In France, Germany, and England, where they are registered and good roads abound, they are, however, more numerous than automobiles. The officers of the National Association of Automobile Manufacturers are as follows: *Pres.*, Windsor T. White; *1st V.-Pres.*, Charles Clifton; *2d V.-Pres.*, E. H. Cutler; *3d V.-Pres.*, G. W. Bennett; *Treas.*, William R. Innis; *Sec.*, J. Wesley Allison; *Gen. Mgr.*, S. A. Miles; *Counsel*, Charles Thaddeus Terry. The offices of the association are at 7 East Forty-second Street, New York city.

The new records made at the international automobile races held at Ormond Beach, Florida, 24–31 Jan. 1905, were as follows: 24 Jan. Arthur McDonald, the Scotch autoist, lowered the 5-mile record to 3.17 with his 90 H. P. car. 25 Jan. H. L. Bowden lowered the 1-mile record to 34 1-5 seconds with his 120 H. P. Mercedes. Arthur McDonald made a new American record in the 1-kilometre time trials with his 90 H. P. Napier car, time 23 seconds. 28 Jan. a new 10-mile world's record was made by E. R. Thomas in his 90 H. P. car, time 6.31 4-5. 30 Jan. H. W. Fletcher, driving the 80 H. P. De Dietrich car owned by O. F. Thomas, won the 100-mile race for the W. K. Vanderbilt, jr., trophy in 1h. 18m. 24s, an average speed of 75 miles an hour. This establishes a record for the distance. 31 Jan. the 50-mile world's record was broken in the 50-mile handicap race by H. W. Fletcher in the De Dietrich car which won the Vanderbilt trophy on 30 Jan. He started at scratch and covered the distance in 38.51. The race was won, however, by Paul Sartori, driving A. G. Vanderbilt's car. Mr. Sartori had a handicap allowance of 4.50, and finished in 40.20, actual time. In the 20-mile open race for the E. R. Thomas trophy, five men lowered the record of 17.02 made last year by W. K. Vanderbilt, jr. The world's record for 1 mile, 34 1-5 seconds, made by H. L. Bowden on 25 Jan., was beaten by himself in a 120 H. P. Mercedes. He covered the distance in 32 4-5 seconds. The hill-climbing record up Mt. Washington, 8 miles, is held by H. Harkness, time 24.57.

autotypog'raphy, a process of producing a metal plate from drawings, made known by Mr. Wallis in Apr. 1863; it resembled NATURE-PRINTING.

Auttose towns. Indian villages in the Creek country, Alabama, attacked and destroyed by brig.-gen. John Floyd, with 950 Georgia militia, 29 Nov. 1813. GEORGIA.

Av'alon or **Avilion,** the earthly paradise of Celtic Mythology, a "green island" in the Atlantic far to the westward.

"I am going a long way . . .
To the island-valley of Avilion;
Where falls not hail, or rain, or any snow,
Nor ever wind blows loudly; but it lies
Deep-meadowed, happy, fair with orchard lawns
And bowery hollows crown'd with summer sea."
—*Tennyson*, "The Passing of Arthur."

Avars, barbarians who ravaged Pannonia, and annoyed the Eastern empire in the 6th and 7th centuries; subdued by Charlemagne about 799, after an 8 years' war.

Avebury or **Abury,** Wiltshire. Here are the remains of the largest so-called Druidical work in England. They have been surveyed by Aubrey, 1648; Dr. Stukeley, 1720; and sir R. C. Hoare in 1812, and by others. Stukeley's "Abury" (1743), and Hoare's "Ancient Wiltshire" (1812–21) give full information. Many theories have been put forth, but the origin of these remains is still unknown. They are considered to date from the "stone age," *i.e.* when weapons and implements were mainly formed of stone. STONEHENGE.

Avein or **Avaine** (Luxembourg, Belgium), where French and Dutch defeated Spaniards, 20 May, 1635.

"Äve Ma-ri'a!" or **"Äve Māry"** the salutation of the angel Gabriel to the Virgin (Luke i. 28), was made a formula of devotion by pope John XXI. about 1326. About 1500 A.D. Vincentius Ferrerius used it before his discourses.—*Bingham.*

"But 'Ave Mary' made she moan,
And 'Ave Mary' night and morn."—*Tennyson.*

Aventine hill, the largest of the 7 hills of Rome, was divided from the Palatine by the valley of the Circus Maximus. Around its northern base flows the Tiber. It was said to have derived its name from Aventinus, an ancient king of Alba, buried here. ROME.

Averasboro, North Carolina. Here on 16 Mch. 1865, gen. Slocum of gen. Sherman's army attacked the confederates under gen. Hardee, who opposed his progress, and compelled them to retreat. Federal loss, 77 killed, 477 wounded.

Avignon (*Ä-ven-yon'*), a city (S.E. France) ceded by Philip III. to the pope in 1273, and made the papal seat by Clement V. in 1309. In 1348 Clement VI. purchased the sovereignty from Jane, countess of Provence and queen of Naples. In 1408, the French, wearied of the schism, expelled Benedict XIII., and Avignon ceased to be the papal seat. Here were held 9 councils (1080–1457). Avignon was seized and restored several times by French kings; the last time restored, 1773. It was claimed by the National Assembly, 1791, and confirmed to France by a congress of sovereigns in 1815. In Oct. 1791, horrible massacres took place here. POPES, 1309–94.

axe, wedge, lever, and other tools, were ascribed to the mythical Dædalus, an artificer of Athens; also the invention of masts and sails for ships, 1240 B.C. Many tools are represented on Egyptian monuments.

axiom (Gr. ἀξίωμα), a self-evident truth, an elementary principle of reasoning; especially applied to the assumptions of geometry which cannot be proved, but are regarded as obvious and indisputable and as the premises of mathematical deduction. The axioms of Euclid (300 B.C.) are still the accepted basis of GEOMETRY.

Axum or **Auxume,** a town in Abyssinia said to have been the capital of a kingdom whose people were converted to Christianity by Frumentius about 330, and were allies of Justinian, 533.

Ayacu'cho, Peru. Here the Peruvians finally achieved their independence by defeating the Spaniards, 9 Dec. 1824.

ayde or **aide,** a tax paid by vassals to a lord upon urgent occasions. In France and England an aide was due for knighting the king's eldest son. One was demanded by Philip the Fair, 1313. The aide due upon the birth of a prince, ordained by the statute of Westminster (Edward I.), 1285, was not to be levied until he was 15 years of age, for the ease of the subject. The aide for marriage of the king's eldest daughter could not be demanded in England until her 7th year. In feudal tenures there was an aide for ransoming the chief lord; so when Richard I. was kept prisoner by the emperor of Germany, an aide of 20*s.* to redeem him was levied upon every knight's fee. BENEVOLENCE.

Ayles'bury, Buckinghamshire, was reduced by the West Saxons in 571. St. O'Syth, beheaded by the pagans in Essex, was buried there, 600. William the Conqueror invested favorites with some of its lands, under the tenure of providing "straw for his bedchambers; 3 eels for his use in winter; and in summer, straw, rushes, and 2 green geese thrice every year." Incorporated by charter in 1554.

Aylesford, Kent. Here, it is said, the Britons were victorious over the Saxon invaders, 455, and Horsa was killed.

Ayllon's (*il-yon'*), **de, Settlement,** in Virginia, 1526. AMERICA.

Az'of, Sea of, the Palus Mæotis of the ancients, communicates by the strait of Yenikalé (the Bosporus Cimmerius) with the Black sea, and is entirely surrounded by Russian territory, Taganrog and Kertch being the principal places. An expedition of British, French, and Turkish troops, under sir G. Brown, arrived at Kertch, 24 May, 1855, when the Russians retired, after blowing up the fortifications. On the 25th, the allies marched upon Yenikalé, which offered no resistance. The same evening the allied fleet entered the sea of Azof, and in a few days completed their occupation of it, capturing a large number of merchant vessels, etc Immense stores were destroyed by the Russians

azoimide, a compound of hydrogen and nitrogen (azote) A very explosive gas, obtained from organic sources, such as benzoyl-glycollic acid and hippuric acid, by prof Curtius in 1890 It forms salts by combination with metals

Azores' or **Western Isles,** N Atlantic, belonging to Portugal, and about 800 miles from its coast, often identified with the fabled Atlantis of the ancients Area, 1005 sq miles, pop 1881, 270 000 These islands are first found distinctly marked in a map of 1351, with names given It has been conjectured that the discoverers were Genoese The so-called Flemish discovery, 1432, by Vanderberg of Bruges, was certainly not the first Gonzalo Velho Cabral, sent by the Portuguese court fell in with St Mary's in 1432, and in 1457 they were all discovered and named Azores from the goshawks found on them They were given by Alfonso V to the duchess of Burgundy in 1466, and colonized by Flemings They were subject to Spain, 1580-1640 The isle of Terceira, during the usurpation of dom Miguel, declared for donna Maria, 1829, and fixed its government at the capital Angra, 1830-33 A volcano at St George's destroyed the town of Ursulina May, 1808, and in 1811 a volcano appeared near St Michael's, in the sea, where it was 80 fathoms deep, an island then formed which gradually disappeared A destructive earthquake, lasting 12 days, occurred in 1591 in St Michael's, the largest island of the group, area, 200 sq miles

az'ote, a name given by Lavoisier and French chemists to NITROGEN

Az'tecs, the ruling tribe in Mexico at the time of the Spanish invasion under Cortes (1519) AMERICA

B

Ba'al (Lord), male deity of the Phœnicians, often worshipped by Israelites, as by Ahab, 918 B.C. His priests and votaries were massacred by Jehu, and his temple defiled, 884 B.C.

Baalbec (*Bal bec'*) **Heliop'olis** (both meaning "City of the Sun"), an ancient city of Syria, of which magnificent ruins remain visited by Wood and Dawkins in 1751, and others Its origin is lost in antiquity The city was sacked by the Moslems, 748, and by Timour Beg, 1400 Here are found the ruins of several temples One called the "Great Temple" was built on a magnificent platform, which extends east and west 1100 feet. The peristyle of the temple proper was of 54 columns, with shafts 62 feet high, 7 feet in diameter at the base, and 5 feet at the top Here Septimius Severus built a temple to the sun, 200 A.D.

Babel, Tower of, built by Noah's posterity, 2247 B.C. (Gen xi) The magnificent temple of Belus, which some identify with this tower, is said to have had lofty spires and many statues of gold, one of them 40 feet high In the upper part of this temple was the tomb of the founder, Belus (Nimrod of scripture), deified after death —*Blair* The Birs Nimroud, examined by Rich, Layard, and others, is by some held to be the remains of the tower of Babel

Babeuf's conspiracy. François Noel Babeuf (Gracchus) and others, in Apr 1796, constituted themselves a "secret directory of public safety," at Paris, aiming to re-establish the revolutionary government, but, arrested, Babeuf was sentenced to death, and was guillotined after attempting suicide, 27 May, 1797. AGRARIAN LAW.

Bâbi-ism, a new sect in Persia, founded in 1843 by Mirza Ali Mahomed, an enthusiast, at Shiraz He termed himself the "Bâb," or "gate," of knowledge, and, giving a new exposition of the Koran, claimed to be the incarnate Holy Spirit His destruction, with most of his followers, was due to Hossein, one of his disciples, combining political and warlike views with their spiritual dogmas. The sect was tolerated by the shah Mahomet, but nearly exterminated by his successor in 1848-49 The Bâb himself was executed 15 July, 1849 The present head of the sect, still numerous, Beheyah Allah, imprisoned in a Turkish fortress, is said to be well conversant with the Bible and to teach a doctrine based on it, termed 'Bâb el Huk" (gate of truth) E G Brown's "Narrative" respecting this sect publ 1892

Babylonia (Babilu Assyrian, Babirush, Persian, the Shinar, Babel, and land of the Chaldees of the Old Testament), a vast plain watered by the Tigris and Euphrates, the seat of a great Asiatic empire, traditionally stated to have been founded by Belus, supposed to have been the Nimrod of Gen x 1, 8 ASSYRIA According to the earliest existing history the country was divided between two races, the Sumir (TURANIAN), and the Accad—ACCADIANS—(Semitic), which became predominant. The city of Babylon was at one time the most magnificent in the world The hanging gardens are described as having been square, rising in terraces as high as the walls of the city, with steps between the terraces The whole was sustained by arches on arches, and on the top were flat stones cemented with plaster of bitumen covered with sheets of lead, supporting the garden mould, with large trees, shrubs flowers, and various vegetables There were 5 gardens, each of about 4 English acres, in the form of an amphitheatre —*Strabo, Diodorus* Pliny said that in his time it was but a wilderness Mr Rich visited the ruins in 1811 and sir R Ker Porter in 1818 The laborious researches of Mr Layard, sir H Rawlinson, M Botta, and others, and the relics excavated and brought to England between the years 1849 and 1855 have drawn attention to the history of Babylon Many inscriptions in the cuneiform or wedge-like character have been translated by sir Henry Rawlinson, George Smith, and others, and published in the Journal of the Royal Asiatic Society In the spring of 1855 Rawlinson brought to England many valuable relics, drawings, etc, now in the British museum He lectured on Babylon at the Royal Institution, London, in 1851, 1855, and 1865 The Rev A H Sayce lectured on Babylonian literature at the same place in 1877 "The fragmentary Canon of Kings," given by Berosus, the Græco-Chaldean priest, 268 B C, has been superseded by the newly-discovered Babylonian canon inscriptions on tablets carefully dated from 2200 to 647 B C, an unequalled chronological series Summaries are given by Mr Boscawen in the articles "Assyria" and "Babylonia," in "Chambers's Encyclopædia," 1888

	B.C.
Earliest astronomical observations at Babylon [2230, *Hales*, 2233, *Clinton*]	2234
Nabonassar governor, 747, his son Nadinu, 734, a revolt, Ukinziru, king about	732
Babylonia conquered by Pul (Tiglath Pileser) king of Assyria, 729, becomes independent, Merodach baladan II king about	722
Sargon king of Assyria, captures Babylon, Merodach baladan returns, but is soon expelled by Sennacherib	705
Babylonia ruled by viceroys. ASSYRIA	
Nabu abla utzar (Nabopolassar), gen, seizes power about 640, proclaimed king	625
Succeeded by his son Nebuchadnezzar, very great and powerful who restores the empire and rebuilds Babylon	604
[His acts are recorded on innumerable tablets and in the Bible, 2 Kings xxiv, xxv, 2 Chron xxxvi, Jer xxxvii-xxxix, lii, Dan i-iv]	
He captures Jerusalem 599, destroys the city and carries most of the inhabitants captives to Babylon, 588, d.	561
Evil Merodach 561, Neriglissar king	559
Labynetus, 556, Nabonadius, a great monarch 551, Belshazzar, king	539
Babylon taken by the Medes and Persians under Cyrus, and Belshazzar slain (Dan v)	538
Babylon revolts, and is taken by Darius	518
Taken by Alexander 331, he dies here	323
Seleucus Nicator who d 280 B C transfers the seat of government to Seleucia, and Babylon is deserted Babylonia is conquered by the Parthians about 140 B C, and becomes part of the Persian empire On the overthrow of the Sassanides by the Mahometans, 650 A D, Babylonia becomes the seat of the caliphs till 1258 Since 1638 it has been subject to Turkey	

Babyngton's conspiracy, to assassinate Elizabeth and make Mary of Scotland queen, devised by John Savage, soldier of Philip of Spain approved by William Gifford and John Ballard, Catholic priests, and embraced by Anthony

Babyngton and others, betrayed by Pooley Aspy 14 were executed, 20, 21 Sept 1586

Bacchana'lia (festivals in honor of Bacchus) arose in Egypt and were introduced into Greece by Melampos, and called *Dionysia*, about 1415 B.C —*Diodorus* In Rome the *Bacchanalia* were suppressed, 186 B.C The priests of Bacchus were called Bacchanals. FESTIVALS, ORGIES

bachelors. The Roman censors often fined unmarried men, and men of full age were required to marry The Spartan women at certain games seized old bachelors, dragged them round their altars, and inflicted on them marks of infamy and disgrace —*Vossius* A tax laid in England upon bachelors 25 years of age (varying from 12*l* 10*s* for a duke to 1*s* for a common person), lasted from 1695 to 1706 Bachelors (Catholic priests excepted) were subjected to an extra tax on their male and female servants in 1785

backgammon. Some call Palamedes of Greece the inventor of this game, about 1224 B.C , others trace it to Wales about the 10th century —*Strutt*

Baconian philosophy, expounded by Francis Bacon in his "Novum Organum" in 1620 Its principles are utility and progress, and its objects the alleviation of suffering and promotion of comfort.—*Macaulay* PHILOSOPHY

Bacon's rebellion. VIRGINIA, 1676.

bacte'ria (Gr. βακτήρια, little rods) ANIMALCULES, GERM THEORY

Bactriana, a province in Asia, was subjugated by Cyrus and formed part of the Persian empire, when conquered by Alexander, 330 B.C About 254 B.C Theodotus or Diodotus, a Greek, threw off the yoke of the Seleucidæ, and became king Eucratides I reigned prosperously about 181 B.C , and Menander about 126 B.C The Greek kingdom seems to have been broken up by irruptions of Scythians soon after

Badajos (*bad-a-hōs'*), S W. Spain, an important barrier fortress, surrendered to the French, under Soult, 11 Mch 1811, invested by the British, under lord Wellington, on 16 Mch 1812, and stormed and taken on 6 Apr following. The French retreated in haste

Bad Axe, Battle of, Wisconsin, U S troops defeated Indians, under Black Hawk, 1-2 Aug 1832

Buddesdown hill or **mount Badon,** near Bath, wher[illegible] Bede says the Britons defeated the Saxons in 493 [illegible] y in 511 or 520.

[illegible] S W Germany The house of Baden is de[illegible] [illegible]rmann, first margrave (1052), son of Berthold [illegible] of Z[illegible]gen, but Hermann II. assumed the title, [illegible] Christopher, who died 1527, proceeded the [illegible]aden-Baden and Baden-Dourlach, united in 1771 [illegible] is a hereditary constitutional monarchy by charter, 26 May, 1818, it joined the German empire by treaty, 15 Nov 1870 Area, 596 sq miles, pop, 1 Dec 1871, 1,461,562, Dec 1875, 1,507,179, 1890, 1,656,817

Louis William, margrave of Baden Baden, gen , b. 1665, sallying from Vienna, defeated Turks 1683 d		1707
Treaty of Baden Landau ceded to France	7 Sept.	1714
Charles William, margrave of Baden Dourlach, b. 1679, d		1746
[Succeeded by his son]		
Charles Frederic, b 1728, margrave of Baden Dourlach, 1738, acquired Baden Baden 1771, made grand duke by Napoleon		1806
Baden [illegible] grand duchy with enlarged territories		"
A representative constitution granted by charter	18 Aug	1818
Baden joins the Zollverein	July,	1867
Chambers meet, liberal measures promised, 24 Sept., universal suffrage adopted by second chamber	29 Oct	1869
Civil marriage made obligatory	17 Nov	"
Baden joins Prussia in war with France	about 20 July,	1870

badge of military merit, established Aug 1781, by Washington, conferred upon non-commissioned officers and soldiers for 3 years' good conduct, or for specially meritorious service, and entitling the bearer "to pass and re-pass all guards and military posts as fully and amply as any commissioned officer whatever"

Baffin's bay, N America, discovered by William Baffin, an Englishman, 1616. Its extent was doubted, until the expeditions of Ross and Parry proved Baffin substantially accurate Parry entered Lancaster sound, and discovered the islands known by his name, 1818 NORTHWEST PASSAGE

bagatelle (*bag-a-tel'*), an indoor game, first described by Cotton in his "Compleat Gamester," 1674

Bagdad, in Asiatic Turkey, supposed to have been built by Al Mansour, and made the seat of the Saracen empire, about 762, but sir H Rawlinson discovered in 1848 that the western bank of the Tigris was lined with an embankment of solid brickwork dating from the time of Nebuchadnezzar, and it has since been found that one of the cities of the time of Sardanapalus bore the name of Bagdad It attained its greatest splendor during the caliphate of Haroun-al-Raschid, 763-809

> "In sooth it was a goodly time,
> For it was in the golden prime
> Of good Haroun Alraschid "—*Tennyson*

Taken by the Tartars, and a period put to the Saracen rule, 1258 Often taken by the Persians, and retaken by the Turks, with great slaughter, the latter have held it since 1638.

bagpipe, an ancient Greek and Roman instrument On a piece of ancient Grecian sculpture, now in Rome, a bagpiper is represented dressed like a modern Highlander Nero is said to have played upon a bagpipe, A D 51. Highland regiments in the English army retain their pipers. Chaucer represents the miller as skilled in playing the bagpipe, and Shakespeare's allusion to "the drone of a Lincolnshire bagpipe" (Henry IV, part i act i sc ii) proves that the instrument has not always been peculiar to Scotland.

Bahama isles, stretching more than 600 miles between the eastern coast of Florida and San Domingo, were the first discovery of Columbus, San Salvador (Cat or, as some suppose, Watling island) being first seen by him on the night of 11 Oct 1492 Ovando, governor of Hispaniola, carried off natives in 1509 for laborers in mines, and the islands were virtually uninhabited until the English, in 1629, settled in New Providence, whence, in 1641, the Spaniards drove them, but made no attempt to settle The English again occupied the islands in 1667, and in 1680 Charles II granted them to settlers In 1703 the French and Spaniards utterly destroyed the settlement on New Providence The islands now became the resort of pirates, especially of the notorious Blackbeard. VIRGINIA, 1718 The English renewed their settlements in 1718. The cultivation of the pineapple and of cotton introduced 1770 In 1776, commodore Hopkins, of the American navy, captured New Providence, but soon abandoned it as untenable. The Spaniards again nominally occupied the Bahamas till 1783, when they were ceded to the English In 1787 the descendants of the original lord proprietors reconveyed their rights to the English crown, receiving therefor 2000*l.* each The cultivation of cotton was quite abandoned in 1800 The islands during the American civil war, 1861-65, profited by the blockade-running trade

Bahar, N India, a province (conquered by Baber in 1530), with Bengal and Orissa, a princely dominion, became subject to the English East India Company in 1765 by the treaty of Allahabad for a quit-rent of about 300,000*l*

Baiæ (*ba'ye*), an ancient town of Campania, Italy, on the *Sinus Baianus*, famous for warm springs and baths. Owing to these, the mild climate, and the beauty of the landscape, it was the resort of the rich of Rome. C. Marius, Lucullus, Pompey, and Julius Cæsar spared no pains to adorn it under the republic, while it was a favorite resort of Nero, Caligula, Hadrian, and Servius It flourished until the days of Theodoric the Goth, 493-526 The castello di Baja was built in the 16th century by Pietro di Toledo.

bail. By ancient common-law, before and since the conquest, all felonies were bailable, till murder was excepted by statute, and by the 3 Edw. I (1275), bail in treason and in divers felonies was taken away Bail was further regulated in later reigns. It is now accepted in all cases except felony, and where a magistrate refuses bail it may be granted by a judge Acts respecting bail passed 1826 and 1852. Exces[illegible] [illegible] forbidden by the constitution of the United States and by those of most of the states

[illegible] sheriff, said to be of Saxon origin London had its *s[illegible]e-reve* prior to the conquest, and this officer was generally appointed for counties in England in 1079. Henry Cornehill and Richard Reynere were appointed bailiffs or sheriffs in London in 1189.—*Stow* Sheriffs were appointed in Dublin under the name of bailiffs in 1308, and the name was changed to sheriff in 1548. There are still places where the chief magistrate is called bailiff, as the high-bailiff of Westminster. Bum-bailiff is a corruption of bound-bailiff, every bailiff giving bonds for his good behavior.—*Blackstone.*

Bairam or **Beiram,** two Mahometan festivals; the greater lasts one day, following the Ramadan or month of fasting; the lesser follows the first at an interval of 60 days, and is the feast of sacrifices which are then made at Mecca, at which all Mahometans offer animals to commemorate Abraham's offering of Isaac; this lasts 4 days.

baize, a manufacture of coarse woollen, was brought into England by some Flemish or Dutch emigrants who settled at Colchester, in Essex, and received privileges from parliament in 1660. The trade was under the control of a corporation called governors of the Dutch baize-hall, who examined the cloth previous to sale.—*Anderson.*

Balakla'va, a small town in the Crimea, with a fine harbor, 10 miles southeast from Sebastopol. After the battle of the Alma, the allies advanced upon it, 26 Sept. 1854.

Battle of Balaklava: About 12,000 Russians, commanded by gen. Liprandi, took some redoubts in the vicinity, which had been intrusted to about 250 Turks. They next assaulted the English, but were driven back, mainly by the charge of the heavy cavalry, led by brigadier Scarlett, under the orders of lord Lucan. After this, from an unfortunate misconception of lord Raglan's order, lord Lucan ordered lord Cardigan, with the light cavalry, to charge the Russian army, which had reformed on its own ground with artillery in front. The order was promptly obeyed, but, of 670 British horsemen, only 198 returned.

"Then they rode back, but not,
Not the Six Hundred."—*Tennyson,* "Charge of the Light Brigade."

The infantry engaged were termed a "thin red line" . . 25 Oct. 1854
A sortie from Sebastopol led to a desperate engagement here; the Russians were repulsed, with the loss of 2000 killed and wounded, the allies losing about 600 . . . . 22 Mch. 1855
A banquet was given to the survivors of the charge at the Alexandra palace . . . . 25 Oct. 1875
6753*l.* raised by subscription for 20 destitute survivors of the Light brigade in the British empire 1891

balance of power, to assure the independency and integrity of states and control the ambition of rulers; a principle first defined, it is said, by Italian politicians of the 15th century on the invasion of Italy by Charles VIII. of France, 1494.—*Robertson.* It was recognized by the treaty of Munster, 24 Oct. 1648. The arrangements for the balance of power in Europe, made in 1815 without consent of the people of the countries interested, have been nearly all set aside since 1830.

baldachin or **baldachino,** more properly CIBORIUM, a canopy over the altar in some ancient churches; first used about 1130, and introduced into England, 1279. The proposal to erect one in St. Barnabas's church, Pimlico, was opposed in the consistory court, Aug. 1873. The trial took place 23, 24 Oct. Dr. Tristram decided against the erection of the baldachin, 15 Dec. 1873.

Balearic islands, in the Mediterranean, called by the Greeks Balearides and by the Romans Baleares, from the dexterity of the inhabitants at slinging: they include Majorca, Minorca, Iviça, Formentera, Cabrera, Conejera, and other islets. They were conquered by the Romans, 123 B.C.; by Vandals, about 426 A.D.; and formed part of Charlemagne's empire in 799. Conquered by the Moors about 1005, and held by them till about 1286, then annexed by Aragon. MAJORCA, MINORCA.

Balize. HONDURAS.

Balkans, the ancient Hæmus, a range of mountains from the Adriatic to the Euxine; the Koja Balkan, west of the Shipka pass, being the highest range, 5900 ft. The passage, deemed impracticable, was made by the Russians under Diebitsch, during the Russian and Turkish war, 26 July, 1829. An armistice followed, and peace was signed at Adrianople, 14 Sept. following. The Balkans were crossed by Russians, under Gourko, 13 July, 1877. RUSSO-TURKISH WAR II. By the treaty of Berlin, 13 July, 1878, the Balkans became the frontiers of European Turkey. The Balkan states are Servia, Bulgaria, and Roumelia.

ballads may be traced in the British history to the Anglo-Saxons.—*Turner.* Adhelme, who died 709, it is said, first introduced ballads into England. "The harp was sent round, and those might sing who could."—*Bede.* Alfred sang ballads.—*Malmesbury.* Canute composed one.—*Turner.* Minstrels were protected by a charter of Edward IV.; but by a statute of Elizabeth were punished with rogues and vagabonds and sturdy beggars.—*Viner.* "Give me the writing of the ballads, and you may make the laws."—*Fletcher of Saltoun.* Dibdin's sea-ballads were popular in the French war; he died 20 Jan. 1833. PERCY'S "RELIQUES," 1765 et seq., prof. Child's great work in course of publication, Boston, Mass.

ballets began through the meretricious taste of the Italian courts. One performed at the interview between Henry VIII. of England, and Francis I. of France in the Field of the Cloth of Gold, at Ardres, 1520.—*Guicciardini.* The Italian ballet was introduced into France in 1581. Ballets became popular in France, and Louis XIV. bore a part in one, 1664. They came to Britain with operas early in the 18th century.

balloons. The proper idea of the balloon was formed by Albert of Saxony, an Augustin monk in the 14th century, and adopted by a Portuguese Jesuit, Francesco Mendoza, who died at Lyons in 1626. It is also attributed to Bartolomeo de Guzmao, who died 1724. The principles of *aeronautics* include: 1, the power of a balloon to rise in the air; 2, the velocity of its ascent; and, 3, the stability of its suspension at any height. The application of sails and rudders has been considered, and found futile; but in 1872 Helmholtz thought steering possible, if moving slowly. Fatal accidents have been estimated at 2 or 3 per cent. The Aeronautical Society of Great Britain, founded to foster and develop aeronautics and aerology, by the duke of Argyll, James Glaisher, sir Charles Bright, and others, 12 Jan. 1866.

Francis Lana, a Jesuit, proposed to navigate air in a boat raised by four hollow balls of thin copper, exhausted of air . . 1670
Joseph Galien suggests filling a bag with fine diffuse air of the upper atmosphere 1755
Henry Cavendish discovered that common air is 14.5 times heavier than hydrogen gas 1766
Black of Edinburgh fills a bag with hydrogen which rose to the ceiling of the room 1767
Cavallo fills soap-bubbles with hydrogen 1782
Joseph Montgolfier makes a silken bag ascend with heated air (first fire balloon) . . . . Nov. "
Joseph and Stephen Montgolfier ascend safely in a fire balloon at Annonay . . . . 5 June, 1783
First ascent in a hydrogen balloon, Paris, by MM. Robert and Charles . . . . 27 Aug. "
Joseph Montgolfier ascends in a balloon inflated with smoke of burned straw and wool . . . . 19 Sept. "
First aerial voyage in a fire balloon—Pilâtre de Rozier and the marquis d'Arlandes . . . . 21 Nov. "
Second ascent of Charles in a hydrogen balloon, 9770 ft. . 1 Dec. "
Mr. Tytler, in a Montgolfier balloon, Edinburgh . . . . 27 Aug. 1784
Ascents of Andreani, 25 Feb.; Blanchard, 2 Mch.; Guyton de Morveau, the chemist, 25 Apr. and 12 June; Fleurant and Madame Thiblé (first female aeronaut), 28 June; duke of Chartres (Philippe Egalité) . . . . 19 Sept. "
First ascent in England, Lunardi, Moorfields, London . . 15 Sept. "
Blanchard and Jeffries ascend at Dover; cross the Channel; alight near Calais . . . . 7 Jan. 1785
First ascent in Ireland, Ranelagh gardens, Dublin . . . . . 19 Jan. "
Rozier and Romain killed in their descent near Boulogne; the balloon takes fire . . . . 15 June, "
Parachutes constructed and used by Blanchard . . . . Aug. "
Garnerin's narrow escape descending in one in London, 2 Sept. 1802
Sadler, after many ascents in England, falls into the sea, near Holyhead, but is rescued . . . . 9 Oct. 1812
Madame Blanchard ascends from Tivoli at night; the balloon, surrounded by fireworks, taking fire, she is thrown down and killed . . . . 6 July, 1819
Charles Green's first ascent (he introduces coal-gas in ballooning) . . . . 19 July, 1821
Lieut. Harris killed in a balloon descent . . . . 25 May, 1824
Sadler, jun., killed, falling from a balloon 1825
Great Nassau balloon, previously exhibited in ascents from Vauxhall gardens, carries 3 persons thence, and after 18 hours in the air descends at Weilburg, duchy of Nassau, 7 Nov. 1836
Mr. Cocking ascends from Vauxhall to try his parachute; in its descent it collapses, and he is thrown out and killed, 24 July, 1837
An Italian aeronaut ascends from Copenhagen; his corpse is found on the shore of an island, dashed to pieces . . . . 14 Sept. 1851
Ascent from Adrian, Mich., Ira Thurston killed . . . . Sept. 1858
J. B. Lassie's model of an "aerial ship," with a screw, submitted to the Academy of Sciences at Paris, 1859; and exhibited at Washington 1859
Mr. Wise and 3 others ascend from St. Louis (travel 1150 miles, and descend in Jefferson county, N. Y., nearly dead), 23 June, "

Nadar's balloon (largest ever made), capacity 215 363 cubic feet of gas, the car, a cottage in wicker work, raises 35 soldiers at Paris, Nadar hopes to steer by a screw, first ascent, with 14 persons successful 4 Oct 1863
Second ascent, voyagers injured, saved by presence of mind of Jules Godard, descend at Nienburg, Hanover 12 Oct "
Nadar with balloon at Crystal palace Sydenham Nov "
Society for Promoting Aerial Navigation formed at M Nadar's, at Paris, president, M Barral 15 Jan 1864
Godard's Montgolfier or fire balloon ascends 28 July and 3 Aug "
Nadar and others ascend in his balloon at Brussels 26 Sept "
Mr Coxwell ascends from Belfast in a new balloon, it is lost and several persons injured 3 July, 1865
Ascent of Nadar in his Geant balloon, Paris 23 June, 1866
Mr Coxwell claims 550 successful ascents to Apr 1867
Aerial screw machine (helicopteric) suggested, Paris, 1863, described by Dr J Bell Pettigrew at the Royal Institution, London 22 Mch "
Mr Hodsman crosses the Channel from Dublin, and descends in Westmoreland 22 Apr "
Great balloon exhibited at Ashburnham park, London, escapes, captured at Bouldon, Bucks 25 May, 1869
Charles Green, aeronaut, said to have made about 600 ascents, d aged 84 27 Mch 1870
Dupuy de Lôme at Vincennes ascends in "navigable" balloon with 13 persons, reported success 2 Feb 1871
Mr Wise proposes to cross the Atlantic from New York to Liverpool in a balloon 100 feet in diameter, 110 feet high, with supplementary balloon 36 feet in diameter, entire lifting power 15 900 lbs carrying power 9500 lbs, disposable ballast 7500 lbs July, balloon reported imperfect Sept, a smaller one, under W J Donaldson, starts (with a life boat) 9 19 A M, 6 Oct, and descends in a storm in Connecticut, narrow escape 7 Oct 1873
Vincent de Groof, Belgian ("flying man"), makes a parachute to imitate a bird in flight, ascends from Cremorne gardens, London, and descends with it more than 300 feet in Essex, 29 June, at his next attempt the parachute becomes disarranged and he is killed 9 July, 1874
Under the Government Balloon Committee Mr Coxwell ascends at Woolwich to try C A Bowdler's apparatus (based on the screw-propeller) for steering balloons, failure reported 25 July, "
[It has been proved that a vertical screw can raise or depress a balloon saving gas and ballast]
M and Mme Duruof ascend from Calais to cross the Channel, 31 Aug, carried out to sea, balloon falls in and drifts towards Norway, rescued by a smack (the *Grand Charge*), aeronauts land at Grimsby 4 Sept. "
Duruof, etc, ascend from Crystal palace 14 Sept "
Menier's hot air balloon fails on trial 5 Sept and 16 Oct "
Ascent of capt. Burnaby at Crystal palace with machine to trace course of wind above clouds, reported success 10 Nov "
MM Tissandier, Croce Spinelli, and Sivel ascend in the "Zenith" from La Villette near Paris, at 26 160 feet Croce throws out ballast, ascend rapidly, he and Sivel are suffocated, Tissandier recovers 15 Apr 1875
Washington J Donaldson, aeronaut, perishes in lake Michigan during a storm 18 July, "
Failure of Carrol's directing apparatus at Paris July, 1878
Frequent ascents in a "captive balloon" Aug "
Giffard's captive balloon, "Paris" burst 16 or 17 Aug 1879
5 balloons from places near London compete for a silver medal of Balloon Society, the "Owl" Mr Wright and commander Cheyne, travels 48 miles in 1 hour 4 Sept 1880
International balloon contest at Crystal palace, England ("Eclipse"), Mr Wright, France, M de Fonvielle, both alight near Portsmouth 21 Oct "
Giffard and De Lôme's aerial ship said to be successful for direction, speed, etc Jan 1881
Mr Eugene (after about 2000 ascents) narrowly escapes death in a storm at Vienna 21 Aug "
Walter Powell, M P, crosses Bristol channel descending at Dingeston goes on to Hereford, 3 Nov, Powell, Templer, and Gardner ascend at Bath in war office balloon "Saladin", descend near Bridport, 2 fall out, Powell drifts to sea, not found 10 Dec "
Remains of the balloon said to have been found on Sierra del Piedroza mountain, Spain about 20 Jan 1882
Col Brine and Mr Simmons start across Channel, picked up half way 4 Mch "
Col Burnaby crosses and lands at Caen 23 Mch "
Mr Simmons goes from Maldon, Essex, to Arras (140 miles) 1 h 20 m 10 June, "
Mr Simmons and sir Claude C. de Crespigny cross from Maldon, Essex, to Oudekerk, near Flushing (140 miles in 6 hours) 1-2 Aug 1883
Mr Simmons and Mr Smale go from Hastings to cape la Hague (6 h 40 m) 13 Sept "
Electrical balloon constructed by Gaston and Albert Tissandier, successful trial reported 8 Oct "
M L'Hoste, from Boulogne to Folkestone, 9 Sept, from Boulogne to Romney, 1 h 30 m 7 Aug. 1884
Gen Brine crosses from Hythe to Hervelinghen 15 Aug "
Aerial navigation said to be effected by M Renard, director of the French military ballooning establishment at Meudon, with an air-ship—length of balloon, 50 42 metres, diameter, 8 40 metres, cubic capacity, 1864 metres, filled with hydrogen, sustaining 2000 kilogrammes—the motors were Faure accumulator of 10 horse power, after going 4 miles and describing a curve of 300 metres radius it returns to the place of starting 9 Aug "
Second trial, result uncertain 12 Sept. 1884
Reported success by M Tissandier 26 Sept. "
Third trial by capt Renard, successful 8 Nov "
Aid to build a vacuum air ship asked by A de Bosset of U S government—to be a steel cylinder 46 yards in diameter, 218 yards in length, weight 260 680 lbs, displacement of air, 719 709 lbs, ascensional force 459,029 lbs with perfect vacuum electric motors, and compound exhaust screw to propel and guide 1889
Reported that prof Samuel P Langley of the Smithsonian Institution, Washington, D C, is perfecting a working model of an air ship Mch 1893
Descent from balloons by means of a parachute at first rarely performed, now common with practical aeronauts 1888-93
[Some descending from a height of 7000 feet.]

MILITARY AND POSTAL APPLICATIONS

Guyton de Morveau ascends twice at the battle of Fleurus obtaining information for Jourdain 17 June, 1794
Balloons devised for postal purposes by C Shepherd, C E 1851
Balloons used at battle of Solferino, 24 June, 1859, by the Federal army, near Washington July, 1861
Balloon corps of U S army employed by gen McClellan at first siege of Richmond 1862
M Duruof conveys mail-bags from Paris to Tours during the siege 23 Sept 1870
Postal balloons from Metz and Paris Sept.-Dec "
" balloon from Crystal palace, Sydenham, successful, 6 Oct "
Gambetta escapes from Paris in a balloon to Rouen 8 Oct "
Many balloons from Paris and other places Oct 1870-Feb 1871
Military experiments ascent of "Univers", very cold weather, valve bursts, several hurt, near Vincennes, no deaths, 8 Dec 1875
Military ascents and balloon equipment for military purposes adopted at Woolwich announced Apr 1879
Captive balloon at the volunteer review, Brighton 29 Mch 1880
Royal Engineers Balloon Corps arrives at Suakin 7 Mch 1885
France and Germany adopt captive balloons for naval purposes 1890

SCIENTIFIC ASCENTS

Gay Lussac and Biot at Paris, 23 Aug, Gay Lussac (to the height of 22 977 feet) 15 Sept. 1804
Bixio and Barral at Paris (19,000 feet, traversing a cloud 9000 feet) . 1850
Mr Welsh ascends. 17, 26 Aug 21 Oct and 10 Nov 1852
Scientific balloon ascents recommended by the British Association and funds provided, begun by James Glaisher, with suitable apparatus, in Mr Coxwell's balloon, at Wolverhampton, 5 miles 17 July, 1862
He ascends at Crystal palace, 18 Apr 11, 21 July, at Wolverhampton 26 June, at Newcastle, during meeting of the British Association 31 Aug 1863
He ascends about 7 miles at Wolverhampton, at 5¾ miles becomes insensible, Mr Coxwell loses use of hands, but opens valve with his teeth, descent in safety 5 Sept.
Glaisher's 16th ascent, surveys London 9 Oct
" 17th ascent at Woolwich, descends at Mr Brandon's, Suffolk 12 Jan 1864
He ascends from Woolwich (24th time) 30 Dec "
His 25th ascent 27 Feb 1865
Other ascents 2 Oct 2 Dec 1865, and in May, 1866
Glaisher's "Travels in the Air" publ Jan 1871
"Astra Castra Experiments and Adventures in the Atmosphere By Hatton Turnor" a copious work appeared . 1865
Mr Coxwell's scientific ascent in the "Nassau" at Hornsey, 22 Sept. 1873
Count von Zeppelin ascends in his air-ship at lake Constance, 2 July, again 17 and 21 Oct 1901
M Santos Dumont's steerable balloon successful in Paris, 12, 29 July, 1901, his air ship was wrecked, 8 Aug, he wins the Deutsch prize 100,000 f, in 30 mins, 19 Oct, his 5th trip at Monaco failed 14 Feb 1902
M Severo makes a trial trip at Vaugirard, Paris, the balloon exploded at the height of 1200 feet, Severo and Sachet were instantly killed 12 May "
Successful trials of dirigible balloons at the St Louis exposition summer of 1904

ballot (Fr *ballotte*, a little ball) Secret voting was practised by the ancient Greeks and Romans (TABELLARIAE LEGES) and modern Venetians, in the United States, in France, and, since 1872, in Great Britain and colonies. SCRUTIN.

A ballot box used in electing aldermen, London 1526
Its use by the Company of Merchant Adventurers in electing an agent, prohibited by Charles I 17 Dec 1637
Ballot box used by the "Rota," a political club at Miles's coffee house, Westminster . . 1659
A tract called "The Benefit of the Ballot," ascribed to Andrew Marvell, publ in the "State Tracts" 1693
Proposed, in a pamphlet, to be used in the election of members of Parliament 1705
Bill authorizing vote by ballot passes the commons, rejected by the lords 1710
George Grote introduced into the commons a ballot bill 6 times 1833-39
House of Commons rejects the ballot—257 being against, and 189 for it 30 June, 1851
Voting secret in the Chamber of Deputies in France from 1840 to 1845, and is so since the coup d'état in Dec "
A test ballot is adopted at Manchester, and Ernest Jones is chosen as a candidate for Parliament. He dies next day, 22, 23 Jan 1869

For many years annually proposed by Henry Berkeley, rejected (by 161 to 112 12 July 1867) He dies 10 Mch 1870
E Leatham introduces a ballot bill in Parliament, Mch, Mr Gladstone speaks for it, bill withdrawn 27 July, "
Ballot employed in electing the London school board in 9 districts 29 Nov "
Ballot recommended in queen Victoria's speech 9 Feb, bill introduced, passed by commons, rejected by lords (97 to 48), 10 Aug 1871
Ballot an open question in Whig governments 1835-72
Bill to amend the law relating to procedure at parliamentary and municipal elections, including the ballot, read in the commons 2d time 109-51, 15 Feb, passed 271-216, 30 May, read 2d time in the lords (86-56), amendments carried in committee making secret voting optional (162-91) passed, 25 June, lords amendments mostly rejected by commons optional clause given up by the lords, 8 July, royal assent (to continue in force till 31 Dec 1880 It has been regularly continued and is now a permanent policy) 18 July, 1872
First election by ballot, at Pontefract, H E Childers re elected very peacefully 15 Aug "
Australian system of ballot This system first proposed by Francis S Dutton member of the Legislature of S Australia, 1851 He is known as the father of the "Australian system" Adopted in Victoria, Australia, 1856, Tasmania New South Wales and S Australia, 1858, New Zealand 1870 England, 1872, British Columbia 1873, Ontario, 1874, Quebec and Nova Scotia 1875
Ballot reform on Australian or English system first advocated in the U S in a pamphlet entitled "English Elections," 1882, by Henry George 1883
George W Walthaw introduces in the lower House of the Michigan Legislature a bill embodying the Australian ballot system (the first presented in the U S) Jan 1887
It is again introduced and passes the House, and the Senate on the last day of the session, 1888 Compromise measures adopted 1889
Ballot reform measures vetoed in New York in 1888 and 1889 by gov Hill, but a bill is approved to enforce the secrecy of the ballot, etc. 1890

[The several STATE RECORDS, 1888]

Ball's Bluff, Battle of Gen McClellan directed brig-gen Chas P Stone to make a slight demonstration towards Leesburg, Va, 20 Oct 1861 Gen Stone thereupon ordered col Devens, of the 15th Mass, to cross the Potomac near Ball's Bluff He did so early on 21 Oct, pushing to near Leesburg with 625 men and 28 officers, meeting some opposition, he fell back to the place of crossing, where he is attacked about noon by confederates. Col Devens retired to the edge of the bluffs, where he was reinforced by col E D Baker with a California regiment and the N Y Tammany, increasing his force to 1900 Col Baker assumed command, fighting continued until about 5 o'clock P M, when col Baker was killed, and the federals gave way, loss about 1000, being 300 killed and 700 wounded, drowned, and prisoners—there being no proper means of transportation in the retreat Confederate loss, 155 The disaster was attributed to mismanagement, and in Feb 1862, gen Stone was arrested on charges of treason STONE, CHAS P, CASE OF

Balmo'ral castle, Deeside, Aberdeenshire, visited by queen Victoria in 1848, 1849, 1850 The estate was purchased for 32,000*l* by prince Albert in 1852 In 1853 the present building, in the Scotch baronial style, was begun, from designs by W Smith of Aberdeen

Baltic sea, Ostsee, or Eastern sea, separates Sweden and the Danish isles from Russia and Germany Declared neutral for commerce by treaty between Russia and Sweden, 1759, and Denmark, 1760 It is often partly frozen Charles X of Sweden, with an army crossed the Belts in 1658, and the Russians passed from Finland to Sweden on the ice in 1809

BALTIC EXPEDITIONS

Against Denmark (ARMED NEUTRALITY) —1 Under lord Nelson and admiral Parker, Copenhagen bombarded, and 28 Danish vessels taken or destroyed 2 Apr 1801
2 Under admiral Gambier and lord Cathcart, 18 sail of the line, 15 frigates, 31 brigs and gunboats surrender to the British, 26 July, 1807
Against Russia.—1 British fleet, sir Charles Napier, sails from Spithead in presence of the queen, who leads in her yacht, the *Fairy* 11 Mch 1854
Arrives Wingo sound, 15 Mch, in the Baltic 20 Mch "
Gulf of Finland blockaded 12 Apr "
10,000 French troops embark at Calais for the Baltic in English ships of war, the emperor present 15 July, "
Capture of Bomarsund, one of the Aland islands, and surrender of the garrison (BOMARSUND) 16 Aug "
English and French fleets start homeward to winter 15 Oct. "
2 Expedition of 85 English ships (2098 guns), under admiral R S. Dundas sails 20 Mch -4 Apr 1855, 16 French ships (408 guns), under admiral Pernand, join it June, 1855
3 vessels silence Russian batteries at Hogland island 21 July 1855
Fleet proceeded towards Cronstadt Many infernal machines discovered Sveaborg attacked (SVEABORG) 9 Aug "
Fleet soon returns to England

Baltimore, the metropolis of Maryland, known as the "Monumental City" covers an area of 31½ sq miles A town of 60 acres, created by act of Assembly, 8 Aug 1729, and bounded approximately by Liberty, Saratoga, and Frederick streets and the Basin was laid out and called Baltimore in honor of Cecilius Calvert, lord Baltimore, 12 Jan 1730 In 1752 the place contained 25 houses and 200 inhabitants Pop in 1790, 13 503 1800, 26,114, 1810, 35,583, 1820, 62,738, 1830, 80,620, 1840, 102 313, 1850, 169,054, 1860, 212,418, 1870, 267,354, 1880, 332,313, 1890, 434,439, 1900, 508,957.

Baltimore laid out 12 Jan 1730
Jones's Town afterwards Old Town east of the falls, laid out. 22 Nov 1732
Parish church built on site afterwards occupied by St Paul's church, cor Saratoga and Charles sts, begun 1730, completed 1739
Baltimore and Jones's Town consolidated and incorporated as Baltimore Town 28 Sept 1745
Subscription of 100*l* by citizens for building a market house and town hall, erected 10 years later on northwest cor Gay and Baltimore sts 23 Apr 1751
32 acres of Coles's harbor annexed 1753
Mount Clare house erected by Charles Carroll, built of imported brick 1754
A number of Acadian exiles settle in Baltimore 1756
Made the county seat and court house erected where Battle monument now stands 1768
Mechanical Company organized, and a fire engine purchased 1769
First umbrella in the U S (brought from India) used here UMBRELLA 1772
Baptist church erected cor Front and Fayette sts, afterwards site of the shot tower 1773
First newspaper, the *Maryland Journal and Baltimore Advertiser* established by William Goddard, first issue 20 Aug "
Stage route opened to Philadelphia "
First Methodist meeting house in Baltimore built in Strawberry alley Nov "
Capt William Perkins arrives at Marblehead with 3000 bush of Indian corn 20 bbls of rye and 21 bbls of bread sent by the people of Baltimore for the poor of Boston 28 Aug 1774
Baltimore contains 564 houses and 5934 inhabitants 1775
St Peter's church (Roman Catholic) on Saratoga and Charles sts built and occupied 1770-75
Continental Congress holds its session in Congress hall cor Baltimore and Liberty sts 20 Dec 1776 to 20 Jan 1777
First notable riot in Baltimore Mr Goddard of the *Maryland Journal* beset in his office by excited members of the "Whig Club" who took exception to an article in his paper lauding king George and Parliament 25 Mch "
Count Pulaski organizes his corps in Baltimore Mch 1778
First custom house erected 1780
Paving of the streets begun 1781
First brick theatre in Baltimore erected in E Baltimore st, nearly opposite the Second Presbyterian church, opened with the play, "King Richard III" 15 Jan 1782
Regular line of stage coaches established to Fredericktown and Annapolis 1783
Policemen first employed "
3 new market houses erected 1784
Streets first lighted with oil lamps "
Methodist church built on northwest cor Light st and Wine alley, begun Aug 1785 dedicated by bishop Asbury 21 May, 1786
First destructive flood recorded 5 Oct "
St Mary's college (seminary of St Sulpice) established 1791
Presbyterian church erected on northwest cor Fayette and North sts (afterwards razed to give place to the U S court house 1860) "
Bank of Maryland organized "
Yellow fever epidemic Aug -Oct 1794
Bank of Baltimore incorporated 24 Dec 1795
First directory of Baltimore Town and Fell's Point pub 1796
Act passed to lay out and establish a turnpike from the city of Washington to Baltimore Town 31 Dec "
Incorporated as a city, pop 20 000 31 Dec "
First mayor, James Calhoun elected 16 Jan. 1797
Library Company of Baltimore afterwards merged with the Maryland Historical Society incorporated 20 Jan "

[Library contained 4000 vols in 1800]

Maryland Society for Promoting the Abolition of Slavery, and the relief of free negroes and others unlawfully held in bondage, formed in Baltimore, the 4th in the U S 8 Sept 1798
Baltimore American and Daily Advertiser first issued 14 May, 1799
Jerome Bonaparte married to Miss Elizabeth Patterson in Baltimore 24 Dec 1803
Union bank of Maryland organized and chartered 1804
Mechanics' bank incorporated 1806
Corner-stone of Roman Catholic church laid 7 July, "
Baltimore Water Company formed with capital of $250,000, 30 Apr 1804, and water first supplied through cast-iron pipes May, 1807
New court house building on North Calvert st cor Lexington, begun 1805, occupied 1809
Mob destroys the office of the *Federal Republican* (UNITED STATES) 27 July 1812

"New Theatre," afterwards called "Holliday Street Theatre," opened....10 May, 1813
First steamboat built in Baltimore, the *Chesapeake*, constructed by William McDonald & Co.... "
British forces under gen. Ross advance against the city, 12 Sept. 1814
Engagement at North Point; gen. Ross killed....13 Sept. "
Fort McHenry bombarded by British fleet....12–13 Sept. "
The "Star-Spangled Banner" printed in the *Baltimore American and Daily Advertiser*....21 Sept. "
Corner-stone of the Washington monument laid (height of monument 180 ft.)....4 July, 1815
Corner-stone of Battle monument laid; erected in honor of Baltimoreans killed in defending the city in 1814, 12 Sept. "
Population of Baltimore increased 16,000 by annexation of the precincts.... 1816
Maryland hospital incorporated....29 Jan. "
St. Andrew's Society incorporated....1 Feb. "
Medical Society of Maryland incorporated....1 Feb. "
New St. Paul's church erected on cor. Saratoga and Charles sts.; corner-stone laid, 4 May, 1814, completed at cost of $126,140.... 1817
Disastrous freshet in Jones's falls; part of the city called the "Meadows" overflowed to depth of 10 to 15 feet. 8 Aug. "
First Odd Fellows' lodge in America, Washington Lodge No. 1, organized at Fell's Point, 13 Apr. 1819, through the efforts of Thomas Wildey. It receives a charter from the duke of York's lodge at Preston, Lancashire, Eng....1 Feb. 1820
First building lighted with gas, Peale's museum, on Holliday st., afterwards Old City Hall, 1816. First public building lighted with gas, the "Belvidere theatre," northwest cor. North and Saratoga sts., and first private house, that of Jacob J. Cohen on North Charles st.... "
Exchange building opened for business....June, "
Roman Catholic cathedral, begun 1806, consecrated by archbishop Mareschal....31 May, 1821
Disastrous fire; 3 lumber-yards and 25 to 30 buildings, mostly warehouses, burned....23 June, 1822
Statue placed on Battle monument....12 Sept. "
Corner-stone of Baltimore Athenæum at southwest cor. St. Paul and Lexington sts. laid....10 Aug. 1824
Gen. Lafayette visits Baltimore....7–11 Oct. "
Mrs. Ellen Moale, first white child born within the city of Baltimore, dies....Mch. 1825
Erection of Barnum's City hotel begun.... "
Maryland Academy of Science and Literature incorporated (continued until 1844)....16 Feb. 1826
First exhibition of the Maryland institute....7 Nov. "
Subscription books for stock of Baltimore and Ohio railroad opened, $4,178,000 taken by 22,000 subscribers, 20–27 Mch. 1827
First bank opened by Evan Poultney in Baltimore st....June, 1828
Foundation stone of the Baltimore and Ohio railroad laid by the Grand Lodge of Maryland, assisted by Charles Carroll of Carrollton....4 July, "
Shot-tower, Phœnix Company, 234 feet high, circular, and of brick, built without scaffolding; completed....25 Nov. "
Corner-stone of the Baltimore and Susquehanna railroad laid, and centennial of Baltimore celebrated....8 Aug. 1829
First public school opened....24 Sept. "
Old Baltimore museum, cor. Baltimore and Calvert sts., opened, 1 Jan. 1830
[Building sold to B. & O. R.R., Mch. 1874.]
Epidemic of cholera....July–Sept. 1832
Charles Carroll of Carrollton, aged 95, dies at Baltimore, 14 Nov. "
Bank of Maryland fails....24 Mch. 1834
Riot, growing out of failure of bank of Maryland....Aug. 1835
First issue of the *Sun*....17 May, 1837
Sudden freshet in Jones's falls; 19 lives lost; Harrison and Frederick sts. 10 feet under water....14 July, "
City of Kingston, first steam vessel from Baltimore to Europe direct, leaves port....20 May, 1838
Baltimore Academy of the Visitation opened, 1837; chartered "
Greenmount cemetery dedicated....13 July, 1839
Mercantile Library Association organized....14 Nov. "
St. Vincent de Paul's church, corner-stone laid by archbishop Eccleston 21 May, 1840; dedicated....7 Nov. 1841
Explosion of steamer *Medora*, just about to start on her trial excursion; 27 killed, 40 wounded....15 Apr. 1842
Historical Society of Maryland organized, Gen. John Spear Smith first president....27 Jan. 1844
Omnibus line established....May, "
Magnetic telegraph from Washington city to the railroad depot in Pratt st., wires covered with rope-yarn and tar, completed; first communication, "What hath God wrought!" (Numbers xxiii. 23), received....27 May, "
Corner-stone of St. Alphonsus's church laid, 1 May, 1842; church dedicated....14 Mch. 1845
Maryland Institute for the Promotion of the Mechanics' Arts organized....12 Jan. 1848
Fire destroys 60 dwellings, breaking out in a cotton factory in Lexington st. above Fremont....28 May, "
Howard Athenæum and Gallery of Art, northeast cor. Baltimore and Charles sts., opened as a theatre....12 June, "
Baltimore Athenæum opened and edifice inaugurated..23 Oct. "
Baltimore Female college opened, 1848; chartered.... 1849
Edgar Allan Poe dies in Baltimore, aged 40 years....7 Oct. "
Jenny Lind arrives in Baltimore (J. H. Whitehurst, "daguerreotypist," bids $100 for first choice of seats at her first concert)....8 Dec. 1850
Reception to Louis Kossuth....27 Dec. 1851
Loyola college, Calvert st. near Madison, opened....15 Sept. 1852
Remains of Junius Brutus Booth, tragedian, arrive in Baltimore, his home, from Louisville, Ky., where he died, 2 Dec., 9 Dec. "
Loudon Park cemetery dedicated....14 July, 1853
Maryland School for the Blind opened.... "
Baltimore orphan asylum, Stricker st. near Saratoga, opened, 10 Nov. "
Excursion train returning to Baltimore from Rider's grove collides with accommodation train from Baltimore, near the Relay house; over 30 killed and about 100 wounded, 4 July, 1854
Water works purchased by the city.... "
Erection of the new First Presbyterian church cor. Madison and Park sts. begun....July, "
Trial of a steam fire-engine, the "Miles Greenwood," built at Cincinnati for the corporation of Boston; the first seen in Baltimore....2 Feb. 1855
Mêlée among the firemen; 2 killed, many injured....18 Aug. "
St. Paul's church burned, 29 Apr. 1854; rebuilt and dedicated, 10 Jan. 1856
Battle between the Rip Rap club and the New Market fire company, many wounded; city election dispute....8 Oct. "
Election riot; Democrats and Know-nothings....4 Nov "
Baltimore *Daily News* established.... 1857
Disastrous fire, 37–41 S. Charles st.; 14 persons killed by a falling wall....14 Apr. "
Strike on the Baltimore and Ohio railroad, and encounter between the militia and rioters....29 Apr.–2 May, "
Banks suspend specie payment....28 Sept. "
Maryland club incorporated....24 Feb. 1858
Clearing-house established....8 Mch. "
Steam fire-engine, the "Alpha," the first owned by the Baltimore fire department, arrives in the city....18 May, "
Flood almost as destructive as that of 1837 occurs....12 June, "
Ordinance passed for a paid city fire department....Sept. "
Reform Association organized at a mass-meeting in Monument square....8 Sept. "
Peabody institute, endowed by George Peabody with $1,300,000, 1857; incorporated, 9 Mch. 1858; corner-stone laid...16 Apr. 1859
Police and fire-alarm telegraph, adopted June, 1858; first put in operation....27 June, "
First car placed on the city passenger railway on Broadway, and line opened....27 Oct. "
Reception to Japanese ambassadors, guests of the United States government....8 June, 1860
Druid Hill park opened....19 Oct. "
A secession mob attacks the 6th Massachusetts and 7th Pennsylvania regiments while passing through the city on their way to Washington. 12 citizens and 3 soldiers killed, 23 soldiers and several citizens wounded....19 Apr. 1861
Gen. B. F. Butler takes military possession....13 May, "
Thomas Wildey, the "father of Odd-Fellowship in the U. S.," dies in Baltimore, aged 80 yrs....19 Oct. "
Corner-stone of St. Martin's Roman Catholic church, southeast cor. Fulton and Fayette sts., laid....9 July, 1865
The Wildey monument, erected by the Odd-Fellows, corner-stone laid, 26 Apr. 1865; is dedicated....20 Sept. "
Southern relief fair, in aid of the suffering poor of the Southern states, held at the hall of the Maryland institute; receipts, $164,569.97....2–13 Apr. 1866
Maryland state normal school opened.... "
Dedication of the Peabody institute....25 Oct. "
Corner-stone of the new Masonic temple laid....20 Nov. "
Maryland Academy of Sciences incorporated....15 Mch. 1867
Corner-stone of the new city hall laid....18 Oct. "
Excessive heat; thermometer 97 to 101° in the shade; 30 cases of sunstroke, 21 fatal....16 July, 1868
Most disastrous flood on record. A street-car floats down Harrison street; the water reaches to the second story of buildings, and most of the bridges over Jones's falls, including the heavy iron bridge at Fayette st., are swept away, 24 July, "
Maryland Institution for the Blind, on North av., near Charles st., dedicated....20 Nov. "
Corner-stone of Mount Vernon Place Methodist Episcopal church laid....26 Sept. 1869
Ford's Grand opera-house inaugurated. Shakespeare's "As You Like It" the opening play....3 Oct. 1871
Third National bank robbed between banking hours, Saturday and Monday; loss over $220,000....17–19 Aug. 1872
Initial number of the *Evening News*....4 Nov. "
Thermometer 10° below zero, night of....29 Jan. 1873
Church of the Ascension, Protestant Episcopal, destroyed by fire....12 May, "
Baltimore and Potomac tunnel, about 1½ miles in length, begun June, 1871, and first passenger train passes through to Calvert station....29 June, "
Union Railroad tunnel begun, May, 1871; completed June, 1873, and first train through....24 July, "
Most extensive fire ever known in the city breaks out in a planing-mill on Park and Clay sts.; 113 buildings destroyed, including 2 churches and 3 school-houses. Loss, $750,000, 25 July, "
Johns Hopkins dies, aged 79....24 Dec. "
Morning Herald established.... 1875
City hall completed.... "
Monument to Edgar Allan Poe unveiled....17 Nov. "

Johns Hopkins university incorporated, 24 Aug. 1867; endowed by its founder with $3,000,000; is opened.................. 1876
150th anniversary of the foundation of the city celebrated, 10-15 Oct. 1880
Over 65 excursionists, principally from Baltimore, drowned by the giving way of the pier at North point, Tivoli, 23 July, 1883
Enoch Pratt free library, founded by Enoch Pratt with $1,250,000 in 1882, formally opened to the public.....5 Jan. 1886
Great fire in Hopkins place, loss $2,000,000, 7 firemen killed and 6 injured..2 Sept. 1888
Asylum for Feeble-minded Children opened ....Jan. 1889
Johns Hopkins hospital, endowed with $3,500,000; opened, 7 May, "
6 days' celebration of 75th anniversary of the defence of the city begun..9 Sept "

MAYORS.

Jas. Calhoun	1797-1804	Saml. Hinks	1854-56
Thorowgood Smith	1804-08	Thomas Swann	1856-60
Edward Johnson	1808-16	Geo. Wm. Brown	1860-61
Geo. Stiles	1816-19	(Arrested and imprisoned by U. S. authorities, Sept. 12, 1861.)	
Edward Johnson	1819-20		
John Montgomery	1820-23		
Edward Johnson	1823-25	John Lee Chapman	1861-67
Jacob Small	1826	Robert T. Banks	1867-71
Wm. Stewart	1826-30	Joshua Vansant	1871-75
Jesse Hunt	1830-32	Ferdinand C. Latrobe	1875-77
Saml. Smith	1832-38	Geo. P. Kane	1877-78
Sheppard C. Leakin	1838-40	Ferd. C. Latrobe	1878-81
Saml. Brady	1840-42	Wm. Pinkney Whyte	1881-83
Solomon Hillin, jr.	1842-43	Ferd. C. Latrobe	1883-85
Jas. O. Law	1843-44	Jas. Hodges	1885-87
Jacob G. Davies	1844-48	Ferd. C. Latrobe	1887-89
Elijah Stansbury	1848-50	Robt. C. Davidson	1889-91
J. H. T. Jerome	1850-52	Ferd. C. Latrobe	1891-93
J. Smith Hollins	1852-54		

Bamberg, Bavaria, said to have been founded by Saxons in 804, and endowed with a church by Charlemagne. Made a bishopric in 1007; the bishop was a prince of the empire till the treaty of Luneville, 1801, when Bamberg was secularized. Incorporated with Bavaria in 1803. The cathedral, rebuilt in 1110, was recently repaired. Bamberg was taken and pillaged by the Prussians in 1759.

Bamborough or **Bamburg,** Northumberland, Engl., according to the "Saxon Chronicle," built by king Ida about 547, and named Bebbanburgh. The castle suffered greatly from the Danes in 933, was taken and retaken in 1463 by the forces of Edward IV. and Henry VI. It is one of the oldest in the kingdom, and has within its keep an ancient draw-well 145 feet deep, first known to modern times in 1770, it having been filled with sand and rubbish. The castle and estate, the property of the Forsters, and forfeited to the crown for aiding the rebellion in 1715, were purchased by Nathaniel lord Crewe, bishop of Durham, and bequeathed by him, 1720, for various charitable purposes, one of which is aid to shipwrecked sailors. The library was founded by the trustees in 1778; books are lent to persons residing within 20 miles.

Bampton lectures (theological), at Oxford annually, began in 1780 with a lecture by James Bandinel, D.D. The lecturer is paid by bequest of rev. John Bampton (d. 1751); the lectures are published. Able courses by White (1784), Heber (1815), Whately (1822), Milman (1827), Hampden (1832), Mansel (1858), Liddon (1866), etc.

Banbury, Oxfordshire, Engl., a Saxon town. The castle, built by Alexander de Blois, bishop of Lincoln, 1125, was often besieged, as by parliamentary troops in 1644 and in 1646, when it was taken, and demolished a few years after. At Edgecot or Danesmore, near Banbury, during an insurrection, the army of Edward IV., under the earl of Pembroke, was defeated, 26 July, 1469; the earl and a brother were soon after taken and executed.—Banbury cakes were renowned in the time of Ben Jonson, and Banbury Cross (that of the nursery rhyme) was destroyed by the Puritans. Cakes presented to the queen at Banbury, 30 Nov. 1866.

Banda isles (10), Eastern archipelago, visited by Portuguese in 1511, who settled, 1521, but were expelled by Dutch about 1600. Rohun island ceded to English in 1616. The Bandas were taken by them in 1796; restored in 1801; retaken in 1811; and restored in Aug. 1816. They form one of the Dutch residencies of the Molucca group.

Banda Oriental (the eastern side), S. America, part of the vice-royalty of Buenos Ayres, of which, in 1828, a division was incorporated with Brazil, while another became independent, as the republic of Uruguay. URUGUAY.

Bangalore, S. India, besieged by British under lord Cornwallis, 6 Mch., and taken by storm, 21 Mch. 1791; restored to Tippoo in 1792, when he destroyed the strong fort, deemed the bulwark of Mysore.

Bangor, Banchor Iskoed, or **Monachorum,** Flintshire, N. Wales, the site of an ancient college, said to have been founded 180, and afterwards converted into a monastery; very populous, if it be true that 1200 monks were slain by Ethelfrid, king of the Angles, for praying for the Welsh in their conflict with him in 607.—*Tanner.*

Bangor, N. Caernarvonshire, N. Wales. The church is dedicated to St. Daniel, bishop, 516. Owen Glendower defaced the cathedral; bishop Bulkeley alienated many lands, and even sold the bells, 1553. An order in council to unite the sees of Bangor and St. Asaph on the next vacancy in either was issued, 1838; rescinded, 1847.

Bangorian controversy, result of a sermon of Dr. Benjamin Hoadley, bishop of Bangor, before George I., 31 Mch. 1717, on the text, "My kingdom is not of this world" (John xviii. 36), expounding the spiritual kingdom of Christ, exciting the indignation of most of the clergy, expressed in hundreds of pamphlets.

Bank holidays.—*United States:* Christmas and New Year's day, 22 Feb., 30 May, 4 July, Thanksgiving day, and in each state all legal holidays.—*England and Ireland:* Easter Monday, Monday in Whitsun week, first Monday in Aug., 26 Dec. (if a week-day).—*Scotland:* New Year's day, Christmas day (if either falls on Sunday, the following Monday), Good Friday, first Mondays in May and Aug.

Bank of England, projected by William Paterson, a Scotch merchant (DARIEN), to assist William III. in raising supplies for the French war. Led by Paterson and Michael Godfrey, 40 merchants subscribed 500,000*l.* towards 1,200,000*l.* to be lent to the government at 8 per cent., in return for a bank charter. Passed against strong opposition, the bill was signed 25 Apr. 1694, and the charter, granted 27 July, made sir John Houblon first governor, and Michael Godfrey first deputy-governor. Business opened 1 Jan. 1695, at Grocers' Hall, Poultry, by issuing notes for 20*l.* and upwards, and discounting bills for 4½ to 6 per cent. The Bank of England does not allow interest on deposits. The average balance of the assets has been from the beginning between 3,000,000*l.* and 4,000,000*l.* The charter was renewed in 1697, 1708, 1713, 1716, 1721, 1724, 1746, 1749, 1764, 1781, 1800, 1808, 1816, 1833, 1844, 1861, 1886.—*Lawson.*

Run on bank; notes at 20 per cent. discount; capital raised to 2,201,171*l.* 10*s*.................................Nov. 1696
Bank monopoly established by forbidding a company exceeding 6 persons to act as bankers (Scotland excepted)........... 1708
Capital raised to 5,559,995*l.* 10*s*.............................. 1710
Bank post bills issued (1st record)..................14 Dec. 1738
Run for gold upon rebellion in the North; bills paid in silver; the city supports the bank..............................Sept. 1745
Richard W. Vaughan, first forger of Bank-of-England notes, hanged.......................................1 May, 1758
10*l.* notes issued.. 1759
Gordon riots; bank since protected by military................ 1780
5*l.* notes issued.. 1793
Cash payments suspended, by order in council.........26 Feb. 1797
1*l.* and 2*l.* notes issued..................................Mch. "
Bank Restriction act ....3 May, "
Voluntary contribution of 200,000*l.* to the government........ 1798
Loss by Aslett's frauds (EXCHEQUER), 342,697*l.*................ 1803
Abraham Newland, 50 years cashier, resigns..........18 Sept. 1807
Bramah's machine for numbering notes adopted.................. 1809
Bank issues silver tokens for 3*s.* and 1*s.* 6*d*..............9 July, 1811
Peel's act for gradual resumption of cash payments.......July, 1819
Cash payments for notes to be in bullion at the mint price, 1 May, 1821; in current coin...........................1 May, 1823
Commercial panic—many 1*l.* notes (accidentally found in a box) issued with beneficial effects.........................Dec. 1825
Act authorizing joint-stock banks ends the monopoly........... 1826
By advice of government, branch banks opened at Gloucester, 19 July; Manchester, 21 Sept.; Swansea, 23 Oct............. "
And at Birmingham, 1 Jan.; Liverpool, 2 July; Bristol, 12 July; Leeds, 23 Aug.; Exeter, 17 Dec........................ 1827
Bank loses 360,000*l.* by Fauntleroy's forgeries................ 1830
Statements of bank pub. quarterly............................. 1833

Peel's Bank Charter act (7 and 8 Vict. c. 32); renews charter till 1 Aug. 1855, and longer, if public debt to the bank (11,015,-100*l*.), with interest, etc., be not paid after notice; establishes issue department; weekly returns to be published; limits issue of notes to 14,000,000*l*., etc. . . . . 19 July, 1844
Commercial panic; lord John Russell suspends restriction of note issue (not acted on); bank discount 8 per cent. . 25 Oct. 1847
Clerks found library and fidelity guarantee fund. . . . . Mch. 1850
Gold bullion in bank (largely from Australia). 21,845,390*l*. 10 July, 1852
Branch bank, Burlington gardens, London, W., opened, 1 Oct. 1856
Committee on the bank acts appointed. . . . . 12 May, 1857
Bank discount 9 per cent.; Palmerston authorizes further issue of notes (2,000,000*l*. were issued). . . . . 12 Nov. "
Committee on bank acts reappointed, 8 Feb.; report recommending no change of policy. . . . . 1 July, 1858
Alarm at bank solicitor's report that bank paper had been stolen from makers (forged notes soon appeared). . . . 16 Aug. 1862
Bank authorized (in accordance with the act of 1844) to increase issue of notes by 250,000*l*. . . . . 11 Feb. 1890
Bank, aided by the Bank of France and others, assists Messrs. Baring and averts a panic. . . . . 15 Nov. "

AVERAGE AMOUNT OF BANK-OF-ENGLAND NOTES IN CIRCULATION.

1718	£1,829,930	1835	£18,215,220
1778	7,030,680	1840	17,231,000
1790	10,217,000	1845	19,262,327
1800	15,450,000	1850	19,776,814
1810	23,904,000	1855	19,616,627
1815	26,803,520	1859	22,705,780
1820	27,174,000	1889	25,263,180
1830	20,620,000	1891	25,851,565

PUBLIC DEBT TO THE BANK OF ENGLAND.

1694	£1,200,000	1742	£10,700,000
1708	2,175,027	1746	11,686,000
1716	4,175,027	1816	14,686,000
1721	9,100,000	1844–89	11,015,700

Bank of Ireland, established at St. Mary's abbey, Dublin, 1 June, 1783. The business removed to the late parliament house, in College green, in May, 1808. Branches formed in most of the provincial towns in Ireland, all since 1828. Irish Banking act passed, 21 July, 1845.

Bankruptcy law. Extracts from the United States Bankruptcy act of 1 July, 1898:

Sec. 4. Who May Become Bankrupts.—(*a*) Any person who owes debts, except a corporation, shall be entitled to the benefits of this act as a voluntary bankrupt. (*b*) Any natural person (except a wage-earner or a person engaged chiefly in farming or the tillage of the soil), any unincorporated company, and any corporation engaged principally in manufacturing, trading, printing, publishing, or mercantile pursuits, owing debts to the amount of $1000 or over, may be adjudged an involuntary bankrupt upon default or an impartial trial, and shall be subject to the provisions and entitled to the benefits of this act. Private bankers, but not national banks or incorporated banks, may be adjudged involuntary bankrupts.

Sec. 7. Duties of Bankrupts.—(*a*) The bankrupt shall (1) attend the first meeting of his creditors, if directed by the court or a judge thereof to do so, and the hearing upon his application for a discharge, if filed; (2) comply with all lawful orders of the court; (3) examine the correctness of all proofs of claims filed against his estate; (4) execute and deliver such papers as shall be ordered by the court; (5) execute to his trustee transfers of all his property in foreign countries; (6) immediately inform his trustee of any attempt, by his creditors or other persons to evade the provisions of this act coming to his knowledge; (7) in case of any person having to his knowledge proved a false claim against his estate, disclose that fact immediately to his trustee; (8) prepare, make oath to, and file in court within ten days, unless further time is granted, after the adjudication if an involuntary bankrupt, and with the petition if a voluntary bankrupt, a schedule of his property, showing the amount and kind of property, the location thereof, its money value in detail, and a list of his creditors, showing their residences, if known (if unknown that fact to be stated), the amount due each of them, the consideration thereof, the security held by them, if any, and a claim for such exemptions as he may be entitled to, all in triplicate, one copy of each for the clerk, one for the referee, and one for the trustee; and (9) when present at the first meeting of his creditors, and at such other times as the court shall order, submit to an examination concerning the con-

FAILURES IN THE UNITED STATES.

	Number.*		Liabilities.*	
	1904.	1903.	1904.	1903.
Manufacturers.				
Iron, foundries, and nails	69	47	$2,083,238	$3,279,355
Machinery and tools	165	178	6,873,342	14,293,898
Woollens, carpets, and knit goods	37	26	1,649,332	1,236,996
Cottons, lace, and hosiery	28	13	1,741,710	699,082
Lumber, carpenters, and coopers	272	257	6,950,429	6,090,559
Clothing and millinery	386	344	3,514,069	5,721,885
Hats, gloves, and furs	39	56	851,034	1,347,478
Chemicals, drugs, and paints	34	41	328,586	736,842
Printing and engraving	157	142	1,392,782	1,995,379
Milling and bakers	180	157	1,118,121	1,846,483
Leather, shoes, and harness	90	110	2,218,856	2,622,871
Liquors and tobacco	101	94	1,828,298	1,763,177
Glass, earthenware, and bricks	75	38	3,514,969	1,566,969
All other	698	818	9,307,522	12,478,097
Total manufacturing	2,325	2,321	$43,372,288	$55,679,071
Traders.				
General stores	1,301	1,144	$9,194,069	$6,728,644
Groceries, meats, and fish	1,844	1,489	6,642,450	5,567,197
Hotels and restaurants	394	326	2,900,214	1,912,573
Liquors and tobacco	831	687	3,903,909	2,976,033
Clothing and furnishing	617	596	4,826,311	4,317,070
Dry goods and carpets	366	361	6,928,992	6,295,476
Shoes, rubbers, and trunks	267	270	1,764,172	2,299,806
Furniture and crockery	193	179	1,535,194	1,325,514
Hardware, stoves, and tools	276	237	2,710,388	1,769,490
Drugs and paints	285	254	1,731,311	1,982,263
Jewelry and clocks	186	131	1,438,940	975,768
Books and papers	54	49	451,304	256,487
Hats, furs, and gloves	40	36	472,061	200,936
All other	707	722	9,827,838	9,202,693
Total trading	7,361	6,481	$54,327,153	$45,809,950
Brokers and transporters	385	460	24,485,492	18,554,401
Total commercial	10,071	9,262	$122,184,933	$120,043,422
Banking	83	88	$21,153,054	$21,806,246

Yearly Failures.		
Year.	No.	Liabilities.
1860	3,676	$79,807,000
1861	6,993	207,210,000
1862	1,652	23,049,000
1863	495	7,899,900
1864	520	8,579,000
1865	530	17,625,000
1866	1,505	53,783,000
1867	2,780	96,666,000
1868	2,608	63,694,000
1869	2,799	75,054,054
1870	3,546	88,242,000
1871	2,915	85,252,000
1872	4,069	121,056,000
1873	5,183	228,499,900
1874	5,830	155,239,000
1875	7,740	201,000,000
1876	9,092	191,117,000
1877	8,872	190,669,936
1878	10,478	234,383,132
1879	6,658	98,149,053
1880	4,735	65,752,000
1881	5,582	81,155,932
1882	6,738	101,547,564
1883	9,184	172,874,172
1884	10,968	226,343,427
1885	10,637	124,220,321
1886	9,834	114,644,119
1887	9,634	167,560,944
1888	10,679	123,829,973
1889	10,882	148,784,337
1890	10,907	189,856,964
1891	12,273	189,868,638
1892	10,344	114,044,167
1893	15,242	346,779,889
1894	13,885	172,992,856
1895	13,197	173,196,060
1896	15,088	226,096,834
1897	13,351	154,332,071
1898	12,186	130,662,899
1899	9,337	90,879,889
1900	10,774	138,495,673
1901	11,002	113,092,376
1902	11,615	117,476,769
1903	12,069	155,444,185

* Ten months to 31 Oct. Other years calendar years. These statistics were prepared for The World by R. G. Dun & Co.

ducting of his business, the cause of his bankruptcy, his dealings with his creditors and other persons the amount, kind, and whereabouts of his property and, in addition, all matters which may affect the administration and settlement of his estate, but no testimony given by him shall be offered in evidence against him in any criminal proceedings Provided, however, that he shall not be required to attend a meeting of his creditors, or at or for an examination at a place more than 150 miles distant from his home or principal place of business, or to examine claims except when presented to him, unless ordered by the court or a judge thereof, for cause shown, and the bankrupt shall be paid his actual expenses from the estate when examined or required to attend at any place other than the city, town, or village of his residence —*Discharge in bankruptcy* relieves the bankrupt from all his provable debts, except taxes due to the U S, state, county or municipality in which he resides, liabilities for money or property obtained by false pretences, wilful and malicious injuries to persons or property, alimony, debts created by fraud or misappropriation, etc The U S Court of Appeals, in the case of Keppel, trustee, against the Tiffin, Ohio, Savings-bank, the U S Supreme Court laid down a new principle in bankruptcy proceedings on 3 Apr 1905 This was that a creditor who has received a merely voidable preference, and who has in good faith retained such preference until deprived thereof by the judgment of a court upon a suit of the trustee, might thereafter prove the debt so voidably preferred Justices Harlan, Brewer, Brown, and Day dissented, and the last named in his opinion said that the bankruptcy law contemplated that a secured creditor who held a security voidable under the law must make his choice while he yet had something to give for the privilege of being placed in the class who should share in the equal distribution of an estate To permit him to prove his claim as a general creditor would tend to defeat the purpose of the act

banks and **banking.** The name is derived from *banco*, a bench in the market-place for the exchange of money Banking reached a high development among the ancients Bankers in Greece and Rome performed nearly the same services as now, but seem not to have issued notes. They received money on deposit, and repaid on demand, with or without interest Banking reappears upon the revival of civilization, first, in Italy, 808, among the Lombard Jews, of whom some settled in Lombard street London, where many bankers still reside The Mint in the Tower of London was anciently the depository for merchants' cash, until Charles I seized the money as a loan, and in 1640 the traders lodged their money with the goldsmiths in Lombard street B C.

Egibe s bank at Babylon, mentioned about 700
Bank of England (1890) possesses a Chinese bank note, supposed to be of the 14th century A D

Bank of A D

Venice formed 1157
Geneva 1345
Barcelona (the earliest existing bank) 1401
Genoa 1407
Amsterdam 1607
Hamburg 1619
Rotterdam 1635
Stockholm 1688
England 1694
Scotland 1695
Copenhagen 1736
Berlin 1765
Caisse d'Escompte France 1776
North America, in Philadelphia. 1780
Ireland 1783
Massachusetts. 1784
New York "
St. Petersburg 1786
In the East Indies 1787
The United States 1791
France laws passed, 1803, 1806, approved. . 1808
United States national banks 1863
Italy 1865
Imperial Bank of Germany (formerly of Prussia) 1 Jan 1876

ENGLISH BANKS

Samuel Lamb London banker, advises Cromwell to establish a public bank 1656-58
Francis Child goldsmith opens a bank about 1663, d 4 Oct 1713
Run on London bankers (said to be the first) 1667
Charles II suspends payments to bankers of their deposits in the exchequer, they lose ultimately 3,321,313*l*. 2 Jan 1672
Hoare s bank begun about . 1680
Bank of England established 1694

BAN

Oldest county bank, Wood's at Gloucester opened 1716
List of bankers given in the "Royal Kalendar" 1765
Forgeries of Henry Fauntleroy banker, executed 30 Nov 1824
Act authorizing joint-stock banks 1826
Rowland Stephenson M P banker and treasurer of St Bartholomew s hospital absconds, defaulter to 200 000*l*, 70,000*l* in exchequer bills, shock to confidence in bankers 27 Dec 1828
Establishment of joint stock banks 1834
Rogers s bank robbed of nearly 40 000*l* (bank notes afterwards returned) 24 Nov 1844
Failure of Strahan Paul & Bates (securities unlawfully used), private banking much injured 11 June, 1855
Check bank in aid of persons not having a banker opened in Pall Mall 23 July, 1873
Number of banks in London alone was 225 in 1892
BANK OF ENGLAND, and BANKS

banks in the United States Before the first U S. bank was chartered, in 1791, there were but 3 banks in the U S, with an aggregate capital of $2,000,000 the Bank of North America, chartered by Congress in 1780 at the instance of Robert Morris, and by Pennsylvania in 1781, with a capital of $400,000, the Bank of Massachusetts, chartered 1784, and the Bank of New York, chartered the same year The charter of the U S bank was limited to 20 years from 1791, its capital was $10,000,000 of which the government could subscribe one fifth, $5 700,000, to be held in Philadelphia, and the remainder to be distributed among the 8 branches Its headquarters were fixed in Philadelphia, with 20 directors. The government sold all its stock at a premium in 1802 Congress was asked to renew the charter in 1808, 3 years before its expiration, but did nothing, and a few weeks before the charter expired the bill for rechartering was defeated UNITED STATES, 1811 It was opposed (1) as unconstitutional, (2) as in the hands of foreigners, (3) as injurious to local banks Specie payments were suspended in 1814, owing largely to this failure to re-charter. An effort was made (1814) to establish a similar bank under another name In 1815 president Madison vetoed a bill chartering a second U S bank, but in 1816 he willingly approved a charter limited to 20 years, with a capital of $35,000,000, of which the government subscribed $7,000 000 and citizens the rest In this bank the government funds were kept on deposit This second U S bank transacted business in Philadelphia from 1817 until Mch 1836 The Suffolk-bank system of redemption began in Boston, Mass, 1825, while the safety-fund system originated in New York in 1828 President Jackson, in his first message, 1829, opposed the bank, and continued the attack in 1830 and 1831 The bank asked a renewal of its charter 1831, the act passed but Jackson vetoed it, 1832 He recommended the removal of the U S deposits from the bank and a sale of the stock (1832), but Congress refused to authorize the measure President Jackson dismissed the sec of treasury, Wm Duane, for refusing to remove the deposits, and appointed Roger B Taney, who removed them, 1833 UNITED STATES. The effect of the failure to renew the charter was disastrous 13 days before the original charter expired Pennsylvania re-chartered it, with the same capital as the U S Bank of Pennsylvania It suspended specie payments in 1837 again in 1839, and in 1840-41 made a final suspension The shares were quoted at 1 25 in 1837, in 1839 at 1 11, and in 1843, after its failure, at 1¼ per cent It proved a total loss to the shareholders New York adopted in 1838 a free-banking system (devised by rev John McVickers, D D prof of political economy in Columbia college in 1827) Ohio, for its state bank, adopted the safety-fund system, under which 10 banks had failed in New York, with a loss of $2 500,000, including all their capital Clearing-house in New York established Oct 1853, and in Boston 29 Mch 1856 CLEARING-HOUSE. Financial embarrassment and suspension of specie payment throughout the U S followed the failure of the Ohio Life and Trust Company, 1857 At the breaking out of the civil war, in 1861, there were 1601 state banks, with aggregate capital of $429 000,000, with 10,000 different kind of notes in circulation, issued in the 34 states then existing, their condition was generally sound, but secretary Chase devised a national-bank system similar to the New York "free-bank system", and the act of 25 Feb 1863 (UNITED STATES), made the paper currency and the banking laws of the country uniform The state banks were induced by privileges, or forced by taxes, to surrender their charters and become national banks. By an act approved 12 June, 1870, the circulation of the national banks was limited to $354,000,000, secured by the deposit of government bonds with the treasurer. This limitation was afterwards repealed. Although the national-bank system has overshadowed the state banks, many of the latter still exist (see table 6 subjoined), mainly under the free-banking laws. The national banks in 22 principal cities—viz., New York, 47; Chicago, 19; St. Louis, 8; Boston, 56; Albany, 6; Brooklyn, 5; Philadelphia, 45; Pittsburg, 26; Baltimore, 19; Washington, 11; New Orleans, 10; Louisville, 10; Cincinnati, 13; Cleveland, 10; Detroit, 8; Milwaukee, 3; St. Paul, 6; Minneapolis, 6; Kansas City, 10; St. Joseph, 4; Omaha, 9; San Francisco, 2—are obliged to keep a reserve of 25% on deposits. These are known as reserve cities. The banks elsewhere hold a reserve of 15% on deposits.

The following tables, 1, 2, 3, 4, and 5, are subjoined to show the condition and growth of the national-bank system up to and including the year 1891-2; table 6, the condition of the other banks:

TABLE 1.

Number and Amount of National-bank Notes Issued and Redeemed since the Organization of the System, and the Amount Outstanding, 31 Oct. 1890.

Denominations.	Number of Notes.			Amount of Notes.		
	Issued.	Redeemed.	Outstanding.	Issued.	Redeemed.	Outstanding.
Ones	23,169,677	22,800,061	369,616	$23,169,677	$22,800,061	$369,616
Twos	7,747,519	7,655,573	91,946	15,495,038	15,311,146	183,892
Fives	108,957,768	98,861,238	10,096,530	544,788,840	494,306,190	50,482,650
Tens	46,124,000	40,362,126	5,761,874	461,240,000	403,621,260	57,618,740
Twenties	14,416,178	12,212,595	2,203,583	288,323,560	244,251,900	44,071,660
Fifties	1,949,362	1,754,196	195,166	97,468,100	87,709,800	9,758,300
One-hundreds	1,472,733	1,305,372	167,361	147,273,300	130,537,200	16,736,100
Five-hundreds	23,894	23,528	366	11,947,000	11,764,000	183,000
One-thousands	7,379	7,333	46	7,379,000	7,333,000	46,000
Total	203,868,510	184,982,022	18,886,488	$1,597,084,515	$1,417,634,557	$179,449,958
Unpresented fractions of notes to be deducted from notes redeemed and added to amount of notes outstanding					25,748	25,748
Total					$1,417,608,809	$179,475,706

TABLE 2.

Number and Authorized Capital of Banks Organized, and the Number and Capital of Banks Closed Each Year ending 31 Oct.

Year.	Organized.		Closed. In voluntary liquidation.		Closed. Insolvent.	
	No.	Capital.	No.	Capital.	No.	Capital.
1863	134	$16,378,700	....	....	....	....
1864	453	79,366,950	3	....	....	....
1865	1014	242,542,982	6	$330,000	1	$50,000
1866	62	8,515,150	4	650,000	2	500,000
1867	10	4,259,300	12	2,160,000	6	1,170,000
1868	12	1,210,000	18	2,445,500	4	410,000
1869	9	1,500,000	17	3,372,710	1	50,000
1870	22	2,736,000	14	2,550,000	1	250,000
1871	170	19,519,000	11	1,450,000	....	....
1872	175	18,988,000	11	2,180,500	6	1,806,100
1873	68	7,602,700	21	3,524,700	11	3,825,000
1874	71	6,745,500	20	2,795,000	3	250,000
1875	107	12,104,000	38	3,820,200	5	1,000,000
1876	36	3,189,800	32	2,565,000	9	965,000
1877	29	2,589,000	26	2,539,500	10	3,344,000
1878	28	2,775,000	41	4,237,500	14	2,612,500
1879	38	3,595,000	33	3,750,000	8	1,230,000
1880	57	6,374,170	9	570,000	3	700,000
1881	86	9,651,050	26	1,920,000	....	....
1882	227	30,038,300	78	16,120,000	3	1,561,300
1883	262	28,654,350	40	7,736,000	2	250,000
1884	191	16,042,230	30	3,647,250	11	1,285,000
1885	145	16,938,000	85	17,856,590	4	600,000
1886	174	21,358,000	25	1,651,100	8	650,000
1887	225	30,546,000	25	2,537,450	8	1,550,000
1888	132	12,053,000	34	4,171,000	8	1,900,000
1889	211	21,240,000	41	4,316,000	2	250,000
1890	307	36,250,000	50	5,050,000	9	750,000
1891	193	20,700,000	41	4,485,000	25	3,662,000
1892	163	15,285,000	53	6,157,500	17	2,450,000
Total.	4811	$698,748,182	844	$114,588,500	181	$33,070,000

Total in operation, 1892, 3786.

TABLE 3.

Number of National Banks whose Charters will expire during Each Year from 1891 to 1902.

Year.	No. of Banks.	Capital.	Circulation.
1891	95	$12,183,900	$3,997,935
1892	100	13,815,100	4,562,760
1893	38	4,701,000	1,982,925
1894	63	7,628,000	2,812,720
1895	76	11,259,000	4,431,610
1896	23	2,173,800	986,650
1897	24	3,419,000	1,171,295
1898	25	2,679,000	1,198,350
1899	39	4,995,000	2,270,700
1900	50	7,807,100	2,153,330
1901	108	14,669,150	3,702,350
1902	132	21,177,300	5,352,350
	773	$106,507,350	$34,622,975

TABLE 4.

Table showing the Number of National Banks, with their Earnings and Dividends, from Mch. 1, 1882, to Mch. 1, 1892.

Year.	No. of Banks.	Capital.	Surplus.	Total Dividends.	Total Net Earnings.
1882	2137	$460,354,485	$131,291,889	$19,915,375	$27,083,599
1883	2267	483,091,342	137,570,105	20,285,102	26,432,934
1884	2491	507,969,300	145,600,849	21,082,806	27,994,764
1885	2650	522,899,715	143,771,121	20,437,650	21,601,202
1886	2708	530,956,195	153,532,919	21,335,436	27,527,666
1887	2855	548,355,770	163,731,900	22,148,587	31,698,794
1888	3044	577,136,748	179,397,147	23,088,607	32,601,294
1889	3147	593,253,850	192,607,500	23,290,978	35,109,889
1890	3294	615,405,545	204,546,434	26,249,766	35,248,539
1891	3542	652,586,585	219,430,741	25,768,775	40,145,974
1892	3671	675,356,310	234,676,901	25,546,853	34,363,020

TABLE 5.

Highest and Lowest Points reached by the National Banks in the Principal Items of Resources and Liabilities, since the Establishment of the System (1866–92).

Items.	January 1, 1866.	Sept. 30, 1892.	Highest point reached.		Lowest point reached.	
			Amount.	Date.	Amount.	Date.
Capital	$403,357,346	$686,573,015	$686,573,015	Sept. 30, 1892	$403,357,346	Jan. 1, 1866
Capital, surplus, and undivided profits	475,330,204	1,027,097,194	1,027,097,194	" "	475,330,204	" "
Circulation	213,239,530	143,423,298	341,320,256	Dec. 26, 1873	122,928,084	Oct. 2, 1890
Total investments in U. S. bonds	440,380,350	183,439,550	712,437,900	Apr. 4, 1879	170,653,050	" "
Individual deposits	520,212,174	1,765,422,983	1,765,422,983	Sept. 30, 1892	501,407,586	Oct. 8, 1870
Loans and discounts	500,650,109	2,153,498,829	2,153,498,829	" "	500,650,109	Jan. 1, 1866
Cash: National-bank notes	20,406,442	19,557,474	28,809,699	Dec. 31, 1883	11,841,104	Oct. 7, 1867
Cash: Legal tender notes	187,846,548	104,267,945	205,793,579	Oct. 1, 1886	52,156,439	Mch. 11, 1881
Cash: Specie	16,909,363	209,116,379	209,116,379	Sept. 30, 1892	8,050,330	Oct. 1, 1875

TABLE 6.

Number, Capital Stock, Surplus and Undivided Profits, and Deposits of all State Banks, Savings (Mutual and Stock), Private Banks, and Loan and Trust Companies (1890–91).

Classes.	No. Banks.	Capital.	Surplus and Undivided Profits.	Deposits.
State banks........	2572	$208,564,841	$81,116,533	$556,637,012
Loan and trust companies......	171	79,292,889	55,503,845	355,330,080
Savings banks (mutual).......	647	....	142,456,741	1,402,332,665
Savings banks (stock)..........	364	32,106,127	13,400,752	252,493,477
Private banks......	1235	36,785,458	12,146,622	94,959,727
Total............	4989	$356,749,315	$304,624,493	$2,661,752,961

banks, joint-stock. The Bank of England was the only joint-stock bank in England until 1826, and in London until 1834. Since the act of 1826, a large number have been established. In Ireland, of similar banks, the first was the Hibernian bank, in 1825. By the new Companies act, passed 15 Aug. 1879, unlimited companies may register as limited. The total capital paid up and reserves of the various joint-stock banks amounted to more than 150,000,000*l.* in 1892.

Chief London Banks.	Founded.
London and Westminster (becomes limited, 1879)............	1834
London Joint-Stock..	1836
Union Bank of London..	1839
Commercial Bank of London...................................	"
London and County (becomes limited, 1879)...................	"
City Bank (becomes limited, 1880)...........................	1855
Bank of London..	"

banks of Scotland. The old Bank of Scotland was set up in 1695 at Edinburgh, and began 1 Nov., the second institution of the kind in the empire; lending money to the crown was prohibited. Royal Bank of Scotland chartered 8 July, 1727.

ban'neret, knight, a dignity between baron and knight, anciently conferred by the king under the royal standard on the field of battle. Its origin is uncertain; Edmondson dates it 736, but it was probably created by Edward I. John Chandos is said to have been made a banneret by the Black Prince and the king of Castile at Najara, 3 Apr. 1367. The dignity was conferred on John Smith, who rescued the royal standard at Edgehill, 23 Oct. 1642. After long disuse, it was revived by George III. for sir William Erskine, in 1764, and for admiral Pye, and capts. Knight, Bickerton, and Vernon, in 1773.

banners were common to all nations. The Jewish tribes had standards or banners (Numb. ii.—1491 B.C.). The standard of Constantine bore the inscription *In hoc signo vinces* ("By this sign thou shalt conquer") under the cross. CROSS. The magical banner of the Danes (a black raven on red ground) was taken by Alfred when he defeated Hubba, 878. St. Martin's cap, and afterwards the celebrated auriflamme, or oriflamme, were the standards of France about 1100. AURIFLAMME, STANDARDS, etc.

Bannockburn', Stirlingshire, the site of 2 battles; (1) between Robert Bruce of Scotland, with 30,000 men, and Edward II. of England, with 100,000 (of whom 52,000 were archers), 24 June, 1314. The English crossed a rivulet to attack, fell into covered pits dug by Bruce, and were thrown into confusion and routed. Edward narrowly escaped, and 50,000 were killed or taken. (2) At Sauchieburn, near here, James III. of Scotland was defeated and slain on 11 June, 1488, by rebellious nobles.

banns, in feudal law, were any solemn proclamation; hence the custom of asking banns, or giving notice before marriage; said to have begun in the English church about 1200. The proper time of publishing banns was much discussed, 1867.

Bantam', Java. Here a British factory was established by capt. Lancaster, in 1603. The English and Danes were driven from their factories by the Dutch in 1683. Bantam surrendered to the British in 1811, but was restored to the Dutch at the peace in 1814.

Bantry bay, S. Ireland, where a French fleet in aid of adherents of James II. attacked the English under admiral Herbert, 1 May, 1689; the latter retired to form and were not pursued. A French squadron of 7 sail of the line, 2 frigates, armed *en flûte*, and 17 transports, anchored here for a few days, without effect, Dec. 1796.—Mutiny of the Bantry bay squadron under admiral Mitchell was in Dec. 1801. In Jan. 1802, 22 of the mutineers were tried on the *Gladiator*, at Portsmouth; 17 were condemned to death, 11 were executed; the others sentenced to receive each 200 lashes. The executions took place on board the *Majestic, Centaur, Formidable, Téméraire*, and *L'Achille*, 8–18 Jan. 1802.

baptism, the ordinance of admission to the church, practised by all Christians except Quakers. John the Baptist baptized Christ, 30 (Matt. iii.). Infant baptism is mentioned by Irenæus about 97. In the reign of Constantine, 319 baptisteries were built, and baptism was performed by immersion. In the west sprinkling was adopted. Much controversy has arisen since 1831 (particularly in 1849 and 1850), in the church of England respecting baptismal regeneration, which the arches court of Canterbury decided to be a doctrine of the church of England. In 1849 the bishop of Exeter refused to install Mr. Gorham at Brampton-Speke, in Devonshire, because he denied spiritual regeneration by baptism. The case was brought before the court of arches. The bishop was justified in his refusal. Mr. Gorham appealed to the judicial committee of the privy council, which pronounced its opinion (1850) that "the doctrine held by Mr. Gorham was not contrary or repugnant to the declared doctrine of the church of England, and that Mr. Gorham ought not, for the reason of the doctrine held by him, to have been refused admission to the vicarage of Brampton-Speke." In the end Mr. Gorham was instituted into the vicarage in question, 7 Aug. 1850.—Demanding fees for baptism was made unlawful in England by an act passed 18 July, 1872.

Baptists. A sect distinguished by holding that (1) the proper subjects of baptism are those who can make profession of faith; (2) the proper mode of baptism is total immersion. There are 7 sections of Baptists: Arminian, Calvinistic (or particular), etc. The first Baptist church formed in London was about 1608. The last execution for heresy in England by burning alive took place at Lichfield, 11 Apr. 1612, the condemned, Edward Wightman, being a Baptist. Baptists published their confession of faith in 1643; revised in 1689. ANABAPTISTS.

Roger Williams baptizes by immersion at Providence, R. I.... 1639
First Baptist church in the North American colonies erected at Dover, N. H.......1639–40
John Clarke founds a Baptist colony on Rhode Island......... 1641
First Baptist church in Massachusetts at Swansey........... 1663
First Baptist church in Connecticut, erected at Groton........ 1705
First incorporated Baptist institution of learning in the U. S. was founded at Warren, R. I., 1764; removed to Providence, 1770
Baptist college at Regent Park, Engl., founded.............. 1810
First theological institution by Baptists, at Hamilton, N. Y.... 1820
Owing to the slavery agitation the Baptist church separates into north and south........ 1845
University of Rochester, at Rochester, N. Y., Baptist, founded, 1850
Rev. C. H. Spurgeon's (b. 19 June, 1834; d. 31 Jan. 1892) great Baptist tabernacle, Newington-Butts, Engl., opened......... 1861

GROWTH OF THE CHURCH IN THE UNITED STATES.

Year.	Churches.	Membership.
1784........	471	35,101
1812........	2164	172,972
1840........	7771	571,926
1860........	12,279	1,016,134
1880........	26.060	2,296,327
1890........	33,588	3,368,381

NUMBER OF CHURCHES AND MEMBERSHIP IN THE WORLD IN 1890.

Location.	Churches.	Membership.
North America........	34,761	3,500,626
Brazil........	6	229
Europe........	3940	404,782
Asia........	743	75,844
Africa........	44	3,039
Australia........	186	15.196
Total.........	39,680	3,999,716

These numbers do not include all who are called Baptists, viz., the DISCIPLES, the FREE-WILL, the SEVENTH-DAY, SABBATARIANS, etc.

Barata'ria, an island-city in Cervantes' romance of

"Don Quixote," of which Sancho Panza was made perpetual governor.

Barataria bay, about 30 miles west of the mouth of the Mississippi river, on the coast of the gulf of Mexico, was the rendezvous of smugglers and pirates for several years prior to 1815. Three brothers, Frenchmen, named Jean, Pierre, and Dominique Laffite, ruled the band, which plundered Spaniards and Englishmen alike, and defied the laws. This resort was broken up without resistance by commodore Patterson, 16 Oct. 1814. LAFFITE, JEAN.

Barba'does, a West India island, one of the Windward isles, discovered by the Portuguese about 1600, taken possession of by the English 1605, and settled by sir Wm. Courteen, who founded Jamestown, 1625. As many royalists settled here, the island was taken by the parliamentarians in 1652. Area, 166 sq. miles. Pop. 1876, 162,042; white, 16,560; colored, 145,482. 1891, 182,322.

A hurricane; more than 4000 perished ....10 Oct. 1780
A large plantation with buildings destroyed by a landslide, 17 Oct. 1784
A flood, Nov. 1795; and 2 great fires....May, Dec. 1796
Bishopric established.... 1824
Thousands of lives and much property destroyed by a hurricane....10 Aug. 1831
Nearly 17,000 persons died of cholera.... 1854
Property about 300,000*l.* burned at Bridgetown....14 Feb. 1860
Great increase in growth of cotton....1864–65
Proposed confederation of the Windward isles; supported by governor's speech, 3 Mch.; opposed by planters....Mch. 1876
Blacks, ignorantly expecting advantage from confederation, rise, plunder and destroy much property and cattle; negroes killed and wounded by police....21, 22 Apr. "
Panic among the planters; the governor and clergy said to have acted judiciously; peace restored....24 Apr. "
Trial of 450 rioters; 82 punished (17 penal servitude; others light sentences)....12-21 Oct. "

Barbary, N. Africa, includes Algeria, Morocco, Fez, Tunis, and Tripoli, with dependencies. Piratical states (nominally subject to Turkey) were founded here by Barbarossa, about 1518.

barbers lived in Greece in the 5th century, and at Rome in the 3d century B.C. In England of old the barber and surgeon were one, a barber-surgeon. A London company was formed in 1308, and incorporated 1462, partially dissolved in 1540, wholly in 1745. "No person using any shaving or barbery in London shall occupy any surgery, letting of blood, or other matter, except only drawing of teeth."—32 Hen. VIII. 1540. SURGERY.

Barca, N. Africa, the Greek Barce, a colony of Cyrene, successively subjugated by Persians, Egyptians, and Saracens. In 1550 sultan Solyman added Barca to the newly conquered pachalic of Tripoli.

Barcelo'na, N.E. Spain, an ancient maritime city, said to have been rebuilt by Hamilcar Barca, father of Hannibal, about 233 B.C. Held by Romans, Goths, Moors, and Franks, and with the province about it made independent about 864 A.D., and incorporated with Aragon, 1164, the last count becoming king. The city has suffered much by war. The siege by the French in 1694 was relieved by an English fleet under admiral Russell; but the city was taken by the earl of Peterborough in 1706. It was bombarded and taken by the duke of Berwick and the French in 1714, taken by Napoleon in 1808, and retained till 1814. It revolted against the queen in 1841, was bombarded and taken in Dec. 1842, by Espartero. Pop. 1887, 272,481.

bards. Demodocus is mentioned as a bard by Homer; and Strabo mentions them among the Romans before Augustus. The Welsh bards formed an hereditary order, regulated, it is said, by laws enacted about 940 and 1078. They lost their privileges at the conquest by Edward I. in 1284. The institution was revived by the Tudor sovereigns; and the EISTEDDFODS (or meetings) have been frequently held: at Swansea, Aug. 1863; at Llandudno, Aug. 1864; in the vale of Conway, 7 Aug. 1865; at Chester, 4 Sept. 1866; at Carmarthen, 3 Sept. 1867; at Ruthin, 5–7 Aug. 1868; at Rhyl, 8–12 Aug. 1870; at Portmadoc, Aug. 1872; at Mold, Aug. 1873; at various places in 1874–76; at Carnarvon, 21 Aug. 1877; at Llanrwst, 1–3 Aug.; at Menai bridge, Aug. 1878; at Conway, 6 Aug., and at other places, 1879. The Cymmrodorion Society held an Eisteddfod at Carnarvon, 23 Aug. 1880. In 1880 the bards decided that the Annual National Eisteddfod should be held alternately in North and South Wales. The Gwyneddigion Society of Bards was founded in 1770. Turlogh O'Carolan, the last of the Irish bards, died in 1738.—*Chambers.*

Barebone's parliament. Cromwell, supreme in the 3 kingdoms, summoned 122 persons, who, with 6 from Scotland and 5 from Ireland, met as a parliament, 4 July, 1653. It bears a nickname of one of its members, a leather-seller, named "Praise-God Barbon." The majority evinced much sense and spirit, proposing to reform abuses, improve the administration of the law, etc. The parliament was suddenly dissolved, 13 Dec. 1653, and Cromwell made lord protector.

Barfleur, N. France, where William, duke of Normandy, equipped his fleet to conquer England, 1066. Near it, William, duke of Normandy, son of Henry I., in his passage from Normandy, was shipwrecked, 25 Nov. 1120; he, his sister, and many others perished. Barfleur was destroyed by the English in the campaign of Crecy, 1346. The French navy was destroyed near the cape by admiral Russell, after the victory of La Hogue, 19 May, 1692.

Bari, S. Italy, the Barium of Horace, in the 9th century a stronghold of the Saracens, was captured by the emperor Louis II., a descendant of Charlemagne, in 871. In the 10th century it became subject to the Eastern empire, till taken by Robert Guiscard, the Norman, about 1060. An ecclesiastical council held here on 1 Oct. 1098, discussed the *filioque* article of the creed and the procession of the Holy Spirit.

Baring island, Arctic sea, discovered by capt. Penny in 1850–51, and named after sir Francis Baring, first lord of the English admiralty in 1849.

barium (Gr. βαρύς, heavy), a metal found abundantly as carbonate and sulphate. The oxide baryta was first recognized as an earth distinct from lime by Scheele in 1774; and the metal was first obtained by Humphry Davy in 1808.—*Watts.*

Barmecides, a powerful Persian family, celebrated for virtue and courage, were massacred through the jealousy of the caliph Haroun-al-Raschid about 802. His vizier Giafar was a Barmecide. The phrase Barmecide (or imaginary) feast originated in the story of the barber's 6th brother, in the "Arabian Nights' Entertainments."

Barnburners. A name for the radical wing of the Democratic party in the state of New York (1844–48). The derivation is doubtful. Thurlow Weed, in a letter to George W. Curtis (1873) assumes that it started in "the Dorr's rebellion," when the followers of Dorr were termed "robbers," "rioters," "incendiaries," and "barnburners." The radicals called the conservative element "Old Hunkers," from their stubborn resistance to active reforms (probably from the Dutch word *honk*, a post or station); the latter retorted by calling the radicals "barnburners," as reckless law-breakers. The story of the ignorant farmer who burned his barn to destroy the rats is another version of its derivation. During the agitation arising out of the slavery question, the "Old Hunkers" maintained their usual conservative attitude, while most of the "Barnburners" joined the Free-soil party of 1848.

Barnet, Hertfordshire, Engl. Here, at Gladsmore heath, Edward IV. defeated the Lancastrians, Easter day, 14 Apr. 1471, when the earl of Warwick, his brother the marquess of Montacute, or Montague, and 10,000 men were slain. A column commemorating this battle stands at the meeting of the St. Albans and Hatfield roads.

barom'eters. Torricelli, a Florentine, first used mercury in a vacuum tube, resembling a pump, and made the first barometer, about 1643. Pascal (1649) made it useful in measuring heights. Wheel barometers were contrived in 1668; pendent barometers in 1695; marine in 1700; and many improvements have been made since. The *aneroid* barometer (from α, no, and νηρός, watery) is without a liquid; the atmospheric pressure acts on a metallic spring. Its invention (attributed to Conté, in 1798, but due to Vidi, who died in Apr. 1866) excited much attention in 1848–49. The sympiesometer, a species of barometer, invented by Adie, of Edinburgh, 1819. Barometers were placed at northeast coast sta-ons, England, in 1860 by the duke of Northumberland and thers.

ames B Jordan's very delicate glycerine barometer, in which 1 inch is expanded to nearly 11 inches, was described to the Royal Society 22 Jan 1880 and was set up during the year at Kew and other places. The publication of two hourly variations begun in the London *Times*, 25 Oct 1880

baron, formerly the only title in the English peerage, ow the lowest Its original name in England, *vavasour*, was hanged by the Saxons into *thane*, and by the Normans into *aron* Many had undoubtedly assisted in or been summoned parliament (in 1205), but the first precept found is of 49 Hen II 1265 The first baron by patent was John de Beauchamp, aron of Kidderminster, by Richard II, 1387 The barons ook arms against king John, and extorted the charter of liberty and the charter of forests, at Runnymede, near Windsor, une, 1215 Charles II granted a coronet to barons on his storation, 1660

baronets, the first in rank among the gentry and the nly knighthood that is hereditary were instituted by James of England, 1611 The rebellion in Ulster seems to have iven rise to this order, it having been required of a baronet his creation, to pay into the exchequer as much as would aintain "30 soldiers 3 years at 8*d* a day, in the province of Ulster, in Ireland" It was further required that a baronet hould be a gentleman born and have a clear estate of 1000*l* er annum The first baronet was sir Nicholas Bacon (whose uccessor is therefore styled *Primus Baronettorum Angliæ*) 22 lay, 1611 The baronets of Ireland were created in 1619, ie first being sir Francis Blundell Baronets of Nova Scotia ere created, 1625 sir Robert Gordon the first baronet All aronets created since the Irish Union in 1801 are of the Inited Kingdom Betham's "Baronetage of England," 5 ols. 4to, 1801-5

barons' war arose from the faithlessness of Henry II of England, and the oppression of his favorites in 1258 he barons, headed by Simon de Montfort, earl of Leicester, nd Gilbert de Clare, earl of Gloucester, met at Oxford in 262, and enacted statutes to which the king objected In 263 their disputes were in vain referred to the decision of ouis IX of France War broke out and on 14 May, 1264, ie king's party was totally defeated at Lewes, and De Montort became the virtual ruler of the kingdom The war was enewed, and at the battle of Evesham, 4 Aug 1265, De Montort was slain and the barons defeated, but they did not submit till 1268 A history of this war was published by Mr W I Blaauw in 1844, 2d ed 1871

Barren hill, near Valley Forge, Pa Gen Washington detached gen Lafayette, 18 May, 1778, with about 2100 nen, to watch the British He occupied Barren hill, where e was approached by about 5000 British troops on 20 May, ntending a surprise Lafayette assuming to be preparing to neet the attack skilfully passed the enemy, retreated across he Schuylkill, and occupied a strong position, whereupon the British retired

barrier treaty, by which the Low Countries were eded to the emperor Charles VI of Germany, was signed by he British, Austrian, and Dutch ministers, 15 Nov 1715

barristers are said to have been first appointed by Edward I of England about 1291, but there is earlier mention of professional advocates They are of various ranks, as king's or queen's counsel, sergeants, etc Students for the bar must keep certain terms at the Inns of Court before being called, and by regulations of 1853 must pass a public examination rish students must keep 8 terms in England

Barrosa or **Barossa,** S Spain The British army, under major-gen sir Thomas Graham, afterwards lord Lynedoch, defeated the French under marshal Victor, 5 Mch 1811, who lost nearly 3000 dead, 6 pieces of cannon, and an eagle, he first taken by British, the British lost 1169 men killed and wounded.

Barrow island, Arctic sea, discovered by capt Penny in 1850-51, and named by him in honor of John Barrow, esq, son of sir John

Barrow, Point, Alaska, the most northerly point of the United States, lat. 71° 20′ N, lon. 155° 50′ W. A relief station was established here in 1889 by the U S government

barrows, circular or oblong mounds found in Britain and other countries, ancient sepulchres Sir Richard Hoare opened several barrows near Stonehenge, finding Celtic ornaments, as beads, buckles, and brooches, in amber, wood and gold, Nov 1808 230 barrows were opened and discoveries made chiefly in Yorkshire 1866 et seq, under the superintendence of the rev canon William Greenwell, who published his elaborate work "British Barrows" in Dec 1878

Barrows at Aldbourne North Wilts were opened by canon Greenwell and rev Walter Money Sept -Oct 1878
Canon Greenwell gave urns and other results of his explorations to the British museum in 1879

Barrow's straits, N Arctic sea, explored by Edward Parry as far as Melville island, lat 74° 26′ N and lon 113° 47′ W The strait, named after sir John Barrow, was entered on 2 Aug 1819 The thermometer was 55° below zero of Fahrenheit

bars in music appear in Agricola's "Musica Instrumentalis" 1529 and in Morley's "Practical Music," 1597, for score music Henry Lawes used them in his "Ayres and Dialogues," 1653

Bar-sur-Aube, N E France Here the French, under Oudinot and Macdonald were defeated by the allies, 27 Feb 1814

Bartholdi's Statue of Liberty Enlightening the World, unveiled on Bedloe's island, N Y. harbor 28 Oct 1886 Soon after the establishment of the French republic, a movement was inaugurated in France to evince the fraternal feeling existing on the part of that country towards the United States Thereupon some of the foremost men of France interested themselves in the formation of the French-American Union Society, and a subscription fund was realized of over 1,000,000 francs for the execution of a suitable memorial Frederic August Bartholdi was the artist selected to do the work $300 000 was raised in the U S to prepare the ground, build the pedestal, etc The statue was formally delivered to the American minister at Paris, 4 July, 1880 Weight, 440 000 lbs from low-water mark to the top of the torch it is 305 ft 11 in The statue is 151 2 ft, pedestal 91 ft and the foundation 52 1 ft in height The statue of Lafayette, in Union square, N Y, is by the same artist

Bartholomew, St., the apostle, martyred 71 The festival (3 Sept) is said to have been instituted 1130

Monastery of St Bartholomew, London (of Austin Friars), founded by Rahere a minstrel of Henry I 1102
Hospital founded by him about 1123
Refounded after dissolution of monasteries (with 100 beds, 1 physician, and 3 surgeons), 1544, incorporated 1546
William Harvey physiologist, physician here 1609-43
Earliest record of medical school 1662
Hospital rebuilt by subscription 1729
Medical college founded 1843
5803 in patients, 160,520 out patients treated, 653 beds 1878
New buildings for medical school, museum, etc, opened by the prince of Wales 3 Nov 1879
Bartholomew Fair Charter was granted by Henry I 1133, long held in SMITHFIELD, shows discontinued, 1850, the fair proclaimed for the last time, 1855 In 1858 H Morley published an illustrated "History of Bartholomew Fair"
Massacre of St Bartholomew began at Paris on the night of the festival 24 Aug 1572
According to Sully 70 000 Huguenots or French Protestants, including women and children, were murdered in the kingdom by secret orders from Charles IX at the instigation of his mother, the queen dowager, Catherine de' Medici
La Popélinière calculates the victims at 20,000, Adriani, De Serres, and De Thou say 30,000, Davila states them at 40 000, and Peréfixe makes the number 100 000 Above 600 persons of rank and 10 000 of inferior condition perished in Paris alone Pope Gregory XIII ordered a *Te Deum*, with other rejoicings

Bartholomew, St., a West Indian island held by Sweden, colonized by French, 1648, several times taken and restored by the British, ceded to Sweden by France in 1785, captured by the English and restored, 1801, ceded to France, 1877.

Bartholomites, a religious order expelled from Armenia, settled at Genoa 1307, where is preserved in the Bartholomite church the image which Christ is said to have sent to king Abgarus The order suppressed by pope Innocent X 1650

base-ball, the American national game, is probably an evolution from the old-time American games of "One-Old-Cat" and "Two-Old Cat" The first permanent base-ball organization, the Knickerbocker club of New York, which played regularly at the Elysian Fields was formed in 1845

First match game of base ball recorded, takes place at Hoboken, N J, between the Knickerbocker and New York clubs 19 June 1846
The Olympic club of Boston the first organized in Massachusetts 1854
Convention of delegates from 16 clubs held in New York, and uniform rules established for the game May 1857
National Association of Base ball Players organized 10 Mch 1858
Excelsior club of Brooklyn plays at Albany, Troy, Buffalo, Rochester, and Newburgh, the first extended trip of a ball club 1860
Nationals of Washington make a western trip 1867
Professional ball players recognized by the National Association and the first regular professional team the Red Stockings of Cincinnati organized 1868
Great success of the Red Stockings champions of the season 1869
Arthur Cummings, of the Star club introduces curved pitching "
Mutuals defeat the Chicagos on their home grounds by score 9 to 0 whence arises the expression "Chicagoed" 23 July, 1870
First game of American base ball is played at the Cricket oval London Engl 27 Feb 1874
First professional match in England, Athletics beat Bostons at Liverpool 30 July, "
The Bostons win the championship of the season, being the fourth season in succession 1875
National League of professional base ball clubs, organized at Louisville 2 Feb 1876
First International Association organized at Pittsburg, Pa 20 Feb 1877
American Association of professional clubs, organized at Cincinnati, O 2 Nov 1881
Triparti, or national agreement made between the National League, American Association, and Northwestern League, 17 Mch 1883
National Brotherhood of Ball players organized in New York 1885, and chapters formed throughout the U S 1886
Game more popular than ever 1894

Basel (Basle, Fr Bâle), a rich city in Switzerland The 18th general council sat here from Dec 1431, to May, 1443 Many church reforms were proposed, but not effected, among others the union of the Greek and Roman churches. The university was founded in 1460 Treaties of peace between France, Spain, and Prussia concluded here in 1795 Made a free imperial city 1392, but joined the Swiss confederation 1501

Basientello, S Naples Here the army of Otho II, in an ambuscade was nearly cut to pieces by Greeks and Saracens, 13 July, 982, Otho barely escaped.

Basilians, an order of monks, named from St Basil (d 380), was re-formed by pope Gregory in 1569 —A sect, founded by Basil, a physician of Bulgaria, which rejected the books of Moses, the eucharist, and baptism, said to have had everything in common, 1110 Basil was burned alive in 1118

basil'ica, a body of law, in Greek, including the Institutes of Justinian, the Pandects, etc, arranged by order of the emperor Basil the Macedonian, and his son Leo the Philosopher, 875-911 —Places of worship of the early Christian emperors were called *basilica* (palace)

Basil'ikon Do'ron (Royal Gift), precepts on the art of government, composed by James I of England for his son Henry, first published at Edinburgh in 1599 James's collected works were published at London, 1616-20, in 1 vol fol

Basque provinces, N W Spain (Biscay, Guipuscoa, and Alava) The Basques were termed Vascones by the Romans, whom they successfully resisted They were subdued with great difficulty by the Goths about 580, and were united to Castile in the 13th and 14th centuries Much speculation has been indulged in regarding their origin without sufficient special knowledge, that they once occupied a great part of Spain and southern France is generally believed Their language is still spoken by about 600,000 Spaniards and French, it appears to be of earlier origin than any Indo-European or Semitic tongue

Basque roads, W. France. 14 French ships of the line, riding at anchor here, were attacked by lords Gambier and Cochrane (the latter commanding the fire-ships), and all destroyed, 11-29 Apr. 1809 Cochrane accused Gambier of neglect to support him, but a court-martial, 26 July-4 Aug, acquitted him

Bassano, N Italy Here the Austrians, under Wurmser, were defeated by the French under Massena, 8 Sept 1796

basset or **bassette,** or *Pour et Contre,* a game at cards, said to have been invented by a noble Venetian, in the 15th century, introduced into France 1674

Basseterre roads, St Christopher's, West Indies Here the French admiral the comte de Grasse, was repulsed with loss in 3 attacks on the British fleet, under sir Thomas Graves, 25, 26 Jan 1782

bassoon, a wooden double-reed wind-instrument, said to have been invented by Afranio, a canon of Ferrara, early in the 16th century

"The Wedding Guest here beat his breast,
For he heard the loud bassoon "
—*Coleridge*, 'The Ancient Mariner "

Bassorah, Bussorah, or **Basrah,** Asia Minor, a Turkish city founded by caliph Omar, about 635, often taken and retaken by the Persians and Turks.

Bass rock, an isle in the frith of Forth, S Scotland, was granted to the Lauders 1316 purchased for a state-prison, 1671, taken by the Jacobites, 1690, surrendered, 1694, granted to the Dalrymples, 1706

Bass's strait, Australia Mr Bass, surgeon of the *Reliance*, in an open boat from Port Jackson, in 1796, penetrated as far as Western Port, and affirmed that a strait existed between New South Wales and Van Diemen's Land Lieut. Flinders circumnavigated Van Diemen's Land and named the strait after Mr Bass, 1799

bastard, a child not born in lawful wedlock An attempt in England, in 1236, to legitimate bastard children by the subsequent marriage of the parents failed The barons assembled in the parliament of Merton answered, *Nolumus leges Angliæ mutari* ("We will not have the laws of England changed") Women concealing their children's birth deemed guilty of murder, 21 James I 1624 In Scotland bastard children could not dispose of their movable estates by will until 1836 A new act, facilitating the claims of mothers and making several provisions for proceeding in bastardy cases, was passed 1845 The Bastardy Laws amendment act was passed 10 Aug 1872 In the United States bastardy is a subject dealt with by the several states acting independently In most of them the bastard inherits only through the mother, and there are statutes for compelling the father of a bastard to support it during minority —Name applied to a section of the Griquas or half-caste Hottentots who migrated with the Boers in the early part of this century from Cape Colony

Bastarnæ, a warlike tribe in Podolia and Moldavia, hired by Perseus, king of Macedon, in his wars with Rome, 168 B C, driven across the Danube by M Crassus for their encroachments, 30 B C Supposed to have been the ancestors of the Russians.—*Anthon's Cl. Dict.*

Bastile' (*bas-teel'*), Paris, a castle built by Charles V, king of France, in 1369, to defend Paris against the English, completed 1383, afterwards a state-prison Henry IV and his veteran army assailed it in vain in the siege of Paris (1587-94) "The man with the iron mask," the mysterious prisoner, died here, 19 Nov 1703 IRON MASK On 14-15 July, 1789, the Bastile was pulled down by the populace, the governor and other officers were conducted to the Place de Grève, their hands and heads were cut off, and the heads carried on pikes through the streets

Basu'to Land, near Orange river, S. Africa, including the Transkei territory, was proclaimed British territory in 1868, and annexed to Cape Colony in 1871 Its inhabitants, the Basutos, are a branch of the Bechuana group of Kafirs. Hostile to the English, 1879 Peace, 1881 Pop, whites, 400, natives, 175,000 Area, 10,293 sq miles

Bata'via, the capital of Java and the Dutch settlements in the East Indies, built by the Dutch about 1619 Taken from the French (who had seized it) by sir Samuel Auchmuty, 26 Aug. 1811, restored to the Dutch in 1814

Bath, Somerset, Engl., named "*Aquæ solis*" by the Romans, remarkable for its hot springs. Coel, a British king, is said to have given this city a charter, and the Saxon king Edgar was crowned here, 973.

Bath plundered and burned in the reign of William Rufus, and again in........ 1137
Abbey church commenced in 1405; finished........ 1609
Beau (Richard) Nash, "king of Bath,' who promoted fame of the waters and amusements, d........Feb. 1761
Bath philosophical society formed........ 1817
Bath royal literary and scientific institution established........ 1825
Victoria park opened by princess Victoria........ 1830
Restoration of the abbey by Sir G. G. Scott........ 1863 et seq.

Bath, Order of the (motto, *Tria juncta in uno*), said to be of early origin, but formally constituted 11 Oct. 1399, by Henry IV. of England, 2 days before his coronation in the Tower, when he conferred the order upon 46 esquires, who had watched the night before and bathed. After the coronation of Charles II. the order was neglected until 18 May, 1725, when it was revived by George I., who fixed the number of knights at 37.

Prince regent (afterwards George IV.) created classes of knights grand crosses (72), knights commanders (180), with an unlimited number of companions........2 Jan. 1815
Existing statutes of this order were annulled; and by new statutes the order, hitherto exclusively military, was opened to civilians........25 May, 1847
Dr. Lyon Playfair and other promoters of the great exhibition received this honor........ 1851

Constitution.		Military.	Civil.
1st Class.	Knights grand cross	50	25
2d Class.	Knights commanders	100	50
3d Class.	Companions	525	200

bathom'eter (Gr. βαθύς, deep), an apparatus invented by Dr. C. William Siemens to measure the depth of water without a sounding-line, 1861-76.

It registers the diminution of gravitation on the surface of the water as compared with that of the earth, since water (of less density) replaces earth (of greater density).

baths were early used in Asia and Greece, and introduced by Agrippa into Rome, where many were constructed by Augustus and his successors. The thermæ of the Romans and gymnasia of the Greeks (of which baths formed merely an appendage) were sumptuous. The marble group of Laocoön was found in 1506 in the baths of Titus, erected about 80, and the Farnese Hercules in those of Caracalla, erected 211.

St. Chad's well, Gray's Inn road, derives its name from St. Chad, the 5th bishop of Lichfield........ 667
In London, St. Agnes le Clere, in Old Street road, was a spring of great antiquity; baths said to have been formed in........ 1502
A bath opened in Bagnio court, now Bath street, Newgate street, London, said to have been the first bath in England for hot bathing........ 1679

bathyb'ius Hæckel'ii (Gr. βαθύς, deep; βίος, life), named by Huxley; a supposed low form of animal life, a gelatinous substance found on stones at the bottom of the sea, in DEEP-SEA SOUNDINGS. Its existence doubted by many naturalists, 1879.

baton', a truncheon borne by generals in the French army, and afterwards by marshals of other nations. Henry III. of France, before he ascended the throne, was made generalissimo of the army of his brother Charles IX., and received the *bâton* as the mark of the high command, 1569.—*Henault.* —The baton used by conductors of concerts is said to have been introduced into England by Spohr in 1820.

Baton Rouge (*bat'on roozh*), La., Battle of, fought 5 Aug. 1862. The town, held by U. S. forces under gen. Thomas Williams, was attacked by Confederates under gen. Breckinridge, who, in a severe engagement, were repulsed. Union loss about 200, among them gen. Williams, killed. The confederate iron-clad gunboat *Arkansas*, designed to engage the naval force in the river, proved useless, and the next day was attacked and destroyed. VICKSBURG CAMPAIGN.

Batoum' or **Batum,** a seaport in Lazistan, on the Black sea. After repulsing Russians, 4 May, 1877, it was ceded to Russia by the treaty of Berlin, 13 July, 1878, to become a free commercial port.

The inhabitants at first resisted, but were persuaded to submit; many emigrating, July-Sept. Russians entered, 6 Sept. 1878.

batteries along the coasts were constructed by Henry VIII. of England. The 10 floating-batteries with which Gibraltar was attacked, in the siege of that fortress, were invented by D'Arcon, a French engineer. They resisted the heavy shells and 32-pound shot, but ultimately yielded to red-hot shot, 13 Sept. 1782. GIBRALTAR. Formidable floating-batteries are now erected. NAVY. The first 2 American floating-batteries were made for the siege of Boston, Oct. 1775.

Plan of floating-battery submitted to Congress by Robert Fulton, the building of which was authorized; launched, 29 Oct. 1814. This battery carried 30 32-pound carronades and 2 columbiads of 100 pounds. Length, 145 ft.; breadth, 55 ft. Never in commission; blew up in 1829. In 1842 Congress commissioned Robert Livingston Stevens to build a floating-battery to protect New York harbor; it was unfinished at his death. New Jersey, 1869-74.

battering-ram (*testudo arietaria*), with other military implements, said to have been invented by Artemon, a Lacedæmonian, and employed by Pericles, about 441 B.C. Sir Christopher Wren used a battering-ram in demolishing old St. Paul's cathedral, 1675.

Battle-abbey, Sussex, Engl., founded by William I., 1067, on the battle-plain of Hastings, dedicated to St. Martin, and given to Benedictine monks, who were to pray for the souls of the slain. The original name of the plain was Hetheland. HASTINGS. After the battle, a list was taken of William's chiefs, amounting to 629, and called the *Battle-roll*, and among these chiefs the lands and titles of the followers of the defeated Harold were distributed.

battle-axe, a weapon of the Celts. The Irish were constantly armed with an axe.—*Burns.* At Bannockburn, king Robert Bruce clove an English champion to the chine at one blow with a battle-axe, 1314. The battle-axe guards, or beaufetiers, vulgarly called beef-eaters, whose arms are a sword and lance, were first raised by Henry VII. in 1485. They were originally attendants upon the king's buffet. YEOMAN OF THE GUARD.

Battle monument. BALTIMORE, 1815.

battles. The Grecian hero, Palamedes (1193 B.C.), is said to have been the first to form an army in regular line of battle, place sentinels round a camp, and excite the soldier's vigilance by giving him a watchword. The following are the most memorable battles, in chronological order; further details are given in separate articles; *n.* signifies *naval.* Those starred in this list are important battles, but those italicised are such that a different result might have changed the history of a nation, possibly of the world.

B.C.
Abraham defeats kings of Canaan (Gen. xiv.)........ 1913
Joshua subdues 5 kings of Canaan (Josh. x.)........ 1451
Gideon defeats the Midianites (Judg. vii.)........ 1245
Trojan war commenced........ 1193
Troy taken and destroyed........ 1184
Jephthah defeats Ammonites and sacrifices his daughter (Judg. xi.)........ 1143
Ethiopians defeated by Asa (2 Chron. xiv.)........ 941
Horatii vanquish Curiatii........ 669
Halys (Medes and Lydians stopped by eclipse)........584 or 585
Thymbra (Cyrus defeats Crœsus)........ 548
Lake Regillus (Romans defeat Latins)........ 499
Marathon (Greeks defeat Persians)........28 or 29 Sept. 490
Thermopylæ (heroism of Leonidas)........7-9 Aug. 480
Salamis, n. (Greeks defeat Persians)........20 Oct. "
Himera (Gelon defeats Carthaginians)........ "
*Mycale (Greeks defeat Persians)........22 Sept. 479
Platæa " " " .... " "
Cremera (Veientes destroy the FABII)........ 477
Eurymedon, *n.* (Greeks defeat Cimon)........ 466
Tanagra (Spartans defeat Athenians)........ 457
Œnophyta (Athenians defeat Bœotians)........ 456
Coronea (Bœotians defeat Athenians)........ 447
Romans totally defeat Veientes........ 437
Naupaktus, *n.* (Athenians defeat Spartans)........ 428
Delium (Bœotians defeat Athenians)........ 424
Amphipolis (Spartans repulse Athenians: Cleon and Brasidas killed)........ 422
Mantinea (Spartans defeat Athenians)........ 418
Athenians defeated before Syracuse........ 413
Cyzicus, *n.* (Alcibiades defeats Spartans)........ 410
Arginusæ, *n.* (Conon defeats Spartan fleet)........ 406
Ægospotamos, *n.* (Athenian fleet destroyed)........ 405
*Cunaxa (Cyrus defeated and killed by Artaxerxes)........ 401
Veii taken by the Romans........ 396
Corinthian war........395-387
Haliartus (Lysander killed)........ 395
Cnidus, *n.* (Conon defeats Spartans)........ 394
Coronea (Argesilaus defeats Athenians and allies)........ "
Allia (Brennus and the Gauls defeat Romans)........16 July, 390
Volsci defeated by Camillus........ 381
Volsci defeat the Romans........ 379
Naxus (Chabrias defeats Lacedæmonians)........376 or 377
Tegyra (Thebans defeat Spartans)........ 375
Leuctra " " " 371
"Tearless victory" of Archidamus over Argives, etc........ 367
Camillus defeats the Gauls........ "

Cynoscephalæ (Thebans defeat Thessalians)		364
Mantinea (Thebans victors. Epaminondas slain)		362
Tamynæ (Æschines there)		358
Crimisus (Timoleon defeats Carthaginians)		339
Chæronea (Philip defeats Athenians, etc.)	Aug	338
Thebes destroyed by Alexander		335
Granicus (Alexander defeats Darius)	22 May,	334
Issus " " "	Oct	333
Arbela " " "	1 Oct	331
Pandosia (Alexander of Epirus defeated and killed)		326
Cranon (Antipater defeats Greeks)		322
Caudine Forks (Roman army captured by Samnites)		321
Gaza (Ptolemy defeats Demetrius)		312
Ecnomus or Himera (Carthaginians defeat Agathocles)		311
Fabius defeats the Etruscans		310
Perusia (Etruscans defeated)		309
Ipsus (Seleucus defeats Antigonus who is slain)		301
Sentinum (Romans defeat Samnites)		295
Gauls defeat Romans at Aretium, 284; defeated by Dolabella		283
Vadimonian lake (Etruscans and Gauls defeated)		"
Corus (Lysimachus defeated and killed)		281
Pandosia (Pyrrhus defeats Romans)		280
Asculum " " "		279
Beneventum (Romans defeat Pyrrhus)		275
First Punic war begins		264
Mylæ, n. (Romans defeat Carthaginians)		260
Carthaginians under Xantippus the Spartan defeat Regulus		255
Panormus (Hasdrubal defeated by Metellus)		250
Drepanum, *n.* (Carthaginians defeat Romans)		249
Lilybæum taken by Romans		241
Ægates *n.* (Romans defeat Carthaginians)		"
Ladocea (Achæans defeated)		226
Clusium or Pisæ (Gauls defeated)		225
Sellasia (Macedonians defeat Spartans)		221
Caphyæ (Achæans defeat Ætolians)		220
Saguntum (taken by Hannibal)		219
Second Punic war.—Ticinus (Hannibal defeats Romans)		218
Trebia (Hannibal defeats Romans)		"
Thrasymene (Hannibal defeats Romans)		217
Raphia (Antiochus defeated by Ptol. Philopator)		"
* Cannæ (victory of Hannibal)	2 Aug	216
Munda (Scipio defeats Hasdrubal)		"
Marcellus surprised and killed by Carthaginian scouts		209
* Metaurus (Nero defeats Hasdrubal, who is killed)		207
* Zama (Scipio defeats Hannibal)		202
Abydos (siége of)		200
Paneas (Antiochus defeats Egyptians, etc.)		198
Cynoscephalæ (Romans defeat Macedonians)		197
Boii defeated at the Vadimonian lake		191
Thermopylæ (Greeks defeated)		"
Magnesia (Scipio defeats Antiochus)		190
Pydna (Romans defeat Perseus)	22 June,	168
Elæsa (Judas Maccabæus killed)		161
Third Punic war		149
Leucopetra (Mummius defeats Achæans)		147
Carthage taken by Publius Scipio		146
Mummius takes Corinth		"
Allobroges defeated by Q. Fabius Maximus		121
Metellus defeats Jugurtha		109
Arausio (Cimbri defeat Romans)		105
Aquæ Sextiæ (Aix, Marius defeats the Teutones)		102
* Cimbri and Teutones defeated by Marius		101
Chæronea (Sulla defeats Mithridates's army)		86
Sacriportus (Marius the younger defeated by Sulla)		82
Cabeira (Lucullus defeats Mithridates)		71
Petelia (Spartacus defeated by Crassus)		"
Tigranocerta (Lucullus defeats Tigranes)		69
Pistoria (Catiline defeated)		62
Cæsar defeats Cassivelaunus in Britain		54
Carrhæ (Crassus defeated and killed by Parthians)	9 June,	53
Alesia (Cæsar defeats Vercingetorix)		52
Pharsalia (Cæsar defeats Pompey)	9 Aug	48
Zela (Cæsar defeats Pharnaces, writes "Veni, vidi, vici")		47
Thapsus (Cæsar defeats Pompeians)		46
* Munda " " "	17 Mch	45
Mutina (Hirtius defeats Antony)	27 Apr	43
Philippi (Brutus and Cassius defeated)		42
Mylæ *n.* (Agrippa defeats Pompey the younger)		36
* Actium, *n.* (Octavius defeats Antony)	2 Sept.	31
		A.D.
* Teutoburg (Varus defeated by Herman)		9
Shropshire (Caractacus taken)		50
Sunbury (Romans defeat Boadicea)		61
Jerusalem taken by Titus		70
Agricola conquers Mona, or Anglesea		78
Ardoch (Agricola defeats Galgacus and Caledonians)		84
Dacians defeated and Decebalus slain		106
Issus (Niger slain)		194
Lyons (Severus defeats Albinus)		197
Verona (emperor Philip defeated and killed)		249
Decius defeated and slain by Goths		251
Valerian defeated and captured by Sapor		260
Naïssus (Claudius defeats Goths, many slain)		269
Châlons (Aurelian victor over rivals)		274
Allectus defeated in Britain		296
Constantine defeats Maxentius (Cross)	27 Oct.	312
Adrianople (Constantine defeats Licinius)	3 July,	323
Aquileia (Constantine II. slain)	Mch.	340
Julian defeats Alemanni		356–357
Thyatira and Nacolea (Procopius defeated)		366
Argentaria (Gratian defeats Alemanni)	May,	378
Adrianople (Gauls defeat Valens)	9 Aug	378
Aquileia (Maximus slain)	28 July,	388
" (Eugenius slain)	6 Sept.	394
Pollentia (Stilicho defeats Alaric)	29 Mch	403
Rome taken by Alaric	24 Aug	410
Ravenna taken by Aspar		425
Franks defeated by Ætius		428
Genseric takes Carthage		439
* Châlons sur Marne (Attila defeated by Ætius)		451
Aylesford (Britons defeat Saxons, Horsa killed)		455
Crayford, Kent (Hengist defeats Britons)		457
Soissons (Clovis defeats Syagrius and Romans)		486
Verona (Theodoric defeats Odoacer)	27 Sept.	489
Tolbiac, or Zulpich (Clovis defeats Alemanni)		496
Vouglé (Clovis defeats Visigoths)		507
Baddesdown hill (Britons defeat Saxons)	? 493,	511
Veseronce (Gondemar defeats Clodomir)		524
Victories of Belisarius in Africa, etc.		533–34
Narses defeats Totila, 552, and Teias		553
Heraclius defeats the Persians (Chosroes)		622
Beder (first victory of Mahomet)		623
Muta (Mahometans defeat Christians)		629
Hatfield (Heathfield, Penda defeats Edwin)		633
Ajnadin (Saracens defeat Heraclius)	13 July,	"
Yermuk (Saracens victors)	23 Aug	634
" (Saracens defeat Heraclius)	Nov	636
Saracens subdue Syria		636–38
Kadseah (Arabs defeat Persians)		638
Saracens take Alexandria		640
Near Oswestry (Penda defeats Oswald of Northumberland),	5 Aug	642
Leeds (Oswy defeats Penda, who is slain)		655
Day of the Camel (Ali victor)	4 Nov	656
Saracens defeated by Wamba in Spain		675
Testri (Pepin defeats Thierry)		687
* Xeres (Saracens defeat Roderic)	19–26 July,	711
Amblef and Vincy (Charles Martel defeats Neustrians)		716–17
Tours (Charles Martel defeats the Saracens)	10 Oct.	732
Victories of Charlemagne		775–800
Roncesvalles (death of Roland)		778
Hengestdown (Danes defeated by Egbert)		835
Charmouth (Ethelwolf defeated by the Danes)		840
Fontenaille, or Fontaneta (Lothaire defeated by Charles and Louis)	25 June,	841
Clavijo (Moors defeated)		844
Albaida (Musa and Moors defeated)		852
Danes defeat king Edmund of East Anglia		870
Assendon, or Ashdown (Danes defeated)		871
Basing and Merton (Danes victorious)		"
Hafsfiord (Harold Hårfager's final victory)		872
Wilton (Danes victorious over Alfred)		"
Andernach (Charles the Bald defeated)	8 Oct.	876
Ethandun (Alfred defeats Danes)		878
Farnham (Danes defeated)		894
Zamora (Alfonso defeats Moors)		901
Bury (Edward defeats Ethelwald and Danes)		905
Tettenhall (Danes defeated)	6 Aug	910
Soissons (king Robert, victor, killed)		923
Merseburg (Germans defeat Hungarians)		934
Brunanburg (Northmen defeated)		937
Simancas (Spaniards defeat Moors)	6 Aug	938
Nicephorus Phocas defeats Saracens		962
Basientello (Otho II. defeated by Greeks)	13 July,	982
Clontarf (Danes defeated in Ireland)	23 Apr	1014
Zetunium (Bulgarians defeated)	29 July,	"
Brentford (Edmund defeats Danes)	May,	1016
Assingdon, Ashdon (Canute defeats Edmund)		"
Sticklestadt (Olaf defeated by Swedes)	29 July,	1030
Civitella (Normans defeat Leo IX.)		1053
Dunsinane (Macbeth defeated)		1054
Fulford (Norwegians defeat English)	20 Sept.	1066
Stanford Bridge (Harold defeats Tostig)	25 Sept.	"
Hastings (William I. defeats Harold)	14 Oct	"
Fladenheim (emperor Henry defeated)		1080
Crusades commence		1090
Alnwick (Scots defeated, Malcolm slain)	13 Nov	1093
Dorylæum (Crusaders defeat Turks)	*1 July,*	1097
Asculon (Crusaders victorious)	12 Aug.	1099
Tinchebray (Robert of Normandy defeated)		1106
Brenneville (Henry I. defeats French)	Aug.	1119
Fraga (Moors defeat Spaniards)	17 July,	1134
Northallerton, or battle of the Standard (Scots under David I. defeated)	22 Aug.	1138
Ourique (Portuguese defeat Moors)	25 July,	1139
Lincoln (Stephen defeated)	2 Feb	1141
Jaen (Moors defeated by Spaniards)		1157
Carcano (Frederic I. defeated by Italians)	9 Aug.	1160
Alnwick (William the Lion defeated)	12 July,	1174
Legnano (Italians defeat emperor)	29 May,	1176
Tiberias (Saladin defeats Crusaders)	3–4 July,	1187
Ascoli (Tancred defeats the army of Henry VI. of Germany)		1190
Acre taken by Crusaders	12 July,	1191
Arsouf (Richard I. defeats Saracens)	6 Sept.	"
Fréteville (Richard I. defeats Philip II.)	15 July,	1194
Arcadiopolis (Bulgarians defeat emperor Isaac)		"
Alarcos (Moors defeat Spaniards)	19 July,	1195
Gisors (Richard I. defeats French)	20 Sept.	1198
Tolosa (Moors defeated)	16 July,	1212
Muret (Albigenses defeated)	12 Sept.	1213
Bouvines (French defeat Germans)	27 July,	1214
Lincoln (French defeated)	20 May,	1217

rte Nuova (Frederic II. defeats Milanese)............27 Nov. 1237

llebourg (French defeat Henry III.)................20 July, 1242

rizmians defeated twice.................................... 1247

ssalta (Ghibellines defeated)........................26 May, 1249

nsourah (Louis IX: and Crusaders defeated) 1250

rgs (Scots defeat Northmen)..........................3 Oct. 1263

wes (English barons victorious)......................14 May, 1264

esham (barons defeated; De Montfort killed).... ....4 Aug. 1265

nevento (Charles of Anjou defeats Maufred).........26 Feb. 1266

gliacozzo (Charles defeats Conradin)................23 Aug. 1268

rchfeld (Austrians defeat Bohemians)...............26 Aug. 1278

er Edw (Llewellyn of Wales defeated) ....11 Dec. 1282

grab (defeat of Charles Martel).............................. 1292

nbar (Scots defeated)....................................27 Apr. 1296

mbuskenneth (Wallace defeats English)............10 Sept. 1297

elheim (Adolphus of Nassau defeated)................2 July, 1298

lkirk (Wallace defeated).................................22 July, "

urtray (Flemings defeat count of Artois).............11 July, 1302

slin, Scotland (Comyn defeats English)..............24 Feb. 1303

phisus (Brienne, duke of Athens, defeated)............Mch. 1311

nnockburn (Bruce defeats English)..................24 June, 1314

rgarten (Swiss defeat Austrians)......................15 Nov. 1315

henry (Irish defeated)...................................10 Aug. 1316

ughard, or Dundalk (Edward Bruce defeated).........5 Oct. 1318

roughbridge (Edward III. defeats barons) ....16 Mch. 1322

hldorf (Bavarians defeat Austrians)..................28 Sept. "

plin (Edward Baliol defeats Mar).......................11 Aug. 1332

lidon hill (Edward III. defeats Scots).................19 July, 1333

rifa (Moors defeated).............................28 or 30 Oct. 1340

beroche (earl of Derby defeats French)...............19 Aug. 1344

recy (English defeat French)..........................26 Aug. 1346

rham, Nevil's Cross (Scots defeated)..................17 Oct. "

Roche Darien (Charles of Blois defeated).................. 1347

oitiers (English defeat French).......................19 Sept. 1356

cherel (Du Guesclin defeats Navarre)..................16 May, 1364

ray (Du Guesclin defeated)..............................29 Sept. "

jara (Navarrete, Logroño) (Black Prince defeats Henry of Trastamare)...................................3 Apr. 1367

ntiel (Peter of Castile defeated).......................14 Mch. 1369

sbecque (French defeat Flemings).......................27 Nov. 1382

ubarrota (Portuguese defeat Spaniards)...............14 Aug. 1385

npach (Swiss defeat Austrians)..........................9 July, 1386

erburn (Chevy Chase; Scots victors)...................10 Aug. 1388

fels (Swiss defeat Austrians)..................................... "

ssova (Turks defeat Albanians, and Amurath I. killed). Sept. 1389

copolis (Turks defeat Christians)......................28 Sept. 1396

sbit (Scots defeated)......................................7 May, 1402

cyra (Timour defeats Bajazet)...........................28 July, "

meldon hill (English defeat Scots.)....................14 Sept. "

rewsbury (Percies, etc., defeated).....................23 July, 1403

ambam moor (Henry IV. defeats rebels)...............19 Feb. 1408

nenberg (Poles defeat Teuton knights) ....15 July, 1410

rlaw (lord of the isles defeated).........................24 July, 1411

gincourt (English defeat French)........................25 Oct. 1415

gue (Hussites under Ziska victors).....................14 July, 1420

jou, Beaugé (English defeated by Scots)..............22 Mch. 1421

vant (English defeat French and Scots)...............11 June, 1423

uila (Aragonese defeated by Italians)...................2 June, 1424

rneuil (English defeat French and Scots)..............17 Aug. "

rrings " " " ....12 Feb. 1429

eans (siege relieved)......................................29 Apr. "

tay (English defeated by Joan of Arc)..................18 June, "

pau, or Böhmischbrod (Hussites defeated)..............28 May, 1434

nobitza (Hunniades defeats the Turks)..................24 Dec. 1443.

Jacob (French defeat Swiss)..............................26 Aug. 1444

rna (Turks defeat Hungarians)............................10 Nov. "

ssova (Turks defeat Hunniades)...........................17 Oct. 1448

rmigni (English defeated by French)....................15 Apr. 1450

venoaks (Jack Cade defeats Stafford)..................27 June, "

par (Agramonts defeat Beaumonts)......................23 Oct. 1452

echin, Scotland (Huntley defeats Crawford)...........18 May, "

stillon, Chatillon (French defeat Talbot).......17 or 23 July, 1453

lgrade (Mahomet II. repulsed)........................... 4 Sept. 1456

ntlhéry (Louis XI. and nobles; indecisive)............16 July, 1465

WAR OF THE ROSES—YORKISTS AND LANCASTRIANS.

Albans (Yorkists victorious)......................22 or 23 May, 1455

oreheath (Yorkists victors)..............................23 Sept. 1459

rthampton (" " Henry VI. taken) ....10 July, 1460

kefield (Lancastrians victors)............................31 Dec. "

rtimer's Cross (Yorkists victorious) ....2 Feb. 1461

Albans (Lancastrians victorious)........................17 Feb. "

wton (Yorkists victorious)................................29 Mch. "

xham (Yorkists victors)...................................15 May, 1464

gecote, or Banbury (Yorkists defeated) ....26 July, 1469

mford (Lancastrians defeated)...........................13 Mch. 1470

rnet " " ....14 Apr. 1471

wkesbury " " ....4 May, "

---

anson (Swiss defeat Charles the Bold)....................3 Mch. 1476

rat " " " " " ....22 June, "

ncy (Charles the Bold killed)..............................5 Jan. 1477

Bosworth (Richard III. defeated)..........................22 Aug. 1485

ke (Lambert Simnel taken)................................16 June, 1487

Aubin (Orleans defeated)..................................28 July, 1488

chieburn, near Bannockburn (James III. defeated by rebels, "

rnovo (French defeat Italians).............................6 July, 1495

minara (French defeat Spaniards)................................ "

ckheath (Cornish rebels defeated).......................22 June, 1497

minara (Gonsalvo defeats French)........................21 Apr. 1503

BAT

Cerignola (Gonsalvo defeats French)......................28 Apr. 1503

Garigliano " " " ....27 Dec. "

Agnadello (French defeat Venetians)......................14 May, 1509

Ravenna (Gaston de Foix, victor, killed)..................11 April, 1512

Novara (Papal Swiss defeat French).......................6 June, 1513

Guinegate (Spurs) (French defeated).......................16 Aug. "

Flodden (English defeat Scots)..............................9 Sept. "

Marignano (French defeat Swiss)......................13–15 Sept. 1515

Bicocca, near Milan (Lautrec defeated)....................29 Apr. 1522

Pavia (Francis I. defeated) ....24 Feb. 1525

Frankenhausen (Anabaptists defeated)....................15 May, "

Mohacz (Turks defeat Hungarians).........................29 Aug. 1526

Cappel (Zwinglius slain).....................................11 Oct. 1531

Lauffen (Hessians defeat Austrians) ....13 May, 1534

Assens (Christian III. defeats Danish rebels)...................... 1535

Abancay (Almagro defeats Alvarado, South America)..12 July, 1537

Solway Moss (English defeat Scots)........................25 Nov. 1542

Ceresuola (French defeat Imperialists)....................14 Apr. 1544

Mühlberg (Charles V. defeats Protestants)...............24 Apr. 1547

Pinkey (English defeat Scots)...............................10 Sept. "

Ket's rebellion suppressed by Warwick.........................Aug. 1549

Marciano (Florentines defeat French)........................3 Aug. 1554

St. Quentin (Spanish and English defeat French)......10 Aug. 1557

Calais (taken)...7 Jan. 1558

Gravelines, *n.* (Spanish and English defeat French)....13 July, "

Dreux, in France (Huguenots defeated)....................19 Dec. 1562

Carberry hill (Mary of Scotland defeated)................15 June, 1567

St. Denis " " " ....10 Nov. "

Langside " " " ....13 May, 1568

Jarnac (Huguenots defeated)..................................13 Mch. 1569

Moncontour (Coligny defeated)................................3 Oct. "

* Lepanto, *n.* (Don John defeats Turks)......................7 Oct. 1571

Dormans (Guise defeats Huguenots)..........................10 Oct. 1575

Alcazar-quiver (Moors defeat Portuguese)..................4 Aug. 1578

Alcantara (Spaniards defeat Portuguese)..................24 June, 1580

Zutphen (Dutch and English defeat Spaniards)........22 Sept. 1586

Coutras (Henry IV. defeats League)..........................20 Oct. 1587

* Spanish Armada defeated, *n.*...............................July, Aug. 1588

Arques (Henry IV. defeats League)..........................21 Sept. 1589

* Ivry, or Yvres (Henry IV. defeats League),...............14 Mch. 1590

Epernay taken by Henry IV. of France.....................26 July, 1592

Fontaine Française (Henry IV. beats Spaniards).........5 June, 1595

Blackwater (Tyrone and rebels defeat Bagnal)...........14 Aug. 1598

Nieuport (Maurice defeats Austrians)................................ 1600

Kinsale (Tyrone reduced by Mountjoy).............................. 1601

Kirchholm (Poles defeat Swedes).................................... 1605

Gibraltar (Dutch defeat Spaniards)................................. 1607

THIRTY YEARS WAR, 1618–48.

Prague (king of Bohemia defeated)...........................8 Nov. 1620

Dessau (Wallenstein defeats Mansfeld).....................25 Apr. 1626

Rochelle (taken)...28 Oct. 1628

Stuhm (Gustavus defeats Poles).. "

* Leipsic, or Breitenfeld (Gustavus defeats Tilly).........7 Sept. 1631

* Lech (Imperialists defeated; Tilly killed)...............5 Apr. 1632

* Lippstadt, Lutzingen, or Lutzen (Swedes victorious; Gustavus slain)..16 Nov. "

Nordlingen (Swedes defeated)...............................27 Aug. 1634

Arras (taken by the French)...................................10 Aug. 1640

Leipsic (Swedes defeat Austrians).............................23 Oct. 1642

Rocroy (French defeat Spaniards)............................19 May, 1643

Friedburg (Condé victor)......................................3–5 Aug. 1644

Nordlingen (Turenne defeats Austrians)............................ 1645

CIVIL WAR IN ENGLAND.

Worcester (prince Rupert victor)..............................23 Sept. 1642

Edgehill fight (issue doubtful)..................................23 Oct. "

Bradock-down (Parliamentarians defeated).....................Jan. 1643

Bramham moor (Fairfax defeated).............................29 Mch. "

Stratton (Royalists victorious).................................16 May, "

Chalgrove (Hampden killed)....................................18 June, "

Atherton moor (Royalists victorious).........................30 June, "

Lansdown " " ....5 July, "

Devizes, or Roundway down (Royalists victorious)....13 July, "

Gainsborough (Cromwell victor)...............................27 July, "

Newbury (favorable to Royalists) ....20 Sept. "

Cheriton, or Alresford (favorable to Royalists)..........29 Mch. 1644

Cropredy bridge (Charles I. victor)..........................29 June, "

* Marston moor (prince Rupert defeated).....................2 July, "

Tippermuir (Montrose defeats Covenanters)..................1 Sept. "

Newbury (indecisive)...27 Oct. "

Naseby (Charles I. totally defeated).......................14 June, 1645

Alford (Montrose defeats Covenanters).......................2 July, "

Kilsyth " " " ....15 Aug. "

Philiphaugh (Covenanters defeat Montrose)................13 Sept. "

Benburb (O'Neill defeats English).............................5 June, 1646

Dungan hill (Irish defeated).....................................8 Aug. 1647

Preston (Cromwell victor)......................................17 Aug. 1648

Rathmines (Irish Royalists defeated)..........................2 Aug. 1649

Drogheda (taken by storm) ....12 Sept. "

Corbiesdale (Montrose defeated) ....27 Apr. 1650

* Dunbar (Cromwell defeats Scots).............................3 Sept. "

Worcester (Cromwell defeats Charles II.) ....3 Sept. 1651

Galway (surrendered).. 1652

Daventry (Lambert defeated by Monk)........................21 Apr. 1660

Arras, France (Turenne defeats Condé)............................ 1654

Dunkirk " " " ....14 June, 1658

Estremoz (Don John defeated by Schomberg).................8 June, 1663

St. Gotthard (Montecuculi defeats Turks).......................1 Aug. 1664

Villa Viciosa (Portuguese defeat Spaniards)................... 1665
Pentland hills (Covenanters defeated)..................28 Nov. 1666
Candia (taken by Turks)....................................6 Sept. 1669
Choczim (Sobieski defeats Turks)......................11 Nov. 1673
Seneffe (French and Dutch; indecisive)...............11 Aug. 1674
Ensisheim (Turenne defeats Imperialists)...............4 Oct. "
Mülhausen " " " ....31 Dec. "
Turckheim " " " ....5 Jan. 1675
Salzbach (Turenne killed)..................................27 July, "
Drumclog (Covenanters defeat Claverhouse)...........1 June, 1679
Bothwell Brigg (Monmouth defeats Covenanters)......22 June, "
Vienna (Turks defeated by Sobieski).....................12 Sept. 1683
Sedgemoor (Monmouth defeated)...........................6 July, 1685
Mohacz (Turks defeated).....................................12 Aug. 1687
Killiecrankie (Highlanders defeat Mackay)..............27 July, 1689
Newtown-butler (Jacobites defeated)......................30 July, "
* Boyne (William III. defeats James II.)...............1 July, 1690
Fleurus (Charleroi, Luxembourg victor)................ " "
Athlone taken by Ginckel..................................30 June, 1691
Aghrim (James II.'s cause ruined).......................12 July, "
Salenckemen (Louis of Baden defeats Turks)..........19 Aug. "
Enghien or Steenkirk (William III. defeated)..........24 July, 1692
Landen (William III. defeated)............................19 July, 1693
Marsaglia (Pignerol) (French victors).....................4 Oct. "
Zenta (prince Eugène defeats Turks).....................11 Sept. 1697
Narva (Charles XII. defeats Russians) ....30 Nov. 1700
Carpi, Modena (allies defeat French).....................9 July, 1701
Chiari (Austrians defeat French)...........................1 Sept. "
Clissau (Charles XII. defeats Poles)......................20 July, 1702
Santa Vittoria (French victors)............................26 July, "
Friedlingen (French defeat Germans)......................14 Oct. "
Pultusk (Swedes defeat Poles)..............................1 May, 1703

WAR OF THE SPANISH SUCCESSION, 1702–13.

Hochstadt (French defeat Austrians)......................20 Sept. "
Donauwerth (Marlborough victor)............................2 July, 1704
Gibraltar (taken by Rooke) ....24 July, "
* Blenheim or Hochstadt (Marlborough victor).......... 13 Aug. "
Tirlemont (Marlborough successful)........................18 July, 1705
Cassano (prince Eugène; indecisive) ....16 Aug. "
Mittau (taken by Russians)...................................14 Sept. "
* Ramillies (Marlborough defeats French)..................23 May, 1706
Turin (French defeated by Eugène)...........................7 Sept. "
Kalitsch (Russians defeat Swedes)..........................19 Nov. "
Almanza (French defeat allies)...............................25 Apr. 1707
Oudenarde (Marlborough victor)..............................11 July, 1708
Liesna, Lenzo (Russians defeat Swedes).....................autumn, "
Lisle (taken by the allies) ....Dec. "
* Pultowa (Peter defeats Charles XII.)......................8 July, 1709
* Malplaquet (Marlborough victor)...........................11 Sept. "
Dobro (Russians defeat Swedes)..............................20 Sept. "
Almenara (Austrians defeat French)..........................28 July, 1710
Saragossa " " " ....20 Aug. "
Villa Viciosa (Austrians defeated)...........................10 Dec. "
Arleux (Marlborough forces French lines)....................5 Aug. 1711
Bouchain (taken by Marlborough).............................13 Sept. "
Denain (Villars defeats allies)................................24 July, 1712
Friburg (taken by French).......................................7 Nov. 1713

Preston (Scotch rebels defeated)..........................12, 13 Nov. 1715
Dumblane or Sheriff-Muir (indecisive) ....13 Nov. "
* Peterwardein (Eugène defeats Turks)......................5 Aug. 1716
Belgrade " " " ....16 Aug. 1717
Bitonto (Spaniards defeat Germans)...........................27 May, 1734
Parma (Austrians and French; indecisive)....................29 June, "
Guastalla (Austrians defeated)..................................19 Sept. "
Erivan (Nadir Shah defeats Turks)................................June, 1735
Krotzka (Turks defeat Austrians)..................................22 July, 1739

WAR OF THE AUSTRIAN SUCCESSION, 1741–48.

Molwitz (Prussians defeat Austrians).........................10 Apr. 1741
Dettingen (George II. defeats French)........................16 June, 1743
* Fontenoy (Saxe defeats Cumberland).........................30 Apr. 1745
Hohenfreiburg (Prussians defeat Austrians)....................4 June, "
St. Lazaro (Sardinians defeat French)..........................4 June, 1746
Placentia (Austrians defeat French).............................16 June, "
Raucoux (Saxe defeats allies).....................................11 Oct. "
Laffeldt (Saxe defeats Cumberland)................................2 July, 1747
Exilles (Sardinians defeat French).................................19 July, "
Bergen-op-Zoom (taken)...15 Sept. "

SCOTS' REBELLION.

Preston Pans (rebels defeat Cope)..................................21 Sept. 1745
Clifton Moor (rebels defeated)..18 Dec. "
Falkirk (rebels defeat Hawley)...17 Jan. 1746
Culloden (Cumberland defeats rebels)................................16 Apr. "

INDIA.

Calcutta (taken by Surajah Dowlah)...................................20 June, 1756
Plassey (Clive's victory) ....23 June, 1757
Wandewash (Coote defeats Lally).......................................22 Jan. 1760
Buxar (Munro defeats army of Oude)...................................23 Oct. 1764

SEVEN YEARS' WAR, 1756–63.

Prague (Frederick defeats allies)..6 May, 1757
Kollin (Frederick defeated)..18 June, "
Norkitten (Russians defeated)...13 Aug. "
*Rosbach (Frederick defeats French)....................................5 Nov. "
Breslau (Austrians victors)..22 Nov. "
Lissa (Frederick defeats Austrians).......................................5 Dec. "
Creveldt (Ferdinand defeats French)....................................23 June, 1758
Zorndorff (Frederick defeats Russians).............................25, 26 Aug. 1758
Hochkirchen (Austrians defeat Prussians)...........................14 Oct. "
Bergen (French defeat allies)..13 Apr. 1759
Zullichau (Russians defeat Prussians).................................23 July, "
Minden (Ferdinand defeats French)..1 Aug. "
Cunnersdorf (Russians defeat Prussians)...............................12 Aug. "
Landshut, Silesia (Prussians defeated)..................................23 June, 1760
Warburg (Ferdinand defeats French)......................................31 July, "
Pfaffendorf (Frederick defeats Austrians)...............................15 Aug. "
Kloster Campen (English and Germans with French; indecisive)...15, 16 Oct. "
*Torgau (Frederick defeats Austrians).......................................3 Nov. "
Kirchdenkern (allies defeat French)..15 July, 1761
Schweidnitz (Frederick II. defeats Austrians).............................16 May, 1762
Johannisberg (French defeat Prussians).....................................30 Aug. "
Freiberg (Prussians defeat Austrians)...29 Oct. 1764

RUSSO-TURKISH WAR.

Choczim (Russians defeat Turks)..........30 Apr. and 13 July, 1769
Galatz (Russians defeat Turks).............................Nov. "
Bender (taken by Russians)...................................28 Sept. 1770
Brailow (Russians defeat Turks)............................19 June, 1773
Silistria (taken by Russians) 1774

FRENCH AND ENGLISH COLONIAL WAR IN AMERICA.

Louisburg (taken from the French by the colonists)...17 June, 1745
Pittsburg, Pa. (then a fort, surrendered to the French)..17 Apr. 1754
Great Meadows (Washington defeats French; Jumonville killed), 28 May, "
Fort Necessity (Washington surrenders to the French)..3 July, "
Braddock's Defeat (French and Indians defeat English)..9 July, 1755
Lake George, N. Y. (first engagement; French defeat English), 8 Sept. "
" " " (second engagement; English defeat French), 8 Sept. "
Oswego (English surrender to Montcalm)..............11 Aug. 1756
Kittanning, Pa. (English defeat Indians)...............8 Sept. "
Fort William Henry, N. Y. (English surrender to Montcalm), 6 July, 1757
Fort Ticonderoga (French repulse English) ....6 July, 1758
Louisburg (French surrender to English)...............26 July, "
Fort Frontenac (French surrender to English).........27 Aug. "
" Duquesne " evacuate.........................25 Nov. "
" Niagara " surrender to English.........24 July, 1759
" Ticonderoga " evacuate.........................26 July, "
Montmorenci (Montcalm defeats English)...............31 July, "
Quebec (Wolf defeats Montcalm).............................13 Sept. "

AMERICAN WAR OF INDEPENDENCE, 1775-82.

Lexington (the first conflict of the war)................19 Apr. 177
Concord (British retreat to Boston).................... " "
Ticonderoga (captured by Ethan Allen)..................10 May, "
*Bunker Hill (Americans retire for want of ammunition), 17 June, "
Montreal (taken by Montgomery)...........................13 Nov. "
Quebec (Montgomery killed).................................31 Dec. "
Norfolk, Va. (burned by British)...........................1 Jan. 177
Moore's Creek Bridge (Tories beaten)....................27 Feb. "
Boston (evacuated by British)...............................17 Mch. "
Fort Sullivan, Charleston, S. C. (British repulsed).....28 June, "
Brooklyn, Long Island (Americans beaten)..............27 Aug. "
Harlem Heights (Americans victorious)...................16 Sept. "
White Plains (Americans retreat)..........................28 Oct. "
Fort Washington (captured by the British)...............16 Nov. "
*Trenton (Americans victorious).............................26 Dec. "
Princeton (Americans victorious)............................3 Jan. 177
Hubbardton, Vt. (Americans beaten).........................7 July, "
Oriskany, N. Y. (Americans defeat Tories and Indians)..6 Aug. "
*Bennington, Vt. (Americans victorious)....................16 Aug. "
Brandywine, Pa. (Americans retreat).........................11 Sept. "
First battle of Bemis's Heights (Americans successful)..19 Sept. "
Paoli (massacre of Americans)...............................20 Sept. "
Philadelphia (occupied by British)..........................25 Sept. "
Germantown (Americans retreat)...............................4 Oct. "
Forts Clinton and Montgomery (taken by British).......6 Oct. "
Second battle of Bemis's Heights (Americans victorious)..7 Oct. "
Saratoga (Burgoyne's surrender).............................17 Oct. "
Fort Mercer (British repulsed)................................22 Oct. "
" Mifflin (Americans evacuate; gallant defence)....16 Nov. "
Monmouth (British retire at night)..........................28 June, 177
Schoharie (Indian massacre)....................................2 July, "
Wyoming " " ....3, 4 July, "
Quaker Hill, R. I. (gen. Sullivan repulses attack of gen. Pigot), 29 Aug. "
Savannah (taken by British)....................................29 Dec. "
Kettle Creek, Ga. (Tories defeated)...........................14 Feb. 177
Brier " " (Americans defeated)...........................3 Mch. "
Stono Ferry, S. C. (Americans repulsed).....................20 June, "
Stony Point (Americans victorious; brilliant exploit)..16 July, "
Paulus's Hook (Americans successful) ....19 Aug. "
Bonhomme Richard and Serapis, *n.* (Americans victorious), 23 Sept. "
Savannah (Americans repulsed)...................................9 Oct. "
Charleston (surrender to British).............................12 May, 178
Washaw (massacre of Buford's men)...........................29 May, "
Springfield, N. J. (British repulsed).........................23 June, "
Rocky Mount, S. C. (Americans repulsed).....................30 June, "
Hanging Rock, S. C. (loyalists dispersed)......................7 Aug. "
Sanders's Creek, near Camden, S. C. (Americans defeated), 16 Aug. "
King's Mountain (loyalists defeated)............................7 Oct. "
Fish Dam Ford, Broad river (Americans victorious)....12 Nov. "

.kstocks (Americans victorious) 20 Nov 1780
pens (British defeated) 17 Jan 1781
an's Ford S C (Americans repulsed) 1 Feb 1781
(total defeat of the loyalists) 25 Feb "
ford Court house (Americans retreat) 15 Mch "
kirk's Hill, S C (Americans retire) 25 Apr "
ety six (besieged by Americans) May and June, "
usta " " " " " "
estown Va (Americans retreat) 9 July, "
London (taken by Benedict Arnold) 5 Sept "
Griswold (captured by the British) " "
aw Springs (undecided) 8 Sept "
rktown (Cornwallis surrendered) 19 Oct "
Licks (Indians victorious) 19 Aug 1782
[Other but inferior actions took place, with varying success both parties.]

MISCELLANEOUS

it (Hyder defeats British) 31 Oct 1780
o Novo (Coote defeats Hyder) 1 July, 1781
ney's victory over De Grasse, n. 12 Apr 1782
ee (Coote defeats Hyder) 2 June, "
ck on Gibraltar fails 13 Sept "
more (taken by Tippoo Sahib) 30 Apr 1783
tinesti (Austrians defeat Turks) 22 Sept 1789
ail (taken by storm by Suwarrow) 22 Dec 1790
galore (taken by storm) 21 Mch 1791
eri (Tippoo defeated) 15 May, "
ngapatam (Tippoo defeated) 6 Feb 1792

FRENCH REVOLUTIONARY WARS

vrain (French repulsed) 28 Apr 1792
ny (French defeat Prussians) 20 Sept "
appes (French victorious) 6 Nov "
winden (French beaten by Austrians) 18 Mch 1793
amand (French defeated by English) 8 May, "
nciennes " " " " 23 May, 26 July, "
elles (Lake defeats French) 18 Aug "
kirk (duke of York defeated) 7, 8 Sept "
noy (reduced by Austrians) 11 Sept "
asens (Prussians defeat French) 14 Sept "
tignies (French defeat Coburg) 14, 15, 16 Oct. "
on (retaken by British) 19 Dec "
bray (French defeated) 24 Apr 1794
sville, Landrecy (taken by allies) 30 Apr "
coing (Moreau defeats allies) 18-22 May, "
erres (taken by allies) 22 May, "
e's naval victory 1 June, "
leroi or Fleurus (French defeat allies) 26 June, "
lon (Vendeans defeated) 28 July, "
le Duc (duke of York defeated) 14 Sept "
tel " " " 17 Sept. "
iejowice (Poles defeated) 10 Oct "
eguen (French victorious), 28 Oct , (defeated) 4 May, "
a (Warsaw taken by Suwarrow) 4 Nov "
port's victory off l'Orient, n 22 June, 1795
eron (emigrants defeated) 21 July, "
nheim (taken by Pichegru) 20 Sept "
io (French defeat Austrians) 23, 24 Nov "
tenotte (Bonaparte victorious) 12 Apr 1796
dovi " " 22 Apr "
" " 10 May, "
nkirchen (Austrians defeated) 4 June, "
stadt (Moreau defeats Austrians). 5 July, "
nkirchen (Austrians victors) 16 Sept "
eredo (French defeat Austrians) 4 Sept "
ano " " " 8 Sept. "
rach " " " 2 Oct. "
ato and Castiglione (French defeat Austrians) 3-5 Aug "
sheim (Moreau defeats archduke Charles) 10 Aug "
ola (Bonaparte victorious) 14-17 Nov "
elnuovo (Bonaparte victorious) 21 Nov "
oli " " 14, 15 Jan 1797
e St Vincent, n (Spaniards defeated) 14 Feb "
iamento (Bonaparte defeats Austrians) 16 Mch "
a Cruz, Canary islands, n , Nelson's unsuccessful attack, ses his right arm 25-26 July, "
iperdown, n (Duncan defeats Dutch) 11 Oct "

IRISH REBELLION

ins. May, 1798
ullen (rebels successful) 23 May, "
s (rebels defeated) 24 May, "
a (rebels defeated) 26 May, "
art (rebels successful) 27 May, "
ey or New Ross (rebels defeated) 4 June, "
rim (rebels defeated) 7 June, "
low (rebels beaten) 10 June, "
ynahinch (Nugent defeats rebels) 13 June, "
egar Hill (Lake defeats rebels) 21 June, "
lebar (French auxiliaries defeated) 27 Aug "
inamuck (French and rebels defeated) 8 Sept. "

NAPOLEONIC WARS.

amids (Bonaparte defeats Mamelukes) 13, 21 July, 1798
e, n (Nelson defeats French fleet) 1 Aug. "
Arisch (French defeat Turks) 18 Feb. 1799
a (stormed by Bonaparte) 7-10 Mch. "
kach (Austrians defeat French) 25 Mch "
ona " " " 28-30 Mch. "
gnano (Kray defeats French) 5 Apr "
unt Thabor (Bonaparte defeats Turks) 16 Apr "
Cassano (Suwarrow defeats Moreau) 27 Apr 1799
Adda (Suwarrow defeats French) " "
Seringapatam (Tippoo killed) 4 May, "
Acre (relieved by sir Sydney Smith) 20 May, "
Zurich (French defeated) 5 June, "
Trebia (Suwarrow defeats French) 17-19 June, "
Alessandria (taken from French) 21 July "
Aboukir (Turks defeated by Bonaparte) 25 July, "
Novi (Suwarrow defeats French) 15 Aug "
Zuyper Sluys (French defeated) 9 Sept "
Bergen and Alkmaer (allies defeated) 19 Sept 26 Oct "
Zurich (Massena defeats Russians) 25 Sept "
Heliopolis (Kleber defeats Turks) 20 Mch 1800
Engen (Moreau defeats Austrians) 3 May, "
Moeskirch " " 5 May, "
Biberach " " " 9 May, "
Montebello (Austrians defeated) 9 June, "
*Marengo (Bonaparte defeats Austrians) 14 June, "
Hochstadt (Moreau defeats Austrians) 19 June, "
Hohenlinden " " " 3 Dec "
Mincio (French defeat Austrians) 25-27 Dec. "
Aboukir (French defeated) 8 Mch 1801
Alexandria (Abercrombie's victory) 21 Mch "
Copenhagen (bombarded by Nelson) 2 Apr "
Ahmednuggur (Wellesley [Wellington] victorious) 12 Aug 1803
Assaye (Wellesley's [Wellington] first great victory) 23 Sept "
Argaum (Wellesley [Wellington] victor) 29 Nov "
Furruckabad (Lake defeats Holkar) 17 Nov 1804
Bhurtpore (taken by Lake) 2 Apr 1805
Elchingen (Ney defeats Austrians) 14 Oct "
Ulm surrenders (Ney defeats Austrians) 17-20 Oct. "
*Trafalgar, n (Nelson destroys French fleet, killed) 21 Oct "
*Austerlitz (Napoleon defeats Austrians and Russians) 2 Dec "
Buenos Ayres (taken by Popham) 27 June, 1806
Maida (Stuart defeats French) 4 July, "
Saalfeld (French defeat Prussians) 10 Oct "
Auerstadt " " " 14 Oct "
Jena " " " " "
Halle stormed by French 17 Oct. "
Pultusk (French and allies, indecisive) 26 Dec "
Mohrungen (French defeat Russians and Prussians) 25 Jan 1807
Montevideo (taken) 3 Feb "
Eylau (indecisive) 7, 8 Feb "
Ostrolenka (French defeat Prussians) 16 Feb "
Friedland (French defeat Russians) 14 June, "
Buenos Ayres (Whitelock defeated) 5 July, "
Copenhagen (bombarded by Cathcart) 2-5 Sept. "
Medina de Rio Seco (French defeat Spaniards) 15 July, 1808
Baylen (Spaniards defeat French) 20 July, "
Vimiera (Wellesley [Wellington] defeats Junot) 21 Aug "
Tudela or Ebro (French defeat Spaniards) 23 Nov "
Corunna (Moore defeats French) 16 Jan 1809
Abenberg (Austrians defeated) 20 Apr "
Landshut " " 21 Apr "
Eckmühl (Davoust defeats Austrians) 22 Apr "
Ebersberg (French defeat Austrians) 4 May, "
Oporto (taken) 29 Mch , 12 May, "
Aspern (Napoleon defeated) 21, 22 May, "
Essling " " " "
*Wagram (Austrians defeated) 5, 6 July, "
Talavera (Wellesley [Wellington] defeats Victor) 27, 28 July "
Silistria (Turks defeat Russians) 26 Sept. "
Ocana (Mortier defeats Spaniards) 19 Nov "
Busaco (Wellington repulses Massena) 27 Sept 1810
Barrosa (Graham defeats Victor) 5 Mch 1811
Badajoz (taken by the French) 11 Mch "
Fuentes de Onoro (Wellington defeats Massena) 3, 5 May, "
Albuera (Beresford defeats Soult) 16 May, "
Ximena (Spaniards defeat French) 10 Sept. "
Merida (Hill defeats French) 28 Oct. "
Albufera (Suchet defeats Spaniards) 4 Jan 1812
Ciudad Rodrigo (stormed by English) 19 Jan "
Badajoz (taken by Wellington) 6 Apr "
Llerena (Cotton defeats Soult) 11 Apr "
Salamanca (Wellington defeats Marmont) 21 July, "
Mohilow (French defeat Russians) 23 July, "
Polotzk (French and Russians) 30, 31 July, "
Krasnoi, Smolensko (French defeat Russians) 15, 19 Aug "
Moskwa (French defeat Russians) 7 Sept. "
*Borodino " " " " "
Moscow (burned by Russians) 16 Sept "
Polotzk (retaken by Russians) 19, 20 Oct. "
Malo Jaroslawatz (French victors) 24 Oct "
Witepsk (French defeated) 14 Nov "
Krasnoi " " 16-18 Nov "
Beresina " " 25-29 Nov "
Kalitsch (Saxons defeated) 13 Feb 1813
Möckern (Eugène defeats Russians) 5 Apr "
Castalla (J Murray defeats Suchet) 13 Apr "
Lutzen (Napoleon checks allies) 2 May, "
Bautzen (Napoleon and allies, indecisive) 20 May, "
Wurschen " " " 21, 22 May, "
Hochkirchen (French defeat Austrians and Russians) 22 May, "
Vittoria (Wellington defeats king Joseph) 21 June, "
Pyrenees (Wellington defeats Soult) 28 July, 2 Aug "
Katzbach (Blücher defeats Ney) 26 Aug "
Dresden (Napoleon checks allies) 26, 27 Aug "
St Sebastian (stormed by Graham). 31 Aug "
Dennewitz (Ney defeated) 6 Sept. "
Möckern (French defeated) 16 Oct "
*Leipsic (Napoleon defeated) 16-18 Oct "

Hanau (Napoleon defeats Bavarians)....30 Oct. 1813
St. Jean-de-Luz (Wellington defeats Soult)....10 Nov. "
Passage of the Nive, 9 Dec.; several engagements between the allies and French....10 to 13 Dec. "
St. Dizier, France (French victors)....26 Jan. 1814
Brienne (allies defeated)....29 Jan. "
La Rothière (Napoleon defeats allies)....1 Feb. "
Bar-sur-Aube (allies victors)....7 Feb. "
Mincio (prince Eugène defeats Austrians)....8 Feb. "
Champ Aubert (French defeat allies)....10–12 Feb. "
Montmirail " " " ....11 Feb. "
Vauchamp " " " ....14 Feb. "
Fontainebleau " " " ....17 Feb. "
Montereau " " " ....18 Feb. "
Orthez (Wellington defeats Soult)....27 Feb. "
Craonne (French victors)....7 Mch. "
Bergen-op-Zoom (Graham defeated)....8 Mch. "
Laon (French defeated)....9–10 Mch. "
Rheims (Napoleon defeats St. Priest)....13 Mch. "
Tarbes (Wellington defeats Soult)....20 Mch. "
Fère Champenoise (French defeated)....25 Mch. "
St. Dizier (French victors)....28 Mch. "
Paris, Montmartre, Romainville (French victors)....30 Mch. "
Battle of the Barriers, 30 Mch. (Marmont evacuates Paris, and the allies enter it)....31 Mch. "
Toulouse (Wellington defeats Soult)....10 Apr. "
Tolentino (Murat defeated)....3 May, 1815
Ligny (Blücher repulsed)....16 June, "
Quatre Bras (Ney repulsed).... " "
*Waterloo (Napoleon finally beaten)....18 June, "

WAR OF 1812 BETWEEN THE UNITED STATES AND GREAT BRITAIN.

War declared....19 June, 1812
Fort Mackinac (captured by the British)....17 July, "
Brownstown (Americans retreat)....5 Aug. "
Maguaga (British retreat)....9 Aug. "
Essex and Alert, *n.* (U. S. Essex captures Alert)....13 Aug. "
Chicago (Indian massacre)....15 Aug. "
Detroit (surrendered)....16 Aug. "
Constitution and Guerrière, *n.* (Guerrière destroyed)....19 Aug. "
Fort Harrison (defence of by capt. Zachary Taylor)..4, 5 Sept. "
Fort Madison (defence of)....5, 6, 7, and 8 Sept. "
Davis's Creek....11 Sept. "
Queenstown Heights (Americans finally defeated)....13 Oct. "
Pimartain's Town....18 Oct. "
Wasp captures Frolic, *n.*.... " "
St. Regis (captured by Americans)....22 Oct. "
United States captures Macedonian, *n.*....25 Oct. "
Fort Niagara (bombarded by British)....21 Nov. "
Ponce Passu....21, 22 Nov. "
Black Rock....29 Nov. "
Constitution captures Java, *n.*....29 Dec. "
Frenchtown (taken by Americans)....18 Jan. 1813
River Raisin (Americans defeated)....22 Jan. "
Elizabethtown (Americans capture)....7 Feb. "
Ogdensburg (British capture)....22 Feb. "
Hornet captures Peacock, *n.*....24 Feb. "
York, Toronto (captured; death of gen. Pike)....27 Apr. "
Fort Meigs (besieged by British and Indians)....May, "
Fort George (captured by Americans)....27 May, "
Sackett's Harbor (Americans repulse attack)....29 May, "
Chesapeake surrenders to Shannon, *n.*....1 June, "
Stony Creek, Burlington Heights (gen. Winder captured), 6 June, "
Hampton (defence of)....13 June, "
Craney Island (British repulsed)....22 June, "
Beaver Dams (Americans surrender)....24 June, "
Fort George (skirmish near)....8 July, "
Black Rock (defence of)....11 July, "
Fort George (defence of outworks)....17 July, "
Fort Stephenson (col. Croghan's gallant defence of)....2 Aug. "
Stonington (bombarded; British repulsed)....9, 10, 11 Aug. "
Fort George (defence of outworks)....24 Aug. "
Enterprise captures Boxer, *n.* (both commanders killed), 4 Sept. "
Battle of lake Erie, *n.* (Perry captures British fleet)..10 Sept. "
Chatham (skirmish)....4 Oct. "
Thames (Harrison defeats Proctor; Tecumseh killed)....5 Oct. "
Fort George (skirmishes near)....6 Oct. "
French Creek (British repulsed)....1, 2 Nov. "
Chrysler's Field (Americans and British both retire)...11 Nov. "
Newark burned by Americans....10 Dec. "
Fort Niagara (surrendered to British)....19 Dec. "
Black Rock (Americans retreat from)....30 Dec. "
Buffalo burned.... " "
Camp Defiance (Indian attack on repulsed)....27 Jan. 1814
Essex, *n.* (surrenders to the Phœbe and Cherub)....28 Mch. "
La Colle Mills (Americans repulsed)....30 Mch. "
Fort Oswego (British capture)....4, 5 May, "
Sandy Creek (British surrender)....30 May, "
Fort Erie (Americans capture)....3 July, "
Chippewa (Americans victorious)....5 July, "
Niagara Falls (Lundy's Lane; indecisive)....25 July, "
Black Rock (British repulsed)....3 Aug. "
Fort Mackinac (Americans repulsed)....4 Aug. "
Fort Erie (bombarded by British)....13–15 Aug. "
Fort Erie (Americans repulse assault)....15 Aug. "
Bladensburg (Americans defeated)....24 Aug. "
Washington (Capitol burned by British).... " "
Moor's Fields, Md. (British repulsed; sir Peter Parker killed), 30 Aug. "
Plattsburg and Lake Champlain (British defeated)....11 Sept. "
North Point, Baltimore (Americans retire)....12 Sept. 1814
Fort McHenry (defence of; British retire)....13 Sept. "
Fort Bowyer (British repulsed)....15 Sept. "
Fort Erie (successful sortie by Americans)....17 Sept. "
Lyon's Creek (skirmish at)....19 Oct. "
Pensacola (Jackson seizes it from the Spaniards)....7 Nov. "
Villeré's Plantation, New Orleans (Jackson stops the approach of the British)....23 Dec. "
Chalmette's Plantation, New Orleans (British repulsed), 28 Dec. "
Rodriguez's Canal, New Orleans (British artillery beaten), 1 Jan. 1815
*New Orleans (British defeated)....8 Jan. "
Fort St. Philip (successful defence of)....9–18 Jan. "
Point Petre, Ga. (surrenders to British)....13 Jan. "
Constitution captures Cyane and Levant, *n.*....20 Feb. "

[For fuller account see separate articles and naval battles.]

THE CREEK INDIAN WAR.

Burnt Corn Creek, Ala. (whites defeated)....27 July, 1813
Fort Mimms (captured by Indians; massacre)....30 Aug. "
Tallasahatchie (Indians defeated by gen. Coffee)....3 Nov. "
Talladega " " " gen. Jackson)....9 Nov. "
Hillabee Town (massacre of Indians by gen. White)....18 Nov. "
Auttose Towns (Indians defeated by gen. Floyd)....29 Nov. "
Econochaco, or "Holy Ground" (Indians defeated by gen. Claiborne)....23 Dec. "
Emucfau (Jackson repulses Indians)....22 Jan. 1814
Enotochopco Creek (Jackson again repulses Indians)..24 Jan. "
Calebee Creek (Indian attack repulsed by gen. Floyd)..27 Jan. "
Horse-shoe Bend (Jackson signally defeats the Indians), 27 Mch. "

BLACK HAWK WAR—MISSISSIPPI WAR.

Stillman's Volunteers (defeat, Rock river)....14 May, 1832
Pickatolica River....15 June, "
Kellogg's Grove (2 skirmishes)....16 June, "
Galena....18 June, "
Kellogg's Grove....24 June, "
Blue Mounds....21 July, "
Warrior, steamer (attack on)....1 Aug. "
Bad Axe (Indians defeated)....2 Aug. "
BLACK HAWK WAR.

SEMINOLE WAR.

Fort King (massacre of gen. Thompson and others)....28 Dec. 1835
Wahoo Swamp (near, massacre of maj. Dade and 100 men), 28 Dec. "
Withlacoochee Ford (U. S. troops with Osceola and Alligator), 31 Dec. "
Dunlawton (maj. Putnam, with Indians under king Philip), 18 Jan. 1836
Withlacoochee Ford (gen. Gaines, 4 skirmishes), 27–29 Feb., 5 Mch. "
Oloklikaha....31 Mch. "
Cooper's Post (defence of by maj. Cooper)....Apr. "
Thlonotosassa....27 Apr. "
Micanopy....9 June, "
Welika Pond....9 July, "
Ridgeley's Mill....27 July, "
Fort Drane....21 Aug. "
San Velasco Hammock....18 Sept. "
Wahoo Swamp....17, 18, 21 Nov. "
Hatcheeluskie....27 Jan. 1837
Camp Monroe (Indian attack repulsed)....8 Feb. "
Fort Mellon " " " ....9 Feb. "
Mosquito Inlet (2 camps of Indians captured)....10 Sept. "
Osceola (seized by order of gen. Jesup)....21 Oct. "
Okechobee Lake (Indians routed by col. Taylor)....25 Dec. "
Waccassassa River....26 Dec. "
Jupiter Creek....15 Jan. 1838
Jupiter Inlet (gen. Jesup wounded)....24 Jan. "
Newmansville....7 June, "
Carloosahatchee (col. Harney wounded)....23 July, 1839
Fort King....28 Apr. 1840
Levi's Prairie....19 May, "
Wacahoota....6 Sept. "
Everglades (expedition into; col. Harney com'd'g)...8–24 Dec. "
Micanopy (lieut. Sherwood killed)....28 Dec. "
Fort Brooke (Indians driven off)....2 Mch. 1841
Hawe Creek....25 Jan. 1842
Pilaklikaha (total defeat of Indians)....19 Apr. "

MEXICAN WAR.

Fort Brown (attack on, relieved by gen. Taylor)....3–5 May, 1846
Palo Alto (gen. Taylor defeats Mexicans)....8 May, "
Resaca de la Palma (gen. Taylor defeats Mexicans)....9 May, "
Monterey (surrenders to gen. Taylor)....21–24 Sept. "
Brazito (col. Doniphan defeats Mexicans)....25 Dec. "
San Gabriel, Cal. (Mexicans defeated)....8, 9 Jan. 1847
Encarnacion (gen. Miñon captures 70 U. S. cavalry)....22 Jan. "
Cañada (col. Price defeats Mexicans)....24 Jan. "
Buena Vista (gen. Taylor defeats Mexicans)....23 Feb. "
Pass of Sacramento (col. Doniphan defeats Mexicans)...28 Feb. "
Vera Cruz (surrendered to the Americans)....29 Mch. "
Alvarado....2 Apr. "
Cerro Gordo (gen. Scott defeats Santa Anna)....18 Apr. "
Tuspan.... " "
Contreras (Scott defeats Mexicans)....20 Aug. "
Cherubusco " " " .... " "
El Molino del Rey (Mexicans defeated)....8 Sept. "
Chapultepec " " ....12–14 Sept. "
City of Mexico (surrenders to gen. Scott)....14 Sept. "
Puebla (col. Childs successfully resists gen. Rea), 18 Sept.–12 Oct. "

Huamantla (gen Lane defeats Santa Anna)	9 Oct	1847
Atlixco (gen Lane defeats gen Rea)	18 Oct	"

MISCELLANEOUS.

Algiers (bombarded by Exmouth)	27 Aug	1816
Chacabuco (Chilians defeat Spaniards)	12 Feb	"
Kirkee (Hastings defeats Pindarrees)	5 Nov	1817
Mehadpore (Hislop defeats Holkar)	21 Dec	"
Valtezza (Turks defeated)	27 May,	1821
Dragaschan (Ipsilanti defeated)	19 June,	"
Tripolitza (stormed by Greeks)	5 Oct	"
Thermopylæ (Greeks defeat Turks)	13 July,	1822
Corinth (taken)	16 Sept	"
Accra (Ashantees defeat sir C Macarthy)	21 Jan	1824
Ayacucho (Peruvians defeat Spaniards)	9 Dec	"
Bhurtpore (taken by Combermere)	18 Jan	1826
Accra (Ashantees defeated)	7 Aug	"
Athens (taken)	17 May,	1827
Navarino (allies destroy Turkish fleet)	20 Oct	"
Brailow (Russians and Turks)	18 June,	1828
Akhalzikh " "	24 Aug	"
Varna (surrenders to Russians)	11 Oct	"
Silistria " " "	30 June,	1829
Kaunly (Russians defeat Turks)	1 July,	"
Balkan (passed by Russians)	26 July,	"
Adrianople (Russians enter)	20 Aug	"
Algiers (captured by French)	5 July,	1830
Paris (days of July)	27-29 July,	"
Grochow (Poles defeat Russians)	19, 20 Feb	1831
Praga " " "	25 Feb	"
Wawz (Skrzynecki defeats Russians)	31 Mch	"
Seidlice (Poles defeat Russians)	10 Apr	"
Ostrolenka " " "	26 May,	"
Wilna (Poles and Russians)	18 June,	"
Warsaw (taken by Russians)	7 Sept	"
Homs (Egyptians defeat Turks)	8 July,	1832
Beylan (Ibrahim defeats Turks)	29 July,	"
Konieh (Egyptians defeat Turks)	21 Dec	"
Antwerp (citadel taken by allies)	23 Dec	"
Hernani (Carlists defeated)	5 May,	1836
St Sebastian " "	1 Oct	"
Bilbao (siege raised, British legion)	24 Dec.	"
Hernani (Carlists repulsed)	16 Mch	1837
Irun (British legion defeats Carlists)	17 May,	"
Valentia (Carlists attacked)	15 July,	"
Herrera (don Carlos defeats Buerens)	24 Aug	"
Constantina, Algiers (taken by French)	13 Oct	"
St Eustache (Canadian rebels defeated)	14 Dec	"
Peñacerrada (Carlists defeated)	22 June,	1838
Prescott (Canadian rebels defeated)	17 Nov	"
Aden (taken)	19 Jan	1839
Ghiznee (taken by Keane)	23 July,	"
Sidon (taken by Napier)	27 Sept.	1840
Beyrout (allies defeat Egyptians)	10 Oct	"
Afghan war INDIA		
Acre (stormed by allies)	3 Nov	"
Kotriah, Scinde (English victors)	1 Dec.	"
Chuen pe (English victors)	7 Jan	1841
Canton (English take Bogue forts)	26 Feb	"
Amoy (taken)	27 Aug	"
Chin hae, etc (taken)	10, 13 Oct	"
Candahar (Afghans defeated)	10 Mch	1842
Ningpo (Chinese defeated)	"	"
Jellalabad (Khyber pass forced)	5, 6 Apr	"
Chin keang (taken)	21 July,	"
Ghiznee (Afghans defeated by Nott)	6 Sept.	"
Meeanee (Napier defeats Ameers)	17 Feb	1843
Maharajpoor (Gough defeats Mahrattas)	29 Dec	"
Isly (French defeat Abd el Kader)	14 Aug	1844
Moodkee (Hardinge defeats Sikhs)	18 Dec.	1845
Ferozeshah " " "	21, 22 Dec.	"
Aliwal (Smith defeats Sikhs)	28 Jan	1846
Sobraon (Gough defeats Sikhs)	10 Feb.	"
St. Ubes (Portugal).	9 May,	"
Flensborg (Danes defeat rebels)	9 Apr	1848
Dannewerke (Prussians defeat Danes)	23 Apr	"
Curtatone (Austrians defeat Italians).	29 May,	"
Custozza " " "	23 July,	"
Velencze (Croats and Hungarians)	29 Sept	"
Mooltan (Sikhs repulsed)	7 Nov	"
Chilianwallah (Gough defeats Sikhs).	13 Jan	1849
Goojerat " " "	21 Feb	"
Gran (Hungarians victors)	27 Feb	"
Novara (Radetzky defeats Sardinians)	23 Mch	"
Velletri (Roman republicans defeat Neapolitans)	19 May,	"
Pered (Russians defeat Hungarians)	21 June,	"
Acs (Hungarians repulsed)	2 and 10 July,	"
Waitzen (taken by Russians)	17 July,	"
Schässberg (Russians defeat Bem)	31 July,	"
Temeswar (Haynau defeats Hungarians)	10 Aug	"
Idstedt (Danes defeat Holsteiners)	25 July,	1850
Nankin (taken by imperialists)	19 July,	1853

RUSSO-TURKISH WAR.

Oltenitza (Turks repulse Russians)	4 Nov	1853
Sinope, n. (Turkish fleet destroyed)	30 Nov	"
Citate (Turks defeat Russians)	6 Jan	1854
Silistria " " "	13-15 June,	"
Giurgevo " " "	7 July,	"
Bayazid (Russians defeat Turks)	29, 30 July,	"
Kuruk Derek " " "	5 Aug.	"
Alma (English and French defeat Russians)	20 Sept.	"
Balaklava (English and French defeat Russians)	25 Oct	1854
Inkermann (English and French defeat Russians)	5 Nov	"
Eupatoria (Turks defeat Russians)	17 Feb	1855
Malakhoff Tower (allies and Russians, indecisive night combats	22-24 May,	"
Capture of the Mamelon etc	7 June,	"
Unsuccessful attempt on Malakhoff tower and Redan (allies and Russians)	18 June	"
Tchernaya or bridge of Traktir (allies defeat Russians)	16 Aug	"
Malakhoff taken by the French	8 Sept	"
Ingour (Turks defeat Russians)	6 Nov	"
Bridau (French defeat Russians)	8 Dec.	"

PERSIAN WAR

Bushire (English defeat Persians)	10 Dec	1856
Kooshab " "	8 Feb	1857
Mohammerah (English defeat Persians)	26 Mch	"

INDIAN MUTINY (INDIA)

Conflicts before Delhi	30, 31 May, 8 June 4, 9, 18, 24 July,	1857
Victories of gen Havelock near Futtehpore, 11 July, Cawnpore, etc	12 July-16 Aug	"
Pandoo Nuddee (victory of Neill)	15 Aug	"
Nujuffghur (death of Nicholson, victor)	25 Aug	"
Assault and capture of Delhi	14-20 Sept	"
Victories of col Greathed	27 Sept, 10 Oct	"
Conflicts before Lucknow	25, 26 Sept, 18, 25 Nov	"
Cawnpore (victory of Campbell)	6 Dec	"
Futtehghur " "	2 Jan	1858
Calpi (victory of Inglis)	4 Feb	"
Alumbagh (victories of Outram)	12 Jan and 21 Feb,	"
Conflicts at Lucknow (taken)	11-19 Mch	"
Jhansi (Rose victorious)	4 Apr	"
Kooneh " "	11 May,	"
Gwalior " "	17 June,	"
Bughur (Mitchell defeats Tantia Topee)	15 Sept	"
Dhoodea Khera (Clyde defeats Beni Madho)	24 Nov	"
Gen Horsford defeats the begum of Oude and Nana Sahib,	10 Feb	1859

ITALIAN WAR (ITALY)

Austrians cross the Ticino	27 Apr	1859
French troops enter Piedmont	May,	"
Montebello (allies victorious)	20 May,	"
Palestro " "	30, 31 May,	"
*Magenta " "	4 June,	"
Malegnano " "	8 June,	"
*Solferino " "	21 June,	"

[Armistice agreed to, 6 July, 1859.]

Taku, at the mouth of the Peiho or Tien tsin ho (English attack on the Chinese forts defeated)	25 June,	1859
Taku forts taken (CHINA)	21 Aug	1860
Chang kia wan, 18 Sept, and Pa li chiau (Chinese defeated),	21 Sept.	"

Castillejo (Spaniards defeat Moors)	1 Jan	1860
Tetuan " " "	4 Feb	"
Guad el Ras " " "	23 Mch	"

Calatafimi (Garibaldi defeats Neapolitans)	15 May,	1860
Melazzo " " "	20, 21 July,	"
Castel Fidardo (Sardinians defeat papal troops)	18 Sept	"
Volturno (Garibaldi defeats Neapolitans)	1 Oct	"
Isernia (Sardinians defeat Neapolitans)	17 Oct.	"
Garigliano (Sardinians defeat Neapolitans)	3 Nov	"
Sardinians defeat Neapolitan reactionists	22 Jan	1861
Gaeta taken by the Sardinians	13 Feb.	"

Insurrection in New Zealand, English repulsed, 14, 28 Mch, 27 June, 10, 19 Sept, 9, 12 Oct.		1860
Mahoetia (Maoris defeated)	6 Nov	"

AMERICAN CIVIL WAR

Fort Sumter, S C (fired upon by confederates)	12 Apr	1861
Surrendered (by maj Robert Anderson)	13 Apr	"
Big Bethel, Va (federals repulsed)	10 June,	"
Booneville, Mo (confederates defeated)	17 June,	"
Carthage, Mo (federals finally retire)	6 July,	"
Rich Mountain, W Va. (gen Rosecrans defeats confederates),	11 July,	"
*Bull Run, Va (confederates defeat federals)	21 July,	"
Wilson's Creek, Mo (federals retire, gen Lyon killed),	10 Aug	"
Hatteras expedition (capture of forts Hatteras and Clark, N C),	26-30 Aug	"
Carnifex Ferry, Va (confederates retreat)	10 Sept	"
Lexington, Mo (taken by confederates)	20 Sept.	"
Santa Rosa Island	9 Oct	"
Ball's Bluff, Va. (federals defeated)	21 Oct.	"
Port Royal expedition (capture of Hilton Head, S C),	29 Oct.-7 Nov	"
Belmont, Mo (confederates reinforced, federals retire),	7 Nov	"
Middle Creek, Ky (Garfield defeats Humphrey Marshall),	10 Jan	1862
Mill Spring, Ky (gen Thomas defeats confederates)	19 Jan	"
Fort Henry, Tenn (captured by com Foote)	6 Feb	"
Roanoke Island, N C (captured by gen Burnside)	7, 8 Feb	"
Fort Donelson, Tenn (surrendered to gen Grant)	16 Feb.	"
Pea Ridge, Ark (gen Curtis defeats Van Dorn)	7, 8 Mch.	"
Hampton Roads, Va (Monitor and Merrimac, Merrimac retires)	9 Mch.	"

Newberne, N C (captured by Burnside) 14 Mch 1862
Kernstown or Winchester Va (gen Shields defeats "Stonewall" Jackson) 23 Mch "
Pittsburg Landing or Shiloh, Tenn (federals defeat confederates) 6, 7 Apr "
Island No 10 (surrenders to Pope) 7 Apr "
New Orleans (com Farragut passes forts St Philip and Jackson) 24 Apr "
New Orleans (occupied by federals) 25 Apr "
Yorktown, Va. (evacuated by confederates) 4 May, "
Williamsburg Va (confederates retire) 5 May, "
Norfolk Va (occupied by federals) 10 May, "
Merrimac (destroyed by confederates) 11 May, "
Winchester Va. (Stonewall Jackson defeats Banks) 25 May, "
Hanover Court house, Va (gen Fitz John Porter defeats confederates) 27 May, "
Corinth Tenn (confederates evacuate) 30 May, "
Seven Pines and Fair Oaks, Va (confederate attack repulsed), 31 May, 1 June, "
Memphis, Tenn (surrendered to federals) 6 June, "
Cross Keys, Va (Stonewall Jackson defeats Fremont) 8 June, "
Port Republic, Va " " " Shields) 9 June, "
Mechanicsville, 26 June, Gaines s Mill 27 June, Savage s Station, 29 June, Glendale 30 June, Frazier's Farm or White Oak Swamp, 30 June, Malvern Hill, 1 July (seven days' battles, federals change base) 26 June-1 July, "
Baton Rouge La (confederates repulsed by gen Williams), 5 Aug "
Cedar Mountain, Va (Banks opposes Stonewall Jackson, who retires) 9 Aug "
Bristow Station, Va (Hooker defeats Ewell) 27 Aug "
Groveton, Va. (unfavorable to federals) 29 Aug "
Manassas or second Bull Run, Va (federals defeated) 30 Aug "
Chantilly, Va (confederate attack repulsed, federal gens Kearny and Stevens killed) 1 Sept. "
South Mountain, Md (Crampton and Turner's Gap, confederates retire) 14 Sept. "
Harper's Ferry, Va (surrenders to Stonewall Jackson, 10,000 federal prisoners) 15 Sept. "
Antietam Md (confederates retreat) 16, 17 Sept. "
Munfordville Ky (surrenders to confederates) 17 Sept. "
Iuka, Miss. (Rosecrans defeats Price) 19 Sept "
Corinth, Miss. (Rosecrans defeats Van Dorn and Price), 3-5 Oct. "
Perryville, Ky (confederates retire) 8 Oct "
Prairie Grove, Ark (gens Blunt and Herron defeat confederate Hindman) 7 Dec. "
Fredericksburg Va. (Lee defeats Burnside) 13 Dec "
Holly Springs, Miss (captured and immense stores destroyed by Van Dorn) 20 Dec. "
Chickasaw Bayou, Miss (Sherman fails to take Vicksburg), 27-29 Dec. "
Stone River (Rosecrans defeats Bragg) 31 Dec 1862-2 Jan 1863
Arkansas Post, Ark. (captured by McClernand) 11 Jan "
Grierson's raid (from Lagrange, Tenn, to Baton Rouge, La), 17 Apr-2 May, "
Streight's raid through northern Alabama (Streight with his command captured) 7 Apr-3 May, "
Port Gibson, Miss (confederates defeated by Grant) 1 2 May, "
Chancellorsville, Va (Lee defeats Hooker, Stonewall Jackson mortally wounded) 1-4 May, "
Raymond, Miss (McPherson and Logan defeat confederates), 12 May, "
Jackson, Miss. (McPherson drives the confederates from Jackson) 14 May, "
Champion Hill Miss (confederates defeated) 16 May, "
Big Black, Miss. " " 17 May, "
Vicksburg, Miss (invested) 19 May, "
Port Hudson, La. (Banks assaults, repulsed) 27 May, "
Milliken s Bend, La (confederates repulsed) 7 June, "
Winchester, Va. (Milroy driven out) 15 June, "
Gettysburg Pa (Meade defeats Lee) 1-3 July, "
Vicksburg, Miss. (surrenders to Grant) 4 July, "
Helena, Ark (confederate assault repulsed) " "
Port Hudson, La (surrendered to Banks) 9 July, "
Fort Wagner, S C (confederates repulse assault) . 10, 18 July, "
Morgan s raid—Ky, Ind, and Ohio (Morgan captured), 24 June-26 July, "
Chickamauga Ga. (Bragg defeats Rosecrans) 19, 20 Sept. "
Wauhatchie Tenn (Hooker repels attack) 29 Oct. "
Campbell Station, Tenn. (Burnside retires before Longstreet), 16 Nov "
Lookout Mountain, Tenn. (Hooker victorious) 24 Nov "
Missionary Ridge, Tenn (Bragg defeated) 25 Nov "
Knoxville Tenn (Longstreet's attack repulsed) 29 Nov "
Olustee, Fla (gen Seymour defeated by confederates) 20 Feb 1864
Sabine Cross Roads, La (confederates defeat Banks) 8 Apr "
Pleasant Hill, La (Banks repels attack) 9 Apr "
Fort Pillow, Tenn (capture and massacre of colored troops), 12 Apr "
Wilderness, Va (Grant attacks Lee, indecisive) 5 6 May, "
Spottsylvania Court house, Va (Grant attacks Lee, indecisive), 7-12 May, "
Petersburg, Va. (Butler's attack fails) 10 May, "
Resaca, Ga. (confederates retreat) 15 May, "
Pumpkin vine Creek, Ga. (Hooker attacks) 25 May, "
Cold Harbor, Va (gen Grant's attack repulsed) 1-3 June, "
Petersburg, Va (W F Smith s attack on, repulsed), 16-18 June, "
Kearsarge sinks the confederate Alabama off Cherbourg, France . ... 19 June, "
Weldon Railroad Va. (federals repulsed) 21-24 June, "
Kenesaw, Ga. (gen Sherman's attack repulsed) 27 June, "
Monocacy, Md (gen Lew Wallace defeated) 9 July, "
Peach tree Creek, Ga (confederate attack repulsed) 20 July, 1864
Atlanta, Ga " " " (McPherson killed) 22 July, "
Ezra's Church, Ga. " " 28 July, "
Petersburg, Va. (mine explosion, failure) 30 July, "
Jonesborough, Ga (confederates defeated) 31 Aug, 1 Sept "
Atlanta, Ga (occupied by Sherman) 2 Sept "
Winchester Va (Sheridan defeats Early) 19 Sept "
Fisher's Hill, Va " " 22 Sept. "
Allatoona, Ga. (gen Corse repels attack) 6 Oct "
Cedar Creek, Va. (gen Sheridan routs Early) 19 Oct. "
Hatcher's Run, Va (Hancock retires) 27 Oct "
*Franklin, Tenn (Hood attacks Schofield, repulsed) 30 Nov "
Fort McAllister, Ga. (gen Hazen captures) 14 Dec "
Nashville, Tenn (gen Thomas defeats Hood) 15, 16 Dec "
Fort Fisher N C (captured by gen Terry) 15 Jan 1865
Hatcher s Run, Va (federals successful) 5 Feb "
Averasboro, N C (confederates retreat) 15 Mch "
Bentonville, " " " 18 Mch "
Five Forks, Va. (Sheridan beats confederates) 31 Mch, 1 Apr "
Sailors' Creek, Va. (gen Ewell surrenders) 7 Apr "
Appomattox, Va (gen Lee surrenders to Grant) 9 Apr "
Mobile, Ala (taken by federals) 12 Apr "
Gen Joseph E Johnston surrenders to gen Sherman, 26 Apr "
Jefferson Davis is captured near Irwinsville Ga 11 May, "

[For details of the important battles, see separate articles, also ATLANTA CAMPAIGN, BULL RUN CAMPAIGN, CHATTANOOGA CAMPAIGN, GRANT S VIRGINIA CAMPAIGN, MARYLAND CAMPAIGN PENINSULAR CAMPAIGN, POPE'S VIRGINIA CAMPAIGN, RED RIVER CAMPAIGN, SHERMAN'S GREAT MARCH, and VICKSBURG CAMPAIGN]

DANISH WAR

Oeversee (Danes and allies) 6 Feb 1864
Duppel (taken by the Prussians) 18 Apr "
Alsen " " " 29 June, "
Rendsburg " " " 21 July, "

SOUTH AMERICAN WAR (BRAZIL.)

Santayuna (allies defeat Paraguayans, Uruguayana taken), 18 Sept 1865
Paso de la Patria (indecisive) 25 Feb, 1866
Parana (allies victors) 16 Apr "
Estero Velhaco (allies victors) 2 May, "
Tuyuty (allies defeated) 16, 18 July, "
Curupaiti " " 17, 19, 22 Sept "
Tuyuty (allies victors) 30 Oct "
Corumba (taken by Brazilians) 13 June, 1867

SEVEN WEEKS' WAR (*Austria and Prussia*)

Custozza (Austrians defeat Italians) 24 June, 1866
Lissa, " " " " 20 July, "

[*Prussian victories* (as inscribed on shield exhibited at Berlin, 30 Sept. 1866) PRUSSIA]

Liebenau, Türnau, Podoll 26 June, "
Nachod, Langensalza, Osweicin, Hühnerwasser 27 June, "
Münchengratz, Soor, Trautenau Skalitz 28 June, "
Gitschin, Königinhof, Jaromier, Schweinschädel 29 June, "
*Königgrätz and Sadowa 3 July, "
Dermbach, 4 July, Hunfeld 5 July, "
Waldaschach, Hausen, Hammelburg, Friedericshall, Kissingen, 10 July, "
Laufach, 13 July, Aschaffenburg 14 July, "
Tobitschau, 15 July, Blumenau, 22 July, Hof 23 July, "
Tauber Bischofsheim, Werbach Hochhausen 24 July, "
Neubrunn, Helmstädt, Gerchsheim 25 July, "
Rossbrunn, Würzburg, Baireuth 28 July, "

Monte Rotondo (Garibaldians victors) 27 Oct. 1867
Mentana (Garibaldi defeated) 3 Nov "
Arogee or Fahla (Abyssinians defeated) 10 Apr 1868
Magdala stormed 13 Apr "
Russians defeat Bokharians and occupy Samarcand 25 May, "
Alcolea (Spanish royalists defeated) 27, 28 Sept "
Villeta (Lopez defeated by Brazilians), etc 11 Dec. "
Lopez defeated .. 12, 16, 18, 21 Aug 1869
Aquidaban (Lopez defeated and killed) 1 Mch 1870

(FRANCO-PRUSSIAN WAR.)

Saarbrück, taken by the French, and Prussians repulsed, 2 Aug 1870
Wissembourg (French defeated) . 4 Aug "
Wörth (French defeated) 6 Aug
Saarbrück or Forbach (French defeated) " "
Courcelles or Pange " " 14 Aug "
Strasburg (French defeated) 16 Aug "
Vionville or Mars la Tour (French defeated) " "
*Gravelotte or Rézonville " " 18 Aug "
Beaumont (French defeated) 30 Aug "
Carignan " " 31 Aug "
Metz " " " "
Sedan " " 31 Aug, 1 Sept "
Before Paris (French defeated) 30 Sept "
Thoury (Germans surprised and repulsed) 5 Oct. "
St. Remy (French defeated) 6 Oct "
Before Metz " " 7 Oct "
Artenay " " 10 Oct. "
Cherizy (Germans repulsed) " "
Orleans (French defeated) 11 Oct "
Ecouis (indecisive) 14 Oct. "
Châteaudun (French defeated) 18 Oct. "
Coulmiers, near Orleans (Germans defeated) 9, 10 Nov "

Near Amiens (French defeated)	27 Nov	1870
Villiers, before Paris (French retreat)	30 Nov, 2 Dec	"
Before Orleans (French defeated)	4 Dec	"
Beaugency " "	7, 8 Dec	"
Nuits (French defeated)	18 Dec.	"
Pont à Novelles (French claim a victory)	23 Dec	"
Bapaume (indecisive)	2, 3 Jan	1871
Le Mans "	6 Jan	"
Le Mans (Chanzy defeated by prince Frederick Charles), 10-12 Jan		"
Belfort (Bourbaki defeated)	15-17 Jan	"
St Quentin (Faidherbe defeated)	19 Jan	"
Paris (Trochu's grand sortie repulsed)	"	"

Oroquieta (Carlists defeated)	4 May	1872
Elmina (Ashantees defeated by British)	13 June	1873
Elgueta (Carlists said to be victorious)	5 6 Aug	"
Mañeru (Carlists and republicans, indecisive)	6 Oct	"
Abrakampra (Ashantees defeated)	5, 6 Nov	"
Borborassie " "	29 Jan	1874
Amoaful " "	31 Jan	"
Becquah " "	1 Feb	"
Fommannah " "	2 Feb	"
Ordahsa " "	4 Feb	"
Before Bilbao (several days, Carlists retreat, Concha enters Bilbao)	2 May,	"
Estella (sharp conflicts, Carlists retreat, Concha killed), 25, 27 June,		"
Irun (Laserna defeats Carlists)	10 Nov	"
Sorota Peru (Pierota and insurgents defeated)	3 Dec.	"
Near Tolosa (Carlists repulse Loma)	7, 8 Dec	"
Khokand (Russians under Kaufman defeat the Khan's troops, etc)	4, 21 Sept.	1875
Abyssinians defeat Egyptians.	Oct	"
Assake (Khokand chiefs defeated)	30 Jan	1876

SERVIAN WAR

Zaitschar (severe conflicts Servians retreat)	2 3 July,	1876
Urbitza (Montenegrins defeat Turks)	28 July,	"
Turkish wars with Servia and Montenegro declared	2 July,	"
Zaicar or Saitschar (Turks and Servians, indecisive)	3 July,	"
Novi Bazar (Turks said to be victors)	6 July,	"
Urbitza (Montenegrins victors)	28 July,	"
Gurgusovatz (Turks victors)	5-7 Aug	"
Medun (Montenegrins victors)	7 or 14 Aug	"
Morava valley, near Alexinatz (severe conflicts, favorable to Turks)	19-27 Aug	"
Podgoritza (Montenegrins victors)	26 Aug	"
Alexinatz (Turks victors), 1 2 28, 29 Sept., captured	31 Oct.	"
Peace between Turkey and Servia	1 Mch	1877

RUSSO-TURKISH WAR

Zabir (Turks defeated)	16 June,	1877
Nicopolis (stormed by Russians, severe fights)	15, 16 July,	"
Plevna (Russians defeated)	19, 20, and 30, 31 July,	"
Valley of Lom (Russians defeated)	22-24 Aug	"
Kurukdara or Kizil Tepe (Russians defeated)	24 25 Aug	"
Shipka Pass (dreadful conflicts, Turks under Suleiman repulsed)	20-27 Aug	"
Karahassankoi, etc, on the Lom (severe, Russians retreat),	30 Aug	"
Lovatz or Luftcha (taken by Russians)	3 Sept	"
Plevna (held by Osman Pacha, severe conflicts, Russians defeated)	11, 12 Sept.	"
Shipka Pass (Suleiman defeated)	17 Sept	"
Near Kars (Russians defeated)	2-4 Oct.	"
Aladja Dagh, near Kars (Turks under Mukhtar totally defeated)	14 15 Oct	"
Deve Boyun, Armenia (Turks under Mukhtar defeated after 9 hours' fighting)	4 Nov	"
Azizi, near Erzeroum (Russians defeated)	9 Nov	"
Kars (taken by storm by Russians)	17, 18 Nov	"
Elena (taken by Turks after sharp conflict)	4 Dec	"
Plevna (Osman Pacha endeavors to break out, totally defeated, surrenders unconditionally)	9, 10 Dec	"
Senova in the Balkans (Turks defeated)	9, 10 Jan	1878
Near Philippopolis " "	14, 15 Jan	"

AFGHAN WAR. (AFGHANISTAN)

Ali Musjid (captured by British)	22 Nov	1878
Peiwar Pass (victory of gen Roberts)	2 Dec	"
Futtehabad (victory of gen Gough).	2 Apr	1879
Char aseab (Afghans defeated)	6 Oct.	"
Severe fighting near Cabul	Dec. 1879-Apr	1880
Ahmed Khel (Stewart defeats Afghans)	19-23 Apr	"
Kuschki-Nakhud or Malwand (Ayoob Khan defeats Burrows,	27 July,	"
Mazra or Baba Wali (Roberts totally defeats Ayoob Khan),	1 Sept.	"

ZULU WAR (ZULULAND)

Isandula (British surprised and defeated)	22 Jan	1879
Rorke's Drift (successfully defended by British)	"	"
Ulundi (Cetewayo totally defeated by lord Chelmsford),	4 July,	"

CHILIAN AND PERUVIAN WAR (CHILI)

Iquique (Chilians defeat Peruvians)	Nov	1879
Chorillos and Miraflores (Chilians defeat Peruvians)	17 Jan	1881

RUSSIAN WAR.

Geok or Denghli Tepé (Russians and Turkomans, indecisive),	9 Sept.	1879
Geok Tepe (besieged by Russians, severe conflicts) 24 Dec 1880, 4, 9, 10 Jan 1881, taken	24 Jan	1881

TRANSVAAL WAR

Laing's Nek (British defeated)	28 Jan	"
Ingogo River " "	8 Feb	"
Majuba Hill " "	27 Feb	"

WAR IN EGYPT

Bombardment of forts at Alexandria	11 July,	1882
Tel el Mahuta and Masameh (natives defeated by British),	24 25 Aug	"
Kassassin (natives defeated by British)	28 Aug and 9 Sept	"
Tel el Kebir " " " decisive)	13 Sept	"

SOUDAN

Arabs in the Soudan defeated by Hicks	29 Apr	1883
El Obeid or Kashgal (Hicks and his army destroyed).	3-5 Nov	"
Tokar (Egyptians defeated)	6 Nov	"
Near Teb, Baker with Egyptians defeated by Arabs	4 Feb	1884
Teb (Graham totally defeats Arabs)	29 Feb	"
Abu Klea (Stewart defeats natives)	17 Jan	1885
Gubat (Arabs defeated)	19 Jan	"
Kerkeben " " gen Earle killed)	10 Feb	"
Hasheen (Arabs defeated)	20 Mch	"
Arab attack near Suakim repulsed	22 Mch	"

Ak Tapa (Russians defeat Afghans)	30 Mar	1885
Chalchuapa, Central America (Barrios defeated and killed)	2 Apr	"
Dagoli, near Massowah (Italians annihilated by Abyssinians)	25 26 Jan	1887
Suakim (Arab dervishes defeated by British)	20 Dec.	1888
Wounded Knee, S Dak (U S troops with Indians) UNITED STATES	29 Dec	1890
Tokar Soudan (Osman Digna defeated)	19 Feb	1891
Placilla Chili (Balmaceda defeated by congressists)	28 Aug	"

[For small conflicts and skirmishes, BASUTO LAND CHILI, EGYPT, FRANCO PRUSSIAN WAR, HERZEGOVINA, INDIA KAFIRS, LAGOS, MANIPUR, RUSSO TURKISH WARS, SALVADOR SENEGAL, SOUDAN SPAIN, SUMATRA TONQUIN, TURKEY, UNITED STATES, ZULULAND, etc and for details of important engagements, see separate articles See also special articles on SOUTH AFRICAN WAR SPANISH AMERICAN WAR RUSSO JAPANESE WAR, CHINO JAPANESE WAR, CHINO-EUROPEAN (BOXERS) WAR

Bautzen, a town in Saxony, near which desperate battles were fought 20, 21, and 22 May, 1813, between the French, commanded by Napoleon, and the allies, under the emperor of Russia and the king of Prussia On the 20th (at Bautzen) the French were more successful, and on the 21st (at Wurschen) the allies were compelled to retire, but Napoleon obtained no permanent advantage

Bavaria (part of ancient Noricum and Vindelicia) a kingdom in S Germany, conquered from the Celtic Gauls (Boii) by the Franks between 630 and 660 The country was afterwards governed by dukes subject to the French monarchs. Tasillon II was deposed by Charlemagne, who established margraves in 788 The margrave Leopold, 895, father of Arnulph the Bad, is styled the first duke Bavaria was made a constitutional monarchy, 26 May, 1818 It joined the German empire, 22 Nov 1870 Pop. 1885, 5,420,199, 1890, 5,589,382 Area, 29,632 sq miles

Bavaria supports Austria in the contest with Prussia	June,	1866
Takes part in the war and makes peace with Prussia.	22 Aug	"
Population (after cessions, 1866), 4 824,421	Dec	1857
An international exhibition in a crystal palace opened	20 July,	1869
The Chambers dissolved, as, through a party struggle, no president was elected	6 Oct	"
Resignation of the ministry, 25 Nov, only partially accepted by the king	9 Dec.	"
Vote of want of confidence in prince Hohenlohe the president, 12 Feb, he resigns	14 Feb	1870
The king announces his intention of joining Prussia in the war with France	about 20 July,	"
Bavarian contingent highly distinguishes itself in the war, Otho, duke of Bavaria killed near Beghe	27 Jan	1871
Dr Döllinger excommunicated for denying papal infallibility, 18 Apr, elected rector of the university of Munich	29 July,	"
President of council, and foreign minister, A de Pfretzschner (FRANCO PRUSSIAN WAR)	22 Aug	"
Government protests against papal infallibility (GERMANY),	27 Sept	"
"Old Catholic" church opened at Munich	end of Sept.	"
The king, in a letter to the king of Saxony proposes the king of Prussia for emperor of Germany, about.	5 Dec	"
The king charges Von Gasser to form an ultramontane ministry, opposed to German unity, 3 Sept., he fails	Sept	1872
Queen dowager, Mary of Prussia, received into the Catholic church	12 Oct.	1874
New ultramontane ("popular Catholic") party formed	6 Mch	1877
International exhibition at Munich opened	19 July,	1879
7th centenary of foundation of the dynasty (Otto of Wittelsbach made duke by Frederick Barbarossa)	25 Aug	1880
The king (insane) drowns himself in a small lake, near one of his castles, after killing Dr Gudden, his physician	13 June,	1886

His brother, Otto, heir to the throne, not being of sound mind, the government appoint as regent prince Luitpold, his uncle, 14 June, 1886

DUKES.

1071. Guelf I., an illustrious warrior.
1101. Guelf II.; son; marries the countess Matilda, 1089.
1120. Henry the Black; brother.
1126. Henry the Proud; son. (He competed with Conrad of Hohenstaufen for the empire, failed, and was deprived of Bavaria.)
1138. Leopold, margrave of Austria; d. 1142.
1142. Henry of Austria; brother; d. 1177.
1154. Henry the Lion (son of Henry the Proud), ancestor of the Brunswick family, restored by the emperor Frederick Barbarossa, but expelled by him 1180 (BRUNSWICK); d. 1195.
1180. Otho, count of Wittelsbach, made duke; d. 1183.
1183. Louis; son.
1231. Otho II., the Illustrious; son; gained the palatinate; assassinated 1231.
1253. Louis II., the Severe; son; d. 1294.
1294. Louis III.; son (without the palatinate), emperor; d. 1347.
1347. Stephen I.; son; d. 1375.
1375. John; brother; d. 1397.
1397. Ernest; brother; d. 1438.
1438. Albert I.; son; d. 1460.
1460. John II. and Sigismund; sons; resigned to
1465. Albert II.; brother; d. 1508.
1508. William I.; son; opposes the Reformation, 1522; d. 1550.
1550. Albert III.; son; d. 1573.
1579. William II.; son; abdicates 1596; d. 1626.
1596. Maximilian the Great; son; the first elector of Bavaria, 25 Feb. 1623; the palatinate restored, 1648; d. 27 Sept. 1651.
1651. Ferdinand Mary; d. 26 May, 1679.
1679. Maximilian Emanuel; son; allies with France, 1702; defeated at Blenheim, 1704; restored to his dominions, 1714; d. 26 Feb. 1726.
1726. Charles Albert; son; elected emperor, 1742; defeated, 1744; d. 20 Jan. 1745.
1745. Maximilian Joseph I.; son; as elector; d. 30 Dec. 1777 (end of younger line of Wittelsbach).
1778. Charles Theodore (the elector palatinate of the Rhine since 1743). French take Munich; he treats with them, 1796; d. 1799.
1799. Maximilian Joseph II.; elector; territories changed by treaty of Luneville, 1801; enlarged when made king, by treaty of Presburg, Dec. 1805.

KINGS OF BAVARIA.

1805. Maximilian Joseph I. He deserts Napoleon, and has his enlarged territories confirmed to him, Oct. 1813; grants a constitutional charter, 22 Aug. 1818; d. 13 Oct. 1825.
1825. Louis I., 13 Oct.; abdicates 21 Mch. 1848; d. 29 Feb. 1868.
[His abdication was mainly caused by his attachment to a woman, known by the assumed name of Lola Montez; who, in the end, was banished for interference in state affairs. She delivered lectures in London in 1859; thence proceeded to the United States, and died in New York, 17 Jan. 1861.]
1848. Maximilian Joseph II.; son; b. 28 Nov. 1811; d. 10 Mch. 1864.
1864. Louis II.; son; b. 25 Aug. 1845; d. 13 June, 1886.
1886. Otto, b. 27 Apr. 1848.
" Prince Luitpold, regent.

Bay Islands (the chief, Rustan), in the bay of Honduras, belonged to Spain till 1821; then to Great Britain, which formed them into a colony in 1852, but ceded them to Honduras, 28 Nov. 1859. HONDURAS.

Bay State, popular name for Massachusetts; so called from the settlements about Boston designated as "The Massachusetts Bay colony," to distinguish it from the "Plymouth colony." MASSACHUSETTS, 1630.

Bayeux (*Bä'yu'*) **tapestry,** said to have been wrought by Matilda, queen of William I. (?). It is 19 inches wide, 214 feet long, and, in compartments, shows events from the visit of Harold to the Norman court to his death at Hastings; now preserved in the public library of Bayeux, near Caen. A copy, drawn by C. Stothard, and colored after the original, was published by the Society of Antiquaries in 1821–23. A reproduction, by autotype process, was published by F. R. Fowke, with notes, 1875.

Baylen, S. Spain, where, on 20 July, 1808, the French, under Dupont and Wedel, were defeated by the Spaniards, under Reding, Coupigny, and other generals.

Baylor's cavalry, massacre of. NEW YORK, 1778.

bayonet, a sharp-pointed instrument of steel for thrusting, fixed at the end of fire-arms, said to have been invented at Bayonne (whence the name), in France, about 1647, 1670, or 1690. It was used at Killiecrankie in 1689, and at Marsaglia by the French, in 1693, "with great success against the enemy, unprepared for the encounter with so formidable a novelty." It was at first inserted in the bore of the gun; but is now made with a ring to slip over the muzzle so that the gun can be fired with the bayonet fixed. The ring-bayonet was adopted by the British, 24 Sept. 1693.

Bayonne', S. France, an ancient city, held by the English from 1295 till it was taken by Charles VII. The queens of Spain and France met the cruel duke of Alva here, June, 1556, it is supposed to arrange the massacre of St. Bartholomew. Charles IV. of Spain abdicated here in favor of "his friend and ally" Napoleon, 4 May; and his sons, Ferdinand, prince of Asturias, don Carlos, and don Antonio, renounced the Spanish throne, 6 May, 1808. Near Bayonne was much fighting between the French and British armies, 9–13 Dec. 1813. Bayonne was invested by the British, 14 Jan. 1814; on 14 Apr. the French rallied and attacked the English vigorously, but were driven back. The loss of the British was considerable, and lieut.-gen. sir John Hope was wounded and taken.

Bayreuth (*bi'royt*), N. Germany, long a margraviate of a branch of the Brandenburg family, but with that of Anspach abdicated by the reigning prince in favor of the king of Prussia, 1790. The archives were brought (in 1783) from Plassenburg to Bayreuth, which was given to Bavaria by Napoleon in 1806.

bazaar', or covered market, an Arabic word. The magnificent bazaar of Ispahan was excelled by that of Tauris, which has held 30,000 men in order of battle.

Bazeilles (*ba-zā'ye*), a village in the ARDENNES, N.E. France. During the battle of Sedan, 1 Sept. 1870, Bazeilles was burned by the Bavarians, and atrocious outrages were said to have been committed. Of nearly 2000 inhabitants, it was asserted, scarcely 50 remained alive, and these indignantly denied having given provocation. Much controversy ensued, and in July, 1871, gen. von der Tann showed that the number of deaths had been grossly exaggerated, that there had been much provocation, and denied the alleged cruelties.

Beachy Head, S.E. Sussex, Engl., a promontory near which the British and Dutch fleet, commanded by the earl of Torrington, was defeated by a superior French force under admiral Tourville, 30 June, 1690; the allies suffered severely. The Dutch lost 2 admirals, 500 men, and several ships—sunk to save them from the enemy; the English lost 2 ships and 400 men. Both admirals were blamed—Torrington for not fighting, Tourville for not pursuing the victory.

Beacon hill, Boston. So called from a pole placed on its summit in 1635, with a torch, said to have been a barrel of tar, to alarm the country in case of attack by the Indians. BOSTON, 1811.

beads, early used in the East for reckoning prayers. St. Augustin mentions them in 366. About 1090 Peter the Hermit is said to have made a series of 55 beads. To Dominic de Guzman is ascribed the invention of the rosary (a series of 15 large and 150 small beads), in honor of the blessed Virgin, about 1202. Beads soon after were in general use. The bead-roll was a list of deceased persons, for the repose of whose souls a certain number of prayers was recited. Beads have been found in British barrows.

beam and **scales.** The apparatus for weighing goods was so called, "as it weighs so much at the king's beam." A public beam was set up in London, and all commodities ordered to be weighed by the city officer, called the weigh-master, who was to do justice between buyer and seller (stat. 3, Edw. II. 1309).—*Stow.* Beams and scales, with weights and measures, were ordered to be examined by the justices at quarter-sessions, 35 Geo. III. 1794. WEIGHTS AND MEASURES.

beans, black and white, were used by the ancients in gathering the votes of the people for the election of magistrates. A white bean signified absolution, and a black one condemnation. The precept ascribed by later writers to Pythagoras, abstain from beans, *abstine a fabis*, has been variously interpreted. "Beans do not favor mental tranquillity."—*Cicero.* The finer kinds of beans were brought to England in Henry VIII.'s reign. We have no certain information that the species of bean, *Phaseolus vulgaris*, existed in the Old World prior to the discovery of America.—*American Naturalist*, vol. 19, p. 447, 1885. The evidence for the antiquity of the bean in America is circumstantial and direct.—*Idem*, p. 448. The Lima bean, *Phaseolus lunatus*, is unquestionably

›f American origin, and De Candolle assigns its original habtat to Brazil. This bean has been found in the mummy ;raves of Peru.—*Idem*, p. 452. The bean is mentioned by arly explorers of America as in use by the aborigines; and he young Indian corn and the unripe shelled bean, boiled ogether, make the savory dish called succotash, which is ndian in origin and name.

bear-baiting, an ancient popular English sport, proibited by Parliament in 1835.

beards. The Egyptians did not wear beards; the Asyrians did. They have been worn for centuries by the Jews, ·ho were forbidden to mar their beards, 1490 B.C. (Lev. xix. 7). The Tartars waged a long war with the Persians, delaring them infidels, because they would not cut their beards, fter the custom of Tartary. The Greeks wore their beards ll the time of Alexander, who ordered the Macedonians to be haved, lest the beard should give a handle to their enemies, 30 B.C. Beards were worn by the Romans, 390 B.C. The emeror Julian wrote a diatribe (entitled "Misopogon") against ·earing beards, 362 A.D. In England they were not fashionble after the Conquest, 1066, until the 13th century, and were iscontinued at the Restoration. Peter the Great enjoined the ussians, even of rank, to shave, but was obliged to keep offi-ers on foot to cut off the beard by force. Since 1851 the ustom of wearing the beard gradually increased in Great ritain. Before 1840 shaving was almost universal in the nited States.—A bearded woman was taken by the Russians t the battle of Pultowa, and presented to the czar, Peter I., 724; her beard measured 1½ yds. A woman is said to have een seen at Paris with a bushy beard, and her whole body overed with hair.—*Dict. de Trévoux.* Margaret of Savoy, aughter of Maximilian I., emperor of Germany, and governess ' the Netherlands, 1507–30, had a very long stiff beard. In avaria, in the time of Wolfius, a virgin had a long black eard. Mdlle. Bois de Chêne, born at Geneva (it was said) 1834, was exhibited in London in 1852–53, when, consequently, 18 years of age; she had a profuse head of hair, a rong black beard, large whiskers, and thick hair on her arms id down from her neck on her back, and masculine features.

Bearn, S. France, the ancient Benecharnum, was held iccessively by the Romans, Franks, Goths, and Gascons, and ecame an hereditary viscounty in 819, under Centule I., son ' Loup, duke of Gascony. From his family it passed to the ouses—of Gabaret, 1134; of Moncade, 1170; of Foix, 1290; id of Bourbon, 1550. Its annexation to France was decreed y Henry IV., 1594; affirmed by Louis XIII., 1620.

Beaulieu, Abbey of (reformed Benedictines), founded y king John, in the New Forest, Hampshire, Engl., in 1204, id dedicated to the blessed Virgin, had the privilege of sanciary. It was the asylum of Margaret, queen of Henry VI., ter the defeat of Warwick, at Barnet, 14 Apr. 1471; and of erkin Warbeck, Sept. 1497.

Beaumont, a village near Sedan, department of Arennes, N.E. France. Near here a part of the army of marial MacMahon under De Failly was surprised, defeated, and riven across the Meuse at Mouzon, 30 Aug. 1870, by the ermans under the crown-prince of Prussia, while retreating ter vainly endeavoring to succor Metz. The French loss icluded about 7000 prisoners, many guns, and much camp quipage. The victory was chiefly gained by the Bavarians.

Beaune-la-Rollande, a village in the Loiret, rance. Here the French army of the Loire, under gen. 'Aurelle de Paladines, was defeated by Germans, under prince rederick Charles, in an attempt to march by Fontainebleau relieve Paris, 28 Nov. 1870. French loss as reported by ermans was 1000 dead, 4000 wounded; above 1700 prisonrs. German loss heavy.

Beauvais (*bō'vā'*), N. France, the ancient Bellovaci, ormerly capital of Picardy. When besieged by Charles the old, duke of Burgundy, with 80,000 men, the women, under eanne Fourquet or Lainé, also de la Hachette, from her weaon, distinguished themselves, and the duke raised the siege, 0 July, 1472. Hence the women of Beauvais head the proession on the anniversary of their deliverance.

Beaver Dams, Ont., now **Homer,** 3 miles east of St. Catharines, was the scene of an engagement, 24 June, 1813, between a body of United States troops over 500 strong, under lieut.-col. Charles G. Boestler, sent out from FORT GEORGE by gen. Dearborn, and a body of British troops and Indians. The Americans, although outnumbering the British force, were deceived and surrendered.

Bechuana-land, S. Africa, proclaimed British territory 8 Oct. 1885. Area, 170,000 sq. miles; chief industry, agriculture.

Becket's murder. Thomas à Becket was born in 1119. His father, Gilbert, was a London trader, and his mother, it is said, a convert from Mahometanism. He was educated at Oxford, and made archdeacon by Theobald, archbishop of Canterbury, who introduced him to king Henry II. He became chancellor in 1155, but when made archbishop of Canterbury, in 1162, resigned the chancellorship, offending the king. He opposed the constitutions of Clarendon in 1164, fled the country, and in 1166 excommunicated all the clergy who agreed to them. He and the king met at Fretville, in Touraine, on 22 July, 1170, and were formally reconciled. On his return he recommenced his struggle with the king, which led to his murder at the altar, 29 Dec. 1170. The king was absolved of guilty knowledge of the crime in 1172, and did penance at the tomb in 1174. The bones of Becket were enshrined in gold and jewels in 1220, but were burned in the reign of Henry VIII., 1539. The Merchant Adventurers were at one time termed "the Brotherhood of St. Thomas à Becket." A Roman Catholic church at Canterbury, dedicated to him, was opened by cardinal Manning, 13 Apr. 1875.

bed. The ancients slept on skins. Beds were afterwards made of loose rushes, heather, or straw. The Romans are said to have first used feathers. An air-cushion is said to have been used by Heliogabalus, 218–222; air-beds were in use in the 16th century. Feather-beds were in use in England in the reign of Henry VIII. The bedsteads of the Egyptians and later Greeks, like modern couches, became common among the Roman upper classes.

The ancient great bed at Ware, Herts, capable of holding 12 persons, was sold, it is said, to Charles Dickens, 6 Sept. 1864.
A bedstead of gold was presented to the queen of England on 2 Nov. 1859, by the maharajah of Cashmere.
Air-beds and water-beds have been made since the manufacture of india-rubber cloth by Clark in 1813; and by Mackintosh in 1823.
Dr. Arnott's hydrostatic bed invented in 1830.

bed of justice, a French court presided over by the king, whose seat was termed a "bed." It controlled the ordinances of the parliament. The last was held by Louis XVI. at Versailles, 19 Nov. 1787, to raise a loan.

Beder, Arabia. Here Mahomet gained his first victory (over the Koreish of Mecca), 623. It was reputed miraculous. BATTLES.

Bedford, a town, N.N.W. London, Engl., renowned for its many free educational establishments, endowed in 1561 by sir William Harpar, a London alderman. Here John Bunyan preached, was imprisoned, and wrote the "Pilgrim's Progress."

A statue of Bunyan, gift of the duke of Bedford, uncovered here, 10 June, 1874. Bronze gates for the Bunyan church, given by the duke, were inaugurated by him 5 July, 1876.

Bedford Level, a portion of the fen districts in the eastern counties, Engl., drained early in the 17th century by the earl of Bedford, aided by the Dutch engineer, sir Cornelius Vermuyden, amid great opposition. LEVELS.

Bedouins, wandering Arabs, living on the plunder of travellers, etc. They profess Mahometanism, are governed by sheiks, and are called descendants of Ishmael. See the prophecy (Gen. xvi. 12), 1911 B.C.

"Beecher's bibles." During the "Kansas trouble," 1854–60, Henry Ward Beecher declared that for the slaveholder of Kansas the Sharpe rifle was a greater moral agency than the Bible; and so those rifles became known as "Beecher's bibles."

bees. Mount Hybla, for its odoriferous flowers, thyme, and abundant honey, is called the "empire of bees." Hymettus, in Attica, was also famous for bees and honey. The economy of bees was admired in the earliest ages; Eumelus of Corinth wrote a poem on bees, 741 B.C. Bees were introduced into Boston in 1670, and have since spread over North [illegible] Mandeville's satirical "Fable of the Bees" appeared in [illegible]. Huber published his observations on bees in 1792. The Apiarian Society had an establishment at Muswell Hill, near London, Engl. (1860–62). The Ligurian honey-bee was successfully introduced into England in 1860.

beet-root is of recent cultivation in England. *Beta vulgaris*, red beet, is used as a salad. Margraff first produced sugar from white beet-root in 1747. M. Achard produced good sugar from it in 1799; and the chemists of France, at the instance of Bonaparte, largely extracted sugar from beet-root in 1800. 60,000 tons of sugar, about half the consumption, are now manufactured in France from beet. It is also largely manufactured in other countries. A refinery of sugar from beet-root has been erected at the Thames bank, Chelsea. The cultivation of beet-root in England and Ireland much advocated, 1871. SUGAR.

beggars were tolerated in ancient times, being often musicians and ballad-singers. In modern times severe laws have been passed against them. In 1572, by 14 Eliz. c. 5, sturdy beggars were ordered to be "grievously whipped and burned through the right ear;" the third offence capital. By the Vagrant act (1824), 5 Geo. IV. c. 83, all public beggars are liable to a month's imprisonment. The "Beggar's Opera," by John Gay, a satire against sir Robert Walpole's ministry, produced at Lincoln's-inn-fields theatre, 29 Jan. 1727–28, ran 63 nights. GUEUX.

be'gums (princesses) of Oude. The spoliation of these princesses was one of the charges against Warren Hastings in his impeachment before the English House of Commons, 1788. CHUNAR and SHERIDAN'S SPEECH. Macaulay's review of Gleig's "Life of Warren Hastings," 1841, gives a full account of the cruelties practised towards them.

beheading, the *decollatio* of the Romans, introduced into England from Normandy (as a less ignominious mode of putting criminals to death) by William the Conqueror, 1076. Waltheof, earl of Huntington, Northampton, and Northumberland, was first so executed. This mode of execution became frequent, particularly in the reigns of Henry VIII., Mary, and Elizabeth, when even women of the noblest blood thus perished: Anne Boleyn, 19 May, 1536; the aged countess of Salisbury, 27 May, 1541; Catherine Howard, 12 Feb. 1542; lady Jane Grey, 17 years of age, 12 Feb. 1554; Mary, queen of Scots, 8 Feb. 1587; Marie Antoinette, queen of France, guillotined 16 Oct. 1793.

Behistun, in Persia. Here a rock has important inscriptions in 3 languages, in cuneiform (or wedge-shaped) characters, which, deciphered and translated by sir H. Rawlinson in 1844–46, were published in the Journal of the Royal Asiatic Society. Each paragraph begins, "I am Darius the Great King."

Behring's sea lies south of Behring's strait and north of the Aleutian islands. Within and about this sea are the most important seal-fisheries in the world. Alaska was purchased from Russia by the United States in 1867, and, as this purchase was considered to include Behring's sea, the United States claimed jurisdiction over these waters, and seized a British Columbia sealer, the *Black Diamond*, as a trespasser, 3 July, 1889.

The British government claimed, as heretofore, the right of fishing in waters beyond the territorial limits. The governments agreed to refer the question to arbitration, Feb. 1890. President Harrison proclaimed the Behring sea closed to unlicensed seal fishing, 25 Mch. A blue-book was published, 15 Aug., containing the correspondence between the two governments from 1 Sept. 1886, to 2 Aug. 1890. The marquis of Salisbury demanded that, pending arbitration, British sealing vessels should not be molested, adding that if so, they should be protected, 2 Aug. 1890. UNITED STATES, 15 Mch., 17 Dec. 1890; 12 Jan., 15 June, 7 Aug., 2 Oct. 1891; 29 Feb.....18 Apr. 1892

The 2 governments agree by treaty to submit the questions in dispute to a tribunal of arbitration.....9 May, "

[The court as finally constituted consisted of 7 members, viz.: justice John M. Harlan and senator John T. Morgan, United States; lord Hannen and sir John S. D. Thompson, Great Britain; baron de Courcel, France; marquis Emilio Visconti Venosta, Italy; judge Gram, Sweden and Norway. Besides these seven there were others connected with the court, viz.: hon. John W. Foster, ex-sec. State, American agent; and E. J. Phelps, James C. Carter, Henry W. Blodgett, F. R. Coudert, and Robert Lansing, counsel for the United States; C. H. Tupper, Canadian minister of Marine, British agent; and sir Charles Russell, sir Henry Webster, hon. W. H. Cross, and C. Robinson, counsel for Great Britain.]

Commissioners of arbitration meet at Paris and adjourn until 23 Mch.....23 Feb. 1893

Court of arbitration held its first session at Paris..... " "

Arguments commenced in the arbitration court.....4 Apr. "

Decision rendered.....15 Aug. "

While the legal questions submitted were decided against the formal claim of the U. S., the policy prescribed for the future regulation of the seal-fisheries was satisfactory to the American people. The principal points were: (1) The close season fixed from 1 May until 31 July. (2) A protective zone established extending 60 miles around the islands in the Behring's sea. Pelagic sealing allowed outside of this zone from 1 Aug. (3) The use of fire-arms prohibited in sealing, etc.

Behring's strait, discovered by capt. Vitus Behring, a Danish navigator in the service of Russia. He proved that the continents of Asia and America are about 39 miles apart, 1728. He died at Behring's island in 1741. In 1778, capt. James Cook surveyed the coasts.

Belfast, capital of Ulster, N. Ireland. Its castle, supposed built by John de Courcy, was destroyed by Scots under Edward Bruce, 1315. ORANGE.

Belfast granted by James I. to sir Arthur Chichester, lord deputy, 1612; and erected into a corporation..... 1613

Long bridge (21 arches, 2562 feet long) built.....1682–86

First edition of the Bible in Ireland printed here..... 1704

Belfort or **Befort**, a fortified town in Alsace, E. France, invested by Germans 3 Nov. 1870; capitulated 16 Feb. 1871; reserved to France when Alsace was ceded, 26 Feb.; quitted by Germans Aug. 1873.

Belgium, the southern portion of the Netherlands, anciently territory of the Belgæ, finally conquered by Julius Cæsar, 51 B.C. Its size is about one eighth of Great Britain, and it is one of the most densely populated countries in the world. Its government is a liberal constitutional monarchy, founded in 1831. For previous history, FLANDERS, HOLLAND, NETHERLANDS. Pop., 31 Dec. 1862, 4,836,566; 1870, 5,087,105; 1900, 6,815,054. Area, 11,400 sq. miles.

Revolution begins at Brussels.....25 Aug. 1830

Provisional government declares independence (M. Van de Weyer active).....4 Oct. "

Antwerp taken (except the citadel).....23 Dec. "

Independence acknowledged by allied powers.....26 Dec. "

Duke de Nemours elected king (his father, the French king, refused consent).....3 Feb. 1831

Surlet de Chokier elected regent.....24 Feb. "

Leopold, prince of Saxe-Coburg, accepts the crown, 12 July; enters Brussels.....19 July, "

War with Netherlands begins.....3 Aug. "

France sends 50,000 troops to assist Belgium; an armistice ensues.....Aug. "

Conference of ministers of 5 powers in London; 24 articles of pacification accepted.....15 Nov. "

Convention; England and France against Holland.....22 Oct. 1832

Antwerp besieged, 30 Nov.; citadel taken by French...23 Dec. "

French army returns to France.....27 Dec. "

Preliminary convention with Holland signed.....21 May, 1833

Treaty of Holland and Belgium at London.....19 Apr. 1839

[Result of a conference in London on Belgium, which decided to maintain the treaty of 15 Nov. 1831, and the compensation of 60,000,000 francs offered by Belgium for territories adjudged to Holland was rejected.]

Increase of army to 100,000 men voted.....10 May, 1853

Opposition to religious charities bill.....June, 1857

[At the revolution in 1830, the Catholic clergy lost the administration of public charities, which they have since struggled to recover. In April, 1857, M. Decker, head of the ministry, brought in a bill for this purpose, but had to withdraw it, and eventually to resign.]

The king proclaims neutrality in Italian war.....May, 1859

Rumors of annexation to France bring loyal addresses to the king.....13 June, 1860

Octrois abolished.....21 July, "

Commercial treaty with France signed.....1 May, 1861

" " " Great Britain, adopted by chambers, 22 Aug. 1862

Dissensions through Catholics, Jan.; ministry resigns, but resumes office, 4 Feb.; dissolution of chambers, 17 July; Protestants succeed in election.....Aug. 1864

Death of Leopold I.....10 Dec. 1865

Mr. Phillips, lord mayor of London, and 1100 English volunteers visit Belgium under col. Lloyd-Lindsay; other foreigners attend; banquet by the king at Brussels.....20 Oct. 1866

About 2400 Belgians (garde civique and volunteers) visit England; arrive, 10 July; received by lord mayor, 12 July; by prince of Wales at Wimbledon, 13 July; dine at Windsor, 16 July; ball at Agricultural hall, 18 July; received by Miss Burdett-Coutts, 19 July; attend review at Wimbledon, 20 July; leave London.....22 July, 1867

New ministry (under M. Frère-Orban); liberal.....3 Jan. 186[illegible]

Monument to Charlemagne at Liège, inaugurated......26 July, 1868
International congress of workmen at Brussels......6-13 Nov. "
Crown-prince Leopold Ferdinand, duke of Brabant, d...22 Jan. 1869
Concession for a Luxembourg railway to a French company, without assent of state, prohibited by Assembly, 13 Feb.; dispute with French government arranged............May, "
Treaty for neutrality between Great Britain and Prussia, signed 9 Aug.; and France, signed.......................11 Aug. 1870
After Sedan, French soldiers enter Belgium; disarmed and interned...1, 2 Sept. "
Comte de Chambord arrives at Antwerp, 17 Feb.; compelled to quit Belgium by popular demonstrations.........27 Feb. 1872
France denounces the treaty of commerce............29 Mch. "
Treaty of commerce with France signed...............5 Feb. 1873
Czar at Brussels.......................................22 May, "
M. Van de Weyer, statesman; active in revolution of 1830; ambassador to England, 1831-67; d.................23 May, 1874
International conference at Brussels on rights of neutrals—no results.................................27 July-28 Aug. "
Notes from German government, complaining of publications favoring censured German ecclesiastics, Feb.; respecting Duchesne's proposal to the archbishop of Paris to assassinate Bismarck..15 Apr. 1875
Dignified Belgian replies........................Mch. and May, "
Popular opposition to religious processions; riots...May, June, "
Catholic successes in elections; riots at Brussels and Antwerp, about 16, 17 June, 1876
Statue of Van de Weyer, at Louvain, inaugurated by the king, 1 Oct. "
International congress on hygiene, etc., at Brussels, 27 Sept.-2 Oct. "
Catholic minority in elections; Malou ministry resign, 13, 14 June; M. Frère-Orban forms a liberal ministry.....20 June, 1878
Gigantic weir for water distribution at La Gileppe, near Verviers, inaugurated by the king.....................28 July, "
Eugene T'Kindt de Rooden Veke, a clerk, convicted of embezzling 20,000,000 francs of the Bank of Belgium (149 thefts); the governor Fortamps, of fraudulently repurchasing shares, etc...3 Dec. "
King sanctions new education law.....................1 July, 1879
Pastoral of Roman Catholic hierarchy against government plan of mixed education (sacraments refused to teachers and parents, etc.) publ. in Germany........................Sept. "
Archduke Rodolph of Austria betrothed to princess Stephanie, Mch. 1880
Permanent international exhibition opened at Brussels. 1 June, "
Elections for Parliament; struggle between liberals and clericals on education; liberals retain moderate majority.......June, "
National exhibition at Brussels opened by the king and queen, 16 June, "
Representative at Vatican recalled through ecclesiastical disputes; diplomatic intercourse suspended...........28 June, "
Jubilee to celebrate national independence............18 July, "
Statue of Leopold I. unveiled at Laeken...............21 July, "
Parliamentary reform-bill passed......................17 Aug. 1883
Henri Conscience, national Flemish poet and novelist, dies, aged 73...9 Sept. "
Death of cardinal Deschamps, abp. of Mechlin, the primate, 29 Sept. "
Elections; majority of clericals through dissension of moderate liberals and reformers, about 10 June; resignation of M. Frère-Orban..11 June, 1884
M. Jules Malou forms conservative Catholic ministry, 12, 13 June, "
Senate dissolved, June; new Senate clerical..............July, "
Meeting of burgomasters at Brussels to oppose M. Jacobs's reactionary education bill, 9 Aug.; it is accepted by the deputies (80-49), 30 Aug.; by the Senate (40-25)..............10 Sept. "
Royal assent to the bill..................................13 Sept. "
Communal elections; great liberal majority............19 Oct. "
MM. Malou, Jacobs, and Woeste (Catholics) resign; M. Bernaert becomes premier...24 Oct. "
Parliament meets...11 Nov. "
Leopold proclaimed sovereign of Congo Free State.....2 May, 1885
Universal exhibition at Antwerp, opened.............. " "
Death of Charles Rogier, aged 85, member of provisional government 1830; 6 times minister....................27 May, "
Castle of Laeken, built 1728, burned; valuable works of art, and historical documents, etc., lost....................1 Jan. 1890
Death of prince Baldwin, aged 21 years.................23 Jan. 1891
Chamber of Representatives adopt universal suffrage, with a provision for a plural vote by property owners, 18 Apr., and the Senate approve...21 Apr. 1893

KINGS.

1831. Leopold, first king of Belgians; b. 16 Dec. 1790; crowned 21 July, 1831, at Brussels; married, 9 Aug. 1832, Louise, eldest daughter of Louis Philippe of France (she d. 11 Oct. 1850). He d. 10 Dec. 1865.
1865. Leopold II., son; b. 9 Apr. 1835; married archduchess Maria Henrietta of Austria, 22 Aug. 1853.
Daughter.—Princess Louise, b. 18 Feb. 1858; married duke Philip of Saxony, 4 Feb. 1875.
Heir brother.—Philip, count of Flanders, b. 24 Mch. 1837; married Mary, princess of Hohenzollern-Sigmaringen, 25 Apr. 1867; son Baldwin, b. 3 June, 1869; d. 23 Jan. 1891; Albert, b. 8 Apr. 1875.

Belgrade, an ancient city in Servia, on the right bank of the Danube, was taken from the Greek emperor by Solomon, king of Hungary, in 1072; gallantly defended by John Hunniades against Turks, under Mahomet II., July-Sept. 1456, who was defeated, with the loss of 40,000 men. Belgrade was taken by sultan Solyman, Aug. 1521, and retaken by Imperialists in 1688, from whom it was again taken by Turks, 1690. It was besieged in May, 1716, by prince Eugène; the Turkish army, 200,000 strong, approached to relieve it, and on 5 Aug., in a battle at Peterwaradein, the Turks lost 20,000 men. Eugène defeated the Turks here, 16 Aug. 1717, and Belgrade surrendered 18 Aug. In 1739 it was ceded to the Turks, after its fortifications had been demolished; was retaken in 1789, and restored at the peace of Reichenbach, in 1790. The Servian insurgents had possession 1806-13. In 1815 it was placed under prince Milosch, subject to Turkey. The fortifications were restored in 1820. On 19 June, 1862, the Turkish pacha was dismissed for firing on the town during a riot. The university was established by private munificence, 1863. The fortress was surrendered by Turks to Servians, 18 Apr. 1867. The independence of Servia proclaimed here, 22 Aug. 1878. SERVIA.

bell, book, and candle. In the Roman Catholic ceremony of EXCOMMUNICATION, the bell is rung, the book is closed, and candle extinguished, to symbolize exclusion from the society of the faithful, divine service, and the sacraments. Its origin is ascribed to the 8th century.

Bell Rock light-house, nearly in front of the Frith of Tay, one of the finest in Great Britain; it is 115 ft. high, upon a rock 427 ft. long and 200 ft. broad, and is about 12 ft. under water. It was erected in 1806-10. It has 2 bells for hazy weather.

Upon this rock, it is said, the abbots of Aberbrothock fixed the *Inchcape bell*, to be rung by the impulse of the sea to warn mariners. It is said that a Dutchman, who took the apparatus away, was here lost with his ship and crew.

Belleisle, an isle on the south of Brittany, France, made a duchy by Louis XV., for marshal Belleisle, in 1742, to reward military and diplomatic services. Belleisle was taken by the British, under commodore Keppel and general Hodgson, after a desperate resistance, 7 June, 1761, but restored to France in 1763.

belles-lettres or **polite learning.** ACADEMIES, LITERATURE.

belligerent act towards France. UNITED STATES, 1798; PROVISIONAL ARMY.

bellmen in London proclaimed the hour at night before public clocks became general; numerous about 1556. They were to ring a bell, and cry, "Take care of your fire and candle, be charitable to the poor, and pray for the dead."

bellows. Anacharsis, the Scythian, is said to have invented them, about 569 B.C.; also tinder, the potter's wheel, anchors for ships, etc. Bellows were not used in the furnaces of the Romans. Great bellows were used in foundries in early times. BLOWING-MACHINES.

bells were used among the Jews, Greeks, and Romans. The responses of the Dodonæan oracle were in part conveyed by bells.—*Strabo.* The monument of Porsenna was decorated with pinnacles, each surmounted by bells.—*Pliny.* Said to have been introduced by Paulinus, bishop of Nola, in Campagna, about 400; and first known in France in 550. The army of Clothaire II., king of France, was frightened from the siege of Sens by the bells of St. Stephen's church. The second excerption of king Egbert of England commands every priest, at proper hours, to sound the church-bells. Bells were rung in churches by order of pope John IX., about 900, as a defence against thunder and lightning. Bells are mythically said to have been cast by Turketul, abbot of England, about 941. The celebrated "Song of the Bell," by Schiller, has been frequently translated, while "The Bells," one of Edgar Allan Poe's most finished poems, is as widely known. The following list is that given by E. Beckett Denison, with the exception of a few later ones, in his discourse on bells at the Royal Institution, 6 Mch. 1857:

	Weight. Tons.	cwt.
Moscow, 1736; broken 1737	250	—
[The metal in this bell has been valued, at the lowest estimate, at 66,565*l.* Gold and silver are said to have been thrown in as votive offerings.]		
Another, 1817	110	—
3 others	16 to 31	—
Novgorod	31	—
Cologne, 1875	26	—
Olmütz	17	18

	Weight. Tons.	cwt.
Vienna, 1711	17	14
London, 1882 (St. Paul's), "Great Paul," note E flat; cost, 3000*l.*	17½	—
Westminster, 1856, "Big Ben"	15	8½

[This bell, the largest in England (named Big Ben, after sir Benjamin Hall, the then chief commissioner of works), cast at Houghton-le-Spring, Durham, by Messrs. Warner, under the superintendence of E. Beckett Denison and the rev. W. Taylor, cost 3343*l.* 14*s.* 9*d.* The composition was 22 parts copper and 7 tin. The diameter was 9 ft. 5½ in.; the height 7 ft. 10½ in. The clapper weighed 12 cwt.—*Rev. W. Taylor.*]

	Tons.	cwt.
Westminster, 1858, "St. Stephen"	13	10¾

[The bell "Big Ben" being cracked, on 24 Oct. 1857, was broken up, and another cast with the same metal, in May, 1858, by Messrs. Mears, Whitechapel. It is different in shape from its predecessor, and about 2 tons lighter. Its diameter is 9 ft. 6 in.; the height, 7 ft. 10 in. It was struck for the first time 18 Nov. 1858. The clapper weighs 6 cwt. Its note is E natural; the quarter-bells being G, B, E, F. On 1 Oct. 1859, this bell was also found to be cracked.]

	Tons.	cwt.
Erfurt, 1497	13	15
Sens	13	—
Paris, Notre Dame, 1680	12	16
Montreal, 1847	12	15
Cologne, 1448	11	3
Breslau, 1507	11	—
Görlitz	10	17
York, 1845	10	15
Bruges, 1680	10	5
St. Peter's, Rome	8	—
Oxford, "Great Tom," 1680	7	12
Lucerne, 1636	7	11
Halberstadt, 1457	7	10
Antwerp	7	3
Brussels	7	1½
Dantzic, 1453	6	1
Lincoln, 1834	5	8

St. Paul's, 1716. The clapper of St. Paul's bell weighs 180 lbs.; the diameter is 10 *ft.* (Mr. Walesby says 6 ft. 9½ in.), and its thickness 10 in. The hour strikes upon this bell, the quarters upon 2 smaller ones. CLOCKS.

	Tons.	cwt.
Ghent	4	18
Boulogne, new	4	18
Exeter, 1675	4	10
Old Lincoln, 1610	4	8
Fourth-quarter bell, Westminster, 1857	4	—

Liberty bell, Philadelphia, first cast by Lester & Peck, 267 Whitechapel, London, 1752, hung in the state-house, Philadelphia. Same year—found to be cracked in the rim—recast 3 times in Philadelphia before it was a success. 23 years afterwards it was rung on Independence day in that city. On 8 July, 1835, it was cracked while tolling for the death of chief-justice Marshall. In 1843 it was removed. It bore this inscription, "Proclaim liberty throughout the land to all the inhabitants thereof" (Lev. xxv. 10). Weight 2080 lbs. Taken to Chicago to be exhibited at the World's Fair......29 Apr. 1893

Baptism of bells.—They were anointed and baptized in churches, it is said, from the 10th century.—*Du Fresnoy.* The bells of the priory of Little Dunmow, in Essex, Engl., were baptized by the names of St. Michael, St. John, Virgin Mary, Holy Trinity, etc., in 1501.—*Weever.* The great bell of Notre Dame of Paris was baptized by the name of Duke of Angoulême, 1816. On the Continent, in Catholic states, they baptize bells as the English do ships, but with religious solemnity.—*Ashe.*

Ringing of bells, in changes of regular peals, is almost peculiar to the English.—*Stow.*

"Companie of the Schollers of Chepeside," 1603; "Society of College Youths," 1637; "Society of Cumberland," 1683; the "Society of Union Scholars," 1713; the "Society of Eastern Scholars," 1733; "London Youths," 1753; "Westminster Youths," 1776.

Fabian Stedman, about 1650, invented "Stedman's principle." Benjamin Anable soon after invented "Grandsire Triples."

720 changes can be rung in an hour upon 12 bells; 479,001,600 changes rung upon them require 75 years, 10 months, and 10 days.

Nell Gwynne left the ringers of the bells of St. Martin's-in-the-Fields money for a weekly entertainment, 1687, and many others have done the same.

Carillons, a collection of bells, in 2 or 3 chromatic scales, played by pedals or keyboards, or by machinery. First said to have been made at Alost, in Flanders, in 1487, and that country and Holland are renowned for carillons. Matthias van den Gheyn was an eminent maker (1721–85). Excellent carillon machines are now made by Messrs. Gillet, Bland & Co., Croydon, Engl. One at Manchester, started 1 Jan. 1879, plays 35 tunes on 20 bells.

Belmont, Mo., Battle of, opposite Columbus, Ky., fought 7 Nov. 1861. Gen. Grant drove the confederates under gen. Pillow from their first position, but they were reinforced from Columbus, finally compelling Grant to withdraw. Union force about 2500 men; loss, killed, wounded, and missing, 485; confederate loss, 642. This was gen. Grant's first battle in the civil war.

Beloo'chistan' or **Beluchistan,** the ancient Gedrosia, S. Asia. The country of the Baluchis, whose name is derived from Belus, king of Babylonia, the Nimrod of the Scriptures.—*Keith Johnston.* Area, 106,800 sq. miles. Pop. 350,000. Khelat, the capital, was taken by the British in the Afghan war, 1839; abandoned, July, 1840; taken and held a short time, Nov. 1840.

The khan was subsidized in 1854, under conditions which were not observed; the arrangement was broken up in 1873; the negotiations of major Sandeman, in 1875, were successful, and Quettah was occupied by the British in 1877, and has since become a prosperous station. The khan proffered assistance after the defeat of gen. Burrows in July, 1880.

Belvoir (*bee'ver*) **castle,** Leicestershire, Engl., built after the Conquest by Robert de Todeni. Its next owner was Robert de Ros, who died 1285. The castle fell into ruins during the wars of the Roses and reign of Richard III. The Manners' family obtained it in the 16th century, and hold it still. In the civil war it was defended for the king. In 1649 the Parliament ordered it demolished. The castle was rebuilt after the Restoration. The last general repairs cost 60,000*l.* It was visited by George IV. as regent, 1814, and by queen Victoria and the prince consort in 1843. Of the cost of living at the castle, the following is a published account of particulars from Dec. 1839 to Apr. 1840: Wine, 200 doz.; ale, 70 hogsheads; wax-lights, 2330; sperm oil, 630 gals. Dined at his grace's table, 1997 persons; in the steward's room, 2421; in the servants' hall, nursery, and kitchen department, including comers and goers, 11,312 persons. There were consumed 8333 loaves of bread; 22,963 lbs. of meats, exclusive of game. The money value of meat, poultry, eggs, and every kind of provision (excluding stores on hand) consumed during this period amounted to 1323*l.* 7*s.* 11¾*d.*, or $6700. There were killed during the season on the estate, 1733 hares, 987 pheasants, 2101 partridges, 28 wild ducks, 108 woodchucks, 138 snipes, 947 rabbits, 776 grouse, 23 black game, and 6 teal.—*Timbs,* "Abbeys and Castles of England and Wales," etc.

Bemis's Heights, First Battle at. Gen. Gates, with the American army, in the autumn of 1777, established a fortified camp on Bemis's heights, near Stillwater, N. Y., where he was attacked by British and Hessians, under gen. Burgoyne, on 19 Sept. Night ended the conflict, and both parties claimed the victory. Burgoyne, however, fell back a few miles to his camp, to wait for reinforcements. The British force engaged was about 3000, and the American about 2500. The former lost, killed, wounded, and missing, a little less than 500; the latter, 319.

Bemis's Heights, *Second Battle at.* Despairing of reinforcements, his army diminishing by desertions, Burgoyne decided to attack Gates, which he did on 7 Oct., almost upon the battle-ground of 19 Sept., but had to fall back to the heights of Saratoga, now Schuylerville, where he was compelled to surrender on 17 Oct. The number of troops surrendered was 5791, of whom 2412 were Hessians, under baron Riedesel; the remainder British regulars and Canadians. NEW YORK, UNITED STATES, and CONVENTION TROOPS.

Bena'res, in India, a holy city of the Hindoos, with many temples, was ceded by the nabob of Oude, Asoph-ud-Dowlah, to the English in 1775. An insurrection here nearly proved fatal to British interests in Hindostan, 1781. (Descriptions of this insurrection introduced in Poe's "Tale of the Ragged Mountains.") The rajah Cheyt Sing was deposed in consequence in 1783. Mr. Che.ry, capt. Conway, and others were assassinated at Benares by vizier Aly, 14 Jan. 1799. In June, 1857, col. Neil suppressed attempts of native infantry to join the mutiny. INDIA.

Benburb, near Armagh, N. Ireland. Here O'Neill defeated the English under Monroe, 5 June, 1646. Moore says, "*the only great victory, since the days of Brian Boru, achieved* by an Irish chieftain in the cause of Ireland."

Bencoo'len, Sumatra. The English East India Company made a settlement here, which preserved the pepper trade after the Dutch had dispossessed them of Bantam, 1682.—*Anderson.* York fort erected by the East India Company, 1690. In 1693 dreadful mortality here, the town being built on a pestilent morass; the governor and council perished. The French, under count d'Estaing, destroyed the English settlement, 1760. Bencoolen was reduced to a residency under the government of Bengal, in 1801; was ceded to the Dutch in 1824, in exchange for possessions in Malacca. INDIA.

Bender, Bessarabia, European Russia. Near it Charles

XII. of Sweden, was permitted to reside by the Turkish sultan after his defeat at Pultowa by Peter the Great, 8 July, 1709. The peace of Bender was concluded in 1711. Bender was taken from the Turks by the Russians in 1770, 1789, and 1809; restored at the peace of Jassy, but retained at the peace of 1812.

Benedict. Fourteen popes have borne the name of Benedict, 573–1740. POPES.

Benedictines, an order of monks founded by St. Benedict (lived 480–543), who introduced monastic life into western Europe, in 529, founding the monastery on Monte Casino, in Campania, and 11 others afterwards. His *Regula Monachorum* (rule of the monks) became the common rule of western monachism. No religious order has been so remarkable for extent, wealth, and men of note and learning as the Benedictine. Among branches, the chief were the Cluniacs, founded in 912; the Cistercians, founded in 1098, and reformed by St. Bernard, abbot of Clairvaux, in 1116; and Carthusians, from the Chartreux (hence charter-house), founded by Bruno about 1080. The Benedictine order was introduced into England by Augustin, in 596; and William I. built an abbey for it on the plain of the battle of Hastings, 1066. BATTLE-ABBEY. William de Warrenne, earl of Warrenne, built a convent at Lewes, in Sussex, in 1077; this order is said to have had 40 popes, 200 cardinals, 50 patriarchs, 116 archbishops, 4600 bishops, 4 emperors, 12 empresses, 46 kings, 41 queens, and 3600 saints. Their founder was canonized. —*Baronius.* The Benedictines have taken little part in politics, but have produced many literary works. The congregation of St. Maur published "L'Art de Vérifier les Dates," in 1750, and edited many ancient authors.

Benedictines with other orders expelled from France by decree, 19 Mch. 1880
14th centenary of the birth of St. Benedict kept at Monte Casino and other places.......Apr. "

benefice (literally, a good deed or favor) or **fief,** a term first applied under the Roman empire to portions of land the usufruct of which was granted by the emperors to soldiers or others for life, as a reward or *beneficium* for past services, and as a retainer for future service. The same method was applied under the feudal system, and in the church, such grants being formally recognized by the council of Orleans, 511. Vicarages, rectories, perpetual curacies, and chaplaincies are termed benefices in distinction from dignities, such as bishoprics, etc. A rector is entitled to all tithes; a vicar, to a small part or none.—All benefices that should become vacant within 6 months were given by pope Clement VII. to his nephew, in 1534.—*Notitia Monastica.*

Beneventum, now **Benevento,** an ancient city in S. Italy, said to have been founded by Diomedes the Greek, after the fall of Troy. Pyrrhus of Macedon, during his invasion of Italy, was defeated near Beneventum, 275 B.C. Near it was erected the triumphal arch of Trajan, 114 A.D. Benevento was formed into a duchy by the Lombards, 571. At a battle here, 26 Feb. 1266, Manfred, king of Sicily, was defeated and slain by Charles of Anjou, who thus became virtually master of Italy. The castle was built 1323; the town was nearly destroyed by an earthquake, 1688, when the archbishop, afterwards pope Benedict XIII., was dug out of the ruins alive, and helped rebuild, 1703. It was seized by the king of Naples, but restored to the pope on the suppression of the Jesuits, 1773. Talleyrand de Périgord, Bonaparte's archchancellor, was made prince of Benevento, 1806. Benevento was taken by French, 1798, and restored to the pope in 1815.

benevolences (aids, free gifts, actually forced loans) appear to have been claimed by Anglo-Saxon sovereigns. Such were levied by Edward IV., 1473, by Richard III., 1485 by Henry VII., 1492, and by James I., 1613, on the marriage of princess Elizabeth with Frederick, elector palatine, afterwards king of Bohemia. In 1615 Oliver St. John, M.P., was fined 5000*l.*, and chief-justice Coke disgraced, for censuring such exactions. Benevolences were declared illegal by the bill of rights, Feb. 1689.

Bengal, chief presidency of British India. Capital, Calcutta. Its governors were appointed by the sovereigns of Delhi till 1340, when it became independent. It was added to the Mogul empire by Baber, about 1529; it forms a lieutenant-governorship, with an area of 203,473 sq. miles and a pop. of 66,691,456.

English first permitted to trade to Bengal........ 1534
They establish a settlement at Hooghly........about 1652
Factories of the French and Danes set up........ 1664
Bengal made a distinct agency........ 1680
English settlement removed to fort William........ 1698
Imperial grant vesting the revenues of Bengal in the company, making it really sovereign........12 Aug. 1765
India bill; Bengal made chief presidency; supreme court of judicature established........16 June, 1773
Bishop of Calcutta appointed........21 July, 1813
Railway opened........15 Aug. 1854

Bennington, Battle of, took place at Hoosick, N. Y., 5 miles from Bennington, Vermont, on 16 Aug. 1777, between British and German detachments, under cols. Baume and Breyman, of Burgoyne's army, and gen. John Stark, with New Hampshire militia. British were defeated, with a loss, in killed, wounded, and prisoners, of almost 1000 men. Americans had 100 killed and as many wounded. Burgoyne sent this expedition to procure cattle and stores. It was a severe blow to him, and led to his final defeat. It is counted one of the important battles of the Revolution. NEW YORK.

Bentonville, N. C. Here on 18 Mch. 1865, the confederates under gen. Joseph E. Johnston fiercely attacked part of Sherman's army under gen. Slocum, especially the corps of gen. Jeff. C. Davis, but were finally repelled. The concentration of gen. Sherman's forces and the fear for his line of retreat compelled gen. Johnston to fall back on Raleigh. Federal loss, killed, wounded, and missing, 1643.

benzole or **benzine,** a compound of hydrogen and carbon, discovered by Faraday in oils (1825), and by C. B. Mansfield in coal-tar (1849). Mansfield died from a burn while experimenting on it (25 Feb. 1855). Benzole has become useful in the arts. Chemists have produced from it ANILINE, the source of the modern dyes mauve, magenta, and many others. ALIZARINE.

Aromatic essences and perfumes have been obtained from benzole by Perkin, Tiemann, Harrmann, and others. Febrifuge medicines, by O. Fischer, Dewar, McKendrick, and others, in 1881. And saccharine, a principle 220 times sweeter than cane-sugar, by Fahlberg and Remsen, patented in Great Britain in 1886; not nutritious, and said to cause indigestion.

Beowulf, an ancient Anglo-Saxon epic poem, describing the deeds of Beowulf, a Scandinavian hero, who probably flourished in the middle of the 5th century; supposed to have been written after 597. The preponderance of opinion now ascribes to this most important surviving monument of Anglo-Saxon poetry a west-Saxon origin, and a date between 705 and 750. An edition by Kemble was published in 1833. It has been translated by Kemble, Thorpe, and Wackerbarth. MANUSCRIPT.

Berengarians, followers of Berengarius, archdeacon of Angers, who, about 1049, opposed the doctrine of transubstantiation or the real presence. Several councils of the church condemned his doctrine, 1050–79. After much controversy, he recanted about 1079, and died, grieved and wearied, 6 Jan. 1088.

Beresi'na, a river in Russia, crossed by the French main army after defeat by the Russians, 25–29 Nov. 1812. The French lost upwards of 20,000 men, and the retreat was ruinous.

Berg, W. Germany, on the extinction of its line of counts, in 1348, was incorporated with Juliers. Napoleon I. made Murat grand-duke in 1806. The principal part is now held by Prussia.

Bergamo, N. Italy, a Lombard duchy, annexed to Venice, 1428; which chiefly held it till it revolted and joined the Cisalpine republic, 1797. It was awarded to Austria in 1814; ceded to Sardinia, 1859.

Bergen, Norway, founded 1070; was the royal residence during the 12th and 13th centuries.

Bergen, Germany, Battle of. French defeated allies, 13 Apr. 1752.—In HOLLAND the allies, under the duke of York, were defeated by the French, under gen. Brune, with great loss, 19 Sept. 1799. In another battle, 2 Oct. same year, the duke gained a victory over Brune; but on the 6th was defeated before Alkmaer, and on the 20th, by a convention, exchanged his army for 6000 French and Dutch prisoners in England.

Bergen-op-Zoom, Holland. This place, deemed impregnable, was taken by the French, 16 Sept. 1747, and again in 1795. An attempt by the British, under gen. sir T. Graham to storm the fortress was defeated; after forcing an entrance their retreat was cut off, and nearly all were cut to pieces or taken, 8 Mch. 1814.

	Weight. Tons.	cwt.
Vienna, 1711	17	14
London, 1882 (St. Paul's), "Great Paul," note E flat; cost, 3000*l.*	17½	—
Westminster, 1856, "Big Ben"	15	8½
[This bell, the largest in England (named Big Ben, after sir Benjamin Hall, the then chief commissioner of works), cast at Houghton-le-Spring, Durham, by Messrs. Warner, under the superintendence of E. Beckett Denison and the rev. W. Taylor, cost 3343*l.* 14*s.* 9*d.* The composition was 22 parts copper and 7 tin. The diameter was 9 ft. 5½ in.; the height 7 ft. 10½ in. The clapper weighed 12 cwt.—*Rev. W. Taylor.*]		
Westminster, 1858, "St. Stephen"	13	10¾
[The bell "Big Ben" being cracked, on 24 Oct. 1857, was broken up, and another cast with the same metal, in May, 1858, by Messrs. Mears, Whitechapel. It is different in shape from its predecessor, and about 2 tons lighter. Its diameter is 9 ft. 6 in.; the height, 7 ft. 10 in. It was struck for the first time 18 Nov. 1858. The clapper weighs 6 cwt. Its note is E natural; the quarter-bells being G, B, E, F. On 1 Oct. 1859, this bell was also found to be cracked.]		
Erfurt, 1497	13	15
Sens	13	—
Paris, Notre Dame, 1680	12	16
Montreal, 1847	12	15
Cologne, 1448	11	3
Breslau, 1507	11	—
Görlitz	10	17
York, 1845	10	15
Bruges, 1680	10	5
St. Peter's, Rome	8	—
Oxford, "Great Tom," 1680	7	12
Lucerne, 1636	7	11
Halberstadt, 1457	7	10
Antwerp	7	3
Brussels	7	1½
Dantzic, 1453	6	1
Lincoln, 1834	5	8
St. Paul's, 1716. The clapper of St. Paul's bell weighs 180 lbs.; the diameter is 10 ft. (Mr. Walesby says 6 ft. 9½ in.), and its thickness 10 in. The hour strikes upon this bell, the quarters upon 2 smaller ones. CLOCKS.		
Ghent	4	18
Boulogne, new	4	18
Exeter, 1675	4	10
Old Lincoln, 1610	4	8
Fourth-quarter bell, Westminster, 1857	4	—

Liberty bell, Philadelphia, first cast by Lester & Peck, 267 Whitechapel, London, 1752, hung in the state-house, Philadelphia. Same year—found to be cracked in the rim—recast 3 times in Philadelphia before it was a success. 23 *years afterwards* it was rung on Independence day in that city. On 8 July, 1835, it was cracked while tolling for the death of chief-justice Marshall. In 1843 it was removed. It bore this inscription, "Proclaim liberty throughout the land to all the inhabitants thereof" (Lev. xxv. 10). Weight 2080 lbs. Taken to Chicago to be exhibited at the World's Fair.......29 Apr. 1893

Baptism of bells.—They were anointed and baptized in churches, it is said, from the 10th century.—*Du Fresnoy.* The bells of the priory of Little Dunmow, in Essex, Engl., were baptized by the names of St. Michael, St. John, Virgin Mary, Holy Trinity, etc., in 1501.—*Weever.* The great bell of Notre Dame of Paris was baptized by the name of Duke of Angoulême, 1816. On the Continent, in Catholic states, they baptize bells as the English do ships, but with religious solemnity.—*Ashe.*

Ringing of bells, in changes of regular peals, is almost peculiar to the English.—*Stow.*

"Companie of the Schollers of Chepeside," 1603; "Society of College Youths," 1637; "Society of Cumberland," 1683; the "Society of Union Scholars," 1713; the "Society of Eastern Scholars," 1733; "London Youths," 1753; "Westminster Youths," 1776.

Fabian Stedman, about 1650, invented "Stedman's principle." Benjamin Anable soon after invented "Grandsire Triples."

720 changes can be rung in an hour upon 12 bells; 479,001,600 changes rung upon them require 75 years, 10 months, and 10 days.

Nell Gwynne left the ringers of the bells of St. Martin's-in-the-Fields money for a weekly entertainment, 1687, and many others have done the same.

Carillons, a collection of bells, in 2 or 3 chromatic scales, played by pedals or keyboards, or by machinery. First said to have been made at Alost, in Flanders, in 1487, and that country and Holland are renowned for carillons. Matthias van den Gheyn was an eminent maker (1721–85). Excellent carillon machines are now made by Messrs. Gillet, Bland & Co., Croydon, Engl. One at Manchester, started 1 Jan. 1879, plays 35 tunes on 20 bells.

Belmont, Mo., Battle of, opposite Columbus, Ky., fought 7 Nov. 1861. Gen. Grant drove the confederates under gen. Pillow from their first position, but they were reinforced from Columbus, finally compelling Grant to withdraw. Union force about 2500 men; loss, killed, wounded, and missing, 485; confederate loss, 642. This was gen. Grant's first battle in the civil war.

Beloo'chistan' or **Beluchistan,** the ancient Gedrosia, S. Asia. The country of the Baluchis, whose name is derived from Belus, king of Babylonia, the Nimrod of the Scriptures.—*Keith Johnston.* Area, 106,800 sq. miles. Pop. 350,000. Khelat, the capital, was taken by the British in the Afghan war, 1839; abandoned, July, 1840; taken and held a short time, Nov. 1840.

The khan was subsidized in 1854, under conditions which were not observed; the arrangement was broken up in 1873; the negotiations of major Sandeman, in 1875, were successful, and Quettah was occupied by the British in 1877, and has since become a prosperous station. The khan proffered assistance after the defeat of gen. Burrows in July, 1880.

Belvoir (*bee'ver*) **castle,** Leicestershire, Engl., built after the Conquest by Robert de Todeni. Its next owner was Robert de Ros, who died 1285. The castle fell into ruins during the wars of the Roses and reign of Richard III. The Manners' family obtained it in the 16th century, and hold it still. In the civil war it was defended for the king. In 1649 the Parliament ordered it demolished. The castle was rebuilt after the Restoration. The last general repairs cost 60,000*l.* It was visited by George IV. as regent, 1814, and by queen Victoria and the prince consort in 1843. Of the cost of living at the castle, the following is a published account of particulars from Dec. 1839 to Apr. 1840: Wine, 200 doz.; ale, 70 hogsheads; wax-lights, 2330; sperm oil, 630 gals. Dined at his grace's table, 1997 persons: in the steward's room, 2421; in the servants' hall, nursery, and kitchen department, including comers and goers, 11,312 persons. There were consumed 8333 loaves of bread; 22,963 lbs. of meats, exclusive of game. The money value of meat, poultry, eggs, and every kind of provision (excluding stores on hand) consumed during this period amounted to 1323*l.* 7*s.* 11¾*d.*, or $6700. There were killed during the season on the estate, 1733 hares, 987 pheasants, 2101 partridges, 28 wild ducks, 108 woodchucks, 138 snipes, 947 rabbits, 776 grouse, 23 black game, and 6 teal.—*Timbs,* "Abbeys and Castles of England and Wales," etc.

Bemis's Heights, First Battle at. Gen. Gates, with the American army, in the autumn of 1777, established a fortified camp on Bemis's heights, near Stillwater, N. Y., where he was attacked by British and Hessians, under gen. Burgoyne, on 19 Sept. Night ended the conflict, and both parties claimed the victory. Burgoyne, however, fell back a few miles to his camp, to wait for reinforcements. The British force engaged was about 3000, and the American about 2500. The former lost, killed, wounded, and missing, a little less than 500; the latter, 319.

Bemis's Heights, Second Battle at. Despairing of reinforcements, his army diminishing by desertions, Burgoyne decided to attack Gates, which he did on 7 Oct., almost upon the battle-ground of 19 Sept., but had to fall back to the heights of Saratoga, now Schuylerville, where he was compelled to surrender on 17 Oct. The number of troops surrendered was 5791, of whom 2412 were Hessians, under baron Riedesel; the remainder British regulars and Canadians. NEW YORK, UNITED STATES, and CONVENTION TROOPS.

Bena'res, in India, a holy city of the Hindoos, with many temples, was ceded by the nabob of Oude, Asoph-ud-Dowlah, to the English in 1775. An insurrection here nearly proved fatal to British interests in Hindostan, 1781. (Descriptions of this insurrection introduced in Poe's "Tale of the Ragged Mountains.") The rajah Cheyt Sing was deposed in consequence in 1783. Mr. Cherry, capt. Conway, and others were assassinated at Benares by vizier Aly, 14 Jan. 1799. In June, 1857, col. Neil suppressed attempts of native infantry to join the mutiny. INDIA.

Benburb, near Armagh, N. Ireland. Here O'Neill defeated the English under Monroe, 5 June, 1646. Moore says, "the only great victory, since the days of Brian Boru, achieved by an Irish chieftain in the cause of Ireland."

Bencoo'len, Sumatra. The English East India Company made a *settlement* here, which preserved the pepper trade after the Dutch had dispossessed them of Bantam, 1682.—*Anderson.* York fort erected by the East India Company, 1690. In 1693 dreadful mortality here, the town being built on a pestilent morass; the governor and council perished. The French, under count d'Estaing, destroyed the English settlement, 1760. Bencoolen was reduced to a residency under the government of Bengal, in 1801; was ceded to the Dutch in 1824, in exchange for possessions in Malacca. INDIA.

Bender, Bessarabia, European Russia. Near it Charles

XII of Sweden, was permitted to reside by the Turkish sultan after his defeat at Pultowa by Peter the Great, 8 July, 1709 The peace of Bender was concluded in 1711 Bender was taken from the Turks by the Russians in 1770, 1789, and 1809, restored at the peace of Jassy, but retained at the peace of 1812.

Benedict. Fourteen popes have borne the name of Benedict, 573-1740 POPES

Benedictines, an order of monks founded by St Benedict (lived 480-543), who introduced monastic life into western Europe, in 529, founding the monastery on Monte Casino, in Campania, and 11 others afterwards His *Regula Monachorum* (rule of the monks) became the common rule of western monachism No religious order has been so remarkable for extent, wealth, and men of note and learning as the Benedictine Among branches, the chief were the Cluniacs, founded in 912, the Cistercians, founded in 1098, and reformed by St. Bernard, abbot of Clairvaux, in 1116, and Carthusians, from the Chartreux (hence charter-house), founded by Bruno about 1080 The Benedictine order was introduced into England by Augustin, in 596, and William I built an abbey for it on the plain of the battle of Hastings, 1066. BATTLE-ABBEY William de Warrenne, earl of Warrenne, built a convent at Lewes, in Sussex in 1077, this order is said to have had 40 popes, 200 cardinals, 50 patriarchs, 116 archbishops, 4600 bishops, 4 emperors, 12 empresses, 46 kings, 41 queens, and 3600 saints Their founder was canonized —*Baronius* The Benedictines have taken little part in politics, but have produced many literary works The congregation of St. Maur published "L'Art de Verifier les Dates," in 1750, and edited many ancient authors

Benedictines with other orders expelled from France by decree, 19 Mch 1880
14th centenary of the birth of St Benedict kept at Monte Casino and other places Apr "

benefice (literally, a good deed or favor) or **fief,** a term first applied under the Roman empire to portions of land the usufruct of which was granted by the emperors to soldiers or others for life, as a reward or *beneficium* for past services, and as a retainer for future service The same method was applied under the feudal system, and in the church, such grants being formally recognized by the council of Orleans, 511 Vicarages, rectories, perpetual curacies, and chaplaincies are termed benefices in distinction from dignities, such as bishoprics, etc A rector is entitled to all tithes, a vicar, to a small part or none.—All benefices that should become vacant within 6 months were given by pope Clement VII to his nephew, in 1534 —*Notitia Monastica*

Beneventum, now **Benevento,** an ancient city in S Italy, said to have been founded by Diomedes the Greek, after the fall of Troy. Pyrrhus of Macedon, during his invasion of Italy, was defeated near Beneventum, 275 B.C. Near it was erected the triumphal arch of Trajan, 114 A D Benevento was formed into a duchy by the Lombards, 571 At a battle here, 26 Feb 1266, Manfred, king of Sicily, was defeated and slain by Charles of Anjou, who thus became virtually master of Italy The castle was built 1323, the town was nearly destroyed by an earthquake, 1688, when the archbishop, afterwards pope Benedict XIII, was dug out of the ruins alive, and helped rebuild, 1703 It was seized by the king of Naples, but restored to the pope on the suppression of the Jesuits, 1773. Talleyrand de Perigord, Bonaparte's archchancellor, was made prince of Benevento, 1806 Benevento was taken by French, 1798, and restored to the pope in 1815

benevolences (aids, free gifts, actually forced loans) appear to have been claimed by Anglo-Saxon sovereigns. Such were levied by Edward IV, 1473, by Richard III, 1485 by Henry VII, 1492, and by James I, 1613, on the marriage of princess Elizabeth with Frederick, elector palatine, afterwards king of Bohemia. In 1615 Oliver St John, M P, was fined 5000*l*., and chief-justice Coke disgraced, for censuring such exactions. Benevolences were declared illegal by the bill of rights, Feb 1689.

Bengal, chief presidency of British India. Capital, Calcutta. Its governors were appointed by the sovereigns of Delhi till 1340, when it became independent. It was added to the Mogul empire by Baber, about 1529, it forms a lieutenant-governorship, with an area of 203,473 sq. miles and a pop of 66,691,456.

English first permitted to trade to Bengal 1534
They establish a settlement at Hooghly about 1652
Factories of the French and Danes set up 1664
Bengal made a distinct agency 1680
English settlement removed to fort William 1698
Imperial grant vesting the revenues of Bengal in the company, making it really sovereign 12 Aug 1765
India bill, Bengal made chief presidency, supreme court of judicature established 16 June, 1773
Bishop of Calcutta appointed 21 July, 1813
Railway opened 15 Aug 1854

Bennington, Battle of, took place at Hoosick N Y, 5 miles from Bennington, Vermont, on 16 Aug 1777, between British and German detachments, under cols Baume and Breyman, of Burgoyne's army, and gen John Stark, with New Hampshire militia British were defeated, with a loss, in killed, wounded, and prisoners of almost 1000 men Americans had 100 killed and as many wounded Burgoyne sent this expedition to procure cattle and stores It was a severe blow to him and led to his final defeat It is counted one of the important battles of the Revolution NEW YORK

Bentonville, N C Here on 18 Mch 1865, the confederates under gen Joseph E Johnston fiercely attacked part of Sherman's army under gen Slocum, especially the corps of gen Jeff C Davis, but were finally repelled The concentration of gen Sherman's forces and the fear for his line of retreat compelled gen Johnston to fall back on Raleigh Federal loss, killed, wounded, and missing, 1613

benzole or **benzine,** a compound of hydrogen and carbon, discovered by Faraday in oils (1825), and by C. B Mansfield in coal-tar (1849) Mansfield died from a burn while experimenting on it (25 Feb 1855). Benzole has become useful in the arts Chemists have produced from it ANILINE, the source of the modern dyes mauve, magenta, and many others ALIZARINE

Aromatic essences and perfumes have been obtained from benzole by Perkin, Tiemann, Harrmann and others. Febrifuge medicines, by O Fischer, Dewar, McKendrick, and others, in 1881 And saccharine a principle 220 times sweeter than cane sugar, by Fahlberg and Remsen patented in Great Britain in 1886, not nutritious, and said to cause indigestion

Beowulf, an ancient Anglo-Saxon epic poem, describing the deeds of Beowulf, a Scandinavian hero, who probably flourished in the middle of the 5th century, supposed to have been written after 597 The preponderance of opinion now ascribes to this most important surviving monument of Anglo Saxon poetry a west-Saxon origin, and a date between 705 and 750 An edition by Kemble was published in 1833. It has been translated by Kemble, Thorpe and Wackerbarth MANUSCRIPT.

Berengarians, followers of Berengarius, archdeacon of Angers, who, about 1049, opposed the doctrine of transubstantiation or the real presence Several councils of the church condemned his doctrine, 1050-79 After much controversy, he recanted about 1079, and died, grieved and wearied, 6 Jan 1088

Beresi'na, a river in Russia, crossed by the French main army after defeat by the Russians, 25-29 Nov 1812 The French lost upwards of 20,000 men, and the retreat was ruinous

Berg, W Germany, on the extinction of its line of counts, in 1348, was incorporated with Juliers Napoleon I made Murat grand-duke in 1806. The principal part is now held by Prussia

Bergamo, N Italy, a Lombard duchy, annexed to Venice, 1428, which chiefly held it till it revolted and joined the Cisalpine republic, 1797 It was awarded to Austria in 1814, ceded to Sardinia, 1859

Bergen, Norway founded 1070, was the royal residence during the 12th and 13th centuries

Bergen, Germany, Battle of French defeated allies, 13 Apr 1752 —In HOLLAND the allies, under the duke of York, were defeated by the French, under gen Brune, with great loss, 19 Sept. 1799 In another battle, 2 Oct same year, the duke gained a victory over Brune, but on the 6th was defeated before Alkmaer, and on the 20th, by a convention, exchanged his army for 6000 French and Dutch prisoners in England

Bergen-op-Zoom, Holland. This place, deemed impregnable, was taken by the French, 16 Sept 1747, and again in 1795. An attempt by the British, under gen. sir T Graham to storm the fortress was defeated, after forcing an entrance their retreat was cut off, and nearly all were cut to pieces or taken, 8 Mch. 1814.

Bergerac, France. Here John of Gaunt, then earl of Derby, defeated French in 1344; here a temporary treaty between Catholics and Protestants, establishing liberty of conscience, was signed 17 Sept. 1577.

Berkeley castle, Gloucestershire, Engl., begun by Henry I. in 1108, was finished in the next reign. Here Edward II. was murdered, 21 Sept. 1327, with circumstances of peculiar atrocity. His queen Isabella (princess of France) and her paramour, Mortimer, earl of March, were held as accessories. Mortimer was hanged at the Elms, near London, 29 Nov. 1330, by Edward III., who also confined his mother in her own house at Castle Rising, near Lynn, in Norfolk, till her death, 1357.

"Mark the year, and mark the night,
When Severn shall re-echo with affright
The shrieks of death through Berkeley's roof that ring,
Shrieks of an agonizing king."—*Gray's Ode*, "The Bard."

Berlin, capital of Prussia, province of Brandenburg, said to have been founded by margrave Albert the Bear, about 1163. Its 5 districts were united under one magistracy in 1714; it afterwards became the capital of Prussia and was greatly improved. It was taken and held by Russians and Austrians, 9-13 Oct. 1760. Establishment of Academy of Sciences, 1702; of the university, 1810. On 27 Oct. 1806, after the battle of Jena, the French entered Berlin, whence Napoleon issued the BERLIN DECREE. Pop. 1890, 1,579,244; 1900, 1,888,848.

BERLIN CONGRESS ON THE EASTERN QUESTION.

Representatives (with resident ambassadors): *Germany*, prince Bismarck, president; *Russia*, prince Gortschakoff; *Turkey*, Alexander Carathéodori; *Great Britain*, lord Beaconsfield and marquis of Salisbury (lord Odo Russell ambassador); *Austria*, count Andrassy; *France*, M. Waddington; *Italy*, count Corti.
First meeting, 13 June; 20th and last; treaty signed. .13 July, 1878
Articles 1-12. Bulgaria constituted an autonomous principality, tributary to the sultan; the Balkans southern limit; the prince to be elected by the people, approved by the sultan and other powers; public laws, and other details.
Articles 13-22. Eastern Rumelia made a province; partly autonomous; boundaries defined; Christian governor-general to be appointed by the sultan; to be organized by an Austrian commission; Russian army of occupation for 9 months.
Article 23. Bosnia and Herzegovina to be occupied and administered by Austro-Hungary.
Articles 24-30. Montenegro independent; new frontiers; Antivari annexed.
Articles 31-39. Servia independent, with new frontiers.
" 40-49. Roumania independent, losing part of Bessarabia to Russia, with compensation.
Articles 50-54. Regulation of navigation of the Danube, etc.
" 55-57. Legal reforms in Crete, etc.
Article 58. The Porte cedes to Russia Ardahan, Kars, and Batoum, and settles boundaries.
Article 59. Batoum to be a free commercial port.
" 60. Alasgird and Bayazid restored to Turkey.
Articles 61, 62. The Porte promises legal reforms, religious liberty, etc.
Article 63. The treaty of Paris (30 Mch. 1856) and of London (13 Mch. 1871) maintained when not modified by this treaty.
Article 64. To be ratified in 3 weeks. Ratified.........3 Aug. "
Circular on delay in executing treaty from earl Granville, foreign secretary, to foreign powers....................May, 1880
Berlin conference..................................16 June-1 July, "
Ambassadors: for Great Britain, lord Odo Russell; France, comte de St. Vallier, etc., president; prince Hohenlohe, German foreign minister.
They agree to a collective note to the sultan of Turkey (urging surrender of Dulcigno and cession of provinces to Greece); presented..15 July, "
DULCIGNO; TURKEY; GREECE, 1880-81; SAMOAN ISLANDS, 1889, *etc.*

Berlin Decree. An interdict issued by Napoleon I. from Berlin against British commerce, 21 Nov. 1806; an attempt to destroy the foreign trade of England as well as a retaliatory measure to offset the British Order in Council issued 16 May, 1806. It declared a blockade of British islands, and ordered all Englishmen in countries occupied by French troops to be treated as prisoners of war. No letters in the English language were to pass through the French post-offices. All trade in English merchandise was forbidden. No vessel directly from England or the English colonies was to be admitted into any French port, and by a later interpretation, all merchandise derived from England and her colonies, by whomsoever owned, was liable to seizure, even on board neutral vessels, and whether even the vessels themselves might not also be liable to confiscation was reserved for future consideration. BRITISH ORDERS IN COUNCIL, MILAN DECREE, UNITED STATES, 1806.

Bermuda Hundred, Va., a peninsula between the Appomattox and James rivers, occupied by gen. B. F. Butler, 6 May, 1864, with between 15,000 and 25,000 men, threatening Petersburg and Richmond on the south. ARMY OF THE JAMES. An attack by Beauregard 17 May, 1864, stopped the advance, and the confederates erected a line of works across the peninsula. Soon after gen. Butler's force was depleted by sending reinforcements to gen. Grant across the James, so that he could not assume the offensive, and his condition was aptly expressed in his own words, "The necessities of the army of the Potomac have bottled me up at Bermuda Hundred."

Bermudas or **Somers's isles,** a group consisting of about 100 coral reefs and rocks with 5 islets, in the N. Atlantic ocean, 32° 26′ n. lat., 64° 37′ w. lon., discovered by Juan Bermudas, a Spaniard, in 1522, but not inhabited until 1609, when sir George Somers was cast away upon them. They were settled by stat. 9 James I. 1612. Among the exiles from England during the civil war was Waller, the poet, who wrote, while here, a poetical description of the islands. There was a hurricane here, 31 Oct. 1780, and by another a third of the houses was destroyed, and the shipping driven ashore, 20 July, 1813. A large iron dry-dock here, which cost 250,000*l.*, was towed from the Medway in June and July, 1869. Pop. 15,534; area about 41 sq. miles.

Bernard′, Great St., a celebrated pass in the Pennine Alps, between Martigny, Switzerland, and Aosta, Piedmont, so called from a hospice supposed to have been founded here by Bernardine Menthon in 962. Height, 8200 ft. On the east side is Mt. Velan, on the west Pointe de Dronaz. Bonaparte crossed by this route in May, 1800. *Little St. Bernard* pass and hospice; height about 7192 ft., about 10 miles south Mt. Blanc, between Savoy and Piedmont, in the Graian Alps. Hannibal probably crossed here into Italy (218 B.C.). ALPS.

Bernardines or **White Monks,** a strict order of Cistercian monks, established by St. Bernard of Clairvaux, about 1115. He founded many monasteries.

Berne, the sovereign canton of Switzerland, joined the Swiss league, 1352; the town Berne was made a free city by the emperor Frederick, May, 1218; it repulsed Rudolph of Hapsburg, 1288. It surrendered to the French under gen. Brune, 12 Apr. 1798. The town has bears for its arms, and still maintains a bear-pit on funds specially provided. It was made capital of Switzerland, 1848.

Berry (the ancient *Biturigum Regis*), central France, held by Romans since Cæsar (58-50 B.C.), till subdued by the Visigoths; from whom it was taken by Clovis in 507 A.D. It was made a duchy by John II. in 1360, and not incorporated into the royal domains till 1601.

Berwick-on-Tweed, a fortified town on the northeast extremity of England, the scene of many bloody contests between England and Scotland; claimed by the Scots because it stood on their side of the river. Upon the treaty entered into between England and Scotland for the ransom of William the Lion, who was taken prisoner near Alnwick in 1174, the castle of Berwick was surrendered to the English, but was restored to Scotland by Richard I. in 1188. Here John Baliol did homage for Scotland, 30 Nov. 1292. It was annexed to England in 1333; was taken and retaken many times, and finally ceded to England in 1482. In 1551 it was made independent. The town surrendered to Cromwell in 1648, and to gen. Monk in 1659. Since the union of the crowns (James I., 1603) the fortifications have been neglected.

Bessara′bia, frontier province of European Russia, part of ancient Dacia; known to the Greeks. After possession by Goths, in the 2d century, and Huns, at the end of the 5th, it came into possession of the Bessi in the 7th century, from whom the country derived its present name.—*Encyc. Brit.* 9th ed. It was conquered by Turks, 1474, seized by Russians, 1770, and ceded to them in 1812. The part annexed to Roumania in 1856 was restored to Russia at the peace of 1878, in exchange for Dobrudscha, by the treaty of Berlin, 13 July, and given up 21 Oct. 1878.

Bessemer. STEAM NAVIGATION, STEEL.

Bethlehem, about 6 miles from Jerusalem, is a place of great antiquity, and under the name of Ephrath is mentioned in Gen. xlviii. 7. Birthplace of David, 1085 B.C., becomes one of the world's most memorable spots as the birthplace of Christ. It now contains a large convent, enclosing, as is said, the birthplace of Christ, a church erected by the empress Helena in the form of a cross, about 325, "The Chapel of the Nativity," where the manger in which Christ was laid is shown, another, called the Chapel of St Joseph, and a third, of the Holy Innocents Bethlehem is much visited by pilgrims.

Bethnal Green, E London, Engl, a poor but populous parish, said to have been the seat of Henry de Montfort, hero of the "Blind Beggar of Bethnal Green" (Percy ballads) Many churches have been recently erected under bishop Blomfield and others, and the district has been favored by the baroness Burdett-Coutts The East London museum, a branch of that at South Kensington, was opened by the prince of Wales, 24 June, 1872. Sir Richard Wallace lent to it for a year a collection of fine pictures and valuable curiosities The gardens opened 19 May, 1875

Beverley, E Yorkshire, Engl, the Saxon Beverlac or Beverlega St. John of Beverley, archbishop of York, founded a monastery here, and died 721, and on his account the town received honors from Athelstane, William I, and other sovereigns It was disfranchised for corruption in 1870, after a long investigation

Beverly Ford, Va UNITED STATES, 1863

Beyrout' (the ancient Berytus), a seaport of Syria, colonized from Sidon It was destroyed by an earthquake, 566, was rebuilt, and was alternately possessed by the Christians and Saracens, and after many changes fell into the power of Amurath IV. It was taken during the Egyptian revolt by Ibrahim Pacha in 1832 The defeat of the Egyptian army by the allied British, Turkish, and Austrian forces, and evacuation of Beyrout (the Egyptians losing 7000 in killed, wounded, and prisoners, and 20 pieces of cannon), took place 10 Oct 1840 Sir C Napier was the English admiral Beyrout suffered from the massacres in Syria in May, 1860 In Nov 1860, above 27,000 were said to be in danger of starving SYRIA

Bianchi (Whites), a political party at Florence in 1300, in favor of the Ghibellines or imperial party, headed by Vieri de' Cerchi, opposed the Neri (or Blacks), headed by Corso de' Donati. The latter banished their opponents, among whom was Dante, in 1302 "Bianchi" were also male and female penitents, clothed in white, who travelled through Italy in Aug 1399, and were suppressed by pope Boniface IX, 1400

Biarchy. Aristodemus, king of Sparta, left twin sons, Eurysthenes and Procles, and the people, not knowing to whom precedence should be given, placed both upon the throne, and thus established the first biarchy, 1102 B.C. Their descendants reigned for about 800 years —*Herodotus*

Biberach, Würtemberg Here Moreau twice defeated the Austrians—under Latour, 2 Oct 1796, and under Kray, 9 May, 1800

Bible (from the Gr βιβλος, a book), the Holy Scriptures. The Old Testament is said to have been collected and arranged by Ezra between 458 and 450 B.C The Apocrypha are considered as inspired writings by Catholics, but not by Jews and Protestants. APOCRYPHA

The division of the Bible into chapters has been ascribed to archbishop Lanfranc in the 11th, and to archbishop Langton in the 13th century, but T Hartwell Horne refers it to cardinal Hugo de Sancto Caro, about 1250 The division into sections was commenced by rabbi Nathan (author of a concordance), about 1445, and completed by Athias a Jew, in 1661 The present division into verses was introduced by the printer Robert Stephens in his Gr Testament (1551) and in his Latin Bible (1556-57)

The original copies of the New Testament writings were probably written on papyrus rolls, and were so soon worn out by frequent use that we do not possess any historical notice of their existence MANUSCRIPTS. They must, however, have been written in uncial or large capital letters without division of words or punctuation, without accents, breathings, etc, and probably without any titles or subscriptions whatever The uncial character held its ground till about the 10th century, when the use of a cursive or running hand became general Euthalius of Alexandria, in the second half of the 5th century, divided the text into lines to suit the sense —*Encyc Brit.* 9th ed

OLD TESTAMENT		B.C.
Genesis contains the history of the world from		4004-1635
Exodus		1635-1490
Leviticus		1490
Numbers		1490-1451
Deuteronomy		1451
Job	about	1520
Joshua		1451-1420
Judges		1425-1120
Ruth		1322-1312
1st and 2d Samuel		1171-1017
1st and 2d Kings		1015- 562
1st and 2d Chronicles		1004- 536
Book of Psalms (principally by David)		1063-1015
Proverbs written	about	1000- 700
Song of Solomon	"	1014
Ecclesiastes.	"	977
Jonah	"	862
Joel	"	800
Hosea	"	785- 725
Amos	"	787
Isaiah	"	760- 698
Micah	"	750- 710
Nahum	"	713
Zephaniah	about	630
Jeremiah	"	629- 588
Lamentations	"	588
Habakkuk	"	626
Daniel	from	607- 534
Ezekiel	"	595- 574
Obadiah	about	587
Ezra	"	536- 456
Esther	"	521- 495
Haggai	"	520
Zechariah	"	520- 518
Nehemiah	"	446- 434
Malachi	"	397

NEW TESTAMENT.	A D
Gospels by Matthew, Mark, Luke, and John	5 B.C -33
Acts of the Apostles	33-65
Epistles—1st and 2d of Paul to Thessalonians.	about 54
To Galatians.	58
1st Corinthians	59
2d Corinthians	60
Romans.	"
Of James	"
1st of Peter	"
To Ephesians, Philippians, Colossians, Hebrews, Philemon	64
Titus, and 1st to Timothy	65
2d to Timothy	66
2d of Peter	"
Of Jude	"
1st, 2d, and 3d of John	after 90
Revelation	96

The most ancient copy of the Hebrew Scriptures was at Toledo, "the Codex of Hillel," it was probably of the 4th century A D, some say about 60 years before Christ. The copy of Ben Asher, of Jerusalem, was made about 1100

Probably the oldest copy of the Old and New Testaments in Greek is the *Codex Sinaiticus*, referred to the 4th century It was discovered by M Constantine Tischendorf at St. Katherine's monastery in 1844 and 1859, and presented to the czar of Russia, at whose cost a splendid edition was publ in 1862 MANUSCRIPTS

The famous *Vatican Codex*, written in the 4th or 5th century, is regarded as substantially equal to the former in antiquity and authority Mai's edition appeared 1857 The next in age is the *Alexandrian Codex* (referred to the 5th century), in the British museum, presented by the Greek patriarch to Charles I in 1628. It has been printed in England, edited by Woide and Baber, 1786-1821. *Codex Ephræmi*, or Codex Regius ascribed to 5th century, in the Royal library, Paris, publ by Tischendorf in 1843

The Hebrew psalter was printed at Bologna in 1477 The complete Hebrew Bible was first printed by Soncino in Italy in 1488, and the Greek Testament (edited by Erasmus) at Rotterdam in 1516 Aldus's edition was printed in 1518, Stephens's in 1546, and the *textus receptus* (or received text) by the Elzevirs in 1624

TRANSLATIONS.

The Old Testament, in *Greek*, termed the SEPTUAGINT, said to have been made by order of Ptolemy Philadelphus, king of Egypt, about 286 or 285 B C., of this many fabulous accounts are given

Origen, after 28 years in collating MSS., began his polyglot Bible at Cæsarea in 231 A D, including the Greek versions of Aquila, Symmachus, and Theodotion, all made in or about the 2d century A D

The following are ancient versions *Syriac*, 1st or 2d century the old *Latin* version early in the 2d century, revised by Jerome in 384, who, however completed a new version in 405, now called the VULGATE, first edition (without date) about 1456, the first dated 1462, *Coptic*, 2d or 3d century, *Ethiopic*, *Armenian* 4th or 5th century, *Slavonic*, 9th century, and the *Mæso Gothic*, by Ulfilas the apostle of the Goths, about 360 (a manuscript copy, called the Codex Argenteus, is at Upsala) MANUSCRIPTS The Psalms were translated into *Saxon* by bishop Aldhelm about 706, Cædmon's metrical paraphrase of a portion of the Bible, about 680, and the Gospels by bishop Egbert, about 721, parts of the Bible by Bede, in the 8th century A complete and literal translation of the Vulgate existed in Germany perhaps as early as the beginning of the 14th century The earliest remains of Romance versions are thought to be as old as the 11th century, but the work of translation assumed important dimensions in the 12th and 13th centuries, though the church of Rome strove to suppress it. The prohibition of the Bible in the vulgar tongue, put forth by the council of Toulouse in 1229, was repeated by other councils in various parts of the church, but failed to quell the rising interest in the Scriptures In England and in Bohemia the Bible was translated by the reforming parties of Wycliffe and Huss, and was printed not only in Latin, but in French, Spanish, Italian, German, and Dutch.

MODERN TRANSLATIONS.

	N. Test.	Bible.
Italian	—	1471
Dutch	—	1475
Flemish	—	1477
Spanish (Valencian)	—	1478
French	—	1487
Bohemian	—	1488
German	1522	1530
English	1526	1535
Swedish	1526	1541
Danish	1524	1550
Polish	1551	1561
Spanish	1543	1569
Welsh	1567	1588
Hungarian	1574	1589
Massachusetts Indians (*Eliot's*)	1661	1666
Irish	1602	1686
Georgian	—	1743
Portuguese	1712	1748
Manx	1748	1767
Turkish	1666	1814
Modern Greek	1638	1821
Russian (parts)	1519	1822
Sanscrit	1808	1822
Chinese	1814	1823

ENGLISH VERSIONS AND EDITIONS.

MS. paraphrase of the whole Bible at the Bodleian library, Oxford, dated by Usher....... 1290

Versions (from the Vulgate) by Wycliffe and his followers (above 170 MS. copies extant).......1356-84

[Part publ. by Lewis, 1731; by Baber, 1810; the whole by Madden & Forshall, at Oxford, 1850.]

William Tyndale's version of Matthew and Mark from the Greek, 1524; of the New Testament, 1525; 6 editions.....1525-30

Miles Coverdale's version of the Bible; printing finished, 4 Oct. 1535

[*Ordered by Henry VIII. to be laid in the choir of every church, "for every man that will to look and read therein."*]

T. Matthews's (said to be fictitious name for John Rogers) version (partly by Tyndale and Coverdale)....... 1537

[Tyndale was strangled and his body then burned at Antwerp, 6 Oct. 1536, at the instigation of Henry VIII. and his council.]

Cranmer's Great Bible (Matthews's revised), the first printed by authority....... 1539

Bible-reading prohibited.......1542-57

Geneva version, "Breeches Bible" (the first with figured verses), 1540-57; publ....... 1560

Archbishop Parker's, called the "Bishops' Bible" (8 of the 14 persons employed being bishops)....... 1568

Catholic authorized version; New Testament at Rheims, 1582; Old Testament at Douay.......1609-10

ENGLISH VERSION OF 1611. (KING JAMES'S BIBLE.)

The English Bible, or "authorized version," is a revision of the "Bishops' Bible," begun in 1604, and published in 1611. It arose out of a conference between the High Church and Low Church parties, held by James I. at Hampton court in 1604. The appointment of the revisers was a work of much responsibility and labor, and 5 months elapsed before they were selected and their respective portions assigned. The 47 who began the work included the leading scholars of England. These were divided into 6 committees. The following table gives the name of each committee, its president, and the work assigned it:

Committees.	Presidents.	Work.
Westminster, Heb.	Bishop Andrewes of Winchester.	Genesis-2 Kings.
Cambridge, "	Prof. Lively, regius prof. of Hebrew.	1 Chron.-Eccles.
Oxford, "	Prof. Harding, regius prof. of Hebrew, and pres. of Magdalen college.	Isaiah-Malachi.
Cambridge, Greek.	Prof. Duport, master of Jesus college, etc.	Apocrypha.
Oxford, "	Bishop Ravis of London.	Gospels, Acts, and Revelation.
Westminster, "	" Barlow of Lincoln.	Epistles.

A set of 15 rules was drawn up to guide the larger body. They comprised 3 general heads (1) To follow the "Bishops' Bible," and to alter as little as the truth of the original will permit. (2) To refrain from marginal notes. (3) To use the utmost diligence in arriving at a true interpretation, sending to any other scholar not directly engaged for his opinion or judgment. The care bestowed upon this translation is shown by the fact that parts of it passed through the committees' hands 17 times. Although the work began in 1604, it was 1611 before Robert Barker, the king's patentee, issued the first volume. Since that time millions of this revised translation have been printed.

[Dr. Benjamin Blayney's revised edition, 1769.]

Authorized Jewish English version.......1851-61

A revision of the English version was recommended by bishops in convocation, 10 Feb. 1870. The committee, eminent scholars of various denominations, appointed in May, met first at Westminster abbey, 22 June, 1870, and consisted finally of 52 members —divided into 2 companies, one for the revision of the Old, and the other of the New Testament. The American clergy and scholars were invited to co-operate. The American house of bishops (Episcopalian) declined to commit itself formally to the enterprise, not restricting, however, the free action of its members. The first meeting of the American Board was in New York, Dec. 1871. The number of American co-operating with English revisers was 32, with Philip Schaff, D.D., LL.D., president, including eminent clergy and scholars of different denominations.

Revision of New Testament completed (103d session, 407 days), 11 Nov. 1880; editions publ. 17 May, 1881. Revision of Old Testament completed, 1884; issued 19 May, 1885.

NOTED AND PECULIAR BIBLES.

Paragraph Bibles published in England by John Reeve, 1808; by the Tract Society, 1848; at Cambridge, Mass., by Dr. Coit, 1834.

Smallest Bible known ($4\frac{1}{4} \times 2 \times \frac{3}{4}$ inches; weight under $3\frac{1}{4}$ oz.), issued from Oxford University press, Oct. 1875.

"Mazarine Bible." PRINTING, BOOKS.

"Bishops' Bible," *see English Versions*, 1568.

"Breeches Bible." The Geneva Bible, often so called from the translation of Gen. iii. 7, where the word "breeches" is used instead of "aprons."

"Bug Bible," an edition of Matthews's Bible, printed in 1551, so called from the rendering of "terror" in Ps. xci. 5, as "bugges," in the sense of a frightful form.

"Wicked Bible." An edition so called from the accident of leaving the word "not" out of the seventh commandment. Similarly a Bible of 1653 omits the word "not" from St. Paul's utterance (1 Cor. vi. 9), rendering it, "Know you not that the unrighteous shall inherit the kingdom of God?"

"Vinegar Bible." So called because in Matt. xx. the "parable of the vineyard" was printed "parable of the vinegar," 1617.

"Placemakers' Bible." Matt. v. 9, was printed "Blessed are the placemakers," instead of "peacemakers."

The first Bible printed in the U. S. (aside from Eliot's Indian translation, 1661-66) was printed at Germantown, Pa., in German, by Christopher Sauer in 1743. The first in English was one at Boston by Kneeland & Green, 1752, with London imprint. First in Philadelphia, 1782, by Robert Aitken.

Bible dictionaries. The most remarkable are Calmet's "Dictionary of the Bible," 1722-28; Kitto's "Cyclopædia of Biblical Literature," 1843 and 1851; Smith's elaborate "Dictionary of the Bible," 1860-63; and McClintock and Strong's "Cyclopædia of Biblical Literature." CONCORDANCES.

Bible societies. The total number of Bibles and Testaments distributed by 80 Bible societies in the world, since the foundation of the British and Foreign Society, has been over 220,000,000 copies. The following is a partial list of the principal and oldest Bible societies:

Society for Promoting Christian Knowledge, organized....... 1698

Society for Propagating the Gospel in Foreign Parts, organized, 1701

Society in Scotland for Promoting Christian Knowledge, organized....... 1709

Society for Promoting Religious Knowledge among the Poor, organized....... 1750

Naval and Military Bible Society, organized....... 1780

Sunday-school Society, organized....... 1785

French Bible Society, organized....... 1792

British and Foreign Bible Society, begun 1803; organized....... 1804

Hibernian Bible Society, organized....... 1806

First Bible society in the U. S. organized at Philadelphia....... 1808

Connecticut Bible Society, organized at Hartford.......May, 1809

Massachusetts Bible Society, organized at Boston.......July, "

New York Bible Society, organized at New York.......Nov. "

New Jersey Bible Society, organized at Princeton, N. J.......Dec. "

Convention of 35 Bible societies meets at New York, and organizes the American Bible Society.......8-13 May, 1816

[The early presidents were:
Hon. Elias Boudinot, LL.D., elected 1816.
Hon. John Jay, " 1821.
Hon. Richard Varick, " 1831.]

A bull from pope Pius VII. against Bible societies appeared in 1817

Bible Association of Friends in America, organized....... 1828

American and Foreign Bible Society, organized....... 1837

American Bible Society, incorporated.......25 Mch. 1841

American Bible Union, organized....... 1850

Bible House at Astor place, N. Y. city, completed and occupied by American Bible Society.......May, 1853

Foundation-stone of new Central hall, of British and Foreign Bible Society, laid in Queen Victoria st., London.......11 June, 1866

Biblia Pauperum (the "Bible for the Poor"), consisting of 40 leaves printed on one side, making 20 when pasted together, and illustrated with engravings of Scripture history, the texts carved in wood—a "block book"—printed early in the 15th century, compiled by Bonaventura, general of the Franciscans, about 1260. Fac-simile published by J. Russell Smith in 1859. BOOKS.

Biblical archæology, Society for, established by Dr. Samuel Birch and others, 1871. Besides a journal, it has published "Records of the Past," translations from the Assyrian, Egyptian, and other languages, 1873-78. PALESTINE.

Bibliography, the science of books.

CATALOGUES AND BIBLIOGRAPHICAL DICTIONARIES.

Gesner's "Bibliotheca Universalis" appeared....... 1545

Ostern's "Bibliothèque Universelle" (list of printed books from 1500 to 1624).... 1625
"Bibliothèque Royale" (French) begun in 1739; 10 vols. finished, 1753
De Bure's "Bibliographie Instructive"..... 1763
Brunet's "Manuel du Libraire" (several editions), first publ.. 1810
Horne's "Introduction to the Study of Bibliography"....... 1814
Peignot's "Manuel du Bibliophile"..... 1823
Watt's "Bibliotheca Britannica"..... 1824
Ebert's "Allgemeines Bibliographisches Lexikon"........ 1830
English translation publ. in Oxford, 4 vols........ 1834
Lowndes's "Bibliographer's Manual," 1834; new ed. by Bohn, 1857–62
Querard's "La France Littéraire".....1828–64
Sampson Low's "British Catalogue".....1835–80
Allibone's "Dictionary of Authors," 1858; last ed.......... 1891
Leypoldt's "American Catalogue," 1876; 1st supplement, 1876–84; 2d.....1884–90
Sabin's "Bibliotheca Americana," 1868, still unfinished, the letter "Q" having been reached in the xcii. part, issued in 1886
Poole's "Index of Periodical Literature".....1882–87
Fletcher's "Co-operative Index to Leading Periodicals," issued quarterly..... 1884

BOOKS, PRINTING.

Bicocca, N. Italy. Lautrec and the French were here defeated by Colonna and the imperialists, 29 Apr. 1522, and Francis thereby lost his conquests in Milan.

bicycle or **velocipede.** A machine of this kind was invented by Blanchard the aeronaut, and described in the *Journal de Paris*, 27 July, 1779; and one was invented by Nicephone Niepce in 1818. The dandy-horse or "Draisena, a machine called a velocipede," was patented for baron von Drais in Paris and London in 1818, and described in "Ackerman's Repository," Feb. 1819. These machines came again into use in 1861, and since 1867 have been common in various forms. In 1869 M. Michaux of Paris conceived the idea of making the front or driving-wheel much larger than the hind wheel.

Pickwick Bicycle Club, organized in England..........about 1869
Cunningham, Heath & Co., of Boston, begin the importation of English bicycles into the United States........ 1877
Publication of the *American Bicycling Journal*, now the *Bicycling World*, the pioneer wheelman's paper, begun....... "
First bicycle manufactory in the U. S. established by A. A. Pope of Boston, Mass...... 1878
League of American Wheelmen (L. A. W.) organized at Newport.....31 May, 1880
James Stanley, inventor of the modern bicycle and tricycle, d. in England, aged 50.....June, 1881
Mr. Terry crosses the English channel on a marine bicycle; leaves Dover at 9 A.M. and arrives at Calais 5 P.M., 28 July, 1883
Safety bicycles begin to come into use.....1886–87
Thomas Stevens, American, makes a trip around the world on a bicycle. Total distance about 30,000 miles, 12,550 on his wheel. He leaves San Francisco, Cal., 22 Apr. 1884, proceeds via Boston, Liverpool, Constantinople, Meshed, returning to Constantinople, Lahore, Calcutta, Canton, Shanghai, Nagasaki, and arrives at San Francisco..........7 Jan. 1887
Providence Ladies' Cycling Club, organized 4 Feb. 1890, and the first ladies' club to join the L. A. W.............4 Mch. 1890
Pneumatic tire safety bicycles introduced into the U. S...... "
International Cyclists' Association organized, London, Engl.; Howard Raymond, American representative, elected president, and it was decided to hold the first annual competitive meeting at Chicago, Ill., during the World's Fair in 1893, 25 Nov. 1892

BICYCLE RECORDS.

Name.	Date.	Place.	Distance. miles.	yards.	Time. d.	h.	m.	sec.	Remarks.
W. J. Morgan......	20 Dec. 1886	Minneapolis, Minn..............	234	—		....			Without dismounting.
H. Higham........	18 Mch. 1880	Agricultural hall, London, Engl...	230.25	—	—	16	59	30	" "
G. P. Mills.........	4–8 Oct. 1891	....	867	—		....			Without sleep in his ride from Land's End to John O'Groat's.

BEST TRACK RECORDS (Safety).

Name.	Date.	Place.	Distance. miles.	yards.	Time. d.	h.	m.	sec.	Remarks.
J. S. Johnson......	31 Oct. 1893	Independence, Ia...............	.25	—	—	—	—	24.4	Amateur, against time (kite track).
H. C. Tyler........	4 Sept. "	Hartford, Conn.................	.25	—	—	—	—	25.8	Amateur, in competition (oval track).
W. C. Sanger......	19 June, "	London, Engl..................	.25	—	—	—	—	27.8	Amateur, against time.
M. F. Dirnberger...	18 Nov. "	Nashville, Tenn.................	.5	—	—	—	—	54	" flying start with pace-maker.
J. S. Johnson......	30 Oct. "	Independence, Ia...............	.5	—	—	—	—	55	Amateur, flying start against time (kite track).
W. W. Windle......	26 Oct. "	Springfield, Mass...............	.5	—	—	—	—	55.8	Amateur, against time (oval track).
A. A. Zimmerman..	6 Sept. 1892	Hartford, Conn.................	.5	—	—	—	1	01.8	Amateur, in competition.
J. S. Prince........	6 Oct. 1893	London, Engl..................	.5	—	—	—	1	05.4	Professional, against time.
J. S. Johnson......	28 Sept. 1894	Waltham, Mass................	1	—	—	—	1	50.6	Amateur, flying start with pacer.
" "	24 Oct. "	Buffalo, N. Y..................	1	—	—	—	1	35.4	" " "
" "	9 Nov. 1893	Independence, Ia...............	1	—	—	—	1	58.2	Amateur, standing start against time.
W. W. Windle......	11 Oct. "	Springfield, Mass...............	1	—	—	—	1	56.8	Amateur, flying start against time.
A. W. Harris.......	2 Oct. "	London, Engl..................	1	—	—	—	2	04.2	Amateur, against time.
W. W. Windle......	17 Oct. "	Springfield, Mass...............	3	—	—	—	6	43	" " "
F. Pope...........	26 Oct. "	London, Engl..................	3	—	—	—	6	53.4	" " "
L. S. Meintjes......	11 Sept. "	Springfield, Mass...............	5	—	—	—	11	09.6	" " "
F. Pope...........	26 Oct. "	London, Engl..................	5	—	—	—	11	33.2	" " "
W. H. Penseyres & C. W. Dorntage...	21 July, 1892	Baltimore, Md..................	5	—	—	—	12	14.8	Tandem, against time.
G. E. Osmond & J. W. Stocks......	1 Sept. 1893	London, Engl..................	5	—	—	—	11	17.2	" " "
L. S. Meintjes......	14 Sept. "	Springfield, Mass...............	10	—	—	—	23	04.6	Amateur, against time.
J. W. Stocks.......	30 Aug. "	London, Engl..................	10	—	—	—	23	20	" " "
L. S. Meintjes......	14 Sept. "	Springfield, Mass...............	15	—	—	—	34	37	" " "
J. W. Stocks.......	30 Aug. "	London, Engl..................	15	—	—	—	35	20.6	" " "
L. S. Meintjes......	14 Sept. "	Springfield, Mass...............	25	—	—	—	57	40.6	" " "
J. W. Stocks.......	30 Aug. "	London, Engl..................	25	—	—	—	59	06.8	" " "
H. Fournier........	13 Aug. 1892	Paris, France..................	25	—	—	1	01	21	Professional, against time.
J. W. Stocks.......	30 Aug. 1893	London, Engl..................	50	—	—	2	05	45.6	Amateur, against time.
L. S. Meintjes......	12 Aug. "	Springfield, Mass...............	50	—	—	2	11	06.8	" " "
Jules Dubois......	17 Sept. 1892	Paris, France..................	50	—	—	2	11	10	Professional, against time.
A. Linton.........	21 Oct. 1893	London, Engl..................	100	—	—	4	29	39.2	Amateur, against time.
F. Waller..........	11 June, 1892	Alameda, Cal..................	100	—	—	5	45	—	Professional, against time.
A. Linton.........	7 Oct. 1893	London, Engl..................	200	—	—	10	01	—	Amateur, against time.
F. E. Spooner......	8–9 July, 1892	Chicago, Ill....................	200	—	—	11	47	15	" " "
F. W. Shoreland...	21–22 July, 1893	London, Engl..................	300	—	—	16	30	21	" " "
F. E. Spooner......	8–9 July, 1892	Chicago, Ill....................	300	—	—	18	29	28	" " "
F. W. Shoreland...	21–22 July, 1893	London, Engl..................	400	—	—	22	43	04.8	" " "
" " ...	" " "	" "	426	440	—	24	—	—	" " "

BICYCLE RECORDS.

BEST TRACK RECORDS (Safety).—*Continued.*

Name.	Date.	Place.	Distance. miles.	Distance. laps.	Time. d.	Time. h.	Time. m.	Time. sec.	Remarks.
Wm. Martin.......	18-24 Oct. 1892	Madison square, N. Y...........	1466	4	6	—	—	—	6 days' race.
Ashinger.........	" " "	" "	1441	1	6	—	—	—	" " "
Lamb.............	" " "	" "	1342	—	6	—	—	—	" " "
Shock............	" " "	" "	1327	5	6	—	—	—	" " "

BEST ROAD RECORDS (Safety).

Name.	Date.	Place.	Distance.	Time. d.	Time. h.	Time. m.	Time. sec.	Remarks.
C. T. Knisely......	24 June, 1893	Louisville, Ky..................	10 miles.	—	—	26	20	Amateur.
W. B. Hurlburt....	" "	Detroit, Mich..................	15 "	—	—	43	18	"
" "	" "	" "	20 "	—	—	57	46	"
H. B. James.......	20 Sept. "	Melbourne, Sydney R'd, Australia.	25 "	—	1	01	—	"
W. B. Hurlburt....	24 June, "	Detroit, Mich..................	25 "	—	1	11	59	"
E. Oxborrow.......	1 Nov. "	Great North Road, Engl.........	25 "	—	1	04	—	Professional.
A. Pellant.........	23 Oct. "	" " " "	50 "	—	2	21	46	Amateur.
F. A. Foell........	26 Aug. "	Buffalo, N. Y..................	50 "	—	2	32	20	"
Miss Dudley.......	12 Sept. 1892	Great North Road, Engl.........	53 "	—	3	19	30	"
E. Hale...........	21 Oct. 1893	" " " "	100 "	—	5	12	02	Amateur.
J. W. Linnemann..	22 Oct. "	Newark, N. J...................	100 "	—	5	37	15	"
Miss Dudley.......	12 Sept. 1892	Great North Road, Engl.........	100 "	—	7	12	04	"
L. Fletcher........	4-5 Sept. 1893	England........................	1000 "	4	23	30	—	Amateur.
H. R. Goodwin.....	1-19 June, 1886	Land's End to John O'Groat's and back, and then to London.....	2054 "	19	—	—	—	"

Biddenden maids. A distribution of bread and cheese to the poor takes place at Biddenden, Kent, on Easter Mondays, supported by the rental of 20 acres of land, in 1875 yielding about 20*l.*, the reputed bequest of two Biddenden maids, sisters named Chulkhurst, joined like the Siamese twins, who died in the 12th century. In 1656, William Horner, the rector, was nonsuited in an attempt to add the "Bread and Cheese lands" to his glebe.

Big Bethel, Va., Battle of, fought 10 June, 1861. Gen. Pierce attacked the confederates in their fortifications, and was repulsed, after a partial success, losing about 40 men. Among them maj. Theodore Winthrop, killed, author of "Cecil Dreeme," "John Brent," etc.

Big Black River, Miss., Battle of. Here the confederates, under Pemberton, made their last stand before retiring into Vicksburg, 17 May, 1863. They were driven from their position and retired into Vicksburg on the 18th. VICKSBURG CAMPAIGN.

bigamy. The Romans branded bigamists with an infamous mark; and in England the punishment, formerly, was death. An act respecting it was passed 5 Edw. I. 1276.—*Viner's Statutes.* Made felony, without benefit of clergy, 1 James I. 1603. Punishable by imprisonment or transportation, 35 Geo. III. 1794; by imprisonment, 24 and 25 Vict. c. 100 (1861). In the United States, by imprisonment.

Bilbao, N.E. Spain, founded about 1300; taken by the French and held a few days, July, 1795; delivered from Carlists by Espartero, assisted by British, 24 Dec. 1836; besieged by Carlists from Feb. to May, 1874; relieved by marshal Concha, who entered Bilbao 2 May.

bill of exceptions. The right of excepting by bill to errors in a judge's charge, or any definition of the law, at a trial provided by the 2d statute of Westminster, 13 Edw. I. 1284, was abolished by the Judicature act, 1875. The practice is maintained in American courts.

bill of rights. The Convention Parliament that gave the crown of England to William and Mary adopted a bill of rights, 13 Feb. 1689, which the new monarchs confirmed by their signatures. It asserted the right of subjects to petition; the right of Parliament to freedom of debate; the right of electors to choose representatives freely, and other privileges. This bill of rights contained the fundamental principles of political liberty, yet the crown would not apply them to the American colonists. Had the bill of rights been extended to the American colonies the principal cause of their final separation would have been removed.

billiards. The origin of the game is uncertain; it was introduced into Europe by knights templars on their return from the first crusade (about 1100), and brought into France in the time of Louis XI. (1461-83).

Billiard-tables with bed of stone covered with cloth, made by Henrique de Vigne, of Paris............................about 1571
M. Mingaud, of Paris, invents the leather-tipped cue.......... 1823
Slate billiard-tables introduced into England.................. 1827
Michael Phelan (American) invents the improved vulcanized rubber cushion.. 1854
First public match of importance in the U. S. at San Francisco, Michael Phelan defeats M. Damon (French).............Feb. 1855
First billiard tournament in New York........................ 1860

BEST BILLIARD RECORDS, 5×10 TABLE.

Three-ball, straight rail. Highest average 333⅓, Jacob Schaefer, Music hall, Chicago, game with George F. Slosson ...15 May, 1879
Three-ball, straight rail. Highest run 1531, by Maurice Vignaux, at Paris, against George F. Slosson..........10-14 Apr. 1880
Cushion carroms, highest run 77, made by William Sexton at Tammany Hall, N.Y., against Jacob Schaefer.........19 Dec. 1881
Champion's game (corner-play barred), highest run 398, made by George F. Slosson at Paris, against Maurice Vignaux, 30 Jan.-3 Feb. 1882
Highest run in America, J. R. Heiser, 351, New York city, in contest with Ed. McLaughlin.......................11 Feb. 1884
Balk-line (8 in.), highest run 329, made by Maurice Vignaux at Paris...Jan. "
Balk-line (14 in.), highest run 230, by Jacob Schaefer at Cosmopolitan Hall, N. Y., against Maurice Vignaux..8-13 Mch. 1886
Three-ball, straight rail; table, 4½×9. Harvey McKenna, highest run 2572 points; game with F. Eames; average, 416⅔, Boston.......................................20, 21 Dec. 1887
[Tables of this size are, however, barred from records.]
Amateur championship of the U. S. and a silver tankard valued at $1000, won by Orville Oddie, Jr., at New York Racquet Club....................................23-28 May, "
Jacob Schaefer (800) beat George F. Slosson (592), match for championship at 14-inch balk-line, New York city...22 Jan. 1892
Frank C. Ives (800) beat Jacob Schaefer (499), 14-inch balk-line, championship, Chicago, Ill...........................19 Mch. "
Frank C. Ives (800) beat Geo. F. Slosson (488), balk-line billiards, Chicago, Ill.......................................21 May, "
Frank C. Ives beat John Roberts at London, Engl., game of 6000 points, in 6 days, 1000 at each meeting; spot and push shots barred. Ives won by 2100 points; highest run, 1540. Roberts highest run, 249..........................29 May-3 June, 1893
Frank C. Ives beat John Roberts at Chicago, Ill. Game, 6000 points; table, 6×12, with pockets; spot and push shots barred. Ives won by 698 points; highest run, 434. Roberts highest run, 166..................................Sept. 18-24, "

Billingsgate, the fish-market in London, is said to be named from Belinus Magnus, a British prince, father of king Lud, 400 B.C., but Stow thinks from a former owner. It was the old port of London, and customs were paid here under Ethelred II., 979 A.D.—*Stow.* Billingsgate was made a free market, 1699.

bills of exchange were invented by the Jews as a means of removing property from nations where they were persecuted, 1160.—*Anderson.* Said to have been used in England, 1307. The only legal mode of sending money from England, 4 Richard II. 1381. Regulated, 1698; first stamped, 1782; duty advanced, 1797; again, June, 1801; and since. It was made capital to counterfeit them in 1734. In 1825, the year of "bubble" speculation, it was computed that there were 400,000,000*l.* represented by bills of exchange and promissory notes. Days of grace were abolished in Great Britain for sight bills of exchange in Aug. 1871; in New York, Jan. 1895. For the laws and regulations in force in the U. S., see Harper's "Cyclopædia of Commerce," p. 167 et seq.

bimetallism, the system of 2 standard metallic currencies in a country—gold and silver—advocated by MM. H. Cernuschi and E. Lavellye and others since 1867. By

56 Geo. III. c. 68 (1816), "gold coins only should be legal-tender in all payments of more than 40s." in Great Britain. A bimetallic currency was established in France in 1803; was recommended for Germany in 1879, and discussed at the monetary conference at Paris, Apr. 1881. A conference of delegates from the United States and the principal countries of Europe on bimetallism met at Brussels, Belgium, 22 Nov. 1892. The proposals and views of the various countries were so divergent that no satisfactory method could be decided upon, and the conference suspended its sittings 17 Dec., and adjourned to 13 May, 1893. The tendency of the conference was unfavorable to bimetallism. SILVER.

binary arithmetic, counting by twos, used in ascertaining the property of numbers and constructing tables, was invented by Leibnitz of Leipsic, about 1703. For the binary theory in chemistry, COMPOUND RADICAL.

binomial expression, in algebra, composed of 2 terms connected with the sign + (plus) or − (minus); a term first used by Recorde about 1557, when he published his "Algebra." The binomial theorem of Newton is said to have been first presented in 1666. ALGEBRA.

biography (Gr. βίος, life, and γράφω, I write), defined as "history teaching by example." Genesis contains the biography of the patriarchs, the Gospels that of Christ. Plutarch wrote the "Lives of Illustrious Men;" Cornelius Nepos, "Lives of Military Commanders;" and Suetonius, "Lives of the Twelve Cæsars" (all three in the first century after Christ); Diogenes Laertius, "Lives of the Philosophers" (about 205).—Boswell's "Life of Johnson" (published 1790), Stanley's "Life of Dr. Arnold" (London, 1845), and Trevelyan's "Life and Letters of Lord Macaulay" (London, 1878), are perhaps the most famous of British biographies.

Chalmers's "Biographical Dictionary," 32 vols. 1812–17
"Nouvelle Biographie Générale," 46 vols. 1852–66
Appleton's "Cyclopædia of American Biography," 6 vols. imp. octavo 1887
Stephen's "Dictionary of National Biography" (Engl.) begun 1885; vol. xxxiv. L.–M., June, 1893. Now (1893) edited by Sidney Lee.

biology, the science of life and living things, so called by Treviranus, of Bremen, in his work on physiology, published 1802–22, includes ZOÖLOGY, ANTHROPOLOGY, and ETHNOLOGY. Herbert Spencer's "Principles of Biology," published 1865–67. T. H. Huxley, "Practical Instruction in Biology," 1875.

In 1831 about 70,000 animals were known and described; in 1881, about 320,000.

birds were divided by Linnæus into 6 orders (1735); by Blumenbach into 8 (1805); and by Cuvier into 6 (1817). Works on birds published by John Gould, F.R.S., consist of nearly 40 folio volumes of colored plates, etc., and include the birds of Europe, Asia, Australia, Great Britain, and New Guinea, besides monographs of humming-birds, etc. John Gould died 3 Feb. 1881. Dr. John Latham's "Synopsis of Birds," 1781–90. John James Audubon's "Birds of America," 1826–40, 4 vols.; later edition, 1869.

Alexander Wilson's great work partially finished; 1st vol. appeared in 1808; 2d in 1810. Work continued by Charles Lucien Bonaparte, 4 vols. 4to, Phila. (1825–33).
British Ornithologists' Union, founded 1858; published the *Ibis*, 1859 et seq.
A morphological classification of birds (based on Huxley's), by professors Parker and Newton; "Encyclopædia Britannica," 9th ed. 1878
International Congress of Ornithologists; 1st meeting at Vienna, Apr. 7–11, 1884; 2d congress met at Buda-Pesth. . May 17, 1891

Birmingham, formerly **Bromwicham** and **Brummegem,** Warwickshire, Engl., existed in the reign of Alfred, 872; and belonged to the Bermengehams, at Domesday Survey, 1086. There were "many smythes" here in the time of Henry VIII. (*Leland*), but its importance began in the reign of William III. Pop. 1891, 429,171.

Grammar-school founded by Edward VI. 1552
Besieged and taken by prince Rupert 1643
Button manufactures established 1689
Soho works established by Matthew Boulton about 1764; and steam-engine works about 1774
Birmingham canal originated 1767
Dr. Ash's hospital founded, 1766; first Birmingham musical festival for it 1768
Riots against Dr. Priestley and others commemorating the French revolution .... 14 July, 1791
Birmingham made a borough by reform act (2 members) 1832
Birmingham and Liverpool "Grand Junction" railway opened, 4 July, 1837
Railway to London opened .... 17 Sept. 1838
Town incorporated, and police act passed 1839
Corn exchange opened .... 27 Oct. 1847
Queen's college organized .... Jan. 1853
Free library opened .... 4 Apr. 1861
Meeting of National Social Science Association .... 7 Oct. 1868
Erdington orphan-houses endowed by Josiah Mason, steel-pen manufacturer; begun 1858; finished .... July, 1869
National Education League meet .... 12, 13 Oct. "
Sir Josiah Mason (knighted 1872) endows a college for practical science 1873
Statue of Priestley (in commemoration of his discovery of oxygen) unveiled by prof. Huxley .... 1 Aug. 1874
Foundation of sir Josiah Mason's college laid by himself and Mr. Bright .... 23 Feb. 1875
Wm. Dudley bequeaths 100,000*l.* for charitable purposes in Birmingham .... Mch. 1876
Birmingham Liberal Federation formed .... May, June, 1877
Central library, chief free reference library, with the Shakespeare library, Cervantes collection, etc., priceless treasures, destroyed by fire .... 11 Jan. 1879
Death of sir Josiah Mason .... 16 June, 1881
Statue of queen Victoria, by T. Woolner (to accompany that of the prince consort, by Foley), in the free library, uncovered, 9 May, 1884
Birmingham created a city .... 14 Jan. 1889
Death of John Bright, M.P. .... 27 Mch. "
His son, J. Albert Bright, elected his successor as M.P., 15 Apr. "

births were taxed in England, viz.: of a duke, 30*l.*; of a common person, 2*s.*, 7 Will. III. 1695. Taxed again, 1783. Instances of 4 children at a birth are numerous; it is recorded that a woman of Königsberg (3 Sept. 1784), and the wife of Nelson, a tailor, of Oxford Market, London (Oct. 1800), had 5 children at a birth. Queen Victoria presents a small sum to a poor woman bearing 3 or more living children at once.

bishop (Gr. ἐπίσκοπος, *overseer*), a name given by the Athenians to inspectors of the city. The Jews and Romans had like officers. St. Peter, styled first bishop of Rome, was martyred 65. Presbyter was the same as bishop.—*Jerome.* The episcopate became an object of contention about 144. The title of pope was anciently assumed by all bishops, and exclusively claimed by Gregory VII. (1073–85).

bishops in England were coeval with Christianity. The see of London is mythically said to have been founded by Lucius, king of Britain, 179.

Bishops have the title of Right Rev. the Lord Bishop of ——. The archbishops of Canterbury and York, taking precedence of dukes, have the title of The Most Rev. His Grace the Lord Archbishop of ——. The bishops of London, Durham, and Winchester have precedence of other bishops; the others rank according to seniority of consecration.
Bishops made barons 1072
Intervention of the pope in regard to bishops, 13th century.
The *congé d'élire* of the king to choose a bishop originated in an arrangement by king John.
Bishops elected by the king's *congé d'élire*, 25 Hen. VIII. 1534
Bishops to rank as barons by stat. Hen. VIII. 1540
Seven deprived for marriage 1554
Several martyred under queen Mary (PROTESTANTS) 1555–56
Bishops excluded from voting in the house of peers on temporal concerns, 16 Char. I. 1641
Several protest against legality of acts passed while they are deprived of votes, 28 Dec.; committed to Tower ..... 30 Dec. "
Order of archbishops and bishops abolished by the Parliament .... 9 Oct. 1646
Bishops regain their seats .... Nov. 1661
Seven bishops (Canterbury, Bath, Chichester, St. Asaph, Bristol, Ely, and Peterborough) sent to Tower for not reading the king's declaration for liberty of conscience (intended to give Catholics ecclesiastical and civil power), 8 June; tried and acquitted .... 29, 30 June, 1688
Archbishop of Canterbury (Dr. Sancroft) and 5 bishops (Bath and Wells, Ely, Gloucester, Norwich, and Peteborough) suspended for rejecting oaths to William and Mary, 1689; deprived 1690
Retirement of bishops: the bishops of London and Durham retired on annuities 1856
Bishop of Norwich resigned 1857
The Bishops' Resignation (for infirmity) act (authorizing the appointment of bishop coadjutors), passed, 11 Aug. 1869; made perpetual by act .... 14 June, 1875
Bishopric of St. Albans created, dioceses of London, Winchester, and Rochester rearranged, 38 and 39 Vict. c. 34, 29 June, "
Bishopric of Truro founded, 39 and 40 Vict. c. 54 ...... 11 Aug. 1876
The Bishoprics act, 41 and 42 Vict. c. 68, authorizes 4 new bishoprics—Liverpool, Newcastle, Wakefield (York), and Southwell (Canterbury). Number of bishops in Parliament not to be increased .... 16 Aug. 1878

ENGLISH BISHOPRICS.

Sees.	Founded.	Sees.	Founded.
YORK (*abpc.*)	4th cent.	Llandaff	5th cent.
Sodor and Man	"	St. David's	"

Sees	Founded	Sees	Founded
Bangor .	about 516	Cornwall (afterwards Devonshire, afterwards Exeter, 1050) . .	909
St Asaph	" 560	Wells	"
CANTERBURY (*abpc*)	598	Bath	1088
Rochester	604	Ely	1108
London	609	Carlisle	1132
East Anglia (afterwards Norwich, 1091)	630	Peterborough	1541
Lindisfarne or Holy Island (afterwards Durham 995),	634	Gloucester	"
West Saxons (afterwards Winchester, 705)	635	Bristol	1542
Mercia (afterwards Lichfield, 669)	656	Chester	"
Hereford	676	Oxford	"
Worcester	680	Ripon .	1836
Lindisse (afterwards Lincoln, 1067)	"	Manchester	1847
Sherborne (afterwards Salisbury, 1042) .	705	St Albans	. 1876
		Truro	1877
		Newcastle, authorized	1878
		Southwell "	"
		Liverpool ..	1880

bishops in Ireland are said to have been consecrated in the 2d century CHURCH OF IRELAND

Prelacies constituted, and divisions of bishoprics in Ireland by cardinal Paparo legate of pope Eugene III 1151
Several prelates deprived by queen Mary 1554
Bishop Atherton suffered death ignominiously 1640
Two bishops deprived for refusing oaths to William and Mary, 1691
Church Temporalities act, reducing number of bishops in Ireland 3 and 4 Will IV c 37, passed . 14 Aug 1833

[Of the 4 archbishoprics of Armagh Dublin Tuam, and Cashel, the last 2 were made to terminate at the deaths of the incumbents, 8 of the then 18 bishoprics should as they became void, be united to other sees which was completed in 1850 The Irish church at present has 2 archbishops (Armagh and Dublin) and 10 bishops]

Sees	Founded	Sees	Founded
Ossory	402	Ferns	about 598
Trim	432	Cloyne	before 604
Killala	about 434	Cork .	about 606
Armagh, 445, *abpc*	1152	Glandalough	before 612
Emly	about 448	Derry .	before 618
·blin .	450	Kilmacduach	about 620
·dagh	454	Lismore .	" 631
Clogher	before 493	Leighlin	632
·wn	about 499	Mayo .	about 665
·dfert and Aghadoe,	before 500	Raphoe .	before 885
·nnor	about "	Cashel, before 901, *abpc*	1152
·am, about 501, *apbc*	1152	Killaloe (*abpc*)	1019
·omore	about 510	Waterford	1096
·ldare	before 519	Limerick	before 1106
·eath	520	Kilmore	1136
·chonry .	530	Dublin (*abpc*)	1152
·outh .	531	Kilfenora	before 1254
Clonmacnois	548	[For the new combinations see the separate articles]	
Clonfert	558		
Ross	about 570		

bishops in Scotland were probably nominated in the 4th century.

The Reformers, self styled "the Congregation of the Lord," having in arms defeated the queen mother. Mary of Guise, called a parliament, which set up a new church polity on the Genevese model, replacing bishops by "superintendents" 1561
Episcopacy restored by regent Morton 1572-73
Three Scottish prelates consecrated at Lambeth (John Spottiswood, Gawin Hamilton, and Andrew Lamb) for Glasgow, Galloway, and Brechin 21 Oct 1610
Episcopacy abolished the bishops deposed, 4 excommunicated by parliament elected by the people (Covenanters), at Glasgow Dec 1638
Episcopacy restored, archbishop (James Sharp) and 3 bishops consecrated by Sheldon, bishop of London 15 Dec 1661
Scottish convention expels the bishops, abolishes episcopacy, declares throne vacant, draws up a claim of right, proclaims William and Mary 11 Apr 1689
Episcopacy abolished, the bishops' revenues sequestrated, 19 Sept "
The Episcopal church was thus reduced to a Nonconformist body, at first barely tolerated Its first congress met 19 May, 1874
Bishop Rose connected the old Episcopal church of Scotland with later tolerated form of it, he was bishop of Edinburgh from 1687 till 1720 when, on his death, Dr Fullarton became the first post revolution bishop of that see Fife (St. Andrews, so called in 1844) now unites the bishopric of Dunkeld (reinstituted in 1727) and that of Dunblane (reinstituted in 1731) Ross (of uncertain date) was united to Moray (reconstituted in 1727) in 1838 Argyll and the Isles never existed independently until 1847, having been conjoined to Moray and Ross or to Ross alone, previously to that year Galloway has been added to the see of Glasgow

Sees	Founded	Sees	Founded.
Orkney .	Uncertain	Aberdeen . .	. 1125
Isles . .	360	Dunkeld .	1130
Galloway	before 500	Dunblane	before 1153
St. Andrews, 800, *abpc*	1470	Argyll	1200
Glasgow, about 560, *abpc*	1488	Edinburgh	1633
Caithness	about 1066		
Brechin .	before 1155	POST-REVOLUTION BISHOPS.	
Moray .	1115	Edinburgh	1720
Ross	1124	Aberdeen and the Isles	1721

Sees	Founded	Sees	Founded.
Moray (and Ross), primus	1727	St. Andrews (Dunkeld, Dunblane, etc.)	1733
Brechin	1731	Argyll and the Isles	1847
Glasgow (and Galloway)	"		

Roman Catholic bishoprics revived by pope Leo XIII 4 Mch 1878
Scotch Protestant bishops protest. 13 Apr "

bishops, British colonial, etc. By 15 and 16 Vict c 52 (1852), and 16 and 17 Vict c. 49 (1853), colonial bishops may perform all episcopal functions in the United Kingdom, but have no jurisdiction

Between 1847-59, Miss (now baroness) Burdett Coutts gave 60,000*l.* to endow colonial bishoprics In 1866 she petitioned Parliament, because some of the bishops claimed independence of the church of England Colonial bishops are since appointed without intervention of the civil power Much discussion took place in 1867, through the deposition of Dr Colenso bishop of Natal, by his metropolitan, Dr Gray, bishop of Cape Town and the attempts of the latter to consecrate a new bishop, in opposition to the law AFRICA, CHURCH OF ENGLAND

Nova Scotia	1787	Nelson N Z	1858
Quebec	1793	Brisbane, Queensland	1859
Calcutta	1814	British Columbia	"
Barbadoes	1824	Goulbourn, N S. W	"
Jamaica	"	St. Helena	"
Madras	1835	Waiapu, N Z	"
Australia (SYDNEY)	1836	Ontario, Canada	1861
Montreal	"	Nassau, Bahamas	"
Bombay	1837	Grafton, Australia	1863
Newfoundland	1839	Dunedin, N Z	1866
Toronto	"	Maritzburg S Africa	1869
Gibraltar	1841	Auckland, N Z.	"
New Zealand (CHRISTCHURCH)	"	Bathurst	"
		Huron	. 1871
Antigua	1842	Trinidad	1872
Guiana S America .	"	Ballarat . .	"
Huron, Canada	"	Moosonee	"
Tasmania	"	Algoma	1873
Colombo Ceylon	1845	St. John's, Kaffraria	"
Fredericton, N B	"	Athabasca	. 1874
Adelaide, S Australia	1847	Saskatchewan ..	"
Cape Town	"	Niagara.	1875
Melbourne	"	Rangoon	1877
Newcastle, N S W	"	Transvaal	"
Sydney (metrop of Australia)	"	Lahore	"
		North Queensland	1878
Rupert's Land	1849	Travancore and Cochin	1879
Victoria, Hong Kong	"	New Caledonia (British Columbia)	"
Sierra Leone	1852		
Graham s Town	1853	New Westminster	"
Natal, S Africa	"	Mid China	1880
Mauritius	1854	Riverina	1883
Labuan	1855	Mackenzie River	1884
Christchurch, N Z.	1856	Qu'Appelle .	"
Perth, W Australia	"	Chota Nagpur	1890
Wellington, N Z	1858	Selkirk	1891

MISSIONARY BISHOPS

Jerusalem	1841	Bloemfontein	1870
Melanesia.	1860	Zululand .	1871
Honolulu	1861	North China	1872
Zanzibar and Central Africa,	1863	Japan	1883
Niger Territory	1864	E Equatorial Africa	1884
Falkland Isles	1869	Corea	1889
Madagascar	1870	Cochin	1890

bishops, Episcopal, in the United States The first was Samuel Seabury, consecrated bishop of Connecticut at Aberdeen, Scotland, by the nonjuring bishops Kilgour, Petrie, and Skinner, 14 Nov 1784. William White, of Pennsylvania and Samuel Provoost, of New York, consecrated bishops in the chapel of Lambeth palace, London, Engl 4 Feb 1787, by the archbishop of Canterbury assisted by the archbishop of York, the bishop of Bath and Wells, and the bishop of Peterborough James Madison, consecrated bishop of Virginia 19 Sept 1790, in the chapel of Lambeth palace, by the archbishop of Canterbury, assisted by the bishop of London and Rochester Madison was the third and last bishop consecrated by bishops of the Anglican church Thomas John Claggett, consecrated bishop of Maryland, 1792, in Trinity church, N Y, by bishop Provoost, assisted by bishops Seabury, White, and Madison, first consecration of a bishop in the U. S CHURCH, METHODISM in the U. S., 1784-87.

bishops, suffragan, to assist metropolitans, existed in the early church 26, appointed by Henry VIII 1534, were abolished by Mary 1553, and restored by Elizabeth, 1558. The last appointed is said to have been Sterne, bishop of Colchester, 1606 The appointment of suffragan bishops was revived in 1869, and archdeacon Henry Mackenzie, suffragan bishop of Nottingham (diocese of Lincoln) was consecrated 2 Feb 1870 and archdeacon Edward Parry, suffragan bishop of Dover (diocese of Canterbury), 23 Mch 1870 Others have been appointed since: Guildford, 1874, Bedford, 1879

bismuth, recognized as a distinct metal by Agricola in 1529, is fusible and brittle, and of a yellowish-white color

bissextile. CALENDAR, LEAP-YEAR

Bithynia, a province in Asia Minor, previously called *Bebricia*, is said to have been invaded by the Thracians under Bithynus, son of Zeus, who gave it its name It was subject successively to Assyrians, Lydians, Persians, and Macedonians Most of the cities were rebuilt by Grecian colonists

	B C
Dydalsus revolted and reigned	about 440-430
Botyras, his son succeeds	378
Bas, or Bias son of Botyras, 376, repulses the Greeks.	328
Zipætes, son of Bias, resists Lysimachus	326
He dies leaving 4 sons of whom the eldest, Nicomedes I succeeds (he invites the Gauls into Asia)	278
He rebuilds Astacus, and names it Nicomedia	264
Zielas, son of Nicomedes, reigns	about 250
Intending to massacre the chiefs of the Gauls at a feast Zielas is detected, is himself put to death, and his son Prusias I made king	about 228
Prusias defeats the Gauls, and takes cities	223
Prusias allies with Philip of Macedon, and marries Apamea, his daughter	208
He receives and employs Hannibal then a fugitive, 187, who poisons himself to escape betrayal to the Romans	183
Prusias II succeeds	180
Nicomedes II kills his father Prusias and reigns	149
Nicomedes III surnamed Philopator	91
Deposed by Mithridates, king of Pontus	88
Restored by the Romans	84
Bequeaths his kingdom to the Romans	74
	A D
Pliny the Younger proconsul	103
Oghusian Tartars settle in Bithynia	1231
Othman Turks take Prusa, the capital, and fix their court here till they possess Constantinople	1327

Bitonto, Naples. Here Montemar and the Spaniards, defeating the Germans, 27 May, 1734, acquired the kingdom of the Two Sicilies for don Carlos

black art. ALCHEMY, WITCHCRAFT

Black Book (*Liber Niger*), a book in the exchequer, which held the orders of the court, publ by Hearne in 1728

A book doubtfully said to have been kept in monasteries, wherein details of enormities practised in religious houses were entered for inspection of visitors, under Hen VIII 1535 The name was given to the list of pensioners, printed 1831, and to other books, ITALY, 1876 The title "Black Book" was given to a list of habitual criminals, 1869-76, pub by lieut col Du Cane of Brixton Engl, Mch 1877

black death. PLAGUES, 1347.

Black Flags. TONQUIN

Black Friars. DOMINICANS

Black Friday, 11 May, 1866, the height of the commercial panic in London, through the stoppage of Overend, Gurney & Co (limited), on 10 May. Messrs John Henry and Edmund Gurney and their partners, committed for trial for conspiracy to defraud, 21 Jan 1869, were tried and acquitted, 13-23 Dec 1869 In the United States the term Black Friday is applied to Friday, 24 Sept 1869, when a group of speculators in New York advanced the price of gold suddenly to 162½, causing a panic

Black Hawk war, the, was an outbreak of the Sacs and Foxes, under the leadership of Black Hawk, one of their chiefs, in 1832 The encroachment of whites on their territory was the principal cause Black Hawk resisted the survey of the land at Rock Island, Ill, although most of the Sacs and Foxes were west of the Mississippi. The trouble commenced in 1831, and after several skirmishes culminated at the battle of Bad Axe river, Wis, 1-2 Aug 1832 Shortly after, Black Hawk was captured by a party of friendly Indians, and taken to the principal cities of the East, to impress him with the greatness of the country He died in 1838

Black Prince, Edward, eldest son of king Edward III, born 15 June, 1330, victor at Poictiers, 19 Sept 1356, at Najara, 3 Apr 1367, died 8 June, 1376

Black Republican, a term of reproach applied to members of the Republican party by the Democrats and Southerners 1856-70, for their advocacy of the abolition of slavery and rights of the blacks.

Black Rock. BUFFALO, NEW YORK, 1813.

black rod with a gold lion at top, is carried by the usher of the Knights of the Garter (instituted 1349), instead of the mace He also keeps the door when a chapter of the order is sitting, and during the sessions of Parliament attends the lords and acts as messenger to the commons

Black sea, the **Euxine** (*Pontus Euxinus* of the ancients), a large inland sea between the S W provinces of Russia and Asia Minor, connected with the sea of Azof by the strait of Yenikale, and with that of Marmora by the Bosporus. It is about 720 miles in length, and 380 in breadth Its total area, including the Sea of Azof (14,000 sq miles) is about 172,500 sq miles

It was much frequented by Greeks and Italians, till closed to all by the Turks after the fall of Constantinople	1453
Russians obtained admission by treaty of Kainardji 10 July,	1774
Partly opened to British and other traders (since when the Russians gradually obtained the preponderance)	1779
Entered by British and French fleets on requisition of the Porte after destruction of Turkish fleet at Sinope by Russians, 30 Nov 1853 3 Jan	1854
Black sea opened to commerce by treaty of	1856
A treaty was signed by all parties to the treaty of Paris 30 Mch 1856, by which the neutralization of the sea was abrogated, but with a special protocol that no nation shall liberate itself from a treaty without the consent of the other signers 13 Mch	1871
Blockade of the Black sea declared by Turkey during the war, about 3 May,	1877

Black Warrior, a steamship, belonging to citizens of the United States, was seized at Havana Cuba, by Spanish authorities, 25 Feb 1854, and with its cargo was declared confiscated The proceeding aroused a bitter feeling against Spain, and a special messenger was despatched instructing the American minister at Madrid to demand as immediate redress indemnification to the owners of $300 000 The reluctance of the Spanish government to accede, with other causes, led to the Ostend Conference. OSTEND MANIFESTO The vessel was finally released on the payment by the owners of a fine of $6000, and amicable relations with Spain were restored

Black Watch, armed companies of the loyal clans (Campbells, Monros etc) employed to watch the Highlands, from about 1725 to 1739 when they were formed into the celebrated 42d regiment, enrolled as "The Royal Highland Black Watch" Their removal for foreign service probably facilitated the outbreak in 1745 They wore dark tartans, and hence were called *Black Watch* They distinguished themselves in the Ashantee war Jan, Feb 1874, and in Egypt, 1882-85

Blackburn, Lancashire, Engl, so called in Domesday-book The manufacture of a cloth called Blackburn check, in 1650, was superseded by Blackburn grays In 1767, James Hargreaves, of this town invented the spinning-jenny, for which he was eventually expelled from the county About 1810 or 1812, the townspeople availed themselves of his discoveries, and engaged largely in the cotton manufacture, now their staple trade

Blackburn's ford, engagement at BULL RUN

Blackheath, Kent, near London, Engl Here Wat Tyler and followers assembled, 12 June, 1381, and here Jack Cade and 20 000 Kentishmen encamped, 1 June, 1450 TYLER, CADE Here the Cornish rebels were defeated and Flammock's insurrection quelled 22 June, 1497 The ancient cavern, on the ascent to Blackheath, popularly termed "the retreat of Cade," and of banditti in the time of Cromwell, was rediscovered in 1780 Several highway robberies were committed near the heath, and youthful culprits punished in 1877

Black-hole. When Suraj-ud-Daula, the nawab of Bengal, besieged fort William at Calcutta, India, the majority of the English officials fled to the mouth of the Hugli river The Europeans who remained were, after a brief resistance, compelled to surrender These prisoners, 146 in number, were thrust into the guard-room prison, scarcely 20 ft. square. Next morning only 23 were taken out alive, among them Mr. Holwell, the annalist of the "Black-hole" This event took place on 20 June, 1756.

black-letter, employed in the first printed books in the middle of the 15th century The first printing-types were Gothic, but were modified into the present Roman type about 1469, Pliny's "Natural History" was then printed in the new characters PRINTING

black-mail, a compulsory payment for protection of cattle, etc., made in the border counties, prohibited by Elizabeth in 1601 It was exacted in Scotland from lowlanders by highlanders till 1745, and checked agricultural improvement

Blackstocks, Battle at. On 20 Nov 1780, Americans under gen. Sumter met British cavalry under col Tarleton, at Blackstock's plantation, on the Tyger river, Union District, S C After a sharp engagement Tarleton fled leaving nearly 200 men dead or wounded upon the field Sumter lost 3 killed and 5 wounded

Blackwater, Battle of, in Ireland, 14 Aug 1598, when the Irish chief O'Neil defeated the English under sir Henry Bagnall. Pope Clement VIII sent O'Neil a consecrated plume, and granted his followers the same indulgence as to crusaders

Bladensburg, engagement at, 24 Aug 1814 This was an attempt to defend Washington from capture by a British force of about 5000 men, under gen Ross and admiral Cockburn The Americans, mostly militia, assembled hastily under gen Winder, upon the rapid approach of the British, and met them at Bladensburg, 4 miles from Washington, but were quickly discomfited, with slight loss to either side The British then occupied Washington and burned the Capitol Here also many duels have been fought, among the most noted that between commodores Decatur and Barron, 22 Mch 1820 The former was mortally, the latter severely wounded DIST OF COLUMBIA

Bland silver bill. A bill introduced 25 July, 1876, by Richard P Bland, M C from Missouri providing for unlimited coinage of silver As finally amended and passed by the Senate, 15 Feb 1878, by 48 to 21, it directed the treasury to purchase and coin not less than $2,000,000 or more than $4,000,000 of silver every month The silver dollar to be 412½ grs. troy, and, with all silver dollars heretofore coined of like weight and fineness, to be legal-tender The House concurred, 203 to 72 President Hayes returned the bill with his veto, 28 Feb 1878, but on the same day both the House and Senate passed the bill over the veto

blankets are said to have been first made at Bristol by Thos. Blanket, in the 14th century This is doubtful

Blarney stone, said to confer on the person kissing it the power to speak agreeably It is built in the wall on the summit of Blarney castle (about 4 miles northwest from Cork) This castle was built by Cormick McCarty, 1449 The true Blarney stone recognized by the natives is not the one commonly saluted, but is in the wall several feet from the top, and can only be kissed with great difficulty and with assistance by leaning over the parapet

blasphemy was punished with death by the law of Moses (Lev xxiv), 1491 B.C, and by the code of Justinian, 529 A D It is punishable by the civil and canon law of England, regulated by 60 George III c 8 (1819) Daniel Isaac Eaton was tried and convicted in London of blasphemy, 6 Mch 1812 Robert Taylor, a Protestant clergyman, was tried twice for the same crime. He was sentenced to 2 years' imprisonment, and heavily fined, July, 1831 In Dec 1840, 2 publishers of blasphemous writings were convicted In the case of Cowan *vs* Milbourn in 1867, the defendant had broken his lease of a lecture-room to the plaintiff, on discovering that the lectures were to maintain that "the character of Christ is defective, and his teaching misleading, and that the Bible is no more inspired than any other book" The court held that the publication of such doctrine was blasphemy, and the contract illegal, reaffirming the dictum of C J Hale that "Christianity is part of the laws of England"

blasting gelatine (a mixture of nitro-glycerine and gun-cotton), a violent explosive prepared by Alfred Nobel and modified by prof Abel, 1879

blazonry. Coats-of-arms were introduced and became hereditary in France and England about 1192, the knights painting their banners with different figures, to distinguish them in the crusades —*Dugdale*

bleaching was known in Egypt, Syria, India, and Gaul —*Pliny* The Dutch introduced chemical improvements into England and Scotland in 1768 There were large bleachfields in Lancashire, Fife, Forfar, and Renfrew, and in the vale of the Leven, in Dumbarton The application of chlorine gas to bleaching is due to Berthollet's discovery, about 1785 Its combination with lime (chloride of lime) was devised by Mr Tennant, of Glasgow, who patented the process in 1798, and by his firm it is still extensively manufactured In 1822 Dr. Ure published elaborate experiments on this substance In 1860 bleaching and dyeing works in Great Britain were regulated by the Factories act

Blenheim or **Plintheim,** a village in Bavaria on the left bank of the Danube, near Hochstett, where, on 13 Aug 1704, the English and Austrians, commanded by the duke of Marlborough and prince Eugene, defeated the French and Bavarians, under marshal Tallard and the elector of Bavaria, the latter losing about 12,000 killed and wounded, and 13,000 prisoners (including Tallard) Bavaria fell to the conquerors. Parliament gave Marlborough the honor of Woodstock and the hundred of Wotton, and built for him the house of Blenheim

> "'Great praise the Duke of Marlborough won,
> And our good prince Eugene'
> 'Why 't was a very wicked thing!'
> Said little Wilhelmine
> 'Nay, nay, my little girl!' quoth he,
> 'It was a famous victory'"
> —*Southey,* "Battle of Blenheim"

Blennerhassett's island, an island in the Ohio river, a few miles below Parkersburg, W Va, purchased in 1798 by Herman Blennerhassett He was born in Hampshire, Engl, 8 Oct 1764, married a daughter of lieutenant-governor Agnew of the isle of Man, 1796, disposed of his estate and came to the United States, 1797 On this island he erected a spacious mansion, where he was visited in 1805 by Aaron Burr, who enlisted him in his schemes of western colonization He was arrested as an accomplice of Burr's, his house and grounds entirely ruined, finally, discharged without trial, he purchased a plantation near Port Gibson, Miss This venture proving unfortunate, he removed to Montreal in 1819, where he began the practice of law, hoping to obtain a judgeship, failing in this, he sailed for Ireland in 1822, to recover, if possible, a part of his estate, unsuccessful, he retired to the island of Guernsey, where he died 1831 In 1842 his wife returned to the U S and petitioned Congress for compensation for the ruined island home The petition was presented by Henry Clay, and in the Senate a favorable report was made, but she died in New York in destitution before a vote on the bill, and was buried by Sisters of Charity BURR'S CONSPIRACY

blind. The first public school for the blind was established by Valentine Haüy, at Paris, in 1784 The first in England was at Liverpool in 1791, in Scotland, at Edinburgh, in 1792, and the first in London in 1799 Printing in raised or embossed characters for the blind was begun at Paris by Haüy in 1786 The whole Bible was printed at Glasgow in raised Roman characters about 1848 A sixpenny magazine for the blind, edited by rev W Taylor, F R.S., so eminent for his 40 years' exertions on behalf of these sufferers, was published in 1855-56 By his aid a college for the wealthy blind was founded at Worcester, Engl, in 1866 In many departments of knowledge blind persons have obtained distinction. Laura Bridgman, born at Hanover, N H, 21 Dec 1829, became through sickness dumb and blind 2 years after She was so well taught by Dr Howe, of Boston, Mass, as to become an able instructor of blind and dumb persons. She died at South Boston, 24 May, 1889

James Holman, the "blind traveller" (b 1786, d. 1857), visited all parts of the world. His travels were publ in 1825 In Apr 1858, a blind clergyman, rev J Sparrow, was elected chaplain to the Mercers Company, London, and read the service, etc., from embossed books.

Viscount Cranborne (blind) wrote interesting historical essays. He died in June, 1865 On 13 July, 1865, Henry Fawcett, the blind professor of political economy at Cambridge, was elected M P for Brighton for Hackney, 1874 and 1880, appointed postmaster general, Apr 1880 F J Campbell (blind) ascended Mont Blanc in 1880

blinding, by consuming the eyeballs with lime or scalding vinegar, was inflicted anciently on adulterers, perjurers, and thieves In the middle ages the penalty was frequently changed from total blindness to a diminution of sight. A whole army of Bulgarians were deprived of sight by the emperor Basil BULGARIA.

blisters, used by Hippocrates (460-357 B.C.), made, it is said, of CANTHARIDES.

blizzard. STORMS.

Block island, Long Island sound MASSACHUSETTS 1 CONNECTICUT, 1636 MANISSES, NEW YORK, 1614

blockade is the closing an enemy's ports to commerce, a practice introduced by the Dutch about 1584 The neiple recognized by European powers is that a blockade, be binding, must be effective The Elbe was blockaded by eat Britain, 1803, the Baltic, by Denmark, 1848-49 and 51, the gulf of Finland by the allies, 1854, and the ports the confederate States by president Lincoln, 19 Apr 1861. e naval force of the United States then consisted of 90 vessels, only 42 were in commission, mounting between 500 and) guns The home squadron consisted of 12 vessels The oclamation of the blockade was a recognition of belligerent hts in the confederates Many vessels succeeded in running e blockade during the war, 1143 were captured by blockng squadrons, valued at $24 500,000, and 355 destroyed, lued at $7,000 000 ALABAMA CLAIMS, BERLIN DECREE, ITISH ORDERS IN COUNCIL, MILAN DECREE, UNITED ATES

Blois, France, the Roman Blesum Stephen of England s earl of Blois through his father, count of Blois, who mard Adela daughter of William the Conqueror The count y II sold it with his domains to Louis, duke of Orleans in 91, and eventually it accrued to the crown The States-neral were held here 1576 and 1588, on account of the relious wars, and here Henry, duke of Guise, and his brother, e cardinal, were assassinated by order of Henry III, 23 Dec 88. Maria Louisa, wife of Napoleon, retired here in 1814

blood. The circulation of the blood was a fact obscurely conjectured by Aristotle, Nemesius, Mondino, and renger, and partly taught by Cæsalpinus, Fabricius, and chael Servetus (b 1509, burnt at Geneva, 1553) The latter st maintained the imperviousness of the septum and the ansition of the blood by what he terms an unknown route, mely, from the right ventricle by the pulmonary artery to e lungs, and thence into the pulmonary vein and left auricle d ventricle, from which, he adds, afterwards it is conveyed the aorta to all parts of the body, but the honor of fully plaining the circulation belongs to William Harvey, who first nounced it in 1619, and published his first work in 1628 memorial window in the church at Folkestone, Kent, Engl, e place of his birth (1578-1657), was uncovered 9 Apr 1874

ting blood was prohibited to Noah (Gen ix), to the Jews (Lev xvii, etc), and to the Gentile converts by the apostles at an assembly at Jerusalem, 52 A D (Acts xv)

ood drinking was anciently tried to give vigor to the system Louis XI in his last illness drank the warm blood of infants, in he vain hope of restoring his decayed strength, 1483 —*Henault* the 15th century an opinion prevailed that the declining vigor of he aged might be repaired by transfusing into their veins the blood of young persons. It was countenanced in France by physicians about 1668, and prevailed for many years, till, fatal effects having ensued, it was suppressed by an edict "An English physician (Louver, or Lower) practised in this way, he died in 1691"—*Freind* It was attempted again in France in 1797, and more recently there, in a few cases, with success, and in England (but rarely) since 1824 Tried at Philadelphia, Pa., Apr 1877, in London, unsuccessful, 10 May, 1877

Blood's conspiracy. Blood, a discarded officer Oliver Cromwell's household, with confederates, seized the ke of Ormond in his coach, intending to hang him, and took m to Tyburn, when he was rescued by his friends, 6 Dec 70. Blood afterwards, disguised as a clergyman, attempted steal the royal crown from the Jewel-office in the Tower, 9 ay, 1671, yet, was not only pardoned by Charles II, but reived a pension of 500*l* per annum, 1671 He died 24 Aug 1680

"bloody assizes," held by Jeffreys in the west of ngland, in Aug 1685, after the defeat of Monmouth at edgmoor Upwards of 300 persons were executed after short ials, many were whipped, imprisoned, and fined, and nearly 00 were sent as slaves to American plantations

Bloody Marsh, Battle of GEORGIA, 1742.

bloomer costume, introduced in the United ates in 1849 by Mrs. Ann Bloomer. It consisted of an pen-fronted jacket and loose trousers, the latter wide like those the Turks, but gathered at the ankles. It never became opular and was soon totally disused

Bloreheath, Staffordshire, Engl., where, 23 Sept. 159, the earl of Salisbury and the Yorkists defeated the Lancastrians, whose leader, lord Audley, was slain with many Cheshire gentlemen A cross commemorates this conflict

blowing-machines. The large cylinders used in blowing-machines were erected by Mr Smeaton at the CARRON IRON-WORKS, 1760 One to supply air for 40 forge-fires was erected at the king's dockyard, Woolwich The hot-air blast, an important improvement, economizing fuel, was invented by James B Neilson, of Glasgow, and patented in 1828. The inventor died 18 Jan 1865

blow-pipe. An Egyptian using one is among the paintings on the tombs at Thebes The blow-pipe was employed in mineralogy by Antony von Swab, a Swede, about 1733, and improved by Wollaston and others In 1802, prof Robert Hare, of Philadelphia, Pa, invented the compound blow-pipe, in which intense heat is produced by a flame of mixed oxygen and hydrogen By Newman's improved blow-pipes, in 1816, Dr E. D Clarke fused the earths, alkalies, metals, etc Books on the blow-pipe, by Plattner and Muspratt, pub 1854, by G Plympton, 1874

blue was the favorite color of the Scotch covenanters in the 17th century Blue and orange or yellow became whig colors after the revolution of 1688, and were adopted on the cover of the whig periodical, the *Edinburgh Review*, first publ in 1802 Prussian-blue dye was discovered by Diesbach, at Berlin, in 1710 Fine blues are now obtained from coal-tar ANILINE Blue-coat schools, so called from the costume of the children The Blue-coat school in Newgate street, London, was instituted by Edward VI in 1552 CHRIST'S HOSPITAL. Blue is the prescribed color of the uniform of the army of the United States Blue-stocking, a term applied to a literary lady, was originally conferred on a society comprising both sexes (1760 et seq) Among its active members was Benjamin Stillingfleet, the naturalist, who wore blue worsted stockings, hence the name The beautiful Mrs. Jerningham is said to have worn blue stockings at the conversaziones of Mrs Montagu.

blue-books, reports and other papers printed by order of the British Parliament, so named from their wrappers, 70 vols were printed for the lords, and 76 vols for the commons in 1871 Blue-book, U S government, contains lists of all persons under the government in the civil, military, and naval departments, including the law office. So called from the color of the cover

blue laws of Connecticut, a code adopted by the settlers as early as 1639 12 "The Blue Laws," edited by J Hammond Trumbull, 1876, gives the several codes of the Connecticut colonies, and S. A Peters's "History of Connecticut," edited by S J McCormick, New York, 1877, gives an exaggerated account of them CONNECTICUT, MASSACHUSETTS, 1631.

Blue Licks, Battle of in Nicholas county, Ky, between 182 Kentucky pioneers and a strong body of Indians under Simon Girty, 19 Aug 1782 Through haste and rashness the Kentuckians were drawn into an ambuscade and defeated with great slaughter losing 62, among them a son of Daniel Boone.

blue lights. During the summer and autumn of 1813, commodore Decatur, with the frigates *United States* and *Macedonian* and the sloop-of-war *Hornet*, was closely blockaded in New London harbor, Conn, by sir Thomas Hardy, with 2 74's, 2 frigates, and several smaller vessels Decatur prepared to run this blockade with great secrecy on the night of 12 Dec Everything was favorable, and he was about to weigh anchor when word was brought that blue lights were burning on both sides of the river Decatur had no doubt they were signals to warn the enemy, so the ships remained imprisoned during the rest of the war The Federalists as the party opposed to the war, were reproached for exhibiting the lights UNITED STATES, 1814

Blue Ridge. APPALACHIAN MOUNTAINS

Blue-stocking. BLUE.

Board of War. UNITED STATES, 12 June, 1776.

boat-races. Thomas Doggett, an eminent actor of Drury lane, at the first anniversary of the accession to the throne of George I, 1 Aug 1715, gave a waterman's coat and silver badge to be rowed for by 6 young watermen in honor of the day, and bequeathed, at his death in 1722, a sum of money to continue the custom. Coat and badge won by Wm. A. Barry, 1 Aug. 1891. On 10 June, 1829, was rowed the first boat-race between the universities of Oxford and Cambridge, Engl.; and boat-racing between Harvard and Yale began in 1852. The following is a list of the Harvard-Yale, Oxford-Cambridge, and international boat-races:

8 OARS—HARVARD-YALE.

Date.	Course.	Distance.	Winner.	Time. Min.	Time. Sec.	Won by
3 Aug. 1852	Centre harbor, lake Winnepesaukee, N. H.	2 miles straight.	Harvard.	—	—	2 lengths.
21 July, 1855	Connecticut river, Springfield.	3 miles with turn.	"	22	—	1 min. 38 secs.
26 " 1859	Worcester, lake Quinsigamond, Mass.	" "	"	19	18	1 min.
24 " 1860	" " " "	" "	"	18	53	12 secs.
29 " 1864	" " " "	" "	Yale.	19	1	42½ secs.
28 " 1865	" " " "	" "	"	17	42½	26½ "
27 " 1866	" " " "	" "	Harvard.	18	43	27 "
19 " 1867	" " " "	" "	"	18	13	1 min. 12½ secs.
24 " 1868	" " " "	" "	"	17	48½	50 secs.
23 " 1869	" " " "	" "	"	18	2	9 "
30 June, 1876	Connecticut river, Springfield, Mass.	4 miles straight.	Yale.	22	3	31 "
30 " 1877	" " " "	" "	Harvard.	24	36	8 "
28 " 1878	Thames river, New London, Conn.	" "	"	20	44¾	44½ secs.
27 " 1879	" " " "	" "	"	22	15	1 min. 43 secs.
1 July, 1880	" " " "	" "	Yale	24	27	42 secs.
1 " 1881	" " " "	" "	"	22	13	6 "
30 June, 1882	" " " "	" "	Harvard.	20	47	3½ secs.
28 " 1883	" " " "	" "	"	24	26	1 min. 33 secs.
26 " 1884	" " " "	" "	Yale.	20	31	15 secs.
26 " 1885	" " " "	" "	Harvard.	25	15½	1 min. 14½ secs.
2 July, 1886	" " " "	" "	Yale.	20	41¼	24½ secs.
1 " 1887	" " " "	" "	"	22	56	14½ "
29 June, 1888	" " " "	" "	"	20	10	1 min. 14 secs.
28 " 1889	" " " "	" "	"	21	30	25 secs.
27 " 1890	" " " "	" "	Yale.	21	29	11 secs.
26 " 1891	" " " "	" "	Harvard.	21	23	34 secs.
1 July, 1892	" " " "	" "	Yale.	20	48	54½ secs.
30 June, 1893	" " " "	" "	"	25	1½	13½ secs.
28 June, 1894	" " " "	" "	"	22	47	53 secs.

8 OARS—OXFORD-CAMBRIDGE. ENGLISH. FIRST RACE, 1829; ANNUAL SINCE 1856. (In 1864, after 20 contests, the opposing parties were equal; up to 1880, Oxford was 1 ahead.)

Date.	Course.	Distance.	Winner.	Time.	Won by
22 Mch. 1880	Putney to Mortlake, Thames, Engl.	4 mls. and 440 yds.	Oxford.	21 m. 23 s.	3¾ lengths.
8 Apr. 1881	" " " "	" "	"	21 " 51 "	3 "
1 " 1882	" " " "	" "	"	20 " 12 "	7 "
15 Mch. 1883	" " " "	" "	"	21 " 18 "	3½ "
7 Apr. 1884	" " " "	" "	Cambridge.	21 " 39 "	2½ "
28 Mch. 1885	" " " "	" "	Oxford.	21 " 36 "	2½ "
3 Apr. 1886	" " " "	" "	Cambridge.	22 " 29 "	⅔ "
26 Mch. 1887	" " " "	" "	"	20 " 52 "	2½ " No. 7 Oxf. broke oar.
24 " 1888	" " " "	" "	"	20 " 48 "	7 "
30 " 1889	" " " "	" "	"	20 " 14 "	2½ "
26 " 1890	" " " "	" "	Oxford.	22 " 3 "	1 "
21 " 1891	" " " "	" "	"	21 " 48 "	½ "
9 Apr. 1892	" " " "	" "	"	19 " 21 "	2¼ "
22 Mch. 1893	" " " "	" "	"	18 " 47 "	2½ "
17 " 1894	" " " "	" "	"	21 " 39 "	3½ "

4 OARS—INTERNATIONAL. HARVARD-OXFORD.

Date.	Course.	Distance.	Winner.	Time. Min.	Time. Sec.	Won by
17 Aug. 1869	Putney to Mortlake, Thames, Engl.	4¼ miles.	Oxford.	22	17	3 lengths.

LONDON R. C.-ATALANTA B. C., NEW YORK, AMATEURS.

Date.	Course.	Distance.	Winner.	Time. Min.	Time. Sec.	
10 June, 1872	Putney to Mortlake, Thames, Engl.	4¼ miles.	London R. C.	21	16	
4-5 July, 1878	Henley, Thames, Engl.	2¼ "	Columbia.	8	42	Wins Visitors' Challenge cup.

LONDON R. C. AND THE SHO-WAE-CAE-METTES, OF MONROE, MICH.

Date.	Course.	Distance.	Winner.	Time. Min.	Time. Sec.	
4-5 July, 1878	Henley, Thames, Engl.	2¼ miles.	London R. C.	8	26	Wins Steward's Challenge cup.

VIENNA, AUSTRIA-CORNELL UNIVERSITY, U. S.

Date.	Course.	Distance.	Winner.	Time. Min.	Time. Sec.	Won by
11 Aug. 1881	Vienna, Danube.	3 miles.	Vienna.	28	30	

THAMES R. C.-HILLSDALE, MICH., R. C., AMATEURS.

Date.	Course.	Distance.	Winner.	Time. Min.	Time. Sec.	Won by
1882	Thames, Engl.	4¼ miles.	Thames R. C.	20	40	

Boat voyage. Alfred Johnson, a young man, started from America in the boat *Centennial*, 20 feet long, 15 June, and landed at Abercastle, Pembrokeshire, Wales ....11 Aug. 1876

Boccaccio's (*bok-kät'cho*) **Decamerone,** a collection of 100 stories (many immoral), severely satirizing the clergy, feigned to have been related in 10 days, during the plague of Florence in 1348. A copy of the first edition (by Valdarfer in 1471) was sold at the duke of Roxburghe's sale to the duke of Marlborough for 2260*l.*, 17 June, 1812, and was afterwards sold by public auction for 875 guineas, 5 June, 1819. LITERATURE.

Bodleian Library, Oxford, founded in 1598, and opened in 1602 by sir Thomas Bodley (d. 28 Jan. 1612). Is open to the public, and receives by the copyright law a copy of every book published in Great Britain In 1868 it contained about 250,000 vols. For rare works and MSS it is said to be second only to the Vatican Mr Macray's "Annals of the Bodleian Library," publ 1868

Bœo'tia, a division of Greece, north of Attica, known previously as Aonia, Messapia, Hyantis, Ogygia, and Cadmeis. Thebes, the capital, was celebrated for the exploits and misfortunes of its kings and heroes The term Bœotian was used by the Athenians as a synonym for dull, but unjustly—since Pindar, Hesiod, Plutarch, Democritus, Epaminondas, and Corinna were Bœotians The early history and dates are mythical THEBES

Arrival of Cadmus, founder of Cadmea (*Hales*, 1494, *Clinton*, 1313) B C 1493
Reign of Polydore 1459
Labdachus ascends the throne 1430
Amphion and Zethus besiege Thebes and dethrone Laius 1388
Myth of Œdipus, he kills in an affray his father Laius, confirming the oracle foretelling his death by the hands of his son, 1276, resolves the Sphinx's enigmas 1266
War of the 7 captains 1225
Thebes besieged and taken 1213
Thersander reigns, 1198, slain 1193
Thebans abolish royalty (ages of obscurity follow) about 1120
Thebans fight with Persians at Platæa 479
Spartans aiding Thebans defeat Athenians near Tanagra 456
Battle of Coronea, Thebans defeat Athenians . 447
Thebans, under Epaminondas and Pelopidas, enroll their sacred band, and join Athens against Sparta 377
Epaminondas defeats Lacedæmonians at Leuctra, and restores Thebes to independence 371
Pelopidas killed at Cynoscephalæ 364
Epaminondas victorious at Mantinea, but slain 362
Philip, king of Macedon, defeats Thebans and Athenians near Chæronea 338
Alexander destroys Thebes, but spares Pindar's house 335
Bœotian confederacy dissolved by the Romans 170
Bœotia henceforth partakes of the fortunes of Greece, and is conquered by the Turks under Mahomet II A D 1456

Boers (peasants), a name given to the Dutch settlers in South Africa, since the 16th century, who still retain their national character Discontented with British rule in the Cape, since 1814 large numbers of them emigrated northward in 1835–37, and founded the Orange Free State (1836) and the Transvaal Republic (1848) SOUTH AFRICAN WAR

bogs, probably the remains of forests, covered with peat and loose soil. An act for drainage of Irish bogs passed Mch 1830 The bog land of Ireland has been estimated at 3,000 000 acres, that of Scotland at upwards of 2,000,000, and that of England at near 1,000,000 acres In Jan 1849, Rees Reece patented certain products from Irish peat Candles and other articles made from peat have been sold in London Fuel for railway engines and other purposes was made from peat (Apr. 1873), and a peat, coal, and charcoal company established

Much destruction has been caused by the motion of bogs. Leland (about 1540) speaks of Chat Moss shifting Mischief was done at Enaghmore, Ireland, 3 Jan 1853, and farm houses and fields near Dunmore were covered, Oct 1873

Bohemia, formerly the Hercynian forest (Boiemum, *Tacitus*), derives its name from the Boii, a Celtic tribe It was governed by dukes (Borzivoi I 891), till Ottocar assumed the title of king, 1198 The kings at first held their territory from the empire, and the crown was elective till it became hereditary in the house of Austria The original Bohemians term themselves Czechs, and, imitating Hungary, now call for autonomy. Prague, the capital, is famous for sieges and battles Pop. in 1857, 4,705,525, in 1870, 5,140,544, in 1890 5,843,250 Area, 20,060 sq miles. PRAGUE.

A D
Czechs (Slavonians) seize Bohemia. about 550
City of Prague founded 795
Introduction of Christianity 894
Bohemia conquered by the emperor Henry III, who devastates the country . . 1041
Ottocar (Premislas) I first king of Bohemia. 1198
Ottocar II rules over Austria, and obtains Styria, etc, 1253, refuses the imperial crown .. 1272
Ottocar vanquished by Rudolph, and deprived of Austria, Styria, and Carniola, 1277, killed at Marchfeld 26 Aug 1278
King John (blind) slain at Crecy 1346
John Huss and Jerome of Prague, early reformers, burned for heresy, an insurrection follows . 1415–16
Ziska, Hussite leader, takes Prague, 1419, dies of plague . 1424
Albert, duke of Austria, marries the daughter of the late emperor, receives the crowns of Bohemia and Hungary 1437
Succession infringed by Ladislas son of the king of Poland, and George Podiebrad, a Protestant chief 1440–58
Ladislas king of Poland, elected king of Bohemia on the death of Podiebrad 1471
Emperor Ferdinand I marries Anne sister of Louis, late king, and obtains the crown 1527
Thirty years' war begun 1618
Emperor Ferdinand II, oppressing Protestants, is deposed, Frederic, elector palatine, elected king 5 Sept 1619
Frederic, defeated at Prague, flees to Holland 9 Nov 1620
Bohemia secured to Austria by treaty 1648
Silesia and Glatz ceded to Prussia 1742
Prague taken by the Prussians 1744
Prussians defeat Austrians at Prague, 7 years' war begins, 6 May, 1757
Revolt of the peasantry 1775
Edict of toleration promulgated 1781
French occupy Prague 1806
Insurrection at Prague, 12 June, submission, siege raised, 20 July, 1848
Prussians enter Bohemia which becomes the seat of war (GERMANY, 1866) 24 June, 1866
Agitation of Czechs that the emperor be crowned king of Bohemia with the crown of St Wenceslas at Prague autumn, 1867
Riots at Prague, habeas corpus act suspended 10 Oct 1868
Bohemian agitation for self government, addresses to the emperor 14 Sept and 5 Oct. 1870
Manifesto of the emperor 14 Sept 1871
Bohemian deputies absent from the Reichsrath Dec. "
"Young Czech" party defeated in elections July, 1874
Czech deputies enter Reichsrath 8 Oct 1879
Motion of the Young Czechs in the assembly for the coronation of the emperor as king of Bohemia negatived after several days warm debate. 9 Nov 1889
Diet reopened 14 Oct, the Young Czechs obstruct legislation Oct. 1890
Young Czechs ask for autonomy like Hungary Dec. "
Gradual dissolution of the Old Czechs party (moderates) " "
Austrian government will make no more concessions to the Czechs, announced in the Diet. 5 Jan 1891
Young Czechs victorious in the elections, the Old Czech party totally defeated Mch "

KINGS

1198 Premislas Ottocar I
1230 Wenceslas III
1253 Premislas Ottocar II
1278 Wenceslas IV, king of Poland
1305 Wenceslas V
1306 Rudolph of Austria
1307 Henry of Carinthia.
1310 John of Luxemburg (killed at Crecy)
1346 Charles I, emperor (1347)
1378 Wenceslas VI, emperor
1419 Sigismund I, emperor
1438 Albert of Austria, emperor
1440 Ladislas V
1458. George von Podiebrad
1471 Ladislas VI, king of Hungary (in 1490)
1516 Louis king of Hungary (killed at Mohatz)
1526 Bohemia united to Austria under Ferdinand I, elected king; GERMANY, emperors

Bohemian Brethren. a body of Christians in Bohemia, appear to have separated from the CALIXTINES, a branch of the Hussites, in 1467. Dupin says, "They rejected the sacraments of the church, were governed by simple laics, and held the Scriptures for their only rule of faith They presented a confession of faith to king Ladislas in 1504 to justify themselves from errors laid to their charge" Though perhaps in sympathy with the Waldenses, they were distinct from them Luther, in 1533, testifies to their purity of doctrine, and Melanchthon commends their discipline They were dispersed during the religious wars of Germany in the 17th century

Boii, a Celtic people of N Italy, who emigrated into Italy, were defeated at the Vadimonian lake, 283 B.C, and were subdued by Scipio Nasica, 191 B.C Recrossing the Alps they betook themselves to what is now Bohemia, but their existence as a separate people was soon lost

boiling of liquids. Dr. Hooke, about 1683, ascertained that liquids cannot increase in heat after beginning to boil, hotter fire only making them boil more rapidly The following are boiling-points

Ether	93° Fahr	Phosphorus	554° Fahr
Alcohol	173 "	Sulphuric acid	600 "
Nitric acid	187 "	Mercury	662 "
Water	212 "	Sulphur	822 "
Oil of turpentine	312 "		

boiling to death, a capital punishment in England, by stat 22 Hen VIII 1531 (repealed 1547), passed when 17 persons had been poisoned by Richard Rosse, otherwise Coke, the bishop of Rochester's cook, 2 of whom died Margaret Davy, a young woman, suffered this penalty for a similar crime, 28 Mch 1542 —*Stow*

Bois-le-duc, Dutch Brabant, where the British were

defeated by a French republican army, and driven from their position to Schyndel, 14 Sept. 1794. The place was captured by the French, 10 Oct. following; surrendered to the Prussian army, under Bulow, in Jan. 1814.

Bokha'ra, central Asia, the ancient Sogdiana, after successively forming part of the empires of Persia, of Alexander, and Bactriana, was conquered by the Turks in the 6th century, by the Chinese in the 7th, and by the Arabs about 705. After various changes of masters, it was subdued by the Uzbek Tartars, its present possessors, in 1505. The British envoys, col. Stoddart and capt. Conolly, were murdered at Bokhara, the capital, by the khan, about June, 1843. In the war with Russia, begun 1866, the emir's army was defeated several times in May et seq. Peace was made 11 July, 1867. The Russians were again victors, 25 May, 1868, and occupied Samarcand the next day. Further conquests were made by the Russians, and Samarcand was secured by treaty, Nov. 1868. A new political and commercial treaty with Russia was published Dec. 1873. Pop. 2,030,000; area, 83,980 sq. miles.

Bolivia, a republic in South America, formerly part of Peru, population in 1875 about 2,000,000; in 1880, 2,325,000; 1890, 2,333,350; area, 784,554 sq. miles, between lat. 10° and 22° S., lon. 58° and 70° W.

An insurrection of the ill-used Indians, headed by Tupac Amaru Andres, takes place here.......... 1780–82
Country declares its independence.......... 6 Aug. 1824
Secured by the victory of Ayacucho.......... 9 Dec. "
Named Bolivia, in honor of gen. Bolivar.......... 11 Aug. 1825
First congress meet.......... 25 May, 1826
General Sucre governs ably.......... 1826–28
Slavery abolished.......... 1836
Santa Cruz rules.......... 1828–39
Free-trade proclaimed.......... 1853
General Cordova, president.......... 1855–57
Succeeded by the dictator José Maria Linares.......... 31 Mch. 1859
George Cordova, constitutional president.......... 1860
Succeeded by José M. de Acha.......... May, 1861
Gen. Melgarejo defeats president De Acha.......... 28 Dec. 1864
Becomes dictator.......... Feb. 1865
Puts down an insurrection under Belzu.......... Mch. "
Routs Arguedas at Viacha and proclaims amnesty.......... 24 Jan. 1866
Suppresses a revolt.......... 17 Oct. "
Proclaims amnesty.......... 21 Dec. 1867
Civil war.......... 1867–70
President A. Morales, 1871, said to have been murdered.......... Jan. 1873
President, Dr. Tomas Frias.......... 14 Feb. 1874
Corral's insurrection suppressed.......... Sept. "
Gen. Hilarion Daza, president.......... 4 May, 1876
Bolivia joins Chili in war against Peru (Chili).......... Apr. 1879
Revolution; Daza deposed; flees; Campero president.......... 1 June, 1880
Peace with Chili finally arranged; loses all of her coast territory.......... Dec. 1883

Bollandists. Acta Sanctorum.

Bologna, central Italy, the ancient Felsina, afterwards Bononia; distinguished for its architecture; made a Roman colony, 189 B.C.

University said to have been founded by Theodosius about 433; really in.......... 1116
Bologna joins the Lombard league.......... 1167
Pope Julius II takes Bologna; enters in triumph.......... 11 Nov. 1506
Added to the states of the church.......... 1513
In the church of St. Petronius, remarkable for its pavement, Cassini draws his meridian line (over one drawn by father Ignatius Dante, 1575).......... 1653
Taken by French, 1796; by Austrians, 1799; by French, after battle of Marengo, 1800; restored to the pope.......... 1815
Revolt suppressed by Austrian interference.......... 1831
Rebellion, 1848; taken by Austrians.......... 16 May, 1849
Austrians evacuate; cardinal Ferretti departs; citizens rise and form a provisional government.......... 12 June, 1859
It decrees that all public acts shall be headed "Under the reign of king Victor Emmanuel," etc.......... 1 Oct. "
He enters Bologna as sovereign.......... 2 May, 1860

bolometer (Gr. *βόλος*, a throw or cast), an electrical instrument invented by prof. S. P. Langley, who also terms it an "actinic balance." By means of it he made discoveries in the ultra red rays of the spectrum. It is much more sensitive to radiant heat than the thermopile.

Bomarsund, a strong fortress on one of the Aland isles in the Baltic sea, taken by sir Charles Napier, with his Baltic expedition, and a French contingent under gen. Baraguay d'Hilliers, 15 Aug. 1854. Gov. Bodisco and the garrison, about 2000 men, prisoners; the fortifications destroyed.

Bombay, the most westerly and smallest of the Indian presidencies, was visited by the Portuguese, 1509, acquired by them, 1530; given (with Tangier in Africa, and 300,000*l.* in money) to Charles II. as the marriage portion of the infanta Catherine of Portugal, 1662. In 1668 it was granted to the East India Company, "in free and common socage," as of the manor of East Greenwich, at an annual rent of 10*l.* Confirmed by William III., 1689. The 2 principal castes at Bombay are Parsees (descendants of ancient Persian fire-worshippers) and Borahs (sprung from early converts to Islamism); both remarkable for commercial activity. Pop. 1891, 26,960,421; area, 188,195 sq. miles.

First British factory established at Ahmednuggur.......... 1612
Mr. Gyfford, deputy-governor, 100 soldiers, and other English die under the climate.......... Oct. 1675–Feb. 1676
Capt. Keigwin usurps the government.......... 1681–84
Bombay made chief of company's settlements.......... 1687
The island, except the fort, seized and held for a time by the mogul's admiral.......... 1690
Bombay a distinct presidency.......... 1708
Additions to the Bombay territory: Bancot river, 1756; island of Salsette.......... 1775
Bishopric established.......... 1837
Lord Elphinstone governor.......... 1853
Pop. of the presidency, 12,034,483.......... 1858
Benevolent sir Jamsetjee Jejeebhoy, a Parsee (who erected hospitals, etc.) dies.......... 15 Apr. 1859
His son sir Cursetjee visits England.......... 1860
Sir G. R. Clerk, governor.......... "
Rioting against the income-tax suppressed.......... Nov. and Dec. "
Sir Henry Bartle Frere governor.......... Mch. 1862
Great speculation in the cotton-trade.......... Nov. 1864
Failure of Byramjee Cama, a Parsee, for 3,300,000*l.*; and others; great depression; project of international exhibition in 1867 abandoned.......... May, 1865
Recovering from commercial crisis.......... Aug. "
W. R. Seymour Fitzgerald appointed governor, Nov. 1866; arrives.......... 28 Feb. 1867
Holds a durbar of native princes at Poona.......... 6 Oct. 1868
Reception of the duke of Edinburgh.......... 11 Mch. 1870
Sir Philip Wodehouse governor.......... Apr. 1872
Riots: Mahometans attack Parsees for publishing part of Washington Irving's "Life of Mahomet;" several lives lost and property destroyed.......... 13–15 Feb. 1874
Culprits punished by British.......... "
Prince of Wales welcomed, 8 Nov. 1875; sails homeward, 13 Mch. 1876
Loyal Mahometans petition queen Victoria in favor of the sultan.......... 24 Sept. "
Famine relieved by government and private subscriptions.......... 1877
Statue of prince of Wales (given by sir Albert Sassoon) uncovered.......... 26 or 27 June, 1879
Sir James Fergusson nominated governor.......... Feb. 1880
A patriotic fund for sufferers by Afghan war subscribed by natives and others.......... Aug. "
Lord Reay appointed governor.......... Dec. 1884
Native troops sail for the Soudan.......... 23 Feb. 1885
New Bombay water-works opened.......... 31 Mch. 1892

bombs (iron shells filled with gunpowder), said to have been invented at Venlo in 1495, and used by the Turks at the siege of Rhodes in 1522, came into general use, 1634 (previously used only by the Dutch and Spaniards). Bomb-vessels were invented in France in 1681.—*Voltaire.* The shrapnel shell (invented by col. Henry Shrapnel, d. 1842) a bomb filled with balls, exploded by a fuse in its flight.

Bonaparte family. The name appears at Florence and Genoa in the 13th century; in the 15th a branch settled in Corsica.

Carlo Maria Bonaparte, b. 29 Mch. 1746; d. 24 Feb. 1785; married, 1767, Letitia Ramolina (b. 24 Aug. 1750; d. Feb. 1836); issue,

1. Joseph, b. 7 Jan. 1768; king of Two Sicilies, 1805; of Naples alone, 1806; of Spain, 1808; in United States, 1815; comes to England, 1832; settles in Italy, 1841; dies at Florence, 28 July, 1844.
2. Napoleon I., emperor, b. 15 Aug. 1769; d. 5 May, 1821. France.
3. Lucien, prince of Canino, born 1775; at first aided his brother's ambition, but later opposed it. He was taken by the English on his way to America, and resided in England till 1814. He died at Viterbo, 30 June, 1840. His son Charles (b. 1803, d. 1857) was an eminent naturalist, and ranks with Audubon and Wilson in ornithology. He resided for some years in the United States, returning to France, 1828. Another son of Lucien was prince Pierre, (b. 1815. In 1870 he shot Victor Noir, and though acquitted, was obliged for a time to leave France, owing to the strong feeling against him; d. 1881).
4. Marie Anne Elisa, b. 3 Jan. 1777, married Felix Bacciochi, 1797; after the fall of Napoleon she lived at Santo Andrea, near Trieste, where she died, 1820.
5. Louis, b. 2 Sept. 1778; king of Holland, 1806; d. 15 July, 1846. Married in 1802 Hortense Beauharnais (daughter of empress Josephine); had 3 sons: 1 Napoleon Louis (b. 1803, d. 1807); 2. Louis Napoleon (b. 1804, d. 1831); and
   3. Charles Louis Napoleon, b. 20 Apr. 1808; educated under his mother at Arenberg, Switzerland, and at Thun, under gen. Dufour.
   Shared in Carbonari insurrection in Papal states.......... Mch. 1831
   Attempted a revolt at Strasburg.......... 30 Oct. 1836
   Sent to America.......... 13 Nov. "

Repairs to London.................................14 Oct. 1838
Lands at Boulogne with 50 followers............ 6 Aug. 1840
Condemned to imprisonment for life...............6 Oct. "
Escapes from Ham.................................25 May, 1846
Arrives at Boulogne...............................2 Mch. 1848
Elected deputy, 8 June, and takes his seat, 27 Aug. "
(FRANCE, 1848–71); d. at Chislehurst..............9 Jan. 1873
Son: Napoleon Eugène Louis Jean Joseph, b. 16 Mch. 1856; educated at Military academy, Woolwich; killed in Zululand..............................1 June. 1879

6. Marie Pauline, b. 1780; married gen. Leclerc and went to San Domingo, 1801, but returned to France on his death in 1802. On 28 Aug. 1803, she married Camillo, prince Borghese. As Napoleon's favorite sister, she wished to share his exile at St. Helena. She lived estranged from her husband nearly until her death, 9 June, 1825. She was extremely beautiful and her statue as Venus Victrix, by Canova, is well known.

7. Marie Annonciade Caroline, b. 1782; married to Murat, 1800; queen of Naples, 1808. She afterwards resided at Trieste with her sister Elisa. In 1838 pensioned by the French government; d. 18 May, 1839.

8. Jerome, b. 15 Nov. 1784; d. 24 June, 1860; king of Westphalia, 1 Dec. 1807–14, married: I. Elizabeth Patterson, in America, 24 Dec. 1803 (she died, aged 94, 4 Apr. 1879; son Jerome, born at Camberwell, London, 7 July, 1805; married Miss Williams, Roxbury, Mass.; d. 1870; his children—Jerome, b. 1832, graduate of West Point, serves U. S. army, 1854; goes to France, serves through Crimean war, Algiers, etc. Charles Joseph, b. 9 June, 1851; graduate Harvard University, 1871; lawyer at Baltimore). II. Princess Catherine of Würtemberg, 12 Aug. 1807. Governor of the Invalides, 1848; and marshal, 1850; issue—

Mathilde, b. 27 May, 1820; married to prince A. Demidoff in 1841.

Napoleon, Joseph Charles Paul Jerome, b. 9 Sept. 1822; d. 17 Mch. 1891 (nicknamed "Plon-Plon," from his own habitual exclamation in the Crimean war—"Du Plomb! du Plomb!"—at every sound like the whizzing of a bullet; others say it was a name he gave himself when young); married princess Clothilde of Savoy, daughter of Victor Emmanuel of Sardinia, 30 Jan. 1859; issue: Victor, b. 18 July, 1862; Louis, b. 16 July, 1864; Marie, b. 20 Dec. 1866; after the death of the Prince Imperial, 1879, prince Victor separates from his father, and is accepted as chief of the Bonapartists; his father publishes painful correspondence, June, 1884; expelled from France, June, 1886; disinherited, Mch. 1891; accepted as head of the family, 31 Mch. 1891.

bondage. VILLANAGE.

bones. The art of softening bones was discovered about 1688, and they are made into handles for cutlery, etc. Bone-dust has been used as a fertilizer since Liebig's researches in 1840.

bonesetting cannot be said to have been practised scientifically until 1620.—*Bell.*

Boniface, the name of 9 popes; first, 418–422, ninth, 1390–1404. POPES.

Bonn, a town on the Rhine (the Roman Bonna), in the electorate of Cologne; often besieged; assigned to Prussia, 1814. The academy founded by the elector in 1777; made a university, 1784; abolished by Napoleon; re-established and enlarged, 1818.

books (Anglo-Saxon, *boc;* Ger. *Buch*), were originally made of boards, or the inner bark of trees; afterwards of skins and parchment. Papyrus, an indigenous plant, was adopted in Egypt long before Herodotus. Books (i. e., rolls or *volumes*), with leaves of vellum were invented by Attalus, king of Pergamus, about 198 B.C. The MSS. in Herculaneum are papyrus rolls, charred and matted together by fire, about 9 in. long, and 1, 2, or 3 in. in diameter, each a separate treatise. The most ancient books are the Pentateuch of Moses and the poems of Homer and Hesiod. Wax tablets continued in use in Europe during the middle ages; the oldest specimen, now in the museum at Florence, is of 1301 A.D. The first printed books were not from movable types, but from solid carved wooden blocks, and consisted of a few leaves only, bearing images of saints or historical pictures with a few explanatory lines. The block was wetted with a thin ink, and the paper then laid on and rubbed with a smooth burnisher till an impression was made. The sheet could be printed only on one side. These are known as "Image" or "Block" books, and form a distinct group in the history of the invention of printing. The best known of the earlier block-books are, "Ars Moriendi" BIBLIA PAUPERUM, "Apocalypse," and the "Canticum Canticorum;" the first and third German, the second and fourth Dutch. The latest block-book of any size, the "Figure del Testamento Vecchio," was printed at Venice, 1510. But the "Speculum Humanæ Salvationis" is the most perfect in design and execution. It was translated into German, Flemish, and other languages, and often reprinted, 1440–50. The "Letters of Indulgence" of pope Nicholas V., printed 1454, fix the earliest period of the impression of metal types with a date subjoined.—*Dibdin.* Probably the first book printed from movable types was the undated *editio princeps* of the Bible (called the "Mazarin Bible," from a copy found in the cardinal's library). It is usually ascribed to a date between 1450 and 1455. It is in 2 volumes of 324 and 317 pages, each page double columns, 42 lines to column, characters Gothic, large and handsome, resembling manuscript. No fewer than 20 copies are known. Before the discovery of this Bible, the Bamberg Bible of Pfister, 36 lines to the page, generally passed for the first. The first printed book with date is the "Psalter" of Faust and Schöffer, printed at Mentz, 1457. Titles of chapters were first used in the "Epistles of Cicero," 1470. The Gothic characters, which were at first uniformly used, were supplanted in 1467 by the Roman type, which was first used in England by Richard Pynson, 1509. Hallam asserts that the price of books was reduced four-fifths by the invention of printing. Jerome (who d. 420) says that he ruined himself by buying the works of Origen. From a letter of Andreas, bishop of Aleria, to the pope, it would seem that 100 golden crowns was the maximum demanded for a valuable MS., and the first printed books were sold for about 4 golden crowns a volume. Much of the value of editions of the 15th century arises from the limited number of impressions. They were seldom more than 300. At the sale of the McCarthy library, the "Psalter" of Faust and Schöffer, on vellum, was bought by Louis XVIII. for 12,000 francs. The Naples edition of "Horace," of 1474, is called by Dibdin the "rarest classical volume in the world," and it was chiefly to possess this book that earl Spencer bought the famous library of the duke of Cassano. At the sale of the first duke of Roxburghe's library, 17 June, 1812, a copy of the first edition of Boccaccio's Decamerone (that of Valdarfer, 1471) fell to the duke of Marlborough, after a spirited competition with earl Spencer, for 2260*l.* (about $11,300). At the sale of the Perkins library, 6 June, 1873, a copy of the Mazarin Bible (see above) on vellum sold for 3400*l.*; one on paper sold for 2690*l.* A copy belonging to sir John Thorold, of Syston-park, sold for 3900*l.*, 13 Dec. 1884; a copy belonging to the earl of Crawford, sold for 2650*l.*, 15 June, 1887; lord Hopetoun's copy sold for 2000*l.*, 25 Feb. 1889; sir John Thorold's copy of the "Book of Psalms" (by Faust and Schöffer, 1457), on vellum, sold for 4950*l.*, 19 Dec. 1884 (formerly sold for 136*l.*). At the duke of Marlborough's sale, 1881, a Bible of 1462 sold for 1600*l.*

TITLES OF THE EARLIEST BOOKS OF CAXTON AND WYNKYN DE WORDE.

THE GAME AND PLAYE OF THE CHESSE. *Translated out of the Frenche and emprynted by me* William Caxton. *Fynysshid the last day of Marche the yer of our Lord God a thousand foure hondred and lxxiiij.* (Probably printed at Cologne.)
[A fac-simile was printed by Vincent Figgins in 1859.]

THE DICTES AND WISE SAYINGS OF THE PHILOSOPHERS is said to be the first book printed by Caxton in England, 1477. (Fac-simile published by Elliot Stock, 1877.)

THE BOKE OF TULLE OF OLDE AGE *Emprynted by me simple persone* William Caxton *into Englysshe as the ‡eysir solace and reverence of men growing in to old age the xij day‸rf August the yere of our Lord* M. CCCC. *lxxxj.—Herbert.*

THE POLYCRONYCON *conteyning the Berynges and Dedes of many Tymes in eyght Bokes. Imprinted by* William Caxton *after having somewhat chaunged th‸ rvde and olde Englysshe, that is to wete* [to wit] *certayn Words which in these Dayes be neither vsyd ne understanden. Ended the second day of Juyll at Westmestre the xxij yere of the Regne of Kynge Edward the fourth, and of the Incarnacion of oure Lord a Thousand four hondred four Score and Tweyne* [1482].—*Dibdin's* "Typ. Ant."

THE CRONICLES OF ENGLOND *Empnted by me* Wyllyam Caxton *thabbey of Westmynstre by london the v day of Juyn the yere of thincarnacion of our lord god* M. CCCC. LXXX.

POLYCRONYCON. *Ended the thyrtenth daye of Apryll the tenth yere of the reyne of kinge Harry the seuenth And of the Jncarnacyon of our lord* MCCCCLXXXXV. *Emprynted by* Wynkyn The worde *at Wesmestre.*

THE HYLLE OF PERFECTION *emprynted at the instance of the reverend relygyous fader* Tho. Prior *of the hous of St. Ann, the order of the charterouse Accomplysshe*[d] *they fynysshe*[d] *att Westmynster the uiii day of Janeuer and ere of our lord Thousande* CCCC. LXXXXVII. *And in the xii yere of kynge Henry the vii by me* wynkyn de worde.—*Ames, Herbert, Dibdin.*

THE DESCRIPCYON OF ENGLONDE *Walys Scotland and Irlond speaking of the Noblesse and Worthynesse of the same Fynysshed and emprynted in Flete strete in the syne of the Sonne by me* Wynkyn de Worde *the yere of our lord a* M *cccc and ij. mensis Mayiis* [mense Maii].—*Dibdin's* "Typ. Ant."

The Festyvall or Sermons on sondays and holidais taken out of the golden legend enprynted at london in Flete-strete at ye sygne of ye Sonne by wynkyn de worde. In the yere of our Lord M. CCCCC. VIII. *And ended the xi daye of Maye.—Ames.*

THE LORD'S PRAYER. [As printed by Caxton in 1483.] *Father our that art in heavens, hallowed be thy name: thy kingdome come to us; thy will be done in earth as is in heaven: our every day bread give us to day; and forgive us oure trespasses, as we forgive them that trespass against us; and lead us not in to temptation, but deliver us from all evil sin, amen.—Lewis's* "Life of Caxton."

A PLACARD. [As printed by William Caxton.] *If it plese ony man spirituel or temperel to bye ony pies of two or three comemoracios of Salisburi use enprynted after the forme of this presēt lettre whiche ben wel & truly correct. late him come to westmonester in to the almonesrye at the reed pale* [red pale] *and he shall have them good there.—Dibdin's* "Typ. Ant."

First book (ALMANAC) printed in the U. S. at Cambridge, Mass. 1639
Bay State Psalm book, Cambridge, Mass. 1640
First books printed in the U. S. (Stephen Daye, publisher).. 1639–49
" " " " " " (Samuel Green, publisher).. 1649–92
[Thomas's "History of Printing in America," pub. 1810.]
Blumenbach's "Physiology by Eliotson," the first book printed by machinery, 1817. The machine employed was König's, one which printed both sides in one operation at the rate of 900 sheets an hour.

BIBLIOGRAPHY, LIBRARIES, LITERATURE, MANUSCRIPTS, PRINTING, etc.

Book-collectors. LIBRARIES.

"Book of the Dead." A collection of prayers and exorcisms written in Egyptian hieroglyphic or hieratic characters, composed for the benefit of the pilgrim soul in his journey through Amenti (the Egyptian Hades). Portions of these papyri were placed with the mummy in his tomb. They are said to form fully one half of the thousands which are extant. The "Book of the Dead" is dated from the 4th dynasty, 3733–3566 B.C. After much toil a pure text with illustrations was published by M. Edouard Naville, 1886. Translations in several European languages have appeared. A fac-simile of the papyrus of Ani in the British museum was printed in 1890.

book-keeping. The system by double-entry, called originally Italian book-keeping, was first taught in the course of algebra published by Luca di Borgo, in 1495, at Venice. John Gowgne, a printer, published a treatise "on the kepyng of the famouse reconynge . . . Debitor and Creditor," London, 1543. This is the earliest English work on book-keeping. James Peele published his "Book-keeping" in 1569. John Mellis published "A Briefe Instruction and Manner how to Keepe Bookes of Accompts," in 1588. Improved systems were published by Benjamin Booth in 1789 and by Edward Thomas Jones in 1821 and 1831.

book-plate, an engraving as a mark of ownership, often elaborate. The earliest book-plates are probably German, of the beginning of the 16th century. Many were fine examples of wood-engraving. Albert Dürer designed book-plates, some earlier than 1511. It is said that one of the earliest English book-plates is that of cardinal Wolsey, about 1525. They have multiplied in later years, and often exhibit quaint and beautiful designs.

booksellers. "The trade in bookselling seems," says Hallam, "to have been established at Paris and Bologna in the 12th century; it is very improbable that it existed in what is known as the Dark Ages. Peter of Blois mentions a book which he bought of a public dealer. These dealers were denominated *stationarii*, perhaps from their practice of having booths or stalls at the corners of streets and in markets." The modern system of bookselling arose soon after the introduction of printing. The earliest printers were also editors and booksellers. Schöffer, about 1469, printed a catalogue of books for sale by himself or agents. It was printed on one side of a sheet, and was meant to be posted as an advertisement in towns visited; the name of the place where the books could be obtained being written at the bottom; there were 21 books thus advertised." — *Duff*, "Early Printed Books." Antony Koburger, who introduced printing into Nuremberg in 1470, was more a bookseller than a printer, for besides his own 16 shops, we are informed by his biographers, he had agents for the sale of his books in every city in Christendom. Wynkyn de Worde, who succeeded the Caxton press in Westminster, had a shop in Fleet street, London.

London Company of Stationers incorporated.................. 1556
Earliest bookseller's catalogue is said to be that published by Andrew Maunsell, of Lothbury, dedicated to queen Elizabeth, 1595
"A catalogue of the most vendible books in England" was publ.. 1658
The chief publishers in London formed an association and fixed the discount, 29 Dec. 1829, and for some years restricted retail booksellers from selling below the publishing price. A dispute arose as to the right of the retailers to sell purchased stock at such less profit as might satisfy them, which was referred to lord chief-justice Campbell, at Stratheden house, 14 Apr. 1852. He decided against the association, which disbanded, 19 May following.

Booneville, Mo., Battle of, 17 June, 1861. Gov. Jackson of Missouri, a confederate sympathizer, had abandoned Jefferson City, which was immediately occupied by gen. Lyon. Before the confederate forces could concentrate about Booneville, 50 miles above Jefferson City, Lyon moved upon Booneville, and with 2000 men defeated Marmaduke, who offered little resistance, in 20 minutes. This compelled the confederate detachments to move to the southern border of the state.

Boothia Felix, a large peninsula, northwest point of America, discovered by sir John Ross in 1830, named after sir Felix Booth, who had given 20,000*l.* to fit out his polar expedition. Sir Felix died at Brighton, Feb. 1850.

Booth's conspiracy. On the morning of 15 Apr. 1865, the whole northern United States was appalled by the intelligence of the assassination of president Lincoln the previous evening (14 Apr.) at Ford's theatre, Washington, by John Wilkes Booth; and at the same time a murderous attack was made upon Mr. Seward by another assassin, the secretary then lying almost helpless from injuries received by the upsetting of his carriage a few days previous. It soon became evident that the head of the conspiracy to assassinate the president, vice-president, gen. Grant, and the secretary of state, was John Wilkes Booth, aided and abetted by George A. Atzerodt, chosen to assassinate vice-pres. Johnson; Lewis Payne (Powell), chosen to assassinate Mr. Seward; Michael O'Laughlin, chosen to assassinate gen. Grant; David E. Herold, John H. Surratt, his mother, Mary E. Surratt, Edward Spangler, Samuel Arnold, and Dr. Samuel A. Mudd. The following is a summary of the events connected with this tragedy:

President Lincoln's messenger engages a private box for the evening for the president, his wife, and gen. and Mrs. Grant, to witness the play of "Our American Cousin," at Ford's theatre.................................morning, 14 Apr. 1865
Atzerodt engages a room at the Kirkwood House, where vice-president Johnson lodges, paying in advance for one day, morning, 14 Apr. "
[Gen. Grant being called to Philadelphia on business by telegram, president Lincoln takes maj. Rathbone and Miss Harris into the presidential party in place of gen. and Mrs. Grant, and they arrive at the theatre about 9 P.M.]
Booth enters the president's box unnoticed shortly after 10 o'clock, and immediately shoots the president, the ball penetrating his skull on the back of the left side of his head and lodging behind the right eye. Maj. Rathbone, who occupied the box with the president, attempting to seize Booth, is severely wounded with a dagger. Booth then leaps from the box to the stage; in so doing his spur catches in the drapery (folds of the American flag), causing him to miss his footing and stumble, fracturing his left leg; crossing the stage brandishing his dagger, and crying "Sic semper tyrannis," he escapes on a horse in waiting in an alley in the rear of the theatre, his exit made easy by Spangler. President Lincoln, unconscious from the moment of shooting, dies at about half past 7 A.M..................................15 Apr. "
The attempt upon the life of Mr. Seward is made about the same time by Lewis Payne (Powell), who enters the secretary's house in the guise of a messenger with a parcel from his physician, Dr. Verdi, and demands a personal interview. Payne succeeds in passing the porter and ascends the stairs, where he is met by the secretary's son Frederick, who refuses his demand. The assassin strikes him down with his pistol, fracturing his skull. He then rushes into the room where the secretary lies. Serg. George F. Robinson meets him at the door; Payne attacks him with his knife, and, rushing to the bed, attempts to stab the secretary, but only succeeds in inflicting several serious cuts about the face and neck, when he is seized by serg. Robinson and maj. Augustus Seward, who enters from an adjoining room. After a severe struggle Payne escapes to the street, wounding E. W. Hansel, a nurse, on the stairs, as he passes out. A horse is in waiting at the door, on which the assassin escapes.
Booth and Herold arrive at Surrattsville, stopping at Lloyd's tavern, about midnight.................................14 Apr. "
Booth and Herold reach the home of Dr. Samuel Mudd, near Bryantown, Md., about 30 miles from Washington, about 4 A.M. Here Booth has his broken leg roughly bandaged, and remains until about 3 P.M.........................15 Apr. "
Samuel Arnold arrested at fortress Monroe..............17 Apr. "
Michael O'Laughlin arrested in Baltimore.................. " "
Payne, who has been in hiding on the outskirts of the city, returns to the house of Mrs. Surratt in the guise of a workman seeking a job, and is arrested by government military police then in charge of the house........midnight, 17 Apr. "
Funeral services of president Lincoln held at the executive mansion at noon.......................................19 Apr. "
Atzerodt arrested in Montgomery county, Md...........20 Apr. "
[Dr. Mudd placed under arrest about the same time.]
Booth and Herold are hidden in the pine woods near Port

Tobacco by Thomas Jones, a contraband trader, for a week. They then cross the Potomac, go to Port Conway, cross the Rappahannock, and take shelter in a barn on the Garret farm, 3 miles from Port Royal, on the road to Bowling Green. 24 Apr. 1865
A cavalry squad detailed from the 16th New York regiment, commanded by lieut. Dougherty and accompanied by E. J. Conger and L. B. Baker, detectives, trace Booth to his hiding-place; Herold surrenders; the barn is fired, and Booth, refusing to surrender, is shot in the head by serg. Boston Corbett, about 2 A.M. ....26 Apr. "
Booth dies from the effects of his wound about sunrise..26 Apr. "
Executive order for trial by military commission of the alleged assassins of president Lincoln, issued....1 May, "
Military commission designated as follows: maj.-gen. David H. Hunter, president; maj.-gen. Lewis Wallace; brevet maj.-gen. August V. Kautz; brig.-gen. Albion P. Howe; brig.-gen. Robert S. Foster; brevet brig.-gen. James A. Elkin (appointed 10 May); brig.-gen. T. M. Harris; brevet col. C. H. Tompkins (appointed 10 May); lieut.-col. David R. Clendennin, 8th Ill. cavalry; brig.-gen. Joseph Holt, judge advocate......6 May, "
Trial of conspirators begins....11 May, "
Trial closes, and sentence pronounced by the commission and confirmed by president Johnson—Herold, Atzerodt, Payne, and Mary E. Surratt to be hanged; O'Laughlin, Arnold, and Mudd imprisoned for life; and Spangler for 6 years in military prison at Dry Tortugas....30 June, "
Herold, Atzerodt, Payne, and Mrs. Surratt hung under direction of gen. Hancock in the yard of the old Capitol........7 July, "
John H. Surratt seen in Washington, 14 Apr. 1865; next heard of at Burlington, Vt., and Montreal, Can., 18 Apr.; sails on the *Peruvian* for Liverpool, 16 Sept.; enlists in the army of the pope in Italy, Apr. 1866; is arrested, but escapes to Alexandria, Egypt, where he is apprehended, and brought to the U. S. on the U. S. man-of-war *Swatara*. His trial begins, 10 June, 1867
Hearing of evidence in the Surratt case begins, 17 June; concludes, 26 July; argument concluded, 7 Aug., and the jury, failing to agree, are discharged....10 Aug. "
Surratt released from custody....22 June, 1868
A second indictment is afterwards found against him, and, the district-attorney entering a *nolle prosequi*, the prisoner is set at large....22 Sept. "
Dr. Mudd pardoned....11 Feb. 1869
Arnold and Spangler pardoned....1 Mch. "

boots, said to have been invented by Carians, were mentioned by Homer, 907 B.C., and often by Roman historians. Many forms appear in Fairholt's "Costume in England." An instrument of torture termed "the boot" was used in Scotland upon the Covenanters about 1666.

borax (boron), known to the ancients, used in soldering, brazing, and casting gold and other metals, was called chrysocolla. Borax is found in the mountains of Thibet, and was brought to Europe from India about 1713. Homberg, in 1702, discovered in borax boracic acid, which was decomposed, 1808, by Gay-Lussac, Thénard, and H. Davy into oxygen and the new element, boron. Borax has lately been found in Saxony. It is largely manufactured from boracic acid, found by Hoefer in gas from certain lagoons in Tuscany, which have enriched their owner, M. Lardarel, since 1818. Its production on the Pacific coast of the United States is confined to California and Nevada. The purest crystallized borax is found in the lakes and springs of Lake county, Cal. 10,000,000 pounds were produced, 1887.

Bordeaux, W. France, the Roman Burdigalla, in Aquitania, was taken by the Goths, 412; by Clovis, 508. It was acquired by Henry II. of England on his marriage with Eleanor of Aquitaine, 1151. Edward the Black Prince brought John, king of France, captive hither after the battle of Poictiers, 19 Sept. 1356, and here held court 11 years; his son, Richard II. of England, was born at Bordeaux, 1366. After several changes Bordeaux surrendered to Charles VII. of France, 14 Oct. 1453. An equestrian statue of Louis XV. was erected in 1743. Bordeaux was entered by the victorious British after the battle of Orthes, 27 Feb. 1814. 13 vessels were burned and others injured in the port by burning petroleum, 28 Sept. 1869. The French delegate government removed here from Tours, 11 Dec. 1870. M. Gambetta remained for a time with the army of the Loire. The "pacte de Bordeaux," among parties of the national assembly, made M. Thiers chief of the executive, 17 Feb. 1871. The French Association for the Advancement of Science held its first meeting here, 5 Sept. 1872; M. Quatrefages, president.

Borgne lake, La., naval battle on. Here, 14 Dec. 1814, the British with about 60 barges and 1200 men under capt. Lockyer, defeated 5 American gunboats with 182 men under lieut. Thomas A. C. Jones. The British, losing about 300 men, gained control of the lake.

Borneo, in the Indian ocean, disputes with NEW GUINEA the title of the largest island in the world. It was discovered by the Portuguese about 1518. It extends more than 800 miles from north to south, is more than 600 miles wide, and contains about 289,000 sq. miles.

Dutch trade here in 1604; establish factories, 1609; abandon them, 1623; re-establish them.... 1776
Sarawak settled by sir James Brooke; appointed rajah.... 1841
Pirates of Borneo chastised by British, 1813; by capt. Keppel, Mch. 1843
By treaty with the sultan, negotiated by sir James Brooke, the island of Labooan, or Labuan (northwest of Borneo), and its dependencies, ceded to Great Britain and formally occupied in presence of Bornean chiefs....2 Dec. 1846
James Brooke, rajah of Sarawak (1846), governor of Labuan and consul-general of Borneo, visits England....Oct. 1847
He destroys many Bornean pirates.... 1849
Labuan made a bishopric; F. J. MacDougall consecrated bishop at Calcutta, the first English bishop consecrated out of England....18 Oct. 1855
Chinese in Sarawak rise and massacre Europeans; sir James Brooke escapes by swimming; returns with Malays, etc., and chastises the insurgents; 2000 are killed.... ...17, 18 Feb. 1857
He comes to England for help from government, without success, 1858
His health being broken, a subscription for him asked.... "
Deputation of merchants proposes to the earl of Derby the purchase of Sarawak, which is declined....30 Nov. "
Sir James Brooke returns to Borneo....20 Nov. 1860
Returns to England; d....11 June, 1868
Rajah of Sarawak, with Malays and Dyaks, suppresses a marauding decapitating tribe of Dyaks....June. 1870
Freedom of trade in the archipelago agreed on by Great Britain, Germany, and Spain, 1877, and further with Spain.... 1884
N. Borneo, with Sarawak and Brunei, constituted a British protectorate.... 1885
Governor appointed.... 1892

Bornou, an extensive kingdom in central Africa, explored by Denham and Clapperton (sent out by the British government) in 1822. Population estimated by Denham at 5,000,000, by Barth at 9,000,000; area, 52,000 sq. miles.

Borodino, a Russian village on the river Moskwa, near which one of the most sanguinary battles of history was fought, 7 Sept. 1812, between the French under Napoleon, and the Russians under Kutusoff, 240,000 men being engaged. Loss 80,000. Each party claimed the victory; but the Russians retreated, leaving Moscow, which the French entered, 14 Sept.

borough or **burgh,** anciently a company of ten families living together; now a town represented in Parliament, since the election of burgesses in the reign of Henry III., 1265. Charters were granted to towns by Henry I., 1132; which were remodelled by Charles II. in 1682-84, but restored in 1688. 22 new English boroughs were created in 1553. Burgesses first admitted into Scottish Parliament by Robert Bruce, 1326; into the Irish, 1365. Acts to amend the representation of the people in England and Wales passed 7 June, 1832, and 15 Aug. 1867; and the act for the regulation of municipal corporations, 9 Sept. 1835. In the United States borough is a corporate town, not a city.—*Worcester.*

Borough-bridge, W. R. of York, Engl. Here Edward II. defeated the earls of Hereford and Lancaster, 16 Mch. 1322. Lancaster was mounted on a lean horse, led to an eminence near Pontefract, and beheaded.

Boscobel, near Donington, Shropshire, Engl. Charles II. (after his defeat at Worcester, 3 Sept. 1651), disguised in the clothes of the Pendrills, remained from 4 to 6 Sept. at White Ladies; on 7 and 8 Sept. he lay at Boscobel house, near an oak, said to be the scion of the royal oak in which the king was part of the time hidden with col. Careless.—*Sharpe.* The "Boscobel Tracts" were published in 1660. In 1861 Mr. F. Manning published "Views," illustrating them. W. H. Ainsworth's "Boscobel," an historical novel, publ. 1872.

Bosnia, in European Turkey, formerly part of Pannonia, was governed by chiefs till a brother-in-law of Louis, king of Hungary, was made king, 1376. He was defeated by the Turks in 1389, and became their vassal. Bosnia was incorporated with Turkey in 1463. Many efforts have been made by the Bosnians to recover their independence. A rebellion, begun in 1849, was quelled by Omar Pacha in 1851. The Bosnians joined the insurgents in Herzegovina, Sept. 1875; revolt was subdued, Aug. 1877. Pop., 1889, 1,504,091.

About 100,000 Bosnian fugitives said to be in Austrian territories....July 1875

Proclamation of the emperor before entering Bosnia (in pursuance of the Treaty of Berlin, 13 July)............27 July, 1878
Advance of Austrians 29 July, resisted by Bosnian begs, aided by Turks..4-6 Aug. "
Bosnians defeated between Zepce and Maglai..........7, 8 Aug. "
Austrians occupy Travnik, the old capital, 11 Aug.; repulsed, 16 Aug. "
Victories of Philippovich at Han Belalovich, 16 Aug.; of Tegethoff..18 Aug. "
Serajevo, the capital, bombarded and taken by storm, 19 Aug.; other successes..........................30 Aug., 5 Sept. "
Fortress Trebinje voluntarily surrenders..............7 Sept. "
Behacs firmly resists, 10 Sept.; taken..................19 Sept. "
Senkovics, a fortress, with arms and ammunition, taken, 21 Sept. "
Zwornik, a stronghold, surrenders..............about 25 Sept. "
Livno bombarded and taken..........................28 Sept. "
Other places surrender.........................about 12 Oct. "
Resistance ended; general amnesty issued........about 9 Nov. "
Austrian loss estimated 5000 killed, wounded, missing....Nov. "
Country adopted gradual political reforms..............Jan. 1880

Bos'porus (improperly Bosphorus), Thracian, now strait of Constantinople, connecting the Black sea with the sea of Marmora, is about 16 miles in length, and varies from 2 miles to 550 yards in width. Darius Hystaspes crossed it on a bridge of boats to invade Greece, 493 B.C.

Bosporus, now **Circassia,** near the Bosporus Cimmerius, now the strait of Kertch or Yenikalé, connecting the Black sea with the sea of Azof or Azov. It was named Cimmerian, from the Cimmerii who dwelt on its borders about 750 B.C. It is spoken of by Herodotus, is conquered by the Scythians, 285 B.C., by Mithridates VI. of Pontus, 80 B.C., and comes under Roman influence, 47 B.C.

Boston, the principal city of New England, and capital of Massachusetts, lies at the head of Massachusetts bay, on peninsula called "Shawmut" by the Indians, meaning "living fountains." It was first named Trimontaine by the English, but soon afterwards Boston, in compliment to Mr. Isaac Johnson, from Boston, Engl., one of the principal promoters of the colony. Pop. 1790, 18,038; 1800, 24,937; 1810, 33,250; 1820, 43,298; 1830, 61,392; 1840, 93,383; 1850, 136,881; 1860, 177,840; 1870, 250,526; 1880, 362,839; 1890, 448,477; 1900, 560,892. By this census it stands the 5th city in the U. S. in point of population. Present area, 37 sq. miles. Lat. 42° 21′ 28″ N., lon. 71° 04′ W.

First settlement at Boston dates from..............17 Mch. 1630
First vessel, *Blessing the Bay*, launched..............4 July, 1632
Made the capital of the Massachusetts colony.............. "
First meeting-house built in Boston on south side of State st., Aug. "
Castle island fortified.. 1633
[These works subsequently rebuilt and named Castle William, in honor of William III. Site now occupied by fort Independence.]
Boston Commons, acres set apart for public use.......... 1634
First Latin school established on part of the ground on School st., afterwards occupied by King's chapel.................. 1635
First military company formed (now known as the "Ancient and Honorable Artillery Company of Boston")............ 1638
Post-office established at the house of Richard Fairbanks for "all letters which are brought from beyond the seas or are to be sent thither"...................................... 1639
First printing-press at Cambridge, Stephen Daye, printer..... "
First printing done in the colonies, "Freeman's Oath" and an almanac for New England (BOOKS, MASSACHUSETTS, PRINTING), "
Ship *Trial* built; makes a voyage to Spain.................. 1644
First mint established, "pine-tree shilling" coined (COINAGE), 1651
Water company incorporated.................................. 1652
First town-house erected; built on pillars, the space underneath used as a market................................ 1658
General court grants Boston 1000 acres for the support of free schools.. 1660
First local Baptist church organized 1662
Old South church, foundation laid..................12 May, 1669
[This stood until 1729, when the present brick one was erected on the same site.]
Oldest man in New England, Boniface Burton, dies at Boston, aged 113 years.. "
Colonial court establish a post-office in Boston, appointing John Heyward postmaster................................ 1676
Great fire, 46 dwellings burned, including North meeting-house in North square.................................2 Nov. "
First fire-engine received from England..............27 Jan. 1679
Great fire; 88 dwellings, 70 warehouses destroyed; loss, 200,000*l*. 8, 9 Aug. "
Episcopalians become permanently established in Boston; King's chapel, on spot occupied by the tower and front of the second chapel, erected at a cost of $1425; first meeting held, 30 June, 1687; building completed..............June, 1689
First brick meeting-house, built by the Quakers on Brattle st. afterwards the site of the Quincy house 1697
Severe winter; Massachusetts bay frozen over............... "

Boston News Letter, first American newspaper pub.; James Campbell, editor. (Year commenced 25 Mch. up to 1717.) First regular issue...............................24 Apr. 1704
Benjamin Franklin born..............................17 Jan. 1706
First public sewer act, specifying that they be built of brick or stone, passed.. 1709
Extensive fire begins in William's court; nearly 100 buildings destroyed, including the First church..............1 Oct. 1711
Act passed providing for a board of 10 fire-wardens, 1711; appointed..Feb. 1712
Old Brick church, built on site afterwards occupied by the Joy building, and later by the Rogers building on Washington st., opposite head of State; first occupied...........3 May, 1713
Library of rev. Ebenezer Pemberton sold at auction; the first of such sales.. 1717
Thomas Fleet publishes "Mother Goose's Melodies" (MASSACHUSETTS, 1715).. 1719
Boston Gazette first pub., William Brookes, editor......21 Dec. "
Five printing-presses running in Boston...................... "
Small-pox first appears in Boston, very severe; inoculation opposed (MASSACHUSETTS) 1721
New England Courant first pub., James Franklin, editor, 17 Aug. "
Christ church (Episcopal) erected............................ 1723
[In its tower was placed a chime of bells, each bearing a separate inscription; that on the 3d bell reads: "We are the first ring of bells cast for the British empire in North America A. R. 1744." From its tower the lantern was hung out which sped Paul Revere on his "midnight ride," 18 Apr. 1775.]
First Masonic lodge established in America.............July, 1733
First market opened..................................4 June, 1734
Corner-stone of Trinity church, erected on site of the "Seven-Star inn," cor. Summer and Hawley sts. (see 1877) laid, 15 Apr. "
FANEUIL HALL, called the "Cradle of Liberty," erected by Peter Faneuil and completed, Sept. 1742. First town-meeting held therein...14 Mch. 1743
[Building destroyed by fire in 1761 and rebuilt.]
Severe riots owing to the acts of the English press-gang...... 1747
Old State-house erected (still standing) 1748
First recorded dramatic entertainment, Otway's "The Orphans; or, the Unhappy Marriage"........................ 1750
[This was almost immediately suppressed; not opened again until 1794.]
King's chapel rebuilt and opened for service..........21 Aug. 1754
Great earthquake....................................18 Nov. 1755
349 houses burned; loss, $500,000....................20 Mch. 1760
Riots in opposition to the stamp-act (MASSACHUSETTS)....Aug. 1765
BOSTON MASSACRE.....................................5 Mch. 1770
Tea thrown overboard in the Boston harbor (MASSACHUSETTS), 16 Dec. 1773
Passing of the "Boston Port bill" by the British Parliament, 7 Mch. 1774; goes into effect (MASSACHUSETTS).......1 June, 1774
Battle of BUNKER HILL...............................17 June, 1775
Washington takes command of the army at Cambridge. 2 July, "
Siege of Boston commences.................................. " "
British evacuate the city and retire to Halifax........17 Mch. 1776
Boston Light, first established, 1715; destroyed by the British, 1776; light-house erected................................ 1783
Massachusetts bank established.............................. 1784
Charles River bridge, 1503 ft. in length, 42 in width, resting on 75 piers and with a 30-foot draw, opened..........17 June, 1786
Massachusetts Historical Society founded..................... 1791
Union bank chartered.. 1792
Federal Street or "Boston" theatre, on northwest cor. Franklin and Federal sts., built and opened..................3 Feb. 1794
[Burned and rebuilt, 1798.]
Haymarket theatre, the second in the city, on Tremont and Boylston sts., opened................................26 Dec. 1796
First Roman Catholic church erected in Boston, afterwards known as the Franklin St. Cathedral of the Holy Cross, dedicated..29 Sept. 1803
Samuel Adams, b. 27 Sept. 1722; d.......................2 Oct. "
South Boston annexed to the city......................6 Mch. 1804
State bank, afterwards State National bank, established....... 1811
Beacon hill levelled .... "
First daily paper, the *Advertiser*, started................... 1813
Handel and Haydn Society (musical) organized 30 Mch. 1815, and constitution adopted..........................20 Apr. 1815
First lodge of Odd Fellows in Boston organized.......26 Mch. 1820
Corner-stone of St. Paul's church, Tremont st., laid 4 Sept. 1819, and church consecrated...........................30 June, "
Massachusetts General hospital, founded 1799, incorporated 1811, and opened for reception of patients.................. 1821
English High school opened..................................May, "
City incorporated, John Phillips first mayor; pop. about 47,000, 23 Feb. 1822
Gas-works erected on Copp's hill............................. "
Corner-stone of Bunker Hill monument laid (BUNKER HILL, Battle of)...17 June, 1825
Boston Athenæum founded, 1804; first public exhibition...... 1826
Corner-stone of Tremont house laid....................4 July, 1828
[Hotel opened, Oct. 1829.]
Massachusetts Horticultural Society organized.........17 Mch. 1829
200th anniversary of the settlement of Boston celebrated, and city government removed from Faneuil hall to the Old State-house ....17 Sept. 1830
Noddle's island, now East Boston, annexed (settlement begun 3 years later)... "
Pasturing of cows on the Commons forbidden by law.......... "

ount Auburn cemetery Cambridge formally dedicated Sept 1831
rst number of the *Boston Post* issued 9 Nov "
rkins Institute and Massachusetts School for the Blind, South Boston, incorporated, 2 May, 1829, opened, with 6 blind pupils, under Dr S G Howe 1832
[Laura Bridgman was educated here]
ederic Tudor ships his first cargo of ice to Martinique 1805-6, o Charleston, S C, 1817, and begins export trade in ice to Calcutta India May, 1833
rning Journal established "
rst locomotive set in motion in Massachusetts on the Boston and Worcester railroad 4 Apr 1834, and first excursion train runs to Davis s tavern in Newton 7 Apr First regular trains begin running from depot in Indiana place, between Washington and Tremont sts 16 May, 1834
y streets first lighted with gas "
ick exchange organized 13 Oct "
erican house opened (rebuilt 1851) 1835
lliam Lloyd Garrison mobbed (SLAVERY) 21 Oct "
ad Street riot between fire companies and Irish 11 June 1837
itannia, first Cunarder, enters Boston harbor 20 July, 1840
ston harbor frozen, the *Britannia* sent to sea through a anal 7 miles long, 100 ft. wide, cut through ice 2 ft thick 3 Feb 1844
ston *Daily Herald* first issued. 31 Aug 1846
ward Athenæum on Howard st, previously known as Miller's Tabernacle, and occupied by the Millerites, opened as a heatre, 13 Oct. 1845 Building burned, 25 Feb. 1846, rebuilt and reoccupied 25 Oct "
ston museum, Tremont st, first opened, June, 1841, new building erected and opened 2 Nov "
vere house built 1847
rest Hills cemetery opened 1848
ter introduced from lake Cochituate, 20 miles west, containing 650 acres 25 Oct. "
olera visits the city, out of a population of 130,000, 5080 die 1849
enæum building E S Cabot, architect, corner stone laid, 847, completed at a cost of $200,000 "
rren Manufacturing Company (Edward Howard and others) egin the manufacture of watches at Roxbury, first made in America 1850
odlawn cemetery opened 1851
is, the negro, seized and returned to the South as a slave MASSACHUSETTS, SLAVERY) "
ston Young Men's Christian Union instituted "
mpletion of railroad lines connecting the city with Canada and the great lakes celebrated 17-19 Sept "
egraphic fire alarm introduced "
ston Young Men's Christian Association organized Dec "
unt Hope cemetery consecrated 24 June, 1852
ston Public library incorporated (540,000 vols 1891) "
nerset club organized "
ston Normal school opened "
ston Music hall dedicated 20 Nov "
ily Globe established 1853
tislavery riot in Court square (TRIALS) 26 May, 1854
"watch," which had existed since 1631, abolished, and police department established, 250 men under chief of police, deputies, and 8 captains 26 May, "
st steam fire engine introduced "
ston Art club organized "
ston theatre opened 11 Sept. "
w city charter adopted 15 Nov "
shington Village annexed 1855
ker house established "
st street railroad chartered, 21 May, 1853 (the Metropolitan) treet railroad lines opened to Cambridge and Roxbury, 1856, and Dorchester Ave. line opened Oct. 1856
aring house established "
antic Monthly established, Ticknor & Fields, publishers 1857
forming of city police begun "
n boxes placed in different sections of the city for deposit f prepaid letters, to be collected by carriers, system goes nto operation 2 Aug 1858
blic garden, 24½ acres, formerly a part of the Commons, and site of Botanic garden, 1837, established 1859
bster statue in the State-house grounds unveiled 17 Sept "
ston college dedicated " 1860
ner stone of new city hall laid 22 Dec. 1862
ion club established 9 Apr 1863
ft riot in the North End, instigated and led at first by women. 14 July, "
y hospital at South End dedicated 24 May, 1864
ssachusetts Institute of Technology, incorporated 1861, and school of Industrial Science opened 1865
rner stone of Horticultural Hall building in Tremont st laid, 8 Aug 1864, and building dedicated 16 Sept. "
w city hall in Sch[illegible] st. begun, 1862, and occupied 18 Sept "
ung Women's C[illegible]an Association established, 1866, incorporated. 1867
rner stone [illegible]ic temple, cor Tremont and Boyl[illegible]
ston st[illegible] 22 June, "
w E[illegible] of Music, the largest school of mu[illegible] the world, established "
[illegible] Nov. "
[illegible]oxbury, 30,000 inhabitants, annexed Jan. 1868
[illegible], on northwest cor of Public garden, dedicated, 27 June, "
[illegible] Woman's club organized "
[illegible]sical Peace Jubilee, concert of 10,371 voices and instruments, with anvils, bells, etc, begun. 15 June, 1869

Colossal equestrian bronze statue of Washington in the Public garden unveiled 3 July, 1869
Horace Mann School for the Deaf opened "
Dorchester annexed Jan 1870
Museum of Fine Arts founded "
Boston University founded 1869 (in theology), Methodist, in medicine, homœopathic), opened 1871
International Peace Jubilee, chorus 20 000 voices, orchestra 1000, with military bands and other performers from different nations, a day allotted to each nation 17 June-4 July, 1872
Great fire in Boston about 80 acres burned over, loss estimated at between 75 and 80 million dollars 9-11 Nov "
Boylston club (vocal music) organized May, 1873
Massachusetts Normal Art school established "
Apollo club organized, 1871 incorporated "
City of Charlestown and towns of Brighton and West Roxbury annexed Jan 1874
Hotel Brunswick built at a cost of nearly $1 000 000 "
New " Old South church " built at cost of $500 000 1874-75
Celebration of the 100th anniversary of the battle of Bunker Hill 16 17 June, 1875
Cathedral of the Holy Cross, corner stone laid, 25 June, 1866, dedicated 8 Dec "
Great elm on Boston Commons blown down 15 Feb 1876
Massachusetts homœopathic hospital, chartered, 1855, new building opened for patients May, "
Museum of Fine Arts, St James ave and Dartmouth st, founded, 1870, first portion opened "
System of public parks established, Apr 1876, and Back bay park project adopted 1877
Trinity church (Episcopal) at intersection of Huntington ave and Boylston and Clarendon sts. Back bay district, the finest Protestant church edifice in America, erected at a cost of $750 000, consecrated 9 Feb "
Prof A Graham Bell telephones from Salem to his laboratory in Exeter place, off Chauncey street 13 Feb "
Army and Navy monument on the Commons, corner stone laid, 18 Sept 1871, dedicated 17 Sept "
Marcella Street Home opened "
Cecilia club (vocal music) established "
Produce exchange organized "
Daily *Evening Record* established 1878
Park theatre opened 14 Apr 1879
Erection of People's church begun "
Boston Society of Natural History, incorporated 1831, celebrates its semi centennial 28 Apr 1880
American Academy of Arts and Sciences, founded 1780, celebrates its centennial May, "
Scollay square lighted by electricity "
[Boston English High and Latin school building begun, 1877, finished, 1880, cost $750,000 (the largest building in the world used as a free public school)]
St Botolph club organized "
250th anniversary of the settlement of Boston celebrated, 17 Sept. "
National Law and Order league organized 22 Feb. 1882
St James hotel purchased for the use of the New England Conservatory of Music "
Foreign exhibition opened 3 Sept. 1883
Wendell Phillips, b 1811, d 2 Feb. 1884
Algonquin club organized 1885
Statue of William Lloyd Garrison (by Olin L Warner) unveiled in Commonwealth ave 1886
Charles Francis Adams b 1807, d 21 Nov "
William Warren the actor, dies 21 Sept 1888
Dr Oliver Wendell Holmes presents his medical library to the Boston Medical Library association Jan 1889
Electric street railway first introduced "
Maritime exhibition opened 4 Nov "
Great fire, loss estimated at $5,000,000 28 Nov "
First annual convention of letter carriers of the U S held (100 delegates) 13 Aug 1890
Centennial celebration of Methodism in New England begins, 21 Oct. "
Centennial celebration of the Massachusetts Historical Society, 24 Jan 1891
First world s convention of the Woman's Christian Temperance Union opened 10 Nov "
Corner stone of State house on Beacon hill, laid 4 July, 1795, occupied, 1798, extension much larger than the original building added 1888-92
Phillips Brooks, bishop of the Protestant Episcopal diocese of Massachusetts, dies 23 Jan 1893
Great fire, loss estimated at $4,500,000 10 Mch. "
Statue of Columbus unveiled "
Public library building, Copley square, facing Public gardens, frontage on Dartmouth st. 225 ft., on St James ave 229 ft., 69 ft high Final plans drawn 1888, completed at a cost of over $2,000,000. 1894

MAYORS.

John Phillips	1822	John P Bigelow	1849
Josiah Quincy	1823	Benjamin Seaver	1852
Harrison Gray Otis	1829	Jerome V C Smith	1854
Charles Wells	1832	Alexander H. Rice	1856
Theodore Lyman, jr	1834	Frederick W Lincoln, jr	1858
Samuel T Armstrong	1836	Joseph W. Wightman	1861
Samuel Atkins Eliot	1837	Frederick W Lincoln	1863
Jonathan Chapman	1840	Otis Norcross	1867
Martin Brimmer	1843	Nathaniel B. Shurtleff	1868
Thomas A. Davis	1845	William Gaston	1871
Josiah Quincy, jr	1846	Henry L. Pierce.	1873

Samuel C. Cobb	1874	Albert Palmer	1883
Frederick O. Prince	1877	Augustus P. Martin	1884
Henry L. Pierce	1878	Hugh O'Brien	1885
Frederick O. Prince	1879	Thomas N. Hart	1889
Samuel A. Greene	1882	Nathan Matthews, jr.	1891

Boston, evacuation of. MASSACHUSETTS, 1775-76.

Boston Massacre. Owing to the unfriendly attitude of the people of Massachusetts, and especially of Boston, towards the British government, 3 regiments were sent over from England in 1768, under gen. Gage, to suppress disturbances. This act, together with the presence of the troops in Boston, was a source of constant irritation to the citizens, so that frequent encounters took place (MASSACHUSETTS, 1770), culminating in "the Boston Massacre" on the evening of 5 Mch. 1770. Several hundred citizens had engaged in a disturbance, attacking with various missiles a sentinel; capt. Preston, going to his assistance with several soldiers, was also attacked, when, without orders, the soldiers fired, killing Crispus Attucks, a mulatto, Samuel Gray, and James Caldwell, and wounding several others, among them Samuel Maverick and Patrick Carr mortally. Further conflict was avoided upon gov. Hutchinson's assurance that justice would be rendered in the morning. Next day the people demanded the immediate withdrawal of the troops, and the trial of capt. Preston and his men for murder. These demands were complied with. The troops removed to Castle William on 12 Mch., and capt. Preston and his men were tried before a Boston jury, but, being ably defended by John Adams and Josiah Quincy, were acquitted, except 2, who were slightly punished. Boston has commemorated this event by the erection of a monument on her Common, on which are inscribed the names of the 5 killed in the affray.

Boston Port bill. MASSACHUSETTS, Mch.-June, 1774.

Bosworth Field, Leicestershire, Engl., site of the 13th and last battle between the houses of York and Lancaster, 22 Aug. 1485, when Richard III., through the desertion of sir William Stanley, was defeated by the earl of Richmond (afterwards Henry VII.) and slain.

botany. Aristotle is considered the founder of the science (about 347 B.C.). "Historia Plantarum," of Theophrastus, was written about 320 B.C. Authors on botany became numerous at the close of the 15th century. Fuchsius, Bock, Bauhin, Cæsalpinus, and others wrote between 1535 and 1600. The system and arrangement of the great Linnæus was made known about 1735; and Jussieu's system, founded on Tournefort's, and called "the natural system," in 1758. At Linnæus's death (1778) the species of plants actually described amounted to 11,800; it cannot now fall short of 100,000. J. C. Loudon's "Encyclopædia of Plants," a comprehensive work, first appeared in 1829. De Candolle's "Prodromus Systematis Naturalis Regni Vegetabilis" (of which vol. i. appeared in 1818) was completed, 1876. An international botanical congress was opened in London 23 May, 1866, A. De Candolle, president; another at Amsterdam, 13 Apr. 1877. Robert Brown, who accompanied Flinders in his survey of New Holland in 1803, and died 10 June, 1858, aged 85, was long acknowledged to be the chief botanist of his day.

Asa Gray, b. Paris, N. Y., 18 Nov. 1810; d. Cambridge, Mass., 30 Jan. 1888; distinguished botanist and professor of natural history in Harvard, author of many works on botany, among them, "Genera of the Plants of the U. S.," and "Manual of the Botany of the Northern U. S.," "Structural and Systematic Botany," the 1st vol. of "The Botany of the U. S. Exploring Expedition under Capt. Wilkes." Alphonso Wood's "Class Book of Botany," 1845, has passed its 50th edition; author also of "American Botanist and Florist," 1870. Chapman's "Flora of the Southern U. S.," 1860. FLOWERS and PLANTS.

BOTANIC GARDENS.

	Established about		Established about
Padua	1545	Coimbra	1773
Montpellier	1558	St. Petersburg	1785
Leyden	1577	Calcutta	1793
Leipsic	1580	Dublin	1800
Paris (Jardin des Plantes)	1624	Horticultural Society's, Chiswick	1821
Jena	1629	Royal Botanic Society's, Regent's park	1839
Oxford	1632	Washington, D. C. (10 acres)	1850
Upsal	1657	Royal Horticultural Society's, S. Kensington	1860
Chelsea	1673-86	Kew, 1760; greatly improved	1841-65
Edinburgh	1680		
Vienna	1753		
Madrid	1755		
Cambridge	1763		

Botany Bay, Australia, discovered by capt. Cook, 28 Apr. 1770, named from the great variety of plants on the shore. Made a colony of convicts from Great Britain. The first governor, capt. Arthur Phillip, who sailed from England in May, 1787, arrived in Jan. 1788. The colony was eventually established at Port Jackson, about 13 miles north of the bay. NEW SOUTH WALES, TRANSPORTATION.

Bothwell Bridge, Lanarkshire, Scotland. The Scotch Covenanters, who took up arms against the tyranny of Charles II., and defeated Claverhouse at Drumclog, 1 June, 1679, were totally routed by the earl of Monmouth at Bothwell Bridge, 22 June, 1679; many prisoners were tortured and executed.

bottles, anciently, were of leather. Glass bottles and drinking-glasses were known to the Romans at least before 79 A.D.; such vessels have been found in the ruins of Pompeii. Bottles were made in England about 1558. A bottle which contained 2 hogsheads was blown, we are told, at Leith, in Scotland, in Jan. 1747-48. Largest bottle-glass works in the United States are the Whitney Glass Works, at Glassboro, N. J., established in 1775. GLASS.

Bouillon (*boo-le-yon'*), Belgium, formerly a duchy, was sold by Godfrey, its ruler, to Albert, bishop of Liége, to obtain funds for the crusade, 1095; was seized by the French in 1672, and held till 1815, then given to the king of the Netherlands, as duke of Luxemburg; awarded to Belgium after the revolution of 1830.

Boulangists. FRANCE, 1886-91.

Boulevards (bulwarks), sites of old fortifications in Paris and other French towns, now planted with rows of trees, and used as avenues. The name is often given to broad streets in England and America.

Boulogne (*boo-lōn'*), a seaport in Picardy, N. France, added to Burgundy, 1435; to France, 1447. Here Henry VIII. and Francis I. concluded a treaty to oppose the Turks, 28 Oct. 1532. Boulogne was besieged by Henry VII., 2 Oct. 1492, for a few days; taken by Henry VIII. on 14 Sept. 1544, but restored for a sum of money, 1550.

Lord Nelson attacked a flotilla here, disabling 10 vessels and sinking 5 .... 3 Aug. 1801
In another attempt he was repulsed with great loss, and capt. Parker of the *Medusa* and two-thirds of his crew were killed, 18 Aug. "
Bonaparte assembled 160,000 men and 10,000 horses, also 1300 vessels and 17,000 sailors, to invade England in 1804; the coasts of Kent and Sussex were covered with martello towers and lines of defence; nearly half the adult males of Britain formed volunteer corps; sir Sydney Smith unsuccessfully attempted to burn the flotilla with fire-machines called catamarans .... 2 Oct. 1804
Army withdrawn on war with Austria 1805
Congreve rockets, in another attack, fired the town .... 8 Oct. 1806
Louis Napoleon (afterwards emperor) made a fruitless descent here with about 50 followers .... 6 Aug. 1840
As emperor, reviewed French troops destined for the Baltic, 10 July, 1854; and entertained prince Albert and the king of the Belgians .... 5 Sept. 1854
Statue of Edward Jenner here inaugurated .... 11 Sept. 1865
Pilgrims adore an image of the Virgin and Child, said to have been miraculously brought hither in a boat in 633 1857-75
Law authorizing construction of a new deep-sea harbor by M. Stoecklin (in 15 years), cost about 680,000*l*.; passed 19 June; first stone laid by M. Freycinet .... 9 Sept. 1878

boundaries. ASHBURTON TREATY, MASON AND DIXON'S LINE, UNITED STATES, and STATES.

bounties. In the French and Indian war of 1754 the French offered bounties for British scalps. The colonists offered 100*l*. for Indian scalp, 1754. In 1755 Massachusetts offered to every soldier enlisting and furnishing his own gun, 3*l*.; also, 40*l*. for the scalp of every male Indian over 12 years of age, and 20*l*. for the scalp of every Indian woman and child. John Penn, grandson of William Penn, and governor of Pennsylvania, offered, for every male Indian captured over 10 years of age, $150, and for every one killed and scalped, $134; for a male under 10, $130, and for a female, $50.—The approximate amount of bounties paid by the loyal states to the soldiers during the civil war was $285,941,036.

Bounty mutiny took place on board the *Bounty*, a British armed ship which quitted Otaheite, with bread-fruit trees, 7 Apr. 1789. The mutineers put their captain, Bligh, and 19 men into an open boat, with a small stock of provisions, ıear Annamooka, one of the Friendly isles, 28 Apr. 1789; :hese reached the island of Timor, south of the Moluccas, in June, after a voyage of nearly 4000 miles. Some of the mu:ineers were tried 15 Sept. 1792; 6 were condemned and 3 ex-ecuted. PITCAIRN ISLAND.

Bourbon, house of, from which came the royal houses of France, Spain, and Naples, derives its name from the rich district in the centre of France called the Bourbonnais, which in the 10th century was one of the 3 great baronies of the kingdom. The first of the long line of Bourbons sketched in history was Adhémar, who was invested with the barony towards the end of the 9th century.

Robert, count of Clermont, son of Louis IX. of France, married the heiress (Bourbon) Beatrice in 1272; d. 1317; and (as the elder branches of the family had become extinct) their son Louis I. was created duke of Bourbon and peer of France by Charles IV.. 1327

In 1488 the line of his descendants ended with Jean II., who died that year. The whole of the estates passed to Jean's brother Pierre, lord of Beaujeu, who married Anne, sister of Louis XI. Pierre d. 1503, leaving only a daughter, Suzanne, who married Charles, duke of Montpensier, 1505, made constable of France by Francis I., but afterwards, offended by his sovereign, entered the service of the emperor Charles V. of Germany, and was killed at the siege of Rome.....6 May, 1527

With the constable ended the direct line from Pierre, duc de Bourbon. But Louis, count of Vendôme, and Chartres, the fourth in descent from Pierre's brother Jacques, became the ancestor of the royal house of Bourbon, and of the noble families of Condé, Conti, and Montpensier. In direct descent and fourth from Louis of Vendôme was Antoine de Bourbon, who married (1548) Jeanne d'Albret, daughter of Henry, king of Lower Navarre, and who became king of that province on the death of Henry, 1554. Their son, Henry, b. at Pau, 14 Dec. 1553, became king of France as Henry IV., 31 July, 1589

Henry was succeeded by his son, Louis XIII., who left 2 sons, Louis XIV. and Philippe, duc d'Orleans, head of the Orleans branch. Louis XIV.'s son, the dauphin, died before his father, leaving 3 sons, one of whom died without issue. Of the others, the elder, Louis of Burgundy, d. 1712, and his only surviving son became Louis XV. of France, while the younger Philippe, duke of Anjou, became king of Spain, and founded the Spanish branch of the Bourbon family. Louis XV. of France was succeeded by his grandson, Louis XVI., who perished on the scaffold, and his son, the dauphin, Louis XVII., in prison. After the Restoration the throne was occupied by Louis XVIII., brother of Louis XVI., who in turn was succeeded by his brother Charles X., who was expelled in 1830. The Orleans branch of the Bourbons then succeeded to the throne of France in the person of Louis Philippe, 1830–48. The second son of Charles X., the duc de Berri, left a son, Henri Charles Ferdinand, duc de Bordeaux and count de Chambord, who was claimant of the throne of France, and was designated by his adherents Henri V. until his death, 1883. Since then, comte de Paris, grandson of Louis Philippe, represents the Orleans branch. *Spanish Branch:* Philippe, duc d'Anjou, grandson of Louis XIV., became king of Spain as Philip V., in 1700. In 1746 he was succeeded by his son Ferdinand VI., who, dying without family, was succeeded by his brother Charles III., 1759, who became king of Naples as well. Charles III. was succeeded by his eldest son, Charles IV., who in turn was succeeded by his son Ferdinand VII., and he by his daughter Isabella. Upon the accession of Isabella, Don Carlos, Ferdinand's brother, claimed the throne of Spain (1833) on the ground of the Salic law, and his descendants have claimed it since. CARLISTS. Isabella abdicated in favor of her son, Alphonso XII., 1870, who d. 1885, leaving as heir to the throne, Alphonso XIII. *Neapolitan Branch:* The first Bourbon on the throne of Naples was Charles III. of Spain, who resigned his kingdom of Naples to his son Ferdinand, on his succession to the Spanish throne, 1759. In 1825 Ferdinand was succeeded by his son Francis I., and he by his son Ferdinand II., 1830, and he by his son Francis II., who was deprived of the kingdom in 1860, when it was gradually incorporated into the kingdom of Italy. FRANCE, NAPLES, SPAIN.

Bourbon, Isle of, in the Indian ocean, discovered by the Portuguese about 1542. The French are said to have first settled here in 1642. It surrendered to the British, under admiral Rowley, 21 Sept. 1809, and was restored to France in 1815. —*Alison.* Hurricane, in Feb. 1829, did much mischief. Bourbon was named "l'Île de la Réunion" in 1848. MAURITIUS.

Bourignonists, a sect founded by Antoinette Bourignon, who, in 1658, took the Augustin habit and travelled in France, Holland, England, and Scotland; in the last she made many converts about 1670. She maintained that Christianity does not consist in faith and practice, but in inward feeling and supernatural impulse. A disciple named Court left her a good estate. She died in 1680, and her works, 21 vols. 8vo, were pub. 1686.

bournous, the Arabic name of a hooded garment worn in Algeria, which has been introduced in a modified form into England and France since 1847.

Bouvines (*boo-veen'*). N. France, scene of a desper[ate] battle, 27 July, 1214, in which Philip Augustus of France [was] victorious over the emperor Otho and his allies, consisting [of] more than 150,000 men. The counts of Flanders and B[ou]logne were taken prisoners, and the earl of Salisbury, bro[ther] of king John.

bowie-knife. The first bowie-knife was made [by] R. P. Bowie, and not by col. James Bowie, as is often inc[or]rectly stated, somewhere about 1820. The blade was [...] in. long and 1½ in. wide, single edge, not curved; to be used [as] a hunting-knife.

bowls or **bowling,** an English game as early as t[he] 13th century. Henry VIII. and Charles I. played at it, a[s] also Charles II. at Tunbridge.—*Grammont.*

Bowyer, Fort, on Mobile bay, 30 miles from Mob[ile,] Ala., was attacked 15 Sept. 1814, by a British force from Pensacola—4 vessels carrying 78 guns and a land force of regulars a[nd] Indians, in all about 1300 men. The garrison, 134 men, un[der] maj. William Lawrence, repulsed the assailants, who lost [...] men, 162 of them killed. The defence lost 5 killed an[d] wounded. UNITED STATES, 1815.

boxing or **prize-fighting** (the *pugilatus* of [the] Romans), once a favorite sport with the strong-armed Briti[sh] and a good school for bayonet fighting.

ENGLISH MATCHES.

Broughton's amphitheatre, behind Oxford road, London, built, [...]
Schools opened in England to teach boxing.................. [...]
Mendoza opened the Lyceum in the Strand, London.......... [...]
Boxing very popular from about 1820 to...................... [...]
Tom Winter (nicknamed "Spring"), besides other victories, beat Langan (for 1000*l.*)..............................8 June, [...]
John Gully, butcher, afterwards prize-fighter, grew rich, and was M.P. for Pontefract, 1835; d.......................9 Mch. [...]
Tom King beat Mace, took the champion's belt, etc....26 Nov. [...]
He beat Goss, 1 Sept., and John C. Heenan, whose friends charged foul play....................................10 Dec. [...]
A trial ensued—culprits discharged on promising not to offend again...5 Apr. [...]
Wormald champion after fighting Marsden.............4 Jan. [...]
Contest for championship between Mace and O'Baldwin, a giant, prevented by the arrest of Mace ....15 Oct. [...]
Railways prohibited carrying persons to a prize-fight, 30 and 31 Vict. c. 119.. [...]

INTERNATIONAL MATCHES.

John C. Heenan, the "Benicia Boy" (American), challenged Thomas Sayers, the champion of England, for the championship of that country and $1000. Sayers was 5 ft. 8 in. and Heenan 6 ft. 1 in. in height. After 42 rounds, lasting 2 h. and 20 min., it was interrupted by fri[ends of Sayers], Farnborough, Engl...17 Apr. [...]
Each man received a silver belt.........................31 May, [...]
Heenan died on his way to California..................25 Oct. [...]
John L. Sullivan and Charles Mitchell (London prize-ring rules); declared a draw after a contest of several hours.....France, [...]

IN THE UNITED STATES.

First distinct match in the U. S. was that of Jacob Hyer (father of "Tom") and Thos. Beasley.................................. [...]
[They parted friends.]
"Tom" Hyer defeated "Yankee" Sullivan (real name, Frank Ambrose Murray) for the championship of America and $10,000. 16 rounds in 17 min. 18 sec., at Rock Point, Md. 7 Feb. [...]
[Hyer died in N. Y. city, 26 June, 1864, aged 45 years.]
"Yankee" Sullivan and John Morrissey fought at Boston Corners, N. Y.; Sullivan defeated ....12 Oct. [...]
[Sullivan went to California; was arrested by the vigilance committee, 1856, and died in prison.]
Bill Poole, of N. Y. city, defeated Morrissey, at Amos Dock, N. Y...27 July, [...]
[Louis Baker, a friend of Morrissey, shot Poole mortally, 24 Feb. 1855, at Stanwix Hall, 579 Broadway, N. Y. city, and took the brig *Isabella Jewett* for the Canary islands. Geo. Law, sr., furnished the clipper-ship *Grapeshot* for pursuit, which intercepted the *Jewett*, 17 Apr. 1855. Baker was brought back and tried, but the jury failed to convict. Poole, who died 8 Mch. 1855, represented the "American" or "Know-nothing" element in N. Y. city, and his funeral, 11 Mch., was largely attended.]
John Morrissey met and defeated John C. Heenan at Long Point, Canada, in 11 rounds; time, 21 min...........20 Oct. [...]
[Morrissey afterwards a leader of New York Democracy; elected to Congress from the 5th district in 1866, and re-elected, 1868; state senator, 1875, and re-elected, 1877. Died at Saratoga, N. Y., 1 May, 1878.]
John L. Sullivan defeated Jack Kilrain, for the championship of America, at Richburg, Miss..........................8 July, [...]
John L. Sullivan met "Jim" Corbett of San Francisco, Cal., for the championship of America, at the "Olympic" arena, New Orleans, on the evening of.........................7 Sept. [...]
[Contest began at 9 P.M. (Queensberry rules); Sullivan was

beaten in 21 rounds; a wager of $10,000 a side was put up, while the "Olympic club" offered $25,000 for the "mill," the entire amount to go to the winner.]

James J. Corbett met Charles Mitchell (English) at Jacksonville, Fla., under the auspices of the Duval Athletic club, 25 Jan. 1894

[Corbett defeated Mitchell in 3 rounds. Club paid $20,000 to winner, and $5000 to cover expenses of both for training.]

Boxtel, a village of Dutch Brabant, Holland, where the British and allied army, under the duke of York, was defeated by the French republicans, who took 2000 prisoners and 8 pieces of cannon, 17 Sept. 1794.

box-tree, indigenous to England. In the United States the tree is common from Massachusetts to Florida. It is called, indifferently, boxwood or dogwood. The wood is largely used by engravers and by mathematical-instrument makers.

boycotting, IRELAND, 1880. A fund to assist capt. Boycott in his trouble was subscribed in 1880-81.

Trades unions and Knights of Labor in the U. S. adopted boycotting to enforce demands and punish opponents.....about 1885

Mrs. Gray and Mrs. Landgraff, two bakers in New York, were boycotted.................................Apr. and May, 1886

[Citizens assisted Mrs. Landgraff by large orders for bread for charity hospitals.]

Paul Wilzig convicted in New York of conspiracy, for boycotting George Theiss, and extorting $1000 from him..26 June, "

George Ehret, a brewer of New York, boycotted for testimony against conspirators.................................June, "

[Boycott ineffective, public sentiment resisting it.]

Boydell's lottery for the Shakespeare gallery of paintings (1786) of alderman Boydell, lord mayor of London. Every ticket was sold, when the alderman died, 12 Dec. 1804, before the drawing.

Boyle lectures, instituted by will (18 July, 1691), by Robert Boyle (son of Richard Boyle, earl of Cork), a distinguished natural philosopher, who died 30 Dec. 1691, leaving 50*l.* a year for lectures to be delivered in London in vindication of the Christian religion; eight lectures to be delivered by each incumbent. The office of lecturer tenable for 3 years.

Boyne, a river in Ireland, near which William III. defeated his father-in-law, James II., 1 July, 1690. The latter lost 1500 (out of 30,000) men; the Protestant army lost about a third of that number (out of 36,000). James fled to Dublin, thence to Waterford, and escaped to France. The duke of Schomberg was killed by mistake by his own soldiers in crossing the river; here also was killed the rev. George Walker, who defended Londonderry in 1689. Near Drogheda is a splendid obelisk, 150 feet in height, erected in 1736 by Protestants to commemorate this victory.

Boyton's swimming apparatus. LIFE-BOAT.

Brabant, part of Holland and Belgium, an ancient duchy in Charlemagne's empire, fell to his son Charles, 806. It became a separate duchy (called at first Lower Lorraine) in 959. It descended to Philip II. of Burgundy, 1429, and in regular succession to the emperor Charles V. In the 17th century it was held by Holland and Austria, as Dutch Brabant and the Walloon provinces, and underwent many changes through the wars of Europe. The Austrian division was taken by the French in 1746 and 1794. It was united to the Netherlands in 1814, but South Brabant was given to Belgium, 1830. The heir of the throne of Belgium is styled duke of Brabant. BELGIUM.

bracelets were worn by the ancients, and *armillæ* were Roman military rewards. Those of pearls and gold were worn by the Roman ladies.

Bradlaugh case. PARLIAMENT, 1880-81.

Braganza, a city in Portugal, gave title to Alfonso, natural son of John I. of Portugal (in 1422), founder of the house of Braganza. When the nation, in a bloodless revolution in 1640, threw off the Spanish yoke, John, duke of Braganza, was called to the throne as John IV., and his descendants now reign over PORTUGAL and until 1889 in BRAZIL.

Bragg's Kentucky campaign. Early in the summer of 1862, the confederates, after their evacuation of Corinth, Miss., 29 May, concentrated about Chattanooga, Tenn., where by August they had between 55,000 and 65,000 men under gen. Braxton Bragg with 3 corps commanders—Hardee, Polk, and Kirby Smith. Deciding to invade Kentucky, Bragg crossed the Tennessee at Harrison, above Chattanooga, 24 Aug., while Kirby Smith advanced from Knoxville more directly across the Cumberland mountains, through Big Creek gap. The Union forces, about 40,000, under maj.-gen. Don Carlos Buell, then stretched from Bridgeport, Ala., to Nashville, Tenn. Concentrating around Nashville, Buell prepared to guard that point or advance into Kentucky. Over difficult mountain-roads Bragg's army entered Kentucky, 5 Sept. Gen. Buell, leaving Nashville strongly garrisoned, 15 Sept., marched towards Louisville, distant 170 miles. Meanwhile Kirby Smith, with his corps, having defeated the Union troops at RICHMOND, Ky., 30 Aug., seized Frankfort, the capital, apparently holding both Cincinnati and Louisville at his mercy, while Bragg compelled J. T. Wilder to surrender Munfordville, Ky., a fortified post, with its garrison of 4000 men, 17 Sept. Elated with these successes, on the next day the confederate commander issued a proclamation, calling the people of Kentucky to his assistance, and declining a battle with Buell, united his forces with Kirby Smith's at Frankfort, 1 Oct. Here on the 4th they inaugurated Richard Hawes provisional governor of Kentucky. By 29 Sept. the Union army reached Louisville. Whence, reinforced by 20,000, mainly new troops, Buell moved his army (now formed into 3 corps under McCook, Gilbert, and Crittenden), 1 Oct., against Bragg, who slowly retreated, covering his immense trains. Nearing Perryville on the afternoon of 7 Oct., Crittenden's corps from scarcity of water was obliged to move some 5 or 6 miles from his intended camp. Bragg, made aware of this separation of the federal troop, now prepared to strike a blow that would, he hoped, defeat, or at least retard, his adversary's advance sufficiently for him to withdraw his trains in safety. On the morning of the 8th there were sharp minor engagements near Perryville, and about 2 P.M. the confederates successfully attacked the left flank of McCook's corps, and for a while seriously threatened the whole left wing, but before night were repulsed at all points. The engagement, though not general, was severe, the federals losing 4348, 916 being killed (among them gens. Jackson and Terrell), 2943 wounded, and 489 missing; and the confederates 510 killed, 2635 wounded, and 251 missing. Next morning (9 Oct.) Buell, having concentrated his forces, expected to renew the battle, but the confederates had retired during the night, leaving 1200 wounded and sick behind. They retreated by Crab Orchard, Mount Vernon, and London to Cumberland gap, and so into E. Tennessee with their immense trains of plunder, the pursuit by the federals stopping at London, 22 Oct. The federal government, dissatisfied with the campaign, superseded Buell, 30 Oct., by maj.-gen. William S. Rosecrans. MURFREESBOROUGH, Battle of.

Brahma, the first person of the Hindu triad. Brahmā (neuter) is not a personality, but designates the universal spirit, the reality and cause of all existence—the creator—and Brahmā (masculine) the personality and supreme being of that creation. Brahma was never worshipped by the people, and only one temple sacred to him is known. He is represented with 4 heads and 4 arms, seated. BRAHMINS.

Brahmins, Hindu priests, the highest of the 4 castes. It is said that Pythagoras learned from them his doctrine of metempsychosis, and that some Greek philosophers went to India to converse with them. The Brahmins derive their name from Brahma, one of the 3 beings (the others being VISHNU and SIVA) whom God, according to their theology, created, and with whose assistance he formed the world.—VEDAS.

Brahmo Somaj. The new theistic church in India owes its origin to Rájá Rám Mohan Rái, born 1772. In 1816 he founded a society, [illegible] 1830 the present Brahmo Somaj. Their principles resem[illegible] Christianity. (1) They believe in one God wit[illegible] personality, etc.; (2) in the immortality of the s[illegible] (3) [illegible] repentance as the only way to salvation; (4) in p[illegible] (5) [illegible] good works as worship; (6) in the providentia[illegible] over his creatures; (7) they reject distinctions [illegible] new society or church grows rapidly in India, [illegible] Bengal, aided by English education and the l[illegible] an missionaries. DEISM.

Bramba[illegible], a village in Java, notable for extensive and remarkable ruins of Hindu temples, ascribed by tradition to 1266 and 1296 A.D. But their chronology and history are very obscure, and probably some of them are much older.

Bramham, W. R., York, Engl. Near here the earl of Northumberland and lord Bardolf were defeated and slain by sir Thomas Rokeby, general of Henry IV., 19 Feb. 1408; and Fairfax was defeated by royalists under the earl of Newcastle, 29 Mch. 1643.

Brandenburg, a city in Prussia, founded by Slavonians, who named it *Bunber* (variously explained as meaning *Guard of the Forest*; burg, or city, of the *Brenus*). Henry I., the Fowler, after defeating the Slavonians, fortified "Brannibor," 926, as a rampart against the Huns, and bestowed it on Sigefroi, count of Ringelheim, with the title of margrave, or protector of the marches or frontiers. The emperor Sigismund gave perpetual investiture to Frederick IV. of Nuremberg, of the house of Hohenzollern, ancestor of the royal family of Prussia, made elector in 1417. For a list of the margraves since 1134, PRUSSIA.

brandy (Ger. *Branntwein,* burned wine), spirit distilled from wine. Alcohol appears to have been known to Raymond Lully in the 13th century, and to have been manufactured in France early in the 14th. It was at first used medicinally, and miraculous cures were ascribed to its influence. The per cent. of alcohol in brandy is 53.4. Manufacture of genuine French brandy almost ceased. Announced, 1885. Fruit brandy produced in the United States in 1880, 129,086 gals.; in 1891, 1,223,725 gals.

Brandy Station, Va., affairs at. (1) A spirited reconnoissance made here, under direction of gen. Hooker, by gen. Pleasanton with gens. Buford's and Gregg's cavalry divisions, 9 June, 1863, which, although forced in the end to retreat with a loss of about 500 men, disclosed the fact that gen. Lee had concentrated his army for an advance north. (2) Gen. Buford with his division of cavalry met the confederate gen. Stuart, 1 Aug. 1863, compelling him to retreat until reinforced, when Buford fell back in turn. (3) Desultory fighting between the Union and confederate forces in this vicinity with cavalry and infantry from 10 to 16 Oct. 1863. Gen. Meade retired.

Brandywine (corruption of Branntwein, Ger. for brandy), a small river emptying into the Delaware near Wilmington, on the banks of which, near Chadd's ford, was fought a battle, 11 Sept. 1777, between 18,000 British, under gens. Howe, Cornwallis, and Knyphausen, and 11,000 Americans, under gen. Washington. It began about 3 P.M. and the Americans were defeated, with a loss of about 1200 men, the British losing about 800. Here gen. Lafayette was wounded. Soon after the battle the British occupied Philadelphia. PENNSYLVANIA.

brass, an alloy of copper and zinc. That mentioned in the Bible was most probably bronze. When Lucius Mummius burned Corinth, 146 B.C., he found immense riches, and, it is said, all the metals in the city melted, which, running together, formed the valuable composition Corinthian brass. But in fact Corinthian artists had long been known for combining gold and silver with copper.—*Du Fresnoy*. Some of the English sepulchral engraved brasses are said to be as old as 1277. Brass was manufactured in England during the reign of Henry VIII., and Parliament prohibited the export of it under severe penalties, repealed 1799. A white brass produced by P. M. Parsons, 1875.

Brauronia, festivals in Attica, at Brauron, now Vraona, where Artemis had a temple; they were attended by young virgins, dedicated to Diana, in yellow gowns, about 10 years of age, and not under 5; and therefore their consecration was called δεκατεύειν, from δέκα, 10; 600 B.C.

Bray, Berks. Fuller says that its vicar, Symon Symonds, was twice a papist and twice a Protestant—in the reigns of Henry VIII., Edward VI., Mary, and Elizabeth (1533-58). When called a turn-coat, he declared his principle, that "of living and dying the vicar of Bray." The modern song called "The Vicar of Bray" refers to political changes of the 17th and 18th centuries.

brazen bull, said to have been contrived by Perillus, at Athens, for Phalaris, tyrant of Agrigentum, 570 B.C. An opening in the side admitted victims, and a fire underneath roasted them to death; their groans resembled the roaring of a bull. Phalaris admired the invention, but ordered the artist to suffer first. The Agrigentes revolted against Phalaris, cut his tongue out, and roasted him in the brazen bull, 549 B.C.

Brazil, a country in South America, extending between lat. 4° 30′ N. to 33° 45′ S., and long. 34° 45′ to 72° 30′ W., being about 2600 miles north and south, and nearly the same distance east and west, with a coast-line on the Atlantic of 3700 miles, was discovered by Vicente Yañez Pinzon in Feb. 1500. Pedro Alvarez de Cabral, a Portuguese, driven upon its coasts by a tempest, Apr. following, called it the land of the Holy Cross; the name Brazil refers to its red wood. The French seized Portugal in 1807, the royal family and nobles embarked for Brazil, and landed 7 Mch. 1808. The dominant religion is Roman Catholic, but others are tolerated. New constitution ratified 25 Mch. 1824; modified 12 Aug. 1834, and 12 May, 1840; new constitution (republican) adopted, 22 June, 1890. Pop. about 14,000,000; area, 3,219,000 sq. miles. PORTUGAL.

Brazil explored by Amerigo Vespucci....................about 1504
Divided into captaincies by the king of Portugal.............. 1530
Martino Affonso de Souza discovers Rio, and founds the first European colony at San Vincente.......................... 1531
Jews banished from Portugal to Brazil.......................... 1548
San Salvador (Bahia) founded by Thomé de Souza............ 1549
French Protestants occupy bay of Rio de Janeiro..........1555-60
Sebastian founded.. 1567
Brazil, with Portugal, becomes subject to Spain.............. 1580
James Lancaster captures Pernambuco.......................... 1593
French establish a colony at Maranham......................... 1594
Belem founded by Calderia..................................... 1615
French expelled... "
Dutch seize the coast, and hold Pernambuco................. 1630
Defeated at Guararapès, 1646; give up Brazil................ 1661
Gold-mining commences... 1693
Destruction of Palmares.. 1697
French assault and capture Rio de Janeiro..................1710-11
Diamond-mines discovered in Sezzo Frio...................... 1729
Jesuits expelled...1758-60
Capital transferred from Bahia to Rio de Janeiro............ 1763
Royal family of Portugal arrive at Brazil..............7 Mch. 1808
First printing-press established................................ "
Brazil becomes a kingdom..................................... 181[illegible]
King John VI. returns to Portugal, dom Pedro regent......... 1821
Brazil declares its independence......................7 Sept. 1822
Pedro I. crowned emperor...............................1 Dec. "
New constitution ratified..............................25 Mch. 1824
Independence recognized by Portugal..................29 Aug. 1825
Revolution at Rio de Janeiro; abdication of dom Pedro I., 7 Apr. 1831
Reform of the constitution.........12 Aug. 1834, and 12 May, 1840
Pedro II. declared of age..............................23 July, "
Steamship line to Europe commenced........................ 1850
Suppression of the slave-trade; railways commenced......... 1852
Rio de Janeiro lit with gas.................................... 1854
The British ship *Prince of Wales* wrecked at Albardas, off coast; plundered by natives; some of the crew killed, about 7 June, 1861
Reparation long refused; reprisals made; 5 Brazilian merchant ships seized by the British.........................31 Dec. 1862
Brazilian minister at London pays 3200*l.* as an indemnity, under protest..26 Feb. 1863
Brazilian government request the British to express their regret for reprisals; declined; diplomatic intercourse suspended..5-28 May, "
Dispute with Great Britain respecting arrest of British officers at Rio de Janeiro (17 June, 1862) referred to arbitration of the king of the Belgians, who decides in favor of Brazil, 18 June, "
New ministry; F. J. Furtado, president; prospect of reconciliation with Great Britain..............................30 Aug. 1864
U. S. war-steamer *Wachusett* seizes the confederate war-vessel *Florida*, in the port of Bahia, under protection of Brazil, 7 Oct.; after remonstrance, the U. S. government disavowed the act (UNITED STATES, Oct. 7)......................26 Dec. "
War with Uruguay; Brazilians take Paysandú, and march upon Montevideo..2 Feb. 1865
Lopez, president of Paraguay, declares war against the Argentine Republic..Apr. "
Treaty between Brazil, Uruguay, and the Argentine Republic against Paraguay, signed.................................1 May, "
Scientific expedition under Agassiz favored by the emperor, July, "
Emperor joins the army against Lopez........................Aug. "
Allies under Flores defeat the Paraguayans at Santayuna on the Uruguay...18 Sept. "
War continues with varied success, though generally in favor of the allies, through..........................1865-66-67-68-69
Lopez defeated and killed near the Aquidaban..........1 Mch. 1870
Treaty of peace; Paraguay subdued....................20 June, "
New ministry under viscount St. Vincent...............29 Sept. "
Emperor and empress in Europe; visit public and scientific institutions, manufactories, etc.....................June-Aug. 1871
Gradual slave-emancipation bill passed by the senate; great rejoicings......................................27, 28 Sept. 1872
Treaty with the Argentine Republic............................Jan. 1873
Prosecution of the archbishop of Pernambuco and other prelates for infraction of the constitution.....................Sept.-Dec. "
Emperor and empress at opening of Philadelphia exhibition, 10 May, 1876; in Europe, etc.; return to Rio de Janeiro...Sept. 1877

Ministerial crisis concerning emancipation of slaves (of whom there were 1,200,000) Sept 1884
Dantas, antislavery minister, resigns 5 May, 1885
Bill for the total abolition of slavery passed by the chambers, 10-14 May, about 700 000 persons freed May, 1888
Revolution at Rio de Janeiro, republic proclaimed, marshal Deodoro da Fonseca head of provisional government, emperor and family forcibly conveyed to the *Alagoas*, sail for Europe 15 Nov 1889
Emperor refuses the offer of the provisional government of 500,000*l.* a year Nov "
Republic recognized informally by France, United States, and Switzerland 29 Nov "
Decree for the separation of church and state 7 Jan 1890
Republic formally recognized by the United States 29 Jan "
New constitution promulgated 22 June, "
Republic formally recognized by Great Britain 20 Oct "
Marshal D da Fonseca elected president for 4 years, installed, 26 Feb 1891
Pres Fonseca resigns and is succeeded by gen Floriano Peixoto, 23 Nov "
Death of gen Deodoro da Fonseca 23 Aug 1892
Growing discontent towards the administration of pres Peixoto on account of his alleged despotic rule throughout "
Southern province in open rebellion, "
RIO DE JANEIRO bombarded by the opposition fleet, under adm Custodio de Mello Sept 1893
Commanders of the foreign war ships request that he refrain from further bombardment, request acceded to. 30 Sept. "

EMPERORS OF BRAZIL

1822. Dom Pedro (of Portugal), abdicated in favor of his infant son, 7 Apr 1831, d 24 Sept. 1834
1831. Dom Pedro II (b 2 Dec. 1825), assumed the government 23 July, 1840, married, 4 Sept 1843, princess Theresa of Naples (b 14 Mch 1822, d. Oporto, Portugal, 28 Dec. 1890) Brazil declared a republic and dom Pedro banished, sails for Portugal, 15 Nov 1889, d in Paris, 4 Dec 1891

PRESIDENTS OF THE REPUBLIC.

Deodoro da Fonseca (resigns, 23 Nov 1891) 26 Feb. 1891
Floriano Peixoto . 23 Nov "
Prudente de Moraes . . . " 1894

Brazito, Chihuahua, Mexico Here col Domphan defeated the Mexicans, 25 Dec 1846

bread. Ching-Noung, successor of Fohi, is reputed the first who taught the Chinese the arts of husbandry, and of making bread from wheat and wine from rice, 1998 B.C.—"Univ Hist." Baking was known in patriarchal ages (Ex xii 15) A profession at Rome, 170 B C. After the conquest of Macedon, 148 B.C, Greek bakers came to Rome, acquired special privileges, and soon obtained a monopoly Public bakeries were throughout the city and grain was distributed directly to the bakers from public granaries, the grain was pounded and sifted at the bakeries. During the siege of Paris by Henry IV, owing to famine, bread, which had been sold while any remained for a crown a pound, was made from the bones of the charnel-house of the Holy Innocents, 1594 A.D —*Hénault*. In the time of James I, barley-bread was used by the poor, and now in Iceland, codfish, beaten to powder, is made into bread, potato-bread is used in Ireland The London Bakers' Company was incorporated in 1307. Bread street was once the London market for bread Until 1302 London bakers were not allowed to sell in their own shops.—*Stow* Bread was made with yeast by the English bakers in 1634. In 1856 and 1857 Dr Dauglish patented a mode of making "aërated bread," in which carbonic-acid gas is combined with water and mixed with flour Aerated bread in the United States successfully produced, 1854. WAGES

bread-fruit tree (*Artocarpus incisa*), a native of the South Sea islands The attention of the English government was directed to the fruit in 1688 by capt. Dampier and later by capt Cook, who recommended its transportation to the West Indian colonies A vessel under capt. Bligh was fitted out to convey some of these trees to various British colonies in 1787 (BOUNTY), and again in 1791 The number taken on board at Otaheite was 1151. Some were left at St. Helena, 352 at Jamaica, and 5 were reserved for Kew gardens, 1793 The tree was successfully cultivated in French Guiana, 1802

breakwaters consist generally of stones or blocks of concrete, deposited or built in deep water to protect an anchorage for vessels during storms. There are 3 types of breakwaters 1 *Sloping* —Deposits of rubble-stone forming a mound are often made when material is plenty. 2 *Composite.*—De[illegible] [illegible] and masonry from the bottom of the sea. The Plymouth breakwater, Engl., an example of the first class, begun 12 Aug. 1812, extends a mile across the sound, in water 58 ft deep at high tide. It is 360 ft. broad at the bottom, 30 ft at the top, 3 ft above high water The architects were John Rennie and his son It cost 1,700,000*l* The Portland breakwater, an example of the second class (began 1849), has a vertical wall rising 25 ft. above high water Another at Alderney island, English channel, of the same kind, cost 1,250,000*l.* The Dover breakwater, Engl., 1847-71, cost 679,300*l*, and that at Aberdeen, Scotland, are examples of the third class There is also an extensive breakwater at Holyhead The Cherbourg breakwater, France, is of the second class, with a wall rising 12½ ft above high water (1784-1830) Cost about $16,000,000 An extensive one at Marseilles, the "Joliette," was begun 1844, and finished 1852 One at Boulogne, 1879, cost $6,400,000 That at Alexandria, Egypt, began 1870, cost nearly $13,000,000 The English have also erected breakwaters at Madras. India, at Colombo, on the island of Ceylon, 1874-85, cost 705,000*l.*, and at Table bay, S. Africa, began 1860 There is also a fine breakwater at Kingstown, at the entrance of Dublin bay, Ireland. The principal breakwater in the United States is the Delaware breakwater, first-class type, at the entrance of Delaware bay (1829-39). Although incomplete it has a surf breaker of 2748 ft., and an ice-breaker of 1710 ft. Cost over $2 000 000. There are others at Galveston, Texas, and on the great lakes at Buffalo, Chicago, and Oswego. There is a natural breakwater at Pernambuco, Brazil, formed by a reef of coral

breastplate. One was worn by the Jewish high-priest, 1491 B C (Ex xxxix) Goliath "was armed with a coat of mail," 1063 B C (Sam xvii) Breastplates dwindled to the diminutive gorgets Ancient breastplates are mentioned as made of gold and silver AARON'S BREASTPLATE

Brechin, Scotland, sustained a siege against Edward III, 1333 The battle of Brechin or Huntly-hill was fought between earls Huntly and Crawford (the latter defeated), 18 May, 1452 The see of Brechin was founded by David I in 1150 One of its bishops, Alexander Campbell, was made prelate when a boy, 1556 The bishopric, discontinued soon after the revolution in 1688, was revived in 1731

Breda, Holland, was taken from the Spaniards by prince Maurice of Nassau in 1590, retaken by the Spaniards, under Spinola, June, 1625, and by the Dutch, Oct. 1637. The "Compromise of Breda" was a proposal to Philip II, deprecating his harsh measures in the Netherlands, presented and refused in 1566 Here Charles II of England resided at the time of the restoration, and issued his declaration of amnesty, 4 Apr 1660 RESTORATION Breda was taken by the French in 1793 The French garrison was expelled by the burgesses in 1813

breeches, among the Greeks, were a badge of slavery. They were worn by the Dacians, Parthians, and other northern nations, and in Italy, it is said, in the time of Augustus In the reign of Honorius, about 394 A.D, the *braccarii*, or breeches-makers, were expelled from Rome. The "Geneva Bible" termed the "Breeches Bible" (from the rendering in Gen iii 7), pub 1560 BIBLE.

brehons. ancient judges in Ireland, said to have administered justice with religious impartiality, but later with a patriotic bias. The statute of Kilkenny forbade English subjects to submit to the brehon laws. 40 Edw III 1365, but they were recognized by the native Irish till 1650 A translation was proposed in 1852, and a commission appointed. The publication of the "Ancient Laws of Ireland," by the government, began 1865.

Bremen, N. Germany, said to have been founded in 788, and long an archbishopric, one of the leading towns of the Hanseatic league, had a seat and a vote in the college of imperial cities in 1640 In 1648 it was secularized and made a duchy, and held by Sweden till 1712, when it was taken by Denmark, who sold it to Hanover in 1731 It was taken by the French in 1757, who were expelled by the Hanoverians in 1758 Bremen was annexed by Napoleon to the French empire in 1810 but its independence was restored in 1813, [illegible] 1866 It entered the North German Confederation [illegible] International agricultural exhibition opened 13 June, 1874 Population of the province, 1871, 122,402, 1890, 180,413, of the city, 125,684 HANSE TOWNS

Brenneville, N W. France Here Henry I of England defeated Louis VI of France, who supported William Clito, son of Robert, duke of Normandy, 20 Aug 1119

Brentford, county town of Middlesex, Engl Here Edmund Ironside defeated the Danes, May, 1016 It was taken by Charles I, after a sharp fight, 12 Nov 1642

Brescia (*bresh e-a*), N Italy (the ancient Brixia), important under the Lombards, suffered by the wars of Italian republics, being attached to Venice It was taken by the French under Gaston de Foix, Feb 1512, when it is said 40,000 of the inhabitants were massacred It was retaken, 26 May, 1516 It surrendered to the Austrian gen Haynau, 30 Mch 1849, on severe terms It was annexed to Sardinia in 1859

Breslau, Silesia, was burned by the Mongols in 1241, and conquered by Frederick II of Prussia, Jan 1741 Here the Austrians routed the Prussians, under prince Bevern, 22 Nov 1757 Breslau was taken, but was regained 21 Dec the same year It was besieged by the French, and surrendered to them, Jan 1807, and again in 1813

Bressa prize. Dr Cesare Antonio Bressa, by will of 4 Sept 1835, bequeathed to the Royal Academy of Sciences, Turin, means for a prize (about $6000) every 2 years for some important discovery or valuable work in physics, natural history, geography, history, statistics, etc, 1st in 1879 to a foreigner, the 2d to an Italian, and so on alternately

Brest, a seaport, N W France, was besieged by Julius Cæsar, 54 B C, possessed by the English, 1378 A D, given up to the duke of Brittany, 1390 Lord Berkeley and a British fleet and army were repulsed here with dreadful loss in 1694 The magazine burned, to the value of some millions of pounds sterling, 1744 The marine hospitals, with 50 galley-slaves, burned, 1766 The magazine again destroyed by fire, 10 July, 1784 From this French naval depot numerous squadrons were equipped against England during the long war among them the fleet which lord Howe defeated on 1 June, 1794 England maintained a large blockading squadron off the harbor from 1793 to 1815, but with little injury to France It is now a chief naval station, and is considered impregnable

Bretigny (*bret'i-ny*), Peace of, concluded with France, 8 May, 1360, England retained Gascony and Guienne, and acquired other provinces, renounced Maine, Anjou, Touraine, and Normandy, was to receive 3,000,000 crowns, and to release king John, taken prisoner at Poictiers 1356 The treaty not being carried out, the king remained and died in England

Bretwalda. A title bestowed upon Egbert in the old English chronicles (cir 855), and (retrospectively) upon seven earlier kings of various old English states, viz Ella, king of Sussex, Ceawlin of Wessex, Ethelbert of Kent, Redwald of East Anglia, Edwin, Oswald, and Oswy of Northumberland. "Its sense can only be 'lord (or ruler) of the Britons,' or 'of Britain'"—*The New English Dictionary.* BRITAIN

breviary (i e., an *abridgment* of the offices used in the Roman Catholic service) contains the 7 canonical hours, viz matins about midnight, lauds (when not joined to matins, about 3 A M), primes (about 6), tierce (about 9), sexts (about 12), nones (about 3 P M.), vespers (4 or 6), complines (about 9) Lord Bute published a translation of the breviary, 1879 The breviary is ascribed to pope Gelasius I about 492. It was first called the custos, and afterwards the breviary, came into use among ecclesiastical orders about 1080, and was reformed by the councils of Trent and Cologne, and by Pius V, Urban VIII, and other popes The type in which it was first printed gave name to *brevier* type

brewers and **brewing.** The art of brewing was practised by the ancient Egyptians, and afterwards by the Greeks, Romans, and Gauls. All nations, whether civilized or savage, have in every age prepared intoxicating drink of some kind, under as many names as there are peoples. Brewing was known to the Anglo-Saxons, and the English have long been pre-eminent in this art It is mentioned in the old English chronicles (cir 893) British monasteries were remarkable for the strength and purity of their ales, brewed from malt prepared by the monks with care and skill As early as the 13th century the waters of Burton-on-Trent began to be famous for brewing purposes, and in 1630 "Burton beer" found its way to London, being sold at "Ye Peacocke" in Gray's Inn lane and according to the *Spectator* was in great demand among the visitors at Vauxhall

> *Fool* "When brewers mar their malt with water"
> —*Shakespeare*, "King Lear," act iii sc 2

In 1585 there were 26 brewers in the city of London, the suburbs, and Westminster, who brewed 648,960 barrels of beer, of which 26,400 barrels were exported to Embden, the Low Countries, and Dieppe —*Stow* The best English colonial beer is made in Tasmania, and shipped frozen to Australia and India The quantity of beer brewed in Great Britain in 186[illegible] was 25,042,664 barrels, of which 521,272 barrels were exported In 1892 over 32,000,000 barrels were brewed in Great Britain and Ireland, and the government collected as taxes on the manufacture and sale more than 9,000,000*l* More beer is brewed in Germany than in any other country, amounting in 1892 to over 16,000,000 barrels Every brewer in the United States pays a tax of $100 if producing 500 barrels or more and $50 if less Total production in 1863, 1,765,827 barrels of 31 gallons, 1873, 9,633,323 barrels, 1880, 13,347,110 barrels, 1892, 39,180,250 barrels.

Briar Creek, Battle of GEORGIA, 177[illegible]

bribery forbidden (Deut. xvi. 19) Samuel's sons were guilty of it, 1112 B.C (1 Sam. viii. 3) In England, Thomas de Weyland banished for bribery in 1288, was chief-justice of the common pleas. William de Thorpe, chief-justice of the king's bench, was convicted of bribery in 1351 Another judge was fined 20,000*l.* for the like offence, 1616. Mr Walpole secretary-at-war, was sent to the Tower for bribery, 1712 Lord Strangford was suspended from voting in the Irish House of Lords for soliciting a bribe, Jan 1784 In 1854 an important act was passed consolidating and amending previous acts relating to bribery at elections By statute of the United States chap 287, 15 Aug 1876, 19 stat at large p 160, § 6, bribery is made punishable Revised statutes of the U. S, §§ 5500-8, prohibit and punish bribery.

Mr Swan, M P for Penryn fined and imprisoned and sir Manasseh Lopez fined 10,000*l* with 2 years' imprisonment for bribery at Grampound Oct 181[illegible]
Sudbury disfranchised, 1844, St Albans also 185[illegible]
Elections at Derby etc, voided for bribery 185[illegible]
In Cooper *v.* Slade, payment of travelling expenses held bribery 17 Apr 185[illegible]
Commissions of inquiry on bribery sit at Great Yarmouth, Totnes Lancaster, and Reigate [illegible] ... cial disclosures, Aug-Nov. 186[illegible]
Reform bill disfranchising boroughs passed 15 Aug 186[illegible]
Parliamentary Elections act, election petitions to be tried by a special court, passed 31 July 186[illegible]
First trials under this act, Mr Roger Fykyn (at Windsor) declared elected, 15 Jan, and sir H Stracey (at Norwich) unseated 18 Jan 186[illegible]
Dr Kinglake Mr Fenelly, and others, fined for bribery in parliamentary elections 10 May, 18[illegible]
Beverly Bridgewater, Sligo, and Cashel disfranchised for bribery and corruption "
New York aldermen in the year 1884, granted a street railway franchise for Broadway under suspicious circumstances Long discussions in the press [illegible] by the legislature in 1886 and little by little the facts were brought out before an investigating committee and in the courts Some of the implicated persons fled the country, some were convicted, some turned informers Following are the dates
A group of aldermen conspire, calling it a "combine," to vote together on railroad franchises 13 May, 188[illegible]
Broadway railroad company applies for franchise 15 July, "
Application approved by railroad committee of aldermen, 10 Aug "
Franchise granted at a special meeting at 9 o'clock A M by 13 aldermen, named Cleary, De Lacy, Dempsey, Duffy, Fullgraff Rothman Waite, McQuade, O'Neill Jaehne Miller, Shiels, Farley, Sayles, McCabe, Wendel, Reilly and Pearson, 30 Aug "
Validity of the franchise being technically doubtful, the company applies anew 15 Sept "
Franchise granted 13 Nov "
Vetoed by the mayor 20 Nov "
Passed over the veto 5 Dec. "
State Senate directs its railroad committee (senator Low, chairman) to investigate 26 Jan 188[illegible]
Committee begins its sittings 6 Feb "
Preliminary report recommends that the franchise be annulled for fraud 9 Mch "
[Franchise annulled and road placed in the hands of a receiver]
Henry Jaehne vice president of the board of aldermen arrested on charge of bribery 18 Mch "

Committee closes investigation 21 Apr 1886
Jaehne put upon trial 10 May, "
Jaehne convicted, 16 May, sentenced to 9 years and 10 months in state-prison 20 May, "
Jaehne lodged in prison at Sing Sing 21 May, "
Alderman McCabe adjudged insane 4 Nov "
Alderman McQuade put upon his trial, Waite, Fullgraff and Duffy giving testimony for the people 15 Nov "
Jury disagree 24 Nov "
Second trial begun 26 Nov "
McQuade convicted 15 Dec, sentenced to 7 years' imprisonment and $5000 fine 20 Dec "
Alderman O Neill put upon trial 24 Jan 1887
O Neill convicted, 1 Feb, sentenced to 4 years' imprisonment and $2000 fine 11 Feb "
James W Foshay, formerly president of the Broadway road, under indictment for bribing aldermen d 17 Feb "
Jacob Sharp one of the principals in bribing aldermen found guilty of bribery, sentenced to 4 years imprisonment and fined $500 14 July, "
Alderman Cleary put upon trial 28 Feb "
Arthur J McQuade the convicted ex alderman brought from Sing Sing to New York, and released on $20,000 bail 4 Oct 1888

bric-à-brac (Fr), old curiosities, such as cabinets, pieces of ironwork, etc Collection became a fashion under queen Anne, 1702-14 The publication of *Bric-a-Brac*, a monthly price-list, began in 1869

[br]ick. Over 2000 years B.C the men on the plains of Shinar said, "Go to, let us make brick, and burn them thoroughly And ... let us build us a city, and a tower, whose top may reach unto heaven" (Gen xi 3) The bricks of Thothmes III (believed to be the prince who reigned in Egypt at the time of the exodus of the Hebrews) are impressed with his cartouch, cir 1600 B C Nebuchadnezzar had his name stamped on the bricks used in erecting his colossal palaces, they are red or pale yellow, and from 12 to 19½ in square, and about 3 in. thick The palaces of Crœsus, king of Lydia (548 B C.), of Mausolus of Halicarnassus (352 B.C), the bath of Titus (79 A D), the pillar of Trajan (98 A.D.), and the bath of Caracalla (212 A D) were of brick Early English brick buildings [illegible] Hurstmonceaux castle, Sussex (cir 1425), Tattershall [illegible], Lincolnshire (1440), Lollards' tower, Lambeth palace [illegible]), and the old part of Hampton court (1514).

A D
[Bric]ks introduced into England by the Romans cir 44
[illegible] under direction of Alfred the Great about 886
[illegible] ar masonry introduced into England shortly before the [Nor]man conquest 1066
[Size] of bricks regulated by order of Charles I 1625
[Brick]s substituted for wood in the erection of buildings in London after the great fire 1666
[Tax] levied on bricks in England 1784
[Mach]ine for making bricks patented in the U S as early as 1792, and about 122 patents granted previous to June, 1836
Duties and drawbacks of excise on bricks in England repealed, 1850
[illegible] Smith patents in the U S a machine capable of making [illegible],000 bricks in a day of 10 hours 9 July, 1868
[Cha]mbers's brick machine, with a capacity of 50 000 bricks per [10] hours, at a cost from the clay bank to the shed of only [illegible]½ cts per 1000, first patented, 20 Aug 1878, and perfected, 1887

Bridewell. Once a palace of king John, near Fleet-ditch London, 1210, was given to the city for a work-house by Edward VI, 1553 The new Bridewell prison, erected in 1829, was pulled down in 1864, that of Tothill-fields was rebuilt in 1831

bridges. The first bridge at Rome, called the Pons Sublicius, was built across the Tiber on piles by Ancus Martius about 620 B.C., noted for the (mythical) defence by Horatius Cocles against Lars Porsenna about 508 B C Abydos is famous for the bridge of boats Xerxes built across the Hellespont, 480 B.C Trestle-bridge on piles built by Julius Cæsar across the Rhine, 55 B C, in 10 days, described in his commentaries The bridge of Trajan, crossing the Danube, was about 4000 ft in length, and was built of timbers resting on stone piers by Apollodorus of Damascus, 105 A D About the same time the bridge at Alcantara, Spain, in honor of Trajan, was built, this bridge was part destroyed by the English in 1809, and by the Carlists in 1836 The Devil's bridge in the canton of Uri, Switzerland, was built on two high rocks, many stories have been invented to account for it At Schaffhausen an extraordinary bridge was built over the Rhine, 400 feet wide, there was a pier in the middle of the river, but it is doubtful whether the bridge rested upon it, a man of light weight felt the bridge totter under him, yet wagons heavily laden passed over without danger The bridge was destroyed by the French in 1799 Trezzo bridge, over the Adda, Italy, built by order of Bernabo Visconti, duke of Milan, in 1380, was the largest masonry arch known, having a span of 251 feet Destroyed by Carmagnola The largest existing masonry arch is in the United States, a span of 220 ft, carrying the Washington Aqueduct over Cabin John creek (AQUEDUCTS), and next in size is the Grosvenor bridge over the Dee at Chester, England, with a span of 200 feet.

A D
Triangular masonry bridge at Coryland abbey, referred to in a charter dated 943
Stone bridge erected at Bow, near Stratford, by queen Matilda, about 1100-18
Religious brotherhoods for building and repairing bridges existed in France during the 13th century, one of them the Fratres Pontis, headed by St. Benezet, built a bridge 3000 ft long, of 18 stone arches, over the Rhone at Avignon 1180
Cast iron for bridges introduced in England 1777
U S patent granted for a wooden bridge, since known as the Burr bridge, to Theodore Burr 14 Feb 1806
James Finley of Fayette county, Pa, erected chain cable suspension bridges as early as 1797 He patented his improvements, 1808, and 2 years later there were 8 of these bridges in existence in the U S, the longest at the falls of Schuylkill, Philadelphia, Pa, 306 ft span, with an intermediate pier, 1810
Town, or lattice truss bridge, patented by Ithiel Town of Conn, 20 Jan 1820
Tension iron bridge believed to be the first of the kind in the U S, patented by Augustus Canfield, of Plainfield, N J, 29 June, 1833
Howe truss bridge patented by William Howe, of Warren, Mass 10 July, 1840
American boiler plate tubular bridge built at Bolton depot, and put in place on the Baltimore and Susquehanna railroad by its inventor, James Millholland Apr 1847
Niagara gorge, 2 miles below the falls crossed by an iron basket or cradle hung on a wire cable suspended over the chasm It was constructed by Charles Ellet, and soon replaced by a slight bridge, a second cable being constructed the same year The first step in the construction of this bridge was the flying of kites across the gorge, one being successfully landed, its string served to carry over a rope and then a cable 1848
Chief Thames bridges freed from toll 24 May, 1879, and 26 June, 1880

NOTED BRIDGES OF THE WORLD — MASONRY ARCH BRIDGES

London bridge One is said to have existed, 978 A bridge built of wood, 1014, was partly burned in 1136 The late old bridge was commenced about 1176 by Peter of Colechurch, with houses on each side connected by large arches of timber which crossed the street, completed 1209
Fire at the Southwark end brought crowds on the bridge, the houses at the north end caught fire, and shut them in, upwards of 3000 persons were killed burned or drowned July, 1212
Bridge restored in 1300, again destroyed by fire in 1471, 13 Feb 1632, and Sept 1725
All the houses pulled down 1756
Water works begun, 1582, destroyed by fire 1774
Toll discontinued 27 Mch 1782
New London bridge, designed by John Rennie, and built by his sons, John and George, total cost, 1,458,311*l*, length of central span, 152 ft The first pile was driven 200 ft to the west of the old bridge, 15 Mch 1824, the first stone was laid by the lord mayor, alderman Garratt 15 June, 1825
Opened by William IV and his queen 1 Aug. 1831
Karlsbrücke (Charles's bridge) over the Moldau at Prague Built by emperor Charles IV of Germany, 1348. 1855 ft long Gate towers at either end ornamented with groups of statuary Greatly damaged by flood, Sept 1890, since repaired
Rialto Masonry arch bridge at Venice over the Grand canal Single span of 98⅓ ft, rise of span, 20 ft, width of foot way, 72 ft. Built by Antonio da Ponte (RIALTO, VENICE) 1588
Westminster bridges Old bridge was built of Portland stone, after a design of M Labelye Begun 13 Sept 1738, opened for passengers, 18 Nov 1750, length, 1223 ft, cost, 426,650*l*
Commissioners of works empowered to rebuild 4 Aug 1853
Work on the new bridge suspended by failure of the contractors, Messrs. Mare. The government eventually undertook the building which was intrusted to Thomas Page. One half of the bridge opened early in 1860, the whole 24 May, 1862
Waterloo bridge over the Thames at London Length within abutments, 1242 ft, width within balustrades, 42 ft, span of each arch, of which there are 9, 120 ft, commenced, 11 Oct. 1811
The present site, plan, and dimensions of the bridge given by G Dodd under act of Parliament in 1806, he was superseded by John Rennie, who completed the structure It was opened on the anniversary of the battle of Waterloo, the duke of Wellington and others being present 18 June, 1817
Bought for 475,000*l* by metropolitan board of works, opened, toll free, 5 Oct 1878, lit by electric light 10 Oct. 1879
Grosvenor bridge, over the Dee at Chester A masonry arch having a span of 200 ft, act for its construction obtained 1825

IRON AND STEEL ARCH BRIDGES

Colebrookdale bridge, over the Severn, between Madeley and Brosely, the first cast iron arch bridge erected in England It has a span of 100 ft, and was completed after designs of Abraham Derby 1777
Sunderland bridge. A cast iron arch 100 ft high, with a span of 236 ft, crossing the Wear, built under superintendence of Thomas Wilson 1796

Southwark bridge, South London was designed by John Rennie It consists of 3 cast iron arches of 210 240, and 210 ft span, resting on massive stone piers and abutments, cost about 800,000*l*, begun 23 Sept 1814, completed Apr 1819

Victoria bridge over the Thames at Pimlico London consists of 4 very wide wrought iron arches. Begun, 1859, completed, 1860, and widened 1865-66

St Louis bridge across the Mississippi at St Louis Mo 3 arches formed of tubes of cast steel and built out from the piers without scaffolding, the centre span 520 ft the others 502 ft each 2200 tons of steel and 3400 tons of iron were used in its construction Built by col James B Eads at a cost of $10,000 000 Begun 1867, and completed 4 July, 1874

Douro bridge, an arched iron structure near Oporto Portugal, total length 1150 ft, span of arch 520 ft height from low water to crown of arch 198 ft Begun, 1875, opened to travel by the king of Portugal Nov 1877

Garabit viaduct over the Truyere in the south of France The total length is 1849 ft, the main portion 1169 ft. in length, is of steel and consists of 5 openings of from 170 to 182 ft, spanned by lattice girders and a trellis parabolic arch with a span of 541 ft and a clear height above the river of 350 ft The rail level is 401 ft above the river (Highest bridge in the world) Designed by M Eiffel and built without scaffold Begun, 1879 completed 1884

Highway bridge over the Harlem river at New York A central stone pier and 2 steel arches having a span of 510 ft. each and a clear headway of 150 ft under the centre of each arch 1888

TUBULAR GIRDER BRIDGES

Conway (Wales) *tubular bridge* A miniature of the Britannia, a single span of 400 ft, erected 1846-48

Britannia tubular bridge carrying the Chester and Holyhead railway across the Menai straits consists of 2 parallel rectangular wrought iron tubes resting on 3 piers There are 2 central spans of 459 ft and 2 shore spans of 230 ft The central pier is built on the Britannia rock and its erection was begun May, 1846 The height of the tube within is 30 ft at the centre diminishing to 23 ft at the shore ends The bridge has a clear headway above high water of 103¾ ft The 4 tubes of the central spans were floated into position and gradually raised to the required height by hydraulic presses First locomotive passes through Mch 1850

Victoria railway bridge, over the St. Lawrence river at Montreal, was erected by James Hodges under the superintendence of Robert Stephenson and A M Ross, engineers It is about 2 miles in length and rests on 24 piers the height being 60 ft above summer level of the river, cost, 1,700,000*l*, work begun 24 May 1854, bridge damaged by floating ice while under construction, 5 Jan 1855, formally opened by the prince of Wales 25 Aug 1860

SUSPENSION BRIDGES

Menai suspension bridge A chain bridge built by Telford across the Menai straits, 102 ft above high water The entire length of the chains is 1710 ft, length of span 570 ft, bridge begun July, 1818, and opened for traffic 30 Jan 1826

Freiburg suspension bridge, over the Sarine valley, Switzerland 870 ft span, 167 ft above the river, built by M Chaley 1833-34

Suspension bridge crossing the Dnieper at Kieff Nearly half a mile in length, having 4 principal spans of 440 ft each, erected 1851

Niagara Falls suspension bridge, across the gorge, 2 miles below the falls Built by John A Roebling Length of span between towers, 800 ft., supported by 4 wire cables, each containing 3640 No 9 wires, height of track above the water, 245 ft, carriage way beneath the track cost of bridge, $400 000, work begun, 1852, first locomotive crosses, 8 Mch 1855

Clifton suspension bridge A chain bridge crossing the Avon below Bristol Engl It was partly constructed of the Hungerford foot bridge, which was taken down in July, 1862 It is said to have the longest span of any chain bridge in the world (702 ft), and is 250 ft. above high water Begun in 1862, opened 8 Dec 1864

Cincinnati and Covington suspension bridge, over the Ohio river at an elevation of 91 ft. above low water and with a span of 1057 ft Built by Roebling, and completed 1867

Clifton suspension bridge at Niagara Falls, a short distance below the falls, built for carriage and foot passengers, has a span of 1260 ft Begun, 1867, completed 1869

Blown down, 10 Jan 1889, and new structure of iron hung on steel cables, opened 7 May, 1889

Brooklyn bridge A wire cable suspension bridge connecting New York city with Brooklyn, designed by John A Roebling, and built by his son W A Roebling It has a total length of carriageway, 5989 ft, and including extensions, 6537 ft, a central span of 1595 ft, and 2 side spans of 930 ft. each, with a clear headway under the centre of the bridge of 135 ft above high water, total height of towers above high water, 278 ft, there are 4 suspension cables, composed of 5296 galvanized steel wires, bound together, but not twisted, width of bridge, 85 ft., cost, $15,000,000, bridge begun, 1870, opened 24 May, 1883

CANTILEVER BRIDGES

Niagara Falls cantilever, over the gorge, a short distance above the old suspension bridge, the first true metal cantilever bridge erected, comprising 2 cantilevers, 395 ft. each in length, extending from the shores to piers and reaching out over the river supporting a central girder 120 ft in length distance between piers, 495 ft, height of bridge, 180 ft above the water, opened 20 Dec 1883

Hooghly bridge, India, carrying the East Indian railway across the Hooghly river at a height of 53 ft above low water It has 1 central span of 5?3½ ft, and 2 end spans of 520 ft It was begun in 1883, and completed at a cost of $1 305 000 1886

Kentucky and Indiana bridge over the Ohio at Louisville has 2 cantilever spans of 480 and 483 ft, begun, 1883, completed "

Sukkur cantilever bridge crossing the Rori branch of the Indus at Sukkur, with a single span of 790 ft, opened June, 1889

Firth cantilever bridge a steel railway bridge across the Firth of Forth at Queensferry Scotl has a total length of 8098 ft., or over a mile and a half It is composed of 3 double cantilevers, a central one of 1620 ft resting on a pier built on the island of Inchgarvie 2 1514¾ ft in length joined to the central cantilever by girders of 350 ft span thus affording 2 openings of 1700 ft each side of the central pier and 2 approach viaducts of 15 girders from 168 to 179 ft in length, resting on masonry piers The highest elevation of the bridge is 361 ft (over the piers), and there is a clear headway under the central spans of 152 ft There were 51 000 tons of steel used in its construction and 56 lives were lost during its erection, which occupied 7 years and gave employment to as many as 5000 men at one time Total cost of the bridge 3 250 000*l*, work begun, Jan 1883, opened 4 Mch 1890

Poughkeepsie bridge crossing the Hudson river at Poughkeepsie, is composed of 2 cantilever spans on each shore of 523 ft and a central cantilever span of 521 ft joined by 2 ordinary girders of 500 ft span with projecting cantilever ends Work begun 1886, opened 1888

DRAWBRIDGES

Newcastle swing bridge, over the Tyne Engl is 281 ft long, weighs 1450 tons, and is lifted by a hydraulic crane Work begun, 1868, completed June, 1876

Arthur Kill bridge, between Staten Island and New Jersey consists of 2 shore spans of 150 ft each, covered by fixed trusses, and a draw 500 ft in length It can be opened and closed in 2 minutes Bridge authorized by act of Congress, 16 June, 1886, completed at a cost of $450 000 13 June 1888

Tower bridge, a bascule bridge crossing the Thames below London bridge. It has a central opening of 200 ft between 2 high towers, connected near the top by a fixed foot bridge 139½ ft above the river and reached by elevators or stairways in the towers There are 2 side spans of 270 ft covered by chain suspension bridges, and between the towers, at a height of 29½ ft above high water a double bascule each leaf 100 ft in length and forming a flat arch when down at a level with the main bridge Foundation laid, 1886, opened, 1894

GIRDER BRIDGES AND MISCELLANEOUS

Wittingen timber bridge, a trussed bridge with a span of 390 ft., was destroyed by fire in 1799 after standing 41 years Erected, 1778

Wooden bridge, over the Connecticut at Hanover, with a single arch of 236 ft, erected 1796

Crumlin viaduct, a Warren girder iron bridge over the Ebbw in Monmouthshire, 1800 ft long with 10 spans of 150 ft. raised 200 ft above the river Begun, 1853, completed 1857

Saltash lenticular girder bridge, built by I K Brunel, across the river Tamar 2 spans of 455 ft with a headway of 100 ft. above high water The platform is supported by small girders carried by suspension chains below and a large arched tube above, strongly braced together It is of wrought iron and has a total length of 2240 ft., opened for traffic 1859

Potomac Run bridge, a famous trestle work 400 ft long and 80 ft. high built in 9 days by soldiers of the army of the Potomac, under the supervision of gen Herman Haupt. It contained more than 2,000,000 ft of lumber, chiefly round sticks, fresh cut from the neighboring woods, erected May 1862

Kuilenburg bridge, a wrought iron girder across the Leck in Holland, has a span of 492 ft, G Van Diesen, architect 1868

Verrugas viaduct, an iron Fink truss bridge on the Oroyo railroad in Peru crosses the valley of the Agua de Verrugas at an altitude of 5478 ft above the sea level Total length, 575 ft., comprising 3 iron piers connected by Fink trusses at a height of about 250 ft from the water Work begun, 17 Sept 1872, and completed in 88 working days early in 1873

Portage bridge, over the Genesee river on the line of the Erie railroad at Portage, N Y An iron truss bridge on iron trestles built in 1875, to replace the original wooden trestle bridge, completed 14 Aug 1852, and burned down, 6 May 1875 The total length is 800 ft, comprising 1 span of 180 ft., 2 of 100 ft., and 7 of 50 ft, height, 230 ft above the river Contract let, 10 May, 1875, opened for traffic 31 July, 1875

Tay bridge, the longest girder bridge in the world, crosses the Tay at Dundee, Scotl. The original bridge consisted of 85 spans, some over 90 ft above water level, and had a total length of 10 612 ft Engineer, sir Thomas Bouch Over 20 lives lost during its construction Work commenced, June, 1871, completed 30 Aug 1877, and opened 31 May, 1878

Bridge much injured by a gale while building 4 Feb 1877

Partly destroyed by a gale while a N British mail train was passing over it, the train and 75 to 90 passengers disappeared, none escaping A gap of about 3000 ft was made in the bridge, about 7 15 P M, Sunday 28 Dec 1879

46 bodies recovered up to 27 Apr. 1880

After the Board of Trade inquiry Mr H C. Rothery reported

"that the bridge had been badly designed, badly constructed, and badly maintained" . 3 July, 1883
Sir Thomas Bouch, engineer, d 30 Oct. "
New Tay bridge, length, 10,700 ft, the 11 longest spans being 245 ft. each, built 1882 to 1887
Wrought iron girder bridge at Cincinnati, over the Ohio river, with a span of 519 ft., 105 ft above low water, built 1877
Kentucky River bridge a trussed girder bridge of iron on the line of the Cincinnati Southern railroad, 3 spans of 375 ft, built without false work, begun, 16 Oct 1876, and completed, at a cost of $404 230 20 Feb "
Railway bridge over the Severn, connecting the forest of Dean with Sharpness Point, Engl. over ¾ of a mile in length Built at a cost of 1 000,000*l*., and formally opened 17 Oct. 1879
Moerdyk bridge, a wrought iron girder bridge carrying the Antwerp and Rotterdam railway across the Hollands Diep by 14 spans of 328 ft, completed . 1880
Kinzua viaduct iron girder and trestle bridge, Warren county, Pa, 301 ft in height (prior to the Garabit viaduct the highest bridge in the world), and built in less than 4 months Work begun, 5 May, opened 29 Aug 1882
Hawkesbury bridge, a steel girder bridge over the Hawkesbury river, New South Wales, 7 miles from the sea It has 7 openings between piers about 416 ft from centre to centre and 40 ft headway at high-water Work begun, 1886, girders floated into position on pontoons at high-water and allowed to rest on the piers as the tide went out Opened for traffic May, 1889
Loa viaduct, a lattice girder iron bridge by which the Antofagasta railway of Bolivia crosses the canon of the Loa at an altitude of 10 000 ft above the sea level The bridge was put together in 9 months under the supervision of Peter and John Fisher, who went from England for the purpose "
Cincinnati iron truss railway bridge across the Ohio river, planned for a double track railroad and 2 roadways and 2 sidewalks in addition. Total structure 1 mile in length, the centre span 550 ft., and 2 spans flanking the main channel 490 ft each Caissons sunk in 1887, completed 1890

Bridgewater, Somersetshire, Engl was incorporated by king John in 1200 In the war between Charles I and the Parliament, the king's forces burned part of the town, 1643 Here stood an ancient castle in which the ill-advised duke of Monmouth lodged when proclaimed king in 1685 The town disfranchised for bribery, 1870

Bridgewater canal, the first great canal in England, 29 miles long, begun by the duke of Bridgewater, the father of canal navigation in Great Britain, in 1759, opened 17 July, 1761 James Brindley was the engineer Starting at Worsley, 7 miles from Manchester, it crosses the Irwell at Barton bridge by an aqueduct upwards of 200 yards long CANALS

Bridgewater treatises. The rev Francis, earl of Bridgewater, died Apr 1829, bequeathing 8000*l* to the author or authors, appointed by the president of the Royal Society, who should write an essay "on the power, wisdom, and goodness of God, as manifested in the creation" The essays by sir Charles Bell, Drs. T. Chalmers, John Kidd, William Buckland, William Prout, Peter M Roget, and the revs William Whewell and William Kirby) were pub. 1833-35

briefs are the letters of the pope despatched to princes and others on public affairs, and usually written short, without preface or preamble, and on paper, thus distinguished from BULLS, which are ample, and written on parchment. Briefs are sealed with red wax and the seal of the fisherman, or St. Peter in a boat, always in the presence of the pope Queen Elizabeth's letters, called "briefs," authorizing collections in churches for charitable purposes, are now discontinued A lawyer's brief is an abridgment of his client's case

Brienne, N E. France Here the allied armies of Russia and Prussia, under Blucher, were defeated by the French, 29 Jan 1814

Bright's disease, a degeneration of the tissues of the kidneys into fat, investigated about 1830 by Richard Bright

Brill or **Briel,** Holland A seaport, seized by the expelled Dutch confederates, became the seat of their independence, 1572 Brill, given to the English in 1585 as security for advances made by queen Elizabeth to Holland, was restored in 1616

Bristol, W England, built by Brennus, a British prince, 380 B.C, is mentioned 430 A D as a fortified city It was called Caer Oder, a city in the valley of Bath, and sometimes Caer Brito, the British city, and by the Saxons Brightstowe, pleasant place Gildas and Nennius speak of Bristol in the 5th and 7th centuries. From the 12th century to the 18th it was, next to London, the most flourishing port in England; since surpassed by Liverpool

Taken by earl of Gloucester in his defence of his sister Maud, the empress, against king Stephen 1138
Eleanor of Brittany (daughter of Geoffrey, son of Henry II) dies in the castle after 39 years' imprisonment 1241
St Mary s church built 1292
Bristol made a distinct county by Edward III . 1373
Bishopric founded by Henry VIII 1542
Taken by prince Rupert, 26 July 1643, by Cromwell 10 Sept 1645
Riot on the entrance of sir Charles Wetherell, the recorder, he opposing the reform bill, the mansion house, bishop's palace, several merchants' stores, some prisons (the inmates liberated), and nearly 100 houses burned, above 500 persons killed 29-31 Oct. 1831
Trial of rioters (4 executed, 22 transported), 2 Jan, suicide of col Brereton, during trial by court martial 9 Jan 1832
Proposed college for science and literature here for the south and west of England, meeting, 13 June, 1874, opened as University college 10 Sept. 1876

Bristol, See of, one of 6 bishoprics erected by Henry VIII out of spoils of dissolved monasteries, 1542 The cathedral was church of the abbey of St Austin, founded by Robert Fitz-Harding, son to a king of Denmark, and a citizen of Bristol, 1148. The see is valued in the king's books at 338*l* 8*s* 4*d*. Paul Bushe, provincial of the Bons-hommes, was the first bishop, in 1542—deprived for being married, 1554 The see was united by an order in council with Gloucester, in 1836 The cathedral (under repair since 1844) was reopened in 1861; a new nave opened, 23 Oct. 1877

Bristow Station, Va, affairs at (1) Here gen. Hooker's division encountered and defeated that of the confederate gen Ewell, 27 Aug 1862, with a loss of about 300 on each side (2) Here, on 14 Oct. 1863, A P Hill's corps (confederate) attacked the 2d corps, maj-gen Warren's, while retreating, but gained no advantage BRANDY STATION

Britain (called by the Romans Britannia, from its Celtic name Prydhain, *Camden*) "The nearest Celtic form is the Irish plural Bretain"—*The New English Dictionary* The earliest records of its history are the manuscripts and poetry of the Cambrians. The Celts, the ancestors of the Britons and modern Welsh, were the first inhabitants of Britain It is referred to as the Cassiterides or tin-islands by Herodotus, 450 B.C, as Albion and Ierne (England and Ireland) by Aristotle, 350 B.C, and Polybius, 260 B.C The Romans divided Britain into *Britannia Prima* (country south of the Thames and Severn), *Britannia Secunda* (Wales), *Flavia Cæsariensis* (between the Thames, Severn, and Humber), *Maxima Cæsariensis* (between the Humber and Tyne), and *Valentia* (between the Tyne and Firth of Forth) Britain, including England, Scotland, and Wales, was anciently called Albion, the name of Britain being applied to all the islands collectively—Albion to only one.—*Pliny* ALBION, ENGLAND, SCOTLAND, WALES

B.C.
Divitiacus, king of the Suessones, in Gaul, said to have supremacy over part of Britain . .. 57
First invasion of Britain by Julius Cæsar .. 26 Aug 55
Second invasion, he defeats Cassivelaunus 54
Cymbeline (Cunobelin), king of Britain 4
A.D.
Aulus Plautus defeats the Britons 43
He and Vespasian reduce S Britain 47
Caractacus defeated by Ostorius, 50, carried in chains to Rome, 51
Romans defeated by Boadicea, queen of the Iceni, 70,000 slain and London burned, she is defeated by Suetonius, 80,000 slain 61
Agricola, governor, conquers Anglesey, overruns Britain in 7 campaigns, and reforms the government 78-84
He defeats the Caledonians under Galgacus, surrenders the islands 84
Emperor Hadrian visits Britain, 120, builds a wall from the Tyne to the Solway (HADRIAN S WALL) 121
Lucius, king of the Britons, said to have sent an embassy on religion to pope Eleutherius. . about 181
Britons (allies of Albinus) defeated at Lyons by Severus 197
Southern Britain subdued and divided by the Romans into 2 provinces 204
Severus keeps his court at York, then called Eboracum, 208, finishes his wall, and dies at York 4 Feb 211
Carausius usurps the throne of Britain . 286
He is killed by Allectus, another usurper . . . 294
Constantius recovers Britain and kills Allectus . 296
St. Alban and 17,000 Christians martyred (*Bede*) 304
Constantius, emperor of Rome, dies at York 25 July, 306
British bishops at the council of Arles . 314
Scots and Picts invade Britain, 360, routed by Theodosius 368
Romans gradually withdraw from Britain 402-436
Reign of Vortigern . . 425
Saxons and Angles aid in expelling Picts and Scots 429

Romans quit Britain 436
Anglo-Saxon invaders drive the Britons into Wales 419–455
Many Britons settle in Armorica (Brittany) 388–457
Saxon heptarchy, Britain divided into 7 or more kingdoms 457
Ella invades S Britain, 477, founds kingdom of Sussex 491
Great Saxon invasion under Cerdic 495
Supposed reigns of Vortimer, 464, Vortigern again, 471, Aurelius Ambrosius 481, and Arthur Pendragon 500
King Arthur said to reign 500-532
Arrival of St Augustin (or Austin), and re establishment of Christianity 597
Cadwallader, last king of the Britons, reigns 678
Lindisfarne church destroyed by the Northmen 794
Egbert, king of Wessex, virtually king of England 827

KINGS OF THE HEPTARCHY (BRETWALDA.)

KENT. [*The shire of Kent*]

454 Hengist. [473 Saxon Chronicle]
488 Æsc, Esca, or Escus, son of Hengist, in honor of whom kings of Kent were often called Æscings
512 Octa son of Æsc
542 Hermenric, or Ermenric son of Octa
560 St Ethelbert, first Christian king (styled *Rex Anglorum*).
616 Eadbald son of Ethelbert.
640 Ercenbert, or Ercombert son of Eadbald
664 Ecbert, or Egbert, son of Ercenbert
673 Lothar, or Lothair, brother of Ecbert
685 Edric, slain in 687 [The kingdom distracted.]
694 Wihtred, or Wihgtred.
725 Eadbert, }
748 Ethelbert II, } sons of Wihtred, succeeding each other
760 Alric, }
794. Edbert or Ethelbert Pryn, deposed
796 Cutbred, or Guthred
805 Baldred, who lost his life and kingdom to
823 Egbert, king of Wessex

SOUTH SAXONS [*Sussex and Surrey*]

491 Ella, a warlike prince, succeeded by
514 Cissa, his son, peaceful reign exceeding 70 years
[The South Saxons became dependent on the kingdom of Wessex]
648 Edilwald, Edilwach, Adelwach, or Ethelwach
686. Authun and Berthun, brothers, reigned jointly, vanquished by Ina, king of Wessex, 689, kingdom conquered in 725

WEST SAXONS. [*Berks, Hampshire, Wilts, Somerset, Dorset, Devon, and part of Cornwall*]

519 Cerdic.
534 Cynric, or Kenric, son of Cerdic
560 Ceawlin, son of Cynric, banished, dies in 593.
591 Ceolric, nephew to Ceawlin
597 Ceolwulf
611 } Cynegils, and in
614 } Cwichelm, his son, reigned jointly
643 Cenwal, Cenwalh, or Cenwald
672. Sexburga, his queen, sister to Penda, king of Mercia, of great qualities, probably deposed
674 Escwine, with Centwine, on his death
676 Centwine rules alone
685 Cædwallo went to Rome, to expiate murders and died there
688 Ina or Inas, brave and wise, visited Rome, left an excellent code of laws.
728 Ethelheard, or Ethelard, related to Ina.
740 Cuthred, brother to Ethelheard
754 Sigebright, or Sigebert, murdered his friend Cumbran, governor of Hampshire, and was slain by one of his victim's retainers
755 Cynewulf, or Kenwulf, or Cenulpe, a noble youth of the line of Cerdic, murdered
784 Bertric, or Beorhtric, poisoned by a cup his queen had prepared for another
800 Egbert, afterwards sole monarch of England

EAST SAXONS [*Essex, Middlesex, and part of Herts*]

526, 527, or 530. Erchenwin, or Erchwine
587 Sledda, his son
597 St Sebert, or Sabert, son, first Christian king
614 Saxred, or Sexted, or Serred, jointly with Sigebert and Seward, all slain
623. Sigebert II the little, son of Seward.
655 Sigebert III the good, brother of Sebert, murdered
661 Swithelm (or Suidhelm), son of Sexbald
663 Sigher or Sigeric, jointly with Sebbi, or Sebba, who became a monk
693 Sigenard, or Sigehard, and Suenfrid.
700 Offa, became a monk at Rome
709 Suebricht, or Selred
738 Swithred, or Swithed, a long reign
792. Sigeric, died in a pilgrimage to Rome.
799 Sigered
823 Kingdom seized by Egbert of Wessex

NORTHUMBRIA. [*Lancaster, York, Cumberland, Westmoreland, Durham, and Northumberland.*]

*** Northumbria was at first in 2 governments, *Bernicia*, from the Tweed to the Tyne, and *Deira*, from the Tyne to the Humber
547 Ida, a valiant Saxon
560. Adda, his eldest son, king of Bernicia
" Ella, king of Deira, afterwards sole king of Northumbria (to 587)
567 Glappa, Clappa, or Elapea, Bernicia
572 Heodwulf, Bernicia
573 Freodwulf, Bernicia.
580 Theodoric, Bernicia
588 Ethelric, Bernicia
593 Ethelfrith, surnamed the Fierce.
617 Edwin, son of Ella, king of Deira in 590, a great prince Slain in battle with Penda, of Mercia
634 Eanfrid rules in Bernicia, and Osric in Deira, both killed
635 Oswald, slain in battle
642. Osweo, or Oswy, a reign of great renown
670 Ecfrid, or Egfrid king of Northumbria.
685 Alcfrid, or Ealdferth
705 Osred, or Ealdferth
716 Cenric, sprung from Ida
718 Osric, son of Alcfrid
729 Ceolwulf, died a monk
737 Eadbert, or Egbert, retired to a monastery
757 Oswulf, or Osulf, slain in a sedition
759 Edilwald or Mollo, slain by Alred
765 Alred Ailred or Alured, deposed
774 Ethelred, son of Mollo, expelled
778 Elwald, or Celwold deposed and slain.
789 Osred, son of Alred, fled
790 Ethelred restored, afterwards slain.
794 Erdulf or Ardulf, deposed
806 Alfwold
808 Erdulf, restored
809 Eanred
841 Kingdom annexed by Egbert.

EAST ANGLES [*Norfolk, Suffolk, Cambridge, Ely*]

526 Uffa lands
571 or 575 Uffa a German said to be first king
578 Titulus, or Tytulus, son of Uffa
599 Redwald, son of Titulus greatest prince of the East Angles
624 Erpwald, Eorpwald, or Eordwald
627 Richbert.
629 Sigebert half brother to Erpwald
632. Egfrid, or Egric, cousin to Sigebert
635 Anna, or Annas, a just ruler, killed
654 Ethelric, or Ethelhere slain in battle
655 Ethelwald, his brother
664 Aldulf or Aldwulf
713 Selred, or Ethelred
746 Alphwald
749 Beorna and Ethelred, jointly
758 Beorna alone
761 Ethelred
790. Ethelbert or Ethelbryght, treacherously killed in Mercia, 792, when Offa king of Mercia, overran the country, which was finally subdued by Egbert
870 St Edmund (vassal king) slain by the Danes

MERCIA [*Gloucester Hereford Chester, Stafford, Worcester, Oxford, Salop Warwick, Derby Leicester, Bucks, Northampton, Notts, Lincoln, Bedford, Rutland, Huntingdon, and part of Herts*]

586 Crida, or Cridda, a noble chieftain
593 [Interregnum—Ceolric.]
597 Wibba, a valiant prince his son
615 Ceorl or Cheorl nephew of Wibba
626 Penda, fierce and cruel, killed in battle
655. Penda son of Penda, killed to make way for
656. Wulfhere (brother), slew his 2 sons.
675 Ethelred, became a monk
704 Cenred or Cendred, became a monk at Rome
709 Ceolred Celred or Chelred, son of Ethelred
716. Ethelbald, slain in a mutiny by his successor,
755. Beornred, or Bernred, himself slain
" Offa, formed the great dike near Wales
794. Egfrid, or Egferth son of Offa, died suddenly
" Cenulph, Cenwulf or Kenulph, slain
819 Kenelm, or Cenelm, a minor, reigned 5 months, killed by his sister Quendred
" Ceolwulf, uncle to Kenelm, expelled.
821 Beornwulf, killed by his own subjects
823 Ludecan, a valiant ruler, slain
825. Withlafe, or Wiglaf
838 Berthulf or Bertulf
852 Burhred or Burdred
874 Ceolwulph, deposed by the Danes 877
[The kingdom merged in ENGLAND]

Britannia tubular bridge. BRIDGES

British America comprises the dominion of CANADA (which includes provinces of Quebec, Ontario, Nova Scotia, New Brunswick, Prince Edward's Island, British Columbia, Manitoba, Northwestern Territories, and Arctic islands) and NEWFOUNDLAND Pop 1891, about 5 000,000

Delegates met at Quebec, 10 Oct, and formed a federal union, with the queen of England as executive (represented by a governor general) a legislative council, members for life, and a house of commons 20 Oct 1864
Secretary for the colonies, Mr Cardwell, approved the plan, 3 Dec "
Plan opposed by New Brunswick 7 Mch 1865
Messrs. Cartier and Galt came to England to advocate it Apr "
Act for union of Canada, Nova Scotia, and New Brunswick, as "the dominion of Canada," introduced by the earl of Carnarvon, 19 Feb., passed 29 Mch 1867

[British government guaranteed a subsidy of 3,000,000*l* to complete the intercolonial railway]
By the British North America act, the Parliament of Canada may establish new provinces 29 June, 1871

British Association for the Advancement of Science was established by sir David Brewster, sir R I Murchison, etc., in 1831 Prof John Phillips was secretary till 1863 It holds annual meetings, the first at York on 27 Sept 1831 A main object is "to promote the intercourse of those who cultivate science with each other" It appoints commissions, makes pecuniary grants for scientific research, and publishes annual reports of proceedings Kew observatory presented to the association by queen Victoria in 1842 AMERICAN ASSOCIATION

British Columbia, N America In June, 1858, news came to California that in April much gold had been found on the mainland of North America, just north and east of Vancouver's Island A great influx of gold-diggers (in a few weeks above 50,000) from all parts followed, and Mr Douglas, governor of Vancouver's Island, ably preserved order The territory with adjacent islands was made a British colony with the above title, with Mr Douglas as governor, under 21 and 22 Vict c. 99 (Aug 1858), a bishop was nominated in 1859 Vancouver's Island was incorporated with the colony in 1866, and Victoria made the capital, 24 May, 1868 The colony was annexed to Canada, 1871 Pop 1891, 92,767

British East Africa. ANGLO-FRENCH-GERMAN AGREEMENT, ZANZIBAR, etc

British museum, originated with the grant by Parliament (5 Apr 1753) of 20,000*l* to the daughters of sir Hans Sloane, in payment for his fine library and collection of the productions of nature and art, valued by himself at 80,000*l* The library contained 50,000 volumes, 4100 valuable MSS, and 69,352 articles of virtu enumerated in the catalogue Montagu House was obtained by government as a place for their reception The museum (including the Cottonian, Harleian, and other collections) was opened 15 Jan 1759, and has since been enormously increased by gifts bequests, and purchases The total expenditure by the government on the British museum for the year ending 31 Mch 1860, was 78,445*l* , 1861, 92 776*l* , 1864, 95,500*l* , 1867, 110,756*l* , 1877, 108,947*l* , 1884, 152,133*l* The number of visitors to the general collection in 1851 (exhibition year), 2,524,754, in 1859, 517,895, in 1862 (exhibition year), 895,007, in 1863, 440,801, in 1866, 516 550, 1871, 418,094, 1875, 663,891 in 1878, 418,516, in 1879, 606,394, in 1880, 655,688 readers, 133,842, 1883 660,557 readers, 152,983 Additions to library in 1880, 27,543 volumes and pamphlets (including books of music and volumes of newspapers). Expenditure on purchases, 1753-1875, 1,070,934*l*

New buildings erected by sir R Smirke 1823-47
Iron railing completed 1852
Great reading room erected by Sydney Smirke on a plan by Antonio Panizzi, the librarian (cost about 150 000*l* , height of dome, 106 ft , diameter, 140 ft , contains about 80.000 volumes, and accommodates 300 readers), opened 18 May, 1857
Incorporation of the 4 library catalogues into one alphabet begun, 3 copies made 1861
Proposed separation of the antiquarian literary, and scientific collections was disapproved by a commission in 1860, a bill to remove natural history collections to South Kensington rejected by the commons. 19 May, 1862
A refreshment room for readers opened 21 Nov 1864
Number of books (estimated), 1,000,000 Jan. 1870
6000*l* voted for a natural history museum at South Kensington 2 Aug "
Photographs of above 5000 objects of antiquity (illustrating man's progress in civilization) published for about 116*l* , Aug 1872
Act of Parliament authorizing removal of natural history collections to South Kensington, passed. 13 Aug 1878
Museum partly opened daily after 11 Feb 1879
Electric light tried in reading room, 25 Feb et seq , adopted for evenings in the winter months . . 20 Oct. "
White bequest (60,000*l*) 1880
New British Museum for Natural History, Cromwell road, South Kensington, building completed Nov "
Part of the collection removed and opened to the public, Easter Monday 18 Apr 1881
John Gould's humming birds, etc , bought about Apr "
New building in Montague st. founded (by means of Wm White's legacy of 63 941*l*.) 23 Sept 1882
New Assyrian room (including Mr Rassam's collection) opened, Jan 1884
New catalogue, 74 volumes, ready. Dec "
New galleries, glass and pottery, Greek sculpture, opened 1889
Open evenings from 8 to 10 Feb 1, 1890

BRI

IMPORTANT ADDITIONS (*bought or given*) —(*Edwards*)
Those marked * were gifts or bequests

* George II , old royal library . 1757
* Solomon Da Costa Hebrew library 1759
* G Thomason, collection (political) from George III 1762
* Solander, fossils 1766
* Birch, library and MSS "
Hamilton vases, etc 1772
* Musgrave library 1790-99
* Cracherode library 1799
Hatchett minerals "
* Alexandrian collection (from George III) 1802
Townley marbles . 1805-17
Lansdowne MSS (state papers) 1804
Greville minerals 1810
Roberts, English coins . "
Hargrave library 1813
Phigaleian marbles . 1815
Elgin marbles 1816
Burney library . 1818
* Banks's archæological collections "
* George III 's library, given by George IV 1823-25
* Payne Knight's collections 1824
* Sir J Banks s library and collections 1827
* Egerton MSS 1829
* Arundelian MSS ... 1831
Mantell, fossils 1839
Syriac MSS 1841-47
* Lycian marbles (by sir C Fellows) 1845
* Grenville library, collected by right hon Thomas Grenville (20,240 vols) 1847
Morrison's Chinese library "
Assyrian collections (by A Layard) 1851-60
Halicarnassian and Cnidian marbles (by C T Newton) 1855-60
Carthaginian antiquities (by N Davis) 1859
Cyrene marbles (by Smith and Porcher) 1860
Cureton, Oriental MSS .. 1864
Duke of Blacas's museum (bought for 48,000*l*) 1866
* Abyssinian antiquities 1868
* Slade collection (glass, etc) "
* George Smith s (of *Daily Telegraph*) Assyrian collections 1873
* Elamite antiquities, by col Ross 1876
* Urns, implements, ornaments, etc , from 234 British barrows (BARROWS), by rev canon Greenwell 1879
300 Babylonian tablets purchased June, 1882
1000 Stowe MSS part of the Ashburnham library 1883
* Slavin and Godman s collection of American birds 1885
* Indian birds and eggs from A O Hume "
* Marquis of Tweeddale's collection of birds Oct 1887
* Morgan's collection of watches, clocks, key rings, etc Oct 1888

PRINCIPAL LIBRARIANS

Dr Gowin Knight	1753	Antonio Panizzi	1856
Dr Matthew Maty	1772	J Winter Jones	1866
Dr Charles Morton	1776	Edward Augustus Bond, Aug 1878, resigned, June,	1888
Joseph Planta	. 1799		
Henry Ellis	1827	Edward Maunde Thompson,	1888

British orders in council. As the sovereign of the United Kingdom can only act through privy-councillors or upon their advice, the more formal acts of administration must proceed from the authority of the sovereign in council, and their performance be directed by orders issued by the sovereign at a meeting of the privy council —*Todd's* "Parliamentary Law of Engl," vol ii p 621 Every "order in council" shall be published in the *London Gazette,* and shall be laid before both Houses of Parliament within 30 days after the making thereof, if Parliament is sitting, and if not, 30 days after the next meeting of Parliament

"British orders in council" of 8 June, 1793, relative to "neutrals," called forth the first embargo act on the part of the United States, 1794
British orders in council of 11 Nov 1807, prohibited any direct trade from the U S to any port or country in Europe from which the British flag was excluded, it allowed direct trade in American productions only between the U S. and Sweden , it ordered all articles of domestic or colonial production exported by the U S to Europe to be landed in England, when their re-exportation on paying duties would be permitted and regulated, and it declared any vessel and cargo good prize if it carried a French consular certificate of the origin of the cargo BERLIN and MILAN DECREES, EMBARGO, UNITED STATES, 1807-09-13.

Brittany, Britanny, or **Bretagne,** N.W. France, the ancient ARMORICA, formed part of the kingdom of the Franks.

Nomenoë revolts and becomes the first count 841
Brittany ravaged by Northmen, 907, ceded to them 921
Geoffroy I the first duke. 992
Alan V , 1008, Conan II 1040
Hoel V , 1066, Alan VI 1084
Conan III 1112
Hoel VI expelled, Geoffroy of Anjou duke 1155
Conan IV duke, 1156, on the death of Geoffroy, cedes Brittany to Henry II of England, and betroths his daughter, Constance, to Henry's son, Geoffroy (both infants) 1159
Geoffroy succeeds, 1171, killed at a tournament 1185

His son, Arthur, murdered by his uncle, John of England; his daughter, Eleanor, imprisoned at Bristol (for 39 years)..Apr. 1203
Alice, daughter of Constance by her second husband, Guy de Thours, proclaimed duchess, 1203; marries Peter of Dreux, made duke........ 1213
John I., duke, 1237; John II........ 1286
John III., 1312; dies without issue........ 1341
Succession disputed between John of Montfort (John IV.), supported by Edward of England, and Charles of Blois, made duke by Philip VI. of France. John is made prisoner; his wife, Jane, besieged at Hennebonne, is relieved by the English, 1343; John dies........ 1345
Charles of Blois defeated and slain at Auray, 29 Sept.; John V., son of Montfort, duke........ 1364
John VI., duke, 1399; Francis I........ 1442
Peter II., 1450; Arthur III........ 1457
Francis II., 1458; takes part with the Orleanists in France; defeated at St. Aubin, 28 July, 1488; dies........ 1488
Anne, his daughter and heiress, marries, 1st, Charles VIII. of France, 1491; 2d, Louis XII., 1499; her eldest daughter, Claude (b. 1499), marries Francis, count of Angoulême, 1514; king of France........1 Jan. 1515
Brittany formally united to the monarchy........ 1532
Brittany held by Spaniards, 1591; recovered by Henry IV..... 1594
Bretons take part in the Vendean insurrection (LA VENDÉE)... 1791

"Britton," an ancient treatise on English law written in French by or in the name of king Edward I., about 1291. Coke attributed the work to John le Breton, bishop of Hereford, who died in 1275. An edition of "Britton," with translation in English by Mr. F. Nicholls, was pub. in 1865.

broad arrow. Origin of this mark is unknown. It is said that timber trees fit for shipping in the forest of Dean in 1639 were marked with the crown and broad arrow. It is said to have been the device of viscount Sydney, earl of Romney, master-general of the ordnance, 1693–1702.—*Brewer.*

"Broad-bottom" administration. The Pelham administration was so called because formed by a coalition of parties (ADMINISTRATIONS OF ENGLAND), Nov. 1744.

Broad-church school in the church of England, with a tendency to reject traditional creeds, became prominent about 1836, through the lectures of Dr. Hampden, and still more through the "Theological Essays" of F. D. Maurice, in 1853; the "Essays and Reviews," in 1860; the works of bishop Colenso on the Pentateuch, etc., 1862 et seq.; and of Dr. Arnold, dean Stanley, canon Kingsley, and others.

brocade, a silken stuff, variegated with gold or silver, and enriched with flowers and figures, originally made by the Chinese; the manufacture was established at Lyons in 1757.

broccoli, a variety of the common cabbage resembling the cauliflower, said to have been brought to England from Italy in the 16th century.

brokers, of money and merchandise, known early in England. APPRAISERS. They were licensed, and their dealings regulated by law in 1695–96, 1816, and 1826. The dealings of stockbrokers were regulated in 1719, 1733, and 1736, and subsequently. Brokers in London placed under the supervision of the lord mayor and aldermen, in 1707; relieved from it by act of 9 Aug. 1870. PAWNBROKER. In the United States they are not licensed, nor do they give bonds.

bromine (from the Gr. βρῶμος, a stink), a poisonous volatile liquid element discovered in salt-water by M. Balardin 1826. It is found in combination with metals and mineral waters.

bronze was known to the ancients, some of whose bronze statues, vessels, etc., are in the British museum. The bronze equestrian statue of Louis XIV., 1699, in the Place Vendôme at Paris (demolished 10 Aug. 1792), the largest ever made, contained 60,000 pounds. Bronze is composed of copper and tin, with sometimes a little zinc and lead. COINAGE.

Brook farm, the location of a society near West Roxbury, Mass., formed in 1841 for a practical test of Christianity as taught by its founder. Up to 1842 it had nothing in common with "Fourierism," after which it became a community and lasted until 1846. It is notable for members eminent in literature: Dr. Channing, Geo. Ripley, Margaret Fuller, Theo. Parker, Geo. W. Curtis, Miss E. P. Peabody, Hawthorne, W. Burton, Chas. A. Dana, R. W. Emerson, etc. It suggested Hawthorne's "Blithedale Romance."

Brooklyn, N. Y., popularly called the "city of churches," ranks (1890) as the fourth city in the United States in point of population, manufacture, and commerce. It is situated on Long Island, opposite New York, and the two cities are practically one. Area, 26.46 sq. miles. The settlement of the present city began at 3 points: In 1636 William A. Bennet and Jacques Bentyn purchased from the Indians 930 acres at Gowanus (between 27th st. and New Utrecht), and John (George) Jansen de Rapalie purchased the piece of land now occupied in part by the U. S. Marine hospital, 16 June, 1637. Jan Evertse Bout in July, 1645, followed in 1646–47 by others, established themselves on what is now Fulton st., near the city-hall, calling the settlement Breuckelen. In 1660 Breuckelen contained 134 inhabitants, disposed in 31 families. In 1738 a census showed a pop. of 721, which increased by annexation, etc. In 1800 it was 2378. Since then by decades it has been: 1810, 4402; 1820, 7175; 1830, 12,406; 1840, 36,233; 1850, 96,838; 1860, 266,661; 1870, 396,099; 1880, 566,663; 1890, 806,343.

Cornelis Dircksen, first regular ferryman, mentioned as proprieter of a ferry between Long Island and New Amsterdam, from the present Fulton st., Brooklyn, to the foot of Peck slip, New York, known as the "old ferry"........ 1642
Breuckelen organized as a town by the colonial council, and Jan Eversen Bout and Huyck Aertsen elected as "schepens," 1646
[Named Breuckelen after a village in Holland, 18 miles from Amsterdam.]
First ferry ordinance, requiring license and establishing fees, enacted, July, 1654, and first ferry-house in Breuckelen built.. 1655
Henricus Selyns, Breuckelen's first minister, formally installed, 7 Sept. 1660
First schoolmaster, Carel de Beauvois, arrives, July, 1661, and a school-house soon after erected at crossing of present North 2d st. and Bushwick ave........ 1661
First Protestant Reformed Dutch church organized, 12 Mch. 1660, and first church edifice in Breuckelen built in the middle of what is now Fulton st., near Lawrence........ 1666
[Pulled down and rebuilt, 1766.]
Gov. Nicolls grants a patent to the inhabitants of Brooklyn, 18 Oct. 1667
Patent confirming that of 1667, obtained from gov. Dongan, under seal of the colony........ 13 May, 1686
Fulton st. and Fulton ave. laid out by commissioners, and known as the main road of the "King's highway"...28 Mch. 1704
General Assembly of the province sits in Brooklyn, owing to the prevalence of small-pox in New York....20 Mch.–8 Oct. 1746
During session of the colonial legislature held in Brooklyn, on account of small-pox in New York, the colonial commissioners cancel 2541 bills of credit issued by the colony of New York, amounting to about 3600*l*........4 June, 1752
Battle of Long Island. NEW YORK........27 Aug. 1776
Fort erected by the British near the junction of Pierrepont and Henry sts........1780–81
A newspaper called the *Brooklyn-Hall Super-Extra Gazette*, the first in the city; only one copy known; pub.....8 June, 1782
First fire-company organized, for which was built the first fire-engine, the "Washington, No. 1," by Jacob Roome of New York........30 Apr. 1785
First Methodist church, built on Sands st. and dedicated, 1 June, 1794
New ferry, afterwards Catharine St. ferry, established by William Furman and Theodosius Hunt........1 Aug. 1795
First fire-alarm bell hung on the storehouse of Jacob Remsen (pulled down 1816), on the cor. of present Fulton and Front sts. 1796
First printing-press established by Thomas Kirk, printing the first regular newspaper in Brooklyn, the *Courier and New York and Long Island Advertiser*........26 June, 1799
Fortitude Lodge No. 19, first permanent Masonic lodge in Brooklyn, organized........4 Dec. "
Brooklyn navy-yard purchased for the U. S.; price paid, $40,000........5 Feb. 1801
Settlement of Brooklyn incorporated as a fire-district....2 Apr. "
St. Ann's church, Episcopal, built........ 1805
Interment with military and civic honors in 13 coffins, one to represent each state, of the bones of the martyrs of the British prison ships, in a vault erected by the Tammany Society, in Jackson st., adjoining the navy-yard........26 May, 1808
Loisian Seminary established, to teach poor children "reading, writing, arithmetic, knitting, and sewing gratis"........ 1813
First steam ferry-boat, the *Nassau*, commences running between Brooklyn and New York........10 May, 1814
Brooklyn Sunday-school Union Society organized.......8 Apr. 1816
That portion of Brooklyn included in the fire-district of 1801, incorporated as a village by act........12 Apr. "
First district school, No. 1, opened on lower floor of Thomas Kirk's printing-office, with 73 scholars (school conducted on the Lancasterian plan and soon removed to cor. Concord and Adams sts.)........6 May, "
Corporate seal adopted........27 June, "
Village trustees sue Jacob Patchen, for refusing to relay the pavement in front of his house in Old Ferry st.........Dec. "
Old Ferry st. renamed Fulton st........June, 1817
First Episcopal Sunday-school opened........spring of 1818
Guy's "Snow Scene of Brooklyn" preserved in the Brooklyn Institute, painted........ 1820
Daily mail to New York and Jamaica established........May, "
First village directory pub. by Alden Spooner........May, 1822
[An incomplete list of residents in Brooklyn appeared in a New York city directory issued in 1796.]
Corner-stone of the first Roman Catholic church (St. James's) laid in Jay st........25 July, "
Fire department of the village of Brooklyn incorporated, 16 Apr. 1823

First Presbyterian church incorporated, 13 Mch 1822, and brick church in Cranberry st dedicated 20 Apr 1822
Brooklyn receives from the state $413 13 for its share of the public school fund "
Apprentices' Library Association organized, 7 Aug and constitution adopted 14 Aug "
Yellow fever epidemic 22 Aug-22 Sept "
St. James church dedicated 28 Aug "
First Baptist church incorporated 15 Oct. "
Corner stone of new St Ann's church laid 31 Mch 1824
Long Island bank incorporated with capital stock $300,000 by act 1 Apr "
Board of Health established 9 Ap. "
Village watch organized and municipal court established "
Corner stone of the Apprentices' Library laid by gen Lafayette, 4 July, 1825

[It stood on the cor of Cranberry and Henry sts afterwards occupied by the armory buildings, and contained the village trustees' room and the post office and was used for preaching service by Elias Hicks and others.]

First parade of the fire department 4 July 1826
Brooklyn Savings bank chartered 7 Apr 1827
Village of Williamsburg incorporated 14 Apr "
First night boat on the Fulton ferry commences running 28 Sept. "
Brooklyn Amphitheatre erected on Fulton st. below Concord, and opened by an equestrian company 10 July, 1828
Explosion of the powder magazine of the steam frigate *Fulton* at the navy yard, 33 killed, 29 wounded 4 June, 1829
Protestant Orphan Asylum Society instituted (incorporated 1835) 1833
Roman Catholic Orphan asylum opened in a house on Jay st 1834
Brooklyn incorporated as a city 8 Apr "
George Hall elected by the board of aldermen, first mayor 20 May, "
First steam railway in Brooklyn, the Brooklyn and Jamaica railroad, completed and opened 18 Apr 1836
Corner stone of the city hall laid (completed 1849) 28 Apr "
Musical instruction introduced in district school No 1, by Theodore Dwight "
Brooklyn Orphan asylum opened 1833, incorporated 13 Feb 1835, and corner stone of building in Cumberland st laid, 6 Oct 1838
Greenwood cemetery incorporated. 1839
First lodge of Odd Fellows in Brooklyn organized, Brooklyn Lodge No 26 12 Nov "
First election of mayor by the people, Cyrus P Smith chosen, 14 Apr 1840
First burial in Greenwood cemetery, John Hanna, near the base of Ocean hill 5 Sept. "
Brooklyn *Eagle*, daily, established 26 Oct 1841
Board of Education of the city of Brooklyn created by act, 23 Mch 1843
Line of omnibuses established between Fulton ferry and E Brooklyn Sept. "
Riot between native Americans and Irish. 4 Apr 1844
Atlantic Dock Company organized, 8 July, 1840, dock construction begun, 3 June, 1841, and building of first warehouse begun 25 May, "
Long Island railroad tunnel in Atlantic st. opened to travel, 3 Dec. "
Holy Trinity church, cor Clinton and Montague sts., erected 1847
Improvement of Washington park begun "
Rev Henry Ward Beecher begins his pastorate in Plymouth church 10 Oct. "
Brooklyn Times established as the *Williamsburg Daily Times*, 28 Feb 1848
Gas first introduced in Brooklyn 27 Mch "
Last of 9000 piles for the Brooklyn dry dock driven 12 May, "
Fire breaks out on Fulton st. near Sands, burns over 7 blocks, loss over $1,500,000, 3 churches and the post office burned, 9 Sept. "
Cypress Hills cemetery dedicated 21 Nov "
Cholera epidemic, 642 deaths, or one to every 155 inhabitants, 29 May-22 Sept. 1849
Cemetery of the Evergreens incorporated 3 Oct. "
Plymouth church burned, 13 Jan 1849, corner stone of new building laid, 29 May, 1849, house first occupied by the congregation. 6 Jan 1850
Brooklyn museum, cor Fulton and Orange sts., opened, 1 July, "
Police department organized, John S. Folk, chief of police. "
Williamsburg chartered as a city 7 Apr 1851
Brooklyn Heights Seminary established by prof Alonzo Gray, LL D "
Brooklyn City hospital incorporated, 8 May, 1845, corner stone of building on old fort Greene laid, 11 June, 1851, and centre building completed and opened 28 Apr 1852
Packer Collegiate Institute incorporated under name of the Brooklyn Female Academy, 1845, and first building dedicated, 4 May, 1846 Building destroyed by fire, 1 Jan. 1853, and interest therein transferred to the Brooklyn Polytechnic Institute 1853
Brooklyn Young Men's Christian Association organized Sept "
Pierrepont house, cor. Montague and Hicks sts, opened May, 1854
Brooklyn City Railroad Company, incorporated 17 Dec 1853, and first street-cars run 3 July, "
Packer Collegiate Institute, new buildings erected and opened, 11 Sept "
Brooklyn Collegiate and Polytechnic Institute incorporated and opened "
Williamsburg and Bushwick annexed to Brooklyn (act of legislature, 17 Apr 1854). 1 Jan 1855
New building of the Brooklyn City hospital opened 31 Jan "
Truant Home founded 12 Apr 1853, opened 1856
Plan prepared by William J McAlpine for supply of water to the city adopted, 28 Apr 1853, and inaugural celebration of building of reservoir in Prospect park occurs 31 July, "
Board of sewer commissioners created 15 Apr 1857
Philharmonic Society of Brooklyn organized 5 May, "
Mercantile Library Association organized, 17 Dec 1857, and library opened with 7000 volumes 7 May, 1858
Long Island College hospital opened May, "
Apprentices' Library sold to the city for $11,000 (1836), occupied until the completion of the city hall (1848) as the city building, torn down and replaced by the city armory buildings "
Plans for sewerage and drainage system reported and adopted, 16 Apr 1859
Water from Ridgewood reservoir first let into the city mains, 4 Dec 1858, event celebrated by the city 28 Apr "
Boiler explosion in hat factory on Nostrand ave, between Myrtle and Park aves, out of 35 persons in the building at the time, 9 killed and 18 wounded 7 A M, 3 Feb 1860
Brooklyn Art Association instituted 5 Jan. 1861
Brooklyn Academy of Music erected at a cost of over $206,000, opened 15 Jan. "
Corner stone of the new county court house (completed Mch 1865) laid 20 May, 1862
Long Island Historical Society, organized 10 Mch 1863, incorporated Apr 1863
Park theatre, Fulton st, the first regularly established theatre in Brooklyn, opened with the comedy by Buckstone, 'Married Life' 14 Sept "
Brooklyn and Long Island fair, net result, $402,943.74, held 22 Feb-8 Mch 1864
Construction of the Erie Basin and Brooklyn Basin begun, June, "
Standard Union established "
Brooklyn Academy of Design instituted 1866
Distribution of medals prepared by order of the common council to every Brooklyn soldier who had returned from the war with an honorable record 25 Oct. "
Corner stone of Roman Catholic cathedral on Lafayette ave, between Clermont and Vanderbilt aves laid by bishop Loughlin 21 June, 1868
Mercantile Library building, corner stone laid, 27 Oct. 1867, opened 18 Jan 1869
John A Roebling, b Prussia, 12 June, 1806, d 22 July, "
[Designer of the Brooklyn Bridge.]
Metropolitan paid fire department created. "
Prospect park provided for by act of legislature, 17 Apr 1860, improvements begun, June 1866, completed about 1871
City ambulance service organized 1873
New city charter June, "
Tabernacle Presbyterian church destroyed by fire, Dec. 1872, and new tabernacle erected and dedicated 22 Feb 1874
Brooklyn theatre burned, 295 lives lost 5 Dec. 1876
Ground broken for municipal building, 21 June, 1876, first occupied. May 1878
Electric light introduced in Brooklyn by F Loeser in his store on Fulton st 14 Dec "
Farewell service in old St. Ann's church 1880
[It was demolished to make way for the approach to the Brooklyn bridge.]
New building of Long Island Historical Society opened, 2 Nov "
St. Mary's General hospital, corner stone laid, 12 Oct 1879, opened for reception of patients 17 Dec. 1882
Work on Brooklyn bridge begun, 3 Jan 1870, and bridge opened (BRIDGES) 24 May, 1883
Panic on Brooklyn bridge, 12 killed, many injured 30 May, "
Brooklyn elevated railway opened 14 May, 1885
Training school for teachers opened (Brooklyn Institute) "
Brooklyn *Citizen*, daily established 1886
Rev Henry Ward Beecher d 8 Mch 1887
Street-railway strike and tie up begins 26 Jan 1889
Brooklyn Tabernacle destroyed by fire. 13 Oct "
Dr Lyman Abbott installed pastor of Plymouth church, 16 Jan 1890
New Brooklyn Tabernacle completed 25 Apr 1891
Statue of Henry Ward Beecher unveiled 24 June, "
New Brooklyn Tabernacle destroyed by fire May, 1894
Street railway (trolley) strike and tie-up begins 10 Jan, and terminates. 2 Mch 1895

MAYORS

George Hall	1834	Samuel S Powell	1857
Jonathan Trotter	1835	Martin Kalbfleisch	1861
Jeremiah Johnson	1837	Alfred M Wood	1864
Cyrus P Smith	1839	Samuel Booth	1866
Henry C. Murphy	1842	Martin Kalbfleisch	1868
Joseph Sprague	1843	Samuel S Powell	1872
Thomas T Talmage	1845	John W Hunter	1874
Francis B Stryker	1846	Fred A Schroeder	1876
Edward Copeland	1849	James Howell	1878
Samuel Smith	1850	Seth Low	1882
Conklin Brush	1851	Daniel D Whitney	1886
Edward A. Lambert	1853	Alfred C Chapin	1888
George Hall	1855	David A. Boody	1892
		Charles A. Schieren	1894

Brooks, Preston S Representative from S. C., 34th Congress. UNITED STATES, 1856.

Brother Jonathan, origin of. CONNECTICUT, 1769

brougham, a popular vehicle said to have been invented in 1839, and adopted by lord Brougham.

Brown, Fort, a work partly completed by the Americans on the Rio Grande, opposite Matamoras, in the spring of 1846 and commanded by major Brown, for whom it was named It was cannonaded from Matamoras on 3 May, 1846 Major Brown was mortally wounded Gen Taylor marched from Point Isabel and relieved it after a cannonade and bombardment of 160 hours This was the opening of the MEXICAN WAR.

Brown Institute, Battersea, Engl, with a hospital for quadrupeds and birds useful to man, established by a bequest of Thomas Brown, of Dublin, first professor Dr Burdon-Sanderson, opened 2 Dec 1871 Dr Greenfield, professor, Dec. 1878.

Brown's Ferry, Tenn CHATTANOOGA CAMPAIGN, 27 Oct 1863

Brown's (John) **insurrection.** An attempt of John Brown to incite the slaves of the south to assert their freedom by force Brown had been zealous in making Kansas a free state, and was known as a bitter enemy of slavery KANSAS, 1855-56 He brought a few followers to near Harper's Ferry, Va., in the summer of 1859, secretly collecting arms and ammunition to arm the slaves whom he expected to join him His party, 23 in number, 17 white and 6 colored men, on Sunday night, 16 Oct. 1859, entered the village of Harper's Ferry about half-past 10 P M, seized without opposition the government armory and railroad bridge, and had the place in their power before daylight Brown arrested many principal citizens as hostages, a desultory combat ensued as soon as the citizens procured arms, and by the afternoon of the 17th Brown was on the defensive and cut off from escape Still he successfully resisted every attempt to dislodge him from the armory In the afternoon col Robert E Lee arrived from Washington with 90 U S. marines and 2 pieces of artillery, too late for attack On the morning of the 18th Brown, still refusing to surrender, although but 4 of his men remained unhurt, an attack was made on the armory and it was easily forced In the final attack Brown was severely wounded The following shows the fate of each of the participants in this enterprise The survivors captured were tried at Charlestown, Va, and executed as follows

John Brown, leader, b 8 May, 1800	hung 2 Dec 1859
John E Cook	" 16 Dec. "
Edwin Coppoc	" " " "
John A Copeland, negro	" " " "
Shields Green negro	" " " "
Aaron C Stephens	" 16 Mch. 1860
Albert Hazlett	" " " "
John Henry Kagi	killed at Harper's Ferry
Watson Brown, son of John	" " " "
Oliver Brown, son of John	" " " "
William H. Leeman	" " " "
Jeremiah G Anderson	" " " "
William Thompson	" " " "
Dauphin Thompson	" " " "
Stewart Taylor	" " " "
Dangerfield Newby, negro	" " " "
Lewis Leary, negro.	" " " "
Charles Plummer Tidd	escaped
Owen Brown	"
Barclay Coppoc.	"
Francis Jackson Merriam.	"
Osborn P Anderson, negro	"
John Anderson, negro	"

Brownian motion, so called from Robert Brown, the celebrated botanist, who in 1827, by the aid of the microscope, observed in drops of dew a motion of minute particles which at first was attributed to rudimentary life, but was afterwards decided to be due to currents occasioned by inequalities of temperature and evaporation.

Browning Society, of England, for the study of the works of Robert Browning, the poet, was organized by F. J. Furnivall and Miss Hickey It held its first meeting in London, 28 Oct 1881.

Brownists or **Barrowists,** the first INDEPENDENTS, named after Robert Brown, a schoolmaster in Southwark, about 1580 Henry Penry, Henry Barrow, and other Brownists were cruelly executed for alleged sedition, 29 May, 1593. Of this sect was Mr Robinson, elder Brewster, and the congregation that settled at Plymouth, Mass., 1620.

Brownstown, Mich, 26 miles below Detroit. Here 200 Ohio volunteers, under major Van Horne, were defeated by some British and Indians on 4 Aug. 1812. The Americans lost 17 killed and 8 wounded.

Bruce's travels. James Bruce, the "Abyssinian traveller," set out in June, 1768, to discover the source of the NILE Proceeding first to Cairo, he navigated the Nile to Syene, thence crossed the desert to the Red sea, and arriving at Jedda, passed some months in Arabia Felix and after various detentions, reached Gondar, the capital of Abyssinia, in Feb 1770 On 14 Nov 1770, he obtained a sight of the sources of the Blue Nile

> "A wanderer proudly stood
> Beside the well spring, deep and lone,
> Of Egypt s awful flood"
> —*Hemans,* "Bruce at the source of the Nile"

He returned to England in 1773, and died 27 Apr 1794

Bruges, Belgium, in the 7th century, was capital of Flanders, and in the 13th and 14th centuries almost the commercial metropolis of the world It suffered much through an insurrection in 1488, and the consequent repression It was subjected to France in 1794 to the Netherlands in 1814, and to Belgium in 1830

> "In the market place of Bruges stands the belfry, old and brown,
> Thrice consumed and thrice rebuilded still it watches o'er the town
> —*Longfellow,* "The Belfry of Bruges"

Brumaire revolution. DIRECTORY

Brunanburg (supposed by some to be near Lord, Northumberland) Anlaf, with an army of Northmen from Ireland, and Constantine III, king of Scots, landed at the mouth of the Humber, and were defeated with very great slaughter at Brunanburg by Athelstan, 937.

Brundisium, now **Brin'disi,** a seaport on the Adriatic sea, S Italy, a Greek city, taken by the Romans, 267 B C, and made a colony, 244 Here Virgil died, 22 Sept. 19 B C Since the establishment of the overland route to India it has become, as the terminus of the Mount Cenis and other railroad routes, a great point of departure of passengers for the East

Brünn, capital of Moravia since 1641, was entered by the French under Murat, 18 Nov 1805, and by the Prussians, 13 July, 1866

Brunswick, House of The duchy of Brunswick, in Lower Saxony, was conquered by Charlemagne, and governed afterwards by counts and dukes Albert-Azzo II, marquess of Italy and lord of Este, died in 1097, and left by his wife Cunegonde (heiress of Guelph, duke of Carinthia in Bavaria), a son, Guelph, who was invited into Germany by Imitza, his mother-in-law, and invested with all the possessions of his wife's step-father, Guelph of Bavaria BAVARIA His descendant, Henry the Lion, married Maud, daughter of Henry II of England, and founded the Brunswick family His dominions were very extensive, but, having refused to assist the emperor Frederick Barbarossa against pope Alexander III., through the emperor's resentment was proscribed at the diet at Wurtzburg, in 1180 The duchy of Bavaria was given to Otho of Wittelsbach, ancestor of the family of Bavaria; the duchy of Saxony to Bernard Ascanius, founder of the house of Anhalt, his other territories to different persons He retired to England, but, at the intercession of Henry II, Brunswick and Luneburg were restored to him The house of Brunswick in 1409 divided into several branches. Brunswick was included by Napoleon in the kingdom of Westphalia in 1806, but was restored to the duke in 1815. Area, 1441 sq miles Pop. in 1871, 312,170, in 1875, 327,493, in 1890, 372,580. Brunswick joined the North German Confederation, 18 Aug. 1866.

DUKES OF BRUNSWICK.

1136 Henry, duke of Bavaria.
1139 Henry the Lion (son)
1195 Henry the Long and William (sons)
1213 Otho I (son of William)
1252. Albert I (son of preceding).
1278 Albert II (son)
1318 Otho, Magnus I, and Ernest (sons)
1368. Magnus II [Torquatus (son of Magnus I.)]

DUKES OF BRUNSWICK-WOLFENBUTTEL.

First Branch.

1409. Henry I (son of Magnus II).
1416. William I and Henry II (sons)
1482 Frederic and William II } sons of William I
1495. Henry III. and Eric } sons of William I
1514. Henry IV (son of Henry II)
1568. Julius (son of preceding)

1589. Henry Julius (son).
1613. Frederic Ulric (son), died without issue.

Second Branch.

1634. Augustus (son of Henry of Luneburg).
1666. Rodolph Augustus; associated his brother, Anthony Ulric, in the government, from 1685; d. 1704.
1704. Anthony Ulric now ruled alone; became a Roman Catholic in 1710; d. in 1714.
1714. Augustus William (son).
1731. Lewis Rodolph (brother).
1735. Ferdinand Albert, duke of Brunswick-Bevern, married Antoinette Amelia, daughter of Lewis Rodolph, and succeeded him.
" Charles (son).
1780. Charles William Ferdinand (son); a great general (served under his uncle Ferdinand in the 7 years' war, 1756-63); married princess Augusta of England; mortally wounded at Auerstadt, 14 Oct., d. 10 Nov. 1806; succeeded by his fourth son (his elder sons, being blind, abdicated).
1806. William Frederick, whose authority practically began with the battle of Leipsic, Oct. 1813; fell at Quatre-Bras, commanding the avantgarde under the duke of Wellington, 16 June, 1815; succeeded by his eldest son.
1815. Charles Frederick William (eccentric); assumed government, 30 Oct. 1823. [Revolution at Brunswick; the duke (declared incapable of reigning by the German diet) retired to England, 7 Sept. 1830; died at Geneva, bequeathing his immense property to that city, 18 Aug. 1873.]
1830. William (brother); b. 25 Apr. 1806; succeeded provisionally, 7 Sept. 1830; and, on the demand of the German diet, definitively, 20 Apr. 1831; unmarried. (His palace was destroyed by fire, 24 Feb. 1865.) His jubilee celebrated 25 Apr. 1881; d. 17 Oct. 1884.
1884. Prince Albert of Prussia, nephew of the emperor, elected, 21 Oct. 1885.

DUKES OF BRUNSWICK-LUNEBURG.

1409. Bernard (son of Magnus II., duke of Brunswick; *see above*).
1434. Otho and Frederic (his sons).
1478. Henry (son of Otho).
1532. Ernest I. (son of Otho). His sons were
1546. Henry (founder of second branch of Brunswick-Wolfenbuttel) and William, whose seven sons cast lots to determine who should marry. The lot fell on George, sixth son. Four of the brothers reigned, viz.:
1592. Ernest II. } no issue.
1611. Christian. }
1633. Augustus. }
1636. Frederic II. }
1648. Christian Lewis (son of George above mentioned).
1665. George William (brother of Christian Lewis), d. in 1705, leaving as heiress Sophia Dorothea, his daughter, who married in 1682 her cousin, prince George Lewis of Hanover, afterwards George I. of England (son of Ernest of Hanover, youngest son of the above-mentioned George).

HANOVER, ENGLAND.

Brussels, once capital of Austrian Brabant, now of Belgium (since 1831), founded by St. Gery, of Cambray, in the 7th century, is celebrated for fine lace, carpets, and tapestry. The *Hôtel de Ville* has a turret 364 ft. in height; and on its top is a copper figure of St. Michael, 17 ft. high, which turns with the wind. Pop. 1890, 448,088. BELGIUM.

Cathedral of St. Gudule (begun 1010?) completed.......... 1273
Made capital of the Low Countries.......... 1507
Ruled tyrannically by Alva.......... 1567
"Union of Brussels" to expel the Spaniards..........1577-78
Bombarded by marshal Villeroi; 14 churches and 10,000 houses destroyed..........Aug. 1695
Taken by the French, 1701; by Marlborough, 1706; by Saxe, 16 Feb. 1746; and by Dumouriez..........Nov. 1792
Revolution commences..........25 Aug. 1830
Maritime conference to obtain uniform meteorological observations held here.......... 1853
International philanthropic congress..........Sept. 1856
" association for social sciences meet...22-25 Sept. 1862
Brussels Conference. The Society for the Amelioration of the Condition of Prisoners of War sent circulars (dated 28 Mch.) to the great powers. On 17 Apr. Russia issued a programme for the conference, consisting of 71 articles, embracing all the "usages of war." Lord Derby (for Great Britain), in a despatch, declined the discussion of international law, 4 July. Gen. sir Alfred Horsford was sent delegate for Great Britain without active powers, reserving liberty of action. Congress opened 27 July; baron Jomini (from Russia) president. United States not represented. Sittings were secret. Conference closed without important results, 28 Aug. 1874. British report published in *London Gazette*..........24 Oct. 1874
Belgian industrial exhibition opened..........5 Sept. "
International exhibition of objects relating to public health and safety, opened by the king, 26 June; congress met 27 Sept.-2 Oct. 1876
International congress of commerce and industry...6-10 Sept. 1880
Antislavery conference meets..........18 Nov. 1889
Arrival of Stanley; entertained by the king..........19-25 Apr. 1890

Bruttium, now **Calabria Olta,** S. Italy. The Bruttians and Lucanians defeated and slew Alexander of Epirus at Pandosia, 326 B.C. They were conquered by Rome, 277.

bubble companies. COMPANIES, LAW'S BUBBLE, SOUTH SEA BUBBLE.

buc'caneers, piratical adventurers, French, English, and Dutch, who began plundering Spaniards of America soon after the latter had taken possession of this continent and the West Indies. Their numbers were much increased by a 12 years' truce between the Spaniards and Dutch in 1609, when many discharged sailors joined the buccaneers. The first levy of ship-money in England, in 1635, was for chastising these pirates. The principal commanders of the buccaneers were Montbar, Lolonois, Basco, Mansvelt, Morgan, and Van Horn, of Ostend; Morgan captured Porto Bello, 1668, and Panama, 1670; Gramont seized Campeachy, 1685; and Pointis took Carthagena, 1697; all gained enormous booty. The buccaneer confederacy was broken up through the peace of Ryswick, 10 Sept. 1697.

Bucen'taur, the vessel in which the doge of Venice wedded the ADRIATIC, from the 12th to the 18th century.

Buchanan, JAMES, administration of. UNITED STATES, 1857-61.

Bu'charest, Wallachia. Preliminaries of peace were ratified here between Russia and Turkey, agreeing on the Pruth as their frontier, 28 May, 1812. Subsequent war between these powers altered many provisions of this treaty. Bucharest was occupied by Russians, Turks, and Austrians, successively, in the Crimean war. The last quitted it in 1856. It is now capital of Roumania, established 26 Mch. 1881.

Buckingham palace, the London residence of the English sovereign. Old Buckingham house was built on the "Mulberry gardens," by John Sheffield, duke of Buckingham, in 1703. In 1761 it was bought by George III., who in 1775 settled it on his queen, Charlotte. She made it her town residence; and here all her children, except the eldest, were born. Here were married the duke of York and princess Frederica of Prussia, in 1791; the duke of Gloucester and princess Mary, 1816; the prince of Hesse-Homburg and princess Elizabeth, 1818; and the duke of Cambridge and princess of Hesse the same year. The house was pulled down in 1825, and the present palace begun on its site. After an expenditure of nearly a million sterling it was completed, and occupied by queen Victoria, 13 July, 1837. Further improvements were made in 1853. The marble arch, from the exterior of this palace, was re-erected at Cumberland Gate, Hyde park, 29 Mch. 1851.

bucklers (shields intended to parry blows but not so large as to cover the body), used in single combat, are said to have been invented by Prœtus and Acricius of Argos, about 1370 B.C. Lucius Papirius defeated the Samnites, taking from them bucklers of gold and silver, 309 B.C.

buckles for the shoe became fashionable and expensive in the reign of Chas. II. of Engl. Disappeared about 1791.

Buckshot war. PENNSYLVANIA, 1838.

Buda or **Ofen,** the ancient Aquincum, on the west bank of the Danube, opposite Pesth, and with it (termed Buda-Pesth) the capital of Hungary. It was taken by Charlemagne in 799; and sacked by Solyman II. after the battle of Mohacz, when the Hungarian king, Louis, was killed and 200,000 of his subjects carried away captives, 1526. Buda was sacked a second time, the inhabitants were put to the sword, and Hungary annexed to the Ottoman empire, 1541. Retaken by imperialists, under the duke of Lorraine, and Mahometans delivered up to the fury of the soldiers, 1686. It suffered much in 1848; was entered without resistance by the Austrians, 5 Jan. 1849; stormed, 20 May; given up by Russians to Austrians, July, 1849. Here the emperor Francis Joseph was crowned king of Hungary, 8 June, 1867. HUNGARY. Buda-Pesth made capital of Hungary, Nov. 1873.

Buddhism, the chief religion in Asia beyond the Ganges, and in China, Japan, and Ceylon, originated with Gautama Siddartha, the Sakya Muni, generally termed Buddha, or "the enlightened," a prince of Kapalivastu, in central India, said to have been born 623, and to have died 543 B.C.

In July, 594 B.C., disgusted with the behavior of the Brahmins, he retired from the world for a time, and, on coming forth, preached a new religion so successfully that it predominated in India till the 10th century, A.D.

Buddhism inculcates strict morality; forbids killing, stealing, adultery, lying, and drunkenness, even in purpose and thought, and

declares charity or love to be the source of virtue. Some writers assert that Buddhism includes belief in the transmigration of souls, and the absorption of the good into God, from whom they have emanated; others reckon annihilation or eternal sleep (the Nirvâna) among Buddhist tenets.
A form of Buddhism, the religion of Fô, exists in China, besides the systems of Confucius and Laot-se. It is said to have been introduced in the reign of Ming-ti, A.D. 68-81.
"Le Bouddha et Ses Religions," by M. J. B. St. Hilaire, was pub. in 1860. T. Rhyl Davids's "Buddhism," in 1878.
Buddhists in the world are estimated at 455,000,000.
Sir Edwin Arnold's "Light of Asia," a poem, 1879.

Bude light (named from Bude, in Cornwall, Engl., the residence of Mr.—afterwards sir Goldsworthy—Gurney, its inventor) consists of 2 or more concentric argand gas-burners, one rising above another, like petals in a rose, producing a brilliant flame. Its illuminating powers were increased by subjecting manganese, etc., to the flame, producing oxygen and hydrogen gas. This light was patented 1839 and 1841.

budget (from the Fr. *bougette*, Lat. *bulga*, a small bag), a term applied to the English chancellor of exchequer's annual statement of the finances of the country, the documents having been formerly presented in a leather bag. In the United States the sec. of the treasury has made an annual report to Congress of receipts and expenditures of the government since 1790. In 1789 the House of Representatives appointed a committee to see that the government is supplied with sufficient revenues, and to devise ways and means for obtaining it, whence the name of "Ways and Means Committee." In 1865 the duties of this committee had become excessive, and a committee of appropriations was appointed to share the work. Estimates for appropriations are prepared by the heads of the several departments and bureaus of the public service for the year ending 30 June, but are often reduced by the House. No appropriations can be made for purposes not sanctioned by the Constitution. APPROPRIATIONS OF CONGRESS.

Buena Vista, Battle of, 22 and 23 Feb. 1847. Gen. Taylor, with only about 5000 men (500 regulars), confronted a Mexican army of 20,000 under gen. Santa Anna, near San Luis Potosi. There was slight skirmishing on the 22d, but on the morning of the 23d the battle opened. The Americans held the field, and that night the Mexicans withdrew, leaving their dead and wounded. The Americans lost 267 killed, 456 wounded, and 23 missing; the Mexicans lost nearly 2000, leaving 500 dead on the field. MEXICAN WAR.

Buenos Ayres (*bway'nos ī'rez*), a province of S. America, now part of the Argentine Republic, was explored by Sebastian Cabot in 1526, and the capital, Buenos Ayres, founded by don Pedro de Mendoza in 1535. In 1585 the city was rebuilt and recolonized, and made a bishopric, 1620, and a viceroyalty, 1775. La Plata, the new capital of the province, founded 24 Nov. 1882; made seat of government, Apr. 1884. Pop. of the province in 1888, 3,793,800; city, 500,000. ARGENTINE CONFEDERATION.

A British fleet and army, under sir Home Popham and gen. Beresford, take the city easily, 27 June; it is retaken by the Spaniards, 12 Aug.; by the British....29 Oct. 1806
Montevideo stormed by sir Samuel Auchmuty, 3 Feb.; evacuated....7 July, 1807
Gen. Whitelock and 8000 British enter Buenos Ayres; repulsed with loss....5 July, "
Independence declared....19 July, 1816
Recognized as part of the Argentine confederation....Feb. 1822
[A prey to civil war through the intrigues of Rosas, Oribe, Urquiza, and others, for many years.]
Urquiza overthrows Rosas; is provisional dictator.... 1851
Oribe defeated by gen. Urquiza, to whom Buenos Ayres capitulates....3 Feb. 1852
Rosas flees, arrives at Plymouth, Engl....25 Apr. "
Urquiza deposed, 10 Sept.; invests the city; after some successes retires....Dec. "
Constitution voted....23 May, 1853
Buenos Ayres secedes from the Argentine confederation, and is independent; 1st governor, Dr. D. Pastor Obligado, elected, 12 Oct. "
Dr. Valentin Alsina elected governor....May, 1857
War breaks out; Urquiza, gen. of the Argentine confederation, has an indecisive conflict with the Buenos Ayres gen. Mitre, 23 Oct. 1859
Buenos Ayres is reunited by treaty with the Argentine confederation....11 Nov. "
Fresh contests: Mitre defeats Urquiza in an almost bloodless contest at Pavon; Urquiza retires....17 Sept. 1861
National congress at Buenos Ayres....25 May, 1862
Mitre installed president....12 Oct. "

Jesuits' college and archbishop's palace burned, priests killed by a mob; martial law proclaimed....28 Feb. 1875
International exhibition....May, 1890

Buffalo, N. Y., situated at the eastern end of lake Erie and at the western terminus of the Erie canal, lat. 42° 53', long. 78° 55', is the 3d city in the state in wealth and population, and the 11th in the U. S. Pop. 1810, 1,508; 1820, 2,095; 1840, 18,213; 1860, 81,129; 1880, 155,134; 1890, 255,664; 1900, 352,387. Area, 42 sq. miles.

GRIFFIN sails past the future site of Buffalo, 7 Aug.... 1679
First dwelling built on the site of Buffalo by Cornelius Winne, 1789
Buffalo laid out as "New Amsterdam," by the Holland Land Company.... 1801
Buffalo creek made a port of entry....3 Mch. 1805
Subscription for first school-house, $127.87½, raised..30 Mch. 1807
Town of Buffalo established.... 1810
Land deeded to county for first court-house....21 Nov. "
Black Rock made a port of entry.... 1811
First newspaper, the *Buffalo Gazette*, now the *Commercial Advertiser*, started....3 Oct. "
First church (Presbyterian) organized by the rev. Mr. Osgood, 2 Feb. 1812
Incorporated a village....2 Apr. 1813
Buffalo and Black Rock burned by British and Indians, 30 Dec. "
[This force, under command of lieut.-gen. Drummond, advanced to nearly opposite Black Rock, 29 Dec.; during the night gen. Riall crossed the river with about 1000 British, Canadians, and Indians, 2 miles below Black Rock; next day he was reinforced by about 800 British regulars. Americans numbered about 2000 men—militia—under gen. Amos Hall. During the night of the 29th nearly half of them decamped and the remainder made a poor defence, so that Black Rock and Buffalo were soon in possession of the British; when they withdrew, but 4 buildings were left, the rest had been burned.]
Village reorganized.... 1815
First library organized....10 Dec. 1816
St. Paul's parish organized....10 Feb. 1817
First vessel registered....26 May, "
First steamboat, *Walk-in-the-Water*, on lake Erie, built at Black Rock, and launched....28 May, 1818
[Although a steam vessel, a yoke of oxen was used in getting the boat into the lake from Black Rock.]
Steamer's first trip to Detroit....23 Aug. "
First church built (Methodist)....24 Jan. 1819
First work on Buffalo harbor.... 1820
Steamer *Walk-in-the-Water* wrecked....1 Nov. 1821
New charter.... 1822
First Presbyterian church built.... 1823
Lafayette visits Buffalo....4 June, 1825
Execution of the "Three Thayers" for the murder of John Love, near Buffalo, Dec. 1824....17 June, "
First billiard table made in the state, by B. I. Staats..21 June, "
Erie canal opened for navigation....26 Oct. "
Ship *Michigan* descends Niagara Falls (NEW YORK)....8 Sept. 1827
Buffalo Republican (dem.), a pioneer of the *Courier*, established, 1828
Universalist and Unitarian churches organized.... 1831
Incorporated as a city....20 Apr. 1832
[Ebenezer Johnson, first mayor.]
Daily Star, now the *Courier*, the oldest daily in the city, started....Apr. 1834
First issue of the *Daily Commercial Advertiser*....1 Jan. 1835
Eagle Street theatre opened....21 July, "
First railroad, "Buffalo and Niagara Falls;" locomotive put on, 19 Aug. 1836
Young Men's Association incorporated....3 Mch. 1837
Western Literary Messenger started.... 1841
[Ceased 1857.]
Burning of steamboat *Erie*, 33 miles out, 170 lives lost, 9 Aug. "
Buffalo Board of Trade organized....18 Jan. 1844
[Incorporated, 7 Mch. 1857.]
Great flood in lower part of city....18 Oct. "
University of Buffalo incorporated....11 May, 1846
Bank of Attica established at Attica, 1836; removed to Buffalo, "
Morning Express first issued....14 Jan. "
Diocese of Buffalo (Catholic) established.... 1847
St. Louis' church (Catholic) dedicated....21 Nov. "
Gas first manufactured....7 Nov. 1848
St. John's church (Episcopal) begun, 1846; completed.... "
First case of cholera....30 May, 1849
[2000 deaths in 3 months.]
Old "Eagle Tavern" burned....14 Nov. "
Corner-stone of St. Paul's church laid....12 June, 1850
[Spire completed, 1870.]
Forest Lawn cemetery dedicated....15 Aug. "
Corner-stone of St. Joseph's cathedral laid....6 Feb. 1851
[Finished, 6 June, 1855.]
Jenny Lind sings at the North church....28 July, "
Buffalo Female Academy opened....15 Sept. "
Great fire in lower part of city, 200 buildings burned..26 Sept. "
Y. M. C. A. incorporated....9 Mch. 1852
Metropolitan theatre, now Academy of Music, opened...11 Oct. "
Erie County savings-bank chartered....10 Apr. 1854
Corner-stone of the Westminster church laid....26 Aug. 1858
Grosvenor library chartered....11 Apr. 1859
First horse-car run, Main st....11 June, 1860
Society of Natural Sciences organized....5 Dec. 1861
Buffalo Fine Arts Academy incorporated....4 Dec. 1862
Historical Society incorporated....10 Jan. 1863

American hotel burned....25 Jan. 1865
Tifft house opened....15 June, "
Decoration day first observed....31 May, 1868
Normal school first opened....13 Sept. 1871
Corner-stone of city and county hall laid....24 June, 1872
[Completed, 1876.]
Corner-stone State Insane Asylum laid....18 Sept. "
International bridge across Niagara river completed....31 Oct. 1873
Ex-president Fillmore dies....8 Mch. 1874
[Born, Cayuga Co., N. Y., 7 Jan. 1800.]
Delaware Avenue Methodist Episcopal church dedicated, 11 Sept. 1876
U. S. life-boat station opened....1 July, 1879
Maj.-gen. S. P. Heintzelman, U. S. A., buried at Forest Lawn, (Died at Washington, 1 May) 4 May, 1880
Brig.-gen. A. J. Meyer, chief signal officer, d. at Buffalo, 14 Aug. "
First issue of the *Evening News*....11 Oct. "
M. H. Birge & Co.'s manufactory destroyed by fire....17 Dec. "
[13 lives lost.]
Pierce's Invalids' hotel burned....16 Feb. 1881
Main st. first lighted by electricity....1 July, 1882
Soldiers' monument completed....4 July, "
[85 ft. high; cost $50,000.]
Music hall (built 1883) and St. Louis' church burned...25 Mch. 1885
[Fire began at 7.30 p.m.]
First incineration at the crematory....27 Dec. "
Great storm; part of new music hall (in construction) blown down; nearly 200 persons homeless by flood....14 Oct. 1886
Natural gas introduced....1 Dec. "
Buffalo library building dedicated....7 Feb. 1887
Richmond hotel (Young Men's Association building, remodeled) opened 21 Feb. 1887, and totally destroyed by fire, with loss of 15 lives....18 Mch. "
Corner-stone of the Church of the Seven Dolors, cor. Genesee and Rich sts., laid....19 June, "
Niagara hotel opened....10 Oct. "
New music hall; corner-stone laid 31 May, 1886; opened with a grand musical festival, Walter J. Damrosch, leader, 18 Oct. 1887, and formally dedicated....7 Feb. 1888
Electric motor tried experimentally on the street railroad, 10 Feb. "
St. Paul's church, Episcopal, burned; fire caused by natural gas....9 May, "
Fort Porter begun, 1841; finished, 1844; demolished and site graded....Oct.–Nov. "
Fire starting cor. Wells and Carroll sts., destroys 30 buildings, burning over nearly 6 blocks; loss, $1,453,500....2 Feb. 1889
First annual commencement of the Buffalo law school, 29 May, "
Trial trip on the electric surface railroad from Cold Springs to the park....20 July, "
Hotel Iroquois opened on site of St. James's hall....2 Aug. "
New St. Louis's church; corner-stone laid, 30 May, 1886; dedicated....25 Aug. "
Old First church and its site sold to the Erie County savings-bank, 28 Mch. 1889, and ground broken for new bank building....11 Sept. 1890
New temple, Beth Zion, dedicated....12 Sept. "
Fire destroys the clothing exchange—loss, $350,000; 2 firemen killed by falling walls....23 Jan. 1891
Free kindergarten movement organized....12 Apr. "
New city charter goes into effect....4 Jan. 1892
Masonic temple; corner-stone laid, 26 July, 1890; dedicated, 19 Jan. "
First board of school examiners appointed....1 Feb. "
Bronze statue of Red Jacket (d. 20 Jan. 1832, aged 78) unveiled in Forest Lawn cemetery....22 June, "
Failure of the National savings-bank, through the defalcation, continued for several years, of its president, Edward S. Dann, (about $500,000 stolen)....29 June, "
Strike of switchmen on the Erie, Lehigh Valley, and Buffalo Creek railroads begins....14 Aug. "
7000 of the National Guard of New York state arrive to protect railroad property against destruction by strikers, 19 Aug. "
Strike declared at an end and troops, except the 4th brigade, leave for their homes....26 Aug. "
New medical college opened....Apr. 1893
New Erie County savings-bank occupied....May, "

MAYORS.

Ebenezer Johnson	1832	James Wadsworth	1851
Major A. Andrews	1833	Hiram Barton	1852
Ebenezer Johnson	1834	Eli Cook	1853
Hiram Pratt	1835	F. P. Stevens	1856
Samuel Wilkeson	1836	T. T. Lockwood	1858
Josiah Trowbridge	1837	Franklin A. Alberger	1860
Ebenezer Walden	1838	William G. Fargo	1862
Hiram Pratt	1839	C. J. Wells	1866
Sheldon Thompson	1840	William F. Rogers	1868
Isaac R. Harrington	1841	Alexander Brush	1870
George W. Clinton	1842	L. P. Dayton	1874
Joseph G. Masten	1843	Philip Becker	1876
William Ketchum	1844	Solomon Scheu	1878
Joseph G. Masten	1845	Alexander Brush	1880
Solomon G. Haven	1846	Grover Cleveland	1882
Elbridge G. Spalding	1847	John B. Manning	1883
Orlando Allen	1848	Jonathan Scoville	1884
Hiram Barton	1849	Philip Becker	1886
Henry K. Smith	1850	Charles F. Bishop	1890
		Edgar B. Jewett	1895

Buffoons were originally mountebanks in Roman theatres. Their shows abolished by Trajan, A.D. 98. JESTERS.

Bulgaria, the ancient Mœsia Inferior, a principality tributary to Turkey. The Bulgarians were a Slavonian tribe, who harassed the Eastern empire and Italy from 499 to 678, when they established a kingdom. They defeated Justinian II., 687; but were subdued, after several conflicts, by the emperor Basil, in 1018. After defeating them in 1014, and taking 15,000 Bulgarian prisoners, he caused their eyes to be put out, leaving one eye only to every hundredth man, to conduct his countrymen home. The kingdom was re-established in 1186; but after several changes was conquered by Bajazet and annexed to the Ottoman empire, 1396. Bulgaria was a chief site of the RUSSO-TURKISH WAR, 1877–78. It contains 5 famous Turkish fortresses, Widdin, Rustchuk, Silistria, Schumla, and Varna. Area, 38,562 sq. miles; pop. 1890, 3,154,000.

Bulgarians said to support the revolt in HERZEGOVINA....1875–76
Insurrection in Bulgaria cruelly suppressed ("Bulgarian Horrors," ENGLAND, 1876). TURKEY....May–Sept. 1876
Zancoff and Balabanow, Bulgarian delegates, in London..9 Oct. "
Bulgaria made self-governing as a principality, tributary to the sultan, by BERLIN TREATY....13 July, 1878
First parliament opened at Tirnova by prince Dondoukoff Korsakoff; new constitution....22 Feb. 1879
Prince Alexander of Hesse elected prince as Alexander I., 29 Apr. "
Visits European courts; received by queen Victoria....5 June, "
Takes oath to the constitution at Tirnova....9 July, "
Bulgaria said to be quitted by the Russians....17 July, "
Ministerial difficulties; Parliament dissolved....18 Dec. "
The prince announces a national assembly, and threatens to resign....9 May, 1881
Zancoff and other liberal ministers arrested for insulting the prince in election addresses (soon released)....21 June, "
Elections for National Assembly; rumored coercion of voters, 27 June et seq. "
Meeting of assembly; prince's proposals unanimously accepted; he promises reforms and adherence to the constitution....13 July, "
Late liberal ministers, Zankoff and Slaviekoff, arrested, about 23 July, "
Prince virtually dictator; opposes Russia, who promotes a liberal reaction against him; a new constitution is proposed; National Assembly meets....16 Sept. 1883
Prince restores Tirnova constitution; Zankoff minister, 20 Sept. "
Dismisses col. Redigher, war minister, and other Russian officers....26 Oct. "
Harmony with Russia restored....about 15 Nov. "
Constitutional changes proposed by government adopted, 17 Dec. "
Dispute with Servia on refugees and boundaries....May–June, 1884
Declaration of war by Servia, 13 Nov.; Bulgaria invaded by Servia....14 Nov. 1885
Cessation of hostilities, after several engagements, through Austrian intervention....28 Nov. "
Peace between Bulgaria and Servia signed at Bucharest, 3 Mch.; ratified by the sultan....13 Mch. 1886
Conspiracy at Sofia; prince Alexander carried off a prisoner, 21–23 Aug. "
Provisional government formed by M. Zankoff and others, 21 Aug. "
Rebel government overthrown....25 Aug. "
Prince Alexander returns; triumphant reception at Rustchuk; issues a proclamation, 29 Aug.; he submits to Russia; announces his intention to abdicate, 4 Sept.; regency appointed....6 Sept. "
Prince Waldemar of Denmark elected prince by the Sobranje; declined....10 Nov. "
Gen. Kaulbars, the Russian agent, and Russian consuls quit Bulgaria....26 Nov. "
Prince Ferdinand of Saxe-Coburg-Gotha invited for election as prince of Bulgaria by delegates, 15 Dec.; prince Nicholas of Mingrelia recommended by Russia.... "
Prince Alexander definitely declines re-election....12 June, 1887
Sobranje elect prince Ferdinand of Saxe-Coburg-Gotha as prince, 7 July; accepts....8 July, "
Prince Ferdinand signs constitution....14 Aug. "
Russia declares prince Ferdinand's position illegal; supported by France and Germany; Austria, England, and Italy maintain reserve....Feb.–Mch. 1888
Maj. Panitza and 6 others arrested on charge of plotting against the prince and government (in 1887 et seq.)....1 Feb. 1890
Tried by court-martial and Panitza sentenced to be shot, and others imprisoned from 3 to 9 years....30 May, "
Government requests of Turkey the recognition of prince Ferdinand and the religious autonomy of Macedonian Bulgaria....26 June, "
Maj. Panitza shot at Sofia....28 June, "
Prince Ferdinand partially recognized by the Porte....5 Feb. 1891

PRINCES.

Alexander (Joseph) I. (son of prince Alexander, uncle of Louis IV., grand-duke of Hesse), b. 5 Apr. 1857; elected....29 Apr. 1879
Deposed....4 Sept. 1886
Ferdinand, duke of Saxe-Coburg-Gotha, b. 26 Feb. 1861; elected, 7 July, 1887

bull, or edict of the pope. The bulla is properly the seal, whether of gold, silver, lead, or wax On one side are represented the heads of St Peter and St Paul with the letters S.PE and S PA, and on the other the name and year of the pope A bull against heresy was issued by Gregory IX, in 1231 Pius V published a bull against Elizabeth, 25 Apr 1570, in 1571 bulls were forbidden to be promulgated in England The bull *Unigenitus* (beginning with this word) against the Jansenists was issued by Clement XI, 1713, confirmed by Benedict XIII, 1725 The GOLDEN BULL of the emperor Charles IV, so called from its golden seal, was made the fundamental law of the German empire, at the diet of Nuremberg, 1356 Pius IX published an encyclical letter censuring modern errors, 8 Dec 1864 ROME, STOCKS

bull-baiting or **bull-fighting** was an amusement at Stamford, Engl, in the reign of John, 1209 and at Tutbury, 1374 In the "Sports of England" we read of the "Easter fierce hunts, when foaming boars fought for their heads and lusty bulls and huge bears were baited with dogs," and near the Clink, London, was the Paris, or bear-garden, celebrated in the time of Elizabeth for bear-baiting, then a fashionable amusement A bill to suppress bull-baiting was thrown out in the commons, chiefly through the influence of Mr Windham, who defended the custom, 24 May, 1802 It was made illegal in 1835 CRUELTY TO ANIMALS Bull-fights were introduced into Spain about 1260, and while abolished "except for pious and patriotic purposes," in 1784, they are still common there as well as in Mexico A bull-fight at Lisbon, attended by 10 000 spectators, on Sunday, 14 June, 1840, one took place at Havre, 5 July, 1868 Theatrical fights with Spanish bulls, at Agricultural hall, London, were stopped 28 Mch 1870, for cruelty

bullets. In 1418, 4000 bullets for cannon were ordered from the quarries of Maidstone, Engl Bullets of stone were in use certainly as late as 1514 Iron ones are mentioned in the "Fœdera," 1550 Leaden bullets were made before 1600 A D The round ball was the only form in use until 1830 The conoidal cup rifle-ball was invented by capt Minie in 1847, a modification (conoidal without cup), by Mr Pritchett (1853), is used with the Enfield rifle Many forms of bullet have since been devised The tendency is towards smaller diameters FIRE-ARMS

Bull Run campaign and **First Battle of.** The first important campaign and battle of the civil war Gen P. G T Beauregard, the confederate commander, selected the plateau at Manassas Junction as the best position to cover Virginia and menace Washington Strong in itself, it was further strengthened by the stream "Bull Run," which covered the front A detachment occupied Centreville, about 3 miles from Bull Run and some 30 from Washington, another was at Fairfax Court-house, still nearer that city The federal army, led by gen Irvin McDowell, but directed from Washington by lieut.-gen Winfield Scott, was ordered, 9 July, 1861, to assume the offensive within 8 days Gen Robert Patterson occupied Martinsburg, in the Shenandoah valley, with 18 000 men, while some 8000 confederates under gen Joseph E Johnston were at Winchester. With the promise from gen Scott that Patterson would prevent Johnston from joining Beauregard, McDowell advanced from Washington with 4 divisions, 16 July, 1861 The 1st division, 9936 men, brig-gen Daniel Tyler commanding, had 4 brigades under col E. D Keyes, col. William Tecumseh Sherman, brig-gen Robert Schenck, and col I. B. Richardson The 2d division, 2648 men, col. David Hunter commanding, had 2 brigades under col Andrew Porter and col. Ambrose E. Burnside. The 3d division, 9777 men, col. S. P. Heintzelman commanding, had 3 brigades—those of col. W. B Franklin, col O B. Wilcox, and col O O. Howard. The 4th division, 5752 men, brig-gen. Theodore Runyon commanding, remained to guard the approaches to Washington The 5th division, 6207 men, col Dixon S Miles commanding, had 2 brigades, col. Lewis Blenker and Thomas A. Davies commanding. The 1st, 2d, and 3d divisions occupied Fairfax Court-house on the evening of 17 July, the confederates retiring to the line of Bull Run Next day gen Tyler advanced Richardson's brigade and engaged the confederates at Blackburn's ford, but retired to Centreville in the evening with a loss of about 80 men Gen McDowell determined to turn the confederate left, where Bull Run is fordable and was poorly guarded On the evening of the 20th he ordered the attack early the next morning The 5th division was to remain at Centreville, while the 1st division was to advance on the road to the stone bridge and force a passage as soon as the confederate left was turned The flanking corps was the 2d and 3d divisions of 12,000 men, and Sudley's ford, about 3 miles above the stone bridge, was the point to cross The 2d federal division reached Sudley's ford about 9 30 A M., July 21, instead of early dawn and supported by the 3d division easily crossed Bull Run, and slowly pushed the confederates back until the stone bridge was uncovered, allowing McDowell to bring into action all his available troops Beauregard had 8 brigades, not formed into divisions in all about 21 000 men, under brig-gens M L. Bonham, R S Ewell, D R Jones, James Longstreet, and cols Philip St George Cocke, J A Early, T H. Holmes, and N G Evans He was reinforced from time to time throughout the day by Johnston, who, concealing his movements from Patterson, succeeded in sending his entire force in detachments by rail, to Beauregard, who, when the battle ended, had about 32 000 men These reinforcements were the brigades of cols T. J Jackson (from this battle known as "Stonewall") F S Barton, brig gen B. E Bee (both killed in this action), cols. A Elzey and C M Wilcox Between 3 and 4 o'clock P M, when everything seemed favorable to the federals, the last [illegible]000 of Johnston's men under Kirby Smith arrived and fell on the unprotected flank of the exhausted federals This attack was followed by another from Early's brigade, the federals were thrown into confusion, and their retreat became a rout The confederates, barely escaping defeat, were unable to follow up their success 5 brigades covered the retreat to Centreville and Washington, which the fugitives reached on the morning of 23 July, unpursued. The defeat was doubtless due to Patterson's failure to check Johnston Federal troops engaged, 28,455, loss, 481 killed, 1011 wounded, 1216 missing, total, 2708 Confederate troops engaged, 32,072, loss, killed, 387, wounded, 1582, total, 1967 PENINSULAR CAMPAIGN

Bulwer-Clayton Treaty, concluded 19 Apr, ratified 4 July, 1850, by which sir Henry Lytton Bulwer for Great Britain, and John M Clayton for the U S government, agreed that neither should alone control the proposed ship-canal through Central America, or erect fortifications in that country UNITED STATES Disputes afterwards arose with respect to this treaty and the connection of Great Britain with the Mosquito territory, which were settled in 1857

Its abrogation was proposed by Americans in 1880, in view of De Lesseps's plan for the Panama canal

Bun'combe, mere talk, or speaking for the gratification of constituents It is said the word received this meaning from a remark of Felix Walker, representative to Congress from North Carolina, 1817-23 While making a speech in the Missouri Compromise debates with little relevancy, as the house thought, he asserted it did not matter, as he was "making a speech for Buncombe," one of the counties he represented.

Bundschuh. JACQUERIE

Bunhill-fields, originally **Bonhill-field,** a burial-ground near Finsbury square, E. London, termed by Southey "the Campo Santo of the Dissenters," first used in 1665. Here lie Thomas Goodwin (1679), John Owen (1683), Isaac Watts (1748), John Bunyan (1688), George Fox, the Quaker (1690), gen Fleetwood, son-in-law of Cromwell (1692), and Daniel De Foe (1731) —*Cunningham.* An act to preserve the ground as an open space was passed 15 July, 1867, and it was reopened by the lord mayor 14 Oct. 1869, and a monument to De Foe, subscribed for by boys and girls, was inaugurated 16 Sept 1870

Bunker Hill, Battle of. MASSACHUSETTS, 16-17 June, 1775

Bunker Hill monument. On the battle-ground a granite obelisk 221 feet in height has been erected, at a cost of $100,000, by subscription The corner-stone was laid by gen Lafayette when guest of the United States, 17 June, 1825, Daniel Webster delivered the principal oration. It was completed and dedicated 17 June, 1843 with imposing ceremonies, president Tyler being present, while Daniel Webster again delivered an oration The base of the obelisk is 30 feet square, and at the spring of the apex 15 feet. The top is reached by 295 stone steps

burgesses, from Fr *bourgeois*, a title coeval in England with corporations They were called to Parliament in England, 1265, in Scotland, in 1326, and in Ireland, about 1365 Burgesses to be resident in the places they represented in Parliament, 1 Hen V (1413) During the colonial period the Virginia House of Representatives was called the House of Burgesses BOROUGH

Burghers. UNITED PRESBYTERIANS

Burgos, Spain, the burial-place of the Cid, 1099 Lord Wellington entered Burgos on 19 Sept after the battle of Salamanca (22 July, 1812) The castle was besieged by British and allies, but the siege was abandoned 21 Oct same year The fortifications were blown up by the French, 12 June, 1813

Bur'gundy, a large province in France, named from Burgundians, a Gothic tribe who overran Gaul in 275, and were driven out by the emperor Probus, they returned in 287, and were defeated by Maximin In 413 they established a kingdom, comprising the present Burgundy, large parts of Switzerland, with Alsace, Savoy, Provence, etc, Gondicar, their first king It was conquered by the Franks, 534 The second kingdom, a part of the first, began with Gontran, son of Clotaire I of France, in 561 The kingdoms of Arles, Provence, and Transjurane Burgundy were formed out of the old kingdom In 877 Charles the Bald made his brother-in-law Richard first duke of Burgundy. In 938, Hugh the Great, count of Paris, founder of the house of Capet, obtained the duchy His descendant Henry, becoming king of France, conferred it on his brother Robert, in whose family it remained till Philippe de Rouvre died without issue, in 1361 In 1363, king John of France made his fourth son, Philip, duke. AUSTRIA, GERMANY.

DUKES.

1363 Philip the Bold, marries Margaret, heiress of Flanders, 1369
1404 John the Fearless (son), joined English invaders of France, privy to assassination of duke of Orleans, 1407, assassinated at Montereau, in presence of dauphin Sept 1419
1419 Philip the Good (son), the most powerful duke.
1467 Charles the Bold, married Margaret of York, sister to Edward IV, 9 July, 1468, invaded France, 1472, Switzerland, 1476, killed, fighting Swiss before Nancy, 4 Jan 1477
1477 Mary (daughter), married, 19 Aug 1477, Maximilian of Austria, d 27 Mch 1482
1479 Louis XI annexed Burgundy to France The other dominions fell to Austria

burials. Abraham buried Sarah at Machpelah, 1860 B.C (Gen xxiii) Places of burial were consecrated under pope Calixtus I. in 210 A.D —*Eusebius* The Greeks had burial-places remote from towns, the Romans near highways, hence the need of inscriptions The first Christian burial-place, it is said, was instituted in 596, burial in cities, 742, in consecrated places, 750, in church-yards, 758 Many early Christians buried in catacombs at Rome CATACOMBS, CEMETERIES, CREMATION, DISSENTERS

Vaults erected in chancels first at Canterbury 1075
Shrouds required to be of wool in England . 1666
Burials taxed in England 1695
Linen scarfs introduced at funerals in Ireland, 1729, and woollen shrouds used . 1733
A tax on burials in England—of a duke 50*l*., of a common person 4s—under William III 1695, and George III 1783
Acts relating to metropolitan burials passed 1850–67
Parochial registers of burials, births, and marriages instituted in England by Cromwell, lord Essex, about 1538 —*Stow*
"Earth to earth" burial advocated by Mr Seymour Haden, wicker coffins shown at Stafford house 17 June, 1875
Consecrated burial grounds in England, 13,673, closed, 1411 1877
Burials act (permitting any Christian service in a parish church yard) passed English Parliament, 7 Sept. 1880

burking, a method of murder, from Burke, who killed his victims by suffocation, and sold the bodies, unmarked by violence, to surgeons for dissection He was executed at Edinburgh, 28 Jan 1829 One Bishop was apprehended in Nov 1831, and executed in London, 5 Dec, with Williams, an accomplice, for burking Carlo Ferrari, a friendless Italian boy They confessed to other similar murders.

Burlingame Treaty, formed by Anson Burlingame and a Chinese embassy, signed at Washington 4 July, 1868, authorizing mutual immigration. California prospered with Chinese labor, till the agitation of 1879–80 led to demands for the abrogation of the treaty Two new treaties between the United States and China, one relating to immigration and the other to commerce, were signed 17 Nov 1880. UNITED STATES, 5 May, 1892

Burlington Heights, Battle of STONY CREEK

Burmah or **Burmese empire,** founded about 1750 A D by Alompra, first sovereign of the present dynasty A British dispute with this power in 1795 was adjusted by gen Erskine Hostilities were commenced by the British in 1824, and they took Rangoon on 11 May The fort and pagoda of Syriam were taken in 1825 After a short armistice, hostilities were renewed, 1 Dec, and pursued until the victories of the British led to the cession of Arracan, and to peace, 24 Feb 1826 For this war, and that of 1851, INDIA. Pegu was annexed to the Indian empire, 20 Dec 1852 The war ended 20 June, 1853 Pop 1891, 7,554,410, area, 156,142 sq miles

Rebellion against the king suppressed by British aid, about Sept 1866
Treaties with Great Britain 1862 and 25 Oct 1867
Burmese embassy in England, 6 June, introduced to Victoria, 21 June, 1872
King Mindone suspected of inciting Chinese to attack British expedition to West China (INDIA) Feb 1875
Sir Douglas Forsyth's mission to the king, arrives at Mandalay, 14 June king submits about 18 June, refuses passage for British troops as convoy to China, Forsyth retires June, "
Col Duncan sent to Mandalay about Aug "
King accedes to the British demands Oct. "
King dies, about 5 Sept, announced 2 Oct 1878
His successor Theebau (Wongyee, prince of Theebau) kills many of the royal family and their friends. Feb. 1879
British resident and others quit Mandalay 8 Oct "
King, attacked by small pox commits atrocities 12 Apr 1880
Prince Nyoung's rebellion, May, June, suppressed, he enters British territory 27 June, "
Political massacres reported at Mandalay 21 Apr 1882
Misgovernment, massacres at Mandalay, 21 Sept, prospect of British intervention Oct 1884
Bhamo captured by the Chinese 8-10 Dec "
Captain Terndrup, of the steamer *Kahbyoi*, rescues missionaries and others 12-13 Dec. "
Commercial treaty with France Feb 1885
Bhamo recaptured by Burmese about 16 Mch "
Dispute between king and the Bombay and Burmah Trading Association, king refuses arbitration of viceroy of India, commissioner of Burmah asks for 8000 men 13 Oct "
Ultimatum sent by lord Dufferin, rejected by king, proclamation of war 8 Nov, British troops advance under gen H N D Prendergast 9 Nov "
King sends flag of truce, agrees to surrender himself army, and Mandalay, Ava forts occupied 27 Nov, and Mandalay occupied without resistance 28 Nov "
King Theebau and court sent to Madras 14 Dec "
Theebau's brother issues a proclamation against British rule, arrival of Mr Bernard, who establishes a provisional government 18 Dec "
DACOITS pillage outside Mandalay, sharp conflicts, Dec. 1885–Jan 1886
Lord Dufferin, the viceroy, arrives at Mandalay 12 Feb. "
British Burmah, including Aracan, Pegu, and Tenasserim, constituted 1862 Upper Burmah annexed by proclamation of the viceroy, lord Dufferin, 1 Jan 1886. Upper and Lower Burmah united in one province, Feb 1886, all Burmah in British India by decree 15 May, "
Increase of "dacoity" in Upper and Lower Burmah, 2 additional regiments sent to Burmah July, "
Continued disturbance and fighting with the Dacoits . 1886–89

Burnett prizes, awarded every 40 years for the 2 best essays on "the evidence that there is a Being all powerful, wise, and good, by whom everything exists," etc., were founded by will of Mr Burnett, a Scotch gentleman, who died 1784 Various amounts have been paid to Dr W. L. Brown, rev J B Sumner, afterwards archbishop of Canterbury, 1815, rev R A Thompson, and Dr J Tulloch, 1855 The establishment of a Burnett lectureship in Aberdeen by the trustees (the lecturer to be chosen in 1883) was sanctioned Aug 1880.

burning alive was inflicted among the Romans, Jews, and other nations, and was countenanced by bulls of the pope Elizabeth Gaunt, an Anabaptist, was burned at Tyburn for treason (concealing rebels under Monmouth), 23 Oct. 1685 AUTO DA FÉ, INQUISITION, PROTESTANTS, WITCHCRAFT

burning the dead. CREMATION.

burning-glass and **concave mirrors.** The former a convex lens of large size and short focus, used for causing intense heat by concentrating the sun's rays on a very small area, the latter so arranged as to produce the same effect. Their power was known to Archimedes, who is said with them to have burned a fleet at Syracuse, 214 B C. They were improved by Settalla, Tschirnhausen, 1680; Buffon, 1747, M de Trudano, 1774, and Parker and others more recently. The following experiments were made in England about 1800 with Mr Parker's lens or burning-mirror which cost $3500, then the largest ever made It was sold to capt Mackenzie, who took it to China, and left it at Pekin

Substances fused	Weight grs	Time sec	Substances fused	Weight grs	Time sec
Pure gold	20	4	A topaz	3	45
Silver	20	3	An emerald	2	25
Copper	33	20	A crystal pebble	7	6
Platina	10	3	Flint	10	30
Cast iron (a cube)	10	3	Cornelian	10	75
Steel	10	12	Pumice stone	10	24
Asbestos	10	10	Lime stone	10	55

Green wood takes fire instantaneously, water boils immediately, bones are calcined, and things not capable of melting at once become red hot

Burns, Negro, Case of MASSACHUSETTS, 1854

Burnt Corn Creek, Battle of ALABAMA, 1813

Burr, Aaron UNITED STATES, 1801, NEW YORK, 1804

Burr's conspiracy. The end of Aaron Burr's term as vice-president of the U S, Mch 1805, found him ruined politically and deeply in debt. Immediately he started for the Mississippi valley with gen Wilkinson Leaving him at Pittsburg, he proceeded down the Ohio, stopping at BLENNERHASSETT'S ISLAND, where he found Blennerhassett and his wife Thence proceeding to Louisville, Ky, he crossed the country to Nashville, where he had a public reception, in which Andrew Jackson participated Returning, he met Wilkinson again at Fort Massac, near the mouth of the Cumberland, proceeded to New Orleans, returned to Natchez, crossed the forest 450 miles to Nashville, where Jackson again entertained him for a week in Aug 1805 Thence he went to St Louis, again visited Wilkinson, turned eastward to Cincinnati, Chillicothe, and Marietta, spent the winter of 1805-6 and the spring and summer in Philadelphia and Washington, holding frequent interviews with gen Eaton, commodore Truxton, etc In Aug 1806 Burr returned to the west, again visited Blennerhassett, and with his financial aid began building 15 boats on the Muskingum In Kentucky he was arrested, but the grand jury, 25 Nov 1806, failed to find a bill On 27 Nov the president issued a proclamation against a supposed conspiracy, warning citizens of the U S not to engage in the contemplated expedition, and directing all authorities to aid in suppressing it The Ohio state government seized the boats on the Muskingum, and a mob destroyed the house of Blennerhassett and desolated the island Meanwhile a few boats passed down the Ohio and were joined by Burr below Louisville At Chickasaw Bluffs, fearing arrest if he should venture to New Orleans, Burr crossed the Mississippi and encamped 30 miles above Natchez Here he surrendered to the civil authorities, but the grand jury of the supreme court of the territory refused to indict him, and presented charges against the governor for his arrest Finding his plans thwarted, he disbanded his followers and attempted to reach the Atlantic coast through the Gulf states, but was arrested near Fort Stoddert, in Alabama, 19 Feb. 1807 He was taken on horseback to Richmond, and indicted in the district of Virginia for treason A trial of several months resulted in his acquittal The principal witnesses against Burr were gen Wilkinson, then commander of the small U S army, who was suspected of plotting with him, gen Eaton, and commodore Truxton Among the lawyers retained to defend Burr was Washington Irving KENTUCKY, MISSISSIPPI, OHIO, UNITED STATES, 1805-7

Bury St. Edmund's, Suffolk, named from St. Edmund, king of East Anglia, who was murdered by the Danes on 20 Nov 870, and buried here, and to whose memory its magnificent abbey was founded Magna Charta was prepared here by the barons on 20 Nov 1214 Henry VI summoned a parliament in Feb. 1447, when Humphry, duke of Gloucester, was imprisoned, and died here, it is supposed by poison It was almost consumed by fire in 1608, and was desolated by plague in 1636.

burying alive. In Bœotia, Creon ordered Antigone, the sister of Polynices, to be buried alive, 1225 B C Unchaste Roman vestals, as Minutia, 337 B.C, Sextilla, 274 B.C, Cornelia, 92 A.D., were buried alive This horrible punishment, that is, immured in brick walls, was still continued and inflicted upon unchaste nuns by the Roman Catholic church.

"And now that blind old Abbot rose,
To speak the chapter's doom,
On those the wall was to enclose
Alive, within the tomb"
—*Scott*, "Marmion" canto ii stanza xxv

Lord Bacon gives instances of the resurrection of persons buried alive, Duns Scotus being one The two assassins of Capo d Istria, president of Greece, were built up in brick walls to their chins, and fed there until they died, Oct 1831 TORTURE

Busaco (*boo-sa'co*) or **Buzaco,** Portugal Here the British, under Wellington, repulsed the French, under Massena, 27 Sept 1810 The latter lost 1000 men killed, and about 3000 wounded, and several hundred prisoners, the loss of the allies did not exceed 1300 The British afterwards retreated to the lines of Torres Vedras, which was too strong for Massena to force

bushel. A measure fixed at 8 gallons of wheat, 12 Hen VIII 1520, the Winchester bushel was regulated 9 Will III 1697, the imperial corn bushel of 2218 192 cubic inches is to the Winchester of 2150 42 as 32 to 31 Regulated by act 5 Geo IV, June, 1824, taking effect 1 Jan 1826 The same in the United States

busts. Lysistratus, the sculptor invented moulds for wax figures, 328 B C —*Pliny* Busts from the face, in plaster of Paris, were first taken by Andrea Verrochi, about 1466 A D Smaller busts and statuettes are accurately produced from larger ones by machinery SCULPTURE

butchers. Among the Romans there were 3 classes the *suarii* provided hogs, the *boarii* or *pecuarii* oxen and sheep, which the *lanii* or *carnifices* killed The Butchers' Company in London is ancient, though incorporated 1604.

butter is said to have been used by the Arabs in early times, but not by the Greeks and Romans who had excellent oil, and never by the Chinese It is not mentioned as food by Galen, 130-200 A D It has long been used by northern nations In Africa, at Kebba, vegetable butter is made from the fruit of the shea-tree, and is of richer taste than any butter made from cows' milk —*Mungo Park*. The amount of butter produced in the United States is given in the following table for the years named

Year	Farms	Factories	Total in pounds
1850	313,345 306		313 345 306
1860	459 681,372		459 681 372
1870	514 092,683		514,092,683
1880	777 250,287	29,421,783	806,672 071
1890	1,024,22[illegible]	181,284,916	1,205,508,384

buttons, an early manufacture in England, those covered with cloth were prohibited, to encourage the manufacture of metal buttons, 8 Geo I 1721 Samuel Williston began the manufacture of covered buttons at Easthampton, Mass., about 1825-26 and removed his works to Haydenville in 1834 It is said that Abel Porter began the manufacture of gilt buttons in one end of a grist-mill at Waterbury, Conn, in 1802 Waterbury has now (1893) the largest button factory in the U S

Buxar, a town in Bengal, near which, 23 Oct 1764, major, afterwards sir Hector Munro, with 857 Europeans and 6215 Sepoys, routed 50.000 troops of the nabob of Oude, etc, 6000 were killed, and 130 pieces of cannon taken. The English loss was trifling

bye plot, of lord Gray of Wilton and others, to imprison James I, and extort liberty of worship to Romanists, was suppressed 1603, called also the "surprise plot"

Byng, Hon Admiral John, was charged with neglect of duty in a fight off Minorca, 20 May, 1756, condemned for an error of judgment, and shot on the *Monarch* at Spithead, 14 Mch 1757

Byron national memorial. The erection of a national memorial to lord Byron was determined on, at a meeting in London, 16 July, 1875, Mr Disraeli in the chair. About $15,000 subscribed The statue, by Richard Claude Belt, on a pedestal near Hamilton place, Hyde park, London, was uncovered privately by lord Houghton, 24 May, 1880 A marble pedestal was promised by Greeks

Byron's voyage. Commodore Byron (grandfather of the poet) left England on his voyage round the globe, 21 June, 1764, and returned 9 May, 1766 He discovered the populous island in the Pacific which bears his name, 16 Aug. 1765 Though brave and intrepid, he was unlucky, and was called by sailors "Foul-weather Jack"

Byzantium, now **Constantinople,** and **Stamboul,** in ancient Thrace, founded by a colony of Megarians, under Byzas, 667 B C, but various dates and persons are given. It was taken successively by the Medes, Athenians, and Spartans In 340 B C, in alliance with the Athenians, the Byzantines defeated the fleet of Philip of Macedon. During wars with Macedon, Syria, etc., it became an ally of the Romans, by whom it was taken, 73 A.D. Rebelling, it was taken after 2 years' siege, and laid in ruins by Severus in 196 It was refounded by Constantine in 324, and dedicated on 22 May, 330, and the heathen temples destroyed; from him it received its name, Constantinople Byzantine art flourished from the time of Constantine to about 1204. The Byzantine or Eastern empire really commenced in 395, when Theodosius divided the Roman empire The "Byzantine Historians," from 325 to 1453, were published at Paris, 1645-1711, and at Venice, 1722-33 EASTERN EMPIRE

C

Ca'aba, a sacred black stone, kept in a temple at Mecca, and venerated by the Arabs, long before the Christian era Its guardians, the tribe of Koreish, were defeated by Mahomet and the worship abolished, 623-30

Cabal'. In English history a term applied to the cabinet of Charles II. 1667-74, formed from the initials of their names sir Thomas, afterwards lord Clifford (C); lord Ashley (A), (afterwards earl of Shaftesbury), George Villiers, duke of Buckingham (B); Henry, lord Arlington (A), and John, duke of Lauderdale (L)

Cab'ala, a Jewish system of philosophy or theosophy, so called from a Hebrew word signifying reception or tradition, said to have been given by God to Adam, transmitted from father to son by his descendants, lost at the Babylonian captivity (587 B.C), but revealed again to Ezra Its supporters assert that the cabalistic book "Sohar," or "Splendor," a mystic commentary on the Pentateuch, was first committed to writing by Simon Ben Jochai, 72-110 A D But the books containing the cabala are believed to have originated between the 9th and the 11th centuries, by mingling Talmudism with the Greek philosophy termed neo-Platonism Some of their dogmas are akin to Christian tenets, such as the trinity, the incarnation etc The cabala exercised much influence upon the Jews, and even captivated great thinkers of the 16th and 17th centuries.

cabbages. Some new kinds were brought to England from Holland about 1510, it is said by sir Arthur Ashley of Dorset, and introduced into Scotland by Cromwell's soldiers. TRUCK FARMING

Cabeiba, Asia Minor Here Mithridates, king of Pontus, was defeated by Lucullus, 71 B.C.

cabinet council. In the United States government the heads of the departments are the president's constitutional advisers, and constitute a cabinet. Each with a salary of $8000 a year They are appointed by the president with the consent of the Senate, hold office at the president's will, and are, under him, the executive officers of the general government. Each department has its official seal for public documents. The departments of state, treasury, and war were created in 1789, and the secretaries were members of the cabinet. The navy department was added in 1798, with its secretary a member of the cabinet The office of attorney-general was created in 1789, but the attorney-general was not a member of the cabinet until 1814, when "Richard Rush was appointed to the attorney-generalship, which now became a cabinet office"—*Hildreth's* "Hist U S.," vol vi p 458 The post-office department was a branch of the treasury until 1829, when W T Barry, the first recognized postmaster-general, was called to the cabinet by president Jackson Department of the interior created, 3 Mch 1849, and its secretary a member of the cabinet. Department of agriculture created, 11 Feb 1889, the secretary a member of the cabinet UNITED STATES —There were councils in England as early as the reign of Ina, king of the West Saxons, 690; Offa, king of the Mercians, 758, and in other reigns of the Heptarchy State councils are referred to Alfred the Great.—*Spelman.* ADMINISTRATIONS Cabinet noir, or "dark closet," the chamber in which letters intrusted to the French post were opened for state purposes The system, which began with Louis XI, was organized under Louis XV., and is said to have been discontinued in 1868.

cabinet, kitchen. A term applied to certain political advisers in the confidence of president Jackson Called "kitchen" because devoid of the public dignity pertaining to the cabinet, and entirely separate and distinct from the cabinet proper The principal members of this "cabinet" were Amos Kendall, Wm B. Lewis, Isaac Hill, Duff Green, and Francis P Blair.

Cabin-John Creek bridge. AQUEDUCTS, BRIDGES

cable, Atlantic. ELECTRICITY.

cables. A machine was invented in 1792 for making them, by which human labor was reduced nine tenths Chain cables were introduced into the British navy about 1812, directions for testing them enacted, 1864 and 1874.

Cabochiens, an armed Burgundian faction, including 500 butchers, named from their leader Simonet Caboche, a skinner, 1412 They ruled Paris with violence, and constrained the doctors of the Sorbonne to become their allies and the dauphin to recognize them as the "WHITE HOODS" and reformers. They were exterminated by the citizens in 1418.

Cabool', on the river Cabul, was made capital of AFGHANISTAN about 1774 by Timsur Shah.

cabriolets (*vulgo* cabs), one-horse vehicles 12 were introduced into the streets of London in 1822 In 1831 they had increased to 165, and then the licenses were thrown open The number in 1862 running in the English metropolis exceeded 6000 (of which about 1800 only plied on Sunday) Previous to throwing open the trade, the number of hackney-carriages was limited to 1200, when there were few omnibuses

Cabs running in London in 1855, 3296, in 1867, 6149, in 1874, 7864, in 1877, about 8000, in 1891, 11,129

cache (*kash*), a concealed place of deposit made for an article or articles—especially a food deposit—and located so as to be easily found by the makers or others informed of it. The word was adopted into English from the Canadian voyagers of the Hudson bay country

cachet (*ka-shā'*). LETTRES DE CACHET.

Caddee, or *League of God's House*, the league of independence in Switzerland, formed by the Grisons to resist domestic tyranny, 1400-19 A second league of the Grisons was called the Grise or Gray League (Graubundten), 1424 A third league, the League of Ten Jurisdictions, was formed in 1436 (GRISONS) They united in 1471.

Cade's insurrection. In May, 1450, Jack or John Cade, an Irishman, assumed the name of Mortimer, and headed about 20,000 Kentish men, who armed "to punish evil ministers, and procure a redress of grievances" He defeated and slew sir Humphry Stafford, at Sevenoaks, 27 June, entered London in triumph, and beheaded the lord treasurer, lord Saye, and several other persons of consequence, 3 July. When the insurgents lost ground, a general pardon was proclaimed, and Cade, deserted by his followers, fled A reward having been offered for his apprehension, he was discovered, and, refusing to surrender, was slain by Alexander Iden, sheriff of Kent, 11 July. For recent biographical notice consult "Dictionary of National (English) Biography"

Cadiz, W Spain, anciently Gadiz, the Roman Gades said to have been built by the Phœnicians about 1100 B.C.

100 vessels of the Spanish armada destroyed in the port by sir Francis Drake 1587
Cadiz taken by English under earl of Essex, and plundered 15 Sept 1596
Vainly attacked by sir George Rooke 1702
Bombarded by the British July 1797
Blockaded by lord St Vincent for 2 years 1797-99
Again bombarded by the British Oct 1800
French squadron of 5 ships of the line and a frigate surrender to the Spanish and British 14 June, 1808
Besieged by the French, but the siege was raised after the battle of Salamanca July, 1812
Insurrection, 1819, massacre by the soldiery 9, 10 Mch 1820
Taken by the French in Oct. 1823, and held till 1828
Declared a free port 1829

cadmium, a metal, discovered by Stromeyer and Hermann in 1818

Caen (*kon*), N France, a place of importance before 912, when it became the capital of the possessions of the Normans It was taken by the English in 1346 and 1417, but recovered by the French 1 July, 1450 Here were buried, in the cathedral of St Etienne, William the Conqueror (1087), who founded it (1066), and his queen (1083)

Caerleon (*ker-le'on*), i e "castle of the legion," Monmouthshire, Wales, the *Isca Silurum* of the Romans, and one of their oldest stations in Britain, and made the seat of an archbishopric by Dubritius His disciple and successor, St David (522), removed it to Menevia, now St. David's, 577 Celebrated in Tennyson's "Idylls of the King" as the chief city of king Arthur's kingdom

Caernarvon (*ker-nar'von*), N. Wales In the castle (founded in 1282) Edward II was born, 25 Apr 1284, the first English Prince of Wales, and the town was then chartered by Edward I That Edward II was born in the castle is disputed by Timbs in his "Abbeys and Castles of England and Wales," but he concedes that he was born somewhere in the town The town suffered by the civil war of Charles, but was finally retained for the Parliament

Cæsarea, Roman capital of Judæa, built by Herod the Great 10 B C. Eusebius the historian was bishop about 315

Cæsarean section, which, it is said (with scarcely sufficient evidence) first gave the name of Cæsar to the Roman family, is performed by cutting the child out of the womb. The case of Alice O'Neal, an Irishwoman, who survived the operation, which was performed by a woman, is authenticated by Dr Gabriel King, of Armagh, and surgeon Duncan Stewart, of Dungannon In Jan 1817, the operation was performed in St. Bartholomew's hospital, London, on a young woman of diminutive stature, under the influence of ether, but she died the next day On 9 Dec 1860, a similar operation was successfully performed by Dr James Edmunds at Bethnal Green On the continent the operation is said to have been more frequent and more successful Cooper's "Surgical Dictionary" (ed 1861) has a table of 2009 cases, with a mortality of 55 4 per cent of mothers and 29.45 per cent of children MEDICAL SCIENCE

Cæsars, Era of. SPANISH ERA

Cæsars, the Twelve

1 Caius *Julius Cæsar*, dictator, b 100 B C , assassinated, 44 B C.
2 Caius Octavius, *Augustus Cæsar*, b 63 B C , emperor 27, d 14 A D , grandson of Julia, sister of Julius Cæsar, adopted by him and made his principal heir
3 *Tiberius*, Claudius Drusus Nero, b. 41 B C , emperor 14 A D , d 37, son of Livia, wife of Augustus, by her former husband Tiberius Claudius Nero, adopted by Augustus.
4. *Caligula*, Caius Cæsar Augustus Germanicus, b 12 A D , emperor, 37, assassinated, 41, son of Germanicus and Agrippina and great grandson of Augustus
5. Tiberius *Claudius* Drusus Cæsar, b 10 B C , emperor, 41 A D , d 54, uncle of Caligula and grand nephew of Augustus
6 *Nero*, Claudius Cæsar Lucius Domitius, b 38 A D , emperor, 54, killed 68, great-grandson of Augustus and of Mark Antony [With Nero ended the line of the Julii]
7 *Galba*, Servius Sulpitius, b 4 B C , emperor, 68 A D , killed, 69, soldier of distinction, commander in Spain, selected by his army for emperor before the death of Nero, and confirmed by the senate after
8 *Otho*, Marcus Salvius, b 31 A D , emperor, 69, kills himself 69
9 *Vitellius* Aulus, emperor, 69 A D , reigns about 8 months, overthrown by Vespasian, 69, and killed at Rome.
10 Titus Flavius *Vespasian*, distinguished soldier, b 10 A D , at the solicitation of his soldiers and of citizens of Rome he overthrows Vitellius and becomes emperor, 69, d 79
11. *Titus*, Flavius Vespasian, son of *Vespasian*, emperor 79 A D , d 81 During his reign Pompeii and Herculaneum were destroyed by an eruption of Vesuvius, and the COLISEUM finished.
12 Titus Flavius Sabinus *Domitian*, 2d son of Vespasian, b 51 A D., emperor 81, assassinated, 96 [These are termed the "Twelve Cæsars," the last 3 the Flavian emperors]

cæsium (Lat bluish), a rare alkaline metal, found in mineral waters by Bunsen in 1861, by SPECTRUM ANALYSIS

cafeine, an alkaline body, discovered in coffee by Runge in 1820, and in tea (and named théine) by Oudry in 1827. Their identity was proved by Jobst and Mulder in 1828

Cagots (*cä-gos*), an outcast race in the Pyrenees, supposed to be descendants of the ancient Goths They were subjected to superstitious persecution so lately as 1755

ça ira! (*sah-ee-rah'*) the burden of a popular song during the French revolution, first heard at Paris 5 Oct 1789

"Ah ça ira, ça ira, ça ira' Malgré les mutins, tout reussira " ("It will proceed' etc In spite of mutineers, all will succeed ") An after addition was Les aristocrates a la lanterne'" ('Hang the aristocrats'")

Cairo (*ki'ro*) or **Grand Cairo,** 5 miles from the Nile delta and on right bank, the modern capital of Egypt, remarkable for its mosques and the sepulchres of its Fatimite caliphs Lat 30° 2' 4" N, lon 31° 15' 36" E Pop 1883, 368,108, 1900, 570,062 EGYPT

Present city founded by the Saracens 969
Taken by the Turks from the Egyptian sultans 1517
Ruined by an earthquake and a fire, when 40,000 persons perished June, 1754
Taken by the French under Napoleon 23 July, 1798
Taken by the British and Turks, 6000 French capitulated, 27 June, 1801
Massacre of the Mamelukes 1 Mch 1811
Visit of the prince of Wales Mch 1862
Riots against Nubar Pacha and the British ministers 18 Feb 1879

Cala'bria, the ancient Messapia of S E Italy, was conquered by the Romans, 266 B C It formed part of the kingdom of the Ostrogoths under Theodoric, 493 A.D , was reconquered (for the Eastern empire) by Belisarius, 536, subdued by the Lombards and joined to the duchy of Benevento, 572. After various changes, it was conquered by Robert Guiscard, the Norman, 1058, who became duke of Calabria, and eventually king of Naples EARTHQUAKES, NAPLES

Calais (*ka-la'*), N W France, fortified by Baldwin IV, count of Flanders, 997, taken by Edward III after a year's siege, 4 Aug 1347 It was at this time that queen Philippa, wife of Edward, prevailed on her husband to spare Eustache St. Pierre and 6 of the chief citizens, who had given themselves up as a sacrifice for the rest of the inhabitants It was retaken by the duke of Guise, in the reign of Mary, 7 Jan 1558, and its loss, it was said, occasioned her death, 17 Nov same year. "When I am dead," said the queen, "Calais will be found written on my heart" It was taken by the Spaniards, Apr. 1596, restored, 1598 Here Louis XVIII landed after his long exile from France, Apr 1814 TUNNELS

Calatrava. KNIGHTHOOD

calcium, the metallic base of lime, discovered at the Royal Institution, London, by Davy, in 1808

calculating-machines. To avoid errors in computing and printing logarithms and tables of figures, machines to calculate and print have been devised Pascal, when 19 years of age, invented one (about 1650). C Babbage's differential machine, begun at the cost of the British government in 1821, was continued till suspended in 1833, after an expenditure of above 15,000*l* The portion completed was placed in the library of King's college, London, it is now at South Kensington Prof Clifford, in a lecture at the Royal Institution, 24 May, 1872, stated that Babbage expended 20,000*l* upon his machines, and that the analytical machine was nearly finished and would eventually be much used In 1857 E and G Scheutz, two Swedish engineers, published in London specimen tables, calculated and printed by machinery constructed between 1837 and 1843, after a study of the account of Mr Babbage's machine Messrs Scheutz brought their machine to England in 1854 It was bought for 1000*l* by J F Rathbone, an American, to be presented to Dudley observatory, in Albany In 1857 Messrs Scheutz were engaged to make one for the British government, which is now completed. Mr Wiberg's machine, exhibited at Paris, Feb 1863, was much commended Tables constructed by Scheutz's machine, and edited by Dr.

W. Farr, were published by the British government in 1864. The arithmometer, patented by M. Thomas (de Colmar) in 1822 (?), was exhibited at the international exhibitions, 1851 and 1862. George B. Grant described a simpler machine in the American *Journal of Science*, Oct. 1874.

Calcutta, capital of Bengal and British India; the first settlement of the English here was made in 1689. Pop. 1876, 776,579; 1891, 840,130.

Purchased as a zemindary, and fort William built............ 1698
Made the head of a separate presidency.................... 1707
Fort attacked and taken by an army of 70,000 horse and foot, and 400 elephants (146 of the British crammed into the BLACK-HOLE)..............................20 June, 1756
Calcutta retaken by Clive..............................2 Jan. 1757
Great cyclone, followed by a "bore" or spring-tide in the Hooghly; water rises 30 feet; immense damage to shipping and houses..............................5 Oct. 1864
Another cyclone; about 30,000 small houses unroofed; much small shipping injured; crops in Lower Bengal destroyed (about 90,000 persons drowned; 75,000 die of cholera)..1 Nov. 1867

Caledonia, now **Scotland.** As its ancient inhabitants appear to have been Celts from the opposite coast of Gaul, the name is perhaps derived from *Gael, Gaelmen*, or *Gadeldoine*, corrupted by the Romans. Tacitus, who died 99 A.D., uses the name Caledonia, and it retained this name until about the beginning of the 4th century, when it was invaded by the SCOTI from the north of Ireland, who, having driven the Picts northward, settled in the Lowlands, giving their name, Scots, to the whole country.

B.C.
Caledonian monarchy, said to have been founded by Fergus I., about 330
Picts from England settle in the south...................... 140

A.D.
Agricola, the Roman, invades Caledonia...................... 79
Defeats Galgacus, builds a wall between the Forth and Clyde... 84
Wall of Antoninus built.................................... 140
Ulpius Marcellus repels their incursions...................... 184
Christianity introduced in the reign of Donald I............. 201
Caledonians invade south Britain, 207; repelled by the emperor Severus, who advances to the Moray Firth............ 209
Caledonia invaded by the Scoti, from Ireland...........about 306
Caledonian monarchy revived by Fergus II..................... 404
Kenneth II., king of the Scoti, subdues the Caledonians and Picts, and founds one monarchy, named Scotland.........838-843

Caledonian canal, from the North sea to the Atlantic ocean. CANALS.

calendar. The Roman calendar was introduced by Romulus, who divided the year into 10 months, comprising 304 days, 738 B.C. This year was 50 days shorter than the lunar year, and 61 than the solar year, and its commencement did not correspond with any fixed season. Numa Pompilius, 713 B.C., added 2 months; and Julius Cæsar, 45 B.C., fixed the solar year at 365 days, 6 hours, every 4th year being bissextile, or LEAP-YEAR. This calendar was defective, as the solar year consists of 365 days, 5 hours, 49 minutes, and not of 365 days, 6 hours. This difference, in the 16th century, amounted to 10 days, the vernal equinox falling on 11 instead of 21 Mch. To obviate this error, pope Gregory XIII. ordained, in 1582, that *that* year should consist of 355 days only (5 Oct. became 15 Oct.); and that a year ending a century should not be bissextile, except that ending each 4th century; thus 1700, 1800, and 1900 are common years, but 2000 will be a leap-year. Thus 3 days are retrenched in 400 years, or about 11 minutes for each year. The year of the calendar is thus made as nearly as possible to correspond with the true solar year. FRENCH REVOLUTIONARY CALENDAR, JEWISH ERA, NEW STYLE.

CORRESPONDENCE OF CALENDARS WITH 1891 A.D.

Julian period... 6604
Year of the world (Jewish year) 15 Sept. 1890-2 Oct. 1891..... 5651
Hegira (17 Aug. 1890-6 Aug. 1891)............................ 1308
Foundation of Rome (*Varro*)................................. 2644
United States' independence..............................115-116
Year of queen Victoria.....................................54-55
Comte, in his "Système de Politique Positive" (instituting the "Religion of Humanity"), published a calendar of 13 months, dedicated successively to Moses, Homer, Aristotle, Archimedes, Cæsar, Paul, Charlemagne, Dante, Guttenberg, Shakespeare, Descartes, Frédéric, and Bichat; an eminent person was commemorated every day. PHILOSOPHY.

calender, a machine used in glazing cloth, introduced into England by the Huguenots, who were driven by persecution from France, Holland, and the Netherlands, about 1685. —*Anderson*.

Calends were the first days of the Roman months. The *Nones* of Mch., May, July, and Oct. fell on the 7th, and their *Ides* on the 15th. The other months had the *Nones* on the 5th and the *Ides* on the 13th. As the Greeks had no *Calends, ad Græcas Calendas* ("on the Greek Calends"), meant *never*. IDES.

Cali Yuga, the Hindu era of the Deluge, dates from 3101 B.C. (according to some, 3102), and begins with the entrance of the sun into the Hindu sign Aswin, now on 11 Apr. N.S. In 1600 the year of this era began on 7 Apr. N.S., from which it has now advanced 4 days, and from the precession of the equinoxes, is still advancing at the rate of a day in 60 years. The number produced by subtracting 3102 from any given year of the Cali Yuga era will be the Christian year in which the given year begins.

cal'ico, cotton cloth, named from Calicut, a city of India, visited by the Portuguese in 1498. Calico was first brought to England by the East India Company in 1631. Calico-printing and the Dutch loom-engine were first used in 1676, when a Frenchman established a factory at Richmond, near London.—*Anderson*. In England, Calicoes were prohibited to be printed or worn in 1700; and in 1721 a penalty of 5*l*. was laid on the wearer, and 20*l*. on the seller of calico. In 1831, by the exertions of Poulett Thompson, afterwards lord Sydenham, and others, the duty of 3½*d*. on the square yard of printed calico was taken off. Since 1834 the manufacture has been greatly increased by inventions. Cylinders for printing are now engraved by galvanism, and many new dyes have been introduced by the discoveries of Liebig, Hofmann, Perkin, etc. The consumption of calico in the United States is greater than in any other country. COTTON, DYEING.

Cal'icut, now **Kol'ikod,** S.W. India, the first Indian port visited by Vasco da Gama, 20 May, 1498. It was seized by Hyder Ali, 1766; taken by the English, 1782; destroyed by Tippoo Saib, 1789; ceded to the English, 1792. CALICO.

California (Sp. *calida formax*, meaning a hot furnace), a Pacific coast state, lies between lat. 32° 28′ and 42° N., and lon. 114° 30′ and 124° 45′ W., having a coast line of over 700 miles. It is bounded on the north by Oregon, east by Nevada and Arizona, south by Mexico, and west by the Pacific. Pop. 1890, 1,208,130; 1900, 1,485,053; area, 158,360 sq. miles, in 54 counties. Capital, Sacramento.

Hernando d' Alarcon sails to the head of the gulf of California, and sends boats up the Colorado river..............May, 1540
Juan Cabrillo, sailing north, discovers a harbor, supposed to be San Diego bay, 28 Sept. 1542, and reaches Monterey, 14 Nov. 1542
After Cabrillo's death at San Miguel, 3 Jan. 1543, Farallo, his pilot, reaches a point recorded as 44° N., but now believed to have been cape Mendocino, 40° 30′ N...............10 Mch. 1543
English explorer sir Francis Drake touches the coast at 43° n. lat., June, 1579; sailing south, he lands in a bay at "Cape of the Kings," about 30 miles northwest of San Francisco, 17 June; received kindly by natives, and calls the country New Albion. Drake leaves..........................July, 1579
Spanish voyageur Sebastian Vizcaino (Biscayer) sails from Acapulco, and is said to have visited the bays of San Diego and Monterey during the latter part of.......................... 1602
After 150 years, with little further exploration, the Spaniards, aroused by priests and by reports of Russian advances southward from Alaska, send to the Pacific coast José de Galvez, who leaves Mexico.................................9 Apr. 1768
Galvez, in Lower California, fits out an expedition for Franciscan fathers, by sea and land; 2 vessels reach San Diego, 11 Apr. and 1 May, 1769
Portola, with land expedition, reaches San Diego, 9 July; leaves 5 days later, arrives at San Pedro, 30 Oct., and thence proceeds nearly to San Francisco bay, but, provisions being exhausted, returns to San Diego........................11 Nov. "
Portola's second expedition from San Diego reaches Monterey bay..24 May, 1770
Mission and presidio of San Carlos at Monterey founded, 3 June, "
Missions of San Antonio de Padua and San Gabriel founded.... 1771
Don Pedro Fages, successor to Portola, sent by viceroy of Mexico, from Monterey, 27 Mch. 1772, with an exploring party, to secure the harbor of San Francisco from foreign aggression; they advance along the shore to San Joaquin river, and unable to cross, return to Monterey..............4 Apr. 1772

CAL

irst interior expedition from Sonora under Juan Bautista de Anza, reaches San Gabriel 22 Mch 1774

ernando Javier de Rivera y Moncada appointed lieut gov of California 23 May, "

uan Perez, in the *Santiago*, explores coast north to lat 45°, 9 July, "

ieut Juan Bautista de Ayala anchors off San Francisco sends a boat in, 1 Aug 1775, he explores the bay for 40 days re turning to Monterey then the capital 22 Sept. 1775

ettlement on the Colorado opposite mouth of the Gila, 17 Dec "

resid o of San Francisco founded 17 Sept 1776

lission established at San Francisco 9 Oct "

ueblo of San José established 29 Nov 1777

ueblo of Concepcion established 1780

ndian massacre at San Pablo and Concepcion, Rivera slain, 17 July, 1781

ueblo of Los Angeles founded 26 Aug "

fleet fitted out by the French government for scientific ex ploration, under Jean François Galaup de la Perouse sailing south from lat 58° 37′ enters Monterey bay 14 Sept 1786, *entertained 10 days by gov Fages and the padres of San* Carlos mission Sept 1786

liss on of Santa Barbara founded 4 Dec "

Spanish scientific expedition from Cadiz under Alejandro Malaspina, explores the coast, anchoring at Monterey 13 Sept 1791

apt George Vancouver with an exploring party, sent by Great Britain around the world, commissioned also to settle the boundary question on the north of California, anchors his vessel the *Discovery*, in San Francisco harbor 14 Nov 1792

ith 7 officers Vancouver, on horseback, visits Santa Clara, under Spanish escort, the first foreigners to penetrate so far into the interior 20 Nov "

ancouver anchors at Monterey, 27 Nov 1792, visits San Car los 2 Dec , puts to sea 15 Jan 1793

eturns from the Hawaiian islands in 1793 and again in 1794, is suspected by the Spanish governor, and coldly received, anchoring at Monterey he visits the Salinas valley, sails away 2 Dec. 1794

irst vessel from the U S in a California port the *Otter*, from Boston, arrives at Monterey, 29 Oct 1796 The captain, Ebenezer Dorr after obtaining supplies, secretly lands 10 Englishmen and 1 woman stowaways from Port Saxon and sails away 6 Nov 1796

y royal orders, the Californias are divided into 2 provinces, Antigua (the peninsula, then under the control of the Domin ican missions) and Nueva California 26 Mch 1804

ussian chamberlain, Nikolai Petrovich Rezanof, royal in spector for Sitka, finding that colony in great need of food, sails to San Francisco with a cargo of goods, which he ex changes for provisions, despite the Spanish restrictions on trade, he wins also the affections of Doña Concepcion, daugh ter of the commandant don José Arguello 21 May, 1806

ndians across the bay from San Francisco troubling Spanish, Alfirez Moraga marches against them and defeats and scat ters the tribe 22 May, 1810

ussians establish a fort at Ross, 18 miles north of Bodega, having settled the vicinity in 1807–10 30 Sept 1812

ov José Joaquin de Arrillaga dies at Soledad mission, capt José Arguello succeeds 24 July, 1814

umors of revolutions in S America, proclamation from gov Pablo Vincente de Sola and preparations for defence, 23 June, 1816

lission of San Rafael founded 14 Dec 1817

rench capt. Hippolyte Bouchard ("the pirate Buchar") ap pears with 2 vessels of 38 and 26 *guns under the flag of* Buenos Ayres, his real purpose is unknown, but, after sum moning Monterey and other places on the coast to surrender, and pillaging the towns, he sails away Dec 1818

alifornia becomes a province of Mexico under the regency of don Augustin Iturbide 1821, and gov Sola is elected deputy to the new Córtes, Iturbide proclaimed emperor 18 May, 1822

ussians warned to abandon California within 6 months, 21 Oct "

turbide surrenders his crown, Mch 1823 and is banished from America, May 1823 , California is substantially independent until the new constitution of the Mexican republic is ratified by the Junta of California 26 May, 1825

lectors, summoned by gov José Maria Echeandia choose capt José de la Guerra y Noriega delegate to Mexican Con gress. 18 Feb 1826

edediah S Smith, a trapper from the U S , the first to make the trip from Salt lake, reaches San Gabriel 26 Dec. "

erritorial Diputacion, 7 members and 3 substitutes chosen by the junta of electors at San Diego in Feb , meets at Monterey, 14 June, 1827

oaquin Solis, a convict ranchero, instigates the troops to re volt against the governor, with a view to give all offices to Californians, soldiers at Monterey seize the presidio, 12-13 Nov , and later meet no opposition at San Francisco. 1829

ov Echeandia by proclamation calls on the Monterey insur gents to surrender, 7 Jan 1830 , recaptures Monterey, 20 Jan , apprehends Solis and other leaders, and sends 15 of them on the bark *Volunteer*, for San Blas 9 May, 1830

ecree for secularization of missions, San Carlos and San Gabriel to be organized as towns, surplus property, after dis tribution to neophytes, passing to secular administrators, other missions the same as far as possible 6 Jan 1831

ecularization accomplished 1834

os Angeles made a city—capital of California 23 May, 1835

fter various attempts at negotiation with the authorities, the warnings of 1822 not being heeded, Russians at Ross, Bode ga, and other points on the coast, sell their rights to col John A Sutter for $30,000, and leave the country Jan. 1842

Placer gold discovered on the San Francisco rancho formerly belonging to the San Fernando mission Mch 1842

Commodore Thomas Ap Catesby Jones, with the U S Pacific squadron of 3 vessels, believing war to exist with Mexico, enters Monterey harbor seizes the fort and declares Cali fornia a territory of the U S 20 Oct 1842, learning next day that there is no war, he restores the territory. 21 Oct "

Col J C Fremont, with exploring expedition reaches Sutter s fort 8 Mch 1844

About 50 Californians under Manuel Castro, Jesus Pico, and others, seize arms and munitions stored at San Juan Bautista and instigate revolt against gov Manuel Micheltorena and his army of convicts from Mexico 14-15 Nov "

Micheltorena is supported by Sutter and other foreigners, but concludes a treaty, agreeing to send away his battalion and return to the capital 1 Dec

First immigrants to California in wagons, the "Murphy com pany " under Elisha Stevens, reach Sutter's fort 13 Dec "

Micheltorena having broken the treaty of 1844, the revolution is renewed, *on the field of Cahuenga he capitulates and Pio* Pico becomes governor in his stead 21 Feb 1845

Col Fremont on a third expedition obtains permission from Mexico, through U S consul Thomas O Larkin, at Mon terey, to continue his explorations of the coast 27 Jan 1846

Col Fremont, in Oregon, receives orders to watch the Mexi can and British relations in California, 9 May, 1846 Re turning to California, he finds gen de Castro prepared to resist American invasion American settlers begin the so called "Bear flag revolt" by occupying Sonoma, with a flag bearing a star and bear and the words, "California Repub lic" 14 June, "

Fremont assumes command of insurgents at Sonoma 5 July, "

Stars and Stripes raised at Monterey 7 July, by order of John D Sloat, commanding U S Pacific squadron, at Sonoma they replace the bear flag, 9 July, and over Sutter s fort 11 July, "

Fremont embarks in the schooner *Cyane*, commodore Dupont, and occupies San Diego 29 July, "

200 Mormon emigrants, recruited in the U S arrive at San Francisco in the ship *Brooklyn*, under elder Brannan, 31 July, "

Americans, under commodore Robert F Stockton and major Fremont, capture Los Angeles 13 Aug "

First number of an American newspaper, the *Californian*, issued at Monterey by Robert Semple and Walter Colton 15 Aug "

Commodore Stockton proclaimed governor 17 Aug "

Mexicans recapture Los Angeles 29–30 Sept "

Gen Stephen W Kearney under orders from Washington to proceed from New Mexico to California and establish a pro visional government arrives at Santa Maria 5 Dec "

Indecisive battle at San Pascual between Mexican general don Andres Pico and gen Kearney, who is twice wounded, 6 Dec "

Battle of San Gabriel, decisive defeat of the Mexicans, 8–9 Jan 1847

Los Angeles regained by the Americans 10 Jan "

Col Fremont assumes the civil government under commission from commodore Stockton 19 Jan "

Gen Kearney, under instructions from the president, issues a proclamation from Monterey as governor, and directs col Fremont to deliver in person, at Monterey, all public documents in his charge, which he does with hesitation, 1 Mch "

Col Richard B Mason appointed governor 31 May, "

First steamboat in California waters leaves San Francisco, reaching Sacramento in 6 days and 7 hours 28 Nov "

Gold discovered near Coloma on col John Sutter's land, by James Wilson Marshall 19 Jan 1848

California and New Mexico ceded to the U S by treaty of Guad alupe Hidalgo 2 Feb 1848, proclaimed in California Aug "

First emigrants from China, 2 men and 1 woman, arrive in the bark *Eagle* "

First gold from California, 1804 59 oz , deposited in the U S mint by David Carter 8 Dec "

Brig gen Bennett Riley, instructed by the secretary of war to assume the civil administration arrives by sea at Monterey, 12 Apr 1849 He issues a proclamation for a temporary government to replace the local provisional governments, 3 June, 1849

A convention to form a state constitution sits at Monterey, 1 Sept 1849, until 13 Oct The constitution adopted and state officers chosen by the people 13 Nov "

New Almaden quicksilver mines opened 1850

California admitted to the Union (the 31st state, pop 92,597) by act approved 9 Sept "

Assay office established at San Francisco "

Of 5 extensive fires in San Francisco since 24 Dec 1849, the greatest destroys a large part of the city (22 blocks) 4 May, 1851

Act of legislature establishing public schools "

Democratic and Whig parties organized in California May, "

Prevalence and immunity of crime, and corruption of officials, prompts the formation of a vigilance committee of leading citizens in San Francisco 6 criminals hanged by them, and nearly 20 banished from the state Gov McDougall issues a proclamation against the committee, 21 July A convicted murderer, reprieved by the governor, is hung by the people at Sacramento 21 Aug "

State prison at San Quentin, Marin co , opened "

University of the Pacific at St. José chartered and opened 1852

California Academy of Sciences founded at San Francisco 1853

CAL

State lunatic asylum established at Stockton.................. 1853
Filibusters under col. Walker sail from San Francisco for Lower California (FILIBUSTERS)......................17 Oct. "
United States branch mint opened at San Francisco......Apr. 1854
Panama railroad opened, facilitating immigration to California, 23 Jan. 1855
College at Santa Clara opened, 1851; chartered.............. "
Law excluding from the courts negro and Indian evidence, amended by adding Chinese.............................. "
James King of William, editor of the San Francisco *Evening Bulletin*, a champion of reform, is shot in the street by James Casey, editor of the *Sunday Times*, a noted politician, 14 May, 1856; d. 20 May. The vigilance committee is revived 15 May, and some 8000 members are enrolled. Casey is taken from jail, 18 May; tried and hung with another man named Cora, convicted of murder..................22 May, 1856
Discovery of gold-mines on the Frazer river...........1 May, 1858
First overland mail west leaves St. Louis, Mo., 16 Sept. 1858; arrives at San Francisco...........................10 Oct. "
42 prisoners escape from state prison in open day, and 100 others following are fired upon and driven back....27 June, 1859
David C. Broderick, wounded by David S. Terry in a duel 12 Sept., d...16 Sept. "
St. Ignatius college at San Francisco opened, 1855; chartered.. "
Industrial school opened at San Francisco................... "
First pony express leaves Sacramento for St. Joseph, Mo..4 Apr. 1860
A Japanese embassy of 72 men are the guests of San Francisco, 29 Mch. "
State Institution for the Deaf, Dumb, and Blind opened at Berkeley.. "
California regiment, col. E. D. Baker, organized........21 Apr. 1861
Citizens' meeting in San Francisco declares for Union, 11 May, "
Daily overland mail established from the Missouri river to San Francisco over the central route, to replace that through northern Texas, New Mexico, Arizona, and Southern California, established in 1858..........................1 July, "
Telegraph line from Denver, Col., to Sacramento, Cal.; completed..Sept. "
Ex-senator Gwin and attorney-general Benham arrested by gen. Summer, charged with complicity in rebellion, 14 Nov. "
State reform school at Marysville opened................Dec. "
150 convicts escape from the state prison. In their recapture 3 are killed and 22 wounded.........................22 July, 1862
Pacific Methodist college at Santa Rosa opened, 1861; chartered, "
Ground broken for the Central Pacific railroad at Sacramento by gov. Stanford (PACIFIC RAILROADS)...............22 Feb. 1863
At San Francisco, U. S. officers seize the schooner *Chapman*, about to sail, as a confederate privateer............15 Mch. "
Congress grants the Yosemite valley and the Mariposa Big-tree grove to California for public use, resort, and recreation; to be inalienable.......................................30 June, 1864
California ratifies the constitutional amendment abolishing slavery..18 Dec. 1865
State Institution for the Deaf, Dumb, and Blind established at Oakland... 1866
St. Vincent's college at Los Angeles opened, 1867; chartered.. 1869
University opened at Berkeley, near San Francisco...23 Sept. "
Riot in Los Angeles; 15 Chinamen hanged and 6 shot by a mob...24 Oct. 1871
State normal school opened at San Francisco, 1862; is removed to San José.. "
Mills college at Mills Seminary, Cal., opened................. "
University of California permanently located at Berkeley, 16 July, 1873
Gen. E. R. S. Canby and commissioner Thomas, while negotiating under a flag of truce for the removal of the Modoc Indians to a reservation, are massacred by capt. Jack and his warriors in the lava beds near fort Klamath............11 Apr. "
Assassins are captured 1 June, tried, and capt. Jack and 2 associates are hung.....................................3 Oct. "
Insane asylum established at Napa............................ "
Central Pacific railroad attempts to obtain from Congress a grant of Goat island, the property of the U. S., on San Francisco bay, opposite Oakland; an independent party in opposition is formed, and Newton Booth, its candidate, elected for the long term to Congress, with judge Johnson S. Hayes, anti-railroad Democrat, for the short term, 20 Dec. "
Law empowering juries to determine between death and imprisonment for life in convicting of a capital crime......... 1874
Compulsory education law passed and school laws revised; a state superintendent of instruction to be elected............ "
State temperance convention at San Francisco........19 Nov. "
State capitol at Sacramento completed......................... 1875
"O'Connor bill" becomes a law, authorizing 3 commissioners of transportation to inspect railroads and require them to be kept in safe condition.................................3 Apr. 1876
Society for the prevention of cruelty to children chartered.... "
Permanent organization of the workingmen's party of California, Dennis Kearney, "the sand-lot orator," president, headquarters at San Francisco............................5 Oct. 1877
Dennis Kearney arrested and imprisoned 2 weeks for incendiary speeches and threats............................3 Nov. "
Act amending the code of civil procedure concerning attorneys, by striking out the words "white male;" Mrs. Clara S. Foltz of San José is admitted to the bar............................ 1878
Act providing for a state labor bureau......................... "
Convention to revise the constitution meets, 28 Sept. 1878; adjourns, 3 Mch. 1879; new constitution takes effect...4 July, 1879
Yacht *Jeannette* sails from San Francisco for the Arctic regions (NORTHEAST and NORTHWEST PASSAGE)..............8 July, "
Popular vote for governor: for Geo. C. Perkins, Rep., 67,970; Hugh J. Glenn, Dem. and new constitution, 47,562; William F. White, workingmen's party, 44,620..............3 Sept. 1879
Normal school at San José destroyed by fire..........10 Feb. 1880
Work begun on the Lick Observatory on mount Hamilton, 4250 ft. above the sea, lat. 37° 21′ 3″ n., and lon. 121° 36′ 40″ w., 13 miles east from San José...................... "
Dennis Kearney arrested for sedition; sentenced to 6 months' imprisonment and a fine of $1000..(SAN FRANCISCO) 15 Mch. "
State viticultural commission founded........................ "
State prison at Folsom opened................................ "
University of Southern California chartered and opened at Los Angeles.. "
"Young débris relief bill" passed, imposing, with a general tax, a special tax on miners, to repair damage done to agriculture by débris washed into the valleys by hydraulic mining; such débris, it is estimated, has destroyed 43,500 acres of good farming land.. "
Convention of miners in Nevada City, 22 July, 1882, to consider the débris question; anti-débris convention of 110 delegates, residents and property holders in the Sacramento and San Joaquin valleys, at Sacramento...............26 Sept. 1882
State normal school at Los Angeles opened.................. "
Acts passed creating a horticultural, sericultural, and forestry commission, and a bureau of labor statistics................ 1885
California Home for the Care and Training of Feeble-minded Children opened at Santa Clara........................... "
36 in. lenses for the great refractor of the Lick Observatory safely brought by rail from Cambridgeport, Mass., and deposited in the observatory vaults.................27 Dec. 1886
Legislature appropriates $5000 for a monument to James W. Marshall, the discoverer of gold, at his grave in Coloma, Eldorado county.. 1887
Tax enacted of 1 cent on each $100 of property for the University of California.. "
Corner-stone of Stanford University laid at Palo Alto, 20 May, "
Asylum for Chronic Insane in Santa Clara county completed.. "
Lick Observatory transferred by the trustees to the regents of the University of California..........................1 June, 1888
Monument erected in Golden Gate park to Francis S. Key, for which James Lick, who died 1 Oct. 1876, bequeathed $60,000... "
Acts passed establishing the South California State Hospital for the Insane, the Mendocino Insane Asylum at Ukiah, and a state reform school for juvenile offenders at Los Angeles.. 1889
Act passed recognizing the veterans' home at Yountville as a state home for disabled veterans and as a beneficiary under the act of Congress providing aid........................ "
David S. Terry, assaulting judge Stephen Field at Lathrop, is shot dead by U. S. marshal Nagle....................14 Aug. "
Pioneer woollen mills close; the last of the large woollen manufactories in the state.. "
State normal school at Chico opened......................... "
Preston School of Industry for Youthful Criminals founded at Ione City... "
Gabriel, the famous mission Indian, dies at Salinas, Monterey county, aged 151 years...........................16 Mch. 1890
29 persons drowned in a train which falls through a drawbridge at Oakland.....................................30 May, "
40th anniversary of the admission of California into the Union, celebrated 6, 8, and 9 Sept., the latter day being a legal holiday in the state by governor's proclamation.......6-9 Sept. "
Act of Congress to reserve as a public park the Big-tree groves in townships 18 and 17 south.........................25 Sept. "
King David Kalakaua of the Sandwich islands lands at San Francisco from the U. S. man-of-war *Charleston*......4 Dec. "
Corner-stone of the Mendocino County Insane Asylum laid at Ukiah...9 Dec. "
Corner-stone of the insane asylum at San Bernardino laid, 16 Dec. "
King David Kalakaua, b. 1836; d. at San Francisco....20 Jan. 1891
Hon. George Hearst, U. S. senator, d. in Washington, D. C., 28 Feb. "
Charles N. Felton, elected U. S. senator..............19 Mch. "
Dr. David S. Jordan, president of Indiana State University, accepts the presidency of Leland Stanford, jr. University, 23 Mch. "
Chilian insurgent transport, the *Itata*, seized at San Diego (UNITED STATES)....................................6 May, "
First shipment of block-tin (7 tons) from the Temescal mines, in San Bernardino county, received in San Francisco, 15 June, "
Australian ballot law takes effect.....................1 July, "
Leland Stanford, jr. University at Palo Alto opened......1 Oct. "
Earthquake; slight elsewhere; damage at Woodland, $50,000, 19-21 Apr. 1892
Train, guarded by U. S. soldiers, with $20,000,000 of government gold leaves San Francisco for New York; has the right of way...5 Aug. "
350th anniversary of the discovery of San Diego bay..28 Sept. "
Leland Stanford, governor, 1862, U. S. senator, 1893, and founder of Leland Stanford, jr. University, d............20 June, 1893

From 1767 up to 1821, California being under Spanish rule, 10 governors were appointed by that power. From 1822 until 1845, being under Mexican domination, her governors (12) were appointed from Mexico. From 1846 her governors have been as follows:

CALIFORNIA REPUBLIC GOVERNORS.

Name.	Term.	Remarks.
John C. Frémont	1846	By the people under the "Bear flag."
PROVISIONAL OR MILITARY GOVERNORS UNDER THE UNITED STATES.		
Com. Robert F. Stockton	1847	13 Jan., date of the surrender to the U. S. government.
John C. Frémont	1847	By appointment of com. Stockton.
Gen. Stephen W. Kearney	1847	Frémont displaced by Kearney, Mch.
Richard B. Mason	1847 to 1849	Appointed from Washington.
Gen. Persifer F. Smith	1849	Temporarily.
Bennett Riley	1849	In office at the adoption of the state constitution.

STATE GOVERNORS.

Name.	Term.	Remarks.	Name.	Term.	Remarks.
Peter H. Burnett	1849 to 1851	Resigned.	Newton Booth	1871 to 1875	Resigned.
John McDougall	1851 " 1852	Lt.-gov. acting	Romualdo Pacheco	1875 " 1875	Lieut.-gov. acting.
John Bigler	1852 " 1856		William Irwin	1875 " 1880	
J. Neely Johnson	1856 " 1858		George C. Perkins	1880 " 1883	
John B. Weller	1858 " 1860		George Stoneman	1883 " 1887	
Milton S. Latham	1860 " 1860	Resigned.	Washington Bartlett	1887 " 1887	Died in office.
John G. Downey	1860 " 1862	Lt.-gov. acting.	Robt. W. Waterman	1887 " 1891	
Leland Stanford	1862 " 1863		Henry H. Markham	1891 " 1895	
Frederick F. Low	1863 " 1867		J. H. Budd	1895 " 1899	
Henry H. Haight	1867 " 1871				

UNITED STATES SENATORS FROM CALIFORNIA.

Name.	No. of Congress.	Date.	Remarks.
John C. Frémont	31st	1849 to 1851	Seated 10 Sept. 1850.
William M. Gwin	31st to 36th	1849 " 1861	" 11 " "
John B. Weller	32d " 34th	1851 " 1857	" 17 Mch. 1852.
David C. Broderick	35th " 36th	1857 " 1859	" 4 " 1857. Died of a wound received in a duel with David S. Terry, 16 Sept. 1859.
Henry P. Hann	36th	1859	*Pro tem.* in place of Broderick.
Milton S. Latham	36th to 37th	1860 to 1863	Elected in place of Broderick.
Jas. A. McDougall	37th " 39th	1861 " 1867	
John Conners	38th " 40th	1863 " 1869	First Republican senator.
Cornelius Cole	40th " 42d	1867 " 1873	
Eugene Casserly	41st " 43d	1869 " 1873	Resigned 29 Nov. 1873.
John S. Hager	43d	1874	Elected in place of Casserly. Seated 9 Feb. 1874.
Aaron A. Sargent	43d to 45th	1873 to 1879	
Newton Booth	44th " 46th	1875 " 1881	
Jas. T. Farley	46th " 48th	1879 " 1885	
John F. Miller	47th " 49th	1851 " 1887	
Leland Stanford	49th " 53d	1885 " 1893	Died 20 June, 1893.
George Hearst	50th " 51st	1887 " 1891	Died 28 Feb. 1891.
Charles N. Felton	52d	1891 " 1893	
Stephen M. White	53d	1893 " ——	Term expires, 1899.
George C. Perkins	53d	1893 " ——	Elected in place of Stanford. Term expires, 1897.

California (Lower or Old), discovered by Ferdnand de Grijalva 1534, is a peninsula extending southward from the state of California, and detached by the gulf of California and the lower reaches of the Colorado river from the rest of Mexico, to which it belongs. It is about 750 miles long, and varies in width from 30 miles to 150. Area about 58,000 square miles; pop. 1890, 31,000.

California (gulf of), once known as the sea of Cortez, by whom it was first explored, separates Lower California from Mexico. It is about 700 miles long and from 40 miles to 100 wide. Into its northern extremity flows the Colorado river.

California (university of), situated at Berkeley, about 9 miles N. E. from San Francisco, was established by an act of the legislature, approved 23 Mch. 1868. It was previously known as the College of California, which was chartered 1855. First class in the university was in 1869, and its first president Henry Durant, LL.D.

cal'iper compass, to measure the bore of cannon, small-arms, etc., is said to have been invented by an artificer of Nuremberg in 1540.

Caliph (*Arab.* Khalifa), *i. e.*, substitute or successor. When Mahomet died, disputes and dissensions arose, until Abu'beckr, his friend and father-in-law, was chosen as his "representative" in 632, but died 634, after a reign of about 2 years. His successor, Omar, began his rule with the remarkable saying: "By Allah, he that is weakest among you shall be in my sight the strongest, until I have vindicated for him his right; but him that is strongest will I treat as the weakest, until he complies with the laws." Omar died 644; his successor, Othman, was killed 656. Ali came next, a cousin and early supporter of Mahomet, but was assassinated in a mosque at Cufa, 661. These first 4 caliphs are followed by 14 known as the Ommiades or Omayyad caliphs (named from a leading family or tribe of Mecca) who reigned for 89 years, 661–750, or an average of 6¼ years. After Merwan II., the last of these, came the ABBASSIDES or Abbasid caliphs, the second of whom founded BAGDAD about 762. As the residence of this dynasty and the capital of the Saracenic empire, it was one of the most magnificent cities of the east. The 37 Abbassides reigned from 750 until the Mongols took Bagdad 1258.

The most famous of the Abbasid caliphs is Harun, surnamed Al-Rashid (the Upright), the 5th of the dynasty, A. D. 786 to 809. The "Thousand and One Nights" has made his name everywhere familiar, and history confirms the fitness of his surname "The Upright." Under this dynasty there were constant dissensions, conspiracies, and rebellions among the different sects of Mahometans. The descendants of the fourth caliph, ALI, the prophet's cousin who married his daughter Fatima, founders of a rival caliphate over Egypt, northern Africa, and later over Syria and Palestine, were the most dangerous opponents to the Abbasid rule. Fourteen of these Fatimite caliphs reigned from about 900 to 1171, when the caliphate was overthrown by the Turks.

In 755 the Saracens of Spain made Abd-al-Rahmin, one of the last survivors of the Omayyads, their head, with the title of Emir of Cordova, although virtually caliph, being entirely independent of Bagdad. Abd-al-Rahmin III., 912, assumed the title of caliph, which title was held until 1031, when the caliphate of Cordova ended with Hisham III., the 5th in order.

The caliphate of Persia dates from 1502, and that of Turkey or the Ottoman Empire from 1517. ABBASSIDES, ALI, MAHOMETANISM.

Calippic period, invented by Calippus about 330 B.C., to correct the Metonic cycle, consists of 4 cycles, or of 76 years, at the expiration of which he incorrectly supposed the new and full moons return on the same day of the solar year. This period began about the end of June, third year or 112th Olympiad, year of Rome 424, and 330 B.C.

Calixtins. 1. A sect derived from the Hussites, about 1420, demanded the cup (Gr. κάλυξ) in the Lord's supper. They were also called Utraquists, as partaking of both elements. They were reconciled to the Roman church at the council of Basle, 1433 —2 The followers of George Calixtus, a Lutheran, who died in 1656 He wrote against the celibacy of the priesthood, and proposed a reunion of Catholics and Protestants under the Apostles' Creed

Cal'lao, Peru After an earthquake the sea retired from the shore, and returned in great waves, destroying the city, in 1687, and on 28 Oct 1746 Attempt of the Spanish admiral Nuñez to bombard Callao, 2 May, 1866, defeated by the Peruvians, blockaded by Chilians, Apr 1880 CHILI

callig'raphy ('beautiful writing') Callicrates is said to have written an elegant distich on a sesamum seed, 472 B.C In the 16th century Peter Bales wrote legibly the Lord's Prayer, Creed, and Decalogue, 2 short Latin prayers, his own name, motto day of the month, year of our Lord, and of the reign of queen Elizabeth (to whom he presented them at Hampton court), all within the circle of a silver penny, enchased in a ring and border of gold, and covered with crystal —*Holinshed*

Calmar, Union of The treaty whereby Denmark, Sweden, and Norway were united under one sovereign, Margaret, queen of Sweden and Norway, ' the Semiramis of the North," June 1397 The union was dissolved by Gustavus Vasa in 1523 RULERS, table of, SWEDEN

Calmucks. TARTARY

cal'omel ("beautiful black"), a compound of mercury, sulphuric acid, and chloride of sodium, first mentioned by Crollius early in the 17th century The first directions given for its preparation were by Beguin in 1608

calorescence. In Jan 1865, prof Tyndall rendered the ultra red rays of the spectrum of the electric light visible by focussing them on a plate of platinum, which they raised to a white heat He termed the phenomenon calorescence FLUORESCENCE.

calor'ic. HEAT

calotype process (from the Gr. καλός, beautiful), by which negative photographs are produced on paper, is the invention of Mr Henry Fox Talbot, about 1840 Also called Talbotype. PHOTOGRAPHY.

Caloy'ers (meaning *good old men*) The monks of the Greek church, of the order of St Basil Their most celebrated monastery in Asia is at Mount Sinai, endowed by Justinian (d 565), the European one is at Mount Athos

Calvary, Mount, the place where the Redeemer suffered death, 5 Apr 30 A.D (*Hales*, 31, *Clinton*, 29, others, 33), see Luke xxiii 33 Hadrian, at the time of his persecution of the Christians, erected a temple of Jupiter on mount Calvary, and a temple of Adonis on the manger at Bethlehem, 142. The empress Helena built a church here about 326 HOLY PLACES

Calvi, Corsica The British forces besieged the fortress of Calvi, 12 June, 1794 After 59 days, it surrendered on 10 Aug. It surrendered to the French in 1796

Calvinists, named after John Calvin (or Chauvin), who was born at Noyon, in Picardy, 10 July, 1509 Adopting the reformed doctrines, he fled to Angoulême, where he composed his "Institutio Christianæ Religionis" in 1533, pub in 1536 He retired to Basle, and settled in Geneva where he died, 27 May, 1564 He took part in burning Servetus for denying the Trinity in 1553 The Calvinists and Lutherans separated after the conference of Poissy in 1561, where the former rejected the 10th and other articles of the Confession of Augsburg, and took the name of Calvinists In France (HUGUENOTS) they took up arms against their persecutors Henry IV, originally a Calvinist, on becoming king, secured their liberty by the EDICT OF NANTES in 1598 Calvinistic doctrines appear in the articles of the church of England and in the confession of the church of Scotland, and are held by many Protestant sects. They include predestination, particular redemption, total depravity, irresistible grace, and the certain perseverance of saints.

Cambodia, a region lying to the southwest of Anam, and south of Siam . Its king, Norodom, recognized French protection by treaty, Oct 1883 Pop 1,800,000, area, 38,000 sq. miles.

Cambray, N France, the ancient Camaracum, was in the middle ages the capital of a prince bishop subject to the emperor It gives its name to CAMBRIC Councils held here 1064, 1303, 1383, 1565

Held by Louis XI of France	1477-78
Taken by Charles V	1544
By the Spaniards.	1595
By the French and annexed	1667
Fénélon made archbishop.	1695
French were defeated at Cæsar's camp in the neighborhood, by the allied army under the duke of York 24 Apr	1794
Invested by the Austrians 8 Aug, the republican general, Declay, replied to the summons to surrender, ' he knew not how to do *that*, but his soldiers knew how to fight " It was taken by Clairfait, the Austrian general 10 Sept	1798
Seized by British under sir Charles Colville 24 June,	1815
League of Cambray against the republic of Venice, comprising pope Julius II, the emperor Maximilian, and Louis XII of France, and Ferdinand of Spain formed 10 Dec	1508
Treaty between Francis I of France and Charles V of Germany (called *Paix des Dames*, because negotiated by Louisa of Savoy mother of the French king, and Margaret of Austria, aunt of the emperor)	1529
Treaty between Charles VI and Philip V of Spain	1724-25

Cambria, ancient name of WALES.

cambric, a fine thin fabric of linen or cotton, first made at CAMBRAY, worn in England, and accounted a great luxury, 1580 —*Stow* Its importation restricted in 1745, prohibited in 1758, readmitted, 1786, prohibited, 1795

Cambridge, the Roman Camboricum and the Saxon Granta bricsir, capital of Cambridge co, Engl., frequently mentioned by the earliest British historians, was burned by the Danes in 870 and 1010

CAMBRIDGE UNIVERSITY

The university, said to have been founded by Sigebert king of the East Angles, about 630 A D, neglected during the Danish invasions from which it suffered much, restored by Edward the elder in 915, began to revive about	1110
Henry I bestows many privileges	"
Henry III grants a charter to the university, about which time the students begin to live together in hostels, which afterwards become colleges named after saints. 1230 or	1231
Wat Tyler s and Jack Straw's rebels enter, seize university records and burn them in the market place.	1381
University press set up	1534
Incorporated by Elizabeth	1571
University authorized to send 2 members to Parliament	1603
University refuses the degree of M A. to father Francis, a Benedictine monk, recommended by the king, and the presidency of Magdalene college to Farmer, a Roman Catholic, notwithstanding the king's mandate.	1680
Mathematical tripos instituted	1747
University tests act passed 16 June,	1877
New code of statutes for the university approved by queen Victoria in council	1882
St Paul's hostelry for Indian students chartered 18 July,	1883
New museum of classical art and archæology opened. 6 May,	1884
Miss A F Ramsay, of Girton, senior and alone in first division of classical tripos. Miss B M Hervey, of Newnham, alone in first division of mediæval and modern languages tripos, 18 June,	1887
Prof G G Stokes, P R.S, elected M P for the university, 17 Nov	"
Miss G P Fawcett, Newnham (daughter of the late professor), above the senior wrangler in mathematics 7 June,	1890
Senate supports compulsory study of Greek (525-185) 29 Oct	1891
Establishment of an engineering school proposed . Dec	"

SEVENTEEN COLLEGES.

Peterhouse college, by Hugo de Balsham, bishop of Ely, founded	1257
Clare hall or college, first founded by Dr Richard Baden in 1326, destroyed by fire and re-established by Elizabeth de Bourg, sister to Gilbert, earl of Clare about	1342
Pembroke college, founded by the countess of Pembroke	1347
Gonville and Caius. by Edmund Gonville	1348
Trinity hall, by William Bateman, bishop of Norwich	1350
Enlarged by Dr John Caius	1558
Corpus Christi, or Benet	1352
King's college, by Henry VI	1441
Queen s college, by Margaret of Anjou, 1448, and Elizabeth Woodville	1449
St. Catherine's college or hall, founded .	1473
Jesus college, by John Alcock, bishop of Ely	1496
Christ s college, founded 1442, endowed by Margaret, countess of Richmond, mother of Henry VII	1505
St. John's college, endowed by Margaret, countess of Richmond	1511
Magdalene college, by Thomas, baron Audley .	1519
Trinity college by Henry VIII .	1546
Emmanuel college, by sir Walter Mildmay	1584
Sidney Sussex college, founded by Frances Sidney, countess of Sussex	1598
Downing college, by sir George Downing by will, in 1717, its charter	1800

HOSTELS.

Non-Coll. students, founded	1869
Cavendish college, opened by duke of Devonshire	1876
Selwyn college, founded	1 June, 1881
Ayerst's Hostel, founded	1884

[*Cambridge University Calendar*, 1891.]

CHANCELLORS.

Charles, duke of Somerset, elected	1688
Thomas, duke of Newcastle	1748
Augustus Henry, duke of Grafton	1768
H. R. H. William Frederick, duke of Gloucester	1811
John, marquis Camden	1834
Hugh, duke of Northumberland	1840
Prince Consort (d. 14 Dec. 1861)	28 Feb. 1847
William, duke of Devonshire	31 Dec. 1861

PRINCIPAL PROFESSORSHIPS.	Founded.
Divinity (Margaret), 1502; Regius	1540
Laws, Hebrew, Greek, and Physic	"
Arabic	1632
Mathematics (Lucasian)	1663
Music	1684
Chemistry	1702
Astronomy	1704, 1749
Anatomy	1707
Modern History, Botany	1724
Natural and Experimental Philosophy	1783
Mineralogy	1808
Political Economy	1863
Slade (fine art)	1869

(Cambridge and Oxford recognize each other's degrees, also those granted by Dublin university, but no others). UNIVERSITIES.

Cambridge, Mass. The town was founded by gov. Winthrop in 1630, and called Newtown. During the British occupation of Boston the American army occupied Cambridge, and there Washington assumed command in 1775. The city of Cambridge, the seat of HARVARD UNIVERSITY, was incorporated in 1846. Pop. in 1880, 52,740; 1890, 70,028.

Cambuskenneth, near Stirling (central Scotland). Here Wallace defeated the English under Warrenne and Cressingham, 10 Sept. 1297.

The abbey, one of the richest in Scotland, was founded by king David I. in 1147; was spoiled and nearly destroyed by the reformers in 1559.

Camden, S. C. Here, 16 Aug. 1780, about 3600 Americans, under gen. Gates, were defeated by from 2000 to 2500 British, under lord Cornwallis, losing 700 men, among them baron de Kalb mortally wounded, nearly all their baggage and artillery.

Camel, Day of the, 4 Nov. 656 (according to some, 658 or 659), when Talha and Zobeir, rebel Arab chiefs, were defeated and slain by caliph Ali. Ayesha, Mahomet's widow, friend of the chiefs, was present in a litter, on a camel; hence the name.

Cam'elot, a legendary city of Britain, famous in king Arthur's time.

> "And thro' the field the road runs by
> To many-tower'd Camelot."
> —*Tennyson*, "The Lady of Shalott."

camera-lucida, invented by Dr. Hooke about 1674; another by Dr. Wollaston in 1807, to facilitate the delineation of distant objects.

camera-obscura or **dark chamber,** constructed, it is said, by Roger Bacon in 1297; improved by Baptista Porta, about 1500; and remodelled by sir Isaac Newton. By the invention of M. Daguerre, in 1839, the pictures of the camera are fixed. PHOTOGRAPHY.

Cameronians, a name frequently given to the Reformed Presbyterian church of Scotland, the descendants of the Covenanters of the 17th century, the established church, 1638-1650. They assumed the name of the "Reformed Presbyterian church" on 25 May, 1876, and soon after united with the Free church of Scotland. Charles II. signed the league and covenant in 1650, in hopes of recovering his kingdoms, but renounced it in 1661, and revived episcopacy. A revolt ensued in 1666, when many Covenanters were slain in battle (in the Pentland hills, etc.); and many, refusing to take the oaths required, and declining to accept the king's indulgence, died on the scaffold, after undergoing cruel tortures. The name Cameronian is derived from Richard Cameron, one of their ministers, who was killed in a skirmish in 1680. On 22 June in that year he and others issued at Sanquathar a declaration for religious liberty. The bi-centenary was kept in 1880. In 1689 they raised a body of soldiers to support William III., who enrolled them under the command of lord Angus, as the 26th regiment, since so famous in British annals. In 1712 they renewed their public covenants, and are described in one of their tracts as "the suffering anti-popish, and anti-prelatical, anti-erastian, true Presbyterian church of Scotland." They have now between 30 and 40 congregations in Scotland.—The 79th regiment (Cameron Highlanders), raised in 1793 by Allan Cameron, has no connection with the Cameronians.

Cameroon, a region in Africa, made a German protectorate in 1884. It has a coast line on the Bight of Biafra, north of the French Congo region, of 120 miles. Its area is about 130,000 sq. miles. Pop. 2,500,000.

Camisards (from *chemise*, Lat. *camisa*, a shirt, which they frequently wore over their dress in night attacks), a name given to the French Protestants in the neighborhood of the Cévennes (mountain-chains in S. France), who, after enduring much persecution after the revocation of the Edict of Nantes, 22 Oct. 1685, took up arms in July, 1702, to rescue some imprisoned brethren. They revenged the cruelties of their enemies, and maintained an obstinate resistance against the royalist armies commanded by marshal Montrevel and other distinguished generals till 1705, when the insurrection was suppressed by marshal Villars. After futile conciliatory efforts, several of the heroic leaders suffered death rather than surrender. Cavalier, an able general, unable to carry out a treaty made with Villars, seceded in 1704, entered the British service, and died governor of Jersey, 1740.

camlet, formerly made of silk and camel's hair, but now of wool, hair, and silk. Oriental camlet first came from Portuguese India in 1660.—*Anderson.*

camp. The Hebrew encampment was first laid out by Divine direction, 1490 B.C. (Numb. ii.). The Romans and Gauls had intrenched camps in open plains; and vestiges of such exist to this day in England and Scotland.

Campagna (*Cam-pan'ya*) **di Roma,** near Rome. A district mostly uncultivated and unhealthy, including the greater part of ancient Latium. The vapors arising from the land produce the pestilential atmosphere called *Aria Cattiva.* This province was not always so unhealthy, but in the early days of the republic contained such cities as Veii and Fidenae, and under the empire many fine villas were built here. Its drainage and planting were authorized by the Italian senate, 31 May, 1878, but little, however, has been done.

Campania, S. Italy, was occupied by Hannibal, and various cities declared in his favor, 216 B.C.; conquered by the Romans, 213. Its capital was CAPUA.

Campbellites or **Rowites,** the followers of the rev. John McLeod Campbell, minister of Row, Dumbartonshire, deposed 24 May, 1831, by the general assembly of the church of Scotland for teaching universal atonement, and other doctrines contrary to the church's standard. Dr. Campbell established a congregation in Glasgow in 1833. The DISCIPLES OF CHRIST are also sometimes termed Campbellites, after Alexander Campbell, their founder.

Campeachy bay, Yucatan, Central America, discovered about 1517, and settled by Spaniards in 1540; taken by the English in 1659, by the buccaneers in 1678, and by the freebooters of St. Domingo in 1685, who burned the town and blew up the citadel. The English logwood-cutters settled here about 1662.

Camperdown, south of the Texel, Holland, near which admiral Duncan, of the English fleet, defeated the Dutch fleet, commanded by admiral De Winter; the latter losing 15 ships, either taken or destroyed, 11 Oct. 1797. The British admiral was made lord Duncan of Camperdown. He died suddenly on his way to Edinburgh, 4 Aug. 1804. Also the name of an English armored battle-ship. WRECKS, 1893.

Campo Formio, N. Italy. Here a treaty was concluded between France and Austria; the latter yielding the Low Countries and the Ionian islands to France, and Milan, Mantua, and Modena to the Cisalpine republic, 17 Oct. 1797. By a secret article the emperor gained the Venetian dominions.

Campus Raudius, near Verona, N. Italy. Here the Cimbri were defeated with great slaughter by Marius and Catulus, 101 B.C.

CAN

Canaan (*ka'nan*) is considered to have been settled by the Canaanites, 1965 B.C (*Clinton*, 2088) Abram, by divine command, went into the land of Canaan, 1921 B.C (Gen xii) The land was divided among the Israelites by Joshua, 1445 B.C (*Hales*, 1602) JEWS, JUDÆA

Canada, N America, was discovered by John and Sebastian Cabot, 24 June, 1497 In 1524, a French expedition under Verazzano formed a settlement named New France, and in 1535 Jacques Cartier (a Breton mariner) ascended the St. Lawrence as far as the site of Montreal Canada has been termed "the Dominion" since its incorporation with the other Anglo American colonies, 1 July (Dominion day), 1867 Capital, Ottawa Pop 1871, 3,788,018, 1881, 4,359,933, 1891, 4,829,411, 1901, 5,371,315 Area, 3,393,320 sq miles. BRITISH AMERICA, FRENCH IN AMERICA.

First permanent settlement Quebec founded 1608

Canada taken by the English, 1629, restored 1632

War begins in 1756, Canada conquered by the English 1759, confirmed to them by the treaty of Paris, signed 10 Feb 1763

Legislative council established the French laws confirmed, and religious liberty given to Roman Catholics 1774

Americans under Montgomery invade Canada, and surprise Montreal, Nov 1775, expelled by Carleton Mch 1776

Canada divided into Upper and Lower 1791

"Clergy reserves" established by Parliament—one seventh of the waste lands of the colony appropriated for the maintenance of the Protestant clergy (during the debates on this bill the quarrel between Mr Burke and Mr Fox arose) "

United States army, under gen Hull, invade Canada from Detroit, 12 July, but retire across the river to Detroit 8 Aug 1812 UNITED STATES 1812-14

First railway in Canada opened July, 1836

Papineau rebellion commences at Montreal by a body called *Fils de la Liberté* 1837

Rebels defeated at St Eustace 14 Dec "

Repulsed at Toronto by sir F Head 5 Jan 1838

Lount and Mathews (rebels) hanged 12 Apr "

Rebellion in Beauharnais, 3 Nov, the insurgents at Napierville, under Nelson, routed, 6 Nov, rebellion suppressed 17 Nov "

Acts for government of Lower Canada passed, Feb 1838, and Aug 1839

Upper and Lower Canada reunited 10 Feb 1840

Riots in Montreal, parliament house burned 26 Apr 1850

Treaty with the U S 7 June, 1854

Grand Trunk railroad of Canada (850 miles), from Quebec to Toronto, opened 12 Nov 1856

On reference to queen Victoria, Ottawa, formerly Bytown, made the capital, this decision unpopular Aug 1858

Canada raises a regiment of soldiers (made one of the line, and called the 100th) "

Prince of Wales duke of Newcastle, etc., arrive at St John's, Newfoundland, 24 July, visit Halifax, 30 July, Quebec, 18 Aug, Montreal, 25 Aug, Ottawa, 1 Sept, leave Canada, 20 Sept., after visiting the U S embark at Portland, 20 Oct., and arrive at Plymouth 15 Nov 1860

In consequence of the *Trent* affair (UNITED STATES, 1861), 3000 British troops sent to Canada, warlike preparations made, Dec 1861

British Parliament grant 50,000*l* for defence of Canada, 2 Mch "

British N American Association founded in London Jan 1862

J Sandfield Macdonald premier 20-23 May, "

Assembly vote only 5000 militia and 5000 reserve for the defence of the country, discontent in England. July, "

Macdonald again premier 20 May, 1863

Meeting of delegates from N American colonies at Quebec, to deliberate on a confederation, 10 Oct, agree on the bases Oct. 1864

Between 20 and 30 armed confederates quit Canada and enter St. Albans, Vt., rob the banks, steal horses and stores, fire, kill one man, and wound others, return to Canada, 19 Oct, 13 are arrested, 21 Oct, but are discharged on technical grounds, by judge Coursol 14 Dec "

Confederation scheme rejected by New Brunswick 7 Mch 1865

St. Albans raiders discharged, 30 Mch., Mr Seward gives up claim for their extradition Apr "

Threatened invasion of the Fenians, 9 Mch, 10,000 volunteers called out 15 Mch 1866

Canadian parliament first meets at Ottawa, the habeas corpus act suspended, many Fenians flee, 35,000 men under arms (FENIANS). . 8 June, "

Discovery of gold in Hastings county, Canada West Nov "

Act for the union of Canada, Nova Scotia, and New Brunswick as "the Dominion of Canada" the executive authority being vested in the sovereign of Great Britain, represented by a gov gen (salary 10 000*l* per annum) and privy council, with parliament, to consist of a senate, members chosen for life, and a house of commons, members chosen for 5 years, passed. . 29 Mch 1867

Canada railway loan act passed 12 Apr "

Lord Monck sworn as viceroy of Canada, under the Union act, 2 July, "

New parliament meets at Ottawa, senate, 72 members, house of commons, 181 6 Nov "

Agitation against the confederation in Nova Scotia Jan 1868

Murder of Darcy McGhee 7 Apr "

A Fenian raid into Canada vigorously repelled by the militia, about 24 May, "

Hudson's bay territories purchased, subject to conditions for 300 000*l* (HUDSON'S BAY) Nov 1869

Some of the settlers resisting (RUPERT'S LAND) an expedition, under col Wolseley arrive at fort Garry, and a conciliatory proclamation is issued 23 July, 1870

Rupert's Land made the province of Manitoba, Adams G A Archibald first governor Aug "

Disputes with U S respecting fishing Nov "

Opposition to the fishery clauses in the treaty of Washington, June, 1871

By the British North America act, the Parliament of Canada may establish new provinces 29 June, "

British Columbia united to the "Dominion" "

Departure of last battalion of royal troops Nov "

Mr Arch, on behalf of British laborers visits Canada autumn, 1873

Canadian and U S fishery commission (sir Alexander Galt for Canada, E T Kellogg for U S, and M Delfosse Belgian U S minister) meet at Halifax 15 June, award $5,500 000 to Canada Mr Kellogg dissenting 23, 24 Nov 1877

American fishermen in Fortune bay attacked for breaking laws respecting fishing 6 Jan 1878

Marquis of Lorne appointed governor general 14 Oct. "

Resignation of ministry, sir John Macdonald forms a new one, about 19 Oct. "

Halifax award paid by the U S (FISH, FISHERIES) 21 Nov "

Marquis of Lorne and princess Louise land at Halifax 25 Nov "

Fortune bay affair (Jan 1878), compensation refused by the earl of Salisbury, granted by lord Granville, but rules affirmed, 26 Oct. 1880

Contract for new Pacific railway ratified by the assembly, 1 Feb 1881

Fortune bay affair, 15 000*l* awarded 28 May, "

Northwest territory beyond Manitoba divided into 4 new territories—Assiniboia, Saskatchewan, Alberta, Athabaska, by order in council July, 1882

Marquis of Lansdowne arrives at Quebec as governor general, 22 Oct. 1884

Canada offers military assistance in the Soudan Feb 1885

Insurrection in northwest territories, led by Louis David Riel, supported by French half breeds and Indians, claiming political and social rights alleged to have been promised in 1870, government stores seized about 24 Mch "

Col Irvine evacuates and burns fort Carleton 25–27 Mch "

Battleford besieged by Indians 1 Apr "

Col Otter, after a fight relieves Battleford 24 Apr "

Gen Middleton defeats the Indians at Fish creek after a severe conflict 24 Apr "

Col Otter defeats Riel's followers near Battleford 3 May, "

Gen Middleton attacks and captures Batoche, on the Saskatchewan well defended by Riel with rifle-pits, etc, British success largely due to the skill and courage of capt. Howard, U S. A, with a Gatling gun 9 May, "

Indian chief Poundmaker, having captured a supply train of 31 wagons, is defeated, but supplies are not recovered, 14 May, "

Riel surrenders with many of his followers 15 May, "

Poundmaker surrenders 26 May, "

Gen Strange attacks Big Bear's intrenched camp, 20 miles from fort Pitt, but retreats 28–29 May, "

Big Bear retreats 7 June, "

Riel tried convicted, and hanged 30 July–16 Nov "

Fisheries dispute between Canada and U S, Canadians put the harshest construction upon the treaty of 1818, seeking to force the U S to a more favorable treaty spring, 1886

U S Congress passes a bill authorizing retaliation against Canadian commerce at the president's discretion 2 Mch 1887

Fisheries Retaliation bill passed by the U S Congress 3 Mch "

Wm O Brien editor of *United Ireland*, arrives at Montreal on a mission, 11 May, visits Ottawa, Toronto, etc., generally unsuccessful and frequently stoned, leaves . 28 May, "

Joint commission on fisheries dispute (3 British, including J Chamberlain, and 3 U S) appointed about 30 Aug "

British vessels seized by U S authorities in N Pacific waters, 2, 9, 12, 17 Aug "

Great railway bridge over the St. Lawrence at Lachine completed 30 July, "

Arrangements made for a fortnightly mail service, etc., from London to the east by the Canadian Pacific railway by government subsidies Sept "

Bill for trade reciprocity with U S negatived after 15 days' debate . 7 Apr 1888

Commissioners report the capability of the great Mackenzie basin, etc (about 1,260,000 sq miles) for colonization, announced . . Sept "

Proposed extension by Manitoba of Red River railway across Canadian Pacific railway, opposed by that company as interfering with their monopoly, and disallowed by the Dominion parliament, a compromise agreed to, Manitoba government determine to proceed, Canadian company resists, Oct, conflict, the company successful, 26 Oct., decision of the supreme court in favor of Manitoba announced, 23 Dec., leave given to cross the line . 28 Jan 1889

Proposed petition to queen to make the governor general independent in foreign affairs negatived by Parliament (94–66), 18 Feb "

Dominion commons unanimously resolve on adhesion to the mother country, a copy to be sent to the queen. . 29 Jan. 1890

Manitoba railway named the Great Northern railway of Canada, Jan. 1890

John Reginald Birchall, an educated Englishman, tried at Woodstock, Ontario, for the murder in Niagara swamp of F. J. Benwell (whom he had decoyed from England into a farming partnership), 17 Feb. Birchall wrote a forged letter to col. Benwell, requesting him to send 500*l.* to his son; evidence circumstantial; 8 days' trial; convicted 11.45 P.M., 29 Sept.; executed, 14 Nov. "

Indians of Ontario and Quebec, at a meeting on 21 Nov., agree to petition the government to release them from the political franchise, and to permit them to elect their own chiefs as formerly, still remaining subject to the government; petition presented, and reserved for consideration, Dec. 1890; Parliament dissolved....................................4 Feb. 1891

Sir John Macdonald, premier, and conservatives, propose reciprocity with the U. S., only of natural products; Mr. Laurier and liberals propose unrestricted reciprocity.................. "

Canadian Pacific railway completed by agreement with New York Central for an entrance to New York..............28 Mch. "

First steamer of the Pacific mail service arrives at Vancouver from Yokohama.................................28 Apr. "

Death of sir John Macdonald, aged 76, greatly lamented, 6 June; public funeral at Kingston.....................10, 11 June, "

Hon. John Joseph C. Abbott becomes premier........14 June, "

Motion in favor of unrestricted reciprocity with the U. S., after 15 days' debate, rejected in the commons, by a government majority of 26....................................29 July, "

Sir Hector Louis Langevin, minister of public works, and his friend, the hon. Thomas McGreevy, an active ministerialist M.P., and other officials, charged by Mr. Tarte, M.P., a journalist, with corruption in contracts for government works in 1890; referred to standing committee on privileges and elections, which met 21 July; sir H. Langevin makes his defence, 11 Aug.; his resignation as minister accepted, 7 Sept.; T. McGreevy makes damaging admissions, and retires to the U. S.; the committee exonerate sir H. Langevin from all charges, except that of negligence; they censure T. McGreevy, and certain officials...............................14 Sept. "

Report adopted by the House............................25 Sept. "

St. Clair tunnel connecting the Canadian and the U. S. railways running to Chicago opened by sir Henry Tyler, chairman of the Grand Trunk railway...................19 Sept. "

Lady Macdonald, widow of sir John Macdonald, premier, created a peeress as baroness Macdonald of Earnscliffe by the British Parliament....................................Oct. "

Meeting at Washington of the representatives of Canada and the U. S. to consider reciprocity; no result.......10–15 Feb. 1892

By order in council, the Dominion discriminates against the U. S. in the use of the Welland canal................4 Apr. "

UNITED STATES, 20 Aug. 1892.

Hon. Alexander Mackenzie, originally a Scotch mason, came to Canada and gradually rose till he became liberal premier, 1873–78; he passed several important acts and promoted great public works; visited Great Britain and was received at Windsor, 1875; d. aged 70........................17 Apr. "

Motion for a new reciprocity tariff with Great Britain, adopted by the commons at Ottawa (98–64)...............25 Apr. "

Canal tolls arranged with the U. S.....................14 Jan. 1893

CANADA PACIFIC RAILROAD.

British Columbia, on entering the confederation, exacts a pledge that a railway to the Pacific shall be built.................. 1871

Government, having begun the work, transfers it to Canada Pacific railroad company, which agrees to complete the work by the year 1891; subsidy 25,000,000 acres of land, exemption from tax for 20 years; free entry for materials imported, and exemption from rival lines for 20 years.......................... 1881

Government further aids the company, guaranteeing 3% interest for 10 years on $65,000,000 of stock......................... 1883

Parliament authorizes loan of $22,500,000 to the company till 1891, on mortgage... 1884

Company embarrassed; government gives 5 years' credit on $7,300,000 due... "

Company still unable to fulfil contract; Parliament cancels the government lien on the property, authorizes a first-mortgage loan of $35,000,000 at 5%; takes $20,000,000 of the mortgage bonds, and renders further aid............................ "

Road opened..18 May, 1885

Main line from Quebec to Port Moody, 3025 miles; branch lines, 4?? miles; total cost to the country, $130,000,000.

canals. Sesostris, 1659 B.C., cut canals for transporting merchandise, running at right angles with the Nile as far as from Memphis to the sea.—*Diodorus Siculus.* Julius Cæsar, Caligula, and Nero each attempted a canal across the isthmus of Corinth. The Grand or Imperial canal of China, nearly 700 miles in length, from Hang-choo-foo to Yan-liang river, dates back to the 13th century. Henry II., about 1555 employed Adam de Crapone to cut the canal of Charolais, Burgundy, near Saone-et-Loire, which was continued by Henry IV. The beginning of general canal navigation in England dates from the opening of the Bridgewater canal between Worsley and Salford, about 29 miles, 17 July, 1761. In 1790 the "canal mania" in England began. The first canal opened in the United States for transportation of passengers and merchandise was the Middlesex canal, connecting Boston with the Concord river, in 1804. But the great era of canal construction in the U. S. was between 1825 and 1830; 13 out of 50 important canals being then under construction. Many of the older canals have been enlarged from time to time, and others have been partly or wholly abandoned, competing railways rendering them unprofitable; hence accurate statistics as to length, size, etc., a obtained with difficulty. Numerous short canals, many of them meriting the name of ship canals, have been constructed in the U. S. and elsewhere, to pass rapids in navigable rivers; such are the Des Moines, the Cascades, the Louisville and Portland, the Lachine, etc. A table of the most important ship canals of the world, not mentioned elsewhere, and of the principal canals of the U. S. and the United Kingdom is here given, showing when first constructed, and present length and capacity.

IMPORTANT CANALS OTHER THAN SHIP CANALS.—(UNITED STATES.)

Name.	Location.	Begun.	Opened.	Length, Miles.	Depth, Feet.	Width, Feet.	No. of Locks.	Size of Largest Locks in Feet.
Erie canal. NEW YORK, 1825	Albany to Buffalo, N. Y.	1817	1825	351.8	7	70	72	208×18
Oswego	Oswego to Syracuse, N. Y.	1825	1828	38	7	70	18	208×18
Cayuga and Seneca	Geneva to Montezuma, N. Y.	1825	1828	22.8	7	70	11	98×18
Black River (main line)	Rome to Carthage, N. Y.	1836	1849	35	4	42	109	78.5×15
Champlain (main line)	Waterford to Whitehall, N. Y.	1817	1824	66	6	58	23	98×18
Delaware and Hudson	Rondout, N. Y., to Honesdale, Pa.	1826	1829	108	6	48	108	92×15
Morris	Jersey City to Phillipsburg, N. J.	1825	1836	102	5	45	33	90×11
Lehigh	Easton to Coalport, Pa.	1821	1829	48	6	60	55	87.5×22
Delaware division	Easton to Bristol, Pa.	....	1830	60	6	44	25	87.5×22
Pennsylvania	Columbia to Wilkesbarre, Pa.	1827	1834	144	6.3	....	35	176×17
West Branch division	....	1828	1833	35	5	....	12	81×17
Juniata division	....	1827	1834	14	5	....	4	81×17
Susquehanna and Tidewater	Susquehanna, Pa., to Havre de Grace, Md.	1827	1840	45	6	....	30	170.7×17
Chesapeake and Ohio	Georgetown to Cumberland, Md.	1828	1850	184.5	6	50–60	73	90×15
Dismal Swamp	Elizabeth river to Pasquotank	1787	1794	29.1	5	....	5	98×17.6
Ohio	Cleveland to Portsmouth, O.	1825	1832	308	4	....	144	78×15
Hocking Branch	....	....	....	41	4	....	19	78×15
Walholding Branch	....	....	....	25	4	....	11	78×15
Miami and Erie (main line). OHIO.	Cincinnati to Toledo, O.	....	1834	264	4	....	93	78×15
Illinois and Michigan	Chicago to Illinois river	1830	1848	97.2	6	....	15	100×18
(UNITED KINGDOM.)								
Aire and Calder navigation	Leeds to Goole	1699	....	36	10	66	10	215×22
Leeds and Liverpool	Leeds to Liverpool	1770	1816	127	4	42	91	76×15
Gloucester and Berkeley	Sharpness to Gloucester	1793	....	17	18	70	....	100×24
Grand Junction	Brentford to Braunston	1873	....	92	....	....	....	80×14.6
Forth and Clyde	Bowling bay to Grangemouth	1768	1790	35	10	56	39	74×20
Grand Canal	Dublin to the Shannon	1765	1788	89	6	40	6	70×14.5
Royal Canal	Dublin to Cloondara	1789	1822	92	6	....	....	....
Shropshire Union canals	Union formed	1846	....	....	....	....	....	....
Chester	River Dee to Nantwich	1772	1776	20	....	....	....	....
Ellesmere	Carreghofa to Hurleston	1793	1806	86	....	....	....	....
Birmingham and Liverpool	Autherly to Nantwich	1826	1835	53	....	....	....	....
Montgomeryshire	Carreghofa to Newton	1794	1820	25	....	....	....	....
Shrewsbury	Wombridge to Shrewsbury	1793	1797	22	....	....	....	....

SHIP CANALS. (SUEZ, PANAMA, NICARAGUA.)

Name.	Location.	Begun.	Opened.	Length, Miles.	Depth, Feet.	Width, Feet.	No. of Locks.	Size of Largest Locks in Feet.
United States.—Sault Ste. Marie canal	Around St. Mary's falls	1855	....	1	20	....	2	800×100
Cape Cod canal	Buzzard's bay to Barnstable bay	....	....	7.6	23	200	....	....
Harlem canal	East river to the Hudson	1888	....	8	....	400	....	....
Canada.—Welland canal	Lake Erie to lake Ontario	1824	1833	27	14	....	....	270×45
England.—Manchester ship canal	Manchester to Eastham	1887	1893	35.5	26	172	3	550×60
Scotland.—Caledonian ship canal	Inverness Forth and loch Eil	1804	1823	60	17–20	120	28	170×40
France.—Havre to Tancarville	Havre to Harfleur Harfleur to Tancarville	....	1887	15.5	19.5 11.5	62 81.5	2	590.5×52.5
Germany.—North Sea and Baltic	Mouth of the Elbe to the gulf of Kiel	1887	....	60	28	197	tidal	1180×196
Belgium.—Ghent [illegible]	Ghent to the river Scheldt	1824	1878	21	20	173	....	....
[illegible]	Amsterdam west to the North sea	1865	1876	15.5	23	197	tidal	390×59
[illegible]	Lake Y to Nieuwe-Diep	1819	1825	52	18.5	123.5	5	237×51
[illegible]	Lake Wener to Göta river	....	1800	22	12.5	....	16	....
[illegible]	Lake Wener to the Baltic sea	1811	1832	115	10	85	58	121.36×22.96
[illegible]	Neva, above St. Petersburg to Cronstadt	1878	1885	18	22	180–240	....	....
[illegible]	Crossing isthmus of Corinth	1882	1893	4	26	77.5	....	....
[illegible]	Crossing isthmus of Suez	1858	1869	90	....	....	....	....

Canary islands, 62½ geographic miles from the N. W. African coast, lying between 27° 40′ and 29° 25′ N. lat., and 13° 25′ and 18° 16′ W. lon., known to the ancients as the *Fortunate isles.* The first meridian was referred to the Canary isles by Hipparchus, about 140 B.C. They were rediscovered by a Norman named Bethencourt about 1400; his descendants sold them to the Spaniards, who became masters, 1483. The canary-bird, a native of these isles, brought to England about 1500. Teneriffe, the largest island, has the "peak of Teneriffe," 12,198 feet high. *Ferro,* the most southwest, was made the French meridian by Louis XIII. in 1632.

Can'dahar, a province of Afghanistan held by Duranis and Ghilzais. Candahar, the capital, is said to have been founded by Alexander the Great (334–323 B.C.). Subject to successive rulers of India, then made capital of Afghanistan by Ahmed Shah, 1747, the seat of government transferred to Cabool in 1774. AFGHANISTAN.

Taken and held by the British.........7 Aug. 1839 to 22 May, 1842
Gen. Nott (with maj. Rawlinson and maj. Lane) defeated the Afghans near here.........................Jan. and June, "
Government of Candahar conferred on Shere Ali (a cousin of the late ameer Shere Ali), with the title of *Wali,* by the viceroy of India.......................................Apr. 1880
Shere Ali resigned, and went to Calcutta in.................Dec. "
After the disaster of Maiwand, 27 July, 1880, Candahar was held by the British during the winter....................1880–81
In the House of Lords, on the earl of Lytton's motion to retain Candahar, 165 voted for its retention, 76 against......5 Mch. 1881
House of Commons, on Mr. Stanhope's motion for retention, 336 voted against it, 216 for it.............24–26 Mch. "
Candahar evacuated by the British................16–21 Apr. "

Candia, the ancient Crete, an island in the Mediterranean sea, celebrated for its 100 cities, its centre Mount Ida, the laws of its king Minos, and its labyrinth to secure the Minotaur (about 1300 B.C.). It was conquered by the Romans, 68 B.C. Area, 2949 sq. miles; pop. estimated, 294,192.

A.D.
Seized by the Saracens.. 823
Retaken by the Greeks... 961
Sold to the Venetians...................................Aug. 1204
Rebelled; reduced... 1364
Gained by the Turks, after a 24 years' siege, during which more than 200,000 men perished...................................... 1669
Ceded to the Egyptian pacha................................... 1830
Restored to Turkey.. 1840
Insurrections suppressed, 1841; by conciliation............... 1858
Persecution of the Christians........................31 July, 1859
Christians demand redress of grievances..................June, 1866
They establish a "sacred battalion"..................12 Aug. "
Publish an address to the powers protecting Greece....21 Aug. "
Cretan general assembly proclaim the abolition of the Turkish authority, and union with Greece...........................2 Sept. "
Commencement of hostilities; the Turkish army commanded by Mustapha Pacha.......................................11 Sept. "
Proposition of Austria, Prussia, Italy, and Switzerland to the sultan to give up Candia, 28 Mch.; declined.........31 Mch. 1867
Collective note from Russia and other powers urging the Porte to suspend hostilities.............................15 June, "
Assembly of delegates meet the vizier.................22 Sept. "
Insurrection subsides; the grand-vizier arrives, 28 Sept.; proclaims an amnesty, and promises reforms............5 Nov. "
Delegates' demands granted...........................11 Dec. "
War renewed (indecisive)...............................Feb. 1868
Provisional government surrendered....................30 Dec. "
New Turkish governor, Omar Fenizi, arrives, and the blockade, began 1866, ends....................................8 Mch. 1869
Insurrection announced, with provisional government, about 20 Dec. 1877
Union with Greece proclaimed, 21 Jan.; decreed by a general assembly..11 Feb. 1878
Insurrection unsubdued; anarchy; Berlin treaty declares for enforcing legal and political reforms...............13 July, 1878
Pacification by Mukhtar Pacha through concession of self-government, etc..Oct. "
Religious insurrection..................................Feb. 1884
Christian notables appeal to the sultan for a Christian governor, and to Greece and other powers for mediation...Mch. "
Anarchy through party strife of Christians and Mahometans, May–June; Turkish troops sent to Crete, 13 June; provisional government formed to restore order..........13 June, 1889
An insurgent assembly demands a constituent assembly, judicial reforms, and dismissal of the governor; the people neutral...about 1 July, "
Insurrection increasing; call for annexation to Greece, or British protection..............................about 25 July, "
Note from the Greek government to the powers, urging intervention in Crete, 6 Aug.; they decline, leaving the settlement to the sultan, 9–12 Aug.; about 17,000 Turkish troops in Crete reported..................................7 Aug. "
Martial law proclaimed...................................14 Aug. "
Partial submission of insurgents; amnesty promised...17 Aug. "
Tranquillity gradually restored by Turkish moderate firmness, Sept. "
Notables address the sultan, thanking him for his good government...28 Jan. 1890
Turkish circular to the great powers, reporting the pacification of Crete, 6 Mch.; amnesty, except to 18 persons convicted of crimes, announced..........................11 Mch. "
Great return of refugees from Greece............about 10 May, "

Candlemas-day, 2 Feb., is kept in the church in memory of the purification of the Virgin, who presented the infant Jesus in the Temple; so called from the candles lit (it is said in memory of Simeon's song, Luke ii. 32, "a light to lighten the Gentiles," etc.). Its origin is ascribed by Bede to pope Gelasius in the 5th century. The practice of lighting the churches was forbidden by order of council, 2 Edw. VI. 1548; but is still continued in the church of Rome. Candlemas is a Scotch quarter-day.

candles. The Roman candles were composed of string surrounded by wax, or dipped in pitch. Splinters of wood fatted were used for light among the lower classes in England, about 1300. Wax candles were little used, and dipped candles were usually burned. The Wax-chandlers' Company was incorporated 1484. Mould-candles are said to be the invention of the sieur Le Brez, of Paris. Spermaceti candles are modern. Candles are also made from wax of the bay or candleberry-tree (*Myrica cerifera*). The duty upon candles made in England, imposed in 1709, amounted to about 500,000*l.* annually, when repealed in 1831. Great improvements in the manufacture of candles are due to the researches on oils and fats carried on by "the father of the fatty acids," Chevreul, since 1811, and published in 1823. At Price's manufactory at Lambeth, the principles involved in many patents are carried into execution; including those of Gwynne (1840), Jones and Price (1842), and Wilson in 1844, for candles which require no snuffing (termed *composite*). Palm and cocoa-nut oils are also used. Paraffine, a substance first discovered in petroleum by Buckner in 1820, and as a product of the distillation of wood by Reichenbach in 1830, is now through the discoveries of Dr. James Young, 1847–50, extensively used in the manufacture of candles. In 1870 the manufacture of candles from a mineral substance named *ozokerit* began. Electric candles of Jablochkoff and Jamin, ELECTRICITY. The Emery Candle Company of Cincinnati are the largest manufacturers of candles in the United States. Incorporated in 1887. The largest in the world are the Price Patent Candle company works near London, Engl

candlesticks or **lamp-stands,** with 7 branches, were regarded as emblematical of the priest's office, and were engraven on their seals, cups, and tombs Bezaleel made "a candlestick of pure gold" for the tabernacle, 1491 B.C. (Exod xxxvii 17) Candlesticks were used in Britain in the days of king Edgar, 959 ("silver candelabra and gilt candelabra well and honorably made")

Candy or **Kandy.** CEYLON

Canicular Period. DOG-DAYS

Can'næ, a small village in Apulia, Italy where, on Aug 2, 216 B.C (or in June, corrected date), Hannibal, with 50 000 Africans, Gauls, and Spaniards, defeated Paulus Æmilius and Terentius Varro, with 88 000 Romans The Roman army was nearly annihilated Among the slain was the consul Æmilius, his chief officers, and above 80 senators. Hannibal lost about 6000 men The consul Varro escaped with a few cavalry, him the Roman senate thanked instead of blaming, because "he had not despaired of the Roman commonwealth."

can'nibal, an Indian term, thought to be a form of Carribal, as Columbus, in 1493, found the CARIBS of the West Indies cannibals *Anthropophagi* (man-eaters) are mentioned by Homer and Herodotus Cannibalism is still practised in some South-sea islands and other savage countries

cannon. Gibbon describes a cannon employed by Mahomet II at the siege of Adrianople, 1453. ARTILLERY, FIRE-ARMS

First cannon cast in England was by Hugget, at Uckfield, Sussex, 1543

Mons Meg, a large cannon (above 13 ft long, 20 in calibre) in Edinburgh castle said to have been cast at Mons, in Hainault, in 1486, but more probably forged at castle Douglas, Galloway, by three brothers named McKim, and presented by them to James II at the siege of Threive castle 1455 It was removed to London 1754, but, at the request of sir Walter Scott restored to Edinburgh, 1829

A cannon of Mahomet II, dated 1464, presented to the British government by the sultan of Turkey, and placed in the Artillery museum Woolwich, 1868

Moolk e-Murdan, an Indian bronze gun of Beejapoor, calibre 23 in, 17th century

At Ehrenbreitstein castle opposite Coblentz, on the Rhine, is a cannon, 18½ ft long, 1½ ft in diameter in the bore, and 3 ft 4 in. in the breech, the ball for it weighs 180 lbs., and its charge of powder 94 lbs It was made by one Simon 1529

In Dover castle is a brass gun (called queen Elizabeth's pocket pistol), 24 ft. long, a present from Charles V to Henry VIII

Fine specimens in the Tower of London

A leathern cannon fired 3 times in the king's park, Edinburgh (Phillips) 23 Oct 1788

Turkish piece now in St. James's park, London, taken by French at Alexandria, was retaken, and placed in the park, Mch 1803

Messrs Horsfall's monster wrought iron gun completed, May, 1856, at Liverpool, is 15 ft. 10 in long, weighs 21 tons 17 cwt. 1 qr 14 lbs, and cost 3500*l*. With a charge of 25 lbs the shot struck a target 2000 yards distant. It has been since presented to government. Wm G Armstrong knighted, 18 Feb. 1859

Armstrong had been working for 4 years on gun making and had succeeded in producing "a breech-loading rifled wrought iron gun of great durability and of extreme lightness, combining a great extent of range and extraordinary accuracy" The range of a 32 lb. gun charged with 5 lbs of powder was a little more than 5 miles. The Armstrong gun is said at equal distances, to be 57 times more accurate than common artillery, which it greatly exceeds, also in destructive effects. The British government engaged the services of sir W Armstrong for 10 years (commencing with 1855) for 20,000*l*., as consulting engineer of rifled ordnance . 22 Feb "

Mr Whitworth's guns and rifles greatly commended 1860–70

An American cannon, weighing 35 tons, then the largest in the world, cast . 1860

Targets like the sides of the English man of war *Warrior*, 3 5 in plates of wrought iron bolted together, pierced 3 times by 156 lb. shot from an Armstrong gun, smooth bore, muzzle loaded with charges of 40 lbs. powder, twice, and once of 50 lbs 8 Apr 1862

Horsfall gun, with a charge of 75 lbs powder and a shot of 270 lbs, smashed a *Warrior* target. 16 Sept "

Armstrong's gun, "Big Will," tried and pronounced to be perfect, weight, 22 tons, length, 15 ft., range with shot weighing 510 lbs., 748 to 4187 yards 19 Nov 1863

Capt. Palliser, by experiment, has shown that iron shot cast in cold iron moulds, instead of hot sand, is much harder and equals steel, he also suggested lining cast-iron guns with wrought iron exits 1864

At Shoeburyness, Palliser's chilled metal shot (250 lbs), by 43 lbs. of powder, in a 9-in muzzle-loading wrought-iron Woolwich rifle gun is sent through a target of 8 in rolled iron 18 in teak and ⅜ in iron, and about 20 ft beyond 14 Sept 1866

[His patent is dated 27 May 1863 James Nasmyth had previously suggested the use of chilled iron]

American 15 in naval gun, with a cast iron spherical shot (453 lbs) greatly damages an 8 in target, other experiments at Shoeburyness 23 July, 1867

Continued experiments at Shoeburyness, Plymouth model fort, with 15 in solid shield plates tried with 23 ton gun of 12 in bore, bearing 600 lb Palliser shot, exterior of fort destroyed interior intact, the 10 in English gun shown to be superior to American and Prussian great guns 16-24 June, 1868

"Woolwich Infant," 35 tons largest gun then ever made, length, 16 ft 3 in, formed of a steel tube with coiled breech piece, designed to fire a 700 lb projectile with 120 lb charge, made at Woolwich in 1870 when tried in Dec 1871, the inner tube cracked others made 1872

"Woolwich Infant" experimental gun constructing at Woolwich—80 tons. 27 ft long. for 1650 lb shot 300 lbs of powder May, 1874

81 ton gun tried at Woolwich, shot, 1250 lbs, 130 lbs of powder, 12 men rammed in the charge shot penetrated 50 ft of sand tried successfully 18 Sept 1875, 24-26 July with 370 lbs of powder 4 Aug 1876

Gen von Uchatius's steel bronze cannon making at Vienna, Sept 1875, reported successful Sept "

Sir William Armstrong's 100 ton gun for Italy tried successfully at Spezzia, 2000 lb shot and 330 lbs of powder 21 Oct "

81 ton (or 80 ton) gun tried at Shoeburyness for sea range with 1700 lb Palliser shell, 27 Sept et seq 1876 and 1 Feb 1877

4 100 ton guns by Armstrong ordered by British government, Mch 1878

A 100 ton gun tried at Woolwich, 13 June, finally proved, 16 July, 1879

Great guns by Krupp successfully tried at Meppen, Hanover, 5-8 Aug "

Breech loading cannon ordered to be made Dec "

A Krupp gun, 130 tons cast for Italy Oct 1884

Sir Wm Armstrong's 111-ton gun tried at Woolwich, length 43 ft. 8 in, charge 960 lbs of gunpowder, weight of projectile 1800 lbs, range of about 8 miles, said to be the largest gun in the world June, 1887

Graydon torpedo projector announced Mch 1889

Zalinski gun for the projection of dynamite adopted by the U S for coast defence, Feb 1889, by the British government, Feb 1890

Messrs Krupp, of Essen, make a gun weighing 270 000 lbs., for Cronstadt, reported 10 Mch "

Giffard gun, in which the propelling agent is liquefied carbonic acid gas, the invention of Paul Giffard a French engineer, the gas is said to be cheaply manufactured liquefied, and stored, many experiments on the continent reported successful 1889-90, M Giffard exhibited and discharged rifles, illustrating his inventions in London before a number of distinguished persons 18 July, "

Hotchkiss Ordnance Company registered 1887, their weapons effective in suppressing the Indian revolt in the U S Dec. "

Lieut James W Graydon, late of U S navy, invents the Graydon dynamite gun, in which dynamite shells are discharged by means of condensed air the force of the dynamite being moderated by means of non conductors of heat, one of these guns manufactured by Taunton & Co, Birmingham Jan 1891

cannon in the United States Cannon were cast at Lynn, Mass., by Henry Leonard, in 1647, and at Orr's foundery, Bridgewater, 1648 In 1735 the Hope furnace was established in Rhode Island, where 6 heavy cannon, ordered by the state, were cast in 1775 The heaviest guns used at this time were 18-pounders

William Denning makes wrought iron cannon of staves bound together with wrought iron bands, and bored and breeched 1790

Board of ordnance established 1812

Col Bomford, of the U S ordnance department, invents a cannon called the *Columbiad*, a long chambered piece for projecting solid shot and shell with a heavy charge of powder . "

West Point foundery established under special patronage of the government 1817

First contract of Gouverneur Kemble, president, for the West Point Foundery Association, for 32 42 pounders, long guns, 11 July, 1820

First gun rifled in America at the South Boston's Iron Company's foundery 1834

Cyrus Alger patents and makes the first malleable iron guns cast and converted in an oven 1836

Earliest piece of heavy ordnance cast at the South Boston foundery, a 10 in columbiad, under the supervision of col Bomford, weight, 14,500 lbs., shot, 130 lbs., shell, 90 lbs., charge of powder, 18 lbs 6 Sept. 1839

Board of ordnance sent to Europe to inspect European ordnance and ordnance works "

Character of "gun iron" definitely fixed by the "metallodynamoter," a testing machine invented by major Wade. 1840

South Boston Iron Company erect the heaviest shops then in the U S for the manufacture of ordnance 1842

First 12 in columbiad, weight, 25,510 lbs., extreme range, 5761 yds, weight of shell, 172 lbs, charge of powder, 20 lbs., cast at the South Boston foundery ..... . 8 July, 1846

Dahlgren gun, of iron, cast solid and cooled from the exterior, very thick at breach and diminishing to muzzle, first cast. May, 1850
Rodman gun a columbiad model smooth bore made by the Rodman process of hollow casting cooled from the interior, adopted by the U S for all sea coast cannon 1860
First 10 pound Parrott gun of iron cast hollow, cooled from the inside and strengthened by an exterior tube made of wrought iron bars spirally coiled and shrunk on, made at the West Point foundery "
15 in Rodman gun weighing 49,000 lbs, cast by the South Boston Iron Company "
Parrott gun first put to test of active warfare in the battle of Bull Run 21 July, 1861
S B Dean, of South Boston Iron Company patents a process of rough boring bronze guns and forcibly expanding the bore to its finished size by means of mandrels. 1869
Pneumatic dynamite torpedo gun built and mounted at fort Lafayette (founded on invention of D M Mefford of Ohio) 1885
Congress makes an appropriation for the establishment of a plant for gun making at the Watervliet arsenal, West Troy 1889
Manufacture of heavy ordnance begun at the Washington navy yard 1890

canoe. In the *Rob Roy*, a lightly-constructed canoe, "giving the pleasure of a yacht without the expense," J Macgregor, in 1865, travelled about 1000 miles on the rivers and lakes of Europe His second cruise was on the Baltic He explored the Suez canal, Nov, and the rivers of Syria, Dec 1868, and the canals and lakes of Holland in the summer of 1871 The *Octoroon* (16 feet long, 23 inches broad) crossed the Channel from Boulogne to Dover in 11 hours, 19 Aug 1867 The Royal Canoe Club founded, 1866, the prince of Wales president, 1876 There are several canoe clubs in the United States, and an annual canoe regatta is held at lake George, N Y The most remarkable canoe voyages made in the U S have been those of N H Bishop, of lake George, who sailed and paddled, upon inland water-ways, from the Canada line, *via* New York, Norfolk, and Charleston, to the Gulf of Mexico on one voyage, and on another, down the Ohio and Mississippi rivers.

New York Canoe Club, first in U S, organized autumn, 1870
Mr Fowler crossed from Boulogne to Sandgate standing in an india rubber twin canoe (the *Podoscaphe*) in 12 hours, 19 Aug 1878
American Canoe Association, organized at lake George, N Y, 3 Aug. 1880

canon, a piece of music in two or more parts, echoing each other "Non nobis, Domine," by Birde (d. 1523), is an early specimen

Canonicus, chief of the Narragansetts MASSACHUSETTS, 1622

canonization of pious men and martyrs as saints was instituted by pope Leo III, 800 —*Tallent* Every day in the calendar is now a saint's day The first canonization by the pope was of St. Udalricus, Ulric, in 993 Previously it was by the bishops and people —*Hénault*. On 8 June, 1862, the pope canonized 27 Japanese, who had been put to death on 5 Feb 1597, near Nagasaki, and 25 others, on 29 June, 1867 Among persons canonized by pope Pius IX in Oct 1872, was the late queen of Naples. Sir Thomas More, bishop John Fisher, and others were canonized, Jan 1887

canons, apostolical, ascribed to the apostles by Bellarmin and Baronius, by others to St. Clement, are certainly of much later date (since 325) The Greek church allows 85, the Latin 50 of them. The first ecclesiastical canon was promulgated 380 —*Usher* Canon-law of the church was introduced into Europe by Gratian about 1140, and into England in 1154 —*Stow* DECRETALS The present canons and constitutions of the church of England, collected from former ordinances, were established in 1603 by the clergy in convocation, and ratified by king James I., 1604 A new body of canons, formed by the convocation in 1640, were declared unlawful by the commons, 16 Dec. 1641 —An intermediate class of religious, between priests and monks, in the 8th century, were termed canons, as living by a rule Canons in some of the English cathedrals and collegiate churches resemble the prebendaries in others Endowment of canonries was facilitated by the Cathedrals act, 1873

Cano'pus, an ancient city of Lower Egypt, now a heap of ruins, on the Mediterranean, about 15 miles to the east of the present city of Alexandria. Said to have been so named by Canopus, the pilot of Menelaus in the Trojan expedition, and who it is said died here ABOUKIR, STARS.

Canossa, a castle in Modena. Here the emperor Henry IV of Germany submitted to penance imposed by his enemy, pope Gregory VII (Hildebrand), then living at the castle, the residence of the countess Matilda Henry was exposed for several days to the inclemency of winter, Jan 1077, till the pope admitted him, and granted absolution Matilda greatly increased the temporal power of the papacy by bequeathing to it her large estates, to the injury of her second husband, Guelph, duke of Bavaria A Canossa monument, near Harzburg, was inaugurated 26 Aug 1877, commemorating the arrogance of the popes

Can'terbury, Kent, Engl, the *Durovernum* of the Romans, and capital of Ethelbert, king of Kent, who reigned 560–616 He was converted to Christianity by Augustin, 596, upon whom he bestowed many favors, giving him land for an abbey and cathedral, 602 St. Martin's church is the oldest Saxon church in Britain The riot at Boughton, near Canterbury, produced by a fanatic called Tom or Thom, who assumed the name of sir William Courtenay, occurred 28–31 May, 1838 THOMITES The railway to London was completed in 1846 —The archbishop is primate and metropolitan of all England, and the first peer in the realm, having precedence of all officers of state, and of all dukes not of the blood royal BISHOPS IN ENGLAND Canterbury had formerly jurisdiction over Ireland, and the archbishop was styled a patriarch This see has yielded to the church of Rome 18 saints and 9 cardinals, and to the civil state of England 12 lord chancellors and 4 lord treasurers. This see was made superior to York, 1073 YORK The revenue is valued in the king's books at 2816*l* 7*s* 9*d*.—*Beatson* Present income, 15,000*l* The cathedral was sacked by the Danes, 1011, and burned down, 1067, rebuilt by Lanfranc and Anselm, and the choir, completed by the prior Conrad in 1130, and in which Becket was murdered, 1170, was burned, 1174 It was partly rebuilt by William of Sens (1174–78), and completed by William Anglus, "English William," 1178–84 A new nave was built and other parts 1378–1410 The great central tower was erected by prior Goldstone about 1495 The gorgeous shrine of Becket, built 1175, was stripped at the Reformation, and his bones burned. This shrine was thronged for 3 centuries by pilgrims and worshippers of all classes, from kings and emperors down, a pilgrimage to the shrine becoming not only a pious exercise, but a fashionable summer excursion Chaucer has given us an admirable picture of one in his "Canterbury Tales." Here were interred Edward the Black Prince, Henry IV, cardinal Pole, and other distinguished persons. Part of the roof was destroyed by an accidental fire, and the edifice narrowly escaped, 3 Sept 1872 The clock-tower was nearly on fire, 2 June, 1876 HUGUENOTS. There have been 95 archbishops of Canterbury, including the present archbishop Benson, of whom the following are conspicuous

St. Augustin or Austin, 1st 602–5
St Dunstan 23d in order 959–88
Stigand 32d in order (deprived by William the Conqueror), 1052–70
Thomas à Becket, 38th in order 1162–70
[BECKET'S MURDER, 29 Dec]
Simon Sudbury, 68th in order 1375–81
[Beheaded by the insurrectionists under Wat Tyler, 14 June, 1381]
Thomas Cranmer, 70th in order 1533–56
[Burned during the reign of Queen Mary, 21 Mch. 1556]
William Laud, 77th in order 1633–45
[Beheaded, 10 Jan 1645, see vacant 16 years.]
Edward White Benson, present archbishop, 95th in order; elected 29 Jan 1883

"Canterbury Tales," by Geoffrey Chaucer, were written before 1400, and first printed about 1475 or 1476 (by Caxton). Chaucer society established, 1867 LITERATURE

canthar'ides, venomous green beetles (called Spanish flies), employed to raise blisters This use is ascribed to Aretæus of Cappadocia, about 50 B C.

Can'ticles, a name given to the Benedictus, Magnificat, Nunc dimittis, etc, in the Book of Common Prayer, and especially to the Song of Solomon.

can'tilever, defined as "a structure overhung from a fixed base" Principle used in bridge-building. BRIDGES.

Canton, founded about 200 B.C, the only city in China with which Europeans were allowed to trade, till the treaty of 29 Aug 1842. Merchants arrived here in 1517. English factory established, 1680 A fire, destroying 15,000 houses,

1822 An inundation swept away 10,000 houses and 1000 persons, Oct 1833 Canton was taken by the British in 1857, restored, 1861 CHINA, 1835, 1839, 1856, 1861 Pop. 1890 estimated at 1,600,000

Canuleian law, permitting the patricians and plebeians to intermarry, was passed at Rome, 445 B C

caoutchouc (*coo'chook*) or **India-rubber,** an elastic resinous substance that exudes from incisions in certain trees in South America, Mexico, Africa, and Asia especially *Castillon Hevea* or *Siphonia elastica*, and *Ficus elastica*.

Observed at Hayti by Columbus (*Herrera*) 1493
Described by Torquemada 1615
Discovered by La Condamine in Quito (termed by natives *cahoutchou*), brought to Europe about 1735
Dr Priestley said that he had seen "a substance excellently adapted to the purpose of wiping from paper the marks of a black lead pencil" It was sold at the rate of 3s the cubic half inch 1770
India-rubber cloth was made by Samuel Peal and patented 1791
Caoutchouc discovered in the Malay archipelago, 1798, in Assam 1810
Vulcanized rubber (India rubber combined with sulphur so that it remains firm at all ordinary temperatures) patented in America by C Goodyear 1839
Invented also by T Hancock (of the firm of Mackintosh & Co), and patented. 1843
Mr Goodyear invented the hard rubber (termed ebonite) as a substitute for horn and tortoise shell 1849
A mode of retaining India rubber in its natural fluid state (by liquid ammonia) patented in England for Henry Lee Norris, of New York 1853
PRINTING
African caoutchouc imported into England 1856
In 1823 500 pairs of shoes were imported into Boston Gum elastic soon became the subject of scientific investigation, and of many experiments In 1832, the manufacture was commenced in Massachusetts by John Haskins and Edwin M Chaffee, who with others, started the Roxbury India rubber Company, soon after incorporated with a capital of $400,000 For this company Mr Chaffee invented the mammoth machine for spreading rubber without a solvent, costing nearly $30,000 Similar machines are now required by all manufacturers of rubber goods The prosperity of this company gave rise to factories in Boston Chelsea Woburn, and Framingham (Mass) New York city, Staten Island, and Troy (N Y), with capitals of from $50 000 to $500,000 These companies made their goods by dissolving the rubber in camphene and other solvents, then mixing lampblack with it, and spreading the paste on cloth from which coats, etc, are made The goods were then dried in the sun or in a warm room until the solvent evaporated, leaving a coating of rubber In 1856 the U S imported crude India rubber to the amount of $97,796, and exported to the amount of $1 093,602 of rubber goods In 1880, the U S imported crude India rubber to the amount of 13,981,964 lbs, valued at $9,606,289

Cape Breton, a large island at the entrance of the gulf of St Lawrence, and separated from Nova Scotia by the narrow strait or gut of Canso, discovered by Cabot, 1497. The French fortress, LOUISBURG, was situated on this island. Island ceded to England, 10 Feb 1763 Incorporated with Nova Scotia, 1819 Pop 1891, 86,914

Cape Coast Castle, on the gold coast of upper Guinea, S W. Africa Settled by the Portuguese in 1610, taken by the Dutch, 1643, demolished by admiral Holmes in 1661 All the British factories and shipping along the coast were destroyed by the Dutch admiral, De Ruyter, in 1665 It was confirmed to the English by the treaty of Breda in 1667 ASHANTEES.

Cape Finisterre, N W Spain. Off this cape admirals lord Anson and Warren defeated and captured a French fleet under De la Jonquiere, 3 May, 1747

Cape of Good Hope, Cape Colony, a promontory on the S point of Africa, called "Cabo Tormentoso" (the stormy cape), the "Lion of the Sea," and the "Head of Africa," discovered by Bartholomew de Diaz, 1487 Its present name was given by John II of Portugal, who augured favorably of future discoveries from Diaz having reached the extremity of Africa. Area of Cape Colony, 221,311 sq miles. Pop in 1856, 267,096, 1891, 1,525,739

Cape doubled, and the passage to India discovered by Vasco da Gama 19 Nov 1497
CAPE TOWN, the capital, founded by the Dutch 1650
Colony taken by the English under admiral Elphinstone and gen. Clarke 16 Sept 1795
Restored at peace of Amiens 25 Mch. 1802
Taken by sir D Baird and sir H Popham. 9 Jan. 1806
Ceded to England 13 Aug 1814
British emigrants arrive Mch 1820
Kaffirs make irruptions on British settlements, and ravage Grahamstown Oct 1834
People defeat attempt to make the cape a penal colony 19 May, 1849
Territories north of Great Orange river placed under British authority, 3 Feb 1848, annexed as the Orange River territory, Mch 1851
Constitution promulgated and joyfully received 1 July 1853
British jurisdiction over Orange River territory abandoned 30 Jan, a free state formed Feb 1854
First parliament meets at Cape Town 1 July "
First railway from Cape Town about 58 miles long opened about Dec 1860
Discovery of diamonds, disputes between free states and the tribes. 1867-70
Colony of Griqualand constituted. 27 Oct 1871
British flag raised over diamond fields 17 Nov "
Great success in diamond fields robbery of diamonds valued between 35,000*l* and 40 000*l*, oppression of natives stopped by sir H Barkly Aug 1872
Transvaal republic annexed 12 Apr 1877
Troublesome disputes between tribes (Fingoes and Galekas) lead to war Sept "
Minister Molteno opposes employing imperial troops in Kaffir war Jan Feb 1878
Kaffir war ended, amnesty to surrendering rebels announced, 2 July, "
Zulu war begins 12 Jan 1879
Insurrection in the Transvaal Dec "
Telegraphic communication with Great Britain completed, telegram from the queen to sir Bartle Frere and others, 25 Dec "
War with Basutos June 1880
Transvaal difficulty settled 1880-81
Railway to Kimberley opened Nov 1885
Conference of delegates from Cape Colony, Natal and Orange Free State, at Cape Town, object, South African federation, 18 Feb 1888
Junction railway between Cape Colony and Orange Free State, 10 Mch 1892
ORANGE FREE STATE, ZULULAND, etc

Cape Horn or **Hoorn,** on the southernmost island of the Fuegian archipelago, south of South America, was discovered and named by Schouten, 1616, after his birthplace in the Netherlands AMERICA

Cape St. Vincent, S W Portugal Sir George Rooke, with 23 ships of war, and the Turkish fleet, was attacked by Tourville, with 160 ships, off cape St. Vincent, 12 English and Dutch men-of-war and 80 merchantmen were captured or destroyed by the French, 16 June, 1693 Sir John Jervis, with the Mediterranean fleet of 15 sail, defeated the Spanish fleet of 27 ships of the line off this cape, taking 4 ships and sinking others, 14 Feb. 1797 For this victory sir John was made earl St Vincent Nelson was engaged in this battle Near this cape the fleet of dom Pedro, under admiral Charles Napier, captured dom Miguel's fleet, 5 July, 1833

Cape Town, 30 miles north of the Cape of Good Hope, capital of Cape Colony, founded, 1650, by the Dutch Pop 1891, 51,083, or with suburbs, 83,718

Cape Verde islands, on the west coast of Africa, off Cape Verde, about 15° n lat, now belonging to Portugal, known to the ancients as Gorgades, were rediscovered by Antonio de Noli, a Genoese navigator in the service of Portugal, 1446, 1450, or 1460 Area of the group, 1700 sq miles. Santiago, the largest and most fertile, runs to a height of 7380 ft, and has the chief town

Capetians, the third race of the kings of France, named from Hugo Capet, count of Paris and Orleans, who seized the throne on the death of Louis V., called the Indolent, 987 —*Henault* The first line of the house of Capet ended with Charles IV, in 1328, when Philip VI of Valois ascended the throne FRANCE

capillarity, the rising of liquids in small tubes, and the ascent of the sap in plants, is said to have been first observed by Niccolo Aggiunti, of Pisa, 1600-35. The theory has been examined by Newton, La Place, and others Dr. T. Young's theory was put forth in 1805, and Mr. Wertheim's researches in 1857

capital punishment. DEATH PENALTY

Capitol, said to have been so called from a human head (*caput*) found when digging the foundations of the fortress of Rome, on Mons Tarpeius. Here a temple was built to Jupiter Capitolinus. The foundation was laid by Tarquinius Priscus, 616 B.C. The building was continued by Servius Tullius, completed by Tarquinius Superbus, but not dedicated till 507 B.C., by the consul Horatius. It covered 8 acres. The ascent to it from the forum was by 100 steps. It was destroyed by lightning, 6 July, 183 B.C., burned during the civil wars, 83 B.C., rebuilt by Sulla, and dedicated by Q Catulus, 69 B.C., it was again burned in the trouble under Vitellius, 69 A.D., part rebuilt and burned again under Titus, 80 A.D., rebuilt for the last time by Domitian, 82 A.D., more grandly than ever, sacked by Genseric, June, 455 The Roman consuls made large donations to this temple, and the emperor Augustus bestowed on it at one time 2000 pounds' weight of gold of which metal the roof was composed. The gilding of the arch of the temple, which was undertaken after the destruction of Carthage, cost 21,000 talents The gates were of brass covered with plates of gold, its thresholds were of brass, and its interior was all of marble, decorated with vessels and shields of solid silver The *Capitoline games*, instituted 387 B.C., to commemorate the deliverance from the Gauls were revived by Domitian, 86 A.D. The Campidoglio contains palaces of the senators, erected on the site of the Capitol by Michael Angelo soon after 1546

capitularies, the laws of the Frankish kings, commencing with Charlemagne (801) Collections have been published by Baluze (1677) and others

Cappadocia, Asia Minor. Its early history is involved in obscurity

	B.C.
Pharnaces said to have founded the kingdom	744
Cappadocia conquered by Perdiccas, regent of Macedon, the king, Ariarathes I, aged 82, crucified	322
Recovers its independence	315
Conquered by Mithridates of Pontus	291
Held by Seleucus, 288, independent	288
Ariarathes V Philopator reigns, 162, dethroned by Holophernes, 158 B.C. but assisted by Attalus, king of Pergamus, he regains his throne, 155 B.C., killed with Crassus in the war against Aristonicus	130
His queen, Laodice, poisons 5 of her sons, the 6th (Ariarathes VI) is saved, she is put to death	"
Ariarathes VI murdered by Mithridates Eupator, who sets up various pretenders, the Roman senate declares the country free, and appoints Ariobarzanes I king	93
He is several times expelled by Mithridates, etc., but restored by the Romans, d	64
Ariobarzanes II supports Pompey, and is slain by Crassus	42
Ariarathes VII deposed by Antony	36
Archelaus is favored by Augustus 20 B.C., but, accused by Tiberius, he comes to Rome and dies there	A.D. 15
Cappadocia becomes a Roman province	17
Invaded by Huns	515
And by Saracens	717
Recovered by emperor Basil I	876
Conquered by Soliman and the Turks.	1074
Annexed to Turkish empire	1360

Cappel, Switzerland Here the reformer Ulric Zwinglius was slain in a conflict between Catholics and the men of Zurich, 11 Oct 1531

Capri (Capreæ), an island near Naples, the sumptuous residence of Augustus, and particularly of Tiberius, memorable for the debaucheries he committed during his last years, 27–37 The whole island is full of Roman remains, and has yielded to the archæologist a rich harvest of coins, inscriptions, etc

capstan, used to work a ship's anchor, perhaps invented, certainly improved, by sir Samuel Morland, who died 30 Dec. 1695

Capua, Naples, capital of Campania, took the part of Hannibal when his army wintered here after the battle of Cannæ, 216 B.C. In 211, when the Romans retook the city, they scourged and beheaded the surviving senators—many had poisoned themselves after a banquet previous to the surrender of the city. Only 2 persons escaped, one woman who had prayed for the success of the Romans, and another who succored some prisoners During the middle ages Capua was successively subjugated by the Greeks, Saracens, Normans, and Germans. Restored to Naples in 1424, captured by Cæsar Borgia, 24 July, 1501; taken by Garibaldi, 2 Nov. 1860

Capuchin friars, Franciscans, so named from wearing a *capuchon*, or cowl, hanging down the back. The order was founded by Matthew Baschi about 1525, and established by pope Clement VII, 1529.

Cara'cas, S. America, part of Venezuela, discovered by Columbus, 1498 It was reduced by arms, and assigned as property to the Welsers, German merchants, by Charles V, but for their tyranny they were dispossessed in 1550, and a crown governor appointed The province declared its independence, 9 May, 1810. In the city Leon de Caracas, on 26 Mch 1812, nearly 12,000 persons perished by an earthquake. VENEZUELA

caravel, a small sea-going vessel of about 100 tons' burden, built somewhat like a galley, formerly used by the Spanish and Portuguese, two of the vessels of Columbus on his first voyage to America were caravels. AMERICA

Carberry hill, S Scotland. Here lord Hume and the confederate barons dispersed the royal army under Bothwell, and took Mary queen of Scots prisoner, 15 June, 1567 Bothwell fled

carbo-dynamite, a powerful explosive of the nitroglycerine class, invented by Reid and Borland, tried in 1888 and 1889, said to be perfect.

carbolic acid or **phenic acid,** obtained by distilling pit-coal by Laurent, 1846-47, is a powerful antiseptic It is largely manufactured for medical purposes, and has been used in England at Carlisle and Exeter to deodorize sewage (1860–61), and as a disinfectant during the prevalence of cholera in London in 1866, and of yellow fever in the Southern States in recent years Used for embalming by prof Seely, in 1868

carbon (symbol, C, atomic weight, 12) was shown to be a distinct element by Lavoisier in 1788 He proved the diamond to be its purest form, and produced carbonic-acid gas by burning it. It is a constituent of all animal and vegetable tissues and coal.

Carbona'ri (charcoal-burners), a powerful secret society in Italy, which became prominent, 1808–14 It sought to drive foreigners, especially the French, from Italy, and establish civil and religious liberty In Mch 1820, it is said that 650,000 joined the society, and an insurrection soon after broke out in Naples, gen Pepe taking the command. The king, Ferdinand, made political concessions, but the allied sovereigns at Laybach induced him to annul them and suppress the liberal party, Jan 1821, when the Carbonari were denounced as traitors The society spread in France, and doubtless hastened the revolutions in 1830 and 1848.

carbonic-acid gas, a gaseous compound of carbon and oxygen, found in the air; a product of combustion, respiration, and fermentation The Grotto del Cane yields 200,000 lbs per annum. No animal can breathe this gas The briskness of champagne, beer, etc., is due to its presence It was liquefied by atmospheric pressure by Faraday in 1823. On exposing the liquid to the air part of it evaporates so rapidly that the remainder is frozen to a solid much like snow.

Carcassonne (*kar-kas-sonn'*), the chief town of the department of Aude, France, the site of *Carcaso*, an ancient city of Gaul From the 9th century till 1300 A.D. it formed a separate countship, and was captured by Simon de Montfort in his crusade against the Albigenses, 1209 Since the 12th century it has been noted for its manufacture of woollen cloth The old town has been restored as a fortress of the middle ages, by the French government, and is the best preserved example of a stronghold of the days before artillery was invented.

Cardiff castle, S Wales, built in the 11th century. Here Robert, duke of Normandy, eldest son of William I, is said to have been imprisoned from 1106 till his death, 10 Feb. 1135. Cromwell (1648) got possession of the castle through treachery, after bombarding it for 3 days, he afterwards hanged the traitor as a warning to his own soldiery.—*Chambers' Encyc.*

Cardiff giant (a noted hoax) discovered on the farm of W C. Newell, near Cardiff, Onondaga Co., New York. NEW YORK, 1869

cardinals, princes in the church of Rome, the council of the pope, and the conclave or "sacred college," at first were the principal priests or incumbents of the parishes in Rome, and said to have been called *cardinales* in 853. They claimed the exclusive power of electing the pope about 1179 They first wore the red hat to remind them that they ought to shed their blood for religion, if required, and were declared princes of the church by Innocent IV., 1243 or 1245. Paul II gave the scarlet habit, 1464, and Urban VIII the title of Eminence in 1623 or 1630. In 1586 Sixtus V. fixed their number at 70, viz., 6 cardinal bishops, 50 cardinal priests, and 14 cardinal deacons, but there are generally vacancies. In 1860 there were 69 cardinals; in 1864, 59; in Nov. 1867, 52; in 1873, 5 of the order of bishops, 34 priests, 6 deacons; 45 in all. 9 cardinals (one a Bonaparte) were made 13 Mch. 1868. 11 new cardinals appointed 12 Mch. 1877. In 1880, 6 cardinal-bishops, 47 priests, 11 deacons; in all 64 (including archbishops Manning, McCloskey, Ledochowski, Edward Howard, and John Henry Newman. *English cardinals:* Henry Stuart, created 1747; Charles Erskine, 1801; Thomas Weld, 1830; Charles Acton, 1839; Nicholas Wiseman, 30 Sept. 1850-65; Henry Edward Manning, 1875 (d. 14 Jan. 1892); Edward Howard, 12 Mch. 1877; John Henry Newman, 12 May, 1879 (d. 21 Aug. 1890); Edward McCabe, 27 Mch. 1882 (d. 11 Feb. 1885). *In the United States:* first cardinal, John McCloskey, 15 Mch. 1875 (d. 10 Oct. 1885); second cardinal, James Gibbon of Baltimore, 7 June, 1886.

cards, playing. The origin of these is uncertain. They are said to have been brought to Viterbo, Italy, in 1379. Cards were illuminated for Charles VI. of France, 1392, then depressed in mind. W. A. Chatto's work on the "History of Playing-cards," pub. 1848. Piquet and all the early names are French.

Caria, Asia Minor, was conquered by Cyrus, 546 B.C.; by Dercyllidas, a Lacedæmonian, 397; his successor Hecatomnus became king, 385 B.C.; for his son Mausolus the MAUSOLEUM was erected. Halicarnassus, the reputed birthplace of Herodotus, was situated in this country. Caria was annexed by the Romans, 129 B.C. It is now part of the Turkish empire.

Caribbee islands. WEST INDIES.

Caribs, the most important and warlike of the Indian tribes inhabiting the islands of the Caribbean sea, to which they gave the name. They were a terror to the other inhabitants of that region at the time of its discovery by Columbus. They are found now mostly in the republic of Honduras, to which place they were transported in a body by the English from the islands of Dominica and St. Vincent in 1796, owing to the continued disturbance they occasioned. They appear to have been addicted to cannibalism, and the word cannibal is not improbably derived from a corruption of the name.

caricatures. Bufalmaco, an Italian painter, about 1330, drew caricatures and put labels with sentences to the mouths of his figures. The modern caricatures of Gillray, Cruikshank, Rowlandson, H. B. (John Doyle $\frac{\text{ID}}{\text{ID}}$ = HB), Richard Doyle, John Leech, John Tenniel, Thomas Nast, and Du Maurier are justly celebrated. The well-known *Punch* was first published in 1841. The most eminent writers of fiction of the day and others (Douglas Jerrold, Thackeray, A'Becket, prof. E. Forbes, etc.) contributed to it. CHARIVARI, PUNCH. T. Wright published a "History of Caricature," 1865; and "The Life and Works of James Gillray," 1873. J. Grego published "T. Rowlandson's Works and Life," 1880. James Parton's "Caricature and other Comic Art in All Times and Many Lands" was published by Harper & Brothers in 1877.

Car'isbrooke castle, isle of Wight, said to have been a British and Roman fortress, was taken, 530, by Cerdic, founder of the kingdom of the West Saxons. Its Norman character has been ascribed to William Fitz-Osborne, earl of Hereford, in William I.'s time. Here Charles I. was imprisoned Nov. 1647, to Nov. 1648; and here his daughter Elizabeth, aged 15, died, probably of a broken heart, 8 Sept. 1650.

Cariz'mians, fierce shepherds living near the Caspian, having been expelled by the Tartars, invaded Syria in 1243. The union of the sultans of Aleppo, Hems, and Damascus was insufficient to resist them, and the Christian military orders were nearly exterminated in a single battle in 1244. In Oct. they took Jerusalem. They were totally defeated in 2 battles in 1247.

Carlaverock castle, S. Scotland, taken by Edward I., July, 1300, the subject of a contemporary poem published, with illustrations, by sir Harris Nicolas in 1828.

Carlisle (I.), a border town between England and Scotland, wherein for years a strong garrison was kept. Just below this town the famous Picts' wall began, which crossed the island to Newcastle-upon-Tyne; here also ended the great Roman highway. ROADS. Of the great church, called St. Mary's, a large part was built by David, king of Scotland, who held Cumberland, Westmoreland, and Northumberland, from the crown of England. The castle, destroyed by the Danes, 875, restored in 1092 by William II., was the prison of Mary queen of Scots in 1568. Taken by the parliamentary forces in 1645, and by the young Pretender, 15 Nov. 1745; retaken by the duke of Cumberland, 30 Dec. same year. The cathedral was founded by Walter, deputy for William Rufus. It was almost ruined by Cromwell, 1648, and partly repaired after the Restoration. It was reopened in 1856 after renovation costing 15,000*l*.—(II.) The county seat of Cumberland county, Penn. Seat of Dickinson college (Methodist). From this point col. Bouquet marched to the relief of fort Pitt in the Pontiac war, 1763. Occupied for a short time by the confederates under Lee, 1 July, 1863.

Carlists. Supporters of the Spanish pretender Don Maria Isidor Carlos de Bourbon (b. 1788, d. 1855), and of his son Don Carlos (b. 1818, d. 1861), and of his nephew Don Carlos (b. 1848), who is now put forward by the ultra legitimists as the true heir to the throne of France as well as Spain. SPAIN, 1830-40, 1872-76. The legitimists of Europe subscribed to their cause, 1873-76. A committee in London supplied arms and money. BOURBONS.

Carlovingians or **Carolingians,** the second dynasty of French kings, 752-987. Charles Martel (715-41) and Pepin his son (741-52) were mayors of the palace. The latter became king, 752. FRANCE.

Carlowitz, Austria. Here was concluded a treaty of peace between Turkey and the allies—Germany, Russia, Poland, and Venice—26 Jan. 1699, after the defeat of the Turks by prince Eugene at Zenta, 11 Sept. 1697, and Hungary was secured to Austria.

Carlsbad ("Charles's bath"), in Bohemia, the celebrated springs, said to have been discovered by the emperor Charles IV. in 1370. The most aristocratic watering-place in Europe. On 1 Aug. 1819, a congress was held here, when the great powers decreed measures to repress the liberal press, etc. Lat. 50° 13′ N., lon. 12° 53′ E.

Carmagnola (*kar-man-yo'la*), a town in Italy in the province of Turin. In the 16th century it was occupied by French, but fell to the Savoyards in 1588. On its capture in 1792 by French revolutionists, its name became famous as the title of a republican dancing-song, written about Aug. 1792; popular in France during the reign of terror, 1793-94. Every verse had the refrain, *Dansons la Carmagnole vive le son du canon.* CONDOTTIERI.

Carmathians, a Mahometan sect. Carmath, a Shiite, about 890, assumed the title of "the guide, the director," etc., including that of the representative of Mahomet, St. John the Baptist, and the angel Gabriel. His followers subdued Bahrein in 900, and devastated the East. Dissensions arose, and their power soon passed away.

Carmel, a rocky promontory of Palestine to the south of the bay of Acre, frequently alluded to in the Scriptures (1 Kings, xviii. 19, scene of Elijah's sacrifice; 2 Kings, ii. 25, iv. 25; Isa. xxxiii. 9, etc.). Here, in the 12th century, originated the order of the CARMELITES.

Carmelites or **White Friars,** of Mount Carmel, one of the 4 orders of mendicants with austere rules, founded by Berthold about 1156, and settled in France in 1252.—*Hénault.* Their rules were modified about 1540. They claimed succession from Elijah. They had numerous monasteries in England, and a precinct in London without the Temple, west of Blackfriars, is called Whitefriars, after a community of their order founded in 1245. A Carmelite church at Kensington was founded by archbishop Manning, July, 1865. The Carmelites, as well as other orders, were expelled from their houses in France in Oct. 1880.

Carnac, a village of France in the department of Morbihan. It owes its celebrity to the rude stone monuments in its vicinity, which are the most extensive and interesting of their kind. They consist of long avenues of standing stones, many of them of great size, some 18 ft. in height. The rock of which these various monuments are composed is the ordinary granite of the district For these and other prehistoric monuments consult sir John Lubbock's "Prehistoric Times" AVEBURY, STONEHENGE.

Carna'tic, a district of southern Hindostan, along the whole coast of Coromandel First invaded and conquered by the Mohammedans, 1370 Hyder Ali entered the Carnatic with 80,000 troops in 1780, and was defeated by the British, 2 June, 1782 It was overrun by Tippoo in 1790. The British acquired it by treaty, 31 July, 1801. INDIA

Carnegie Institution of Washington, founded by Andrew Carnegie, was incorporated 4 Jan. 1902, and endowed with $10,000,000 The conduct of the institution was intrusted to a board of 27 trustees chosen by the founder The purpose of the institution is to encourage investigation, research, and discovery, show the application of knowledge to the improvement of mankind, provide such buildings, laboratories books, and apparatus as may be needed, and afford instruction of an advanced character to students properly qualified to profit thereby Dr R S Woodward elected pres, Dec 13, 1904, vice D C Gilman, resigned

Carneian games, observed in many Grecian cities, particularly at Sparta (instituted about 675 B.C, in honor of Apollo, surnamed Carneus), lasted 9 days.

Carnifex Ferry, West Va, Battle of, fought Sept 10, 1861 McClellan, when assigned to the army of the Potomac, left the command in West Virginia to Rosecrans Floyd commanded the confederate forces on the Gauley river, and was attacked by Rosecrans at Carnifex Ferry It was rather a manœuvre than a battle, and during the night Floyd retreated

Carnival. A festival time in Roman Catholic countries at Shrovetide, or just before Lent

Carolinas. NORTH and SOUTH CAROLINA

Caroline, Amelia Augusta, queen. QUEEN CAROLINE.

Caroline islands, S Pacific, said to have been discovered by the Portuguese, 1525, also by the Spaniard Lopez de Villalobos, 1545, and named after Charles II of Spain, 1686 These islands were virtually given up to Spain in 1876 The Germans occupying some of the islands, Spain protested in Aug 1885 Spanish vessels arrived at the island of Yop, 21 Aug, the Germans landed and set up their flag, 24 Aug Dispute referred to the pope, the sovereignty awarded to Spain, with commercial concessions to Germany and Great Britain Agreement signed, 25 Nov, confirmed at Rome, 17 Dec 1885 Natives subdued, Spaniards in full possession, Feb 1891

carpet-baggers, a name of reproach given by the South to citizens of the North who went South after the war, 1861-65 Many of them went there with the best intentions, some in hope of political advancement by the aid of negro votes The movement served to retard rather than hasten reconciliation between the sections

carpets are of ancient use in the East In Egypt they were first applied to religious purposes by the priests of Heliopolis, and were used to garnish the palaces of the Pharaohs. The carpets of the Homeric age were generally white or plain cloths The manufacture of woollen carpets was introduced into France from Persia, in the reign of Henry IV, between 1589 and 1610. Some artisans who had quitted France in disgust established the English carpet manufacture, about 1750 A cork-carpet company was formed in 1862 The manufacture of carpets in the United States is very extensive and rapidly growing. GOBELIN, TAPESTRY

Carpi, N Italy. Here prince Eugene and the imperialists defeated the French 9 July, 1701

carrack or **karrack** (Ital. *caracca*), a large ship in the middle ages. The *Santa Anna*, the property of the knights of St. John, of about 1700 tons, sheathed with lead, was built at Nice about 1530 She was literally a floating fortress, and aided Charles V in taking Tunis in 1535 She carried a crew of 300 men and 50 pieces of artillery.

carriages. Erichthonius of Athens is said to have produced the first chariot about 1486 B.C. Rude carriages were known in France in the reign of Henry II., 1547 A.D.; in England in 1555 Henry IV of France had one without straps or springs They were made in England in the reign of Elizabeth, and then called whirlicotes. The duke of Buckingham, in 1619, drove 6 horses and the earl of Northumberland, in rivalry, drove 8 Carriages were let for hire in Paris in 1650, at the hôtel Fiacre hence the name *fiacre* Carlo Bianconi successfully introduced cars into Ireland about 1815. G A. Thrupp's "History of Coaches," pub 1877 CABRIOLETS, COACHES, etc

Carrickfergus, Antrim, Ireland Its castle is supposed to have been built by Hugh de Lacy in 1178 The town surrendered to the duke of Schomberg, 28 Aug 1689, the castle to the French admiral Thurot, Feb 1760

Carrick's ford, W Va Here, 14 July, 1861, the confederate gen Robt S. Garnett, having been defeated at Rich Mountain by gen McClellan, attempted on the retreat to check the Union advance, lost his life, and his command was routed Gen Garnett was a graduate of West Point, and the first general killed in the war

carrocium, a vehicle containing a crucifix and a banner, usually accompanied Italian armies in the middle ages The Milanese lost theirs at Cortenuova, 27 Nov 1237.

Carron ironworks, on the banks of the Carron, in Stirlingshire, established in 1760 The works in 1852 employed about 1600 men Here, since 1776, have been made the pieces of ordnance called *carronades* or *smashers*

carrots and other edible roots were imported into Great Britain from Holland and Flanders, about 1510

cartes de visite (*kärt'-dĕ-vĭ-zēt'*). The small photographic portraits thus termed are said to have been first taken at Nice, by M Ferrier, in 1857. The duke of Parma had his portrait placed upon his visiting-cards, and his example was soon followed in Paris and London.

Cartesian doctrines. PHILOSOPHY

Carthage, north coast of Africa, near Tunis, founded by Dido or Elissa, 878 B.C (869, *Blair*, 826, *Niebuhr*) She fled from her brother Pygmalion, king of Tyre, who had killed her husband, and took refuge in Africa. Carthage disputed the empire of the world with Rome, hence the Punic wars. The Carthaginians were reputed faithless, hence the term Punic faith. Cato the censor (about 146 B.C) always ended his speeches in the senate with "*Carthago delenda est!*" (Carthage must be destroyed!) Many councils held here, 200-535 A D.

	B C.
First alliance of Carthaginians and Romans	503
Carthaginians in Sicily defeated at Himera by Gelo, the elder Hamilcar perishes	480
They send 300 000 men into Sicily	407
Take Agrigentum	406
Siege of Syracuse	396
Carthaginians land in Italy	379
Their defeat by Timoleon at the Crimesus	339
Defeated by Agathocles, they immolate their children on the altar to Saturn	310
First Punic war begins (lasts 23 years)	264
Carthaginians defeated by the Roman consul Duilius in a naval engagement	260
Xanthippus defeats Regulus	255
Hasdrubal defeated by Metellus at Panormos	251
Regulus put to death	250
Romans defeated before Lilybæum	"
The great Hannibal born	247
Hasdrubal founds New Carthage (Carthagena)	242
End of first Punic war, Sicily lost by Carthage	241
War between the Carthaginians and African mercenaries	"
Hamilcar Barcas sent into Spain, takes his son, Hannibal at the age of 9 years, having first made him swear an eternal enmity to the Romans	238
Hamilcar killed	229
Hasdrubal assassinated	220
Hannibal conquers Spain as far as the Iberus	219
Second Punic war begins (lasts 17 years)	218
Hannibal crosses the Alps, and enters Italy	"
He defeats the Roman consuls at the TICINUS and TREBIA, 218, at the lake THRASYMENUS, 217, and at CANNÆ 2 Aug	216
Publius Scipio carries war into Spain and takes New Carthage	210
Hasdrubal, Hannibal's brother, arrives in Italy with his army, defeated and slain at the METAURUS	207
Carthaginians expelled from Spain by Scipio	206
Scipio arrives in Africa, and lays siege to Utica	204
Hannibal recalled to Carthage	203
Totally defeated at ZAMA	202
End of the second Punic war	201
Third Punic war, Scipio invades Africa	149

Carthage taken and burned, by order of the senate......July,	146
Colony settled at Carthage by C. Gracchus....................	122
Its rebuilding planned by Julius Cæsar.......................	46
And executed by his successors...........................	19 et seq.
	A.D.
A Christian bishopric..	200
Cyprian holds a council here.................................	252
Taken by Genseric the Vandal..........................9 Oct.	439
Retaken by Belisarius..	533
Ravaged by the Arabs...	647
Taken and destroyed by Hassan, the Saracenic governor of Egypt..	698
Carthaginian antiquities (excavated by Nathan Davis) brought to the British museum....................................	1861
His excavations about to be renewed..................Aug.	1876
Bosworth Smith's "Carthage" pub..............................	1878

Carthage, Mo., Battle of, fought 6 July, 1861. Sigel attacked the confederates under Price, Rains, and Jackson. Until 2 P.M. it was an artillery duel, and confederates were worsted. Sigel was then obliged to retreat, which he did skilfully, saving his baggage.

Carthagena or **New Carthage,** S.E. Spain, built by Hasdrubal, the Carthaginian general, 242 B.C.; taken by Scipio, 210 B.C. The modern Carthagena was taken by a British force under sir John Leake, June, 1706; retaken by the duke of Berwick, Nov. It was the last place held by the Intransigentes and Internationalists of Spain; was besieged by gen. Martin Campos, about 22 Aug. 1873. Bombardment begun 26 Nov., taken by gen. Lopez Dominguez, 12 Jan. 1874. SPAIN.

Carthagena, Colombia, South America, was founded in 1533 by Pedro de Heredia; in 1544 it was taken by the French; it was taken by sir Francis Drake in 1585; pillaged by the French buccaneers in 1697, who obtained from it over $5,000,000. The English admiral Vernon unsuccessfully besieged the town in 1741.

Carthusians, a religious order (springing from the Benedictines) founded by Bruno of Cologne, who retired with 6 companions about 1084 to CHARTREUSE, in the mountains of Dauphiné. Their austere rules were formed by Basil VII., their general. They appeared in England about 1180, and a monastery was founded by sir William Manny, 1371, on the site of the present Charter-house, London. CHARTER-HOUSE. The Carthusian powder of father Simon, at Chartreuse, was first compounded about 1715.

cartoons, large chalk drawings preparatory to oil painting. Those of Raphael (25 in number) were designed (for tapestries) in the chambers of the Vatican, under Julius II. and Leo X. about 1510 to 1516. The 7 preserved (what became of the other 18 has never been ascertained) were purchased in Flanders by Rubens for Charles I. of England, for Hampton-court palace in 1629. They were removed to South Kensington, 28 Apr. 1865. The tapestries executed at Arras from these designs are at Rome. They were twice carried away by invaders, in 1526 and 1798, and were restored in 1815. Besides the cartoons of Raphael, were those executed in competition by Leonardo da Vinci and Michael Angelo, two of which, the "Battle of the Standard," by the former, and the "Cartoon of Pisa"—soldiers bathing, surprised by the approach of the enemy—by the latter, were justly celebrated in art history. Both have perished, but the general design of them has been preserved. Cartoons for the British Houses of Parliament were exhibited in July, 1843.

RAPHAEL'S CARTOONS.

1. The Miraculous Draught of Fishes.
2. The Charge to Peter.
3. Peter and John Healing the Lame at the Gate of the Temple.
4. The Death of Ananias.
5. Elymas the Sorcerer Struck with Blindness.
6. The Sacrifice to Paul and Barnabas, at Lystra.
7. Paul Preaching at Athens.

Cashmere. KASHMIR.

Cassano, N. Italy. Site of an indecisive conflict between prince Eugene of Savoy and the French, 16 Aug. 1705.

Cassation, Court of, a supreme court of appeal in France, established 10 Nov. 1790, by the National Assembly.

Cassel, formerly the capital of Hesse-Cassel, central Germany, acquired importance by becoming the refuge of French Protestants after the revocation of the edict of Nantes, 1685. It was the capital of Jerome Bonaparte, king of Westphalia, 1807-13, and Wilhelmshöhe, a neighboring castle, became the residence of Napoleon III. after his surrender to the king of Prussia, 2 Sept. 1870, arriving at 9.35 P.M. 5 Sept. He went to England in 1871.

Castel Fidardo, near Ancona, central Italy. Near here gen. Lamoricière and the papal army of 11,000 men were totally defeated by the Sardinian general, Cialdini, 18 Sept. 1860. Lamoricière with a few horsemen fled to Ancona, then besieged. On 29 Sept. he and the garrison surrendered, but were soon set at liberty.

castes, distinct classes of society in India. By the laws of MENU, the Hindus are divided into the Brahmins, or sacerdotal class; the Kshatrya or Chuttree, military class; the Vaisya, or commercial class; and the Sudras, or Sooders, servile class.

Castiglione (*kas-teel-yo'-na*), N. Italy. Here the French, under Augereau, defeated the Austrians, commanded by Wurmser, with great loss, 5 Aug. 1796.

Castile, central Spain. A Gothic government was established here about 800. Roderick, count of Castile, 860; Ferdinand, a count, became king, 1035. Ferdinand, king of Aragon, married Isabella, queen of Castile, in 1474, and formed one monarchy, 1479. SPAIN.

Castillejos (*cas-til-le'-hos*), N. Africa. Here, on 1 Jan. 1860, was fought the first decisive battle in the war between Spain and Morocco. Gen. Prim, after a vigorous resistance, repulsed the Moors under Muley Abbas, and advanced towards Tetuan.

Castillon, Guienne, S. France. Here the army of Henry VI. of England was defeated by that of Charles VII. of France, and an end put to the English dominion in France, Calais alone remaining, 17 or 23 July, 1453. Talbot, earl of Shrewsbury, was killed.

Castine, Me. MAINE, 1814.

Castlebar, Ireland. About 1100 French troops, under Humbert, landed at Killala and, assisted by Irish insurgents here, compelled the king's troops, under Lake, to retreat, 27 Aug. 1798; but surrendered at Ballinamuck, 8 Sept.

castles. The castle of the Anglo-Saxon was a tower keep, either round or square, with an entrance so elevated that a long flight of steps was necessary to reach it. William I. erected 48 strong castles. Several hundreds, built by permission of Stephen, between 1135 and 1154, were demolished by Henry II. 1154. Many were dismantled in the civil wars. Richborough, Studfall, and Burgh are existing specimens of Roman castles. For the history of the different castles of England, consult Timbs, "Abbeys and Castles of England," 3 vols., London, 1872.

catacombs (Gr. κατά, down, and κύμβη, hollow), early depositories of the dead. The first Christians at Rome met for worship in the catacombs; and here are said to have been the tombs of the apostles Peter and Paul. Belzoni in 1815-18 explored many Egyptian catacombs, built 3000 years ago. He brought to England the sarcophagus of Psammetichus, of oriental alabaster, exquisitely sculptured. In the Parisian catacombs (formerly stone quarries) bones from the cemetery of the Innocents were deposited in 1785; and many victims of the revolution in 1792-94 are interred in them. On 31 May, 1578, some laborers digging on the Via Salaria, 2 miles from Rome, discovered the celebrated catacombs described, with engravings, by Antonio Bosio, in his "Roma Sotteranea" (1632), and by Aringhi (1659), and others. Elaborate accounts have been published recently by De' Rossi, an abstract of whose researches will be found in the "Roma Sotteranea" of the rev. J. S. Northcote and W. R. Brownlow, 1869 and 1879.

catalogues. BOOKS, LIBRARIES.

Catalonia, N.E. Spain, was settled by the Goths and Alani about 409; conquered by the Saracens, 712; recovered by Pepin, and by Charlemagne, 788. It formed part of the Spanish marches and the territory of the count of BARCELONA. The natives were able seamen; being frequently unruly, their peculiar privileges were abolished in 1714.

catalytic (Gr καταλυτικός, able to dissolve) **force.** The discovery in 1819, by Thenard, of the decomposition of peroxide of hydrogen by platinum, and by Dobereiner in 1825 of its property to ignite a mixture of hydrogen and oxygen, formed the groundwork of the doctrine of catalytic force, also termed "action of contact or presence," put forth by Berzelius and Mitscherlich Their view has not been adopted by Liebig and other chemists

cat'amarans or **carcasses,** fire-machines for destroying ships, tried in vain by sir Sydney Smith, 2 Oct 1804, on the Boulogne flotilla destined by Bonaparte to invade England Also a vessel with 2 keels used on the coast of Ceylon, of India, the eastern coast of South America, etc, and of late years common in the lumber districts of northwestern America.

Cata'nia (the ancient Catana), a town near Etna Sicily, was founded by a colony from Chalcis, about 753 B.C Ceres had a temple here, open to none but women Catania was almost totally overthrown by an eruption of Etna in 1669, and in 1693 was nearly swallowed up by an earthquake, in a moment more than 18,000 of its inhabitants were buried in the ruins. An earthquake did great damage, 22 Feb 1817 In Aug 1862, the town was held by Garibaldi and his volunteers, against Italian troops He was captured on 29 Aug

cataphrygians, heretics in the 2d century, who followed the errors of Montanus They are said to have baptized their dead, forbidden marriage, and mingled the bread and wine in the Lord's supper with the blood of children

catapultæ, military engines of the crossbow kind, for throwing arrows javelins, and sometimes stones Said to have been invented by Dionysius, the tyrant of Syracuse, 399 B.C. These engines are often confounded with the ballista, which was more used to hurl huge stones either into a city or against its walls These engines were in use until the invention of gunpowder, the catapulte being mentioned by Irving as operative in the siege of Granada, 1492

Catawbas. INDIANS.

Cateau Cambrésis, N. France, where, on 2, 3 Apr 1559, peace was concluded between Henry II of France, Philip II of Spain, and Elizabeth of England France ceded Savoy, Corsica, and nearly 200 forts in Italy and the Low Countries to Philip

catechisms are said to have been compiled in the 8th or 9th century Luther's were published 1520 and 1529 The catechism of the church of England in the first book of Edward VI, 7 Mch 1549, contained merely the baptismal vow, the creed, the ten commandments, and the Lord's prayer, with explanations, but James I ordered the bishops to add an explication of the sacraments, 1612 The catechism of the council of Trent was published in 1566, those of the assembly of divines at Westminster, 1647 and 1648

Cathari (from the Gr καθαρος, pure), a name given to the Novatians (about 251), Montanists, and other early Christian sects PURITANS.

Cathay', an old name for China.

"Better fifty years of Europe than a cycle of Cathay "
—*Tennyson*, "Locksley Hall "

cathedral, the chief church of a diocese as containing the *cathedra*, or seat of the bishop, obtained the name in the 10th century. CANTERBURY, COLOGNE, DURHAM, LINCOLN, NOTRE DAME, ROUEN, SALISBURY, STRASBURG, ST STEPHENS, VIENNA, ULM, YORK, and others throughout

Catherine. The order of knights of St Catherine was instituted in Palestine, 1063 An order of ladies of the highest rank in Russia was founded by Peter the Great, 1714, in honor of the bravery of his empress Catherine They were to be distinguished, as the name implied (from καθαρός, pure), for purity of life and manners

Catholic majesty. This title was given by pope Gregory III. to Alphonso I. of Spain, 739, and to Ferdinand V and his queen in 1474 by Innocent VIII. in recognition of their zeal for religion and the establishment of the inquisition

Catholic Union of Great Britain; president, the duke of Norfolk, constituted in 1871 A Catholic union in Dublin was formed Dec 1873. ROMAN CATHOLICS.

Catiline's conspiracy. Lucius Sergius Catiline, a Roman citizen of patrician rank, having been refused the consulship (65 B.C), conspired to overthrow the government. This conspiracy was discovered and frustrated A second plot for the same purpose, and in which he was again the principal, was detected by Cicero, then consul, in 63 Catiline's daring appearance in the senate-house, after his guilt was known, drew forth Cicero's celebrated invective, "Quousque tandem abutere Catilina, patientia nostra?" 8 Nov On the arrest of 5 of his accomplices, Catiline left Rome and joined his forces already collected. The 5 conspirators arrested were put to death, and Catiline defeated by Petreius, and himself slain, at Pistoria in Etruria, Jan 62 B C

Cato-street conspiracy. A gang of desperate men, headed by Arthur Thistlewood, assembled in Cato street, Edgware Road, and proposed to assassinate the ministers at a cabinet dinner They were betrayed and arrested, 23 Feb. 1820, and Thistlewood Brunt, Davidson, Ings, and Tidd were executed as traitors on 1 May

Catskill mountains, N. Y. A group of the Appalachian range on the west bank of the Hudson river Highest point, Round Top, 3804 ft On a terrace of Pine Orchard mount is the Mountain house, 2400 ft higher than the Hudson

Catti, a German tribe, attacked but not subdued by the Romans 15 and 84 A D, absorbed by the Franks, 3d century

cattle. Of horned cattle only the buffalo or bison is native of America, and this has never been domesticated. Columbus, in 1493, brought the first tame cattle to America, a bull and several cows As the various parts of North and South America were settled by Europeans, cattle were introduced, and from these have descended all the vast herds which now roam over the plains of Texas and South America Of improved neat-cattle there are 2 distinct classes, (1) beef stock, (2) dairy Of the first, the short-horns or Durham, Herefords, Aberdeen-angus, Galloways, Sussex, West Highland, and Devons are the principal, although the short-horns and Devons are also included in the second or dairy stock, with the Jerseys, Guernseys, Ayrshires, Holstein-Frisian, Brown-Swiss, and the different kinds of polled (without horns) cattle. In 1611 Sir Thomas Yates brought into Virginia from England 100 cows and other cattle, and in 1624 1 bull and 3 heifers were brought into Massachusetts, the first neat-cattle in New England Imported short-horns from England introduced into South Carolina by Wade Hampton, 1782, and into Virginia by Mr Miller, 1797, and from Virginia into Kentucky the same year Stock greatly improved in New England by importations, 1818-20 In 1816 Henry Clay imported 2 Hereford cattle into the U. S. for his farm at Ashland, Ky, but this stock was largely increased by the importations of Erastus Corning, of Albany, N Y, in 1841 First record of the importation of Devons into the U S was for Caton and Patterson, of Baltimore, Md, 1817 Herd-book opened 1851 Jerseys were imported early in this century into the U S, but notably in numbers by John A. Taintor, of Hartford, Conn, in 1850 They are sometimes incorrectly called Alderneys (the cattle of that island are rarely exported) The Jersey stock require the utmost care, and do not mature under 4 or 5 years. The stock is maintained pure in the island of Jersey by the strictest exclusion of foreign importation Guernseys imported into the U. S. about the same time as the Jerseys Ayrshires first brought to the U S in 1831 J P Cushing, of Watertown, Mass., imported largely of this stock in 1837 Brown-Swiss brought to the U S. by Henry M Clark, Belmont, Mass, 1869. Holstein-Frisian, Holland cattle, long known in the U S, as they were brought over by the Dutch settlers of New York, about the beginning of the 18th century Lewis F. Allen, of Buffalo, N Y, began the publication of the American Association's Herd-book in 1846, since 1883, published in Chicago Through the extraordinary attention given to the selection and crossing of the best breeds in Great Britain and in the U S, great improvement has been made both in weight of carcass, quality of meat, and in abundance and richness of milk, since the beginning of this century. The importation of horned cattle from Ireland and Scotland into England was prohibited by a law, 1663; but the export of cattle from Ireland became very extensive In 1842 the importation of cattle into England from foreign countries was subjected to a moderate duty, in 1846 they were made duty free, and since then the numbers imported have enormously increased The export trade of U S in neat-cattle for the year 1880 amounted to $13,344 195, in 1890 it was $31,261,131, in 1892, $35,099,095 AGRICULTURE For sums paid for improved stock at some of the great cattle sales in the U S, see NEW YORK, 1873 During the years 1865-70 there raged an epidemic among cattle, especially in England, so deadly there as to be termed the plague Its seriousness is shown by the following English statistics

- Cattle plague appears at Laycock's dairy, Barnsbury, London, N, rapidly spreads — about 24 June 1865
- 27,432 beasts had been attacked, 12 680 died, 8998 slaughtered up to — 21 Oct "
- A royal commission to inquire into the causes of cattle plague and suggest remedies met first 10 Oct, majority consider the disease to have been imported and recommend slaughter of animals and stringent prohibition of passage of cattle on public roads, etc, 31 Oct 1865, second report, 6 Feb, third report — 1 May, 1866
- Orders in council for regulating the cattle plague (in conformity with the act of 1850), 23 Nov and 16 Dec 1865, and — 20 Jan "
- Disease raging, official report cattle attacked, 120 740, killed, 16,742, died, 73 750, recovered, 14,162, unaccounted for, 16 086 — 1 Feb "
- Cattle Disease acts passed — 20 Feb and 10 Aug "
- Orders in council making uniform repressive measures throughout the country — 27 Mch "
- Disease materially abates — Apr "
- Privy council return cattle attacked, 248 965, killed 80,597, died, 124,187, recovered, 32,989, unaccounted for, 11,192, — 22 June, "
- Disease nearly "stamped out" — 27 Oct "

Caucasus, a lofty mountain, a continuation of the ridge of Mount Taurus, between the Euxine and Caspian seas In mythology, Prometheus was said to have been tied on the top of Caucasus by Jupiter, where his vitals were continually devoured by vultures (1518 B.C.) The passes near the mountain were called *Caucasiæ Portæ*, and it is supposed that through them the Sarmatians or Huns invaded the provinces of Rome, 447 A D CIRCASSIA

caucus, an American term A private meeting of politicians to make plans for an election or session of a legislative body The word is now applied to private meetings of the members of Congress, or of a legislature, belonging to one political party to determine its policy or select its candidates. The word is said to be derived from "ship"-caulkers' meetings. A "caucus club" is mentioned by John Adams, in 1763 —*Bartlett* Similar meetings are occasionally held in London by conservatives and liberals, one was held by Mr Gladstone respecting the ballot bill, 6 July, 1871 Jealousy respecting the system was aroused in 1878

Caudine forks, according to Livy, the *Furculæ Caudinæ* (in Samnium, S Italy), were 2 narrow defiles or gorges, united by a range of mountains on each side The Romans went through the first pass, but found the second blocked up, on returning they found the first similarly obstructed Being thus hemmed in by the Samnites, under the command of C Pontus, they surrendered at discretion, 321 B.C (after a fruitless contest, according to Cicero) The Roman senate broke the treaty.

cauliflower (Lat. *caulis*, cabbage, and flower), a plant of the cabbage family, whose young flowers are eaten as a vegetable, said to have been brought from Cyprus to England about 1603.

caustic, in painting, a method of burning colors into wood or ivory, invented by Gausias of Sicyon He painted his mistress Glycerē sitting on the ground making garlands with flowers, the picture was hence named *Stephanoplocon* It was bought by Lucullus for 2 talents, 335 B.C.—*Pliny*

cautionary towns, Holland (the Briel, Flushing, Rammekins, and Walcheren), were given to queen Elizabeth in 1585 as security for their repaying her for assistance in their struggle with Spain. They were restored to the Dutch republic by James I. in 1616

Cavalier. The appellation given to the supporters of Charles I. of England during the civil war, from a number of gentlemen forming themselves into a body-guard for his protection in 1641 They were opposed to the ROUNDHEADS, or parliamentarians.

cavalry. Used by the Canaanites in war, 1450 B.C. (Josh xi 4) Attached to each Roman legion was a body of 300 horse, in 10 turmæ, the commander always a veteran. The Persians had 10,000 horse at Marathon, 490 B C, and 10,000 Persian horse were slain at the battle of Issus, 333 B C —*Plutarch* In the wars with Napoleon I the British cavalry reached 31,000 men ARMY OF THE UNITED STATES

Cavendish experiment. In 1798 the hon Henry Cavendish described his experiment for determining the mean density of the earth, by comparing the force of terrestrial attraction with that of the attraction of leaden spheres of known magnitude and density, by the torsion balance —*Brande* The Cavendish Society for the publication of chemical works, which ceased with Gmelin's "Chemistry" (1848-67), was established 1846

Cave-of-the-winds, Niagara falls a cave so called formed by the solid wall of rock on one side and a wall of rushing water as it pours over and down the fall on the other side With proper water-proof clothing it can be visited with safety

caves are frequently mentioned in the Bible as dwellings, refuges, and burying-places W B Dawkins's "Cave-hunting Researches on the Evidence of Caves respecting the Early Inhabitants of Europe," was published 1874 The MAMMOTH CAVE, Kentucky the largest in the world, Weyer's cave Virginia, discovered 1804, Wyandotte cave, Indiana; Oreston cave, Devon, Engl, 1816, Kirkdale, Yorkshire, 1821; Kents hole, Torquay, 1825, Brixham cave, 1858, Wookey hole, Somerset, 1859, and many others, have been well explored

Cawnpore, a town in India, on the Doab, a peninsula between the Ganges and Jumna During the mutiny in June, 1857 it was garrisoned by native troops under sir Hugh Wheeler These revolted An adopted son of the old Peishwa Bajee Rao, Nana Sahib, who had long lived on friendly terms with the British, came apparently to their assistance, but joined the rebels The English residents, about 1000 in number, of whom 465 were men of all ages and professions, the rest women and children, attempted to defend themselves in an entrenched camp After sustaining a siege for 3 weeks, they were compelled to surrender, 26 June, and, in spite of a treaty, were all massacred except 2 officers and 2 privates, who escaped Gen Havelock defeated Nana Sahib, 16 July, at Futtehpore, and retook Cawnpore, 17 July, but too late to rescue any prisoners Sir Colin Campbell defeated the rebels here on 6 Dec following A column was erected here, in memory of the killed, by their relatives of the 32d regiment INDIA, 1857.

Caxton Society, for the publication of chronicles and literature of the middle ages, published 16 volumes, 1844-54.

Cayenne, capital of French Guiana, South America, settled by the French, 1604-35 It afterwards came successively into the hands of the English (1654), French, and Dutch The last were expelled by the French in 1677 Cayenne was taken by the British, 12 Jan 1809, but was restored to the French in 1814 Here is produced the *Capsicum baccatum*, or cayenne pepper Many French political prisoners were sent here in 1848. Pop in 1880, 10,000.

Cayugas. INDIANS

Cedar Creek, Va, Battle of Here, 19 Oct 1864, the confederates, under gen Early, were signally defeated by the federals, under gen Sheridan. The confederate forces, previously defeated at WINCHESTER and FISHER HILL, being strongly reinforced, Early, smarting under his recent defeats, and hearing that Sheridan was away in Washington, resolved to surprise the federal force This he succeeded in doing on the morning of the 19th The result was the discomfiture and retreat first of the 19th and then of the 6th corps, by 10 A M., with a loss of 24 guns and 1500 prisoners At this juncture Sheridan, who had stopped at Winchester over-night on his return from Washington, met the first of the retreating troops With words of cheer he halted the fugitives, and, slowly re-forming the line, was ready to advance at 3 P M, the final result being a complete overthrow of the confederates, so that there was no more fighting in the Shenandoah valley. Federal loss 3000 in both engagements. This battle furnishes the subject of "Sheridan's Ride," a poem by Thomas Buchanan Read.

Cedar Mountain, Va., Battle of. POPE'S VIRGINIA CAMPAIGN.

cedar-tree. The red cedar (*Juniperus Virginiana*) introduced into England from North America before 1664; the Bermudas cedar from Bermudas before 1683; the cedar of Lebanon (*Pinus Cedrus*) from the Levant before 1683. In 1850 a grove of venerable cedars, about 40 ft. high, remained on Lebanon. The cedar of Goa (*Cupressus lusitanica*) was brought to Europe by the Portuguese about 1683. CYPRESS.

celery is said to have been introduced into England by the French marshal, Tallard, during his captivity in England, after his defeat at Blenheim by Marlborough, 2 Aug. 1704.

celibacy (from *cœlebs*, unmarried) was preached by St. Anthony in Egypt about 305. His early converts lived in caves, etc., till monasteries were founded. The doctrine was rejected in the council of Nice, 325. Celibacy was enjoined on bishops only in 692. The decree was opposed in England, 958-78. The Romish clergy generally were enjoined to vow celibacy by pope Gregory VII. in 1073-85; sustained by the council of Placentia, held in 1095. Marriage was restored to the English clergy in 1547. The marriage of the clergy was proposed, but negatived, at the council of Trent (1563); also at a conference of the Old Catholics at Bonn, June, 1876. Sir Bartle Frere termed the Zulu army "a *celibate* man-slaying machine," 1878.

cell theory (propounded by Schwann in 1839) supposes that the ultimate constituents of all animal and vegetable tissues are small cells. The lowest forms of animal and vegetable life are said to consist of merely a single cell, as the germinal vesicle in the egg and the red-snow plant.

Celts or **Kelts,** a group of the Aryan family. GAULS. Above 8000*l.* subscribed to found a Celtic professorship at the university of Edinburgh, Oct. 1876; 11,937*l.* subscribed Apr. 1879. One was established at Oxford in 1876.

cemeteries. The burying-places of the Jews, Greeks, Romans, were outside their towns (Matt. xxvii. 60). Many public cemeteries, resembling "Père-la-Chaise," at Paris, have been opened in all parts of Great Britain since 1856. CATACOMBS.

cemeteries in the United States. By an act of the legislature of New York state, 27 Apr. 1847, land devoted to cemetery purposes in that state is exempt from taxation. Statistics of 6 of the largest cemeteries in the neighborhood of New York city show a total area of 2288 acres, and a total of 1,336,546 burials up to 1891, distributed as follows: Calvary, 585,000; Greenwood, 259,893; Lutheran, 208,000; Cypress Hills, 130,000; Evergreens, 115,701; and Woodlawn, 37,952. The principal cemeteries of the larger cities in the U. S. are here mentioned, with name, date of opening, and estimated area as near as can be ascertained. As a rule these cemeteries are so beautified and kept in such perfect order under perpetual contracts with the lot owners as to be an ornament to the cities to which they belong.

CEMETERIES.

City.	Name.	Area in acres.	Established.
Brooklyn, N. Y.	Greenwood	474	1840
	Cypress Hills	400	1848
	Calvary	214	1848
	Evergreens	400	1851
	Lutheran	400	1852
New York, N. Y.	Woodlawn	400	1865
Boston, Mass.	Mount Auburn	125	1831
	Forest Hills	225	1848
	Woodland	100	1851
	Mount Hope	106	1852
Philadelphia, Pa.	Laurel Hill	80	1836
	Woodlands	80	1851
	West Laurel Hill	200	1869
Chicago, Ill.	Rose Hill	500	1859
	Calvary	100	1859
	Graceland	125	1861
	Oakwood	300	1864
Baltimore, Md.	Green Mount Park	350	18[illegible]
	London Park	200	185[illegible]
Buffalo, N. Y.	Forest Lawn	280	18[illegible]

CEMETERIES—*Continued.*

City.	Name.	Area in acres.	Established.
Cincinnati, O.	Spring Grove	600	1845
Cleveland, O.	Lake View	300	1870
Detroit, Mich.	Woodmere	200	1869
Georgetown, D. C.	Oak Hill	35	1849
Hartford, Conn.	Cedar Hills	254	1868
Indianapolis, Ind.	Crown Hill	360	1863
Louisville, Ky.	Cave Hill	200	1845
Memphis, Tenn.	Elmwood	80	1852
Milwaukee, Wisc.	Forest Home	200	1850
Newark, N. J.	Fairmount	60	1855
New Orleans, La.	Metairie Ridge	108	1836
Pittsburg, Pa.	Allegheny	360	1845
Providence, R. I.	Swan Point	250	1858
Richmond, Va.	Hollywood	95	1847
Rochester, N. Y.	Mount Hope	217	1854
St. Louis, Mo.	Belle Fontaine	332	1849
San Francisco, Cal.	Lone Mountain	300	1865
Washington, D. C.	Congressional	40	1812

cemeteries, national. The United States government has established national cemeteries in various parts of the country for the burial of men who died in the naval or military service. There are 82 national cemeteries scattered throughout 21 states and territories, mostly in the southern states; 21 of these have over 2000, not exceeding 5000, graves; 9 have over 5000, not exceeding 10,000; 11 have over 10,000. Total number of graves in all the cemeteries, 322,851; of these 9438 are confederates. A marble headstone marks each grave, with name and rank of occupant when known. The following is a list of the 11 largest, each containing over 10,000 graves:

Name.	Known.	Unknown.	Total.
Andersonville, Ga.	12,781	921	13,702
Arlington, Va.	11,853	4,349	16,202
Chalmette, La.	6,851	5,674	12,525
Chattanooga, Tenn.	8,012	4,963	12,975
Fredericksburg, Va.	2,487	12,771	15,258
Jefferson's Barracks, Mo.	8,647	2,906	11,553
Marietta, Ga.	7,192	2,963	10,155
Memphis, Tenn.	5,163	8,818	13,981
Nashville, Tenn.	11,825	4,701	16,526
Salisbury, N. C.	97	10,032	11,129
Vicksburg, Miss.	3,899	12,701	16,600

The national cemetery at Gettysburg, Pa., while not containing as many graves as those mentioned, there being only 3575, is noted as having been dedicated by President Lincoln, 1863. It is adorned with numerous memorials of the dead, among them a national monument. The government took charge of the cemetery in 1872.

Cenis, Mount. TUNNELS.

censors, Roman magistrates, to survey and rate the property, and correct the manners of the people. The first two censors were appointed, 443 B.C. Plebeian censors were first appointed, 131 B.C. The office, abolished by the emperors, was revived by Decius, 251 A.D. PRESS.

censuring the President of the United States. Congress has twice censured the president: Jackson in 1834, and Tyler in 1843. UNITED STATES.

census. The Israelites were numbered by Moses, 1490 B.C., and by David, 1017 B.C.; Demetrius Phalereus is said to have taken a census of Attica, 317 B.C. Servius Tullius enacted that a general estimate of every Roman's estate and personal effects should be delivered to the government upon oath every 5 years, 566 B.C. A census of the people is said to have been taken at Florence, 1527; at Venice, 1584; in France, 1700; in Sweden, 1794. The proposal in England for a census in 1375 was opposed as profane. In the United Kingdom the census is now taken at decennial periods since 1801; 1811, 1821, 1831, 1841, 1851, 1861 (7 Apr.), 1871 (3 Apr.), 1881 (3 Apr.), 1891 (5 Apr.). The first United States census was made in 1790. The constitution requires that a new census shall be made every 10 years. The latest census year was 1890. POPULATION.

centennial exhibition, an international exhibition, in celebration of the hundredth year of American independence, was held at Philadelphia, 1876. 38 foreign countries were represented by their products. 5 principal buildings, with "annexes," or supplementary buildings, were erected; and, including foreign and state buildings, the total number of structures was 199. The main building covered 21 acres, and the 5 principal buildings, with their annexes, covered

75 acres Number of persons admitted to the exhibition, 9,910,966, largest number admitted on one day, 274,919

First bill providing for the exhibition signed by the president, 3 Mch 1871
Centennial commission formed 24 Mch 1872
Centennial board of finance created by act of congress, 1 June,
Exhibition opened by president Grant 19 May, 1876
Exhibition closed 10 Nov "

Central America. AMERICA, WRECKS, 1857

centre of population. POPULATION, U S

centurion, the captain head, or commander of a subdivision of a Roman legion which consisted of 100 men, and was called a *centuria* By the Roman census 556 B C, each hundred of the people was called a centuria

century. The Greeks computed time by the Olympiads, beginning 776 B C., and the Roman church by Indictions, the first of which began 21 Sept 312 A D The reckoning of time by centuries from the incarnation of Christ was adopted in chronological history first in France —*Dupin*

Cephalo'nia, one of the Ionian islands, was taken from the Ætolians by the Romans 189 B C, and given to the Athenians by Hadrian 135 A D IONIAN ISLES

Cephi'sus, a river in Attica near which Walter de Brienne, duke of Athens, was defeated and slain by the Catalans, 1311

Ceremonies, Master of, an office instituted for the more honorable reception of ambassadors and persons of quality at court, 1 James I 1603 The order maintained by the master of ceremonies at Bath, "Beau Nash," the "king of Bath," led to the adoption of the office in ordinary assemblies "Beau Nash" died, 1761, in his 88th year —*Ashe.*

Ceres, an asteroid, 160 miles in diameter, was discovered by M Piazzi, at Palermo, Italy, 1 Jan 1801, he named it after a goddess highly esteemed by the ancient Sicilians

Ceresuola (*ce-re-swo'-la*), N Italy Here Francis de Bourbon, count d'Enghien, defeated the imperialists under the marquis de Guasto, 14 Apr 1544

Cerignola (*ce-rin'-yo-la*), S Italy Here capt Gonsalvo de Cordova and the Spaniards defeated the duc de Nemours and the French, 28 Apr. 1503

Cerinthians, followers of Cerinthus, a Jew, who lived about 80 A D, are said to have combined Judaism with pagan philosophy

cerium, a very rare metal, discovered by Klaproth and others in 1803

Cerro Gordo, Battle of With about 8500 men, gen Scott, after capturing VERA CRUZ, marched towards the Mexican capital At Cerro Gordo, a difficult mountain pass at the foot of the eastern chain of the Cordilleras, he found Santa Anna strongly posted and fortified, with 12,000 men Scott attacked him 18 Apr 1847, drove him from his position, and dispersed his army Santa Anna escaped on the back of a mule More than 1000 Mexicans were killed, or wounded, and 3000 were made prisoners The Americans lost in killed and wounded 431 Scott pushed on towards the Mexican capital MEXICAN WAR.

Ceuta (the ancient Septa), a town on north coast of Africa, stands on the site of the ancient Abyla, the southern pillar of Hercules It was taken from the Vandals by Belisarius for Justinian, 534, by the Goths, 618, by the Moors, about 709, from whom it was taken by the Portuguese, 1415 With Portugal, it was annexed in 1580 to Spain, which retains it

Ceylon (the ancient Taprobane), an island in the Indian ocean, called by the natives the Seat of Paradise It became a seat of Buddhism, 307 B.C, and was known to the Romans about 41 A D Area, 25,364 sq. miles, pop. 1873, 2,323,760, 1891, 3,008,239

Invaded by the Portuguese Almeyda 1505
Dutch land in Ceylon, 1602, capture the capital, Colombo 1603
Frequent conflicts, peaceful commercial relations established 1604
Intercourse with the British begun 1713
A large portion of the country taken by them in 1782, restored, 1783
Dutch settlements seized by the British, Trincomalee, 26 Aug, Jaffnapatam Sept. 1795
Ceylon ceded to Great Britain by the peace of Amiens 1802
British troops treacherously massacred or imprisoned by the adigar of Candy, at Colombo 26 June, 1803
Complete sovereignty of the island assumed by England 1815

Chærone'a, Bœotia Here Greece was ruined by Philip, 32 000 Macedonians defeating 30,000 Thebans, Athenians, etc, 6 or 7 Aug 338 B.C Here Archelaus, lieutenant of Mithridates, was defeated by Sylla, and 110,000 Cappadocians were slain, 86 B C CORONEA

chain, the great This chain was stretched across the Hudson river at West Point just below fort Clinton, 1 May, 1778, to prevent the British war-ships from ascending the river Its links were 2½ in square, and over 2 ft long, each weighing 140 pounds Total weight, 180 tons, length, 450 yds Portions of this chain are still at West Point

chain-bridges. The largest and oldest chain-bridge in the world is said to be that at Kingtung, in China, where it forms a perfect road from the top of one mountain to the top of another Mr Telford constructed the first chain-bridge on a grand scale in England over the strait between Anglesey and the coast of Wales, 1818-25 MENAI STRAIT

chain-cables, pumps, and **shot.** Iron chain-cables were in use by the Veneti, a people intimately connected with the Belgæ of Britain in the time of Cæsar, 57 B.C These cables came into use generally, in the navy of England, in 1812 Acts for the proving and sale of chain-cables and anchors in England were passed in 1864, 1871, and 1874 —*Chain-shot* to destroy the rigging of an enemy's ship were invented by the Dutch admiral De Witt in 1666 —*Chain-pumps* were first used on board the British frigate *Flora*, in 1787

chains, hanging in. By 25 Geo II 1752, it was enacted that judges should direct the bodies of pirates and murderers to be dissected and anatomized, or hung in chains. The custom of hanging in chains was abolished in England in 1834

Chalce'don, Asia Minor, opposite Byzantium, colonized by Megarians, about 681 B C It was taken by Darius, 505 B C, by the Romans, 74, plundered by the Goths, 259 A D, taken by Chosroes, the Persian, 609, by Orchan, the Turk, 1338 Here was held the "Synod of the Oak," 403, and the fourth general council, which annulled the act of the "Robber Synod," 8 Oct 451

Chalcis-Eubœa. ALPHABET.

Chaldæ'a, the ancient name of Babylonia, but afterwards restricted to the southwest portion The Chaldæans were devoted to astronomy and astrology (Dan ii etc) — The *Chaldean Registers* of celestial observations, said to have commenced 2234 B.C were brought down to the taking of Babylon by Alexander, 331 B.C (1903 years) These registers were sent to Aristotle by Calisthenes —*Chaldæan characters* the Bible was transcribed from the original Hebrew into these characters, now called Hebrew, by Ezra, about 445 B.C

Chalgrove, Oxfordshire At a skirmish here with prince Rupert, 18 June, 1643, John Hampden, of the parliament party, was wounded, and died 24 June A column was erected to his memory, 18 June, 1843.

"Challenger." DEEP-SEA SOUNDINGS

Chalmette plantation, La, a few miles below New Orleans on the Mississippi river, where gen Jackson repulsed an advance of the British, 28 Dec 1814

Châlons-sur-Marne (*sha-lon'-sur-marn'*), N E France Here the emperor Aurelian defeated Tetricus, the last of the pretenders to the throne, termed the Thirty Tyrants, 274, and here in 451 Aëtius, the Roman general, assisted by the Visigoths, under their king Theodoric, checked the advance of Attila the Hun, causing him to retire into Pannonia, after one of the most desperate and gigantic contests recorded in history

chamberlain, early a high court officer in France, Germany, and England The office of chamberlain of the exchequer was discontinued in 1834

Hereditary Lord Great Chamberlain of England —The sixth great officer of state, whose duties, among others, relate to coronations and public solemnities

Lord Chamberlain of the Household —An ancient office The title is from the Fr *chambellan*, in Lat *camerarius*

Chambersburg, Pa. PENNSYLVANIA, 1862-64

"Chambers's Journal" was first published at Edinburgh in Feb 1832

Chambre Ardente ("fiery chamber"), an extraordinary French tribunal, so named from the punishment frequently awarded by it Francis I in 1535, and Henry II. in 1549, employed it for the extirpation of heresy, which led to the civil war with the Huguenots in 1560, and in 1679 Louis XIV appointed one to investigate the poisoning cases which occurred after the execution of the marchioness Brinvilliers.

Champ de Mars (*shän de märs*), an open square in front of the military school at Paris, with artificial embankments on each side, extending nearly to the river Seine The ancient assemblies of the Frankish people, the germ of parliaments, held annually in March, received this name In 747 Pepin changed the month to May Here was held, 14 July 1790 (the anniversary of the capture of the Bastile), the "federation," or solemnity of swearing fidelity to the "patriot king" and new constitution, great rejoicings followed On 14 July 1791, a second great meeting was held here, directed by the Jacobin clubs, to sign petitions on the "altar of the country," praying for the abdication of Louis XVI A commemoration meeting took place, 14 July, 1792 Another constitution was sworn to here, under the eye of Napoleon I, 1 May, 1815, at a ceremony called the *Champ de Mai* The prince president (afterwards Napoleon III) held a review in the Champ de Mars, and distributed eagles to the army, 10 May, 1852 Here also were held the international exhibitions, opened 1 Apr 1867, and 1 May, 1878 PARIS

Champagne, an ancient province, N E France once part of the kingdom of Burgundy, was governed by counts from the 10th century till it was united to Navarre, count Thi[illegible] becoming king in 1234 The countess Joanna married Philip IV of France in 1284, and in 1361 Champagne was annexed by their descendant king John The effervescing wine, termed champagne, made in this province, became popular in the latter part of the 18th century

Champion Hills, Miss, Battle of VICKSBURG CAMPAIGN

champion of the king of England (most honorable), an ancient office, since 1377 has been attached to the manor of Scrivelsby, held by the Marmion family Their descendant, sir Henry Dymoke, the 17th of his family who held the office died 28 Apr 1865, succeeded by his brother John, he died, and his son Henry Lionel succeeded, who died Dec 1875 At the coronation of an English king, the champion used to challenge any one that should deny his title

Champlain, Lake. LAKE CHAMPLAIN and NEW YORK, 1609, 1776, 1814

chancellor of England, lord high, the first lay subject after the princes of the blood royal Anciently the office was conferred upon some dignified ecclesiastic termed *cancellarius*, or doorkeeper, who admitted suitors to the sovereign's presence Arfastus or Herefast, chaplain to the king (William the Conqueror) and bishop of Elmham, was lord chancellor in 1067 —*Hardy* Thomas à Becket was made chancellor in 1154 The first person qualified by education to decide causes upon his own judgment was sir Thomas More, appointed in 1529, before which the officer was rather a state functionary than a judge Sir Christopher Hatton, appointed lord chancellor in 1587, was very ignorant, and the first reference was made to a master in 1588 Salary, 1875, 6000*l*., as speaker of the House of Lords, 4000*l* The great seal has been frequently put in commission In 1813 the office of vice-chancellor was established KEEPER, VICE-CHANCELLOR

chancellor of Ireland, lord high The earliest nomination was by Richard I, 1189, that of Stephen Ridel The office of vice-chancellor was known in Ireland in 1232, Geoffrey Turvillo, archdeacon of Dublin being so named The Chancery and Common Law Offices (Ireland) act was passed 20 Aug 1867

chancellor of Scotland, lord The laws of Malcolm II (1004) say "The chancellar sall at al tymes assist the king in giving him counsall mair secretly nor the rest of the nobility . The chancellar sall be ludgit neir unto the kingis grace, for keiping of his bodie, and the seill, and that he may be readie, baith day and nicht, at the kingis command." —*Sir James Balfour* Evan was lord chancellor to Malcolm III, Canmore, 1057, and James, earl of Seafield, afterwards Findlater, was the last lord chancellor of Scotland, the office having been abolished in 1708 KEEPER

Chancellorsville, Va, Battle of On 26 Jan 1863, maj-gen Joseph Hooker assumed command of the army of the Potomac, and by 1 Apr that army was in excellent condition for a forward movement, numbering 100,000 infantry, 10,000 artillery, and 13,000 cavalry On 27 Apr gen Hooker despatched gen Stoneman with most of the cavalry on a raid to the rear of the confederate army From Falmouth, opposite Fredericksburg, gen Hooker, 28 Apr, moved about 70,000 of his forces towards the U S ford on the Rappahannock, leaving gen Sedgwick with some 30,000 opposite Fredericksburg, where the confederate army was encamped Gen Hooker succeeded in crossing the Rappahannock in the vicinity of Chancellorsville (that place being a single hotel, at some time kept by a Mr Chancellor), almost without molestation, by the evening of 30 Apr The movement thus far was a success, and a surprise to the confederate commander On 1 May, Hooker advanced a division of the 5th corps on the road towards Fredericksburg, which soon became engaged with the confederate advance from that place. Gen Hooker now recalled this advance, and the day closed with the confederates occupying the better position Early in the morning of 2 May, gen. Lee detached "Stonewall" Jackson with about 25 000 men for an attack on the federal extreme right, occupied by the 11th corps, under command of gen O O Howard This movement of Jackson's culminated a little before 6 P M by a swift and overwhelming attack on the right wing, breaking it in panic This attack was finally repelled During this fighting in the darkness "Stonewall" Jackson was mortally wounded by his own men, dying on the 10th The conflict was again renewed on 3 May (Sunday), around the Chancellor house, with a general confederate success. In the meanwhile gen Sedgwick at Fredericksburg was ordered, late on the evening of the 2d, to cross the Rappahannock at that point, move towards Chancellorsville, and thus strike the rear of the confederate army Sedgwick moved as ordered, early on the morning of the 3d, but was not able to carry the heights beyond Fredericksburg until noon, then, advancing towards Chancellorsville about 4 miles, he was stopped by a strong force of the confederates about 5 P M. During the 4th, gen Lee was able to still further reinforce the troops in front of Sedgwick, and at the same time keep Hooker engaged at Chancellorsville Sedgwick was pushed back during the day, and recrossed the river during the night with a loss of 5000 men The federals also at Chancellorsville recrossed the Rappahannock during the night of the 4th unmolested Hooker's loss was 17,197, including Sedgwick's, of whom 5000 were prisoners, while the confederate loss was some 13,000, of whom 3000 were prisoners This battle places Lee in the front rank of military leaders Hooker's army was composed of the best material, was well equipped and full of spirit, and numbered 120,000, while Lee's force was 62,000 Hooker succeeded in turning Lee's position, and in forcing him out of his fortified camp into the open field, where a complete victory for the national forces seemed easy and well-nigh certain. That it was not won was due to the activity and masterly combinations of the confederate commander For a careful criticism of the battle see "The Campaign of Chancellorsville" by lieut-col Theodore Dodge, U S A, pub. 1881

chancery, English court of, is said to have been instituted either in 605, or by Alfred, 887, refounded by William I, 1067 (*Stow*) or 1070 This court had its origin in the desire to render justice complete, and to moderate the rigor of other courts that are bound to the strict letter of the law It gives relief to or against infants, notwithstanding their minority, and to or against married women, notwithstanding their coverture, and all frauds, deceits, breaches of trust and confidence, for which there is no redress at common-law, are relievable here.—*Blackstone* CHANCELLOR OF ENGLAND The delays in chancery proceedings having long given dissatisfaction, the subject was brought before Parliament in 1825, and frequently since, which led to important acts in 1852, 1853, 1855, 1858, and 1867, to amend the practice in the court of chancery. The chancery division of the high court of justice now consists of the lord chancellor and 5 judges. The first court of this character in the colonies was established in New York in 1698, by gov. Bellomont, under authority of the Board of Trade and Plantations. In the United States the terms *Equity* and *Courts of Equity* are more frequently used than the corresponding terms *Chancery* and *Courts of Chancery.* COURTS OF THE UNITED STATES.

Chantilly, Va., Battle of. POPE'S VIRGINIA CAMPAIGN.

chanting the psalms was adopted by Ambrose from the pagan ceremonies of the Romans, about 350.—*Lenglet.* About 602, Gregory the Great added tones to the Ambrosian chant, and established singing-schools. John Marbeck's "Book of Common Praier noted" (1559) is the first adaptation of the ancient Latin music to the Reformed church; Clifford's "Common Tunes" for chanting, 1664. MUSIC.

chapel. There are free chapels, chapels of ease, the chapel royal, etc.—*Cowell.* The gentlemen pensioners (formerly poor knights of Windsor, who were instituted by the direction of Henry VIII. in his testament, 1546–47) were called knights of the chapel. POOR KNIGHTS OF WINDSOR. The Private Chapels act passed in England 14 Aug. 1871.—The place of conference among printers, and the conference itself, are by them called a *chapel,* it is said, because the first work printed in England by Caxton was executed in a ruined chapel in Westminster abbey.

chaplain, a clergyman who performs divine service in a chapel, for a prince or nobleman. In the U. S. one who holds divine service in the army or navy or any public body, or in a family. About 70 chaplains are attached to the chapel royal of England. The chief personages in Great Britain invested with the privilege of retaining chaplains are the following, with the number that was originally allotted to each rank, by 21 Hen. VIII. c. 13 (1529):

Archbishop	8	Knight of the Garter	3
Duke	6	Duchess	2
Bishop	6	Marchioness	2
Marquis	5	Countess	2
Earl	5	Baroness	2
Viscount	4	Master of the Rolls	2
Baron	3	Royal almoner	2
Chancellor	3	Chief-justice	1

chapter. Anciently in Great Britain the bishop and clergy lived in the cathedral, the latter to assist the former in performing holy offices and governing the church, until the reign of Henry VIII. The chapter is now an assembly of the clergy of a collegiate church or cathedral.—*Cowell.* The chapter-house of Westminster abbey was built in 1250. By consent of the abbot, the commoners of England held parliaments there from 1377 until 1547, when Edward VI. granted them the chapel of St. Stephen.

Chapultepec, Battle of. Chapultepec castle stands on a lofty hill, strongly fortified, and is the seat of the military school of Mexico. It was the last place defended outside the capital towards the middle of Sept. 1847, the invading Americans, under Scott, having taken every other stronghold from Vera Cruz to Chapultepec. Scott brought 4 heavy batteries to bear upon it on the night of 11 Sept., and on the 12th commenced a heavy cannonade. On the 13th the Americans made a furious assault, routed the Mexicans, and unfurled the Stars and Stripes over the shattered castle. On the following day Scott and his army entered the city of Mexico in triumph.

charcoal air-filters were devised by Dr. John Stenhouse, F.R.S., in 1853. About the end of the last century Löwitz, a German chemist, discovered that charcoal (carbon) possessed the property of deodorizing putrid substances, by absorbing and decomposing offensive gases. Air-filters, based on this property, have been successfully applied to public buildings, sewers, etc. Dr. Stenhouse also invented charcoal respirators. FIREMAN'S RESPIRATOR.

Charing Cross. At the village of Charing, London, Engl., stood the last of the memorial crosses erected in memory of Eleanor, queen of Edward I. of England, in conformity with her will. ELEANOR'S CROSSES. She died 28 Nov. 1290. The cross remained till 1647, when it was destroyed as a monument of popish superstition. The present cross was erected for the Southeastern Railway company in 1865 by E. M. Barry. The houses at Charing Cross were built about 1678; alterations began in 1829. The first stone of Charing-cross hospital was laid by the duke of Sussex, 15 Sept. 1831. Hungerford-bridge (or Charing-cross bridge) was opened 1 May, 1845; taken down July, 1862, and the materials employed in erecting Clifton suspension bridge, beginning Mch. 1863.

chariots. Chariot racing was a Greek and Roman exercise. The price of an Egyptian war-chariot in the time of Solomon, 1015 B.C., was 600 shekels of silver (about $300). The chariot of an Ethiopian officer is mentioned, Acts, viii. 28. Cæsar relates that Cassivelaunus, after dismissing his other forces, retained no fewer than 4000 war-chariots about his person. CARRIAGES, etc.

Charitable Brethren, an order founded by St. John of God, and approved by pope Pius V. 1572; introduced into France, 1601; settled at Paris, 1602.—*Hénault.*

charities and **charity schools.** EDUCATION. The British charity commission reported to Parliament that the endowed charities alone of Great Britain amounted in 1840 to 1,500,000*l.* annually. Charity schools were instituted in London to keep the infant poor from Roman Catholic seminaries 3 James II., 1687–88. Mr. Low's "Charities of London" was pub. 1862. Newest ed., 1880.

First charity commission, originated by Mr. (afterwards lord) Brougham, in 1816, appointed in 1818; issued reports in 38 vols. (income of charities, 1,209,395*l.*)....1819–40
New commissioners appointed, 1853; office, Gwydyr house, Whitehall; powers increased.... 1860
A meeting was held at the Mansion-house, London, to consider objections to charity electioneering....30 Oct. 1873
Additional commissioners appointed upon the abolition of the Endowed School Commission.... 1874
Charity Voting Association held its first annual meeting, 18 Feb. 1875
Metropolitan charities received about 3,195,181*l.*, 1874; 4,114,489*l.*.... "
Charity commissioners' scheme for the Campden estates, Kensington, much opposed; confirmed by chancery, 27 May, 1881
Henry Quinn bequeaths 50,000*l.* to London charities.... 1888

charity organization in the United States. The banding together of municipal, institutional, and private charities for better administration, and for a study of the causes and cure of pauperism, was introduced into London, England, in 1869, and into the U. S. in 1877. POOR. As reported at the 17th national conference of charities and corrections at Baltimore (14–21 May, 1890), there were 78 societies in the U. S. operated under charity organization either wholly or in part.

The principal charity organization societies with date of organization are as follows:

Name.	Place.	Organized.	
Charity Organization Society.	Buffalo, N. Y.	11 Dec.	1877
Society for Organizing Charity	Philadelphia, Pa.	13 June,	1878
Bureau of Charities	Brooklyn, L. I.	26 Nov.	"
Associated Charities	Boston, Mass.	26 Feb.	1879
" "	Cincinnati, O.	18 Nov.	"
Charity Organization Society.	Indianapolis, Ind.	12 Dec.	"
Association of Charities	Detroit, Mich.	11 Feb.	1880
Society for Organizing Charities	Cleveland, O.	14 Jan.	1881
Charity Organization Society.	Baltimore, Md.	30 Apr.	"
Associated Charities	Washington, D. C.	7 June,	"
Charity Organization Society.	Newark, N. J.		"
" " "	Milwaukee, Wis.	22 Dec.	"
" " "	New York city, N. Y.	26 Jan.	1882
" " "	Chicago, Ill.		"
" " "	Louisville, Ky.		1883
" " "	New Orleans, La.		"
" " "	Minneapolis, Minn.		1884

Saving societies for the poor through regularly appointed collectors, instituted by Charity Organization Society of Newport, R. I.... 1879
First law procured by charity organization was that regulating the sale and use of intoxicating liquors in New Haven, Conn. 1880
Massachusetts passes a law for bringing children of worthless parents before the court and giving them into proper guardianship.... 1883
System of central registration of all travelling mendicants and impostors at Buffalo, N. Y., instituted.... 1886
Charity organizations in various cities memorialize Congress in favor of postal savings-banks.... "
Boston secures a law prohibiting begging and peddling by children.... 1887

"Charivari" (Fr. for "clattering of pots and pans," etc., noise made to annoy obnoxious persons), the name assumed by the French illustrated satirical journal, first published 1 Dec. 1832, edited by Louis Desnoyers, Altaroche, and Albert

Clerc Among the artists were "Cham," a name taken by the comte de Noé, who contributed from 1842 till his death, 6 Sept 1879 PUNCH, "the London *Charivari*"

Charleroi, in Belgium, fortified and named by the Spanish governor Rodrigo, 1666 Several great battles have been fought near it, especially in 1690 and 1794 FLEURUS Charleroi was besieged in vain by the prince of Orange 1672 and 1677 Near here, at Ligny, Napoleon attacked the Prussian line, and drove it back upon Wavres, 16 June, 1815

"Charles-et-Georges," a French vessel, professedly conveying free African emigrants (really slaves) seized by the Portuguese in Conducia bay, 29 Nov 1857, sent to Lisbon, and condemned as a slaver The French government sent 2 ships-of-war to the Tagus, and the vessel was surrendered under protest, but the emperor of France gave up the free-emigration scheme

Charleston, S C. SOUTH CAROLINA

Charlestown, Mass MASSACHUSETTS, 1629, 1630, 1775

Charlestown, West Va Here on 2 Dec 1859, John Brown was hung, and on the 16th, Green, Copeland, Cook, and Coppoc, and on 16 Mch 1860, Stephens and Hazlett BROWN'S INSURRECTION

"Charte Constitutionnelle," the French political constitution acknowledged by Louis XVIII, 4-10 June, 1814 The infraction of this constitution led to the revolution of 1830 The amended "Charte" was promulgated by Louis Philippe, 14 Aug 1830, and set aside by the revolution of 1848

Charter-house (a corruption of CHARTREUSE). London, formerly a Carthusian monastery founded in 1371 by sir William Manny, one of the knights of Edward III, now a charitable establishment The last prior, John Houghton, was executed as a traitor, for denying the king's supremacy, in May, 1535 After the dissolution of monasteries in 1539, the Charter-house passed through various hands till 1 Nov 1611, when it was sold by the earl of Suffolk to Thomas Sutton for 13,000*l.*, who obtained letters-patent directing that it should be called "the hospital of king James, founded in the Charter-house," and that "there should be forever 16 governors," etc. On the foundation are 80 poor brothers and 41 poor scholars. Sutton died 12 Dec 1611 In Sept 1872, the school was opened in new buildings, at Godalming, Surrey The old buildings, adapted for the Merchant Taylors' (day) school, were opened by the prince of Wales, 6 Apr. 1875 The buildings for the poor "brethren" were also modified, and in Nov. entirely new arrangements for them were proposed The "Charter House, Past and Present," by Dr. Wm Haig Brown, head-master, pub 1879

Charter Oak. CONNECTICUT, 1687, 1856

charters, granted to corporate towns to protect their manufactures by Henry I in 1132, modified by Charles II in 1683, the ancient charters restored in 1698 Alterations were made by the Municipal Reform act in 1835 Ancient Anglo-Saxon charters are printed in Kemble's "Codex Diplomaticus," 1829 BOROUGHS, MAGNA CHARTA For colonial charters in the U S, see the different State Records

chartists, the name assumed in England by large bodies of workingmen soon after the passing of the Reform bill in 1832. They demanded the people's charter, with 6 points *Universal Suffrage, Vote by Ballot, Annual Parliaments, Payment of the Members, the Abolition of the Property Qualification* (this was enacted June, 1858), and *Equal Electoral Districts* In 1838 the chartists assembled in many places, armed with guns, pikes, and other weapons, and carrying torches and flags. A proclamation was issued against them, 12 Dec Their petition (agreed to at Birmingham, 6 Aug 1838), was presented to Parliament by T. Attwood, 14 June, 1839. They committed outrages at Birmingham, 15 July, 1839, and at Newport, 4 Nov 1839. They held for some time a sort of parliament, called the "National Convention," the leading men being Feargus O'Connor, Henry Vincent, Mr Stephens, etc. On 10 Apr 1848, they proposed to hold a meeting of 200,000 men on Kennington Common, London, to march in procession to Westminster, and present a petition to Parliament, but only about 20,000 came The bank and other establishments were fortified, preventive measures adopted, and not less than 150,000 volunteers of all ranks (including Louis Napoleon, afterwards emperor) were sworn to act as special constables. The chartists dispersed after slight encounters with the police, and the monster petition, in detached rolls, was sent in cabs to the House of Commons. From this time the proceedings of the chartists became insignificant

Chartreuse (*shar-truz'*), **La Grande,** chief of the monasteries of the Carthusian order, among the rugged mountains near Grenoble, in France, was founded by Bruno of Cologne about 1084 At the revolution in 1792 the monks were expelled and their valuable library destroyed They returned to the monastery after the restoration of 1815 In Nov 1880, they declined to accept exemption from the decrees expelling the religious orders from France —An aromatic cordial is so called from being made at this monastery

chart. A representation of a portion of the earth's surface, projected on a plane Specifically it is a map for navigators' use, on which merely the outlines of coasts, islands, rocks, etc, are shown Marine charts were introduced by Henry, son of John I of Portugal, about 1400, and brought to England about 1489 by Bartholomew Columbus, to illustrate his brother's theory respecting a western route to India. First magnetic chart constructed by Dr Halley, 1701 It noted the Atlantic and Indian oceans MAPS

Chassepot (*shas-po'*) **rifle,** a modified needle-gun, breech-loading (named after its inventor, Alphonse Chassepot), adopted by France in 1866 In Apr 1867, 10,000 had been issued to the troops In his report on the battle of MENTANA, 3 Nov 1867, gen de Failly said, "the chassepot has done wonders." It was considered successful in the war, 1870-71 "The range of the chassepot being 1800 paces, and that of the needle-gun only between 600 and 700, the Germans in all their charges had to traverse 1200 paces before their arms could be used to purpose" Many Germans carried the chassepot after the surrender of Sedan, 2 Sept 1870. FIRE-ARMS

chastity. The Roman laws justified homicide in defence of one's self or relatives, and by the laws of all civilized nations a woman may kill a man in defence of her chastity, or a husband or a father him who attempts to violate his wife or daughter In 1100 years (from Numa, 710 B C, to Theodosius, 394 A D), only 18 Roman vestals had been condemned for incontinence ACRE, COLDINGHAM, VESTALS.

Chat Moss, Lancashire, Engl., a peat bog, 12 miles square, in most places too soft to support a man or horse, over which George Stephenson, engineer, carried the Liverpool and Manchester railway, overcoming difficulties considered invincible The road (literally a floating one) was completed by 1 Jan 1830, when the first experimental train was drawn by the Rocket locomotive. BOGS

Châteaudun, an old city, N C France, the residence of the heroic Dunois, who died 1468. Here were massacred, 20 July, 1183, about 7000 Brabançons. fanatic mercenaries hired to exterminate the Albigenses by cardinal Henry, abbot of Clairvaux, in 1181 They had become the scourge of the country, and the "Capuchons" were organized for their destruction.—Châteaudun was captured by the Germans after a severe conflict of about 9 hours, 18 Oct 1870 Barricades had been erected in the town, and the Garde Mobile fought bravely The town was reoccupied by the French, 6 Nov

Chatham, Kent, Engl., a principal station of the British navy, the dockyard, commenced by queen Elizabeth, was much extended in 1872. The Chatham Chest, for wounded and decayed seamen, established here by queen Elizabeth and admirals Drake and Hawkins in 1588, was removed to Greenwich in 1803. On 10 June, 1667, the Dutch fleet, under admiral de Ruyter, sailed up to this town, and burned several men-of-war, but the entrance into the Medway is now defended by Sheerness and other forts, and additional fortifications were made at Chatham New docks and a basin, said to be the largest and finest in the world, opened by Mr Göschen, 21 June, 1871

Chatillon (*sha-til-yon'*), on the Seine, France Here at a congress of the 4 great powers allied against France,

Caulaincourt attended for Napoleon, 4 Feb. 1814; the negotiations for peace were broken off on 19 Mch. following.

Chattanooga campaign. The campaign of Chattanooga, following closely that of CHICKAMAUGA, may properly be termed a continuation of it, with a change of commanders, a new formation of the army corps, and an increase of the army by reinforcements.

Immediately after the battle of Chickamauga the army of the Cumberland falls back to Chattanooga..........21-22 Sept. 1863

[The confederate army follows at once, and occupies the strong positions of Missionary Ridge and Lookout mountain. Chattanooga is thus practically invested, the federal army having but one route whereby it can obtain its supplies, and that over the Cumberland mountains by an obscure wagon road maintained with difficulty.]

The 11th and 12th corps, under command of maj.-gen. Hooker, ordered from the army of the Potomac to aid the army of the Cumberland..................................23 Sept. "

Maj.-gen. Grant is placed in command of the military division of the Mississippi, including the armies and departments of the Tennessee, Cumberland, and the Ohio. Maj.-gen. Rosecrans is relieved of command of the army of the Cumberland, and maj.-gen. George H. Thomas placed in command by general order No. 337, War Dept....................16 Oct. "

This order relieving gen. Rosecrans left optional with gen. Grant. Gen. Rosecrans is relieved.................19 Oct. "

Gen. Grant reaching Chattanooga takes command......23 Oct. "

He orders gen. Sherman at once from Corinth, Miss., to Chattanooga...24 Oct. "

Gen. Hooker, now at Bridgeport, Ala., with the 11th and 12th corps, is ordered to cross the Tennessee at that place and reach the Wauhatchie valley by....................27 Oct. "

To support this movement and open another route for supplies, gen. Grant decides on a pontoon bridge across the Tennessee at Brown's ferry, a few miles below Chattanooga. It is placed by brig.-gen. W. F. Smith on the night of 27 Oct. "

On the morning of the 28th a sufficient force has passed over and intrenched to hold the position. During the day gen. Hooker moves down the Wauhatchie valley to within a mile of the U. S. force at Brown's ferry. The confederates, watching Hooker's advance from Lookout mountain, plan a night attack on him. It begins about 1 A.M., and at 4 they retire, repulsed. This battle is known as that of Wauhatchie. Gen. Hooker loses nearly 500 killed and wounded. This occupation of the Wauhatchie valley opens an excellent route for supplies, removing all danger of famine, and prepares the way for gen. Sherman's advance from Bridgeport. Grant, before further attack on the besieging forces, awaits Sherman, who is hastening from Corinth, while Bragg detaches from his army some 16,000 men under Longstreet to move against Burnside, at Knoxville, 4 Nov. Sherman's advance arrives at Bridgeport, 13 Nov., but as the position assigned his command on the extreme left necessitates moving his forces above Chattanooga, they are not in position with facilities for crossing the Tennessee until the afternoon of 23 Nov. "

Gen. Thomas advances his centre and occupies "Orchard Knob," a slight eminence midway between the defences of Chattanooga and the foot of Missionary Ridge.......23 Nov. "

To cover Sherman's crossing, Grant orders gen. Hooker, 24 Nov., to make a diversion by attacking the confederates on the slope of Lookout mountain towards the Wauhatchie valley. Gen. Hooker, with about 10,000 men, by 4 o'clock P.M. has driven the confederates from the Wauhatchie valley around the slope of Lookout mountain into the Chattanooga valley, and connected with gen. Thomas in Chattanooga on his left. This is called the battle of Lookout mountain. Gen. Sherman crosses the Tennessee and intrenches on the morning of..24 Nov. "

Battle of Chattanooga or Missionary Ridge the decisive battle of the campaign..25 Nov. "

Gen. Sherman is ordered to turn the confederate right at the extreme north end of Missionary Ridge. At early dawn, Nov. 25, he attacks the strong position of the confederates, but up to 3 P.M. has made no decided advance. Gen. Hooker meanwhile advances from the foot of Lookout mountain towards Rossville against the confederate left. Up to 3 P.M. the confederate line on the ridge remains intact, when gen. Thomas advances the division of Baird, of the 14th corps, and Wood's, Sheridan's, and Johnson's, of the 4th corps, on the confederate centre occupying the heights of the ridge, well defended by rifle-pits at the foot and on the slope. The intrenchments at the foot of the ridge are carried, and the troops continue, without orders, to ascend and carry the heights, breaking the confederate centre. The pursuit ceases because of darkness. The confederate loss is over 9000 (of which 6000 are prisoners), 40 pieces of artillery, and 7000 stands of small-arms. The federal loss is between 5000 and 6000. Gen. Grant detaches gen. Sherman's command with the 4th corps of the army of the Cumberland to relieve Knoxville (KNOXVILLE, SIEGE OF)..................28 Nov. "

[Gen. Bragg was beaten by his inaction, and by detaching Longstreet's command in the midst of an aggressive movement of the federals. The federal forces in the final battle were about 65,000; the confederates about 45,000 (in a position almost impregnable).

Chaumont (on the Marne, France), Treaty of, between Great Britain, Austria, Russia, and Prussia, 1 Mch. 1814; succeeded by that of Paris, 11 Apr., by which Napoleon renounced his sovereignty. PARIS.

chauvinism, said to be derived from Chauvin, the principal character in Scribe's "Soldat Laboureur," a veteran soldier of the first empire, worshipper of Napoleon. Scribe was born 24 Dec. 1794; died 20 Feb. 1861.

checkers. DRAUGHTS.

cheese is mentioned by Aristotle about 350 B.C. It is supposed by Camden and others that the English learned cheese-making from the Romans about the Christian era. Wilts, Gloucester, and Cheshire make vast quantities. The total production of cheese in the United States for the several years mentioned, beginning with 1850, have been:

Year.	On farms.	In factories.	Total pounds.
1850................	....	....	105,535,893
1860................	....	....	103,663,927
1870................	53,492,153	109,435,229	162,927,382
1880................	27,272,489	215,885,361	243,157,850
1890................	18,726,818	238,035,065	256,761,883

The first cheese factory in the U. S. was established at Rome, N. Y., by Jesse Williams in 1851. 9 years later there were 37 factories in operation. The number increased to 946 in 1870, and to 2532 in 1880. Previous to 1851 American cheese was made by the wives and daughters of farmers in their home dairies. A mammoth cheese weighing 1400 pounds, 13 ft. in circumference, 18 in. thick, and made from the milk of 700 cows collected at a single milking, was sent to president Jefferson by the ladies of Cheshire, Mass., through the rev. John Leland, in 1801; it bore the motto, "Rebellion to Tyrants is obedience to God." The exportation of cheese from the U. S. began about 1826, Harry Burrell of Herkimer county, N. Y., being one of the first to open a regular cheese trade with England in that year. The number of pounds of cheese exported from the U. S. has been as follows:

1820–21............	766,431	1860–61........about	25,000,000
1830–31............	1,131,817	1870–71............	63,698,867
1840–41............	1,748,471	1880–81............	147,995,614
1850–51............	10,361,189	1890............	95,376,053

New York State Cheese Manufacturers' Association organized at Rome..4 Jan. 1864

Mr. Willard, as agent for the American Dairymen's Association, visits England, Scotland, France, and Switzerland, and reports that the Cheddar system of cheese-making, at Cheddar, Somersetshire, Engl., is the best for American export manufacture.. 1866

[This system has been largely adopted in the U. S.]

Chelsea, Middlesex, Engl. A council held here 27 July, 816.—*Nicolas.* A theological college here founded by James I. in 1609, by Charles II. in 1682 made an asylum for wounded and superannuated soldiers. The erection was carried on by James II., and completed by William III. in 1690. The projector was sir Stephen Fox, grandfather of the orator C. J. Fox; the architect sir Christopher Wren; cost 150,000*l.* In 1850 there were 70,000 out- and 539 in-pensioners. The body of the duke of Wellington lay here in state, 10–17 Nov. 1852. The physic garden of sir Hans Sloane, at Chelsea, was given to the Apothecaries' Company, 1721. The first stone of the Military Asylum, Chelsea, was laid by Frederick, duke of York, 19 June, 1801.

Cheltenham, Gloucestershire, Engl. Its mineral spring was discovered in 1718. The king's well was sunk in 1778; and other wells by P. Thompson in 1806. Magnesian salt was first found in the waters in 1811.

chemical societies. One formed in London in 1780 did not long continue. The Chemical Society of London was established in 1841; that of Paris in 1857; that of Germany at Berlin, 1867. The Institute of Chemistry of Great Britain formed, prof. Edward Frankland first president, 1877; first meeting, 1 Feb. 1878. American Chemical Society incorporated, 10 Nov. 1877. Chemical Industry Society founded, 4 Apr. 1881.

chemistry was introduced into Spain by the Moors, about 1150. The Egyptians and Chinese claim an early acquaintance with chemistry. The first chemists were the alchemists (ALCHEMY); but chemistry was not a science till the 17th century; its study was promoted by Bacon, Hooke, Mayow, and Boyle. Early in the 18th century Dr. Stephen Hales laid the foundation of pneumatic chemistry, and Boerhaave combined the study of chemistry with medicine. These were succeeded by Bergman, Stahl, Black, etc. In 1772, Priestley published his researches on air, having discovered oxygen, ammonia, etc, a new chemical era He was ably seconded by Cavendish, Scheele, Lavoisier, Chaptal, and others The 19th century opened with the discoveries of Davy, continued by Dalton, Faraday, Thomson etc Organic chemistry has been advanced by Berzelius, Liebig, Dumas, Laurent, Hofmann, Cahours, Frankland, and others, since 1830 In 1828 Wohler produced artificially *urea*, hitherto known only as an animal product Since then acetic acid, alcohol, grape-sugar, various essential oils, similar to those of the pineapple, pear, garlic, etc, have been formed by combining oxygen, hydrogen, and carbonic acid The barrier between organic and inorganic bodies is thus broken down Indigo artificially formed by Bayer, 1878. ATMOLYSIS, DIALYSIS, ELECTRICITY, GALVANISM, PHARMACY, and SPECTRUM ANALYSIS The Royal College of Chemistry, Oxford street, London, was established in 1815 (now at South Kensington) Henry Watts's "Dictionary of Chemistry," begun 1863, has supplements (new ed 1888 et seq) M Ad Wurtz's "Dictionnaire de Chimie," 1868 Prof T E. Thorpe's "Dictionary of Applied Chemistry," 1890

Cherbourg, the naval fortress and arsenal of France on the coast of Brittany, equidistant from Portsmouth and Plymouth, Engl It was captured by Henry V. of England in 1418, and lost in 1450 Under Louis XIV, some works were erected here by Vauban, which, with some shipping, etc, were destroyed by the British, 6, 7 Aug 1758 The works, resumed by Louis XVI, were interrupted by the French revolution. The breakwater, commenced in 1783, resumed by Napoleon I. about 1803, completed in 1813, forms a secure harbor, affording anchorage for nearly the whole navy of France, and protected by strong fortifications On 4, 5 Aug 1858, the railway and the Grand Napoleon docks were opened Just outside of the harbor of Cherbourg the U S ship *Kearsarge* sunk the *Alabama*, 15 June, 1864 NAVAL BATTLES

Cheriton Down, Hants, Engl Here sir William Waller defeated the royalists under lord Hopton, 29 Mch 1644.

cherry, the *Prunus Cerasus* (from Cerasus, a city of Pontus, whence the tree was brought by Lucullus to Rome about 70 B.C), first planted in Britain, it is said, about 100 A D Fine kinds were brought from Flanders, in 1540, and planted in Kent

Cherry Valley, N Y, so named from the wild cherries found growing there by early settlers Made historical by a massacre there by a body of about 700 Indians and tories, under Joseph Brant and Walter Butler, who burned the settlement and killed between 40 and 50 of the inhabitants, mostly women and children, 11 Nov 1778

Cherubusco, Battle of Cherubusco was a strongly fortified place near the city of Mexico Towards this the Americans advanced after the battle at Contreras Santa Anna, who commanded 12,000 men near the walls of Mexico, advanced, and the whole region became a battle-field, 21 Aug 1847. Cherubusco was taken, and Santa Anna fled towards the city, sending a flag asking an armistice of 3 days, preparatory for negotiations for peace It was granted, but he violated the agreement, and hostilities were reopened MEXICAN WAR

Chesapeake. At the mouth of this bay a contest took place between the British admiral Graves and the French admiral de Grasse aiding the American colonies against Great Britain, the former was obliged to retire, 5 Sept 1781 The Chesapeake and Delaware were blockaded by the British fleet in the war of 1812, and the bay was, at that period, the scene of hostilities with various results. MARYLAND, UNITED STATES, VIRGINIA

Chesapeake and Shannon. NAVAL BATTLES.

Chesapeake and Leopard. UNITED STATES, 1807.

chess, a game attributed to Palamedes, 680 B.C., by Hyde and sir William Jones to the Hindus.

- Caxton printed "the Game and Playe of the Chesse" . 1474
- Chess club formed at Slaughter's coffee house, St. Martin's lane, London 1747
- Automaton chess player (machine) exhibited in England 1783
- M. F A Danican, known as Philidor, played 3 matches blindfolded at the Salopian, d 1795
- London Chess club founded, 1807, St George's 1833
- Des Chappelles noted chess player, d, Paris 27 Oct 1847
- Chess congress New York 1857
  [Paul Morphy, the greatest genius of chess, becomes known]
- Morphy won a match with Löwenthal in London 1858
- Played 8 games simultaneously, without seeing the boards, winning 6, at Birmingham, Engl 26 Aug "
- Defeated Harrwitz in Paris Sept "
- And Anderssen 20 Dec. "
- Staunton cannot be induced to meet Morphy "
- Morphy crowned chess king at a banquet in his honor, Paris, 4 May, 1859
- Paulsen played 10 games at once, won 5, lost 1, 3 were drawn, and 1 not ended Dec 1861
- International chess congresses 1, 2, London (winner, M Anderssen, of Breslau), 1851, 1862, 3, Paris (M Kolisch), 1867, 4, Paris (M Anderssen), 1870, 5, Vienna (M Steinmetz), Aug 1873
- Automaton chess player at the Crystal palace (a youth concealed in perforated box) exhibited "
- Howard Staunton, English player, d June, 1874
- Third American chess congress, Chicago, G H Mackenzie best player 7-14 July, "
- J J Löwenthal, Hungarian player, d 20 July, 1876
- Centennial chess tournament, Philadelphia, J Mason best player 16 Aug "
- J H Zukertort of Riga gains first prize at the International Chess Congress, Paris June, July, 1878
- "Mephisto," a mechanical chess player, exhibited at the Westminster aquarium, London 2 Oct. "
- Adolph Anderssen d . 14 Mch 1879
- Fifth American Chess Congress at New York, Mackenzie best player Jan 1880
- Chess tournament at Wiesbaden 9 July, "
- Herr Steinitz, opposing 30 competitors simultaneously, won 27 games, 2 draw, 1 lost, Baltimore, Md 22 Dec 1882
- Chess match, New York city, 6 games—Steinitz, 3 games, Mackenzie, 1, draw 2 7 Feb 1883
- Tournament at Berlin, 30 Aug 1881, at Vienna 24 June, 1882, in London. 26 Apr-23 June, "
- Morphy d at New Orleans (aged 47 years) 10 July, 1884
- Match between Steinitz and Zukertort in New York, St Louis, and New Orleans, begun 11 Jan 1886
  [Stakes, $2000 a side, Steinitz wins.]
- Geo. H Mackenzie, chess champion of America, awarded first prize, 1000 marks, at International Chess Congress at Frankfort on the Main. Aug 1887
- Chess match, Havana, Cuba, Tschigorin, Russian, first, Gunsberg, second 11 Feb 1890
- Mackenzie d in New York city 14 Mch 1891
- Louis Paulsen d 19 Aug "
- International Chess Match Championship of the World, Havana, Cuba, W Steinitz of New York city beats M Tschigorin, 10 to 8 28 Feb 1892

Chester, England, N W, the British Caerleon and the Roman Deva, station of the 20th legion, *Valeria Victrix*, quitted about 406 The city wall was first built by Edelfleda, about 908, Hugh Lupus, the earl, nephew of William I, rebuilt the Saxon castle in 1084, and the abbey of St. Werburgh Chester was incorporated by Henry III and made a county. The palatine jurisdiction was abolished by Parliament, 23 July, 1830 The see anciently part of Lichfield, whose bishop, Peter, removed hither in 1075, so that his successors were styled bishops of Chester, it was made a distinct bishopric by Henry VIII. in 1541, and the church of the abbey of St. Werburgh became the cathedral

- Chester ravaged by Danes . 980
- Taken, after 3 months' siege, for the parliament. 1645
- Fatal gunpowder explosion 1772
- Exchange and town hall burned . 30 Dec. 1862
- Projected attack of Fenians on Chester castle defeated by the police and the arrival of the military 11, 12 Feb. 1867
- Cathedral reopened, restored by sir Gilbert G Scott 7 Aug 1876
- Ancient tower of St John's church fell 15 Apr 1881

Chester, Pa., first town settled in Pennsylvania. PENNSYLVANIA, 1643-82 The Delaware River Iron Ship-building and Engine Works established here in 1872 by John Roach Here the *City of Pekin* and *City of Tokio* were built for the Pacific mail service.

Chevy Chase. OTTERBURNE.

Chicago, Ill., the 2d city in the United States in population, is first mentioned in Hennepin's account of the building of a new fort on the river Illinois in 1680, as Checaw-gou The town of Chicago was surveyed, and a plat, covering the portion of the present city bounded by Madison, Desplaines, Kinzie, and State streets, filed by James Thompson, 4 Aug. 1830 Population at that time was about 50, population since by decades 1840, 4470, 1850, 29,963; 1860, 109,260; 1870, 298,977, 1880, 503,185, 1890, 1,099,850; 1900, 1,698,575. Area, 1893, 197 sq. m, lat. 41° 56' N, lon 87° 40' W.

Baptiste Point de Saible, a well-educated negro, settles on the north bank of the Chicago river............................ 1779

De Saible sells his cabin to Le Mai, a French trader, and returns to Peoria.. 1796

A company of U. S. soldiers, under command of capt. John Whistler, arrive at Chicago river, July, 1803, and erect fort Dearborn on the south side of the river.................... 1803

John Kinzie, "father of Chicago," emigrates from near Niles, Mich., and purchases the property of Le Mai.............. 1804

U. S. Indian agency established at Chicago.................. "

First white child of Chicago, Ellen Marion Kinzie, born in the Le Mai cabin...Dec. "

FORT DEARBORN evacuated and garrison massacred by Indians, 15 Aug. 1812, and the fort burned..................16 Aug. 1812

Fort Dearborn rebuilt; site, near the present junction of River st. and Michigan ave.. 1816

First regular school opened by William L. Cox, in a small log-house near present crossing of Pine and Michigan sts...... "

Archibald Clybourne appointed first constable.........6 Sept. 1825

Rev. Isaac McCoy, a Baptist minister from near Niles, Mich., preaches the first sermon in English in Chicago......9 Oct. "

Town surveyed and platted by James Thompson........4 Aug. 1830

First frame hotel, kept by Mark Beaubien and called the "Sauganash," erected at the southeast cor. of the present Lake and Market sts... "

Chicago made county seat of Cook county by act of.....15 Jan. 1831

First post-office established, in a log-store near present cor. of Lake and South Water sts., Jonathan N. Bailey postmaster, 31 Mch. "

First frame business structures erected: one by George W. Dole on southeast cor. of Water and Dearborn sts., and one by Mr. Peck on southeast cor. Water and La Salle sts........... 1832

Improvement of the harbor, and building of the south pier commenced..1 July, 1833

Chicago incorporated as a town, 10 Aug., and first election of town officers held, Thomas J. V. Owen chosen president; pop. about 150....................................12 Aug. "

First Catholic church, erected near southwest cor. of Lake and State sts., by J. I. St. Cyr, and dedicated..............Aug. "

First newspaper, the *Chicago Democrat*, issued by John Calhoun..26 Nov. "

First Protestant church, on southwest cor. of Lake and Clark sts., dedicated..4 Jan. 1834

First steamboat to enter the river below Dearborn st., the *Michigan*...June, "

First lake schooner, the *Illinois*, of nearly 100 tons, from Sackett's Harbor, N. Y., sails up the river to Wolf Point, 12 July, "

First drawbridge across the river built by Nelson R. Porter; a double bascule of primitive form, completed............Aug. "

Fire wardens first appointed and fire limits defined by board of town trustees...................................25 Sept. "

First building erected especially for school purposes, built by John S. Wright on Clark st., south of Lake.................. 1835

First cemeteries established: one of 10 acres on the north side, near Chicago ave., east of Clark st., and one on south side, 16 acres, near the lake shore and 23d st..............26 Aug. "

One-story and basement brick court-house erected on northeast cor. of square in Clark and Randolph sts.................. "

Hook and Ladder company formed, Oct. 1835; fire department reorganized, 4 Nov., and fire-engine purchased........1 Dec. "

"Engine Company No. 1" (disbanded in Feb. 1860) organized, 12 Dec. "

First bank, a branch of the Illinois State bank, opened at the cor. of La Salle and South Water sts..................Dec. "

Saloon building on southeast cor. Lake and Clark sts., used as a city-hall from 1837-42, erected by J. B. F. Russell and G. W. Doan... 1836

City of Chicago incorporated by legislature.............4 Mch. 1837

First city election; William B. Ogden elected mayor....2 May, "

First brick church edifice, St. James's Episcopal, erected at cor. of Clark and Illinois sts., and dedicated............25 June, "

First theatre opened in the Sauganash hotel............Nov. "

"Metamora Engine Company No. 2" (disbanded 1859) organized...4 Dec. "

First permanent theatre, the "Rialto," established in building on west side of Dearborn, between Lake and South Water sts; license given.....................................20 May, 1838

First daily paper issued, the *Daily American*, now the *Evening Journal*...................................9 Apr. 1839

Regular line of steamboats between Chicago and Buffalo established..July, "

Tremont house built on present site, and completed...20 May, 1840

First public execution, that of John Stone, for murder of Mrs. Lucretia Thompson..............................10 July, "

School system reorganized and public free schools established, "

Water-works of the Chicago Hydraulic company (incorporated 18 Jan. 1836) in successful operation (wooden pipes)....May, 1842

First propeller built on lake Michigan, launched at Averell's ship-yard..July, "

Hogs prohibited from running at large in the streets of the city by ordinance...................................21 Apr. 1843

First Chicago Masonic lodge, Lafayette Lodge No. 18, chartered..2 Oct. "

First session of Rush Medical College held, 22 Nov. 1843, and first lecture in the college building.................11 Dec. "

First beef packed in Chicago for the English market.......1844-45

First permanent public school building erected on Madison st., opposite site of McVicker's theatre, at a cost of $7500...... 1845

Chicago Volksfreund, the first newspaper in a foreign language in Chicago, begins publication.....................26 Nov. "

Rice's first theatre on Dearborn cor. Randolph st., opened, 28 June, 1847

CHI

Great River and Harbor convention opens in Chicago..5 July, 1847

Chicago Tribune started as a Whig paper............10 July, "

Board of Trade organized at the office of W. L. Whiting, 13 Mch. 1848

Illinois Staats-Zeitung founded..........................Apr. "

First telegram received in Chicago, a message from Milwaukee, 15 Jan. 1848, and first through telegram from the east, 6 Apr. "

First boat locked through the Illinois and Michigan canal, the *General Frye*, arrives at lake Michigan, 10 Apr. 1848; canal formally opened....................................16 Apr. "

First cattle-yards, located in the vicinity of Madison st. and Ashland ave., and known as the "Bull's Head," opened.... "

Market building on State st. erected, and rooms first occupied by the common council............................13 Nov. "

Galena and Chicago Union railroad, begun June, 1848; completed 10 miles to the Desplaines river, and opened..20 Nov. "

Planking of principal streets and general numbering of houses begun... 1849

Great flood in Chicago river.........................12 Mch. "

Epidemic of cholera; 30 deaths in one day (1 Aug.), 25 July–28 Aug. "

Opening of Chicago and Galena railroad to Elgin celebrated by a grand excursion....................................1 Feb. 1850

First season of opera opens at Rice's theatre on Randolph st.; theatre burned..30 July, "

City first lighted with gas............................4 Sept. "

Corner-stone of new court-house and city-hall laid....12 Sept. 1851

Marine bank, the first under state general banking laws, organized..13 Jan. 1852

First through train from the east, via Michigan Southern railroad, enters Chicago................................20 Feb. "

New court-house occupied..............................7 Feb. 1853

First season of opera at Rice's new theatre opens with "Lucia di Lammermoor"....................................27 Oct. "

Chicago Orphan Asylum, organized 5 Nov. 1849; present location occupied... "

Chicago City Hydraulic company incorporated, 15 Feb. 1851, and water supply for the city begun..................Feb. 1854

Corner-stone of first Masonic temple, on Dearborn st., between Washington and Randolph, laid.....................18 May, "

Chicago and Rock Island railroad completed to Chicago, 5 June, "

New seal adopted for the city..........................June, "

Office of superintendent of schools created by ordinance, 23 June, "

Chicago Times started as a Democratic paper................ "

Cholera epidemic.....................................July, "

Police department organized, Cyrus P. Bradley, chief....June, 1855

Government post-office building, on Monroe st., begun......... "

State agricultural fair held for first time in Chicago.....9 Oct. "

Chicago Historical Society organized.................24 Apr. 1856

Steam tugs first used in the river and harbor............May, "

First suburban trains run from Chicago to Hyde Park..1 June, "

Chicago High School organized; C. A. Dupee, principal..8 Oct. "

First wooden pavement laid on Wells st., between Lake and South Water sts.......................................Nov. "

Free evening schools first held............................ "

Board of Sewerage Commissioners incorporated, 14 Feb. 1855, and first city sewers, a total of 6.2 miles, constructed........ "

McVicker's "New Chicago Theatre" opened...........5 Nov. 1857

Grade of city streets changed 1856–58

First steam fire-engine tried in 1855; proves unsatisfactory. First steam fire-engine bought by the city, the "Long John," tested at foot of South La Salle st.....................5 Feb. 1858

Paid fire department organized.........................2 Aug. "

First street railway, on State st., opened...............25 Apr. 1859

Chicago Academy of Science, founded 1857; incorporated..... "

Board of Trade incorporated................................ "

City charter amended, Feb. 1861, and Board of Public Works established...6 May, 1861

Graceland cemetery founded................................. "

Camp Douglas, on Cottage Grove st., between 31st and 33d sts., located..Sept. "

Cook County Hospital founded.............................. 1865

German Männerchor organized................................ "

Christ church erected...................................... "

Union stock-yards opened.............................25 Dec. "

Water-works tunnel begun, 17 Mch. 1864; last brick laid, 6 Dec. 1866, and water first let into the tunnel........25 Mch. 1867

Washington-street tunnel under Chicago river formally opened, 1 Jan. 1869

West Side Park Commission incorporated.............27 Feb. "

South Park Commission act ratified at election.......23 Mch. "

Chicago club founded....................................... "

Chicago Base-ball club organized........................... 1870

Foundlings' Home opened.............................31 Jan. 1871

La Salle St. tunnel under Chicago river opened to the public, 1 July, "

Great fire breaks out in a barn in the rear of lot No. 137 De Koven st., owned by Patrick O'Leary, about 8.45 P.M. Sunday (FIRES)...8 Oct. "

Union Park Congregational church building completed........ "

Inter-Ocean first issued..............................25 Mch. 1872

Apollo Musical club organized.............................. "

Grand Pacific hotel opened............................3 June, 1873

Palmer house opened..................................1 Nov. "

New Tremont house opened................................... "

St. James's church (Episcopal) erected...................... "

Unity church organized, 23 Dec. 1857; present building dedicated...7 Dec. "

Chicago Public library established, 1873; circulating department opened to the public.........................1 May, 1874

Second Presbyterian church, new edifice, dedicated....7 June, 1871
Trinity church (Methodist Episcopal), completed and opened for service..12 Mch. 1875
Cathedral of the Holy Name, foundation stone laid, 19 July, 1874; opened..1 Nov. "
Chicago Avenue church, "Moody's church," cor. Chicago and La Salle aves., completed.................................... "
Chicago *Daily News* first published.....................20 Dec. "
Exposition building opened.. 1877
Union club organized......................................Feb. 1878
Calumet club organized....................................4 Apr. "
Illinois club organized.......................................Apr. "
Art Institute incorporated as the Chicago Academy of Fine Arts, 20 May, 1879
Central Music hall opened.....................................5 Dec. "
U. S. government building, post-office and custom-house, completed at a cost of $6,000,000...........................3 May, 1880
St. James's church (Roman Catholic) dedicated.......24 May, "
St. John's church (Roman Catholic) established, 29 June, 1859; present edifice dedicated.. 1881
Immanuel Baptist church dedicated.......................25 Dec. "
First public trial of new cable street railway on State st. 28 Jan. 1882
Washington Park club organized 1883
McCoy's European hotel opened.............................1 June, 1884
Third Presbyterian church destroyed by fire..............9 Oct. "
County court-house and city-hall, began, 1877; completed and occupied...3 Jan. 1885
Chicago opera house opened to the public..............18 Aug. "
New Board of Trade building completed.............................. "
A force of 180 policemen, endeavoring to disperse a mob of anarchists at the Haymarket, are attacked with dynamite and revolvers; 7 are killed and 60 wounded..........4 May, 1886

[Of the anarchists, 8—Engle, Fielden, Fischer, Lingg, Neebe, Parsons, Schwab, Spies—are tried and convicted; 4—Engle, Fischer, Parsons, and Spies—are hung; 3 imprisoned, Schwab and Spies for life, Neebe for 15 years; and Lingg commits suicide.]

Auditorium building completed 1889, and opera-house dedicated; Adelina Patti sings; president Harrison present.......9 Dec. 1889
Area of city increased to 172.18 sq. miles..............29 July, "
Chicago secures the World's Fair, the vote in the House of Representatives being: Chicago, 157; New York, 107; St. Louis, 26; Washington, 18..............................24 Feb. 1890
Panic in the Chicago Board of Trade......................12 Apr. "
Illinois World's Fair constitutional amendment to permit the city to issue 5-per-cent. bonds to an amount not to exceed $5,000,000 in aid of the World's Columbian Exposition, passes the legislature..31 July, "
City area increased to 180.2 sq. miles....................4 Nov. "
Equestrian statue of gen. Grant unveiled...................7 Oct. 1891
Wergeland, a steel propeller, 400 tons, from Bergen, Norway, 12 Apr., arrives at Chicago, via St. Lawrence and Welland canal, 26 May, 1892

[The second vessel from a foreign port, the *Rosedale*, from England, in 1886, being the first.]

First elevated railway opened.............................27 May, "
University of Chicago opens *without formal ceremony*, with 500 students..1 Oct. "
World's Columbian Exposition, opening exercises held on the Exposition grounds; orations by Chauncey M. Depew and Henry Watterson..21 Oct. "
In the "Chicago Lake Front Case" the U. S. *Supreme Court* affirms the judgment of the U. S. Circuit Court adverse to the claims of the Illinois Central railroad company to title in the submerged lands...5 Dec. "
WORLD'S COLUMBIAN EXPOSITION formally opened by president Cleveland..1 May, 1893
A granite monument to the memory of Spies, Parsons, Fischer, Lingg, and Engle, anarchists in the Haymarket massacre, 1886, unveiled in Waldheim cemetery...................25 June, "
Gov. Altgeld pardons the anarchists Fielden, Neebe, Schwab, in *prison as principals* in the Haymarket massacre.....26 June, "
Mayor Harrison assassinated at his residence by Patrick E. Prendergast on the evening of...........................28 Oct. "
Prendergast executed......................................13 July, 1894

MAYORS.

William B. Ogden	1837	Thomas Dyer	1856
Buckner S. Morris	1838	John Wentworth	1857
Benjamin W. Raymond	1839	John C. Haines	1858
Alexander Loyd	1840	John Wentworth	1860
Francis C. Sherman	1841	Julian S. Rumsey	1861
Benjamin W. Raymond	1842	F. C. Sherman	1862
Augustus Garrett	1843	John B. Rice	1865
A. S. Sherman	1844	R. B. Mason	1869
Augustus Garrett	1845	Joseph Medill	1871
John P. Chapin	1846	Harvey D. Colvin	1873
James Curtiss	1847	Monroe Heath	1876
James H. Woodworth	1848	Carter H. Harrison	1879
James Curtiss	1850	John A. Roche	1888
Walter S. Gurnee	1851	Dewitt C. Cregier	1890
Charles M. Gray	1853	Hemp. Washburne	1891
Ira L. Milliken	1854	Carter H. Harrison	1893
Levi D. Boone	1855	John P. Hopkins	1894

Chichester, Sussex, Engl., built by Cissa, about 540. The first cathedral was completed about 1108, burned with the city in 1114, and rebuilt by bishop Seffrid about 1187. The second was erected during the 13th century. The spire fell 20 Feb. 1861; a new one was begun 2 May, 1865; completed June, 1866. The cathedral reopened after repairs, 14 Nov. 1867. The bishopric originated thus: Wilfrid, archbishop of York, compelled to flee by Egfrid, king of Northumberland, preached the gospel in this country, and built a church in the isle of Selsey, about 673. In 681 Selsey became a bishopric, and so continued until it was removed to Chichester; then called Cissan-Caester, from its builder, Cissa, by Stigand, about 1082. This see has yielded to the church 2 saints, and to the nation 3 lord chancellors.

Chickahominy battles. PENINSULAR CAMPAIGN and UNITED STATES, 1862.

Chickamauga, Ga., **campaign** and **battle of.** Having procured the necessary supplies for his army after the TULLAHOMA CAMPAIGN, gen. Rosecrans again assumed the offensive, advancing against the confederate forces still under gen. Bragg, and now mostly concentrated in and around Chattanooga, Tenn.

Campaign begins with the advance of the army of the Cumberland, numbering about 55,000 men, infantry, cavalry, and artillery, in 3 corps—14th, maj.-gen. George H. Thomas; 20th, maj.-gen. Alexander McD. McCook; 21st, maj.-gen. Thomas L. Crittenden. It moves from middle Tennessee over the Cumberland mountains towards Chattanooga.....16-19 Aug. 1863
Crosses the Tennessee river at different points without serious opposition..29 Aug.-7 Sept. "
Confederates, under gen. Bragg, retire *from Chattanooga*, 7-8 Sept., towards Lafayette, Ga., about 25 miles southeast. The 21st corps occupies Chattanooga.....................9 Sept. "
Leaving 1 brigade as garrison it advances towards Ringgold, 9-12 Sept. "
20th corps *crosses* Lookout mountain, south *of* Chattanooga, and moves towards Alpine.........................10-14 Sept. "
14th corps crosses Lookout mountain and threatens Lafayette by Cattlet's and Dug's gaps in the Pigeon mountain, 10-17 Sept. "
Gen. Rosecrans, learning that the confederates are in force near Lafayette, concentrates his army near Lee and Gordon's mill, 10 miles southeast from Chattanooga.......17-18 Sept. "
Meanwhile Longstreet, with reinforcements from Virginia, has joined Bragg, who strikes the 21st corps near Lee and Gordon's mill..P.M., 18 Sept. "

Confederates on the morning of the 19th seek to turn the federal left, strongly reinforced by gen. Thomas during the night. Bragg aims to crowd the federals away from Chattanooga by occupying Rossville. There is continuous and desperate fighting all day without *definite results.* The confederates attack, while the federals maintain their ground, and at night still hold the road contended for all day. The federals have used almost every available man; while the confederates begin the 20th with fresh troops and elated by reinforcements. The confederates continue the same tactics on the 20th, and gen. Rosecrans is *obliged to shift* his troops to the left, where the confederate attack is persistent and desperate. Intending to obey the following order from gen. Rosecrans, "The general commanding directs that you close up on Reynolds as fast as possible and support him," gen. Wood moves his division of the 21st corps out of the line of battle before its place is filled. The defeat of the federals is at least greatly accelerated by this order and movement, for Longstreet, already prepared, now advances 8 brigades, attacking successfully, and enters with little or no resistance at the gap thus made, enabling him to crush the federal right, so that it takes no part in the battle thereafter. It causes the separation of gens. Rosecrans, McCook, and Crittenden for the rest of the day from the fighting portion of the army. But gen. Thomas still holds the left, and here earns the well-won title of "Rock of Chickamauga." Reinforced during the afternoon by gen. Gordon Granger from Rossville with 3700 men, he holds his position until dark, when he retires to Rossville. The federals, prepared to renew the contest, await the confederates along Missionary Ridge, at Rossville, throughout the 21st, but there is no pursuit and no fighting, and at night they retire to Chattanooga and fortify it. Federal loss: killed, 1647; wounded, 9262; missing, 4945, cavalry, 500; total, 16,351. CHATTANOOGA CAMPAIGN.

Chickasaw bayou, Miss., Battle of. Here on 29 Dec. 1862, gen. Sherman assaulted the confederate works in order to gain the rear of Vicksburg, but was repulsed. Federal loss about 2000; confederate, 207. VICKSBURG CAMPAIGN.

Chickasaws. INDIANS.

children. Many ancient nations exposed their infants—the Egyptians on the banks of rivers, and the Greeks on highways—when they could not support or educate them; in such cases they were protected by the state. The old custom of English parents selling their children to the Irish for slaves was prohibited by Canute, about 1017. FOUNDLING, INFANTICIDE. ORPHAN-HOUSES and FOUNDLING HOSPITALS are ancient, but the methods of dealing with dependent and delinquent children as well as children in general have vastly improved within a half-century, as witness the reformatories, homes for feeble-minded children, newsboys' and bootblacks' homes, boys' clubs, free kindergartens fresh-air missions, crèches, etc A complete Factory and Workshop act, regulating the hours of labor for women and children and the age under which the latter may not be employed in factories, etc., was passed in England in 1878 In the United States, compulsory education laws and the legal regulation of factories and labor fall to each state separately, hence the provisions regulating child labor, etc, are various In general, by the existing laws, the ages under which children cannot be employed vary from 10 to 14 years, and attendance at school for from 12 to 16 weeks during the previous year is required in all cases where minors are employed The legal hours of labor vary from 8 to 18

Cotton Mills act, passed in England fixing the working age of children at 9 years and limiting the hours of labor for children under 16 to 12 hours daily 1819
Night work forbidden to minors in England 1831
First law dealing with child labor enacted by Connecticut 1842
American Female Guardian Society incorporated in New York, 1849
Children s Aid Society of New York founded 1853
First effective law limiting child labor in Massachusetts 1866
Society for the Prevention of Cruelty to Children organized in New York under statute enacted 1875
Fresh air movement begun by rev Willard Parsons of Sherman Pa 1877
First boys club in New York started in the Wilson mission St Mark's place about 1878
Children s Dangerous Performance act passed in England 24 July 1879
Tribune fresh air fund, the continuation of the *Evening Post* fund, begun 1882
[Up to 1892 more than 94 000 children of New York were given a 2 weeks' vacation each year in the country as the guests of philanthropic farmers and village residents]
Act passed in the English Parliament for the prevention of cruelty to and protection of children 26 Aug 1889

Chili or **Chilé,** South America discovered by Diego de Almagro, one of the conquerors of Peru, 1535 Chili was partially subdued in 1546 It extends from about 21° to 56° S lat, or along the whole of the west coast of South America from Peru south about 2500 miles between the Andes and the Pacific ocean, and is from 40 to 200 miles in breadth Area, 124,000 sq miles Pop. in 1865, 1,068,447, in 1875, 2,068,447, 1878, 2,136,724, 1889, 2,766,747

Chili declares its independence of Spain 18 Sept 1810
War with varying success, decisive victory by San Martin over the royal forces at Chacabuco, 12 Feb 1817, the province declared independent 12 Feb. 1818
Present constitution formed after the constitution of the U S, 22 May, 1833
Rupture with Bolivia over the "Guano" isles 1 Mch 1864
Disputes with Spain respecting Peru settled by the Spanish minister, 20 May, disavowed by his government 25 July, "
Religious toleration enacted July, 1865
J J Perez again president, vigorous prosecution of the war, Oct. "
Spanish admiral Pareja at Valparaiso claims satisfaction for intervention in the war with Peru 17 Sept., refused, 21 Sept, he declares a blockade, 24 Sept, Chili declares war against Spain, 29 Sept, joins Peru 5 Dec "
Spaniards bombard Valparaiso 31 Mch 1866
End of the blockade 14 Apr "
Gold mines discovered near Iquique Oct. 1871
Chili refuses to recognize a boundary treaty between Peru and Bolivia (6 Feb. 1873), they declare war against Chili Apr 1879
Chilian wooden vessels *Esmeralda* and *Covadonga* blockade Iquique, the Peruvian iron clad turret-ships (with rams) *Huascar* and *Independencia* attempt relief, *Esmeralda* sunk by *Huascar* (about 110 perish), *Independencia* runs ashore chasing *Covadonga*, capt. Platts and 6 men climb up *Huascar* and are killed fighting on deck 21, 23 May, "
Huascar enters port of Iquique, and captures 2 vessels, 29 July, "
Blockade of Iquique raised, announced 4 Aug. "
Huascar captured by Chilian fleet off Mejillones, after 6 hours' fight, the admiral and many officers killed 8 Oct. "
Pisagua bombarded and captured by Chilians 2 Nov "
Combined Peruvian and Bolivian army defeated near Iquique (which surrenders), Nov, again near Tarapaca, which is taken about 27 Nov "
Naval engagement, gallant conduct of Peruvians. 27 Feb 1880
Callao blockaded by Chilians, alarm at Lima about 18 Apr "
Battle of Tacna, captured by Chilians. 26 Apr "
Arica taken by the Chilians 8 June, "
Pierola dictator of Peru, declares for perseverance in the war, excitement at Lima, levy *en masse* 28 June, "
Chilian transport *Loa* sunk by torpedo of a Peruvian launch apparently laden with fruit, Callao greatly shaken 3 July, "
Chilian vessel *Covadonga*, bombarding town, sunk by Peruvian torpedoes off Chancay, about 115 perish, reprisals 14 Sept. "
Chilians storm Lurin, 4 Jan., defeat Peruvians at Chorillos, 13 Jan, at Miraflores, 15 Jan, occupy Lima without resistance, Pierola flees about 17 Jan, Callao taken Jan. 1881
Conditions of peace reported cession of territory, $730,000,000 indemnity, occupation of Callao, working of mines till indemnity paid, announced 30 Jan. "
England and France requested to mediate by Peru Feb 1881
U S. seeks to adjust relations between Chili and Peru "
Treaty of peace with Spain confirmed Sept.
Domingo Santa Maria becomes president 18 Sept.
Treaty of peace with Bolivia 25 Jan 1882
Peace protocol between Chili and Peru agreed to Mch "
War resumed, skirmishes, Chilians generally successful July, "
Peruvians defeated by Chilians 13 15 and 16 July, also 8 Aug "
Peruvians defeated with great loss at Huamachuca 10 July 1883
Peruvians defeated at Huanchuco by col Gorostiago 19 July "
Peace with Peru signed at Ancon 20 Oct "
Lima evacuated 23 Oct. "
Señor don José Manuel Balmaceda president 18 Sept 1886
Congress issues a declaration deposing the president for treason against the constitution tyranny and misuse of the public moneys, and designates sen Jorge Montt as its assistant in restoring the due observance of the constitution 1 Jan 1891
The navy (under capt J Montt) revolts against the president, the army remains faithful to him about 7 Jan "
Valparaiso held for the president blockaded by the navy frequent skirmishes contradictory reports 16 Jan "
President s troops defeated at Pozo Almonte 4 Mch, the province of Tarapaca held by the congress party about 8 Mch "
Part of the army joins the congress party which holds all southern Chili reported 12 Mch "
A provisional government or junta established by the congress party at Iquique 19 Apr "
Part of the regular army (2400) crosses the Argentine territory to reach Santiago reported 14 Apr "
Newly elected congress (his nominees) opened by the president 21 Apr "
Itata surrenders to the American cruisers at Iquique 4 June, "
UNITED STATES, 7-9 May and 4 June 1891
Provisional junta at Iquique in a circular note to the powers denounce Balmaceda as a dictator, and ask recognition as a belligerent 7 May published 11 June, "
Congress party occupy the Atacama province 25 July, "
Congressist army about 10 000, with artillery, etc commanded by col Canto land at Quinteros bay 20 Aug and after a night's march they completely defeat Balmaceda's army at Colmo, the congressists have about 300 killed, Balmaceda has about 1000 killed, 21 Aug, they advance and take Salto, 24 Aug, and Quilpue, 25 Aug, march towards Valparaiso, receiving large numbers of deserters from the enemy, and encamp in a farm house 27 Aug "
Battle of Placilla, Balmaceda s army totally defeated, about 1000 killed and 3000 prisoners, congressists, 400 killed, the battle lasted from 7 30 to 10 30, and the congressists took possession of Valparaiso at 1 P M 28 Aug "
The great powers recognize the congressist provisional government about 16 Sept "
Balmaceda, concealed at the Argentine legation in Santiago, commits suicide, leaving a justificatory letter, and is secretly buried 19 Sept "
National holiday with great rejoicings 18-20 Sept. "
Patrick Egan the U S minister charged with breach of neutrality by favoring Balmaceda s party during the war Oct "
At Valparaiso some of the populace assault the boats' crews of the U S ship *Baltimore*, 2 of the crew killed, 16 Oct, the U S government demands reparation, the Chilian government promises investigation 22 Oct. "
UNITED STATES Oct 1891, Jan and July, 1892.
Sen Jorge Montt elected president 4 Nov "
Patrick Egan concludes a convention between Chili and the U S Aug 1892

Chillianwallah, India, Battle of, between strong Sikh forces and the British under lord (afterwards viscount) Gough, 13 Jan 1849 The Sikhs routed, but with great loss to the British 26 officers killed, 66 wounded, 731 rank and file killed, and 1446 wounded The Sikhs lost 3000 killed and 4000 wounded. On 21 Feb lord Gough routed the Sikh army, under Shere Singh, at Goojerat, capturing its camp.

Chiltern Hundreds (viz Burnham, Desborough, and Stoke), an estate of the British crown on the chain of chalk hills that pass from east to west through Buckinghamshire The stewardship, a nominal office with salary of 25*s*, is given to a member of Parliament who wishes to vacate his seat The strict legality of the practice is questioned

Chimborazo. ANDES.

chimneys. Chafing-dishes were in use in Great Britain till 1200, when chimneys were introduced, only in the kitchen and large hall The family sat round a stove, with a funnel through the ceiling, in 1300. Chimneys were general in domestic architecture in 1310.

Act to regulate chimney sweeping, 28 Geo III 1789
Chimney sweeping machine invented by Smart 1805
A statute regulating the trade, the apprenticeship of children, construction of flues, forbidding calling "sweep" in the streets, etc., passed 1834
By 3 and 4 Vict. c 85 (1840), no master sweep may take apprentices under 16, no person under 21 to ascend a chimney after 1 July, 1842
Enforcement of this law made more stringent 1864

Joseph Glass, inventor of sweeping-machine now in general use, not patented, d. ....29 Jan. 1868
New Chimney-sweepers' act passed ....11 Aug. 1875

China (*Tsing*), the "Celestial Empire," in eastern Asia, for which the Chinese annals claim an antiquity of from 80,000 to 100,000 years B.C., is said to have commenced about 2500 B.C.; by some to have been founded by Fohi, supposed to be the Noah of the Bible, 2240 B.C. The 3 religions of China are CONFUCIANISM, TAOISM, and BUDDHISM. It is said that the Chinese were astronomers in the reign of Yao, 2357 B.C. The historical period of China begins about 650 B.C. 22 dynasties have reigned, including the present. Area of China proper, 1,554,000 sq. miles; other territory, 2,985,750 sq. miles; total, 4,539,750 sq. miles. Pop. of the empire estimated at 190,348,228 in 1757, at 414,607,000 in 1860, and at 434,600,000 in 1877. The "Statesman's Year-book" puts the population at 402,680,000, but the truth is, but little is known as to it. Gen. James H. Wilson in his book on China, 1887, puts it as low as 300,000,000.

B.C.

Chinese state their first cycle begun 2700
First dates fixed to his history, by Se-ma-tsien, begin 651
Supposed age of Confucius (Kungfutze), the philosopher 550
Wall of China completed (CHINESE WALL) 211
Dynasty of Han 206
Literature and art of printing encouraged (?) 202
Battle between Phraates and Scythians; Chinese aid the latter, and ravage the coasts of the Caspian; their first appearance in history—*Lenglet* 129
Religion of Laot-se begun 15

A.D.

Buddhism, or religion of Fŏ, introduced ....about 68–81
Nankin becomes the capital 420
Atheistical philosopher, San-Shin, flourishes 449
Nestorian Christians permitted to preach 635
They are proscribed and extirpated 845
China ravaged by Tartars ....9th and 11th centuries
Seat of government transferred to Pekin 1260
Marco Polo introduces missionaries 1275
Kublai Khan establishes the Yuen or Mongol dynasty...about "
Ming dynasty 1368
Canal, called the Yu Ho, completed ....about 1400
Europeans first arrive at Canton 1517
Macao is granted to the Portuguese 1536
Jesuit missionaries are sent from Rome 1575
Country is conquered by the eastern or Mantchou Tartars, who establish the present Tsin dynasty 1616–44
Tea brought to England 1660
General earthquake; 300,000 persons buried at Pekin alone.... 1662
Galdan, a prince of Jangaria, conquers Kashgaria and becomes supreme in central Asia, 1678; checked by Kang-hi, 1689; totally defeated 1695
Commerce with East India Company begins 1680
Jesuit missionaries preach 1692
Commercial relations with Russia 1719–27
Jesuits expelled 1724–32
Another general earthquake destroys 100,000 persons at Pekin, and 80,000 in a suburb 1731
Successful war in central Asia; Davatsi and his opponent Amursana, subdued by Keen-lung, 1755 et seq.; Kashgar, Khokand, the Khirgez, etc., annexed 1760
In a salute by a British ship in a Chinese harbor, a shot inadvertently kills a native; the government demands the gunner; he is soon strangled 1785
Earl Macartney's embassy arrives at Pekin; his reception by the emperor ....14 Sept. 1793

[This embassy threw light on the empire; it appeared to be divided into 15 provinces, with 4402 walled cities; a population of 333,000,000; annual revenues, 66,000,000*l.*; and army, including Tartars, 1,000,000 infantry and 800,000 cavalry; religion pagan, and government absolute. Arts and sciences were encouraged, and ethics studied.]

He is ordered to depart ....7 Oct. "
And arrives in England ....6 Sept. 1794
Affair of the company's ship *Neptune*, a Chinaman killed..... 1807
Edict against Christianity 1812
Chinese rule in central Asia weakened .... "
Lord Amherst's embassy; he leaves England ....8 Feb. 1816

[He failed in his mission, having refused to make the prostration of the kotou, lest he compromise the majesty of England.]

Opium dispute begins; the trade prohibited by the emperor, Nov. 1834
Chinese seize the *Argyle* and crew ....31 Jan. 1835
A British commissioner settled at Canton ....Mch. 1837
Commissioner Lin orders seizure of opium, 18 Mch.; foreign residents forbidden to leave Canton, 19 Mch.; factories surrounded, and outrages committed ....24 Mch. 1839
Capt. Elliot, British commissioner, requires British subjects to surrender all opium, promising full value, 27 Mch.; half is given up as contraband to the Chinese, 20 Apr.; the remainder (20,283 chests) surrendered, 21 May; capt. Elliot and the British merchants leave Canton, 24 May; the opium destroyed by the Chinese ....3 June, "
Affair between British and U. S. seamen and the Chinese; a native killed ....7 July, "

Hong-Kong taken ....23 Aug. 1839
British boat *Black Joke* attacked, the crew murdered, 24 Aug.; British merchants retire from Macao ....26 Aug. "
Affairs at Kow-lung between British boats and Chinese junks, 4 Sept. "
Attack by 28 armed junks on the British frigates *Volage* and *Hyacinth*; several junks blown up ....3 Nov. "
British trade with China ceases, by edict of the emperor; the last servant of the company leaves ....6 Dec. "
Emperor's interdict against intercourse with England forever ....5 Jan. 1840
Ship *Hellas* attacked by armed junks, 22 May; blockade of Canton by a British fleet, by order of sir Gordon Bremer, 28 June; blockade of the Chinese coast ....10 July, "
Capt. Elliot, on a British steamship, enters the Pei-ho river, near Pekin ....11 Aug. "
Ship *Kite* lost on a sand-bank; the captain's wife and part of the crew captured by natives and confined in cages..15 Sept. "
Lin degraded; Keshin appointed imperial commissioner, 16 Sept.; capt. Elliot's truce with him ....6 Nov. "
Admiral Elliot's resignation announced ....29 Nov. "
Negotiations ended by emperor's breach of faith ....6 Jan. 1841
Chuen-pe and Tae-coc-tow, and 173 guns (some sent to England) captured ....7 Jan. "
Hong-Kong ceded by Keshin to Great Britain, $6,000,000 to be paid within 10 days to the British ....20 Jan. "
Hong-Kong taken possession of ....26 Jan. "
The emperor rejects Keshin's treaty, 11 Feb.; hostilities resumed, 23 Feb.; Chusan evacuated, 24 Feb.; rewards proclaimed at Canton for the bodies of Englishmen, dead or alive; $50,000 to be given for chiefs ....25 Feb. "
Bogue forts taken by sir G. Bremer; admiral Kwan killed; 459 guns captured ....26 Feb. "
British squadron proceeds to Canton, 1 Mch.; sir H. Gough takes command of the army, 2 Mch.; hostilities suspended, 3 Mch.; and again resumed, 6 Mch.; Keshin degraded by the emperor ....12 Mch. "
Flotilla of boats destroyed; Canton threatened, foreign factories seized, and 461 guns taken by the British ....18 Mch. "
Hong-Kong Gazette first published ....1 May, "
Capt. Elliot prepares to attack Canton ....17 May, "
City ransomed for $6,000,000; $5,000,000 paid down; hostilities cease ....31 May, "
British trade reopened ....16 July, "
Sir Henry Pottinger reaches Macao, as plenipotentiary; proclaims the objects of his mission; capt. Elliot superseded, 10 Aug. "
Amoy taken, and 296 guns destroyed ....27 Aug. "
Bogue forts destroyed ....14 Sept. "
Ting-hae taken, 136 guns captured, and Chusan reoccupied by the British, 1 Oct.; they take Chin-hae, 10 Oct.; Ning-po, 13 Oct.; Yu-yaou, Tsze-kee, and Foong-hua ....28 Dec. "
Chinese attack Ning-po and Chin-hae, are repulsed with great loss, 10 Mch.; 8000 Chinese routed near Tsze-kee....15 Mch. 1842
Cha-pou attacked; defences destroyed ....18 May, "
British squadron enters river Kiang, 13 June; captures Woosung and 230 guns and stores, 16 June; Shang-Haï taken, 19 June, "
British armament anchors near the "Golden Isle," 20 July; Chin-Keang taken; the Tartar general and many of the garrison commit suicide, 21 July; advanced ships reach Nankin, 4 Aug.; fleet arrives, and disembarkation commences, 9 Aug.; Keying arrives, with full powers to treat ....12 Aug. "
Treaty of peace signed before Nankin, on the *Cornwallis*, by sir Henry Pottinger for England, and Keying Elepoo and Neu-Kien on the part of the Chinese emperor—[Conditions: Lasting peace and friendship between the 2 empires; China to pay $21,000,000; Canton, Amoy, Foochoofoo, Ning-po, and Shang-Haï to be thrown open to the British, and consuls to reside at these cities; Hong-Kong ceded in perpetuity to England, etc.; Chusan and Ku-lang-su to be held by the British until the provisions are fulfilled] ....29 Aug. "

[The non-fulfilment of this treaty led gradually to the war of 1856–57.]

Ratifications formally exchanged ....22 July, 1843
Canton opened to the British ....27 July, "
Bogue forts captured by the British ....5 Apr. 1847
Hong-Kong and neighborhood visited by a typhoon; immense damage to shipping; upwards of 1000 boat-dwellers on the Canton river drowned ....Oct. 1848
British steamship *Medea* destroys 13 pirate-junks in the Chinese seas ....4 Mch. 1850
Rebellion breaks out in Quang-si ....Aug. "
Appearance of the pretender Tien-teh ....Mch. 1851
Emperor Taou-Kwang d. 25 Feb. 1850. He had of late grown liberal, and favored the introduction of European arts; but his son, a rash and narrow-minded prince, abandoned this policy, and particularly opposed English influence. An insurrection broke out in consequence, Aug. 1850, and quickly became alarming. The insurgents at first proposed only to expel the Tartars; but in Mch. 1851, a pretender was announced, first called Tien-teh (Celestial Virtue), but afterwards assuming other names. He was said to be a native of Quang-si, of obscure origin, but to have obtained some literary knowledge at Canton about 1835, and to have learned the principles of Christianity from a Chinese Christian named Leang-afa, and also from the missionary Roberts in 1844. He announced himself as the restorer of the worship of the true God, Shang-ti, and derived many of his dogmas from the Bible. He declared himself to be the monarch of all beneath the sky, the lord of China (and thus of all the world), the brother of Jesus, the second son of God, and demanded universal

submission He sought alliance with lord Elgin in Nov 1860 His followers are termed Tae Pings, "princes of peace," a title belied by their atrocious deeds The rebellion was virtually terminated 18 July 1864, by the capture of Nankin, suicide of Tien Wang, and execution of the leaders

Defeat of Leu, the imperial commissioner, and destruction of half the army 19 June, 1852

Progress of the rebels, the emperor vainly asks the Europeans for help Mch and Apr 1853

Rebels take Nankin, 19, 20 Mch , Amoy 19 May, Shang Haï 7 Sept "

Outrage on the British lorcha *Arrow* in Canton river 8 Oct. 1856

[It was boarded by the Chinese officers 12 men out of the crew of 14 carried off, and the national ensign taken down Sir J Bowring governor of Hong Kong applied to India and Ceylon for troops On 3 Mch 1857, the *House of Commons*, by a majority of 19, censured sir John for "violent measures " The ministry (who took his part) dissolved Parliament but obtained a large majority in the new one]

After vain negotiations with commissioner Yeh Canton forts attacked and taken 23 Oct "

A Chinese fleet destroyed and Canton bombarded by sir M Seymour 3, 4 Nov "

Imperialists defeated, quit Shang Haï 6 Nov "

And murder the crew of the *Thistle* 30 Dec "

Mahometans of Panthay, in Yunan, become independent during Tae Ping rebellion "

Troops arrive from Madras and England, and lord Elgin appointed envoy Mch 1857

Chinese fleet destroyed by commodore Elliot, 25 27 May , and sir M Seymour and commodore Keppel 1 June "

Blockade of Canton Aug "

Canton bombarded and taken by English and French, 28, 29 Dec 1857, who enter it 5 Jan 1858

Allies proceed towards Pekin, and take the Pei ho forts, 20 May, "

Negotiations commence, 5 June, treaty of peace signed at Tien tsin by lord Elgin, baron Gros, and Keying (who signed the treaty of 1842), ambassadors to be at both courts, freedom of trade, toleration of Christianity, expenses of war to be paid by China, a revised tariff, term *I* (*barbarian*) to be no longer applied to Europeans 26, 28 29 June, "

Lord Elgin visits Japan, and concludes an important treaty with the emperor 28 Aug "

Mr Bruce, British envoy, on his way to Pekin, is stopped in the river Pei ho (or Tien tsin) admiral Hope, attempting to force a passage, is repulsed, with the loss of 81 killed and about 390 wounded 25 June 1859

U S envoy Ward arrives at Pekin, and refusing to submit to degrading ceremonies does not see the emperor 29 July, "

[Frederick Townshend Ward was born at Salem, Mass , Nov 1831 He was educated at the Salem high school, saw service in the Mexican war and as a lieutenant in the French army in the Crimea Going to China in 1859, he became admiral general in the service of the emperor, trained the Chinese into good soldiers, and at their head won many victories over the rebels, but was killed at Kah sing, 7 Oct 1862]

Commercial treaty with the U S 24 Nov "

English and French prepare an expedition against China, Oct "

War begins, British under sir Hope Grant, French, gen Montauban. Chinese defeated in a skirmish near the Pei ho, 12 Aug 1860

Allies repulse Tae Ping rebels at Shang Haï, 18-20 Aug , take Taku forts, losing 500 killed and wounded, Tartar gen San ko lin sin retreats 21 Aug "

After vain negotiations, allies advance towards Pekin, defeat Chinese at Chang kia wan and Pa li chiau 18 and 21 Sept "

Consul Parkes, capts. Anderson and Brabazon, Mr De Norman, Mr Bowlby (London *Times* correspondent), and 14 others (Europeans and Sikhs), advancing to Tung chow to arrange a meeting of the ministers, are captured by San ko lin sin, Brabazon and abbé de Luc beheaded and said to be thrown into the canal, others carried to Pekin 21 Sept. "

Allies march towards Pekin, French ravage emperor's summer palace, 6 Oct., Parkes, Loch and others restored, 8 Oct., Anderson De Norman, and others die of ill usage 8-11 Oct "

Pekin invested, surrenders, 12 Oct., severe proclamation of sir Hope Grant 15 Oct. "

Summer palace (Yuen ming yuen) burned by British 18 Oct. "

Convention signed in Pekin by lord Elgin and the prince of Kung, treaty of Tien tsin ratified apology for attack at Pei ho (25 June, 1859), indemnity to be paid immediately, compensation to the families of the murdered prisoners, etc., Kowloon ceded in exchange for Chusan, treaty and convention to be proclaimed throughout the empire 24 Oct. "

Allies quit Pekin 5 Nov "

Treaty, Russia and China—the former obtaining free trade, territories, etc 14 Nov "

English and French embassies fixed at Pekin Mch 1861

Emperor Hienfung d . 21 Aug "

Canton restored to Chinese . 21 Oct. "

Advance of rebels, they seize and desolate Ning po and Hang-chow Dec. "

They reach Shang Haï, it is placed under protection of the English and French, and fortified Jan. 1862

English and French assist against rebels, Ning po retaken, 10 May, "

Imperialists gain ground, take Kah sing, etc , gen Ward killed (see 1859) 7 Oct. "

Tungani (Mahometan) revolt in central Asia, massacre of Buddhists . . "

Commercial treaty with Prussia ratified 14 Jan 1863

Imperialists under col Charles Gordon defeat the Tae-Pings under Burgevine, etc Oct. "

Gordon captures Sow chow (after a severe attack, 27, 28 Nov), rebel chiefs butchered by Chinese 4, 5 Dec "

Capt Osborne comes to China, retires, the Chinese government breaking its engagements 31 Dec "

Gordon s successes continue Jan to Apr 1864

Takes Nankin (in ruins), Hun seu tseun the Tien wang (rebel emperor) commits suicide by eating gold leaf, 30 June, Ching wang and Kan wang rebel generals are "cut into a thousand pieces" 18 July, "

Tae Pings hold Ming chow, Mahometan rebellion (Dounganes) progressing in Honan Jan -Mch 1865

Rebellion in the north advancing June, "

Pekin in danger July "

Chinese newspaper, *Messenger of the Flying Dragon*, appears in London 14 Jan 1866

Chinese commissioners visit London June, "

Mahomed Yakoob Beg defeats the Tungani, supreme in Kashgar 1866, recognized by Europe "

Chinese embassy (Anson Burlingame Chin Kang and Sun Chia Su) received by president at Washington, 5 June, sign a treaty (BURLINGAME TREATY and UNITED STATES), 4 July, arrive in London, Sept , received by queen 20 Nov 1868

People at Yang chow, incited by "literati" (learned classes), destroy Protestant mission houses, 22 Aug , redress not obtained, British squadron proceeds to Nankin, 8 Nov , viceroy superseded, British demands acceded to 14 Nov "

Chinese embassy received by emperor at Paris 24 Jan 1869

Supplementary convention to treaty of Tien tsin (June 1858) for commercial freedom signed 23 Oct "

Burlingame dies at St Petersburg 22 Feb 1870

Massacre at Tien tsin of French consul, Roman Catholic priests, sisters of mercy (22 persons), many native converts and above 30 children in the orphanage, by a mob said to be favored by authorities, missionaries accused of kidnapping children 21 June, "

Increased hatred of people to foreigners at Tien tsin, government lukewarm against the murderers July, "

Chapels destroyed at Fatshan 21 Sept. "

French ultimatum refused, murderers of nuns unpunished, Chinese warlike preparations reported 26 Sept. "

Mandate from the mandarin Tseng kwo fan, exculpates missionaries, and condemns their massacre Oct "

Sixteen coolies beheaded 15 Sept , and 23 exiled, indemnity to the sufferers ordered, reported 26 Oct "

End of the difficulty announced 3 Nov "

Chung How, an envoy, arrives in London Aug 1871

Received at Paris, apologizes for Tien tsin massacres, and assures redress 23 Nov "

Memorial to the Chinese government by Mr Hart British inspector of customs, recommending changes in civil and military administration autumn, "

Young emperor married 16 Oct "

Russia annexes Kuldja "

William Armstrong Russell consecrated Anglican bishop of North China Dec 1872

Emperor of age, assumes the government 23 Feb 1873

Talifoo, capital of the insurgent Panthay Mahometans, captured, thousands massacred Feb. "

Foreign ministers first received by emperor 29 June, "

Dispute with Japan (FORMOSA), July-Aug , settled by treaty, 31 Oct. 1874

Death of the emperor 12 Jan 1875

Proclamation of Tsai tien, son of Chun, seventh son of Taou-Twang (nephew of Kung) 4 Feb. "

British exploring expedition under col. Horace Browne to open passage from Burmah into S W China, Dec 1874, Mr Margary and 5 Chinese in advance killed at Manwyne, 21 Feb , col Browne repulses an attack by Chinese, retreats to Rangoon, 22 Feb 12 Mch "

First railway in China Shang Haï to Oussoon (Woo sung) 11 miles, trial trip, 16 Mch (at first opposed), opened 30 June, 1876

Chee foo convention, difficulties in negotiations removed (the government to compensate Mr Margary's family, remove commercial grievances, open 4 ports, proper official intercourse), signed, 13 Sept , ratified 17 Sept "

Chinese envoy (Quo ta Zhan) lands at Southampton 21 Jan 1877

Decree of equal rights to Chinese Christians 1 Feb "

Four more ports opened 1 Apr "

Opium smoking interdicted after 3 years Aug "

Quo ta Zhan (or Kuo ta Jén) first accredited minister at London, Liu ta Jén at Berlin about Nov "

Yakoob Beg of Kashgaria defeated by the Chinese general, Tso tsung tang, is assassinated, May, Kashgar and other towns captured, end of war Dec "

Chinese immigrants excluded from Australia by a poll tax 1878

Treaty with Russia, who agrees to evacuate the Kuldja territory, China to pay an indemnity about June, 1879

Chinese from Kashgar invade Russian territory May, 1880

Prospect of war, col Gordon goes to China from Bombay, June, "

New treaties with U S signed 17 Nov "

Peace with Russia, who makes concessions negotiated by marquis Tseng 1881

Complication with France respecting Tonquin Sept. 1883

Chinese claim Anam as dependency Nov "

Coup d'état at Pekin by prince Chun, father of emperor, he becomes dictator, prince Kung and the viceroy, Li Hung Chang, deposed 11 Apr et seq 1884

Treaty with France, signed by capt Fournier and Li Hung Chang at Tien-tsin, French protectorate of Anam and Tonquin recognized, 3 southern provinces opened to commerce, 11 May, 1884

Chinese break the treaty by attacking French marching to occupy Langson "

French demand evacuation of Tonquin frontier forts, and 10,000,000*l* indemnity July, "

War party at Pekin oppose the empress and Li Hung Chang the viceroy July, "

Kelung in Formosa bombarded, and forts destroyed by alleged treachery of admiral Lespès 5, 6 Aug "

France declines mediation, issues circular to the powers 17 Aug "

Indemnity claimed by France reduced to 3,200,000*l*, 19 Aug, refused by China "

French ambassador, Semallé, leaves Pekin, war ensues 21 Aug "

Admiral Courbet with fleet sails up the Min river unattacked, destroys Chinese fleet, 23 Aug, bombards arsenal at Foo chow, dismantles and destroys forts and batteries at Mingan and Kinpai, French killed, about 7, Chinese said to be about 1000 26-28 Aug "

Li Hung Chang deprived of his highest offices about 28 Aug "

Chinese declaration of war announced 6 Sept "

Preliminaries of peace signed at Pekin Apr 1885

Treaty signed 9 June, "

Introduction of railways authorized, new policy Aug "

Emperor agrees to receive a papal agent to protect Roman Catholic missionaries July, "

Chinese annul French protectorate over all Christians Nov 1886

Decanville railway opened 21 Nov "

General proclamation for protection of Christian missionaries and converts Jan 1887

Emperor, aged 16, assumes the government 7 Feb "

Convention between Great Britain and China respecting Burmah and Thibet ratified 25 Aug "

Commercial treaty with France signed and ratified Aug "

Chinese Exclusion act vigorously carried out at San Francisco, and at other places (UNITED STATES, 13 Sept 1888) Oct. 1888

Railway from Tien tsin to Taku opened Nov "

Conventions with Italy and Germany for them to protect their missionaries, announced Dec "

New Roman Catholic cathedral at Pekin consecrated 8 Dec "

Marriage of the emperor 25 Feb 1889

An imperial decree, granting audience of the emperor to representatives of foreign powers issued 12 Dec 1890

China formally objects to Henry W Blair as minister to that country from the U S. 28 Apr 1891

Anti European riots at Wuhu, much destruction, British consulate wrecked, the consul and his wife escape, quiet restored by force 12, 13 May, "

Increased anti foreign agitation throughout China, June, diplomatic body appeal to the government, emperor decrees protection of foreigners about 15 June, "

Continued persecution of foreigners, the imperial decree ineffectual, the diplomatic body press the government about 18 Aug "

Kolao Hui, a secret society, strongly opposed to foreigners and Christianity, active summer, "

American mission at Ishang destroyed 11 Sept. "

Outrages against foreigners increase, the diplomatic body report to their respective governments about 15 Sept. "

Great Britain, France, Germany and U S. unite to protect their people against Chinese violence, reported 21 Sept "

Sufferers in Wuhu compensated by viceroy about 23 Oct "

British squadron and other vessels at Nagasaki and other ports, about 23 Oct. "

A *modus vivendi* with the Chinese authorities arranged by the European ministers, reported 11 Nov "

Insurrection in Mongolia and N China against foreigners and native Christians, reported massacres, Nov, suppressed by government troops after battles, with much slaughter, 28, 29 Nov "

Agreement of the Hunan societies against Europeans etc, published at Shang Hai about 7 Dec "

Memorials of the viceroys of Nankin and Hukuang (attributing the anti foreign outrages to baseless rumors circulated by conspirators) issued Dec "

Government pays indemnities amounting to 100 000*l* to Christian missions and others, and punishes the Chinese officials and offenders, reported 27 Dec. "

Chauhan, the agitator ordered to be arrested, 25 Mch, not arrested, the right of audience by the emperor requested by the foreign ministers, rejected early Apr 1892

Stringent exclusion measures adopted by the U S government against the Chinese (UNITED STATES) May, "

Great inundation by the Yellow river, 12 towns said to be destroyed 23 Sept. "

Chinese exclusion amended bill passed by the U S senate. 2 Nov "

FOR WAR WITH JAPAN, SEE CHINO JAPANESE WAR

Treaty between China and U S. ratified Aug 1894

Imperial edict for the protection of foreigners. 15 Oct "

Li Hung Chang superseded by prince Kung 4 Nov "

Prince Kung appointed president of the grand council, virtually dictator, Li-Hung Chang returns to power... 13 Dec. "

Treaty of peace with Japan 17 Apr 1895

Loan of 400,000,000 francs, 4 per cent., guaranteed by Russia, signed at Pekin, 4 July, at St. Petersburg 6 July, "

Japan demands an indemnity for giving up the Liao-tung peninsula, evacuations to begin on first payment, Aug, supplementary treaty signed 8 Nov "

Insurrection of the Dungans, Chinese troops defeated near Su chau, gen Sou beheaded, reported 22 Sept. 1895

British ultimatum demanding the degradation of the viceroy of Szu chuan and others, 28 Sept., accepted by China, 30 Sept. "

China agrees to pay compensation to Germany for the plundering of a mission station at Swatau, an agreement concluded at Shang-Hai for a crown concession to Germany at Han Kow, 6 Oct, and at Tien tsin, reported 30 Oct "

An explosion on the transport *Kung Pai*, near Kinchau, 500 soldiers killed 14 Oct. "

Li Hung Chang charged with orders to suppress the insurrection, mutiny of troops at Kiu-kiang Khiang Nov "

Anglo German loan for 16,000,000*l*. at 5 per cent. signed at Pekin 24 Mch 1896

Sir Robert Hart appointed superintendent of posts and telegraphs, reported 30 Mch. "

China enters the postal union 2 Apr "

Tidal wave at Hai chau, 4000 lives lost. 26 July, "

Sheng Ta Jên, director of railways, contract for the construction of the Han Kow railway signed 30 May, 1897

Reparation demanded by Germany for the recent murder of 2 German missionaries, troops landed at Kiao-chau, 14 Nov "

[Kiao chau ceded to Germany, with adjacent territory, 99 years' lease, 5 Jan, ratified, 24 Jan 1898.]

Russian fleet arrives at Kinchau, near Port Arthur, with China's approval 18 Dec "

Li Hung Chang recalled to power 3 Jan 1898

Japan claims payment of the indemnity (11,008,857*l* paid by the bank of England on behalf of China, 7 May) 9 Feb "

Inland waters to be opened to British and other steamers, with regulations, in June 20 Feb. "

Chinese loan of 16,000,000*l* at 4½ per cent, between Hong-Kong and other banks, ratified 3 Mch. "

German Chinese agreement relating to privileges in Shantung, signed 6 Mch "

The Yangtse trade regulations, drawn up by sir Robert Hart, agreed to 13 May, "

Death of prince Kung, aged 68 29 May, "

Wei hai wei occupied by the British 30 May, "

Prince Henry and the German squadron visit Kiao chau, 5 May, received by the emperor and empress at Pekin 15-18 May, "

Convention signed at Pekin leasing extension of boundaries to Hong Kong 9 June, "

Concession for Grand-central railway from Han Kow to Pekin secured by Franco Belgian syndicate, reported 15 June, "

Li Hung Chang dismissed from the Tsung li Yamên 7 Sept "

Coup d'état, regency of the empress restored, reactionary policy, flight of Kang Yu Wei, reformer (saved by British consuls, and conveyed to Hong Kong) 22 Sept "

The marquis Ito visits Pekin, received by the emperor, 20 Sept. "

Six members of the reform party executed 28 Sept. "

Great fire at Han-Kow, 1000 deaths reported 1 Oct "

Reformers in office dismissed 10 Oct. "

Russian troops (1300) at Port Arthur and neighborhood, Feb, fight between Russians and Chinese at Ta lien wan, many Chinese killed, reported 19 Feb 1899

Yu Hsien, founder of the anti foreign and anti Christian sect the "Boxers," made governor of Shantung Mch "

Boundary of territory leased by Russia near Port Arthur settled, mid Mch anti foreign disturbances by the Boxers (Red Fist) and the Big Knife societies, in Shantung, Mch., German punitive expedition, villages burned, Yi chau occupied Apr "

Coup d'etat by the empress dowager, edict issued, naming Po Ching (14), son of prince Tuan, the heir designate 24 Jan 1900

The "open door" in China for the world's commerce successfully promoted by Mr Hay, U S secretary of state Mch "

The Tsung li-Yamên reorganized under prince Tuan and 3 Manchus 10 June, "

Baron von Ketteler murdered by Chinese troops in Pekin, the legations besieged 20 June, "

The dowager empress and prince Tuan issue anti foreign decrees 22 or 23 June, "

SEE CHINO-EUROPEAN (BOXERS) WAR for events not given here.

Li Hung Chang maintains order in Canton, frequent executions of robbers and pirates, reported 6 July, "

The Russians seize Hailar, Harbin relieved, Chinese defeated at Blagovestchensk, Sakhalin, and Niu-Chwang captured, 3, 4 Aug "

Emperor, empress, and court fly from Pekin after ordering the execution of 5 pro-foreign members of the Yamên, 14 Aug "

Russians seize both banks of the Amur, massacre of about 4800 Chinese at Blagovestchensk 14 Aug "

Total allies in Pekin, 62,000 (22,000 Russians, 19,000 Japanese, 5000 British) 14 Sept. "

Kirin, a rich town in Manchuria, occupied by the Russians, 21 Sept, An suan jan captured 26 Sept. "

Degradation and punishment of prince Tuan and 4 others, ordered by imperial edict (reported a forgery, 15 Oct) 25 Sept. "

Imperial court reported at Si-ngan fu 15 Oct. "

Anti dynastic rebellion in S. China, reported mid. Oct. "

Russian *de facto* protectorate over Feng tien and Mukden, Manchuria-Russo-Chinese agreement signed about 31 Dec "

Peace protocol signed at Pekin, 14 Jan; ratified by the emperor 17 Jan 1901

Departure of foreign troops May et seq. "

Count von Waldersee leaves Pekin for Germany. 3 June, "

Great fire in the Forbidden city at Pekin 4 June, "

"Allied villagers," new anti foreign movement spreading, reported 24 June, 1901
Prince Chun's mission received at Potsdam, 4 Sept., Chinese envoy sent to Japan Sept "
Peace protocol with China signed by the 11 foreign ministers, 15 Aug, by prince Ching and envoys 7 Sept "
The court leaves Si ngan fu for Pekin 6 Oct "
Death of Li Hung Chang, diplomatist, friend of Russia, aged about 78, 7 Nov, succeeded by Yuan Shih kai as governor of Chi li 8 Nov "
Imperial edicts favoring reorganization and reforms issued, Pu Chun, heir apparent disinherited 10 Nov "
The imperial court returns to Pekin, the dowager empress again supreme 7 Jan. 1902
Edicts protecting missionaries and native Christians, and ordering punishment of officials complicated in the Boxer movement, issued 14 Jan "
U S note protesting against Russian encroachments in Manchuria 1 Feb "
Anglo Japanese agreement, maintaining the *status quo*, the "open door" policy, independence and territorial integrity of China and Corea, signed in London 30 Jan "
Manchurian convention revised, the *status quo* to be maintained, Russia to withdraw gradually in 18 months, signed and ratified 8, 9 Apr "
[Russia's non compliance with the terms of this treaty led to the Russo-Japanese war, which see]
Kai Chi, Chinese cruiser, blown up by an explosion in the powder magazine near Nankin, 150 lives lost 22 June, "
Tien tsin transferred to the Chinese 15 Aug "
Evacuation of Shang Hai completed by departure of last detachment of German troops 3 Jan 1903
Agreement for construction of a railway from Shang Hai to Nankin early Jan "
Memorial arch erected at Pekin by Chinese government as atonement for murder of baron von Ketteler in 1900, formally dedicated by prince Chun in presence of baron Goltz and large number of foreigners and natives 18 Jan "
Russia presents 7 demands as conditions for carrying out the Manchurian convention and the evacuation of Niu Chwang and the 2 southern provinces of Manchuria. Chief provisions No new treaty ports to be opened in Manchuria and no new foreign consuls permitted, all customs revenues to be paid into Russo Chinese bank, no portion of Manchuria to be alienated to any other power, none but Russians to be employed in any administrative capacity, civil or military, in Manchuria, reported 23 Apr "
Demand rejected by China 29 Apr "
Settlement of a Chinese customs at Dalny, on the Russian frontier of leased territory 12 June, "
Negotiations with Japan for revision of commercial treaty, in consequence of the insistence of Japan on clause in treaty opening Mukden, Taku shen, and other Manchurian centres to foreign trade, announced 12 June, "
Secret agreement between China and Russia regarding Manchuria, reported 22 June, "
Commercial treaties with the U S and Japan, signed 8 Oct "
Russia fails to evacuate Manchuria according to agreement on appointed date 8 Oct "
Commercial treaty by which U S consuls may be sent to Mukden and Antung, in Manchuria, signed by the emperor, ratified by telegraph, and consuls appointed by U S government Commercial treaty with Japan, for opening the foreign trade and settlement of 2 treaty ports, Mukden and Ta tung Ku, in Manchuria, ratified 13 Jan 1904
First train on railroad from Tsing tow to Tsian fu 26 Feb "
SEE RUSSO-JAPANESE WAR for events in Manchuria in 1904-1905
Russian gun boat *Mandjur* dismantled at Shang Hai 31 Mch "
Wei shien, Chow cheen, Chwan fu, and Chou tsun opened to commerce 18 May, "
Roman Catholic bishop and two priests murdered at Hupe, 24 July, "
Rebellion near Shan tung 11 Oct "
Rebellion in Kwang si 16 Nov "
China threatened by Russia on account of contraband trade with Japan 17 Jan 1905
China reported to be opposed to the Japanese plan to open Manchuria 7 May, "

CHINESE EMPERORS

1627 Chwang lei
1644 Shun che (first of the Tsin dynasty)
1662. Kang-hi an able sovereign, consolidated the empire, compiled a Chinese dictionary
1723 Yung ching
1736. Keen lung, warlike, fond of art, embellished Pekin
1795 Kea king
1820 Taou Kwang
1850 Hien fung 25 Feb
1861 Ki tsiang (altered to Toung chi), 24 Aug; b 27 Apr 1856, married 16 Oct. 1872, d 12 Jan 1875
1875 Tsai T'ien (altered to Kwang Su), aged 4. Jan
[China was ruled by 2 empresses (Tsze An and Tsze Chi), 1861-81, and by one (Tsze Chi), an able woman, 1881-87]
1887 Emperor assumed the government, 7 Feb

China grass or **rhea.** A prize of 5000*l* was offered by the Indian government for machinery to prepare and cleanse the fibre, 11 Jan 1870. John Greig's machine was exhibited in Edinburgh, Dec 1871 RAMIE

China porcelain, introduced into England about 1531 POTTERY

China rose, etc. *Rosa Indica* was brought from China, and successfully planted in England, 1786, the Chinese apple-tree, or *Pyrus spectabilis*, about 1780

chincho'na or **cincho'na,** discovered, it is said, by a Jesuit about 1535 (and used by the order) It was called by the Spaniards "fever-wood," and also "Jesuit's bark" Its virtues were not generally known till 1633 or 1638 It was sold at one period for its weight in silver Was introduced into France in 1649 and is said to have cured the dauphin, afterwards Louis XIV, of a fever It came into general use in 1680, and sir Hans Sloane introduced it into England about 1700 The chinchona has been largely planted in the Neilgherry hills, India, and already its culture has spread over a wide area in southern India, in Ceylon, and in British Burmah The preparation of its bark, most extensively employed in medicine, is the alkaloid quinine in the form of a sulphate QUININE

Chinese wall, said to have been erected about 211 B.C Reported in 1879 to be 1728 miles long, extending from the sea shore on the gulf of Pe-che lee westward beyond Soo-Choo, on the borders of Turkestan, by a zigzag through a belt over 300 miles in width, its northern limit being north of Pekin, in the province of Pe-che lee, where it reaches 41° N lat., and its southern limit is the province of Kan soo, near the city of Lan-Choo, lat 36° 5' N No pains were taken to select the most practicable route, for it passes up steep mountains, down into gorges and ravines, crosses rivers, valleys, and plains, seemingly regardless of obstacles Some idea of the labor expended on this work can be formed when it is known that this wall is 20 feet thick at the bottom and 15 feet at the top and from 25 to 30 feet high, with flanking turrets 35 to 40 feet high every 200 or 300 yards. The exterior faces are of blocks of well cut granite, laid in excellent mortar, within it is filled with close-packed earth and stones, its upper surface is paved with bricks a foot square, laid several layers thick, forming an excellent passageway That it was well and strongly built is proved by its present condition, after more than 2000 years.

Chino-European (Boxers) war. By the treaty of Shimonoseki, in 1895, China gave Japan the island of Formosa and the peninsula of Liao-tung (Port Arthur) and acknowledged the independence of Corea Russia intervened and, backed by France and Germany, and unopposed by England, forced Japan to accept a pecuniary compensation in place of Port Arthur and the adjoining territory In Nov 1897, Germany seized the port of Kiau-chau, in the province of Shantung, and in Jan 1898 received from China a 99 year lease of the town, harbor, and district In Mch 1898, Port Arthur and the Liao-tung peninsula were leased by China to Russia for 25 years, with the right to build fortifications, and also important railway concessions in Manchuria England followed in Apr 1898 by demanding and obtaining a lease of Wei hai-wei for 25 years and also a 99 year lease of territory on the mainland opposite Hong-Kong At the same time France obtained a 99 year lease of 2 small islands and of territory on the mainland opposite to Hainan Italy also demanded the lease of a part, but this was refused by China The Boxer movement was the result of an intense hatred of all foreigners, excited by these successive occupations of Chinese territory Their first overt act was to murder foreigners wherever they were to be found unprotected The Chinese government could not, or would not, put down the Boxers, who soon obtained control of the empress The immediate result was an attack on the European legations in Pekin, in which the imperial troops took part.

Yu Hsien, founder of the anti foreign and anti Christian sect the Boxers, made governor of Shantung Mch 1899
Boundary of territory leased by Russia near Port Arthur settled, mid Mch, anti foreign disturbances by the Boxers (Red Fist) and the Big Knife societies, in Shantung, Mch, German punitive expedition villages burned Apr "
Coup d'état by the empress-dowager, edict issued, naming Po Ching (14), son of Prince Tuan the heir designate, 24 Jan 1900
Foreign ministers demand the suppression of the Boxers and other hostile secret societies 27 Jan "
The "open door" in China for the world's commerce successfully promoted by Mr Hay, U S secretary of state, Mch "

Attacks on the Wei hai wei boundary commission repulsed by Chinese under col Bower and capt Watson 5, 6 May, 1900

Massacre of native Christians by Boxers between Pao ting-fu and Pekin mid May, "

Insurrection spreads, railway property, etc, destroyed, Chinese employes killed 27 May, "

Feng tai railway station burned by the Boxers, refugees arrive at Pekin 28 May, "

Evasive edict, practically encouraging the Boxers, issued 29 May, "

Emphatic protests *re* the Boxer movement from the legations to the Yamen 20-30 May, "

Foreign marine guards (340) arrive at the Pekin legation 31 May, "

Pao-ting fu refugees attacked by Boxers, 4 killed and many missing 31 May, "

Huang tsun station burned, employés killed by the Boxers, 4 June, "

German and Austrian guards arrive in Pekin 3-5 June, "

Foreign reinforcements land at Tien tsin 5 June, "

Railway communication stopped at Pekin 6 June, "

Massacres and destruction of railway and mission stations spreading from Pekin district to other provinces, 7, 8 June, "

Imperial edict decreeing a massacre of foreigners, issued 9 June (changed into a protective edict by 3 members of the Tsung li Yamen, who were afterwards cruelly executed, 14 Aug)

The Tsung li Yamen reorganized under prince Tuan and 3 Manchus 10 June, "

Adm sir Edw Seymour's force defeats the Boxers at Lang-fang 11 June, "

M Sugiyama, Japanese chancellor, murdered by Chinese troops in Pekin 11 June, "

Massacre of native converts and foreign employés in Pekin, buildings burned 13, 14 June, "

Disbandment of troops in the Taku forts demanded by allies, 16 June, the forts open fire on allied fleets, but are captured 17 June, "

Tien tsin foreign settlement attacked 17 June, "

Foreign legations ordered to quit Pekin 19 June, "

Baron von Ketteler murdered by Chinese troops in Pekin, 20 June, "

Siege of the Pekin legations begins, total guards 18 officers, 389 men, the British legation filled with refugees, outposts fiercely attacked, prof J Huberty and others killed 20 June, "

Sir Claude Macdonald takes command at the British legation, *the Hanlin academy burned by Chinese* 22 June, "

Seymour captures arsenal near Tien tsin 22 June, "

Chinese driven back, capt Beyts killed 23 June, "

Tien-tsin relieved by allies after hard fighting 23 June, "

The Japanese repulse a fierce attack, many Chinese killed, 24 June, "

Seymour returns to Tien tsin 26 June, "

Edict issued at Pekin virtually declares war on all foreigners, and their expulsion ordered . 26 June, "

Arsenal N E of Tien tsin captured by the allies 27 June, "

Combined attack of Boxers and troops repulsed with severe loss . 27 June, "

Insurrection spreads to Manchuria in the north and Shantung in the south, slaughter of Chinese near Tien tsin, reported 29 June, "

Adm Seymour's advance to Pekin checked, retires to Tien tsin .. . 29 June, "

Anarchy in Manchuria, missions destroyed, bishop Guillon, R C, and others, burned alive in the cathedral of Mukden, July, "

Edict from Pekin ordering the extermination of foreigners, issued . July, "

Li Hung Chang *maintains order in Canton, frequent executions of robbers and pirates* July, "

Brilliant sortie, many Chinese killed 3 July, "

Co operation of the powers, Japan allowed a free hand, about 6 July, "

Massacre of about 64 missionaries, men, women, and children, at Tai yuen fu in Shang si, by Yu-Hsien, the governor's, orders 28 June and 9 July, "

Li Hung Chang made viceroy of Chi li 9 July, "

Fierce fighting at Tien tsin, 6 July, the allies seize an arsenal, about 386 Chinese killed . 9 July, "

Tien-tsin, native city and forts, captured, a fort and 48 guns seized by the Japanese 13, 14 July, "

[Allies, casualties about 800]

Fighting on the Russian frontier of the Amur, Blagovestchensk bombarded . 16 July, "

Captain Strouts killed . . 16 July, "

Armistice concluded, but siege continued 17 July, "

Li Hung Chang confers with the governor in Hong Kong, 18 July, "

Capt. Watts Jones and 10 or 12 Europeans murdered at Kwei-hua cheng by the governor's order, about 20 July, "

Li-Hung Chang arrives at Shang Hai . 21 July, "

The emperor appeals in vain for mediation to France, Germany, U S., and Japan . . 19, 21 July, "

Further massacres of missionaries and others in Shang si at Pao ting fu, Chu Chau, and other places in the north, 21 July, "

Severe fighting at Niu Chwang . . 19-26 July, "

Two progressive Yamên ministers beheaded in Pekin by the empress's order, and the exiled Chang Yin Huan executed in Kashgaria 29, 31 July, 1900

The Russians seize Hailar, Harbin relieved, Chinese defeated at Blagovestchensk, Sakhalin, and Niu Chwang captured, 3, 4 Aug "

Allies advance to Pekin, Japanese victory, Chinese driven out of Pei tsang, many killed, 4, 5 Aug, Yang tsun captured 6 Aug "

Field marshal von Waldersee, of the German army was unanimously selected to lead the allied armies in China 6 Aug "

British troops land at Shang Hai 9 Aug "

Emperor empress, and court fly from Pekin after ordering the execution of 5 pro foreign members of the Yamên, 14 Aug "

Russians seize both banks of the Amur, massacre of about 4800 Chinese by Gribsky and his Cossacks at Blagovestchensk 14 Aug "

The allies relieve the legations 14 Aug "

[*Total casualties during the siege about 67 killed, 120 wounded, and 5 other deaths*]

Pei tang R C bishopric, in Pekin, nobly defended by mgr Favier 133 priests and 42 French and Italian marines, with about 3000 refugees, 20 June, till relieved by the Japanese and allies 17 Aug "

(Total deaths during the siege, 400)

Imperial city entered, palace gates held by allies 17 Aug "

Forbidden city closely guarded by allies 17 Aug "

Boxers defeated near Tien tsin, 300 killed, 64 captured, 19 Aug "

Sir Robert Hart resumes his office in Pekin 21 Aug "

Li-Hung Chang's peace overtures rejected by the powers, 22 Aug "

The allies forbid looting and call on the Chinese to return, 22 Aug, they march through the Forbidden city and occupy the imperial palace 28 Aug "

Continued Russian successes in Manchuria 24-29 Aug "

Wholesale massacres of missionaries and native converts at Fu chau fu, 15 Aug, and many other places July, Aug "

Four Boxer leaders executed at Tien tsin 30 Aug "

British troops occupy Feng tai, near Pekin early Sept. "

Liang hsiang, S W *of Pekin, stormed by German marines and* Bengal lancers, 500 Boxers killed . 11 Sept "

20 Germans killed in an encounter with Boxers near Pekin, 13 Sept "

Boxers routed and over 200 killed by Americans and Bengal lancers, at Mo tao mid Sept "

Total allies in Pekin, 62,000 . 14 Sept "

Boxers defeated at Pa ta chu 17 Sept "

Ti lin occupied by the allies and afterwards burned, mid Sept. "

Russians occupy the Manchurian frontier and 6 towns, columns penetrating the interior, much slaughter, reported 18 Sept. "

Pei tang and Lutai captured with heavy losses by the allies, 20, 21 Sept "

Anti Christian riots in the south, converts slaughtered, reported 21 Sept "

Boxers routed by the British, 16 m S of Pekin 25 Sept "

Kirin, in Manchuria, occupied by the Russians 24 Sept., An shan jan captured 26 Sept "

Degradation and punishment of prince Tuan and 4 others, ordered by imperial edict (reported a forgery, 15 Oct), 25 Sept. "

Count von Waldersee appointed commander-in chief of the allies, Aug, arrives at Tien tsin 27 Sept "

Shan hai kwan forts surrender to the British 29 Sept "

Russian garrison in Pekin reduced 29 Sept. "

The German emperor, in reply to the emperor Kwang su's message, insists on full reparation for the crimes committed and punishment of the guilty officials. 1 Oct. "

Mukden taken by the Russians 1 Oct. "

Summer palace looted by the Russians, Sept., occupied by the British and Italians . 3 Oct "

French note, demanding punishment of the chief culprits, indemnities, establishment of permanent legation guards at Pekin, dismantlement of the Taku forts, etc (accepted as the basis of negotiations), issued 4 Oct. "

Pekin-Tien tsin railway held by the British, Russian claim to left bank of river at Tien tsin disputed 8 Oct. "

Conference of ministers in Pekin, Chinese proposals pronounced inadequate 8 Oct "

Prince Ching, Li Hung Chang, Liu Kun yi, and Chang Chih tung appointed peace negotiators, by edict 13 Oct "

Imperial court reported at Si ngan fu 15 Oct "

Anti dynastic rebellion in S. China, reported mid Oct. "

Anglo German agreement—chief points the "open door" and the integrity of China to be maintained 16 Oct. "

Allies (4000, under gens. Campbell and Bailloud) enter Pao-ting fu . . . 15-21 Oct "

Joint note, after long negotiations, demanding China's compliance to "12 irrevocable conditions," preliminary to the withdrawal of the allies from Pekin and provinces, signed by the ministers in Pekin, 20 Dec., presented, 22 Dec., accepted by the emperor in his decree .... . 27 Dec "

Prince Chun's mission received at Potsdam, 4 Sept. 1901, Chinese envoy sent to Japan . . . . . . Sept. 1901

Peace protocol with China (signed by the 11 foreign ministers), 15 Aug., by prince Ching and envoys. . . 7 Sept "

The Summer palace occupied by the British and Italians, 12 Oct, 1900, transferred to the Chinese 14 Sept. 1901
The Japanese and Americans hand over the Forbidden city to the Chinese, the evacuation of Pekin completed 17 Sept "

Chino-Japanese war. By the treaty of 1885 between Japan and China, neither power was to send armed men into Corea without previous notification to the other This treaty was violated by China 7 June, 1894, by sending a Chinese force into Corea "to protect our tributary state," thus defying Japan, and forcing her to maintain her rights if she could Japan replied on 12 June that she would send a body of troops into Corea, and at the same time Japan invited China to jointly undertake needed reforms in Corea This was refused by China, and war between the two powers was inevitable

Difficulty between Japan and China settled by European mediation, treaty 18 Apr 1885
British flag set up at Port Hamilton, announced 13 May, 1885, *decided to be kept* Nov 1886
Port Hamilton restored to Corea, subject to China Jan 1887
Corea endeavors to enter into independent diplomatic relations with U S and European powers May, 1888
Treaty with Russia 8 Aug "
China reasserts by proclamation her suzerainty over Corea, 7 June, 1894
Invasion of Corea by Japanese troops, Seoul occupied 25 June, "
China remonstrates 27 June, "
Corea renounces all subjection to China, and calls on the Japanese for help 30 June, "
Japan demands extensive reforms, and claims observance of treaty of 1885, opposed by China July, "
Hostilities begin between China and Japan, the *Kowshing*, a British despatch-boat conveying Chinese troops, attacked by Japanese warships and sunk off Asan 25 July, "
Japanese victories at Chan hon and at Asan under gen. Oshima 29 July, "
Chinese declaration of war 4 Aug "
The emperor of China transmits a justificatory circular to the great powers 23 Aug "
Japanese army increased, they hold Seoul and some provinces guerilla warfare, treaty of alliance between Japan and Corea signed at Seoul 26 Aug "
Asan recaptured 30 Aug "
The Chinese surrounded and defeated with great loss at Ping Yang, on the Tatong river, gen Tso (Chinese) killed, 15, 16 Sept "
Great naval battle at the mouth of the Yalu river, much slaughter, 8 Chinese vessels destroyed 17 Sept "
Japanese occupy Wi-ju without resistance, reported 9 Oct. "
Indecisive battle near Wi ju, great slaughter 23 Oct. "
The Japanese cross the Yalu and enter Manchuria, Chinese fort taken after sharp fighting 25 Oct "
Kiu lien tcheng taken by marshal Yamagata 26 Oct. "
Gens. Yeh and Wei (Chinese) tried at Shang Hai for cowardice, etc, at Ping Yang, 15 Sept, and degraded 30 Oct. "
Tung huan-tcheng surrenders 31 Oct. "
Prince Kung acknowledges the defeat of China, and requests foreign intervention 3 Nov "
Kinchou and Talienwan captured 6, 7 Nov "
Chinese routed at the Namquan Pass 9 Nov "
Port Arthur, a strong naval arsenal, taken by the Japanese under marshal Oyama by storm 20, 21 Nov
[Great massacre of Chinese after the battle, owing to their having killed some captive Japanese, 21-26 Nov]
Vigorous attack of Chinese on marshal Yamagata's army at *the Fen Shui pass repulsed* 25 Nov "
Kinchou reoccupied by marshal Oyama . 3 Dec "
Fuchou taken without resistance 5 Dec "
Chinese defeated at Kinkuahu and Yih man shan 10, 14 Dec "
Hai tcheng taken by gen Katsura 13 Dec "
Chinese defeated under gen Sung by gen Katsura, near Hai-tcheng 19 Dec. "
Rebellion of the Tonghaks, 3 towns burned, rebels defeated, 23 Dec, again defeated 8 Jan 1895
Japan refuses an armistice 5 Jan "
Desolation in Manchuria, Chinese routed at Kai phing, 10 Jan "
Tung chou bombarded and taken 18, 19 Jan "
Yung tcheng and Ning-hai occupied 20, 24 Jan "
Bombardment of Wei hai wei and the island fortress Leu kung tau by adm Ito and marshal Oyama, began, 30 Jan, fierce fighting, adm Ting, gen Chang, capt Liu surrender ships and forts under honors of war, and commit suicide from grief and shame ....12 Feb. "
Adm McClure accepts the Japanese conditions .. 13 Feb "
Japanese successful advances .. Feb "
Niu-Chwang and port of Ying kow taken after fierce fighting by gen Nodzu .. 4, 6 Mch "
Denshodai burned by the Japanese, much slaughter 9 Mch "
Li Hung Chang, Chinese minister plenipotentiary, with Mr Foster, American adviser, sent to treat for peace, received by visct. Mutsu, Japanese minister, at Shimonoseki, in Manchuria . 19 Mch "
Li Hung Chang fired at in the face by Koyama, a young Japanese, a lunatic 24 Mch "
Haichow, on the Kiangsu coast, taken 24 Mch 1895
The Pescadores islands taken 26-31 Mch "
Armistice (21 days) proclaimed at Tokio 29 Mch "
Peace signed, conditions the independence of Corea, Japan retains conquered places, the Pescadores, and part of the Liao tung peninsula, Liao, and Formosa, an indemnity of 200,000,000 taels, 4 new ports opened to commerce, Li Hung Chang departs 17 Apr "
The ministers of Russia, Germany, and France protest against the annexation of Chinese continental territory to the Japanese empire by the treaty 23 Apr "
Japan abandons the claim to the Liao tung peninsula, 6 May, ratifications of the treaty exchanged 8 May, "
Count Inouye employed by Japan to promote reforms, May *et seq* "
Mutiny of Corean soldiers, the palace invaded by an anti reform mob, the queen of Corea and 2 ladies murdered reported 8 Oct, H M S *Edgar* ordered to Chemulpo 13 Oct, visct. Miura and other Japanese ministers and soldiers recalled from Seoul 18 Oct "
Evacuation of the Liao tung peninsula by the Japanese, 30 Nov "
Withdrawal of Japanese troops completed 7 Jan 1896
Insurrection at Seoul, the king and his son take refuge in the Russian legation, Russian marines landed at Chemulpo, march to Seoul 10, 11 Feb "
Two Corean ministers executed for treason, anti Japanese cabinet formed, Russian influence predominant 14 Feb "
Fighting between the Japanese and rebels near Fusan reported 23 Mch "
Treaty between Russia and Japan providing for the maintenance of the independence of Corea under their military protection, text published 24 Feb 1897
Convention signed between Russia and Japan respecting Corea Apr 1898
Attempt to poison the emperor and crown prince of Corea frustrated, 16 Sept Tim Khunyuk, interpreter at the Russian legation, executed on a false charge, his wife and others tortured, 10, 12 Oct., the minister of justice dismissed 13 Oct "
Political riot at Seoul 23 deaths reported 23 Nov "
Seoul and Chemulpo railway taken over by Japan, Jan, 1899 (opened 5 July, 1900)
Cabinet dismissed and 2 ministers banished on account of changes in provincial offices Mch 1899
Ports (3) on the E coast leased to Russia for 12 years May, "
Japanese influence again paramount in Seoul Aug "
Russia obtains an exclusive settlement at Masampho harbor, agreements signed 30 Mch 1900
Two Corean officials, under Japanese protection, suspected of complicity in the murder of the queen (1895), tortured and put to death . May, "
Corean judicial officials punished to appease Japan mid June, "
Land at Masampho, Corea, leased to Japan by government, May, 1901
Anglo Japanese agreement, the *status quo* and independence of Corea to be maintained, signed . 30 Jan 1902
Corea gives its adhesion to the Geneva convention 8 Jan 1903
Russian demand for concession to Russo-Chinese bank of the Seoul Wi ju railway rejected 25 Feb "
Dispute with Japan (RUSSO-JAPANESE WAR)

Chios, now **Scio,** an isle in the Greek archipelago, revolted against Athens, 412 and 357 B C It partook of the fortunes of Greece, being conquered by the Venetians, 1124 A D, by the crusaders, 1204, by the Greek emperor, 1329, by the Genoese, 1346, and finally by the Turks in 1594 About 40,000 inhabitants were massacred by the Turks 11 Apr 1822, during the Greek insurrection EARTHQUAKES

Chip'pewa, Canada, a short distance above Niagara falls. Here the British, under Riall, were defeated by the Americans, under Brown, 5 July, 1814 American loss, 61 killed, 255 wounded, and 19 missing British loss, 236 killed, 322 wounded, and 46 missing Gen Winfield Scott commanded a brigade here

Chip'pewas or **Ojib'ways.** INDIANS.

chivalry arose out of the feudal system in the latter part of the 8th century (*chevalier* or knight, from *caballarius*, the equipped feudal tenant on horseback) From the 12th to the 15th century it refined manners. The knight swore to the duties of his profession, as champion of God and ladies, to speak truth, maintain right, protect the distressed, practise courtesy, fulfil obligations, and vindicate at every peril his honor and character Chivalry proper expired with the feudal system. KNIGHTHOOD, TOURNAMENTS By letters-patent of James I, 1623, the earl-marshal of England had "the like jurisdiction in the courts of chivalry, when the office of lord high constable was vacant, as this latter and the marshal did jointly exercise"

chloral hydrate, a combination of chlorine and

alcohol, discovered by Liebig, produces deep sleep, but not insensibility to pain. Its property was discovered by Oscar Liebreich, and reported to the French Academy of Sciences, 16 Aug. 1869. It is often deleterious.

chloral'um, or chloride of alumina, a compound of chlorine and alumina, an antiseptic disinfectant, made by Dr. Gamgee about 1870; said to be safe and efficacious, useful in medicine for gargles, washing wounds, etc.

chlorine (Gr. χλωρός, pale green), a gas first obtained by Scheele in 1774, by treating manganese with muriatic (hydrochloric) acid. Sir H. Davy, in 1810, discovered the gaseous element, and named it chlorine. Combined with sodium it forms common salt (chloride of sodium), and with lime, the bleaching powder and disinfectant, chloride of lime. BLEACHING. In 1823 Faraday condensed chlorine into a liquid.

The supposed dissociation of oxygen from chlorine by heat, by V. and H. Meyer of Zurich, was announced Aug. 1879. Afterwards chlorine was proved to exist in 2 states at high temperatures.

chloroform (ter-chloride of the hypothetical radical formyl), a compound of carbon, hydrogen, and chlorine, and made from alcohol, water, and bleaching powder, was discovered by Samuel Guthrie of Sackett's Harbor, N. Y., in 1831, and independently by Liebig in 1832. It was analyzed by Dumas in 1834. Chloroform was first applied as an anæsthetic experimentally, by Jacob Bell in London in February, and Simpson in Edinburgh in Nov. 1847. A committee of the Royal Medical and Chirurgical Society reported, July, 1864, that mortality was not increased by anæsthetics.

chlo'rozone, a disinfectant, introduced 1873.

choc'olate, made of the cocoa berry, introduced into Europe (from Mexico and the Brazils) about 1520, was sold in the London coffee-houses soon after their establishment, 1650. First factory for the preparation of chocolate in the United States established at Dorchester, Mass., 1765; still continues.

Choctaws. INDIANS.

Choczim, Bessarabia, S. Russia. Here Turks were defeated by John Sobieski, king of Poland, 11 Nov. 1673; and by Russians, 30 Apr. and 13 July, 1769.

choir was separated from the nave of the church in Constantine's time. The choral service was first used in England at Canterbury, 677. CHANTING.

cholera (Asiatic), described by Garcia del Huerto, a physician of Goa, about 1560, appeared in India in 1774, and often, and became endemic in Lower Bengal, 1817; gradually spread till it reached Russia, 1830, Germany, 1831, carrying off more than 900,000 persons on the Continent in 1829-30; in England and Wales in 1848-49, 53,293 persons; in 1854, 20,097.

IN EUROPE.

Cholera appears at Sunderland........................26 Oct. 1831
And at Edinburgh..6 Feb. 1832
First observed at Rotherhithe and Limehouse, London, 13 Feb.; and in Dublin..3 Mch. "
Mortality very great, but more so on the Continent; 18,000 deaths at Paris....................between Mch. and Aug. "
Rages in Rome, the Two Sicilies, Genoa, Berlin, etc., July and Aug. 1837
Again in England.. 1849
Newcastle-upon-Tyne, Hexham, Tynemouth, and other northern towns, suffer much from cholera..................Sept. 1853
Rages in Italy and Sicily.................................. 1854
Severe for a short time in south London, Soho, and St. James's, Westminster..............................Aug. and Sept. "
Cases at Marseilles, Toulon, Southampton............end of Sept. 1865
Prevalent at Marseilles, Paris, Madrid, Naples........July-Oct. "
International meeting at Constantinople, for preventive measures, proposed, Oct. 1865, meet 18 Feb. 1866, conclude that cholera may be propagated from great distances, and preventive measures recommended....................26 Sept. 1866
Cholera appears at Bristol, 24 Apr.; at Liverpool, 13 May; at Southampton and London..............................July, "
Cholera severe in Vienna, Aug.; Paris.....................Sept. 1873
Cholera appears in France, a few cases in Paris............. 1884
Very severe in Naples and Turin............................ "
In 1892 it made its appearance in European Russia, Vienna, Buda-Pesth, Berlin, Paris, but in Hamburg states it was especially fatal, where, out of a population of 640,000, there were 18,757 cases, of which some 7,839 were fatal up to Oct.

IN THE UNITED STATES.

First death by cholera in North America, 8 June, 1832, in Quebec. In New York, 22 June, 1832. Cincinnati to New Orleans, Oct. 1832 (very severe throughout the U. S.). Again in the U. S. in 1834, slightly in 1849, severely in 1855, and again slightly.......................................1866-67.
By the prompt and energetic enforcement of quarantine it was prevented from entering the U. S., 1892. The German steamship *Moravia* reached New York harbor, 31 Aug., having had 22 deaths from cholera during the voyage. The president ordered 20 days' quarantine for all immigrant vessels from cholera-infected districts, 1 Sept. On 3 Sept. the *Normannia* and *Rugia*, from Hamburg, were put in quarantine. On 10 Sept. the *Scandia* arrived with more cholera cases. Surf hotel property on Fire island bought for quarantine purposes, 10 Sept. 1892

Cholu'la, Mexico, first visited by Cortez in 1519, and given up to pillage and massacre. Here was one of the largest Mexican temples to the god Quetzalcoatl, on a truncated pyramid 160 ft. high. The pyramid remains.

chora'gus, the regulator of the chorus in Greek feasts, etc. Stesichorus (or Tysias), so called, first taught the chorus to dance to the lyre, 556 B.C.—*Quintil.*

chorus-singing, was early practised at Athens, forming an important part of the Greek dramas, beginning in the 6th century B.C., and has been continued in modern oratorios and operas. Hypodicus, of Chalcides, carried off the prize for the best voice, 508 B.C. MUSIC.

chrism, consecrated oil, used early in Greek and Roman churches. Musk, saffron, cinnamon, roses, and frankincense were used with the oil in 1541. It was ordained, 1596, that chrism should consist of oil and balsam only; the one representing the human nature of Christ, and the other his divine nature.

Christian Commission, United States, organized 14 Nov. 1861 at New York city. Object sought to be attained was the spiritual welfare of the soldier in the field, and incidentally thereto his social and physical comfort. Headquarters of the commission was at Philadelphia, with 31 subordinate offices. It was indirectly connected with the SANITARY COMMISSION of the U. S. during the years 1861-65, disbursing over $5,000,000 to relieve the suffering and improve the condition of the soldier. Last meeting held at Representative Hall, 11 Feb. 1866.

Christian Endeavor Society, Young People's. Formed 2 Feb. 1881, by rev. F. E. Clark, pastor of the Williston church, Portland, Me., for the purpose of training converts for the duties of church membership. It includes all denominations of Christians, under the motto "For Christ and the church." 1 Jan. 1905, there were 64,804 societies, with a membership of 3,888,240, chiefly in the United States, Canada, Great Britain and Australia.

Christian era. ANNO DOMINI.

Christian Science. The total membership of the mother church (1904), was 30,534. In the *Christian Science Journal* directory for Aug. 1904, 850 churches and societies of this denomination are listed. The estimated membership of these branch churches is approximately 40,000. There are 102 institutes for teaching Christian Science, and upward of 4000 practitioners of Christian Science mind-healing. Mrs. Eddy says in her book, "Retrospection and Introspection": "I claim for healing scientifically the following advantages: 1. It does away with all material medicines and recognizes the antidote for all sickness, as well as sin, in the immortal mind; and mortal mind is the source of all the ills which befall mortals. 2. It is more effectual than drugs, and cures when they fail, or only relieve, thus proving the superiority of metaphysics over physics. 3. A person healed by Christian Science is not only healed of his disease, but he is advanced morally and spiritually. The mortal body being but the objective state of the mortal mind, this mind must be renovated to improve the body." Hypnotism, mesmerism, spiritualism, theosophy, faith-cure, and kindred systems are foreign to true Christian Science.

Christia'nia, the capital of Norway, built in 1624, by Christian IV. of Denmark, to replace Opslo (the ancient capital founded by Harold Haardrade, 1058), which had been destroyed by fire. Pop. 1891, 150,444.

Christianity. The name Christian was first given to the disciples of Christ at Antioch, in Syria, 43 (Acts xi. 26; 1 Pet. iv. 16). The first Christians were divided into *episcopoi* (bishops or overseers) or *presbyteroi* (elders), *diaconoi* (ministers or deacons), and *pistoi* (believers), afterwards also *catechumens*, or learners, and *energumens*, to be exorcised PERSECUTIONS, RELIGION

Christianity preached in Jerusalem, 33 A D , Samaria 34, Damascus, 35, Asia Minor 41, Cyprus 45, Macedonia 53, Athens Corinth etc , 54, Ephesus 56, Troas, etc 60 Rome, 63
Said to be taught in Britain, about 64, and propagated with some success (*Bede*) 156
Said to be introduced in Scotland under Donald I about 212
Constantine the Great converted 312
Frumentius preaches in Abyssinia about 346
Introduced among the Goths by Ulfilas . 376
Into Ireland in the 2d century, but with more success after the arrival of St Patrick 432
Established in France by Clovis 496
Tradition says that Gregory the Great before he became pope passing through the slave market at Rome saw beautiful children for sale inquired about their country and finding they were English pagans cried out "*Non Angli sed Angeli forent, si essent Christiani*" ("They would not be English, but angels, if they were Christians") From that time he ardently desired to convert the nation, and sent a monk named Austin, or Augustin, and others on a mission to Britain 596
Conversion of the Saxons by Augustin 597
Introduced into Helvetia by Irish missionaries 613
Into Flanders in the 7th century
Into Saxony by Charlemagne 785
Into Denmark, under Harold 827
Into Bohemia, under Borsivoi 894
Into Russia by Swiatoslaf about 940
Into Poland, under Mecislaüs I 992
Into Hungary under Geisa 994
Into Norway and Iceland, under Olaf I 998
Into Sweden, between 10th and 11th centuries
Into Prussia, by Teutonic knights returning from holy wars 1227
Into Lithuania, paganism abolished about 1386
Into Guinea, Angola, and Congo, 15th century
Into China (where it was afterwards extirpated, and thousands of Chinese Christians put to death) 1575
Into India and America, in the 16th century
Christianity re established in Greece 1628
Into Japan by Xavier and the Jesuits, 1549, but the Christians were exterminated . 1638

Christmas day, 25 Dec (from *Christ*, and the Saxon *mæsse*, signifying the *mass* and a *feast*), a festival in honor of Christ's birth, said to have been first kept 98, and ordered to be held as a solemn feast, by pope Telesphorus, about 137 By the 5th century, whether from the influence of some tradition or from a desire to supplant heathen festivals of that period of the year, as the *Saturnalia*, the 25 Dec was generally observed. Augustin expressly mentions this date, and Chrysostom seems to speak of it as a custom imported from the west within 10 years It seems earlier to have been kept with the feast of the EPIPHANY, on 6 Jan , as now in the eastern church The holly and mistletoe used at Christmas are said to be relics of religious observances of Druids. ANNO DOMINI Diocletian, Roman emperor, keeping court at Nicomedia, hearing that the Christians assembled on this day in multitudes to celebrate Christ's birth, ordered the doors shut, and the church set on fire, and 600 perished This began the 10th persecution, which lasted 10 years, 303

Christopher's, St., or St. Kitt's, a West India island, discovered in 1493 by Columbus, who gave it his own name. Settled by the English and French, 1623 or 1626 Ceded to England by the peace of Utrecht, 1713 Taken by the French in 1782, but restored the next year Area, 65 sq miles, pop 24,137

Christ's Hospital (the *Blue-coat* school) was established by Edward VI 1553, on the site of the Gray Friars' monastery, England A mathematical ward was founded by Charles II 1672 The *Times* ward was founded in 1811 The edifice decaying, was rebuilt, in 1822 a new infirmary was completed, and in 1825 (25 Apr) the duke of York laid the first stone of the new hall The subordinate school at Hertford, for 416 younger boys and 80 girls, was founded in 1863 Annual income (1870) about 70,000*l* The charity commissioners' scheme to reform the administration was issued Aug 1880

Christ's thorn, conjectured to be the plant of which our Saviour's crown of thorns was composed, came to England from the south of Europe before 1596

chro'mium (Gr χρῶμα, color), a rare metal, discovered by Vauquelin in 1797 It is found combined with iron and lead, and gives color to the emerald

chromo-lithography. PRINTING IN COLORS

chronicles. The earliest are of Jews, Chinese, and Hindus In Scripture there are 2 "Books of Chronicles" BIBLE. Collections of British chronicles have been published by Camden, Gale etc , since 1602, in this century by the English Historical Society, etc In England in 1858 the master of the rolls began to publish "Chronicles and Memorials of Great Britain and Ireland during the Middle Ages" (still progressing, 1893), in 1845 Macray's "Manual of the British Historians" was published

chronology (the science of time) means the arrangement of the events of history in order of succession, showing the intervals between them Among the numerous works on chronology, the following are some of the most valuable "De Emendatione Temporum," by Joseph Scaliger, 1583, in which were laid the foundations of modern chronological science. "De Doctrina Temporum" by Petavius, 1627, with supplement 1630, and "Rationarium Temporum," an abridgment, 1633. "Annales Veteris et Novi Testamenti," by archbishop Usher, 1650, the most widely received chronology of the Bible "The Chronology of Ancient Kingdoms, amended," by sir Isaac Newton 1728. "L'Art de Vérifier les Dates," compiled by the Benedictines (1st ed 1750, 3d ed in 38 vols 8 vo, 1818-1831) Playfair's "Chronology," 1784 Blair's "Chronology" 1754 (new editions by sir H Ellis in 1844, and by Mr Rosse in 1856) C G Zumpt's "Annales Veterum Regnorum," 1819 The Oxford "Chronological Tables" 1838 Sir Harris Nicholas's "Chronology of History," 1833, new edition 1852 Hales's "Chronology," 1809-1814, 2d edition, 1830, Woodward and Cates's "Encyclopædia of Chronology," 1872 H Fynes-Clinton's "Fasti Hellenici" and "Fasti Romani" (1824-50) "The Assyrian Eponyme Canon," by Geo Smith, 1875 EPOCHS, ERAS

chronoscope, an apparatus invented by prof Wheatstone in 1840, to measure small intervals of time It has been applied to the velocity of projectiles and of the electric current One was invented by Pouillet in 1844, others since Capt Andrew Noble (engaged by sir William *Armstrong*) invented an apparatus to determine the velocity of a projectile within a gun, a second is divided into millionths, and the electric spark records the rate of the passage It was exhibited at Newcastle-on-Tyne in Aug 1869, and in London in Apr 1870

chrysanthemums were introduced into England from China, about 1790, and many varieties since

Chrysler's Field, Canada Battle of This battle was fought near Cornwall, some 90 miles above Montreal, 11 Nov 1813, when the Americans attempted to capture Montreal Gen Wilkinson commanded the expedition, which utterly failed, the defeat here being its culmination The American force engaged was probably not far from 5000, loss, 339, British loss, 187 Immediately after, Wilkinson recrossed the St. Lawrence into winter quarters

Chunar or Chunarghur, N W. India, taken by the British, 1763, ceded to them, 1768 Here was concluded a treaty, 19 Sept. 1781, between the nabob of Oude and governor Hastings, relieving the nabob of his debts to the East India Company, on condition of his seizing and delivering to the English the property of his mother and grandmother (begums) It enabled the nabob to take the lands of Fyzoola Khan, a Rohilla chief, settled at Rampoor under guarantee of the English The nabob gave Mr Hastings 100,000*l* BEGUMS, HASTINGS'S TRIAL, SHERIDAN.

church (probably derived from the Gr κυριακός, pertaining to the Lord, Κύριος) signifies both a collected body of Christians and the place where they meet. In the New Testament, it signifies "congregation," in the original ἐκκλησία Christian architecture commenced with Constantine, who erected at Rome churches called basilicas (from the Gr βασιλεύς, a king), old St. Peter's about 330. His successors erected others, and adopted heathen temples as places of worship ARCHITECTURE, CHURCH OF ENGLAND, etc , POPES.

church congresses, English, meet annually since 1861.

Church of England has 3 orders of clergy—bishops, priests, and deacons, 1892, 2 archbishops, 32 bishops, with 13 suffragans and 5 assistants, and 81 colonial and missionary bishops The other dignitaries are chancellors, deans (of cathedrals and collegiate churches), archdeacons, prebendaries, canons, minor canons, and priest-vicars these and the incumbents of rectories, vicarages, and chapelries, make the number of preferments of the established church, according to official returns, 1892, 14,250 Estimated average income from all sources—endowments, tithe, glebe, rent value of residences, pew-rents, etc.—may be stated, 1892, at 7,250,000*l* In Sept 1880, the archbishop of Canterbury said that he was in communion with 162 bishops. The following are leading facts in her history for details, refer to separate articles

Britain converted to Christianity ("Christo subdita," *Tertullian*) 2d century

Invasion of the Saxons, 477, converted by Augustin and his companions 596

Dunstan establishes the supremacy of the monastic orders, about 960

Aggrandizement of the church, fostered by Edward the Confessor, checked by William I and his successors 1066 et seq

Contest between Henry II and Becket respecting "Constitutions of Clarendon" 1164–70

Contest between national or English party and Roman party (chiefly Norman) 11th and 12th centuries

John surrenders his crown to the papal legate 1213

Rise of the Lollards, Wickliffe publishes tracts against errors of the church of Rome, 1356, and a version of the Bible about 1383

Clergy regulated by Parliament, 1529, they lose the first-fruits, 1534

Royal supremacy imposed on the clergy by Henry VIII, 1531, many suffer death for refusal 1535

Coverdale's Bible commanded to be read in churches "

"Six Articles of Religion" promulgated 1539

First Book of Common Prayer issued 1549

Clergy permitted to marry "

"Forty two Articles of Religion" issued 1552

Roman forms restored, Protestants persecuted by Mary 1553–58

Protestant forms restored by Elizabeth, Puritan dissensions begin 1558-1603

"Thirty nine Articles" pub 1563

Hampton Court conference with the Puritans 1604

New translation of the Bible pub 1611

Book of Common Prayer suppressed and Directory established by Parliament. 1644

Presbyterians established by the Commonwealth 1649

Act of uniformity (14 Chas II c 4) passed, 2000 non conforming ministers resign their livings 1662

Attempts of James II to revive Romanism, "Declaration of Indulgence" pub 1687

Acquittal of the 7 bishops on a charge of "seditious libel" 1688

Non juring bishops and others deprived (they formed a separate communion) 1 Feb 1691

"Queen Anne's Bounty" augmenting poor livings 1704

Fierce disputes, low church and high church, Henry Sacheverell tried for seditious sermons, riots 1710

Bangorian controversy begins . 1717

John Wesley and George Whitefield begin preaching 1738

Rise of the Evangelical party under Newton, Romaine, and others latter part of 18th century

Churches of England and Ireland united at the union 1800

Clergy Incapacitation act passed 1801

"Tracts for the Times" mostly by John Henry Newman (Nos 1-90) pub (much controversy ensues) 1833-41

Newman joins the Roman Catholic church 9 Oct 1845

English Church Union, established 1859

"Essays and Reviews" pub 1860, numerous replies issued 1861-62

[The church of England is now said to be divided into High, Moderate, Low (or Evangelical), and Broad church the last including persons who hold the opinions of the late Dr Arnold, the late rev F D Maurice, dean Stanley, the late canon Kingsley, and others] ESTABLISHED CHURCH

First church congresses began at Cambridge, 1861, and at Oxford July, 1862

Dr Colenso, bishop of Natal, publishes his work on "The Pentateuch," about Oct 1862, the bishops, in convocation, declare that it contains "errors of the gravest and most dangerous character" 20 May, 1863

Bishop Colenso deposed by his metropolitan, Dr Gray, bishop of Cape Town 16 Apr 1864

"Oxford Declaration" (authorship ascribed to archdeacon Denison and Dr Pusey) respecting eternal punishment, signed on 25 Feb, and sent by post to the clergy at large for signature about 3000 are said to have signed, presented to the archbishop of Canterbury 12 May, "

Bishop of London's Fund, to relieve spiritual destitution in London, established, queen Victoria promises (in 3 years) 3000*l*., and prince of Wales 1000*l* 7 Mch "

100,456*l* received, 70,003*l* promised 31 Dec. "

Bishop Colenso's appeal before the privy council, which declared bishop Gray's proceedings void (a colonial bishop has no authority not granted by Parliament or by the colonial legislature) 21 Mch 1865

Queen Victoria engages to give 15,000*l*. in 10 years. Apr "

Meeting in London of 3 bishops, Dr Pusey, and nearly 80 of the clergy and laity, with counts Orloff and Tolstse, and the Russian chaplain, to consider union of English and Russian churches . . 15 Nov "

Church Association (against popery and ritualism) established, "

Bishop Colenso publicly excommunicated at Maritzburg cathedral by bishop Gray 5 Jan 1866

Bishop Gray declares independence, establishes synods calls his see "The Church of South Africa" early in "

Church Missionary Society refuses to support colonial bishops unless they keep within the formularies of the church of England early in "

Excitement over the progress of ritualism Sept -Nov "

Bishop Colenso *v* Gladstone and others (trustees of the Colonial Bishopric fund) for his salary Verdict of master of the rolls for plaintiff with costs 6 Nov "

Unqualified condemnation of ritualism by bishops in convocation, 13 Feb, lower house concur 15 Feb 1867

Bishop of Salisbury (Dr Hamilton), in a church, asserts the supernatural gifts of priests, and divine presence in the sacrament, public protest 16 May, "

Trial in Court of Arches Martin *v* Mackonochie respecting extreme ritualistic practices at St Alban's, Holborn, case deferred 21 May, "

Royal Ritualistic commission to consider rubrics in the prayer book, table of lessons, etc, 3 June, first report, censuring innovation, signed 19 Aug "

PAN ANGLICAN SYNOD at Lambeth 24-27 Sept. "

Ritualists meet in St James's hall, claim liberty 19 Nov "

Case of Martin *v* Mackonochie, begun 4 Dec, lasted 14 days, resumed 15-18 Jan 1868

Proposal of bishop Gray of Cape Town to consecrate Mr Macrorie bishop of Natal instead of bishop Colenso, disapproved by English and Scotch bishops Jan "

Bishop of London's Fund received 312 309*l*. 31 Jan "

Martin *v* Mackonochie decided for plaintiff, use of incense, mixing water with the wine, and elevation of the elements, in the sacrament, forbidden 28 Mch "

Great meeting at St James's hall in defence of Irish church establishment, 23 bishops present 6 May, "

Martin *v* Mackonochie appeal case, verdict for plaintiff, declaring certain ritualistic practices illegal 23 Dec. "

Warm meeting of ritualists at St James's hall 12 Jan 1869

Martin *v* Mackonochie defendant censured by privy council for evading sentence 4 Dec. "

Bishop of London's Fund—111 839*l* received July, 1870

Rev Mr Mackonochie suspended for 3 months by privy council for evading former sentence 25 Nov "

Rev C Voysey sentenced to be deprived for heresy, appeal to judicial committee of privy council disallowed, 10 Feb 1871

Hebbert *v* Purchas, of Brighton, verdict against defendant for breach of ecclesiastical law, a great defeat of the ritualists, causes excitement 23 Feb "

Mr Miall's resolution for disestablishing the church of England defeated in the commons (374–89) 9 May, "

Sheppard *v* Bennett (for teaching the divine presence in the sacrament), appeal to privy council, 28 Nov, judgment adjourned 2 Dec. "

Bishop of London's Fund—received 441,109*l* 31 Dec "

Convocation authorized to consider alterations in Prayer book, Feb 1872

Rev John Purchas, of Brighton suspended for one year from [He died 18 Oct] 18 Feb "

Sheppard *v* Bennett, judgment for defendant, who is censured, 8 June, "

Memorial (signed by 60,200 persons) against Romanist teaching etc, in the church, presented at Lambeth to the archbishop by the Church Association 5 May, 1873

Archbishops in reply admit the danger, and recognize their duty, as well as the difficulties of action, saying, "We live in an age when all opinions and beliefs are keenly criticised, and when there is less inclination than ever was before to respect authority in matters of opinion. In every state, in every religious community, almost in every family, the effect of this unsettled condition may be traced" 1 June, "

Mr Miall's motion for disestablishing the church lost (356-61), 16 May, "

Archdeacon Denison, Dr Pusey, canons Liddon and Liddell, and others, publish a declaration in favor of confession and absolution in *Times* 6 Dec "

Archdeacon Denison attacks the bishops in a Latin pamphlet, "Episcopatus Bilinguis" Dec. "

Public Worship Regulation act brought in by the archbishops, 20 Apr, royal assent 7 Aug 1874

Addresses to archbishops largely signed for and against a distinctive dress for minister during holy communion Sept "

New society formed by bishops of Manchester, Carlisle, and Edinburgh, and others, to promote union with orthodox dissenters Oct "

Bishop of London's Fund—500,187*l* received or promised Nov "

Martin *v* Mackonochie new suit in Court of Arches (see 1867, etc) 26 Nov, Mackonochie to be suspended for 6 weeks and pay costs 7 Dec "

Pastoral of archbishops and bishops (bishops of Salisbury and Durham excepted) to clergy and laity (counselling moderation and forbearance) dated 1 Mch 1875

Mackonochie declines to appeal, excitement at his church, rev A Stanton and congregation celebrate communion at St Vedast's, Foster lane . 27 June et seq "

Several clergymen secede to Rome Oct. "

Public Worship Regulation act new court, under lord Penzance, meet at Lambeth palace, first case the parish of Folkestone *v* rev Charles Joseph Ridsdale, 4 Jan, verdict for plaintiffs . 3 Feb 1876

Reported negotiation of ritualistic ministers with Rome dis

claimed by Mr. Mackonochie and about 100 others in *Times*, 4 Feb. 1876
"English Church Union" deny authority of secular court in matters spiritual, at a meeting ... 16 Jan. 1877
Address to archbishops and bishops (signed by Dr. Church, dean of St. Paul's, and other deans and canons) against Public Worship Regulation act, etc., requiring legislation in ecclesiastical affairs to be made by church synods and adopted by Parliament ... 3 Apr. "
Both archbishops vote for permitting dissenters' funeral service in church-yards ... 17 May, "
Bishop of London's Fund received 571,597*l*. ... June, "
Declaration of above 41,000 (clergy and laity) and proposed petition to queen Victoria against judgment in the Ridsdale case, July, "
Ninety-six peers (duke of Westminster and others) address archbishop of Canterbury against auricular confession, "Priest in Absolution," etc ... about 9 Aug. "
Pan-Anglican Congress at Lambeth, etc ... 2-27 July, 1878
New rubrics in prayer-book agreed to by the convocation, 4 July; act passed by convocation ... Aug. 1879
Dr. Julius *v.* bishop of Oxford (for not prosecuting rev. Mr. Carter, of Clewer), Queen's Bench; verdict against bishop, 1879; reversed by House of Lords; bishop may, but is not compelled to, prosecute ... 22 Mch. 1880
John Baghot de la Bere, jun., vicar of Prestbury, Gloucestershire, deprived for disobedience in ritualism, etc., by Court of Arches ... 21 Dec. 1880, and 8 Jan. 1881
Memorial to archbishop of Canterbury from 5 deans (Dr. Church, dean of St. Paul's, and other clergymen) for toleration of divergence in ritualistic practice ... 10 Jan. "
Counter-memorial from bishops Parry and Ryan, dean Close, and other deans and clergymen, opposing toleration of unscriptural practices ... 31 Jan. "
Mr. Mackonochie's appeal to the lords dismissed; sentence of 3 years' suspension affirmed ... 7 Apr. "
Catholic league formed ... June, 1882
Death of Dr. E. B. Pusey ... 16 Sept. "
Rev. A. Mackonochie resigns living of St. Alban's, Holborn, at request of archbishop of Canterbury ... 1 Dec. "
"Official Year-book of the Church of England" first pub ... 1883
Church of England Purity Society (White Cross Army) ... 1884
Proposed disestablishment of the church of Wales negatived in the commons (241-220) ... 9 Mch. 1886
Twenty-eighth Church Congress at Manchester; disputed questions boldly discussed ... 1 Oct. 1888
Thirty-first Church Congress at Rhyl ... 6 Oct. 1891
A declaration of faith in the inspiration of the Bible on the testimony of the universal church, independently of human criticism. Signed by dean Goulburn and 37 other eminent clergymen ... "

Church of France. St. Pothinus preached Christianity to the Gauls about 160; became bishop of Lyons, and suffered martyrdom with others, 177. For the reformed church, Huguenots, Protestants.

Mission of 7 bishops arrived in 245; followed by severe persecution ... 286-288
Christianity tolerated by Constantius Chlorus ... 292
Council of Arles convoked by Constantine, about 600 bishops present; the Donatists condemned ... 314
Christianity established by Clovis ... 496
Pragmatic sanction of St. Louis restraining the pope's impositions, and restoring the election of bishops, etc ... 1269
Pragmatic sanction of Bourges, setting general councils above pope, and prohibiting appeals to him ... 1438
Concordat of Leo X. and Francis I. annulling the pragmatic sanction ... 18 Aug. 1516
Disputes between Jesuits and Jansenists ... 1640
Declaration of clergy (drawn by Bossuet) in accordance with pragmatic sanctions, confirmed by king ... 23 Mch. 1682
Jansenists excommunicated by bull Unigenitus ... 1713
Concordat with Pius VII. and Napoleon ... 1801 and 1813
Principles of concordat of Leo X. restored by Pius VII. and Louis XVIII ... 1817
Archbishop of Paris and other prelates resist dogma of papal infallibility at council at Rome ... 1870
Clergy at first support Napoleon III.; but oppose his Italian policy, 1852-70; support MacMahon's ministry, in elections, Sept., Oct. 1877
Eighteen archbishops, 77 bishops ... "
Abbé Bougaud reckons 2658 parishes without priests, and 3000 parishes without churches ... 1878

Church of Ireland, founded by St. Patrick in 5th century; accepted Reformation about 1550; United Church of England and Ireland formed in 1800. Bishops; Ireland, 1868.

"An act to put an end to the establishment of the church of Ireland," introduced by Mr. Gladstone, 1 Mch.; vote for second reading, 368; against, 250; 2 A.M., 24 Mch.; for third reading, 361; against, 247 ... 31 May, 1869
Introduced in lords by earl Granville, 1 June; read third time, 12 July; some amendments by the lords accepted, others rejected by the commons; royal assent (to come into effect, 1 Jan. 1871) ... 26 July, "
Address of bishops to clergy and laity ... dated 18 Aug. "
Meeting of general synod of Irish church in St. Patrick's cathedral, Dublin, for reorganization of general council ... 14 Sept. "
Conference of laity; duke of Abercorn chairman ... 13 Oct. 1869
Church of Ireland disestablished ... 1 Jan. 1871
A sustentation fund established (well supported) ... "
First elected bishop (Dr. Maurice Day, bishop of Cashel) consecrated at St. Patrick's, Dublin ... 14 Apr. 1872
New ecclesiastical court meets; tries a case of ritual practices, 26 June, "
Irish Church act amended ... June, "
Received for the sustentation fund, 33,573*l*. up to ... 31 Dec. "
First bishop elected by clergy and laity of Kilmore, etc., archdeacon Darley (12 candidates) ... 23 Sept. 1874
Alleged migration of clergy to England ... autumn, "
Warm discussion upon revision of the liturgy ... May, 1875

Church of Scotland. Bishops in Scotland. On the abolition of Episcopacy, in 1638, Presbyterianism became the established religion. Its formulary of faith, said to have been compiled by John Knox in 1560, was approved by Parliament and ratified in 1567, settled by act of the Scottish senate in 1696, and secured by treaty of union with England in 1707. The church is regulated by 4 courts—the general assembly, the synod, the presbytery, and kirk sessions. Presbyterians. For important secessions, Burghers, 1732; Free Church, 1843.

First general assembly of the church ... 20 Dec. 1560
[General assembly is the highest ecclesiastical court; it meets annually in Edinburgh in May, and sits about 10 days. It consists of a grand commissioner, appointed by the sovereign, and delegates from presbyteries, royal boroughs, and universities, some being laymen. To it all appeals from inferior ecclesiastical courts lie, and its decision is final.]
Patronage abolished after 1 Jan. 1875; act passed ... 7 Aug. 1874

Church, Protestant Episcopal, in the United States. Immediately after the Revolution action was taken by the members of the Anglican church in the U. S. to establish a church conforming to the English church as near as was practicable under another government. Connecticut independently called a convention at Woodbury in 1783, and chose Samuel Seabury bishop, provided he should be consecrated by Anglican bishops. Seabury proceeded to England and remained there a year, but failed to secure consecration. He went to Scotland, where he was consecrated by nonjuring bishops. Bishops, Nonjurors. An informal meeting, held at New Brunswick, N. J., May, 1784, called a conference of churchmen at New York, Oct. 1784. This conference was attended by members from Pennsylvania, New York, New Jersey, Delaware, Maryland, Virginia; also by Connecticut, which, however, took no part. The general principles adopted for the regulation of the church were: (1) it should be a federal constitutional church; (2) the several states to be its units; (3) its governing body to include both clergy and laymen; (4) the forms of worship of the church of England to be followed, making only such changes in worship and discipline as the changed political situation rendered necessary; (5) to confer no powers on the general governing body but such as could not be exercised by the local church. This convention assumed the power to summon the members of the churches in the different states to send delegates to a constitutional convention to be held at Philadelphia, Sept. 1785. This convention—the first regular convention of the Protestant Episcopal church in the U. S.—met at Philadelphia, 27 Sept.-7 Oct. 1785. New York, New Jersey, Pennsylvania, Delaware, Maryland, Virginia, and South Carolina were represented; the rev. William White, D.D., of Pennsylvania (afterwards bishop), chosen president. The second convention was held at Philadelphia, 20-26 June, 1786; rev. David Griffith, president. At the third, held at Wilmington, Del., 10-11 Oct. 1786, rev. William White, of Pennsylvania, and rev. Samuel Provoost, of New York, were sent to England for consecration. Bishops, Episcopal. The fourth convention, held at Philadelphia, 28 July-8 Aug. 1789; bishop White, president. First house of bishops organized, 5 Oct. 1789. The general convention is held triennially, and is composed of the house of bishops and house of deputies; the deputies consist of 4 clergymen and 4 laymen from each diocese.

LIST OF THE DIOCESES OF THE CHURCH, WHEN ORGANIZED, AND THEIR FIRST BISHOPS.

Name of diocese.	Organized.	First bishop.	
Connecticut	1783	Samuel Seabury	1784
Pennsylvania	1784	William White	1787
New York	1785	Samuel Provoost	"
Virginia	"	James Madison	1790
Maryland	1783	Thomas John Claggett	1792
South Carolina	1785	Robert Smith	1795

CHU

Name of diocese.	Organized.	First bishop.	
Massachusetts	1784	Edward Bass	1797
Eastern (including all the New England states except Connecticut)		Alexander Viets Griswold (the only bishop)	1811
New Jersey	1782	John Croes	1815
Ohio	1818	Philander Chase	1819
North Carolina	1816	John Stark Ravenscroft	1823
Vermont	1790	John Henry Hopkins	1832
Kentucky	1829	Benjamin Bosworth Smith	"
Tennessee	1828	James Hervey Otey	1834
Chicago, Ill.	1835	Philander Chase	1835
Michigan	1832	Samuel Allen McCoskry	1836
Western New York	1838	William Heathcote De Lancey	1839
Georgia	1823	Stephen Elliott	1841
Louisiana	1838	Leonidas Polk	"
Delaware	1786	Alfred Lee	"
Rhode Island	1790	John Prentiss Kewly Henshaw	1843
New Hampshire	1802	Carlton Chase	1844
Alabama	1830	Nicholas Hamner Cobbs	"
Missouri	1839	Cicero Stephens Hawks	"
Maine	1820	George Burgess	1847
Indiana	1838	George Upfold	1849
Mississippi	1825	William Mercer Green	1850
Florida	1838	Francis Huger Rutledge	1851
Milwaukee (formerly Wisconsin)	1847	Jackson Kemper	1854
Iowa	1853	Henry Washington Lee	"
California	1850	William Ingraham	1857
Texas	1849	Alexander Gregg	1859
Minnesota	1857	Henry Benjamin Whipple	"
Kansas	1859	Thomas Hubbard Vail	1864
Pittsburg, Pa.	1865	John Barrett Kerfoot	1866
Nebraska	1868	Robert Harper Clarkson	1868
Oregon	"	Benjamin Weston Morris	"
Long Island	"	Abraham Newkirk Littlejohn	1869
Albany	"	William Croswell Doane	"
Central New York	"	Frederic Dan Huntington	"
Easton, Md.	"	Henry Champlin Lay	"
Central Pennsylvania	1871	Mark Antony De Wolf Howe	1871
Western Michigan	1874	George De Normandie Gillespie	1875
Southern Ohio	1875	Thomas Augustus Jagger	"
Fond du Lac	"	John Henry Hobart Brown	"
Quincy, Ill.	1877	Alexander Burgess	1878
West Virginia	"	George William Peterkin	"
Springfield, Ill.	"	George Franklin Seymour	"
Newark, N. J.	1874	Thomas Alford Starkey	1880
East Carolina	1883	Alfred Augustine Watson	1884
Colorado	1887	John Franklin Spalding	1887
The Platte	1890	Anson Roger Graves	1890
West Missouri	"	Edwin Robert Atwill	"

The church has also (1893) 12 domestic missions, extending from Alaska to New Mexico, each with a missionary bishop, besides 7 foreign missions, 5019 churches, 532,054 communicants; value of church property, $82,000,000.

Church, Roman Catholic. This church claims to be the only true beatific church, and finds its adherents chiefly among the Latin nations. It further claims an unbroken line of pontiffs from St. Peter (the present pope Leo XIII. being the 263d successor). The metropolitan position of the city of Rome at the time of the introduction of Christianity fostered the idea of supremacy. The chief ecclesiastic, the bishop of Rome, assumed the control of the church in Italy, and to some extent in Gaul and Africa, during the 2d and 3d centuries. The emperors leaving Rome, its prestige exalted the popes. Its growth was helped by the wide diffusion of the Latin tongue and the eminence of the fathers of the first 5 centuries; the cross taking the place of the crown, the pope of the emperor. For many centuries this was the church of all western Europe. Its history quite naturally falls into 3 divisions: (1) Græco-Latin Catholicism, from the 2d to the 7th century, the inheritance of all churches, and some of the theology of the later Greek, Protestant, and Roman Catholic churches. (2) The Roman Catholic church proper, from the 7th to the 15th century, still the church of all western Europe, with the conversion of barbarians and the growth of the papal hierarchy, of secular in connection with spiritual power. (3) Modern Romanism from 1563; divided into Tridentine Romanism (the church as against the Reformation) and Vatican Romanism (as against Rationalism and Gallicanism). The title of the pope is "supreme pontiff of the universal church, bishop of Rome, vicar of Jesus Christ, successor of St. Peter, prince of apostles, patriarch of the west, primate of Italy, archbishop and metropolitan of the Roman province, sovereign of the temporal dominions of the Holy Roman church." COUNCILS, EARLY FATHERS, EDICTS, JESUITS, POPES, REFORMATION, ROMAN CATHOLICS IN ENGLAND, etc.

Church, Roman Catholic, in the United States. This church began in early colonial days, and formally occupied the south and west as early as 1520. Its recent rapid growth is largely due to immigration from Catholic countries of Europe. The Spanish Catholics, as early as 1520, established, in what is now Arizona and New Mexico, the diocese of Mexico, called Guadalajara (1548–1620) and Durango (1620–1850). The diocese of Guadalajara (1548–1777) is now Texas; the diocese of Quebec (French Catholics) extended east and west of the Mississippi from its mouth (1670–1776). The part west of the Mississippi was annexed to the diocese of Santiago de Cuba (Spanish, 1777–87), which included Spanish Florida (1522–1787). Along the line of the great lakes, including northern New York, New Hampshire, Vermont, and Maine, was the diocese of Rouen (French, 1609–57); changed to the vicariate-apostolic of New France, 1657–70; and to the vicariate-apostolic of Quebec, 1670–1789. In Maryland was established the vicariate-apostolic of England, 1632–88; afterwards the vicariate-apostolic of London, 1688–1785. In 1790 John Carroll of Baltimore, the first Roman Catholic bishop in the U. S., assumed supervision of the whole country as the diocese of Baltimore, by bull issued by pope Pius VI. under the seal of the Fisherman's ring, 6 Nov. 1789. In 1808 it was divided, by bull issued by pope Pius VII., 8 Apr., and the sees of New York, Philadelphia, Boston, and Bardstown, Ky., erected, with Richard Luke Concanen as bishop of New York (he, however, never reached New York; dying at Naples, 1810); Michael Egan, bishop of Philadelphia, 1810; John Cheverus, bishop of Boston, 1810; Benedict Joseph Flaget, bishop of Bardstown, 1810; and John Connolly, bishop of New York, 1814. John McCloskey, archbishop of New York, was made a cardinal, 15 Mch. 1875, the first in the U. S. The present cardinal is James Gibbon, Baltimore, from 7 June, 1886. The following is a list of the several provinces, archdioceses, and dioceses in the U. S., 1893, with the year of their establishment, and their first archbishop or bishop.

HIERARCHY.

Province of Baltimore.—See erected, 1789. 1st bishop, John Carroll.
Archdiocese of Baltimore.—Established, 1808. 1st archbishop, John Carroll.

Diocese.	Established.	1st bishop.
Charleston	1820	John England.
Richmond	1821	Patrick Kelly.
Savannah	1850	Francis X. Gartland.
St. Augustine	1870	Augustin Verot.
Wheeling	1850	Richard Vincent
Wilmington	1868	Thos. A. Becker.

Province of Boston.—See erected, 1808. 1st bishop, John Cheverus.
Archdiocese of Boston.—Established, 1875. 1st archbishop, John Joseph Williams.

Diocese.	Established.	1st bishop.
Burlington	1853	Louis De Goesbriaud.
Hartford	1844	William Tyler.
Manchester	1884	Denis M. Bradley.
Portland	1855	David W. Bacon.
Providence	1872	Thos. F. Hendricken.
Springfield	1870	Patrick Thos. O'Reilly.

Province of Chicago.—See erected, 1844. 1st bishop, William Quarters.
Archdiocese of Chicago.—Established, 1880. 1st archbishop, Patrick A. Feehan.

Diocese.	Established.	1st bishop.
Alton	1857	Henry D. Juncker.
Belleville	1887	John Janssen.
Peoria	1877	John L. Spalding.

Province of Cincinnati.—See erected, 1821. 1st bishop, Edward Dominic Fenwick.
Archdiocese of Cincinnati.—Established, 1833. 1st archbishop, John Baptist Purcell.

Diocese.	Established.	1st bishop.
Cleveland	1847	Amadeus Rappe.
Columbus	1868	S. H. Rosecrans.
Covington	1853	George Aloysius Carrell.
Detroit	1832	Frederick Rese.
Fort Wayne	1857	J. H. Luers.
Grand Rapids	1882	Henry J. Richter.
Louisville (Bardstown)	1808	Benedict Jos. Flaget.
Nashville	1837	Richard Pius Miles.
Vincennes	1834	Simon Gabriel Burte.

Province of Milwaukee.—See erected, 1844. 1st bishop, John Martin Henni.
Archdiocese of Milwaukee.—Established, 1875. 1st archbishop, John Martin Henni.

Diocese.	Established.	1st bishop.
Green Bay	1868	Joseph Melcher.
La Crosse	"	Michael Heiss.
Marquette	1857	Frederic Baraga.

Province of New Orleans.—See erected, 1793 1st bishop, Luis Penalver y Cardenas.

Archdiocese of New Orleans.—Established, 1835 1st archbishop Anthony Blanc

Diocese	Established	1st bishop
Galveston	1847	John Mary Odin
Little Rock	1843	Andrew Byrne
Mobile	1824	Michael Portier
Natchez	1837	John M J Chanche
Natchitoches	1853	Augustus M Martin
San Antonio	1874	Anthony D Pellicer

Province of New York.—See erected, 1808 1st bishop, R Luke Concanen (Dominican)

Archdiocese of New York.—Established, 1850 1st archbishop (1850), John Hughes.

Diocese	Established	1st bishop
Albany	1847	John McCloskey
Brooklyn	1853	John Loughlin
Buffalo	1847	John Timon
Newark	1853	Jas R Bayley
Ogdensburg	1872	Edgar P Wadhams
Rochester	1868	Bernard I McQuaid
Syracuse	1886	P A Ludden
Trenton	1881	M J O Farrell

Province of Oregon. See erected (archbishopric) 1846, including portions of British America 1st archbishop Francis N Blanchet.

Archdiocese of Oregon City 1st archbishop under the United States, 1853 Francis N Blanchet

Diocese	Established	1st bishop
Helena Mont.	1884	John B Brondel
Nesqually, Wash	1850	A M A Blanchet
Vancouver s island, B C	1847	Modeste Demers

Province of Philadelphia.—See erected 1808 1st bishop, Patrick Michael Egan

Archdiocese of Philadelphia — Established, 1875 1st archbishop, James Frederic Wood

Diocese	Established	1st bishop
Erie	1854	Michael O Connor
Harrisburg	1868	J F Shanahan
Pittsburg	1843	Michael O'Connor
Scranton	1868	Wm O'Hara

Province of St Louis.—See erected 1826 1st bishop Joseph Rosati

Archdiocese of St Louis.—Established, 1847 1st archbishop, Peter Richard Kenrick

Diocese	Established	1st bishop
Cheyenne	1887	M F Burke
Concordia Kans	"	Richard Scannell
Davenport,	1881	John McMullen
Dubuque	1837	Mathias Loras
Kansas City and St Joseph's,	1940 / 1868	John J Hogan
Leavenworth	1877	Louis M Fink
Lincoln	1887	Thos Bonacum
Omaha	1885	Jas O'Connor
Wichita	1887	John Joseph Hennessy

Province of St. Paul.—See erected, 1850 1st bishop, Joseph Cretin

Archdiocese of St. Paul.—Established, 1888 1st archbishop, John Ireland.

Diocese	Established	1st bishop
Duluth	1889	Jas McGolrick
Jamestown, N Dak	"	John Shanley
St Cloud	"	Otto Zardetti
Sioux Falls	"	M Martin Marty
Winona	"	J B Cotter

Province of California.—See erected, 1840 1st bishop, Francis G D y Moreno

Archdiocese of San Francisco.—Established, 1853 1st archbishop, Joseph Sadoc Alemany

Diocese	Established	1st bishop
Monterey and Los Angeles	1850	Jos Sadoc Alemany
Sacramento	1886	P Manogue.

Province of Santa Fé.—See erected, 1850 1st bishop, J B Lamy

Archdiocese of Santa Fé.—Established, 1875. 1st archbishop, J B Lamy

Diocese	Established	1st bishop
Denver	1887	Nicholas Chrysostome Matz

There are also the vicariate apostolics of North Carolina, of Brownsville, Tex, of Idaho, of Utah, and of Arizona, and the prefecture-apostolic of the Indian Territory According to the census of 1890 there were 10,221 churches Value of church property, $118,381,516, number of communicants, 6,250,045

church services were ordered by pope Vitellianus to be read in Latin, 663, by queen Elizabeth, in 1558, to be read in English.

church-rates. Church repairs, in the church of England, belong to the parishioners, who alone, in vestry, tax themselves for the cost. Payment, which is continually disputed by dissenters and others, was enforced by ecclesiastical courts. Many attempts were made to abolish church-rates before Mr Gladstone's "Compulsory Church-rate Abolition" bill passed, 31 July, 1868

Compulsory church rates for Scotland repealed in the commons (204–143) . . . . . 11 July, 1877

church-wardens, officers of the church of England, appointed by the first canon of the synod of London in 1127 Parish overseers were appointed by the same body, and they continue nearly as then constituted.—*Johnson's Canons* Church-wardens, by canons of 1603, are chosen annually In the U S annually at Easter

ciborium, in early Christian times, a protection to the altar-table, first a tabernacle, afterwards a baldachin over the altar, and a canopy in solemn processions, also a vessel for the eucharist.

cider (Ger *Zider*), first made in England and called wine, about 1284 The earl of Manchester, ambassador in France, is said to have passed off cider for wine It was subjected to excise duty in 1763, taken off in 1830 Many orchards were planted in Herefordshire by lord Scudamore, ambassador from Charles I to France John Philips published his poem "Cyder" in 1706 The cider of Newark, N J, is superior, and much of it is sold as champagne

Cilicia, in Asia Minor, became a Roman province about 64 B C, and was conquered by the Turks, 1387 A D

Cimbri, a Teutonic race from Jutland, invaded the Roman empire about 120 B.C They defeated the Romans, under Cneius Papirius Carbo, 113 B C, under the consul Marcus Silanus, 109 B C, and under Cæpio Manlius, at Arausio, on the banks of the Rhine, where 80,000 Romans were slain 105 B C. Their allies, the Teutones, were defeated by Marius in 2 battles at Aquæ Sextiæ (Aix) in Gaul, 200,000 were killed, and 70,000 made prisoners, 102 B C The Cimbri were defeated by Marius and Catulus, at Campus Raudius, when about to enter Italy, 120,000 were killed, and 60,000 taken prisoners, 101 B.C Afterwards merged in the Teutones or Saxons

Cimento (It *experiment*) The "Accademia del Cimento," at Florence, held its first meeting for scientific experiments, 18 June, 1657 It was patronized by Ferdinand, grand duke of Tuscany The *Nuovo Cimento*, a scientific periodical, first issued at Pisa, 1855

cinchona. CHINCHONA

Cincinnati, the 1st city in Ohio and the 9th in the United States (1890) in point of population, is situated on the north bank of the Ohio river, first known as Losanteville (L'osante-ville), "the town opposite the mouth," being established opposite the mouth of the Licking river, in the winter of 1788-1789 It received its present name in 1790 In 1795, it contained 94 cabins, 10 frame houses, and about 500 inhabitants, and in 1800 its population was 750, 1810, 2540, 1820, 9602, 1830, 24,831, 1840, 46,338, 1850, 115,436, 1860, 161,044, 1870, 216,239, 1880, 255,139, 1890, 296,908, 1900, 325,902. Area, 24¼ sq miles, lat 39° 9′ N, lon 84° 25′ W.

Israel Ludlow and about 20 others cross the Ohio from the mouth of the Licking and commence the settlement of Losanteville 28 Dec. 1788

First log cabin erected, on present Front, east of Main st, Jan 1789

Major Doughty arrives with about 140 men from fort Harmar, on the Muskingum, June, 1789, and erects fort Washington on line of Third st, between Broadway and Lawrence sts., fort completed Nov "

A Presbyterian house of worship erected on lot bounded by Main, Walnut, Fourth and Fifth sts 1792

First post office established, Abner Dunn postmaster 1793

William Maxwell establishes the *Centinel of the North Western Territory*, first newspaper 9 Nov "

Nova Cesarea Harmony Lodge of Free Masons organized, 27 Dec. 1794

Western Spy and Hamilton Gazette first pub 28 May, 1799

First recorded celebration of Independence day 4 July, "

Contract made for a new court house, to replace the old one of logs, on west side of Main near Fifth st 1801

First sea going vessel to descend the Ohio, built at Marietta, and of 100 tons, passes Cincinnati bound for the West Indies, (Ohio) 27 Apr "

Cincinnati theatre established 30 Sept "

Bill passes legislature to remove seat of government from Chillicothe to Cincinnati, by vote of 12 to 8. 19 Dec "

Town of Cincinnati incorporated Jan 1802

Town library company formed 6 Mch "

Plat of town of Cincinnati recorded 29 Apr "

U S. reservation around fort Washington sold by direction of the secretary of the treasury 1808

First steamboat built in Cincinnati 1816

Branch of U S bank opened 28 Jan 1817

Christ church, the oldest Episcopal society in Cincinnati, of which William Henry Harrison, afterwards president of the U S., was a vestryman, organized 18 May "

Cincinnati college incorporated by legislature at session 1818-19

Cincinnati incorporated as a city 1819

Col Samuel W Davis obtains a charter, May, 1817, granting the exclusive privilege of laying water pipes, etc , in the streets of the city for 99 years, and erects a pumping station on the river above Deer creek, supplying water to the city through wooden pipes 1819

Western Methodist Book Concern established 1824

Residence of Jacob Burnet, distinguished citizen, on northwest cor of Seventh and Elm sts , built "

Medical college of Ohio chartered Dec 1825

Cincinnati Gazette issued as a daily 1826

Cincinnati Water Company incorporated "

Ohio Mechanical Institute chartered and established in north wing of Cincinnati college 1828

First lodge of Odd Fellows in Ohio instituted in Cincinnati, 23 Dec 1830

Common school system founded 1831

St Xavier college established "

Flood which submerged the whole lower level of the city so that steamboats passed through Second st , winter of 1831-32

Pearl st first opened 1832

Cincinnati Orphan asylum at Mount Auburn, the oldest charity of the kind in the west, chartered 1833

Lane theological seminary incorporated, 1829, opened "

First city bonds issued 1834

Locks on the Miami and Erie canal at Cincinnati completed "

Ohio Life Insurance and Trust Company bank incorporated, banking house cor Main and Third sts "

Young Men's Mercantile Library Association chartered, 5 Jan. 1836

Daily paper, the Cincinnati *Times-Star*, established "

Daily *Volksblatt* established 1838

Superior court established "

Cincinnati Academy of Fine Arts organized 18 Oct. "

Chamber of Commerce instituted 22 Oct 1839

Little Miami railroad built 1840

Cincinnati Gaslight and Coke Company, with exclusive right to lay gas mains in the city for 25 years, incorporated 1841

Cincinnati *Commercial Gazette*, daily, established "

Cincinnati *Enquirer* first issued 1842

Cincinnati Wesleyan college founded "

Cincinnati Astronomical society organized, May, 1842 and corner stone of observatory laid by John Quincy Adams, on summit of Mount Adams 9 Nov 1843

[Building sold in 1872 to the Passionist Fathers.]

St Peter's cathedral begun, 1839, consecrated 1844

[The altar, of Carrara marble, is the work of Hiram Powers]

Spring Grove cemetery consecrated 1845

Cincinnati Law library chartered, 1834, established 1846

Pleasant Hill academy founded, 1833, incorporated as Farmer s college "

Law enacted to prevent hogs running at large in the streets. 1848

Burnet house, on northwest corner Third and Vine sts., built, 1849

German Protestant Orphan asylum established . "

Literary club organized "

Cincinnati Relief Union founded 1850

Cincinnati House of Refuge opened "

Cincinnati *Volksfreund* established "

Chime of 13 bells presented to St Peter s cathedral by Reuben R. Springer . . "

Miami Medical college established 1852

Jacob Burnet dies 27 Apr 1853

City building erected . "

Court house of Hamilton county erected . "

Hughes's High school built at a cost of $25,000 . . "

Erection of Woodward high-school begun . "

Paid steam fire department organized "

Cincinnati public library and reading room established 1856

Mount Auburn Young Ladies' Institute chartered and opened "

Erection of Masonic temple begun 1859

Gen Kirby Smith advances on Cincinnati, and martial law is proclaimed and citizens prepare for defence 2 Sept. 1862

Soldiers' monument in Spring Grove cemetery erected . 1864

Old Pike's opera-house destroyed by fire 1866

Cincinnati Clearing house Association organized . "

Cincinnati and Covington suspension bridge, 1057 ft span, completed and opened . . 1 Jan 1867

Cincinnati normal school established 1868

New building of Cincinnati Wesleyan college, on site of the old Catherine St burying ground, completed "

Cincinnati hospital first occupied . Jan 1869

Harmonic society organized "

College building burned, 1845, rebuilt, and damaged by fire, and remodelled "

Cincinnati College of Pharmacy organized 1870

Total area of city 19 75 sq miles, 12 75 being annexed "

First Cincinnati industrial exposition held . . Sept "

University of Cincinnati organized under Act 16, Apr 1870, and University board appointed . . Jan. 1871

Unveiling of the Tyler-Davidson fountain on Fountain square, designed by August von Kreling of Nuremberg, and cast by Ferdinand von Müller, director of the Royal bronze foundery of Bavaria, cost $105,000 . 6 Oct. "

Reading rooms of the public library first opened on Sunday, 12 Mch. "

Union Railroad Stock yards Company incorporated. "

Cincinnati cotton exchange established . "

Eden park, 206 acres, first improved 1872

Pork Packers' Association of Cincinnati organized 30 Oct. "

St. Mary's hospital established, 1869, building completed. 1873

Total area of city increased to 24 sq miles by annexation of 4.25 sq miles . "

Queen City club organized 1874

Grand hotel opened 1874

Woman s Christian Temperance Union organized . 1875

Burnet woods park purchased, 1873, improvements begun "

Miami stock yards opened 1876

Hotel Emery opened Nov 1877

Wrought iron girder bridge across the Ohio built. "

St. Francis de Sales church, corner stone laid 30 June, 1878

Eden Park middle service reservoir begun, 1866, completed, upper basin, 1875 lower "

College of Music of Cincinnati incorporated "

Corner stone of Widows' and Old Men s Home on Walnut Hills laid 2 July, 1879

Cincinnati *Daily Post* established 1880

A 6 days' riot begins, after a verdict of manslaughter in the Berner and Palmer murder trial, both having confessed the murder, there being about 20 untried murderers in jail in the city, the court house is set on fire etc , 45 killed, 138 wounded 28 Mch 1884

MAYORS

J G Burnet	1827–31	Charles F Wilstach	1867–69
Elisha Hotchkiss	1831–33	John F Torrence	1869–71
Samuel W Davies.	1833–43	S S Davis	1871–73
Henry E Spencer	1843–51	George W Johnston	1873–77
Mark P Taylor	1851–53	R M Moore	1877–79
D T Snellbaker	1853–55	Charles Jacob, jr	1879–81
James J Farran	1855–57	William Means	1881–83
N W Thomas	1857–59	Thomas J Stephens	1883–85
R M Bishop	1859–61	Amos Smith, jr	1885–89
George B Hatch	1861–63	John B Mosby	1889–91
L A Harris	1863–67	"	1891–94

All the above for 2 years' term, except the last, as under the new charter (1891) the term is for 3 years

Cincinna'ti, Order of, formed in 1783 by officers of the American army NEW YORK, 1783 The first general meeting, held at Philadelphia, May, 1784, made amendments to the constitution, which were ratified by the state societies At the second general meeting, 1787, Washington was chosen president-general, and was re-elected every 3 years while he lived, he was followed by Alex Hamilton The society was accused of tending to establish an hereditary military aristocracy, and the state societies of Connecticut, Delaware, New Hampshire, Virginia, and Georgia were dissolved about 1804 The general society and 7 state organizations still exist—viz those of Massachusetts, Rhode Island, New York, New Jersey, Pennsylvania, Maryland, and South Carolina The general society meets triennially Next meeting, Boston, Mass , 1893 Number of living members reported 1890, 439

cin'namon, a species of laurel, mentioned among perfumes of the sanctuary (Exod xxx 23), 1491 B C , found in American forests by don Ulloa, 1736, cultivated in Jamaica and Dominica, 1788, and now in Ceylon.

Cinque Ports, on the south coast of England, were originally 5 (hence the name)—Dover, Hastings, Hythe, Romney, and Sandwich, Winchelsea and Rye were afterwards added —*Jeake* Their jurisdiction was vested in barons, called wardens, to protect the coast, these ports being nearest France, and considered the keys of the kingdom, said to have been instituted by William I in 1078.—*Rapin*. Their peculiar jurisdiction was abolished in 1855, the lord-wardenship being now a merely honorary dignity

Cintra, a town of Portugal. Here was signed an agreement on 22 Aug 1808, between the French and English the day after the battle of Vimeira As the basis of a convention of 30 Aug following, it is called the convention of Cintra It permitted Junot to evacuate Portugal free, in British ships The convention was denounced, but a court of inquiry at Chelsea exonerated the British commanders. Both Wellington and Napoleon justified sir Hew Dalrymple

cipher, secret writing. Julius Cæsar and Augustus in secret despatches are said to have used for each letter the second or third after it. This cipher was in use till Sixtus IV. (1471–84), when it was divulged by Leon Battista Alberti, and a new cipher devised The father of Venetian cipher was Zuan Soro, who flourished about 1516 —*Rawdon Brown* Edgar Allan Poe introduces an ingenious cipher in his tale of the "Gold Bug" CRYPTOGRAPH and CRYPTOGRAM

cipher despatches. The result of the presidential election of 1876 in the United States depended upon the electoral votes of Louisiana, South Carolina, and Florida, long in dispute Mr. Hayes needed all 3 states, while any one of them would have elected Mr Tilden Pending the result, many despatches in cipher passed between Mr Tilden's friends and persons in the south, which, when translated and published in the New York *Tribune* (Rep), 1877, suggested attempted bribery A great scandal arose, and Mr Tilden publicly disclaimed all knowledge of the despatches

Circassia, Asia, on north side of the Caucasus The Circassians, said to be descended from the Albanians, were unsubdued even by Timour In the 16th century they submitted to czar Ivan II of Russia, and about 1745 the princes of Kabarda took oaths of fealty Many Circassians became Mahometans in the 18th century

Circassia ceded to Russia by Turkey by the treaty of Adrianople (but Circassians, under Schamyl, long resist) 14 Sept 1829
Victories of Orbelliani over them June, Nov, Dec 1857
He subdues much country, and expels the inhabitants April, 1858
Schamyl, Circassian leader, captured, and treated with respect, 7 Sept 1859
About 20 000 Circassians reach Constantinople in distress, and are relieved 28 Apr 1860
Caidar, last Circassian stronghold captured, grand duke Michael declares the war at an end 8 June, 1864
Many thousand Circassians enter Turkey, partly relieved by the government June et seq "
Schamyl and his son at marriage of czarowitch, 9 Nov 1866, Schamyl d March, 1871
Revolt against Russia, suppressed, many Circassians flee to Turkey and join the army July, Aug 1877

Circensian games were combats in the Roman circus (at first in honor of Consus, god of councils, afterwards of Jupiter, Neptune, Juno, and Minerva), said to have been instituted by Evander, and established at Rome, 732 B C, by Romulus Tarquin named them Circensian; they lasted from 4 to 12 Sept

circle. Its quadrature, or ratio of the diameter to the circumference, has exercised mathematical ingenuity in all ages Archimedes, about 221 B C, gave it as 7 to 22, Abraham Sharp (1717) as 1 to 3 and 72 decimals, and Lagny (1719) as 1 to 3 and 122 decimals

circles of Germany (formed by Maximilian I, about 1500, to distinguish the members of the diet of the empire) were, in 1512, Franconia, Bavaria, Upper Rhine, Suabia, Westphalia, and Lower Saxony, in 1789, Austria, Burgundy, Lower Rhine, the Palatinate, Upper Saxony, and Brandenburg were added All were merged in the CONFEDERATION OF THE RHINE, in 1806.

circuits in England were divided into 3, with 3 justices in each, 1176 They were afterwards 4, with 5 justices in each, 1180 —*Rapin* They have been frequently altered England and Wales long had 8 judges travelling in spring and summer to try civil and criminal cases, the larger towns are visited in winter for trials of criminals only, this is called "going the circuit." The circuits were settled by order in council, 5 Feb 1876 The courts sit monthly for the city of London and county of Middlesex COURTS IN THE UNITED STATES.

circular letter. MASSACHUSETTS, 1768.

circulating library. Stationers lent books on hire in the middle ages. A public circulating library in England, opened by Samuel Fancourt, a dissenting minister of Salisbury, about 1740, failed, but similar institutions at Bath and in London succeeded, and others were established throughout the kingdom. There was a circulating library at Crane court, London, in 1748, and a catalogue in 2 vols was published.—No books can be taken from the British museum except for judicial purposes, but the libraries of the Royal Society and the principal scientific societies, except that of the Royal Institution, London, are circulating The London library (circulating), which was founded 24 June, 1840, is useful to literary men Of private subscription libraries, that founded by C. E Mudie, in New Oxford street, London, is remarkable for quantity and quality—sometimes thousands of copies of a new work being in circulation It began 1842, and gained celebrity, Dec. 1848, by supplying the unprecedented demand for the first 2 vols. of Macaulay's "History of England" The hall, its walls covered with shelves of new books, was opened Dec. 1860. The "Circulating Library Company," London, was founded Jan 1862, and other companies since The Boston Public library, the largest collection of books in the United States, except the Congressional library, was organized 1852, and its building delivered to the trustees 1 Jan. 1858. It is a free circulating library. BOSTON, 1894 LIBRARIES.

circumcision (instituted 1897 B.C) was the seal of the covenant made by God with Abraham It was practised by the ancient Egyptians, and is still by Jews, the Copts, and some Oriental nations The custom is also found among some of the savage tribes of Africa, South America and islands of the Pacific The Festival of the Circumcision (of Christ), originally the octave of Christmas, is mentioned about 187, and has been introduced into the liturgy of the Roman Catholic, Greek, and Anglican churches

circumnavigators. It became evident after the discovery of America by Columbus that the earth was a globe and could be circumnavigated At first considered one of the *most daring enterprises it soon ceased to be so, as first one and* then another of the navigators of the 16th century accomplished it. The following is a list of the early circumnavigators

Magellan, or Magalhaens a native of Portugal in the service of Spain sailed from San Lucar 20 Sept 1519 with 5 ships, only 1 of which succeeded in circumnavigating the globe (AMERICA) 1519-22
Grijalva, Spaniard 1537
Alvarado, Spaniard "
Mendana, Spaniard 1567
Sir Francis Drake, first English 1577-80
Cavendish first voyage 1586-88
Le Maire, Dutch 1615-17
Quiros Spaniard 1625
Tasman, Dutch (VAN DIEMEN'S LAND) 1642
Cowley, British 1683
Dampier, British 1689
Cooke, British 1708
Clipperton British 1719
Roggewein Dutch 1721-23
Anson, British (ACAPULCO) 1740-44
Byron, British 1764-66
Wallis, British 1766-68
Carteret, British 1766-69
Bougainville French "
James Cook, British (HAWAII) "
On his death the voyage was continued by King 1779
Portlocke, British 1788
Robert Gray, in the ship *Columbia*, from Boston, the first American ship 1790
King and Fitzroy, British 1826-36
Belcher, British 1836-42
Wilkes, American 1838-42
DEEP SEA SOUNDINGS, EXPEDITIONS, NORTHEAST AND NORTHWEST PASSAGE

circus (Gr. κιρκος) There were 8 (some say 10) circuses at Rome, the largest, the Circus Maximus, built by the younger Tarquin, 605 B.C It was an oval, length, 3½ stadia, or more than 3 English furlongs, breadth 960 Roman ft It was enlarged by Julius Cæsar, restored after a fire by Augustus, and rebuilt by Domitian and Trajan It is supposed to have seated 250,000 people It was surrounded by a canal 10 ft wide and 10 ft deep, which supplied the water for naval exhibitions AMPHITHEATRES, FACTIONS.

Cirrha, a town of Phocis, N Greece, for sacrilege razed to the ground in the Sacred War, 586 B C

Cisalpine republic, N Italy, formed by the French in May, 1797, from the *Cispadane* and *Transpadane* republics, acknowledged by the emperor of Germany by treaty of CAMPO FORMIO, 17 Oct. 1797. It received a new constitution in Sept. 1798, was remodelled, and named the Italian republic, with Napoleon Bonaparte president, 1802, merged into the kingdom of Italy, Mch 1805. ITALY

Cispadane republic, with the Transpadane republic, merged into the Cisalpine republic, Oct 1797

Cistercians (the order of Citeaux), a powerful order of monks founded about 1098 by Robert, a Benedictine, abbot of Molesme, named from Citeaux, in France, site of the first convent, near the end of the 11th century The monks cultivated their lands, observed silence, abstained from flesh, lay on straw, and wore neither shoes nor shirts. Its power was such as to crush Abelard, Arnold of Brescia, and the Cathari, it originated the 2d crusade and inaugurated many of the military orders of the church BENEDICTINES, BERNARDINES, FEUILLANTS, TRAPPISTS

Citate. The Russian general Gortschakoff, intending to storm Kalafat, threw up redoubts at Citate, close to the Danube, which were stormed by the Turks under Omar Pacha, 6 Jan 1854 The fighting continued the 7th, 8th, and 9th, when the Russians were compelled to retire to their former position at Krajowa, having lost 1500 killed and 2000 wounded

The loss of the Turks was estimated at 338 killed and 700 wounded

Cities of Refuge. 6 Levitical cities appointed by Mosaic law (Num xxxv 13) as asylums for involuntary manslayers. Within the walls of either of these cities, or 1000 yards around them, the homicide was safe from the "avenger of blood," but if slain without these limits the slayer was held guiltless The roads leading to these cities were well defined and in good order These cities under Joshua (xx 3) were Kedesh, Shechem, and Hebron on the west of the river Jordan, and Bezer, Ramoth-Gilead, and Golan on the east side

citizen. It was not lawful to scourge a citizen of Rome, much less to crucify him In England a citizen is a person who is free of a city, or who doth carry on a trade therein —*Camden*. Various privileges have been conferred on citizens as freemen in several reigns The wives of citizens of London (not aldermen's wives, nor gentlewomen by descent) were obliged to wear minever caps, being white woollen knit, three-cornered, with peaks projecting 3 or 4 in beyond the foreheads, aldermen's wives wore caps of velvet, 1 Eliz 1558 —*Stow* On 10 Oct 1792, the convention decreed "citoyen" and "citoyenne" as the only titles in France In the United States all male persons over 21, except Indians and foreigners not naturalized, are citizens Before the 14th and 15th amendments to the Constitution, proclaimed 20 July, 1868, and 30 Mch 1869, citizenship was restricted to white men DRED SCOTT Every citizen of the United States is a voter, unless disfranchised

city (Lat *civitas*, Fr *cité*, It *città*) The word has been used in England only since the Conquest, when London was called *Londonburgh* Cities were first incorporated, 1079 In England, a town corporate is called a city when the seat of a bishop with a cathedral church —*Camden*

Ciudad Rodrigo, a fortified town in Spain invested by French, 11 June, 1810, surrendered, 10 July, and held by them until stormed by the British, under Wellington, 19 Jan 1812

civil law. CODES The civil law was restored in Italy, Germany, etc, 1127 —*Blair* It was introduced into England by Theobald, a Norman abbot, afterwards archbishop of Canterbury, in 1138 It is now used there in the spiritual courts only, and in maritime affairs DOCTORS' COMMONS, LAWS

civil list. This is the revenue given to the crown of England in lieu of its ancient hereditary income The entire revenue of Elizabeth was not more than 600,000*l*, and that of Charles I. was about 800,000*l* After the English revolution of 1688, a civil-list revenue was settled on William and Mary of 700,000*l*., parliament having assumed the support of the army and navy in 1690 The civil list of George II was increased to 800,000*l*, and that of George III, in 1815, was 1,030,000*l*

In 1831, the civil list was fixed at 510 000*l*., and in Dec. 1837, at 385,000*l* (This does not include the various amounts paid the royal family apart from the sovereign, which in 1892 were more than 250,000*l*.)
Sir H. Parnell's motion for inquiry into the civil list led to resignation of Wellington cabinet . 15 Nov. 1830
Prince Albert obtained an annuity from Parliament of 30,000*l*, 7 Feb 1840
A select committee of inquiry appointed by the commons, 2 Feb. 1860

civil service in Great Britain While this service dates back over 2 centuries, it is only within the last hundred years that it has assumed a national importance The civil service now comprises all who serve the government in a civil capacity as opposed to those in the military or naval service. In all, including the treasury, home, foreign, colonial, post, despatch, and revenue officers, etc, at least 500,000 persons (1892) Within the last 50 years several commissions have been appointed to examine into the methods of appointments, etc. In 1855 a commission reported against the existing system of appointments, and on 21 May of that year commissioners were appointed to examine the qualifications of candidates and report annually In Apr 1859, the Civil-service Superannuation act was passed. On 4 June, 1870, by order in council, competitive examinations were made general after 1 Oct 1870. Through a report made by a select committee, June, 1874, important changes were made by order in council, Feb 1876. There are 2 grades of examinations, in the first the examinations are severe, with positions and salaries to correspond, attracting many university men as candidates, in the second or lower grade the examinations are comparatively easy and salaries limited from 4 Feb. 1890, to be from 70*l* to 250*l* per annum The civil service for the year ending 31 Mch. 1855, cost 7,735,515*l*, 1865, 10,205,413*l*, 1871, 13,176,659*l*., 1880, 15,155,522*l*, 1892-1893, 17,310,920*l*

civil-service reform in the United States During the years 1866-71, the climax of the patronage system, there were 1678 removals in the New York custom-house, more than one for each secular day President Grant asked Congress, in 1870, to aid him in reforming the civil service, and by the law of 3 Mch 1871, the president appointed a civil-service commission, which instituted competitive examinations for appointments and promotions in certain branches of the service, 1 Jan 1872 In Mch 1871, however, col Silas W. Burt, deputy naval officer, had, on his own responsibility, made the first trial of these examinations in the civil service of the United States, in reorganizing the naval office It was eminently successful Politicians opposed the system, and in 1873 Congress refused to appropriate the $25,000 needed for them President Grant repeatedly urged these appropriations, once, in April, 1874, by special message, but in vain 31 Aug 1874, president Grant issued executive order No 4, as follows "It appearing to me, from their trial at Washington and at the city of New York, that the farther extension of the civil-service rules will promote the efficiency of the public service, it is ordered that such rules be and they are hereby extended to the several federal offices at the city and in the custom-house district of Boston, and that the proper measures be taken for carrying this order into effect." The rules were not fully carried out, patronage still prevailing In 1877 president Hayes appointed the Jay commission, consisting of John Jay (chairman), Lawrence Turnure, of New York, and J H Robinson, of the Department of Justice, Washington, whose elaborate report led to the removal of collector Arthur and naval officer Cornell. On 6 Mch. 1879, an executive order established competitive examinations for the clerical offices of the New York custom-house, and it is still enforced.

On 16 Jan 1883, Congress authorized the president to appoint a civil-service commission of 6 members, "to regulate and improve the civil service of the U S" At this time there were subject to examination in the executive department at Washington, 5652, in custom districts, 2573, and in post office department, 5699
Convention of civil service reformers at Baltimore 22 Feb 1889
List of "eligibles" for appointment to government service made public after 25 May, "
Portions of the Indian service classified under the civil service rules, school superintendents, teachers, physicians, etc, by order of president Harrison 14 Apr. 1891
[On 4 Jan 1889, the civil service regulations were extended to the railway mail service by order of president Cleveland.]

civil wars. CONFEDERATE STATES, ENGLAND FRANCE, UNITED STATES, 1861-65, etc.

Clan-na-Gael ("brotherhood of Gaels"), an Irish secret society formed in 1881 to succeed the Fenians It belonged to the Irish National League in the United States, of which it was the extreme violent part The ultimate object of the Clan-na-Gael was said to be Ireland's independence of England For murder of Dr Cronin, TRIALS, 1889

clans are said to have arisen in Scotland, in the reign of king Malcolm II, about 1008 The legal power of chiefs and all heritable jurisdiction were abolished in Scotland, and liberty granted to clansmen in 1747, after the rebellion of 1745 The chief of each clan wears 2 eagle feathers in his bonnet, in addition to the badge.—*Chambers* A history of the clans by Wm Buchanan was pub in 1775. The following is a list of the known clans of Scotland, with their ancient badges.

Name	Badge	Name	Badge
Buchanan	Birch.	Frazer	Yew
Cameron	Oak	Gordon	Ivy
Campbell	Myrtle	Graham	Laurel
Chisholm	Alder	Grant	Cranberry heath.
Colquhoun	Hazel	Gun	Rosewort.
Cumming	Common sallow	Lamont	Crab apple tree.
Drummond	Holly	M'Alister	5 leaved heath
Farquharson	Purple fox glove.	M'Donald	Bell-heath
Ferguson	Poplar	M'Donnell	Mountain heath.
Forbes	Broom.	M'Dougall	Cypress.

Name	Badge	Name	Badge
'Farlane	Cloudberry bush	M'Quarrie	Blackthorn
Gregor	Pine	M'Rae	Fir-club moss
'Intosh	Boxwood	Menzies	Ash
'Kay	Bulrush	Munro	Eagle's feathers
Kenzie	Deer grass	Murray	Juniper
'Kinnon	St John's wort	Ogilvie	Hawthorne
'Lachlan	Mountain ash	Oliphant	Great maple
'Lean	Blackberry heath	Robertson	Fern, or brechans
'Leod	Red whortleberries	Rose	Brier rose.
'Nab	Rose blackberries	Ross	Bear berries.
'Neil	Sea ware	Sinclair	Clover
'Pherson	Variegated boxwood	Stewart	Thistle
		Sutherland	Cat's tail grass

Clare was the first place in Ireland since 1689 to elect Roman Catholic M P (ROMAN CATHOLICS), when, at Ennis e county town, Daniel O'Connell was returned, 5 July 1828 e did not sit till after the Catholic Emancipation act in 1829, ing re-elected 30 July 1829

Clare and **Clarence,** Suffolk, Engl Richard de Clare, rl of Gloucester, is said to have seated here a monastery of e order of Friars Eremites, the first of these mendicants who me to England, 1248 —*Tanner* Lionel, 3d son of Edward I, obtaining the honor of Clare by marriage, was created ke of Clarence, a title since in a branch of the royal family

Clarendon, Constitutions of, enacted at a council held Jan 1164, at Clarendon, in Wiltshire, Engl, to *retrench* the wer of the clergy They led to Becket's quarrel with Henry , were annulled by the pope, and abandoned by the king, pr 1174

All suits concerning advowsons to lie in civil courts
Clergy accused of crime to be tried by civil judges
I No person of rank to leave the realm without royal license
Laics not to be accused in spiritual courts, except by legal and reputable promoters and witnesses.
No chief tenant of the crown to be excommunicated, nor his lands put under interdict
I Revenues of vacant sees to belong to the king
II Goods forfeited to the crown not to be protected in churches
III Sons of villeins not to be *ordained* clerks without the consent of their lord
. Bishops to be barons, with the burdens of that rank
Churches belonging to the king's see not to be granted in perpetuity against his will
I Excommunicated persons not to be bound to give security for continuing in their abode
II No inhabitant in demesne to be excommunicated for non appearance in a spiritual court
III If any tenant *in capite* refuse submission to spiritual courts, the case to be referred to the king
IV The clergy to abandon all right of enforcing debts contracted by oath or promise
V Causes between laymen and ecclesiastics to be determined by a jury
VI Appeals to be ultimately carried to the king, and no further without his consent

Clarendon Press, Oxford, Engl The building was ected by sir John Vanbrugh, in 1711-13, out of the copyght of lord Clarendon's "History of the Rebellion," given to e university by his son The original building was conrted into a museum, lecture-rooms, etc, and a new printingfice erected by Blore & Robertson, 1825-30

clarion, said by Spanish writers to have been invented the Moors in Spain, about 800, at first a trumpet, serving a treble to trumpets sounding tenor and bass.—*Ashe*

clarionet or **clarinet,** a wind-instrument of the ed kind, said to have been invented by Johann Christoph enner, in Nuremberg, about 1690

classis, a name first used by Tullius Servius (6th ing) for a division of the Roman people, 573 B C The first the 6 classes were called *classici*, by way of eminence, and ence authors of the first rank (especially Greek and Latin) me to be called classics.

clav'ichord, a keyed stringed musical instrument of arious forms, in use in France, Spain, and Germany, in the 5th and 17th centuries. PIANO, SPINET, VIRGINALS

clavicythe'rium, an upright musical instrument, robably like the harpsichord of the 16th century

clearing-house. The *Chambre de Compensation Lyon* as reorganized in 1667, it is claimed, was similar to the odern clearing-house The London Bankers' clearing-house as instituted previous to 1773, the building in Lombard street, nce known as the clearing-house was opened in 1810. Joint ock-brokers were admitted in 1854, and country check clearing was begun in 1858. The Bank of England entered in 1864, but only clears against the other banks The association consists of 27 banks The records show as the amount of clearings for various years as follows 1839, 954,000,000*l*, 1868, 3,425,000 000*l*, 1874, 5,937,000,000*l*, 1881, 6,357,000,000*l*, 1888, 6,942,000,000*l*, 1890, 7,801 000,000*l* There are now clearing-houses in most of the large towns of England The London railway clearing-house was organized in 1842, and the Stock Exchange clearing-house in 1874 *La Chambre de Compensation des Banquiers de Paris* was formed Mch 1872, the clearing-house in Vienna in 1864, and in Berlin in 1883 The first clearing-house in the United States was started in New York city, 11 Oct 1853 The membership of the New York Clearing-house Association, in 1892 comprised 46 national banks, 18 state banks, and the sub-treasury of the U S at New York The total clearing-house transactions in the 57 associations existing in the U S for the year ending 30 Sept 1892, was $61,017,839,067, an increase over the corresponding year ending 30 Sept 1891, of $3,836,491,783, and this volume of business was accomplished with the use of only about 8 per cent in currency or money Of the 57 associations in the U S, those showing transactions amounting to over $1,000,000,000 in 1892 are as follows New York, $36 279 905,236, Boston, $4,901,096,976, Chicago, $4,959,861,142, Philadelphia, $3,671,149,047, St Louis, $1,211,370,719

A stock clearing house association was organized in the city of New York 17 May, 1892

Clementines, apocryphal pieces, attributed to Clemens Romanus, a contemporary of St Paul, and said to have succeeded St Peter as bishop of Rome He died 102.—*Niceron* Also the decretals of pope Clement V, who died 1314, published by his successor —*Bowyer* Also Augustin monks, each of whom, having been a superior 9 years, became a common monk.—*Clementines* were the adherents of Robert, son of the count of Geneva, who, as Clement VII succeeded Gregory XI, 1378, and *Urbanists*, those of pope Urban VI Christendom was divided, France, Castile, Scotland, etc, adhering to Clement, Rome, Italy, and England to Urban The schism ended in 1409, when Alexander V was elected pope, and his rivals resigned ANTI-POPE

Cleopatra's Needle. OBELISKS

clergy (from the Gr. κλῆρος, a lot or inheritance), in the first century termed presbyters, elders, or bishops and deacons. The bishops (ἐπίσκοποι or overseers) elected from the presbyters, assumed higher functions about 330, and, under Constantine, obtained the recognition and protection of the secular power Under the Lombard and Norman-French kings in the 7th and 8th centuries, the clergy acquired temporal power as owners of lands, and after monachism arose, regular clergy, who lived apart from the world, by a *regula*, or rule, were distinguished from secular (worldly) or beneficed clergy The English clergy write *clerk* after their names in legal documents BISHOPS, CHURCH OF ENGLAND

Clergy were first styled clerks, judges being chosen from them after the Norman custom and the officers being clergy, they keep the name to this day —*Blackstone*

As the Druids kept the keys of religion and of letters, so did the priests keep both to themselves, they alone profess letters, and a man of letters was called a clerk, hence learning was called clerkship.—*Pasquier*

Benefit of clergy, *privilegium clericale*, arose in regard of princes to the church, and consisted of 1st an exemption of places consecrated from criminal arrests, as sanctuaries, 2d, exemption of persons of clergymen from criminal process before the secular judge, in particular cases—the original meaning of the *privilegium clericale* The benefit of clergy was afterwards extended to every one who could read, and it was enacted that if any man who could read were condemned to death, the bishop of the diocese might claim him as a clerk and dispose of him in certain places as he might deem meet. The ordinary gave the prisoner a Latin book, in a black Gothic character, to read a verse or two, and if the ordinary said, "*Legit ut clericus*" ("He reads like a clerk"), the offender was burned in the hand, otherwise he suffered death (3 Edw I 1274)

Privilege was restricted by Henry VII in 1489, and abolished, for murderers and great criminals, by Henry VIII, 1512 —*Stow.*

Reading was discontinued, 5 Anne, c 6 (1706)

Benefit of clergy was repealed, 7 and 8 Geo. IV c. 28 (1827)

CLERGY CHARITIES IN ENGLAND.

William Assheton, theological writer, first proposed a plan to provide for families of deceased clergy He died Sept. 1711.—*Watts's "Life of Assheton"*

Festival of "Sons of the Clergy," held annually at St. Paul's, insti tuted about 1655; from it sprang the charity called "Sons of the Clergy" (Clergy Orphan and Widow Corporation), incorporated 1 July, 1678.

Clergy Orphan Corporation, 1749.

Friend of the Clergy Corporation, 1849.

St. John's Foundation School for Sons of Poor Clergy, 1852.

Poor Clergy Relief Corporation, established 1856; *incorporated* 1867.

There are other charities for relatives of the clergy.

Clergy excluded from Parliament, 1801.

A bill to repeal this lost in the commons (110–101), 11 May, 1881.

Clerkenwell, a parish, N.E. London, from a well (*fons clericorum*) in Ray street, where parish clerks occasionally acted mystery-plays; once before Richard II. in 1390. Hunt's political meetings in 1817 were held in Spa-fields in this parish. In St. John's parish are remains of the priory of the knights of St. John of Jerusalem. Clerkenwell prison was built in 1615, in lieu of that called "the Cage," taken down in 1614, the then Bridewell being insufficient. The House of Detention, erected in 1775, was rebuilt in 1818; again, 1844. For an explosion here, FENIANS, Dec. 1867. At Clerkenwell-close stood the house of Oliver Cromwell, where some suppose the death-warrant of Charles I. was signed, Jan. 1649.

Clermont, a town of France. Here was held the council under pope Urban II. in 1095, which approved the first crusade against the infidels, and named Godfrey of Bouillon to command it. In this council the name pope, previously assumed by other bishops, is said to have been limited to the bishop of Rome; and Philip I. of France was (a second time) excommunicated.—*Hénault.*

Cleveland, the most important port of Ohio, on lake Erie, was named after gen. Moses Cleaveland, director of the Connecticut Land Company, who arrived at the present site of Cleveland, 22 July, 1796, and began the settlement at the mouth of Cuyahoga river. In 1800 the population was only 7; in 1810 it was 57; 1820, 150; 1830, 1075; 1840, 6071; 1850, 17,034. In 1854, Ohio City, on the opposite bank of the river, was united with Cleveland, and in 1860 the population of the united cities was 43,838; in 1870, 92,829; 1880, 159,404; and 1890, 261,353; 1900, 381,768. By this census the 1st city in the state and the 7th of the U. S. In 1890 the city covered an area of 34 sq. miles. Lat. 41° 36′ N., lon. 81° 38′ W.

Meeting of Pontiac with maj. Rogers and his rangers occurs at the mouth of Cuyahoga river, the present site of Cleveland (*Parkman*)....7 Nov. 1760
Gen. Moses Cleaveland and party arrive....22 July, 1796
Surveys begun, 16 Sept., and first plat of the city of Cleveland made by Amos Spafford....1 Oct. "
Storehouse for the Connecticut Land Company erected a short distance south of St. Clair st., and a cabin built on the east side of Bank st., for Job P. Stiles, who was left in charge of the company's stores....fall of "
First white child in Cuyahoga county born to Mr. and Mrs. Stiles.... 1797
Second surveying party arrives, 1797; one of the party, David Eldridge, drowned the day previous to their arrival, and buried in the cemetery lot cor. Ontario and Prospect sts., 4 June, "
Edward Paine opens a general store.... "
W. W. Williams and maj. Wyatt build a grist-mill at Newburg.. 1799
Miss Sarah Doan opens a township school.... 1800
Celebration ball held at maj. Carter's double log-house..4 July, 1801
City re-surveyed by maj. Amos Spafford, and corners of the streets marked by oak posts.... "
Elisha Norton opens a store in Carter's house under the hill, near the west end of Superior st.... "
First town meeting held at the house of James Kingsbury; Rodolphus Edwards chairman of the board of trustees...5 Apr. 1802
First permanent frame house built by Amos Spafford, near west end of Superior st., on south side, 1802. A house erected by maj. Carter previously was burned before completion.... "
Mouth of the Cuyahoga made a port of entry.... 1805
First postmaster, Elisha Norton, appointed....2 Oct. "
A 30-ton schooner, the *Zephyr*, built by maj. Carter and launched at the foot of Superior st.... 1808
Cleveland chosen as the seat of justice for Cuyahoga county... 1809
Alfred Kelly, the first lawyer, and David Long, the first doctor in Cleveland, arrive.... 1810
Maj. Carter erects the first warehouse, a log structure, on the lake shore, near the junction of Meadow and Spring sts.... "
Elias and Harvey Murray, first regular merchants, open a store on Water st.... "
Court of common pleas holds its first session in the store of E. and H. Murray....5 June, "
The *Ohio*, a vessel of 60 tons, built and launched.... "
A court-house which served also as country jail and residence erected on the public square (it stood till 1828).... 1812
Omic, an Indian, for murder of 2 trappers, Buel and Gibbs, near Sandusky, is hung on the public square....24 June, "
Village of Cleveland incorporated by charter dated....23 Dec. 1814
First village election; Alfred Kelly chosen president....June, 1815

CLE

Total assessed value of real estate in Cleveland, $21,065.... 1816
Commercial Bank of Lake Erie opened; Leonard Case, president, "
First frame warehouse built by Leonard Case and capt. William Gaylord a little north of St. Clair st. on the river....about "
Euclid st. laid out.... "
First school-house, a 1-story frame, owned by the corporation, erected cor. Bank and St. Clair sts.... 1817
First religious organization, holding services in private residences, organized, with rev. Roger Searls (Episcopal) as pastor, "
First number of the first newspaper, the *Cleveland Gazette and Commercial Record*, issued by Andrew Logan....31 July, 1818
First steamboat on lake Erie, the *Walk-in-the-Water*, enters the harbor, from Buffalo, N. Y....1 Sept. "
Cleveland Herald first issued by Ziba Wiles.... 1819
Joseph Barber erects a cabin in Brooklyn.... "
First stage coach line between Cleveland and Columbus established, 1820, and between Cleveland and Buffalo, N. Y.... 1821
Ohio canal opened to Akron.... 1827
Coal first used for fuel.... "
New court-house erected on southwest quarter of the square, a 2-story brick.... 1828
Improvement of harbor begun.... "
Old Trinity church, cor. St. Clair and Seneca sts., built.... "
Market house established.... 1829
First fire-engine purchased.... "
Prospect st. laid out.... 1831
First iron-works, a foundery, erected by John Ballard & Co.. "
Brooklyn "boom" begins; Massasoit house erected, ship-canal built, etc.... "
New jail built on Champlain st., in rear of court-house.... 1832
Presbyterian society organized, 1820, and build their first church, the "Stone church," cor. Ontario st. and the square.... 1834
First Catholic church built, a frame structure, on Columbus st., 1835
Village of Brooklyn incorporated as Ohio City....3 Mch. 1836
Cleveland incorporated as a city....5 Mch. "
John W. Willey elected first mayor, and first meeting of city council....15 Apr. "
Public-school system adopted.... "
Fire department organized; Henry Cook, chief.... "
"City Watch" established.... "
Baptist society (organized 1832) erect a church cor. Champlain and Seneca sts.... "
Columbus st. bridge war, 1837; James S. Clark builds a bridge over the river, and gives it to the city; Ohio City people object and attempt to destroy the bridge; they are met by residents of Cleveland with fire-arms and force; the matter is finally settled in court.... 1837
St. Clair St. academy purchased for $6000.... 1839
[Site afterwards occupied as fire department headquarters.]
Ohio and Pennsylvania canal opened to Pittsburg.... 1841
Cleveland *Plain Dealer* established.... "
Cuyahoga Steam Furnace Company organized, 1835; builds the first locomotive west of the Alleghany mountains.... 1842
State bank of Ohio created by act of legislature, and Commercial, Merchants', and City banks organized.... 1845
Lake Erie Telegraph Company file the first request to erect poles and wires in the streets.... 1847
Cleveland Leader established.... "
Wedell house erected.... 1848
Case library founded.... "
Cleveland Gas-light and Coke Company, incorporated, 6 Feb. 1846; lays its first pipes in Superior and other streets.... 1849
Young Men's Christian Association organized.... 1850
Cleveland, Columbus, and Cincinnati railroad opened to Columbus.... 1851
Cleveland, Painesville, and Ashtabula railroad chartered, 1849; opened....20 Nov. 1852
Cleveland, Norwalk, and Toledo railroad chartered, 1850; opened....24 Jan. 1853
[Completing line between New York and Chicago.]
Cleveland and Ohio City united....6 June, 1854
Government buildings, post-office, etc., erected.... 1856
Kennard house erected.... "
Waterworks begun, 1849, and water first supplied....10 Sept. "
Cleveland Rolling Mills Company founded by Henry Chisholm, 1857
Third court-house erected.... 1858
Central high-school building erected on Euclid ave., near Erie st.... "
Board of Education created.... 1859
First line of street-cars on Woodland ave. starts....10 Sept. 1860
Statue of commodore Perry unveiled, Public sq., Superior st., on the 47th anniversary of the battle of lake Erie....10 Sept. "
Western Reserve Historical Society organized.... 1867
Bessemer steel first made at the Cleveland rolling mills.... 1868
Standard Oil Company founded.... "
Cleveland public library founded.... "
First iron vessel on the lakes launched from Blaisdell's shipyard, "
Cleveland *Evening News and Herald* established.... 1869
Lake View cemetery established.... 1870
Village of East Cleveland annexed....14 Oct. 1872
Lake View park purchased and improved.... 1873
Newburg annexed as the 18th ward....16 Sept. "
Waterworks tunnel, under lake Erie, begun, 1869; completed, Oct. "
Cleveland training-school opened.... 1874
Harbor improvement begun.... 1875
Iron and stone viaduct, connecting east and west sides, completed.... 1878
Cleveland *Press* established.... "
High-school on Wilson ave. first occupied, and old high-school on Euclid ave. given to Board of Education and public library, "
South Side park purchased.... 1879

Case School of Applied Science, chartered, 1800, opened 1881
Western Reserve college removes from Hudson to Cleveland, and re named Adelbert college (Ohio) 1882
Electric car begins regular trips over the East Cleveland st railway, the first in regular operation in the U S 27 July, 1884
Case School of Applied Science and Adelbert College building erected 1885-86
City treasurer Thomas Axworthy embezzles half a million dollars of city funds 1888
Contract for new waterworks tunnel let 24 Mch "
Cleveland *Daily World* established 1889
Garfield Memorial dedicated at Lake View cemetery 30 May, 1890

MAYORS

John W Willey	1836-38	Edward S Flint	1861-63
Joshua Mills	1838-40	Irvine W Master / George B Senter	1863-65
Nicholas Dockstader	1840-41		
John W Allen	1841-42	Herman M Chapin	1865-67
Joshua Mills	1842-43	Stephen Buhrer	1867-71
Nelson Hayward	1843-44	Frederick W Pelton	1871-73
Samuel Starkweather	1844-46	Charles A Otis	1873-75
George Hoadly	1846-47	Nathan P Payne	1875-77
Josiah A Harris	1847-48	William G Rose	1877-79
Lorenzo A Kelsey	1848-49	R R Herrick	1879-83
Flavel W Bingham	1849-50	John H Farley	1883-85
William Case	1850-52	George W Gardner	1885-87
Abner C Brownell	1852-55	B D Babcock	1887-89
William B Castle	1855-57	George W Gardner	1889-91
Samuel Starkweather	1857-59	William G Rose	1891-93
George B Senter	1859-61	Robert Blee	1893-95

Cleveland's administration. UNITED STATES, 1885-89, 1893-97

Cleves, a town of Germany about 40 miles north of Dusseldorf and the birth-place of Anne of Cleves, one of the wives of Henry the VIII. of England Rutger, count of Cleves, lived at the beginning of the 11th century Adolphus, count of Mark, was made duke of Cleves by emperor Sigismund, *1417* John William, duke of Cleves, Berg, Juliers, etc., died without issue, 25 Mch 1609, which led to a war of succession Cleves was assigned to the elector of Brandenburg in 1666, seized by the French in 1757, restored at peace in 1763, and now belongs to Prussia

Clifton suspension bridge, over the Avon BRIDGES

climacteric, the term applied to any year of life (a multiple of 7 or 9), when great changes in the health and constitution are supposed to occur Cotgrave says, "Every 7th or 9th or 63d year of a man's life all very dangerous, but the last most" The grand climacteric is 63 Hippocrates is said to have referred to these periods, 383 B C

climate. METEOROLOGY, TEMPERATURE

Clinton and Montgomery, forts (about 6 miles below West Point, on the Hudson), Surrender of Sir Henry Clinton, wishing to make a diversion in favor of gen Burgoyne, who was hard pressed by gen Gates, advanced up the Hudson on 4 Oct 1777, with about 3000 men, and deceiving gen Putnam as to his purpose, took these forts, feebly garrisoned, before they could be reinforced They were commanded by gens James and George Clinton, who escaped in the darkness with about 200 men American loss, 300, British, 140

Clio, the muse of history. The letters C L I O, in consecutive order, were signed to the best papers of Addison, in the London *Spectator*, in 1713 —*Cibber*

Cloaca Maxima, one of the ancient sewers of Rome, still in existence, said by Livy to have been constructed by Tarquinius Priscus (assassinated, 578 B C.) and Tarquinius Superbus It was originally 12 ft 4 in high, and 10 ft. 8 in wide, but one third is now choked with mud It was intended as a sewer and drain for the marsh of the Velabrum, and the land springs of the Forum It extends from near the church of S. Giorgio, where it is fed by 7 cloacæ, to the Tiber, near the Ponte Rotto

clock. The clepsydra, or water-clock, was introduced at Rome about 158 B.C. by Scipio Nasica Toothed wheels were placed in it by Ctesibius, about 140 B.C The only clock then known was sent by pope Paul I to Pepin, king of France, 760 A.D. Pacificus, archdeacon of Genoa, invented one in the 9th century. Originally the wheels were 3 ft. in diameter. The earliest complete clock of which there is certain record was made by a Saracen mechanic in the 13th century.

Escapement ascribed to Gerbert 1000
A clock placed in the old palace yard, London, that remained until the 16th century 1288

A great clock put up at Canterbury cathedral, cost 30*l* 1292
One made by Richard, abbot of St Alban's about 1326
John Visconti sets up a clock at Genoa 1353
One put up at Bologna 1356
A striking clock in Westminster 1368
A perfect one made at Paris by Vick 1370
A clock placed on the Strasburg cathedral 1370, greatly improved by Conradus Dasypodus (STRASBURG) 1571
First portable one made 1530
First accurate clock in England at Hampton Court (maker's initials, N O) 1540

"　like a German clock,
Still a repairing, ever out of frame,
And never going aright"
—*Shakespeare*, "Love's Labor's Lost," 1598

Pendulum in clocks ascribed to the younger Galileo, 1639, and Richard Harris (who erected a clock at St. Paul's, Covent Garden, London) 1641
Christian Huyghens said he made his pendulum clock previous to 1658
Fromantil, a Dutchman, improved the pendulum about 1669
Repeating clocks and watches invented by Barlow about 1676
Spiral pendulum spring invented by Robert Hooke, about 1658, cylinder and escapement, by Thomas Tompion 1695
Dead beat and horizontal escapements, by Graham, about 1700, compensating pendulum 1715
A spiral balance spring suggested, and the duplex escapement invented, by Dr Hooke, pivot holes jewelled by Facio, detached escapement invented by Mudge and improved by Berthould, Arnold, Earnshaw, and others in the 18th century
HARRISON'S TIME PIECE constructed 1735
First illuminated church clock St Bride's, London 2 Dec 1826
Horological institute established 1858
Great Westminster clock set up 30 May, 1859
Barraud and Lund's electric synchronizing clocks, city of London circuit of 108 clocks Nov 1878
Victor Popp of Vienna applies compressed air as a motive power to clocks, announced Mch 1881
One of the earliest clock makers in the U S. was William Tenny, who made brass clocks at "Nine Partners," Dutchess county, N Y, *about 1790, Eli Terry began to make wooden clocks* about the same time, and in 1802 to make them by machinery with water power, at Plymouth, Conn., and in 1816, shelf and mantel clocks, selling for $2 and upwards. ELECTRICITY, TIME, WATCHES

Clogher, Ireland St Macartin, a disciple of St Patrick, fixed a bishopric at Clogher, where he built an abbey "in the street before the royal seat of the kings of Ergal" He died in 506. Clogher is named from a golden stone, from which, in times of paganism, the devil gave juggling answers, like the oracles of *Apollo Pythius —Sir James Ware* In 1041, the cathedral was rebuilt, and dedicated to its founder Clogher merged, on the death of its last prelate, Dr Tottenham, into the archiepiscopal see of Armagh, by the act of 1833

Clonfert, Ireland St Brendan founded an abbey at Clonfert in 558, his life is extant in jingling monkish metre in the Cottonian library at Westminster In his time the cathedral, famous in ancient days for its seven altars, was erected, and Colgan makes St Brendan its founder and first bishop, but it is said in the "Ulster Annals," under the year 571, "Mæns, bishop of Clonfert Brenain, went to rest" Clonfert is Irish for a "wonderful den," or retirement. In 1839 the see merged in that of Killaloe

Clontarf, near Dublin, site of a battle, Good Friday, 23 Apr 1014, between Danes and Irish, headed by Bryan Boroimhe, monarch of Ireland, who though victorious, was mortally wounded, his son Murchard also fell, with many nobles, 13,000 Danes are said to have perished.

Closterseven, Hanover, Convention of, 8 Sept 1757, between the duke of Cumberland, 3d son of George II, hardly pressed, and the duke of Richelieu, commanding the French, by it 38,000 Hanoverians surrendered, and were dispersed The treaty was disavowed by the king, the duke resigned his commands, and the convention was soon broken.

clôture, in 6th of new rules of British Parliament put forth, 9 Feb 1881, power given the speaker of the House of Commons to close debate, under rules adopted, Nov 1882 First used in Parliament, 24 Feb 1884 PARLIAMENT.

Cloud, St., a palace near Paris, named from prince Clodoald, or Cloud, who became a monk there in 533, after the murder of his brothers, and died in 560. In the present palace, built in the 16th century, Henry II was assassinated by Clement, 2 Aug 1589 Long the property of the dukes of Orleans, it was bought by Marie Antoinette, 1785 It was a favorite residence of the empress Josephine, of Charles X and his family, and of Napoleon III It was burned, 13 Oct 1870, having been fired upon by the French

cloud-bursts. STORMS.

clouds consist of minute particles of water, often frozen, floating in the air In 1803, Mr Luke Howard published a classification of clouds, generally adopted, in 3 primary forms—cirrus, cumulus, and stratus, 3 compounds of these forms, and the nimbus, or black rain-clouds (cumulo-cirro-stratus) A new edition of his "Essay on the Clouds" appeared 1865

Cloveshoo, now **Cliff,** Kent, Engl Here was held a council of nobility and clergy on government and discipline of the church, Sept 747; and others, 800, 803, 822, 824

Cloyne, S Ireland, a bishopric, founded in the 6th century by St Colman in 1431 united to Cork, and so continued for 200 years It was united with Cork and Ross, 1834 BISHOPS

club-foot, a deformity due to the shortened muscles. Lorenz, in 1784, cut the *tendo Achillis* to relieve it, but the cure was not effectual till 1831, when Strohmeyer, of Erlangen, cured Dr Little by dividing the tendons of the contracted muscles with a very thin knife

clubs, originally a few persons of kindred tastes and pursuits, meeting at stated times for social intercourse. The club at the Mermaid tavern, London, late in the 16th century, consisted of Raleigh, Shakespeare, and others Ben Jonson set up a club at the Devil tavern Addison, Steele, and others, frequently met at Button's coffee-house, as described in the *Spectator* London clubs, often of from 300 to 1500 members, have many luxuriously furnished edifices in or near Pall Mall The members obtain choice viands and wines at moderate charges, and many clubs possess excellent libraries, particularly the ATHENÆUM. They may be political, literary, scientific, fine-arts, business or commercial, athletic, etc, and clubs of these classes are established in all of the principal cities of the United States and Europe Political clubs often exert great influence in public affairs COBDEN, JACOBINS, etc The oldest club in the U S is the Wistar club, Philadelphia, 1833, and the next, the Union club of New York city, 1836 See the Record of the different cities of the U S

clubs, French The first arose about 1782 They were mainly political, and concerned in the revolution The *Club Breton* became the celebrated *Club des Jacobins*, and the *Club des Cordeliers* comprised Danton and Camille Desmoulins From these two came the Mountain party, which overthrew the Girondists in 1793, and fell in 1794. The clubs disappeared with the Directory in 1799 Many were revived in 1848, but with less importance, and were suppressed by decrees, 22 June, 1849, and 6 June, 1850.—*Bouillet*

Clugny or **Cluny,** abbey of, in France, formerly magnificent, founded by Benedictines, under abbot Bern, about 910, sustained afterwards by William, duke of Berry and Aquitaine Its library, one of the richest in France, was greatly injured when the abbey was sacked by the Huguenots, 1562, and almost destroyed by the revolutionists in 1793 English foundations for Cluniac monks were instituted soon after

Clyde and Forth wall was built by Agricola, 84. HADRIAN'S WALL. The Forth and Clyde canal was commenced by Mr Smeaton, 10 July, 1768, and was opened 28 July, 1790 It connects the seas on the east and west of Scotland

Cnidus (*ni'dus*), in Caria, Asia Minor Near here Conon the Athenian defeated the Lacedæmonian fleet under Peisander, 394 B C

coach (from Sp. *coche*) Beckmann states that Charles of Anjou's queen entered Naples in a *caretta* (about 1282). Under Francis I there were but 2 in Paris one the queen's, the other that of Diana, natural daughter of Henry II There were but 3 in Paris in 1550, and Henry IV had one without straps or springs. John de Laval de Bois-Dauphin set up a coach to carry his enormous bulk The first coach in England was about 1553 Others were introduced by Fitz-Alan, earl of Arundel, in 1580—*Stow* A law in England forbade riding in coaches as effeminate, 43 Eliz 1601.—*Carte.* Repealed 1625. The coach of the duke of Buckingham had 6 horses, that of the earl of Northumberland 8, 1619. The English coach-tax commenced in 1747 Of recent years there has been a revival especially in England of the fashion of journeying by coach, as it is not a necessity, and more expensive than by rail, it is not indulged in except for pleasure. G. Thrupp's "History of Coaches," pub 1877. CARRIAGES, CHARIOTS, STAGE-COACHES, etc

coal. There are 4 kinds of the fossil fuel called "cole" in old English, now known as coal anthracite, bituminous, cannel or gas-coal, and lignite or brown coal The composition of wood is about 49 1 carbon, 6.3 hydrogen, 44 6 oxygen, while the best anthracite coal contains more than .90 of carbon, with about 03 of hydrogen and 025 of oxygen "It is plausibly contended that coal, although not mentioned by the Romans in notices of Britain, was used by the ancient Britons."—*Brandt.* Henry III is said to have granted a license to dig coals near Newcastle-upon-Tyne in 1234, some say earlier, others in 1239. Burning sea-coal was prohibited in and near London, as "prejudicial to human health;" and even smiths were obliged to burn wood, 1273.—*Stow* In 1306 the gentry petitioned against coal. Coal was first made an article of trade from Newcastle to London, 4 Rich II 1381—*Rymer's Fœdera* Notwithstanding many previous complaints against coal as a public nuisance, it was generally burned in London in 1400; but was not in common use in England until Charles I, 1625 Coal was brought to Dublin from Newry in 1742 Anzin coal-mines, near Valenciennes, N France, first worked 24 June, 1734, output in 1872, 2,200,000 tons. Anthracite coal, mined chiefly in Pennsylvania, was first used as fuel by two Connecticut blacksmiths, named Gore, in 1768-69, first used as domestic fuel by judge Jesse Fell, of Wilkesbarre, Pa, in 1808 PENNSYLVANIA, 1791, 1812, '20, '21, '22, '39 Except the diamond, anthracite coal is the purest natural carbon The coal-fields of Great Britain are estimated at 5400 sq miles, of Durham and Northumberland, 723 sq. miles—*Bakewell.*

MINED IN GREAT BRITAIN AND IRELAND.

1861	83,635,214 tons	
1870	110,431,192 "	Value, 27,607,798*l.*
1879	133,808,000 "	" 46,832,000*l.*
1890.	181,614,288 "	" 74,953,997*l.*

Women were prohibited from working in English collieries . 1842

A commission (duke of Argyll, sir R I Murchison, Dr John Percy, prof Ramsay, and others) appointed to investigate the probable quantity of coal in the United Kingdom, etc, 28 June, 1866, reported, 27 July, 1871

Attainable quantity in known coal fields	90,207,000,000 tons.
Probable available coal in other places	56,273,000,000 "
Total	146,480,000,000 "

A commission to inquire into causes and remedies for coal-mine explosions appointed (Messrs. W. Warington Smyth, Tyndall, F A Abel, and others) Feb. 1879

Accidents.—About 1000 lives are lost annually by accidents in mines (1856–76) 1877, 1208, 1878, 1413, 1879, 973, 1880, 1318, 1885, 1150, 1890, 1206, 1891, 1030

IN THE UNITED STATES

Anthracite is found mostly in Pennsylvania, while the bituminous is widely distributed. Cannel is found in Pennsylvania, Virginia, Kentucky, Ohio, Indiana, Illinois, and Missouri Lignite in Vermont and west. No workable coal is found in Maine, New Hampshire, New York, New Jersey, Delaware, South Carolina, Florida, Mississippi, Louisiana, Minnesota The anthracite coal fields of Pennsylvania are estimated at 382 sq miles, and this is practically all there is in the U S The bituminous coal-fields are estimated at 203,336 sq miles. The anthracite output in Pennsylvania from 1820 to 1880 was 409,597,748 tons. The amount of coal mined was

1869	Anthracite, Pa.	13,866,180 tons
	Bituminous, Pa. and other states	17,211,814 "
	Total	31,077,994 "
1876	Anthracite, Pa.	21,436,667 "
	Bituminous, Pa and other states	27,569,081 "
	Total	49,005,748 "
1881.	Anthracite, Pa	31,500,000 "
	Bituminous, Pa.	20,000,000 "
	" other states	28,405,000 "
	Total	79,905,000 "
1889	Anthracite, Pa.	45,544,970 "
	Bituminous, Pa.	36,174,089 "
	" other states	59,011,229 "
	Total	140,730,288 "
1890	Anthracite, Pa	46,468,641 "
	Bituminous, Pa	42,302,173 "
	" other states	69,017,842 "
	Total	157,788,656 "

coalitions against France mostly promoted by British subsidies of other powers. TREATIES

Austria, Prussia, and Great Britain	1793
Great Britain, Germany, Russia, Naples, Portugal, and Turkey, signed	22 June, 1799
Great Britain, Russia, Austria, and Naples	5 Aug. 1805
Great Britain, Russia, Prussia, and Saxony	6 Oct. 1806

Great Britain and Austria 6 Apr 1809
Russia and Prussia, treaty ratified at Kalisch 17 Mch 1813

coast survey of the United States. A complete survey upon a uniform system, of the whole coast was first proposed by the late prof Patterson in 1806 Its objects were the astronomical determination of prominent points, triangulation to connect those points, and a hydrographic survey based upon this triangulation Mr Gallatin, secretary of the treasury, encouraged the project, and consulted learned men as to the best methods He adopted the plans of Mr F R Hassler, first superintendent of the coast survey The work was begun in 1817, on a small scale, only since 1832 has it been actively pressed While the government neglected it, commerce was chiefly indebted to the hydrographers Messrs Blunt of New York (father and son), for charts, etc In 1844, the first year of prof A D Bache's superintendence, 9 states on the Atlantic seaboard were reached by the coast survey, in 1845, 13 states, in 1846, 15, and in 1847, 18 states It has since been extended to the Pacific coast, to Alaska, and through the great lakes, under prof Benjamin Peirce He was succeeded by capt Carlile P Patterson, who carried the work into the interior, and it is now extending across the continent The present superintendent, T. C. Mendenhall, succeeded prof J E Hilgard, long the general manager, 1889 Capt Patterson died in 1882, and Hilgard in 1891 The whole work is under the control of the treasury department, while a superintendent directs all the details, governs the movements of parties, and controls the expenditures

cobalt, a rare mineral, early found among veins of ores, or in fissures of stone, in Cornwall mines, where workmen call it mundic —*Hill.* It was classed as a metal by Brandt in 1733.

Cobden club, instituted to spread and apply Cobden's principles, held first dinner, London, W E Gladstone in the chair, 21 July, 1866 The statue of Richard Cobden, at Camden Town, was inaugurated, 27 June, 1868 12 out of 14 cabinet ministers were members, July, 1880 It has for honorary members several American economists and statesmen

coca, a powerful medicinal agent found in the *Erythoxylon coca*, a South American plant, the leaves of which are chewed by the people of South America A little of the coca taken internally is said to enable one to endure hard labor without food for 6 or 7 days and nights The poet Cowley wrote in 1700

> "Our *Varicocha* first this *coca* sent,
> Endowed with leaves of wondrous nourishment,
> Whose juice succ'd in, and to the stomach tak'n,
> Long hunger and long labor can sustain"

Dr Mantegazza's prize essay in German on coca was published at Vienna in 1849

cocaine (*ko-ka-in*), a powerful anæsthetic obtained from the coca plant, first used in ophthalmic and other surgical operations, 1884.

Cocceians (*cox-ē'-ans*), a small sect founded by John Cocceius (d. 1665), of Bremen, in the 17th century They look for a visible reign of Christ on earth, after conversion of the Jews and all other people to Christian faith

Cocherel, near Evreux, N W France. Here Bertrand du Guesclin defeated the king of Navarre, and took prisoner the captal de Buch, 16 May, 1364.

Cochin, India, held by the Portuguese, 1503, by the Dutch, 1663, by Hyder Ali, 1776, taken by the British, 1796, ceded to them, 1814. For Cochin China, ANNAM

cochineal insect (*Coccus cacti*), deriving its scarlet color from feeding on a certain kind of cactus, became known to the Spaniards soon after the conquest of Mexico, in 1518. Cochineal was brought to Europe about 1523, but was not known in Italy in 1548, although the art of dyeing then flourished there In 1858, it was cultivated successfully in Teneriffe, the vines in Europe having failed through disease

Cock-lane ghost. In 1760-62, great excitement was produced in London by unaccountable noises in a house occupied by William Parsons, No 33 Cock lane. A luminous figure, resembling a deceased lady who formerly resided in the house, was said to have been seen The duke of York, Mr Walpole, Dr Samuel Johnson, and many others visited the house and investigated Imposition was detected, and the parents of the medium (a girl of about 12) were condemned to the pillory and imprisonment, 10 July, 1762

cocoa (*kō-kō*) or **cacao** (*ka-kā-ō*), the kernel or seed of *Theobroma cacao* (Linn), was brought to England soon after the discovery of Mexico, where it is an article of diet From cocoa is produced chocolate

cocoa-nut palm (*Cocos nucifera*, Linn) supplies the natives of Central America with almost all they need, as bread, water, liquor, vinegar, milk, oil, honey, sugar, needles, clothes, thread, cups, spoons, basins baskets, paper, masts for ships, sails, cordage, covering for houses, etc —*Ray* In Sept 1829, Mr Soames patented a mode of extracting stearine and elaine from cocoa-nut oil

cod (*Morrhua vulgaris*), the most common species of anaranthine fishes, is caught in immense numbers in many parts of the northern temperate zone, most largely on the banks of Newfoundland, and about the outer Hebrides The Dutch, English, and French engaged in this fishery before 1350

codes. LAWS Alfrenus Varus, the civilian, first collected the Roman laws about 66 B.C , and Servius Sulpicius, the civilian codified them about 53 B.C The Gregorian and Hermogenian codes were published 290 A D , the Theodosian code commenced by order of Theodosius II in 429, and published for the eastern empire in 438 In 447 he transmitted to Valentinian his new constitutions, promulgated as the law of the west in 448 The code of the emperor Justinian in 529 —a digest from it made in 533, BASILICA Alfred's code, a selection from existing laws, is the foundation of the common-law of England, 887 The *Code Napoleon*, the civil code of France, was promulgated from 1803 to 1810 The emperor considered it his most enduring monument It was prepared under his supervision by eminent jurists, from 400 earlier systems, and has been adopted by other countries

A conference of jurists and publicists to consider an international code at Brussels July, Aug 1874

codex. BIBLE, MANUSCRIPT

cod-liver oil, an oil obtained mostly from the liver of the cod, and recommended as a remedy for chronic rheumatism by Dr Percival in 1782 and for diseases of the lungs about 1833 De Jongh's treatise on cod-liver oil was published in Latin, 1844, in English, 1849 Great improvement made in its preparation since 1853, and very important discoveries as to its constituents, 1891.

Cœur de Lion, or the Lion-hearted, a surname of Richard I of England, on account of his courage, about 1192, and of Louis VIII of France, distinguished in crusades, and in wars against England, about 1223

coffee, seeds of the tree *Coffea arabica* The tree was conveyed from Mocha, in Arabia, to Holland about 1616, and to the West Indies in 1726 First cultivated at Surinam by the Dutch, 1718. The culture was encouraged in the plantations about 1732, and British and French colonies now grow coffee abundantly. Its use as a beverage is traced to the Persians Not known to the Greeks or Romans It came into great repute in Arabia Felix, about 1454, and passed into Egypt and Syria, and thence (in 1511) to Constantinople, where a coffee-house was opened, 1551. M Thevenot, the traveller, first brought it to France, 1662 —*Chambers.* CAFFEINE.

Coffee brought to England by Nathaniel Canopus, a Cretan who made it his common beverage at Baliol college, Oxford (*Anderson*) . . . 1641
First coffee house in England kept by a Jew, named Jacobs, in Oxford 1650
Mr Edwards, a Turkey merchant, brought home with him Pasquet a Greek servant, who opened the first coffee house in London George yard, Lombard st 1652
[Pasquet afterwards went to Holland, and opened the first house in that country —*Anderson*]
Rainbow coffee house, Temple Bar, represented as a nuisance 1657
Coffee houses suppressed by proclamation, 1675, the order revoked on petition of traders . . 1676
Licenses to sell coffee abolished . 1869
Duty on coffee reduced in England to 1½*d.* the pound from 2 May, 1872
U S. duty removed from coffee . 6 June, "

Importations of coffee into U. S. for 1880 valued at $60,360,769; for 1891, 519,528,432 lbs., value, $96,123,777; 1892, 640,210,788 lbs., value, $128,041,930. Total production in the world, 1889, 1,249,000,000 lbs., of which Brazil produced, 812,000,000 lbs.; other parts of America, 253,000,000 lbs.; East Indies and Africa, 184,000,000 lbs.

coffins. Athenian heroes were buried in coffins of cedar, owing to its aromatic and incorruptible qualities.—*Thucydides.* Coffins of marble and stone were used by the Romans. Alexander is said to have been buried in one of gold; and glass coffins have been found in England.—*Gough.* The earliest record of wooden coffins in England is that of king Arthur, an entire trunk of oak hollowed, 542.—*Asser.* Patent coffins were invented in 1796; air-tight metallic coffins advertised at Birmingham in 1861.

cohort, a division of the Roman army consisting of about 420 men, with 300 cavalry, divided into centuries. It was the 6th part of a legion. LEGION.

coif. The coif was introduced before 1259, and used to hide the tonsure of renegade clergymen, who acted as advocates in the secular courts, notwithstanding their prohibition by canon.—*Blackstone.* The coif was at first a thin linen cover gathered in the form of a skull or helmet, the material afterwards changed for white silk, and the form eventually becoming a black patch at the top of the forensic wig, now the distinguishing mark in England of the sergeant-at-law.—*Foss's* "Lives of the Judges."

Coimbra was made capital of Portugal by Alfonso, the first king, 1139. The only Portuguese university was transferred from Lisbon to Coimbra in 1308; finally settled in 1527. In a convent here, Alfonso IV. had Iñez de Castro, once mistress and afterwards wife of his son Pedro, murdered in 135[illegible].

coin and **coinage.** Homer speaks of brass money, 1184 B.C., but says nothing of coined money. Herodotus tells us that the Lydians first coined gold, and the "Parian Chronicle" (ARUNDELIAN MARBLES) records that Pheidon of Argos first coined silver in Ægina about 862 B.C. The most ancient known coins bearing the name of a prince are those of Alexander I. of Macedon, 500 to about 460 B.C. Very little if any gold is supposed to have been coined in Athens or Greece proper until after Alexander the Great, 356–23 B.C. The Romans coined copper or bronze under Servius Tullius, 578–34 B.C. Silver first coined by them, 269 B.C., and gold about 206 B.C.—*Dye's* "Coin Encyclopædia." The earliest Roman coinage was that of the republic. The imperial coinage of Rome began with Augustus, 16 B.C., and lasted to the fall of the western empire, 476 A.D. The material of the earliest coins of Lydia was a compound of gold and silver. When Cæsar landed in Britain, 55 B.C., coins of brass and iron were found in use among the natives. There is no absolute proof that the Jews coined money before the Maccabees, 139 B.C. The earliest coins known among the Anglo-Saxons were the *sceattæ* of silver, and the *stycas* of brass or copper—the latter equal to about one half-farthing. The coins of Norway begin with the pennies of Harold Haardrada, slain at Stamford Bridge, 1066, and those of Denmark with Canute. Russian coinage began in the 15th century. COPPER, GOLD, SILVER, and coins under their names. An international conference upon a universal system of coinage met in Paris, 1867, and a royal commission was appointed in London, Feb. 1868. At present the great monetary systems of (1) France and her allies, (2) England and the larger part of her colonies, and (3) the United States are firmly established in their several countries; no one of them is likely to become universal. The arguments in favor of the franc are its perfect decimal divisions, and the wide area of the Latin union; those in favor of the British unit of value, the pound, are its greater value, and the immense extent of the English colonies and trade; and the arguments in favor of the dollar are its convenient size, and the prospective growth of the U. S. The gold and silver coinage of France, Germany, Spain, Italy, Belgium, and the U. S., contains nine tenths of pure metal, that of Great Britain and Russia containing eleven twelfths. A mint was established at Camulodunum (Colchester) by Cunobelinus (the Cymbeline of Shakespeare), about the time of Augustus Cæsar. The coins of this king far surpass those of other early British kings, both in workmanship and artistic design.—"Dict. of National Biog." (English).

COINAGE IN ENGLAND.

English coins made sterling (PENNY, STERLING)............... 1216
First English gold coin on certain record struck, reign of Henry III.. 1275
Edward III. introduced a regular gold currency, first, of florins (name of the gold coin of Florence), 1337; second, of gold six-shilling pieces, and nobles of six shillings eightpence; also half and quarter nobles (NOBLES)........................ 1344
Edward IV. coined angels with the figure of St. Michael and the dragon, the original of St. George and the dragon....... 1465
Pound sovereign first minted by Henry VII., 1489; shillings..1503–4
Crowns and half-crowns coined, Edward VI................. 1553
Queen Elizabeth causes the base coin to be recalled and genuine issued.. 1560
[In the reign of Elizabeth the coins of England attained their highest number, including 20 distinct denominations.]
Modern milling introduced................................ 1631
Guineas (value 20*s.*), 2-guinea, and 5-guinea pieces coined...1663–64
[The sovereign, first called the *broad* under James I., was valued at 21 silver shillings under Charles II., and as the gold then came mostly from Guinea, this coin was called GUINEA.]
Half-pence and farthings first coined...................... 1665
Pennies, half-pennies, and farthings (*copper*) coined.......... 1672
Quarter-guinea coined, George I........................... 1716
Twopenny copper pieces coined............................. 1797
Gold 7-shilling pieces authorized .... "
George III. reintroduces the sovereign, new coinage, St. George and dragon.. 1817
[The guinea was abandoned save as money of account.]
Fourpenny pieces (GROAT) coined...........................1836–56
Half-farthings first coined, 1843; silver florin (two shillings).. 1849
Bronze coinage first issued, 1860; threepenny pieces first coined.. 1861
St. George and the dragon sovereigns reissued.........14 Jan. 1871
Sale of Whittall's great collection of Greek and other coins, 1668 lots, realized about $20,000.......................July, 1884

COINAGE IN ENGLAND FROM 1196 TO 1890 INCLUSIVE.

Reign.	Silver.	Gold.	Total.
Henry III..................	£3,898	....	£3,898
Edward I..................	38,603	....	38,603
Edward II..................	46,756	....	46,756
Edward III..................	85,701	£11,340	97,041
Richard II..................	2,228	3,988	6,216
Henry IV..................	314	396	710
Henry V..................	6,924	19,746	26,670
Henry VI..................	404,677	38,317	442,994
Edward IV..................	89,704	230,760	320,464
Henry VII..................	138,280	189,232	327,512
Henry VIII..................	355,403	292,916	648,319
Elizabeth..................	6,359,583	795,138	7,154,721
James I..................	1,641,005	3,666,390	5,307,395
Charles I..................	8,776,544	3,319,677	12,096,221
Cromwell..................	1,000,000	154,512	1,154,512
Charles II..................	3,722,180	4,177,254	7,899,434
James II..................	518,316	2,113,639	2,631,955
William and Mary..........	7,093,074	3,418,889	10,511,963
Anne..................	207,095	2,484,531	2,691,626
George I..................	233,045	8,492,876	8,725,921
George II..................	304,360	11,662,216	11,966,576
George III..................	6,827,818	75,447,489	82,275,307
George IV..................	2,216,163	36,147,701	38,363,864
William IV..................	1,111,298	11,435,334	12,546,632
Victoria up to 1890.........	32,791,443	323,807,622	356,599,065
		Total.......	£561,884,375

Equal to $2,729,758,062.

COIN AND COINAGE IN THE UNITED STATES.

Earliest coinage for America (for the Virginia company), about 1612–15
[The coin was used in the Bermudas, and is known as the "Hogge money," a hog being shown on it. It was issued in shillings and sixpences. But 2 of the shillings are known to exist, and but 1 sixpence.]
General court of Massachusetts passes an act establishing at Boston the first mint in the U. S, 27 May, 1652, John Hull, mint-master. Denominations, shilling, sixpence, and threepence. This is known as the "Pine-tree money." Coining discontinued on the death of the mint-master..........1 Oct. 1683
Maryland has shillings, sixpences, and pennies coined in England for her use, by lord Baltimore...................May, 1661
William Wood, of Wolverhampton, Engl., obtains a monopoly for coining "tokens" for currency in America............ 1722
[These tokens were made of a mixed metal resembling brass. (It was also coined for Ireland.) This is known as the "Rosa Americana" coinage or "Wood's money," and obtained quite a circulation (WOOD'S HALF-PENCE).]
Connecticut had in circulation a private or unauthorized coinage, issued by John Higley of Granby, known as the "Granby" or Higley token................................ 1737
Copper coin, one cent, issued by Vermont.................. 1785
Copper coined in New Jersey by act of legislature......1 June, 1786
A law of Massachusetts establishes a mint to coin gold, silver, and copper.....................................16 Oct. "
[No gold or silver ever coined in this mint.]
Coinage discontinued ....21 Jan. 1789
Following coins were decided upon by Congress: Gold: eagle, half-eagle, and quarter-eagle. Silver: dollar, half-dollar,

quarter-dollar, dime, and half-dime. Copper: cent and half-cent (TABLE OF U. S. COINAGE) 1786
First U. S. mint established ..... 2 Apr. 1792
First U. S. coinage 1793
No gold coined in the years ..... 1816 and 1817
No minor coinage in the years ..... 1815 and 1823
First steam-power press in the U. S. mint 1836
[Previous to this the mill and screw were used.]
Rare coins of the U. S. are the double eagles of the issue of ... 1849
[But one is known: in the cabinet of the U. S. mint; this is the rarest U. S. coin.]
Half-eagles of the issue of 1815
[But 7 of this date are known.]
Silver dollars of 1794
Silver dollars of 1804
[There were issued from the mint in 1804, 19,570 silver dollars, and it has been a "standing mystery" why the dollar of this issue is so scarce (it being styled the king of rare American coin). It has been said that the mintage of 1805 included this mintage, or a part of it, although the mintage of 1805 shows an issue of but $321. Others assert that a vessel bound for China with almost the entire mintage was lost at sea.]
Half-dollars of 1796-97
Quarter-dollars of 1827
Dimes of 1804
Half-dimes of 1802

The following statistics of coinage are estimates from the report of the director of the mint to the secretary of the treasury from 1793-1890:

Greatest amount of gold coined in one year, $96,850,890.00.... 1881
" " silver " " " 39,202,908.20.... 1890
" " minor coin coined in one year ..... 1,819,910.00.... 1867
Greatest amount of gold, silver, and minor coin coined in one year ..... 125,219,205.50.... 1881
Least amount of gold coined in one year.... 3,175.00.... 1815
" " silver " " " .... 14,550.45.... 1797
" " minor coin (cents and half-cents only) coined in one year ..... 2,495.95.... 1811
Least amount of gold, silver, and minor coin coined in one year ..... 20,483.00.... 1815

Total coinage of the U. S. from 1793 to 1890 inclusive:

Gold	$1,531,999,915
Silver	623,746,536
Minor coin	22,634,500
Total	$2,178,380,951

COINS OF THE UNITED STATES, AND THE YEARS OF ISSUE.

Name.	Years of Issue.	Kind of Metal.	Present Weight.	Remarks.
Double eagle	1850 et seq.	gold	516 grs.	
Eagle	1795-1804 1838 et seq.	"	258 "	Act of Congress, 28 June, 1834.
Half-eagle	1795-1815 1818 et seq.	"	129 "	" " " "
Three dollars	1854-90	"	77.4 "	" " 21 Feb. 1853. Coinage discontinued, 1890.
Quarter-eagle	1796-99 1802-08 1821 — 1824-27 1829 et seq.	"	64.5 "	" " 28 June, 1834.
Dollar	1849-90	"	25.8 "	" " 3 Mch. 1849. Coinage discontinued, 1890
Trade dollar	1874-78	silver	420 "	Coinage discontinued, 1878.
Dollar	1793-1805 1836 — 1839-57 1859-73 1878 et seq.	"	412.5 "	Act of Congress, Jan. 1837.
Half-dollar	1793-96 1801-14 1816 et seq.	"	192.9 "	Act of Congress, 1873.
Quarter-dollar	1796, 1797 1804-07 1815, 1816 1818-23 1825 — 1827, 1828 1831 et seq.	"	96.45 "	Act of Congress, 1873.
Twenty cents	1875-78	"	77.16 "	Coinage discontinued, 1878.
Dimes	1796-98 1800-1805 1807 — 1809-11 1814 — 1820-23 1825 — 1827 et seq.	"	38.58 "	
Half-dimes	1793-97 1800-1803 1805 — 1829-73	"	19.29 "	Coinage discontinued, 1873.
Three cents	1851-56 1858-73	"	11.52 "	Coinage discontinued, 1873.
Five cents	1866 et seq.	copper and nickel	77.16 "	Act of Congress, 16 Mch. 1866.
Three cents	1865-76 1878-90	"	30 "	" " 3 Mch. 1865. Coinage discontinued, 1890.
Two cents	1864-72	bronze	96 "	Coinage discontinued, 1872.
One cent	1793-1814 1816-22 1824-53	copper	168 "	As nickel from 1857 to 1864, 72 grs.; both discontinued, 1864.
One cent	1864 et seq.	bronze	48 "	Act of Congress, 22 Apr. 1864.
Half-cent	1793-97 1799, 1800 1802-11 1825, 1826 1828, 1829 1831 — 1833-36 1849-51 1853-57	copper	84 "	Coinage discontinued, 1857.

COINAGE OF CONFEDERATE STATES.

When Louisiana seceded and seized the U. S. mint at New Orleans, there were thousands of dollars' worth of gold and silver bullion in store. The state issued jointly with the confederate government a gold coinage of $254,820 in double eagles, and a silver coinage of $1,101,316.50 in half-dollars, using the U. S. dies of 1861, the dies of 1860 having been destroyed. The bullion, when nearly exhausted, was transferred to the confederate government, May, 1861, and all the U. S. dies were destroyed, the confederate government ordering a new die for its use. When completed it was of such high relief as to be useless in the press. As there was but little if any bullion to coin, no attempt was made to engrave another. Four pieces, however, half-dollars, were struck, which formed the entire coinage of the Confederate States. The coin shows—*obverse:* A goddess of liberty within an arc of 13 stars, Exergue, 1861. *Reverse:* An American shield beneath a liberty-cap, the upper part of the shield containing 7 stars, the whole surrounded by a wreath: to the left, cotton in bloom; to the right, sugar-cane. *Legend:* Confederate States of America. Exergue, Half Dol. Borders, milled; edge, serrated.

VALUE OF FOREIGN COINS IN UNITED STATES MONEY.

Country.		Monetary Unit.	Value in U. S. Money.	Remarks.
Argentine Republic	100 centesimos =	1 peso	$0.965	
Austria	100 kreutzers =	1 florin	0.48	Present system introduced in 1870.
Belgium	100 centimes =	1 franc	0.193	System the same as France.
Bolivia	100 centavos =	1 peso	0.96	
Brazil	1000 reis =	1 milrei	0.55	
Canada	100 cents =	1 dollar	1.00	
Chili	100 centavos =	1 peso	0.91	Most of the South American states issue standard coin corresponding to the peso of Chili, which is identical with the 5-franc piece of France.
China	1000 cash =	tael	1.61	Has no national coin.
Cuba	......	peso	0.93	
Denmark	100 ore =	1 crown	0.27	
Egypt	100 piastres =	1 pound	4.94	
France	100 centimes =	1 franc	0.193	
German Empire	100 pfennig =	1 mark	0.24	The substitution of the *mark* for the older *thaler* came into force 1 Jan. 1875.
Great Britain	20 shillings =	1 pound	4.86	
Greece	100 leptas =	1 drachma	0.193	Monetary system same as France.
Guatemala	......	peso	0.70	
Hayti	......	gourde	0.965	
Honduras	......	peso	0.70	
India	16 annas =	1 rupee	0.40	
Italy	100 centesimi =	1 lira	0.193	Monetary system same as France.
Japan	100 sen =	1 yen	1.00	Monetary system recast in 1871.
Liberia	100 cents =	1 dollar	1.00	
Mexico	100 " =	1 dollar	0.98	
Netherlands	100 " =	1 florin	0.40	
Nicaragua	......	peso	0.70	
Norway	100 ore =	1 crown	0.27	Monetary system same as Denmark.
Peru	100 centesimos =	1 sol	0.96	
Portugal	1000 reis =	1 milrei	1.08	
Russia	100 copecks =	1 ruble	0.77	
Spain	100 centesimos =	1 peseta	0.193	Monetary system same as France.
Sweden	100 ore =	1 crown	0.27	" " " Denmark.
Switzerland	100 centimes =	1 franc	0.193	" " " France.
U. S. of Colombia	100 centavos =	1 peso	0.96	
Turkey	100 piastres =	1 lira	4.40	

In the table above, the value assigned to the monetary unit of each nation is that which its gold coinage has in the gold coin of the United States, by comparison of the amounts of pure gold contained in each. The actual value of the silver coins of all nations, such as Italy, Mexico, and Russia, which do not redeem these coins at their nominal equivalent in gold, depends on the current value of silver bullion, and fluctuates widely. In July, 1893, it fell to less than half the values assigned above.

The present coinage system of France came into force 6 May, 1790, and was extended to Belgium, Italy, and Switzerland in the convention of 1865. It has since been adopted by Greece, Roumania, Servia, and Spain. The units in the different states have different names: in France, Belgium, and Switzerland, franc and centime; in Italy, lira and centesimo; in Greece, drachma and lepta; in Roumania, lei and bani; in Servia, dinar and para; in Spain, peseta and centesimos; but the value is the same.—"Encyclopædia Britannica."

coining. Originally the metal was placed between 2 steel dies, and struck by a hammer. In 1553, a mill was invented by Antoine Brucher, introduced into England, 1562. An engine invented by Balancier, 1617. Great improvements effected by Boulton and Watt, at Soho, London, 1788. The erection of the mint machinery, London, began 1811. The machinery was reorganized in 1869. COIN and COINAGE.

coke, the residue obtained from bituminous coal by distillation, or by heating with the air almost entirely excluded—used largely in melting pig-iron; first successfully used for this purpose by Darby at Coalbrookdale, Engl., 1735, its use soon became general there. First successfully used for the same purpose in the United States, 1835, but not extensively until about 1860. The principal producing state is Pennsylvania, which, in 1889, produced nearly 7,000,000 tons.

Colchester, Essex, Engl. The *Camulodunum* of the Romans obtained its first charter from Richard I., 1189. It was captured by the parliamentary forces under Fairfax, after a 10 weeks' siege, June-Aug. 1648. Two of its defenders, sir George Lisle and sir Charles Lucas, were tried and shot after surrendering. The baize manufacture was established here, 1660.—*Anderson.*

cold. The extremes of heat and cold are found to produce similar perceptions on the skin; and the touch of mercury frozen at −40° is like that of red-hot iron. TEMPERATURE.

Cold Harbor, Va. Here gen. Grant, after much fighting on 1-2 June, 1864, for position, assaulted the confederates, under gen. Lee, behind defences, at sunrise, 3 June, along the whole line. It resulted in a bloody repulse, although Grant advanced his line somewhat and held it. The federal loss, while occupying this position, 1-12 June, was 14,931, of whom 1905 were killed, 10,570 wounded, and 2456 missing. Confederate loss, 1700. On the night of 12 June the army of the Potomac was withdrawn towards the James. Of this assault gen. Grant says, "I have always regretted that the last assault at Cold Harbor was ever made."—"Autobiography." GRANT'S VIRGINIA CAMPAIGN.

Coldingham, near Berwick, Engl., celebrated for the heroism of its nuns, who, on the attack of the Danes, to preserve their chastity, cut off their noses and lips. The Danes burned them all, with the abbess Ebba, in their monastery, 870.

Coldstream guards. Gen. Monk, before marching from Scotland into England to restore Charles II., raised this regiment at Coldstream, at the confluence of the Leet and Tweed, 1660. For its services in suppressing Venner's insurrection in 1661 it was not disbanded, but constituted the 2d regiment of *foot-guards.*

Colise'um, more properly **Colosseum,** an elliptical amphitheatre at Rome, commenced by the emperor Vespasian and finished by his son Titus, 75-80 A.D. Its height is 160 ft., its major diameter 615 ft. and its minor diameter 510 ft. The length and breadth of its arena are 281 and 176 ft. respectively. 87,000 spectators were accommodated by it. The name Colosseum first occurs in the writings of Bede in the 7th century. It is probably derived from the Colossus of Nero, which stood in the square before its entrance. The name of its architect is not known. It is said to have cost 10,000,000 crowns, and 12,000 Jews, who were made slaves at the conquest of Jerusalem, were employed upon it.—Anthon, "Classical Dict."

collar, a very ancient ornament. The Roman hero Titus Manlius slew a gigantic Gaul in single combat, and put his *torques* (twisted chain or collar) on his own neck, and was surnamed Torquatus, 361 B.C.—A collar is part of the ensigns of the order of knighthood.

collects, short prayers, very ancient, introduced into the Roman service by pope Gelasius, about 493, and into the English liturgy in 1548. The king of England, coming into Normandy, appointed a collect for the relief of the Holy Land, 1166.—*Rapin.*

colleges (from the Lat. *collegium*, assemblages of persons for sacred, civil, literary, or scientific purposes). The word is now commonly used to mean an institution for the higher education. They were first founded within universities to relieve students from the expense of living at lodging-houses and at inns. Collegiate or academic degrees are said to have been first conferred at the University of Paris, 1140; but some say not before 1215. In England, it is contended that the date is much higher, and some hold that Bede obtained a degree formally at Cambridge, and John de Beverley at Oxford, and that they were the first doctors of these universities. ABERDEEN, CAMBRIDGE, HERALDS, OXFORD, QUEEN'S COLLEGES, WORKING-MEN'S COLLEGES, etc.

COLLEGES IN GREAT BRITAIN.

	Founded
Winchester	1387
St. Andrews, Scotland	1410
Eton college	1441
Glasgow college, now university	1451
Physicians', London	1523
Highgate	1564
Gresham	1581
Trinity college, Dublin	1591
Dulwich	1619
Sion, incorporated	1630
Physicians', Dublin	1667
Doctors' Commons, civil law	1670
Physicians', Edinburgh	1681
Naval college, Portsmouth	1722
Surgeons', London	1745
Surgeons', Dublin	1786
Cheshunt college	1792
Maynooth college	1795
Military college, Sandhurst	1799
Surgeons', Edinburgh (new)	1803
University, London	1826
Highbury college	"
King's college, London	1829
New college, St. John's Wood	1850
Birmingham, Queen's college	1853
Owen's college, Manchester	1870

PRINCIPAL COLLEGES IN THE UNITED STATES.

Name.	Location.	Opened.	Denomination.
Harvard	Cambridge, Mass.	1638	Non-sectarian.
William and Mary's	Williamsburg, Va.	1693	"
Yale	New Haven, Conn.	1701	"
College of New Jersey	Princeton, N. J.	1746	"
Washington and Lee university	Lexington, Va.	1749	"
University of Pennsylvania	Philadelphia, Pa.	1751	"
Columbia, formerly Kings	New York	1754	"
Brown's university	Providence, R. I.	1765	"
Dartmouth	Hanover, N. H.	1770	Congregational.
Rutgers, formerly Queens	New Brunswick, N. J.	"	Reformed.
Dickinson	Carlisle, Pa.	1783	Now Methodist Episcopal.
Franklin and Marshall's	Lancaster, Pa.	1787	Reformed.
St. Johns	Annapolis, Md.	1789	Non-sectarian.
Georgetown college	Washington, D. C.	"	Roman Catholic.
Williams	Williamstown, Mass.	1793	Non-sectarian.
Union	Schenectady, N. Y.	1795	"
University of North Carolina	Chapel Hill, N. C.	"	"
University of Georgia	Athens, Ga.	1801	"
Bowdoin	Brunswick, Me.	1802	Congregational.
Ohio university	Athens, O.	1809	Non-sectarian.
Hamilton	Clinton, N. Y.	1812	Presbyterian.
Madison university	Hamilton, N. Y.	1820	Baptist.
Amherst	Amherst, Mass.	1821	Congregational.
Hobart	Geneva, N. Y.	1825	Protestant Episcopal.
Kenyon	Gambier, O.	"	" "
Trinity	Hartford, Conn.	1826	" "
Adelbert	Cleveland, O.	"	Presbyterian and Congregational.
Wesleyan	Middletown, Conn.	1830	Methodist Episcopal.
University of the City of New York	New York	"	Non-sectarian.
Oberlin	Oberlin, O.	1833	Congregational.
Tulane university	New Orleans, La.	1834	Non-sectarian.
Marietta	Marietta, O.	1835	
University of Michigan	Ann Arbor, Mich.	1841	"
Ohio Wesleyan university	Delaware, O.	1844	Methodist Episcopal.
University of Rochester	Rochester, N. Y.	1850	Baptist.
Antioch	Yellow Springs, O.	1853	Non sectarian.
Tufts	College Hill, Mass.	1855	Universalist.
Hillsdale	Hillsdale, Mich.	"	Free Baptist.
Northwestern university	Evanston, Ill.	"	Methodist Episcopal.
University of California	Berkeley, Cal.	"	Non-sectarian.
Vassar, exclusively for Women	Poughkeepsie, N. Y.	1865	Evangelical.
Fisk university	Nashville, Tenn.	1867	Congregational.
Cornell university	Ithaca, N. Y.	1868	Non-sectarian.
Wellesley, exclusively for Women	Wellesley, Mass.	1875	"
Johns Hopkins university	Baltimore, Md.	1876	"
Stanford university	Palo Alto, Cal.	1891	"

There are more than 430 collegiate institutions for males or for both sexes, many of which are under the patronage of some religious denomination, and 200 for females alone in the U. S. Many are richly endowed, such as Harvard, Columbia, Northwestern university, Ill., University of California, University of Pennsylvania, Tulane University of Louisiana, Yale, Cornell, and Michigan university. Many possess fine LIBRARIES. As to students, Harvard stands first with 2970; Columbia, over 1564; University of Michigan, over 2800; Oberlin, 1462; Northwestern university, 1618; Yale, 1930; University of Pennsylvania, 1990; Cornell, 1592; University of the City of New York, 1288; Tulane university, La., 1284; Ohio Wesleyan, Delaware, O., 1217; Princeton, N. J., 1160; Washington university, St. Louis, Mo., 1714. For these and other colleges and educational institutions consult separate states and separate articles.

college fraternities. The principal Greek-letter societies in the United States are as follows:

Name.	Greek letters.	Where founded.	Date.
Kappa Alpha	Κ Α	Union	1825
Delta Phi	Δ Φ	"	1827
Sigma Phi	Σ Φ	"	"
Alpha Delta Phi	Α Δ Φ	Hamilton	1832
Psi Upsilon	Ψ Υ	Union	1833
Delta Upsilon	Δ Υ	Williams	1834
Beta Theta Pi	Β Θ Π	Miami	1839
Chi Psi	Χ Ψ	Union	1841
Delta Kappa Epsilon	Δ Κ Ε	Yale	1844
Zeta Psi	Ζ Ψ	New York University	1846
Delta Psi	Δ Ψ	Columbia	1847
Theta Delta Chi	Θ Δ Χ	Union	"
Phi Delta Theta	Φ Δ Θ	Miami	1848
Phi Gamma Delta	Φ Γ Δ	Jefferson	"
Phi Kappa Sigma	Φ Κ Σ	University of Pennsylvania	1850
Phi Kappa Psi	Φ Κ Ψ	Jefferson	1852
Chi Phi	Χ Φ	Princeton	1854
Sigma Chi	Σ Χ	Miami	1855
Sigma Alpha Epsilon	Σ Α Ε	Alabama	1856
Delta Tau Delta	Δ Τ Δ	Bethany	1860
Alpha Tau Omega	Α Τ Ω	Virginia Military Institute	1865
Kappa Alpha (south)	Κ Α	Washington and Lee	1867
Kappa Sigma	Κ Σ	Virginia	"
Sigma Nu	Σ Ν	Virginia Military Institute	1869

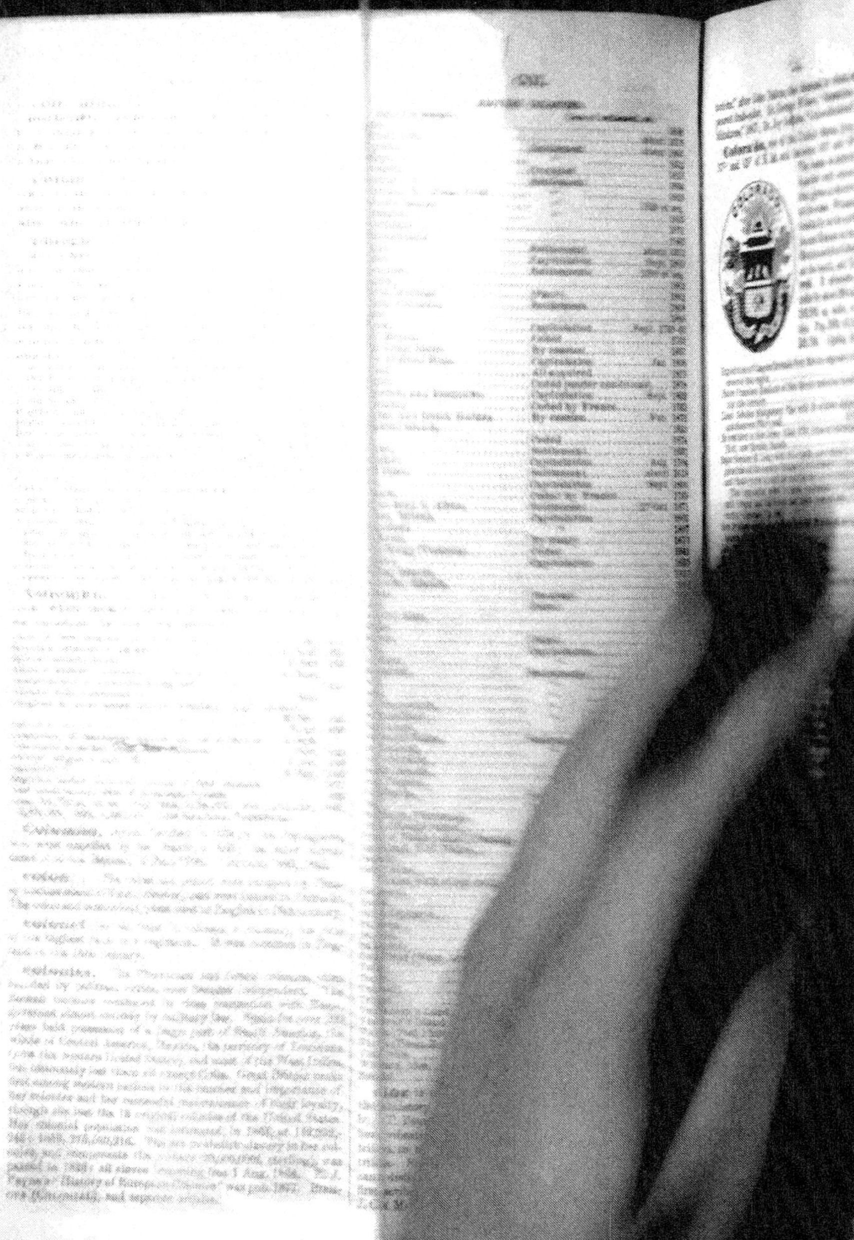

tonism," after John Dalton, the chemist, to whom scarlet appeared drab-color. Dr. George Wilson, "Researches on Color-blindness," 1847; Dr. Joy Jeffries, "Color-blindness," 1879.

Colora'do, one of the United States, lying between 37° and 41° of N. lat. and between 102° and 109° W. lon. The name is derived from the Spanish verb *colorar*, and was first given to the *river* and later to the state. Wyoming and Nebraska lie on the north, Nebraska and Kansas on the east, New Mexico and the Indian Territory on the south, and Utah on the west. It measures about 380 miles by about 280 miles. Area, 103,925 sq. miles, in 56 counties. Pop. 1890, 412,198; 1900, 539,700. Capital, Denver.

Expedition of Vasquez Coronado from Mexico, supposed to have entered this region.... 1541

Padre Francisco Escalante of New Mexico makes an expedition into this territory.... 1776

Lieut. Zebulon Montgomery Pike with 23 soldiers explores it and discovers Pike's peak.... 15 Nov. 1806

He was born in New Jersey, 5 Jan. 1779; killed at the taking of York, now Toronto, Canada.... 1813

Major Stephen H. Long visits this region, and reports to Congress that all the country drained by the Missouri, Arkansas, and Platte rivers is unfit for cultivation and uninhabitable 1819

[This impression aided to delay settlement of Colorado until Oregon and California had [illegible] settled. Bancroft's "Colorado," p. 349.]

Bent brothers [illegible] the north branch of [illegible] 1832

John C. Fre[illegible] 1842-44

Fort Ma[illegible]

Discovery [illegible]

W. Green [illegible] pedition [illegible]

Denver [illegible]

[illegible]

Denver selected as permanent capital of the state.... [illegible] 1881

[illegible] appointed secretary of the interior [illegible] 1882

Act passed providing for the establishment of a state Home and Industrial School for girls at Denver, and the first Monday [illegible] ... 1887

[illegible] 1889

[illegible] 1890

[illegible] 1891

[illegible]

TERRITORIAL GOVERNORS OF COLORADO.

Name	Term	Remarks
[illegible]	1861-62	appointed by president Lincoln
[illegible]	1862-65	
Alexander Cummings	1865-67	" " " Johnson
A. C. Hunt	1867-69	" " "
Edward M. McCook	1869-73	" " " Grant
Samuel H. Elbert	1873-74	" " " "
Edward M. McCook	1874-75	" " " "
John L. Routt	1875-76	" " " "

GOVERNORS OF THE STATE.

Name	Term
John L. Routt	1876-78
F. W. Pitkin	1879-83
James B. Grant	1883-85
B. H. Eaton	1885-86
[illegible]	1887-88
[illegible] Cooper	1889-91
[illegible] Routt	1891-93
[illegible] Waite	1893-95
[illegible] McIntyre	1895-97

UNITED STATES SENATORS FROM THE STATE OF COLORADO.

Name	No. of Congress	Date	Remarks
[illegible] B. Chaffee	44th to 48th	1876 to 1879	Republican
[illegible] M. Teller	44th " 47th	1877 " 1882	"
[illegible] P. Hill	46th " 49th	1879 " 1885	"
[illegible] M. Bowen	48th " 50th	1883 " 1889	"
[illegible] M. Teller	47th [illegible]	1885	"
[illegible] O. Wolcott	51st	1889	"

[illegible]lossus of Rhodes, a brass statue of Apollo, 70 [illegible] high, one of the "wonders of the world," erected at the [illegible] Rhodes in honor of the sun, by Chares of Lindus, the [illegible] of Lysippus, 290 or 280 B.C.; thrown down by an earth[illegible] about 224 B.C. The figure is said to have stood upon [illegible], a leg on each side of the harbor, so that a vessel [illegible] sail could enter between. The statue was in ruins for [illegible] centuries, when the Saracens, taking Rhodes, pulled [illegible] down, and sold the metal, 720,900 lbs., to a Jew, who is [illegible] have taken it, on 900 camels, to Alexandria about 668. [illegible]

[illegible]olumbia. District of Columbia.

[illegible]olumbiad. Cannon in the U. S.

[illegible]olumbian Exposition. World's Columbian [illegible]sition.

[illegible]lum'bium, a metal discovered by C. Hatchett, in [illegible] mineral columbite, in 1801. It is identical with niobium, [illegible] with tantalum, as some suppose.—*Watts.*

[illegible]manches. Indians.

[illegible]mbat, single, trial by, began among the Lombards, [illegible] *Burgundians.* It was introduced into England for treason [illegible] if neither accuser nor accused had good evidence. Ar[illegible] of battle, Constable of England.

[illegible] combat was fought before the king, William II., and the [illegible] between Geoffrey Baynard and William, earl of Eu, accused [illegible] of high treason; Baynard conquering, Eu was deemed [illegible], blinded and mutilated, 1096.

[illegible] proposed between Henry of Bolingbroke (afterwards Henry IV.) [illegible] Thomas, duke of Norfolk, was forbidden by Richard II., Sept. [illegible]. Shakespeare introduces this incident in "King Richard [illegible] act i. sc. iii.

collo'dion, a film obtained from the solution of gun-cotton in ether *Iodized* collodion, for photography, invented by F Scott Archer, was announced in the London *Chemist*, in Mch 1851 On the premature death of himself and wife, a pension of 50*l* was granted to his 3 orphan children

Colmar, W Germany, an imperial city, 13th century, taken by the Swedes, 1632, by Louis XIV of France, who destroyed the fortifications, 1673, ceded to France, 1697, with Alsace, restored to Germany, 1871

Cologne (Ger *Koln*, Lat *Colonia Agrippina*), on the Rhine, a colony founded by the empress Agrippina, about 50 A D, an imperial town, 957, a member of the Hanseatic League, 1260 Many ecclesiastical councils held here, 782-1536 The Jews were expelled from it in 1485, and the Protestants in 1618, and it fell into decay It was taken by French under Jourdan, Oct 1794 The archbishopric secularized, 1801, assigned to Prussia, 1814 Pop 1890, 281,273

Cathedral or *Dom* (containing many supposed relics, such as the heads of the magi or 3 kings), founded by archbishop Conrad von Hochstade or Hochstettin, architect, Gerhard von Richl or Rile	15 Aug	1248
Building intermittent, suspended		1509
Collections made for resuming it by Prussia		1814 et seq
Repairs completed, new buildings founded	4 Sept	1842
Body of the cathedral opened in the presence of the king, 600th anniversary of the foundation	15 Aug	1848
International industrial exhibition opened by the crown prince,	2 June,	1865
Dispute between the king and chapter on election of an archbishop, settled, the pope appoints Melchers	Jan	1866
Congress of Old Catholics meet	20, 22 Sept	1872
Archbishop Melchers arrested by government.	30 Mch	1874
A colossal statue of Frederick William III, 22 ft. high, with pedestrian figures at the base (Blucher, Humboldt, and others), the work of Blaser and Calendrelli, subscribed for by Rhinelanders, unveiled by the emperor William I	26 Sept	1878
Cathedral reported finished, 14 Aug, height, 510 ft, solemnly opened by the emperor and other German sovereigns, 15 Oct		1880

Colombia, a republic of South America, formed of states which declared their independence, Dec. 1819, civil war ensued and the union was dissolved

Union of New Granada and Venezuela	17 Dec.	1819
Royalists defeated at Carabobo	24 June,	1821
Bolivar named dictator	10 Feb	1824
Alliance between Colombia and Mexico	30 June,	"
Independence of Colombia recognized		1825
Alliance with Guatemala	Mch.	"
Congress at Lima names Bolivar president, Aug, dictator,	23 Nov	1826
Padilla's insurrection	9 Apr	1828
Conspiracy of Santander against the life of Bolivar	25 Sept.	"
Venezuela separates from New Granada.	Nov	1829
Bolivar resigns, 4 Apr, d	17 Dec	1830
Santander d	26 May,	1840
Republic named Colombia instead of New Granada		1871
New constitution, term of president 6 years.		1885

Area, 504,773 sq miles Pop 1864, 2,794,473, 1870, 2,910,329, 1880, 3,878,000, 1892, 4,200,000 NEW GRANADA, VENEZUELA

Colombo, Ceylon, fortified in 1638 by the Portuguese, who were expelled by the Dutch in 1666, the latter surrendered it to the British, 15 Feb 1796 CEYLON, 1803, 1845.

colon (:). The colon and period were adopted by Thrasymachus about 373 B C. (*Suidas*), and were known to Aristotle. The colon and semicolon (;) first used in English in 16th century

colonel (*kur'nel*, from It. *colonna*, a column), the title of the highest rank in a regiment. It was common in England in the 16th century

colonies. The Phœnician and Greek colonies, often founded by political exiles, soon became independent The Roman colonies continued in close connection with Rome, governed almost entirely by military law Spain for over 200 years held possession of a large part of South America, the whole of Central America, Mexico, the territory of Louisiana (now the western United States), and most of the West Indies, but ultimately lost them all except Cuba Great Britain ranks first among modern nations in the number and importance of her colonies and her successful maintainance of their loyalty, though she lost the 13 original colonies of the United States Her colonial population was estimated, in 1861, at 142,952,243, 1888, 275,520,216 The act to abolish slavery in her colonies, and compensate the owners (20,000,000*l.* sterling), was passed in 1833 all slaves becoming free 1 Aug 1834. E. J Payne's "History of European Colonies" was pub. 1877. BISHOPS (COLONIAL), and separate articles.

BRITISH COLONIES.

Colony or possession	Date of settlement, etc	
Aden		1838
African forts		about 1618
Anguilla	Settlement	about 1666
Antigua.	"	1632
Ascension	Occupied	1815
Australia, S	Settlement	1834
Australia, W (Swan river)	"	1829
Bahama islands	"	1629 et seq
Barbadoes	"	1605
Basutoland		1871
Bechuanaland		1885
Bengal	Settlement	about 1652
Berbice	Capitulation	Sept. 1803
Bermudas	Settlements	1609 et seq
Bombay		1662
British Burmah	(PEGU)	1862
British Columbia	Settlement.	1858
Brunei		1888
Canada	Capitulation	Sept. 1759-60
Cape Breton	Ceded	1763
Cape Coast Castle	By cession	1667
Cape of Good Hope	Capitulation	Jan 1806
Ceylon	All acquired	1815
Cyprus	Ceded (under conditions)	1878
Demerara and Essequibo	Capitulation	Sept. 1803
Dominica	Ceded by France	1763
Elmina and Dutch Guinea	By cession	Feb 1872
Falkland islands		1833
Fiji	Ceded	1874
Gambia	Settlement	1631
Gibraltar	Capitulation	Aug 1704
Gold Coast	Settlement	about 1618
Gozo	Capitulation	Sept. 1800
Grenada	Ceded by France	1763
Griqua land, S Africa	Settlement	27 Oct. 1871
Guiana, British	Capitulation	1803
Heligoland	"	1807
Honduras	By treaty	1670
Hong-Kong (Victoria)	Ceded	1841
Jamaica	Capitulation	1655
Keeling islands		1857
Kermadec islands		1886
Labuan	(BORNEO)	1846
Lagos	Ceded	1861
Leeward isles		1626
Madras		1639
Malacca.	Ceded	1825
Malta	Capitulation	Sept. 1800
Mauritius	"	Dec 1810
Montserrat.	Settlement.	1632
Natal	"	1823
Nevis	"	1628
New Brunswick	"	1622-1713
Newfoundland	"	about 1500
New Guinea		1884
New South Wales.	Settlement	1787
New Zealand.	"	1840
Niger districts		1885
Norfolk islands		1787
North Borneo		1840
Nova Scotia.	Settlement.	1622
Pegu	Conquered	1852
Port Philip (VICTORIA)		
Prince Edward island.	Capitulation	1745
Prince of Wales island (Penang)	Settlement	1786
Queensland, N S Wales.	"	1860
Sarawak		1888
Sierra Leone	Settlement	1787
[United with other settlements as West Africa, Feb 1866]		
Singapore	Purchased	1819
Socotra		1886
St. Christopher's.	Settlement	1623
St. Helena.	Capitulation	1600
St Lucia.	Capitulation.	June, 1803
St. Vincent	Ceded by France	1763
Swan River (WEST AUSTRALIA)		
Tobago	Ceded by France	"
Tortola	Settlement.	1666
Transvaal	Annexed	1877
Trinidad	Capitulation.	Feb. 1797
Van Diemen's Land	Settlement.	1803
Vancouver's island	"	1781
Victoria (Port Philip)	"	1850
Victoria (HONG-KONG)		
Virgin isles	Settlement.	1666
Windward isles		1605-1803
Zululand		1886

color is to light what pitch is to sound, according to the undulatory theory of Huyghens (about 1678), established by Dr T. Young, and others. The shade varies with the number of vibrations 458 trillions of vibrations in a second attributed to the red end of the spectrum, to the violet, 727 trillions. SPECTRUM. Some persons (about 65 out of 1154) cannot distinguish colors, and are termed color-blind, a defect first described by Priestley.—*Phil Trans*, 1777 In 1859, prof. J. Clerk Maxwell invented spectacles for what is called "Daltonism," after John Dalton, the chemist, to whom scarlet appeared drab-color. Dr. George Wilson, "Researches on Color-blindness," 1847; Dr. Joy Jeffries, "Color-blindness," 1879.

Colora'do, one of the United States, lying between 37° and 41° of N. lat. and between 102° and 109° W. lon.

The name is derived from the Spanish verb *colorar*, and was first given to the river and later to the state. Wyoming and Nebraska lie on the north, Nebraska and Kansas on the east, New Mexico and the Indian Territory on the south, and Utah on the west. It measures about 380 miles by about 280 miles. Area, 103,925 sq. miles, in 55 counties. Pop. 1890, 412,198; 1900, 539,700. Capital, Denver.

Expedition of Vasquez Coronado from Mexico, supposed to have entered this region.... 1541

Padre Francisco Escalante of New Mexico makes an expedition into this territory.... 1776

Lieut. Zebulon Montgomery Pike with 23 soldiers explores it and discovers Pike's peak....15 Nov. 1806

He was born in New Jersey, 5 Jan. 1779; killed at the taking of York, now Toronto, Canada.... 1812

Major Stephen H. Long visits this region, and reports to Congress that all the country drained by the Missouri, Arkansas, and Platte rivers is unfit for cultivation and uninhabitable 1819

[This impression aided to delay settlement of Colorado until Oregon and California had both been settled. Bancroft's "Colorado," p. 349.]

Bent brothers erect a stockade called fort William on the north branch of the Arkansas river.... 1832

John C. Fremont's expedition touches Colorado....1842-44

Fort Massachusetts erected on Ute creek.... 1850

Discovery of gold in what is now Colorado, reported....1852-57

W. Green Russell, a miner of Dahlomega, Ga., organizes an expedition to search for gold in Colorado.... 1858

Denver founded.... "

[Named after the governor of Kansas.]

Gold discovered at Boulder creek....15 Jan. 1859

First saw-mill erected on Plum creek by D. C. Oakes, and lumber furnished for building the town....21 Apr. "

Great influx of gold-seekers.... "

John H. Gregory discovers gold on the north fork of Clear creek, the richest mine in Colorado, and one of the richest in the world....10 May, "

[Gregory, a lazy fellow from Gordon county, Ga., drove a government team from Leavenworth to Fort Laramie in 1858. He sells his claim for $22,000, expecting easily to find another; disappears in 1862, and is never seen again.—*Bancroft.*]

Discovery of silver in Colorado.... "

Pueblo laid off on the site of the old town of Pueblo....1859-60

Increased immigration into Colorado.... 1860

Act erecting a new territory to be called Colorado....28 Feb. 1861

[Name suggested by William Gilpin, first governor.]

William Gilpin commissioned governor.... "

Hiram P. Bennett first delegate to Congress.... "

First legislature meets at Denver.... "

Great suffering from cold during the winter and drought during the summer of.... 1863

Great flood at Denver....Apr. 1864

Col. Chivington with 900 men attacks an Indian camp at Sand creek, Larimer county, and kills 131 persons, men, women, and children....27 Nov. "

First national bank at Denver established.... 1865

Alexander Cummings, governor....Oct. "

Nathaniel P. Hill organizes the "Boston and Colorado Smelting Company," and erects a furnace at Black Hawk, near Central City.... 1866

[This furnace (removed to Denver, 1879), reduces refractory ores and makes abandoned mines of value.]

The state adopts for the courts the "Illinois practice code." The capital was Colorado City, but changed to Golden City in 1862, and back to Denver.... 1868

Greeley, Weld county, located and settled.... 1870

First street railroad at Denver completed.... 1872

Act admitting Colorado as a state....3 Mch. 1875

Admission of Colorado proclaimed by president Grant..1 Aug. 1876

[38th in order.]

Leadville settled....Aug. 1877

University of Colorado incorporated 1860, and opened at Boulder "

Massacre at White River agency of N. C. Meeker and 12 others by Indians....29 Sept. 1879

On the same day the Ute Indians ambush and attack 160 troops at Milk creek, in Rio Blanca county. Capt. Thornbury, the commander, killed; capt. Payne of the 5th cavalry takes command. After being invested 5 days, they are relieved by col. Merritt....5 Oct. "

[The troops lost 14 killed and 43 wounded.]

First important discovery of silver in Gunnison county, the Forest Queen lode, made near Crested Butte.... "

State Industrial school at Golden City provided for by act of legislature.... 1881

Denver selected as permanent capital of the state....4 Nov. 1881

Henry M. Teller appointed secretary of the interior in president Arthur's cabinet....6 Apr. 1882

Act passed providing for the establishment of a State Home and Industrial School for Girls at Denver, and the first Monday in September of each year designated as "labor day," a public holiday, by legislature in session....5 Jan.-4 Apr. 1887

A Soldiers and Sailors' home at Monte Vista, a State Normal school at Greeley, and a State reformatory in Chaffee county provided for by legislature in session....2 Jan.-1 Apr. 1889

Last spike of the Pike's Peak mountain railroad driven, 20 Oct. 1890

Troops called out to suppress disorder in the legislature owing to collision of rival factions in the lower house....14 Jan. 1891

Australian ballot law passed in session....7 Jan.-7 Apr. "

Verdict of "Not guilty" in the Millington murder trial at Denver....29 Apr. "

Trans-Mississippi Commercial congress, 1200 delegates, opens at Denver....19 May, "

First passenger train ascends Pike's Peak....30 June, "

National Mining congress, 10,000 delegates, opens at Denver, 18 Nov. "

Forest preserve, Pike's peak, set apart by proclamations of president Harrison, 11 Feb., and supplementary....18 Mch. 1892

Conclave of the grand encampment of the Knights Templar of the U. S. formally opens at Denver....9 Aug. "

Death at Wilmington, O., of gen. James W. Denver, in whose honor Denver was named....9 Aug. "

TERRITORIAL GOVERNORS OF COLORADO.

Names.	Date.	Remarks.
William Gilpin.......	1861-62	Appointed by president Lincoln.
John Evans..........	1862-65	" " " "
Alexander Cummings.	1865-67	" " " Johnson.
A. C. Hunt..........	1867-69	" " " "
Edward M. McCook...	1869-73	" " " Grant.
Samuel H. Elbert.....	1873-74	" " " "
Edward M. McCook...	1874-75	" " " "
John L. Routt.......	1875-76	" " " "

GOVERNORS OF THE STATE.

Names.	Date.
John L. Routt....	1876-78
Fred. W. Pitkin....	1879-82
James B. Grant....	1883-85
Benj. H. Eaton....	1885-86
Alva Adams....	1887-88
Job A. Cooper....	1889-90
John L. Routt....	1891-93
Davis H. Waite....	1893-95
A. W. McIntyre....	1895-97

UNITED STATES SENATORS FROM THE STATE OF COLORADO.

Names.	No. of Congress.	Date.	Remarks.
Jerome B. Chaffee........	44th to 45th	1876 to 1879	Republican.
Henry M. Teller..........	44th " 47th	1877 " 1883	"
Nathaniel P. Hill.........	46th " 48th	1879 " 1885	"
Thomas M. Bowen........	48th " 50th	1883 " 1889	"
Henry M. Teller.........	49th	1885	"
Edward O. Wolcott.......	51st	1889	"

Colossus of Rhodes, a brass statue of Apollo, 70 cubits high, one of the "wonders of the world," erected at the port of Rhodes in honor of the sun, by Chares of Lindus, disciple of Lysippus, 290 or 288 B.C.; thrown down by an earthquake about 224 B.C. The figure is said to have stood upon 2 moles, a leg on each side of the harbor, so that a vessel in full sail could enter between. The statue was in ruins for nearly 9 centuries, when the Saracens, taking Rhodes, pulled it to pieces, and sold the metal, 720,900 lbs., to a Jew, who is said to have taken it, on 900 camels, to Alexandria about 653. —*Dufresnoy.*

Columbia. DISTRICT OF COLUMBIA.

Columbiad. CANNON in the U. S.

Columbian Exposition. WORLD'S COLUMBIAN EXPOSITION.

colum'bium, a metal discovered by C. Hatchett, in the mineral columbite, in 1801. It is identical with niobium, not with tantalum, as some suppose.—*Watts.*

Comanches. INDIANS.

combat, single, trial by, began among the Lombards, 659.—*Baronius.* It was introduced into England for treason cases, if neither accuser nor accused had good evidence. APPEAL OF BATTLE, CONSTABLE OF ENGLAND.

A single combat was fought before the king, William II., and the peers, between Geoffrey Baynard and William, earl of Eu, accused by Baynard of high-treason; Baynard conquering, Eu was deemed convicted, blinded and mutilated, 1096.

One proposed between Henry of Bolingbroke (afterwards Henry IV.) and Thomas, duke of Norfolk, was forbidden by Richard II., Sept. 1398. Shakespeare introduces this incident in "King Richard II." act i. sc. iii.

A trial was appointed between the prior of Kilmainham and the earl of Ormond, whom the prior impeached of high-treason; but the quarrel was settled by the king without fighting, 1446.

A combat was proposed between lord Reay and David Ramsey in 1631, but the king prevented it.

In a combat in Dublin castle, before the lords justices and council, between Connor MacCormack O'Connor and Teig Mac-Gilpatrick O'Connor, the former's head was cut off, and presented to the lords, 1553.

combination. Laws were enacted in England from the time of Edward I. regulating prices of labor and relations between masters and workmen, and prohibiting workmen's combinations, but all were repealed, 6 Geo. IV. c. 129, 1825, protection being given to both parties. The act was amended in 1859 by 22 Vict. c. 34, when attention was drawn to the subject by strikes in building trades. SHEFFIELD, STRIKES.

combs, found in Pompeii. Comb-makers' company incorporated in England, 1636 or 1650.

comedy. Thalia is the muse of comedy and lyric poetry. Susarion and Dolon, supposed inventors of theatrical exhibitions, 562 B.C., performed the first comedy at Athens, on a wagon or movable stage, on 4 wheels, and were rewarded with a basket of figs and a cask of wine. DRAMA, LITERATURE, SHAKESPEAREAN PLAYS.

Comedy prohibited at Athens as libellous, 440 B.C.

Aristophanes, prince of old comedy, 434 B.C., Menander of new, 320 B.C.

Of Plautus, 20 comedies are extant; he flourished 220 B.C.

Statius Cæcilius wrote more than 30 comedies; at Rome 180 B.C.

Comedies of Lælius and Terence first acted 154 B.C.

First regular comedy in England about 1551 A.D.

Sheridan said to have written the best comedy ("The School for Scandal"), best opera ("The Duenna"), and best afterpiece ("The Critic") in the language, 1775–79.

comets (Gr. κόμη, a hair).

"... A blazing star
Threatens the world with famine, plague, and war;
To princes death; to kingdoms many crosses;
To all estates inevitable losses;
To herdmen rot; to ploughmen hapless seasons;
To sailors storms; to cities civil treasons."
—*Sylvester*, "Du Bartas."

"... Satan stood
Unterrified, and like a comet burned,
That fires the length of Ophiucus huge
In the arctic sky, and from his horrid hair
Shakes pestilence and war." —*Milton*, "Paradise Lost."

A comet consists of 3 parts: head or nucleus, coma, and tail. According to Chambers no effect produced on the earth by cometary influence. The first described accurately was by Nicephorus, 1337. The identity and periodicity of comets are considered in Chambers's "Hand-book of Astronomy," 1889–1890, and in W. T. Lynn's "Celestial Motions," 1891. Amédée Guillemin's "World of Comets," by J. Glaisher, pub. 1877.

1140 B.C. "At the time that Nebuchadnezzar overran Elar a comet arose whose body was bright like day, while from its luminous body a tail extended like the sting of a scorpion."—*A. H. Sayce*, "Babylonian Inscriptions."

Aristotle described the probable course of a comet which appeared 370 B.C.

At the birth of Mithridates 2 comets were seen for 72 days together, whose splendor eclipsed the mid-day sun, covering one fourth of the heavens, about 135 B.C.—*Justin.*

A grand comet seen, 1264. Its tail said to have extended 100°. Perhaps the same one in 1556, with diminished splendor; expected again about Aug. 1858 or Aug. 1860.—*Hind.*

A remarkable one seen in England, June, 1337.—*Stow.*

Tycho Brahe proved comets extraneous to our atmosphere, about 1577

A comet which caused terror seen from 3 Nov. 1679, to 9 Mch. 1680; enabled Newton to prove comets subject to the law of gravitation, and probably in elliptic orbits, 1704.

A brilliant comet in 1769 passed very swiftly within 2,000,000 miles of the earth. It was seen in London; its tail, 36,000,000 miles long, stretched across the sky like a luminous arch.

Comet of 1811, on 15 Oct. was supposed by Herschel to stretch 100,000,000 miles, and its greatest breadth 15,000,000 miles. It was visible all the autumn to the naked eye.—*Philos. Trans. Royal Soc.* for 1812. Another comet, discovered by M. Pons, 29 Dec. 1823, had, besides the tail turned from the sun, another turned towards it.

Halley's Comet, 1682. Named after the great English astronomer, who first proved the periodical returns of comets, identifying the comet of 1682 with that of 1456, 1531, and 1607 by careful observations in 1682, and comparisons with records of earlier appearances. Halley's comet traverses its orbit in about 75 years; it appeared (as he had predicted) in 1759, reaching its perihelion on 13 Mch.; its last appearance was 1835; its next will be 1910.

Encke's Comet. First discovered by M. Pons, 26 Nov. 1818, but named for prof. Encke, who determined its orbit, motions, and perturbations; like Halley's, it has reappeared according to prediction, its period being 3 years and 15 weeks. 13th return observed at Copenhagen by M. d'Arrest, 20 July, 1863; in England, 14 Oct. 1871; seen 13 Apr. 1875; in New South Wales, 3 Aug. 1878.

Biela's Comet is remarkable for its close approach to the earth's orbit. It was discovered by M. Biela, an Austrian officer, 28 Feb. 1826. It has also reappeared as predicted, its period being 6 years and 38 weeks. Its second appearance was in 1832; its perihelion passage 27 Nov.; its third was in 1839; its fourth in 1845; and its fifth in 1852; it has since vanished.

Great Comet of 1843, the brightest of this century, was distinctly visible to the naked eye beside the sun. After sunset, its tail stretched in a double broad band of intense white light from the horizon more than half way to the zenith, as seen in the U. S.

Donati's Comet, one of the finest comets of the present century, first observed by Dr. Donati, of Florence, 2 June, 1858, 228,000,000 miles from our earth. It was very brilliant in the U. S. in the end of Sept. and Oct. following, when the tail was said to be 40,000,000 miles long. On 10 Oct. it was nearest the earth; on the 18th it was near Venus. Opinions varied as to this comet's brilliancy compared with that of 1811. Its period of return is about 2000 years.

Great Comet of 1861 was first seen by Mr. Tebbutt at Sydney, in Australia, 13 May; by M. Goldschmidt and others in France and England on 29, 30 June. The nucleus was about 400 miles in diameter, with a long bush-like tail; it moved about 10,000,000 miles in 24 hours. On 30 June it was suggested that we were in the tail—there being "a phosphorescent auroral glare."

A tailless comet was discovered in Cassiopeia, by M. Seeling, at Athens, 2 July, and by M. Tempel, at Marseilles, 2 and 3 July, 1862.

M. Babinet regards cometary matter as so rare that a comet's tail, traversed by the earth, might be unnoticed, 4 May, 1857.

Schiaparelli, of Milan, identifies the path of August meteors round the sun with orbit of second comet of 1862–66.

Coggia's Comet, seen by him at Marseilles, 18 Apr.; (near Polar star) in London about 4 July; gradually grew brighter, but, lost to sight in Europe, appeared at Melbourne, 1 Aug. 1874.

Most important work on these comets was the successful photographing by prof. Henry Draper, of New York, 1880–81.

Spectra show carbon; in one case the greater part of the comet's light was proved to be reflected.

Of about 270 comets whose orbits have been computed with approximate accuracy, nearly 200 appear to move in parabolas, and therefore, after their one visit to the solar system, have passed away into the depths of space. About 50 are known to have oval or elliptic orbits, and are erratic members of our own system. But the attraction of a planet, especially of Jupiter, may sometimes change a comet's orbit from a parabola to an ellipse, or conversely. The close connection of comets with the periodical showers of meteors (usually observed 12 Aug., 13, 27, and 28 Nov., etc.), first demonstrated in 1864 by prof. H. A. Newton, of Yale college, is now universally admitted. Several streams of meteors are known to move in long elliptic orbits about the sun, each the orbit of a known comet, and most astronomers suppose the meteors to be the result of the gradual disintegration of the comets.

COMETS REVOLVING ABOUT THE SUN IN LESS THAN 20 YEARS.

Name.	Orbital movement. Years.	Appearance.
1. Encke's	3.29	Oct. 1891
2. Tempel's, 2d	5.15	Feb. 1894
3. Winnecke's	5.54	Dec. 1891
4. Brorsen's	5.58	Apr. 1890
5. Tempel's, 1st	5.98	Apr. 1891
6. Swift's	6.	Oct. 1892
7. Barnard's	6.	1890
8. D'Arrest's	6.64	Sept. "
9. Finlay's	6.67	1893
10. Wolfe's	6.76	Aug. 1891
11. Faye's	7.44	Dec. 1895
12. Denning's	8.86	July, 1890
13. Tuttle's	13.66	Mch. 1899

COMETS REVOLVING ABOUT THE SUN IN LESS THAN 100 YEARS.

Name.	Years.	Next appearance.
1. Westphal's	67.7	1920
2. Pons's	70.68	1954
3. De Vico's	73.25	1919
4. Olbers's	74.05	1961
5. Brorsen's	74.97	1922
6. Halley's	76.78	1910

(Halley's comet has been traced as far back as 11 B.C. by Hind).

YEARS OF REMARKABLE COMETS.

1066
1106
1145
1265
1378
1402
1456
1531
1556
1577
1607
1618
1661
1680—Period estimated at 8814 years.—*Guillemin.*
1682—Halley's.
1689
1729
1744
1759—Halley's.
1769
1811 {The most remarkable of modern times. Period, 3065 years. Discovered 26 Mch. 1811.
1823
1835—Halley's.
1843 {One of the most brilliant ever observed. It approached the sun to within 450,000 miles of its centre and less than 30,000 from its surface.
1858—Donati's. See notice in this article.
1861—See notice in this article.
1882

TABLE OF RECORDED COMETS.

Period	No observed	Orbits calculated	Identified
Before A D	79	4	1
0-100.	22	1	1
101-200	22	2.	1
201-300.	39	3.	2
301-400	22	0	1
401-500	19	1	1
501-600	25	4	1
601-700	29	0	2
701-800	17	2	1
801-900	41	1	0
901-1000	30	2	3
1001-1100	37	4	2
1101-1200	28	0	1
1201-1300	29	3	3
1301-1400	34	7	3
1401-1500	43	12	1
1501-1600	39	13	4
1601-1700	32	20	5
1701-1800	72	64	8
1801-1888	270	249	68
	929	392	109

commander-in-chief. ARMY OF THE UNITED STATES

commerce early flourished in Arabia, Egypt, and among the Phœnicians, see the description of Tyre, 588 B.C, Ezek xxvii Later it was spread over Europe by a confederacy of maritime cities, 1241 (HANSE TOWNS), by the discoveries of Columbus, and by the enterprises of the Dutch and Portuguese EXPORTS, IMPORTS, and articles connected with this subject

England's first treaty of commerce with a foreign nation was with the Flemings 1 Edw I 1272 The second with Portugal and Spain, 2 Edw II 1308 —*Anderson*. TREATIES Hertslet's "Collection," in 12 vols 8vo, pub 1827-59, has a copious index
Chambers of commerce originated at Marseilles in the 14th century and in the chief cities in France about 1700
Suppressed in 1791, restored by decrees 3 Sept 1851
Chamber of commerce at Glasgow established 1783, at Edinburgh 1785, Manchester, 1820, Hull 1837
International congress of commerce at Brussels 6-10 Sept 1880
A minister of commerce in England proposed, 1880, dropped 1881

common council of London, organized about 1208. The charter of Henry I mentions the *folk-mote*, Saxon for a court or assembly of the people Its general place of meeting was in the open air at St Paul's cross, St. Paul's churchyard In Henry III 's reign representatives were chosen out of each ward, who, with the lord mayor and aldermen, constituted the court of common council At first 2 were returned for each ward, the number was enlarged in 1347, and since This council, consisting of 206 members, meets every Thursday, and is elected annually 21 Dec., St Thomas's day It supported the prince of Orange in 1688, and queen Caroline in 1820.—Most of the cities of the United States are governed by a "common council," consisting of aldermen elected from the different wards.

Common Pleas, Court of, in England, in ancient times followed the king's person, and is distinct from the King's Bench; but on the grant of Magna Charta by king John, in 1215, it was fixed at Westminster, where it remains. In 1833 procedure in all superior courts was made uniform In England, no barrister under the degree of sergeant could plead in Common Pleas, but in 1846 the privilege was extended to barristers practising in the superior courts at Westminster Sat last, July, 1875. The common-pleas division of the high court of justice now consists of the chief-justice and 4 judges SUPREME COURT, COURTS IN THE U. S.

"Common Prayer, Book of," first ordered by Parliament printed in English, 1 Apr 1548, was published 7 Mch. 1549; reformed by act of uniformity, 6 Apr. 1552, abolished under queen Mary, Oct 1553, restored, with changes, 24 June, 1559, revised, 1604, abolished, 1644, and its use prohibited under heavy penalties, till the new act of uniformity, 19 May, 1662, since when it has been continuously in use. With a few changes, this prayer-book is used by Episcopal churches in Scotland, Ireland, and North America

"King's Primer" pub. 1545
First book of Edward VI printed 7 Mch 1549
Second book of Edward VI 1552
First book of Elizabeth (revised) 1559
King James's book " 1604
Scotch book of Charles I 1637
Charles II 's book (*Savoy conference*) now in use 1662
State services (never part of the prayer book but annexed to it at the beginning of every reign) for 5 Nov (gunpowder treason), 30 Jan (Charles I 's execution), and 29 May (Charles II 's restoration), were ordered discontinued 17 Jan 1859
Public Worship Regulation act (to check ritualism) passed Aug 1874
Wesleyan Methodists who had used the prayer book appoint a committee to revise it Aug "

common-law of England, including unwritten maxims and customs (*leges non scriptæ*), of British, Saxon, and Danish origin, immemorial in that kingdom, though somewhat impaired by the Norman conquest, is still recognized by the courts At the parliament of Merton, 1236, "all the earls and barons," says the parliament roll "with one voice answered that they would not change the laws of England which have hitherto been used and approved" BASTARD The process, practice, and mode of pleading in the superior courts of common-law were amended 1852 and 1854 In the United States the term common-law means that of England, and statutes passed by the English Parliament, before the first settlements in the colonial states were made, and with the exception of Louisiana, is the basis of the jurisprudence of all the states, in so far as it conforms to the circumstances and institutions of the country, and has not been otherwise modified by statutory provisions

Commons, House of, originated when Simon de Montfort, earl of Leicester, by the provisions of Oxford, ordered returns of 2 knights from every shire and deputies from certain boroughs, to meet his friends of the barons and clergy, to strengthen his power against Henry III, 1258.—*Stow* PARLIAMENT In 1832 the house had 658 members In 1844 Sudbury, and in 1852 St Albans, were disfranchised for bribery and corruption, each having returned 2 members; the number then became 654 In 1861 the forfeited seats were given—2 additional to the West Riding of York, 1 to South Lancashire, and 1 to a new borough, Birkenhead In 1859 Mr Newmarch estimated the voters of England and Wales at 934,000 The number was largely increased by the Reform act of 1867 Registered parliamentary electors, 1872 England and Wales, boroughs, 1,250,019, counties, 801,109 Scotland, burghs, 49,025, counties, 79,919 Ireland, boroughs, 171,912, counties, 175,439 Total, 2 526,423 Parliamentary electors England and Wales, 1875, 2,301,266, 1878, 2,416,222, 1879 (May), 2,459,999 Scotland, 1875, 289,789, 1878, 304,-268, 1879, 307,941 Ireland, 1875, 230,436, 1878, 231,515, 1879, 231,289 Total, 1875, 2,821,491; 1878, 2,952,005, 1879, 2,999,229 Disfranchised and replaced, 1867 · Lancaster, Yarmouth, Totnes, and Reigate Disfranchised, 1870 Beverley and Bridgewater, each 2 members, Cashel and Sligo, each 1 member · 652 members, 1878, 12 members short, through void elections. Aug 1880 The Reform bill of 1885 makes manhood suffrage almost universal The registered electors in England, 1891, number 4,469,630, Wales, 261,117; Scotland, 576,213, Ireland, 760,173 Total, 6,067,133, an average of 9055 electors to every member Salary of the speaker of the house, 5000*l* Number of members at different times:

Old House.	Members	By the Reform act of 1832	Members.
England	489	England	472
Wales	24	Wales	28
Scotland.	45	Scotland	53
Ireland	100	Ireland .	105
Total	658	Total	658

By the acts of 1867–68.	Members	By the Reform act of 1885.	Members
England.	463	England.	465
Wales	30	Wales	30
Scotland	60	Scotland	72
Ireland.	105	Ireland	103
Total	658	Total	670

common schools in the United States EDUCATION

Common-sense pamphlet, Paine's. PENNSYLVANIA, 1776

Commonwealth of England, the term applied to the interregnum between the death of Charles I and the restoration of Charles II A republic was established at the execution of Charles I, 30 Jan. 1649—a new oath, called the "Engagement," framed, which all officials must take—*Salmon*. They swore to be true and faithful to the Commonwealth, without king or house of lords. The statues of Charles were next day demolished, particularly that at the royal exchange, and one at the west end of St. Paul's, and in their room the following inscription was conspicuously set up: "*Exit Tyrannus Regum ultimus, Anno Libertatis Angliæ Restitutæ Primo. Anno Dom.* 1649, Jan. 30." Oliver Cromwell was made protector 16 Dec. 1653; succeeded by his son Richard, 3 Sept. 1658. Monarchy was restored 8 May, and Charles II. entered London, 29 May, 1660.

commun'alists or **com'munists,** propose to divide France into about 1000 independent states, with councils elected by all; Paris to be the ruling head; capital and its holders to be adapted to nobler uses, or cease to exist. They are said to be atheists and materialists. They are intimately connected with the international society of workmen, and the communists or socialists (1871–73). SOCIALISM.

communes, in France, are territorial divisions under a mayor. In the 11th century the name was given to combinations of citizens, favored by the crown, against the exactions of the nobles. In 1356 Stephen Marcel, during English invasion, endeavored to form a confederation of sovereign cities, having Paris as governing head; and for 6 months it was governed by a commune in 1588. After the insurrection of July, 1789, the revolutionary committee replaced the city council, taking the name of "Commune of Paris," Péthion being mayor. It met at the Hôtel de Ville, and organized 21 May, 1791. It had great power under Robespierre, and fell with him, 17 July, 1794, being replaced by 12 municipalities. The commune was proclaimed in Paris, 28 Mch. 1871, during the insurrection which began 18 Mch. and ended with the capture of the city by the government, 28 May. 2245 communists were pardoned by decree issued 17 Jan. 1879; and many others afterwards. A number re-entered Paris 4 Sept. following. For the communal rule in Paris, FRANCE, 1871; SOCIALISM.

communion, the ordinance of the Lord's supper (1 Cor. x. 16). Communicating under the form of bread alone is said to have begun under pope Urban II. 1096. The cup was first denied to the laity by the council of Constance, 1414–1418. The fourth Lateran council (1215) decreed that every believer should receive the communion at least at Easter. The communion service of the church of England was set forth in 1549.

companies. The London trade companies were gradually formed out of the trade or craft guilds, mainly by the exertions of Walter Harvey, mayor in 1272. The original religious element in the companies gradually disappeared. The first commercial company in England was probably the Steelyard society, established 1232. The second was the Merchants of St. Thomas à Becket, in 1248.—*Stow.* The third was the Merchant Adventurers, incorporated by Elizabeth, 1564. Of bubble companies, Law's bubble, in 1720–21, was perhaps the most famous, and the South Sea bubble, in the same year, was scarcely less memorable for the ruin of thousands of families. LAW'S and SOUTH SEA BUBBLE, LONDON and PLYMOUTH COMPANIES.

compass, mariner's, said to have been known to the Chinese, 1115 B.C., and brought to Europe by Marco Polo, a Venetian, 1260 A.D. Flavio Gioja, of Amalfi, a navigator of Naples, is said to have introduced the suspension of the needle, 1302. The statement that the fleur-de-lis was placed at the northern point of the compass in compliment to Charles, king of Naples at the time of the discovery, has been contradicted. The compass is said to have been known to the Swedes under king Jarl Birger, 1250. Its variation was discovered first by Columbus, 1492; afterwards by Sebastian Cabot, 1540. The compass-box and hanging-compass used by navigators were invented by William Barlowe, an English divine and natural philosopher, in 1608. MAGNETISM.—The measuring compass (dividers) was invented by Jost Bing, of Hesse, in 1602.

Compiegne (*kom-pe-ān'*), a French city north of Paris, residence of the Carlovingian kings. During its siege, JOAN OF ARC was captured here by Burgundians, 25 May, 1430, and given up to the English. Napoleon III. and the king of Prussia met here 6 Oct. 1861.

Composite order, a mixture of Corinthian and Ionic, also called the Roman order; of uncertain date.

composite portraits. By photography, in 1877–1878, Francis Galton combined from 2 to 9 portraits; often improving the features of the components.

compound radical, in organic chemistry, is a substance containing 2 or more elements, but often acting as one element. The radical or binary theory was propounded by Berzelius, 1833, and by Liebig, 1838; and modified in the nucleus theory of Aug. Laurent, 1836. The first compound radical isolated was cyanogen, by Gay-Lussac, 1815. AMYL, ETHYL, METHYL.

Comte's (*kŏnt's*) **philosophy.** PHILOSOPHY.

Conception, Immaculate. A festival (8 Dec.) appointed 1389, observed in the Roman Catholic church in honor of the Virgin Mary's conception and birth without original sin. Opposition to this doctrine was forbidden by decree of pope Paul V. in 1617, which was confirmed by Gregory XV. and Alexander VII.—*Hénault.* On 8 Dec. 1854, pope Pius IX. promulgated a bull, declaring this dogma an article of faith, and making it heresy to doubt or speak against it.—The Conceptionists were an order of nuns in Italy, established in 1488. SANTIAGO.

concept'ualism. Philosophic thought intermediate between realism and nominalism. PHILOSOPHY, Abelard.

concertina (*con-ser-tee'na*), a musical instrument invented by prof., afterwards sir, Charles Wheatstone, about 1825, and improved by G. Case. The sounds are produced by free vibrating metal springs.

concerts. The Filarmonia gave concerts at Vicenza in the 16th century. The first public subscription concert was at Oxford in 1665; the first in London is said to have been in 1672, by John Banister, afterwards by Thomas Britton till his death, 1714. The academy of ancient music began concerts in London, 1710; the concerts of ancient music in 1776; and the Philharmonic society of London in 1813. CRYSTAL PALACE, HANDEL, MUSIC. Colossal peace concerts were held at Boston, Mass., 15 June, etc., 1869; 17 June to 4 July, 1872. BOSTON.

conchol'ogy, the science of shells, mentioned by Aristotle and Pliny, was reduced to a system by John Daniel Major, of Kiel, Holstein, Germany, who published his classification of the *Testacea* in 1675. Lister's system was published 1685; that of Largius 1722. Johnson's "Introduction" (1850) and Sowerby's "Manual of Conchology" (1842) are useful. Forbes and Hanley's "British Mollusca and their Shells" (1848–53) is a magnificent work. "British Conchology," by J. G. Jeffreys, pub. 1862–69.

conclave. A range of small cells in the hall of the Vatican, where the cardinals usually meet to elect a pope; also the assembly of cardinals shut up for the purpose. Clement IV. died at Viterbo in 1268; the cardinals were nearly 3 years unable to agree, and were about to disperse, when the magistrates, by advice of St. Bonaventura, shut the city gates, and locked up the cardinals till they agreed, 1271.

Concord. MASSACHUSETTS, 1775.

concor'dance. An index or alphabetical catalogue of the words, or a chronological account of the facts in a book. The first was made of the Bible under Hugo de St. Caro, who employed 500 monks upon it, 1247.—*Abbé Lenglet.* It was based on one compiled by Anthony of Padua. Thomas Gibson's "Concordance of the New Testament," pub. 1535. John Marbeck's "Concordance" (for the whole Bible), 1550. Two concordances, by Robert F. Herrey, appeared in 1578. Cruden's "Concordance" was published in London in 1737. Dr. Robert Young's "Analytical Concordance to the Bible," 1879. The "Index to the Bible," published by queen Victoria's printers, prepared by B. Vincent, was completed May, 1848.

Verbal indexes accompany good editions of ancient classics. An "Index to Shakespeare," by Ayscough, appeared in 1790; another by Twiss in 1805; and Mrs. Cowden-Clarke's "Concordance to Shakespeare's Plays" (after 16 years' labor) in 1847. Mrs. Horace Furness's "Concordance to Shakespeare's Poems," 1874. Todd's "Verbal Index to Milton," 1809. Cleveland's "Concordance to Milton," 1867. Brightwell's "Concordance to Tennyson," 1869. Abbott's "Concordance to Pope," 1875. Dunbars to Homer, 1880. Ellis to Shelley, 1892.

concor'dat. An agreement between a prince and the

pope, usually concerning benefices. That between the emperor Henry V. of Germany and pope Calixtus II., in 1122, has been regarded as fundamental law of the church in Germany. The concordat between Bonaparte and Pius VII., at Paris, 15 July, 1801, re-established the papal authority in France. Napoleon was made in effect the head of the Gallican church, bishops to be appointed by him, and invested by the pope. Another concordat between the same persons was signed at Fontainebleau, 25 Jan. 1813. These were almost nullified by another, 22 Nov. 1817. A concordat, 18 Aug. 1855, between Austria and Rome, by which the liberty of the Austrian church was largely given up to the papacy, caused dissatisfaction. In 1868 it was virtually abolished by the legislatures of Hungary and Austria.

concubines were tolerated among the Jews, Greeks, and Romans, but strictly forbidden to Christians (Mark x.; 1 Cor. vii. 2). They are mentioned as having been allowed to priests, 1132. MORGANATIC MARRIAGES.

condottieri (*con-dot-te-ā'ree*), conductors or leaders of mercenaries, termed free companies or lances. The first to give a definite form to these lawless bands was Montreal d'Albarno of Provence. This body, named the "Grand Company," numbered 7000 cavalry and 1500 select infantry, mostly Germans, and was for some years the terror of Italy. After the peace of Bretigny, in 1360, sir John Hawkwood, an able general, after ravaging France, led his army of English mercenaries, called the "White Company," into Italy, which first in the service of Pisa, and afterwards of Florence, took a prominent part in the confused Italian wars of that period. The first who formed an exclusively Italian company was Alberico da Barbiano. In his school the great condottieri Braccio da Montone and Attendolo Sforza were formed. The greatest condottieri during the first half of the 15th century were Francesco Bussone, count of Carmagnola, who was beheaded between the columns at Venice, 1432, Niccolo Piccinino, who died at Milan, 1444, and Francesco Sforza, son of Attendolo Sforza, who, marrying the daughter of the duke of Milan, seized that duchy on the death of his father-in-law, 1450, the only condottiere who obtained territory of importance. He exhibited rare qualities as a ruler. Towards the end of the 15th century, when the large cities had gradually absorbed the smaller states, and Italy itself, drawn into European politics, became the battle-field of powerful armies, French, Spanish, and German, the condottieri disappeared.

conduits. Two remarkable conduits, among others in London, existed early in Cheapside. The "great conduit," the first cistern of lead in London, was built 1285. At the procession of Anne Boleyn, on her marriage, it ran with white and claret wine all afternoon, 1 June, 1533.—*Stow.*

Confederate States of America. An organization of slave-holding states in an attempt to secede from the Union and establish an independent government. During the 4 years of its existence its history is confined almost wholly to the battle-field. The following table gives the dates of legislative action for secession in the several states:

State.	Act of Secession.		Vote.
South Carolina.............	20 Dec.	1860	Unanimous.
Mississippi.................	9 Jan.	1861	84 yeas, 15 nays.
Florida.....................	10 "	"	62 " 7 "
Alabama....................	11 "	"	61 " 39 "
Georgia.....................	19 "	"	208 " 89 "
Louisiana..................	26 "	"	113 " 17 "
Texas.......................	1 Feb.	"	166 " 7 "
Virginia....................	17 Apr.	"	88 " 55 "
Arkansas...................	6 May,	"	69 " 1 "
North Carolina............	21 "	"	Unanimous.
Tennessee..................	8 June,	"	....

Legislatures of Missouri, Kentucky, Maryland, and Delaware refused to pass an ordinance of secession, and declared themselves neutral.

Convention of South Carolina, after passing the ordinance of secession, issues a call, 27 Dec. 1860, for a convention at Montgomery, Ala., of such slave-holding states as should secede, Feb. 4, 1861. At that date the following delegates met:

South Carolina: R. B. Rhett, Jas. Chesnut, jr., W. P. Miles, T. J. Withers, R. W. Barnwell, C. G. Memminger, L. M. Keitt, W. W. Boyce.

Georgia: Robert Toombs, Howell Cobb, Benj. H. Hill, Alex. H. Stephens, Francis Barbour, Martin J. Crawford, E. A. Nisbett, Augustus B. Wright, Thos. R. R. Cobb, Augustus Keenan.

Alabama: Richard W. Walker, Robert H. Smith, Colin J. McRae, John Gill Shorter, S. F. Hale, David P. Lewis, Thomas Fearn, J. L. M. Curry, W. P. Chilton.

Mississippi: Wiley P. Harris, Walker Brooke, A. M. Clayton, W. S. Barry, J. T. Harrison, J. A. P. Campbell, W. S. Wilson.

Louisiana: John Perkins, jr., Duncan F. Kenna, C. M. Conrad, E. Sparrow, Henry Marshall.

Florida: Jackson Morton, J. Patton Anderson, Jas. B. Owens.

This convention, with Howell Cobb as permanent president, adopted, on 9 Feb. 1861, a provisional constitution for the Confederate States of America. On the same day, Jefferson Davis of Mississippi was elected president, Alexander H. Stephens of Georgia vice-president, by a unanimous vote of the delegates (42 in number). Davis was inaugurated 18 Feb. 1861; oath of office being administered by Howell Cobb. The delegates from the other states of the confederacy took seats in the provisional congress as follows:

Texas, 1st session, 2 Mch. 1861: Louis T. Wigfall, John H. Reagan, John Hemphill, T. H. Waul, William B. Ochiltree, W. S. Oldham, John Gregg.

Arkansas, 2d session, May, 1861: Robert W. Johnson, Albert Rust, Augustus H. Garland, Wm. W. Watkins, Hugh F. Thomasson.

Virginia, 2d session, May, 1861: Jas. A. Soddon, Wm. Ballard Preston, Robt. M. T. Hunter, John Tyler, sen., Wm. H. McFarland, Roger A. Pryor, Thos. S. Bocock, Wm. C. Rives.

Tennessee, 2d session, May, 1861: Jos. B. Heiskill, Thomas Menees, Wm. G. Swan, —— Meeker, —— House, Geo. W. Jones, John D. C. Atkins, —— De Witt, —— McIlhery.

North Carolina, 3d session, July, 1861: Geo. Davis, Wm. W. Avery, Wm. N. H. Smith, Thos. Ruffin, Thos. D. McDowell, Abram W. Venable, John M. Morehead, Robt. C. Puryear, Burton Craige, Andrew J. Davidson.

Kentucky, 4th session, Dec. 1861: Henry C. Burnett, —— Thomas, Willis B. Machen, Thomas B. Munroe.

Missouri, 4th session, Dec. 1861: Wm. H. Cook, Thos. A. Harris, Casper W. Bell, A. H. Conrow, Geo. C. Vest, Thos. W. Freeman, Samuel Hyer.

The permanent constitution of the Confederate States (that of the United States with slight alterations) was submitted to the provisional congress 11 Mch. and unanimously adopted, and was ratified by the following states: Alabama, 13 Mch. 1861; Georgia, 16 Mch.; Louisiana, 21 Mch.; Texas, 23 Mch.; South Carolina, 3 Apr.; Virginia, 25 Apr.; North Carolina, 21 May.

The confederate (provisional) congress held four sessions: (1) 4 Feb. 1861, to 16 Mch. 1861; (2) 29 Apr. 1861, to 22 May, 1861; (3) 20 July, 1861, to 22 Aug. 1861; (4) 18 Nov. 1861, to 17 Feb. 1862.

The government was removed from Montgomery, Ala., to Richmond, Va., 24 May, 1861, where the 3d session of its congress opened 20 July, 1861, and remained until driven out by Grant in Apr. 1865.

The government, under its permanent constitution, was organized at Richmond, Va., 22 Feb. 1862.

Jefferson Davis of Miss., president........................1862-65
Alexander H. Stephens of Ga., vice-president................ "

CABINET.

Judah P. Benjamin, La., secretary of state.
Charles G. Memminger, S. C., secretary of treasury.
Geo. W. Randolph, Va., secretary of war.
Stephen R. Mallory, Fla., secretary of navy.
Thos. H. Watts, Ala., attorney-general.
John H. Reagan, Tex., postmaster-general.

First Congress, session (1) 18 Feb. 1862, to 22 Apr. 1862.
" (2) 12 Aug. " " 13 Oct. "
" (3) 12 Jan. 1863, " 8 May, 1863.
" (4) 7 Dec. " " 18 Feb. 1864.

Senate: Alexander H. Stephens, Ga., vice-president.
R. M. T. Hunter, Va., president *pro tem.*

Members from Ala.: Clement C. Clay, William L. Yancey.
" " Ark.: Robt. W. Johnson, Chas. B. Mitchell.
" " Fla.: Jas. M. Baker, Augustus E. Maxwell.
" " Ga.: Benj. H. Hill, John W. Lewis.
" " Ky.: Henry C. Burnett, Wm. E. Simms.
" " La.: Thos. J. Semmes, Edward Sparrow.
" " Miss.: Albert G. Brown, Jas. Phelan.
" " Mo.: John B. Clark, R. L. Y. Peyton.
" " N. C.: Wm. T. Dortch, Geo. Davis.
" " S. C.: Robt. W. Barnwell, Jas. L. Orr.
" " Tenn.: Gustavus A. Henry, Landon C. Haynes.
" " Va.: Robt. M. T. Hunter, Wm. Ballard Preston.
" " Tex.: Louis T. Wigfall, Williamson S. Oldham.

House: Thos. S. Bocock, Va., speaker.

Members: Alabama 9, Arkansas 4, Florida 2, Georgia 10, Kentucky 12, Louisiana 6, Mississippi 7, Missouri 6, North Carolina 10, South Carolina 6, Tennessee 11, Texas 7, Virginia 16; total, 106.

Second Congress, session (1) 2 May, 1864, to 15 June, 1864.
" (2) 7 Nov. " " 18 Mch. 1865.

Senate: Alex. H. Stephens, Ga., vice-president.
R. M. T. Hunter, Va., president *pro tem.*

Members from Ala.: Robt. Jennson, jr., Richard W. Walker.
" " Ark.: Robt. W. Johnson, Augustus H. Garland.
" " Fla.: Jas. M. Baker, Augustus E. Maxwell.
" " Ga.: Benj. H. Hill, Herschel V. Johnson.
" " Ky.: Henry C. Burnett, Wm. E. Simms.
" " La.: Edward Sparrow, Thos. J. Semmes.
" " Miss.: J. W. C. Watson, Albert G. Brown.
" " Mo.: Waldo P. Johnson, L. M. Louis.
" " N. C.: Wm. T. Dortch, Wm. A. Graham.

Members from S C · Robt. W Barnwell, Jas. L. Orr
" " Tenn Gustavus A Henry, Landon C Haynes
" " Tex Louis T Wigfall, Williamson S. Oldham
" " Va Robert M T Hunter, Allen T Caperton
House Thos S Bocock, speaker

Members Alabama 9 Arkansas 3 Florida 2, Georgia 10 Kentucky 12, Louisiana 5, Mississippi 7, Missouri 7, North Carolina 10, South Carolina 6, Tennessee 11, Texas 6, Virginia 16, total 104

Kentucky and Missouri were represented though as states they never seceded This government lasted 4 years, 1 month, and 14 days after which the seceding states gradually returned to their allegiance, and by 23 May, 1872, all were again represented in Congress UNITED STATES, 1861-65

Before the first year ended in Dec. 1861 gold was worth 120 in confederate notes, in Dec 1862, 300, in Dec 1863, 1900, in Dec 1864, 6000, in Mch 1865, 6000

confederation at Paris, 14 July, 1790 BASTILE, CHAMP DE MARS

Confederation and Perpetual Union, Articles of. At the second Continental Congress at Philadelphia a committee was appointed, 11 June, 1776, to draft a form of confederation for the states It consisted of one member from each state, viz John Dickinson, Pa, chairman, Joseph Bartlett, N H, Samuel Adams, Mass, Roger Sherman, Conn, Stephen Hopkins, R I, R R Livingston, N Y, Francis Hopkinson, N J, Thomas McKean, Del, Thomas Stone, Md, Thomas Nelson, Va, Joseph Hewes, N C, Edward Rutledge, S C., Button Gwinnett, Ga

This committee presents a draft to Congress	12 July,	1776
Debated until laid aside	20 Aug	"
Taken up for reconsideration	8 Apr	1777
Adopted with amendments as "Articles of Confederation and Perpetual Union between the States"	15 Nov	"

The confederacy to be styled "The United States of America" These articles, 13 in number, were ratified by the states as follows

South Carolina	5 Feb	1778	Massachusetts	10 Mch	1778
New York	6 Feb	"	North Carolina	5 Apr	"
Rhode Island	9 Feb	"	New Jersey	19 Nov	"
Connecticut	12 Feb	"	Virginia	15 Dec.	"
Georgia	26 Feb	"	Delaware	1 Feb	1779
New Hampshire	4 Mch	"	Maryland	30 Jan	1781
Pennsylvania	5 Mch	"	MARYLAND, 1781		

Formally announced by all the states	1 Mch	1781
Congress assembles	2 Mch	"

UNITED STATES

Confederation of the Rhine. By the Act of Federation, subscribed to 12 July, 1806 the king of Bavaria and Würtemberg, the elector of Baden, and 13 minor princes united themselves in the league known as the "Confederation of the Rhine," under [illegible] of the French emperor, and undertook to furnish contingents amounting to 63,000 men in all wars in which the French emperor should engage It was joined by others, until, in 1808, it consisted of 4 kingdoms, 7 grand-duchies, 6 duchies, and 20 principalities This league ended with the fall of the French emperor, 1814, and in 1815 was replaced by the GERMANIC CONFEDERATION The Confederation of the Rhine put an end to the ancient German empire, after an existence of 1006 years, from Charlemagne (800) to Francis II, who soon after abdicated a sovereignty and title ended *de facto* in a great part of Germany, and assumed the title of emperor of Austria

conferences, ecclesiastical. One was held at Hampton court by prelates of the church of England and Puritan ministers, to effect a general union, at the instance of James I, 14, 16, 18 Jan 1604. It led to the authorized version of the Bible, made 1607-11 Some alterations in the church liturgy were agreed upon, but, these not satisfying the dissenters, no more was done — A conference of bishops and Presbyterian ministers, with the same view, was held in the Savoy, London, 15 Apr to 25 July, 1661. The dissenters' objections were generally disallowed, but some alterations were recommended in the prayer-book.—In the United States the Methodist Episcopal church calls its ecclesiastical bodies conferences. The general conference, once in 4 years, is the supreme legislative body Annual conferences in fixed territorial divisions, and quarterly conferences in presiding elders' districts, are subsidiary bodies.

First American conference	1773
First general conference..	24 Dec. 1784

confessional. AURICULAR CONFESSION.

confessions of faith, or *creeds.* "APOSTLES', ATHANASIAN, NICENE CREEDS J R Lumby's "History of the Creeds," pub 1874.

Confession of the Greek church was presented to Mahomet II in 1453 Superseded 1643 to one composed by Mogila, metropolitan of Kiev, the present standard	
Creed of Pius VI, i e, the Nicene creed, with addition of the peculiar dogmas of the Roman Catholic church, published by council of Trent	1564
Church of England retains the Apostles', Nicene, and Athanasian creeds with articles—42 in 1552, reduced to 39	1563
Confession of Augsburg (Lutheran) drawn up principally by Melanchthon, 1530, since modified, last by the "Form of Concord"	1579
WESTMINSTER CONFESSION framed 1643, adopted by the Presbyterian church of Scotland	1647
Congregational dissenters publish declaration of faith	1833

confirmation, or **laying on hands,** was practised by the apostles in 34 and 56 (Acts viii 17, xix 6), and general, some assert, in 190 In the Episcopal church it is the public profession of religion by an adult previously baptized It is a sacrament of the church of Rome

Conflans (*kon-flon'*), near Paris, Treaty of, between Louis XI of France and the dukes of Bourbon, Brittany, and Burgundy, 5 Oct 1465 Normandy was ceded to the duke of Berry, and an end put to the "War of the Public Good" It was confirmed by the treaty of Peronne, 1468.

Confu'cianism, the doctrines or system of morality taught by Confucius (K'ung Fû-tze or "the master K'ung"), 551-479 B.C., which has long been adopted in China as the basis of jurisprudence and education It inculcates no worship of a God and doubts a future state

congé d'élire ("permission to elect"), the license of a sovereign, as head of the church, to chapters and other bodies, to elect dignitaries, particularly bishops; the right asserted by Henry VIII, 1535 After the interdict of the pope upon England was removed in 1214, king John arranged with the clergy for electing bishops.

congela'tion, the act of freezing. Ice was produced in summer by chemical process, by Mr. Walker in 1783. Quicksilver was frozen without snow or ice in 1787. In 1810 Leslie froze water in an air-pump by evaporating sulphuric acid under it. Numerous freezing mixtures have been discovered since Intense cold is produced by evaporating liquefied carbonic acid gas. In 1857 Mr Harrison patented a machine for manufacturing ice by ether and salt-water, and made large blocks. In 1860 M Carré devised a method of freezing to − 60° by making water in a close vessel absorb and give off the gas ammonia. Siebe's ice-making machine was exhibited at the International Exhibition of 1862

In R. Reece's ice making machine (made known Dec 1868), liquefied ammonia is vaporized in a close vessel surrounded by water

Congo Free State, the result of discoveries by Henry M Stanley, was constituted and defined by the general act of the International Congo conference, signed at Berlin, 26 Feb 1885, and declared neutral and free to the trade of all nations The boundaries were defined by convention between the International Association of the Congo and Germany, 8 Nov 1884, Great Britain, 16 Dec 1884, Netherland, 27 Dec. 1884, France, 5 Feb 1885, and Portugal, 14 Feb. 1885. It includes a small section on the north bank of the Congo, from its mouth to Manyanga, from Manyanga to the mouth of the Mobangi the French occupy, from this point the state extends north to 4° N lat., thence eastward to 30° E lon, thence southward to lake Bangweolo 12° S. lat, thence west to 24° E lon, then northward to 6° S. lat., then westward to the south bank of the Congo at Nokki This area is estimated at 1,056,200 sq miles, with a population of from 8 000,000 to 10,000,000 The Congo and its navigable tributaries are its leading geographical feature. The state was formed under the sovereignty of the king of the Belgians individually, 1885, but in Aug 1889, he bequeathed to Belgium his sovereign rights in it. He has endowed it from his private fortune to the extent of $200,000 annually. On 31 July, 1890, its territories were declared inalienable, and a convention of 3 July, 1890, between Belgium and the state, reserved to Belgium the right to annex it after 10 years In 1890 the expenditures of the state above the Belgian subsidies exceeded its income by $125,000 The same year the "Congo Commercial Company" sent out an expedition to explore the Congo

Congregation of the Lord, a name taken by Scotch reformers, headed by John Knox, about 1546. Their leaders (earls of Glencairn, Argyle, Morton, etc.), called "lords of the congregation," signed the first bond or covenant which united the Protestants in one association, 3 Dec. 1557.—*Tytler.*

Congregationalists. English Congregationalism is not merely a development of English Puritanism; it is an independent system of church government, as distinct from Episcopacy and Presbyterianism as they are from each other. —*Schaff-Herzog's* "Encyc. of Religious Knowledge," p. 534.

Robert Browne defends separation from the English church..1575-82
[Termed Brownists or Separatists—unlike Puritans, who aimed to reform the church of England, they denounced it as idolatrous, false to Christianity and to truth.]
Henry Barrowe, Greenwood, and Penry, leaders in the movement, executed....6 Apr. 1593
Church retires to Amsterdam....1593-1600
Here under John Robinson (1575-1625), they plan a settlement in America, and a part of his congregation under elder Brewster start from Leyden....22 July, 1620
Arrival of the *Mayflower* at Plymouth....16 Dec. "
1. Church in America at Plymouth.... 1620
2. " " " " Salem....6 Aug. 1629
3. " " " " Dorchester....June, 1630
4. " " " " Boston....30 July, "
5. " " " " Watertown.... " "
6. " " " " Roxbury.... 1632
7. " " " " Lynn....July, "
8. " " " " Duxbury, 9. Marshfield, 10. Charlestown.... "
11. Church in America at Cambridge.... 1633
12. " " " " Ipswich.... 1634
First churches in New Hampshire at Dover and Exeter.... 1638
In Connecticut at New Haven and Milford.... 1639
Ten years after the arrival of the *Mayflower* there were but 5 Congregational churches on the continent, and 20 years after, 35.
Creative era of American Congregationalism....1620-48
Leading writers and ministers of this time were John Cotton, 1585-1652; Thomas Hooker, 1586-1647; John Norton, 1606-1663; John Davenport, 1597-1670; Richard Mather....1596-1669
General synods have been held: in 1637, at Newtown, now Cambridge, Mass., on the antinomian teachings of the rev. John Wheelwright and Mrs. Ann Hutchinson. MASSACHUSETTS. At Cambridge, 1646-48, when the Westminster Confession was adopted, and a platform of church discipline framed; at Albany in 1852, abrogating a plan of union with the Presbyterians; at Boston, 1865, dealing particularly with the growth of the church.
Important local synod at Boston, 1662, and another on reform at Boston.... 1679
Saybrook platform adopted by a synod called at Saybrook, Conn., by the legislature of Connecticut.... 1708
National council meets triennially since.... 1871
The following are the principal theological seminaries: Andover, Mass., opened 1808; Bangor, Me., 1817; Yale, 1822; Hartford, 1834; Oberlin, O., 1835; Chicago, 1858; Pacific, Oakland, Cal., 1869.
In 1880 the Congregational churches in the U. S. were 3743; members, 384,332; in Sabbath-schools, 444,628; ministers, 3577.
In 1890, churches, 4868; members, 512,771; value of church property, $43,335,427. INDEPENDENTS.

congress. An assembly of representative men, to confer on the affairs of one or more nations. Among the chief congresses of Europe were those of

Münster.... 1643-48
Nimeguen.... 1676-78
Ryswick.... 1697
Utrecht.... 1713
Soissons.... 1728
Antwerp....8 Apr. 1793
Rastadt....9 Dec. 1797-99
Chatillon....5 Feb. 1814
Vienna....3 Nov. "
Aix-la-Chapelle....9 Oct. 1818
Carlsbad....1 Aug. 1819
Troppau....20 Oct. 1820
Laybach....6 May, 1821
Verona....25 Aug. 1822
Paris....16 Jan.-22 Apr. 1856
Frankfort (GERMANY)....16-31 Aug. 1863
Constantinople....23 Dec. 1876-20 Jan. 1878
Berlin....13 June-13 July, "
ALLIANCES, CHURCH, CONVENTIONS, etc.

Congress, Confederate. CONFEDERATE STATES.

Congress, United States. UNITED STATES throughout. REPRESENTATIVES and SENATE.

Congress, United States, characterized. UNITED STATES. 1st congress, 1791; 31st, 1849; 34th, 1855; 37th, 1863.

Congreve rockets. ROCKETS.

conic sections. Certain properties were probably known to the Greeks 4 or 5 centuries before the Christian era, and their study was cultivated in the time of Plato, 390 B.C. The earliest treatise on them was written by Aristæus, about 330 B.C. Apollonius's 8 books were written about 240 B.C. The investigation of the parabola of projectiles was begun by Galileo, that of the ellipse in the orbit of planets by Kepler, and of comets by Newton.

"Connaissance des Temps" (*ko-ne'-sān-s dê tan*), the French nautical almanac, continuing Hecker's "Ephemerides," first published by Picard, 1679.

Connaught, W. Ireland; long a nominal kingdom, divided into counties, 1590.

Connecticut, U. S. (Ind. *Quonecktacut,* i.e. Long River or River of Pines), one of the 6 New England and of the 13 original states, lies between 41° and 42° 3′ N. lat. and 71° 55′ and 73° 50′ W. lon. Massachusetts lies on the north, Rhode Island on the east, Long Island sound on the south, and New York on the west. The southwest corner projects along the sound for about 13 miles. Area, 4990 sq. miles, in 8 counties. Pop. 1890, 746,258; 1900, 908,420. Capital, Hartford.

Adrian Block, a Dutch navigator, first explores the Connecticut river as far as Hartford.... 1614
Robert, earl of Warwick, president of the council of Plymouth, grants to lord Say and Seal, and 11 others, among them John Hampden and John Pym, all that part of New England which lies west from the Narragansett river, 120 miles on the coast, and thence in latitude and breadth aforesaid to the Pacific ocean....19 Mch. 1631
[The council of Plymouth the previous year had granted the whole tract to the earl of Warwick, and the grant had been confirmed to him by a patent from king Charles I.]
Wahquimacut, a sachem from the Connecticut river, visits Plymouth and Boston, asking colonial governors to send settlers to that river.... "
[Governor Winthrop of Massachusetts does not favor the movement.]
John Oldham, from Dorchester, Mass., and 3 others visit the Connecticut....Sept. 1633
William Holmes of Plymouth prepares the frame of a house with a board covering, places it on a vessel, and sails for the Connecticut river; passes a small Dutch fort, "The House of Good Hope," at Hartford, and landing on the west bank erects the first English house in C[illegible] (now Windsor). Oct. "
Dutch at New Netherlands, with 70 men, make a feeble attempt to drive the settlers away.... 1634
Rev. Thomas Hooker, of Newtown (now Cambridge), Mass., advocates new settlements on the Connecticut river.... "
About 60 men, women, and children, with horses, cattle, and swine, start through the wilderness from near Boston to the Connecticut river....15 Oct. 1635
They reach the river about the middle of....Nov. "
Colonists from Massachusetts, led by John Winthrop, son of gov. Winthrop, fortify the mouth of the Connecticut, and call the fort Saybrook, in honor of lords Say and Brooke..9 Nov. "
A Dutch vessel appears off the mouth, but is not suffered to land....Nov. "
Great suffering at Windsor, on the Connecticut, during the winter of....1635-36
[Some return through the wilderness to Massachusetts settlements, others by water. A few remain. The settlers lose in cattle alone about $1000.]
First court in Connecticut held at Newtown (Hartford), 26 Apr. 1636
Rev. Thomas Hooker, "the light of the western churches," and rev. Mr. Stone, with 100 men, women, and children, and 160 head of cattle, leave Cambridge, Mass., for the Connecticut river through the wilderness....June, "
They reach the river early in....July "
John Oldham murdered by the Indians near Block Island (MASSACHUSETTS)....July, "
War with the Pequots.... "
[The Pequots, with at least 700 warriors, then occupied eastern Connecticut, and ruled part of Long island.]
An expedition against the Pequots and Indians on Block island is sent from Massachusetts under John Endicott, 25 Aug.-14 Sept. "
[It exasperated but did not subdue the Indians.]
Roger Williams of Rhode Island prevents a league between the Pequots and Narragansetts.... "
Fort at Saybrook, at the mouth of the Connecticut, beleaguered by the Pequots all the winter of....1636-37
About 30 colonists of Connecticut killed by the Pequots during the winter of (HILDRETH, U. S.).... "
Court at Newtown (Hartford) applies to Massachusetts for aid against the Pequots....21 Feb. 1637

[The name Newtown is changed to Hartford, Watertown to Wethersfield, and Dorchester to Windsor by this court. Hartford was so named in honor to the rev Mr Stone, who was born at Hartford, Engl]

Wethersfield attacked by the Pequots, several killed Apr 1637

The court at Hartford, bent on offensive war against the Pequots call for 88 men—42 from Hartford, 30 from Windsor, 16 from Wethersfield 1 May, "

These are joined by Uncas, sachem of the Mohegans, with 70 warriors at Saybrook fort 15 May, "

[The plan was to attack the Pequots in their 2 strongholds, one on Fort hill, in Groton, about 4 miles east of New London, the other on the west side of Mystic hill, near Mystic village.]

Captain John Mason of Windsor commanding, the expedition sails from fort Saybrook for Narragansett bay, to surprise the Pequot fort 19 May, "

At Narragansett bay about 200 Narragansett warriors join him He approaches the Pequot fort on the evening of 25 May, and next morning at early light, he attacks and completely destroys it, together with about 600 Indians, men, women, and children, losing 2 killed and about 20 wounded, 26 May "

Court of Connecticut calls for 40 more men for the war against the Pequots 26 June, "

Pequots attempt to escape into the wilderness westward Capt. Stoughton, with a Massachusetts company, pursues along Long Island sound With Sassacus, their sachem, the Pequots take shelter in a swamp near Fairfield, and after another severe fight surrender, but their sachem and a few followers escape 13 July "

[These fled to the Mohawks, who treacherously murdered them The prisoners were sold into slavery or incorporated with other tribes "There remained not a sannup nor a squaw, not a warrior nor a child "]

The *Hector* lands at Boston rev John Davenport, Theophilus Eaton, and Edward Hopkins 26 July, "

Mr Eaton and others explore the lands and harbors of Connecticut on the sea coast, and select Quinnipiack (now New Haven) for a settlement in the autumn of "

Rev John Davenport, Mr Eaton, and others sail from Boston and arrive at Quinnipiack about the middle of Apr 1638

Gloomy prospects of the colonists Great earthquake 1 June, "

Colonists purchase land in and about New Haven of the Indians 24 Nov "

[The New Haven colonists were the most opulent company that came into New England.—*Trumbull's* "History of Connecticut."]

All free planters convene at Hartford and frame a constitution for civil government 14 Jan 1639

First constitution of Connecticut adopted at Hartford Apr "

General election held at Hartford " "

[John Haynes chosen governor]

General election held at Quinnipiack (New Haven) 25 Oct. "

[Theophilus Eaton chosen governor]

Milford and Guilford purchased of the Indians and settled. "

[Laws founded upon and administered according to the Scriptures]

Settlement made at Saybrook by George Fenwick "

Fourteen capital laws of Connecticut enacted, founded on passages of Scripture. 2 Apr 1642

Boundary line between Connecticut and Massachusetts first run by Woodward and Saffery "

Colonies of Massachusetts Bay, Plymouth, Connecticut, and New Haven confederate under the name of the United Colonies of New England 19 May, 1643

Connecticut purchases of col George Fenwick the old Connecticut patent for 1600*l*, and assumes jurisdiction over the whole territory 1644

New London settled 1648

Governors and magistrates receive no salaries in Connecticut up to "

[Then the governor's salary was fixed at 30*l*.]

Governor Stuyvesant, of the New Netherlands, visits Hartford to settle certain boundary questions with the New England United Colonies 11 Sept. 1650

Norwalk settled 1651

Middletown settled "

French agents from Quebec visit the Connecticut colonists, asking aid against the 5 nations of New York (the Iroquois) "

Alarm and distress of the colonists owing to trouble with the Dutch 1653

Commissioners are for war, but Massachusetts refuses assistance "

They address Parliament and Cromwell for aid "

Colony, ordered by Parliament to treat the Dutch as enemies, seize the Dutch house and lands at Hartford 1654

Death of gov Haynes "

Law against Quakers to be fined and sent out of jurisdiction, Oct. 1656

Gov John Winthrop obtains for Connecticut a charter, with ample privileges, from Charles II 20 Apr 1662

[This charter united New Haven with Hartford in one colony, extending from Narragansett river to the Pacific, and gave the colonists entire self government.]

Charles II grants a patent to his brother, the duke of York, of extensive tracts, including the west side of Connecticut river, 12 Mch 1664

Col Richard Nichols, governor of New York, and commissioners from Connecticut, fix the western boundary of Connecticut, beginning on the east side of Mamaroneck creek and, thence north-northwest to the Massachusetts line. The southern line was determined to be the sound, Connecticut losing her possessions on Long island 30 Nov. 1664

United colony elects John Winthrop governor 1665

[This union was at first opposed by New Haven, under the rev Mr Davenport]

Lyme made a town May, 1667

Haddam made a town Oct 1668

Maj Andros the new governor of New York, claims under the duke of York all land west of the Connecticut river 1675

Maj Andros appears before the fort at Saybrook with an armed force, and demands its surrender 11 July, "

[It is refused by capt Bull, and the patent and commission forbidden to be read]

War with Philip, sachem of the Wampanoags. "

Connecticut furnishes 315 men in the fight at Narragansett fort (MASSACHUSETTS) 19 Dec "

Death of gov John Winthrop 5 Apr 1676

Boundary between Connecticut and New York of 1664 superseded by that of 1683

[At this time the quadrilateral at the southwest corner of the state first appears]

Sir Edmund Andros, the royal governor, comes to Hartford and demands the charter in the name of king James II 31 Oct 1687

[After a long discussion in the assembly early in the evening the lights are extinguished, and the charter is taken from the table and secreted by capt William Wadsworth of Hartford in a hollow oak tree, known since as the "charter oak," on the estate of the Wyllyses, across the river]

Sir Edmund Andros assumes the government, selects councillors, seizes the records of the colony, and rules arbitrarily 31 Oct. "

QUO WARRANTO ACT

Overthrow of sir Edmund Andros's government at Boston on hearing of the revolution in England and flight of James II, 18 Apr 1689

Charter recovered and free government restored in Connecticut, 9 May, "

William and Mary proclaimed at Hartford with great ceremony and joy 13 June, "

Col Benjamin Fletcher, governor of New York, comes to Hartford while the assembly is in session and demands command of the militia under commission from the king 26 Oct 1693

[The assembly refusing, he orders the militia under arms, and attempts to read his commission to them and assume command Capt Wadsworth prevents this by ordering the drums to beat, threatening death to the governor if he persists]

Charter ratified by William III Apr 1694

Boundary of 1683 between New York and Connecticut confirmed by William III 1700

Charter for a college at New Haven granted by the general court (YALE COLLEGE) 9 Oct 1701

First Baptist church formed in Connecticut at Groton 1705

First issue of bills of credit by Connecticut, 8000*l* for an anticipated expedition against Canada 1709

First printer in the colony, Thomas Short, from Boston, at New London "

He publishes the "Saybrook Platform of Church Discipline" 1710

[He was followed by Timothy Green, 1714, a descendant of Samuel Green, of Cambridge, Mass., the first printer in North America —*Trumbull's* "History of Connecticut "]

Settlement of the boundary with Massachusetts 1713

[Massachusetts grants to Connecticut 107,793 acres, the amount that Massachusetts had encroached upon Connecticut. The tract was sold by Connecticut in 1716 for about $2274, given to Yale college. Boundary run as it now is 1826, leaving indentation to Massachusetts about 2 miles square, as compensation for towns previously lost.]

First state house built at Hartford 1720

["A condition of society so happy as that enjoyed by Connecticut at this period has been rare in the experience of mankind "—*Palfrey's* "History of New England," vol iv]

Gurdon Saltonstall, governor for 16 years, d. 20 Sept. 1724

First church steeple raised in Connecticut at Guilford 1726

Final boundary established with Rhode Island 1728

Joint survey made between New York and Connecticut 1731

Connecticut furnishes 1000 men for land and marine service against Louisburg 1745

First silk coat and stockings of New England production were worn by governor Law of Connecticut 1747

Phineas Lyman maj-gen of the Connecticut forces, second in command at the battle of lake George. 6 Sept 1755

[Sir William Johnson being disabled, gen Lyman conducted the engagement successfully to Dieskau's defeat]

Citizens of Connecticut, known as the Susquehanna company, purchase from the 6 nations land, 70 miles in length, on the Susquehanna river, and extending from 10 miles east of that river west 140 miles, for about $10,000, 11 July, 1754. It includes the Wyoming valley, where they make a settlement 1763

[This leads to a long controversy between Connecticut and Pennsylvania. "But for the Revolution and the check occasioned by the Wyoming massacre, and the appearance of popular government in place of Penn's, nothing could have prevented the establishment of Connecticut's authority over all the region embraced in her western claim "—*Alexander Johnston's* "Connecticut" SUSQUEHANNA SETTLERS]

Connecticut *Courant*, published by Thomas Green, at Hartford, first issued 26 Oct. 1764

[Continued till now without interruption or change of name]

Jared Ingersoll sent by Connecticut to England to oppose the stamp act "

He accepts the position of stamp master, and is compelled by the citizens to resign 19 Sept. 1765

CON

Gov. Thomas Fitch consents to take the oath for the support of the stamp-act.. 1766

[He is dismissed at the next election.]

Connecticut *Journal* first published at New Haven............ 1767

Jonathan Trumbull elected governor.......................... 1769

[The only colonial governor who favored independence in 1776. He was elected governor annually until 1784. The name "Brother Jonathan," humorously bestowed upon him by gen. Washington, has been applied to the U. S.]

First manufacture of tin-ware by Edward Patterson, commenced at Berlin, Conn.. 1770

Eliphalet Dyer, Roger Sherman, and Silas Deane, elected at Norwich to the first Continental Congress...........6 June, 1774

Israel Putnam, of Pomfret, Conn., hastens to Boston on hearing of the battle of Lexington; arrives.....................21 Apr. 1775

[Riding on one horse 100 miles in 18 hours.]

Col. Samuel H. Parsons and Benedict Arnold, at Hartford, plan the capture of Ticonderoga.............................27 Apr. "

Benedict Arnold marches from New Haven with his company and reaches Boston...29 Apr. "

Surrender of TICONDEROGA to col. Ethan Allen and Benedict Arnold...10 May, "

General assembly authorize bills of credit to $500,000 to equip 8 regiments..11 May, "

Ex-gov. Tryon with 2000 men destroys Danbury.......26 Apr. 1777

[Gen. David Wooster of Connecticut is mortally wounded.]

Gen. Tryon lands at New Haven with about 3000 men and plunders it...5 July, 1778

Fairfield, Green's Farm, and Norwalk burned................. "

Gen. Tryon, from Kingsbridge, N. Y., with 1500 troops destroys the salt-works at Horseneck, Conn. Here gen. Putnam is said to have ridden down a declivity in escaping..........26 Mch. 1779

Benedict Arnold plunders and burns New London......6 Sept. 1781

[Fort Griswold across the river is captured the same day, and out of a garrison of 150 men, 73 are killed, including their commander, col. Ledyard, and 30 wounded, mostly after the surrender. Connecticut furnished during the Revolution 31,959 troops, only Massachusetts furnishing more.] ARMY.

Samuel Seabury, D.D., seeks in England consecration as bishop of Connecticut; being refused, he is consecrated by 3 bishops of the Episcopal church in Scotland ....14 Nov. 1784

Connecticut frees her slaves.................................. "

Connecticut makes a qualified cession to the U. S. of all territory south of 41° N. lat. and west of a line 120 miles west of Pennsylvania.....................................14 Sept. 1786

[The space left to Connecticut in Ohio is known as the Western Reserve, and is claimed as a compensation for the territory relinquished in Pennsylvania.]

Constitution of the U. S. ratified by Connecticut; vote 128 to 40, 9 Jan. 1788

First Methodist church established in Connecticut at Stratford, 26 Sept. 1789

Wooden clocks first made at Waterbury...................... 1790

Gen. Israel Putnam dies at Brookline, Conn...........19 May, "

Connecticut bestows upon citizens, especially those of Danbury, Fairfield, Groton, New London, and Norwalk, who had suffered during the Revolution, half a million acres at the west end of the Western Reserve in Ohio, hence known as "Fire lands".. 1792

Connecticut sells to the Connecticut Land Company, of 320 citizens, 3,200,000 acres, the remainder of the tract between lake Erie and 41° N. lat.................................. 1795

[The price, $1,200,000, was made a state school fund.]

Connecticut through gov. Trumbull, executes surrender to the U. S. of jurisdiction over the Western Reserve, Ohio.30 May, 1800

Connecticut opposed to war of............................. 1812

New London blockaded by sir Thomas Hardy with British ships for 20 months.................................June, 1813

Stonington bombarded by sir Thomas Hardy's fleet..9–12 Aug. 1814

Delegates from the several New England legislatures meet in convention at Hartford to consider the grievances caused by the war, and to devise measures for its termination..15 Dec. "

[This convention remained in secret session 3 weeks. The war ended before the convention published its resolutions. "The convention was legitimate in its origin, in no respect violating any provisions of the Constitution of the U. S., either in its letter or its spirit."—Theo. Dwight's "Hist. Hartford Convention."]

Connecticut adopts a state constitution in place of the royal charter, by a vote of 13,918 to 12,361.................5 Oct. 1818

Washington college (Episcopal) chartered at Hartford........ 1823

[Name changed to Trinity, 1845.]

Wesleyan university at Middletown (Methodist) chartered.... 1831

Prudence Crandall opens a school for colored children at Canterbury, Windham county.. 1833

[She is arrested and sent to jail. On failure to convict her, the school-house is sacked by a mob, and the inmates expelled.]

Henry Barnard first state superintendent of public instruction, 1838

Ship *Amistad*, Spanish, brought into New London by lieut. Geding, of the U. S. brig *Washington* (AMISTAD)......29 Aug. 1839

John W. Niles appointed postmaster-general in Van Buren's cabinet..25 May, 1840

Amendment to art. viii. of the state constitution abolishing freehold qualification for electors, etc., ratified.............Oct. 1845

State Teachers' association organized..................7 Apr. 1846

Sheffield Scientific school of Yale university opened........ 1847

Act passed for registering births, marriages, and deaths....... 1848

Isaac Toucey appointed attorney-general.............21 June, "

Connecticut normal and training school opens at New Britain, 15 May, 1850

Samuel Colt begins the manufacture of revolvers at Hartford. 1852

Samuel D. Hubbard appointed postmaster-general......31 Aug. 1852

State reform school at Meriden opened..................1 Mch. 1854

Legislature establishes the Supreme Court of Errors and the Superior court, and abolishes the county courts........May, 1855

Amendment to state constitution ratified, making ability to read the constitution a qualification for electors.........Oct. "

Act abolishing school societies and putting the support of schools upon towns, who are to elect a board of school visitors of 3, 6, or 9 members..................................1 July, 1856

Charter oak at Hartford blown down.....................21 Aug. "

State constitution amended by vote of 7290 to 6062, so that judges of the Supreme Court of Errors and Superior court shall sit 8 years, but may be removed by impeachment..Oct. "

Isaac Toucey appointed secretary of the navy..........6 Mch. 1857

Connecticut School for Imbeciles opened at Lakeville......... 1858

Gov. Buckingham issues a proclamation ordering the purchase of equipments for an army of 5000 men, and urging militia companies to fill their ranks ....17 Jan. 1861

Gideon Welles appointed secretary of the navy........5 Mch. "

First infantry, 780 3-months' men, leaves New Haven for Washington, under col. Daniel Tyler.....................9 May, "

First regiment enlisted for 3 years, the 4th Connecticut infantry, leaves Hartford under col. Levi Woodhouse.....10 June, "

Brig.-gen. Nathaniel Lyon, b. Ashford, 14 July, 1819; killed in battle of Wilson's Creek, Mo.........................10 Aug. "

Gen. Joseph K. F. Mansfield, b. New Haven, 22 Dec. 1803; killed in battle of Antietam...................................17 Sept. 1862

Rear-admiral Andrew Hull Foote, b. New Haven, 12 Sept. 1806; d. in New York city.....................................26 June, 1863

Maj.-gen. John Sedgwick, b. Cornwall, 13 Sept. 1813; killed in battle of Spottsylvania.................................9 May, 1864

50,623 3-years' troops furnished during the war........... 1861–65

State Board of Fish Commissioners created.................. 1865

State Board of Education organized, with Daniel C. Gilman as secretary .... "

Lydia Sigourney, poet, d. in Hartford.................10 June, "

Legislature, which convened at Hartford, 3 May, adjourns after the longest session on record up to date..................21 July, "

An exciting election for governor; pres. Johnson's influence favoring James E. English; Joseph R. Hawley, Republican, elected by only 541 majority...............................Apr. 1866

Legislature ratifies the 14th amendment to the Constitution, 30 June, "

Legislature ratifies the 15th amendment to the Constitution, 16 Mch. 1869

Normal school at New Britain, closed for 2 years for lack of appropriation, is reopened................................Sept. "

State Industrial School for Girls, at Middletown, opened, June, 1870

Election for governor being close, a joint committee of the General Assembly appointed to examine returns, 3 May; report total vote 94,860; for Marshall Jewell, Republican, 47,473; for James E. English, 47,373; scattering, 14; and declare Jewell elected...10 May, 1871

Gov. Jewell assumes office.............................16 May, "

Morgan school at Clinton opened .... "

Noah Porter elected president of Yale university in place of Theodore D. Woolsey, resigned.................................. "

Temperance party, represented by about 100 delegates, meets at New Haven, and nominates a full state ticket.....13 Dec. "

Labor-reform party holds a state convention at Bridgeport, and nominates a state ticket...............................3 Jan. 1872

Jesse Olney, geographer, b. 1798; d. at Stratford.......30 July, "

State constitution amended; all sessions of the General Assembly, from May, 1875, to be held at Hartford........7 Oct. 1873

Ex-gov. and U. S. senator W. A. Buckingham, d. at Norwich, 4 Feb. 1875

State constitution amended: Tuesday after 1st Monday in Nov. made general election day; Wednesday after 1st Monday in Jan. the day of meeting of General Assembly.........2 Oct. "

Orris S. Ferry, U. S. senator from Connecticut, d. in Norwalk, 21 Nov. "

"Greenback men" meet in convention at New Haven, 22 Feb. 1876

William H. Barnum, Democrat, elected to fill the unexpired term of U. S. senator Ferry, deceased..................17 May, "

Agricultural experiment station established by law........... 1877

Gideon Welles, ex-secretary of navy, d. at Hartford....11 Feb. 1878

Act passed for state board of health, of 6 members....13 Mch. "

Legislature occupies the new capitol for the first time, 26 Mch. "

There being no choice for state officers, Nov. 1878, the legislature elects Charles B. Andrews governor.................9 Jan. 1879

Boundary dispute between New York and Connecticut, begun in 1856, is settled, the southern boundary being fixed through the middle of Long Island sound; the "oblong tract," 4.68 sq. miles in area, lying 20 miles east of the North river, goes to NEW YORK.. 1880

Board of Pardons, consisting of the governor, a judge of the Supreme Court of Errors, and 4 persons appointed by the General Assembly, who must all concur in a pardon, is created by legislature.................................3 Jan.–3 May, 1883

Bronze memorial statue of William A. Buckingham, Connecticut's war governor, is unveiled in Hartford.........18 June, 1884

State constitution amended: biennial legislative sessions to begin in 1887; ratified by 30,520 to 10,380...............6 Oct. "

Benjamin Silliman, chemist, b. 1816; d. at New Haven, 14 June, 1885

President Noah Porter of Yale university resigns............ 1886

Republican candidates for state offices elected by the legislature, there being no choice in state election of 2 Nov. 1886, Jan. 1887

First text-book ever published by the state, a small treatise on the effect of alcohol on the human system, is issued and distributed to the schools.......................................Sept. "

Equestrian statue of gen. Israel Putnam erected at Brooklyn, Windham county, and unveiled..................14 June, 1888

t Monday in Sept. designated a public holiday (Labor-day)
state normal school established at Willimantic, and
anti-screen" saloon law, and modified Australian ballot
w passed by legislature in session.........9 Jan.–22 June
ed H. Terry, maj.-gen. U. S. A., b. 1827; d. at New Haven
16 Dec.

dlock between the two houses of the legislature on the
vernorship...7 Jan.
nocratic candidates for state offices sworn in by the Senate
fused possession by Republican incumbents.........13 Jan.
Bulkeley by proclamation warns the citizens against rec-
gnizing the Democratic state officers..................19 Jan.
Barnum, b. 1810; d. at Bridgeport..................7 April
erior court decides in favor of gov. Bulkeley.........24 June
h claimants to governorship agree to take the matter into
e State Supreme court.................................1 Oct.
gov. Hobart B. Bigelow d. at New Haven...............12 Oct.
he suit of Morris, Democrat, versus Bulkeley, Republican,
e Supreme court holds Bulkeley to be governor.....5 Jan.
iel Grant, one of the famous triplets of Torrington, d.
ged 71 years, his 2 brothers surviving..................5 Oct.
ebration of the 250th anniversary of the founding of Stam-
ord...15 Oct.

GOVERNORS OF THE CONNECTICUT COLONY.

Name.	Date.
...n Haynes	1639
...ward Hopkins	1640
...n Haynes	1641
...orge Wyllys	1642
...n Haynes and Edward Hopkins, alternately from	1643
...omas Welles	1655
...n Webster	1656
...n Winthrop	1657
...omas Welles	1658
...n Winthrop	1659

Until this time no person could be elected to a second term im-
diately following the first.

GOVERNORS OF THE NEW HAVEN COLONY.

Name.	Date.
...ophilus Eaton	1639
...ncis Newman	1658
...lliam Leete	1661

GOVERNORS OF CONNECTICUT.

Name.	Date.	Remarks.
...n Winthrop	1665 to 1676	
...lliam Leete	1676 " 1683	
...bert Treat	1683 " 1687	
...mund Andros	1687 " 1689	Royal governor.
...bert Treat	1689 " 1698	
.... John Winthrop	1698 " 1707	

UNITED STATES SENATORS...

Name.	No. of Congress.
...ver Ellsworth	1st to 4th
...lliam S. Johnson	1st
...ger Sherman	2d
...phen Nix Mitchell	3d
...mes Hillhouse	4th to 11th
...nathan Trumbull	4th
...iah Tracy	4th to 8th
...auncey Goodrich	10th " 12th
...muel W. Dana	11th " 16th
...vid Daggett	13th " 15th
...mes Lanman	16th " 18th
...ijah Boardman	17th
...enry W. Edwards	18th to 19th
...lvin Willey	19th " 21st
...muel A. Foote	20th " 22d
...deon Tomlinson	22d " 24th
...athan Smith	23d
...hn M. Niles	24th to 25th
...rry Smith	25th " 27th
...addeus Betts	26th
...bez W. Huntington	26th to 29th
...hn M. Niles	28th " 30th
...oger S. Baldwin	30th " 31st
...ruman Smith	31st " 33d
...saac Toucey	32d " 34th
...rancis Gillett	33d
...afayette Foster	34th to 39th
...ames Dixon	35th " 40th
...rris S. Ferry	40th " 44th
...illiam A. Buckingham	41st " 43d
...illiam W. Eaton	43d " 46th
...ames E. English	44th
...illiam H. Barnum	44th to 45th
...rville H. Platt	46th
...oseph R. Hawley	47th

CON

GOVERNORS OF CONNECTICUT.—(Continued.)

Name.	Date.	Remarks.
Gurdon Saltonstall	1707 to 1724	
Joseph Talcott	1724 " 1741	
Jonathan Law	1741 " 1750	
Roger Wolcott	1750 " 1754	
Thomas Fitch	1754 " 1766	
William Pitkin	1766 " 1769	
Jonathan Trumbull	1769 " 1784	The only one of the colonial governors that remained true to the people against Great Britain.
Mathew Griswold	1784 " 1786	
Samuel Huntington	1786 " 1796	Federal.
Oliver Wolcott	1796 " 1798	"
Jonathan Trumbull	1798 " 1809	"
John Treadwell	1809 " 1811	"
Roger Griswold	1811 " 1813	"
John Cotton Smith	1813 " 1817	"
Oliver Wolcott	1817 " 1827	Democrat-Republican.
Gideon Tomlinson	1827 " 1831	
John S. Peters	1831 " 1833	
H. W. Edwards	1833 " 1834	Democrat.
Samuel A. Foote	1834 " 1835	"
H. W. Edwards	1835 " 1838	"
W. W. Ellsworth	1838 " 1842	Whig.
C. F. Cleveland	1842 " 1844	Democrat.
Roger S. Baldwin	1844 " 1846	Whig.
Clark Bissell	1846 " 1849	"
Joseph Trumbull	1849 " 1850	"
Thomas H. Seymour	1850 " 1853	Democrat.
Charles H. Pond	1853 " 1854	"
Henry Dutton	1854 " 1855	Whig.
W. T. Minor	1855 " 1857	Republican.
A. H. Holley	1857 " 1858	"
William A. Buckingham	1858 " 1866	" war governor.
Joseph R. Hawley	1866 " 1867	"
James E. English	[illegible] " 1869	Democrat.
Marshall Jewell	[illegible] " 1870	Republican.
James E. English	[illegible] " 1871	Democrat.
Marshall Jewell	[illegible]	Republican.
Charles R. Ingersoll	[illegible]	Democrat.
R. D. Hubbard	[illegible]	...Governors chosen ...ually until 1876, ...annually since.
...les B. Andrews	[illegible]	...lican.
...Bigelow	[illegible]	
...M. Waller	[illegible]	...ocrat.
...B. Harrison	[illegible]	...lican.
...C. Lounsbury	[illegible]	
...G. Bulkeley	[illegible]	
...D. Morris	[illegible]	
...ncent Coffin	[illegible]	

Connor, Ireland. The bishopric was united to Down, 1442. The first prelate, Ængus Macnisius, died 507. Both sees were added to Dromore on the death of its last bishop, 1842, under the Irish Church Temporalities act, 1833.

conquest, in British history, when William, duke of Normandy, overcame Harold II. at Hastings, 14 Oct. 1066, and obtained the crown which he claimed under the will of Edward the Confessor (Edgar being the rightful heir). William, though styled the Conqueror, succeeded to the crown by compact. He defeated Harold, himself a usurper, but much of the kingdom held out against him; and he swore to observe the laws and customs of the realm, in order to win the people. Formerly, English judges used to reprehend a barrister who said casually William the Conqueror, instead of William I.—*Selden*. Maclise exhibited 42 drawings on the events of the Norman conquest, in May, 1857. E. A. Freeman's "History of the Norman Conquest," 6 vols., 1870-79.

conscience, liberty of, a principle of Christianity (1 Cor. x. 29); repudiated by Romanism; proclaimed by James II. for political purposes, 1687. MASSACHUSETTS, 1635, regarding Roger Williams.

conscript fathers (*patres conscripti*). Roman senators were so called because their names were in registers of the senate.

conscription, a mode, derived from the Romans, of recruiting armies. On 5 Sept. 1798, a military conscription was ordained in France, of all men from 20 to 25 years of age, from whom selections were made. A conscription for 350,000 men took place in Jan. 1813, after the Russian disasters, and in Dec. same year another for 300,000 after the battle of Leipsic. Estimated conscriptions, 1793-1813, 4,103,000. The law of 1818 (modified in 1824, 1832, and 1868) assigned an annual contingent to each department. The conscription was enlarged and modified by the army bill of Feb. 1868. A reorganization of the army began in 1871, after the war with Germany; substitutes were allowed under certain conditions. Conscription for Great Britain was discussed in 1875. MILITIA. In the American civil war (1861-65) conscription was resorted to by both governments. The national armies, however, were less dependent on the measure, as large bounties brought them [illegible] volunteers. The first confederate conscription law, [illegible] 1862, annulled all contracts with volunteers for short [illegible] holding them for 2 additional years, and made every [illegible] male between 18 and 35 liable to service at a moment's [illegible] On 27 Sept. the law was extended to men between [illegible] 45 years of age. In July, 1863, all between 18 and 45 [illegible] called into active service. In Feb. 1864, the law was [illegible] to all between 17 and 50. DRAFT RIOTS.

[illegible]ecration. Aaron and his sons were consecrated [illegible] B.C. (Lev. viii.). The Jewish tabernacle was ded[illegible] B.C., and Solomon's temple, 1004 B.C. (1 Kings viii.). [illegible] of churches began in the 2d century. Anciently [illegible] of popes was deferred until the emperor as[illegible] election. Gregory IV. desired to have his elec[illegible] by the emperor Louis in 828.—*Hénault*. The [illegible] of churches, places of burial, etc., is permitted by [illegible] An act relating to the consecration of church[illegible] church of England, passed 29 Aug. 1867, was [illegible] 1868. A form of consecration was adopted by [illegible] but not sanctioned by the crown, Apr. 1712. It [illegible], but is not compulsory.—*Burn*. The form [illegible] bishops in the church of England is in the [illegible] of 1549.—*Stow*. BISHOPS, Episcopal.

[illegible]vation of force. The doctrine that no [illegible] can be created or destroyed, though it may be [illegible] maintained by Faraday, Grove, Helmholtz, [illegible] other philosophers. CORRELATION.

[illegible]atives, a name of modern date, given in [illegible] to a political party whose leading principle is [illegible] of national institutions, said to have been in[illegible] Wilson Croker in 1830. Conservative (a Tory), [illegible] usage, is now opposed to Liberal. It was termed [illegible] by Macaulay in *Edinburgh Review*, July, 1832. [illegible] acknowledged himself a conservative when re[illegible] Irish party in Parliament as an Orangeman; but [illegible] wards separated from him called their principles conservative, opposed to those he had now adopted. A meeting of the National Union of Conservative Associations was held at the Crystal Palace, London, 24 June, 1872. The party in the minority at elections in 1868, in England, obtained a majority in Feb. 1874, and came into office. They were again in a minority, and resigned, 28 Apr. 1880. The marquis of Salisbury became leader of the party, 9 May, 1881, succeeding the earl of Beaconsfield, who died 19 Apr. previous. ADMINISTRATIONS.

conservatoires, institutions for cultivating music and the arts on the European continent. One was established at Naples in 1537. The singing-school at Paris, founded in 1784, closed in 1789, was reopened in 1793 as the "Institut National de Musique," and, as reorganized, was renamed "Conservatoire de Musique" in 1795, and flourished under Cherubini (1822-42). The "Conservatoire des Arts et Metiers," established in 1784, has museum and library, and provides lectures to workmen.

consistories, for regulating discipline and worship in the Lutheran church in Germany, were established at the Reformation—first, Wittenberg, in 1542; others after the peace of Augsburg in 1555.

consols (contraction of consolidated (annuities), same as cab for cabriolet, pants for pantaloons, etc.), the interest of 3 per cent. which the British government pays on its debt. The loans were negotiated at various times and at different rates of interest, and finally consolidated into one fund. The consolidated annuities act passed 1857.

conspiracies. Among recorded conspiracies, real or supposed, the following are remarkable:

	B.C.
Of Catiline, suppressed by Cicero	63
Of Brutus, Cassius, and others; death of Cæsar [illegible] most famous of all.]	44

England.

	A.D.
Of Anthony Babyngton and others against Elizabeth (BABYNGTON)	1586
GUNPOWDER PLOT	1605
Of Blood, who seized the duke of Ormond, wounded him, and would have hanged him, Dec. 1670, and who afterwards attempted to steal the regalia (BLOOD'S CONSPIRACY) ... 9 May,	1671
Pretended conspiracy of French, Spanish, and English Jesuits to assassinate Charles II. revealed by the infamous Titus Oates (OATES), Bedingfield, and others ... Aug.	1678
MEAL-TUB PLOT	1679
RYE-HOUSE PLOT to assassinate the king on his way to Newmarket	1683
Of Col. Despard (DESPARD)	1802
Of Thistlewood and others to assassinate the king's ministers (CATO-STREET CONSPIRACY)	1820

Scotland.

Of Robert Graham and the earl of Athol; murder of James I. (PERTH) ... 20 Feb.	1437
Of Gowrie's attempt to seize James IV. of Scotland (GOWRIE'S CONSPIRACY) ... 5 Aug.	1600

France.

Of St. Bartholomew and massacre ... 24 Aug.	1572
Of Georges, against the life of Bonaparte ... 15 Feb.	1804
To assassinate the vice president Napoleon ... 1 July,	1852
To assassinate Napoleon III. (FRANCE) ... 14 Jan.	1858

Germany.

For the assassination of emperor William I. by the socialists	1878

Russia.

Of the STRELITZ	1698
Against Peter III., murdered	1762
Against Paul I., murdered ... 24 Mch.	1801
Of Pestal against Nicolas I. ... 26-29 Dec.	1825
Of socialists among the students ... Jan.	1870
Of nihilists for the death of the czar by blowing up the Winter palace ... 17 Feb.	1880
Of nihilists; death of the czar by the explosion of a bomb (NIHILISTS) ... 13 Mch.	1881

Bulgaria.

Major Panitza against prince Ferdinand ... Feb. et seq.	1890

United States.

Of Aaron Burr (BURR CONSPIRACY)	1805-6
Of John Wilkes Booth, for the assassination of pres. Lincoln, vice-pres. Johnson, Mr. Seward, and gen. Grant (BOOTH'S CONSPIRACY) ... 14 Apr.	1865

ASSASSINATIONS, REBELLIONS, etc.

constable of England, lord-high, the 7th great officer of the crown, and, with the earl marshal, formerly a judge of the court of chivalry, called, in the time of Henry IV., *curia militaris* and subsequently the court of honor. His power was so great that in 1389 a statute was passed to lessen it and that of the EARL MARSHAL. The office existed before the conquest, after which it went by inheritance to the earls

First Monday in Sept. designated a public holiday (Labor-day), a state normal school established at Willimantic, and an "anti-screen" saloon law, and modified Australian ballot law passed by legislature in session........9 Jan.–22 June, 1889
Alfred H. Terry, maj.-gen. U. S. A., b. 1827; d. at New Haven, 16 Dec. 1890
Deadlock between the two houses of the legislature on the governorship.......................................7 Jan. 1891
Democratic candidates for state offices sworn in by the Senate, refused possession by Republican incumbents.......13 Jan. "
Gov. Bulkeley by proclamation warns the citizens against recognizing the Democratic state officers...............19 Jan. "
P. T. Barnum, b. 1810; d. at Bridgeport...............7 Apr. "
Superior court decides in favor of gov. Bulkeley.......24 June, "
Both claimants to governorship agree to take the matter into the State Supreme court..............................1 Oct. "
Ex-gov. Hobart B. Bigelow d. at New Haven............12 Oct. "
In the suit of Morris, Democrat, versus Bulkeley, Republican, the Supreme court holds Bulkeley to be governor.....5 Jan. 1892
Daniel Grant, one of the famous triplets of Torrington, dies, aged 71 years, his 2 brothers surviving...............5 Oct. "
Celebration of the 250th anniversary of the founding of Stamford...16 Oct. "

GOVERNORS OF THE CONNECTICUT COLONY.

Name.	Date.
John Haynes	1639 to 1640
Edward Hopkins	1640 " 1641
John Haynes	1641 " 1642
George Wyllys	1642 " 1643
John Haynes and Edward Hopkins, alternately from	1643 " 1655
Thomas Welles	1655 " 1656
John Webster	1656 " 1657
John Winthrop	1657 " 1658
Thomas Welles	1658 " 1659
John Winthrop	1659 " 1665

Until this time no person could be elected to a second term immediately following the first.

GOVERNORS OF THE NEW HAVEN COLONY.

Name.	Date.
Theophilus Eaton	1639 to 1657
Francis Newman	1658 " 1660
William Leete	1661 " 1665

GOVERNORS OF CONNECTICUT.

Name.	Date.	Remarks.
John Winthrop	1665 to 1676	
William Leete	1676 " 1683	
Robert Treat	1683 " 1687	
Edmund Andros	1687 " 1689	Royal governor.
Robert Treat	1689 " 1698	
Fitz John Winthrop	1698 " 1707	

GOVERNORS OF CONNECTICUT.—(*Continued.*)

Name.	Date.	Remarks.
Gurdon Saltonstall	1707 to 1724	
Joseph Talcott	1724 " 1741	
Jonathan Law	1741 " 1750	
Roger Wolcott	1750 " 1754	
Thomas Fitch	1754 " 1766	
William Pitkin	1766 " 1769	
Jonathan Trumbull	1769 " 1784	The only one of the colonial governors that remained true to the people against Great Britain.
Mathew Griswold	1784 " 1786	
Samuel Huntington	1786 " 1796	Federal.
Oliver Wolcott	1796 " 1798	"
Jonathan Trumbull	1798 " 1809	"
John Treadwell	1809 " 1811	"
Roger Griswold	1811 " 1813	"
John Cotton Smith	1813 " 1817	"
Oliver Wolcott	1817 " 1827	Democrat-Republican.
Gideon Tomlinson	1827 " 1831	
John S. Peters	1831 " 1833	
H. W. Edwards	1833 " 1834	Democrat.
Samuel A. Foote	1834 " 1835	"
H. W. Edwards	1835 " 1838	"
W. W. Ellsworth	1838 " 1842	Whig.
C. F. Cleveland	1842 " 1844	Democrat.
Roger S. Baldwin	1844 " 1846	Whig.
Clark Bissell	1846 " 1849	"
Joseph Trumbull	1849 " 1850	"
Thomas H. Seymour	1850 " 1853	Democrat.
Charles H. Pond	1853 " 1854	"
Henry Dutton	1854 " 1855	Whig.
W. T. Minor	1855 " 1857	Republican.
A. H. Holley	1857 " 1858	"
William A. Buckingham	1858 " 1866	" war governor.
Joseph R. Hawley	1866 " 1867	"
James E. English	1867 " 1869	Democrat.
Marshall Jewell	1869 " 1870	Republican.
James E. English	1870 " 1871	Democrat.
Marshall Jewell	1871 " 1873	Republican.
Charles R. Ingersoll	1873 " 1876	Democrat.
R. D. Hubbard	1876 " 1879	" Governors chosen annually until 1876, and bi-annually since.
Charles B. Andrews	1879 " 1881	Republican.
H. B. Bigelow	1881 " 1883	"
Thomas M. Waller	1883 " 1885	Democrat.
Henry B. Harrison	1885 " 1887	Republican.
Phineas C. Lounsbury	1887 " 1889	"
Morgan G. Bulkeley	1889 " 1891	"
"	1891 " 1893	"
Luzon B. Morris	1893 " 1895	Democrat.
O. Vincent Coffin	1895 " 1897	Republican.

UNITED STATES SENATORS FROM THE STATE OF CONNECTICUT

Name.	No. of Congress.	Date.	Remarks.
Oliver Ellsworth	1st to 4th	1789 to 1797	Term expired 3 Mch. 1791. Reappointed. Resigned 1796.
William S. Johnson	1st	1789 " 1791	Resigned 1791.
Roger Sherman	2d	1791 " 1793	Elected in place of W. S. Johnson. Died 1793.
Stephen Nix Mitchell	3d	1793 " 1795	Elected in place of Sherman. Seated Dec. 1793.
James Hillhouse	4th to 11th	1796 " 1811	Elected in place of Ellsworth. Seated 5 Dec. 1796. Elected president *pro tem.* 28 Feb. 1801. Resigned 1810.
Jonathan Trumbull	4th	1795 " 1796	Resigned 1796.
Uriah Tracy	4th to 9th	1796 " 1807	Elected in place of Trumbull. Seated 6 Dec. 1796. Elected president *pro tem.* 14 May, 1800. Died, 1807.
Chauncey Goodrich	10th " 12th	1807 " 1813	Elected in place of Tracy. Seated 27 Nov. 1807. Resigned 1813.
Samuel W. Dana	11th " 16th	1810 " 1821	Elected in place of Hillhouse. Seated 3 Dec. 1810.
David Daggett	13th " 15th	1813 " 1819	Elected in place of Goodrich. Seated 24 May, 1813.
James Lanman	16th " 18th	1819 " 1825	
Elijah Boardman	17th	1821 " 1823	Died 1823.
Henry W. Edwards	18th to 19th	1823 " 1827	Appointed in place of Boardman. Seated 1 Dec. 1823.
Calvin Willey	19th " 21st	1825 " 1831	Elected in place of Lanman.
Samuel A. Foote	20th " 22d	1827 " 1833	Democrat. Senator Foote offered the resolutions "on the public lands," in the 21st Congress, 29 Dec. 1829, the principal subject of the great debate between Hayne of South Carolina and Webster, 1830.
Gideon Tomlinson	22d " 24th	1831 " 1837	
Nathan Smith	23d	1833 " 1835	Whig.
John M. Niles	24th to 25th	1835 " 1839	Democrat. Elected in place of Smith, 1835.
Perry Smith	25th " 27th	1837 " 1843	Democrat.
Thaddeus Betts	26th	1839 " 1840	Died 1840.
Jabez W. Huntington	26th to 29th	1840 " 1847	Whig. Elected in place of Betts. Seated 2 June, 1840. Died 1847.
John M. Niles	28th " 30th	1843 " 1849	Democrat.
Roger S. Baldwin	30th " 31st	1847 " 1851	Whig. Appointed in place of Huntington, 1847.
Truman Smith	31st " 33d	1849 " 1854	Whig. Resigned 1854.
Isaac Toucey	32d " 34th	1852 " 1857	Democrat. Seated 14 May, 1852.
Francis Gillett	33d	1854 " 1855	Elected in place of Truman Smith, 1854.
Lafayette Foster	34th to 39th	1855 " 1867	Whig. Elected president *pro tem.* 1865.
James Dixon	35th " 40th	1857 " 1869	Republican. Seated 1857.
Orris S. Ferry	40th " 44th	1867 " 1875	" Died 23 Nov. 1875.
William A. Buckingham	41st " 43d	1869 " 1875	" Died 5 Feb. 1875.
William W. Eaton	43d " 46th	1875 " 1881	Democrat. Appointed in place of Buckingham, 1875.
James E. English	44th	1875 " 1877	" Appointed in place of Ferry, 1875.
William H. Barnum	44th to 45th	1875 " 1879	" Elected in place of Ferry, 1875.
Orville H. Platt	46th	1879	Republican.
Joseph R. Hawley	47th	1881	"

Connor, Ireland. The bishopric was united to Down, 1442. The first prelate, Ængus Macnisius, died 507. Both sees were added to Dromore on the death of its last bishop, 1842, under the Irish Church Temporalities act, 1833.

conquest, in British history, when William, duke of Normandy, overcame Harold II. at Hastings, 14 Oct. 1066, and obtained the crown which he claimed under the will of Edward the Confessor (Edgar being the rightful heir). William, though styled the Conqueror, succeeded to the crown by compact. He defeated Harold, himself a usurper, but much of the kingdom held out against him; and he swore to observe the laws and customs of the realm, in order to win the people. Formerly, English judges used to reprehend a barrister who said casually William the Conqueror, instead of William I.—*Selden.* Maclise exhibited 42 drawings on the events of the Norman conquest, in May, 1857. E. A. Freeman's "History of the Norman Conquest," 6 vols., 1870–79.

conscience, liberty of, a principle of Christianity (1 Cor. x. 29); repudiated by Romanism; proclaimed by James II. for political purposes, 1687. MASSACHUSETTS, 1635, regarding Roger Williams.

conscript fathers (*patres conscripti*). Roman senators were so called because their names were in registers of the senate.

conscription, a mode, derived from the Romans, of recruiting armies. On 5 Sept. 1798, a military conscription was ordained in France, of all men from 20 to 25 years of age, from whom selections were made. A conscription for 350,000 men took place in Jan. 1813, after the Russian disasters, and in Dec. same year another for 300,000 after the battle of Leipsic. Estimated conscriptions, 1793–1813, 4,103,000. The law of 1818 (modified in 1824, 1832, and 1868) assigned an annual contingent to each department. The conscription was enlarged and modified by the army bill of Feb. 1868. A reorganization of the army began in 1871, after the war with Germany; substitutes were allowed under certain conditions. Conscription for Great Britain was discussed in 1875. MILITIA. In the American civil war (1861–65) conscription was resorted to by both governments. The national armies, however, were less dependent on the measure, as large bounties brought them enough volunteers. The first confederate conscription law, 16 Apr. 1862, annulled all contracts with volunteers for short terms, holding them for 2 additional years, and made every white male between 18 and 35 liable to service at a moment's notice. On 27 Sept. the law was extended to men between 35 and 45 years of age. In July, 1863, all between 18 and 45 were called into active service. In Feb. 1864, the law was extended to all between 17 and 50. DRAFT RIOTS.

consecration. Aaron and his sons were consecrated priests, 1490 B.C. (Lev. viii.). The Jewish tabernacle was dedicated 1490 B.C., and Solomon's temple, 1004 B.C. (1 Kings viii.). Consecration of churches began in the 2d century. Anciently the consecration of popes was deferred until the emperor assented to the election. Gregory IV. desired to have his election confirmed by the emperor Louis in 828.—*Hénault.* The consecration of churches, places of burial, etc., is permitted by Protestants. An act relating to the consecration of churchyards of the church of England, passed 20 Aug. 1867, was amended in 1868. A form of consecration was adopted by convocation, but not sanctioned by the crown, Apr. 1712. It is generally used, but is not compulsory.—*Burn.* The form of consecrating bishops in the church of England is in the prayer-book of 1549.—*Stow.* BISHOPS, Episcopal.

conservation of force. The doctrine that no physical force can be created or destroyed, though it may be transformed, is maintained by Faraday, Grove, Helmholtz, Tyndall, and other philosophers. CORRELATION.

conservatives, a name of modern date, given in Great Britain to a political party whose leading principle is the preservation of national institutions, said to have been invented by John Wilson Croker in 1830. Conservative (a Tory), in popular language, is now opposed to Liberal. It was termed a new cant word by Macaulay in *Edinburgh Review*, July, 1832. Sir Robert Peel acknowledged himself a conservative when reproached by the Irish party in Parliament as an Orangeman; but a party that afterwards separated from him called their principles conservative, as opposed to those he had now adopted. A meeting of the National Union of Conservative Associations was held at the Crystal palace, London, 24 June, 1872. The party in the minority at elections in 1868, in England, obtained a majority in Feb. 1874, and came into office. They were again in a minority, and resigned, 22 Apr. 1880. The marquis of Salisbury became leader of the party, 9 May, 1881, succeeding the earl of Beaconsfield, who died 19 Apr. previous. ADMINISTRATIONS.

conservatoires, institutions for cultivating music and the arts on the European continent. One was established at Naples in 1537. The singing-school at Paris, founded in 1784, closed in 1789, was reopened in 1793 as the "Institut National de Musique;" and, as reorganized, was renamed "Conservatoire de Musique" in 1795, and flourished under Cherubini (1822–42). The "Conservatoire des Arts et Métiers," established in 1784, has a museum and library, and provides lectures to workmen.

consistories, for regulating discipline and worship in the Lutheran church in Germany, were established at the Reformation—first at Wittenberg, in 1542; others after the peace of Augsburg, in 1555.

consols (clip form of consolidated (annuities), same as cab for cabriolet, pants for pantaloons, etc.), the interest of 3 per cent. which the British government pays on its debt. The loans were negotiated at various times and at different rates of interest, and finally consolidated into one fund. The consolidated annuities act passed 1857.

conspiracies. Among recorded conspiracies, real or supposed, the following are remarkable:

B.C.
Of Catiline, suppressed by Cicero........ 63
Of Brutus, Cassius, and others; death of Cæsar........ 44
[Most famous of all.]

England.

A.D.
Of Anthony Babyngton and others against Elizabeth (BABYNGTON)........ 1586
GUNPOWDER PLOT........ 1605
Of Blood, who seized the duke of Ormond, wounded him, and would have hanged him, Dec. 1670, and who afterwards attempted to steal the regalia (BLOOD'S CONSPIRACY)...9 May, 1671
Pretended conspiracy of French, Spanish, and English Jesuits to assassinate Charles II. revealed by the infamous Titus Oates (OATES), Dr. Tongue, and others........Aug. 1678
MEAL-TUB PLOT........ 1679
RYE-HOUSE PLOT to assassinate the king on his way to New-market........ 1683
Of Col. Despard (DESPARD)........ 1802
Of Thistlewood and others to assassinate the king's ministers (CATO-STREET CONSPIRACY)........ 1820

Scotland.

Of Robert Graham and the earl of Athol; murder of James I. (PERTH)........20 Feb. 1437
Of Gowrie's attempt to seize James IV. of Scotland (GOWRIE'S CONSPIRACY)........5 Aug. 1600

France.

Of ST. BARTHOLOMEW and massacre........24 Aug. 1572
Of GEORGES, against the life of Bonaparte........15 Feb. 1804
To assassinate the prince president Napoleon........ 1 July, 1852
To assassinate Napoleon III. (FRANCE)........14 Jan. 1858

Germany.

For the assassination of emperor William I. by the socialists... 1878

Russia.

Of the STRELITZ........ 1698
Against Peter III., murdered........ 1762
Against Paul I., murdered........24 Mch. 1801
Of Pestal against Nicholas I........26–29 Dec. 1825
Of socialists among the students........Jan. 1870
Of nihilists for the death of the czar by blowing up the Winter palace........17 Feb. 1880
Of nihilists, death of the czar by the explosion of a bomb (NIHILISTS)........13 Mch. 1881

Bulgaria.

Major Panitza against prince Ferdinand........Feb. et seq. 1890

United States.

Of Aaron Burr (BURR'S CONSPIRACY)........1805–6
Of John Wilkes Booth, for the assassination of pres. Lincoln, vice-pres. Johnson, sec. Seward, and gen. Grant (BOOTH'S CONSPIRACY)........14 Apr. 1865

ASSASSINATIONS, REBELLIONS, etc.

constable of England, lord-high, the 7th great officer of the crown, and, with the earl marshal, formerly a judge of the court of chivalry, called, in the time of Henry IV., *curia militaris*, and subsequently the court of honor. His power was so great that in 1389 a statute was passed to lessen it and that of the EARL MARSHAL. The office existed before the conquest, after which it went by inheritance to the earls of Hereford and Essex, and next in line of Stafford In 1521 it was forfeited by Edward Stafford, duke of Buckingham, attainted for high-treason, and has since been granted only *pro hâc vice* (for this occasion) to attend at a coronation or trial by combat The only trial by combat ordered since this office fell to the crown was between lord Reay and David Ramsey, in Nov 1631, but the king prevented it

constable of France, first officer of the kings of France and afterwards commander-in-chief of the army and highest authority in all questions of chivalry and honor. Office suppressed, 1627

constable of Scotland, lord-high The office was instituted by David I about 1147. The holder was keeper of the king's sword, which the king, at his promotion, delivered to him naked (hence the badge of the lord-high constable is a naked sword), and had the command of the king's armies in the field, in the king's absence The office was made hereditary, 1321, in sir Gilbert Hay, created earl of Erroll by Robert Bruce, and with his descendants it remains, being preserved by the treaty of union in 1707 The present earl of Erroll is the 22d lord high constable (1881)

constables of Hundreds and Franchises, instituted in the reign of Edward I, 1285, are now called high-constables in England There are 3 kinds of constables, *high*, *petty*, and *special* the high-constable's jurisdiction extends to the whole hundred, the petty constable's, to his parish or liberty, and the special constable is appointed for particular emergencies (as in Apr 1848, on account of the Chartists) The general appointment of parish constables was made unnecessary by an act, Aug 1872 In the United States a local official of a town or village

Constance, a city in Baden, S Germany Here sat the 17th general council, 1414-18, which condemned John Huss, and here he was burned, 6 July, 1415 HUSSITES

Constanti'na, the ancient capital of Numidia, was taken by the French, 13 Oct 1837 During the assault on 12 Oct the French general Damremont was killed Achmet Bey retired with 12,000 men as the victors entered Constantina

Constantinople (formerly BYZANTIUM), founded 667 B.C., named for Constantine the Great, who fixed the seat of the Eastern empire here, dedicating it 11 May, 330 A D. Its Turkish name *Stamboul* is said to be a corruption of the Gr *εἰς τὴν πόλιν* Estimated pop. 1893, 925,000. EASTERN EMPIRE

General ecclesiastical councils against heresy were held here in 381, 553, 680, and . .	869
Seized by Procopius	365
City suffered from religious dissensions, and was burned during the "Nika" conflicts .	532
Rebuilt by Justinian with great splendor . .	"
St Sophia dedicated . .	537
Resisted the Saracens successfully	675, 718
And the Russians. ..	865, 904, 941, 1043
Taken by the crusaders	1203, 1204
Recovered by the Greeks	1261
Vainly besieged by Amurath the Ottoman June-Aug	1422
Taken by Mahomet II after 53 days' siege 29 May,	1453
Conference on Turkish affairs representatives *Great Britain*, marquis of Salisbury, *Russia*, gen Ignatieff, *France*, Chaudordy, *Austria*, Zichy, *Germany*, Von Werther, *Italy* Corti, ordinary meetings began 23 Dec	1876
Turkey rejecting the propositions, conference closed 20 Jan	1877
Treaty of peace with Russia 12 articles, Turkey accepted modifications of treaty of San Stefano, an indemnity of about 802,500,000 francs to be paid by Turkey (settlement deferred), Russian troops to quit within 40 days, etc, signed (TURKEY) 8 Feb	1879

Era of Constantinople, dating the creation 5508 years B.C., was used by the Russians until Peter the Great, and is still in the Greek church The civil year begins 1 Sept, the ecclesiastical year in March, the day not exactly determined To reduce it to our era, subtract 5508 years from January to August, and 5509 from September to December —*Nicolas*

constellations. Groups of fixed stars, supposed to resemble the forms of living beings or other objects *Arcturus*, *Orion*, the *Pleiades*, and *Mazzaroth* are mentioned (Job ix 9, and xxxviii 31) about 1520 B C. Homer and Hesiod notice constellations, but the first definite record is that of Claudius Ptolemæus, about 140 A.D Hipparchus (about 147 B C.) made a list of 48 constellations, others were added by Tycho Brahe, Hevelius, Halley, etc. There are now recognized 29 northern, 45 southern, and 12 zodiacal The zodiacal constellations are Aries, Taurus, Gemini, Cancer, Leo, Virgo, Libra, Scorpio, Sagittarius, Capricornus, Aquarius, and Pisces. STARS.

Constitution of England. It comprehends the whole body of laws by which the British people are governed, and to which it is presumptively held that every individual has assented —*Lord Somers* It is thus distinguished from the term government—the constitution is the rule by which the sovereign ought to govern at all times, and government is that by which he does govern at any particular time —*Lord Bolingbroke* The king of England is not supreme, he sees his equals in the coexisting branches of the legislature, and his superior in the law —*Sheridan* Hallam's "Constitutional History of England" was first pub in 1827, May's in 1861-63, Stubbs's in 1875

Constitution of the United States. The "Articles of Confederation" (CONFEDERATION, ARTICLES OF) which had carried the country through the Revolution were felt to be inadequate when peace was proclaimed. The government was without defined limits in its executive, legislative, or judiciary There was no treasury, but a heavy debt. During the winter of 1784-85 Noah Webster began a series of political essays, "Sketches of American Policy," showing the necessity of a new government, vesting in Congress legislative powers, etc. On 5 Mch 1785, commissioners from Virginia and Maryland, appointed through the influence of Washington, assembled at Mount Vernon to consider a scheme for a canal connecting the Potomac and the Ohio, and a national tariff and other topics were discussed A convention of all the states was called at Annapolis in Sept 1786, but only 5 were represented, viz New York, New Jersey, Pennsylvania, Delaware, Virginia, too few for national action It adjourned after recommending to the legislatures represented the calling of another convention at Philadelphia, on the 2d Monday in May, 1787, the delegates to it to be empowered "to devise such further provisions as shall appear to them necessary to render the constitution of the federal government adequate to the exigencies of the Union" This report was referred by Congress to a committee, which reported a resolution, 21 Feb 1787, that Congress, believing the "Articles of Confederation" inadequate for the purposes of the Union, strongly recommended the legislatures to send delegates to the proposed convention on the 2d Monday in May, 1787. Delegates were accordingly chosen in the several states "for the purpose of revising the articles of confederation and reporting to Congress and the several legislatures such alterations and provisions therein as shall, when agreed to in Congress, and confirmed by the states, render the federal Constitution adequate to the exigencies of the government" Although called for the 2d Monday, 14 May, 1787, the delegates came late and only organized 25 May, with Washington as president. On the 29th, the main business was opened by Edmund Randolph of Virginia, who set forth the defects of the "Articles of Confederation" in order, and offered 15 resolutions, drawn by Madison, embodying the "Virginia" or "national plan" These were discussed until 15 June, when Patterson of New Jersey brought forward the "New Jersey plan" of the State-rights party, which preserved the Continental Congress as the federal legislature with certain additional powers. Its advocates insisted that the convention must make no fundamental changes, and that the states would not ratify a closer union Alexander Hamilton of New York dissented from both plans. He doubted the stability of a republic, but public sentiment demanded republican forms, and he sketched a system devised by himself He proposed a national legislature in 2 branches, the assembly to be elected for 3 years, the senate to serve during good behavior, as could the governor or president; state laws contrary to the Constitution to be void, a governor of each state, appointed by the general government, to have a veto upon laws in the state, no state to have a land or naval force, the militia of all the states to be under the exclusive control of the U S., who should appoint and commission the officers. The resolutions first submitted by Randolph were substantially adopted, and formed the skeleton of our present Constitution. The convention appointed a committee of detail, 26 July, to report a constitution embodying the proposals it had approved, and adjourned for 10 days. This committee, Nathaniel Gorham, Oliver Ellsworth, Jas. Wilson, Edmund Randolph, and John Rutledge, reported on 6 Aug. a rough sketch of the Constitution. The convention made many amendments and submitted the report to Congress, 12 Sept. 1787. Congress resolved, 28 Sept. 1787, unanimously "that the said report, with the resolution and letter accompanying the same, be transmitted to the several legislatures, in order to be submitted to a convention of delegates chosen in each state by the people thereof, in conformity to the resolves of the convention made and provided in that case." This convention adjourned 17 Sept. 1787. It sat with closed doors, and the injunction of secrecy was never removed. At the adjournment the journal, under a previous vote, was intrusted to Washington, who deposited it in the department of state. It was first printed in 1818 by order of Congress. The notes of Madison, with less full ones by Yates of New York and Luther Martin of Maryland, with the official journal, furnish the only information of the different views and contests in the convention during the long struggle which resulted in the Constitution of the U. S. The Constitution was submitted to the state conventions, and the debates in several were protracted and exciting. The following list shows the dates of ratification in the several state

Delaware, unanimously .... 7 De
Pennsylvania, vote 46 to 23 .... 12 De
New Jersey, unanimously .... 18 D
Georgia, " .... 2 Ja
Connecticut, vote 128 to 40 .... 9 Jan. "
Massachusetts, vote 187 to 168 .... 6 Feb. "
Maryland, vote 63 to 12 .... 28 Apr. "
South Carolina, vote 149 to 73 .... 23 May, "
New Hampshire, vote 57 to 46 .... 21 June, "
Virginia, vote 89 to 79 .... 25 June, "
New York, vote 30 to 28 .... 26 June, "
North Carolina, vote 193 to 75 .... 21 Nov. 1789
Rhode Island, vote 34 to 32 .... 29 May, 1790

After ratification by the 9th state, Congress passed, 13 Sept. 1788, the following resolution:

"*Resolved*, That the 1st Wednesday in Jan. next be the day for appointing electors in the several states which, before the said day, shall have ratified the said Constitution; that the 1st Wednesday in Feb. next be the day for the electors to assemble in their respective states, and vote for a President; and that the 1st Wednesday in Mch. next be the time, and the present seat of Congress (New York) the place for commencing the proceedings under the Constitution." UNITED STATES UNDER THE CONSTITUTION.

MEMBERS OF THE CONVENTION FRAMING THE CONSTITUTION, 25 May–17 Sept. 1787.

Elected.	Serving.	Signing.	Representing.	Remarks.
Baldwin, Abraham	Served	Signed	Georgia	Seated, 11 June.
Bassett, Richard	"	"	Delaware	" 25 May.
Bedford, Gunning, jr.	"	"	"	" 28 May.
Blair, John	"	"	Virginia	" 25 May.
Blount, William	"	"	North Carolina	" 20 June, in place of Caswell.
Breasley, David	"	"	New Jersey	" 25 May.
Broom, Jacob	"	"	Delaware	" "
Butler, Pierce	"	"	South Carolina	" "
Carroll, Daniel	"	"	Maryland	" 9 July.
Caswell, Richard	....	....	North Carolina	Resigned. BLOUNT.
Clark, Abraham	....	....	New Jersey	
Clymer, George	Served	Signed	Pennsylvania	Seated, 28 May.
Dana, Francis	....	....	Massachusetts	Could not attend.
Davie, Wm. Richardson	Served	....	North Carolina	Seated, 25 May. Called away by sickness.
Dayton, Jonathan	"	Signed	New Jersey	" 21 June.
Dickinson, John	"	"	Delaware	" 28 May.
Ellsworth, Oliver	"	....	Connecticut	" 29 May. Called away by sickness.
Few, William	"	Signed	Georgia	" 25 May.
Fitzsimons, Thomas	"	"	Pennsylvania	" "
Franklin, Benjamin	"	"	"	" 28 May. The oldest signer, 81 years old.
Gerry, Elbridge	"	....	Massachusetts	" 29 May. Refused to sign. Feared a civil war.
Gilman, Nicholas	"	Signed	New Hampshire	" 23 July. The youngest signer, 25 years old.
Gorham, Nathaniel	"	"	Massachusetts	" 28 May.
Hamilton, Alexander	"	"	New York	" 25 May.
Henry, Patrick	....	....	Virginia	Declined for private reasons.
Houston, W. Churchill	Served	....	New Jersey	Seated, 25 May.
Houstoun, William	"	....	Georgia	" 1 June.
Ingersoll, Jared	"	Signed	Pennsylvania	" 28 May.
Jenifer, Daniel, of St. Thomas	"	"	Maryland	" 2 June.
Johnson, Wm. Samuel	"	"	Connecticut	" "
Jones, Willie	....	....	North Carolina	WILLIAMSON.
King, Rufus	Served	Signed	Massachusetts	Seated, 25 May.
Langdon, John	"	"	New Hampshire	" 23 July.
Lansing, John, jr.	"	....	New York	" 2 June. Opposed the constitution and withdrew.
Livingston, William	"	Signed	New Jersey	Seated, 5 June.
Madison, James	"	"	Virginia	" 25 May. Called the "Father of the Constitution."
Martin, Alexander	"	....	North Carolina	" 15 May.
Martin, Luther	"	....	Maryland	" 9 June. Withdrew. Opposed to the constitution.
Mason, George	"	....	Virginia	Seated, 25 May. Refused to sign. Too monarchical.
McClurg, James	"	....	"	" " Substitute for Patrick Henry, absent on day of signing.
McHenry, James	"	Signed	Maryland	Seated, 29 May.
Mercer, John Francis	"	....	"	" 6 Aug. Withdrew without signing.
Mifflin, Thomas	"	Signed	Pennsylvania	" 28 May.
Morris, Gouverneur	"	"	"	" 25 May. Framed the Constitution.
Morris, Robert	"	"	"	" "
Neilson, John	....	....	New Jersey	
Patterson, William	Served	Signed	"	" "
Pendleton, Nathaniel	....	....	Georgia	
Pickering, John	....	....	New Hampshire	
Pierce, William	Served	....	Georgia	" 31 May. Absent on day of signing.
Pinckney, Charles	"	Signed	South Carolina	" 25 May.
Pinckney, C. Cotesworth	"	"	"	" "
Randolph, Edmund, jr.	"	....	Virginia	" " Refused. Objected to powers conferred on president and Senate.
Read, George	"	Signed	Delaware	Seated, 25 May.
Rutledge, John	"	"	South Carolina	" "
Sherman, Roger	"	"	Connecticut	" 30 May.
Spaight, Richard Dobbs	"	"	North Carolina	" 25 May.
Strong, Caleb	"	....	Massachusetts	" 28 May. Absent on day of signing.
Walton, George	....	....	Georgia	Declined.
Washington, George	Served	Signed	Virginia	Seated, 25 May. President of the convention and first signer.
West, Benjamin	....	....	New Hampshire	
Williamson, Hugh	Served	Signed	North Carolina	" " Substitute for Willie Jones.
Wilson, James	"	"	Pennsylvania	" "
Wythe, George	"	....	Virginia	" " Absent on day of signing.
Yates, Robert	"	....	New York	" " Withdrew. Opposed to the constitution.

Rhode Island not represented.

of He **nstitution of the United States,** Amend-it was to During the debates on the ratification of the Con-tainte m, many amendments were offered Massachusetts pro-*hác vic*9, South Carolina 4, New Hampshire 12, Virginia 20, combat.ork 32, North Carolina 26, the Pennsylvania minor-fell t?, the Maryland minority 28, in place of which the As-sembly agreed upon 17, which the Senate reduced to 12 These were passed by two thirds of both branches of Congress, 25 Sept 1789 The first 2 were not ratified, and the remaining 10, though rejected by Massachusetts, Connecticut, and Georgia, were ratified by the other states.

I to X inclusive declared in force, 15 Dec 1791

XI This amendment passed by two thirds of both branches of Congress, 5 Mch 1794, declared in force 8 Jan 1798

[It covered such cases as Chisholm *vs* Georgia (2 Dall 470) It was construed in the case of Cohens *vs* Virginia (6 Wheat. 264)]

XII This amendment relates to elections, and was adopted by the House, 1 May 1802, by 47 to 17, but rejected by the Senate 15 to 8 At the next session of Congress it was again lost. On the third trial, Oct. 1803, after a long debate, it passed the Senate, 22 to 10, and the House, 84 to 42 The speaker, Mr Macon, voting aye, made the necessary two thirds Of the 42 votes in the minority, 24 came from New England It was declared in force 25 Sept 1804

[Ratified by Georgia Kentucky, Maryland, New Jersey, New York, North Carolina, Ohio Pennsylvania, Rhode Island, South Carolina, Tennessee Vermont, Virginia, rejected by Connecticut, Delaware, Massachusetts and New Hampshire]

XIII This amendment, carrying out the emancipation proclamation, passed the Senate 8 Apr 1864, by a vote of 38 to 6, but failed in the House, 15 June vote 95 to 66, but on reconsideration, 31 Jan 1865, it passed, 119 to 56. It was ratified by 31 out of the 36 states, rejected by Delaware and Kentucky, not acted on by Texas, and conditionally ratified by Alabama and Mississippi It was proclaimed 18 Dec 1865

XIV This amendment, an essential part of the reconstruction plan passed the Senate, 8 June, 1866, by 33 to 11 and the House, 13 June, 138 to 36, rejected by Delaware, Kentucky, Maryland, not acted on by California, and ratified by the other states—33 out of 37 10 of the Southern states at first rejected it, but the reconstruction act of 2 Mch 1867, declared these state governments provisional only until its ratification They then ratified it, and it was declared in force 28 July, 1868

XV This amendment bestows citizenship on the negro It was proposed in Congress, 26 Feb 1869, passed the Senate, 39 to 13, and the House, 144 to 44 It was not acted on by Tennessee, rejected by California, Delaware, Kentucky, Maryland, New Jersey, and Oregon, and ratified by the remaining 30 states New York rescinded its ratification 5 Jan 1870 This amendment was declared in force . 30 Mch 1870

Constitution, the frigate NAVY.

Constitutions of Clarendon. CLARENDON

Constitutions of France, enacted 1789-91, 1795, 1799 (charter), 1814, 1848, 1852, 1875.

consubstantiation. TRANSUBSTANTIATION.

consuls (meaning colleagues), Roman. At the expulsion of the Tarquins, a republic was established, to be ruled by 2 consuls elected annually, the first being Lucius Junius Brutus and Lucius Tarquinius Collatinus, husband of the injured Lucretia, 509 B.C The consular power was in emergencies superseded by dictators and tribunes In modern times, consuls are public officers commissioned by a government to manage and protect the commercial interests of its citizens in other countries, and formally recognized by the government within whose jurisdiction they act. In some countries, particularly in the Levant, it is customary for consuls to exercise certain judicial powers in cases affecting their countrymen

B C.

Government of the Decemviri . 451-49

Three military tribunes with consular power 444

A plebeian elected consul . 366

(Under Tiberius consuls were nominated by the senate, the office being henceforth honorary)

French consulate established when the directory was abolished, Bonaparte, Sieyès, and Roger Ducos made provisional consular commissioners, 10 Nov , Bonaparte, Cambacérès, and Lebrun made consuls 13 Dec. 1799

Bonaparte first consul for 10 years, 6 May, for life, 2 Aug 1802, emperor . . 18 May, 1804

Commercial agents were first called consuls in Italy Lorenzo Strozzi appointed by Richard III 1485

A British consul first appointed in Portugal ... 1633

Continental army. ARMY.

Continental Congress. UNITED STATES.

Continental money. The bills of credit issued by Congress during the war for independence When that war broke out, Spanish coin was the principal metallic currency in the colonies, but the quantity was inadequate, and, after the battle of Bunker Hill, Congress, imitating some of the colonial governments, issued bills of credit. During 1775, bills for $3,000,000 were issued PAPER MONEY Other issues were made, until, at the beginning of 1780, these bills of credit amounted to $200,000,000, promising payment "in Spanish milled dollars" After 1777 they depreciated rapidly, the prospect of redemption appearing remote. Efforts to sustain their credit were in vain In 1780, 40 paper dollars were worth only 1 in specie, and in 1781 they were valueless. They afforded temporary relief, but finally occasioned much public evil and individual suffering. These bills are now curiosities in collections

continental system, Napoleon's plan to exclude British merchandise from the European Continent. It began with his BERLIN DECREE in 1806, and occasioned the ORDERS IN COUNCIL.

continuity. W R. Grove (afterwards sir), in an address as president of the British Association, on 22 Aug 1866, at Nottingham, Engl., expressed the opinion of many philosophers that all past changes in the world have been produced by the continuous action of causes now in operation—that "continuity is a law of nature, the true expression of the action of Almighty power"

contraband of war, a term said to have been first employed in the treaty of Southampton between England and Spain in 1625 During the war between Spain and Holland, both powers acted with rigor towards ships of neutrals conveying goods to belligerents This provoked England A milder policy was adopted by the treaty of Pyrenees, 1650, and by the declaration of Paris, 26 Apr 1856. The subject was discussed during the American civil war, 1861-64, whether slaves could be regarded as contraband VIRGINIA, 27 May, 1861

contre-danse (Engl. country dance), a dance with the dancers in opposite files, introduced into France (probably from England) about 1715

Contreras (Mexico), Battle of, between U. S. troops and Mexicans, 20 Aug 1847 Americans stormed and took a fortified camp defended by 6000 Mexicans, capturing 80 officers, 3000 soldiers, and 35 guns. MEXICAN WAR.

convent, a building for the use of an association or a community of persons generally limited to women (nuns) devoted to a religious life They were first founded, some say, 270 The first in England was erected at Folkestone, by Eadbald, in 630 —*Camden*. The first in Scotland was at Coldingham, where Ethelreda took the veil in 670 They were founded earlier in Ireland They were repeatedly suppressed in England, most severely by Henry VIII , many have been suppressed in Europe in this century. The king of Prussia secularized the convents in the duchy of Posen Dom Pedro put down 300 convents in Portugal in 1834, and Spain abolished 1800 convents Many were abolished in Italy and Sicily in 1860, 1861, and 1866, and many in Russia, 31 July, 1832, and Nov 1864

In 1597, lady Mary Percy founded a convent at Brussels, which flourished till 1794, when the nuns were driven to England. They were received by bishop Milner, and placed at Winchester, where they remained till their removal to East Bergholt, in Suffolk, June, 1857, this was the first English convent on the European Continent after the Reformation.

The Emancipation act of 1829, 10 Geo IV , prohibits convents and religious communities in the United Kingdom, but it has been a dead letter . . . 1829

[There were, in 1832, 16 convents in England, in 1870, 233, and 70 monasteries in Great Britain]

A select committee of the commons upon the revenues of British convents, 10 May, 1870, reappointed Feb. 1871

Committee reported the evidence . June, "

Mr Newdegate's motion for an inquiry into convents negatived, 12 June, 1874

Large convent at Bournemouth, under church of England, opened . . . .. 3 Oct. 1875

A Carmelite convent, patronized by the duke of Norfolk and family, at St. Charles's square, Notting Hill, London, W , opened by cardinal Manning .... 29 Sept. 1878

Many convents in France abolished by decree . 29 Mch. 1880

conventicles, private assemblies for religious worship, held by dissenters, a term first applied to the schools of Wycliffe. They were strictly forbidden by Elizabeth in 1593.

and by Charles II, 1664; and persons attending were liable to severe punishment The statutes were repealed by the Toleration act, 24 May, 1689

convention, Hartford CONNECTICUT, 1814

convention parliaments assembled without the king's writ upon extraordinary occasions. One on 25 Apr 1660, voted the restoration of Charles II A second, met 22 Jan 1689 offered the crown to William and Mary, 13 Feb, and dissolved in Feb 1690 NATIONAL CONVENTION

convention troops. When Burgoyne's army surrendered to gen Gates, these generals agreed that the prisoners (over 5000) (NEW YORK) should be marched to Cambridge, near Boston, to embark for England, on their parole not to serve again against the Americans Suspecting that the parole would be violated, Congress after ratifying, revoked it As the British government did not recognize the authority of Congress, these troops remained near Boston until Congress, owing to the scarcity of supplies in New England, ordered them to Virginia, whither they went, Oct and Nov 1778, 4000 remaining at Charlottesville until Oct 1780, when the British were removed to fort Frederick, in Maryland, and the Germans to Winchester, their numbers reduced to 2100 Soon after they were removed to Lancaster, and some to East Windsor, Conn In the course of 1782 they were dispersed by exchange or desertion

conventions. TREATIES.

convocation, a general assembly of clergy in Engl., called by the sovereign's writ, on the affairs of the church, the writ, directed to the archbishops, requires them to summon all the bishops, archdeacons, etc The convocation is in 2 houses—the upper, of bishops, the lower, of deans, prebendaries, archdeacons, and delegates from the inferior clergy The clergy were summoned to meet the king by writ, 23 Edw I 1294 The power of convocation was limited at its reorganization by a statute of Henry VIII It was deprived of various privileges in 1716, and ceased to meet The clergy have held formal meetings annually during the sessions of Parliament since 1854, and have in vain sought power to deal summarily with ecclesiastical affairs, but in Feb 1872, convocation was authorized to consider changes in the Liturgy, upon which it acted, 5 Mch , and again in 1889

convol'vulus (Lat *convolvere*, to twine together) The Canary convolvulus (*Convolvulus canariensis*) came to England from the Canary isles, 1690, the many-flowered, 1779 The *Convolvulus japonicus*, another elegant variety, is a native of China FLOWERS AND PLANTS.

Conway cabal, the Thomas, count de Conway, was born in Ireland, but taken to France while young In 1777, through the influence of Silas Deane, he came to the United States, was commissioned brig-gen, 13 May, 1777, and fought at Brandywine and Germantown, 1777 Washington's defeats caused widespread discontent in 1777, especially when the British occupied Philadelphia Burgoyne's surrender gave Gates the prestige of a great success Such men as John Adams, Samuel Adams, Richard Henry Lee, Thomas Mifflin, etc, began to doubt Washington's fitness for the chief command Conway did not originate the cabal for Washington's removal, but was so active in it that it bears his name Gates willingly lent his influence, in the hope of obtaining the command himself There was correspondence derogatory to Washington between Gates, Mifflin, and Conway during the summer and autumn of 1777. In the new board of war, organized Nov 1777, the faction was represented by Gates as president, and Mifflin and others as members Conway, against Washington's remonstrance, was promoted maj-gen, and made inspector-general of the army A vain attempt was made to win Lafayette by offering him an army to invade Canada, but these intrigues, when known to the army, were heartily reprobated, nor did the state legislatures approve them. In spite of disasters to the army, Washington retained the confidence and affection of soldiers and people, and most of the conspirators shrank from avowing their share in the plot Conway, ordered to the northern department, complained to Congress, and offered his resignation It was accepted, and he tried in vain to obtain a reinstatement. He was wounded soon after in a duel with gen Cadwallader, and, believing his end near, wrote an apology to Washington for his course He recovered, however, and returned to France

cookery, as an art, belongs to civilized life Animals were granted as food to Noah, 2348 B.C, but eating blood was forbidden (Gen ix 3, 4) In 1898 B.C a calf was cooked by Abraham to entertain his guests (Gen xviii 7, 8) "The Forme of Cury" (i e cookery) is dated 1390 An English cookery-book was printed 1498

Three medals were awarded to the Norwegian self acting cooking apparatus (Sorensen s patent) at the Paris Exhibition, 1867 Cooking is effected by boiling water the heat of which is maintained by enclosing it in a non conducting substance

In the U S, schools of cookery have become common in large cities since 1874

Cook's excursions. Thomas Cook in 1841 began his tourist system by arranging with the Midland Railway Company (England) for the conveyance of a party of 570 persons from Leicester to Loughborough and back for 1s each He gradually extended the system to the Continent, to America, India, Egypt, Holy Land, etc. He died 18 July, 1892, aged 83

Cook's voyages. James Cook, accompanied by Joseph Banks (afterwards sir), sailed from England in the *Endeavor* on his first voyage, 30 July, 1768, and after circumnavigating the globe, arrived at Deal 12 June, 1771 This expedition was proposed by the Royal Society to observe the transit of Venus, 3 June, 1769 Capt Cook sailed to explore the southern hemisphere 13 July, 1772 In his last expedition (begun 12 July, 1776) he was killed by the savages of Owhyhee, 14 Feb 1779 His ships, the *Resolution* and *Discovery*, arrived at Sheerness 4 Oct 1780

coolies (Hindu, *kuli*, laborer), the hill-tribes of India, are much employed as laborers in Australia and California, especially since 1861, about 30,000 of them were brought, conveyed by M Koopmanschap to work on the great Pacific railway He proposed in 1869 to replace the negroes of the cotton states with coolies, but the proposition was not accepted "The Coolie, his Rights and Wrongs," by E Jenkins, was pub 1871 Coolie emigration has been the subject of negotiation between the British and Chinese governments since 1855 "In spite of his utility, the coolie has become an offence to the working classes of the United States and Australia He is accused of various bad habits, but his principal offence is in working for low wages, and thus lowering the market value of labor"—*Chambers's Ency*

cooperage, the art of making casks and barrels out of staves bound by hoops, to hold liquids, etc It was practised in ancient times, being mentioned by Pliny It is only in very recent times that machinery has largely superseded hand labor in cooperage The coopers of London were incorporated in 1501

co-operative societies (England) of working-men sell articles of daily consumption to members at low prices. The Rochdale Equitable Pioneers' Society began in 1844, with a capital of 28*l* In 1860 the business done amounted to 152,063*l*, the profits being 15,906*l* These societies (332 in 1862) are registered pursuant to 13 and 14 Vict. c 115 (1849) On 31 Dec. 1866, 749 industrial, provident, and co-operative societies were registered By an act of 1867 they must make a return A congress of delegates is held annually. International congress held at Bologna, 1 Oct 1888

Co operative cotton mills in south Lancashire were reported successful in 1875

Ouseburn Co operative Engineering Works, established 1871, failed through want of capital, wound up, 1875

Much discontent among London tradesmen on account of the numerous co operative stores, 1878–80

Co operative Union included 1500 societies with a share capital of 11,000,000*l*, Nov 1890.

Copan', Ruins of, situated in the extreme western part of Honduras, supposed to be those of a city of unknown antiquity, first discovered in 1576 AMERICA Baldwin's "Ancient America," Charnay's "Ancient Cities of the New World," and Stephens's "Travels in Central America," are the best works published on these and other ruins of America.

Copenhagen, Denmark, built by Waldemar I, 1157, made the capital, 1443, the university founded, 1479 In 1728 more than 70 streets and 3785 houses were burned Its palace, valued at 4,000,000*l.*, was burned, Feb. 1794; 100 persons lost their lives. In a fire which lasted 48 hours, the arsenal, admiralty, and 50 streets were destroyed, June, 1795. A new national theatre was founded by the king, 18 Oct. 1872. Copenhagen was bombarded by English under lord Nelson and admiral Parker; and of 23 Danish ships of the line, 18 were taken or destroyed by the British, 2 Apr. 1801. Again, after a bombardment of 3 days, the city surrendered to admiral Gambier and lord Cathcart, 7 Sept. 1807, with the fleet of 18 sail of the line, 15 frigates, 6 brigs, 25 gunboats, and immense naval stores. Pop. with suburbs, 1880, 273,727; 1890, 375,251.

Copernican system, from its author, Nicolas Copernicus, born at Thorn, west Prussia, 19 Feb. 1473; died, 24 May, 1543, a few days after the printing of his book on the "Revolution of the Celestial Bodies," which marks one of the greatest steps ever taken in science. The system, which resembles "the Pythagorean," was condemned by pope Paul V. in 1616; decree revoked 1818 by Pius VII. It has been advanced from time to time by Kepler, Galileo, Newton, and the whole body of modern astronomers.

copophone, a musical instrument formed of glass tumblers on a sounding-board. The sounds are produced by wet fingers on the edge of the glasses. It was played at parties in London in June, 1875, by chevalier Furtado Coelho, the inventor.

copper. One of the 6 primitive metals, said to have been first discovered in Cyprus.—*Pliny.* We read in the Scriptures of 2 vessels of fine copper (or brass), "precious as gold," 457 B.C. (Ezra viii. 27). The mines of Fahlun, in Sweden, are surprising excavations. In England, copper-mines were discovered in 1561; there are more than 50 mines in Cornwall, where mining has grown from the reign of William III. In 1857, 75,832 tons of copper ore were taken to England, and 25,241 tons mined. In 1865, 198,298 tons of copper ore were extracted from British mines, and 11,888 tons smelted; 82,562 tons were imported. In 1856, 24,257 tons of pure copper (worth 2,983,611*l.*); in 1870, 8291 tons (worth 644,065*l.*); in 1875, 4332 tons (worth 388,984*l.*); in 1876, 4694 tons (worth 391,130*l.*); in 1879, 3462 tons (worth 222,507*l.*); in 1890, 936 tons were produced in the United Kingdom. The Burra-Burra copper-mines in S. Australia, discovered 1842, are valuable. The copper production of the United States for 10 years (1880–89) was over 733,061 tons, valued at $192,237,714; for 1891, 147,905 tons, valued at $38,455,300. The richest mine in the world is the Calumet and Hecla on lake Superior, Michigan, having paid in dividends $32,000,000 in 20 years.

Copper money. The Romans, before Servius Tullius, used rude pieces of copper for money. COIN.
In England copper money was made at the instance of sir Robert Cotton, in 1609; but was first coined (when Miss Stewart sat for the figure of Britannia) 1665
Its regular coinage began 1672; largely issued 1689
In Ireland, copper was coined, 1339; in Scotland, 1406; in France 1580
Wood's coinage in Ireland commenced 1723
Copper coinage largely manufactured at Birmingham, by Boulton and Watt 1792
Penny and twopenny pieces extensively issued 1797
Half-farthing was coined, but disused (FARTHING) 1843
10,000*l.* voted for replacing the copper coinage .... July, 1855
Copper coinage discontinued in U. S., a mixed metal substituted, 21 Feb. 1857
Bronze coinage issued .... Dec. 1860
French syndicate formed to raise the price of copper by a monopoly, Feb. 1888; fails .... Mch. 1889
Copper-plate printing invented in Germany, about 1450; rolling-presses for working the plates .... about 1545
Messrs. Perkins, of Philadelphia, invented engraving on soft steel, from which, when hardened, copper plates and impressions are made indefinitely (ENGRAVING) 1819
Copper sheathing first applied to the British ship *Alarm*, at Woolwich, 1761; all the navy copper-bottomed by 1780
Electrotyping with copper printing types and casts from wood-cuts, began .... about 1850
Copper-zinc couple, a voltaic arrangement of Dr. J. H. Gladstone and A. Tribe in 1872; a mixture of the 2 metals is finely subdivided, with points of junction exposed; any binary liquid containing this is rapidly decomposed, its resistance being greatly reduced. The couple is formed by immersing zinc-foil in a solution of sulphate of copper; the copper being deposited on the zinc in minute particles. By this couple impurities in water are readily detected, many peculiar analyses have been made, and new organic bodies formed.

copperas, a mineral composed of copper or iron with sulphuric acid (vitriol), found in copper-mines, commonly a green or blue color; said to have been first produced in England by Cornelius de Vos, a merchant, in 1587.

Copperheads. In and after 1863 members of the Democratic party in the U. S. who favored peace on any terms.—Copperhead, a poisonous serpent, the *Trigonocephalus contortrix*, also named dumb-rattlesnake, red viper, etc.

Copts, in Egypt, the supposed descendants of the ancient Egyptians, mingled with Greeks and Persians. Their religion is a form of Christianity derived from the Eutychians.

copying-machines (for letters, etc.) were invented in Engl. by James Watt in 1778; patented in May, 1780; and 150 machines were sold before the end of the year. Wedgwood's "manifold writer" was patented in 1806; and in 1855 Terry patented a copying-machine to be combined with the cover of a book. Other inventions patented since. Zuccato's papyrograph is much esteemed.

copyright in England. Decree of the star-chamber regarding it, 1556. Every book and publication ordered to be licensed, 1585.

Ordinance forbids printing of any work without the consent of the owner 1649
First copyright act (for 14 years, and for the author's life if then living), 8 Anne 1709
This act sustained by the lords, and the claim of perpetual copyright overruled .... 22 Feb. 1774
Copyright in prints and engravings, 17 Geo. III 1777
Copyright Protection act (for 28 years, and for the author's life), 54 Geo. III 1814
Dramatic Authors' Protection act, 3 Will. IV. c. 15 1833
Act protecting lecturers, 6 Will. IV. c. 65 1835
International Copyright bill, 1 Vict. c. 59 1838
5 and 6 Vict. c. 45 (Talfourd's or lord Mahon's act), to amend the Copyright act, passed 1842
[Copyright is for the life of the author, and 7 years after; but for 42 years in any case; posthumous works protected for 42 years.]
Colonies' Copyright act, 10 and 11 Vict. c. 95, passed 1847
Canada Copyright act, passed .... 2 Aug. 1875
Copyright of 14 years conferred on sculpture 1798, 1814
Photographs protected as works of art .... July, 1862

INTERNATIONAL COPYRIGHT.

First movement in the U. S. for international copyright in 1837, when Henry Clay presented a petition. Referred to Senate committee, including Clay, Webster, and Buchanan who reported for full protection.
Lord Palmerston invites the U. S. to co-operate 1838
British acts secure to authors, in certain cases, international copyright (1 and 2 Vict. c. 59, 7 and 8 Vict. c. 12, and 15 Vict. c. 12); conventions entered into with France, Prussia, etc., 1838, 1852
Proposal again before the U. S. Congress, supported by Edward Everett, secretary of state 1853
Claim of a foreigner to British copyright negatived by the House of Lords, reversing the court of exchequer, on appeal by defendant in Boosey *v.* Jeffrey. (In 1831 Mr. Boosey purchased the copyright of Bellini's opera, "La Sonnambula," from which Mr. Jeffrey published a cavatina. 6 judges for the copyright; 7 against) .... Aug. 1854
Baldwin's bill introduced in British Parliament 1868
International copyright bill introduced in the U. S. Congress, 21 Feb. "
In Routledge *v.* Low, the House of Lords on appeal uphold copyright of a foreign author .... 29 May, "
Discussion at the Literary Congress, Paris .... 18 June, "
Sir Edward Thornton submits a proposed treaty to publishers in the U. S. 1870
Copyright Association of England, founded by eminent London booksellers .... 19 Mch. 1872
Senator Morrill, chairman of joint library committee, report against international copyright 1873
Messrs. Harper & Brothers, N. Y., submit a suggestion to the department of state of a treaty on the subject .... 25 Nov. 1878
Harper treaty approved by prominent American authors .. Aug. 1880
Congress passes an international copyright law .... 3 Mch. 1891
President Harrison proclaims that Switzerland, France, Belgium, Great Britain, Germany, and Italy, having complied with the conditions, the benefits of copyright in the U. S. are extended to their citizens .... 1 July, "
[There is no treaty of international copyright between the U. S. and other countries. A citizen of the U. S., to secure copyright in Great Britain, must (1) enter the title at Stationer's Hall, London, fee, 5*s.*; (2) the work must be first published in Great Britain. A foreigner may copyright a publication in France by depositing 2 copies at the Ministry of the Interior at Paris. In Germany, by entering the work in the general copyright registry at Leipzig and publishing it within the German empire. In Canada, by registry with the minister of agriculture, fee $1, and publication in Canada.]

COPYRIGHT IN THE UNITED STATES.

First copyright law passed 1790
Copyrights granted for 28 years, with a renewal for 14 years 1831
Copyrights granted in plays for exclusive representation 1856
Law granting any author, inventor, designer, or proprietor a copyright for his work for 28 years, with renewal for himself, his widow, or children for 14 years 1870

An act of Congress amending sections 4952, 4954, 4956, 4958, 4959, 4963, 4964, 4965, and 4967, Revised Statutes passed, 3 Mch 1891
To take effect 1 July, "

[As an international copyright law it "only applies to a citizen or subject of a foreign state or nation, when such foreign state or nation permits to citizens of the U S. of America the benefit of copyright on substantially the same basis as its own citizens, or when such foreign state or nation is a party to an international agreement which provides for reciprocity in the granting of copyright, by the terms of which agreement the U S of America may at its pleasure become a party to such agreement The existence of either of these conditions aforesaid shall be determined by the president of the U S by proclamation made from time to time as the purposes of this act may require "]

coral, a production of the *Actinozoa coralligena*, and confined to the warmer latitude of the globe The most valuable kind is the *Corallium rubrum* of the Mediterranean sea, having been from remote times greatly prized for personal ornamentation and decorative purposes generally The most important fisheries extend along the coast of northern Africa, but it is also obtained near Naples, Leghorn, and Genoa, and off the coasts of Sardinia, Corsica, etc The price of the finest tints varies from $400 to $600 per oz

Corbiesdale, Caithness, N Scotland Here, on 27 Apr 1650, the marquis of Montrose was defeated by Covenanters He was taken soon after, treated with contumely, and hanged at Edinburgh, 21 May

Corcy'ra, now **Corfu,** chief of the Ionian isles, a colony founded by Corinthians about 734 B.C It had frequent wars with the mother-country, one for Epidamnus (431 B C.) led to the Peloponnesian war It was subdued by the Spartans in 373, and by the Romans, 230. At the decline of the eastern empire it fell to the Venetians, about 1119 A D The Turks vainly attacked Corfu in 1716 It was taken from the French by the allied Russian and Turkish fleets, 3 Mch. 1799, and formed (with the other isles) into the Ionian republic. IONIAN ISLES

Cordeliers (*kor'-de-lyar'*), friars of the order of St Francis d'Assisi (the Minorites) instituted about 1223, wearing coarse gray cloth and a girdle of cord, hence the name, first given by St Louis of France, about 1227

Cordeliers, a political club formed in Paris, 1790, so called for its meeting in the chapel of that name It included among its leaders some of the most violent of the revolutionists, viz Danton, Marat, Hébert, Camille Desmoulins, and others It was first allied with, but afterwards opposed, the Jacobins, was overthrown in Mch 1794, and several members guillotined, formally closed 23 Aug 1795

cordilleras (Sp *kor'-dēl-yā'-ra*), a continuous range of mountains ANDES

Cor'dova, the Roman Corduba, S Spain, founded about 152 B C, taken by the Goths, 572 A D., and made capital of an Arab kingdom by Abderahman in 756, who founded the great mosque (now the cathedral), 786 Here Seneca, Lucan, and the Arabian physician Averrhoes were born In the 10th century it contained nearly 1,000,000 inhabitants and 300 mosques. It was rescued from the Arabs by Ferdinand III of Castile, in 1236, taken by French under Dupont and ravaged, 7-9 June, 1808, surrendered to Joseph Bonaparte, Jan. 1810, abandoned by the French in 1813; plundered by Carlists, Oct 1836 Pop. 1890 about 56,000

Core'a or **Kore'a,** a peninsula, E Asia, tributary to China, which excluded all foreigners until 1882, when 4 ports were opened to commerce through the agency of the United States and China by treaty. Area, 82,000 sq miles, pop estimated about 10,000,000

President Arthur receives officially at the Fifth Avenue hotel, New York, the Corean ambassadors 18 Sept. 1883
Treaty with Great Britain 1884
With Germany "
With Italy and Russia "
With France 1886
Invaded by Japanese troops, and Chinese driven out, July–Sept 1894

Corces. INDIANS.

Corfu. CORCYRA.

Cor'inth, Greece, a city said to have been built 1520 B.C., and named Ephyra. It was defended by a lofty and strongly walled fortress called Acrocorinth. Cicero named it the *Eye of Greece* Its history is fabulous or legendary, and all dates in it are conjectural, until the 7th century B.C

B C
Isthmian games, mythically ascribed to Sisyphus, who founded a kingdom 1326
Return of the Heraclidæ or Dorians 1107
Their dynasty established by Aletes 1074
Corinthians invent *triremes* (ships with 3 benches of oars), 786 or 758
Reign of Bacchis, 925, oligarchy of Bacchidæ 747–657
Thelestes deposed, government of Prytanes instituted Automenes, first about 745
Corinthian colonies, Syracuse and Corcyra founded about 734
Corcyreans revolting, defeat Corinthians at sea 664
Cypselus a despot, sets aside the Prytanes 655
His son Periander rules, and favors learning 627–585
Psammetichus deposed, and a republic formed 580
Corinth engaged in the Persian war 480
Defeated by Corcyreans 435
CORINTHIAN WAR 395
Timoleon kills his usurping brother Timophanes 344
Acrocorinth taken by Aratus, given to the Achæan league 243
Roman ambassadors first appear at Corinth 228
Greeks defeated at Cynoscephalæ 197
Corinth sacked by Lucius Mummius, who sends to Italy the first fine paintings there seen (*Livy*) 146
Rebuilt by Julius Cæsar 46
A D
Visited by St Paul (Acts xviii) 54
His two *Epistles to the Corinthians* about 59–60
Ravaged by Alaric 396
Plundered by Normans from Sicily 1146
Taken by Turks 1446, by Venetians, 1687, by Turks, June, 1714, from them by Greeks 1823
Nearly destroyed by an earthquake 21 Feb 1858
A concession for 99 years to a French company for canal through the isthmus, to be completed in 6 years by MM E G Piat and Chollet, Apr 1870, transferred to baron de Lesseps and gen Turr (to be begun in spring, 1882) 28 May, 1881
Work begun 5 May, 1882
Completed 1893
CANALS

Corinth, Miss. After the battle of Shiloh, or PITTSBURG LANDING, 6, 7 Apr 1862, gen Halleck took command of the forces, about 120,000 men, and 3 weeks later moved towards Corinth, then held by the confederate gen. Beauregard, taking from 30 Apr to 30 May for the advance of 20 miles He was unopposed until within 4 or 5 miles of Corinth, and while he prepared for a siege Beauregard quietly evacuated the place on the 29th May, taking his stores, and Halleck occupied it on the 30th Corinth was also the scene of a severe battle, when 35,000 or more confederates, under Price and Van Dorn, attacked Rosecrans's army of 20,000, in a strong and fortified position, 3 Oct 1862 in the afternoon. The main fighting was next forenoon, when the attack was repulsed. Federal loss, 315 killed, 1812 wounded, 232 missing Confederate loss, supposed about 1423 killed, 5692 wounded, and 2225 prisoners.

Corinthian order, the richest order of ancient architecture, called by Scamozzi the virginal order, attributed to Callimachus, 540 B.C. ABACUS.

Corinthian war began 395 B.C, so called because mostly fought near Corinth, by a confederacy of Athenians, Thebans, Corinthians, and Argives, against the Lacedæmonians. It was closed by the peace of Antalcidas, 387 B C The chief battles were at CORONEA and LECHÆUM

Cori'oli, a Latin city, capital of the Volscians, taken by Romans, 493 B.C The exploits of Caius Marcius or Coriolanus are mythical

Cork, S. Ireland, built in the 6th century The principality of the M'Cartys was converted into a shire by king John, as lord of Ireland The foundation of the see is ascribed to St Barr, or Finbarr, early in the 7th century About 1431 it was united to Cloyne, but in 1678 separated, Ross having been added to Cork, 1582. Cork and Cloyne were reunited (by the act of 1833), 1835

Garrisoned by Henry II 1172
First charter, from Henry II 1185
Supported Perkin Warbeck, who landed here 1492
A large part of the town burned 1621
Taken by Cromwell 1649
Marlborough took Cork by siege, the duke of Grafton, a son of Charles II, was slain 1690
Cathedral rebuilt from a coal duty between 1725 and 1735
One of 3 colleges, endowed under act 8 and 9 Vict. c. 66, passed, 31 July, 1845, inaugurated (QUEEN'S COLLEGES) 7 Nov 1849

cork-tree (*Quercus suber*), a species of oak, cork is part of its bark. The Egyptians made coffins of cork. The tree grows in abundance on the Pyrenees and in other parts of Spain and in France It was brought to England about 1690 A cork-carpet company was formed, 1862

corn. A general term for the seed of cereal plants, including all grains used as food But it has also a specific sense, as in England it generally means wheat, in Scotland oats, and in the United States MAIZE The origin of its cultivation is attributed to Ceres, who having taught the art to the Egyptians, was deified by them, 2409 B C —*Arundelian Marbles* Husbandry, and making bread from wheat, and wine from rice, are attributed by Chinese to Ching Noung, successor of Fohi, and second monarch of China, 1998 B.C.—*Univ Hist* Corn was a common article of food from the earliest ages, and bread was baked in patriarchal times (Ex xii 15) The first known importation of corn into England was in 1347. Laws restricting it were made in 1361, and often afterwards. Bounties were granted on its importation into England in 1689. WHEAT

CORN LAWS OF ENGLAND

Restrictions on importing corn became oppressive as manufactures increased about 1770, relaxed 1773
Mr Robinson's act passed, permitting importation when wheat is 80s a quarter 1815
While this bill was pending mobs assembled in London and many houses of its supporters were damaged, 28 Jan, a riot in Westminster 6-9 Mch
A corn bill passed by commons rejected by lords amended by the duke of Wellington, and carried by a majority of 4, 1 June, 1827
An act (the sliding scale) permits wheat to be imported at a duty of 1*l* 5*s* 8*d*. per quarter, when the average price is under 62*s*, from 62*s* to 63*s* 1*l*. 4*s* 8*d*., and so gradually reduced to 1*s*, when the average price is 73*s* and upwards passed 15 July 1828
Act 5 Vict. c. 14, the second "sliding scale act," regulates the duty on wheat, passed 29 Apr 1842
Corn Importation bill (introduced by sir Robert Peel) 9 and 10 Vict. c 22 (the duty reduced to 4*s* when imported at or above 53*s*, until 1 Feb 1849, after that the duty to be 1*s* per quarter on all grain imported, at any prices), approved, 26 June, 1846
The 1*s* duty repealed by act passed 24 June, 1869

corn, Indian MAIZE

Cornell University, Ithaca, N. Y In 1862 the national government gave to each of the states certain public lands, the proceeds to establish schools of agriculture and the mechanic arts, 990,000 acres was New York's share Ezra Cornell generously offered to add $500 000 to the fund if it should all be used to found one institution Largely through the efforts of state senator Andrew D White of Syracuse, the offer was accepted, and Ithaca was selected as the site, Mr Cornell further giving 200 acres of land for an experimental farm The institution, taking his name, was opened for students in 1868, with Andrew D White as president The first year it had 388 students Women have been admitted since 1873 COLLEGES IN THE UNITED STATES

Cornwall, southwest extremity of England, originally *Kernou*, a term connected with Latin *cornu*, a horn, from its numerous promontories After the retreat of the Britons, Cornwall is said to have formed a kingdom, for many years, under different princes, among them Ambrosius Aurel us and "king Arthur" Cornwall is said to have been made an earldom by Alfred The eldest son born to the reigning sovereign is duke of Cornwall

Bishopric of Cornwall, founded 909, united to Devonshire, 1040, removed to Exeter 1046
Cornwall given by the conqueror to Robert de Mortein, his half brother, 1068, killed 1087
Cornwall made a duchy, by Edward III., for Edward, his eldest son, the Black Prince 17 Mch 1337
Insurrection of Cornishmen under lord Audley, Thomas Flammock, etc, against taxes, they march to London, defeated at Blackheath 22 June, 1497
Insurrection in Devon and Cornwall against the Protestant liturgy, defeated by lord Russell Aug 1549
Rev R Polwhele's "History of Cornwall" pub 1803-8

coronation. Leo I, emperor of the east, crowned by Anatolius, patriarch of Constantinople, the first Christian sovereign crowned by a priest, 457 Majorian, emperor of the west, said to have been crowned in the same year in a similar manner

Charlemagne crowned emperor of the west by pope Leo III. (with the words "*coronatus a Deo*"—"crowned by God"), 25 Dec. 800
Edward I, son of Alfred, crowned .16 May, 902
William I crowned at Westminster. 25 Dec 1066
Anointing at coronations introduced into England 872, and Scotland 1097
Coronation of Henry III, at Gloucester A plain circle was used, the crown having been lost with the baggage of king John, in passing the marshes of Lynn, or the Wash near Wisbeach 28 Oct 1216
William and Mary crowned by Compton, bishop of London (Sancroft, archbishop of Canterbury, refused the oaths), 11 Apr 1689
George IV crowned 19 July, 1821
William IV crowned, with his queen 8 Sept 1831
Victoria crowned 28 June, 1838
Coronation chair In the cathedral of Cashel, formerly the metropolis of the kings of Munster, was deposited the *Lia Fail* or Fatal Stone on which they were crowned Tradition says that in 513 Fergus of the royal line, obtaining the Scottish throne, procured this stone for his coronation at Dunstaffnage, where it remained until Kenneth II removed it to Scone, and in 1296 it was removed by Edward I from Scone to Westminster, the present chair being made to receive it
A coronation oath was administered by Dunstan, archbishop of Canterbury, to Ethelred II in 978 An oath, much like that now in use, was administered in 1377
Oath prescribed by 1 Will and Mary, c 6 (1689), was modified in 1706 and again in 1821, on account of the union of the churches of England and Ireland

Coronea, Battles of I (or Chæronea) The Athenians defeated and their general, Tolmides, slain by the Bœotians at Coronea near Chæronea, 447 B C II The Athenians, Thebans, Argives, and Corinthians forming a league against Sparta, Agesilaus, after many victories, even in Upper Asia, engaged and defeated the allies at Coronea, 394 B C

coroners (anciently crowner), officers of the English realm, mentioned in a charter, 925 Coroners for every county in England were first appointed by statute of Westminster, 3 Edw I 1275.—*Stow* They are chosen for life by the freeholders, to inquire into the cause of unnatural death, upon view of the body The same applies to the office in the United States, except as to length of term

coronets, caps or inferior crowns of the English nobility. The coronets for earls were first allowed by Henry III., for viscounts by Henry VIII, and for barons by Charles II.—*Baker* But authorities conflict Sir Robert Cecil, earl of Salisbury, was the first earl who wore a coronet, 1604. It is uncertain when the coronets of dukes and marquises were settled.—*Beatson.*

corporations. Numa, to break the force of the rival factions, Sabines and Romans, is said to have instituted separate societies of manual trades —*Plutarch.* In England, bodies politic, authorized by the king's charter to have a common seal, one head officer, or more, and members, who, by common consent, may grant or receive in law any matter within the compass of their charter —*Cowell.* Charters of rights were granted by the kings of England to various towns, first by Edward the Confessor Henry I granted charters, 1100, and succeeding monarchs gave corporate powers to numerous communities throughout the realm, subject to tests, oaths, and conditions —*Blackstone.*

corpulence. In Germany some fat monks have weighed 18 stone —*Render*

Mr Bright a tallow chandler and grocer of Maldon, in Essex, died in his 29th year His waistcoat easily held 7 persons of common size; buried at All-Saints, Maldon 12 Nov 1750
Daniel Lambert, supposed the heaviest man that ever lived, died in his 40th year at Stamford, in Lincolnshire, weighing 52 stone (a stone 14 lbs.) 11 pounds, (10 stone 4 pounds more than Mr Bright) 21 June, 1809
James Mansfield, died at Dobden, aged 82, weighing 34 stone, 9 Nov 1856
William Banting published a letter on corpulence, recommending, from experience, as a remedy, great moderation in sugar and starch as food. 50,000 copies were speedily circulated 1863

Corpus Christi (*Fête Dieu* in France), a splendid festival in the Roman Catholic church, in honor of transubstantiation, kept on the Thursday after TRINITY SUNDAY. It was instituted by pope Urban IV. between 1262 and 1264, and confirmed by the council of Vienne in 1311

"Correlation of the Physical Forces," a book by Mr (afterwards sir) W. R. Grove, F.R.S, who in 1842 explained the correlation or mutual dependence and convertibility of the forces of nature (viz, heat, light, electricity, magnetism, chemical affinity, and motion).

Cor'sica, an island in the Mediterranean (called by the Greeks Κυρνος), held by the French It is 114 miles long and 52 broad Area, 3378 sq miles, pop 1890, about 280,000 The ancient inhabitants were robbers, liars, and atheists, according to Seneca Corsica was colonized by Phocæans 561 B C, and afterwards held by the Carthaginians till taken by the Romans, 231 B.C It has been held by Vandals, 456 A D, by Saracens, 852, by Pisans, 1077 It belonged to Genoa from 1559 till ceded to France in 1768

During a revolt made a kingdom under Theodore Neuhoff, its first and only king 1736

He came to England lay in the King's Bench prison for debt, supported by private friends but was released, gave in his schedule the kingdom of Corsica to his creditors and died in Soho 1756

[The Earl of Orford wrote the following epitaph for a tablet near his grave in St Anne's church, Dean street

"The grave, great teacher! to a level brings
Heroes and beggars, galley slaves and kings
But Theodore this moral learn'd ere dead,
Fate pour'd its lesson on his living head,
Bestowed a kingdom and denied him bread "]

Pascal Paoli chosen general by Corsicans. 1753

Defeated by the count de Vaux he fled to England 1769

Napoleon Bonaparte born at Ajaccio (5 Feb 1768, baptismal register, doubtful) 15 Aug "

People acknowledge George III king 17 June, 1794

Sir Gilbert Eliott viceroy opened parliament 1795

Revolt suppressed June, the island relinquished by the British, 22 Oct., the people declare for the French 1796

Corte Nuova (*kōr'-tā noo'-vā*), near Milan, N Italy Here the emperor Frederic II defeated the Milanese after a severe conflict, 27 Nov 1237

Cortes, the Spanish parliament, grew out of the old Gothic councils. The Cortes were assembled after a long interval of years, 24 Sept 1810, and settled the new constitution, 16 Mch 1812, which was set aside by Ferdinand VII, who banished many members in May, 1814 The Cortes were reopened by him, Mch 1820, dissolved Oct 1823, again assembled Apr 1834, and have since met regularly The Cortes of Portugal assembled under dom Pedro's charter, 30 Oct 1826, they were suppressed by dom Miguel in 1828, and restored in 1833

Corunna, N W Spain The British army, about 15,000 men, under sir John Moore, were attacked in retreat at Corunna, by more than 20,000 French, who were repulsed, but the loss of the British was immense, 16 Jan 1809 Sir John being struck by a cannon-ball, which carried away his left shoulder and part of the collar-bone, died universally lamented, and was buried at Corunna by his soldiers The remains of the army embarked under sir David Baird, 17 Jan "The Burial of Sir John Moore," called by Charles Knight "the noblest dirge ever written," is by Charles Wolfe, born in Ireland, 1791, died 1823

Co'rus, Corupe'dion, or **Cyrope'dium,** a plain in Phrygia, Asia Minor, where the aged Lysimachus was defeated by Seleucus, and slain, 281 B.C. These 2 were the only survivors of Alexander the Great's generals.

corvée, forced labor and service under the feudal system in France, was alleviated by Louis XVI, at the suggestion of Turgot, 27 June, 1787, by the constituent assembly, 18 Mch. 1790, and abolished by the convention, 17 July, 1792

coryphæus (*kōr'-y-phe'-us*), the principal person of the chorus in ancient tragedy. Tysias or Stesichorus, who first instructed the chorus to dance to the lyre, 556 B C., was so called

cosmog'ony, a theory of the origin of the world PHILOSOPHY.

Cossacks (armed horsemen), a people of Russia, extending from the confines of Poland through Siberia. They are termed Cossacks of the Don, Azof, Danube, Dnieper, Caucasus, Ural, Orenboorg etc They have finally submitted to the state control of Russia Mazeppa, a hetman (ruler) of the Dnieper Cossacks, joined Charles XII. of Sweden against Russia 1708, which led to their subjugation The Cossack serves in the Russian army as light cavalry, forming one of the most valuable elements in it, as a protection of the frontier from the Caucasus to the Pacific.

Cosso'va, a plain in Servia Here Amurath I defeated the Christian army (Servians, Hungarians, etc.), Sept 1389, but was killed by an expiring soldier Here John Hunniades was defeated by a Turkish army 4 times his strength, 17 Oct 1448

Costa Rica, a republic in Central America, part of Guatemala, independent Nov 1848 Constitution, 27 Dec 1859 Area, 21,000 sq miles Pop. 1891, estimated, 238,782 AMERICA, CENTRAL

Cotopaxi (*kō tō päks'-e*) ANDES

cottage. Originally a small house without land, 4 Edw I, 1275 "No man may build a cottage, except in towns, unless he lay 4 acres of land thereto," etc., 31 Eliz 1589 This was repealed, 15 Geo III 1775

cotton, a vegetable wool, produce of the *Gossypium*, a shrub indigenous to tropical India and America Indian cotton cloth is mentioned by Herodotus, was known in Arabia in time of Mahomet, 627, and brought to Europe by his followers It was perhaps first used by the Chinese in the 13th century, to them we owe the cotton fabric nankeen Cotton was the chief material of clothing among the American Indians visited by Columbus It was grown and manufactured in Spain in the 10th century, and in the 14th was introduced into Italy Indian muslins, chintzes, and cottons were largely imported into England in the 17th century, but a law of 1700 prohibited their introduction Cotton became the staple commodity of England in the present century About 1841 the "cotton" or "Manchester" interest grew to political importance, which led to the repeal of the corn laws in 1846 CALICO, MUSLIN, etc

COTTON IN GREAT BRITAIN

Fustian and *velveteen* made of cotton, about 1641

Calico sheeting, etc The fly shuttle was invented by John Kay of Bury 1738, the drop box by Robert Kay, 1760, spinning by rollers (also attributed to John Wyatt) patented by Louis Paul, 1738, the spinning jenny, by Hargreaves, 1767, the water frame by Arkwright, 1769, the power loom by rev Dr Edmund Cartwright 1785, the dressing machine by Johnson and Radcliffe, 1802-4, another power loom by Horrocks, 1803-13 A combing machine was patented by Joshua Heilmann, in 1845

British muslin (superseding that of India) is due mainly to the MULE invented by Samuel Crompton, 1774-79 and to the self acting mule of Mr Roberts, 1825

Calico printing commenced, 1764

Steam engine first applied to cotton manufacture (by Boulton and Watt), 1785

Bleaching by chloride of lime introduced by Mr Tennant, of Glasgow 1798

Stockings The stocking frame invented by William Lee, 1589 *Cotton stockings* first made by [illegible] 1730, Jedediah Strutt patented Derby ribbed stockings in 1759, Horton his knotter frame in 1776, Crompton's mule was employed in making thread for the stocking manufacture about 1770

Cotton lace—Bobbin net The stocking frame of Lee was applied to lace making by Hammond, about 1768, the process perfected by John Heathcoat, 1809

COTTON-FIBRE IMPORTED INTO THE UNITED KINGDOM.

	Pounds		Pounds.
1710	715,008	1865	978 502 000
1730	1,545,472	1866	1,377,514,096
1790	31,500,000	1872	1,408,837,472
1810	132 500 000	1879	1,469,358,464
1860	390,938,75_	1885	1 425 816,336
1862	523,973,296	1890	1,793,495,200

IMPORTED FROM THE UNITED STATES.

	Pounds		Pounds
1795	5,250,000	1871	1,038,677,920
1820	89,999,174	1872	625,600,080
1830	210,885,358	1873	832,573,616
1840	487,856,504	1874	874,926,864
1847	364,599,291	1875	841,333,472
1859	961,707,264	1876	932,800,176
1860	1,115,890,608	1877	912,244,592
1861	819,500,528	1879	1,082,462,080
1866.	520 057,440	1885	1,050,546,000
1870	716,248,848	1890	1,316,756,896

In 1862-65 it nearly ceased

Australian cotton said by Manchester manufacturers to be superior to the best American, Jan 1861

Company formed at Manchester to obtain cotton from India, Africa, and other places (arose out of the Cotton Supply association, formed in 1857), Sept 1860

Since 1861, the cultivation of cotton in India, Egypt, Italy, etc., has greatly increased

Cotton factories regulated by law, 1825, 1831, 1833, and 1844 The hours of labor limited, the employment of children under 9 prohibited The number of spindles in operation in 1892 45,350,000, and the cotton manufactured, estimated at 4,977,000 bales of 400 lbs. each

COTTON IN THE UNITED STATES

Before 1795, England obtained her cotton fibre from the East and West Indies, the Levant, and a little from the U S About 1786 the cultivation of cotton began in Georgia In 1784, 8 bags, entered as American cotton were seized at Liverpool on the ground that so much could not have been produced in the U S Sea island cotton was first grown in 1786

First cotton factory in America at East Bridgewater Mass. 1787

First Arkwright machinery used in America, in Providence, R I, Dec 1790

By the end of 1809, 62 mills were in operation, 48 by water and 14 by horse power, with 31 000 spindles, many others in process of erection Their products were bed tickings, at from 53 to 90 cents per yard, stripes and checks, at from 30 to 40 cents, ginghams, from 40 to 50 cents, shirtings and sheetings, 35 to 75 cents, and counterpanes $8 each Some attempts had been made at printing calicoes, but with little success.—*Hildreth*, "Hist U S.," vol vi p 210 At the end of 1816 it was claimed that the cotton industry invested $40 000 000, and gave employment to 100,000 persons mostly boys and females, consuming annually 27,000,000 lbs, and producing 81,000,000 yds of cloth at an average price of 30 cents per yard —*Hildreth* In 1892 there were 15,277,000 spindles in operation in the U S, consuming 1,316,000,000 lbs of cotton

The cotton crop of the U S for the year ending 30 Sept. 1880, was 5,757,397 bales of 481 55 lbs. each Of this there were exported 3,865,621 bales, while 1,760,000 bales were manufactured in the U S For 1889-90 it was 7,434,487 bales, and for the year ending Sept. 1, 1891, it amounted to 8,652 579 bales. The total exports, excluding Canada, were 5,778,822 bales, of which Great Britain received 3,329,432 and France 559,099 In the U S the Northern spinners consumed 2,632,023 bales, and the Southern spinners 604,661 For 1892 the crop was 9,038,707 bales, average net weight 440 lbs The estimated production of the world being 12,353,000 bales of 400 lbs each

cotton-gin, a machine by which the cotton is separated from the seed and cleaned with great expedition. Invented and constructed by Eli Whitney (b. Westborough, Mass, 8 Dec. 1765, d New Haven, Conn, 8 Jan 1825) while engaged as a teacher in Georgia, 1792, and patented 1793 Although one of the most important of inventions, Whitney never realized much pecuniary benefit from it. This invention is said greatly to have promoted the growth of slavery in the United States

cotton-seed oil, largely manufactured from seeds of the cotton plant in the southern states, year 1876-77, 3,316,000 gallons, 1878-79, 8,175,000 gallons, 1889-90, 41,-250,000 gallons (crude), exported, 13,385,000 gallons

Cottonian library, formed by sir Robert Bruce Cotton, 1600 et seq He died 6 May, 1631 It was rescued from the republicans during the protectorate, 1649-60, and secured to the public by law in 1700 It was removed to Essex-house in 1712, in 1730 to Dean's yard, Westminster (where on 23 Oct 1731, it was damaged by fire), to the British museum in 1757

Coul'miers, a village 10 miles west of Orleans, central France. Here the Bavarians, under gen. von der Tann, were defeated by the French army of the Loire, under gen D'Aurelle de Paladines, who took about 2000 prisoners, 9 Nov. 1870, and regained Orleans

councils. King Alfred, in about 886, is said to have arranged legislative business so that all resolutions passed 3 councils The first was a select council to prepare matters for the second council, which consisted of bishops and nobles appointed by the king, like the present privy council The third was a general assembly of the nation, called, in Saxon, Wittenagemot, in which quality and office gave a right to sit. In these 3 councils we behold the origin of the cabinet, privy councils, and parliaments

councils of the church. The following are among the principal Those numbered are the *œcumenical* or *general* councils. Sir Harris Nicolas, in his "Chronology of History," enumerates 1604 councils, and gives an alphabetical list.

Of the church at Jerusalem (Acts xv) 50

Of western bishops at Arles, France, to suppress Donatists, 3 fathers of the English church attended 314

I First œcumenical or general, at Nice (Constantine the Great presided), decreed the consubstantiality of the Son, condemned Arianism, composed the Nicene creed 325

At Tyre, against Athanasius 335

First at Constantinople, when the Arian heresy gained ground, 337

At Rome, in favor of Athanasius 342

At Sardis 370 bishops attended, Arians condemned 347

At Rimini 400 bishops attended, Constantine forced on them a new confession 359

II Constantinople Oriental council, 150 orthodox bishops met, presided over, *first*, by Meletius, *second*, by Gregory Nazianzen, *third*, by Nectarius, added to the Nicene creed, declared the bishop of Constantinople next in rank to Rome, Constantinople being New Rome 381

III. Ephesus Cyril of Alexandria presided, anathematized and deposed Nestorius, denounced additions to the Nicene creed 431

IV Chalcedon 520 bishops present, declared the 2 natures of Christ, divine and human, as defined by Leo of Rome, accepted and decreed the Constantinopolitan addition to the Nicene creed 451

V Constantinople Eutyches, patriarch of Constantinople presided, condemned the 3 chapters (of Theodore of Mopsuestia, Theodoret, and others), Vigilius, bishop of Rome first protested, later assented 553

VI Constantinople pope Agatho presided, against Monothelites 7 Nov 680-16 Sept 681

Authority of 6 general councils re established by Theodosius 715

VII Second Nicene 350 bishops against Iconoclasts, 24 Sept -23 Oct. 787

VIII Constantinople emperor Basil attended, against Iconoclasts and heresies 5 Oct 869-28 Feb 870

At Clermont, convened by Urban II to authorize crusades, 310 bishops 1095

IX First Lateran right of investiture settled by treaty of pope Calixtus II and emperor Henry V 18 Mch.-5 Apr 1123

X Second Lateran Innocent II presided, chief topic, preservation of temporalities of ecclesiastics, 1000 church fathers 20 Apr 1139

XI Third Lateran against schismatics 5-19 Mch 1179

XII Fourth Lateran 400 bishops and 1000 abbots, Innocent III presided, against Albigenses, etc 11-30 Nov 1215

XIII Lyons under Innocent IV, emperor Frederick II deposed 28 June-17 July 1245

XIV Lyons under Gregory X, temporary union of Greek and Latin churches 7 May-17 June 1274

XV Vienne in Dauphine Clement V presided, kings of France and Aragon attended, Knights Templars suppressed, 16 Oct 1311, 3 Apr and 6 May 1312

XVI Pisa Gregory XII and Benedict XIII deposed, Alexander elected 5 Mch -7 Aug 1409

XVII Constance Martin V elected pope, John Huss and Jerome of Prague condemned to be burned 1414-18

XVIII Basel 1431-43

XIX Fifth Lateran begun by Julius II 1512

Continued under Leo X to suppress pragmatic sanction of France, against council of Pisa, etc, till 1517

XX. Trent to condemn doctrines of Luther, Zwinglius, and Calvin (TRENT) 13 Dec 1545-3 Dec 1563

XXI Rome called by encyclical letter, 8 Sept. 1868, met, 8 Dec 1869

Six archbishop princes, 49 cardinals, 11 patriarchs, 680 archbishops and bishops, 28 abbots, 29 generals of orders—803 in all, held 4 public sessions, and between 90 and 100 congregations. New canons were issued 24 Apr 1870, and, after much opposition, the pope's infallibility, as head of the church, was affirmed by 547 placets against 2 non placets, and promulgated 18 July, 1870

[Many bishops withdrew from the discussion The council adjourned to 11 Nov ROME.]

councils, French. The Council of ANCIENTS, the upper chamber of the legislature, of 250 members, each at least 40 years of age, with the Council of FIVE HUNDRED, instituted at Paris, 1 Nov 1795, the executive was a directory of FIVE. Bonaparte dispersed the Five Hundred at St Cloud, 9 Nov 1799, declaring himself, Roger Ducos, and Sieyès, consuls *provisoires* FRANCE

counsel are supposed to be coeval with the *curia regis.* Advocates are referred to the time of Edward I., but mentioned earlier Counsel guilty of deceit or collusion were punishable by the statute of Westminster, 13 Edw. I. 1285 Counsel were allowed to persons charged with treason, by 8 Will III 1696 An act allowing counsel to persons indicted for felony, passed in England Aug 1836 BARRISTERS

count (Lat *comes*, a companion, Fr *comte*), a title equivalent to English earl (whose wife is still termed a countess), and to the German *Graf*

counterpoint (in music), the chords to a melody The earliest known contrapuntal writing is by Adam de la Halle in the 12th century.

counties or **shires.** The division of England into counties began, it is said, with king Alfred, but some counties bore their present names a century earlier Ireland was formed into counties, 1562 Lord-lieutenants were appointed in 1549 in England, and in 1831 in Ireland Counties first sent members to Parliament (knights met previously in their own counties), 1285 By Chandos Clause, sec. 20 of the Reform act, 2 Will IV. c. 45 (1832), inserted on motion of the marquis of Chandos, occupiers as tenants of land not in a borough, paying an annual rent of 50*l*, had a vote for knight of the shire. It increased Tory voters, and attempts were made to repeal it. It was superseded by the Reform act of 15 Aug. 1867.

By Winter Assizes act 1876, certain counties were united (by order in council, first, 23 Oct. 1876) to facilitate speedy trials
In the U S the division of states into counties dates from the colonial period In Louisiana counties are called "parishes," and until 1868 those in South Carolina were called "districts"

county courts or **schyremotes,** in Saxon times were important tribunals Alfred is said to have divided England into counties and hundreds, but county courts seem to have existed much earlier

County courts, for recovery of debts under 20*l*, superseding courts of requests, instituted by 9 and 10 Vict. c 95 26 Aug 1846
Counties of England and Wales divided into 60 districts each with a county court, a barrister is judge, and juries when necessary Jurisdiction extended by 13 and 14 Vict c 61, to 50*l* 1850
Their proceedings facilitated in 1852 and 1854, 60 county courts in England and Wales 1868-72
County courts in the U S exist in each county first established in Virginia, 1622 to relieve the governor and council of business First in Connecticut, May, 1666, when the General Assembly divided the colony into 4 counties—Hartford, New Haven, New London, and Fairfield—a county court in each

coup-d'état (*coo'-da-tah'*), in France, *pronunciamento* in Spain A sudden change in government effected by a ruler or high officer Many in French history, the most celebrated that of Louis Napoleon 2 Dec 1851, by which he assumed the title and power of emperor of France

couriers. Xenophon attributes the first to Cyrus, and Herodotus says that they were common among the Persians (Esther iii 15) about 510 B C The Greeks and Romans had no regular couriers till the time of Augustus, when they travelled in cars, about 24 B C Couriers or posts are said to have been instituted in France by Charlemagne about 800 A D Couriers for letters were employed by Louis XI. of France, 1463 —*Henault* POST-OFFICE

Courland, a duchy of Livonia, conquered by Danes, 1218, by Teutonic knights, 1239, subjected to Poland in 1561, conquered by Charles XII of Sweden in 1701, Ernest Biren, duke, 1737, his son, Peter, 1769, annexed to Russia, Mch 1795

Court of Chancery. CHANCERY

Court of Honor. In England the court of chivalry, of which the lord high constable was a judge, was called *Curia Militaris* in the time of Henry IV, and later the Court of Honor In Bavaria, to prevent duelling, a court of honor was instituted in Apr 1819 Joseph Hamilton long advocated a similar institution in Britain

Court of Session, the highest civil tribunal in Scotland, instituted by statute of James V, 17 May, 1532, consisted of 14 judges and a president, and replaced a committee of Parliament In 1830 the number was reduced, and it now consists of the lord president, lord justice-clerk, and 11 ordinary judges

Court Party—Country Party, politicians in British Parliament, beginning about 1620 At the end of the 17th century the latter was a Tory and high-church party, maintaining "the land," as opposed to Whig and trading interests. Its most distinguished statesman was sir Thomas Hanmer (the *Montalto* of Pope's "Satires"), who died in 1746 —*Ashe*

Courtrai (*koor-trā'*), a fortified town of Belgium Here Robert, count of Artois, who defeated the Flemings in 1297, was defeated and slain by them, 11 July, 1302, in the "Battle of Spurs," so called from the gilt spurs collected

Courts of Justice were instituted at Athens 1507 B C (AREOPAGUS), by Moses, 1491 B C. (Exod. xviii 25), and in Rome. For England, CHANCERY, COMMON PLEAS, EXCHEQUER, KING'S BENCH, etc. Citizens of London were privileged to plead their own cause in the courts of judicature, without employing lawyers, except in pleas of the crown, 41 Hen III. 1257 —*Stow*. The rights of the Irish courts were established by the British Parliament in Apr. 1783.

Courts of the United States. *Supreme Court.* Under the confederation there was no national judicial department. The Supreme Court was organized in 1789, with 1 chief-justice and 5 associate judges. JUSTICES. It holds one term annually at the seat of government, commencing on the 2d Monday in Oct. The U S are divided for judicial purposes into 9 circuits, and these circuits are subdivided into 2 or more districts The 1st circuit consists of the states of Maine, Massachusetts, New Hampshire, and Rhode Island, 2d, Connecticut, New York, and Vermont, 3d, Delaware, New Jersey and Pennsylvania, 4th, Maryland North Carolina, South Carolina, Virginia, and West Virginia, 5th, Alabama, Florida, Georgia, Louisiana, Mississippi, and Texas, 6th Kentucky, Michigan, Ohio, and Tennessee, 7th, Illinois, Indiana, and Wisconsin, 8th, Arkansas, Colorado, Iowa, Kansas, Minnesota, Missouri, Nebraska, North Dakota, South Dakota, and Wyoming, 9th, California, Idaho, Nevada, Oregon, Montana, and Washington Each judge of the Supreme Court is allotted a circuit, and is required to attend that circuit at least one term every 2 years Salary of chief-justice, $10,500, each justice, $10,000 a year —*Circuit Courts*, established and organized by Congress Each of the circuits has allotted to it one of the judges of the Supreme Court, and has a local judge appointed termed circuit judge There are 10 circuit judges, the 2d circuit having 2 Salary, $6000 a year —*Circuit Court of Appeals* established and organized by Congress 1891, for the relief of the Supreme Court The justice of the Supreme Court presiding over the circuit, the circuit judge, and a judge appointed for this special court constitute it. Salary, $6000 a year —*District Courts*, established and organized by Congress Of these districts there are now (1893) 65, each presided over by a judge, termed district judge Salary, $5000 a year —*Court of Claims*, established and organized by Congress 1855, to hear and determine claims against the U S It consists of 1 chief-justice and 4 associate judges The solicitor-general appears before this court Salary of judges $4500 per annum —*Court of Private Land Claims*, established and organized by Congress, consists of 1 chief-justice and 4 associate judges Salary, $5000 per annum *Supreme Court of the District of Columbia*, established and organized by Congress, consists of 1 chief-justice and 4 associate judges Salary of chief-justice, $4500, associate judges, $4000 —*Territorial Courts*, established and organized by Congress Alaska, 1 judge, Arizona, 1 chief-justice and 3 associate judges, Indian Territory, 1 judge, New Mexico, 1 judge and 4 associate judges, Utah, 1 chief-justice and 3 associate judges, Oklahoma, 1 chief-justice and 2 associate judges. Salary, $3000 per annum When any judge of any court of the U S resigns his office, after having held his commission as such at least 10 years and having reached 70 years of age during his service, he shall receive during life the same salary as at the time of his resignation This right is given to no other class of civil officers under the government of the U S. The attorney-general appears in the Supreme Court of the U S in behalf of the government There is also a U S district attorney appointed for each district in which circuit and district courts are held, to look after the interest of the government in all cases that concern it. Women were admitted to practice in the Supreme Court of the U S by act of Congress approved 15 Feb 1879

Coutras (*koo-tra'*), S W France Here Henry of Navarre defeated the duc de Joyeuse and royalists, 20 Oct 1587

Cov'enanters, in the reign of Charles I, signers of the solemn league and covenant, engaged to stand together against the king in 1638 The *covenant*, or league between England and Scotland (the preceding one modified), adopted by Parliament, 25 Sept 1643, was accepted by Charles II 16 Aug 1650, but repudiated on his restoration in 1661, and declared to be illegal by Parliament, and ordered to be burned

Covenant consisted of 6 articles
1 Preservation of the reformed church in Scotland, and the reformation of religion in England and Ireland
2 Extirpation of popery, prelacy, schism, etc.
3 Preservation of the liberties of Parliament and the king's person and authority
4 Discovery and punishment of all malignants, etc
5. Preservation of "a blessed peace between these kingdoms"
6. Assisting all who enter into the covenant "*This will we do as in the sight of God.*" BOTHWELL BRIDGE, CAMERONIANS.

Cov'ent Garden, London, corrupted from "Convent Garden," once the garden of St. Peter's convent The square was built about 1633, the piazza on the north and the church designed by Inigo Jones. The fruit and vegetable markets were rebuilt in 1829-30, from designs by Mr Fowler (on ground of the duke of Bedford)

Covent Garden theatre sprang out of one in Lincoln's-inn Fields, through a patent granted 14 Chas. II 1662, to sir William Davenant, whose company was denominated the "duke's servants," as a compliment to the duke of York, afterwards James II THEATRES

Coventry, Warwickshire, Engl Leofric, earl of Mercia, lord of Coventry, is said to have relieved it from heavy taxes at the intercession of his wife Godiva, on condition of her riding naked through the town about 1057

"'Alas'' she said.
'But prove me what it is I would not do'
And from a heart as rough as Esau's hand,
He answered, 'Ride you naked through the town,
And I repeal it'" —*Tennyson*, "Godiva"

Processions in her memory took place in 1851, 23 June, 1862, 4 June, 1866, 20 June, 1870, and 4 June, 1877 A parliament was held here in the reign of Henry IV, called *parliamentum indoctum*, the unlearned parliament, because lawyers were excluded, 1404, and in the reign of Henry VI another met called *parliamentum diabolicum*, from acts of attainder passed against the duke of York and others, 20 Nov 1459 The town had strong walls, 3 miles in circumference, and 26 towers, which were demolished by Charles II in 1662 The ribbon-makers here suffered from want of work in the winter of 1860-1861 The bishopric was founded by Oswy, king of Mercia, 656, under the double name of Coventry and Lichfield, later Lichfield and Coventry It was so wealthy that king Offa, by the favor of pope Adrian, made it archiepiscopal, but this title was laid aside on the death of that king In 1075 the see was removed to Chester, in 1102 to Coventry, and afterwards back to Lichfield, under opposition from the monks of Coventry Coventry merged into the bishopric of Lichfield

Cowan's Ford, on the Catawba river, N C Lord Cornwallis, in rapid pursuit of the Americans under gen Morgan, was prevented from crossing by a sudden rise after the Americans had crossed Cornwallis moved down a few miles towards Cowan's Ford, where Morgan had stationed 300 militia under gen Davidson to oppose his crossing The British forced a crossing 1 Feb 1781, and the militia were dispersed, gen Davidson being killed

cowboys. British marauders and Tories who plundered the people east of the Hudson river, in New York, during the occupancy of New York city by the British, 1776-82, were so called The word is now applied to herdsmen on the ranches of the western states and territories. NEUTRAL GROUND

Cowpens, Battle at the Here, in Spartanburg district, South Carolina, among the Thickety mountains, on 17 Jan 1781, a severe battle was fought between the Americans under gen Daniel Morgan, and the British under col Tarleton After a hard fight of more than 2 hours, the British were defeated, with a loss of about 300 killed and wounded, 500 prisoners, and much ammunition, stores, and baggage The Americans lost 70 men, only 12 killed Congress voted Morgan a gold medal for his brilliant victory The name Cowpens is thus explained Before the Revolution this region, abounding in grass and fine springs, was devoted to pasture, and as the cows were shut in small yards at night, this place became known as "The Cowpens"

cow-pock inoculation. SMALL-POX, VACCINATION

Cracow (*krā'-kō*), a city in Austrian Poland The Poles elected Cracus duke, who built Cracow with spoils of the Franks, about 700 It was their capital, 1320-1609 Cracow was taken by Charles XII in 1702, and later several times by the Russians and other confederates. The sovereign was crowned at Cracow until 1764 The Russians, who had taken it, 1768, were expelled by Kosciusko, 24 Mch 1794, but it surrendered to the Prussians, 15 June, and in 1795 was awarded to Austria Cracow became a republic, June, 1815. Occupied by 10,000 Russians, who followed here the defeated Poles, Sept 1831. Its independence was extinguished, and it was seized and incorporated by Austria, 16 Nov 1846, against the protest of England, France, Sweden, and Turkey. Fire destroyed most of the city, 18 July, 1850 The discovery on 22 July, 1869, of Barbare Abryk, a nun, secluded for 21 years in a convent cell, led to riots. Pop 1890, 75,593

Cradle of Liberty. FANEUIL HALL.

Crampton's Gap, Battle of MARYLAND CAMPAIGN

Cranberry, FLOWERS AND PLANTS

cranes, machines for moving weights, with a horizontal and a vertical movement, are of early date, for the engines of Archimedes may be so called A crane at Woolwich, England (4 years in building), exceeds 1800 tons in weight, and lifts 1200 tons DERRICKS

Craney island, Defence of This island, about 5 miles below Norfolk, Va, was attacked by British, 22 June, 1813, and defended by col Beatty and maj Faulkner The British were repulsed, losing about 200 men, the Americans losing none Occupied by the confederates for a short time, but evacuated 11 May, 1861

craniology. PHRENOLOGY.

Cranmer, Latimer, and **Ridley,** martyrdom of PROTESTANTS

crannoges. LAKE-DWELLINGS.

Crannon or **Cranon**, a city of Thessaly, N Greece Near here the Macedonians, under Antipater and Craterus, defeated the confederated Greeks, twice by sea and once by land, 322 B.C The Athenians demanded peace, and Antipater put their orators to death, among them Hyperides, who, not to betray secrets of his country under torture, cut out his tongue, and Demosthenes is said to have taken poison shortly after

Craonne (*kra-onn'*), a town of N France Here Victor and Ney defeated the Prussians, under Blucher, after a severe contest, 7 Mch 1814

crape. A thin, semi-transparent stuff made of silk finely crinkled, especially appropriate for mourning purposes It is said some crape was made by Ste Badour, when queen of France, about 680 It is said to have been first made at Bologna

Crayford, Kent, Engl Hengist the Saxon is said to have defeated the Britons here, 457

crayons, pencils made of colored paste, were known in France about 1422, and improved by L'Oriot, 1748

cre'asote or **kreasote** (discovered by Reichenbach about 1833), an antiseptic and coagulator of albuminous tissue, is obtained by destructive distillation of wood and other organic matters. It has been used to preserve meat, timber, etc

cre'atine (from the Gr κρέας, flesh), the chemical principle of flesh, discovered in 1835 by E Chevreul, investigated by Liebig, Gregory, and others.

Creation of the world The date given by the English Bible, and by Usher, Blair, and some others, is 4004 B.C Countless dates have been assigned to the creation, varying from 3616 to 6984 B.C Dr. Hales gives 5411 ERAS, MUSIC

crèches, establishments for temporarily protecting the children of working mothers, begun at Paris about 1844, in London (in Rathbone place, etc.) about 1863, in the United States about 1870.

Crécy (*krā-sē'*), or **Cressy**, a town of N. France, where Edward III. and his son, Edward the Black Prince, with about 36,800 men, routed Philip, king of France, with about 130,000, 26 Aug 1346 John, king of Bohemia (nearly blind), James, king of Majorca, Ralph, duke of Lorraine (sovereign princes), and many French nobles, with 30,000 privates, were slain, while the loss of the English was small. The crest of the king of Bohemia (3 ostrich-feathers, with the motto *Ich dien*—in English, "I serve") has been adopted by princes of Wales.

crédit foncier (*kra-dee' fon-see-a'*), etc. A plan of providing loans to land-owners was introduced by Frederick the Great of Prussia in 1763, in some Prussian provinces, to alleviate the distresses of the landed interest. Loans are made on the security of estates, from capital provided by selling debentures charged upon the aggregate mortgaged estates. This may be done (1) by means of an association of land-owners, (2) by means of a proprietary public company The former plan obtains in eastern Prussia, only the latter in western Europe.

Crédit foncier companies have been founded in Hamburg (1782), western Prussia (1787), Belgium (1841), France (1852), England

1863). Similar companies were formed in all the states of Eu-rope, in India, and in our colonies and dependencies.—*Henriques.*

Crédit Mobilier (*kra-dee' mo-bee-lee-a'*) (i.e., credit personal property). A joint-stock company with this name is established at Paris by Isaac and Emile Péreire and others, Nov. 1852.

promoted trading enterprises of all kinds, on the principle of *commandité*, or limited liabilities; and was authorized to supersede or buy in any other companies (replacing their shares or bonds with its own scrip), and also to carry on the ordinary business of banking. Funds were to be obtained by a paid-up capital of 2⅖ millions sterling, the issue of obligations at not less than 45 days' date or sight, and the receipt of money on deposit. The society apparently prospered; but was considered by many to resemble Law's bank of 1716.
veral directors failed, Sept. 1857; no dividend.........May, 1858
any companies on like principles established in London..... 1863
nile and Isaac Péreire withdrew from the management; the company failed, the capital disappeared..................Oct. 1867
gh court of appeal held MM. Péreire and other directors responsible, and adjudged damages to the shareholders, 1 Aug. 1868
nile Péreire d. 6 Jan. 1875; Isaac d..................12 July, 1880

Crédit Mobilier of America. A joint-stock company under this name was organized May, 1863, with a capital of $2,500,000. The charter was purchased, Jan. 1867, by company constructing the Union Pacific railroad, and the ock, which was increased to $3,750,000, rose to a high price, ying enormous dividends, earned in connection with Pacific ilroad construction. In 1872, in certain legal proceedings, appeared that several members of Congress and vice-president Schuyler Colfax were holders of this stock, a fact which used great scandal, as the profits of the company largely depended upon the action of Congress. The suspicion was general that some members had received stock as an indirect bribe, d a prolonged investigation followed during the session of 72-73. The Senate committee, 27 Feb. 1873, recommended e expulsion of one senator; but no action was taken, and s term expired five days later. The House of Representatives passed resolutions censuring 2 of its members. UNITED ATES, Dec. 1872; Jan., Feb. 1873.

Creedmoor, a post-hamlet on Long Island, 12 miles st of New York city. Here an extended rifle range has en established (1871), the most perfectly appointed in the S.

creeds. CONFESSIONS OF FAITH. J. R. Lumby's History of the Creeds" appeared 1874.

Creek war. In 1813, while the United States were war with Great Britain, the Creek Indians of Alabama were cited to hostility by Tecumseh, who visited them for that rpose, and by British agents in Florida. A war followed, in hich the Creeks, led by William Weatherford (Red Eagle), re overcome by gen. Jackson. The war endangered the tegrity of the nation; and, the Creeks being intelligent and rtly civilized, many well-planned and stoutly contested bat-s were fought. ALABAMA, 1813-14; UNITED STATES, 13-14.

Creeks. INDIANS.

cremation. Before and at the beginning of the ristian era, cremation prevailed in the civilized world, except among the Egyptians, Chinese, and Jews, but gradually ve place to earth burial. Descriptions given by Homer. odern sanitation is largely responsible for the revival of emation within the last two decades. The crematories in e world have increased from 1 in 1874 to 4 in 1880 and over in 1890. 17 of these are in the United States, and in em, up to May, 1891, about 2200 bodies have been incinerated. There are 6 public crematories in Tokio, Japan, and out 10,000 bodies a year are burned in that city. It is estimated that 47 per cent. of the dead in Japan are incinerated. The first crematory in the U. S. was built at Washington, Pa., by Dr. F. Julius le Moyne, and the first incineration ere, that of the body of baron de Palm, took place in Dec. 76. This crematory was built for private use, but being e only one in the U. S. up to 1884, it was used for 38 or 40 cinerations, and was closed to the public, 1 Aug. 1884.

. Coletti, rector of the University of Padua, prepares a memoir for the Academy of Science and Literature in that city, strongly commending the practice of cremation............ 1856
ofs. Coletti and Castiglioni introduce the subject of cremation n the Medical International Congress at Florence.......... 1869
Royal Institute of Science and Letters of Lombardy offers a prize for the best practical method of cremation........... 1872
Cremation society of England founded; sir Henry Thompson, president...Jan. 1874
"Cremation of the Dead: its History," etc., pub. by William Eassie.. "
Crematory at Milan, Italy, erected.......................... "
Crematory at Lodi, Italy, built............................. 1876
Crematory at Gotha, Germany, built by the municipal council and opened to the public............................Nov. 1878
First cremation in England, that of Mrs. Hanham, at Manston House, county Dorset..............................8 Oct. 1882
Second crematory in the U. S. opened at Lancaster, Pa., 25 Nov. 1884
Crematory built at Woking, Engl., in 1879. First incineration takes place 6 years later, the interval being devoted to proving that no law, ancient or modern, in England forbade the practice. First incineration......................26 Mch. 1885
First incineration in crematory at Fresh Pond, L. I., Dec. 4, and at Buffalo, N. Y...................................27 Dec. "
University of Pennsylvania erects a crematory for incinerating the remains of those dissected in the medical department, 1886
Crematory with 2 furnaces built at a cost of $50,000 in the cemetery of Père la Chaise at the suggestion of the municipal council of Paris. First incineration takes place..22 Oct. 1887
Legislature of New York state appropriates $20,000 for building and equipping a crematory on Swinburne island for the use of the commissioners of quarantine (1888). This was the first state action on record; crematory built............ 1888
Crematory in Oakwood cemetery, Troy, N. Y., one of the finest buildings of its kind in the world, erected as a memorial to Gardiner Earl; built of granite in Romanesque style, 136 ft. in length, 70 in width, and with a tower 90 ft. high.....Nov. 1889
New England Cremation Society organized.................. 1892

Cremera, Battle of. FABII.

Cremo'na, N. Italy, a city founded by the Romans, 221 B.C. It became an independent republic in 1107, but was frequently subjugated by its neighbors, Milan and Venice, and partook of their fortunes. In Nov. 1859, it became part of the kingdom of Italy. Cremona was eminent for violin-makers from about 1550 to 1750.

cre'ole. In the United States (Louisiana), any native of French or Spanish descent by either parent, especially French.

Creole (the ship), Case of. UNITED STATES, 1841.

crescent, a symbol of sovereignty among the Greeks and Romans, and the device of Byzantium, now Constantinople. While besieged, 340 B.C., by Philip, father of Alexander the Great, in a night attack their danger was revealed to the Greeks by the light of the moon, then in crescent; in gratitude they assumed the crescent as a symbol of their city. It is also a symbol of certain tribes of Central Asia, among them the Turks. The crescent has given name to 3 orders of knighthood: founded by Charles I. of Naples, 1268; by René of Anjou, in 1448; by the sultan Selim, in 1801. The last is still in existence.

Crespy, a town of N. France. Here was signed a treaty between Charles V. of Germany and Francis I. of France, 18 Sept. 1544. The former renounced Burgundy and the latter Italy.

crests are ascribed to the Carians. Richard I. (1189) had a crest on the helmet like a plume of feathers. The English kings generally had crowns above their helmets; that of Richard II., 1377, was surmounted by a lion on a cap of dignity. CRECY. Alexander III. of Scotland, 1249, had a plume of feathers; the helmet of Robert I. was surmounted by a crown, 1306; and that of James I. by a lion, 1424. In the 15th and 16th centuries, the crest was described as a figure placed upon a wreath, coronet, or cap of maintenance.—*Gwillim.*

Crete, now CANDIA.

cribbage, a game at cards, usually played by 2 persons in 61 points. Probably of English origin, formerly called *noddy*, mentioned 1616. The earliest description of the game is in "The Compleat Gamester," 1674.

cricket, the national game of England. The earliest allusion to the game is found in the wardrobe account of king Edward I. in 1300. The word "cricket" occurs first about 1550. It was played at Winchester college as early as 1650.

First recorded match between Kent and All England, held at the Artillery ground, Finsbury.......................4 Aug. 1746
Hambledon club, which existed 21 years, founded.............. 1750
First collection of rules for playing framed.................. 1774
Marylebone Cricket-club organized........................... 1787
Round or straight-arm bowling accepted and comes into use.. 1825
Union Cricket-club of Philadelphia, Pa., organized........... 1832
All England Eleven commence playing.......................... 1846

International matches, generally won by English team, held in America, in 1859, 1868, 1872, 1881, and.................... 1882
Australian club victors in a match with the "Players of England" at the Crystal palace.................27, 28, 29 Sept. 1880
Australians defeated at Manchester, Engl., by the North of England team..................................16 Sept. 1882

crime, England and Wales. From the "Judicial Statistics" of England and Wales it is shown that during the 20 years previous to 1890 there was a notable increase in the following crimes: murder, assault with intent to ravish and abuse, burglary and house-breaking, breaking into shops and warehouses, etc., and attempts to commit suicide, the latter crime having more than quadrupled. On the contrary, a marked decrease took place in attempts to murder, shooting, stabbing, etc., with intent to maim, assault on officers, receiving stolen goods, and larceny. In 1887 it was announced that the number of female convicts had fallen nearly 50 per cent. in 10 years. The number of criminals in England and Wales at various periods, and the number and classification of sentences passed, is shown in the following tables:

NUMBER OF CRIMINALS IN ENGLAND AND WALES AT VARIOUS PERIODS, AND PROPORTION OF POPULATION TO CRIMINALS.

Criminal class.	1868–69	1872–73	1877–78	1882–83	1887–88
At large, suspected, etc.....	54,249	45,201	40,626	38,420	32,910
In local prisons, except debtor and military prisons...	19,927	17,511	17,625	16,751	13,973
In convict prisons..........	8,864	9,582	10,358	9,640	5,583
In reform schools..........	4,318	4,515	4,883	4,517	4,203
Totals.......	87,358	76,809	73,492	69,328	56,669
Proportion of total population to each criminal....	254.3	304.3	340.6	386.1	506.3

Showing a large decrease in crimes in relation to the increase of population.

NUMBER AND CLASSIFICATION OF SENTENCES PASSED ON OFFENDERS IN ENGLAND AND WALES IN YEARS NAMED, AND MEAN OF 20 YEARS.

Criminals sentenced.	1869	1873	1878	1883	1888	Mean for 20 years
To death..........	18	18	20	23	36	26.9
Life imprisonment..	8	8	14	10	4	10.25
Over 15 years......	15	18	25	28	4	19.5
Under 15 years.....	13,728	10,608	11,813	10,795	9,930	10,975
Sent to Reformatory..........	257	236	210	160	103	168.85
Fined, etc..........	314	201	391	331	484	339.45
Totals......	[illegible]	11,089	12,473	11,347	10,561	11,581

crime, United States. The total number of prisoners on 1 June, 1890, was 82,329. As to parentage, there were 57,310 of purely white blood, 24,277 negroes, 407 Chinese, 13 Japanese, and 322 Indians; and from carefully prepared statistics of the nativity of both parents of the 57,310 white prisoners, it is found that 43.19 per cent. of crime committed in the U. S. by white men and women is chargeable to the native white element of the population, and 56.81 per cent. to the foreign element. The distribution of the 82,329 prisoners in the U. S. 1 June, 1890, was as follows: In penitentiaries, 45,233; county jails, 19,861; city prisons, 3264; workhouses, 9968; leased out, 2308; in military prisons, 794; in insane hospitals, 901. The statistical table given below shows in the aggregate the number convicted and under various sentences, according to the U. S. census of 1880 and 1890.

PRISONERS OF ALL KINDS IN THE UNITED STATES, 1880–90.

Sentenced.	1 June, 1880.	1 June, 1890.
Death..................................	80	162
Imprisonment for life..................	1,615	2,766
" 20 years and over....	1,112	1,697
" 1–20 years...........	29,258	43,442
" under 1 year.........	11,100	18,539
Fine only..............................	2,031	3,691
....	....	....
Held for trial, witnesses, etc.............	5,564	10,835
Not stated.............................	7,849	1,197
Totals............	58,609	82,329

Of the above number for 1890, 7351 were in prison for the crime of homicide (6958 males and 393 females), and not included in the above table (1890) were 14,846 juveniles in reformatories (11,535 boys and 3311 girls).

NUMBER AND NATIVITY OF PRISONERS IN THE UNITED STATES FROM CENSUS STATISTICS, 1850–90.

Date.	Native.	Foreign.	Totals.
1 June, 1850..........................	4,326	2,411	6,737
" 1860..........................	10,143	8,943	19,086
" 1870..........................	24,173	8,728	32,901
" 1880..........................	45,802	12,807	58,609
" 1890..........................	65,070	17,259	82,329

The number of executions and lynchings reported by the sheriffs as taking place in the U. S. during the calendar year 1890 was as follows:

Locality.	Executions.	Lynchings.
North Atlantic Division......................	17	....
South Atlantic Division......................	43	40
North Central Division......................	28	12
South Central Division......................	51	54
Western Division...........................	17	11
Totals........	156	117

Crimea (*krim-ee'-a*) or **Crim Tartary,** a peninsula in the Euxine or Black sea, area about 10,000 sq. miles, pop. 1890, about 250,000. The ancient *Taurica Chersonesus*, colonized by Greeks about 550 B.C. The Milesians founded the kingdom of Bosporus, now Kertch, which, about 108 B.C., was subject to Mithridates, king of Pontus, whose descendants ruled it, under Roman protection, till the irruption of the Goths, Huns, etc., about 258 A.D. About 1237 it fell to the Mongols under Genghis Khan; soon after the Venetians established commercial stations, with lucrative trade, but were supplanted by the Genoese, who were permitted to rebuild and fortify Kaffa about 1261. In 1475 Mahomet II. expelled the Genoese, and the Ottomans, leaving the government to the native khans, closed the Black sea to western Europe. In 1774, by the intervention of the empress Catherine II., the Crimea recovered its independence; but on the abdication of the khan in 1783 the Russians took possession, after a war with Turkey, and retained it by the treaty of Jassy, 9 Jan. 1792. The Crimea (now a part of the province of Taurida) was divided into 8 governments in 1802. War having been declared against Russia by England and France, 28 Mch. 1854, large masses of troops sent to the East, after remaining some time at Gallipoli and other places, sailed for Varna, where they disembarked 29 May. The allies deciding to attack the Crimea, British, French, and Turkish forces of 58,000 men (25,000 British), under lord Raglan and marshal St. Arnaud, sailed from Varna 3 Sept., and landed on the 14th, 15th, and 16th, without opposition, at Old Fort, near Eupatoria, about 30 miles from Sebastopol. On the 20th they attacked the Russians, between 40,000 and 50,000 strong (under prince Menschikoff), intrenched on the heights of Alma, supposed impregnable, and after a sharp contest routed them. ALMA and RUSSO-TURKISH WARS. Peace was proclaimed Apr. 1856, and the allies quitted the Crimea 12 July following.

Crimi'sus, a river in Sicily, near which Timoleon defeated the Carthaginians, 339 B.C.

crin'oline (a French word, meaning stuff made of *crin*, hair), is the modern name of the "farthingale" of the time of queen Elizabeth, hoop-like petticoats made of whalebone, steel, etc.; fashion revived, 1855–70, since disappeared entirely. Hoops frequently extended to 12 and 15 feet in circumference. In No. 116 of the *Tatler*, pub. 5 Jan. 1710 in London, is an amusing trial of the hoop-petticoat then in fashion.

Cripplegate, London, was so called from the lame beggars who sat there, so early as the year 1010. The gate was newly built by the brewers of London in 1244; and was pulled down and sold for 91*l.* in July, 1760. The poet Milton was buried in the church near it, 12 Nov. 1674. LONDON.

"Crisis, The," a series of 14 patriotic papers by Thomas Paine during the Revolution, extending from 1775 to 1783. The first, in reply to gen. Gage's proclamation, is dated 9 Aug. 1775; the second, written just after Congress leaves Philadelphia, fearing its capture by the British, to meet at Baltimore, is dated 19 Dec. 1776. It begins with the well-known words, "These are the times that try men's souls." The third is dated Jan. 1777; most, if not all, were published in Philadelphia. PENNSYLVANIA, 1776.

crisis, commercial and monetary Those that have most affected England were in the following years, to wit 1763 1783, 1793, 1797, 1810, 1816, 1825, 1837-38, 1847, 1857, 1864-66, 1875 In the United States, 1816, 1825, 1837, 1847, 1857, 1873, 1893 A crisis in Holland was caused by the Tulip speculation, which lasted from 1634-39, and during which a certain kind of tulip was quoted at 5500 florins The state put a stop to the craze A crisis in France, 1620, caused by the Mississippi scheme of John Law LAW'S BUBBLE The crisis of 1837 the most disastrous in the U S, followed general and excessive land speculation

Crispin and **Crispian** are said to have been 2 saints, born at Rome, who travelled to Soissons, in France, to propagate the Christian religion They worked as shoemakers (hence the patron saint of that trade), but the governor of the town, discovering them to be Christians, ordered them to be beheaded, about 288 Their day is 25 Oct, the date of the battle of Agincourt

> 'This day is called—the feast of Crispian'
> —*Shakespeare*, 'Henry V' act iv sc iii

crith (from the Gr κριθή, a barley corn, or small weight), term suggested by dr A W Hofmann (about 1864) to express the volume-weight of gases, a cube containing 1 litre of hydrogen (0 0896 gramme) to be the unit Hydrogen being 1 crith, oxygen will be 16, nitrogen 14 criths

critics. The first society of them was formed 276 B C —*Blair* Varro, Cicero, Apollonius, and Aristarchus were ancient critics In modern times the *Journal des Sçavans*, the earliest critical periodical, founded by Denis de Sallo, ecclesiastical councillor in the parliament of France, was first published at Paris, 30 May, 1655 and is still continued Jean le Clerc's "Ars Critica," pub 1696, is said to be the earliest systematic treatise The first work of this kind in England was the 'Review" of Daniel Defoe (the term being invented by himself), pub in Feb 1703 The *Works of the Learned* began 1710, and the *Wares of Literature* in 1711, discontinued in 1722 REVIEWS

The legality of fair criticism was established in the English courts in Feb 1794, in an action that excited great attention, brought by an author against a reviewer for a severe critique Judgment was given for the defendant, on the principle that criticism is allowable, however sharp, if just, and not malicious.

Croa'tia, conquered by Coloman, king of Hungary, in 1102, was with that country united to Austria in 1526 The Croatian Diet was abolished Nov. 1861 The Croats protested against incorporation with Hungary, 25 May, 1867, and their diet (including Croatia and Slavonia) at Agram was dissolved 27 May. The union of Croatia with Hungary was recognized by a Croatian deputation 27 May, 1868, and Croatian delegates entered the Hungarian Diet 24 Nov Area of Croatia and Slavonia about 16,785 sq miles, pop 1890, about 2 184,419

crofters and **cottars,** the holders of small portions of land, and the laborers in the highlands and islands of Scotland

A royal commission appointed 22 Mch 1883 (Francis, baron Napier and others), to inquire into their condition, report their state as not worse than formerly, but disclose many grievances relating to the tenure of land, high rents, deficiency of education, of postal communication, of roads etc They recommend among other remedies, the revival of ancient highland townships with common privileges, limiting the power of superior lords, etc 28 Apr 1884
Meeting at Inverness of chief landlords, conciliatory favorable changes proposed 14 Jan 1885
Crofters colonization commission appointed by British and Canadian governments. Dec 1888
Canadian settlements reported prosperous 1891

Croix, St. (*sent kroi'*), a West India island, purchased from the French by Christian VI, king of Denmark, in 1733, taken by sir Alexander Cochrane, 22 Dec. 1807, restored in 1814

cromlechs, ancient monuments, formerly considered to be Druidical altars, but now believed to be connected with burials One is in Anglesey, similar structures have been found in Ireland, India, Arabia, and other countries AVEBURY, CARNAC, STONEHENGE.

Cronstadt, Russia, founded by Peter the Great, 1710, and received its name (Crown-town) in 1721 It was not attacked by the fleets in the war with Russia, 1854-55

Cropredy Bridge, near Banbury, Oxfordshire Here the royalists defeated sir William Waller and the army of the parliament, 29 June, 1644

croquet (*krō-kay'*) This game, which became common in Britain about 1850, is said to be a revival of the old "pall-mall" It has been largely superseded by lawn-tennis, 1887-93

crosier, a staff supporting a cross, borne before an archbishop was in use in the 4th century The bearing of a crosier before ecclesiastics is mentioned in the life of St Cæsarea of Arles about 500

cross (Lat *crux*) an instrument for inflicting the punishment of death, originally a tree, on which the culprit was tied or impaled, and left to perish, later, an upright stake with a horizontal bar, to which the victim was bound and nailed with spikes through the outstretched extremities CRUCIFIXION The cross on which the Redeemer suffered on Calvary was said to have been found buried at Jerusalem, with 2 others, by St Helena 3 May, 328 (termed the *Invention of the Cross*), Christ's, it is alleged, being distinguished by the cure of a sick woman from its touch It was carried away by Chosroes, king of Persia, on plundering Jerusalem but recovered by the emperor Heraclius (who defeated him in battle), 14 Sept 615, a day since commemorated in some churches as "the festival of the Exaltation of the Cross," established in 642

Church writers say that a great shining cross seen in the heavens by Constantine led him to adopt it on his standard, with the inscription "*In hoc signo vinces*"—'Under this sign thou shalt conquer' With this (labarum) he advanced to Rome, where he vanquished Maxentius, 27 Oct 312 —*Lenglet*
Signing with the Cross first practised by Christians to distinguish themselves from pagans. about 110
In the time of Tertullian, it was deemed efficacious against poison, witchcraft, etc 200
Crosses in churches and chambers were introduced about 431, and set up on steeples about 568
Crosses in honor of queen Eleanor were set up in places where her hearse rested, between 1290 (when she died) and 1307
Crosses and idolatrous pictures removed from churches, and crosses in streets demolished by order of Parliament 1641
Maids of the Cross, a community of young women who made vows of poverty, chastity, and obedience, instituted 1625
Order of *Ladies of the Star of the Cross*, instituted by the empress Eleonora di Gonzaga, wife of Leopold I 1668

Cross-Keys, Va Here on 8 June, 1862, gen Fremont engaged part of "Stonewall" Jackson's command under gen Ewell, with indecisive results Ewell retired during the night PENINSULAR CAMPAIGN

Croton aqueduct, which supplies New York city with water from the Croton river, was begun in 1837, and finished in 1842 at a cost of $12,500,000 It is of brick, and extends from Croton river dam about 30 miles from Harlem river along the Hudson, crossing the Harlem by the High bridge Its capacity is about 98,000,000 gallons in 24 hours The population of the city when it was finished was quite 350,000 By 1880 the rapid increase of population made an increased water supply necessary A plan was submitted to the mayor by the commissioners of public works, 22 Feb 1882, for a new aqueduct A resolution of the state senate, 9 Jan 1883, requested the mayor of New York to appoint 5 commissioners to examine plans, etc The commissioners reported 7 Mch 1883 recommending a new aqueduct The Aqueduct act passed by the legislature authorizing the work, 1883 The aqueduct commission permanently organized, 8 Aug 1883 Benj S Church appointed chief engineer, 15 Aug 1883 Expense of the commissions, 1883 $22,747 90, 1884, $185,730 63, 1885, $2,265,147 58, 1886, $5,020 684 21 Total from 8 Aug 1883, $7,503,310 32, 1887, $7,242,293.75 Total from the first to Jan 1888, $14,745,604.27 The work of sinking the first shaft began about 15 Jan 1884, and the new aqueduct was opened for use 15 July, 1890 Total cost, $24,767,477 25 The cross-section of the aqueduct is equal to a circle 14 feet in diameter, in its length of 33½ miles its fall is 33.8 feet Its discharging capacity is 318,000,000 gallons in 24 hours, or with the old aqueduct, 415,000,000 gallons in 24 hours In connection with the aqueduct the dam at Quaker Bridge was built, 1887-91, at a cost of $3,000,000 It is 1350 feet long, 277 feet high, and 216 feet wide at the bottom. The capacity of this dam is nearly 70,000,000,000 gallons, and it impounds the water of 300 sq. miles.

Croto'na, S. Italy, a city founded by the Achæan Greeks about 710 B.C. Here Pythagoras taught about 520. The Crotons destroyed Sybaris, 510. Its medical school was, in the days of Herodotus and long after, the most renowned in Greece.

crown. An Amalekite brought Saul's crown to David, 1056 B.C. (2 Sam. i.). The first Roman who wore a crown was Tarquin the Elder, 616 B.C. The crown was first a fillet tied round the head; afterwards it was formed of leaves and flowers, and also of stuffs adorned with jewels. TIARA.

Crown of Alfred bore 2 little bells (872); it is said to have been long preserved at Westminster, and perhaps was that described in the parliamentary inventory of 1649.
Athelstan's crown resembled an earl's coronet, 929.
William I. wore his crown on a cap, adorned with points, 1066.
Richard III. introduced the crosses, 1483.
Henry VII. introduced the arches, 1485.
Crown and regalia of England were pledged to the city of London by Richard II. for 2000*l.* in 1386; see the king's receipt on redeeming them.—*Rymer.*
Crown of Charles II., made in 1660, is the oldest existing in England. BLOOD'S CONSPIRACY.
Imperial state crown of England was made by Rundell & Bridges in 1838, principally of jewels from old crowns. It contains 1 large ruby, 1 large sapphire, 16 sapphires, 11 emeralds, 4 rubies, 1363 brilliant diamonds, 1273 rose diamonds, 147 table diamonds, 4 drop-shaped pearls, and 273 pearls.—*Prof. Tennant.*

crown lands. The revenue from those in England is now nearly all subject to Parliament, which appropriates to the sovereign and government about 375,000*l.* a year. The revenue of the duchy of Cornwall belongs to the prince of Wales even during minority. Henry VII. (1485) resumed the lands given to followers by sovereigns of the house of York. The hereditary crown estates were largely bestowed on courtiers by sovereigns—especially by the Stuarts.

Crown of India, Imperial Order of, instituted by queen Victoria (on assuming the title of empress, 1 Jan. 1877), for princesses of the royal family, distinguished Indian and British ladies, and wives of viceroys and governors and secretaries of state for India, 31 Dec. 1877. Twelve ladies (the marchioness of Salisbury and others) invested, 29 Apr. 1878.

Crown Point, on lake Champlain, Essex county, N. Y. First fortified by the French in 1731 as fort Frederick; evacuated by them and occupied by the English under gen. Amherst, 1759; fortified at a cost of $10,000,000, but fortifications never completed, and after the peace of 1763 not kept in repair. It was occupied by 1 sergeant and 11 men, with 114 cannon (61 serviceable), when captured by "Green Mountain Boys" under col. Seth Warner, from the British, 12 May, 1775. Abandoned by the Americans on the approach of Burgoyne, 1777. Reoccupied same year.

crowns and **half-crowns** of silver were coined in England by Edward VI., 1553; none in 1861, and they were gradually withdrawn from circulation. The coinage of half-crowns was resumed, 1874, after an inquiry as to their utility.

Crows. INDIANS.

crucifix, an imitation of the cross bearing the figure of Christ, first known in the 4th, came into general use in the 8th century.

crucifixion. A cruel mode of execution among the Assyrians, Egyptians, Persians, Carthaginians, Greeks, Jews, and Romans. Ariarathes, of Cappadocia, aged 80, vanquished by Perdiccas, when identified among the prisoners, was flayed alive and nailed to a cross, with his principal officers, 322 B.C. Jesus Christ was crucified 3 Apr. 33 A.D. by the Romans, instigated by the Jews, in its most cruel form, namely, by piercing the hands and feet with nails.—*Usher* (15 Apr. 29 A.D., *Clinton;* 28 Mch. 31 A.D., *Hales*). Crucifixion discontinued by Constantine, 330.—*Lenglet.*

cruelty to animals. ANIMALS, VIVISECTION.

crusades (Fr. *croisades*), wars to drive infidels from Jerusalem and the "Holy Land." Peter Gautier, the Hermit, an officer of Amiens, returning from pilgrimage, incited pope Urban II. to expel infidels from the holy city. Urban convened a council of 310 bishops at Clermont in France, ambassadors of the chief Christian potentates assisting, and gave Peter commission to summon Europe to a general war, 1094. The first crusade was proclaimed; an army of 300,000 men raised, with Godfrey de Bouillon as commander under Peter's guidance, 1095. The warriors wore a red cross on the right shoulder, and their motto was *Volenté de Dieu*—"God's will." The French government has published chronicles of the crusades in a magnificent form (1844–77).

I. Crusade (1095) ended, Jerusalem taken by assault, 15 July, 1099; Godfrey de Bouillon made king.
II. Preached by St. Bernard in 1146, headed by emperor Conrad II. and Louis VII. of France. Crusaders defeated; Jerusalem lost in 1187.
III. Emperor Frederick Barbarossa, etc., in 1188, joined by Philip II. of France and Richard I. of England in 1190. Glorious, but fruitless.
IV. 1195, by emperor Henry VI.; successful till his death in 1197.
V. Proclaimed by Innocent III., 1198. Baldwin, count of Flanders, attacked the Greeks, and took Constantinople in 1203. His companions returned.
VI. In 1216. In 1229, emperor Frederick II. obtained possession of Jerusalem by truce for 10 years.
VII. In 1240 Richard, earl of Cornwall, arrived at Palestine, but soon departed.
VIII. By Louis IX. (St. Louis), 1248; defeated and taken prisoner at Mansourah, 5 Apr. 1250; released by ransom; truce of 10 years.
IX., and last, 1270, by St. Louis, who died of a contagious disease, at Carthage, in Africa, 25 Aug. Prince Edward, afterwards Edward I. of England, was at Acre, 1271. In 1291, the sultan took Acre; Christians driven out of Syria.
In 1212 occurred the "children's crusades." In France, under the boy Stephen, 30,000 encamped around Vendome, and in moving to Marseilles 10,000 were lost. Thence about 5000 sailed for Palestine, only in the end to be sold into slavery. In the same year 20,000 German boys and girls set out from Cologne for Palestine, under the peasant lad Nicholas; 5000 reached Genoa; the rest mostly dispersed; some sailed for Palestine from Brindisi, only to be soon forgotten. The Genoese persuaded their visitors to remain, and some rose to distinction in the state. ALBIGENSES.

cry'olite, a Greenland mineral, a fluoride of aluminium and sodium, used in extracting aluminium in 1855.

cryoph'orus, an instrument (invented by dr. Wollaston about 1812) to demonstrate the effects of evaporation in producing cold.

Cryp'togram, The Great. SHAKESPEARE'S PLAYS.

cryp'tograph, an apparatus for writing in cipher, invented by sir Charles Wheatstone, and made known in 1868, designed, by using different key-words, to insure absolute secrecy. A cryptographic machine was patented 1860. CIPHER.

A system of secret writing described in "Archiv der Mathematik" 1795
Prof. J. F. Lorenz published a system at Magdeburg 1806
Joseph Ludwig Kluber published "Kryptographik" 1809
Messrs. Thos. De la Rue published Wm. Henry Rochfort's system of secret writing termed "Arcanography," resembling Lorenz's 1836
A. L. Flamm patented an improvement on this system, about Oct. 1875

Crystal palace, New York. This building, in Reservoir square, was opened 14 July, 1853, by president Pierce, for a universal industrial exhibition. Its main buildings and galleries covered 173,000 sq. feet. After the exhibition the American Institute fairs and other meetings were held there. On 5 Oct. 1858, it was destroyed by fire, with many articles for exhibition at the Institute. The palace, built by a stock company, was designed by Messrs. Carstensen & Gildemeister, of New York, and was considered a beautiful piece of architecture.

Crystal palace, Sydenham, Engl. The exhibition building of 1851 was surrendered to Messrs. Fox & Henderson, 1 Dec. 1851, and the materials sold for 70,000*l.* to a company, who soon rebuilt the Crystal palace on its present site, near Sydenham in Kent, under the direction of sir Joseph Paxton, Owen Jones, Digby Wyatt, and others. The proposed capital of 500,000*l.* (in 100,000 shares of 5*l.* each) was increased Jan. 1853, to 1,000,000*l.*

crystallog'raphy is the science of symmetrical forms assumed by substances passing from the liquid to the solid state. Romé de Lisle published his "Essai de Cristallographie" in 1772; but René-Just Haüy is regarded as the founder of the modern school of crystallography (1801).—*Whewell.* Dana, Dufresnoy, and Miller are eminent modern writers on this subject.

Ctes'iphon (afterwards *Al Madayn*), on the Tigris, the capital of Parthia, was taken by Trajan in 116, and by Alex-

CUB

ander Severus (who made 100,000 captives), 198. Its defences deterred Julian from siege, 363. It was taken by Omar and Saracens, 637, and destroyed, and Cufa, near it, built of the remains.

Cuba (the original name), an island in the Caribbean sea, the largest of the Antilles, discovered by Columbus on his first voyage, 28 Oct. 1492; settled by Velasquez, 1511-12. Area, 43,220 sq. miles. Population, 1870, 765,000 whites, 250,000 colored, 368,000 slaves; in 1877, about 1,400,000; 1889, 1,518,650 (480,000 negroes and 50,000 Chinese); 1900, 1,572,797.

Buccaneer Morgan took Havana (BUCCANEERS).................. 1669
A British expedition lands and remains.......20 July-20 Nov. 1741
Havana taken by admiral Pococke and lord Albemarle, 1762; restored at the Peace of Paris.......................10 Feb. 1763
"LONE STAR" society for the acquisition of Cuba, etc., formed, 1848
Pres. Taylor of the U. S. publishes a strong proclamation, denouncing the object of the invaders.................11 Aug. 1849
Expedition of gen. Lopez and a large body of Americans, with the view of wresting this island from the dominion of Spain, landed at Cuba (defeated)...........................17 May, 1850
Cuba again invaded by Lopez and others..............13 Aug. 1851
They are defeated and taken; 50 shot, and Lopez garroted at Havana (FILIBUSTERS)..............................1 Sept. "
U. S. steamer *Black Warrior* seized by the Cuban authorities at Havana (BLACK WARRIOR)........................28 Feb. 1854
Pres. Pierce of the U. S. issues a proclamation against an intended expedition against Cuba.....................31 May, "
Messrs. Buchanan, Mason, and Soulé, U. S. envoys, meet at *Ostend* and *Aix-la-Chapelle*, and report, recommending the purchase of Cuba (OSTEND MANIFESTO)...............18 Oct. "
Spanish minister in Cortes declares that the sale would be "the sale of Spanish honor itself"..................19 Dec. "
Insurrection of creoles, under Carlos Manuel de Cespedes, to expel Spaniards after revolution in Spain; volunteers raised for gov. Lersundi.............................Sept.-Nov. 1868
A filibusters' attack on Cuba repelled.................17 May, 1869
U. S. refuse to recognize insurgents as belligerents......June, 1870
About 2000 lives lost by a hurricane............about 14 Oct. "
Capt.-gen. De Rodas resigned, left Cuba...............15 Dec. "
Insurrection mostly subdued; volunteers insubordinate; military despotism; local reign of terror; massacres, Jan.-Nov. 1871
Don Gonzalo Castañon murdered by Cubans; his tomb desecrated by medical students, 25 Nov.; 8 tried and shot at Havana...27 Nov. "
F. Delano sent by the U. S. government to report on the state of Cuba..9 Dec. 1872
War still continues; no quarter given.....................Dec. "
Suspended hostilities by establishment of Spanish republic, Feb. 1873
Much fighting reported..................................June, "
Virginius, American steamer, conveying men and arms from New York to the insurgents, is captured by the Spanish gunboat *Tornado*, 31 Oct.; conveyed to Cuba; above 90 insurgents and sailors (some British and Americans) tried; many insurgents and about 6 British and 30 Americans (captain and crew) shot...................................4-7 Nov. "
After correspondence the *Virginius* surrendered to Americans, 19 Dec.; foundered on her way to New York..about 26 Dec. "
Bascones defeats marquis Santa Lucia and 5000 insurgents at Naranjo...Feb. 1874
Gen. Martinez Campos governor, with plenary powers....Oct. 1876
Struggle going on less actively...................summer, 1877
A "Cuban league" in U. S. said to seek recognition of the insurgents as belligerents, etc.........................Sept. "
Estrada, the Cuban president, said to be captured........Oct. "
Reported surrender of many insurgents............23, 24 Dec. "
Surrender of insurgent government; end of insurrection announced...21 Feb. 1878
Amnesty, with freedom to slaves presenting themselves before 31 Mch. (gradual abolition)............................Mch. "
Campos and Jovellar enter Havana triumphantly.....14 June, "
Insurrection; state of siege; amnesty promised.......19 Sept. 1879
Insurgents defeated at Placeta; announced.............3 Dec. "
Bill for gradual emancipation passes Spanish senate, 21 Dec. 1879; Chambers of Deputies (230-10, 21 Jan.); promulgated, 18 Feb. 1880
Cuba reported tranquil....................................Sept. "
Slavery abolished absolutely.................................. 1886
Destructive cyclone, with great loss of life by inundations, etc.; about 1000 lives lost..................................4 Sept. 1888
Cuba suffers much by the McKinley tariff bill, and appeals to the queen-regent for help..........................7 Jan. 1891
Gov.-gen. Calleja in Cuba...................................... 1894
Insurrection in Santiago; reported........................Feb. 1895
Gen. Calleja resigns; reported.........................28 Mch. "
Insurgents defeated near Palmarito....................12 Apr. "
Arrival of marshal Campos.............................16 Apr. "
Gen. Salcedo defeats the insurgents under gen. Maceo in Parra Hueco...28 Apr. "
The insurgents defeated near Guantanamo..............13 May, "
The insurgents capture Cristo........................16 May, "
Gen. Salcedo defeats the insurgents in Porto Principe; their leader, José Marti, killed.............................21 May, "
Yellow-fever epidemic, great mortality....................July, "
Cuba demands autonomy under Spain.........................July, "
Gen. Martinez Campos attacked by insurgents near Bayamo, gen. Cildes killed....................................12 July, "
Gen. Salcedo resigns; leaves for Spain, 9 Aug.; the insurgent delegates proclaim a federal republic, and the Autonomista party petitions the Spanish government for a constitution resembling the Dominion of Canada.....................Aug. 1895
Antonio Maceo defeated at Holguin....................30 Sept. "
The insurgent leader Cantero killed in a skirmish; reported, 17 Sept.; defeat of the insurgents; Mejon, their leader, killed at Limpias; reported.................................1 Oct. "
Capt. Borrega's party (72) surprised by 800 insurgents near Porto Principe; lieut. Ardieta and 29 Spaniards killed..Dec. "
Insurgents under Gomez severely defeated by gen. Campos at Coliseo...24 Dec. "
Gen. Campos defeats the insurgents near Havana.......6 Jan. 1896
Guerilla warfare, with varying results................14 Jan. "
Gen. Martinez Campos recalled (leaves Havana 21 Jan.); succeeded by gen. Weyler................................19 Jan. "
The *Hawkins*, U. S. filibustering steamer from Philadelphia, wrecked, 75 miles off Long Island; 10 deaths; reported.28 Jan. "
Main body of Gomez's army defeated, with heavy loss, at St. Lucia...29 Jan. "
Fierce fight on the borders of Havana, the Spanish column, under gen. Canella, saved..............................1 Feb. "
Gen. Canella defeats the united bands of Maceo and others (6000), near Candelaria; reported......................8 Feb. "
The Spaniards entrapped and defeated by Maceo, near Lechuzo; reported.......................................4 Apr. "
U. S. filibustering schooner *Competitor* captured; 5 men sentenced to death, 8 May; intervention of the U. S. government... 10 May, "
Insurgents defeated by gen. Valdes near Consolacion..26 May, "
Again by gen. Castellano near Porto Principe.........14 June, "
Reinforcements, 14,000, arrive........................12 Sept. "
Fighting at Soroa, Pinar del Rio, near Guanajay; Reyes, the rebel leader, and other officers killed; reported......27 Oct. "
Guaimaro, in Porto Principe, surrendered to the insurgents under Calixto Garcia.....................................7 Nov. "
Insurgents defeated by gen. Castellano at San Miguel; the town of Pagsanjuan captured by the Spaniards; reported, 24 Nov. "
Col. Aldea defeats insurgents (300 killed) in Matanzas; reported...5 Dec. "
Antonio Maceo, insurgent leader, killed in a hot fight; and death of Francisco Gomez at San Pedro, in Havana..17 Dec. "
Convoy captured by insurgents under Calixto Garcia; 6 Spanish officers and 158 men killed near Manzanillo; reported, 27 Dec. "
Filibustering expedition of the *Three Friends* failed; 2 boats wrecked and 51 deaths; reported........................1 Jan. 1897
Col. Luque defeats Maximo Gomez at Arroyo Blanco, 106 killed, and 205 submit...5 Jan. "
Reform scheme drawn up by señ. Canovas; signed by the queen-regent at Madrid (refused by the Cubans, who demand independence)..4 Feb. "
Filibustering expedition under capt. Roloff landed by the *Laurada* at Banes...Mch. "
Gen. Rius Rivera, insurgent leader in the ten years' war, wounded at Cabezadas, and taken prisoner; reported, 29 Mch. "
Gen. Weyler's campaign destructive and indecisive, situation little changed since Apr. 1896; pacification of the west of the island...29 Apr. "
Application of reforms published at Havana..........6 June, "
Train blown up with dynamite by insurgents, about 100 killed, near Havana; reported................................10 June, "
Gen. Weyler proclaims an amnesty to all who surrender, 6 July, "
Desultory fighting, 202 insurgents killed, 700 surrender; 20 Spaniards killed; reported...........................16 Aug. "
Victoria de las Lunas besieged by the insurgents under García, 14 Aug.; captured....................................28 Aug. "
Señ. Domingo Mendez Capote elected president of the Cuban Insurgent republic at Havana; announced..........12 Sept. "
Gen. Weyler recalled, and succeeded by marshal Blanco.7 Oct. "
Gen. Weyler signs a general amnesty; reported........11 Oct. "
The *Triton*, an overloaded steamer, wrecked off Pinar del Rio; 181 deaths..16 Oct. "
Several engagements: 303 insurgents killed, 400 captured, and 69 surrendered; 3 Spanish officers and 23 soldiers killed (during 10 days)...Dec. "
Guisa, in Santiago, captured by the insurgents under Calixto Garcia; Spanish loss heavy; announced.............2 Dec. "
Insurgents defeated near Manzanillo; Maximo Gomez defeated in Santa Clara; reported...............................8 Dec. "
33 out of 60 filibustering expeditions frustrated by the U. S. during the rebellion; reported........................9 Dec. "
Fort Guamo besieged by insurgents, under Rabi, 11 days; siege raised on the arrival of Spanish column.......11 Dec. "
Decrees granting constitutional rights to Cubans, etc., approved by council, 6 Nov.; published, 27 Nov.; at Havana..17 Dec. "
Col. Ruiz sent to Aranguren, rebel chief, to induce him to surrender and accept autonomy; is executed by his orders; reported..19 Dec. "
Gen. Gonzalez Munoz appointed captain-general of Porto Rico, 23 Dec. "
First cabinet under the autonomy scheme: señ. José M. Galvez, president; established...........................1 Jan. 1898
Lieut.-col. Soto, maj. Nuñez, and other insurgent leaders, with their men, submit, declaring themselves satisfied with the new autonomous régime; reported.....................9 Jan. "
Gen. Masso, insurgent, with 11 officers and 100 men, surrenders to gen. Aguirre in Santa Clara; 115 rebels killed and 379 surrendered, 34 prisoners; 12 Spaniards killed (in 2 weeks); reported..21 Jan. "
Maximo Gomez's second squadron surrenders; reported, 23 Jan. "

Marshal Blanco publishes manifesto of the new autonomous government	24 Jan	1898
An armistice granted	Apr	"
[For events of the war see SPANISH AMERICAN WAR]		
Gen Lee, U S ambassador, leaves Havana	10 Apr	"
Blockade of Cuba by the U S fleet, ordered	22 Apr	"
The first Cuban autonomous congress opened by gen Blanco,	4 May,	"
Starvation round Havana, many deaths, gen Fernandez appointed acting governor	13 May	"
Gen Blanco holds a meeting in Havana of generals and officers on the question of peace negotiations or extension of the war,	12 July,	"
Havana occupied by U S troops	7 Oct	"
Mutiny of Spanish troops at Havana, order restored	14 Nov	"
Gen Blanco leaves succeeded by gen Castellanos	30 Nov	"
The remains of Columbus taken to Spain	26 Sept -Dec	"
Desperate fighting at Najasa, Cartagena, and Camaguez, Calixto Garcia defeated by gen Luque, Mch , Garcia dies in Washington	11 Dec	"
Gen Brooke arrives in Havana	27 Dec	"
American flag hoisted	1 Jan	1899
New tariff, 6 per cent. average reduction	1 Jan	"
Gen Gomez insurgent leader, accepts the U S terms, $3.000 000 to be distributed to the soldiers	Feb	"
The Cuban assembly votes disbandment of the army and its own dissolution (21 to 1), reported	1 Apr	"
Pres McKinley issues a proclamation regarding a system of Cuban self-government, a census to be taken etc	17 Aug	"
Cuban constitutional convention opened, reported	5 Nov	"
American terms accepted	June,	1901
Señ Estrada Palma and Estèvez chosen president and vice-president of the Cuban republic	24 Feb	1902
Señ Palma's ministry formed, announced	17 May,	"
Transfer of Cuba to the new republican government under American suzerainty, gen Wood, retiring U S governor, and troops leave Havana	20 May,	"
Commercial treaty with U S , signed	12 Dec	"
Treaty with U S ratified by Cuban senate	28 Mar	1903
Permanent treaty between Cuba and U S signed, secures the right of U S to intervene for the preservation of the independence of the republic	end of May,	"
Treaty providing for perpetual naval bases for U S and placing Isle of Pines under Cuban sovereignty signed	July,	"
Custom house established at Nueva Gerona, Isle of Pines	9 Dec	"
U S flag raised at Camp McCalla Guantanamo	11 Dec.	"
Pres Roosevelt signs the Cuban reciprocity bill	23 Dec	"
Pres Palma vetoes the lottery bill	7 Jan	1904
Duties to be increased by not more than 30 per cent. authorized by the legislature	13 Jan	"
Congress closed by pres Palma	19 Jan	"
Last American soldiers leave Cuba	5 Feb	"
The new tariff published	5 Feb	"
Cuban loan of $35 000,000, to pay the revolutionary soldiers, is taken by Speyer & Co., New York	15 Feb	"
Treaty conferring Cuban sovereignty over Isle of Pines, signed,	2 Mch	"
Cuban congress lacks a quorum	5 Apr	"
Extradition treaty with the U S , published	22 Apr	"
Cyclone in Santiago, over 100 persons killed	16 June,	"
Congress appropriates $190,000 for street cleaning, 14 Dec , and $326,000 for sanitation	17 Dec.	"
The moderate party forms a new cabinet	3 Mch	1905
Celebration of third anniversary of Cuban independence.	20 May,	"

THE CUBAN GOVERNMENT

President of the Republic—Tomas Estrada Palma
Vice President—dr Luis Estevez y Romero
Speaker of the Senate—dr Domingo Méndez Capote
Speaker of the House of Representatives—dr Santiago Garcia Canizares
President of the Supreme Court of Justice—dr Juan Hernandez Barreiro
Secretary of the Interior—Eduardo Yero Buduen
Secretary of the Treasury—José Maria Garcia Montes
Secretary of Public Instruction—Leopoldo Cancio
Secretary of Public Works—Manuel L Diaz.
Secretary of State and Justice—dr Carlos Eugenio Ortiz
Secretary of Agriculture, Industry, and Commerce—Vacant.
Postmaster General—Fernando Figueredo.

cubit, by which Noah's ark was measured (2448 B C), was the distance from a man's elbow to the extremity of the middle finger According to Arbuthnot, the Hebrew cubit was a little under 22 inches, the Roman cubit 17½ inches, and the English cubit 18 inches.

cucking-stool or **ducking-stool**, for shrews, one at Kingston on-Thames was used in Apr 1745, and another at Cambridge in 1780 —*Chambers*

cucumbers, noticed by Vergil and other ancient poets, brought to England from the Netherlands about 1538

Cud'dalore, India, on the coast of the Carnatic, acquired by the English in 1681, reduced by the French in 1758, recaptured in 1760 by sir Eyre Coote Again lost in 1781, it underwent a destructive siege by the British under gen Stuart, in 1783, which lasted until peace was signed, when it reverted to them, 1784

Cuen'ca, New Castile, Spain, 80 miles from Madrid, attacked by the Carlists 13 July, and captured 14 July, 1874, and garrison and inhabitants barbarously used Gen Lopez Pinto rescued the prisoners, 19 July

cuirass (*kwee'-ras*), a part of Greek and Roman armor Skins, and afterwards tanned leather, formed the cuirass of Britons until the Anglo-Saxon era. It was afterwards made of iron and brass The cuirass was worn by cavalry of Henry III, 1216 et seq Napoleon had regiments of cavalry wearing cuirasses, and most European armies have picked corps of such

Culdees, said to derive their name from *cultores Dei*, worshippers of God, monks in Scotland and Ireland, with their principal seat at St Andrews It is said that in 1185 at Tipperary, a Culdean abbey had monks "attached to simple truth and pure Christian worship, and had not yet conformed to the reigning superstition" They were eventually subjected to the pope

Cullen's-wood, Ireland An English colony from Bristol, at Dublin going for diversion to Cullen's-wood, the O'Byrnes and O Tooles fell upon them, and destroyed 500 men, with women and children, 30 Mch 1209 (on Easter, afterwards called Black Monday)

Cullo'den, near Inverness, where the English, under William, duke of Cumberland, defeated the Scotch, headed by the young Pretender, last of the Stuarts, 16 Apr 1746 The Scots lost 2500 killed upon the field or in the pursuit, while the loss of the English did not far exceed 200 Prince Charles, who wandered among the wilds of Scotland for 6 months, while 30,000*l* were offered for taking him, at length escaped from Uist to Morlaix, and died at Rome, 3 Mch 1788

culture, according to Matthew Arnold ("the Apostle of Culture"), is the knowledge of "the best that has been thought and said in the world" (1880)

culverin (from the Fr *couleuvrine*) a kind of cannon, said to have been introduced into England from a French model in 1534, originally 5¼ inches diameter in the bore, with a ball of 18 pounds.—*Bailey*.

Cumæ, S Italy, a Greek colony, 1050 B.C., reputed residence of the ancient Sibyl, was taken by Samnites 420 B.C., and annexed by Rome 338 B C.

Cumberland, a northwest county of England, was granted to Malcolm I of Scotland in 945, by king Edmund, "on condition that he should be his fellow-worker." It was seized by William I, but restored to Malcolm III, "who became his man," 1072. William the Lion, after defeat at Alnwick, resigned Cumberland to Henry II, and it was annexed to England in 1237.

Cumberland and **Merrimac**, NAVAL BATTLES, 1862.

Cumberland Presbyterians. PRESBYTERIANS

Cumberland road. An act of U. S. Congress, 29 Mch 1806, authorized the president to appoint 3 commissioners to lay out a public road from Cumberland, Md , on the Potomac to the Ohio river, and appropriated $30,000 for that purpose The road was continued from time to time, reaching Illinois in 1838, when railroads superseded it. The total cost of building and repairs up to that time was $6,821,246. 60 acts passed Congress relating to this road

Cunaxa, in Mesopotamia, near the Euphrates, where Cyrus the younger was defeated and slain by his brother Artaxerxes II, against whom he conspired (401 B.C), told in Xenophon's "Anabasis" His Greek auxiliaries retreated safely. RETREAT OF THE GREEKS.

cune'iform or **cu'niform inscriptions** (from *cuneus*, Lat for a wedge), in characters resembling arrow-heads, inscribed on bricks or clay tablets, found at Babylon, Behistun, etc., some dating as far back as 2000 B.C. ACCADIANS, ASSYRIA, BABYLON, BEHISTUN.

Cunnersdorf, Prussia, where, on 12 Aug 1759, Frederick II. of Prussia, with 50,000 men, attacked the Austrian and Russian army of 90,000 in camp, at first with success, but, when rashly pursued, the Austrians and Russians rallied and gained a complete victory The Prussians lost 200 pieces of cannon and 30,000 killed and wounded

cupping, a mode of blood-letting The skin is scarified by lancets, and a glass cup with its air rarefied by heat is applied, when blood flows into the cup This operation was known to the ancients and is described by Hippocrates (413 B.C.) and Celsus (20 B.C.) It was common in England about 1820

Curaçoa (*ku-ra-sō'-a*), an island in the Caribbean sea, settled by the Spaniards about 1527, was seized by the Dutch in 1634 In 1800 the French, settled on this island, quarrelled with the Dutch, who surrendered it to a British frigate It was restored to the Dutch in 1802, taken by the British in 1807, and again restored in 1814

curates were early appointed as coadjutors in the Catholic church, and are mentioned in England in the 7th century Among the acts passed for the relief of these laborious clergy are the 12th Anne, 1713, and 36th, 53d, and 58th Geo III, and especially the beneficent act, 2 Will IV, Oct 1831 It appeared by parliamentary reports that there were, in 1831, 5230 curates in England and Wales, with stipends of 424,695*l* The greatest number in one diocese was in Lincoln, 629, and the smallest in St Asaph, 43 The Pastoral Aid Society was established in 1836, the Society for Promoting the Employment of Additional Curates, in 1837, the Curates' Augmentation Fund, 1866

curfew bell (from the Fr *couvre feu*) was revived or introduced in England by Will I 1068 When it rang at 8 P M all fires and candles were to be extinguished, under a severe penalty —*Rapin* The curfew was abolished 1 Hen I 1100 A so-called curfew bell was rung at West Ham so lately as Nov 1859

Curiatii. ROME, 669 B.C

curling, a Scotch national game with stones on the ice, said to have been introduced from the Low Countries in the 16th century The Duddingstone curling club was instituted 1795 The royal Caledonian curling club, founded in 1838, owns a large artificial pond at Strathallan, Perthshire

Montreal curling club organized 1807
Quebec curling club organized 1821
Curling introduced into Ontario about 1830, and Toronto curling club organized 1837
First "bonspiel" or tournament of Canadian and U S clubs held at Buffalo, N Y 1865
Grand National curling club of America organized 1867

currants, from *Corinth*, whence, probably, the bush was first brought to England about 1533 The name is also given to a small dried grape, from the Levant and Zante. The hawthorn currant (*Ribes oxyacanthoides*) was brought to England from Canada in 1705. FLOWERS AND PLANTS

Curtatone, near Mantua, N Italy Here the Austrians, under Radetzky, crossed the Mincio, and defeated the Italians after a severe conflict, 29 May, 1848

cushee pieces, invented by Richard Leake, master-gunner of the British man-of-war *Royal Prince*, renowned for bravery in fighting the Dutch admiral Van Tromp in 1673

custom is law not written (*lex non scripta*), established by long usage and consent, distinguished from *lex scripta*, or written law It is law when derived from 1189 downwards In England 60 years' custom is binding in civil law, and 40 years' in ecclesiastical cases.

customs were collected upon merchandise in England, under Ethelred II in 979 The king's claim to them by grant of Parliament was established 3 Edw I 1274 The customs were farmed to sir Thomas Smith for annual sums varying from 14,000*l* to 50,000*l* in the reign of Elizabeth —*Stow* They were farmed by Charles II for 390,000*l*. in 1666 —*Davenant.* In 1671 commissioners were appointed. The customs were consolidated by Mr Pitt in 1787 Many changes have been made since REVENUE

Customs in Ireland a sack of wool, 3*d*, a last of hides, 6*d*., a barrel of wine, 2*d* 1224
Customs business of Ireland was transferred to the London board. . . . 6 Jan. 1830
Customs receipts in Great Britain from 1872 to 1890 vary between 19,000,000*l*. and 21,000,000*l* yearly

CUSTOMS AND CUSTOM-HOUSES IN THE UNITED STATES

Act of Parliament establishing custom houses in the American colonies under English commissioners of customs 1672
Further enforced 1676-77
Customs collected in New York prior to 1677
First custom house in Boston Edward Randolph, commissioner 1680
First custom house in Charleston S C 1685
"Plantation duties" collected in the colonies paid the custom house expenses, leaving a surplus of from $5000 to $6000 (*Hildreth*) 1690-1700
Court of vice admiralty established 1696-97
Enumerated articles greatly increased 1767

LOCATION OF CUSTOM-HOUSES IN THE UNITED STATES, 1890

Alabama—Mobile
Alaska—Sitka
California—Eureka, San Diego San Francisco, Wilmington
Colorado—Denver
Connecticut—Fairfield, Hartford, New Haven, New London, Stonington
Delaware—Wilmington
District of Columbia—Georgetown
Florida—Appalachicola Cedar Keys, Fernandina, Jacksonville, Key West Pensacola St Augustine Tampa
Georgia—Atlanta, Brunswick St Mary's, Savannah
Illinois—Chicago Galena
Indiana—Evansville, Indianapolis, Michigan City
Iowa—Burlington, Dubuque
Kentucky—Louisville Paducah
Louisiana—Brishear, New Orleans
Maine—Bangor, Bath, Belfast, Castine Eastport Ellsworth Houlton, Kennebunk, Machias Portland, Saco, Waldoborough Wiscasset York
Maryland—Annapolis, Baltimore Crisfield
Massachusetts—Barnstable, Boston Edgarton Fall River, Gloucester, Marblehead Nantucket, New Bedford, Newburyport Plymouth Salem
Michigan—Detroit, Grand Haven, Grand Rapids, Marquette, Port Huron
Minnesota—Duluth St Paul
Mississippi—Natchez Shieldsborough, Vicksburg
Missouri—Kansas City, St Joseph, St Louis
Montana—Fort Benton
Nebraska—Omaha
New Hampshire—Portsmouth
New Jersey—Bridgeton Newark, Perth Amboy, Somers Point, Trenton, Tuckerton
New York—Albany, Buffalo Cape Vincent, Dunkirk, New York, Ogdensburg Oswego, Patchogue, Plattsburg, Port Jefferson, Rochester Sag Harbor, Suspension Bridge.
North Carolina—Beaufort Edenton, Newberne, Wilmington
Ohio—Cincinnati, Columbus, Cleveland Sandusky, Toledo
Oregon—Astoria Empire City Portland Yaquina.
Pennsylvania—Erie Philadelphia Pittsburg
Rhode Island—Bristol Newport, Providence
South Carolina—Beaufort Charleston, Georgetown.
Tennessee—Chattanooga. Memphis
Texas—Brownsville, Corpus Christi, Eagle Pass, El Paso, Galveston
Vermont—Burlington
Virginia—Alexandria Cherry Stone, Newport News, Norfolk, Petersburg Richmond, Tappahannock
Washington—Port Townsend
West Virginia—Wheeling
Wisconsin—La Crosse, Milwaukee
For custom receipts in the U S REVENUE

custos rotulorum, keeper of the rolls or records of the sessions of the peace, England, previously nominated by the lord chancellor, was in 1545 directed to be appointed by a bill signed by the king The act was confirmed in 1689.

Custozza (*koos-tot'-za*), near Verona, N Italy Here the Italians were defeated by marshal Radetzky, 23 July, 1848, and here they were again defeated, 24 June, 1866, after a series of desperate attacks on the Austrian army The Italians were commanded by their king, Victor Emmanuel, and the Austrians by the archduke Albrecht The Italian loss was computed to be 720 killed, 3112 wounded, and 4315 missing, the Austrian loss, 960 killed, 3690 wounded, and nearly a thousand prisoners The Italians soon recrossed the Mincio

Cutch (*kŭtch*), W India, a principality under the government of Bombay In consequence of the depredations of the natives, the East India government resorted to hostile measures, which resulted in a stringent treaty with the rao in Jan 1816. In 1819 he was deposed for misgovernment, and replaced by his infant son, supported by a British contingent The traffic in children, detected in Dec. 1835, was suppressed by the British Many persons perished by an earthquake in July, 1819 —*Thornton.*

Cuttack (*ku-tak'*), E India, a British province ceded to the East India company in 1803 Cuttack, the capital, was taken by col Harcourt, 14 Oct same year The Mahrattas conquered it in 1750 —*Thornton*

cutting-out machines. Wearing apparel was first cut out by machinery in England by Messrs Hyams in 1853 The machine, invented by Frederick Osbourn, consists of a reciprocating vertical knife working through a slot in the table that supports the pile of cloth to be cut The cloth is pressed by the attendant up to the edge of the knife, which divides it along lines marked on the upper layer

Cuzco (*koos'-ko*), capital of Peru, was entered by Pizarro in Nov 1533 and taken by him in Aug 1536, after 5 months' siege

cyan'ogen, a colorless gas (composed of nitrogen and carbon), irritating to the nose and eyes, derived from Prussian blue, was first obtained in the free state by Gay-Lussac in 1815, being the first instance of the isolation of a compound radical

cycle of the sun, the 28 years before the days of the week return to the same days of the month, that of the moon is 19 lunar years and 7 intercalary months, or 19 solar years The cycle of Jupiter is 60 years The Paschal cycle, or the time of keeping Easter, was first calculated for the period of 532 years by Victorius, 463.—*Blair* CALIPPIC PERIOD, METONIC CYCLE.

cyclones. STORMS

Cyclope'an, from Cyclopes, a fabled race of gigantic size, a term given to certain ancient works of masonry from the great size of the stones, found in Greece, Italy, and Asia Minor, erected probably before 1000 B.C

cymbal, the oldest known musical instrument, made of brass Xenophon says the cymbal was invented by Cybele, and used in her feasts about 1580 B C

Cymri or **Kymri** (hence Cambria), the great Celtic family to which the Britons belonged, came from Asia and occupied much of Europe perhaps before 1500 B C About 640 A D Dyvnwal Moelmud reigned "King of the Cymry" WALES

cynics, a sect of philosophers founded by Antisthenes (about 396 B C, *Diog Laert*, *Clinton*), who professed to contemn all worldly things, even sciences, except morality, and lived in public Diogenes, the eminent cynic, died 323 B.C. PHILOSOPHY

cynosceph'alæ (*dogs' heads*, so named from the shape of the heights), in Thessaly, where Pelopidas and the Thebans defeated Alexander, tyrant of Pheræ and the Thessalians, 364 B.C Pelopidas was slain Here also the consul Flaminius defeated Philip V of Macedon, 197 B C., and ended the war PHALANX.

cypress, *Cupressus sempervirens*, a tree of Cyprus The Athenians buried heroes in coffins of cypress, of which Egyptian mummy-chests were also made The ancients planted it in cemeteries. The cypress was taken to England about 1441. The deciduous cypress, *C disticha*, exported from North America before 1640.

Cyprus, an island 148 miles long and about 40 wide, in the Mediterranean, near the coasts of Asia Minor and Syria, present capital Levkosia or Nikosia, seaports, Larnaka and Famagosta Here the ancients found copper (*æs Cyprium*), silver, and precious stones. The country was fertile and well-wooded in ancient times, and under Venice its commerce was important Area, 3584 sq miles. Population, two thirds Greek, 1891, 209,300, under Venice, said to have been 1,000,000.

	B.C
Phœnician colonists introduced the worship of Ashtaroth (Gr Aphrodite, Rom Venus)	about 569
Conquered by Amasis, king of Egypt, revolted at the invasion of Cambyses, and submitted to Persia	525
Revolted and subjected	500-499
Partly independent under Evagoras and Nicocles, kings of Salamis	387 et seq
Supported Alexander the Great	333
Taken from Demetrius by Ptolemy of Egypt.	295
Became a Roman province	58
	A D
Visited by Paul and Barnabas (Acts xiii)	45
Great revolt of the Jews.	117
Seized by Arabs 646 recovered by Greeks	648
Isaac Comnenus king	1184
Seized by Richard I of England, 1191, and given to Guy de Lusignan, as king	1192
"Order of the Sword" established (erased with 8th king)	1195
Guy's descendant, Catherine de Cornaro, sold it to Venice	1487
Cruelly subdued by the Turks	1570-71
Insurrections suppressed 1764 with massacre	1823
Gen di Cesnola, a Genoese, American consul, by excavations discovers Babylonian Egyptian Phœnician, and Greek gold and silver ornaments and relics (sold to Metropolitan Museum, New York)	1866 et seq
His work, "Cyprus its Ancient Cities, Tombs and Temples," pub in London and New York	Dec 1877
Given to Great Britain for administration by the Anglo Turkish convention	4 June, 1878
Possession taken by admiral lord John Hay, 12 July, by sir Garnet J Wolseley as lord high commissioner	22 July, "
British buy the government lands except the sultan's estate	1879
Excavations on the site of the temple of Aphrodite, discoveries of inscriptions etc	1888

Cyr, St., near Versailles, France Here a college for ladies was founded by Madame de Maintenon, in 1686, and here she died, 15 Apr 1719. It was made a military college in 1803

Cyrena'ic Sect, founded by Aristippus the Elder, 365 B C, taught that the supreme good is pleasure, particularly of the senses, and virtue is commended only as causing pleasure.

Cyrene (*si-ree'-nee*), N W Africa, a Greek colony, founded by Battus about 630 B.C. Aristæus, chief of the colonists, gave the city his mother's name It was also called Pentapolis, from its 5 towns—Cyrene, Ptolemais, Berenice, Apollonia, and Arsinoe It was conquered by Ptolemy Soter I, who placed many Jews here (286 B C) It was a Jew of Cyrene whom Roman soldiers compelled to bear the cross of Jesus Cyrene was left by Ptolemy Apion to the Romans, 97 B C It is now a desert Some Cyrenaic sculptures were placed in the British museum in July, 1861.

Cyz'icus, Asia Minor In the Peloponnesian war, the Lacedæmonian fleet under Mindarus, assisted by Pharnabazus, the Persian, was defeated by Athenians under Alcibiades, with great slaughter, near Cyzicus, Mindarus being slain, 410 B C. —*Plutarch*

czar (the title of the emperor of Russia), probably from Cæsar, said to have been assumed by Ivan Basilowitz after defeating the Tartars, about 1482. The empress is termed czarina, and the eldest son czarowitch

Czechs (*tcheks*), a branch of the Slavonic race, native in BOHEMIA and MORAVIA. The antagonism between Germans and Czechs is milder in Moravia than in Bohemia Czech representatives entered the Reichsrath at Vienna, 8 Oct. 1879. AUSTRIA.

D

D in the English alphabet is the fourth letter, as it also is in the Hebrew, Chaldee, Syriac, Greek, and Latin alphabets. Its form is the same as that of the Latin, and the Latin is no other than the Greek Δ This symbol is again from the ancient Phœnician, and so from the Egyptian ALPHABET, GRIMM'S LAW

Dacca, N E India, a province of Bengal, acquired by the East India company in 1765, and ruled under them by a nawab till its annexation in 1845 —*Thornton.*

Da'cia, a Roman province including parts of Hungary, Transylvania, Wallachia, Moldavia, and Galicia, after many contests, was subdued by Trajan, 106, when Decebalus, the Dacian leader, was killed Dacia was abandoned to the Goths by Aurelian, in 270, subdued by Huns, 376, by Scythians, 566, by Charlemagne, and by Magyars, in the 9th century.

dacoits', hereditary robbers of N. India, formerly employed in war by native sovereigns.

It is said that between 1818 and 1834, one tribe alone, in 118 "dacoitees," or expeditions killed 172 persons, and obtained plunder valued at 115,000*l*. In 1838 lord Auckland did much to suppress the dacoits and many settlements were broken up, but they are not quite extinct in Bengal and Burmah. Several dacoitees were suppressed in 1879. BURMAH.

Daghistan' (mountain-land), in Asiatic Russia on the west coast of the Caspian sea, was conquered by czar Peter, 1723, restored to Persia, 1735, reannexed to Russia by Alexander I, 1813. Area, 11,425 sq. miles. Pop. 1890, 540,000.

Dagobert, name of several of the Merovingian kings of France, the first, 628-38. FRANCE.

Da'gon, a national god of the Philistines, spoken of in Judg. xvi. 23, 1 Sam. v. 2. His principal temples were at Ashdod (1 Sam. v. 1) and Gaza (Judg. xvi. 1 23). His image had the head and hands of a man and the tail of a fish.

Daguerrotype (*da-gĕr'-o-tip*) **process,** invented by Daguerre, pub. 1838. PHOTOGRAPHY.

Dahlgren gun. CANNON.

dah'lia, a flower, native in Mexico brought to Europe about 1787, and cultivated by the Swedish botanist, Dahl. About 1814 it was introduced into France and England; Andre Thouine suggested improvements in its culture, and it soon became a favorite. Georgi introduced it at St. Petersburg, hence it is known in Germany as the *Georgina*.

Daho'mey, a negro kingdom, W. Africa, became known to Europeans early in the last century, when Trudo Audati or Guadjor Trudo, a man of energy and talent, was king. He died in 1732, and was succeeded by a series of cruel tyrants, whose revenue was largely derived from the slave-trade. Abbeokuta, a robbers' haunt in 1825, has, since 1829, become a strong-walled town, inhabited by free blacks. The king of Dahomey has repeatedly attacked it and been repulsed and once, 16 Mch. 1864, a great number of his Amazons were slain. During the last few years Dahomey has been visited by capt. Burton and other travellers, who have described the royal sanguinary customs.

King ordered to pay a fine (for an outrage on Mr. Turnbull at Whydah, 23 Jan.) Mch. 1876
He refuses in insulting terms, Apr.; the coast about to be blockaded July, "
King threatens massacre of Europeans if attacked Aug. "
He makes concessions, blockade removed 12 May, 1877
Renewed massacres of natives ("customs") and outrages on foreigners at Whydah, reported 26 Sept. 1879
French in Dahomey 1890
Dahomey coast blockaded by the French Apr. "
Whydah bombarded by the French, 29-30 Apr.; surrender of French prisoners 5 May, "
New king Behanzin installed, continued difficulty with France. 1892

Dah'ra, Algeria. On 18 June, 1845, above 500 Kabyles at war with the French were suffocated in a cave in a fire kindled by order of gen. Pelissier, afterwards duke of Malakoff. They had fired on a messenger bearing an offer of a truce. The massacre was condemned by marshal Soult, minister of war, but justified by marshal Bugeaud.

Daimios (*dī'-myō*), nobles of Japan who enjoyed almost absolute power before the revolution of 1871, when they were deprived of their privileges. JAPAN, 1868.

dairy. BUTTER, CATTLE, CHEESE.

Dakota. NORTH DAKOTA and SOUTH DAKOTA.

Dakotas. INDIANS.

Dalecar'lians, Sweden, revolted against Christian of Denmark, 1521, and placed Gustavus Vasa on the throne of Sweden.

Dallas, Ga. In this vicinity, in Sherman's advance on Atlanta, the confederates held him in check, gen. Hooker's command having a severe engagement with them on the afternoon of 25 May, 1864, while on the 28th Hardee attacked McPherson on the right, with loss. The confederates retired 6 June. ATLANTA CAMPAIGN.

Dalmatia, an Austrian province, N. E. of the Adriatic, conquered and made a province by the Romans, 34 B.C. The emperor Diocletian, who was born in this province, erected his palace at Spalato or Spalatro, and retired there, 305 A.D. Dalmatia was held in turn by the Goths, Hungarians, and Turks till ceded to Venice in 1699. By the treaty of CAMPO FORMIO in 1797 it was given to Austria, but in 1805 it was incorporated with Italy, and gave the title of duke to marshal Soult. In 1814 it reverted to Austria. Area, 4937 sq. miles. Pop. 1890, 527,426.

Dalton, northern Ga. Here the confederates, under gen. Joseph E. Johnston, strongly fortified, checked the advance of gen. Sherman, until forced to evacuate by a flank movement by gen. McPherson, 10-12 May, 1864. ATLANTA CAMPAIGN.

Daltonism. COLOR.

Dam'araland. GERMAN EAST AND WEST AFRICA.

Damascus, Syria, a city in the time of Abraham, 1913 B.C. (Gen. xiv.), now the capital of a Turkish pachalic.

Taken by David (1040 B.C.) but soon retaken; capital of Syria under Benhadad and his successors B.C. 951
Recovered by Jeroboam II about 822
Taken by Tiglath Pileser, king of Assyria 740
From the Assyrians it passed to the Persians, and from them to the Greeks under Alexander 333
To the Romans about 64
A.D.
Paul converted, preaches here (Acts ix.) 52
Taken by the Saracens, 634, by the Turks in 1075, destroyed by Tamerlane Jan. 1401
Taken by Ibrahim Pacha 1832
Disappearance of a Greek priest named father Tommaso, here, 1 Feb. 1840, led to torture and persecution of the Jews, who were accused of his murder, which caused remonstrances from many states of Europe 1840
Damascus restored to Turkey 1841
In a dispute between Druses and Maronites the Mahometans massacred above 3000 Christians and destroyed houses, rendering vast numbers of persons destitute, many rescued by Abd-el-Kader, who held the citadel 9, 10, 11 July, 1860
These crimes punished by Fuad Pacha: 160 persons executed, including the Turkish governor, and 11,000 made soldiers, Aug.-Sept. "

damask linens and **silks,** first manufactured at Damascus, have been beautifully imitated by the Dutch and Flemish. The manufacture was brought to England by artisans who fled from the persecutions of Alva, 1571-73. The damask rose was brought to England from the south of Europe by dr. Linacre, physician to Henry VIII, about 1540.

Damiens's attempt. Louis XV of France was stabbed with a knife in the right side by Robert François Damiens, a native of Arras, 5 Jan. 1757. The culprit endured frightful tortures, and was then broken on the wheel, 28 Mch. TORTURE.

Damiet'ta, a town of Lower Egypt, was taken by the crusaders, 5 Nov. 1219, lost, 1221, retaken by Louis IX, 5 June, 1249, surrendered as his ransom when a prisoner, 6 May, 1250. The present town was built soon after. Here, it is said, dimity was first manufactured. Pop. 1888, 34,044.

Da'mon and **Pyth'ias** (or **Phintias**), Pythagorean philosophers. Damon was condemned to death by Dionysius of Syracuse, about 387 B.C. He obtained leave to settle some domestic affairs, promising to return at the time of execution, and Pythias became his surety. When Damon did not appear, Pythias surrendered and was led to execution, but at this moment Damon returned. Dionysius remitted the sentence, and desired to share their friendship.

Dan'ăi, a name originally given to the Argives, as having been subjects of Danaus, king of Argos, 1474 B.C. In consequence, however, of the warlike character of the race and their high renown, Homer uses the name Danai (*Δαναοί*) as a general appellation for the Greeks.

Dance of Death. The triumph of death over all men was a favorite subject with artists of the middle ages, in rude carvings and pictures in various countries.

Chorea Machabæorum or *Danse Macabre*, the first printed representation, published by Guyot Marchand, a bookseller of Paris 1485
Holbein's "Dance of Death" (53 distinct sketches for engraving, called "Imagines Mortis." They are now at St. Petersburg, the authorship has been much controverted), printed at Lyons in 1538, and at Basel 1594
Many editions have since appeared, one with introduction and notes by Russell Smith 1849
The term *Dance of Death* was also applied to the frenzied movements of flagellants, who had sometimes skeletons depicted on their clothing, about the end of the 14th century

dancing was invented by the Curetes, 1534 B C — *Eusebius* As a mark of rejoicing, Ex xv 20, xxxii 19, Judg xi 34, 2 Sam vi 14, etc For favors granted, Matt xiv 6, Mark vi 22 The Greeks combined the dance with their dramas, and pantomimic dances were introduced on the Roman stage 22 B C — *Usher* Dancing by cinque paces was introduced into England from Italy, 1541 A D Dancing was one of the amusements of the North American Indians They have religious, martial, and social dances For dancing in modern times BALLET CONTRE-DANSE, MORICE DANCE, POLKA, QUADRILLE, WALTZ

dancing mania. A kind of dervish frenzy that raged among the people of middle Europe, 1021, 1278 1374, and less severe in the 15th and 16th centuries In Germany this malady first bore the name of St John's dance, but later was known as St Vitus's dance St Vitus, a Sicilian youth, was invoked for relief He is said to have suffered martyrdom 303, during the persecution of Diocletian, and his remains were brought to France in 836 and buried in the church of St Deny This half-religious frenzy spread rapidly from city to city, through Germany, Flanders, and France, hundreds and even thousands were seized with it, and engaged in the wild movements until many died from exhaustion and exposure In Italy it was termed tarantism, because erroneously supposed to be produced by the bite of the tarantula spider It was found that music had a tendency to subdue the frenzy The mania first made the subject of medical research by Paracelsus This dancing mania should not be confounded with the disease of the muscles, known in medical science as chorea (St Vitus's dance)

Dane-geld or **Danegelt,** a tribute paid the Danes to stop their ravages in England, first raised by Ethelred II in 991, and again in 1003, and levied after the expulsion of the Danes to pay fleets for clearing the seas of them The tax was suppressed by Edward the Confessor in 1051, revived by William I 1068, and formed part of the revenue of the crown till abolished by Stephen, 1136 Every hide of land, i e., as much as one plough could plough, or, as Bede says, as much as could maintain a family, was taxed at first 1*s* afterwards as much as 7*s* Camden says that once 24,360*l* was raised

Danes or **Northmen.** DENMARK During their attacks upon Britain and Ireland they made a descent on France, where in 895, under Rollo, they received presents under the walls of Paris. They returned and ravaged the French territories as far as Ostend in 896 They attacked Italy in 903. Neustria was granted by the king of France to Rollo and his Normans (Northmen), hence Normandy, in 911 The invasions of England and Ireland were as follows

First hostile appearance of the Danes. 783
They land near Purbeck, Dorset. 787
Descend in Northumberland, destroy the church at Lindisfarne, are repelled, and perish by shipwreck 8 Jan 794
Invade Scotland and Ireland 795, 796
Enter Dublin with 60 sail, and seize also Fingal, etc 798
Take the isle of Sheppey 832
Defeated at Hengeston, in Cornwall, by Egbert 835
Land in Kent from 350 vessels, and take Canterbury and London 851
Descend on the north, and take York 867
Defeat the Saxons at Merton 871
Take Wareham and Exeter 876
Take Chippenham, but 120 ships are wrecked 877
Defeated Guthrum, their leader, becomes Christian, and many settle in England 878
Alfred enters into a treaty with them 882
Their fleet destroyed by Alfred at Appledore 894
Defeated near isle of Wight 897
Invade and waste Wales 900
Defeated by Edward the Elder 922
Defeat the people of Leinster 956
Ravage Cornwall, Devon, and Dorset 982
Ravage Essex and Suffolk . 990
Said to assume the title *lord dane* about 991
Their fleet defeated after a breach of treaty, purchased by money 992
Anlaf and Sweyn ravage Kent and the south (erroneously said to have been paid 16 000*l*. for peace) . 994
A general massacre of the Danes, by Ethelred II 13 Nov 1002
Sweyn revenges it, and *receives* 36,000*l* (as annual *tribute*) to depart. 1003
Their fleet anchors at Isle of Wight. 1006
They make fresh inroads and defeat the Saxons in Suffolk, 1010, sack Canterbury and kill the inhabitants, 1011, receive 48,000*l*. as tribute, and murder Alphege, archbishop, 1012
Vanquished at Clontarf, Ireland (CLONTARF) 1014
Conquest of England completed, Canute king 1017
Settle in Scotland 1020
Land again at Sandwich, carrying plunder to Flanders. 1047
Defeated by Harold II at Stamford bridge 25 Sept 1066
Burn York and kill 3000 Normans. 1069
Once more invade England to aid a conspiracy, but compelled to depart 1074

Dan'ite ("Dan shall be a serpent by the way, an adder in the path," Gen xlix 17), a member of an alleged secret society or order of the Mormons connected with the early history of that people, accused of various crimes in the interest of Mormonism Denied by the Mormons

Danne'werke or **Danna'wirke,** a series of earthworks, considered almost impregnable, stretching across the long, narrow peninsula of Schleswig Holstein, and Jutland —said to have been constructed during the "stone age," long before the art of metal-working They were rebuilt in 937 by Thyra, queen of Gormo the Old, for which she was named "Dannabod," the pride of the Danes Repaired by Olaf Tryggveson between 995 and 1000 Near here the Prussians, helping the duchies, defeated the Danes, 23 Apr 1848 The retreat of the Danes from it, 5 Feb 1864, occasioned much dissatisfaction at Copenhagen

Dante's "Divina Commedia" was first printed in 1472 Dante was born 14 May, 1265, died at Ravenna, 14 Sept 1321 A *festival in his honor, at Florence*, was opened by the king, 14 May, 1865, when a large statue of Dante by Pazzi of Ravenna was uncovered LITERATURE

Dantzic, N Germany, a commercial city in 997, built, others say, by Waldemar I in 1165. Poland obtained the sovereignty in 1454 It was seized by the king of Prussia, and annexed in 1793 It surrendered to the French, May, 1807; and by the treaty of Tilsit was restored to independence, under the protection of Prussia and Saxony, July, 1807 Dantzic was besieged by the allies in 1812, and surrendered 1 Jan 1814 By the treaty of Paris it reverted to Prussia The Vistula breaking through its dikes, destroyed many lives, 10,000 heads of cattle, and 4000 houses, 9 Apr 1829

Danube (Ger *Donau*, anciently Ister, in its lower part), the largest river in Europe except the Volga, rises in the Black forest and falls into the Black sea Trajan's bridge at Gladova was destroyed by Hadrian, to prevent the barbarians crossing south BRIDGES Steam navigation was projected on this river, by count Szechenyi, in 1830; the first steamboat was then launched at Vienna, and the Austrian company was formed soon after The Bavarian company was formed 1836 A canal between the Danube and the Maine was completed by Louis I of Bavaria. Charlemagne, in the 8th century, contemplated uniting the Danube and Rhine by a canal At the peace of 30 Mch 1856, the free navigation of the Danube was secured, and an independent European commission, appointed to make it navigable from Isaktchi to the sea, has worked with good effect. The British government, in 1868, lent 135 000*l* to complete the works The treaty respecting the navigation of the Danube renewed for 12 years, 13 Mch 1871 The river suddenly took possession of a new bed, near Vienna, 17 Apr., which was formally opened 30 May, 1875.

Navigation of the Danube was regulated by articles 50–54 of Berlin treaty 13 July, 1878
"Iron Gates," huge rocks in the lower Danube, blown up, 15 Sept 1890
Great bridge commenced at Tchernavoda 21 Oct. "

Danubian principalities. WALLACHIA and MOLDAVIA (capitals, Bucharest and Jassy) were united and named Roumania, 1859. Population of the two, 1860, 3,864,848; 1866, 4,424,961, 1887, 5,500,000 These provinces formed part of the ancient DACIA

Part of Moldavia ceded to Russia . . 1812
Provinces having joined in the Greek insurrection in 1821, were oppressed by the Turks, but by the treaty of Adrianople were placed under the protection of Russia 1829
Porte appointed as hospodars prince Stirbey for Wallachia, and prince Ghika for Moldavia June, 1849
They retire from their governments when the Russians enter Moldavia (RUSSO TURKISH WARS) . 2 July, 1853
Russians quit the provinces and Austrians enter, Sept. 1854, retire . . . . . Mch 1857
Government of the principalities finally settled at the Paris conference (there were to be 2 hospodars, chosen by elective assemblages, but under the suzerainty of Turkey) 19 Aug 1858

Alexander Couza elected hospodar of Moldavia, 17 Jan.; of Wallachia ... 5 Feb. 1859
Election acknowledged by the allies ... 6 Sept. "
Union of the provinces (as Roumania) proclaimed and acknowledged by the Porte ... Dec. 1861

[For continuation, ROUMANIA.]

Dardanelles', a narrow strait, about 47 miles in length and from 3 to 4 in width, between Europe and Asiatic Turkey, connecting the sea of Marmora with the Ægean sea, named Dardanelles from the contiguous town Dardanus. The passage of the strait is easily defended by the fortifications built on its banks; especially by the two castles, Sestos on the European and Abydos on the Asiatic shore, built by Mahomet IV. in 1659, and commanding the entrance to the sea of Marmora at Gallipoli. The strait was passed by the British squadron under sir John Duckworth, 19 Feb. 1807; but he repassed with great loss, 3 Mch., the castles of Sestos and Abydos hurling stone shot upon the ships. The allied English and French fleets passed the Dardanelles, at the sultan's request, Oct. 1853. The British squadron passed the Dardanelles against the protest of the Porte, 13 Feb. 1878. HELLESPONT, XERXES.

Dar'dani, inhabitants of the territory about the ancient city of Troy. Their first king was Dardanus, whence the name, from whom was descended Priam, king of Troy at the time of its siege and capture by the Greeks. TROY.

daric, a Persian gold coin, issued by Darius, about 538 B.C. About $5.56.—*Knowles.* It weighed 2 grains more than the English guinea.—*Dr. Bernard.*

Da'rien, Isthmus of, Central America, discovered by Columbus, 1494. Crossed by Balboa, 1513. In 1694 William Paterson, founder of the Bank of England, published his plan for colonizing Darien. A company was formed in 1695, and in 1698-99 3 expeditions sailed thither from Scotland, where 400,000*l.* had been raised. The first consisted of 1200 young men of all classes, besides women and children. The enterprise not being recognized by the English government, the settlements were threatened by the Spaniards, to whom they were surrendered, 30 Mch. 1700. Paterson and a few survivors from famine and disease left just before the arrival of the second expedition. Several years after, 398,085*l.* were voted by Parliament to the survivors as "equivalent money." 18,000*l.* were also voted to Paterson; but the bill was rejected in the House of Lords. The average breadth 40 miles; least breadth 30 miles. AMERICA, PANAMA.

dark ages, a term applied to the middle ages; according to Hallam, about 1000 years—from the invasion of France by Clovis, 486, to that of Naples by Charles VIII., 1495. Learning was at a low ebb. Hallam's "View of the Middle Ages," pub. 1818, supplement 1848.

dark day. MASSACHUSETTS, 19 May, 1780.

Dartford, Kent, Engl. Here commenced the insurrection of Wat Tyler, 1381. A convent of nuns, of the order of St. Augustin, endowed here by Edward III., 1355, was converted by Henry VIII. into a royal palace. The first paper-mill in England was erected at Dartford by sir John Spielman, a German, in 1590 (*Stow*), and about the same period the first mill for splitting iron bars.

Dartmoor prison, Devonshire, Engl., founded Mch. 1806. At the close of the war 1812-14, this prison contained several thousand U. S. prisoners, as well as impressed U. S. sailors, who would not serve against their country. On Apr. 6, 1815, several months after peace was declared, a disturbance took place among the prisoners; the prison authorities fired on them, killing 7 and wounding 33. This act, regarded by the citizens of the U. S. as a wanton outrage, was justified by the British authorities.

Dartmouth, Devon, Engl. Burned by the French in the reigns of Richard I. and Henry IV. In a third attempt (1404), the invaders were defeated. The French commander, Du Chastel, 3 lords, and 32 knights, were made prisoners. In the war of the parliament, Dartmouth was taken after a siege of 4 weeks, by prince Maurice, who garrisoned the place for the king (1643); but gen. Fairfax retook it by storm in 1646.

Dartmouth college, N. H., grew out of an earlier school established by rev. Eleazar Wheelock, D.D., a Congregationalist, at Lebanon, Conn., 1754-55, designed for Indian children. To carry the design out more fully, it was transferred to Hanover, N. H., in 1770, having been chartered by gov. Wentworth in 1769. It was named Dartmouth in honor of lord Dartmouth, one of its first patrons. In 1816 it successfully resisted, under the leadership of Daniel Webster, the creation of a new corporation called Dartmouth university. COLLEGES, TRIALS.

Darwinism. This term is commonly used to mean the doctrine of the origin of species by "natural selection," or the "survival of the fittest;" first taught by the British naturalist Charles R. Darwin and A. R. Wallace in 1858, and elaborately expounded by Darwin in his book on "The Origin of Species," 1859. DEVELOPMENT, EVOLUTION THEORY, SPECIES.

dates were affixed to grants and assignments, 18 Edw. I. 1290. Before this time it was usual, at least, to pass lands without dating the deed.—*Lewis.* Many assignments enrolled among early records in England establish this. The date is then determined by the names of the parties, particularly that of the grantor: the possession of land was proof of title.—*Hardie.* A useful glossary of dates given in old charters and chronicles will be found in Nicolas's "Chronology of History," J. J. Bond's "Handy-book for Verifying Dates," pub. 1866.

Dauphiné (*dō-fee-nā'*), a province of S.E. France—so called from the fact that one of the counts of Vienne placed a dolphin (dauphin) in his coat-of-arms and assumed the title of dauphin—was successively held by the Allobroges, Burgundians, and Lombards. In 732-34 it was delivered from the invading Saracens by Charles Martel. After forming part of the kingdom of Arles, it was much subdivided among counts. One of these, Humbert II., ceded Dauphiné and the Viennois to Philip VI. in 1343, for his eldest son, on condition that the prince should be styled dauphine, which took effect in 1349, when Humbert became a monk. Louis Antoine, duke of Angoulême, son of Charles X., the last dauphin who assumed the title at his father's accession, 16 Sept. 1824, died 3 June, 1844.

Dav'entry, a town of Northamptonshire, Engl. Near here Lambert, having escaped from the Tower, was defeated and retaken in his attempt to enkindle war, by Monk, 21 Apr. 1660. The dissenting academy removed here from Northampton in 1752, was transferred to Wymondley in 1789, thence to London as Coward college, and finally united with Homerton and Highbury colleges as New college, in 1850.

David's, St., S.W. Wales, the ancient Menapia, now a poor, decayed place, but once the metropolitan see of Wales, and archiepiscopal. When Christianity was planted in Britain, 3 archbishops' seats were appointed—viz., London, York, and Caerleon upon Usk, in Monmouthshire. That at Caerleon, being too near the dominions of the Saxons, was removed to Mynyw, and called St. David's, in honor of the archbishop who removed it, 522. St. Sampson was the last archbishop of the Welsh; for he, withdrawing himself on account of a pestilence to Dôle, in Brittany, carried the pall with him. In the reign of Henry I. the archbishops submitted to the see of Canterbury.—*Beatson.* Present income, 4500*l.*

David's day, St., 1 Mch., is annually commemorated by the Welsh, in honor of St. David. Tradition states that on St. David's birthday, 540, a great victory was obtained by the Welsh over their Saxon invaders; and that the Welsh soldiers were distinguished, by order of St. David, by a leek in their caps. LEEKS.

Davis, Jefferson, Capture of. UNITED STATES, 1865.

Davis's, Jefferson, order regarding gen. Benj. F. Butler and the officers of his command. UNITED STATES, 23 Dec. 1862.

Davis's strait, North America, connects Baffin's bay with Atlantic ocean; discovered by John Davis, 11 Aug. 1585, on his voyage to find a northwest passage, 1585-87. He made 2 more voyages for this purpose, and 5 to the East Indies; but was killed by Japanese pirates, on the coast of Malacca, 27 or 29 Dec. 1605.

Davy lamp, etc. SAFETY LAMP.

Davy medal, furnished by the sale of sir Humphry Davy's plate, was first awarded (Nov. 1877) by the Royal society to profs. Bunsen and Kirchhoff for their discovery of SPECTRUM ANALYSIS.

da'vyum, a new metal, announced as discovered by Sergius Kern, 28 June, 1877, in the residuum of platinum ore, said to be hard, infusible, and rather ductile It has been suspected to be ruthenium

day. Day began at sunrise among most of the northern nations, at sunset among the Athenians and Jews, and among the Romans at midnight as with us The Italians in some places reckon the day from sunset to sunset, making their clocks strike 24 hours The Chinese divide the day into 12 parts of 2 hours each. The astronomical day begins at noon, is divided into 24 hours (instead of 2 parts of 12 hours), and is used in the nautical almanac. Thus the astronomical day 8 Dec. begins at noon of 8 Dec and ends at noon 9 Dec At Greenwich, from 1 Jan 1885, the day of 24 hours began at midnight, the reckoning was recommended for railways, etc The Washington Prime Meridian Conference adopted a resolution declaring the universal day to be the mean solar day, beginning, for all the world, at the moment of mean midnight of the initial meridian, coinciding with the beginning of the civil day, and that meridian to be counted from zero up to 24 hours, 21 Oct. 1881 The scheme for universal time was advocated by W H M Christie, the astronomer royal at the Royal British institution, 19 Mch 1886 STANDARD TIME

deaconesses, or ministering widows, have their qualifications given in 1 Tim v 9, 10 (65) Their duties were to visit the poor and sick, assist at the *agapæ* or love-feasts, admonish the young women, etc The office was discontinued in the Western church in the 5th and 6th centuries, and in the Greek church about the 12th, but again revived by pastor Fliedner, of the United Evangelical church of Prussia, at Kaiserswerth, in 1836 The appointment of deaconesses in the Anglican church, subject to the parochial clergy, was advocated by the bishop of Ely, England, about 1853, and some were appointed The Diocesan Deaconess institution, London, was established in 1861 The largest institution in the United States is in the Episcopal diocese of Long Island, established in 1872

deacons (literally, *servants*), an order of Christian ministers, began with the Apostles, about 53 (Acts vi.). Their qualifications are given by St. Paul (65), 1 Tim iii 8-14. This order or office is established in the church of Rome, Anglican, Presbyterian, Congregational, Baptist, Methodist, and others.

dead. Prayers for their benefit were probably offered in the 2d century being referred to by Tertullian, who died 220 The practice was protested against by Aërius, and defended by Epiphanius, who died 403 It is generally objected to by the church of England, but is not expressly forbidden, so decided in the court of arches, 1873-76.

dead weight loan acquired its name from its locking up the capital of the Bank of England, which in 1823 advanced 11,000,000*l.* to the government (to construct new ordnance, etc), in exchange for an annuity of 585,740*l.* for 44 years, which ceased in June, 1867

deaf and dumb. Comparing the figures of 1885, there were in the United States, Great Britain, and France, 179 schools for the deaf and dumb, employing about 1200 teachers and having over 12,500 pupils Of these schools, 61 were in the U S., 48 in Great Britain and Ireland, and 70 in France. There were in the U. S. in 1891, 73 schools with an aggregate attendance of 8000 scholars, and employing over 600 teachers, the value of the buildings and grounds belonging to these 73 institutions is about $10,000,000. The estimated deaf population of the U S. is 40,000, about 2000 of whom live in New York and Brooklyn. The first systematic attempt to instruct the deaf and dumb was made by Pedro de Ponce, a Benedictine monk of Spain, on Jerome Cardan's system, about 1570

Bonet, a monk, publishes a system of deaf mute instruction at Madrid . . . 1620
Dr John Wallis Savilian professor of mathematics in the university of Oxford, taught the deaf and dumb, and published a work on the subject . . . 1650
"Didascalocophus, or Deaf and Dumb Man's Tutor," by George Dalgrano (the first English writer who gives a manual alphabet) pub. . . . 1680
Abbé de l'Epée establishes his school in Paris . . . 1765
First school for deaf mutes in Great Britain started in Edinburgh by Thomas Braidwood . . . 1773
Dr W Thornton, of Philadelphia, Pa., published an essay on "Teaching the Deaf to Speak" . . . 1793
Unsuccessful attempts made by Braidwood to establish schools for the deaf in New York and Virginia . . . 1811
Asylum for deaf and dumb children opened in London through the exertions of Mr Townsend in 1792, one in Edinburgh by J Braidwood in 1810, and one in Birmingham by T Braidwood, 1815
Asylum at Claremont, Dublin, opened . . . 1816
First institution for the instruction of deaf mutes in America, opened under dr T H Gallaudet, at Hartford, Conn., 15 Apr 1817
New York institution chartered, 15 Apr 1817, Pennsylvania institution, 1820, Kentucky institution . . . 1823
[Provision for the education of deaf mutes is now made in every state.]
Rev dr T H. Gallaudet vicar of St Ann's church, New York, begins holding services in the sign language in his church 1852
Statue to the memory of rev T H Gallaudet erected at a cost of $2500 by the deaf of the U S, is unveiled at Hartford, Conn . . . 6 Sept. 1854
National college for deaf mutes, dr E M Gallaudet, president, established at Washington D C . . . 1864
Alex Melville Bell expounds his system of VISIBLE SPEECH to the Society of Arts London . . . 14 Mch 1866
An English deaf and dumb debating club (Wallis club) closed its 3d session . . . Apr 1869
Foundation stone of St Saviour's church, near Oxford st., London, for the deaf and dumb, laid by the prince of Wales, 5 July, 1870
Association for the oral instruction of deaf and dumb, founded in England on the German system introduced by William van Praagh . . . 1871
[Taught by speech and lip movement only, the finger alphabet and artificial signs excluded]
Oral Association school and Training college on Fitzroy square, London, Engl, established . . . 16 July, 1872
Church mission to deaf mutes incorporated in the U S. . . . "
Monument to Laurent Clerc erected in Hartford, Conn, and unveiled . . . 16 Sept. 1874
Ordination of the first deaf person to the ministry of the Episcopal church, rev Henry Winter Syle, occurs in Philadelphia, 1876
International congress at Milan, great majority in favor of oral teaching of deaf-mutes . . . Sept. 1880
A deaf mutes' home begun as a branch of the church mission, removed to Wappinger's Falls N Y, and established as the Gallaudet home for aged and infirm deaf mutes . . . 1885
Bronze statue, emblematic of the meeting between Gallaudet and Alice Cogswell, and called the "Gallaudet Centennial Memorial," is unveiled at Washington, D C . . 26 June, 1889
Convention of deaf mutes from all parts of the world at Paris, "

dean (*decanus*), a name commonly given to the arch-presbyter, or eldest presbyter, in the 12th century, originally a military title, an officer over 10 soldiers. In the church of England the dean and chapter of a cathedral nominally elect the bishop and form his council. By 13 and 14 Car. II. (1662), a dean must be in priest's orders. The office had sometimes been held by a layman, under special dispensation. The ancient office of "rural dean," often revived in England since 1850 The Deans and Canons' Resignation act passed 13 May, 1872 The Five Deans' memorial, and counter-memorial, CHURCH OF ENGLAND, 1881.

Dean, Forest of, Gloucestershire, Engl., anciently all wooded, in the last century, though much curtailed, was 20 miles long and 10 wide It was famous for its oaks, the material of ships of war Riots in this district, when more than 3000 persons assembled in the forest, and demolished upwards of 50 miles of wall and fence, throwing open 10,000 acres of plantation, took place on 8 June, 1831 The Dean Forest (mines) act passed 16 Aug 1871.

death penalty, ordained for murder, 2348 B.C. (Gen. ix 6).

B C.
Jews generally stoned their criminals (Lev xx 2) . . . 1490
Draco's code punished every offence with death . . . 621
It was limited to murder by Solon . . . 594
A.D
Maurice, son of a nobleman, hanged, drawn, and quartered, for piracy, the first such execution in England, 25 Hen III . . . 1241
Capital punishment abolished in Russia by Catherine II., except for treason. . . . 1767
Abolished for most offences in England by sir Robert Peel's acts, 4 to 10 Geo. IV . . . 1824-29
By the Criminal Law Consolidation acts, death was confined to treason and wilful murder . . . 1861
British commission on capital punishment (appointed 1864) recommend penal servitude instead of death for unpremeditated killing, and that executions be private. . . . Dec. 1865
Capital punishment practically abolished in Italy. . . . Apr. "
Its proposed abolition in Belgium negatived. . . . 18 Jan 1867
["Capital Punishment within Prisons bill" passed May, 1868, 1st case, 13 Aug 1868. EXECUTIONS.]
Capital punishment abolished in Saxony . . . 1 Apr. 1868
Vote for its abolition in Switzerland, 1874, for its restoration (191,197-177,263) . . . May, 1879
Abolition of it in Great Britain proposed by Mr Gilpin in the commons, negatived (127-23), 21 Apr. 1868, negatived (118-58), 29 July, 1869, negatived (167-54), 24 July, 1872; (155-50), 12 June, 1877, (263-64), 13 Mch. 1878; proposed by Mr Pease, negatived (175-79). . . . 22 June, 1881

half of the Church of Rome (then accounted *Domicilium fidei Catholicæ*).

degrees. Eratosthenes attempted to determine the length of a geographical degree about 250 B.C. GEODESY, LATITUDE, LONGITUDE.—*Collegiate* degrees are coeval with universities. Masters and doctors existed 826. Those in law are traced up to 1149; in medicine, to 1384; in music, to 1463. Middle-class examinations for degrees were instituted at Oxford, 18 June, 1857; at Cambridge, 24 Nov. 1857; and girls were allowed to compete for degrees, Oct. 1863. Bill to enable Scotch universities to grant degrees to women rejected by the commons, 3 Mch. 1875. WOMEN.

Deira (*dī'ra*), a part of the Anglo-Saxon kingdom of Northumbria. BRITAIN.

deism, theism, or **monotheism** (Lat. *Deus;* Gr. *Θεός*, God), the belief in one God, opposed to polytheism or to the doctrine of the Trinity. About the middle of the 16th century the term deist began to be applied in France and Italy to men who disputed the doctrine of the Trinity. The most distinguished deists were Herbert, baron of Cherbury, in 1624; Hobbes, Tindal, Morgan, lord Bolingbroke, Gibbon, Hume, Holcroft, Paine, and Godwin.

High-caste Brahmin, Rammohun Roy, founded a Brahmin monotheistic church ....about 1830
"Progressive Brahmins," termed the BRAHMO SOMAJ, or theistic church of India, opened a place of worship at Calcutta, 24 Aug. 1869
Their leader, Baboo Keshub Chunder Sen, was received at a public meeting in London as a reformer, 12 Apr., and subsequently preached in a Unitarian chapel, Finsbury, London.. 1870
Schism in his church; new church formed.................... 1880
PHILOSOPHY, UNITARIANS.

Delago'a bay, S.E. Africa, claimed by Great Britain and Portugal. Having been referred to arbitration, it was warded to Portugal by marshal MacMahon, Aug. 1875.

Delaware, one of the middle Atlantic states, is, next Rhode Island, the smallest state in the Union. Its southern boundary is a line drawn due west from the Atlantic on lat. 38° 28′ N., half way to the Chesapeake bay. Its western boundary is a line drawn north from this point, tangent to a circle having a radius of 12 miles and with New Castle as its centre. An arc of this circle forms the northern boundary of the state, and separates it from Pennsylvania in about lat. 39° 50′. Delaware river and bay separate it from New

sey on the east, and Maryland lies to the south and west. ea, 2050 sq. miles, in 3 counties. Pop. 1890, 168,493; 1900, 735. Capital, Dover.

y Hudson discovers the Delaware river...........28 Aug. 1609
De la Warr, governor of Virginia, enters the bay called this name.. 1610
d Godyn, a director in the Dutch West India company, ases 16 Dutch sq. miles from the natives, at the mouth Delaware..................................25 July, 1630
etersen de Vries makes a small settlement at the kill, now Lewes, just within the entrance to Delaware d calls it Swanendael..................................Mch. 1631
having left the colony soon after, returns to find it ed by the Indians; all the settlers killed......5 Dec. 1632
f Swanendael transfer all their interest in the property directors of the Dutch West India company....7 Feb. 1635
rmanent settlement of Europeans in Delaware by es under Peter Minuit, a former director of the Dutch India company at Manhattan. They locate at Christi- within the present limits of Wilmington, build a fort and a church within its walls, and name the territory "New den"..Mch. 1638
t buys from 5 chiefs of the Minquas territory on west of the Delaware, from Bombay Hook to the river Schuylkill, with no western boundary specified............29 Mch. "
est against Swedish settlement by William Kieft, director-neral of the New Netherlands, on claim of prior possession the Dutch...6 May, "
er Minuit having been drowned in a storm at sea off the West Indies, lieut. Peter Hollender, commissioned governor f New Sweden, arrives with new immigrants at Christiana, st as the colony had resolved to break up.........11 Apr. 1640
ch settlement made a few miles from Christiana under a reditary fief grant from the crown of Sweden......2 Nov. "

Johan Printz, a Swede, appointed governor of New Sweden, arrives at Christiana with 2 vessels of war..........15 Feb. 1643
Fifth Swedish expedition arrives at Christiana.........11 Mch. 1644
Dutch States-general and West India company secure from the Indians a deed to all lands between Christiana creek and Canarosse, the same which had been sold to the Swedes by the Indians, and erect fort Casimir, now New Castle....19 July, 1651
Gov. Printz, returning home, appoints his son-in-law, Johan Pappegoia, governor of the colony.......................Oct. 1652
Johan Claudii Rising, arriving at fort Casimir in the ship *Eagle*, direct from Sweden, with reinforcements for the colony in New Sweden, demands its surrender, takes the fort without bloodshed, and renames it fort Trinity.........May, 1654
Vice-gov. Pappegoia returning to Sweden soon, Rising assumes supreme authority as director-general of New Sweden...... "
Gov. Peter Stuyvesant of Manhattan captures forts Trinity and Christiana, sends to Europe all Swedes refusing allegiance to Holland, and brings the colony under Dutch rule, 16-25 Sept. 1655
Gov. Rising and companions embark for Sweden on the *De Waag*, and bid farewell to Delaware..................1 Oct. "
Stuyvesant commissions Johan Paul Jaquet governor of the Dutch colony on the Delaware, who selects fort Casimir as his residence.......................................29 Nov. "
Swedes arriving on the ship *Mercurius*, not knowing of the change in government, attempt to ascend the river and land, but are dismissed by the Dutch without bloodshed...24 Mch. 1656
Gov.-general and council give 75 deeds for land, chiefly for lots in New Amstel, now New Castle. The first made....12 Apr. "
Dutch West India company transfers to the city of Amsterdam fort Casimir and the adjacent territory of New Amstel, which becomes known as the Colony of the City............16 Aug. "
Jaquet is removed for mismanagement, and Jacob Alrich appointed in Holland as governor of New Amstel..........Apr. 1657
William Beekman appointed vice-governor of the Colony of the Company, with headquarters at Altena, now Wilmington, 28 Oct. 1658
Beekman secures a deed of land from the Indians, and erects a fort at the Hoorn-kill............................23 May, 1659
Gov. Alrich dies; Alexander Hinoyosa succeeds........30 Dec. "
Colony of the Company surrenders its rights to the Colony of the City...7 Feb. 1663
Colony passes into British control under the duke of York, 1 Oct. 1664
New Amstel surrendered to sir Robert Carr, sent to subject the country by Charles II., and called New Castle.....3 Nov. "
Swedish church erected at Crane-hook, 1½ miles from fort Christiana.. 1667
Temporary council of deputy-gov. Carr and 6 others, swearing allegiance to the duke of York, established at New Castle.. 1668
Konigsmarke, better known as the "Long Finn," instigating rebellion against the duke of York in Delaware, is arrested and imprisoned in New York; afterwards transported to the Barbadoes.......................................20 Dec. 1669
George Fox, the Friend, holds a large meeting in New Castle.. 1672
New Castle incorporated and a constable's court erected..May, "
Anthony Clove appointed governor of Delaware under the Dutch, who retake New York......................12 Aug. 1673
By treaty of Westminster, Delaware reverts to the English, and sir Edmund Andros reappoints magistrates who had been removed by the Dutch.................................. 1674
William Penn arrives at New Castle with deed from duke of York for a circle of 12 miles around New Castle, and lands between this tract and the sea......................28 Oct. 1682
Act of union and naturalization passed at the first assembly in Upland (now Chester, Pa.), annexing to Pennsylvania the 3 lower counties on the Delaware: New Castle, Kent, and Sussex...7 Dec. "
Lords of Trade and Plantations decide in favor of Penn against lord Baltimore's claim to Delaware........................ 1685
Delaware, under its charter from Penn, forms a legislative assembly, first meeting at New Castle........................ 1703
Willingtown, now Wilmington, laid out by Thomas Willing, Oct. 1731
After 20 years of litigation, the boundaries of Delaware are defined... 1733
James Adams introduces printing into Delaware, publishing at Wilmington, for 6 months, the *Wilmington Courant*........ 1761
Thomas McKean and Cæsar Rodney sent as delegates to the first Colonial Congress at New York.................7 Oct. 1765
Cæsar Rodney chosen commissioner to erect state-house and public buildings in Dover.. 1772
Thomas McKean, George Read, and Cæsar Rodney elected delegates to the first Continental Congress................ 1774
Assembly unanimously approves resolution of Continental Congress of 15 May, and overturns the proprietary government, substituting the name of the province on all occasions for that of the king, and directs the delegates to vote on independence according to their own judgment.......15 June, 1776
Convention at New Castle frames a new constitution, assumes the name "The Delaware State," and designates Dover as capital...27 Aug. "
Evening after battle of Brandywine, pres. McKinley captured by a party of British; George Read, speaker of assembly, succeeds him...12 Sept. 1777
Thomas McKean of Delaware elected president of Continental Congress..10 July, 1781
Richard Basset, Gunning Bedford, jr., Jacob Broom, John Dickinson, and George Read, sign the Constitution of the U. S. as representatives from Delaware..............17 Sept. 1787
Delaware first state to adopt the federal Constitution, and without amendments.......................................7 Dec. "
New constitution, framed by a convention at Newcastle, changes

the name to "The State of Delaware," and goes into operation without submission to the people.....................June, 1792
Act appropriating receipts from marriage and tavern licenses for a school-fund.. 1796
James A. Bayard of Delaware appointed minister plenipotentiary to France....................................19 Feb. 1801
Du Pont powder mills near Wilmington, established by Eleuthère Irénée Du Pont de Nemours........................... 1802
Cæsar Rodney of Delaware appointed attorney-general of U. S..20 Jan. 1807
"The Wilmington Turnpike company" incorporated....1 Feb. 1808
James A. Bayard of Wilmington, one of the negotiators of the treaty of Ghent, signed............................24 Dec. 1814
Cæsar Rodney of Delaware appointed minister plenipotentiary to Buenos Ayres.............................27 Jan. 1823
Act passed establishing free schools.......................... 1829
Chesapeake and Delaware canal completed at cost of $2,250,000 "
Locomotive introduced on New Castle railroad................ 1831
Louis McLane of Delaware appointed U. S. secretary of the treasury...8 Aug. "
State constitution revised by a convention of 30 delegates at Dover...8 Nov. "
Wilmington made a city.. 1832
New Castle and Frenchtown railroad, 16⅛ miles long, completed.. "
Louis McLane appointed U. S. secretary of state.......29 May, 1833
Explosion of 5000 pounds of powder at Du Pont's powder mills, Wilmington..18 Apr. 1847
Title to Pea Patch island, derived from Delaware by U. S. and from New Jersey by James Humphrey, many years in litigation, awarded to U. S. by hon. John Sergeant, referee, 15 Jan. 1848
John Middleton Clayton of Delaware negotiates the Clayton-Bulwer treaty with the British government............Apr. 1850
A new constitution framed and submitted to the people, but rejected...11 Oct. 1853
Amendment to constitution changing day of state elections, 30 Jan. 1855
Henry Dickinson, commissioner from Mississippi, invites the state to join the confederacy; proposition rejected unanimously by the House and by a majority of the Senate.3 Jan. 1861
Delaware declares for the Union.........................15 Apr. "
Delaware added to the military department of Washington, 19 Apr. "
Gov. Burton calls for volunteers for U. S. army, and obtains a regiment of about 775 3-months' men. (Subsequently 2 regiments of about 1000 each were enlisted for the war)..23 Apr. "
A peace convention at Dover resolves against the war, and for a peaceable recognition of the confederacy.........27 June, "
Delaware raises its quota for volunteer army, under calls of July and August, without drafting; in all about 5000 men furnished by the state... 1862
Gov. Cannon undertakes military supervision for the U. S. of election for congressman; opposition in public meeting at New Castle decide not to vote, as a protest against the interference...17 Nov. 1863
Delaware creates her first state debt, by issuing bonds for $1,000,000 for obtaining substitutes for the draft........... 1864
Equal-rights convention held at Wilmington...........4 Sept. 1867
General tax act passed, including corporation tax on railroad capital stock, net earnings, and rolling-stock..........Apr. 1869
Woman's Suffrage convention at Wilmington............Nov. "
Delaware State college at Newark organized................ 1870
Ratification of 15th amendment celebrated by colored people of Delaware with much enthusiasm.....................14 Apr. "
New Castle, with a population of 2300, incorporated as a city.. 1875
School bill passed; board of education to consist of the president of Delaware college, secretary of state, and state auditor, "
State Temperance convention at Smyrna..............26 Dec. 1878
Act passed imposing a fine on any person taking part in any political torch-light parade................................ 1881
High-license bill passed by legislature........................ 1889
Pillory and whipping for female convicts abolished........... "
Provision made for a state hospital for the insane at Wilmington...Aug. "
Monument over grave of Cæsar Rodney, 1728–84, member of Continental Congress; signer of Declaration of Independence, and president (gov.) of the state, unveiled............30 Oct. 1889

DEL

A secret-ballot law passed, and the governor made president of the state board of education instead of the president of Delaware college at session of the legislature, 6 Jan.–16 May, 1891
Ex-gov. John W. Hall dies at Frederica...............23 Jan. 1892

GOVERNORS OF DELAWARE.

UNDER THE SWEDES.

Name.	Date.	Remarks.
Peter Minuit............	1638 to 1640	Formerly governor of New York.
Peter Hollender..........	1640 " 1642	
Johan Printz............	1643 " 1652	
Johan Pappegoia.........	1653 " 1654	
Johan C. Rising..........	1654 " 1655	Swedish colony surrenders to the Dutch from Manhattan.
UNDER THE DUTCH.		
Peter Stuyvesant.........	1655 to 1664	Surrendered to the English.

ENGLISH COLONIAL.

From 1664 up to 1683, under the government of New York; and from 1683 up to 1773, under the proprietary government of Pennsylvania.

STATE.

Name.	Date.	Remarks.
John McKinley..........	1776 to 1777	Termed president.
Cæsar Rodney...........	1778 " 1781	
John Dickinson..........	1782 " 1783	Chosen president of Pennsylvania.
John Cook..............	1783 " 1783	
Nicholas Van Dyke.......	1784 " 1786	
Thomas Collins..........	1786 " 1789	
Joshua Clayton..........	1789 " 1792	
Joshua Clayton..........	1792 " 1796	First governor elected under new constitution.
Gunning Bedford.........	1796 " 1797	Died in office.
Daniel Rogers...........	1797 " 1798	Acting.
Richard Bassett..........	1798 " 1801	Appointed circuit judge.
Jas. Sykes..............	1801 " 1802	Acting.
David Hall..............	1802 " 1805	
Nathaniel Mitchell........	1805 " 1808	
Geo. Truitt.............	1808 " 1811	
Joseph Hazlett...........	1811 " 1814	
Daniel Rodney...........	1814 " 1817	
John Clark..............	1817 " 1820	
Jacob Stout.............	1820 " 1821	Acting.
John Collins............	1821 " 1822	Died in office.
Caleb Rodney............	1822 " 1823	Acting.
Joseph Hazlett...........	1823 " 1824	Died in office.
Sam'l Paynter...........	1824 " 1827	Acting.
Chas. Polk..............	1827 " 1830	
David Hazzard...........	1830 " 1833	
Caleb P. Bennett.........	1833 " 1836	Died in office.
Chas. Polk..............	1836 " 1837	Acting.
Cornelius P. Comegys.....	1837 " 1840	
Wm. B. Cooper...........	1840 " 1844	
Thomas Stockton.........	1844 " 1846	Died in office.
Joseph Maul.............	1846 " 1846	Acting. Died in office.
Wm. Temple.............	1846 " 1846	Acting.
Wm. Thorp..............	1847 " 1851	
Wm. H. Ross............	1851 " 1855	
Peter F. Cansey..........	1855 " 1859	
Wm. Burton.............	1859 " 1863	
Wm. Cannon.............	1863 " 1867	Republican.
Grove Saulsbury.........	1867 " 1871	Democrat.
Jas. Ponder.............	1871 " 1875	"
John P. Cochran..........	1875 " 1879	"
John W. Hall............	1879 " 1883	"
Chas. C. Stockley.........	1883 " 1887	"
Benj. T. Biggs...........	1887 " 1891	" No Rep. nom.
Robt. J. Reynolds.........	1891 " 1895	"
Joshua H. Marvil.........	1895 " 1899	Republican.

UNITED STATES SENATORS FROM THE STATE OF DELAWARE.

Name.	No. of Congress.	Date.	Remarks.
Richard Bassett...........	1st and 2d	1789 to 1793	
George Read.............	1st " 2d	1789 " 1793	Resigned.
Henry Latimer............	3d to 6th	1793 " 1801	Elected in place of Read.
John Vining..............	3d " 5th	1793 " 1798	Resigned 1798.
Joshua Clayton...........	5th	1798	Elected in place of Vining; died 1798.
Wm. Hill Wells...........	5th to 8th	1799 to 1805	Elected in place of Clayton. Seated 4 Feb. 1799. Resigned 1805.
Samuel White............	7th " 11th	1801 " 1809	Died 1809.
James A. Bayard..........	8th " 12th	1805 " 1813	Elected in place of Wells. Resigned 1813.
Outerbridge Horsey........	11th " 16th	1810 " 1821	Elected in place of White. Seated 29 Jan. 1810.
Wm. Hill Wells...........	13th " 14th	1813 " 1817	Elected in place of Bayard.
Nicholas Van Dyke........	15th " 19th	1817 " 1827	Died 1828.
Cæsar A. Rodney..........	17th	1821 " 1823	Resigned 1823.
Thomas Clayton...........	18th to 19th	1824 " 1827	
Daniel Rodney............	19th	1826	Appointed *pro tem.* in place of Van Dyke, 1826.
Henry M. Ridgely.........	19th to 20th	1827 to 1829	Elected in place of Van Dyke, 1827.
Louis McLane............	20th " 21st	1827 " 1829	Resigned 1829.
John M. Clayton..........	21st " 23d	1829 " 1835	Resigned.
Arnold Naudain...........	21st " 23d	1830 " 1836	Elected in place of McLane. Seated 1830. Resigned.
Richard H. Bayard........	24th " 28th	1836 " 1845	Elected in place of Naudain, 1836.

UNITED STATES SENATORS FROM THE STATE OF DELAWARE.—(*Continued.*)

Name.	No. of Congress.	Date.	Remarks.
Thomas Clayton	24th to 29th	1837 to 1847	Elected in place of J. M. Clayton. Seated 19 Jan. 1837.
John M. Clayton	29th " 30th	1845 " 1849	Resigned 1849.
John Wales	30th " 31st	1849 " 1851	Elected in place of J. M. Clayton, 1849.
Presley Spruance	30th " 32d	1847 " 1853	
James A. Bayard	32d " 38th	1851 " 1864	
John M. Clayton	33d " 34th	1853 " 1856	Died 9 Nov. 1856.
Joseph P. Comegys	34th	1856	Appointed *pro tem.* in place of Clayton, 1856.
Martin Bates	35th	1858	Elected in place of Clayton, 1858.
Willard Saulsbury	36th to 41st	1859 to 1871	
Geo. Read Riddle	38th " 40th	1864 " 1867	Elected in place of Bayard. Seated 2 Feb. 1864; died 29 Mch. 1867.
James A. Bayard	40th	1867 " 1869	Appointed *pro tem.* in place of Riddle, 1867.
Thomas Francis Bayard	41st to 48th	1869 " 1885	Elected in place of Riddle. Seated 4 Mch. 1869. Resigned 1885. Appointed sec. of state by pres. Cleveland.
Eli Saulsbury	42d " 50th	1871 " 1889	
George Gray	49th " ——	1885 " ——	Elected in place of Bayard, 1885.
Anthony Higgins	51st " ——	1889 " ——	

Delawares, INDIANS.

Delft, S. Holland, a town founded by Godfrey le Bossu about 1074; famous for "Delft earthenware;" first manufactured here about 1310. The sale of delft greatly declined after the introduction of potteries into Germany and England. Grotius was born here, 10 Apr. 1583; here William, prince of Orange, was assassinated by Gerard, 10 July, 1584.

Delhi (*dĕl'-lee*), the once great capital of the Mogul empire, and chief seat of the Mahometan power in India; it was taken by Timour in 1398. It is now in decay, but contained a million inhabitants in 1700. In 1739, when Nadir Shah invaded Hindostan, he entered Delhi; 100,000 of the inhabitants perished, and plunder worth 62,000,000*l.* sterling is said to have been collected. Similar calamities were endured in 1761, on the invasion of Abdalla, king of Candahar. In 1803, the Mahrattas, aided by the French, took Delhi; but were defeated by gen. Lake, 11 Sept., and the aged Shah Aulum, emperor of Hindostan, was restored to his throne with a pension. INDIA, 1803. On 10 May, 1857, a mutiny arose in the sepoy regiments at Meerut. It was soon checked; but the fugitives fled to Delhi on 11 May, and, with other troops, seized the city, proclaimed a descendant of the Mogul king, and committed frightful atrocities. The rebels were anxious to possess the chief magazine; but, after a gallant defence by the British, it was exploded by order of lieut. Willoughby, who died of his wounds shortly after. Other heroes of this exploit were lieutenants Forrest and Rayner, and the gunners Buckley and Scully. Delhi was soon after besieged by the British, but was not taken till 20 Sept. following. The final struggle began on the 14th, brigadier (since sir) R. Archdale Wilson being the commander. Much heroism was shown; the gallant death of Salkeld at the explosion of the Cashmere gate created much enthusiasm. The old king and his sons were captured soon after. The latter were shot, and the former, after a trial, was sent for life to Rangoon, where he died 11 Nov. 1862. INDIA, 1857. A camp formed at Delhi by the earl of Mayo, the viceroy, Dec. 1871, was visited by the king of Siam, Jan. 1872. The prince of Wales visited Delhi, 11 Jan. 1876. Queen Victoria was proclaimed empress of India here, 1 Jan. 1877. Pop. 1891, 193,580.

"delicate investigation" into the conduct of the princess of Wales (afterwards queen of England, as consort of George IV.) was commenced by a committee of the privy council, under a warrant of inquiry, dated 29 May, 1806. The members were lord Grenville, lord Erskine, earl Spencer, and lord Ellenborough. The inquiry, asked for by the countess of Jersey, sir J. and lady Douglas, and others, led to the publication called "The Book;" afterwards suppressed. The charges against the princess were disproved in 1807 and in 1813; but, not being permitted to appear at court, she went on the Continent in 1814. QUEEN CAROLINE.

De'lium, Bœotia, N. Greece, the site of a celebrated temple of Apollo. Here, in a fight in which the Athenians were defeated by the Bœotians, Socrates is said to have saved the life of his pupil Xenophon, 424 B.C.

Della Crusca academy of Florence merged into the Florentine in 1582.—The Della Crusca school, certain English residents at Florence, who printed sentimental poetry and prose in 1785. They came to England, where their works, popular for a short time, were so severely satirized by Gifford in his "Baviad" and "Mæviad" (1792-95), as to fall into general disrepute.

De'los, a Greek isle in the Ægean sea. Here the Greeks, during the Persian war, 477 B.C., established their common treasury, which was removed to Athens, 461 B.C.

Delphi, now **Kastri,** N. Greece, celebrated not only in Greece but among neighboring nations for enigmatical oracles delivered by the Pythia, or priestess in the temple of Apollo, which was built, some say, by the council of the Amphictyons, 1263 B.C. The Pythian games were first celebrated here 586 B.C. The temple was burned by the Pisistratidæ, 548 B.C. A new temple was raised by the Alcmæonidæ. The Persians (480 B.C.) and the Gauls (279 B.C.) were deterred from plundering the temple by awful portents. It was robbed and seized by the Phocians in whose state it stood, 357 B.C., which led to the Sacred war, and Nero carried from it 500 costly statues, 67 A.D. The oracle was consulted by Julian, but silenced by Theodosius.

Delphin classics, a collection of 39 Latin authors in 60 volumes, made for the use of the dauphin (*in usum Delphini*), son of Louis XIV., and pub. in 1674-91. Ausonius was added in 1730. The duc de Montausier, the young prince's governor, proposed the plan to Huet, bishop of Avranches, the dauphin's preceptor, and he edited all the Latin classics except Lucan, assisted, however, by other learned persons, including the beautiful and gifted Madame Dacier, who, at the age of 23, had translated Callimachus, as well as Anacreon, Sappho, Plautus, Terence, and Homer. She died in 1720. Each author is illustrated by notes and an index of words. An edition of the Delphin classics, with additional notes, etc., was pub. by Mr. Valpy of London, 1818 et seq.

Delta metal, a modern bronze resembling gold, containing a small proportion of iron, invented by A. Dick. Watch-cases were made of it at Geneva in 1885.

Deluge. The Deluge, it is supposed, was threatened in the year of the world 1536; and began 7 Dec. 1656, and continued 377 days (Gen. vi., vii., and viii.). The ark rested on Mount Ararat 6 May, 1657; and Noah left the ark 18 Dec. following. The year corresponds with that of 2348 B.C. —*Blair*. The following is the date of the Deluge according to different chronologies (*Hales*):

	B.C.		B.C.
Septuagint	3246	Clinton	2482
Jackson	3170	Playfair	2352
Hales	3155	Usher and English Bible	2348
Josephus	3146	Marsham	2344
Persian	3103	Petavius	2329
Hindoo	3102	Strauchius	2293
Samaritan	2998	Hebrew	2288
Howard	2698	Vulgar Jewish	2104

In the reign of Ogyges, king of Attica, 1764 B.C., a deluge so inundated Attica that it lay waste for nearly 200 years.—*Blair*. Buffon imagined that the Hebrew and Grecian deluges were the same, and arose from the Atlantic and Bosporus bursting into the valley of the Mediterranean.

The deluge of Deucalion, in Thessaly, is dated 1503 B.C. according to Eusebius. It was often confounded by the ancients with the general flood; but some regard it as merely a local inundation, occasioned by the overflowing of the river Peneius, whose course was stopped by an earthquake between the mounts Olympus and Ossa. Deucalion, who then reigned in Thessaly, with his wife Pyrrha, and some of their subjects, are said to have saved themselves by climbing up Mount Parnassus.

A general deluge was predicted for 1524, and arks were built; but the season proved to be fine and dry in England.

Demera'ra and **Essequi'bo,** colonies in British Guiana, South America, founded by the Dutch, 1580, were taken by the British, under maj.-gen Whyte, 22 Apr. 1796, but were restored at the peace of Amiens, Mch 1802. They again surrendered to the British under gen Grinfield and commodore Hood, Sept 1803, and became English colonies in 1814.

Demeter (*di-me'-ter*) MYTHOLOGY

Democratic-Republican party. POLITICAL PARTIES

democrats, advocates for government by the people (δῆμος, people, and κρατεῖν, to govern), a term adopted by the French republicans in 1790 (who termed their opponents *aristocrats*, from ἄριστος, bravest or best) For Democrats in the United States, POLITICAL PARTIES

demog'raphy. A modern term, signifying "the natural history of society."

demonol'ogy. DEVIL-WORSHIP.

• **Denain** (*de-năn'*), N France Here marshal Villars defeated the imperialists, 24 July, 1712

dena'rius, the chief silver coin among the Romans weighing the seventh of a Roman ounce, worth 7¾*d* sterling, about 16 cents U. S currency, first coined about 269 B C, when it exchanged for 10 ases As In 216 B C it exchanged for 16 ases. A pound weight of silver was coined into 100 denarii.—*Digby* A pound weight of gold was coined into 20 denarii aurei in 206 B.C, and in Nero's time into 45 denarii aurei —*Lempriere*

Denis, St. (*săn dnē'*), an ancient town of France, north of Paris, famous for its abbey and church, the former abolished at the revolution, 1789, the latter the burial-place of French kings, from its foundation by Dagobert, about 630, the remains of St. Denis were placed there in 636 On 6, 7, 8 Aug 1793, the republicans demolished most of the royal tombs, and in Oct following the bodies were taken from coffins and cast into a pit, the lead was melted, and the gold and jewels taken to Paris By a decree of Bonaparte, dated 20 Feb 1806, the church (then a cattle-market) was cleansed out and redecorated as "the future burial-place of the emperors of France" On the return of the Bourbons other restorations were effected, and the duc de Berri and Louis XVIII were buried here The damage sustained in the war of 1870–71 has been repaired

Denmark, N Europe The most ancient inhabitants were Cimbri and Teutones, who were driven out by the Jutes or Goths The Teutones settled in Germany and Gaul, the Cimbrians invaded Italy, where they were defeated by Marius The peninsula of Jutland obtained its name from the Jutes, and the name of Denmark is supposed to be derived from *Dan*, the founder of the Danish monarchy, and *mark*, a German word signifying country For their numerous invasions of Britain, etc, DANES Population of the kingdom of Denmark in 1860, 1,600,551, of the duchies of Schleswig, Holstein, and Lauenburg, 1,004,473, of the colonies, 120,283 By the treaty of peace, signed 30 Oct 1864, the duchies were taken from Denmark, Schleswig and Holstein were to be made independent, and Lauenburg was to be incorporated, by its desire, with Prussia For the result, GASTEIN, PRUSSIA, 1866 Area, 14,760 sq miles. Population of the monarchy, 1870, 1,784,741, 1876, 1,903,000, 1880, 1,969 454, 1890, 2,172,205, of the colonies, 1860, 127,401, 1876, 129,000, 1880, 130,350, 1890, 115,988

B C

Reign of Skiold, alleged first king . . 60

A D

Danish chronicles mention 18 kings to the time of Ragnor Lodbrog, killed in an attempt on England 794

Canute the Great conquers Norway 1016–28

By the union of Calmar, Denmark, Norway, and Sweden made 1 kingdom under Margaret 12 July, 1397

Copenhagen made the capital 1440

Accession of Christian I (of Oldenburg), from whom the late royal family sprang 1448

Christian II deposed, independence of Sweden under Gustavus Vasa acknowledged 1523

Lutheranism introduced in 1527, established by Christian III 1530

Danish East India Company established 1612

Christian IV chosen head of the Protestant league against the emperor 1629

Charles Gustavus of Sweden invades Denmark, besieges Copenhagen, and makes conquests 1658

Crown made hereditary and absolute 1665

Frederick IV takes Holstein, Schleswig Tonningen, and Stralsund, reduces Weismar, and drives the Swedes from Norway, 1716 et seq

Copenhagen nearly destroyed by fire 1728

Peaceful reign of Christian VI 1730–46

Plot of the queen dowager against the ministers and Matilda (sister of George III and queen of Christian VII) Matilda, entrapped into a confession of criminality to save the life of her supposed lover Struenzee, condemned to imprisonment for life in the castle of Zell 18 Jan 1772

Count Struenzee and Brandt beheaded 28 Apr "

Queen Matilda dies, aged 24 1775

Christian VII becomes deranged, and prince Frederick is appointed regent 1784

One fourth of Copenhagen burned 9 June, 1795

Admirals Nelson and Parker bombard Copenhagen. (Confederacy of the north [ARMED NEUTRALITY] dissolved) 2 Apr 1801

Admiral Gambier and lord Cathcart bombard Copenhagen, the Danish fleet surrenders 7 Sept 1807

Peace of Kiel, Pomerania and Rügen annexed to Denmark for Norway 14 Jan 1814

Pomerania and Rügen ceded to Prussia for Lauenburg 1815

Commercial treaty with England 1824

Frederick VI grants a new constitution 1831

Christian VIII declares the right of the crown to Schleswig, Holstein etc. 11 July, 1846

Accession of Frederick VII 20 Jan, he proclaims a new constitution, uniting the duchies (Schleswig and Holstein) more closely with Denmark 28 Jan 1848

Insurrection in the duchies a provisional government founded, 23 Mch "

Rebels seize fortress of Rendsburg 24 Mch "

They are defeated near Flensburg 9 Apr "

Danes defeated by the Prussians (helping the duchies) near Dannawerke, Schleswig 23 Apr "

North sea blockaded by Denmark 1 Aug "

Hostilities suspended the European powers recommend peace, 26 Aug "

Hostilities recommence 25 Mch 1849

Victory of the Danes over the Holsteiners and Germans, 10 Apr "

Several conflicts with varying success June, "

King sanctions a new liberal constitution 5 June, "

Armistice renewed at Malmo 10 July, "

Separate peace with Prussia 2 July, 1850

Integrity of Denmark guaranteed by England, France, Prussia, and Sweden 4 July, "

Battle of Idstedt, and defeat of the Schleswig-Holsteiners by the Danes 25 July, "

Procotol signed in London by the ministers of all the great powers 23 Aug "

Bombardment of Friedrichstadt by the Holsteiners, the town almost destroyed but not taken 29 Sept–6 Oct. "

Proclamation of the stadtholders of Schleswig Holstein placing the rights of the country under the protection of the Germanic confederation 10 Jan 1851

Integrity of the Danish monarchy and the independence of Schleswig and its old union with Holstein guaranteed by treaty 18 Feb 1852

Austrians evacuate Holstein, etc 2 Mch. "

Treaty of European powers 8 May, "

[Succession in the line of Sonderburg Glücksburg settled, and the integrity of the Danish kingdom guaranteed Christian, duke of Augustenburg Holstein, renounces his rights for a compensation in money]

King promulgates a new constitution, 29 July, 1854, adopted, 1 Oct 1855

Sound dues abolished for compensation (SOUND) 14 Mch 1857

Dissension between government and the duchies Oct 1857–62

Fortification of Copenhagen decreed 27 Mch 1858

New ministry appointed 3 Dec. 1859, resigns 9 Feb, bishop Monrad forms a ministry 24 Feb. 1860

Assembly of Schleswig complain that the promise of equality of national rights in 1852 has not been kept, 11 Feb., protest against the annexation to Denmark 1 Mch "

Prussian Chamber of Deputies receive a petition from Schleswig. and declare that they will aid the duchies, 4 May, Danish government protests 16 May, "

Correspondence between the Prussian, Danish, and British governments, the Danish government declares for war, if German forces enter the duchies Jan 1861

Warlike preparations in Denmark Feb "

Decimal coinage adopted June, "

Agitation for union with Sweden, June, the king of Sweden visits Denmark, and is warmly received 17 July, 1862

Earl Russell advises the government to give to Holstein and Lauenburg all that the German confederation desire for them, and to give self government to Schleswig 24 Sept. "

M Hall, the Danish minister, declines to accede, because it would imperil the existence of the monarchy 20 Nov "

Princess Alexandra of Denmark married to the prince of Wales at Windsor . 10 Mch 1863

King grants, by patent, independent rights to Holstein, but annexes Schleswig 30 Mch "

Austria and Prussia protest against it 17 Apr "

Further diplomatic correspondence. May, "

King accepts the crown of Greece for his relative, prince William George 6 June, "

Crown prince Frederick Ferdinand, the king's uncle, d 29 June, "

German Diet demands annulment of patent of 30 Mch (Holstein and Schleswig to be united with the same right), threatens an army of occupation 9 July, "

King replies that he will consider occupation an act of war, 27 Aug. 1863
Vain efforts for alliance with Sweden....................Aug. "
Extra levy for the army decreed......................1 Aug. "
New constitution (uniting Schleswig with Denmark) proposed in the rigsraad..29 Sept. "
Death of Frederick VII. and accession of Christian IX., 15 Nov. "
Prince Frederick of Augustenburg claims the duchies of Schleswig and Holstein.................................16 Nov. "
Great excitement in Holstein; many officials refuse to take oath to Christian...........................21 Nov. et seq. "
Saxony, Bavaria, Hesse, and other German powers resolve to support the prince of Augustenburg..........26 Nov. et seq. "
New constitution affirmed by the rigsraad, 13 Nov.; signed by king, 18 Nov.; pub.................................1, 2 Dec. "
Austrian and Prussian ministers say that they will quit Copenhagen if the constitution of 18 Nov. is not annulled, Dec. "
Great excitement in Norway; proposals to support Denmark, Dec. "
Prince Frederick's letter to the emperor Napoleon, 2 Dec.; an ambiguous reply..10 Dec. "
Denmark protests against federal occupation..........19 Dec. "
Nine hundred representatives of German states meet at Frankfort-on-the-Main, resolve to support prince Frederick as duke of Schleswig and Holstein, and the inseparable union of those duchies...21 Dec. "
Federal occupation takes place; a German regiment enters Altona, 24 Dec.; and the federal commissioners assume administrative powers.................................25 Dec. "
Danes retire from Holstein to avoid collision with federal troops.....................................26 Dec. et seq. "
Prince Frederick enters Kiel as duke of Schleswig and Holstein..30 Dec. "
Danes evacuate Rendsburg..............................31 Dec. "
Ministerial crisis: Hall retires, and bishop Monrad forms a cabinet...31 Dec. "
Dissension among Germans; the Austro-Prussian proposition rejected by the diet..................................14 Jan. 1864
Austria and Prussia demand abrogation of the constitution (of 18 Nov.) in 2 days, 16 Jan.; the Danes require 6 weeks' time, 18 Jan. "
German troops under marshal Wrangel enter Holstein..21 Jan. "
Prussians enter Schleswig, and take Eckernförde.......1 Feb. "
They bombard Missunde, 2 Feb.; which is burned......3 Feb. "
Danes abandon the Dannewerke to save their army, 5 Feb.; great discontent in Copenhagen.......................6 Feb. "
Danes defeated by marshal Gablénz at Oversee; Schleswig taken; prince Frederick proclaimed....................6 Feb. "
Allies occupy Flensburg, 7 Feb.; commence their attack on Düppel..13 Feb. "
Federal commissioners protest against the Prussian occupation of Altona..13 Feb. "
Prussians enter Jutland; take Kolding, 18 Feb.; Danes fortify Alsen....................................18 Feb. et seq. "
Conference on Danish affairs proposed by England; agreed to by allies...23 Feb. "
Subscription for the wounded Danes begun in London, 24 Feb. "
De Gertach, general of the Danes......................1 Mch. "
Defeated at Sonderbygaard and Veill..................8 Mch. "
Rigsraad vote a firm address to the king, 26 Feb.; adjourned, 22 Mch. "
Prussians bombard and take Düppel, or Dybböl, 16, 17 Mch.; bombard Fredericia, 20 Mch.; repulsed in an attack on the fortress...28 Mch. "
Opening of the conference adjourned from.......12 to 20 Apr. "
Prussians take the fortress of Düppel by assault, with much slaughter..18 Apr. "
Meetings of the conference at London; result unfavorable to Denmark.......................................25 Apr. et seq. "
Danes retreat to Alsen; evacuate Fredericia and fortresses of Jutland..29 Apr. "
Agreement for an armistice for 1 month from 12 May..9 May, "
Jutland subjected to pillage for not paying a war contribution to Prussians.................................6 May et seq. "
Danes defeat the allies in a naval battle off Heligoland..9 May, "
Armistice prolonged a fortnight......................9 June, "
Conference ends.......................................22 June, "
Hostilities resumed, 26 June; the Prussians bombard Alsen; take the batteries and 2400 prisoners.............29 June, "
Monrad ministry resigns; count Moltke charged to form an administration..8-10 July, "
Alsen taken; Jutland under Prussian administration; prince John of Denmark sent to negotiate at Berlin........9 July, "
Formation of the Bluhme ministry......................11 July, "
Armistice agreed to...................................18 July, "
Conference for peace at Vienna........................26 July, "
Treaty of peace at Vienna; king of Denmark resigns the duchies to the allies, and agrees to a rectification of his frontier, and to pay a large war indemnity.......................30 Oct. "
Proclamation of the king to the inhabitants of the duchies, releasing their allegiance..............................16 Nov. "
Project of a new constitution presented to the chambers, 21 Dec.; rejected......................................25 Feb. 1865
New ministry formed under count Frijsenborg, 6 Nov.; a new constitution proposed, 7 Nov.; approved by the 2 chambers, 19 and 27 July; sanctioned by the king...........28 July, 1866
Princess Dagmar married to prince Alexander of Russia, 9 Nov. "
New rigsraad opened...................................12 Nov. "
King visits England...................................Mch. 1867

Danish West Indies, St. Thomas and St. John, proposed to be sold to the United States for $7,500,000; proclamation in the islands dated...25 Oct. 1867
Proposed sale of St. Thomas to the U. S. approved by the assembly (not carried out)..............................30 Jan. 1868
Marriage of the crown-prince Frederick to the princess Louisa of Sweden...28 July, 1869
New ministry formed by M. Holsteinborg.............20 May, 1870
Denmark remains neutral in the Franco-Prussian war; fruitless visit of the duc de Cadore to Copenhagen.....4-11 Aug. "
Birth of a son to the crown-prince...................27 Sept. "
Negro outbreak at Santa Cruz (VIRGIN ISLES)..........1-5 Oct. 1878
Marriage of princess Thyra with the duke of Cumberland, 11 Dec. "
Lower house dismissed by the king as incapable and idle, about 10 May, 1881
Amnesty granted to political prisoners on the king's 70th birthday..15 Nov. 1888
National celebration of the king's golden wedding....26 May, 1892

SOVEREIGNS.

A.D.
794. Sigurd Snogoje.
803. Hardicanute.
850. Eric I.
854. Eric II.
883. Gormo, the Old; reigned 53 years.
941. Harold, surnamed Blue Tooth.
991. Suenon, or Sweyn, the Forked-beard.
1014. Canute II. the Great, king of Denmark and England.
1035. Canute III., son (Hardicanute of England).
1042. Magnus, surnamed the Good, of Norway.
1047. Suenon, or Sweyn II. (Denmark only).
1073. [Interreguum.]
1076. Harold, called the Simple.
1080. Canute IV.
1086. Olaus IV. the Hungry.
1095. Eric I., styled the Good.
1103. [Interregnum.]
1105. Nicholas I., killed at Sleswick.
1135. Eric II., surnamed Harefoot.
1137. Eric III. the Lamb.
1147. {Suenon, or Sweyn III.; beheaded. {Canute V. until 1157 (civil war).
1157. Waldemar, styled the Great.
1182. Canute VI., surnamed the Pious.
1202. Waldemar II. the Victorious.
1241. Eric IV.
1250. Abel: assassinated his elder brother Eric; killed in an expedition against the Frisons.
1252. Christopher I.; poisoned.
1259. Eric V.
1286. Eric VI.
1320. Christopher II.
1334. [Interregnum of 7 years.]
1340. Waldemar III.
1375. [Interregnum.]
1376. Olaus V.
1387. Margaret, styled the "Semiramis of the North," queen of Sweden, Norway, and Denmark.
1397. Margaret and Eric VII. (Eric VII. of Sweden).
1412. Eric VII. reigns alone; obliged to resign both crowns.
1438. [Interregnum.]
1440. Christopher III. king of Sweden.
1448. Christian I. count of Oldenburg; elected king of Denmark, 1448; of Sweden, 1457; succeeded by his son,
1481. John; succeeded by his son,
1513. Christian II., called the Cruel, and the "Nero of the North;" he caused all the Swedish nobility to be massacred; dethroned for tyranny in 1523; died in a dungeon in 1559. [Sweden separated from Denmark.]

DENMARK AND NORWAY.

1523. Frederick I. duke of Holstein, son of Christian I.; a liberal ruler.
1533. Christian III., son of Frederick; established the Lutheran religion; esteemed the "Father of his People."
1559. Frederick II., son of Christian III.
1588. Christian IV., son.
1648. Frederick III.; changed constitution from an elective to an hereditary monarchy, in his own family, 1665.
1670. Christian V., son of Frederick III.; succeeded by his son.
1699. Frederick IV.; leagued with czar Peter and king of Poland against Charles XII. of Sweden.
1730. Christian VI., his son.
1746. Frederick V., his son; married princess Louisa of England, daughter of George II.
1766. Christian VII., his son.
1784. Prince Frederick regent, his father being deranged.
1808. Frederick VI., previously regent.
1814. Norway annexed to Sweden, 14 Jan.

DENMARK.

1839. Christian VIII. (son of Frederick, brother of Christian VII.).
1848. Frederick VII., son of Christian VIII.; 20 Jan.; b. 6 Oct. 1808; separated from his first wife, Sept. 1837; from his second wife, Sept. 1846; married morganatically Louisa, countess of Danner, 7 Aug. 1850; d. 15 Nov. 1863.
1863. Christian IX., son of William, duke of Schleswig-Holstein-Sonderburg-Glücksburg; 15 Nov. (succeeded by virtue of the protocol of London, 8 May, 1852, and of the law of the Danish succession, 31 July, 1853). He was born 8 Apr. 1818; married princess Louisa of Hesse-Cassel, 26 May, 1842. [He

is descended from Christian III, and she from Frederick V, both from George II of England]

Heir Frederick (his son) born 3 June, 1843, married princess Louisa of Sweden, 28 July, 1869 Son Christian, born 26 Sept 1870

Dennewitz, a village of Prussia Here a victory was obtained by the allies under marshal Bernadotte (afterwards Charles XIV king of Sweden) over marshal Ney, 6 Sept. 1813 The loss of the French exceeded 13,000 men out of 70,000, several eagles, and 43 cannon, of the allies, 6000 out of 50,000 The defeat of Napoleon at Leipsic, on 18 Oct. following, closed this disastrous campaign

dentistry is the art of treating teeth and of supplying substitutes for them when lost Treatment of the teeth by the Egyptians mentioned by Herodotus, and some evidence that the Egyptians and also the Etruscans at least attempted to supply teeth by artificial means is found in mummies and in skulls exhumed, etc Galen is the first physician who speaks of treating the teeth Ambrose Paré notices the treatment of teeth in his work on surgery, 1550 It is only within the last 60 years that dentistry has become a recognized branch of surgical science The teeth were only cared for so far as to have them extracted when troublesome—mere tooth-drawing constituting dentistry early in this century The science of the teeth may be said to date from the researches of prof Richard Owen who, in 1839, first clearly demonstrated the organic connection between the vascular and the vital soft parts of the frame and the hard substance of the teeth His work was pub 1840-45 The English Odontological society was established 1856 The first dental school chartered in the United States was at Baltimore, 1839, one at Cincinnati, 1845, another at Philadelphia, 1856, etc In 1892 there were 38 dental schools in the U S.

de'odand (Lat *to be given to God*) By the old common-law of England anything which had caused the death of a human being became forfeit to the sovereign or lord of the manor, and was to be sold for the benefit of the poor The forfeiture was abolished by 9 and 10 Vict c 62 (1846)

D'Éon (*da-on'*), Chevalier, who had acted in a diplomatic capacity in several countries, and been minister plenipotentiary from France in London, was affirmed to be a woman, at a trial at the King's Bench in 1771, in an action to recover wagers as to his sex He subsequently wore female attire, but at his death he was proved to be a man

deontol'ogy, the knowledge of what is right, or the science of duty (from the Gr τὸ δέον, that which is proper), the Utilitarian philosophy propounded by Jeremy Bentham in his "Deontology," pub by dr Bowring in 1834

De Pauw university. INDIANA, 1837

Deptford, a town, suburb of London The hospital here incorporated by Henry VIII about 1512, was called the Trinity-house of Deptford Strond, the brethren of Trinity-house hold their corporate rights by this hospital The dock-yard, founded about 1513, was closed 31 Mch 1869, having been purchased by T P Austin for 70,000*l.* He sold part of it to the corporation of London for 94,640*l*, for a market for foreign cattle, which was opened for use 28 Dec 1871 On 4 Apr 1581, queen Elizabeth dined at Deptford on board the *Golden Hind*, the ship in which Drake had made his voyage round the globe Peter the Great of Russia lived at Evelyn's house, Say's court, while learning ship-building here, etc, in 1698

Deputies, Chamber of, the title borne by the French legislative assembly, from the restoration of the Bourbons in 1814 till Jan 1852, when it was named *Corps Legislatif*

Derby, Engl (name given it by the Danes), was made a royal burgh by Egbert (about 828). Alfred expelled the Danes and planted a colony in 880 His daughter, Ethelfleda, again expelled the Danes in 918 William I gave Derby to his illegitimate son, William Peveril. Here is a free grammar-school, founded 1162. Lombe's silk-throwing machine was set up in 1718; and in 1756 Jedediah Strutt invented the Derby ribbed stocking-frame The young Pretender reached Derby 3 Dec. 1745, and retreated thence soon after Pop 1891, 94,146.

Derby-day (RACES), generally (not always) the Wednesday in the week preceding Whitsunday, the second day of the grand spring meeting at Epsom, Engl.

RECENT WINNERS OF "THE DERBY" AT EPSOM.

1846 Pyrrhus
1847 Cossack
1848 Surplice
1849 Flying Dutchman
1850 Voltigeur
1851 Teddington
1852 Daniel O'Rourke
1853 West Australian
1854 Andover
1855 Wild Dayrell.
1856 Ellington
1857 Blink Bonny
1858 Beadsman
1859 Musjid
1860 Thormanby
1861 Kettledrum.
1862 Caractacus
1863 Macaroni
1864 Blair Athol
1865 Gladiateur (31 May), a horse reared in France the property of the comte de la Grange He also won the St Leger at Doncaster, 13 Sept.
1866 Lord Lyon (16 May)
1867 Hermit (22 May)
1868 Blue Gown (27 May)
1869 Pretender (26 May)
1870 Kingcraft (1 June)
1871 Favonius (24 May)
1872 Cremorne (29 May)
1873 Doncaster (28 May)
1874 George Frederick (3 June)
1875 Galopin (26 May)
1876 Kisbér, or Mineral Colt (Hungarian owner, Alex Baltazzi), 31 May
1877 Silvio (30 May)
1878 Sefton (5 June)
1879 Sir Bevys (baron Rothschild's), 28 May
1880 Bend Or (duke of Westminster's), 26 May
1881 Iroquois (Mr Lorillard's, an American), 1 June
1882. Shotover (duke of Westminster's)
1883. St Blaise (sir F Johnstone's)
1884. { St. Gatien (Mr J Hammond's) / Harvester (sir J Willoughby's) }
1885 Melton (lord Hastings's)
1886 Ormonde (duke of Westminster's)
1887 Merry Hampton (Mr Abingdon s)
1888 Ayrshire (duke of Portland's)
1889 Donovan (duke of Portland's)
1890 Sainfoin (sir J Miller's)
1891 Common (sir F Johnstone's)
1892 Sir Hugo (lord Bradford's)

derricks (said to have been named from Derrick, hangman at Tyburn about 1606), are lofty, portable, crane-like structures, used on land and water for lifting heavy loads They are extensively used in the United States, and floating-derricks for raising sunken vessels were introduced into England by their inventor, A. D Bishop, in 1857

Desaix's (*deh-sa'*) **arrival.** MARENGO

Descartes's (*da-kart'*) **Cartesian philosophy.** PHILOSOPHY

descent of man. DEVELOPMENT

"Deserted Village," a poem by dr. Oliver Goldsmith, first pub May, 1770 LITERATURE

des'erts. SAHARA

Des'pard's conspiracy. Col Edward Marcus Despard (a native of Ireland), Broughton, Francis, Graham, Macnamara, Wood, and Wratten conspired to kill George III. of England, and establish a republic on the day of opening Parliament, 16 Nov 1802 Above 30 persons, including soldiers, were taken in custody, of those tried, 20 Jan 1803, Despard and 6 others were executed, 21 Feb He had been a distinguished officer under Nelson.

Detroit, the capital of Michigan from 1836 to 1847 and the present commercial metropolis of that state, was visited by French traders early in the 17th century On 24 July, 1701, Antoine Laumet de la Mothe Cadillac arrived with 50 soldiers and 50 Canadian traders and artisans, and established fort Pontchartrain on the bank of the river, south of what is now Jefferson ave, and between Griswold and Shelby streets On 26 July, he laid the foundations of St Anne's church, which was burned in 1703, and rebuilt in 1709 On 2 Feb 1704, the first white child, a daughter of Cadillac, was baptized in the place, which was called by the French "La Ville d'Etroit." The settlement was increased in 1749 by 46 immigrants, who came in response to a proclamation of the governor-general of Canada offering a subsidy to new settlers, and in 1755 many fugitives from ACADIA found a refuge in Detroit The population reached 500 in 1796, and 770 in 1810 Since that date the decennial censuses have shown as follows 1820, 1442, 1830, 2222, 1840, 9192, 1850, 21,019, 1860, 45,619, 1870, 79,577, 1880, 116,342, 1890, 205,876, 1900, 285,704 Area, 23 sq miles Lat 42° 20′ N, lon. 83° W.

French surrender fort Pontchartrain to the English (MICHIGAN), 29 Nov 1760
Fort at Detroit besieged by the Indians under Pontiac (MICHIGAN) . . . . 9 May, 1763
News of treaty of peace and cession of Detroit by France to England received . . . 3 June, "
Warrant issued for Lodge of Masons No. 1 at Detroit ...27 Apr 1763

irst civil government provided by the British for Detroit and surrounding territory........22 June, 1774

ohn Coutincinau and Ann Wyley convicted of stealing $50, and hanged on the public square........26 Mch. 1777

ort Lernoult or Shelby, between the present fort Lafayette, Griswold and Wayne sts., erected........ 1778

ampus Martius (from which the principal avenues radiate) so named........2 July, 1788

ast session of the English court of general quarter-sessions held in Detroit........29 Jan. 1796

merican troops occupy Detroit........11 July, "

. S. schooner *Wilkinson* (80 tons) built at Detroit........ 1797

etroit constituted a port of entry........2 Mch. 1799

own of Detroit incorporated........18 Jan. 1802

irst town-tax voted........17 Apr. "

irst town election; James Henry appointed chairman of board of trustees........3 May, "

lias Wallen appointed the first city marshal........Oct. "

ost-office established........1 Jan. 1803

rst fire company organized........19 Sept. "

etroit declared the seat of territorial government of Michigan........11 Jan. 1805

etroit almost entirely destroyed by fire........11 June, "

rst session of district court *held on* the *open* square. 19 Aug. "

overnor and judges authorized to lay out a new town and to dispose of town lands........21 Apr. 1806

etroit bank, in a brick building on northwest cor. Jefferson ave. and Randolph st., incorporated........19 Sept. "

rst brick dwelling erected........ 1807

ark lots ordered surveyed........14 Dec. 1808

corporated as a city, 13 Sept. 1806; act repealed........24 Feb. 1809

ark lots, lying on both sides of Woodward ave. north from Adams ave., laid out and 41 of them sold at auction..6 Mch. "

rst paper printed in Detroit, the *Michigan Essay or Impartial Observer*, issued........31 Aug. "

rst Protestant church society organized........ 1810

en. Hull arrives at Detroit, 7 Aug., and surrenders to the British (MICHIGAN)........16 Aug. 1812

ort Detroit evacuated by British. 28 Sept., and gen. Duncan McArthur takes possession of the town........29 Sept. 1813

rst seal adopted........3 Jan. 1815

illage charter vesting local government in the people, 24 Oct., and 5 trustees elected; Solomon Sibley chairman....30 Oct. "

heatre opened in brick storehouse at foot of Wayne st........ 1816

etroit *Gazette*, weekly, first issued........25 July, 1817

own library incorporated........26 Aug. "

orner-stone of university building laid on west side of Bates, near Congress st........24 Sept. "

rst school in the university building opened........10 Aug. 1818

eamboat *Walk-in-the-Water* arrives from Buffalo, N. Y., 27 Aug. "

oard of trustees organize a fire company........23 Sept. "

rst Protestant Sunday-school held........4 Oct. "

ank of Michigan opens........2 Jan. 1819

oodworth's Steamboat hotel, conducted by "Uncle Ben" Woodworth since 1812, rebuilt and opened (burned 9 May, 1848)........Mch. "

rst Protestant church building within the city limits, on Woodward ave., near Larned st., dedicated........27 Feb. 1820

rst brick store erected by Thomas Palmer, on southwest cor. Jefferson ave. and Griswold st........ "

etroit *Lodge of* Freemasons organized........21 Dec. 1821

ublic stages first run to and from Detroit........June, 1822

orner-stone of the capitol laid........22 Sept. 1823

ity chartered; boundary extended and common council created; John R. Williams first mayor........5 Aug. 1824

rst street-paving contracted for........24 May, 1825

ire-engine "Protection No. 1" purchased........21 Sept. "

ire company organized........28 Sept. "

ongress donates the military reserve to the city........20 May, 1826

ity cemetery, on Beaubien farm, bounded by what is now Paton, Gratiot, and Clinton sts. (closed 1855), is purchased, 22 Mch. 1827

ermanent seal for the city adopted........26 Mch. "

orporate name of Detroit changed to "The Mayor, Recorder, and Aldermen of the City of Detroit"........4 Apr. "

ansion house, near northwest cor. Jefferson ave. and Cass st., erected by James May, 1805, opened as a hotel........3 May, "

rst steam ferry-boat in operation........May, "

ort Shelby demolished........" "

rst city water supply, by hydraulic company, furnished from pump-house on Berthelet wharf and reservoir 16 ft. square on Randolph st., by wooden pipes supplying portions of Jefferson ave., Larned and Congress sts........ "

apitol building first occupied........5 May, 1828

istorical society organized at the Mansion house........3 July, "

orthwestern Journal first issued........20 Nov. 1829

aily mails from the east begin........9 Jan. 1831

emocratic Free Press and Michigan Intelligencer first issued, 5 May, "

rst county poor-house completed........31 Dec. 1832

etroit Young Men's Society organized........18 Jan. 1833

eamboat *Michigan* launched at Detroit........27 Apr. "

ity cemetery, on Guoin farm, Russel st., near Gratiot road (vacated 14 May, 1879), is purchased........31 May, 1834

rst hose company organized........8 Oct. "

ichigan Exchange hotel opened........27 June, 1835

aily Free Press first issued........28 Sept. "

d city-hall east of Woodward ave., in middle of Grand ave., erected at a cost of $14,747, and first occupied........18 Nov. "

ichigan admitted into the Union, Detroit the capital of the state........26 Jan. 1836

DET

Works of hydraulic company purchased by city........18 May, 1836

Detroit *Daily Advertiser* first issued........11 June, "

First underground sewer, "the grand," built........ "

Michigan Central railroad opened to Ypsilanti *with a large* excursion from Detroit........3 Feb. 1838

Detroit boat club, the *first in the city, organized*........18 Feb. 1839

City divided into wards........27 Mch. "

Board of education created........17 Feb. 1842

Michigan Lodge No. 1 of Odd Fellows, instituted........4 Dec. 1843

Office of city auditor created........11 Mch. 1844

Free school for boys and girls opened by 4 Sisters of Charity who arrive in May........10 June, "

St. Vincent's (now St. Mary's) hospital, the first in the city, *opened on Larned st.*........9 June, 1845

First power-press in Michigan set up in the office of the *Free Press*, 1846

Elmwood cemetery opened........8 Oct. "

Last session of the legislature held in Detroit closes. (Capital removed to Lansing)........17 Mch. 1847

Board of Trade organized........20 Oct. "

First telegraphic despatch sent to Ypsilanti........29 Nov. "

First telegraphic despatch from New York received....1 Mch. 1848

Detroit Savings-bank incorporated........5 Mch. 1849

Harmonie Society, the oldest musical association in the city, organized........1 June, "

Cholera epidemic; nearly 300 deaths........July-Sept. "

First annual fair of the Michigan State Agricultural Society held on Woodward ave., near Duffield st........25-27 Sept. "

Daily Tribune first issued........19 Nov. "

Police court created........2 Apr. 1850

Young Men's hall, Jefferson ave., between Bates and Randolph sts., dedicated........27 Nov. "

First grain elevator erected........ 1851

Steam power first applied to printing........ "

Streets first lighted with gas........24 Sept. "

Board of Water Commissioners established........14 Feb. 1853

Daily Free Democrat first issued........3 Apr. "

First railroad ferry-boat; the *Transit's* trial trip........27 Feb. 1854

New Odd Fellows' hall on Campus Martius dedicated..13 Sept. 1855

Present Board of Trade organized........15 July, 1856

New charter, as "City of Detroit," and city enlarged...5 Feb. 1857

Masonic hall dedicated........24 June, "

First telegraphic cable laid across Detroit river........16 July, "

Russel house, on site of National hotel (opened 1 Dec. 1836), enlarged and opened........28 Sept. "

Water-works reservoir on the Dequindre farm completed. Nov. "

Marine hospital opened........30 Nov. "

Corner-stone of new post office and custom house laid, 18 May, 1858

First session of the high-school held in upper story of Miami Ave. school building........30 Aug. "

First trial of steam fire-engine........2 Sept. "

Daily meetings of the Board of Trade begun........3 May, 1859

Detroit female seminary opened........Sept. "

Grand Trunk railroad opened to Port Huron........21 Nov. "

U. S. custom-house and post-office, cor. Griswold and Larned sts., opened........30 Jan. 1860

First steam fire-engine purchased by city........26 June, "

Detroit House of Correction established........15 Mch. 1861

Detroit Light Guards organized........17 Apr. "

First regiment leaves for Washington........13 May, "

Second regiment leaves the city........2 June, "

Paid fire department established........25 June, "

Young Men's hall in Biddle House block first opened..21 Nov. "

Street-cars start on Jefferson and Woodward aves........3 Aug. 1863

Second National bank opened........11 Oct. "

First National bank........16 Nov. "

Detroit Young Men's Christian Association organized...1 Aug. 1864

Mail delivery by carriers begun........Oct. "

Harper hospital opened........12 Oct. "

Board of Trade building dedicated........22 Feb. 1865

Metropolitan police commission established by law....28 Feb. "

Public library opened in the old capitol........25 Mch. "

Police force organized........15 May, "

Round-house reservoir, built 1838 with a capacity of 422,979 gallons, in use until 1860, is torn down; work begun, 27 Mch. 1866

Detroit *Daily Post*, the first 8-page paper, issued........27 Mch. "

Fire-alarm telegraph inaugurated........4 Jan. 1867

Board of Fire Commissioners established........26 Mch. "

Corner-stone of soldiers' monument in East Grand Circus park laid........4 July, "

Corner-stone of new city-hall laid........6 Aug. 1868

Detroit medical college opened........2 Feb. 1869

Detroit Opera-house opened........29 Mch. "

Memorial day observed for the first time........29 May, "

Woodmere cemetery association organized, 8 July, 1867, and cemetery dedicated........14 July, "

People's Savings-bank organized........1 Jan. 1871

Act providing for and appointing park commissioners passed by the legislature........15 Apr. "

New city-hall formally opened; cost $600,000........4 July, "

Soldiers' monument unveiled; 55 feet high; cost $75,000, 9 Apr. 1872

Board of public works created........29 Apr. 1873

Superior court established, 28 Mch., and first formal session held in the Seitz block........11 June, "

Evening News established........23 Aug. "

St. Joseph's church consecrated........16 Nov. "

Corner-stone of new Odd Fellows hall laid........20 Aug. 1874

Corner-stone of public library building laid........29 May, 1875

Whitney's Grand Opera-house opened........13 Sept. "

Building of the Harmonie Society dedicated........11 Nov. "

New high-school building erected........ "

Public Library building dedicated........22 Jan. 1877

Office of fire marshal created	23 May, 1877
Water first supplied from new water works in Hamtramck	15 Dec "
Telephones come into general use	15 Aug 1878
Recreation park first opened	10 May 1879
Brush electric light first exhibited in Detroit	4 June, "
Belle Isle purchased for park purposes	25 Sept "
Michigan College of Medicine opened	17 Nov "
Detroit Association of Charities organized	22 Apr 1880
White's Grand theatre (formerly Music hall) opened	31 Aug "
Board of councilmen (originally the city council) created by act	12 Apr 1881
New ward boundaries erected by act of legislature	5 May, "
Soldiers' monument completed	19 July, "
Board of park commissioners for Belle Isle park created,	29 Aug "
Electric lighting becomes general	Sept "
Clearing house established	1 Feb 1883
New city charter enacted	5 June, "
Detroit *Evening Journal* first issued	1 Sept "
Contract made to light the entire city by electricity	June 1884
Twenty fifth annual reunion of the Grand Army of the Republic opens at Detroit	4 Aug 1891

MAYORS

John R Williams	1824-26	Charles Howard	1849-50
Henry J Hunt	1826-27	John Ladue	1850-51
John Biddle	1827-29	Zachariah Chandler	1851-52
Jonathan Kearsley	1829-30	John H Harmon	1852-54
John R Williams	1830-31	Oliver M Hyde	1854-55
Marshall Chapin	1831-32	Henry Ledyard	1855-56
Levi Cook	1832-34	O M Hyde	1856-58
Marshall Chapin	1834	John Patton	1858-60
C C Trowbridge	1834	Christian H Buhl	1860-62
Andrew Mack	1834-35	William C Duncan	1862-64
Levi Cook	1835-37	K C Barker	1864-66
Henry Howard	1837-38	Merrill I Mills	1866-68
Augustus S Porter	1838	William W Wheaton	1868-72
Asher B Bates	1838-39	Hugh Moffat	1872-76
De Garmo Jones	1839-40	Alexander Lewis	1876-78
Zina Pitcher	1840-42	George C Langdon	1878-80
Douglas Houghton	1842-43	William G Thompson	1880-84
Zina Pitcher	1843-44	Stephen B Grummond	1884-86
John R Williams	1844-47	M H Chamberlain	1886-88
James A Van Dyke	1847-48	John Pridgeon, jr	1888-90
Frederick Buhl	1848-49	H S Pingree	1890-93

Det'tingen, Bavaria, Battle of, 27 June, 1743, between the British, Hanoverian, and Hessian army (52,000), under king George II of England and the earl of Stair, and the French army (60,000), under marshal Noailles and the duc de Grammont, in the war of the AUSTRIAN SUCCESSION The French passed a defile, which they should have merely guarded The duc de Grammont, with his cavalry, charged the British foot with great fury, but was obliged to give way and to repass the Maine, losing 3000 men This was the last time an English king took personal command of an army in battle Handel's "Dettingen Te Deum" first performed 27 Nov 1743

development or **evolution.** Wolff put forth a theory of epigenesis in 1759, Lamarck, the naturalist, in 1809, propounded a theory that all animals had been developed from "monads," living minute particles SPECIES, VESTIGES Buffon held a similar doctrine In 1827 Ernst von Baer of Konigsberg demonstrated that every mammal is developed from a minute egg not a hundredth of an inch in diameter C Darwin's views are given in his "Origin of Species," 1859, and "Descent of Man," 1871. He supposes that man was gradually evolved from the lowest created form of animal life Haeckel, his most advanced follower, published in German a "History of Creation," 1873, a translation in English, 1875. Alfred Wallace published his work on Natural Selection in 1870 EVOLUTION

A theory of the development of living beings out of the earth was put forth by Lucretius in his "De Rerum Natura," about 57 B C.

"We cannot teach, we cannot pronounce it to be a conquest of science, that man descends from the ape or from any other animal. We can only indicate it as a hypothesis"—*Prof Virchow*, 1877

"The primitive monads were born by spontaneous generation in the sea"—*Prof Haeckel*, 1878

devil, according to Swedenborg, a more debased and lower form of evil than SATAN, pertaining more to the will than the understanding, to action than to thought, and without distinctive form aside from the personality of man Superstitious thought has given it a locality and a form which it by no means possesses, and thus suggested many mediæval myths and traditions DEVIL WORSHIP

devil-fish (*Octopus vulgaris*, the eight-armed cuttle-fish) Many old writers have given exaggerated accounts of the size of these sea animals They are now known to attain a length of 15 ft. and upward, head and body, and, measuring the long tentacles, from 30 to 40 ft Graphic description given of its form and habits in Victor Hugo's "Toilers of the Sea"

devil-worship. (Devil—Gr διάβολος, false accuser, Heb *satan*, an adversary, *abaddon*, destroyer, etc) The worship of devils is frequently mentioned in the Bible (Lev xvii 7, 2 Chron xi 15, 1 Cor x 20, Rev ix 20, etc.) Mr Layard describes the Yezidees as recognizing one supreme being, yet reverencing the devil as a king or mighty angel, to be conciliated (1841)

Moncure Conway's "Demonology and Devil lore," first pub Dec 1878

Devi'zes, a borough of Wilts, Engl At Roundway Down, near here, sir William Waller and the parliamentarians were defeated, 13 July, 1643

Devonshire, Engl, the country of the Damnonii, or Dumnonii Odun, earl of Devon, in 878 defeated the Danes, slew Ubbo, or Hubba, their chief and captured his magic standard A bishopric of Devonshire was founded in 909 EXETER

Richard de Redvers first earl of Devon, son of Baldwin, sheriff of Devonshire, d 1137

William Courtenay the present earl is descended from Robert de Courtenay and Mary de Redvers, daughter of William de Redvers, earl of Devon in 1184

William Cavendish, created first earl of Devonshire, 1618

William Cavendish (his great grandson), created first duke of Devonshire, 1684

> "The brave Geraint, a knight of Arthur's court,
> A tributary prince of Devon one
> Of that great Order of the Table Round"
> —*Tennyson*, "Geraint and Enid"

"Devout Life." "Introduction a la Vie Devote," written by St François de Sales, and published 1608 He was born 21 Aug 1567, bishop of Geneva, 1602, died 28 Dec 1622

dew, the modern theory that dew is atmospheric vapor deposited on the surface of bodies, generally during the night, was put forth by dr Wells in his book, 1814 The point of temperature at which the vapor in the air begins to condense is called the dew-point

diadem, the band or fillet worn by the ancients instead of the crown, and consecrated to the gods At first it was made of silk or wool set with precious stones, and was tied round the temples and forehead, the 2 ends knotted behind fell on the neck Aurelian was the first Roman emperor who wore a diadem, 272 —*Tillemont.*

dials. "The sun dial of Ahaz," 713 B C (Isa xxxviii 8). A dial invented by Anaximander, 550 B C —*Pliny* The first dial of the sun seen at Rome was placed on the temple of Quirinus by L. Papirius Cursor, when time was divided into hours, 293 B C.—*Blair* Dials set up in churches about 613 A D.—*Lenglet.* Mrs. Alfred Gatty's "Book of Sun-dials" pub 1872

dial'ysis (Gr διάλυσις, dissolution), a branch of chemical analysis, depending on the different degrees of diffusibility of substances in liquids, made known in 1861 by its discoverer, prof Thomas Graham, then master of the mint

diamag'netism, the property possessed by nearly all bodies of behaving differently to iron when placed between 2 magnets The phenomena, previously little known, were reduced to a law by Faraday in 1845, and confirmed by Tyndall and others.

diamonds were first brought to Europe from the east, where the mine of Sumbulpoor was the first known, and where the mines of Golconda, the realm of diamonds, were discovered in 1534. The mines of Brazil were discovered in 1728 From these last a diamond weighing 1680 carats, or 14 ounces, was sent in 1741 to the court of Portugal, known as the Braganza diamond (never cut), and was valued by Romeo de l'Isle at 224,000,000*l*, by others at 56,000,000*l.* and at 3,500,000*l.*, its true value (not being brilliant) was 400,000*l.*

Great *Russian* or *Orloff* diamond weighs 193 carats, or 1 oz 12 dwts. 4 gr troy The empress Catherine II offered for it 104,166*l.* 13*s* 4*d* and an annuity for life of 1041*l.* 13*s* 4*d*, which was refused, but sold to Catherine's favorite, count Orloff, for the first mentioned sum, without the annuity, and presented to the empress on her birthday, 1772, it is now in the sceptre of Russia

Pitt diamond 136 carats, or, after cutting, 106 carats, was sold to the king of France for 125,000*l* in 1720

Pigott diamond (bought by Mr Pitt, grandfather of William Pitt) was sold for 9500 guineas, 10 May, 1802.

Diamond called the *Kohinoor* or *Mountain of Light*, was found in the mines of Golconda, in 1550, and is said to have belonged in turn to Shah Jehan, Aurungzebe, Nadir Shah, the Afghan rulers, and the Sikh chief Runjeet Singh Upon the abdication of Dhuleep Singh, the last ruler of the Punjab, and the annexation of his dominions to the British empire, in 1849 the Kohinoor was surrendered to the queen, and was presented to her, 3 July, 1850 It was shown in the great exhibition, 1851 Its original weight was nearly 800 carats, but it was reduced by the unskilfulness of the artist Hortensio Borghese, a Venetian, to 279 carats Its shape and size resembled the pointed half (rose cut) of a small hen's egg The value is scarcely computable, though 2 000,000*l* have been mentioned as a justifiable price, on the scale employed in the trade This diamond was recut in 1852, and now weighs 102¼ carats

ancy diamond, which belonged to Charles the Bold duke of Burgundy, was bought by sir C. Jejeebhoy from the Demidoff family for 20,000*l* in Feb 1865

diamond the *Star of the South*, was brought from Brazil in 1855, weighing 254½ carats, half of which was lost by cutting

ther diamonds of note are the *Rajah of Mattan* Borneo 367 ..., carats *Florentine*, emperor of Austria 139½ carats, 138½ carats king of Portugal, 80 carats czar of Russia 78½ carats marquis of Westminster, 288½ carats uncut the *Stewart* diamond

iamonds were discovered in Cape Colony S Africa, in Mch 1867 A fine one, the *Star of South Africa*, brought to England in 1869, was purchased by Messrs Hunt & Roskell After cutting, it weighed 46½ carats, and was valued at 25 000*l* in June 1870

ich diamond fields discovered near the Vaal and Orange rivers, Sept 1870

reat influx of diggers, and many fine diamonds found Nov Value of 141 diamonds found in 1869 7405*l* of 5661 found in 1870, 124,910*l*, about 2 000 000*l* worth said to have been exported in 1877

rgest African diamond found, weighing 302 carats, at Kimberley, named *Victoria* 27 Mch 1884

everal other magnificent S African diamonds since found one 400 carats cut to 180 Estimated value of S African diamonds up to 1886 $200 000,000

iamond necklace Affair —In 1785, Bohmer, the court jeweller of France, offered the queen, Marie Antoinette, a diamond necklace for 56,000*l* The queen desired the necklace, but feared the expense The countess de la Motte (of the ancient house of Valois) forged the queen's signature and pretending that the queen had an attachment for him persuaded the cardinal de Rohan, the queen's almoner to buy the necklace for 56,000*l*. She then made away with the necklace For this she was tried in 1786, and sentenced to be branded on the shoulders and imprisoned for life. She accused in vain the Italian adventurer Cagliostro of complicity he being intimate with the cardinal She made her escape and went to London where she was killed by falling from a window in attempting to escape an arrest for debt De Rohan was tried and acquitted, 14 Apr 1786 The public in France suspected the queen of being a party to the fraud Talleyrand wrote that he should not be surprised if this miserable affair overturned the throne Best account, Carlyle's "French Revolution"

rtificial diamonds Prepared by Mr MacTear of Glasgow, examined by Story Maskelyne, and declared not to be diamonds, 30 Dec 1879, acknowledged by Mr MacTear, Jan 1880

iamonds said to have been made by J Ballantine Hannay at Glasgow, announced in *Times*, 20 Feb 1880

iamonds said to have been made at Paris, 1880

INFLAMMABILITY OF DIAMONDS

oetius de Boot conjectured that the diamond was inflammable, 1609 When exposed to a high temperature it gave an acrid vapor, and part of it was dissipated 1673 —*Boyle*

r Isaac Newton concluded from its great refracting power, that it must be combustible 1675

verani concentrated the rays of the sun upon the diamond which was exhaled in vapor and entirely disappeared, while other precious stones merely grew softer, 1695

has been ascertained by Guyton, Davy, and others, that diamonds, like charcoal, are pure carbon Diamonds were charred by the heat of the voltaic battery—by M Dumas, in Paris, and by prof Faraday, in London, in 1848

Dia'na, Temple of at Ephesus, Asia Minor, accounted ne of the 7 wonders of the world, was built at the common harge of all the Asiatic states, 552 B.C , the chief architect being Ctesiphon. Pliny says that 220 years were occupied in completing it. It was 425 ft. long, 225 broad, and was supported by 27 columns (60 ft high, each weighing 150 tons) of Parian arble, furnished by many kings It was set on fire the night lexander the Great was born, by Herostratus or Eratostratus, ho confessed that his motive was the desire of transmitting is name to future ages, 356 B C The temple was rebuilt, but gain burned by the Goths in their naval invasion, 256 or 32 A D In Apr, 1869, J T. Wood discovered the site of the econd temple, and since then sculptured marble columns have een removed to the British museum Diana was the Roman ame of the Greek *Artemis* The *three-formed* goddess ruling s Selene in the sky, as Artemis or Diana on earth, as Hecate r Proserpina in Erebus

"Goddess whom all gods love with threefold heart,
Being treble in thy divided deity,
A light for dead men and dark hours, a foot
Swift on the hills as morning and a hand
To all things fierce and fleet that roar and range
Mortal " —*Swinburne*, "Atalanta in Calydon"

RCHITECTURE, MYTHOLOGY

dice. The invention of dice is ascribed to Palamedes of Greece, about 1244 B.C. The game of tali and tessera among the Romans was played with dice Stow mentions 2 entertainments given by the city of London, at which dice were played Act to regulate the licenses of makers and the sale of dice in England, 9 Geo IV 1828

In 1357 the kings of Scotland and France being prisoners, and the king of Cyprus on a visit to Edward III, a great tournament was held in Smithfield, and afterwards Henry Picard mayor of London, "kept his hall against all comers that were willing to play at dice and hazard The lady Margaret his wife, did keepe her chamber to the same intent " The mayor restored to the king of Cyprus 50 marks which he had won from him, saying, "My lord and king, be not aggrieved, for I covet not your gold, but your play," etc —*Stow*

di'chroscope (Gr δίχροος, two-colored, and σκοπεῖν, view), an optical apparatus, invented by prof Dove of Berlin, in 1860, to represent interferences, spectra in colored lights polarization of light etc

dictators were supreme magistrates of Rome, appointed to act in critical times Titus Lartius Flavius, the first dictator, was appointed 501 B C Caius Marcius Rutilus was the first plebeian dictator, 356 B.C This office became odious by the usurpations of Sylla and Julius Cæsar, and after the death of the latter the Roman senate, on motion of the consul Antony, passed a law forbidding a dictatorship, 44 B C

dictionary. A standard dictionary of the Chinese language, containing about 40,000 characters, most of them hieroglyphic, was perfected by Pa-out-she, who lived about 1100 B C —*Morrison* ENCYCLOPÆDIAS, MUSIC, etc

	B C
A Latin dictionary was compiled by Varro, b	116
Varro's work "De Lingua Latina," he d	28
	A D
"Onomasticon," a collection of vocabularies in Greek by Julius Pollux, was pub about	177
"Catholicon" an attempt at a Latin lexicon, by friar Johannes Balbus Januensis, printed at Mentz	1460
A noted polyglot dictionary, perhaps the first, is by Ambrose Calepini, a Venetian friar, in Latin, he wrote one in 8 languages (*Necron*) about	1500
John L Avenar's "Dictionarium Hebraicum" was published at Wittenberg in 1589 Buxtorf's great work, "Lexicon Hebraicum" etc. appeared	1621
"Lexicon Heptaglotton" was published by Edmund Castell	1669
English dictionary by Samuel Johnson appeared	1755
Francis Grose's "Dictionary of the Vulgar Tongue" was compiled	1768
Following academies have published large dictionaries of their respective languages the French academy (the first, edited by Vaugelas), 1694 new editions, 1718, 1740, 1762, 1835, and 1878 the Spanish 1726, the Italian academy (della Crusca), 1729, and the ...	1789-94
Schwan's great German French dictionary appeared	1782
Walker's (English), popular for half a century	1791
Webster's American dictionary first pub (often revised)	1828
Smart's dictionary pub	1836
Richardson's English dictionary appeared	1836
Lemprière's classical dictionary, 1788, now superseded by Dr W Smith's classical series	1842-57
Worcester's dictionary	1860
Great German dictionary by Jacob and Wilhelm Grimm	1854 et seq
Hensleigh Wedgwood's "Dictionary of English Etymology"	1859-67
Smith's "Dictionary of the Bible" pub	1860-63
Earliest known English Latin dictionary is the "Promptorium Parvulorum," compiled by Galfridus Grammaticus a preaching friar of Norfolk in 1440, ... printed by Pynson, as "Promptorius Puerorum," in 1499 A new edition, by Albert Way from MSS, published by Camden Society	1843-65
Great French dictionary, by E Littré 1863-72 supplement	1877
"Bona fide French and English Dictionary (4½ inches by 2¾, weight 4 oz), printed by Bellows	1873
"Harper's Latin Dictionary" (founded upon Andrews's translation of Freund's "Latin German Lexicon"), standard authority in English and American universities, pub	1879
"Encyclopædic Dictionary" (English), by Robert Hunter, M A, F G S	1879-88
"Imperial Dictionary" (English) 4 vols 8vo	1882
"Century Dictionary" (named after the company publishing it) 6 vols. imperial octavo, edited by Wm Dwight Whitney, Ph D, LL D, of Yale	1891
Philological Society of London issued "proposals for a new English dictionary," on the historical method 1859 after long delay work began systematically, editor, dr J H Murray, [About 5000 authors, dating from 1150 to 1853, have been read by about 13 000 persons (British and American), who made about 3,000,000 extracts Part I, pub Feb 1884, was considered to promise the grandest lexicographical work ever produced. Vol III part I 1892]	1879
A, B, and parts of C and D, completed	Jan 1893

didym'ium, a rare metal, discovered by Mosander in 1841, appears to be always associated with lanthanum and cerium

Dieppe (*dée-ep'*), N. France. This town was bombarded

by an English fleet, under admiral Russell, and laid in ashes, July, 1694 It was again bombarded in 1794, and again, together with Granville, by the British, 14 Sept 1803

"Di'es Iræ" ("Day of Wrath"), a Latin mediæval hymn on the day of judgment, is ascribed to various authors, among others to pope Gregory the Great (d about 604), St. Bernard (d 1153); but was doubtless composed by Thomas of Celano (d 1255), and used in the Roman service of the mass before 1385

"Dies iræ dies illa
Solvet sæclum in favilla,
Teste David cum Sibylla," etc.

Many translations of this hymn have been made, but none express the force of the original

Diet of the German empire (the body which exercised supreme authority in the empire) was composed of 3 colleges one of electors, one of princes, and one of imperial towns, and originated with the edict or Golden Bull of Charles IV 1356 AUGSBURG, 1530, FRANKFORT-ON-THE-MAIN, 1806 et seq, GERMANY, GOLDEN BULL, NUREMBERG, 1467, RATISBON, 1541, SPIRES, 1529, WORMS, 1521, WURZBURG, 1180

diether'oscope, an apparatus for geodesy and teaching optics, constructed by G Luvini of Turin, and announced Apr 1876

Dieu et mon droit ('God and my right'), the royal motto of England, was the pass-word of the day, given by Richard I of England to his army at the battle of Gisors, in France, 20 Sept 1198, in which the French army was signally defeated It seems to have been first assumed as a motto by Henry VI (1422-61) SEMPER EADEM

"Dieu-donné" ("God-given"), the name given in his infancy to Louis le Grand, king of France, the queen, his mother, having been barren for 23 years previous to 1638 Also to the late comte de Chambord, son of the duchess of Berri, born 29 Sept 1820 His father was assassinated 14 Feb 1820 One of the popes (672) was named *Adeodatus*, or God's gift.

diffusion of gases. In 1825, Döbereiner observed the transmission of hydrogen gas through a crack in a glass vessel and prof Thomas Graham discovered the passage of gases through porous porcelain, graphite, and other substances, and established laws in 1832 He also discovered ATMOLYSIS and DIALYSIS He died 16 Sept 1869

Digest. The first collection of Roman laws under this title was prepared by the civilian Alfrenus Varus, of Cremona, 66 B C.—*Quintil.* The "Digest," so called by way of eminence, was the collection made by order of the emperor Justinian, 529, it made the first part of the Roman law and the first volume of the civil law Quotations from it are marked with a ff.—*Pardon.* The "Digest of Law" commissioners signed their first report 13 May, 1867, recommending the immediate preparation of a digest of the English common-law, statute law, and judicial decisions.

digits are properly the fingers (Lat *digitus*, a finger) The figures representing any whole number under 10 (1, 2, etc.) are called the 9 digits Arithmetical figures were known to the Arabian Moors about 900, and were introduced by them into Spain in 1050, and thence into England about 1253.—In astronomy, the digit as a measure of eclipses, is the twelfth part of the luminary eclipsed ARITHMETIC NUMERALS

Dijon (*de'-zhon'*), E. France, the ancient capital of Burgundy, said to have been founded by Julius Cæsar, fortified by the emperor Marcus Aurelius, and named *Divio*, about 274 It has been several times captured, and a castle was erected here by Louis XI Dijon became the capital of the dukes of Burgundy about 1180 It was attacked by the Germans, under gen Beyer, 30 Oct 1870 The high suburbs were taken by prince William of Baden, and the town surrendered on 31 Oct

Dilettan'ti, Society of, established in 1734 by the viscount Harcourt, lord Middlesex, duke of Dorset, and others who had travelled and were desirous of encouraging the fine arts in Great Britain The society aided in publishing Stuart's "Athens" (1762-1816), Chandler's "Travels" (1775-76), and other illustrated works. The members dine together from time to time at the Thatched-house tavern, St. James's R. P Pullan on behalf of this society, excavated the temple of Bacchus at Teos, of Apollo Smintheus in the Troad, and of Minerva Polias at Priene, between 1861-70. Pub "Antiquities of Ionia," 4 parts, 1769-1881

dim'ity, a cotton fabric, generally figured or striped The term is derived from the Gr δίς, twice, and μίτος, thread DAMIETTA

Dinornis (δεινός, terrible, and ὄρνις, bird), an extinct gigantic bird, the remains of which are found in certain parts of New Zealand From the size of its bones the bird must have measured at least 10 feet in height. It was called the Moa by the natives of New Zealand, and the Maoris have traditions of hunting it, so that its extinction has been of comparatively recent date.

di'ocese. The first division of the Roman empire into dioceses, then civil governments, is ascribed to Constantine, 323, but Strabo remarks that the Romans had the departments called dioceses long before In England the principal dioceses are coeval with the establishment of Christianity, of 28 dioceses, 20 are suffragan to the diocese of Canterbury, and 6 to that of York BISHOPS, and the sees severally Diocesan conferences of the clergy and laity now frequent CHURCH, English, Protestant-Episcopal, and Roman Catholic.

Diocle'tian Era (called also the Era of Martyrs, from the persecution in his reign) was used by Christian writers until the introduction of the Christian era in the 6th century, and is still by the Abyssinians and Copts. It dates from the day on which Diocletian was proclaimed emperor at Chalcedon, 29 Aug 284.

dioptric system (from the Gr διόπτρα, an optical instrument for measuring), an arrangement of lenses for refracting light in light-houses, devised by Fresnel about 1819, based on discoveries of Buffon, Condorcet, Brewster, and others LIGHT-HOUSES

diorama (Gr διά, through, and ὅραμα, vision), paintings viewed through a large aperture or proscenium, invented by Daguerre and Bouton, and first exhibited in Paris, 1822

diphthe'ria (from the Gr. διφθέρα, leather), a disease resembling croup which develops a false membrane on the mucous lining of the throat It was named *diphtheritis* by Brétonneau of Tours in 1820 From its prevalence in Boulogne it has been termed the Boulogne sore-throat, many persons were affected with it in England at the beginning of 1858 It has been often epidemic in Russia

Directory, the French, established by the constitution of the 5th of Fructidor, an III (22 Aug 1795), and nominated 1 Nov, was composed of 5 members (MM Lépeaux, Letourneur, Rewbel, Barras, and Carnot) It ruled in conjunction with 2 chambers, the Council of Ancients and Council of Five Hundred (COUNCILS, FRENCH). At the revolution of the 18th of Brumaire (9 Nov 1799), it was deposed by Bonaparte, who, with Cambacérès and Lebrun, assumed the government as 3 consuls, himself the first, 13 Dec 1799. CONSULS.

"Directory," the first London, is said to have been printed in 1677. The "Post-office Directory" first appeared in 1800 For cities of the United States see under their respective heads.

Disciples of Christ, formerly known in the United States as Campbellites, from their founders Thomas and Alexander Campbell, father and son, who came from Ireland to the U S in 1809 Originally Presbyterians, they preached at Bush Run, Pa, but united with the Baptists in 1812, who, protesting against their creed, excluded them from their fellowship in 1827 The early success of the sect is almost entirely due to the efforts of Alexander, who, educated at the university of Glasgow, was able to formulate a theology. They profess adherence to pure scriptural doctrine and practice, reject human creeds and formularies, and admit to their communion all who recognize Christ's obedience and death as "the only meritorious cause of the sinner's acceptance with God," and are baptized (by immersion) in his name They number, according to the statistics of 1892, 8416 churches, with 789,497 members, and possess church property valued at $12,206,038. James A. Garfield was a member of this church, and, prior to his entry into military and political life, was active in promoting its tenets

discipline, ecclesiastical, originally conducted spiritually recording to the divine commands in Matt. xviii. 15,

1 Cor. v., 2 Thess. iii. 6, and other texts, gradually became temporal, as it now is in the Roman, Greek, and other churches. The "First Book of Discipline" of the Presbyterian church of Scotland was drawn up by John Knox and 4 ministers in Jan. 1560-61. The more important "Second Book" was prepared with great care in 1578 by Andrew Melville and a committee of the leading members of the general assembly. It lays down a Presbyterian form of government, defines the position of the ecclesiastical and civil powers, etc.

disestablishment. CHURCH OF IRELAND.

Dismal swamp, a morass in southern Virginia, extending into North Carolina. It was formerly 40 miles long and 25 miles wide, but has become somewhat reduced in area by drainage of its border. It is densely timbered with cypress, juniper, cedar, pine, etc. Lake Drummond, near its centre, covers about 6 square miles. This swamp rises towards its centre, which is considerably higher than its margin. It is now traversed by a canal and two narrow-gauge railroads from Suffolk. Thomas Moore the poet, while at Norfolk, Virginia, put into verse an Indian legend, under the title of "The Lake of the Dismal Swamp."

dispensations, ecclesiastical, were first granted by pope Innocent III. in 1200. These exemptions from the discipline of the church, with indulgences, absolutions, etc., led eventually to the Reformation in Germany in 1517.

dispensing power of the crown (for setting aside laws or their power) asserted by some British sovereigns, especially by Charles II. (in 1672 for the relief of non-conformists), and by James II. in 1786, was abolished by the bill of rights, 1689. It has been exercised in the case of embargoes upon ships, the Bank Charter act, etc. INDEMNITY.

Disraeli (*diz-rā'l-ē*) **administrations.** ADMINISTRATIONS, ENGLISH. Benjamin Disraeli (son of Isaac D'Israeli, author of "Curiosities of Literature," etc.), born 21 Dec. 1805; published "Vivian Grey," 1825; M.P. for Maidstone, 1837-41; Shrewsbury, 1841-47; Bucks, 1847-76. Chancellor of exchequer, Feb. 1852; Feb. 1858; July, 1866; installed lord rector of Glasgow university, 19 Nov. 1873; created earl of Beaconsfield, Aug. 1876; plenipotentiary at the Berlin congress, 13 June-13 July, 1878; K.G., invested by the queen, 22 July, 1878; received freedom of London, 3 Aug. 1878 ("at the pinnacle of ministerial renown; the favorite of his sovereign, and the idol of society."—London *Times*, 8 Aug. 1878). Resigned (after Liberal victory in elections), 22 Apr. 1880; published "Endymion," Dec. 1880; died 19 Apr. 1881; buried at Hughenden, prince of Wales and many present, 26 Apr.; monument in Westminster abbey voted, 9 May, 1881. His wife created viscountess Beaconsfield, 28 Nov. 1868; died Dec. 1872.

Dissenters, the modern name of PURITANS, NON-CONFORMISTS, and English Protestants generally who dissent from the church of England. In 1851, in London, the number of chapels, meeting-houses, etc., for all classes of dissenters, amounted to more than 554. (The church of England had 458; Roman Catholics, 35.) The great act (9 Geo. IV. c. 17) for the relief of dissenters from disabilities, passed 9 May, 1828, and called the Corporation and Test Repeal act, repealed all laws requiring the sacrament of the Lord's Supper as a qualification for certain offices, etc. By 6 and 7 Will. IV. c. 85 (1836), dissenters acquired the right of solemnizing marriages at their own chapels, or at a registry office. WORSHIP.

A burials bill to permit dissenting ministers to officiate at funerals in church-yards several times rejected; in the commons, 248-234, 21 Apr. 1875; 279-248, 3 Mch. 1876; earl Granville's resolution in the lords rejected, 148-92, 15 May, 1876.

Lord Harrowby's additional clause to the government burials bill (permitting dissenters to have religious services in church-yards), was supported by the archbishops, and carried against government (127-111), 18 June; the bill withdrawn, 25 June, 1877.

Osborne Morgan's resolution for reforming burial laws (i. e., permitting other services), rejected (242-227), 15 Feb. 1878.

Act to amend the burial laws, permitting dissenters to have their own service or no service in church-yards; passed commons (258-79), 13 Aug.; royal assent, 7 Sept. 1880.

Rev. W. H. Fremantle having proposed to preach at Dr. Parker's city temple, and the bishop of London having disapproved, the opinion of 2 counsel (Fitzjames Stephen and Benjamin Shaw) was taken. They declared it to be illegal for the clergy of the English church to take part in worship of dissenters, June, 1875.

Several Episcopal clergymen take part in the dedication services of Christ church (formerly Surrey chapel), Blackfriars, middle of July, 1876.

dissolving views, a name given to pictures thrown on a background or scene in such manner as to appear to dissolve or vanish into the one following without any break or interval between them. Henry Langdon Childe, the alleged inventor, died 15 Oct. 1874, aged 92.

dis'taff or **rock,** the staff to which flax or any substance to be spun is fastened. The art of spinning with it at the small wheel first taught to Englishwomen by Anthony Bonavisa, an Italian.—*Stow*. St. Distaff's or Rock day was formerly in England the first free day after the Epiphany (6 Jan.), when the Christmas holidays were over and women's work was resumed.

distillation, and the various processes dependent on it, are believed to have been introduced into Europe by the Moors about 1150. ALCOHOL, BRANDY. The distillation of spirituous liquors was in practice in Great Britain in the 16th century.—*Burns*. The processes were improved by Adam of Montpellier in 1801. M. Payen's work (1861) contains the most recent improvements. An act to prevent the use of stills by unlicensed persons was passed in 1846. 118 licenses to distillers were granted in the year ending 31 Mch. 1858, for the United Kingdom.

M. Raoul Pictet announces a method of distillation by use of ice made by the air-pump, Apr. 1881.

District of Columbia. The District of Columbia, containing the capital of the United States, is on the east side of the Potomac river, and was formerly part of Maryland. It contains about 64 sq. miles, and being under the "exclusive legislation of Congress," according to art. i. sec. 8 of the U. S. Constitution, its citizens do not vote for president or vice-president of the U. S., nor in the affairs of the District. The centre of the dome of the Capitol is in lat. 38° 53′ 20″ N., and lon. 77° 00′ 29″ W. Pop. 1900, 278,718.

Georgetown laid out under act of assembly in 80 lots, comprising 60 acres....15 May, 1751
Constitution of the U. S. gives Congress power to "exercise exclusive legislation in all cases whatever over such district (not exceeding 10 miles sq.) as may, by cession of particular states and the acceptance of Congress, become the seat of government of the U. S."....17 Sept. 1787
Act of Maryland to cede to Congress 10 miles sq. in the state for the seat of government of the U. S....23 Dec. 1788
Act of Virginia ceding 10 miles sq. or less upon the Potomac for the seat of government of the U. S....3 Dec. 1789
Georgetown incorporated....25 Dec. "
Act of Congress locating the district for a seat of government, 16 July, 1790
Pres. Washington appoints Thomas Johnson, Daniel Carroll of Maryland, and David Stuart of Virginia, commissioners to survey the federal district....22 Jan. 1791
Nineteen proprietors agree upon terms for sale of lands to the government. Lots, for public buildings, to be paid for at $125 per acre, streets free; other lots to be the joint property of the owners and the public trustees....30 Mch. "
Pres. Washington proclaims the lines and boundaries of the district. A square comprising 64 sq. miles in Maryland and 36 in Virginia....30 Mch. "
First stone marking boundary of the district set in Jones's Point, Hunting Creek, Va....15 Apr. "
Commissioners agree to call the federal district the "Territory of Columbia," and the federal city the "City of Washington," and to name the streets of the latter alphabetically one way and numerically the other....9 Sept. "
Corner-stone of president's house in Washington laid...13 Oct. 1792
Corner-stone of north wing of the Capitol laid....18 Sept. 1793
First newspaper, the *National Intelligencer*, published in Washington.... 1800
Congress first meets in Washington....17 Nov. "
Superintendence of Washington placed in the hands of 3 commissioners.... "
Congress assumes jurisdiction of the district, and continues in force the existing laws of Maryland and Virginia....27 Feb. 1801
Thomas Jefferson inaugurated president at Washington..4 Mch. "
Washington incorporated by Congress; with a mayor appointed by the president and a council elected by the people, 3 May, 1802
Navy-yard at Washington established....27 Mch. 1804
Public buildings in Washington burned and destroyed by the British after the battle of Bladensburg....24 Aug. 1814
Georgetown college, founded in 1789, chartered as a university....1 May, 1815
American Colonization society for colonizing free people of color in Liberia, founded at Washington.... 1817

New charter granted Washington, and mayor elected by the people 15 May, 1820
Columbian college Washington incorporated 1821
Corner stone of first lock in Chesapeake and Ohio canal laid near Georgetown in presence of president Jackson 29 May 1829
Building of the government post office, designed by Robert Mills commenced 1839
U S Treasury building designed by Robert Mills, completed 1841
U S naval observatory founded 1842
Congress retrocedes the 36 sq miles received from Virginia, 9 July, 1846
Corner stone of the Smithsonian institution laid. 1 May. 1847
Corner stone of the Washington monument laid 4 July, 1848
National soldiers home, 2 miles north of Washington established by act of Congress 3 Mch 1851
Corner stone of south extension of the Capitol laid 4 July, "
Principal room of the library of Congress burned, 35,000 volumes destroyed 24 Dec. "
Louis Kossuth visits Washington 31 Dec "
First national agricultural convention, 151 members from 22 states Marshall P Wilder of Mass, president, meets at Washington 24 June, 1852
Congress appropriates $50,000 for an equestrian statue of Washington on public grounds near the Capitol 25 Jan 1853
Government hospital for the insane of the army and navy established near Uniontown, 1853, opened 1855
Columbia Institution for the Deaf and Dumb, founded by Amos Kendall chartered by Congress. 1857
Peace conference of 5 commissioners from each state assembles at Washington 4 Feb 1861
Balloon ascension for military purposes made at Washington, and first telegraph message from a balloon sent by Mr Lowe to pres. Lincoln 18 June,
Congress emancipates all slaves, to be valued by commissioners and paid for at a maximum of $300 16 Apr 1862
Collegiate department of the Columbia Institution for the Deaf and Dumb known as the National Deaf Mute college, the only one in the world, publicly opened 28 June, 1864
General Jubal Early confederate attacks fort Stevens, 6 miles north of Washington and is repulsed 12 July, "
Pres Lincoln assassinated in Ford s theatre Washington, 14 Apr 1865
Suffrage granted to colored citizens in the District. 8 Jan 1867
The extensions of the capitol finished Nov "
Howard university chartered "
Corcoran Art Gallery deeded to trustees by W W Corcoran, the founder 10 May, 1869
Congress repeals the charters of Washington and Georgetown, and forms a territorial government for the district, with a governor and council of 11 members appointed by the president of U S for 4 years, and a House of Delegates elected by the people Henry D Cooke first governor 21 Feb 1871
Alexander R Shepherd appointed governor 1873
Congress abolishes the territorial government, substituting a board of 3 regents appointed by the president 20 June, 1874
Permanent government of district constituted by Congress, in a board of 3 commissioners with no local legislative body Josiah Dent, president of board 11 June, 1878
Pres. Garfield assassinated in the Baltimore and Potomac railroad station at Washington 2 July, 1881
Joseph R West, president of board of commissioners. 1882
James B Edmonds president of board of commissioners 1883
Remains of John Howard Payne, who died in Tunis, Africa, in 1852, interred in Oak Hill cemetery, Washington 9 June, "
Capstone of the Washington monument placed (monument 555 ft. high) 6 Dec. 1884
William B Webb, president of board of commissioners 1886
American college of the Roman Catholic church opened at Washington 13 Nov 1889

divination was forbidden to the Jews, 1451 B.C (Deut. xviii 10) It was common among their neighbors, and is described by Ezekiel (xxi. 21) 493 B C

divine right of kings, to the absolute and unqualified obedience of subjects, a doctrine foreign to the genius of the English constitution, was defended by many writers of various schools of thought, e g, by Hobbes the free-thinker (1642), by Salmasius (1640), by sir Robert Filmer (about 1653), in his "Patriarcha," pub in 1680, and by the High Church party generally about 1714, but opposed by Milton (1651), Algernon Sydney, and others

diving-bell (first mentioned, though obscurely, by Aristotle, about 325 B.C) was used in Europe about 1509 A D It is said to have been used on the coast of Mull, Scotland, in searching for the wreck of part of the Spanish Armada, before 1662. Halley (about 1716) greatly improved this machine, and was, it is said, the first who, by means of a diving-bell, set his foot on the ground at the bottom of the sea Smeaton made use of the diving-bell in improving Ramsgate harbor, 1779-88 Mr Spalding and his assistants going down in a diving-bell on the Irish coast were drowned, 1 June, 1783 The British man-of-war *Royal George*, sunk off Portsmouth in 1782, was first surveyed by means of a diving-bell, in May, 1817 Latterly it has been employed in submarine surveys and harbor works The "*talpa marina*," or sea-mole, a diving machine for laying down torpedoes, etc., being a cylinder provided with compressed air sufficient for 2 persons for 50 hours, was invented by Toselli, a Venetian, and was successfully tried in the bay of Naples, 26 Aug 1871 —*Diving-dress*, a close dress made by Mr Siebe about 1836, used by sir C W Pasley in 1838 M Cabirol, maker of one, died Dec 1874

Mr Fleuss invented a helmet with a mouthpiece into which he introduced enough oxygen to last 5 hours, and thus was enabled to remain under water several hours He exhibited his method at the Polytechnic Institution, London, Nov 1879, and at the Society of Arts, 6 May, 1880

divining rod (*virgula divina, baculatorius*), formed of wood or metal, was formerly believed, even by educated persons, to have the property of indicating the position of minerals and springs of water Instances were alleged in 1851 by Dr H Mayo, in his work on "Popular Superstitions"

divorce was permitted by the law of Moses (Deut xxiv. 1), 1151 B.C, but forbidden by Christ, except for unchastity (Matt v 31, 32) It was put in practice by Spurius Carvilius Ruga at Rome, 234 B.C At this time morals were so debased that 3000 prosecutions for adultery were enrolled Divorces are of two kinds one, *a vinculo matrimonii* (total divorce), the other, *a mensâ et thoro* (from board and bed). It was sought to make divorces easier in England in 1539. The Judicature act, 1873, constituted the probate, divorce and admiralty division of the High Court of Justice, with two judges SUPREME COURT, PROBATE

Bill to prevent women marrying their seducers brought into Parliament 1801
Commissioners on law of divorce issue their first report Apl 1857
In 1857 there had been in England, since the Reformation, 317 divorces by act of Parliament, in Scotland, by the law, 174 divorces since 1836, 1858–67, 1279 dissolutions of marriage, 213 judicial separations
From the establishment of the divorce court, to Mch 1859, 37 divorces had been granted out of 288 petitions, from Nov 1860, to July 1861, 164
By 20 and 21 Vict c 85, the jurisdiction of the ecclesiastical courts over divorce, etc, was abolished, and the Divorce and Matrimonial Causes court instituted, to consist of 3 judges, the judge of the Probate court to be one (if possible) "
A full court sat—lord Campbell, chief baron Pollock sir Cresswell Cresswell (judge of the Probate court)—when 5 marriages were dissolved 10 May, 1859
Act amended by acts passed in consequence of the increase of the business of the court 1858–60
An act respecting divorces in Scotland passed 1861
Divorce Amendment act passed 21 July, 1868
On appeal, the lords decide that action will lie for divorce from a wife insane (TRIALS 1870, Mordaunt case) 22 June, 1874
Legalized by the French republic, about 7000 divorces in Paris alone, 1793-94, prohibited by the civil code, but Napoleon divorced Josephine 16 Dec 1809, again prohibited, 1816, again legalized, with conditions, July, many suits Aug 1884

In the United States divorce is regulated by the states As a consequence the laws vary greatly, and confusion arises from their conflict. A man may be the lawful husband of one woman in one state, while the law of another state may hold him to be the husband of another The necessity of providing some uniform system was discussed, 1881 The violation of the marriage vow is, however, a cause for absolute divorce in all the states and territories having divorce laws South Carolina has no divorce laws According to the divorce statistics of the U S for 20 years ending 1886, there were 328,716 divorces granted, of which 129,382 were of couples with children, and 57,524 without. The causes were desertion, 126,676, adultery, 67,686, cruelty, 51,595, drunkenness, 13,866, neglect to provide, 7955.—A divorce bill for Victoria, Australia, having received the assent of the home government, the bishop of Victoria forbade the clergy marrying divorced persons, May, 1890

Dix's order. This celebrated order was issued by John A Dix, sec of the treasury, 1861, to Hemphill Jones, who was in New Orleans trying to prevent the seizure of the U S revenue cutter, the *Robert McClelland*, by the Louisiana state government Capt Breshwood was in command of the *McClelland*, and refused to take the vessel north as ordered, in anticipation of delivering it to the Louisiana government The order reads as follows:

"TREASURY DEPARTMENT "*Jan.* 29, 1861

"Tell lieut Caldwell to arrest capt. Breshwood assume command of the cutter, and obey the order I gave through you If capt Breshwood, after arrest, undertakes to interfere with the command of the cutter, tell lieut Caldwell to consider him as a mutineer, and treat him accordingly If any one attempts to haul down the American flag, shoot him on the spot "JOHN A DIX,
"Secretary of the Treasury"

Dixie's Land. Songs of the Civil War.

Dizier, St., N.E. France. Here a siege was sustained for 6 weeks against the army of the emperor Charles V., 1544. The allies here defeated Napoleon, 27 Jan. and 26 Mch. 1814.

Doce'tæ, a sect of the 1st century, said to have held that Jesus Christ was God, but that his body was an appearance, not a reality.

docks, artificial basins for the reception of ships for safety or repairing. Those for the safety of the ship are termed wet, and those for repairing dry, and these may be floating as well as stationary. The Athenian docks in the Piræus cost 1000 talents. The docks of ancient Rome (*navalia*) were attached to the emporium outside of the Porta Trigemina and were connected with the Tiber. The following are the principal commercial docks:

ENGLISH DOCKS.

Commercial docks, Rotherhithe, originated about 1660, covers in all 70 acres.
West India docks, commenced 3 Feb. 1800; opened 27 Aug. 1802, when the *Henry Addington*, West Indiaman, first entered them, decorated with the colors of the different nations of Europe.
London docks were commenced 26 June, 1802, and opened 20 Jan. 1805, Mr. Rennie superintending engineer; cost $7,500,000.
East India docks commenced 1803; opened 4 Aug. 1806; covers 32 acres.
St. Katharine's docks began 3 May, 1827; 2500 men were daily employed on them until they were opened, 25 Oct. 1828; covers 24 acres; cost over $10,000,000.
Royal Victoria docks (in Plaistow marshes) completed and opened Nov. 1855; great enlargement proposed July, 1876; completed and named Royal Albert docks by the duke and duchess of Connaught, 24 June, 1880.
Magnificent docks at Liverpool and Birkenhead erected 1810-57, at a cost of $20,500,000.
Milwall docks, near London, formerly opened, 14 Mch. 1868.
A great floating iron dry-dock, which cost $1,250,000, was launched at North Woolwich, 3 Sept. 1868, and towed from the Medway by 2 ships of war, 23 June, 1860, and arrived at the Bermudas (in 36 days), 30 July.
Construction of floating docks for repairing ships advocated by lord Brassey, Jan. 1887.
Erection of docks at Tilbury determined on 30 Sept. 1881; begun 8 July, 1882; opened 17 Apr. 1886.
New Barry docks, 7 miles west of Cardiff, Bristol channel (which with breakwater, etc.), cost $4,250,000; opened 18 July, 1889.

PRINCIPAL UNITED STATES DOCKS.

Boston, Mass., dry-dock, built 1833; cost $1,000,000.
Atlantic dock, Brooklyn, N. Y., completed 1851; covering 42 acres; cost nearly $2,000,000. Brooklyn, 1844.
Portland, Me., dry-dock.
Red Hook, Brooklyn, N. Y., dry-dock.
Norfolk, Va., dry-dock.
Savannah, Ga., dry-dock.
Mare island, Cal., dry-dock, has cost $3,000,000; not completed 1893.
Detroit, Mich., dry-dock, completed 1891; cost $200,000.
One building at Puget sound, Washington, larger than any yet built in the U. S.

doctor. Doctor of the church was a title given to Athanasius, Basil, Gregory Nazianzen, and Chrysostom in the Greek church; and to Jerome, Augustin, Ambrose, and Gregory the Great in the Latin church. Fathers. Afterwards the title was conferred on certain persons with distinguishing epithets—viz.: Thomas Aquinas (Angelicus), Bonaventura (Seraphicus), Alexander de Hales (Irrefragabilis), Duns Scotus (Subtilis), Roger Bacon (Mirabilis), William Occam (Singularis), Joseph Gerson (Christianissimus), Thomas Bradwardine (Profundus), and so on.—*Doctor of the Law* was a title of honor among the Jews. The degree of doctor was conferred in England, 8 John, 1207.—*Spelman.* Some give it an earlier date, referring it to the time of the venerable Bede and John de Beverley, the former of whom, it is said, first obtained the degree at Cambridge, in the 8th century.

Doctors' commons, the college for the professors of civil and canon law in the 8th century. In Feb. 1568, Dr. Henry Hervie, dean of the arches and master of Trinity hall (a seminary founded at Cambridge, Engl., chiefly for the study of the civil and canon laws), procured from the dean and chapter of the diocese of London a lease of Montjoy house and buildings in the parish of St. Benet, Paul's wharf, for the accommodation of the society. Other courts being held here, the whole place was called "Doctors' Commons." The original college was destroyed in the great fire of 1666; in 1672 it was rebuilt. After the great fire, until 1672, the society held its courts at Exeter house, in the Strand. It was incorporated by charter in June, 1768.—*Coote.* The buildings of the College of Advocates, which included all the courts of Doctors' Commons (arches, admiralty, consistory, etc.), were purchased by the Metropolitan Board of Works, and pulled down in Apr. 1867, for the new Queen Victoria street; some new buildings were erected. Till 1857 the causes taken cognizance of here were blasphemy, divorces, bastardy, adultery, penance, tithes, mortuaries, probate of wills, etc. The building in Knightrider street being dilapidated and too small, the wills were removed to Somerset house, where the office was opened 24 Oct. 1874. Civil law, Ecclesiastical Courts, etc.

doctor's mob. New York, 1788.

doctrinaires (*dok-tri-narz'*), a name given since 1814 to a class of politicians in France (Guizot, Molé, the duc de Broglie, and others), who upheld constitutional principles, in opposition to arbitrary monarchical power. The party came into office in 1830 under Louis Philippe, and fell with him in 1848. The term has been applied in England to the writers in the *Westminster Review* (1824 et seq.), Bentham, Molesworth, and others.

do'do (*Didus ineptus*), an extinct member of the order *Columbae.* The remains of this bird are found only on the island of Mauritius. It was incapable of flying, and stupid, and somewhat larger than the swan. It was exterminated about 1693. Our principal knowledge of it is based upon a few bones found, and drawings made in Holland, where it was brought alive before extermination.

Dodo'na, Epirus. The temple of Jupiter here, renowned for its ancient oracle, delivered by the sound of wind in a grove of oak trees, was destroyed by the Ætolians, 219 B.C. Foundation of the temple, etc., excavated by M. Carapanos, 1883.

dog. Buffon considers the shepherd's dog as "the root of the tree," as having naturally the greatest share of instinct. Dr. Gall asserts that a dog, taken from Vienna to England, escaped to Dover, got on a vessel, landed at Calais, accompanied a man to Mentz, and returned to Vienna.

Statute against dog-stealing, 10 Geo. III ... 1770
Use of dogs to draw carts, etc., abolished in London, 1839; in the United Kingdom ... 1854
Dog-tax imposed, 1796; again in 1808; 12s. a year realized 219,313*l.* ... 1866
Dog-tax repealed, 29 Mch. 1867; annual excise duty of 5s. imposed on all dogs more than 6 months old, to begin ... 5 Apr. 1867
Dog show in London, 1861; since 1862 at the Agricultural hall, Islington, the Crystal palace, and other places.
"Dogs' temporary home" opened, Hollingsworth street, London, N., 1861; removed to Battersea in 1871; about 2200 animals have been sheltered in a year.
As a nuisance, dogs at large unmuzzled in London ordered to be seized by the police ... July-27 Nov. 1868
New act, more stringent, passed ... 24 July, 1871
Dog licenses (annual 5s.) issued in financial year, 1871-72, produced 279,425*l.*; in 1875-76, 343,257*l.*; in 1876-77, 349,613*l.*; 1877-78, 372,699*l.*
Dogs licensed in United Kingdom: in 1866, 445,656; in 1876, 1,362,-176.
There are in England 12 packs of stag-hounds, containing 295 couples; 4 packs in Ireland, containing 100 couples. The largest pack is the queen's, 40 couples; master, the earl of Coventry; kennels at Ascot Heath. Of fox-hound packs there are 155 in England and Wales, containing 6239 couples: in Scotland, 9 packs with 326 couples, and in Ireland, 17 packs with 635 couples. There are also 124 packs of harries and beagles in England and Wales, with 1997 couples; 40 packs in Ireland with 512 couples, and 6 packs in Scotland with 116 couples. Thus more than 20,000 hounds are maintained exclusively for hunting in the United Kingdom.

dog-days (the Canicular period). The rising and setting of Sirius, or the dog-star, with the sun has been erroneously regarded as the cause of excessive heat and of consequent calamities. These days have been spoken of by the earliest observers. Hippocrates (450 B.C.) speaks of them as the hottest and most unhealthy part of summer, and Pliny says they began with the heliacal rising of Procyon on what is now 19 July, and this date has been widely accepted. But he also says the sun was then entering Leo, which would make the days begin 28 July. This has also been used as the starting-point. If the time is given from 3 July to 11 Aug. it is probably of Babylonian origin. Various durations from 30 to 54 days have been assigned to them.

doge or **duke.** Venice was first governed by a doge named Anafesto Paululio, or Paoluccio, 697. Venice. The Genoese chose their first doge, Simone Boccanegra, in 1339. Genoa.

Dogger-bank, a sand bank in the North sea, 170 miles in length, and average width 40 miles. Here an indecisive battle was fought between the British, under admiral sir Hyde Parker, and the Dutch 5 Aug 1781.

Doggett's coat and **badge.** BOAT-RACES

doit. A silver Scottish penny 12 made a penny sterling Some struck by Charles I and II are in cabinets The circulation of "doydekyns" (small Dutch coins) was prohibited in England by statute in 1415

dollar (Ger *Thaler*) Stamped Spanish dollars (value 4s 9d) were issued from the British mint in Mch 1797, but called in in Oct following The dollar is the unit of United States money It is coined in silver, formerly also in gold, and is worth 4s 1¼d. English money COIN AND COINAGE in the U S

dolphin, a cetaceous mammal of the genus *Delphinus delphis* Also the name of the caravel of Verrazzani, in which he entered the bay of New York in 1524, and of the U S despatch boat carrying president Cleveland while reviewing the navies of the world in New York harbor, 27 Apr 1893

Dom-boc or **Doom-book** (*Liber Judicialis*), the code of law compiled by king Alfred (871-901 A D) from the West Saxon collection of Ina and other sources.

Domesday, or **Doomsday, book** (*Domus Dei book—Stow*) (*Liber Censualis Angliæ*), a book of the general survey of England, commenced under William I, 1080 (or 1085), completed in 1086, designed as a register to determine the right in tenure of estates sir Martin Wright says "to discover the quantity of every man's fee, and to fix his homage," i e the question of military aid he was bound to furnish, and from it the question whether lands be ancient demesne or not is sometimes still decided The book, formerly kept in the chapter-house of Westminster, is now in the public record office It consists of two volumes, a greater and a less, applying to all counties of England except Northumberland, Durham, Westmoreland, and Cumberland "This Dome's-day Book was the tax-book of kinge William"—*Camden.* The taxes were levied by it till 13 Hen VIII, 1522, when a more accurate survey was taken, called by the people the "New Doomsday Book" It was printed in 4 vols. fol , with introductions, etc , 1783-1816 Photo-zincographic copies of various counties have been published since 1861. In Sept 1872, the British government ordered a return of all owners of land in England and Wales—a new domesday-book, to be made by the local government board

The return for Sc[illegible]-73, was published by government, Apr 1874, for England and Wales (exclusive of the metropolis) in 1875, for Ireland, 1876

domestic economy, or the study of food and clothing, was introduced into the government educational department of England in 1874, the congresses began at Birmingham, 16 July, 1877, Manchester, 26 June, 1878, London (Society of Arts), 26 June, 1879, 21 June, 1881

Domin'go, St. HAYTI

Domin'ica, one of the Leeward islands, West Indies, discovered by Columbus in his second voyage, and so called because first sighted on Sunday, 3 Nov 1493, was taken by the British in 1761, and confirmed to them by the peace of Paris, Feb 1763 The French took Dominica in 1778, but restored it at the peace of 1783 Their admiral Villeneuve ineffectually attacked it in 1805. It suffered damage by a hurricane in 1806 Pop 1892, 29,500, area 291 sq miles Capital Roseau.

domin'ical letter, noting the Lord's day, or Sunday The 7 days of the week, reckoned as beginning on 1 Jan , are designated by the first 7 letters of the alphabet, A (1 Jan), B, C, D, E, F, G; and the one of these which denotes Sunday is the dominical letter If the year begin on Sunday, A is the dominical letter, if on Monday, G, if on Tuesday, F, and so on. To find the dominical letter call New year's day A, the next B, and so on to the first Sunday, and the letter that answers to it is the dominical letter, in leap-years count 2 letters The letter for 1893, A; 1894, G, 1895, F, 1896, E, D (leap-year).

Domin'icans, formerly a powerful religious order (called in France Jacobins, from Rue St. Jacques (Jacobus), where they first established themselves, and in England Black friars), founded to put down the Albigenses and other heretics by St. Dominic (b. Old Castile 1170, d. Bologne 1221; canonized by pope Gregory IX 1234), approved by Innocent III in 1215, and confirmed by Honorius III in 1216, under St Augustin's rules and the founder's particular constitution In 1220 they declared for complete poverty, renouncing the possession of property in every form, and begging for daily bread In 1276 the corporation of London gave the Dominicans two streets near the Thames, where they erected a large convent, in the neighborhood still called Blackfriars. A Dominican establishment at Haverstock hill, near London, was consecrated 16 Oct 1867

Dominion of Canada. CANADA.

dom'inos. This game has been variously traced to Greek, Hebrew, and Chinese origin Early in the 18th century it was introduced into France from Italy, and the Cafe de l Opera in Paris was long the headquarters for expert players. From France it spread to Germany, England, and America

"Don Quixote" (*don kee-ho'-ta*), by Saavedra Miguel de Cervantes (b 1547, d 1616) The first part appeared in 1605, the second in 1608, first complete edition, 1637 It is said that upwards of 12 000 copies of the first part were circulated before the second was printed.—*Watts* Best English edition, Ormsby's, 4 vols, London 1885

Do'natists, an ancient strict sect, formed about 313-18, by an African bishop, Donatus, jealous of Cæcilian, bishop of Carthage, which became extinct in the 7th century They held that the Father was above the Son, the Son above the Holy Ghost Their discipline was severe, and those who joined them were rebaptized

Donauwerth, a town of Bavaria, where French and Bavarians were defeated by Marlborough, 2 July, 1704.

Don'caster, Yorkshire, Engl , the Roman *Danum*, the Saxon *Donne ceastre*. The races here (held annually in September) began about 1703 RACES

Donelson, Fort. FORT DONELSON.

Doomsday-book. DOMESDAY-BOOK

Dorchester, Dorsetshire, Engl , the Roman *Durnovaria*, the Saxon *Dorneceaster*, with remains of a Roman theatre and a British camp Here Jeffrey held his 'bloody assize" (after Monmouth's rebellion), 3 Sept 1685

Dorchester Heights. MASSACHUSETTS, 1776.

Dorians, Greeks, who claimed descent from Dorus, son of Hellen. GREECE. The return of the Dorians, named Heraclidæ, to the Peloponnesus, is dated 1104 B.C. They sent out many colonies From this race is named the Doric architecture, the second of the 5 orders, and the Doric dialect.

Dorking, Surrey, Engl, an ancient town; the manor given by the Conqueror to earl Fitzwarren Imaginary "Battle of Dorking," in which the German invaders totally defeat the British army is a clever article attributed to col George Chesney, in *Blackwood's Magazine* for May, 1871. It occasioned much controversy and several pamphlets

Dormans, a town of N.E France. The Huguenots and allies, under Montmorency, were here defeated by the duke of Guise, 10 Oct 1575.

Dorr's rebellion. From 1663, the people of Rhode Island had lived under a charter from Charles II., according to which only those owning a certain amount of property could vote. In 1841 the desire to change this provision gave rise to 2 parties, the "Suffrage" and the "Law and Order." Each party determined to secure the administration of affairs, and each elected its own state officers. Thomas W. Dorr was chosen governor by the "Suffrage" party, and took possession of the state arsenal, the militia were called out, and he was compelled to flee In a second attempt the party was overpowered by U. S. troops, and Dorr was arrested, brought to trial, convicted of treason, and sentenced to imprisonment for life, but some time after he was pardoned. A free constitution was adopted in the meantime by the people, and is now in force. RHODE ISLAND.

Dort or **Dordrecht,** an ancient town in Holland By an inundation of the Meuse in 1421, on the breaking-down of the dikes, in the territory of Dordrecht 10,000 persons perished, and more than 100,000 round Dollart, in Friesland, and in Zealand.—The independence of the 13 provinces was de-

Dresden china was invented by John Frederick Böttger (or Böttcher), an apothecary's boy, about 1709 He died 13 Mch 1719

dress. The attire of the Hebrew women is censured in Isaiah iii, about 760 B.C Excess in dress among the early [illegible] was restrained by laws, and in England by numerous statutes, in 1363, 1465, 1570, etc —*Stow* F W Fairholt's "Costume in England" (1846) contains a history of dress, with illustrations from MSS., the works of Strutt, etc J R Planché's elaborate "Cyclopædia of Costume" first appeared in 1876 A "dress-making company" was established in London, 6 Feb 1865, to improve the condition of workwomen

Sir Walter Raleigh wore a white satin pinked vest close sleeved to the wrist, and over the body a doublet finely flowered, embroidered with pearls, in the feather of his hat a large ruby and pearl drop at the bottom of the sprig in place of a button His breeches with his stockings and ribbon garters, fringed at the end, all white, and buff shoes which on great court days, were gorgeously covered with precious stones worth over 6000*l*, he had armor of solid silver, with sword and belt blazing with diamonds, rubies, and pearls

King James's favorite, the duke of Buckingham, had diamonds tacked so loosely on that he could shake a few off on the ground and obtained all the fame he desired from the pickers up who were generally *les dames de la cour*

Court dress of civilians, previously that of the time of the Georges, was modified by the lord chamberlain, lord Sydney, in 1869 Bloomer costume BLOOMER

Dreux, a town of N W France. Here Montmorenci defeated the Huguenots under Condé, 19 Dec 1562 Here is the burying-place of the Orleans family since 1816 The bodies of king Louis Philippe and his family were brought here from England and buried, 9 June, 1876

Dreyfus Case. FRANCE, Dec 1894–99

Drogheda (*droh'-he-da*), E Ireland, formerly Tredagh, a borough of great importance, having the privilege of coining money Here was passed POYNINGS' LAW in 1494 An act of Edward VI was passed for the foundation of a university here The town was besieged several times between 1641 and 1691, and Cromwell took it by storm, and put the governor, sir A Aston, and the whole of the garrison to the sword, 12 Sept 1649 More than 3000 men, mostly English, perished. It surrendered to William III in 1690.

Drontheim, ~~capital~~ of Norway, founded by Olaf I about 998

drowning, an ancient punishment. The Britons inflicted death by drowning in a quagmire, before 450 B.C.—*Stow* It is said to have been inflicted on 80 intractable bishops near Nicomedia, 370 A D, and to have been adopted as a punishment in France by Louis XI. The wholesale drownings of royalists in the Loire at Nantes, by command of the brutal Carrier, Nov 1793, were termed *Noyades* 94 priests were drowned at one time. Carrier was condemned to death Dec 1794. Societies for the recovery of drowning persons were first instituted in Holland in 1767 The second society is said to have been formed at Milan in 1768, the third at Hamburg in 1771, the fourth at Paris in 1772, and the fifth in London in 1774. The motto of the Royal Humane Society in England is *Lateat scintillula forsan* ("A small spark may perhaps lie hid"). François Texier of Dunkerque, after saving 30 lives at different times, was drowned in a storm, Oct 1871 LIFE-SAVING SERVICE

Druids, priests among the ancient Germans, Gauls, and Britons, so named from their veneration for the oak (Brit. *derw*) They administered sacred things, were the interpreters of the gods, and supreme judges They headed the Britons who opposed Cæsar's first landing, 55 B C, and were exterminated by the Roman governor, Suetonius Paulinus, 61 A D

drum. Its invention is ascribed to Bacchus, who, according to Polyænus, "gave his signals of battle with cymbals and drums" It was used by the Egyptians, and brought by the Moors into Spain, 1713.—The drum, or drum capstan, for weighing anchors, was invented by sir S Morland in 1685.—*Anderson*

Drumclog, a hill in W. Scotland Here the Covenanters defeated Graham of Claverhouse on 1 June, 1679. The conflict is described by sir Walter Scott in "Old Mortality."

Drummond light. LIME-LIGHT.

drunkards were excommunicated in the early church, 59 (1 Cor. v. 11) In England, a canon law forbade drunkenness in the clergy, 747 Constantine, king of Scots, punished it with death, 870 By 21 James I c 7, 1625, a drunkard was fined 5 shillings, or set 6 hours in the stocks TEETOTALER, TEMPERANCE

A society for promoting legislation for the control and cure of habitual drunkards formed in England — 22 Sept 1876
Dr Leslie E Keeley's hypodermic injections of bichloride of gold as a cure for habitual drunkenness, first used in the United States — 1891

Drury-lane theatre derives its origin from a cockpit, made a theatre under James I It was rebuilt and called the Phœnix, and Charles II granted an exclusive patent to Thomas Killigrew, 25 Apr 1662 The actors were called "the king's servants," and 10 of them, called "gentlemen of the great chamber," had an annual allowance of 10 yards of scarlet cloth, with lace. THEATRES

Druses, a warlike people in the mountains of Lebanon, originally a fanatical Mahometan sect which arose in Egypt about 996, and fled to Palestine to avoid persecution They now retain hardly any of the religion of their ancestors they eat pork and drink wine, and do not practise circumcision, pray, or fast In the middle of 1860, the Druses attacked their neighbors the MARONITES, whom they massacred, it was said, without regard to age or sex Peace was made in July, meantime a religious fury seized the Mahometans of neighboring cities, and a general massacre of Christians ensued Fuad Pacha with Turkish troops, and gen Hautpoul with French auxiliaries, invaded Lebanon in Aug and Sept. The Druses surrendered, giving up their chiefs, Jan 1861 DAMASCUS, SYRIA

Dry Tortu'gas (Sp *tortuga*, a tortoise), a group of several small barren islands, about 40 miles west of the most westerly of the Florida Keys They belong to Monroe county, Fla, and served for a place of imprisonment for certain offenders during the United States civil war Lat 24° 38' N, lon 82° 53' W BOOTH'S CONSPIRACY

du'alin, a new explosive substance (said to be from 4 to 10 times more powerful than gunpowder), composed of varying proportions of cellulose (woody fibre), nitro-starch, nitro-mannite, and nitro-cellulose, invented by Carl Ditmar a Prussian, and made known in 1870 This name is also given to another explosive compound, invented by Mr Nobel, composed of ammonia and sawdust, acted on by nitro-sulphuric acid

Dublin, capital of Ireland, anciently called Ashcled, said to have been built 140 Auliana, daughter of Alpinus, a lord or chief among the Irish, having been drowned at the ford where now Whitworth bridge is built, he changed the name to Auliana, by Ptolemy called Eblana (afterwards corrupted into Dublana) Alpinus is said to have brought "the then rude hill into the form of a town," about 155 Pop 1891, 254,709 city proper, 361,891 metropolitan police district IRELAND, TRINITY COLLEGES.

Christianity established by St. Patrick, and St Patrick's cathedral founded — about 448
Dublin environed with walls by the Danes — 798
Named by king Edgar in the preface to his charter "Nobilissima Civitas" — 964
Battle of Clontarf — 23 Apr 1014
Dublin taken by Raymond le Gros, 1170, for Henry II, who soon after arrives — 1171
Charter granted by this king — 1173
Christ church built by Danes, 1038, rebuilt — about 1180–1225
Slaughter of 500 British by Irish citizens near Dublin (CULLEN'S WOOD) — 1209
Assembled Irish princes swear allegiance to king John — 1210
Dublin castle founded by Henry de Loundres, 1205, finished — 1213
John de Decer first provost, Richard de St Olave and John Stakebold first bailiffs (MAYOR) — 1308
Thomas Cusack first mayor — 1409
Besieged by the son of the earl of Kildare, lord deputy — 1500
Christ church made a deanery and chapter by Henry VIII — 1541
Bailiff changed to sheriffs, John Ryan and Thomas Comyn first, — 1548
Trinity college founded — 1591
Charter granted by James I — 1609
Convocation frames 39 articles of religion — 1614
Besieged by the marquess of Ormond, defeated at battle of Rathmines — 2 Aug. 1649
Cromwell arrives in Dublin with 9000 foot and 400 horse, Aug — "
Chief magistrate styled lord mayor — 1665
Royal hospital, Kilmainham, founded — 1683
James II arrives in Dublin, 24 Mch, proclaimed — 4 May, 1689
Lamps first erected in the city — 1698
St. Patrick's spire erected (ST PATRICK) — 1749
Act for a general pavement of the city — 1773
Royal Exchange begun 1769, opened — 1779
Order of St Patrick instituted — 1783

Bank of Ireland instituted (BANK) 1783
Police established by statute 1786
Custom house begun 1781, opened 1791
Dublin Library instituted .
Dublin lighted with gas 5 Oct 1825
Phœnix Park murders (IRELAND) 6 May, 1882
Statue of D O'Connell unveiled and the exhibition of Irish arts and manufactures (not patronized by queen Victoria and loyalists) opened by the lord mayor Dawson. 15 Aug 1882, closed 6 Jan 1883
Burial of Charles S Parnell in Glasnevin cemetery 11 Oct 1891

Dublin, Archbishopric of It is supposed that the bishopric of Dublin was founded by St Patrick in 448 Gregory, bishop in 1121, became archbishop in 1152 It was united to Glandalagh in 1214 George Browne, an Augustin friar of London (deprived by queen Mary in 1554), was the first Protestant archbishop Dublin has 2 cathedrals, Christ church and St Patrick's

duc'at, a coin so called because struck by dukes.—*Johnson* First coined by Longinus governor of Italy —*Procopius* First struck in the duchy of Apulia, 1140 —*Du Cange* Coined by Robert, king of Sicily, in 1240

ducking-stool. CUCKING-STOOL

duelling took its rise from the judicial combats of the Celtic nations. The first formal duel in England, between William count d'Eu and Godfrey Baynard, took place 1096 Duelling in civil matters was forbidden in France, 1305 Francis I challenged the emperor Charles V in vain, 1528 The fight with small-swords was introduced into England, 1587 Proclamation that no person should be pardoned who killed another in a duel, 1679 Duelling was checked in the British army, 1792, and has been abolished in England by the influence of public opinion, aided by the late prince-consort A society "for the discouraging of duelling" was established in 1845 "The British Code of Duel," pub in 1824, was approved by the duke of Wellington and others. COMBAT, JARNAC

MEMORABLE DUELS IN EUROPE

Between the duke of Hamilton and lord Mohun, fought 15 Nov 1712
[Fought with small swords in Hyde park Lord Mohun was killed on the spot, and the duke died of his wounds while carried to his coach] Attempt made at this time to suppress duelling, bill passed in the House of Commons to its 3d reading—defeated
Lord Byron killed Mr Chaworth 26 Jan 1765
Lord Townsend wounded lord Bellamont 1 Feb 1773
Comte d'Artois wounded by duc de Bourbon, at Paris, 21 Mch 1778
Charles James Fox wounded by Mr Adam 30 Nov 1779
Rev Mr Allen killed Lloyd Dulany 18 June, 1782
Mr M'Keon killed George N Reynolds, 1787, executed, 16 Feb 1788
Duke of York and col Lennox, afterwards duke of Richmond (for an insignificant cause) 26 May, 1789
Mr Curran and major Hobart 1 Apr 1790
Wm Pitt and George Tierney 27 May, 1798
Henry Grattan wounded Isaac Corry 15 Jan 1800
M de Granpré and M Le Pique, in balloons, near Paris and the latter killed 3 May, 1808
Major Campbell and capt. Boyd, latter killed (former hanged, 2 Oct. 1808) 23 June, "
Lord Castlereagh wounded Geo Canning 21 Sept. 1809
Capt Stackpole (of Engl frigate *Statira*) and lieut Cecil (be cause of words spoken 4 years previously), the captain killed, Apr 1814
D O'Connell killed Mr D'Esterre 31 Jan 1815
Mr O'Connell and Mr Peel, an affair, no meeting 31 Aug "
Mr Grattan and the earl of Clare 7 June, 1820
Rev Mr Hodson wounded Mr Grady Aug 1827
Duke of Wellington and the earl of Winchelsea, no injury, 21 Mch 1829
Sir Colquhoun Grant and lord Seymour, no fatality 29 May, 1835
Earl of Cardigan and capt Tuckett, 2 shots each, the latter wounded (the earl acquitted in House of Lords, 16 Feb. 1841), 12 Sept. 1840
Duc de Grammont Caderousse kills Mr Dillon at Paris, for a newspaper attack Oct 1862
Paul de Cassagnac and M Lissagaray, journalists (latter run through) 4 Sept 1868
Don Enrique de Bourbon killed by the duc de Montpensier, near Madrid, after much provocation 12 Mch 1870
Paul de Cassagnac (wounded) and M Ranc, Paris 7 July, 1873
Prince Soutza kills N Ghika at Fontainebleau 27 Nov "
MM Gambetta and De Fortou, neither hit 21 Nov 1878
Gen Boulanger (seriously wounded) and M Floquet 13 July, 1888

IN THE UNITED STATES

First duel in America, between 2 serving men, Plymouth, Mass (MASSACHUSETTS) 1621
Button Gwinnett and gen McIntosh . 1777
Gen Conway and gen Cadwallader (CONWAY CABAL) 1778
De Witt Clinton and John Swartwout . 1802
De Witt Clinton and gen Dayton . 1803
Alexander Hamilton (killed) and Aaron Burr (NEW YORK) 1804
Gen Jackson and col Dickenson, Dickenson killed 1806
Henry Clay and Humphrey Marshall 1808
Col Benton and gen Jackson Sept 1813
Commodore Decatur and commodore Barron (Decatur killed) (UNITED STATES) 22 Mch 1820
Henry Clay and John Randolph (UNITED STATES) 1826
Graves and Cilley (killed) congressmen (UNITED STATES), 24 Feb. 1838
Preston S Brooks, S C challenges Anson Burlingame, member of Congress from Massachusetts (UNITED STATES) 1856
David C. Broderick, U S senator from California, mortally wounded by Judge Terry (UNITED STATES) 16 Sept 1859
Col Calhoun and major Rhett (confederate officers), Calhoun killed, at Charleston, S C 1862
[Gen Beauregard refused to enforce military law against Rhett who was promoted to Calhoun's place]

duke (from Lat *dux*, a leader) In Saxon times, the commanders of English armies were called dukes, *duces.—Camden.* In Gen xxxvi some of Esau's descendants are termed *dukes. Duke-duke* was a title of the house of Sylvia, in Spain, from its many duchies

Edward the Black Prince made duke of Cornwall 17 Mch 1337
Robert de Vere created marquess of Dublin and duke of Ireland 9 Rich II 1385
Robert III created David, prince of Scotland, duke of Rothsay, afterwards a title of the king's eldest son, 1398, now borne by the prince of Wales
Cosmo de' Medici created grand duke of Tuscany, the first of the rank, by pope Pius V 1569

Dulcigno (*dool-cheen'-yō*), a port in Albania, on the Adriatic

Taken by Turks . 1571
In the 17th century a den of pirates, and residence of Sabbatai Zewi a Smyrnese Jew who declared himself the Messiah, but became Mahometan, d 1676
Taken by Venetians and held for a short time 1722
Montenegrins take it by storm, but give it up 1878
Assigned to them by the Berlin conference June, July, 1880
Turks expelled by 8000 Albanians about 18 Sept "
Sultan cedes it to Montenegro 12 Oct "
Dervish Pacha repulses Albanians 22 Nov, occupies it 24 Nov, surrenders it to the Montenegrins 26, 27 Nov "

dumb. DEAF AND DUMB

Dumblane or **Dunblane,** Perth, Scotland, an ancient city, near which was the battle of Sheriffmuir, between royalists under duke of Argyll, and Scots rebels under earl of Mar, 13 Nov 1715 Both claimed victory

Dunbar', Haddington, Scotland Here Warrenne, earl of Surrey, 27 Apr 1296, defeated John Baliol with his Scots. Near here, also, Cromwell crushed the Scots of Charles II, 3 Sept. 1650

"Dun'ciad," satirical poem by Alexander Pope, was pub in 1728.

Dundalk, Louth, Ireland. On 5 Oct 1318, at Fougbard, near this place, was defeated and slain Edward Bruce, who had invaded Ireland in 1315 Its fortifications were destroyed in 1641 It was taken by Cromwell in 1649. Here cambric manufacture was first established in Ireland by artisans from France in 1727.

Dundee, E Scotland, on the Tay On a site given by William the Lion (reigned 1165-1214) his brother David, earl of Huntingdon, built or strengthened the castle, and built a church, whose tower, 156 feet high, still remains The town was taken by the English in 1385, pillaged by Montrose, 1645, stormed by Monk in 1651 Claverhouse, viscount Dundee (killed 1689), had a house here Population in 1861, 90,-425, in 1871, 118,974

Tay bridge completed Aug 1877, opened 31 May, 1878, destroyed by a gale (between 80 and 90 lives lost), 7 15 P M (BRIDGES) 28 Dec. 1879
New university founded by sir D Baxter, professor appointed Nov 1882. Endowed by Miss Mary Ann Baxter, sister of sir David, 1882 (she d. 19 Dec. 1884), college opened by earl of Dalhousie 5 Oct. 1883

Dungan-hill, Ireland Here the English army, under col. Jones, defeated the Irish, 6000 said to have been slain, the English loss inconsiderable, 8 Aug 1647.

Dunkers or **Dunkards.** TUNKERS.

Dunkirk, a town on strait of Dover, extreme north of France, founded 7th century; taken by the Spaniards, Sept. 1652, and retaken by the English and French after Turenne defeated them under Condé on the dunes, 14 June, 1658, and given to the English, 25 June following It was sold by Charles II for 500,000*l* to Louis XIV, 17 Oct., restored 1662, was one of the best-fortified ports of France, but the works were demolished under the treaty of Utrecht in 1713, in 1783 ey were rebuilt. The duke of York attacked Dunkirk, but is driven away by Hoche, with loss, 7 Sept. 1793. It was ide a free port in 1826.

Dunmow, a town of Essex, Engl., famous for the tene of the manor (made by Robert Fitz-Walter, 1244), "that atever married couple will go to the priory, and, kneeling 2 sharp-pointed stones, will swear that they have not arrelled nor repented of their marriage within a year and lay after its celebration, shall receive a flitch of bacon."

rliest recorded claim for the bacon was 1445, and up to 1855 it is said to have been claimed only 5 times.
st claimants, before 1855, John Shakeshanks and wife, 20 June, 1751, sold slices to witnesses of the ceremony (5000 persons).
tches awarded to Mr. and Mrs. Barlow of Chipping-Ongar, and chevalier Chatelaine and wife, 19 July, 1855.
rd of the manor opposed the revival; but W. Harrison Ainsworth, the novelist, and some friends, defrayed the expense and superintended the ceremonies.
ard in 1860; 9 July, 1873; 17 July, 1876, to James Henry and Mary Boosey; to others, 23 July, 1877.

Dunse, a town of S. Scotland. Here, 18 June, 1639, arles I., by treaty, acceded to the demands of the Scots mmission to disband their army. Disputes arose, and the aty was not carried into effect.

Dunsinane, Perthshire, Scotland. On this hill was e battle between king Macbeth, formerly thane of Glamis, d Siward, earl of Northumberland, 27 July, 1054. Edward e Confessor had sent Siward on behalf of Malcolm III., ose father, Duncan, the usurper had murdered. Macbeth s defeated, and it was said was pursued to Lumphanan, in erdeenshire, and there slain, 1056 or 1057.

"Macbeth shall never vanquished be, until
Great Birnam wood to high Dunsinane hill
Shall come against him."
—*Shakespeare*, "Macbeth," act iv. sc. i.

Duomo. MILAN.

Dupes, Day of, 11 Nov. 1630, when Richelieu energetlly and adroitly frustrated the plan for his ruin formed by een Marie de Medicis, Gaston, duke of Orleans, and others, ring the king's illness.

Dupplin, a town of Perthshire, Scotland. Here Edrd Baliol and English allies defeated Scots under earl of ir, 11 Aug. 1332, obtaining the crown for 3 months.

Duquesne (*du-kain'*), Fort. FORT DUQUESNE; PENNSYLVANIA, 1753, '54, '55, '56, '58; VIRGINIA, 1753, '54, '55.

durbar, an East Indian term for an audience-chamber reception. On 18 Oct. 1864, at a durbar at Lahore, the vicey of India, sir John Lawrence, received 604 illustrious princes d chieftains of the northwest province, magnificently clothed, hers since.

Durham, Engl., an ancient city, the *Dunholme* of the xons, and *Durême* of the Normans. The bishopric was ought, 995, from Chester-le-street, whither it had been transred from Lindisfarne, or Holy Island, on the coast of Northiberland in 875, on an invasion of the Danes. The bones of Cuthbert, the 6th bishop, were brought from Lindisfarne d interred in Durham cathedral. This see, deemed the hest in England, was valued in the king's books at 2821*l*. esent income 8000*l*.

llege founded (abolished at the Reformation) 1290
ar Durham was fought the decisive battle of Neville's Cross STRIKES) .... 17 Oct. 1346
rham ravaged by Malcolm of Scotland, 1070; occupied by northern rebels 1569
Scots 1640
omwell quartered Scotch prisoners in the cathedral 1650
omwell established a college, 1657; which was suppressed at the Restoration 1660
latine privileges, granted the bishop by the Danish Northumbrian prince Guthrum, taken by the crown .... June, 1836
esent university established in 1831; opened Oct. 1833; chartered .... June, 1837
hedral renovated; reopened .... 18 Oct. 1876

Durham letter. PAPAL AGGRESSION.

dust and disease. In a lecture, prof. Tyndall, at the yal Institution, London, 21 Jan. 1870, demonstrated the presce of organic matters in the dust of the atmosphere in conmity with the experiments of Pasteur and other eminent ilosophers. The agency of dust in promoting fires and exosions was asserted by Faraday in relation to coal-mines in 15, and by Rankine and MacAdam in relation to flour-mills in 1872. Atkins's dust-converting apparatus set up on Ben-Nevis, Scotland, Feb. 1890. GERM THEORY.

Dustin, Hannah, capture of. MASSACHUSETTS, 1697.

Dutch republic. HOLLAND.

duties. CUSTOMS, REVENUE, TARIFF.

duum'viri, 2 Roman patricians appointed by Tarquin the Proud, 520 B.C., to take care of the books of the Sibyls, supposed to contain the fate of the Roman empire. The books were buried in a chest under the capitol. The number of keepers was increased to 10 (decemviri), 365 B.C., afterwards to 15; the added 5 called *quinque viri*.

dwarfs, ancient. Philetas of Cos, about 330 B.C., a poet and grammarian, said to have carried weights in his dress to prevent his being blown away. He was preceptor to Ptolemy Philadelphus.—*Ælian*. Julia, niece of Augustus, had a dwarf named Coropas, 2 feet and a hand's-breadth high; and Andromeda, a freed-maid of Julia's, was of the same height.—*Pliny*. Aug. Cæsar exhibited in plays a man not 2 feet in stature.—*Sueton.* Alypius of Alexandria, a logician and philosopher, was but 1 foot 5½ inches high.—*Vos. Instit.*

MODERN DWARFS.

John d'Estrix of Mechlin was brought to the duke of Parma in 1592, when he was 35 years of age, having a long beard. He was skilled in languages, and not more than 3 feet high.
Geoffrey Hudson, an English dwarf, when a youth, 18 inches high, was served in a cold pie to the king and queen by the duchess of Buckingham in 1626. He challenged Mr. Crofts, but the latter came armed with a squirt. At another time the dwarf shot an antagonist dead, 1653.
Count Borowlaski, a Polish gentleman of great accomplishments, well known in England, where he resided for many years, was born Nov. 1739. His height was, at 1 year of age, 14 inches; at 6, 17 inches; at 20, 33 inches; and at 30, 39 inches. He had a sister named Anastasia, 7 years younger, and so much shorter that she could stand under his arm. He visited many courts of Europe, and died in England in 1837.
Charles Stratton (gen. Tom Thumb), an American, exhibited in England, 1846. In Feb. 1863, in New York, when 25 years old and 31 inches high, he married Lavinia Warren, aged 21, 32 inches high. He, his wife and child, and commodore Nutt, another dwarf, went to England in Dec. 1864.
Mr. Collard, aged 22, smaller than Stratton, sang at concerts in London, and was termed the "Pocket Sims Reeves," May, June, 1878.
Several dwarfs (said to be smaller than the preceding) exhibited at the Westminster aquarium, July, 1878.
Che-mah, a Chinese, 42 years old, 25 inches high, exhibited at the Westminster aquarium, 11 June, 1880.
Lucia Zarate, born 2 Jan. 1863, in Mexico; height 20 inches, weight 4¾ lbs.
Gen. Mite (Francis Joseph Flynn), born 2 Oct. 1864, in New York state; height 21 inches, weight 9 lbs.; exhibited in Piccadilly, London, 22 Nov. 1880 et seq. Exhibited in New York in company with the preceding, under the collective term of "The Midgets," 1879 et seq.
Gen. Mite married Milly Edwards, weight 7 lbs., at Manchester, Engl., 28 May, 1884.

dyeing is attributed to the Tyrians, about 1500 B.C. The English are said to have sent fine goods to be dyed in Holland till the art was brought to them, probably in 1608. "2 dyers of Exeter were flogged for teaching their art *in the north*" (of England), 1628. A statute against abuses in dyeing passed in 1783. The art has been greatly improved by chemical research. A discovery of dr. Stenhouse in 1848 led to M. Marnas procuring *mauve* from lichens; and dr. Hofmann's production of aniline from coal-tar has led to the invention of a number of beautiful dyes (mauve, magenta, red, green, black, etc.). ANILINE.

Dyer, Mary, Case of. MASSACHUSETTS, 1656-60.

dy'namite, a portable explosive invented by Alfred Nobel about 1866, consisting of 25 parts of silicious earth saturated with 75 parts of NITRO-GLYCERINE. It is useful in mining, and was tried and approved at Merstham, 14 July, 1868. Its manufacture is very dangerous. Dynamite which cannot be frozen invented by Edward Liebert of Berlin, reported Aug. 1890. CANNON.

dynamo-electric machines. ELECTRICITY.

Dzoungaria or **Soongaria,** a region of Central Asia, north of China, with about 2,000,000 inhabitants—fierce, warlike Mahometans. After being long tributary to China, they rebelled in 1864, massacred the Chinese residents, and set up Abel Oghlan as sultan. As he was unable to restrain predatory attacks upon the Russians, the czar declared war in Apr. 1871. After a brief campaign in May and June, and several defeats, the sultan surrendered to gen. Kolpakoviskie, 4 July, and the country was annexed to Russia.

E

eagle. The standard of the eagle was borne by the Persians at Cunaxa, 401 B.C. The Romans carried gold and silver eagles as ensigns, sometimes represented with a thunderbolt in the talons, on the point of a spear, 102 B.C. Charlemagne added the second head to the eagle for his arms, to denote that the empires of Rome and Germany were united in him, 802 A.D. The eagle was the standard of Napoleon I. and Napoleon III., as it is now of Austria, Russia, and Prussia.—The great seal of the UNITED STATES, adopted 20 June, 1782, shows a shield of 13 perpendicular red and white stripes, upholding a blue field. This shield is borne on the breast of the American eagle (bald), displayed proper, holding in his dexter talon an olive branch, and in his sinister a bundle of 13 arrows, and in his beak a scroll inscribed with the motto, E PLURIBUS UNUM.—An ancient coin of Ireland, of a base metal, current in the first years of Edward I., about 1272, was so named from the figure impressed upon it.—The United States gold coinage of eagles, half-eagles, and quarter-eagles, began 6 Dec. 1792; an eagle is of the value of $10. COIN and COINAGE.

earl. Old Norse, *earl, jarl*, chief, nobleman; Fr. *compte*, from Lat. *comes; Engl. count;* the latter title introduced into England at the Norman conquest, and so long as the Norman-French continued to be spoken, earls were styled counts; hence the term countess as the feminine of earl. Earls were the highest rank in England until Edward III. created dukes in 1337 and 1351, and Richard II. created marquesses (1385), both ranking above earls. Alfred bore the title of earl as synonymous with king. William Fitz-Osborn was made earl of Hereford by William the Conqueror, 1066. Gilchrist was created earl of Angus, in Scotland, by king Malcolm III., in 1037, and sir John de Courcy was created baron of Kinsale and earl of Ulster in Ireland, by Henry II., 1181.

Earl marshal of England, the 8th great officer of state. This office, until it was made hereditary, passed by grant from the king. Gilbert de Clare was created lord marshal by king Stephen, 1135. The last lord marshal was John Fitz-Alan, lord Maltravers.—*Camden.* Richard II., in 1397, granted letters-patent to the earl of Nottingham as earl marshal. In 1672, Charles II. granted to Henry, lord Howard, the dignity of hereditary earl marshal. The earl marshal's court was abolished in 1641. HOWARD.

Earl marischal of Scotland was an officer who commanded the cavalry, whereas the constable commanded the whole army; but they seem to have had a joint command, as all orders were addressed to "our constable and marischal." The office was never out of the Keith family. It was reversed at the Union, and when the heritable jurisdictions were bought, it reverted to the crown, being forfeited by the rebellion of George Keith, earl marischal, in 1715.

There are 118 English earls, 42 Scotch, and 63 Irish.—*Whitaker*, 1892.

ear-rings were worn by Jacob's family, 1732 B.C. (Gen. xxxv. 4).

earth. GLOBE.

earthquake, a trembling or shaking of the ground, produced by subterranean forces. Anaxagoras supposed that earthquakes were produced by subterraneous clouds bursting into lightning, which shook the vaults that confined them, 435 B.C.—*Diog. Laert.* Kircher, Des Cartes, and others supposed that there were many vast cavities underground which have a communication with each other, some of which abound with water, others with exhalations arising from inflammable substances, as nitre, bitumen, sulphur, etc. Drs. Stukeley and Priestley attributed earthquakes to electricity. Some are probably due to steam generated by subterraneous heat; others to a contraction of the earth's crust. An elaborate catalogue of earthquakes (from 1606 B.C. to 1842 A.D.), with commentaries on the phenomena, by R. and J. W. Mallet, was published by the British Association in 1858. In 1860 the velocity of their propagation was estimated by J. Brown at between 470 and 530 feet per second. Reports of earthquakes commonly exaggerate the loss of life. Until of late years such reports were usually accepted without criticism, and the numbers given of lives lost in many of the disasters in this list are without doubt greatly exaggerated.

B.C.
One which made Eubœa an island.......... 425
Helice and Bura in Peloponnesus swallowed up.......... 373
Duras, in Greece, buried with all its inhabitants; and 12 cities in Campania also buried.......... 345
Lysimachia and its inhabitants buried..........about 283

A.D.
Ephesus and other cities overturned.......... 17
One accompanied the eruption of Vesuvius when Pompeii and Herculaneum were buried.......... 79
Four cities in Asia, 2 in Greece, and 2 in Galatia overturned, 105 or 106
Antioch destroyed.......... 115
Nicomedia, Cæsarea, and Nicea overturned.......... 126
In Asia, Pontus, and Macedonia, 150 cities and towns damaged, 157
Nicomedia again demolished, with its inhabitants.......... 358
At Constantinople; edifices destroyed; thousands perished... 557
In Africa; many cities destroyed.......... 560
Awful one in Syria, Palestine, and Asia; more than 500 towns destroyed, with immense loss of life.......... 742
In France, Germany, and Italy.......... 801
Constantinople overturned; all Greece shaken.......... 936
One felt throughout England.......... 1089
One at Antioch; many towns destroyed.......... 1114
Catania, in Sicily, overturned; 15,000 persons buried.......... 1137
One severely felt at Lincoln, Engl.......... 1142
In Syria, etc.; 20,000 perished.......... 1158
At Calabria; a city with its inhabitants overwhelmed in the Adriatic sea..........Sept. 1186
In Cilicia; 60,000 perished.......... 1268
One again felt throughout England; Glastonbury destroyed... 1274
In England; the greatest known there..........14 Nov. 1318
At Naples; 40,000 persons perished..........5 Dec. 1456
Constantinople; thousands perished..........14 Sept. 1509
At Lisbon; 1500 houses and 30,000 persons buried in the ruins; several neighboring towns engulfed..........26 Feb. 1531
In London; part of St. Paul's and Temple churches fell..6 Apr. 1580
In Japan; several cities ruined, thousands perish......2 July, 1596
In Naples; 30 villages ruined, 70,000 lives lost..........30 July, 1626
Awful one at Calabria..........27 Mch. 1638
Ragusa ruined, 5000 perished..........6 Apr. 1667
At Schamaki; lasted 3 months, 80,000 perished.......... "
At Rimini; above 1500 perished..........14 Apr. 1672
One severely felt at Dublin, etc..........17 Oct. 1690
At Jamaica, houses of Port Royal engulfed, 3000 perished, June 7, 1692
One in Sicily destroyed 54 cities and towns and 300 villages; of Catania, with 18,000 inhabitants, not a trace remained; more than 100,000 lives lost..........Sept. 1693
Aquila, in Italy, ruined; 5000 perished..........2 Feb. 1703
Jeddo, Japan, ruined; 200,000 perished.......... "
In the Abruzzi; 15,000 perished..........3 Nov. 1706
At Algiers; 20,000 perished..........May and June, 1716
Palermo almost destroyed; nearly 6000 lives lost..........1 Sept. 1726
In China; 100,000 persons swallowed up at Pekin.....30 Nov. 1731
In Naples, etc.; 1940 perished..........29 Nov. 1732
Lima and Callao demolished; 18,000 persons buried....28 Oct. 1746
In London, etc., a slight shock..........19 Feb. 1750
Port-au-Prince, St. Domingo, ruined..........21 Nov. 1751
Adrianople nearly overwhelmed..........29 July, 1752
At Grand Cairo; half the houses and 40,000 persons lost..Sept. 1754
Quito destroyed..........Apr. 1755
Kaschan, N. Persia, destroyed; 40,000 perished..........7 June, "
Great earthquake at LISBON. In about 8 minutes most of the houses and 50,000 inhabitants were destroyed, and whole streets buried. The cities of Coimbra, Oporto, and Braga suffered much, and St. Ubes was destroyed. In Spain a large part of Malaga became ruins. One half of Fez, in Morocco, was destroyed, and more than 12,000 Arabs perished. Above half of the island of Madeira became waste; and 2000 houses in Mitylene, in the Archipelago, were overthrown; was felt over 5000 miles, even in Scotland..........1 Nov. "
In Syria, over 10,000 sq. miles; Baalbec destroyed; here 20,000 perished..........30 Oct. 1759
Comorn, Pesth, etc., much damaged..........28 June, 1763
At Martinique; 1600 persons perished..........Aug. 1767
At Guatemala; Santiago with its inhabitants swallowed, 7 June, 1773
A destructive one at Smyrna..........3 July, 1778
At Tauris; 15,000 houses thrown down, and multitudes buried, 1780
Messina and other towns in Italy and Sicily overthrown; thousands perished..........4 Feb. 1783
Ezinghian, near Erzeroum, destroyed, and 5000 persons buried in its ruins..........23 July, 1784
St. Lucia, West Indies; 900 perished..........12 Oct. 1788
At Borgo di San Sepolcro; many houses and 1000 persons lost, 30 Sept. 1789
In Naples; Vesuvius overwhelmed city of Torre del Greco. June, 1794
Country between Santa Fé and Panama destroyed, including Cuzco and Quito; 40,000 people buried suddenly......4 Feb. 1797
Cumana, South America, ruined..........14 Dec. "
At Constantinople; destroyed the royal palace and many buildings..........26 Sept. 1800
From Cronstadt to Constantinople..........26 Oct. 1802
A violent one felt in Holland..........end of Jan. 1804
At Frosolone, Naples; 6000 lives lost..........26 July, 1805
At the Azores; a village of St. Michael's sunk, and a lake of boiling water appeared in its place..........11 Aug. 1810
Many earthquakes in the lower Mississippi valley, especially at New Madrid, opening great chasms.......... 1811
Awful one at CARACAS..........26 Mch. 1812
Several throughout India; district of Kutch sunk; 2000 persons buried..........16 June, 1819

Genoa, Palermo, Rome, and many other towns damaged, thousands perish 1819
Aleppo destroyed, above 20,000 perish, shocks on 10 and 13 Aug and 5 Sept 1822
Coast of Chili permanently raised 19 Nov "
In Spain, Murcia and numerous villages devastated, 6000 perish 21 Mch 1829
Canton and neighborhood, above 6000 perished 26 and 27 May, 1830
In duchy of Parma, 40 shocks at Borgotaro, and at Pontremoli many houses thrown down 14 Feb 1834
Concepcion etc in Chili, destroyed 20 Feb 1835
In Calabria, Cosenza and villages destroyed, 1000 persons buried 20 Apr "
In Calabria, 100 perish at Castiglione 12 Oct "
At Martinique nearly half of Port Royal destroyed, nearly 700 persons killed and the whole island damaged 11 Jan 1839
At Ternate, the island laid waste, thousands lost 14 Feb 1840
Destructive earthquake at Mount Ararat, in Armenia, 3137 houses overthrown hundreds perished 27 July, "
Great earthquake at Zante, many perished 30 Oct "
At Cape Haytien, St Domingo, nearly two thirds of the town destroyed, between 4000 and 5000 lives lost 7 May, 1842
Point à Pitre Guadeloupe entirely destroyed 8 Feb 1843
At Rhodes and Macri, a mountain fell in at Macri crushing a village and destroying 600 persons 28 Feb–7 Mch 1851
At Valparaiso more than 400 houses destroyed 2 Apr "
In S Italy, Melfi almost laid in ruins, 14,000 lives lost, 14 Aug "
Philippine isles, Manilla much injured 16–30 Sept 1852
In northwest of England, slight 9 Nov "
Thebes, in Greece, nearly destroyed 18 Aug 1853
St Salvador S America, destroyed 16 Apr 1854
Anasaca, in Japan, and Simoda, in Niphon, destroyed, Jeddo much injured 23 Dec "
Broussa, in Turkey, nearly destroyed 28 Feb 1855
Several villages in central Europe destroyed 25, 26 July, "
Jeddo Japan nearly destroyed 11 Nov "
At the island of Great Sauger, one of the Moluccas, volcanic eruption and earthquake, nearly 3000 lives lost 2 Mch 1856
In the Mediterranean, at Candia, 500 lives lost, Rhodes 100, and other islands, 150 12 Oct "
In Calabria, Montemurro and other towns in the kingdom of Naples destroyed, and about 10,000 lives lost 16 Dec 1857
[In 75 years, from 1783 to 1857, the kingdom of Naples lost at least 111,000 inhabitants by earthquakes or more than 1500 per year, of an average population of 6 000,000'—*Lacaita*]
Corinth nearly destroyed 21 Feb 1858
At Quito, about 5000 persons killed, and much property destroyed 22 Mch 1859
Erzeroum, Asia Minor, thousands perished 2 June–17 July, "
At San Salvador, many buildings destroyed no lives lost, 8 Dec "
In Cornwall slight 21 Oct 1859, 13 Jan 1860
At Mendoza, S America, about two thirds of the city and 7000 lives lost 20 Mch "
In Perugia, Italy, several lives lost 8 May, 1861
In Greece, N Morea Corinth and other places injured, 26 Dec "
Guatemala, 150 buildings and 14 churches destroyed 19 Dec 1862
Rhodes, 13 villages destroyed, about 300 persons and much cattle and property lost 22 Apr 1863
Manilla, Philippine isles, great destruction of property, about 1000 persons perished 2, 3 July "
Central, west, and northwest of England, at 3 22 A M 6 Oct "
At Macchia Bendinella, etc., Sicily, 200 houses destroyed, 64 persons killed 18 July, 1865
Slight earthquake near Tours and Blois, in France 14 Sept. 1866
Argostoli, Cephalonia, above 50 perished 4 Feb 1867
At Mitylene, about 1000 killed 8, 9 Mch "
Djocja, Java, above 400 perished, town destroyed 10 June, "
Cities of Arequipa, Iquique, Tacna, and Chincha, and many small towns in Peru and Ecuador destroyed, about 25,000 lives lost, and 30,000 rendered homeless, damage estimated at $300,000,000 13–15 Aug 1868
[About 11,000*l* collected in London to relieve sufferers.]
Slight earthquake in W England and S Wales, felt at Bath, Swansea, etc 30 Oct "
In Santa Maura, an Ionian isle, the town Santa Maura destroyed, about 17 persons perished 28 Dec. 1869
At Quebec not much damage 20 Oct 1870
In Calabria, several villages destroyed, early Oct. "
Northwest of England, houses shaken, crockery broken, evening, 17 Mch, slight in Yorkshire 22 Mch 1871
California Inyo valley, several small towns destroyed, about 30 killed 26, 27 Mch 1872
Lehree, Eastern Catchi, Sinde frontier, India, destroyed, about 500 killed 14, 15 Dec "
San Salvador nearly destroyed, about 50 killed, the rest escaped through timely warning 19 Mch 1873
North of Italy, at Feletto, near Conegliano, Venetia, church destroyed, about 50 killed, lives lost at Belluno, etc., shock at Venice, Verona, etc 29 June, "
Azagra, Spain, 200 killed by a landslip 22 July, 1874
Antigua and other places in Guatemala destroyed, great loss of life 3 Sept. "
Kara Hissa and other places in Asia Minor, great destruction of life 3–5 May, 1875
Smyrna and neighborhood, many perish 12 May, "
San José de Cucuta and other towns near Santander, on the boundary of Colombia, destroyed, about 14,000 lives said to be lost 16–18 May, "
Lahore and vicinity, India, several killed 12 Dec. "
At Scheibs, on the Danube, felt throughout Austrian empire, 17 July, 1876

Earthquake and tidal wave near Callao, went southward much shipping and several towns destroyed, not much mortality, 9, 10 May, 1877
Cua, Venezuela, nearly destroyed, about 300 killed, loss about $150 000 14 Apr 1878
Shocks at Cologne and other parts of Germany and Holland, houses shaken, bells rung etc 9–11 A M 26 Aug "
Aci Reale, Catania, Sicily 5 villages destroyed, 10 persons killed 17 June, 1879
Severe shock at Brieg, in Switzerland, felt at Berne, Zurich, Geneva, etc, several killed 4 July, 1880
Manilla, etc, Philippines, cathedral destroyed, several killed, many hurt 18–24 July, "
Smyrna and neighborhood, many houses destroyed, 2 persons killed 29, 30 July, "
Valparaiso at Illapel, Chili, about 200 perish 15 Sept "
S Austria, much damage with loss of life at Agram, etc., 9–16 Nov–8 Dec "
Slight shocks at Inverary and other places W Scotland, 28 Nov "
Berne and other places, Switzerland, houses split up, etc, 27 Jan and 3 Mch 1881
Severe shocks in S Italy, at Casamicciola in the isle of Ischia, 280 houses destroyed 114 lives lost, about $180,000 loss 4 Mch, another destructive shock 15 Mch "
Scio—the town and several villages destroyed, about 4000 perish much destitution ensues, successive shocks, beginning 1 30 P M 3 Apr "
Panama, railway partially destroyed 7 9, 10 Sept. 1882
Slight shock in Cornwall and Devon 25 June, 1883
Casamicciola, and several villages in the island of Ischia, almost entirely destroyed, 1990 lives lost, 28 July, slight shocks since, one severe 3 Aug "
Java and neighboring isles desolated by a series of violent eruptions from the volcanoes (JAVA SUMATRA) 25–28 Aug "
Anatolia coast of Asia Minor, Ischesne and about 30 small towns and villages destroyed about 100 lives lost, and 30 000 destitute, Smyrna much shaken about 16 Oct. "
Shocks felt at Gibraltar 20 Oct et seq "
Severe shocks in eastern counties of England proceeding from N E to S W, centre Colchester, where the Congregational church steeple fell, as well as many chimneys, damage estimated at $50 000, much destruction in neighboring villages, many inhabitants homeless, Langenhoe church wrecked, much damage at Abberton, a child killed at Rowhedge, an invalid died, the shock felt at Coggeshall, Sudbury, Ipswich, Cambridge Bishop's Stortford Northampton Leicester, Woolwich Sheerness different parts of London Hampstead, etc, (MANSION HOUSE FUNDS) 22 Apr 1884
Severe shocks for several days on Asiatic shore of sea of Marmora, about 20 deaths reported 19 May, "
Violent shock on the island of Kishm near the mouth of the Persian gulf, 12 villages destroyed, about 200 people killed, 19, 20 May, "
Slight shocks in the Alban hills, near Rome 7 Aug "
Slight shocks in U S, from Washington to New York, 10, 11 Aug "
At Genoa 27 Nov, at Marseilles Lyons etc 29 Nov "
Severe shocks in Andalusia Malaga, many houses destroyed about 266 persons killed, felt at Madrid 25 Dec. "
Several towns destroyed, Alhama, Granada, many killed, Periana, about 900 killed 26, 27 Dec "
Shocks, intermitting 26–31 Dec "
Slight shocks in Carinthia and Styria 28 Dec et seq "
Shocks, 1-27 Jan, much camping out 1885
Slight shocks in Styria 27 28 Jan "
Slight shocks at Alhama 12 Feb "
Alarming shocks at Malaga and other towns 27 Feb "
In province of Granada 690 killed (SPAIN 1884) 28 Feb "
Shocks throughout eastern U S, at Charleston, S C, 41 lives and $5 000 000 worth of property lost 31 Aug 1886
Slight shocks at and around Charleston, causing panic, Sept.–Dec "
Terrible earthquake in southern Europe especially in the Riviera, estimated loss of 2000 lives 23 Feb 1887
Severe shock at San Salvador 9 Sept. 1891
Shock felt at San Francisco 14 Oct "
Severe earthquake in Japan 28 Oct "
[The official estimate places the killed at 4000, injured at 5000, and 50 000 houses destroyed]
Slight shocks in New South Wales, Victoria, and Tasmania, 27 Jan 1892
Islands of Zante and Stromboli (the former west of Greece, the latter one of the Lipari group west of Calabria, Italy) severely shaken, 31 Jan, and again 12 Feb and 17 Apr 1893
[Zante suffered a great loss in lives and property, especially on the latter date] VOLCANOES
Meshed and Kuchan Persia, destroyed, many lives lost, 20 Nov "
Slight shock felt in New Hampshire and Vermont 27 Nov "

East Angles, the 6th kingdom of the Heptarchy, commenced by Uffa, 526, ended with Ethelbert in 792 BRITAIN The bishop's see founded by St. Felix, who converted the East Angles in 630, was eventually settled at Norwich, about 1094.

East India Company. INDIA, INDIA COMPANY, EAST

East Indies. INDIA

East Saxons. BRITAIN

Easter, instituted about 68, the festival of the church in commemoration of our Saviour's resurrection, so called in

England from the Saxon goddess *Eostre*, whose festival was in April. After much contention between the eastern and western churches, it was ordained by the council of Nice, 325, to be observed on the same day through the Christian world. "Easter-day is the Sunday following that 14th day of the calendar moon which happens upon or next after 21 Mch., so that, if the said 14th day be a Sunday, Easter-day is not that Sunday, but the next." Easter-day may be any Sunday of the 5 weeks which commence with 22 Mch. and end with 25 Apr. During the 19th century, Easter occurred but once on 22 Mch. (1818), and but once on 25 Apr. (1886). The dispute between the old British church and the new Anglo-Saxon church respecting Easter was settled about 664.—Easter Sunday, 1892, 17 Apr.; 1893, 2 Apr.; 1894, 25 Mch.; 1895, 14 Apr.; 1896, 5 Apr.; 1897, 18 Apr.; 1898, 10 Apr.; 1899, 2 Apr.; 1900, 15 Apr.

Easter island, in the Pacific ocean, was discovered by Davis in 1686; it was visited by Roggewein, Apr. 1722, and from him obtained its name; visited by captain Cook, Mch. 1774. At the southeast extremity is the crater of an old volcano, about 2 miles in circuit and 800 ft. deep.

Eastern, or Greek, church. GREEK CHURCH.

Eastern empire. After the death of the emperor Jovian, Feb. 364, the generals at Nice elected Valentinian as his successor, who, in June, made his brother Valens emperor of the West; the final division was in 395, between the sons of Theodosius. The Eastern empire ended with the capture of Constantinople, and death of Constantine XIII., 29 May, 1453. TURKEY.

Nestorius, the bishop, nominated the first patriarch of Constantinople.......9 July, 381
Theodosius the Great succors Valentinian II., the Western emperor, and defeats the tyrant Maximus, at Aquileia....... 388
Valentinian II. slain by Arbogastes the Frank, who makes Eugenius emperor....... 392
Eugenius defeated and slain by Theodosius, who reunites the 2 empires.......6 Sept. 394
Death of Theodosius; the empire finally divided between his sons—Arcadius receives the East, Honorius the West. 17 Jan. 395
Alaric the Goth begins to ravage the empire....... 396
Constantinople walled by Theodosius II....... 413
Violent religious dissensions; Theodosius II. establishes schools and revives learning....... 425
Theodosian Code promulgated....... 438
Councils of Ephesus, 431, 449; of Chalcedon....... 451
Frequent sanguinary conflicts between Blues and Greens, circus factions at Constantinople.......498–520
Justinian Code published....... 529
War with Persia; victorious career of Belisarius, imperial general, begins.......529–531
He suppresses the "Nika" ("conquer") insurrection of the circus factions; 30,000 Greeks slain, Constantinople burned, 532
Dedication of St. Sophia....... 537
Victories of Belisarius in Africa, Italy, and the east.......533–541
Recalled through Justinian's jealousy, 542; again, 548; again, 549; disgraced....... 562
Beginning of the Turkish power in Asia....... 545
Slavonians ravage Illyria....... 551
Narses defeats Totila and the Goths near Rome....... 552
Disaffection of Narses....... 561
Death of Belisarius (aged 84), of Justinian (aged 83)....... 565
Victories of Maurice and Narses in the east.......579 et seq.
Severe contests with the Avars.......594–620
Narses burned at Constantinople....... 606
Flight (Hegira) of Mahomet from Mecca to Medina, where he establishes himself as a prophet and prince.......16 July, 622
Victorious career of Heraclius II.......622 et seq.
He recovers his lost territories....... 627
Saracens invade the empire, 632; defeat Heraclius at Aiznadin, 633; at Yermuk, 636; take Alexandria, 640; and the Greek provinces in Africa....... 648
Constans purchases peace with them....... 660
They besiege Constantinople 7 times.......672–77
Bulgarians establish a kingdom in Mœsia (now Bulgaria), 678; they ravage the country up to Constantinople....... 711
Saracens vainly invest Constantinople, 716, 718; defeated....... 720
Leo III. the Isaurian forbids the worship of images (hence the Iconoclast controversy, and eventually the separation of the Eastern and Western churches)....... 726
Arab invaders (90,000) defeated by Acronius....... 739
Monasteries dissolved....... 770
Destruction of images throughout the empire decreed, 754; image worship restored by the empress Irene (for which she was canonized)....... 787
Empire loses the exarchate of Italy, 752; Dalmatia, 825; Sicily and Crete....... 827
Image-worship persecuted, 830; restored, 842; forbidden at Constantinople by one council, 860; restored by another....... 879
S. Italy annexed to the empire....... 890
Five emperors reigning at one time....... 928
Naples added to the empire....... "
Basil subdues the Bulgarians.......987, 1014
Bulgaria annexed to the empire....... 1018
Turks invade Asia Minor....... 1068
Normans conquer S. Italy....... 1080
First crusade; Alexis I. recovers Asia....... 1097
Venetians victorious over Greeks....... 1125
Hungarians repelled, 1152; peace made with Normans in Sicily, 1156
Wars with Turks and Venetians....... 1172
Cyprus lost to the empire....... 1190
Fourth crusade begins....... 1202
Revolt of Alexis against his brother Isaac; crusaders take Constantinople, and restore Isaac and his son Alexis IV. 19 July, 1203
Alexis Ducas murders Alexis IV. and usurps the throne; crusaders take Constantinople, kill Alexis, and establish the Latin empire, under Baldwin, count of Flanders.......9 May, 1204
Empire of Nice founded by Theodore Lascaris....... "
Kingdom of Epirus and Ætolia established....... 1208
Constantinople recovered, and the empire re-established by Michael Palæologus.......25 July, 1261
Establishment of the Turkish empire in Asia, under Othman I. 1299
Genoese trade in the Black sea....... 1303
Turks ravage Mysia, etc., 1340 and 1345; and settle on the coast of Thrace....... 1353
Sultan Amurath takes Adrianople, and makes it his capital, 1362; and, by treaty, greatly reduces the empire....... 1373
All the Greek possessions in Asia lost....... 1390
Sultan Bajazet defeats the Christians under Sigismund of Hungary, at Nicopolis.......28 Sept. 1396
Emperor Manuel vainly solicits help from the western sovereigns....... 1400
A Turkish pacha established at Athens....... 1401
Greek empire made tributary to Timour, 1402, who subjugates the Turkish sultan, and dismembers his empire, 1403; death of Timour, on his way to China....... 1405
Dissension among the Turks defers the fall of Constantinople, 1403–12; Mahomet I., aided by the emperor Manuel, becomes sultan....... 1413
Amurath II. in vain besieges Constantinople, 1422; peace made, 1425
John Palæologus visits Rome, etc., soliciting help in vain...1437–40
Accession of Constantine XIII., last emperor....... 1448
Accession of Mahomet II., 1451; begins the siege of Constantinople, 6 Apr.; takes it.......29 May, 1453

[He granted the Christians personal security and free exercise of their religion.]

EMPERORS OF THE EAST.

364. Valens.
379. Theodosius I. the Great.
395. Arcadius, the son of Theodosius.
408. Theodosius II. succeeded his father.
450. Marcian, a Thracian of obscure family.
457. Leo I. the Thracian.
474. Leo II. the Younger (died the same year).
" Zeno, called the Isaurian.
491. Anastasius I., an Illyrian, of mean birth.
518. Justin I., originally a private soldier.
527. Justinian I., compiler of the Digest.
565. Justin II., nephew of Justinian.
578. Tiberius II., renowned for his virtues.
582. Maurice, the Cappadocian, murdered, with all his children, by
602. Phocas the Usurper, a centurion, whose crimes and cruelties led to his own assassination in 610.
610. Heraclius, by whom Phocas was dethroned.
641. (Heracleonas) Constantine III. reigned a few months; poisoned by his stepmother, Martina.
" Constans II.; assassinated in a bath.
668. Constantine III. (or IV.) Pogonatus.
685. Justinian II., son of the preceding; abhorred for exactions, debaucheries, and cruelties; dethroned and mutilated by
695. Leontius; dethroned and mutilated by Tiberius Aspimar.
698. Tiberius III. Aspimar.
705. Justinian II. restored. Leontius and Tiberius degraded in the Hippodrome, and put to death. Justinian slain in 711.
711. Philippicus Bardanes; assassinated.
713. Anastasius II.; fled on the election of Theodosius in 716; afterwards delivered up to Leo III. and put to death.
716. Theodosius III.
718. Leo III., the Isaurian.

[In 726 began the Iconoclastic controversy; alternate prohibition and restoration of images embroil several reigns.]

741. Constantine IV. (or V.) Copronymus, son of the preceding; succeeded by his son,
775. Leo IV.
780. Constantine V. (or VI.) and his mother, Irene.
790. Constantine alone, by desire of people, Irene unpopular.
792. Irene again, jointly with her son, and afterwards alone, 797; deposed for cruelties and murders, and exiled.
802. Nicephorus I. Logothetes; slain.
811. Stauracius; reigns a few days only.
" Michael I.; defeated, abdicates, and enters a monastery.
813. Leo V. the Armenian; killed in the temple at Constantinople on Christmas day, 820, by conspirators in the interest of
820. Michael II. the Stammerer.
829. Theophilus, son of Michael.
842. Michael III. Porphyrogenitus, and the Sot, son of the preceding, murdered by his successor.
867. Basil I. the Macedonian.
886. Leo VI. the Philosopher.
911. Alexander and Constantine VI. (or VII.) Porphyrogenitus, Leo's brother and son, the latter only 6 years of age; the former dying in 912, Zoe, mother of Constantine, assumes the regency.
919. Romanus Lecapenus, usurper, associates with him his sons,
920. Christopher, and

928. Stephen and Constantine VII (or VIII)
[Five emperors now reign. Christopher d 931. Romanus exiled by Constantine and Stephen, who are banished]
945 Constantine VII (or VIII) reigns alone, poisoned by his daughter in law, Theophania, 959
959 Romanus II, son of preceding, contrives his father's death, banishes his mother, Helena
963 Nicephorus II Phocas, marries Theophania, his predecessor's consort who has him assassinated
969 John I Zimisces, celebrated general, takes Basil II and Constantine VIII (or IX) sons of Romanus II, as colleagues, John dies, supposed by poison and
976. Basil II and Constantine VIII reign, the former dies in 1025, the latter in 1028
1028. Romanus III Argyropulus, poisoned by his profligate consort Zoe, who raises
1034 Michael IV the Paphlagonian to the throne, on his death, Zoe places
1041 Michael V Calaphates as his successor, Zoe dethrones him, has his eyes put out and marries
1042 Constantine IX (or X) Monomachus, they reign jointly, Zoe d 1050
1054 Theodora, widow of Constantine
1056 Michael VI Stratiotes or Strato, deposed
1057 Isaac I Comnenus, abdicates
1059 Constantine X (or XI) Ducas
1067 Eudocia, consort of the preceding, and Romanus IV Diogenes, whom she marries, reign to the prejudice of Michael, Constantine's son
1071. Michael VII Parapinaces recovers his throne, and reigns jointly with Constantine XI (or XII)
1078. Nicephorus III, dethroned by
1081 Alexis or Alexius I Comnenus, succeeded by
1118 John Comnenus, his son Kalos, dies of a wound from a poisoned arrow
1143. Manuel I Comnenus, son of John
1180 Alexis II Comnenus, son of the preceding, under the regency of the empress Maria his mother
1183. Andronicus I Comnenus, causes Alexis to be strangled, and seizes the throne, put to death by
1185 Isaac II Angelus Comnenus, who is deposed, imprisoned, and deprived of his eyes by his brother
1195. Alexis III Angelus, the Tyrant, deposed, and his eyes put out, dies in a monastery
1203. Isaac II again with his son, Alexis IV deposed
1204 Alexis V Ducas, murders Alexis IV, killed by crusaders

LATIN EMPERORS

1204. Baldwin I, earl of Flanders, on the capture of Constantinople by the Latins, elected emperor, made prisoner by king of Bulgaria, and not heard of after
1206 Henry I, his brother (d in 1217)
1216 Peter de Courtenay his brother in law
1221 Robert de Courtenay, his son
1228. Baldwin II, his brother (a minor), and John de Brienne, of Jerusalem regent and associate emperor
1261. [Constantinople recovered, and the empire of the Franks or Latins terminates]

GREEK EMPERORS AT NICE

1204 Theodore Lascaris I
1222 John Ducas Vataces
1255 Theodore Lascaris II, his son
1259 John Lascaris, and (1260) Michael VIII Palæologus

GREEK EMPERORS AT CONSTANTINOPLE

1261 Michael VIII, now at Constantinople, puts out the eyes of John, and reigns alone
1282. Andronicus II Palæologus, the Elder, son of preceding, deposed by
1328 Andronicus III, the Younger, his grandson
1341 John Palæologus I, under the guardianship of John Cantacuzenus, the latter proclaimed emperor at Adrianople
1347 John Cantacuzenus abdicates
1355 John I Palæologus restored.
1391 Manuel II Palæologus, his son, succeeded by his son and colleague
1425 John II Palæologus. The throne claimed by his 3 brothers
1448 Constantine Palæologus XII (XIII or XIV, other emperors called Constantine by some writers), killed and Constantinople taken, 29 May, 1453

Ebel'ians, a German revivalist sect, founded at Königsberg, in Prussia, about 1836, its leaders archdeacon Ebel and dr. Diestel, who were condemned for unsound doctrine and impure lives in 1839 The sentence was annulled in 1842, it is said by royal influence The sect is popularly termed "Mucker," German for hypocrites Their theory and practice of spiritual marriage are described by Hepworth Dixon, in his "Spiritual Wives," 1868

E'bionites (etym doubtful), heretics, in the 1st century, a branch of the Nazarenes, of 2 kinds one believed our Saviour born of a virgin, observed precepts of the Christian religion, but added ceremonies of Jews, the other believed Christ born after the manner of man, and denied his divinity Photinus revived the sect in 342.

eb'onite, vulcanized India-rubber CAOUTCHOUC

Ebro, a river in Spain, scene of a signal defeat of Spaniards by French, under Lannes, near Tudela, 23 Nov 1808, and of important movements of the allied British and Spanish armies in the Peninsular war (1809-13)

ecarté (*ā'kar'tā'*), a game at cards, of modern origin, probably first played in the Paris salons in the first quarter of the 19th century, a development of a very old card game called la triomphe or French ruff

Ecclesias'tes, the Book of In Hebrew tradition one of the 3 canonical books of Solomon, the others being Proverbs and the Song of Songs or Canticles Its later origin has many advocates, while able scholars defend it as the production of Solomon, son of David

ecclesiastical courts. There was no distinction between lay and ecclesiastical courts in England until 1085, after the Norman conquest The most important and most ancient of the English ecclesiastical courts is the Court of Arches, chiefly a court of appeal from inferior jurisdictions within the province of Canterbury, name derived from the church of St. Mary-le-Bow (*Sancta Maria de Arcubus*), London, where it was formerly held Appeals from this court lie to the judicial committee of the privy council, by statute, 1832 Till the establishment of the divorce and probate courts in 1857, the following were causes cognizable in ecclesiastical courts blasphemy, apostasy from Christianity, heresy schism, ordinations, institutions to benefices, matrimony divorces, bastardy, tithes, incest, fornication, adultery, probate of wills, administrations, etc CHURCH OF ENGLAND, Martin *v* Mackonochie, 1867, etc

Echo (Gr 'Ηχώ) In Greek mythology one of the oreades or mountain nymphs The word denotes mere sound The time which elapses between the utterance of a sound and its return must be more than one twelfth of a second to form an echo The whispering-gallery of St. Paul's, London, is a well-known example ACOUSTICS.

Eckmühl, a village of Bavaria, site of a battle between the main armies of France (75,000) and Austria (40,000), Napoleon and marshal Davoust (hence prince d'Eckmühl) defeated archduke Charles, 22 Apr 1809

Eclectics (from Gr ἐκλέγω, I choose), ancient philosophers (called *Analogetici*, and also *Philalethes*, the lovers of truth), who, not joining any sect, chose what they judged good from each, of them was Potamon of Alexandria, about 1 A D Also a Christian sect, who considered the doctrine of Plato conformable to the spirit of Christianity MEDICAL SCIENCE, PHILOSOPHY, Victor Cousin

eclipse, in astronomy, the obscuration of any heavenly body by entering the shadow of another body Anaxagoras, the Stoic, of Klazomenæ, was the first to explain the physical cause of eclipses, about 450 B.C., but Nicias sacrificed the Athenian army at Syracuse to his superstitious dread of the lunar eclipse of 27 Aug 413 B C Columbus is said to have awed the Indians of Jamaica by predicting the time of an eclipse of the moon, 1504 The Egyptians said they had accurately observed 373 eclipses of the sun, and 832 of the moon, in the period from Vulcan to Alexander, who died 323 B.C The theory of eclipses is said to have been known to the Chinese before 120 B.C The first eclipse recorded happened 19 Mch 721 B C at 8 40 P M, according to Ptolemy, it was lunar, and was observed with accuracy at Babylon There may be as many as 7 eclipses in a year and 4 will then be solar There cannot be less than 2, if but 2 then they will be solar.

A list of eclipses to the year 2000 is given in "L'Art de Vérifier les Dates"

Royal Astronomical Society published a volume of "Observations made during Total Solar Eclipses," 1880.

ECLIPSES OF THE SUN

		B C
Nineveh eclipse (recorded, according to sir Henry Rawlinson, on a Nineveh tablet in the British museum)	15 June,	763
That predicted by Thales (*Pliny*, lib. ii 9) believed to have occurred (HALYS) .	28 May,	585
[Sir G B. Airy astronomer royal, thinks the date should be 610, others say 603 or 584 B C It is recorded by Herodotus as interrupting a battle between Medes and Lydians]		
Eclipse of Xerxes, when setting out against Greece	17 Feb	478
One at Athens (*Thucydides*, lib iv) .		424
Eclipse of Agathocles (*Airy*)	15 Aug	310
Total 3 days' supplication decreed at Rome (*Livy*)		188
		A D
One at the death of Jesus Christ (*Josephus*)	3 Apr	33
One observed at Constantinople .		968
At the battle of Sticklestadt.	29 July,	1030

In France, when it was dark at noon (*Du Fresnoy*)	29 June,	1033
In England a total darkness (W Malmsb)	20 Mch	1140
Again, stars visible at 10 in the morning (*Camden*)	23 June,	1191
True sun and the appearance of another, so that astronomers alone could distinguish the difference by colored glasses		"
One observed in Scotland, termed the "black hour"	7 June,	1433
Another in Scotland, termed "Mirk Monday"	8 Apr	1652
Total in England, stars shone and birds roosted at noon	3 May,	1715
Last total eclipse in England, seen near Salisbury	22 May,	1724
One central and annular in middle Europe	7 Sept	1802
Total eclipses 17 July, 1833, 8 July, 1842,	28 July,	1851
Annular, photographed at Oundle, not seen well at other places,	15 Mch	1858
Total eclipse of the sun, well seen by sir G B Airy and others in Spain, Warren de la Rue took photographs	18 July,	1860
Total, of longest possible duration (observed for British Royal Society in India, by col Walker, Mr Herschel, and others),	18 Aug	1868

[During this eclipse in India, M Janssen invented a method of studying the sun at any time by several spectroscopes, multiplying the length of the spectrum and diffusing its brilliancy Joseph Norman Lockyer had suggested a similar method in 1866, but did not use it till 20 Oct 1868, being then not aware of M Janssen's discovery]

One well observed in North America	7 Aug	1869
Two expeditions sent out by the British government, not successful, to observe eclipse of	22 Dec	1870
One well observed at Ceylon and in southern India, 12 Dec 1871, and in North America	29 30 July,	1878

[Similar eclipses (about 70) recur after 18 years, 10⅓ days]

Solar eclipse well observed in Egypt	17 May,	1882
Eclipse well observed at Caroline islands, Pacific	6 May,	1883

[Except on 12 Aug 1999, no total eclipse of the sun will be visible in England for 250 years —*Hind*, July, 1871]

One observed in the Pacific states of the U S	1 Jan	1889

ECLIPSES OF THE MOON

	B C
First, observed by the Chaldæans at Babylon (*Ptolemy*, iv)	721
Total one observed at Sardis (*Thucydides*, vii)	413
Again, in Asia Minor (*Polybius*)	219
One at Rome, predicted by Q Sulpitius Gallus (*Livy*, xliv)	168
One terrified the Roman troops and quelled their revolt (*Tacitus*)	A D 14

Économistes (*ā-ko'-no-mists*), a philosophical sect, founded by François Quesnay (1694-1774), who exalted agriculture above other arts, he asserted that it gave 2 things, the support of the laborer, and an excess of value which belonged to the proprietor of the land ("product net"), and which alone should be taxed He favored freedom for industry and trade His "Physiocratie" (1768) and other works were very popular, even at court, and influenced Adam Smith, author of "The Wealth of Nations"

Écorcheurs (*ā-kōr-sheur'*) ("flayers"), bands of armed adventurers who desolated France and Belgium during the 15th century, beginning about 1435 Among their leaders were Chabannes, comte de Dammartin, the bastard of Armagnac, and Villandras, and they at one time numbered 100,000. They are said to have stripped their victims to their shirts, and flayed the cattle They were favored by the English invasion and the civil wars

ec'rasite, an explosive invented by Siersch and Kubin, Austrian engineers, impervious to damp, shock, or fire, Oct 1889

Ec'uador, a South American republic, formerly Quito and other provinces, part of Colombia, 1821, independent in 1831, when the Colombian republic was divided into 3, the other 2 being Venezuela and New Granada. Area, 144,000 sq miles. The population of Ecuador is about 1 146,000 (1890), of Quito, the capital, 76,000 EARTHQUAKES, 1868

Eddas (thought formerly to mean *Oldemoder*, or "mother of mothers," by others, "art"), 2 books of songs and sagas (prose and verse), the former, the prose Edda, also called the Younger Edda, or Snorri's Edda, the latter, the poetic or Elder Edda, a collection of old Norse poems, contain the Scandinavian mythology (or history of Odin, Thor, Frea, etc), written by skalds, or bards, about the 11th or 12th century Translations have been made into French, English, etc. MSS of the Eddas exist at Copenhagen and Upsal LITERATURE.

Eddystone, or Edystone, light-house, off the port of Plymouth, English channel, erected by the Trinity house to enable ships to avoid the Eddystone rock. The first light-house was commenced under Mr Winstanley, in 1696, finished in 1699, and destroyed in the tempest of 27 Nov 1703, when Winstanley and others perished A wooden one, by Rudyerd, was built by order of Parliament, and ships were ordered to pay one penny per ton inwards and outwards towards supporting it, 1708 This was burned 4 Dec. 1755, and a better, erected by Mr Smeaton, finished 9 Oct. 1759 The woodwork of this, burned in 1770, was replaced by stone.

Foundation having given way, a new one was designed by James N Douglass, engineer of the Trinity house The foundation stone was laid by the duke of Edinburgh in the presence of the prince of Wales, 19 Aug 1879 The corner stone was placed by the duke on 1 June, 1881, successfully lighted, 3 Feb 1882, opened, 18 May, 1882 LIGHT HOUSES

Edes'sa, now **Orfah,** a town in Mesopotamia, said to have been built by Nimrod, by Appian, to have been built by Seleucus, famous for its schools of theology in the 5th century. It was made a principality by the crusaders, and was taken by the Saracens, 1145, by Nur-ed-deen, in 1144, and the Turks, in 1181 Its ancient kings or rulers were named Abgarus and Mannus

Edgehill fight (23 Oct. 1642), Warwickshire, Engl, between royalists under Charles I and the parliament army under the earl of Essex, was the first of importance in the civil war Prince Rupert, who led the right wing of the royalists and headed the cavalry, broke the left wing of the parliament forces, but, pursuing too far, lost his advantage Earl Lindsay, who headed the royal foot, was mortally wounded Royalists forces, 12,000, parliament army, 10,000 The action was indecisive, though parliament claimed the victory.

Edict of Nantes, by which Henry IV of France granted toleration to his Protestant subjects, 13 Apr 1598, was confirmed by Louis XIII in 1610, and by Louis XIV. in 1652 It was revoked by Louis XIV 22 Oct. 1685 This act cost France 50,000 Protestant families, and gave England and Germany thousands of industrious artisans. It also caused a fierce insurrection in Languedoc CAMISARDS Some of the refugees settled in Spitalfields, where descendants yet remain, others in Soho and St. Giles's, pursuing the art of making crystal glasses, and the silk manufacture and jewelry, then new in England.

edicts, public ordinances and decrees, usually by sovereigns, originated with the Romans. The PERPETUAL EDICT Salvius Julianus, of Milan, a civilian at Rome (author of several treatises on public right), was employed by the emperor Adrian to draw up this body of laws for the prætors, promulgated 132

Edinburgh, the metropolis of Scotland, derives its name—in ancient records *Edinbure* and *Dun Edin*, "the hill of Edin"—from its castle, founded or rebuilt by Edwin, king of Northumbria, after greatly extending his dominions, to protect them from incursions of Scots and Picts, 626. But it is said the castle was first built by Camelon, king of the Picts, 330 B C. It is conspicuous, standing on a rock 300 ft high at the west end of the old town, and, before the invention of great guns, had considerable strength. Pop. 1891, 261,970.

Christianity introduced (reign of Donald I)		201
City fortified, and castle rebuilt by Malcolm Canmore		1074
Improved by David I	1124 to	1153
Holyrood abbey founded by David I		1128
Edinburgh constituted a burgh	about	"
Castle held by England.		1174-86
Parliament held here under Alexander II		1215
City taken by the English		1296
Grant of the town of Leith to Edinburgh		1329
Surrenders to Edward III		1355
St Giles's cathedral built		1359
City burned by Richard II, 1385, and by Henry IV.		1401
James II first king crowned here		1437
Execution of the earl of Athol		"
Annual fair granted by James II		1447
City strengthened by a wall		1450
Charter of James III		1477
Edinburgh made the metropolis by James III		1482
Royal College of Surgeons incorporated		1505
Charter of James IV		1508
[The palace of Holyrood was built in this reign]		
High school founded	about	1518
British, from 200 ships, burn Edinburgh and Leith	May,	1544
Leith is again burned, but Edinburgh is spared.		1547
Tolbooth built		1561
Edinburgh university chartered	14 Apr	1582
James VI leaves Edinburgh as king of England	5 Apr	1603
He revisits it	16 May,	1617
George Heriot's hospital founded by his will		1624
Charles I visits Edinburgh	June,	1633
Riots in Greyfriars church against English liturgy	23 July,	1637
Charles again visits the city		1641
Castle is surrendered to Cromwell	Dec	1650
Mercurius Caledonius, first Edinburgh newspaper, appeared		1661
Coffee houses first opened		1677
College of Physicians incorporated		1681
African and East India company incorporated		1695

Bank of Scotland founded 1695
Royal bank founded 1727
Royal Infirmary incorporated 1736
Medical Society instituted 1737
Modern improvements "New town" commenced 1753
Royal exchange completed 1761
Calton hill observatory founded 25 July, 1776
Society of Antiquaries 1780
Royal Society of Edinburgh incorporated 1783
Robertson the historian, dies here 11 June, 1793
Holyrood an asylum of Louis XVIII and his brother, afterwards Charles X 1795 to 1799
Edinburgh Review first published 10 Oct 1802
Nelson's monument completed 1815
Gas company incorporated 1818
Water company incorporated 1819
Society of Arts instituted 1821
Union canal completed 1822
Royal Institution erected 1823
Royal Scottish academy of painting, sculpture, and architecture founded 1826
Edinburgh and Dalkeith railway opened July, 1831
Death of sir Walter Scott 21 Sept 1832
Chambers's Edinburgh Journal pub "
Association of the Fine Arts 1833
Edinburgh and Granton railway begun 183?
Art Union of Scotland 1837
Society of Arts founded 1821 incorporated 1842
Edinburgh and Glasgow railway opened Feb "
Secession and formation of the Free church 18 May, 1843
New college instituted "
North British railway commenced 1844
Monument to political martyrs of 1793-94 by Mr Hume 21 Aug "
Sir Walter Scott's monument completed (begun 1840) 1845
Edinburgh Philosophical Association (established 1832) reorganized as the Edinburgh Philosophical Society 1846
North British railway opened 18 June, "
Prince Albert lays the foundation stone of the Scotch National Gallery 30 Aug 1850
National Gallery opened 21 Mch 1859
Lord Brougham elected chancellor of the university, Edinburgh, 1 Nov "
Prince consort lays foundation of new post office and Industrial museum 23 Oct 1861
Statues of Allan Ramsay and John Wilson inaugurated, 25 Mch 1865
National Museum of Science and Art opened by prince Alfred (created duke of Edinburgh etc, the first royal prince whose leading title was Scotch 24 May) 19 May, 1866
Prince of Wales installed patron of Freemasons of Scotland, 12 Oct, laid foundation of new Royal Infirmary 13 Oct 1870
Scott centenary celebrated 9 (for 15) Aug 1871
Lady Burdett Coutts made a burgess 15 Jan 1873
Earl of Derby elected lord rector of the university 14 Nov 1874
Statue of Dr Livingstone unveiled 15 Aug 1876
New water works (Portmore reservoir at the Moorfoot hills) opened by the lord provost 13 June, 1879
Academy of Music for Scotland (at Edinburgh) founded Sept 1882
Death of William Chambers, bookseller, restorer of St Giles's (which is reopened 23 May) 20 May, 1883
Tercentenary of the university celebrated 16-18 Apr 1884
Ancient cross restored by Gladstone Nov 1885
Freedom of the city presented to Parnell (18,000 vote against it), 20 July, 1889
[His name erased from the roll, 1891]
Free public library opened 9 June, 1890
[Andrew Carnegie of Pittsburg Pa, U S, gave it $250 000]
Henry M Stanley receives the freedom of the city 11 June, "
SCOTLAND

"Edinburgh Review" (a Whig quarterly started by Francis Jeffrey, rev Sydney Smith, Henry Brougham, and others), published first on 10 Oct 1802

Edmonton, a large suburban village of London, Engl Charles Lamb spent his last years here, and is buried in its churchyard Here also is the "Bell inn," made famous by Cowper

> "To morrow is our wedding day,
> And we will then repair
> Unto the Bell at Edmonton
> All in a chaise and pair"
> —*Cowper*, "History of John Gilpin."

Edom. IDUMÆA

education, the art of developing the physical, intellectual, and moral faculties of man, has occupied the greatest minds in all ages—Socrates, Plato, Aristotle, Cicero, Quintilian, Bacon, Milton, Locke, Rousseau, etc. In England the earliest schools for the poor were attached to monasteries, for the well-to-do halls and colleges were gradually founded CAMBRIDGE, COLLEGES, OXFORD, UNIVERSITIES, etc

IN ENGLAND.

William of Wykeham planted the school at Winchester, whence arose his colleges at that place and Oxford 1370
Eton college founded by Henry VI 1443
After the Reformation education improved, many grammar schools erected and endowed by Edward VI and Elizabeth, 1535-65
Christ's Hospital, the Blue coat school, established 1553

Westminster school founded by Elizabeth 1560
Foundation of Rugby school by Lawrence Sheriff, 1567, of Harrow school by John Lyon 1571
Charterhouse founded by Thomas Sutton 1611
Protestant charity schools founded about 1687
Queen Anne, zealous for education, founded the Grey coat school Westminster, and supported parochial charity schools (one established at St Margaret's, Westminster, 1688) 1698
Nearly 2000 of these schools established in Great Britain and Ireland principally through the Society for the Promotion of Christian Knowledge 1698-1741
Robert Raikes began Sunday schools about 1781
[In 1833 there were 16,828 of these with 1,548 890 scholars]
Joseph Lancaster a young Quaker began to instruct the children of the poor 1796
To provide teachers, he invented the monitorial system His exertions gave rise to the British and Foreign School Society as the "Royal Lancasterian Institution" etc 1805
This was followed by the church of England "National Society for Educating the Poor," on dr Bell's system 1811
Infant schools began about 1815
Charity commission appointed at the instance of Brougham published their "Reports on Education" in 37 vols folio, 1819-40
Irish national school system (for Catholics and Protestants) organized mainly by archbishop Whately and the Catholic archbishop Murray 1831
City of London school, Honey lane opened 1834
In 1834 the government began annual grants (the first 20 000*l*), continued till the Committee of the Privy Council on Education was formed to distribute the money 1839
Ragged School Union established 1844
Middle class examinations from the university of Oxford began, June 1858 The examiners granted the degree of A A to many persons at Liverpool, Leeds, etc, similar examinations from Cambridge in the autumn 1858
Report of Commissioners on Popular Education (appointed 1858), pub 18 Mch 1861 led to the minute of the Committee of the Privy Council on Education establishing a revised code of regulations, adopted 21 July, 1861 to come into operation after 31 Mch 1862. It decreed regular examinations, payment by results, evening schools for adults, and other changes under opposition from the clergy and schoolmasters After agitation in Parliament (25, 28 Mch 1862) a compromise was effected 6 May, 1862
Suggestion of 4 establishments in England France Germany, and Italy ascribed to Mr Cobden and Michel Chevalier "
"Conscience clause" founded on Endowed Schools act, Mch 1860, introduced by Committee of Council on Education for parishes with only one school, children of dissenters to be admitted without religious teaching or attendance at public worship Nov 1863
[Report 10 June, 1865 Opposed by the clergy, it created much controversy in 1866-67]
Parliamentary committee to consider the best mode of benefiting schools unassisted by the state 28 Feb 1865
Committee appointed at a meeting for establishing higher schools for middle classes in London by funds of lapsed charities, etc, 7 Nov, nearly 28,000*l.* subscribed by end of Dec 1865, 51,349*l* received Oct 1866
Subscribers chartered first school opened by lord mayor and others in Bath st, St Luke's 1 Oct "
Resolutions moved in the lords by earl Russell (that every child has a right to education, and recommending appointment of a cabinet minister of education), withdrawn 2 Dec 1867
Conference at Manchester recommend compulsory education, to be paid for by rates 15 Jan 1868
Technical Education —Committee of Education recommend scholarships for scientific instruction to artisans 21 Dec "
Joseph Whitworth's (now sir) offer to found 30 scholarships, each of 100*l* a year, in mechanics, etc., 18 Mch, accepted by the lords of the council 27 Mch. "
Foundation of the first new building for a middle class school in London laid by the lord mayor, Lawrence. 15 Dec "
National Education League for compulsory secular education by the state, first met at Birmingham 12, 13 Oct 1869
National Education Union to supplement the denominational system first met at Manchester 3 Nov "
Elementary Education bill introduced by W E Forster, 17 Feb, opposed by dissenters, signed 9 Aug 1870
[Amended in 1872, 1873, and 1876]
Education (Scotland) act passed 10 Aug 1872
Dublin University bill introduced by Mr Gladstone 13 Feb 1873
College for northern counties at Knutsford, foundation laid, 24 Sept "
College for higher education of women opened at GIRTON Oct. "
Domestic Economy —Study of food and clothing introduced into government educational department 1874
Mr Dixon's compulsory attendance bill lost (320-156) 1 July, "
Nuneham college at Cambridge for women opened 18 Oct. 1875
First annual conference of teachers 14 Jan 1876
Mr Dixon's bill for universal school boards and compulsory education rejected by the commons (281-260) Apr "
Intermediate Education act for Ireland passed 16 Aug 1878
Technical college for north of England opened at Newcastle, 24 Sept. 1880
Ascham Society formed "
Technical Education —City and Guilds of London Institute for the advancement of technical education, plan recommended by a committee lord Selborne chairman, pub June, the institute formally constituted, 11 Nov 1878, foundation of the building laid by prince Leopold 10 May 1881

Lord Aberdare, W. E. Forster, sir John Lubbock, and others form a committee to instruct electors of school-board..23 Oct. 1882
Fifth Metropolitan school-board elected (old policy affirmed; E. M. Buxton, chairman)............................24 Nov. "
Boys' public day-school company founded, 5 Dec. 1882; first school opened.....................................12 Sept. 1883
Technical college, Finsbury, opened....................19 Feb. "
Art for school societies formed in London and the provinces.. "
New education code (much attacked) takes effect.......3 Apr. 1884
Royal commission on technical instruction appointed, 5 Aug. 1881 (Bernhard Samuelson, prof. H. E. Roscoe, and 4 others), to inquire abroad and at home; 1st report, preliminary, 17 Feb. 1882; 2d report issued, reassuring as to English work, recommends advance in education, etc........about 16 May, "
Committee on relieving children coming to school unfed, Nov. 2; London School Dinner Association formed..........Dec. 1889
Grant for free or assisted education, $10,000,000 annually, proposed by Mr. Goschen..............................23 Apr. 1891
Irish Free Education act passed.......................27 June, 1892
Metropolitan school-board children on the rolls: 1871, 1117; 1890, 443,143.
Primary schools in Great Britain: in 1854, 3825; in 1860, 7272; in 1870, 10,949; in 1880, 20,670; in 1890, 22,495; average attendance, 4,927,987.
Annual grant for primary schools in Great Britain: in 1861, $4,067,-210; in 1870, $4,201,680; in 1880, $14,274,690; in 1890, $21,295,-400; in 1891, $21,964,685.
Grant for public education in Great Britain, in 1852, was $750,000; 1867, $3,529.325; 1884–85, $15,080,835 (for 18,540 schools, 4,670,000 pupils); 1891–92, $19,595,660.
Grant for education, science, and art, in 1861, was $6,794,980; 1872, $7,757,800; 1879–80, $14,274,690; 1891–92, $31,244,950.

education in the United States. Here popular education is provided for by the several states; their systems differ only in details. Early in the history of the northern colonies, free district schools were common, and out of these has grown a system of free, popular education in all the states; every child may have elementary secular education, without cost. The common-school system is supplemented by state normal schools, and the higher education is provided for by colleges. As early as 1647 Massachusetts passed laws authorizing public and grammar schools. Connecticut followed in 1650, and New Haven in 1655 enforced such laws by penalties. Rhode Island acted in 1690. Maine was a part of Massachusetts until 1820; New Hampshire until 1693. New Jersey, by law, 1693, left the establishment of schools to the majority of the inhabitants of each township; but, if decided upon, made the school-tax binding upon all. The Penn Charter school was established in 1698. New York, while slower in this movement than her neighbors until after the Revolution, organized a general school system by commissioners in 1812. District-school libraries were instituted in 1838, and a state normal school in 1844. The more southern states did little for education, except to aid a few colleges, until after the civil war. But in all the colonies the methods and instruments of instruction were of the simplest character; a brief inventory of the text-books in use in early colonial days will show this. The "New England Primer," used from the first in New England colonies, reached its 15th edition in 1720, and held its place as late as 1777. The "New England Psalm Book," in use until after the Revolution. "Dilworth's Spelling-book," succeeded by that of Noah Webster, pub. 1783, and still in print. John Woolman's "First Book for Children." The readers for the more advanced were Bingham's "American Preceptor," the "Columbian Orator," and later, Murray's "English Reader" (1800–45). Mathematics were not neglected, and "Hodder's Arithmetic," 1719, followed by Pike's, 1785, and later by Daboll's, 1790, and "Dellworth's Assistant," were found in all common schools of those times. Of grammars, Lindley Murray's was the first, followed later by Goold Brown's. These, with "Morse's Geography," 1784, and, later, Olney's, were the chief text-books in public or district schools throughout the U. S. up to 1840.

National Aid.—As early as 1785 the Continental Congress, foreshadowing the permanent policy of the nation in encouraging education, enacted that lot No. 16 of every township of public lands, consisting of 640 acres, or 1 mile square, be reserved for the maintenance of public schools. No method of managing this endowment was prescribed. It, however, established a principle, and dedicated $\frac{1}{36}$ part of all the public lands of the U. S. (with certain exceptions as to minerals, etc.), to the cause of education. This act was strengthened by the act of 23 July, 1787, making the reservation perpetual. Whether the public schools thus endowed were to remain under the control of the nation or the state remained a question until after the admission of Ohio in 1802. This income is supplemented by state and local taxation, so that it constitutes on an average about 5½ per cent. of the total school revenue of all the states. The total amount expended on elementary public schools in the U. S., for 1870, was $63,396,666; 1880, $78,094,687; 1890–91 it was $148,724,647 for the average attendance of 8,373,264 pupils for 134.7 days, out of 13,010,136 pupils enrolled from a school population of 18,812,766. The amount expended *per pupil* in the U. S. ranges from $3.38 in South Carolina to $43.43 in Colorado (Rept. of Com. of Ed. 1889–90). The number of pupils enrolled in private and parochial elementary schools, not included in these numbers, was estimated at 1,516,300. The private middle-class schools numbered 99,849 pupils. The following tables show the number of acres granted to the different states and territories by the U. S., for school purposes, arranged, as near as possible, according to the date of grant:

UNITED STATES LAND GRANTS FOR PUBLIC SCHOOLS.

State.	Date of Grant.	No. of Acres.
Ohio	3 Mch. 1803	704,488
Louisiana	21 Apr. 1806 15 Feb. 1843	786,044
Mississippi	3 Mch. 1803 19 May, 1852 3 Mch. 1857	837,584
Indiana	19 Apr. 1816	650,317
Illinois	18 Apr. 1818	985,066
Alabama	2 Mch. 1819	902,774
Missouri	6 Mch. 1820	1,199,139
Michigan	23 Jan. 1836	1,067,397
Arkansas	23 Jan. 1836	886,460
Florida	3 Mch. 1845	908,503
Iowa	3 Mch. 1845	905,144
Wisconsin	6 Aug. 1846	958,649
Washington	2 Mch. 1853	2,488,675
California	3 Mch. 1853	6,719,344
Minnesota	26 Feb. 1857	2,969,990
Oregon	14 Feb. 1859	3,329,706
Kansas	29 Jan. 1861	2,801,306
Montana	28 Feb. 1861	5,112,035
North Dakota South Dakota	2 Mch. 1861	8,554,560
Idaho	3 Mch. 1863	3,068,231
Nevada	21 Mch. 1864	3,985,428
Wyoming	25 July, 1868	3,480,281
Nebraska	19 Apr. 1869	2,702,044
Colorado	3 Mch. 1875	3,715,555
Territories.		
New Mexico	9 Sept. 1850 22 July, 1854	4,309,368
Utah	9 Sept. 1850	3,003,613
Arizona	26 May, 1864	4,050,347
	Total	71,082,048

UNIVERSITY GRANTS AND RESERVATIONS.

State	Date of Grant	No. of Acres
Ohio	21 Apr. 1792 3 Mch. 1803	69,120
Mississippi	3 Mch. 1803 20 Feb. 1819	46,080
Illinois	26 Mch. 1804 18 Apr. 1818	46,080
Indiana	26 Mch. 1804 19 Apr. 1816	46,080
Louisiana	26 Apr. 1806 3 Mch. 1811 3 Mch. 1827	46,080
Missouri	17 Feb. 1818 6 Mch. 1820	46,080
Alabama	20 Apr. 1818 2 Mch. 1819	46,080
Michigan	23 June, 1836	46,080
Arkansas	23 June, 1836	46,080
Florida	3 Mch. 1845	92,160
Iowa	3 Mch. 1845	46,080
Wisconsin	6 Aug. 1846 15 Dec. 1854	92,160
California	3 Mch. 1853	46,080
Washington	17 July, 1854 14 Mch. 1864	46,080
Minnesota	2 Mch. 1861 26 Feb. 1867 8 July, 1870	82,640
Oregon	14 Feb. 1859 2 Mch. 1861	46,080
Kansas	29 Jan. 1861	46,080
Nebraska	19 Apr. 1864	46,080
Nevada	4 July, 1866	46,080
Colorado	3 Mch. 1875	46,080
Territories.		
New Mexico	22 July, 1854	46,080
Utah	21 Feb. 1855	46,080
	Total	1,165,520

By act of Congress, 2 July, 1862, there was awarded 30,000 acres of public land to each state (no mineral lands to be selected) for each senator and representative in Congress, under the apportionment of 1860, to establish agricultural colleges and schools of the mechanic arts. The following table shows the location of colleges, with the number of acres granted and sum which the state received, with other information. UNITED STATES, 1890.

UNITED STATES LAND GRANTS FOR AGRICULTURAL COLLEGES AND SCHOOLS OF THE MECHANIC ARTS.

Location and name of College.	No. of acres.	Amt. received.	No. of pupils, 1890.
Auburn, Ala.—Alabama Polytechnic College	240,000	$216,000	247
Fayetteville, Ark.—Arkansas Industrial University	150,000	135,000	592
Berkeley, Cal.—University of California with branches	150,000	750,000	....
Fort Collins, Col.—State Agricultural College	90,000	112,500	74
New Haven—Sheffield Scientific School of Yale University	180,000	135,000	284
Newark, Del.—Delaware College	90,000	83,000	82
Lake City, Fla.—Florida Agricultural College	90,000	110,806	162
Athens, Ga.—State College of Agriculture and Mechanic Arts has branches at Cuthbert, Dahlonega, Milledgeville, and Thomasville	270,000	243,000	1010
Urbana, Ill.—University of Illinois, Agricultural department	480,000	319,494	463
Lafayette, Ind.—Pardee University, Agricultural department	390,000	212,238	429
Ames, Ia.—Iowa Agricultural College and Farm	240,000	500,000	226
Manhattan, Kan.—Kansas State Apricultural College	90,000	290,000	504
Lexington, Ky.—Agricultural and Mechanical College of Kentucky	330,000	165,000	532
Baton Rouge, La.—State Agricultural College	210,000	210,000	....
Orono, Me.—Maine State College of Agricultural and Mechanic Arts	210,000	116,359	131
College Hill, Md.—Maryland Agricultural College	210,000	112,500	45
Amherst, Mass.—Massachusetts Agricultural College }	360,000	157,538	135
Boston, Mass.—Massachusetts Institute of Technology }		78,769	873
Lansing, Mich.—State Agricultural College	240,000	275,104	378
Minneapolis, Minn.—University of the State of Minnesota, Agricultural department	120,000	178,000	150
Rodney, Miss.—Alcorn Agricultural and Mechanical College for colored pupils }	210,000	113,000	248
Starkville, Miss.—Mississippi Agricultural College }		115,000	330
Columbia, Mo.—University of the State of Missouri }	330,000	170,000	....
Rolla, Mo.—Missouri State School of Mines and Metallurgy }			67
Lincoln, Neb.—University of Nebraska, Agricultural department	90,000	39,504	....
Reno, Nev.—Nevada State University	90,000	95,000	....
Hanover, N. H.—New Hampshire College of Agriculture and Mechanic Arts	150,000	80,000	31
New Brunswick, N. J.—Rutgers Scientific School	210,000	116,000	80
Ithaca, N. Y.—Cornell University, Agricultural department. The national land grant of 1862 amounted to over $6,000,000 for this college. Valuable timber lands were located and held until 1881, through the advice and aid of Ezra Cornell, when 990,000 acres realized over $6 an acre	990,000	6,600,000	608
Chapel Hill, N. C.—North Carolina College of Agriculture and Mechanic Arts	270,000	125,000	72
Columbus, O.—Ohio State University, Agricultural department	630,000	507,913	....
Corvallis, Ore.—Oregon State Agricultural College	90,000	93,985	177
State College, Bellefonte, Pa.—Pennsylvania State College; farm, 400 acres	780,000	439,186	196
Providence, R. I.	120,000	50,000	....
Orangeburg, S. C.—Claflin University, College of Agriculture and Mechanic Institute	180,000	191,800	167
Knoxville, Tenn.—State Agricultural and Mechanic College	300,000	271,875	....
Bryan, Tex.—State Agricultural and Mechanic College	180,000	209,000	272
Burlington, Vt.—State Agricultural College, with the University of Vermont	150,000	122,626	....
Blacksburg, Va.—Virginia Agricultural and Mechanical College }	300,000	190,000	127
Hampton, Va.—Hampton Agricultural Institute }		95,000	692
Morgantown, W. Va.—West Virginia University, Agricultural department	150,000	90,000	....
Madison, Wis.—University of Wisconsin, Agricultural department	240,000	363,738	....
Total	9,600,000		
Total for universities	1,165,520		
" " public schools	71,082,048		
Grand total	81,847,568		

LIST OF THE LARGER INDIVIDUAL BENEFACTIONS, WITH NAME OF COLLEGE OR UNIVERSITY ENDOWED OR BENEFITED.

Benefactor.	College or University.	Amount.
Stephen Girard	Girard College, Pa.	$8,000,000
George Peabody	For educating in the U. S.	6,000,000
Leland Stanford	Leland Stanford, jr., University, Cal.	5,000,000
Asa Packer	Lehigh University, Pa.	3,500,000
Johns Hopkins	Johns Hopkins University, Md.	*3,500,000
Paul Turlane	Turlane University, La.	2,500,000
Isaac Rich	Boston University, Mass.	2,000,000
Jonas G. Clark	Clark University, Mass.	2,000,000
The Vanderbilts	Vanderbilt University, Tenn.	1,775,000
James Lick	University of California	1,650,000
John D. Rockefeller	University of Chicago	1,600,000
John C. Green	Princeton College, N. J.	1,500,000
Wm. C. De Pauw	De Pauw University, Ind.	1,500,000
A. J. Drexel	Drexel Industrial Institute, Pa.	1,500,000
Leonard Case	School of Applied Sciences, Cleveland, O.	1,200,000
Peter Cooper	Cooper Union, N. Y.	1,200,000
Ezra Cornell	Cornell University, Ithaca, N. Y.	1,000,000
Henry W. Sage	" " " "	1,100,000
Matthew Vassar	Vassar College, Poughkeepsie, N. Y.	998,000
George I. Seney	Wesleyan University, Conn.	700,000
S. W. Phenix	Columbia College, N. Y.	650,000
E. P. Greenleaf	Harvard University, Mass.	630,000
Amasa Stone	Adelbert College, O.	600,000
Ario Pardee	Lafayette College, Pa.	500,000
Benj. Bussey	Bussey Institute, Harvard University, Mass.	500,000
Joseph Sheffield	Yale College, Conn.	500,000
J. P. Jones	Haverford, Pa.	500,000
Joseph W. Taylor	Bryn Mawr College, Pa.	450,000

* A like bequest to the Johns Hopkins hospital.

educational institutions. COLLEGES, UNIVERSITIES, etc.; for academies and state normal schools, see each state separately.

Edward, Fort. FORT EDWARD.

Egypt, N.E. Africa; area, 400,000 sq. miles; pop. 1890, 6,817,265. The earliest-known seat of civilization, the hieroglyphic and Coptic Kemi; Hebrew, Mazor (Lower Egypt), Mizraim (Upper and Lower Egypt); Greek, Αἴγυπτος; Arabic for all Egypt, Misr or Masr. Three magnificent works on Egypt have been published: in France (commenced by Napoleon and the savans who accompanied him to Egypt), "Description de l'Égypte," 1809-22; in Italy, Rosellini's "Monumenti dell' Egitto," 1832-44; and in Prussia, Lepsius's "Denkmäler aus Aegypten," 1848-56. For our present knowledge of the early history of Egypt we are almost wholly indebted to discoveries in the present century, and to the interpretation of monumental inscriptions, and the papyri found in the tombs. Among the most recent investigators are Brugsch, Maspero, Lepsius, De Rougé, Mariette, Chabas, Lieblein, Birch, Naville, Le Page, Renouf, and Petrie. ABYDOS, EGYPTIAN EXPLORATION FUND, ROSETTA STONE, etc.

Manetho, a high-priest of On or Heliopolis, in the 2d century B.C., at the request of king Ptolemy Philadelphus, wrote a history of Egypt, under 30 dynasties from Menes to the Persian conquests; of his work only lists of kings were preserved, by Julius Africanus, a writer who lived about 300 A.D. Eusebius died about 340, Georgius Syncellus, 800.

Fabulous god-kings, including the sun-god Osiris, god of Hades, and Isis his wife, Typhon; Horus (the last) was said to have reigned 13,900 years, the demigods and manes, 4000 years.

Following table of dynasties, including the more important kings, is derived from various sources; the names and dates vary. B. stands for Brugsch, and M. for Mariette.

I. Thinite (from This, near Abydos), M. 5004; B. 4400 B.C.

Mena or Menes; first known king and law-giver, founder of Memphis. M. 5004; B. 4455. Tola or Athothis—Onenephes I., conjectured to have built the Stepped pyramid of Sakkárah.

II. Memphite. M. 4751; B. 4133.

Kakaoo or Kaiechos. The worship of Apis the bull established at Memphis. B. 4160.

III. Memphite (monumental history properly begins). M. 4449; B. 3966.

Seneferoo—soldier, architect, and patron of literature and art.

IV. Memphite. M. 4235; B. 3733.

Shoofoo or Khufa, the Cheops of Herodotus, built the great pyramid of Gizeh. M. 4235; B. 3733. The great limestone rock at the foot of the Libyan mountains was converted into the form of a man-headed lion, termed by the Greeks SPHINX. Khafra built the second Gizeh pyramid. B. 3666. Menkaura (Mycerinus III.). B. 3633. High state of civilization and art, and the vast cemetery of Memphis erected. The book or ritual of the dead (papyri) found in tombs. BOOK OF THE DEAD.

V. Memphite. M. 3951; B. 3566.

Raenooser. B. 3433. Katkara. B. 3366. Unas truncated pyramid near Sakkárah built. B. 3333.

VI. Memphite (history nearly a blank to the 11th dynasty). M. 3703; B. 3300.

Pepi I.—powerful—long reign. B. 3233. Romantic story of queen Nitocris in Herodotus.

VII. Memphite. B. 3100.

Petty kings.

VIII. Memphite.

IX. Heracleopolite. M. 3358.

X. Heracleopolite. M. 3249.

XI. Theban. M. 3064.

Sankhkara, expedition to Ophir and Punt (S. Arabia?). B. 2500.

XII. Theban (Egypt very prosperous). B. 2466.

Amenemhat I. M. 3064; B. 2466.

Osirtasen I. (obelisk of On or Heliopolis erected).

Osirtasen II. (memorial temple discovered in 1889).

Osirtasen III., important national works, excavated the lake Moeris and made the labyrinth and the Nilometer. B. 2300.

XIII. Theban. M. 2851; B. 2233.

Sebekhotep, name of several kings.

XIV. Xoite. M. 2398.

XV. Hyksos or Shepherd kings. M. 2214.

Invaders from Asia take Memphis and settle in Lower Egypt.

XVI. Hyksos or Shepherd kings.

XVII. Hyksos or Shepherd kings.

Nub—arrival of Joseph. B. 1750.

Dynasties XIII.-XVII. history very obscure; probably Theban kings reigned in southern, while the Hyksos reigned in Lower Egypt.

XVIII. Theban. M. 1703; B. 1700.

Achmes I. conquers the Hyksos. M. 1703; B. 1700. Amenhotep I. B. 1666. Thothmes I. B. 1633. Thothmes II. and Hatasoo, sister. B. 1600. Thothmes III., great king, victor in western Asia, etc.; his exploits recorded in his temple at Karnak. B. 1600. Amenhotep II. B. 1566. Thothmes IV. B. 1533. Amenhotep III. victorious in Ethiopia; the Colossi or vocal Memnon bear his name. B. 1500. Amenhotep IV. introduced Semitic worship. 2 or 3 heretical successors. Haremhebi or Horus restores the old worship.

XIX. Theban. M. 1462; B. 1400.

Rameses I. M. 1462; B. 1400. Seti or Sethos (Menetah I.) victorious in Asia; made first canal from the Red sea to the Nile; many monuments of him at Karnak, etc. B. 1333. Rameses II., son, the legendary Sesostris, took Salem, conquered Ethiopia, and built a fleet about 1322. Maneptah, son, probably the Pharaoh of the Exodus, 1300; Seti II. and 2 or 3 unimportant kings.

XX. Theban. M. 1288; B. 1200.

Rameses III. (Rhampsinitus of Herodotus) victorious, cultivated navigation and commerce. M. 1288; B. 1200. Inglorious line of kings named Rameses.

EGY

XXI. Tanite. M. 1110; B. 1100.

History obscure—Hirhor, high-priest of Amen, probably first of priest kings—Assyrian governors.

XXII. Bubasite. M. 980; B. 966. Shashank or Sheshonk I., Shishak, 1 Kings xiv. 25-28.

XXIII. Tanite, probably only 3 petty kings. M. 810; B. 766.

XXIV. Saite. M. 721; B. 733.

Bocchoris (Bokenranef), taken prisoner by Sabaco, king of Ethiopia, and burned alive. During the last 3 dynasties, the Ethiopians appear to have ruled in the south.

XXV. Karnak. Ethiopian. M. 715; B. 700.

Shabat or Sabaco. M. 715; B. 700. Takaraka or Tirhakah (2 Kings xix. 9). B. 693. Egypt frequently invaded by the Assyrians; subdued and divided into 12 governments.

XXVI. Saite. M. 665; B. 666.

Psammetichus I. (Greek), governor under the Assyrians, restored the monarchy and revived art. M. 665; B. 666. Necho II. son, attempted a canal across isthmus of Suez; defeated Josiah, king of Judah, at Megiddo (2 Kings xxiii. 29); defeated by Nebuchadnezzar at Carchemish, 612. Psammetichus II.; inglorious. B. 596. Uahbra or Hophra (Jer. xliv. 30), son; went to help Zedekiah, but deserted him. B. 591. Apries loses the conquests and is strangled by Amasis, who has a long, prosperous reign and increased intercourse with the Greeks. B. 572. Psammetichus III. son (defeated by Cambyses, son of Cyrus, king of Persia). B. 528.

XXVII. Persian. M. 527; B. 527.

Cambyses conquers Egypt; his army lost invading Ethiopia. M. 527; B. 527. Darius I. Hystaspes, greatly favored Egypt, 521. Xerxes I., severe (Egyptian revolt subdued), 486. Artaxerxes I. Longimanus (another revolt), 465. Darius II. Nothos, 424. Egypt regained its independence by Armyrtæus, 424.

XXVIII. Saite. M. 406.

Armyrtæus, 406.

XXIX. Mendesian. M. 399; B. 399.

Nepherches and Achoris maintain Greek alliance.

XXX. Sebennyte. M. 378; B. 378.

Nectanebes I. Nectanebes II. conquered by Artaxerxes Ochus, king of Persia.

XXXI. Persia, 340.

Darius III. Codomanus—defeated by Alexander the Great and killed.

Alexander conquered Egypt and founded Alexandria.......... 332

Empire divided, 323. One of Alexander's generals, Ptolemy I. (the son of Lagus) Soter became king of Egypt.............. 323

Ptolemy II. Philadelphus (with his father), 285; alone (museum of Alexandria founded; Septuagint version of Hebrew Scriptures made; Pharos completed)....................283-247

Ambassadors first sent to Rome.............................. 269

Ptolemy III. Euergetes reigns............................... 247

Overruns Syria; returns laden with rich spoils and 2500 statues and vessels of gold and silver, which Cambyses had taken from Egyptian temples (*Blair*).............................. 246

Ptolemy IV. Philopator.............................Nov. 222

Battle of Raphia; Ptolemy defeats Antiochus, king of Syria.... 217

Ptolemy V. Epiphanes...............................Nov. 205

Embassy to Rome.. 200

Egypt under the protective influence of Rome................ "

Ptolemy VI. Philometor..............................Oct. 181

At the death of Philometor, his brother Physcon (Ptolemy VII. Euergetes) marries his queen, and on the same day murders Philometor's infant son in the mother's arms...........Nov. 146

His subjects, wearied by cruelties and crimes, expel him....... 130

He defeats the Egyptians and recovers his throne, 128; d....... 117

Ptolemy VIII. Soter II. and Cleopatra his mother.............. "

Alexander I. and Cleopatra.................................. 107

Ptolemy VIII. restored...................................... 89

Revolt in Upper Egypt; Thebes destroyed after a siege of 3 years (*Diod. Siculus*)...................................... 82

Alexander II. and Cleopatra I............................... 81

Ptolemy IX. Auletes... 80

Berenice and Tryphæna....................................... 58

Auletes restored, 55; leaves his kingdom to Ptolemy and Cleopatra.. 51

Pompeius (Pompey) slain by the order of Ptolemy........Sept. 48

During a civil war between Ptolemy and Cleopatra II., Alexandria is besieged by Julius Cæsar, and the library nearly destroyed by fire (*Blair*)............................... 47

Cæsar defeats the king, who, in crossing the Nile, is drowned; the younger Ptolemy and Cleopatra reign................... 46

Cleopatra poisons her brother, and reigns alone............... 43

She appears before Mark Antony to answer the crime; fascinated by her beauty, he follows her into Egypt............. 41

Cleopatra in Syria.. 36

Antony defeated by Octavianus Cæsar at Actium (*Blair*)..2 Sept. 31

Octavianus enters Egypt; Antony and Cleopatra kill themselves; Egypt a Roman province..................Sept. 30

Octavianus (Augustus) Cæsar introduces the Julian year........ 24

A.D.

Egypt visited by Hadrian, 122; by Severus................... 200

By Caracalla (MASSACRES).................................... 215

Egypt conquered by Zenobia, queen of Palmyra................ 270

Reconquered by emperor Aurelian.............................. 272

Severe Christian persecution by Diocletian................... 303

Monachism begun in Egypt by Antony.......................... 305

Destruction of the temple and worship of Serapis............. 389

Egypt conquered by Chosroes II. of Persia.................... 616

Invasion of the Saracens under Amrou................June, 638

Conquest of Alexandria..........................22 Dec. 640

Cairo founded by the Saracens................................ 969

Conquest by the Turks...................................1163-96

Government of the Mamelukes established..................... 1250

Selim I, emperor of the Turks, conquers Egypt 1517

It is governed by beys till a great part is conquered by the French under Bonaparte (ALEXANDRIA) 1798–99

French expelled by British, Turks restored 1801

Mehemet Ali massacres the MAMELUKES, and reigns 1 Mch 1811

Arrival of Belzoni, 1815, he removes statue of MEMNON, 1816, explores temples, etc 1817

Mahmoud canal, from Alexandria to the Nile, built 1820

Mehemet Pacha revolts and invades Syria 1831

His son Ibrahim takes Acre, 27 May, overruns Syria, defeats the Turks at Konieh 21 Dec 1832

He advances on Constantinople, which Russian auxiliaries enter, 3 Apr, peace by convention of Kutayah 4 May, 1833

Mehemet again revolts claiming hereditary power, Ibrahim defeats the Turks at Nezib 24 June, 1839

England, Austria, Russia, and Prussia undertake to expel Ibrahim from Syria, Napier bombards Beyrout, 10 Oct, Acre taken by the British and Austrian fleets under sir R Stopford, 3 Nov, the Egyptians quit Syria 21 Nov. et seq 1840

Peace restored by treaty, Mehemet made hereditary viceroy of Egypt but deprived of Syria 15 July, 1841

Ibrahim Pacha d 10 Nov 1848

SUEZ CANAL begun 1858

Hereditary succession and right of coining money granted but tribute raised from 400,000*l.* to 750,000*l* 27 May, 1861

Malta and Alexandria telegraph opened 1 Nov "

Viceroy Saïd visits Italy, France, and England, May to Sept, returns to Alexandria 1 Oct. 1862

Sultan of Turkey visits Egypt 7 Apr 1863

Increased cultivation of cotton in Egypt 1863–67

At the demand of the sultan, the viceroy sends troops to repress the insurgents in Arabia May, 1864

Opening of part of Suez canal 15 Aug 1865

Direct succession to the viceroyalty granted by the Porte, 21 May, 1866

Opening of the Suez canal 17 Nov 1869

Differences with the sultan respecting prerogatives arranged, the viceroy giving up power over taxes and loans. Dec "

Sir Samuel Baker commissioned to suppress the slave trade up the Nile, with absolute authority south of Gondokoro (for 4 years from 1 Apr 1869) 10 May, 1869

Departure from Khartoum 8 Feb. 1870

After long delay, starts to explore White Nile 11 Aug "

Arrives at Gondokoro 15 Apr, names it Ismailia, and officially annexes it to Egypt. . 26 May, 1871

Advances south Jan.–Feb. 1872

Arrives at the African paradise, Faliko, 6 Mch, at Masindi, in Unyoro 25 Apr "

Received by Kabba Rega, the young king, who attempts to poison Baker's party, and attacks them in the night, he is defeated and Masindi burned 8 June, "

Baker marches to Foweera, 18 July, returns to Faliko 2 Aug "

Slave trade apparently subdued. . 31 Dec. "

Baker returns to Gondokoro, 1 Apr, honors from the khedive at Cairo, 25 Aug, reaches London 9 Oct. 1873

Col Gordon appointed successor, Abou Saoud subordinate . "

Baker's work, "Ismailia," pub Nov 1874

First stone of new port laid by khedive. . 15 May, 1871

Khedive's son, prince Hassan, made D.C.L. at Oxford 13 June, 1872

Sultan, by firman, renders khedive practically independent (he must not coin money, make treaties, or build iron-clads), 8 June, 1873

First Egyptian budget produced, asserted revenue, $50,830,000, expenditure, $45,200,000 Oct "

International court of justice opened by the khedive 28 June, 1875

Khedive's shares of Suez canal purchased by the British government, announced Nov "

British Egyptian expedition into Abyssinia surprised and defeated with much slaughter . . . 16 Oct. "

New (Gregorian) style adopted, mixed courts opened 1 Jan. 1876

War with Abyssinia 1875–77

Col Gordon, after great success, reaches England Feb. 1877

Peace with Abyssinia negotiating by col Gordon, June, terms said to be accepted. Oct "

Definitive peace between the khedive and Abyssinia announced, Feb. 1879

Col Gordon's lieutenant, Gessi (Nov 1878), defeats rebel slave-dealers in Soudan, central Africa 5 May, "

England and France, by note, require the appointment of European ministers. about 5 May, "

England, France, Germany, Austria, and Italy recommend the khedive to abdicate about 20 June, "

He refers to the sultan, who declines to interfere, the khedive offers to pay his debts in full 22 June, "

Khedive deposed by the sultan, prince Tewfik, his son, proclaimed successor 26 June, "

Khedive leaves for Naples 30 June, "

Tewfik succeeds as khedive 8 Aug "

Col Gordon, negotiating with Abyssinia to prevent war, reported successful Oct. "

He resigns governorship of the Soudan, Oct. 1879, accepted, Jan 1880

Peace with Abyssinia announced . end of June, "

Decree for abolition of slavery end of July, 1881

Insurrection in the SOUDAN July, "

Ministerial crisis, khedive calls for Riaz Pacha Aug "

Ahmed Arabi Bey and about 4000 soldiers surround the khedive's palace, demanding increased pay—agreed to, Cherif Pacha made minister 9 Sept 1881

EGY

Arabi Bey appointed under secretary of war Jan 1882

Crisis continues, 9–13 May, khedive firm, ministry submits, about 16 May, English and French squadron arrive at Alexandria, 20 May, Arabi Pacha refuses to resign, 23 May, ultimatum of English and French consuls, Arabi Pacha to retire, khedive's authority to be restored etc 25 May, "

Ministry resigns, Cherif Pacha appointed, May, officers resist, Arabi Pacha reinstated, 27–28 May, anarchy, Europeans quitting the country, 29 May, 6000 Egyptian soldiers said to be massacred June, "

Commencement of rebellion, riots at Alexandria, Arabs attack Europeans, quelled by Egyptian troops great loss of life (about 60 Europeans killed), town ravaged and deserted, 11 June, "

Powers agree to a conference at Constantinople, Turkey objects, 19 June, "

Conference opened 24 June, "

English and French admirals protest against the fortifying of Alexandria about 4 July, "

British subjects warned to quit Egypt about 6 July, "

Bombardment of forts at Alexandria threatened by admiral Seymour, if works threatening the British fleet are not stopped 9 July, "

Bombardment begun, its object fully obtained, bombardment ceases, 5.30 P.M., Egyptian loss heavy in forts and part of the town British loss 6 killed, 28 wounded 11 July, "

Arabi Pacha and part of his army abandon Alexandria and retreat into the interior, he releases convicts, who with the Arab mob plunder and set fire to the city, and massacre it is said, many Christians 12 July, "

European portion entirely destroyed 13 July, "

Khedive at palace Ras el Tin guarded by British marines degrades Arabi Pacha from his office, sends for Cherif Pacha, Riaz Pacha etc. about 16 July, "

Arabi Pacha attempts to cut off water supply, denounces the khedive, and calls on the people about 20, 21 July, "

Proclamation of khedive declaring Arabi a rebel, etc, about 23 July, "

Arabi proclaims a Jihad or holy war, said to have 30,000 men, about 24 July, "

British troops landed at Alexandria 24 July, "

Troops sent to Egypt from England and India about 25 July, "

Duke of Connaught sails in the *Orient* for Egypt 31 July, "

Sir Evelyn Wood sails for Egypt 3 Aug "

Reconnoissance by gen sir A Alison, British success, near Mahmoudieh canal, lieut. Howard Vyse and 3 others killed, about 30 wounded, Egyptian loss about 300 5 Aug "

Conference agrees to the international protection of the Suez canal, and adjourns *sine die* 14 Aug "

Sir Garnet Wolseley assumes command at Alexandria, khedive empowers British commanders to establish order "

Troops, etc., under gen Willis embark as if for Aboukir, but proceed eastward and occupy Port Saïd, Ismailia, and Kantara, thus command the canal 19, 20 Aug, skirmishes near Mahmoudieh canal sir Evelyn Wood successful, the enemy shelled out of Nefiche. 20 Aug "

Total British force in Egypt, 31,4[illegible] " "

Twenty six British ironclads at Alexandria " "

Gen Macpherson with Indian troops arrives at Suez 21 Aug "

From Ismailia 2 squadrons of household cavalry, with 2 guns, and detachment of 19th hussars, mounted infantry, etc, move on Nefiche, met by 10,000 Egyptians with artillery, 21 Aug "

Cavalry and artillery engagement, enemy routed, capture of 5 Krupp guns and train of ammunition and provisions, Egyptian camps at Tel el Mahuta and Mahsameh occupied, British loss, 6 killed, 30 wounded 25 Aug "

Suez canal held by the British 26 Aug "

Gen Graham at Kassassin vigorously attacked by 13,000 Egyptians, signals for assistance rendered by gen Drury Lowe with household cavalry, brilliant charge and capture of 11 guns (afterwards lost), rout of the enemy, disorderly flight, British loss, 7 killed, 70 wounded 28 Aug "

Capture of TEL-EL KEBIR, Egyptians routed under Arabi Pacha, surrender of Zagazig with railway trains etc 13 Sept "

British enter Cairo, Arabi Pacha and his officers surrender unconditionally with about 10,000 Egyptian soldiers. 14 Sept "

Khedive dissolves the Egyptian army 17 Sept "

Surrender of Aboukir, 17 Sept., re establishment of khedive's authority 19 Sept "

Abd el Al holding Damietta with about 7000 men, 21 Sept, sir Evelyn Wood sent against him, 22 Sept, he surrenders, 23 Sept. "

Valentine Baker Pacha nominated commander of a new Egyptian army (10,900) end of Sept "

Twelve thousand British to remain in Egypt, sir A Alison commander 30 Sept "

Prophet El Mahdi said to hold all the country south of Khartoum 25 *Oct* "

Anglo French control abolished 9 Nov "

Arabi Pacha tried, secret examination of witnesses (defence supported by Wilfred Blunt) Nov "

Pleads guilty of rebellion, sentence of death commuted to banishment for life 3 Dec "

Letters from Arabi Pacha to Wilfred Blunt, expressing gratitude to, and confidence in, England 4 Dec, *Times*, 5 Dec "

Mahoud and other rebel leaders sentenced to banishment, 7 Dec. "

Riaz Pacha resigns, succeeded by Nubar Pacha 7, 8 Dec "

Sir Evelyn Wood appointed commander of the new Egyptian army, arrives at Cairo 22 Dec 1882
Arabi and others sail for Ceylon, 27 Dec., arrive 10 Jan 1883
End of dual control 11 Jan "
British circular to the powers laid before the Porte, etc. (the Suez canal to be free, with restrictions in time of war, formation of Egyptian army, etc.) 11 Jan et seq "
Powers, except France and Turkey, consent, about 27 Jan "
Constitution signed by khedive 30 Apr., promulgated, 1 May, "
Suleiman Sami convicted of firing, massacring and plundering at Alexandria (11 June, 1882), hanged 9 June, "
Ex khedive Ismail in London 28 June, "
Parliamentary grants to lord Alcester (Seymour), 25,000*l.*, lord Wolseley 30,000*l.* 29 June, "
Departure of some British troops countermanded on account of the destruction of gen. Hicks's army (SOUDAN) Nov "
British government require a limitation of the line of defence in regard to the Soudan 6 Jan 1884
British army total killed, 255 July, 1882–Mch "
Conference on Egyptian finance invited by England, Germany, Austria, Russia, Italy, France, and Turkey accept May, "
Conference meets 28 June, "
Conference adjourns without result *sine die* 2 Aug "
British force in Egypt and Soudan, about 16,000 men Nov "
Ancient necropolis discovered at Assouan Feb 1886
Sudden death of gen. Valentine Baker Pacha, aged 62 17 Nov 1887
Ismail Pacha permitted to reside at Constantinople. Dec "
Equatorial province lost by the retirement of Emin Pacha. 1888–89
Forced labor (*corvee*) of peasantry (*fellaheen*) abolished, tax proposed to general assembly, 15 Dec., enacted 17 Dec. 1889
Discovery of a vast tomb of a high priest of Ammon, west of Thebes (MUMMIES) Feb 1891
Sudden death of khedive Tewfik 7 Jan 1892
Abbas, his eldest son recognized by the Porte 8 Jan "
New railway bridge over the Nile opened by the khedive, 5 May, "

KHEDIVES, OR HEREDITARY VICEROYS
(nearly independent)

1806 Mehemet Ali Pacha, abdicated Sept 1848, d. 2 Aug 1849
1848 Ibrahim (adopted son) Sept., d. 9 or 10 Nov 1848
" Abbas (his son) 10 Nov., d. 14 July, 1854.
1854 Saïd (brother) 14 July, d. 18 Jan 1863
1863. Ismail (nephew) 18 Jan (b. 31 Dec 1830), deposed by the sultan at the request of England, France, and other powers, 26 June, 1879
1879. Mechmet Tewfik, b. 10 Nov 1852, invested with the Star of India by the prince of Wales 25 Oct 1875, proclaimed 26 June acceded 14 Aug., d. 7 Jan 1892.
1892 Abbas Pacha (son of Tewfik), b. 14 July, 1874, acceded 8 Jan

Egyptian Era, etc The old Egyptian year was the era of Nabonassar of 365 days, dating from 26 Feb 747 B.C. It was reformed 30 B.C., when the new year had receded to 29 Aug., thenceforth made the first day of the year To reduce to the Christian era, subtract 746 years, 125 days The canicular or heliacal period of the Egyptians and Ethiopians (1460 years) began when Sirius, or the dog-star, emerged from the rays of the sun, on 20 July, 2785 B.C., and extended to 1325 B.C. This year comprised 12 months of 30 days, with 5 supplementary days.

Egyptian Exploration Fund, originated by Miss Amelia B. Edwards, a learned Egyptologist, and promoted by sir Erasmus Wilson, 1st president (d. 8 Aug 1884), and R. S. Poole, secretary, 1881, to elucidate by excavations the history and arts of ancient Egypt and biblical history Miss Edwards died 15 Apr. 1892 She bequeathed property to endow a professorship of Egyptology in University college, London

M. Edouard Naville's explorations began 19 Jan 1883. The excavations conducted by M. Naville, 1883–84, led to many important discoveries, including the site of Goshen W. M. F. Petrie examined more than 20 sites in 1884–85, and made remarkable discoveries. Some of the results were given to British and foreign museums He disclosed Naucratis, which was a flourishing Greek commercial and manufacturing city, on the Canopic arm of the Nile, about 550 B.C., and declined after the Persian invasion and the founding of Alexandria 332 B.C. Explorations carried on by F. Llewellyn Griffith at Tanis, 1886, Mr Petrie, in the mounds of Tel Defenneh, discovered the remains of "Pharaoh's house in Tahpanhes" (588 B.C., Jer xliii 8–11), May, 1886

Ernest A. Gardner reported excavations in the spring at Naucratis, and exhibited statuettes, pottery, etc., from temples, cemeteries, etc., 6 July, 1886 M. Naville's explorations at the city of Onia and the "Mound of the Jews" continued spring 1887 He discovers the great temple of Bubastis (about 1300 B.C.), granite monolithic colums, sculpture, etc., Apr.–June, 1887, resumes his excavations, Mch. 1888.

Exhibition of Egyptian antiquities at the Egyptian Hall, Piccadilly, London, by Flinders Petrie, of his excavations at Fayoum, July, 1888.

Mr Petrie forces an extrance into the sepulchral chamber of the pyramid of Anenemhat III at Hawara, Jan., exhibits the results of his explorations, at the Oxford Mansions, London, mummies, ornaments, implements, etc., Sept. 1889 et seq

A monograph on the results of M. Naville's excavations at Bubastis in 1887–89, pub. in the "Memoirs" Feb 1891

Mr Petrie discovers fragments of a lost play of Euripides, of the "Phædo" of Plato and other writers, which have been published by prof. Mahaffy after study by himself and prof. Sayce, reported July, 1891 Mr Petrie's "Ten Years' Digging in Egypt, 1881 to 1891," pub May, 1892

Egyptology. Much attention has been given of late years to this science, and great interest excited through the interpretation of monumental inscriptions, discoveries, etc. Consult "BOOK OF THE DEAD," EGYPT, EGYPTIAN EXPLORATION FUND, MUMMIES, etc

Ehrenbreit'stein ("honor's broad stone"), a Prussian fortress on the Rhine, formerly belonged to the electors of Treves It was often besieged It surrendered to the French general Jourdain, 24 Jan 1799 The fortifications were destroyed on its evacuation, 9 Feb 1801, at the peace of Luneville The works have been restored since 1814

Eiffel tower, so called from its builder, a colossal iron structure, erected on the Champ-de-Mars, Paris, 1887–89. One of the principal curiosities of the great exposition at Paris, 1889 It is 985 ft high, contains 7000 tons of iron, and cost $1,000,000

"Eikōn Basil'ikē" ("The Portraiture of His Sacred Majesty in his Solitudes and Sufferings"), a book of devotion formerly attributed to king Charles I, but now generally believed to have been written mainly by bishop Gauden, and approved by the king, it was pub. in 1648, and sold quickly.

Eisteddfod, from the Welsh verb *eistedd*, to sit; meaning a session or muster First appointed by Gryffith ap Conan to reform the Welsh bard system, 1078 BARDS.

El-Arisch, a village of Egypt, captured by French under Reynier 18 Feb 1799 A convention was signed here between the grand-vizier and Kleber for the evacuation of Egypt by the French, 28 Jan 1800 Kleber beat the Turks at Heliopolis on 20 Mch., and was assassinated 14 June following

Elba, Isle of, on the coast of Tuscany, Italy, about 6 miles from the mainland, area 90 sq miles, taken by admiral Nelson in 1796, but abandoned 1797 Elba was conferred upon Napoleon (with the title of emperor) on his abdication in France, 5 Apr 1814. He secretly embarked hence, with about 1200 men in hired feluccas, on the night of 25 Feb 1815, landed in Provence, 1 Mch., and soon after recovered the crown FRANCE, 1815 Elba was resumed by the grand-duke of Tuscany, July, 1815 Annexed to Italy in 1860, and now forms part of the Italian province of Livorno

Elchingen, a village of Bavaria Here Ney beat the Austrians, 14 Oct 1805, and was made duke of Elchingen

elders (Gr πρεσβύτεροι), in the early church one with ἐπίσκοποι, or bishops (see 1 Tim. iii and Titus i), who afterwards became a distinct and superior order Elders in the Presbyterian churches are laymen

El Dora'do ("the Gilded Man") When the Spaniards had conquered Mexico and Peru, they began to look for new sources of wealth, and having heard, through Orellana, a companion of Pizarro and the explorer of the Amazon, of a city ruled by a king whose garments, changed daily, were woven gold, they organized expeditions into the interior of South America about 1560, in search of this fabulous region, which they and other nations continued to believe in and search for quite to the 18th century Raleigh's expeditions were in search of this region, in 1596 and 1617.

"But he grew old—this knight so bold—
And o'er his heart a shadow
Fell, as he found no spot of ground
That looked like El Dorado "—*Poe*

Eleanor's crosses. 12 memorial crosses erected, in conformity with the will of Eleanor of Castile, wife of Edward I of England, in the places where her bier rested on its way from Hornby in Lincolnshire, Engl., where she died (1290) to Westminster Abbey, where she was buried. The 12 places are here given in their order, from Hornby to Westminster Lincoln, Grantham, Stamford, Geddington, Northampton, Stony Stratford, Woburn, Dunstable, St. Albans, Waltham, West Cheap, Charing But 3 now remain, Geddington, Northampton, and Waltham CHARING CROSS

Eleasa, Palestine Here Judas Maccabæus was defeated and slain by Bacchides and Alcimus and the Syrians, about 161 B.C. (1 Macc. ix.).

Eleatic sect, founded at Elea, in Sicily, by Xenophanes of Colophon, about 535 B.C., whither he had been banished on account of his wild theory of God and nature. He supposed that the stars were extinguished every morning and rekindled at night, that eclipses were occasioned by partial extinction of the sun, that there were several suns and moons for the convenience of the different climates of the earth, etc.—*Strabo*. Zeno (about 163 B.C.) was an Eleatic. PHILOSOPHY.

elections, United States. The presidential election takes place on the 1st Tuesday after the 1st Monday of Nov. in every 4th year preceding the year in which the presidential term expires. UNITED STATES. The state elections are held on the same day of the month, with the following exceptions: Alabama, 1st Monday in Aug.; Arkansas, 1st Monday in Sept.; Georgia, 1st Wednesday in Oct.; Louisiana, 3d Monday in Apr.; Maine, 2d Monday in Sept.; Oregon, 1st Monday in June; Rhode Island, 1st Wednesday in Apr.; Vermont, 1st Tuesday in Sept.

Electoral Commission. UNITED STATES, 1876.

electoral vote. UNITED STATES throughout.

electors in England for members of Parliament for counties were obliged to have 40*s.* a year in land, 8 Hen. VI. 1429. Among the acts relating to electors are the following: Act depriving excise and custom-house officers and contractors with government of their votes, 1782. CUSTOMS. Act to regulate polling, 1828. Great changes were made by the Reform acts of 1832, 1867, and 1868. County Elections act, 1836. BRIBERY. The 40*s.* freeholders in Ireland lost their privilege in 1829. By Dodson's act, passed in 1861, university electors are permitted to vote by sending balloting papers. Hours of polling in metropolitan boroughs extended (from 8 A.M. to 8 P.M.) by act passed 25 Feb. 1878.

electors of Germany. In the reign of Conrad I., king of Germany (912–18), the dukes and counts, from being merely officers, became gradually independent of the sovereign, and subsequently elected him. In 919 they confirmed the nomination of Henry I., duke of Saxony, by Conrad as his successor. In the 13th century 7 princes (the archbishops of Mentz, Treves, and Cologne, the king of Bohemia, the electors of Brandenburg and Saxony, and the elector palatine) assumed the exclusive privilege of nominating the emperor.—*Robertson*. An 8th elector (Bavaria) was made in 1648, and a 9th (Hanover) in 1692. The number was reduced to 8 in 1777 (by the elector palatine acquiring Bavaria), and increased to 10 at the peace of Luneville in 1801. On the dissolution of the German empire, the crown of Austria was made hereditary, 1804–6. GERMANY.

electors, United States. By the constitution (art. ii. sec. 1), the president and vice president are chosen every 4 years by electors. As many are appointed by each state, "in such manner as the legislature thereof may direct," as the state has representatives and senators in Congress. By the TWELFTH ARTICLE OF AMENDMENTS, the electors meet in their respective states and vote by ballot for 2 persons, of whom one at least shall not be an inhabitant of the same state with themselves. The result, duly certified, is then transmitted to the president of the Senate, who shall, in the presence of both houses, open the certificates and the votes shall then be counted. The person having the greatest number of votes is declared president, "if such number be a majority of the whole number of electors appointed; and if there be more than one who have such majority, and have an equal number of votes," then the House of Representatives chooses one of them for president, the votes being taken by states. After this vote, the person having the greatest number of electoral votes is declared vice-president. If the House in such a case should not before 4 Mch. following choose a president, then the former vice-president becomes acting president. In case there is no majority of electoral votes for vice-president, he is, in like manner, chosen by the Senate. The 49th Congress enacted that the presidential electors meet and vote on the 2d Monday in Jan. next following the election, and that Congress count the ballots on the 2d Wednesday in Feb. succeeding.

electricity (from the Gr. ἤλεκτρον, electrum, amber). The electrical properties of amber while being rubbed are said to have been known to Thales, 600 B.C., and Pliny, 70 A.D. MAGNETISM.

FRICTIONAL OR STATIC ELECTRICITY.

Gilbert records that other bodies besides amber generate electricity when rubbed, and that all substances may be attracted. He was the first to use the term *electric*, as electric force, electric attraction, etc. 1600
Otto von Guericke constructed the first electric machine (a globe of sulphur) about 1647
Robert Boyle published his electrical experiments 1676
Stephen Gray, aided by Wheeler, discovered that the human body conducts electricity; that electricity acts at a distance (motion in light bodies being produced by frictional electricity at a distance of 666 feet), the fact of electric induction, and other phenomena 1720–36
Du Fay stated his theory of 2 electric fluids, *vitreous*, from rubbed glass, etc., and *resinous*, from rubbed amber, resin, etc., and showed that bodies similarly electrified repel while those oppositely electrified attract each other about 1733
Désaguliers classified bodies as electrics and non-electrics 1742
Leyden jar (vial or bottle) discovered by Kleist 1745, and by Cunæus and Muschenbroek of Leyden; Winckler constructed the Leyden battery 1746
Researches of Watson, Canton, Beccaria, and Nollet 1740–47
At a picnic, Franklin "killed a turkey by the electric spark and roasted it by an electric jack before a fire kindled by the electric bottle" 1748
He announced his theory of a single fluid, terming vitreous electricity *positive*, and resinous *negative*, 1747, and demonstrated the identity of the electric spark and lightning, drawing electricity from a cloud by a kite June, 1752
Prof. Richman killed at St. Petersburg while repeating Franklin's experiments Aug. 1753
Beccaria published his researches on atmospheric electricity, 1758, and Æpinus his mathematical theory 1759
Electricity developed by fishes investigated by Ingenhousz, Cavendish, and others about 1773
Lichtenberg produced his electrical figures 1777
Electro statics. Coulomb applied the torsion balance to the measurement of electric force 1785
Electro chemistry. water decomposed by Cavendish, Fourcroy, and others 1787–90
Discoveries of Galvani and Volta (VOLTAIC ELECTRICITY, next page) 1791–93
Oersted, of Copenhagen, discovered electro magnetic action (ELECTRO MAGNETISM, next page) 1819
Thermo electricity (currents produced by heat) discovered by Seebeck, produced by heating pieces of copper and bismuth soldered together, 1821. The thermo electrometer invented by William Snow Harris, 1827, the thermo multiplier constructed by Melloni and Nobili 1831
[Marcus constructed a powerful thermo electric battery in 1865.]
Faraday produced a spark by the sudden separation of a coiled keeper from a permanent magnet (MAGNETO ELECTRICITY, next page) "
Wheatstone calculated the velocity of electricity, on the double fluid theory, to be 288 000 miles a second; on the single fluid theory, 576,000 miles a second . 1834
Armstrong discovered, and Faraday explained, electricity in high pressure steam, used in the hydro electric machine 1840
Electric Machines.—Otto von Guericke obtained sparks by rubbing a globe of sulphur, about 1647; Newton, Boyle, and others used glass, about 1675; Hawksbee improved the machine, about 1709; Bose introduced a metallic conductor, 1733; Winckler contrived the cushion for the rubber, 1741; Gordon employed a glass cylinder, 1742, for which a plate was substituted about 1770; Canton introduced amalgam for the rubber, 1751; Van Marum constructed an electric machine at Haarlem, said to have been the most powerful ever made, 1785; Dr. H. M. Noad set up at the Panopticon, Leicester square, London, a very powerful electric machine and Leyden battery (in possession of Edwin Clark, 1862) 1855
Hydro electric machine, by Armstrong, was constructed 1840
Electrophorus, a useful apparatus for obtaining frictional electricity, was invented by Volta in 1775, and improved by him 1782
C. F. Varley's "reciprocal electrophorus" invented 1862
Holtz's induction machine 1866
Sir William Thomson's "electric replenisher" described Jan. 1868
Mr. Apps's great inductorium, or induction coil, giving the largest sparks ever seen, exhibited at the Royal Polytechnic Institution . . 29 Mch. 1869
Electroscope and *electrometer*, apparatus for ascertaining the presence and quantity of electrical excitation. Pith balls were employed in various ways as electroscopes by Gilbert, Canton, and others. Dr. Milner invented an electrometer similar to Peltier's, 1783. The gold leaf electrometer was invented by rev. A. Bennet, 1789, and improved by Singer, about 1810. Lane's discharging electrometer is dated 1767, Henley's, 1772, Bohnenberger's electroscope, 1820, Peltier's induction electrometer . about 1848

GALVANISM, OR VOLTAIC ELECTRICITY, ELECTROLYSIS, AND ELECTRO-MAGNETISM

Sulzer noticed a peculiar sensation in the tongue when silver and lead were brought into contact with it and each other 1762
Mad Galvani observed the convulsion in the muscles of frogs when brought into contact with 2 metals, in 1789, and M Galvani, after studying the phenomenon, laid the foundation of the galvanic battery 1791
Volta announced his discovery of the "voltaic pile," disks of zinc and silver, and moistened card 1800
By the voltaic pile, Nicholson and Carlisle decomposed water, and Dr Henry decomposed nitric acid, ammonia, etc "
Transfer of acids and alkalies by Hisinger and Berzelius 1803
Behrens formed a dry pile of 80 pairs of zinc, copper, and gilt paper 1805
By a large voltaic battery in the Royal Institution London, Davy decomposed potash and isolated the metal potassium (soda and other substances soon after) 6 Oct 1807
Zamboni s dry pile of paper disks coated with tin on one side and peroxide of manganese on the other 1809
Children's battery fused platinum, etc "
J W Ritter constructed his "secondary pile" about 1812
Davy exhibited the voltaic arc 1813
Wollaston s thimble battery ignited platinum wire 1815
[Multipliers or rheometers, popularly termed "galvanometers," invented by Ampère and by Schweigger, 1820, by Cumming, 1821, De la Rive, 1824, Ritchie (torsion) 1830, Joule (magnetic), 1843]
Faraday explains electro magnetic rotation Jan 1822
Ohm enunciated his formulæ for galvanic currents. 1827
[Improvements in the *voltaic battery* by Wollaston, 1815, Becquerel, 1829, Sturgeon 1830, J F Daniell, 1836, Grove (nitric acid etc), 1839, Jacobi, 1840, Smee, 1840, Bunsen (carbon, etc) 1842, Grove (gas battery), 1842]
Faraday read the first series of his "Experimental Researches on Electricity" at the Royal society, London 21 Nov 1831
Faraday demonstrated the nature of electro chemical decomposition, and *the principle that the quantity and intensity* of electric action of a galvanic battery depend on the size and number of plates employed . 1834
Wheatstone invented his electro magnetic chronoscope 1840
Copper zinc couple (COPPER) constructed by Dr J H Gladstone and A Tribe 1872
Batteries Bichromate of potash battery—a modification of Dr Leeson's, very powerful, now much used (Gaston Planté's lead battery, powerful, 1860) Chloride of silver battery (14,400 cells)—results of its discharge published by drs. *Warren de la Rue and Hugo Müller Powerful results* exhibited at Royal Institution, London 21 Jan 1881
Dr Byrne's pneumatic battery (air blown in), very effective, announced 1878
E. J Atkins's method of separating metals from their alloys by electrolysis, announced Nov 1883
Electric accumulator, a modification by M Faure of Gaston Planté's lead battery of 1860, was exhibited at Paris, May, 1881 In June, a box 1 cubic foot in size, containing 4 cells, enclosing thin sheets of lead surrounded with felt saturated with dilute acid, etc., was conveyed from Paris to London Sir William Thomson found it to possess electric energy of 1,000,000 foot pounds, and said, in the London *Times* of 9 June, 1881, "This solves the problem of storing electricity in a manner and in a state useful for many important applications" 6 June, 1881
James Wimshurst invents a "continuous electrophorus" and an "influence machine" . 1882
Faure's accumulator patented in the U S., Jan. 1882, Julien's improvements attract attention 1885–86
Electrical Accumulator company establish a large factory at Newark, N J 1889
Electro magnetism began with Oersted's discovery of the action of the electric current on the magnetic needle, 1819, proved by Ampère, who exhibited the action of the voltaic pile on the magnetic needle, and of terrestrial magnetism on the voltaic current, he also arranged the conducting wire in the form of a helix or spiral, invented a galvanometer, and imitated the magnet by a spiral galvanic wire 1820
Arago magnetized a needle by the electric current, and attracted iron filings by the connecting wire of a galvanic battery "
First electro magnet . 1825
Electric induction discovered by Faraday announced . 1831
Becquerel invented an electro magnetic balance "
Faraday discovered the electro magnetic rotative force developed in a magnet by voltaic electricity, 1831, experiments on the induction of a voltaic current, etc 1834–35
Sturgeon made a bar of soft iron magnetic by sending an electric current through coils of wire surrounding it 1837
Induction coil made by prof G C. Page, of Salem, Mass "
Joseph Henry announced his discovery of secondary currents, 2 Nov 1838
Breguet used electro magnetic force to manufacture mathematical instruments about 1854
Magneto electricity (the converse of Oersted's discovery of electro magnetism) discovered by Faraday, who produced an electric spark by suddenly separating a coiled keeper from a permanent magnet, and found an electric current in a copper disk rotated between the poles of a magnet. 1831
Magneto electric machine first made at Paris by Pixii, 1832, and in London by Saxton .. 1833
Magneto electricity applied to electro plating by Woolwich . 1842
Ruhmkorff's magneto electric induction coil constructed, about 1850
Siemens's armature produced 1854
H Wilde's description of his machine (a powerful generator of dynamic electricity, by permanent magnets) and the magneto electric machine (constructed in 1865) sent to the Royal society by prof Faraday 26 Apr 1866
Principle of accumulation by successive action discovered by Wilde, 1865, by mutual action (by which permanent steel magnets are dispensed with), independently by Wheatstone and Siemens "
Light (resembling bright moonlight) exhibited on top of Burlington house 2 Mch 1867
"Faraday as a Discoverer," by prof Tyndall, pub. Mch 1868
W Groves s electro induction balance 1879
Proposed International Electrical Congress at Paris with exhibition 1 Aug -15 Nov 1881
Dynamo magneto electric machines, by Wheatstone and Siemens, described at the Royal society, London, 14 Feb., by Ladd 14 Mch 1867
Trial of Siemens's dynamo magneto electric light in the torpedo service at Sheerness reported successful 18 Dec. 1871
Two of Siemens s machines ordered for the Lizards, announced, 1878
Gramme's magneto electric machine described . 1875

APPLICATIONS.—*Electric Telegraph*

Transmission of electricity by an insulated wire was shown by Watson and others 1747
Telegraphic arrangements were devised by Lesage, 1744, Betancourt, 1787, Cavallo 1795, Salva, 1796, Soemmering, exhibited 29 Aug 1809, Ronalds 1816
Ampère invents his telegraphic arrangement, employing the magnetic needle and coil, and the galvanic battery 1820
F Ronalds publishes an account of his electric telegraph (d aged 85, 8 Aug 1873) 1823
Prof Wheatstone, by electro magnetic apparatus, conveys 30 *signals through nearly 4 miles of wire* June, 1836
Telegraphs invented by Schilling Gauss, Weber, and prof Henry (magneto electric), 1833, by Steinheil and by Masson, 1837, by Morse 1837
[Morse system of telegraphy is now established in France, Germany, Denmark, Sweden Russia, Austria, and Australia]
Magnetic needle telegraph patented by William F Cooke (aft sir) and Charles Wheatstone (aft. sir) 12 June, "
[Society of Arts Albert gold medal was awarded to them, June, 1867]
Mr Cooke set up the telegraph line on the Great Western railway, from Paddington to West Drayton, Engl , 1838–39 , on the Blackwall line, 1840, and in Glasgow . . 1841
Wheatstone s alphabetical printing telegraph patented "
First telegraph line in U S. set up from Washington to BALTIMORE (UNITED STATES) 1844
Electric telegraph company established (having purchased Cooke's and Wheatstone's telegraphic inventions) . 1846
Gutta percha suggested as an insulator by Faraday 1847
Duplex telegraphy, 2 messages transmitted along a single wire at the same time in opposite directions, first accomplished by dr Gintl, Austrian, 1853, Carl Frischen of Hanover, 1854, by Messrs Siemens, 1857, in the same direction, by Stark of Vienna, 1855, apparatus perfected by Joseph B Stearns of Boston, Mass, 1872, applied to British telegraphs. . 1873
Quadruplex telegraphy, 4 messages along 1 wire, successful experiments between London and Liverpool 25 Sept. 1877
House's printing telegraph, 1846, Bain's electro chemical telegraph, 1846, Hughes's system . 1855
Wheatstone's automatic printing telegraph patented . 1860
Bonelli's typo electric telegraph made known and company established, 1860, and trial between Liverpool and Manchester, 1863, promised revival June, 1864
[Electro chemical automatic of Bain (1846–50) was brought to public notice in the U S as a system of great speed, in 1869. The Atlantic and Pacific Telegraph company adopted it in 1874, in competing with the Western Union, claiming to transmit 500 to 800 words per minute against 25 per minute in the Morse system It proved a failure and an expensive experiment An improved form was taken up in 1879 by the American Rapid Telegraph company, after a trial of 5 years it was again abandoned. An effort was made by the Postal Telegraph company to introduce the automatic system of Leggo between New York and Chicago in 1883, but it was abandoned after a trial of 3 years. It is asserted that 4000 words a minute can be sent over a single wire by this system. The Western Union Telegraph company now control the electro-chemical system, but do not utilize it.]
Economical systems of electrical distribution inventors, Gaulard and Gibbs, 1882, Zipernowski and Deri . 1883
Telegraphing by induction, from moving railway trains to stations, by ordinary wire The idea of telegraphing to moving trains was contemplated as early as 1853 (William Wiley Smith of Indianapolis proposed to communicate between moving cars) 1881
This was effected by the inventions of Thomas A Edison, L. J Phelps, and Gilliland, first published exhibition 15 Feb. 1885
Used on the Lehigh Valley railroad with success 1887
T A Edison's quadruplex instrument, by which 4 messages, 2

from each end, may be transmitted upon 1 wire simultaneously, and prof Delaney s synchronous multiplex instrument, by which 6 messages may be so transmitted on 1 wire, were exhibited at the Post office Jubilee Fête, London, 2 July, 1890

SUBMARINE TELEGRAPHY —*Atlantic Telegraph*, and others

Prof Charles Wheatstone drew plans of a projected submarine telegraph between Dover and Calais 1840

John Watkins Brett (on behalf of his brother, Jacob Brett, the inventor and patentee), submitted a similar plan to Louis Philippe without success 1847

He obtained permission from Louis Napoleon to make a trial, 1847, took place 28 Aug 1850

[Connecting wires (27 miles long) were placed on the government pier in Dover harbor, and in the steamer *Goliath* were coiled about 30 miles of telegraph wire, in a covering of gutta percha half an inch in diameter The *Goliath* started from Dover, unrolling the wire and dropping it to the bottom of the sea In the evening it arrived at cape Grisnez, and messages were sent to and fro between England and the French coast, but the wire, in settling into the sea bottom, crossed a rocky ridge, and parted, and the enterprise failed]

New arrangements were made on a larger scale, and the telegraph was opened, the opening and closing prices of the funds in Paris were known on the London stock exchange within business hours, and guns were fired at Dover by wire from Calais 13 Nov 1851

Project of the Atlantic cable was conceived in 1853, when the magnetic telegraph had been in operation 10 years The original projectors were Americans, including, besides prof Morse, Peter Cooper, Cyrus W Field, Moses Taylor Marshal O Roberts, etc The company succeeded in building the line from St John's across Newfoundland, and under the gulf of St Lawrence to the mainland They obtained subsidies from the British and U S governments, which have since expired 2500 miles of wire were manufactured and tested . . . . Mch 1857

Laying commenced at Valentia, Ireland 5 Aug. "

Vessels employed were the *Niagara* and *Susquehanna* (U S vessels), and the *Leopard* and *Agamemnon* (British vessels) After sailing a few miles the cable snapped, this was soon repaired, but on 11 Aug, after 300 miles of wire had been paid out, it snapped again, and the vessels returned to Plymouth 11 Aug "

A second attempt failed through a violent storm 20-21 June, 1858

Third voyage was successful Junction of the continents was completed by 2050 miles of wire from Valentia, in Ireland, to Newfoundland, 5 Aug First 2 messages were from queen Victoria to pres Buchanan, and his reply (UNITED STATES) 16 Aug "

This event caused great rejoicing, but the insulation of the wire gradually became more faulty, and the power of transmitting intelligence utterly ceased 4 Sept. "

[Name of operator at western terminus of cable was De Sauty, who, with a hope born of extreme desire for the success of the cable, maintained to the last that it was *All right!*—

"Till the land was filled with loud reverberations
Of 'All right!'"
"*De Sauty*"

But with the disappearance of the power to transmit, De Sauty disappeared also, this disappearance furnished dr Holmes material for his humorous poem "De Sauty" (1858), quoted from above

A new company formed . 1860

Steamer *Great Eastern* (capt. Anderson) engaged to lay 2300 miles of wire, sailed for Valentia, Ireland, from the Thames, work supervised by prof Wm Thomson and Cromwell F Varley . 15 July, 1865

After connecting the wire, sailed from Valentia. 23 July, "

Telegraphic communication with the vessel (interrupted by 2 faults, quickly repaired, due to defective insulation, from pieces of metal pressed into the gutta-percha coating) ceased, 2 Aug Apparatus for raising the wire proving insufficient, the vessel returned, reaching the Medway, 19 Aug "

Atlantic Telegraph company reconstituted as the Anglo-American Telegraph company, limited Mch 1866

Great Eastern, with a new cable, sailed from the Medway, 30 June, the end at Valentia was spliced and the laying began, 13 July, 1200 miles of cable had been laid, 22 July, landed at Heart's Content, Newfoundland, and a message sent to lord Stanley, 27 July, from queen Victoria to pres. Johnson, 28 July, "From the queen, Osborne, to the president of the U S, Washington The queen congratulates the president on the successful completion of an undertaking which she hopes may serve as an additional bond of union between the U S. and England" To which he replied . . . . 30 July, "

Lost cable of 1865 recovered, 2 Sept., and its laying completed at Newfoundland . 8 Sept. "

Great Eastern arrived at Liverpool 19 Sept. "

Samuel Canning, Daniel Gooch, and capt. Anderson knighted, Oct "

[It was stated (Sept 1866) that the engineer of the cable passed signals through 3700 miles of wire from a battery in a lady s thimble.]

U S Congress voted a gold medal to Cyrus W Field for exertions connected with Atlantic telegraphs 7 Mch. 1867

At a dinner given to Cyrus W Field at Willis's rooms, London, telegraphic messages were exchanged between the company and lord Monck, viceroy of Canada, and pres Johnson 1 July 1868

French Atlantic Telegraph company formed, French government grant concession for 20 years, from 1 Sept 1869 to Julius Reuter and baron Emile d'Erlangen 8 July, "

Anglo Danish telegraph (Newbiggin to Copenhagen) completed, 31 Aug "

European end of French Atlantic cable laid at Brest, 17 June, American end at Duxbury, Mass 23 July, 1869

Reported union between Anglo American and French Atlantic telegraph companies Jan 1870

Telegraph between Bombay and Suez completed "

Telegraph between Adelaide and Port Darwin, Australia, completed 22 Aug 1872

Message from the mayor of Adelaide received by the lord mayor of London, and replied to 21 Oct "

Fourth Atlantic cable laid by *Great Eastern* Valentia, Ireland, to Heart's Content Newfoundland 8 June-3 July, 1873

Brazil telegraph cable completely laid 22 Sept "

Faraday, a great electric cable ship, built for Siemens Bros, launched at Newcastle, Engl (STEAM), 17 Feb, sails to lay the "Direct U S company's" cable, 16 May, laid shore end in Nova Scotia, 31 May, in New Hampshire, 8 June, connected with Newfoundland July, 1874

Sixth Anglo American telegraph laid by the *Great Eastern*, Aug-Sept. "

E A Cowper's writing telegraph quick plain writing (36 miles), exhibited at Royal Institution, London, etc May, 1879

Sixth international telegraph conference opened in London, 18 June, "

South African line laid between Mozambique and Natal, 23 Aug, connected with Cape Town, telegrams sent by queen Victoria to sir Bartle Frere and others, 25 Dec., opened to the public 29 Dec. "

New French transatlantic cable to be laid from Brest to St Pierre by the *Faraday*, sailed June, connected with Halifax, Oct. 1879, line from Paris to New York opened 1 June, 1880

International congress of electricians to be opened at Paris, 15 Sept, exhibition on 11 Aug 1881

New Atlantic cable laid by the *Faraday* 22 Aug et seq "

Telegraph from England to Panama completed Sept 1882

International submarine telegraph conference, Paris 16 Oct "

International conference for protection of submarine cables, Paris, closed convention agreed to, 26 Oct 1883, signed at London 14 Mch 1884 signed for U S 26 Mch 1884

Commercial Cable company s cables opened 24 Dec "

Another international conference for the protection of submarine cables 1 Dec. 1886

For statistics, TELEGRAPH

ELECTRIC LIGHT.

Humphry Davy produced electric light with carbon points 1802

[Apparatus for regulating the electric light was devised in 1845 by J W Star, and by W Staite's patents, 1846, 1849, Staite (at Sunderland, Engl, 25 Oct. 1847), and Petrie in 1848, by Foucault soon after]

Jules Duboscq's *electric lamp* (the most perfect of the kind) appeared at the Paris exhibition in 1855, and was employed by prof Tyndall, at the Royal Institution, London, to illustrate lectures on light and colors 1856

Works of new Westminster bridge, London, illuminated by Watson's electric light 1858

Magneto electric light (the most brilliant artificial light yet produced), devised by prof Holmes, successfully tried at the South Foreland light house, Dover 1858 and 1859

French government ordered 8 light houses illuminated by electric light Apr 1861

M Serrin, of Paris, exhibited his improved electric lamp 1862

Electric candle, invented by Paul Jablochkoff (an electric current passed through 2 carbons side by side with a slip of kaolin between them, produces a steady, soft, noiseless light, the carbons burn like wax), reported to the Academy of Sciences, Paris, by M Dénayrouze Oct. 1876

Electric light successfully employed for photography by H Van der Weyde "

Head, Wrightson & Co., of Stockton on Tees, use Siemens's electric light for bridge building "

At the Magasin du Louvre, 8 electric lights replaced 100 Carcel gas burners, as manageable as coal gas supply, tried at West India docks, London 15 June, 1877

Tyndall's experiments at South Foreland, Engl, demonstrate superiority of Siemens's dynamo electric machine, Aug 1876–July, "

Gramme's machine (light equal to 758 candles) "

Serrin's and Jablochkoff's lights improved by Rapieff, a Russian, taken up by E J Reed, M P, a small magneto electric machine, worked by steam, conducting wires replace the gasworks and pipes . July, 1878

Mr Stayton reports that the light is much dearer than gas, and not suitable for street lighting in London Sept "

Electric light tried at Westminster palace 28 Mch "

Two of Siemens's dynamo magneto electric machines ordered for the Lizards light-houses "

Gaiety theatre, London, lighted by Lontin's machine and modification of Jablochkoff's Aug. "

Hippolyte Fontaine's treatise on Electric Lighting, 1877, translated by Paget Biggs, pub. "

T A. Edison announces his method of producing lights and power from a Ritchie inductive coil, a dynamo electric machine, which he terms "telemachon," worked by water-

power or steam; panic among gas companies in London in value of shares..........Sept., Oct. 1878
Wm. E. Sawyer and A. Man produce their first successful incandescent lamp.......... "
Edison's plan of subdividing lights filed at patent office, 23 Oct. "
National Electric Light company forming..........Nov. "
Richard Werdermann's electric light subdivided; a number of jets lit simultaneously; shown by British Telegraph company, 2 Nov. "
Electric light used for large workshops at Woolwich, etc., Engl., and throughout the country..........Nov. "
London *Times* machine-room lit by 6 lights from 1 current; Rapieff system..........Oct., Nov. "
Three systems trying at New York by Edison, Sawyer, and Brush..........Nov. "
Wallace lamp (American) introduced in London by Mr. Ladd, autumn, "
Jablochkoff candle tried at Westgate-on-Sea, Engl., by E. F. Davis, 2-26 Dec.; light successful; difficulty in practice; given up..........Dec. "
Formation of nitric acid in the air by electric light; announced by T. Wills, 13 Dec. 1878; of hydrocyanic or prussic acid by prof. J. Dewar..........autumn, 1879
Machines of *Farmer & Wallace*, Lontin, De Meritens, Browning, Carré, and others, in use in London.......... "
Edison obtains beautiful light from platinum; used 600 horse-power to obtain 20,000 lights at 1 station; his patent registered..........23 Apr. "
M. Jamin's electric candle exhibited at Academy of Sciences, Paris..........about 17 Mch. "
Dynamo-magneto-electric machine patented by lord Elphinstone and C. W. Vincent.......... "
[Committee of the House of Commons, appointed "to consider whether it is desirable to authorize municipal corporations or other local authorities to adopt any schemes for lighting by electricity" (dr. Lyon Playfair, chairman), reports: "The energy of 1 horse-power converted into gaslight, yields a luminosity equal to 12 candle-power. But the same amount of energy transformed into electric light produces 1600 candle-power. . . . Scientific witnesses thought that electricity might be used to transmit power as well as light to a distance, furnishing mechanical power by day and light by night. . . . The electric light has established itself for light-house illumination, that of large places, such as squares, public halls, railway stations, and workshops. . . . Compared with gas, the economy for equal illumination is not conclusively established."—London *Times*.]
St. George Lane Fox's invention to light lamps by electricity tried at Fulham, Engl., and reported successful.......... "
Dr. C. William Siemens reports to Royal Society that electric light acts like solar light on vegetation..........2 Mch. 1880
Electric light applied by him to grow vegetables and fruit in greenhouses.......... "
J. W. Swan exhibits his system of dividing light, etc., at Newcastle-on-Tyne (afterwards in London)..........20 Oct. "
Trial of 3 systems in London: Lontin's, Southwark bridge, etc.; Brush, Blackfriars bridge, etc.; Siemens's, Guildhall, etc., 31 Mch. 1881
New lamp (the "Sun") by Louis Clerc, a combination of the arc and incandescent systems..........June, 1882
Electric "sun" lamp and power company was formed....July, "
G. C. V. Holmes, F. E. Burke, and F. Cheesewright's invention for electric light in railways tried on Great Northern line, reported successful..........25 Oct. "
Ferranti system of electric lighting (invented by sir William Thomson, S. Ziani de Ferranti, and Alfred Thomson) successfully tried..........Dec. "
Domestic electric lighting by the Beeman, Taylor, and King system tried at Colchester, Engl..........11 June, 1884
Electric light in Liverpool and Manchester trains..........Aug. "
Electric light adopted at Milan, Rome, Paris, Tours, Marseilles, and other large European cities.......... 1890
Most large cities in the U. S. partly lighted by electricity....1882-85
"Liberty Enlightening the World," New York harbor, lighted by electricity.......... 1886
Most of the large hotels and public halls of the larger cities of the U. S. lighted by electricity..........1885-90
First permanent electric lights in the city of London set up in Queen Victoria st.......... 1891

ELECTRIC RAILWAYS.

Stratingh and Becker of Groeningen, in 1835, and Botto of Turin, in 1836, construct rude electric carriages. Davidson, a Scotchman, in 1838-39, builds an electric car, of several tons' weight, which runs 4 miles an hour. Thomas Davenport of Brandon, Vt., exhibits a model of a circular railway at Springfield, Mass., traversed by an electro-magnetic locomotive.......... 1835
Alfred Vail, aided by an appropriation from Congress, constructs an electric locomotive, which runs from Washington, D. C., to Bladensburg, Md., on the Washington branch of the B. and O. R. R., 29 Apr. 1851; attains a speed of 19 miles an hour. Jean Henry Cazal, a French engineer, proposes to utilize the natural powers, as water, etc., for operating railways by electrical transmission of power.......... 1864
Dr. Werner Siemens exhibits an electric railway at the Industrial Exhibition at Berlin.......... 1879
Meanwhile Stephen D. Field of San Francisco, dr. Jos. R. Finney of Pittsburg, and Thos. A. Edison of N. Y., were independently at work. Edison was the first to construct a dynamo-electric railway in America, at the expense of Henry Villard, at Menlo Park, N. J., on a tract 80 rods in length.......... 1880
First electric street-railway in Europe was the "Lichterfelde line," constructed by dr. Siemens, at Berlin..........1881
First electric tram-way cars in England run at Leytonstone, Essex..........4 Mch. 1882
New electric railway opened at Berlin..........1 May, "
Prof. Fleeming Jenkin invents the telpherage system.......... "
Finney exhibits and successfully operates experimental electric motor on ordinary street car at Alleghany, Pa.......... "
Field's electric locomotive first exhibited at the Exposition of Railway Appliances at Chicago..........June, 1883
Siemens's electrical tram-way between Portrush and Giant's Causeway, Ireland, completed, Dec. 1882; opened by earl Spencer..........28 Sept. "
Electric tram-cars first run from Kew to Hammersmith, Engl., 10 Mch. "
First electric street railway in America from Baltimore to Hampden, Md., 2 miles. The current ran in an insulated rail midway between the other two. The electrical machinery was designed and constructed by Leo Daft of Jersey City, N. J. The line opened..........1 Sept. 1885
A successful electric street railroad at Scranton, Pa., was designed by Charles J. Van Depoele of Chicago, and went into operation..........Dec. 1886
There are 3 systems whereby the electric current is supplied to the motor upon the car, the *overhead system*, the *underground system*, and the *storage-battery system*. The first is in general use; while the last, if it could be made economical, would soon supersede the others.
Growth of electric railway and of electrical transmission of power very rapid from 1881 to 1886. Chief inventors in electric railways: Siemens, Ayrton and Perry, Daft, Field, Sprague, Bentley and Knight, and Van Depoele; chief inventors of telpherage system, Jenkin, Ayrton, and Perry.

ELECTRICAL MEASUREMENTS.

The following terms (after great electricians) were adopted by the electrical congress at Paris, 22 Sept. 1881: ohm, volt, ampère, coulomb, and farad. (ELECTRICIANS, under this article.) Important resolutions were passed by the international conference on electrical units at Paris (the "congress ohm" agreed to)..........Apr.-May, 1884
Electrical standard committee (consisting of lord Raleigh, sir Wm. Thomson, and others) appointed, Dec. 1890; it was recommended that new denominations of standards be made, and determined with reference to the centimetre, gramme, and second, of the Board of Trade; the ohm to be the standard of resistance; the ampère, the standard of electrical current; the volt, the standard of electrical pressure; all being scientifically defined..........20 Feb. 1891
Committee's report printed..........Aug. "
The electrical congress adopted the henry as the unit of electrical induction in honor of prof. Henry at the World's Fair, Chicago.......... 1893

ELECTRO-PHYSIOLOGY.

Aristotle and Pliny refer to the powers of the torpedo; Walsh and Ingenhousz, the discoveries of Galvani in 1790, and the researches of Matteucci, about 1830, advanced the science.
Fowler experimented on animals with galvanism, 1793; Aldini, 1796, produced muscular contractions in a criminal recently executed, 1803; Ure did the same.......... 1818
Du Bois-Reymond lectured on animal electricity at the Royal Institution, and showed an electric current, developed by action of human muscles..........May, 1855
Dr. Burdon Sanderson announced discovery of electricity in plants to British Association at Bradford..........Sept. 1873

ELECTRIC USE IN GENERAL.

William Kemmler executed by electricity at Auburn, N. Y., the first in the world, 6 Aug. 1890; several since at Sing Sing, N. Y., among them Carlyle W. Harris..........8 May, 1893

ELECTRICAL TRANSMISSION OF FORCE.

M. Marcel Deprez' experiments at Creil (1876-86), supported by M. Rothschild, reported successful: mechanical power transmitted 35 miles for industrial purposes..........23 July, 1886
Elieson company's electric engines reported successful at Stratford; tram-cars driven 5 miles..........Oct. et seq. "
Electrical traction on tram-ways at Northfleet; successful demonstration..........14 Mch. "
Successful trial of electric tram-car at Birmingham.....23 Oct. 1889
M. Immisch's electric motors successful in pumping and hauling at St. John's colliery, Normanton..........Nov. "
City and South London Electric railway opened by the prince of Wales, 4 Nov., to the public..........18 Dec. 1890
Nickola Tesla, at the Royal Institution, exhibited his alternate-current motor, by which currents are transformed by constantly reversing the direction into mechanical power. It was stated that, with the increase of physical power, the effect upon the human frame is diminished..........3, 4 Feb. 1892
[By means of Mr. Tesla's apparatus, the force of about 77.7 horse-power was transmitted from the rapids of the Neckar to Frankfort-on-Maine, 110 miles, Sept. 1891.]
Work began on the Niagara Falls tunnel (American side), 4 Oct. 1890. Object, to develop electric power for transmission. Source of power practically unlimited. Tunnel finished and most machinery in place..........May, 1893
PHONOGRAPH, PHOTOPHONE, TELEGRAPH, TELEPHONE, etc.

ELECTRICITY—LATEST DEVELOPMENTS.

Wireless Telegraphy—Sir W. H. Preece, at the Royal Institution, after some remarks on the propagation of waves in the ether, described and illustrated his own method of "Signalling through Space without Wires," by means of electro-magnetic waves of low frequency and 2 parallel circuits, established on each bank of a river; this system was successfully used in 1895 to telegraph across the sound of Mull, when the submarine cable had broken down; sir Wm. Preece next exhibited and explained the apparatus by which Hertzian waves of high frequency are utilized in the new system invented by Mr. Marconi, a young Italian, who brought it to England in July, 1896, and who assisted at the lecture....4 June, 1897

Prof. Hughes in 1879-80 and in 1888 telephoned messages across space; capt. Jackson succeeded in getting Morse signals across the air, Dec. 1895.

By Marconi's system, signals had been transmitted across the Bristol channel, between Penarth and Brian Down, about 9 miles; sir Wm. Preece considered the invention valuable for shipping and light-house purposes; further experiments by the post-office authorities between Dover and Ft. Burgoyne, 17 Sept. *et seq.* 1897; and by prof. Slaby with balloons (13½ miles)....Mch. 1898

Very successful experiments between the S. Foreland light-house and the E. Goodwin light-ship (12 miles); current not affected by stormy weather, mid. Jan.; again....30 Jan. 1899

The first press message, by Marconi's system, from Wimreux, near Boulogne, to S. Foreland....28-31 Mch. "

Lord Rayleigh and members of Trinity House inspect sig. Marconi's system at S. Foreland....6 Apr. "

Experiments in the presence of a French commission between a moving ship and the land; messages sent between the French gun-boat *Isis*, the S. Foreland, the E. Goodwin light-ship, and Boulogne. It was clearly shown by a new device discovered by sig. Marconi that not only can moving ships communicate with each other at sea, but that the messages can be concentrated on the point intended to be reached....24 Apr. "

Similar experiments carried on before the Chinese minister and others....25 Apr. "

The E. Goodwin light-ship being run into and damaged by *F. F. Matthews*, steamer, a wireless message from the light-ship to the S. Foreland procured assistance....28 Apr. "

Experiments by prof. Tuma, between 2 balloons at Vienna, fairly successful....14 July, "

Messages sent from Dover town-hall to S. Foreland and E. Goodwin light-ship....16 Aug. "

Experiments with the Popoff system arranged under conditions of warfare, successfully carried on between the Black Sea fleet and the Crimean shore, reported....25 Sept. "

"History of Wireless Telegraphy," by J. J. Fahie, published.. "

Rapid development, successful long-distance transmissions from the Poldhu station at the Lizard, Cornwall, to St. Catharine's, Isle of Wight....22 Jan. 1901

Across the Atlantic to St. John's, Newfoundland..13, 14 Dec. "

And at night 2000 miles to and from the ship *Philadelphia*, 25 Feb. 1902

Correspondence as to whether prof. Oliver Lodge (in 1894) or sig. Marconi (about June, 1902) was the first inventor, London *Times*....5 and 15 July, "

Messages sent from the Lizard received by the *Carlo Alberto*, Italian cruiser, at Kronstadt, 1600 miles....14 July, "

And from there to the Mediterranean, Aug.-Sept.; various patents taken out by sir O. Lodge, M. Righi Branley, Popoff, Slaby, Arco, Braun, Solari, Guarini, Cervera, Ducretet, Castelli, Rutherford, Jackson, and Willoughby Smith.... "

Messages (sent from Cape Breton to Poldhu, Cornwall) exchanged....21 Dec. "

Used successfully between Aldershot and the channel squadron off Portsmouth....12 Jan. 1903

Pres. Roosevelt sends a greeting to king Edward....19 Jan. "

Two telegrams from the U. S. received by "Marconigraph," Poldhu....28, 29 Mch. "

The Orling-Armstrong system shown....2 Apr. "

Italian legation begin installation of Marconi system at Pekin to communicate direct with ships in the gulf of Pe-chi-li, reported....11 June, "

International conference on wireless telegraphy opened in Berlin....4 Aug. "

New system of radio-telegraphy originated by prof. Alessandro Artom; successful experiments made by Italian naval authorities, reported....14 Nov. "

German government adopts the Pollak and Virag wireless system.... "

Mr. Chamberlain's speech on the fiscal question, at the Guild-hall, reproduced simultaneously to a large assembly at Queen's hall by wireless telegraphy....19 Jan. 1904

The English government accepts messages at all post-offices for wireless telegrams to ships at sea at 13 cts. per word, 1 Jan. 1905

Communication established between Key West, Florida, and Chicago; and between Key West and New York City. 26 Feb. "

Telephone—The Pulsion telephone, in which sounds are sent over a wire, without electricity, invented by Mr. Lemuel Mellett, successfully used on railways in America.... 1888

Mr. Edison, said to have invented a process of combining photography with the telephone....Feb. 1890

Telephonic communication between London and Paris opened to the public (day and night)....1 Apr. 1891

Telephonic communication from London to Marseilles and Brussels, completed 19 Apr. 1891; between Dublin and Belfast, opened....5 Apr. 1892

The government authorized to raise 1,000,000*l.* to purchase the trunk lines of the telephone companies (in Great Britain) by the telegraph act passed....June, "

Telephone from New York to Chicago (950 miles), opened Oct. "

Telephone from Berlin to Vienna (410 miles), opened..20 Nov. 1894

Telephone between the post-office, London, Edinburgh, and other principal towns, inaugurated....12 June, 1895

The Apostoloff automatic telephone, system described in the London *Times*....17 Aug. 1896

All the trunk telephone lines in the United Kingdom transferred to the post-office....6 Feb. 1897

Second telephone cable (24 miles long), between Abbot's-cliff, near Dover, and Sangatte, near Calais, laid....8 May, "

Telephone communication with and through Ireland, begun 9 Sept. "

Report of telephone committee issued....12 Aug. 1898

Communication between farms by instruments on wire fences used in Australia, announced....Sept. "

The history of the telephone service, from 1877 to 1892, London *Times*....20, 23 Jan. 1899

Successful experiments with the Brussels-London telephone, reported....3 Oct. 1900

Telephone convention between Great Britain and France signed....29 July, 1902

"Automatic" (really a selector) system of telephony installed in New York and Chicago.... 1903

Telegraph—International conferences (commercial) have been held at Brussels, 1858; Paris, Mch. 1865; Vienna, 1868; Rome, 1871-72; St. Petersburg, 1 June, 1875; London, 18 June, 1879; Paris, 16 Oct. 1882; Berlin, 10 Aug.-17 Sept., 1885; Paris (114 delegates, representing 38 states and 23 great companies)....15 May-21 June, 1890

Great progress made, messages and returns sent all round the world in a few minutes from New York during an electrical exposition....June, 1896

Sir John Pender, an energetic promoter of submarine telegraphy, b. 1815; d....7 July, "

Submarine telegraph cable between Emden and Vigo, opened, reported....24 Dec. "

Successful experiments in rapid telegraphing in Buda-Pesth and Berlin, 220 words sent in 10 secs....Sept. "

Prof. Rowland's multiplex system of printing to telegraphy, successful....Apr. 1900

German-American cable between Emden and New York, opened....1 Sept. "

Submarine cable between Cornwall and St. Vincent, Cape de Verd islands, opened....30 Jan. 1901

Cable from S. Africa to W. Australia, opened....Oct. "

British Pacific cable bill passed....16 Aug. "

All British Pacific cable from Vancouver to Queensland, connecting New Zealand, Norfolk island, and Australia..1 Nov. "

Cable between San Francisco and Manila completed...July 5, 1903

Cable between Australia and Vancouver completed.... "

Second cable between Germany and the U. S. completed.... 1904

MISCELLANEOUS

Successful experiments made with prof. Elisha Gray's Telautographic machine, June, 1894; messages transmitted in facsimile writing (83 miles), 22 July, 1894; further improvements in....1898-1905

International electro-technical congress at Frankfort-on-Main, opened....8 Sept. 1891

Electrical exhibition at the Crystal Palace, near London, opened....9 Jan. 1892

Electrical exhibition at St. Petersburg, opened....23 Jan. "

Continuous to alternating current transformer, invented by sir David Salomons and Mr. L. Pyke, exhibited....1 Dec. "

M. Heilmann's electric-motor traction-engine in France attained the speed of 65 miles an hour....9 May, 1894

Trial trip from Paris to Mantes of an electric locomotive devised by M. Heilmann....12 Nov. 1897

Central London electric railway (Bank to Shepherd's Bush) opened by the prince of Wales....27 June, 1900

New York Electro-Chemical society, organized.... 1902

Sault Ste. Marie (American) 50,000 horse-power electric plant opened....25 Oct. "

New York Central and Pennsylvania Central railroads to spend over $50,000,000; tunnel and suburban trains to be worked by electrical power.... "

New York elevated roads use electric power only.... "

Electrification of Mersey railway completed....1 May, 1903

South London electric tramways system opened by prince of Wales....15 May, "

Application of X-rays and Finsen or ultra violet rays, reported beneficial in lupus, cancer, etc....19 May, "

Peter Cooper Hewitt electric light (vapor of mercury) exhibited in public.... "

Miami and Erie canal install the electric trolley for haulage.. "

Electric installation at Niagara Falls, on both the American and Canadian sides; increased largely 1902-1905.

New York subway opened....27 Oct. 1904

LIST OF THE PRINCIPAL INVESTIGATORS AND INVENTORS IN ELECTRICITY AND MAGNETISM.

Names.	Born.	Died.	Remarks.
Æpinus, Franz Maria T. W.	Germany 1724	1802	Investigator. Established the affinity between electricity and magnetism; discovered the polarity of the tourmaline, etc.
Aldini, Giovanni	Italy 1762	1834	Experimenter with galvanism.
Ampère, Andre Marie	France 1775	1836	Electro-dynamics. Unit of electrical current named in his honor *ampère*.
App	England	....	Investigator. Induction coil giving the largest spark ever seen, 1869.
Arago, Dominic F.	France 1786	1853	Rotary magnetism, etc.
Aristotle	Greece 384 B.C.	322 B.C.	Acquainted with phenomena of electro-physiology.
Armstrong, Sir Wm. Geo	England 1810	....	Hydro-electric machine, etc.
Atkins, E. J.	....	....	Separates metals from their alloys by electrolysis, 1883.
Ayrton, W. E.	England 1847	....	Inventor of electric railway, telpherage system, etc.
Bain, Alexander	Scotland 1810	1877	Automatic chemical telegraph, 1846. ELECTRIC TELEGRAPH.
Barlow, Wm. H.	England 1812	....	Electric motor.
Beccaria, Giovanni B.	Italy 1716	1781	Published researches on atmospheric electricity, 1758.
Becker	Germany	....	Electric railway, etc.
Becquerel, Antoine C.	France 1788	1878	Improves the voltaic battery, 1829; invents electro-magnetic balance, 1831.
Beeman	....	....	Electric lighting.
Behrens	....	....	Forms a dry pile of 80 pairs of zinc, copper, and gilt paper, 1805.
Bell, Alexander Graham	Scotland 1847	....	In the United States, 1872, telephone and photophone.
Bennet, Rev. A.	England	....	Invents the "doubler of electricity," 1786, and the gold-leaf electrometer, etc.
Bentley, Edward M.	....	....	Electric railways, etc.
Berzelius, Johan Jakob	Sweden 1779	1848	Investigator.
Betancourt	....	....	Investigator in electric telegraphy, 1787.
Bláthy, Otto T.	Hungary 1860	....	Dynamos.
Bohnenberger	....	....	Invents an electroscope, 1820.
Bonelli	*Italy*	....	Typo-electric telegraph made known, 1860. Inventor of an electric loom, railway, etc.
Botta	Italy	....	Constructs a rude electric carriage, 1836.
Boyle, Robert	Ireland 1626	1691	Published his electrical experiments, 1676.
Boys, C. Vernon	England	....	Thermopile quartz fibre.
Breguet, A. L.	Switzerland 1747	1823	Uses electro-magnetism in making mathematical instruments.
Brett, Jacob	....	....	Submarine telegraphy, 1847.
Browning	....	....	Electric lighting.
Brush, Chas. Francis	Ohio 1849	....	Dynamos, electric lights, etc.
Bunsen, Robert W.	Germany 1811	....	Improves the voltaic battery (carbon, etc.), 1842.
Burke, F. E.	....	....	Electric lights, etc.
Byrne	....	....	Pneumatic battery (air blown in), 1878.
Canton, J.	England 1718	1782	Investigator.
Carlisle, Sir Anthony	England 1768	1840	Decomposed water by the voltaic pile, 1800.
Carré	....	....	Electrophorus machine.
Cavallo, Tiberio	Italy 1749	1809	Investigator. Electric telegraphy, 1795.
Cavendish, Henry	England 1731	1810	Eminent investigator.
Cazal, Jean Heury	France	....	Electric railway.
Cheesewright, F.	....	....	Electric lighting in railways.
Clerc, M. Louis	France	....	Electric lamp "Sun."
Cooke, Sir Wm. F.	England	....	Magnetic needle telegraph, patented 1837.
Coulomb, Chas. A. de	France 1736	1806	Electro-statics. Unit of electrical quantity named in his honor *coulomb*.
Cowper, E. A.	....	....	Writing telegraph, 1879.
Crookes, Wm.	England 1832	....	Investigator.
Crosby, O. T.	United States	....	Investigator and writer on electricity.
Cruickshank	England	....	Voltaic battery, 1801.
Cummings	....	....	Galvanometer or rheometer, 1821.
Cunæus	....	....	Leyden jar, alleged discoverer.
Daft, Leo	New Jersey	....	Electric motor for railroads.
Dal Negro, Salvatore Abbé	Italy	....	Electric motor, 1830, experiment.
Daniell, J. F.	England 1790	1845	Improver of the voltaic battery, 1836.
Davenport, Thomas	Vermont 1802	1851	Electric motor for railroad, 1835.
Davidson, Robert	Scotland 1804	....	Electric motor for railroad, 1838–39; experiment.
Davy, Sir Humphry	England 1778	1829	Experiments with electricity in chemistry, and the discoverer of electric light.
Delaney, P. B.	Ireland 1845	....	Telegraphy. Invents a synchronous multiplex instrument. Came to the U. S. 1855.
De la Rive, Auguste	Switzerland 1801	1873	Galvanometer, 1824.
De Meritens	....	....	Electric light, etc.
Deprez, M. Marcel	France 1843	....	Investigator of the electrical transmission of force.
Deri, Max	Hungary 1854	....	Inventor of economic distribution of electricity.
Desaguliers, J. Theophile	France 1683	1744	Investigator. Classifies bodies as electric and non-electric.
Dolbear, Amos E.	Connecticut 1837	....	Inventor, investigator, etc.
Duboscq, Jules	France	....	Electric light (in Paris exhibition, 1855).
Du Bois-Reymond, Emil H.	Germany 1818	....	Animal electricity.
Du Fay, Chas. François	France 1698	1739	Discovered two-fold nature of electricity.
Dyar, Harrison G.	United States	....	Electric telegraph, Long Island, N. Y., 1828.
Edison, Thomas Alva	Milan, O. 1847	....	Inventor of telephone, phonograph, electric light, electric railroad, etc.
Faraday, Michael	England 1791	1867	Eminent investigator. Unit of electrical capacity named in his honor *farad*.
Farmer, Moses G.	Massachusetts 1820	1893	Electric light, etc.
Faure, Camille A.	France	....	Electric accumulator, 1881; patented in the U. S. 1882.
Ferranti, S. Zianide	England 1864	....	Dynamos, electric lighting, etc.
Field, Cyrus W.	Massachusetts 1819	1892	Zealous in placing the Atlantic telegraph.
Field, Stephen D.	California	....	Electric railroad.
Finney, Joseph R.	Pittsburg, Pa.	....	Electric railroad.
Fleming, J. A.	England 1849	....	Eminent investigator, etc.
Fontaine, H.	France	....	Electric lighting.
Foucault, Leon	France 1819	1868	Electric light, regulating it.
Fourcroy, Antoine F.	France 1755	1809	Electro-chemistry, decomposed water, 1787–90.
Fowler	....	....	Experiments on animals with galvanism, 1793.
Fox, St. Geo. L.	....	....	Inventor of lighting lamps by electricity, 1879. Eminent investigator.
Franklin, Benjamin	Boston, Mass. 1706	1790	Eminent and original investigator. Identifies lightning with electricity.
Frischen, Carl	Germany	....	Duplex telegraphy.
Galvani, Aloisio	Italy 1737	1798	Animal electricity, galvanic arc, etc.
Gaulard	....	....	Inventor of a system of economical electrical distribution, 1882.
Gauss, Karl Friedrich	Germany 1777	1855	Electro-magnetism. Applied electro-magnetism to telegraphy.

LIST OF THE PRINCIPAL INVESTIGATORS AND INVENTORS IN ELECTRICITY AND MAGNETISM.—(*Continued.*)

Names.	Born.	Died.	Remarks.
Gay-Lussac, Jos. Louis	France 1778	1850	Electro-magnetism.
Gibbs			System of economical electrical distribution, etc., 1882.
Gilbert, Dr. Wm.	England 1540	1603	The "Galileo of magnetism;" uses the terms "electric force," "electric attraction," etc.
Gilliland, Arthur			Inductive telegraphy, telephone, etc.
Gintl, Dr.	Austria		Duplex telegraphy, *first accomplished*, 1853.
Gladstone, J. H.	England 1827		Constructs copper-zinc couple, 1872.
Gordon			Electrical machine with glass cylinder, 1742.
Gore, George	England		Eminent investigator in voltaic electricity and electro-chemistry.
Gramme	France		Magneto-electric machine, 1870.
Gray, Elisha	Illinois		Inventor of telephones, etc., and of the graphophone.
Gray, Stephen	England	1736	Investigator; discovers the fact of electric induction.
Grove, Wm. R.	England 1811		Improves voltaic battery, etc., 1839.
Guericke, Otto von	Germany 1602	1686	First electrical machine, 1647.
Hall, Thomas	England		Electric locomotive.
Harris, Sir Wm. Snow	England 1791	1867	Investigator. Invents lightning conductors for ships, thermo-electrometer.
Hawksbee			Electrical machine, 1709.
Helmholtz, Hermann L. F.	Germany 1821		Electro-dynamics, etc.; invents the tangent compass, 1849.
Henley			Invents an electrometer, 1772.
Henry, Prof. Joseph	Albany, N. Y. 1797	1878	Eminent investigator; electro-magnetism. Unit of electrical induction named in his honor *henry*.
Hisinger			Transfer of acids and alkalies by the voltaic pile, 1803.
Hjorth	Sweden		Discovers the reaction principle of magnetization, 1854.
Holmes, F. H.	England		Electric light.
Holmes, G. C. V.	England		Electric light, London, 1882.
Holtz, W.	Germany		Induction machine, 1865.
Hooke, Robert	England 1635	1703	Investigator.
House, Royal E.			Electric telegraph, printing, 1846–48.
Houston, Ed. Jas.	Virginia 1844		Investigator; electric light, railway, etc.
Hughes, D. E.	England 1831		Electric telegraph, 1855.
Humboldt, Friedrich H. Alexander	Germany 1769	1859	Eminent investigator of electricity and magnetism.
Immisch, M.			Electric motor, 1889.
Ingenhousz, Jan	Holland 1730	1799	Electro-physiologist, etc.
Jablochkoff, Paul	Russia	1894	Electric candle, etc.
Jacobi, Moritz Herman	Germany 1801	1874	Electric motor, experimental, 1838. Improves the voltaic pile.
Jamins, M.	France		Electric candle, etc.
Jenkin, Fleeming	England		Telpherage system.
Joulé, Dr. James Prescott	England 1818		Investigator. Invents magnetic galvanometer, 1843.
Julien, Edmond	Belgium		Electric motor. Improved electric accumulator, 1885.
Kapp, Gisbert	Austria 1852		Electric light, dynamos, etc.
Kerr, Dr. John			
King	England		Domestic electric lighting.
Kirchhoff, Gustav R.	Germany 1824		
Kleist (a German monk)	Germany		Leyden jar, discovered 1745. See CUNÆUS, above, MUSCHENBROEK, below.
Knight, Walter H.			Electric railways, etc., Bentley-Knight electric railroad.
Kohlrausch			Eminent investigator of electro-dynamics, etc.
Ladd			Magneto-electric machine, 1867.
Lane	England		Invents a discharging electrometer, 1767.
Legg			Automatic system of telegraphy.
Lemonnier, Pierre C.	France 1715	1799	
Lesage, Geo. Louis	Switzerland 1724	1803	Devises telegraphic arrangements, 1774.
Lichtenberg, Geo. Christoph	Germany 1742	1799	Investigator. Electrical dust figures, etc.
Lontin			Electric lighting.
Marcus			Thermo-electric battery, 1865.
Masson, Antoine Philbert	France 1806		Investigator and inventor of electric telegraphy, 1837.
Matteucci, Carlo	Italy 1811	1868	Electro-physiology, electrolysis, etc.
Maxim, Hiram S.	Maine 1840		Electric lighting. Also fire-arms, "Maxim Gun," etc.
Maxwell, J. C.	England 1831	1879	Work on electricity and magnetism, London, 1873, etc.
Melloni, M.	Italy 1801	1854	Investigator. Thermo-multiplier constructed, 1831.
Milner, Isaac	England 1751	1820	Invents an electrometer, 1783.
Mordey, W. M.	England 1856		Victoria dynamo.
Morse, Samuel F. B.	Massachusetts 1791	1872	Electric telegraph, 1837.
Muschenbroek, Peter van	Holland 1692	1761	Leyden jar.
Neumann, F. E.	Germany		Discovers a function called the "potential," from which he deduces a theory of induction, 1845.
Newton, Sir Isaac	England 1642	1727	Eminent investigator. Electrical machine, 1675.
Nicholson, Wm.	England 1755	1815	Decomposes water by the voltaic pile, 1800.
Noad, H. M.	England		Investigator. Powerful electrical machine, 1855.
Nobili, Leopoldo	Italy 1784	1835	Investigator. Constructs a thermo-multiplier, 1831.
Nollet, Jean Antoine	France 1700	1770	Investigator. Contemporary with Beccaria, Canton, and Watson.
Oersted, Hans Christian	Denmark 1777	1851	Eminent investigator. Discovers electro-magnetic action.
Ohm, Georg Simon	Germany 1789	1854	Investigator. States his formulæ relating to galvanic currents, 1827. Unit of electrical resistance named in his honor *ohm*.
Pacinotti, Antonio	Italy		Electro-magnetic machine, 1864.
Page, Dr. C. G.	Massachusetts 1812	1868	Investigator. Electric locomotive, etc., 1851–52.
Peltier			Inventor; discovers what is termed the "Peltier effect," 1834; electrometer, etc., 1848.
Perry, John	Ireland 1849		Electric railways, etc.
Petrie			Electric light, apparatus for regulating, 1848.
Phelps, L. J.			Inventor inductive telegraphy, 1885.
Pixii			First maker of the magneto-electric machine, Paris, 1832.
Plante, Gaston	France 1834		Investigator. Lead battery, 1860.
Pliny (the Elder)	Italy 23	79	Electro-physiology.
Pope, F. L.	United States		Investigator.
Priestley, Joseph	England 1733	1804	History of electricity.
Rapieff	Russia		Improves the Jablochkoff light.
Richman, G. Wilhelm	Germany 1711	1753	Killed at St. Petersburg while attempting Franklin's experiment.
Riess			Eminent investigator in electricity of high potential, etc., 1861.
Ritchie			Galvanometer (torsion), 1830.
Ritter, J. Wilhelm	Germany 1776	1810	Constructs a "secondary pile."
Ronalds, F.		1873	Electric telegraph, pub. 1823.
Ruhmkorff, N.	France [illegible]		Magneto-electric induction coil, constructed 1850.

LIST OF THE PRINCIPAL INVESTIGATORS AND INVENTORS IN ELECTRICITY AND MAGNETISM.—(*Concluded.*)

Names.	Born.	Died.	Remarks.
Salva, Francisco	Spain 1747	1808	Devises telegraphic communications, 1796.
Sanderson, Burdon	England..........	....	Electricity in plants, 1873.
Sawyer, Wm. E.	....	....	Incandescent lamp, termed the Sawyer-Man.
Saxton, Joseph	Pennsylvania ..1799	1873	Magneto-electric machine, London, 1833.
Schilling, Gustavus	Germany 1805	....	Investigator and inventor in electric telegraphy, 1833.
Schweigger, John S. C.	Germany 1779	1857	Invents a galvanometer, 1820. The parent of the needle system.
Seebeck, John T.	Germany 1770	1831	Thermo-electricity discovered, 1821.
Serrin, M.	France	....	Electric lighting.
Siemens, Chas. W.	Germany 1823	....	Eminent investigator and inventor electric railway, lights, etc., in London.
Siemens, Dr. E. Werner	Germany 1816	1892	Eminent investigator, etc.
Singer	....	....	Electrometer improved, 1810.
Smee, Alfred	England 1818	1877	Investigator. Improves the voltaic battery, 1840.
Smith, Wm. Wiley	Indiana...........	....	Communication by induction between moving trains by telegraph.
Soemmering, S. T.	Germany 1755	1830	Exhibits telegraphic arrangements of communication, 1809.
Sprague, Lt. F. J.	United States......	....	Electric railroad, etc.
Staite, W. E.	....	....	Electric light, experimental, 1846, patent.
Stark	Austria...........	....	Duplex telegraphy, etc.
Starr, John W	United States......	....	Electric light, regulating it, 1845.
Stearns, Jos. B.	Massachusetts......	....	Duplex telegraphy, etc.
Steinheil, C. A	Germany	....	Investigator and inventor in electric telegraphy, 1837. Discovers the "earth circuit."
Stratingh	Germany	....	Electric railway. Experiment, 1836.
Sturgeon, William	England 1783	1850	Eminent investigator. Improves the voltaic pile, 1830.
Sulzer, John Geo	Switzerland....1720	1779	Investigator in electro-physiology.
Swan, J. W.	England 1828	....	Inventor electric lighting, etc.
Symmer, Robert	....	....	Investigator, 1759. Maintained the theory of 2 distinct fluids, etc.
Tainter, Sumner	....	....	Photophone.
Taylor	England...........	....	Domestic electric lighting.
Tesla, Nickola	Austria........1857	....	Investigator of high potentials and of currents of great frequency.
Thales	Greece.....636 B.C.	546 B.C.	Acquainted with electricity.
Thomson, Alfred	England...........	....	Inventor. Electric lighting.
Thomson, Sir Wm.	England 1824	....	Investigator and inventor. Electric replenisher, 1868.
Thomson, Elihu	Manchester, Engl..... 1853	....	In U. S., electric railways, electric welding, Thomson-Houston motor, etc.
Tissandier	....	....	
Topler	....	....	Inventor inductive machine, etc.
Tribe, A.	England...........	....	Constructs a copper-zinc couple, 1872. COPPER.
Tyndall, John	England.......1820	1893	Investigator.
Ure, Andrew	Scotland.......1778	1857	Experimenter with galvanism, 1818.
Vail, Alfred	United States......	....	Electric railway. Constructs a locomotive, 1851.
Van Depoele, C. J.	Belgium 1846	....	Electric street railroad, Scranton, Pa., 1886.
Van Marum, Martin	Holland.......1750	1857	Electric mechanician. Said to have constructed the most powerful electric machine ever made, 1785.
Varley, C. F.	England...........	1883	Investigator and inventor. Reciprocal electrophorus.
Vincent, C. W.	England...........	....	Dynamo-magneto-electric machine, 1878.
Voss	....	....	
Volta, Alessandro	Italy 1745	1826	Eminent investigator. Inventor of the voltaic battery, electrophorus, etc. Unit of electrical pressure called in his honor *volt*.
Wallace	....	....	Electric lighting.
Walsh	England...........	....	Electro-physiology, etc.
Watson, Sir William	England 1715	1787	Investigator during the years 1740-50; Copley medal. Transmission of electricity by an insulated wire, 1747.
Weber, Wilhelm E.	Germany 1804	1891	Investigator. Inventions in electric telegraphy, electro-dynamometer, etc.
Weems, David G.	....	....	
Werdermann, Richard	....	....	Electric light.
Weston, Edward	....	....	Dynamo-electrical machine.
Wheatstone, Sir Chas.	England 1802	1875	Eminent investigator and inventor. Electric telegraph, etc.
Wheeler	England...........	....	Associated with Gray in the discovery of electric induction.
Wilde, Henry	England...........	....	Discovers the principle of accumulation by successive action, 1865.
Wills, T.	England...........	....	Announces the formation of nitric acid in the air by electric light, 1878.
Wilson, Benjamin	....	....	
Wimshurst, James	England 1832	....	Inventor. Continuous electrophones and an influence machine, 1882.
Winckler, John Heinrich	Germany 1703	1772	Constructed the Leyden battery, 1746.
Wollaston, Wm. H.	England 1766	1828	Eminent investigator and inventor. Demonstrates the identity of galvanism with electricity.
Wright	....	....	
Zamboni, G.	Italy 1777	1846	Investigator of galvanism and voltaic electricity.
Zipernowski, Carl	Austria........1853	....	Dynamos. Alternate current transformation.

elegy. Elegiac verse (hexameters and pentameters alternately) was the first variation from the hexameter or epic measure, used by Tyrtæus and other early poets. Elegies by Ovid and Catullus are celebrated. Gray's "Elegy, written in a Country Churchyard," pub. 1749. LITERATURE.

elements were anciently reckoned as 4: earth, air, fire, and water. Lavoisier enunciated the principle that all bodies which cannot be proved to be compounded are to be regarded as elements (see table opposite, and separate articles). The chemical elements now known are about 80; with the exception of bromine and fluorine all the elements enter into combination directly or indirectly with oxygen to form oxides. Joseph Norman Lockyer, in a paper read at the Royal society, 12 Dec. 1878, expressed doubts of the elementary character of some of the following substances, based on his spectroscopic experiments. His views were not supported by the researches of profs. Dewar and Liveing, 1880-81. CHLORINE.

LIST OF THE ELEMENTS,

Their atomic weight, specific gravity, chemical symbols, year of their discovery as element or isolation, and name of the discoverer.

[Hydrogen is taken as the unit of atomic weight, and also the unit of specific gravity for gases, the unit of specific gravity for other elements is water. Those elements noted (?) are still doubtful.]

Name.	Atomic weight.	Specific gravity.	Chem. symbol.	Discoverers.	Year.
Aluminum	27.4	2.6	Al.	Wöhler	1827
Antimony.....	120	6.7	Sb.	B. Valentine....	1490
Arsenic.......	75	5.7	As.	G. Brandt......	1733
Barium.......	136.9	4	Ba.	Davy........; Berzelius.....; Ponton.......	1808
Bismuth	207.5	9.8	Bi.	....	1530
Boron	11	2.6	B.	Davy ....; Gay Lussac...; Thénard......	1808
Bromine	79.76	3	Br.	Balard.	1826
Cadmium	111.7	8.65	Cd.	Hermann ....; Stomeyer	1818
Cæsium........	132.7	..	Cs.	Kirchhoff ....; Bunsen.......	1860

LIST OF THE ELEMENTS.—(*Continued.*)

Name.	Atomic weight.	Specific gravity.	Chem. symbol.	Discoverers.	Year.
Calcium	39.9	1.57	Ca.	Davy; Berzelius; Pontin	1808
Carbon	11.97	3.4; 2.2	C.	....	..
Cerium	141	6.7	Ce.	Berzelius; Hisinger; Klaproth	1803
Chlorine	35.37	35.5	Cl.	Davy	1810
Chromium	52.4	6.8	Cr.	Vauquelin	1797
Cobalt	58.74	8.9	Co.	G. Brandt	1733
Copper	63.8	8.9	Cu.	....	..
Davyum (?)	..	..	..	Kern	1877
Decipium (?)	..	..	..	Delafontaine	1878
Didymium	142.1	6.5	Di.	Mosander	1841
Erbium	166	..	Er.	"	1843
Fluorine	19.1	..	F.	Ampère	1810
Gallium	70	..	Ga.	Boisbeadran	1875
Germanium	73.32	..	Ge.	....	1886
Glucinum	9.1	2.1	Gl.	Wöhler	1828
Gold	196.2	19.3	Au.	....	..
Holmium (?)	..	..	Ho.	Soret	1879
Hydrogen	1	.1	H.	Cavendish	1766
Ilmenium (?)	..	..	..	Hermann	1877
Indium	113.4	7.4	In.	Reich; Richter	1863
Iodine	126.54	5	I.	Courtois	1811
Iridium	192.5	22.4	Ir.	Tennant	1804
Iron	55.88	7.8	Fe.	....	..
Lanthanum	138.5	6.1	La.	Mosander	1839
Lead	206.4	11.4	Pb.	....	..
Lithium	7.01	.59	L.	Arfwedson	1817
Magnesium	23.94	1.74	Mg.	Davy	1808
Manganese	54.8	8	Mn.	Gahn	1774
Mercury	199.8	13.56	Hg.	....	..
Molybdenum	95.9	8.6	Mo.	Scheele (?)	1778
Mosandrum (?)	..	..	..	L. Smith	1879
Neptunium (?)	..	..	..	Hermann	1877
Nickel	58.6	8.2	Ni.	Cronstedt	1751
Niobium	94	6.3	Nb.	H. *Rose*	1846
Nitrogen	14.01	14	N.	Rutherford	1772
Norwegium (?)	..	..	Ng.	Dahll	1879
Osmium	191	22.4	Os.	Tennant	1804
Oxygen	15.96	16	O.	Priestley	1774
Palladium	106.2	12	Pd.	Wollaston	1803
Philippium (?)	..	..	..	Delafontaine	1878
Phosphorus	30.96	1.82	P.	Brandt	1669
Platinum	194.3	21.5	Pt.	Woods	1741
Potassium	39.04	.86	K.	Davy	1807
Rhodium	104.1	12.1	Ro.	Wollaston	1803
Rubidium	85.2	1.52	Rb.	Kirchhoff; Bunson	1860
Ruthenium	103.5	11.4	Ru.	Claus	1844
Scandium (?)	..	..	..	....	..
Selenium	79	4.5	Se.	Berzelius	1817
Silicon	28	..	Si.	Berzelius	1823
Silver	107.66	10.5	Ag.	....	..
Sodium	23	.97	Na.	Davy	1807
Strontium	87.2	2.5	Sr.	Davy	1808
Sulphur	31.98	2.05	S.	....	..
Tantalum	182	10.8	Ta.	Hatchett	1801
Tellurium	128	6.2	Te.	Klaproth	1798
Thallium	203.64	11.8	Tl.	Crookes	1861
Thorium	232	7.7	Th.	Berzelius	1828
Thulium (?)	..	..	..	Soret	1879
Tin	117.8	7.3	Sn.	....	..
Titanium	48	..	T.	Klaproth	1795
Tungsten	183.6	18.2	W.	Scheele	1781
Uralium (?)	..	..	..	A. Guyard	1879
Uranium	239.8	18.4	U.	Klaproth	1789
Vanadium	51.2	5.5	V.	Sefstrom	1830
Vesbium (?)	..	..	..	Scacchi	1879
Ytterbium (?)	172.6	..	Yb.	Marignac	1879
Yttrium	88.9	..	Y.	Wöhler	1828
Zinc	65.1	7.15	Zn.	Paracelsus	1541
Zirconium	90.4	4.1	Zr.	Berzelius	1824

Of these, 17 are non-metals, viz.: hydrogen, chlorine, bromine, iodine, fluorine, oxygen, sulphur, selenium, boron, nitrogen, phosphorus, carbon, silicon, tellurium, arsenic, antimony, bismuth.

elephant, a pachydermatous animal, the largest of living quadrupeds, was in the earliest times trained to war. The history of the Maccabees informs us that "to every elephant they appointed 1000 men armed with coats of mail, and 500 horse; and upon the elephants were strong towers of wood," etc. The elephants in the army of Antiochus were provoked to fight by showing them the "blood of grapes and mulberries." The first elephant said to have been seen in England was one of enormous size, presented by Louis IX. to Henry III. in 1238.—*Baker's Chron.* Polyænus states that Julius Cæsar brought one to Britain 54 B.C., which terrified the inhabitants greatly.

Mr. Barnum, the American showman, bought, for $10,000, the large male African elephant Jumbo, 6 tons' weight, of the Zoological Society, Regent's park, London. Jumbo refused to go, 18 Feb. After much trouble he was removed in the night, 22-23 Mch., and placed on board the *Assyrian Monarch*, 24 Mch.; arrived at New York, 9 Apr. 1882; killed by a locomotive in Canada.....16 Sept. 1885

Eleusin'ian mysteries. The institution of these annual secret religious ceremonies (in honor of Demeter) at Athens is attributed to Cadmus, 1550; to Erechtheus, 1399; or to Eumolpus, 1356 B.C. If any one revealed them, he was to be put to death. They were introduced from Eleusis into Rome, in honor of Ceres, lasted about 1800 years, and were abolished by Theodosius, 389 A.D. The laws were—1. To honor parents; 2. To honor the gods with the fruits of the earth; 3. Not to treat brutes with cruelty. Cicero regards civilization as promoted by the Eleusinian mysteries.

Elgin marbles, brought chiefly from the Parthenon, a temple of Pallas Athene (Minerva), on the Acropolis at Athens, of which they formed part of the frieze and pediment, the work of Phidias, under the government of Pericles, about 440 B.C. Thomas lord Elgin began the collection of these marbles during his mission to the Ottoman porte, in 1802; and from him they were purchased by the British government for 35,000*l.*, and placed in the British museum in 1816. The ship conveying them was wrecked near Cerigo, and W. R. Hamilton, who was on board, remained several months at Cerigo, and recovered them from the sea.

Elis, a Greek state termed the "Holy Land," in the Peloponnesus, founded by the Heraclidæ, 1103 B.C. Here Iphitus revived the Olympic games, 884, which were regularly celebrated after Corœbus gained the prize in 776. Elis surrendered many towns to the Spartans in war, 400. After various changes, Elis joined the Achæan league, 274; and with the rest of Greece was subjugated by the Romans in 146.

ell (so named from *ulna*, the arm) was fixed at 45 inches by king Henry I. of Engl., in 1101. The old French ell, or *aune*, was 46.79 inches.

Ello'ra or **Elo'ra,** central India; remarkable for a very ancient rock-cut temple, excavated according to Hindu legends nearly 7000 years ago; more probably about 800 A.D. The town was ceded to the British by Holkar in 1818, and transferred by them to the nizam of the Deccan in 1822.

Elmi'na and **Dutch Guinea,** W. Africa, were ceded by the Dutch government by treaty, signed Feb. 1872, and consolidated with the West African settlements; first governor, Pope Hennessy, Apr. 1872. ASHANTEES.

El Moli'no del Rey, Battle at. On the morning of 8 Sept. 1847, less than 4000 U. S. troops attacked over 14,000 Mexicans under Santa Anna, at El Molino del Rey (the King's Mills), near the fortress of Chapultepec, close by the city of Mexico. They were at first repulsed with slaughter; but, returning to the attack, fought desperately for an hour, and conquered. The Americans lost about 800; the Mexicans left more than 1000 dead on the field. CHAPULTEPEC.

Elphin, Ireland. St. Patrick founded a cathedral near Elphin, "by a river issuing from 2 fountains," in the 5th century, and placed over it St. Asicus, whom he created bishop, who soon after filled it with monks. After many centuries, Roscommon, Ardcarn, Drumclive, and others were annexed to Elphin, making one of the richest sees in Ireland. It is valued in the king's books, by an extent returned 28 Eliz., at 103*l.* 18*s.* sterling. The see was united to Kilmore in 1841, under the Church Temporalities act, passed Aug. 1833.

El'sinore (Zealand, Denmark), formerly the station for collecting sound dues. The scene of Shakespeare's "Hamlet."

"*Hamlet.* Gentlemen, you are welcome to Elsinore."
—Act ii. sc. ii.

E'ly, an island in Cambridgeshire, Engl., on which a church was built about 673, by Etheldreda, queen of Egfrid, king of Northumberland; she also founded a religious house, filled it with virgins, and became first abbess. The 1200th anniversary was celebrated 17-21 Oct. 1873; about 60,000*l.* had then been spent in restoring the cathedral. The Danes ruined the convent about 870; but a monastery was built in 879, on which king Edgar and succeeding monarchs bestowed privileges and grants of land, whereby it became the richest in England.

Richard, the 11th abbot, wishing to free himself from the bishop of Lincoln, made great interest with Henry I. to get Ely erected into a bishopric, 1108, and his successor Hervæus was the first prelate, 1109. Hereward le Wake defended the island against William the Conqueror until 1074. Its defence is described in canon Kingsley's novel, "Hereward the Wake; or, the Last of the Saxons."

El'zevir or **Elsevier,** a family of printers, in Holland, famous for fine pocket editions of the classics.

Louis, the founder, was b. in 1540; began business at Leyden in 1580; he printed about 150 works, and d. 4 Feb. 1617. His sons (especially Bonaventure) and grandsons were celebrated for their work. No fewer than 15 members of this family carried on the business in succession until 1712. Their Pliny (1635), Vergil (1636), and Cicero (1642), are the masterpieces of their press. Their texts, however, were without authority, not resting like those of Aldus and the Stephenses on ancient MSS.

Emancipation in the United States, and **Proclamation of.** While every one knew in 1861, north as well as south, that the only basis of lasting peace was the abolition of slavery, it was after a year of war that Congress took notice of slavery, first by act 13 Mch. 1862, forbidding the use of troops to return fugitive slaves. This was followed by an act, 16 July, 1862, that slaves escaping to the federal line should be free. In a preliminary proclamation, 22 Sept. 1862, pres. Lincoln announced that on 1 Jan. 1863, all persons held in slavery by men in arms against the United States would be declared free. Final proclamation issued 1 Jan. 1863. The number of slaves set free by the president's proclamation, being those in Alabama, Arkansas, Florida, Georgia, Louisiana (part), Mississippi, North Carolina, South Carolina, Texas, Virginia (part), was 3,063,392. Slavery was not disturbed by the proclamation in Delaware, Kentucky, Louisiana (part), Maryland, Missouri, Tennessee, Virginia (part), West Virginia; slave pop. 831,780. These were emancipated by the XIIIth Amendment to the Constitution, making the total number set free 3,895,172. SLAVERY, UNITED STATES.

embalming. The ancient Egyptians, believing that their souls, after many thousand years, would reinhabit their bodies if preserved entire, embalmed the dead. Some of the bodies, called *mummies*, buried 3000 years ago, are still perfect. "The physicians embalmed Israel," 1689 B.C. (Gen. l. 2). MUMMIES. Carbolic acid was successfully employed by prof. Seely in the United States in 1868.

The most perfect specimens of modern embalming are in the museum of the Royal College of Surgeons, London, one, the wife of Van Butchell, preserved by John Hunter by injecting camphorated spirits of wine, etc., into the arteries and veins; and the other the body of a young woman, who died about 1780 of consumption, in the Lock hospital. The method of embalming royal personages in modern times is fully described in Hunter's "Posthumous Works." He died in 1793.—During the U. S. civil war many soldiers' bodies were embalmed and sent home.

embankments of earth were erected by the ancients for protection from their enemies and from inundations. Those of the Egyptians and Babylonians are described by Herodotus and Strabo. To the Romans are attributed the first dikes of Holland, and the embankments of Romney marsh, considered to be the oldest in Britain. In 1250, Henry III. issued a writ enforcing the support of these works, and his successors followed his example. James I. greatly encouraged the embankment of the Thames. Sir W. Dugdale's "History of Embanking" first appeared in 1662. DRAINAGE, LEVEES, LEVELS, MOUND BUILDERS, THAMES.

embargo (from the Sp. *embargar*, to detain), an order restraining ships from sailing. In Great Britain this power is vested in the crown, but is exercised only in extreme cases, sometimes as a prelude to war. The most memorable instances of embargo in Great Britain were those to prevent exports of corn in 1766; and for the detention of all Russian, Danish, and Swedish ships in the several ports, owing to the armed neutrality, 14 Jan. 1801. On account of insults to the United States flag by British cruisers, U. S. Congress, in Dec. 1807, decreed an embargo, detaining with few exceptions all vessels, U. S. and foreign, then in U. S. ports, and ordering all U. S. vessels home. The decree was repealed in Mch. 1809, and the Non-intercourse act passed. Another embargo, for 90 days, was laid in Apr. 1812. UNITED STATES, 1807.

Ember-weeks, instituted, it is said, by pope Calixtus I. (219–223) to implore the blessing of God on the produce of the earth by prayer and fasting, penitents sprinkling ashes (embers) of humiliation on their heads. In the Episcopal church *Ember days* are the Wednesday, Friday, and Saturday after the following days: the first Sunday in Lent, Whitsunday, 14 Sept. (Holy Cross), and 13 Dec. (St. Lucia).

embroidery is usually ascribed to the Phrygians; but the Sidonians excelled in it, and it is mentioned in 1491 B.C. (Exod. xxxv. 35, and xxxviii. 23). BAYEUX TAPESTRY. Embroidery is now largely done by machinery. The first embroidery machine is said to have been invented by John Duncan, of Glasgow, in 1804. Heilman's was patented by Köchlin. *Berlin wool-work* has been improved by elegant patterns, first pub. by Mr. Wittich in Berlin, about 1810.

emerald, a green, precious stone, found in the East and in Peru. It has been erroneously alleged that there were no true emeralds in Europe before the conquest of Peru, 1545; there is one in the Paris museum, taken from the mitre of pope Julius II., who died in 1513.

Em'esa, now **Hems,** a town of Syria, renowned for a temple of the sun, whose priest, Bassianus, was proclaimed emperor as Heliogabalus or Elagabalus, 218. His atrocities led to his assassination, 11 Mch. 222.

emigrants (Lat. *emigrare: e*, out; and *migrare*, to remove one's abode). The French aristocracy and clergy (*émigrés*) began to leave their country in July, 1789, at the breaking-out of the revolution: their estates were confiscated in Dec. A large number returned in 1802 by an amnesty granted after the peace of Amiens. Many were indemnified after the restoration in 1815.

emigration. Phœnician and Greek emigrants colonized the coasts of the Mediterranean and the Black sea. MAGNA GRÆCIA, MARSEILLES, etc. The discovery of America opened a vast field for emigration. IMMIGRATION.

eminence, a title conferred upon cardinals by pope Urban VIII., 10 Jan. 1631, more honorable than "excellency." Previous cardinals had the title of *illustrissimi.—Ashe.* The grand-master of Malta obtained this title.—*Pardon.*

emir (*e-mēr'*), a title of the caliphs among the Turks and Persians, first awarded to the descendants of Mahomet's daughter Fatima, about 650. To such only was originally given the privilege of wearing the green turban.

emission theory of light (advocated by Newton, about 1672) supposes that particles pass from the luminous body to the eye, and that each ray of light from the sun consists of matter in transit. It is opposed to the *undulatory theory*, now generally received.

empalement, or transfixing by a pale or stake, a mode of executing criminals, mentioned by Juvenal, and often inflicted in Rome; still used in Turkey and Arabia. In England, the dead bodies of murderers were sometimes staked; abolished 1823. SUICIDE.

emperor, from *imperator* (ruler), a title first conferred on victorious Roman generals, and afterwards upon the sovereign of that people.

	B.C.
Augustus Cæsar first Roman emperor	27
	A.D.
Valentinian I. first emperor of the west, and Valens first emperor of the east	364
Charlemagne first emperor of Germany, crowned by Leo III.	800
Othman I. founder of Turkish empire, first emperor of Turkey,	1299
Peter I. first emperor of Russia......22 Oct.	1721
Francis II. of Germany first emperor of Austria......11 Aug.	1804
Napoleon Bonaparte first emperor of the French	"
Napoleon III., his nephew, founded the second French empire, Dec. 1852; deposed......4 Sept.	1870
Iturbide emperor of Mexico, Feb. 1822; shot......19 July,	1824
Dom Pedro IV. of Portugal first emperor of Brazil	1825
Faustin I. first emperor of Hayti, in 1849; deposed	1859
Maximilian I. emperor of Mexico, 10 Apr. 1864; shot..19 June,	1867
King of Prussia proclaimed emperor of Germany at Versailles, France......18 Jan.	1871
Queen Victoria proclaimed empress of India......1 May,	1876

Empirics, a sect of physicians, dating from the 3d century before Christ, who rejected all theories of the animal economy, accepting experience as the only foundation of medicine. The sect adopted the principles of Acron of Agrigentum, who flourished about 430 B.C.

Emuc'fau and **En'otochop'eo,** Alabama, Battles of, on 22 and 24 Jan. 1814. These were fought by 930 'ennessee volunteers and 200 or 300 friendly Indians, under en Jackson, against 900 Creeks The U.S troops lost 20 killed nd 75 wounded The Creeks left 190 warriors dead on the eld

enamelling was practised by the Egyptians, Chinese, nd other nations, and was known in England in the time of he Saxons At Oxford is an enamelled jewel which be- onged to Alfred, made, as the inscription shows, by his order, bout 887 Limoges enamelled ware was popular in the 16th entury Magnificent specimens by Lepec, Elkington, Eman- el, etc, at the exhibition at Paris, 1867 MOSAIC

Encænia, Greek festivals kept on days on which cities 'ere built and temples consecrated, and in later times, as at)xford, at the celebration or commemoration of founders and enefactors.—*Oldsworth* The public commemoration at Ox- ord suspended in 1875, restored, 21 June, 1876 They were he origin of church-wakes in England, about 600 They 'ere also feasts celebrated by the Jews on the 25th of the inth month, in commemoration of the Maccabees cleansing he temple, which had been polluted by Antiochus Epiphanes, 31 B C

encaustic painting, enamelling by fire Painting ith burned wax is said to have been known to Praxiteles bout 360 B.C This art was revived by M Bachelier, 1749, y count Caylus, 1765, and by Miss Greenland, 1785 and 792

Encke's (*enk-eh'*) **comet.** COMETS

Encratites, followers of Titian, about 170, denounced iarriage, and abstained from flesh, and from wine even at the ord's supper.

Encyc'lical letter. ROME, 1864

encyclopædia or **cyclopædia**, a general dic- onary of art, science, and literature This name has been iven to a work by Abulpharagius in the 13th century

lsted s Encyclopædia 1620
ouis Moreri's Dictionnaire Historique 1673
ofmann's Lexicon Universale 1677
orneille's Dictionnaire des Arts 1694
ayle's Dictionnaire 1696
exicon Technicum of John Harris (earliest English encyclo pædia), 1704, supplements 1710, 1741
phraim Chambers's Cyclopædia 1728
edler s Universal Lexicon 1732-50
ncyclopédie (by Didérot and D'Alembert) 1751-80
[The contributors were termed *encyclopédistes* and their daring writings are believed to have hastened the French rev olution in 1789]
ncyclopædia Britannica (1st edition by William Smellie) 1771
[The 8th completed, 1861, 9th begun, 1875, finished, 1887 25 vols 4 vols. American supplement.]
ncyclopédie Methodique (by Pancoucke) 1782-1832
hambers's Cyclopædia (edited by Rees) 1785
ees's Cyclopædia 1802-19
rockhaus s Conversations Lexikon, 1st edition 1818
[Later editions frequent]
ncyclopædia Metropolitana 1817-45
ncyclopædia Americana (by F Lieber, etc) 1829-32
abinet Cyclopædia (a collection of treatises) 1829-46
enny Cyclopædia. 1833-46
night's English Cyclopædia (4 divisions) 1853-61-70
uyckinck's Cyclopædia of American Literature 1855-66
llibone's Dictionary of Authors 1858-80
lew American Cyclopædia begun 1858
Iomans s Cyclopædia of Commerce 1859
ell's Popular Cyclopædia 1872 et seq
IcClintock and Strong's Cyclopædia of Biblical, Theological, and Ecclesiastical Literature 1867 et seq
hambers's Cyclopædia 1859-68, 1874-75, 1889
ppletons' Annual Cyclopædia 1861 et seq
rsch and Gruber's Allgemeine Encyclopädie, begun 1818, 153 vols pub 1881
hinese Cyclopædia, 6109 vols (all the valuable books then ex isting), printed by order of the emperor between 1661-1721
'opy bought for British museum 1877
merican Cyclopædia, by George Ripley and Charles A Dana 16 vols. 1873-78
arousse's Grand Dictionnaire Universel du XIX Siècle, 15 vols, imp. octavo, 1865, 1st and 2d supplement 1878 et seq
[One of the best of the encyclopædic works of the 19th century]
ohnson's Universal Cyclopædia, 1873, revised 1893-94
lobe Encyclopædia, completed 1879
ossing's Cyclopædia of American History 1881
ncyclopædic Dictionary, completed 1889

Enderby Land. SOUTHERN CONTINENT.

endosmo'sis. M. Dutrochet, about 1826, found that if 2 fluids, gases, or vapors, of unequal density, are separated by an animal or vegetable membrane, the less dense will pass through This property he called *endosmose*, when the move ment is from the outside to the inside, and *exosmose* when from the inside to the outside Many natural phenomena are thus explained —*Brande*

energy. In an address to the British association at York, Engl, 1 Sept. 1881, sir William Thomson declared all energy in nature available for mechanical effects, as tides, food, falls, wind, and rain, to be derived from the sun

Engen, a town of Baden Here Moreau defeated the Austrians, 3 May, 1800

Enghien (*ong-ghe-an'*) or **Steenkirk**, a town of S W. Belgium Here the British, under William III, were defeated by the French under marshal Luxembourg, 21 July 1692 —The duc d'Enghien, a descendant of the great Condé, was seized in Baden by order of Bonaparte, conveyed to Vin- cennes, and, after a hasty trial, shot by torchlight, immediately after condemnation, 21 Mch 1804 The body was exhumed 20 Mch 1816

engineering and **engineers.** "Engineering is the art of directing the great sources of power in nature for the use and convenience of man"—*Thomas Tredgold* It embraces a very wide range of subjects, and the different departments into which the profession is now divided do not admit of very strict definition But it may be classified as *civil*, including the design and construction of canals, river navigation, har- bors, docks, roads, bridges, railways, lighthouses, water supply, irrigation, sewerage, etc , as *mechanical*, including machinery of all kinds, steam-engines, iron shipbuilding, agricultural implements, etc., as *mining*, including all the detail of open- ing and working mines, and as *military*, including the build- ing of fortifications, use of artillery, etc The military en- gineers were formerly called trench-masters in England, sir William Pelham being so called in 1622, and the chief-engi- neer was called camp-master-general in 1634 Capt Thomas Rudd had the rank of chief-engineer to the king of England about 1650 The British corps of engineers was formerly a civil corps, but was made a military corps and directed to rank with the artillery, 25 Apr 1787 It has a colonel-in- chief, 16 colonels-commandant, and 16 colonels In the army of the United States the highest rank in the corps of engi- neers is colonel, of which there are 6, and 12 lieut-colonels *Civil engineering* improved rapidly after the middle of the 18th century, when Smeaton began the Eddystone lighthouse, and Brindley the Bridgewater canal Since then the Rennies, Stephensons, Brunels, and Telford, Locke, Hawkshaw, Lyster, Fowler, Baker, and Coode in England, and the Roeblings (fa- ther and son), gen Newton, Eads, C Shaler Smith, C C Schneder, and many others in the U S, have improved navi- gation and constructed breakwaters, docks, bridges, railways, tunnels, etc, which are the marvel of the age

ENGINEERS, SOCIETIES, ETC., IN ENGLAND

First society of civil engineers formed by Smeaton and others, afterwards termed the Smeatonian Society of Civil Engineers, 1793
Institution of Civil Engineers, established in England, 2 Jan 1818, obtained a charter 3 June, 1828
[1472 members, Jan 1868]
Institution of Mechanical Engineers, which had its headquar ters in Birmingham moved to London 1877, established 1847
Isambard Kingdom Brunel, projector of the *Great Eastern*, aged 53, d 15 Sept 1859
Robert Stephenson, railway engineer, aged 59, d 12 Oct. "
Engineers' Amalgamated Society Engl in 1867, consisted of above 30,000 members, annual income 86,000*l*, disbursed to disabled workmen, etc., about 50,000*l*, amassed capital, about 125,000*l*
Engineer (London), weekly journal, established 4 Jan 1856
Engineering (London), weekly journal established Jan 1866
College of Practical Engineers, Muswell hill, near London, opened by sir Henry Bessemer, sir Joseph Whitworth, dr C Wm Siemens, and others Sept 1881
Sir John Hawkshaw, engineer of the Severn tunnel, d aged 80, 2 June, 1891
Sir John Coode, eminent for breakwaters and other works, b 1816, d 2 Mch 1892

IN THE UNITED STATES

American Society of Civil Engineers organized 1852
American Institute of Mining Engineers organized 1871
[Home members 2200, foreign 38, 1893]
American Society of Mechanical Engineers organized 1880
[Total membership 1569, 1893]

American Institute of Electrical Engineers organized 1884
[Membership 642, 1893]
Principal periodicals published in the interest of engineering are *The Engineering Magazine*, *The Engineering and Mining Journal*, *The Engineering News*, and *The Engineering Record*, all pub in New York
BREAKWATERS, BRIDGES, DOCKS, RAILROADS, TUNNELS, etc

England (from *Angles* and *lond*, land), so named, it is said, by Egbert, first king of the English in a general council held at Winchester, 829, or by Athelstan, 925 ANGLO-SAXONS England was united to Wales, 1283, to Scotland in 1603, they have had the same legislature since 1707, when the 3 were styled Great Britain Ireland was incorporated with them, by the act of legislative union, 1 Jan 1801, and the whole was called the United Kingdom of Great Britain and Ireland England contains 40 counties The British empire is computed to contain about 7,000,000 sq miles of territory, with 340,220 000 inhabitants Statistical details are given under the respective headings, ARMY, NAVY, REVENUE, etc Pop of England and Wales, 1891, 27,482,104, 1901, 32,527,843 For previous history, BRITAIN, histories of England, by Rapin, 1725-31, Carte, 1747-55, Hume, 1755-62, Tobias Smollett, 1757-65, John Lingard, 1819-30, Charles Knight, 1856-62, J R Green, 1874-80 Parts by T. B. Macaulay, earl Stanhope, J A Froude, Miss H Martineau, and others. CHRONICLES, IRELAND, SCOTLAND, WALES

Egbert, "king of the English" 828, defeats the Welsh, Danes, etc, at Hengestdown 835
Alfred, king 871, after many vicissitudes, vanquishes the Danes 871-896
He frames a code of laws 890, forms a militia and navy, surveys and subdivides the country, and promotes education 896
Athelstan crushes Danes Scots, etc, at Brunanburg 937
Predominance of Dunstan, he promotes monachism and the celibacy of the clergy about 952
Ethelred compounds with the Danes for peace 991
Causes their massacre 13 Nov 1002
Avenged by Sweyn, king of Denmark, Ethelred flees to Normandy 1003
Sweyn dies, and Ethelred returns, 1014, d 1016
Canute, the Dane, sole monarch 1017
Edward the Confessor, king, Saxon dynasty restored, Norman language, customs, and laws introduced 1042
Harold II crowned, 6 Jan, defeats the Norwegians at STAMFORD BRIDGE, 25 Sept, defeated and slain at HASTINGS by William of Normandy 14 Oct 1066

NORMAN CONQUEST

William I crowned at Westminster abbey 25 Dec 1066
Northern counties rebel, ravaged from the Humber to the Tyne. 1069-70
Introduction of the feudal system about 1070
Justices of peace appointed 1076
Domesday-book compiled 1085-86
William II crowned 26 Sept. 1087
Crusades begin 1096
William II killed by an arrow (NEW FOREST) 2 Aug 1100
Henry I crowned, restores Saxon laws, etc 5 Aug "
Defeats his brother Robert and gains Normandy 1106
Prince William and nobles drowned (BARFLEUR) 25 Nov 1120
Stephen crowned 26 Dec 1135
Civil war between the empress Maud, Henry's daughter, and Stephen, her Scots defeated at the battle of Standard, 22 Aug 1138
She lands in England and is successful 1139
Crowned at Winchester 3 Mch. 1141
Defeated, retires to France. 1147
Concludes a peace with Stephen 1153
Henry II crowned 19 Dec 1154
CONSTITUTIONS OF CLARENDON enacted Jan. 1164
Arrogance of Becket, murdered (BECKET) 29 Dec. 1170
Conquest of Ireland 1171, 1172
England divided into 6 judicial circuits 1176
English laws digested by Glanville. about 1181
Richard I crowned 3 Sept. 1189
He joins the crusades 1191
Defeats Saladin 1192
Made prisoner by duke of Austria, and sold to Henry VI of Germany Dec. "
Ransomed for about 300,000*l* 1194
John crowned May, 1199
Normandy lost to England 1204
England put under an interdict 1208
MAGNA CHARTA granted 15 June, 1215
Henry III crowned 28 Oct. 1216
BARONS WAR 1262-68
First regular parliament 1265
Edward I crowned 20 Nov 1272
Wales subdued, united to England 1283
Death of Roger Bacon 1292
Scotland subdued, 1296, revolts 1297
Edward II crowned. 8 July, 1307
Defeated by Bruce at Bannockburn 24 June, 1314
Insurrection of the barons against his favorites... 1308, 1315, 1325
Edward III. crowned 25 Jan. 1327
Edward II murdered (BERKELEY CASTLE) 21 Sept. 1327
Defeat of the Scots at Halidon hill 1333
Invades France, victorious at Crecy 26 Aug 1346
Takes Calais 1347
Order of the Garter instituted 1349
Victory at Poitiers 19 Sept. 1356
Peace of Bretigny 8 May, 1360
Law pleadings in English 1362
Richard II crowned 22 June, 1377
Insurrection of Wat Tyler suppressed 15 June, 1381
Death of Wickliffe 1385
Henry IV crowned 30 Sept 1399
Order of the Bath instituted by Henry IV "
Insurrection of the Percies and the Welsh 1402-5
Henry V crowned 21 Mch 1413
France invaded by Henry V, victor at Agincourt 25 Oct 1415
Treaty of Troyes, the French crown gained 1420
Henry VI crowned at Paris Dec 1430
English conquests lost in France except Calais (JOAN OF ARC), 1429-31
Cade's insurrection June, 1450
War of the Roses (BATTLES, ROSES) 1451-57
Edward IV deposes Henry VI 4 Mch 1461
Printing introduced by Caxton 1471
Edward V, accession 9 Apr 1483
Murdered in the Tower soon after "
Richard III deposes Edward V 25 June, "
Valuable statutes enacted 1484
Henry VII, accession, Richard defeated and slain at Bosworth field 22 Aug 1485
Yeomen of the guard, the first standing army in England instituted "
Henry marries Elizabeth daughter of Edward IV 1486
Insurrection of Lambert Simnel quelled 1486-87
Court of Star chamber instituted 1487
Insurrection of Perkin Warbeck quelled 1492-98
Gardening introduced, principally from the Netherlands about 1502
Death of prince Arthur 2 Apr "
Henry VIII, accession 22 Apr 1509
Rise of Wolsey 1514
Henry VIII's interview with Francis I at Ardres (FIELD OF THE CLOTH OF GOLD) 4-25 June, 1520
First map of England drawn by G Lilly about "
Henry VIII becomes "Defender of the Faith" 1521
Fall of Wolsey, d 29 Nov 1530
Henry VIII marries Anne Boleyn privately, Nov 1532, or Jan 1533, divorced from Catherine. 23 May, 1533
Henry VIII styled "head of the church" 1534
Pope's authority in England abolished "
Sir Thomas More beheaded 6 July, 1535
Queen Anne Boleyn beheaded. 19 May, 1536
Queen Jane Seymour d 24 Oct. 1537
Monasteries suppressed 1538
Statute of Six Articles passed. 1539
Abbots of Glastonbury, Reading, etc., executed "
First authorized edition of the Bible (Cranmer's) printed "
Cromwell lord Essex, beheaded 1540
Anne of Cleves divorced 9 July, "
Queen Catherine Howard beheaded 1542
Ireland declared a kingdom, and the title of "king of Ireland" confirmed to the English sovereigns 1543
Henry marries Catherine Parr 12 July, "
Edward VI, accession, 28 Jan, promotes the Reformation (Somerset, protector) 1547
"Book of Common Prayer" authorized 1548
Somerset deprived of power, 1549, beheaded 1552
Mary, accession, 6 July, restores popery 1553
Execution of lady Jane Grey and her husband, Lord Guilford Dudley 1554
Mary marries Philip of Spain, persecutes the Protestants "
Ridley, Latimer and Cranmer burned (PROTESTANTS) 1555 and 1556
Calais retaken by the French. 7 Jan. 1558
Elizabeth, accession, church of England re established, 17 Nov. "
Mary, queen of Scots, seeks refuge in England, 1568, executed, 8 Feb. 1587
Spanish armada repulsed (ARMADA) July, 1588
Devereux, earl of Essex, beheaded 25 Feb 1601
James I, accession, union of the 2 crowns 24 Mch 1603
Styled "king of Great Britain" 24 Oct. 1604
Gunpowder plot Nov 1605
Authorized version of the Bible completed. 1611
Baronets first created May, "
Overbury murder 15 Sept. 1613
Shakespeare d 23 Apr 1616
Raleigh beheaded 29 Oct 1618
Book of Sports published 24 May, "
Charles I accession 27 Mch 1625
Death of lord Bacon 9 Apr 1626
Duke of Buckingham assassinated 23 Aug 1628
Hampden's trial respecting "ship money" 1637
Contest between the king and parliament, impeachment and execution of lord Strafford 1641
Attempted "arrest of the 5 members" 4 Jan 1642
Civil war begins. Charles I. sets up his standard at Nottingham (BATTLES) 22 Aug "
Battle of Edgehill 23 Oct. "
Archbishop Laud beheaded 10 Jan 1645
Charles defeated at Naseby 14 June, "
He flees to the Scotch, 5 May, is given up 21 Sept. 1646
Execution of Charles I 30 Jan. 1649
Cromwell's victory at Worcester 3 Sept 1651

Oliver Cromwell, protector of the Commonwealth...16 Dec. 1653
Naval victories of Blake...1652-57
Richard Cromwell, protector...3 Sept. 1658
Richard resigns...25 May, 1659
Charles II.; monarchy re-established...29 May, 1660
Act of uniformity passed; church of England restored... 1662
Great plague... 1665
Great fire of London...2, 3 Sept. 1666
Disgrace of lord Clarendon...Nov. 1667
Death of John Milton...8 Nov. 1674
Oates's "popish plot" creates a panic...13 Aug. 1678
Sir Edmond Berry Godfrey found murdered...17 Oct. "
Many Roman Catholics executed...1678-79
Habeas corpus act for protecting English subjects against false arrest and imprisonment, passed...27 May, 1679
"Rye-house plot;" William, lord Russell, executed, 21 July, and Algernon Sydney executed...7 Dec. 1683
James II., accession...6 Feb. 1685
Duke of Monmouth's rebellion defeated at Sedgemoor, 6 July; he is beheaded...15 July, "
Acquittal of the 7 bishops...30 June, 1688
Abdication of James II...11 Dec. "
William III. and *Mary* proclaimed by the convention parliament...13 Feb. 1689
National debt begins... 1692
Bank of England incorporated...27 July, 1694
Death of the queen regnant, Mary...28 Dec. "
Peace of Ryswick... 1697
Death of James II. in exile...16 Sept. 1701
Anne, accession...8 Mch. 1702
Victory of Marlborough at Blenheim...13 Aug. 1704
Union of the 2 kingdoms as Great Britain...1 May, 1707
Sacheverell riots... 1710
Treaty of Utrecht, advantageous to Great Britain...11 Apr. 1713
George I. of Hanover, accession...1 Aug. 1714
Scots' rebellion quelled... 1715
South-sea bubble... 1720
Death of the duke of Marlborough...16 June, 1722
Order of the Bath revived... 1725
George II., accession...11 June, 1727
Death of Newton...20 Mch. "
George II. at the victory of DETTINGEN...16 June, 1743
Second Scots' rebellion; prince Charles-Edward gains Edinburgh, 17 Sept.; victor at Preston Pans...21 Sept. 1745
Victory at Falkirk, 17 Jan.; defeated totally at Culloden, 16 Apr. 1746
Death of prince Frederick Louis, son of George II. and father of George III...20 Mch. 1751
New style introduced into England, 3 Sept. (made 14)... 1752
Seven years' war begins (BATTLES)...May, 1756
Conquest of India begins, under col. (afterwards lord) Clive (INDIA)... 1757
Victory and death of gen. Wolfe (QUEBEC)... 1759
George III., accession...25 Oct. 1760
Marries Charlotte Sophia, of Mecklenburg-Strelitz, 8 Sept.; is crowned...22 Sept. 1761
Peace of Paris; Canada gained...10 Feb. 1763
Isle of Man annexed to Great Britain... 1765
Death of the Old Pretender, "chevalier de St. George" (PRETENDERS)...30 Dec. "
Royal Marriage act passed... 1772
American war for independence begins (UNITED STATES)... 1775
Death of earl of Chatham...11 May, 1778
"No Popery" riots...2-7 June, 1780
Preliminary treaty recognizing the independence of the U. S. signed...30 Nov. 1782
Definitive treaty signed...3 Sept. 1783
Margaret Nicholson attempts life of George III...2 Aug. 1786
Trial of Warren Hastings begins...13 Feb. 1788
Death of the Young Pretender at Rome...3 Mch. "
King's malady made known...12 Oct. "
He recovers, and offers thanks at St. Paul's...23 Apr. 1789
First coalition against France...26 June, 1792
Habeas Corpus act suspended...23 May, 1794
Howe's victory...1 June, "
Prince of Wales marries princess Caroline of Brunswick.8 Apr. 1795
Warren Hastings acquitted...23 Apr. "
Princess Charlotte of Wales b...7 Jan. 1796
Cash payments suspended...25 Feb. 1797
Death of Edmund Burke...9 July, "
Irish rebellion...May, 1798
Habeas Corpus act again suspended... "
Battle of the Nile; Nelson victor...1 Aug. "
Hatfield's attempt on the king's life...11 May, 1800
Union of Great Britain with Ireland...1 Jan. 1801
Nelson's victory at Copenhagen...2 Apr. "
Habeas Corpus act again suspended...19 Apr. "
Peace of Amiens concluded...1 Oct. "
War against France under Bonaparte...18 May, 1803
Nelson's victory and death at Trafalgar...21 Oct. 1805
Death of Mr. Pitt...23 Jan. 1806
"DELICATE INVESTIGATION"...May, "
Lord Melville impeached, 29 Apr.; acquitted...12 June, "
Death of Charles James Fox...13 Sept. "
Orders in council against Berlin decree...7 Jan. 1807
Abolition of the slave-trade by Parliament...25 Mch. "
Victory and death of sir J. Moore (CORUNNA)...16 Jan. 1809
Duke of York impeached by col. Wardle...Jan. "
Jubilee celebrating king's accession...25 Oct. "
Unfortunate Walcheren expedition...Aug.-Nov. "
Sir Francis Burdett's arrest, and riots...6 Apr. 1810
King's malady returns...2 Nov. "

ENG

General commercial embarrassment...Dec. 1810
Regent.—The prince of Wales...5 Feb. 1811
Luddite riots...Nov. "
Assassination of Mr. Perceval, premier...11 May, 1812
Earl of Liverpool premier...9 June, "
War with the U. S. commenced...18 June, "
Peace with France, etc...14 Apr. 1814
Emperor of Russia and king of Prussia visit England...7 June, "
Centenary of the house of Hanover...1 Aug. "
Peace with the U. S. (treaty of Ghent)...24 Dec. "
Battle of Waterloo (close of French war)...18 June, 1815
Princess Charlotte marries prince Leopold of Saxe-Coburg, 2 May, 1816
Death of R. B. Sheridan...9 July, "
Spa-fields meeting...2 Dec. "
Green-bag inquiry...2 Feb. 1817
Habeas Corpus act suspended...24 Feb. "
Cash payments resumed (suspended 1797)...22 Sept. "
Queen Charlotte dies at Kew...17 Nov. 1818
Queen Victoria b...24 May, 1819
Manchester reform meeting (Peterloo) (MANCHESTER)...16 Aug. "
Duke of Kent d...23 Jan. 1820
George IV., accession...29 Jan. "
Cato-st. conspirators arrested, 23 Feb.; executed...1 May, "
Trial of QUEEN CAROLINE...19 Aug.-10 Nov. "
Coronation of George IV...19 July, 1821
Queen Caroline dies at Hammersmith...7 Aug. "
Lord Byron d...19 Apr. 1824
Commercial panic...1825-26
Duke of York d...5 Jan. 1827
Mr. Canning, premier, 30 Apr.; d...8 Aug. "
Battle of Navarino...20 Oct. "
Roman Catholic Relief bill passed...13 Apr. 1829
Political panic in London; riots...Nov. "
William IV. accession...26 June, 1830
Mr. Huskisson killed at the opening of the Liverpool and Manchester railway...15 Sept. "
Grey administration formed...Nov. "
King opens new London bridge...Aug. 1831
Reform bill rejected by lords, 7 Oct.; Bristol riots...29 Oct. "
English Reform act passed...7 June, 1832
Assault on William IV. by a discharged pensioner at Ascot, 19 June, "
Sir Walter Scott d...21 Sept. "
Samuel T. Coleridge d...25 July, 1834
Slavery ceases in the colonies...1 Aug. "
Corporation Reform act passed...9 Sept. 1835
Victoria, accession; Hanover separated from Great Britain...20 June, 1837
Coronation of queen Victoria...28 June, 1838
Beginning of war with China...Mch. 1839
Penny postage begins...10 Jan. 1840
Queen marries prince Albert of Saxe-Coburg...10 Feb. "
Oxford's assault on the queen...10 June, "
Prince of Wales b...9 Nov. 1841
King of Prussia visits England...24 Jan. 1842
John Francis fires at the queen...30 May, "
Bean presents a pistol at her...3 July, "
Income-tax act passed...Aug. "
Peace of Nankin (with China)...Dec. "
Death of duke of Sussex...21 Apr. 1843
Tractarian or Puseyite controversy...1844-45
Anti-corn law agitation... 1845
Peel's new tariff, 1845; railway mania...Nov. "
Commercial panic...Mch. 1846
Corn laws repealed...26 June, "
Chartist demonstration in London...10 Apr. 1848
Cholera reappears in England...1848 and 1849
Adelaide, queen dowager, d...2 Dec. "
"Exhibition of 1851" announced...3 Jan. 1850
Death of Wordsworth (aged 80)...23 Apr. "
Pate's assault on the queen...27 June, "
Death of sir Robert Peel (aged 62)...2 July, "
Duke of Cambridge d...8 July, "
Great excitement occasioned by the pope's establishment of a Roman Catholic hierarchy in England...Nov. "
Sixth census of the United Kingdom (POPULATION), 27,637,761, 30 Mch. 1851
First "Great Exhibition" opened...1 May, "
Australian gold arrives...Dec. "
Death of the poet Thomas Moore...26 Feb. 1852
John Camden Neild, an eccentric miser, bequeathed about 250,000*l.* to the queen; d...30 Aug. "
Death of Wellington (aged 83), Sept. 14; public funeral, 18 Nov. "
Death of sir Charles Napier, conqueror of Scinde...29 Aug. 1853
English and French fleets enter Bosporus...22 Oct. "
Protocol between England, France, Austria, and Prussia for peace between Russia and Turkey...5 Dec. "
Conferences on Eastern question favor Turkey...Sept.-Dec. "
Alliance between England, France, and Turkey signed..12 Mch. 1854
War declared against Russia (RUSSO-TURKISH WARS)...28 Mch. "
Resignation of Aberdeen ministry...29 Jan. 1855
Formation of Palmerston ministry...Feb. "
Death of Joseph Hume (aged 78)...20 Feb. "
Peace with Russia proclaimed, 19 Apr.; thanksgiving day, 4 May; illuminations, etc...29 May, 1856
War with China...Oct. "
War with Persia...Nov. "
Mutiny of Indian army begins (INDIA)...Mch. 1857
Death of duchess of Gloucester (aged 81), the last of George III.'s children...30 Apr. "

ENG

Princess royal marries prince Frederick William of Prussia, 25 Jan. 1858
Jewish Disabilities bill passed........................23 July, "
India bill passed....................................2 Aug. "
Association for the Promotion of Social Science meet at Liverpool...12 Oct. "
Derby ministry defeated on the Reform bill; dissolve Parliament, 23 Apr.; again defeated, they resign, 11 June; the Palmerston-Russell administration formed..........18 June, 1859
Lord Macaulay d. (aged 59)...........................28 Dec. "
Sir Charles Barry d. (aged 65)......................12 May, 1860
Peace with China signed.............................24 Oct. "
Thomas Cochrane, earl of Dundonald, d. (aged 82)......31 Oct. "
Prince of Wales visits Canada and United States, 24 July–20 Oct.; returns.....................................15 Nov. "
Seventh census taken (29,192,419)......................8 Apr. 1861
Excitement, capt. Wilkes (of U. S. navy) having seized Messrs. Slidell and Mason from British mail steamer *Trent* (TRENT AFFAIR)...8 Nov. "
Death of the prince consort of "typhoid fever, duration 21 days," 14 Dec.; buried...........................23 Dec. "
U. S. government release Messrs. Slidell and Mason....28 Dec. "
Prince Alfred declared king of Greece at Athens (throne declined)...23 Oct. 1862
Great distress in the cotton-manufacturing districts begins, Apr.; contributions received, Central Relief fund, 407,830*l.*; Mansion-house fund, 236,926*l.*.........................20 Dec. "
Rupture with Brazil......................................Jan. 1863
Prince Alfred elected king of Greece...................3 Feb. "
Princess Alexandra of Denmark enters London, 7 Mch.; married to the prince of Wales.........................10 Mch. "
British, French, and Austrian governments remonstrate with Russia on cruelties in Poland........................7 Apr. "
Capts. Grant and Speke return from exploring the sources of the Nile...June, "
Government declines the French emperor's proposal for a congress of sovereigns..................................Nov. "
Death of William M. Thackeray (aged 52)........... 24 Dec. "
Judicial committee of privy council decide that government had no authority to seize the *Alexandra* (confederate steamer), 8 Feb. 1864
Garibaldi's visit to England.........................3–27 Apr. "
Ionian isles made over to Greece......................1 June, "
European conference at London on the Schleswig-Holstein question; no result......................24 Apr.–25 June, "
Death of John Leech (aged 47).........................29 Oct. "
Death of Richard Cobden (aged 61)......................2 Apr. 1865
Death of lord Palmerston, 18 Oct.; public funeral......27 Oct. "
Earl Russell premier.....................................3 Nov. "
New Reform bill introduced by Mr. Gladstone.........12 Mch. 1866
Commercial panic in London..........................11 May et seq. "
Ministry defeated on Reform bill, 18 June; resign....26 June, "
Atlantic telegraph (ELECTRICITY) completed; messages sent to lord Stanley...27 July, "
Cable of 1865 recovered, and communication established with Valentia, 2 Sept.; and with Newfoundland...........8 Sept. "
Visit of the sultan (TURKEY).......................12–23 July, 1867
New Reform act passed (REFORM).......................15 Aug. "
Michael Faraday, natural philosopher (nearly 76), d....25 Aug. "
Preparations for the expedition to Abyssinia (ABYSSINIA)..Aug. "
Fenian outrages; rescue of prisoners at Manchester (FENIANS), 18 Sept. "
Synod of bishops at Lambeth (PAN-ANGLICAN)......24–27 Sept. "
Earl of Derby resigns, 25 Feb.; Disraeli ministry formed, 29 Feb. 1868
Mr. Gladstone's resolution for disestablishing the Irish church adopted by the Commons...........................30 Apr. "
Death of lord Brougham (aged 89)........................7 May, "
Irish and Scotch Reform acts passed...................13 July, "
Disraeli ministry resigns, 2 Dec.; Gladstone ministry take office, 9 Dec. "
Convention with the U. S. respecting the ALABAMA CLAIM signed (afterwards rejected by the U. S.)...................14 Jan. 1869
Irish church bill introduced into the Commons, 1 Mch.; royal assent...26 July, "
Earl of Derby d. (aged 70)............................23 Oct. "
Charles Dickens d. (aged 58)...........................9 June, 1870
Earl of Clarendon d. (aged 70)........................27 June, "
Irish land bill brought in, 15 Feb.; signed.............8 July, "
Neutrality in FRANCO-PRUSSIAN WAR proclaimed......19 July, "
Treaty with Prussia and France for neutrality of Belgium signed...9, 11 Aug. "
Election of elementary school-boards....................Nov. "
Excitement over Russian note announcing Russian war vessels in Black sea (RUSSIA)..................................Nov. "
Princess Louise marries marquess of Lorne...........21 Mch. 1871
Death of sir John F. Herschel, astronomer and philosopher (aged 79)..11 May, "
Death of George Grote, historian of Greece (aged 77)..18 June, "
Black sea conference met 17 Jan.; closed (neutralization of Black sea abrogated, etc.)...........................13 Mch. "
Disestablishment of the church of England bill rejected in the Commons (374–89), 1 May; Parliament prorogued....21 Aug. "
Prince of Wales ill with typhoid fever; began to recover, 14 Dec. "
Excitement over U. S. claims under treaty of Washington, Feb. "
Queen, entering Buckingham palace, threatened by Arthur O'Connor, aged about 18, with an unloaded pistol, and a paper to be signed; immediately apprehended............29 Feb. "
Arthur O'Connor pleads guilty (sentenced to imprisonment and flogging)...9 Apr. "
British and U. S. governments correspond on claims for indirect losses from confederate cruisers, which the former rejects, 3 Feb.–May, 1871
Supplemental treaty proposed; accepted by U. S. senate, 25 May; further discussion in Parliament; unsatisfactory correspondence; the U. S. Congress adjourns............10 June, "
Strikes among builders and other trades................June, "
Final meeting of arbitrators; damages awarded (ALABAMA), 14 Sept. "
Death of Edward Bulwer, lord Lytton, orator, poet, and novelist (aged 66)......................................18 Jan. 1873
Mr. Gladstone defeated on the Dublin university bill (287–284); resigns, 13 Mch.; resumes office...................17 Mch. "
Visit of the shah of Persia....................13 June–5 July, "
Duke of Edinburgh marries grand-duchess Marie of Russia, 23 Jan. 1874
Parliament dissolved.....................................26 Jan. "
General election; conservative majority about 50, Feb.; Gladstone ministry resigns, 17 Feb.; Disraeli ministry formed, 21 Feb. "
Close of Tichborne trial (TRIALS)......................28 Feb. "
Sir Garnet Wolseley returns from his successful expedition against the Ashantees.............................21 Mch. "
Queen receives a testimonial of gratitude from the French nation for British assistance during the war (FRANCE)...3 Dec. "
Moody and Sankey, U. S. revivalists, arrive in London, 9 Mch.; sail from Liverpool (REVIVALS).......................4 Aug. 1875
Khedive's shares in the Suez canal bought by the British government (SUEZ), 1 Nov.; announced.............25 Nov. "
Queen proclaimed "empress of India"..................1 May, 1876
Mr. Gladstone's "Horrors in Bulgaria" pub..............6 Sept. "
Meeting against war to defend Turkey, St. James's hall..8 Dec. "
Proclamation of neutrality in Russo-Turkish war......30 Apr. 1877
Debate on Mr. Gladstone's resolutions, expressing dissatisfaction and complaint at the conduct of the Ottoman porte with regard to the despatch written by the earl of Derby, 21 Sept. 1876, relating to the massacres in Bulgaria (for the resolution, 225; against, 354).............................7–14 May, "
Fleet sent to Besika bay..................................3 July, "
Statue of king Alfred by count Gleichen, at Wantage, unveiled by the prince of Wales, his descendant..............14 July, "
Early meeting of Parliament on account of Russo-Turkish war, 17 Jan. 1878
Vote of 6,000,000*l.* asked for before entering into conference respecting Eastern affairs, 24 Jan.; debate..........31 Jan. "
Liberal amendment withdrawn on report of Russian advance on Constantinople, 7 Feb.; vote passed (204–124)......8 Feb. "
Warlike policy of the ministry; resignation of lord Carnarvon, 24 Jan.; and earl of Derby.........................28 Mch. "
Earl of Salisbury's circular indicting the treaty of San Stefano, 2 Apr.; moderate reply of Gortschakoff printed......10 Apr. 1878
Indian troops ordered to Malta..................about 17 Apr. "
Censured by the opposition; debate in Commons: for government, 347; against, 226.........................20–23 May, "
Earl Russell d. (aged 85).............................28 May, "
Ministry announce a European congress on the Eastern question, to meet on 13 June; the earl of Beaconsfield and the marquess of Salisbury to attend for England (BERLIN), 3 June, "
Anglo-Turkish convention (TURKEY) signed............4 June, "
Conference meets at BERLIN 13 June; treaty signed...13 July, "
10,000*l.* a year voted the duke of Connaught on his marriage with princess Louise Margaret of Prussia...........25 July, "
Debate on the Berlin treaty in the Commons; speech of Mr. Gladstone, 30 July; majority for government (338–195), 29 July–3 Aug. "
Parliament prorogued...................................16 Aug. "
Meeting of Parliament on account of Afghan war........5 Dec. "
Majority for ministers on vote of censure, Lords (201–65), 10 Dec.; Commons (328–227).........................13–14 Dec. "
Princess Alice dies of diphtheria at Darmstadt, after attending her husband and children, 7.30 A.M..................14 Dec. "
Edward Byrne Madden (? lunatic) arrested for threatening the queen in letters to the Home office, 12 Dec. 1878; judged insane...13 Jan. 1879
1,500,000*l.* voted for Zulu war..........................27 Feb. "
Expedition sent (between 8000 and 9000 men, 1800 horses, etc.), Feb.–Mch. "
Marriage of duke and duchess of Connaught at Windsor, 13 Mch. "
Proposed censure of government respecting Zulu war, etc., negatived, Lords (156–61), 25 Mch.; Commons (306–246), 31 Mch.–1 Apr. "
Commons debate on the budget; for government, 303; against, 230...28–29 Apr. "
Parliament opened by the queen, 5 Feb.; dissolved....23 Feb. 1880
General election, great liberal majority, 30 Mch.–16 Apr.; resignation of ministry.................................22 Apr. "
Gladstone ministry formed..............................29 Apr. "
New Parliament meets 29 Apr.; Bradlaugh difficulty (PARLIAMENTS)..3 May et seq. "
Court and general mourning for death of gen. Garfield, president of U. S.......................................21–27 Sept. 1881
Great hurricane throughout England, causing destruction of life, property, and shipping......................13–15 Oct. "
Queen shot at, at Great Western railway station, Windsor, by Roderick Maclean, aged 27, 2 Mch.; he is committed for high treason...10 Mch. 1882
Queen dedicates Epping forest to the people for all time, 6 May, "
Detection of secret manufacture of explosives at Birmingham, 4 Apr.; arrest of Alfred Whitehead, Thos. Gallagher, physician, Wm. Norman, H. H. Wilson, H. D. E. and Henry Dalton, otherwise John O'Connor..........................5, 6 Apr. 1883

Other arrests in Liverpool, Glasgow and London about 6, 7 Apr 1883

Egypt and the Soudan censure of government for its "vacillating and inconsistent policy," voted by the lords (181-81) 12 Feb, rejected by the Commons (311-262) 12-20 Feb 1884

Prince Leopold, duke of Albany, dies, age nearly 31, 28 Mch, buried at Windsor 5 Apr "

Vote of censure of government for not supporting Gordon negatived in the Commons (303-275) 12-14 May, "

Vote of censure on the government respecting Egypt passed by the Lords (189-58), negatived by the Commons (302-288), 27, 28 Feb 1885

Day of mourning for gen Gordon and the killed in the Soudan, 13 Mch "

Reserves to be called out in prospect of war with Russia 27 Mch "

Mr Gladstone declines an earldom on retiring 15 June, "

Princess Beatrice marries prince Henry of Battenberg 3 July, "

Sir Moses Montefiore dies at London age 101 28 July, "

Funeral services in Westminster abbey for gen U S. Grant, attended by representatives of the royal family 4 Aug "

Great Eastern steamship sold at auction at Lloyds' for 26,000*l* to a private merchant 29 Oct "

Mersey tunnel formally opened, connecting Birkenhead and Liverpool 20 Jan 1886

Edinburgh Courant the oldest newspaper in Scotland to which Scott, Wilson, Lockhart, Aytoun De Quincey, and Hogg had been contributors, appears for the last time 6 Feb "

Bell's Life (London), the oldest sporting paper in the world, after having existed 64 years, ceased to appear 28 May, "

In digging for the foundation of a building in upper Kirkgate, Aberdeen, a bronze pot found containing 15,000 pieces of silver coin of the reign of Edward I 31 May, "

First stone of the Tower bridge laid, designed to cost 750,000*l*. Crossing the Thames near Wapping, without impeding the navigation of the river by the largest ships 21 June, "

Oliver Wendell Holmes receives the degree of honorary D C L from Oxford 30 June, "

In an excavation at Cannon Street road and Cable street, London, a skeleton found impaled on a stake It was believed to be that of Williams, who hanged himself in Coldbath Fields prison in 1811, when accused of 7 murders, referred to in De Quincey's essay on "Murder as a Fine Art" (RATCLIFFE HIGHWAY) 28 July, "

Henry M Stanley left England for Alexandria and Zanzibar, to head expedition to relieve Emin Pacha, governor of the equatorial province of Egypt 21 Jan 1887

Times asserted that Charles S. Parnell, M P, had long resided in London suburbs, under the name Preston 26 Nov "

Major Barttelot, who left Stanley falls, on the Congo, to relieve Stanley, shot by one of his carriers 19 July, 1888

Great Eastern, after a career of 30 years beached at New Ferry, on the Mersey, to be broken up (GREAT EASTERN) 25 Aug "

First sitting of Parnell commission in the probate court, Palace of Justice The attorney general opened for the *Times*, 22 Oct "

British protectorate proclaimed over British north Borneo, Brunei, and Sarawak, about 70,000 sq miles 24 Oct "

Before the Parnell commission, Richard Pigott's confession of forgery is read, the attorney general, for the *Times*, withdraws the case founded on the forged letters 27 Feb 1889

Pigott commits suicide in Madrid 1 Mch "

John Bright d 27 Mch "

House of Lords rejects the Deceased Wife's Sister bill—the prince of Wales voting with the minority 9 May, "

Snowdon, the highest of the Welsh mountains containing about 1500 acres, with fishing, mineral, and other rights, sold at public auction for 5750*l*., to sir E W Watkin, M P, 10 July, "

Marriage of the earl of Fife with the princess Louise, daughter of the prince of Wales . 27 July, "

First Mahometan mosque in England, completed at Woking, 13 Aug "

Parnell commission meets for the 128th and last time 22 Nov "

Martin Farquhar Tupper, the poet, d (aged 80) 29 Nov "

Robert Browning, the poet, dies in Venice (aged 77) 12 Dec "

Long pending trial of Parnell *v* Walter, editor of the *Times*, settled, 5000*l*. paid by the *Times* (PARNELL) 3 Feb 1890

Firth bridge formally opened. BRIDGES (John Fowler, the engineer, created baronet) 4 Mch "

Henry M Stanley reaches England (AFRICA) 26 Apr "

Marries Miss Dorothy Tennant in Westminster abbey, 12 July, "

England transfers HELIGOLAND to Germany . 9 Aug "

Cardinal John Henry Newman d. (aged 90) 11 Aug "

O'Shea divorce case begins in London, no defence 15 Nov "

Mr Gladstone denies an assertion in Parnell's manifesto (PARNELL) 29 Nov "

Justin McCarthy and 44 others withdraw from the Nationalist parliamentary meeting, and form a separate body 6 Dec "

Archbishop's and bishop's letter denouncing Parnell read in all the Catholic churches of Ireland 7 Dec "

Parnell seizes the office of *United Ireland* in Dublin 10 Dec "

Parnell, while stumping Ireland, temporarily blinded by lime thrown at Castle Comer 16 Dec "

Kilkenny election held, sir John Pope Hennessy, the McCarthyite candidate, elected 22 Dec. "

Alexander Wm Kinglake (historian) d 2 Jan 1891

Charles Bradlaugh d 30 Jan "

Sir William Gordon Cumming the plaintiff in the baccarat trial, married to Miss Florence Garner of New York, 10 June, "

Parnell and Mrs O'Shea secretly married 25 June, "

Charles Stewart Parnell dies at Brighton, Engl. 6 Oct. "

Widow of sir John A Macdonald, premier of Canada, created a peeress . .. . 22 Oct. "

Cardinal Manning d............ ... . .14 Jan 1892

ENG

Eldest son of the prince of Wales, Albert Victor, duke of Clarence and Avondale. d 14 Jan 1892

Cardinal Howard dies at Brighton 16 Sept "

Alfred (lord) Tennyson d (aged 82) 6 Oct "

Marriage of princess Marie of Edinburgh and prince Ferdinand of Roumania, at Sigmaringen 10 Jan 1893

Mr Gladstone takes the oath as premier 31 Jan "

Algernon Sartoris, Nellie Grant's husband, d in Italy 7 Feb "

Mr Gladstone introduces Home Rule bill in Commons 13 Feb "

Home Rule bill passes first reading 17 Feb "

Passes second reading by 347 to 304 21 Apr "

British battle ship *Victoria* collides with the *Camperdown* off Tripoli, Syria, while manœuvring, loss, including vice-admiral sir George Tryon, 22 officers and 336 crew 23 June, "

Duke of York, son of the prince of Wales, and princess May of Teck, married, St James palace, London 6 July, "

Court martial on surviving officers of the *Victoria* opened at Valetta, upon the *Hibernia* 17 July, "

[Found, 27 July, vice admiral Tryon responsible for the calamity, exonerating surviving officers]

Duke of Saxe Coburg and Gotha dies, duke of Edinburgh succeeds 23 Aug "

Home Rule bill passes the Commons by 301 to 267, first read in the House of Lords 1 Sept. "

House of Lords rejects the bill by 419 to 41 8 Sept. "

Manchester ship canal finished 6 Nov "

Memorial to James Russell Lowell, 2 stained glass windows in Westminster abbey unveiled with ceremonies 28 Nov "

Prof John Tyndall, scientist, d (aged 73) 4 Dec. "

The overhead electrical railway, at the docks of Liverpool, about 7 miles long, completed "

Manchester ship canal, public opening 1 Jan 1894

Disagreement of the Commons and the Lords on the employers' liability and local government bills Feb "

Anarchist society in London raided 16 Feb "

Visit of the empress Frederick to Osborne 2 Feb -19 Mch "

Resignation of Mr Gladstone as premier, succeeded by the earl of Rosebery 3 Mch "

Parliament prorogued, 5 Mch, reopened 12 Mch "

The unification of London report adopted by the royal commission 16 Mch "

The Commons adopts resolution for payment of members (176-158) 22 Mch "

William C Gully succeeds A W Peel as speaker 10 Apr "

The queen inaugurates the Manchester ship canal 21 May, "

Cabmen's strike in London 16 May-11 June, "

Birth of prince Edward Albert Christian, etc, of York 23 June, "

Tower bridge, London, opened . 30 June, "

Equalization of rates (London) bill passed 25 Aug "

Parliament prorogued 25 Aug "

James Anthony Froude, historian, b 23 Apr 1818, d 20 Oct. "

Dispute between British Guiana and Venezuela as to the boundary line 1895

Death of lord Randolph Churchill (b 13 Feb 1849) 24 Jan "

Meeting of Parliament 5 Feb "

Apostolic letter of pope Leo XIII to the English people, 14 Apr "

Resignation of the Rosebery ministry 22 June, "

New cabinet formed by the marquis of Salisbury, 4th administration 25 June, *et seq* "

Visit of the German emperor to the queen, the fleet at Cowes, 5 Aug "

Parliament dissolved, 8 July, meets 12 Aug -5 Sept "

Reassuring speech of the marquis of Salisbury at the lord mayor's banquet in reference to Turkey, etc., unity of the great powers, the sultan warned 9 Nov "

[For dispute with the U S. see VENEZUELA, 1895]

England sends an ultimatum to Venezuela demanding reparation for insults to British officers at Uruan ... Dec "

[1500*l* indemnity was paid to England Jan 1897]

Falls on the stock exchange, London 17, 18 Dec "

General displeasure at the German emperor's message to pres Krüger respecting the defeat of dr Jameson . 4 Jan 1896

Naval force ordered to Delagoa bay 7 Jan "

Sir Frederick (lord) Leighton, painter sculptor, and scholar (b 3 Dec 1830, d 25 Jan 1896), public funeral at St Paul's, 3 Feb "

Death of prince Henry of Battenberg, 20 Jan, buried at Whippingham . 5 Feb "

Dr Jameson and his troopers (350 officers and men) arrive at Plymouth, 23 Feb, at London 25 Feb "

Blue book containing diplomatic correspondence with Venezuela since 1822 presented to the arbitration commission sitting at Washington 10 Mch "

Marriage of princess Maud of Wales and prince Charles of Denmark, at Buckingham palace . 22 July, "

Naval manœuvres, 4 fleets engaged 24-30 July, "

[These manœuvres, on a grand scale, occur annually in the summer]

Visit of Li Hung Chang . 1 Aug *et seq* "

Lord Rosebery proposes non party public meetings to protest against the massacre of Armenians 14 Sept. "

Meetings held at London, Liverpool, Birmingham, and Manchester, urging the government to take stronger measures, 15 Sept. *et seq* "

British association meets at Liverpool 16-23 Sept. "

Lord Rosebery resigns the leadership of the Liberal party through differences with Mr Gladstone and others on the Eastern question .. .. 6 Oct. "

Venezuela treaty with England signed in Washington by sir Julian Pauncefote and señor Andrade . ... 2 Feb 1897

Lady Wallace bequeaths her husband's collection of pictures, etc., to the nation conditionally 25 Feb 1897
Completion of the 60th year of the queen's reign great rejoicings 20 June, *et seq* "
Grand naval review at Spithead 26 June, "
Close of the 7 months engineering dispute 28 Jan 1898
A lease of Wei-hai-wei granted by China to Great Britain 2 Apr "
Death of Mr Gladstone 19 May, "
Birmingham university opened July, "
Death of the princess Mary of Cambridge, duchess of Teck, 27 Oct "
Split in the Liberal party Dec "
Mr Joseph Choate appointed U S ambassador 11 Jan 1899
Tercentenary of the birth of Oliver Cromwell celebrated 25 Apr "
The queen's message to Parliament, vote of 30 000*l* to lord Kitchener for services in the Soudan, carried, with vote of thanks to the officers and men 5-8 June, "
The duke of York opens the new general post office in Liverpool 19 July, "
Prince Alfred (duke of Edinburgh), duke of Saxe Coburg and Gotha, d near Coburg (aged 55) 30 July, "
Transvaal crisis Parliament affirms the duty of the imperial power to protect the Uitlanders against oppression, and demands the minimum of reforms laid down by sir A Milner 28 July, Parliament prorogued, 9 Aug, mobilization of troops, reserves called out, well responded to, 7 Oct *et seq*, steady growth of national prosperity during 1898, 1899, meetings throughout the country and empire supporting the government's policy in S Africa, 13 Oct, gen sir Redvers Buller leaves to take command in S Africa, 14 Oct, Parliament summoned 17 Oct "
[For events of the war see SOUTH AFRICAN WAR]
German emperor visits England 25 Nov "
City subway between the Mansion House, Bank of England and Royal Exchange opened 8 Jan 1900
Death of the duke of Teck 21 Jan "
Attempt on life of the prince of Wales at Brussels 28 Apr "
Visit of the khedive 21 June, "
Death of lord Russell of Killowen, lord chief justice (aged 68), 13 Aug "
Letters from Mr Labouchere, Mr Ellis, dr Clark, and others to Boer officials found in S Africa, published as a Parliamentary paper and greatly discussed 23 Aug *et seq* "
Parliament prorogued, 8 Aug, dissolved, 25 Sept, 4th Salisbury administration, cabinet reconstructed 12 Nov "
Lord Wolseley retires from command in chief 12 Nov "
Sir Arthur Sullivan, popular composer, d (aged 58) 22 Nov "
New Parliament meets 3 Dec "
Lord Roberts received by the queen at Osborne and created an earl and K G 2 Jan 1901
Death of the queen at Osborne after a few days' illness, the German emperor, her children, and grandchildren being with her 6 30 P M 22 Jan "
King Edward VII, accession 23 Jan "
Parliament meets 25 Jan "
Punitive expedition against the Somalis Feb "
[The British defeat the "Mad Mullah" 30 May, again 17 July, 3 Sept and 6 Oct, 1901, and 15 Apr 1903, in a second expedition, fighting continued during 1903, 1904, and until Mch 1905, when England was finally victorious, at England's request, Italy assumed the protectorate of Somaliland in Mch 1905]
Funeral of queen Victoria 4 Feb "
The German emperor (made a field marshal in the army and the crown prince a K G) leaves 5 Feb "
The king and queen open Parliament in state 14 Feb "
Roman Catholic peers protest formally against the terms of the accession oath 14 Feb "
The duke and duchess of Cornwall start on a colonial tour, 16 Mch "
Reorganization of the Yeomanry 18 Apr "
Transvaal loan of 35,000 000*l* agreed upon 6 May, "
New botanical laboratories in Liverpool opened by sir W T Dyer 10 May, "
Sir Alfred Milner, high commissioner of S Africa, made a peer 24 May, "
Great Indian famine through drought 1899-1901
[During the entire period India and England co operated in relieving distress, but several millions of the natives died of starvation]
Pro Boer meeting in the Queen's hall, London (Mr Labouchere, M P, chairman), addressed by the Afrikander bond delegates and others 19 June, "
Blue book issued on S African war 10 July, "
Mass meeting at the Guild hall in favor of the government's S African policy 10 July, "
Vote of 100,000*l* to lord Roberts for his eminent services in S Africa, passed 31 July, "
Great unionist demonstration at Blenheim palace, speakers, Mr Chamberlain, Mr Balfour, and others 10 Aug "
Parliament prorogued 18 Aug "
King Alfred millenary, celebration 18 Sept "
Torpedo boat *Cobra* sank in a gale, 68 lives lost 16 Oct "
The duke of Devonshire opens a new technical school in Liverpool 26 Oct "
Lord Rosebery, at Chesterfield, urges the Liberals to throw off their own Toryism, and offers his services, appealing solely to the tribunal of public opinion 16 Dec. "
The marquis Ito, eminent Japanese statesman, arrives 24 Dec. "
Lord Derby's motion for a university in the city of Liverpool adopted 27 Jan 1902

ENG

Dutch government's proposals for negotiations with the Boers in S Africa presented, 25 Jan, firmly declined by the British government 29 Jan 1902
Death of lord Dufferin 12 Feb "
Lord Rosebery exhorts the Liberals to wipe the slate clean and make a new start 14 Feb "
Great Liverpool bank frauds 17-22 Feb "
Princess Louise opens the navy league exhibition in Liverpool, 12 Mch "
New loan on consols 320,000,000*l* 16-18 Apr "
Lord Pauncefote d (aged 74) 24 May, "
Peace signed at Pretoria 31 May, "
Peace rejoicings 2 June, "
Lord Acton, prof of modern history, Cambridge, eminent scholar, d (aged 68) 19 June, "
The king made an admiral of the German navy 26 June, "
Grand colonial and Indian reviews (the duke of Connaught in command) held by the prince of Wales. 1, 2 July, "
The king's dinner to 500,000 poor of London 5 July, "
The queen's teas to 10,000 maid servants of London 7 July, "
Colonial reception held by the prince and princess of Wales, 10 July, "
Lord Salisbury, over 13½ years prime minister and lord privy seal 4 times foreign secretary resigns 11 July, "
Lord Kitchener welcomed from S Africa 12 July, "
The king's dinner to the blind of London 12 July, "
Mr Arthur J Balfour made prime minister and lord privy seal 12-14 July, "
Debate in the Commons on the case of sir Redvers Buller, his message to sir George White at Ladysmith, Spion Kop, etc 17 July "
Ministerial changes 8 Aug "
Parliament adjourns 8 Aug "
Coronation of king Edward VII and queen Alexandra at the abbey 9 Aug "
The king receives the Indian princes and colonial premiers, 12 Aug, holds investiture parades of the colonial and Indian troops, London 12, 13 Aug "
Coronation review at Spithead, 20 battle ships, 24 cruisers, 15 torpedo boats, 32 torpedo-boat destroyers, etc, 103 vessels exclusive of special service vessels, etc 16 Aug "
Visit of the shah of Persia 17-25 Aug "
The Boer generals—Botha De Wet, and Delarey—received by lords Kitchener and Roberts and Mr Chamberlain at Southampton, 16 Aug, they leave for the continent. 18 Aug "
The king inspects the fleet 18 Aug "
Conference between Mr Chamberlain and the Boer generals, the Vereeniging terms signed (31 May) unaltered 5 Sept "
Nonconformist agitation against the education bill Aug -Oct "
Royal commission of inquiry into the conduct of the S African war Oct. "
Carnegie library in Liverpool opened 15 Oct. "
Parliament meets 16 Oct. "
Royal progress through London 25-27 Oct "
Grant of 8,000,000*l* voted for the Transvaal and Orange River Colony 5 Nov "
Visit of the emperor of Germany 8-20 Nov "
Death of prince Edward of Saxe Weimar, G C B (aged 79), served in the Crimea, 1854-55, a general, 1879, commander of forces in Ireland, 1885-90, field marshal, 1897 16 Nov "
Mr Chamberlain leaves on his mission to Africa 25 Nov "
Visit of the king of Portugal 17 Nov -8 Dec "
Education bill powers and duties of school boards and control of all secular instruction transferred to local authorities, religious training to be according to parents' faith, 3 Dec 1902 received royal assent 18 Dec "
[This bill is met with "passive resistance" by the nonconformists, agitation continues 1905.]
Death of dr Temple archbishop of Canterbury (aged 81), 23 Dec "
The queen's Christmas dinner to the widows and orphans of soldiers killed in S Africa 27 Dec "
Mr W W Astor gives $250,000 to the hospital for sick children Jan. 1903
Coronation durbar at Delhi 1-9 Jan "
Sale of relics of Newgate prison 4 Feb "
Grenadier guards scandal 10 Feb "
Dr Davidson, archbishop of Canterbury 12 Feb "
Demonstrations of the unemployed of London in Trafalgar square 14 Feb "
The king opens Parliament, address agreed to 17 Feb. "
Mr Chamberlain returns from Africa 14 Mch "
Dr Farrar, dean of Canterbury, d. (aged 71) 22 Mch "
Royal Geographical Society celebrates the tercentenary of queen Elizabeth's death 23 Mch "
Maj gen sir Hector Macdonald, "Fighting Mac," found dead in Paris 25 Mch "
Royal commission of inquiry in the matter of food imports, etc, during the S African war, appointed Apr "
Mr Chas Booth's "Life and Labor of the People in London" 3d series. "Religious Influences" published mid Apr "
London Education bill, first reading (House of Commons), 7 Apr "
Demonstrations against the educational bill May, "
Reorganization of the fleets and naval reserves May, "
The king visits Portugal 7 Apr -5 May, "
Transvaal loan, 35,000,000*l*., 3 per cent, issued, well taken up 7 May, "
Mr Chamberlain's speech on preferential tariffs, at Birmingham 15 May, "
South London electric tramway opened 15 May, "

Mr Chamberlain's inter imperial tariff scheme much discussed in England and on the continent, generally approved in the colonies May–June, *et seq* 1903
Stationers' company celebrate the 500th anniversary of their foundation 10 June, "
Lord Rosebery speaks at liberal league dinner against the tariff scheme 12 June, "
The king receives Mr Austen Chamberlain M P, and nearly 300 members of the international telegraph convention, at Windsor 15 June, "
Bicentenary of John Wesley's birth celebrated 17 June, "
Cardinal Vaughan, archbishop of Westminster, d (aged 71) 19 June, "
Khedive visits England, arrives 24 June, "
Meeting of unionist members of Parliament against Mr Chamberlain's proposals for a protective tax on food 1 July, "
Centenary of the Sunday school union, great international bazaar, Portman rooms opened by lady Aberdeen, 2 July, speech by Mr Choate, U S ambassador, at public meeting, 6 July, festival at the Crystal palace 8 July, "
M Loubet, president of the French republic, visits the king, arrives at Dover, 6 July, returns 9 July, "
Death of Mr Whistler, distinguished artist 17 July, "
Visit of U S squadron to Portsmouth 6-17 July, "
Tariff reform league inaugurated 21 July, "
Irish land bill passed the third reading by 317 votes to 20, 21 July, "
Visit of the king and queen to Ireland 20-25 July, "
Royal naval college opened at Osborne by the king 4 Aug "
Death of Phil May 5 Aug "
Irish land bill agreed to 13 Aug "
London education bill, royal assent 14 Aug "
Death of lord Salisbury (aged 73) 22 Aug "
Royal commission on S African war, report 25 Aug "
Resignation of Mr Chamberlain, Mr Ritchie, and lord George Hamilton, announced 18 Sept "
Lord Milner arrives in England 28 Sept. "
Death of sir Michael Herbert, British ambassador to the U S, 30 Sept "
Old Roman wall discovered on the site of Newgate prison Oct. "
Meeting of the National Conservative association at Sheffield, 1 Oct "
Duke of Devonshire's resignation, and new cabinet appointments announced 6 Oct "
Mr Chamberlain opens his "fiscal campaign" by a speech on "Colonial Preference," at St Andrew's hall, Glasgow, 6 Oct "
Mr John Morley's biography of Mr Gladstone published, 8 Oct. "
Mr Chamberlain speaks at the Hippodrome, in Liverpool on preferential tariffs 27 Oct. "
Progressive and Labor parties win at the London municipal elections 2 Nov "
King of Italy visits England 19 Nov "
Anglo Italian permanent arbitration treaty approved 19 Nov "
Joseph Chamberlain's tariff commission met in London 15 Jan 1904
Mrs Florence Maybrick after 15 years' imprisonment, released on parole 25 Jan "
Whitaker Wright, sentenced to 7 years' penal servitude commits suicide 26 Jan "
Thibet demands withdrawal of the English expedition 29 Jan "
Office of commander in chief abolished 31 Jan "
Defeat of the government in the Commons by a majority of 11 on an Irish bill 15 Mch "
The Commons pass bill allowing women to vote for members of Parliament 16 Mch "
Death of the duke of Cambridge 17 Mch "
Col Younghusband defeats the Thibetans 21 Mch "
Anglo French colonial treaty, covering all disputed questions, signed in London 8 Apr "
House of Commons passes bill legalizing picketing, and amended law of conspiracy as relating to trades unions 22 Apr "
British foreign office agrees to set aside 5000 sq miles near the Victoria Nyanza, in E Africa, for Zionists 23 Apr "
The Karo pass, in Thibet, captured by col Younghusband, 6 May, "
Death of Henry M Stanley (aged 64) 10 May, "
England protests against the U S coastwise law in the Philippines 13 June, "
Anglo German arbitration treaty signed 12 July, "
House of Lords decide the Free Church of Scotland case, property to the value of $50,000,000 involved 1 Aug "
The British army enter Lhassa unopposed 7 Aug "
Announced in Parliament that Germany, Italy, Austria, and Russia recognize English paramountcy in Egypt 8 Aug "
Russia protests against the Anglo Thibetan treaty 20 Sept. "
Irish Reform association, lord Dunraven, chairman provides for a financial council of 24, the lord lieutenant of Ireland to be president, the chief secretary for Ireland vice president, 25 Sept "
The Russian Baltic fleet attacks a British fishing fleet in the North Sea, 2 men killed, many wounded 22 Oct "
Russia and England agree to arbitrate the North Sea difficulty, 28 Oct "
Anglo French colonial treaty ratified by France 12 Nov "
North Sea commission opens in Paris 19 Jan 1905
A parcels post treaty is signed between U S and England, 17 Feb. "
The North Sea commission finds there were no hostile vessels, but that the Russian admiral's fear of attack justified his course 25 Feb "
Manuel Garcia celebrates his 100th birthday 17 Mch 1905
[He sang in the Italian opera company of his father in New York in 1825, his sister was the famous Malibran]
England arranges with Italy to have latter assume the protectorate of Somaliland 20 Mch "
Venezuela agrees to pay Germany and England $26,000,000 of their claims 21 Mch "
Increase in naval expenditure defended by the government in Parliament 21 Mch "
Russia invites London newspapers to verify the existence of a gold reserve of $325,000 000, accepted by the *Daily Mail*, 26 Mch "
Queen of England visits Gibraltar 28 Mch "
The secretary of war in Parliament refuses to reduce military forces as they are needed to protect the frontiers 28 Mch "
England proposes to place Macedonian finances under international control 28 Mch "
Vote of censure of premier Balfour's fiscal policy unanimously carried, Ministerialists abstain from voting 28 Mch "
British foreign secretary accuses Germany of violating the agreement to protect British traders in the Marshall and Caroline islands 4 Apr "
Cunard line withdraws from the Atlantic shipping trust, 13 Apr "
The new Transvaal constitution is made public 21 Apr "
Mr Balfour designates 30 May for debate on proposed vote of censure 25 May "
J Pierpont Morgan buys a 16th century drinking cup at auction for $32 000 26 May, "
Ambassador Joseph Choate returns to the U S, is succeeded by Whitelaw Reid June, "

KINGS AND QUEENS OF ENGLAND

BEFORE THE CONQUEST

827 Egbert, styled "king of England" in 828
837 Ethelwolf, his son
857 Ethelbald his son
860 Ethelbert, brother
866 Ethelred, brother
871 Alfred the Great brother, d 21 or 28 Oct. 901
901 Edward the Elder, son, d 925
925 Athelstan eldest son, d 17 Oct 940
940 Edmund I, 5th son of Edward the Elder, died from a wound received in an affray 26 May, 946
946 Edred, brother, d 955
955 Edwy, eldest son of Edmund, died of grief in 958
958 Edgar the Peaceable, brother, d 1 July, 975
975 Edward the Martyr, his son, stabbed at Corfe castle, at the instance of his stepmother, Elfrida, 18 Mch 979
979 Ethelred II half brother, retired
1013 Sweyn, proclaimed king, d 3 Feb 1014
1014 Canute the Great his son
" Ethelred restored in Canute's absence, d 24 Apr 1016
1016 Edmund Ironside his son divided the kingdom with Canute, murdered at Oxford, 30 Nov 1016, reigned 7 months
1017 Canute sole king married Emma, widow of Ethelred, d 12 Nov 1035, age 40
1035 Harold I, son, d 17 Mch 1040
1040 Hardicanute, son of Canute and Emma, died of repletion at a marriage feast 8 June, 1042
1042 Edward the Confessor, son of Ethelred and Emma, d. 5 Jan 1066, age 62.
1066. Harold II, son of earl Godwin, reigned 9 months, killed near Hastings. 14 Oct. 1066

THE NORMANS

The dates are those of sir H Nicolas The early Norman and Plantagenet kings reckoned reigns from their coronation, the later Plantagenets from the day after death of the predecessor From Edward VI the reign has dated from the death of the preceding sovereign

1066 William the Conqueror, crowned 25 Dec., d. at Rouen, 9 Sept. 1087, age 60
Queen Matilda, daughter of Baldwin, earl of Flanders, married in 1054, d 1083
1087 William II Rufus, reign began 26 Sept, killed by an arrow, 2 Aug 1100, age 40
1100 Henry I Beauclerc, his brother, reign began 5 Aug, died of a surfeit, 1 Dec 1135, age 67
Queens Matilda, daughter of Malcolm III king of Scotland, married 11 Nov 1100, d 1 May, 1119 2 Adelais, daughter of Godfrey, earl of Louvaine, married 29 Jan 1129, d 1151
1135 Stephen, earl of Blois, nephew of Henry, reign 26 Dec, d 25 Oct 1154, age 50
Queen Matilda, daughter of Eustace, count of Boulogne, married 1128, d 3 May, 1151
[Maud, daughter of Henry I and rightful heir to the throne, b 1101, betrothed, 1109, at 8 years of age, to Henry V, emperor of Germany, who d 1125. She married, secondly, Geoffrey Plantagenet, earl of Anjou, 1130. Was set aside from the English succession by Stephen, 1135, landed in England and claimed the crown 1139 Crowned, but soon after defeated at Winchester, 1141, concluded a peace with Stephen, making her son Henry successor, 1153, d 1165]

THE PLANTAGENETS.

1154. Henry II Plantagenet, grandson of Henry I and son of Maud, reign began 19 Dec, d 6 July, 1189, age 56
Queen Eleanor, the repudiated queen of Louis VII, king of France, and heiress of Guienne and Poitou, married to Henry, 1151, d 26 June, 1202 ROSAMOND

1189. Richard I. Cœur de Lion, son; reign began 3 Sept.; died of a wound, 6 Apr. 1199; age 42. ARCHERY.
Queen: Berengaria, daughter of the king of Navarre; married 12 May, 1191; survived the king.

1199. John, the brother of Richard; reign began 27 May; d. 19 Oct. 1216; age 49.
Queens: Avisa, daughter of the earl of Gloucester; married 1189; divorced. 2. Isabella, daughter of the count of Angoulême, virgin wife of count de la Marche; married to John 1200. Survived the king, and remarried count de la Marche.

1216. Henry III., son of John; reign began 28 Oct.; d. 16 Nov. 1272; age 65.
Queen: Eleanor, daughter of the count de Provence; married 14 Jan. 1236; survived the king; and d. 1291, in a monastery.

1272. Edward I., son of Henry, surnamed *Longshanks;* reign began 20 Nov.; d. 7 July, 1307; age 68.
Queens: Eleanor of Castile; married 1253; died of a fever, on her journey to Scotland, at Hornby, in Lincolnshire, 1290 (ELEANOR'S CROSSES). 2. Margaret, sister of the king of France; married 12 Sept. 1299; survived the king; d. 1317.

1307. Edward II., son of Edward I.; reign began 8 July; dethroned 20 Jan. 1327; murdered at BERKELEY CASTLE, 21 Sept. following; age 43.
Queen: Isabella, daughter of the king of France; married 1308. After the execution of her favorite Mortimer, she was confined at Castle Rising, near Lynn, and d. 1357.

1327. Edward III., son; reign began 25 Jan.; d. 21 June, 1377; age 65.
Queen: Philippa, daughter of the count of Hainault; married 1326; d. 15 Aug. 1369.

1377. Richard II., son of Edward the Black Prince, and grandson of Edward III.; reign began 22 June; dethroned 29 Sept. 1399; said to have been murdered at Pomfret castle, 10 Feb. 1400; age 34.
Queens: Anne of Bohemia, sister of the emperor Wenceslaus of Germany; married Jan. 1382; d. 7 June, 1394. 2. Isabella, daughter of Charles V. of France; married when only 7 years old, 1 Nov. 1396. On the deposition of her husband she returned to her father.

HOUSE OF LANCASTER.

1399. Henry IV., cousin of Richard II.; reign began 30 Sept.; d. 20 Mch. 1413; age 47.
Wives: Mary, daughter of the earl of Hereford; d. 1394. 2. Queen Joan of Navarre, widow of the duke of Bretagne; married 1403; survived the king; d. 1437.

1413. Henry V., son; reign began 21 Mch.; d. 31 Aug. 1422; age 34.
Queen: Catherine, daughter of the king of France; married 30 May, 1420. She outlived Henry, and was married to Owen Tudor, grandfather of Henry VII., in 1423; d. 1437.

1422. Henry VI., son; reign began 1 Sept.; deposed 4 Mch. 1461; said to have been murdered by Richard, duke of Gloucester, in the Tower, 20 June, 1471; age 49.
Queen: Margaret, daughter of the duke of Anjou; married 22 Apr. 1445; survived the king; d. 25 Aug. 1481.

HOUSE OF YORK.

1461. Edward IV.; d. 9 Apr. 1483; age 41.
Queen: Lady Elizabeth Grey, daughter of sir Richard Woodville, and widow of sir John Grey, of Groby; married 1463 or 1464. Suspected of favoring the insurrection of Lambert Simnel; and closed her life in confinement, 8 June, 1492.

1483. Edward V., son; deposed 25 June, 1483; said to have been murdered in the Tower; reigned 2 months 13 days; age 13.

" Richard III., brother of Edward IV.; began to reign 26 June, slain at Bosworth, 22 Aug. 1485; age 35.
Queen: Anne, daughter of earl of Warwick, widow of Edward, prince of Wales, murdered 1471. Said to have been poisoned by Richard (died suddenly, 16 Mch. 1485), to make way for him to marry princess Elizabeth of York.

HOUSE OF TUDOR.

1485. Henry VII. son of Edmund Tudor, earl of Richmond (son of Owen Tudor and queen Catherine, widow of Henry V.), and Margaret, daughter of John Beaufort, duke of Somerset, legitimated descendant of John of Gaunt, duke of Lancaster; began to reign 22 Aug.; d. 21 Apr. 1509; age 53.
Queen: Elizabeth of York, princess of England, daughter of Edward IV.; married 18 Jan. 1486; d. 11 Feb. 1503.

1509. Henry VIII., son; from 22 Apr.; d. 28 Jan. 1547; age 56.
Queens: Catherine of Aragon, widow of Henry's elder brother, Arthur, prince of Wales; married 11 June, 1509; mother of queen Mary; repudiated, and afterwards formally divorced, 23 May, 1533; d. 7 Jan. 1536.
2. Anne Boleyn, daughter of sir Thomas Boleyn, and maid of honor to Catherine; privately married, before Catherine was divorced, 14 Nov. 1532; mother of queen Elizabeth; beheaded at the Tower, 19 May, 1536.
3. Jane Seymour, daughter of sir John Seymour, and maid of honor to Anne Boleyn; married 20 May, 1536; died in childbirth, of Edward VI. 24 Oct. 1537.
4. Anne of Cleves, sister of William, duke of Cleves; married 6 Jan. 1540; divorced 10 July, 1540; d. 1557.
5. Catherine Howard, niece of the duke of Norfolk; married 28 July, 1540; beheaded 12 Feb. 1542.
6. Catherine Parr, daughter of sir Thomas Parr, and widow of Nevill, lord Latimer; married 12 July, 1543; survived the king, and married sir Thomas Seymour, created lord Sudley; d. 5 Sept. 1548.

1547. Edward VI., son (by Jane Seymour); d. 6 July, 1553; age 16.

1553. Jane, daughter of the duke of Suffolk, and wife of lord Guildford Dudley; proclaimed queen on the death of Edward; 10 days afterwards returned to private life; was tried 13 Nov. 1553; beheaded 12 Feb. 1554, 17 years of age.

" Mary, daughter of Henry (by Catherine of Aragon); married Philip of Spain, 25 July, 1554; d. 17 Nov. 1558; age 43.

1558. Elizabeth, daughter of Henry (by Anne Boleyn), d. 24 Mch. 1603; age 70.

HOUSE OF STUART.

1603. James I. of England and VI. of Scotland, son of Mary queen of Scots; d. 27 Mch. 1625; age 59.
Queen: Anne, princess of Denmark, daughter of Frederick II.; married 20 Aug. 1590; d. Mch. 1619.

1625. Charles I., son; beheaded at Whitehall, 30 Jan. 1649; age 48.
Queen: Henrietta Maria, daughter of Henry IV., king of France; married 13 June, 1625; survived the king; died in France, 10 Aug. 1669.

1649. *Commonwealth.* Oliver Cromwell made protector, 16 Dec. 1653; d. 3 Sept. 1658; age 59.

1658. Richard Cromwell, his son, made protector, 4 Sept.; resigned 22 Apr. 1659.

1660. Charles II., son of Charles I.; d. 6 Feb. 1685; age 55.
Queen: Catherine of Braganza, infanta of Portugal, daughter of John IV. and sister of Alfonso VI.; married 21 May, 1662; survived the king; returned to Portugal; d. 21 Dec. 1705.

1685. James II., brother of Charles II., abdicated by flight, 11 Dec. 1688; died in exile, 6 Aug. 1701; age 68.
[*1st wife*, Ann Hyde, daughter of Edward Hyde, earl of Clarendon; married Sept. 1660; d. 1671; mother of queens Mary II. and Anne.]
Queen: Mary Beatrice, princess of Modena, daughter of Alfonso d'Este, duke; married 21 Nov. 1673; in 1688 retired with James to France; died at St. Germain, 1718.

1689. William III., prince of Orange, king, and Mary, queen, daughter of James; married 4 Nov. 1677; began their reign 13 Feb. 1689; Mary d. 28 Dec. 1694; age 33.

1694. William III.; died of a fall from his horse, 8 Mch. 1702; age 51.

1702. Anne, daughter of James II.; married George, prince of Denmark, 28 July, 1683; succeeded, 8 Mch. 1702; her 13 children all died young; lost her husband 28 Oct. 1708; d. 1 Aug. 1714; age 49.

HOUSE OF HANOVER; family name GUELPH or GUELP. (BRUNSWICK, ESTE.)

1714. George I., elector of Hanover and duke of Brunswick-Luneburg; son of Sophia, daughter of Elizabeth, daughter of James I.; d. 11 June, 1727; age 67.
Queen: Sophia Dorothea, daughter of the duke of Zell; died in prison, 2 Nov. 1726.

1727. George II., son; d. 25 Oct. 1760; age 77.
Queen: Wilhelmina Carolina Dorothea of Brandenburg-Anspach; married 1705; d. 20 Nov. 1737.

1760. George III., grandson of George II.; d. 29 Jan. 1820; age 82.
Queen: Charlotte Sophia, daughter of the duke of Mecklenburg-Strelitz; married 8 Sept. 1761; d. 17 Nov. 1818.

1820. George IV., son; d. 26 June, 1830; age 68.
Queen: Caroline Amelia Augusta, daughter of the duke of Brunswick; married 8 Apr. 1795; d. 7 Aug. 1821 (QUEEN CAROLINE).

1830. William IV., brother of George IV.; d. 20 June, 1837; age 72.
Queen: Adelaide Amelia Louisa Theresa Caroline, sister of the duke of Saxe-Meiningen; married 11 July, 1818; d. 2 Dec. 1849.

1837. Victoria, the reigning queen.

THE PRESENT ROYAL FAMILY OF GREAT BRITAIN.

The queen, and empress of India by proclamation 28 Apr. 1876, Alexandrina Victoria, only daughter of Edward, duke of Kent (4th son of king George III.), b. 24 May, 1819; succeeded on the decease of her uncle, William IV., 20 June, 1837; crowned at Westminster, 28 June, 1838; married (10 Feb. 1840) to her cousin,

Francis Albert Augustus Charles Emmanuel, duke of Saxe, prince of Saxe-Coburg and Gotha; b. 26 Aug. 1819; naturalized, 24 Jan. 1840 (ordered to be styled Prince Consort 25 June, 1857); elected chancellor of the university of Cambridge, 28 Feb. 1847; d. 14 Dec. 1861.

Issue.

1. Victoria Adelaide Mary Louisa, princess royal, b. 21 Nov. 1840; married to the crown-prince Frederick William of Prussia, 25 Jan. 1858 (dowry 40,000*l.* and annuity of 8000*l.*); dowager empress of Germany. Issue: William, present emperor of Germany (succeeded his father Frederick William, June, 1888); b. 27 Jan. 1859; and 5 other children living.
2. Albert Edward, prince of Wales, duke of Saxony, duke of Cornwall and Rothsay, earl of Chester, Carrick, and Dublin, baron of Renfrew, and lord of the Isles; b. 9 Nov. 1841; married princess Alexandra of Denmark (b. 1 Dec. 1844) 10 Mch. 1863. Issue: Albert Victor, b. 8 Jan. 1864, d. 14 Jan. 1892; George, b. 3 June, 1865, married princess Mary of Teck 6 July, 1893; Louise, b. 20 Feb. 1867, married duke of Fife 27 July, 1889; Victoria, b. 6 July, 1868, married prince Ferdinand, crown-prince of Roumania, 10 Jan. 1893; Maud, b. 26 Nov. 1869; Alexander John, b. 6 Apr., d. 7 Apr. 1871. WALES.
3. Alice Maud Mary, b. 25 Apr. 1843; married prince Louis (since grand-duke) of Hesse-Darmstadt, 1 July, 1862 (dowry 30,000*l.*, annuity 6000*l.*). Issue: Victoria, 5 Apr. 1863; and 5 other children; died of diphtheria, 14 Dec. 1878.
4. Alfred Ernest, b. 6 Aug. 1844; entered the *Euryalus* as midshipman, 31 Aug. 1858; created duke of Edinburgh, etc., 24 May,

1866, married archduchess Marie of Russia (b 17 Oct 1853), 23 Jan 1874 Issue Alfred, b 15 Oct 1874, Mary 29 Oct 1875 Victoria, 25 Nov 1876, Alexandrina, 1 Sept 1878, Beatrice, 20 Apr 1884
Helena Augusta Victoria b 25 May 1846 married to prince Christian of Schleswig Holstein 5 July, 1866 Issue Christian Victor, b 14 Apr 1867, and other children
Louise Carolina Alberta, b 18 Mch 1848, married to John, marquis of Lorne (b 6 Aug 1845), 21 Mch 1871
Arthur William Patrick Albert, b 1 May, 1850, created duke of Connaught, earl of Sussex and Strathearn 23 May 1874, married 13 Mch 1879, to princess Louise Margaret of Prussia (b 25 July, 1860), his issue
Leopold George Duncan Albert, b 7 Apr 1853, married 27 Apr 1882, to princess Helen, daughter of prince of Waldeck, d 28 Mch 1884, has issue
Beatrice Mary Victoria Feodore b 14 Apr 1857, married 23 July, 1885, prince Henry Maurice of Battenberg, has issue

HOUSE OF SAXE COBURG.

dward VII, b 9 Nov 1841, married princess Alexandra of Denmark, 10 Mch 1863, succeeded to the throne 22 Jan 1901

Issue

Albert Victor, b 8 Jan 1864, created duke of Clarence and Avondale, etc, 23 May, 1890, died at Sandringham, 14 Jan 1892
George Frederick, b 3 June, 1865, created duke of York, earl of Inverness and baron Killarney, 24 May, 1892, married princess Victoria Mary (May) of Teck, 6 July, 1893, duke of Cornwall, Jan 1901, prince of Wales and earl of Chester, 9 Nov 1901 Issue Edward Albert Christian, b 23 June 1894, Albert Frederick, b 14 Dec. 1895, Victoria Alexandra, b 25 Apr 1897, Henry William, b 31 Mch 1900, George b 20 Dec 1902
Louise, princess royal, b 20 Feb 1867, married Alexander William George, duke of Fife, 27 July, 1889 Issue Alexandra, b 17 May, 1891, Maud, b 3 Apr 1893
Victoria, b 6 July, 1868

ROYAL ARMS OF ENGLAND

illiam I, William II, and Henry I —2 lions or leopards passant
tephen—Sagittarius, the archer, a sign of the zodiac (traditional)
enry II to Edward II —3 lions passant
dward III and his successors—the preceding with fleurs de lis
enry V used only 3 fleurs de lis
ary I —the preceding with the arms of Philip II of Spain

ROYAL ARMS OF UNITED KINGDOM

ames I and his successors combined the arms of England and France (1st and 4th quarters), 2d, the lion rampant of Scotland, 3d, the harp of Ireland He introduced the unicorn as a supporter of the arms
eorge I introduced the arms of Brunswick (modified in 1816 by Hanover being made a kingdom)
1801 the arms of France were omitted
ictoria.—In 1837 the arms of Hanover were omitted

English language is traced from the Frisian ariety (Low German) of the Teutonic or Germanic branch of he great Indo-European family, and is closely related to those ialects spoken on the north shores and lowlands of Germany ts origin due to the immigration of the Angles, Jutes, and axons A number of words still remain of the Celts, the riginal inhabitants, as *basket*, *bran*, *breeches*, *crock*, etc

	A D
eltic prevailed and Latin introduced in England	1
irst period —Saxon prevails (Beowulf, Cædmon, Alfred)	450-1066
atin reintroduced by missionaries	596
econd period —Norman French combining with English	1066-1250
illiam I and his successors used English in their laws, etc., it was superseded by Latin in the reign of Henry II Norman French was first used in law deeds under Henry III	
hird Period —Early English	1250-1500
ourth period —Present English settled in the 16th century	
aw pleadings were made in English by order of Edward III instead of in French	1362
nglish tongue and English apparel were ordered to be used in Ireland, 28 Hen VIII	1536
nglish ordered used in lawsuits, Latin disused	May, 1731
ercentage of Anglo Saxon words in the English Bible, 97, Swift, 89, Shakespeare and Thomson, 85, Addison, 83, Spenser and Milton, 81, Locke, 80, Young, 79, Pope, 76, Johnson, 75, Robertson, 68, Hume, 65, Gibbon, 58.—*Marsh.*	
f 100,000 English words, 60 000 are of Teutonic origin, 30,000 Greek and Latin, and 10,000 from other sources.	
arly English Text Society began publishing	1864
nglish Dialect Society formed to print old glossaries	May, 1873
nglish literature and authors, LITERATURE	

engraving on signets is mentioned Exod xxviii. 11 1491 B.C). Engraving on plates and wood began about the iddle of the 15th century Engraving on glass was perfected y Bourdier, of Paris, 1799 The British copyright to enravings has been protected by several statutes, among the rincipal are the acts 16 and 18 Geo. III. 1775 and 1777, and he acts 7 and 8 Vict., 6 Aug. 1844, and 15 Vict., 28 May, 1852 process of enlarging and reducing engravings by means of heets of vulcanized india-rubber was shown by the Electrorinting Block Company, in England, in 1860. LITHOGRAPHY, PHOTO-GALVANOGRAPHY In "Lyra Germanica" pub 1861, are illustrations engraved upon blocks photographed from negatives taken by John Leighton, F S A

Engraving on Copper —Prints from engraved copper plates first appeared about 1450 in Germany Masso surnamed Finiguerra, is called the first Italian engraver about 1440 NIELLO
Earliest date known of a copper plate engraving is 1461
Rolling presses for working the plates were invented in 1545
Of etching on copper by aqua fortis, Francis Mazzuoli, or Parmegiano is the reputed inventor, about 1532 —*De Piles*
Etching was practised by Albert Dürer, especially by Rembrandt, revived about 1860 Eminent modern etchers Lalanne P G Hamerton F Seymour Haden, Bracquemond, Jacquemart, Martial, etc. Etching club established in London in 1838
Society of Painter etchers formed, opened an exhibition Apr 1881
Engraving on wood, long known in China, began in Europe with the *Briefmahlers* or manufacturers of playing cards about 1400 PRINTING The art is referred by some to a Florentine, and by others to Reuss a German, it was greatly improved by Durer (1471-1528) and Lucas van Leyden (1497) and in England by Bewick and his brother and pupils Nesbitt, Anderson, etc, 1789 et seq The earliest wood engraving preserved represents St Christopher carrying the infant Jesus over the sea, date 1423 W J Linton's "Masters of Wood Engraving," with 250 fine examples, pub July, 1890
Engraving on soft steel, to be hardened afterwards was introduced into England by Messrs Perkins and Heath, of Philadelphia, 1819
John Pye, "father of English landscape engraving," d 6 Feb 1874
Mezzotinto is said to have been discovered by col von Siegen, who engraved a portrait of princess Amelia of Hesse in mezzotinto in 1643, it was improved by prince Rupert in 1648, and by sir Christopher Wren about 1662
Aquatinta, with a soft and beautiful effect, was invented by the French artist St. Non about 1662, he communicated it to Le Prince Barabbe of Paris was distinguished for his improvements in it 1763 *Chiaroscuro* engraving originated with the Germans, and was first practised by Mair, one of whose prints bears date 1491 ZINC, etc

Enniskillen, N W Ireland This town made an obstinate defence against the army of Elizabeth, 1595, and resisted James II, 1689 1500 Enniskilleners met his gen. M'Carthy at Newtown-butler with 6000 men (of whom 3000 were slain, and nearly all the rest made prisoners), losing but 20 men, 30 July 1689 The dragoon regiment "Inniskillingers" was originally recruited here

Enoch, Book of, an apocryphal work, quoted in Jude, 14th and 15th verses, and by the early fathers, disappeared about the 8th century A MS. Ethiopic version was found in Abyssinia by Bruce, and brought to England in 1773 Of this, archbishop Lawrence published an English translation in 1821, and the Ethiopic text in 1838

En'sisheim, a town of Alsace Here Turenne defeated the Imperial army, and expelled it from Alsace, 4 Oct 1674

entail of estates began in England with the statute of Westminster, 1285 Subsequent legislation broke the entail in cases of treason (1534), when the estate is to revert to the crown, and of bankruptcy (1833 and 1849), when it is to be sold The law of entail in Scotland was amended in 1875 Entail abolished in Virginia, 1776

Enterprise and **Boxer.** NAVAL BATTLES.

entomology, the science of insects, now mainly based upon the arrangement of Linnæus, 1739 Ray's "Methodus Insectorum," 1705, "Insectorum Historia," 1710 The Entomological Society of London was instituted in 1833. A national entomological exhibition at the Westminster aquarium was opened 9 Mch 1878

envelopes for letters are mentioned by Swift, 1726 Stamped adhesive envelopes came into general use in Great Britain soon after the penny postal system, 10 Jan 1840. Machinery for their manufacture was patented by George Wilson in 1844, and by Messrs. E Hill and Warren De La Rue, 17 Mch. 1845

envoys at courts, in dignity below ambassadors, enjoy the protection, but not the ceremonies, of ambassadors Envoys-extraordinary are of modern date —*Wicquefort.* The court of France denied envoys the ceremony of conduct to court in royal carriages, 1639

eozoön (*e-o-zo'-on*) **Canadense,** asserted to be the earliest known form of life, is a species of foraminifera, found by prof J. W. Dawson, of Montreal, in Laurentian limestone, in 1858.

epact (Gr ἐπακτός, added) is the excess of the solar month above the lunar synodical month, 1 day, 11 hours, 15 minutes, 57 seconds, the lunar month being only 29 days, 12 hours, 44 minutes, 3 seconds; and the excess of the solar year above the lunar synodical year (nearly 11 days), the lunar year being 354 days. The number of the Gregorian epact for 1877, 15; 1878, 26; 1879, 7; 1880, 18.

Eph'esus, Asia Minor, a city founded by the Ionians about 1043 B.C. It was subdued by Cyrus in 544 B.C.; revolted from the Persians, 501 B.C.; and was nearly destroyed by an earthquake in 17 A.D. DIANA, Temple of; SEVEN CHURCHES. Paul preached here 55, 56 A.D. (Acts xviii., xix.). His epistle to the Ephesians is dated 64 A.D. The 3d general council was held here in 431. After investigation, begun in 1863, J. T. Wood discovered the site of the temple of Diana (Artemis) in Apr. 1870; and about 60 tons of marble were shipped at Smyrna for the British museum, Jan. 1872. Mr. Wood published an illustrated account of his discoveries in 1876. The site of the temple was purchased for the British museum.

eph'ori, powerful magistrates of Sparta, 5 in number, said to have been first created by Theopompus to control the royal power, about 757 B.C.

epic poems (from Gr. ἔπος, a song), narratives in verse. Eminent examples:

Homer's "Iliad" and "Odyssey" (*Greek*), between 8th and 10th century B.C. HOMER.	
Māhā-bhārata (*Sanscrit*), very ancient; by several authors; the longest epic known (220,000 lines).	B.C.
Virgil's "Æneid" (*Latin*) ... about	19
	A.D.
Ovid's "Metamorphoses" (*Latin*) ... about	1
Dante (d. 1321), "Divina Commedia" (*Italian*) pub.	1472
Ariosto, "Orlando Furioso" (*Italian*)	1516
Camoens, "Lusiad" (*Portuguese*)	1569
Tasso, "Jerusalem Delivered" (*Italian*)	1581
Spenser's "Faerie Queene"	1590–96
Milton's "Paradise Lost"	1667
Voltaire, "Henriade" (*French*)	1728
Walter Scott, "Lay of the Last Minstrel," etc.	1805

LITERATURE.

Epicure'an philosophy. Epicurus of Gargettus, near Athens, about 300 B.C., taught that the greatest good consists in peace of mind springing from virtue; but the name epicurean is frequently given to those who derive happiness from sensual pleasure. ATOMS, PHILOSOPHY.

Epidau'rus, a seaport village of Greece, celebrated as the site of the temple of Asclepius, or Æsculapius, god of medicine, and enriched by gifts from persons healed. The Romans sent an embassy to seek the help of the god during a pestilence, and his worship was introduced at Rome, 293 B.C. The temple was visited by Æmilius Paulus, after his conquest of Macedonia, 167 B.C.

epigen'esis. SPONTANEOUS GENERATION.

epigrams, originally inscriptions, especially on tombs. Marcus Valerius Martialis, the Latin epigrammatist, who flourished about 83 A.D., is allowed to have excelled all others, ancient or modern. The following epigram on Christ's turning water into wine (John ii.) is an example: "Vidit et erubuit lympha pudica Deum" ("the modest water saw its God, and blushed").—*Crashaw* (d. 1650).

"The Epigrammatists," a collection by rev. H. P. Dodd, pub. 1870 and 1875.

Epiph'any (Gr. ἐπιφανής, manifest), a feast (Jan. 6), termed Twelfth-day, celebrates the manifestation of the Saviour by the appearance of the star which conducted the magi to him; instituted 813.—*Whately.*

Epi'rus, a country of N. Greece. Its early history is obscure.

	B.C.
First Pyrrhus (Neoptolemus) settled in Epirus, after the Trojan war, 1170 B.C.; killed in the temple of Delphi ... about	1165
Pyrrhus the Great reigns, 295; he takes Macedon from Demetrius, 290; compelled to yield to Lysimachus	287
He invades Italy; defeats the Romans, 280; again, 279; subdues Sicily	278
He invades Italy again, and is totally defeated by Curius Dentatus at Beneventum	275
He takes Macedon from Antigonus	273
He unsuccessfully invades Sparta; enters Argos, and is killed by a tile, thrown by a woman	272
Philip unites Epirus to Macedon	220
Its conquest by the Romans	167
	A.D.
Epirus annexed to the Ottoman empire	1[illegible]
An insurrection against the Turks put down	[illegible]4

Epis'copacy. BISHOPS, CHURCH OF ENGLAND.

epistles or **letters.** An Egyptian letter, about 1300 B.C., is translated in "Records of the Past," vol. vi. A letter was sent to Joab by David by the hands of Uriah, about 1035 B.C. (2 Sam. xi. 14). Horace Walpole, renowned for letters, was born 5 Oct. 1717; died 2 Mch. 1797. The collection entitled "Elegant Epistles," commencing with Cicero, pub. 1790, ends with an essay on letter-writing by dr. Johnson.

epitaphs were inscribed on tombs by the Egyptians, Jews, Greeks, and Romans. T. J. Pettigrew published a collection entitled "Chronicles of the Tombs," in 1857.

epithala'mium, a nuptial song at marriage. Tisias the lyric poet, is said to have written the first. He received the name of Stesichorus, from the alterations made by him in music and dancing, about 536 B.C.—*Bossuet.*

epocha, a point of time made remarkable by some event, from which subsequent years are reckoned by historians and chronologers. ERAS.

	B.C.
Creation	4004
Deluge	2348
First Olympiad	776
Building of Rome	753
	A.D.
Birth of Christ	1
Hegira (or flight of Mahomet)	622

Epsom, Surrey, Engl. The mineral springs were discovered in 1618. The races began about 1711, and have been held annually since 1730.

equestrian order in Rome began with Romulus, about 750 B.C. KNIGHTHOOD.

equinox. When the sun crosses the equator, day and night are equal all over the globe. This occurs twice in the year: about 21 Mch. the *vernal* equinox, and 22 Sept. the *autumnal* equinox. The crossings, called equinoctial points, move backwards about 50 seconds yearly, in about 26,000 years making a complete revolution. This is called the *precession* of the equinoxes. The axis of the earth does not remain rigorously parallel to itself, but varies in direction, describing an entire cone in about 26,000 years. The northern extremity of the earth's axis is now quite near the polestar, Polaris, and is still approaching that star. It will continue to do so until the year 2120, when it will point to within half a degree of it. The axis will then recede from it and pass from the Little Bear to Cepheus, then across the border of the Swan, and in about 13,000 years Vega in Lyra will be the polestar. After another 13,000 years Polaris will again be the polestar. Hipparchus of Alexandria about 2000 years ago is said to have been the first to note the precession of the equinoxes. It was fully explained by D'Alembert and Laplace as a result of gravitation.

eras. The principal are more fully noticed in their alphabetical order.

	B.C.
Era of CONSTANTINOPLE ... 1 Sept.	5508
Mundane Era of Antioch (ALEXANDRIA, etc., JULIAN PERIOD)	5493
Julian Era (CALENDAR, YEAR).	
ALEXANDRIAN ERA, same as ABYSSINIAN ERA	"
Common Era of the creation (English Bible, *Usher*, etc.)	4004
JEWISH ERA	3761
Romans reckoned from the founding of their city, A.U.C. (*anno urbis conditæ*)	753
Era of *Nabonassar*, after which the astronomical observations made at Babylon were reckoned ... began 26 Feb.	747
ALEXANDER, ERA OF	325
Era of the *Seleucidæ* or *Macedonian* (used by the Maccabees), commenced	312
Era of *Tyre* (INDICTION)	125
AUGUSTAN ERA	27
Olympiads belong to the Grecians, and date from 1 July, 776 B.C.; they subsequently reckoned by indictions, the first beginning 313 A.D.; these, among chronologers, are still used (INDICTIONS).	
	A.D.
Spanish Era (of the conquest of Spain), *Varro*, 752, *Cato the Elder*, the 16th year of the emperor Augustus (CÆSARS), long used by the Spaniards ... 1 Jan.	38
DIOCLETIAN ERA, or Era of Martyrs ... began 29 Aug.	284
Mahometans began their era from the *Hegira*, or flight of their prophet from Mecca ... 16 July,	622
Persian or YEZDEGIRD ERA	632

ANNO DOMINI, CALENDAR, CREATION, and the names of eras throughout.

Erastianism, the belief of Thomas Lieber (Greek equivalent *Erastus*), a German physician (1524–83), that the hurch had no right to exclude any person from church ordinances, to inflict excommunication, etc Persons who acknowledge the jurisdiction of the civil power in spiritual matters and the law of patronage are now termed Erastians

Er'furt, a city of central Germany, was founded in 476, and its university established about 1390 Erfurt was ceded to Prussia in 1802 It capitulated to Murat, when 14 000 Prussian troops surrendered, 16 Oct 1806 Here Napoleon and Alexander met, and offered peace to England, 27 Sept 1808 The French retreated to Erfurt from Leipsic, 18 Oct 1813 A German parliament met here in Mch and Apr 1850

Er'icsson's caloric engine. HEAT

Erie canal. NEW YORK, 1817-25

Erie, Fort FORT ERIE

Eries. OHIO, 1656

Erivan', Armenia in the 16th century the residence of the shahs of Persia was taken by the Turks in 1553 and 1582, but was recovered by Abbas the Great, 1604 After being several times captured, it was ceded to Persia 1769 It was taken by Paskiewitch in 1827 and annexed to Russia by treaty 1 Feb 1828

Erzeroum (*erz-room'*), principal city in Armenia in Asiatic Turkey, a city built by Theodosius II, 415, taken by the Seljuk Turks in the 13th century and by the Ottoman Turks in 1517 It was captured by the Russian general Paskiewitch, June, 1829, but restored in 1830 It was almost totally destroyed by earthquakes, 2 June to 17 July, 1859 Pop 1885, 60,000

Escu'rial, properly **Esco'rial,** 25 miles N W of Madrid, the palace of the sovereigns of Spain, termed the 8th wonder of the world, was begun by Philip II in 1563, and completed in 1586 at a cost of about $50,000,000 It is in the form of a gridiron, in honor of St Lawrence, on whose day (10 Aug 1557) the Spaniards gained the victory of St Quentin According to Francisco de los Santos, the total length of its rooms is above 120 English miles The Escurial comprises a church, mausoleum, monastery, palace, library, and museum It was struck by lightning and caught fire 11 30 P M, 1 Oct 1872, and was much damaged, but the grand library and other treasures were preserved

Espierre (*es-pe-air'*), Belgium At Pont-a-Chin, near this village, the French, under Pichegru, attacked the allied English and Austrian army (100,000 men), commanded by the Duke of York, and were repulsed after a long and desperate engagement, losing the advantages gained by the victory at Tourcoing, 22 May, 1794

esquires, among the Greeks and Romans, were armor-bearers to, or attendants on, a knight —*Blount* In England, the king created esquires by putting about their necks the collars of SS, and bestowing upon them a pair of silver spurs. John de Kingston was created a squire by patent, 13 Richard II, 1389-90

Essenes, an ascetic Jewish sect at the time of Christ, representing the highest culture of the Jewish nation.

Essex, U S. ship. For engagement with the British ships *Phœbe* and *Cherub*, NAVAL BATTLES

established church, the state religion of a country, a church exclusively recognized by the state During the first 3 centuries of the Christian era there was no established or state church During the reign of Constantine (323-337) the state and church were first united. During mediæval times up to the Reformation the Roman Catholic faith was the state religion of all western Europe, in fact, every government was in vassalage to papacy The Reformation introduced more freedom, so that now each state or government decides upon its own establishment In England, while the Episcopal service is the established form, there is a Broad Church party, which advocates freedom of belief enough to take in all churches, and even other religions In the United States, as in all true republics, there is not and cannot be an established church CHURCH

Este, House of Boniface, count of Lucca and duke of Tuscany, about 811, is said to have descended from Odoacer, king of Italy From Boniface sprang Albert-Azzo II, marquess of Italy and lord of Este, born about 996, who married—first, Cunegonde of the house of Guelf, mother of Guelf, duke of Bavaria, ancestor of the house of Brunswick (BAVARIA, BRUNSWICK), and, secondly, Gersonda, mother of Fulk, ancestor of the Estes, dukes of Ferrara and Modena

Esthonia or **Revel,** a Russian province, said to have been conquered by Teutonic knights in the 12th century, after various changes it was ceded to Sweden by the treaty of Oliva, 3 May, 1660, and finally to Russia by the peace of Nystadt 30 Aug 1721, having been conquered by Peter the Great in 1710

etching. ENGRAVING

ether was known to the earliest chemists Nitric ether was discovered by Kunkel, in 1681, and muriatic ether, from the chloride of tin, by Courtanvaux, in 1759 Acetic ether was discovered by count Lauraguais, same year, and hydriotic ether was first prepared by Gay-Lussac Phosphoric ether was obtained by M Boullay The discovery that by inhaling ether the patient is rendered unconscious of pain is due to Dr Charles T Jackson, of Boston, Mass. Thomas Morton of the same place, first introduced it into surgical practice, under dr Jackson's directions (1846) AMYLENE, CHLOROFORM The term "ether" was applied to a transparent and extremely sparse fluid, supposed to fill celestial space by the German astronomer Encke, about 1829, when studying the elements of Pons's comet, discovered in 1818

ethics (Gr ἠθικα, term for morals) Pythagoras, 500 B.C, was the first of the Greeks who recognized it as a social force He was followed by Socrates, 450 B C, Plato, 374 B C, Aristotle, 334 B.C, Epicurus, 306 B.C, Zeno the Stoic, 290 B C, and others, each with a different system Jewish ethics, represented by Moses and the Old Testament, Christian ethics, by the New Testament, mediæval, by St Augustin and Thomas Aquinas, modern, by Grotius, 1583-1645, Hobbes, 1588-1679, Descartes, 1595-1650, Spinoza, 1632-77, Locke, 1632-1704, Leibnitz, 1646-1716, Reid, 1710-96 Hume, 1711-1776, Kant, 1724-1804, Paley, 1743-1805, Bentham, 1747-1832, Fichte, 1762-1814, Hegel, 1770-1831, Schelling, 1775-1854, Cousin, 1792-1867, Whewell, 1795-1866, Comte, 1798-1857, John Stuart Mill, 1806-73, and others PHILOSOPHY

Ethiopia. The name was applied anciently rather vaguely to countries the inhabitants of which had sunburned complexions, in Asia and Africa, but applied properly to the modern Nubia, Sennaar, and northern Abyssinia Many pyramids are at Napata, the capital of Meroë, the civilized part of ancient Ethiopia EGYPT

	B C
Ethiopians settle near Egypt	1615
Zerah, the Ethiopian, defeated by Asa	941
A dynasty of Ethiopian kings reigned over Egypt	765 to 715
Tirhakah, king of Ethiopia, marches against Sennacherib	710
Unsuccessful invasion of Cambyses	525-22
Ptolemy III Euergetes extends conquests in Ethiopia	225
Candace queen of Meroë advancing against the Roman settlement of Elephantine, defeated by Petronius	A D 22-23

ethnology, a branch of anthropology, is defined as the science "which determines the distinctive characters of the persistent modifications of mankind, their distribution, and the causes of the modifications and distribution" The study of the relations of the different divisions of mankind to each other is of recent origin Balbi's "Ethnographic Atlas" was published in 1826, and dr Prichard's great work, "Researches on the Physical History of Mankind," 1841-47 Dr R G Latham's works appeared in 1851-52 Charles Pickering's "The Races of Men, and Their Geographical Distribution," Philadelphia, 1848, Antoine Desmoulin's "Histoire Naturelle des Races Humaines," Paris, 1826, J. J Virey's "Histoire Naturelle du Genre Humain," Paris, 1824, A de Quatrefages's "Histoire Generale des Races Humaines" Paris, 1887, Nott and Gliddon's "Types of Mankind," 1854, and "Indigenous Races of the Earth," Philadelphia, 1857, Paul Broca's "Memoires d'Anthropologie," Paris, 1883, Paul Topinard's "Éléments d'Anthropologie Générale," Paris, 1885, Huxley's "Geographical Distribution of Mankind," London, 1870 The Ethnological Society, England, established in 1843, published transactions. On 17 Jan 1871, it was amalgamated with the Anthropological Society, and named the Anthropological Institute Bureau of Ethnology, Washington, D C, began to publish annual reports, 1879 This bureau is the highest authority on the language, sociology, and customs of the American aborigines. The International Congress of the Ethnographic Sciences met at Paris, 30 Sept. 1889. Many naturalists have attempted to describe the races or varieties into which man is divided; some resting with the simplest and most palpable differences, others extending the comparisons to the most complex: (1) color; (2) hair; (3) shape of skull and facial angle; (4) features; (5) constitution and character; (6) language, etc. The following shows the classification of some of the most eminent naturalists. Cuvier: *Caucasian*, *Mongolian*, *Ethiopian* or *Negro*. Buffon and Blumenbach: *Caucasian*, *Mongolian*, *Ethiopian*, *American*, *Malayan* (this division was long generally accepted). Linnæus: *European* or *whitish*, *American* or *coppery*, *Asiatic* or *tawny*, *Negro* or *black*. Dr. Prichard divided them into 7 races; Pickering into 11; Desmoulins, at first into 11, and afterwards 16; dr. Latham, 3 primary divisions and 16 subdivisions; De Quatrefages, a single stem with 3 trunks, *White*, *Yellow*, and *Black*; White subdivided into 3 parts, Yellow into 2, and Black into 4, and these again subdivided; Bory de St. Vincent, into 15; Nott, 8 families, as also Agassiz; Huxley, 2: 1, Ulotrichi, woolly hair (Negroid); 2, Leiostrichi, smooth hair; subdivided—Australoid, Mongoloid, Hanthrochroic, Melanochroic. Keith Johnson classifies after Buffon as follows (3 types):

1. CAUCASIAN.

Shemitic, Georgian, Circassian, Armenian, Iranian, Hindu, Gypsies, Celtic, Grecian, Italic, Teutonic, Goths or Germans, Sclavonic.

2. MONGOLIAN (central Asian).

Tibetans, Chinese, Burmese, Anamese, Siamese, Cambodians (northern Asian), Samoeids, Ostiaks, Yeniseians, Tungus (Turanians), Finns, Lapps, Magyars, Koreans, Japanese, Kamtchatdales, Korjaks, Esquimaux, Mongolians, and Turks.
Malay (subdivision), Malayan, Polynesian, Papuan, Australian.
American (subdivision), includes all Indians in North and South America.

3. ETHIOPIAN.

All the inhabitants of Africa. Subdivisions: Kaffirs, Hottentots, tribes of northern Africa (partially Caucasian), Berbers, Copts, Nubians, Gallas, Abyssinians, etc.
LANGUAGE.

TABLE OF RACES (after Brinton's classification).

Race.	Traits.	Branch.	Stock.	Groups or Peoples.
Eurafrican.	Color, white. Hair, wavy. Nose, narrow.	I. South Mediterranean	Hamitic	1. Libyan. 2. Egyptian. 3. East African.
			Semitic.	1. Arabian. 2. Abyssinian. 3. Chaldean.
		II. North Mediterranean	Euskaric	Euskarian.
			Aryac	Indo Germanic or Celtindic.
			Caucasic	Peoples of the Caucasus.
Austafrican.	Color, black or dark. Hair, frizzly. Nose, broad.	I. Negrillo	Central African	Dwarfs of the Congo.
			South African	Bushmen, Hottentots.
		II. Negro	Nilotic, Soudanese, Senegambian, Guinean	Nubian.
		III. Negroid	Bantu	Kaffirs, Congo tribes, etc.
Asian.	Color, yellow or olive. Hair, straight. Nose, medium.	I. Sinitic	Chinese	Chinese.
			Tibetan	Tibetan.
			Indo-Chinese	Burmese, Siamese, Anamese, etc.
		II. Sibiric	Tungusic	Manchus, Tungus.
			Mongolic	Mongols, Kalmucks.
			Tartaric	Turks, Cossacks.
			Finnic	Finns, Magyars.
			Arctic	Chukchis, Ainos.
			Japanic	Japanese, Koreans.
American.	Color, coppery. Hair, straight or wavy. Nose, medium.	I. Northern	Arctic	Eskimos.
			Atlantic	Tinneh, Algonkin, Iroquois.
			Pacific	Chinooks, Koloshes, etc.
		II. Central	Mexican	Nahuas, Tarascos.
			Isthmian	Mayas, Chapanecs.
		III. Southern	Atlantic	Caribs, Arawaks, Tupis.
			Pacific	Chibchas, Quichuas.
Insular and littoral peoples.	Color, dark. Hair, wavy or frizzly. Nose, medium or narrow.	I. Negritic	Negrito	Mincopies, Aetas.
			Papuan	New Guineans.
			Melanesian	Feegeeans, etc.
		II. Malayic	Malayan	Malayan, Tagalas.
			Polynesian	Pacific islanders.
		III. Australic	Australian	Australians.
			Dravidian	Dravidians, Mundas.

ethyl, a compound radical, a colorless gas, with a slightly ethereal odor, a compound of carbon and hydrogen, first obtained in the free state by prof. Edward Frankland in 1849. Several of its compounds with metals take fire on exposure to the air.

Etna, Mount, Sicily. Here were the fabled forges of the Cyclopes, and it is called by Pindar the pillar of heaven. Eruptions are mentioned by Diodorus Siculus as happening 1693 B.C., and Thucydides speaks of 3 eruptions as occurring 734, 477, and 425 B.C. There were eruptions, 125, 121, and 43 B.C.—*Livy*. VOLCANOES.

Eruptions, 40, 254, and 420 A.D.—*Carrera*.
One in 1012.—*Geoffrey de Viterbo*.
One overwhelmed Catania, when 15,000 inhabitants perished.. 1169
Eruptions, 1329, 1408, 1445, 1536, 1537, 1564, *et seq*.
In 1669, tens of thousands of persons perished in streams of lava which rolled along for 40 days.
Eruptions in 1766, 1787, 1809, 1811, and in May, 1830, when several villages were destroyed, and showers of ashes reached near to Rome.
Town of Bronte was destroyed....18 Nov. 1832
Violent eruption occurred....Aug. and Sept. 1852
An eruption began 1 Feb., and ceased....July, 1865
Violent eruption began....28 Nov. 1868
Another eruption began....29 Aug. 1874
Violent eruption....26 May–7 June, 1879
Eruption, severe....31 May, 1886
Another....July, 1892

Eton college, Buckinghamshire, Engl., founded by Henry VI. in 1440, and designed as a nursery to King's college, Cambridge.

"Ye distant spires, ye antique towers
That crown the watery glade,
Where grateful Science still adores
Her Henry's holy shade."
—*Gray*, "Ode on a Distant Prospect of Eton College."

John Stanbery, confessor to Henry VI. (bishop of Bangor, in 1448), was nominated the first provost. One of the provosts, William Waynflete (bishop of Winchester, 1447), greatly promoted the erection of the buildings. Besides about 300 noblemen's and gentlemen's sons, there were 70 king's scholars on the foundation, who, when properly qualified, were formally elected, on the first Tuesday in August, to King's college, Cambridge, and removed there when there were vacancies, according to seniority. The establishment of the montem is nearly coeval with the college. It consisted in the procession of the scholars, arrayed in fancy dresses, to Salt-hill once in 3 years, the donations collected on the road (sometimes as much as 800*l*) were given to the senior or best scholar, their captain, for his support at Cambridge. The montem was discontinued in 1847. The college system was modified by the Public Schools act, 1868. In 1873 the practice of electing students to King's college, Cambridge, ceased, the scholars to be students at Cambridge being chosen there. In 1880 there were 853 students.

Etru'ria or **Tuscia** (hence the modern name Tuscany), a province of Italy, whence the Romans derived many laws, customs, and superstitions. Herodotus asserts that the country was conquered by a colony of Lydians. Its subjugation forms an important part of early Roman history. It was most powerful under Porsena of Clusium, who attempted to reinstate the Tarquins, 506 B.C. Veii was taken by Camillus, 396 B.C. A truce between the Romans and Etrurians for 40 years was concluded, 351 B.C. The latter were defeated at the Vadimonian lake, 310, with the Boii, their allies, 283 B.C., and lost their independence about 265 B.C. Vases and other works of the Etruscans still remaining show their civilization. Napoleon I. established a kingdom of Etruria, 1801, and suppressed it 1807. TUSCANY. "The Cities and Cemeteries of Etruria," by George Dennis, pub. 1848 and 1878.—Etruria, Staffordshire, Engl., the site of Josiah Wedgwood's porcelain works, etc., was founded in 1771.

Eubœ'a, the largest island in the Ægean sea. Two of its cities, CHALCIS and Eretria, were very important, till the former was subdued by Athens, 506 B.C., and the latter by the Persians, 490. After the Persian war Eubœa became wholly subject to Athens, and was its most valuable possession. It revolted in 445, but was soon subdued by Pericles. After the battle of Chæronea, 338, it became subject to Macedon. It was made independent by the Romans in 194, but was afterwards incorporated in the province of Achaia. It now forms part of the kingdom of Greece.

Eucalyp'tus glob'ulus, or blue-gum-tree, a very fast-growing Tasmanian evergreen, of the order *Myrtaceæ*. From the extraordinary power of its roots to absorb moisture, and the salutary aromatic odor of its leaves, it has been found highly beneficial in counteracting the malaria of marshy districts of hot climates, and hence has been named the fever-destroying tree. M. Ramel (d. 1881) first sent seeds from Melbourne to Paris in 1854, and subsequently seeds were distributed over the south of Europe, the north and south of Africa, and elsewhere.

So rapid is the growth of this tree that a forest may be formed in 20 years. It sometimes reaches the height of 350 feet, with a circumference of 100 feet, rivalling WELLINGTONIA GIGANTEA.

Timber, bark, and oils of the eucalyptus are highly valuable, and prof. Bentley says that the genus is one of the most important to man in the vegetable kingdom. In 1874 its medicinal value was said to have been exaggerated.

Eucharist, thanksgiving, an early name for the Lord's supper. SACRAMENT.

Euclid's "Elements." Euclid, a native of Alexandria, Egypt, flourished about 300 B.C. The "Elements" are not wholly original, many of the demonstrations were derived from Thales, Pythagoras, Eudoxus, and others. Euclid reduced them to order, and probably inserted many theorems of his own. The "Elements" were first printed at Basle by Simon Grynæus, in 1533.

eudiom'eter, an apparatus to ascertain the purity of air, or the quantity of oxygen gas in it; one was invented by dr. Priestley in 1772.

Eugubine tables, 7 tablets of brass, probable date about 400 B.C. (with inscriptions relating to sacrifices, etc.—4 in Umbrian, 2 in Latin, and one partly in both dialects), were discovered in 1444 at Gubbio, the ancient Eugubium, or Iguvium. The inscriptions are accurately given by Lepsius, in his "Inscriptiones Umbricæ et Oscæ," 1841.

eunuchs, first mentioned among the Egyptians and Assyrians, are said to have been first employed by Semiramis, queen of Assyria, about 2007 B.C. Eunuchs frequently attained to political power in the later Eastern empire.

eu'phuism, an affected style of language, prevalent in the time of Elizabeth, arose from "Euphues, the Anatomy of Wit," by John Lyly, pub. 1579.

Eurasian plain, the great central plain of Europe and Asia, so named by ethnologists (1865). ETHNOLOGY.

Europe, the smallest of 3 continents of the old world, really an appendage of Asia; area, nearly 3,800,000 sq. miles; pop. 1872, 301,700,000; 1891, 380,000,000. For the history, GREECE, ROME, and the modern kingdoms.

Eurym'edon, a river in Pamphylia, near which Cimon, son of Miltiades, destroyed the fleet of the Persians at Cyprus, and defeated their land forces, 466 B.C.

Eusta'tius, St., a West India island, settled by the Dutch, 1632; taken by the French in 1689, by the British in 1690, again by the British forces under Rodney and Vaughan, 3 Feb. 1781. It was recovered by the French under the marquess de Bouillé, 26 Nov. same year; recaptured by the British, 1801, 1810; restored to the Dutch, 1814.

Eutaw Springs, Battle of. One of the most sanguinary battles of the American Revolution was fought at Eutaw Springs, near the Santee river in South Carolina, on 8 Sept. 1781. The Americans were commanded by gen. Greene, and the British by col. Stewart. The conflict was indecisive. Stewart kept the field, but at night retreated towards Charleston. Next morning Greene took possession of the battle-ground, and sent detachments in pursuit. Congress presented a gold medal and a British flag then captured to Greene, in appreciation of his valor. American loss in killed, wounded, and missing, 555. British loss, 693. UNITED STATES.

Euty'chians, from Eutyches, an abbot of Constantinople, who asserted in 446 that there was but one nature in Christ, the human having been absorbed in the divine. This doctrine was condemned by a council at Constantinople in 448, and at Chalcedon in 451. It has been also called *Monophysite* (of one nature), and *Jacobite*, from Jacobus Baradæus, its zealous defender in the 6th century. It is the form of Christianity among the Copts and Armenians.

Eux'ine. BLACK SEA.

Evangelical (Gr. εὐαγγέλιον, good news), of or pertaining to the gospel of Jesus Christ, and specifically applied in England to a portion of the clergy of the Anglican church (also called the low church), who profess to preach the gospel more purely than their brethren termed the high-church party. CHURCH OF ENGLAND.

Evangelical Alliance was founded by sir Culling Eardley Smith and others at Liverpool in 1845, to promote unity among Protestants against Romanism and infidelity. It holds annual meetings. It met in Sept. 1857, at Berlin, where it was well received by the king. The 19th meeting was held at Hull, 3 Oct. 1865, the 20th at Bath 16 Oct. 1866, the 21st at Amsterdam, Aug. 1867, at Derby, 23-28 Nov. 1869. Lord Ebury presided at a day of united prayer for the issue of the general election about to take place, 1 Oct. 1868. The proposed conference at New York in Sept. 1870, deferred on account of the Franco Prussian war, took place Oct. 1873. The Alliance met at Geneva, 23-28 Sept. 1872, at Brighton, 22-24 Apr. 1873, at Oxford 29 Aug. 1874, at Constantinople, March 1875, at Southport, 3 Oct. 1876, at Oxford, 25 Oct. 1877, at Basle, 2 Sept., and at Edinburgh, 28 Oct. 1879.

"Evangelical church" in Germany began with a fusion of the Lutherans and Calvinists in Nassau, 1817, followed by similar movements in different parts of Germany, 1818-22.

Evangelical Association or **Albrecht Brethren.** A sect founded by rev. Jacob Albrecht or Albright, a German Lutheran of Pennsylvania, in 1803. They held their first conference in 1807, and soon after adopted the name of *Die evangelische Gemeinschaft von Nord Amerika*. Their first general conference was held in 1816. In doctrine they are Arminian. They have a college at Plainfield, Ill., and a publishing house at Cleveland, O., with a branch at Stuttgart, Germany. Their strength in 1890 was 26 conferences and missions, 1845 preachers, 145,703 members, and 1958 churches.

Evangelists, preachers of the "gospel," or good news. GOSPELS.

Eves'ham, a town of Worcestershire, Engl., where prince Edward, afterwards Edward I., defeated the barons headed by Simon de Montfort, earl of Leicester, 4 Aug. 1265, when the earl, his son Henry, and most of his adherents were slain. Henry III., when about to be cut down by a soldier who did not know him, was saved by exclaiming, "Do not kill me, soldier, I am Henry of Winchester, thy king!" This victory broke up the combination of the barons.

evolution theory includes the nebular theory and Darwin's doctrine of natural selection DEVELOPMENT, PROGRESSIONISTS

In 1877, 3 forms of evolution were discussed —1 That of all animals gradually from the lowest form, the amœba, up to man, in contrast with the Biblical account of the creation, 2 that of every animal from protoplasm in a cell, or egg, 3 that of all the parts of an animal from its blood

exarchs, appointed by the Byzantine emperors of the east, to govern central Italy after its conquest by Belisarius and Narses, 518 They ruled Ravenna from 568 to 752, when Eutychius, the last, was overcome by Astolphus the Lombard

exchange, formerly *bourse*, the Royal Exchange being "Britain's Burse," that at Paris is still named *La Bourse*, from *bursa*, a purse One called *Collegium Mercatorum* existed at Rome, 495 B.C The Exchange at Amsterdam was reckoned the finest structure of the kind in the world The Stock exchange of New York occupies a marble building on Wall street and numbers 1100 members, with a membership fee or seat at a cost of $21,000 The Produce exchange has a membership of 3000 and the Consolidated Stock and Petroleum exchange a membership of 2362 There are also a Cotton exchange, a Coffee exchange, etc

exchequer, an ancient institution of England, consisting of officers with financial and judicial functions, the chancellor of the exchequer, the financial officer, formerly sat in the court of exchequer above the barons The first chancellor was Eustace de Fauconbridge, bishop of London, in the reign of Henry III, about 1221. Sir Robert Walpole was the last chancellor of the exchequer who acted judicially (1735). The legal function of the chancellor was abolished by the Judicature act, Aug 1873

CHANCELLORS OF THE EXCHEQUER.

Henry Addington (afterwards lord Sidmouth)	21 Mch. 1801
William Pitt (premier)	16 May, 1804
Lord Henry Petty (afterwards marquis of Lansdowne)	10 Feb 1806
Spencer Perceval	31 Mch 1807
Premier 6 Dec 1809, assassinated	11 May, 1812
Nicholas Vansittart (afterwards lord Bexley)	9 June, "
Fred J Robinson (afterwards lord Goderich and earl of Ripon),	31 Jan 1823
George Canning (premier)	Apr 1827
John C. Herries.	17 Aug "
Henry Goulburn	26 Jan 1828
Viscount Althorp (afterwards earl Spencer)	22 Nov 1830
Sir Robert Peel (premier)	10 Dec 1834
Thomas Spring Rice (afterwards lord Monteagle)	18 Apr 1835
Francis T Baring (afterwards baronet)	26 Aug 1839
Henry Goulburn	3 Sept 1841
Charles Wood (afterwards baronet, lord Halifax, 1866)	6 July, 1846
Benjamin Disraeli (afterwards lord Beaconsfield)	21 Feb 1852
William Ewart Gladstone	28 Dec. "
Sir George Cornewall Lewis	5 Mch 1855
Benjamin Disraeli, again	27 Feb 1858
William Ewart Gladstone, again.	June, 1859
Benjamin Disraeli, again	6 July, 1866
George Ward Hunt.	29 Feb 1868
Robert Lowe.	9 Dec "
William Ewart Gladstone (and premier)	Aug 1873
Sir Stafford Northcote	21 Feb 1874
William Ewart Gladstone (and premier)	28 Apr 1880
Hugh Culling E Childers	Dec. 1882
Sir Michael Hicks Beach	24 June, 1885
Sir William V Harcourt	6 Feb 1886
Lord Randolph Henry Spencer Churchill (resigned)	26 July, "
George J Goschen	3 Jan 1887
Sir William V Harcourt	18 Aug 1892

Exchequer, Court of (*Curia Regis*), instituted by William I on the model of the transmarine exchequer of Normandy, in 1079, according to some authorities by Henry I It included the common pleas until they were separated (16 John, 1215).—*Coke's Reports* The exchequer was so named from a checkered cloth which anciently covered the table where the judges and chief officers sat Here are tried causes relating to the king's revenue, to accounts, disbursements, customs, and fines imposed, as well as all matters at common-law between subject and subject The judges are styled barons, first appointed in 1234 There are a chief and 4 puisne barons, the fifth judge having been added 23 July, 1830

excise. The system was established in England by the Long Parliament in 1643, duties being levied on wines, beer, etc., and tobacco, to support the army against Charles I It was continued under Charles II. The present system was enacted about 1733 The old excise office was built on the site of Gresham college in 1744, the present is at Somerset house The officers of excise and customs were deprived of votes for members to Parliament in 1782, but received them again in 1868 In 1849 the boards of excise, stamps, and taxes were united as "the board of commissioners of inland revenue" Notwithstanding the abolition of the excise duty upon numerous articles, and the reduction of duty upon various others of late years, the total excise revenue has progressively advanced Additional excise duties were charged by 17 and 18 Vict c. 27 3 July, 1851 The excise duties were further modified in 1860 REVENUE. For the United States, CUSTOMS, REVENUE

REVENUE FROM EXCISE IN THE UNITED KINGDOM

1786.	£ 5 540 114	1850	£15,278,203
1808	19,867 914	1860	20,240,467
1820	26 364,702	1870	21,579,238
1830	18 644,385	1880.	25,218,303
1840	12,607,766	1890	24,723,917

excommunication, or separation from Christian communion (Matt xviii 17, 1 Cor v, etc), was instituted to preserve the purity of the church The Roman church excommunicated by BELL, BOOK, and CANDLE INTERDICT.

Gregory VII excommunicated the emperor Henry IV, and absolved his subjects from their allegiance	1077
Innocent III excommunicated John of England, placing the country under an interdict.	1208–14
Gregory IX excommunicated the emperor Frederick II 4 times, between	1228–45
Louis XII of France was excommunicated by Julius II 1510, Luther by Leo X 1521, Henry VIII of England by Paul III in 1535, and Elizabeth by Pius V	25 Apr 1570
Emperor of France, king of Sardinia, and others were virtually excommunicated (but not by name) on account of the annexation of the Romagna by Sardinia	29 Mch 1860

executions. In the reign of Henry VIII (38 years), it is said that no less a number than 72,000 criminals were executed —*Stow.* In the 10 years between 1820 and 1830, there were executed in England alone 797 criminals, but as laws were mitigated the number of executions decreased In the 3 years ending 1820, the executions in England and Wales amounted to 312, in the 3 years ending 1830, they were 178, in the 3 years ending 1840, they were 62 In England from 1850-60, 93 executions, from 1860-70, 136, from 1870-80, 163. The place of execution in London (formerly generally at Tyburn) was in front of Newgate from 1783 to 1868, when an act directed executions to take place within the walls of prisons. The dissection of bodies of executed criminals was abolished in 1832 John Calcraft, born 1800, executioner for London, 1828-74, died 13 Dec 1879.—For remarkable executions, TRIALS.—In the United States the legal executions reported for 1891 were 123—52 white, 65 negroes, 1 Mexican, 4 Indians, and 1 Japanese The lynchings reported were 195, all in the western and southern states (Alabama reporting 26 and Mississippi 23) Of these 121 were negroes and 69 were white, with a few Indians, Chinese, and Mexicans Of the 195, 6 were women CRIME, DEATH.

Exeter, a town of Devonshire, Engl., said to have been named *Augusta* from having been occupied by the second Augustan legion commanded by Vespasian, its present name is derived from *Excestre* It was for a considerable time the capital of the West Saxon kingdom The bishopric anciently comprised 2 sees—Devonshire (founded about 909) and Cornwall The church of the former was at Crediton, of the latter at Bodmin, and afterwards at St. German's About 1040 the sees were united. *St Petroc was the first bishop of Cornwall, before* 900, Eadulphus, the first bishop of Devonshire, 905, and Leofric, the first bishop of Exeter, in 1049 The cathedral originally belonged to a monastery founded by Athelstan, Edward the Confessor removed the monks to his new abbey of Westminster, and gave their church for a cathedral to the united see, 1049

Alfred invested the city, held by the Danes, and compelled them to capitulate.	877, 894
Exeter sacked by Sweyn	1003
Besieged by William the Conqueror	1067
Castle surrendered to king Stephen	1136
City first governed by a mayor	1200
Celebrated nunnery founded	1236
Ancient bridge built	1250
Edward I holds a parliament here	1286
Besieged by sir William Courtenay	1469

City assaulted by Perkin Warbeck........................... 1497
Exeter constituted a county of itself.......................... 1536
Welsh, vicar of St. Thomas's, hanged on the tower of his church as a Cornish rebel...............................2 July, 1549
Prince Maurice takes Exeter for king Charles I..........Sept. 1643
It surrenders to the parliamentarians.................Apr. 1646

Exeter college, Oxford, Engl., was founded by Walter Stapleton, bishop of Exeter, in 1314. The buildings are mainly a quadrangle in the later Gothic style.

Exeter hall, Strand, London, erected in 1830-31 for the meetings of religious and philanthropic institutions, concerts, oratorios, and musical societies, a large apartment with orchestra and organ, and rooms attached for committees, etc., opened 29 Mch. 1831. MUSIC. Religious services were held here in 1856 by rev. C. Spurgeon, and in 1857 by ministers of the church of England, on Sundays.

Hall was purchased for the Young Men's Christian Association for 25,000*l*., July, 1880; reopened (jubilee)..........29 Mch. 1881

exhibitions, industrial, began with the French. Expositions having been organized and opened at Paris in 1798, 1801, '02, '06, '19, '23, '27, '34, '39, '44, and '49. The first exhibition of the kind in England was the National Repository, opened under royal patronage in 1828, near Charing Cross. In the United States at New York in 1853. CRYSTAL PALACE. The following is a list of the principal World's Industrial Exhibitions:

Place.	Year.	Acres, Building.	Exhibitors.	Visitors.	Open days.
London........	1851	21	13,937	6,039,195	141
New York.....	1853	4¾	4,000	....	...
Paris..........	1855	24½	20,839	5,162,330	200
London........	1862	23½	28,653	6,211,103	171
Paris..........	1867	37	50,226	8,805,969	217
Vienna	1873	40	50,000	6,740,500	186
Philadelphia...	1876	70.08	30,864	10,164,489	159
Paris..........	1878	60	40,366	16,032,725	194
Paris..........	1889	75½	55,006	28,149,353	185
Chicago.......	1893	142.12	....	27,539,041	158

WORLD'S COLUMBIAN EXHIBITION.

Exodus (Gr. ἔξοδος, way out), the departure of the Israelites from Egypt, 1491 B.C.; and described in the book of Exodus. Chronologers vary in the date of this event: the Septuagint gives 1614; Hales, 1648; Wilkinson, 1495; Bunsen, 1320 or 1314.

expeditions. Lat. *ex*, out, and *pes*, *pedis*, foot; a sending or setting forth of a body of persons on any important enterprise.

MILITARY AND NAVAL EXPEDITIONS. B.C.

Jason and the Argonauts in the ship *Argo* to Colchis.......... 1263
[William Morris' poem "Jason" pub. 1867. ARGONAUTS.]
Greek expedition against Troy, and siege.................1193-84
[Described in the "Iliad" of Homer. TROY.]
Darius into Greece; battle of Marathon...............29 Sept. 490
Xerxes into Greece; battle of Thermopylæ. Salamis (naval), Platæa..480-79
Cyrus against Artaxerxes; retreat of 10,000 Greeks.......... 401
Alexander the Great into Asia; overthrow of the Persian monarchy; battles of Granicus, 334; Issus, 333; Arbela........ 331
Hannibal into Italy; battles of Thrasymene, 217; Cannæ...... 216
Julius Cæsar into Britain; first, 55; second..................... 54
A.D.
Saracens into France; battle of Tours..................10 Oct. 732
Crusades.. 1095-1291
Edward III. of England into France; battle of Crecy.......... 1346
Henry V. of England into France; battle of Agincourt........ 1415
Philip II. of Spain into England; the Armada................ 1588
Napoleon into Russia and retreat (Moscow)................... 1812
British into ABYSSINIA..1867-68

EXPEDITIONS OF DISCOVERY AND COLONIZATION.

Egyptian, of Pharaoh-Necho, Phœnician, down the Arabian gulf around the southern extremity of Africa into the Mediterranean by the strait of Gibraltar, arriving in Egypt after an interval of about 3 years (*Herodotus*).................... B.C. 604
Hanno the Carthaginian along the western coast of Africa..... 570
A.D.
Northmen discover Iceland.. 861
Christopher Columbus discovers America....................... 1492
Vasco de Gama, western coast of Africa, cape of Good Hope, passage to the East Indies.................................... 1497
Fernando de Magellan's voyage around the world...........1520-21
Lewis and Clark, to the mouth of the Columbia river (UNITED STATES)...1805-6
John C. Fremont, throughout the west to the Pacific (UNITED STATES)...1842-46
Lieut. Wilkes, with 6 small vessels of the U. S. navy (*Vincennes*, *Peacock*, *Porpoise*, *Relief*, *Flying-fish*, and *Sea-gull*), sails from Hampton Roads, Va., to explore the southern seas, 19 Aug. 1838
They discover an antarctic continent.................19 July, 1839
Peacock lost on the bar at the mouth of the Columbia river, July, 1841
Vincennes, Wilkes's flag-ship, returns to New York after an absence of almost 4 years...................................June, 1842
[Wilkes's "Narrative" was pub. in 6 vols. illustrated. The scientific reports form 20 quarto and folio vols.]
Voyage of the British steamer *Challenger* to examine into the physical and biological condition of the great ocean basins and oceanic currents (DEEP-SEA SOUNDINGS)................ 1872

EXPEDITIONS OF SEARCH AND RELIEF.

In search of sir John Franklin...................................1848-60
Henry M. Stanley in search of David Livingstone (AFRICA).... 1872
Engineer Melville in search of the survivors of the U. S. yacht *Jeannette*...24 Mch. 1882
Commander W. S. Schley in search of lieut. A. Greely (NORTHEAST and NORTHWEST PASSAGE)................................ 1884
Henry M. Stanley to relieve Emin Pacha.......................1887-90
For minor expeditions, AMERICA, NORTHEAST and NORTHWEST PASSAGE, and separate governments throughout the work.

expenditures of the United States. The principal objects of expenditure in the U. S. are civil, army, navy, Indians, pensions, interest. Premiums on bonds purchased were also quite an important source of expenditure during the years 1867-74, and 1889-91.

EXPENDITURE FOR EACH OF THE YEARS NAMED, AND THEREFROM ITS GENERAL INCREASE.

Year.	Civil and Miscellaneous.	War.	Navy.	Indians.	Pensions.	Premiums.	Interest.	Total.
1789-91	$1,083,972	$632,804	....	$27,000	$175,814	....	$1,177,863	$3,097,453
1800	1,337,613	2,560,879	$3,448,716	31	64,131	....	3,402,601	10,813,971
1810	1,101,145	2,294,324	1,654,244	177,625	83,744	....	3,163,671	8,474,753
1820	2,592,022	2,630,392	4,387,990	315,750	3,208,376	....	5,151,004	18,285,534
1830	3,237,416	4,767,129	3,239,429	622,262	1,363,297	....	[illegible],212,575	15,142,108
1840	5,995,399	7,095,267	6,113,897	2,331,795	2,603,562	....	174,598	24,314,518
1850	16,043,763	9,687,025	7,904,725	1,663,591	1,866,886	....	3,782,393	40,948,383
1860	27,977,978	16,472,203	11,514,650	2,991,122	1,100,802	....	3,144,121	63,200,876
1865	42,989,383	1,030,690,400	122,617,434	5,059,360	16,347,621	1,717,900	77,395,090	1,296,817,188
1870	53,237,462	57,655,675	21,780,230	3,407,938	28,340,202	15,996,556	129,235,498	309,653,561
1880	54,713,530	38,116,916	13,536,985	5,945,457	56,777,174	2,795,320	95,757,575	267,642,958
1890	81,403,256	44,582,838	22,006,206	6,708,047	106,936,855	20,304,244	36,099,284	318,040,711
TOTAL EXPENDITURES FROM 1789 TO 1891 INCLUSIVE.								
....	2,368,670,150	4,777,863,340	1,207,598,473	264,471,240	1,373,889,939	122,902,713	2,682,025,768	12,797,421,623

As there was no national debt in 1836-37 there was no interest—the only years without interest.

The expenditures for the United Kingdom of Great Britain show as follows for the years given—gross amount.

1860	£69,502,289
1865	66,462,207
1870	68,864,752
1875	74,328,040
1880	84,105,754
1887	90,869,282
1891	87,377,000

REVENUE.

explosives. BLASTING, DUALINE, DYNAMITE, GELATINE, GLYOXILINE, GUN-COTTON, GUNPOWDER, LITHOFRACTEUR, NITRO-GLYCERINE, etc.

exports, United States. Specie value, from 1790.

	Domestic Merchandise.	Domestic Gold and Silver.
1790	$19,666,000	....
1800	31,840,906	....
1810	42,366,675	....
1820	51,683,640	....
1830	58,524,878	$937,151
1840	111,660,561	2,235,073
1850	134,900,233	2,046,679
1860	356,242,423	56,946,851
1870	455,208,341	43,883,803
1880	823,946,353	9,347,893
1890	845,293,828	35,782,189

The greatest amount of domestic merchandise exported in any one year was in 1881, amounting to $883,925,947. The greatest amount of gold and silver, in 1875, $83,857,129, and in 1889, $80,214,994. The percentage of exported agricultural products was, in 1860, 81.13; 1870, 79.35; 1880, 83.25; 1890, 74.51 of the whole amount. The exports of the U. S. to the principal foreign countries were, to

Great Britain	1880	$453,796,497
	1890	447,895,662
Germany	1880	57,062,263
	1890	85,563,312
France	1880	100,063,044
	1890	49,977,024
Canada	1880	30,775,871
	1890	41,503,812
Belgium	1880	34,154,180
	1890	26,630,444
Netherlands	1880	17,207,098
	1890	22,657,795
Spain	1880	14,657,884
	1890	12,758,463
Italy	1880	12,352,642
	1890	13,068,096
Cuba	1880	11,225,699
	1890	13,084,415
Mexico	1880	7,866,493
	1890	13,285,287

The next in order are Australia, Brazil, and Japan.

AMOUNT OF DOMESTIC EXPORTS FROM THE UNITED KINGDOM.

	Exports to Foreign Countries.	Exports to British Colonies.	Exports. Totals.
1856–60 average	£84,000,000	£40,000,000	£124,000,000
1861–65 average	97,000,000	47,000,000	144,000,000
1866–70 average	137,000,000	51,000,000	188,000,000
1871–75 average	175,000,000	64,000,000	239,000,000
1876–80 average	134,000,000	67,000,000	201,000,000
1881–85 average	151,000,000	81,000,000	232,000,000
1886–90 average	155,000,000	81,000,000	236,000,000

IMPORTS.

Extradition, Treaty of. Treaties on the subject of criminals arise from the universal practice of nations to surrender criminals only under special treaty with the country which claims them. Treaties of this character have been made between the United States and Great Britain, 9 Aug. 1842; with France, 9 Nov. 1843; and later supplemented Switzerland, 25 Nov. 1850; Austria, 3 July, 1856; Sweden and Norway, 21 Mch. 1860; Mexico, 11 Dec. 1861; Italy, 23 Mch. 1868, and later; Ottoman empire, 5 Jan. 1877. In the treaty with Belgium, 1882, attempted assassination of a ruler made an extraditable offence; treaty with Spain, 1887; with Uruguay, 1887, with Prussia, 1892, and others. The crimes for which extradition is usually granted are forgery, burglary, embezzlement, counterfeiting, grand larceny, manslaughter, murder, perjury, rape, and other felonies. In modern states, particularly in England and the U. S., political offences have always been excepted from extradition. Great Britain refused to surrender Ezra D. Winslow, of Boston, who, charged with forgery, escaped to London, 1872, unless it was agreed that the prisoner should be tried only for that offence, according to the treaty. Mr. Fish, the secretary of state, stood on the Ashburton treaty of 1842. The British government yielded, 27 Oct. 1876. William M. Tweed escaped from New York to Spain, was arrested there, and returned to the U. S., although there was no extradition treaty between the countries, Sept. 1876. Difficulty arose with Mexico, 1877, regarding the pursuit of criminals across the border. The Sicilian bandit Randazzo was captured in New Orleans, 1881, and taken to New York, whence he was extradited on the requisition of the Italian government.

extreme unction. ANOINTING.

Eylau, a town of E. Prussia, where, on 7–8 Feb. 1807, the French defeated the Russians in a bloody contest. Napoleon commanded in person. Both armies, by this and other battles, were so much reduced that the French retired to the Vistula and the Russians on the Pregel.

F

Fa'bii. A noble family of Rome, the name said to come from *faba*, a bean, because their ancestors cultivated beans; or from Fabius, a son of Hercules. They made war against the people of Veii, and near the Cremera all the grown-up males of the family (306 men) were slain in a sudden attack, 477 B.C. From one, Q. Fabius Vibulanus, whose tender age had detained him at Rome, arose the noble Fabii of the following ages. Q. Fabius Maximus Verrucosus, a celebrated general of Rome, successfully opposed Hannibal, 216 B.C. He devised a system of defensive warfare since known as "Fabian," and was himself called *Cunctator*, the delayer.

fables. "Jotham's fable of the trees (Judg. ix., about 1209 B.C.) is the oldest extant, and as beautiful as any made since."—*Addison.* Nathan's fable of the poor man (2 Sam. xii., about 1034 B.C.) is next in antiquity. The oldest collection of fables is of Eastern origin, and in Sanscrit. The fables of Vishnoo Sarma, or Pilpay, are the most beautiful, if not the most ancient, in the world.—*Sir William Jones.* Prof. Max Müller traced La Fontaine's fable of the "Milkmaid" to the early Sanscrit. ÆSOP'S FABLES, dated about 565 or 620 B.C., were versified by Babrius, a Greek poet, about 130 B.C. (*Coray*), and rewritten in prose by Maximus Planudes, a Greek monk, about 1320, who added other fables and a worthless life of Æsop. The fables of Phædrus, in Latin iambics (about 8 A.D.), of La Fontaine (1700), and of Gay (1727), are esteemed.

facial angle (contained by a line from the middle of the ear to the edge of the nostrils, and another thence to the ridge of the frontal bone) was devised by Peter Camper to measure the elevation of the forehead. In negroes this angle is about 70°; in Europeans varies from 75° to 85°. Camper died 7 Apr. 1789. His book on "Characteristic Marks of Countenance" was pub. 1791.

factions of the circus, among the Romans, were parties of racers with chariots in the circus, distinguished by colors, as green, blue, red, and white; Domitian added gold and scarlet, about 90 A.D. In Jan. 532, an insurrection occurred at Constantinople, called the *Nika sedition*, which lasted 5 days, about 30,000 lives were lost, and Justinian was indebted for his life and throne to the heroism of his empress Theodora. The blues and greens (political parties named for the colors worn in the races of the circus) united for a day or two against the emperor, taking *Nika!* (conquer) for a watchword. The blues soon turned, and massacred the greens. The conflict was suppressed by Belisarius with difficulty, and the games were abolished for a time. Described fully by the contemporary historian Procopius; briefly in Gibbon's "Decline and Fall of the Roman Empire."

Faen'za, a city of central Italy, the ancient Faventia, submitted to the emperor Frederick I., 1162; was taken by Frederick II., 12 Apr. 1241; held by the pope, 1275; by the Bolognese, 1282; by Cæsar Borgia, 1501; by Venice, 1504; by the papacy, 1509; by the French, 1512. After various changes early in the 16th century it was held by the papacy till the annexation by Sardinia, 1859. Hence Faïence pottery is named, first made here.

"Faerie Queene," by Edmund Spenser; a part was pub. in England in 1590; the whole, 1611.

Fahrenheit. THERMOMETER.

Fainéants (*fa-na-on'*). MAYORS OF THE PALACE.

Fairlop oak, with a trunk 48 feet in circumference, the growth of 5 centuries, in Hainault forest, Essex, Engl., was blown down in Feb. 1820. Beneath its branches an annual fair was long held on the 1st Friday in July, founded by the eccentric Mr. Day, a pump and block maker of Wapping, who, having a small estate in the vicinity, annually came here with friends to dine on beans and bacon

Fair Oaks, near Richmond Va, the site of an indecisive battle between confederates, under gen Joseph E Johnston, and a part of the army of the Potomac, 31 May and 1 June, 1862 PENINSULAR CAMPAIGN, VIRGINIA

fairs and **wakes** were instituted in Italy about 500, in England by Alfred, 886.—*Spelman* At wakes, established by Gregory VII in 1078, and termed *feriæ*, monks celebrated the festival of their patron saint the concourse of people occasioned a great demand for goods Fairs were established in France about 800 by Charlemagne, and encouraged in England about 1071 by William the Conqueror Many statutes were made for the regulation of fairs (1328-1868) The "Fairs act," passed 25 May, 1871, abolishes fairs, in 1872, Charlton and Blackheath fairs, and in 1873 Clapham fair, were abolished as nuisances.—In the United States the term *fair* has mostly lost its Old World meaning, and is applied to industrial exhibitions including township, county, and state fairs Certain state fairs have assumed an importance almost national WORLD'S COLUMBIAN EXHIBITION

falconry, or **hawking,** the use of trained birds of prey in the pursuit of smaller game, in England cannot be traced with certainty before the reign of king Ethelbert, the Saxon monarch, 858 —*Pennant* The grand seignior at one time kept 6000 falconers in his service Juliana Berners's book on "Hawkynge and Huntynge" was printed in 1496 ANGLING Recent attempts have been made in England to revive falconry. Hawking was practised in Thrace —*Aristotle*

Falczi (*fal'-shee*), a town on the Pruth, Turkey Here was concluded a peace between Russia and Turkey, 21 July, 1711, the Russians giving up Azof, and all possessions on the Black sea, to the Turks The Russians were saved from destruction by the address of Catherine, the empress In 1712 the war was renewed, until the peace of Constantinople, 16 Apr 1712

Faler'ii, a city of the Falisci, Etruscans who joined the Veii against Rome, and were beaten by Cornelius Cossus, 437 B.C When the city was besieged by Camillus in 394, a schoolmaster offered to betray the children of the principal citizens into his hands. On his refusal, the citizens from gratitude surrendered They opposed Rome in the first Punic war, and in 241 the city was taken and destroyed

Falernian wine, celebrated by Virgil and Horace, was the produce of Falernus, or, as called by Martial, Mons Massicus, in Campania Horace, in his ode "Ad Amphoram" —"To a jar of wine"—probably 31 B C, speaks of the wine as born with him in the consulate of Manlius Torquatus, "*O nata mecum Consule Manlio,*" which makes its age 34 years, as Horace was born 65 B.C

Falkirk, a town of Stirlingshire, Scotland, the site of a victory by the English under Edward I over the Scots, under Wallace, part of whose forces deserted It is said from 20,000 to 40,000 Scots were slain, 22 July, 1298 In a battle at Falkirk muir royal forces under Hawley were defeated by prince Charles Edward Stuart, 17 Jan 1746

Falkland islands, a group in the South Atlantic, about 100 in number (the 2 principal being East and West Falkland) between lat 51° and 52° S., and lon. 57° and 62° W, belonging to Great Britain, seen by Americus Vespucius, 1502, and visited by Davis, 1592, explored by Hawkins, 1594, seized by France, 1764 The French were expelled by the Spaniards, and in 1771 Spain yielded to England. The republic of Buenos Ayres afterwards claimed the islands, and a colony from that country settled at Port Louis, but in a dispute with the U S the settlement was destroyed in 1831 In 1833 the British flag was hoisted at Port Louis, and a British officer has since resided there Area of East Falkland 3000 sq miles, and of West Falkland 2300 sq. miles, of the whole group 6500 sq miles. Pop 1893 about 2000

famines. The famine of the 7 years in Egypt began 1708 B C.—*Usher, Blair*

	B C
At Rome, thousands threw themselves into the Tiber	436
	A D.
Awful in Egypt	42
At Rome, attended by plague	262
In Britain, people ate the bark of trees	272
In Scotland, thousands died	306
In England, 40,000 perished	310
Awful in Phrygia	370
In Italy parents ate their children (*Dufresnoy*)	450
In England, Wales and Scotland	739
Again, when thousands starve.	823
Again which lasts 4 years	954
Awful throughout Europe.	1016
In England 21 William I	1087
In England and France, followed by pestilential fever	1193-95
Again in England	1251
Again people devoured horses, dogs cats, and vermin	1315
Occasioned by long rains	1336
In England and France (*Rapin*)	1353
Again, bread made from fern roots (*Stow*)	1438
Throughout Britain	1565
Awful in France (*Voltaire*)	1693
General in Britain	1748
Devastates Bengal	1771
At Cape Verd, 16,000 persons perish	1775
Grievous in France, hastened the French revolution	1789
Severe in England	1795
Throughout Britain	1801
At Drontheim, Sweden intercepting the supplies	1813
Scarcity of food for Irish poor, 1814, 16, 22 '31, '46 by failure of the potato crop Grants by Parliament, to relieve suffering made in 1847, in all $50 000 000	
In N W India, above 800 000 perish	1837-38
In N W India, thousands perish	*1860-61*
In Bengal and Orissa, about 1,000 000 perish	1865-66
In Rajpootana etc, about 1,500,000 perish	1868-69
In Persia very severe	1871-72
In Bengal through drought	1874
In Asia Minor	1874-75
In Bombay, Madras Mysore, etc, about 500,000 perish	1877
In N China, very severe, 9,500,000 said to have perished ($225,000 collected in England for relief)	1877-78
In Cashmere	1879
Very severe in Taurus, etc, in Asia Minor	July, 1880
Very severe in Russia	1891-92

fan. Used by the ancients, *Cape hoc flabellum, et venta um hunc sic facito*—"Take this fan, and give her thus a little air"—*Terence's* "Eunuchus," 166 B.C Fans, together with muffs, masks, and false hair, were first devised by demi-monde in Italy, and were brought to England from France —*Stow* In the British museum are Egyptian fan-handles

Faneuil (*fan'-el*) **hall,** the "Cradle of Liberty," built by Peter Faneuil a Huguenot merchant of Boston, in 1742, and presented to the city It was rebuilt in 1768 The lower story was used as a market It was a meeting-place of the people during the disputes with Great Britain which led to the War of Independence, hence the name "Cradle of Liberty"

faradiza'tion, the medical application of magneto-electric currents which Faraday discovered in 1837 The apparatus was first made by M Pixii, and employed by dr Neef of Frankfort on-the-Main *Farad*, name taken for a unit of electric capacity, 1875 ELECTRICITY

farce, a short comic drama, usually of one or two acts. One by Otway is dated 1677. The best English farces (by Foote, Garrick, Bickerstaff, etc) appeared from 1740 to 1780 They originated in droll shows exhibited by charlatans and buffoons in the streets DRAMA

Farmers' Alliance. POLITICAL PARTIES.

farmers-general. FERMIERS.

Farnese family became important through the elevation of Alexander Farnese to the papacy as Paul III He gave his natural son Peter the duchy of Parma, Italy, and his descendants ruled till Antony died, without issue, 1731 Alexander, prince of Parma, was governor of the Netherlands in 1579

farthing, an early English coin. Farthings in silver were coined by king John, the Irish farthing of his reign (1210) is rare. Farthings were coined in England in silver by Henry VIII First coined in copper by Charles II, 1665, again in 1672, in a large coinage of copper money Half-farthings were first coined in 1843. QUEEN ANNE'S FARTHINGS

Fasti Capitolini, marble tablets found in the forum at Rome, 1547, contain a list of consuls and other officers from the year of Rome 250 to 765 Other fragments were found in 1817 and 1818. The "Fasti Consulares," from 509 B C to 235 A D, are given in Smith's "Dictionary of Greek and Roman Antiquities."

fasts, observed by many nations from remote antiquity by the Jews (2 Chron xx 3), by the Ninevites (Jonah iii), see Isa lviii A fast of the Jews was the great day of atonement, Lev xxiii, 1490 B C Moses fasted 40 days and nights on Sinai (Exod xxiv), 1491 B C The first Christian ministers were ordained with fasting (45 A D) Acts xiii 2 Annual fasts, as that of Lent, and at other stated times, and fasts on particular occasions to appease the anger of God, began in the church in the 2d century (138) The Mahometan fast is termed RAMADAN —Days of humiliation, fasting, and prayer appointed by the presidents of the United States

Wednesday	9 May, 1798,	by president	John Adams.
Thursday	12 Jan 1815,	" "	Madison
Last Thursday of	Sept. 1861,	" "	Lincoln
Thursday	30 Apr 1863,	" "	"
First Thursday in	Aug 1864,	" "	"
Thursday	1 June, 1865,	" "	Johnson
Monday	26 Sept 1881,	" "	Arthur

fathers of the church. The following are the principal

1st century —Greek
Apostolical

Hermas	
Barnabas	
Clemens Romanus	d 100
Ignatius	d 115
Polycarp	d about 169

2d century —Greek

Justin Martyr	d about 166
Irenæus	d about 200
Athenagoras.	

3d century —Greek

Clemens Alexandrinus,	d abt 217
Hippolytus	d 230
Origen	d about 253

Latin

Tertullian	d about 220
Minutius Felix	fl about 230
Cyprian	d about 258

4th and 5th centuries.—Greek

Eusebius	d about 340
Athanasius	d 373
Ephrem Syrus	d about 378
Basil	d 379
Cyril of Jerusalem	d 386
Gregory Nazianzen	d 389
Macarius	d about 391
Gregory Nyssen	d about 394
Epiphanius	d 403
John Chrysostom	d. 407
Cyril of Alexandria	d 444
Theodoret	d 457

Latin

Arnobius	fl 303
Lactantius	d about 330
Ambrose	d 397
Jerome	d 420
Augustine	d 430

Fat'imites. ALI, MAHOMETANISM

fats are oils solid at ordinary temperatures The researches of Chevreul since 1811 on their chemical nature are very important. CANDLES

Faustus, a professor of magic, renowned in chap-books, flourished about 1500 A D Goethe's dramatic poem "Faust" appeared in 1790

feasts and **festivals.** The "Feasts of the Lord"—viz, those of the Passover, Pentecost, Trumpets, and Tabernacles—were instituted 1490 B C (Lev xxiii)

Feast of Tabernacles, at dedication of Solomon s temple, 1004 B C
Hezekiah (726 B C) and Josiah (623) kept the feast of Passover
In the Christian church, the feasts of Christmas Easter Ascension, and the Pentecost or WHITSUNTIDE, are said to date from the 1st century
Rogation days appointed 469
Jubilees in the Romish church were instituted by Boniface VIII in 1300 JUBILEES

The Christian festivals of the church are·

Fixed	All Saints or All Hallows	1 Nov
"	All Souls	2 Nov
"	Christmas or the Nativity	25 Dec
"	Innocents	28 Dec.
"	Circumcision	1 Jan
"	Epiphany or Twelfth day	6 Jan
"	Candlemas-day	2 Feb
"	Lady day	25 Mch

Movable Ascension day or Holy Thursday
Ash Wednesday, Easter Sunday, Good Friday, Palm Sunday, Sexagesima Sunday, Trinity Sunday, see under separate articles. The date of these days depends on the date of Easter Besides these there are the Saints or Red Letter days, fixed
Of the festivals of the Greeks the principal were The Agraulia, in honor of the daughter of Cecrops. Artemisia, in honor of Artemis (Diana) Dionysia in honor of Dionysus (Bacchus)—the Bacchanalia of the Romans, Eleusinia, the most celebrated of any in Greece, latter part of Sept. and first part of Oct, Panathenaia, in honor of Athene (Minerva)
Of the Romans Agonalia, in honor of Janus Bacchanalia, in honor of Bacchus, suppressed in 186 B C. Faunalia, in honor of Faunus, celebrated 13 Feb, or the ides of the month (on this date occurred the slaughter of the Fabii) Lupercalia, in honor of the god Pan, 15 Feb Liberalia in honor of Liber, the Roman Bacchus Cerealia in honor of Ceres Persons in mourning could not attend this celebration, and therefore it was not observed in the year after the battle of Cannæ. Bona Dea ("the Good Goddess"), she was worshipped by the Roman matrons in the house of the chief pontiff, and the male sex was carefully excluded, no man ever entered her temple Saturnalia, in honor of Saturn, the most remarkable one in the Roman year, at first lasting but 1 day (19 Dec), but afterwards extended to 7 During its continuance the senate did not sit, the schools were closed, no war was proclaimed, no criminal executed, while the utmost liberty and good will prevailed

February (Lat. *Februum*, originally from the Sabine language, signifying a purgative), the 2d month, in which the Romans celebrated Februa, festivals of purification and expiation on the 15th of the month, for the manes of the dead This month with January, was added to the year by Numa, about 713 B C

fecia'les or **fetia'les,** 20 in number, heralds of Rome to announce war or proclaim peace, appointed by Numa, about 712 B C

federal, federalists. POLITICAL PARTIES.

felony, in English law (Blackstone, 1723-80), comprises every species of crime which occasions the forfeiture of land and goods

fencing, recently revived in England and the United States as a sport, was introduced into England from France, but to prevent duelling, fencing-schools were prohibited by law in 1285 Scott's "Fencing Master" was pub. in Edinburgh by sir W Hope in 1687, and a society to encourage the art was formed in Scotland in 1692

Fe'nians (the name of ancient Irish militia, Fianna Eirin), a "brotherhood" in the United States and Ireland united to liberate Ireland and establish a republic The agitation was begun, it is said, by Stephens, in Mch 1858, and in 1864 enlistments and secret drillings took place The leaders were called "head-centres" A convention was formed in 1863 in the U S The movement was opposed by the Roman Catholic clergy IRELAND

Fenian riot at the Rotondo, Dublin 22 Feb. 1864
Twenty five persons arrested in Dublin, and the newspaper *Irish People* (established Sept 1863) seized, 15 Sept, others arrested at Cork, etc 16-30 Sept 1865
Fenians in the U S assert in an address that officers are going to Ireland to organize an army of 200,000 Sept "
Allocution of the pope, condemning secret societies. 30 Sept. "
O Donovan and 5 others committed for high treason 2 Oct "
A Fenian provisional government at New York, and a congress of 600 members held at Philadelphia Oct "
Capture of James Stephens, Irish head-centre, 11 Nov, he escapes from jail 24 Nov "
Habeas corpus act suspended in Ireland, about 250 suspected persons arrested immediately 17 Feb 1866
Mass meeting in New York, threats to invade Canada 4 Mch. "
Fenian schooner *Friend* captures British schooner *Wentworth*, and scuttles her near Eastport Me 1 May, "
James Stephens arrives in New York 10 May, "
Col O Niel and Fenians cross the Niagara and enter Canada, 31 May, met by volunteers, with bloodshed 2 June, "
Sweeny and others arrested . 6, 7 June, "
Pres Johnson's proclamation against the Fenians 7 June, "
Spear and others cross boundary near Vermont, 7 June, corps demoralized, many return 9 June, "
Trials in Canada—col Lynch and rev John MacMahon (sentenced to be hanged on 13 Dec) reprieved 24-26 Oct. "
James Stephens, "central organizer of the Irish republic," said to sail from U S 24 Nov "
Britain offers 2000*l* for his apprehension . Nov "
Sweeny (released) rejoins the U S army Jan 1867
Fenians enter Chester, repulsed 11, 12 Feb "
Outbreak in Kerry, Killarney threatened, capt Moriarty and others captured 12 Feb. "
Gen Massey captured 4 or 6 Mch "
Proclamation of the Irish republic sent to the London *Times* and other papers 6 Mch "
Fenian rising near Dublin, telegraph destroyed, attack on police station at Tallaght repelled, several shot, 208 prisoners taken into Dublin 7 Mch. "
One thousand Fenians hold market place at Drogheda, but retreat at approach of police 7 Mch. "
Capt. Maclure captured 31 Mch. "
Special commission to try 230 Fenians—Whiteside, chief-justice, Deasy and Fitzgerald, begin (Massey, Keogh, Corydon, and McGough, approvers) 9 Apr et seq "
Burke and Doran sentenced to death 1 May, reprieved, 26 May, "
Many convictions of treason (M'Afferty, M'Clure, and others) and treason felony, and many discharged May, "
Pres Roberts retires, party in U S said to be demoralized, July, "
Many arrests, 23 on charge of murder, tried, 5 condemned to death (2 reprieved), 7 sentenced to 7 years' imprisonment, 29 Oct.-12 Nov "
Allen, Gould, and Larkin executed at Salford 23 Nov "
Address of Fenian brotherhood of U S to "liberty loving people of England," dated New York 12 Dec "
Explosion at Clerkenwell House of Detention, London, to release Burke and Casey, leading Fenians, at 3 45 (A cask of gunpowder was fired close to the prison wall, Timothy Desmond, Jeremiah Allen, and Ann Justice arrested on suspicion) 13 Dec. "

Reunion of Roberts and Stephens parties under a new president about 20 Dec 1867
Mullany a prisoner turns queen's evidence, and accuses Barrett or Jackson (captured at Glasgow, 14 Jan) of firing the barrel at Clerkenwell 28 Jan 1868
O'Farrell, a Fenian, wounds the duke of Edinburgh at Port Jackson, 12 Mch , sentenced to death 31 Mch "
Darcy M Gee, M P shot dead by a Fenian at Ottawa 7 Apr "
Trial of Wm and Timothy Desmond, Nicholas English John O Keefe, Michael Barrett and Ann Justice, for murder (Clerkenwell outrage) begun 20, acquittal of Justice, 23, of O Keefe, 24, and of the 2 Desmonds and English 27 Conviction of Barrett 27 Apr "
Michael Barrett executed 26 May, "
O Donovan Rossa and others released Mch 1869
Fenian raid into Canada repelled by militia, gen Neill captured by U S marshal 26 May, 1870
Michael Davitt and John Wilson convicted of treason felony 18 July, "
Pres Grant s proclamation against Fenian raids into Canada, 13 Oct "
Mr Gladstone promises release of Fenian convicts 15 Dec "
Convicts released Jan 1871
Fenians favor the French in the war Aug 1870–Feb "
Fenian raid into Manitoba suppressed by U S troops and gen Neill arrested (IRELAND) about 12 Oct "
Gen Cluseret (a short time in the service of the Fenians) describes them in *Fraser's Magazine*, he says "Their insurrection was foolishly planned and still more foolishly executed," and advises reconciliation with England July, 1872
Escape of Fenian prisoners from W Australia in the *Catalpa*, American ship, 17 Apr , arrive at New York 19 Aug 1876
O'Mahony, head centre d at New York, grand funeral service, 6 Feb. 1877
Michael Davitt and other Fenian convicts released Jan -Sept 1878
Again arrested and committed to prison 3, 4 Feb 1881
Michael Davitt elected M P for county Meath 22 Feb 1882
Convention at Philadelphia opened, 25 Apr , denounced by O'Donovan Rossa, who revives the Irish Revolutionary Brotherhood 6 May, 1883
Capt Thos Phelan stabbed (not killed) as a suspected traitor by Richard Short, in Rossa s office, New York, 9 Jan , O Donovan Rossa shot in the street by Lucille Yseult Dudley, an English widow (declared insane), aged 25, 2 Feb , Phelan and he recover, in the same hospital Feb 1885
Great Fenian congress at Paris . 23 Feb 1888
Michael Davitt elected M P for N Meath July, 1892

Fere-Champenoise (*fare-shamp-nwas'*), a village of France Here the French army under Marmont, Mortier, and Arrighi were surprised and defeated by the allies under the prince of Schwarzenberg, 25 Mch 1814, after an heroic resistance Paris surrendered 6 days after

Fergus MacIvor of Scott's "Waverley " The original was maj Donald MacDonald, executed 18 Oct 1746, with 8 others

Feriæ Latinæ, Roman festivals ascribed to Tarquin the Proud, about 531 B C The principal magistrates of 47 Latin towns met on a mount near Rome, and with the Roman authorities offered a bull to Jupiter Latialis.

fermentation, termed by Gay-Lussac one of the most mysterious processes in nature, he showed in a memoir, 1810, that in the process 45 lbs of sugar are resolved into 23 of alcohol and 22 of carbonic acid In 1861 Pasteur showed that fermentation depends on minute organisms in the fermenting fluid, derived from the atmosphere For his researches he was awarded an annual pension of 12 000 francs in 1874

fermiers généraux (*fair-me-ay' ja-na-rau'*), officers who farmed the French revenues before 1789, often oppressively There were 60 of them at the beginning of the French revolution Lavoisier and 27 of these were executed 8 May, 1794

Ferozeshah', a town of the Punjab, India. The British, under sir Hugh Gough, attacked the entrenched Sikhs, and carried their first line, 21 Dec 1845, but night coming on, the operations were suspended till daybreak, when the second line was stormed by gen Gilbert, and 74 guns captured The Sikhs advanced to retake their guns, were repulsed with great loss, and retreating to the Sutlej, 22 Dec , recrossed the river unmolested, 27 Dec British loss reckoned at 2415

Ferra'ra, part of the exarchate of Ravenna, under the emperors of the East, subdued by the Lombards in the 8th century, and taken about 752 by Pepin, who gave it to pope Stephen II. About 1208 it fell to the house of ESTE, and became the principal seat of literature and fine arts in Italy Pope Clement VIII obtained the sovereignty in 1598, on the death of duke Alphonso II, last legitimate male of the Este family. His illegitimate nephew, Cæsar, became duke of Modena The French under Massena took Ferrara in 1796, but it was restored to the pope in 1814 An Austrian garrison held it from 1849, it retired in June, 1859, and the people demanded annexation to Sardinia, which was accomplished in Mch 1860

Ferrars's arrest. In Mch 1542, George Ferrars a member of Parliament, while at the house, was seized by a sheriff's officer for debt, and committed to the Compter prison The house despatched a sergeant to require his release, which was resisted and, in the affray, his mace was broken The house in a body repaired to the Lords to complain, when the contempt was adjudged to be great, and the punishment was referred to the lower house On another message to the sheriffs by the Commons they delivered up the member and the civil magistrates and creditor were committed to the Tower, the inferior officers to Newgate, and an act passed released Ferrars from liability for the debt Henry VIII approved all these proceedings, from which dates the rule of Parliament exempting members from arrest —*Holinshed*

Ferro, the most western Canary isle, from whose west point some geographers take their first meridian, was known to the ancients, and was rediscovered in 1402

Ferrol, a seaport town of N W Spain Upwards of 10,000 British landed near Ferrol under sir James Pulteney, in Aug 1800, and occupied the heights, but, despairing of success, from the strength of the works, sir James re-embarked His conduct was condemned Soult captured Ferrol, 27 Jan 1809 An insurrection of about 1500 men in the arsenal, headed by brigadier Pozas and capt Montojo, raised the red flag, 11 Oct 1872 They dispersed or surrendered, fearing attack 17 Oct.

Fescen'nine verses were rude extemporary dialogues, frequently licentious, in favor among the ancient Etruscans at weddings, and still popular in Italy

festivals. FEASTS, MUSIC

Fête Dieu, a feast of the Roman church in honor of the real presence in the Lord's supper, on the Thursday after Trinity Sunday CORPUS CHRISTI Berengarius, archbishop of Angers opposed transubstantiation and to atone for his crime a yearly procession was made at Angers, called *la fête de Dieu*, 1019

feudal laws. The tenure of land by suit and service to lord or owner, in use in England by the Saxons, about 600, was extended by William I in 1066 The kingdom was divided into baronies, given on condition of furnishing the king men and money The vassalage, limited by Henry VII., 1495, was abolished by statute, 1660 The feudal system was introduced in Scotland by Malcolm II in 1008, and the hereditary jurisdictions were abolished in that kingdom, 1746-47. Feudal laws, established in France by Clovis I about 486, were discountenanced by Louis XI in 1470

Feuillants (*feu yäns'*), a religious order of reformed Cistercians, founded by Jean de la Barrière in 1577 at the abbey of Feuillant (whence the name), near Toulouse, and settled in Paris in 1587 The Feuillant club, formed in Paris by Lafayette and others in 1789, to counteract the intrigues of Jacobins was named from the convent where they met. A body of Jacobins burst into their hall and dispersed them, 25 Dec 1791, and the club broke up in 1792

Fez (in the ancient Mauritania, Africa), a city of Morocco, founded by Edris, a descendant of Mahomet, about 787, was long capital of the kingdom of Fez After long struggles, it was annexed to Morocco about 1550 Leo Africanus describes it as containing more than 700 temples, mosques, and other public edifices, in the 12th century

fictions. ROMANCES Fictions in law are the formal or pretended observance of a rule of law which is really obsolete, such as the plea of citizenship in Roman courts, which was necessary to the jurisdiction, but could not be disputed, even if known to be false See Maine, "Ancient Law," p 26 Lord Mansfield, in the court of King's Bench, declared that "no fiction of law shall ever so far prevail against the real truth as to prevent the execution of justice," 31 May, 1781 They have been mostly abolished

"Fidelio," Beethoven's only opera, composed in 1804, produced first at Vienna, 20 Nov 1805

Fide'næ, a Sabine city, often at war with Rome It was captured and the inhabitants enslaved, 426 B C, by the Romans, whose ambassadors they had slain

Field of the Cloth of Gold, a plain near Ardres and Calais, in France, on which Henry VIII met Francis I of France, 7-25 June, 1520 The nobility of both kingdoms displayed their magnificence, and many involved themselves in debt Paintings of the embarkation and interview are at Windsor castle CHAMP DE MARS

Fieschi's (*fe-es'-kee*) **attempt** on the life of Louis Philippe FRANCE, 1835.

Fifth-monarchy men, about 1645, supposed the Millennium to be at hand, when Jesus Christ from heaven should erect the 5th universal monarchy They elected him king at London Cromwell dispersed them, 1653 —*Kearsley* Another rising with loss of life, was suppressed 6 Jan 1661 Thos Venner, a cooper, their leader, and 16 others, were soon after executed

Fi'ji, Fee'jee, or **Viti isles,** in the South Pacific ocean, between lat 15° 30′ and 19° 30′ S and lon 177° E and 178° W, discovered by Tasman, Dutch navigator, 1643 There are above 200 isles, 80 inhabited, the largest about 360 miles in circumference, with a population of 124,658, 2100 European, 1890 Capital Suva

Islands offered by the king Thakombau, and chiefs to the British government but not accepted	July 1859
House of Commons granted 1680*l* for expenditure in them, and European settlements made	1860
Annexation to Great Britain proposed in Parliament, declined 25 June, 1872, but unconditional cession to the British government accepted by sir Hercules Robinson, July, and announced by him	25 Oct. 1874
His club presented to the queen by king Thakombau	"
Sir Arthur Hamilton Gordon first governor	1875
Many deaths by epidemic measles	early in "
Outbreak of cannibal devil worshippers suppressed by military, about 20 ringleaders executed	about June, 1876

files are mentioned (1 Sam xiii 21) 1093 B.C They are manufactured in great perfection by file-cutting machinery That set up by T Greenwood of Leeds, in 1859, was invented by M. Bernot of Paris It is said that the price of files by it is reduced from 32*d.* to 4*d.* per dozen

fil'ibusters (properly *flibustiers*), originally freebooters who plundered coasts of America in the 16th and 17th centuries, also applied to Narcisco Lopez and his followers. Lopez, born in Venezuela, 1799, went to Cuba and entered the army Distinguished himself in Spain, joined the revolutionists in Cuba in 1848, organized an expedition to invade Cuba at New York, but stopped by a proclamation of president Taylor, 1849 Organized another expedition and landed at the town of Cardenas, 19 May, 1850, with 600 men, took the town, but soon after evacuated it and returned to New Orleans. Prepared another expedition, and, sailing from New Orleans, 3 Aug 1851, he landed at Bahia Hondo, to the west of Havana, 11 Aug, he was accompanied on this expedition by col William L. Crittenden of Kentucky, whom he left at the landing-place with 130 men, while he moved on Las Pozas with 323 men He here appealed to the people in vain for a general rising, he was obliged to surrender shortly after (28 Aug), having accomplished nothing He was tried for high treason at Havana and garroted 1 Sept 1851 Col Crittenden was captured while attempting to escape to New Orleans and with 50 others shot at Havana, 16 Aug —William Walker, another filibuster, was born at Nashville, Tenn, in 1824. Going to California in 1850, he led an expedition into lower California, landing at La Paz, 4 Nov. 1853, his plans failing, he retreated northward, and in May, 1854, surrendered to the United States authorities at San Diego, taken to San Francisco he was tried under the neutrality laws and acquitted, 15 May, 1854. Early in 1855 Walker was invited to Nicaragua by one of the factions, "The Liberals," with a promise of 52,000 acres of land. On 4 May, 1855, with 60 men, he arrived at San Juan del Sur on the Pacific coast of Nicaragua from San Francisco. Gained the battle of Virgin bay or La Virgin, 1 Sept 1855, with 170 men against 540 Nicaraguans. On 13 Oct. he occupied Grenada, a town on lake Nicaragua, here he ordered gen. Corral shot, 8 Nov 1855 War began with Costa Rica. Walker was defeated at Guana Castro, 20 Mch 1856, but defeated the Costa Ricans at Rivas 11 Apr. He forced his election as president of Nicaragua, Sept 1856, and his minister, Padre Vijil, was recognized at Washington by president Pierce. His government, however, soon ended, and on 1 May, 1857, he surrendered with 16 officers to com Charles H Davis of the U S sloop-of-war *Mary*, which conveyed him to Panama, whence he returned to New Orleans, where he was received with great enthusiasm There were engaged in this undertaking 2288 men, of whom 61 were officers On 25 Nov 1857, he again invaded Nicaragua with about 200 men, landing near Greytown, but was soon compelled to surrender to com Hiram Paulding of the U S frigate *Wabash*, and was conveyed to New York, but escaped punishment by *nolle prosequi*, 2 June, 1858, while com Paulding was censured Again Walker, intending to create a revolution, on 5 Aug 1860, landed at Truxillo, Honduras, and took the fort on the 6th On the next day he issued a proclamation stating he made war on the government, and not on the people He was summoned to surrender by the captain of the British man-of-war *Icarus*, but refused and fled, he was caught 30 Sept 1860, delivered up to the Honduras government, tried, and shot 12 Oct. 1860 His followers were liberated —The term "filibustering" has of late been applied to all forms of irregular and predatory warfare and to methods of delaying the decision of debated questions in deliberative assemblies, by raising false or trivial issues, or wasting time in useless motions and roll-calls.

Filio'que, "and from the Son," inserted in the NICENE CREED, in respect to the procession of the Holy Ghost from the Father and the Son, in a council at Toledo, 589, adopted by the western, but rejected by the eastern church since 662 The omission of the phrase was considered at the Old Catholic conference at Bonn, Aug 1875 ATHANASIAN CREED.

fine arts. ARTS, ENGRAVING, PAINTING, SCULPTURE

Finland, a Russian grand-duchy, in the middle of the 12th century was conquered by Eric IX of Sweden, who introduced Christianity Often taken by the Russians (1714–1742, and 1808), and restored (1721 and 1743), but after 1809 retained by treaty ABO Its political constitution was confirmed by the czar in 1800, 1825, and 1855 Area 144,255 sq. miles Pop 1862, 1,746,229, 1875, 1,912,647, 1889, 2,358,404 During a famine whole villages were starved, Mch 1868.

fire. The ancient poets supposed that fire was stolen from heaven by Prometheus Heraclitus, about 596 B.C., maintained that the world was created from fire, and deemed it to be a god omnipotent. PARSEES, PHILOSOPHY

fire-annihilator, an apparatus invented by T Phillips, in 1849 When put in action, steam and carbonic acid are formed, which extinguish flame. It was not successful commercially. *L'Extincteur* was invented by dr F Carlier, and patented by A Vignon in July, 1862 It is an iron cylinder filled with water and carbonic-acid gas, generated by bicarbonate of soda and tartaric acid The apparatus was developed and improved by W B Dick in his manual and chemical fire engines, which give a continuous flow of water and gas, patented Apr 1869

"Mata fuego," or "fire killer," of M Banolas of Paris, was successfully exhibited at the Alexandra palace, 16 Oct 1880. Great bodies of flame were almost instantaneously extinguished.

fire-arms. The first fire-arms were cannon, and the first small fire-arms were a species of cannon borne by 2 men ARTILLERY, CANNON, CHASSEPOT RIFLE, PISTOLS, REVOLVERS.

Fire arms made at Perugia in Italy	1364
Employed by the Burgundians at Arras	1414
Arquebus in use about	1465
Edward IV of England landed at Ravenspur, it is said, with 300 Flemings armed with hand guns	1471
At Morat the Swiss are said to have had 10,000 *arquebusiers*	"
A fire arm known as the petronel (from *poitrine*, the chest), a kind of large "pistol," came into use	1480
Fire-arms said to have been used at the siege of Berwick	1521
Musket used in the armies of Charles V	about 1521
Earliest breech loaders	about 1537
(During the 17th and 18th centuries numerous)	
[These were of rude construction, the first discharged by a lighted match, later forms (about 1517) by a wheel lock. Loading and firing took much time At Kuisyingen, in 1636, only 7 shots were fired by soldiers in 8 hours, and at Wittenmergen, 1638, the musketeers of the duke of Weimar fired 7 times from noon until 8 P M.]	
Match lock and wheel lock superseded by the flint-lock, which is of Spanish origin, prior to.	1630
[Introduced into England during the reign of William III,	

remained in use in the British army until 1840, and manufactured as late as 1842. The best were manufactured in 1815 by Joseph Manton, the "king of gun-makers."]

Rifles not in repute or much used until the 17th century. William, landgrave of Hesse, armed his companies with the rifle-carbine... 1631

[The most famous rifle-barrel maker was Nicholas Bis, goldsmith to Philip V. of Spain; the lowest price for his single rifle-barrel was $200.]

Fergusson rifle, breech-loader, in use in the American revolution...1775-82
Percussion principle patented by rev. Mr. Forsythe........... 1807
First patent in the U. S. for a breech-loading fire-arm was to Thornton & Hall, of North Yarmouth, Mass. (10,000 of which were made for the U. S.)....................21 May, 1811
Copper percussion caps made in England................... 1818
Revolvers invented by Samuel Colt, 1829; patented.......... 1835
Percussion musket in use in the British army................. 1842
Old musket, "Brown Bess," superseded in England by the Enfield rifle (so called from the place of manufacture).......... 1857
Before the civil war in the U. S., 1861-65, the principal breech-loading rifles were Maynard's, patented 1851; Merrill's, 1856; Burnside's, 1856; Sharp's, 1859; Spencer, 1860. While the Springfield rifle-musket, muzzle-loader, was the principal fire-arm in use among the northern troops during the civil war, the following breech-loaders were purchased by the U. S. government from 1 Jan. 1861 to 30 Jan. 1866. The "Spencer," 8-shooter, being most in demand.

Ballard	1,500	Maynard	20,002
Ball	1,002	Palmer	1,001
Burnside	55,567	Remington	20,000
Cosmopolitan	9,342	Sharp	80,512
Gallagher	22,728	Smith	30,062
Gibbs	1,052	Spencer	94,156
Hall	3,520	Starr	25,603
Joslyn	11,261	Warner	4,001
Lindner	892	Wesson	151
Merrill	14,495		

The weight and calibre of the modern army rifle has been much reduced, as shown below.

RIFLES USED BY THE PRINCIPAL NATIONS.

Nation.	Gun.	Weight.		Calibre.	No. of Rounds.
		lbs.	oz.	inch.	
Austria	Mannlicher	9	0	0.315	5
Belgium	Mauser	8	2	0.31	5
China	Lee	9	0	0.433	5
Denmark	Mannlicher	9	0	0.315	5
England	Lee-Speed	9	9	0.303	8
France	Lebel	9	4	0.315	8
Germany	Mannlicher	9	0	0.315	5
Italy	Mannlicher	9	0	0.315	5
Japan	Murata	10	10	0.3	5
Portugal	Kropatchek	10	10	0.3	5
Russia	Lebel	9	4	0.304	8
Spain	Mannlicher	9	0	0.315	5
Sweden and Norway	Krag-Jorgensen	8	12	0.3	5
Switzerland	Schmidt	9	8	0.295	12
Turkey	Mauser	8	4	0.31	5
United States	Krag-Jorgensen	8	12	0.3	5

Gatling, Maxim, Mitrailleuse.

fire-engines are said to have been invented by Ctesibius, 250 B.C. They are mentioned by Pliny, 70 A.D. A "water-bow" was patented by Thomas Grent in 1632; one was constructed by John Van der Heyden about 1663. Bramah's engine was patented in 1793. John Braithwaite constructed a steam fire-engine in 1830.

W. Dennis's portable self-acting pneumatic fire-engine tried successfully at gas-works near the Thames, Engl.....30 Nov. 1876
Number of fire-engines in the principal cities of the U. S.: New York, 57, including 3 fire-boats; Chicago, 63; Philadelphia, 40; Boston, 34; St. Louis, 31; Cincinnati, 26; Brooklyn, 34, including 3 fire-boats; San Francisco, 23; Buffalo, 21; New Orleans, 20; Pittsburg, 19; Cleveland, 18; Detroit, 17; Milwaukee, 16; Baltimore, 14; Louisville, 14.

fire-escapes were patented by David Marie (1766) and Joachim Smith (1773) and many since. Versmann's composition for rendering wash dresses fire-proof was made public about 1860. Many devices patented in the U. S. since 1870.

fire insurance. Insurance.

fireman's respirator, the invention of dr. Tyndall (1870-71), is a combination of his respirator of cotton-wool moistened with glycerine, and dr. Stenhouse's charcoal respirator. Armed with it a man may remain long in dense smoke.

fires. The conflagration of a city, with all its tumult of concomitant distress, is one of the most dreadful spectacles which this world can offer to human eyes.—*Dr. Johnson.* Liverpool, 1862, etc.; Santiago.

IN LONDON.

Much of the city, with St. Paul's cathedral, destroyed..962 and 1087
One at London bridge began on the Southwark side, extended to the other side and hemmed in a crowd; about 3000 were drowned, and much of the city, north and south, burned... 1212
Great Fire, whose ruins covered 436 acres, extended from the Tower to the Temple church, and from the northeast gate to Holborn bridge. It began in a baker's house in Pudding lane, behind Monument yard, and destroyed, in 4 days, 89 churches (including St. Paul's), the city gates, the Royal exchange, the Custom-house, Guildhall, Sion college, and many other public buildings, besides 13,200 houses, laying waste 400 streets. About 200,000 persons encamped in Islington and Highgate fields (Monument).........2-6 Sept. 1666
In Cornhill ward, 200 houses burned; began in Change alley; most terrible since 1666.................................25 Mch. 1748
There were 953 fires in 1854; 1113 in 1857; 1114 in 1858 (38 lives lost); 1183 in 1861. 1303 fires in 1862; 1404 in 1863; and 1715 in 1864. In 1866, 1338 fires (326 serious); in 1867, 1397 fires (245 serious); in 1868, 1668 fires (235 serious); in 1869, 1572 fires (199 serious); in 1870, 1946 fires (276 serious); in 1871, 1842 (207 serious); in 1872, 1494 (120 serious); in 1873, 1548 (166 serious; 35 lives lost); in 1874, 1573 (154 serious; 23 lives lost); in 1875, 1668 (163 serious; 29 lives lost); in 1876, 1787 (166 serious; 35 lives lost); in 1877, 1708 (159 serious; 29 lives lost); in 1878, 1659 (170 serious); in 1879, 1718; 1880, 1871 (162 serious; 33 lives lost). In but few cases were the premises totally destroyed.
In 1890 there were 2555 fires (153 serious; 61 lives lost). The fires in London are far more numerous in December than in any other month.

IN THE UNITED STATES.

Theatre at Richmond, Va.; the governor and many leading citizens perished (Virginia).........................26 Dec. 1811
New York city, 600 warehouses, etc; loss, $20,000,000, 16 Dec. 1835
Washington city, destroying general post-office and patent-office, with 10,000 valuable models, drawings, etc.....15 Dec. 1836
Charleston, S. C., 1158 buildings, covering 145 acres....27 Apr. 1838
New York city, 46 buildings; loss, $10,000,000.........6 Sept. 1839
Pittsburg, Pa., 1000 buildings; loss about $6,000,000....10 Apr. 1845
New York city, 1300 dwellings destroyed.............28 June, "
New York city, 302 stores and dwellings, 4 lives, and $6,000,000 of property......................................19 July, "
Albany, N. Y., 600 buildings, besides steamboats, piers, etc.; 24 acres burned over; loss, $3,000,000.....................9 Sept. 1848
St. Louis, Mo., 15 blocks of houses and 23 steamboats; loss estimated at $3,000,000..............................17 May, 1849
San Francisco, Cal., nearly 2500 buildings burned; estimated loss about $3,500,000; many lives lost.............3-5 May, 1851
San Francisco, Cal., 500 buildings; estimated loss, $3,000,000, 22 June, "
Congressional library, Washington city, 35,000 volumes, with works of art.......................................24 Dec. "
Syracuse, N. Y., 12 acres of ground burned over, about 100 buildings; loss, $1,000,000...........................8 Nov. 1856
New York Crystal palace destroyed, with an immense amount of property on exhibition.............................5 Oct. 1858
Portland, Me., nearly destroyed; 10,000 people rendered homeless; loss, $15,000,000..................................4 July, 1866
Great Chicago fire, burning over about 3¼ square miles, destroying 17,450 buildings, killing 200 persons, and rendering 98,500 homeless; loss over $200,000,000. The most destructive fire ever known...................................8, 9 Oct. 1871
Great fire in Boston; over 800 buildings burned; loss, $80,000,000...9 Nov. 1872
Brooklyn theatre (Brooklyn, N. Y.) burned; 295 lives lost (Theatres)...5 Dec. 1876
For smaller fires, see articles on different cities.

fire-ships. Among the most formidable of such contrivances was an explosion vessel to destroy a bridge of boats at the siege of Antwerp in 1585. The first use of them in the British navy was by Charles, lord Howard, of Effingham, against the Spanish Armada, July, 1588.—*Rapin.*

fireworks are said to have been made by the Chinese in remote ages. They were invented in Europe, at Florence, about 1360, and were exhibited as a spectacle in 1588. In the United States most used in celebrating the anniversary of the Declaration of Independence, 4 July.

fire-worshippers. Parsees.

first-fruits as offerings were a large part of the revenues of the Hebrew priesthood. First-fruits (called Annates, from *annus*, a year), in the Roman church, originally the profits of one year of every vacant bishopric, afterwards of every benefice, were first claimed by pope Clement V. in 1306, and were collected in England in 1316; but chronologers differ. In 26 Henry VIII., 1534, the first-fruits were assigned by Parliament to the king and his successors. Mary gave the annates to the popes (1555); but Elizabeth resumed them (1559). They were granted, together with the tenths, to the poor clergy, by queen Anne, in 1703. The offices of first-fruits, tenths, and queen Anne's bounty were consolidated by 1 Vict. c. 20 (1838). Annates were long resisted in France, and totally suppressed in 1789.

Fish Dam ford, S. C., Battle at, between Americans under Sumter and British under Wemyss, 12 Nov. 1780. American victory.

fish, fisheries, etc. Laws for the protection of fisheries were enacted by Edward I. in 1284, and by his successors. The rights of the English and French fishermen were defined by treaty in 1839. The known species of fish are about 7000. —*Günther*, 1871.

First experiments in artificial propagation of fish in the U. S. were made in South Carolina in 1804. In 1853 successful efforts to hatch trout were made at Cleveland, Ohio. Many large establishments for hatching are now in operation; and there are fish commissioners in about half the states. Much has been done to stock or restock rivers, creeks, lakes, and ponds; and laws for the protection of fish are general. By act of Congress of 9 Feb. 1871, a U. S. commissioner of fish and fisheries was provided for; and great progress has been made in the propagation and conservation of food fishes.

Fishmongers' company of London (salt), 1433; (stock), 1509; united... 1536
Fishing towns in England regulated by an act passed... 1542
Fishing on the English coast forbidden to strangers... 1609
Dutch paid 30,000*l.* for right to fish on British coasts... 1636
Corporation of free British fisheries instituted... 1750
Fish-machines, for conveying fish by land to London, set up in 1761; and supported by Parliament... 1784
British society of fisheries established in London... 1786
Irish Fishery company formed... Dec. 1818
In 1849, 2 peasants, Remy and Gehin, obtained medals for cultivating fish in France, and the government set up an establishment for this purpose at Huningue, under M. Coumes.
In 1860 great progress had been made by M. Coste and others.
Commission to examine British fisheries appointed... 1860
Acts to amend British fishery laws...1861, 1862, 1863, 1868, 1869
In Apr., Mr. Ponders placed in the Thames 76,000 young fish (salmon, trout, char, and grayling); and on 17 Apr., Frank Buckland demonstrated the importance of fish-culture before members of the Royal Institution, London... 1863
In 1853 Mr. Buist began the culture of fish at Stormontfield, Perthshire; reported highly successful...Sept. 1866
Convention with France on sea-fisheries signed at Paris, 11 Nov. 1867; ratified by Sea-Fisheries act, passed.....13 July, 1868
Act for the protection of fresh-water fish passed........8 Aug. 1878
International fish and fishing exhibition at Berlin opened by the crown-prince...20 Apr. 1880
National fisheries exhibition at Norwich opened by the prince of Wales...18-30 Apr. 1881

American Sea-Fisheries.—Sebastian Cabot first directed attention to American fisheries in 1498. The earliest fishing voyages to American coasts were made in 1517. Bartholomew Gosnold explored the New England coast in 1602; and, catching cod near the southern cape of Massachusetts, named it Cape Cod. A shipload of fish was sent from Massachusetts to England in 1624. Fish were exported from Boston in 1633. An act to encourage fishing was passed by Massachusetts in 1639, and the industry grew rapidly until the Revolution. By the treaty of peace in 1783, the right of U. S. citizens to fish on the banks of Newfoundland, in the gulf of St. Lawrence, etc., was conceded. But, to injure the U. S. fishing industry, the British government, in July, 1783, prohibited the importation of its fish into the British West Indies. The U. S. government passed a bounty act to encourage fishing in 1789, and another in 1790, imposing duties on imported fish. Other acts to encourage this industry were passed 16 Feb. 1792, 2 May, 1792, 1797, and 1799. The bounties were abolished in 1807, but restored in 1813. There has been much legislation since, with the general policy of encouraging the industry. After the war of 1812-15, the British maintained that hostilities had abrogated the fishing rights of 1783; and in 1818, by a convention, the fishing privileges of U. S. citizens were defined. Disputes concerning bay and inlet fishing arose in 1852, which were settled by the reciprocity treaty of 1854. The U. S. gave notice, 17 Mch. 1865, of the abrogation of this treaty, taking effect 17 Mch. 1866. In consequence of disputes which arose in 1870, the subject was included in the treaty of Washington, 1871, the fisheries provisions of which took effect 1 July, 1873. By it the fisheries of both countries were opened equally to the citizens of both; but the difference of value, in the respective concessions, was referred to arbitration. This commission met at Halifax, Nova Scotia, in 1877, and awarded to Great Britain $5,500,000. The justice of this decision was disputed in the U. S.; but Congress promptly made the appropriation, and the money was paid in London by the American minister, 23 Nov. 1878, who protested against the award as excessive.

Seal Fisheries Dispute.—The coast of Alaska has valuable seal fisheries. The Russian American Fur company, under grant from Russia, annually exported about 25,000 skins of the seal, sea-otter, beaver, etc. In 1867 the U. S. purchased ALASKA. To prevent the extinction of seals threatened by the rapid increase of fishers, Congress, in 1868, placed Alaska under the treasury department, and forbade the killing of any mink, marten, sable, or fur-seal in Alaska or its waters. The breeding-grounds of seal were leased to the Alaska Commercial company of San Francisco for $60,000 a year, and $2 for every seal-skin shipped, the number limited each year to 100,000. But the company could not protect its territory; vessels from British Columbia and the U. S. took seals with impunity, and the extinction of the seal in a few years was threatened. The government sent cruisers into the Behring sea in 1876, checking the slaughter. But poaching continued; the natives especially capture seals, and take them in boats to vessels awaiting them at sea. The U. S. claimed the Behring sea as *mare clausum*, with jurisdiction over half of it, asserting that Russia had maintained this doctrine, and that Great Britain had once admitted it. But in 1822, in answer to the Russian claim, both Great Britain and the U. S. insisted that a sea whose entrance is 1000 miles wide or more cannot be other than open to all, and the claim of the U. S. has been met by Great Britain and Russia with the same rule. However, the U. S. revenue cutter *Corwin* was sent to the Behring sea with instructions to seize all sealers found east of a line drawn from between the Diomede islands in Behring sea, straight southwesterly to a point equidistant from Copper and Otter islands in the Aleutian group. In 1886 the British schooners *Caroline*, *Onward*, and *Thornton* were captured and taken to Sitka. The vessels were condemned, their masters fined, the cargoes of seal-skins confiscated and sent to San Francisco. The British government demanded the release of the prisoners and an indemnity of $160,000. In Jan. 1887 the president directed the authorities of Alaska to release the imprisoned men and surrender the vessels and property; but it was not until Sept. that the order was complied with. U. S. vessels still guarded the waters, and in 1887 the *Rush* seized the British vessels *Dolphin*, *Annie Beck*, *W. P. Saywood*, *Grace*, and *Alfred*, besides 7 American vessels at various distances from the shore, varying from 30 to 70 miles. The British vessels were again released. In 1889 Congress provided for the better protection of the Alaskan fisheries, tacitly receding from the claim that the Behring sea is *mare clausum*. Arbitration between the U. S. and Great Britain was proposed and practically accepted, and, as this would take much time, a *modus vivendi* for the protection of the seals meanwhile was proposed in a correspondence begun 4 May, 1891, and closed 15 June, 1891, when the president proclaimed the terms. For final settlement consult BEHRING SEA.

Fisher's Hill, Va. Here, on 21 Sept. 1864, gen. Sheridan again defeated the confederates under gen. Early (whom he had defeated 2 days before at WINCHESTER), capturing 1100 prisoners and 16 guns. GRANT'S VIRGINIA CAMPAIGN.

Fiume (*fe-oo'-ma*) (meaning river), the port of the kingdom of Hungary, on the Adriatic; built on the supposed site of Tersatica, destroyed by Charlemagne about 799, afterwards known as Vitopolis, Civitâ Sancti Viti ad Flumen, and finally Fiume. It was successively subject to the Greeks, Romans, the eastern emperors, the pope, and the house of Hapsburg. It was captured by the French early in the century, taken by the English in 1813, and given to Austria in 1814. It was transferred to Hungary in 1822; to Croatia in 1848; restored to Hungary in 1868. A new port and railways were constructed in 1877. Pop. 1880, 13,314.

Five Forks, Battle of, near Richmond, Va. Here gen. Sheridan turned the front of the confederates and defeated them after a fierce struggle, 1 Apr. 1865. GRANT'S VIRGINIA CAMPAIGN.

Five Hundred, Council of, under new French constitution, 22 Aug. 1795; rudely dissolved by Napoleon, 10 Nov. 1799. COUNCIL, FRENCH.

Five-mile act, 17 Chas. II. c. 2 (Oct. 1665), forbade nonconformist teachers who refused the non-resistance oath to come within five miles of any corporation where they had preached since the act of Oblivion (unless travelling), under penalty of 40*l.* They were relieved by Will. III. in 1689.

Fladenheim or **Flatheim,** Saxony. Here Rodolph of Swabia defeated the emperor Henry IV., 27 Jan. 1080.

flag. The flag acquired its present form in the 6th century, in Spain; it was previously small and square.—*Ashe.* Introduced, it is said, by the Saracens, before whom the ensigns of war were extended on cross-pieces of wood. CARROCIUM. The *honor-of-the-flag salute* at sea, exacted by England from early times, was formally conceded by the Dutch in 1673 after many defeats. Louis XIV. obliged the Spaniards to lower their flag to the French, 1680.—*Hénault.* After an engagement of 3 hours between Tourville and the Spanish admiral Papachin, the latter yielded, firing a salute of nine guns to the French flag, 2 June, 1688.—*Idem.*

flag, United States. The earliest legislation on a national flag was a resolution of Congress, 14 June, 1777, "that the flag of the 13 United States be 13 stripes alternate red and white; that the union be 13 stars, white in a blue field, representing the new constellation." In 1794 Congress ordered that after 1 May, 1795, "the flag of the United States be 15 stripes, alternate red and white, and that the union be 15 stars, white in a blue field." This was to note the admission of Vermont and Kentucky. In 1816 a committee was appointed to inquire into the expediency of changing the flag, and 4 Apr. 1818, an act was approved reducing the number of stripes to 13, and increasing the number of stars to represent at all times the number of states in the Union. 44 stars in the U. S. flag in 1893.

First U. S. flag raised was that over Fort Schuyler, N. Y., then a military post on the site of the village of Rome (FORT SCHUYLER)....3 Aug. 1777
It was first seen in a foreign country aboard the *Ranger*, capt. Paul Jones, at Quiberon bay, France, where it received the salute of that government....14 Feb. 1778
First displayed in a British port on board the *Bedford*, of Massachusetts, which arrived in the Downs....3 Feb. 1783
First trip around the world in the ship *Columbia* (UNITED STATES)....1787-90
Carried farthest south in the schooner *Flying Fish*, lieut. W. M. Walker, U. S. N. (Wilkes U. S. exploring expedition), lat. 70° 14' S., lon. 100° W....24 Mch. 1839
Carried farthest north by lieut. J. B. Lockwood, U. S. N. (Greely expedition), lat. 83° 23' 8" N., lon. 40° 46' W. (NORTHEAST AND NORTHWEST PASSAGES AND POLAR EXPEDITIONS)....13-15 May 1882
Before 1866 all American flags were of English bunting. SALUTE AT SEA and UNION JACK.

Flagel'lants, at Perouse, Italy, about 1268, during a plague, maintained there was no remission of sins without flagellation, and publicly lashed themselves. Clement VI. declared them heretics in 1349; and 90 of them, and their leader, Conrad Schmidt, were burned, 1414. In 1574 Henry III. of France became a Flagellant for a short time.

flage'olet, a musical instrument ascribed to Juvigny, about 1581; double flageolet patented by William Bainbridge, 1803; improved 1809 and 1819.

Flanders, part of ancient Belgium, which was conquered by Julius Cæsar, 51 B.C. It became part of France, 843 A.D., and was governed by counts subject to the king, from 862 till 1369, the first being Baldwin, *Bras de Fer*, who is said to have introduced the cloth manufacture. In 1204 Baldwin IX. became emperor at Constantinople. In 1369 Philip, duke of Burgundy, married Margaret, the heiress of count Louis II. After this Flanders was subjected successively to Burgundy (1384), Austria (1477), and Spain (1555). In 1580 it declared independence, but afterwards returned to its allegiance to the house of Hapsburg. In 1713 it was in the German empire. France obtained part of Flanders by treaty in 1659 and 1679. Natives of Flanders were called Flemings. BELGIUM, BURGUNDY, and NETHERLANDS.

Flattery, Cape, at the entrance of the strait Juan de Fuca, west coast of the state of Washington, U.S., so named by capt. Cook because it looked like a distant harbor, 1778.

Flavian Cæsars, the Roman emperors Vespasian, Titus, and Domitian, 66-96 A.D. CÆSARS, THE TWELVE.

flax. The manufacture in Egypt in very early times was carried thence to Tyre about 588 B.C., and to Gaul about 1 B.C.; and thus reached Britain. It was encouraged in England, by statue 24 Hen. VIII. 1533. For many ages the core was separated from the flax, the bark of the plant, by hand. A mallet was next used; but the old methods of breaking and scutching the flax yielded to a water-mill which was invented in Scotland about 1750. FLOWERS AND PLANTS, HEMP.

Fleet prison, London, was built over the small river Fleta (whence the name fleet), now a sewer. In the reign of Henry VII. this river is said to have been navigable to Holborn bridge.

It was founded in the 1st year of Richard I., was allotted for debtors, 1640; and persons were committed here by the star-chamber, and for contempt of court of chancery. It was burned during the Gordon riots, 7 June, 1780, rebuilt 1781-82, pulled down 1845 (debtors removed to Queen's Bench prison). The site was sold to the London, Dover, and Chatham railway company for 60,000*l.* on 2 June, 1864. Last vestige removed....Feb. 1868

Fleet marriages. Between 19 Oct. 1704 and 12 Feb. 1705 there were celebrated 295 marriages in the Fleet without license or certificate of banns. 20 or 30 couples were sometimes joined in one day, and their names concealed by private marks if they chose to pay an extra fee. Pennant says that in his youth he was often accosted with, "Sir, will you please to walk in and be married?" Painted signs of joined hands, with the inscription, "Marriages performed within," were common on the building.

This abuse abolished by the Marriage act....1753

Flemish school. PAINTING.

Flensburg, a city of Schleswig. Here the Danes defeated the allied Schleswig and German troops, 9 Apr. 1848. It was entered by the allies, 7 Feb. 1864. DENMARK.

fleur-de-lis (*fler-de-le'*), the emblem of France, said to have been brought from heaven by an angel to Clovis on his vow that, if victorious in a pending battle with the Alemanni near Cologne, he would embrace Christianity, 496. It was the national emblem till the revolution in 1789, when the tricolor (blue, white, and red) was adopted.

Fleurus, a village of Belgium, the site of several battles.

Between the Catholic league under Gonzales de Cordova and the Protestant union (indecisive)....30 Aug. 1622
Prince of Waldeck defeated by marshal Luxemburg....1 July, 1690
Allies under the prince of Coburg defeated by the French revolutionary army under Jourdan, who joined the armies of the Moselle, the Ardennes, and the North. (The French said to have profited by a balloon reconnoissance.)..26 June, 1794
Here Napoleon defeated Blücher (LIGNY)....16 June, 1815

floating batteries. BATTERIES; GIBRALTAR, 1781.

Flodden field, Northumberland, Engl. Site of a battle on 9 Sept. 1513, between English and Scots; James IV. of Scotland having joined Louis XII. of France against Henry VIII. of England. James, many nobles, and 10,000 men were slain—scarce a Scotch family of eminence but had a member of it killed in this battle—while the English, under the earl of Surrey, lost only persons of small note.

"Tradition, legend, time, and song,
Shall many an age the wail prolong:
Still from the sire the son shall hear
Of the stern strife and carnage drear
Of Flodden's fatal field,
Where shivered was fair Scotland's spear,
And broken was her shield."
—*Scott*, "Marmion," canto vi. stanza 34.

flogging, by the Jewish law, was limited to forty stripes, "lest thy brother should seem vile unto thee," 1451 B.C. (Deut. xxv. 3). William Cobbett in 1810, and John Drakard in 1811, were punished for publishing severe censures on flogging in the British army.

Flogging abolished in the U. S. navy and on vessels of commerce....28 Sept. 1850
Abolished in the U. S. army....5 Aug. 1861
Abolished in British army by Army Discipline act....Apr. 1881

floods. INUNDATIONS.

Flora'lia, annual games at Rome in honor of Flora, lasting from 28 Apr. to 2 May, instituted about 752, but not celebrated with regularity till about 174 B.C.

Florence (*Florentia*), capital of TUSCANY, and from 1864 to 1871 of Italy, is said to have been founded by the soldiers of Sulla (80 B.C.), and enlarged by the Roman triumviri. In its palaces, universities, academies, churches, and libraries are many of the rarest works of sculpture and painting. The Florentine academy and *Academia della Crusca* (established 1582) were instituted to enrich literature and improve the language of Tuscany; the latter was so named because it rejects like *bran* all words not pure Tuscan: both are now united under the former name. Pop. 1890, 191,453.

Destroyed by Totila....about 541
Rebuilt by Charlemagne....about 800
Becomes an independent republic....about 1198
Wars of the Guelphs and Ghibellines....1215 et seq.
Dante born here....14 May, 1265
Arti or guilds established....1266
Factions of the Bianchi and Neri....1300
Great plague, the Black Death....1348
Influence of the Medici begins with Cosmo de' Medici, "the father of his country"....about 1420
Death of Lorenzo de' Medici....8 Apr. 1492
Savonarola strangled and burned....23 May, 1498
Alexander de' Medici perpetual governor....1530
Cosmo de' Medici created grand-duke of Tuscany; makes Florence his capital (TUSCANY)....1569
Revolution at Florence....27 Apr. 1859
Annexation to Sardinia voted by people, 11, 12 Mch.; the king enters Florence....7 Apr. 1860
King opens the exhibition of the industrial products of Italy, 15 Sept. 1861
Florence decreed the capital of Italy till the acquisition of Rome....11 Dec. 1864
King and court remove there....13 May, 1865

Dante festival (the 600th anniversary of his birth) opened by the king....................................14 May, 1865
First assembly of Italian parliament here.............18 Nov. "
Capital removed to Rome..................................July, 1871
Fourth centenary of Michel Angelo....................12 Sept. 1875
Brick duomo, begun by Arnulfo, 1294; dedicated by pope Eugenius IV., 1436; completed by Brunelleschi, 1447; the façade cased with marble by government, uncovered in presence of the king....................................12 May, 1887
Equestrian statue of king Victor Emmanuel unveiled, 20 Sept. 1890

Flores, or Isle of Flowers, one of the AZORES, discovered by Vanderberg in 1439, and settled by the Portuguese in 1448.

Florida, one of the United States, lies between 31° and 24° 30′ N. lat., and 79° 48′ and 87° 38′ W. lon. The Perdido river separates it from Alabama on the west. It is mostly a peninsula, 275 miles long and averaging 90 miles in width, extending south to the strait of Bimini, and separating the gulf of Mexico from the Atlantic ocean. Georgia and Alabama are on the north. Area, 54,240 sq. miles, in 45 counties. Pop. 1890, 391,422; 1900, 528,542. Capital, Tallahassee.

Juan Ponce de Leon, sailing from Porto Rico in search of new lands, discovers Florida 27 Mch., lands near St. Augustine, plants the cross, and takes possession in the name of the Spanish monarch..............................2 Apr. 1512
Diego Miruelo, a pilot, sails from Cuba with one vessel, touches at Florida, and obtains pieces of gold from the natives...... 1516
Spaniards, under Francis Hernandez de Cordova, land in Florida, but are driven off by the natives, and return to Cuba..... 1517
Ponce de Leon having returned to Porto Rico and obtained title and privileges of Adelantado of Florida, fits out 2 vessels and revisits Florida. Driven off by the natives, he soon after dies in Cuba.. 1521
Panfilo de Narvaez, commissioned to conquer and govern the mainland from the river of Palms near Tampico to cape Florida, lands at Tampa bay with 400 men and 80 horses, 15 Apr. 1528
Fernando de Soto, leaving Cuba, lands at Tampa bay, which he calls Espiritu Santo, with about 1000 men and 350 horses, and passing north through Florida erects a cross of wood near the northern boundary. He lands............25 May, 1539
Don Tristan de Luna, with about 1500 soldiers and many zealous friars, anchors in Santa Maria bay (probably Pensacola), establishes a camp, from which he makes excursions, 14 Aug. 1559
Expedition fitted out by admiral Coligni, under capt. Jean Ribault, on the way north along the coast, place at the entrance of St. John's river a monument of stones, bearing the arms of France, and build fort Charles.......................... 1562
René de Laudonnière, with 3 vessels sent from France by Coligni, settles at point now known as St. John's bluff..22 June, 1564
Sir John Hawkins, with 4 vessels, anchors at Laudonnière's settlement, and seeing the settlers in great need, offers to take them back to France. Laudonnière refuses, but buys a vessel of Hawkins, who sets sail..................15 Aug. 1565
Seven vessels, under Ribault, from Dieppe, 23 May, with 500 men and families of artisans, land at river St. John..29 Aug. "
Don Pedro Menendez de Avilla arrives from Spain with an expedition at St. Augustine, 28 Aug. 1565. Re-embarking, they discover 4 large vessels of the French anchored at the mouth of the St. John. Being fired upon by the Spanish the French put to sea, and Menendez returns to St. Augustine, lands, and takes possession of the country in the name of the king of Spain...........................8 Sept. "
Menendez, with 500 men, attacks and massacres the settlers of Laudonnière at fort Caroline, few of the French escaping. He calls the fort San Mateo..........................19 Sept. "
Ribault sails to surprise the Spanish, 10 Sept., but by a tempest is driven ashore near Mosquito inlet and followed up by Menendez, and all who reject the Catholic faith are massacred..Sept. "
Laudonnière, with 18 or 20 fugitives, the survivors of the massacre at fort Caroline, sails for France..........25 Sept. "
Menendez sails for Spain, having in 18 months established forts and block-houses at St. Augustine, San Mateo, Avista, Guale, St. Helena, Tequesta, Carlos, Tocobayo, and Coava....spring, 1567
Father Sedeño and brother Baez begin a mission among Indians on Guale (Amelia island); the latter compiles a catechism in Indian language.................................. 1568
Dominic de Gourgues lands near the mouth of St. Mary's river, at Fernandina, with 184 men. Befriended by Indians hostile to the Spanish, and seeking revenge for the French, he surprises the Spanish, destroys fort San Mateo, and sets sail for France......................................3 May, "
Menendez, having returned, spends a few years in Florida, then leaves the government to his relative, marquis de Menendez, and again goes to Spain.............................. 1572
Sir Francis Drake lands at St. Augustine and destroys the fort which the Spaniards abandoned, but rebuilt immediately after his departure....................................8 May, 1586
Twelve brothers of the order of St. Francis sent to Florida to continue the mission on the island of Guale................ 1593
Son of the chief of Guale incites a general conspiracy, and the missionaries are massacred.................................. 1598
War between the Spanish and Apalachee Indians, who are conquered, and a large number set to work on the fortifications of St. Augustine...................................... 1638
Diego de Rebellado succeeds to the house of Menendez as captain-general of Florida.................................... 1655
St. Augustine pillaged by buccaneers under capt. John Davis, an Englishman.. 1665
Don Juan Hita de Salacar, captain-general of Florida......... 1675
Don Juan Marquez de Cabrera, captain-general of Florida..... 1680
Marquez Cabrera attempts to remove tribes of Florida Indians from the interior to the islands on the coast; an insurrection follows, and some tribes removing to Carolina make incursions into Florida.....................................about 1681
Three galleys of Spaniards from St. Augustine break up the colony of Scots on Port Royal island, S. C.................. 1686
Don Laureano de Torres, governor of E. Florida............. 1693
Andres de Arriola appointed first governor of a Spanish colony at Pensacola, with a fort, "Charles," and other public buildings, 1696
Don Joseph Cuniga governor of St. Augustine................ 1701
St. Augustine besieged by a land expedition from Carolina under col. Daniel, and a naval force under gov. Moore; 2 Spanish vessels appearing off the harbor, gov. Moore raises the siege, 1702
Carolina troops under col. Moore move against the Indians in N. Florida and fight the Spaniards under Don Juan Mexia, at fort San Luis near Tallahassee.....................15 Jan. 1703
Combined attack of French and Spaniards unsuccessfully made upon Charleston, S. C................................Aug. 1706
Don Gregorio de Salinas, governor of Pensacola, succeeded by Don Juan Pedro Metamoras.................................. 1717
Don Antonio de Benavuedi y Malina appointed governor of E. Florida to succeed Don Juan de Ayala....................... 1718
Expedition against Pensacola fitted out by M. de Bienville, the French commander at Mobile, captures the fort, and takes the garrison to Havana in 2 French vessels; gov. Metamoras immediately equips an expedition and recaptures the fort...... 1719
French under Desnade de Champmeslin besiege Pensacola, destroying the fortifications and public buildings and capturing the fort and Santa Rosa island.........................18 Sept. "
Pensacola restored to Spain by peace with France; Spaniards rebuild the town on Santa Rosa island near where fort Pickens now stands.. 1722
Col. Palmer of Carolina, with 300 men and a band of friendly Indians, makes a rapid, unexpected, and effectual descent upon Indian and Spanish settlements in Florida............ 1727
Don Francisco Moral Sanchez, governor of St. Augustine, for an unsatisfactory treaty with the English under gen. Oglethorpe, is recalled to Spain and executed.................... 1736
Don Manuel Joseph de Justis, sent in place of gov. Moral, is succeeded by Don Manuel de Monteano.......................... 1737
Gen. Oglethorpe, governor of Georgia, arrives at the mouth of St. John's river and captures fort San Diego........24 May, 1740
Gen. Oglethorpe destroys fort Moosa which he finds deserted, but afterwards places there a garrison of Highlanders under col. Palmer..June, "
English reinforced by a Carolina regiment, open the siege of St. Augustine......................................24 June, "
Three hundred Spaniards capture fort Moosa; col. Palmer killed in action..25 June, "
Gen. Oglethorpe hearing of the arrival of Spanish vessels with supplies for besieged, and many of his men being sick and discouraged, raises the siege..........................20 July, "
Spanish fleet of 36 sail under gov. Monteano enters harbor of St. Simons, Ga., and after 4 hours' engagement, Oglethorpe abandons the works and retires to Frederica.........5 July, 1742
After an unsuccessful attack on Frederica, gov. Monteano, scared by a decoy letter sent by Oglethorpe, and by 3 vessels from Charleston, sails away for Florida.............14 July, "
Oglethorpe makes a sudden descent upon St. Augustine, but captures only a few Spaniards..........................9 Mch. 1743
Noted Indian chief Secoffee, with his tribe, settles in Alachua, about the centre of Florida; founder of the Seminole nation. 1750
Don Alonzo Fernandez de Herrera appointed governor of Florida, 1755
Treaty ceding E. and W. Florida to Great Britain in exchange for Havana and the west part of Cuba ratified........10 Feb. 1763
Temporary command of province given to maj. Ogilvie....... "
By proclamation, king of Great Britain divides Florida into 2 provinces, east and west, by the Apalachicola river; W. Florida extending to the Mississippi and N. from gulf to lat. 31°..7 Oct. "
Gen. James Grant appointed first English governor of E. Florida, "
Pensacola laid out as a city, with streets at right angles, making squares 400×200 feet.. "
Dennis Rolle, obtaining from British government a grant of 40,000 acres, embarks from England with 100 families and settles on east side of the St. John's river at Rollstown...... 1765
King's road, from fort Barrington to St. Augustine constructed by subscription from public-spirited men in Florida........ "
Forty families from Bermuda emigrate to Mosquito to engage in ship-building.. 1766
Fifteen hundred Greeks, Italians, and Minorcans, indentured to work for a company organized in England by sir William Duncan and dr. Andrew Turnbull, form a settlement at Mosquito called New Smyrna.................................... 1767
Gen. Grant, returning to England, is succeeded by lieut.-gov. John Moultrie.. 1771
Col. Patrick Tonyn, sent from England to assume the governorship of E. Florida, arrives..............................Mch. 1774
British vessel, *The Betsy*, from London, with 111 barrels of powder, captured off St. Augustine by a privateer from Carolina..Aug. 1775

Colonists at New Smyrna institute proceedings to annul their indentures, and, being successful, remove to St. Augustine... 1776
Governor of E. Florida calls out the militia to join the royal troops in resisting "the perfidious insinuations" of the neighboring colonies...... "
Sixty of the most distinguished citizens of Carolina are seized by the British and transported as prisoners to St. Augustine, 1780
Gov. Tonyn, owing to the state of public affairs, is forced to call a general assembly which meets..........17 Mch. 1781
Don Bernardo de Galvez, assisted by a naval force under admiral Solana, invests Pensacola; forts St. Michel and St. Bernard garrisoned by 1000 English under gen. Campbell; the magazine of fort exploding, gen. Campbell capitulates, Mch. "
Country west of Pensacola as far as the Mississippi river receded to Great Britain by Spain...... "
Expedition under col. Devereux sails from St. Augustine, and with 50 men captures the Bahama islands from Spanish..... 1783
By treaty, Great Britain cedes to Spain E. and W. Florida, evacuation to take place within 3 months..........3 Sept. "
Gov. Zespedez, the new Spanish governor, arrives at St. Augustine and takes possession of Florida in the name of the king of Spain..........June, 1784
Alexander McGillivray, chief of the Creeks, forms a treaty with the Spanish governor in behalf of the Creek and Seminole Indians, engaging to prevent white men from entering the country without a Spanish permit...... "
William Augustus Bowles, in British employ, who had won the favor of the Creeks at Pensacola, captures fort St. Marks and holds it for several weeks until gov. O'Neil of Pensacola drives him out, arrests and sends him prisoner to Cuba.......... 1789
Gen. McIntosh, after imprisonment for a year in Cuba because of the jealousy of the Spanish governor, Quesada, returns to Florida, gathers followers, destroys a Spanish fort at Jacksonville and several Spanish galleys; returns to Georgia.... 1794
Spain recedes to France all of W. Florida lying west of the Perdido river...... 1795
Band of Seminole Indians, or "runaways," from the Creek nation, settle near the present site of Tallahassee...... 1808
Congress authorizes the president to seize W. Florida if a foreign power attempts to capture it..........15 Jan. 1811
Settlers on the northern border of Florida organize a provisional government, with gen. John H. McIntosh governor of the republic and col. Ashley military chief...... 1812
Fernandina, at this time a depot of neutral trade, garrisoned by Spanish troops under Don José Lopez, is besieged by gen. McIntosh and capitulates..........17 Mch. "
Gov. Kindelan, sent from Spain to succeed col. Estrada, acting-governor of Florida, demands withdrawal of U. S. troops.... "
Company of U. S. troops, mostly invalids, under command of lieut. Williams, is attacked by negroes under Prince, sent by the governor of St. Augustine; negroes are dispersed after mortally wounding lieut. Williams..........12 May, "
Monument erected in the public square at St. Augustine by order of the Spanish Cortes, to commemorate the liberal constitution granted to Spain and her colonies.......17 Oct. "
British fleet enters Pensacola harbor and garrisons forts Michel and Barrancas with British troops, by consent of the Spanish governor..........Aug. 1814
Gen. Jackson, with 5000 Tennessee volunteers, captures Pensacola and fort Michel; fort Barrancas is blown up by the British..........7 Nov. "
U. S. troops, under col. Duncan L. Clinch, unexpectedly reinforced by Creek Indians on the same errand, and aided by 2 gunboats, attack a fort on the Apalachicola river established by the British as a refuge for runaway negroes, and commanded by a negro named Garcia; a hot shot from gunboat "154" entering the magazine blows it up; out of 350 men, women, and children in the fort not over 50 escape..24 Aug. 1816
By order of the president of the U. S. capt. Henly invests and breaks up a depot for smugglers and buccaneering privateers on Amelia island, under the Spanish flag, and led by Gregor McGregor and Louis Aury..........23 Dec. 1817
Gen. Jackson, aided by Creeks under a treaty, attacks the Seminoles in Florida, destroying the Miccosukee and Fowl towns and fort Marks...... 1818
Gen. Jackson, the Spanish governor at Pensacola furnishing arms to the hostile Indians, and blockading his supplies up the Escambia, marches to Pensacola and captures it....... "
Gen. Jackson hangs Arbuthnot and Ambrister (ARBUTHNOT and AMBRISTER, case of)..........30 Apr. "
E. and W. Florida ceded to U. S. by treaty and purchase, Spain receiving \$5,000,000..........22 Feb. 1819
Change of flags at St. Augustine under gov. Coppinger, on the part of Spain, and col. Robert Butler, of the U.S.....10 July, 1821
Change of flags at Pensacola, gov. Callava representing Spain, and gen. Jackson the U.S..........21 July, "
Gen. Jackson appointed governor of Florida on change of flags, "
Juan P. Salas sells to John W. Simonton his title to Key West obtained from the Spanish government in 1815......20 Dec. "
Gen. Jackson in W., and capt. Hanham in E. Florida, wrest papers and archives from the Spanish governors.......... "
Act for a territorial government in Florida of all territory ceded by Spain to U. S., known as E. and W. Florida, 30 Mch. 1822
William P. Duval appointed territorial governor...... "
First legislative council meets at Pensacola..........June, "
Key West made a naval depot and station of the U. S., under command of com. Porter...... "
By Congress E. and W. Florida are united, and legislative council meets at St. Augustine..........30 Mch. 1823
Treaty of fort Moultrie; the Indians of Florida agree to remove within certain limits, the northern line being about 20 miles south of Micanopy..........18 Sept. 1823
Dr. William H. Simmons and John L. Williams, commissioners of legislative council, select Tallahassee as capital......Oct. "
First house in new capital erected...... 1824
Name of the castle of St. Marks at St. Augustine changed to fort Marion..........7 Jan. 1825
Florida Institute of Agriculture, Antiquities, and Sciences organized at Tallahassee, and holds its first public meeting, 4 Jan. 1827
Treaty of Payne's landing between col. James Gadsden, U. S. commissioner, and the Seminole Indians; who surrender their lands in Florida for an equal area in Indian territory, agreeing to remove within 3 years..........9 May, 1833
Additional treaty made at fort Gibson, Indian territory, with representative chiefs of Seminoles, assigning them a tract in the Indian territory..........28 Mch. 1834
Proclamation of pres. Jackson announcing the ratification of the treaty of Payne's landing and fort Gibson.......12 Apr. "
State-house in Tallahassee begun, 1826; finished...... "
John H. Eaton appointed territorial governor...... "
U. S. officer at fort King notifies gen. Thompson, Indian agent for Florida, of the determination of influential chiefs of Florida Indians not to emigrate..........Oct. "
Severest cold ever known in Florida; the St. John's river frozen several rods from the shore, and thermometer marks 7° above zero, a northwest wind for 3 days.....about 8 Feb. 1835
A council at the Indian agency extends time for removal to 1 Jan. 1836; 8 chiefs agree to emigrate, 5 refuse......24 Apr. "
Battle near Wahoo swamp; U. S. troops attacked by Indians under Micanopy, Jumper, and Alligator, and maj. Dade's command massacred..........28 Dec. "
Seminole chief Osceola, seeking revenge for recent imprisonment by the whites, with about 20 Indians, surprises gen. Thompson and a friend while walking near the Indian agency, and kills and scalps them..........28 Dec. "
Battle of gen. Clinch with Indians under Osceola and Alligator, near the Withlacooche river..........31 Dec. "
Battle at Dunlawtown of maj. Putnam with Indians under king Philip..........18 Jan. 1836
Gen. Gaines, with troops from New Orleans, attacked by Indians while seeking to ford the Withlacoochee........29 Feb. "
Richard Keith Call appointed territorial governor......Mch. "
Defence of Cooper's post west of the Withlacoochee by Georgia volunteers under maj. Cooper against 250 Seminole warriors, 5-7 Apr. "
Railroad from St. Joseph to bayou Columbus opened......... "
Battles between the U. S. troops and Indians in Florida, at Micanopy, 9 June; Welika pond, 9 July; Ridgely's mills, 27 July; fort Drane, 21 Aug.; San Velasco..........18 Sept. "
Battle of Wahoo swamp ends the campaign of 1836; results of the year encourage the Seminoles..........17-21 Nov. "
Gen. Call relieved; gen. Thomas S. Jesup takes command, Nov. "
Attack on camp Monroe by 400 Seminoles under king Philip repulsed..........8 Feb. 1837
Four hundred Seminoles attack fort Mellon, on lake Monroe, and retire..........9 Feb. "
Indians assembled in large numbers at fort Dade, by articles of capitulation agree to withdraw south of the Hillsborough river, and prepare at once to emigrate to the west....6 Mch. "
Gen. Hernandez captures 2 camps of Indians and negroes, 10 Sept. "
Gen. Hernandez, by order of gen. Jesup, captures Osceola and sends him to fort Moultrie, S. C., as a prisoner.......21 Oct. "
Gen. Taylor routs a large Indian force at Okeechobee lake, 25 Dec. "
Battle at Wacassassa river..........26 Dec. "
Action with Seminoles at Jupiter inlet; gen. Jesup wounded, 24 Jan. 1838
Gen. Jesup offering peace, many Indians come into camp, agreeing to let the president decide whether they remain in the country or not..........Feb. "
President determining to enforce the treaties, gen. Jesup captures about 700 Indians and negroes..........22 Mch. "
Over 1000 Indians removed to the western reservation........ "
Gen. Zachary Taylor takes command in Florida, gen. Jesup retiring..........15 May, "
Territory of Florida, in convention at St. Joseph, forms a state constitution..........3 Dec. "
Robert H. Reid appointed territorial governor...... 1839
Indians attack col. Harney's post on the Carloosahatchee, 23 July, "
During this and 4 years previous Florida furnished 5342 volunteers for the Indian war...... "
Gen. Taylor asking to be relieved, brevet brig.-gen. W. R. Armistead is assigned to command in Florida..........6 May, 1840
Battles with Indians at fort King, Marion co., 28 Apr.; Waccahoota, 6 Sept.; Everglades, 3-24 Dec.; Micanopy...28 Dec. "
Battle at fort Brooke..........2 Mch. 1841
Gen. Armistead relieved at his request, and gen. William J. Worth takes command..........31 May, "
Richard K. Call reappointed territorial governor...... "
Battle at Hawe creek, 25 Jan.; at Pilakikaha..........19 Apr. 1842
Gen. Worth, by general order, announces the cessation of hostilities with Indians in Florida..........14 Aug. "
Officers and soldiers who died in the Florida war buried at St. Augustine with military honors, and a monument erected by their comrades..........15 Aug. "
John Branch, territorial governor...... 1844
Congress grants 8 sections of public lands in Florida for seat of government, 1 section in each township for public schools, 2 townships for 2 seminaries of learning, and 5 per cent. from sales of public lands for educational purposes; state admitted to the Union..........3 Mch. 1845

William D. Moseley, governor of the new state............... 1845

Destructive hurricane passes over Key West...........11 Oct. 1846

Thomas Brown, governor.................................... 1849

Public meeting in St. Augustine petitions the federal government for removal of all Indians from the state.......25 Aug. "

Chief and 6 sub-chiefs of the Seminoles and Micasukies, and a delegate from the Tallahassees, meet gen. Twiggs in council and agree to remove west of the Mississippi and try to persuade their people to do so....................21 Jan. 1850

James E. Broome, governor................................. 1853

Madison S. Perry, governor................................ 1857

Two state seminaries of learning organized, one at Palatka, known as the seminary east of the Suwanee, and the other at Tallahassee, known as the seminary west of the Suwanee.... "

Most of the Florida Indians emigrate to the Indian territory; U. S. troops mustered out.................................. 1858

Fort Marion seized by confederates of St. Augustine by order of the governor.....................................7 Jan. 1861

Fort Clinch, in construction on Amelia island, seized by confederates...Jan. "

Apalachicola arsenal, established in 1833, captured by confederates...Jan. "

State convention at Tallahassee passes an ordinance of secession—yeas 62, nays 7—amending the Constitution by inserting the words "Confederate States" in place of "United States," 10 Jan. "

Forts Barrancas and McRae and the navy-yards at Pensacola seized by confederates.............................12 Jan. "

John Milton, governor..................................... "

Forts McRae and Barrancas dismantled..................Apr. "

Federals in fort Pickens, near Pensacola, are reinforced by troops from New York and Illinois, on steamer *Atlantic*..16–23 Apr. "

Confederate "Coast Guard" seize the light-house and all U. S. government property at Key Biscayne, Fla..........23 Aug. "

Confederates attack the Wilson Guards on Santa Rosa island, 9 Oct. "

Frigates *Niagara* and *Richmond* bombard forts McRae, Barrancas, and Pickens...................................23 Nov. "

Electoral vote cast for Jefferson Davis.................12 Feb. 1862

Federal fleet under admiral Dupont, with slight resistance, takes St. Mary's, Fernandina, and fort Clinch.................... "

St. Augustine taken by federals without resistance....11 Mch. "

Jacksonville, Fla., surrendered to Dupont.............12 Mch. "

Jacksonville evacuated by federals.....................9 Apr. "

Confederate fort on St. John's bluff, St. John's river, captured by federals...3 Oct. "

Federals again take Jacksonville........................5 Oct. "

St. Mary's shelled and burned by federal gunboat *Mohawk*, 9 Nov. "

Jacksonville taken by federals under col. Higginson...10 Mch. 1863

Federals badly defeated at Olustee.....................20 Feb. 1864

Regarding Florida as still a state of the Union, a convention at Jacksonville appoints delegates to the presidential convention at Baltimore.................................24 May, "

By proclamation, pres. Johnson appoints William Marvin provisional governor..................................13 July, 1865

Delegates elected to state convention at Tallahassee....10 Oct. "

Convention at Tallahassee adopts a new constitution without submission to the people and repeals the ordinance of secession...28 Oct. "

David S. Walker elected governor.....................29 Nov. "

Pres. Johnson proclaims that "the insurrection which heretofore existed in the state of Florida is at an end and is henceforth to be so regarded"...........................2 Apr. 1866

Meeting at Tallahassee forms a state educational association, 20 May, 1867

Col. Sprague, military commander of district of Florida; headquarters at Tallahassee (later at Jacksonville)......31 May, "

Republican convention at Tallahassee; 129 delegates..11 July, "

Convention organizing a Conservative party (Constitutional Union) at Tallahassee appoints a state committee...25 Sept. "

Forty-one out of 46 delegates elected to constitutional convention at Tallahassee; organize, but disagree as to the eligibility of 4 of their number..........................20 Jan. 1868

Fifteen members of the constitutional convention decide not to attend the meetings..............................1 Feb. "

D. Richards, president of convention, announces for 20 or 22 delegates that they, a legal quorum, have framed and adopted a constitution ignoring the constitution of 1865....6 Feb. "

Fifteen members meet at Tallahassee and elect Horatio Jenkins president...8 Feb. "

Gen. Meade calls the delegates together, and col. Sprague, acting as chairman, Richards and Jenkins resign, and Jenkins is appointed president of the convention...............18 Feb. "

State constitution adopted; 8 delegates sign under protest, 9 refuse..25 Feb. "

New constitution ratified by the people.................May, "

Harrison Reed elected governor......................... " "

Legislature meets and adopts the XIV. Amendment.....June, "

Military and civil government surrendered to Harrison Reed, who is inaugurated as governor.......................4 July, "

Unsuccessful attempt to impeach gov. Reed of high crimes and misdemeanors in office...................................... "

Legislature provides for a state board of education...........1869

XV. Amendment ratified by House and Senate, 11 and 16 June, "

Harvey S. Harmon admitted to the bar at Alucha circuit court, by judge J. H. Gross; first negro admitted in Florida........ "

People of Florida west of the Choctawhatchee river vote by a majority for annexation to Alabama, the conditions fixed by commissioners being "the consent of Congress and consideration of $1,000,000 paid to Florida by Alabama," 2 Nov. "

Equalization act passed by legislature.................27 Jan. 1871

Taxation felt to be unnecessarily heavy; delegates from nearly all the counties meet at Lake City and appoint a finance committee to "examine into the financial condition of the state" and to call on the governor to interfere.......6 Sept. 1871

Proclamation of governor calling on the people not to bring the law into contempt by refusal to pay taxes, and promising enforcement of the Equalization act till declared unconstitutional or repealed.....................................6 Nov. "

Attempt to remove gov. Reed by impeachment unsuccessfully renewed..Feb. 1872

Act reorganizing the state agricultural college, proposed by a former legislature, and making the superintendent of public instruction its president.................................. "

Brown's Theological Institute incorporated.................. "

Ossian B. Hart elected governor.........................5 Nov. "

Act at special session of the legislature refunding the state indebtedness (total bonded debt, $1,430,223.48)...........Feb. 1873

Marcellus L. Stearns succeeds gov. Hart, who d........18 Mch. 1874

Florida Fruit Growers' association opens a few days' session at Jacksonville....................................20 Jan. 1875

At a special election, amendments to the constitution are ratified by the people.................................4 May, "

George F. Drew, Democrat, elected governor...........7 Nov. 1876

After the November presidential election 3 sets of certificates of electoral votes were sent to Washington: (1) that of Republican electors, signed by gov. Stearns; (2) that of Democratic electors, signed by attorney-gen. Cocke; (3) that of Democratic electors made under act of the legislature and signed by gov. Drew.........................Dec. 1876–Jan. 1877

Act authorizing state adjutant-general to lease convicts, 3 Mch. "

Florida state-prison made an asylum for lunatics........1 Apr. "

Convention of colored men at Tallahassee addresses the colored people of the state on education and acquiring homesteads and fostering habits of industry and sobriety, 4 July, "

Gov. Drew procures conveyance to the state of nearly 1,800,000 acres of government land under act of Congress relating to swamp and overflowed lands.............................. 1880

William D. Bloxham, Democrat, elected governor........Nov. "

State sells 4,000,000 acres of state land south of Ocala and east of the Kissimmee river to Hamilton Disston and associates of Philadelphia for $1,000,000....................... 1881

Active work begun on a contract with Philadelphia capitalists for draining lake Okeechobee and reclaiming land; half of reclaimed land to go to the contractors................... 1882

Trustees remove the state university from Eau Gallie to Lake City and incorporate the "Florida University"............ 1883

State institution for blind and deaf and dumb located at St. Augustine.. 1884

Edward A. Perry, Democrat, elected governor..........4 Nov. "

At the November election a new constitution, formed by the convention of 1885, ratified by the people............2 Nov. 1886

Francis P. Fleming, Democrat, elected governor..........Nov. 1888

Discovery of phosphate rock in abundance near Dunnellen, Marion co..June, 1889

Sub-tropical exposition opens at Jacksonville...........9 Jan. 1890

Constitutional amendment adopted providing that the election of state officers shall be held on the Tuesday after the first Monday in October every 2d year......................Nov. "

Supreme council of the National Farmer's Alliance begins its session at Ocala..2 Dec. "

Gen. Francis E. Spinner, ex-secretary of the treasury of the U. S., born 1802, dies at Jacksonville................31 Dec. "

Monument to the confederate dead unveiled at Pensacola, 17 June, 1891

U. S. senator Wilkinson Call secures renomination on the 86th ballot in caucus, by vote of 52 to 42 for D. H. Mayo and 2 for ex-gov. Bloxham.....................................25 May, "

Senator Call declared re-elected by 51 votes in joint session, a majority of both houses; but as only 15 senators and 39 members of the House attended, his election is disputed, there being no quorum of the Senate...............26 May, "

Governor appoints R. H. M. Davidson U. S. senator to fill the supposed vacancy..................................15 Sept. "

Ex-gov. Marcellus L. Stearns dies at Palatine Bridge, N. Y., aged 53..8 Dec. "

Senator Wilkinson Call seated in U. S. Senate........... " "

TERRITORIAL GOVERNORS.

Names.	Term.	Names.	Term.
Andrew Jackson....	1821 to 1822	Robert R. Reid......	1839 to 1841
William P. Duval....	1822 " 1834	Richard K. Call.....	1841 " 1844
John H. Eaton......	1834 " 1836	John Branch........	1844 " 1845
Richard K. Call.....	1836 " 1839		

STATE GOVERNORS.

Names.	Term.	Remarks.
William D. Moseley...............	1845 to 1849	
Thomas Brown.....................	1849 " 1853	
James E. Broome..................	1853 " 1857	
Madison S. Perry.................	1857 " 1861	
John Milton......................	1861 " 1865	
William Marvin...................	1865 " 1866	Provisional.
David S. Walker..................	1866 " 1868	
Harrison Reed....................	1868 " 1872	
Ossian B. Hart...................	1872 " 1874	Died in office
Marcellus L. Stearns.............	1874 " 1877	
George F. Drew...................	1877 " 1881	
William D. Bloxham...............	1881 " 1885	
Edward A. Perry..................	1885 " 1889	
Francis P. Fleming...............	1889 " 1893	
Henry L. Mitchell................	1893 " 1897	

UNITED STATES SENATORS FROM THE STATE OF FLORIDA.

Name.	No. of Congress.	Date.	Remarks.
James D. Westcott, jr.	29th to 30th	1845 to 1849	Seated 1 Dec. 1845.
David L. Yulee	29th " 31st	1845 " 1851	" " "
Jackson Morton	31st " 33d	1849 " 1855	
Stephen R. Mallory	32d " 36th	1851 " 1861	Yulee contests this seat unsuccessfully.
David L. Yulee	34th " 36th	1855 " 1861	
[37th, 38th, and 39th Congress, seats vacant.]			
Thomas W. Osborn	40th to 42d	1868 to 1873	Seated 30 June, 1868.
Adonijah S. Welch	40th	1868 " ——	" 2 July, "
Abijah Gilbert	41st " 43d	1869 " 1875	
Simon B. Conover	43d " 45th	1873 " 1879	
Charles W. Jones	44th " 49th	1875 " 1887	
Wilkinson Call	46th " ——	1879 " ——	Term expires 1897.
Samuel Pasco	50th " ——	1887 " ——	" " 1899.

florin, a coin first made by the Florentines. A florin issued by Edward III. was current in England for 6*s.* in 1337. —*Camden.* This English coin was called floren, after the Florentine coin, because the latter was of the best gold. COIN and COINAGE.

flowers and plants. Many flowers now common in England were introduced between Henry VII. and Elizabeth (1485-1603). The art of preserving flowers in sand was discovered in 1633. A mode of preserving them from frost in winter, and hastening vegetation in summer, was invented in U. S. by George Morris, in 1792.—The floraculture of the United States has rapidly increased since 1870. Besides the Society of American Florists, there are over 1000 state and local ones, and above 400 horticultural societies. This pleasant industry has become remunerative.

NAMES OF THE PRINCIPAL PLANTS OF THE UNITED STATES, SHOWING THEIR NATIVITY.

Names.		Nativity.	Remarks.
Popular.	Botanical.		
Almond	*Amygdalus pumilia*	China.	
Apple	*Pyrus malus*	Europe and Asia	Over 1000 varieties now in the U. S. The Romans had 22 varieties (*Pliny*).
Apricot	*Prunus armeniaca*	Asia.	
Arbor-vitæ	*Thuja* {*occidentalis*	United States.	
	Thuja *orientalis*	China.	
Arbutus, trailing	*Epigæa repens*	United States	One of the most beautiful and fragrant of early spring wood-flowers of the northern U. S.
Artichoke	*Cynara scolymus*	Europe, S.	
Artichoke, Jerusalem	*Helianthus tuberosus*	Brazil.	
Ash	*Fraxinus americana*	United States.	
Asparagus	*Asparagus officinalis*	Europe, W.	Praised by Pliny and Cato. One of the oldest culinary vegetables.
Aster, China	*Callistrephus chinensis*	China.	
Azalea	*Azalea* {*calendulacea*	United States.	
	Azalea *pontica*	Asia Minor.	
Bachelor's button	*Centaurea cyanus*	Europe, central	Botanical name from Centaur. Chiron, one of the Centaurs, being wounded in his foot by Hercules, cured it with this plant. A hardy and popular annual.
Balm of Gilead	*Populus candicans*	United States.	
Balsam	*Impatiens balsamine*	India.	
Banana	*Musa sapientum*	India	Cultivated in all tropical and sub-tropical climates. No specific difference between it and the plantain.
Barley	*Hordeum vulgare*	Egypt	Native country conjectural. "Their steeds beside the cars— Champing their oats and their white barley—stood, And waited for the golden morn to rise." —*Homer,* "Iliad," viii. 686-88, Bryant's trans.
Basswood (Linden)	*Tilia* {*americana*	United States.	
	Tilia *europæa*	Europe	"The topmost linden gathered green From draughts of balmy air." —*Tennyson.*
Bayberry	*Myrica cerifera*	United States, E.	Furnishes the bayberry tallow of commerce.
Bean	*Faba vulgaris*	Egypt.	
Bean (Kidney)	*Phaseolus vulgaris*	America	BEANS.
Bean (Lima)	*Phaseolus lunatus*	South America.	
Beech	*Fagus silvatica*	United States	The beech of Virgil's "Pastorals": "Patulæ recumbans sub tegmine fagi," was not a beech, but the *Quercus esculus.*
Beet	*Beta vulgaris*	Europe, S.	
Birch	*Betula* {*lenta*, *excelsa*, *populifolia*, *papyracea*, *laciniata*}	United States, N.	The species *Papyracea* furnishes the bark for the Indian canoe.
Blackberry	*Rubus villosus*	United States	Much cultivated of late years in U. S.
Bluebell	*Hyacinthus nutans*	Europe and Asia.	
Blue-grass	*Poa compressa*	United States, Middle	Celebrated in Kentucky.
Boxwood	*Buxus sempervirens*	Europe.	
Broom-corn	*Sorghum saccharatum*	Abyssinia	"It is said that Benj. Franklin introduced it into U. S."—*Geo. Thurber.*
Buckwheat	*Fagopyrum esculentum*	Asia	Its flour an important article of food in the U. S. AGRICULTURE.
Bulrush	*Juncus effusus*	United States.	
Buttercup	*Ranunculus acris*	Europe.	
Butternut	*Juglans cinerea*	United States.	
Cabbage	*Brassica oleracea*	Europe, N.	In its wild state without head.
Cactus, night-blooming	*Cereus grandiflorus*	Mexico	Its magnificent flower expands by night and blooms but a few hours. The order is exclusively American.
Cale	*Brassica campestris*	Europe, N.	
Candytuft	*Iberis umbellata*	Europe, S.	
Caraway	*Carum carvi*	Caria.	
Cardinal-flower	*Lobelia* {*cardinalis*, *fulgens*}	United States.	
Carnation	*Dianthus caryophyllus*	Europe, S.	
Carrot	*Daucus carota*	Europe and Asia.	
Castor-oil plant	*Ricinus communis*	India	In India it becomes a tree. In the southern U. S. a stout shrub, where it is extensively cultivated for the oil extracted from its seed.

NAMES OF THE PRINCIPAL PLANTS OF THE UNITED STATES, SHOWING THEIR NATIVITY.—(*Continued.*)

Names.		Nativity.	Remarks.
Popular.	Botanical.		
Catnip	*Nepeta cataria*	Europe, S.E.	Said to be eaten by cats. The dried herb in infusion is slightly sudorific.
Cat-tail	*Typha latifolia*	United States.	
Cauliflower	*Brassica botrytis—cauliflora*	Europe, N.	In the cauliflower we eat the fleshy flower-stalks and undeveloped buds, which are crowded together in a compact mass forming the head.
Cedar, red	*Juniperus virginiana*	United States.	
Celery	*Apium graveolis*	Egypt.	
Century-plant	*Agave americana*	Central and S. America.	The largest of all herbaceous plants. That it flowers but once in a hundred years is a popular fallacy.
Cherry	*Cerasus vulgarum*	Europe, E.	
Chestnut	*Castanea vesca*	United States.	
Chiccory (succory)	*Cichorum intybus*	Central Asia.	
Choke-cherry	*Cerasus virginiana*	United States, E.	
Chrysanthemum	*Chrysanthemum sinense*	China.	Of late years, through cultivation, has become one of the most showy and popular of the autumn flowers.
Citron	*Citrus medica*	Asia.	
Clematis	*Clematis virginiana*	United States.	
Clover {white red	*Trifolium* {*repens* *pratense*	Europe and Asia.	Introduced into the U. S. before 1774. With other grass it makes the best of hay. Its cultivation, when "turned in," improves the soil.
Clover, sweet	*Mililotus alba*	Europe and Asia.	
Cockscomb	*Celosia cristata*	India.	
Columbine	*Aquilegia* {*vulgaris* *canadensis*	Europe and Asia. United States.	
Corn, Indian	*Zea mays*	America.	MAIZE.
Corn-cockle	*Agrostemma githago*	Europe.	
Cotton-plant	*Gossypium* {*herbaceum* *barbadense*	India. West Indies.	COTTON.
Crab-apple	*Pyrus coronaria*	United States.	
Cranberry	*Oxycoccus macrocarpus*	United States, N.	Its fine acid fruit has become a staple article of commerce, and on the bog-lands of Massachusetts, New Jersey, and Wisconsin, its cultivation has proved a success.
Cress, water	*Nasturtium officinale*	Europe.	
Crocus	*Crocus vernus*	Europe, S.	
Cucumber	*Cucumis sativus*	Asia.	
Cucumber-tree	*Magnolia acuminata*	United States.	
Currants	*Ribes* {*alba* *rubrum*	Europe.	
Cypress	{*Cupressus thyoides* *Taxodium distychum*	United States. United States, S.	White cedar.
Daffodil	*Narcissus, Pseudo-narcissus*	Europe.	"Daffodils, That come before the swallow dares, and take The winds of March with beauty." —*Shakespeare*, "Winter's Tale," act iv. sc. iii.
Dahlia	*Dahlia variabilis*	Mexico.	
Daisy	*Bellis perennis*	England.	"When daisies pied and violets blue, And lady-smocks all silver-white, And cuckoo-buds of yellow hue Do paint the meadows with delight." —*Shakespeare*, "Love's Labor's Lost," act v. sc. ii.
Dandelion	*Taraxacum dens-leonis*	Europe, N., and Asia.	
Dewberry	*Rubus* {*canadensis* *trivialis*	United States, N. United States, S.	
Dogwood	*Cornus florida*	United States, N.	An excellent tree for cultivation. Wood close-grained and firm. Bark sometimes used as a tonic. Very ornamental when in flower.
Egg-plant	*Solanum esculentum*	Central Africa.	
Elder	*Sambucus* {*canadensis* *pubens*	United States.	
Elm {white slippery	*Ulmus* {*americana* *fulva*	United States.	The white elm is one of the most magnificent of trees.
Fennel	*Anethum fœniculum*	England.	
Filbert, hazelnut	*Corylus* {*americana* *avellana*	United States. Asia.	
Fir	*Abies* {*balsamea* *fraseri*	United States, N. United States.	
Flax	*Linum usitatissimum*	Asia.	From the fibres of its bark linen is made, and its seeds yield "linseed oil." Mentioned by Virgil, "Urit enim *lini* campum seges, urit avenæ.—"Georg." i. 76. FLAX.
Four-o'clock	*Mirabilis jalapa*	Peru.	
Foxglove	*Digitalis purpurea*	Central Europe.	
Fuchsia	*Fuchsia coccinea*	Chili.	
Garlic	*Allium sativum* (common)	Asia.	
Geranium	*Pelargonium* {*graveolens* {rose-scented *zonale* (horse-shoe)	Cape of Good Hope.	A thrifty plant, many varieties largely cultivated.
Ginseng	*Panax quinquefolium*	United States.	Its root used medicinally.
Gladiolus	*Gladiolus communis*	Europe, S.	
Goldenrod	*Solidago* {*canadensis* *altissima*	United States.	"But on the hill the goldenrod, and the aster in the wood, And the yellow sunflower by the brook in autumn beauty stood." —*Bryant.*
Gooseberry, garden	*Ribes uva—crispa*	Europe.	
Gourd	*Lagenaria vulgaris*	India.	
Grape	{*Vitis labrusca* {Isabella, Catawba, Concord, and others. *Vitis vulpina* (Scuppernong) *Vitis vinifera* {European wine-grape.	United States. United States. Asia.	"This song of mine is a song of the vine, To be sung by the glowing embers Of wayside inns, when the rain begins To darken the drear November." —*Longfellow*, "Catawba Wine."
Hawthorn	*Cratægus* {*oxyacantha* *cordata*	England. United States.	"And every shepherd tells his tale Under the hawthorn in the dale." —*Milton.*
Heliotrope	*Heliotropium peruvianum*	Peru.	
Hemlock	*Abies canadensis*	United States, N.	"This is the forest primeval, the murmuring pines and the hemlocks." —*Longfellow*, "Evangeline."
Hemp	*Cannabis sativa*	India.	HEMP.
Hickory	*Carya alba*	United States.	
Holly	*Ilex* {*opaca* (American holly) *aquifolium* (English holly)	United States. England.	"Heigh, ho! sing heigh, ho! unto the green holly." —*Shakespeare*, "As You Like It," song, act ii. sc. vii.
Hollyhock	*Althæa rosea*	Asia Minor, China.	

NAMES OF THE PRINCIPAL PLANTS OF THE UNITED STATES, SHOWING THEIR NATIVITY.—*(Continued.)*

Names. Popular.	Names. Botanical.	Nativity.	Remarks.
Honeysuckle	*Lonicera japonica*	China.	
	Lonicera periclymenum (woodbine)	Europe.	
	Lonicera caprifolium (common)	Europe.	
Hop	*Humulus lupulus*	Europe	Hops.
Horse-chestnut	*Æsculus hippocastanum*	Asia, N.	
Horse-radish	*Amoracia rusticana*	Europe.	
House-leek	*Sempervivum tectorum*	Europe.	
Huckleberry	*Gaylussacia frondosa* (blue), *resinosa* (black)	United States	Botanically it is named in honor of Gay-Lussac.
Hyacinth	*Hyacinthus orientalis*	Levant.	
Hydrangea	*Hydrangea hortensis*	China.	
Ironwood	*Ostrya virginica*	United States.	
Ivy	*Hedera helix*	England	"A rare old plant is the ivy green." —*Dickens*
	Rhus toxicodendron (poison ivy), *radicans* (climbing ivy)	United States.	
Jack-in-the-pulpit	*Arisæma triphylum*	United States.	
Jasmine	*Jasminum fruticans* (yellow)	Europe, S.	"The jessamine clambers in flower o'er the thatch." —*Dimond*, "The Mariner's Dream."
	Jasminum officinale (white)	Asia.	
Jingko-tree	*Salisburia adiantifolia*	Japan	Introduced into the U. S.; very rare.
Juniper	*Juniperus communis*	United States.	
Larch	*Larix americana*	United States.	
Larkspur	*Delphinium consolida*	Europe.	
	Delphinium elatum	Siberia.	
	Delphinium grandiflorum	Siberia.	
Laurel, American	*Kalmia latifolia* (calico-bush)	United States, E.	
Lavender	*Lavandula spica*	Europe, S.	The plant is fragrant, and by distillation yields oil of lavender.
Leek	*Allium porrum*	Switzerland.	
Lemon	*Citrus limonum*	Asia.	
Lentils	*Ervum lens*	Asia	This legume, as an article of food, is of the greatest antiquity (Gen. xxv. 34).
Lettuce	*Lactuca scariola*	Europe and Asia.	
Lilac	*Syringa vulgaris*	Hungary.	
Lily	*Lilium candidum*	Levant.	
	Lilium bulbiferum	Italy.	
	Lilium tigrinum	China.	
Lily, calla	*Richardia æthiopica*	Cape of Good Hope.	
Lily, white day	*Funkia subcordata*	Japan.	
Lily-of-the-valley	*Convallaria majalis*	United States & Europe.	
Lime	*Citrus limenta*	Asia, E.	
Linden. (Basswood.)			Formerly much prized as a shade tree.
Live-for-ever, common orpine	*Sedum telephium*	Europe.	
Locust	*Robinia pseudacacia* (common)	United States	"I can see his sickle gleaming, Cheery-voiced can hear him teaming Down the locust-shaded way." —*Whittier.*
	Robinia hispida (rose acacia)	United States, S.	
Locust, honey	*Gleditschia tracanthus*	United States.	
Love-lies-bleeding	*Amarantus melancholicus*	Asia, E.	
Magnolia	*Magnolia grandiflora*	United States, S.	A stately and beautiful tree, in height 70-90 ft., flowers pure white, very fragrant.
	Magnolia conspicua	China.	
Mallow	*Malva rotundifolio*	Europe.	
Maple	*Acer rubrum*, *dasycarpum*, *saccharinum*, *nigrum*	United States	Eminently American, the sugar maple especially, one of the most valuable and interesting of our trees. The sugar and syrup made from its sap is highly prized. Each variety esteemed as shade trees.
Marigold	*Calendula officinalis*	Asia, E.	
Marjoram	*Origanum majorana*	Portugal.	
May-flower. (Trailing arbutus)			
Mignonette	*Receda odorata*	Africa, N.	
Milkweed	*Asclepias cornuti*	United States.	
Mint. (Peppermint and Spearmint)			
Mistletoe	*Phorodendron flavescens*	United States, Middle	A parasitic plant. Many varieties foreign. "The mistletoe hung in the castle hall, The holly branch shone on the old oak wall." —*Bayly*, "The Mistletoe Bough."
Morning-glory	*Pharbitis purpura*, *nil*	Central America.	
	Convolvulus japonicus	China.	
Mountain ash	*Pyrus americana*	United States	Much admired, especially the European variety, for its clusters of beautiful scarlet berries in the autumn.
	Pyrus aucuparia	Europe	
Mulberry	*Morus rubra*	United States	A tree 40 ft. in height, fruit resembles the blackberry.
	Morus alba	China	Cultivated for the sake of its leaves as food of the silkworm.
	Morus nigra	Persia.	
Mullein	*Verbascum thapsus*	United States.	
Muskmelon	*Cucumis melo*	Asia, into Eng. 1570	Varieties numerous.
Mustard	*Sinapis alba*, *nigra*	Europe.	
Myrtle	*Myrtus communis*	Europe, S.	
Narcissus	*Narcissus poeticus*	Europe, S.	
Nasturtion	*Tropæolum majus*	Peru.	
Oak	*Quercus virens*	United States, S.	Timber formerly in great demand for ship-building.
	Quercus nigra, *rubra*, *tinctoria*	United States.	
	Quercus alba	United States	A tree pre-eminent for grandeur, strength, and usefulness.
Oat	*Avena sativa*	Island of Juan Fernandez.	The island of Juan Fernandez is given as its native place, but that of none of our cultivated grains is clearly known.
Oleander	*Nerium oleander*	Palestine	A splendid shrub, almost a tree in the East. Green-bay-tree supposed to be the plant referred to in Ps. xxxvii. 35.
Onion	*Allium cepa*	Syria and Persia.	
Orange	*Citrus aurantium*	India and West Indies.	

NAMES OF THE PRINCIPAL PLANTS OF THE UNITED STATES, SHOWING THEIR NATIVITY.—(*Continued.*)

Names.		Nativity.	Remarks.
Popular.	Botanical.		
Orchis, showy	*Orchis spectabilis*	United States	The order Orchidaceæ, with its 400 genera and several thousand species, is among the most interesting and curious of plants, being remarkable for the grotesque form of stem, root, and flower; they are natives of nearly every part of the world. Great attention of late years given to their cultivation.
Osage-orange	*Maclura aurantiaca*	United States, S.W.	
Pæony	*Pæonia officinalis*	Italy.	
Pansy	*Viola tricolor*	England	"*Ophelia.*—. . . And there is pansies, that's for thought." —*Shakespeare*, "Hamlet," act iv. sc. v.
Parsley	*Apium petroslienum*	Europe, S.	
Parsnip	*Pastinaca sativa*	Europe, W.	
Pea	*Pisum sativum*	Europe and Asia.	
Peach	*Persica vulgaris*	Persia.	
Peanut	*Arachis hypogæa*	United States, S.	The pods, as they first form, force themselves into the soil, where they ripen. Its cultivation furnishes profitable employment where it can be grown. Tennessee, North Carolina, N. Georgia, etc., produce hundreds of thousands of bushels annually.
Pear	*Pyrus communis*	Europe	A fruit next in popularity and value to the apple. The Romans had many varieties.
Pecan nut	*Carya olivæformis*	United States, S.W.	Its nuts much esteemed.
Pennyroyal	*Hedeoma pulegioides* *Mentha pulegium*	United States. Europe.	
Pepper, red	*Capsicum annum*	India.	
Pepper, black	*Piper nigrum*	India.	
Peppermint	*Mentha piperita*	Europe	This plant is largely cultivated in the U. S., especially in Wayne Co., central N. Y., for the manufacture of the oil of peppermint.
Pepper-root	*Dentaria diphylla*	United States.	
Persimmon	*Diospyros virginiana*	United States, S. and W.	
Petunia	*Petunia violacea*	Brazil.	
Phlox	*Paniculata maculata* {many varieties}	United States.	
Pine	*Pinus* { *strobus* (white) *palustris* (turpentine) *mitis* (yellow) *resinosa* (Norway)	United States, N. U. S., S. Atlantic United States United States, N.	Of the highest importance. Lumber, turpentine, tar, pitch, and resin are products of the pine.
Pineapple	*Bromelia ananas*	U. S., S., and West Indies.	
Pink. (CARNATION and SWEET-WILLIAM.)	*Dianthus* { *chinensis* *plumarius*	China. Europe.	
Plum	*Prunus* { *domestica* (many varieties) *americana*	Europe, S. United States.	
Poison ivy. (IVY.)			
Pokeweed	*Phytolacca decandra*	United States.	
Pomegranate	*Punica granatum*	Europe, S.	
Pond-lily. (WATER-LILY.)	*Nuphar advena*	United States.	
Poplar. (BALM OF GILEAD.)	*Populus* { *tremuloides* *dilatata* (Lombardy) *alba*	United States Italy Europe	"Hard by a poplar shook alway, All silver-green with gnarled bark." —*Tennyson*, "Mariana."
Poppy	*Papaver* { *somniferum* *rhœas*	Asia, S. Europe	"*Iago.*—Not poppy, nor mandragora, Nor all the drowsy syrups of the world, Shall ever med'cine thee to that sweet sleep Which thou ow'dst yesterday." —*Shakespeare*, "Othello," act iii. sc. iii.
Potato. (SWEET-POTATO.)	*Solanum tuberosum*	South America	POTATO.
Prince's feather	*Polygonum orientale*	India.	"Ah! on Thanksgiving day, when from east and from west, From north and from south, come the pilgrim and guest, ... What moistens the lip and brightens the eye— What calls back the past like the rich pumpkin-pie?" —*Whittier*, "The Pumpkin."
Pumpkin	*Cucurbita pepo*	Levant	
Quince	*Cydonia vulgaris*	Levant.	
Radish	*Raphanus sativa*	China.	
Raspberry	*Rubus* { *idæus* (garden) *strigosus* (wild red) *occidentalis* (black)	China United States United States	Now extensively cultivated in the U.S.
Rhubarb, garden	*Rheum rhaponticum*	Siberia	Cultivated for its fleshy acid petioles as a substitute for fruit in the spring.
Rice	*Oryza sativa*	India.	
Rose	*Rosa* { *setigera* (prairie) *multiflora* (Japan) *rubiginosa* (Eglantine) *cinnamonea* (cinnamon) *canina* (dog) *centifolia* (Provens) *damascena* (damask) *alba* (white) *judica* (Chinese monthly) *eglantaria* (yellow) *gallica* (French)	United States. Japan. Europe. Europe. Europe. Europe, S. Levant. Germany. India. Germany. France.	
Rue	*Ruta graveolens*	Europe, S.	"*Ophelia.*—There's rue for you; and here is some for me; We may call it herb-grace o'Sundays." —*Shakespeare*, "Hamlet," act. iv. sc. v.
Rye	*Secale cereale*	Europe, N. and E.	This is the principal cereal for bread in the northern parts of Europe.
Saffron	*Crocus sativa*	Asia.	
Sage	*Salvia officinalis*	Europe, S.	
Sago-plant	*Cycas circinalis*	Asia, S.	
Sarsaparilla	*Smilax sarsaparilla*	United States	This is regarded as the true medicinal sarsaparilla.
Sassafras	*Sassafras officinale*	United States.	
Scuppernong. (GRAPE.)			
Snow-ball	*Viurnum opulus roseum*	Central Europe.	
Sorghum. (BROOM-CORN.)			SORGHUM, SUGAR.
Sorrel	*Rumex acetosella*	United States.	

NAMES OF THE PRINCIPAL PLANTS OF THE UNITED STATES, SHOWING THEIR NATIVITY.—(*Concluded.*)

Names.		Nativity.	Remarks.
Popular.	Botanical.		
Spearmint	*Mentha viridis*	United States.	
Spikenard	*Aralia racemosa*	United States, N.	This now well-known pot-herb is said to have been brought into Spain by the Arabs.
Spinach	*Spinacia oleracea*	Europe	
Spring-beauty	*Claytonia* {*caroliniana*, *virginica*}	United States	One of the first, as well as the most delicate, of our early spring wood flowers.
Spruce	*Abies* {*alba*, *nigra*, *excelsa*}	United States, N.; United States, N.; Europe, N.	
Squash	*Cucurbita* {*melopepo*, *verrucosa*}	(?); United States.	
Star-of-Bethlehem	*Orinthogalum umbellatum*	Europe.	
Strawberry	*Fragaria vesca*	U. S. and Europe	Extensively cultivated for its fruit.
Sugar-cane	*Saccharum officinarum*	Asia, S.	SUGAR.
Sumach. (IVY.)	*Rhus* {*glabra*, *typhina*, *venenata* (poison)}	United States.	
Sunflower	*Helianthus annuus*	South America.	
Sweet-cicely	*Osmorhiza longistylis*	United States, N.	
Sweet-flag	*Acorus calamus*	United States.	
Sweet-pea	*Lathyrus odoratus*	Sicily.	
Sweet-potato	*Batatas edulis*	Both Indies	First brought to Spain from the West Indies by Columbus. It is the potato of Shakespeare (mentioned twice, "Merry Wives of Windsor," act. v. sc. v., "Troilus and Cressida," act. iv. sc. ii.) and contemporary writers, the *Solanum tuberosum* being then almost unknown in Europe.
Sweet-william	*Dianthus barbatus*	Europe, E.	
Sycamore	{*Platanus occidentalis*, *Acer pseudo-platanus*}	United States.; Europe, N.	
Syringa	*Syringa persica*	Persia.	
Tamarack. (LARCH.)			
Tansy	*Tanacetum vulgare*	Europe and Asia.	
Tea-rose	*Camellia japonica*	China and Japan.	
Teasel	*Dipsacus* {*sylvestris*, *fullonum*}	Europe.	
Thistle	*Cirsium* {*lanceolatum*, *arvense* (Canada)}	United States.	
Thyme	*Thymus serpyllus*	Europe, N.	
Timothy, herdsgrass	*Phelum pratense*	Europe	Extensively cultivated for fodder in the eastern and middle U. S.
Tobacco	*Nicotiana tabacum*	Central America	TOBACCO.
Tomato	*Lycopersicum esculentum*	Central and S. America	TOMATO.
Tree-of-heaven	*Ailanthus glandulosa*	China	Rapid growth and rather graceful appearance favored its cultivation at first, but its disagreeable odor when in flower stopped it. Congress forbade further planting of it in public grounds of the U. S., 3 Mch. 1863.
Trillium. (WAKEROBIN.)			
Trumpet-flower	*Tecoma* {*radicans*, *capensis*, *grandiflora*}	United States.; Cape of Good Hope.; China and Japan.	
Tuberose	*Polyanthes tuberosa*	Ceylon.	
Tulip	*Tulipa gesneriana*	Persia.	
Tulip-tree. (WHITE-WOOD.)			
Turnip, common rutabaga	*Brassica* {*rapa depressa*, *campestris rutabaga*}	Europe and Asia.	
Vegetable oyster	*Tragopogon porrifolius*	Europe.	
Verbena	{*Aubletia*, *Chamædrifolia*}	United States.; South America.	
Violet. (PANSY.)	*Viola* {*grandiflora*, English, *cucullata* (wild) and many other varieties}	Switzerland, England; U. S. throughout.	"Violets, dim, But sweeter than the lids of Juno's eyes, Or Cytherea's breath." —*Shakespeare*, "Winter's Tale," act iv. sc. iii.
Virginia creeper	*Ampelopsis quinquefolia*	United States	A vigorous climber, occupying nearly the same position in the U. S. that the ivy does in England, being cultivated as a covering for walls, etc.
Wakerobin	*Trillium erythrocarpum*	United States.	
Walnut, black	*Juglans nigra*	U. S., Middle and W.	The dense dark-brown wood of this species is among the most valuable in the northern U. S. Its nuts are also esteemed. It is becoming scarce.
Water-lily	*Nymphæa* {*odorata*, *tuberosa*}	United States.	
Watermelon	*Citrullus vulgaris*	India	Extensively cultivated in the U. S. for its delicious, cooling fruit.
Wheat	*Triticum vulgare*	Europe and Asia	WHEAT.
White-wood	*Liriodendron tulipifera*	U. S., Middle and W.	A magnificent forest tree; wood extensively used as a substitute for pine; becoming scarce.
Wild cherry, black	*Cerasus serotina*	United States.	
Willow, weeping	*Salix babylonica*	Central Asia	WEEPING WILLOW.
Wintergreen	*Gaultheria procumbens*	United States, N.	A little plant of the woods, with spicy leaves and scarlet berries.
Wistaria	{*Frutescens*, *Consequana*}	U. S., S. and W.; China.	A splendid flowering vine of rapid growth; flowers in long pendulous clusters.
Witch-hazel	*Hamamelis virginiana*	United States	Medicinal extract from its leaves and bark esteemed.
Woodbine. (HONEYSUCKLE.)			
Yew	*Taxus* {*canadensis*, *baccata*}	U. S., N. and Middle.; England	

fluorescence. When the invisible chemical rays beyond the blue end of the spectrum pass through uranium glass or solutions of quinine, horse-chestnut bark, or stramonium datura, they become luminous by what was termed "fluorescence" by its discoverer, prof. Stokes, in 1852. By fluorescence, drs. Bence Jones and Dupré detected the presence of quinoidine in animal tissues. CALORESCENCE.

fluorine, a gaseous element obtained from fluor-spar; first collected over mercury by Priestley; named by Ampère, 1810. It is so corrosive that it is separated with great difficulty. Its chemical history was elucidated by Davy (1809), Berzelius (1824), and succeeding chemists. The corrosive properties of fluoric acid were applied in the arts in 1760 by Schwankhard of Nuremberg.—*Gmelin.*

Flushing, a seaport of the Netherlands, on the isle of Walcheren. For the siege, WALCHEREN EXPEDITION. It was fortified by Napoleon I., but the works were finally dismantled in 1867. The port improved, and new dock opened by the king of Holland, 8 Sept. 1873.

flute. The transverse flute (called the "German," but

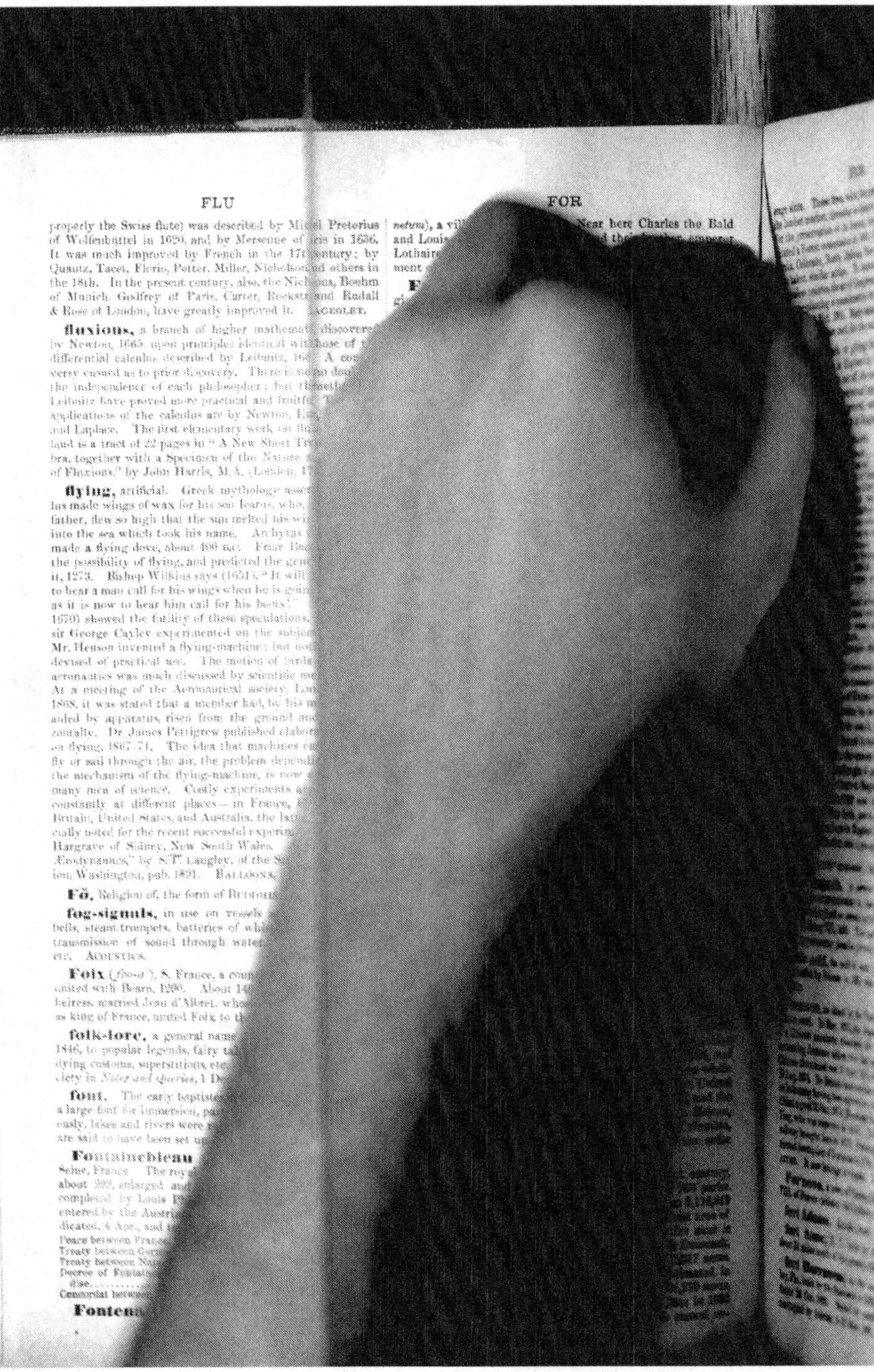
FLU
FOR
properly the Swiss flute) was described by Mi Pretorius
of Wolfenbüttel in 1620, and by Mersenne of ris in 1636.
It was much improved by French in the 17t entury; by
Quantz, Tacet, Florio, Potter, Miller, Nicholson nd others in
the 18th. In the present century, also, the Nich ons, Boehm
of Munich, Godfrey of Paris, Carter, Rocksti and Rudall
& Rose of London, have greatly improved it.
fluxions, a branch of higher mathemat discovere
by Newton, 1665, upon principles identical with those of
differential calculus described by Leibnitz, 16 A con
versy ensued as to prior discovery.
the independence of each philosopher;
Leibnitz have proved more practical and fruitf
applications of the calculus are by Newton,
and Laplace. The first elementary work on
land is a tract of 22 pages in "A New Short Tre
bra, together with a Specimen of the Nature
of Fluxions," by John Harris, M.A. (London, 1
flying, artificial. Greek mythology asser
lus made wings of wax for his son Icarus, who,
father, flew so high that the sun melted his wi
into the sea which took his name. Archytas
made a flying dove, about 400 B.C. Friar Ba
the possibility of flying, and predicted the gen
it, 1273. Bishop Wilkins says (1651), "It will
to hear a man call for his wings when he is goin
as it is now to hear him call for his boots!"
1670) showed the futility of these speculations,
sir George Cayley experimented on the subjec
Mr. Henson invented a flying-machine; but no
devised of practical use. The motion of birds
aeronautics was much discussed by scientific me
At a meeting of the Aeronautical society, Lon
1868, it was stated that a member had, by his m
aided by apparatus, risen from the ground and
zontally. Dr James Pettigrew published elabor
on flying, 1867-71. The idea that machines ca
fly or sail through the air, the problem dependi
the mechanism of the flying-machine, is now
many men of science. Costly experiments a
constantly at different places—in France,
Britain, United States, and Australia, the lat
cially noted for the recent successful experim
Hargrave of Sidney, New South Wales.
Ærodynamics," by S.P. Langley, of the S
ion, Washington, pub. 1891. BALLOONS.
Fŏ, Religion of, the form of BUDDHI
fog-signals, in use on vessels
bells, steam-trumpets, batteries of wh
transmission of sound through water
etc. ACOUSTICS.
Foix (fwa), S. France, a coun
united with Béarn, 1290. About 14
heiress, married Jean d'Albret, wh
as king of France, united Foix to th
folk-lore, a general name
1846, to popular legends, fairy ta
dying customs, superstitions, etc.
ciety in Notes and Queries, 1 D
font. The early baptiste
a large font for immersion, p
ously, lakes and rivers were
are said to have been set u
Fontainebleau
Seine, France. The roy
about 999, enlarged
completed by Louis
entered by the Austri
dicated, 4 Apr., and
Peace between Fran
Treaty between
Treaty between
Decree of Fontai
Concordat betwe
Fonten
netum), a vil Near here Charles the Bald
and Louis
Lothair
ment

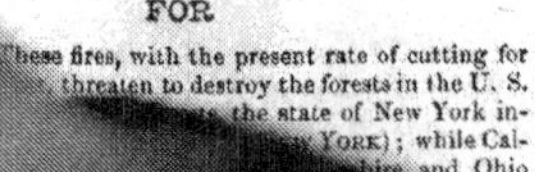

These fires, with the present rate of cutting for [illegible] threaten to destroy the forests in the U. S. [illegible] the state of New York in- [illegible] York); while Cal- [illegible] hire, and Ohio [illegible] ting on [illegible] 1878, [illegible] ds, [illegible]

[illegible] S [illegible] [illegible] ties [illegible] wood [illegible] sacola [illegible] United [illegible] 1861; [illegible]

FOR

fort Booe, built by Daniel Boone on the present site of Boonesbough, Ky., as a defence against Indians, 1775, withstood severattacks from them during 1777–78.

fort Bower. BOWYER, FORT.

fort Brown, Texas, on the Rio Grande, opposite Matamoras, built by [illegible]n. Taylor, 1846, defended by major Brown against a fierce [illegible] of Mexicans, 6 May, 1846, until relieved by gen. Taylor [illegible] the 10th. Major Brown was killed.

fort Clinon. CLINTON and MONTGOMERY, FORTS.

fort Crown Point. CROWN POINT.

fort Cumerland, Md., on the Potomac, built 1754, a rendezvous f[illegible] troops under gen. Braddock in his expedition against fort [illegible]uquesne in 1755.

fort Deborn, Chicago, built 1805–6, under the superintendence [illegible] maj John Whistler (who also built fort Wayne); [illegible] in 1812 by capt Nathan Heald, with a garrison of 54 [illegible]; evacuated by orders from gen. Hull, 15 Aug. 1812. Th[illegible] Indians slew many of the garrison and residents immediat[illegible] after. Fort burned same day. ILLINOIS.

fort De [illegible]ussy, La., on the Red river, a short distance below Al[illegible]andria, built by the confederates. Captured [illegible] adm. Porter [illegible] gen. A. J. Smith, 14 Mch. 1864.

fort Donelson, Tenn., built when the rebellion be[illegible] by the c[illegible]ederates on the Cumberland river, east of [illegible] Henry, to [illegible]tect Nashville and the heart of the confed[illegible]acy. But i[illegible]mportance was not appreciated by the con[illegible]erates, who [illegible]pected a federal advance in 1862 into east [illegible]nnessee. Ft Henry was captured 6 Feb. Com. Foote [illegible]acked Donels[illegible] with flotilla on the 14th, but was repulsed. [illegible]attle was f[illegible]ght on the 15th, the garrison trying to cut its [illegible] through [illegible] line. It was successful at first against [illegible] federal rig[illegible] but failed to press its advantage, and on the [illegible] the fort [illegible]rendered, with 10,000 prisoners and 40 guns. [illegible] the origina[illegible] garrison of about 18,000 men, 2000 were killed [illegible] wounded, [illegible] many escaped by the river, among them [illegible] Floyd, P[illegible]ow, and Forrest. The defence was misman[illegible]d. The fe[illegible]eral loss was about 2000; the confederate [illegible]ewhat larg[illegible]. The immediate result was the confederate [illegible]cuation of [illegible]ashville and Columbus.

fort Duaesne. PENNSYLVANIA, 1754, '55, '57.

fort Edward, N. Y. This fort, built on east bank of [illegible] Hudson [illegible]ver, about 45 miles north of Albany, by the [illegible]itish in 175[illegible] under gen. Lyman, and was first called fort [illegible]yman, but nae changed soon after to fort Edward by sir [illegible]illiam Johns[illegible]. The village of fort Edward now covers its [illegible], and take[illegible]s name from it. Near it Jane McCrea was [illegible]led while be[illegible]g taken to the camp of Burgoyne, 1777. NEW [illegible]ORK.

fort Er[illegible], in Ontario, Canada, on the Niagara river [illegible]pposite Buffa[illegible], was taken, with its garrison of 200 men, on [illegible]uly 3, 1814, [illegible]he Americans under gens. Brown, Scott, and [illegible]ipley. Ear[illegible] in Aug. the fort, garrisoned by 2500 men under gen. Gaes, was besieged by 5000 British under gen. Drummond. [illegible] 15 Aug. Drummond made a desperate assault, but was [illegible]pulsed, losing 600 men killed, wounded, and prisoners. A[illegible]erican loss, 84 killed, wounded, and missing. The siege co[illegible]ued until Sept. 17, when gen. Brown, then in command, ma[illegible] a sortie to destroy the enemy's outer defences, and drive D[illegible]mmond to relinquish the siege. It was made by 2000 men [illegible]d with complete success, inflicting a loss of 1000 men. A[illegible]erican loss, 79 killed, 216 wounded. On the night of Se[illegible] 21, Drummond precipitately retired; and on 5 Nov. 1814, [illegible]e Americans abandoned and destroyed this fort. Its rui[illegible] which now mark its site, are scarcely discernible. NEW [illegible]RK, UNITED STATES.

fort Fiser, N. C., built by the confederates at one of the entrances [illegible] Cape Fear river, was the main defence of the seaward app[illegible]ch to Williamston, N. C. Attempt to blow up the fort by e[illegible]oding 250 tons of gunpowder, near its seaward wall (plan c[illegible]ceived by gen. Benj. F. Butler) failed, 23 Nov. 1864. Capt[illegible]d by gen. Alfred H. Terry, supported by the fleet, 15 Jan. [illegible]65; 2083 prisoners, 169 heavy guns.

fort Fety or **Forty fort,** Pa., erected by Connecticut settlers [illegible] Wyoming valley in 1769, was the rendezvous

properly the Swiss flute) was described by Michael Pretorius of Wolfenbüttel in 1620, and by Mersenne of Paris in 1636. It was much improved by French in the 17th century, by Quantz, Tacet, Florio, Potter Miller, Nicholson, and others in the 18th In the present century, also, the Nicholsons, Boehm of Munich, Godfrey of Paris, Carter, Rockstro, and Rudall & Rose of London, have greatly improved it FLAGEOLET

fluxions, a branch of higher mathematics, discovered by Newton, 1665, upon principles identical with those of the differential calculus described by Leibnitz, 1684 A controversy ensued as to prior discovery There is now no doubt of the independence of each philosopher, but the methods of Leibnitz have proved more practical and fruitful The finest applications of the calculus are by Newton Euler Lagrange, and Laplace The first elementary work on fluxions in England is a tract of 22 pages in "A New Short Treatise of Algebra, together with a Specimen of the Nature and Algorithm of Fluxions," by John Harris, M A (London, 1702)

flying, artificial. Greek mythology asserts that Dædalus made wings of wax for his son Icarus, who, disobeying his father, flew so high that the sun melted his wings, and he fell into the sea which took his name Archytas is said to have made a flying dove, about 400 B C Friar Bacon maintained the possibility of flying, and predicted the general practice of it, 1273 Bishop Wilkins says (1651), "It will yet be as usual to hear a man call for his wings when he is going on a journey as it is now to hear him call for his boots!" Borelli (about 1670) showed the futility of these speculations. About 1800 sir George Cayley experimented on the subject, and in 1813 Mr Henson invented a flying-machine, but nothing has been devised of practical use The motion of birds in relation to aeronautics was much discussed by scientific men in 1867-68 At a meeting of the Aeronautical society, London, 26 Mch 1868, it was stated that a member had, by his muscular force, aided by apparatus, risen from the ground and flown horizontally. Dr James Pettigrew published elaborate researches on flying, 1867-71 The idea that machines can be made to fly or sail through the air, the problem depending merely on the mechanism of the flying-machine, is now entertained by many men of science Costly experiments are made almost constantly at different places — in France, Germany, Great Britain, United States, and Australia, the latter country especially noted for the recent successful experiments of Lawrence Hargrave of Sidney, New South Wales "Experiments in Ærodynamics," by S P Langley, of the Smithsonian Institution, Washington, pub 1891 BALLOONS.

Fō, Religion of, the form of BUDDHISM existing in China.

fog-signals, in use on vessels and along coasts, are bells, steam trumpets, batteries of whistles blown by steam, transmission of sound through water, the sirene, fog-horn, etc ACOUSTICS.

Foix (*foo-a'*), S France, a county established 1050, and united with Béarn, 1290 About 1494 Catherine de Foix, the heiress, married Jean d'Albret, whose descendant, Henry IV, as king of France, united Foix to the monarchy, 1589

folk-lore, a general name given by W J Thoms, in 1846, to popular legends, fairy tales, local traditions, old outlying customs, superstitions, etc He proposed a Folk-lore society in *Notes and Queries*, 1 Dec. 1877, formed 1878.

font. The early baptistery was part of the church, with a large font for immersion, partitioned from the rest. Previously, lakes and rivers were resorted to for immersion Fonts are said to have been set up in churches in the 6th century.

Fontainebleau (*fon-tain-blo'*), a town near the Seine France The royal palace, founded by Robert le Pieux about 999, enlarged and adorned by successive kings, was completed by Louis Philippe, 1837-40 Fontainebleau was entered by the Austrians, 17 Feb. 1814 Here Napoleon abdicated, 4 Apr, and took leave of the army, 20 Apr 1814

Peace between France, Denmark, etc	2 Sept.	1679
Treaty between Germany and Holland	8 Nov	1785
Treaty between Napoleon and Spain	27 Oct.	1807
Decree of Fontainebleau for destruction of British merchandise	19 Oct.	1810
Concordat between Napoleon and pope Pius VII	25 Jan	1813

Fontenaille (*font'e-na*) or **Fontenay** (*Fontanetum*), a village in Burgundy Near here Charles the Bald and Louis the German totally defeated their brother, emperor Lothaire I, 25 June, 841 This victory, termed "the judgment of God," helped to form the French monarchy

Fontenoy (*font-noi'*), a village near Tournay, Belgium site of a sanguinary battle, 30 Apr (11 May, N S), 1745, between French, under marshal Saxe, and English, Hanoverians, Dutch, and Austrians, under duke of Cumberland The king, Louis XV, and the dauphin were present The opening success of the British illustrates the power of a column, and the advance of the Austrians at Marengo (14 June, 1800) was compared to it by Bonaparte The allies lost 12 000, the French nearly as many, but the allies retreated Marshal Saxe (ill of the disorder of which he died) was carried about the posts in a litter, assuring his troops of success

foot-ball. The first distinct mention of foot ball in England is by William Fitzstephen, in his "History of London," 1175 To prevent the decadence of archery in England, foot-ball and other games were prohibited (1365) In 1458, James III of Scotland decreed that foot-ball and GOLF be utterly put down Shrove Tuesday was known in England as "Foot-ball day" as late as 1830

Foot ball revived among university men	about	1860
Foot ball association (no handling or touching the ball except by kicking) formed in England		1863
Rugby Foot ball union founded		1871
Harvard and Yale adopt 11 as the number of a foot ball team,		1880
R Young, by place kick with run sends the ball 137 ft 10 in,	2 July,	1881
Best distance by drop kick 172 ft 8 in, made by F Hardgrave, at Queen's park, Brisbane, Australia	Oct.	1882
American Foot ball association organized		1884
J E Duffy, Ann Arbor, Mich, by drop kick, sends the ball 168 ft 7½ in	22 May	1886
Greatest score made on the American point system, Harvard 158 to Exeter 0		"
William P Chadwick at Exeter, N H, by place kick with run, sends the ball 200 ft 8 in	29 Nov	"
Harvard defeats Yale for the first time since 1875, at Hampden park Springfield Mass Score, 12-6.	22 Nov	1889
Intercollegiate association, Princeton beats Yale, 10-0, N Y city	28 Nov	"
Intercollegiate association, Yale beats Princeton, 32-0, Eastern park, Brooklyn, N Y	27 Nov	1890
Yale beats Harvard, 6-0, Springfield Mass	19 Nov	1892
Intercollegiate association, Yale beats Princeton, 12-0, N Y city	24 Nov	"
Yale beats Harvard 6-0, Springfield, Mass	25 Nov	1893
Princeton beats Yale, 6-0, N Y city	30 Nov	"
Yale beats Harvard, 12-4, Springfield, Mass	24 Nov	1894
Pennsylvania beats Harvard, 18-4, Philadelphia, Pa	29 Nov	"
Yale beats Princeton, 24-0, N Y city	1 Dec	"

foreign orders. No British subject may accept an order from a foreign sovereign, or wear his insignia, without the sovereign's consent, by orders issued in 1812 and 1834, regulations published in London *Gazette*, 10 May, 1855 In the United States "No title of nobility shall be granted by the U S., and no person holding any office of profit or trust under them shall, without the consent of the Congress, accept any present, emolument, office, or title of any kind whatever, from any king, prince, or foreign state."—*Constitution U S*, art. I. sec. IX.

Foresters, Ancient Order of, a species of benefit society, founded on the principle that many can help one, religious and political discussions are excluded. The American branch, founded 1864, has grand-courts 16, sub courts 900, and 90,000 members The membership of the order in the whole world was (31 Dec 1890) 816,176 It has lodges in the United States, Canada, Great Britain, Ireland, Holland, India, and the West Indies, Spain, Malta, E, W, and S Africa, St Helena, New South Wales, Australia, New Zealand, British Columbia, Peru, Nicaragua, and Colombia, etc The funds of the order are $25,288,825, assets, $70,000,000

forests. There were in England, in the last century, as many as 68 forests, 18 chases, and upwards of 780 parks. NEW FOREST In the United Kingdom there are 3,116,819 acres of forest Of the European countries the forest area of Russia is the greatest, being 503,880,000 acres, the next is Sweden and Norway, with 62,315,939, the least is Denmark, with 464,360 The total for all Europe is 726,685,617 acres. The total forest area in the United States was estimated, in 1891, at 481,764,599 acres, included in farms 185,794,219 acres, besides Alaska and Indian reservations. Forest fires in 1880 burned over 432,464 acres, this is probably the annual average since. These fires, with the present rate of cutting for the lumber market, threaten to destroy the forests in the U S For the preservation of its forests, the state of New York instituted a Forest commission in 1885 (NEW YORK), while California, Colorado, North Dakota, New Hampshire, and Ohio have taken similar action To encourage forest-planting on the treeless prairies, the act of Congress, approved 14 June, 1878, made tree-planting a consideration for grants of public lands Act repealed 3 Mch 1891 Many states have appointed a holiday, known as ARBOR DAY, for the voluntary planting of trees

forgery of deeds, or giving forged deeds in evidence, was made punishable in England by fine, by standing in the pillory, having both ears cut off, the nostrils slit up and seared, the forfeiture of land, and perpetual imprisonment, 5 Eliz 1562 Since paper credit became general, many statutes have been enacted, the latest Forgery act in England passed 9 Aug 1870

IN ENGLAND

Forgery first made punishable by death 1634
Forging letters of attorney made capital 1722
Mr Ward, M P, expelled the House of Commons for forgery, 16 May, 1726, and consigned to the pillory 17 Mch 1727
First forger on the Bank of England was Richard William Vaughan, once a linen draper of Stafford He employed a number of artists on different parts of notes, filled up twenty and gave them to a young lady whom he was to marry, as a proof of wealth, no suspicion entertained One of the artists informed and Vaughan executed at Tyburn 1 May, 1758
Forged notes presented to the bank 1801-10, for 101,661*l*
Bank prosecutes 142 persons for forgery or uttering forged notes 1817
Thos Maynard, the last person executed for forgery 31 Dec 1829
One act all forgeries henceforth punished with death 1830
Punishment of forgery with death ceases except of wills or powers of attorney to transfer stock 1832
These cases also reduced to transportable offences 1837

forks were in use on the Continent in the 13th and 14th centuries — *Voltaire* This is reasonably disputed In Fynes Moryson's "Itinerary," reign of Elizabeth, he says, "At Venice each person was served (besides his knife and spoon) with a fork to hold the meat while he cuts it, for there they deem it ill manners that one should touch it with his hand" Thomas Coryate solemnly describes the manner of using forks in Italy, and adds, "I myself have thought it good to imitate the Italian fashion since I came home to England," 1608 2 pronged forks were made at Sheffield soon after 3-pronged forks are more recent. Silver forks, previously only used by the rich, came into general use in England about 1814.

G Smith found a bronze fork with 2 prongs at Kouyunjik, Assyria, 1873
A "flesh hook of 3 teeth" mentioned 1 Sam ii 13, about 1165 B C

forma pauperis. A person having a just cause of suit, yet too poor to maintain it, has attorney and counsel assigned him in England on swearing that he is not worth 5*l*, by statute 11 Henry VII, 1495. This act has been remodelled, and now any person may plead *in formâ pauperis* in the courts

formic acid, the acid of ants (*formicæ*) Its artificial production by Pelouze in 1831 was an epoch in organic chemistry

Formo'sa, an island in the Pacific, 90 miles from the Chinese coast In May, 1874, the Japanese, with the consent of a Chinese mandarin, chastised the savage tribes here for massacring Japanese sailors who had settled on the isle The Chinese threatened war if they did not quit within 90 days, 18 Aug 1874. By British interposition the Japanese withdrew, an indemnity having been agreed on, treaty between Japan and China signed 31 Oct. 1874 Formosa flourished under the rule of Ting, who was removed in 1878 The plant of the Woosung railway brought here in 1878 Psalmanazar published his fabricated description of Formosa in 1704 FORGERIES OF LITERATURE. It now belongs to Japan. Pop. in 1880, 3,000,000.

For'novo, a town of Parma, Italy. Near here Charles VIII of France defeated the Italians, 6 July, 1495.

fort Adams. ADAMS, FORT

fort Anne, N. Y, built by the British, 1757, stood about 14 miles south of the present village of Whitehall.

fort Barrancas, on the south side of Pensacola bay, Fla., built by the Spaniards in 1669. Ceded to the United States 24 Oct 1820 Seized by confederates 13 Jan. 1861, reoccupied by federals, 9-10 May, 1862.

fort Boone, built by Daniel Boone on the present site of Boonesborough, Ky, as a defence against Indians, 1775, withstood several attacks from them during 1777-78

fort Bowyer. BOWYER, FORT

fort Brown, Texas on the Rio Grande, opposite Matamoras, built by gen Taylor, 1846, defended by major Brown against a fierce assault of Mexicans, 6 May, 1846, until relieved by gen Taylor on the 10th. Major Brown was killed

fort Clinton. CLINTON and MONTGOMERY, FORTS

fort Crown Point. CROWN POINT

fort Cumberland, Md, on the Potomac, built 1751, a rendezvous for troops under gen Braddock in his expedition against fort Duquesne in 1755

fort Dearborn, Chicago, built 1805-6, under the superintendence of maj John Whistler (who also built fort Wayne), occupied in 1812 by capt Nathan Heald, with a garrison of 54 men, evacuated by orders from gen Hull, 15 Aug 1812 The Indians slew many of the garrison and residents immediately after Fort burned same day. ILLINOIS

fort De Russy, La, on the Red river, a short distance below Alexandria, built by the confederates Captured by adm Porter and gen A J Smith, 11 Mch 1864

fort Donelson, Tenn, built when the rebellion began by the confederates on the Cumberland river, east of fort Henry, to protect Nashville and the heart of the confederacy But its importance was not appreciated by the confederates, who expected a federal advance in 1862 into east Tennessee Fort Henry was captured 6 Feb Com Foote attacked Donelson with flotilla on the 14th, but was repulsed. A battle was fought on the 15th, the garrison trying to cut its way through Grant's line It was successful at first against the federal right, but failed to press its advantage, and on the 16th the fort surrendered, with 10,000 prisoners and 40 guns Of the original garrison of about 18,000 men, 2000 were killed or wounded, and many escaped by the river among them gens Floyd, Pillow, and Forrest. The defence was mismanaged The federal loss was about 2000, the confederate somewhat larger The immediate result was the confederate evacuation of Nashville and Columbus

fort Duquesne. PENNSYLVANIA, 1754, '55, '57

fort Edward, N Y. This fort, built on east bank of the Hudson river, about 45 miles north of Albany, by the British in 1755, under gen Lyman, and was first called fort Lyman, but name changed soon after to fort Edward by sir William Johnson The village of fort Edward now covers its site, and takes its name from it Near it Jane McCrea was killed while being taken to the camp of Burgoyne, 1777 NEW YORK

fort Erie, in Ontario, Canada, on the Niagara river opposite Buffalo, was taken, with its garrison of 200 men, on July 3, 1814 by the Americans under gens Brown, Scott, and Ripley Early in Aug the fort, garrisoned by 2500 men under gen Gaines, was besieged by 5000 British under gen Drummond On 15 Aug Drummond made a desperate assault, but was repulsed, losing 600 men killed, wounded, and prisoners American loss, 84 killed, wounded, and missing The siege continued until Sept 17, when gen Brown, then in command, made a sortie to destroy the enemy's outer defences, and drive Drummond to relinquish the siege It was made by 3000 men, and with complete success, inflicting a loss of 1000 men American loss, 79 killed, 216 wounded On the night of Sept. 21, Drummond precipitately retired, and on 5 Nov. 1814, the Americans abandoned and destroyed this fort. Its ruins which now mark its site, are scarcely discernible. NEW YORK, UNITED STATES.

fort Fisher, N C., built by the confederates at one of the entrances to Cape Fear river, was the main defence of the seaward approach to Wilmington, N C Attempt to blow up the fort by exploding 250 tons of gunpowder, near its seaward wall (plan conceived by gen Benj F Butler) failed, 23 Nov 1864 Captured by gen. Alfred H Terry, supported by the fleet, 15 Jan 1865, 2083 prisoners, 169 heavy guns

fort Forty or **Forty fort,** Pa, erected by Connecticut settlers in Wyoming valley in 1769, was the rendezvous of the Americans when the valley was invaded by Tories and Indians, 3 July, 1778 Fort surrendered, 4 July WYOMING

fort Frederick, Md, built 1755-56, on the north bank of the Potomac, 50 miles below fort Cumberland

fort Frontenac, near the present site of Kingston Ont built by Frontenac, governor of Canada, 1673, was for 80 years the strongest fort in America The French held it until 1758, when it was taken by the British under col Bradstreet without resistance It had been the main rendezvous of French expeditions against the English

fort George, N Y, near the site of fort William Henry, built 1758-60, has no historic reputation

fort George, at the mouth of the Niagara river on the Canada side, and opposite fort Niagara, occupied by the British, was captured by the U S troops under gen Dearborn 27 May, 1813 British garrison numbered about 3000 U S troops lost 34 killed and 88 wounded, the British lost 108 killed, 163 wounded, and 622 made prisoners On 8 July following a U S foraging party near fort George was attacked by a superior force of British and Indians Only a corporal and 9 men escaped to the fort, the remainder (29) were killed or wounded On the 17th the outworks of fort George were attacked by 200 British and Indians, they were gallantly defended by a detachment from the garrison under col (afterwards lieut.-gen) Winfield Scott The U S troops lost 4 killed and 4 wounded Again, on 24 Aug, these outworks were attacked by a British party They were repulsed by a detachment under capt Davenport The loss on both sides was inconsiderable Evacuated by the U S. force 10 Dec 1813 NEW YORK, UNITED STATES

fort Griswold, on the east bank of the Thames river, Conn, defended by some 150 men under col William Ledyard, was captured by the British, 6 Sept. 1781, who, under Benedict Arnold, acted cruelly after the surrender, col. Ledyard being killed when delivering his sword

fort Harrison, on the Wabash, about 2 miles above Terre Haute, Ind, built by gen Harrison, 1811 Gallantly defended by capt. Zachary Taylor, with a garrison of 50 men, from an attack by the Indians, 4 Sept 1812

fort Henry, W Va., built on the south bank of the Ohio, just above Wheeling, as a place of refuge from the Indians, 1774 Attacked by Simon Girty with 400 Indians in summer of 1777 It was garrisoned by 40 men, 23 of whom were killed in an attempted reconnoissance, the remainder stood a siege until reinforced by 54 men, when their assailants retired Here Elizabeth Zane, in the midst of the attack, undertook the dangerous task of procuring a keg of powder concealed in a distant outhouse for the garrison

fort Henry, Tenn., on the Tennessee river, was captured by gen U S Grant and com A. H Foote, 6 Feb 1862, with 7 gun-boats, 4 of them iron-clad. Gen Grant, with 11 regiments, moved to the rear of the fort, when gen Tilghman, commanding, sent most of his men, about 3000, to fort Donelson, retaining 83 in the fort. 21 of these were killed or wounded and the remainder, including Tilghman, with 17 guns, were captured.

fort Hindman, Arkansas post, on the Arkansas river, captured by the federals under gen John A McClernand, 11 Jan 1863 ARKANSAS.

fort Independence, on Castle island, in Boston harbor, was first built in 1634, and called Castle William It was ceded to the United States by Massachusetts in 1798, and received its name from pres John Adams while visiting it in 1799 It is one of the finest forts in the U S

fort Independence, N Y, a small fort built 1776 on the east bank of the Hudson, a little below and on the opposite side of the river from forts Clinton and Montgomery

fort Jackson, La., about 65 miles below New Orleans, on the Mississippi was begun in 1814 It was seized by the confederates 10-13 Jan 1861 Com Farragut passed this fort and St Philip 24 Apr 1862, it surrendered to gen. B F Butler 28 Apr

fort Lafayette (formerly fort Diamond, name changed 1823), on the left of the Narrows in New York harbor, used during the civil war as a military prison

fort Le Bœuf, Pa, built by the French on French creek about 30 miles southeast of the present city of Erie, Pa, 1753 Here Washington met the French commander when sent by gov Dinwiddie of Virginia to learn regarding the occupancy of the Ohio valley by the French PENNSYLVANIA.

fort Lee, N J, on the Hudson, opposite fort Washington Occupied by gen Greene when it was captured by Cornwallis, 19 Nov 1776, gen Greene, however, escaped with his force, but lost all the stores, cannon, etc

fort Mackinac, Mich, on an island in the strait between lakes Huron and Michigan, built by the French, 1670-1680, occupied by the English, 1760 Capture and massacre of the English garrison by Indians during the Pontiac war, 4 June, 1763, turned over to the United States by the British, 1795 Captured by the British without resistance, 17 July, 1812 U S troops, 500 regulars and 400 militia, under col Croghan, unsuccessfully attempted to recapture it, 4 Aug 1814

fort Macon, N C., on Rogue's island, commands the entrance to Newport river, begun in 1826 and finished in 1834 Seized by gov Ellis of N C. early in 1861 for the confederates Surrendered to the federals under gen. Parke and adm Dupont, 25 Apr 1862

fort McAllister, Ga., on the Ogeechee river, built by the confederates; captured by assault by gen Hazen, 13 Dec 1864

fort McHenry, Md, 3 miles southeast from the city of Baltimore First work built 1775, present work 1794. Sustained, with a garrison of 1000 men under gen Armistead, a severe bombardment from the British fleet of 16 vessels, 13 Sept 1814 It was during this bombardment that Francis S Key composed the song, "STAR SPANGLED BANNER." British retired, loss slight on both sides.

fort McRee, Fla, opposite fort Pickens, Pensacola bay, begun in 1833, seized by the confederates, 12-13 Jan 1861, re-occupied by the federals, 9-10 May, 1862

fort Meigs, at the foot of the Maumee rapids, Ohio, built early in 1813 by gen Harrison, and named after gov. Meigs of Ohio. Here gen Harrison was besieged by a strong force of British and Indians under gen Proctor, 28 Apr.-8 May, 1813 Gen Green Clay, attempting to reinforce Harrison, lost most of his command, but part of it entered the fort, and Proctor retired. Again assaulted by the same leader with about 4000 British and Indians, 21 July, 1813, repulsed, gen. Clay in command of the fort

fort Mercer, N J, built on the east bank of the Delaware, not far below Philadelphia, under command of col Christopher Green Assaulted by British under count Donop, 22 Oct 1777, repulsed, Donop mortally wounded and captured, dying on the 25th Evacuated 20 Nov 1777 Cornwallis dismantled the fort and demolished the works.

fort Mifflin, Pa., on Mud island, 7 miles below Philadelphia, under lieut.-col Smith of Maryland, bombarded by a British fleet, 23 Oct 1777, which retired baffled, but renewed the attack on 10 Nov, and on the 16th the garrison evacuated it American loss 250 killed and wounded

fort Mimms, Ala., near Montgomery, celebrated for the Indian massacre of 30 Aug. 1813. ALABAMA.

fort Montgomery, N. Y, on the west bank of the Hudson, a little below West Point, built at the same time as fort Clinton, completed 1776. It held a garrison of 800 men. Captured with fort Clinton by a British force under sir Henry Clinton, 6 Oct 1777. CLINTON and MONTGOMERY, FORTS

fort Morgan, Ala., entrance to Mobile bay, begun 1819, seized by the Alabama troops, 5 Jan 1861, surrendered to the federals—fleet under adm Farragut, and land forces under gen. Gordon Granger—23 Aug 1864

fort Motte, S. C., near the Congaree river, the residence of Mrs Rebecca Motte, fortified by the British, captured by the Americans under gen. Marion, 12 May, 1781.

fort Moultrie, S. C., on Sullivan's island, in Charleston harbor, built in 1776, first called fort Sullivan, but name changed to Moultrie in honor of its commander, bombarded by a British fleet under sir Peter Parker, 28 June, 1776, of 10 vessels, 2 of 50 guns each, 7 of 28, and 1 of 22 After 10 hours of firing it withdrew During this bombardment, serg William Jasper distinguished himself by replacing the flag, the staff of which had been shot away, the flag falling outside of the fort Fort rebuilt in 1812 Evacuated by maj Robert Anderson by night, 26 Dec 1860, and FORT SUMTER occupied Fort Moultrie occupied by confederates on the 27th, until abandoned 18 Feb 1865, upon the evacuation of Charleston

fort Necessity. VIRGINIA, 1754

fort Niagara, N Y, at the mouth of the Niagara river on its east bank A fortification was erected here by La Salle in 1679, improved by the French, 1725, captured by the British, 1759 Further enlarged, it was the rendezvous of Tories and Indians during the Revolution, and held by the British until turned over, 1795, to the United States. Bombarded by the British across the river, 21 Nov 1812, captured by them, 19 Dec 1813 NEW YORK

fort Ninety-six, on the site of the village of Cambridge, S C, built by the British, named because 96 miles from the frontier fort Prince George Occupied by a garrison of American loyalists under lieut-col Cruger, besieged by gen Greene from 22 May to 19 June, 1781, when, on approach of Rawdon, he raised the siege Soon after abandoned by the British.

fort Ontario, N Y, at the mouth of the Oswego river East bank built by the English, 1727, strengthened in 1755 Surrendered to the French under Montcalm, 14 Aug 1756, 1400 men, 120 cannon, 14 mortars, with ammunition and stores Fort dismantled by the French and partly destroyed The British rebuilt it in 1759 and held it through the Revolution, but was delivered up to the United States, 1796 The fort, with a garrison of about 300 men under lieut-col Mitchell, attacked by the British fleet with 3000 men under sir James L Yeo, 6 May, 1814 The garrison withdrew from the fort, which the British immediately occupied, but abandoned the next day after dismantling it

fort Orange, built by the Dutch at Albany, N Y, 1623 NEW YORK.

fort Pickens, Fla, on Santa Rosa island, commanding the entrance to the harbor of Pensacola bay. While most of the forts in the south were seized by the confederates during the spring of 1861, this fort was held by lieut Adam J Slemmer, with a garrison of but 81 officers and men, and retained by the federals throughout the civil war It was besieged from 18 Jan 1861, until the middle of April, when it was reinforced with several hundred troops under col Henry Brown

fort Pillow, Tenn, on the east bank of the Mississippi, 40 miles above Memphis, built by the confederates, evacuated by them 4 Jan 1862, occupied by the federals, 5 Jan, and garrisoned by 577 men, 262 of whom were negroes, captured by the confederates under Forrest, 12 Apr 1864 From number killed both of black and white troops, after surrender, this event is known as the Fort Pillow massacre

fort Pitt. FORT DUQUESNE

fort Pulaski, Ga, on Cockspur island, built to guard the entrance to the Savannah river, was seized by confederates early in 1861 With difficulty gen Quincy A. Gillmore established batteries on Tybee island, which commanded it. On 9 Apr. 1862, these opened on the fort at a distance of about 1650 yards, and compelled its surrender on the 11th

fort Putnam, N Y, built 1778, on an eminence back of the present site of West Point.

fort Sanders, an unfinished but important work in the fortifications erected for the defence of Knoxville, E Tenn, assaulted by the confederates under gen. Longstreet on the night of 28–29 Nov 1863, repulsed with a loss of 800

fort Schuyler, N Y, built in 1758 as fort Stanwix, under the direction of gen Stanwix, where the city of Rome now stands. In 1776 it was extensively repaired, and called Schuyler in honor of gen. Philip Schuyler The fort invested by a force of British and Indians, 1700 strong, under St Leger, 2 Aug 1777 The garrison of 750 men, under command of col Gansevoort, having no flag, made one after the pattern adopted by the Continental Congress FLAG Gen Herkimer advanced with 800 men and fought the battle of ORISKANY, but while not defeated, he was unable to relieve the fort Schuyler now sent Benedict Arnold forward with a relieving force The latter, by stratagem, excited a panic in the force of St Leger, who hastily retired Fort abandoned 12 May, 1781

fort Stephenson, at lower Sandusky now Fremont, Ohio, was built in 1812, and garrisoned by 150 men under command of maj George Croghan, then 21 years of age It was invested by a large force of British and Indians under command of Proctor, 31 July, 1813, but in an assault, 2 Aug, they lost 120 men and retired early on the morning of the 3d On 13 Feb 1835, 22 years after, Congress awarded a gold medal to col Croghan for his gallant defence UNITED STATES, 1835

fort Stony Point, N Y, a partly finished fort on the Hudson river, captured by the British with its small garrison, 1 June, 1779 They further strengthened the fort and garrisoned it with about 600 men under lieut.-col Johnson Gen Washington assigned the task of recapturing it to gen Anthony Wayne, who, on the night of 16 July, stormed the works with Massachusetts light infantry, capturing the entire garrison, with a loss of 15 killed and 83 wounded The Americans, however, evacuated it on the 18th, after destroying the works Wayne's assault was one of the most brilliant exploits of the Revolution

fort St. Philip, La., about 65 miles below New Orleans, on the opposite (east) bank, and a little above fort Jackson, on the Mississippi, built by the Spaniards about 1750 Seized with fort Jackson by the confederates, 10-13 Jan 1861, and bombarded by Farragut on his way up the river to New Orleans, 24 Apr 1862 It surrendered to gen Benj F Butler, 28 Apr

fort Sumter, in Charleston harbor, nearly midway between Sullivan and Morris islands, and 3½ miles from Charleston city Begun in 1828, and originally a casemated brickwork of 5 faces, designed for 2 tiers of guns in embrasure and *en barbette* In the spring of 1861 maj Robert Anderson, commanding in Charleston harbor, in view of the secession of South Carolina (20 Dec. 1860), and of her preparations to seize the forts in the harbor, evacuated FORT MOULTRIE on the night of 26 Dec and occupied fort Sumter The *Star of the West*, sent to reinforce Sumter, was fired upon off Morris island (9 Jan 1861), and returned to New York For 4 months preparations were made by the confederates at Charleston—7000 men under gen G T Beauregard—for an attack on fort Sumter On 11 Apr Beauregard demanded its surrender, which was refused by maj Anderson That night the relieving flotilla reached the offing, and at 3.20 A.M on the 12th Anderson was notified that fire would be opened upon him in one hour At that time the bombardment began from fort Moultrie 2 batteries at fort Johnson, an iron-clad battery on Cumming's Point, another near Charleston, and others formed for this purpose The first gun was fired by Edmund Ruffin, an aged Virginian UNITED STATES, 1861 After about 3 hours the garrison answered the fire 3 times during the day the quarters were set on fire by the shells At noon the relieving fleet was discerned from the fort and saluted The bombardment was continued till dark, and renewed on the 13th No reinforcements could reach the fort. The fires again broke out, and the fort becoming untenable, maj Anderson surrendered it, and the next day (14 Apr) evacuated the work, lowering his flag with a salute, and with the garrison sailed northward In this first conflict of the civil war there were no casualties on either side On 7 Apr 1863, an attempt by adm Dupont, with a fleet of monitors, to reduce fort Sumter, failed on account of obstructions in the harbor, which prevented the vessels from reaching the weakest side of the fort The monitor *Keokuk* was sunk, and other vessels sustained serious injuries The bombardment was renewed by adm Dahlgren after the occupation of Morris island in the summer of 1863, but the fort, though reduced to an earthwork, and rendered temporarily harmless as an offensive work, was not captured It was held by the confederates until they evacuated Charleston, 17 Feb 1865 On 18 Feb 1865, the U S flag was again raised over fort Sumter by maj.-gen Hennessy, while on 14 Apr 1865, the same flag which had been lowered by maj Anderson just 4 years before (14 Apr 1861) was again raised by him above the fort with appropriate ceremonies

fort Ticonderoga, N Y, on the west side of lake Champlain and at the outlet of lake George into that lake, built by the French in 1756, and named by them fort Carillon, but the Indian name was generally applied to it—Ticonderoga, a corruption of Cheonderoga, an Iroquois word signifying *sounding* or *brawling water* It was from the first a strong work, but afterwards much strengthened, and served as the starting-place and general rendezvous for the French expeditions under Montcalm and others. An attack was made on the fort 8 July, 1758, by gen James Abercrombie, who had moved against it from the lower end of lake George with 7000 regulars, 9000 provincials, and a large train of artillery, and although the French commander had but 4000 men, the British were signally defeated with a loss of 2000, including gen Geo. A Howe. Abercrombie retreated In 1759 it was again invested by gen Amherst with 11,000 men, the French, without resistance, retired to Crown Point, 27 July, 1759 At the commencement of the Revolution, Ticonderoga was garrisoned by 48 men under capt. Delaplace. It was surprised on the morning of 10 May, 1775, by Ethan Allen with 83 men, and taken with 120 iron cannon, 50 swivels, 2 10-inch mortars, 1 howitzer, 1 cohorn 10 tons of musket-balls, 3 cartloads of flints, 100 stands of small-arms, etc Benedict Arnold accompanied this expedition. Maj.-gen Arthur St. Clair was in command at Ticonderoga when it was approached by Burgoyne in 1777. His force consisted of 2546 continentals and 900 militia Owing to the superior position of the British, St Clair abandoned the fort on the night of 6 July, 1777

fort Wagner, S C, built by confederates at the north end of Morris island about 2600 yards from fort Sumter Assaulted by the federals, 11 July, 1863, grand assault made after a bombardment by batteries and fleet from noon until dark, 18 July, 1863, which failed, with a loss to the federals of 1500 men From this time it was under an almost continuous fire until 7 Sept 1863, when it was evacuated, the federals having advanced their parallels nearly to the fort. Although 122,300 pounds of metal had been hurled at the fort during the last 2 days of the siege at short range from breaching guns, none of them less than 100-pounders, the bomb-proofs were found intact, showing the power of resistance in sand.

fort Warren, Boston harbor, Mass, on George's island, begun in 1833, famous as a prison for confederate officers during the civil war

fort Washington, site between 181st and 186th sts, New York, was built 1776 on the highest elevation on Manhattan island On 16 Nov 1776, it was captured by the British under Howe, with its garrison of more than 2000 men under command of col Robert Magaw.

fort Wayne, Ind, where the town of Fort Wayne now stands, was built in 1794 by gen Wayne, soon after his defeat of the Indians at "Fallen Timbers." It was successfully defended against 600 Indians, 28 Aug.-12 Sept 1812, by a garrison of 70 men under capt James Rhea, on 12 Sept the Indians fled on the approach of a relieving party under gen Harrison

fort William Henry, erected at the head of lake George, N Y, by gen Johnson, late in 1755, after a battle there with the French under Dieskau, was attacked by the French and Indians, under Montcalm, 16 Mch 1757, but the defence was so vigorous that Montcalm retired to Ticonderoga, where, being reinforced, he again marched to the fort, with a force of over 9000 men and a train of artillery, while the garrison under col Monroe numbered some 3000 To a summons from Montcalm to surrender, 3 Aug, Monroe refused After a siege of 6 days, col Monroe, his ammunition and stores quite exhausted, agreed to surrender under a promise of protection from the Indians No sooner, however, had the garrison marched out (9 Aug), than the Indians commenced an indiscriminate slaughter, which was continued half-way to fort Edward, 1500 of the garrison perished or were carried into captivity Montcalm burned or otherwise destroyed everything connected with the fort. It was never again rebuilt. FORT GEORGE

fortifications and **fortresses.** The Phœnicians were the first people to fortify cities Apollodorus says that Perseus fortified Mycenæ, where statues were afterwards erected to him CHINESE WALL, HADRIAN'S WALL The modern system was introduced about 1500 Albert Durer wrote on fortification in 1527, and improvements were made by Vauban, who fortified many places in France, he died 1707 The following is a list of principal fortresses of Europe

Austria Hungary.—First class fortresses at Cracow, Przemysl, Karlsburg, Arad, Temesvar Komorn, Peterwardein Buda Pesth, Pola, and Trieste, the 2 last naval harbors as well There are lesser fortresses at Josephstadt, Theresienstadt, Brod-Karlstadt, Zara, Ragusa, Cattaro, besides numerous defences on the Alpine frontier in Tyrol, etc

Belgium—First class, Antwerp, and the fortified towns of Dendermonde and Diest, on the Meuse, Liége, Huy, and Namur, and on French frontier, Mons Tournay, and Ypres

Denmark—Copenhagen is the only fortress of importance

France—On the German frontier 3 first class fortresses, Belfort, Verdun, and Briançon, besides less important ones at Langres, Toul Auxonne, and 9 fourth class places On the Belgian frontier 4 first class, Lille, Dunkirk, Arras, and Douay, 8 second class, 6 third class, and others of less note On the Italian frontier 3 first class, Lyon, Grenoble, and Besançon, and 11 detached forts Mediterranean coast, Toulon (naval), first-class, Antibes second-class, and 21 forts Spanish frontier, first class, Perpignan and Bayonne and 12 lesser fortifications. On the Atlantic coast 3 first class, Rochefort, Lorient, and Brest, 5 second class and 17 forts. Channel coast, first class Cherbourg, 2 second class and 16 forts

Germany—On the Baltic, 2 first class, Königsberg and Danzig, 3 second class, Boyen, Memel and Pillau On the Polish frontier, Posen and Neisse, first class, Glogau and Klatz, second class Central Germany 3 first class, Spandau, Magdeburg, and Küstrin, second class, Torgau Southern Germany, 4 first class, Mainz, Ingolstadt, Rastatt, and Ulm French frontier, first class, Metz and Strasburg, second-class, Dienhofen, Bitsch, and New Breisach Belgian frontier, first class, Cologne and Koblenz, second class, Wesel and Saar Louis. Lower Baltic and North sea, first class, Kiel, second class, Friedrichsort Cuxhaven Geestemünde, Wilhelmshaven, and Swinemünde Vistula district, second class, Thorn, Graudenz, and Dirschau The German fortresses are all connected by underground telegraphs

Italy.—First class fortresses at Casale, Placentia, Cremona, Peschiera, Verona Mantua, Legnago (the last 4 forming the old Austrian Quadrilateral), all in the valley of the Po, besides Pavia, Venice, Alessandria, and Bologna On the coasts are Ventimiglia, Vado, Genoa, Spezzia, Gaeta, Civita Vecchia Tarentum, Brindisi, Ancona, Brindolo, etc

Russia.—Has an extensive frontier of land and sea protected by numerous fortresses. The principal on the west (Polish) frontier are Novo Georgievsk, Warsaw, Kief Ivangorod Brest Litovsk, and Vilna Baltic coast Riga, Dunamünde, Revel, Narva, Kronstadt, Viborg, Fredericksham, Helsingfors, Abo, and others Black sea coast, Odessa and Nikolaiev In the Crimea, Sebastopol and isthmus of Perekop, while others less important extend eastward to the Pacific ocean, where is found Nikolaifsk and Vladivostok, at the mouth of the Amour

Turkey—In Bulgaria are the 5 famous fortresses, viz Rustchuk, Silistria, and Widden on the Danube, Varna on the Black sea, and Shumla in the interior

Principal fortresses in the Mediterranean are MALTA and GIBRALTAR, both belonging to Great Britain

United States—The only fortress is fortress Monroe at Old Point Comfort, Va., built to defend the navy yard at Norfolk It was commenced in 1817 after designs by gen Simon Bernard (b France 1779, d Paris 1839, eminent military engineer under Napoleon, etc, served in U S army, 1816-31) Its area is about 80 acres, surrounded by a moat, with tide water from 8 to 15 feet deep and from 75 to 150 feet wide A full armament would consist of 371 guns. Its plan is an irregular heptagon, it has cost about $3,000,000

Fortunate isles. CANARY ISLANDS.

fortune-telling is traced to early astrologers, by whom the planets Jupiter and Venus were supposed to betoken happiness The Sibyllæ were women said to be inspired by Heaven. GYPSIES, SIBYLS In England the laws against fortune-telling were long severe A severe decree was published in France, 11 Jan 1680, against fortune-tellers and poisoners, under which several suffered death—*Hénault* Fortune-tellers in England are liable by acts of 1743 and 1824 to be imprisoned as rogues and vagabonds

forum, at Rome, originally a market-place, became about 472 B.C. the place of assembly of the people in their tribes (the Comitia), and was gradually adorned with temples and public buildings.—Near Forum Trebronii, in Mœsia, the Romans were defeated by the Goths, Nov 251 A D After a struggle in the morass, the emperor Decius and his son were slain and their bodies not recovered

Fossalta, near Bologna, central Italy. Here Enzo or Enrico, titular king of Sardinia, natural son of the emperor Frederick II, was defeated and made prisoner, 26 May, 1249. He was kept in honorable captivity till his death, 14 Mch. 1272.

Fotheringhay castle, Northamptonshire, Engl, built about 1400 Here Richard III of England was born in 1450, and here Mary queen of Scots was tried, 11-14 Oct 1586, and beheaded, 8 Feb 1587 It was demolished by her son, James I of England, in 1604

Foughard, near Dundalk, N Ireland Here Edward, brother of Robert Bruce, after invading Ireland in 1315, was defeated by sir John Bermingham, 5 Oct 1318 Bruce was killed by Roger de Maupis, a burgess of Dundalk

foundling-hospitals are ancient Public buildings for receiving foundlings existed in Rome in the 6th century One was set up at Milan in 787, and in the middle ages others in the principal cities of Europe One founded in Florence in 1317 still flourishes The French government in 1790 declared foundlings "children of the state"

No foundling hospital in England when Addison wrote 1713
London foundling hospital, projected by Thomas Coram, a sea-captain, incorporated Oct 1739, opened 2 June, 1756
Handel gave an organ, opened it 1 May, 1750
It succors about 500 infants, Coram s statue put up 1856
Foundling hospital in Dublin instituted in 1704, internal department closed by order of government 31 Mch 1835
Foundling hospital at Moscow, founded by Catherine II in 1772, about 12 000 children are received annually

fountains. The fountain of Hero of Alexandria was invented about 150 B C Among remarkable fountains at Rome are the Fontana di Trevi, constructed for pope Clement XII in 1735, the Fontana Paolina, for pope Paul V in 1612, and Fontana dell' Acqua Felice, called also the Fountain of Moses Those in the palace gardens at Versailles, made for Louis XIV, and the Grand Jet d'Eau at St Cloud, are beautiful There are above 100 public fountains in Paris, the most striking being the Château d'Eau on the Boulevard St Martin (by Girard, 1811), and that at the Palais Royal

Fourierism, a social system devised by M Charles Fourier (d 1837) The phalanstery (from *phalanx*), an association of 400 families living in one edifice, designed to secure the highest amount of happiness at lowest cost. The system failed, its advocates say, because tried on a small scale

"Four Masters," a name given to Michael, Conary, and Cucogry O'Clery and Ferfeasa O'Mulconry, who, in the first half of the 17th century, compiled from original documents the annals of Ireland from 2242 B.C to 1616 A D An edition of these, from autograph MSS, with a translation edited by dr John O'Donovan, was published at Dublin, 1851

foxglove (folks' or fairies' glove), a handsome indigenous flower The canary foxglove (*Digitalis canariensis*) came from the Canary islands, 1698 The Madeira foxglove introduced into England in 1777 The fox-grape, the scuppernong (*Vitis vulpina*), from Virginia to England before 1656

Fraga, a town of N.E. Spain Near here the Christians, under Alfonso I. of Aragon, were defeated by the Moors, 17 July, 1134.

franc, the current silver French coin (19 4 cents), superseded the *livre tournois* by law in 1795

France, the Roman GAUL In the 5th century it was conquered by the Franks, a German people of Franconia in Germany, where they became known about 240. The country was gradually named *Franken ric*, Franks' kingdom For dynastic changes, see tables Before the revolution France was divided into 40 governments In 1790 it was divided into 83 departments, and later into 130, including Corsica, Geneva, Savoy, and other conquests. In 1815 the departments were reduced to 86, in 1860 they were raised to 89 by the acquisition of Savoy and Nice, in 1871 reduced to 86 by the loss of Alsace and Lorraine France, since the overthrow of Napoleon III, 4 Sept. 1870, has been a republic, confirmed 25 Feb. and 16 June, 1875, by an organic law (*Constitution Wallon*), modified June, 1879, Aug 1884, June, 1885, and July, 1889 The legislative power is vested in a Chamber of Deputies and a Senate, and the executive in a president and a ministry. President elected for 7 years by the Senate and the Chamber of Deputies united in a congress. The president promulgates the laws and enforces them He selects a ministry from the chamber, appoints all civil and military officers, has the right of individual pardon, and is responsible only in case of high-treason. He concludes treaties with foreign powers, but cannot declare war without previous assent of both chambers In case of vacancy the 2 chambers meet immediately and unitedly elect a new president Area, 204,092 sq miles. Pop in 1700, 19,669,320, 1762, 21,769,163, 1801, 27,349,003, 1820, 30,451,187, 1836, 33,540,910, 1846, 35,401 761, 1856, 36 039,364, 1861, including the new departments, 37,382,225, 1872 (after the war), 36 102,921 (Alsace and Lorraine lost with 1,597,219 in 1871), 1876, 36,905,788, 1886, 38,218,903, 1891, 38,343,192, 1901, 38,961,945

Franks settle in that part of Gaul afterwards called Flanders, about 418
Clovis 481, defeats Syagrius and the Gauls at Soissons, 486, the Alemanni at Tolbiac, near Cologne, embraces Christianity, 496
He kills Alaric the Goth at the battle of Vouglé, near Poitiers, unites his conquests from the Loire to the Pyrenees and makes Paris his capital 507
He proclaims the Salic law, and dies, leaving 4 sons 511
Frequent invasions of the Avars and Lombards 562-84
Mayors of the palace assume sovereign authority 584
Charles Martel, mayor of the palace 714
Invasion of Saracens. 720, defeated by Charles Martel near Tours 10 Oct 732
Reign of Pepin the Short 752
Charlemagne king, 768, conquers Saxony and Lombardy, 773-774, crowned emperor of the West 25 Dec. 800
Normans invade Neustria, 876, part of which is granted Rollo, as Normandy, by Charles the Simple 911
Reign of Hugh Capet. 987
Paris made capital of all France 996
Letters of franchise granted to cities and towns by Louis VI 1135
Louis VII joins in the crusades. 1146
Philip Augustus defeats the Germans at Bouvines 1214
Louis VIII, Cœur de Lion, frees his serfs 1224
Charles of Anjou conquers Naples and Sicily 1266
Louis IX conducts an army into Palestine, takes Damietta, 1249 (CRUSADES), d before Tunis 25 Aug 1270
Tyranny of Charles of Anjou causes massacre called SICILIAN VESPERS 1282
Philip the Fair's quarrels with the pope 1301-2
Knights templars suppressed 1307-8
Union of France and Navarre 1314
English invasion—Philip VI defeated at Crecy 26 Aug 1346
Calais taken by Edward III 3 Aug 1347
Dauphiny annexed to France 1349
Battle of POITIERS, king John taken (brought prisoner to England) 19 Sept 1356
France laid under an interdict by the pope. 1407
Battle of AGINCOURT 25 Oct 1415
Massacre of the Armagnacs by the Burgundians June, 1418
Henry V of England acknowledged heir to the throne 1420
Henry VI crowned at Paris, duke of Bedford regent. 1422
Siege of Orleans, 8 May, battle of Patay, English defeated by Joan of Arc. 18 June, 1429
Joan of Arc burned at Rouen 30 May, 1431
England lost all France (but Calais) . 1434 and 1450
"League of the Public Good" against Louis XI by the nobles, Dec 1464-Oct 1465
Edward IV of England invades France . 1475
Charles VIII conquers Naples, 1494, loses it 1496
League of Cambray against Venice 1508
Pope Julius II forms the Holy League against France 1511
English invasion—battle of Spurs. 16 Aug 1513
Interview on the FIELD OF THE CLOTH OF GOLD between Francis I and Henry VIII of England 1520
Francis I defeated and taken at Pavia 24 Feb. 1525
Peace of Cambray 5 Aug 1529
Persecution of Protestants begins 1530
Royal printing press established, 1531, Robert Stephens prints Latin Bible 1532
Brittany annexed to France "
League of England with emperor Charles V, Henry VIII invades France 1544
Peace with England 7 June, 1546
Successful defence of Metz by the duke of Guise 1552
He takes Calais 1558
Religious wars, massacre of Protestants at Vassy 1 Mch 1562
Guise defeats Huguenots at Dreux 19 Dec "
Guise killed at siege of Orleans, 18 Feb, temporary peace of Amboise 19 Mch 1563
Huguenots defeated at St. Denis . 10 Nov 1567
At Jarnac, 13 Mch, at Moncontour 3 Oct. 1569
Massacre of St Bartholomew 24 Aug 1572
"Holy Catholic League" established 1576
Duc de Guise assassinated by king's order, 23 Dec, and his brother the cardinal 24 Dec. 1588
Henry III stabbed by Jacques Clement, a friar, 1 Aug., d 2 Aug 1589
Henry IV defeats the league at Ivry 14 Mch. 1590
He becomes a Roman Catholic 25 July, 1593
League leaders submit to him Jan 1596
He promulgates the edict of Nantes . 13 Apr 1598
Silk and other manufactures introduced by him and Sully 1606-10
Quebec, in North America, settled . 1608
Murder of Henry IV by Ravaillac 14 May, 1610
Regency of Mary de' Medici 1610-14
States general complain of the management of finances 27 Oct. 1614
Rise of the Concinis, 1610, their fall and death 1617
Navarre annexed to France 1620

Vigorous administration of Richelieu, begins with finance. 1624
Rochelle taken after a long siege 1628
"Day of Dupes," Richelieu defeats machinations of enemies, 11 Nov 1630
[Bulwer's drama "Richelieu" founded on the events of this time]
Richelieu organizes the *Academie de France* (ACADEMIES) 1634–35
His death (aged 58) 4 Dec 1642
Louis XIV, king, aged 4 (Anne of Austria regent) 14 May 1643
Administration of Mazarin, victories of Turenne 1643–46
Civil wars of the Fronde 1648 et seq
Death of Mazarin, 9 Mch, Colbert financial minister 1661
War with Holland etc 1672
Canal of Languedoc constructed 1664–81
Peace of Nimeguen 10 Aug 1678
Edict of Nantes revoked 22 Oct 1685
Louis marries madame de Maintenon "
War with William III of England 1689 et seq
Peace of Ryswick 20 Sept 1697
WAR OF THE SPANISH SUCCESSION Sept 1701
French defeated at Blenheim 2 Aug 1704
At Ramillies 23 May, 1706
Peace of Utrecht 11 Apr 1713
Dissensions of Jesuits and Jansenists, the bull Unigenitus Sept "
Accession of Louis XV, stormy regency of the duke of Orleans 1 Sept 1715 et seq
LAW'S BUBBLE in France 1716
French defeated at Dettingen 16 June, 1743
Successful campaign of marshal Saxe 1746
Peace of Aix la Chapelle 18 Oct 1748
SEVEN YEARS' WAR begins May, 1756
Damiens's attempt on life of Louis XV 5 Jan 1757
Canada lost—battle of Quebec 13 Sept 1759
Jesuits banished from France, their effects confiscated 1762
Peace of Paris, Canada ceded to England 10 Feb 1763
Louis XV under the influence of madame du Barry 1769
Death of Louis XV 10 May, 1774
Famine riots at Versailles May, 1775
Minister Turgot dismissed May, 1776
Ministry of Necker Nov "
Louis XVI assists American colonies against England, at first secretly 1778
Torture abolished in French judicature 1780
Peace of Versailles with England 3 Sept. 1783
Diamond necklace affair (DIAMONDS) 1785
Meeting of the assembly of notables 22 Feb 1787, again, 6 Nov 1788
Opening of STATES-GENERAL (308 ecclesiastics, 285 nobles, 621 deputies, Tiers Etat) 5 May, 1789
Tiers Etat constitute National Assembly 17 June, "
FRENCH REVOLUTION begins, destruction of BASTILE 14 July, "
National Assembly changes title "king of France" to "king of the French" 16 Oct "
Property of the clergy confiscated 2 Nov "
Emigration of nobles. Oct-Dec "
Confederation of Champ de Mars, France declared a limited monarchy, Louis XVI swears to maintain the constitution, 14 July, 1790
Silver plate taken from churches and coined 3 Mch 1791
Death of Mirabeau aged 42 years 2 Apr "
King, queen, and royal family arrested at Varennes, in flight, 21 June, "
Louis (a prisoner) sanctions national constitution 15 Sept "
War declared against the emperor 20 Apr 1792
Jacobin club declare their sittings permanent 18 June "
Multitude, with red bonnet of liberty march to Tuileries to make demands on king 20 June, "
First coalition against France, great French war begins (BATTLES 1792–1815) June, "
Swiss GUARDS cut to pieces, massacre of 5000 10 Aug "
Revolutionary tribunal set up 19 Aug "
Decree of National Assembly against priests, 40,000 exiled, 26 Aug "
Massacre in Paris, prisons broken open and 1200 persons (100 priests) slain 2–5 Sept "
Murder of the princess de Lamballe (FRENCH REVOLUTION), 3 Sept. "
National convention opened . 17 Sept. "
Duke of Brunswick defeated at Valmy 20 Sept "
Convention decrees a republic, 20 Sept, proclaimed 22 Sept. "
French people declare fraternity with all nations who desire to be free, and offer help 19 Nov "
Flanders conquered Dec "
Decree of perpetual banishment of Bourbons, those confined in Temple excepted 20 Dec "
Louis imprisoned in the Temple apart from the queen, brought to trial 19 Jan, condemned to death, 20 Jan, beheaded in the Place de Louis Quinze 21 Jan 1793
Committee of public safety established "
War with England and Holland declared 1 Feb "
War in LA VENDÉE Mch "
Reign of Terror—proscription of Girondists, 31 May, establishment of convention 23 June, "
Marat stabbed by Charlotte Corday 13 July, "
Charlotte Corday guillotined 17 July, "
Queen Marie Antoinette beheaded 16 Oct "
Execution of the Girondists 31 Oct "
Philip Egalité, duke of Orleans, who voted for the king's death, guillotined at Paris (ORLEANS), 6 Nov, madame Roland, 8 Nov "
Worship of Goddess of Reason . 10 Nov "
Adoption of new republican calendar 24 Nov "

Execution of Danton and others, 5 Apr, of madame Elizabeth, 12 May, 1794
Robespierre president, 4 June, he and 71 others guillotined, 28 July, "
Abolition of the revolutionary tribunal 15 Dec "
Peace with Prussia 5 Apr 1795
Insurrection of the Faubourgs 20, 21 May, "
Louis XVII dies in prison (WILLIAMS ELEAZAR) 8 June, "
French directory chosen 1 Nov "
Bonaparte marries Josephine, widow of vicomte de Beauharnais 8 Mch 1796
Bonaparte's successful campaigns in Italy 1796 et seq
Babeuf's conspiracy suppressed 12 May, 1796
Pichegru's conspiracy fails May, 1797
Expedition to Syria and Egypt July, 1798
European coalition against France Apr 1799
Council of Five Hundred deposed by Bonaparte, who is declared first consul 10 Nov "
He defeats the Austrians at Marengo 14 June, 1800
His life attempted by an infernal machine 24 Dec. "
Peace of Amiens (with England, Spain, and Holland) signed, 25–27 Mch. 1802
Amnesty to the emigrants Apr "
Legion of Honor instituted . 19 May, "
Bonaparte made consul for life 2 Aug "
Bank of France established 14 Apr 1803
Declaration of war against England 22 May, "
Conspiracy of Moreau and Pichegru against Bonaparte, 15 Feb, Pichegru strangled in prison (GEORGES) .6 Apr 1804
Duc d'Enghien executed 21 Mch. "
France an empire, Napoleon emperor, 18 May, crowned by the pope 2 Dec "
He is crowned king of Italy 26 May, 1805
Another coalition against France . Aug "
Napoleon defeats the allies at Austerlitz 2 Dec "
Prussians at Jena 14 Oct. 1806
Russians at Eylau . 8 Feb 1807
Meets the czar at Tilsit, 26 June, peace signed 7 July, "
His Milan decree against British commerce 17 Dec. "
New nobility of France created 1 Mch 1808
Abdication of Charles IV of Spain and his son in favor of Napoleon, 5 May, insurrection in Spain 27 May, "
Commencement of the Peninsular war (SPAIN) July, "
Alliance of England and Austria against France Apr 1809
Victories in Austria, Napoleon enters Vienna May, "
Peace of Vienna 14 Oct "
Divorce of Josephine decreed by the Senate 16 Dec "
Napoleon marries Maria Louisa of Austria . 1 Apr 1810
Holland united to France 9 July, "
Birth of the king of Rome (since styled Napoleon II) 20 Mch 1811
War with Russia declared 22 June, 1812
Victory at Borodino . 7 Sept "
Disastrous retreat from Moscow, French army destroyed Oct. "
Austria, Russia, and Prussia allied against France Mch 1813
British enter France 7 Oct "
Surrender of Paris to the allies 31 Mch. 1814
Abdication of Napoleon negotiated . 5 Apr "
Bourbons restored, Louis XVIII arrives in Paris 3 May, "
Napoleon arrives at Elba 4 May, "
Constitutional charter decreed . . 4–10 June, "
Quits Elba, and lands at Cannes 1 Mch 1815
Arrives at Fontainebleau (HUNDRED DAYS) 20 Mch "
Joined by all the army 22 Mch. "
Allies sign a treaty against him Mch. "
He abolishes the slave trade 29 Mch "
Leaves Paris for the army . . 12 June, "
Defeated at WATERLOO 18 June, "
Returns to Paris, 20 June, abdicates in favor of his infant son 22 June, "
Intending to embark for America arrives at Rochefort, 3 July, "
Louis XVIII enters Paris " "
Napoleon surrenders to capt. Maitland of the *Bellerophon* at Rochefort . .15 July, "
Transferred at Torbay to the *Northumberland*, and with adm sir George Cockburn sails for St Helena . 8 Aug "
Arrives at St. Helena to remain for life 15 Oct. "
Execution of marshal Ney . . 7 Dec. "
Family of Bonaparte excluded forever from France by the law of amnesty 12 Jan. 1816
Duc de Berri murdered 13 Feb. 1820
Death of Napoleon I (WILLS) . . . . 5 May, 1821
Louis XVIII dies, Charles X. king. . 16 Sept. 1824
National guard disbanded 30 Apr 1827
War with Algiers, dey's fleet defeated 4 Nov "
Seventy six new peers created 5 Nov "
Election riots at Paris, barricades, several killed 9, 20 Nov "
Villèle ministry replaced by the Martignac . 4 Jan 1828
Béranger imprisoned for political songs 10 Dec "
Polignac administration formed 8 Aug 1829
Chamber of Deputies dissolved . . . . 16 May, 1830
Algiers taken 5 July, "
Obnoxious ordinances regarding press, and reconstruction of Chamber of Deputies . 26 July, "
Revolution commences with barricades . . 27 July, "
Conflicts in Paris between the populace (ultimately aided by the national guard) and the army . 28–30 July, "
Charles X retires to Rambouillet, flight of his ministry, 31 July, he abdicates . . . 2 Aug "
Duc de Orleans accepts the crown as Louis Philippe I 7 Aug "
Constitutional charter of July pub . . . . 14 Aug "
Charles X. retires to England. . . . . 17 Aug. "

Polignac and other ministers tried and sentenced to perpetual imprisonment 21 Dec 1830
Abolition of hereditary peerage decreed, the peers (36 new peers created) concurring by 103 to 70 27 Dec 1831
A B C (*abaisses*) insurrection in Paris suppressed 5, 6 June, 1832
Charles X leaves Holyrood house, London, for Continent, 18 Sept "
Ministry of Soult, duke of Dalmatia 11 Oct "
Bergeron and Benoit tried for an attempt on the life of Louis Philippe, acquitted 18 Mch 1833
Duchess de Berri, who has been delivered of a female child, and asserts her secret marriage with an Italian nobleman, sent to Palermo 9 June, "
Death of Lafayette 20 May, 1834
Marshal Gerard takes office 15 July, "
M Dupuytren d 8 Feb 1835
Duc de Broglie minister Feb "
Fieschi attempts the king s life 28 July, "
[He fired an infernal machine as the king and his sons rode along the lines of the national guard on the Boulevard du Temple It had 25 barrels, charged with missiles, lighted simultaneously by a train of gunpowder The king and his sons escaped, but marshal Mortier, duke of Treviso, was shot dead, many officers dangerously wounded, more than 40 persons killed or injured]
Fieschi executed 19 Feb 1836
Louis Alibaud fires at the king on his way from the Tuileries, 25 June, guillotined 11 July, "
Ministry of count Molé *vice* M Thiers 6 Sept "
Death of Charles X 6 Nov "
Attempted insurrection at Strasburg by Louis Napoleon (planned, it is said, by Filain de Persigny), 29, 30 Oct, he is sent to America 13 Nov "
Prince Polignac and others set at liberty from Ham and sent out of France 23 Nov "
Meunier fires at the king on his way to open the French chambers 27 Dec. "
Amnesty for political offences 8 May, 1837
"Idées Napoleoniennes," by prince Louis Napoleon, pub 1838
Talleyrand d 20 May, "
Marshal Soult at the coronation of the queen of England, 28 June, "
Birth of the comte de Paris . 24 Aug "
Death of duchess of Würtemberg (daughter of Louis Philippe), a good sculptor 2 Jan 1839
Insurrection of Barbès and Blanqui at Paris 12 May, "
M Thiers minister of foreign affairs 1 Mch 1840
Chambers decree the removal of Napoleon s remains from St Helena to France 12 May, "
[By permission of the British government these were taken from tomb at St. Helena 15 Oct 1840 and embarked next day on board the French frigate *Belle Poule* under prince de Joinville, reached Cherbourg 30 Nov, and 15 Dec were deposited in the Hôtel des Invalides The ceremony was witnessed by 1,000 000 persons, 150 000 soldiers assisted in the obsequies, and the royal family and all notables were present, the relatives of the emperor were in exile or in prison The body was placed in its crypt on 31 Mch 1861]
Descent of prince Louis Napoleon, gen. Montholon and 50 followers, at Vimereux near Boulogne, 6 Aug, the prince sentenced to imprisonment for life 6 Oct "
Darmes fires at the king 15 Oct "
M Guizot minister of foreign affairs. 29 Oct. "
Project of law for an extraordinary credit of 140,000,000 francs for fortifications of Paris 15 Dec "
Copyright fixed at 30 years after author s death 30 Mch 1841
Bronze statue of Napoleon placed on the column of the Grande Armée, Boulogne 15 Aug "
Attempt to assassinate the duc d'Aumale (king's son) on return from Africa 13 Sept "
Duc de Orleans, heir to the throne, killed by a fall from his carriage 13 July 1842
Queen of England visits royal family at Chateau d Eu, 2-7 Sept 1843
Extradition treaty with England signed. "
War with Morocco, May, peace 10 Sept 1844
Lecompte attempts to assassinate king at Fontainebleau, 16 Apr 1846
Louis Napoleon escapes from Ham 25 May, "
Seventh attempt on life of the king, by Joseph Henri, 29 July, "
Spanish marriages queen of Spain with her cousin, and infanta with duc de Montpensier . 10 Oct. "
Disastrous inundations in the south 18 Oct "
Praslin murder (PRASLIN) 18 Aug 1847
Death of Marshal Oudinot (duc de Reggio) at Paris, in his 91st year, 13 Sept, Soult succeeds as general of France. 26 Sept "
Jerome Bonaparte returns to France after an exile of 32 years. 10 Oct "
Surrender of Abd-el Kader 23 Dec. "
Death of the ex empress, Maria Louisa, 18 Dec, and of madame Adelaide . 30 Dec. "
Grand reform banquet at Paris prohibited 21 Feb 1848
Revolutionary tumult, impeachment and resignation of Guizot, 22 Feb., barricades thrown up Tuileries ransacked, prisons opened and frightful disorders 23 24 Feb "
Louis Philippe abdicates in favor of his infant grandson, the comte de Paris, royal family and ministers escape 24 Feb "
Republic proclaimed from steps of Hôtel de Ville 26 Feb "
Ex king and queen arrive at Newhaven, Engl 3 Mch. "
Funeral procession for the victims of the revolution 4 Mch. "
Provisional government resigns to an executive commission, elected by the National Assembly 7 May, "
[The members were MM Dupont de l'Eure, Arago, Garnier Pagès, Marie, Lamartine, Ledru-Rollin, and Crémieux. The secretaries Louis Blanc, Albert, Flocon, and Marrast]
People s attack on the assembly suppressed 15 May 1848
Perpetual banishment of Louis Philippe and family decreed 26 May, "
Louis Napoleon elected to the National Assembly for the Seine and 3 other departments 13 June "
Rise of the Red Republicans, war against troops and national guard, more than 300 barricades thrown up, firing in all parts of Paris during the night 23 June, "
Troops under Cavaignac and Lamoricière with immense loss drive insurgents from left bank of Seine 24 June "
Paris declared in a state of siege 25 June, "
Faubourg du Temple carried with cannon and the insurgents surrender 26 June "
[The outbreak said to cost the nation 30 000,000 francs, 16 000 persons killed and wounded 8000 prisoners taken Archbishop of Paris killed while tending the dying, 26 June]
Cavaignac, president of the council 28 June, "
Louis Napoleon takes seat in National Assembly 26 Sept "
Paris relieved after a state of siege of 4 months 20 Oct "
Constitution of 4 Nov promulgated from Tuileries 12 Nov "
Louis Napoleon elected president, 11 Dec, proclaimed 20 Dec "
[He had 5,587,759 votes, Cavaignac 1,474 687 Ledru Rollin 381 026, Raspail 37,121, Lamartine, 21,032, Changarnier, 1975]
Military demonstration deters Reds from insurrection 29 Jan 1849
Louis Philippe dies at Claremont Engl 26 Aug 1850
Liberty of the press restricted 26 Sept "
Gen Changarnier, commander of national guard, removed, 10 Jan 1851
Death of the duchess d Angoulême, daughter of Louis XVI at Frohsdorf 19 Oct "
Death of marshal Soult 26 Oct "
Telegraph between England and France opened 13 Nov "
Coup d'etat, legislative assembly dissolved, universal suffrage proclaimed, Paris declared in a state of siege, president for 10 years proposed, and a second chamber or senate 2 Dec "
MM Thiers, Changarnier Cavaignac, Bedeau, Lamoricière, and Charres arrested and sent to castle of Vincennes 2 Dec "
About 180 members of the assembly, with M Berryer attempting to meet, arrested, Paris occupied by troops 2 Dec "
Fighting in Paris, troops victorious 3 4 Dec "
Consultative commission founded 12 Dec "
Vote for president for 10 years, 7,473,431, against, 641 351. 21 22 Dec "
Prince president installed at Notre Dame, a national holiday, Louis Napoleon occupies Tuileries 1 Jan 1852
Gens Changarnier, Lamoricière, and others conducted to the Belgian frontier 9 Jan "
Eighty three members of legislative assembly banished, 575 persons arrested for resisting *coup d'etat* of 2 Dec, and sent to Havre for transport to Cayenne 10 Jan "
[The inscription "Liberty, Fraternity, Equality" ordered erased throughout France and old names of streets public buildings, etc, restored Trees of liberty hewn down and burned]
National guard disbanded reorganized, and placed under executive, the president appointing officers 10 Jan "
New constitution pub . 14 Jan "
Orleans family required to sell all their property in France within a year 22 Jan "
Second decree, annulling family settlement by Louis Philippe at his accession, confiscating the property 22 Jan "
Birthday of Napoleon I (15 Aug) made the only national holiday 17 Feb "
Crystal palace authorized in Champs Elysées Paris 30 Mch "
M Thiers and others permitted to return to France 8 Aug "
Senate prays "the re establishment of hereditary sovereign power in the Bonaparte family" 13 Sept "
Prince president at Toulon, 27 Sept., at Bordeaux, says "*L'empire c'est la paix*" ("the empire is peace") 7 Oct "
Releases Abd el Kader (ALGIERS) 16 Oct "
Convokes senate for November to consider changes of government and prepare a decree for ratification by the people, 19 Oct "
By message to the senate he promises restoration of the empire and orders the people to be consulted 4 Nov "
Votes for the empire 7,824,189, nays, 253,145, null, 63,326. 21 Nov "
Prince president declared emperor as Napoleon III 2 Dec "
Marries Eugénie de Montijo, countess of Téba, at Notre Dame. 29 Jan 1853
Statue of Marshal Ney unveiled on the spot where he died, exactly 38 years before 7 Dec "
War declared against Russia (RUSSO TURKISH WARS) 27 Mch 1854
Industrial exhibition at Paris opened 15 May, 1855
Attempted assassination of emperor by Pianori 28 Apr "
By Bellemarre 8 Sept "
Peace with Russia signed 30 Mch 1856
Death of Beranger, popular poet 16 July, 1857
Longwood the residence of Napoleon I at St. Helena, bought for 180 000 francs "
Death of Eugène Cavaignac (aged 55) 28 Oct. "
Death of mdlle Rachel (aged 38) 4 Jan 1858
Attempted assassination of emperor by Orsini, Pieri, Rudio, Gomez, etc, by explosion of 3 shells (2 persons killed, many wounded) 14 Jan "
[Felix Orsini, a man of talent and energy, earnest for Italian independence b Dec. 1819, studied at Bologna in 1837, joined a secret society in 1843, condemned to the galleys for life in 1844, released in 1846, took part in the Roman revolution in 1848, elected to the assembly, on the fall of the

republic, fled to Genoa 1849, to England 1853 For fresh conspiracies, arrested in Hungary, Jan 1855, and sent to Mantua, escaped to England in 1856, where he associated with Kossuth, Mazzini etc , delivered lectures, and devised the plot for which he suffered By will he acknowledged the justice of his sentence]

"Napoleon III et l'Angleterre" pub 11 Mch 1858

Orsini and Pieri executed 13 Mch "

Dispute with Portugal on CHARLES ET GEORGES settled 23 Oct. "

Trial of comte de Montalembert 25 Nov "

[In Oct 1858, the comte in a pamphlet, "Un Debat sur l'Inde," eulogized English institutions depreciating those of France He was sentenced to 6 months imprisonment and fined 3000 francs, but pardoned by the emperor 2 Dec He appealed was acquitted of a part of the charge, and his sentence again remitted (21 Dec) In Oct 1859, the comte published a pamphlet entitled "Pie IX et la France en 1849 et 1850," censuring England for opposition to Romanism]

Publication of "Napoleon III et l Italie" Feb 1859

Austria invading Sardinia France declares war, and the French enter, the empress appointed regent, the emperor arrives at Genoa 12 May, "

Victories of French and Sardinians at Montebello, 20 May, Palestro, 30, 31 May, Magenta, 4 June, Melegnano (Marignano), 8 June, Napoleon enters Milan, 8 June, at Solferino, 24 June, "

Armistice 6 July, "

Emperors of France and Austria meet at Villa Franca, 11 July, "

Peace agreed on 12 July, "

Austrian and French envoys confer at ZURICH 8 Aug -Nov "

Emperor announces a free trade policy, Mr Cobden at Paris 5 Jan 1860

Treaty for annexation of Savoy and Nice signed 24 Mch "

Jerome Bonaparte, the emperor's uncle, d (aged 76) 24 June, "

New tariff comes into operation 1 Oct "

Public levy of Peter s pence forbidden, and issue of pastoral letters checked Nov "

Jerome (son of Jerome Bonaparte and Elizabeth Patterson, of Baltimore) sues for legitimate rights, nonsuited, 25 Jan -15 Feb 1861

[The marriage in the U S 24 Dec. 1803, was annulled, and Jerome married princess Catherine of Würtemberg, 12 Aug 1807, their children were prince Napoleon and princess Mathilde (BONAPARTE)]

Principality of Monaco bought for 4,000,000 francs, 2 Feb , announced 5 Feb "

"La France, Rome, et l'Italie" pub. 15 Feb. "

Prince Napoleon speaks for Italian unity, English alliance, and against the pope's temporal power 1 Mch "

Pope s temporal government advocated in the chambers, French army has 687 000 men Mch "

Circular forbidding priests to meddle with politics 11 Apr "

Declaration of neutrality in U S. conflict 11 June, "

Recognition of kingdom of Italy 24 June, "

Convention of France, Great Britain, and Spain, on intervention in Mexico, signed (MEXICO) 31 Oct. "

Embarrassment in finances, Achille Fould finance minister, 14 Nov , with enlarged powers 12 Dec. "

Emperor reminds clergy of their duty "to Cæsar" 1 Jan 1862

French army lands at Vera Cruz 7 Jan "

French masters of the province of Bienhoa, in Anam 20 Jan "

Victories in Cochin China (6 provinces ceded to France), 28 Mch "

Spanish and British plenipotentiaries decide to quit Mexico, French declare war against MEXICO 16 Apr "

Treaty of peace between France and Anam signed 3 June, "

Camp at Chalons formed because of Garibaldi's movements in Sicily, broken, when he is taken prisoner 29 Aug "

Sympathy for him in France Sept "

Emperor proposes a European congress, and invites sovereigns or their deputies by letter 4 Nov 1863

Invitation declined by England 25 Nov "

Convention of France, Brazil, Italy, Portugal, and Hayti for a telegraph between Europe and America 16 May, 1864

Death of marshal Pelissier, duke of Malakoff, governor of Algeria (b 1794) 22 May, "

Convention with France signed by Japanese ambassadors at Paris 20 June, "

Convention (France and Italy) to evacuate Rome, etc., 15 Sept "

Clergy forbidden to read pope's encyclical letter of 8 Dec in churches, archbishop of Besançon and other prelates disobey 5 Jan 1865

Death of Proudhon (b 1809), who said "La propriété c'est le vol" 19 Jan. "

Prince Jerome Napoleon vice president of privy council Jan "

Decree for an international exhibition of agriculture, industry, and the fine arts, at Paris, on 1 May, 1867 1 Feb. "

Duc de Morny (reported half brother of emperor), d. 10 Mch "

Inauguration of statue of Napoleon I at Ajaccio, with imprudent speech by prince Napoleon, 15 May, censured by emperor, 23 May, prince resigns offices 9 June, "

U S protest against intervention in Mexico—prolonged correspondence (MEXICO) Aug 1865-Feb. 1866

At Auxerre, Napoleon denounces the treaties of 1815 6 May, "

By letter says that in the German war "France will observe an attentive neutrality" 11 June, "

Emperor of Austria cedes Venetia to France, and invites emperor's intervention with Prussia 4 July, "

Empress Charlotte of Mexico arrives at Paris. 8 Aug. "

Note to Prussia desiring restoration of frontier of 1814; declared by Prussia to be inadmissible .. . . Aug "

Letter from comte de Chambord to his adherents in favor of the pope s temporal power, dated 9 Dec 1866

Richelieu's head after many removals, deposited in the Sorbonne 17 Dec. "

International exhibition opened (PARIS) 1 Apr 1867

Three provinces in Anam annexed to the empire 25 June, "

International conference at Paris on money 17 June-9 July, "

Protectorate over Cambodia assured by treaty 15 July, "

Abolition of imprisonment for debt adopted by senate, 18 July, "

Emperors of France and Austria meet at Salzburg, 18-21 Aug "

Emperor by letter recommends expenditure in railways, canals, and roads 15 Aug "

French troops enter ROME 30 Oct "

Garibaldians defeated at Mentana 3 Nov "

"Napoleon III et l Europe en 1867" pub Nov "

In the legislative assembly, Rouher the minister, says, "We declare that Italy shall never seize upon Rome" (government supported by 238 votes to 17) 5 Dec "

New army bill (allowing 100,000 recruits annually, a new national guard, etc , providing for an army of 1,200 000 men), passed in the *corps legislatif* (206 to 60) 1 Jan 1868

M Magne announces deficiency in the budget, and a loan for 90 000.000 francs 29 Jan "

Army bill passes senate—125 to 1 (Michel Chevalier, who spoke warmly against it), 30 Jan , becomes law 4 Feb "

"Les Titres de la Dynastie Imperiale" appeared about 20 Mch "

Rochefort's weekly *La Lanterne* suppressed, he and his printer condemned to fine and imprisonment, escapes to Belgium Aug "

Death of Lamartine (b Oct 1792), 28 Feb , of Troplong president of the senate 1 Mch 1869

Dissolution of legislative assembly of 1863 26 Apr "

Laying of French Atlantic telegraph completed 23 July, "

Père Hyacinthe (Loyson), Carmelite preacher at Paris protests against papal infallibility, etc. and resigns 20 Sept. "

Agitation against free trade Oct , Nov , Dec "

Victor Noir a journalist, killed by Pierre Bonaparte, at Auteuil, in meeting for a challenge to M Rochefort 10 Jan. 1870

Charles, comte de Montalembert author, d (*see* 1858) 13 Mch "

Trial of Pierre Bonaparte at Tours, acquitted (but ordered to pay 25,000 francs to Noir's family). 21-27 Mch "

Emperor proclaims proposed changes in constitution 24 Apr "

Plebiscite. Do the people approve the changes? (yes, 7,527,379, no, 1,530,909) 8 May, "

Orleans princes address legislative assembly, demanding return to France, 19 June, refused, 173 to 31 2 July, "

Prince Leopold of Hohenzollern Sigmaringen nominated for Spanish throne, warlike speeches of ministers 5, 6, 7 July, "

Prince Leopold withdraws, guarantees required by France from Prussia refused, France decides on war, 15 July, declaration signed (FRANCO PRUSSIAN WAR) 17 July, "

Empress appointed regent 23 July, "

Emperor joins army 28 July, "

Government declares that France is only "at war with the policy of Bismarck" 2 Aug "

State of siege proclaimed in Paris after defeat of MacMahon at Woerth 7 Aug "

Government appeals to France and Europe against Prussia, 8 Aug "

Stormy debate in the *corps legislatif* (M de Kératry called on emperor to abdicate, Guyot Montpeyroux said the army were "lions led by asses"), resignation of Ollivier and ministry 9 Aug "

New ministry gen Cousin Montauban, comte de Palikao (distinguished in China) minister of war, chief, M Chevreau, interior, M Magne, finance, Clement Duvernois, commerce and agriculture, adm Rigault de Genouilly, marine, baron Jerome David, public works, prince de La Tour d'Auvergne, foreign affairs, etc 10 Aug "

Decree enlarging army for the war, and appointing a "defence committee" for Paris 10 Aug "

Orleans princes (duc d'Aumale, prince de Joinville, duc de Chartres) offer services in the army, declined Aug "

Government declares against any negotiations for peace, 14 Aug "

Murder of Allain de Moneys, suspected of republicanism and Germanism (badly beaten and burned to death by peasants at Hautefaye, Dordogne, near Bordeaux) 16 Aug "

Gen Trochu (Orleanist), author of "L'Armée Française en 1867," governor of Paris, 17 Aug , issues proclamation, 18 Aug "

Decrees expulsion of all foreigners not naturalized 28 Aug "

Deputation from 10,000 persons call on Trochu to assume the government, he declines 8 P M 3 Sept "

Palikao announces to assembly defeat at Sedan, surrender of emperor and MacMahon s army (90,000) Jules Favre declares for defence to the last gasp, attacks the empire, and proposes dictatorship of gen. Trochu 3.35 A M 4 Sept. "

On motion of Thiers, a commission of government and national defence named, and a constituent assembly called, 3 10 P M 4 Sept. "

Assembly invaded by the crowd, demanding a republic, most deputies retire. Gambetta and other liberals assume to depose the emperor and establish a republic 4 15 P M. 4 Sept. "

Last meeting of senate, it adheres to the emperor " "

"Government of defence" proclaimed, gen Trochu president, Léon Gambetta, interior, Jules Simon, public instruction, Jules Favre, foreign, Crémieux, justice, Jules Picard, finance, gen Leflo war, Fourichon, marine, Magne, agriculture, Dorian, public works, Étienne Arago, mayor of Paris, Kératry, police . 4 Sept. "

Informal meeting of assembly, M Thiers, president. Jules

Favre reports formation of provisional government, some protest, Thiers recommends moderation evening. 4 Sept 1870

Empress, the comte de Palikao, and ministers secretly leave Paris and enter Belgium evening 4 Sept "

Legislative chamber dissolved, senate abolished, regular troops and national guard fraternize, perfect order reigns, 5 Sept "

Napoleon III reaches Wilhelmshöhe, near Cassel 9.35 P.M. 5 Sept "

Republican deputies in Spanish Cortes greet republic " "

Red Republican flag raised at Lyons " "

Victor Hugo and Louis Blanc arrive in Paris 6 Sept "

Jules Favre in a circular to French diplomatic representatives, says, "We will not cede either an inch of our territories or a stone of our fortresses" 6 Sept "

Proffered services of Orleans princes again declined " "

Republic recognized by the U. S. 8 Sept "

Defence committee summon king of Prussia to quit France at once 8 Sept "

Decree convoking constituent assembly of 750 members (to be elected on 16 Oct.) 8 Sept "

Prince imperial at Hastings 7 Sept., joined by empress. " "

Republic recognized by Spain 8 Sept., by Switzerland 9 Sept. "

Elections for constituent assembly ordered 2 Oct 16 Sept "

Diplomatic circular from Jules Favre, France makes no claim on Prussia for disinterestedness statesmen should hesitate to continue a war in which more than 200 000 men have fallen, a freely elected assembly is summoned, and the government will abide by its judgment, France, left to free action, asks the cessation of the war, but prefers disaster to dishonor, France has been wrong, and acknowledges its obligation to repair the wrong 17 Sept "

Government delegation under M. Crémieux, minister of justice, and foreign ambassadors, at Tours 18 Sept. "

Manifesto of Red Republicans by gen. Cluseret placarded in Paris about 18 Sept. "

Bronze statues of Napoleon ordered to be made into cannon, about 19 Sept "

M. Duruof in a post balloon quits Paris with mail bags, arrives at Evreux, and reaches Tours 23 Sept "

Failure of negotiations for peace between Bismarck and Jules Favre, manifesto of government at Tours, people must either disavow ministry or "fight to the bitter end," elections for assembly suspended 24 Sept "

All Frenchmen between 20 and 25 years of age prohibited leaving France about 26 Sept "

Enthusiasm in provinces on failure of negotiations, "war to the knife," and *levee en masse* proclaimed by prefects, war like ardor in Brittany stirred by M. Cathelineau, 26, 27 Sept. "

Disorder by Red Republicans at Lyons quieted by national guards, gen. Cluseret disappears 28 Sept. "

All between 21 and 40 to form a national garde mobile, all men in arms at disposal of minister of war 30 Sept "

All Frenchmen under 60 forbidden to quit France 8 Oct. "

M. Gambetta escapes from Paris in a balloon, 7 Oct., arrives at Rouen and declares for "a pact with victory or death," 8 Oct., arrives at Tours and becomes minister of war as well as of the interior 9 Oct "

Address from comte de Chambord, his whole ambition to found with the people a really national government 9 Oct. "

Blanqui, Gustave Flourens, Ledru Rollin, Félix Pyat, etc., Red Republicans, defeated in attempts to establish commune at Paris, 10, 11 Oct., reconciliation by Rochefort. about 14 Oct "

Circular of Gambetta stigmatizing surrender of Metz (on 27 Oct.) as a crime 28 Oct "

M. Thiers brings Paris news of surrender of Metz and proposals for an armistice 30 Oct "

Riots in Paris, gen. Trochu threatened, principal members of the defence government imprisoned in Hôtel de Ville, Ledru Rollin, Victor Hugo, and Gustave Flourens, etc., made a committee of public safety and of the commune under M. Picard, national guard releases the government 31 Oct. "

Empress arrives at Wilhelmshöhe, interview of Bazaine with emperor 31 Oct. "

Marshals Canrobert and Lebœuf and many generals at Wilhelmshöhe 1 Nov "

Government proclaims a *plebiscite* in Paris on 3 Nov Do the people uphold the government of national defence? 1 Nov "

Plébiscite for government, 557,976, against, 62,638 3 Nov "

Mobilization of all able bodied men between 20 and 40 4 Nov "

Failure of negotiations for an armistice 6 Nov "

"France can but carry on with such courage and strength as remain to her a war *à outrance*."—*Guizot.* 8 Nov "

Alexandre Dumas, novelist and dramatist, d 10 Dec "

Delegate government removed from Tours to Bordeaux, 11 Dec. "

Gambetta at Bordeaux declares that the government only holds office for the defence of the country, demonstration in honor of republic 1 Jan 1871

Foreigners not permitted to leave Paris by Germans 19 Jan "

Fierce speech of Gambetta at Lille, demanding continuance of war 22 Jan "

Disturbances at Paris suppressed by army 23 Jan "

Resignation of Trochu, Vinoy governor of Paris 24 Jan "

Capitulation of Paris, armistice signed by Favre and Bismarck. 28 Jan "

Disavowed by Gambetta at Bordeaux 31 Jan "

Duc d'Aumale declares for constitutional monarchy 1 Feb. "

Food from London reaches Paris (MANSION HOUSE) 3 Feb "

Government publish reasons for capitulation (2,000,000 people in Paris with only 10 days' provisions), 4 Feb., annul Gambetta's decree, 4 Feb., he and his ministry resign 5, 6 Feb. "

Proclamation of Napoleon III. "Betrayed by fortune," he condemns the government of 4 Sept. says that his government was 4 times confirmed in 20 years submits to the judgment of time, saying that a nation cannot long obey those who have no right to command" 8 Feb 1871

General election of a National Assembly " "

F. P. J. Grévy elected president Feb "

First meeting of new National Assembly 12 Feb "

Supplementary armistice signed 15 Feb "

Garibaldi resigns his election, 13 Feb., Grevy elected president by 519 out of 538 16 Feb "

Termination of war, Belfort garrison (12,000) marches out with military honors 16 Feb "

Pact of Bordeaux Thiers made chief of executive by agreement of parties in assembly, 17 Feb., voted 18 Feb "

Thiers ministry Dufaure justice, Jules Favre, foreign, Picard, interior, Jules Simon public instruction, Lambrecht commerce, gen. Leflo, war, adm. Pothuau, marine, De Larcy, public works 17 Feb "

Government recognized by the great powers 18 Feb "

Duc de Broglie appointed minister at London 21 Feb "

Thiers and Bismarck negotiate 22, 23, 24 Feb "

Preliminaries of peace accepted by MM. Thiers and Favre and 15 delegates to National Assembly (cession of parts of Alsace and Lorraine, including Strasburg and Metz and payment of 5 milliards of francs—$1,000,000,000), 25 Feb., signed, 26 Feb "

Preliminaries accepted by assembly (546 to 107), deposition of Napoleon III unanimously confirmed 1 Mch "

National guards seize cannon and plant them at Montmartre and Belleville against Germans entering Paris 1 Mch "

Emperor of Germany reviews about 100,000 troops at Longchamps near Paris 1 Mch "

Germans, 30 000 enter Paris, 1 Mch., depart 3 Mch "

National Assembly remove to Versailles (461-104) 10 Mch "

Blanqui, Floureus, etc., condemned for insurrection of 31 Oct 1870 12 Mch "

Central committee of republican confederation of national guards ("government of the Buttes") meet, depose Vinoy, appoint Garibaldi general in chief 15 Mch "

Insurrection at Paris, regular troops occupying Buttes Montmartre and Belleville, attacked by national guards soon fraternize with insurgents who capture and shoot gens. Lecomte and Clément Thomas, and seize the Hôtel de Ville, barricades erected in Belleville and other places, gen. Vinoy, with gendarmerie retires across the Seine 18 Mch "

Insurgents nominate a central committee of national guard, headed by Assy, a workman who seize public offices, Thiers by circular enjoins obedience to the assembly 19 Mch "

Central committee orders communal election in Paris, 19 Mch., liberates 11 000 political prisoners in Paris 20 Mch "

National Assembly at Versailles, propose conciliation, appoint committee to support the government 20 Mch "

Napoleon III arrives at Dover, Engl " "

Bank of France saved by courage of marquis de Plœuc, the governor and the forbearance of citizen Beslay 20 Mch "

Assembly appeal to nation and army 21 Mch "

Unarmed demonstration of Friends of Order, fired on by insurgents, 10 killed, 20 wounded 22 Mch "

Municipal elections at Paris, 200,000 out of 500 000 vote, two thirds in favor of insurgents 26 Mch "

Commune proclaimed at Hôtel de Ville 28 Mch "

Conference for peace meets at Brussels " "

Gustave Flourens, Blanqui, and Félix Pyat head the commune, wish to imitate Italian republics of middle ages 29 Mch "

Part remission of overdue rents ordered, standing army named national guard 29 Mch "

Reign of terror "Paris has no longer liberty of the press, of public meeting, of conscience, or of person."—*Le Soir*, 1 Apr "

Fighting begins 9 A.M. at Courbevoie, Flourens marches to Versailles *via* Rueil 2 Apr "

Corps of gen. Bergeret at Rond Point, near Neuilly, stopped by artillery of Mont Valérien, insurgents in forts Issy and Vanves exchange shots with Meudon 3 Apr "

Gen. Duval taken in fight at Châtillon, and shot, death of Flourens at Chatou, Delescluze, Cournet, and Vermorel succeed Bergeret, Eudes, and Duval on executive commission, Cluseret delegate of war, Bergeret commandant of Paris forces 4 Apr "

Gen. Cluseret takes offensive, military service compulsory for citizens under 40, the archbishop of Paris arrested 5 Apr "

Extension of lines to Neuilly and Courbevoie, "complicity with Versailles" made penal, hostages arrested, Dombrowski succeeds Bergeret in command of Paris, guillotine burned on Place Voltaire 6 Apr "

Federals abandon Neuilly, commission of barricades created and presided over by Gaillard senior, railway termini seized by insurgents. 8 Apr "

Marshal MacMahon, commander in chief for assembly, disposes his forces and invests fort Issy 11 Apr "

Versailles batteries established on Châtillon, Orleans railway and telegraph cut, southern communications of insurgents intercepted, decree to destroy column Vendôme 12 Apr "

Redoubt of Gennevilliers taken, troops of Versailles advance to Château de Bécon, Assy at bar of commune 14 Apr "

Communists appeal to the nation 19 Apr "

Bagneux occupied by Versaillais, reorganization of commissions, Eudes appointed inspector general of southern forts, moves from Montrouge to palace of Legion of Honor, 20 Apr "

Versailles batteries at Breteuil, Brimborion, Meudon, and Moulin de Pierre trouble the federal fort Issy, battery between Bagneux and Châtillon shells fort Vanves, truce at

Neuilly 9 A.M. to 5 P.M., inhabitants of Neuilly enter Paris by Porte des Ternes 25 Apr 1871

Les Moulineaux outpost of insurgents, taken by troops, fortified on the 27th and 28th 26 Apr "

Cemetery and park of Issy taken by Versaillais at night, free masons attempt reconciliation again, commune levies 2,000,000 francs from railway companies 29 Apr "

Flag of truce to fort Issy from the Versaillais calling federals to surrender, gen. Eudes, with fresh troops takes command, Cluseret imprisoned at Mazas by commune, Rossel made provisional delegate of war 30 Apr "

Versaillais take station of Clamart and Chateau of Issy, committee of public safety formed Antoine Arnauld, Leo Meillet Ranvier, Felix Pyat Charles Gérardin, alleged massacre of communist prisoners 1 May, "

Central committee of national guard charged with administration of war, Chapelle Expiatore ordered destroyed, materials to be sold by auction 5 May, "

Battery of Montretout (70 marine guns) opens fire, Thiers calls Parisians to rise against commune 8 May, "

Morning insurgents evacuate fort Issy, committee of public safety renewed—Ranvier Antoine Arnauld Gambon Eudes, Delescluze, Rossel resigns 8 May, "

Peace with Germany signed at Frankfort on the Main 10 May, "

Cannon from fort Issy taken to Versailles, decree to destroy Thiers's house, Delescluze made delegate of war 10 May "

Thiers opposed, offers to resign, assembly vote confidence in him (495–10) 11 May, "

Troops occupy Couvent des Oiseaux at Issy, and lyceum at Vanves, Auber the composer d (aged 89) 12 May, "

Triumphal entry of troops into Versailles with flags and cannon from convent, evacuation of Issy completed, fort Vanves taken by troops 13 May, "

Cannonade from batteries of Courbevoie Becon Asnieres on Levallois and Clichy, both villages evacuated, demolition of house of M Thiers begun 14 May, "

Column Vendôme overthrown 16 May, "

Secession from communist government, central club formed, a battalion of women formed 17 May, "

Silver ornaments in churches seized, cartridge factory near Champ de Mars explodes 100 killed 17 May, "

Assembly adopts treaty of peace 18 May, "

Rochefort brought prisoner to Versailles, last session of the commune 21 May, "

Noon explosion of powder magazine of Manége d'Etat major (staff riding school), hostages transferred from Mazas to La Roquette, Assy arrested in Paris by Versaillais, assembly votes to restore column Vendôme, M Ducatel, at risk of life, signalling that the way is clear the Versaillais enter Paris by gates of St Cloud and Montrouge, 2 P.M. 21 May, take possession of south and west, and about 10,000 prisoners after some fighting 22 May, "

Montmartre taken by Douai and Ladmirault, death of Dombrowski Morning Assy arrives at Versailles, gendarmes and Gustave Chaudey executed at prison of Sainte Pélagie Night Tuileries fired, Delescluze and committee of public safety sit at Hôtel de Ville 23 May, "

Morning Palais Royal Ministry of Finance Hôtel de Ville, etc, fired 1 P.M., powder magazine at Palais du Luxembourg blown up, committee of public safety organize detachments of fusee bearers, petroleum pumped into burning buildings, Raoul Rigault shot by soldiers Evening At prison of La Roquette archbishop, abbé Deguerry, president Bonjean, and 64 others, hostages, shot 24 May, "

Forts Montrouge, Hautes Bruyères, Bicêtre, evacuated by insurgents, death of Delescluze reported, at Avenue d'Italie the Pères Dominicains of Arcueil shot 25 May, "

Sixteen priests and 38 gendarmes shot at Belleville by insurgents, many women fighting, and casting petroleum into fires, shot 26, 27 May, "

Buttes Chaumont, heights of Belleville and cemetery of Père la Chaise carried by troops, prison of La Roquette by marines, deliverance of 169 hostages, investment of Belleville complete, last position captured by MacMahon, fighting ends 5 P.M. 28 May, "

Federal garrison of Vincennes surrendered 29 May, "

Reported results of 7 days' fighting regular troops—877 killed, 645 wounded, 183 missing, insurgents—about 50,000 dead, 25,000 prisoners, nearly all leaders killed or prisoners, about a fourth of Paris destroyed 22-27 May, "

Estimated loss of property, 800,000,000 francs Apr.-May, "

Thiers's decree disarming Paris and abolishing national guard of Seine 29 May, "

Victor Hugo expelled from Belgium 30 May, "

Reported wholesale execution of prisoners by marquis de Gallifet, Paris put under martial law, about 50,000 insurgents still at large 30 May, "

Solemn funeral of Darboy, archbishop of Paris 7 June, "

Abrogation of proscription by assembly (484–103), elections of duc d'Aumale and prince de Joinville legalized 8 June, "

Thiers advocates maintaining republic " "

New taxes (463 000,000 francs) and loan proposed by M Pouyer Quertier 12 June, "

Trochu's speech defending "government of national defence," 13, 14 June, "

Theatres, etc., reopened in Paris about 20 June, "

Letter of M Guizot to M Grévy, recommending political moderation and maintenance of present government 22 June, "

Loan of 2,000,000,000 francs decreed, 26 June, subscription opened, 27 June, about 4,000,000,000 subscribed in France, 28 June, "

One hundred and thirty two members elected to assembly, includes Gambetta, a few legitimists and Bonapartists, the rest support government 2 July, 1871

Letter from comte de Chambord at Chambord, professing devotion to France, modern policy and liberality, but declining to give up the white flag of Henry IV, he retires to Germany to avoid agitation, dated 5 July, "

Government said to have 500 votes in the assembly, bill for new taxes passed (483–5) 8 July, "

Five hundred million francs, part of indemnity to Germany, paid about 14 July, "

Prince Jerome Napoleon expelled from France (at Havre), 15 July "

Full compensation for losses of invaded provinces refused by Thiers, who acknowledges no debt, but proposes to act generously Aug "

Trial of communist prisoners at Paris begun about 8 Aug "

Dissensions in assembly between monarchists and republicans, resignation of Thiers not accepted, 24 Aug., his power continued and the sovereign and constituent authority of the assembly voted (443–227) about 25 Aug "

Thiers named president of the republic while the assembly shall continue (the Rivet Vitet proposition), 491–93 31 Aug "

Ferré and Lullier sentenced to death, others to transportation or imprisonment, 2 Sept., 3 women (pétroleuses) to death for throwing petroleum on fires 5 Sept. "

Assembly assumes for the nation the losses of invaded provinces 6 Sept "

Rossel, communist general sentenced to death 8 Sept "

Law carrying out treaty with Germany on imports from Alsace and Lorraine, and reducing German troops in France to 50,000 men, 14 Sept., passed (533–33), session closed, 2 A.M. 17 Sept. "

Germans evacuate Paris forts about 20 Sept "

Rochefort (of *La Lanterne* and *Le Mot d'Ordre*) sentenced to life imprisonment 21 Sept. "

Difficulty in Alsace and Lorraine treaty " "

Eight murderers of gens. Lecomte and Thomas condemned, 18 Nov "

Rossel, Ferré and Bourgeois, communists, shot at Satory before 3000 soldiers 28 Nov "

Gaston Crémieux executed at Marseilles 30 Nov "

Territory held by Germans declared under siege 4 Dec "

Thiers's message to assembly, deprecates free trade, proposes moderate protection 7 Dec "

Long debate, proposed taxes on raw materials opposed, government defeated (377–307) 19 Jan 1872

Resignation of Thiers and ministry, MacMahon writes, "Army will obey orders of a majority of assembly, but not dictatorship," Thiers resumes office 20 Jan "

Assassins of archbishop Darboy and others (on 24 May, 1871) convicted 23 Jan "

Manifesto of comte de Chambord, he will not become a legitimate king by revolution 29 Jan. "

General subscription to indemnity to Germans begins Feb "

Manifesto for constitutional monarchy signed by about 280 of the Right about 21 Feb. "

Ex emperor assumes by letter responsibility of surrender at Sedan 12 May, "

Majority of assembly propose MacMahon as president in room of Thiers July, "

Pilgrimage of about 20,000 to grotto of Virgin at Lourdes (where miraculous appearance of Virgin to 2 girls was reported, 14 Feb 1858) 6 Oct "

Comte de Chambord writes De la Rochette, protesting against a republic, that France can be saved by a monarchy alone, he is Catholic and monarchical, etc. 15 Oct "

National Assembly meets again, 11 Nov., Thiers, in his message, declares republic legal, urges conservatism, proposes changes 12 Nov "

Attack of gen. Changarnier on Thiers's policy and Gambetta's speech at Grenoble, majority for government, 150 (300 did not vote) 18 Nov "

Government project becomes law 19 Nov "

Report of commission read by M Batbie, claiming right of assembly to frame constitution with responsible ministry, president not to speak in the assembly, etc 26 Nov "

M Thiers addresses assembly, prefers English to American system, monarchy now impossible, adheres to republic, wishes it conservative Dufaure's amendment carried by 370 to 334 (royalists with Bonapartists against radicals) 29 Nov "

Manifesto of Left, proposing a legal dissolution of assembly, 10 Dec. "

Negatived (490-201) 14 Dec "

Powerful speech of Thiers to the commission of 30 16 Dec "

Debt (before the war, about 11,512,500,000 francs), 18,717,500,000 francs Dec "

Meeting of National Assembly 6 Jan 1873

Death of Napoleon III at Chiselhurst 9 Jan "

Bonapartist manifesto "The emperor is dead, but the empire is living and indestructible" 15 Jan "

Thiers addresses commission of 30 against proposed changes, 2 Feb "

Letter of comte de Chambord published; destroys prospects of fusion of Bourbons Feb. "

Debate begins on report of commission, which preserves legislative rights of present assembly, and the provisional state of the "pacte de Bordeaux," 27 Feb. Thiers supports this "truce of parties," adopted (475–199) 4 Mch "

Convention at Berlin for final evacuation of departments in Sept. on payment of indemnity 15 Mch. "

Declaration in the assembly, "that M Thiers has deserved well of his country" 17 Mch 1873

Resignation of Thiers and his ministry accepted (368-339), 24 May, marshal MacMahon duc de Magenta (b 1808), elected president by 390 votes (the Left did not vote), he accepts declaring independence of party, 24 May, in his message he says, "The post in which you have placed me is that of a sentinel, who has to watch over the integrity of your sovereign power" 26 May, "

France, except Verdun evacuated by Germans 2 Aug "

Fusion of legitimists and Orleanists, comte de Paris meets comte de Chambord who is accepted as chief 5 Aug "

Prince imperial Napoleon declares policy of his family, "Everything by the people for the people" 15 Aug "

Last instalment 250,000,000 francs of indemnity of 5,000 000 000 francs paid 5 Sept "

Verdun quitted by Germans 13 Sept "

Last quitted French territory 16 Sept "

Letter from comte de Chambord to the vicomte de Rodez Benavent, tendency to concession, says "I want the co operation of all and all have need of me" dated 19 Sept "

Prince Jerome Napoleon joins republicans 26 Sept "

Trial of marshal Bazaine commander on the Rhine in 1870, for treachery and misconduct at Metz begins, duc d Aumale president of court 6 Oct "

Manifesto of monarchists proposing restoration, guaranteeing liberties etc 18 Oct "

Léon Say and Left Centre decline negotiation with monarchists, who threaten abstention in next elections 23 Oct "

Letter of comte de Chambord to M Chesnelong "I retract nothing and curtail nothing of my previous declarations. I do not wish to begin a reign of reparation by an act of weakness, if enfeebled to day. I should be powerless to morrow, I am a necessary pilot, the only one capable of guiding the ship to port, because I have for it a mission of authority," 27 Oct "

Léon Say and Left Centre say the time has come to organize a conservative republic 30 Oct "

Meeting of National Assembly, president's message asks increased and prolonged power (10 years), referred to a committee of 15, voted urgent (by 360-350) 5 Nov "

Eight of committee favor extending presidency 5 years after meeting of next legislature, under existing conditions till the passing of constitutional laws, the others favor 10 years without conditions 13 Nov "

M Laboulaye presents report of committee, MacMahon by message, suggests 7 years 17 Nov "

Warm debate, majority of 68 for ministers, 18 Nov, 7 years' power voted to president MacMahon (383-317) 19 Nov, decree 20 Nov "

Bazaine found guilty of capitulating (with 170,000 men) in open field, of negotiating dishonourably with enemy, and surrendering a fortified place, sentence, death and degradation 10 Dec, commuted to 20 years' imprisonment 12 Dec "

"Comte Albert de Bourbon," claiming to be son of Louis XVII, discredited (IMPOSTORS) 27 Feb 1874

Prince Louis Napoleon's majority (at 18) celebrated at Chiselhurst by 6000 Frenchmen, he awaits the 8th *plebiscite*, 16 Mch "

Dahirel, legitimist, moves that on 1 June the assembly vote between monarchy and republic, negatived (330-256) 27 Mch "

Disputes of republicans and Bonapartists, Left Centre demand the republic, or dissolution of assembly 8, 9 June, "

Bonnard, communist, condemned for murder, 25 Feb, shot, 6 June, "

Electoral bill, age of electors fixed at 21, not 25 (defeat of ministry) 10 June, "

Casimir Périer (leader of Left Centre) moves recognition of republic, MacMahon president till 20 Nov 1880, and revision of constitution, voted "urgent" (345-341) 14, 15 June, "

Duc de Rochefoucauld Bisaccia moves restoration of legitimate monarchy, negatived, he resigns British embassy, 15 June "

By order of the day, president MacMahon declares that with army he will maintain authority for the 7 years 29 June, "

Manifesto of comte de Chambord, "France has need of monarchy My birth has made me your king The Christian and French monarchy is in its very essence limited (*temperee*) It admits of the existence of 2 chambers, one nominated by the sovereign, the other by the nation I do not wish for those barren parliamentary struggles, whence the sovereign too frequently issues powerless and enfeebled I reject the formula of foreign importation, which all our national traditions repudiate, with its king who reigns and does not govern"—Signed Henry V 2 July, "

Debate on manifesto, legitimists defeated, ministers, defeated on motion for septennate, resign (368-331), resignation not accepted by president 8 July, "

President by message declares determination to maintain law of 20 Nov, calls for constitutional laws 9 July, "

Reports of committee, by Ventavon (bill proposes maintenance of authority of president, ministerial responsibility, 2 legislative assemblies, dissolution of Chamber of Deputies by president, etc), suspended 16 July, "

Casimir Périer's motion for republic rejected (375-333), 23 July, "

Malleville's motion for dissolution rejected (374-332) "

Assembly adjourns (to 30 Nov) 5 Aug "

Bazaine escapes from isle of Ste Marguerite 10 P M 9 Aug "

[His wife asserted that he descended by an old gutter on a knotted rope, was taken in a boat by her and her nephew, Alvarez de Rul, to steamer *Baron Ricasola*, which landed him at Genoa (see Dec 1873)]

Vendôme column restored 31 Aug 1874

Death of M Guizot 12 Sept "

Bazaine's defence sent by him to the New York *Herald* dated 6 Sept, pub in London 14 Sept "

Trials for complicity in Bazaine's escape, col Villette and others sentenced to imprisonment 17 Sept "

Thiers, at Vizille near Grenoble, upon an address says, "Since you cannot establish monarchy, establish the republic frankly and sincerely" 27 Sept "

Political parties were—Extreme Right legitimists, adherents of Henry V Moderate Right monarchists Right Centre septennates imperialists or Bonapartists Left Centre moderate republicans (chief, Thiers) Left more pronounced Extreme Left radicals (chief Gambetta) Nov "

St Genest's pamphlet, "L'Assemblee et la France," inciting to a *coup d'etat* end of Nov "

Comte de Chambord requests friends not to vote so as to prevent or delay restoration of monarchy Nov "

Addresses from towns, etc, in France with thanks for relief during war 1870-71 (inscribed "*Britanniae grata Gallia*"), with about 12 000,000 signatures presented to queen Victoria by M d Agiout and comte de Serrurier (placed in British museum for inspection) 3 Dec "

Assembly meets president s firm moderate message " "

Sudden death of M Ledru Rollin 31 Dec "

President recommends a senate motion against it passed (420-230), 6 Jan, ministers' resignation not accepted 7 Jan 1875

Cost of war (9 885,000,000 francs or $1,977,000,000) announced, Jan "

Laboulaye s amendment rejected (359-335) 29 Jan "

Wallon's amendment (president to be elected by majority of 2 chambers for 7 years eligible for re election, republic virtually established), passed 1 A M 31 Jan "

Rejoicing through the country Feb "

Duprat's amendment carried (senate chosen by universal suffrage), 11 Feb, 3d reading of constitutional bill rejected (357-345), dissolution of assembly negatived (407-266), 12 Feb, president s message disapproving of last votes 13 Feb "

Senate bill (senate of 300, 225 elected by departments, 75 by National Assembly) 22 Feb "

Union of moderate monarchists and republicans, legitimists and Bonapartists defeated, senate bill passed (448-241), 24 Feb, final vote for republic, constitutional laws passed (436-262), 5 P M 25 Feb, pub 1 Mch "

New ministry Buffet, interior, Dufaure, justice, Léon Say, finance, Wallon, instruction, De Meaux agriculture and commerce, Cissey war, Decazes, foreign, Montaignac, marine, Caillaux public works 10 Mch "

Duc d'Audiffret Pasquier elected president of assembly almost unanimously 15 Mch "

Assembly adjourns to 11 May 20 Mch "

Meeting of assembly 11 May, ministry propose to refer a bill to committee of 30, defeated, part of committee resign 18 May, new committee elected (republican majority) 26 May "

Assembly adjourns 4 Aug "

Plon having lost by publishing "Julius Cæsar," by Napoleon III, sues emperor's executors, fails, and is adjudged to pay costs Aug "

Assembly ballots for senators for life, duc d'Audiffret Pasquier elected, breach between legitimists and Orleanists disclosed, government defeated 9 Dec "

Seventy five senators for life (52 republicans) elected, 9-21 Dec. "

Communist trials report, 9596 convicted, 110 sentenced to death Dec "

Estimated result of elections moderate republicans, 270, radicals, 60, Bonapartists, 92, Orleanists, 58, legitimists, 36, 7 Mch 1876

Amnesty for communists introduced in senate by Victor Hugo, in assembly by Raspail 21 Mch "

Debate on amnesty, 14 May, rejected (394-52), 17 May, Victor Hugo s speech for amnesty, proposal rejected almost unanimously 22 May, "

Gambetta's resolution for parliamentary government carried (355-154), 17 May, 363 liberal deputies protest 18 May, 1877

President prorogues chambers for a month, firm manifesto by the Left 18 May, "

Thiers accepted as leader by republicans, Broglie's circular for repressing the press issued about 29 May, "

President in an order of the day, after a review at Longchamps, says, "I appeal to the army to defend the dearest interests of the country" 2 July, "

Prosecution of Gambetta (and Murat, editor of *République Française*) for saying at Lille (29 July) the president must, if the elections be against him, "se soumettre ou se démettre" ("submit or resign") about 25 Aug "

Thiers d, aged 80, 3 Sept, public funeral no disorder, 8 Sept "

Gambetta and Murat sentenced to 3 months in prison and fine of 2000 francs, 11 Sept, on appeal, sentence affirmed, 22 Sept. "

Pres. MacMahon, in manifesto on elections, claims success for government, and says, "I cannot obey the injunctions of the demagogy, I can neither become the instrument of radicalism nor abandon the post in which the constitution has placed me" 19 Sept. "

Thiers's manifesto to electors (an historical defence of the republic and late chamber) pub 24 Sept. "

Gambetta convicted for placarding his address, fine, 3750 francs and 3 months' imprisonment 12 Oct. "

General election quiet, defeat of Bonapartist and clerical parties (of 506 official candidates about 199 elected, republicans, 320) 14 Oct "

Final result 325 republicans, 112 Bonapartists, 96 monarchists 28 Oct 1877
Census for 1876 announced, 36,905,788 (increase of 802,867 over 1872) 8 Nov "
MacMahon will not resign, ministry remains temporarily, announced 8 Nov "
F P Jules Grévy re elected president of chamber 10 Nov "
Albert Grévy s resolution for commission of 33 upon government interference in elections, 13 Nov, carried after warm debate (312-205) 15 Nov "
Commercial men meet in Paris, petition president 2 Dec "
President submits unconditionally, 13 Dec. A republican ministry formed, Dufaure, president of council and minister of justice, De Marcere, interior, Waddington (Protestant), foreign affairs, Bardoux, public instruction, gen Borel war, vice adm Pothuau, marine, Léon Say, finance, Teisserenc de Bort, commerce, De Freycinet, public works, the president in message accepts the will of the country 14 Dec. "
Limoges affair, gen Rochebouet said to have issued orders to gen de Bressoles for a military movement, 12 Dec, major Labordère denounces orders as illegal, 13 Dec, orders nullified by change of ministry, 14 Dec, De Bressoles suspended for mistake, Labordère cashiered, excitement in Paris over suspected preparations for a *coup d'etat* Jan 1878
Gen Ducrot dismissed, suspected of conspiring for *coup d'etat*, 10, 11 Jan "
International exhibition at Paris opened by president (Paris), 1 May, "
Joan of Arc and Voltaire centenaries celebrated 30 May, "
Death of Thiers commemorated at Notre Dame, etc 3 Sept. "
Twelve thousand national lottery tickets of 1 franc sold (Lotteries) up to Nov "
Letter from comte de Chambord to M de Mun, maintaining his rights, pub 25 Nov "
Elections for senate 64 republican, 16 opposition 5 Jan 1879
Chamber votes confidence in the ministry (223-121) 30 Jan "
Ministerial programme pardons to communists, clerical influence upon education checked, officials opposed to republic dismissed, etc 16 Jan. "
Drawing of the national lottery begun 26 Jan "
Pres MacMahon refuses to supersede military officers, resigns, 28 Jan, F P Jules Grévy elected president by senate and deputies united as "The National Assembly" (536 for Grévy, 99 for gen Chanzy) 30 Jan "
Gambetta president of chamber 31 Jan "
Communist amnesty passed by Chamber of Deputies 21 Feb. "
Proposed return of assemblies to Paris, congress to be appointed (315-128) 22 Mch "
M Ferry s education bills to check clerical influences, abolishing Jesuit colleges, etc Mch "
Blanqui (a convict) elected for Bordeaux 20 Apr "
Prince imperial Louis Napoleon killed while reconnoitring in Zululand . 1 June, "
Blanqui's election annulled by chamber (372-33), 4 June, pardoned and released . 11 June, "
Senate and deputies vote return to Paris (526-249) 20 June, "
M Ferry's law of superior public instruction passed by the deputies 9 July, "
President Grévy's first military review at Longchamps. 13 July, "
Fête of the republic 14 July, "
Prince Jerome Napoleon coldly accepted as chief by Bonapartists 20 July, "
Comte de Chambord s letter "With the co operation of all honest men, and with the grace of God, I may save France, and will" 26 July, "
Senate and assembly meet again at Paris 27 Nov "
Death (ex foreign ministers) duc de Grammont, 16 Jan, Jules Favre 20 Jan. 1880
Debate in senate 7th clause of Ferry's education bill (abolishing Jesuit schools, etc), Jules Simon speaks against it, rejected (148-129) 9 Mch. "
Decree dissolving Jesuits and other orders in France 29 Mch. "
Letter from prince Jerome Napoleon in favor of the decree, offends Bonapartists about 5 Apr "
Bishops and others protest against the decree Apr "
Amnesty bill for political offences, presented by M de Freycinet, 19 June, passed by chambers (333-140) 21 June, "
Otaheite formally annexed to France . 29 June, "
Expulsion of religious orders (officially opposed) carried into effect with Jesuits . 30 June, "
Amnesty bill passed for all, except incendiaries and assassins, by senate (143-138) 3 July, "
President Grévy grants general amnesty, 10 July, Rochefort warmly received in Paris 12 July, "
First grand republican national fête 14 July, "
Carmelites and other religious orders expelled 16 Oct.-Nov "
Loan of 1 000,000,000 fr offered (public debt about 3,000,000,000 fr), 30 times the amount subscribed Mch 1881
Scrutin de liste advocated by Gambetta, opposed by president, who yields. 21, 22 Mch "
Expedition to N Africa to chastise the Kroumirs; invasion of Tunis. Mch, Apr "
Treaty with the bey signed (Tunis) 12 May, "
Excitement at Marseilles and in Italy . 13 May et seq "
M Bardoux's bill for the *scrutin de liste* passed by deputies (243-235) . 18 May, "
Tunis treaty ratified by chamber (453-1) 23 May, "
Scrutin de liste rejected by senate (148-114) 9 June, "
Election addresses. M Rouher retires from politics (virtual end of Bonapartism), about 31 July, prince Napoleon Jerome advocates progress—"everything for and by the people"—about 31 July, Gambetta speaks at Tours, Belleville, 12 Aug, for revision of constitution, Aug, Jules Ferry at Nancy deprecates division about 11 Aug 1881
General elections, republican triumph, many extremists rejected 21 Aug et seq "
Capuchins and other orders relieved from monastic vows by the pope Oct. "
New ministry Gambetta, minister of foreign affairs and premier, Cazot, justice, Waldeck Rousseau, interior, Allain-Targé, finance, gen Campenon, war, Gougeard, marine, Paul Bert, education and worship, Raynal, public works, Rouvier commerce and colonies, Cochery, post and telegraph, Devès, agriculture, and Proust, arts. 12 Nov "
Defeat of government, *scrutin de liste* rejected (305-119), Gambetta resigns 26 Jan 1882
New ministry De Freycinet, president of council and minister for foreign affairs, Léon Say, finance, Jules Ferry, public instruction, Goblet, interior and public worship, Humbert, justice, gen Billot, war, adm Jauréguiberry, marine, Varroy public works, Tirard, commerce, De Mahy, agriculture, Cochery, post and telegraph 30 31 Jan "
Credit to protect Suez canal refused on motion of Clémenceau (416-75), ministry resigns . 29 July, "
New ministry Duclerc, president of the council and minister for foreign affairs, Tirard, finance, Devès, justice, De Fallieres, interior, Pierre Legrand, commerce and *ad interim* public works, gen Billot, war, adm Jauréguiberry, marine, Cochery, post and telegraph, De Mahy, agriculture, Duvaux, public instruction . 1 Aug. "
Bonapartists select prince Victor chief about 31 Aug. "
Compulsory Education act takes effect 2 Oct. "
Death of Gambetta, aged 44, after weeks of suffering from accidental wound, midnight 31 Dec. "
Prince Napoleon arrested for manifesto against government, 16 Jan 1883
Floquet s bill to exile Bourbons and Bonapartists " "
Government bill of De Fallières for power to expel same, 20 Jan "
Expulsion bill adopted by committee 25 Jan "
Fabre's bill permitting princes to remain without civil rights discussed, 29 Jan, passed by chamber (343-163), 1 Feb "
Prince Napoleon's indictment quashed, released .. 9 Feb "
Senate rejects expulsion bill, adopts amendment of Say and Waddington (165-127), expelling princes only after trial, 12 Feb "
Decree to retire Orleanist princes from army under law of 1834 (duc d'Aumale, duc de Chartres, and duc d'Alençon), approved by deputies (295-103) . 24 Feb. "
Marshal Bazaine publishes his defence at Madrid . . "
Museum of revolution established at Versailles 20 June, "
National fete, colossal statue of Republic uncovered 14 July, "
Death of comte de Chambord, aged nearly 63 24 Aug "
Statue of Lafayette unveiled at Lepuy 6 Sept. "
Government awards 25,000 francs to Mr Shaw (Madagascar, 1883) . . about 15 Oct. "
François Mignet historian, d (aged 87) . 24 Mch 1884
Prince Victor acknowledged chief of Bonapartists, his father publishes painful correspondence June, "
Colossal statue of Liberty by Bartholdi given to United States, unveiled by Jules Ferry at Paris 4 July, "
Death of Victor Hugo, poet, dramatist, and novelist (aged 83), 22 May, buried in Panthéon, all Paris spectators 1 June, 1885
Scrutin de liste bill with senate amendments.. . 8 June, "
Madagascar under French protection by treaty of 12 Dec. "
Senate votes expulsion of Bonaparte family (141-107) 22 June, 1886
Mobilization of army on the Spanish frontier 30 Aug 1887
[The troops were from 2 to 6 days in concentrating.]
Marie François Sadi Carnot elected president 3 Dec. "
Gen Boulanger minister of war "
Daniel Wilson, son in law of ex-president Grévy, sentenced to 2 years' imprisonment and a fine of 3000 francs for complicity in sale of army decorations. 1 Mch 1888
Duel between M Floquet, premier, and gen Boulanger, the latter severely wounded . "
French seize the Marquesa group in the Pacific ocean 20 Sept. "
Marshal Bazaine dies at Madrid . 23 Sept. "
Senate passes bankruptcy bill as desired by Panama Canal company 17 Jan 1889
Gen Boulanger proclaims devotion to the republic on the eve of the election 26 Jan. "
Boulanger elected deputy in the department of the Seine by plurality of 81,550 over M Jacques, republican 27 Jan "
Old Panama company dissolved 4 Feb "
Cabinet decides to prosecute gen Boulanger 29 Mch "
Boulanger flees from Paris to Brussels. 1 Apr "
In public statement says he left France rather than be tried by the senate. . . . 3 Apr "
He issues manifesto . ... 5 Apr "
His trial begun before the senate . ... . 12 Apr "
Boulanger leaves Brussels for England .. . 24 Apr "
Formal opening of French exposition. ... 6 May, "
Carlotta Patti, singer, sister of Adelina, d at Paris 28 June, "
Boulanger defeated in election, out of 1344 cantons he carries but 12 . . . . 29 July, "
Boulanger's trial before high court of senate begun 7 Aug. "
Boulanger, Henri Rochefort, and count Dillon sentenced to be *deported to some fortified place* 14 Aug "
Boulanger issues manifesto from London. . 16 Aug "
Names of Boulanger and count Dillon erased from the Legion of Honor ... . 26 Aug "

Return of 158 republican deputies and 89 opposition, Boulanger elect on claimed from Montmartre 23 Sept 1889
Paris municipal commission declare votes for Boulanger in Montmartre and Henri Rochefort in Belleville void 26 Sept "
Electoral bureau decide Boulanger not elected deputy 27 Nov "
Duke of Orleans sentenced to 2 years' imprisonment 12 Feb 1890
Pardoned by pres Carnot 3 June, "
Panama Canal commission report 20 years and 1 737,000,000 francs needed to complete canal 27 June "
International congress opens at Paris 16 Sept "
Meissonier celebrated painter, d 31 Jan 1891
Prince Jerome Napoleon (son of Jerome, brother of Napoleon I) dies at Rome (BONAPARTE FAMILY) 17 Mch "
[Bonapartist leaders recognize Victor his eldest son, as heir to the empire, Jerome by will names Louis, his second son, head of the house of Bonaparte]
François Jules P Grévy ex president d (aged 84) 9 Sept "
Gen Boulanger (b 1837) shoots himself at the grave of his mistress Mme de Bonne Main, near Brussels 30 Sept "
Senate adopts a duty on American pork in place of prohibition, 30 Oct "
Decree admitting American pork at 4 ports 5 Dec. "
Encyclical of pope to French bishops enjoining submission to republic 16 Feb 1892
Chamber votes 300,000,000 francs for an expedition against Dahomey 11 Apr "
Order to prosecute archbishop of Avignon and bishops of Nimes, Montpellier, Valence, and Viviers, for concerted addresses to Catholic electors against the state about 22 Apr "
Investigation of the Panama canal scandal begun 23 Nov "
Loubet ministry resigns on the Panama scandal issue 28 Nov "
Ribot ministry succeeds 5 Dec. "
Charles de Lesseps arrested for complicity in canal frauds, 16 Dec. "
Ferdinand and Charles de Lesseps Fontane Cottu and Eiffel, sentenced to prison and fine by court of appeals for fraud in the Panama canal 9 Feb 1893
M Taine, historian, d 5 Mch "
Trial of those accused of corruption in the Panama Lottery Bond bill begun in the assize court, Paris 8 Mch "
Jules Ferry, president of the senate, d 17 Mch "
Arton, an anarchist, is sentenced to 20 years' hard labor and 400,000 francs fine, for complicity in frauds and dynamite explosions 23 May, "
French court of cassation quashes the sentence of Charles de Lesseps and others convicted of fraud in the Panama affair, and all released from prison 15 June, "
Active hostilities with the Siamese government begun July, "
France, by ultimatum to Siam, demands reparation for outrages, answer required within 48 hours 19 July, "
Siam accepts French ultimatum in full 29 July, "
Letter from the pope to the Catholics severely censuring malecontents 3 Aug "
M Millevoye, a Boulangist, accuses M Clemenceau and others of complicity in the publication in the *Concorde* of forged documents alleged to have been stolen from the British embassy, after a stormy debate, the chamber passes to the order of the day, 22 June, Norton, for forgery, sentenced to 3 years' imprisonment, Ducret to 1 year 5, 9 Aug "
Conflicts between French and Italian salt workers at Aigues Mortes 16 Aug "
General election for government, 292, socialists, 187 "rallied" (to republicanism), 35, monarchists, 58, M Clemenceau and M Floquet rejected, many socialists, M Réne Goblet, leader, elected for Paris 20 Aug -3 Sept "
The coal miners in the Pas de Calais, etc , demand increase of wages, leads to a strike of about 42,000 men 18 Sept "
Marshal MacMahon, duke of Magenta, ex president, d 17 Oct "
M Gounod, great French composer, d at Paris. 18 Oct "
Visit of the Russian fleet to Toulon 13-29 Oct "
Strike ends by submission 4 Nov "
The new chamber opens 14 Nov "
Difference between M Carnot and the ministry, M Dupuy resigns after a crisis 26 Nov "
New ministry premier, M Casimir Perier 3 Dec. "
M Dupuy elected president of the chamber 5 Dec "
Auguste Vaillant, a violent anarchist, throws a dynamite bomb from the gallery of the French Chamber of Deputies among the members below while they were in session 9 Dec "
A restrictive press law in relation to anarchists passed by the chamber (413-63) 11 Dec "
The "rallied" agree to call themselves "independent republicans" about 13 Dec "
Nearly 2000 domiciliary visits on anarchists in Paris and provinces, many arrests and seizure of explosives 1 Jan et seq 1894
Bill for the conversion of the 4½ per cent rentes to 3½ per cent , passed by the senate 17 Jan "
Chanzy armored cruiser launched at Bordeaux 24 Jan "
M Maurice Charney sentenced to 6 years' imprisonment for publishing "Le catéchisme du soldat," inciting to mutiny, 27 Jan "
Vaillant, the anarchist, tried during Jan , condemned to death and guillotined 5 Feb "
Émile Henry, an anarchist, aged 20, throws a bomb into the café of the Terminus hôtel, many injured, 2 deaths, 12 Feb "
Another bomb explosion in a private house, several injured and a woman killed 19 Feb. "
M Jean Grave sentenced to 2 years' imprisonment and a fine for writing "La société mourante," and "L'anarchie," 24 Feb "

Duty on corn, 7 francs per quintal, passed by the senate, 27 Feb 1894
Joseph Pauwels killed by his own bomb at the Madeleine, 15 Mch "
Budget introduced, deficit 139,000,000 francs, met by conversion of the debt increased taxation, etc 16 Apr "
Fetes in honor of Joan of Arc at Orleans, Marseilles, etc , 6-8 May, "
Émile Henry, anarchist, convicted 28 Apr , executed 21 May, "
Defeat of the ministry in the chamber by the radicals in relation to the restraining of workmen on state railways from attending a congress (251-217), resigned 23 May, "
New ministry premier, interior, and public worship, M Dupuy 29 May, "
M Casimir Perier elected president of the chamber 2 June, "
Pres Carnot warmly received at Lyons, stabbed in his carriage on his way to the theatre by Caserio Santo Hieronymo 9 30 P M , 24 June, d at 12 45 A M 25 June, "
M Casimir Perier, president of the chamber, elected president of the republic by the senate and chamber 27 June, "
National state funeral of M Carnot at the Panthéon, after service at Notre Dame 1 July, "
M Dupuy and his cabinet agree to remain in office 1 July, "
M Burdeau elected president of the chamber 5 July, "
New anti anarchist bill passed by the chamber 26 July, by the senate 27 July, "
Chamber prorogued 28 July, "
Socialist Radical manifesto 30 July, "
Execution of the abbé Bruneau at Laval for the murder of the abbé Fricot 30 Aug "
Death of the comte de Paris at Stowe, Bucks 8 Sept "
65,000 000 francs voted, etc , for the Madagascar expedition (26 Nov), by the senate 6 Dec "
Ferdinand de Lesseps (b 19 Nov 1805) d 7 Dec. "
Death of M Auguste Burdeau (aged 42), president of the chamber of deputies, 12 Dec , funeral at Paris 16 Dec. "
M Brisson elected president of the chamber 18 Dec "
Dreyfus case, 1894-99, capt Alfred Dreyfus arrested, 14 Oct (trial within closed doors), convicted of delivering to a foreign power, in 1894, documents connected with the defence of France, sentenced to perpetual imprisonment 23 Dec "
Resignation of M Dupuy s ministry through an adverse vote in the chamber 14 Jan 1895
Resignation of pres Casimir Perier 15 Jan "
M Felix Faure, minister of marine in the Dupuy cabinet, elected president of the republic by 430 votes in the convention against 361 for M Brisson 17 Jan "
A ministry formed by M Ribot (finance) 26 Jan "
The amnesty bill passed by the chamber 28 Jan "
Death of marshal Canrobert (aged 86) 28 Jan "
Return of Henri Rochefort, 6 years an exile. 3 Feb "
M Hanotaux's moderate speech in the senate respecting English influence in Africa 5 Apr "
Bursting of a dam on the Eastern canal, at Bousey, in the Vosges, 2 villages and bridges swept away, 110 deaths, estimated damage above 50,000,000 francs 27 Apr "
Naval manœuvres at Toulon 1 July et seq "
Meetings of the clergy against the monastic tax, declared illegal July, "
M Louis Pasteur, chemist, physicist, and biologist (b 27 Dec 1822), d 28 Sept. "
Treaty of peace with the Hovas 1 Oct "
Resignation of the Ribot ministry through a vote of censure relating to a railway scandal 28 Oct "
Huahine and Bolabola, 2 islands in the S. Pacific, annexed by France Oct "
New cabinet (radical but pacific) premier and minister of interior, M Bourgeois 31 Oct "
M Barthelemy Saint Hilaire, statesman, philosopher, and savant (b 19 Aug 1805) d 24 Nov "
M Alexandre Dumas (fils), dramatist and novelist (b 29 July, 1824), d 27 Nov "
M Loubet elected president of the senate 16 Jan 1896
The government income tax, replacing the house tax, passed by the chamber 26 Mch "
Resignation of M Berthelot, duties assumed by M Bourgeois, 29 Mch "
M Jean Baptiste Léon Say, eminent political economist (b 1826), d 22 Apr "
M Bourgeois and his ministry resign with a protest 23 Apr , the senate adopts the Madagascar credits 24 Apr "
New cabinet (moderate) premier and minister of agriculture, M Meline 29 Apr "
Proposed revision of the constitution rejected by the chamber and senate 30 Apr "
Bill for the annexation of Madagascar and its dependent islands, proposed by M Hanotaux 30 May, "
Death of M Jules Simon (aged 82) 8 June, "
The chamber prorogued 11 July, "
National fête, the president fired at by a lunatic 14 July, "
The *Ernest Bazin*, new roller ship, launched at St Denis, 19 Aug "
State visit of the czar and czarina, he gives 100,000 francs to charities, 402 criminals released 5-9 Oct "
The chamber and senate meet 27 Oct "
Émile Arton, alias Baron, sentenced, in connection with the Panama scandals, to 8 years' imprisonment 6 Nov "
Vote of confidence passed in the chamber, reinforcements sent to Crete 15 Mch 1897
M Gerault Richard, socialist, expelled from the chamber for disorderly conduct 5 June, "

FRA

Franco Russian alliance confirmed . Aug 1897

Duel between prince Henry of Orleans and the count of Turin, 15 Aug "

Pres Faure received by the czar at Cronstadt, arrives at Peterhof, 23 Aug , leaves, 26 Aug , returns to Paris, 31 Aug "

The chambers reassemble 19 Oct "

Government inquiry of Dreyfus case instituted 16 Nov "

Debates in the chamber on the Dreyfus affair 4, 7 Dec. "

M Alphonse Daudet, novelist, d. (aged 57) 16 Dec "

Count Esterhazy tried by court-martial for treason, 10 Jan , acquitted 11 Jan 1898

Letter *J'accuse* to the president from M Zola in the *Aurore*, denouncing the conviction of capt Dreyfus 13 Jan "

Violent scene in the chamber on the discussion of the Dreyfus case, sitting closed 22 Jan "

Declarations of the government against further discussion in the chamber, adopted (376-133) 24 Jan "

Herr von Bülow, foreign secretary, asserts in the Reichstag at Berlin that there never had been any relations between ex capt Dreyfus and any German representative, 24 Jan , Italy declares the same. 31 Jan "

M Zola and M Perreux tried for defamation of the Dreyfus court martial, sentence, M Zola, 1 year, and M Perreux, 4 months. 23 Feb "

Interpellation in the chamber, government largely supported, "disciplinary measures" introduced by M Méline, 24 Feb , col Picquart and others punished for intervention, 25 Feb "

Lease of a bay, S E coast, etc , granted by China, 5 Apr , Kwang chau wan occupied . 22 Apr "

Anglo-French agreement . 14 June, "

New ministry premier, M Brisson 28 June, "

General elections government *net* majority (4), 8 May, the chamber meets, 1 June, M Méline resigns, 15 June, M Brisson forms a cabinet, 28 June, the chambers meet, 30 June, "

Flachat French liner, lost, 16 Feb., *La Bourgogne*, French liner, lost . 4 July, "

Legal proceedings respecting M Zola, 2 Apr , he escapes to England . 18 July, "

Lieut. col Henry, after confessing to forgery of documents against Dreyfus, is arrested, and commits suicide 31 Aug. "

Col Picquart arrested for disclosing state papers, 13 July, his trial postponed 21 Sept. "

Proposed revision of the Dreyfus case agreed to M Cavaignac, minister of war resigns 3 Sept., succeeded by gen Zurlinden, 5 Sept , he and M Tillaye, both against revision of the Dreyfus case, resign, 17 Sept , revision commission meets, 21 Sept et seq , divided in opinion, the Dreyfus case referred to the cour de cassation 27 Sept. "

New conciliation ministry premier and minister of interior, M Dupuy . 31 Oct. "

New commercial treaty with Italy, signed 21 Nov "

Fashoda, on the White Nile, occupied by capt Marchand, with 8 officers and 120 Sengalese (who had crossed from the French Congo), 10 July, Dervish attack repulsed, 25 Aug , diplomatic correspondence blue book published, 9 Oct , the Marchand mission recalled by the French government, 4 Nov , they leave Fashoda 11 Dec "

Demonstration in Paris against col Picquart and in honor of the army , stormy scene in the chamber, 12 Dec , chambers closed . . . . 24 Dec. "

"League de la Patrie Française" (anti revision of the Dreyfus case) founded, "L'Union Nationale," opposition league, started .. . Jan 1899

Anarchist disorder in Paris suppressed . .. 10 Feb "

Sudden death of pres Faure 16 Feb "

M Émile Loubet elected president of the republic by 483 votes against 279 for M Méline . . . . 18 Feb "

M Méline elected president of the chamber. . . 25 Feb. "

M Fallières elected president of the senate 3 Mch "

Domiciliary visits to royalist houses, etc., 25-28 Feb , treasonable leagues dissolved and prosecuted Mch -Apr. "

M de Freycinet (minister of war), after a stormy debate in the chamber, resigns, 5 May, succeeded by M Krantz, 6 May, "

Anglo French convention signed in London, 21 Mch., ratified, 30 May, "

Anti Dreyfus demonstration at the Auteuil races, pres. Loubet assaulted, ringleaders arrested 4 June, "

The ministry resigns 12 June, "

New (concentration) cabinet. premier and minister of the interior, M Waldeck Rousseau. . . 22 June, "

Stormy debate in the chamber, M Déroulède s proposal for the revision of the constitution refused urgency, 379-70, 27 June, chamber prorogued 4 July, "

Gen Zurlinden, military governor of Paris, superseded by gen. Brugère .. . .. 7 July, "

Suffren, first class battle ship, launched at Brest; displacement, 12 728 tons . 25 July, "

Gen de Negrier dismissed from the supreme council of war for inciting to insubordination in the army, 26 July, succeeded by gen Pierron . Aug "

Pisson condemned to 3 years' imprisonment for attempting to sell to foreigners documents relating to national defences, 12 Aug "

M Paul Déroulède and others arrested on a charge of plotting against the republic . . . . 12 Aug. "

Anarchist demonstration in Paris, rioting, 380 persons injured, 2 churches pillaged, many arrests... . 20 Aug "

Suppression of the embassy to the Vatican voted by the budget committee 30 Oct. 1899

Gen de Galliffet's army reforms sanctioned by the cabinet and president 31 Oct "

Major Esterhazy tried for embezzlement, sentenced to 3 years' imprisonment . 6 Nov "

The *Aurore* petition, demanding "justice for Dreyfus," 44,-760 signatures, sent to the president 17 Jan 1900

Stipends of several bishops suspended by government Jan "

Senatorial elections, republican victory (99 seats, 92 gained by the government), nationalists gen Mercier and 2 others, 28 Jan "

MM Buffet and Déroulède charged with conspiracy against the state, 9 Nov , sentenced to 10 years' banishment, M Jules Guérin to 10 years' detention in a fortress, 4 Jan , M Marcel Habert banished for 5 years 23 Feb. "

Death of count Benedetti, diplomatist, ambassador in Berlin, 1864-70 (aged 83) 28 Mch "

Paris (international) exhibition opened by pres. Loubet 14 Apr "

Chamber meets, amendment opposing a revival of the Dreyfus case carried (457-78), 22 May, amnesty bill (stopping further prosecution connected with the Dreyfus case) passed by the senate . 2 June, "

The shah of Persia visits Paris 28 July-11 Aug "

[Fired at by Salsou, an anarchist, 2 Aug . Salsou sentenced to life imprisonment, 10 Nov , d Sept. 1901]

The *Framee*, torpedo boat destroyer, sunk in collision with the *Brennus* war ship off Trafalgar, 42 deaths, including all the officers . 11 Aug "

Banquet to 22,000 mayors (23,000 guests) in the Tuileries gardens, speech by pres Loubet. 22 Sept "

M Waldeck-Rousseau announces the religious associations bill and other important measures 6, 8 Nov "

International exhibition in Paris closed 12 Nov "

Popular ovations to Mr Krüger, ex president of the Transvaal, at Paris, received by pres. Loubet 24 Nov "

Resolutions of sympathy to Mr Krüger passed by the chamber and senate 29, 30 Nov "

Amnesty amendment bill, against a revival of the Dreyfus agitation, and stopping prosecutions pending against M Zola, col Picquart, and others, passed . 24 Dec "

Chambers meet, MM Deschanel and Fallières re elected presidents 8, 9 Jan 1901

M Waldeck Rousseau s declaration that the pope has no power to intervene in state affairs carried by a large majority, 14 Jan "

Death of the duc de Broglie, historian and statesman (aged 80), 19 Jan "

Army reorganization, M de Montebello's plan adopted by army committee early Feb. "

The associations (21 clauses) bill (against unauthorized religious tutelage and communities) introduced, 15 Jan ; passed by the chamber after long debates (303-224) 29 Mch. "

Pres Loubet visits Nice, and entertains the Italian fleet at Toulon 8-10 Apr "

Scene in the chamber, M Drumont, an anti Semite, expelled, 14 June, "

Associations (religious) bill passed . . 28 June, "

Prince Henry of Orleans, eminent explorer, d at Saigon (aged 34) 9 Aug "

Sugar bounties reduced by 55 per cent to cover 14,000,000 francs deficit 25 Aug "

Diplomatic rupture with Turkey . Aug.-3 Sept. "

President meets the czar and czarina off Dunkirk, naval review held . . 18 Sept "

8800 R. C religious establishments, out of a total of 16 468, apply for authorization under the new associations law, the Jesuits, Passionists, Assumptionists, Benedictines, and others leave France, many for England July-3 Oct. "

M de Lanessan (marine minister) abolishes compulsory attendance at mass .. Nov "

Abrogation of the Falloux law, guaranteeing liberty of instruction, voted in the chamber . . . 14 Feb 1902

New ministry premier and minister of interior and public worship, M Combes . 7 June, "

Cabinet council decides that no official is to be appointed until questioned as to politics . . 20 June, "

Protests of the episcopate against the closing of conventual schools, July, M Combes's defence issued . .. 21 July, "

M Émile Zola, d 29 Sept. "

Petition of 74 bishops, in favor of the religious orders, declared illegal, reported . 28 Nov "

Two years military service bill, to come into operation 1904, passed . . 29 Nov "

Brussels sugar convention ratified . 24 Jan 1903

Dispute with the Vatican concerning vacant bishopric nominations . Feb. "

Motion for the suppression of the budget of public worship rejected . . . 21 Mch "

Territory on the right bank of the lower Senegal added to French colonial possessions, announced Aug "

Terrible fire and explosion on the Underground railway in Paris, 84 lives lost 10 Aug "

Outbreak of French bubonic plague at Marseilles mid Sept "

Anglo French arbitration agreement signed, London 14 Oct. "

Chambers opened, 20 Oct., resolution on M Combe's policy against clerical and monarchist reactionaries, carried, 22 Oct. "

Amendment to the education bill, excluding members of religious bodies, whether authorized or unauthorized, from teaching, passed by the senate (147-136) .. .. .. 20 Nov. "

Second revision of the Dreyfus case decided upon, commission appointed by M Valle, minister of justice, announced, 27 Nov 1903

Baron Arthur de Rothschild (he bequeathed his valuable collection of paintings to the Louvre, and collection of ancient rings to the Cluny museum) d 10 Dec "

Franco Italian arbitration treaty, signed 25 Dec "

Labor riots at Lyons 25 Dec "

The government threatens the Vatican, by prohibiting the collection of "Peter's pence" 15 Jan 1904

Court of cassation investigates the Dreyfus case 7 Mch "

The French chamber of deputies (316-269) debars the religious orders from teaching in France 28 Mch "

All forms of religious teaching by religious orders prohibited, 28 Mch "

Great strike in the department of the north, which is declared under martial law 29-31 Mch "

The courts remove all legal obstacles to the transfer of the Panama canal to the U S 31 Mch "

Premier Combe orders the removal of religious emblems from the French courts of justice 1 Apr "

Anglo French colonial treaty, covering all disputed questions, signed in London, Morocco to be in the sphere of French influence 8 Apr "

Sale of Panama canal ratified by the stockholders at Paris 23 Apr "

President Loubet and king Victor Emmanuel review the French and Italian ships at Naples 29 Apr "

The protest made by the Vatican to pres Loubet's visit to the king of Italy rejected by France 6 May, "

The French ambassador to the Vatican recalled 21 May "

Mob wrecks a church at Toulon 2 June, "

Papal nuncio at Paris notified that his usefulness as a representative from the Vatican was ended 29 July, "

Bishop of Dijon violates the concordat by going to Rome, his salary discontinued by the government 29 July, "

Death of ex premier Waldeck Rousseau 10 Aug "

Death of Bartholdi the sculptor, designer of the statue "Liberty Enlightening the World" in New York harbor 4 Oct "

Arbitration treaty between France and the U S signed at Washington 1 Nov "

Riot in the Chamber of Deputies, gen André struck in the face because he refused to resign 4 Nov "

Anglo French colonial treaty ratified by France 12 Nov "

Gen André minister of war, resigns 21 Nov "

Louise Michel communist, d at Marseilles (aged 75) 9 Jan 1905

The cabinet resigns 15 Jan "

The new Rouvier cabinet announced 22 Jan "

A committee's report to the French assembly urges speedy separation of church and state 15 Mch "

The Chamber of Deputies votes to reduce the active term of service in the army to 2 years 17 Mch "

Jules Verne, novelist, d (aged 77) 24 Mch "

German emperor visits Tangier, in a speech demands an open door, refuses to recognize the right of France and England alone to settle the Morocco question 31 Mch "

The continued use of French harbors by the Russian fleet at Madagascar and Indo-China lead to protests by Japan May, "

Germany's request for an international congress to consider reforms in Morocco leads to negotiations between France, England, and Germany . June, "

SOVEREIGNS OF FRANCE

MEROVINGIAN RACE

Pharamond (existence doubtful)
428. Clodion the Hairy, his supposed son, king of the Salic Franks
447 Merovæus, or Merovée, son in law of Clodion
458 Childeric, son of Mérovée.
481 Clovis, his son, real founder of the monarchy
His 4 sons divided the empire
511 Childebert, Paris.
" Clodomir, Orleans
" Thierry, Metz
" Clotaire, Soissons
534 Theodebert, Metz
548 Theodebald, succeeded in Metz
558 Clotaire I, sole ruler Upon his death, the kingdom divided between 4 sons, viz
561 Charibert, ruled at Paris
" Gontram, in Orleans and Burgundy
" Sigebert, at Metz, and } Both assassinated by Fredegond
" Chilperic, at Soissons }
575 Childebert II
584 Clotaire II, Soissons
596 Thierry II, son of Childebert, in Orleans
" Theodebert II, Metz.
613 Clotaire II, became sole king
628. Dagobert I, the Great, son of Clotaire II, divided the kingdom between his 2 sons
638 Clovis II, Burgundy and Neustria.
" Sigebert II, Austrasia.
656 Clotaire III, son of Clovis II
670 Childeric II, sole king, assassinated, with his queen and his son Dagobert, in the forest of Livri
" Thierry III, Burgundy and Neustria
674. Dagobert II, son of Sigebert in Austrasia, assassinated 679
691. Clovis III (Pepin, mayor of the palace, rules in his name)
695 Childebert III, the Just, brother of Clovis, Pepin supreme
711 Dagobert III, son of Childebert
715 Chilperic II, deposed by Charles Martel, mayor of the palace
717 Clotaire IV, of obscure origin raised by Charles Martel to the throne, dies soon after, Chilperic is recalled from Aquitaine
720 Chilperic II restored, soon dies at Noyon
" Thierry IV, son of Dagobert III surnamed *de Chelles*, d 737 Charles Martel reigns under the new title of "duke of the French"—*Henault*
737 Interregnum, till the death of Charles Martel, in 741
742 Childeric III, son of Chilperic II, surnamed the Stupid Carloman and Pepin, sons of Charles Martel, share the crown.

THE CARLOVINGIANS

752 Pepin the Short, son of Charles Martel, succeeded by his 2 sons
768 Charles the Great (Charlemagne) and Carloman Charles crowned emperor of the West, by Leo III 800 Carloman reigned but 3 years Charlemagne d 28 Jan 814, age 72
814 Louis I, *le Debonnaire* emperor, dethroned but restored
840 Charles surnamed the Bald king, emperor in 875, poisoned by Zedechias a Jewish physician
877 Louis II, the Stammerer son of Charles the Bald king
879 Louis III and Carloman II, the former d 882, and Carloman reigned alone
884 Charles III, *le Gros*, usurps right of Charles the Simple
887 Eudes or Hugh count of Paris
898 Charles III (or IV) the Simple, deposed and died in prison in 929, he married Edgiva, daughter of Edward the Elder, of England by whom he had a son, king Louis IV
922 Robert brother of Eudes, crowned at Rheims, Charles killed him in battle.—*Hénault*
923 Rudolph, or Raoul duke of Burgundy, elected king, but never acknowledged by the southern provinces —*Henault*
936 Louis IV, *d'Outremer*, or Transmarine son of Charles III (or IV), taken by his mother into England, died by fall from his horse
954 Lothaire, his son, with his father from 952 succeeds him at 15 years of age protected by Hugh the Great, poisoned
986. Louis V, the Indolent, son of Lothaire, poisoned (supposed by his queen, Blanche), last of race of Charlemagne

THE CAPETS

987 Hugh Capet, the Great, count of Paris, etc, eldest son of Hugh the Abbot 3 July, usurps the rights of Charles of Lorraine, uncle of Louis Transmarine From him this race of kings is called Capevingians and Capetians He d 24 Oct
996 Robert II, surnamed the Sage, son, died lamented 20 July, age 61
1031 Henry I son, d 29 Aug
1060 Philip I, the Fair, *l'Amoureux*, son, succeeded at 8 years of age, ruled at 14, d 3 Aug, age 55
1108. Louis VI, surnamed the Lusty, or *le Gros*, son d. 1 Aug 1137, age 59
1137 Louis VII, son, surnamed the Young, reigned with his father for some years, d 18 Sept 1180, age 60
1180 Philip II (Augustus), son, succeeds at 15, crowned at Rheims in his father's lifetime, d 14 July, 1223 age 58
1223 Louis VIII *Cœur de Lion*, son, d 8 Nov 1226, age 39
1226 Louis IX, son, called St. Louis, succeeded at 15 under his mother as guardian and regent, died in camp before Tunis, 25 Aug 1270, age 55
1270 Philip III, the Hardy, son, died at Perpignan, 6 Oct 1285, age 40
1285 Philip IV, the Fair, son, king in his 17th year, d 29 Nov 1314, age 47
1314. Louis X, son, surnamed *Hutin*, an old word for headstrong, or mutinous, d 5 June 1316, age 27
1316 John I, posthumous son of Louis X, b 15 Nov, d 19 Nov
" Philip V the Long (on account of his stature), brother of Louis, d 3 Jan 1322, age 28
1322 Charles IV, the Handsome, brother, d 31 Jan 1328, age 34

HOUSE OF VALOIS

1328 Philip VI de Valois, the Fortunate, grandson of Philip III, d 23 Aug 1350, age 57
1350 John II, the Good, son, died suddenly in the Savoy in London, 8 Apr
1364 Charles V, the Wise, son, d 16 Sept 1380, age 43
1380 Charles VI, the Beloved, son, d 21 Oct 1422, age 54
1422. Charles VII, the Victorious, son, d 22 July, 1461, age 58
1461 Louis XI, son, able but cruel, d 30 Aug 1483, age 60
1483. Charles VIII, the Affable, son, d 7 Apr 1498, age 28
1498 Louis XII, duke of Orleans, the Father of his People, great grandson of Charles V, d 1 Jan 1515, age 53.
1515 Francis I of Angoulême, called the Father of Letters, great great grandson of Charles V, d 31 Mch 1547, age 52.
1547 Henry II, son, died of accidental wound by comte de Montmorency at a tournament for nuptials of his sister with the duke of Savoy, 10 July, 1559, age 40
1559 Francis II, son, married Mary Stuart, queen of Scots, d 5 Dec 1560, age 17
1560 Charles IX, brother, Catherine de' Medici, his mother, regent, d 30 May, 1574, age 24.
1574 Henry III, brother, elected king of Poland, last of the house of Valois, stabbed by Jacques Clément, a Dominican friar, 1 Aug, d 2 Aug 1589, age 38

HOUSE OF BOURBON

1589 Henry IV, the Great, of Bourbon, king of Navarre, son in law of Henry II, assassinated by Francis Ravaillac, 14 May, 1610, age 57
1610 Louis XIII, the Just, son, d. 14 May, 1643, age 42.
1643 Louis XIV, the Great, *Dieudonné*, son, d 1 Sept 1715, age 77

1715 Louis XV, the Well beloved, great grandson, d 20 May, 1774, age 64

1774 Louis XVI, his grandson, ascended the throne in his 20th year, married the archduchess Marie Antoinette, of Austria, May, 1770 dethroned 14 July, 1789, guillotined, 21 Jan 1793, age 39, and his queen, 16 Oct following

[Louis was executed Monday, 21 Jan 1793, at 8 o'clock A M On the scaffold he said, "Frenchmen, I die innocent of the offences imputed to me I pardon all my enemies, and I implore of Heaven that my beloved France—" At this instant Santerre ordered the drums to beat, and the executioners to perform their office When the guillotine descended the priest exclaimed "Son of St Louis! ascend to heaven" The head was held up, and a few shouted, "*Vive la Republique!*" The body was interred, the grave immediately filled with quicklime, and a guard set until it should be consumed]

1793 Louis XVII, son of Louis XVI, never reigned, but died in prison, supposed by poison, 8 June, 1795, aged 10 years 2 months Owing to the uncertainty of his death quite a number of impostors have laid claim to being Louis XVII, or his son It has been asserted that he escaped to England, and lived there as Augustus Meves Even as late as 1874 one Naundorf claimed to be Albert de Bourbon son of Louis XVII and with Jules Favre as counsel, he brought his claim to trial Verdict strongly against his claim, 27 Feb 1874 WILLIAMS, ELEAZER

FIRST REPUBLIC

1792 National Convention (750 members), first sitting 21 Sept.

1795 Directory (Larevellière Lépaux, Letourneur, Rewbell Barras, and Carnot) nominated 1 Nov, abolished and Bonaparte, Ducos, and Sieyès appointed an executive commission, Nov 1799

1799 Consulate Napoleon Bonaparte, Cambacérès, and Lebrun appointed consuls, 24 Dec Napoleon appointed consul for 10 years. 6 May, 1802, for life, 2 Aug 1802.

FIRST EMPIRE. (BONAPARTE FAMILY)

[Established by the senate 18 May, 1804]

1804 Napoleon (Bonaparte) I, b 15 Aug 1769 He married,
1st, Josephine, widow of Alexis, vicomte de Beauharnais, 8 Mch 1796 (who was divorced 16 Dec 1809, d 29 May, 1814)
2d, Maria Louisa of Austria, 2 Apr 1810 (d 17 Dec 1847) Son, Napoleon Joseph, duke of Reichstadt, b 20 Mch 1811, d 22 July 1832
He renounced the thrones of France and Italy, and accepted the isle of Elba for his retreat, 5 Apr 1814
Again appeared in France, 1 Mch 1815
Was defeated at Waterloo, 18 June, 1815
Abdicated in favor of his infant son, 22 June, 1815 Banished to St. Helena, where he d 5 May, 1821, age 52 FRANCE, 1840

BOURBONS RESTORED

1814 Louis XVIII (comte de Provence) brother of Louis XVI, b 17 Nov 1755, married Marie Josephine Louise of Savoy, entered Paris, and took possession of the throne 3 May, 1814, obliged to flee, 20 Mch 1815, returned 8 July, same year, died without issue, 6 Sept 1824, age 69

1824 Charles X (comte d'Artois), his brother, b 9 Oct 1757, married Marie Thérèse of Savoy, deposed 30 July, 1830 He resided in Britain till 1832, and died at Gratz, in Hungary, 6 Nov 1836, age 79
Heir Henry, duc de Bordeaux, called comte de Chambord, son of duc de Berry, b 29 Sept. 1820, married princess Theresa of Modena, Nov 1846, no issue, styled himself Henri V, d 24 Aug 1883, age 63 FRANCE, 1870 et seq

HOUSE OF ORLEANS (ORLEANS.)

1830. Louis Philippe, son of Louis Philippe duke of Orleans, called *Egalite*, descended from Philippe, duke of Orleans, son of Louis XIII, b 6 Oct. 1773, married 25 Nov 1809 Maria Amelia, daughter of Ferdinand I (IV), king of the 2 Sicilies (d 24 Mch 1866) Raised to the throne as the king of the French, 9 Aug 1830, abdicated 24 Feb 1848 Died in exile, in England, 26 Aug 1850, age 77
Heir Louis Philippe, count of Paris, b 24 Aug 1838, d. 8 Sept 1894

SECOND REPUBLIC, 1848.

Revolution began in a popular insurrection at Paris, 22 Feb 1848. The royal family escaped to England, a provisional government was established, monarchy abolished and a republic declared

Charles Louis Napoleon Bonaparte, declared by the National Assembly (19 Dec) president of the republic of France, and proclaimed next day, 20 Dec, elected for 10 years, 22 Dec. 1851

FRENCH EMPIRE REVIVED (BONAPARTE FAMILY)

[1821. Napoleon II (so termed by decree of Napoleon III on accession) Napoleon Joseph, son of Napoleon I and Maria Louisa archduchess of Austria, b 20 Mch 1811, created king of Rome At his father's abdication he was made duke of Reichstadt in Austria, died at Schönbrunn, 22 July, 1832, age 21]

1852 Napoleon III, president of French republic, elected emperor, 21, 22 Nov 1852, proclaimed 2 Dec. 1852, surrendered to king of Prussia at Sedan 2 Sept 1870, deposed at Paris, 4 Sept, arrives at Wilhelmshöhe, near Cassel 5 Sept, deposition confirmed by National Assembly 1 Mch, he protested against it, 6 Mch 1871, died at Chiselhurst, England, 9 Jan. 1873, buried there 15 Jan, age 65

Empress Eugènie Marie (a Spaniard, countess of Téba), b 5 May, 1826, married 29 Jan 1853.
Heir Napoleon Eugène Louis Jean Joseph son, styled Napoleon IV, b 16 Mch 1856, killed in Zululand 1 June, 1879, buried beside his father at Chiselhurst (prince of Wales and other princes present), 12 July, 1879 WILLS
At the celebration of the fete Napoleon, 15 Aug 1873, the prince declared the policy of his family to be "Everything by the people, for the people"

[On 18 Dec 1852 the succession, in default of issue from the emperor was determined in favor of prince Jerome Napoleon and his heirs male] FRANCE, 1883-91

THIRD REPUBLIC

I Louis Adolphe Thiers (b 16 Apr 1797) appointed chief of the executive, 17 Feb, and president of the republic 31 Aug 1871, resigned, 24 May, 1873, d 3 Sept 1877, age 80

II Marshal M E Patrice Maurice MacMahon duc de Magenta (b 13 July 1808), elected president, 24 May, nominated for 7 years 20 Nov 1873, d 17 Oct 1893

III François Paul Jules Grévy (b 15 Aug 1813), elected 30 Jan 1879, d 9 Sept 1891

IV Marie François Sadi Carnot (b 11 Aug 1837), elected 3 Dec 1887

France, Isle of. MAURITIUS

Franche-Comté (*fransh con-ta'y*), a province in upper Burgundy, E France, was conquered by Julius Cæsar about 45 B.C., by Burgundians, early in the 5th century A D, and by Franks about 534 It was made a county for Hugh the Black in 915, and named, because taken from Renaud III (1127-48) and restored to him By marrying the count's daughter Beatrice, the emperor Frederick I acquired it, 1156 Their descendant, Mary of Burgundy, marrying the archduke Maximilian, conveyed it to the house of Austria, 1477 It was conquered by the French, 1668, restored by treaty of Aix-la-Chapelle, 2 May, 1668, again conquered, and annexed to France by treaty, 1678

franchise. A privilege or exemption from ordinary jurisdiction, anciently an asylum or sanctuary for the person In Spain, churches and monasteries were, until lately, franchises for criminals, as formerly in England SANCTUARIES. In 1429, the elective franchise, or right to vote for rulers and magistrates, for counties in England, was restricted to residents having at least 40*s* a year in land The elective franchise is conferred upon male citizens in each of the United States, with certain conditions of previous residence, at the age of 21 years Women possess it only in Wyoming, and in some states at school elections. WOMAN'S SUFFRAGE The conditions of the franchise vary slightly in the different states. For instance, in Vermont deserters from the U S army or navy during the civil war and ex-confederates are excluded from voting In New York and Wyoming no man can vote at any election on the result of which he has a bet Residents of the District of Columbia cannot vote for president of the U S DISTRICT OF COLUMBIA

Franciscans. Gray or Minor Friars, an order founded by St Francis d'Assisi about 1209 Their rules were chastity, poverty, obedience, and an austere regimen About 1220 they appeared in England, where, at the dissolution of monasteries by Henry VIII, they had 55 abbeys or other houses, 1536-38

Francis's assault on the queen John Francis, a youth, fired a pistol at queen Victoria as she passed down Constitution hill, London, in an open barouche, accompanied by prince Albert, 30 May, 1842. The queen was uninjured Warned of an attack, the queen had forbidden the ladies of her court to attend her Francis was condemned to death, 17 June, following, but was transported for life, and liberated on ticket-of-leave in 1867.

Franco'nia or **Frank'enland** (on the Maine), formerly a circle of the German empire part of Thuringia, was conquered by Thierry, king of the Franks, 530, and colonized. Its count or duke, Conrad, was elected king of Germany, 912, and was ancestor of emperor Conrad III, elected 1138, and another duke Franconia was made a distinct circle from Thuringia in 1512 At its subdivision in 1806 various German princes obtained parts, but in 1814 the largest share fell to Bavaria.

Franco-Prussian war originated in the French emperor's jealousy of the growing power of Prussia, by the defeat of Denmark in 1864, and of Austria in 1866. These successes destroyed the German confederation, and led to the North German confederation under the control of the king of

Prussia, who acquired besides Hanover, Hesse-Cassel, Nassau, Frankfort, and other provinces This aggrandizement of Prussia was largely due to the policy of count Bismarck-Schonhausen, prime minister from Sept 1862

In a draught treaty secretly proposed to Prussia by Napoleon III in 1866 "1 The emperor recognizes the acquisitions which Prussia has made in the last war, 2 The king of Prussia promises to facilitate the acquisition of Luxembourg by France, 3 The emperor will not oppose a federal union of the northern and southern states of Germany excluding Austria, 4 The king of Prussia in case the emperor should enter or conquer Belgium will support him in arms against any opposing power, 5 They enter into an alliance offensive and defensive "

[This draught appeared in the London *Times*, 25 July 1870 After discussion, its authenticity was admitted, Bismarck asserting that it emanated from the French emperor and had never been seriously entertained by himself]

In Mch 1867, a dispute arose, the French emperor seeking to purchase Luxembourg from the king of Holland was opposed by Prussia, the province had formed part of the German confederation At a conference of representatives of the great powers in London, the neutrality of Luxembourg was determined, with the withdrawal of the Prussian garrison and the destruction of the fortifications 7-11 May 1867

Prince Leopold of Hohenzollern Sigmaringen (connected with the Prussian dynasty and brother of Charles, prince of Roumania), a candidate for the throne of Spain 4 July, 1870

Remonstrances by France, threatening speeches in the chamber by duc de Grammont, foreign minister, after negotiation and intervention of Great Britain prince Leopold with the consent of his sovereign, declined the crown 12 July, "

France not satisfied, demanded a pledge that the candidacy should not be renewed This irritated Prussia and ended the negotiations, the king refusing to receive the count Benedetti, the French minister 13 July, "

Fruitless efforts to avert war by earl Granville, British foreign minister about 15 July, "

War announced by the emperor, the great majority of chambers approving, Lefts or Republicans, opposing M Thiers and a few others protested against it as premature 15 July "

[After Sedan the emperor told Bismarck that he was forced into war by public opinion He was deceived as to the strength of his army and its preparation.]

[" The greatest national crime that we have had the pain of recording since the days of the first French revolution has been consummated War is declared—an unjust but premeditated war "—London *Times* 16 July, 1871]

[For details of battles, see separate articles]

French army, about 300 000
1st corps, under marshal MacMahon
2d corps, under gen Frossard
3d corps, under marshal Bazaine
4th corps, under gen Ladmirault.
5th corps under gen de Failly
6th corps, under marshal Canrobert
Imperial guard, under gen Bourbaki
Commander-in chief, the emperor, gen le Bœuf, second, succeeded by marshal Bazaine

Prussian army, about 640,000
1 Northern, under gen Vogel von Falckenstein, about 220,000, defending the Elbe, Hanover, etc
2 Right, under prince Frederick Charles, about 180,000
3 Centre, under gens von Bittenfeld and von Steinmetz, about 80 000
4 Left, under crown prince of Prussia, about 166,000
Commander in chief, king William, second, gen von Moltke

North German army, Aug, contained 1st, 550,000 line with 1200 guns and 53,000 cavalry, 2d, 187,000 reserve, with 234 guns and 18,000 cavalry, and 3d, 205,000 landwehr, or militia, with 10,000 cavalry, in all 944,000 men, with 1680 mobilized guns and 193 000 horses.

Add to these the Bavarians, 69,000 line, with 192 guns and 14,800 horses—25,000 reserve with 2400 horses, and 22,000 landwehr, Würtembergers—22,000 line, with 54 guns and 6200 horses, 6500 reserve, and 6000 landwehr, and Badenese —16,000 line with 54 guns 4000 reserve, and 9600 landwehr

Total of German troops, 1,124,000 Aug "

Four weeks sooner, on peace footing, there were only 360,000

Both French and German soldiers were brave and efficient, but the French generals acted largely upon impulse The Germans had usually a well matured plan, massing forces at critical points. From Saarbrück to Sedan, Moltke's plans were ably carried out.

Causes of the ruin of the French army were "(1) superiority of the Germans in numbers, (2) unity of their command and concert of operation, (3) their superior mechanism in equipment and supplies, (4) superior intelligence, steadiness, and discipline of the soldiers, (5) superior education of the officers, and the dash and intelligence of the cavalry "—*Quarterly Review*

Estimated cost of the war to France, 9,885,000,000 francs Jan. 1875

War resolved on by France, 15 July, declaration delivered at Berlin . 19 July, 1870

North German parliament meet at Berlin, and engage to support Prussia in the war 19 July, "

Würtemberg Bavaria, Baden and Hesse Darmstadt declare war against France, and send forces . 20 July, "

War proclamation of emperor Napoleon 23 July, 1870

Part of bridge at Kehl blown up by Prussians " "

Proclamation of king promising as results of the war, a durable peace and the liberty and unity of Germany 25 July, "

Napoleon joins the army, at Metz assumes command and proclaims that the war will be long and severe 28 29 July "

King of Prussia proclaims amnesty for political offences, 31 July, "

French government announce that "they make war, not against Germany but against Prussia, or rather against the policy of count Bismarck " 2 Aug "

French under Frossard bombard Saarbrück emperor and his son present, Prussians dislodged, with little loss 2 Aug "

King leaves Berlin for the army, 1 Aug, and announces that "all Germany stands united in arms 3 Aug "

Crown prince crosses the Lauter into France and defeats Frossard storming the lines of Wissembourg and Geisburg, gen Douay killed 4 Aug "

Battle of Woerth, crown prince defeats MacMahon's army of Rhine they retire to Saverne to cover Nancy 6 Aug "

Battle of Forbach, Saarbrück recaptured and Forbach (in France) taken by gens. von Göben and von Steinmetz, the French retreat 6 Aug "

Germans occupy Forbach Haguenau and Sarreguemines, 7 Aug "

Bazaine appointed to command at Metz (about 130 000 men), MacMahon has about 50 000 near Saverne, Canrobert about 50 000 near Nancy 8 Aug "

Bombardment of Strasburg begun 14 Aug "

Emperor retires to Verdun " "

Bazaine defeated in several sanguinary battles before Metz

1 Battle of Courcelles (Pange, or Longeville) by Von Steinmetz and the 1st army 14 Aug "
2 Battle of Vionville or Mars la Tour by prince Frederick Charles and the 2d army 16 Aug "
3. Battle of Gravelotte by king's combined armies 18 Aug "

MacMahon reaches Châlons 16 Aug, joined by emperor, his army between 130 000 and 150,000 20 Aug "

MacMahon's army of the Rhine retreats, Prussians under king and crown prince advance, prince Frederick Charles opposed to Bazaine at Metz (German armies in France about 500,000, French armies about 300 000, communications between Bazaine and MacMahon difficult) about 20 Aug "

MacMahon at Rheims with shattered corps of Failly and Canrobert, starts to join Bazaine, 23 Aug crown prince and prince of Saxony pursue, 23 Aug, march upon Châlons, 24 Aug "

Three armies of reserve formed in Germany and a 4th army, under crown prince of Saxony, to co operate with crown prince of Prussia against Paris 26 Aug "

Two German armies (220 000) marching on Paris 28 Aug "

Continued retreat of MacMahon's army, severe fighting at Dun, Stenay and Mouzon 28 Aug "

MacMahon, with about 150 000, and the emperor retreat northwards part of army under De Failly surprised and defeated near Beaumont, between Mouzon and Moulins, French beaten in several engagements during the day 30 Aug "

Germans enter Carignan, attack French in plain of Douzy, after a repulse, drive them to Sedan 31 Aug "

Bazaine striving to escape, driven back into Metz 31 Aug, 1 Sept "

Battle round Sedan, began at 4 A M between Sedan and Douzy, French at first successful, after a severe struggle Germans victorious, MacMahon wounded 5 30 P M., gen de Wimpfen refuses terms offered by king of Prussia. 1 Sept. "

Sedan and MacMahon's army capitulate, emperor surrenders to the king (SEDAN) 2 Sept. "

Revolution at Paris, republic proclaimed (FRANCE) 4 Sept "

Gen Vinoy and a corps sent too late to aid MacMahon, retreat and arrive in Paris 6, 7 Sept. "

Siege of Paris begun, ingress and egress prohibited without a permit 15 Sept "

Three French divisions under gen Vinoy attack Germans on heights of Sceaux, repulsed with loss of 7 guns and 2500 prisoners, defeat attributed to disorder of Zouaves, national guard behave well 19 Sept "

Bismarck consents to receive Jules Favre (about 16 Sept), they meet at Chateau de la Haute Maison 19 Sept, and at king's headquarters, Ferrieres, near Lagny 20 Sept. "

Versailles surrenders, 19 Sept, entered by crown prince of Prussia 20 Sept. "

Jules Favre reports his interviews with Bismarck Prussia demands cession of departments of upper and lower Rhine and part of Moselle, with Metz, Chateau Salins, and Soissons, would grant an armistice while a French constituent assembly might meet, French to surrender Strasburg Toul, and Verdun (or Phalsburg, according to Favre) and Mont Valérien if assembly meet at Paris, terms rejected 21 Sept. "

Gen von Steinmetz sent to Posen as governor general, prince Frederick Charles commands before Metz 21 Sept "

Levee en masse of men under 25 in France 23 Sept. "

Desperate ineffective sallies from Metz 23, 24, 27 Sept. "

All departments of the Seine and Marne occupied by Germans, 26 Sept. "

Iron cross given by crown prince of Prussia to more than 30 soldiers under statue of Louis XIV at Versailles 26 Sept. "

Capitulation of Strasburg, 27 Sept., formal surrender 28 Sept "

Sortie of gen Vinoy's army (at Paris), repulsed, after 2 hours' fighting—crown prince present, above 200 prisoners taken, gen Guilhem killed 30 Sept. "

Circular from Bismarck disclaiming any intention of reducing France to a second rate power 1 Oct. "

Gen. Burnside, U S A., visits M Favre " "

FRA

M Thiers's fruitless visit to Vienna, 23 Sept , to St Petersburg, 27 Sept , dined with the czar 2 Oct 1870

M Favre, in the name of the diplomatic body, requests Bismarck to give notice before bombarding Paris and to allow a weekly courier, count declines both requests, but permits passage of open letters, reported 3 Oct "

Battle of Thoury, van of gen Reyau's army of Loire under gen. la Motte Rouge, defeats Germans between Chaussy and Thoury, and captures prisoners and cattle 5 Oct "

M Thiers s mission to foreign courts reported abortive 6 Oct "

Part of army of Lyons, under gen Dupré, defeated by Badenese under gen von Gegenfeld near St Remy , French loss about 1500, and 660 prisoners, German loss about 430 6 Oct "

Gen Burnside leaves Paris to meet Bismarck 7 Oct "

Great sortie from Metz, Germans surprised, 40 000 French engaged, repulsed after severe conflicts, French loss about 2000, German about 600 7 Oct. "

M Thiers again at Vienna 8 Oct. "

Garibaldi arrives at Tours, enthusiastically received, reviews national guard at Tours 9 Oct. "

Russia, Great Britain and Spain refuse mediation 10 Oct "

Prussian circular to European powers regretting obstinate resistance of French government to peace, and foretelling social disorganization and starvation 10 Oct "

Ablis near Paris, burned for alleged treachery (killing sleeping soldiers) 10 Oct. "

Gambetta escapes from Paris by a balloon 7 Oct , proclaims at Tours that Paris has 560 000 troops , that cannon are cast daily, and that women are making cartridges, demands co operation in war 10 Oct "

Part of army of Loire defeated at Arthenay, near Orleans, by Bavarians under Von der Tann, 2000 prisoners taken 10 Oct "

First three shots fired at Paris 11 Oct "

Orleans captured by gen von der Tann, after 9 hours fighting, army of Loire defeated retires behind the Loire 11 Oct. "

Gen Bourbaki accepts command at Tours, gen la Motte Rouge superseded in command of army of the Loire by gen d'Aurelle de Paladines 12 Oct "

Garibaldi appointed commander of French irregulars " "

St Cloud fired on by French and burned 13, 14 Oct "

Emperor Napoleon declares that " there can be no prospect of peace, on the basis of ceding to Prussia a single foot of French territory , and no government in France can attach its signature *to such a treaty* and *remain in power a day* " 17 Oct. "

Circular of Jules Favre asserting that Prussia " coldly and systematically pursues her task of annihilating us. France has now no illusions left For her it is now a question of existence We prefer our present sufferings, our perils, and our sacrifices to the consequences of the inflexible and cruel ambition of our enemy France needed, perhaps to pass through a supreme trial—she will issue from it transfigured " 18 Oct. "

British government (supported by neutral powers) asks an armistice to elect a national assembly 21 Oct "

Reported failure of suggestions for an armistice, Prussia demanding consent of France to cession of territory 24 Oct "

Gambetta informs mayors of towns that " resistance is more than ever the order of the day " 24 Oct "

Reported negotiation for surrender of Metz " "

Thiers undertakes mission for an armistice about " "

Bazaine surrenders Metz and his army, " conquered by famine " (FRANCE Oct.-Dec 1873, METZ) 27 Oct. "

Safe conduct to Thiers to enter Paris for negotiation 28 Oct. "

Bismarck to earl Granville, expresses desire for a French national assembly to consider terms of peace, but overtures must come from the French 28 Oct. "

Gen von Moltke created a count on his 70th birthday " "

Thiers enters Paris 30 Oct. "

Thiers receives powers from French defence government to treat for armistice and meets Bismarck 31 Oct , 1 Nov "

Bismarck offers armistice of 25 days for election of a French national assembly 3 Nov "

Favre declares to the national guard that the government has sworn not to yield an inch of territory, and will remain faithful to this engagement. 3 Nov "

Failure of negotiation, as Bismarck will not permit food to enter Paris during the armistice without any military equivalent, Thiers ordered to break off negotiation 6 Nov "

Permission for election of a French national assembly declined by French government 7 Nov "

Orders that no one shall enter or quit Paris " "

Capitulation of Verdun 8 Nov "

Germans, under gen von der Tann, defeated between Coulmiers and Baccon, near Orleans, retire to Thoury 9 Nov "

Continued fighting, Orleans retaken by gen d'Aurelle de Paladines, French losses, 2000, German, about 700 and 2000 prisoners 10 Nov "

Armies in central France now under prince Frederick Charles and the grand duke of Mecklenburg 14 Nov "

Grand duke of Mecklenburg repulses army of Loire, near Dreux, which is captured by Von Treskow 17 Nov "

Paris engirdled with a second line of investment 20 Nov "

Manteuffel defeats French army of north, between Villers Bretonneux and Soleur, near Amiens 27 Nov "

Amiens occupied by Von Göben after a battle 28 Nov "

Severe engagement near Beaune la Rolande (Loiret) between part of army of Loire, under D'Aurelle de Paladines, and the Germans under Voigts-Rhetz, prince Frederick Charles arrives and turns the day, French retire 28 Nov "

De Kératry resigns, accusing Gambetta of misconduct, 28 Nov , Bourbaki appointed to an army corps 29 Nov "

Fruitless endeavors of army in Paris and army of the Loire to unite 29 Nov -4 Dec 1870

Great sortie of 120,000, under gens Trochu and Ducrot, who cross the Marne, severest conflict between Champigny-sur-Marne Brie sur Marne, and Villiers sur Marne, French retain ground gained, but advance is checked, (chiefly Saxons and Würtembergers engaged) 30 Nov "

Contest resumed at Avron, Germans retake Champigny and Brie, French retreat 2 Dec. "

Army of the Loire, Chanzy defeated by grand duke of Mecklenburg at Bazoche des Hautes, 2 Dec. , near Chevilly (French call the affair indecisive) 3 Dec "

Gen d'Aurelle de Paladines intrenched before Orleans , proposes to retreat, government opposes him, but yields, he determines to await attack, part of his army defeated by prince Frederick Charles and grand duke of Mecklenburg, he retreats with 100,000 men, Orleans threatened with bombardment, surrenders at midnight 4 Dec "

Ten thousand prisoners, 77 guns, and 4 gunboats captured at Orleans 5 Dec "

Rouen occupied by Manteuffel 6 Dec "

General order of king of Prussia, " We enter on a new phase of the war Every attempt to break through the investment or relieve Paris has failed " 6 Dec "

Grand duke of Mecklenburg attacks gen Chanzy and army of Loire near Beaugency, indecisive, 7 Dec , the Germans victorious, taking 1100 prisoners and 6 guns, and occupying Beaugency, but with severe loss 8 Dec. "

Gen Manteuffel's army part occupies Evreux, and marches to Cherbourg, part to Havre 8 Dec. "

Whole army of the Loire engaged, under gen Chanzy and others, it retreats but obstinately resists 5-10 Dec "

Brilliant action by Chanzy 11 Dec "

Delegate government transferred from Tours to Bordeaux, Gambetta remains with army of Loire 11 Dec. "

Vigorous sortie from Paris repulsed—artillery action 21 Dec. "

Tours partly shelled, submits, but not occupied by Germans, 21 Dec "

Seven hours' battle at Pont à Noyelles between Manteuffel and army of north under Faidherbe, both claim victory, Faidherbe retreats. 23 Dec "

Mont Avron fort near Paris, after a day's bombardment, abandoned and occupied by Germans. 29 Dec. "

Severe battles near Bapaume, between army of the north under Faidherbe and Germans under Manteuffel and Von Göben, victory claimed by both, French retreat 2, 3 Jan 1871

Bombardment of eastern front of Paris and of southern forts, 4 Jan , forts Issy and Vanves silenced 6 Jan. "

Bombardment of Paris, buildings injured, and people killed, France appeals to foreign powers 9, 10 Jan "

Chanzy retreating, defeated near Le Mans by prince Frederick Charles and grand duke of Mecklenburg 11 Jan "

Prince Frederick Charles enters Le Mans after 6 days' fighting (about 20,000 French prisoners , German loss about 3400), 12 Jan "

Vigorous sorties from Paris repulsed 13 Jan. "

Chanzy retreating 14 Jan , defeated near Vosges 15, 16 Jan "

St Quentin recaptured by Isnard, under Faidherbe " "

Bourbaki defeated near Belfort after 3 days' fighting, 15-17 Jan , retreats south 18 Jan. "

Grand-duke of Mecklenburg enters Alençon 17 Jan. "

Bombardment of Longwy begun " "

Faidherbe defeated near St. Quentin, after 7 hours' fighting, by Von Göben, 4000 prisoners taken 19 Jan. "

Great sortie from Paris of Trochu and 100.000 men, repulsed with loss of about 1000 dead and 5000 wounded 19 Jan "

Armistice for 2 days at Paris refused . 22 Jan "

Bombardment of St. Denis and Cambrai " "

Resignation of Trochu, Vinoy governor of Paris. 23, 24 Jan. "

Favre opens negotiations with Bismarck " "

Longwy capitulates, 4000 prisoners, 200 guns . 25 Jan "

Letter from M Guizot to Mr Gladstone proposing demolition of fortresses on both sides of Rhine, and maintenance of balance of power by congresses, pub 26 Jan "

Capitulation of Paris, armistice for 21 days signed by count Bismarck and Jules Favre . 28 Jan "

Forts round Paris occupied by the Germans. 29 Jan "

Advance of German troops into France suspended 30 Jan "

Bourbaki with about 80 000 men driven by Manteuffel into Switzerland, near Pontarlier, about 6000 captured, 30 Jan., 1 Feb. "

French loss about 350,000 men, 800 guns up to Jan "

Dijon occupied by Germans . . 1 Feb "

Belfort capitulates with military honors. 13 Feb "

Negotiations for peace, Thiers and Bismarck 22–24 Feb "

Preliminaries of a treaty accepted by Thiers, Favre, and 15 delegates from National Assembly France to cede parts of Lorraine, including Metz and Thionville, and Alsace less Belfort, and pay 5,000,000,000 francs, 25 Feb., signed 26 Feb , accepted by National Assembly 1 Mch "

[German loss in battles throughout the war killed or died soon after, 17.570, died of wounds eventually, 10,707, total killed and wounded, 127 867]

German troops enter Paris and remain 48 hours . 1–3 Mch "

They quit Versailles . 12 Mch "

Conference for peace open at Brussels . 28 Mch. "

Treaty of peace signed at Frankfort on the Main, 10 May, ratified by French National Assembly 18 May, "

francs-tireurs (*frang-tee-rurr'*, free-shooters), armed men unattached to any body of regular troops, guerillas, active in the Franco-Prussian war from about 14 Aug 1870, especially after the surrender of MacMahon's army at Sedan, 2 Sept

Frankenhausen, N Germany Near this place Philip, landgrave of Hesse, and allies defeated insurgent peasant, headed by Munzer the anabaptist, 15 May, 1525

Frankfort-on-the-Main, a city of central Germany, founded in the 5th century, was the residence of Charlemagne in 794, walled by Louis I, 838, a capital city, 843, an imperial city, 1245

Union of Frankfort treaty between France Sweden, Prussia, and other German states led to war with Austria	22 May	1744
Frankfort captured by French by surprise	2 Jan	1759
Captured by Custine 28 Oct retaken by Prussians	2 Dec	1792
Bombarded by French, surrendered to Kleber	16 July,	1796
Made part of confederation of the Rhine		1806
A grand duchy under Carl von Dalberg		1810
Republic restored, made capital of German confederation		1815
Vain attempts at insurrection by students	Apr 1833 May,	1834
Frankfort diet publish a federative constitution	30 Mch	1848
Plenipotentiaries of Austria Bavaria, Saxony, Hanover, Würtemberg, Mecklenburg, etc, here constitute council of the German diet	1 Sept	1850
German sovereigns (except king of Prussia) meet at Frankfort (at invitation of emperor of Austria) to consider federal reform, 17 Aug, plan not accepted by Prussia	22 Sept.	1863
Meeting of diet of German confederation, condemn treaty of Gastein	1 Oct.	1865
Diet adopts the Austrian motion that Prussia has broken the treaty, Prussian representative declares the confederation at an end, and proposes a new confederation	14 June,	1866
Entered by the Prussians, who exact heavy supplies	16 July,	"
Annexed to Prussia by law of 20 Sept, promulgated at Frankfort (the legislative corps and 15 000 citizens protest) 8 Oct		"
Visited by king of Prussia, cathedral of St Bartholomew (founded 1315, completed 1512) burned	14, 15 Aug	1867
Frankfort supported Prussia in the war	July	1870
Peace between France and Germany signed here	10 May,	1871

Pop in Dec 1867, 78,277, in 1890, 179,985 GERMANY

Frankfort-on-the-Oder, a city of N Germany, a member of the Hanseatic league, suffered much from marauders in the middle ages and in the Thirty Years' war The university was founded in 1506, and incorporated with that of Breslau in 1811 Near Frankfort, 12 Aug 1759, Frederick of Prussia was defeated by the Russians and Austrians Pop in 1890, 55,738 CUNNERSDORF

franking letters, sending letters free of postage, right claimed by members of Parliament about 1660 In England the privilege was restricted in 1839, and abolished under uniform penny postage, 10 Jan 1840 Queen Victoria was among the first to relinquish the privilege The franking privilege in the United States formerly belonged to the president during life, and to senators and members of Congress during their terms of office It was abolished July 1, 1873, but certain mail matter on public business may be sent free in "penalty envelopes."

Frankland, State of After North Carolina ceded to the United States her western territory, the people of east Tennessee, thus disposed of without their consent, met in convention at Jonesborough in 1784, to form an independent state And although North Carolina repealed the act of cession, and erected the Tennessee counties into a separate judicial and military district with a supreme court and brigadier-general of their own, a second convention assembled at Jonesborough and organized an independent government under the name of Frankland The provisional organization was based on that of North Carolina—a permanent constitution to be framed the next year Under the provisional arrangement an assembly met, John Sevier was chosen governor, laws were passed, courts were constituted, new counties were erected, and the government of North Carolina was notified that the people of the state of Frankland had declared themselves independent of North Carolina, and were no longer under her jurisdiction To this North Carolina objected In the meanwhile disputes upon the constitution divided the convention, while a third party, in favor of adhering to North Carolina, appeared The convention of the new state delegated William Cocke to Congress, with a memorial asking admission into the Union. But he met with no encouragement The party adhering to North Carolina rallied, and in the spring of 1786 elections were held in all counties for members of its assembly. The state of Frankland also held elections, and thus 2 sets of officers claimed authority, threatening civil war Virginia became interested, as one of her counties, Washington, adjoining the state of Frankland, looked to a union with it, this alarmed the Virginia assembly, which passed a resolution making it treason to attempt to erect a new state in her territory without permission of the assembly The state government of Frankland continued to maintain a *quasi* existence throughout the year 1787, under frequent collisions with the North Carolina government, which constantly grew stronger, until, in May, 1788, Sevier the leader of the new state party (afterwards first governor of the state of Tennessee), fled and with his flight the state of Frankland expired A few weeks after, a supreme court of North Carolina, was held at Greeneville without interruption Among attorneys then admitted to practice was Andrew Jackson

franklin, the English freeholder in the middle ages See "The Franklin's Tale" in Chaucer's "Canterbury Tales" (written about 1364)

Franklin, Battle of Gen Sherman confided to gen Geo H Thomas, 28 Sept 1864, the defence of Tennessee with unlimited discretion He also detached gen Stanley with the 4th corps, and gen Schofield with the 23d and most of the cavalry under gen Wilson, from his command, to report to Thomas at Nashville Gen A J Smith, from west of the Mississippi, was also ordered to report to him All this was done to meet the threatened advance of the confederate gen Hood upon Nashville Hood crossed the Tennessee river at Florence with about 35,000 infantry and 10,000 cavalry, on 29 Oct 1864 On 17 Nov, having learned that Sherman had gone south from Atlanta, he left the Tennessee and started northward towards Nashville His army was formed in 3 corps, under maj-gen B F Cheatham, lieut.-gens A P Stewart and S D Lee and his cavalry under Forrest, each corps having three divisions Gen Thomas was at Nashville, while gen Schofield commanded at the front Schofield fell back from Pulaski to Columbia, Tenn, as Hood advanced, and concentrated his forces, Nov 24 As Hood declined to bring on an engagement, Schofield directed Stanley to retire to Spring Hill, where Hood attacked him late on 29 Nov, without decisive results, although the confederates were enabled to bivouac within a few rods of Schofield's line of retreat and controlled it The latter, however, pushed forward his train during the night of the 29th so that on the morning of 30 Nov the whole army was well on its way towards Franklin Franklin lies in a bend of the Harpeth river, some 20 miles south from Nashville Here Schofield, with his force of about 17,000 men, was compelled to halt till his trains could cross the river Defences were hastily erected, and as the federal troops moved into Franklin they were posted behind them, except the 3d division of the 4th corps, which was placed on the extreme left across the Harpeth, and the 2d and 3d brigades of the 2d division, 4th corps, which were halted about 400 yards in advance of the line of defence, the 2d brigade on the right of the Columbia pike, and the 3d brigade on the left of that pike and deployed in a weak line of battle, and left without orders The federals were in position at 3 P M or earlier, but the confederates had not formed for assault before half-past 3 or 4 P M, when they advanced directly in front on the Columbia pike The blunder of placing troops in front of the works helped the confederates, so that they gained them quite as soon as the fleeing brigades They entered on the Columbia pike directly in the centre, and would soon have occupied the whole line but for the brilliant charge of the 1st brigade of the 2d division, 4th corps, under gen Emerson Opdycke, "who, acting entirely upon his own judgment," succeeded in repelling the dangerous assault.* Others followed, equally determined but even less successful, until 10 P M., when the battle ceased Schofield hastily with-

* When, in reviewing this battle, one considers the disaster that might have followed this unmilitary formation but for the foresight and bravery of gen Opdycke, he is apt to inquire why these 2 brigades were thus left, not only exposed themselves, but jeopardizing the whole command If the army had been defeated, this objectless arrangement must have been investigated, and it would be known who was the delinquent Maj gen John M Schofield commanded the field, maj gen David S Stanley the corps to which these troops belonged and gen Wagner the division, Conrad the 3d brigade, and Lane the 2d brigade of the troops in front, while other officers of distinction were looking on It would seem among so many military men with an experience of nearly 4 years of active service, many of them with a West Point education, that some one would have detected and at least attempted to correct this blunder

drew the troops across the river, and by daylight they were well on their way towards Nashville. The loss to the federals in this battle was 189 killed, 1033 wounded, and 1104 missing (captured from the 2 brigades halted in front of the works); total, 2326. The confederate loss was 1750 killed, 3800 wounded, and 702 prisoners; total, 6252, and was especially heavy in general officers. The killed were, maj.-gen. P. R. Cleburne, brig.-gens. Gist, Adams, Strahl, and Granbury; wounded, maj.-gen. Brown, brig.-gens. Carter, Manigault, Quarles, Cockrell, and Scott; captured, brig.-gen. Gordon. The battle of Franklin shows the greatest loss in killed for the number engaged on the part of the assailing force of any battle in history, and adds additional testimony to the superb fighting qualities of the confederate soldier.

Franklin, Search for. Sir John Franklin (1786-1847) served under Nelson at Copenhagen, 1801. First arctic expedition of exploration, 1819, overland from York factory, Hudson's bay, down the Coppermine river to the Arctic ocean and return, traversing 5550 miles. Second arctic expedition descends the Mackenzie river and traverses and surveys 37° of lon. of the arctic coast; for this he was knighted by the British government, 1829, and the university of Oxford conferred on him the degree of D.C.L. With capts. Crozier and Fitzjames, in the British ships *Erebus* and *Terror* (carrying a crew of 138), he sailed from Greenhithe, Engl., on his 3d arctic expedition of discovery, 24 May, 1845. NORTHWEST PASSAGE. Their last despatches were from the Whalefish islands, dated 12 July, 1845. Their prolonged absence caused intense anxiety, and several expeditions were sent from England and elsewhere in search of them; and coals, provisions, clothing, and other necessaries were deposited in various places in the arctic seas by the English and by the United States government, by lady Franklin, and private persons. The *Truelove*, capt. Parker, which arrived at Hull 4 Oct. 1849, from Davis's strait, brought intelligence (not afterwards confirmed) that the natives had seen sir John Franklin's ships the p[...] vious Mch., frozen up by ice in Prince Regent's inlet. O[...] accounts were equally illusory. The British governme[...] 7 Mch. 1850, offered a reward of 20,000*l.* to any party [...] country that should render efficient assistance to the [...] crews. Sir John's first winter-quarters were found at [...] island by capts. Ommanney and Penny.

1. British ship *Plover*, capt. Moore (afterwards under capt. [...]guire), sailed from Sheerness to Behring's strait, in sear[...] 1.
2. Land expedition under sir John Richardson and dr. [...] of Hudson's Bay company, left England..........25
   [Sir John Richardson returned to England in 1849 dr. Rae continued his search till 1851.]
3. Sir James Ross, with the *Enterprise* and *Investigat*[...] June, 1848), having also sailed in search to Barrow's [...] returned to England (Scarborough)..................
4. *Enterprise*, capt. Collinson, and *Investigator*, comm[...] M'Clure, sailed from Plymouth for Behring's strait..[...]
   [Both ships went through to the eastward.]
5. Capt. Austin's expedition, viz., *Resolute*, capt. Austin, *Assistance*, capt. Ommanney; *Intrepid*, lieut. Bertie [...] and *Pioneer*, lieut. Sherard Osborn, sailed from Engla[...] Barrow's strait......................................2
   [Returned Sept. 1851.]
6. *Lady Franklin*, capt. Penny; and *Sophia*, capt. St[...] sailed from Aberdeen for Barrow's strait............1[...]
   [Returned home Sept. 1851.]
7. U. S. expedition in the *Advance* and *Rescue*, under [...] De Haven and dr. Kane (son of the judge), towards whic[...] Grinnell subscribed $30,000, sailed for Lancaster sound [...] Barrow's strait; after drifting in the pack down Ba[...] bay, the ships were released in 1851 uninjured......25 [...]
8. *Felix*, sir John Ross, fitted out chiefly by the Huds[...] Bay company, sailed to the same locality..........22 M[...]
   [Returned in 1851.]
9. British ship *North Star*, commander Saunders, which b[...] sailed from England in 1849, wintered in Wolstenholm[...] sound, and returned to Spithead...................28 Se[...]
10. British ship *Herald*, capt Kellett, C.B., which had sailed [...] 1848, made 3 voyages to Behring's strait, and returned..
Lieut. Pim went to St. Petersburg meaning to travel thr[...] Siberia to the mouth of the river Kolyma; but wa[...] suaded from proceeding by the Russian government. 1[...]
   [*Enterprise* and *Investigator* (see No. 4 above) [...] been heard of for 2 years.]
11. Sir Edward Belcher's expedition—consisting of *A*[...] sir Edward Belcher, C.B.; *Resolute*, capt. Kellett, C.[...] *Star*, capt. Pullen; *Intrepid*, capt. M'Clintock; a[...] capt. Sherard Osborn—sailed from Woolwich..[...]
   [This expedition arrived at Beechy island [...] The *Assistance* and *Pioneer* proceeded thro[...]

[...]chan[ne]l, and the *Resolute* and *Intrepid* to Melville island; the [No]rth Star remaining at Beechy island.]

LADY FRANKLIN'S EQUIPMENTS.

Lady [Fr]anklin, with a few friends (and the "Tasmanian tribute, 1500*l.*), equipped 4 expeditions (Nos. 12, 13, 14, 16).

12. *P*[rin]ce *Albert*, capt. Forsyth, sailed from Aberdeen to Barrow strait..........................5 June, 1850
   [Returned 1 Oct. 1850.]
13. *P*[rin]ce *Albert*, Mr. Kennedy, accompanied by lieut. Bellot, of the French navy, and John Hepburn, sailed from Stromness [for] Prince Regent's inlet..........................4 June, 1851
   [Returned Oct. 1852.]
14. *I*[sabe]l, commander Inglefield, sailed for the head of Baffin's bay, [Jo]nes's sound, and the Wellington channel, 6 July; and ret[urn]ed...........................Nov. 1852
15. Mr. Kennedy sailed again in the *Isabel*, on a [...] to Behring's strait.....................1853
16. [Brit]ish ship *Rattlesnake*, commander T[...] sle [...] the *Plover*, capt. Maguire (who suc[...] at Barrow in Apr.; met with her [...]
17. [...] and U. S. expedition [...] *Advance* [...]
18. [...]

another)—the *Fox*, screw steamer, under capt. (since sir F. L. M'Clintock, British navy (see No 11)—sailed from Aberdeen, 1 July, 1857; returned......................22 Sept. 1[illegible]

[On 6 May, 1859, lieut. Hobson found at point Victory, near cape Victoria, beside a cairn, a tin case containing a paper signed 25 Apr. 1848, by capt. Fitzjames, which certified that ships *Erebus* and *Terror*, on 12 Sept. 1846, were beset in lat. 70° 50′ N. and lon. 98° 23′ W.; that sir John Franklin died 11 June, 1847; that the ships were deserted 22 Apr. 1848. Capt. M'Clintock continued the search, and discovered skeletons and other relics. His "Journal" was pub. in Dec. 1859; and on 28 May, 1860, gold medals were given to him and to lady Franklin by Royal Geographical Society.

Mr. Hall, arctic explorer, reported, in Aug. 1865, a hope that capt. Crozier and others were surviving.

A national monument by Noble, set up in Waterloo place, London, was inaugurated 15 Nov. 1866. It is inscribed to "Franklin, the great navigator, and his brave companions who sacrificed their lives in completing the discovery of the North west Passage, 1847-48 A.D."

Sir John Franklin discovered the *northwest passage* by sai-
[illegible]ing down Peel and Victoria (now Franklin) straits.
[illegible]anklin search expedition," under lieut. Schwatka, of the
[illegible]S. army, overland in summer and autumn of 1879, discov-
[illegible] remains of the crews, etc.; he set up memorials, brought
[illegible]emains of lieut. John Irving, of the *Terror*, and returned
[illegible]ston, Mass.........................about 28 Sept. 1[illegible]
[illegible]ns of lieut. John Irving buried at Edinburgh......7 Jan. [illegible]

[illegible]**anks** (or freemen), a name of a combination of nth-
[illegible] German tribes about 240 A.D., which invaded [illegible]ul
[illegible] parts of the Roman empire with various succe[illegible] in
[illegible]tury. FRANCE, GAUL.

[illegible]**hofer's lines.** SPECTRUM.

[illegible]**cksburg,** Campaign and Battle of. [illegible]ter
[illegible]tietam (MARYLAND CAMPAIGN), McClen,
[illegible] of the army of the Potomac, occupied ar-
[illegible]ot. 1862. After a delay of over a mon[illegible] he
[illegible]c—26 Oct.-2 Nov.—in pursuit of Lee, ho
[illegible]he Rappahannock. Warrenton wa[illegible]the
[illegible]Clellan for the concentration of the[illegible]my,
[illegible]y of the Potomac manœuvred bet[illegible] or
[illegible]r a great struggle, and never ha[illegible]the
[illegible]en general and soldiers been gater
[illegible]*Count de Paris*, "History of th[illegible]ivil
[illegible]. 555. On the evening of 7 N[illegible], a
[illegible]Clellan, relieving him of the[illegible]om-
[illegible] Ambrose E. Burnside in his [illegible]ead.
[illegible] that Burnside assumed [illegible]trol.
[illegible] was changed. Burnside[illegible]plan
[illegible]lpeper, descend the left[illegible]bank
[illegible] Falmouth, in front of[illegible]red-
[illegible], to occupy Fredericksburg.
[illegible]rders for an advan[illegible]from
[illegible] already divided th[illegible]army
[illegible]ions, each of 2 corps. The
[illegible]anklin, consisted of [illegible] 1st
[illegible]; the centre, under [illegible]oker,
[illegible] Stoneman; and th[illegible]right
[illegible] and 9th corps, Co[illegible] and
[illegible]15 Nov. and arrived [illegible] Fal-
[illegible] Falmouth with F[illegible]nklin's
[illegible]re until 25 Nov. [illegible] army
[illegible]m Washington by [illegible]ter to
[illegible]een at Falmouth [illegible]on as
[illegible] confederates to [illegible] and
[illegible]icksburg. It was [illegible] until
[illegible]ain, that Burnside [illegible] or-
[illegible]ksburg, and attack [illegible] con-
[illegible] laid with great [illegible]ficulty
[illegible]e whole of the [illegible] being
[illegible]d by the fire of co[illegible]ferates
[illegible]sburg. Gen. Frankli[illegible]rossed
[illegible] loss, on the mornin[illegible] of the
[illegible] 80,000 strong, lay [illegible]nched
[illegible]ksburg, with an ope[illegible]lain in
[illegible]ing the height know[illegible] Mary's
[illegible], while Stonewall Ja[illegible]son lay
[illegible] Franklin's grand divis[illegible]. The
[illegible]ner on the right, Hoo[illegible] in the
[illegible]ft. The battle was [illegible]ned by
[illegible], and continued, in [illegible]ries of
[illegible] attacks on the enemy works,
[illegible] of the 14th Burnside [illegible]as only

prevented from renewing the attack by the united disapproval of his corps commanders. On the 14th and 15th the armies were quiet, a truce of a few hours being obtained by the federals for burying the dead. On the night of 15 Dec. the federals retired across the river, and on the 16th the confederates again occupied Fredericksburg. The federal losses were 1180 killed, 9028 wounded, 2145 missing; total, 12,353. Confederates lost 593 killed, 3961 wounded, 653 missing; total, 5297. Soon after the discomfiture of the Potomac army at Fredericksburg, Burnside proposed another campaign, crossing the Rappahannock above Fredericksburg. Every arrangement was made for crossing at Banks ford, about 15 miles above Fredericksburg, on 20 Jan. 1863. The weather was fine and the confederates were evidently deceived, but a storm broke out on the night of the 20th, such as to render movement impossible. Burnside relinquished the campaign and went into winter-quarters at Falmouth. This movement is known as the Mud campaign. Burnside was relieved at his own request, 26 Jan. 1863.

Fred'erickshald, a maritime town of Norway. Charles XII. of Sweden was killed by a cannon shot before its walls, while examining the works, 11 Dec. 1718. His hand was on his sword and a prayer-book in his pocket.

free companies and **lances.** CONDOTTIERI.

Freedmen's Bureau. At the close of the civil war in the United States a bureau was created in the war department to care for the freedmen, who had been the wards first of the war and then of the treasury department. It had four divisions: I. Lands; II. Records; III. Financial affairs; IV. Medical. It was under the management of a commissioner, appointed by the president, and an assistant commissioner from each of the states declared *to be in insurrection.* The bureau received in 1865 768,590 acres of land acquired by the U. S. by confiscation or sale, not more than 40 acres of which was to be assigned to each of the freedmen or refugees for use for three years at a maximum annual rental of six per cent. of its appraised value. About $400,000 were collected for rents. Under the workings of the bureau, during 4 years, 20,897,431 rations were issued, 1,000,000 freedmen received hospital treatment, and schools were established throughout the south. Its work latterly was largely educational, and entirely so after 1 Jan. 1869, except that the collection of pay and bounties for colored soldiers and sailors was continued until 1872. The total expenditures of the bureau from Mch. 1865 to 30 Aug. 1870 were $15,359,692.27.

A "Bureau of Refugees, Freedman, and Abandoned Lands" created by Congress..........................3 Mch. 1865
Major gen. Oliver O. Howard appointed commissioner....May, "
School superintendent for each state appointed........12 July, "
"Inspector of Schools" or general superintendent appointed, Sept. "
Supplementary Freedmen's Bureau bill, passed 6 Feb. 1866, vetoed..........................19 Feb. 1866
Act enlarging powers of the bureau passed over the president's veto..........................16 July, "
Act passed to continue the bureau for one year from 16 July, 1868, passed..........................July, 1868
Bureau ordered withdrawn 1 Jan. 1869, with exceptions above noted, by act of..........................3 Aug. "
Educational supervision ceases..........................1 July, 1870

Freemasonry. Writers on Masonry, themselves Masons, affirm that it has had a being "ever since symmetry began and harmony displayed her charms." It is traced by some to the patriarchs, to the pagan mysteries, to Solomon's temple, to the crusades, to Knights Templars, to the Roman college of artificers, to masonry as a craft in the middle ages, to the Rosicrucians, to Cromwell, to prince Charles for political purposes, to sir Christopher Wren, to dr. Desaguliers and his friends, 1717. Its introduction into Britain has been fixed by some as early as 674; and into Scotland 1140.

First grand-lodge was founded at York, Engl.................. 926
[The York rite is the basis of all rites of a Masonic character.]
Grand-lodge of England established, London (George Payne, grandmaster)..................1717
Masonry introduced in France..................1725-25
First lodge in Paris founded by the earl of Derwentwater...... 1725
Grand-lodge of Ireland established.................. 1729
Grand-lodge at York partially accepts the constitution of the grand-lodge of England.................. 1732
First provincial grand-lodge in America established at Boston.. 1733
Freemasons persecuted in Holland by the States-general...... 1735
Scottish grand-lodge reformed at Edinburgh.................. 1736

drew the troops across the river, and by daylight they were well on their way towards Nashville. The loss to the federals in this battle was 189 killed, 1033 wounded, and 1104 missing (captured from the 2 brigades halted in front of the works); total, 2326. The confederate loss was 1750 killed, 3800 wounded, and 702 prisoners; total, 6252, and was especially heavy in general officers. The killed were, maj.-gen. P. R. Cleburne, brig.-gens. Gist, Adams, Strahl, and Granbury; wounded, maj.-gen. Brown, brig.-gens. Carter, Manigault, Quarles, Cockrell, and Scott; captured, brig.-gen. Gordon. The battle of Franklin shows the greatest loss in killed for the number engaged on the part of the assailing force of any battle in history, and adds additional testimony to the superb fighting qualities of the confederate soldier.

Franklin, Search for. Sir John Franklin (1786-1847) served under Nelson at Copenhagen, 1801. First arctic expedition of exploration, 1819, overland from York factory, Hudson's bay, down the Coppermine river to the Arctic ocean and return, traversing 5550 miles. Second arctic expedition descends the Mackenzie river and traverses and surveys 37° of lon. of the arctic coast; for this he was knighted by the British government, 1829, and the university of Oxford conferred on him the degree of D.C.L. With capts. Crozier and Fitzjames, in the British ships *Erebus* and *Terror* (carrying a crew of 138), he sailed from Greenhithe, Engl., on his 3d arctic expedition of discovery, 24 May, 1845. NORTHWEST PASSAGE. Their last despatches were from the Whalefish islands, dated 12 July, 1845. Their prolonged absence caused intense anxiety, and several expeditions were sent from England and elsewhere in search of them; and coals, provisions, clothing, and other necessaries were deposited in various places in the arctic seas by the English and by the United States government, by lady Franklin, and private persons. The *True-love*, capt. Parker, which arrived at Hull 4 Oct. 1849, from Davis's strait, brought intelligence (not afterwards confirmed) that the natives had seen sir John Franklin's ships the previous Mch., frozen up by ice in Prince Regent's inlet. Other accounts were equally illusory. The British government, on 7 Mch. 1850, offered a reward of 20,000*l.* to any party of any country that should render efficient assistance to the missing crews. Sir John's first winter-quarters were found at Beechy island by capts. Ommanney and Penny.

1. British ship *Plover*, capt. Moore (afterwards under capt. Maguire), sailed from Sheerness to Behring's strait, in search, 1 Jan. 1848
2. Land expedition under sir John Richardson and dr. Rae, of Hudson's Bay company, left England..........25 Mch. "
   [Sir John Richardson returned to England in 1849, and dr. Rae continued his search till 1851.]
3. Sir James Ross, with the *Enterprise* and *Investigator* (12 June, 1848), having also sailed in search to Barrow's strait, returned to England (Scarborough)..................3 Nov. 1849
4. *Enterprise*, capt. Collinson, and *Investigator*, commander M'Clure, sailed from Plymouth for Behring's strait..20 Jan. 1850
   [Both ships went through to the eastward.]
5. Capt. Austin's expedition, viz., *Resolute*, capt. Austin, C. B.; *Assistance*, capt. Ommanney; *Intrepid*, lieut. Bertie Cator; and *Pioneer*, lieut. Sherard Osborn, sailed from England for Barrow's strait..................................25 Apr. "
   [Returned Sept. 1851.]
6. *Lady Franklin*, capt. Penny; and *Sophia*, capt. Stewart, sailed from Aberdeen for Barrow's strait...........13 Apr. "
   [Returned home Sept. 1851.]
7. U. S. expedition in the *Advance* and *Rescue*, under lieut. De Haven and dr. Kane (son of the judge), towards which Mr. Grinnell subscribed $30,000, sailed for Lancaster sound and Barrow's strait; after drifting in the pack down Baffin's bay, the ships were released in 1851 uninjured......25 May, "
8. *Felix*, sir John Ross, fitted out chiefly by the Hudson's Bay company, sailed to the same locality...........22 May, "
   [Returned in 1851.]
9. British ship *North Star*, commander Saunders, which had sailed from England in 1849, wintered in Wolstenholme sound, and returned to Spithead..................28 Sept. "
10. British ship *Herald*, capt. Kellett, C.B., which had sailed in 1848, made 3 voyages to Behring's strait, and returned..... 1851

Lieut. Pim went to St. Petersburg, meaning to travel through Siberia to the mouth of the river Kolyma; but was dissuaded from proceeding by the Russian government, 18 Nov. "

[*Enterprise* and *Investigator* (see No. 4 above) had not been heard of for 2 years.]

11. Sir Edward Belcher's expedition—consisting of *Assistance*, sir Edward Belcher, C.B.; *Resolute*, capt. Kellett, C.B.; *North Star*, capt. Pullen; *Intrepid*, capt. M'Clintock; and *Pioneer*, capt. Sherard Osborn—sailed from Woolwich........15 Apr. 1852
    [This expedition arrived at Beechy island 14 Aug. 1852. The *Assistance* and *Pioneer* proceeded through Wellington channel, and the *Resolute* and *Intrepid* to Melville island; the *North Star* remaining at Beechy island.]

LADY FRANKLIN'S EQUIPMENTS.

Lady Franklin, with a few friends (and the "Tasmanian tribute," 1500*l.*), equipped 4 expeditions (Nos. 12, 13, 14, 16).

12. *Prince Albert*, capt. Forsyth, sailed from Aberdeen to Barrow's strait....................................5 June, 1850
    [Returned 1 Oct. 1850.]
13. *Prince Albert*, Mr. Kennedy, accompanied by lieut. Bellot, of the French navy, and John Hepburn, sailed from Stromness to Prince Regent's inlet.......................4 June, 1851
    [Returned, Oct. 1852.]
14. *Isabel*, commander Inglefield, sailed for the head of Baffin's bay, Jones's sound, and the Wellington channel, 6 July; and returned...Nov. 1852
15. Mr. Kennedy sailed again in the *Isabel*, on a renewed search to Behring's strait.. 1853
16. British ship *Rattlesnake*, commander Trollope, sent to assist the *Plover*, capt. Maguire (who succeeded capt. Moore), at Point Barrow in Apr.; met with her................Aug. "
17. Second U. S. expedition, the *Advance*, under dr. Kane, early in June, "
18. *Phœnix* (with the *Bredalbane* transport), commander Inglefield, accompanied by lieut. Bellot, sailed in May; returned, bringing despatches from sir E. Belcher, etc............Oct. "
    [*Investigator* and sir E. Belcher's squadron were safe; but no traces of Franklin's party had been met with. Lieut. Bellot was drowned in August while conveying despatches for sir E. Belcher. Capt. M'Clure had left the *Herald* (10) at Cape Lisburne, 31 July, 1850. On 8 Oct. the ship was frozen in, and so continued for 9 months. On 26 Oct. 1850, on an excursion, the captain discovered an entrance into Barrow's strait, and thus established a N.E.-N.W. passage. In Sept. 1851 the ship was again fixed in ice, and so remained till lieut. Pim and a party from capt. Kellett's ship, the *Resolute* (11), fell in with them in Apr. 1853. The position of the *Enterprise* (4) was still unknown.]

A monument to Bellot's memory was erected at Greenwich. His "Journal" was pub...................................... 1854

Dr. Rae, spring of 1853, again approached the magnetic pole; July, 1854, he reported to the admiralty purchase from Esquimaux of articles which had belonged to sir J. Franklin and his party—sir John's star or order, part of a watch, silver spoons, and forks with crests, etc. Natives told him that they had met white men about 4 winters previous, and had sold them a seal; and that 4 months later, they had found the bodies of 30 men (some buried), who had evidently perished from starvation; the place appears to have been near the Great Fish river of Back. Dr. Rae arrived in England on 22 Oct. 1854, with the relics, which were deposited in Greenwich hospital. He and his companions were awarded 10,000*l.* for their discovery.

19. *Phœnix*, *North Star*, and *Talbot*, under capt. Inglefield, sailed in May, and returned...........................Oct. "

Sir E. Belcher (No. 11), after deliberation, in Apr. 1854, ordered all his captains to abandon the ships; and capt. Kellett gave similar orders to capt. M'Clure, of the *Investigator*. The vessels had been abandoned 15 May when the crews of the *Phœnix* and *Talbot* (under capt. Inglefield) arrived (19). On their return to England all the captains were tried by court-martial and honorably acquitted.......................17-19 Oct. 1855

[Capt. Kellett's ship, the *Resolute*, adrift 1000 miles from where she was left, was found by George Henry, commanding an American whaler, who brought her to New York. The British government having abandoned their claim on the vessel, she was bought by order of Congress, repaired and equipped, and intrusted to com. H. J. Hartstene, to be presented to queen Victoria. She arrived at Southampton, 12 Dec. 1856; was visited by the queen on the 16th, and formally surrendered on the 30th. When the ship was broken up a desk was made of the wood, and presented by the queen to pres. Hayes, 29 Nov. 1880.]

Capt. Collinson's fate was long uncertain, and another expedition was planned, when intelligence came, Feb. 1855, that he had met the *Rattlesnake* (16) at fort Clarence on 21 Aug. 1854, and had sailed immediately, in hopes of getting up with capt. Maguire in the *Plover* (1), which had sailed 2 days previously. Capt. Collinson, having failed in getting through the ice in 1850 with capt. M'Clure, returned to Hong-Kong to winter. In 1851 he passed through Prince of Wales's strait, and remained in the arctic regions without hearing of Franklin till July, 1854, when, again released from the ice, he went to fort Clarence, as above mentioned. Capts. Collinson and Maguire arrived in England.............May, "

20. Third U. S. expedition in search of dr. Kane, in the *Advance*, consisted of the *Release* and the steamer *Arctic*, the bark *Eringo*, and another vessel under com. H. J. Hartstene, accompanied by a brother of dr. Kane as surgeon, 31 May, "
    [On 17 May, 1855, dr. Kane and his party quitted the *Advance*, and journeyed over the ice, 1300 miles, to the Danish settlement; on their way home in a Danish vessel they fell in with com. Hartstene, 18 Sept.; and arrived with him at New York, 11 Oct. 1855. Dr. Kane visited England in 1856; he died in 1857.]

Hudson's Bay company, under advice of dr. Rae and sir G. Back, sent an overland expedition, June, 1855, which returned Sept. following. More remains of Franklin's party were discovered.. "

21. Eighteenth British expedition (equipped by lady Franklin and her friends, the government having declined to fit out

another)—the *Fox*, screw steamer, under capt. (since sir) F. L. M'Clintock, British navy (see No. 11)—sailed from Aberdeen, 1 July, 1857; returned ....22 Sept. 1859

[On 6 May, 1859, lieut. Hobson found at point Victory, near cape Victoria, beside a cairn, a tin case containing a paper signed 25 Apr. 1848, by capt. Fitzjames, which certified that ships *Erebus* and *Terror*, on 12 Sept. 1846, were beset in lat. 70° 50′ N. and lon. 98° 23′ W.; that sir John Franklin died 11 June, 1847; that the ships were deserted 22 Apr. 1848. Capt. M'Clintock continued the search, and discovered skeletons and other relics. His "Journal" was pub. in Dec. 1859; and on 28 May, 1860, gold medals were given to him and to lady Franklin by Royal Geographical Society.

Mr. Hall, arctic explorer, reported, in Aug. 1865, a hope that capt. Crozier and others were surviving.

A national monument by Noble, set up in Waterloo place, London, was inaugurated 15 Nov. 1866. It is inscribed to "Franklin, the great navigator, and his brave companions who sacrificed their lives in completing the discovery of the North-west Passage, 1847–48 A.D."

Sir John Franklin discovered the *northwest passage* by sailing down Peel and Victoria (now Franklin) straits.

"Franklin search expedition," under lieut. Schwatka, of the U. S. army, overland in summer and autumn of 1879, discovers remains of the crews, etc.; he set up memorials, brought the remains of lieut. John Irving, of the *Terror;* and returned to Boston, Mass. ....about 23 Sept. 1880

Remains of lieut. John Irving buried at Edinburgh.....7 Jan. 1881

Franks (or freemen), *a name of a combination of north*-western German tribes about 240 A.D., which invaded Gaul and other parts of the Roman empire with various success in the 5th century. FRANCE, GAUL.

Fraunhofer's lines. SPECTRUM.

Fredericksburg, Campaign and Battle of. After the battle of Antietam (MARYLAND CAMPAIGN), McClellan, still in command of the army of the Potomac, occupied Harper's Ferry, 22 Sept. 1862. After a delay of over a month, he crossed the Potomac—26 Oct.–2 Nov.—*in pursuit of Lee, who* rapidly retired to the Rappahannock. Warrenton was the place selected by McClellan for the concentration of the army. "Never had the army of the Potomac manœuvred better or been better prepared for a great struggle, and never had the mutual confidence between general and soldiers been greater than at this moment."—*Count de Paris*, "History of the Civil War in America," vol. ii. p. 555. On the evening of 7 Nov. a despatch was handed McClellan, relieving him of the command, and appointing gen. Ambrose E. Burnside in his stead. It was with great reluctance that Burnside assumed control. McClellan's plan of campaign was changed. Burnside's plan was to leave the enemy at Culpeper, descend the left bank of the Rappahannock as far as Falmouth, in front of Fredericksburg, and crossing the river, to occupy Fredericksburg. On 14 Nov. Burnside issued his orders for an advance from Warrenton to Falmouth. He had already divided the army of 127,574 men into 3 grand divisions, each of 2 corps. The left grand division, under gen. Franklin, consisted of the 1st and 6th corps, Reynolds and Smith; the centre, under Hooker, 3d and 5th corps, Butterfield and Stoneman; and the right grand division, under Sumner, 2d and 9th corps, Couch and Wilcox. Sumner left Warrenton 15 Nov. and arrived at Falmouth the 17th. Burnside was at Falmouth with Franklin's grand division on the 19th. Here until 25 Nov. the army lay awaiting the pontoon-train from Washington by water to Aquia creek, which should have been at Falmouth as soon as the army. This delay allowed the confederates to seize and fortify the heights behind Fredericksburg. It was not until Dec. 11, owing to the incessant rain, that Burnside gave orders to cross the river at Fredericksburg, and attack the confederates. The pontoons were laid with great difficulty and considerable loss, nearly the whole of the 11th being consumed in the effort, thwarted by the fire of confederates concealed in houses of Fredericksburg. Gen. Franklin crossed below Fredericksburg, without loss, on the morning of the 12th. The confederate forces, 80,000 strong, lay intrenched along the hills behind Fredericksburg, with an open plain in front, Longstreet's corps occupying the height known as Mary's hill, directly behind the town, while Stonewall Jackson lay farther to the right in front of Franklin's grand division. The federals were formed with Sumner on the right, Hooker in the centre, and Franklin on the left. The battle was opened by Franklin about 9 A.M. 13 Dec., and continued, in a series of disconnected and unsuccessful attacks on the enemy's works, until night. On the morning of the 14th Burnside was only prevented from renewing the attack by the united disapproval of his corps commanders. On the 14th and 15th the armies were quiet, a truce of a few hours being obtained by the federals for burying the dead. On the night of 15 Dec. the federals retired across the river, and on the 16th the confederates again occupied Fredericksburg. The federal losses were 1180 killed, 9028 wounded, 2145 missing; total, 12,353. Confederates lost 593 killed, 3961 wounded, 653 missing; total, 5207. Soon after the discomfiture of the Potomac army at Fredericksburg, Burnside proposed another campaign, crossing the Rappahannock above Fredericksburg. Every arrangement was made for crossing at Banks ford, about 15 miles above Fredericksburg, on 20 Jan. 1863. The weather was fine and the confederates were evidently deceived, but a storm broke out on the night of the 20th, such as to render movement impossible. Burnside relinquished the campaign and went into winter-quarters at Falmouth. This movement is known as the Mud campaign. Burnside was relieved at his own request, 25 Jan. 1863.

Fred'erickshald, a maritime town of Norway. Charles XII. of Sweden was killed by a cannon-shot before its walls, while examining the works, 11 Dec. 1718. His hand was on his sword and a prayer-book in his pocket.

free companies and **lances.** CONDOTTIERI.

Freedmen's Bureau. At the close of the civil war in the United States a bureau was created in the war department to care for the freedmen, who had been the wards first of the war and then of the treasury department. It had four divisions: I. Lands; II. Records; III. Financial affairs; IV. Medical. It was under the management of a commissioner, appointed by the president, and an assistant commissioner from each of the states declared to be in insurrection. The bureau received in 1865 768,590 acres of land acquired by the U. S. by confiscation of sale, not more than 40 acres of which was to be assigned to each of the freedmen or refugees for use for three years at a maximum annual rental of six per cent. of its appraised value. About $400,000 were collected for rents. Under the workings of the bureau, during 4 years, 20,897,431 rations were issued, 1,000,000 freedmen received hospital treatment, and schools were established throughout the south. Its work latterly was largely educational, and entirely so after 1 Jan. 1869, except that the collection of pay and bounties for colored soldiers and sailors was continued until 1872. The total expenditures of the bureau from Mch. 1865 to 30 Aug. 1870 were $15,359,092.27.

A "Bureau of Refugees, Freedman, and Abandoned Lands" created by Congress..............................3 Mch. 1865
Major-gen. Oliver O. Howard appointed commissioner....May, "
School superintendent for each state appointed.......12 July, "
"Inspector of Schools" or general superintendent appointed, Sept. "
Supplementary Freedmen's Bureau bill, passed 6 Feb. 1866, vetoed..19 Feb. 1866
Act enlarging powers of the bureau passed over the president's veto..16 July, "
Act passed to continue the bureau for one year from 16 July, 1868, passed..July, 1868
Bureau ordered withdrawn 1 Jan. 1869, with exceptions above noted, by act of..3 Aug. "
Educational supervision ceases..........................1 July, 1870

Freemasonry. Writers on Masonry, themselves Masons, affirm that it has had a being "ever since symmetry began and harmony displayed her charms." It is traced by some to the patriarchs, to the pagan mysteries, to Solomon's temple, to the crusades, to Knights Templars, to the Roman college of artificers, to masonry as a craft in the middle ages, to the Rosicrucians, to Cromwell, to prince Charles for political purposes, to sir Christopher Wren, to dr. Desaguliers and his friends, 1717. Its introduction into Britain has been fixed by some as early as 674; and into Scotland 1140.

First grand-lodge was founded at York, Engl................. 926
[The York rite is the basis of all rites of a Masonic character.]
Grand-lodge of England established, London (George Payne, grandmaster).. 1717
Masonry introduced in France................................1722–25
First lodge in Paris founded by the earl of Derwentwater...... 1725
Grand-lodge of Ireland established............................ 1729
Grand-lodge at York partially accepts the constitution of the grand-lodge of England.. 1732
First provincial grand-lodge in America established at Boston.. 1733
Freemasons persecuted in Holland by the States-general...... 1735
Scottish grand-lodge reformed at Edinburgh.................. 1736

Pope Clement XII. by bull excommunicates Freemasons, and an edict of Charles VI. of Germany forbids Masonic meetings in the Netherlands or in Austria 1738
Frederick the Great of Prussia initiated .... "
Explanation of the pope's bull given by cardinal Ferraro: "Any one joining the Freemasons subject to death and confiscation of property without hope of remission or pardon" 1739
Grand Royal Mother lodge of the Three Globes erected at Berlin 1740; made grand-lodge 1744
Severe edicts against Masonry in Russia, Holland, France, Portugal, Naples, etc. 1731-51
Chapter of Clermont formed at Paris 1754
English grand-lodge of France founded, 1736; assumes the title of grand-lodge of France 1756
Foundation of the national grand-lodge of Italy (dissolved 1790), "
Grand-lodge of Holland established .... "
Rite of "Strict Observance" introduced in Germany 1762
Royal York grand-lodge founded at Berlin 1765
Swedish rite promulgated 1767
"Grand Orient" of France founded 1772
Masonic charity instituted in England 1788
Ancient and accepted Scottish rite, 33°, first introduced in Europe (Paris) from Charleston, S. C., by De Grasse Tilly, son of adm. De Grasse .... about 1802-4
Union of the 2 grand-lodges of England, York and London, making the ancient and true Freemasonry consist of but 3 degrees: apprentice, fellow-craft, and master 1813
Edict of pope Pius VII. against Freemasonry 1814
Rite of Mizraim introduced in Paris 1815
Edict of the king of Portugal against Freemasonry 1824
Dispute in Germany as to receiving Jews as members 1836
[Still unsettled.]
Gould's "History of Freemasonry" pub. London 1887

FREEMASONRY IN THE UNITED STATES.

"Documentary evidence and tradition are alike silent as to the time of the introduction of Freemasonry into the U. S."—*Gould*, "History of Freemasonry," 1887, vol. vi. p. 424.
Pennsylvania Gazette, 8 Dec. 1730, contains the earliest printed notice of the craft in America. It says: "As there are several lodges of Freemasons erected in the province, and people have lately become much amused with conjectures concerning them, we think the following account of Freemasonry from London will not be unacceptable to our readers."
According to many Masonic writers a provincial grand-lodge (St. John's) and also a private lodge were established at Boston, Mass., by Henry Price .... 30 July, 1733
This obtained a place on the roll of the grand-lodge of England, 1734
Benj. Franklin, probably initiated in England, writes to grand-lodge of Massachusetts as grandmaster of Pennsylvania .... "
Franklin publishes the Masonic constitution .... "
Henry Price constituted grandmaster over all North America .. "
George Washington initiated at Fredericksburg, Va. .... 4 Nov. 1752
St. Andrew's lodge constituted at Boston .... 30 Nov. "
Washington made master Mason .... 4 Aug. 1753
First Masonic hall built in the U. S. (Philadelphia) 1754
Second lodge in Philadelphia constituted 1758
Joseph Warren initiated at St. Andrew's lodge, Boston, 10 Sept. 1761
" provincial grandmaster 1769
" provincial grandmaster of America 1772
Order of the "Eastern Star" established in the U. S. 1778
[It belongs to "Adoptive Masonry," introduced into France about 1775 to convert women with Masonry. It can be conferred only on master Masons in good standing, their wives, widows, sisters, daughters, and mothers. Its degrees are Jephthah's Daughter, for daughter; Ruth, widow; Esther, wife; Martha, sister; Electa, mother.]
During the revolution there were as many as 10 field or travelling lodges with the army.
In New York the first provincial grandmaster was Daniel Coxie, 1730; and the earliest lodge on record was in working order certainly before 24 Jan. 1738.
A grand-lodge established in New York during its occupancy by the British, 1781; and by the citizens about 1785.
Grand-lodge established in Pennsylvania 1786
De Witt Clinton initiated in the Holland lodge, New York 1793
[Made grandmaster of the grand-lodge of New York, 1806.]
First grand-chapter in the U. S. at Philadelphia .... 24 Oct. 1797
Imposing ceremonies at Boston, Mass., by the Freemasons in honor of brother Lafayette 1825
Abduction and supposed murder of William Morgan by Freemasons for revealing secrets of the order .... Sept. 1826
New York; Morgan, William.

LIST SHOWING THE DATE OF THE INTRODUCTION OF FREEMASONRY INTO THE OLDER STATES.

State	Introduced		1st grand-lodge
Georgia	1735	1st grand-lodge	1786
[2d American lodge on the English rolls.]			
South Carolina	1736	1st grand-lodge	1787
New Hampshire	1736	"	1789
Maryland	1737	"	1781
Rhode Island	1749	"	1791
Connecticut	1750	"	1789
Virginia	1750 (?)	"	1778
North Carolina	1756	"	1787
New Jersey	1761	"	1786
Delaware	1765	"	1806
Vermont	1781	"	1794
Kentucky	1788	"	1800
Ohio	1790-95 (?)	"	1808
Mississippi	1801	"	1818
Louisiana	1807	"	1812
[There were probably lodges in Louisiana prior to 1807, but the above lodge, established by the grand-lodge of New York, was the first lodge working in the English language.]			
Michigan	1794 (British?),	1st grand-lodge	1826
District of Columbia	—	"	1810

[There are now (1893) 49 grand-lodges in the U. S. and about 10,000 lodges with a membership of 667,000.]

MASONS, BLACK OR COLORED.

The blacks, or negro population, of Boston, Mass., applied to England for a charter—their lodge having existed in Boston for 8 years—in 1784. The request was granted 29 Sept. 1784, but the warrant did not arrive in Boston until 1787. Its number was "459," and the title "African lodge." Prince Hall was the first master. He established a lodge by his own authority at Philadelphia, 1797, and a second at Providence, R. I., soon after. The "African lodge" was shown on the English list until 1813. Formally declared its independence of foreign control, 1827. Organized a national grand-lodge in 1847. They have grand-lodges in several states, which are more or less recognized as legal in France, Italy, Germany, Hungary, Peru, Liberia, etc., but not in the U. S.
The degrees of the Ancient Arabic Order of Nobles of the Mystic Shrine conferred on colored Masons for the first time in the U. S., Washington, D. C., 25 June, 1893, when the highest degree in that order was conferred upon John G. Jones.

Free-soil party. Political parties.

free-trade principles, advocated by Adam Smith in his "Wealth of Nations" (1776), triumphed in England when the corn-laws were abolished in 1846, and the commercial treaty with France was adopted in 1860. Richard Cobden, termed "Apostle of Free Trade," who advocated these measures, died, 2 Apr. 1865. Since 1830 British exports have been tripled. In the United States the Democratic party has of late years advocated a reform of the tariff, in the direction of free-trade; while the Republicans defend extreme protection. Tariff.

Free-will Baptists. A denomination of Baptists in the United States, Arminian in doctrine. The first church was organized by elder Benjamin Randall, a convert of Whitefield, in New Durham, N. H., 30 June, 1780. The first general congress was held in 1827. The society sustains colleges at Lewiston, Me., Hillsdale, Mich., and elsewhere. Its strength in the U. S. and Canada in 1890 was: Churches, 1613; ministers, 1600; members, 86,300.

French in America.

Island of cape Breton discovered by fishermen from Brittany .. 1504
Rude chart of gulf of St. Lawrence by Dennys of Harfleur 1506
Verazzano in the interest of France skirts eastern coast of North America and enters New York and Newport harbors. 1524
Jacques Cartier, a mariner of St. Malo, crosses gulf of St. Lawrence and enters the bay which he names Des Chaleurs, from the heat of mid-summer 1534
[He enters the gulf again in 1535, naming it St. Lawrence. He ascends to the island of Orleans, and sends a boat as far as Montreal.]
Francis de la Roque, lord of Roberval, obtains from Francis I. viceroyalty of Canada, Saguenay, Newfoundland, Belle Isle, cape Breton, and Labrador, with authority to plant a colony 1540
Cartier makes his 3d voyage and passes the winter in the St. Lawrence, but returns to France 1541
[Roberval proceeds to the St. Lawrence 1542, but returns the next year. The discoveries of the French fishermen, of Verazzano and Cartier, give France her claim to the northern portion of America.]
Jean Ribault, under the patronage of adm. de Coligny, explores the coast of Florida and discovers the river St. John and the inlet Port Royal .... May, 1562
On an island in this harbor he erects a fort (soon abandoned), which he names Carolina, after Charles IX. of France .... "
French, under Ribault and Rene de Laudonnière, establish a settlement on the river St. John, and build a fort which is also named fort Carolina 1564
Fort Carolina attacked by the Spaniards under Menendez and the entire garrison and inhabitants of the settlement put to death as Protestants 1565
In turn Dominic de Gourges, a French soldier of fortune, attacks the Spaniards at fort Carolina, which he captures, and hangs the entire garrison "as robbers and murderers. 3 May, 1568
[Ending the attempt of the French to colonize Florida.]
Marquis de la Roche commissioned by France to conquer Canada and adjacent countries not possessed by any Christian prince. 1598
Chauvin, a naval officer, obtains a similar commission on the death of Roche 1600
M. de Chatte commissioned as governor 1602
[The name Canada, first confined to a small district opposite the mouth of the Saguenay, was extended to all territory watered by the St. Lawrence and its tributaries.]
Pontgravé, accompanied by Samuel Champlain, ascends the St. Lawrence 1603
Patent to Pierre de Gast Sieur de Monts for "Acadia," being North America between 40° and 46° N. lat. .... "
De Monts, attended by Champlain and Poutrincourt, discovers the harbor of Port Royal, now Annapolis, Nova Scotia 1604
Champlain explores the bay of Fundy, discovers and names the river St. John, and enters Passamaquoddy bay .... "

De Monts enters the Penobscot the Kennebec Casco bay, and the Saco, and examines the coast as far south as cape Cod 1605
Poutrincourt establishes the first permanent French settlement in America at Port Royal 1607
Champlain establishes the post of Quebec 3 July, 1608
He joins a war party of Hurons against the Iroquois enters and coasts the lake that now bears his name 1609
[A series of explorations now secures to the French the later "New France" including Canada and Acadia]
French Jesuits, under father Biart reach Port Royal, Mount Desert, and the Kennebec and ascend that river 1611-12
Argall from Virginia destroys the fortifications of De Monts on the isle of St. Croix, and burns the settlement at Port Royal 1613
Champlain visits lake Huron 1615
He enters New York with a war party of Hurons and attacks a village of the Seneca Indians near the foot of Seneca lake and is repulsed "
Etienne Brulé of Champigny penetrates the region beyond lake Huron 1616-18
Champlain governor of Canada 1620
Organization of the company of the Hundred Associates" or of the "New France" ratified by France 6 May, 1628
Port Royal occupied by the English
Quebec surrenders to sir David Kirke 1629
["Not a port in North America remained to the French, from Long Island to the Pole, England was without a rival" —*Bancroft* Hist of U. S," vol i p 335]
By treaty with England Richelieu obtains restitution of all territory as prior to the war 29 Mch 1632
Champlain publishes his consolidated narrative, and on his map the falls of Niagara are first noted "
"Jesuit Relations of Canada" begun "
Jesuits active among the Indians, the Micmac mission started, Brébeuf, Daniel, and Lallemand establish missions on lake Huron and other places 1634-35
Champlain, governor of Canada, d 1635
French occupy the islands of Martinique and Dominique 1636
Madame de la Peltier, with the aid of 3 nuns, establishes the Ursuline convent at Quebec. 1639
Jean Nicolet at Green Bay, Wis 1640
Montreal founded 1641
Charles Raymbault and Isaac Jogues reach the strait that forms the outlet of lake Superior 4 Oct. "
François de Montmorency Laval, first bishop of Quebec, arrives 16 June, 1659
[He was vicar apostolic of New France, and made bishop of Quebec 1674]
Groseillers and Radisson, fur traders, explore lake Superior "
Augustin de Saffray de Mesy, 7th governor of Canada 1663-65
Jacques Marquette places a mission at Sault Ste Marie Apr 1668
La Salle, perhaps, tracks the Ohio river to the Mississippi (Ohio) 1669-71
Maine, east of the Penobscot surrendered to the French 1670
French occupy about lakes Huron and Superior 1671
Daniel de Remi, seigneur de Courcelles, governor of Canada 1666-72
Louis de Buade, count de Frontenac, arrives at Quebec as governor of Canada 1672
Fort Frontenac built on the present site of Kingston, Ont 1673
Marquette and Joliet in Iowa "
Marquette and Joliet sail down the Mississippi below the Arkansas river and return "
Joliet's map of the Mississippi "
Marquette d (aged 38) 18 May, 1675
La Salle at fort Frontenac 1676
La Salle Tonty, and Hennepin at Niagara falls 8 Jan 1679
Griffin launched on lake Erie (NEW YORK) "
Hennepin at the falls of St. Anthony May, 1680
La Salle descends the Mississippi, erects a cabin on the Chickasaw bluff, raises the cross at the mouth of the Arkansas, and at the mouth of the Mississippi plants the arms of France and calls the whole valley LOUISIANA 1682
Frontenac recalled to France (succeeded by De la Barre) 1682
Hennepin publishes his explorations 1683
French in Texas under La Salle 1685
French on the Hudson bay
La Salle shot by Duhaut and L'Archeveque while on his way from Texas to the Illinois country 20 Mch 1687
Frontenac reappointed governor of Canada 1689
France declares war against England ("King William's war"), 25 June, 1689
French occupy the Hudson bay territory "
Indians fall on Cocheco (Dover), N H, murder maj Richard Waldron and 23 others, carrying captive 29 27 June, "
Iroquois capture Montreal and Lachine 25 Aug "
French and Indians destroy Schenectady, N Y (NEW YORK), 8 Feb., settlement at Salmon Falls, N H., 27 Mch., and Falmouth, on Casco bay (MAINE) May, 1690
Sir William Phipps conquers Acadia "
His expedition by water against Quebec utterly fails as well as the invasion by land Oct. "
Schuyler's raid into Canada against the French settlement on the Sorrel 1691
Acadia retaken by the French 26 Nov "
York, Me, attacked by the French and Indians (MAINE) Jan. 1692
Frontenac's last invasion of western New York July, 1696
Peace of Ryswick, France retains the coast and adjacent islands from Maine beyond Labrador and Hudson's bay, also Canada and Mississippi valley without boundary lines 20 Sept. 1697
Hennepin publishes a further account of his exploration
Death of Frontenac, aged 78 years 28 Nov 1698

D'Iberville enters the Mississippi from the gulf (LOUISIANA), 2 Mch 1699
["The Mississippi as yet, had never been entered from the sea"—*Bancroft* Hist of U S," vol iii p 200]
Treaty of Canada with the Iroquois 8 Sept 1700
La Motte Cadillac establishes a post at Detroit July, 1701
Bienville in command of the settlements in LOUISIANA "
Chief fortress removed from Biloxi to the western bank of the Mobile river, the first settlement of Europeans in ALABAMA 1702
"War of the Spanish Succession," or Queen Anne's war, 4 May "
Philippe de Rigaud marquis de Vaudreuil governor of Canada, 1703
French and Indians surprise unprotected villages, Wells Scarborough, Casco, Spurwink, and others, in Maine, killing or carrying off inhabitants to Quebec 10 Aug "
Deerfield Mass attacked and destroyed 28 Feb 1704
Death of Henri de Tonty, companion of La Salle Sept "
Attack on Haverhill Mass, partially destroyed 29 Aug 1708
French surrender Port Royal Acadia, to an English fleet 2 Oct 1710
[The English change the name to Annapolis]
Sir Hovenden Walker's expedition against Quebec fails 1711
Truce established between England and France 1712
Treaty of Utrecht (Spanish Succession war ends) gives Acadia to the English, boundary lines still undefined 1713
French establish a trading post at Natchez "
Fort Toulouse built in Alabama 1714
Death of Louis XIV of France 1715
French in the Ohio valley 1716
Illinois joined to Louisiana 1717
New Orleans founded 1718
Five hundred negroes brought from Guinea to Louisiana 1719
French begin to fortify Louisburg 1720
Joncaire establishes a post at Niagara among the Senecas 1721
[Trade with the valley of the Mississippi established (1) by way of lake Erie, the Maumee and the Wabash, and so down the Ohio, (2) by lake Michigan, the Chicago river to the Illinois, to the Mississippi, (3) by the way of Green bay, Fox river, and the Wisconsin]
Postal arrangements between Montreal and Quebec "
New Orleans made the capital of the Louisiana colony 1722
Vaudreuil gov of Canada, d 1725
Massacre of the French at Natchez by the Indians 29 Nov 1729
M Varennes de Verendrye reaches lake Winnipeg 1731
French establish themselves on lake Champlain "
Verendrye builds fort Rouge near the present site of the city of Winnipeg and discovers the Rocky mountains 1736
Explorations between lake Superior and Hudson bay 1738-42
AUSTRIAN SUCCESSION war begins between England and France (known in the colonies as King George's war) 15 Mch. 1744
Capture of Louisburg by the English (MASSACHUSETTS) 1745
Montreal island raided by the English 1747
Treaty of Aix la Chapelle (Austrian Succession war ends) 1748
Roland, M B, marquis Galissonière, governor of Canada 1745-49
Expedition of Céloron de Bienville down the Ohio, burial of plates (OHIO) 1749
Fort Rouillé (Toronto) built by the French "
Sugar cane introduced into Louisiana 1751
Virginia treats with the Indians at Logstown June, 1752
English trading post at Pickawillany, or Piqua O, broken up by the French June, "
French occupying the Ohio country build a fort at Presque isle, now Erie, Pa, and fort Le Bœuf on French creek about 25 miles southeast from Erie 1753
Washington at fort Le Bœuf (PENNSYLVANIA, VIRGINIA) "
Ohio Company begin a fort at the forks of the Ohio, but are driven away by the French, who complete the work and call it fort Duquesne 1754
Washington attacks the French under Jumondville, builds fort Necessity and surrenders to the French (VIRGINIA) "
English fleet going to Acadia transports the French inhabitants to the Atlantic colonies (ACADIA) 1755
Dieskau defeated at lake George (NEW YORK) "
Gov Shirley's failure in the Niagara expedition "
[French forts and posts north of the Ohio at this time were Le Bœuf and Venango on French creek, Pa., Presque Isle and Duquesne, Pa., Sandusky and Miami, Ohio, St Joseph's, near lake Michigan, Pontchartrain (Detroit), Michillimackinac, Fox river, Creve Cœur and fort St Louis on the Illinois, Vincennes, Cahokia, and Kaskaskia]
Braddock defeated (PENNSYLVANIA) 9 July, "
De Menneville, marquis Duquesne, governor of Canada, 1752-55
Montcalm in Quebec 1756
Montcalm captures Oswego 14 Aug "
Montcalm takes fort William Henry (FORTS, NEW YORK) 9 Aug 1757
French defeat Rogers on lake Champlain Mch 1758
Abercrombie defeated in his assault on Ticonderoga 8 July, "
Amherst captures Louisburg July, "
Col. Bradstreet attacks fort Frontenac, the garrison surrenders, 27 Aug "
Gen Forbes advances on fort Duquesne, the French blow up the works and retire (PENNSYLVANIA) Nov "
Gen Johnson captures fort Niagara (NEW YORK) 1759
Amherst captures Ticonderoga 26 July, "
Gen Wolfe's victory at Quebec, his death and that of Montcalm, 13 Sept ; Quebec surrenders 18 Sept. "
Pierre François, marquis de Vaudreuil, governor (and last French) of Canada, 1755-60, surrenders Montreal to gen Amherst, Canada passes to the English 8 Sept 1760
Belétre surrenders Detroit 29 Nov "
By secret treaty Louis XV cedes to Spain Louisiana west of the Mississippi with island of Orleans east of it. 3 Nov 1762

Acadia confirmed to the English by treaty of Paris. 10 Feb 1763
Spain cedes Louisiana to France by treaty of St Ildefonso Oct 1800
U S purchases Louisiana of the French government for $15,000,000, 30 Apr , ratified by Napoleon in May and by the U S (LOUISIANA, UNITED STATES) Oct. 1803

French Association for the Advancement of Science was established by the General Assembly 22 Apr 1872, its chief founders being MM Balard, Claude, Bernard, Delaunay, Dumas, Pasteur, Berthelet, Wurtz, and others M de Quatrefages was elected first president, and the first annual meeting was held at Bordeaux, 5 Sept 1872, when many foreign scientific men were present

French language is mainly based on rude Latin of western nations subjugated by Rome German was introduced by Franks in the 8th century In the 9th the Gallo-Romanic dialect became divided into the *langue d'oc* of the south and the *langue d'oïl* of the north The dialect of the Isle of France became predominant in the 12th century The French language as written by Froissart assimilates more to modern French, and its development was almost completed when the Académie Française (established by Richelieu in 1634) published a dictionary of it in 1674. The French language, laws, and customs were introduced into England by William I, 1066. Law pleadings were changed from French to English in the reign of Edward III, 1362 —*Stow*

French literature and **authors.** LITERATURE

French revolution of 1789-95 The condition of the laboring poor in France had grown rapidly worse during the reigns of Louis XIV and XV, and at the accession of Louis XVI was desperate Starvation threatened whole provinces, and disaffection towards the crown was increased by the unpopularity of the king's marriage with Marie Antoinette, daughter of Maria Theresa of Austria, an alliance which indicated the persistent adherence of the monarchy to its arbitrary and oppressive traditions After the dismissal of Calonne, 1787, a feeling prevailed that the country was on the eve of a revolution, that the financial confusion, the spread of poverty, the helplessness of the government, the feebleness of the king, and the extravagance and luxury of his court could not continue without a catastrophe The first assembly of "the notables" was called 22 Feb 1787, the second, 1788 The States-general met May, 1789 The National Assembly was formed 30 June, 1789 The revolution began with the destruction of the Bastile, 14 July, 1789 FRANCE, 1789-95 The names given below are the best known of the revolution, either for their tragic fate or for their prominence FRANCE, 1785, etc

Bailly, Jean Sylvain, b Paris, 15 Sept. 1736 Eminent scientist, as tronomer, etc., favored the revolution, mayor of Paris, 1789, resist the sanguinary revolutionists, guillotined 12 Nov 1793

Barbaroux (*bar ba roo'*), Charles Jean Marie, b at Marseilles, France, 6 Mch 1767 Joined the Girondists, escaped until 25 June, 1794, when he was captured and guillotined at Bordeaux One of the few lovable characters of the revolution

Barère de Vieusac (*bä'rĕr deh ve uh zak'*), Bertrand, b Tarbes, France, 10 Sept. 1755. Notorious for meanness, cowardice, and atrocious cruelty, supporting always the strongest party, he escaped the vengeance of all, and d 15 Jan 1841 the last of the Committee of Public Safety See Macaulay's famous essay "Barère."

Barnave (*bär näv*), Antoine Pierre Joseph Marie, b Grenoble, France, 1761, member of Tiers Etat of States-general, 1789, member of assembly, and, except Mirabeau, its most powerful orator, president of assembly, Oct 1790, maintained the inviolability of the king's person, favored a constitutional monarchy At the end of the Constituent Assembly he returned to Grenoble, 1792 His sympathy for the royal family brought him under suspicion, and he was arrested Aug 1792 After a years' confinement he was brought before the revolutionary tribunal, condemned, and guillotined, 30 Nov 1793 One of the noblest actors and victims of the revolution

Barras (*bä-rä'*), Paul François Jean Nicolas, comte de, b France, June, 1755. In the national convention voted for the king's death. Successfully opposed Robespierre, 27 July, 1794 Gave Napoleon Bonaparte command against the insurrection of 5 Oct 1795. Prominent in national affairs until 1799, d 1829

Beauharnais (*bō-ar na'*) Alexandre de, b. Martinique, 1760, married at Paris mdlle Josephine Tacher de la Pagerie (afterwards wife of Napoleon Bonaparte), member of the States general and national convention Joined the army of the north, retired because of noble birth, condemned by the revolutionary tribunal, and guillotined 23 June, 1794

Billaud Varennes (*be-yo' vä-ren'*), Jacques Nicolas, b Rochelle, France, 1762, active in the massacre of Sept. 1792 In the national convention voted for the death of the king, and against allowing him counsel, deserted Robespierre, but was banished to Cayenne, whence he escaped, and d. at Port-au-Prince, Hayti, 1819

Brissot (*bré so*), Jean Pierre b Chartres, France, Jan 1754. A leading Girondist, guillotined 31 Oct 1793.

Calonne (*ka lon'*), Charles Alexandre de, b Douai, France, 1734. State minister before the revolution (1783-87), recommending a redistribution of taxes, abolition of *corvées* and the gabelle, etc, he was dismissed and exiled He returned to France, 1802, and d 30 Oct of that year

Cambacérès (*kon bah sa-res'*), Jean Jacques Regis de, b Montpellier, France, 18 Oct. 1753, member of National Assembly, 1792. In the trial of the king, advocated all latitude of defence for the king's advocate, and while voting the king guilty, moved for delay in the execution of the sentence Enjoyed the confidence of Napoleon throughout his reign, retired to Belgium, 1815, recalled and restored to his rights, 1818, d 1824

Cambon (*kon bon'*), Joseph, b 1754 Member of the assembly, 1791, voted for the king s death, accused Robespierre in the assembly, 1794, etc, d. 1820.

Carnot (*kar no'*). Lazare Nicolas Marguerite b Nolay, France, 13 May, 1753 Member of the National Assembly, 1791, and of the Committee of Public Safety under Robespierre, voted for the overthrow of the nobility and the death of the king Defended Collot d'Herbois and Barère after the fall of Robespierre In 1795 he became one of the 5 directors of the republic, minister of war for a short time before Napoleon became consul for life, 1806 retired to private life During the "hundred days" again minister of war, retired to Warsaw, d at Magdeburg, 1823.

Carrier (*kä re a'*), Jean Baptiste, b Yolai, France, 1756, a cruel leader in the "reign of terror", active Jacobin, member of the National Assembly, voted for the king's death Prominent in the arrest of the duc d Orleans and in the overthrow of the Girondists. Best known for his wholesale butchery of men, women, and children at Nantes, 1793-94 After the fall of Robespierre he was condemned by the revolutionary tribunal and guillotined 16 Dec 1794

Chaumette (*sho-met'*), Pierre Gaspard, b Nevers, France, 1763, a violent and brutal revolutionist, insulted the imprisoned king, and, with Hébert, accused the queen of infamous crimes, devised the "Fêtes de la Raison", was guillotined through the jealousy of Robespierre, 1794

Clootz, Jean Baptiste, better known as Anacharsis Clootz, b Prussia, 1755, of a wealthy and aristocratic family, sent to Paris to be educated, 1766, embraced republican principles, and, upon the opening of the revolution, became a violent fanatic In the national convention he voted the death of the king but exciting the jealousy of Robespierre, was guillotined, with Hebert, Chaumette, and others, 1794

Collot d'Herbois (*ko-lo der bwä'*), Jean Marie, b Paris, 1750, a sanguinary leader active in the conflicts of 10 Aug and in the massacre of Sept. 1792, noted for ordering 600 inhabitants of Lyons shot in one day Supported Robespierre, voted for the death of the king, abandoned Robespierre but was tried with Billaud and transported to Cayenne, where he d 8 June, 1796 Called the Tiger of the Revolution

Condorcet (*kon dor sa'*), Marie Jean Antoine Nicolas Caritat, marquis de, b Picardy, 17 Sept. 1743 Eminent in literature and science He greeted with enthusiasm the revolution in the interests of liberty, member of the legislative assembly and of the national convention, 1792, voted the king guilty, opposed his death, voted for an appeal to the people, denounced the arrest and execution of the Girondists, and incurred the hatred of the "Mountain" Fleeing from proscription, he was captured 7 Apr. 1794, and died the next day in prison from exhaustion

Corday d'Armans, Marie Anne Charlotte b Normandy, France, 1768, assassinated Marat in a warm bath in his house, guillotined July, 1793

Cottereau, Jean (called Chouan, *screech owl*), grateful to Louis XVI for a pardon for some slight offence, he led a loyalist band of peasantry in his district against the revolutionists, 1792-94, mortally wounded, 28 July, 1794

Couthon (*koo ton'*), George, b. Auvergne, France 1756 In the National Assembly voted for the death of the king, opposed the Girondists, engaged in the massacre at Lyons, on the fall of Robespierre was guillotined, July, 1794 Called the Panther of the Triumvirate

Danton (*don'ton'*), George Jacques, b. Arcis sur-Aube, France, 1759 His public career began as president of the club Cordeliers, in which he showed himself one of the most extreme of the early revolutionists, and fully equalled either Marat or Robespierre in his bloody work In 1792 he led the struggle against the Girondists In the national convention he voted for the death of the king His ability was the greatest force in accomplishing the destruction of the Girondists, but Robespierre and the Jacobins were too strong for him, and he was arrested, with his followers, 30 Mch 1794, and guillotined 5 Apr 1794 He was an orator, and has been termed the Mirabeau of the Sans Culottes

Desmoulins (*da-moo lan'*), Lucie Simplice Camille Benoist, b. Picardy, France, 2 Mch 1760. Active revolutionist and journalist. In the national convention voted for the abolition of royalty and death of the king, at first intimate with Robespierre, but afterwards joined Danton, and with him was arrested and guillotined, 5 Apr 1794 His wife was guillotined a few days after

Dumouriez (*du-moo re ä'*), Charles François, b at Cambray, France, 1739, advocated reform in the government with the Girondists. Commanding the army of the north, he gained the battle of Jemappes, 1792, and was successful in the Netherlands until defeated at Neerwinden, 1793, when, being recalled by the convention under a charge of treason he took refuge in the Austrian camp. In 1804 he settled in England, and was pensioned by George III with $6000 a year, d. 1823

Fauchet (*fō-shä*), (Abbé) Claude, b Dornes, department Nièvre, France, 1744, devoted to the service of the church, rapidly promoted, preached before the king, for too liberal a tone in his sermons he was deposed, 1788, earnest and active in the revolution a leader of the attack on the Bastile, member of the commune, figured in the extreme clubs blessed the tricolor, appointed constitutional bishop, 1791, organized the "Cercle Social" 1791, member of the assembly and convention, disgusted with the excesses of the Jacobins he sided with the Girondists, opposed the death of the king and voted for an appeal to the people for imprisonment and banishment suspected by the more violent of the Revolutionists he was accused of complicity with Charlotte Corday in the murder of Marat, and guillotined with the Girondists, 31 Oct 1793 Called the Priest of the Revolution

Fouché (*foo sha*) Joseph, b Nantes, France, 29 May, 1763 Attached to the most violent party in the national convention, he voted for the king's death, took part in the massacre at Lyons Best known as minister of police before and under Napoleon, treacherous and unscrupulous, d in exile at Trieste 25 Dec 1820

Foulon', Joseph François, b France 1715. Held office under the monarchy, counselled reform in some departments of the government Hated by the populace for sayings ascribed to him, such as, "If the people have no bread let them eat hay," he was seized by the mob on the day of the destruction of the Bastile, 1789, killed, and his head with the mouth filled with hay, paraded on a pole through the streets

Fouquier Tinville (*foo ke a' tan vel'*), Antoine Quentin, b Heronel, France 1747, an infamous public accuser From the first an extreme revolutionist, friend of Danton and Robespierre Persons of both sexes and of all ages, innocent and guilty, royalists, Girondists, Jacobins, friend or foe, his own associates, Hébert, Clootz, Danton, and Desmoulins, were indifferently accused by him On the fall of Robespierre he was condemned and guillotined 1794

Freteau (*fre to'*), St Just Emmanuel Marie Michel Philippe de, b France 1745, moderate revolutionist, favored a constitutional monarchy, retired to his estate, but fell a victim to the revolutionary frenzy, 1794.

Gensonne (*zhan-so-na'*), Armand, b Bordeaux, France, 10 Aug 1758 Helped organize the Gironde, member of convention, voted for the king's death, but afterwards, with his party, became more moderate He was guillotined, 31 Oct 1793

Guadet (*ga da'*), Marguerite Elie, b Bordeaux, France, 1758, member of the national convention, spoke against the death of the king, but voted for it. A leader of Girondists, on the fall of that party he took refuge with friends at Bordeaux, but was discovered and executed there, July, 1794.

Guillotin (*ge-yo tan'*), Joseph Ignace, b Sautes, France, 1738, moderate revolutionist, known as the person who first proposed in the legislative assembly, 1789 some machine to be used for capital punishment other than the sword or axe Although not its inventor, he gives name to the machine (guillotine), d 1814

Hébert (*a ber'*), Jacques René, b Alençon, France, 1755, poor and vile, the scum of the revolution, and, with Chaumette the most unprincipled of accusers Witness against the queen, charges too revolting for even the revolutionary tribunal Denounced by Saint Just, 13 Mch 1794, he was guillotined on the 22d, died like a coward His widow was guillotined a few days after, on the same day as the widow of Desmoulins

Herault de Sechelles (*a ro' deh sa-shel'*), Marie Jean, b Paris 1760, extreme revolutionist, friend of Danton, member of "Cordeliers", guillotined, with Hebert, Clootz, Danton, and others, Apr 1794

Hoche (*osh*), Lazare, b Montreuil, France, 1768. As a soldier, with the revolutionists, he successfully opposed the Austrians, 1793, but having incurred the displeasure of Saint Just, he was arrested, and only escaped death by the fall of Robespierre Again, as a commander, he distinguished himself, but d 1797 One of the most skilful of the generals of the revolution

Isnard (*is nar'*), Maximin, b Grasse, France, 1751, member of assembly, 1791 United with the Girondists, member of the Committee of Public Safety On the fall of the Girondists he escaped death by concealment, afterwards a member of the Five Hundred, returned to private life, 1800, d 1830

Jourdan (*zhoor don'*), Jean Baptiste, b France, 1762 One of the generals of the revolutionary period, successful in 1794. Not being properly supported by the government, he resigned. With the army under Napoleon, made peer of France, 1819, d 1833

Kellermann, François Christophe, b Strasburg, 30 May, 1735, ardent revolutionist, gains the battle of Valmy, 20 Sept. 1792 Employed by Napoleon, d 12 Sept. 1820.

Lafayette, Jean Marie Paul Roch Yves Gilbert Motier, marquis de, b at the château of Chavagniac, Auvergne, France, 6 Sept 1757 An ardent republican, he heartily embraced the American cause, and served through the War of Independence In France he was a member of the Assembly of Notables, 1787, of the National Assembly, 1789 His name is prominent in revolutionary annals until 1792, when he took refuge in the neutral territory of Liege to escape the revolutionists, but was seized by Austrians and held prisoner for 5 years under great hardship Napoleon stipulated for his release at the treaty with Austria of Campo Formio, 1797 His was the purest character of the revolutionary period, but failed to influence the revolutionary party, and by his advocacy of a constitutional monarchy he forfeited the confidence of the royalists. His life of patriotic service ended 20 May, 1834.

Lamballe (*lon'bal'*) Marie Thérèse Louise de Savoie Carignan de, princess of, b. Turin, 1749 Distinguished for beauty and virtue, married prince of Lamballe, 1767, a widow, 1768. Favorite attendant of the queen Marie Antoinette, whose dangers and adversities she shared. Imprisoned in La Force, and murdered, Sept. 1792, with great brutality, her remains mutilated beyond recognition, and her head carried on a pike through the streets

Lavoisier (*la vwa se-a'*), Antoine Laurent, b. Paris, 1743. Eminent scientist, one of the founders of modern chemistry, a prominent member of the Farmers general, on 2 May, 1794 one Dupin in the convention presented a frivolous charge against the whole body of ex Farmers-general, on 6 May, 1794, Lavoisier with 27 others of them was condemned, and 2 days afterwards they were guillotined A petition in his favor evoked the reply "the republic has no need of savants"

FRE

Lebas (*leh ba*) Philippe François, b Arras 1765, violent revolutionist, devoted personal friend and partisan of Robespierre, on whose fall he committed suicide, 1794

Louis XVI FRANCE, 1775-93 House of Bourbon

Louis XVII FRANCE, House of Bourbon

Louvet de Couvray (*loo veh' deh koo vra'*), b Paris, 1760 Prominent member of the Gironde, elected to national convention 1792 Proscribed with his party but escaped the guillotine, member of the Council of Five Hundred, d 1797

Marat (*ma ra'*) Jean Paul, b Baudry, Switzerland, 24 May, 1743. Educated he obtained some notice in several departments of science. In 1788 he entered the political arena and engaged in issuing pamphlets Edited a paper, *L'Ami du Peuple*, 12 Sept 1789 Offending parties in power he sought safety for a while in England and on his return in the cellars and sewers of Paris After 10 Aug 1792, he took his seat in the commune, and demanded a tribunal to try the royalists in prison As no tribunal was formed, the massacre of the prisoners followed in Sept As member of the national convention, he maintained that the king should be tried for no act prior to his acceptance of the constitution, but that he must die In his struggle with the Girondists Marat, aided by Danton, was successful in the end Assassinated by Charlotte Corday, 13 July, 1793 That Marat was insane through most of his public career there is no question Under the insanity of "suspicion" he became a monster of cruelty, albeit naturally humane

Marie Antoinette, Josephe Jeanne, queen of France, b Austria, 2 Nov 1755, married Louis, afterwards Louis XVI of France, 1770, became queen, 1775 The hatred of the people for her frivolity, selfishness, extravagance, and obstinacy hastened the revolution Many false accusations brought against her found support in her conduct The diamond necklace scandal, in which she was not to blame brought her name into disrepute Her self will hampered the good intentions of the king She would not consent to any limit of the royal power Her sufferings during the last year of her life excited universal sympathy She was tried Oct 1793, and on the 16th was sentenced and guillotined

Mirabeau (*mer-a bo*), Honoré Gabriel Riquetti comte de, b Bignon, France, 9 Mch 1749 The small pox when he was but 3 years old disfigured his face for life In 1789 he was returned a member of the States general from Aix—in the Tiers Etat. Here his political life commenced, and for the next 2 years he was the principal leader of the revolution He d 2 Apr 1791, too soon to shape the government or the future of France He was an orator of the highest order, but his statesmanship was never fully tested Some imagine that, had he lived, France would have escaped the horrors of the revolution, through a constitutional monarchy

Necker (*nek ker'*), Jacques, b Geneva, Switzerland, 1732, celebrated as the father of madame de Staël and as minister of finance under Louis XVI, at the opening of the revolution He was twice dismissed by the king but recalled at the demand of the people His second dismissal excited the populace to destroy the Bastile, and the king recalled him He soon showed himself unable to cope with political or financial questions, and in Sept. 1790, resigned office, unregretted, d at Coppet Switzerland 1804

D'Orléans (*dor la on*), Louis Philippe Joseph duc called *Egalite*, b Saint Cloud, 1747, by marriage became one of the richest men in France He was a pronounced liberal, and his dissensions with the court of Louis XVI, where he was cordially disliked, probably led him to make his Palais Royal in Paris a focus of liberal ideas His popularity in Paris was greatly increased by his liberality during the famine Was elected to the States general, 1780, and joined the Tiers Etat with others of the nobility Allied himself with the Dantonists and assumed the title *Egalite* Member of the national convention, he voted for the death of the king—a standing disgrace to his name He was arrested and guillotined during the "reign of terror," Nov 1793, merely on account of his rank

Petion de Villeneuve (*pa te on' deh vel nuv'*), Jerome, b. Chartres, France, 1753 Radical member of the National Assembly, 1790, elected mayor of Paris, 1791 Having acted in the convention with the Girondists, he escaped their destruction, but was found dead in a field in the department of the Gironde, June, 1794

Pichegru (*pesh gru'*), Charles, b Arbois, France, 1761 Joined the revolutionists, general in chief of the army of the north, 1794. Aided materially in suppressing the insurrection of the Faubourgs, Apr 1795 Suspected of sympathy with royalists he retired from the army President of the Council of Five Hundred, again suspected of complicity with the royalists, he was condemned and transported to Cayenne Escaped to England, and returned secretly to Paris, 1804, where he was arrested, and a few days after (6 Apr) was found dead in his prison

Robespierre (*rob es pe er'*), François Joseph Maximilien Isidore, b Arras, France, 1759 From the first a prominent figure of the revolution, connected with many sanguinary and brutal acts From the Sept massacre of 1792 he was virtually dictator, until his overthrow July, 1794 He was arraigned by the Girondists, and his fate was in their hands, but by their vacillation he obtained the ascendency, and 31 Oct 1793, saw the leaders of that party executed In the deaths of the king and queen in the overthrow of the Gironde and of Danton, his was the ruling hand. He was most abhorred among the many monsters of this period He was at last assailed in the tribune by members made desperate through fear of their own lives, 27 July, 1794, condemned and guillotined the next day (28th), already half dead with a broken jaw received in the mêlee the day previous.

Roland de la Platière (*ro lon' deh la pla te air'*), Jean Marie, b Villefranche, France 1734, moderate revolutionist Girondist, minister of state, minister of the interior under the republic, Aug. 1792–

Jan 1793 resigned and returned to Rouen, on hearing of the death of his wife (guillotined), he committed suicide, Nov 1793

Roland, Marie Jeanne, madame, b Paris, 17 Mch 1754 Although her beauty and grace attracted many suitors, she married M Roland, 20 years her senior, in 1780 She was zealous in the cause of liberty, and enlisted in the early movement of the revolution with enthusiasm By her manners, genius, and conversational powers she acquired great influence among the Girondists She was guillotined 9 Nov 1793

Saint Just (*san zhust'*) Antoine Louis Leon de b Decize France, 1767 Violent revolutionist, intimate friend of Robespierre, whose measures he always supported, member of the national convention voted for the death of the king without delay or appeal to the people Prominent in overthrowing the Girondists and Danton's party, and with Robespierre and Couthon formed the triumvirate of the "reign of terror" Guillotined, with Robespierre July, 1794

Santerre (*son ter'*) Antoine Joseph, b Paris, 1752, a revolutionary leader, commanded national guards, 1792 and guards at execution of the king, etc, d 1809 FRANCE, House of Bourbon

Sieyes (*se yais'*), Emmanuel Joseph known as abbé Sieyés, b Fréjus, France, 3 May 1748 Zealous revolutionist, member of the convention of 1792, voted for the king's death, but, shocked by the "reign of terror" temporarily retired from public life Later, member of the Committee of Public Safety, and of the Directory, and one of the first consuls, 1799 Unable to cope with Napoleon, he again retired, d Paris, 20 June, 1836 Famous as a constitution maker

Tallien (*ta le an'*) Jean Lambert, b Paris 1769, conspicuous at the outbreak of the revolution as a "patriot" Intimate with Danton and Marat Participated in the massacres of Sept and other atrocities Being suspected by Robespierre he opposed his domination for a time, and on 9 Thermidor (27 July, 1794) Robespierre was overthrown Tallien then sunk into obscurity, and died in Paris in great poverty, Nov 1820

Vergniaud (*vern ye o'*), Pierre Victurnien b Limoges, France, 31 May, 1759 Elected to the Legislative Assembly, Sept 1791 attacked the king in a brilliant speech, July, 1792 Member of the national convention, in the trial of the king voted for an appeal to the people, but, defeated in this, voted for the king's death, and as president of the convention passed the sentence on him, Jan 1793 As a Girondist he defended his party ably but unsuccessfully against Robespierre and the "Mountain," Apr 1793, arrested June 1793, guillotined, 31 Oct. 1793 One of the most brilliant leaders of the revolution

French revolutionary calendar. In 1792, the French nation adopted a calendar professedly founded on philosophical principles The first year of the era of the republic began at midnight, between 21 and 22 Sept 1792, but its establishment was not decreed until the 4th Frimaire of the year II, 24 Nov 1793 The calendar existed until the 10th Nivose, year of the republic XIV, 31 Dec 1805, when the Gregorian mode of calculation was restored by Napoleon I

	AUTUMN	
Vendemiaire	Vintage month	22 Sept to 21 Oct
Brumaire	Fog month	22 Oct to 20 Nov.
Frimaire	Sleet month	21 Nov to 20 Dec
	WINTER.	
Nivose	Snow month	21 Dec. to 19 Jan
Pluviose	Rain month	20 Jan to 18 Feb
Ventose	Wind month	19 Feb. to 20 Mch.
	SPRING.	
Germinal.	Sprouts' month	21 Mch to 19 Apr
Floréal	Flowers' month	20 Apr to 19 May
Prairial	Pasture month	20 May to 18 June
	SUMMER.	
Messidor	Harvest month	19 June to 18 July
Fervidor, or Thermidor	Hot month	19 July to 17 Aug.
Fructidor	Fruit month	18 Aug to 16 Sept

SANSCULOTIDES, OR FEASTS DEDICATED TO

Les Vertus	The Virtues	17 Sept
Le Génie	Genius	18 "
Le Travail	Labor	19 "
L'Opinion	Opinion	20 "
Les Récompenses.	Rewards	21 "

French revolutions. FRANCE, 1830, 1848, 1870.

Frenchtown, now **Monroe,** Mich, was taken from the British by gen Winchester, 18 Jan. 1813 It was retaken by the British under gen Proctor, 22 Jan, and Winchester and his force captured Known as the RIVER RAISIN massacre

fresco paintings are executed on fresh plaster. Ancient ones exist in Egypt, Italy, and England, and modern ones in the British houses of parliament, at Berlin, and other places The fresco paintings by Giotto and others at the Campo Santo, a cemetery at Pisa, executed in the 13th century, are justly celebrated. STEREOCHROMY.

Frétaval, a town of central France. Here Richard I of England defeated Philip II. of France, and captured his royal seal, archives, etc., 15 July, 1194. Frétaval was taken by the Germans, 14 Dec. 1870, and soon abandoned.

friars (from Fr *frère*, a brother) BENEDICTINES, CARMELITES, CISTERCIANS, DOMINICANS, FRANCISCANS, MINORITES, and other orders

Friday, the 6th day of the week, so called from Friga, or Frea the Scandinavian Venus, wife of Thor, and goddess of peace, fertility, and riches, who with Thor and Odin formed the supreme council of the gods GOOD FRIDAY

Friedland, a town of N Prussia Here the allied Russians and Prussians were beaten by French, commanded by Napoleon, on 14 June, 1807. The allies lost 80 pieces of cannon and about 18,000 men, the French about 10,000 The peace of Tilsit followed, Prussia surrendering nearly half her dominions. This battle furnished a subject for one of Meissonier's greatest war-pictures

Friendly isles, in the southern Pacific, between lat 13° and 25° S and lon 172° W. and 177° E, more than 150 in number, form a large archipelago They were discovered by Tasman, in 1643, visited by Wallis, who called them Keppel isles, 1767, and by capt. Cook, who named them from the friendly disposition of the natives, 1773, though later voyagers found them very ferocious.

Friesland, East, N Germany, ancient Frisia, formerly governed by its own counts On the death of its prince, Charles Edward, in 1744, it became subject to the king of Prussia, Hanover disputed its possession, but Prussia prevailed. It was annexed to Holland by Bonaparte in 1806, to the French empire, 1810, and awarded to Hanover in 1815. The English language is said to be mainly derived from the old Frisian dialect.—*Friesland, West,* in Holland, was part of Charlemagne's empire in 800 It passed under the counts of Holland about 936, and was one of 7 provinces which renounced the Spanish yoke in 1580 The term *chevaux-de-frise* (or *cheval-de-frise*, a Friesland horse) is derived from Friesland, where it was invented

Friuli (*free-oo'-lee*), Venetia, made a duchy by Alboin the Lombard when he established his kingdom, about 570 It was conquered by Charlemagne Duke Henri, a Frenchman, was assassinated in 799, as was duke Berengarius, king of Italy and emperor, in 924. The emperor Conrad gave the duchy to his chancellor, Poppo, patriarch of Aquileia, in the 11th century, it was conquered by Venice in 1420, annexed to Austria, 1797, to France, 1805, to Austria, 1814, to Italy, 1866

Fro'bisher's strait, discovered by sir Martin Frobisher, who sought a northwest passage to China, and after exploring the coast of New Greenland, entered this strait, 11 Aug. 1576. He returned to England, bringing with him black ore, supposed to contain gold, which induced queen Elizabeth to patronize a second voyage. This led to a third fruitless expedition. He was mortally wounded at Brest, Nov. 1594.

Froebel (*fro'-bel*) **Society,** established to promote the KINDERGARTEN SYSTEM, 1874.

Fronde, Civil wars of the, in France, in the minority of Louis XIV (1648-52), during the government of queen Anne of Austria and cardinal Mazarin, between the followers of the court and nobility, and the parliament and citizens The latter were called *Frondeurs* (slingers), it is said, from an incident in a street quarrel. In a riot on 27 Aug 1648, barricades were erected in Paris.

fruits. FLOWERS AND PLANTS.

fuchsia (*few'-zhe-a*), an American plant named after the German botanist Leonard Fuchs, about 1542. The *Fuchsia fulgens*, the most beautiful variety, was introduced from Mexico, about 1830

Fuen'tes-de-Ono're, a town of central Spain On 2 May, 1811, Massena crossed the Agueda with 40,000 infantry, 5000 cavalry, and about 30 pieces of artillery, to relieve Almeida. He expected every day to be superseded in command, and wished to make a last effort for his own military character. Wellington had but 32,000 men, of which 1200 were cavalry. He, however, determined to fight rather than raise the blockade of Almeida After much fighting, on 3 May, night stopped the conflict. Next day Massena was joined by Bessières with a body of the Imperial Guard, and on 5 May made his grand attack. In all the war there was no more dangerous hour for England. The fight lasted until evening, when the lower part of the town was abandoned by both parties—the British maintaining the chapel and crags, and the French retiring a cannon-shot from the stream —*Napier*

fugitive-slave law. Slavery in the United States.

fugue (*feug*), in music (in which one part seems to chase another), is described in Morley's "Introduction to Practicall Musicke," 1597 Sebastian Bach and Handel were eminent fugue-writers

Fulford, a town of Yorkshire England Here Harold Hardrada of Norway, and Tostig brother of Harold of England, defeated the earls Edwin and Morcar, 20 Sept 1066, and the people near York submitted to them Stamford bridge

funerals. David lamented over Saul and Jonathan, 1056 B.C, and over Abner, 1048 B C (2 Sam i and iii) In Greece, Solon first pronounced a funeral oration, according to Herodotus, 580 B C The Romans made harangues over their illustrious dead Theopompus obtained a prize for the best funeral oration in praise of Mausolus, 353 B C. Popilia was the first Roman lady at whose funeral an oration was delivered It was done by her son Crassus Cicero says that Julius Cæsar did the like for his aunt Julia and his wife Cornelia.—Funeral games, among the Greeks and Romans, included horse-races, dramatic representations, processions, and mortal combats of gladiators These games were abolished by the emperor Claudius, 47 A D. A tax was laid on funerals in England, 1793

furniture. Specimens of Egyptian furniture, represented on the interior walls of the pyramids, appear in Rosellini's "Monumenti dell' Egitto," vol ii 1832-44 J G Pollen's "Ancient and Modern Furniture and Woodwork," in the South Kensington museum, London, 1874, illustrated by photographs and engravings, was pub July, 1874 Many interesting examples will be found in Fosbroke's "Encyclopædia of Antiquities," vol i 1825

Fur'ruckabad', N India, a province acquired by the East India company in June, 1802 Near the capital of the same name, 16 Nov 1804, lord Lake defeated the Mahratta chief Holkar, and about 60,000 cavalry, himself losing 2 killed and about 20 wounded

furs were worn in England by Henry I about 1125 Edward III enacted that persons who could not spend 100*l* a year should not indulge in them, 28 Mch 1336-37

fusiliers, British foot-soldiers, formerly armed with fusees with slings to sling them The 7th regiment (or Royal English Fusiliers) was raised, 11 June, 1685, the 21st (or Royal North British), 23 Sept 1679, the 23d (or Royal Welsh), 17 Mch 1688 —*Grose*

Fut'tehghur', a town of British India. Here Nana Sahib massacred both the English defenders of the fort and their Sepoy assailants, July, 1857, and here the Sepoy rebels were defeated by sir Colin Campbell, 2 Jan. 1858

G

gabelle (*ga-bel'*), (from *Gabe*, a gift), a term applied to various taxes, but afterwards restricted to the duty upon salt, first imposed by Philip the Fair on the French in 1286 —*Duruy* Edward III of England, termed Philip of Valois, who exacted the tax rigorously, the author of the salic law (from *sal*, salt), 1340 The heavy assessments, though in some provinces lightened by exemptions purchased from the sovereigns, produced 38,000,000 francs under Louis XVI This grievous burden hastened the revolution It was abolished 1790

Gadsden purchase. United States, 1853

Gaelic (*gā'lic*), the northern branch of the Celtic languages, Irish, Erse or Highland Scottish, and Manx The "Dean of Lismore's Book" (written 1511-51) contains Gaelic poetry, specimens were published, with translations, in 1862, by rev T. M'Lachlan Celts. Gaelic society of London founded 1777 Gaelic society, to extend acquaintance with the Gaelic languages and history, established in New York 1879

Gaeta (*ga-ā'-ta*), the ancient Cajeta, a fortified Neapolitan seaport, has undergone several remarkable sieges It was taken by the French, 4 Jan 1799, by the English, 31 Oct 1799, by the French, 18 July, 1806, and by the Austrians in 1815 and 1821 Here pope Pius IX took refuge, 24 Nov 1848, and resided more than a year Here also Francis II of Naples, with his queen and court, fled when Garibaldi entered Naples, 7 Sept 1860, and remained till the city was taken by the Sardinian gen. Cialdini, 13 Feb 1861, after a siege, uselessly prolonged by a French fleet in the harbor Cialdini was created duke of Gaeta.

Gaines's Mill, Va, Battle of. Peninsular campaign

Galapa'gos or **Tortoise islands,** ceded to the United States by Ecuador, 3 Nov 1854, under protest of Britain, France, and other powers. Area, 2400 sq. miles, pop 200

Gala'tia, a province of Asia Minor In the 3d century B C., Gauls under Brennus invaded Greece, crossed the Hellespont, and conquered the Troas, 278; were checked by Attalus I. in battle about 241; and settled in what was afterwards Gallogræcia and Galatia The country was ravaged by Cneius Manlius, 189 B C., and was annexed to the Roman empire, 25 B.C, on the death of king Amyntas. Paul's epistle to the Galatians was probably written 58 A.D.

Galatz, a town of Roumania Preliminaries of peace between Russia and Turkey signed here, 11 Aug 1791, led to treaty of Jassy, 9 Jan 1792 The site of several conflicts, Russians defeating Turks, Nov. 1769 10 May, 1828 Pop 1876, 80,763.

Galicia (*gal-ish'-e-a*), a province of N W Spain, conquered by D. Junius Brutus, 136 B C, and by Vandals, 419 A.D., and by successive invaders. In 1065, Ferdinand I, king of Castile and Leon, died, his dominions were divided, and his son Garcia became king of Galicia. Ruling tyrannically, he was expelled by his brother Sancho, returned at latter's death, 1072, was again expelled by his brother Alfonso, 1073, and died in prison, 1091 The dissolute Urraca, queen of Castile, gave Galicia to her son Alfonso in 1109 He defended her against her husband, Alfonso VII, and at her death, in 1126, acquired Castile, reuniting the kingdoms

Galicia, a province of Austro-Hungary East Galicia was acquired by Germany at the partition in 1772 and West Galicia at that of 1795 The latter was ceded to the grand-duchy of Warsaw in 1809, but recovered by Austria in 1815 The appointment of count Goluchowski, a Pole, as governor, in Oct. 1866, pleased the Poles About 2,000,000 in this province. Poland

galleries. Louvre, Luxembourg, National, Painting, Versailles

galleys with 2 rows of rowers, *biremes*, with 3 rows of rowers, *triremes*, and with 4 rows of rowers, *quadriremes*, were in use among the Greeks, Romans, Carthaginians and more modern nations Generally the rowers were slaves or criminals The phrases "galley-slave" and "condemned to the galleys" refer to these sea-vessels with 25 to 30 oars on each side, manned by 4 or 5 slaves to each oar In France they had a general of galleys, of whom the baron de la Garde was the first, 1544 The punishment of the galleys (*galeres*) in France has been superseded by the *travaux forces*, forced labor, regulated by a law of 1854, the men being called *forçats*.

Gallican, (1) of or pertaining to France (2) Specifically pertaining to the Roman Catholic church in France.

Gallicanism, the spirit of nationalism within the church of France as opposed to the power of the papal see—the spirit of the Gallican church as distinguished from the

Romish It has existed in France from the introduction of Christianity This spirit culminated during the reign of Louis XIV, when in Mch. 1682, the French clergy demanded that the papal authority in France be limited to spiritual matters and be subject to the decision of a general council This was condemned by successive popes in 1682-90, 1706-94 The Gallicanists have been overpowered by the ULTRAMONTANISTS during the 19th century

gallium, new element, a metal, discovered by Lecoq de Boisbaudran, by the spectroscope, reported to French Academy of Sciences 20 Sept and 6 Dec 1875.

galoches (*ga-loshes'*), French for overshoes, formerly of leather, since 1843 of vulcanized India-rubber The importation into England was prohibited by 3 Edw IV c 4 (1463)

galvanism. ELECTRICITY

Galway, W Ireland The ancient settlers here formed 13 tribes, a distinction not yet forgotten It was conquered by Richard de Burgo in 1232. In 1690 Galway city declared for king James, but was taken by gen Ginckel soon after the decisive battle of Aughrim, 12 July, 1691

Gambia, a British colony of WEST AFRICA. The proposed cession of Gambia to France, in exchange for other territories, was opposed in Jan. 1876, and eventually given up. Erected into an independent colony, Dec 1888, with an administrator and legislative council Area, 2700 sq miles, pop 50,000 Area of settlement, 69 sq miles, pop 14,266

gamboge', a medicine and pigment, brought from India by the Dutch about 1600 Hermann, in 1677, announced that it was derived from trees of Ceylon, since ascertained to belong to the order *Guttifera* The gamboge of commerce is mainly derived from Siam, Cambodia, and Cochin China

game laws are a remnant of the forest laws of William the Conqueror, who, to preserve game, made it forfeiture of property to disable a wild beast, and loss of eyes for a stag, buck, or boar. The clergy protested against ameliorations of these laws under Henry III The first game act passed in 1496 Game certificates were first granted with a duty in 1784 The Game act (1 and 2 Will IV. c 32), modifying all previous laws, passed in 1831, permits the sale of game at certain seasons The game laws throughout the United States differ widely, but all inflict a penalty of from $5 to $50 for killing song-birds. In New York the killing of moose is illegal. Some game are protected for a limited time, as quail in Niagara county, N Y, which could not be lawfully killed for 3 years from 17 May, 1886. Duck, geese, and brant cannot be killed in the state of New York between sunset and daylight, nor with any net, device, or other instrument than guns fired from the shoulder, and lanterns or other light must not be used

games. Candidates for athletic games in Greece were dieted on new cheese, dried figs, and boiled grain, with warm water, and no meat. The sports were leaping, foot-races, quoits, wrestling, and boxing CAPITOLINE, ISTHMIAN, OLYMPIC, PYTHIAN, SECULAR GAMES, SPORTS, etc.

gaming was introduced into England by the Saxons; the loser was often made a slave to the winner, and sold in traffic, like other merchandise.—*Camden*.

Act prohibiting gaming to all gentlemen (and tennis, cards, dice, bowls, etc, to inferiors, except at Christmas time)	1541
Gaming-houses licensed in London	1620
Losses by betting or play of more than 100*l*. at any one time, not collectible by law, 16 Chas II	1663
Bonds or other securities given for money won at play not enforcible, and any person losing more than 10*l*. may sue the winner to recover it back, 9 Anne, c. 14	1710
Act to prevent excessive and fraudulent gaming, suppressing private lotteries and faro, basset, and hazard	1739
Betting houses suppressed	1853
Public gaming tables suppressed at Wiesbaden, Homburg, etc., 31 Dec	1872
Revenue of Monaco is mainly derived from its gaming-tables (MONACO)	

gam'ut. The scale of musical intervals (commonly termed *do* or *ut*, *re*, *mi*, *fa*, *sol*, *la*, to which *si* was added afterwards), for which the first 7 letters of the alphabet are now employed, is mentioned by Guido Aretino, a Tuscan monk, about 1025. MUSIC.

Ganges canal, irrigating the country between the Ganges and the Jumna. The main line (525 miles long) was opened 8 Apr. 1854 Great difficulties were overcome by its engineer, sir Proby Cautley. In Oct. 1864, sir Arthur Cotton asserted that the work was badly done, and the investment only paid 3 per cent

gardening. The first garden, Eden, planted by God (Gen ii) The Scriptures abound with allusions to gardens, particularly the Song of Solomon and the prophets, and Christ's agony took place in a garden Xenophon describes the gardens at Sardis, and Epicurus and Plato taught in gardens Theophrastus's "History of Plants" was written about 322 B.C Horace, Virgil, and Ovid derive many images from the garden (50 B.C. to 50 A D), and Pliny's Tusculan villa is circumstantially described (about 100 A D) The Romans introduced gardening into Britain, religious orders maintained it, and its practice increased in the 16th century, when many Flemings came to England to escape persecutions of Philip II Miller's dictionary was pub 1724, the British Horticultural Society was established in 1804, London's "Encyclopædia of Gardening" was first pub 1822, and his "Encyclopædia of Plants" in 1829 FLOWERS AND PLANTS, TRUCK-FARMING

Garfield monument. The memorial stands on a wide stone terrace in Lake View cemetery, Cleveland, O It is a circular tower 148 feet high, with a diameter of 50 feet It is highly decorated with allegorical and other designs In the centre of the tower is a heroic marble statue of Garfield, modelled by George Doyle of New York The memorial was designed by George Keller of Hartford, Conn, dedicated 30 May, 1890, and cost $134,755, of which 38 states contributed $130,380, 10 territories, $3166, France, $1149, Belgium, $40, Australia, $12, England, $5, Canada, $3.

Gargarus, a mountain in Asia Minor, 10 miles northwest of Adramyti, the highest of the range of Ida, near the supposed site of ancient Troy

> "There lies a vale in Ida, lovelier
> Than all the valleys of the Ionian hills
>
> Behind the valley topmost Gargarus
> Stands up and takes the morning, but in front
> The gorges, opening wide apart, reveal
> Troas and Ilion's column'd citadel,
> The crown of Troas" —*Tennyson*, "Œnone."

Garigliano (*ga-reel-yah'-no*), a river, S W Italy. After long waiting and refusing to recede, Gonsalvo de Cordova bridged this river, 27 Dec 1503, and surprised and defeated the French army Gaeta surrendered a few days after

Garter, Order of the Edward III, when at war with France and eager to obtain the best soldiers of Europe, projected a revival of king Arthur's round-table On New-Year's day, 1343-44, he published letters of protection for the safe coming and return of foreign knights who would venture their reputation at his jousts and tournaments. These took place 23 Apr. 1344 A table was erected in Windsor castle of 200 feet diameter, and the knights were entertained at the king's expense. In 1346 Edward gave his garter for the signal of a successful battle (probably Crecy), and being victorious, and having David, king of Scotland, a prisoner, he, in memory of these exploits, is said to have instituted this order, 23 Apr. 1349

Edward III made the chief badge of the order a garter of blue velvet bordered with gold, inscribed in old French, "*Honi soit qui mal y pense*" (Evil be to him who evil thinks) Knights are installed at Windsor, and styled *Equites aureæ periscelidis* (knights of the golden garter) —*Beatson*

The order, until Edward VI's time, was called the order of St. George, patron saint of England His figure on horseback, holding a spear, and killing the dragon, was first worn by the knights suspended by a blue ribbon across the body from the shoulder

Instituted according to Selden, 23 Apr 1344, according to Nicolas, 1347, to Ashmole.	1349
Office of "Garter king of arms of Englishmen" instituted, between May and July,	1417
Additions to the statutes decreed	1421, 1423
Order of the Garter in Ireland instituted by Edward IV, 1466, abolished	1494
Collar and George of the order instituted by Henry VII., about	1497
Statutes reformed by order, 28 May, 1519, issued 23 Apr	1522
Ceremonies changed, because of the Reformation 20 Apr	1548
Revision of the statutes	1560
Annual feast of St. George discontinued	1567
Escutcheon converted into a star	1629
Number of knights increased by 7	1786
Order reconstituted, to consist of the sovereign, prince of Wales, 25 knights companions, and lineal descendants of George III, when elected 17 Jan.	1805

Several European sovereigns elected......................1813–14
Abdul-Aziz, sultan of Turkey, receives the Garter from queen Victoria on her yacht at a naval review.............17 July, 1867
Shah of Persia invested at Windsor...................20 June, 1873

ORIGINAL KNIGHTS.

King Edward III., sovereign.	Thomas, earl of Kent.
Edward, prince of Wales (called the Black Prince).	John, lord Grey, of Rotherfield.
Henry, duke of Lancaster.	Sir Richard Fitz-Simon.
Thomas, earl of Warwick.	Sir Miles Stapleton.
John, captal de Buch.	Sir Thomas Wale.
Ralph, earl of Stafford.	Sir Hugh Wrottesley.
William, earl of Salisbury.	Sir Nele Loryng.
Roger, earl of Mortimer.	Sir John Chandos.
Sir John Lisle.	Sir James Audeley.
Bartholomew, lord Burghershe.	Sir Otho Holand.
John, lord Beauchamp.	Sir Henry Eam.
John, lord Mohun, of Dunster.	Sir Sanchet d'Abrichecourt.
Sir Hugh Courtenay.	Sir Walter Paveley.

gas, in chemistry, a permanently elastic aeriform fluid. CHLORINE, ELEMENTS, HYDROGEN, NITROGEN, OXYGEN, etc.

Monge and Clouet, it is said, condensed sulphurous acid before 1800; Northmore liquefied chlorine........................ 1805
Faraday determined a gas to be the vapor of a volatile liquid at a temperature above the boiling-point of the liquid; and that the condensing-point of the gas is the boiling-point of the liquid; he, by pressure, liquefied chlorine.............. 1823
Furnaces with gases as fuel invented by C. W. Siemens, and employed in glass-works, etc............................ 1861
Lenoir's gas engine, motive power obtained by combined gases ignited by electricity, patented.......................... "
One hundred and forty-three of these engines working in Paris; introduced into England.............................Dec. 1864
Prof. Thomas Graham's paper on diffusion of gases, 1834; he showed that platinum and other metals absorb gases........ 1866
Pierre Hugon's gas-engine (said to be superior to Lenoir's, 1861) exhibited.. 1867
Oxygen liquefied by cold and pressure (predicted by Faraday); by Cailletet, at Paris, 2 Dec.; by Raoul Pictet at Geneva, 22 Dec. 1877
Nitrogen, hydrogen, and air liquefied by Cailletet...........1877–78
Process exhibited at Royal Institution, London, by prof. James Dewar..14 June, 1878
Ozone liquefied by Hautefeuille and Chappuis, Paris.......Oct. 1880
Gas from gas-wells used as fuel in western Pennsylvania...... 1884
Extensively used throughout western Pennsylvania, New York, Ohio, Indiana, and Illinois................................. 1890
In province of Ontario.. 1891

gas-light, the inflammable aeriform fluid, carburetted hydrogen, evolved by combustion of coal; described by dr. Clayton in 1739.

Coal-gas for illumination tried by Mr. Murdoch, in Cornwall... 1792
Gas-light introduced at Boulton & Watt's foundery in Birmingham... 1798
Lyceum theatre, London, experimentally lit with gas by Mr. Winsor... 1803
Adopted at cotton-mills of Phillips & Lee, Manchester (1000 burners lighted)...................................... 1805
Introduced in London, at Golden lane, 16 Aug. 1807; Pall Mall, 1809; generally through London.......................1814–20
David Pollock, father of the late chief baron, was governor of the first "chartered" gas company....................... 1812
Attempt fails to introduce gas into Baltimore..............1816–20
Gas-lighting introduced in Paris............................ 1819
Successfully introduced into Boston.......................... 1822
Gas-lighting introduced into New York......................1823–24
Gas first used in Dublin, 1818; the streets generally lighted, Oct. 1825
First used in Philadelphia.................................. 1835
Sidney, Australia, first lighted with gas.................... 1841
Moscow first lighted.. 1866
Gas successful as fuel for the generation of steam by Jackson's patent...Apr. 1868
Processes to obtain illuminating gas from water patented by Cruickshanks (1839); White (1849), and others. Water-gas, by Ruck's process, mixed with ordinary gas, reported successful at Chichester...................................Aug. 1873
[Gas-meters patented by John Malam (1820), sir W. Congreve (1824), Samuel Clegg (1830), Nathan Defries (1838), and others.]
By the London Gas act, passed 13 July, 1868, ordinary gas charged 3*s*. 9*d*. the 1000 cubic feet after 1 Jan. 1870. Charges raised because of dear coal and labor..................Jan. 1874
Street gas lit by electricity, by St. G. Lane Fox's method; a trial, partly successful, Pall Mall, etc..............13 Apr. 1878
Electric light replacing gas for street illumination in the U.S., 1891–94

Gaspee, Affair of the. The British revenue schooner *Gaspee* annoyed American seamen in Narragansett bay by demanding the lowering of their flags in passing. While trying to enforce the demand the *Gaspee* went ashore at what is known as "Gaspee's Point." On the same night, 9 June, 1772, 64 armed men boarded the boat, captured the crew, and burned the vessel. Although a large reward ($5000) was offered for the apprehension of the leader, Abraham Whipple, he was never betrayed. He was afterwards a commodore in the Continental navy.

Gastein, a city of Salzburg, Austria. The long discussion between Austria and Prussia respecting the disposal of the duchies conquered from Denmark was closed by a provisional agreement signed here by their ministers (Blum for Austria and Bismarck for Prussia) 14 Aug. 1865. This agreement was censured by other powers and abrogated by war in 1866.

Austria was to have the temporary government of Holstein, and Prussia that of Schleswig; the establishment of a Prussian fleet was proposed, with Kiel as a federal harbor, held by Prussia; Lauenburg was absolutely ceded to Prussia, and the king was to pay Austria as a compensation 2,500,000 Danish dollars.
Emperors of Austria and Germany met at Gastein, Aug. 1886.

Gatling gun, named after its inventor, a citizen of the United States, exhibited at Paris in 1867; designed to discharge at once a number of projectiles smaller than the shells of field guns; it has as many locks as barrels. It was tried at Shoeburyness, Engl., and rejected as inferior to a field gun firing shrapnel. The gun has since been greatly improved, and is believed to be one of the best arms of its class in use. A powder for the Gatling, invented by M. Pertuiset, was tried in London, Aug. 1870.

gauges (*ga'-ges*) (in railways). A discussion (termed "the battle of the gauges") began in England among engineers about 1833. I. M. Brunel approved the broad gauge adopted on the Great Western railway; R. Stephenson, Joseph Locke, and others, chose the narrow, now almost universal. A 2-foot gauge was recommended in Feb. 1870, as successful on the Festiniog railway, Wales, with Fairlie's engine. About 200 miles of the southwestern lines of the Great Western were altered from the broad to the narrow gauge in a few days, June, 1874. In the United States the broad (6 feet) gauge formerly used by the Erie, Grand Trunk, and other roads, has been abandoned. The southern railroads, originally 5 feet, and the Ohio railroads, originally 4 feet 10 inches, have conformed to the standard gauge of 4 feet 8½ inches; now in use throughout the country, except upon a few unimportant lines, where, for the sake of economy, very narrow gauges (3 feet, or 2 feet 6 inches) have been adopted.

gauging, measuring the liquid contents of a barrel or other vessel, regulated in England by law, 27 Edw. III. 1352.

Gaul and **Gauls**. Gallia was the ancient name of France and Belgium. The Gauls (whom Greeks called Γαλάται; Romans, Galli or Celtæ) came from Asia, invading eastern Europe; were driven westward, and settled in Spain (in Galicia), north Italy (Gallia Cisalpina), France, Belgium (Gallia Transalpina), and the British isles (lands of the Cymry or Gaels).

B.C.
Phocæans found Massilia, now Marseilles..................... 600
Galli Senones under Brennus defeat Romans at the river Allia; sack Rome; defeated and expelled by Camillus.....13 July, 390
Again defeated.. 367
Gauls defeated by the Romans at Sentinum................... 295
Senones defeat Romans at Arretium; nearly exterminated by Dolabella.. 283
Gauls overrun northern Greece, 280 B.C.; beaten at Delphi, 279; and by Antigonus, king of Macedon......................... 273
Gauls defeated with great slaughter near Pisa................ 225
Insubres overthrown by Marcellus; king Viridomarus slain.. 222
They assist Hannibal.................................218 et seq.
Romans conquer Gallia Cisalpina, 220; invade Gallia Transalpina, with varied success..................................121–58
They colonize Aix, 123 B.C.; and Narbonne.................... 118
Julius Cæsar subdues Gaul in 8 campaigns.....................58–50
Lyons (Lugdunum) founded.................................... 41

A.D.
Druids' religion proscribed by Claudius...................... 43
Adrian visits and favors Gaul; called Restorer of the Gauls... 120
Introduction of Christianity.................................. 160
Christians persecuted.......................177, 202, 257, 286, 288
Franks and others defeated by Aurelian....................... 241
By Probus, 275, 277; who introduces vine culture............ 280
Maximian defeats the Franks.................................. 281
Constantine proclaimed emperor of Gaul....................... 306
Julian relieves Gaul, desolated by barbarians; defeats Alemanni at Strasburg.. 357
Julian proclaimed emperor at Paris, 360; d.................... 363
Gaul harassed by Alemanni...................................365–77
Invasion and settlement of Burgundians, Franks, Visigoths, etc...378–450
Clodion, chief of the Salian Franks, invades Gaul; defeated by Aëtius... 447
Huns under Attila defeated by Aëtius near CHALONS........... 451
Ægidius, Roman commander, murdered.......................... 464
Childeric the Frank takes Paris.............................. "
All Gaul west of the Rhone ceded to Visigoths................. 475
End of Roman empire of the West; kingdom of the Franks begins (FRANCE)... 476

gauntlet, an iron glove, introduced in the 13th century, perhaps about 1225, it was thrown down as a challenge to an adversary

gauze (from Gaza, a city of Palestine, where first made), a fabric much prized among the Romans "Brocades and damasks and tabbies and gauzes have been lately brought over" (to Ireland) —*Dean Swift*, in 1698 The manufacture of gauze and articles of a light fabric at Paisley, in Scotland, began about 1759

gavel-kind (derived from the Saxon *gif eal cyn*, "give all suitably," or from *gafolcynd*, land yielding rent), a custom in Kent of dividing estates in land, the wife to have half, the rest equally among male children, 500 By Irish gavel-kind, even bastards inherited —*Davies* Not only a father's lands were equally divided among sons, but a brother's among brethren, if he had no issue —*Law Dict*

Gaza, a city of Philistines, whose gates Samson carried off about 1120 B.C (Judg xvi) It was taken by Alexander after a long siege, 332, and near it Ptolemy defeated Demetrius Poliorcetes, 312 B.C It was taken by Saladin, 1170 A D, by Bonaparte, Mch 1799, and by Egyptians under Ibrahim Pacha, 1831

gems. The Greeks excelled in cutting precious stones, and many ancient specimens remain. The art was revived in Italy in the 15th century In Feb 1860, Herz's collection of gems was sold for $50,000 Rev C King's "Antique Gems" appeared in 1860, and his "Natural History of Precious Stones and Gems" in 1865 Dr A Billing's "Science of Gems," 1868. Artificial gems have been produced by chemists (Ebelmen, Deville, Wohler, and others), 1858-65

Duke of Marlborough's collection, valued at 60,000*l*, sold by auction to Mr Bromilow for 36,750*l*. 28 June, 1875

AARON'S BREASTPLATE, DIAMOND, etc

genealogy (Gr γενεαλογία—from γενεά, birth, descent, and λογος, discourse) The earliest pedigrees are contained in the 5th 10th, and 11th chapters of Genesis The 1st book of Chronicles contains many genealogies The pedigree of Christ is given in Matt i and Luke iii There are many books on the subject, one was issued at Magdeburg, "Theatrum Genealogicum," by Henninges, in 1598 Anderson, "Royal Genealogies," London, 1732 Sims's "Manual for the Genealogist," etc., 1586, will be found a useful guide The works of Collins (1756 et seq), Edmondson (1764-84) and Nicolas (1825 and 1857), on the British peerage, are highly esteemed. The Genealogical Society, London, established in 1853

generals. Matthew de Montmorency was the first general of French armies, 1203.—*Henault* Balzac says cardinal Richelieu coined the word *generalissimo*, on taking command of the French armies in Italy, in 1629 Ulysses S Grant became the first general of the army of the United States in 1866 ARMY, UNITED STATES

generation, in chronology, the interval between the birth of a father and the birth of his child 33 years on the average Harvey's thesis "*Omne vivum ex ovo*" (every living being springs from an egg) has been disproved by the researches of Von Siebold and others SPONTANEOUS GENERATION

Gene'va (Ger *Genf*), a town of Allobroges, a Gallic tribe, 58 B.C., capital of the kingdom of Burgundy, 426 A D, part of the empire of Charlemagne, about 800 Pop 1888, 71,807.

Republic founded	1512
Emancipated from Savoy	1526
Calvin settling here, Geneva was termed the "Rome of Calvinism"	about 1536
Servetus was burned for heresy	27 Oct. 1553
Geneva allied to Swiss cantons	1584
Incorporated with France	26 Apr 1798
Admitted to Swiss Confederation	30 Dec. 1813
Constitution made more democratic	1846
Revolution, Catholic cantons seeking to introduce Jesuit teachers, provisional government.	7 Oct 1848
[The scheme was withdrawn]	
Alabama arbitration commission met, received cases and adjourned to 15 June, 1872	18 Dec. 1871
Formal meeting of commission	15 June, 1872
Monsignor Mermillod nominated bishop of Geneva (in the diocese of bishop of Lausanne) and vicar apostolic, his arrest proposed, 2 Feb, ordered to quit, or submit to civil government by 15 Feb, expelled	17 Feb. "
Ex duke of Brunswick dies here and bequeaths his vast property, above $3,820,000, to the city	18 Aug 1873

Geneva convention. RED CROSS.

Gen'oa (It. *Genova*), the ancient Genua, N. Italy. Its inhabitants were Ligures, who submitted to Romans, 115 B.C It partook of the revolutions of the Roman empire Pop. 1881, 138,081

Genoa becomes a free commercial state	about 1000
Frequent wars with Pisa	1070-1284
Frederick II captures 22 galleys, and vainly besieges Genoa	1241
University founded	1243
Doria and Spinola families rule	about 1270
Genoese destroy naval power of Pisa at MELORA	6 Aug 1284
Frequent wars with Venice	1218-32, 1293-99
Rafaele Doria and Galeotto Spinola appointed captains	1335
Simon Boccanegra made first doge, 1339, set aside by the nobles, 1344, reappointed	1356
Discord, many doges appointed	1394
Genoa under protection of France, 1396, of Naples, 1410, of Milan 1419, losing and regaining freedom	1421-1512
Sacked by Spaniards and Italians under Prosper Colonna	1522
Andrew Doria deserts French service, and restores independence of his country	1528
Genoa bombarded by French	May, 1684
By British	Sept 1745
Taken by imperialists, soon expelled	" 1746
Another siege raised	10 June, 1747
Celebrated bank failed	1750
Genoa made the Ligurian republic	May 1797
Blockaded by British fleet and Austrian army until starved, evacuated by capitulation, 5 June, but surrendered to French after victory at Marengo	14 June, 1800
Genoa annexed to French empire	4 June, 1805
Surrenders to English and Sicilians	18 Apr 1814
United to kingdom of Sardinia	Dec "
Insurgents after a murderous struggle, drove out garrison and proclaimed the Ligurian republic, 3 Apr, surrendered to gen La Marmora	11 Apr 1849
Columbus's first voyage, 1492, celebrated	Sept 1892

gens-d'armes (*zhan-darms'*), anciently in France the king's horse guards only, afterwards the king's *gardes-du-corps*, musketeers and light horse were reckoned among them. There was also a company of gentlemen (about 250) bearing this name Scots guards were about the persons of kings of France from St Louis, 1226 They were organized as a royal corps by Charles VII about 1441, younger sons of Scottish nobles being usually captains In England the name gens-d'armes was at one time given to the police, but was changed to "municipal guard" in 1830

gentleman (from *gentilis*, of a *gens*, a race or clan) The Gauls, observing that of the Roman soldiers *scutarii* and *gentiles* had the best appointments, called them *écuyers* and *gentilshommes* The "grand old name" of gentleman in England was given to the well-descended about 1430 —*Sidney*. Gentlemen by blood were those who could show 4 descents from a gentleman created by the king by letters-patent.

gentlemen-at-arms, formerly the Band of Gentlemen Pensioners, the oldest corps in England, except Yeomen of the Guard It was instituted by Henry VIII in 1509, entirely of gentlemen of noble blood, whom he named his pensioners or spears William IV commanded that it be called his majesty's honorable corps of gentlemen-at-arms, 7 Mch. 1834 —*Curling*

geod'esy (from Gk γῆ, the earth, and δαιω, I divide), the art of measuring the surface and determining the figure of the earth, etc Col. A. Clarke's "Geodesy" pub 1880

Seventh international geodetic congress met at Rome, 15-24 Oct 1883, recommended the adoption of Greenwich as zero of longitude, and of uniform time International congress at Washington, 1 Oct. 1884, recommends Greenwich as the prime meridian (France and Brazil dissent)	13 Oct. 1884
Terms of a universal day agreed upon (DAY, LATITUDE) 1 Nov	"

geog'raphy. The first geographical records are in the Pentateuch and the book of Joshua. Homer describes the shield of Achilles as representing the earth surrounded by the sea, and also the countries of Greece, islands of the archipelago, and site of Troy.—*Iliad* The priests taught that the temple of Apollo at Delphos was the centre of the world Anaximander of Miletus devised geographical maps, about 568 B C. Hipparchus attempted to reduce geography to a mathematical basis, about 135 B.C. Strabo, the great Greek geographer, lived 71-14 B.C Ptolemy flourished about 139 A D The science was brought to Europe by Moors of Barbary and Spain, about 1240.—*Denglet* Maps and charts were introduced into England by Bartholomew Columbus to illustrate his brother's theory of a western continent, 1489. Geography is now divided into mathematical, physical, political, and commercial; and its study has been promoted during this century by expeditions at the expense of governments and societies. The Royal Geographical Society of London was established in 1830; that of Paris in 1821. The American Geographical Society, New York, was organized 1852. AFRICA, NORTHWEST PASSAGE, MAPS.

International congress of geographers at Antwerp in 1871; at Paris, 1 Aug. 1875; at Brussels....................12 Sept. 1876
Dr. August Heinrich Petermann, founder and editor of "Mittheilungen über wichtige neue Erforschungen auf dem Gesammtgebiete der Geographie" in 1855, and an eminent cartographer, d..26 Sept. 1878
Congress on commercial geography at Brussels...........Oct. 1879
E. H. Bunbury's "History of Ancient Geography among the Greeks and Romans," pub. 1879. He refers especially to Hecatæus, Herodotus, Hanno, Pytheas (discoverer of Britain), Eratosthenes (b. 276 B.C.; made a map), and to Ptolemy, about 130 A.D.
E. A. Freeman's "Historical Geography of Europe" pub...... 1881
International congress of geographers at Venice, 15 Sept. 1881; at Bordeaux..4 Sept. 1882
British Commercial Geographical Society; founded at the Mansion House, London, 15 July; met.....................27 Oct. 1884
Scottish Geographical Society, Edinburgh, inaugurated..3 Dec. "
Manchester Geographical Society established............Jan. 1885

geol'ogy, the science of the earth, said to have been cultivated in China before Christ, as well as by Aristotle, Theophrastus, Pliny, Avicenna, and the Arabian writers.

In 1574 Mercati wrote of fossils in the pope's museum: Cesalpino Majoli and others, 1597; Steno, 1669; Scilla, 1670; Quirini, 1676; Plot and Lister, 1678; Leibnitz, 1680, wrote observations and theories on changes in the earth's crust.
Hooke (1668), in a work on earthquakes, declared fossils "as monuments of nature, more certain tokens of antiquity than coins or medals; and though difficult, it would not be impossible *to raise a chronology out of them.*"
Burnet's "Theory of the Earth," 1690; Whiston's in 1696.
Buffon's geological views (1749), censured by the SORBONNE in 1751, were recanted. He said that the present condition of the earth is due to secondary causes, which will produce further changes. His eminent fellow-laborers and successors were Gesner, 1758; Michell, 1760; Raspe, 1762–73; Pallas and Saussure, 1793–1800.
Werner (1775) ascribed rocks to an *aqueous* origin, denied the existence of volcanoes in primitive geological times, and had many followers—Kirwan, De Luc, etc. Hutton (1788), supported by Playfair (1801), opposed Werner's views, referring the principal changes in the earth's crust to the energy of *fire.* The parties were termed Neptunists and Vulcanists.
William Smith, father of British geology (who had walked over a large part of England), published a "Tabular View of British Strata" in 1799, and his "Geological Map of England and Wales," 1812–15; d. 28 Aug. 1839. Rev. Adam Sedgwick d. 27 Jan. 1873, aged 87. Sir Charles Lyell d. 22 Feb. 1875.
In 1803 the Royal Institution had the best geological collection in London, collected by H. Davy, C. Hatchett, and others; proposal of sir John St. Aubyn, sir Abraham Hume, and the right hon. C. F. Greville to aid government in establishing a school of mines there in 1804–7; declined 13 Nov. 1807.
Geological Society of London established 1807. By collecting new facts it checked the disposition to theorize, and led to views midway between those of Werner and Hutton.
Geological Society of Dublin, 1832; of Edinburgh, 1834; of France, 1830; of Germany, 1848.
In 1835 Mr. (afterwards sir Henry) De la Beche suggested the present Museum of Geology, which began at Craig's court, and was removed to Jermyn street, London. To him are due valuable geological maps formed on the ordnance survey. The building was erected by Mr. Pennethorne, and formally opened by the late prince consort, 14 May, 1851. Attached to the museum are the Mining Records office, a lecture theatre, laboratories, etc. Sir H. De la Beche, the first director, d. 13 Apr. 1855; succeeded by sir Roderick Murchison, who d. 22 Oct. 1871; by prof. A. C. Ramsay, Mch. 1872.
A similar institution established at Calcutta by the East India company in 1840.
International Geological congress at Paris, 1878; at Bologna, 29 Sept. 1881.
English standard works on geology are those of Lyell, Murchison, Phillips, De la Beche, Mantell, and Austed.
Cuvier and Brongniart's work on "Geology of Paris," 1808 et seq.
L. Agassiz, "Poissons Fossiles," 1833–45.
Dana's "Manual of Geology," 1874.

Strata composing the earth's crust form 2 great classes:

I. {Those generally attributed to the action of fire; Igneous formations unstratified, crystalline,
 1. Volcanic, as basalt, etc.
 2. Plutonic, as granite, etc.

II. {Those generally attributed to the agency of water; Aqueous formations stratified, rarely crystalline,
 1. Metamorphic or unfossiliferous rocks.
 2. Sedimentary or fossiliferous rocks, divided into 4 great series:

I. Neozoic, latest forms of life	Post-tertiary,	Man.
II. Cainozoic, recent forms of life	Tertiary,	Mammals.
III. Mesozoic, middle-life period	Secondary,	Reptiles.
IV. Palæozoic, most ancient forms of life	Primary,	Fish. Invertebrates.

TABLE OF STRATA (*chiefly from Lyell*).

NEOZOIC—I. POST-TERTIARY.

A. *Post-Pliocene:*
 1. *Recent:* marine strata, with *human remains;* Danish peat; kitchen middens; bronze and stone implements; Swiss lake-dwellings; temple of Serapis at Pozzuoli.
 2. *Post-Pliocene:* Brixham cave, with flint knives, and bones of living and extinct quadrupeds; ancient valley gravels; glacial drift; ancient Nile mud; post-glacial North American deposits; remains of *mastodon;* Australian breccias.

II. TERTIARY, OR CAINOZOIC, SERIES.

B. *Pliocene:*
 3. *Newer Pliocene* (or Pleistocene), mammalian beds, Norwich crag (*marine shells*).
 4. *Older Pliocene:* red and coralline crag (Suffolk, Antwerp).
C. 5, 6. *Miocene,* upper and lower: Bordeaux; Virginia sands and Touraine beds; Pikermé deposits near Athens; volcanic tuff and limestone of the Azores, etc.; brown coal of Germany, etc. (*mastodon, gigantic elk, salamander,* etc.).
D. 7, 8, 9. *Eocene,* upper, middle, and lower: fresh-water and marine beds; Barton clays; Bracklesham sands; Paris gypsum; London plastic, and Thanet clays (*palms, birds,* etc.).

III. SECONDARY, OR MESOZOIC, SERIES.

E. 10. *Cretaceous,* upper: British chalk; Maestricht beds.—Chalk with and without flints, chalk marl, upper green sand, gault, lower green sand (*mesosaurus; fish, mollusks,* etc.).
 11. Lower (or *Neocomian* or *Wealden*): Kentish rag; Weald clay; Hastings sand (*iguanodon, hylæosaurus,* etc.).
F. 12. *Oölite,* upper: Purbeck beds, Portland stone and sand, Kimmeridge clay; lithographic stone of Solenhofen with *archæopteryx* (*fish*).
 13. Middle: Calcareous grit, coral rag, Oxford clay, Kelloway rock (*belemnites* and *ammonites*).
 14. Lower: Cornbrash, forest marble, Bradford clay, great oölite, Stonesfield slate, fuller's earth, inferior oölite (*ichthyosaurus, plesiosaurus, pterodactyl*).
G. 15. *Lias:* Lias clay and marl stone (*ammonites, equisetum, amphibia, labyrinthodon*).
H. 16. *Trias,* upper: White lias, red clay, with salt in Cheshire, coal-fields in Pennsylvania (*fish,-dromatherium*).
 17. Middle, or Muschelkalk (wanting in England) (*Encrinus; Placodus gigas*).
 18. Lower: New red sandstone of Lancashire and Cheshire (*labyrinthodon, footprints of birds and reptiles*).

IV. PRIMARY, OR PALÆOZOIC, SERIES.

I. 19. *Permian:* magnesian limestone, marl slates, red sandstone and shale, dolomite; Kupferschiefer (*firs, fishes, amphibia*).
K. 20, 21. *Carboniferous,* upper and lower: Coal measures, millstone grit, mountain limestone (*ferns, calamites, coal*).
L. 22, 23, 24. *Devonian,* upper, middle, and lower: tilestones, cornstones, and marls, quartzose, conglomerates (*shells, fish, trilobites*).
M. 25, 26, 27. *Silurian,* upper, middle, and lower: Ludlow shales, Aymestry limestone, Wenlock limestone, Wenlock shale, Caradoc sandstone, Llandeilo flags; Niagara limestone (*sponges, corals, trilobites, shells*).
N. 28, 29. *Cambrian,* upper and lower: Bala limestone, Festiniog slates. Bangor slates and grits, Wicklow rock, Hasleets grits, Huronian series of Canada (*zoöphytes, lingula, ferns, sigillaria, stigmaria, calamites,* and *cryptogamia*).
O. 30. *Laurentian,* upper gneiss of the Hebrides (?): Labradorite series, north of the St. Lawrence; Adirondack mountains, New York.
 31. Lower: Gneiss and quartzites, with interstratified limestones, in one of which, 1000 feet thick, occurs a foraminifer, *eozoön Canadense,* the oldest known fossil.

NORTH AMERICA'S GEOLOGIC AGES, PERIODS, AND EPOCHS (according to Dana).

"The history of the ages of each continent has its periods and epochs, which may or may not correspond in their limits with those of the other continents."—*Dana.*

Time.	Age.	Period.	Epoch.
Cenozoic	Quaternary, or of man	Recent	Modern. Second Glacial.
		Champlain	Aluvian. Deluvian.
		Glacial	Glacial.
	Tertiary, or of mammals	Sumter	Pliocene.
		Yorktown	Miocene.
		Alabama	Upper Eocene. Middle "
		Lignitic	Lower "

NORTH AMERICA'S GEOLOGIC AGES, PERIODS, AND EPOCHS.—(*Continued.*)

Time.	Age.		Period.	Epoch.
Mesozoic	Of reptiles		Cretaceous	Upper. Middle. Lower.
			Jurassic	Wealden. Oölitic: Upper. Middle. Lower. Liassic: Upper lias. Marlstone. Lower lias.
			Triassic	Keuper (mottled clays). Muschelkalk (shell limestone). Bunter Sandstein (variegated sandstone).
Palæozoic	Carboniferous		Permian	Permian—from ancient kingdom of Permia, Russia.
			Carboniferous	Upper coal measure. Lower coal measure. Millstone grit.
			Sub-carboniferous	Upper. Lower.
	Devonian or of fishes		Catskill	Catskill.
			Chemung	Chemung. Portage.
			Hamilton	Genesee. Hamilton. Marcellus.
			Corniferous	Corniferous. Schoharie. Canda-Galli.
	Silurian or of invertebrates	Upper silurian	Oriskany	Oriskany.
			Lower Helderberg	Lower Helderberg.
			Salina	Salina.
			Niagara	Niagara. Clinton. Medina.
		Lower silurian	Trenton	Cincinnati. Utica. Trenton.
			Canadian	Chazy. Quebec. Calciferous.
			Cambrian	Potsdam. Acadian.
Archæan	Eozoic		Including the earliest forms of life.	See Nos. 30 and 31, Table of Strata, p. 320.
	Azoic		Previous to the appearance of life.	

geom'etry (Gr. *γεωμετρία*, earth measurement) is ascribed to Egyptians; annual inundations of the Nile made it necessary by carrying away landmarks and boundaries. B.C.

Thales introduced geometry into Greece....................about 600
Pythagoras cultivated it.......................................about 580
Doctrine of curves arose from conic sections; considered by Plato..about 390
Euclid's "Elements" compiled..............................about 300
Archimedes, a discoverer in geometry.......................287–212
Conchoid curve discovered by Nicomedes........................ 220
Ptolemy, the astronomer, 2d century, A.D.
Geometry taught in Europe in the 13th century.
Books on geometry and astronomy were destroyed in England as infected with magic, 7 Edw. VI.—*Stow*...................... 1552
Descartes published his "Analytical Geometry"................ 1627
Sir Isaac Newton ("Arithmetica Universalis," etc.)......1642–1727
Simson's edition of Euclid first appeared...................... 1756
La Place's "Mécanique Céleste"..............................1799–1805

George, St., tutelary saint of England, adopted as patron of the order of the Garter by Edward III. His day is 23 Apr. GARTER, KNIGHTHOOD.

St. George, a tribune in the reign of Diocletian, being a man of courage, was a favorite; but, complaining to the emperor of his severities towards the Christians, and arguing in their defence, he was beheaded 23 Apr. 290.—On that day, in 1192, Richard I. defeated Saladin.

Georges' conspiracy, in France. Gen. Moreau, gen. Pichegru, Georges Cadoudal, who was commonly known by the name of Georges, and others, were arrested at Paris, charged with conspiracy to kill Bonaparte and restore Louis XVIII., Feb. 1804. Pichegru was strangled in prison, 6 Apr. 12 conspirators, including Georges, were executed, 25 June, and others imprisoned. Moreau was exiled, and went to America. In 1813 he was killed before Dresden.

Geor'gia, ancient Iberia, now a province of S. Russia, near the Caucasus, submitted to Alexander about 331 B.C., but threw off the yoke of his successors. It was subjugated to Rome by Pompey, 65 B.C., but retained its sovereigns. Christianity was introduced in the 3d century. In the 8th century, after a severe struggle, it was subdued by the Arab caliphs; by the Turkish sultan Alp-Arslan, 1068; and by Tartar hordes, 1235. From the 14th to the 18th century, Georgia was successively held by Persian and Turkish monarchs. In 1740 Nadir Shah made part of it a principality, whose last ruler, Heraclius, surrendered it to the czar in 1799, and in 1802 Georgia became a Russian province.

Georgia, the southernmost and youngest of the 13 original states of the United States, is bounded north by Tennessee and North Carolina, east by the Savannah river (which separates it from South Carolina), and by the Atlantic ocean, which forms a coast line of about 128 miles; Florida bounds it on the south, and Alabama and a small part of Florida on the west. It lies between lat. 30° 20′ and 35° N., and lon. 80° 40′ and 85° 38′ W. Area, 59,475 sq. miles, in 137 counties. Pop. 1890, 1,837,353; 1900, 2,216,-331. Capital, Atlanta.

De Soto enters the state from Florida; travels northeast through the pine barrens, erects a cross of wood near the Ocmulgee; hears from Indians on the Etowah of gold to the north, and proceeds westward to the Mississippi, entering Alabama by the Coosa.. 1540
Tristan de Luna, with 300 Spaniards, spends the summer in what is now Habersham county, searching for gold......... 1560
Jean Ribault of Dieppe, with 2 ships fitted out by Gaspard de Coligni, high admiral of France and leader of Huguenots, anchors off mouth of Satilla, discovers Altamaha river, Ossabaw sound, and the Savannah river....................May, 1562
Second expedition sent out by Coligni, 3 ships under René de Laudonnier anchor in St. Andrew's sound.............June, 1564
Land between lat. 31° and 36° N., and westward to the ocean, granted by first charter of Charles II. to the lords proprietors of Carolina...24 Mch. 1663
A 3 years' grant of lands between Savannah and Altamaha rivers obtained from lords proprietors of Carolina by sir Robert Montgomery, bart., who issues proposals for settlement of his province, the "Margravate of Azilia"......... 1717
Montgomery fails to colonize and forfeits grant................ 1720
Lords proprietors of Carolina sell seven eighths of their grant to Parliament, and all south of Savannah river is reserved by British crown... 1729
Lord Carteret, owner of one eighth, sells it to trustees for establishing the colony of Georgia in America.........28 Feb. 1732
Trustees receive their charter granting "all those lands between Savannah and Altamaha, and westerly from heads of said

GEO

rivers in a direct line to the South seas, including islands within 20 leagues of the coast." The trustees serving without pay, offer to all "and gent persons who would be willing to seek a livelihood in the colony if provided with a passage thither and means of getting settled" free citizenship and free exercise of religion (Papists excluded) Charter granted 9 June, 1732

Ship *Ann*, capt John Thomas, with gen Oglethorpe (OGLETHORPE gen James) rev Henry Herbert D D, and 35 families, anchors in Rebellion roads, S C 13 Jan 1733

Obtaining consent of Creek Indians through Mary Musgrove, interpreter, rev Thomas Bosomworth, Oglethorpe and colonists land at Yamacraw bluff on south side of Savannah river the present site of Savannah 12 Feb "

First clapboard house in Georgia begun in Savannah 19 Feb "

Two thousand religious books received by trustees from unknown person in England for use in colony 18 Apr "

Ship *James* capt Yoakly, first ship to sail up the Savannah and unload at the town May, "

Treaty of Oglethorpe with lower Creek tribes and Yamacraw Indians who agree ever to protect the English and restore runaway negroes receiving for each 4 blankets and 2 guns, or an equivalent 21 May, "

Ten families sent from Savannah to fort Argyle on Ogeechee river previously garrisoned by rangers June, "

Public designation of town and wards with religious exercises, town court of record established, first session of magistrates held, and first jury in Georgia impanelled 7 July, "

Forty Jews arrive at Savannah, sent by the committee appointed by the trustees July, "

Trustees prohibit rum in Georgia 11 Aug "

Forty two families of Salzburgers, sent from Augsburg, Bavaria, by the Society for the Propagation of Christian Knowledge, settle at Ebenezer 17 Mch 1734

Oglethorpe sails for England, leaving Thomas Causton in authority 7 Apr "

Ten persons, under rev Gottlieb Spanzenberg, sent over from Saxony to begin a Moravian settlement in America, locate on north side of the Ogeechee river, near fort Argyle Jan 1735

Fifty nine Salzburgers under Mr Vat 22 British emigrants, and some Indian chiefs whom Oglethorpe had taken to England, arrive at Savannah early in "

Small quantity of Georgia silk taken to England and court dress made, worn by queen Caroline at levee on king's birthday, 2 Apr "

Augusta laid out and garrisoned at trustees' expense, Roger de Lacy, an Indian agent one of its first settlers "

First issue of 4000*l* of Sola bills, or bills of exchange of various denominations, made by trustees' agents in Georgia, 21 July, "

About 100 Highlanders, sent from Scotland by trustees, settle on north side of the Altamaha river, calling it New Inverness, Jan 1736

Two ships convoyed by British sloop *Hawk*, bringing Oglethorpe, John and Charles Wesley, 25 Moravians, and a number of Salzburgers, anchor near Tybee island 5 Feb "

Fort on St. Simon's island at Frederica, as marked out by Oglethorpe begun 19 Feb "

John Wesley first preaches at Savannah 7 Mch "

First Sunday school in Georgia held by Mr Delamotte and John Wesley at Savannah "

Fort St Andrews erected on Cumberland island by Highlanders and fort William planned "

Treaty ending hostilities between Spanish and English colonies, and referring all disputes as to boundaries between Georgia and Florida to the home governments 27 Oct. "

Oglethorpe appointed general of forces in South Carolina and Georgia June, 1737

John Wesley sails for England 24 Dec "

Uprising of negroes, incited by the Spanish at Stono, quelled 1738

Arrival of ship bringing rev George Whitefield and a regiment recruited by Oglethorpe in England, the regiment, under col Cochran, locating at Frederica. 3 May, "

Many Moravian emigrants remove to Pennsylvania (the rest follow 2 years later) "

Attempted assassination of gen Oglethorpe while inspecting fort St. Andrews on Cumberland island Nov "

Articles of convention between the British and Spanish governments, disputed territories to be retained by present possessors 14 Jan. 1739

Treaty of peace at Coweta Town between chiefs of Creek Indians and Oglethorpe 21 Aug "

George Whitefield lays first brick of central building of orphan house "Bethesda," 9 miles from Savannah 25 Mch 1740

Spanish fort St. Diego, near St Augustine, defended by 57 men, taken by Oglethorpe. 10 May, "

Being joined at St. John's by Carolina troops, Oglethorpe marches upon fort Moosa, which Spaniards evacuate and retreat to St. Augustine 15 May, "

Foundation for Christ church Savannah, commenced 11 June, "

Fort Moosa recaptured by 300 Spaniards under don Antonio Salgrado after a bloody conflict 26 June, "

After an ineffectual siege of 3 weeks Oglethorpe retires from before St Augustine and reaches Frederica about 20 July, "

Georgia divided into 2 counties Savannah, comprising all territory north of Darien, and Frederica, covering the settlements on St Simon's island and the Altamaha, and col William Stephens chosen president of Savannah 15 Apr 1741

Nine Spanish vessels, attempting to enter Amelia sound, are repulsed by cannon of fort William, on Cumberland island, aided by armed schooner of 14 guns and 80 men 21 June, 1742

Spanish squadron of 36 vessels enters St Simon's harbor in spite of battery of fort and a few English ships, lands about 500 men within 4 miles of Frederica . . 5 July, "

English having abandoned fort St Simon, the Spanish occupy it, march against Frederica, and are driven back to an open marsh bordering on a forest, where they stack arms and are surprised and completely routed by a platoon and company of rangers under lieuts Sutherland and Mackay in a battle known as "Bloody marsh" 7 July, 1742

Rum act repealed in Georgia by order of House of Commons 14 July, "

Gen don Manuel de Montiano alarmed by a decoy letter sent by Oglethorpe with his fleet, fearful of being hemmed in by sea and land, hastens to sea about 20 July, "

Oglethorpe returns with detachment of Highlanders from a fruitless incursion into Florida 9 Mch 1743

Magazine at Frederica blown up 22 Mch

Trustees abrogate part of constitution appointing board for Frederica, and counties are consolidated, col Wm Stephens elected first president of colony of Georgia, under government established at solicitation of people, by the king 18 Apr

Chas Harris and James Habersham in partnership establish first commercial house in Georgia 1744

Thomas Bosomworth obtains deed from Indian chief and emperor, Malatchee, to islands of Ossabaw, Sapelo, and St Catharine 14 Dec 1747

Small ship (the first) chartered in England by Harris and Habersham to bring Georgia products May 1749

In response to petitions the act of 1735, prohibiting importation and use of negro slaves, was repealed by trustees 26 Oct "

Trustees abolish tail male tenure of grants and make them absolute 25 May, 1750

Henry Parker commissioned vice president of Georgia, 26 June, "

Christ church (Anglican) Savannah, dedicated 7 July "

Provincial assembly of delegates to propose debate, and refer matters to the trustees first meets at Savannah 15 Jan 1751

Henry Parker chosen president of colony 8 Apr "

First general muster of militia in lower districts at Savannah, 13 June "

Trustees hold last meeting surrender charters and the government passes to the Board of Trade and Plantations 23 June, 1752

Community of Anglican church people, after preliminary examination of lands in 1752-53 and procuring grant of about 32 000 acres of land between Ogeechee and Altamaha, settle at Midway, Ga. Mch 1754

Patrick Graham elected president of colony "

Silver seal made for colony under king's direction 21 June, "

Capt John Reynolds, of the British navy, appointed governor of Georgia in Aug, arrives at Savannah 29 Oct "

Reynolds dissolves board and forms a royal council under letters patent from the crown 30 Oct "

First General Assembly, of freeholders of estates of not less than 500 acres, meets at Savannah 7 Jan 1755

Governor assents to 12 acts of assembly, the second was for issuing 3000*l* in paper bills of credit 7 Mch "

Two transports arrive at Savannah with about 400 Acadians, banished from Nova Scotia (ACADIA) As Papists could not remain in Georgia under charter, they were sent to South Carolina the next spring Dec "

By machinations of his secretary, William Little, gov Reynolds is charged with maladministration and resigns office to Henry Ellis, elected lieutenant governor 16 Feb. 1757

Treaty of peace with council of upper and lower Creeks by lieut. gov Ellis 3 Nov "

Georgia divided into 8 parishes, and church of England worship established. 17 Mch 1758

Islands of Ossabaw, St Catharine, and Sapelo formally ceded to England by Creek nation 22 Apr "

Ellis appointed governor in chief by lords of trade 17 May, "

Grant of 300 acres for site of Sunbury by Mark Carr, part of his 500 acre grant from the king in 1757 20 June, "

Claims of Thomas and Mary Bosomworth settled by order of the king 9 Feb 1759

First wharf built in Savannah "

Act for issuing 7410*l* in paper bills of credit 1 May, 1760

Lieut gov James Wright succeeds gov Ellis. 2 Nov "

George III proclaimed king with civil and military pomp, the only event of the kind ever witnessed in Georgia, 10 Feb 1761

Commission creating James Wright captain general and governor in chief of Georgia reaches Savannah 28 Jan 1762

William Grover, first chief justice of Georgia, removed from office for maladministration Mch 1763

Protest and caveat issued by gov Wright against grants of land south of the Altamaha by South Carolina 30 Mch "

First newspaper in Georgia, the *Georgia Gazette*, issued at Savannah by James Johnson 17 Apr "

By royal proclamation, southern boundary of Georgia is made the St Mary's river, including lands between this and the Altamaha claimed by South Carolina 7 Oct. "

Congress of Creeks, Cherokees, Catawbas, Chickasaws, and Choctaws, meet governors of Virginia, North Carolina, South Carolina, and Georgia at Augusta, and conclude treaty and cede additional land to Georgia 5 Nov "

New commission granted gov Wright for the new Mississippi territory of Georgia 20 Jan 1764

Four additional parishes laid off between Altamaha and St. Mary's rivers 1765

Sixteen members of assembly at Savannah consider a circular from Massachusetts assembly, proposing a general congress at New York on the stamp act. 2 Sept. "

Letter sent general congress in New York announces hearty co-operation of Georgia assembly, but opposition of gov Wright prevents attendance of delegates Oct "

British ship *Speedwell* arrives in Savannah river with stamps,

which are secretly transferred to fort Halifax to avoid destruction threatened by "Liberty Boys" 5 Dec. 1765
South Carolina aroused because Georgia accepts stamps to clear 60 or 70 vessels waiting at Savannah Dec "
Two hundred Liberty Boys threatening to break open fort and destroy stamps, the governor removes them under military escort to the guard house 2 Jan 1766
Mr Agnus stamp distributer, arrives at Tybee, is secretly conveyed to the governor's house takes the oath, but in a few days leaves town convinced of his insecurity 3 Jan "
A body of 600 men threatening fort George and the governor's house the stamps are placed on the *Speedwell* 3 Feb "
Effigy of gov Wright, with offensive circular of sec. Conway in his hand burned on the commons in Savannah 4 Feb "
Official announcement of repeal of stamp act received by governor 6 July, "
Assembly refuses governor's call for supplies for British troops in Georgia and gen Cage withdraws all troops from province soon after 20 Jan 1767
One hundred and seven Irish Protestants settle at forks of Lambert creek and Great Ogeechee Mch 1768
Benjamin Franklin appointed agent for Georgia in Great Britain, 11 Apr "
King rejects as irregular and disrespectful a petition of the assembly presented by Franklin, protesting against acts of Parliament taxing America, under date of 24 Dec. "
Merchants and traders of Savannah meet and resolve that importers of articles subject to parliamentary duties are enemies to the country 16 Sept 1769
Unanimous election of dr Wimberly Jones as speaker of assembly, vetoed by governor, who dissolves assembly, 22 Feb 1770
James Habersham president of the council, assumes executive duties on Wright's departure for England and twice vetoes election of dr Jones as speaker of assembly July 1771
Works for filature in Savannah, erected 1751, discontinued, end of silk industry in Georgia 1772
Gov Wright returns from England with title of baronet. Feb 1773
Creeks and Cherokees convene at Augusta and cede to king over 2,100,000 acres in Georgia, to liquidate indebtedness to traders of over $200,000 1 June, "
Meeting in Savannah, resolves to concur with sister colonies in every constitutional measure to obtain redress of American grievances This meeting was afterwards pronounced illegal and punishable by gov Wright 10 Aug 1774
Resolutions of fealty to Continental Congress drawn up by representatives of Darien in district congress 12 Jan 1775
Provincial congress in Savannah elects dr Jones, Archibald Bulloch, and John Houstoun, delegates to the Continental Congress in Philadelphia . 18 Jan "
Delegates send patriotic letter, but cannot attend during struggle in Georgia with royal power 8 Apr "
General Assembly convenes, no quorum, royal government in Georgia suspended 9 May, "
Noble Wimberly Jones, Joseph Habersham, Edward Telfair, and a few others appropriate to colonial use 500 pounds of powder from king's magazine 11 May, "
Lyman Hall, delegate from parish of St. John, to Continental Congress, arrives at Philadelphia with present for patriots in Massachusetts of 1[illegible] barrels of rice and 50*l* 13 May, "
Other delegates from the state not taking their seats in Congress Georgia, except parish of St John is placed under ban of colonial intercourse by Continental Congress 17 May, "
Ship *Juliana* leaves Savannah with gift of 63 barrels of rice and 120*l*. in specie for Massachusetts 1 June, "
Gov Wright having issued orders for celebration of king's birthday, Liberty people spike the cannon on the bay, dismount them, and roll them to the bottom of bluff 2 June "
First liberty pole in Georgia erected at Savannah, on king's birthday . 5 June, "
Claim of George Galphin, a prominent and liberal trader, audited before governor and approved, for 9791*l*. 6 June, "
Provincial congress at Tondee's Long Room Savannah, elect Archibald Bullock president, adopt the "American Declaration or Bill of Rights" of Continental Congress, and resolve on non importation of British merchandise 4 July, "
First provincial vessel commissioned for naval warfare in the Revolution, is sent out by Georgia under command of capt. Bowen and Joseph Habersham Discovering an English vessel bringing powder for Indians and royalists, they board her and secure the powder 10 July, "
Continental Congress officially notified that Georgia acceded to general association, it is thenceforth one of the United Colonies .. .. 20 July, "
Messrs Zubley, Bullock, and Houstoun, take seats as delegates from Georgia to Continental Congress . . 13 Sept. "
English ship with 250 barrels of gunpowder seized off Tybee island by the Liberty people 17 Sept "
Provincial congress takes under supervision all courts of law, 1 Dec. "
Council of safety fully organized, George Walton, pres, 11 Dec. "
Battalion of troops ordered raised at continental expense for protection of Georgia, organized .. . . 7 Jan 1776
Gov Wright arrested by maj Joseph Habersham and put under parole 18 Jan. "
Provincial congress organize, elect hon Archibald Bullock president, issue bills of credit for military stores, and draw up temporary constitution for Georgia. 22 Jan "
Gov Wright escapes to English ship *Scarborough*, and writes a letter to people, offering peace but is not heeded 11 Feb. "
Capt Rice, charged by the council of safety to dismantle shipping at Savannah to prevent capture by the British, is surprised and imprisoned on a vessel which the British had boarded. To accomplish his release the council of safety fired several vessels arrested all members of royal council in Savannah, and menaced officers of ships at Tybee 2 Mch 1776
Lord North's bill prohibiting trade with the colonies in rebellion is announced in Georgia. Mch "
Temporary constitution ratified by provincial congress. 15 Apr "
Declaration of Independence signed by Lyman Hall, Button Gwinnett, and George Walton, members from Georgia, 3 July, "
Declaration of Independence received in Savannah, read by Archibald Bullock at liberty pole, and acknowledged by national salute 8 Aug "
First constitution of Georgia ratified in convention, parishes abolished and counties erected instead 5 Feb 1777
Fort McIntosh on St Illa river surrendered to British 17 Feb. "
Pres Bullock invested with the executive power, with assistance of 5 persons of his own choosing 22 Feb "
Mr Bullock dying within a month, is succeeded by Button Gwinnett, who was soon after killed in a duel with gen. McIntosh 4 Mch "
Act of attainder of enemies of American liberty as traitors, and confiscating their estates, passes the assembly 1 Mch 1778
Executive council invests the governor with sole executive power independent of council 16 Apr "
British under col Prevost advance north into Georgia to join lieut.-col Campbell who sailed from New York 27 Nov "
Campbell anchors off Tybee 27 Dec. "
Campbell lands, attacks rear of Americans under gen Howe, who retreats across the Savannah, abandoning the city American loss, nearly 100 killed and wounded, 30 drowned in swamps, 7 officers, 416 non commissioned officers and privates taken prisoners British loss, 2 captains and 5 privates killed, 8 privates wounded , 29 Dec. "
Col. Campbell takes possession of Cherokee hill and Ebenezer, 1, 2 Jan. 1779
Maj Lane surrenders garrison at Sunbury to Prevost 9 Jan "
Augusta surrendered to British under Campbell Jan "
Americans under Pickens, Dooly, and Clarke repulse British at battle of Kettle creek, Wilkes county 14 Feb. "
Prevost surprises and defeats Americans under gen Ashe at Briar creek Loss, American, 340 killed, wounded, and prisoners, British, 16 killed and wounded 3 Mch "
Civil government renewed by British under col Prevost, 4 Mch "
Gov Wright returns to Georgia. 13 July, "
As British invasion prevented carrying the constitution into effect, the supreme executive council is clothed with plenary power and elects John Wereat president 6 Aug "
Count d'Estaing with fleet of 33 war vessels, surprises and captures part of British fleet under sir James Wallace commanding Tybee station 3 Sept. "
Armies of Lincoln and D'Estaing besiege Savannah 23 Sept. "
Capt French with 111 British, and 5 vessels with crews and ammunition frightened by bonfires and voices, surrender to col John White of Georgia line and 6 Americans 1 Oct "
Americans and French attack Savannah, lose 1100 killed and wounded out of 4000 and abandon siege, bearing away count Pulaski, mortally wounded 9 Oct. "
A dissatisfied faction elects George Walton governor, appoints executive councillors, and elects delegates to Congress, producing great confusion 4 Nov "
Assembly at Augusta elects Richard Howley governor and George Wells president of executive council 4 Jan 1780
Gov Howley by proclamation calls on people to support and defend the government. 2 Feb "
Assembly adjourns to Heard's Fort, Wilkes county, which becomes temporary capital of the state. 5 Feb "
Gov Howley leaves for Continental Congress, pres. Wells dying soon after, Stephen Heard becomes executive, 18 Feb "
House of Assembly of only 15 members (18 being a quorum) passes acts attainting rebels of high treason 9 May. "
Augusta taken by col Clarke, 14 Sept., retaken by British, 17 Sept "
Fort Grierson, one of the defences of Augusta, taken by Clarke, Pickens, and Lee 24 May, 1781
Col Brown, who with British forces stands a protracted siege of Augusta by Americans, capitulates (AUGUSTA) 5 June, "
Assembly convenes at Augusta and elects Nathan Brownson governor . 16 Aug "
John Martin elected governor at Augusta. 1 Jan 1782
Legislature consults with gen Wayne at Sister's Ferry on the Savannah, and by proclamation invites desertion from British army and return of citizens to Georgia. 12 Jan "
Gov Martin, in destitution, is supplied by legislature by sale of forfeited negroes and supplies 4 May, "
British forces, advancing 7 miles from Savannah to escort Creek Indian allies into camp, are routed by Wayne 21 May, "
Orders received by sir James Wright at Savannah for evacuation of the province 14 June, "
Seat of provincial government removed to Ebenezer, headquarters of gen Wayne, where assembly meets 1 July, "
Savannah evacuated by British, col. James Jackson selected to receive the keys . 11 July, "
Executive council establish themselves in Savannah, and legislature convenes 14 July, "
Last blood of Revolution shed in Georgia, col John Laurens, killed in a skirmish at Combahee Ferry 27 Aug "
Gen Pickens and col Clarke drive a party of marauding Tories from settlement on Etowah into Florida 17 Oct "
Gen McIntosh, John Houstoun, and Edward Telfair appointed agents to adjust the northern boundaries 15 Feb. 1783
Treaty ratified at Augusta, Creeks cede country west of Tugaloo, including head waters of Oconee river .. 31 May, "

Legislature convenes at Augusta. 8 July, 1783

Franklin and Washington counties laid out on land ceded by the Creek Indians Feb 1784

Executive council notified of ratification by Congress of treaty of peace with Great Britain 1 Mch "

Land court opened at Augusta to issue warrants "Citizens' Rights" "Refugee certificates," "Continental certificates," "Minute men certificates" and "Marine certificates" Apr "

University of Georgia receives charter and 40,000 acres of wild land 1785

Legislature grants count d'Estaing 20,000 acres of land and free citizenship of Georgia "

Hostile Creeks subjected by col Clarke, and treaty concluded at Galphington 12 Nov "

Chatham artillery of Savannah organized 1 May, 1786

Col Gunn breaks up camp of runaway negroes, trained to arms by the British and ravaging country 6 May, "

Gen Nathaniel Greene dies at "Mulberry Grove," 14 miles from Savannah, the home presented him by the legislature 19 June, "

Assembly directs paper bills of credit not to exceed 30,000*l* struck off under direction of governor 14 Aug "

Abram Baldwin and hon William Few, delegates from Georgia, sign draught of constitution proposed for ratification 17 Sept 1787

Legislature at Augusta ratifies the federal Constitution the 4th state 2 Jan 1788

George Handly elected governor to succeed gen James Jackson (age 30) elected 9 Jan, who resigned on account of his youth. 25 Jan "

Differences between South Carolina and Georgia settled, northern boundary of Georgia fixed in line west from head of most northern branch of Tugaloo river to the Mississippi river, Feb. "

First bag of cotton exported from Georgia, raised by Alexander Bissel of St Simon's island "

New constitution to take effect in following Oct, formally accepted by governor 6 May, 1789

First general assembly under new constitution meets 3 Nov "

General assembly meets for public worship in St. Paul's church, Augusta, on the first national thanksgiving under the constitution 26 Nov "

Col Willet gains the confidence of Creek Indians and Alexander McGillivray, son of a Scotchman by a half breed Creek, an enemy to the Americans and acknowledged head of the Creeks, McGillivray with 8 warriors accompanies Willet to Philadelphia and New York, when a treaty is concluded, ceding land south of Oconee and Ocmulgee rivers 13 Aug 1790

Two brass cannon taken at Yorktown, are presented to the Chatham artillery of Savannah, by gen Washington, in appreciation of their part in his reception in Savannah, one bears the inscription "Surrendered by the capitulation of York Town, 19 Oct. 1781. *Honi soit qui mal y pense*—G R." with the imperial crown 1791

Gen Washington on a presidential tour, arrives at Savannah and is received with enthusiasm 13 May, "

Eli Whitney of Connecticut, while residing in Georgia, invents the cotton-gin 27 May, 1793

Gen Clarke claiming that by the treaty of 1790 certain lands on the south side of the Oconee river had been improperly ceded to the Creeks by the U S., takes possession, defying Georgia and U S, but is driven out 12 Oct 1794

Seat of government removed from Augusta to Louisville, now county seat of Jefferson county 16 May, 1795

Rescinding act signed by gov Irwin, who was elected the previous month (YAZOO SPECULATIONS) 13 Feb 1796

U S grants to Georgia pre-emption rights to lands obtained by joint treaty made with the Creek Indians by U S and Georgia in previous year Mch. 1797

Mississippi territory set off from Georgia by act of Congress, 7 Apr 1798

Revised constitution signed by delegates at Louisville, proclaimed by 16 rounds of artillery 30 May, "

"Senatus Academicus" of university of Georgia first meets at Louisville Nov 1799

Moravian mission among the Cherokees begun at Spring Place, Murray county 1801

First building erected for university of Georgia. "

James Jackson resigns to take seat in U S Senate, David Emanuel acting governor 7 Dec "

Georgia cedes her western territory to the U S for $1 250 000 and stipulation that the Indian title to lands in Georgia should be extinguished by U S., but no time for completion of contract is specified 24 Apr 1802

First commencement at university of Georgia May, 1804

Treaty at Washington, Creek Indians cede land between Oconee and Ocmulgee to the U S 14 Nov 1805

First session of legislature at Milledgeville, the new capital 1807

Battle between Georgia volunteers under col Daniel Newman and Lotchaway and Alligator Indians in E Florida 5 Oct. 1812

Attack and destruction of Auttose towns by 950 Georgia militia under gen Floyd, and battle with Creeks on Tallapoosa river, Indian loss, 200 killed, Americans, 11 killed, 54 wounded, 29 Nov 1813

Gen Floyd repulses a large body of Creek Indians at camp Defiance, 48 miles west of the Chattahoochee, after a loss of 17 killed and 132 wounded 27 Jan 1814

Treaty ceding territory to U S between Creek Indians and gen. Jackson, at fort Jackson 9 Aug "

Point Petric, near St Mary's, defended by about 90 men under capt. Massias, is surrendered to 1000 British 13 Jan 1815

William H Crawford appointed secretary of war. 3 Mch. "

Frederic Tudor of Boston ships first load of ice to Savannah 1817

GEO

First mission of American Board of Commissioners among the Cherokees commenced at Spring Place, Murray county 1817

William H Crawford appointed secretary of treasury 22 Oct "

David B Mitchell resigns governorship and is succeeded by William Rabun president of the senate 4 Nov "

Three hundred Georgia infantry under lieut. col Arbuckle repulse Fowltown Indians 12 miles from fort Scott on Flint river 23 Nov "

Ex gov Mitchell, U S agent to the Creek Indians, concludes treaty, ceding lands in N W Georgia to the U S to be annexed to Georgia 22 Jan 1818

First transatlantic steamship *Savannah* sails from Savannah for Liverpool (passage took 26 days) 26 May, 1819

Gov Rabun dying is succeeded by Matthew Talbot, president of the senate 24 Oct "

Macon laid out, and first court held 20 Mch 1823

Wilson Lumpkin appointed by president commissioner of boundary between Georgia and Florida "

By amendment to the constitution the election of governor is transferred from the legislature to the people 17 Nov 1824

Treaty at Indian Springs with Creeks—represented by gen William McIntosh and 50 others They cede to U S all the Creek country in Georgia and several millions of acres in Alabama 12 Feb 1825

Savannah and Ogeechee canal begun the state subscribing for $40 000 of stock "

Governor orders a survey of Indian lands in Georgia "

U S government sends gen. Gaines to Georgia to protect the Indians. "

Treaty with Creek Indians at Washington annuls treaty of 1825 and cedes only lands in Georgia, the Creeks agreeing to emigrate 24 Jan 1826

Threatening correspondence between gov Troup and the U S on jurisdiction in Indian matters within the state 1826–27

State extends criminal jurisdiction over part of Georgia claimed by the Cherokees 20 Dec 1828

John M Berrien appointed attorney general 9 Mch 1829

Legislation annuls all laws and ordinances made by Cherokees, 19 Dec "

First gold from Georgia mines received at the U S mint 1830

Law forbidding any white person to enter the Cherokee country without license and oath of allegiance to Georgia, 22 Dec "

Cherokee Georgia surveyed by order of governor, laid out in small sections, and distributed by lottery to the people of Georgia Apr 1831

Rev Samuel A Worcester and Elizur Butler, M D, missionaries to Cherokees refusing oath of allegiance to Georgia, are imprisoned in state penitentiary 16 Sept. "

Supreme court of the U S pronounces authority assumed by Georgia unconstitutional, declares void laws depriving Indians of their rights, and orders release of missionaries Mch 1832

Gospel of Matthew printed at New Echota in Cherokee language "

Altamaha and Brunswick railroad 12 miles long, commenced "

Anti tariff convention meets at Milledgeville 12 Nov "

Imprisoned missionaries pardoned by gov Lumpkin 14 Jan 1833

John Forsyth appointed secretary of state 27 June, 1834

William Schley elected governor, recommends a state lunatic asylum at Milledgeville and geological survey Nov 1835

Treaty at New Echota between U S and Cherokee nation fixes 24 May, 1838, for Georgia to take possession of territory ceded by Cherokees. 29 Dec. "

Battle of Chickasawhachee in Baker county between Creek Indians on their way to join the Seminoles, and Georgia militia 3 July, 1836

Wesleyan female college, the oldest for women in the U S, chartered 1837

U S branch mint opened at Dahlonega Lumpkin county "

Southern convention, 180 delegates from 5 states, at Augusta for establishing direct trade with Europe 2 Apr 1838

Cherokee Indians 1560 in number, escorted out of Georgia to Ross Landing, Tenn, by Georgia militia. 3 June, "

Bonds for $1,579,875 issued by state for the Western and Atlantic railroad 1839

Georgia Historical Society incorporated. "

First settlement on site of Atlanta. "

Gov McDonald advocates the Missouri compromise "

Great flood in Georgia, the Savannah river the highest in a century, boats pass through streets of Augusta 28 May, 1840

Law reducing state tax 20 per cent 1841

After much opposition bill passes, adding 25 per cent to state tax of previous year 1842

Suspension from office of bishop Andrews of Methodist Episcopal church, for marrying a slave holder, results in the formation of the Methodist Episcopal church, South, organized at Louisville, Ky 1 May, 1845

Opening of Georgia Institution for Education of Deaf and Dumb in a log cabin at Cave Springs 1846

Settlement previously known as Marthasville and Terminus is named Atlanta 1847

Macon and Atlanta telegraph line in operation 1849

George W Crawford appointed secretary of war 6 Mch "

Wallace, Iverson, and Lumpkin of Georgia issue a manifesto to people of the U S, declaring emancipation certain unless prevented by the slave states and calling upon the latter for union and concert in self defence "

Gen Narciso Lopez, having fled from Cuba to New York under charges of conspiracy, organizes an expedition against Cuba, lands at Savannah, is arrested, but discharged amid the cheers of the people and allowed to proceed 27 May, 1850

State convention of delegates called by the executive at Milledgeville adopts the "platform of 1850" "*Resolved* That the state of Georgia, even to the disruption of every tie that binds her to the Union, will resist any act of Congress abolishing slavery" 10 Dec 1850

Extension of slavery into California and New Mexico being advocated by the Southern Extremists, the Union party nominate and elect Howell Cobb governor Oct. 1851

By joint resolution the governor is requested to withdraw the block of marble bearing the inscription, 'The Constitution as it is, the Union as it was," contributed to the Washington monument and substitute one bearing the state arms 31 Dec "

Formation of the "Know Nothing" or American party in Georgia 1852

Southern convention meets in Savannah 12 Dec 1856

Appropriation of $200,000 made by Congress for purchase of site for a naval depot at Brunswick on Blythe island, 28 Jan 1857

Howell Cobb appointed secretary of the treasury 6 Mch "

Gov Brown vetoes bill suspending forfeiture proceedings against banks for one year, the banks in Augusta and elsewhere resume specie payment 1 May, 1858

Georgia schooner yacht *Wanderer* seized in New York on suspicion of being a slave trader, but released 16 June, "

Gov Brown seizes forts Pulaski and Jackson 16 days before Georgia secedes 3 Jan 1861

Ordinance of secession passed (yeas, 208, nays, 89) 19 Jan "

[Alex H Stephens and Herschel V Johnson vote nay]

Members of Congress from Georgia withdraw 23 Jan "

Iverson withdraws from the Senate (UNITED STATES) 28 Jan "

Mint at Dahlonega seized by confederate authorities of Georgia 28 Feb "

Georgia adopts confederate constitution 16 Mch "

Georgia adopts a state constitution 23 Mch "

Gov Brown by proclamation forbids the people of Georgia to pay northern creditors 26 Apr "

Admiral Dupont, U S navy, takes Tybee island Nov "

Draft of troops made in Savannah, at call of pres. Davis for 1200 volunteers from Georgia 4 Mch 1862

Fort Pulaski bombarded by federals and taken 10 Apr "

Conscript act, annulling previous contracts by volunteers and making all men over 18 years and under 35 soldiers for the war, sustained by supreme court of Georgia 11 Nov "

First general council of the Protestant Episcopal church of the confederate states assembles at Augusta 19 Nov "

Federals under col Montgomery capture and burn Darien, 11 June, 1863

Confederate war vessel *Atlanta* leaves Savannah to attack the blockading fleet, meets federal monitor *Weehawken*, and in 15 minutes is disabled and captured 17 June, "

Battle of CHICKAMAUGA 19-20 Sept. "

Battle of Ringgold 27 Nov "

First detachment of federal prisoners received at ANDERSONVILLE PRISON 15 Feb 1864

Battle of Tunnel hill 22-25 Feb "

Resolutions passed by legislature recommending the tender of peace to the U S after every victory Mch "

Confederates under gen Johnston evacuate Resaca (ATLANTA CAMPAIGN) and cross the Oostenaula, speedily followed by federals under gen Sherman 15 May, "

Sherman attacks Johnston at bluffs of Kenesaw mountain and is repulsed (ATLANTA CAMPAIGN) 27 June, "

Johnston evacuates Marietta 1 July, "

Johnston succeeded by Hood in defence of Atlanta 17 July, "

First battle (Peach tree creek) near Atlanta 20 July, "

Second battle (Decatur) near Atlanta 22 July, "

Third battle near Atlanta 28 July, "

Battle of Jonesboro 31 Aug "

Hood evacuates Atlanta after burning all machinery, supplies, and munitions of war not portable 1 Sept. "

Pres. Jefferson Davis, on a tour of inspection, delivers an address on the crisis, at Macon 23 Sept. "

Battle of ALLATOONA PASS 6 Oct "

Sherman begins his march to the sea with 2 corps of the army of the Tennessee under Howard and 2 corps of the army of the Cumberland under Slocum 14 Nov "

[City of Atlanta burned at the same time (SHERMAN'S GREAT MARCH)]

Gov Brown and Georgia legislature, in session at Milledgeville, leave hurriedly for Augusta 18 Nov "

Fort McAllister captured by the federals under Hazen, 13 Dec. "

Confederates evacuate Savannah 20 Dec. "

Legislature assembles at Macon 11 Feb 1865

James Johnson appointed provisional governor by president Johnson 17 June, "

Convention of state delegates at Milledgeville repeal ordinance of secession 30 Oct "

War debt declared void by convention, and revised constitution adopted 7 Nov "

Legislature assembled at Milledgeville adopts amendment to federal Constitution abolishing slavery 5 Dec. "

Charles J Jenkins inaugurated governor of Georgia 14 Dec "

Legislature appropriates $200 000 to buy corn for indigent poor of the state, and distributes it to 45,000 people, 12 Mch 1866

Legislature passes over the governor's veto a stay law forbidding levy or sale under execution upon any contract or liability made or incurred prior to 1 Jan 1865, or any subsequent renewal, except for one third of the principal and interest after 1 Jan 1868, and one third after each subsequent year "

New constitution set aside by Congress. Mch. 1867

Maj gen John Pope assumes command of third military district 1 Apr "

Use of "chain gang" as a legal mode of punishment except in penitentiary discontinued 1 May, "

Republican state mass convention held at Atlanta adopts the name "Union Republican Party of Georgia," and pledges hearty support of reconstruction measures 4 July, "

Convention of native white citizens of Georgia, at Macon, under name of "Conservative Party of Georgia" 5 Dec "

Constitutional convention, called by order of gen Pope meets at Atlanta 9 Dec "

Convention makes Atlanta the capital 8 Jan 1868

Gov Jenkins refusing warrant for expenses of constitutional convention, is removed by gen Meade military governor, maj gen Thomas H Ruger made provisional governor, 13 Jan "

State central committee of conservative party meets at Macon and adopts the title, "The Central Executive Committee of the National Democratic Party of Georgia" 13 Feb "

New constitution ratified 11 Mch "

Rufus B Bullock, republican elected governor 20 Apr "

"Farming out" of penitentiary convicts begun by gen Ruger, 11 May, "

Gov Bullock inaugurated to serve 4 years 22 July, "

Convention of negroes held at Macon 6 Oct "

Right of negroes to hold office settled by the Supreme court, 22 June, 1869

Act of Congress completes reconstruction of Georgia 22 Dec. "

Georgia senate refuses to ratify the XV th Amendment "

Gen A H Terry assigned to military command of district of Georgia 24 Dec. "

Legislature elected 1868 assemble in Atlanta by gov Bullock's proclamation, to perfect organization of state 10 Jan 1870

XIV th and XV th Amendments ratified in legislature Feb "

Georgia readmitted to the Union 15 July, "

System of public instruction established by law 13 Oct "

Gov Bullock accused of fraudulent negotiation of bonds indorsed by the state, resigns and leaves the state, Benjamin Conley, pres of the senate, succeeds 30 Oct. 1871

James M Smith elected governor by special election 19 Dec "

Macon and Brunswick railroad seized by the state for nonpayment of interest 2 July, 1873

Amendment to bonding law prohibits payment of $8,000,000 bonds indorsed by gov Bullock, and pronounced fraudulent (Being ambiguously worded, it failed of its purpose) Passed, Feb. 1874

Commissioner of agriculture authorized by law Feb "

State board of health organized 9 June, 1875

Alfred H Colquitt, Democrat, elected governor 4 Oct. 1876

New constitution adopted 25 July, 1877

Confederate monument unveiled at Augusta 31 Oct 1878

Legislature votes bounties to soldiers who had lost limbs in the confederate service, appoints a commission to regulate railroad charges, and adopts a state flag July-Oct. 1879

Macon and Brunswick railroad sold at auction by the state for $1,125,000 13 Jan 1880

Nugget of gold weighing over a pound found in Nacoochee valley spring of "

Revision of state code regulating time for voting by the electoral college "

State temperance convention meets at Atlanta. 4 July, 1881

International cotton exposition held at Atlanta, 5 Oct.-31 Dec "

One hundred and fiftieth anniversary of settlement of Savannah celebrated 13 Feb 1883

Gov Stephens dying, is succeeded by James S Boynton, president of the senate 5 Mch. "

Henry D McDaniel, Democrat, elected governor at special election 24 Apr

Legislature prohibits Sunday excursion trains "

General local option law passed by legislature 1885

First election under local option law in Fulton county, majority of 225 for prohibition in vote of about 7000 25 Nov "

Interstate farmers' convention held at Atlanta Aug 1887

At local option election in Fulton county, Prohibitionists are defeated by 1122 votes out of a total of 9244 "

Legislature increases Supreme court from 3 judges to 5 "

Opening of the Technological school at Atlanta, a branch of the state university Oct. 1888

New capitol at Atlanta finished and accepted by state, cost, $1,000,000 20 Mch 1890

National military park established at Chickamauga battle field by Congress 19 Aug "

Direct trade convention held at Atlanta 10 Sept "

Direct trade convention, delegates from 6 cotton producing states, organizes at Atlanta 10 Sept. "

William J Northen, president of State Agricultural Society, nominated by Farmers' State Alliance in June, and by Democratic State Convention in Aug, is elected governor, 1 Oct. "

Corner stone of Normal and Technological school for girls at Milledgeville laid Nov "

Ex gov Gordon elected U S senator 19 Nov "

Ex gov James Milton Smith dies at Columbus 25 Nov "

Monument to Henry W Grady unveiled at Atlanta 21 Oct. 1891

Southern states exposition opens at Augusta 2 Nov "

Charles F Crisp elected speaker U S. Congress 8 Dec. "

First state convention of People's party at Atlanta, nominates W L Peck for governor and a full state ticket 20 July, 1892

L Q C Lamar, of U S Supreme court, dies at Macon 23 Jan. 1893

GOVERNORS OF GEORGIA—COLONIAL.

Name.	Date.	Remarks.
John Reynolds	1754	
Henry Ellis	1757	
James Wright	1760	
Archibald Bulloch, acting	1776	Appointed by the Georgia assembly.
Button Gwinnett, acting	1777	" " "
John A. Treutlen	1777	Under the new state constitution.
John Houstoun	1778	" " "
Georgia in the hands of the British, with Sir James Wright as royal governor	1779-81	
John Martin	1782	Chosen by assembly.
Lyman Hall	1783	
John Houstoun	1784	
Samuel Elbert	1785	
Edward Telfair	1786	
George Matthews	1787	
George Handley	1788	

UNDER THE FEDERAL CONSTITUTION.

Name	Date	Name	Date
George Walton	1789-90	William Schley	1835-37
Edward Telfair	1790-93	Geo. R. Gilmer	1837-39
George Matthews	1793-96	Chas. J. McDonald	1839-43
Jared Irwin	1796-98	Geo. W. Crawford	1843-47
James Jackson	1798-1801	Geo. W. B. Towns	1847-51
David Emanuel	1801	Howell Cobb	1851-53
Josiah Tattnall	1801-2	Herschel V. Johnson	1853-57
John Milledge	1802-6	Joseph E. Brown	1857-65
Jared Irwin	1806-9	James Johnson	1865
David B. Mitchell	1809-13	Chas. J. Jenkins	1865-67
Peter Early	1813-15	Gen. T. H. Ruger	1867-68
David B. Mitchell	1815-17	Rufus B. Bullock	1868-72
William Rabun	1817-19	James Milton Smith	1872-77
Matthew Talbot, act.	1819	Alfred H. Colquitt	1877-82
John Clark	1819-23	Alex. H. Stephens	1882-83
Geo. M. Troup	1823-27	Henry D. McDaniel	1883-86
John Forsyth	1827-29	John B. Gordon	1886-90
Geo. R. Gilmer	1829-31	William J. Northen	1890-94
Wilson Lumpkin	1831-35	William Y. Atkinson	1895-99

UNITED STATES SENATORS FROM THE STATE OF GEORGIA.

Name.	No. of Congress.	Date.	Remarks.
William Few	1st and 2d	1789 to 1793	
James Gunn	1st to 7th	1789 " 1801	
James Jackson	3d	1794 " 1795	Resigned 1795. Opposed bill to suppress slave-trade.
George Watson	4th	1795	Appointed in place of Jackson, 1795.
Josiah Tattnall	4th to 5th	1796 to 1799	Elected in place of Jackson, 1796.
Abraham Baldwin	6th " 9th	1799 " 1807	Died 1807. Elected president *pro tem.* 1801-2 and 1807.
James Jackson	7th " 8th	1801 " 1806	Died 18 Mch. 1806.
John Milledge	9th " 12th	1806 " 1809	Elected president *pro tem.* 1809. Resigned 1809.
George Jones	10th	1807	Appointed in place of Baldwin, 1807.
William H. Crawford	10th to 12th	1807 to 1813	Elected in place of Baldwin, 1807. Elected president *pro tem.* 1812. Resigned 1813, being appointed minister to France.
Charles Tait	11th	1809	Elected in place of Milledge.
William B. Bullock	13th	1813	Appointed in place of Crawford.
William Wyatt Bibb	13th to 14th	1813 to 1816	Elected in place of Crawford. Resigned 1816.
George M. Troup	14th " 15th	1816 " 1819	Elected in place of Bibb. Resigned 1819.
John Forsyth	15th	1819	Resigned 1819.
John Elliott	16th to 18th	1819 to 1824	
Freeman Walker	16th	1819 " 1821	Elected in place of Forsyth. Resigned 1821.
Nicholas Ware	17th to 18th	1821 " 1824	Died 1824.
Thomas W. Cobb	18th " 20th	1824 " 1828	Elected in place of Ware, 1824. Resigned 1828.
John McPherson Berrien	19th " 20th	1825 " 1829	Resigned 1829.
Oliver H. Prince	20th	1828	Elected in place of Cobb.
John Forsyth	21st to 23d	1829 to 1834	Elected in place of Berrien. Resigned 1834.
George M. Troup	21st " 22d	1829 " 1833	
Alfred Cuthbert	23d " 27th	1834 " 1843	Elected in place of Forsyth.
John P. King	23d " 24th	1833 " 1837	Resigned 1837.
Wilson Lumpkin	25th " 26th	1837 " 1841	Elected in place of King.
John McPherson Berrien	27th " 32d	1841 " 1852	Resigned 1852.
Walter T. Colquitt	28th " 30th	1843 " 1848	Resigned 1848.
Herschel V. Johnson	30th	1848	Appointed in place of Colquitt.
William C. Dawson	31st to 33d	1849 to 1855	
Robert M. Charlton	32d	1852	Appointed in place of Berrien.
Robert Toombs	33d to 36th	1853 to 1861	Expelled 14 Mch. 1861.
Alfred Iverson	34th " 36th	1855 " 1861	Withdrew from the Senate 28 Jan. 1861. UNITED STATES.
....	36th " 41st	1861 " 1871	No representation in the United States Senate.
Joshua Hill	41st " 42d	1871 " 1873	
H. V. M. Miller	41st	1871	
Thomas M. Norwood	42d to 43d	1871 to 1875	
John B. Gordon	43d " 46th	1873 " 1881	
Benjamin H. Hill	45th " 47th	1877 " 1882	Died 16 Aug. 1882.
Joseph E. Brown	47th " 51st	1881 " 1891	
Pope Barrow	47th	1882	Elected in place of Hill.
Alfred H. Colquit	48th to 53d	1883 to 1894	Died 26 Mch. 1894.
John B. Gordon	52d	1891	Term expires 1897.

Georgium sidus, the first name of the planet URANUS, discovered 13 Mch. 1781.

Gerberoi, an ancient town of Normandy, N. France. Here William the Conqueror was wounded in battle by his son Robert, who had joined the French king, Philip I., 1078.

germ theory of disease supposes "many diseases due to the presence and propagation in the animal system of minute organisms having no part in its normal economy."—*Maclagan*, 1876.

Doctrine of *contagium animatum* was held in the middle ages and put forth in the 16th century, but the organisms were first discovered in the 19th by profs. Lister, Tyndall, and others, 1875-78. At the British association, 14 Sept. 1870, prof. Huxley expressed his concurrence with the "germ theory." DUST AND DISEASE.

Dr. Koch identified the microscopical germs of cattle disease, of consumption, of cholera, and other diseases........1879 et seq.

Dr. E. Klein reported his investigations on the relation of bacteria to cholera........Feb. 1885

Numerous specimens of these germs were exhibited at the British Royal Institution in illustration of prof. Tyndall's discourse on "Living Contagia"........16 Jan. "

By excluding these germs from wounds, etc., sir Joseph Lister introduced antiseptic surgery........about 1870

"Louis Pasteur," by M. Radot, his son-in-law, gives an account of Pasteur's success in mitigating some diseases by inoculation. A translation by lady Claud Hamilton pub., Feb. 1885

M. Engelmann demonstrates the action of microbes in the development of vegetable cells from carbonic acid and moisture in the atmosphere........1889

Profs. Behring and Kissasato of Berlin announce their method of treating tetanus and diphtheria........Jan. 1891

Discovery of influenza bacillus by dr. Richard Pfeiffer announced (MEDICAL SCIENCE)........Jan. 1892

German confederation, North, established in room of the GERMANIC CONFEDERATION. Pop. 1867, estimated 29,906,092; merged in the German empire, 1 Jan. 1871.

King of Prussia invites the states of North Germany to form a new confederation........16 July, 1866

Treaty of alliance, offensive and defensive, between Prussia and Saxe-Weimar, Oldenburg, Brunswick, Saxe-Altenburg, Saxe-Coburg-Gotha, Anhalt, 2 Schwarzburgs, Waldeck, the younger Reuss, 2 Lippes, Lubeck, Bremen, and Hamburg; signed........18 Aug. "

Two Mecklenburgs........21 Aug. "

Hesse (for country north of the Main)........3 Sept. "

Elder Reuss........26 Sept. "

Saxe-Meiningen........8 Oct. "

Saxony........21 Oct. "

Meeting of North German parliament (295 deputies from the 22 states) at Berlin........24 Feb. 1867

German East Africa. The German sphere of influence in E. Africa, with an estimated area of 345,000 sq. miles, and an estimated pop. of 1,760,000, extends southward from the equator to about the 12° of latitude, and between the 30° and 40° of E. longitude, having a coast line east on the Indian ocean of about 400 miles. On its north-northeast lies British E. Africa, W. Congo State, S.W. British Central Africa, and S. Portuguese E. Africa. The following is a summary of the events of settlement, etc.:

Dr. Carl Peters goes to Africa as chief agent for the committee for German colonization and concludes treaties with 10 sultans; German flag hoisted......................Nov.-Dec. 1884
German E. African company, mainly founded by dr. Peters at Berlin, chartered..................................12 Feb. 1886
Settlements founded in the valley of Kingani......Mch.-Apr. "
Treaty with the sultan of Zanzibar comes into force...19 Aug. "
Dr. Peters, with a party of 23 engineers, medical men, etc., leaves Germany as the agent of the German Emin Pasha Relief Society..Apr. 1887
Germans attack Bogamoya and kill natives...........23 Sept. 1888
Collapse of the German settlement, attributed to the Arab slave-dealers; reported...............................Oct. "
E. African bill passed by the parliament, granting money for the defence of German interests and suppression of slave-trade...30 Jan. 1889
Germans defeat Arabs at Bogamoya...................6 Mch. "
Capt. (afterwards maj.) Wissmann appointed imperial commissioner in E. Africa, 21 Feb. (dissension with dr. Peters), 31 Mch. "
German flag hoisted at the consulate; capt. Wissman assumes command..5 Apr. "
Dr. Peters organizing his Emin Relief expedition; men and camels engaged.................................Mch.-Apr. "
Capt. Wissmann captures Pangani.....................8 July, "
Adm. Freemantle, of the British navy, seizes the steamship *Neera*, belonging to the Emin Relief expedition at Lamu, and takes it to Zanzibar, June; dr. Peters remonstrates, 29 June; after a trial the ship is released, the owners paying costs, 6 Aug.; dr. Peters directed by his committee to proceed no farther..31 Oct. "
Differences between the sultan of Zanzibar and the Germans respecting territory.........................about 8 Nov. "
Maj. Wissmann receives H. M. Stanley, Emin Pasha, and party at Bogamoya..5 Dec. "
After fights, Busbiri captured and hanged............16 Dec. "
Maj. Wissmann, after severe fighting, captures Bwana Heri's fortified position near Saadani........................5 Jan. 1890
Arab tribes come to Bogamoya and submit......about 18 Jan. "
Bwana Heri holds a considerable force against maj. Wissmann; reported..16 Feb. "
Emin Pasha enters the German service and proceeds with a military expedition to Victoria Nyanza............31 Mch. "
German parliament votes 4,850,000 marks to E. African service..24 June, "
Mahomed Bin Cassim and 3 companions were hanged at Bogamoya, after trial for murder of a German merchant about 8 years previously.....................................27 June, "
Anglo-German convention signed at Berlin by the emperor, 1 July, "
Maj. Wissmann ennobled and warmly received in Berlin and other places, June; unwell, enjoined absolute rest...14 July, "
Dr. Peters and party arrive at Zanzibar about 10 July; telegraphs to his company...............................18 July, "
[His treaty with the king of Uganda invalid; he is accused of living by raids on the natives.]
Advance of Emin Pasha; severe fighting with the Masai in Ugogo; reported...................................31 July, "
Dr. Carl Peters arrives in Berlin......................25 Aug. "
German E. African company cedes all its territorial rights to the imperial government; reported...................28 Oct. "
Emperor contributes 3000 marks towards the building of the steamer *Wissmann*, to be placed on lake Victoria Nyanza. about 5 Dec. "
Emin Pasha Relief committee dissolves itself..........15 Dec. "
Emin Pasha (refractory) recalled to the coast by maj. von Wissmann, imperial commissary; reported..........19 Dec. "
German imperial flag hoisted at Bogamoya, 1 Jan.; maj. von Wissmann established there.............................26 Jan. 1891
Baron von Soden appointed governor of German E. Africa, dr. Carl Peters his commissary, Feb., with a peaceful, progressive programme....................................Mch. "
Maj. von Wissmann severely punishes the Kishobo tribe for robbery; reported....................................6 Mch. "
Returns to Bogamoya, 15 Mch.; recalled for rest; reported, 14 Apr. "
Dr. Peters's "New Light on Dark Africa," pub........spring, "
German expeditionary colonial troops under lieut. von Zelewski attacked by the natives (about 3000) south of the Ruaha river; lieutenant and other officers killed; 10 Europeans and about 300 native members of the expedition massacred near the station Mpwapwa, Kondora; large capture of arms and ammunition...17 Aug. "
Capt. Ruediger appointed acting-governor of German E. Africa about 1 Oct. "
Movements of Emin Pasha about Albert Nyanza, repudiated by German government, July; resignation of maj. von Wissmann...Oct. "
Revolt of the Wadigoes against taxation; Germans under capt. Krenzler defeated 12 Dec.; defeated again..............19 Dec. "
Baron von Soden pursues a peaceful policy in opposition to maj. von Wissmann.................................Jan. 1892
He meets lieut. C. S. Smith and dr. Peters, joint commissioners for the delimitation of the territories at Wanga.....Feb. "
German parliament votes 2,500,000 marks for German interests in E. Africa and suppression of the slave-trade, 5 Mch. "
Dr. Kayser sent to E. Africa to examine the state of the colony..May, "

German language has 2 great branches: *Hochdeutsch* and *Plattdeutsch*, High and Low German. The former became the literary language, largely by its use in Luther's translation of the Bible and other works, 1522-34. There are many dialects; the satirical epic in Low-German, "Reineke Fuchs," appeared in 1498. REYNARD THE FOX.

German literature and authors. LITERATURE.

German West Africa. The German sphere of influence in W. Africa (aside from CAMEROONS) extends along the Atlantic coast about 950 miles from the Orange river on the south, to the Cunene river on the north, including the native province of Damaraland and Nemaqualand. The Portuguese territory of Angola bounds it on the north, while to the east lies British S. Africa, and on the south the British territory of Cape Colony. Total estimated area, 342,000 sq. miles, with a pop. of 250,000. An imperial commissioner exercises a nominal authority in the protectorate.

German government sends an exploring expedition into southwest African coast, Damaraland (visited by German missionaries since 1840); Mr. Luderitz acquires some lands at Angra Pequeña from the chiefs; dr. Nachtigall's official visit to this place in a German man-of-war failed; after this dr. Goering obtained a treaty ceding land from the chief Kamaherero, afterwards denied, having previously in 1885 transferred all his rights to Robert Lewis, a British subject, long known to the Damaras. Mr. Lewis's rights were set aside by the German Colonial company of S.W. Africa, and he and other English were expelled; claims of Messrs. Lewis, Ford, and Bam, set forth at Berlin by the British government.......1885-91
Germans disallow Mr. Lewis's claims; reported.........3 Apr. 1891

Germanic confederation, superseding the CONFEDERATION OF THE RHINE, was constituted 8 June, 1815; held its first diet at Frankfort-on-the-Main, 16 Nov. 1816, and its last, 24 Aug. 1866. GERMANY. It comprised:

1. Austria; 2. Prussia; 3. Bavaria; 4. Saxony; 5. Hanover; 6. Würtemberg.
7. Baden; 8, 9. Hesse (electorate and grand-duchy).
10. Denmark (for Holstein and Lauenburg).
11. Netherlands (for Luxemburg).
12. Saxe-Weimar, Saxe-Coburg, Saxe-Meiningen, and Saxe-Altenburg.
13. Brunswick and Nassau.
14. Mecklenburg-Schwerin and Mecklenburg-Strelitz.
15. Oldenburg, 3 Anhalts, and 2 Schwarzburgs.
16. Two Hohenzollerns, Liechtenstein, 2 Reuss, Schaumburg-Lippe, Lippe, and Waldeck.
17. Free cities: Lubeck, Frankfort-on-the-Main, Bremen, and Hamburg.

Diet calls a constituent assembly, 30 Mch., which met 18 May, 1848
Diet remits its functions to the archduke John, vicar of the empire (GERMANY)...............................12 July, "
Diet re-established, meets............................30 May, 1851
Emperor of Austria proposes reform of confederation, 17 Aug.; accepted by diet, 1 Sept.; rejected by Prussia.......22 Sept. 1863
Diet celebrates its 50th anniversary....................8 June, 1865
Majority of diet supports Austrian claims on Schleswig and Holstein; Prussia withdraws and dissolves the confederation; diet declares itself indissoluble, and protests..14 June, 1866
Diet removes to Augsburg during the war..............14 July, "
Confederation renounced by Austria at Nikolsburg....26 July, "
Diet holds its last sitting...............................24 Aug. "

Germantown, Pa., Battle of. After occupation of Philadelphia by British, Sept. 1777, Howe stationed his main forces at Germantown, while the continental army was at Skippock creek, about 20 miles from Philadelphia. Learning that Howe's force was weakened, Washington decided to attack, and moved on the night of 3 Oct. 1777, with Sullivan and Wayne and about 10,000 men. The battle was opened about 7 A.M., 4 Oct., by Sullivan near Germantown, and the British advance column was obliged to retire after a sharp engagement, but on the retreat 5 companies occupied Judge Chew's stone house and held the Americans in check. The attempt to dislodge the enemy caused delay and embarrassment. After 3 hours of severe fighting the Americans were obliged to retreat, with a loss of about 600. The British loss was [illegible] to be 800. Washington retired to his former camp [illegible] pursuit.

Germany (*Germania, Alemannia*), an empire of Europe, anciently divided into independent states. The Germans long resisted the Romans, and although that people conquered parts of the country, they were expelled before 300 A.D. In the 5th century the Huns and other eastern tribes overran most of Germany. In the latter part of the 8th century, Charlemagne subdued the Saxons and other tribes, and was crowned emperor at Rome, 25 Dec. 800. At the extinction of his family, 911, the empire became elective, and was held mostly by the Hapsburgs from 1437 till 1804. Germany was divided into circles, 1501–12. The CONFEDERATION OF THE RHINE was formed 12 July, 1806; GERMANIC CONFEDERATION, 8 June, 1815; NORTH GERMAN CONFEDERATION, 18 Aug. 1866; the treaty ratified 8 Sept. 1866. FRANCO-PRUSSIAN WAR, 1870–71. The re-established empire of Germany (1 Jan. 1871) founded upon treaties concluded between the North German confederation and (1) the grand-duchies of Baden and Hesse, 15 Nov. 1870; (2) the kingdom of Bavaria, 23 Nov. 1870; (3) the kingdom of Würtemberg, 25 Nov. 1870; ratified, 29 Jan. 1871. William I., king of Prussia, was proclaimed emperor at Versailles, 18 *Jan.* 1871. *Area*, 208,738 sq. miles. Pop. in 1871 (including Alsace-Lorraine, acquired 1870), 41,069,846; 1881, 45,194,172; *1890*, 49,416,476; *1900*, 56,367,178. The parliament is elected by manhood suffrage and ballot. ARMY.

B.C.

Teutones, with Cymry, defeat Romans in Illyria.............. 113

After varying success are defeated by Marius.............. 102

Drusus invaded Germany.............. 12–9

Battle of Teutoburg; Hermann, or Arminius, destroys Romans under Varus.............. A.D. 9

Hermann assassinated.............. 19

Franks invade Gaul.............. 238

Great irruption of Germanic tribes into *Gaul*..............*450 et seq.*

Charlemagne subdues and Christianizes the Saxons..............772–85

Crowned emperor of the West at Rome by the pope....25 Dec. 800

He adds a second head to the eagle, standard of the double empire of Rome and Germany.............. 802

Louis (*le Débonnaire*) separates Germany from France..............839–40

Germans under Arnulf take Rome.............. 896

German princes assert independence, and Conrad I. of Franconia reigns..............8 Nov. 911

[The electorate began about this time. ELECTORS.]

Reign of Henry I. (king), the *Fowler*; he vanquishes the Huns, Danes, Vandals, and Bohemians..............918–31

Otho I. crowned emperor by the pope.............. 962

Otho II. conquers Lorraine.............. 978

Henry III. conquers Bohemia.............. 1042

Contest between *Henry IV.* and *pope Gregory VII.* (Hildebrand).............. 1075

Henry's humiliation at CANOSSA.............. 1077

He takes Rome, 1084; Gregory dies in exile at Salerno.............. 1085

Disputes with pope on ecclesiastical investitures..............1073–1123

GUELPH and Ghibelline feuds begin.............. 1140

Conrad III. leads a crusade; baffled by Greek treachery.............. 1147

Frederick Barbarossa emperor, 1152; wars in Italy..............1154–77

He destroys Milan.............. 1162

Ruins Henry the Lion (BAVARIA).............. 1180

Is drowned during the crusade in Syria..............10 June, 1190

Teutonic order of knighthood.............. "

Hanseatic league established..............about 1245

Rudolph, count of Hapsburg, chosen by electors.............. 1273

Edict called the GOLDEN BULL, by Charles IV.............. 1356

Tyrol acquired.............. 1363

Sigismund, king of Bohemia, elected. He betrays John Huss and Jerome of Prague, who are burned alive (BOHEMIA)...1414–16

Sigismund deposed; Albert II., duke of Austria, succeeds.............. 1437

Pragmatic sanction settles the empire in house of Hapsburg.............. 1439

Peasants' wars..............1502, 1514, 1524

Era of Reformation (LUTHERANISM).............. 1517

Luther excommunicated by diet at Worms..............17 Apr. 1521

German Bible and liturgy published by Luther..............1522–46

War with pope—the Germans storm Rome.............. 1527

Diet at Spires; *Protestants* condemned..............13 Mch. 1529

Confession of Augsburg pub..............25 Jan. 1530

Protestant league of Smalcald..............31 Dec. 1531

ANABAPTISTS seize Münster, 24 June, 1535; defeated, and John of Leyden slain.............. 1536

Death of Luther..............18 Feb. 1546

War with Protestants..............26 June, "

Who are helped by Henry II. of France—Peace of Religion at Passau..............31 July, 1552

Abdication of Charles V. announced..............25 Oct. 1555

Hungary joined to empire.............. 1570

THIRTY YEARS' war begins between Evangelic union und elector-palatine, and Catholic league under duke of Bavaria. 1618

Battle of Prague, which ruined the elector-palatine.....8 Nov. 1620

Gustavus Adolphus of Sweden invades Germany..............June, 1630

Gustavus Adolphus, victor, killed at Lutzen..............16 [illegible] 1632

Treason of Wallenstein; he is assassinated..............25 Feb. 1634

End of Thirty Years' war; treaty of Westphalia, establishing religious toleration..............24 Oct. 1648

War with France.............. 1674

John Sobieski, king of Poland, after defeating the Turks obliges them to raise the siege of Vienna..............12 Sept. 1683

Peace of Ryswick (with France)..............20 Sept. 1697

Peace of Carlowitz (with the Turks)..............26 Jan. 1699

War with France, etc., 6 Oct. 1702; Marlborough's victory at Blenheim..............13 Aug. 1704

Peace of Utrecht..............11 Apr. 1713

PRAGMATIC SANCTION.............. 1722

Francis I., duke of Lorraine, marries the heiress of Austria, Maria Theresa (1736); she succeeds her father, and becomes queen of Hungary..............20 Oct. 1740

Elector of Bavaria elected as Charles VII..............22 Jan. 1742

Dies 20 Jan.; Francis I., duke of Lorraine, elected....13 Sept. 1745

Seven Years' war between Austria and Prussia and their allies begins Aug. 1756; ends with peace of Hubertsburg...15 *Feb.* 1763

Lorraine ceded to France.............. 1766

Joseph II. extends his realm by partition of Poland, 1772; civil reforms and liberal changes.............. 1782

War with Turkey.............. 1788

Victory of Austrians and Russians at Rimnik..............22 Sept. 1789

J. G. Basedow, educational reformer, d..............25 July, 1790

Rhenish *provinces revolt*.............. 1793

Francis I. joins in 2d partition of Poland.............. 1795

In wars with France loses Netherlands, all territories west of the Rhine, and states in Italy..............1793–1803

Territory ceded to France by treaty of Luneville..............9 Feb. 1801

Francis II. resigns the imperial crown of Germany (AUSTRIA), 11 Aug. 1804

Napoleon establishes kingdoms of Bavaria and Würtemberg, 1805; of Westphalia, 1807; German empire *dissolved, confederation* of Rhine formed..............12 July, 1806

North Germany annexed to France..............13 Dec. 1810–11

Commencement of war of independence; order of the Iron Cross instituted..............Mch. 1813

Defeat of French at Leipsic..............16–19 *Oct.* "

Congress of Vienna..............1 Nov. 1814 and 25 May, 1815

GERMANIC CONFEDERATION formed..............8 June, "

ZOLLVEREIN formed.............. 1818

"Society for Promoting Knowledge of Ancient German History" founded by Stein.............. 1819

A German scientific association formed, "Naturforscher-Verein"..............Sept. 1822

General depression in trade.............. 1824

Death of J. H. Voss, poet, etc..............29 Mch. 1826

Revolution at Brunswick (*flight of the duke*)..............7 Sept. 1830

In Saxony (abdication of the king)..............13 Sept. "

Death of Goethe, poet, novelist, philosopher..............22 Mch. 1832

Becker's song, the free German RHINE; and Alfred de Musset's song, "Le Rhin Allemand," appear.............. 1841

Excitement about Ronge, Catholic *reformer*, and the holy coat of Treves.............. 1844

Insurrection at Vienna and throughout Germany (AUSTRIA, HUNGARY, etc.).............. 1848

Revolt in Schleswig and Holstein (DENMARK)..............Mch. "

King of Prussia makes *proclamation as an agitator* for reconsolidation of the German empire..............27 Mch. "

National Assembly meets at Frankfort-on-the-Main....18 May, "

Archduke John of Austria elected vicar of the empire..12 July, "

National Assembly elects the king of Prussia emperor, 28 Mch.; he declines..............3 Apr. 1849

Recalls the Prussian members of assembly..............14 May, "

Frankfort assembly adjourns to Stuttgart..............30 May, "

Treaty of Vienna; Austria and Prussia agree to form a new central power for a limited time; appeal to be made to governments of Germany..............30 Sept. "

Austria protests against alliance of Prussia with smaller German states..............12 Nov. "

Treaty of Munich; Bavaria, Saxony, and Würtemberg to revise German Confederation..............27 Feb. 1850

Parliament at *Erfurt*..............Mch. "

King of Würtemberg denounces insidious ambition of king of Prussia..............15 Mch. "

German diet at Frankfort..............10 May, "

Hesse-Cassel not represented at Erfurt, 7 June; Hesse-Darmstadt withdraws *from* Prussian league..............20 June, "

Austria calls an assembly of German Confederation, 19 July; it meets at Frankfort..............2 Sept. "

Austrian, Bavarian, and Prussian forces enter HESSE-CASSEL, 12 Nov. "

Conferences at Dresden..............23 Dec. 1850, to 15 May, 1851

Max Schneckenburger, author of "Die Wacht am Rhein," d., "

Diet of Germanic Confederation renewed at Frankfort, 30 May, "

New liberal party meet in Eisenach, Saxe-Weimar, 17 July; *in* 7 resolutions recommend reform of federal constitution; diet replaced by a *strong* central government; a national assembly summoned; Prussia invited to take the initiative....14 Aug. 1859

Proposal not accepted by Prussia, opposed by Hanover....Sept. "

Dispute with Denmark on Holstein and Schleswig..............Nov. 1860

National association at Berlin recommends a federal government with central executive, under leadership of Prussia, 13 Mch. 1862

Meetings of plenipotentiaries from German states on federal reform..............*8 July–10 Aug.* "

Deputies from German states at Weimar declare that Germany *should form one* federal state..............28, 29 Sept. "

Deputies declare in favor of unity..............21 Aug. 1863

Emperor of Austria invites German sovereigns to congress at Frankfort, 31 July; king of Prussia declines, 4 Aug.; nearly all the sovereigns meet, 16, 17 Aug.; approve Austrian plan *of federal reform*, 1 Sept.; rejected by Prussia..............22 Sept. "

Diet determines on federal execution in Holstein if Denmark does not fulfil her obligations..............1 Oct. "

Fiftieth anniversary of the battle of *Leipsic celebrated*..18 Oct. "

 GER

German troops enter Holstein for "federal execution" (DENMARK)....23 Dec. 1863

Death of Maximilian II. of Bavaria....10 Mch. 1864

Prussia retains duchies; discussion between Austria and Prussia; diet adopts resolution of Bavaria and Saxony, requesting Austria and Prussia to give Holstein to duke of Augustenburg; rejected....6 Apr. 1865

Austria declares that Prussia has broken treaty by invading Holstein, 11 June; diet approves by 9 votes; Prussian representative declares Germanic Confederation at an end and proposes a new one, excluding Austria....14 June, 1866

Prussians enter Saxony; war begins....15 June, "

Diet determines for war, 16 June; proclaims prince Charles of Bavaria general of confederation....27 June, "

[For the war, etc., PRUSSIA; GERMAN CONFEDERATION, NORTH.]

Alliance of Prussia and northern states; ratified....8 Sept. "

Disputes between diet and Austria and Prussia on Schleswig-Holstein....Oct. and Nov. "

Luxemburg evacuated by Prussian garrison....9 Sept. 1867

Inauguration of Luther monument at Worms by king of Prussia....25 June, 1868

Count Arnim, German representative at Rome, protests against papal infallibility....May, 1870

Count Bismarck, announcing declaration of war by France, terms it groundless and presumptuous....19 July, "

Bavaria, Würtemberg, Hesse-Darmstadt, and Baden support Prussia in war....20 July, "

Munich, Stuttgart, and other cities declare for union with North Germany....about 6 Sept. "

Baden and Hesse-Darmstadt join North German confederation by treaty, about 15 Nov.; Bavaria, 23 Nov.; and Würtemberg, 25 Nov.; retaining certain military and diplomatic powers....Nov. "

King of Bavaria, in a letter to king of Saxony, nominates king of Prussia for emperor of Germany....about 4 Dec. "

Parliament in an address requests king to become emperor (votes for, 188; against, 6)....10 Dec. "

Address solemnly presented to king in an assembly of princes by dr. Simson....18 Dec. "

German empire restored, 1 Jan.; William I. of Prussia proclaimed emperor at Versailles....18 Jan. 1871

Preliminaries of peace signed at Versailles....26 Feb. "

First Reichstag, or imperial council, opened at Berlin by the emperor....21 Mch. "

New constitution of empire comes into force....4 May, "

Chancery of empire; prince Bismarck chancellor....12 May, "

Treaty of peace ratified....16 May, "

Dr. Döllinger of Munich excommunicated for opposing dogma of papal infallibility, 18 Apr.; made D.C.L. of Oxford..June, "

Ultramontane agitation against government; excitement among Polish Romanists; Bismarck carries school-inspection bill against Roman clergy....Mch. 1872

Bill for expulsion of Jesuits passed in Parliament (181–93) session ends 19 June; the law pub....5 July, "

Last payment of French war indemnity....5 Sept. 1873

Count Harry Arnim, formerly ambassador at Rome and Paris, arrested and imprisoned in Berlin, ostensibly for detaining official papers, 4 Oct., released on bail....28 Oct. 1874

Bismarck resigns after an adverse vote in the Parliament, 16 Dec.; on a vote of confidence (199–71) remains....18 Dec. "

Civil-marriage bill passed....25 Jan. 1875

Bismarck resigns again, 3 Apr.; withdrawn....8 Apr. 1877

Attempted assassination of emperor by Hödel, 11 May; stringent bill to repress socialism introduced and rejected (251–57), 24, 25 May, 1878

Emperor fired at and wounded by prof. Karl Eduard Nobiling, a socialist, at Berlin....2 June, "

Crown-prince charged with public affairs....4, 5 June, "

Emil Heinrich Max Hödel condemned....10 July, "

Hödel executed at Berlin....16 Aug. "

Dr. Nobiling dies of self-inflicted wounds....10 Sept. "

Bismarck's resignation tendered, not accepted by the emperor; the states yield....Apr. 1880

New army bill passed (186–96)....9 Apr. "

Imperial rescript against parliamentary government pub., 7 Jan. 1882

Death of prince Charles, emperor's brother....21 Jan. 1883

Germania, a colossal statue, etc., by prof. Schilling, a national memorial of German unity and victories of 1870–71, set up in Niederwald at Rudesheim on the Rhine, uncovered by emperor William in presence of German sovereigns and 5000 spectators; Von Moltke there, but not Bismarck. 28 Sept. "

Bismarck refuses to present to the chamber a letter of condolence from the U. S. Congress on the death of dr. Lasker, formerly his supporter, afterwards his opponent....Feb. 1884

German Parliament opened; disputes on Lasker affair, 6, 7 Mch. "

Mr. Sargent, obnoxious U. S. minister, appointed to St. Petersburg, 26 Mch.; declined....27 Mch. "

German colony founded at Cameroons, and Bimbia, west coast of Africa, by Herr Nachtigall....Aug. "

German flag said to be hoisted on north coast of New Guinea, New Britain, and other islands....Dec. "

German colonization society constituted at Frankfort, 6 Dec. 1882. By charter of the emperor, dr. Carl Peters and others authorized to acquire Usagara, N'Gury, and other territories west of Zanzibar....27 Feb. 1885

Prince Frederick Charles d....15 June, "

Leopold von Ranke, historian, d. (aged 90)....23 May, 1886

Foundation-stone of the opening lock of a canal from the Baltic to the North sea, 61 miles long, laid at Holtenau, near Kiel, by the emperor; estimated cost, 168,000,000 marks..3 June, 1887

Indisposition of the crown-prince. Winters in Italy and S. France, under the care of sir Morell Mackenzie, 1887; said *to have malignant growth of the larynx*; tracheotomy performed (the German doctors and Mackenzie differ)....Feb. 1888

Serious illness of the emperor; prince William (grandson) intrusted with official powers....8 Mch. "

Emperor d. (nearly 91 years old)....9 Mch. "

Emperor Frederick III. arrives at Berlin....11 Mch. "

Solemn national funeral of the deceased emperor....16 Mch. "

Rescript empowering the crown-prince William to act for the emperor in state affairs when required....21 Mch. "

Emperor Frederick III. d. (cancer of the larynx)....15 June, "

Emperor William II. opens Parliament....25 June, "

Sir Morell Mackenzie publishes "The Fatal Illness of Frederick the Noble." The German surgeons' report of the case differs....about 15 Nov. "

E. African bill, granting money to defend German interests and suppress slave-trade, adopted by federal council (AFRICA, ANGLO-FRENCH AGREEMENTS)....1 Feb. 1889

Three German war-vessels lost, 9 officers and 87 men drowned at SAMOA....16 Mch. "

Bismarck's bill to compel the working class, with the assistance of the state and their employers, to provide for sickness (passed 1883), for accidents (passed 1884), for old age and infirmity, passed....24 May, "

Emperor and empress present at the marriage of his sister to the duke of Sparta....27 Oct. "

Dr. Dollinger d. at Munich....10 Jan. 1890

Two rescripts of emperor for improving condition of the working classes, and suggesting co-operation of France, England, Belgium, and Switzerland....4 Feb. "

Delegates with ambassadors and ministers meet....15 Mch. "

[Delegates: Great Britain, sir John Gorst; France, Jules Simon; Italy, senator Boccardo, and others. The conference opened by the baron von Berlepsch, Prussian minister of commerce, elected president 15 Mch.; closed 29 Mch. 1890. Subjects discussed: regulation of labor in mines, of Sunday labor, and of the labor of children and youths. Recommendations adopted referred to the respective legislatures.]

Resignation of prince Bismarck, chancellor....18 Mch. "

He declines title of duke of Lauenburg....about 23 Mch. "

He is succeeded by gen. George von Caprivi de Caprera de Montecucculi....about 20 Mch. "

Count Herbert Bismarck, secretary for foreign affairs, resigns, succeeded by baron Marschall von Biederstein..about 1 Apr. "

New Parliament opened by the emperor; while desiring peace he asks 18,000,000 marks for army supplies....6 May, "

Vote of 4,500,000 marks, and an annual subsidy of 350,000 marks, for the suppression of slavery, and protection of German interests in E. Africa proposed by gen. von Caprivi....12 May "

First German national horse-show (at Berlin)..12 June, et seq. "

New army bill passed by the Parliament....28 June, "

Anglo-German convention respecting E. Africa signed at Berlin....1 July, "

HELIGOLAND formally transferred to Germany by England, 9 Aug. "

Sudden death of field-marshal von Moltke, aged 90, 24 Apr.; military funeral, attended by emperor, German sovereigns, state officers, ambassadors, etc., Berlin, 28 Apr.; quiet interment at Kreisau, in Silesia....29 Apr. 1891

Prince Bismarck elected deputy to Reichstag for Geestemünde, 1 May, "

Emperor's speech at Brandenburg censures political opponents as "grumblers"....24 Feb. et seq. 1892

Several newspapers at Berlin confiscated for reprinting the *Times* leader on the emperor's speech....3 Mch. "

Rioting at Berlin, Hanover, Dantzig, and other places, through distress....25 Feb. et seq. "

Ministerial crisis in Prussia....22 Mch. "

Government defeated in the Parliament; the vote for an imperial corvette negatived....29 Mch. "

Parliament prorogued....31 Mch. "

Cholera severe at Hamburg through Aug., Sept., and....Oct. "

Army bill rejected by a vote of 210–162. Reichstag immediately dissolved by the emperor....6 May, 1893

New German Reichstag opened by the emperor; his speech asks passage of army bill without delay....4 July, "

Army bill passed the Reichstag by 201–185; peace effective fixed at 479,220 men for 2 years....15 July, "

Russian duty on German imports raised 50 per cent.; German reprisals....2 Aug. *et seq.* "

Army banquet at Coblentz; speech by the emperor; crown-prince of Italy present....1 Sept. "

The army bill comes into force....1 Oct. "

[Two years' service substituted for three; the peace footing of the army is fixed at 479,229 men, from 1 Oct. to 31 Mch. 1899; being an increase of 70,000.]

50th anniversary of the doctorate of prof. Mommsen; celebrated....8 Nov. "

Anti-Jesuit law of 4 July, 1872; bill for its repeal introduced; passed (173–136)....1 Dec. "

Degony and Delguey-Malvas arrested as French spies at Kiel, 28 Aug.; *Degony sentenced to 6 years'*, *Delguey-Malvas to 4 years' imprisonment*....16 Dec. "

Reconciliation between the emperor and prince Bismarck, 26 Jan. 1894

Commercial treaty with Russia for 10 years; signed, 10 Feb.; comes into force....20 Mch. "

Two French officers (*see above*, Aug. 1893) released by the emperor....1 July, "

The emperor visits the queen at Osborne, etc 6-14 Aug 1891
Death of prof von Helmholtz (aged 73) 8 Sept "
Resignation of the chancellor, count von Caprivi 26 Oct "
Prince Clovis von Hohenlohe appointed chancellor of the empire and president of the Prussian ministry 29 Oct. "
The new parliament house opened by the emperor at Berlin, 5 Dec "
Imperial finance (reform) bill introduced 27 Jan 1895
The emperor presents to prince Bismarck a sword of honor for his 80th birthday 26 Mch "
Tobacco taxation bill rejected 13 May, "
The North sea and Baltic canal opened by emperor William II, 20 June, "
Prof von Gneist, jurist and statesman (b 13 Aug 1816), d 21 July, "
Christian Bernhard Tauchnitz, eminent publisher (b 25 Aug 1816) d 11 Aug "
The emperor intervenes in the Transvaal difficulty 2 Jan 1896
Celebration of the 25th anniversary of the foundation of the German empire 18 Jan "
Prof von Treitschke, historian and poet (b 15 Sept 1834), d 28 Apr "
The new civil code (to come into force 1 Jan 1900), passed, 1 July, "
Discussion in the reichsrath respecting the so called Bismarckian "revelations" on a Russo German treaty of William I and the triple alliance, affair closed 11-16 Nov "
New stock and produce regulations come into force, 1 Jan, much opposed, business transacted under the auspices of the new "free commercial union" 2 Jan 1897
New commercial code passed 7 Apr "
The *Kaiser Wilhelm der Grosse*, of the N German Lloyd steamship company, launched 4 May, "
Emergency bill, declaring that associations of every kind may enter into union, and repealing all provisions to the contrary in the laws of other states, passed in the reichstag (207-33), 20 May, "
Denunciation of the Anglo German treaty of commerce (30 May, 1865) by the British government 30 July, "
New coinage completed Dec. "
Bill for the reform of military judicial procedure, civil code and navy act, passed 28 Mch 1898
Kiao chau treaty with China, ratified, 6 Mch, prince Henry arrives there 1 June, "
Death of prince Bismarck (b 1 Apr 1815) 30 July, "
New German imperial 3 per cent loan and the new Prussian 3 per cent consols well taken up Feb. 1899
Gen count von Caprivi, chancellor 1890-94 (b 24 Feb 1831), d 6 Feb. "
Bill prolonging the most favored nation treatment to the commerce of the British empire (except Canada), and one ratifying treaty with Spain for the acquisition of the Caroline islands, passed, penal servitude (labor strikes) bill rejected by a large majority in the diet 21, 22 June, "
The Dortmund Ems canal opened 11 Aug "
Reichstag meets, 14 Nov, labor (penal servitude) bill again rejected 20 Nov "
Herzog and *Bundesrath*, German vessels, seized by English cruisers on suspicion of carrying contraband of war Dec "
Navy (increase) bill introduced 8 Feb 1900
Prince Henry of Prussia warmly received in Berlin after 2 years' naval duty in the far East 13 Feb "
Navy bill passed, 201-103, the Reichstag adjourns 12 June, "
North German Lloyd disaster 30 June, "
Tariff agreement between Germany and the U S 10 July, "
Prince Hohenlohe, imperial chancellor (aged 81), resigns, 16 Oct, succeeded by count von Bülow 18 Oct. "
The emperor declines to receive Mr Krüger, ex president of the Transvaal 1 Dec "
Count von Bülow announces German intervention in S Africa to be impossible 10 Dec. "
Field marshal count von Blumenthal d (aged 90) 21 Dec "
The emperor present at the queen's death, 22 Jan, made field marshal, the crown prince, K G, 27, 28 Jan, returns, about 7 Feb 1901
Death of prince Hohenlohe, ex chancellor (aged 82) 6 July, "
Death of the empress Frederick (the princess royal of Great Britain and Ireland), aged 60 ... 5 Aug "
Prince Chun, Chinese envoy, presents a letter to the emperor from the Chinese emperor, and expresses regret for the revolutionary events of 1900, and particularly for the death of baron von Ketteler 4 Sept. "
Celebrations in honor of prof Virchow's 80th birthday, 12 Oct. "
Dr Leyds, Transvaal envoy, arrives in Berlin 11 Nov "
Anti-British agitation, Mr Chamberlain's speech at Edinburgh denounced mid Nov "
Count Hatzfeldt, 16 years ambassador in London, d (aged 70), 22 Nov "
Prince Henry of Prussia visits America 23 Feb.-11 Mch 1902
King Albert of Saxony, eminent commander in the war of 1870, d (aged 74) .... 19 June, "
The triple alliance renewed 28 June, "
New articles of war promulgated by the emperor Sept "
Prof Rudolf Virchow, the great scientist and politician, d (aged 81) 5 Sept "
Congress on German colonial enterprise, Berlin 10 Oct. "
New rule of procedure in the Reichstag, vote by ballot instead of roll call, adopted 14 Nov "
Death of Friedrich Alfred Krupp (aged 48) 22 Nov "
Parliamentary crisis indignation at an attempt to pass the new tariff *en bloc*, sitting adjourns, 4 5 Dec, changes in the rule of procedure passed (206-92), 9 Dec, tariff bill read second time *en bloc* (183-136), 11 Dec, passed 14 Dec 1902
Herr Bebel, the social democratic leader, calls attention to duelling in the army and the ill treatment of soldiers by non commissioned officers 9 Mch 1903
General order on subject of the maltreatment of private soldiers by their superiors issued early Apr "
Trust of sugar refiners formed with reference to the situation created by the Brussels convention mid Aug "
Socialist congress opened at Dresden 13 Sept "
Army scandal 50 officers, 525 non commissioned officers, and 52 others convicted between 8 July, 1902, and 8 July, 1903, for ill treatment of soldiers, Breitenbach sentenced to 8 years imprisonment 20 Sept. "
Congress of non socialist democratic workmen at Frankfort, 25 Oct "
Death of prof Mommsen (aged 85) 1 Nov "
Lieut Bilse sentenced to 6 months' imprisonment for libelling officers in a novel 11 Nov "
General revolt of tribes in Great Namaqua land Dec "
The emperor pronounced recovered from his severe illness, 15 Dec "
Emperor congratulates the German legion "on having saved the British army from destruction at Waterloo" 19 Dec "
Herero rebels besiege Windhuck Jan 1904
Hereros driven back 28 Jan "
German steel trust organized 1 Mch "
Serious riots between German and Bohemian students at the university of Vienna 11 Mch "
30 Russian students at Berlin deported 16 Mch "
Hereros defeat the Germans at Owikokorero 19 Mch "
German troops defeat 3000 Hereros in S W Africa 11 Apr "
$500 000 appropriated for assistance of German settlers in S W Africa 22 Apr "
Franz von Lenbach, artist d at Munich 6 May, "
6000 soldiers sent to S W Africa. 14 May, "
Cable between Germany and America, completed 2 June, "
International women's congress meets at Berlin 13 June, "
Commercial treaty between Germany and Russia, signed, 28 July, "
Hereros broke through the surrounding German troops 12 Sept. "
Death of prince Herbert Bismarck 18 Sept "
Death of the king of Saxony 14 Oct "
Arbitration treaty between U S and Germany, signed at Washington 15 Nov "
Statue of Frederick the Great unveiled at Washington, 19 Nov "
Hottentots murder 50 German settlers 29 Nov "
First trackless trolley, speed 10 miles an hour, began running in Berlin 5 Dec "
Great coal strike, 300,000 miners affected, efforts of the emperor and the minister of commerce to mediate fail, Jan-Feb 1905
Adolf von Menzel, artist, d at Berlin (aged 90) 9 Feb "
The Evangelical cathedral is dedicated at Berlin 27 Feb "
Venezuela agrees to pay Germany and England $26,000,000 of their claims 21 Mch "
Count von Bülow declares that Germany stands firm for the "open door" in Morocco 29 Mch "
German emperor visits Tangier, makes a speech to the German merchants. 31 Mch "
France declares for the "open door" in Morocco despite the German emperor's speech 4 Apr "
Emperor William visits Corfu 11 Apr "
German ambassador to France and the French premier confer on the Moroccan question 15 Apr "
Germany demands exclusive mining rights in Shantung, China, 17 Apr "
Germany expresses willingness to negotiate with the U S for new reciprocity treaty (the existing agreement expiring 1 Mch 1906) 26 Apr "
Röntgen international congress meets at Berlin 3 May, "
Centennial of Schiller's death celebrated 7 May, "
The emperor sends the grand cross of the order of the red eagle to the sultan of Morocco 16 May, "
The sultan of Morocco refuses predominance to any nation, but invites a council of all the powers to suggest reforms, 5 June, "
Marriage of the crown prince to the duchess Cecilia of Mecklenburg Schwerin 7 June, "
Count von Bülow created a prince 7 June, "

KINGS AND EMPERORS OF GERMANY

CARLOVINGIAN RACE.

800 Charles I, the Great, or Charlemagne
814. Louis I, *le Debonnaire*, king of France
840 Lothaire I, or Lother, son of Louis, died in a monastery at Treves, Sept. 855
855. Louis II, son of Lothaire
875 Charles II, the Bald, king of France, d 877
881 Charles III, the Fat, crowned king of Italy, deposed, succeeded by
887 Arnulf, or Arnoul, crowned emperor of Rome, 896
899 Louis III, the Blind
" Louis IV, the Child, son of Arnulf, last of Carlovingian race in Germany

SAXON DYNASTY.

911. Otho, duke of Saxony, refuses because of age.
" Conrad I, duke of Franconia, king

918 Henry I, the Fowler son of Otho, duke of Saxony, king
936 Otho I, the Great, son of Henry, crowned by pope John XII, 2 Feb 962, beginning of holy Roman empire
973 Otho II, the Bloody, massacred his chief nobility at an entertainment 981, wounded by a poisoned arrow
983 Otho III, the Red his son a minor, poisoned
1002 Henry II, duke of Bavaria, surnamed the Holy and the Lame

HOUSE OF FRANCONIA

1024 Conrad II, surnamed the Salique
1039 Henry III the Black, son
1056 Henry IV, son, a minor, Agnes, regent, deposed by his son and successor, Rudolph (1077), Herman (1082) nominated by the pope, Conrad (1087)
1106. Henry V, married Maud, or Matilda daughter of Henry I of England
1125. Lothaire II, surnamed the Saxon

HOUSE OF HOHENSTAUFEN, OR OF SUABIA

1138. Conrad III, duke of Franconia
1152 Frederick I, Barbarossa, drowned, his horse throwing him into river Saleph, 10 June, 1190
1190 Henry VI, son, surnamed Asper or Sharp, detained Richard I of England a prisoner, d 1197
[Interregnum throne contested by Philip of Suabia and Otho of Brunswick]
1198 Philip brother to Henry, assassinated at Bamberg by Otto of Wittelsbach
1208 Otho IV, surnamed the Superb, excommunicated and deposed, d 1218
1215. Frederick II, king of Sicily, son of Henry VI, deposed by subjects who elected Henry, landgrave of Thuringia 1246, Frederick died 1250, naming his son Conrad his successor, but the pope appointed
1247 William, earl of Holland (nominal)
1250 Conrad IV, son of Frederick
[His son Conradin was proclaimed king of Sicily, which was however surrendered to his uncle Manfred, 1254, and at his death given by the pope to Charles of Anjou in 1266 Conradin, on invitation of the Ghibellines, entered Italy with a large army, was defeated at Tagliacozzo, 23 Aug 1268, and beheaded at Naples, 29 Oct, ending the Hohenstaufen family]
1256 [Interregnum]
1257 Richard, earl of Cornwall, and Alphonso of Castile merely nominated

HOUSES OF HAPSBURG, LUXEMBURG, BAVARIA, ETC

1273 Rudolph, count of Hapsburg.
1291 [Interregnum]
1292 Adolphus, count of Nassau to exclusion of Albert son of Rudolph, deposed, slain at Gelheim, 2 July, 1298, by
1298 Albert I, duke of Austria Rudolph s son, killed by his nephew at Rheinfels, 1 May, 1308
1308 Henry VII of Luxemburg
1313 [Interregnum]
1314 Louis IV of Bavaria and Frederick III of Austria, son of Albert rival emperors, Frederick d. 1330.
1330 Louis reigns alone
1347 Charles IV of Luxemburg (At Nuremberg, in 1356, the *Golden Bull* became the fundamental law of the empire)
1378 Wenceslas, king of Bohemia, son, twice imprisoned, forced to resign, but continued to reign in Bohemia
1400 Frederick III duke of Brunswick, assassinated as soon as elected, seldom in list of emperors.
" Rupert, count palatine of the Rhine, crowned at Cologne, d 1410
1410 Jossus, marquess of Moravia, chosen by a party of electors, died next year
" Sigismund, king of Hungary, elected by a party, on the death of Jossus recognized by all, king of Bohemia, 1419.

IMPERIAL HOUSE OF AUSTRIA

1438 Albert II, the Great, duke of Austria, and king of Hungary and Bohemia, d. 27 Oct. 1439
1439 [Interregnum]
1440 Frederick IV, surnamed the Pacific, elected emperor 2 Feb, not crowned until June, 1442.
1493. Maximilian I, son, d 1519 In 1477 he married Mary of Burgundy
Francis I of France and Charles I of Spain compete for the empire
1519 Charles V (I of Spain), son of Joan of Castile and Philip of Austria, elected, resigned both crowns, 1556, retired to a monastery, where he d. 21 Sept 1558
1556 Ferdinand I brother; succeeded by his son
1564. Maximilian II, king of Hungary and Bohemia.
1576. Rudolph II, son
1612 Matthias, brother
1619 Ferdinand II, cousin, king of Hungary
1637 Ferdinand III, son.
1658. Leopold I, son
1705 Joseph I, son
1711 Charles VI, brother
1740 Maria Theresa, daughter, queen of Hungary and Bohemia, sustained by England
1742 Charles VII, elector of Bavaria, rival emperor, supported by France, d Jan 1745.
[Hence a general war AUSTRIAN SUCCESSION]
1745. Francis I of Lorraine, grand duke of Tuscany, consort of Maria Theresa.
1765. Joseph II, son.
1790 Leopold II., brother
1792 Francis II, son, emperor of Austria only, as Francis I, 1804 AUSTRIA.

HOUSE OF HOHENZOLLERN (PRUSSIA)

1871 William I, king of Prussia, 18 Jan (b 22 Mch 1797, d 9 Mch 1888), empress, Augusta, b 30 Sept 1811, d 7 Jan 1890
1888 Frederick William b 18 Oct 1831 Married Victoria Adelaide Mary Louise, princess royal of England, 25 Jan 1858, d 15 June, 1888
" William II, eldest son of Frederick William, b. 27 Jan 1859 married princess Victoria of Schleswig Holstein Sonderburg Augustenburg (b 22 Oct 1858) 27 Feb 1881
Heir Frederick William Victor August Ernest, b 6 May, 1882. PRUSSIA

gerrymander, an unfair division of a community into representative districts in the interest of a political party The term originated in Massachusetts in 1812, when the Democratic-Republicans, to secure the United States senator, framed the senatorial districts so as to control most of them The apportionment was approved by Elbridge Gerry, then governor A district was formed which was thought to resemble on the map a salamander, but the Federalists called it "gerrymander," from the governor's name The word is now in common use

"Gesta Romanorum," a collection of popular tales from Oriental and classical sources, written in Latin by an unknown author, about 1350 A.D One of the first books printed in the 15th century These tales were largely used by early English poets and dramatists, including Shakespeare An English translation, by the rev C Swan (from an edition printed at Hagenau, 1508), appeared 1824

Gettysburg, Pa, Battle of, fought 1-3 July, 1863 After the confederate victory at Chancellorsville the South called on Lee to invade the northern states. As early as May Lee's movements foreshadowed such an invasion. Early in June his army concentrated at Culpeper, except A. P. Hill's division, which was at Fredericksburg At the middle of June the movement fairly commenced, with full 100,000 men. On 12 June, Hooker began to fall back from the Rappahannock to cover Washington Lee advanced, and on 15 June dispersed Milroy's force at Winchester (7000 strong), capturing 2300 prisoners. He then crossed the Potomac (24, 25 June), and advanced to Chambersburg Hooker also crossed on 26 June, and the next day was relieved by gen. Meade Lee, in the meantime, was pushing on into Pennsylvania. The federal army moved in a parallel direction east of the Blue Ridge Lee was in advance, and threatened Harrisburg. As in the former invasion (1862), the passes of South mountain afforded access to the confederate rear. Meade took advantage of them, and (28 June) Lee saw that he must halt and stake the campaign upon a battle The time and place of battle were not selected by either side, but determined by accident and the physical character of the country. Lee concentrated his army at Gettysburg, whither Ewell marched southwardly from Carlisle, and Longstreet and Hill eastwardly from Chambersburg Meade's right (30 June) was near Gettysburg, and gen Pleasanton, perceiving the importance of that place, advanced and occupied it—anticipating the confederates. On 1 July there was a collision, in which gen. Reynolds was killed, but, after losing 10,000 men, the federal forces still held a position which was the key of the field of operations. On 2 July (both armies being well up and in position) there was a second battle, with heavy loss on both sides. Sickles was driven from a position of no great importance. At night the Union forces still held Cemetery hill from Culp's hill to Round Top. On 3 July after a bombardment of Cemetery hill from Seminary ridge, Lee again assaulted. The assaulting column, under Pickett and Heth, numbered 18,000. It was almost annihilated After this decisive repulse Lee retreated (Sunday, 5 July) His army might have been utterly demoralized and dispersed by prompt and relentless pursuit. The forces were about equal at Gettysburg, each numbering from 70,000 to 80,000 infantry and artillery The federal loss was 23,190, of whom nearly 7000 were missing The confederate loss was about 36,000, of whom 13,733, wounded or unwounded, remained as prisoners. Lee's entire loss, from commencement to close of the invasion, was nearly 60,000 men —On 19 Nov. 1863, the battle-ground was consecrated as a national cemetery for soldiers who fell in the July battles. It was on this occasion that president Lincoln made the most famous of his speeches. CEMETERIES, UNITED STATES

Ghent (*gant*), Belgium, an ancient city built about the 7th century, during the middle ages became very rich John, 3d son of Edward III of England, is said to have been born here in 1340 (hence named John of Gaunt) during the revolt under Jacob van Artevelde, a brewer, whose son Philip revived the insurrection against Louis, count of Flanders, 1379-1382 Pop 1891, 153,740

Ghent rebelled against Philip of Burgundy 1451, against the emperor Charles V, 1539, severely punished 1540

"Pacification of Ghent" (when the north and south provinces of the Netherlands united against Spain) proclaimed 8 Nov 1576, broken up, 1579 The 300th anniversary celebrated 3-10 Sept 1876

Ghent taken by Louis XIV of France, 9 Mch 1678, and by the duke of Marlborough 1706

Ghent seized by French, 1793, annexed to Netherlands, 1814, made part of Belgium, 1830

Peace of Ghent, between Great Britain and U S, signed 24 Dec 1814

Ghibellines. GUELPHS

ghosts, produced by optical science Mr Dircks described his method at the British Association meeting in 1858 Dr John Taylor produced ghosts scientifically in Mch, and Mr Pepper exhibited the ghost illusion at the Royal Polytechnic Institution, London, July, 1863 COCK-LANE GHOST

giants are mentioned in Gen vi 4 Bones of reputed giants, 17, 18, 20, and 30 ft high, have been proved to be remains of animals.—The battle of Marignano (1515) has been termed "battle of the giants" DWARFS.

Og king of Bashan, of the remnant of the giants his bedstead was 9 cubits long (about 16½ ft) 1451 B C (Deut iii 11)

Goliath of Gath's "height was 6 cubits and a span" Killed by David about 1063 B C (1 Sam xvii 4)

Four giants, sons of Goliath, killed (2 Sam xxi 15-22) about 1018

Emperor Maximin (235 A D) was 8½ ft in height, and of great bulk Some say between 7 and 8 ft, others above 8.

"The tallest man that hath been seen in our age was one named Gabara, who in the days of Claudius, the late emperor, was brought out of Arabia He was 9 ft 9 in high"—*Pliny*

John Middleton (b 1578), commonly called the Child of Hale (Lancashire), whose hand from the carpus to the end of his middle finger, was 17 in long, his palm 8½ in broad, his whole height 9 ft 3 in.—*Plot*, "Nat Hist of Staffordshire" p 295

Patrick Cotter, Irish giant, b in 1761 was 8 ft 7 in in height, his hand to the extremity of the middle finger, measured 12 in, and his shoe was 17 in. long, d. Sept. 1806

Charles Byrne, called O'Brien, 8 ft 4 in high, d 1783, his skeleton is in the museum, Royal College of Surgeons England

Big Sam porter of prince of Wales at Carlton palace near 8 ft high, performed as a giant in "Cymon," at the Opera house, London, 1809

M Brice a native of the Vosges, 7 ft 6 in. high, exhibited himself in London, Sept. 1862 and Nov 1863

Robert Hales, the Norfolk giant, d at Great Yarmouth, 22 Nov 1863 (aged 43) He was 7 ft 6 in high, and weighed 452 lbs

Chang Woo Gow, a Chinese, aged 19, 7 ft 8 in high exhibited himself in London in Sept et seq, 1865 Grown to 8 ft, exhibited at Westminster aquarium, with him Brustav, a Norwegian, 7 ft 9 in, aged 35, 11 June, 1880

Capt. Martin Van Buren Bates, of Kentucky, and miss Ann Hanen Swann, of Nova Scotia, each about 7 ft. high, exhibited in London in May, married at St Martin's in the-Fields, 17 June, 1871

Marian, "the Amazon queen," 8 ft 2 in high, born in Thuringia, 21 Jan. 1866, exhibited in London, July, 1882

giaour (*jowr*), Turkish for infidel, an unbeliever in Mahometanism.—Byron's poem, "The Giaour," was pub in 1813

Gibral'tar. The ancient Calpe (with Abyla, on the opposite shore of Africa, called the Pillars of Hercules), a town and strongly fortified rock in S. Spain, at the entrance of the Mediterranean, belonging to Great Britain and considered impregnable. The height of the rock, according to Cuvier, is 1437 English ft. It was taken by the Saracens under Tarik, whence its present name (derived from *Gibel el-Tarik*), in 711. Area of town, $1\frac{9}{10}$ sq miles; pop. 1891, 25,755, including a garrison of 6737.

Taken from the Moors, 1309, surrendered to them 1333, taken from them by Henry IV of Castile, 1462, strengthened by Charles V . . . 1552

Attacked by British under sir George Rooke, the prince of Hesse Darmstadt, sir John Leake, and admiral Byng, 21 July, taken . . . 24 July, 1704

Besieged by Spanish and French, they lose 10,000 men, the victorious British but 400 . . . 11 Oct. "

Sir John Leake captured several ships, and raised the siege, 10 Mch. 1705

Ceded to England by treaty of Utrecht . . . 11 Apr 1713

Spaniards repulsed in an attack with great loss . . . 1720

They again attack with 20,000 men, and lose 5000, British loss, 300 . . . 22 Feb 1727

Siege by Spaniards and French, whose armaments (the greatest brought against a fortress) were overthrown 16 July 1779

In one night their floating batteries were destroyed with red hot balls, and their line of works by a sortie of gen Eliott, the enemy's loss in munitions of war was estimated at 2,000,000*l*, the army was 40 000 men 27 Nov 1781

Grand defeat by a garrison of only 7000 British 13 Sept 1782

[Duke of Crillon commanded 12 000 of the best troops of France 1000 pieces of artillery were brought against the fortress, besides 47 sail of the line, all 3 deckers, 10 great floating batteries esteemed invincible carrying 212 guns, innumerable frigates, xebecs, bomb-ketches, cutters and gun and mortar boats small craft for disembarking forces covered the bay For weeks 6000 shells were daily thrown into the town]

Blockade ceased 5 Feb 1783

Royal battery destroyed by fire Nov 1800

Engagement between French and English fleets in the bay, British ship *Hannibal*, 74 guns, lost 6 July, 1801

Royal Carlos and *St Hermenegildo*, Spanish ships each of 112 guns, blew up with crews, at night time, in the strait, all on board perished 12 July, "

Gil'bertines, an order of canons and nuns established at Sempringham, Lincolnshire, Engl, by Gilbert of that place, 1131-48 At the dissolution by Henry VIII there were 25 houses of the order in England and Wales

gilding on wood formed part of decorations of the Jewish tabernacle, 1490 B.C (Exod xxv 11), was practised at Rome about 145 B.C The capitol was the first building thus adorned —*Pliny* Of gold-leaf for gilding, the Romans made but 750 leaves, 4 fingers square, out of an ounce —*Pliny* Gilding with leaf gold on *bole ammoniac* was first introduced by Margaritone in 1273

gin, ardent spirit, made from bigg, a kind of barley, and from rye flavored with the essential oil of the juniper berry

gin (contracted from engine), a machine for separating cotton-wool from the seed COTTON-GIN

ginger, the root of the *Amomum zinziber*, a native of India and China, now cultivated in the West Indies

gingham (Jav. *ginggang*), a woven cotton fabric the yarn colored before weaving Its manufacture introduced into England from the East about the middle of the 18th century Largely used in the United States and the West Indies First manufactured in the U S at Clinton, Mass, by Erastus Bigelow, 1846

giraffe' or **camel'opard,** a quadruped of interior Africa, known to the ancients In 1827 one was brought to England first, as a present to George IV It died in 1829 On 25 May, 1835, 4 giraffes, obtained by M Thibaut, were introduced into the Zoological gardens, Regent's park, London, where a young one was born in 1839 The bones of the leg differ from those of other ruminants in being solid

Girard college. COLLEGES, EDUCATION

Girgen'ti. AGRIGENTUM

Giron'dists, a party during the French revolution, led by deputies from the Gironde They were ardent republicans, but after the cruelties of Aug and Sept 1792, failed to restrain the cruelties of Robespierre and the Mountain party, and the leaders, Brissot, Vergniaud, and others, were guillotined 31 Oct 1793 Lamartine's "Histoire des Girondins," pub 1847, hastened the revolution of 1848. FRENCH REVOLUTION

Girton college, Cambridge, Engl, for the higher education of women It began at Hitchin, 1869, removed here, and was opened Oct. 1873 Newnham college, Cambridge, in connection with it, was opened 18 Oct 1875

Miss Charlotte Angas Scott, aged about 22, attained the position of "wrangler" (for mathematics) Jan 1880

Miss A F Ramsay of this college, senior, and alone in first division of classical tripos at Cambridge 18 June, 1887

Gisors (*zhee-zor'*), France, Battle of, on 20 Sept or 10 Oct 1198, when Richard I of England defeated the French His parole for the day, "*Dieu et mon droit*" ("God and my right"), afterwards became the motto of the arms of England

gladiators were originally malefactors who fought for their lives, or captives who fought for freedom They were first exhibited at the funeral ceremonies of the Romans, 263 B.C., and afterwards at festivals, about 215 B.C Their revolt under Spartacus, 73 B.C, was quelled by Crassus, 71 When Dacia was reduced by Trajan, 10,000 gladiators fought at Rome in celebration of his triumph, for 123 days, 103 A D.—

Anthon These combats were suppressed in the East by Constantine the Great, 325, and in the West by Theodoric in 500 In these gladiatorial combats, the spectators decided the fate of the vanquished, and indicated their will by pointing the thumb at the desired victim (*pollice verso*), or by shutting it down upon the hand (*pollice presso*) as as sign of mercy

Gladstone's administrations, (1st) 9 Dec 1868-20 Feb 1874, (2d) 28 Apr 1880-9 June, 1885, (3d) 26 Feb 1886-20 July, 1886, (4th) 18 Aug 1892-4 March, 1894. ADMINISTRATIONS William Ewart Gladstone, born 29 Dec. 1809, master of the mint, Sept 1841, president of the board of trade, May, 1843-Feb 1845, secretary for colonies, Dec 1845-July, 1846, chancellor of the exchequer, Jan 1853-Feb 1855, June, 1859-June, 1866, lord high commissioner extraordinary to the Ionian isles, Nov 1858, M P for Newark 13 Dec 1832-46, for Oxford, 1847-65, for South Lancashire, 1865-68, for Greenwich, Nov 1868, announced the dissolution of Parliament, 23 Jan 1874, resigned, 17 Feb 1874, temporarily resigned leadership of liberal party, 13 Jan 1875, elected M P for Mid-Lothian (1579-1368), 5 Apr 1880, his ministry resigned on account of minority on the budget bill (264-252), 9 June, 1885, he declined an earldom, 16 June, 1885. Among measures carried by Gladstone ministries are The Irish Church Disestablishment act, the Irish Land act of 1870, the Education act, the Ballot act, the Irish Land Law act of 1881, the Employers' Liability act, the Agricultural Holdings act, the Burials act, the Ground Game act, the Franchise act He introduced his Irish bill, 8 Apr 1886, rejected (343-313), 7-8 June, minority in general election, resigned, 20 July, 1886, opposed the government crimes bill unsuccessfully, Feb-July, 1887, received silver trophy presented to him by Joseph Pulitzer of the New York *World*, the result of subscriptions, etc., 9 July, 1887 The term "grand old man" is said to have been first applied to Mr Gladstone by Henry Labouchere, M P, about Apr 1881, and soon generally adopted ENGLAND, 1893

Glas'gow, Lanarkshire, the largest city in Scotland, grew rapidly after the union in 1707, obtaining some of the American trade. Pop 1707 about 12,000, in 1861, 394,857, in 1871, 477,144, in 1891, with suburbs, 792,728

Cathedral or high church, dedicated to St Kentigern, or Mungo, began about 1181
Erected into a burgh 1190
Charter was obtained from James II 1451
University founded by bishop Turnbull about "
Made a royal burgh by James VI 1611

Glasites in Scotland and **Sandemanians** in England In 1727, John Glas, a minister of the church of Scotland, published "The Testimony of the King of Martyrs concerning his Kingdom (John xviii. 36)," opposing national churches, and describing the original constitution of the church, its doctrines, ordinances, officers, and discipline, as in the New Testament. Having been deposed in 1728, he and others formed several churches upon the primitive models A series of letters on Hervey's "Theron and Aspasio," published by Robert Sandeman, in 1755, gave rise to churches in London and other places in England, and also in North America. The meeting-house at Barnsbury, London, N., was erected in 1862

glass. The Egyptians are said to have been taught glass-making by Hermes The discovery of glass took place in Syria.—*Pliny* Glass-houses were erected in Tyre. Glass was used by Romans in the time of Tiberius, and the ruins of Pompeii show windows of glass used before 79

Glass is said to have been brought to England by Benedict Biscop, abbot of Wearmouth 676
Glass manufacture established in England at Crutched friars and in the Savoy —*Stow* 1557
Chemical discoveries have greatly improved the manufacture in this century Faraday published researches on the manufacture of glass for optical purposes 1830
Glass painting was known to the ancient Egyptians. It was revived about the 10th century, and is described in the treatise by the monk Theophilus, was practised at Marseilles in a beautiful style, about 1500, most perfect about 1530 Specimens of the 13th century exist in England, C Winston's work is the best on the subject, 1846, new edition 1867
"Marvels of Glass-making in All Ages," A. de Sanzay, Engl transl 1870
Glass plate, for coach windows, mirrors, etc., made at Lambeth by Venetian artists, under patronage of Villiers, duke of Buckingham . 1673
Manufacture was improved by French, who made large plates, and in Lancashire, when the British Plate glass company was established 1773
Manufacture of British sheet glass introduced by Messrs Chance of Birmingham about 1832
Tempered or toughened glass M De la Bastie's process (plunging heated glass into a hot bath of oleaginous or alkaline compounds) announced Apr 1875, largely manufactured in France, and sold cheap in London 1876
Oldest bottle glass manufactory in the U S established at Glassboro, N J 1775
Cut-glass manufactory established at White s Mill, Wayne county Pa 1852
Largest plate glass manufactory at New Albany Ind
Frederick Siemens described his process for producing strong homogeneous tempered glass at the British Society of Arts, 26 Feb 1885
Application of glass for rails proposed by H Lindsay Bucknall, and for railway sleepers proposed by F Siemens 1885-86
[This glass asserted to be much stronger than iron]

Glastonbury, a market-town of Somerset, Engl said to have been the residence of Joseph of Arimathea, and the site of the first Christian church in Britain, about 60

" From our old books I know
That Joseph came of old to Glastonbury

And there he built with wattles from the marsh
A little lonely church in days of yore."
—*Tennyson*, "The Holy Grail"

Traditional burial-place of king Arthur, about 544 A church was built here by Ina about 708 The town and abbey were burned, 1184, and an earthquake did great damage in 1275 Richard Whiting, the last abbot, who had 100 monks and 400 domestics was hanged on Tor hill in his pontificals for refusing the oath of supremacy to Henry VIII, 14 Nov 1539. The monastery was suppressed 1540

glee, a piece of unaccompanied vocal music, in at least 3 parts, first composed early in the 18th century. Eminent composers, Samuel Webbe (1740-1816), Stevens, Callcott, Horsley, Danby, Paxton, lord Mornington, Spofforth, etc MUSIC

Glencoe massacre of the Macdonalds, a Jacobite clan, of Scotland, for not surrendering before 1 Jan 1692, the time stated in king William's proclamation Sir John Dalrymple, master (afterwards earl) of Stair, their enemy, obtained a decree "to extirpate that set of thieves," which the king is said to have signed without perusing Every man under 70 was to be slain This mandate was treacherously executed by 120 soldiers of a Campbell regiment, hospitably received by the Highlanders, 13 Feb 1692 About 60 men were slain, and many women and children, turned out naked in a freezing night, perished This excited great indignation, and an inquiry was set on foot, May, 1695, but no capital punishment followed The account of this massacre, as given by Macaulay in his history, is highly colored.

Glendale, Battle of. PENINSULAR CAMPAIGN

globe or **earth.** The globular form of the earth, the 5 zones, some of the principal circles of the sphere, the opacity of the moon, and the true causes of lunar eclipses were taught, and an eclipse predicted, by Thales of Miletus, about 640 B.C Pythagoras argued, from the varying altitudes of the stars by change of place, that the earth must be round, that there might be antipodes on the opposite part of the globe, that Venus was the morning and evening star, that the universe consisted of 12 spheres—those of the earth, water, air, fire, the moon, the sun, Venus, Mercury, Mars, Jupiter, Saturn, and the stars—about 506 B.C—Aristarchus of Samos's theory that the earth turned on its own axis and revolved about the sun seemed to his contemporaries so absurd that the philosopher nearly lost his life, 280 B.C. It revolves around the sun at a speed of over 68,000 miles an hour, in 365 d 6 h 9 m 9 6 s; this is termed the sidereal year. The mean solar year is somewhat less, being 365 d 5 h. 48 m. 46 7 s It revolves on its axis once in 23 h 56 m 4 1 s. mean solar time, equivalent to 24 h. SIDEREAL TIME. Its axis, which is inclined 23° 27′ from a perpendicular to the ecliptic (so called because solar and lunar eclipses can only take place when the moon is very near this plane), continually points in the same direction, thus causing the change of seasons and difference in length of day and night. Eccentricity of its orbit around the sun, 0 01679 Greatest distance from the sun (aphelion, about 8 July), 94,450,000 miles, nearest (perihelion, about 31 Dec), 91,330,000 miles, mean distance, 92,890,000 miles ECLIPSE, EQUINOX, LATITUDE, LONGITUDE, PLANETS, STARS, SUN, YEAR, etc.

Copernicus explaining the movement of the earth and planets around the sun, laid the foundation of modern astronomy 1543
To determine the figure of the earth, degrees of latitude have frequently been measured by Bouguer and La Condamine in Peru and by Maupertuis and others in Lapland 1735
In France and Spain by Méchain, Delambre, Biot, and Arago between 1792 and 1821
In India by col (afterwards sir George) Everest, pub 1830
Measurements made on a meridian by astronomical observations at points connected by telegraph, at Calais, Me, and Nantucket Mass by the U S Coast Survey 1866–67

The following table, from "Guillemin's Astronomy," edited by J Norman Lockyer, and revised by Richard A Proctor, shows the length of arcs, measured in the northern hemisphere, at gradually increasing latitudes

Place	Mean lat of arc	Length of deg in ft
India	12° 32′ 20″	362,956
"	16° 8′ 21″	364,044
America	39° 12′ 0″	363,786
Italy	42° 59′ 0″	364,262
France	44° 51′ 2″	364,572
England	52° 2′ 19″	364,951
Denmark	54° 8′ 14″	365,087
Russia	56° 3′ 55″	365,291
Sweden	66° 20′ 10″	365,744

Equatorial diameter	41,848,380 feet	=7925 83+ miles
Polar "	41,708,710 "	=7899 40+ "
Difference	139,670 "	=26 43+ "

Recent geodesists show that the equatorial diameter from lon 14° 23′ east to 194° 23′ east of Greenwich is 2 miles longer than that at right angles to it —*Mem Roy Ast Soc* vol xxix 1860
Surface of the earth contains about 196,626,000 sq miles, of which over three quarters is water
Experiments by pendulums to demonstrate the earth's rotation by Foucault in 1851, and to determine its density by Maskelyne, Bailly, and others, and in 1826, 1828, and 1854 by Mr (afterwards sir) G B Airy the astronomer royal
Estimated density 5 6 times that of water, weight, 6,000,000,000,000 000,000 000 tons —*Proctor*, 1875
[This does not include the air, which weighs 5,178,000,000,000 000 tons]
Artificial globes It is said that a celestial globe was brought to Greece from Egypt, 368 B.C , and that Archimedes constructed a planetarium about 212 B.C
Earliest preserved globe, in the Bibliothèque Nationale de Paris, is of copper engraved in Arabic Cufic characters of the 11th century
Earliest post Columbian globe extant is in the Lenox library of New York city, supposed 1506–7
[Copper, 4½ inches in diameter and engraved]
That of Johann Schöner of Bamberg showing North and South America as large islands (now at Nuremberg) 1520
Illustrious Gerard Mercator constructed and published a terrestrial globe at Louvain in 1541, and a celestial globe 1551
[These were the most celebrated globes of the 16th century Of many published, only 2 sets are now known, one in the royal library at Brussels, one at Vienna]
Globe of Euphrosynus Ulpius 1542
[Made in Rome and preserved in the museum of the New York Historical Society]
Mollineux, globes of 1592
[Only 1 extant in the library of the Middle Temple, London]
Globe of Gottorp, a concave sphere, 11 feet in diameter containing a table and seats for 12 persons, the inner surface representing the visible heavens, the stars and constellations, all distinguished according to magnitude and, turned by curious mechanism, their true position, rising and setting, are shown The outside is a terrestrial globe The original globe of Gottorp, at the expense of Frederick II , duke of Holstein, was erected at Gottorp, under the direction of Adam Olearius, after a design found among the papers of Tycho Brahe Frederick IV of Denmark presented it to Peter the Great in 1713 It was nearly destroyed by fire in 1757, but was reconstructed —*Coxe*
Globe at Pembroke hall, Cambridge, Engl., erected by dr Long (master, 1733), 18 feet in diameter
In 1851, Mr Abrahams erected in Leicester square London, for Mr Wyld, a globe 60 feet 4 inches in diameter, lighted from the centre by day, and by gas at night It was closed in July, 1861, the models were sold, and the building taken down

Globe theatre, Bankside, London THEATRES

glory, the nimbus drawn by painters round the heads of saints, angels, and holy men, and the circle of rays on images, adopted from the Cæsars and their flatterers, were used in the first century.—The doxology, "*Gloria Patri*," is very ancient, and originally without the clause "as it was in the beginning," etc In the Greek it began with *Δοξα*, glory.

Gloucester (*glos'ter*), the capital city, on the river Severn, of Gloucestershire, England Known to the Britons as *Caer-Glou*, to the Romans as *Glevum*, to the Saxons as *Gleaun-Ceastre*, whence its modern name Its abbey, founded by king Wulfhere in the 7th century, has been burned and rebuilt several times. In the 16th century it was converted into a cathedral, and of its kind is one of the finest in England, it being 440 ft long, 154 ft wide, and 85½ ft high, with tower and pinnacles 280 ft Here are the tombs of Robert, son of William I , and of Edward II Here Henry III was crowned, 1216 The city received its first charter from Richard III

gluci'num (from γλυκυς, sweet) In 1798 Vauquelin discovered the earth glucina (so termed from the sweet taste of its salts) It is found in the beryl and other crystals From glucina Wohler and Bussy obtained the rare metal glucinum in 1828 —*Gmelin*

glucose. SUGAR

gluten, an ingredient of grain, particularly wheat, termed the vegeto-animal principle (containing nitrogen) Its discovery is attributed to Beccaria in the 18th century

glyc'erine, discovered by Scheele about 1779, and termed by him the "sweet principle of fats," and further studied by Chevreul, termed the "father of the fatty acids" It is obtained pure by saponifying olive-oil or animal fat with oxide of lead or litharge Glycerine is now much employed in medicine and the arts

glyox'yline (invented by F A Abel, the chemist of the British war department, in 1867), an explosive mixture of gun-cotton, pulp, and saltpetre saturated with nitro-glycerine. It was abandoned for compressed gun-cotton

Gnostics (*nos-tiks*) (from the Gr γνῶσις, knowledge), a sect who, soon after the preaching of Christianity, endeavored to combine its principles with the Greek philosophy Among their teachers were Saturnius, 111, Basilides, 134, and Valentine, 140 Priscillian, a Spaniard, was burned at Treves as a heretic, in 384, for endeavoring to revive Gnosticism

Goa, a maritime city of S W Hindostan, was taken by the Portuguese under Albuquerque in 1510, and made their Indian capital Area of the colonial possessions, 1447 sq miles Pop 1881, 415,450

Gobelin (*gobe-lan'*) **tapestry,** so called from a house in Paris, formerly possessed by wool dyers, whereof the chief (Jehan Gobelin), in the reign of Francis I , is said to have found the secret of dyeing scarlet This house was purchased by Louis XIV about 1662 for a manufactory of works for adorning palaces (under the direction of Colbert), especially tapestry, designs for which were drawn by Le Brun, about 1666

"God save the king." This melody is said to have been composed by John Bull, mus doc in 1606, for a dinner given to James I at Merchant Taylors' hall, others ascribe it to Henry Carey, author of "Sally in our alley," who died 4 Oct 1743 It was much sung 1745–46 It has been claimed by the French The controversy is summed up in Chappell's "Popular Music of the Olden Times" (1859) The melody has been adopted for the German national anthem ("Heil dir im Siegerkranz"), and also adapted to the Danish

godfathers and **godmothers,** or **sponsors.** The Jews are said to have had them at circumcision, but they are not mentioned in Scripture Tradition says sponsors were first appointed by Hyginus, a Roman bishop, about 154, during a persecution In Roman Catholic countries bells have godfathers and godmothers at their baptism

gods, Greek and Roman MYTHOLOGY.

Godwin sands, sand-banks off the east coast of Kent, on land which belonged to Godwin earl of Kent, the father of Harold II This ground was afterwards given to the monastery of St Augustin at Canterbury , but the abbot neglecting to repair the wall that defended it from the sea the tract was submerged about 1100, leaving the sands, upon which many ships have been wrecked —*Salmon*

"If a skipper stands out by sen' George s channel, making for the Downs, what s right ahead of him? The Goodwins. He isn't forced to run upon the Goodwins, but he may "—*Dickens*, "Dombey and Son "

Godwin's oath. "Take care you are not swearing Godwin's oath " This caution, to a person taking a voluntary and intemperate oath, or making violent protestations, refers to a monkish tradition that Godwin, earl of Kent, tried for the murder of prince Alfred, brother of Edward the Confessor, and pardoned, died at the king's table while protesting with oaths his innocence 1053 , supposed to have been choked with a piece of bread, as a judgment from heaven, having prayed it might stick in his throat if he were guilty of the murder

gold (mentioned Gen ii 11), the most ductile of metals, considered by all nations the most valuable It is too soft to be used pure, and to harden it it is alloyed with copper or silver English coin consists of 22 carats of pure gold and 2 of copper

Value of gold compared with silver is said to have been in the time of Herodotus, 450 B C, about 10 to 1, of Plato, 38 B C, 12 to 1, 1876 A D, more than 15 to 1

The ratio in the U S. in 1862 was 15 35, in 1872, 15 63, in 1882, 18 19, in 1889, 22 03, in 1891, 20 92

Amalgamation of gold is described by Vitruvius (about 27 B C) and Pliny (about 77 A D) The alchemist Basil Valentine (in the 15th century) knew the solution of chloride of gold and fulminating gold Andreas Cassius, in 1685, described the preparation of gold purple, then adapted by Kunkel to make red glass, and to other purposes —*Gmelin* The chemical properties of gold have been investigated by eminent chemists, such as Berzelius and Faraday

Gold mines —Gold was found most abundantly in Africa, Japan and in South America, where it was discovered by the Spaniards in 1492 From that time to 1731 they imported into Europe 6 000 000 000 pieces of eight, in registered gold and silver, exclusive of what were unregistered

Peter the Great reopened ancient gold mines in Russia, 1699

Ural or Oural mountains of Russia long produced much gold

A piece of gold weighing 90 marks, equal to 60 lbs. troy (the mark being 8 ounces) was found near La Paz a town of Peru, 1730

Gold discovered in Malacca in 1731, in New Andalusia in 1785, in Ceylon, 1800, 2887 ounces of gold value 9991*l*, obtained from mines in Britain and Ireland in 1864, it has been found in Cornwall, Engl and in the county of Wicklow, in Ireland

Gold discovered in California, 19 Jan 1848, on col Sutter's place, by James Wilson Marshal

First deposit of gold from California weighing 1804 59 ounces, valued at $18 055 per ounce, made at U S mint 8 Dec 1848

Gold discovery in Australia —Edward Hargraves went to California in search of gold, and observed there rocks and strata resembling those of his own district of Conobolas 30 miles west of Bathurst New South Wales On his return home, he examined the soil and after 1 or 2 months' digging, found gold, 12 Feb 1851 He obtained a reward from the colonial government, and was made commissioner of crown lands. The excitement spread through New South Wales, Victoria, and other places, and in the first week of July 1851, a native, formerly attached to the Wellington mission then in the service of dr Kerr, of Wallawa, discovered, while tending sheep, a mass of gold in a heap of quartz 3 blocks of quartz (from 2 to 3 cwt), found in the Murroo creek 50 miles to the north of Bathurst, contained 112 lbs of pure gold valued at 4000*l* The "Victoria nugget," a magnificent mass of virgin gold weighing 340 oz, was taken to England from the Bendigo diggings, and a piece of pure gold of 106 lbs. weight was also found From the gold fields of mount Alexander and Ballarat, in the district of Victoria, up to Oct 1852, there were taken 2,532,422 oz, or 105 tons 10 cwt. of gold, and gold was exported worth 8 863 477*l*. In Nov 1856, the *James Baines* and *Lightning* brought gold from Melbourne valued at 1,200,000*l*. The "Welcome nugget" weighed 2019¾ oz, value, 8376*l* 10*s* 3*d*, found at Baker's hill, Ballarat, 11 June, 1858. Between May, 1851, and May 1861 96,000,000*l* of gold were taken to England from New South Wales and Victoria

Amount of gold produced in the U S. since its discovery in California in 1848, to 1890, $1,837,170 000 The greatest amount in any one year 1853, $65,000,000, the least amount, 1883, $30,000,000 Gold production of the world in 400 years, $7,240,000,000 Gold production of the world for 1890, $116,008,900. COIN AND COINAGE SILVER

Gold wire was first made in Italy about 1350 An ounce of gold is sufficient to gild a silver wire above 1300 miles in length, and such is its tenacity that a wire the one eighteenth part of an inch will bear the weight of 500 pounds without breaking —*Fourcroy*

Gold leaf —A single grain of gold may be extended into a leaf of 56 sq inches, and gold leaf can be reduced to the 300,000th part of an inch, and gilding to the 10,000,000th part.—*Kelly's Cambist* GILDING

Gold Coast, a British colony in W Africa, settlements made by the Dutch, transferred to Great Britain by treaty, signed 2 Feb 1872, joined with Lagos to form the "Gold Coast Colony" Area, 46,600 sq miles, pop estimated, 1,905,000, of whom about 150 are Europeans

Golden Bull, or *Bulla Aurea*, of emperor Charles IV of Germany, one of the most peculiar public documents of the middle ages After a prayer for divine assistance, etc., and the questioning of Satan, the emperor proceeds as follows "Inasmuch as we, through the office by which we possess the imperial dignity, are doubly—both as emperor and by the electoral right which we enjoy—bound to put an end to future danger of discords among the electors themselves, to which number we, as king of Bohemia, are known to belong we have promulgated, decreed, and recommended for ratification the subjoined laws for the purpose of cherishing unity among the electors and of bringing about a unanimous election, and of closing all approach to the aforesaid detestable discord and to various dangers which arise from it This we have done in our solemn court at Nuremberg, in session with all the electoral princes, ecclesiastical and secular, and amid a numerous multitude of other princes, counts, barons, magnates, nobles, and citizens, after mature deliberation and fulness of our imperial power, sitting on the throne of our imperial majesty, adorned with the imperial bands, insignia, and diadem, in the year of our Lord 1356, in the 9th Indiction, on the 4th day before the ides of January, in the 10th year of our reign as king—the 1st as emperor"

The following is a list of the subjects for which specific directions or laws are given

1 The proper escort of electors and by whom furnished
2 Of electing the king of the Romans.
3 Of seating the bishops of Treves, Cologne, and Mainz
4 Of the princes' elections in common
5 Of the rights of the count palatine and the duke of Saxony
6 Of comparison of prince electors with ordinary princes
7 Of the successors of the princes.
8 Of the immunity of the king of Bohemia and his subjects.
9 Of mines of gold, silver, and other specie
10 Of money
11 Of the immunity of prince electors.
12 Of the coming together of the princes
13 Of revoking privileges
14 Of those from whom, as unworthy, their feudal possessions are taken
15 Of conspiracies
16. Of "Pfalzburgers" (citizens of one place who reside in another)
17 Of challenges of defiance
18 Of letters of intimidation
19 Formula of representation sent by a prince elector with an envoy or proxy
20 Of the unity of the electorial principalities and of the rights connected with them
21 Of the order of marching as regards the archbishops
22. Of the order of proceeding of the prince electors and by whom the insignia shall be carried
23 Of the benediction of the archbishop in the presence of the emperor
24 Of conspiracies.
25. Of the succession of the different kingdoms and provinces.
26 Of the order of procession
27 Of the offices of the prince electors in the solemn courts of the emperor or king of the Romans.
28 Of the arrangement of the imperial table
29 Of election, coronation, and first imperial court when held
30 Of the rights of the officials when princes receive their fiefs from the emperor or king of the Romans
31. Of the necessity of teaching the Italian and Slavic tongues.

golden fleece. According to the Greek legend, Phrixus and Helle were children of Athamas, king of ORCHOMENUS Through the designs of their step-mother, Ino, Phrixus was about to be sacrificed to Zeus, when Hermes sent a golden-fleeced ram which carried the children in safety over land and water as far as the sea between Sigæum and the Chersonese, when Helle fell and was drowned in its waters, whence named Hellespontus (*Helle's sea*) Phrixus went on to Colchis, to king Æetes, who received him kindly. Phrixus here sacrificed the ram to Zeus, and its golden fleece was hung in a grove sacred to Ares To bring back the golden fleece to Greece was the object of the ARGONAUTS.—Philip the Good, duke of Burgundy, at his marriage in 1429, instituted the military order of *Toison d'or*, or "golden fleece," on account it is said, of his profit from wool The number of knights was 31. The king of Spain, as duke of Burgundy, became grandmaster of the order The knights wore a scarlet cloak lined with ermine, a collar opened, and the duke's cipher, a B, to signify Burgundy, together with flints striking fire, and the motto, "*Ante ferit, quam flamma micat.*" On the collar hung a golden fleece, with this device, "*Pretium non vile laborum.*" The order afterwards became common to all princes of the house of Austria, as descendants of Mary, daughter of Charles the Bold, last duke of Burgundy, who married Maximilian of Austria in 1477. It now belongs to both Austria and Spain, by treaty made 30 Apr. 1725

Golden Horde, a name of Mongolian Tartars, who established an empire in Kaptchak (or Kibzak), now S E Russia, about 1224, under Batou, grandson of Genghis Khan. Invading Russia, they made Alexander Newski grand-duke, 1252 At the battle of Bielawisch, in 1481, they were crushed by Ivan III and the Nogai Tartars.

"Golden Legend" ("Legenda Aurea"). The lives of our Lord and the saints, written by Giacomo Varaggio, or

Jacobus de Voragine, a Dominican monk, about 1260, first printed 1470, a translation printed by Caxton, 1483 Longfellow's "Golden Legend," a lyric drama based upon a story of self-sacrifice, appeared in 1851

golden number, the number that shows the year of the moon's cycle of 19 years, its discovery is ascribed to Meton of Athens, about 432 B C—*Pliny* To find the golden number or year of the lunar cycle, add one to the date and divide by 19, the quotient is the number of cycles since Christ, and the remainder the golden number This is now the 99th cycle, and the golden number for 1892 is 12, 1893, 13, 1894, 14, 1895, 15

gold-fish (the golden carp, *Cyprinus auratus*), taken to England from China in 1691, but not common till about 1728

golf, the national game of Scotland, has spread to England, Europe, India, America, and Cape of Good Hope It is played with rubber balls and a golf club, along a series of links or downs, in which are small round holes at intervals of 100 to 400 yards With other games it was prohibited by the king in 1457 The royal golf club of St Andrews is now the national club of Scotland

Gutta percha balls substituted for those made of leather and stuffed with feathers 1848
Allan Robertson the greatest golfer that ever lived d 1859

gonfalonier (*gon'-fal-o-neer'*) or **standard-bearer of justice,** originally a subordinate officer in Florence, instituted 1292, became paramount in the 15th century, and was suppressed 27 Apr 1532, when the constitution was changed and Alexander de' Medici made duke

Good Friday (probably God's Friday), the Friday before Easter day, a solemn fast of the church in remembrance of the crucifixion of Christ on Friday, 3 Apr 33, or 15 Apr 29 Its appellation of *good* appears to be peculiar to the church of England the Saxons denominated it *Long Friday*, from the long offices and fastings enjoined on this day. For its date, EASTER

Good Templars (order originated in the United States in 1851) pledge themselves not to make, buy, sell, furnish, or cause to be furnished, intoxicating liquors to others as a beverage The first English lodge was formed at Birmingham in May, 1868 In 1891 there were 100 grand lodges in the world, and the membership was 410,996, with a juvenile branch of 159,106 members.

Goorkhas (*goor'kas*), a warlike tribe of Nepaul, India, became prominent in the 17th century Their invasions were defeated about 1791 by Chinese, whose vassals they became In a war with British in 1814 they were at first successful, but were subdued, and a treaty of peace was signed in Feb 1816 Since 1841 the native regiments have been largely recruited by Goorkhas, who have rendered valuable service in nearly all British-Indian wars, and in Afghanistan, 1878-79

Gordian knot, said to have been made of thongs used as harness to the wagon of Gordius, a husbandman, afterwards king of Phrygia. Whosoever loosed this knot the ends of which were not discoverable, the oracle declared should be ruler of Persia Alexander the Great cut away the knot with his sword until he found the ends of it, and thus, in a military sense at least, interpreted the oracle, 330 B.C.

Gordon's "No Popery" riots, London, occasioned by the zeal of lord George Gordon, 2-9 June, 1780

On 4 Jan 1780, he tendered the petition of the Protestant association to lord North
On Friday, 2 June, he headed the mob of 40,000 persons who assembled in St. George's fields, under the name of the Protestant association, to carry a petition to Parliament for repeal of an act which granted indulgences to the Roman Catholics The mob proceeded to pillage, burn, and pull down the chapels and houses of the Roman Catholics first, but afterwards of others, for nearly 6 days The bank was attempted jails opened (the King's Bench, Newgate, Fleet, and Bridewell prisons) On the 7th, 36 fires were blazing at once By the aid of armed associations of citizens, the horse and foot guards, and militia of several counties, embodied and marched to London, the riot was quelled on the 8th
Two hundred and ten rioters were killed and 248 wounded, of whom 75 died in hospitals, and many were convicted and executed
Loss of property was estimated at 180,000*l*.
Lord George was tried for high treason and acquitted, 5 Feb 1781 He died a prisoner for libel, 1 Nov 1793.
Dickens gives a vivid description of these riots in "Barnaby Rudge"

gorget (*gor'-jet*), the ancient breastplate was very large, varying in size and weight The present diminutive breastplate came into use about 1660 ARMOR

gorilla, a powerful ape of W Africa, about 5 ft 7 in high It is a match for the lion, and attacks the elephant with a club Perhaps identical with the hairy people *Gorillai*, mentioned by the Carthaginian navigator Hanno, in his "Periplus," about 570 B C EXPEDITIONS In 1847 a sketch of a gorilla's cranium was sent to prof Owen by dr Savage, then at the Gaboon river, and preserved specimens have been brought to Europe, a living one died on its voyage to France In 1851 prof Owen described specimens to the Zoological Society, in 1859 he gave an account of the species at the Royal Institution London, and in 1861 several skins and skulls were there exhibited by M du Chaillu, who killed 21 of them while in central Africa A young one brought to New York in 1890 The gorilla was not known to Cuvier

Gospellers, a name given to the followers of Wickliffe, who attacked popery about 1377 Wickliffe opposed the pope's supremacy, temporal jurisdiction of bishops, etc, and is called father of the Reformation

Gospels (Sax *god-spell*, good story) Matthew's and Mark's are conjectured to have been written between 38 and 65 A D, Luke's, 55 or 65, John's, about 97 Irenæus in the 2d century refers to each gospel by name Dr Robert Bray was one of the authors of the Society for the Propagation of the Gospel in Foreign Countries, incorporated in 1701 A body termed "Bray's Associates" still exists, meant to aid in forming and supporting clerical parochial libraries

Gotha (*go'-ta*), capital of the duchy of Saxe-Coburg-Gotha Here is published the celebrated *Almanach de Gotha*, which first appeared in 1764, in German, and which is the best and most complete account of the descent and kindred of all the royal families of the world

Gothenburg system, in Sweden A plan first devised and executed by the municipal government of this city for the regulation of the liquor traffic It begins by limiting licenses closely, with the view of ultimately vesting a monopoly of the sale in the municipality itself, and excluding from the trade all who derive a profit from it It was advocated in England by Mr Chamberlain, M P, and much discussed, 1876-77

Gothic architecture arose about the 9th century A D, and spread over Europe Its characteristic is the pointed arch, hence it has been called the *pointed style* "Gothic" was originally a term of reproach given it by Renaissance architects of the 16th century Its invention has been claimed for several nations, particularly for the Saracens The following list is from Godwin's "Chronological Table of English Architecture"

Anglo Roman—55 B C to about 250 A D—St Martin's church, Canterbury
Anglo Saxon—800 to 1066—Earl's Barton church, St Peter's, Lincolnshire
Gothic Anglo Roman—1066 to 1135—Rochester cathedral nave, St Bartholomew's, Smithfield, St Cross, Hants, etc
Early English, or Pointed—1135 to 1272—Temple church, London, parts of Winchester Wells, Salisbury, and Durham cathedrals, and Westminster abbey
Pointed, called pure Gothic—1272 to 1377—Exeter cathedral Waltham Cross, etc, St Stephen's, Westminster
Florid Pointed—1377 to 1509—Westminster hall, King's college Cambridge, St. George's chapel, Windsor, Henry VII's chapel, Westminster
Elizabethan—1509 to 1625—Northumberland house, Strand, part of Windsor castle, Hatfield house, schools at Oxford
Revival of Grecian architecture about 1625 Banqueting house, Whitehall, etc
Revival of Gothic architecture began about 1825, mainly through the exertions of A W Pugin Controversy on its value was rife in 1860-61

Gothland, an isle in the Baltic sea, was conquered by the Teutonic knights, 1397-98, given up to the Danes, 1524, to Sweden, 1645, conquered by the Danes, 1677, and restored to Sweden, 1679

Gothard, St. (Fr *san go-tar'*). TUNNELS.

Goths, a warlike nation between the Caspian, Pontus, Euxine, and Baltic seas They entered Mœsia, took Philippopolis, massacring thousands, defeated and killed the emperor Decius, 251, but were defeated at Naissus by Claudius, hence surnamed Gothicus, 320,000 being slain, 269 Aurelian ceded Dacia to them in 272, but they long troubled the empire After the destruction of the Roman western empire by the Heruli, the Ostrogoths, or Eastern Goths, under Theodoric, subdued most of Italy, and retained it till 553, when they were conquered by Narses, Justinian's general The Visigoths, or Western Goths, founded a kingdom in Spain, which continued until the Saracen conquest.

Gotthard, St. (*san got'-hart*) a Cistercian convent near the river Raab, Hungary Here the Turks, under grand-vizier Kuprult, were routed by imperialists and their allies, commanded by Montecuculi, 1 Aug 1664 Peace followed

Göttingen, a town of Hanover, a member of the Hanseatic League about 1360 The university "Georgia Augusta," founded by George II of England in 1734, was opened 1737 It was seized by the French, 1760, and held till 1762 In 1837 several able professors were dismissed for expressing political opinions

"Gouvernour, The," a moral and educational work, full of anecdotes, by sir Thomas Elyot, first pub 1531, an annotated edition with glossary by H H S Croft pub 1880

governor, an instrument attached to steam-engines, etc, for the purpose of preserving regularity of motion by adjusting the amount of power The centrifugal governor or the fly-ball governor, as it is called, was invented by Huyghens about 1650 Watt applied it to the regulating of steam-engines, 1784, many improvements since

Gowrie conspiracy. John Ruthven, earl of Gowrie, in 1600, reckoning on the support of the burghs and the kirk, conspired to dethrone James VI of Scotland, and seize the government. and the king was decoyed into Gowrie's house in Perth, on 5 Aug 1600 The plot was frustrated, and the earl and his brother Alexander were slain on the spot At the time, many believed that the young men were rather victims than authors of a plot Their father, William, was treacherously executed in 1584 for his share in the raid of Ruthven, in 1582, and he and his father, Patrick, were among the assassins of Rizzio, 9 Mch 1566

grace, a title assumed by Henry IV of England, on his accession in 1399 Excellent grace was assumed by Henry VI about 1425 Till James I, 1603, the king was addressed by that title, but afterwards by the title of majesty only "Your grace" is the form of address to an archbishop or a duke The term "Grace of God" is said to have been taken by bishops at Ephesus, 431 (probably from 1 Cor xv 10), by the Carlovingian princes in the 9th century, by popes in the 13th century, and about 1440 it was assumed by kings as signifying their supposed divine right "*Dei gratia*" was put on his great seal by William II of England, and on his gold coin by Edward III The king of Prussia's saying that he would reign "by the grace of God" gave much offence, 18 Oct 1861.

grace at meat. The ancient Greeks would not partake of meat until they had offered part of it, as first-fruits, to the gods. The short prayer said before, and by some persons after meat, in Christian countries, is in conformity with Christ's example, John vi 11, etc "The custom of saying grace at meals had probably its origin in the early times of the world"—*Lamb*, "Grace before Meat, Essays of Elia"

Græcia Magna, colonies planted by the Greeks, 974–748 B.C ITALY

graffiti (*graf-fee'-tee*), the scribblings found on the walls of Pompeii and other Roman ruins, selections were published by Wordsworth in 1837, and by Garrucci in 1856

Graham's dike, Scotland, a wall built in 209 A.D by Severus Septimus, the Roman emperor, or by Antoninus Pius It reached from the Firth of Forth to the Clyde Buchanan mentions considerable remains of this wall in his time, and vestiges are still to be seen

"Grail, Holy" (Sangreal) Tennyson's poem with this title, Dec. 1869, led to much discussion. Tennyson treats it as the cup in which Christ drank at the Last Supper

> "The Holy Grail! What is it?
> The phantom of a cup that comes and goes?
> The cup the cup itself, from which our Lord
> Drank at the last sad supper with his own"
> —*Tennyson*, "The Holy Grail"

Mediæval romances treat it as the dish which held the paschal lamb The word is probably old French, *gréal*, from the old Latin *gradalis*, a dish

grain. Henry III of England is said to have chosen a grain of wheat from the middle of the ear as the standard of weight 12 grains to be a pennyweight, 12 pennyweights one ounce, and 12 ounces a pound troy —*Lawson.*

grammarians, those versed in grammar or the structure of language A society of grammarians was formed at Rome as early as 276 B.C —*Blair* Apollodorus of Athens, Varro, Cicero, Messala, Julius Cæsar, Nicias, Ælius Donatus, Remmius, Palemon, Tyrannion of Pontus, Athenæus, and other distinguished men were of this class A Greek grammar was printed at Milan in 1476, Lily's Latin grammar ("Brevis Institutio"), 1513, Lindley Murray's English grammar, 1795, Cobbett's English grammar, 1818 Harris's "Hermes" was pub. 1750, Horne Tooke's "Epea Pteroenta, or, The Diversions of Purley," in 1786, treatises on the philosophy of language and grammar Cobbett declared Mr Canning to have been the only purely grammatical orator of his time, and dr Parr, speaking of a speech of Mr Pitt's, said, "We threw our whole grammatical mind upon it, and could not discover one error" Among the English grammars first published in the United States were Ross's, Hartford, 1782, "British Grammar," London and Boston, 1784, Buchanan's English, pub Philadelphia, 1792, Ticknor's, Boston, 1794, Dearborn's, Boston, 1795, Bingham's, Boston, 1801, Cochran's, Boston, 1802, Noah Webster's, 1807, Gurney's, 1808, Judson's, Boston, 1808, Alden's, Boston, 1811, Smith's, Philadelphia, 1812, Lindley Murray's, American edition, New York, 1814, Goold Brown's, 1823, Peter Bullions's, 1834

gramme. METRICAL SYSTEM

Gramme's magneto-electric machine, invented 1870 ELECTRICITY.

Grampian hills, central Scotland At Ardoch, near *Mons Grampius* of Tacitus, Scots and Picts under Galgacus were defeated by Romans under Agricola, 84 or 85 A.D.

Granada, a city, S Spain, was founded by Moors in the 8th century, and was then in the kingdom of Cordova. In 1236, Mohammed-al-Hamar made it capital of his new kingdom of Granada, which prospered till its subjugation by the "great captain," Gonsalvo de Cordova, 2 Jan 1492 In 1609 and 1610 the industrious Moors were expelled from Spain by the bigoted Philip III, to the lasting injury of his country. Granada was taken by marshal Soult in 1810, and held till 1812 Pop 1888, 73,006. In the province of Granada, 5 towns were destroyed, 914 persons killed, with a great loss of property through the earthquake of 25 Dec et seq 1884

granaries were formed by Joseph in Egypt, 1715 B.C (Gen xli 48) There were 327 granaries in Rome —*Univ Hist*

grand alliance between the emperor Leopold I and the Dutch States-general (principally to prevent the union of the French and Spanish monarchies in one person), signed at Vienna, 12 May, 1689, to which England, Spain, and the duke of Savoy afterwards acceded.

Grand Army of the Republic. This society of Union veteran soldiers of the civil war was first organized at Springfield, Ill, during the winter of 1865-66, under the leadership of dr. B. F. Stephenson, surgeon of the 14th Illinois infantry A national encampment is held by the society annually. Total membership, 1893, 403,024 in 45 departments

First post formed at Decatur, Ill 6 Apr 1866
A national convention was called and met at Indianapolis, Ind, 20 Nov "

[The following states represented New York, Pennsylvania, Illinois, Missouri, Kentucky, Wisconsin, Ohio Iowa, Kansas Indiana and the District of Columbia Gen Stephen A Hurlbut of Illinois was elected commander in chief, with dr Stephenson as adjutant general.]

NATIONAL ENCAMPMENTS AND COMMANDERS OF THE GRAND ARMY OF THE REPUBLIC.

No.	Commander.	Encampment.	Year.
1	Stephen A. Hurlbut, Ill.	Indianapolis, Ind.	20 Nov. 1866
2	John A. Logan, Ill.	Philadelphia, Pa.	15 June, 1868
3	John A. Logan, Ill.	Cincinnati, O.	12 May, 1869
4	John A. Logan, Ill.	Washington, D. C.	12 " 1870
5	Ambrose E. Burnside, R. I.	Boston, Mass.	10 " 1871
6	Ambrose E. Burnside, R. I.	Cleveland, O.	8 " 1872
7	Charles Devens, jr., Mass.	New Haven, Conn.	14 " 1873
8	Charles Devens, jr., Mass.	Harrisburg, Pa.	13 " 1874
9	John F. Hartranft, Pa.	Chicago, Ill.	12 " 1875
10	John F. Hartranft, Pa.	Philadelphia, Pa.	30 June, 1876
11	John C. Robinson, N. Y.	Providence, R. I.	26 " 1877
12	John C. Robinson, N. Y.	Springfield, Mass.	4 " 1878
13	William Earnshaw, Ohio.	Albany, N. Y.	17 " 1879
14	Louis Wagner, Pa.	Dayton, O.	8 " 1880
15	George S. Merrill, Mass.	Indianapolis, Ind.	15 " 1881
16	Paul Van Der Voort, Neb.	Baltimore, Md.	21 " 1882
17	Robert B. Beath, Pa.	Denver, Col.	25 July, 1883
18	John S. Kuntz, Ohio.	Minneapolis, Minn.	23 " 1884
19	S. S. Burdette, Washington, D.C.	Portland, Me.	24 June, 1885
20	Lucius Fairchild, Wis.	San Francisco, Cal.	26 Aug. 1886
21	John P. Rea, Minn.	St. Louis, Mo.	27 Sept. 1887
22	William Warner, Mo.	Columbus, O.	10 " 1888
23	Russell A. Alger, Mich.	Milwaukee, Wis.	27 Aug. 1889
24	Wheelock G. Veazey, Vt.	Boston, Mass.	12 " 1890
25	John Palmer, N. Y.	Detroit, Mich.	4 " 1891
26	A. G. Weissert, Wis.	Washington, D. C.	20 Sept. 1892
27	J. G. B. Adams, Mass.	Indianapolis, Ind.	5 " 1893
28	Thomas G. Lawler	Pittsburg, Pa.	10 " 1894

grand pensionary, a chief state functionary in Holland in the 16th century. In the constitution given by France to the Batavian republic, before the kingdom of Holland was formed, the title was revived and given to the head of the government, 29 Apr. 1805, Rutger Jan Schimmelpenninck being made grand pensionary. HOLLAND.

Grange, National, organized at Washington, D. C., Dec. 1867, to protect the interests of farmers and improve their condition. Reorganized at St. Louis in 1874. It is strictly non-political and numbered 250,000 members in 1891, among them not a few women. The chief officer is termed master, 2d officer, overseer, etc.

Grani'cus, a river in N.W. Asia Minor, near which, on 22 May, 334 B.C., Alexander the Great defeated the Persians. The Macedonian troops (30,000 foot and 5000 horse) crossed the Granicus in the face of the Persian army (600,000 foot and 20,000 horse).—*Justin.* The victors lost 55 foot and 60 horse. Sardis capitulated, Miletus and Halicarnassus were taken by storm, and other great towns submitted. BATTLES.

Granson, near the lake of Neufchâtel, Switzerland, where Charles the Bold, duke of Burgundy, was defeated by the Swiss, 3 Mch. 1476.

Grant, Ulysses S., administration of. UNITED STATES, 1869–77.

Grant's campaign in Virginia (4 May, 1864 to 9 Apr. 1865). The grade of lieutenant-general was revived 2 Mch. 1864, and on the 9th Grant was appointed with this rank commander, under the president, of the armies of the United States. Under him Sherman acted, and a plan was agreed upon for a simultaneous advance in May against the armies of Johnston in Georgia and Lee in Virginia. In April, Grant transferred Sheridan from the army of the Cumberland to command the cavalry in Virginia, while gen. Meade still led the army of the Potomac. The confederate army under Lee, at the opening of this campaign, was on the south bank of the Rapidan, 60,000 to 70,000 strong, never under better discipline, or more alert and active. As this was the culminating campaign of the war, a list is given of the principal officers of the 2 federal armies which co-operated in it, with their aggregate strength for duty, and a table of their losses.

ARMY OF THE POTOMAC.

Maj.-gen. George G. Meade.

2d Army Corps, maj.-gen. Winfield S. Hancock.
1st div., brig.-gen. Francis C. Barlow; 2d div., brig.-gen. John Gibbon; 3d div., brig.-gen. David B. Birney; 4th div., brig.-gen. Gershom Mott.

5th Army Corps, maj.-gen. Gouverneur K. Warren.
1st div., brig.-gen. Charles Griffin; 2d div., brig.-gen. John C. Robinson; 3d div., brig.-gen. Samuel W. Crawford; 4th div., brig.-gen. James S. Wadsworth.

6th Army Corps, maj.-gen. John Sedgwick.
1st div., brig.-gen. Horatio G. Wright; 2d div., brig.-gen. George W. Getty; 3d div., brig.-gen. James B. Ricketts.

9th Army Corps, maj.-gen. Ambrose E. Burnside.
1st div., brig.-gen. Thomas G. Stevenson; 2d div., brig.-gen. Robert B. Potter; 3d div., brig.-gen. Orlando B. Wilcox; 4th div., brig.-gen. Edward Ferrera.

Cavalry, maj.-gen. Philip H. Sheridan.
1st div., brig.-gen. Alfred T. A. Torbert; 2d div., brig.-gen. David McM. Gregg; 3d div., brig.-gen. James H. Wilson.

Artillery, brig.-gen. Henry J. Hunt.

Aggregate Strength for Duty.

	Officers.	Enlisted men.	Guns.
Infantry	4459	91,420	
Artillery	226	7,554	192 / 92 Reserve.
Cavalry	607	12,257	32
Total	5292	111,231	316

ARMY OF THE JAMES.

Maj.-gen. Benjamin F. Butler.

10th Army Corps, maj.-gen. Quincy A. Gillmore.
1st div., brig.-gen. Alfred H. Terry; 2d div., brig.-gen. John W. Turner; 3d div., brig.-gen. Adelbert Ames.

18th Army Corps, maj.-gen. W. F. Smith.
1st div., brig.-gen. William T. H. Brooks; 2d div., brig.-gen. Godfrey Weitzel; 3d div., brig.-gen. Edward W. Hinks.

Cavalry, brig.-gen. August V. Kautz.

Aggregate Strength for Duty.

	Officers.	Enlisted men.	Guns.
Infantry	1337	30,453	
Artillery	61	2,065	82
Cavalry	128	4,604	8
Total	1526	37,122	90

Grant moves against Lee, the army of the Potomac crossing the Rapidan .... 4 May, 1864

Warren with the 5th corps leading at Germania ford, followed by Sedgwick with the 6th, pushes directly into the WILDERNESS. Hancock crosses at Ely's ford and moves on Chancellorsville.

Battle of the Wilderness .... 5-6 May, "

It was not the intention of Grant to fight Lee here, but the attack of the confederates compelled it. The severe fighting of the 5th and the battle of the 6th were indecisive. On the morning of the 7th Lee was intrenched, awaiting attack. Grant withdrew, directing the column towards Spottsylvania Court-house; Warren leading at 7 A.M.

Battle of Spottsylvania .... 10-12 May, "

Warren, nearing Spottsylvania Court-house, finds that confederates have anticipated him; he intrenches, and awaits other troops. On the 9th Grant has cleared the Wilderness and concentrated near Spottsylvania; Hancock on the right, Warren in the centre, and Sedgwick on the left. On this day, while placing his artillery, Sedgwick is killed, and Wright takes the 6th corps. On the 10th and 11th there is severe but desultory fighting. On the 12th occurs the gallant assault of Hancock's corps on the confederate works, capturing 20 guns and some 3000 prisoners. The desperate attempt of the confederates to retake these works, known as the "Fight at the Salient" or "Bloody Angle," was unsuccessful. After several days of manœuvring, on the night of 20-21 May, the army marches on towards Richmond.

North Anna crossing.—Warren's corps crosses the North Anna at Jericho ford on the 23d. Hancock crosses at Chesterfield bridge on the morning of the 24th. Here again Grant is confronted by Lee; after a spirited reconnoissance it is found that the confederate position is too strong to be forced. Grant withdraws from its front and moves towards the Pamunkey river on the night of .... 26-27 May, "

Sheridan meets Fitzhugh Lee and Hampton at Hawes's shops in a severe cavalry engagement....................28 May, 1864

Battle of Cold Harbor..................................3 June, "

Grant again moves south to Cold Harbor, 31 May-2 June, where he finds Lee strongly intrenched; a partial engagement takes place on the afternoon of the 2d. On 3 June, the army of the Potomac being reinforced by the 18th corps (army of the James), Grant assaults the confederate works at early sunrise for 30 minutes, resulting in a disastrous repulse and a loss of over 10,000 men. The armies face each other until 12 June, when Grant decides to approach Richmond from the south. Accordingly from 12-15 June the army passes from the Chickahominy to the James; Petersburg, 22 miles south of Richmond, is now its objective point.

Sheridan's first raid..................................8-24 May, "

Grant despatches Sheridan to harass the confederate rear. He passes to the left of the confederate army, with an engagement at Todd's tavern on the 8th. Crosses the North Anna and captures Beaver-dam station, destroying the railroad for 10 miles, and 1,500,000 rations, on the 9th; Allen station, Ashland, and Yellow tavern, 11th. At Yellow tavern the confederate cavalry commander, gen. Stuart, is killed. Engagements follow at Meadow bridge, Mechanicsville, Strawberry hill, Richmond fortifications, 12th. Resting 3 days at Haxhall's landing, on the James, Sheridan returns to the army of the Potomac on 24 May, having passed completely around the confederate army.

Sheridan's second raid..................................4-24 June, "

Sheridan's object was to join Hunter at Gordonsville, and with him to destroy the confederate communications and threaten Richmond. But Hunter failed to reach Gordonsville, and Sheridan was not strong enough to meet the enemy. His cavalry engagements were those at Trevillian station and Newton's cross-roads, 11-12 June; King and Queen Court-house, 18th to 20th; White House and Tunstall's station, 21st; Jones's bridge, 23d; St. Mary's church, 24th.

Movement against Petersburg, army of the James.—Gen. Butler, commanding the army of the James, moves from fortress Monroe towards Petersburg, 5 May, to support the army of the Potomac. Butler occupies BERMUDA HUNDREDS, 6 May. Petersburg is immediately occupied by Beauregard; and Butler is checked at Bermuda Hundreds by Beauregard's works across the neck of the peninsula, 12-31 May, 1864

Eighteenth corps of the army of the James transferred to Grant at Cold Harbor..................................2 June, "

Butler attempts Petersburg, but fails..................10 June, "

Army of the Potomac advances, joining Butler....15-16 June, "

Hancock advances on Petersburg, failing to take it through imperfect co-operation and misunderstanding......15 June, "

Assaults on defences of Petersburg repulsed....16-17-18 June, "

Failure of 2d and 6th corps to sever the Weldon railroad, 21-22 June, "

Affair at Deep Bottom, 2d corps engaged............26 July, "

Explosion of mine and assault on confederate works; total failure (MINE EXPLOSION)..........................30 July, "

Warren with 5th corps seizes and holds the Weldon railroad, 18-21 Aug. "

Hancock with 2d corps driven from Reams's station, on the Weldon railroad, with severe loss..................25 Aug. "

Gen. Butler, with 10th corps under Birney and 18th corps under Ord, assaults and takes fort Harrison...........29 Sept. "

Warren with 5th and Parke with 9th corps capture confederate works at Peebles's farm................30 Sept.-1 Oct. "

Failure of Hancock to seize south-side railroad at Boydton Plank-road or Hatcher's Run.......................27 Oct. "

Second attempt to turn confederate right at Hatcher's Run fails..5-6 Feb. 1865

Lee attacks and captures fort Stedman, which is immediately retaken; confederate loss 4000.....................25 Mch. "

Sheridan joins the army of the Potomac from his raid in the Shenandoah valley with some 10,000 cavalry.......27 Mch. "

Battle of Five Forks; Sheridan with 5th corps and cavalry defeats the confederates.....................31 Mch.-1 Apr. "

Sheridan removes Warren from command of the 5th corps late on the afternoon of 1 Apr., and substitutes Griffin. Grant assaults and carries the works about Petersburg. Gen. A. P. Hill, confederate, killed...................2 Apr. "

Richmond evacuated...................................." "

" occupied by gen. Weitzel....................3 Apr. "

Pursuit of Lee; affair at Sailor's creek.................6 Apr. "

" " " " Farmville......................7 Apr. "

Army of northern Virginia surrenders at Appomattox..9 Apr. "

FEDERAL LOSSES (POTOMAC ARMY) FROM THE WILDERNESS TO THE JAMES, 4 May-16 June.

Battles.	Killed.		Wounded.		Captured or missing.		Totals.
	Officers.	Men.	Officers.	Men.	Officers.	Men.	
Wilderness	143	2103	569	11,468	138	3,245	17,666
Spottsylvania	174	2551	672	12,744	62	2,196	18,399
North Anna	41	550	159	2,575	17	644	3,986
Cold Harbor	143	1702	433	8,644	35	1,780	12,737
Sheridan's 1st raid	7	57	16	321	10	214	625
" 2d "	14	136	43	698	25	600	1,516
Totals	522	7099	1892	36,450	287	8,679	54,929
Army of the James, May-15 June............Totals	**38**	**596**	**181**	**3,722**	**45**	**1,633**	**6,215**
About Petersburg (army of the Potomac and army of the James) 15-30 June	111	1902	525	9,410	168	4,458	16,569
July	76	849	221	3,587	91	1,553	6,377
Aug. and Sept	137	1384	544	7,112	301	8,539	18,017
Oct., Nov., and Dec	48	603	194	3,288	62	2,409	6,604
Totals	372	4738	1484	23,397	622	16,954	47,567
Jan., Feb., Mch., and Apr. 1865............Totals	81	1085	384	7,298	70	1,941	10,859
Grand totals	1013	13,518	3941	70,867	1024	29,207	119,570

OPERATIONS IN THE SHENANDOAH VALLEY.

Campaign of Grant against Lee embraced movements up the Shenandoah valley. Sigel, commanding department of West Virginia, is sent up the valley with 10,000 men, supported by gen. Crook, who leaves Charlestown, W. Va., at the same time..1 May, 1864

Breckinridge easily defeats Sigel at Newmarket......15 May, "

Grant relieves Sigel and appoints Hunter, who defeats the confederates under gen. W. E. Jones at Piedmont.......5 June, "

Hunter, joined by Crook and Averill, advances to Staunton, and instead of proceeding to Gordonsville to join Sheridan, goes to Lexington, and on 18 June threatens Lynchburg with 20,000 men; but opposed by a much stronger force, escapes into West Virginia, where his force for the time is useless.

Confederate forces, now under gen. Early, move rapidly down the Shenandoah to the Potomac, and spread consternation from Baltimore to Washington..................2, 3 July, "

Gen. Lew. Wallace attempts to check the confederates at Monocacy, but is defeated with a loss of 98 killed, 579 wounded. and 1280 missing..................................9 July, "

Confederate cavalry approach Baltimore..............10 July, "

On the 11th Early is within 6 or 7 miles of Washington, and menaces the capital on the 12th, but retires on the 13th. The 19th corps (Emory's), arriving at fortress Monroe from Louisiana, and the 6th corps from before Petersburg, sent by Grant under Wright to attack Early, pursue him some distance up the valley, and return to Leesburg, and are ordered back to Petersburg. Early returns as soon as the pursuit ceases; strikes Crook at Martinsburg, defeats him, and holds the Potomac from Shepardstown to Williamsport.

Early now sends B. R. Johnston and McCausland with some 3000 cavalry on a raid into Pennsylvania...........30 July, "

Approaching Chambersburg, Pa., they demand $100,000, which is not paid, and burn the town.

Sixth and 19th corps, on their way to Petersburg, return. Grant relieves gen. Hunter, organizes the army of the middle division, and gives the command to Sheridan (ARMY).....7 Aug. 1864

Sheridan attacks and defeats Early, strongly fortified at Opequan creek, near Winchester.........................19 Sept. "

Early falls back to Fisher's hill, south of Winchester, where Sheridan routs him, taking 1100 prisoners and 16 guns, 23 Sept. "

Sheridan pushes Early to the mountains; returns to Cedar creek, and leaving his command, visits Washington..15 Oct. "

Early, reinforced, returns to Fisher's hill, and learning Sheridan's absence, sets out to attack on the evening of...18 Oct. "

Surprises the federals under Wright, driving them back with a loss of 24 guns and 1200 prisoners, morning of......19 Oct. "

Sheridan at Winchester on the night of the 18th. On his way to the front news of the rout of his army reaches him. His arrival on the field stops the retreat. The line of battle re-formed at 3 P.M., he attacks, and by dark recovers the ground lost in the morning. Early is crushed, and the campaign in the valley ended. CEDAR CREEK.

Sheridan, with 10,000 cavalry, drives the confederates from Waynesboro, 27 Feb., and advancing, joins Grant before Petersburg (see *supra*)................................27 Mch. 1865

grapes. Before Edward VI.'s time grapes were brought to England in quantities from Flanders, where they were first cultivated about 1276. The vine was introduced into England 1552, being first planted at Bloxhall, in Suffolk. In the gardens of Hampton court palace is a vine planted 1769, said to surpass any in Europe, it is 72 feet by 20, and has in one season produced 2272 bunches of grapes, weighing 18 cwt, the stem is 13 inches in girth —*Leigh* FLOWERS AND PLANTS

"Graphic, London," an illustrated weekly journal, established 4 Dec 1869

graphite (from the Gr *γράφειν*, to write), a form of mineral carbon, with a trace of iron, improperly termed black-lead and plumbago In 1809 sir Humphry Davy investigated the relations of 3 forms of carbon—the diamond, graphite, and charcoal A rude kind of black-lead pencil is mentioned by Gesner, 1565 Interesting results of sir B C Brodie's researches on graphite appeared in the international exhibition of 1862 Fresh discoveries were made in the nearly exhausted Borrowdale mines, Cumberland, in 1875

graph'oscope, an optical apparatus for magnifying engravings, photographs, etc, with fine effect, invented by C J Rowsell, exhibited in 1871

graph'otype, a process for making blocks for surface-printing, invented by De Witt Clinton Hitchcock in 1860, and described by Mr Fitz-Cook at the Society of Arts, England, 6 Dec 1865 Drawings were made on blocks of chalk with silicious ink, when dried the soft parts were brushed away, and the drawings remained in relief, stereotypes were then taken from the block

grates. The Anglo-Saxons had arched hearths, and chafing-dishes were in use until the introduction of chimneys about 1200 CHIMNEYS, STOVES

Gravelines (*grav leen'*), a fortified seaport town of N France. Here the Spaniards, aided by an English fleet, defeated the French on 13 July, 1558

Gravelotte (*grav-lot'*), Battle of, 18 Aug 1870 METZ

gravitation, as a supposed innate power, was noticed by the Greeks, and also by Seneca, who speaks of the moon attracting the waters, about 38 A.D Kepler investigated the subject about 1615, and Hooke devised a theory of gravitation about 1674 The principles of gravity were demonstrated by Galileo at Florence, about 1633, but the law laid down by Newton in his 'Principia," in 1687, is said to have been proved by him in 1670 The fall of an apple from a tree in 1666 is said to have directed his attention to the subject

Newton says, " I do not anywhere take on me to define the kind or manner of any action, the causes or physical reasons thereof or attribute forces in a true and physical sense to certain centres, when I speak of them as attracting, or enduced with attractive powers "

On 15 July, 1867, M Chasles laid before the Paris Academy of Sciences some letters alleged to be from Newton to Pascal and others to show that to Pascal was due the theory of gravitation The authenticity of these letters was denied, and their forgery and his own delusion were acknowledged by M Chasles before the academy, 13 Sept 1869

gravity, specific ELEMENTS

Great Bridge, Battle of VIRGINIA, 1775.

Great Britain, the name given in 1604 to ENGLAND, SCOTLAND, and WALES

Great Eastern. This colossal paddle and screw steamship justly called "Leviathan," was built by Messrs. Scott Russell & Co, from designs of I K Brunel, and after 3 months' effort was launched at Millwall, Engl, 31 Jan 1858 Her dimensions were length, 691 ft., breadth, 83 ft, and depth, 48 ft, tonnage, 18,915 Steam was generated in 10 boilers, with 100 furnaces. When launched she had cost about 720,000*l*.

She leaves her moorings at Deptford for Portland Roads (10 firemen were killed by an explosion during the trip), 7 Sept 1859
Wintering at Southampton, she sails for New York under capt. Vine Hall with 38 passengers and 8 guests 17 June, 1860
Remaining at New York on exhibition 28 June to 16 Aug, she returns to England, arriving 26 Aug "
On one of several trips between Liverpool and New York in 1862, she runs on a rock near Long Island Aug 1862
Bought by Glass, Elliot & Co in spring of 1864, and chartered to lay the second Atlantic telegraph cable . 1864
Sails for Valentia, Ireland, with over 2000 miles of cable, with prof William Thomson and Cromwell F Varley to superintend the paying out (ELECTRICITY) 15 July, 1865
Cable breaks 2 Aug, and the *Great Eastern* returns to Medway, arriving 19 Aug "
With a new cable she sails from Medway . 30 June, 1866
New cable completed at Heart's Content, Newfoundland, and messages exchanged between the U S and England 30 July, 1866
Recovers the lost cable of 1865, 2 Sept 1866 and completes the laying at Newfoundland 8 Sept "
Great Eastern returns to Liverpool, arriving 19 Sept "
Sails for New York prepared for 2000 passengers for the Paris exposition and returns with 191 She is seized on her arrival by the seamen claiming their wages May 1867
Successfully lays the French Atlantic cable leaving Brest with 2725 miles of cable 22 June, reaching the island of St Pierre, near gulf of St Lawrence 13 July 1869
Arrives at Bombay with the Bombay and Suez cable 27 Feb 1870
Completes the laying of the 5th Atlantic cable 3 July 1873
Lays the 6th Atlantic cable Aug –Sept 1874
Sold at auction at Lloyds' to Frederick de Mattos for 26,200*l*, 29 Oct 1885
Beached at New Ferry on the Mersey to be broken up, 25 Aug 1888

Great Meadows. VIRGINIA 1754

great seal of England. The first seal used by Edward the Confessor was called the broad seal, and affixed to the grants of the crown, 1048 —*Baker's Chron* The most ancient seal with arms is that of Richard I James II, when fleeing from London in 1688, dropped the great seal in the Thames The great seal of England was stolen from the house of lord chancellor Thurlow in Great Ormond street, London, and carried away, with other property, 24 Mch 1784, a day before the dissolution of Parliament, it was never recovered, and was replaced the next day A new seal was brought into use on the union with Ireland, 1 Jan 1801 A new seal for Ireland was brought into use and the old one defaced, 21 Jan 1832 The Great Seal Offices act, passed 7 Aug 1874, abolished certain offices, transferred duties, etc The Great Seal act, passed 2 Aug 1880, relates to appointment of judges, patents, etc

great seal of the Confederacy. Joint resolution to establish a seal for the Confederate States passed by the Confederate congress, and approved 30 Apr 1863 Made in England, and completed July, 1864, at a cost of $600 It reached Richmond in Apr 1865, about the time of its evacuation, and was never used It is now in the office of the state secretary of South Carolina

great seal of the United States. Immediately after the adoption of the Declaration of Independence, 4 July, 1776, a committee was appointed to prepare a device for a seal, but the matter was not consummated until 20 June, 1782, when the present seal was adopted The device is, on one side a spread eagle with a shield with 13 stripes paleways, and a chief azure, in one talon a bundle of arrows, in the other an olive branch, in its beak a scroll with the motto *E pluribus unum*, and over its head a glory breaking from the clouds, surrounding 13 stars On the reverse is an unfinished pyramid, symbolling the growth and strength of the states, over it the all-seeing eye in a triangle, surrounded by a glory, and around the rim the words *Annuit cœptis* (God has favored the undertaking), and *Novus ordo seclorum* (a new order of things) This seal has never been changed, and is in charge of the secretary of state.

Greece, anciently termed **Hellas,** a kingdom in the southeastern part of Europe The Greeks are fabled to have been the progeny of Javan, 4th son of Japheth Mythology derived the name Greece from an ancient king, Græcus, and Hellas from another king, Hellen, son of Deucalion From Hellen's sons, Dorus and Æolus, came the Dorians and Æolians, another son, Xuthus, was father of Achæus and Ion, progenitors of the Achæans and Ionians Homer calls the inhabitants indifferently Myrmidons, Hellenes and Achaians They were also termed Danaï, from Danaus, king of Argos, 1474 B.C Greece anciently consisted of the peninsula of PELOPONNESUS, containing the states of ACHAIA, ARCADIA, Argolis, chief city ARGOS, ELIS, LACONIA, chief city SPARTA, MESSENIA The other states of Greece separated from the Peloponnesus by the isthmus of Corinth (which isthmus constituted the state of Corinthia, chief city CORINTH), were ACARNANIA, ÆTOLIA, ATTICA, chief city ATHENS, BŒOTIA, chief city THEBES, Dolopia, Doris (inhabitants DORIANS), EPIRUS, EUBŒA, an island, Locris (inhabitants LOCRIANS), MACEDON, Megaris, chief city MEGARA, PHOCIS, chief city DELPHI, Thessaly, and the islands The limits of modern Greece are much more confined Greece became subject to the Turkish empire in the 15th century The population of the kingdom, established in 1829, 96,810, in 1861,

1,096,810, with the Ionian isles (added in 1864), about 1,348,522, in 1870 1,457,894 Area, including Thessaly, 25,041 sq miles, pop. 1889, 2,187,208 The early history is mythic B C

Sicyon founded (*Eusebius*) 2089
Uranus arrives in Greece (*Lenglet*) 2042
Revolt of the Titans, war of the Giants * *
Inachus, king of the Argives 1910
Kingdom of Argos begun by Inachus (*Eusebius*) 1856
Reign of Ogyges in Bœotia (*Eusebius*) 1796
Sacrifices to the gods introduced by Phoroneus 1773
Sicyon now begun (*Lenglet*) "
Deluge of OGYGES. 1764
A colony of Arcadians emigrate to Italy under Œnotrus the country first called Œnotria, afterwards Magna Græcia (*Eusebius*) 1710
Pelasgi hold the Peloponnesus, 1700-1550, succeeded by the Hellenes 1550-1300
Chronology of the Arundelian marbles commences (*Eusebius*) 1582
Cecrops arrives from Egypt about 1550
AREOPAGUS established 1504
Deluge of Deucalion (*Eusebius*) 1503
Panathenæan games instituted 1495
Cadmus with the Phœnician letters settles in Bœotia, and founds Thebes about 1493
Lelex, first king of Laconia, afterwards called Sparta 1490
Danaus, king of Argos (DANAI), said to have brought the first ship into Greece and to have introduced pumps 1485
Reign of Hellen (*Eusebius*) 1459
First Olympic games at Elis, by the *Idæi Dactyli* 1453
Who are said to have discovered iron 1406
Corinth rebuilt and so named 1384
Eleusinian mysteries instituted by Eumolpus (1356) and Isthmian games 1326
Kingdom of Mycenæ created out of Argos 1313
Pelops, from Lydia, settles in south Greece (Peloponnesus), about 1283
Argonautic expedition (ARGONAUTS) 1263
Pythian games begun by Adrastus. "
War of the 7 Greek captains against Thebes 1225
Amazonian war 1213
Rape of Helen by Theseus (SPARTA) "
Rape of Helen by Paris 1204
Commencement of the Trojan war 1193
Troy taken and destroyed on the night of the 7th of the month Thargelion (27 May or 11 June) 1184
Æneas said to have arrived in Italy about 1182
Migration of Æolians, who build Smyrna, etc 1123
Return of the Heraclidæ about 1103
Settlement of the Ionians in Asia Minor 1044
Rhodians begin navigation laws 916
Lycurgus flourishes 846
Olympic games revived at Elis, 884, the first Olympiad, the beginning of authentic chronology in Greece 776
Messenian wars 743-669
Sea-fight, first on record, between Corinthians and the inhabitants of the island of Corcyra . . 664
Byzantium built. 657
Seven sages of Greece (Solon, Periander, Pittacus, Chilo, Thales, Cleobulus, and Bias) flourish about 590
Persian conquests in Ionia . 544
Sybaris in Magna Græcia destroyed, 100,000 Crotonians under Milo defeat 300,000 Sybarites 508
Sardis burned by Greeks, provoking Persian invasion 504
Thrace and Macedonia conquered 496
Athens and Sparta resist demands of king of Persia 490
Persians defeated at MARATHON 28 Sept. 491
Xerxes invades Greece, but is checked at THERMOPYLÆ by Leonidas . Aug 480
Battle of SALAMIS 20 Oct. "
Mardonius defeated and slain at PLATÆA, Persian fleet destroyed at MYCALE 22 Sept. 479
Battle of Eurymedon (end of Persian war) 466
Athens begins to tyrannize over Greece 459
SACRED WAR begun 448
War between Corinth and its colony Corcyra 435
Leads to the Peloponnesian war 431-404
Disastrous Athenian expedition to Syracuse 415-413
Athenian fleet defeated by Lysander the Spartan at Ægospotami Sept 405
RETREAT OF THE 10,000 under Xenophon 400
Death of Socrates 399
Sea fight at CNIDUS 394
Peace of Antalcidas 387
Rise and fall of the Theban power in Greece 370-360
Battle of Mantinea, death of Epaminondas . 362
Ambitious designs of Philip of Macedon . 353
Sacred wars ended by Philip, who subdues the Phocians 348
Battle of CHÆRONEA 338
Philip assassinated by Pausanias 335
Alexander, his son, subdues Athenians, and destroys Thebes "
Alexander conquers the Persian empire 334-331
Rise of Pyrrhus the Great (EPIRUS, ROME) 295
Greece harassed by Alexander's successors, revive the Ætolian and Achaian leagues (ACHAIA) 284-280
Greece invaded by Gauls, 280, they are defeated at Delphi, 279, and expelled 277
Dissensions lead to Roman intervention . 200
Greece conquered by Mummius and made a Roman province, 147-146
Greece visited and favored by Augustus, 21 B C., and by Hadrian . . . . A D 122-133

GRE

Invaded by Alaric 396
Plundered by the Normans of Sicily 1146
Conquered by Latins, and divided into small governments 1204
Turks under Mahomet II conquer Athens and part of Greece 1456
Venetians hold Athens and the Morea 1466
Greece mainly subject to the Turks. 1540
Morea held by Venice 1687-1715
Struggle for independence with Russian help, 1770 et seq, fruitless insurrection of the Suliotes 1803
Secret society, the Hetairia, established 1815
Insurrection in Moldavia and Wallachia, in which Greeks join, suppressed 1821
Proclamation of prince Alexander to shake off Turkish yoke, Mch, he raises the standard of the cross against the crescent, and war of independence begins 6 Apr "
Greek patriarch put to death at Constantinople 23 Apr "
Morea gained by the Greeks June, "
Missolonghi taken by Greeks Nov "
Independence of Greece proclaimed 27 Jan 1822
Siege of Corinth by the Turks Jan "
Bombardment of Scio, its capture, most horrible massacre recorded in modern history (CHIOS) 11 Apr "
Greeks victors at Thermopylæ, etc 13 July, "
Massacre at Cyprus July, "
Corinth taken . 16 Sept "
National congress at Argos 10 Apr 1823
Victories of Marco Bozzaris June, killed 10 Aug "
Lord Byron in Greece, embraces its cause Aug "
First Greek loan Feb 1824
Death of lord Byron at Missolonghi 19 Apr "
Defeat of the capitan pacha at Samos 16 Aug "
Provisional government of Greece set up 12 Oct "
Ibrahim Pacha lands, 25 Feb, takes Navarino, 23 May, Tripolitza 30 June, 1825
Greek fleet defeats the capitan pacha June, "
Provisional government asks protection of England July, "
Ibrahim Pacha takes Missolonghi by assault, after a long and heroic defence 23 Apr 1826
Seventy thousand pounds raised in Europe for the Greeks "
Reschid Pacha takes Athens 2 June, 1827
Egypto Turkish fleet destroyed at NAVARINO 20 Oct "
Treaty of London, between Great Britain, Russia, and France, on behalf of Greece, signed 6 July, "
Count Capo d'Istria president of Greece 18 Jan 1828
Panhellenion Grand Council of State, established 2 Feb "
National bank founded 14 Feb "
Convention of viceroy of Egypt with sir Edward Codrington for evacuation of Morea and delivery of captives 6 Aug "
Patras, Navarino, and Modon surrender to French 6 Oct. "
Turks evacuate the Morea Oct. "
Missolonghi surrendered to Greece 16 May, 1829
Greek National Assembly meets at Argos. 23 July, "
Porte acknowledges independence of Greece by treaty of Adrianople 14 Sept "
Prince Leopold of Saxe Coburg declines the sovereignty, 21 May, 1830
Count Capo d'Istria, president of Greece, assassinated by the brother and son of Mavromichaelis, a Mainote chief whom he had imprisoned 9 Oct 1831
Assassins built into close brick walls to their chins, and supplied with food until they die 29 Oct "
Crown offered to and accepted by Otho of Bavaria, previously under a regency 7 May, 1832
Otho I assumes the government 1 June, 1835
University at Athens established 1837, building commenced 1839
Leopold of Bavaria proposed as heir to the throne Jan 1862
Insurrection at Patras and Missolonghi, 17 Oct., provisional government at Athens deposes the king, 23 Oct., he and the queen flee, arrive at Corfu, 27 Oct, European powers neutral, general submission to provisional government. 31 Oct. "
Demonstrations in favor of prince Alfred of Great Britain, who is proclaimed king at Lamia in Phthiotis, 22 Nov, excitement in his favor at Athens 23 Nov "
Provisional government grants universal suffrage . 4 Dec "
National Assembly meets at Athens 22 Dec "
National Assembly elects M Balbis president, 29 Jan, prince Alfred chosen king by 230 016 out of 241,202 votes 3 Feb 1863
Assembly offers crown to prince William of Schleswig Holstein, 18 Mch, proclaims him as king George I 30 Mch "
Protocol between the 3 protecting powers—France, England, and Russia—signed at London, consenting to offer on condition of annexation of the Ionian isles to Greece 5 June, "
King of Denmark accepts from the aged adm Canaris the Greek crown for prince William, whom he advises to adhere to the constitution and gain the love of his people 6 June, "
King arrives at Athens, 30 Oct., takes oath to the constitution, 31 Oct "
Balbis ministry formed 28 Apr 1864
Protocol annexing Ionian isles to Greece, signed by M Zaïmis and sir H. Storks, 28 May, Greek troops occupy Corfu, 2 June, king arrives there 6 June, "
New ministry under Canaris formed . . 7 Aug "
Assembly recognizes the debt of 1824 5 Sept. "
After delay and remonstrance from the king, 19 Oct, a new constitution (no upper house) passed by assembly, 1 Nov, accepted by king 28 Nov "
Agitation in favor of Cretan insurrection (CANDIA) Aug-Dec 1866
Great sympathy with insurrection in Candia, blockade run by Greek vessels with volunteers, arms, and provisions, Apr et seq 1867
King marries grand duchess Olga of Russia . . . . 27 Oct "

Rupture between Turkey and Greece in consequence of Greek armed intervention in CANDIA Dec 1868
After conference of western powers at Paris, Jan, their requisitions accepted, and diplomatic relations between Turkey and Greece resumed 26 Feb 1869
Law for cutting isthmus of Corinth passed 7 Nov "
Concession to cut a canal through isthmus of Corinth granted to a French company Apr 1870
Lord and lady Muncaster and a party of English travellers seized by brigands at Oropos, near Marathon, lord Muncaster and the ladies sent to treat, 25,000*l* demanded as ransom, with pardon 11 Apr "
Brigands retreating, surrounded by troops, kill Mr Vyner, Mr Lloyd, Mr Herbert and count de Boyl 21 Apr "
Great excitement, influential persons charged with connivance at brigandage May, June, "
Several brigands killed, 7 captured, tried and condemned 23 May, 5 executed 20 June, "
Decree for suppression of brigandage issued Oct "
Discovery of relics at Spata, near Athens, tombs containing bones, precious metal ornaments, etc (removed to Athens by M Stamataki) about 1 July, 1877
Revival of Theban "sacred band," instituted by Epaminondas (to be 1000 instead of 300) about July, "
Insurrection in Thessaly against Turks 28 Jan, 10,000 Greeks enter the country, retire at the armistice early in Feb 1878
Insurrection struggling, battles at Macrinitza, 28, 29 Mch., C Ogle, *Times* correspondent, killed by Turks (investigation led to no result) 29 Mch "
Insurrection closed through British intervention, announced, 6 May "
Greece disappointed by Berlin treaty, 13 July, rectification of frontiers by sultan, proposed about 24 July, "
Convention of Turkey and Greece at Constantinople, Thessaly ceded to Greece, 24 May, signed 2 July, 1881
Carried into effect, Greek flag raised in Arta. 6 July, "
Railway from Athens to Corinth opened 15 Apr 1885
Great discovery of statuary near the Acropolis, Athens 1886
Crown prince Constantine, duke of Sparta, marries princess Sophie of Prussia, sister of emperor of Germany 27 Oct. 1889
Statues, etc, supposed to be the work of Phidias at Rhamnus in Attica, discovered Oct. 1890
Seventieth anniversary of Greek independence 6 Apr 1891
Canal across the isthmus of Corinth begun 5 May, 1882, completed 1893
This canal is about 4 miles long 27 ft deep, 71 ft. wide at the top, and 69 ft at the bottom The lease to the company extends for 99 years, when the canal falls to the government on payment of $1,000,000 to the company This canal shortens the route from the Adriatic to Constantinople by 185 nautical miles, and effects a great saving in distance to other ports of the Mediterranean

KINGS OF GREECE.

1832 Otho I, prince of Bavaria, b. 1 June, 1815, elected king, 7 May, 1832, under regency till 1 June, 1835, married, 22 Nov 1836, to Maria Frederica, daughter of grand-duke of Oldenburg, deposed 23 Oct 1862, d in Bavaria, 26 July, 1867
1863 George I (son of Christian IX of Denmark), king of the Hellenes, b 24 Dec 1845, accepted the crown, 6 June, 1863, declared of age, 27 June, 1863, married grand duchess Olga of Russia, 27 Oct. 1867
Heir Constantine, duke of Sparta, b 2 Aug. 1868, married to princess Sophie of Prussia, 27 Oct. 1889
Heir George, b. 19 July, 1890

Greek architecture. ARCHITECTURE.

Greek church, or Eastern church. While disowning the supremacy of the pope and rejecting many doctrines and practices of the Roman church, the Greek church is both the source and background of it. The council of Nicæa (325) recognized 3 patriarchs—the bishop of Rome, of Alexandria, and of Antioch, to these were afterwards added the bishops of Constantinople and Jerusalem The relation of the Greek church to the Roman is one of growing estrangement from the 5th century to its final separation in 1054 with several abortive attempts to unite since The estrangement and final rupture may be traced to the overweening pretensions of the Roman bishops and to Western innovations in the doctrine of the Holy Spirit, accompanied by an alteration of the creed, etc, strengthened by a difference in the religious spirit and ideas of each "Greek theology had its root in Greek philosophy, while a great deal of Western theology was based on Roman law. The Greek fathers succeeded the Greek sophists, while the Latin theologian succeeded the Roman advocate "—*Stanley*, "Eastern Church," ch. i. The prime difference in the doctrine of the two churches lies in the procession of the Holy Ghost from the Father only, or from the Father and the Son, the Greek church teaching the former doctrine, and the Roman the latter. In the Greek church, too, patriarchs of equal dignity have higher rank among the bishops, instead of pope; and priests are allowed to marry once. The number of sacraments is also different The orthodox Greek church includes various churches produced by jealousy of race or by territorial division which are independent or autocephalous, and yet one in doctrine with their head The most important of these are, the churches of Russia, Georgia, Servia, Roumania, Bulgaria, Greece, Montenegro, etc The orthodox Greek church (1893) is estimated to contain 98,000,000 people FATHERS OF THE CHURCH

Catechetical school at Alexandria (Origen, Clemens, etc) 180-254
Rise of monachism about 300
Foundation of churches of Armenia, about 300, of Georgia or Iberia 318
First council of Nice (COUNCILS OF THE CHURCH) 325
Rivalry between Rome and Constantinople begins about 340
Ulphilas preaches to the Goths about 376
Nestorius the bishop nominated the first patriarch of Constantinople 9 July, 381
On the death of Theodosius the Roman empire finally divided between his sons Arcadius and Honorius, the former receiving the East and the latter the West 17 Jan 395
[When the empire was divided there was one patriarch in the West (bishop of Rome), while in the East there were at first 2, then 4 and later 5]
Nestorius condemned at the council of Ephesus 431
Jerusalem made a patriarchate with jurisdiction over Palestine 451
Monophysite controversy, churches of Egypt, Syria, and Armenia part from church of Constantinople 461
Close of school of Athens, extinction of Platonic theology 529
Jacobite sect founded in Syria by Jacobus Baradæus 541
Struggle with Mahometans begins 634
FILIOQUE in the Nicene creed rejected by the Eastern church 662
Maronite sect begins to prevail about 676
Paulicians severely persecuted 690
Iconoclastic controversy begins about 726
Pope Gregory II excommunicates emperor Leo, hence the separation of the Eastern (Greek) and Western (Roman) churches, 729
Image worship condemned 734
Foundation of church in Russia, conversion of princess Olga, 955, of Vladimir 988
Pope Leo IX excommunicates the Eastern church 1054
Maronites join the Roman church 1182
Reunion of Eastern and Western churches at council of Lyons, 1274 (more political than ecclesiastical), again separated 1277
Orthodox confession of faith put forth in 1643
Proposed union with church of England 1723
Patriarchate of Moscow established, 1582, suppressed 1762
Archimandrite Nilos, representing Constantinople and 4 patriarchates visits London on behalf of Greek clergy in Danubian principalities 1863
Pope's invitation to an œcumenical council, 8 Dec 1869, declined by patriarch of Constantinople about 3 Oct. 1868
Letter from patriarch Gregory to archbishop of Canterbury acknowledging receipt of English prayer book, and objecting to some of "Thirty nine Articles" dated 8 Oct 1869
Greek church at Liverpool consecrated by an archbishop, 16 Jan 1870

Greek empire. EASTERN EMPIRE

Greek fire, a combustible composition (unknown, thought to have been principally naphtha) thrown from engines, said to have been invented by Callinicus, an engineer of Heliopolis, in Syria, in the 7th century, to destroy the Saracens' ships, which was effected by the general of the fleet of Constantine Pogonatus, and 30,000 men were killed A so-called "Greek fire," probably a solution of phosphorus in bisulphide of carbon, was employed at siege of Charleston, S. C., Sept. 1863

Greek language. The study was revived in W Europe about 1450, in France, 1473 William Grocyn, or Grokeyn, an English professor of this language, introduced it at Oxford, about 1491, where he taught Erasmus, who taught it at Cambridge in 1510.—*Wood's Athen Oxon* England has produced many eminent Greek scholars, such as Richard Bentley, died 1742, prof Richard Porson, died 1808, dr. Samuel Parr, died 1825, and dr Charles Burney, died 1817 "Society for Promoting Hellenic Studies" formed 16 June, 1879. A "Greek Club," for the study of the language and literature of ancient Greece, was founded in New York by prof Henry Drisler, rev dr Howard Crosby, and others, in 1857, and is still maintained. Modern Greek literature is now cultivated.

Greek literature and authors. LITERATURE

Greeley's peace mission. UNITED STATES, 1864

Greely's arctic expedition. ABSTINENCE, NORTHEAST AND NORTHWEST PASSAGES.

greenbacks, a name given, from the predominating color of the ink, to notes for a dollar and upwards, first issued by the United States government in 1862 Notes for lower sums (even 3 cents) were termed "fractional currency"

Greene's famous retreat. UNITED STATES, 1781

Greenland is the name applied to a large continental island separated from North America by Davis strait, lying mostly within the arctic circle belonging to Denmark, and supposed to extend from lat 59° 49′ N to lat 81° N It was discovered by Icelanders, under Eric Raude, about 980, and named from its verdure It was visited by Frobisher in 1576 The first ship from England to Greenland was sent for the whale-fishery by the Muscovy company, 2 James I 1604 In a voyage in 1630 8 men were left behind by accident, who suffered incredible hardships till the following year, when the company's ships brought them home —*Tindal* The Greenland Fishing company was incorporated 1693 Hans Egede, a Danish missionary, founded a new colony, called *Godhaab*, or Good Hope, in 1720-23, and other missionary stations have been since established Partially surveyed by Scoresby in 1821, and by capt Graah, for Denmark, in 1829-30 Pop in 1878, about 9408, 1888, 10,221, area estimated at between 400,000 and 600,000 sq miles NORTHEAST PASSAGES, 1892-94

Greenwich, Kent, Engl., anciently Grenawic, an ancient manor, near which Danes murdered archbishop Elphege, 1012 The hospital stands on the site of a royal residence erected in the reign of Edward I, and enlarged by his successors Here were born Henry VIII, his daughters Mary and Elizabeth, and here his son Edward VI died Charles II. planned a new palace here, but erected one wing only

William III and Mary converted the palace into a royal hospital for seamen, 1694, and added new buildings, erected by Wren 1696

By act of Parliament, about 900 indoor pensioners received additions to their pensions, quitted the hospital 1 Oct 1865, henceforth to be an infirmary The remaining inmates, except 31 bedridden persons, had left previously 1 Oct 1869

Greenwich observatory, built at the solicitation of sir Jonas Moore and sir Christopher Wren, by Charles II, on the summit of Flamsteed hill, so called from the first astronomer-royal The building was founded 10 Aug 1675, and Flamsteed commenced his residence 10 July, 1676 In 1852, an electric telegraph signal-ball in the Strand, London, was completed, and connected with Greenwich observatory.

ASTRONOMERS-ROYAL.

John Flamsteed	1675	Nevil Maskelyne	1765
Edmund Halley	1719	John Pond	1811
James Bradley	1742	George Biddell Airy	1835
Nathaniel Bliss	1762	Wm H M Christie	1881

Gregorian calendar. CALENDAR, NEW STYLE.

Gregorian chant and **modes** received their name from pope Gregory I., who improved the Ambrosian chant, and increased the number of modes (musical scales) to 8 about 590 On these the ritual music of the Western churches is founded MUSIC.

grenade (Sp *granada*), an explosive missile, invented 1594, is a hollow globe or ball of iron, filled with fine powder, and fired by a fusee

Hand grenades are about 2½ inches in diameter Rampant grenades, of various sizes, are rolled over the parapet in a trough

grenadiers. The grenadier corps was a company, consisting of the tallest and strongest men in an infantry regiment, armed with a pouch of hand-grenades. Established in France in 1667, and in England in 1685 —*Brown* GUARDS

Gretna Green, a village of Dumfries, S. Scotland, near the border Here runaway marriages were contracted for many years, as Scotch law ruled that an acknowledgment before witnesses made a legal marriage John Paisley, a tobacconist, and termed a blacksmith, who officiated from 1760, died in 1814. His first residence was at Megg's hill, on the common or green between Gretna and Springfield, to the last of which villages he removed in 1782. A man named Elliot was lately the principal officiating person. The General Assembly, in 1826, in vain attempted to suppress this system, but Parliament, in 1856, made these marriages illegal after that year, unless one of the parties had lived in Scotland 21 days.

Greytown, Attack upon. UNITED STATES, 1854.

Griffin or **Griffon,** The. NEW YORK, 1679.

Grimm's law of the transmutation of consonants in the Aryan family of languages, propounded by Jacob L Grimm in his "History of the German Languages," in 1848.

	Labials			Dentals			Gutturals		
Greek, Latin, Sanskrit	*p*	*b*	*f*	*t*	*d*	*th*	*k*	*g*	*ch*
Gothic	*f*	*p*	*b*	*th*	*t*	*d*		*k*	
Old High German	*b* (*v*)	*f*	*p*	*d*	*z*	*t*	*g*	*ch*	*k*

Examples Sanskrit *pitri*, Greek and Latin, *pater*, Italian, *padre*, Spanish, *padre*, French, *pere*, Gothic, *fadrein* (*pl.*), Old High German, *vatar*, English, *father*

Gri'qualand, W and E., 2 districts in British S Africa, containing diamond fields. The first diamond was discovered in W Griqualand in Mch 1867, and caused a great influx of immigrants from all nations, and the formation of many settlements Diamonds to the value of 12,000,000*l* were found there between 1871 and 1880, and about 15,000,000*l* between 1883 and 1887 The district was annexed to Cape Colony 27 Oct. 1871, and incorporated with it in 1880 Kimberley, the capital, was founded in 1871, population in 1890, about 6000 Europeans and 10 000 natives. Griqualand E, between the Kaffir border and southern Natal, was annexed to Cape Colony in 1875, pop 1890, 152,618.

Grisons (*gre-zon'*), a Swiss canton CADDEE. It was overrun by the French in 1798 and 1799 The ancient league was abolished, and Grisons became a member of the Helvetic confederation, 19 Feb. 1803

groat, from the Dutch *groot*, value fourpence, was the largest silver coin in England until after 1351. Fourpenny pieces were coined in 1836 to the value of 70,884*l.*, in 1837, 16,038*l*, discontinued since 1856

grocers anciently meant "ingrossers or monopolizers," as appears by a statute 37 Edw III 1363 "Les marchauntz nomez engrossent totes maners de merchandises vendables" The Grocers' company, one of the 12 chief companies of London, was established in 1345, and incorporated in 1429.

Gro'chow, a suburb of Warsaw Here took place a desperate conflict between the Poles and Russians, 19, 20 Feb 1831. The Russians are said to have lost 7000 men, and the Poles 2000 POLAND, 1861

grog, sea term for rum and water, derived its name from adm Edw Vernon, who wore grogram breeches, and was hence called "Old Grog" About 1745, he ordered his sailors to dilute their rum with water

Groveton, Battle of. POPE'S VIRGINIA CAMPAIGN

Guadalupe Hidalgo, a city of San Luis Potosi, Mexico, where, on 2 Feb. 1848, the Mexican and United States commissioners concluded peace By that treaty, New Mexico and Upper California were ceded to the United States for $15,000,000 and the assumption of debts of $3,500,000 due from Mexico to U S. citizens for property destroyed. ANNEXATIONS, MEXICAN WAR, UNITED STATES, Feb 1848

Guadeloupe, a West India island, discovered by Columbus in 1493. The French took possession in 1635, and colonized it in 1664. Taken by the English in 1759, and restored in 1763 Again taken by the English in 1779, 1794, and 1810 Restored to France in 1814 Taken by the British in 1815, restored to the French in 1816.

Guam, the largest of the Marianne or Ladrone archipelago, was ceded by Spain to the United States by art 2 of the treaty of peace concluded at Paris 10 Dec. 1898. It lies in a direct line from San Francisco to the southern part of the Philippines, and is 5200 miles from San Francisco and 900 miles from Manila It is about 32 miles long and 100 miles in circumference, and has a population of about 8661, of whom 5249 are in Agana, the capital The inhabitants are mostly immigrants or descendants of immigrants from the Philippines, the original race of the Ladrone islands being extinct. The prevailing language is Spanish. Nine-tenths of the islanders can read and write. The island is thickly wooded, well watered, and fertile, and possesses an excellent harbor. The productions are tropical fruits, cacao, rice, corn, tobacco, and sugar-cane.

guano, the excrement of sea-birds that swarm on the coasts of Peru and Bolivia, and of Africa and Australia. The importation of guano into Great Britain appears to have commenced in 1839. AGRICULTURE, UNITED STATES, 1840.

guards. The custom of having guards is said to have been introduced by Saul, 1093 B.C

Body guards were appointed for kings of England, 1 Hen VII 1485
Horse guards were raised 4 Edw VI 1550
Royal regiment of guards was first raised by Charles II in Flanders in 1656, col lord Wentworth, another regiment was raised by col John Russell, 1660, under whom they were combined in 1665 The Coldstream Guards raised by gen Monk, were constituted the 2d regiment in 1661 COLDSTREAM GUARDS These guards were the beginning of the British standing army
Gen sir F Wm Hamilton's "History of the Grenadier Guards," an elaborate work, appeared 1874
IMPERIAL GUARD, LIFE GUARD, Washington's, MILITIA, NATIONAL GUARDS

Guatema'la A republic in Central America, revolted from Spain 1821, and declared independent 21 Mch 1847, after having formed for 26 years part of the confederation of Central America Constitution settled, 2 Oct 1859 President (1862), gen Raphael Carrera, elected 1851, appointed for life, 1854, died 14 Apr 1865, succeeded by Vincent Cerna, 3 May, 1865-69, Manuel Garcia Granedos, Dec. 1872, R Barrios 7 May, 1873. A war between Guatemala and San Salvador broke out in Jan 1863, and on 16 June the troops of the latter were totally defeated An insurrection became formidable, July, 1871 Alliance with Honduras against San Salvador Mch 1872 It is now governed under a constitution proclaimed Dec 1879, modified Oct 1885, Nov 1887, and Oct 1889 The National Assembly consists of members chosen for 4 years The president is elected for 6 Area, 46,800 sq miles, pop. 1890, estimated 1,452,000

Guelphs (*gwelfs*) and **Ghibellines** (*gib-e-leens'*), the papal and imperial factions who destroyed the peace of Italy from the 12th to the end of the 15th century (the invasion of Charles VIII of France in 1495) The origin of the names is ascribed to the contest for the imperial crown between Conrad of Hohenstaufen, duke of Swabia, lord of Wiblingen (hence *Ghibelin*), and Henry, nephew of Welf, or Guelf, duke of Bavaria, in 1138 The former was successful, but the popes and several Italian cities took the side of his rival *Hie Guelf* and *Hie Ghibelin* are said to have been used as war-cries in 1140, at a battle before Weinsberg, in Würtemberg, when Guelf of Bavaria was defeated by the emperor Conrad IV, who came to help the rival duke, Leopold It is a tradition that upon the surrender of Weinsberg the emperor condemned all the men of that city to death, but permitted the women to bring out whatever they most valued, on which they carried out their husbands on their shoulders. The Ghibellines were mostly expelled from Italy in 1267, when Conradin, last of the Hohenstaufens, was beheaded by Charles of Anjou Guelph is the name of the present royal family of England BAVARIA, duke of, BRUNSWICK, ENGLAND, HANOVER

guerilla (Sp *guerrilla*, "little war"), a term first applied to armed peasants who worried the French armies during the Peninsular war, 1808-14

Gueux (*geh*, "beggars"), a name given by the comte de Barlaimont to the 300 Protestant deputies from the Low Countries, headed by Henri of Brederode and Louis of Nassau, who petitioned Margaret, governess of the Low Countries, to abolish the Inquisition, 5 Apr 1566 The deputies at once assumed the name as honorable, and organized armed resistance to the government HOLLAND

Guiana (*ḡe-a'-na*), northeast coast of South America, discovered by Columbus in 1498, visited by the Spaniards in the 16th century, and explored by sir Walter Raleigh in 1596 and 1617 The French settlements here were formed in 1626-1643, and the Dutch, 1627-67. At the peace of Breda, 1667, Dutch Guiana was assured to the Netherlands in exchange for the colony New Netherland (New York), and this was confirmed by the treaty of Westminster, Feb. 1674 Since then Surinam has been twice in the power of England—1799 till 1802, and again in 1804 to 1814, when it was returned, with other Dutch colonies, except Berbice, Demerara, and Essequibo, which remain to the British. Area, British Guiana, 109,000 sq miles, pop. 1891, 284,887 CAYENNE, DEMERARA, SURINAM

guide-books for travellers are an English invention Paterson's "British Itinerary" appeared in 1776, the last edition in 1840, when it was superseded by railways. Galignani's "Picture of Paris," 1814 Murray's "Handbook for Travellers on the Continent," the parent of the series, appeared in 1836 Appleton's "General Guide to the United States and Canada," 1879, and since

Guienne (*ḡe-en'*), a French province, was part of the dominions of Henry II in right of his wife Eleanor 1152 Philip of France seized it in 1293, which led to war It was alternately held by England and France till 1453, when John Talbot, earl of Shrewsbury, in vain attempted to retake it from the latter

Guildhall, London, was built in 1411 When it was rebuilt (in 1669), after the great fire of 1666, no part of the ancient building remained, except the interior of the porch and walls of the hall The front was erected in 1789, a new roof built, 1861-65 Beneath the west window are colossal figures of Gog and Magog, said to represent a Saxon and an ancient Briton, replaced older ones, 1708, renewed 1837 The hall holds 7000 persons Here were entertained the allied sovereigns in 1814, and Napoleon III 19 Apr 1855 A library existed in the Guildhall in 1426, from which books were taken by protector Somerset in the reign of Edward VI The library was again set up, and reopened, Jan 1828

guilds (of Saxon origin, about the 8th century), associations in towns for mutual benefit resembling British religious and friendly societies, chartered in Great Britain by the sovereign since the time of Henry II

Guild of Corpus Christi, York, had 14,800 members when a return of these guilds was ordered, 1388
Revival of religious guilds began in 1851, with that of St Alban

Guilford Court-house, Battle at Gen Greene retreated from the Catawba river, in South Carolina, into Virginia, before pursuing Cornwallis, in the winter of 1781 He soon returned, and at Guilford Court-house, in North Carolina, he fought Cornwallis and the British for more than 2 hours desperately The Americans were repulsed, and the British took possession of the field, but at a cost that made the victory a sad disaster "Another such victory," said Fox, in the British Parliament, "will ruin the British army" The British lost over 600, the Americans about 400 killed and wounded, and 1000 who deserted to their homes

guillotine (*ḡil-lo-teen'*), an instrument for immediate and painless death named after its supposed inventor, a physician named Joseph Ignatius Guillotin FRENCH REVOLUTION In 1866 M Dubois, of Amiens, stated that the idea only was due to Guillotin, who at a meeting of the legislative assembly in 1789 expressed an opinion that capital punishment should be the same for all classes Accordingly, at the request of the assembly, M Louis, secretary of the "Academie de Chirurgie," submitted to that body, on 20 Mch 1792, his invention of a mode of capital punishment, "sure, quick, and uniform" The first person executed by it was a highway robber named Pelletier, on 25 Apr; and Dangremont was its first political victim, 21 Aug following Guillotin died in 1814 The guillotine at Paris was burned by the communists, 7 Apr. 1871. A similar instrument (called the *Mannaia*) is said to have been used in Italy, at Halifax in England (HALIFAX) and in Scotland, there called the Maiden and the Widow.

Guinea (*ḡin'-ee*), a geographical division of W Africa, was discovered by the Portuguese about 1446 From their trade with the Moors originated the slave-trade, sir John Hawkins being the first Englishman who engaged in this traffic Assisted by other Englishmen with money, he sailed from England in Oct. 1562, with 3 ships, to the coast of Guinea, purchased or forcibly seized 300 negroes, sold them profitably at Hispaniola, and returned home richly laden with hides, sugar, ginger, and other merchandise, in Sept. 1563 This voyage led to similar enterprises.—*Hakluyt* SLAVE-TRADE An African company to trade with Guinea was chartered 1588 The Dutch settlements here were transferred to Great Britain, 6 Apr 1872 ASHANTEES, ELMINA

guinea, English gold coin, so named from having been first coined of gold brought by the African company from the coast of Guinea in 1663, valued then at 20*s*, but worth 30*s* in 1695. Reduced at various times, in 1717 to 21*s* In 1810 guineas were sold for 22*s* 6*d*, in 1816, for 27*s*. In 1811 an act was passed forbidding their exportation, and their sale at a price above the current value, 21s The first guineas bore the impression of an elephant, having been coined of African gold Since the issue of sovereigns, 1 July, 1817, guineas have not been coined COIN and COINAGE

"Gulliver's Travels," by dean Swift, first pub. 1726-27

gun. ARTILLERY, FIRE-ARMS.

gun-boats. UNITED STATES, 1807.

gun-cotton, a highly explosive substance, invented by prof Schonbein, of Basel, and made known in 1846 It is purified cotton, steeped in a mixture of equal parts of nitric acid and sulphuric acid, and dried, retaining the appearance of cotton-wool COLLODION Its nature was known to Braconnot and Pelouze

gunpowder. The invention of gunpowder is ascribed to Bertholdus or Michael Schwartz, a Cordelier monk of Goslar, south of Brunswick, in Germany, about 1320 But some maintain that it was known much earlier Some say that the Chinese and Hindus possessed it centuries before Its composition is mentioned by Roger Bacon, in his treatise "De Nullitate Magiæ." He died in 1292 or 1294 Various substitutes for gunpowder have been recently invented, such as the white gunpowder of Mr Horsley and dr Ehrhardt, and gun-paper by Mr Hochstodten A new gunpowder by M Newmayer of Toya, near Leipsic, was discussed in Nov 1866 "Pellet gunpowder" was ordered to be used in gun-charges in the British army, Mch 1868. An act to amend the law concerning the making, keeping, and carriage of gunpowder, etc, was passed in England, 28 Aug 1860, and other acts since BIRMINGHAM, 1870 In May, 1872, a company was formed to manufacture R Punshon's patent cotton gunpowder, asserted to be very safe and controllable. Common gunpowder when burned produces much smoke The invention of a smokeless powder has long been sought "The great majority of smokeless powders (over 20 in all) may be classed under 2 heads, (1) those consisting of nitro-cellulose, and (2) those in which nitro-glycerine forms a part"—*Engineering Journal*, London, 20 May, 1892, p. 629 Of the different kinds the principal ones are apyrite, chosen by Sweden after exhaustive and protracted experiments, 1891, Nobel's (German), 1889-91, French, "B N," nitro-glycerine, English, cordite. CHRONOSCOPE

The use of gunpowder was denounced by Ariosto, 1516, by Jean Marot, 1532, by Cervantes 1604, termed "villanous saltpetre," by Shakespeare, about 1598

English war gunpowder 75 parts nitrate of potash (saltpetre), 10 sulphur, 15 carbon These proportions may be slightly varied

W Hunter, after a careful examination of the question, in 1847, says "July and August, 1346, may be safely assumed to be the time when the explosive force of gunpowder was first brought to bear on the military operations of the English nation."

gunpowder plot, a conspiracy to spring a mine under the British houses of Parliament, and destroy the king, lords, and commons, was discovered 4 Nov. 1605. It was projected by Robert Catesby early in 1604, and several Roman Catholics of rank were in the plot. Guy Faux was found in the vaults under the House of Lords, hired for the purpose, preparing a train to be fired the next day Catesby and Percy (of the family of Northumberland) were killed at Holbeach house, whither they had fled, 8 Nov, and Guy Faux, sir Everard Digby, Rookwood, Winter, and others were executed, 30, 31 Jan 1606. Henry Garnet, a Jesuit, suffered as an accomplice, 3 May following The discovery was occasioned by an anonymous letter sent to lord Monteagle, which said "Though there be no appearance of any stir, yet I say they shall receive a terrible blow this parliament, and yet they shall not see who hurts them." In 1825, the vault called Guy Faux cellar, in which barrels of gunpowder were lodged, was converted into offices

Gunter's chain, 66 ft. long, divided into 100 links, is used in measuring land. It was invented by Edmund Gunter in 1606

gutta-percha, a gum from the sap of the *Isonandra gutta*, a large forest-tree of the Malay peninsula and neighboring islands It was made known in England by drs. De Almeida and Montgomery, at the Society of Arts, in 1843 Being a non-conductor of electricity, it is invaluable as an insulator, and its use in submarine telegraphs was suggested by Faraday and Werner Siemens independently, 1847

gymna'sium, a place where the Greeks performed public exercises, and where philosophers, poets, and rhetoricians repeated their compositions In wrestling and boxing the athletes were often naked (*gymnos*), whence the name —The *gymnasia* in Germany are the classical schools preparing pupils in a nine years' course for the universities and the learned professions

gypsies, gipsies, or **Egyptians** (Fr. *Bohémiens;* It *Zingari*, Sp *Gitanos*, Ger *Zigeuner*), vagrants, supposed to be descendants of low-caste Hindus expelled by Timour, about 1399. They appeared in Germany and Italy early in the 15th century, and at Paris in 1427. In England an act was passed to suppress them as vagabonds in 1530, and under Charles I 13 persons were executed at one assizes for having associated with gypsies for a month The gypsy settlement at Norwood, England, was broken up, and they were treated as vagrants, May, 1797. There were in Spain alone, before 1800, more than 120,000 gypsies, and there are communities of them in England. Notwithstanding their intercourse with other nations, their manners, customs, visage, and appearance are almost wholly unchanged, and their pretended knowledge of futurity gives them power over the superstitious Esther Faa was crowned queen of the gypsies at Blyth, England, on 18 Nov 1860 The Bible has been translated into gypsy dialects. Gypsy parliaments are occasionally held.

George Borrow fraternized with the gypsies and wrote several works describing his adventures, especially "The Zincali" (1841), "The Bible in Spain" (1842), "Lavengro" (1850), and a "Dictionary of the Gypsy Language" (1874) He was b in 1803, and d. in Aug 1881

gy'roscope (from Gr. γῦρος, *ring*, and σκοπέω, *to observe*), a rotatory apparatus invented by Fessel of Cologne (1852), improved by prof Wheatstone and M. Foucault of Paris It is similar in principle to the rotatory apparatus of Bohnenberger of Tübingen (b. 1765, d 1831) The gyroscope, by exhibiting the combination and counteraction of centrifugal and centripetal forces, illustrates the laws of motion.

H

H. This letter of the alphabet has varied in form from the Phœnician and old Hebrew symbol 𐤇, called Cheth, only by the removal of the upper and lower horizontal lines.

Haarlem (*har'lem*), an ancient town in Holland, mentioned in the register of the 10th century. Through count William II, it obtained a charter in 1245. For a short time in 1492 it was occupied by the insurgents called the "bread-and-cheese folk." Its inhabitants took a prominent part in the revolt of the Netherlands. It was invested by the duke of Alva with a force of 30,000, Dec. 1572, and surrendered after a heroic defence July, 1573 Alva violated his capitulation promises [illegible] nearly half the inhabitants. It was recovered from the Spaniards by the prince of Orange in 1577 The lake was drained 1848-52, liberating 42,000 acres of land, estimated cost of drainage, $3,600,000. Pop 1890, 51,626.

Habak'kuk, one of the minor prophets of the Old Testament, 606 B.C.—*Usher*

habeas corpus (in England). The subjects' *Writ of Right*, passed "for the better securing the liberty of the subject," 31 Charles II. c. 2, 27 May, 1679 If any person be imprisoned by the order of any court, or of the queen, he may have a writ of habeas corpus to bring him before the queen's bench, or common pleas, which shall determine [illegible] committal be just This act (founded on the old common-law) is next in importance to *Magna Charta* Parliament may suspend the *Habeas Corpus* act for a specified time in a great emergency Then the nation parts with a portion of liberty to secure its permanent welfare, and suspected persons may then be arrested without cause assigned.—*Blackstone*

Act suspended for a short time 1689, 1696 1708
Suspended for Scots' rebellion 1715-16
Suspended for 12 months 1722
Suspended for Scots' rebellion 1744-45
Suspended for American war 1777-79
Again by Mr Pitt, owing to French revolution 1794
Suspended in Ireland in the great rebellion 1798
Suspended in England 28 Aug 1799, and 14 Apr 1801
Again, on account of Irish insurrection 1803
Again, on alleged secret meetings. 21 Feb. 1817
Bill to restore *habeas corpus* introduced 28 Jan 1818
Suspended in Ireland (insurrection) 24 July, 1848
Restored there 1 Mch 1849
Suspended again (FENIANS), 17 Feb 1866, 26 Feb and 31 May 1867, and 28 Feb 1868, till 25 Mch 1869
Because of the affair of John Anderson (SLAVERY IN ENGLAND), an act of 1862 enacted that no writ of *habeas corpus* should issue out of England to any colony, etc, having a court with authority to grant such writ

habeas corpus (in the United States) The Constitution of the U S provides that "the privilege of *habeas corpus* shall not be suspended, unless when, in cases of rebellion or invasion, the public safety may require it," but does not specify what department of the government may suspend it A series of contests on this subject began with the civil war and continued throughout, both as to the legality of suspension and the jurisdiction The writ of *habeas corpus* was first suspended by pres. Lincoln between Washington and Philadelphia, 27 Apr 1861, in instructions to gen Scott (it had been suspended by state authority in Rhode Island for a brief time during DORR'S REBELLION)

President suspends the writ in Key West, Tortugas, and Santa Rosa 10 May, 1861
Further extension 2 July, "
Chief justice Taney issues a writ of *habeas corpus* 27 May to gen Geo Cadwallader on appeal by John Merryman of Baltimore then confined in fort McHenry 25 May, "
[On the general's refusal to obey the writ Taney attempts to arrest him, but fails]
Theophilus Parsons supports president s power to suspend, 5 June, "
Attorney general Bates asserts the president's power to declare martial law and suspend the writ of *habeas corpus* 5 July, "
One hundred and seventy four persons committed to fort Lafayette July to Oct. "
Suspension of the writ made general 24 Sept 1862
Congress by act upholds this power 3 Mch 1863
Vallandigham arrested (UNITED STATES) 4 May, "
President suspends by proclamation 15 Sept "
All persons held under suspension of the writ discharged May, 1864
Suspends in Kentucky 5 July, "
Pres. Johnson restores the writ of *habeas corpus* except in the late insurrectionary states, District of Columbia, New Mexico, and Arizona, by proclamation 11 Dec 1865
In all states and territories except Texas 2 Apr 1866
Throughout the U S 20 Aug "
Thirty eight thousand arrests were made according to the provost marshal's record, Washington, during the rebellion MILLIGAN CASE, STONE, BRIG GEN CHARLES P, Case of

Hades (Gr Ἅιδης) (α, not, and εἴδω, to see), originally the god of the lower world, and only in this sense in Homer Hence the place of departed spirits The word *Sheol* of the Hebrews expresses the same idea The later Greek as well as Hebrew thought divided the place into 2 parts Later still the idea developed into the contrasted spheres of Heaven and Hell, including the Purgatory of the church

Hadrian's wall, built to prevent irruptions of Scots and Picts into the northern counties of England, then under Roman government, extended from the Tyne to Solway frith It was 80 miles long, 12 feet high, and 8 feet thick, with mile castles and smaller sentry boxes between Along its whole northern side was a ditch or fosse about 36 feet wide and 15 feet deep, while on the southern side was a Roman road connecting the garrisons of the different stations. It was probably from 10 to 15 years in building, and required 10,000 men to garrison its stations Probably built under Hadrian 121 A D., and extended by Servius 207-10

Hafsflord (*hafs-fe-ord'*), Norway. Here Harold Härfager, in a sea-fight, defeated his enemies and consolidated his kingdom, 872 A millenary festival was held throughout Norway, and a monument to his memory set up at Haugesund, by prince Oscar of Sweden, 18 July, 1872

Hague, the, capital of Holland, once called the finest *village* in Europe, the place of meeting of the States-general, and residence of the former earls of Holland since 1250, when William II built the palace here Pop 1890, 160,531

Here the states abjured the authority of Philip II of Spain 1580
A conference upon the 5 articles of remonstrants, which occasioned the synod of Dort 1610
Treaty at the Hague (to preserve equilibrium of the North) of England, France and Holland 21 May, 1659
De Witts torn in pieces here 4 Aug 1672
French took possession of the Hague, inhabitants and troops declared in their favor, revolution ensued 19 Jan 1795
The Hague evacuated by the French Nov 1813

Hague Tribunal. PEACE CONFERENCE

"Hail, Columbia!" This patriotic song was written by Joseph Hopkinson, 29 Apr 1798, when the United States were threatened with a war with France It was composed to the air of the "President's March," for a young actor and singer in the Philadelphia theatre, and became at once highly popular LITERATURE, NEW YORK CITY, 1789

hail-storms. STORMS

Hainault forest, Essex, Engl, disafforested in 1851. Here stood the FAIRLOP OAK.

Hainaut (*hā'-no'*), a frontier province of Belgium, anciently governed by counts hereditary after Regnier I, who died in 916 The count John d'Arsenes became count of Holland in 1299 Hainaut henceforth partook of the fortunes of Flanders

Haines's Bluff, Operations at VICKSBURG CAMPAIGN

hair. In Gaul, hair was much esteemed, hence the appellation *Gallia comata*, cutting off the hair was a punishment The royal family of France held it a privilege to wear long hair artfully dressed and curled. "The clerical tonsure is of apostolic institution!"—*Isidorus Hispalensis* Pope Anicetus forbade the clergy to wear long hair, 155 Long hair was a distinctive mark of the cavaliers or followers of Charles I of England, as short hair was of the ROUNDHEADS, during the civil war and protectorate of Cromwell, 1642-60 Of late years the hair is worn much shorter than formerly.

Hakluyt (*hăk'-loot*) **Society,** England, for the publication of rare voyages and travels, 15 Dec 1846, was named after Richard Hakluyt, who published his "Principal Navigations, Voyages, and Discoveries made by the English Nation," in 1589, and died 23 Nov. 1616, aged 63 VIRGINIA, 1606.

halcyon (Gr ἀλκυών, king-fisher), a poetic name for the king-fisher, and since that bird was fabled to lay its eggs on the waves, and to keep the sea calm during incubation, "halcyon days" are days of calm and peace

Hale, capt. Nathan, the American spy, belonged to Knowlton's regiment and accepted the perilous service of exploring the British camp on Long Island under instructions from gen. Washington, then retreating to Harlem Heights. With the desired information, he was discovered before reaching the American lines, through a Tory kinsman, and hanged next morning, 22 Sept. 1776, without trial and with insult and cruelty He was a graduate of Yale, 1773, and died at the age of 22 His statue erected in City Hall park, N. Y., Dec. 1893. NEW YORK, 1776

Half-breeds. POLITICAL PARTIES

Hal'icarnas'sus, now **Boodroom,** an ancient town of Caria, Asia Minor, reputed birthplace of Herodotus, 484 B C, site of the tomb of Mausolus, erected 352, taken by Alexander, 334. MAUSOLEUM

Halidon hill, near Berwick, where, on 19 July, 1333, the English defeated the Scots, killing more than 14,000, with the regent Douglas and many nobles, the English loss was small. Edward Balliol thus became king of Scotland for a short time.

Halifax, capital of Nova Scotia, lat 44° 37′ N., lon 63°

38′ W., was founded by the hon. Edward Cornwallis in 1749, and named after the earl of Halifax. Pop. 1891, 38,556.

Halle, Prussian Saxony, N. Germany, first mentioned 801, made a city by the emperor Otho II., in 981. University founded by Frederick I., 1694, recognized as one of the principal schools of Protestant theology. The orphan-house was established by August Francke, 1698–99. Halle suffered much by the Thirty Years' and Seven Years' wars. It was stormed by the French, 17 Oct. 1806, and added to Westphalia; but given to Prussia in 1814. Pop. 1890, 101,401.

hallelujah and **amen** (*Praise the Lord*, and *So be it*), expressions in Hebrew hymns, ascribed to Haggai about 520 B.C. Their introduction into Christian worship is ascribed to St. Jerome, about 390 A.D.

Halloween or **Hallow-eve,** the evening before All-Saints' day, the night of Oct. 31, in many countries a time for superstitious ceremonies, and in Scotland especially devoted by young people to playful divination for predicting future husbands or wives.

"Amang the bonny, winding banks,
  Where Doon rins, wimplin', clear,
Where Bruce ance ruled the martial ranks,
  And shook his Carrick spear,
Some merry, friendly, country folks
  Together did convene,
To burn their nits, and pou their stocks,
  And haud their Halloween
      Fu' blythe that night."
        —*Burns*, "Halloween."

halo, a circle of light around the sun or moon, produced by refraction through minute ice crystals suspended in the atmosphere.

Ha'lys, a river in Asia Minor, near which a battle between Lydians and Medes was interrupted by an almost total eclipse of the sun, which led to peace, 28 May, 585 B.C. (the 4th year of the 48th Olympiad).—*Pliny*, "Nat. Hist." ii. Others date it 584, 603, or 610 B.C. This eclipse is said to have been predicted many years before by Thales of Miletus. —*Herodotus*, i. 75.

Ham, a town on the Somme, N. France. The castle was built in 1470 by the constable Louis of Luxembourg, comte de St. Pol, beheaded by Louis XI., 19 Dec. 1475. Here were imprisoned the ex-ministers of Charles X., 1830, and Louis Napoleon after his attempt at Boulogne, from Oct. 1840, till 25 May, 1846, when he escaped by the aid of Mazzini.

Hamburg, a free city of N.W. Germany, on the right bank of the Elbe, founded by Charlemagne about 809. It joined the Hanseatic league (HANSE TOWNS) in the 13th century, and became a flourishing commercial city. Pop. in 1860, 229,941; 1871, 338,974; 1875, 338,618; 1890, 323,923. Its territory includes 158 sq. miles, with a pop., 1900, of 705,738.

A free imperial city by permission of dukes of Holstein, 1296; subject to them till 1618; purchased total exemption from their claims.... 1768
French declared war upon Hamburg for treachery in giving up Napper Tandy (TANDY)....Oct. 1799
British property sequestrated....Mch. 1801
Hamburg taken by French after battle of Jena.... 1806
Incorporated with France.... 1810
Evacuated by French on Russian advance into Germany.... 1813
Restored to independence by the allies....May, 1814
Hamburg joined North German confederation....21 Aug. 1866
Joined German empire, Jan.; privileges as free port confirmed, 16 Apr. 1871
Visitation of CHOLERA.... 1892

Hamburg, S. C., **massacre.** SOUTH CAROLINA, 1876.

Hamilton and **Burr.** NEW YORK, 1804.

Hampton Court palace, Middlesex, Engl., built by cardinal Wolsey on the site of the manor-house of the knights hospitallers, and in 1525 presented to Henry VIII. Here Edward VI. was born, 12 Oct. 1537; here his mother, Jane Seymour, died, 24 Oct. following; and here Mary, Elizabeth, Charles, and other sovereigns resided. Much was pulled down, and the grand inner court built by William III. in 1694, when the gardens, occupying 40 acres, were laid out. The vine was planted 1769. A conference here, 14–16–18 Jan. 1604, between Puritans and established church clergy, led to a new translation of the Bible. CONFERENCE.

Hampton Roads, Va., Conflict between the *Monitor* and the *Merrimac*. The United States war ship *Merrimac*, sunk when Norfolk navy-yard was abandoned by the federals, 20 Apr. 1861, was raised by confederates, converted into an iron-clad ram, and named *Virginia*. John Ericsson contracted to build the *Monitor* 5 Oct. 1861; completed it early in the following January. On 5 Mch. 1862, she was despatched to fortress Monroe. Just before she arrived the *Virginia*, commanded by Franklin Buchanan, came out (8 Mch.) and attacked the federal vessels in Hampton Roads. She sunk the *Cumberland*, captured the *Congress*, and pushed the *Minnesota* aground, and at night returned to Norfolk. Next morning she reappeared, but was met by the *Monitor*, commanded by lieut. John L. Worden. After a short conflict the *Virginia*, finding the odds against her, again retired. After evacuation of Norfolk by the confederates, she was blown up by her commander, Josiah Tatnall, 11 May, 1862. The *Monitor* sank on her passage to Charleston, 31 Dec. 1862. MONITOR, NAVY.

Hampton Roads conference. In Jan. 1865, Francis P. Blair twice visited Richmond, Va., to confer with Jefferson Davis. He believed that a suspension of hostilities, and an ultimate settlement by restoration of the Union, might be brought about, by the common desire, north and south, to enforce the Monroe doctrine against the French in Mexico. Out of Mr. Blair's visits grew a conference, held on a vessel in Hampton Roads, 3 Feb. 1865, between Mr. Lincoln and Mr. Seward upon one side, and Messrs. A. H. Stephens, R. M. T. Hunter, and John A. Campbell on the other. It was informal, and no basis for negotiation was reached.

Hanau (*ha'-now*), a town of Hesse-Cassel, incorporated 1303. Here a division of the armies of Austria and Bavaria of 30,000 men, under gen. Wrede, encountered the French, 70,000 strong, under Napoleon I., on their retreat from Leipsic, 30 Oct. 1813. The French suffered severely, though the allies were compelled to retire. Hanau was made a principality in 1803; seized by the French in 1806; incorporated with the duchy of Frankfort in 1809; restored in 1813 to Hesse; which was annexed to Prussia in 1866.

Handel's commemorations. The first was held in Westminster abbey, London, 26 May, 1784; above 3000 persons present. The band contained 268 vocal and 245 instrumental performers, and the receipts of 3 days were 12,746*l.* These concerts were repeated in 1785, 1786, 1787, and 1791.

Second great commemoration, with 644 performers, 24, 26, 28 June, and 1 July, 1834.
Great Handel festival (at the Crystal palace) on the centenary of his death, projected by Sacred Harmonic Society. Grand rehearsal at Crystal palace, 15, 17, 19 June, 1857, and 2 July, 1858.
Performances: "Messiah," 20 June; selections, 22 June; "Israel in Egypt," 24 June, 1859, 26,827 persons present, with 2765 vocal and 393 instrumental performers. The receipts were about 33,000*l.*, expenses 18,000*l.*; of the residue (15,000*l.*), 2 parts accrued to the Crystal Palace company, and 1 part to the Sacred Harmonic Society. Handel's harpsichord, original scores of his oratorios, and other relics were exhibited.
Handel festivals (at the Crystal palace): 4000 performers, highly successful, 23, 25, 27 June, 1862; again, 26, 28, 30 June, 1865; again, 15, 17, 19 June, 1868 (about 25,000 present); also, 19, 21, 23 June, 1871 (about 84,000 persons subscribed); also, 22, 24, 26 June, 1874 (total present, 78,839); also, 25, 27, 29 June, 1877 (present, 74,124); 18, 21, 23, 25 June, 1880 (present, 70,643).
Handel and Haydn Society, Boston, Mass., for performances only; founded 1816. MUSIC.

handkerchiefs, wrought and edged with gold, used to be worn in England by gentlemen in their hats, as favors from young ladies; worth from 5*d.* to 12*d.* each, in the reign of Elizabeth, 1558.—*Stow's Chron.* Paisley handkerchiefs were first made in 1743.

hands, Imposition of, first performed by Moses in setting apart his successor Joshua (Numb. xxvii. 23); in reception into the church, and in ordination, by the Apostles (Acts viii. 17; 1 Tim. iv. 14).

hanging, drawing, and **quartering,** said to have been first inflicted upon William Marise, a pirate, a nobleman's son, 25 Hen. III. 1241. 5 gentlemen of the duke of

Gloucester were arraigned and condemned for treason, and at the place of execution were hanged, cut down alive instantly, stripped naked, their bodies marked for quartering, and then pardoned, 25 Hen IV 1447 —*Stow* The Cato-street conspirators (CATO-STREET CONSPIRACY) were beheaded after death by hanging, 1 May, 1820 Hanging in chains was abolished in 1834 DEATH PENALTY

Hanging Rock, S C, Battle of A few miles eastward of ROCKY MOUNT, on the Catawba river, a large bowlder on a high bank, called Hanging rock gives name to the place There a large body of British and Tories were attacked and dispersed by gen Sumter on 6 Aug 1780, after a desperate engagement of about 4 hours Sumter lost 12 killed and 41 wounded

Hanover, N W Germany, successively an electorate and a kingdom, chiefly territories which once belonged to the dukes of Brunswick It was annexed to Prussia, 20 Sept 1866 Pop 1859, 1,850,000, 1861, 1 888,070, 1875, 2 017,393, 1890, 2,278,361

Hanover became the 9th electorate	19 Dec 1692
Suffered much during the Seven Years war	1756–63
Seized by Prussia	3 Apr 1801
Occupied and hardly used by the French	5 June, 1803
Delivered to Prussia	1805
Retaken by the French	1807
Part of it annexed to Westphalia	1810
Regained for England by Bernadotte	6 Nov 1813
Made a kingdom, George III of England king	12 Oct 1814
Duke of Cambridge viceroy, representative government established	Nov 1816
Visited by George IV	Oct 1821
Ernest, duke of Cumberland king	20 June, 1837
He granted a constitution with electoral rights, 1848, annulled by decree of the federal diet	12 Apr 1855
King claims from England crown jewels of George III (value about 120,000*l*), 1857, arbitration the jewels given up Jan	1858
STADE—dues given up for compensation	12 June, 1861
King takes side with Austria, the Prussians enter and occupy Hanover	13 June et seq 1866
Hanoverians defeat Prussians at Langensalza, 27 June, but surrender	29 June, "
Hanover annexed to Prussia by law, 20 Sept , promulgated,	6 Oct. "
Protest of king of Hanover to Europe	23 Sept "
Arrangement with Prussia by a treaty ratified.	18 Oct. 1867

ELECTORS

1692. Ernest Augustus, youngest son of George, that son of William, duke of Brunswick Luneburg, who obtained by lot the right to marry (BRUNSWICK) He became bishop of Osnaburg in 1662 and in 1679 inherited the possessions of his uncle John, duke of Calenberg, created elector of Hanover in 1692
   [He married, in 1659, princess Sophia, daughter of Frederick, elector palatine, and of Elizabeth, daughter of James I of England. In 1701 Parliament settled the British crown in her descendants "being Protestants," after failure of descendants from William III and Anne]

1698. George Lewis, son of the preceding, married his cousin Sophia, heiress of duke of Brunswick Zell, became king of Great Britain, 1 Aug 1714, as George I

1727 George Augustus, his son (George II of England), 11 June

1760. George William Frederick, his grandson (George III of England), 25 Oct.

KINGS.

1814 George III of England became first king of Hanover 12 Oct.

1820 George Augustus Frederick, his son (George IV of England), 29 Jan

1830 William Henry, his brother (William IV of England), 26 June, d 20 June, 1837
   [Hanover separated from crown of Great Britain.]

1837 Ernest Augustus, duke of Cumberland, brother to William IV of England, succeeded (as a distinct inheritance) to the throne of Hanover 20 June

1851. George V (b 27 May, 1819), son of Ernest, ascended the throne on the death of his father, 18 Nov His states annexed to Prussia, 20 Sept 1866, visited England, May, June, 1876, d 12 June, 1878

1878. Ernest Augustus II, son, b 21 Sept. 1845, maintained his claims in a circular to the sovereigns of Europe, dated 11 July, 1878, married princess Thyra of Denmark, 20 Dec. 1878

Hanse towns. The Hanseatic league (from *hansa*, association), formed by port towns in Germany against the piracies of Swedes and Danes, began about 1140, the league signed 1241 At first only of towns on the coasts of the Baltic, in 1370 it included 66 cities and 44 confederates. The league proclaimed war against Waldemar, king of Denmark, about 1348, and against Eric, in 1428, with 40 ships and 12,000 regular troops, besides seamen On this several princes ordered the merchants of their kingdoms to withdraw their effects. The Thirty Years' war in Germany (1618–48) broke the strength of the league, and in 1630 only BREMEN, HAMBURG, and LUBECK retained the name The league suffered also by the rise of the commerce of the Low Countries in the 15th century Their privileges by treaty in England were abolished by Elizabeth in 1578

Hapsburg, Habsburg, or **Habichtsburg** (Hawk's castle), House of, the family from which the imperial house of Austria sprang in the 11th century, Werner being the first-named count of Hapsburg 1099 Hapsburg was an ancient castle of Switzerland, on a lofty eminence near Schintznach Rudolph, count of Hapsburg, became archduke of Austria and emperor of Germany, 1273, through the support of archbishop Werner elector of Mentz, and the duke of Bavaria AUSTRIA, GERMANY.

hard-cider and **log-cabin campaign.** UNITED STATES, 1840

Harfleur (*har-flur'*), seaport, N W France, taken by Henry V, 22 Sept 1415

Harlaw, Aberdeenshire, Scotland, site of a desperate, indecisive battle between the earl of Mar, with the royal army, and Donald, the lord of the Isles, who aimed at independence, 24 July, 1411 It was disastrous to the nobility, some houses losing all their males.

Harleian (*har-lē'-an*) **library,** with 7000 MSS., besides rare books, bought by Edward Harley, afterwards earl of Oxford and Mortimer, 1705 et seq , is now in the British museum Much of his life and wealth was spent on the collection He died 21 May, 1724 The "Harleian Miscellany," a selection from MSS and tracts of his library, was pub 1744 and 1808.

Harlem Heights, Battle of A severe skirmish, on 16 Sept 1776, between American troops under col Knowlton and major Leitch, and detachments of the British army, then in possession of New York city Knowlton and Leitch were killed, but the Americans were victorious. Of Knowlton, Washington said, "He was an honor to any country"

Harlem River Aqueduct bridge. AQUEDUCTS.

Harmar's Indian expedition. OHIO, 1790.

harmonic strings, said to have been invented by Pythagoras about 540 B.C , through hearing 4 blacksmiths working with hammers, in harmony, whose weights he found to be 6, 8, 9, and 12

harmon'ica, or musical glasses (tuned by regulating the amount of water, and played by a moistened finger on the rim), were played on by Gluck in London, 23 Apr 1746, "arranged" by Puckeridge and Delaval, and improved by dr. Franklin in 1760 Mozart, Beethoven, and others composed for this instrument COPOPHONE.

harmon'ichord, a keyed instrument, in which sounds are produced by friction, invented by Th Kauffmann in 1810.

Harmonists, a sect founded in Wurtemberg by George and Frederick Rapp, about 1780 Not much is known of their tenets, but they held their property in common, and considered marriage a civil contract. They emigrated to America, and settled first in Butler county, Pa 1805, but removed to Indiana, and purchased 27,000 acres of land, and called it New Harmony, 1814. In 1824 they sold their land to Robert Owen, and, returning to Pennsylvania, settled at Economy, a few miles north of Pittsburg NEW HARMONY Robert Owen failed in his scheme for a "social" community, and returned to England SOCIALISM

harmo'nium, a keyed instrument, resembling the accordion, its tones produced by wind upon metallic reeds The Chinese were well acquainted with the effects of vibrating tongues of metal M Biot stated, in 1810, that they were used musically by M Grenié, and in 1827–29 free reed-stops were employed in organs at Beauvais and Paris. The best-known harmoniums in England are those of Alexandre and Debain, the latter claiming to be the original maker of the

French instrument. In 1841, W. E. Evans, of Cheltenham, produced his English harmonium, then termed the "organ-harmonica," which, by successive improvements, became a fine instrument, with diapason quality, and great rapidity of speech, without loss of power.

harmony, the combination of musical notes of different pitch; not understood by the ancient Greeks. MUSIC.

harness, originally defensive armor; now applied to working-tackle of animals. Chariots, and leathern dressings for horses to draw them, are ascribed by mythology to Erichthonius of Athens, who was made the constellation *Boötes* (ploughman) after his death, about 1487 B.C.

harp. Invented by Jubal, 3875 B.C. (Gen. iv. 21). David played it before Saul, 1063 B.C. (1 Sam. xvi. 23). The Cimbri, or English Saxons, had this instrument. The celebrated Welsh harp was strung with gut; and the Irish harp, like more ancient harps, with wire. Erard's improved harps were patented in 1795.

One of the most ancient harps is that of Brian Boroimhe, monarch of Ireland, given by his son Donagh to pope John XVIII., with the crown and other regalia of his father, to obtain absolution for the murder of his brother Teig. Adrian IV. alleged this as one of his titles to the kingdom of Ireland in a bull transferring it to Henry II. This harp was givén by Leo X. to Henry VIII., by him to the first earl of Clanricarde; it then came to the family of De Burgh; next to that of MacMahon of Clenagh, county Clare; afterwards to that of MacNamara of Limerick; and was deposited by the right hon. William Conyngham in the College museum, Dublin, in 1782.

Harper's Ferry, W. Va., at the outlet of the Shenandoah valley, where the Shenandoah joins the Potomac. The town in 1860 had a population of 10,000. John Brown seized the place 16 Oct. 1859. BROWN'S INSURRECTION. On 18 Apr. 1861, the day after the secession of Virginia, a confederate force marched upon the town. Lieut. Roger Jones, unable to hold the post, abandoned it, after destroying the arsenal and workshops. The place was held by gen. Patterson just before and during the first battle of Bull Run. On 15 Sept. 1862, it was surrounded and captured by "Stonewall" Jackson. Col. Dixon S. Miles, commanding the post, was killed; 12,520 men fell into the hands of the confederates. MARYLAND CAMPAIGN and UNITED STATES and VIRGINIA, 1859-62.

harpsichord. PIANO-FORTE.

Harrison, Fort. FORT HARRISON.

Harrison, William Henry, Administration of. UNITED STATES, 1840-41.

Harrison, Benjamin, Administration of. UNITED STATES, 1889-93.

Harrison's timepiece, made by John Harrison, of Foulby, near Pontefract, Engl. In 1714, the British government offered rewards for methods of determining longitude at sea. Harrison came to London, and produced his first timepiece in 1735; his second in 1739; his third in 1749, and his fourth, which procured him the reward of 20,000*l.* offered by the Board of Longitude, a few years after. He obtained 10,000*l.* of his reward in 1764; and other sums, more than 24,000*l.* in all, for later improvements.

Patent museum at South Kensington has an 8-day clock made by Harrison in 1715. It strikes the hour, indicates the day of the month, and, except the escapement, its wheels are entirely made of wood. It was going in 1871.

Harrow-on-the-Hill school, Middlesex, Engl., founded and endowed by John Lyon in 1571. To encourage archery, the founder instituted a prize of a silver arrow, to be shot for annually on 4 Aug.; but the custom has been abolished. Lord Palmerston, sir R. Peel, and lord Byrón were educated here. The school arrangements were modified by the Public-schools act, 1868. Charles II. called Harrow church "the visible church."

Hartford convention. Delegates from the New England states politically opposed to pres. Madison, and to the war with Great Britain, met at Hartford in Dec. 1814, to consider public affairs. Peace soon made further action unnecessary. The convention excited acrimonious discussion. It was alleged that secession or obstruction to the government in prosecuting the war was contemplated; but this was stoutly denied. CONNECTICUT, 1814.

"Hartford (or **Connecticut) Courant"** first pub. 26 Oct. 1764. CONNECTICUT.

harus'pices, priests or soothsayers, of Etruscan origin, who foretold events by observing entrails of animals, were introduced in Rome by Romulus (about 750 B.C.), and abolished by Constantine 337 A.D., then 70 in number.

Harvard college, now **Harvard university,** the oldest institution of learning in the United States, was founded by act of the general court of Massachusetts granting 400*l.* towards a school or college, 28 Oct. 1636. Number of graduates from all departments to 1893, 18,300.

John Harvard, a graduate of Emmanuel college, Cambridge, Engl., dying at Charlestown, Mass., bequeaths his library and half of his estate, about 700*l.*, for a college..........14 Sept. 1638
Cambridge (then Newtown) the place selected as the site of the college, to be known as Harvard....................13 Mch. 1639
Its first head was Nathaniel Eaten, soon deposed for ill-treating and starving the students and beating his assistant, a Mr. Briscoe. Succeeded by Henry Dunster, its first president..27 Aug. 1640
[The school soon acquires a high reputation under him.]
First commencement..................................Aug. 1642
[Graduates, Benj. Woodbridge, George Dowing, John Bulkley, William Hubbard, Samuel Bellingham, John Wilson, Henry Saltonstal, Tobias Barnard, Nathaniel Brewster.]
Overseers of the college established.......................... "
Thirty graduates in all to.. 1646
First charter.. 1650
Pres. Dunster is indicted for disobeying the ordinance of infant baptism in the Cambridge church, and among other inflictions is compelled to resign his office...................Oct. 1654
Charles Chauncy accepts the presidency..............27 Nov. "
New building of brick erected, cost 3000*l.*, from contributions throughout New England, mostly in Massachusetts.......... 1669
[The bequests to the college up to 1700 amounted to over 6000*l.* besides 2000 acres of land, and 320 books.]
Medical school in connection with the college established..... 1783
Divinity " " " " " 1815
Law " " " " " 1817
Observatory built.. 1846
Abbott Lawrence founds the Lawrence Scientific school...... 1847
Election of overseers transferred to B.A.'s, M.A.'s, and honorary graduates instead of state officials, etc............... 1865
Museum built, and chair of American archæology and ethnology endowed by a gift of $150,000 from George Peabody...... 1866
Dental school established.. 1868
School of agriculture established through aid from Benj. Bussey, 1871
School of forestry established.................................. 1872
Memorial hall, with a classic theatre, erected in commemoration of the 136 Harvard men who died in the war for the Union, 1861-65.. 1874
Harvard Annex, now Radcliffe college, founded for the collegiate education of women............................... 1879
Veterinary school established.................................. 1882

PRESIDENTS OF HARVARD.

Name.	Term of office.	Remarks.
Rev. Henry Dunster.........	1640 to 1654	Forced to resign.
" Charles Chauncy........	1654 " 1672	Died in office.
" Leonard Hoar..........	1672 " 1675	Obliged to resign.
" Urian Oakes............	1675 " 1681	Not formally installed until 1680.
" John Rogers............	1682 " 1684	Died in office.
" Increase Mather........	1685 " 1701	
" Samuel Willard.........	1701 " 1707	Vice-president until his death.
" John Leverett..........	1707 " 1724	Died in office.
" Benjamin Wadsworth...	1725 " 1737	" " "
" Edward Holyoke........	1737 " 1769	" " "
" Samuel Locke..........	1770 " 1773	Resigned.
" Samuel Langdon........	1774 " 1780	"
" Joseph Willard..........	1781 " 1804	Died in office. Salary, $1400 a year.
" Samuel Webber.........	1806 " 1810	Died in office.
" John Thornton Kirkland.	1810 " 1828	Resigned.
" Josiah Quincy..........	1829 " 1845	Wrote a history of the college up to 1840.
Edward Everett.............	1846 " 1849	
Jared Sparks................	1849 " 1853	
James Walker...............	1853 " 1860	
Cornelius C. Felton.........	1860 " 1862	Died in office.
Thomas Hill.................	1862 " 1868	
Charles W. Eliot............	1869	

COLLEGES.

Hastings, one of the Cinque-ports, Sussex, Engl.; said to owe its name to a Danish pirate Hastinge, who built forts here about 893; but Mr. Kemble thinks it was the seat of a Saxon tribe named Hastingas. William, duke of Normandy, occupied Hastings, 29 Sept. 1066, in his invasion of England, and at Senlac, now Battle, near Hastings, defeated Harold II. of England, taking his life and kingdom, 14 Oct. 1066. His 2 brothers were slain with him, and were interred at Waltham

Abbey, Essex The severity of this battle attests the courage and determination of the combatants, and it is regarded as one of the decisive battles of the world It is described in Bulwer's novel "Harold, the Last of the Saxons," also in Kingsley's "Hereward the Wake" STAMFORD BRIDGE

Hastings's trial. Warren Hastings, governor-general of India, was tried by the peers of Great Britain for high crimes and misdemeanors Among other charges was his acceptance of a present of 100,000*l* from the nabob of Oude, CHUNAR TREATY OF The trial occupied 145 days, during 7 years and 3 months, commencing 13 Feb 1788, terminating in his acquittal, 23 Apr 1795 SHERIDAN'S SPEECH on the impeachment excited great admiration

Hastings was born in 1732 went to India as a writer in 1750 became governor general of Bengal in 1772, of India, 1773, governed ably but tyrannically till he resigned in 1785 The expenses of his trial (70 000*l*) were paid by the East India company, and a pension was granted to him He died a privy councillor in 1818

Hatcher's Run, Battle of GRANT'S CAMPAIGN IN VIRGINIA, 1864-65

Hatfield's attempt. On 11 May, 1800, during a review in Hyde park, an undiscovered hand fired, wounding a young man who stood near king George III In the evening, at Drury-lane theatre, Hatfield fired a pistol at the king Hatfield was confined as a lunatic till his death, 23 Jan 1841, aged 69

hats, first made by a Swiss at Paris, 1404 When Charles VII of France entered Rouen in triumph, in 1449, he wore a hat lined with red velvet, bearing a rich plume of feathers Henceforward, hats and caps, at least in France, began to take the place of chaperons and hoods.—*Henault* Hats were first manufactured in England by Spaniards, in 1510 —*Stow*. Very high-crowned hats were worn by Queen Elizabeth's courtiers, and were again introduced in 1783 Silk hats began to supersede beaver about 1820

None allowed to sell any hat for above 20*d* nor cap for above 2*s* 8*d*, 5 Hen VII 1489 Every person above 7 years to wear on Sundays and holidays a cap of wool, knit, made, thickened, and dressed in England by some of the trade of cappers, under forfeiture of 3 farthings for every day s neglect, 1571 Excepted maids, ladies, and gentlewomen, and every lord, knight, and gentleman of 20 marks of land, and their heirs, and such as had borne office of worship in any city, town, or place, and the wardens of London companies, 1571

Hatteras expedition. UNITED STATES, Aug 1861, Jan. 1862, etc.

Hauser, Casper, Case of There appeared in the streets of Nuremberg, 20 May, 1828, a boy in the garb of a peasant, helpless and bewildered He carried 2 letters. One purporting to be by a laborer said that the boy was given into his custody on 7 Oct 1812, and by agreement he had instructed him in reading, writing, and the Christian religion, and kept him in close confinement from that time. The other letter purported to be from his mother, saying he was born on 30 Apr 1812, that his name was Casper, and that his father, an officer in the 6th Nuremberg regiment, was now dead The appearance of the youth corresponded with these credentials He was detained in prison as a vagrant until July, 1828, when he was given into the care of prof Daumer, who, as guardian, took charge of his education. On 17 Oct. 1829, he was found wounded on his forehead, as he said, by a man with a blackened face. He was placed under surveillance The earl of Stanhope became interested, and sent him to Anspach to school After this he became clerk to the president of the court of appeals The case again attracted notice by his receiving a death wound at the hands of some person unknown to him while walking in the outskirts of the town on the afternoon of 14 Dec 1833 Prof Daumer, and Feuerbach, president of the court of appeals, believed that he was son of the grand-duke Charles of Baden, kidnapped by the countess of Hochberg to secure succession to the children of the grand-duke Charles Frederick, but this was contradicted in 1875, and an official record of the baptism, post-mortem examination, and burial of the heir were published It is still uncertain who the boy was, but the prevailing belief connects him closely with the grand-duke of Baden. Much interest has been excited among students of psychology by prof. Daumer's record of Casper's intellectual growth after his release from solitude A monument was erected to him at Anspach.

Havana, capital of Cuba, West Indies, founded by Velasquez, 1511, taken by a British force under lord Albemarle, 14 Aug 1762, restored, 1763 The remains of Columbus, brought from St Domingo, were deposited in the cathedral here, 1795 Pop 1893, 200,000

Haverhill, Mass (celebrated its 250th anniversary 2 July, 1890), Indian massacre at MASSACHUSETTS, 1697-1708, DUSTIN

Havre-de-Grace (*a'vr-deh-gras*), or **Le Havre,** a seaport town of N W France, was defended for the Huguenots by the English in 1562, who were expelled in 1563 It was bombarded by Rodney, 6 to 9 July, 1759, by sir Richard Strachan, 25 May, 1798, and blockaded, 6 Sept 1803 Attempts of the British to burn the shipping here failed, 7 Aug 1804 Pop 1891, 116,369

Havre-de-Grace (*hav'-er-de-gras*), a post-village of Maryland, ravaged by the British under adm Cockburn, 3 May, 1813

Hawaii, the chief of the 12 islands which constitute the territory of Hawaii situated in the N Pacific ocean. The islands are said to have been discovered in 1542 by Gaetano, and were rediscovered by capt. Cook in 1778, who named them the Sandwich islands after lord Sandwich, then the first lord of the admiralty of Great Britain Capt Cook was killed at Owhyhee (Hawaii) by the natives, 1779 King Kamehameha I, who died, 1819, united the 12 islands into one monarchy, and under his successor, Kamehameha II, idolatry was abolished (1819-20). In 1840, Kamehameha III established a constitution, which included an assembly of nobles, and a representative council The independence of the kingdom was guaranteed by the English and French governments in 1843 In 1893 a revolution broke out, and a republic was proclaimed in 1894 Hawaii was formally annexed to the U S in 1898, and became one of its territories in 1900

Money takes the place of barter 1817

King Kamehameha I, a chieftain of the island Hawaii, subdued the other isles, and ruled from . 1780-1819

Idolatry gradually superseded by Christianity . .. . "

The first printing press established by the missionaries . 1822

Kamehameha II, with his queen, visit England, both d of measles in London . . 1824

Ship building established in Honolulu . . 1825

The first newspaper in the islands 1836

Sugar growing established in the islands (this business has grown to be the industrial backbone of the islands . 1837

The sandal wood business prosperous . 1800-1840

Kamehameha III, promulgation of constitution, 1840, independence of the state recognized by the great powers 1843

Daniel Webster declared that "no other power ought either to take possession of the islands as a conqueror, or for the purpose of colonization" "

Clayton, U S secretary of state, notifies France that "we could never, with indifference, allow the Hawaiian islands to pass under dominion or exclusive control of any other country" 1850

The Hawaiian islands supplied California with potatoes, meat, and flour .. . 1848-1854

The U S requested to annex the Hawaiian islands by the reigning sovereign, the U S refuses "

Reciprocity treaty between the U S and Hawaii, not ratified by the U S .. . 1855

Kamehameha IV married Miss Emma Rooker (she went to England and was received by the queen 9 Sept 1865) 1856

An inter island steamboat service established 1859

The king d, Kamehameha V king . . Nov 1863

Reciprocity treaty between the U S and Hawaii, ratified by the Hawaiian government but refused by the U S 1867

The king requests annexation, but U S refuses 1868

The duke of Edinburgh warmly received at Honolulu 21 July 1869

Honolulu the centre of the whaling industry 1819-1871

The whaling fleet crushed in the Arctic region . "

Kamehameha V d, unmarried 11 Dec 1872

The U S again requested to annex the islands. 1874

William C Lunalilo crowned, 8 Jan 1873, d . . 3 Feb "

Reciprocity treaty concluded between Hawaii and the U S 1875

David Kalakau (b. 16 Nov 1836) elected king in opposition to queen Emma, 12 Feb, visits the president at Washington, 12 Dec. 1876, visits Europe, at Rome, 1 July, received by the queen at Windsor, 12 July, 1881, crowned 12 Feb 1883

8000 Portuguese are assisted to immigrate into Hawaii, each workingman costs the government from $240 to $400 1878-1887

Queen Kapiolani arrives at Liverpool to be present at the royal jubilee service . .. . 2 June, "

Revolution against a corrupt ministry, 25 June, the ministry deposed, 30 June, the king, powerless appeals to the foreign representatives, who recommend the formation of a new constitution, the king signs a new constitution 7 July, "

17,000 Chinese are brought in as contract laborers up to...... 1888
Mr. Robert Wilcox, with 100 men, attempts the seizure of the palace at Honolulu, 30 July; 6 rebels killed; Wilcox surrenders..31 July, 1889
Death of the king David Kalakau at San Francisco, 20 Jan.; succeeded by his sister, Lydia Liliuokalani; proclaimed, 29 Jan. 1891
Political troubles: the late king's ministers refuse to resign, Feb.; opposition to the queen; American intervention against civil war ....about 4 Mch. "
The ministry resigns; new one formed, 26 Feb.; princess Kaiulani declared heir-apparent ....9 Mch. "
The queen nominates her privy council of 40 members, including her husband, Mr. John Owen Dominis, Mch.; Mr. Dominis d...27 Aug. "
Mr. Robert Wilcox heads a native party against the government, desiring a republic.............. ....Dec. "
Conspiracy of Wilcox and others suppressed..........20 May, 1892
John L. Stevens, U.S. minister at Hawaii, writes to his government in favor of annexation ....19 Nov. "
The queen, proposing to change the constitution, is dethroned, and a provisional government set up (justice S. B. Dole and others), 17 Jan.; order maintained by troops from the U.S. warship *Boston;* the provisional government recognized by the British minister..................................19 Jan. 1893
A mission sent to Washington desiring annexation, 14-16 Jan.; the commissioners received at Washington....4 Feb. et seq. "
John L. Stevens, U. S. minister at Hawaii, assumes a protectorate pending instructions from Washington.........9 Feb. "
Pres. Harrison, by message to the Senate, recommends annexation of the islands under a treaty concluded between sec. Foster and the Hawaiian commissioners............15 Feb. "
An envoy of queen Liliuokulani arrives at Washington.17 Feb. "
Commissioners from the queen oppose the treaty, Feb.; appeal of the princess Kaiulani; published, 21 Feb.; she arrives at New York..1 Mch. "
Treaty for the annexation of the islands to the U.S.; proposed, 16 Feb.; the treaty withdrawn from the Senate by pres. Cleveland...9 Mch. "
Ex-representative James H. Blount of Georgia sent on a special mission to Hawaii from the U.S. government...20 Mch. "
Commissioner Blount orders the U.S. flag lowered at Hawaii, 13 Apr. "
Commissioner Blount appointed envoy extraordinary and minister plenipotentiary to the Hawaiian islands........9 May, "
Lorin A. Thurston, Hawaiian minister to the U.S., presented to pres. Cleveland...................................9 June, "
Commissioner Blount arrives at Washington..........22 Aug. "
Albert S. Willis of Kentucky appointed minister.......8 Sept. "
Minister Willis presents his credentials to pres. Dole of the provisional government ....7 Nov. "
The U.S. decline the annexation; the restoration of the queen opposed by the provisional government; reported......Jan. 1894
U.S. adm. Walker authorized to establish an American naval station at Honolulu..............................24 Mch. "
The U.S. Senate affirm the sole right of Hawaii to fix its own form of government ....31 May, "
Republic proclaimed and a constitution adopted..........4 July, "
[Sanford B. Dole elected president for the term 1894-1900.]
Land act, making special homestead provision; passed....... 1895
Rising of the Hawaiians against the republican government; Mr. C. L. Carter, late U. S. commissioner, killed; martial law proclaimed...................................6, 7 Jan. "
The ex-queen arrested for complicity, 19 Jan.; sentenced to 5 years' imprisonment and fine of $5000; 3 of her adherents sentenced to death (remitted); many to long imprisonment, 24 Feb.-Mch. "
Ex-queen Liliuokalani renounces her right to the throne of Hawaii...30 June, "
All political prisoners released.........................1 Jan. 1896
The ex-queen and most of her supporters pardoned, 13 Sept. 1895; the queen restored to civil rights..............29 Oct. "
Treaty between the U. S. and Hawaii providing for annexation, 16 June, 1897
The ex-queen protests; announced..................18 June, "
Ratified by Hawaii.................................14 Sept. "
30,000 Japanese immigrate into Hawaii from............1886-1898
[In 1898 the Chinese numbered about 24,000; the Portuguese 16,000.]
Pres. Dole of Hawaii arrives in Washington as the guest of the U.S...26 Jan. "
Joint resolution for the annexation of Hawaii; passed, 17 June, "
Pres. McKinley approves the joint resolution annexing the Hawaiian islands.................................7 July, "
Transfer of sovereignty..............................12 Aug. "
Princess Kaiulani dies at Honolulu.....................6 Mch. 1899
Act providing a government for the territory of Hawaii; to take effect 14 June, 1900; approved ....30 Apr. 1900
Gov. Dole inaugurated..............................14 June, "
Wilcox elected territorial representative in the U. S. House of Representatives ....Nov. "
First territorial legislature opened...................20 Feb. 1901

GOVERNORS.

Sanford B. Dole.......................................1900-1904
George R. Carter.......................................1904-

Hawaii was annexed to the U. S. by a joint resolution of Congress, 6 July, 1898. A bill to create Hawaii a territory of the U. S. was passed by Congress and approved 30 Apr. 1900. The area of the several islands of the Hawaiian group is as follows: Hawaii, 4210 square miles; Maui, 760; Oahu, 600; Kauai, 590; Molokai, 270; Lanai, 150; Niihau, 97; Kahoolawe, 63. Total, 6740 square miles. At the time of the discovery of the islands by capt. Cook, in 1778, the native population was about 200,000. This has steadily decreased, so that at the last census the natives numbered but 31,019 which was less than that of the Japanese and Chinese immigrants settled in the islands. A census taken early in 1897 revealed a total population of 109,020, distributed according to race as follows:

	Males.	Females.	Total.
Hawaiians..........................	16,399	14,620	31,019
Part Hawaiians....................	4,249	4,236	8,485
Japanese...........................	19,212	5,195	24,407
Chinese	19,167	2,449	21,616
Portuguese........................	8,202	6,898	15,100
Americans.........................	1,975	1,111	3,086
British	1,406	844	2,250

The remainder were Germans, French, Norwegians, South Sea Islanders, and representatives of other nationalities. The American population was 2.73 per cent. of the whole. The American population has increased since annexation. The first U. S. census of the islands was taken in 1900 with the following result: Hawaii island, 46,843; Kauai island, 20,562; Niihau island, 172; Maui island, 25,416; Molokai island and Lanai island, 2504; Oahu island, 58,504. Total of the territory, 154,001. The population of the city of Honolulu is 39,306. Nearly all the natives are Christians. In 1896 there were 23,773 Protestants, 26,362 Roman Catholics, 4886 Mormons, 44,306 Buddhists, etc., and 10,192 not described. There are 71 miles of railroad and about 250 miles of telegraph in the islands. Honolulu has most of the local features of an enterprising American city. The bulk of the business is done by Americans and Europeans. Of sugar, of which it is said the Hawaiian islands are much more productive in a given area than those of the West Indies, the exportation was 545,370,537 pounds in 1899. Of coffee, the exportation was 337,158 pounds in 1897; of rice, the exportation was 5,499,499 pounds in 1897. In the matter of imports, nearly all of the necessities of life, aside from sugar, fruits, and vegetables, are imported, the products of the U. S. being given the preference in nearly all cases. The exports from Hawaii to the U. S. in the 12 months ending 30 June, 1903, were valued at $26,201,175, of which the item of sugar figured at $25,310,684. The imports into Hawaii from the U. S. for the same period were valued at $10,787,666. The imports from foreign countries for the same period were $3,142,013; exports, $27,029. The new territorial government was inaugurated at Honolulu, 14 June, 1900, and the first territorial legislature began its sessions at Honolulu 20 Feb. 1901. The legislature is composed of 2 houses—the senate of 15 members, holding office 4 years, and the house of representatives of 30 members, holding office 2 years. The legislature meets biennially, and sessions are limited to 60 days. The executive power is lodged in a governor, a secretary, both appointed by the president, and hold office 4 years, and the following officials appointed by the governor, by and with the consent of the senate of Hawaii: an attorney-general, treasurer, commissioner of public lands, commissioner of agriculture and forestry, superintendent of public works, superintendent of public instruction, auditor and deputy, surveyor, high sheriff, and members of the boards of health, public instruction, prison inspectors, etc. They hold office for 4 years, and must be citizens of Hawaii. The judiciary of the territory is composed of the supreme court, with 3 judges, the circuit court, and such inferior courts as the legislature may establish. The judges are appointed by the president. The territory is a federal judicial district, with a district judge, district attorney, and marshal, all appointed by the president. The district judge has all the powers of a circuit judge. The territory is represented in congress by a delegate, who is elected biennially by the people. Provision is made in the act creating the territory for the residence of Chinese in the territory, and prohibition as laborers to enter the U. S.

hawking. FALCONRY.

hay. AGRICULTURE.

Hayes's administration. UNITED STATES, 1877.

Hayti (*ha'-tī*), or **Haiti,** Indian name of a West Indian island discovered by Columbus in Dec 1492 and named Hispaniola, and afterwards St Domingo Before the Spaniards fully conquered it, they are said to have destroyed, in battle or cold blood, 3 000,000 of its inhabitants, 1495 It now comprises the republics of St Domingo in the east, and Hayti in the west Area of Hayti 10,204 sq miles, pop about 572,000, area of St Domingo, 18,045 sq miles, pop about 610,000

Hayti seized by the fil busters and French buccaneers		1630
French government took possession of colony		1677
Negroes revolt against France	23 Aug	1791
And massacre nearly all the whites	21-23 June,	1793
French directory recognize Toussaint l'Ouverture as general in chief		1794
Eastern part of the island ceded to France by Spain		1795
Toussaint founds an independent republic in St Domingo,	9 May,	1801
Surrenders to the French	7 May,	1802
Is conducted to France where he dies		1803
New insurrection under Dessalines, French quit the island	Nov	"
Dessalines proclaims massacre of all whites, 29 Mch, crowned emperor of Hayti, as Jacques I	Oct	1804
He is assassinated, the isle divided	17 Oct	1806
Henry Christophe, colored president Feb 1807 crowned emperor as Henry I, while Pethion rules as president at Port au Prince	Mch	1811
Numerous black nobility and prelates created		"
Pethion dies, Boyer elected president	May,	1818
Christophe commits suicide Oct 1820, the 2 states united under Boyer as regent for life, Nov 1820, who is recognized by France		1825
[Re]volution, Boyer deposed		1843
[St] Domingo and eastern Hayti proclaim the "Dominican republic," Feb 1844, recognized by France, 1848, Buenaventura Baez, president		1849-53
Hayti proclaimed an empire under its late president, Solouque, as Faustin I, 26 Aug 1849, crowned	18 Apr	1852
Santana, president of the Dominican republic, 1853-56, succeeded by B Baez		1856-58
Faustin attacks republic of St. Domingo, repulsed	1 Feb	1856
Jose Valverde elected president of Dominican republic.		1858
Revolution in Hayti, gen Fabre Geffrard proclaims republic,	22 Dec	"
Faustin abdicates	15 Jan	1859
Geffrard takes oath as president of Hayti	23 Jan	"
Sixteen executions for conspiracy against Geffrard	Oct	"
Spanish emigrants land, a declaration for reunion with Spain signed 18 Mch decreed by the queen	20 May,	1861
Insurrection against Spain in St. Domingo	18 Aug	1863
Spanish force sent, insurgents generally defeated		1864
St Domingo renounced by Spain	5 May,	1865
New constitution proclaimed in Hayti	June,	1867
President of the republic of St Domingo gen Ulisses Heureaux, elected		1886
President of the republic of Hayti, gen Hyppolite	Oct	1889

Health, National Board of, established by act of Congress approved 3 Mch 1879 National quarantine law passed, 3 June, 1879

hearth, or **chimney, tax,** on every fireplace or hearth in England, was imposed by Charles II in 1662, when it produced about 200,000*l* a year It was abolished by William and Mary in 1689, imposed again, and again abolished

heat (called by French chemists caloric). Little progress was made in the science of heat till about 1757, when Joseph Black put forward his theory of latent heat (heat, he said, being absorbed by melting ice), and of specific heat Cavendish, Lavoisier, and others continued Black's researches. Sir John Leslie published his views on radiant heat in 1804. Count Rumford proposed the theory that heat consists in motion among particles of matter, and supported it by experiments on friction (recorded in 1802) This theory (called the dynamical or mechanical theory of heat, and used to explain numberless phenomena of physics and chemistry) has been established by independent researches of dr J Meyer of Heilbronn, Germany, and of Mr Joule of Manchester, Engl. (about 1840), showing that heat is the equivalent of work done In 1854, prof. William Thomson of Glasgow published researches on the dynamical power of the sun's rays. Thermo-electricity, produced by heating pieces of copper and bismuth soldered together, was discovered by Seebeck in 1823 A powerful thermo-electric battery was constructed by Marcus of Vienna in 1865 Prof Tyndall's "Heat, a Mode of Motion," first pub Feb. 1863, 3d edition, 1868

Sir George Cayley invented a heated air engine in 1807, and Mr Stirling applied it to raising water in Ayrshire, Scotland, in 1818 One invented by Mr Wenham was described in 1873 Improvements have been made by C William Siemens

Capt Ericsson constructed a ship, in which caloric or heat was the motive power On 4 Jan 1853 it sailed down the bay of New York at 14 miles an hour it is said at a cost of 80 per cent less than steam Although caloric engines were not commercially successful, capt Ericsson continued his experiments, and patented an improved engine in 1856

Heb'rides (the *Ebudæ* of Ptolemy and the *Hebudes* of Pliny), western isles of Scotland, long subject to Norway, ceded to Scotland in 1264, and annexed to the Scottish crown in 1540 by James V The heritable jurisdictions were abolished in 1747 Johnson's "Journey to the Hebrides" pub in 1775

He'bron, a town of Palestine Here Abraham resided, 1860 B C, and here David was made king of Judah, 1048 B C. Near Hebron is the cave of Machpelah, where were buried Abraham and his descendants

hec'atomb, an ancient sacrifice of 100 oxen, particularly observed by the Lacedæmonians when they possessed 100 cities The sacrifice was subsequently reduced to 23 animals and goats and lambs were substituted

Heck'ewelder, Mary, the first white child born in Ohio, 1781 OHIO.

Hecla, mount, Iceland Its first recorded eruption is 1004 About 22 eruptions have taken place, according to Olasson and Paulson Great convulsions of this mountain occurred in 1766, since when a visit to the top in summer is not attended with great difficulty Perhaps the most awful volcanic eruption on record took place in 1784-85 when rivers were dried up and villages destroyed The mount was in violent eruption from 2 Sept 1845, to Apr 1846. 3 new craters were formed, from which pillars of fire rose to the height of 14,000 English feet The lava formed several hills, and pieces of pumice-stone and scoriæ of 2 cwt were thrown a league and a half, the ice and snow which had covered the mountain for centuries melted in great floods

Hegira (*hej'-i-ra*, Arab *hejra*), **era of the,** dates from the flight of Mahomet from Mecca to Medina on the night of Thursday, 15 July, 622 The era commences on the 16th Some begin from the 15th, but Cantemir proves that the 16th was the first day 33 of its lunar years are equal to 32 of our reckoning

Heidelberg (*hī'-dl-burg*), Germany, capital of the Palatinate 1362-1719 The Protestant electoral house becoming extinct in 1693, war ensued, in which the castle was ruined, and the elector removed to Mannheim It was annexed to Baden in 1802 Here was the celebrated tun, constructed 1343, containing 21 pipes of wine Another was made in 1664, which held 600 hogsheads. It was destroyed by the French in 1688, but a larger one, fabricated in 1751, which held 800 hogsheads, and was formerly kept full of Rhenish wine, is said to be mouldering in a damp vault, empty since 1769 The university here is the oldest in the empire, founded in 1356 by the elector Rupert In 1891, it had 123 professors and teachers, and 970 students

Hel'ena, Ark, Affair at ARKANSAS, 1863

Hele'na, St., an island in the S Atlantic Ocean, discovered by the Portuguese under Juan de Nova Castilla, on St. Helena's day, 21 May, 1502 The Dutch afterwards held it until 1600, when they were expelled by the English The British East India company settled here in 1651, and the island was alternately possessed by the English and Dutch until 1673, when Charles II, on 12 Dec, assigned it to the company once more St Helena was the place of Napoleon's captivity, 16 Oct 1815, and here he died, 5 May, 1821 His remains were removed in 1840, and interred at the Hôtel des Invalides, Paris FRANCE, 1840 The house and tomb have been purchased by the French government. Area, 47 sq miles, pop 1891, 4116

Heligoland (*hel'-ig-o-land*), an island in the North sea, taken from the Danes by the British 5 Sept 1807, made a depot for British merchandise, confirmed to England by the treaty of Kiel, 14 Jan 1814. In a naval engagement off Heligoland, between the Danes and the Austrians and Prussians, the allies were compelled to retire, 9 May, 1864. Transferred to the German government, 9 Aug 1890, and united with the province of Schleswig-Holstein Area, 3/4 sq mile, its average height, 198 ft, pop 1890, 2086

heliog'raphy (from Gr ἥλιος, the sun, and γραφω, to describe)

A system of telegraphing by mirrors flashing solar rays said to have been employed in the time of Alexander, about 330 B C

A portable heliograph invented by H Mauce of the Persian telegraph department was described 1875 It was employed in India, 1877-78, and in the Afghan and Zulu campaigns 1879-80 PHOTOGRAPHY

heliom'eter, an instrument for measuring the diameters of the sun, moon, planets, and stars, invented by Savary in 1713, applied by M Bouguer in 1744 A fine heliometer by Repsold of Hamburg, was set up at the Radcliffe, Engl, observatory, Oct. 1849

he'lioscope, a peculiar telescope for protecting the eye while observing the sun, invented by Christopher Scheiner in 1625.

he'liostat, an instrument to make a sunbeam apparently stationary, invented by Gravesande about 1719, and greatly improved by Malus and others. One constructed by MM Foucault and Dubosq was exhibited at Paris in Oct. 1862

Hell. HADES.

Hell Gate. NEW YORK, 1876, etc

Hellas, Thessaly, the home of the Hellenes and the Greek race, which supplanted the Pelasgians from the 15th to the 11th century B C., named for Hellen, king of Phthiotis, about 1600 B C The Hellenes separated into the Dorians, Æolians Ionians, and Achaians The present king of Greece is called "king of the Hellenes." GREECE

Hel'lespont (now strait of the Dardanelles), named after Helle, daughter of Athamas, king of Thebes, who was drowned here It is celebrated for the story of the loves of Hero, priestess of Aphrodite at Sestos, and Leander of Abydos Leander was drowned on a tempestuous night swimming across the Hellespont (about 1 mile), and Hero, in despair, threw herself into the sea, about 627 B C Lord Byron and lieut Ekenhead also swam across, 3 May, 1810 GOLDEN FLEECE, XERXES.

helmets. Romans had a vizor of grated bars to raise above the eyes, and a beaver to lower for eating, the Greek helmet was round, the Roman square. Richard I of England wore a plain round helmet, but most of the English kings had crowns above their helmets Alexander III of Scotland, 1249, had a flat helmet, with a square grated vizor, and the helmet of Robert I was surmounted by a crown, 1306.—*Gwillim.* In the 16th century the beaver was confounded with the vizor

"*Hamlet* Then saw you not his face?
"*Horatio* O, yes, my lord, he wore his beaver up"
—*Shakespeare*, "Hamlet," act. iv sc. ii

hel'ots, captives (so called from the Gr ἑλεῖν, to take, or from Helos, a city which refused tribute to Sparta, 883 B.C.) The Spartans, it is said, ruined the city, reduced the Helots to slavery, and called all slaves and prisoners of war *helotæ* The number of helots was much enlarged by the conquest of Messenia, 668 B C, they are said to have formed four fifths of the inhabitants of Sparta In the Peloponnesian war the helots behaved bravely, and were rewarded with liberty, 431 B.C., but the sudden disappearance of 2000 manumitted slaves was attributed to Lacedæmonian treachery —*Herodotus*

Helvetian republic. Switzerland having been conquered by the French in 1797, a republic was established Apr 1798, with this title SWITZERLAND

Helvetii, a Celto-Germanic people who inhabited what is now Switzerland Invading Gaul, 61 B C., they were defeated and massacred by Julius Cæsar, 58 B.C., near Geneva.

hemp (*Cannabis sativa*), an annual plant, with an angular rough stem and alternate lobed leaves, probably a native of central Asia Its fibre was made into cloth in early times—mentioned by Herodotus The Anglo-Saxons had hempen cloth, and it was in common use in central and southern Europe in the 13th century Hemp-seed was ordered for the Plymouth colony, Massachusetts, 1629, and has been cultivated in the United States ever since, most largely in Kentucky, Tennessee, Missouri Ohio, Indiana, and Illinois It is extensively used in cables, ropes, cordage, twine, sacking, tarpaulins, canvas, sail-cloth, etc The process of preparation of the fibre is similar to that of flax The finest hemp grows in Italy and Russia The *Cannabis indica*, or Indian hemp, from which the intoxicating drug hashish is obtained, is but a variety of the common hemp

Hennepin, Louis FRENCH IN AMERICA, 1680, '83, '97

henot'icon (from Gr ἑνοτης, unity), an edict of union to reconcile the Eutychians with the church, issued by emperor Zeno at the instance of Acacius patriarch of Constantinople, 482 It was zealously opposed by the popes, and was annulled by Justin I in 518 The orthodox party triumphed, and many heretic bishops were expelled from their sees

Henry, John, Case of UNITED STATES, Mch 1812

hep'tarchy (government of 7 rulers) in England was gradually formed from 455, when Hengist became king of Kent, and ended 828, when Egbert became sole monarch of England There were at first 9 or 10 Saxon kingdoms, but Middlesex soon ceased to exist, and Bernicia and Deira were generally governed by one ruler, as Northumbria. BRITAIN, OCTARCHY.

Heracli'dæ, descendants of Hercules, expelled from the Peloponnesus about 1200 B.C., they reconquered it in 1048, 1103-4, or 1109 B C, a noted epoch in chronology, preceding history being accounted fabulous.

heraldry. Marks of honor were used in the first ages.—*Nisbet* The Phrygians had a sow, the Thracians, Mars, the Romans, an eagle, the Goths, a bear, the Flemings, a bull, the Saxons, a horse, and the ancient French, a lion, and afterwards the FLEUR-DE-LIS Heraldry, as an art, is ascribed first to Charlemagne, about 800, and next to Frederick Barbarossa, about 1152, it began and grew with the feudal law —*Mackenzie* The great English works on heraldry are those of Barcham or Barkham, pub by Gwillim, 1610, Edmonson, 1780, and Burke's "Armory," 1842, new ed 1878, contains history and the arms of above 60,000 British families

Edward III appointed 2 heraldic kings at arms for the south and north (Surroy, Norroy) . 1340

Richard III incorporated and endowed the Heralds' college, 1483-84

Philip and Mary enlarged its privileges, and confirmed them by letters patent 15 July, 1554

Formerly, in many ceremonies, the herald represented the king's person, and therefore wore a crown, and was always a knight.

College has an earl marshal, 3 kings of arms (Garter, Clarencieux, and Norroy), 6 heralds (Richmond, Lancaster, Chester, Windsor, Somerset, and York), 4 pursuivants, and 2 extra heralds EARL, KINGS OF ARMS.

He'rat, on the confines of Khorasân, a strong city, called the key of Afghanistan, conquered by Persia early in the 16th century, by the Afghans, 1715, by Nadir Shah, 1731, recovered by the Afghans, 1749 The Persians, baffled in an attempt in 1838, took it 25 Oct 1856, in violation of the treaty of 1853, and war ensued between Great Britain and Persia Peace was made in Apr 1857, and Herat was restored 27 July following It was seized again by Dost Mahomed, 26 May, 1863, taken by Yakoob Khan, rebelling against his father, 6 May, 1871 Yakoob, reconciled to his father, was made governor, 16 Sept. 1871 AFGHANISTAN

Herculaneum, an ancient city of Campania, overwhelmed, with POMPEII, by an eruption of lava and also from Vesuvius, 23 or 24 Aug 79 Successive eruptions covered the site, it was lost until excavations began in 1711, in 1713 many antiquities were found. In 1738 excavations were resumed and continued until 1780, and works of art, monuments, and memorials of the ancient city discovered, resumed again in 1828, but without encouraging results. 150 rolls of MS. papyri were found in 1754, many antiquities were purchased by sir William Hamilton, and sold to the British museum, but the principal relics are preserved in the museum of Portici. The "Antichità di Ercolano," 8 vols folio, were published by the Neapolitan government, 1757-92

heredity. The transmission of qualities from parents has been specially studied by Francis Galton, F R S, who published "Hereditary Genius," 1869, and "Records of Family Faculties," containing tabular forms to be filled with authentic data for his new science of "Eugenics" Money prizes, 5*l* and upwards, were offered for the best records. His 'Inquiries into Human Faculty" was pub in 1883, and 'Natural Inheritance" in 1889

heretics (from Gr αἵρεσις, choice) Paul says, "After the way which they call heresy, so worship I the God of my fathers" (Acts xxiv 14,60) Heresy was unknown to the Greek and Roman religions Simon Magus is said to have broached the Gnostic heresy about 41. This was followed by the Manichees Nestorians, Arians, etc INQUISITION It is said that laws for prosecuting heretics began with emperor Frederick II in 1220, and were immediately adopted by pope Honorius III

Epiphanius chosen bishop of Constantius in Cyprus, 367, wrote "Panarium," a d scourse against heresies, d 402
Thirty heretics came from Germany to England to propagate their opinions, and were branded in the forehead, whipped, and thrust naked into the streets in the depth of winter, where none daring to relieve them, they died of hunger and cold (*Speed*) 1160
[Highest point reached by ecclesiastical power in England was in the act *De hæretico comburendo* (2 Hen IV c 15) This enabled the diocesan to pronounce sentence of heresy and the sheriff to execute it by burning the offender without waiting for consent of the crown]
Laws against heretics repealed, 25 Hen VIII 1534-35
Last person executed for heresy in Great Britain was Thomas Aikenhead at Edinburgh 1696
[Orthodox Mahometans are Sonnites, the heretics, Shiites, Druses etc]

Hermas, author of "The Shepherd," a Christian apocryphal book, probably written about 131 Some believe Hermas to be mentioned in Rom xvi 14

Hermitage, the, about 12 miles from Nashville, Tenn, on the Cumberland river, the residence of Andrew Jackson The vault in which lie his remains and those of his wife is marked by a simple, elegant monument

hermits. MONACHISM

Herne's oak, Windsor park, Engl So called from an old tradition that one Herne, a keeper in the park, hung himself upon it, and it was ever after haunted by his ghost Said to have been cut down inadvertently in 1796 Others say that it stood until blown down in 1863 Celebrated by mention in Shakespeare's "Merry Wives of Windsor," act iv sc iv

"*Mrs Page.* There is an old tale goes that Herne the hunter,
Sometime a keeper here in Windsor forest,
Doth all the winter time at still midnight
Walk round about an oak, with great ragg'd horns

"*Page* Why, yet there want not many, that do fear
In deep of night to walk by this Herne's oak"

herrings, Battle of the, fought 12 Feb 1429, when the duc de Bourbon was defeated while attempting to intercept a convoy of salt fish, on the road to the English besieging Orleans. Sir John Fastolff commanded the English

Herrn'huters. MORAVIANS

Her'uli, a German tribe which ravaged Greece and Asia Minor in the 3d century Odoacer, their leader, overwhelmed the Western empire and became king of Italy, 476 He was defeated and put to death by Theodoric the Ostrogoth, 491-93 ROME

Herzegovina (*hert'-se-gō-vē'-nă*) or **Hertsek,** a province of Austria, originally part of Croatia, was united with Bosnia in 1326, and made the duchy of St Saba by the emperor Frederick III in the following century It was ceded to Turkey in 1699 at the peace of Carlowitz In Dec 1861, an insurrection against the Turks broke out, fostered by the prince of Montenegro It was subdued, and on 23 Sept 1862, Vucatovitch, chief of the insurgents, surrendered, on behalf of his countrymen, to Kurschid Pacha, and an amnesty was granted. Another insurrection against the Turks broke out, 1875, and continued until the provinces of Bosnia and Herzegovina were, by the treaty of Berlin, 13 July, 1878, handed over to the Austro-Hungarian government Herzegovina was occupied by the Austrians, Aug 1878, in conformity with the treaty of Berlin, 13 July, 1878 Pop about 250,000 BOSNIA

Hesse, W Germany, seat of the Catti part of the empire of Charlemagne, its present rulers are descended from those of that day It was joined to Thuringia till about 1263, when Henry I (son of a duke of Brabant and Sophia, daughter of the landgrave of Thuringia) became landgrave of Hesse The most remarkable of his successors was Philip the Magnanimous (1509), an eminent warrior and supporter of the Reformation, who signed the Augsburg Confession in 1530, and the league of Smalcald in 1531 At his death, in 1567, Hesse was divided into Hesse-Cassel and Hesse-Darmstadt, under his sons William and George, and their descendants were eminent in the convulsions of Germany during the 17th and 18th centuries HESSIANS In 1803 Hesse-Cassel became an electorate, and in 1806 Hesse-Darmstadt a grand-duchy, titles retained in 1814 In 1807 Hesse-Cassel was incorporated with Westphalia, but in 1813 the electorate was re-established. Area, 2965 sq miles Pop 1875 (grand-duchy), 884,218, 1880, 936,340, 1890, 993,659

ELECTORS

1803. William I, b 3 June 1743, succeeded as landgrave, 1785, made elector, 1803, deprived of his states, 1806, restored 1813, d 27 Feb 1821
1821 William II, b 28 July, 1777, d 20 Nov 1847
1847 Frederick William, b 20 Aug 1802
The elector, in 1850, remodelled constitution of 1831 giving the chamber exclusive right of voting taxes, and convened the chamber only at the usual time for closing the session, making demand for money for 1851 The chamber asked a regular budget for discussion Elector dissolved the chamber, and declared dominions in a state of siege, 7 Sept 1850
He fled to Hanover later to Frankfort, on 14 Oct he called on the Frankfort diet to help re establish his authority On 6 Nov 10,000 Austro Bavarians entered Hesse Cassel, under prince Thurn und Taxis with headquarters in Hanau, next day a Prussian force entered Cassel Elector returned to his capital, taxes having been collected under threats of imprisonment, 27 Dec 1850
Constitution of 1831 abolished, and a new one established, 1852
Conflict resumed, till, by law of 20 Sept 1866, Hesse Cassel was annexed to Prussia, 8 Oct 1866.
Ex elector's property sequestrated for intrigues against Prussia 2 Nov 1868, and Feb 1869 He d 6 Jan 1875.
Pop of Hesse Darmstadt, Dec 1875, 884,218

GRAND-DUKES

1806 Louis I, b 14 June, 1753, d 6 Apr 1830
1830 Louis II, b 26 Dec 1777, d 16 June, 1848
1848 Louis III, b 9 June 1806 By treaty 15 Sept. 1866, he ceded northern Hesse Darmstadt to Prussia and paid a war contribution, supported Prussia against France, Aug 1870, d 13 June, 1877
1877 Louis IV, nephew b 12 Sept 1837, married princess Alice of Great Britain (b 25 Apr 1843) 1 July, 1862, d of diphtheria after nursing her husband and children, 14 Dec 1878.
Heir Ernest Louis b 25 Nov 1868
Frederick William, 2d son, killed by a fall 29 May, 1873, and other children
Hesse Homburg a landgraviate, established by Frederick, son of George of Hesse Darmstadt in 1596 His descendant, Augustus Frederick, married (7 May, 1818) Elizabeth, daughter of George III of England, who had no issue
Landgraviate was absorbed into the grand duchy of Hesse in 1806, but re established in 1815 with additional territories Landgrave Ferdinand succeeded his brother, 8 Sept. 1848, and d 24 Mch 1866
Hesse-Homburg annexed to Prussia, 8 Oct 1866

Hessian fly (*Cecidomyia destructor*), the American wheat midge, very destructive to wheat in the United States in 1786, whither it is said to have been brought by the Hessian soldiers in British pay—hence its name

Wheat crop suffered severely in the U S in 1846 and 1886. Fly appeared in England in 1788, and was described by sir Joseph Banks Its appearance in England in 1887 occasioned much alarm through out the country
Its action said to be checked by a parasite—saw fly (*Ceraphron destructor*) —*W Fream*, Aug 1887 Very prevalent in eastern coast of Britain not much inland —*Ormerod*, Aug 1887
In 20 English and 10 Scotch counties, the alarm considered to be exaggerated —*Parl. Rep* Sept 1887
Presence of the insect reported in Lincoln, Suffolk, Herts, Perthshire, 28 July, 1890.

Hessians. During the War of Independence, Great Britain hired a large number of auxiliaries from the landgrave of Hesse, to serve against the colonies In Nov 1786, Great Britain paid him 471,000*l*. in 3 per cent. consols, as compensation for the loss of 15,700 of his subjects in this war, or about $150 for each life. It was with the proceeds of this traffic in the lives of his people that the famous water-works and pleasure grounds at Cassel were constructed. BEMIS'S HEIGHTS

hexameter, the measure of Greek heroic verse, of 6 feet, each containing 2 long syllables (a spondee), or a long one and 2 short (a dactyl), the verse of the "Iliad" and "Odyssey," and of Virgil's "Æneid"

Hexham or **Hagulstad,** Northumberland The see of Hexham, founded about 678, had 10 bishops successively, but the rapine of the Danes destroyed it, the last prelate appointed 810 At the battle of Hexham the Yorkist army of Edward IV defeated the Lancastrian army of Henry VI 15 May, 1464

Hi-a-wa'-tha, reputed founder of the Iroquois confederacy Longfellow's "Song of Hiawatha" was pub in 1855 LITERATURE.

Hibbert fund. Robert Hibbert on 19 July, 1847, established a trust fund "for the promotion of comprehensive learning and thorough research in relation to religion as it appears to the eye of the scholar and philosopher, and wholly apart from the interest of any particular church or system"

Hibbert lectures, first course of, 7 by prof Max Müller (given at Westminster) "On the Origin and Growth of Religion, as illustrated by the Religions of India" 25 Apr -30 May, 1878

Since given by M Renouf in 1879, by Ernest Renan, 6-14 Apr 1880, by T W Rhys Davids, 26 Apr -24 May, 1881, by prof Kuenen, 25 Apr -May, 1882, by C Beard 1883, by prof Albert Reville, 21 Apr et seq 1884, by prof O Pfleiderer, 1885, by J Rhys, 1886, by prof A H Sayce Apr 1887

Hibernia, Ibernia, Ivernia, and **Ierne,** a name of Ireland in ancient writers (Aristotle, Ptolemy, etc) IRELAND

Hicksites. QUAKERS

hieroglyph'ics, literally sacred sculptures or engravings, the representation of objects to express language, used by the ancient Egyptians, Mexicans, and other nations. The Egyptians used about 1700 hieroglyphs, engraved on stone, painted on wood, and written on papyri They were either phonetic or ideographic Their invention is mythically ascribed to Thoth (Logos) That they were entirely ideographic was the opinion held until 1787, when Zoega stated that the ovals or cartouches contained royal names In 1818 Dr Young deciphered the named Ptolemy in the Rosetta Stone Young Champollion, Rosellini, Lepsius, Brugsch, Mariette, Chabas, Birch, and others (in the present century) have elucidated Egyptian hieroglyphics ABYDOS, "BOOK OF THE DEAD," EGYPT, ROSETTA STONE, TELL-EL-AMARNA TABLETS

High and **Low Church,** sections in the church of England, became prominent in the reign of Anne Dr. Sacheverell, preacher at St. Saviour's, Southwark, was prosecuted for 2 seditious sermons preached (14 Aug and 9 Nov 1709) exciting apprehension for the safety of the church, and hostility against dissenters His friends were called High-church and his opponents Low-church, or moderate men, 1720. The queen favored Sacheverell, and made him rector of St Andrew's, Holborn He died 1724

High Commission, Court of, an ecclesiastical court, established by 1 Eliz c. 1, 1559, by which all spiritual jurisdiction was vested in the crown It originally had no power to fine or imprison, but under Charles I and archbishop Laud it assumed illegal powers, was complained of by the Parliament, and abolished in 1641

Highlands of Scotland, long held by semi barbarous clans, were greatly improved by gen Wade's military roads, about 1725-26, by the abolition of heritable jurisdiction of feudal rights in 1747, and by the establishment of the Highland and Agricultural Society in 1784 REGIMENTS

highness. The title of "highness" was given to Henry VII, and this, and sometimes "your grace," was the manner of addressing Henry VIII, but about the end of his reign, the titles of "highness" and "your grace" were absorbed in that of "majesty" Louis XIII of France gave the title of "highness," in 1664, to the prince of Orange, who was previously called "excellency." Louis XIV gave the princes of Orange the title of "high and mighty lords," 1644. —*Henault*

high-priest. PRIEST

high-treason. To regulate trials for this crime and protect liberty in England, the 25th of Edward III 1352, was enacted, requiring 2 living witnesses, Parliament having refused to sanction the sentence of death against the duke of Somerset. By 40 Geo. III 1800, where the overt act is a direct attempt upon the life of the sovereign, the trial is conducted in the same manner as for murder TREASON.

Last 2 executions in England for high treason

I William Cundell, alias Connell and John Smith, 2 of 14 British subjects taken in the enemy's service in the isles of France and Bourbon tried by special commission, 6 Feb 1812 Mr Abbot, afterwards lord Tenterden and chief justice, and sir Vicary Gibbs, attorney general, conducted the prosecution and Mr (afterwards lord) Brougham defended the prisoners. The defence was that they had assumed the French uniform to aid their escape to England They were hanged and beheaded on the lodge of Horsemonger lane jail on 16 Mch 1812

All the other convicts were pardoned, on condition of serving in colonies beyond seas

II Cato street conspirators (CATO STREET CONSPIRACY) executed 1 May, 1820.

Hillabee towns, Attack on, by gen White, with 300 mounted Tennessee militia and some friendly Cherokees This place is on the Tallapoosa, in Alabama The attack was made on 18 Nov 1813 61 warriors were killed and 256 made prisoners without loss of a man.

Himalaya (*him-a'-la-ya*) **mountains.** MOUNTAINS.

Him'era, a town of Sicily Here Theron and Gelon of Agrigentum defeated the Carthaginians, 480 B.C., and at Ecnomus, near here, the latter defeated Agathocles of Syracuse, 311 B.C

Hindostan'. INDIA.

Hindu era began 3101 B.C, or 756 before the Deluge of 2348 The Hindus count months by the progress of the sun through the zodiac The Samoat era begins 56 B.C, the Saca era 79 A D.

hippopot'amus (Gr ἱπποποταμος, river-horse), a native of Africa, known to, but incorrectly described by, ancient writers. Hippopotami were exhibited at Rome by Antoninus, Commodus, and others, about 138, 180, and 218 The first brought to England arrived 25 May, 1850, and was placed in the Zoological gardens, Regent's park, London (d 11 Mch. 1878), another, a female, 4 months old, was placed there in 1854. One born there, 21 Feb 1871, and another born 1 Jan 1872, lived a few days only, another born 5 Nov 1872 Two young ones, born at Paris in May, 1858, and June, 1859, were killed by their mother. One born at Amsterdam, 29 July, 1865 One born in Central Park, New York 1893

Hispani'ola. HAYTI.

histology (from Gr ἱστος, a web), the science which treats of the tissues in animals and vegetables, mainly dependent on the microscope Schwann, Valentin, Kölliker, Quekett, and Robin are celebrated for their researches. Prof Quekett's "Lectures on Histology" were pub. in 1852 and 1854. MEDICAL SCIENCE

history. The Bible, the Parian Chronicle, the histories of Herodotus ("the father of history") and Ctesias, and the poems of Homer are the foundations of early ancient history Later ancient history is considered as ending with the destruction of the Roman empire in Italy, 476 Modern history dates from the age of Charlemagne, about 800 There was not a professorship of modern history in either English university until the years 1724 and 1736, when "regius" professorships were established by George I and George II —*Royal Historical Society*, London, established 1868, earl Russell, president, 1872 A commission was appointed in England 31 Aug 1869 to examine historical MSS held by institutions and private families, and to publish any considered desirable. It has issued several reports, 1870 et seq.

Hittites, descendants of Heth, second son of Canaan, a commercial tribe, from whom Abraham bought a grave for his wife, 1860 B C. (Gen xxiii.) They opposed Joshua, 1451 B.C, and the Egyptians, about 1340 B.C.

Castle of Jerablus a mound and ruins 20 miles below Beredjik, on the Euphrates, was visited by Henry Maundrell 1699, by dr Pococke, 1745, and by J H Skene and George Smith (d 1876), who agreed in considering the remains to be those of Carchemish, the ancient capital of the Hittites, captured and annexed by Sargon king of Assyria (about 721 B C) The site had been held successively by Hittites Assyrians Babylonians, Greeks, Romans, and Arabs A rich harvest may be expected from its exploration

Capt C R Conder's discovery of a key to the language of Hittite inscriptions on bas-reliefs gems etc, some of which were discovered by Burckhardt, 1808, and rediscovered by Mr Palmer in 1870, announced 26 Feb 1887, they consist of invocations hymns etc, to the sun etc His "Altaic Hieroglyphs and Hittite Inscriptions" pub 1887

Prof A H Sayce, in 1879 considered the Hittites to have been in very early times the predominant power in Asia Minor and N Syria The investigations of Ramsay Hogarth and Headlam, in 1890, supported by the English Asia Minor Exploration Fund, led to many discoveries which are described in the London *Times* of 25 July, 1891

Hobkirk's Hill, S C, Battle of, fought 25 Apr. 1781, between the British under lord Rawdon, and the Americans under Greene The Americans were worsted and retired British loss, 258, American, 266

Hochelaga (*hok-a-la'-ga*), the chief town of the Hurons, on the site of Montreal, Canada, when the French first entered the St Lawrence in 1535

Hochkirchen, Saxony Here the Prussian army of Frederick II was surprised and defeated by the Austrians under count Daun, 14 Oct 1758 The French here defeated the Russians and Prussians, 21 May, 1813

Hochstadt, a city on the Danube in Bavaria, near which several important battles have been fought (1) 20 Sept. 1703, when the imperialists were defeated by the French and Bavarians, under marshal Villars and the elector of Bavaria (2) 2 [N S 13] Aug 1704, called the battle of BLENHEIM (3) 19 June, 1800, when Moreau defeated the Austrians, and avenged the defeat of the French at Blenheim

Hohenlinden, a village of Bavaria. Here the Austrians, commanded by archduke John, were beaten by the French and Bavarians, commanded by Moreau, 3 Dec. 1800 The peace of Luneville followed Campbell commemorated this battle in his lyric of "Hohenlinden," published soon after

Hohenstaufen. GERMANY, GUELPHS

Hohenzollern (*hō-en-tsol'-lern*), the reigning family in Prussia Its origin is referred to Thassilo, about 800, who built the castle of Hohenzollern. In 1417, Frederick of Nuremberg, his descendant, was made elector of Brandenburg. The princes of Hohenzollern-Hechingen and Hohenzollern-Sigmaringen abdicated in favor of the king of Prussia, 7 Dec. 1849 Charles, son of the prince of Hohenzollern-Sigmaringen, was elected prince of Roumania, 20 Apr 1866. DANUBIAN PRINCIPALITIES His brother Leopold, nominated candidate for the throne of Spain, withdrew July, 1870 BRANDENBURG, PRUSSIA

Holbein Society, England, for obtaining photo-lithographic representations of ancient wood engravings, established in 1868, sir William Stirling Maxwell president. DANCE OF DEATH, PAINTING (German school)

holidays. LEGAL HOLIDAYS.

Holland (*hollow land*, or some say, *wooded land*), a kingdom in N W Europe (now known as Netherlands), composed of land rescued from the sea, and defended by immense dikes. It was inhabited by the Batavi in the time of Cæsar, who made a league with them It became part of Gallia Belgica, and afterwards of the kingdom of Austrasia From the 10th century to the 15th it was governed by counts under the German emperors. In 1861 the population of the kingdom in Europe was 3,521,416, of the colonies, 18,175,910; of both in 1863, 21,805,607, of the kingdom, Jan 1873, 3,767,263, 1876, 3,865,456, colonies, about 25,110,000, 1879, kingdom, 4,037,010, colonies, 1889, 29,765,031, kingdom, 1890, 4,564,565 BELGIUM, FLANDERS.

Parties termed Hooks (followers of Margaret, countess of Holland) and Codfish (supporters of her son William, who endeavored to supplant her) begin civil war, which lasted many years. . . . 1347
Holland united to Hainaut, 1299, and Brabant. . . . 1416
Annexed to Burgundy by duke Philip, who wrests it from his niece Jaqueline of Holland, daughter of the last count . . . 4136
Annexed to Austria through marriage of Mary of Burgundy with archduke Maximilian . . . 1477
Government of Philip of Austria . . . 1495
Of Margaret of Austria and Charles V . . . 1506
Of Philip II . . . 1555
Philip II establishes the Inquisition, Hollanders having embraced Reformed doctrines confederacy of GUEUX (Beggars) formed by nobles against it . . . 1566
Compromise of Breda presented . . . Jan "
Revolt under William prince of Orange begins . . . 1572
Elizabeth of England declines offered sovereignty, but promises help . . . 1575
Pacification of Ghent—union of north and south provinces . . . 1576
League of Utrecht between 7 northern provinces . . . 1579
Their independence declared . . . 29 Sept 1580
Assassination of William of Orange . . . 10 July, 1584
Ten southern provinces conquered by prince of Parma . . . 1585
Provinces solicit help from England and France, expedition of earl of Leicester, English and Dutch disagree . . . 1585–87
Battle of Zutphen—sir Philip Sidney mortally wounded, . . . 22 Sept 1586
Prince Maurice appointed stadtholder . . . 1587
Death of Philip II His son Philip III cedes the Netherlands to Albert of Austria and the infanta Isabella . . . 1598
Campaigns of Maurice and Spinola . . . 1599–1604
Maurice defeats the archduke at Nieuwport . . . 2 July 1600
Independence of the United Provinces recognized, truce of Antwerp for 12 years . . . 9 Apr 1609
Batavia in Java built . . . 1610
Religious dissensions between Arminians and Gomarists . . . 1610–19
Maurice favors the latter and intrigues for royal power . . . 1616
Synod of Dort, persecution of the Arminians . . . 1618–19
Execution of Barneveldt . . . 13 May, 1619
Renewal of war, Maurice saves Bergen op Zoom . . . 1622
His tyranny, plot against him, 16 persons executed . . . 1623
His death, his brother Frederick succeeds, and annuls the persecution . . . 1625
Manhattan (now New York), North America founded, massacre of English at Amboyna, India . . . 1624
Victories of Van Tromp, who takes 2 Spanish fleets off the Downs . . . 16 Sept and 21 Oct. 1639
Peace of Westphalia, republic recognized by Europe . . . 1648
War with England—naval actions Blake defeats De Ruyter, 22 Oct, is surprised by Van Tromp who takes some English ships and sails the Channel with a broom at his mast head, . . . 29 Nov 1652
Indecisive sea fights, 12-14 June, death of Van Tromp, 21 July, peace follows . . . 1653
Victorious war with Sweden . . . 1659
Another war with England . . . 1665
Indecisive sea fights, 1-4 June, victory of Monk over De Ruyter, . . . 25 July, 1666
Triple alliance—England, Holland, and Sweden against France, 1668
Charles II deserts Holland, joins France . . . 1670
French overrun Holland . . . 1671
Desperate condition of the states—populace massacre the De Witts—William III made stadtholder . . . 1672
French repelled by the sluices being opened . . . "
Indecisive campaigns . . . 1673–77
William marries princess Mary of England . . . 1677
Peace with France (Nimeguen) . . . 1678
William becomes king of England . . . 1689
Sanguinary war with France . . . 1689–96
Peace of Ryswick signed . . . 20 Sept 1697
Death of William . . . 8 Mch 1702
No stadtholder appointed—administration of Heinsius . . . "
War against France and Spain, campaigns of Marlborough, 1702–13
Peace of Utrecht . . . 30 Mch 1714
Holland supports the empress Maria Theresa . . . 1743–48
William Henry hereditary stadtholder . . . 1747
Peace of Aix la Chapelle . . . 18 Oct 1748
War with England—Holland loses colonies . . . 1781–83
Civil wars in the Low Countries . . . 1787–89
French republicans enter Holland, people support them . . . 1793
Unsuccessful campaign of the duke of York . . . 1794
Batavian republic established in alliance with France . . . 1795
Battle of Camperdown, Duncan defeats Dutch . . . 11 Oct. 1797
Texel fleet—12 ships of the line, with 13 Indiamen—surrenders to the British admiral, without firing a gun . . . 30 Aug 1799
New constitution in Batavian republic, chief officer (R. J Schimmelpenninck) called grand pensionary . . . 26 Apr 1805
Holland erected into a kingdom, and Louis Bonaparte, father of Napoleon III, declared king . . . 5 June, 1806
Ill fated WALCHEREN EXPEDITION . . . July, Sept 1809
Louis abdicates . . . 1 July, 1810
Holland united to France . . . 9 July, "
Restored to the house of Orange, Belgium annexed . . . 17 Nov 1813
Prince of Orange proclaimed sovereign prince of the united Netherlands . . . 6 Dec. "
New constitution . . . 1815
Revolution in Belgium . . . 25 Aug 1830
Belgium separated from Holland . . . 12 July, 1831
Holland makes war against Belgium . . . 3 Aug "
Treaty between Holland and Belgium signed in London 19 Apr 1839
Abdication of William I . . . 7–10 Oct 1840
King agrees to political reform, Mch, a new constitution granted . . . 17 Apr 1848
Death of William II . . . 17 Mch 1849
Roman Catholic hierarchy restored, announced . . . 12 Mch 1853

States general pass a law for the abolition of slavery in the Dutch West Indies (after 1 July, 1863) 6 Aug 1862
Slavery ceases in the Dutch West Indies 1 July, 1863
Canal from Amsterdam to North sea began 8 Mch 1865
Government undertakes a canal to connect Rotterdam with the sea Mch "
New ministry (protectionist) 1 June, 1866
Correspondence with Prussia respecting the Prussian garrison in Luxemburg July-Aug "
Alleged treaty with France to cede LUXEMBURG 22 Mch 1867
Fortifications of Luxemburg razed May, 1868
International exhibition opened at Amsterdam by prince Henry, 15 July, 1869
Meeting of the chambers, strict neutrality in the Franco Prussian war to be maintained 19 Sept 1870
Cession of Dutch possessions in Guinea to Great Britain, voted, 7 July, 1871
Expedition against the Achinese (SUMATRA) embarks. Dec. 1873
Canal between the North sea and Amsterdam passed by a monitor (see 1865), 4 Oct, inaugurated by the king 1 Nov 1876
International exhibition at Amsterdam opened 1 May, 1883
Committee for revising the constitution appointed 12 May, "
Death of the prince of Orange 24 June, 1884
Queen appointed by a congress to be regent if necessary 1 Aug "
Death of William III 23 Nov 1890
Queen Emma takes oath as regent during minority of her daughter, queen Wilhelmine, b 31 Aug 1880 9 Dec. "

PRINCES OF ORANGE (ORANGE), STADTHOLDERS.

1502 Philibert de Chalons
1530 René de Nassau his nephew
1544 William of Nassau, styled the Great, cousin to Rene, recovers the principality of Orange in 1559 Nominated stadtholder, 1570, killed by an assassin hired by Philip II of Spain, 10 July, 1584
1584 Philip William, his son, stolen from the university of Louvain, Dutch excluded him from their provinces, d 1618
1618 Maurice renowned general, stadtholder in 1587, a younger son of William by second marriage
1625 Frederick Henry (brother), stadtholder
1647 William II, stadtholder, married Mary, daughter of Charles I of England, his son succeeded in 1672
1650–72 John De Witt, grand pensioner, no stadtholder
1660 William Henry, stadtholder 1672, married Mary, eldest daughter of James II of England, 1677
1702–47 No stadtholder
1702 John William, nephew of William III, loses the principality of Orange, which is annexed to France
1747 William Henry, hereditary stadtholder, married princess Anne of England, succeeded by his son
1751 William IV, retired on French invasion 1795, d 1806.
1795. Holland and Belgium united to French republic

KINGS

1806. Louis Bonaparte made king of Holland by his brother Napoleon, 5 June, 1806, abdicated, 31 July, 1810
1810 Holland again united to France
1813 House of Orange restored William Frederick, prince of Orange (b 1772, proclaimed 6 Dec 1813, took oath of fidelity as sovereign prince, 30 Mch 1814, assumed style of king of the Netherlands, 16 Mch 1815, abdicated in favor of his son, 7 Oct 1840, d. 12 Dec 1843
1840 William II, b 6 Dec 1792, succeeded on his father's abdication, d 17 Mch 1849, succeeded by
1849 William III, son, b 19 Feb 1817, married Sophia of Würtemberg, 18 June, 1839 (She d 3 June, 1877) Married Emma of Waldeck Pyrmont, 7 Jan 1879, issue Wilhelmine, b 31 Aug 1880
1890. Wilhelmine, queen, b 31 Aug 1880

Holland Land company and **purchase.** NEW YORK, 1796, etc.

Holland, New. AUSTRALIA, AUSTRALASIA

Holloway hospitals and **college.** Thomas Holloway, proprietor of the popular ointment, etc., offered the British government 250,000*l.* to erect, for the use of the middle classes, a sanatorium or asylum for the insane, and hospitals for incurables and convalescents The asylum was erected at St Anne's Hill, Egham, near Virginia Water, 1873 et seq Opened by the prince of Wales, 16 June, 1885

Royal Holloway College for the Higher Education of Women, Egham, Engl First brick laid, 12 Sept. 1879 Opened by queen Victoria, 30 June, 1886. It includes library, reading-room, museum, and picture gallery Estimated cost 600,000*l*, endowment 200,000*l* The princely buildings are in the French renaissance style, *temp* Francis I (1515–47), architect, W Crossland There is good accommodation for 250 students. The session opened 4 Oct. 1887 Mr Holloway gave 250,000*l*, and promised 100,000*l*. additional for endowment He d 26 Dec. 1883, aged 83, leaving an immense fortune, although he was exceedingly generous during his lifetime, he is said to have expended 45,000*l* a year in advertisements

hol'ophote, a form of lamp in which the light is converged and directed to a particular spot to prevent collisions at sea, etc. Different kinds have been invented by Stevenson, Macdonald, Preece and others (1889).

Holstein (*hōl'-stīn*) and **Schles'wig,** N W Germany, duchies once belonging to Denmark The country, inhabited by Saxons, was subdued by Charlemagne early in the 9th century, and afterwards was part of the duchy of Saxony. In 1106 or 1110 Adolphus of Schauenberg became count of Holstein, his descendants ruled till 1459, when Adolphus VII died without issue, and Holstein and Schleswig, fearing his nephew Christian, king of Denmark, elected him duke In 1544 his grandson, Christian II, divided his states among his brothers, the duchies to remain subject to Denmark The eldest branch of the family reigned in Denmark till the decease of Frederick VII, 15 Nov 1863 From a younger branch (dukes of Holstein-Gottorp) descended the kings of Sweden from 1751 to 1818, and the reigning family in Russia since 1762, when duke, as husband of Anne, became czar In 1773 Catherine II of Russia ceded Holstein-Gottorp to Denmark in exchange for Oldenburg, etc The duchies were occupied by the Swedes in 1813, but restored to Denmark in 1814, and on 28 May, 1831, constituent assemblies were granted to them. Since 1844 disputes have been rife between the duchies and Denmark, and in 1848 the States-general of the duchies voted annexation to the German confederacy, supported by Prussia, war ensued till 1850, when they submitted to Denmark The agitation in the duchies, encouraged by Prussia, revived in 1857 The Germans in Schleswig wished to join the German confederation, like Holstein, but both duchies demanded greater independence of Denmark, that power opposing the change. DENMARK By the convention of GASTEIN, 14 Aug 1865, the government of Holstein was left with Austria, and that of Schleswig with Prussia. The whole of Holstein and part of Schleswig were ceded to Prussia by the treaty of Prague, 23 Aug 1866 The 5th clause, directing N Schleswig to be given to Denmark if the people voted for it, was not acted on, and was abrogated, Feb 1879 Area, 7273 sq miles. Pop. in 1860, 1,004,473, 1890, 1,217,437. HELIGOLAND DENMARK

Holy Alliance, ratified at Paris, 26 Sept 1815, between emperor of Russia (its originator), emperor of Austria, and king of Prussia, bound them, among other things, to be governed by Christian principles in all political transactions, with a view to perpetuating peace The compact was severely censured in England as opposed to liberty.

Holy Grail. "GRAIL, HOLY"

Holy Maid of Kent. Elizabeth Barton was incited by Catholics to oppose the Reformation by pretending inspiration from heaven She foretold the speedy and violent death of Henry VIII. if he divorced Catherine of Spain and married Anne Boleyn, and direful calamities to the nation. Executed, with confederates, at Tyburn, 5 May, 1534

holy places in Palestine have stirred contention between the Greek and Latin churches for several centuries. In the reign of Francis I. they were placed under Latin monks, protected by the French government, but the Greeks from time to time obtained firmans from the Porte invalidating the rights of the Latins, who were at last (in 1757) expelled from the sacred buildings, which were committed to the care of the Greeks by a hatti-scherif, or imperial ordinance.

Holy sepulchre partly destroyed by fire and rebuilt by Greeks, who claim additional privileges. 1808
Russian and French governments sent envoys (M Dashkoff and M Marcellus) to adjust the dispute, arrangement prevented by the Greek revolution 1821
Subject again agitated and the Porte proposed mixed commission to adjudicate all claims M Titoff the Russian envoy, for the Greeks, and M Lavalette, the French envoy, for the Latins, took up the question 1850
A firman of the Porte confirms the rights previously granted to Greek Christians, and denies to the Latins exclusive possession of certain holy places but leaves them a key of the church at Bethlehem, etc, as in former times 9 Mch. 1852
French government acquiesced with dissatisfaction, but the Russian envoy still desired the key withheld from the Latin monks M d'Ozeroff declared the right of Russia to protect the orthodox under the treaty of Kainardji in 1774 and demanded that the firman of 9 Mch 1852, be read at Jerusalem, though it militated against his pretensions, which was accordingly done The dispute continued, the Porte exposed to attacks of the Russian and French governments. Mch 1853
Prince Menschikoff arrives at Constantinople as envoy extraordinary, and besides claims respecting the holy places, demands a protectorate of Greek Christians in Turkey, leading to the war of 1854–56 (RUSSO-TURKISH WARS). 28 Feb. "

Holy Roman Empire. The German empire received this title under the emperor Otho I the Great, crowned at Rome by pope John XII, 2 Feb 962 GERMANY, ROME

Holy Rood or **Cross.** A festival for the recovery, by the emperor Heraclius, of a large piece of the cross, taken away, on the plundering of Jerusalem, about 615 The feast of the Invention (or Finding) of the Cross is on 3 May, that of the Exaltation of the Cross, 14 Sept At Boxley abbey, in Kent, Engl, was a crucifix, called the Rood of Grace, at the dissolution it was broken in pieces as an imposture by Hilsey, bishop of Rochester, at St Paul's cross, London, 1536

Holy Sepulchre, a Byzantine church in modern Jerusalem Fergusson, Robinson, and others consider the true site of the Holy Sepulchre to be the mosque of Omar, the "dome of the Rock" The question is undecided The Order of the Holy Sepulchre was founded by Godfrey of Bouillon, 1099, revived by pope Alexander VI 1496, reorganized 1847 and 1868

holy water is said to have been used in churches as early as 120 A D.—*Ashe*

Holy Week, or the "Week of Indulgences," is the week before Easter

Holyrood palace, Edinburgh, formerly an abbey, for several centuries the residence of the monarchs of Scotland The abbey, of which vestiges remain, was founded by David I in 1128, and contains the burial-place of several of his successors. The palace is a large quadrangular edifice of hewn stone, around a court surrounded by piazzas In the north-west tower is the bedchamber of queen Mary, and from an adjoining cabinet David Rizzio, her favorite, was dragged and murdered, 9 Mch 1566 The northwest towers were built by James V, and the rest of the palace was added during the reign of Charles II

home-rule. The Home Government Association (for home-rule), established in Dublin in 1870 held its first anniversary meeting, 26 June, 1871 It includes both Catholics and Protestants among its members.

Isaac Butt, home-ruler elected M P for Limerick 20 Sept 1871
Home rule advocated by archbishop McHale and others of the Romanist clergy in Ireland 1873
Programme of the party requiring an Irish parliament of queen, lords, and commons, and other powers, pub 25 Oct. "
A conference at the Rotondo, Dublin, reported a failure, 18-21 Nov "
A motion in the commons in favor of home rule defeated (314 to 52) 20 Mch 1874
Isaac Butt's motion for a committee on the subject, 30 June, was negatived (458 to 61), 2, 3 July, 1875, again (291 to 61), 30 June, 1 July, 1876, again (417 to 67) 24 Apr 1877
Stormy convention at Dublin, Mr Butt chairman 21, 22 Aug "
Home-rulers obstruct business in commons (PARLIAMENT) "
Home rule M P 's meet at Dublin, Mr Butt still leader 9 Oct. "
He yields to the obstructionists, Jan, resigns Apr 1878
Meeting at Dublin, 14 Oct, dissensions between moderate party (Mr Butt and others) and obstructives (Charles Stewart Parnell and others) Oct-Nov "
Death of Mr Butt, 5 May, succeeded as leader by William Shaw, 1879
Mr Parnell proposes a convention to meet at Dublin, 11 Sept, opposed by William Shaw, Mitchell Henry, and others, Sept. "
Meeting at Dublin, pronounced opposition to British government 20, 21 Jan. 1880
About 65 home rulers in the new Parliament, led by Mr Shaw and Mr Parnell Apr "
Mr Parnell chosen by 45 as parliamentary chairman 17 May, "
Thirty one home rulers voted with the government, 16 with Mr Parnell 13 July, "
Home rule convention at Newcastle on Tyne 9 Aug "
Meeting at Dublin, Justin McCarthy appointed vice president, resolution to resist coercion in Ireland adopted 27 Dec. "
Trial of Mr Parnell and others at Dublin (TRIALS), 28 Dec 1880-25 Jan 1881
Strong manifesto of Parnell, a counter one by Shaw Feb. "
Lord Salisbury in a speech ridicules the agitation in favor of home rule in Ireland 23 Apr 1889

ENGLAND, IRELAND, PARNELL.

"Home, sweet home." LITERATURE, American, 1792, MUSIC

Homer's "Iliad" and **"Odyssey,"** the oldest Greek epic poems. The first begins with the wrath of Achilles, and ends with the funeral of Hector, the second recounts the voyages and adventures of Ulysses, after the destruction of Troy. Various dates are assigned to these works, from 962 to 500 B.C. Among the thousands of volumes burned at Constantinople, 477 A D., are said to have been a Homer, written in gold on the great gut of a dragon, 120 feet long

F A Wolf, in his "Prolegomena" in 1795, regarded the poems as a composite of epic songs formed by Pisistratus about 550 B C This was the beginning of "the Homeric controversy," in which the leading scholars of Europe have been engaged ever since The Germans have generally accepted the theory of Wolf, with some modifications, while the British have until very recently defended the unity of each epic, and the individuality of Homer, under the lead of col Mure, the historian of Grecian literature, Mr Gladstone ("Homer and the Homeric Age") and others Grote the historian of Greece, believed that the Iliad was originally a poem of moderate length on "the wrath of Achilles" and had been pieced out, after the art of writing became general, with several shorter poems More recently Paley and others in England have adopted extreme views as to the late date of the poems in their present form, and the multiplicity of authors of their constituent parts

First English version of the "Iliad" by Arthur Hall appeared in 1581 The most celebrated versions of Homer's works are Chapman's, 1616, Hobbes's, 1675, Pope's, 1715-25, Cowper's 1791, and Bryant's 1870-71 The translation of the "Iliad" by the earl of Derby (1864) is much commended

hom'icide was tried at Athens by the Areopagites, 1507 B.C Killing in any public exercise of skill, or killing one who lay in wait to do injury, or one taken with another's wife, sister, daughter, or concubine, or one who, without just grounds, assaulted another violently, was not murder Among the Jews wilful murder was capital, but he who killed in chance-medley might flee to one of the CITIES OF REFUGE, and there continue till the death of the high priest (Numb xxxv), 1451 B C 9 Geo. IV c 31 (1828) defines justifiable homicide and homicide in its various degrees of guilt, and circumstances of provocation and wilfulness MURDER

Homildon Hill, Northumberland, Engl, where the Scots, under earl Douglas, were defeated by the Percies (among them Hotspur), 14 Sept 1402 Douglas and the earls of Angus, Murray, Orkney, and the earl of Fife, son of the duke of Albany, and nephew of the Scottish king, with many nobility and gentry, were taken

homilies, in early Christian times, were discourses delivered by the bishop or presbyter, in a homely manner, for the common people Charlemagne's "Homilarium" was issued 809 In England the "Book of Homilies," drawn up by abp. Cranmer, and pub 1547, and another prepared by order of convocation, 1563, were directed to be read in churches that had no minister able to compose proper discourses.

homœop'athy, a system of therapeutics taught in his "Organon of Medicine," 1810, and other works, by dr Samuel Hahnemann of Leipsic (d 2 July, 1843). He held that every medicine has a specific power of inducing a diseased state of the system (*similia similibus curantur*, like cures like), and that if such medicine be given to a person suffering under the disease which it has a tendency to induce, the disease disappears, because 2 similar diseased actions cannot simultaneously subsist in the same organ —*Brande* He used infinitesimal doses of medicine, such as the millionth of a grain of aloes, and required the patient to regulate his diet and habits carefully Introduced into England, 1827, and into United States about the same time by dr Hans B Gram The Hahnemann hospital was opened in Bloomsbury square, London, 16 Sept 1850 The World's Convention of Homœopathic Physicians opened at Philadelphia, Pa., 26 June, 1876. London School of Homœopathy founded 15 Dec 1876 Homœopathic congress met at Liverpool, 14 Sept 1877 There were said to be 12,500 practitioners in the U. S, 15 colleges with 1200 students, in 1890 American Institute of Homœopathy met in Washington, D C, June, 1892. MEDICAL SCIENCE.

homoousion (*ho'-mo-ö'-si-on*) and **homoiousion** (*ho'-moi-ü'-si-on*) (Gr. ὁμοούσιον, same essence, ὁμοιούσιον, similar essence or being), terms employed with respect to the nature of the Father and the Son in the Trinity The orthodox party adopted the former term as a party cry at the council of Nice, 325, the Arians adopted the latter at Seleucia, 359

Hondu'ras, discovered by Columbus in 1502, and conquered by the Spaniards 1523, is one of the republics of Central America, established 5 Nov 1838, and is governed under a charter proclaimed in Nov. 1865 A new constitution 1 Nov 1880 The executive authority rests in a president elected for 4 years Gen Pariano Leista elected president,

10 Nov 1891 Area, 46,400 sq miles, pop. 1889, 431,917 — *British Honduras*, Central America, was settled by English from Jamaica soon after a treaty with Spain in 1667 They were often disturbed by the Spaniards, and sometimes expelled, till 1783 Balize, or Belize, the capital, has a large mahogany trade Area, 7560 sq miles, pop 1891, 31,471 The English governor's salary is 2400*l* a year

honeymoon. It was a custom to drink of diluted honey for 30 days, or a moon's age, after a wedding, and hence the term honeymoon, of Teutonic origin Attila the Hun drank, it is said, so freely of *hydromel* on his marriage-day that he died of suffocation, 453

Hong-Kong, an island off the coast of China, was taken by capt Elliott, 23 Aug 1839, and ceded to Great Britain 20 Jan 1841 Its chief town is Victoria, built in 1842 Hong-Kong is separated from the mainland by a strait half a mile wide and contains about 29 sq miles The opposite peninsula of Kowloon, part of the mainland of China, was ceded to Great Britain by treaty, 1861, and is now part of Hong-Kong The governor's salary is 5000*l* Pop 1891, 221,441

"Honi soit qui mal y pense" ("Evil to him who evil thinks") Tradition says that the countess of Salisbury, at a ball at court, dropping her garter, the king, Edward III, took it up and presented it to her with these words, afterwards the motto of the order of the GARTER

Honor. Temples were erected to Honor by Scipio Africanus, about 197 B C, and by C Marius, about 102 B.C —The Legion of Honor was created by Bonaparte in 1802

Hood's invasion of Tennessee, 1864 FRANKLIN and NASHVILLE, Battles of

Hoosac tunnel. TUNNELS

hops, in use in England in 1425 —*Harleian MS* Introduced from the Netherlands into England about 1524, and used in brewing, but the physicians having represented that they were unwholesome, their use was prohibited in 1528 —*Anderson* The duty on hops was repealed in 1862, after many applications. Hops are largely cultivated in the United States They were introduced about 1640, but were not an article of commerce until about 1810-20 In 1840 there was produced some 1,240,000 lbs, 1850, 3,497,029 lbs, 1860, 10,991,996 lbs, 1870, 25,456,669 lbs, 1880, 26,546,378 lbs., 1890, 39,171,270 lbs 17 of the states produce hops, especially California, New York, Oregon, Washington, and Wisconsin, which in 1890 raised 99 48 per cent. of the whole The U S in 1879, had 46,800 acres of hops, in 1889, 50,212 acres California, in 1879, had 1119 acres, and in 1889, 3971, Oregon, in 1879, had 304 acres, in 1889, 3130, and Washington, in 1879, had 534 acres, in 1889, 5113

Horatii and Curiatii. ROME, 669 B.C

horn, hornpipe. The horn is thought to be, next to the reed, the earliest wind-instrument, and is known to most savage nations. It was first made of horn, hence the name, afterwards of brass, with keys for the semitones, in the last century.—The dance called the hornpipe is supposed to be so named from its having been performed to the Welsh *pib-corn*, that is, hornpipe, about 1300 —*Spencer* Many hornpipes were composed in the 18th century The "College Hornpipe" was very popular

Hornet, Battles of the NAVAL BATTLES

horse. The remains of the earliest known animal, *eohippus* (not larger than a fox), to which it is possible to trace back the modern horse, are found in the lowest Eocene strata (GEOLOGY) in New Mexico, Wyoming, and Utah In Europe wild horses were abundant in the Neolithic or polished-stone age The people of Thessaly were excellent equestrians, and probably first among the Greeks who broke horses in for service in war, whence the fable that Thessaly was originally inhabited by centaurs. "Solomon had 40,000 stalls of horses for his chariots, and 12,000 horsemen" (1 Kings iv 26), 1014 B.C The Greeks and Romans had some covering to secure their horses' hoofs from injury First mention of the British horse—*Cæsar*, "De Bello Gallico," iv 24-33, v 15-16. In the 9th century horses were shod only in time of frost Shoeing was introduced into England by William I, 1066 Horses were not used for agricultural labor until a comparatively recent time A law in Wales forbade ploughing with the horse The crusades introduced the eastern horse into Europe The use of post-horses introduced into England during the reign of Richard III Queen Elizabeth reputed an accomplished horse-woman Introduction of famous eastern horses into England during the reign of William III The Darley Arabian brought over during the reign of queen Anne

First horses in Massachusetts.	1629-30
J S Rarey, an American, in London publicly tamed vicious horses, and even a zebra from the Zoological gardens His system is founded on study of the disposition of the animal, and on kindness He taught many his method (20 Mch, lord Palmerston and 20 others), under pledge of secrecy, released in June, when his book was reprinted in England with out his consent	1858
He was engaged to instruct cavalry officers and riding masters of the army	July, 1859
He gave a lecture to the London cabmen, 12 Jan 1860, and received 20 guineas from the Society for the Prevention of Cruelty to Animals	May, 1860
Horse tax in England was imposed in 1784 It was extended and increased in 1796, and again in 1808 The duty upon "horses for riding" only, in England, amounts to about 350,000*l* per year	1862
An establishment for the sale of horse flesh as food was opened at Paris 9 July 1866 with success. About 150 persons (including sir Henry Thompson and sir John Lubbock) dined on horse flesh at the Langham hotel, London	6 Feb. 1868
Annual license duty in England on horses and mules 10s 6d each, horse dealers' license, 12*l* 10s (act passed 1869)	1870
Horse epidemic ("epizooty"), from Canada, at New York, Boston, etc	Oct. 1872
Banquet on flesh of horse, mule, and donkey at Paris	3 Apr 1875

RACING

Hortensian law, passed by Q Hortensius, dictator, 286 B C., after the secession of the plebeians to the Janiculum, affirmed the legislative power granted them by previous laws in 446 and 336 B.C

horticulture (from *hortus* and *cultura*), the art of cultivating gardens GARDENING.

Royal Horticultural Society of London founded by sir Joseph Banks and others in 1804, incorporated 17 Apr 1809, transactions first pub	1812
Massachusetts State Horticultural Society, the oldest in America, established (FLOWERS AND PLANTS)	1829

Hospitallers. KNIGHTS, MALTA.

hospitals, originally *hospitia* for the reception of travellers Among the earliest hospitals were the one founded by Valens in Cæsarea, 370-80 A D, and that built at Rome in the time of St. Jerome The earliest date of a hospital in England is 1080, when Lanfranc, archbishop of Canterbury, founded 2, 1 for leprosy and 1 for ordinary diseases. One at Jerusalem, built by the Knights of St John, 1112, had room for 2000 inmates, with an infirmary Of the first of English hospitals was St Bartholomew's. It was built as a priory, 1102, handed over to citizens of London, 1547, rebuilt in 1729 St. Thomas's, founded as a priory, 1213, purchased by the city of London, 1551, and opened for the sick. After various changes it was transferred to Lambeth, its present site, 1871 Bethlehem (or Bedlam), a priory built 1247, was given to king Henry VIII. for the reception of lunatics, 1547 (the oldest lunatic asylum in Europe except that at Granada) The present building was constructed in 1810. CHRIST'S HOSPITAL early ceased to serve as a hospital A great movement for founding hospitals in England commenced in the 18th century The oldest hospital in the United States is the Pennsylvania hospital, Philadelphia, 1750, followed by the New York hospital, 1770, Charity hospital, New Orleans, 1784, Boston dispensary, 1796. Of recent hospitals the Johns Hopkins hospital of Baltimore, opened 1889, is noted for the care bestowed upon its plans. It is a result of years of study of European hospitals, with the advice of distinguished American doctors. It is the largest hospital in America and as perfect as any in the world Capacity, 400 patients Endowed by Johns Hopkins, a merchant of Baltimore, with $3,500,000

Hounslow, Engl., formerly a market-town, is on a branch of the London and Southwestern railway, 9 miles from Hyde Park Corner Before the railway was opened 500 coaches passed through the town daily. West of the town there was "Hounslow heath," containing some 4293 acres, for many years a favorite resort of highwaymen, who when executed were exposed in gibbets along the way

hour. The early Egyptians divided day and night each into 12 hours, a custom adopted by Jews or Greeks probably from the Babylonians The day is said to have been first divided into hours from 293 B C, when L Papirius Cursor erected a sun-dial in the temple of Quirinus at Rome Before WATER-CLOCKS were invented, 158 B C, time was called at Rome by public criers In England, the measurement of time was, in early days, uncertain one expedient was by wax-candles, 3 inches burning an hour, and 6 wax candles burning 24 hours—ascribed to Alfred, 886 A D DAY

House of Commons, Lords, etc COMMONS, LORDS, PARLIAMENT

Howard Association, United States. This voluntary organization distinguished itself for courage in caring for sick of Southern cities during yellow-fever epidemics, 1878-79 The members nursed 21,000 patients in New Orleans alone between 17 Aug and 26 Oct 1868, and expended in charity $380 185.83 The association makes no distinction among sufferers of race or religion, and judiciously dispenses funds contributed by the charitable throughout the country

howitzer, a German piece of ordnance, ranking between a cannon and a mortar, came into use early in the 18th century

Hubbardton, Vt., Battle at St Clair, after evacuating FORT TICONDEROGA, retired towards Hubbardton, leaving a rear-guard there of 1200 men under col Seth Warner, he marched towards Castleton At Hubbardton the rear-guard was overtaken by the British, 7 July, 1777, when a sharp engagement took place, in which the Americans were beaten and dispersed with a loss of 120 killed and wounded, and 200 prisoners St Clair, with about 2000 men, made his way through the forest to fort Edward

"Hudibras." The first 3 cantos of this political satire, by Samuel Butler, appeared in 1663, the other parts in 1664 and 1678 LITERATURE

Hudson, Henry, Fate of It was the intention of Hudson to winter in Hudson's bay, 1610, but his crew were mutinous and obliged him to sail for England While still near Hudson's bay he was seized by mutineers, and with 8 others, including his son, sent adrift in an open boat and never heard from afterwards. His fate was revealed by one of the mutineers NEW YORK, 1609.

Hudson's sea, misnamed **bay,** North America, discovered by Sebastian Cabot, 1517, and rediscovered by capt Henry Hudson when in search of a northwest passage to the Pacific ocean, 1610 Connected with the Atlantic ocean by Hudson strait, and with the Arctic ocean by Hecla and Fury straits With Fox channel, its length on lon 80°, from the lower end of James's bay, is about 1350 miles, and in breadth it extends through 17° on lat 60° Its distance inland from the Atlantic ocean is about 13° on lat 62°. The "governor and company of adventurers of England trading to Hudson's bay" obtained a charter from Charles II in 1670. The "fertile belt" was settled by lord Selkirk in 1812 For these territories the bishopric of Rupert's Land was founded, 1849 The charter having expired, the chief part of the company's territories, on the proposition of earl Granville, the colonial secretary (9 Mch 1869), were transferred to the Dominion of Canada for 300,000*l*, and a right to a portion of land within 50 years, and other privileges, the company having consented to this 9 Apr 1869. Some of the people resisted annexation, and gen Louis Riel proclaimed independence and seized the company's treasury, Jan 1870 On 3 or 4 Mch he tried and shot Thomas Scott, a Canadian, who had escaped from his custody. Col. (afterwards sir) Garnet J Wolseley conducted a Canadian expedition to the territories (now named Manitoba), and issued a proclamation to the loyal inhabitants, 23 July, saying "our mission is one of peace" Riel was unsupported and offered no resistance MANITOBA.

hue and **cry,** the old common-law process in England of pursuing "with horn and voice," from hundred to hundred, and county to county, all robbers and felons Formerly the hundred was bound to make good losses by robberies therein, unless the felon were taken, but by subsequent laws it is answerable only for damage by riotous assemblies The pursuit of a felon was aided by a description of him in the *Hue and Cry*, a gazette for the purpose, founded 1710 —*Ashe.*

Huguenots (*hū'-ge-not*), a term (derived by some from the Ger *Eidgenossen*, oath-companions, by others from Hugues, a Genevese Calvinist) applied to the Reformed party in France, followers of Calvin They took up arms against their persecutors in 1561 After a delusive edict of toleration, many were massacred at Vassy, 1 Mch 1562, when civil wars began, which lasted, with some intermission, till the edict of Nantes in 1598 (revoked in 1685) On the revocation of the edict many Huguenots fled to the United States, settling in South Carolina, Virginia, and New York The massacre of St Bartholomew's day 24 Aug 1572, occurred during a truce BARTHOLOMEW, CALVINISTS, CAMISARDS, EDICT OF NANTES, PROTESTANTS Smiles's 'History of the Huguenots" appeared in 1867 Baird's "Rise of the Huguenots" was pub 1879 The crypt in Canterbury cathedral assigned to French Protestants in 1550 is still used by them for divine worship

Hull, Gen William, Trial of UNITED STATES, 1812, Jan. and Mch. 1814

Humaitá, a strong post on the river Paraguay, fortified with a battery of 300 cannon by Lopez, the president of Paraguay, and believed to be impregnable, was passed by the Brazilian iron-clads 17 Feb 1868 On the 19th Caxias, the Brazilian general, stormed a work north of Humaitá, and captured many stores Humaita itself, after a siege, was abandoned, 24 July, 1868

Humane Society, Royal, London, for recovery of persons apparently drowned, was founded in 1774 by drs Goldsmith, Heberden Towers, Lettsom, Hawes and Cogan, principally by the last 3 The society has above 280 depots, with apparatus The principal one was erected in 1794 on ground given by George III, north of the Serpentine river, Hyde park DROWNING

humanism, the philosophical study of man's personality as the most important subject of culture, the pursuit of an ideal in mind and character as the end of all education and progress, advocated by Petrarch and other disciples of ancient classic literature, termed the "new learning" ("*literæ humaniores*"), and the *renaissance*, in the 14th, 15th, and 16th centuries.

Humanitarians, a small sect in London, founded by Mr Kaspary, a German Jew Their principles, set forth in "The Fifteen Doctrines of the Religion of God," written 1866, include pantheism and transmigration of souls.

Humanity, Religion of POSITIVE PHILOSOPHY, SECULARISM.

hundred, a Danish institution, was a part of a shire, composed, it is said, of a hundred families when the counties were first divided, about 897. The hundred-court is a court-baron for all the inhabitants of a hundred instead of a manor

Hundred Days, the term of Napoleon's restoration, from his arrival in Paris, 20 Mch, to his departure 29 June, 1815.

Hundred Years' war, in French history, began with the English invasion in 1337

Hungary, a kingdom of central Europe, forming with Austria the Austro-Hungarian monarchy, formerly part of ancient Pannonia and Dacia, subjected to the Romans about 106, retained till the 3d century, then seized by the Goths, who were expelled about 376 by the Huns ATTILA, HUNS After Attila's death in 453, the Gepidæ, and in 500 the Lombards, held the country It was acquired by the Avars about 568, and retained till their destruction by Charlemagne in 799 About 890 it was settled by a Scythian tribe named Vingours, or Ungri (whence the Ger name *Ungarn*), and Magyars, of Finnish origin The chief of the latter, Arpad (889), was ancestor of a line of kings ending in 1301 The progress of Magyars westward ended with their defeat by the emperor Henry the Fowler, 934 Area, 125,039 sq miles Population of the kingdom, including Transylvania, Fiume, Croatia, and Slavonia, 31 Dec 1869, 15,509,455, 1890, 17,335,929 AUSTRIA

Stephen, founder of the monarchy, establishes Christianity, subdues Slavs etc, entitled Apostolic king by the pope 997
Poles overrun Hungary 1061
Bela III introduces Greek civilization 1174 et seq
Ravages of Tartars under sons of Genghis Khan, throughout Hungary, Bohemia, and Russia 1241 et seq
Golden bull of Andrew II granting personal rights 1222
Death of Andrew III, end of the Arpad dynasty 1301
Victories of Louis the Great in Bulgaria Servia, and Dalmatia, 1344-82
Invading Italy, he avenges the murder of his brother Andrew, king of Naples 1348
Sanguinary anarchy, Elizabeth, queen of Louis, is drowned, king Mary, the daughter marries Sigismond of Brandenburg, they govern with severity 1382
[The Hungarians disliked the name queen, and when a female came to the throne, called her king]
Sigismond's cruelties, his subjects appeal to the Turks. 1393
Battle of Nicopolis, Bajazet vanquishes Sigismond and a large army 28 Sept. 1396
Sigismond obtains crown of Bohemia, and is elected emperor of Germany 1410
Albert of Austria succeeds to throne of Hungary 1437
Victories of John Hunniades (reputed illegitimate son of Sigismond) over the Turks 1442-44
Who obtain a truce of 10 years 1444
Broken by Ladislas, king of Hungary (at the pope's instigation), he is defeated and slain with the papal legate, at Varna 10 Nov "
John Hunniades escapes, becomes regent. 1444-53
Raises siege of Belgrade 14 July, d 10 Sept 1456
Hungarians insult Turkish ambassadors, war ensues, Solyman II takes Buda 1526
Disastrous battle of MOHATZ 29 Aug "
Hungary subject to Austria "
Peace of VIENNA, Protestants tolerated 23 June, 1606
John Sobieski defeats Turks in several battles, and raises siege of Vienna 12 Nov 1683
Duke of Lorraine retakes BUDA 1686
Prince Louis of Baden defeats Turks at Salenckemen 19 Aug 1691
Prince Eugene defeats them at Zenta 11 Sept 1697
Peace of Carlowitz 26 Jan 1699
PRAGMATIC SANCTION, authorizing female succession 1722-23
Servia and Wallachia ceded to Turkey at peace of Belgrade 1739
Hungarians enthusiastically support Maria Theresa against France and Bavaria 1740
Protestants permitted to have churches 1784
Independence of Hungary guaranteed 1790
Diet meets, Hungarian academy established 1825
People, discontented with Austrian rule rebel 11 Sept 1848
Murder of military governor, count Lamberg, by a mob at Pesth, Hungarian Diet appoints provisional government under Kossuth and Louis Batthyany, 28 Sept, Hungarians defeat the ban of Croatia 29 Sept "
Diet denounces as traitors all who acknowledge the emperor of Austria as king of Hungary 8 Dec. "
Insurgents defeated by Austrians at Szaikszo, 21 Dec., at Mohr by the ban Jellachich 29 Dec "
Buda-Pesth taken by Windischgrätz 5 Jan 1849
Bem defeats Austrians at Hermannstadt 21 Jan "
Hungary declares itself free, Kossuth governor 14 April, "
Hungarians defeat Imperialists before Gran 18 April, "
Russian army crosses Galicia to join Austrians 1 May, "
Austro Russian troops defeat Hungarians at Pered. 20 June, "
Battles of Acs, Austrians defeat Hungarians 2, 10 July, "
Hungarians defeat Jellachich 14 July, "
Hungarians defeated by Russians, Görgey retreats after 3 days' battle 15 July, "
Battle before Komorn with Austro Russian army. 16 July, "
Insurgents under Bem enter Moldavia, 23 July, defeated by the Russians at Schässburg 31 July, "
Haynau defeats Hungarians before Temesvar 10 Aug "
Görgey and army surrender to Russians 13 Aug "
Kossuth, Andrassy, Bem, etc., escape to Turkish frontiers, placed under protection at New Orsova (TURKEY) 21 Aug. "
Komorn surrenders to Austrians, war ends 27 Sept. "
Louis Batthyany tried at Pesth, and shot, many insurgent chiefs put to death 6 Oct. "
Amnesty to Hungarian insurgents, who return home 16 Oct. "
Bem dies at Aleppo 10 Dec. 1850
Crown of St. Stephen and royal insignia discovered and sent to Vienna. 8 Sept 1853
Amnesty for political offenders of 1848-49. 12 July, 1856
During the Italian war in 1859, an insurrection was planned in Hungary, communications between Louis Napoleon and Kossuth, it is said, led the emperor of Austria to the sudden peace of Villafranca, and afterwards to promise reforms and to grant liberty to Protestants in Hungary Aug.-Oct. 1859
Recall of archduke Albert, gen Benedek governor April, 1860
Demand for restoration of old constitution, reunion of the Banat and Voivodina with Hungary, etc Oct. "
Meeting of Reichsrath at Vienna, no deputies from Hungary or Croatia 29 April, 1861
Imperial rescript refusing entire independence of Hungary, 21 July, Diet protesting, 20 Aug, is dissolved 21 Aug "
Archbishop of Gran, primate, protests against the act of imperial government Sept.-Oct "
Summoned to Vienna, he stands firm 25 Oct 1861
Magistrates in comitat of Pesth resign, military government established, passive resistance of nobility Dec "
Emperor visits Buda Pesth, well received, a new policy announced, rights of Hungary to be restored 6-9 June, 1865
Imperial rescript, abolishing representative constitution of the empire, restoring independence of Hungary, etc 21 Sept "
Hungarian legions join Prussian army, June (after peace allowed to return to their allegiance) Oct 1866
Constitution of 1848 restored, independent ministry appointed under count Julius Andrassy 17 Feb 1867
Croats protest against incorporation with Hungary 25 May, "
Emperor and empress crowned at Buda with ancient ceremonies 8 June, "
Bills for financial arrangement with Austria and for Jewish emancipation receive royal assent 29 Dec "
First trial by jury of press offences (fine and imprisonment for publishing a letter of Kossuth) 27 Feb 1868
Kossuth (elected to the legislature) resigns by letter 14 April, "
Croatian deputation accepts union with Hungary 27 May, "
Congress of Hungarian Jews opened, Joseph Eötvos minister, 14 Dec "
Louis Batthyany (executed and privately buried, Oct. 1849), reinterred in public cemetery, Pesth 9 June, 1870
Count Andrassy succeeds count von Beust, foreign minister at Vienna, count Lonyay, Hungarian premier 14 Nov 1871
Buda Pesth formally constituted the capital Nov 1873
Joseph Scharf and 9 other Jews tried at Nyireghyhaza for murder of a Christian maid, Esther Solymosi (on 1 April, 1882) June, 1883
Acquitted 3 Aug "
Violent anti Jewish riots Pesth, Zala, Egersseg, etc, July, Aug, martial law proclaimed 29, 30 Aug "
Count Julius Andrassy dies in Istria 18 Feb 1890
Unveiling at Arad of the national monument of the 13 generals executed 6 Oct 1848, currency reform bill (gold to be the basis) introduced into the Diet. 14 May, 1892

SOVEREIGNS

997 St. Stephen, duke of Hungary (son of Geisa), established Catholic religion (1000), with title from the pope of apostolic king still borne by emperor of Austria, as king of Hungary
1038 Peter, the German, deposed
1041 Aba, or Owen
1044 Peter, again, deposed, and his eyes put out.
1047 Andrew I, deposed
1061 Bela I, killed by the fall of a tower
1074 Salamon, son of Andrew
1075 Geisa I, son of Bela
1077 Ladislas I, the Pious
1095 Coloman, son of Geisa
1114 Stephen II, named Thunder
1131 Bela II, had his eyes put out.
1141 Geisa II, succeeded by his son,
1161 Stephen III, and Stephen IV (anarchy)
1173 Bela III, succeeded by his son,
1196 Emeric, succeeded by his son,
1204 Ladislas II, reigned 6 months only
1205 Andrew II, son of Bela III
1235. Bela IV
1270 Stephen IV (or V), his son
1272 Ladislas III, killed
1290 Andrew III, surnamed the Venetian, son in law of Rudolph of Hapsburg, emperor of Germany (last of the house of Arpad), d 1301
1301 Wenceslas of Bohemia, and (1305) Otho of Bavaria.
1309 Charobert, or Charles Robert, of Anjou
1342. Louis I, the Great, elected king of Poland, 1370.
1382 Mary, called king Mary, daughter of Louis.
1385-86. Charles Durazzo
1387 Mary and her consort Sigismond the latter became king of Bohemia, and was elected emperor in 1410
1392 Sigismond alone (on the death of Mary)
1437 Albert, duke of Austria, marries Elizabeth, daughter of Sigismond, and obtains the thrones of Hungary, Bohemia, and Germany, dies suddenly
1439 Elizabeth alone, she marries
1440 Ladislas IV, king of Poland, of which kingdom he was Ladislas VI, slain at Varna.
1444. [Interregnum]
1445. John Hunniades, regent.
1458. Ladislas V, posthumous son of Albert, poisoned
" Matthias Corvinus, son of Hunniades
1490 Ladislas VI, king of Bohemia the emperor Maximilian laid claim to both kingdoms
1516 Louis II of Hungary (I of Bohemia), loses his life at the battle of Mohatz.
1526. { John Zapolski, voivode of Transylvania, elected by Hungarians, and supported by sultan Solyman, by treaty with Ferdinand, he founds principality of Transylvania, 1536
Ferdinand I, king of Bohemia, brother to the emperor Charles V, rival kings (with Ferdinand the Hapsburg period began, the sovereign rulers of Austria after him succeeding to the title of the Hungarian crown) }
1540 Ferdinand alone, elected emperor, 1558
1563 Maximilian, son, emperor in 1564
1572. Rudolph, son, emperor in 1576
1608 Matthias II brother, emperor in 1612.
1618. Ferdinand II, cousin, emperor
1625 Ferdinand III, son, emperor, 1637
1647 Ferdinand IV, son, d in 1654, 3 years before his father

1655. Leopold I., brother; emperor, 1657.
1687. Joseph I., son; emperor, 1705.
1712. Charles VI. (of Germany), brother, and nominal king of Spain.
1741. Maria Theresa, daughter, empress; survived her consort, emperor Francis I., from 1765 until 1780. GERMANY.
1780. Joseph II., son; emperor in 1765; succeeded to Hungary on the death of his mother.
1790. Leopold II., brother; emperor; succeeded by his son.
1792. Francis I., son (Francis II. as emperor of Germany); in 1804 he became emperor of Austria only.
1835. Ferdinand V., son; Ferdinand I. as emperor of Austria.
1848. Francis Joseph, emperor of Austria; nephew; succeeded on the abdication of his uncle, 2 Dec. 1848; crowned king of Hungary, 8 June, 1867.

Hunker, Hunkerism, a term applied to the conservative element in the Democratic party of New York, 1835–60, which accepted the pro-slavery doctrine of the south without question. BARNBURNERS.

Huns, a race of warlike Asiatics, said to have conquered China about 210 B.C., and to have been expelled therefrom about 90 A.D. They invaded Hungary about 376, and drove out the Goths. Marching westward, under Attila, they were thoroughly beaten at CHÂLONS by the consul Aëtius, 451; on the death of ATTILA they ceased to be formidable and gradually disappeared.

hunting. The Assyrian kings maintained game preserves, and with the Egyptians were partial to the chase. Herod, says Josephus, was a successful sportsman. The ancient Greeks loved the chase, and Xenophon wrote a work on hunting, especially the hare, with dogs.

Alfred the Great is said by Asserius, his biographer, to have been an expert hunter at 12 years of age 860
"Bokys of Hawking and Huntyng," by dame Julyana Berners, was printed at St. Albans........ 1486
Famous among modern hunters are Rowaleyn Gordon Cumming, Scottish sportsman of Altyre, who spent 5 years hunting in S. Africa, between 1843 and 1849; and Jules Gérard, surnamed the "Lion-killer," a French officer in Africa, who killed his 25th lion........ 1855
Stag hunting.—A pack of stag-hounds is recorded as kept by Hugh Rolland, queen Elizabeth's ranger, at Simonsbath.... 1598
This pack was sold in London........ 1825
Sir Arthur Chichester establishes a pack of stag-hounds in Exmoor district........ 1827
Fox hunting.—Lord Wilton says: "About the year 1750 hounds began to be entered solely to fox." Previous to this time the fox was not considered an animal of the higher chase.
Lord Arundel (English) kept a pack of fox-hounds........1690–1700
Fox-hunting has come into some prominence in the U. S. since 1876, when the "Livingston County (N. Y.) Hunt" was organized by W. A. Wadsworth and C. C. Fitzhugh, and the "Queens County Drag Hounds" was established. Other hunt-clubs in the U. S. and Canada are: Rockaway, at Cedarhurst, L. I.; Essex County, at Orange, N. J.; Meadowbrook, at Hempstead, L. I.; Myopia, Wenham, Mass.; Radnor, Bryn Mawr, Pa.; Rose Tree, Media, Pa.; Elk Ridge, near Baltimore; Dutchess County Hunt-Club, N. Y.; Dunblane Hounds, Washington, D. C.; Montreal Hunt-Club, Quebec; and Toronto Hunt-Club, Ont. DOGS.

hurricanes. STORMS.

hussars', Hungarian mounted militia, provided by land-holders; instituted by Matthias Corvinus, about 1359. (Hussar is derived from *huss*, 20, and *ar*, price). The British hussars were enrolled in 1759.

Huss'ites. The clergy having instigated the pope to issue a bull against heretics, John Huss (b. in Bohemia, 1373), a zealous reformer, was cited before the council of Constance, the emperor Sigismond sending him a safe-conduct. He appeared, but was thrown into prison, and after some months' confinement was condemned and burned alive, with heroic endurance, 6 or 7 July, 1415. Jerome of Prague, his intimate friend, who came to support and second him, was also burned, 30 May, 1416, although under a safe-conduct. Many followers of Huss took up arms in 1419, formed a political party under John Ziska, and built the city of Tabor. Ziska defeated emperor Sigismond, 11 July, 1420, and a short truce followed. Ziska, blinded at the siege of Rabi, beat all the armies sent against him. He died of the plague, 18 Oct. 1424, and is said to have ordered a drum made of his skin to terrify his enemies. 2 Hussite generals, named Procopius, defeated the imperialists in 1431, and a temporary peace ensued. Divisions took place among the Hussites, and on 30 May, 1434, they were defeated, and Procopius the elder slain at Bömischbrod or Lippau. Toleration was granted by the treaty of Iglau, and Sigismond entered Prague 23 Aug. 1436. The Hussites opposed his successor, Albert of Austria, and called Casimir of Poland to the throne; but were defeated in 1438. Hussites still existed in the time of Luther, and were called "BOHEMIAN BRETHREN."

hustings (said to be from *house-court*, an assembly of the Anglo-Saxons), an ancient court of London, its supreme court of judicature, as the court of common council is of legislature. The court of *hustyngs* was granted to the city of London, to be holden and kept weekly, by Edward the Confessor, 1052. One was held to outlaw defaulters, 6 Dec. 1870. Winchester, Lincoln, York, etc., were also granted hustings courts.

Hutchings, William. REVOLUTION, SURVIVORS OF THE.

Hutchinson, Anne. MASSACHUSETTS, 1636; NEW YORK, 1643.

Hutchinsonians included many eminent clergy of England, who did not form a sect, but held the opinions of John Hutchinson of Yorkshire (1674–1737); they rejected the Newtonian system, and sought in the Scriptures a complete natural philosophy. Hutchinson's work, "Moses's Principia," was pub. 1724. He derived all things from air, whence, he said, proceeded fire, light, and spirit, types of the Trinity. In 1712 he invented a timepiece for finding longitudes, and died in 1737.

Hydas'pes, a river in India, where Alexander the Great defeated Porus, after a severe engagement, 327 B.C.

Hyde park, London, W., the ancient manor of Hyde, belonging to Westminster abbey, became crown property at the dissolution, 1535. It was sold by Parliament in 1652; but resumed by the king at the restoration in 1660. The Serpentine was formed 1730–33.

Colossal statue of Achilles, cast from cannon taken at Salamanca, Vittoria, Toulouse, and Waterloo, inscribed to "Arthur, duke of Wellington, and his brave companions in arms, by their countrywomen," erected........18 June, 1822

hydraulic press. HYDROSTATICS.

hydrochlo'ric acid or **chlorhy'dric acid,** the only known compound of chlorine and hydrogen, discovered by dr. Priestley, 1772; its constitution determined by Davy, 1810. It is also called muriatic acid and spirits of salt. ALKALIES.

hydrodynam'ics, that branch of hydromechanics that treats of the motion of fluids. HYDROSTATICS.

hy'drogen (from Gr. ὕδωρ, water, and γεννάω, I generate). Paracelsus observed a gas rise from a solution of iron in oil of vitriol, about 1500; Turquet de Mayerne discovered its inflammability, 1656; as did Boyle, 1672; Lemery noticed its detonating power, 1700. In 1766 Cavendish proved it to be an element, and in 1781 he and Watt first showed that when combined with oxygen, by burning, water is produced. Subsequently Lavoisier decomposed water, and gave hydrogen its present name instead of "inflammable air." One volume of oxygen combines with 2 volumes of hydrogen to form water. Hydrogen is never found in the free state. It was liquefied by Raoul Pictet and Cailletet, end of 1877. ELEMENTS.

hydroge'nium, a hypothetical metal. In a paper before the Royal Society, London, 7 Jan. 1869, Thomas Graham, master of the mint, suggested that a piece of the metal palladium, into which hydrogen had been pressed, became an "alloy of the volatile metal hydrogenium."

hydrog'raphy is the description of the surface waters of the earth. The first sea-chart is attributed to Henry the Navigator, in the 16th century. CHARTS, COAST SURVEY, MAPS.

hydrom'eter, an instrument to measure gravity, density, and other properties of liquids. The oldest mention of it occurs in the 5th century in the letters of Synesius to Hypatia; but it is not improbable that Archimedes was the inventor of it.—*Beckmann.* Archimedes was killed in 212 B.C., and Hypatia was torn to pieces at Alexandria 415 A.D. Robert Boyle described a hydrometer in 1675. Baumé's (1762) and Sykes's (about 1818) have been much employed.

hydrop'athy, a term applied to the treatment of disease by cold water, practised by Hippocrates in the 4th century B.C., by the Arabs in the 10th century A.D., and revived by dr Currie in 1797 A system was taught in 1825 by Vincenz Priessnitz, of Grafenberg, in Austrian Silesia Similar doctrines were outlined by dr Sydenham before 1689 Priessnitz died 26 Nov 1851 —*Brande* MEDICAL SCIENCE (Theories, Systems, and Schools)

hydropho'bia (Gr *ὕδρο*, water, *φόβος*, fear), properly, a horror of water, a disease originating in dogs, but communicable to men by the saliva of the dog entering the blood, and characterized by great nervous disturbance, muscular rigors It was regarded as inevitably fatal, until the first inoculation of the human subject for hydrophobia was performed by Louis Pasteur upon Joseph Meister at Paris, 7-16 July, 1885 First on natives of the United States, 4 children from Newark, N J, sent to him for treatment 21 Dec 1885, successful First performed in the U S by dr Valentine Mott of New York, Oct 1886, virus procured at Pasteur's laboratory

hydrostat'ics. Theory and practice of the pressure and equalization of fluids, etc. were probably first studied in the Alexandrian school about 300 B.C

		B C
Pressure of fluids discovered by Archimedes	about	250
Forcing-pump and air fountain invented by Hero	about	120
		A D
Water mills were known	about	1
Science revived by Galileo Castellio Torricelli, and Pascal (who suggested the principle of the hydraulic press) 17th century		
Theory of rivers scientifically understood		1697
Oscillation of waves correctly explained by Newton		1714
Scientific form given to hydro dynamics by Bernoulli		1738
Joseph Bramah's hydrostatic or hydraulic press patented		1785
Sir William Armstrong's hydraulic crane patented		1846
John Crowther's		1825

hygiene (*hy'-geen*), from Hygieia, goddess of health The science of the preservation of health. LIFE, SANITARY.

hygrom'eter, an instrument to measure moisture in the atmosphere That by Saussure (d 1799) is most employed It consists of a human hair boiled in caustic lye, and acts by absorption —*Brande.* Daniell's hygrometer (1820) is much esteemed

hymns. The song of Moses is the most ancient, 1491 B.C. (Exod xv) The Psalms date from about 1060 B.C. to about 444 B.C (from David to Ezra) The Jews often accompanied hymns with instrumental music Paul (64 A D) speaks of Christians admonishing one another "in psalms and hymns and spiritual songs" (Col iii 16) Hilary, the bishop of Arles, in France, is said first to have composed hymns to be sung in Christian churches, about 431 The hymns of dr Watts (d 1784), of John Wesley (d 1791), and of his brother Charles (d 1788), are used by English churchmen and dissenters. "Hymns, Ancient and Modern," edited by rev sir Henry Baker, first appeared in 1860 "Dictionary of Hymnology," by rev John Julian, pub 1892

hyp'notism (Gr *ὕπνος*, sleep), or nervous sleep, terms given by Mr Braid (in 1843) to a sleep-like condition produced by steadily fixing the mind on one object. Minor surgical operations have, it is said, been performed without pain on persons in this state "It may be regarded as an artificial catalepsy"—*Encycl Brit*, 9th ed, vol xv., p 282.

hypsom'eter, a thermometrical barometer for measuring altitudes, invented by F J Wollaston in 1817, much improved by Regnault about 1847

Hyrca'nia, Asia, near the Caspian, a province subject to Persia, 334 B.C, held by Parthians, 244 It is now Mazenderan, a Persian province

---

I

I, the 9th letter of the English alphabet, corresponding to the Greek *iota*, which was derived from Semitic source, and possibly ultimately from Egypt ALPHABET

iambic verse, a verse consisting wholly or mainly of iambic feet, each of which consists of one short followed by a long syllable, on which the stress falls It is the common verse of dramatic dialogue, both in Greek and in Latin, and the iambus is the fundamental foot in all epic and heroic poetry, in the Italian, French, German, and other languages, as well as in English The word iambus was mythically derived from Iambe, in Greek mythology an attendant of Metanira, wife of Celeus, king of Eleusis, who entertained Demeter, while seeking through Attica her daughter Perserphone, with jokes, stories, and poetical effusions, and hence free and satirical verses were called iambics —*Apollodorus* Iambic verses were first written about 700 B.C by Archilochus, who courted Neobule, the daughter of Lycambes, but, after a promise of marriage, the father preferred a richer suitor, whereupon Archilochus wrote so bitter a satire on the old man's avarice that he hanged himself.—*Herodotus.*

Ibe'ria. GEORGIA, SPAIN

Icarians. A communistic society, founded in France by Etienne Cabet in 1840 3 Feb 1848, the van-guard sailed for Texas and settled in Fannin county Decimated by fever, the remnant joined a second colony from France, and settled at Nauvoo, Ill, in Mch 1849 In 1853 they purchased 3000 acres in Adams county, Iowa, to which they removed in 1859

ice. Water in the solid state, which it assumes under ordinary conditions of atmospheric pressure at a temperature of 32° Fahrenheit. Galileo observed ice to be lighter than water, about 1597, specific gravity being 92 The ice trade first started in Boston, Mass., in 1805, when a man named Tudor shipped ice to Martinique Ice is now made artificially, especially in the southern states and in Australia.

Iceland, an island situated between the N Atlantic and the Arctic oceans, subject to Denmark, discovered by Norwegian chiefs about 861, according to some accounts, it had been previously visited by a Scandinavian pirate. Area, 39,756 sq miles, pop 69,224

Colonized by Norwegians		874
Christianity introduced	about	1000
[Annual general assembly was termed Althing 4 great schools, like universities, were founded in the 11th century, and education was general]		
Warrior, statesman, and poet Snorri Sturluson was murdered,	22 Sept	1241
Had a republican government and a flourishing literature till subjected to Hakon, king of Norway		1264
Protestantism introduced	about	1551
New constitution signed by the king 5 Jan, took effect 1 Aug, on a visit of king Christian of Denmark, when the 1000th anniversary of the colonization was celebrated at the capital, Reykjavik		1874
Cleasby's Icelandic English Dictionary pub in England		1869-73

Iceland has suffered by volcanic eruptions, especially in 1783, and on 29 Mch 1875, whole districts of pasture land were devastated. AMERICA, EDDAS, HECLA

Ice'ni, a British tribe, chiefly in Suffolk and Norfolk. In 61 A D, while Suetonius Paulinus was reducing Mona (Anglesey), incited by their queen Boadicea they marched southwards and destroyed Verulam, London, and other places, with the Roman inhabitants; but were defeated by Suetonius, with great slaughter, near London

"While about the shores of Mona those Neronian legionaries
Burnt and broke the grove and altar of the Druid and Druidess,
Far in the East Boădicéa, standing loftily charioted,
Mad and maddening all that heard her in her fierce volubility,
Girt by half the tribes of Britain, near the colony Cámulodúne,
Yell'd and shriek'd between her daughters o'er a wild confederacy"
—*Tennyson*, "Boădicéa"

ice-yachting. SAILING.

"Ich dien" ("I serve"), the motto under the plume of ostrich feathers found in the helmet of the king of Bohemia, slain at the battle of Cressy while a volunteer in the French army, 26 Aug. 1346 Edward the Black Prince, who won the battle, in respect to his father, Edward III, who commanded in chief, adopted the motto, since borne with the feathers by heirs to the crown of England.

ichnol'ogy, the science of footprints, or impressions in mud or sand of animals of former ages. Dr Duncan discovered the footprints of a tortoise in the sandstone of Annandale, in 1828, many discoveries have since been made by Owen, Lyell, Huxley, and others.

ichthyol'ogy, the science of fishes. Eminent writers ire Willoughby, Ray, Valenciennes, Cuvier, Owen, Agassiz, etc. Farrell's "British Fishes" (1836-59) is a classical work. FISH.

Ico'nium, now **Ko'niyeh,** a town of Syria. Here Paul and Barnabas preached, 38. Soliman the Seljuk founded a kingdom here in 1074, which lasted till conquered by Turks, 307, but subdued by crusaders in 1097 and 1190.

icon'oclasts ("image-breakers"). The controversy respecting images (introduced into churches for popular instruction about 300) began about 726, and caused disturbance and oss of life in the Eastern empire. Leo Isauricus issued 2 edicts for demolishing images in churches in that year, and enforced them with rigor in 736. Defenders of images were again persecuted in 752 and 761, when Constantine forbade his subjects becoming monks. The worship of images was restored by Irene in 780. This schism occasioned the second council of Nice, 787. Theophilus banished painters and statuaries from the Eastern empire, 832. The iconoclasts were excommunicated at the 8th general council at Constantinople, 869-70. This controversy led to the separation of the Greek and Latin churches. Many images in churches were destroyed in England and Scotland during the Reformation and the English civil war, 1641-48.

Idaho (Ind. *Edah hoe*), one of the states of the north-western division of the Union. Its name signifies "light on the mountains." It lies between 42° and 49° N. lat., and 111° and 117° W. lon. The Dominion of Canada bounds it on the north, Montana and Wyoming on the east, Utah and Nevada on the south, and Oregon and Washington on the west. Area, 84,800 sq. miles, pop. 1890, 84,385; 1900, 161,772. Capital, Boisé City.

First white men in Idaho, Lewis and Clark's exploring expedition (UNITED STATES)....1805-6
First settlement at fort Hall by N. J. Wyeth.... 1834
Cœur d'Alene mission established.... 1842
Gold discovered on the Oro Fino creek, followed by a large immigration....1858-60
Idaho created a territory....3 Mch. 1863
General school law passed....12 Jan. 1877
Test-oaths abjuring polygamy, plural and celestial marriages required of all county and precinct officers....1884-85
New capitol completed at Boisé City.... 1887
Insane asylum erected at Blackfeet.... "
Legislature unseats 3 members as ineligible under the anti-Mormon test-oaths.... 1888
University at Moscow, authorized by the legislature....Jan. 1889
Convention frames a state constitution....4 July-6 Aug. "
Constitution ratified and state officers elected....5 Nov. "
Supreme court sustains the Idaho anti-Mormon test-oath law for voters....3 Feb. 1890
Admitted as the 43d state by proclamation of president.3 July, "
Gov. Shoup takes the oath of office, 3 Nov., and convenes the legislature at Boisé City....8 Dec. "
Legislature elects U. S. senators; gov. Shoup for term ending 4 Mch. 1891 (also F. T. Dubois to succeed him), and W. J. McConnell....18 Dec. "
Lt.-gov. Willey succeeds gov. Shoup resigned....20 Dec. "
Election of Dubois being deemed illegal, William H. Claggett is chosen Shoup's successor....11 Feb. 1891
Law allowing verdict by three-fourths of a jury in a civil action, and an Australian ballot law enacted at session ending 14 Mch. "
U. S. senate seats Dubois (vote 55-5)....3 Mch. 1892
Lockout involving 3000 striking miners begins in the Cœur d'Alene mining district in Shoshone county, 1 Apr. An attack on men employed in the Gem mines, made by union men, results in the killing of several miners....11 July, "
Martial law put in force in Shoshone county....14 July, "
Proclamation of pres. Harrison commanding all persons in insurrection in Idaho to disperse....16 July, "
Two thousand U. S. troops, by order of pres. Harrison, occupy Wardner, 14 July; suppress disturbance; withdraw. 23 July, "
Trial of insurrectionary miners at Cœur d'Alene city for conspiracy; 4 convicted, 10 acquitted....29 Sept. "

TERRITORIAL GOVERNORS.

Name.	Date.	Name.	Date.
Wm. H. Wallace....	1863 to 1864	Thomas W. Bennett..	1871 to 1876
Caleb Lyon....	1864 " 1866	Mason Brayman....	1876 " 1880
David W. Ballard....	1866 " 1867	John B. Neil....	1880 " 1883
Samuel Bard....	1870	John N. Irwin....	1883
Gilman Marston....	1870 " 1871	Wm. N. Burn....	1884 " 1885
Alexander Connor....	1871	Edwin A. Stevens....	1885 " 1889
Thomas M. Bowen....	1871		

STATE GOVERNORS.

Name.	Date	Remarks.
George L. Shoup....	1890	Elected U. S. senator.
N. B. Willey....	1890 to 1893	Lt.-gov. acting
Wm. J. McConnell....	1893 " 1895	Republican.
" "	1895 " 1897	"

UNITED STATES SENATORS FROM IDAHO.

Name.	No. of Congress.	Date.	Remarks.
George L. Shoup....	Fifty-first	1890	Term expires, 1897
Fred. T. Dubois....	"	"	" " 1895

idealism. PHILOSOPHY.

ides (Lat. *idus*), in the Roman and church calendar the 15th day of Mch., May, July, and Oct.; the 13th day in every other month. Dates were reckoned backward from the ides, as from the calends and the nones. On the *idus* of Mch., 44 B.C., Julius Cæsar was assassinated.

idols. Images or similitudes of a divinity, as objects of worship. The public worship of idols was introduced by Ninus, king of Assyria, 2059 B.C.—*Vossius*. Images are mentioned in Gen. xxxi. 19, 30, 1739 B.C. The Jews frequently deserted the worship of God for idols till their captivity, 588 B.C. Constantine, emperor of Rome, ordered heathen temples destroyed, and all sacrifices to cease, 330 A.D.—*Dufresnoy*. Idolatry was revived in Britain by Saxons about 473, but died out after the coming of Augustin, about 597. ICONOCLASTS, WEEK.

Idumæ'a, the country of the Edomites, descendants of Esau, brother of Jacob (Gen. xxxvi., Josh. xxiv. 4). B.C.
Edomites refuse the Israelites a way through their country.. 1453
They are subjugated by David.... 1040
Revolt against Ahaziah, 892; are defeated by Amaziah.... 827
They join the Chaldæans against Judah, and are anathematized in Ps. cxxxvii....about 570
John Hyrcanus, the Maccabee, subjugates and endeavors to incorporate them with the Jews.... 125
Herod the Great, son of Antipater, an Idumæan, king of Judæa, 40

Ildefon'so, San, a town of Spain. Here was signed a treaty between France and Spain, 19 Aug. 1796; and another, by which France regained Louisiana, 1 Oct. 1800. UNITED STATES.

Ilerda, a town of N.E. Spain, founded by the Carthaginians, now Lerida on the Segre. Here Cæsar defeated Afranius and Petreius, lieutenant of Pompey, after a brave resistance, 49 B.C.

Il'ium, Asia Minor. A city was built here by Dardanus and called Dardania, 1480 B.C. TROY, another city, was founded by Troas, about 1341 B.C.; and Ilus, his successor, called the country Ilium. HOMER.

Illinois, one of the northern central states of the United States, its western boundary the Mississippi river, which separates it from Iowa and Missouri; Wisconsin bounds it on the north, lake Michigan touching the northeastern corner; Indiana on the east, and Kentucky on the south. It is limited in lat. by 36° 59′ to 42° 30′ N., and in lon. by 87° 35′ to 91° 40′ W. Area, 56,650 sq. miles. Pop. 1890, 3,826,351; 1900, 4,821,550. Capital, Springfield.

Louis Joliet and Jacques Marquette descend the Mississippi river from the mouth of the Wisconsin to the Arkansas. Returning, they ascend the Illinois, making their way to lake Michigan *via* the Desplaines and Chicago rivers, 1673
Marquette, purposing to establish a mission among the Illinois Indians, makes a portage from the Chicago to the Desplaines, descends the Illinois river nearly to Utica, where he meets a large concourse of chiefs and warriors....8 Apr. 1675
Father Claude Allouez, successor to Marquette, who d. 18 May, 1675, enters the Chicago river on his way to the Indian mission....Apr. 1676
Robert Cavalier Sieur de la Salle, with Henry Tonti, father Hennepin, and a party of 33, descending the Kankakee and Illinois rivers, pass through Peoria lake 3 Jan. 1680, and erect fort Crevecœur on the east shore of the outlet.... 1680
Father Hennepin descends the Illinois from the fort to explore the upper Mississippi....28 Feb. "

vived by dr. Currie in 1797. A system was taught in 1825 by Vincenz Priessnitz, of Grafenberg, in Austrian Silesia. Similar doctrines were outlined by dr. Sydenham before 1689. Priessnitz died 26 Nov. 1851.—*Brande.* MEDICAL SCIENCE (Theories, Systems, and Schools).

hydropho'bia (Gr. ὕδωρ, water, φόβος, fear), properly, a horror of water, a disease originating in dogs, but communicable to men by the saliva of the dog entering the blood, and characterized by great nervous disturbance, muscular rigors. It was regarded as inevitably fatal, until the first inoculation of the human subject for hydrophobia was performed by Louis Pasteur upon Joseph Meister at Paris, 16 July, 1885. First inoculations of the United States, 4 children from Newark, N. J., sent to him for treatment 21 Dec. 1885; successful. First performed in the U. S. by dr. Valentine Mott of New York, Oct. 1886, virus procured at Pasteur's laboratory.

hydrostat'ics. Theory and practice of the pressure and equalization of fluids, etc., were probably first studied in the Alexandrian school about 300 B.C.

	B.C.
Pressure of fluids discovered by Archimedes ....about	250
Forcing-pump and air fountain invented by Hero ......about	120
	A.D.
Water mills were known ....about	1
Science revived by Galileo, Castelli, Torricelli, and Pascal (who suggested the principle of the hydraulic press) 17th century	
Theory of rivers scientifically understood	1697
Oscillation of waves correctly explained by Newton	1714
Scientific form given to hydro dynamics by Bernoulli	1738
Joseph Bramah's hydrostatic or hydraulic press patented	1785
Sir William Armstrong's hydraulic crane patented	1846
John Crowther's	1825

hygiene (*hy'-jeen*), from Hygieia, goddess of health. The science of the preservation of health. LIFE, SANITARY.

hygrom'eter, an instrument to measure moisture in the atmosphere. That by Saussure (d. 1799) is most employed. It consists of a human hair boiled in caustic lye, and acts by absorption.—*Brande.* Daniell's hygrometer (1820) is much esteemed.

hymns. The song of Moses is the most ancient, 1491 B.C. (Exod. xv.). The Psalms date from about 1060 B.C. to about 444 B.C. (from David to Ezra). The Jews often accompanied hymns with instrumental music. Paul (64 A.D.) speaks of Christians admonishing one another "in psalms and hymns and spiritual songs" (Col. iii. 16). Hilary, the bishop of Arles, in France, is said first to have composed hymns to be sung in Christian churches, about 431. The hymns of dr. Watts (d. 1748), of John Wesley (d. 1791), and of his brother Charles (d. 1788), are used by English churchmen and dissenters. "Hymns, Ancient and Modern," edited by rev. sir Henry Baker, first appeared in 1860. "Dictionary of Hymnology," by rev. John Julian, pub. 1892.

hyp'notism (Gr. ὕπνος, sleep), or nervous sleep, terms given by Mr. Braid (in 1843) to a sleep-like condition produced by steadily fixing the mind on one object. Minor surgical operations have, it is said, been performed without pain on persons in this state. "It may be regarded as an artificial catalepsy."—*Encycl. Brit.*, 9th ed., vol. xv., p. 282.

hypsom'eter, a thermometrical barometer for measuring altitudes, invented by F. J. Wollaston in 1817; much improved by Regnault about 1847.

Hyrca'nia, Asia, near the Caspian, a province subject to Persia, 334 B.C.; held by Parthians, 244. It is now Mazenderan, a Persian province.

I

I, the 9th letter of the English alphabet, corresponding to the Greek *iota*, which was derived from Semitic source, and possibly ultimately from Egypt. ALPHABET.

iambic verse, a verse consisting wholly or mainly of iambic feet, each of which consists of one short followed by a long syllable, on which the stress falls. It is the common verse of dramatic dialogue, both in Greek and in Latin; and the iambus is the fundamental foot in all epic and heroic poetry, in the Italian, French, German, and other languages, as well as in English. The word iambus was mythically derived from Iambe, in Greek mythology an attendant of Metanira, wife of Celeus, king of Eleusis, who entertained Demeter, while seeking through Attica her daughter Persephone, with jokes, stories and poetical effusions; and hence free and satirical verses were called iambics.—*Apollodorus.* Iambic verses were first written about 700 B.C. by Archilochus, who courted Neobule, the daughter of Lycambes; but, after a promise of marriage, the father preferred a richer suitor; whereupon Archilochus wrote so bitter a satire on the old man's avarice that he hanged himself.—*Herodotus.*

Ibe'ria. GEORGIA, SPAIN.

Icarians. A communistic society, founded in France by Etienne Cabet in 1840. 3 Feb. 1848, the vanguard sailed for Texas and settled in Fannin county. Decimated by fever, the remnant joined a second colony from France, and settled at Nauvoo, Ill., in Mch. 1849. In 1853 they purchased 3000 acres in Adams county, Iowa, to which they removed in 1859.

ice. Water in the solid state, which it assumes under ordinary conditions of atmospheric pressure at a temperature of 32° Fahrenheit. Galileo observed ice to be lighter than water, about 1597; specific gravity being .92. The ice trade first started in Boston, Mass., in 1805, when a man named Tudor shipped ice to Martinique. Ice is now made artificially, especially in the southern states and in Australia.

Iceland, an island situated between the Atlantic and the Arctic oceans, subject to Denmark, discovered by Norwegian chiefs about 861; according to some accounts, it had been previously visited by a Scandinavian pirate. Area, 39,756 sq. miles; pop. 69,224.

Colonized by Norwegians	874
Christianity introduced ....about	1000
[Annual general assembly was termed Althing: 4 great schools, like universities, were founded in the 11th century; and education was general.]	
Warrior, statesman, and poet Snorri Sturluson was murdered, 22 Sept.	1241
Had a republican government and a flourishing literature till subjected to Hakon, king of Norway	1264
Protestantism introduced ....about	1551
New constitution signed by the king, 5 Jan., took effect 1 Aug., on a visit of king Christian of Denmark, when the 1000th anniversary of the colonization was celebrated at the capital, Reykjavik	1874
Cleasby's Icelandic-English Dictionary pub. in England	1869–74
Iceland has suffered by volcanic eruptions, especially in 1783; and on 29 Mch. 1875, whole districts of pasture-land were devastated.	

AMERICA, EDDAS, HECLA.

Ice'ni, a British tribe, chiefly in Suffolk and Norfolk. In 61 A.D., while Suetonius Paulinus was reducing Mona (Anglesey), incited by their queen Boädicéa they ma[illegible] wards and destroyed Verulam, London, and [illegible] the Roman inhabitants; but were defeat[illegible] great slaughter, near London.

> "While about the shores of Mona those [illegible]
> Burnt and broke the grove and alt[illegible]
> Far in the East Boädicéa, stand[illegible]
> Mad and maddening all that h[illegible]
> Girt by half the tribes of [illegible]
> Yell'd and shriek'd [illegible]
> cy."

ice-yacht[illegible]

"Ich die[illegible] ostrich feathe[illegible] slain at the b[illegible] army, 26 A[illegible] battle, in [illegible] in chief, [illegible] heirs to[illegible]

Ich[illegible] in m[illegible] disc[illegible] na[illegible]

ichthyol′ogy, the science of fishes. Eminent writers are Willoughby, Ray, Valenciennes, Cuvier, Owen, Agassiz, etc. Yarrell's "British Fishes" (1836-59) is a classical work. FISH.

Ico′nium, now **Ko′niyeh,** a town of Syria. Here Paul and Barnabas preached, 88. Soliman the Seljuk founded a kingdom here in 1074, which lasted till conquered by Turks, 1307, but subdued by crusaders in 1097 and 1190.

icon′oclasts ("image-breakers"). The controversy respecting images (introduced into churches for popular instruction about 300) began about 726, and caused disturbance and loss of life in the Eastern empire. Leo Isauricus issued 2 edicts for demolishing images in churches in that year, and enforced them with rigor in 736. Defenders of images were again persecuted in 752 and 761, when Constantine forbade his subjects becoming monks. The worship of images was restored by Irene in 780. This schism occasioned the second council of Nice, 787. Theophilus banished painters and statuaries from the Eastern empire, 832. The iconoclasts were excommunicated at the 8th general council at Constantinople, 869-70. This controversy led to the separation of the Greek and Latin churches. Many images in churches were destroyed in England and Scotland during the Reformation and the English civil war, 1641-48.

Idaho (Ind. *Edah hoe*), one of the states of the northwestern division of the Union. Its name signifies "light on the mountains." It lies between 42° and 49° N. lat., and 111° and 117° W. lon. The Dominion of Canada bounds it on the north, Montana and Wyoming on the east, Utah and Nevada on the south, and Oregon and Washington on the west. Area, 84,800 sq. miles, pop. 1890, 84,385; 1900, 161,-772. Capital, Boise City.

First white men in Idaho, Lewis and Clark's exploring expedition (UNITED STATES) ... 1805-6
First settlement at fort Hall by N. J. Wyeth ... 1834
Cœur d'Alene mission established ... 1842
Gold discovered on the Oro Fino creek, followed by a large immigration ... 1858-60
Idaho created a territory ... 3 Mch. 1863
General school law passed ... 12 Jan. 1877
Test-oaths abjuring polygamy, plural and celestial marriages required of all county and precinct officers ... 1884-85
New capitol completed at Boisé City ... 1887
Insane asylum erected at Blackfoot ... "
Legislature unseats 3 members as ineligible under the anti-Mormon test-oaths ... 1888
University at Moscow, authorized by the legislature ... Jan. 1889
Convention frames a state constitution ... 4 July-6 Aug. "
Constitution ratified and state officers elected ... 3 Nov. "
Supreme court sustains the Idaho anti-Mormon test-oath law for voters ... 3 Feb. 1890
Admitted as the 43d state by proclamation of president, 3 July, "
Gov. Shoup takes the oath of office, 3 Nov., and convenes the legislature at Boisé City ... 8 Dec. "
Legislature elects U. S. senators; gov. Shoup for term ending 4 Mch. 1891 (also F. T. Dubois to succeed him), and W. J. McConnell ... 18 Dec. "
Lt.-gov. Willey succeeds gov. Shoup resigned ... 20 Dec. "
Election of Dubois being deemed illegal, William H. Claggett is chosen Shoup's successor ... 12 Feb. 1891
Law allowing verdict by three-fourths of a jury in a civil action, and an Australian ballot law enacted at session ending 11 [illegible]
U. S. senate seats Dubois (vote 55-5) [illegible]
Lockout, ensuing from striking miners [illegible] Cœur d'Alene mining district in Shoshone county [illegible] on men employed in the Gem mines, made [illegible] results in the killing of several miners [illegible]
Martial law put in force in Shoshone county [illegible]
Proclamation of pres. Harrison commanding [illegible] insurgents in Idaho to disperse [illegible]
Two thousand U. S. troops, by [illegible] Wallace, in July, suppressed [illegible]
Trial of insurrectionary miners [illegible] spiracy; 4 convicted, 13 [illegible]

TERRI[illegible]

Name.	[illegible]
Wm. H. Wallace	[illegible]
[illegible]	[illegible]

STATE GOVERNORS.

Name.	Term.	Remarks.
George L. Shoup	1890	Elected U. S. senator.
N. B. Willey	1890 to 1892	[illegible]
Wm. J. McConnell	1893 " 1896	Rep. [illegible]
[illegible]	1897 " 1898	

UNITED STATES SENATORS FROM IDAHO.

Name.	No. of Congress.	Date.	Remarks.
George L. Shoup	Fifty-first	1890	[illegible]
Fred. T. Dubois	"	[illegible]	[illegible]

idealism. PHILOSOPHY.

ides (L. *idus*), in the Roman and church calendar the 15th day of Mch., May, July, and Oct.; the 13th day in every other month. Dates were reckoned backward from the ides, as from the calends and the nones. On the *ides* of Mch., 44 B.C., Julius Cæsar was assassinated.

idols, images or similitudes of a divinity, as objects of worship. The public worship of idols was introduced by Ninus, king of Assyria, 2059 B.C.—*Usher*. Images are mentioned in Gen. xxxi. 19, 30, 1739 B.C. The Jews frequently deserted the worship of God for idols till their captivity, 588 B.C. Constantine, emperor of Rome, ordered heathen temples destroyed, and all sacrifices to cease, 330 A.D.—*Lenglet*. Idolatry was revived in Britain by Saxons about 473, but died out after the coming of Augustin, about 597. ICONOCLASTS, WEEK.

Idumæa, the country of the Edomites, descendants of Esau, brother of Jacob (Gen. xxxvi., Josh. xxiv. 4).

	B.C.
Edomites refuse the Israelites a way through their country	1453
They are subjugated by David	1040
Revolt against Judah, 892; are defeated by Amaziah	827
They join the Chaldeans against Judah, and are anathematized in Ps. cxxxvii ... about	575
John Hyrcanus the Maccabee subjugates and endeavors to incorporate them with the Jews	125
Herod the Great, son of Antipater, an Idumæan, king of Judæa,	40

Ildefon′so, San, a town of Spain. Here was signed a treaty between France and Spain, 19 Aug. 1796; and another, by which France regained Louisiana, 1 Oct. 1800. UNITED STATES.

Ilerda, a town of N.E. Spain, founded by the Carthaginians, now Lerida on the Segre. Here Cæsar defeated Afranius and Petreius, lieutenant of Pompey, after a brave resistance, 49 B.C.

Il′ium, Asia Minor. A city was built here by Dardanus and called Dardania, 1480 B.C. TROY, another city, was founded by Tros, after 1341 B.C.; and Ilus, his successor, called the country Ilium. HOMER.

Illinois, one of the northern central states of the United States, its western boundary [illegible] Mississippi river, which separates [illegible] from Iowa and Missouri [illegible] Wisconsin bounds it [illegible] north, lake Michigan [illegible] the northeastern corner [illegible] Indiana on the east, and Kentucky on the south. It is [illegible] ted in lat. by 36° 59′ to 42° [illegible] N., and in lon. by 87° 35′ to 91° 40′ W. Area, 56,650 sq. miles. Pop. 1890, 3,826,351; 1900, 4,821,550. Capital, Springfield.

Louis Joliet and Jacques Marquette descend the [illegible] from the mouth of the Wisconsin to the [illegible] returning, they ascend the Illinois, making their [illegible] via the Desplaines and Chicago rivers, 1673
[illegible] to establish a mission among the Illinois [illegible] a portage from the Chicago to the Desplaines [illegible] Illinois river nearly to Utica, where he [illegible] large concourse of chiefs and [illegible] Apr. 1675
[illegible] Claude Allouez, successor [illegible] [illegible] the Illinois [illegible]
[illegible] Cavalier Ro[illegible] [illegible] ... [illegible] ch. 1682
[illegible] of a [illegible] "
[illegible] "
[illegible] ... 21 June, "
[illegible] mony, with [illegible] ... 1 Oct. "

La Salle, returning from Montreal with supplies for fort Creve cœur, finds the town of the Illinois Indians burned by the Iroquois, the fort destroyed, and the garrison dispersed 1680

La Salle and Tonti, seeking the mouth of the Mississippi descend the Illinois, arriving at its mouth 6 Feb 1682

They build fort St Louis on Starved Rock on the Illinois, near the site of Utica. Nov "

La Salle returns to France, 1683, sails for the mouth of the Mississippi in Aug 1684 Tonti, with 25 Frenchmen and 5 Indians intending to meet him at the mouth of the Mississippi, leaves fort St Louis 13 Feb. 1686

Fort Chicago, probably built by M de la Durantaye in 1685, appears on a map of lake Michigan dated 1688

Mission established at the great town of the Illinois is removed down the river to the present site of Kaskaskia before 1690

Philip Renault, with 200 mechanics and laborers and 500 negro slaves for working supposed mines in Illinois, founds St Philipps, a village a few miles above Kaskaskia 1719

Pierre Duque Boisbriant, sent by the Western company, builds fort Chartres on the east side of the Mississippi, 22 miles from Kaskaskia 1720

Jesuits establish a monastery and college at Kaskaskia 1721

Kaskaskia becomes an incorporated town 1725

Renault sells his slaves to the French colonists in Illinois 1744

Fort Massac, or Massacre on the Ohio, about 40 miles from its mouth, established by the French about 1711, is enlarged and garrisoned 1756

British flag raised over fort Chartres 10 Oct. 1765

Col Wilkins, sent to fort Chartres to govern the Illinois country assumes by proclamation the civil administration, appointing 7 magistrates or judges 21 Nov 1768

First court held in Illinois opens at fort Chartres 6 Dec "

Land grant of 30,000 acres in the present county of Randolph made by col Wilkins, to John Baynton, Samuel Wharton, and George Morgan, merchants of Philadelphia 12 Apr 1769

A freshet destroying a part of fort Chartres, it is abandoned by the British garrison who occupy fort Gage, opposite Kaskaskia, and fix the government there 1772

Deed to the Illinois Land company from the chiefs of Indian tribes in Illinois for 2 immense tracts of land in southern Illinois, bought 5 July, recorded at Kaskaskia 2 Sept 1773

American expedition under George Rogers Clark conquers Illinois without bloodshed occupying Kaskaskia 4 July 1778

Territory conquered by col Clark is made by the legislature of Virginia into Illinois county Oct. "

Col John Todd proclaims from Kaskaskia a temporary government for Illinois 15 June, 1779

Illinois included in the Virginia act of cession to the U S. 20 Dec 1783, the deed of which is executed 1 Mch 1784

Illinois included in Northwest territory, organized by act of Congress 13 July, 1787

Maj gen Arthur St. Clair, elected by Congress governor of the Northwest territory, arrives at Kaskaskia Feb 1790

By act of Congress 400 acres are granted to every head of family who had improved farms in Illinois prior to 1788 1791

By the treaty of Greenville, 16 tracts 6 miles square in Illinois are ceded by the Indians, one at the mouth of the Chicago river, "where a fort formerly stood" 3 Aug 1795

Site of Peoria fixed by the abandonment of a settlement called La Ville de Maillet, located farther up the lake in 1788 1796

Jean Baptiste Point de Saible, a negro who settled at Chicago about 1779, sells his cabin to a French trader named Le Mai and moves to Peoria "

Illinois part of Indiana territory, created by act of 7 May, 1800

Memorial to Congress by a committee called to Vincennes by gov Harrison, requesting repeal of the 6th article of the organic act prohibiting slavery 20 Dec 1802

By treaty of fort Wayne, 7 June, ratified at Vincennes 7 Aug 1803, the Indians cede to the U S *1,634,000 acres of land*, 336,128 in Illinois, and by treaty of Vincennes, 13 Aug, the Kaskaskias cede most of southern Illinois 1803

Fort Dearborn built on the south side of Chicago river by the federal government and garrisoned The corner of Michigan ave and River st, Chicago, marks the site "

Congress establishes land offices at Kaskaskia, Vincennes, and Detroit 15 Mch 1804

John Kinzie of the American Fur company buys Le Mai's trading house, is the first permanent settler at Chicago. "

By the treaty of St. Louis, 3 Nov 1804, the united Sac and Fox Indians cede to the U S land on both sides of the Mississippi river, extending on the east from the mouth of the Illinois to its head and thence to the Wisconsin 3 Nov "

Western Star Lodge of Freemasons established at Kaskaskia, 24 Sept. 1805

Piankeshaw Indians cede to the U S. 2,616,921 acres west of the Wabash, opposite Vincennes. 30 Dec. "

Territory of Illinois created with Kaskaskia as the seat of government 3 Feb 1809

Ninian Edwards commissioned governor by Madison 24 Apr "

Mail route established by law from Vincennes to St. Louis *via* Kaskaskia Prairie du Rocher and Cahokia. 1810

Illinois raised to second grade of territorial government, 21 May, 1812

Owing to Indian murders and outrages a cordon of forts and blockhouses is erected in Illinois, the most noted is fort Russel, near Edwardsville "

Garrison of FORT DEARBORN by order of gen Hull, 7 Aug 1812, though reinforced by capt Wells and 15 friendly Miamis, evacuate the fort 15 Aug They are attacked and massacred by Indians, 39 killed, 27 taken prisoners, and the fort burned 15–16 Aug. "

Capt. Craig of Shawneetown, under instructions from gen. Samuel Hopkins, burns Peoria and removes the captured French inhabitants suspected of complicity with the Indians, to Alton Oct. 1812

Legislature convenes at Kaskaskia 25 Nov "

Illinois Herald established at Kaskaskia by Matthew Duncan 1814

Laws of the territory revised by Nathaniel Pope, and printed by Matthew Duncan under date 2 June, 1815

Bank of Illinois incorporated at Shawneetown 1816

Fort Dearborn rebuilt "

Charter for Cairo city granted by the legislature 1817-18

Enabling act for the state of Illinois approved 18 Apr 1818

Northern boundary of Illinois extended 50 miles to lat. 42° 30', "

Convention at Kaskaskia to frame a constitution adopts an ordinance accepting the Enabling act 26 Aug "

Illinois Emigrant, afterwards the *Illinois Gazette*, established at Shawneetown by Henry Eddy and Singleton H Kimmel "

First general *assembly under the constitution meets* at Kaskaskia 5 Oct. "

Illinois admitted into the Union, approved 3 Dec. "

State bank of Illinois incorporated with 4 branches 22 Mch 1819

Legislature re-enacts the "black laws" respecting free negroes, mulattoes, servants, and slaves 30 Mch "

Spectator founded by Hooper Warren at Edwardsville "

Ferdinand Ernst, from Hanover, locates a colony of 25 or 30 families at Vandalia "

John Kelly and family the first white settlers at Springfield "

A Frenchman named Boutilier settles on the Fever river "

Seat of government removed to Vandalia 1820

State house at Vandalia destroyed by fire 9 Dec 1823

General election, proposed convention to amend constitution, permitting slavery, defeated by 4972 to 6640 Aug 1824

Illinois and Michigan Canal Association incorporated 19 Jan 1825

Reception given gen Lafayette at Kaskaskia 30 Apr "

Congress grants 224,322 acres to the state of Illinois to aiding the Illinois and Michigan canal 2 Mch 1827

Father of Abraham Lincoln removes from Indiana with his family to Macon county, Ill 1830

Towns of Chicago and Ottawa surveyed and *laid* out by a board of canal commissioners and maps prepared by James Thompson bearing date 4 Aug "

State penitentiary at Alton constructed 1831

"Reports of the Supreme Court of Illinois," the first book published *in the state, by Sidney Breese* "

U S troops under gen Gaines, having burned the old Sac village on the Mississippi, deserted by Black Hawk and his warriors, encamp at Rock island where Black Hawk, summoned to a council, signs an agreement not to recross the Mississippi to the Illinois side without permission from the governor, or the president of the U S 30 June, "

Rock Springs Theological seminary and high school, founded by rev John M Peck, D D, is transferred to Alton and becomes the nucleus of Shurtleff college "

Black Hawk, with 150 warriors, unsuccessfully attacks Apple River fort, 12 miles from Galena 6 June, 1832

Battle of Kellog's grove, 50 miles from Dixon, col Demont attacked by Indians under Black Hawk 26 June, "

Chicago incorporated as a town Aug 1833

New state bank with 6 branches, incorporated 1834

Abraham Lincoln elected to the state legislature "
[Also 1836, '38, '40]

First number of the *Alton Observer*, an antislavery newspaper, published by rev Elijah P Lovejoy 8 Sept. 1836

Abraham Lincoln admitted to practise law "

Act to establish and maintain a general *system of internal improvement* appropriates $10,230,000 27 Feb. 1837

Chicago chartered as a city 4 Mch "

Corner stone of state capitol at Springfield laid 4 July, "

Rev Elijah P Lovejoy, publisher of the *Alton Observer*, shot *dead by a mob at his office* (ALTON RIOT) 7 Nov "

First rail on Northern Cross railroad laid at Meredosia, 9 May, and first locomotive in Mississippi valley put on the track 8 Nov "

Legislature first meets at Springfield, the new capital Assembly in second Presbyterian church, Senate in first Methodist, and the superior court in the Episcopal 9 Dec 1839

Mormons locate on the east bank of the Mississippi, in Hancock county and found Nauvoo 1840

Knox college, at Galesburgh, chartered 1837, opened 1841

Laws passed, "to diminish the state debt and put the state bank into liquidation," 24 Jan 1843, and "to reduce the public debt $1,000,000 and put the bank of Illinois into liquidation" 1843

Mormon leaders Joe and Hyrum Smith, the former mayor of Nauvoo, imprisoned for treason in levying war against the state by declaring martial law in Nauvoo and by ordering out the Nauvoo Legion to resist a *posse comitatus*, assassinated in jail at Carthage by conspirators 27 June, 1844

Jacksonville Female academy, at Jacksonville, opened 1830, chartered 1845

Two thousand Mormons, the van of the general exodus, cross the Mississippi on the ice 15 Feb. 1846

Illinois Institute for the Deaf and Dumb, at Jacksonville, opened "

Abraham Lincoln elected to Congress "

Illinois Female college at Jacksonville opened and chartered 1847

Illinois Institution for the Blind at Jacksonville opened "

Convention met at Springfield 7 June, 1847, and completed a constitution 31 Aug, which is adopted by the people, 59,887 to 15,859 and takes effect 1 Apr 1848

Illinois Staats Zeitung founded by Robert Hoeffger, at Chicago, Apr "

Illinois and Michigan canal, begun in 1836, opened 16 Apr "

Bloody Island dike built at E St Louis "

Rockford seminary at Rockford chartered in 1847, is opened, 1849

Jefferson Davis challenges col W H Bissell, afterwards governor, to a duel, he accepts the challenge, but the matter is amicably settled Feb 1850

Geological survey authorized by act of 17 Feb 1851

Central Hospital for the Insane at Jacksonville opened Nov "

Law providing that any negro or mulatto, bond or free, who comes into the state and remains 10 days, may be fined $50 or sold into slavery until the fine is worked out 12 Feb 1853

Act passed incorporating the State Agricultural Society "

Mount Carrol seminary, at Mount Carrol, chartered 1852, opened "

Illinois Wesleyan university, at Bloomington, chartered and opened "

State common school convention meets at Bloomington Dec "

Hon N W Edwards appointed state superintendent of common schools 15 Mch 1854

Attempt of senator Stephen A Douglas to address the people of Chicago from an open balcony in defence of the Kansas Nebraska bill is met with hisses, groans, and continued noise for 4 hours, when Douglas retires 1 Sept "

Law for a system of free schools in the state 15 Feb 1855

Trial of some 30 German saloon keepers in Chicago for violating the prohibitory liquor law just passed leads to a riot 21 Apr, city placed under martial law 22 Apr "

Eureka college opened at Eureka in 1849, receives its charter, "

Northwestern university at Evanston, chartered in 1851, is opened "

Illinois state university at Normal opened 1857

Monmouth college at Monmouth opened in 1856, chartered "

Many prisoners from the old penitentiary at Alton removed to the new penitentiary at Joliet 22 May, 1858

Debate between Lincoln and Douglas throughout the state on slavery summer and autumn, "

Gov Bissell dies, lieut gov John Wood succeeds 18 Mch 1860

Abraham Lincoln nominated for president by the Republican national convention at Chicago 16 May, "

Abraham Lincoln inaugurated president 4 Mch 1861

Gen Swift, with 6 companies and 4 cannon, leaves Chicago to occupy Cairo, under telegraphic order from the secretary of war to gov Yates of 19 Apr 21 Apr "

Twenty one thousand stands of arms seized at the St Louis arsenal by forces under capt. Stokes, and removed to Alton by boat thence to Springfield by rail 26 Apr "

U S Grant tenders his services to gov Yates and is assigned to command of camps Yates, Grant, and Douglas Apr "

Stephen A Douglas dies at Chicago, aged 48 3 June, "

Dr Newberry organizes the northwestern branch of the U S. Sanitary Commission at Chicago "

A convention chosen to form a new constitution meets 7 Jan 1862, assumes legislative powers ratifies the XIII th Amendment to the Constitution, votes $500,000 of state money for the relief of sick and wounded Illinois soldiers, and frames a constitution which was rejected by the people June, 1862

Arsenal established by act of Congress on Rock island, where fort Armstrong was erected in 1816 1863

Chicago Times suppressed for one day by order from gen Burnside, No 84, dated 1 June, and revoked 4 June, "

Democratic mass convention, 40,000 delegates, held at Springfield 17 June, "

Political disturbance at Charleston, Coles county, between citizens attendant upon the circuit court and veterans of the 54th Illinois regiment, 7 lives are lost 22 Mch 1864

Discovery of fraudulent reissue of $224 182 66 of 90 days redeemed canal scrip dating back some 30 years, by the use of checks signed in blank at that time Suspicion points to ex-gov Matteson, who offers to indemnify the state against loss, 9 Feb 1859 Other evidences of fraud in office coming to light, under a decree rendered in the Sangamon circuit court against Matteson for $255,500, the state secures $238,000 at a master's sale of the ex governor's property 27 Apr "

Democratic national convention meets at Chicago 29 Aug "

Plot to liberate confederate prisoners at camp Douglas, Chicago, is exposed, and leaders, arrested Nov 1864, are tried by court martial and convicted at Cincinnati Jan 1865

Legislature ratifies the XIII th Amendment to the Constitution and repeals the "black laws" "

Burial of pres. Lincoln at Springfield 4 May, "

Sanitary Commission fair at Chicago, $250,000 raised May, "

Illinois Asylum for Feeble minded Children, at Lincoln opened, "

First post of the Grand Army of the Republic mustered in at Decatur (GRAND ARMY) 6 Apr 1866

Orville H Browning appointed secretary of the interior 1 Sept "

Tunnel under lake Michigan to supply Chicago with water completed, length 2 miles Dec. "

Law passed abolishing capital punishment 1867

Horace Capron, U S commissioner of agriculture 4 Dec "

University of Illinois at Urbana, chartered 1867, opened Mch 1868

U S Grant nominated for president by the Republican national convention at Chicago 20 May, "

Cook county normal school at Englewood opened "

Corner stone of the new capitol at Springfield laid 5 Oct. "

First river tunnel in this country completed under the Chicago river, 810 ft long Dec "

U S Grant inaugurated president 4 Mch 1869

Legislature ratifies the XV th Amendment to the Constitution, vote, in Senate 17 to 7, in House 52 to 2[illegible] 5 Mch "

Elihu B Washburne appointed secretary of treasury " "

John A Rawlins appointed secretary of war " "

Appropriation made by legislature for the Northern Illinois Hospital for the Insane at Elgin "

Constitution framed by a convention at Springfield, May, 1870, ratified by the people, 134 227 to 35 443 2 July, 1870

Evangelical proseminary at Elmhurst, chartered 1868, opened, "

Seminary of the Sacred Heart at Chicago opened in 1858, chartered "

Remains of pres Lincoln transferred from the temporary tomb to the crypt of the monument at Oak Ridge cemetery, May, 1871

Deepening of the Illinois and Michigan canal to create a current from lake Michigan to the Illinois river, begun in 1865, is completed 18 July "

Illinois and Michigan canal turned over to the state Aug "

Sovereign Grand Lodge of Odd Fellows meets at Chicago, 18 Sept "

Chicago fire, which burns over 2124 acres and destroys 17,500 buildings, begins (FIRES) 8-9 Oct "

New building for the U S Marine hospital established at Chicago, May, 1852 completed 1872

Gov Oglesby elected U S senator, lieut gov John L Beveridge succeeds him 4 Mch 1873

St Francis Solanus college at Quincy, opened in 1860, is chartered "

Northwestern Farmers' convention of 150 delegates from Indiana, Iowa, Michigan, New York, and Illinois, meets at Chicago 22 Oct "

North wing of the Southern Hospital for the Insane at Anna opened 13 Dec "

Southern Illinois normal university at Carbondale opened 1874

Monument to Abraham Lincoln at Oak ridge, Springfield dedicated (LINCOLN'S MONUMENT) 15 Oct "

National convention of the Grand Army of the Republic held at Chicago 12 May, 1875

National temperance association meets at Chicago 3 June, "

Chicago day schools for the deaf opened "

Lake Forest university at lake Forest, opened 1876

Parade of 1500 armed Communists carrying the red flag in Chicago, winter of "

Appropriation by the legislature for the Eastern Hospital for the Insane, at Kankakee 1877

State Board of Health organized 1878

Illinois Industrial School for Girls, at South Evanston, opened "

Militia law, entire male population to be enrolled, and 8000 organized and armed, no other military organizations to parade or drill unless licensed 28 May, 1879

Board of Fish Commissioners created by legislature "

Bureau of labor statistics established "

Republican national convention meets at Chicago 2 June, 1880

Greenback national convention meets at Chicago " "

Robert T Lincoln secretary of war 5 Mch 1881

St Joseph's Diocesan college, at Teutopolis, opened 1862, chartered "

Aurora the first city in the world to light its streets with electricity "

State penitentiary at Chester ready for occupation "

St. Mary's school, Knoxville, opened 1868, chartered 1882

Gov Cullom, elected U S senator, is succeeded by John M Hamilton 7 Feb 1883

Chicago Voice and Hearing School for the Deaf opened at Englewood "

Ephphatha School for the Deaf opened at Chicago 1884

Haymarket massacre by anarchists (CHICAGO) 4 May, 1886

Illinois Soldiers and Sailors' Home at Quincy, organized 1885, and dedicated 20 Oct "

Gen John A Logan U S senator, dies at Washington 26 Dec "

Appropriation by the legislature for the Industrial Home for the Blind in Cook county 1887

Illinois asylum for insane criminals established at Chester 1889

Chicago university endowed with $1 600,000 by J D Rockefeller, and a gift of land by Marshall Field 1890

Convention of Afro American leagues opens in Chicago 15 Jan "

Chicago secures the World's Fair the vote on the site in the House of Representatives being Chicago, 157, New York, 107, St Louis, 26, Washington, 18 24 Feb "

Panic in the Chicago Board of Trade 12 Apr "

Constitutional amendment, to permit the city of Chicago to issue 5% bonds to $5,000,000 to aid the World's Columbian Exposition adopted by legislature 31 July, "

Governor signs the World's Fair bill 5 Aug "

George R Davis selected as director general of the World's Columbian Exposition 19 Sept "

Gen John M Palmer, democrat, elected U S senator on the 154th ballot. 11 Mch 1891

Laws reducing the legal rate of interest from 6 to 5%, and making the first Monday in Sept (Labor Day) and 12 Feb (Abraham Lincoln's Birthday) legal holidays, passed at session ending 12 June, "

Gov Fifer signs the Ballot Reform bill 23 June, "

First reunion of survivors of the Black Hawk war of 1832 held at Lena, 17 veterans present 28 Aug "

Equestrian statue of gen Grant unveiled at Chicago 7 Oct. "

World's Fair amendment to state constitution adopted by vote of 500,299 to 15,095 Nov "

Alien land law pronounced unconstitutional 23 Dec "

Train of 28 cars containing 12 000 bushels of shelled corn, the contribution of residents of McLean county to the Russian famine sufferers is made up at Bloomington 10 Mch 1892

Eighty sq miles of territory inundated by the breaking of a levee on the Mississippi "

Democratic national convention meets at Chicago 21 June, "

University of Chicago opens, without formal ceremony, with 600 students 1 Oct. "

World's Columbian Exposition, preliminary exercises at Chicago; orations by Chauncey M. Depew and Henry Watterson, 21 Oct. 1892

U. S. supreme court affirms the judgment of the U. S. circuit court adverse to the claims of the Illinois Central Railroad company to the submerged lands.....5 Dec. "

World's Columbian Exposition opened at Chicago......1 May, 1893

Gov. Altgeld pardons the anarchists Fielden, Neebe, and Schwab, serving sentence in the penitentiary for complicity in the Haymarket riot (CHICAGO)..........26 June, "

Carter H. Harrison, mayor of Chicago, assassinated (CHICAGO), 28 Oct. "

World's Columbian Exposition closed..........30 Oct. "

Prendergast, the murderer of the mayor of Chicago, hanged, 13 July, 1894

TERRITORIAL GOVERNOR.

Ninian Edwards.........commissioned..............24 Apr. 1809

STATE.

Shadrach Bond..........assumes office.................... 1818
Edward Cowles..........assumes office.................... 1822
Ninian Edwards......... " " 1826
John Reynolds.......... " " 1830
William L. D. Ewing.....acting.................... 1834
Joseph Duncan..........assumes office.................... "
Thomas Carlin.......... " " 1838
Thomas Ford............ " " 1842
Augustus C. French...... " " 1846
Joel A. Matteson........ " " 1853
William H. Bissell....... " " 1857
John Wood..............acting....................18 Mch. 1860
Richard Yates..........assumes office..............Jan. 1861
Richard J. Oglesby.................................... " 1865
John M. Palmer.. " 1869
Richard J. Oglesby.................................... " 1873
John L. Beveridge.......acting....................4 Mch. "
Shelby M. Cullom.......assumes office..............Jan. 1877
John M. Hamilton.......acting....................7 Feb. 1883
Richard J. Oglesby....................................Jan. 1885
Joseph W. Fifer....................................... " 1889
John B. Altgeld....................................... " 1893

UNITED STATES SENATORS FROM THE STATE OF ILLINOIS.

Name.	No. of Congress.	Date.	Remarks.
Ninian Edwards	15th to 18th	1818 to 1824	Seated 4 Dec. 1818. Resigned 1824.
Jesse B. Thomas	15th " 19th	1818 " 1826	Seated 4 Dec. 1818.
John McLean	18th " 20th	1824 " 1830	Elected in place of Edwards. Died 14 Oct. 1830.
Elias Kent Kane	19th " 23d	1826 " 1835	Died 11 Dec. 1835.
David J. Baker	21st	1830	Appointed in place of McLean, 1830.
John M. Robinson	21st to 27th	1831 to 1841	Elected in place of McLean.
William L. D. Ewing	24th	1836	Elected in place of Kane, 1836.
Richard M. Young	25th to 27th	1837 to 1843	
Samuel McRoberts	27th	1841 " 1843	Died 27 Mch. 1843.
Sidney Breese	28th to 31st	1843 " 1849	
James Semple	28th	1843 " 1846	Appointed in place of McRoberts, 1843.
Stephen A. Douglas	29th to 37th	1847 " 1861	Nominated for the presidency 1860 by the Democratic party. Died 3 June, 1861.
James Shields	31st " 33d	1849 " 1855	
Lyman Trumbull	34th " 42d	1855 " 1871	
Orville H. Browning	37th	1861	Appointed in place of Douglas.
William A. Richardson	37th to 39th	1863 to 1865	Elected in place of Douglas.
Richard Yates	39th " 42d	1865 " 1871	
John A. Logan	42d " 45th	1871 " 1877	
Richard J. Oglesby	43d " 46th	1873 " 1878	
David Davis	45th " 47th	1877 " 1883	
John A. Logan	46th " 49th	1879 " 1886	Nominated for vice-president 1884. Died 26 Dec. 1886.
Shelby McCullom	48th ——	1883 ——	Term expires 1895.
Charles B. Farwell	50th " 51st	1887 " 1891	
John M. Palmer	52d ——	1891 ——	Term expires 1897.

illuminated books. The practice of decorating MSS. with drawings, emblematical figures, and portraits, is of great antiquity. Varro wrote the lives of 700 illustrious Romans, embellished with their portraits, about 70 B.C.—*Plin.* "Nat. Hist." Beautiful missals and other works were printed in the 15th and 16th centuries, and fine imitations have appeared. MANUSCRIPTS.

Illumina'ti, heretics in Spain, where they were called Alombrados, about 1575. Suppressed there, they appeared in France. One of their leaders was friar Anthony Buchet. They professed to obtain grace and perfection by prayer. A secret society bearing this name, opposed to tyranny and priestcraft, founded in Ingolstadt, Bavaria, by dr. Adam Weishaupt, in May, 1776, was suppressed in 1784–85.

illustrated papers. NEWSPAPERS.

Illyr'ia, now including Dalmatia, Croatia, and Bosnia, Austrian provinces, after several wars (from 230 B.C.) was made a Roman province, 167 B.C. In 1809 Napoleon I. gave the name of Illyrian provinces to Carniola, Dalmatia, and other provinces, then part of the French empire, now Carinthia, Carniola, etc.

ilme'nium, a metal of the tantalum group, announced by R. Herrmann, about 1847, but rejected by chemists; its claims were reasserted by him in 1867.

image-worship. ICONOCLASTS.

"Imitation of Jesus Christ" ("*De Imitatione Christi*"), a devotional work of unknown authorship. It has been attributed to an abbot Gersen (whose existence is doubtful); to Jean Gerson, chancellor of Paris; and to Thomas à Kempis, said to have been merely a compiler and editor; he died 25 July, 1471.

immaculate conception. CONCEPTION.

immigration into the United States. Owing to the increased immigration into the U. S. of paupers and criminals, Congress in 1885 and 1891 enacted laws regulating immigration, and in the latter year created the office of Superintendent of Immigration. UNITED STATES, 1885–91, etc.

NUMBER OF IMMIGRANTS AND THEIR NATIONALITY BY DECADES FROM 1821 TO 1890, INCLUSIVE.

Immigrants from	1821–30	1831–40	1841–50	1851–60	1861–70	1871–80	1881–90	Total. 1821–90	Grand Total.
Great Britain (not specified)	22,167	73,143	263,332	385,643	568,128	460,479	657,488	2,430,380	
Scotland	2,912	2,667	3,712	38,331	38,768	87,564	149,869	323,823	
Ireland	50,724	207,381	780,719	914,119	435,778	436,871	655,482	3,481,074	
Total	75,803	283,191	1,047,763	1,338,093	1,042,674	984,914	1,462,839		6,235,277
Germany	6,761	152,454	434,626	951,667	787,468	718,182	1,452,970	4,504,128	
Norway and Sweden	91	1,201	13,903	20,931	109,298	211,245	568,362	925,031	
Austro-Hungary	......	......	......	......	7,800	72,969	353,719	434,488	
Italy	408	2,253	1,870	9,231	11,728	55,759	307,309	388,558	
France	8,497	45,575	77,262	76,358	35,984	72,206	50,464	366,346	
Russian Poland	91	646	656	1,621	4,536	52,254	265,088	324,892	
Switzerland	3,226	4,821	4,644	25,011	23,286	28,293	81,98[illegible]	171,269	
Denmark	169	1,063	539	3,749	17,094	31,771	[illegible]	142,517	
Netherlands	1,078	1,412	8,251	10,789	9,102	[illegible]	53,701	100,874	
Belgium	27	22	5,074	4,738	6,7[illegible]	7,221	20,177	43,993	
Spain and Portugal	2,622	2,954	2,759	10,353	[illegible]	9,893	6,535	43,609	
All others	43	96	155	[illegible]	210	656	10,318	11,594	
Total	23,013	212,497	549,739	1,114,[illegible]64	1,021,733	1,276,990	3,258,763		7,457,299

NUMBER OF IMMIGRANTS AND THEIR NATIONALITY BY DECADES FROM 1821 TO 1890 INCLUSIVE.—(*Continued.*)

Immigrants from	1821-30	1831-40	1841-50	1851-60	1861-70	1871-80	1881-90	Total, 1821-90	Grand total.
Asia:									
China	2	8	35	41,397	64,301	123,201	61,711	290,655	
All others	8	40	47	61	308	622	6,669	7,755	
Total	10	48	82	41,458	64,609	123,823	68,380		298,410
Africa	16	52	55	210	312	229	437		1,311
America:									
British America	2,277	13,624	41,723	59,309	153,871	383,269	392,802	1,046,875	
West Indies	3,834	12,301	13,528	10,660	9,043	13,957	29,042	92,365	
Mexico	4,817	6,599	3,271	3,078	2,191	5,362	1,913	27,231	
South America	531	856	3,579	1,224	1,396	928	2,304	10,818	
Central America	105	44	368	449	96	210	462	1,734	
Total	11,564	33,424	62,469	74,720	166,597	403,726	426,523		1,179,023
Islands:									
Atlantic	325	103	337	3,090	3,446	10,056	15,798	33,155	
Pacific	2	9	29	158	221	10,913	12,574	23,906	
All others	32,679	69,802	52,777	25,921	15,232	1,540	1,299	199,250	
Total	33,006	69,914	53,143	29,169	18,899	22,509	29,671		256,311
Totals	143,412	599,126	1,713,251	2,598,214	2,314,824	2,812,191	5,246,613		15,427,631
From 1789 to 1820, estimated									250,000
Grand total									15,677,631

Of the immigrants during the last decade (1881–90) 61.1 per cent. were males and 38.9 per cent. females; 21.4 per cent. were under 15 years, 68.1 per cent. were between 15 and 40, and 10.5 per cent. were over 40. The number of immigrants, irrespective of nationality, for the year 1891, was 560,319; 1892, 623,084; 1893, 502,917. The greatest number of immigrants in any one year was in 1882, when the number 788,992 was reached.

Immortals (Gr. ἀθάνατοι), the flower of the Persian army, limited to 10,000, and recruited from the nobility alone, about 500 B.C. The name was also given to the body-guard of the emperors at Constantinople in the 4th and 5th centuries.

Immortals, The forty. The Institute of France is composed of 5 ACADEMIES. The highest is the French academy of 40 members, a chair in which is the highest honor in the French literary world. The others are the Academy of Inscriptions and Belles-Lettres, 40 members; Academy of Science, 66 members; of Fine Arts, 40 members (14 painters, 8 sculptors, 8 architects, 4 engravers, 6 musicians); and the Academy of Moral and Political Science, 40 members. Members of each are elected for life.

impeachment in England. The first impeachment by the commons and the first of a lord chancellor, Michael de la Pole, earl of Suffolk, was in 1386. By statute 12 and 13 Will. and Mary, 1700, no pardon under the great seal shall be pleaded to an impeachment by the commons.

Impeachment of Warren Hastings, 13 Feb. 1788–25 Apr. 1795; acquittal.
Impeachment of lord Melville, 9 Apr.; acquittal, 12 June, 1806.
Inquiry into the charges preferred by col. Wardle against the duke of York, 27 Jan. to 20 Mch. 1809; acquittal.
Trial of Caroline, queen of George IV., by bill of pains and penalties, before the House of Lords, commenced 16 Aug.; Mr. Brougham began her defence, 3 Oct.; the last debate on the bill took place 10 Nov. 1820. QUEEN CAROLINE.

impeachment in the United States. The Constitution of the U. S. gives the House of Representatives sole power to impeach the president, vice-president, and all civil officers of the U. S. by a numerical majority only. It also gives the Senate sole power to try all impeachments. The Senate then sits as a court, organizing anew, senators taking a special oath or affirmation applicable to the proceeding. From their decision there is no appeal. A vote of two thirds of the Senate is necessary to convict. When the president is tried the chief-justice shall preside. The punishment is limited by the Constitution, (1) to removal from office; (2) to disqualification for holding and enjoying any office of honor, trust, or profit under the U. S. government. Important cases: (1) William Blount, U. S. senator from Tennessee, for conspiring to transfer New Orleans from Spain to Great Britain, 1797–98; acquitted for want of evidence. UNITED STATES. (2) John Pickering, judge of the district court of New Hampshire, charged with drunkenness, profanity, etc.; convicted 12 Mch. 1803. (3) Judge Samuel Chase, impeached 30 Mch. 1804; acquitted 1 Mch. 1805. UNITED STATES. (4) James H. Peck, district judge of Missouri, impeached 13 Dec. 1830, for arbitrary conduct, etc.; acquitted. (5) West H. Humphreys, district judge of Tennessee, impeached and convicted for rebellion, 26 Jan. 1862. (6) Andrew Johnson, pres. of the U. S., 1868. UNITED STATES. (7) W. W. Belknap, sec. of war, impeached for receiving money of post-traders among the Indians, 2 Mch. 1876; resigns at the same time; acquitted for want of jurisdiction.

"Impending Crisis," a book written by Hinton R. Helper, a North Carolinian, pointing out the evil effects of slavery upon the whites, first pub. 1857. It had a large sale (140,000 copies) and great influence. UNITED STATES, 1859.

Imperial guard of France was created by Napoleon from the guard of the Convention, the Directory, and the Consulate, when he became emperor in 1804. It consisted at first of 9775 men, but was afterwards enlarged. Subdivided in 1809 into the old and young guard. In Jan. 1814 it numbered 102,706. It was dissolved by Louis XVIII. in 1815; revived by Napoleon III. in 1854. It surrendered with Metz to the Germans, 27 Oct. 1870; and was abolished by the defence government soon after. It took part in the Crimean war in 1855.

imports of merchandise into the United States from 30 Sept. 1789, for the years shown, are given in following table. As the treasury accounts did not separate merchandise from specie until 1821, they are shown together up to that year.

Year.	Imports.		Totals.
	Merchandise.	Coin and bullion.	
1790	....	....	$23,000,000
1800	....	....	91,252,768
1810	....	....	85,400,000
1820	....	....	74,450,000
1821	$54,520,835	$8,064,890	62,585,724
1831	95,885,179	7,305,945	103,191,124
1841	122,957,544	4,988,633	127,946,177
1851	210,771,429	5,453,503	216,224,932
1861	289,310,542	46,339,611	335,650,153
1871	520,223,684	21,270,024	541,493,708
1881	642,664,628	110,575,497	753,240,125
1891	844,916,196	36,259,447	881,175,643

LIST AND VALUE OF THE PRINCIPAL ARTICLES OF IMPORT FOR 1891.

Articles.	Value.
Sugar	$105,728,216
Coffee	96,123,777
Wool, and manufactures of	59,291,452
Iron and steel, and manufactures of	55,974,531
Chemicals, drugs, dyes, and medicines	47,317,031
Silk manufactures	37,880,143
Flax, hemp, jute, etc., and manufactures of	30,005,100
Cotton manufactures	29,712,624
Hides and skins	27,930,759
Fruits and nuts	25,983,136
Wood, and manufactures of	19,888,186
Silk, raw	19,077,366
India-rubber, and manufactures of	18,375,449
Tobacco, and manufactures of	16,763,141
Tea	13,828,993
Precious stones	13,217,602
Leather, and manufactures of	12,683,303
Wines	10,007,060
Furs, and manufactures of	9,828,849
Earthen-ware and china	8,381,388
Glass and glass-ware	8,364,312
Tin	7,977,545
All other articles	178,584,433
Total	$844,916,196

TOTAL VALUE OF IMPORTS INTO GREAT BRITAIN

Year	Imports	Year	Imports
1800	£30 570,605	1879	£362 991 875
1810	36 514 564	1881	397,022 489
1830	46,245 241	1883	426,891,579
1840	62,004 000	1885	370,967 955
1850	95 252,084	1887	362,227,564
1861	217 485,024	1889	427,637,595
1870	303,296,082	1891	435 441,264

impostors. The following are among the most extraordinary

Mahomet promulgated his creed, 604 MAHOMETANISM
Aldebert a Gaul in 743, pretending to have a letter from the Redeemer which fell from heaven at Jerusalem seduced multitudes into woods and forests to live in imitation of John the Baptist He was condemned by a council at Rome in 745.
Gonzalvo Martin a Spaniard claimed to be the angel Michael in 1359, burned by the Inquisition in Spain in 1360
George David, son of a waterman at Ghent, styled himself son of God sent into the world to adopt children worthy of heaven, he denied the resurrection, preached a community of women and taught that the body only could be defiled by sin, he had many followers, d at Basle, 1556, promising to rise again in 3 years
Otrefief a monk pretended to be Demetrius, the son of Ivan, czar of Muscovy killed by the usurper Boris. He maintained that another child had been substituted He was supported by Poland, his success led the Russians to invite him to the throne and deliver into his hands Feodor, the reigning czar, and all his family, his imposition was discovered, and he was assassinated in his palace 1606
Sabbatai Levi, a Jew of Smyrna long amused Jews and Turks at Constantinople etc., by personating Christ, 1666
Joseph Smith MORMONS
Apparition of Our Lady of Salette, imposture exposed and several persons prosecuted, Apr 1846 The superstition revived and flourishing, Aug 1872
Pilgrimage of about 20 000 persons to Lourdes, in the Pyrenees, on account of alleged miracles (the Virgin said to have appeared to 2 girls 11 Feb 1858), 6 Oct 1872 FRANCE, LORETTO
Louis XVII FRANCE list of sovereigns

IN BRITISH HISTORY

Man pretending to be the Messiah, and woman assuming to be the Virgin Mary, were burned, 1222
Jack Cade assumed the name of Mortimer CADE'S INSURRECTION, 1450
In 1487 Lambert Simnel, tutored by Richard Simon, a priest, supported by the duke of Burgundy, personated the earl of Warwick Simnel's army was defeated by Henry VII, and he was made a scullion in the king's kitchen
For Warbeck's imposture in 1492 WARBECK.
Elizabeth Barton styled the Holy Maid of Kent claimed inspiration, foretelling that the king would have an early and violent death if he divorced Catherine of Spain and married Anne Boleyn She and confederates were executed at Tyburn 21 Apr 1534
In 1553 (first year of Mary's reign, after her marriage with Philip), Elizabeth Croft, a girl 18 years of age, was secreted in a wall, and with a whistle uttered seditious speeches against the queen and the prince, and also against the mass and confession, for which she did penance
William Hacket, a fanatic, personated our Saviour, and was executed for blasphemy, 1591
Valentine Greatrix, an Irish impostor, pretended to cure diseases by stroking the patient, he deceived many, and occasioned warm disputes in Ireland and England about 1666 Boyle and Flamsteed believed in him
Dr Titus OATES.
Robert Young, a prisoner in Newgate forged the writing of the earls of Marlborough, Salisbury, and other noblemen to a pretended association for restoring king James, the earls were imprisoned, but the imposture being detected, Young was fined 1000*l* and put in the pillory 1692 and afterwards hanged for coining
Mary Tofts of Godalming, pretending to breed rabbits within her, imposed upon many persons (among others, Mr St Andre, surgeon to the king), who espoused her cause 1726
Cock lane ghost impostures by William Parsons, his wife, and daughter, 1762 COCK LANE GHOST
Johanna Southcote, claiming conception of the Messiah, had many followers, d 27 Dec 1814
W Thom THOMITES.
Tichborne case TRIALS
ABSTINENCE

impressionistes, artists who aim at producing rapid unstudied effects independent of the canons of art, as Manet, Duez, and others in France In England Mr Whistler exhibited such pictures in 1877, including moonlight scenes etc, painted in two days, showing great sense of color For Mr Ruskin's criticisms, TRIALS, 1878

impressment of seamen, affirmed by sir M Foster to be an ancient practice The stat 2 Rich II speaks of impressment as well known, 1378 The first commission for it was issued 29 Edw III 1355 Pressing for sea or land service declared illegal by Parliament, Dec. 1641, but practised till recently Impressment was not resorted to in the Anglo-Russian war, 1854-55 Impressment by the British government of seamen, citizens of the colonies, was a cause of irritation in America before the Revolution In 1707 Parliament prohibited impressment in colonial ports.—*Hildreth*, vol ii p 58 But notwithstanding this a riot in Boston, 1747, grew out of the impressment of citizens MASSACHUSETTS In 1775 Great Britain authorized impressment for the navy of all crews of captured colonial vessels. As Great Britain claimed the right of pressing into her service any British-born seaman not within the immediate jurisdiction of some foreign state, after the Revolution native born seamen of the United States were often taken by force from their own ships to serve in the British navy The procedure was arbitrary, and careful discrimination was not made between British subjects and citizens of the U S This was the main cause of the war of 1812 The Jay treaty of 1794 was unpopular, because the wrongs of our seamen were not noticed A vigorous attempt was made by the U S in 1796 to stop the impressment of U S seamen by diplomacy —*Hildreth*, vol iv p 629 After certain U S seamen were taken from the U S sloop-of-war *Baltimore*, 18 Nov 1798, by a British war vessel, the U S government directed its commanders to resist such impressments if possible, and otherwise to surrender their ships. Renewed outrages 1804 Renewed attempt to treat on this subject 1806 Affair of the *Chesapeake* and *Leopard*, 1807, 12 June, 1812 UNITED STATES Impressment was earnestly debated in Congress 1811, when 3500 impressed U S seamen were asserted to be in the British navy The British government admitted the number to be 1600 2500 impressed seamen were committed to Dartmoor and other prisons in England during the war of 1812 for refusing to serve against the U S., of which they claimed to be citizens Yet the general desire for peace was so strong in the U S that the subject was ignored in the treaty of peace with Great Britain, 1814.

imprisonment for debt. ARRESTS, DEBTORS, FERRARS'S ARREST

Incas. PERU

incendiaries. The punishment for arson was death by Saxon laws and Gothic constitutions Under Edward I of England, incendiaries were burned This crime was made high-treason by statute 8 Hen VI 1429, and was denied benefit of clergy, 21 Hen VIII 1528 In Great Britain the punishment of death was remitted, except in special cases, in 1827 ARSON

incest. Marriage with a very near relation, almost universally forbidden elsewhere, was permitted in most Oriental countries and Greece For recent cases, PORTUGAL, 1760, 1777, 1826, and ITALY, 1888 The table of kindred in the "Book of Common Prayer" was set forth in 1563 For the Hebrew law, see Leviticus, chap xviii (1490 B C)

inch. It was defined in 1824, by act of Parliament, 39 13929 inches being the length of a seconds pendulum in the latitude of London, vibrating *in vacuo* at the sea-level, at the temperature of 62° Fahrenheit CANDLES, STANDARD and METRIC SYSTEM

Inchcape bell. BELL ROCK LIGHT-HOUSE

income-tax in the United Kingdom In 1512 Parliament granted a subsidy of two fifteenths from the commons and two tenths from the clergy, to begin war with France In Dec 1798, Mr Pitt carried, amid great opposition, resolutions for increased taxes "as an aid for the prosecution of the war" with France

Graduated duties on income imposed, beginning with 60*l* per annum, by the act passed 9 Jan 1799
"Property tax" passed, levying 5 per cent on incomes above 150*l* and lower rates on smaller incomes, 11 Aug 1803
Gross annual value of property and profits assessed to the income tax in the United Kingdom in 1871 was 465,478,688*l*, in 1890 it was 669,358,613*l*., of which England returned 572,128,525*l*., Scotland, 60,030,510*l*, Ireland, 37,199,578*l*.

REVENUE FROM INCOMES SINCE 1882

Year	Tax per £	Amount in £
1882	5*d*.	9,945 000
1883	6½*d*.	11,900,000
1884	5*d*.	10 718 000
1885	6*d*.	12,000,000

Year	Tax per £	Amount in £
1886	8d	15 160 000
1887	8d	15 900 000
1888	7d	14 440 000
1889	6d	12,700,000
1890	6d	12,770 000
1891	6d	13,250 000

Since 1877 only incomes of and above 150*l* are charged, with an abatement of 120*l* on those under 400*l*

income-tax in the United States The first income-tax was enacted by Congress 1 July, 1862, to take effect 1863 It taxed all incomes over $600 and under $10,000 3 per cent., and over $10 000 5 per cent By the act of 3 Mch 1865, the rate was increased to 5 and to 10 per cent on the excess over $5000, the exemption of $600 remaining the same On 2 Mch 1867, the exemption was increased to $1000, and the rate fixed at 5 per cent on all excess above $1000, the tax to be levied only until 1870 After a contest in Congress the tax was renewed for one year only by act of 14 July 1870 at the reduced rate of 2½ per cent on the excess of income above $2000 A bill to repeal it passed the Senate 26 Jan 1871, by 26 to 25 The House refused to take up the Senate bill 9 Feb 1871, by a vote of 104 to 105, but on 3 Mch 1871, concurred in the report of a committee which endorsed the Senate bill and repealed the tax The last tax levied under the law was in 1871 TARIFF, UNITED STATES, 1894 Income-taxes assessed and due in 1871 and for preceding years, however, continued to be collected 1872-74 as seen by the subjoined table

AMOUNT OF REVENUE FROM INCOME-TAX EACH YEAR

1863	$2,741,857
1864	20 294,733
1865	32,050,017
1866	72 982,160
1867	66,014 429
1868	41,455,599
1869	34,791,857
1870	37,775,872
1871	19,162 652
1872	14,436,861
1873	5,062,312
1874	140,391
Total	$346,908,740

indemnity bill relieves a minister of the crown or a government from responsibility for measures adopted in urgent cases, without the sanction of Parliament One was passed in England 19 Apr 1801, another, to indemnify ministers for acts during the suspension of the Habeas-Corpus act, was carried in the commons (principal divisions, 190 to 64), and in the lords (93 to 27), 10 Mch 1818 In 1848 and 1857 bills of indemnity were passed for the suspension of the Bank Charter act by the ministry An indemnity bill is passed at the end of every session of Parliament for persons who transgress through ignorance of the law The practice began in 1715

Independence, Declaration of. DECLARATION OF

Independents or **Congregationalists** hold each church or congregation an independent community They ascribe no supreme authority to synods or councils, but respect them as advisory bodies A church may reprove another, but cannot excommunicate Robert Browne preached these doctrines about 1585, but, after 32 imprisonments, he eventually conformed to the Established church A church was formed in London in 1593, when there were 20,000 Independents. They were driven by persecution to Holland, where they formed several churches, that at Leyden was under Mr Robinson, by some called the founder of Independency In 1616 Henry Jacobs returned to England and founded a meeting-house Cromwell, himself an Independent, obtained them toleration, in opposition to the Presbyterians. The Independents published an epitome of their faith, drawn up at the Savoy in 1658, and the Congregational Union of England and Wales, formed in 1831, published their "declaration of faith, order, and discipline" in 1833 In 1851 they had 3244 chapels for 1,067,760 persons in England and Wales WORSHIP The first Independents in Scotland were the GLASITES The first Independent church in America was founded by followers of John Robinson, at Plymouth, New England, in 1620. CONGREGATIONALISTS.

Index Expurgato'rius, a catalogue of books proscribed by the church of Rome, first made by inquisitors, and approved by the Council of Trent, 1559 The index by which reading the Scriptures was forbidden (with certain exceptions) to the laity was confirmed by a bull of pope Clement VIII in 1595 Many works of great authors of France, Spain, Germany, and England were thus prohibited On 25 June, 1864, Hugo's "Les Miserables" and other books were added, and many since

Index Society, established by the librarians of various London scientific and literary institutions and societies, and literary men, to form a library of indexes, and to make indexes to rare serial works, important books, etc, 17 Dec 1877 Poole's "Index to Periodical Literature," first pub 1848

India or **Hindostan,** the most southern portion of Asia Its histories claim an antiquity far greater than the reach of common chronologies A race of kings is mentioned as reigning 2300 B C, and Buddhism is said to have been introduced 956 B.C Several ancient nations particularly the Tyrians and Egyptians, carried on commerce with India It was partly conquered by Darius Hystaspis, who formed an Indian satrapy, in 512 B C, and by Alexander, 327 B C, and afterwards intercourse with the Roman empire extended The authentic history of Hindostan commences with the conquest of Mahmud Ghuzni, 1001 A D.—*Rennell* British India comprises all the territory ruled by the governor-general, whether in the Indian peninsula or beyond it The present form of government was established 2 Aug 1858, all the former authority of the East India company being vested in the queen The executive authority is a governor-general appointed by the British crown India extends from 8° to 31° N lat. and from 70° to 90° E lon, and contains about 1,587,104 sq miles, with a population of 286,696,960 in 1891 Of this population 220,529,100 belong to the British territory, while the native or feudatory states number 66,167,860 There are 27 cities in India, each with 100 000 inhabitants or more, and 76 with over 50,000 Calcutta is the largest with 840 000, Bombay second with 805,000 The revenue in 1890 was 85,085,203*l*, expenditures, 82,473,170*l* The army consists of European and native soldiers, the Europeans number 73,405, the natives, 144,839, total, 218,244 Miles of railway 1890-91, 16 996. BENGAL, BOMBAY, CALCUTTA, MADRAS and OUDE for further details GANGES CANAL

	B.C.
Religion of Brahma introduced	about 2000
Buddhism introduced	about 956
Invasion of Alexander	327
Irruptions of Mahometans, under Mahmud Ghuzni, 1001-24	A D.
He captured Somnath	1024
House of Ghuzni extinct, 1186, slave kings of Delhi rule, 1206-88, Kilgiis and house of Toghlak, 1288-1412, Syuds 1412-50, house of Lodi	1450-1526
Patan, or Afghan empire, founded	1205
Invasion of Moguls under Genghis Khan, 1219, he d	1227
Mogul Tartars, under Timour (Tamerlane), invade Hindostan, take Delhi, defeat Indian army, 1397, conquer Hindostan and butcher 100 000 people	1398-99
Passage to India discovered by Vasco de Gama	1497
First European settlement (Portuguese) by him at Cochin (south coast)	1502
Albuquerque governor general, 1508, d at Goa	1514
Conquest of India completed by sultan Baber, founder of the Mogul empire	1519-26
Reign of his son Humayun	1531-56
Reign of Akbar, greatest sovereign of Hindostan	1556-1605
Portuguese introduce tobacco	1600
Dutch first visit India, 1601, establish a United East company,	1602
Tranquebar granted to the Danes	1619
Reign of Jehanghir	1605-27
Reign of Shah Jehad, golden age of the Moguls	1627-58
Aurungzebe dethrones his father and murders his brothers 1658, reigns	1658-1707
French East India company established	1664
Rise of Mahratta power under Sevajee, 1659, he assumes royalty, 1674, d	1680
Aurungzebe conquers Golconda, etc	1687
His prosperity wanes, 1702, d 21 Feb	1707
Bahadoor Shah succeeds 1707, d	1712
Jehander Shah, 1713, dethroned and killed	1718
Accession of Mahomed Shah	1719
Independence of the Nizam of the Deccan	1723
Rise of Mahratta families, Holkar and Sindiah	1730
Invasion of Persian Nadir Shah or Kouli Khan at Delhi he orders a massacre, and 150,000 persons perish, carries away treasure amounting to 125,000,000*l*.	1739
Mahomed Shah d	1748

[The Mogul empire was now nominal, petty princes being independent. In 1761 Shah Alum II, attacking the English was defeated at Patna, 15 Jan In 1764, after the battle of Buxar, he was protected by the English at Allahabad After the victory at Delhi, in 1803 gen Lake restored the aged monarch to a nominal sovereignty, which his son, Akbar

Shah inherited. He d. 1837. His son, the last king of Delhi, who received a pension of about 125,000*l*. per annum, joined the mutiny in 1857, was tried in 1858, and transported to Rangoon; d. there, 11 Nov. 1862.]

BRITISH POWER IN INDIA

Attempts to reach India by north-east and north-west. 1528
Sir Francis Drake's expedition 1579
Levant company's land expedition 1580
First commercial adventure from England 1591
London Company of Merchants chartered (INDIA COMPANY) 1600
Factories established at Surat, etc. 1612
Sir Thos. Roe, first English ambassador 1615
Madras founded 1640, made a presidency 1652
Bombay ceded to England as part of dowry of Catherine, queen of Charles II. 1662
French company established 1664
They settle at Pondicherry 1668
Calcutta purchased 1698
War between the English and French in India 1746–49
English besiege Pondicherry, seat of the French government, without success 1748
Clive takes Arcot 1751
Peace made 1754
Severndroog and other strongholds of the pirate Angria taken, 11 Feb. 1756
Capture of Calcutta by Surajah Dowla; suffocation of English in the BLACK HOLE 20 June, "
Clive retakes Calcutta, 2 Jan.; defeats the Soubah at Plassey, 23 June, 1757
Fort William, the strongest fort in India, built "
French successful under Lally 1758
But lose nearly all their power 1759
French under Lally defeated by sir Eyre Coote near Wandewash 2 July, 1760
Hyder Ali usurps the sovereignty of Mysore 1763–64
Conquest of Patna 6 Nov. 1763
Battle of BUXAR 23 Oct. 1764
Nabob becomes subject to the English 1765
Lord Clive obtains the Dewanny by imperial grant, making the company receivers of revenue in Bengal, Bahar, and Orissa, with virtual sovereignty 12 Aug. "
Treaty with Nizam Ali; the English obtain the northern Circars 12 Nov. 1766
Hyder Ali ravages the Carnatic. Jan. 1769
Frightful famine in Bengal 1770
Warren Hastings governor of Bengal 13 Apr. 1772
India bill; supreme court established 1773
Treaty with Bhootan 1774
Death of Clive "
Warren Hastings accused of taking a bribe from a concubine of Meer Jaffier (HASTINGS) 30 May, 1775
Nuncomar, a Brahmin, accuses Hastings of receiving bribes, 11 Mch. 1776
Is hanged for forgery . 5 Aug. "
Pondicherry taken 11 Oct. 1778
Fortress of Gwalior taken by Popham 4 Aug. "
Hyder Ali overruns the Carnatic, and defeats the British 10 Sept.; takes Arcot 31 Oct. 1780
Hyder Ali defeated by sir Eyre Coote 1 July, 1781
Further charges against Warren Hastings (CHUNAR) 19 Sept. "
Bussy lands with a French detachment. Mch. 1782
War with Hyder Ali aided by the French "
Hyder Ali overthrown by Coote . 2 June, "
Death of Hyder; his son, Tippoo Sahib, succeeds Dec. "
Tippoo, after seizing Cuddalore, takes Bednore Apr. 1783
Pondicherry restored to French, Trincomalee to Dutch "
Fox's India bill thrown out "
Pitt's India bill . 1784
Ignoble peace with Tippoo 11 Mch. "
Charges against Warren Hastings . 1786
His trial begun . 13 Feb. 1788
War with Tippoo renewed. 1790
Bangalore taken (BANGALORE) . . 21 Mch. 1791
Cornwallis defeats Tippoo at Arikera 15 May, "
Fortress of Severndroog taken 21 Dec. "
Definitive treaty with Tippoo; his 2 sons hostages 19 Mch. 1792
Civil and criminal courts erected 1793
Pondicherry again taken . "
Tippoo's sons restored 29 Mch. 1794
First dispute with Burmese, adjusted by gen. Erskine 1795
Warren Hastings acquitted 23 Apr. "
Government of lord Mornington, afterwards marquess Wellesley . . . 17 May, 1798
Seringapatam stormed by gen. Baird; Tippoo Sahib killed 4 May; Mysore divided 22 June, 1799
Victories of the British; the Carnatic conquered . 1800
Nabob of Furruckabad cedes his territories to the English for a pension . 4 June, 1802
Important treaty of Bassein (with Mahrattas) 31 Dec. "
Mahratta war. Victories of sir Arthur Wellesley and gen. Lake, 1803
Wellesley's great victory at Assaye 23 Sept. "
Pondicherry (restored 1801) retaken . Dec. "
War with Holkar 1804–5
Capture of Bhurtpore . 2 Apr. 1805
Marquess Cornwallis succeeds Wellesley; d. 5 Oct. "
Mahratta chief, Scindiah, defeated by British; treaty of peace, 23 Nov. "
Treaty of peace with Holkar . 24 Dec. "
Sepoy mutiny at Vellore; 800 executed .. July, 1806
Cumoona surrenders. .. . . 21 Nov. 1807
Mutiny at Seringapatam quelled 23 Aug. 1809
Act opening the trade to India July, 1813
War with Nepaul 1814–15
Holkar defeated by sir T. Hislop 21 Dec. 1817
Pindaree war. English successful 1817–18
Peace with Holkar 6 Jan. 1818
Burmese war. British take Rangoon 5 May, 1824
Peace with the Burmese 24 Feb. 1826
[They pay 1,000,000*l*. and cede a great extent of territory.]
Abolition of SUTTEES (the burning of widows) 7 Dec. 1829
Act opening the trade to India, and tea trade, etc., to China, a new era in British commerce 28 Aug. 1833
Coorg annexed; rajah deposed 10 Apr. 1834
Natives admitted to magistracy 1 May, "
Slavery abolished 1 Aug. 1838
Afghan war. Proclamation against Dost Mahomed 1 Oct. "
British occupy Candahar 21 Apr. 1839
Victory at GHIZNEE of sir John (afterwards lord) Keane 23 July, "
Wade forces the Khyber pass 26 July, "
English defeat Dost Mahomed 18 Oct. 1840
At the funeral of Kurruck Singh, king of Lahore, his successor is killed by accident; Dost Mahomed, next heir, surrenders to England 5 Nov. "
Rising against British at Cabul; sir Alex. Burnes and others murdered 2 Nov. 1841
Sir Wm. Macnaghten assassinated . 23 Dec. "
Jellalabad held by sir R. Sale 1841–42
British under convention evacuate Cabul, placing lady Sale, etc., as hostages with Akbar Khan; a massacre ensues of about 16,000 persons 6–13 Jan. 1842
British evacuate Ghiznee 1 Mch. "
Sortie from Jellalabad; gen. Pollock forces the Khyber pass, 5 Apr. "
Ghiznee retaken by gen. Nott 6 Sept. "
Gen. Pollock enters Cabul 16 Sept. "
Lady Sale and other prisoners rescued by Sir R. Shakspeare, arrive at gen. Pollock's camp 21 Sept. "
Cabul evacuated after destroying fortifications 12 Oct. "
Scinde war. Ameers defeated by sir Charles Napier at Meanee, 17 Feb. 1843
Scinde annexed to British empire; sir Charles Napier governor June, "
Gwalior war. Battles of Maharajpoor and Punniar; the fort of Gwalior, "Gibraltar of the East," taken 29 Dec. "
Danish possessions in India purchased 1845
Sikh war. Sikhs cross the Sutlej river and attack the British at Ferozepore 14 Dec. "
Sir H. Hardinge, by a rapid march, reaches Moodkee; Sikhs (20,000) attack; after a hard contest they retire, abandoning their guns (MOODKEE) . 18 Dec. "
Sir Hugh Gough seizes citadel of Lahore and ends the war, 20 Feb. 1846
Treaty of Lahore signed 9 Mch. "
Shere Singh, intrenched on right bank of the Chenab, with 40,000 men and 28 guns; gen. Thackwell crossing with 8 infantry regiments, cavalry, and cannon, 1 Dec., attacks his left flank at Sadoolapore 3 Dec. 1848
Lord Gough attacks enemy's advanced position; victory of CHILLIANWALLAH 13 Jan. 1849
Sir Charles Napier commander-in-chief 7 Mch. "
Punjaub annexed to British dominions; Dhuleep Singh obtains a pension of 40,000*l*. 29 Mch. "
Sir Charles Napier resigns his command 2 July, 1850
Burmese war. Death of Bajee Rao, ex-peishwa of the Mahrattas (his nephew Nana Sahib's claim for continuance of the pension of 80,000*l*. refused) . 28 Jan. 1851
A British naval force reaching Rangoon, in the Burman empire, commodore Lambert allows the viceroy 35 days to obtain instructions from Ava. 29 Oct. "
Viceroy of Rangoon interdicts communication between the shore and the British ships of war, and erects batteries to prevent their departure 4 Jan. 1852
[Commodore Lambert blockades the Irawaddy; the *Fox*, *Hermes*, etc., attacked by batteries, destroy the fortifications, killing nearly 300 men.]
Pegu annexed to Indian empire by proclamation of the governor-general 20 Dec. "
First Indian railway opened (Bombay to Tannah) 16 Apr. 1853
End of war . . . June, "
Opening of the Calcutta railway 3 Feb. 1855
Treaty of friendship with Dost Mahomed of Cabul 30 Mch. "

MUTINY OF THE NATIVE ARMY

For the improved (Enfield) musket in the Indian army cartridges greased with the fat of pigs were brought from England. These were offensive to native soldiers on religious grounds, and were recalled by orders in Jan. 1857. A mutinous spirit appeared in the Bengal native army. In Mch. several regiments were disbanded, and by June the army had lost by disbandment and desertion about 30,000 men. On 5 Apr. a sepoy, and on 20 Apr. a jemadar, or native lieutenant, were executed. At the end of May, 34 regiments were lost. In April, 85 of the 3d Bengal native cavalry at Meerut refused to use their cartridges. On 9 May they were committed to jail. On Sunday, the 10th, a mutiny in the native troops broke out; they fired on officers, killing col. Finnis and others, released their comrades, massacred many Europeans, and fired public buildings. The European troops rallied and drove them from their cantonments. The mutineers then fled to DELHI.
Mutinies in Bengal army; at Barrackpore, etc.; regiments disbanded. . . . . Mch. 1857

Mutiny at Meerut (near Delhi) 10 May. The mutineers seize Delhi, commit outrages, and proclaim the king of Delhi emperor....................11–12 May, etc. 1857

Mutiny at Lucknow....................30 May, "

Neill suppresses the mutiny at Benares, 3 June, and recovers Allahabad....................4 June, "

Mutiny spreads through Bengal; fearful atrocities.......... "

[At the end of June native troops were in open mutiny at *Meerut*, *Delhi*, Ferozepore, Allyghur, Roorkee, Murdaun, Lucknow, *Cawnpore*, *Nusseerabad*, *Neemuch*, *Hansi*, *Hissar*, *Jahnsi*, Mehidpore, Jullundur, Azimghur, Futtehghur, Jaunpore, *Bareilly*, Shahjehanpore, *Allahabad*. At the stations in italics, European women and children were massacred.]

Residency at Lucknow besieged by rebels..........1 July, "

Sir H. Lawrence dies of wounds at Lucknow..........4 July, "

Cawnpore surrenders to Nana Sahib, who kills garrison, etc., 28 June; he is defeated by gen. Havelock, 16 July, who recaptures CAWNPORE..........17 July, "

Mutinies suppressed at Hyderabad, 18 July; at Lahore.20 July, "

Assault of Delhi, 14 Sept.; taken, 20 Sept.; king captured, 21 Sept.; his son and grandson slain by col. Hodson...22 Sept. "

Sir James Outram joins Havelock and serves under him.16 Sept. "

Havelock, relieving besieged residency at Lucknow, retires, leaving Outram in command; Neill killed.......25, 26 Sept. "

Col. Greathed defeats rebels at Bolundshohur, 27 Sept.; destroys fort at Molaghur, 29 Sept.; takes Allyghur, 5 Oct.; defeats rebels at Agra....................10 Oct. "

Sir Colin Campbell (afterwards lord Clyde) commander-in-chief, 11 July; arrives at Cawnpore..........3 Nov. "

Joined by Havelock, he attacks rebels and rescues besieged in residency..........18–25 Nov. "

Havelock dies of dysentery at Alumbagh..........24 Nov. "

[Born 5 Apr. 1795; educated at Charterhouse, London, where he was called "Old Phlos"; went to India, 1823; served in the Burmese war, 1824, and in the Sikh war, 1845. He was a Baptist.]

Sir Colin Campbell arrives at Cawnpore, which he retakes, 28 Nov., and defeats the Gwalior rebels..........6 Dec. "

Lucknow strongly fortified by the rebels..........Jan. 1858

Sir Colin Campbell marches to Lucknow, 11 Feb.; siege commences, 8 Mch.; taken by successive assaults; the enemy retreat; Hodson killed..........14–19 Mch. "

Government of the East India company ceases..........1 Sept. "

Queen Victoria proclaimed in India; lord Canning to be first viceroy..........1 Nov. "

Punjaub made a distinct presidency..........1 Jan. 1859

Thanksgiving in England for pacification of India......1 May, "

Sir Hugh Rose takes command of Indian army, amalgamated with the British..........July, 1860

Nana Sahib, supposed to have died of jungle fever in Aug. 1858, is said to be living in Thibet..........Dec. "

Famine in N.W. provinces through failure of crops; government and others strive to relieve the sufferers....Jan.–June, 1861

British subscriptions for relief of famine open at Mansion house, London, with 4000*l*., 28 Mch.; 52,000*l*. subscribed 20 Apr.; closes with 114,807*l*..........Nov. "

Order of "STAR OF INDIA" instituted..........25 June, "

Law of property in India altered; sale of waste lands authorized..........Oct. "

Lord Elgin, governor-general, installed at Calcutta....12 Mch. 1862

Hindu religion deprived of government support..........Dec. 1863

Death of the viceroy, lord Elgin..........20 Nov. "

Sir John Lawrence, his successor, assumes office.......12 Jan. 1864

Hindus excited by government suppressing funeral rites on sanitary grounds..........Mch. "

Gold currency (a sovereign = 10 rupees) ordered introduced at Christmas..........July, "

Cyclone, great loss of life, property, and ships at Calcutta and elsewhere..........5 Oct. "

Opening of Indo-European telegraph; a telegram from Kurrachee received..........1 Mch. 1865

Settlement of dispute on marriage of Hindu converts.....Apr. 1866

Rise of the religious reformers termed BRAHMO SAMAJ....Aug. 1869

Act for better governing India and defining governor-general's powers passed..........11 Aug. "

Viceroy arrives at Rangoon, 28 Jan.; returning, visiting convict establishment in Andaman islands, is assassinated at Port Blair by Shere Ali, a convict, while about to embark in the *Glasgow*..........8 Feb. 1872

Shere Ali hanged, without naming associates..........12 Mch. "

Annual pension from Indian government to lady Mayo, 1000*l*.; grant of 20,000*l*. for children..........Mch. "

Christian marriage bill passed..........July, "

Begum of Bhopal made knight of the Star of India at Bombay, 16 Nov. "

Lord Lytton, viceroy, takes oath at Calcutta..........12 Apr. 1876

Queen Victoria proclaimed empress of India in London..1 May, "

Viceregal proclamation of the queen's title, "Empress of India" (to be proclaimed at Delhi, 1 Jan. 1877)......19 Aug. "

Queen Victoria proclaimed empress of India at Delhi, by the viceroy; also at Calcutta, Madras, and Bombay.......1 Jan. 1877

Creation of the "Order of the Empire of India" announced, 1 Jan. "

"Imperial Order of the Crown of India" for ladies, instituted, 31 Dec. "

War with AFGHANISTAN..........Sept. 1878

England holds passes to India by land..........Feb. 1879

Sirhind canal (502 miles, for irrigation) opened by the viceroy, 24 Nov. 1882

Budget—revenue, 70,690,681*l*.; expenditure, 71,077,127*l*....1884–85

Sir Donald Stewart, with 50,000 men, ordered to advance to Quettah..........Mch. 1885

IND

Meeting of the ameer of Afghanistan and the viceroy at Rawul Pindi conference and durbar..........2–12 Apr. 1885

Nawab of Moorshedabad and other princes offer their jewels, etc., for money to aid the British in India against Russia, Apr.–May, "

Thorough defence of India determined on by the British government, declared..........12 May, "

Proposed loan of 10,000,000*l*. 21 May, et seq.; act passed.22 July, "

Sir Frederick Roberts appointed commander-in-chief; announced..........30 July, "

Upper Burmah annexed by proclamation of the viceroy, lord Dufferin..........1 Jan. 1886

Grand military review at Delhi held by the viceroy (35,000 troops, 709 officers, etc.)..........19 Jan. "

National Indian congress at Calcutta, 400 delegates (Hindus) to promote native advancement, 28 Dec. 1886; and again early, 1887

Queen's jubilee celebrated; honors distributed; 25,000 prisoners of good character released..........16 Feb. et seq. "

Thirteen thousand three hundred and ninety miles of railway in India; reported.......... "

Nizam of Hyderabad offers lord Dufferin, viceroy, 20 lakhs of rupees for 3 years, total 600,000*l*., to defend the northwest, Sept.; acknowledged with thanks; announced......10 Oct. "

Rajah of Kaparthala offers his army and 5 lakhs of rupees for the defence of India; announced..........31 Oct. "

Four lakhs offered by rajah of Nabha..........Nov. "

Similar offers by other princes.......... " "

Lady Dufferin's jubilee fund subscribed for medical aid to women amounts to 478,465 rupees in India, and 1770*l*. in England, 15 Oct.; amount received 50,000*l*..........25 Oct. "

Quettah with districts of Pishin, Thal Chotiali, and Sibi in BELOOCHISTAN annexed and placed under a chief commissioner; announced..........Nov. "

India 4 per cent. stock converted into 3½ per cent. by act, 23 May, "

Maharajah of Darbhanga in Bengal establishes a medical hospital for women in aid of lady Dufferin's fund......autumn, "

Lord Dufferin at a durbar at Patiala announces that government declines money from the princes; but recommends to improve their armies and fit them with the British for defence of India..........18 Nov. 1888

Installation of the marquess of Lansdowne as viceroy; departure of lord Dufferin..........10 Dec. "

Fortress of Quettah, a bulwark of India, finished..........Jan. 1889

Sukkur bridge opened..........27 Mch. "

Arthur Travers Crawford, commissioner for 34 years in Bombay, after a long investigation, was acquitted of serious charges of financial misconduct, but was for indiscreet borrowing dismissed the service. After correspondence sentence confirmed by lord Cross, secretary for India..........29 Mch. "

Tantia Bheel, robber chief of the central provinces, a kind of Robin Hood, in the Holkar territory, began his career about 1874; robbed the rich and helped the poor; lately suffered much, captured about 18 Aug., convicted of murder (in 1879) about 20 Oct., executed at Jubbulpore..........4 Dec. "

Increased agitation in India and England against Hindu child marriages..........Aug. 1890

Insurrection in Cambay with bloodshed, the nawab appeals to the British for help; they restore order; reported...23 Sept. "

Sixth national congress of mixed character, no government officials present, 26–30 Dec. 1890; sir A. Scoble introduces a bill into the legislative council to raise the age of consent to marriage by girls from 10 to 12..........9 Jan. 1891

After much public discussion, the "age of consent to marriage bill" is passed by the legislative council..........19 Mch. "

Sir D. Barbour's financial statement; reported surplus 29 Mch.; he recommends a commission to consider the currency and the introduction of a gold standard, etc.....Mch. "

Deficiency of rain causes famine, especially in Madras, Rajputana, the Punjaub, and the south..........middle of July, "

Gen. sir Frederick Sleigh Roberts created a peer as baron Roberts of Candahar..........Feb. 1892

Famine relief works; persons employed: Madras, 48,000; Bombay, 2000; Bengal, 17,000; Burmah, 28,000; Mysore, 13,000; Rajputana, 33,000; reported..........2 Apr. "

Indian Currency Association formed to promote the abolition of silver as the sole standard in India..........May, "

Value of the rupee reduced to 1*s*. 3*d*.; great anxiety......Aug. "

GOVERNORS-GENERAL OF INDIA, ETC.

Warren Hastings assumes the government..........13 Apr. 1772

Sir John Macpherson..........1 Feb. 1785

Lord Cornwallis..........12 Sept. 1786

Sir John Shore (afterwards lord Teignmouth)..........28 Oct. 1793

[Lord (afterwards marquess) Cornwallis again; he relinquished the appointment.]

Sir Alured Clarke..........6 Apr. 1798

Lord Mornington (afterwards marquess Wellesley)....17 May, "

Marquess Cornwallis again..........30 July, 1805

Sir George Hilaro Barlow..........10 Oct. "

Lord Minto..........31 July, 1807

Earl of Moira (afterwards marquess of Hastings)........4 Oct. 1813

Hon. John Adam..........13 Jan. 1823

George Canning; relinquished the appointment.......... "

William, lord (afterwards earl) Amherst..........1 Aug. "

Hon. W. Butterworth Bayley..........13 Mch. 1828

Lord William Cavendish Bentinck..........4 July, "

[First governor-general of India, under the act 3 and 4 Will. IV. c. 85, Aug. 28. 1833.]

Sir Charles Theophilus Metcalfe (afterwards lord Metcalfe), 20 Mch. 1835

William, lord Heytesbury; did not proceed.......... "

George, lord Auckland (afterwards earl of Auckland)....4 Mch. 1836

Edward, lord Ellenborough............................28 Feb. 1842
William Wilberforce Bird...........................15 June, 1844
Sir Henry (afterwards viscount) Hardinge...........23 July, "
James Andrew, earl (afterwards marquess) of Dalhousie..12 Jan. 1848
Charles John, viscount Canning, appointed.............July, 1855
Proclaimed the first viceroy throughout India.........1 Nov. 1858
James, earl of Elgin, appointed Aug. 1861; d..........20 Nov. 1863
Sir John Lawrence appointed...........................Dec. "
Richard, earl of Mayo, appointed......................Oct. 1868
[Assassinated 8 Feb. 1872.]
Thomas George Baring, lord Northbrook................Feb. 1872
Edward Robert Bulwer Lytton, lord Lytton, took oath at Calcutta..12 Apr. 1876
George Frederick Samuel Robinson, marquess of Ripon..May, 1880
Frederick Temple Hamilton Blackwood, earl of Dufferin..Sept. 1884
Henry Charles Keith Petty Fitzmaurice, marquess of Lansdowne...Dec. 1888

India, Empress of, queen Victoria so proclaimed in London, 1 May, 1876; in India, 1 Jan. 1877. Order of the Indian Empire instituted, 1 Jan. 1878.

India Company, East. The first commercial intercourse of the English with India was a private adventure of 3 ships fitted out in 1591. Only 1 reached India; and, after a voyage of 3 years, the commander, capt. Lancaster, was brought home in another ship, the sailors having seized his own; but his information gave rise to a mercantile voyage, and a company, whose first charter, in Dec. 1600, was renewed in 1609, '57, '61, '93, and 1744. Its stock in 1600 consisted of 72,000*l.*, when it fitted out 4 ships. Meeting with success, it continued to trade, and India stock sold at 500*l.* for a share of 100*l.* in 1683.

A new company (the "English"), was chartered in 1698, and the old (the "London") suspended trading for 3 years; the 2 were united.. 1702
New East India Company established........................ 1708
Privileges of the company continued till 1783................ 1744
Affairs of company brought before Parliament; a committee exposed intrigues and crimes.........................Aug. 1772
Two acts (one authorized a loan of 1,000,000*l.* to the company; the other celebrated as the India bill) reformed the constitution of the company. A governor-general was to reside in Bengal, the other presidencies to be subordinate; a supreme court of judicature was instituted at Calcutta; the salary of the governor was fixed at 25,000*l.* per year; that of the council at 10,000*l.* each; and of the chief judge at 8000*l.*; the affairs of the company were controlled; all the departments reorganized; all territorial correspondence to be laid before the British ministry.................................June, 1773
Mr. Pitt's act appointing the Board of Control.........18 May, 1784
Company's charter was renewed for 20 years................ 1793
Trade with India opened..................................... 1813
Trade to China opened; charter renewed till 1854............ 1833
Government of India continued in the company till Parliament otherwise provided.. 1853
After the mutiny of 1857, and the disappearance of the company's army, the government was transferred to the crown, the Board of Control abolished, and a Council of State for In[illegible] [illegible]nstituted by 21 and 22 Vict. c. 106, approved.....2 Aug. 1858
[illegible]ny's political power ceased 1 Sept.; Victoria proclaimed [illegible] of Great Britain and colonies, etc..............1 Nov. "
[illegible] India House built, 1726; enlarged and a new front erected, [illegible] sold with furniture, 1861; razed Sept. and Oct......... 1862
[illegible] to be dissolved 1 June, 1874, and dividends redeemed, by the "East India Stock Dividend Redemption act," passed, 15 May, 1873

India-rubber. CAOUTCHOUC.

Indian civilization in the United States. Not including the 5 civilized tribes of the Indian territory and the New York Indians, there are, according to the report of the secretary of the interior, 1888–89, 27,394 Indians engaged more or less in civilized pursuits: 17,203 occupy houses; 26,223 speak English; 62,625 wear civilized dress; 251,858 acres cultivated; 242,647 rods of fence built; 267,400 feet of lumber sawed; 93,082 cords wood cut; 83,426 lbs. butter made; 727,859 bu. wheat raised; 600,203 bu. oats, barley, and rye; 1,306,961 bu. of corn; 129,171 tons of hay. They possess 417,328 horses, ponies, and mules; 128,766 cattle; 40,343 swine; and 860,336 sheep. INDIAN EDUCATION, INDIAN TERRITORY.

Indian education in the United States. Efforts were early made for the education of the American Indians. John Eliot in Massachusetts translated the Bible into the Indian tongue, 1660–1675; and a chief purpose of William and Mary college in Virginia (1693) was to educate the red men. The policy of the U. S. government is to induce the Indians to abandon tribal relations and accept citizenship. Under pres. Hayes much was done for the education of Indian children, and the work is still pursued, with a view to the gradual civilization of the wild tribes. INDIAN TERRITORY. The following is a brief summary of the Indian schools (government) in 1891:

Government training and boarding schools, average attendance, 1891.......... 6,738
Government day schools, average attendance, 1891.......... 1,661
Contract schools (mostly sectarian, aided by government):
Boarding schools, average attendance, 1891.................. 4,667
Day schools, average attendance, 1891........................ 502
Total........... 13,568

Cost to the government of the Indian contract schools was as follows: 1886, $228,259; 1887, $363,214; 1888, $376,264; 1889, 530,905; 1890, $562,640; 1891, $570,218; 1892, $604,240.

LIST OF ESTABLISHED GOVERNMENT TRAINING-SCHOOLS FOR INDIANS IN THE U. S.

Name.	Location.	Average attendance.	Cost.
Carlisle School......	Carlisle, Pa...........	754	$106,393
Harrison Institute...	Chemawa, Or..........	164	31,338
Haworth " ...	Chillocco, Ind. Ter.....	164	24,220
Howard " ...	Fort Stevenson, N. Dak.	98	14,420
Grant " ...	Genoa, Neb...........	190	41,897
Haskell " ...	Lawrence, Kan.......	487	82,632
Fisk " ...	Albuquerque, N. Mex..	188	29,245
Teller " ...	Grand Junction, Col...	35	....
Dawes " ...	Santa Fé, N. Mex......	45	10,065
Stewart " ...	Carson, Nev..........	84	13,129
Pierre " ...	Pierre, S. Dak.........	49	5,851
Fort Mohave " ...	Fort Mohave, Ariz....	79	15,546
Ramona Indian School for Girls ..	Santa Fé, N. Mex......	....	....

Indian history. The following are the principal events in the history of the Indians in the U. S. For further information consult the state records severally as well as the topics noted and article Indians.

Indians carried from South Carolina for slaves by Spaniards (SOUTH CAROLINA).. 1520
De Soto's expedition through country of southern Indians, 1539–42
Capt. John Smith, captured by Indians of Virginia, is condemned to death, but is saved by Pocahontas, daughter of Powhatan (VIRGINIA).................................. 1607
Pocahontas marries John Rolfe, visits England, and dies there (VIRGINIA).. 1616–17
Samoset welcomes the English (MASSACHUSETTS)............ 1620
Indian massacre of whites in VIRGINIA..................... 1622
Pequot war, and destruction of that nation by the English (CONNECTICUT, MASSACHUSETTS).......................... 1637
Dutch massacre Indians at Hackensack (NEW YORK)......... 1643
During this war Mrs. Anne Hutchinson is murdered (NEW YORK) "
Powhatan confederacy destroyed (VIRGINIA).................. 1644
Wyandots or Hurons driven from the St. Lawrence valley by Iroquois.. 1659
Eliot translates the Bible into the Indian tongue............ 1661
War with king Philip of the Wampanoags................ 1675–76
First blow struck by Indians at Swanzey (MASSACHUSETTS), July, 1675
Indians defeat whites at Bloody Brook, near Deerfield (MASSACHUSETTS)...18 Sept. "
"Great Swamp Fight;" defeat of the Narragansetts (MASSACHUSETTS)...19 Dec. "
Canonchet, chief of Narragansetts, killed by English.....Apr. 1676
English beaten at Turner's Falls (MASSACHUSETTS).....18 May, "
Hatfield attack; Indians repulsed (MASSACHUSETTS)...30 May, "
Hadley surprised (MASSACHUSETTS)..................12 June, "
King Philip killed at Mount Hope (MASSACHUSETTS)....17 Aug. "
Total destruction of the Wampanoags and Narragansetts....1676–77
[Iroquois or Five Nations generally hostile to the French (NEW YORK), 1609–10.]
English treaty with Iroquois at Albany.................July, 1684
War with eastern Indians; Dover, N. H., surprised, and maj. Waldron killed (NEW HAMPSHIRE)....................27 Jan. 1689
Iroquois capture Montreal...........................25 Aug. "
Schenectady burned (NEW YORK)............................ 1690
French and Indians burn Salmon Falls, Me...........18 Mch. "
French and Indians burn Falmouth, Me.................May, "
Haverbill, Mass., surprised; Hannah Dustin's escape (MASSACHUSETTS).. 1697
Appalachian Indians of Georgia suffer in a war with South Carolina.. 1703
"Queen Anne's war;" Indians burn Deerfield, Mass.....Mch. 1704
Haverhill, Mass., surprised and burned..................... 1708
Massacre of whites in North Carolina by Tuscaroras and Corees...2 Oct. 1711
Tuscaroras, driven from North Carolina, join the Iroquois in New York.. 1713
Creeks, Yemassees, Appalachians, with the Cherokees, Catawbas, and Congarees, unite against whites in South Carolina; Indians defeated.. 1715
"Lovewell's war," with eastern Indians of MAINE..........1722–26
Chickasaws successfully resist encroachments of French...... 1740
Eastern Indians join French in war of.................... 1745–48
Treaty with them (MAINE)...............................7 Oct. 1748
Delawares retire from the Delaware and Susquehanna rivers towards the Ohio.. 1752
Indians of entire central frontier join French in war.......1754–63
Assist the French to defeat Braddock (PENNSYLVANIA)..9 July, 1755
Indians surprised and defeated at Kittanning, on the Alleghany river, by col. John Armstrong (PENNSYLVANIA).......7 Sept. 1756

Indians massacre the surrendered garrison of fort William Henry (FORTS, NEW YORK) . 9 Aug 1757

Christian Indians of Pennsylvania retire to the Muskingum Ohio 1759-60

Cherokees attack the Carolinas frontier 1760

Subdued 1761

PONTIAC CONSPIRACY and war 1763-64

[The principal tribes engaged in this were the Ottawas, Miamis, Wyandots, Chippewas Pottawatomies, Shawnees, Foxes, and Winnebagoes, the Senecas of the Six Nations also joined]

Fort Pitt (formerly Duquesne) besieged by Indians, June-July, 1763

Relieved by col Bouquet, battle of Bushy Run (PENNSYLVANIA), 5 Aug "

Massacre of Christian Indians at Conestoga (PENNSYLVANIA), 27 Dec "

Col Bouquet's expedition into Indian country of OHIO 1764

Pontiac besieges Detroit (MICHIGAN) from May, 1763-May, "

Gov Dunmores war, battle of Point Pleasant on the Ohio (VIRGINIA) 10 Oct. 1774

Iroquois join British during the Revolution 1775-83

Indians join Burgoyne, death of Jane McCrea (NEW YORK) 27 July, 1777

Cherokees again subdued "

Massacre at WYOMING 3-5 July, 1778

Massacre at CHERRY VALLEY 10 Nov "

Gen Sullivan s expedition against the Six Nations (NEW YORK), Aug 1779

Massacre of Christian Indians at Gnadenhütten on the Tuscaroras river (OHIO) 8 Mch 1782

Defeat of col Crawford (OHIO) 5-6 June, "

Boone and Kentuckians defeated by Indians at BLUE LICKS, 19 Aug "

Six Nations cede all claims west of Pennsylvania to U S by treaty at fort Schuyler 4 Oct 1784

Shawnees limited by treaty to lands between the Miami and the Wabash 31 Jan. 1786

Cherokees, Choctaws, and Chickasaws by treaty to retain most of Tennessee, Alabama, and Mississippi 3 Jan "

Treaty with Creek Indians (GEORGIA) . 1790

Partial defeat of gen Harmar near the Miami villages (OHIO), 22 Oct. "

Defeat of gen St Clair (OHIO) 4 Nov 1791

Indians defeated by gen Wayne (OHIO) 20 Aug 1794

Wayne's treaty with Indians of the Northwest territory at Greenville, O 3 Aug 1795

[Tribes represented Chippewas, Delawares, Eel River Kaskaskias, Kickapoos, Miamis, Ottawas, Piankeshaws, Pottawatomies, Shawnees, Weas and Wyandots.]

Harrison defeats Indians at TIPPECANOE 7 Nov 1811

Massacre of whites at FORT MIMMS, Ala. (ALABAMA) 30 Aug 1813

Death of Tecumseh at battle of the THAMES 5 Oct. "

Creek war (ALABAMA) . 1813-14

Treaty with Creeks 1814

Treaty with Indians at Detroit 1 Sept. 1815

War with Seminoles (BATTLES, FLORIDA) 1817-18

Indians of Ohio cede all their remaining land 1818

Indians cede lands south of Grand river, Michigan, to U S 1821

Sequoyah, a Cherokee, invents the Cherokee alphabet 1821-22

Treaty with Creek Indians at Indian Spring 1825

Choctaws cede their lands to U S 1820-30

Measures for removing Indians west of the Mississippi adopted . . 1832

BLACK HAWK WAR, battle of BAD AXE 1 Aug "

Commissioner of Indian affairs appointed "

Chickasaws cede their lands to U S., and agree to remove west of the Mississippi (ALABAMA) . "

Creeks cede their lands to U S "

Black Hawk is taken through the principal eastern cities 1833

Treaty with Seminole Indians at Payne's Landing . 9 May, "

Indian territory established (INDIAN TERRITORY) . 1834

Seminole war (FLORIDA) . 1835-42

Cherokees cede all their lands to state of ALABAMA 1836

Sioux (Winnebagoes) cede lands east of the Mississippi to U S., 1837

Osceola, the Seminole chief, captured (FLORIDA, UNITED STATES), 22 Oct. "

War between Sioux and Chippewas . "

Cherokees, 1560 in number, leave Georgia for lands west of the Mississippi 3 June, 1838

Sioux cede all lands in Iowa and in Minnesota east of the Red river, etc , to U S . . 23 July, 1851

War with Indians of Rogue river, Oregon . .. 1853

Massacre of whites in the Rogue River valley . 1855

Chief John surrenders (OREGON) June, 1856

Most of the Seminole Indians of Florida emigrate to Indian Territory 1858

Sioux in Minnesota, led by Little Crow, massacre 500 persons, including women and children 17 Aug et seq 1862

[Gen Sibley, and afterwards gen. Pope, beat the Indians and rescued many captives, 38 Indians executed as assassins. MINNESOTA]

Little Crow killed by a settler . 1863

Fight with Cheyennes in Colorado 11 Apr 1864

Col. Chivington's Sand Creek massacre of 500 Indians who had asked protection and submitted to military authority, near fort Lyon, Colorado 27 Nov "

A fierce war ensues 1865-66

Fifty U S soldiers massacred at fort Phil Kearney 21 Dec. 1866

Indians plunder along line of Union Pacific railroad and impede construction summer, 1867

Severe fight near fort Phil. Kearney . 2 Aug "

And at Plum Creek, near Omaha 16 Aug 1867

Congress by law forbids treaties with Indians 29 Mch "

Repealed June, "

Law authorizing peace commission 20 July, "

Commission organized 6 Aug "

Secured a general suspension of hostilities autumn, "

Treaty with the SIOUX 2 Mch 1868

Indians troublesome in Colorado and Kansas summer, "

Severe fighting, 17 Sept , 18 Oct , 27 Nov , 25 Dec , conquering the Indians "

Board of Indian Commissioners established 1869

Modoc war began autumn, 1872

Canby massacre (gen Canby and commissioner Thomas, who with Mr Meacham had met capt Jack and other Modocs to negotiate, were treacherously killed, Meacham wounded), 11 Apr 1873

Capt. Jack and his fellows captured about 1 June, "

Capt Jack and 2 others hanged (CALIFORNIA) 3 Oct. "

Sioux war began winter, 1876

Gen Custer with his command 5 companies of the 7th cavalry (276 men) killed by Sioux under Sitting Bull on the Little Big Horn river Montana 26 June, "

War with the Nez Percés under chief Joseph and White Bird began 14 June, 1877

Joseph's retreat 17 July-30 Sept. "

Joseph captured, with 500 followers 1 Oct "

Standing Bear, a Ponca chief and 25 followers arrested in Dakota for abandoning reservation and returning to their former home, taken from military authorities by *habeas corpus* the first ever issued for an Indian 8-18 Apr 1879

Indians, legal status as persons and right of *habeas corpus* affirmed in the U S. district court at Lincoln Neb by judge Dundy, 12 May, 1879 Standing Bear and followers released by secretary of war, under this decision 12 May, "

Ute outbreak in Colorado, maj Thornburgh's command ambushed, and agent Meeker killed at the agency (COLORADO), 29 Sept. "

Apache outbreak, New Mexico Sept -Oct "

Apaches under Victoria chased into Mexico, Victoria killed and most of his band killed or captured spring, 1880

Fifteen hundred of Sitting Bull s Indians return to U S from British America and surrender Nov "

Indian Rights association organized Dec 1882

Courts established on reservations by Interior department, judges to be Indians, to take cognizance of theft, polygamy, barbarous dances, etc , under rules given by the department, 1883

Choctaws adopt freedmen (negroes) into their tribe "

Indians allowed to avail themselves of the homestead laws without fees or commissions, lands to be inalienable for 25 years, 1884

Lands allotted in severalty to the Omahas in Nebraska "

U S laws touching murder, manslaughter, rape, assault with intent to kill, arson, burglary, and larceny made applicable to Indians 1885

Lands allotted in severalty to the Santees in Nebraska "

Instruction on effects of alcohol, etc , in the human system made obligatory in Indian schools 1886

Land allotted to most of the hitherto wild Crows in Montana "

[A band of Apaches under Geronimo and Natchez left their reservation in Arizona, spring of 1882, and maintained irregular warfare for 3 years Gen Crook captured the band 1 Sept. 1885, but they escaped a few days later, Crook was transferred and gen Miles succeeded him Pursuit was resumed, and capt Crawford was killed by Mexican troops through alleged mistake, 21 Jan 1886, the Indians continued depredations until Sept 1886, when they surrendered under pledges which prevented a trial for murder, they were soon after removed to Florida, where the leaders are kept.]

Creeks cede half their domain in Oklahoma to the U S for $2,280,857 1 Mch 1889

Sioux dissatisfied in South Dakota, stated to be suffering from reduced government rations, incited by fanatical medicine men, who predict a conquering Messiah, they begin ghost war dances, attack outlying white settlers and friendly Indians, causing great alarm, troops and supplies of food sent to the Dakota frontier, the Sioux are soon joined by other tribes, Nov , col Wm F Cody ("Buffalo Bill") sent to the front 23 Nov 1890

Gen Miles commanding in Dakota, aided by gen Brook, with troops ordered for active service 25 Nov "

Old Sioux chief Sitting Bull captured 14 Dec., and in an attempt to rescue him, his son Crow Foot and himself are killed with others, and his camp seized .. 15 Dec. "

Gen Miles's headquarters at Rapid City 18 Dec "

Red Cloud, at a great council, recommends surrender and warns resisters 19 Dec "

Battle of Wounded Knee Creek.—To revenge Sitting Bull's death, remains of his band join Big Foot's band on Cheyenne river, start for Bad Lands, and, joined by other Indians, making about 160 warriors, are met and captured by the 7th cavalry under lieut Hawthorne, and artillery under maj Whiteside, 28 Dec , in the evening maj Forsyth with other troops arrives While pretending to surrender their arms, at the command of maj Whiteside, the Indians suddenly attack the dismounted troopers, and a murderous hand to-hand fight ensues, the Indians are joined by others, and additional troops arrive, the Indians flee to the ravines, are pursued by the artillery, in confused fight Big Foot and his band are nearly exterminated, together with many women and children (about 200) Capt Wallace, lieuts Casey and Mann, and several non commissioned officers and privates killed. 29 Dec "

Vigorous attack on Pine Ridge agency repulsed, 29 Dec. et seq.; sharp skirmish, Indians dispersed by maj. Forsyth, 29, 30 Dec. 1890
Large body of Indians near Pine Ridge agency surrounded by the 2d infantry under gen. Brook...........2 Jan. et seq. 1891
Gen. Miles receives the submission of the rebel chiefs of the Brules; provisions sent to the Indians............14 Jan. "
About 4000 Indians, nearly surrounded by the troops, come in and surrender their arms...................15 Jan. et seq. "
Gen. Miles, in an address, commends his troops and declares the war at an end.................................19 Jan. "
He takes 40 Indians and also some friendly chiefs to Washington, Feb.; they have a conference with Mr. Noble, secretary of the interior, 7 Feb., and pres. Harrison..........12 Feb. "
Delegates return to Pine Ridge from Washington dissatisfied with reception; their loyal chief, "American Horse," complains of the injustice and harshness of the government and officials, but commends gen. Miles...................23 Feb. "

Indian reservations. RESERVATIONS.

Indian Territory, a division of the United States definitely set apart for the Indians, 30 June, 1834, lat. 33° 35′ to 37° N., lon. 94° 20′ to 103° W. Oklahoma and Kansas are on the north, Missouri and Arkansas to the east, and Texas on the south and west. Area, 31,400 sq. miles. Pop. 1890, about 75,000; 1900, 392,060. Its area has been further reduced by the loss of the "Cherokee Strip," added to OKLAHOMA.

Cherokees get lands west of the Mississippi by treaty...6 May, 1828
Grant (5,000,000 acres in the north and northwest) further confirmed by treaty..................................4 Feb. 1833
Their final removal effected by treaty..................29 Dec. 1835
Choctaws receive lands (6,668,000 acres in the southwest) by treaty..27 Sept. 1830
Their removal was gradual, mostly in.............................. 1838
Creeks are granted land in the territory by treaty......24 Mch. 1832
Grant defined, 3,215,495 acres in the eastern part by a further treaty..14 Feb. 1833
Their removal was gradual, mostly in.............................. 1838
Seminoles are allotted lands here by treaty..........28 Mch. 1833
It was not until after the SEMINOLE WAR that they were removed to the territory, the last leaving Florida............ 1858
[They have some 200,000 acres, central.]
Chickasaws receive land in the territory by treaty.....24 May, 1834
[Removal effected gradually, mostly in 1838. They occupy about 4,377,000 acres in the south.]
Besides these 5 civilized tribes, Congress has from time to time located other tribes and fragments of tribes in this territory. INDIANS. Large sections of the territory being unoccupied, the Creek, Seminole, and other tribes cede lands to the U. S. which are incorporated into OKLAHOMA.

EDUCATION.

Cherokees spend $80,000 yearly in education. They have 2 high-schools, 110 common and 15 denominational schools; also 2 seminaries, one for girls and one for boys, at Tahlequah, where the higher branches are taught. Teachers mostly Indians. One newspaper, the *Advocate*, published partly in Cherokee.
Chickasaws have 14 common schools and 3 academies.
Creeks spend $80,000 in education, sending some young people to schools in the states, although they support 4 boarding-schools, 40 public schools, and several denominational schools. Indian university near Muscogee was founded by the Baptist Indians in 1880; there are also a Methodist and a Presbyterian school.
Choctaws.—Their school property is valued at $200,000; yearly educational expenses, $83,000; 4 boarding schools, 170 common, and several denominational schools. A newspaper published at Ataka.
Seminoles have 5 free schools, 3 mission schools, and one of the finest school buildings in the territory.

Indiana, one of the north central states of the United States, extends from the Ohio river, which separates the state from Kentucky on the south, to lake Michigan and the state of Michigan, which bound it on the north. Ohio lies to the east and Illinois bounds it on the west. It is limited in lat. by 37° 47′ to 41° 46′ N., and in lon. by 84° 49′ to 88° 2′ W. Area, 36,350 sq. miles in 92 counties. Pop. 1890, 2,192,404; 1900, 2,516,462. Capital, Indianapolis.

Robert Cavalier de la Salle and Henri Tonti with a party of 33, ascend the St. Joseph river to the site of South Bend, thence by portage to the Kankakee and down the Illinois river...Dec. 1679
La Salle, returning from Montreal with supplies for Tonti at fort Crevecœur, makes the portage from the St. Joseph to the Kankakee..Nov. 1680
Mention made of one Sieur Dubinson as commandant at a post near the site of Lafayette, called Ouiatenon......................1719
Sieur de Vincennes mentioned as commandant at the poste de Ouabache (Eng. Wabash), now Vincennes.......................1727
[Supposed to have been settled 1702.]
Mission established at post Vincennes by Sebastian L. Meurin, 1749
Garrison at Ouiatenon, under lieut. Jenkins, surrenders to Indians, who distribute the English prisoners among neighboring French traders.. 1763
On a proclamation by the British commandant, Edward Abbott, many inhabitants of post Vincennes swear allegiance to Great Britain..May, 1777
Inhabitants of Vincennes throw off allegiance to Great Britain and declare themselves citizens of the U. S., at the suggestion of col. Clark....................................18 July, 1778
Capt. Helm placed in charge of post Vincennes by col. Clark, and his garrison of 1 man surrenders, "with the honors of war," to British force under gov. Henry Hamilton...15 Dec. "
Gov. Hamilton surrenders Vincennes to the Americans under col. Clark..24 Feb. 1779
Court of civil and criminal jurisdiction organized at Vincennes, June, "
An expedition against Detroit organized by La Balme, a Frenchman of Kaskaskia, who plunders British traders at site of fort Wayne, is dispersed by an attack of Miami Indians, Sept. 1780
One hundred and fifty thousand acres of land in Indiana opposite the falls of the Ohio presented to col. George R. Clark and his regiment by Virginia legislature...3 Oct. 1779 and 5 Oct. "
Spaniards under capt. Eugenio Puerre march across Indiana from St. Louis, and capture fort St. Joseph.................. 1781
Indiana included in the Virginia act of cession, 20 Dec. 1783; deed conveying to the U. S. the territory northwest of the Ohio executed...1 Mch. 1784
Gen. Clark makes an unauthorized seizure of Spanish property at fort Vincennes, which he garrisons.............................. 1786
By resolution of Congress, the secretary of war is directed to order the commanding officer on the Ohio to dispossess "a body of men who had, in a lawless and unauthorized manner, taken possession of post Vincennes"...........24 Apr. 1787
Indiana part of Northwest territory, created by law....13 July, "
Maj.-gen. Arthur St. Clair elected by Congress governor of the territory northwest of the Ohio......................5 Oct. "
By act of Congress, 400 acres are granted to each person who, in 1783, was head of a family at Vincennes...........3 Mch. 1791
Brig.-gen. Scott, with 800 men, sent against Wea Indian towns on the Wabash, destroys Ouiatenon..................1 June, "
Second expedition against the Indian villages on the Wabash under brig.-gen. James Wilkinson, who leaves fort Washington 1 Aug. 1791, destroys the Eel river Indian village near Logansport, and over 400 acres of corn, and reaches the rapids of the Ohio..21 Aug. "
Treaty of peace and friendship with the Indians at Vincennes, by brig.-gen. Rufus Putnam........................27 Sept. 1792
FORT WAYNE, on the site of an ancient Miami village and an English fort erected 1764, built and garrisoned.......22 Oct. 1794
Northwestern territory divided: that part west of a line from the mouth of the Kentucky river to fort Recovery, and thence north to be called Indiana territory, and Vincennes the seat of government, by act approved.............7 May, 1800
William Henry Harrison, appointed governor of Indiana territory, 13 May, 1800, arrives at Vincennes.............10 Jan. 1801
General court of the territory first held, Vincennes......3 Mch. "
Town of Jeffersonville laid out on plan proposed by pres. Thomas Jefferson... 1802
Memorial to Congress by a convention called at Vincennes, 20 Dec. 1802, by gov. Harrison, 22 Nov., asks repeal of the VI. th Article of the Organic act, which prohibits slavery......... "
Congress establishes land offices at Kaskaskia, Vincennes, and Detroit...15 Mch. 1804
Western Sun, edited by Elihu Stout, first published at Vincennes as the *Indiana Gazette*.........................4 July, "
By treaty at Vincennes, the Delaware Indians cede to the U. S. land between the Wabash and Ohio rivers, and south of the road from Vincennes to the falls of the Ohio, 18 Aug., and the Piankeshaw Indians relinquish their claim to this territory..27 Aug. "
First general assembly of Indiana territory meets at Vincennes..29 July, 1805
Delaware, Pottawatomie, Miami, Eel River, and Wea Indians cede to the U. S. land in eastern Indiana, by treaty at Grouseland near Vincennes.......................................21 Aug. "
Laws of Indiana published at Vincennes by Messrs. Stout & Smoot.. 1807
Property qualification of 50 acres, or a town lot valued at $100, required of electors in territory by act of Congress...26 Feb. 1808
Illinois territory set off from Indiana, comprising all west of the Wabash river and a line drawn north from post Vincennes..3 Feb. 1809
By treaty at fort Wayne, 30 Sept. 1809, the Delaware, Pottawatomie, Miami, and Eel River tribes, cede to the U. S. about 2,900,000 acres south of the Wabash; treaty confirmed by the Weas, who meet gov. Harrison in council at Vincennes...26 Oct. "
"An act for the introduction of negroes and mulattoes into the territory of Indiana," approved 17 Sept. 1807; repealed, 4 Dec. 1810
Property qualification for voters abolished by Congress, 3 Mch. 1811
FORT HARRISON, on the Wabash, near the site of Terre Haute, completed..28 Oct. "
Battle of Tippecanoe; a sudden attack before sunrise of Indians under the Prophet, a brother of Tecumseh, on gen. Harrison's camp at Burnet's creek, about 7 miles northeast from Lafayette in Tippecanoe county. Loss to the Americans, 37 killed, 151 wounded. Indians defeated......7 Nov. "
Prophetstown, deserted by the Prophet, is destroyed together with a quantity of corn.................................8 Nov. 1811

IND

One *man* and 21 women and children massacred at the Pigeon Roost settlement, Scott county, by Shawnee Indians, 3 Sept. 1812

Night attack of Indians on fort Harrison successfully resisted by the garrison under capt. Zachary Taylor........4–5 Sept. "

FORT WAYNE *invested* by the Indians about 1 Sept., and the garrison relieved by 2000 Kentucky troops and 700 citizens of Ohio under *gen.* Harrison.........................12 Sept. "

Deserted Indian villages in the vicinity of fort Wayne destroyed by *detachments of troops*...............13–19 Sept. "

Expedition under lieut.-col. John B. Campbell leaves Dayton, O., 14 Dec. 1812; *burns the Indian villages* on the Mississinewa river...Dec. "

Seat of government fixed at Corydon, Harrison county, by act approved...11 Mch. 1813

Books, papers, and records destroyed by the *burning* of the office of the recorder of Knox county..................Jan. 1814

One thousand Miamis, reduced to destitution, assemble at *fort* Wayne to obtain food....................................Jan. "

Settlement of Harmony, on the Wabash, *50* miles from its mouth, formed by a German community under Frederick Rapp, from Pennsylvania (HARMONISTS, NEW HARMONY).... "

Farmers and Mechanics' bank of Indiana at Madison, incorporated by legislature.................................6 Sept. "

Bank of Vincennes incorporated........................10 Sept. "

Congress passes an enabling act for Indiana; the northern boundary a line drawn east and west 10 miles north of the southern extremity of lake Michigan..................19 Apr. 1816

Ordinance accepting the enabling act passed by a convention which met at Corydon, 10 June..........................29 June, "

State constitution adopted by convention............ " "

Jonathan Jennings inaugurated first governor at Corydon, 7 Nov. "

Indiana admitted into the Union by act approved.......11 Dec. "

Act to appoint superintendents of school sections authorized to lease school lands, every lessee required to set out 100 apple and *100 peach trees within 4 years*..............14 Dec. "

Bank of Vincennes adopted as state bank of Indiana, empowered to adopt *the Farmers and Mechanics'* bank of Indiana as one of its branches.................................1 Jan. 1817

Thomas Lincoln, the *father of Abraham Lincoln*, with his family, moves from Kentucky to what is now Spencer county.. "

By treaty at St. Mary's, O., the *Delaware* Indians cede to the U. S. all claims to land in Indiana.......................3 Oct. 1818

Site for capital of Indiana located by a committee, which met at the house of William Conner, on the west fork of the White river, 22 May, 1820, accepted and confirmed by the legislature, and the capital named Indianapolis ......6 Jan. 1821

First general school law of Indiana in revised statutes of 1824, drawn by committee appointed by legislature........9 Jan. "

Proceedings against the state bank for fraudulent management, which results in forfeiting its franchise, begun, 31 Dec. "

Southern state prison at Jeffersonville established............ 1822

Indiana university at Bloomington, chartered 1820, opened.... 1824

Mr. Rapp and associates sell their property at Harmony to Robert Dale Owen, of Scotland, a philanthropist, who attempts to establish a community, naming the place NEW HARMONY 1825

State road from lake Michigan to Madison on the Ohio, begun 1830

Thomas Lincoln, with his family, removes to Macon county, Ill... "

Indiana Historical Society incorporated....................... 1831

Hanover college, at Hanover, *opened* in 1828, chartered....... 1832

Wabash and Erie canal in Indiana, begun..............22 Feb. "

Wabash college at Crawfordsville, opened 1833, chartered..... 1834

Internal Improvement law, a state loan of $10,000,000 to be expended by a Board of Internal Improvement.........Jan. 1836

Madison and Lafayette railroad commenced.................. "

Indiana Asbury university (since 1884 *De Pauw*), at Greencastle, chartered and opened.............................. 1837

Indiana Institution for the Deaf and *Dumb*, at Indianapolis, opened.. 1844

University of Notre Dame (R. C.), at Notre Dame, chartered 1844, and opened.. 1845

State failing to pay its interest on the public debt for several years, compromises with creditors, who release one half of the indebtedness... 1846

Earlham college at Richmond opened......................... 1847

Fort Wayne college for women, at Fort Wayne, chartered and opened.. "

Indiana Institution for the Education of the Blind, at Indianapolis, opened...................................1 Oct. "

Central Insane hospital at Indianapolis opened..........Dec. 1848

Constitution, framed by a convention which met at Indianapolis, 7 Oct. 1850, adopted...............................10 Feb. 1851

New constitution, ratified by vote, 109,319 to 26,755, goes into operation..1 Nov. "

Butler university, at Irvington, chartered in 1850, opened..... 1855

Lieut.-gov. A. A. Hammond succeeds gov. Willard, who died at St. Paul, Minn...3 Oct. 1860

Gov. Lane elected U. S. senator; lieut.-gov. Morton succeeds, Jan. 1861

Caleb B. Smith appointed secretary of the interior.....5 Mch. "

Six regiments *raised and mustered* in within a week after the call of the president for troops, made................15 Apr. "

John P. Usher appointed secretary of the interior........8 Jan. 1863

Second Kentucky cavalry, confederate, capt. Hines, cross the Ohio at *Flint Rock*, *plunder* Leavenworth, Corydon, and Paoli, and retreat across the river..........................16 June, "

Confederates under Morgan cross the *Ohio* at Brandenburg, Ky., 8 July, pursued by federals under gen. Hobson. They move eastward, covering 700 miles in 20 days (MORGAN'S RAID)...July, 1863

Hugh McCulloch appointed secretary of the treasury...7 Mch. 1865

Law making colored people competent witnesses............ "

Indianapolis normal school opened............................ 1866

Convention of colored citizens of Indiana at Indianapolis to devise means to obtain full citizenship..................6 Nov. "

National convention of the Grand Army of the Republic held at Indianapolis.......................................20 Nov. "

Gov. Morton resigns, being elected U. S. senator, and is succeeded by lieut.-gov. Conrad Baker.........................Jan. 1867

Legislature ratifies the XIV.th Amendment to the Constitution, 29 Jan. "

Corner stone of the Soldiers' Home at Knightstown laid, 4 July, "

Indiana Reform School for Boys, at Plainfield, opened...1 Jan. 1868

Robbers of an express-car on the Jeffersonville railroad, 22 May, 1868, are arrested, and on their way to Jackson for trial the train is stopped by a so-called vigilance committee of Seymour, a confession extorted from the prisoners, who are hung, 20 July. 4 other prisoners lodged in jail at New Albany, are hung by 70 masked men.......................12 Dec. "

Legislature ratifies the XV.th Amendment to the Constitution, 13–14 May, 1869

State Woman's *Suffrage* convention at Indianapolis....8 June, "

State Normal school at Terre Haute opened..................... 1870

Seizing and hanging of *certain negroes* suspected of the murder of a family in Clark county, by a mob of disguised persons, calls forth a *proclamation from gov.* Baker, expressing his determination to suppress mob violence..............23 Nov. 1871

Indiana State Grange organized................................ 1872

Portion of the Northern state prison at Michigan City, in erection from 1863 to 1870, is *destroyed by fire*.......13 July, "

Amendment to the constitution, providing that "no law or resolution shall ever be passed that *shall recognize* any liability of this state to pay or redeem any certificate of stock" issued in 1846 for the completion of the Wabash and Erie canal, ratified..18 Feb. 1873

Second annual meeting of the National Congress of Agriculture at Indianapolis; 200 delegates from 25 states........28 May, "

Reform School for Girls and Woman's prison, at Indianapolis, opened..Sept. "

Jeffersonville depot of the quartermasters' department of the U. S. completed.. 1874

Purdue university, the land grant college of Indiana, at Lafayette, chartered 1862, opened................................ "

Commission appointed by the legislatures of Indiana and Kentucky, *governed* by the U. S. survey of 1806, determine that Green island, near Evansville, belongs to Kentucky.....July, 1875

James N. Tyner *postmaster*-general...................12 July, 1876

Richard W. Thompson secretary of the navy..........12 Mch. 1877

Office of *mine inspector* created by act of legislature.......... 1879

Indiana School for Feeble-minded Youth, at Richmond, opened, "

Corner-stone of *new state-house* at Indianapolis laid...28 Sept. 1880

Nine amendments to the state constitution adopted by the people. The 2d and 4th *making* the constitution conform to that of the U. S. as to the rights of colored citizens, 14 Mch. 1881

National convention of the Grand Army of the Republic held at Indianapolis.......................................15 June, "

Walter Q. Gresham postmaster-general....................3 Apr. 1883

Rose Polytechnic Institute, at Terre *Haute*, chartered in 1874, is opened.. "

Walter Q. Gresham secretary of the treasury.........24 Sept. 1884

Hugh McCulloch secretary of the treasury.............28 Oct. "

First Natural Gas company in Indiana chartered.......5 Mch. 1886

Evansville School for the Deaf opened......................... "

Indiana Normal college at Covington opened................. "

School for Feeble-minded Youth established at Fort Wayne by law... 1887

Legislature appropriates $200,000 for a soldiers and sailors' monument in Clyde park, Indianapolis........................ "

State Normal school at Terre Haute burned............9 Apr. 1888

Northern Insane hospital at Logansport opened................ "

Australian ballot system substantially adopted by law......... 1889

Offices of state geologist, mine inspector, and state inspector of oils abolished, and a department of geology and natural resources created... "

Secret organization of so-called White Caps in southern Illinois is investigated by the government of the state in 1888, and *a law passed to suppress riotous* conspiracy................. "

Hospital for the Insane, at Evansville, completed............ "

Eastern *Hospital for* the Insane, at Richmond, completed...... "

William H. Miller appointed attorney-general.........5 Mch. "

Marion *branch of the National* Soldiers' Home opened......... 1890

Monument to vice-pres. Hendricks unveiled at Indianapolis, 1 July, "

Supreme council of the Farmers' Alliance convenes at Indianapolis...17 Nov. 1891

Gov. Hovey dies at Indianapolis, 23 Nov.; lieut.-gov. Chase acting..Nov. "

State female reformatory destroyed by fire..............1 Mch. 1892

John W. Foster, secretary of state.......................29 June, "

Burial of the wife of pres. Harrison at Indianapolis.....28 Oct. "

Popular welcome at Indianapolis to ex-pres. Harrison on his arrival at the close of his administration.............6 Mch. 1893

GOVERNORS—TERRITORIAL.

William Henry Harrison........appointed.............13 May, 1800

John Gibson....................acting......................... 1812

Thomas Posey.................appointed...............3 Mch. 1813

GOVERNORS—STATE.

Jonathan Jennings............assumes office..........7 Nov. 1816
William Hendricks............ " " ....4 Dec. 1822
James B. Ray.................. " " ....12 Feb. 1825
Noah Noble.................... " " ....7 Dec. 1831
David Wallace................. " " ....6 Dec. 1837
Samuel Bigger................. " " ....9 Dec. 1840
James Whitcomb................ " " ....6 Dec. 1843
Joseph A. Wright.............. " " ....6 Dec. 1849
Ashbel P. Willard............. " " ....12 Jan. 1857
Abraham A. Hammond........assumes office............Oct. 1860
Henry S. Lane...............elected U. S. senator......Jan. 1861
Oliver P. Morton............assumes office............ " "
Conrad Baker................ " " .... " 1867
Thomas A. Hendricks......... " " .... " 1873
James D. Williams........... " " .... " 1877
Albert G. Porter............ " " .... " 1881
Isaac P. Gray............... " " .... " 1885
Alvin P. Hovey.............. (d. in office) .... " 1889
Ira J. Chase, lieut.-gov.........acting..................Nov. 1891
Claude Matthews.............assumes office............Jan. 1893

UNITED STATES SENATORS FROM THE STATE OF INDIANA.

Name.	No. of Congress.	Date.	Remarks.
James Noble	14th to 22d	1816 to 1831	Seated 12 Dec. 1816. Died 26 Feb. 1831.
Waller Taylor	14th " 19th	1816 " 1825	Seated 12 Dec. 1816.
William Hendricks	19th " 24th	1825 " 1837	
Robert Hanna	22d	1831 " 1832	Appointed in place of Noble, 1831.
John Tipton	22d to 25th	1832 " 1837	Elected in place of Noble.
Oliver H. Smith	25th " 27th	1837 " 1843	
Albert S. White	26th " 28th	1839 " 1844	
Edward A. Hannegan	28th " 30th	1843 " 1849	
Jesse D. Bright	29th " 37th	1845 " 1861	Seated 27 Dec. 1845. President *pro tem.* 5 Dec. 1854, 11 June, 1856, and again 12 June, 1860. Expelled from the Senate, 5 Feb. 1861, as a secessionist.
James Whitcomb	31st " 32d	1849 " 1852	Died 4 Oct. 1852.
Charles W. Cathcart	32d	1852 " 1853	Appointed in place of Whitcomb.
John Petit	32d to 33d	1853 " 1855	Elected in place of Whitcomb.
Graham N. Fitch	34th " 36th	1857 " 1860	Seated 9 Feb. 1857.
Henry S. Lane	37th " 39th	1861 " 1867	
Joseph A. Wright	37th	1861 " 1862	Appointed in place of Bright. Seated 3 Mch. 1861.
David Turpie	37th	1863	Elected in place of Bright. Seated 22 Jan. 1863.
Thomas A. Hendricks	38th to 40th	1863 to 1867	Nominated for vice-president by the Democratic party, 1876, and again in 1884.
Oliver P. Morton	40th " 45th	1867 " 1877	Died 1 Nov. 1877.
Daniel D Pratt	41st " 43d	1869 " 1875	
Joseph E. McDonald	44th " 46th	1875 " 1881	
Daniel W. Voorhees	45th " —	1877 " —	Term expires 1897.
Benjamin Harrison	47th " 49th	1881 " 1888	Elected president of the U. S., 1889–93.
David Turpie	50th " —	1888 " —	Term expires 1899.

Indians, the aboriginal inhabitants of America. So called by Columbus, who supposed he had discovered the eastern shores of India. The following remarks and tables refer to Indians within the present area of the United States. In manners, customs, and general features the difference between the Indians of the Gulf states and those of the shores of the northern lakes is scarcely perceptible; it is only by languages that they can be grouped into great families. East of the Mississippi there were not more than 8 radically distinct languages, 4 of which are still in existence, while the others have disappeared.

NAMES AND LOCATION OF THE PRINCIPAL TRIBES OF THE 8 GREAT FAMILIES IN THE PRESENT AREA OF THE UNITED STATES EAST OF THE MISSISSIPPI, AT THE TIME OF THE FIRST SETTLEMENTS.

Name.	Location.
I. *Algonquin tribes:*	
Micmacs	East of the state of Maine.
Etchemins or Canoemen	Maine.
Abenakis	New Hampshire and Maine.
Narragansetts; Pokanokets or Wampanoags	E. Massachusetts and Rhode Island.
Pequots	Central Massachusetts and Rhode Island.
Mohegans	W. Massachusetts and Connecticut.
Delawares or Lenni Lenape	New Jersey, the valley of the Delaware and Schuylkill.
Nanticokes	Eastern shores of Chesapeake bay.
Powhatan Confederacy	E. Virginia and Maryland.
Corees	E. North Carolina.
Shawnees	South of the Ohio, W. Kentucky, and Tennessee.
Miamis	S. Michigan, N. Indiana, and N.W. Ohio.
Illinois	S. Illinois and Indiana.
Kickapoos	N. and central Illinois.
Pottawatomies	N. Illinois.
Ottawas	Michigan.
Sacs and Foxes	N. Wisconsin.
Menomonees	Southern shore of lake Superior.
Chippewas or Ojibways	" " " "
II. *Wyandot or Huron-Iroquois tribes:*	
Eries (Huron or Wyandot-Iroquois)	Southern shore of lake Erie.
Andastes (Huron or Wyandot-Iroquois)	Head-waters of the Ohio.
Wyandots (Huron or Wyandot-Iroquois)	Territory north of lakes Erie and Ontario.
Senecas (Iroquois proper)	W. New York. LONG HOUSE.
Cayugas " "	Central New York.
Onondagas " "	" " "
Oneidas " "	E. New York.
Mohawks " "	" " "

NAMES AND LOCATION OF THE PRINCIPAL TRIBES OF THE 8 GREAT FAMILIES, ETC.—(*Continued.*)

Name.	Location.
Tuscaroras (Iroquois proper)	S.W. Virginia and North Carolina. Join the Iroquois of New York, 1713.
Chowans (Huron or Wyandot-Iroquois)	S. Virginia.
Meherrins (Huron or Wyandot-Iroquois)	"
Nottaways (Huron or Wyandot-Iroquois)	"
III. *Catawbas*	W. North and South Carolina.
IV. *Cherokees*	Mountainous regions of Tennessee, Georgia, North and South Carolina.
V. *Uchees*	About Augusta, Ga.
VI. *Natchez*	N. W. Mississippi.
VII. *Mobilian or Muskhogees:*	
Chickasaws	W. Tennessee and N. Mississippi.
Choctaws	E. Mississippi and W. Alabama.
Creeks or Muskhogees	Alabama and Georgia.
Seminoles	Florida.
VIII. *Winnebagoes*	About Green Bay, Wis.

PRINCIPAL TRIBES WEST OF THE MISSISSIPPI IN 1800–30.

Name.	Location.
Dakotas (Sioux)	Wisconsin, west to Rocky mts.
Arapahoes	Wyoming, head-waters of Platte.
Cheyennes	Wyoming and Nebraska.
Kansas	Kansas, west.
Poncas	Dakota.
Omahas	Nebraska.
Mandans	Montana.
Assiniboins	Montana and Dakota.
Minnetaries (Gros Ventres)	Montana.
Missouris	Lower Missouri.
Iowas	Iowa.
Osages	Kansas, west.
Crows	Dakota.
Kaws	Kansas.
Pawnees	Kansas and Nebraska.
Caddos	Red river and Arkansas.
Shoshones or Snakes	Kansas to Oregon.
Kiowas	Kansas, west.
Utes	Utah and Colorado.
Comanches	Texas and New Mexico.
Apaches	New Mexico and Arizona.
Navajos and Mosquis	Arizona.
Yumas	Arizona and California.
Pueblos	Nevada and New Mexico.
Pimas	Arizona.
Bannocks	Idaho and Oregon.
Modocs	Nevada and Oregon.
Nez Percés	" "
Flatheads	California, Oregon, and Nevada.
Klamaths	Oregon and N. California.

SITUATION, NUMBERS, AND TRIBES OF INDIANS WITHIN THE UNITED STATES IN 1893.

State.	Tribe.	Number.
Maine	Penobscot Passamaquoddy	385 525
Massachusetts		145
Connecticut		24
New York reservations:		
Alleghany	Mostly Senecas	955
Cattaraugus	" "	1,574
Tonawanda	" "	561
Tuscarora	Tuscaroras	455
St. Regis	St. Regis	1,058
Onondaga	Onondagas	469
Oneida	Oneidas	237
North Carolina, Tennessee, and Georgia	Cherokees	2,885 mostly in North Carolina.
Florida	Seminoles, transferred Apaches	269
Indiana	Miamis	71
Michigan	Ottawas, Chippewas, and Pottawatomies	6,991 not on reservation.
Mississippi		1,404 " "
Louisiana		132 " "
Wisconsin	Munsees, Oneidas (from New York), Chippewas, Menomones, and Stockbridge (from Massachusetts)	7,915 on reservation. 981 off "
Iowa	Sacs and Foxes	397
Minnesota	Chippewas mostly	6,263 on reservation. 802 off "
Nebraska	Winnebagoes, Poncas, Omahas, and Pawnees	3,751 on " 113 off "
Kansas	Munsees, Miamis, Kansas or Kaws, Kickapoos, Pottawatomies, and Chippewas	1,016 on " 421 off "
North and South Dakota	Sioux, Poncas, Arickarees, Gros Ventres, and Mandans	26,880 on " 917 off "
Montana	Blackfeet, Blood, Peigan, Assiniboins, Gros Ventres, Crows, Flatheads, Shoshones, Bannocks, and Roving Sioux	10,336 on " 237 off "
Wyoming	Shoshones and Arapahoes	1,806 on "
Idaho	Nez Percés, Bannocks, and Shoshones	3,640 on " 269 off "
Colorado	Utes	985 on " 49 off "
Nevada	Utes, Shoshones, and Bannocks	1,552 on " 3,404 off "
Washington	Cœur d'Aline, Spokane, Yakama, and others	7,938 on " 2,899 off "
Oregon	Klamaths, Walla-Wallas, Shoshones, and others	3,708 on " 574 off "
California	Yumas, Klamaths, and others	5,020 on " 10,263 off "
Utah	Utes	1,854 on " 635 off "
New Mexico	Pueblos Navajos, Apaches, and Utes	8,278 citizens. 20,521 on reservation.
Arizona	Pimas, Yumas, and Apaches	15,414 on " 1,326 off "
Oklahoma	Pottawatomies, Sacs and Foxes, Osages, Kansas, Pawnees, Poncas, Otoes, and Missouris	5,689 on "
Indian Territory	The five civilized tribes: Cherokees 25,357; Chickasaws 4,625; Choctaws 10,253; Creeks 9,291; Seminoles 2,539	52,065
	Colored population and claimants	14,224
	Cheyennes, Arapahoes, Apaches, Kiowas, Comanches, Wichitas, Delawares, Caddos, Shawnees, Miamis, Modocs, Ottawas, Peorias, Quapaws, Senecas, Cayugas, Wyandots	8,708 on reservations.
Indians in prison, etc.		288
	Total	249,273

indiction, a cycle of tributes of corn demanded every 15 years, not known before Constantine. The first examples in the Theodosian code are of the reign of Constantius, who died 361.—In memory of Constantine's victory over Mezentius, 8 Cal. Oct. 312, the council of Nice ordained that years should be no longer reckoned by Olympiads, but by the indiction, dating from 1 Jan. 313. It was first used by the Latin church in 342.

in'digo, a dye from the woad plant, *Isatis tinctoria*, used by the Egyptians and other ancient nations; the processes are described by Pliny. After the passage of the Cape of Good Hope, in 1497, it was gradually superseded by Eastern indigo, from the *indigofera*. Indigo is named in English statutes in 1581. Its cultivation began in South Carolina in 1743.

After long experiments, especially by prof. A. Baeyer, the dye has been prepared artificially from coal-tar. . . . 1869–80
Prof. H. E. Roscoe, at the Royal institution, London, demonstrates identity of artificial and natural indigo. . . . 27 May, 1881

indirect claims. ALABAMA CLAIMS.

in'dium, a metal discovered in arsenical pyrites of Freiburg, by F. Reich and T. Richter in 1863; named from giving an indigo-blue ray in its spectrum.

induction of electric currents, discovered by Faraday, announced in his "Experimental Researches," in 1831–32. Ruhmkorff's magneto-electric induction coil constructed in 1850. ELECTRICITY.

inductive philosophy, based on observations and experiments, really common-sense, is expounded by Bacon in "Novum Organum," pub. 1620, Book II. The term philosophy, which is more correctly applied to the investigation of mental and spiritual truth, has been loosely bestowed on this method. The senses are never philosophic. PHILOSOPHY.

indulgences, in the early church, were the moderation of ecclesiastical punishment. Papal grants of absolute pardon of sin, commenced by Leo III. about 800, were granted in the 11th century by Gregory VII., and by Urban II. and by others in the 12th century, as rewards to the crusaders. Clement V. was the first pope who made public sale of indulgences, 1313. In 1517 Leo X. published general indulgences, and resistance to them led to the Reformation

industrial exhibitions. EXHIBITIONS, FAIRS

infallibility of the pope, in regard to faith and morals, was decreed by the Vatican council, and promulgated 18 July, 1870 Extensive opposition to the doctrine in Germany led to the constitution of the church named "OLD CATHOLICS" Mr Gladstone's pamphlets, 'The Vatican Decrees in their Bearing on Civil Allegiance,' pub Nov 1874, and "Vaticanism," Feb 1875

infant schools. KINDERGARTENS

infantry, foot-soldiers, their organization much improved during the wars of Charles V and Francis I, in the 16th century The British army comprises 109 regiments, now merged into line battalions with a rifle brigade For the United Kingdom 1891, 69,274 men For the United States, 25 regiments, 13,002 men ARMY

infirmaries. Ancient Rome had no houses for the cure of the sick, diseased persons were carried to the temple of Æsculapius for cure Institutions for the accommodation of travellers, the indigent, and sick were founded by the emperor Julian about 362, and infirmaries or hospitals were frequently added to cathedrals and monasteries The emperor Louis II caused infirmaries on mountains to be visited, 855 In Jerusalem knights and brothers attended the sick There were hospitals for the sick at Constantinople in the 11th century Physicians and surgeons in infirmaries are first mentioned 1437 —*Beckmann.* HOSPITALS

influenza, a name given in Italy about 1741 to an epidemic febrile catarrh with variations, probably known to the ancients

It prevailed in Europe in 1510 and has since frequently appeared, generally commencing in Russia and thence spreading over the continent It appeared in Britain in 1762 and frequently since, especially in 1830-31, 1833 1836-37, and 1847 It appeared at Paris in 1866-67, and at Berlin 1874-75 In Oct 1889, it was severe at St Petersburg, and thence spread over Europe, reaching Great Britain, Canada and the U S, Jan 1890, causing indirectly the death of several eminent persons. In the spring the disease was severe in India and Australia In 1891 the disease was severe in the west of the U S and in London and other parts of England, and also on the continent The disease reappeared in Jan 1892, in much the same localities In London the general mortality was much increased, all classes being attacked The death of the duke of Clarence and Avondale, 14 Jan 1892, was attributed to pneumonia following influenza Report of the epidemic of 1889-1890, by dr Parsons issued by British government, about 3 July, 1891 Special government inquiry into the disease ordered in England, early Feb 1892

infuso'ria. ANIMALCULES

ink. The ancient black inks were made of soot and ivory-black (Vitruvius and Pliny mention lamp-black), but they had ink of various colors, as red, gold, silver, and purple Red ink was made of vermilion and gum Indian-ink was brought from China, and must have been in use by the people of the east from the earliest ages Invisible or sympathetic inks were early known Ovid (2 A D) teaches young women to write with new milk Receipts for invisible ink were given by Peter Borel in 1653, and by Le Mort in 1669 —*Beckmann.*

Ink'erman, a village and seaport in the Crimea. The Russian army (about 40,000) reinforced and encouraged by the presence of grand-dukes Michael and Nicholas, attacked the British (8000) near the old fort of Inkerman, before daybreak, 5 Nov 1854 They were kept at bay 6 hours till the arrival of 6000 French, and then repulsed, leaving 9000 killed and wounded The allies lost 462 killed, 1952 wounded, and 191 missing Sir George Cathcart, and gens. Strangways, Goldie, and Torrens, were among the slain

Innocents' Day, 28 Dec. in the Western church, 29 Dec in the Greek or Eastern church.

inns or **houses** for the lodgement and entertainment of travellers, at Rome, were regulated by laws. Edward III enacted that they should be subjected to inquiry, 1353

"Now spurs the lated traveller apace
To gain the timely inn"
—*Shakespeare,* "Macbeth," act iii sc. iii.

"One autumn night, in Sudbury town,
Across the meadows bare and brown
The windows of the wayside inn
Gleamed red with fire light through the leaves
Of woodbine hanging from the eaves,
Their crimson curtains rent and thin"
—*Longfellow,* "Wayside Inn," Prelude

TAVERNS

inns of court, London, were established at different periods, in some degree as colleges for teaching the law. Annual revenue in 1872 said to be about 25,000*l.*

"*Shallow* He is at Oxford still, is he not?"
"*Silence* Indeed sir to my cost."
"*Shallow* He must then to the inns of court shortly I was once of Clement's inn, ' etc
—*Shakespeare,* "2 Henry IV," act iii sc. ii

Temple founded, church built by Knights Templars.	1185
Lincoln's inn, 4 Edw II	1310 or 1312
Clifford's inn, 20 Edw III.	1345
Gray's inn, 32 Edw III	1357
Staples' inn, 4 Hen V	1415
Lyon's inn	1420
Sergeants' inn, Fleet street.	1429
Barnard's inn, an inn of chancery	1445
Clement's inn, 18 Edw IV	1478
New inn, 1 Hen VII	1485
Thavies's inn, 10 Hen VIII	1519
Inner and Middle Temple made inns of law about 1340, Outer about (*Stow*)	1560
Furnival's inn, 5 Eliz	1563
Sergeants' inn, Chancery lane (sold for 57 000*l*, 23 Feb 1877)	1666

inoculation. The communication of a disease to a person by inserting contagious matter in his skin or flesh Inoculation with the small-pox was introduced into England from Turkey by lady Mary Wortley Montagu In 1718 she had her son inoculated at Adrianople with success She was allowed to have it first tried in England on 7 condemned criminals, 1721, and in 1722 2 of the royal family were inoculated. The practice was preached against by many of the bishops and clergy until 1760 Dr Mead inoculated successfully up to 1754, and dr Dimsdale of London inoculated Catherine II, empress of Russia, in 1768 Of 5964 inoculated in 1797-99 only 3 died An inoculation hospital was established in 1746. *Vaccine* inoculation, called VACCINATION, was introduced by dr Jenner, 21 Jan 1799, he discovered its virtue in 1796, and experimented on it for 3 years Inoculation in Great Britain was forbidden by law in 1840 First introduced into America in Boston, Mass, about 1721 through the influence of dr Cotton Mather. First inoculation in the family of dr Zabdiel Boylston. It was denounced by the clergy and by many physicians MEDICAL SCIENCE, SMALL-POX.

inquests. CORONERS.

Inquisition, or **holy office.** Before Constantine (306) heresy and spiritual offences were punished by excommunication only, but soon after his death capital punishments were added, and inquisitors were appointed by Theodosius, 382 Priscillian was put to death in 384 Justinian decreed the doctrine of the 4 holy synods as to the Scriptures and their canons to be observed as laws, 529; hence the penal code against heretics. About 800 the power of Western bishops was enlarged, and courts were established to try and punish spiritual offenders, even with death, the punishment being termed in Spain *auto da-fé,* "an act of faith." In the 12th century many heresies arose, and during crusades against the Albigenses, Gregory IX in 1233 established rules for inquisitorial missions sent out by Innocent III, 1210-15, and committed them to the Dominicans. Pietro da Verona (Peter Martyr) the first inquisitor who burned heretics, assassinated by an accused gonfalonier, 6 Apr. 1252, was canonized

Pierre de Castelnan sent against the Albigenses, 1210, St. Dominic, first inquisitor general	1215
Inquisition constituted by Gregory IX, 1233, in Aragon, 1233, Venice, 1249, France, 1255, Castile	1290
Inquisition revived by a bull 1 Nov	1478
Holy office reinstituted in Spain by Ferdinand and Isabella, Torquemada inquisitor general	1480
Nearly 3000 persons burned in Andalusia, and 17,000 suffer other penalties	1481

"Instructions" of new tribunal promulgated.........29 Nov. 1484
New articles added.................................1488 and 1498
Established in Portugal.. 1520
Resisted in Naples; permitted elsewhere in Italy under restrictions by the temporal power.........................1546–47
New ordinances in 81 articles compiled by inquisitor-general Valdez.. 1561
Suppressed in France by edict of Nantes.................... 1598
Carnesecchi executed at Rome, 1567; Galileo called to Rome and admonished not thenceforward to "hold, teach, or defend" the doctrine condemned by the church, "that the sun is the centre of the solar system, and that the earth has a diurnal motion of rotation," 1616; compelled to abjure these views and read his recantation of them in the church of Santa Maria, Rome..22 June, 1633
Louis XIV. revokes edict of Nantes, but refuses to introduce the Inquisition.. 1685
Twenty persons perish at an *auto-da-fé* at Goa................ 1717
Gabriel Malagrida, a Jesuit, burned at Lisbon................. 1761
A woman accused of contract with the devil burned at Seville..7 Nov. 1781
Tribunal abolished in Tuscany and Lombardy.................. 1787
Suppressed in Spain by Napoleon, 4 Dec. 1808, and by the Cortes..12 Feb. 1813
Restored by Ferdinand VII..........................21 July, 1814
Finally abolished by Cortes...................................... 1820

[Llorente reckons about 32,000 persons put to death in Spain by the Inquisition in 236 years; 291,000 otherwise punished.]

insanity (defined by sir William Hamilton as "the paralysis of the regulating or legislating faculties of the mind"), in 1000 male patients, has been traced to—

Drunkenness	110	Accidents	39
Consequences of disease	100	Religious enthusiasm	29
Epilepsy	78	Unnatural practices	27
Ambition	78	Political events	26
Excessive labor	73	Poisonous effluvia	17
Born idiots	71	Ill-usage	12
Misfortunes	69	Crimes, remorse, and despair	9
Old age	69	Malformation of the skull	4
Chagrin	54	Unknown causes	88
Love	47	Pretended insanity	5

"The king shall have the custody of the lands of natural fools," etc., 17 Edw. II.. 1324
Marriages with lunatics declared void, 15 Geo. II. c. 30........ 1742
Act regarding criminal lunatics passed.....................Aug. 1840
Numerous laws respecting lunatics consolidated and amended by 16 and 17 Vict., cc. 70, 96, 97................................ 1853
A new lunacy act for Scotland passed......................... 1858
Law for commissions of lunacy amended (after the Wyndham case. TRIALS, 1862)... 1862

TREATMENT OF THE INSANE IN GREAT BRITAIN.

Earliest notice of lunatics having been received at Bethlem... 1403
Forty-four lunatics were maintained at Bethlem............... 1644
Till about 1800 lunatics were treated with cruelty. See Conolly "On the Treatment of the Insane," 1856.
Insane at Bethlem made a show for 1*d.* or 2*d.* till............ 1770
Enlightened treatment introduced by William Tuke at Society of Friends' "Retreat," at York, and by Pinel, at the Bicêtre, Paris, with success.. 1792
Esquirol succeeds Pinel, and recommends instruction in management of mental disorders................................... 1810
Exposure of cruelties in the Bethlem hospital................ 1815
Gradual improvements, and total abolition of mechanical restraints at Lincoln, 1837, and at Hanwell Asylum (under dr. John Conolly) and other places................................ 1839
Psychological Journal issued by dr. Forbes Winslow.......... 1848
Journal of Mental Science, by dr. J. C. Bucknill.............. 1852
HOSPITALS.

PERSONS OF UNSOUND MIND, LUNATICS, IDIOTS, ETC., IN ENGLAND AND WALES.

1 Jan.		Registered.
1860		38,058
1870		54,713
1878	Male lunatics	31,024
	Female lunatics	37,514
1880		71,191

Until 1840 the insane poor in the United States were cared for almost exclusively by the township and county authorities. It was estimated that in 1833 there were 2500 lunatics in jails and other prisons, besides hundreds in the county poor-houses and private families. One of the very earliest asylums for the insane was that opened in 1797 at Bloomingdale in the suburbs of New York city, by the New York Hospital Society. To the labors of Miss Dorothea L. Dix (b. Worcester, Mass., about 1802; d. Trenton, N. J., 1887), is largely due the establishment of state asylums. Miss Dix devoted herself after 1837 to the investigation of the subject, and visited every state east of the Rocky mountains, appealing to the state legislatures to provide for the care of the insane. In Apr. 1854, a bill appropriating 10,000,000 acres of public lands to the several states for the relief of the pauper insane, passed by Congress under her appeals, was vetoed by pres. Pierce. VETOES. Her efforts, however, led to the establishment of state insane asylums, and it is now recognized as the duty of each state to care for its insane. New York state has 15 corporate institutions of this class. The following statistics show the number of insane, etc., in the U. S. Until 1850 there are no reliable statistics:

Year	Population of U. S.	No. of insane.	To each million of inhabitants.
1850	21,191,876	15,610	673
1860	31,443,321	24,642	783
1870	38,558,371	37,432	971
1880	50,155,783	91,997	1834
1890	62,622,250	106,252	1697

insects. About 400,000 species known, 1881. An exhibition, illustrating their structure, food, and habits, opened in Tuileries gardens at Paris, 7 Sept. 1874; in England, at the Westminster aquarium, 9 Mch. 1878, and in the Zoological gardens, Regent's park, 1881. ENTOMOLOGY.

insolvency. The first insolvent act was passed in 1649, of limited operation; acts more extensive were passed later, particularly in the reign of George III. The benefit of the Great Insolvent act was taken in England by 50,733 insolvents from its passage in 1814 to Mch. 1827. Since then these acts have been several times amended. Persons not traders, or traders whose debts are less than 300*l.*, might petition the court of bankruptcy, and propose compositions, and have *pro tem.* protection from process against their persons and property, by 1 Vict. c. 116 (1842). In 1861, by a new bankruptcy act, the business of the insolvent debtors' court was transferred to the court of bankruptcy; and a number of imprisoned debtors were released in Nov. 1861.—In May, 1837, a commercial crisis occurred in the United States. Failures to the amount of more than $100,000,000 occurred. Banks generally suspended specie payment. A general bankrupt law was passed by Congress, 9 Aug. 1841. Another crisis occurred in 1857. The banks throughout the U. S. suspended specie payment, but soon resumed. During the civil war of 1861–65 the banks suspended specie payment, but resumed 1 Jan. 1879. CRISIS.

Institute of France. On 25 Oct. 1795, all royal academies—viz., the French Academy, the Academy of Inscriptions and Belles-lettres, that of mathematical and physical sciences, of fine arts, and of moral and political sciences—were combined in one "Institut National," afterwards Royal, Imperial, and now National. ACADEMIES, IMMORTALS, PARIS.

insurance. The object of insurance is to indemnify the insured to the extent of the agreement for losses which may be incurred from causes beyond his control. Its chief branches are accident, fire, life, and marine, and of late hail, wind or tornado insurance. Suetonius conjectures that Claudius, the Roman emperor, was the first contriver of the insurance of ships, 43 A.D.

Insurance in use in Italy, 1194, and in England................ 1560
Insurance policies first used in Florence....................... 1523
First law of insurance in Britain enacted...................... 1601
Insurance against fire, in London, began the year after the great fire of London... 1667
Office for insuring buildings opened, chiefly on the plan of dr. Barton, one of the first great builders of London........ "
First regular office in London, the Hand-in-Hand.............. 1696
Sun fire-office established..................................... 1710
Union second fire-office in England............................ 1714
First marine insurance the Royal Exchange and the London Insurance.. 1720
First fire-office in Scotland.................................... "
In Germany, 1750; in France, 1816; and in Russia............ 1827

Insurance, fire, marine, etc., in the United States. First insurance in the Colonies was at Boston by the Sun (English), 1728. Some insurance done in Philadelphia in 1752. First fire-insurance policy issued in the United States at Hartford, Conn., 1794, under the unofficial title of "Hartford Fire-Insurance Co." 16 years after, in 1810, the Hartford Fire-Insurance Co. was organized. From 1801–10 there were 60 charters issued; 1811–20, 43; 1821–30, 149; 1831–40, 467; 1841–50, 401; 1851–60, 896; 1861–70, 1041.

INCREASE OF FIRE, MARINE, AND TORNADO INSURANCE IN THE UNITED STATES SHOWN BY A COMPARISON OF THE YEAR 1880 WITH 1889.

		Number of companies.	Risks written and renewed.	Premiums and assessments received in cash.	Losses paid in cash.	Average amount of losses paid to each dollar of premium received.	Kind of insurance.
Alabama.......	1880..	47	$40,219,820	$486,703	$312,181	0.6414	41 Fire, 2 O. Marine, 4 I. Marine.
	1889..	81	68,429,106	966,425	312,651	0.3235	73 “ 3 “ 5 “
Arkansas......	1880..	26	10,191,665	204,546	51,788	0.2532	23 “ 2 I. Marine, 1 Tornado.
	1889..	71	30,495,143	636,690	296,740	0.4661	67 “ 2 “ 2 “
California......	1880..	130	309,266,249	4,396,883	1,555,279	0.3537	96 “ 32 O. Marine, 2 I. Marine.
	1889..	172	516,282,686	7,919,878	3,908,600	0.4935	124 “ 46 “ 2 “
Colorado.......	1880..	44	17,330,798	282,481	104,151	0.3687	43 “ 1 Tornado.
	1889..	130	75,329,774	1,321,096	554,624	0.4198	129 “ 1 “
Connecticut....	1880..	135	166,796,209	1,494,121	673,969	0.4511	134 “ 1 O. Marine.
	1889..	144	244,732,602	2,257,657	990,547	0.4467	139 “ 3 “ 2 I. Marine.
North and South Dakotas.....	1880..	39	6,113,903	111,074	29,773	0.2680	38 “ 1 Tornado.
	1889..	80	40,137,434	846,640	488,192	0.5766	76 “ 4 “
Delaware......	1880..	61	29,614,399	145,122	95,755	0.6598	58 “ 1 O. Marine, 2 I. Marine.
	1889..	77	46,043,696	234,647	140,860	0.6003	76 “ 1 Tornado.
District of Columbia......	1880..	65	45,583,365	230,032	80,312	0.3491	64 “ 1 O. Marine.
	1889..	126	85,911,641	434,520	83,060	0.1912	124 “ 1 “ 1 Tornado.
Florida........	1880..	20	6,846,921	99,013	149,286	1.5077	19 “ 1 I. Marine.
	1889..	41	22,861,420	410,817	286,657	0.6978	40 “ 1 “
Georgia........	1880..	46	89,176,709	904,605	393,319	0.4348	45 “ 1 O. Marine.
	1889..	72	140,826,192	1,706,650	1,372,703	0.8043	67 “ 4 “ 1 Tornado.
Idaho..........	1880..	9	219,627	5,001	186	0.0372	9 “
	1889..	43	2,522,173	72,009	117,770	1.6355	43 “
Illinois.........	1880..	344	607,608,550	6,302,741	2,203,691	0.3496	320 “ 1 O. Marine, 22 I. Marine, 1 Tor.
	1889..	436	905,469,110	9,850,539	4,758,078	0.4830	406 “ 4 “ 20 “ 6 “
Indiana........	1880..	147	137,939,059	1,605,479	804,644	0.5012	142 “ 1 “ 4 “
	1889..	178	222,378,423	2,774,638	1,555,981	0.5608	168 “ 1 “ 3 “ 6 Tor.
Iowa...........	1880..	181	141,496,566	1,885,903	772,303	0.4095	176 “ 4 I. Marine, 1 Tornado.
	1889..	268	240,521,193	3,589,398	1,613,872	0.4496	257 “ 1 O. Marine, 2 I. Marine, 8 Tor.
Kansas........	1880..	61	44,677,100	671,024	261,798	0.3901	59 “ 1 I. Marine, 1 Tornado.
	1889..	119	140,955,028	1,983,611	1,108,685	0.5589	112 “ 1 “ 6 “
Kentucky......	1880..	120	111,701,347	1,328,570	621,082	0.4675	111 “ 9 “
	1889..	144	183,239,656	2,377,975	1,912,759	0.8044	135 “ 5 “ 4 Tornado.
Louisiana......	1880..	68	335,674,073	3,171,888	1,171,703	0.3694	42 “ 12 O. Marine, 14 I. Marine.
	1889..	122	320,034,632	2,803,374	1,063,003	0.3792	92 “ 15 “ 14 “ 1 Tor.
Maine.........	1880..	135	85,861,024	1,190,582	732,139	0.6149	126 “ 9 “
	1889..	147	115,045,506	1,724,124	900,637	0.5224	139 “ 8 “
Maryland......	1880..	159	296,360,062	1,833,139	986,652	0.5382	149 “ 9 “ 1 I. Marine.
	1889..	180	260,502,950	1,964,843	1,006,026	0.5120	164 “ 14 “ 1 “ 1 Tor.
Massachusetts..	1880..	222	883,893,466	9,089,434	5,450,067	0.5996	196 “ 24 “ 2 “
	1889..	245	1,125,781,420	11,411,928	10,417,399	0.9129	221 “ 23 “ 1 “
Michigan.......	1880..	194	202,614,931	2,292,695	1,019,564	0.4447	175 “ 1 “ 18 “
	1889..	238	291,945,425	4,325,422	2,042,667	0.4722	221 “ 2 “ 12 “ 3 Tor.
Minnesota......	1880..	135	110,552,224	1,303,925	1,340,304	1.0279	128 “ 1 “ 5 “ 1 “
	1889.	281	245,578,295	3,471,266	1,722,863	0.4962	261 “ 1 “ 15 “ 4 “
Mississippi.....	1880..	9	13,016,985	249,615	89,940	0.3603	9 “
	1889..	37	38,801,862	684,569	356,348	0.5205	33 “ 2 O. Marine, 1 I. Marine, 1 Tor.
Missouri.......	1880..	187	296,389,697	3,053,891	1,702,529	0.5575	163 “ 1 “ 22 “ 1 “
	1889..	235	396,644,927	4,793,341	3,014,298	0.6289	215 “ 2 “ 12 “ 6 “
Montana.......	1880..	13	1,626,682	29,018	7,506	0.2509	13 “
	1889..	66	19,982,848	489,720	294,478	0.6013	66 “
Nebraska......	1880..	66	25,830,246	430,709	336,082	0.9803	65 “ 1 Tornado.
	1889..	148	113,426,886	1,779,019	832,535	0.4680	140 “ 1 I. Marine, 7 Tornado.
Nevada........	1880..	17	2,988,281	82,512	83,776	1.0153	17 “
	1889..	46	4,976,720	134,306	105,409	0.7848	46 “
New Hampshire	1880..	95	50,099,635	570,736	369,947	0.6478	95 “
	1889..	88	86,488,988	927,970	308,770	0.3327	88 “
New Jersey....	1880..	153	236,546,019	1,829,559	840,744	0.4595	150 “ 1 O. Marine, 2 I. Marine.
	1882..	165	374,083,724	2,943,481	1,402,426	0.4765	163 “ 1 “ 1 “
New York......	1880..	304	3,895,710,856	24,404,773	14,565,103	0.5968	251 “ 24 “ 29 “
	1889..	351	4,893,753,969	28,316,202	18,991,389	0.6707	305 “ 23 “ 22 “ 1 Tor.
North Carolina.	1880..	28	23,517,021	287,115	135,750	0.4728	26 “ 2 “
	1889..	78	66,625,893	676,917	290,185	0.4287	75 “ 2 “ 1 Tornado.
Ohio...........	1880..	251	425,786,647	4,390,834	2,681,770	0.6101	221 “ 2 “ 28 I. Marine.
	1889..	307	608,574,153	6,925,840	3,891,877	0.5619	279 “ 2 “ 21 “ 5 Tor.
Oregon.........	1880..	17	12,424,523	193,643	78,921	0.4076	16 “ 1 “
	1889..	52	40,768,484	784,983	199,208	0.2538	52 “ 3 “
Pennsylvania..	1880..	402	679,624,970	6,730,439	4,236,876	0.6295	380 “ 4 “ 18 I. Marine.
	1889..	418	1,010,130,180	10,300,732	5,696,752	0.5483	399 “ 8 “ 7 “ 4 Tor.
Rhode Island...	1880..	146	146,832,438	1,343,748	330,504	0.2460	140 “ 5 “ 1 “
	1889..	140	300,189,064	2,741,440	765,047	0.2791	134 “ 4 “ 2 “
South Carolina.	1880..	44	41,034,380	400,380	202,081	0.5047	41 “ 3 “
	1889..	95	59,425,875	711,604	254,221	0.3574	86 “ 7 “ 1 I. Marine, 1 Tor.
Tennessee......	1880..	74	54,803,187	702,283	308,340	0.4391	67 “ 1 “ 6 “
	1889..	119	123,247,138	1,712,659	808,113	0.4718	106 “ 3 “ 7 “ 3 Tor.
Texas..........	1880..	59	84,779,854	1,156,274	476,831	0.4124	53 “ 4 “ 2 “
	1889..	97	171,370,363	2,664,295	1,028,012	0.3858	88 “ 6 “ 1 “ 2 Tor.
Vermont.......	1880..	51	28,972,180	442,613	274,075	0.6192	51 “
	1889..	67	42,797,923	615,837	476,224	0.7733	67 “
Virginia........	1880..	47	56,645,602	547,538	367,346	0.6709	42 “ 4 O. Marine, 1 I. Marine.
	1889..	84	121,656,891	1,446,472	965,395	0.6674	76 “ 6 “ 1 “ 1 Tor.
Washington ...	1880..	17	2,002,693	42,814	28,570	0.6673	16 “ 1 “
	1889..	87	32,724,810	1,012,011	3,639,186	3.5985	86 “ 1 “
West Virginia..	1880..	37	10,723,794	128,724	52,675	0.4092	35 “ 2 I. Marine.
	1889..	73	28,956,437	351,075	148,302	0.4224	70 “ 2 O. Marine, 1 I. Marine.
Wisconsin......	1880..	271	179,560,399	1,879,986	1,224,414	0.6513	263 “ 1 “ 6 “ 1 Tor.
	1889..	351	249,296,261	3,571,047	2,020,418	0.5658	337 “ 1 “ 8 “ 5 “
Wyoming......	1880..	18	3,979,200	58,420	10,986	0.1881	18 “
	1889..	53	5,653,524	105,901	34,008	0.3211	53 “

From 1 Jan. 1880 to 31 Dec. 1889, property of the citizens of the United States was insured against fire and accident on ocean, lake, and river, and by tornado, to the amount of over $120,000,000,000, for premiums of $1,156,675,391, and losses were paid of $647,726,051, being 56 per cent. of the premiums. —*Census Insurance Report*, 1890.

Life insurance was not known before the 16th century. The first life insurance company, "The Amicable," was established in London, England, 1706, and insured at uniform rates persons between 12 and 45 years of age. In 1734 it guaranteed a dividend for each deceased member not less than 100*l.* This was the first insurance for a definite sum at death, whenever that might occur. In 1762 the Equitable Assurance Society of London began to rate members according to age. At the close of the 18th century there were 8 companies transacting in a more or less complete form the business of life insurance in Great Britain and Ireland. ANNUITIES. The Presbyterian Annuity and Life Insurance Company of Philadelphia, the first life insurance company in the United States, received its charter from Thomas Penn in 1759. The Penn Company for Insurance on Lives was chartered 1812. Massachusetts Hospital Life Insurance Company, Boston, 1818.

LIST, WITH DATE OF CHARTER OF THE EARLIER "OLD-LINE" INSURANCE COMPANIES IN THE UNITED STATES.

Company	Date	Company	Date
New York Life-insurance and Trust Co.	1830	Berkshire	1851
Baltimore Life	"	Massachusetts Mutual	"
New England Mutual	1835	Northwestern	1858
Girard Life Assurance, Annuity, and Trust Co.	1836	Equitable	1859
Mutual Life of New York	1842	Home	1860
New York Life	1845	Germania	"
Connecticut Mutual	1846	John Hancock	1862
Penn Mutual	1847	Continental	1864
Ætna Life	1850	Brooklyn	"
Manhattan	"	Connecticut General	1865
Phenix Mutual	1851	Hartford Life	1867
		Metropolitan	"

Introduction of the TONTINE system of insurance has added largely to the business of some of the companies.

Assessment system of life insurance is based on the plan of collecting assessments on living members to pay death losses as they occur. In this plan the assessments during early years are less than the premiums of regular companies; but they increase rapidly, and often become impossible to collect in later years. Since its appearance (about 1865) as an insurance business aside from fraternal organizations, this system has rapidly extended.

Total amount of insurance in force in the U. S. 1 Jan. 1893, was in the "regular" or "old-line" companies, $4,895,724,691
Assessment companies 6,974,520,000
Total $11,870,244,691

First accident insurance company established in the U. S. was the Traveller's, of Hartford, Conn. 1863
First steam-boiler insurance company, Hartford, Conn.; chartered 1866
Plate-glass first insured 1870

Most of the states have established departments or bureaus of insurance, for the supervision of the companies and the enforcement of the laws requiring their solvency to be maintained. The maintenance of these departments, and all expenses of supervision are charged to the companies, and sometimes amount to a serious burden, increasing the cost of insurance to the people. The belief of most insurance experts and of political economists is that the effort to regulate the business by law has been carried much too far, and has done at least as much harm as good.

insurrections. CONSPIRACIES, MASSACRES, REBELLIONS, RIOTS, etc.

interdict or **ecclesiastical censure,** seldom decreed in Europe till Gregory VII. (1073), but often afterwards. When a prince was excommunicated, subjects continuing allegiance were excommunicated also, and the clergy were forbidden to perform any divine service or clerical duties, save baptism of infants and confession of dying penitents. In 1170, pope Alexander III. put England under interdict for the complicity of Henry II. in murder of Becket; and when king John was excommunicated in 1208, the kingdom lay under a papal interdict for 6 years. England was put under an interdict on Henry VIII. shaking off the pope's supremacy, 1535; and pope Sixtus V. proclaimed a crusade against queen Elizabeth of England in 1588. EXCOMMUNICATION.

interest. USURY. The word interest was first used in an act of Parliament of 21 James I. 1623, for a lawful increase as compensation for the use of money lent. The rate fixed by the act was 8*l.* for the use of 100*l.* for a year, in place of usury at 10*l.* before taken. The Commonwealth lowered the rate to 6*l.* in 1651; confirmed in 1660; and by an act of 13 queen Anne, 1713, it was reduced to 5*l.* The restraint being found prejudicial to commerce, it was totally removed by 17 and 18 Vict. c. 90 (1854).

INTEREST IN THE UNITED STATES.

State.	Legal rate.	Rate allowed by contract.	Penalty for usury.
	Per cent.	*Per cent.*	*Forfeiture*
Alabama	8	8	Of all interest.
Arizona	7	Any rate	None.
Arkansas	6	10	Of principal and interest.
California	7	Any rate	None.
Colorado	8	"	"
Connecticut	6	6	"
Delaware	6	6	Of contract.
District of Columbia	6	10	Of all interest.
Florida	8	Any rate	None.
Georgia	7	8	Of all interest.
Idaho	10	18	Of 3 times excess of interest.
Illinois	5	7	Of all interest.
Indiana	6	8	Of excess of interest.
Iowa	6	8	Of interest and costs.
Kansas	7	12	Of excess of interest.
Kentucky	6	6	Of interest.
Louisiana	5	8	"
Maine	6	Any rate	None.
Maryland	6	6	Of excess of interest.
Massachusetts	6	Any rate	None.
Michigan	7	10	Of excess of interest.
Minnesota	7	10	Of contract.
Mississippi	6	10	Of interest.
Missouri	6	10	"
Montana	10	Any rate	None.
Nebraska	7	10	Of interest and costs.
Nevada	10	Any rate	None.
New Hampshire	6	6	Of 3 times the excess.
New Jersey	6	6	Of interest and costs.
New Mexico	6	12	None.
New York	6	6	Of principal and interest.
North Carolina	6	8	Of twice interest.
North Dakota	7	12	Of contract.
Ohio	6	8	Of excess of interest.
Oklahoma	7	12	Of interest.
Oregon	8	10	Of principal and interest.
Pennsylvania	6	6	Of excess of interest.
Rhode Island	6	Any rate	None.
South Carolina	7	10	Of interest.
South Dakota	7	12	Of contract.
Tennessee	6	6	Of excess of interest.
Texas	8	12	Of interest.
Utah	8	Any rate	None.
Vermont	6	6	Of excess of interest.
Virginia	6	6	" "
Washington	10	Any rate	None.
West Virginia	6	6	Of excess of interest.
Wisconsin	7	10	Of entire interest.
Wyoming	12	Any rate	None.

The effect of stringent usury laws, wherever tried, has been to make loans more difficult and more costly to the borrower. This is beginning to be understood by legislators, and many states, beginning with Massachusetts, have made contracts for loans as free as any others. The average rate of interest received by 20 leading American life insurance companies from 1870 to 1879 inclusive was 5.9 per cent.; from 1880 to 1889 inclusive it was 4.8 per cent., showing a gradual decline in interest earnings.

Interim of Augsburg, a decree of the emperor Charles V. in 1548 to reconcile Catholics and Protestants, which entirely failed. It was revoked in 1552. The term *interim* has been applied to other decrees and treaties.

internal revenue. REVENUE.

international law. NEUTRAL POWERS.

Association for the Reform and Codification of the Law of Nations first met at Brussels, 10 Oct. 1873; Geneva, 2-5 Sept. 1874; the Hague, Sept. 1875; Bremen, 1876; Antwerp, 30 Aug.-3 Sept. 1877; Frankfort, about 20 Aug. 1878; London, 11 Aug. 1879; Berne, 24 Aug. 1880; Cologne, 16-19 Aug. 1881; Turin, 11 Sept. 1882; Milan, 11 Sept. 1883.

Institute of International Law was organized at Ghent by dr. Lieber and M. Moynier, in 1873. It has since met at Geneva; the Hague; Zurich, 1877; Paris; Brussels, Sept. 1879; Oxford, 6-10 Sept. 1880; Turin, 1882; Munich, 4 Sept. 1883.

interoceanic canal between the Atlantic and Pacific. NICARAGUA, PANAMA.

Interstate Commerce Commission. UNITED STATES, 1887.

inundations. Among the most remarkable were:

	A.D.
Inundation of the sea in Lincolnshire over many thousand acres (*Camden*)	245
Another in Cheshire; 3000 persons and countless cattle perished	353
At Glasgow; more than 400 families drowned (*Fordun*)	758
On the English coasts; number of seaport towns destroyed	1014

Earl Godwin's lands, exceeding 4000 acres, overflowed by the sea, an immense sand bank formed on the coast of Kent, now known as the GODWIN SANDS (*Camden*) 1100
Flanders inundated by the sea, and the town and harbor of Ostend immersed 1108
More than 300 houses overwhelmed at Winchelsea by the sea 1280
At the Texel, which first raised the commerce of Amsterdam 1400
Sea at DORT, drowned 72 villages and 100 000 people 17 Apr 1421
Severn overflowed 10 days carried away families in their beds, and covered hills, the flood was called the Great Waters for 100 years after, 1 Richard III (*Holinshed*) 1483
General inundation by failure of dikes in Holland, 400,000 said to be drowned 1530
At Catalonia, 50,000 persons perished 1617
Part of Zealand overflowed, 1300 inhabitants drowned, vast damage at Hamburg 1717
In Yorkshire a dreadful inundation, called Ripon Flood 1771
In Navarre, 2000 persons lost by torrents from the mountains, Sept 1787
Inundation of the Liffey, immense damage in Dublin, 12 Nov 1787, again 2 3 Dec 1802
Lorca, a city of Murcia in Spain destroyed by a bursting reservoir, inundated more than 20 leagues, and killed 1000 persons, besides cattle 14 Apr "
At Pesth, near Presburg, the Danube destroyed 24 villages and their inhabitants Apr 1811
Inundations in Hungary, Austria, and Poland, summer of 1813
Danube overwhelmed a Turkish corps of 2000 men on a small island near Widdin 14 Sept "
In Silesia 6000 inhabitants perished, the ruin of Macdonald's French army accelerated by the floods, in Poland 4000 lives supposed to have been lost "
In Germany Vistula overflowed, many villages laid under water, with great loss of life and property 21 Mch 1816
In England, 5000 acres deluged in the Fen countries. June, 1819
At Dantzic the Vistula breaking dikes, 10 000 head of cattle and 4000 houses destroyed, numerous lives lost 9 Apr 1829
"Moray floods," in Scotland, caused by rainfall, the Spey and Findhorn rose in places 50 ft above ordinary level, with great destruction of property and life, whole families taking refuge on elevated places, were with difficulty rescued (*sir T Dick Lauder*) 3, 4, 27 Aug "
At Vienna the dwellings of 50,000 under water Feb 1830
Ten thousand houses swept away, and about 1000 persons perished, at Canton, in China, in an inundation from incessant rains Similar calamity in other parts of China Oct 1833
Awful inundation in France, the Saône and Rhone broke their banks, and covered 60 000 acres, Lyons inundated, in Avignon 100 houses swept away, 218 at La Guillotière, and upwards of 300 at Vaise, Marseilles, and Nimes, the Saone higher than for 238 years 31 Oct -4 Nov 1840
Inundation in the centre, west, and southwest of France numerous bridges with the Orleans and Vierzon viaduct (cost 6,000,000 francs) swept away The damage exceeded 100,000,000 francs The Loire rose 20 ft in one night. 22 Oct 1846
Great inundation at New Orleans, La , 1600 houses flooded 12 May, 1849
Bursting of the Bradfield reservoir (SHEFFIELD), about 250 persons drowned 11 Mch. 1864
Floods in north of England, in Yorkshire, Lancashire, and Derbyshire, farms destroyed, mines flooded, mills thrown down, railways stopped, much suffering at Leeds (about 20 drowned), Manchester Preston, Wakefield, etc 16, 17 Nov 1866
Inundations from mountains in N Italy, Po and other rivers overflow, thousands of people unhoused, Mantua, Ferrara, etc , suffer latter part of Oct. 1872
Mill River valley, near Northampton, Mass , several villages destroyed by bursting reservoir, above 144 perished 16 May, 1874
Eureka, Nevada, through rain and a waterspout, between 20 and 30 persons perish 24 July, "
Pittsburg and Alleghany W Pennsylvania storm of rain, rivers overflow, about 220 persons drowned 26 July, "
Toulouse partly destroyed by the Garonne, about 1000 lives lost and much property (St Cyprien quarter a sepulchre) June, 1875
Szegedin, Hungary, through storms dams of the Theiss gave way, town nearly destroyed, of 6566 houses, only 331 stood, about 77 persons drowned, thousands homeless 12, 13 Mch. 1879
Inundations in Murcia, Spain, through heavy rains, provinces of Andalusia, Alicante, Almaria, and Malaga, about 1000 lives lost and much property, about 2000 houses 16 17 Oct "
Floods in Iowa, Kansas, Minnesota, Missouri 12 June, et seq 1881
Ohio and Mississippi valleys flooded, lives lost and much property, Feb 1882 Governor of Mississippi appeals for aid 22 Feb 1882
In Pennsylvania, Ohio, and Kentucky, very severe at Cincinnati Feb 1883
Ohio river, about 15 deaths and 5000 homeless about 7 Feb 1884
Floods in Pennsylvania, New York, and New England, great loss of property 5 Jan 1886
Storm and flood in Texas, houses in Galveston washed away, 38 lives lost and more than $5 000,000 damage 20 Aug "
Johnstown flood, Pa. (JOHNSTOWN) 1 June, 1889

Invalides', Hôtel des, founded in 1671 by Louis XIV , the body of Napoleon I. deposited there 15 Dec 1840.

invasions. EXPEDITIONS

inventions. AGRICULTURE, COTTON, ELECTRICITY See also names of machines and implements, subjects of invention

Inverness', N.W. Scotland, a city of the Picts up to 843, taken by Edward I , retaken by Bruce, 1313 , burned by the lord of the Isles, 1411 , taken by Cromwell, 1649 , and by prince Charles Edward in 1746 The last totally defeated at Culloden, about 5 miles from Inverness, 16 Apr 1746

investiture of ecclesiastics was a cause of discord between the pope and temporal sovereigns in the middle ages, and led to war between Gregory VII and the emperor Henry IV, 1075-85 The pope endeavored to deprive the sovereign of nomination of bishops and abbots, and of investing them with cross and ring Henry V gave up the right, by treaty, Feb 1111, but other sovereigns refused to concede it

Invincible Armada, or Spanish Armada. ARMADA

invocation of the Virgin and saints to intercede with God, a practice of the Catholic church traced to the time of Gregory the Great, 593 The Eastern church began (in the 5th century) calling upon the dead, and demanding their suffrage in divine offices.

i'odine (from the Gr ἰώδης, violet-like), discovered by M de Courtois, a manufacturer of saltpetre at Paris in 1812, and investigated by M Clement, 1813, when heated it rises as a dense violet-colored vapor, easily evaporates, and melts at 220 degrees, it changes vegetable blues to yellow, and a seven-thousandth part gives water a deep yellow color, and starch a purple

Io'na, I'colmkill, or **Hii,** one of the Hebrides About 565 St Columba founded a monastery here, which flourished till the 8th and 9th centuries, when it was frequently ravaged by the Norsemen Other religious bodies were afterwards formed here, and the isle was long esteemed sacred

Io'nia, Asia Minor About 1040 B.C the Iones, a Pelasgic race, emigrated from Greece, and settled here and on the adjoining islands They built Ephesus and 12 other cities, among them Chios, Teos, Smyrna, Samos, and Miletus. They were conquered by the great Cyrus about 548 B.C., revolted 501, but were again subdued After the victories of Cimon, Ionia was independent till 387 B C, when it was again subjected to Persia It formed part of the dominions of Alexander and his successors, was annexed to the Roman empire, 133 B C., and conquered by the Turks. Ionia was renowned for historians, poets, and philosophers The poets Homer and Anacreon were Ionians, as well as Parrhasius the painter and the philosophers Thales and Anaxagoras

Ionian islands, on west coast of Greece Corfu (the capital), Cephalonia, Zante, Ithaca, Santa Maura, Cerigo, and Paxo. They were colonized by Iones, and partook of the fortunes of the Greeks, were subject to Naples in the 13th century, and in the 14th to Venice

Islands ceded to France by treaty of Campo Formio 17 Oct. 1797
Formed into the republic of the 7 islands under Russia and Turkey 21 Mch. 1800
Restored to France by treaty of Tilsit 7 July, 1807
Taken by the English 3-12 Oct 1809
Formed an independent state under protection of Great Britain (sir Thomas Maitland lord high commissioner) 5 Nov 1815
Constitution ratified . 11 July, 1817
University established at Corfu . 1823
Constitution liberalized under lord Seaton 1848-49
In consequence of complaints, W E Gladstone went out on a commission of inquiry etc Nov 1858
Sir H. Storks, lord high commissioner . Feb. 1859
Parliament vote annexation to Greece Mch 1861 and Apr 1862
Islands annexed to Greece, 28 May, British troops retired, 2 June, king George I arrived at Corfu (GREECE) 6 June, 1864

Ion'ic order of architecture, an improvement on the Doric, invented by Ionians about 1350 B C.—*Vitruvius* Its distinguishing characters are slenderness and flutings of its columns, and volutes of rams' horns that adorn the capital. ARCHITECTURE

Ionic sect of philosophers, founded by Thales of Miletus about 600 B C, distinguished for abstruse speculations under his successors and pupils, Anaximander, Anaximenes, Anaxagoras, and Archelaus, the master of Socrates. They held the world a living being, and water the origin of all things PHILOSOPHY

Iowa, a state of the north central United States, separated on the east by the Mississippi river from Wisconsin and Illinois. Minnesota bounds it on the north, South Dakota and Nebraska on the west—the Missouri river forming the boundary line of the latter state—and Missouri on the south. It is limited in lat. by 40° 36′ to 43° 30′ N., and in lon. by 89° 5′ to 96° 31′ W. Area, 56,025 sq. miles. Pop. 1890, 1,911,896; 1900, 2,231,853. Capital, Des Moines.

Father Marquette and Louis Joliet descend the Wisconsin river, reaching its mouth 17 June, 1673; 100 miles below, on the western shore of the Mississippi, they discover an Indian trail, which they follow to an Indian village, where Marquette "publishes to them the one true God".....June, 1673
Father Louis Hennepin, M. Dugay, and 6 other Frenchmen ascend the Mississippi from the mouth of the Illinois to the falls of St. Anthony, leaving fort Crevecœur, Ill......28 Feb. 1680
Wife of Peosta, a Fox warrior, discovers lead in Iowa, on the west bank of the Mississippi..... 1780
At a council at Prairie du Chien, Julien Dubuque, a French-Canadian trader, obtains from Indians permission to work lead mines at the place now bearing his name, and a grant of 140,000 acres of land..... 1788
Land grant to Julien Dubuque by Indians is confirmed by baron Carondelet, and a king's title issued..... 1796
Lands on both sides of the Mississippi, including a large part of Iowa, ceded to U. S. by Sac and Fox Indians, by treaty at St. Louis.....3 Nov. 1804
Territory of Louisiana, including Iowa, framed by law of 3 Mch. 1805
Iowa included in territory of Missouri, erected by act, 4 June, 1812
Fort Madison, built in 1808 on the site selected by lieut. Pike in 1805, is abandoned by the garrison and burned to prevent its falling into the hands of Indians and British..... 1813
Sioux annihilate Sac and Fox tribes near Dubuque; whites occupy deserted villages, but are driven out by U. S. troops under lieut. Jefferson Davis, by order of col. Zachary Taylor, 1830
David Tothers makes the first settlement in Des Moines county, 3 miles southwest from the site of Burlington..... 1832
Treaty at Rock Island; the Sacs and Foxes cede to the U. S. Iowa and a part of Wisconsin, known as the Black Hawk purchase, reserving 40 miles square to Keokuk.....21 Sept. "
Zachariah Hawkins, Benjamin Jennings, and others settle a colony at fort Madison..... "
First permanent settlement in Scott county by Antoine le Claire..... 1833
Dubuque founded..... "
Iowa included in territory of Michigan, erected by act approved.....28 June, 1834
Aaron Street founds Salem, first Quaker settlement in Iowa... "
Iowa included in territory of Wisconsin, erected by act approved.....20 Apr. 1836
Treaty at East Davenport between gov. Dodge, U. S. commissioner, and the Sacs and Foxes; Indians sell to U. S. the Keokuk reserve, 256,000 acres, at 75 cents per acre.....Sept. "
Burlington, settled in 1833, is incorporated..... 1837
Treaty with the Sacs and Foxes extends the western boundary of the Black Hawk purchase in lat. 45° 40′ to include the principal sources of the Iowa river.....21 Oct. "
Territory of Iowa erected, including all Wisconsin, west of the Mississippi.....12 June, 1838
Penitentiary located at fort Madison..... "
Territorial government inaugurated at Burlington......4 July, "
Black Hawk, who had settled on the Des Moines river, d., 3 Oct. "
Seat of government removed to Iowa City..... 1839
Boundary disputes between Missouri and Iowa cause fighting on the border; 1 Iowan is killed in resisting the Missouri sheriff's collection of taxes..... "
Constitution adopted by a convention which meets at Iowa City, 7 Oct. 1844.....1 Nov. 1844
Enabling act for Iowa approved.....3 Mch. 1845
Boundary defined in the Enabling act rejected by the people; 7235 for, and 7656 against..... "
Mormons remove from Nauvoo, Ill., and settle at Council Bluffs, 1846
Constitution framed by a convention which meets at Iowa City, 4 May, 1846, completing its labors, 19 May, 1846, is ratified by a vote of the people, 9492 to 9036.....3 Aug. "
Act of Congress, fixing boundaries for Iowa, referring the Missouri boundary to the Supreme court.....4 Aug. "
Iowa admitted into the Union by act approved.....28 Dec. "
Iowa college at Grinnell, chartered in 1847, is opened..... 1848
Iowa College for the Blind at Vinton opened..... 1852
Antoine le Claire breaks ground at Davenport for the Mississippi and Missouri railroad, now the Chicago, Rock Island, and Pacific.....1 Sept. 1853
Hospital for the Insane at Mount Pleasant established..... 1855
Iowa Wesleyan university at Mount Pleasant chartered and opened..... "
Corner-stone of the first railroad bridge over the Mississippi river, between Rock Island and Davenport, laid 1 Sept. 1854; and first locomotive, the "Des Moines," to cross the Mississippi passes over.....21 Apr. 1856
Massacre of white settlers at Spirit Lake by a predatory band of Indians under the Sioux chief Ink-pa-duta.....Mch. 1857
Cornell college at Mount Vernon chartered and opened..... "
Constitutional convention meets at Iowa city, 19 Jan. 1857, completes its labors, 6 Mch. 1857; constitution ratified by the people, 40,311 to 38,681.....3 Aug. "
State capital removed to Des Moines..... "
Iowa Institution for Deaf and Dumb at Council Bluffs opened, 1859
State university of Iowa at Iowa City, chartered 1847, opened, Silas Totten, pres..... 1860
Legislature votes a war loan of $600,000.....June, 1861
Soldiers' Orphans' Home and Home for Indigent Children at Davenport opened..... 1862
Upper Iowa university at Fayette, opened 1857; chartered.... "
James Harlan appointed secretary of the interior.....15 May, 1865
Legislature ratifies XIII.th Amendment to Constitution...Jan. 1866
Legislature ratifies XIV.th Amendment to Constitution..3 Apr. 1868
An amendment to the state constitution, striking out the word "white" from the qualifications of electors, is adopted by a vote of the people, 105,384 to 81,119..... "
State Board of Immigration created by act of legislature..... 1869
Iowa Agricultural college at Ames, chartered 1857, opened.... "
William W. Belknap appointed secretary of war......25 Oct. "
Legislature ratifies XV.th Amendment to Constitution..3 Feb. 1870
Corner-stone of new capitol laid.....22 Nov. 1871
Law passed restricting sale of liquors and limiting licensees' profit to 33 per cent..... 1872
State penitentiary at Anamosa created by act of..... "
Act passed abolishing penalty of death (see below, 1878)..... "
Maj. Samuel E. Rankin, late treasurer of the state and agricultural college, proves a defaulter for $38,301.46..... "
State convention of Patrons of Husbandry at Des Moines..Jan. 1873
Hospital for Insane at Independence opened.....1 May, "
Iowa Industrial School for Girls at Mitchellville, and for boys at Eldora, established..... 1874
Gov. Kirkwood, elected U. S. senator, resigns, and is succeeded by Joshua G. Newbold.....Jan. 1876
Iowa Institution for Feeble-minded Children at Glenwood opened..... "
Iowa state normal school at Cedar Falls opened..... "
Geo. W. McCrary appointed secretary of war.....12 Mch. 1877
Canal around Des Moines rapids at Keokuk, 7½ miles long, and costing $4,500,000, is formally opened .....Aug. "
Bill abolishing capital punishment repealed, and the jury empowered to hang convicted murderers, or imprison for life.. 1878
State Board of Health organized..... 1880
Dexter Normal college at Dexter opened..... "
Western Normal college at Shenandoah, Iowa, opened..... 1881
Drake university at Des Moines opened and chartered..... "
West Des Moines Training-school at Des Moines opened..... 1882
Prohibitory liquor law goes into effect.....4 July, 1884
State capitol dedicated; cost $3,000,000..... "
Frank Hatton appointed postmaster-general.....14 Oct. "
Woodbine Normal school at Woodbine opened..... "
Storm Lake Normal and Business school at Storm Lake opened, "
Soldiers' Home at Marshalltown opened.....30 Nov. "
Eastern Iowa School for the Deaf at Dubuque opened..... "
Hospital for the Insane at Clarinda opened.....15 Dec. 1889
Sioux city Training-school for teachers opened..... "
Lower house of legislature assembles, 13 Jan. 1890, having 2 factions, the Republicans with 50 votes, and the combined Democratic, Union labor, and Independent, with 50 votes; no organization until 27 Jan.; by compromise, a Democratic temporary speaker and a Republican clerk are elected; permanent organization with a Democratic speaker and Republican clerk; minor offices divided.....19 Feb. 1890
Horace Boies, Democrat, inaugurated as governor......27 Feb. "
Legal rate of interest reduced from 10 to 8 per cent., and the first Monday in Sept. (Labor Day) made a public holiday.... "
Beer sent in sealed kegs from Peoria, Ill., to Keokuk, Ia., and there sold in "original packages" by agents, being seized under the prohibitory laws of the state, the Supreme court decides such seizure was in violation of the clause of the Constitution giving to the U. S. the exclusive right to regulate inter-state commerce.....28 Apr. "
Wilson "Original Package bill," as amended, making all intoxicating liquors imported into a state subject to its laws, passes Congress and is approved.....8 Aug. "
Legislature passes an Australian Ballot Reform act..... 1892

GOVERNORS—TERRITORIAL.

Robert Lucas.....assumes office.....July, 1838
John Chambers..... " " 1841
James Clark..... " " 1845

STATE.

Ansel Briggs.....assumes office..... 1846
Stephen Hempstead..... " " .....Dec. 1850
James W. Grimes..... " " ..... " 1854
Ralph P. Lowe..... " " ..... " 1858
Samuel J. Kirkwood..... " " .....Jan. 1860
William M. Stone..... " " ..... " 1864
Samuel Merrill..... " " ..... " 1868
C. C. Carpenter..... " " ..... " 1872
Samuel J. Kirkwood..... " " ..... " 1876
Joshua G. Newbold.....acting..... " "
John H. Gear.....assumes office..... " 1878
Buren R. Sherman..... " " ..... " 1882
William Larrabee..... " " ..... " 1886
Horace Boies..... " " ..... " 1890
Frank D. Jackson..... " " ..... " 1894

UNITED STATES SENATORS FROM THE STATE OF IOWA.

Name.	No. of Congress.	Date.	Remarks.
Augustus C. Dodge	30th to 33d	1848 to 1855	Seated 26 Dec. 1848.
George W. Jones	30th " 36th	1848 " 1859	Seated 26 Dec. 1848.
James Harlan	34th " 38th	1855 " 1865	Resigned 1865. Appointed secretary of interior.
James W. Grimes	36th " 40th	1859 " 1869	Resigned 1869.
Samuel J. Kirkwood	39th	1865 " 1867	Elected in place of Harlan, 1865.
James Harlan	40th to 43d	1867 " 1873	
James B. Howell	41st	1869 " 1871	Elected in place of Grimes.
George G. Wright	42d to 44th	1871 " 1877	
William B. Allison	43d ——	1873 ——	Term expires 1897.
Samuel J. Kirkwood	45th to 46th	1877 " 1881	
James W. McDill	47th	1881 " 1883	
James F. Wilson	48th ——	1883 ——	Term expires 1895.

Ipsus, Phrygia, Battle of, Aug. 301 B.C., when Seleucus was confirmed in his kingdom of Syria by the defeat and death of Antigonus, king of Asia. The latter led into the field an army of about 70,000 foot and 10,000 horse, with 75 elephants. The former had 64,000 foot, besides 10,500 horse, 400 elephants, and 120 armed chariots.—*Plutarch.*

Ipswich, a town of Suffolk, the Saxon Gippeswic, was ravaged by the Danes, 991 and 1000. Wolsey was born here, 1471; and founded a school in 1525.

Ipswich, Mass. AGAWAM.

Ireland, anciently named Eri or Erin, Ierne and Hibernia, said to have been first colonized by Phœnicians. Some assert that Partholani landed in Ireland about 2048 B.C.; that the descent of the Damnonii was made about 1463 B.C.; followed by the descent of Heber and Heremon, Milesian princes, from Galicia, in Spain, who conquered Ireland, and gave to its throne a race of 171 kings. SCOTT. Area, 32,531 sq. miles, or 20,819,982 acres, in 32 counties. Pop. 1891, 4,706,162; 1901, 4,458,775.

Arrival of St. Patrick.....about 432

Christianity established.....about 448

Danes and Normans, called Easterlings, or Ostmen, invade Ireland..... 795

They build Dublin and other cities.....about 800

Brian Boroimbe defeats the Danes at Clontarf; and is killed, 23 Apr. 1014

[In the 12th century Ireland had 5 kingdoms, viz.: Ulster, Leinster, Meath, Connaught, and Munster, besides petty principalities, whose sovereigns were at continual war.]

Adrian IV. permitted Henry II. to invade Ireland, he to compel every Irish family to pay a carolus to the holy see, and hold it as a fief of the church..... 1155

Dermot MacMurrough, king of Leinster, driven from his throne for oppression..... 1166

Flees to England; takes oath of fidelity to Henry II., who promises to restore him..... 1168

Invasion of the English under Fitz-Stephen..... 1169

Landing of Strongbow at Waterford..... "

Dermot d..... 1171

Henry II. lands near Waterford, and receives submission of the princes; settles the government, and makes his son John lord of Ireland.....May, 1177

Many English settlers adopt Irish names and manners...about 1200

Ireland reduced to temporary obedience by king John..... 1210

Invasion of Edward Bruce, 1315; crowned king..... 1316

Defeated and slain at Foughart, near Dundalk..... 1318

Lionel, duke of Clarence, 3d son of Edward III. marries Elizabeth de Burgh, heiress of Ulster..... 1361

Statute of Kilkenny passed by him..... 1367

Richard II. lands at Waterford with nobles, 4000 men-at-arms, and 30,000 archers; gains affection of the people by munificence, and confers knighthood on chiefs..... 1394

Richard again lands in Ireland..... 1399

Sanguinary Head act passed at Trim by the earl of Desmond, deputy; act ordained "That it shall be lawful to all manner of men that find any theeves robbing by day or night, or going or coming to rob or steal, or any persons going or coming, having no faithful man of good name and fame in their company, in English apparell, that it shall be lawful to take and kill those, and to cut off their heads, without any impeachment of our sovereign lord the king. And of any head so cut off in the county of Meath, that the cutter and his ayders there to him cause the said head so cut off to be brought to the portreffe to put it upon a stake or spear, upon the castle of Trim; and that the said portreffe shall testify the bringing of the same to him. And that it shall be lawful for the said bringer of the said head to distrain and levy by his own hand (as his reward) of every man having one ploughland in the barony, two pence; and of every man having half a ploughland, one peny; and of every man having one house and goods, value forty shillings, one peny; and of every other cottier having house and smoak, one half peny," etc. Much slaughter is said to have ensued..... 1465

Apparel and Surname act (the Irish to dress like the English, and to adopt surnames)..... "

"Poynings's law," subjecting Irish parliament to the English council..... 1494

Great rebellion of the Fitzgeralds subdued..... 1534

Henry VIII. assumes title of king, instead of lord, of Ireland..... 1542

Reformed religion embraced by English settlers in the reign of Edward VI..... 1547

Ireland finally divided into shires..... 1569

Printing in Irish characters introduced by N. Walsh, chancellor of St. Patrick's..... 1571

Seven hundred Italians, headed by Fitzmaurice, land in Kerry; treacherously butchered by earl of Ormond..... 1580

O'Neill revolts, 1597; defeats English at Blackwater...14 Aug. 1598

He invites the Spaniards, and settles them in Kinsale; defeated by lord deputy Mountjoy.....1601–2

Through rebellions and forfeitures 511,465 acres of land in Ulster became vested in the crown; and James I., after removing the Irish from hills and fastnesses, divides the land among English and Scottish Protestant settlers.....1609–12

Ulster civil war: More and Maguire's rebellion; the Catholics said to conspire to expel the English, and massacre Protestant settlers in Ulster, commenced on St. Ignatius's day (some doubt the massacre).....23 Oct. 1641

O'Neill defeats English under Monroe at Benburb.....5 June, 1646

Massacre and capture of Drogheda by Cromwell.....11 Sept. 1649

Cromwell and Ireton reduce Ireland.....1649–56

Landing of James II.....12 Mch. 1689

Three thousand Protestants attainted.....July, "

William III. lands at Carrickfergus.....14 June, 1690

Battle of the Boyne; James defeated.....1 July, "

Treaty of Limerick.....3 Oct. 1691

Linen manufacture encouraged..... 1696

Popery act passed..... 1704

Excitement against WOOD'S HALF-PENCE..... 1724

Thurot's invasion; a small French naval force plunders Carrickfergus.....Feb. 1760

Indulgences granted Catholics by the relief bill..... 1778

Ireland admitted to a free trade..... 1779

Released from submission to an English council; Poynings's law repealed..... 1782

Genevese refugees received in Ireland, and asylum given them in Waterford..... 1783

Order of St. Patrick established..... "

Society of United Irishmen founded..... 1791

Orange clubs, etc., formed..... 1795

Irish rebellion commenced, 4 May, 1798; cost 150,000 Irish lives, 20,000 English; gradually suppressed..... 1799

Legislative Union of Great Britain and Ireland.....1 Jan. 1801

Emmett's insurrection.....23 July, 1803

Robert Emmett executed for high-treason at Dublin...20 Sept. "

Roman Catholic Emancipation act passed.....13 Apr. 1829

"Young Ireland" party formed..... 1840

Population by census, 8,196,597..... 1841

Potato crop fails in Ireland; relief by Parliament..... 1846

O'Connell's last speech in the commons.....8 Feb. 1847

Parliament grants 10,000,000*l.* to relieve the people..... "

Death of O'Connell at Genoa, on his way to Rome, in his 73d year; he bequeathed his heart to Rome.....15 May, "

Habeas Corpus act suspended.....26 July, 1848

O'Brien's rebellion suppressed.....29 July, "

Census taken; population, 6,574,278.....30 Mch. 1851

Great emigration to America.....spring, 1860

Census taken; population, 5,798,967.....8 Apr. 1861

Appearance of the FENIANS.....Jan. 1864

Death of Smith O'Brien, descendant of king Brian Boroimhe, 16 June, "

Fenian trials begun at Dublin, 27 Nov.; Thomas Clarke Luby sentenced for treason-felony to 20 years' penal servitude, 1 Dec. 1865

O'Leary and others convicted, Dec.; O'Donovan Rossa sentenced to imprisonment for life.....13 Dec. "

Habeas Corpus act suspended; many Fenians flee.....17 Feb. 1866

Declaration of Roman Catholic clergy professing loyalty, but claiming self-government for Ireland.....23 Dec. 1867

George Francis Train on arrival from the U. S., arrested as a Fenian; soon discharged (claimed 10,000*l.*).....18 Jan. 1868

Habeas Corpus act suspended till 1 Mch. 1869 (83 persons detained on suspicion).....Feb. "

George Francis Train arrested for debt.....3 Mch. "

Four nights' debate on Ireland in commons ended (Gladstone declared for disestablishment of Irish Protestant church), 16 Mch. "

Irish Reform bill introduced into the commons.....19 Mch. "

Debate on committee on disestablishment (carried, 328–272), 30 Mch. to early morning of.....4 Apr. "

Mr. Gladstone's first resolution passed in commons (by 330-265) early on 1 May; second and third resolutions, 7 May, 1868

Irish archbishops and bishops address queen at Windsor on behalf of Irish church establishment ....14 May, "

Irish church commission recommend consolidation of dioceses and other reforms (first report)..............27 July, "

Earl Spencer lord lieutenant..............Dec. "

Irish Church bill introduced in commons, 1 Mch.; after much opposition passed..............26 July, 1869

Irish mixed schools denounced by abp. Cullen; support for a Catholic university demanded in a circular dated..18 Aug. "

Irish Land bill read a second time in commons (442-11), 1 A.M., 12 Mch.; second time in the lords..........17 June, 1870

Reported growth of a "Nationality" party among the Protestants..............July, "

Irish Land act passed..............1 Aug. "

"Home Government Association," to include all parties, meet at Dublin ....1 Sept. "

John Martin, a nationalist, elected M.P. for Meath.......5 Jan. 1871

Census taken; population, 5,402,759..............3 Apr. "

Isaac Butt, leader of home-rule movement, elected M.P. for Limerick..............20 Sept. "

Roman Catholic bishop of Derry, the O'Donoghue, and others, declare against the movement, Jan.; members in its favor elected for Galway and Kerry..............Feb. 1872

Mr. Gladstone brings into the commons the Irish University bill (rejected and withdrawn)..............13 Feb. 1874

Home-rule and amnesty associations active..............Oct. "

Motions for HOME-RULE defeated..........20 Mch. and 3 July, "

Centenary of the birth of Daniel O'Connell celebrated at Dublin, many foreign Roman Catholic dignitaries present; much dissension at the banquet between the clerical and home-rule parties..............6 Aug. 1875

Mr. McSwiney, lord mayor of Dublin, advocates a party for "faith and fatherland," opposed to home-rule, Aug.-Sept. "

Catholic synod at Maynooth; mixed education censured, Sept. "

An Irish University bill introduced by Mr. Butt (withdrawn), 16 May, 1876

Bill to abolish the Queen's university, and to establish a new university (for Roman Catholics), introduced by lord chancellor Cairns, 30 June; carried in commons (257-90), 25 July; passed..............15 Aug. 1879

Irish national convention at Dublin proposed by Mr. Parnell (HOME-RULE)..............11 Sept. "

Progresses of Mr. Parnell; anti-rent agitation........autumn, "

Appeal for Irish National Land League by Mr. Parnell; subscriptions to buy land for tenants..............9 Oct. "

Exciting speeches of Mr. Parnell at Navan..........11, 13 Oct. "

Mr. Parnell arrives at New York to agitate for help to relieve Ireland politically and pecuniarily..............2 Jan. 1880

Contributions to famine funds arrive from Canada, Australia, India, U. S., etc..............Jan.-Feb. "

Charter for new Irish university signed by queen Victoria, 19 Apr. "

Relief for Irish distress brought in the *Constellation* from U. S.; arrives at Cork..............20 Apr. "

Violent speech of Mr. Dillon, M.P., at Kildare, in favor of the Land League, 15 Aug.; termed "wicked and cowardly" by W. E. Forster, who justifies the terms in Parliament, 23 Aug. "

Mr. Parnell proposes that tenant become owner of land after paying 35 years' just rent..............Sept. "

Progress of agitation; exciting speeches of Messrs. Parnell, Redpath, Dillon, and others..............Sept.-Oct. "

Timothy M. Healy, Mr. Parnell's secretary, and Mr. Walsh arrested for intimidating Mr. Manning (on 16 Oct.), 26, 27 Oct. "

Parnell and others arrested for conspiracy and intimidation to prevent tenants paying rent, etc. (19 counts); notices served, 3 Nov. et seq. "

Mr. Boycott of Lough Mask farm, near Ballinrobe, Mayo, besieged; his laborers threatened; his tradesmen refuse to supply him; his crops gathered by immigrant laborers, protected by military, etc..............11, 12 Nov. "

W. Bence Jones of Ballinascorthy "boycotted"..........Dec. "

Parnell and others tried for conspiracy (TRIALS).......28 Dec. "

Jury disagree; discharged..............25 Jan. 1881

About 25,000 soldiers in Ireland..............Jan. "

Report of *agricultural commission (for Ireland) issued; great* distress, 1877-79; good harvest, 1880; recommends emigration in some districts..............Jan. "

Bill for protection of life and property brought in by Mr. Forster, 24 Jan.; long debates; much obstruction (PARLIAMENT); passed commons (281-36), 25, 26 Feb.; passed lords, 1-3 Mch.; royal assent..............3 Mch. "

Many agitators arrested; 23 in Kilmainham jail.......10 Mch. "

Peace Preservation bill (Arms bill); introduced 1 Mch.; passed commons, 11, 12 Mch.; passed lords, 18 Mch.; royal assent, 21 Mch. "

"Clan-na-Gael" secret society to replace Fenians said to be formed..............Mch. "

Irish Land bill ("legalized confiscation"—*Beaconsfield*) introduced in the commons by Mr. Gladstone..............7 Apr. "

Land bill in House of Lords; read second time, 2, 3 Aug.; third time (with amendments), 8 Aug.; commons reject some amendments, 12 Aug.; lords resist, 13 Aug.; commons modify amendments, 15 Aug.; lords yield, 16 Aug.; royal assent, 22 Aug. "

IRE

Delegates from Land League meet; denounce Land act as a sham; Mr. Parnell present..............17-19 Sept. 1881

Mr. Parnell arrested for inciting to intimidation and non-payment of rent; put into Kilmainham jail, Dublin.....13 Oct. "

This arrest "legal, merited, and expedient" (*Times*)...15 Oct. "

More troops sent to Ireland from Chatham, etc.; manifesto of Land League, denouncing government and ordering non-payment of rent..............18 Oct. "

Lord lieutenant proclaims suppression of Land League as illegal and criminal, 20 Oct.; leaders declare for passive resistance; abp. McCabe's pastoral against Land League manifesto read in Roman Catholic churches in Dublin..............30 Oct. "

Home-rule meeting at Dublin..............8 Nov. "

Death of dr. McHale, archbishop of Tuam, "Lion of the fold of Judah"..............8 Nov. "

Above 40,000 applications to the land courts..........12 Nov. "

Committee to inquire into working of Land act voted by lords (96-53, 17 Feb.), earl Cairns, chairman.........23 Feb. 1882

Mr. Gladstone's resolution against the lords' committee, 27 Feb.; carried (303-235)..............9, 10 Mch. "

Lords' committee sit..............Mch. "

Mr. Forster confesses failure of government policy through influence of secret societies..............27 Mch. "

Mr. Parnell released *en parole* for 10 days..............10 Apr. "

New government policy; resignation of W. E. Forster; release of Mr. Parnell and other suspects; earl Spencer lord lieutenant about 2 May, 1882; release of Michael Davitt, 5 May, "

Earl Spencer enters Dublin; lord Frederick Cavendish, new chief secretary, and T. H. Burke, permanent under-secretary, assassinated by stabbing, by 4 men, about 7 P.M., in Phœnix park, Dublin, 6 May; manifesto expressing abhorrence of the deed signed by C. S. Parnell, J. Dillon, and M. Davitt, 7 May, "

Government offers 10,000*l.* reward for the murderers; G. O. Trevelyan appointed chief secretary..............9 May, "

Bill for prevention of crime in Ireland, introduced by sir W. V. Harcourt (new tribunal of 3 judges without jury, for special occasions; powers of police increased; Alien act revived; supervision of newspapers and of assemblies, etc.), 11 May, 1882; second reading (383-45)..............19, 20 May, "

Alleged agreement of government with Parnell party, early May, 1882, sarcastically termed treaty of Kilmainham; Arrears of Rent bill, second reading (269-157)......23, 24 May, "

Walter Bourke and corporal Wallace, his escort, shot dead by 5 men near Gort, Galway..............8 June, "

John Henry Blake, agent to marquis of Clanricarde, and his steward, Mr. Kane, shot dead near Loughrea.......29 June, "

Discussion in commons on Prevention of Crime bill; 23 Irish members suspended..............30 June-1 July, "

Mr. Parnell and home-rulers withdraw, July, 1882; 22 arrests at Loughrea, 4 July; government defeated in amendment checking domiciliary visits of suspected persons at night (207-194); *Prevention of Crime bill read third time,* 7, 8 July; passed by the lords, 11 July; royal assent, 12 July, "

Seventeen counties proclaimed..............about 13 July, "

Arrears bill passed in commons (285-177), 21 July; by lords, with amendments (169-98), 31 July; which are modified or negatived by the commons, 8, 9 Aug.; revision accepted by the lords, 10 Aug.; royal assent..............18 Aug. "

John Joyce, wife, son, and daughter shot dead by band of men, near Maamtrasma, in Clonder district, Galway, for informing police..............17, 18 Aug. "

Expiration of Coercion act; suspects released........30 Sept. "

Land League fund in North America closed..........6 Oct. "

Nationalist conference at Dublin forms new Irish National League (ultra) for self-government and land-law reform......17 Oct. "

Conviction of murderers of Joyce family; Patrick Joyce, 15 Nov.; Patrick Casey, 17 Nov.; Myles Joyce, 18 Nov. (all executed, 15 Dec.); *Michael Casey, Thomas Joyce, John Casey,* and Martin Joyce confess; sentence commuted; Thomas Casey and Philbyn, informers..............21 Nov. "

Assault on detectives in Dublin; Cox killed; his murderer, Dowling, severely wounded..............25 Nov. "

Mr. Field, a juryman, stabbed, 27 Nov.; reward of 500*l.* for assassin; Dublin under martial law..............28 Nov. "

Emigration from Ireland; 89,566 in.............. "

Pope's letter to archbishop McCabe, exhorting clergy against secret societies, etc..............about 20 Jan. 1883

Eight men charged with complicity in murder of lord Frederick Cavendish and Mr. Burke..............3 Feb. "

Irish National League, first meeting..............7 Feb. "

Revelations of James Carey, implicating the Land League (Thomas Brennan, secretary, and P. J. Sheridan): statement respecting Irish Invincibles; Mrs. F. Byrne charged with transmitting arms, etc., 17 Feb.; discharged........20 Feb. "

Accused prisoners committed for *trial*.............. " "

W. E. Forster's defence in the commons, and charges against Mr. Parnell; Mr. O'Kelly suspended for a week for giving him the lie..............22, 23 Feb. "

Mr. Parnell's unsatisfactory reply.............. " "

Phœnix park murders: Robert Farrell, James Carey, and others, informers; trial of Joseph Brady, convicted, 11-13 Apr.; Timothy Kelly, third trial, 7-9 May; Thomas Caffrey pleads guilty, 2 May; Patrick Delany and Daniel Curley, 16-18 Apr.; Michael Fagan..............25-27 Apr. "

Irish convention at Philadelphia; Parnell's policy adopted; *dynamitors defeated*..............25-27 Apr. "

Circular from the pope, enjoining the bishops to abstain from favoring disaffection to the government, not to subscribe to

testimonials, etc (archbishop Croke, of Cashel, h. 50*l* to the Parnell testimonial etc) 11 May, 1883
Executed Joseph Brady (actual murderer), 14 May, Daniel Curley 18 May, Michael Fagan 28 May, Thomas Caffrey, 2 June, Timothy Kelly 9 June, "
James Carey, informer, shot dead by Patrick O'Donnell, on board the *Melrose Castle*, near Port Elizabeth, South Africa, 29 July, "
Thirty eight thousand pounds presented to Mr Parnell (" as a national tribute " from the Irish people) at a banquet at the Rotunda Dublin 11 Dec "
Parnellite Land Law Amendment bill rejected by commons (as tending to confiscation) by 235-72 5 Mch 1884
Wm O Brien arrested at Manchester 29 Jan 1889
[Taken to Ireland and confined in Clonmel jail 30 Jan , refusing to wear the prison garb, is roughly treated]
Gladstone and Parnell speak on the Morley amendment to the reply to the queen s speech (amendment defeated), 1 Mch "
Pigott, forger of the Parnell letter, commits suicide at Madrid, 1 Mch "
Sir Charles Russell defends the Parnellites before the commission, tracing the history of agitation for home rule, 18 Mch "
Freedom of city of Edinburgh conferred on Parnell by a vote of 14-13 23 Apr "
Wm O'Brien again arrested with John Dillon for advising tenants not to pay rent 17 Sept 1890
They escape, reach France 10 Oct., sail for U S 25 Oct. "
Trial of the O Shea divorce case begun in London, neither Mrs O Shea nor Parnell offers any defence 15 Nov "
O Shea secures his divorce 17 Nov "
John Dillon and O'Brien convicted and sentenced to 6 months in jail 19 Nov "
Parnell notifies his colleagues that he will not resign leader ship while supported by the Irish people 20 Nov "
Parnell elected unanimously to the leadership of the Irish Nationalist members of Parliament 25 Nov "
Parnell issues a manifesto to the Irish people, stating reasons for continuing in the leadership of the Irish party 28 Nov "
Gladstone denies the statement made concerning him by Parnell 29 Nov "
Catholic hierarchy declare against Parnell 3 Dec "
Justin McCarthy and 44 others withdraw from the meeting of Nationalist members of Parliament and organize as a separate body 6 Dec "
Archbishop and bishops' letter denouncing Parnell read in the Catholic churches in Ireland 7 Dec. "
Parnell leaves London for Ireland, 7 Dec , enthusiastically received at Dublin, 9 Dec , seizes the office of *United Ireland* and ejects the acting editor 10 Dec. "
Anti Parnellites issue a manifesto " "
Parnell begins a stumping tour of Ireland at Cork 11 Dec "
Parnell at Kilkenny 13 Dec. "
McCarthy leaves London for Ireland 15 Dec "
Parnell temporarily blinded at Castle Comers by lime thrown in his eyes 16 Dec "
Sir John Pope Hennessy the McCarthyite candidate, elected at the Kilkenny elections by 1171 votes over Vincent Scully, the Parnellite 22 Dec. "
Parnell and O'Brien hold a secret conference at Boulogne, 30 Dec "
And another 6 Jan 1891
McCarthy and O Brien hold a conference at Boulogne 10 Jan "
Gladstone denies the statement of Parnell that he knew the substance of Parnell s manifesto 13 Jan "
Dillon and O'Brien land at Folkestone and deliver themselves up to the English police 12 Feb "
They are taken to Ireland and placed in Clonmel jail 13 Feb "
Seven Parnellites sail from Queenstown for the U S to raise funds 8 Mch "
National federal convention meets at Dublin, Justin McCarthy presiding 10 Mch "
Gladstone declares in a speech at Hastings that the Liberal party will never support Parnell 17 Mch "
McCarthyites win the North Sligo elections, 780 majority, 2 Apr "
Parnell secretly married 25 June, "
Parnell addresses the League convention at Dublin 23 July, "
Wm O Brien and John Dillon released from jail 30 July, "
Parnell d at his home at Brighton, Engl 7 Oct. "
Parnell buried at Dublin 11 Oct "
Parnellite members issue a manifesto declaring their hostility to the McCarthyites 12 Oct "
Mr Flavin McCarthyite candidate, elected M P to succeed Parnell by a plurality of 1512 6 Nov "
Irish Education bill introduced (opposed by the Roman Catholic clergy) 22 Feb. 1892
Ulster convention at Belfast against home rule 17 June, "
Bill passed 27 June, "
ENGLAND, PARNELL.

KINGS OF IRELAND

979 or 980 Maol Ceachlin II (Malachi) deposed
1001 or 1002 Brian Baromy or Boromhe, slain after defeating Danes at Clontarf 23 Apr 1014
1014 Maol Ceachlin II restored, d 1022 or 1023
[Disputed succession]
1058. Donough or Denis, O Brian, son
1072. Tirloch or Turlough nephew, d 1086.
1086–1132. Kingdom divided, fierce contests for it
1166 Roderic, or Rory, …
1172 Henry II king of England
[English monarchs were styled "Lords of Ireland" until the reign of Henry VIII , who first styled himself king]

Ireland forgeries. In 1786 W H Ireland made public Shakespeare manuscripts which he had forged, and deceived many critics The play "Vortigern" was performed at Drury-lane theatre on 2 Apr 1796 He shortly after acknowledged the forgery, and published his "Confessions" in 1805 He died in 1835 SHAKESPEARE AND HIS PLAYS.

irid'ium and **osmium.** In 1804 Tennant discovered these metals (the heaviest known) in the ore of platinum, in which, in 1844, Claus discovered a third, ruthenium. ELEMENTS

iron found on Mount Ida by the Dactyles, the forest having been burned by lightning, 1432 B.C.—*Arundelian Marbles* [1407, *Hales*, 1283, *Clinton*] The Greeks claimed the discovery of iron, and referred glass to the Phœnicians. Iron was wrought by Tubal-Cain (Gen iv 22) Swedish iron is very celebrated, and Dannemora is the greatest mine of Sweden STEEL.

Belgium an early seat of the iron manufacture, coal said to have been employed at Marche les dames, 1340
British iron cast by Ralph Page and Peter Baude in Sussex, 1543 — *Rymer's Fœdera*
Iron mills used for slitting iron into bars for smiths by Godfrey Bochs, 1590.
Tinning of iron introduced from Bohemia, 1681 Till about 1730 iron ores were smelted with wood charcoal which did not wholly give way to coal and coke till 1788
Operation termed *puddling*, and other improvements in the manufacture, invented by Henry Cort about 1781, who did not reap the due reward of his ingenuity He d in 1800
Henry Bessemer patented his method of manufacturing iron and steel 17 Oct., 5 Dec 1855, 12 Feb. 1856
Wm Robinson announced a method of making wrought iron from cast iron by magnetism July, 1867
John Heaton s process for making steel announced about Nov. 1867, discussed Oct 1868

IN THE UNITED STATES

The first recorded discovery of iron in the U S was in North Carolina, 1585, and the first attempt to manufacture it was in Virginia, 1619 The works were destroyed by the Indians, 1622. The next attempt was at Lynn Mass , where a blast furnace was started, 1643, which produced some "sow" iron, 1645; and a forge was built, 1648 Bog ore was generally used in New England in colonial days The first export of iron ("bar") to England was in 1717, the first pig iron, 1728. Up to 1720 Massachusetts was the chief seat of the iron industry in the colonies. In 1750, Pennsylvania became the leading iron producing state, and maintained the supremacy until after 1880
Great Britain imposes a duty of 10*s* per ton on all iron imported into the American colonies . 1679
Board of Trade (Great Britain) report to Parliament that iron works had been for many years established in Massachusetts, Rhode Island, Connecticut New York Pennsylvania Maryland Virginia and the Carolinas, and from the progress they had made it was expedient to encourage the manufacture in the colonies 1732
Act of Parliament permitting pig-iron and bar iron to be imported into London from the American colonies free of duty, but prohibiting them from erecting any rolling or slitting mill, or forge, to work with a tilt hammer, and from manufacturing steel for exportation 1750
[Duty on bar iron at this time was 2*l.* 1*s* 6*d.* per ton, and on pig iron 3*s* 9*d* per ton]
Furnace, on the Sterling estate, Orange co , N Y , which produced annually 1500 tons of pig iron, worked into bar iron, was built . . 1751
[Great iron chain which crossed the Hudson river during the Revolution to prevent the British from ascending it was made here CHAIN]
Mt. Etna furnace, near Hagerstown, Md , was among the first to cast cannon
Largest amount of iron exported by the American colonies to Great Britain, between 1761 and 1776, was in 1771, when 2222 tons of bar and 5302 tons of pig iron were exported. The manufacturing of iron fell off rapidly after the Revolution, and between 1789-90 the U S. only exported 200 tons of bar and 3500 tons of pig iron.
Report of the Secretary of the Treasury, 1810 shows from $15,000 000 to $20,000 000 invested in the business. There being 153 furnaces, making 53,908 tons of pig iron, 330 forges, making 24,541 tons bar iron, 316 trip hammers and 34 rolling and slitting mills using 6500 tons, and 410 nail factories producing 15 000 000 lbs of nails Iron was then made exclusively with charcoal from the smelting to the finished bar
Hot blast introduced 1832-38
Mauch Chunk Pa., the first successful furnace in smelting iron ore with anthracite coal in the U S , built and in operation 1838

PRODUCTION OF PIG-IRON AND STEEL IN METRIC TONS.

Year.	Austria-Hungary		Belgium.		Canada.	France.		Germany.	
	Pig-Iron.	Steel.	Pig-Iron.	Steel.	Pig-Iron.	Pig-Iron.	Steel.	Pig-Iron.	Steel.
1898.	1,286,338	605,500	979,755	567,728	69,248	2,525,100	1,174,000	7,215,927	5,734,307
1899.	1,323,999	1,127,104	1,036,185	729,820	95,582	2,578,400	1,240,000	7,160,203	6,290,434
1900.	1,311,949	1,145,654	1,161,180	655,199	87,612	2,714,298	1,566,164	7,549,655	6,645,869
1901.	1,300,000	1,142,000	765,420	526,670	248,896	2,400,240	1,465,071	7,835,204	6,394,222
1902.	1,335,000	1,443,000	1,102,910	776,875	324,670	2,427,427	1,635,300	8,402,660	7,780,682
1903.	1,355,000	1,146,000	1,216,500	981,740	265,418	2,827,668	1,854,620	10,085,634	8,801,515

Year.	Italy.		Russia.		Spain.		Sweden.	
	Pig-Iron.	Steel.	Pig-Iron.	Steel.	Pig-Iron.	Steel.	Pig-Iron.	Steel.
1909.	23,990	115,887	2,895,636	1,830,260	289,788	144,355	526,868	300,536
1901.	25,000	120,000	2,807,972	1,815,000	294,118	122,954	528,375	269,897
1902.	24,500	119,500	2,566,000	1,730,250	278,000	124,000	524,400	283,500
1903.	28,250	116,000	2,210,000	1,525,000	380,284	199,642	489,700	310,000

Year.	United Kingdom.		United States.		All Other Countries.		Totals.	
	Pig-Iron.	Steel.	Pig-Iron.	Steel.	Pig-Iron.	Steel.	Pig-Iron.	Steel.
1898.	8,819,968	4,639,042	11,963,317	9,075,793	545,000	355,000	36,418,900	23,710,432
1899.	9,572,178	5,080,000	13,838,634	10,832,765	625,000	400,000	39,722,260	27,520,966
1900.	9,003,046	5,130,800	14,009,870	10,382,064	625,000	400,000	40,198,892	28,315,793
1901.	7,886,019	5,080,000	16,132,408	13,689,173	635,000	405,000	40,800,680	31,029,987
1902.	8,653,976	5,102,420	18,003,448	15,186,406	615,000	412,000	44,557,991	36,479,783
1903.	8,952,183	5,114,647	18,297,400	14,756,691	625,000	418,000	46,733,039	35,356,355

This table shows the changes in the principal iron producing states. In 1860 Michigan stood 5th in order; 2d in 1880; and 1st in 1889. Alabama first appears in 1880, when she ranked 7th; 2d in 1889. Pennsylvania ranked 1st until 1889, when it took 3d place, etc. The principal varieties of ore mined are: Red hematite (Gr. αἱματίτης; sc. λίθος, stone), red iron ore, anhydrous sesquioxide of iron; brown hematite (hydrated sesquioxide of iron); magnetite, ores in which the magnetic oxide of iron (Fe_3O_4) is predominant; carbonite (protoxide of iron). Red hematite, the most valuable of the different varieties, is mined extensively in Michigan, Wisconsin, Alabama, Tennessee, and Missouri; the brown hematite in Virginia and W. Virginia, and quite largely in Pennsylvania; magnetite in New York, Pennsylvania, and New Jersey; carbonite in Kentucky and Ohio, although all the iron-producing states mine red and brown hematite. Total number of persons employed in iron mining in 1889 was, above ground, 18,000, below, 19,709.

AMOUNT OF IRON ORE MINED BY THE PRINCIPAL NATIONS, 1889.

Great Britain	14,546,105 tons.	Sweden	985,904 tons.
Germany	11,001,042 "	Algeria	475,000 "
Spain	5,067,144 "	Cuba	256,278 "
France	2,500,000 "	Belgium	220,000 "
Austro-Hungary	2,300,000 "	Italy	173,489 "
Russia	1,400,000 "	Canada	75,162 "

[This amount has not materially changed up to 1894.]

Amount of pig-iron produced in the U. S. in 1870 was 2,052,821 tons; in 1880, 3,781,021 tons; in 1890, 9,579,779 tons, or about 35 per cent. of the production of the world, valued at over $134,000,000. In the production of pig-iron for the year 1890 the principal states rank as follows:

1. Pennsylvania	4,712,511 tons.	8. Michigan	224,908 tons.
2. Ohio	1,302,299 "	9. Wisconsin	210,037 "
3. Alabama	890,432 "	10. New Jersey	145,040 "
4. Illinois	674,506 "	11. West Virginia	108,764 "
5. New York	359,040 "	12. Missouri	99,131 "
6. Virginia	302,447 "	13. Maryland	96,246 "
7. Tennessee	290,747 "	14. Kentucky	44,199 "

Iron Cross, an order of merit established by Frederick William III. of Prussia, 10 Mch. 1813, for patriotic bravery in war against France; revived by William I. in the Franco-Prussian war, and awarded by him to his son for victory at Wissembourg, 4 Aug. 1870. About 40,000 persons were decorated in 1870-71.

iron crown (of Italy), of gold and precious stones, set in a thin ring of iron, said to have been forged from a nail of Christ's cross, by order of Theudelinde for her husband, Agilulf, king of the Longobards, 591, and deposited in the church at Monza. Charlemagne was crowned with it, and later all emperors who were kings of Lombardy; Napoleon I. at Milan, on 26 May, 1805, put it on his head, saying, "*Dieu me l'a donnée; gare à qui y touchera*" ("God has given it to me; woe to him who touches it"). The crown was removed from Monza to Mantua by the Austrians on 23 Apr. 1859. After the peace of Vienna, in 1866, it was given up to gen. Menabrea on 11 Oct., and presented to king Victor Emmanuel at Turin on 4 Nov. It is now kept in the cathedral at Monza.—The order of the "Iron Crown of Italy," instituted by Napoleon, 26 May, 1805, was abolished in 1814, but revived by the emperor of Austria, 12 Feb. 1816. The order of the Crown of Italy was instituted by king Victor Emmanuel, 20 Feb. 1868.

iron mask, the man with the. A mysterious prisoner in France, wearing a mask and closely confined under M. de St.-Mars, at Pignerol (1679), Exilles (1681), Sainte-Marguerite (1687), and at the Bastile (1698), where he died, 19 Nov. 1703. He was of noble mien, and was treated with respect; but his keepers had orders to despatch him if he uncovered. M. de St.-Mars himself always placed the dishes on his table, and stood in his presence. The following conjectures have been made as to his identity: An Armenian patriarch forcibly carried from Constantinople (who died 10 years before the mask); the duc de Vermandois, son of Louis XIV., reported to have perished in the camp before Dixmude; the duc de Beaufort, reported beheaded before Candia; James, duke of Monmouth, executed on Tower hill; a son of Anne of Austria, queen of Louis XIII., either by cardinal Mazarin or by the duke of Buckingham; the twin brother of Louis XIV. (a conjecture of Voltaire and others); Foucquet, an eminent statesman in the time of Louis XIV., and a count Matthioli, secretary of state to Charles III., duke of Mantua. M. Delort and the right hon. Agar Ellis (afterwards lord Dover) tried to prove Matthioli to have been the person; and later investigations makes this more probable. Recently a general de Burlonde has been cited as wearer of the mask, for raising the siege of Conti (an improbable story). The mask was of velvet, strengthened with whalebone.

Iroquois. INDIANS.

irrigation, practised in the east and in Egypt from remote ages. It was strenuously advocated for India by sir A. Cotton and others at the Social Science congress at Manchester, Oct. 1866. Of late irrigation has been widely practised in the western United States, where large tracts of fertile land cannot be cultivated unless irrigated; and a great deal of land that was worthless owing to the scarcity of water has been brought under cultivation, especially in California, Colorado, Utah, Wyoming, Nevada, Idaho, Montana, and the territories of Arizona and New Mexico.

NUMBER OF ACRES IRRIGATED DEVOTED TO CROPS (NOT PASTURAGE), AND COST, ETC.

Areas.	Idaho.	Utah.	Wyoming.	Montana.	Nevada.	Arizona.	New Mexico.
Total irrigated acreage in crops, 1890	217,005	263,473	229,676	350,582	224,403	65,821	91,745
Number of irrigators	4,323	9,724	1,917	3,706	1,167	1,075	3,085
Average size of farms irrigated in crop acres	50	27	119	95	192	61	30
Average size of crop areas of 160 acres and upwards in acres	270	312	494	307	513	287	312
Per cent. of acreage of irrigated crop areas of 160 acres and upwards to total irrigation	26	10	65	50	79	34	21
Average size of irrigated crop areas under 160 acres	[illegible]	25	50	56	58	43	24

NUMBER OF ACRES IRRIGATED DEVOTED TO CROPS (NOT PASTURAGE), AND COST, ETC.—(*Continued.*)

Areas.	Idaho.	Utah.	Wyoming.	Montana.	Nevada.	Arizona.	New Mexico.
Average first cost of water per acre cultivated by irrigation.	$4.74	$10.55	$3.62	$4.63	$7.58	$7.07	$5.58
" annual cost " " "	.80	.91	.44	.95	.84	1.55	1.54
" first cost of preparation per acre for cultivation...	9.31	14.85	8.23	8.29	10.57	8.60	11.71
" value of irrigated lands per acre including buildings, etc..............................	46.50	84.25	31.40	49.50	41.00	48.68	50.98
" annual value of products per acre of irrigated lands..	12.93	18.03	8.25	12.96	12.92	13.92	12.80
Per cent. of irrigated crop lands to total area of state......	.25 of 1%	.5 of 1%	.4 of 1%	.4 of 1%	.3 of 1%	.1 of 1%	.1 of 1%

Irvingites, followers of Edward Irving, who was born 15 Aug. 1792, and became assistant to dr. Chalmers, at Glasgow, in 1819. In 1823 he attracted crowds of distinguished persons to his sermons at the Scotch church, Hatton garden, London. A new church was built for him in Regent square in 1827. Soon after he propounded new doctrines on the human nature of Christ; and the "Utterances of Unknown Tongues," which began in his congregation with a Miss Hall and Mr. Taplin, 16 Oct. 1831, were countenanced by him as of divine inspiration. He was expelled from the Scotch church 15 Mch. 1833. His church, "reconstituted with the threefold cord of a sevenfold ministry," was removed to Newman street. Irving was in his early manhood an ardent admirer of Jane Welsh, afterwards the wife of Carlyle. He died 8 Dec. 1834. The church established by him is now called the "Holy Catholic Apostolic Church." It uses a liturgy (framed in 1842 and enlarged 1853), and its officers are named apostles, angels, prophets, etc. In 1852 lighted candles were placed on the magnificent altar, and burning of incense during prayers was prescribed. The Gothic church, in Gordon square, London, was solemnly opened, 1 Jan. 1854. It is said that all who join the church offer it a tenth of their income. They had 30 chapels in England in 1851.

Isan'dula, Isandla'na, or **Isandlwa'na,** termed the "English Cremera." ZULULAND, 22 Jan. 1879.

Isauria, a province in Asia Minor, conquered by the Romans 78 B.C.; by the Saracens 650 A.D.; retaken by the emperor Leo III., who founded the Isaurian dynasty, 718, which ended with Constantine VI. in 797. Isauria was incorporated with Turkey 1387.

[illegible] mission to God, the name given [illegible]

[illegible] ucky). An island in the Missis- [illegible] Madrid, Mo., was strongly forti- [illegible] the beginning of the civil war. It surrendered to gen. Pope and commodore Foote 7 Apr. 1862, with about 7000 prisoners and over 100 pieces of artillery.

islands, imaginary. Besides the Hesperides, there were many islands scattered over the Atlantic by the fancies of navigators and cosmographers. Such islands are described in the Arabic geography of Edrisi, 1153-54 A.D. To these may be added the island of St. Brandon, supposed to have been discovered in the 6th century. Also Antilia and the Islands of the Seven Cities, as well as Mayda and the isle Verda; but none more famous or longer-lived than the isle of Brazil. It first appeared on a Venetian map of Andrea di Bianco, 1436, as the I. de Brazi, near the present Azores. This, with Antilia, St. Brandon, and others, was conspicuous on maps in the time of Columbus. Antilia still lives by name in the Greater and Lesser Antilles, as applied to the West Indies; and the isle of Brazil is remembered in the name of the largest state of South America.

Isle of France. MAURITIUS.

Ismail, Bessarabia. After a long siege by the Russians, who lost 20,000 men, the town was taken by storm, 22 Dec. 1790; when Suwarrow, the most merciless warrior of modern times, put the brave Turkish garrison (30,000 men) to the sword, delivered Ismail to pillage, and ordered the massacre of 6000 women. It was again captured by the Russians 26 Sept. 1809, and retained till the treaty of Paris in 1856, when it was ceded to Moldavia.

Ispahan' was made the capital of Persia by Abbas the Great, in 1590. It lost its supremacy in 1796, when Teheran became the capital.

Israel, kingdom of. JEWS.—Händel's oratorio "Israel in Egypt" first performed 4 Apr. 1739.

Issus, Asia Minor, the site of Alexander's second great battle with Darius, whose queen and family were captured, Oct. 333 B.C. The Persian army, according to Justin, consisted of 400,000 foot and 100,000 horse; 61,000 of the former and 10,000 of the latter were left dead on the field, and 40,000 were taken prisoners. Here the emperor Septimius defeated his rival Niger, 194 A.D.

Isthmian games received their name from the isthmus of Corinth, where they were observed; instituted by Sisyphus about 1406 B.C., in honor of Melicertes, a sea-god.—*Lenglet.* Reinstituted in honor of Neptune by Theseus about 1239 B.C.; and their celebration was held so sacred that even a public calamity did not prevent it. The games were revived by Julius Cæsar, 60 B.C.; and by the emperor Julian, 362 A.D.

Istria, a peninsula in the Adriatic sea, was finally subdued by the Romans, 177 B.C. After various changes it came under the rule of Venice in 1378, and was annexed 1420. It was obtained by Austria, 1796; by France, 1806; by Austria, 1814.

Italian language, based on Latin, is said by Dante to be formed of a selection of the best forms from the different dialects. Elegant poetry was written by Guido Cavalcanti, who died 1301; and good prose by Malespini, about 1250.

Italian literature and **authors.** LITERATURE.

Italian Republic was the name given to the remodelled Cisalpine republic. Napoleon Bonaparte president, Jan. 1802.

Italy (either from Italus, an early king, or *italus*, a bull calf), a kingdom in S. Europe, consisting of a peninsula and numerous islands, was called the garden of Europe. The Pelasgians, Umbrians, Oscans, and Etruscans combined are regarded as the progenitors of the Latins; a predominant element in the nations still known as the Latin races in southern Europe. The history of Italy is soon absorbed into that of Rome, founded 753 B.C. Previous to the 15th century it was desolated by intestine wars and the interference of the German emperors. GUELPHS. Since then Spain, France, and Germany struggled for the possession of the country, which has been divided among them several times. Spain predominated in Italy during the 16th and 17th centuries; yielded to the house of Hapsburg at the beginning of the 18th. The victories of Bonaparte in 1797-98 changed the government of Italy; but the Austrian rule was re-established at the peace in 1814. In 1848 the Milanese and Venetians revolted and joined Piedmont, but were subdued by marshal Radetzky. The hostile feeling between Austria and Piedmont gradually increased till war broke out in April, 1859. The Austrians were defeated, and the kingdom of Italy, comprising Piedmont, Sardinia, Lombardy, Tuscany, Modena, Parma, the Romagna, Naples, and Sicily, was re-established 17 Mch. 1861, by the Italian parliament (443 deputies from 59 provinces). On 29 Oct. 1861, the internal government was reorganized; the 59 provinces were placed under prefects, subject to 4 directors-general. In 1861 the population was 21,728,529. War with Austria was declared 18 June, 1866; and on 3 Oct. peace was signed at Vienna, and Venetia was ceded to Italy, on the payment of 40,000,000 florins. The kingdom of Italy was completed by the occupation of Rome as the capital, 1870. Estimated population of the kingdom, 1862, 25,003,635 (Rome was added in 1870); 1878, 28,209,620; 1890, 30,158,408; 1901, 32,475,000. Area, 114,410 sq. miles. For other details, aside from this record, ROME and the various Italian cities.

	B.C.
Italy (Saturnia), fabled rule of Saturn, the golden age........	2450
Arrival of Œnotrus from Arcadia, 1710; and of Evander; reign of Latinus..about	1240
Æneas the Trojan said to land in Italy, defeat and kill Turnus;	

marry Lavinia, daughter of king Latinus, and found Lavinium in S. Italy 1182 et seq
Greek colonies (MAGNA GRÆCIA) founded 974-443
Romulus builds Rome 753
[For subsequent history, ROME] A.D.
Odoacer, leader of Heruli, establishes the kingdom of Italy 476
Ostrogoths invade Italy 489, and retain it till 491
They are expelled by the imperial gens Narses and Belisarius (IRON CROWN, KINGS OF ITALY) 552
Narses, governor of Italy invites Lombards from Germany, 568, who overrun Italy 596
Invasion and defeat of Constans II 662
Venice first governed by a doge 697
Pepin gives Ravenna to the pope 754
Charlemagne invades Italy 774, overcomes Lombards, crowned emperor of the West at Rome by pope Leo III 25 Dec 800
Saracens invade Italy and settle at Bari 842
Invasion of Otho I 951, crowned emperor 2 Feb 962
Genoa becomes important 1000
Saracens expelled by the Normans 1016-17
Normans acquire Naples from the pope 1051
Pope Gregory VII, Hildebrand pretends to universal sovereignty, assisted by Matilda, countess of Tuscany, mistress of greater part of Italy 1073-85
Disputes between popes and emperors as to ecclesiastical investitures begin to agitate Italy and Germany about 1073
Rise of Lombard cities about 1120
Who war with each other 1144
Venetians obtain many victories over Eastern emperors 1125
Wars of GUELPHS and GHIBELLINES begin about 1161
Frederick I (Barbarossa) interferes, his wars 1154-75
Lombard league formed 1167
His defeat at Legnano 29 May, 1176
Peace of Constance 1183
Civil wars again 1199 et seq
Rise of the Medici at Florence about 1251
Wars of Frederick II and the Lombard league 1236-50
His natural son Manfred king of Sicily, defeated and killed at Benevento by Charles of Anjou 26 Feb 1266
Who defeats Conradin at Tagliacozzo 23 Aug 1268
Visconti rule at Milan 1277
SICILIAN VESPERS, massacre of French, who are expelled from Sicily 30 Mch 1282
Clement V (pope, 1305) fixes his residence at Avignon in France, 1309
Louis Gonzaga master of Mantua with title of imperial vicar, 1328
First doge of Genoa appointed 1339
Lucca independent 1370
Rome again the seat of the pope 1377
Charles VIII of France invades Italy, 1494, and conquers Naples, 1495, loses it 1496
Louis XII joins Venice and conquers Milan (soon lost) 1499
League of Cambray (1508) against Venice, which is despoiled of Italian possessions 1509
Leo X pope, patron of literature and art 1513-22
Wars of Charles V and Francis I 1515-21
Francis defeated and prisoner at Pavia 24 Feb 1525
Parma and Placentia made a duchy for his family by pope Paul III (Alexander Farnese) 1545
Peace of Cateau Cambresis 1559
War of the Mantuan succession 1627-31
Catinat and the French defeat duke of Savoy at Marsaglia, 4 Oct 1693
War of Spanish succession commences in Italy 1701
Battle of Turin 7 Sept. 1706
Division of Italy at the peace of Utrecht 11 Apr 1713
Duke of Savoy becomes king of Sardinia 1720
Successful French campaign in Italy 1745
Milan, etc., obtained by house of Hapsburg, 1706, confirmed by treaty of Aix la Chapelle 1748
Italy overrun by French May-Dec 1796
Venetian states divided by France and Austria by treaty of Campo Formio, Cisalpine republic founded 17 Oct 1797
Pius VI deposed by Bonaparte Feb 1798
Russians, under Suwarrow, defeat French at Trebia, etc 1799
Bonaparte crosses Alps, 16-20 May, defeats Austrians at Marengo 14 June, 1800
Cisalpine, Italy, becomes the Italian republic (Bonaparte president) Jan 1802
Napoleon crowned king of Italy 26 May, 1805
Eugène Beauharnais viceroy of Italy "
Austria loses Italian possessions by treaty of Presburg, ratified, 1 Jan 1806
Kingdom ceases at fall of Napoleon, 1814, Lombardo Venetian kingdom established for Austria 7 Apr 1815
Formation of Young Italy party by Mazzini, insurrections 1831-33
Italian Association for Science first met (at Pisa) 1837
Insurrection in Lombardy and Venice, Mch, supported by king of Sardinia and pope Apr 1848
King, defeated at Novara, abdicates, 23 Mch, and Lombardy reverts to Austria (AUSTRIA, SARDINIA) May, 1849
"Napoleon III et l'Italie" pub Feb. 1859
Austrian ultimatum, rejected by Sardinia 26 Apr "
Austrians cross the Ticino, 27 Apr, French enter Genoa, 3 May, "
Peaceful revolution at Florence, 27 Apr, Parma, 3 May, Modena 15 June, "
Austrians defeated at Montebello, 20 May, Palestro, 30, 31 May, Magenta, 4 June, Marignano, 8 June, Solferino 24 June, "
Provisional governments at Florence, 27 Apr, Parma, May, and Modena (sovereigns retire) 15 June, "
Insurrection in papal states Bologna, Ferrara, etc. 13-15 June, "

ITA

Massacre of insurgents at Perugia by Swiss troops 20 June, 1859
Allies cross the Mincio 1 July, "
Armistice between Austria and France 8 July "
Preliminaries of peace at Villafranca, Lombardy surrendered to Sardinia 11 July, "
Italy dismayed at peace, agitation at Milan Florence, Modena, Parma, etc, count Cavour resigns as minister July "
Pope appeals to Europe against king of Sardinia 12 July, "
Tuscany Modena, Parma, and Romagna form a defensive alliance and ask annexation to Piedmont 20 Aug-10 Sept., trade made free between them and Piedmont 10 Oct "
Treaty of Zurich (Italian confederacy, etc), signed 10 Nov "
Garibaldi retires from Sardinian service 18 Nov "
New Sardinian constitution proclaimed 7 Dec "
Pope condemns pamphlet "Le Pape et le Congres" 31 Dec "
Napoleon III recommends pope to give up legations " "
Pope refuses and denounces emperor 8 Jan 1860
Count Cavour charged to form a ministry 16 Jan "
Annexation to Sardinia voted (by universal suffrage) in Parma, Modena and the Romagna, 11 Mch, Tuscany, 16 Mch, accepted by the king 18-22 Mch "
Treaty ceding Savoy and Nice to France signed, 24 Mch approved by Sardinian parliament 29 May, "
French troops retire from Italy May, "
Vain insurrections in Sicily 4 Apr, 2 May, "
Garibaldi lands at Marsala in Sicily 11 May, assumes office of dictator 14 May, defeats Neapolitans at Calatafimi, 15 May, and at Melazzo 20 July, by convention Neapolitans agree to evacuate SICILY 30 July, "
Garibaldi lands at Reggio in Calabria, 18 Aug, enters Naples, Francis II retires 7 Sept "
Insurrection in Papal States 8 Sept, Sardinians enter 11 Sept, defeat papal troops at Castel Fidardo, 18 Sept, take Ancona, 17-29 Sept "
Victor Emmanuel takes command of army 4 Oct "
Sardinians enter kingdom of Naples, 15 Oct, defeat Neapolitans at Isernia 17 Oct. "
Garibaldi defeats Neapolitans at the Volturno 1 Oct "
By universal suffrage (plebiscitum), Sicily and Naples vote for annexation to Sardinia 21 Oct. "
Capua bombarded, Neapolitans retire, 2 Nov, and are defeated at the Garigliano 3 Nov "
Victor Emmanuel enters Naples as king, 7 Nov, Garibaldi resigns dictatorship, retires to Caprera 9 Nov "
Victor Emmanuel receives homage from Neapolitan clergy etc, gives money to encourage education, appoints a ministry, including Poerio, etc. Nov "
Siege of Gaeta commences attack by sea prevented by the presence of the French fleet 3 Nov et seq "
Treaty of ZURICH signed 10 Nov "
Decree in honor of Garibaldi's army 16 Nov "
Reactionary movements suppressed Nov-Dec "
Prince of Carignan Savoy appointed lieutenant of Naples Jan 1861
French fleet retires from Gaeta, 19 Jan, after bombardment it surrenders, Francis II retires to Rome 13 Feb "
Monastic establishments in Naples abolished, with compensation to the inmates, schools established Feb "
First Italian parliament meets, 18 Feb, decrees Victor Emmanuel king 26 Feb and 14 Mch "
Italy recognized by Great Britain 31 Mch "
Order for the levy of 70 000 soldiers Apr "
Cavour forms a new ministry, with members from all parts of Italy Apr "
Pope protests against the kingdom 15 Apr "
Death of count Cavour, aged 52. 6 June, "
Kingdom recognized by France 24 June, "
Kingdom recognized by Portugal and Belgium, 1 Oct, divided into 59 prefectures etc 13 Oct. "
Kingdom recognized by Prussia 1 Mch 1862
Kingdom recognized by Russia. 3 July, "
Garibaldi enters Sicily, at Marsala calls for volunteers, giving the watchword "Rome or death!" 19 July, "
King issues a proclamation against his proceedings as tending to rebellion 3 Aug "
Garibaldi at Catania, organizes provisional government, 19 Aug "
Sicily proclaimed in a state of siege, 21 Aug, put under gen Cialdini 22 Aug "
Garibaldi issues his last proclamation, embarks at Catania, lands at Melito, in Calabria, and marches towards Reggio, 25 Aug, La Marmora proclaims a state of siege 26 Aug, Garibaldi and followers meet royalists under Pallavicini, at Aspromonte, after a short skirmish, he is wounded and taken, 29 Aug., removed to Varignano, near Spezzia 1 Sept. "
Gen Durando in diplomatic circular condemns Garibaldi's proceedings, asserting the necessity of the Italian government possessing Rome 10 Sept "
Amnesty to Garibaldi and followers 5 Oct. "
Father Passaglia and 10 000 (out of 80,000) Italian priests sign declaration against pope's temporal authority Nov "
Garibaldi removed to Pisa, 9 Nov, ball extracted from his foot, 23 Nov "
Grand Cavour canal for irrigation of Piedmont opened. 1 June, 1863
Army of Piedmont (50,000) consolidated by La Marmora and expanded into the "army of Italy" (250,000) Oct. "
Franco Italian convention (French troops to quit Rome in 2 years [from 6 Feb 1865], Florence to be capital) 15 Sept. 1864
King and court proceed to Florence, 13 May, he opens the festival, the 600th anniversary of Dante's birth 14 May, 1865
Kingdom recognized by Spain June, "
French troops leaving Italy, general election, moderate party pr[illegible]te. Nov "

Alliance with Prussia. 12 May, 1866

War declared against Austria 18 June, "

Army, headed by the king, crosses the Mincio, 23 June, defeated at Custozza 24 June, "

Venetia ceded to France by emperor of Austria 3 July, "

Fruitless conflicts, volunteers under Garibaldi defeated at Monte Suello 4 July, "

Bill for suppression of monasteries and confiscation of property passed 7 July, "

Cialdini crosses the Po and enters Venetia 8 July, "

Naval battle near Lissa Italians defeated by Austrians (*Re d'Italia* and *Palestro* blown up) 20 July, "

Italians beaten at Versa the last conflict 26 July "

Armistice for 4 weeks signed 12 Aug "

Peace with Austria signed at Vienna 3 Oct, ratified 12 Oct "

Austrians retire from Peschiera, 9 Oct., Mantua, 10 Oct, Verona, 16 Oct., Venice 17 Oct "

Plebiscitum in Venetia, for annexation with Italy, 641,758, against, 69 21 Oct "

Result reported, the IRON CROWN presented to the king at Turin, 4 Nov "

Parliament opened by king, who declares that "Italy is now restored to herself" 15 Dec. "

Government proposal to invest property of religious bodies for support of clergy (Free Church and Ecclesiastical Liquidation bill) brought forward Jan 1867

Church Property bill passed Aug "

Garibaldi, about to enter the Roman territory with volunteers, captured by Italian government at Sinalunga (or Asinalunga) and sent to Alessandria 23 Sept "

Sent to Caprera, 27 Sept, escapes to Leghorn and is sent back, 2 Oct "

Bands of Garibaldians invade Roman territories Sept-Oct "

Garibaldi escapes from Caprera 15 Oct "

Embarkation of French troops at Toulon suspended by resignation of Rattazzi and ministry 20 Oct. "

Garibaldi at Florence proclaims expedition against Rome, 22 Oct "

Garibaldians defeated at Viterbo 25 Oct. "

Enter Roman territories, defeat papal troops and take Monte Rotondo 26, 27 Oct. "

Menabrea's ministry formed, proclamation of Victor Emmanuel against the Garibaldian invasion 27 Oct. "

French army arrives at Cività Vecchia, 28 Oct, 2 brigades enter Rome 30 Oct "

Royal Italian troops enter papal territory, Menabrea's justificatory circular, suppression of insurrectional committees in Italy 30 Oct "

Garibaldi defeated at Mentana, 3 Nov, retreats into Italy with his son captured and sent to Varignano, gulf of Spezzia, 4 Nov "

Garibaldi sent to Caprera 25 Nov "

Meeting of parliament, judicious firmness, amnesty for Garibaldians proclaimed 5 Dec. "

New order of knighthood, the "Crown of Italy," constituted, 20 Feb. 1868

Victor Emmanuel Ferdinand, son of prince Humbert, born at Naples 11 Nov 1869

Œcumenical council at Rome (COUNCILS OF THE CHURCH, ROME) opened 8 Dec "

Neutrality in Franco Prussian war announced, 18 July, additional armaments ordered . 4 Aug 1870

Fruitless mission of prince Napoleon to obtain help for France, 21-25 Aug "

Circular note from government recounting failure to conciliate the pope since 1860, proposes favorable terms 29 Aug "

French vessel *Orenoque* placed at Cività Vecchia on behalf of the pope . Aug "

Letter from king to pope, announcing occupation of Rome necessary to order . 8 Sept. "

Italian troops enter papal territories (ROME), occupy Viterbo and other places 12 Sept "

Gen Bixio marches towards Rome 18, 19 Sept. "

After short resistance, Italians under gen Cadorna enter ROME, 20 Sept "

Plébiscite in papal territories for union with kingdom of Italy (out of 167,548 voters), 133,681, against, 1507 2 Oct. "

King receives the result of the plébiscite 8 Oct "

Rome incorporated with Italy by royal decree, gen La Marmora governor 9 Oct "

Diplomatic circular announcing occupation of Rome as capital of Italy 18 Oct "

Roman provinces united in one, with 5 sub prefectures, 19 Oct. "

Amadeus, duke of Aosta, the king's second son, elected king by the Spanish Cortes 16 Nov "

Parliament meets, king declares Rome capital of Italy, 5 Dec "

Bills introduced for transfer of capital and preservation of pope's rights . about 10 Dec "

Cenis tunnel completed 25 Dec "

King and ministers remove to Rome, 1, 2 July, proclaimed the capital 3 July, 1871

Law for expulsion of JESUITS passed 25 June, 1873

Accoltellatori (secret assassinating societies) reported in Ravenna and other places Sept.-Oct. 1874

About 80 secret extortioners (camorra) in Naples seized and transported . Sept.-Oct "

Jesuits ordered to quit their establishments . 15 Oct. "

Garibaldi declines money (3500*l*.) voted to him 31 Dec. "

He enters Rome amid excitement, takes seat in Chamber of Deputies, and takes oath to the king 24 Jan 1875

Devotes sum voted to improvement of the Tiber, etc 12 Feb "

Elections of parish priests declared valid in opposition to bishops . July-Aug 1875

Discovery near Verona of above 50,000 coins of Gallienus and others, chiefly bronze Jan 1877

Bill for repressing clerical abuses adopted by deputies, pope expresses displeasure in circular to foreign powers, 21 Mch, bill rejected by senate 7 May, "

Antonelli case.—Countess Loreta Lambertini claims property of her alleged father cardinal Antonelli, resisted by his brothers, 30 June, trial, case not proved 6 Dec. "

Father Curci (JESUITS) publishes "Dissidio Moderno fra la Chiesa e l'Italia," against pope's temporal power Dec. "

Death of La Marmora (aged 74), 5 Jan, death of king Victor Emmanuel II 9 Jan, his funeral, procession 2 miles long, buried in the Pantheon, Rome 17 Jan 1878

Death of pope Pius IX, 7 Feb., election of Leo XIII 20 Feb "

Antonelli case.—Countess permitted to appear in court, case deferred . Feb "

Popular discontent at Berlin treaty, desire for acquiring Trent and Trieste, cry of "Italia irredenta!" meetings at Rome, etc about 21 July "

David Lazzaretti "the saint," a peasant, aged 48, founder of a religious socialistic sect in 1868 with 12 apostles, etc., and creed somewhat Protestant, proposed to erect 7 hermitages, marched towards Arcidosso, in Tuscany, with between 2000 and 3000 followers, David, clad in a half regal, half pontifical costume proclaiming the Christian republic, resisted police, who, when fired on, fired and killed David and another, his followers carry off David's body 18 Aug "

Attempted assassination of king at Naples by Giovanni Passanante, an internationalist, aged 29, king and Cairoli, minister, slightly wounded 17 Nov "

Passanante condemned to death at Naples, 7 Mch, to perpetual imprisonment (by the king) 29 Mch 1879

Antonelli case.—Countess Lambertini's appeal rejected, 8 July, "

Aurora a papal daily newspaper, appears at Rome. 1 Jan 1880

Garibaldi and his son Menotti resign as deputies on account of imprisonment of his son in-law gen Canzio, for republican manifestations, 27 Sept., Garibaldi goes to Genoa, Oct, Canzio released 10 Oct "

St Gothard railway opened, Lucerne to Milan 20, 21 May, 1882

Death of Garibaldi at Caprera deeply lamented 2 June, "

Buried there in presence of thousands 8 June, "

Four hundredth anniversary of Raphael's birth celebrated at Rome 28 Mch. 1883

Army, 2,113,969 men 1 Jan 1885

Navy consists of 112 vessels afloat or building " "

Expedition to Assab to avenge the massacre of Giuletti and Bianchi . "

Ironclad *Castel Fidardo* arrives at Beilul 25 Jan. "

Ministry determine to assist Great Britain in the Soudan, 6 Feb. "

Italian flag hoisted at Massowah (SOUDAN) " "

Additional expeditions sent to the Red sea Feb. "

Sig Crispi, premier Aug 1887

Duke Torlonia, syndic of Rome, dismissed for congratulating the pope on his jubilee 2 Jan 1888

Abolition of capital punishment passed by the chambers, June, "

War with Abyssinia (MASSOWAH) 1887-88

Duke of Aosta, ex king of Spain, marries his niece, princess Lætitia, daughter of his sister Clotilde and prince Napoleon Jerome . 11 Sept 1888

Treaty of peace with Abyssinia . 2 Oct 1889

Italian protectorate over Abyssinia announced 14 Oct "

Maj Gaetani Casati returns from African explorations, received at Rome (AFRICA) . 14 July, 1890

Great ironclad *Sardegna* launched at Spezia (NAVY) 20 Sept "

Treaty for delimitation of British and Italian sphere of influence in E Africa signed at Rome 15 Apr 1891

Sig Crispi retires from public office. 15 Feb 1892

Difficulty with U S. relative to massacre of Italians at New Orleans La, settled (MAFFIA) 14 Apr 1893

UNITED STATES

KINGS OF ITALY

476 Odoacer, king of the Heruli, invades Italy, and becomes king, conquered and slain by

493. Theodoric, king of the Ostrogoths, an able prince. He put to death the philosophers Boëthius and Symmachus, falsely accused about 525

526 Athalaric, his grandson, dies of the plague.

534. Theodatus elected, assassinated.

536 Vitiges elected

540. Theodebald (Hildibald) elected, assassinated

541 Totila, or Baduila, a great prince, killed in battle against imperial army under Narses.

552 Theias falls in battle

Italy subject to the Eastern empire till

568. Alboin, king of the Lombards, with a huge mixed army, conquers Italy, poisoned by his wife Rosamond for compelling her to drink wine out of a cup formed of her father's skull

573 Cleoph, assassinated.

575 Autharis, poisoned.

591 Agilulph.

615 Adaloald, poisoned

625 Arioald.

636 Rotharis; married Arioald's widow, published a code of laws.

652 Rodoald (son), assassinated

653 Aribert I (uncle)

661. Berthari and Godebert (sons), dethroned by

662 Grimoald, duke of Benevento.

671. Berthari re established.

686 Cunibert (son)
700 Luitbert, dethroned by
701 Ragimbert
" Aribert II (son)
712 Anspraud elected
" Luitprand (son) a great prince and a favorite of the church
744 Hildebrand (nephew), deposed
" Rachis, duke of Friuli, elected, became a monk
749 Astolph (brother)
756 Desiderius (Didier) quarrelled with pope Adrian, who invited Charlemagne into Italy, who deposed Desiderius, and ended the Lombard kingdom
781 Pepin or Carloman (son of Charlemagne)
812 Bernard
820 Lothaire (son of Louis le Debonnaire)

EMPERORS

875 Charles the Bald
877 Carloman
879 Charles the Fat
888 Berenger I
889 " and Guy
891 " and Lambert.
921 " and Rudolph of Burgundy
926 Hugh of Provence
945 Lothaire II
950 Berenger II and Adalbert his son, deposed in 961 by emperor Otho the Great, who added Italy to German empire

MODERN KINGS OF ITALY

1805 Napoleon I proclaimed king of Italy, 18 Mch, crowned at Milan, 26 May, abdicated 1814
1851 Victor Emmanuel II (of SARDINIA) b 14 Mch 1820 declared king of Italy by parliament, 17 Mch 1861, d 9 Jan 1878
1878 Humbert (son) b 14 Mch 1844, married his cousin, Margherita (b 20 Nov 1851), 22 Apr 1868
Heir Victor Emmanuel (son), prince of Naples, b 11 Nov 1869

Ith'aca, a small island in the Ionian sea, kingdom of Ulysses IONIAN ISLANDS It was explored by dr Schliemann, in 1878, few discoveries being made Area, 44 sq miles

itineraries. The Roman Itinerarium was a table of stages between important places The "Itineraria Antonini" of the whole Roman empire, usually ascribed to the emperor Aurelius Antoninus and his successors, 138-180 A D, was probably based upon the survey made by Julius Cæsar 44 B.C. The Itinerarium Hierosolymitanum" was drawn up for pilgrims about 333 A D

Iu'ka, a post-village of N E Mississippi Near here Rosecrans attacked the confederates under Price, 19 Sept 1862, losing 782 men, killed and wounded The confederates about a like number The general movement was under direction of gen Grant, but the failure of subordinates to co-operate allowed Price to retreat without severe loss.

ivory is essentially equivalent to dentine, the principal constituent of teeth By usage however, its application is restricted to the tusks of the elephant the hippopotamus, the walrus, the narwhal, the sperm-whale, and of the mammoth embedded in the ice along the northern coast of Siberia It was brought to Solomon from Tarshish, about 992 B.C (1 Kings x 22) The colossal statues of Jupiter Minerva, etc. by Phidias, were formed of ivory and gold, 444 B C SCULPTURE Ivory tusk, 7 ft long, sent by the Zulu king Cetywayo to lord Chelmsford as a token of peace, summer, 1879 A pair of African elephant's tusks at the London exhibition of 1851 measured 8 ft 6 in in length, 22 in in circumference, and weighed 325 pounds

ivory, vegetable, the ripened seed of the plant known to botanists as *Phytelephas macrocarpa* It is a native of South America The hard ripened seed is valuable as a substitute for animal ivory

Ivry, a town near Evreux, N W France Here Henry IV totally defeated the duc de Mayenne and the League army, 14 Mch 1590 Macaulay makes this victory of the Huguenots over the French Catholics the subject of a poem, "Battle of Ivry"

J

J, the latest addition to the English alphabet, was distinguished from **I** by the Dutch scholars of the 16th century, and introduced into the alphabet by Giles Beys, printer, of Paris, 1550 —*Dufresnoy* It was not, however, until the middle of the 17th century that it came into general use in English books. The dot remains as a witness that the letter was developed out of the i

Jac'obins, original name of the DOMINICANS —The Jacobin club (first called "Club Breton") of about 40 members met in the hall of the Jacobin friars at Paris, in Oct 1789, to discuss political and other questions. It became the most violent of the revolutionary societies, including among its members Marat and Robespierre FRENCH REVOLUTION Similar societies were instituted in all the principal towns of the kingdom The club was closed 11 Nov 1794

Jac'obites, a Christian sect, so called from Jacobus Baradæus, a Syrian, about 541 EUTYCHIANS —The partisans of James II (Lat Jacobus II) were so named after his expulsion from England in 1688

Jackson, Andrew, Administration of UNITED STATES, 1829-37

Jackson in New Orleans. Gen. Jackson had proclaimed martial law in New Orleans, Dec 1814, while it was threatened by British troops, and continued it after their defeat and departure with no apparent necessity A complaint appearing in a New Orleans newspaper, Jackson compelled the publisher to disclose the author, committed him to prison, and proposed to try him by military court Judge Hall, of the U S. district court, issued a *habeas corpus* Jackson arrested the judge and sent him from the city Judge Hall, on his return, summoned Jackson to show cause why attachment should not issue against him for contempt. The general answered to the summons 30 Mch. 1815 The hearing finished, the judge held Jackson guilty of contempt, and fined him $1000 This was immediately paid by the general The people of New Orleans proposed to reimburse Jackson, but he refused the money, it was, however, afterwards refunded by Congress.

Jaco'bus, a gold coin, named from king James I of England, in whose reign it was struck, 1603-25

Jacquerie (*zhak-rē'*), bands of revolted peasants (headed by one Caillot, called Jacques Bonhomme), who ravaged France during the captivity of king John in 1358, and were quelled with much bloodshed Similar insurrections occurred in Germany One was termed the *Bundschuh*, from a large shoe worn by peasants, in 1502, and another termed the Bund (or league) of the Poor Conrad, 1514 and 1524, which cost about 100,000 lives, and led to the insurrection of Anabaptists

Jaffa, a seaport of Syria, in Scripture, Joppa, whence Jonah embarked (about 862 B C), and where Peter raised Tabitha from the dead (38 A D), in mythology, the place whence Perseus delivered Andromeda Jaffa was taken by caliph Omar in 636 by crusaders, 1099, by Saladin, 1193, by Louis IX, 1252, and by Bonaparte, 7 Mch 1799, the French were driven out by British in June, 1799 Here, according to sir Robert Wilson, were massacred 3800 prisoners by Bonaparte, but this is doubted Jaffa suffered by earthquake in Jan 1837, when, it is said, 13,000 persons were killed

Jagellons, a dynasty which at times reigned over Lithuania, Poland, Hungary, and Bohemia, beginning with Jagellon, duke of Lithuania (husband of Hedwig, daughter of Louis of Hungary, 1384), who became king of Poland as Ladislas III or V. in 1399, and ending with Sigismund II, who died in 1572

Jains, a religious sect in India whose tenets are somewhat analogous to the Buddhists (inasmuch as they deny the divine origin of the Veda), and to the Brahmins in recognizing the institution of caste Their creed is highly fantastical They numbered 450,000 in 1881

Jamaica (*ja-mā'-ka*), one of the largest of the West India islands, belonging to Great Britain, 90 miles south of Cuba, discovered by Columbus, 3 May, 1494, and named in 1514 *Isle de San Jago*. It was taken from the Spaniards by the English under adm Penn, with land forces under Venables, 3 May, 1655, and settled soon after Area, 4200 sq miles, pop. in 1861, 13,816 whites, 81,074 mulattoes, 346,374 blacks; in 1871, 506,154: whites, 13,101; mulattoes, 100,346; blacks, 392,707; 1881, 585,582; 1891, 639,491.

An earthquake here.....2 June, 1692
Maroons (runaway slaves) permitted to settle in the north of the island..... 1738
Desolating hurricanes.....1722, 1734, and 1751
In June, 1795, the maroons rose against the English, and were not quelled till.....Mch. 1796
Many transported to Sierra Leone..... 1800
Slave-trade abolished.....1 May, 1807
Hurricane, the whole island deluged, hundreds of houses washed away, vessels wrecked, 1000 persons drowned...Oct. 1815
Insurrection of slaves; numerous plantations burned; the governor, lord Belmore, declares martial law.....22 Dec. 1831
Emancipation of slaves.....1 Aug. 1834
About 50,000 die of cholera..... 1850
Edward John Eyre appointed governor.....July, 1864
Negro insurrection begins at Morant bay in resisting capture of a negro criminal, 7 Oct.; the court-house fired on; baron Ketelholdt, rev. V. Herschell, and others murdered; many wounded.....11 Oct. 1865
Rebellion spreads; many atrocities; it is suppressed by the governor, military, and naval officers, volunteers, maroons, and loyal negroes.....13–24 Oct. "
George William Gordon, colored member of legislature, convicted of encouraging rebellion, 21 Oct., executed.....23 Oct. "
Paul Bogle executed.....24 Oct. "
Numerous executions.....Oct. and Nov. "
Sir Henry Storks summoned from Malta to England, and sent to Jamaica, with Russell Gurney and John B. Maule as commissioners, to inquire into disturbances, and the measures for suppressing them.....11 Dec. et seq. "
Gov. Eyre temporarily suspended; sir Henry Storks arrives in Jamaica.....6 Jan. 1866
Legislative assembly of Jamaica dissolves and abrogates constitution (which had existed 200 years).....17 Jan. "
Sixteen hundred pounds sterling subscribed at Jamaica for defence of gov. Eyre.....Feb. "
Commission opened 23 Jan.; closed.....21 Mch. "
They take evidence of widespread discontent during 1865; report that 439 persons had suffered by martial law; about 1000 dwellings had been burned; about 600 (many women) had been flogged; they considered the punishments excessive, the executions unnecessarily frequent, the burning of houses wanton; they saw no proof of Gordon's complicity in the outbreak, or in an organized conspiracy.....9 Apr. "
"Jamaica committee," J. S. Mill, chairman, propose prosecution of gov. Eyre.....27 July, "
He arrives at Southampton, 12 Aug.; welcomed by a banquet, 21 Aug. "
Committee for his defence formed.....Sept. "
Gov. sir J. P. Grant promulgates the new constitution; legislative council (governor and 6 members) opened.....16 Oct. "
Warrants issued against gov. Eyre, col. Nelson, and lieut. Brand, Feb.; the grand jury discharges the bills against Eyre, 29 Mch., and the others.....11 Apr. 1867
Bill of indictment for misdemeanor against gov. Eyre brought in, 15 May; discharged by grand-jury.....2 June, 1868
Chief-justice Cockburn disclaimed agreement with part of justice Blackburn's charge; an almost unexampled case, 8 June, "
Trial of Phillips *v.* Eyre (for beating and imprisonment during rebellion of 1866); Eyre pleaded act of indemnity; verdict for defendant.....29 Jan. 1869
Legal expenses of Mr. Eyre ordered to be paid, after discussion in the commons.....8 July, 1872

James's palace, St., etc., London, was built by Henry VIII. on the site of a hospital of the same name, 1530-36. It has been the official town residence of the English court since the fire at Whitehall in 1698.

Park a marsh till Henry VIII. enclosed and laid it out in walks. 1530
Much improved by Charles II., who employed Le Nôtre to plant lime-trees, and to lay out "the mall," for a game with a ball called a mall..... 1668

Jamestown. VIRGINIA, 1607, etc.

jan'izary (Turk. *iéni tchéri*, new soldiers), an order of infantry in the Turkish army; originally, young prisoners trained to arms; first organized by Orcan, about 1330, and remodelled by his son Amurath I., 1360; their numbers increased by the succeeding sultans; later they degenerated from strict discipline, and several times deposed and killed sultans. During an insurrection, 14, 15 June, 1826, when nearly 3000 of them were killed, the Ottoman army was reorganized by Mahmud II., and a firman was issued on 17 June abolishing the janizary.

Jan'senists, followers of Cornelius Jansen, bishop of Ypres, who died in 1638. His "Augustinus," pub. 1640, maintaining the doctrine of free grace, kindled a fierce controversy, and was condemned by a bull of pope Urban VIII. in 1642. Through the Jesuits, Jansenism was condemned by Innocent X. in 1653, and by Clement XI. in 1713, by the bull Unigenitus. This bull the French church rejected. Jansenism still exists at Utrecht and Haarlem.

Jan'uary, named from Janus, an early Roman divinity, was added to the Roman calendar by Numa, 713 B.C. He placed it about the winter solstice, and made it the first month, because Janus presided over the beginning of all business. In 1751 the legal year in England was ordered to begin on 1 Jan. instead of 25 March.

Janus, Temple of, at Rome, was erected by Romulus, and kept open in time of war, and closed in time of peace. During 700 years and over it was shut only under Numa, 714 B.C.; at the close of the first Punic war, 235 B.C.; and under Augustus, 29, 25, and 5 B.C.

Japan, an insular Asiatic empire, composed of Niphon, area 87,485 sq. miles; Yezo, 36,299 sq. miles; Kinshin, 16,840 sq. miles; Shikoku, 7031 sq. miles, and many smaller islands. The Japanese claim that their empire was founded 660 B.C., and under a dynasty which still reigns. It was visited by Marco Polo, the Venetian traveller, in the 13th century, and by Mendez Pinto, a Portuguese, about 1535 or 1542, whose countrymen soon after obtained permission to found a settlement. The Jesuit missionaries followed, and made converts, who sent a deputation to pope Gregory XIII. in 1585; but a fierce persecution of Christians began 1590, aggravated, it is said, by the indiscreet zeal and arrogance of Jesuits; thousands of converts suffered death, and Portuguese were utterly expelled, 1637-42. Dutch trade with Japan commenced about 1600 under restrictions, and has since been frequently suspended; other nations, except Chinese, being excluded until 1853. The learned Kæmpfer visited Japan in 1690, and published an account of it. Government greatly changed in 1870-71, and a new constitution promulgated in 1889. Area, 155,520 sq. miles. Pop. 1890, 40,072,020; 1903, 46,732,841.

American expedition under com. Perry reaches Jeddo, and is favorably received, but remains only a few days (UNITED STATES).....8 July, 1853
Treaty of commercial alliance concluded between the 2 countries (UNITED STATES).....31 Mch. 1854
Similar treaty with Great Britain.....14 Oct. "
With Russia.....26 Jan. 1855
Nagasaki and Hakodadi opened to European commerce..... 1856
Commercial treaty with Russia.....19 Aug. 1858
Lord Elgin visits Japan, with a present of a steamer for the emperor, and is honorably received, July; obtains treaty of Jeddo, opening Japan to British commerce.....26 Aug. "
Secular emperor d. (aged 36).....16 Sept. "
Japanese embassy visits Washington, New York, etc., 14 May–30 June, 1860
Embassy received at Paris, 13 Apr.; London, June; in Holland, Prussia, etc.....July–Sept. 1862
Batteries and vessels of the prince of Nagato fire on an English and a French vessel at the entrance of the strait of Simonosaki.....15, 19 Nov. "
Japanese minister announces closing of the ports opened by treaties.....24 June, 1863
Some English, French, and American vessels bombard his forts and his vessels.....15–19 July, "
Reparation demanded; $500,000 paid by the government; the prince of Satsuma resists payment of $125,000, his portion; adm. Kuper enters the bay of Kagosima, and is fired upon; he bombards the town and burns the prince's steamers, 15 Aug. "
Prince of Satsuma pays the $125,000.....11 Dec. "
Sir Rutherford Alcock's "Japan" pub..... "
Japanese government refuses to abide by treaties; a combined fleet enters strait of Simonosaki, 4 Sept., and destroys Japanese batteries.....5, 6 Sept. 1864
Treaties with England, France, etc., ratified.....25 Nov. 1865
Two more ports opened.....Jan. 1866
Jeddo and other ports opened to trade by government..25 Apr. 1867
Osaka and Niogo opened to European commerce.....1 Jan. 1868
Insurrection of the Daimios; rivalry between mikado and tycoon, Dec.; foreigners neutral.....27 Jan.–Feb. "
Japanese outrages on French sailors; culprits executed, 16 Mch.; further outrages punished.....23 Mch. "
Mikado's troops defeat the tycoon's, who flies, 26–30 Jan.; the mikado's defeated near Jeddo.....10–17 May, "
After long war and varying success the rebellion ends; the mikado re-established.....July, "
Feudal system suppressed; internal improvements and assimilation to European civilization; proposed railways, telegraphs, etc.....1870–71
Embassy of distinguished Japanese arrives at Washington, 4 Mch.; in London.....17 Aug. 1872
First railway (Yokohama to Shinagawa) opened, 12 June, to Jeddo; opened by the mikado.....Oct. "
English proposed as the national tongue.....Dec. "
Successful expedition against FORMOSA; Japanese withdraw, Nov. 1874
Mikado decrees a new constitution; 2 chambers, etc...14 Apr. 1875
Mikado opens parliament of officials, nominated by himself, in Jeddo.....20 June, "
Foo-Soo, iron-clad man-of-war, launched at Poplar, London; Chinese ambassador present.....14 Apr. 1877

Insurrection of the Daimios suppressed................13 Oct. 1877

Ex-pres. Grant arrives at Nagasaki....................21 June, 1879

Entertainments prepared in his honor were memorable in the history of the nation. He sails from Yokohama.....3 Sept. "

Scientific works in English pub. by Tokio university........1879-80

Sir Edward J. Reed's "Japan," and Miss Isabella Bird's "Unbeaten Tracks in Japan," pub.............................. 1880

Japan to be thrown open to foreign trade, with mixed tribunals, announced......................................Nov. 1883

Death of the last tycoon....................................Apr. 1884

New order of hereditary nobility instituted...............Sept. "

National religion disestablished; freedom given to other religions..11 Aug. "

Gradual adoption of alphabetical in place of ideographic writing by agency of the Roma-ji-Rai, or Roman Alphabet Association, 1885

Japanese dictionary printed in Roman characters completed.. "

Decree giving enlarged power to the prime-minister solely responsible to the mikado..............................1 Dec. "

Count Ito, the prime-minister, energetically introduces western dress and habits...............................spring, 1887

Japanese commission to examine the fine arts in Europe and U. S.; reports in favor of Japan; "pure art is asleep in Japan, but dead in Europe"................................1886-87

Japanese fine art exhibitions opened in London............1887-88

Completion of the translation of the Bible into Japanese celebrated..3 Feb. 1888

New constitution promulgated by the mikado at Tokio; the houses of lords and commons established; religious liberty and general freedom granted; succession to the throne fixed upon the male descendants; if wanting, the throne devolves upon the nearest prince and his descendants.........11 Feb. 1889

Government desires new commercial treaties with the European powers; they hesitate; one with U. S. promptly signed, Feb.; with Russia, 8 Aug.; with Italy, with Germany, with France. "

Japanese commission of inquiry respecting parliamentary procedure in Europe arrives in London early in...........Oct. "

Nine non-treaty ports opened to commerce, early in...... " "

N. Japan, destructive gales, 11 Sept.; total loss, 12 prefectures devastated; 2419 persons killed, above 90,000 destitute, 50,000 houses swept away; 150,000 acres of crops destroyed, 6000 bridges destroyed, reported.....................about 18 Nov. "

Volcanic eruption of the Zoo, Bingo district, Fukuyama buried, inhabitants escape..................................16 Jan. 1890

National Industrial and Fine Arts exhibition opened at Tokio by the mikado..27 Mch. "

New civil code promulgated..............................21 Apr. "

Mikado institutes a new order of knighthood, "the Golden Falcon," to commemorate the 2555th anniversary of the coronation of Jimmû Tenno, the semi-mythical first sovereign of Japan, reported..............................12 May, "

First Japanese Parliament opened by the emperor with great rejoicing..29 Nov. "

Czarewitch travels in Japan; wounded by a fanatic at Otsa, 11 May; visited by the mikado..........................13 May, 1891

Very destructive earthquake on the Niphon islands; about 84,000 houses and railways, bridges, etc. destroyed; about 10,000 persons killed and 300,000 homeless; minor shocks follow; estimated loss $10,000,000......................28 Oct. "

Parliament, opposing the government, dissolved.......25 Dec. "

Japanese Parliament opened by the mikado.............6 May, 1892

Japanese guards at Seoul, capital of Korea, fired on by troops in the interest of China. The Japanese, after a short conflict, occupy the palace and overthrow the Chinese faction in the Korean government..........................23 July, 1894

Japanese warship *Naniwa* sinks the Chinese war-steamer *Kow-Shing*, transporting troops to Korea, in the Yellow sea, 25 July, "

Chinese forces driven out of Asan, Korea, by the Japanese, 29 July, "

War formally declared against China....................3 Aug. "

[The immediate cause of this war was the question of the right of both parties to keep an armed force on Korean soil and the opposition of the Chinese faction to the introduction of reforms in the Korean government advocated by Japan.]

(CHINO-JAPANESE WAR).

Loan of $50,000,000 authorized, 17 Aug.; the nobles subscribe $80,000,000..22 Aug. "

Anglo-Japanese treaty signed, 16 July; ratified; the tariff modified and the foreign jurisdiction at the treaty ports to be abolished; British residents equalized with the Japanese; treaty to remain in force 5 years....................25 Aug. "

Parliament opened by the mikado with a firm speech against China; a large loan authorized, 17 Oct.; session closed, 22 Oct. "

Earthquake in Yamagata and Akita; the town of Sakata nearly destroyed, with great loss of life......................22 Oct. "

Treaty with U. S. signed..................................23 Nov. "

Parliament opened..24 Dec. "

Treaty of peace with China; concluded 17 Apr.; ratifications exchanged..8 May, 1895

Train on a sea-wall wrecked during a gale, 140 soldiers killed, 27 July, "

Counts Ito, Yamagata, Oyama created marquises; others raised to dignity..Aug. "

Parliament opened by the emperor.......................28 Dec. "

Yashima, warship, launched on the Tyne at Elswick...28 Feb. 1896

Fuji, warship, launched on the Thames..................31 Mch. "

Treaty of commerce, etc., with Germany, signed at Berlin, 4 Apr. "

Kamaishi, in N. Japan, almost completely destroyed by earthquakes, about 1000 lives lost, 150 shocks in 20 hours; about 20,000 persons drowned by a seismic wave, and many towns destroyed..15-17 June, "

Resignation of the marquis Ito and ministry.............Aug. 1896

Count Matsukata appointed premier and minister of finance; count Okuma, foreign minister; announced........18 Sept. "

Parliament opened, 25 Dec.; closed......................24 Mch. 1897

Typhoon at Yokohama, with loss of life.................9 Sept. "

Parliament opened, 21 Dec.; the ministry resigns, 27 Dec.; an independent ministry formed by the marquis Ito, 12 Jan.; he resigns; succeeded by count Okuma............28 June, 1898

The *Yara*, transport vessel, wrecked on her way to the Pescadores, 85 deaths; reported...........................16 Jan. "

Chinese war indemnity paid, 11,008,857*l*..................7 May, "

Terrible gale on N.E. coast, 1500 fishermen drowned..11 May, "

New commercial and civil code comes into operation..16 July, "

Count Okuma's cabinet resigns, 31 Oct.; the marquis Yamagata forms one...6 Nov. "

Shikishima, battleship, launched at Blackwall..........1 Nov. "

Parliament opened with an imperial message..........3 Dec. "

Lord Charles Beresford visits Yokohama; urges an alliance between Great Britain, Japan, Germany, and U.S.N.A., to prevent war in the Far East; leaves................25 Jan. 1899

Asaki, battleship, launched at Glasgow...............13 Mch. "

Loan of 10,000,000*l*. issued in London.......................June, "

New press law (1897), free press restrictions removed, 1 July, "

Imperial rescript issued, 30 June; foreign treaties revised; Japan open to Europeans; consular jurisdiction abolished, 17 July; ratified...15 Aug. "

Chinese mission to treat for a treaty of alliance fails..mid. Aug. "

Copper-mine flooded at Besshi Ihikoku, 600 deaths; reported, 1 Sept. "

Grand naval review (30 warships) off Kobe, the emperor present..30 Apr. 1900

Mobilization of 20,000 troops ordered, owing to Chinese crisis, 26 June, "

Eruption of mount Adsuma, near Bandai San, 200 persons reported killed or injured..........................17 July, "

Yamagata's ministry resigns, succeeded by the marquis Ito, 29 Sept. "

Mikasa, warship, launched at Barrow...................8 Nov. "

Dr. Kitasato's new method of treating dysentery by inoculation very successful...............................1895-Nov. "

Political crisis, early Mch.; taxation bills passed by the peers, 16 Mch. 1901

Bill recognizing the titles of foreign landholders; passed, Mch. "

Financial panic, 20 banks suspend payment; reported..25 Apr. "

Crisis; cabinet resigns, 3 May; visct. Katsura forms a ministry, 3 June, "

M. Hoshi Toru, liberal leader, assassinated by Iba Sotaro in the Tokio city council...............................21 June, "

Baron Iwasaki buys and presents prof. Max Müller's library (about 13,000 vols. and 81 Sanscrit MSS.) to Tokio university, July, "

Surplus for 1900, 3,000,000 yen; reported............10 Sept. "

Infantry detachment (210) lost in the snow, only 13 survived, 23 Jan.-2 Feb. 1902

Anglo-Japanese treaty of alliance signed, London......30 Jan. "

Marquis Ito received by the emperor...................9 Mch. "

Issues of bonds, over 7½ million yen, for railways and public works..29 Mch. "

Herring fleet lost in a gale off Yezo, 250 deaths.......30 Apr. "

British naval squadron fêted at Tokio...................26 May, "

Russian grand-duke Boris visits Tokio.............2-12 July, "

Insurgents defeated in S. Formosa......................26 July, "

Tori Shima, a small island, overwhelmed by a volcanic eruption, the inhabitants (over 150) killed..........13-15 Aug. "

Typhoon at Yokohama, great loss of life, Odawara swept by a wave, about 200 drowned..............................29 Sept. "

Japanese loan of 5,000,000*l*. issued London...........7 Oct. "

Naval expansion scheme, budget, 3,700,000*l*., 1901-02, settled, early Oct. "

Consent of Korean government to grant to Japanese subjects equal whaling privileges on the eastern coast as have been granted to Russian government since 1899, including 3 stations on shore...................................early May, 1903

The Formosan camphor monopoly extended to the whole empire..4 June, "

Increasing excitement over the Manchurian question in Japan; reported...June, "

Dispute between Japan and Korea respecting the opening of Wi-ju, for which Japan presses and Korea refuses on ground of Russian objection..............................early July, "

Pressure put upon Korea for the opening of Wi-ju; plea that Russia objects regarded by Japan as irrelevant, about 10 July, "

Cabinet changes; the marquis Ito closes his connection with the Seiyu-Kai, and accepts office of president of privy council, which will in future assume great importance in state affairs; the marquis Yamagata and count Matsugata appointed privy councillors; the premier resumes office; end of crisis..13 July, "

Strained relations caused by rivalry of Russia and Japan in Korea in consequence of Russian activity having secured a position on the Korean side of the Yalu and Tuman rivers. Russia seeks for the right to assist in the construction of a railway through Wi-ju to Seoul; Japanese proposal for a *modus vivendi* regarding Russian policy in Korea and Manchuria presented at St. Petersburg..................12 Aug. "

Strained relations between Japan and Russia on the question of the non-evacuation of Manchuria by the latter by 8 Sept. according to the terms of the convention, and Japanese interests in Korea.....................................Oct.-Nov. "

Ministry censured in the lower house, 10 Dec.; house dissolved by emperor.....................................11 Dec. "

Unsatisfactory reply of Russia to Japanese Korean proposals; received ....11 Dec. 1903

Japanese reply to Russian proposals; increasing tension, 22 Dec. "

Japan grants $10,000,000 for the completion of the Seoul-Fusan railway in Korea ....28 Dec. "

War preparations; 2 Argentine warships bought by Japan; the government is invested with unlimited credit for the defence of Japan.......................28, 29 Dec. "

Reported Japanese warning to the powers that she will fight if her demands are not conceded; mobilization of troops, 31 Dec. "

Russia vaguely states her intention to respect Japanese rights in Manchuria, but repeats her request for the neutralization of a third part of the territory of Korea.............6 Jan. 1904

Japanese reply, claiming an "open door" in Manchuria, demands perfect equality in all respects for her subjects in that province; and absolutely declines the proposal for a diplomatic partition of Korea.......................13 Jan. "

Field-marshal Yamagata appointed president of military council.......................15 Jan. "

Korea declares her neutrality in case of war between Russia and Japan.......................23 Jan. "

Loan of $50,000,000 authorized.......................24 Jan. "

Ordinance issued at Tokio empowering the government to take over all private railway lines for military purposes..25 Jan. "

100 Japanese soldiers sent to Ping-Yang, Korea, to preserve order.......................26 Jan. "

Japan severs diplomatic relations with Russia...........5 Feb. "

[Japanese interests in Russia were left in charge of the U. S. ambassador.]

Cable between Japan and Korea cut by Togo...........8 Feb. "

The U. S. send an identical note to Russia, Japan, and the powers, asking the two belligerents to unite with the neutral powers in a guarantee to preserve the integrity of China, and to localize the hostilities to Korea and Manchuria..8 Feb. "

[The belligerents and all the neutral powers send favorable replies.]

The Russian fleet at Port Arthur attacked by Togo, and badly damaged.......................9 Feb. "

Declaration of war by Japan.......................11 Feb. "

[For events of the war see RUSSO-JAPANESE WAR.]

Offer of Anita N. McGee to provide American army nurses accepted by Japan.......................21 Feb. "

Japan notifies the U. S. of the defensive alliance between Korea and Japan.......................24 Feb. "

Parliamentary elections.......................1 Mch. "

Marquis Ito sent on a special mission to the emperor of Korea, carrying an autograph letter from the emperor of Japan, 7 Mch. "

Japan denies the Russian charges that she had violated the neutrality of Korea.......................8 Mch. "

Special session of the Japanese parliament...........27 Mch "

Perry memorial relief fund in commemoration of the 50th anniversary of the signing of the Perry treaty, organized in Tokio.......................31 Mch. "

First Japanese war loan of $50,000,000, one-half taken in the U. S.; price 93½ per cent, interest 6 per cent........10 May, "

Second issue of exchequer bonds oversubscribed......18 June, "

Death of gen. Yamaguchi in Tokio.......................7 Aug. "

Chinese governor of Mukden issues a proclamation of friendship for the Japanese.......................13 Aug. "

Death of Lafcadio Hearn in Tokio.......................26 Sept. "

Conscription law gazetted; the term of the second reservists extended from 5 to 10 years.......................29 Sept. "

Second loan of $60,000,000 at 90½ per cent., rate 6 per cent., taken one-half in the U. S.......................14 Nov. "

Seoul-Fusan railroad completed.......................Dec. "

Transfer of prisoners from Port Arthur to Japan; 878 officers, 23,481 men.......................Jan. 1905

Japanese parliament vote thanks to gen. Nogi and the third army.......................6 Jan. "

Blockade of Liao-Tung peninsula raised.......................7 Jan. "

Third loan of $150,000,000 at 90 per cent., interest 4½ per cent., one half taken in the U. S.......................28 Mch. "

Kelung, Formosa, closed to trade.......................11 Apr. "

Pescadores islands closed to trade, and powers are notified that the passages are defended by mines.......................16 Apr. "

China warned to preserve neutrality.......................24 Apr. "

Feast in Tokio on the enshrinement of the names of 30,886 Japanese soldiers who died in battle previous to......1 May, "

N. Y. *Sun* publishes a despatch, refused by the French authorities, showing violation of neutrality by French officials in Cochin China.......................8 May, "

Formosa declared under martial law.......................13 May, "

Japanese press denounce France for violation of neutrality by permitting the Russian fleet to remain in French waters at Kamranh Bay from.......................12 Apr–14 May, "

Japan protests officially to France for permitting the violation of neutrality by the Russian fleet during.....Apr. and May, "

Togo's fleet sail to meet Russian fleet; no news of Togo's ships, April–May, "

Arbitrators decide that houses of foreigners in the old concession of land are not subject to the Japanese land tax...May, "

REIGNING EMPEROR OR MIKADO.

Mutsu Hito, b. 3 Nov. 1852; succeeded his father, Kōmei Tenno, 13 Feb. 1867; married to princess Haruko, 9 Feb. 1869.

Heir: prince Yoshi Hito, b. 31 Aug. 1877; proclaimed crown-prince (Kotaishi), 3 Nov. 1878.

Jarnac, a town of W. France. On 13 Mch. 1569, the duke of Anjou, afterwards Henry III. of France, here defeated the Huguenots under Louis, prince of Condé, who was killed in cold blood by Montesquieu. The victor (17 years of age), on account of his success here and at Moncontour, was chosen king of Poland.

A Jarnac stroke, a term of opprobrium, from seigneur de Jarnac, who, in a duel or judicial combat for a great insult, disabled La Chataigneraye by a wound in the thigh, of which he shortly after died.......................1547

jasmine or **jessamine** (*Jasminum officinale*), native of Persia, etc., was brought to England from Circassia before 1548. The Catalonian jasmine came from India in 1629, and the yellow Indian jasmine in 1656. FLOWERS AND PLANTS.

Java, an island in the Malay archipelago, next to Borneo and Sumatra the largest in the Sunda group, is said to have been reached by the Portuguese in 1511, and by the Dutch in 1595. The latter, who now possess it, built Batavia, the capital, about 1619. BATAVIA. The massacre of 20,000 unarmed natives by Dutch, sparing neither women nor children, to possess their effects, took place in 1740. The island capitulated to the British, 18 Sept. 1811. The sultan was dethroned by the English, and the hereditary prince raised to the throne, in June, 1813. Java was restored to Holland in 1814. The English promoted free labor instead of forced; but the Dutch reverted to the old system, and in 1830 abolished free labor, introducing the "culture system," by which the government controls the cultivation of the land and buys the produce at its own price. In Aug. 1860, the Swiss soldiers here, aided by the natives, mutinied, but were soon reduced, and many suffered death. The diminished prosperity of Java led to warm discussions in the Dutch chamber in 1866. Area, 50,848 sq. miles; pop. 1890, 23,064,086.

Java has 46 volcanoes; has been devastated by eruptions and earthquakes, 5 Jan. 1699, 21 Oct. 1876, and 10 June, 1877.

Java and neighboring isles desolated by violent eruptions from about two thirds of the 46 volcanoes, beginning with Krakatoa. Disturbance began with rumbling noises, 25 Aug. 1883; violent eruption of Krakatoa, 26 Aug.; great submarine disturbance and a tidal wave which destroyed Anjer and other places, 27 Aug.; the lighthouses in the strait of Sunda were swallowed up, 25–28 Aug.; atmospheric, electrical, and oceanic disturbances for thousands of miles. SUN, 1883.

Jeannette, Voyage of the. NORTHEAST AND NORTHWEST PASSAGES.

Jeddo or **Yeddo.** TOKIO.

Jefferson, Thomas, Administrations of. UNITED STATES, 1801–9.

Jefferson's letter to Philip Mazzei, dated 24 Apr. 1796. Mazzei published an Italian translation of it in Florence, 1 Jan. 1797. It was retranslated into French and published in the *Moniteur*, 25 Jan., and found its way through the English press into the American newspapers about the beginning of May. In this letter he opposed the Jay treaty, and commented freely against Washington and his administration as Anglican, monarchical, and aristocratic, etc. This letter destroyed Washington's faith in Jefferson.

"Je maintiendrai"—"I will maintain," the motto of the house of Nassau. When William III. came to the throne of England, he retained it, adding "the liberties of England and the Protestant religion," also ordering that the old motto of the royal arms, "*Dieu et mon droit*," should be retained on the great seal, 1689.

Jemmapes (*jem-map'*), a town of N.W. Belgium, site of the first pitched battle gained by French republicans (under Dumouriez), in which 40,000 French troops drove out 19,000 Austrians, intrenched in woods and mountains, defended by redoubts and many cannon, 6 Nov. 1792. The number killed on each side was reckoned at 5000.

Jena (*yā'-ne*) and **Auerstadt** (*ow'-er-stat*), towns of central Germany, where 2 battles were fought, 14 Oct. 1806, between French commanded at Jena by Napoleon, and at Auerstadt by Davoust, and Prussians under prince Hohenlohe at the former place, and the king of Prussia at the latter. The Prussians were defeated, losing nearly 20,000 killed and wounded, and nearly as many prisoners, and 200 field-pieces; the French lost 14,000 men. Napoleon advanced to Berlin, and issued the BERLIN DECREE.

"Jephthah," Handel's last oratorio; composed 21 Jan.–30 Aug. 1751; first performed 26 Feb. 1752. JUDGES.

Jersey, the chief island of the Channel archipelago hich includes Guernsey, Sark, Alderney, etc.), belonging to eat Britain, held by the Romans in the 3d and 4th centuries er Christ—Jersey being termed Cæsarea. The isles were ptured by Rollo, became an appanage of the duchy of Normndy, and were united to the crown of England by his demndant, William the Conqueror. The inhabitants of the annel islands preferred to remain subjects of king John at e conquest of Normandy by Philip Augustus, and, while reing the laws, customs, and (until lately) the language of eir continental ancestors, have remained firm in their alleince to England. Almost every war with France has been aracterized by an attack on Jersey; the most formidable, unr the baron de Rullecour, was defeated by the English garrison d Jersey militia, under maj. Pierson, 6 Jan. 1781. J. Bertrand yne, in his "Armorial of Jersey" and his "Gossiping Guide," s treated the general and family history of the island. Area, ,717 acres; pop. 1881 52,445; 1891, 54,518. CATTLE.

Jeru'salem, called also **Salem,** 1913 B.C. (Gen. xiv.). Its king Adonizedek (also one of the kings of the Amors) was slain by Joshua, 1451 B.C. It was taken by David, en in possession of the Jebusites, 1048 B.C., who dwelt in the t, calling it the city of David. HOLY PLACES, JEWS. p. 1891, about 28,000.

	B.C.
rst temple founded by Solomon, 1012 B.C.; and solemnly ledicated on Friday (JEWS)........................30 Oct.	1004
	A.D.
usalem taken by Chosroes the Persian, 614 A.D.; retaken by the emperor Heraclius, 628; by Saracens, 637; and by crusaders, when 70,000 infidels were put to the sword; a new kingdom founded........................15 July,	1099
Assize of Jerusalem," a code of laws, established by Godfrey of Bouillon, king........................	1100
ng Guy defeated at Tiberias; Jerusalem taken by Saladin, 2 Oct.	1187
the Turks, who drive away the Saracens.........1217 and	1239
rrendered to the emperor Frederick II. by treaty..........	1228
rrendered to the crusaders........................	1243
ken by Carismians........................	1244
ken from the Christians........................	1291
ken by the Turks........................	1516
ld by the French under Bonaparte........................Feb.	1799
nvention to preserve the holy sepulchre signed on behalf of Russia, France, and Turkey........................5 Sept.	1862
itish survey of Jerusalem and neighborhood began....Sept.	1864
sited by crown-prince of Prussia, 4 Nov.; by emperor of Austria........................9 Nov.	1869
railway from Jerusalem to Jaffa built by a French company; opened........................13 Sept.	1892

CHRISTIAN KINGS.

dfrey of Bouillon (styled himself "baron of the holy sepulchre")........................	1099
ldwin I........................	1100
ldwin II........................	1118
lk of Anjou........................	1131
ldwin III........................	1144
nauri (or Almeric)........................	1162
ldwin IV........................	1173
byl, then his son Baldwin V........................	1185
ly de Lusignan........................	1186
enry of Champagne........................	1192
nauri de Lusignan........................	1197
an de Brienne........................	1210
nperor Frederick II........................	1229-39
otestant Bishopric of Jerusalem, erected under the protection of Great Britain and Prussia:	
M. S. Alexander consecrated bishop........................7 Nov.	1841
muel Gobat, bishop, 1846; d........................11 May,	1879
seph Barclay, LL.D., consecrated........................25 July,	"

"Jerusalem Delivered," the great Italian epic Tasso, was pub. in 1580. LITERATURE.

jester, or the "KING'S FOOL," is described as "a witty and cose person kept by princes to inform them of their faults, d of those of others, under the disguise of a waggish story." everal of the English kings, particularly the Tudors, kept jests. Rahere, the founder of St. Bartholomew's priory, West nithfield, London, 1133, is said to have been a court jester and instrel. There was a jester at court in the reigns of James I. d Charles I., but probably no licensed jester afterwards.

"'What art thou?' And the voice about his feet
Sent up an answer, sobbing, 'I am thy fool,
And I shall never make thee smile again.'"
—*Tennyson*, "The Last Tournament."

Viola. Art not thou the lady Olivia's fool?
Clown. No, indeed, sir . . . she will keep no fool, sir, till she be married." —*Shakespeare*, "Twelfth Night," act iii. sc. i.

"This same skull, sir, was Yorick's skull, the king's jester."
—*Shakespeare*, "Hamlet," act v. sc. i.

Jesuits, the Society or Company of Jesus, founded by Ignatius Loyola, a page to Ferdinand V. of Spain, later an officer in his army, and canonized after death. Being wounded in both legs at the siege of Pampeluna, in 1521, he abandoned the army, and embraced the ecclesiastical profession. He dedicated his life to the blessed Virgin as her knight; made a pilgrimage to Holy Land, and on his return founded his society at Paris, 16 Aug. 1534. He presented his institutes in 1539 to pope Paul III., who made objections; but Ignatius adding to the vows of chastity, poverty, and obedience a fourth of implicit submission to the holy see, the institution was confirmed by a bull, 27 Sept. 1540. The number of members was not to exceed 60, but that restriction was taken off by another bull, 14 Mch. 1543; and popes Julius III., Pius V., and Gregory XIII. granted many privileges. Loyola died 31 July, 1556. Francis Xavier and other missionaries, the first brethren, carried the order everywhere; but it met with great opposition in Europe, particularly in Paris. The order still exists in many European states contrary to the laws. FRENCH IN AMERICA, JANSENISTS, PARAGUAY.

Society condemned by the Sorbonne, Paris, 1554; expelled from France, 1594; readmitted, 1604; but after several decrees suppressed in France and its property confiscated.....	1764
Ordered by Parliament expelled from England 1579, 1581, 1586, 1602; and by the Catholic Relief act........................	1829
Expelled from Venice, 1607; Holland, 1708; Portugal, 1759; Spain........................	1767
Abolished by Clement XIV........................21 July,	1773
Restored by Pius VI........................7 Aug.	1814
Father Pierre J. Beckx elected general........................	1853
Expelled from Belgium, 1818; Russia, 1820; Spain, 1820, 1835; France, 1831, 1845; Portugal, 1834; Sardinia, Austria, and other states, 1848; Italy........................	1860
Chief of the order appeals to the king of Sardinia for redress of grievances........................24 Oct.	"
Report: total number of Jesuits, 8167; in France, 2422......	1868
Order actively advocating papal supremacy, a bill for its expulsion from Germany passed by parliament at Berlin (131-93), 19 June; promulgated........................5 July,	1872
Proposed removal of headquarters from Rome to Malta....Oct.	1873
Expulsion of Jesuits from Italy, decreed 25 June; carried into execution........................20 Oct.-2 Nov.	"
Father Curci, orthodox and eloquent, resigned (virtually expelled) for advising pope to yield temporal power, Oct. 1877; publishes "Il Moderno Dissidio fra la Chiesa e l'Italia," Dec. 1877; reconciled to the new pope, Leo XIII............	1878
Twenty-seven Jesuits' colleges in France; 848 teachers.......	1879
Order in France dissolved by decree........................30 Mch.	1880
Decree for expulsion of Jesuits and other orders from France, 30 Mch.; carried out........................30 June,	"

Jesuit's bark. CHINCHONA OR CINCHONA.

Jesus Christ, the Saviour of the world, whose birth is celebrated 25 Dec. in each year. The date of his birth is uncertain, but was probably 4 years before the common era. NATIVITY. The following dates are given by ecclesiastical writers:

	A.D.
Christ's baptism by John and first ministry........................	27
Last passover, institution of the eucharist..............2 Apr.	33
Crucified on 3 Apr. at 3 o'clock in the afternoon; arose..5 Apr.	"
Ascended to heaven from mount Olivet..............14 May,	"
Holy Spirit descended on his disciples on Sunday, the day of Pentecost........................24 May,	"
Divinity of Christ, denied by the Arians, was affirmed by the council of Nice........................	325

Jeu de Paume ("the tennis-court"). Louis XVI. having closed the hall of the assembly at Versailles, the Third Estate (*Tiers État*) met in this place, and swore not to dissolve till a constitution was established, 20 June, 1789. (It is the subject of a painting by David.)

Jew, The Wandering, a legendary character condemned to wander from place to place until the Day of Judgment. According to Matthew Paris and Roger Wendover ("Chronicles of St. Albans," 13th century) he was Cartaphilus, door-keeper of the Judgment hall of Pilate; others say Ahasuerus, a cobbler; others, Judas, etc. In Germany the tradition of the wandering Jew became connected with John Beltadœus, a real personage. The story of this Jew was published in 1602 and frequently since. The wandering Jew is the subject of Southey's "Curse of Kebama," Croly's "Salathiel," and Sue's "Le Juif Errant," though in violation of the entire legend. The legend derives a pathetic poetical suggestiveness and meaning from the wanderings through the world of the scattered Jewish race, of which its hero is the representative.

Jewelry was received by Rebekah as a marriage gift, 1857 B.C. (Gen. xxiv. 53). Pliny the elder says he saw Lollia

Paulina (wife of Caius Cæsar, and afterwards Caligula) wearing ornaments valued at 322,916*l*. Jewels were worn in France by Agnes Sorel in 1434, and encouraged in England about 1685. The standard of gold for jewelry, except wedding-rings, was lowered by Parliament in 1854.

Jewish disabilities. JEWS, 1269–1867.

Jewish era and **calendar.** The Jews usually dated from the era of the Seleucidæ until the 15th century, when a new mode was adopted, reckoning from the Creation, 3760 years and 3 months before the commencement of our era. To reduce Jewish time to ours, subtract 3761 years. The Jewish year consists of either 12 or 13 months, of 29 or 30 days. The civil year commences with the month Tisri, immediately after the new moon following the autumnal equinox; the ecclesiastical year begins with Nisan. The year 1892 A.D. compares with the Jewish year 5652–53 A.M. as follows:

Tebet........began 1 Jan. 1892		Ab..........began 25 July, 1892
Sebat........ " 30 Jan. "		Elul........ " 24 Aug. "
Adar........ " 29 Feb. "		Tisri, 1st day of the year 5653.......began 22 Sept. "
Nisan........ " 29 Mch. "		Hesvan..... " 22 Oct. "
Yiar........ " 28 Apr. "		Kislev....... " 20 Nov. "
Sivan........ " 27 May, "		Tebet....... " 20 Dec. "

Year 5652 commenced.................................8 Oct. 1891

All Jewish Sabbaths, festivals, and feasts commence at sunset.

Jews, successively called Hebrews, Israelites, and Jews, the descendants of Abraham, with whom God made a covenant, 1898 B.C. (Gen. xvii.). Computed number of Jews in the world, 1893, between 7,000,000 and 8,000,000, mostly in Europe, in eastern Russia and Austro-Hungary. JERUSALEM, JUDÆA.

	B.C.
Call of Abram	1921
Isaac born to Abraham	1896
Birth of Esau and Jacob	1837
Death of Abraham	1822
Joseph sold into Egypt	1729
Jacob and all his family go into Egypt	1706
Male children of the Israelites thrown into the Nile; Moses b..	1571
Passover instituted; Israelites go out of Egypt, and cross the Red sea	1491
Law promulgated from mount Sinai	"
Tabernacle set up	1490
Moses dies, aged 120 years	1451
Joshua leads Israelites into Canaan	"
Joshua dies, aged 110 years	1443
First bondage (Othniel, judge, 1405)	1413
Second bondage (Ehud, 1325)	1343
Third bondage (Deborah and Barak, 1285)	1305
Fourth bondage (Gideon, 1245)	1252
Fifth bondage (Jephthah, 1187)	1206
Sixth bondage	1157
Samson slays the Philistines	1136
Samuel governs as judge.....about	1120
Samson pulls down the temple of Dagon	1117
Saul made king	1095
David slays Goliath.....about	1063
Death of Saul; David made king	1055
David captures JERUSALEM, and makes it his capital	1048
Absalom's rebellion	1023
Solomon king, 1015; founds the TEMPLE, 1012; dedicated	1004
Death of Solomon; kingdom divided	975

KINGDOM OF ISRAEL (254 years).

Jeroboam establishes idolatry	975
Bethel taken from Jeroboam; 500,000 Israelites slain	957
Israel afflicted with the famine predicted by Elijah	906
Syrians besiege Samaria	901
Elijah translated to heaven	896
Miracles of Elisha the prophet	895
Assyrian invasion under Phul	771
Pekah besieges Jerusalem	741
Samaria taken by king of Assyria; 10 tribes are carried into captivity; kingdom of Israel ends	721

KINGDOM OF JUDAH (387 years).

Shishak, king of Egypt, takes Jerusalem, and pillages the temple	971
Abijah defeats king of Israel; 50,000 men slain	957
Asa defeats Ethiopians; abolishes idolatry	941
Jehoshaphat orders the law to be taught, 912; defeats Ammonites, etc.	896
Usurpation and death of Athaliah	884
Hazael desolates Judah	857
Pekah, king of Israel, lays siege to Jerusalem; 120,000 men of Judah slain in one day	741
Hezekiah abolishes idolatry	726
Sennacherib invades Judea; the destroying angel enters the Assyrian camp and in one night destroys 185,000	710
Holofernes said to have been killed at the siege of Bethulia by Judith	656
In repairing the temple, Hilkiah discovers the book of the law, and Josiah keeps a solemn passover	624
Nebuchadnezzar subjugates Judea	605
He takes Jerusalem after a long siege	588
Jerusalem fired, temple burned, the walls razed	587

JEW

KINGS.	B.C.	PROPHETS.
Saul began to reign	1095	Samuel.
David, king of Judah, 1055; of all Israel	1048	Nathan.
Solomon, king of all Israel	1015	

B.C.	KINGS OF JUDAH.	KINGS OF ISRAEL.	
975.	Rehoboam	Jeroboam I.	Abijah.
958.	Abijah	"	
955.	Asa	Nadab (954)	Azariah.
953.	"	Baasha (954)	Hanani.
930.	"	Elah (954)	Jehu.
929.	"	Zimri	"
925.	"	Omri	"
918.	"	Ahab	Elijah.
914.	Jehoshaphat	"	"
897.		Ahaziah	Elisha.
896.		Jehoram, or Joram	Jahaziel.
889.	Jehoram	" "	
885.	Ahaziah	" "	
884.	Athaliah	Jehu.	
878.	Joash, or Jehoahaz	"	
857.	" "	Jehoahaz.	
839.	Amaziah	Jehoash (841).	
825.	"	Jeroboam II.	Jonah.
810.	Uzziah or Azariah	"	Hosea. Amos.
784.	" "	[Anarchy.]	
773.	" "	Zechariah	Joel.
772.	" "	Shallum. Menahem.	
761.	" "	Pekahiah.	
759.	" "	Pekah.	
758.	Jotham	"	Isaiah and Micah.
742.	Ahaz	"	
730.	"	Hoshea.	
726.	Hezekiah	[Captivity, 721]	Nahum.
698.	Manasseh.		
643.	Amon		Jeremiah.
641.	Josiah		Zephaniah.
610.	Jehoahaz (Shallum). Jehoiakim.		Habakkuk.
599.	Jehoiachin (Coniah).		Daniel.
	Zedekiah		Ezekiel.

BABYLONISH CAPTIVITY.

	B.C.
Daniel taken to Babylon	607
Daniel prophesies at Babylon	603
Shadrach, Meshach, and Abed-nego, refusing to worship the golden image, are cast into a fiery furnace, but are delivered by the angel	587
Obadiah prophesies	"
Daniel declares the meaning of the handwriting against Belshazzar; cast into the lion's den; prophesies return from captivity, and coming of the Messiah	538

RETURN FROM CAPTIVITY.

Cyrus, sovereign of Asia, decrees the return of the Jews and rebuilding of the temple	536
Haggai and Zechariah prophets	520
Second temple finished.....10 Mch.	515
Jews delivered from Haman by Esther	510
Ezra, the priest, arrives in Jerusalem to reform abuses	458
Here begin the 70 weeks of years predicted by Daniel, being 490 years before the crucifixion of the Redeemer	457
Walls of Jerusalem built	445
Malachi the prophet	415

[The Scripture history of the Jews ends, according to Eusebius, in 442 B.C.; afterwards Josephus and Roman historians give the best account of the Jews.]

Alexander the Great marches to besiege Jerusalem, but, it is said, on seeing Jaddus, the high-priest, in his robes, declares he had seen such a figure in Macedonia, inviting him to Asia, and promising to deliver the Persian empire into his hands; he enters the temple, and sacrifices to the God of the Jews..	332
Jerusalem taken by Ptolemy Soter	320
Ptolemy Philadelphus said to employ 72 Jews to translate the Scriptures.....about	285
Sadducee sect formed	250
Jews massacred at Alexandria	216
Antiochus takes Jerusalem, pillages temple, and slays 40,000 inhabitants	170
Government of Maccabees begins	166
Treaty with Romans; first on record with Jews	161
Judas Hyrcanus Aristobulus assumes title of "king of the Jews"	107
Alexander Jannæus suppresses a rebellion of Pharisees cruelly,	86
Jerusalem taken by Roman legions under Pompey	63
Temple plundered by Crassus	54
Antipater made intendant of Judea by Julius Cæsar	49
Herod, son of Antipater, marries Mariamne, granddaughter of the high-priest	42
Invasion of Parthians	40
Herod supported by the senate; they decree him king	"
Jerusalem taken by Herod and the Roman Sosius	37
Herod kills Mariamne, 29; rebuilds temple	29–18
Jesus Christ b.	4
	A.D.
Pontius Pilate made procurator of Judea	26

ohn the Baptist begins to preach 26
hrist s ministry and miracles, 27–33, his crucifixion and resurrection 33
ews persecuted *for refusing to worship Caligula* 38
eceive the right of Roman citizenship 41
laudius banishes Jews from Rome 50
nvasion of Vespasian 68
ews settle at Merida Spain 69
itus takes Jerusalem, city and temple sacked and burned, and 1 100 000 Jews perish 8 Sept 70
osephus b 37 A D , died about 100
argum of Onkelos written about 100
Iadrian rebuilds Jerusalem (calling it Ælia Capitolina) and erects a temple to Jupiter 130
Rebellion of Barchochebas takes Jerusalem 132, killed in war with Julius Severus 135, desolation of Judea 135–36
Iore than 580 000 Jews are slain by Romans "
ews favored by Antoninus Pius, college of Jamnia opened 138
Iishna (TALMUD) *written by rabbi Judah the prince* 141
ews favored by Severus, 196, by Constantine, 310, by Julian, 363, persecuted by Constans 353
ews massacred at Alexandria 415
Babylonian Talmud completed 504
erusalem taken by Omar, ceases to be the city of the Jews 655
ews first mentioned in English chronicles 740
ect of KARAITES formed by Anan about 754
ewish college founded at Cordova 948
almud translated into Arabic 1005
ews said to be banished from England by Canute 1020
Polygamy in Christian countries prohibited by the Jewish synod at Worms 1030
ews return to England 1066

[Chiefly settled in London and Lincoln]

ews massacred in London, on coronation day of Richard I, at the instigation of priests 1189
ive hundred Jews, besieged in York castle by the mob, cut each other's throats to avoid their fury 1190
ews of both sexes imprisoned, eyes or teeth plucked out, and numbers butchered, by king John 1204
Rabbi Moses Maimonides d "
even hundred Jews slain in London, a Jew having forced a Christian to pay him more than 2s per week as interest on a loan of 20s (*Stow*) 1262
tatute that no Jew should enjoy a freehold 1269
Every Jew lending money on interest compelled to wear a plate on his breast, signifying that he was a usurer, or to quit the realm (*Stow*) 1274
wo hundred and sixty seven Jews hanged and quartered, accused of clipping coin 1278
ll Jews (16,511) banished from England (*Rapin*) 1290
Pillaged and persecuted in France during 14th and 15th centuries.
A fatal distemper raging in Europe, many are slain for poisoning springs (*Lenglet*) 1348
ews banished from Spain Portugal, and France, they consider it as great a calamity as the destruction of Jerusalem 1492–94
Edicts against Jews rescinded by *pope Sixtus V* 1585
ews favored in Holland 1603
After banishment from England 370 years, permitted to return by Cromwell 1650
Who grants a pension to Manasseh ben Israel 1655
First Portuguese synagogue, King street, Duke s place, erected 1656
Statute to compel them to maintain their Protestant children enacted 1702
ews acquire right to possess land in England 1723
Bill to naturalize professors of Jewish religion in Ireland (where 200 Jews resided) refused royal assent 1746
Statute to naturalize them in England passed 1753
Repealed on the petition of all the cities 1754
Jews of Spain, Portugal, and Avignon declared citizens of France, 1790
Sitting of the great Sanhedrim of Paris convened by the emperor Napoleon . 18 Sept. 1806
Jews' hospital, London, founded . "
London Society for Promoting Christianity among the Jews established 1808
Jews' free school, Spitalfields, London, established 1817
Alexander of Russia grants land on the sea of Azof to converted Jews . . . . . . 1 Sept. 1820
Rothschild brothers made barons of the Austrian empire 1822
Jews' Orphan Asylum founded . . . 1831
David Salomons elected sheriff of London (first Jew), Enabling act passed for him . 24 June, 1835
Bill for Jewish emancipation in England lost on second reading in the commons (228–165) . 17 May, 1836
Moses Montefiore elected sheriff of London, first Jew knighted by the queen . . . 9 Nov 1837
Ukase of emperor of Russia permitting the title of citizen of the first class to be held by any Jew worthy of it . 1839
On disappearance of a Greek priest, persecution of the Jews began at DAMASCUS . . 1 Feb 1840
Jewish mission to the east under sir Moses Montefiore "
Congregation of British Jews formed (see below) 1840–41
Act to relieve Jews elected to municipal offices from oaths, etc., 9 Vict. . 1846
Baron Lionel de Rothschild returned to Parliament for the city of London by a majority of 6619, his opponent, lord John Manners, polling only 3104. . . . 3 July, 1849
Alderman Salomons elected for Greenwich . . 28 June, 1851
Neither permitted to sit . . . . . . "
Jews' Oaths of Abjuration bill passed commons 3 July, "
Baron Rothschild again returned for London at general elections, July, 1852, Mch. 1857, July, 1857, and July, 1865

Violent outbreak against Jews in Stockholm 3 Sept 1852
Jewish Oath bill passed in commons, 15 Apr , thrown out in the lords 29 Apr 1853
Alderman Salomons, first Jewish lord mayor of London 9 Nov 1855
Jewish Oath bill several times passed in the commons and thrown out in the lords 1854–57
Edgar Mortara a Jewish child forcibly taken from parents by order of archbishop of Bologna on plea of baptism when an infant by a Roman Catholic maid servant 24 June, 1858
Act passed enabling Jews to sit in Parliament by resolution of the house July, "
Baron Rothschild takes seat as M P for London 26 July, "
To commemorate this event he endowed a scholarship in the City of London school "
French government having in vain urged Mortara s restoration to parents sir Moses Montefiore proceeds to Rome (but obtains no redress) 22 Dec "
Alderman Salomons elected M P for Greenwich (d 18 July, 1873), baron Meyer de Rothschild for Hythe 15 Feb 1859
Protest on seizure of the boy Mortara signed at London by archbishop of Canterbury, bishops noblemen and gentlemen, sent to French ambassador, Oct , presented to lord John Russell Nov "
Laws oppressing Jews in Austria annulled 6 10 Jan 1860
Act passed permitting Jewish M P s to omit from the oath the words "on the faith of a Christian" 6 Aug "
Additional political privileges granted Jews in Russia, 26 Jan , in Poland June, 1862
Jews persecuted at Rome Dec 1864
Alderman Benjamin Samuel Phillips 2d Jewish lord mayor, 9 Nov 1865
Persecution of Jews at Bucharest reported July, 1866
A synagogue at Berlin, said to be the largest and most beautiful *in the world, consecrated* 5 Sept "
Jewish Emancipation bill, Hungary approved 29 Dec 1867
Benjamin Disraeli, of Jewish extraction, premier of England 29 Feb 1868
Jews' synagogue at Barnsbury, London N , founded by baron F Rothschild, 24 Dec 1867 , consecrated 29 Mch "
Jews permitted to return to Spain Oct "
Jewish congress at Pesth opened by minister of public worship Eötvös 14 Dec. "
It closes presenting new statutes to ministers 25 Feb 1869
Jewish reform convention at Philadelphia, alterations in rituals, etc , resolved on Oct "
Alfred Davis, a Jew, promoter of education, Jewish and Christian, d 7 Jan. 1870
New Central synagogue in Great Portland st , London, W , founded by baron Rothschild, 18 Mch 1869 7 Apr "
"Hebrew Literature society" established in London 29 June, "
Anglo Jewish Association for moral social, and intellectual progress of Jews (a branch of the Universal Israelitish Alliance whose seat is Paris) founded 2 July "
Emperor of Brazil attended worship at the West Central London synagogue 8 July, "
Jews permitted to work on Sundays by a Workshops act "
Society formed at Birmingham to resist proselytism "
Congregation of British Jews formed in 1840 and 1841 by families of Spanish and German Jews, for uniting 2 sections of the community, opposing Talmudism, and simplifying rituals, recognizing the Mosaic Scriptures as sole standard for faith and practice and rejecting the oral or Talmudic law as not binding on Reformed Jews. Their West London synagogue in Burton st opened 1 Jan 1842, removed to Margaret st , Regent st., 1849, superseded by a synagogue, Berkeley st , consecrated (KARAITES) 22 Sept. "
A Jew made M A at Oxford (after abolition of tests) 22 June, 1871
Sir George Jessel, a Jew, solicitor general, Nov 1871, master of the rolls 29 Aug 1873
Estimated number of Jews in Great Britain, 51,520, in London, 39,833 1876
New synagogue founded at Bayswater 7 June, 1877
Movement against Jews in Berlin, etc. (JUDENHASSE and JUDENHETZE), opposed by Mommsen Virchow, the crown-prince, etc , debate in chambers, no vote, 22 Nov Many Jews leave Berlin Dec 1880
Anti Semitic league formed, petition to Bismarck, signed by 255 000 13 Apr 1881
About 60,000 Russian Jews request permission to return to Spain, granted. June, "
Persecution in Prussia, the emperor interferes to stop it Aug "
Renewal of persecution in Russia, Apr 1882, June, Nov -Dec 1884 denounced as barbarous at a meeting at Mansion house, London 1 Feb 1882
Many Jews go to America Feb. "
Jews attacked at [illegible]burg, Hungary, martial law proclaimed, 29 Sept. "
Trial of Jews (HUNGARY) 1883
Attacks on Jews at St Petersburg, Pesth, Zala Egerszeg etc , July, Aug "
Death of Charlotte, baroness de Rothschild 13 Mch 1884
Jews persecuted in Russia Aug et seq "
Commission to consider the condition and rights of Jews, Oct. "
Jews enjoy full citizenship in Europe (except Portugal, Roumania, Russia and Spain), also in the United States "
Sir Moses Montefiore completes his 100th year, celebrated by Jews all over the world as a benefactor (27 Oct. Jewish calendar), 25–26 Oct 1884, d. . . 28 July, 1885
Estimated number of Jews in the world, 6 377,602 "
Exhibition of Anglo-Jewish antiquities at the Royal Albert hall opened ... . 4 Apr 1887

Expulsion of Jews from Odessa and Finland decreed Apr 1888
Sir Nathaniel de Rothschild, son of Lionel, created a peer, takes his seat, 9 July, 1885, made lord-lieut of Buckinghamshire, May, 1889
Henry Aaron Isaacs, 3d Jewish lord mayor of London Nov "
Enforcement of the severe edict of May, 1882 against the Jews in Russia, many Jews expelled from Russia Dec. 1890
At a great meeting in the Guildhall London an appeal to the czar to mitigate the laws against the Jews agreed to, 10 Dec "
Expulsion of Jews from S Russia ordered about 29 May, 1891
Relaxation of the persecution enforcement of the decree of expulsion from St Petersburg adjourned about 18 July, "
Three thousand acres of land at Hulberton, Cumberland county, N J purchased by Leon Lait, a Russian, for a Hebrew colony about 20 July, "
Jewish Colonization Association founded about 11 Sept "

Jew's-harp (probably jaws' harp), an ancient instrument Charles Eulenstein produced remarkable effects with Jew's-harps at the Royal Institution, London, 15 Feb 1828.

Jeynes. Jains

Jihad (*yee-had'*), or religious warfare against unbelievers, although inculcated in the Mahometan law, was prohibited by the Sheeahs, and rarely permitted by the Sonnites, not with any nation in treaty relations The jihad was preached by fanatics in India in 1871, and prohibited by government

A jihad against the Russians announced by the sheikh ul Islam, at Constantinople about 28 May, 1877
A jihad against the British in Afghanistan, proposed by Shere Ali Oct. 1878
A jihad against the British proclaimed by Arabi Pacha, 24 July, 1882

Jingo party, a name given in Great Britain in 1878 to persons who favored war with Russia "in pursuance of a vigorous foreign policy" A popular song said—

"We don't want to fight, but, by jingo, if we do,
We've got the ships, we've got the men, and we've got the money too"

"By jingo" occurs in Jarvis's "Don Quixote," and in the "Vicar of Wakefield"

Joan of Arc, Maid of Orleans, born at Domremy, imagined that she had a divine commission to expel the English, who, under the earl of Salisbury, were besieging Orleans. Charles VII intrusted her with some French troops, she raised the siege, and entered Orleans with supplies, 29 Apr 1429, and the English, who were before the place from 12 Oct preceding, abandoned the enterprise 8 May following She took several towns from the English, whom she defeated in a battle near Patay, 18 June, 1429 She was wounded several times, but never shed blood with her own hand She was taken at the siege of Compiegne, 25 May, 1430, and, after trial, burned for a witch at Rouen, 30 May, 1431 A statue of her, the work of the princess Marie of France, was inaugurated at Orleans, 13 Sept. 1851, and the 435th anniversary of the deliverance of the city celebrated on 14 May, 1865 Patay The anniversary of her death celebrated 30 May, 1878 Her statue unveiled at Beaurevoir 9 Aug, and at Domremy 26 Aug. 1891

John Bull, a nickname of England and of Englishmen, is said to be derived from dr Arbuthnot's satire "John Bull," pub. 1712.—*Brewer* —"John Bull," a comedy, by George Colman the younger, was performed 1805 —The *John Bull*, a Tory newspaper, supported by Theodore Hook, was first pub 1820

John Doe and **Richard Roe,** names used in legal fictions, especially as standing pledges for the prosecution of suits. In early times real and substantial persons were required to pledge themselves to answer to the crown for an amercement, or fine, set upon the plaintiff, for raising a false accusation, if he brought action without cause, or failed in it, and in 1285, 13 Edw I., sheriffs and bailiffs were, before deliverance of a distress, to receive pledges for pursuing a suit, and for the return of the property, if awarded But this becoming a matter of form, the fictitious names of Doe and Roe were used, until the form was abolished by the Common-law Procedure act, 1852

John O'Groat's house, an ancient house, stood on Duncansby Head, the most northerly point of Scotland, deriving its name from John of Groat, or Groot, and his brothers, from Holland, said to have settled here about 1489.

House was of an octagon shape, being 1 room, with 8 windows and 8 doors, to admit 8 members of the family, the heads of different branches of it to prevent quarrels for precedence at table. Each came in at his own door, and at an octagon table, of course, there was no chief place or head. Bicycle records

John, St., Knights of. Malta.

Knights of St John (*Johanniterritter*), a Lutheran order of high rank, founded by Frederick William III of Prussia, 23 May, 1812, and reorganized 15 Oct 1852 These knights co operated with the Knights of St. John of Malta and other bodies in ministering to the wounded during the Franco Prussian war in 1870-71, the chief office being at the ancient gate of the priory of St John Clerkenwell, London, E C, the duke of Manchester being a prior of the order

John's, St., night, or Midsummer-eve, 23 June, bonfires are still made in Ireland, and in some parts of England, and thought to be the relic of a pagan custom—resembling the Phœnician worship of Baal.

John's Gate, St. (St John's square, Clerkenwell, London), a fine vestige of monastic building, once the gate of the priory of St. John of Jerusalem (suppressed in 1540) was the place where the *Gentleman's Magazine* was first published, 6 Mch 1731 The house was often visited by dr Johnson, Garrick, and their friends. The gate was purchased for the Order of the Knights of St John by sir Edmund A H Lechmere, Bt., secretary of the English league The first meeting held here 24 June, 1874

Johnson, Andrew, administration of United States, 1865-66.

Johnson's club. Literary clubs.

Johnstown flood, the most disastrous to life that ever occurred in the United States, was at Johnstown, Pa., a city of about 28,000 inhabitants, on the Pennsylvania railroad, about 39 miles from Altoona and 78 from Pittsburg, and on the Conemaugh river or creek About 18 miles above Johnstown was Conemaugh lake, formerly a reservoir, owned by the South Fork Fishing and Hunting Club, with a level about 275 feet higher than the town, and about 2½ miles long by 1¼ miles wide The river had been rising for several days, under incessant rains, until the lake poured over the dam in unusual volume Warning had been given to people below that the dam might break at any moment, but little heed was given to it. The break occurred at 3 P M 31 May, 1889, and the distance of 18 miles to Johnstown was traversed by the advancing column of water in 7 minutes It met no obstacle until it reached the Pennsylvania railroad bridge immediately below the city which dammed the waters back and greatly increased the loss of life, while it collected a huge mass of débris which soon after took fire and added to the destruction Aid was sent to the sufferers by all the states, and many cities and countries of Europe contributed The following is a brief statement of the contributions received and turned over to the Flood Relief Commission appointed by the governor of Pennsylvania.

By gov Beaver		$1,236,146 45
Philadelphia Relief Committee	..	600,000.00
Pittsburg " "		560,000 00
New York " "	.	516 199 85
	Total	$2,912,346 30
Expended in the valley	$2,592,936 68	
" outside	246,475.26	
" general and office	5,728 89	2,845,140.83
	On hand	$67,205 47

Total number of lives lost 2142, of these 1115 were found and identified, 636 found and not identified, 319 missing, 99 whole families were lost, 124 women made widows, 965 children orphans or half orphans The sum of $183 281 was distributed among the widows, giving each about $1500, and $108,500 was set apart for the children Each orphan will receive about $50 annually until the age of 16 Loss of property by the flood estimated at $9,674,105.

Jonathan, Brother. Brother Jonathan

Jonesboro', Ga. Battle of Hardee (confederate) attacked Howard 31 Aug 1864, was repulsed with a loss of 2500 men. The confederates retreated to Lovejoy's Station during the night. Atlanta campaign

Joshua, successor of Moses, led the Israelites into Canaan, 1451 B.C Jews.—Handel's 14th oratorio, "Joshua," was finished 19 Aug 1747, produced 9 Mch 1748 It contained "See the Conquering Hero Comes," afterwards transferred to "Judas Maccabæus"

Journals of Congress, United States, have been kept and published from the first meeting of the Continental Congress at Philadelphia, Sept 1774 Annals.

Journals of the House of Commons, commenced in 1547, first ordered printed in 1752, 5000*l* being voted to Mr Hardinge for the work The journals of the House of Peers (commencing 1509) were ordered printed in 1767.

Ju'an Fernan'dez, an island in the Pacific, named ·om its discoverer in 1567. Alexander Selkirk, a native of ·cotland, left on shore here by his captain in Nov. 1704, lived lone till discovered by capt. Rogers in 1709. He died lieu-enant of the British ship *Weymouth*, 1723. A monument to is memory was erected on the island in 1868, then colonized y Germans. On his narrative De Foe founded the "Adven-ures of Robinson Crusoe," first pub. in 1719.

Juan, San, a small island near Vancouver's island. 'he possession of this island, commanding the strait between British Columbia and the United States, was disputed, under onflicting interpretations of the treaty of Washington re-pecting the boundaries, 12 June, 1846. UNITED STATES, uly and Oct. 1859. The matter (by treaty of Washington, May, 1871) was referred for arbitration to the emperor of Germany, who decided in favor of the U. S., Oct. 1872. The sle was evacuated by the British 22 Nov. following.

jubilees. The Jews were commanded to celebrate a ubilee every 50 years, 1491 B.C. (Lev. xxv. 8). Among the Christians a jubilee every century was instituted by pope Boniface VIII. in the year 1300. Clement VI. ordered it cel-brated every 50 years; Urban VI. every 33d year; Sixtus V. very 25th year.

hakespeare's jubilee, projected by David Garrick, celebrated at Shakespeare's birthplace, Stratford-on-Avon.....6, 7, 8 Sept. 1769
ational jubilee in England; George III. entering the 50th year of his reign.....25 Oct. 1809
ubilee of the general peace, and of the centenary of accession of Brunswick family.....1 Aug. 1814
'iftieth anniversary of signing the Declaration of Independence celebrated as a jubilee.....4 July, 1826
[Thomas Jefferson, who wrote the document, and John Adams, its earnest supporter, both signers, and both afterwards presidents of the U. S., d. on that day.]
hakespeare festival at Stratford.....23 Apr. 1836
" " ".....1865
cott centenary celebrated (he was b. 15 Aug. 1771).....9 Aug. 1871
nternational musical jubilee at Boston, Mass. (MUSIC), 17 June–4 July, 1872
entennial celebration..... 1876
'our hundredth anniversary of discovery of America.....1892–93

Judæa, the southern division of Palestine, received his name after the Jewish captivity. On returning (536 B.C.) he tribe of Judah settled first at Jerusalem, but gradually pread over the country. The following table shows the ivisions of the country from the first:

Canaanitish (1451 B.C.).	Israelitish (1451–63 B.C.).	Roman (63 B.C.).
idonians	tribe of Asher	Upper Galilee.
	" Naphtali.	
anaanites	" Zebulon.	Lower Galilee.
	" Issachar.	
Iivites	half-tribe of Manasseh	Samaria.
erizzites	tribe of Ephraim	
ebusites	" Benjamin	Judæa.
morites, Iittites	" Judah	
hilistines	" Simeon	
	" Dan	
Ioabites	" Reuben	Peræa.
mmonites, ileadites	" Gad	
ashanites	half-tribe of Manasseh	

Judah. JEWS.

"Judas Maccabæ'us," Handel's 12th oratorio, omposed 9 July–11 Aug. 1746; produced 1 Apr. 1747. MAC-ABEES.

Judenhasse and **Judenhetze** ("hatred of ews"), a term applied to the movement against them in Germany in 1880, through jealousy of their prosperity and lleged obtrusiveness. JEWS.

judge advocate-general and **judge mar-ial of all the forces,** an ancient office in England, eld by patent from the crown. He is the legal adviser of the ommander-in-chief in military cases, and by his authority all eneral courts-martial are held. The office of judge advocate-eneral in the English army was constituted soon after the Restoration.—In the United States, Congress enacted that he president shall appoint a judge advocate-general with the ank and pay of a colonel of cavalry, approved 17 July, 1862. Bureau of military justice established by Congress 20 June, 864, under control of the judge advocate-general, with the ank of brigadier-general, with 1 assistant judge advocate-eneral, with the rank of colonel of cavalry. Joseph Holt of Kentucky, first judge advocate-general as colonel, 1862; as brigadier-general, 1864. ARMY.

judges appointed by God, when the Israelites were in bondage, ruled from 1402 B.C. till the election of Saul as king, 1095. They were Othniel, Ehud, Deborah and Barak, Gideon, Abimelech, Tola, Jair, Jephthah, Ibzan, Elon, Abdon, Samson, Eli, Samuel.

judges of the United States Supreme court. JUSTICES.

Juggernaut, or "Lord of the World," one of the in-carnations of Vishnu as Krishna, an idol in the temple at Puri in Orissa, India, formed of an irregular pyramidal black stone, with 2 rich diamonds for eyes; the nose and mouth painted vermilion. The pilgrims that formerly visited the temple and god were reckoned at 1,200,000 annually, and it was customary for many of the fanatics to throw themselves before the car bearing the idol to be crushed by its wheels. The temple of Juggernaut was built 1198 A.D. at a cost esti-mated at $2,500,000. The state allowance to the temple was suspended by the Indian government in June, 1851. The festi-val was kept June, 1872. 12 persons were said to be killed by accident, Aug. 1878. The festival of 1878 reported a failure.

Jugurthine war. Jugurtha murdered his cousin, Hiempsal, king of Numidia, and usurped his throne, 118 B.C. He gave Adherbal a share in the government, but killed him in 112. He then provoked the Romans to war. Cæcilius Metellus was first sent against him, and defeated him in 2 battles; and Marius brought him in chains to Rome to adorn his triumph, 106 B.C., where he was put to death in 104. This war has been immortalized by the pen of Sallust.

Julian Period (by Joseph Scaliger, about 1583), a term of years produced by the multiplication of the lunar cycle 19, solar cycle 28, and Roman indiction 15. It consists of 7980 years, and began 4713 years before our era. Therefore the Ju-lian period for 1894 A.D. will be 4713 + 1894 = 6607 years, and the Julian period for 1894 B.C. will be 4714 − 1894 = 2820 years. By subtracting 4713 from the Julian period, our era is found; if before Christ, subtract the Julian period from 4714. It has been employed in computing time to avoid the ambiguity at-tendant on reckoning any period antecedent to our era, an ad-vantage in common with the mundane eras used at different times. For Julian era, CALENDAR, YEAR.

July, the 7th, originally 5th, Roman month, named by Marc Antony from Julius Cæsar, the dictator of Rome, who was born in it.

June, the 6th month, owes its name to Junius, which some derive from Juno, and others from Juniores, this being the month for the young, as May was for aged persons. Ovid, in his "Fasti," introduces Juno as claiming this month.

Junius's letters began in the London *Public Ad-vertiser*, 21 Jan. 1769.

They have been ascribed to Mr. Burke, William Gerard Hamilton, commonly called Single-speech Hamilton, John Wilkes, Mr. Dunning (afterwards lord Ashburton), sergeant Adair, the rev. J. Rosenhagen, John Roberts, Charles Lloyd, Samuel Dyer, gen. Lee, the duke of Portland, Hugh Boyd, and lord George Sackville; but sir Philip Francis is generally admitted to have been the author. Junius said, "I am the depository of my own secret, and it shall perish with me." The work of Mr. Chabot and hon. E. T. B. Twisleton is considered decisive of sir Philip Francis being Junius, May, 1871. "Junius is as much unknown as ever."—London *Athenæum*, 8 Sept. 1888. Sale of MSS. papers of sir Philip Francis, inconclusive respecting Junius, reported June, 1892.

Juno, the planet discovered by M. Harding, of Lilienthal, near Bremen, 1 Sept. 1804. It is 254,000,000 miles from the sun, and its period is 4 years and 128 days, moving nearly 42,000 miles an hour. Its diameter is estimated at 1424 Eng-lish miles.—The Roman name of the queen of heaven, wife of Jupiter, identical with the Greek goddess Hera.

Junonia, festivals in honor of Juno (the Greek Hera, or Here) at Rome, and instituted 431 B.C.

Junta. The Spanish provincial juntas, or councils, de-clared against the French in 1808, and incited insurrection.

Jupiter, known as a planet to the Chaldeans, 3000 B.C., and noted in a chart of the heavens made about 600 B.C., now in the national library at Paris. Its diameter is 85,000 miles, and it revolves on its axis once in 9 hours, 55 minutes,

26 seconds. It makes one revolution around the sun in 12 of our years, travelling in its orbit at the rate of 29,000 miles an hour. Its year is made up of 10,478 of its days; as compared with the earth it is 1233 times larger, but its weight is only 301 times greater, its mean density being less than a quarter of the earth's, the strata forming its surface being at most of the density of water. Its mean distance from the sun is 475,692,000 miles. It is accompanied by 5 satellites, 4 discovered by Galileo, 8 Jan. 1610, which are respectively 2352, 2099, 3436, and 2929 miles in diameter. The 5th, the nearest of the five to the planet, was discovered from the Lick observatory, 9 Sept. 1892.—The supreme Roman deity, the Greek Ζεύς. The most famous temple erected to this god was at Olympia, in Elis, where every 4th year the Olympic games were celebrated in his honor. He had also a splendid fane in the island of Ægina, and one in Libya, said to have been erected to him by Bacchus out of gratitude for water found there. Cambyses sent a force to bring away the immense treasures kept there, but they perished in the desert, 525 B.C. MYTHOLOGY. It was visited by Alexander 332 B.C. to consult the oracle as to his divinity.

juries. Trial by jury was introduced into England during the Saxon heptarchy, 6 Welsh and 6 *Anglo-Saxon freemen* being appointed to try causes between Englishmen and Welshmen of property, and made responsible with their whole estates, real and personal, for false verdicts.—*Lambard.* By most authorities the institution is ascribed to Alfred about 886. In Magna Charta, juries are insisted on as a bulwark of the people's liberty. An act for trial by jury in civil cases in Scotland was passed in 1815. The constitution of 1791 established trial by jury in France. An imperial decree abolished trial by jury throughout the Austrian empire, 15 Jan. 1852. Trial by jury began in Russia, 8 Aug. 1866; in Spain 1889. In Scotland, Guernsey, Jersey, and France, juries decide by a majority; in France, since 1831, a majority of two thirds is required. Under the original Constitution of the United States provision is made for the trial of criminal cases by jury, but not of civil cases. This caused dissatisfaction, people claiming that the omission was intended to abolish trial by jury in civil cases, hence the VII.th Amendment was adopted at an early day (CONSTITUTION OF THE U.S., AMENDMENTS TO), securing the rights of trial by jury in suits at common-law where the value in controversy shall exceed $20. *Grand juries* (of not less than 12 or more than 23 persons) decide whether sufficient evidence is adduced to put the accused on trial.

justices, chief and associate, of the Supreme court of the United States. Ever since the organization of this court, 1789, there has been 1 chief justice. But the number of associate justices has varied by act of Congress. At first the number was 5; 3 Mch. 1837 it was increased to 8; 3 Mch. 1863 to 9; 10 Apr. 1869 reduced to 8 again. This court holds one term a year in the city of Washington.

LIST OF THE JUSTICES SINCE THE ADOPTION OF THE CONSTITUTION.

(Chief-justices in *italics*, associate in roman.)

Name.	Appointed from	Term of service.	Remarks.
John Jay	New York	1789 to 1795	Resigned.
John Rutledge	South Carolina	1789 " 1791 1795	Resigned as associate judge. Appointed chief justice; served one term; not confirmed by Senate.
Caleb Cushing	Massachusetts	1789 to 1810	Appointed chief-justice 1796, but declined; died in office.
James Wilson	Pennsylvania	1789 " 1798	Died in office.
John Blair	Virginia	1789 " 1796	Resigned.
Robert H. Harrison	Maryland	1789 " 1790	"
James Iredell	North Carolina	1790 " 1799	Died in office.
Thomas Johnson	Maryland	1791 " 1793	Resigned.
William Petterson	New Jersey	1793 " 1806	Died in office.
Samuel Chase	Maryland	1796 " 1811	" " "
Oliver Ellsworth	Connecticut	1796 " 1801	Resigned.
Bushrod Washington	Virginia	1798 " 1829	Died in office.
Alfred Moore	North Carolina	1799 " 1804	Resigned.
John Marshall	Virginia	1801 " 1835	Died in office.
William Johnson	South Carolina	1804 " 1834	" " "
Brockholst Livingston	New York	1806 " 1823	" " "
Thomas Todd	Kentucky	1807 " 1826	" " "
Joseph Story	Massachusetts	1811 " 1845	" " "
Gabriel Duval	Maryland	1811 " 1836	Resigned.
Smith Thompson	New York	1823 " 1845	Died in office.
Robert Trimble	Kentucky	1826 " 1828	" " "
John McLean	Ohio	1829 " 1861	" " "
Henry Baldwin	Pennsylvania	1830 " 1846	" " "
Jas. M. Wayne	Georgia	1835 " 1867	" " "
Roger B. Taney	Maryland	1836 " 1864	" " "
Philip P. Barbour	Virginia	1836 " 1841	" " "
John Catron	Tennessee	1837 " 1865	" " "
John McKinley	Alabama	1837 " 1852	" " "
Peter V. Daniel	Virginia	1841 " 1860	" " "
Samuel Nelson	New York	1845 " 1872	Resigned.
Levi Woodbury	New Hampshire	1845 " 1851	Died in office.
Robert C. Grier	Pennsylvania	1846 " 1869	Resigned.
Benjamin R. Curtis	Massachusetts	1851 " 1857	"
John A. Campbell	Alabama	1853 " 1861	"
Nathan Clifford	Maine	1858 " 1881	Died in office.
Noah H. Swayne	Ohio	1861 " 1881	Resigned.
Samuel F. Miller	Iowa	1862 " 1890	Died in office.
David Davis	Illinois	1862 " 1877	Resigned.
Stephen J. Field	California	1863	
Salmon P. Chase	Ohio	1864 to 1873	Died in office.
William Strong	Pennsylvania	1870 " 1880	Resigned.
Joseph P. Bradley	New Jersey	1870 " 1892	Died in office.
Ward Hunt	New York	1872 " 1882	Resigned.
Morrison R. Waite	Ohio	1874 " 1888	Died in office.
John M. Harlan	Kentucky	1877	
William B. Woods	Georgia	1880 to 1887	" " "
Stanley Matthews	Ohio	1881 " 1889	" " "
Horace Gray	Massachusetts	1881	
Samuel Blatchford	New York	1882 to 1893	" " "
Lucius Q. C. Lamar	Mississippi	1888 " 1893	" " "
Melville W. Fuller	Illinois	1888	
David J. Brewer	Kansas	1889	
Henry B. Brown	Michigan	1890	
George Shiras, jr.	Pennsylvania	1892	
Howell E. Jackson	Tennessee	1893 to 1895	Died in office
Edward D. White	Louisiana	1894	
Rufus W. Peckham	New York	1895	

Justinian code compiled by a commission for emperor Justinian I. Feb. 528, including what may be termed the statute law (2000 volumes reduced to 50), was promulgated Apr. 529. To this Justinian added the Digest or Pandects, the Institutes, nd Novels, promulgated 16 Nov. 534. These compilations are alled, collectively, the Body of Civil Law (*Corpus Juris Civilis*).

Jute, the fibres of 2 plants, the chonch and isbund (*Corhorus olitorius* and *Corchorus capsularis*), since 1830 cultiated in Bengal for making gunny-cloth, etc. Jute has been ɪanufactured at Dundee as a substitute for flax, tow, etc., and ı July, 1862, assertions were made that it could be employed s a substitute for cotton. It is now successfully cultivated in the southern United States, so that the large importation will be diminished.

Jutland, a low, flat peninsula of Denmark, the home of the Jutes who settled in the southern counties of Great Britain. South Jutland, or Schleswig, was taken by the allies in 1813, and restored in 1814; again taken from Denmark by the allies in 1861, and in 1866 merged into the Prussian province Schleswig-Holstein.

K

Kainardji, a village of Bulgaria. Here a treaty was igned, July, 1774, between the Turks and Russians, opening he Black sea and giving Crimea to Russia.

Kaffra'ria, or land of the Kafirs, an extensive country ı S. Africa, extending from the north of Cape Colony to the)range river. Now included in Cape Colony and NATAL. 'his name, signifying unbeliever or infidel, was given by the ırabs. CAPE OF GOOD HOPE, ZULULAND, etc.

Kalafat', a town on the Danube, opposite the fortress f Widdin, was fortified by the Turks under Omar Pacha when hey crossed the river, 28 Oct. 1853. In Dec., prince Gortchakoff, with the Russian army, determined to storm the inrenchments. The conflict lasted from 31 Dec. to 9 Jan. 1854, vhen the Russians were compelled to retire. One of these onflicts occurred at CITATE, 6 Jan. Kalafat was invested 28 'an.; gen. Schilders attacked it on 19 Apr. without success, ınd the blockade was raised 21 Apr.

Kalakh, ancient capital of middle ASSYRIA; where ,ayard and others made many discoveries.

kalei'doscope, an optical instrument, with a comıination of mirrors, symmetrically reflecting transparent subtances placed between, was devised by dr. (afterwards sir)avid) Brewster of Edinburgh in 1814 and perfected in 1817.)EBUSSCOPE.

Kalisz, a city of Russian Poland. Here the Russians lefeated the Swedes, 19 Nov. 1706; and here the Saxons unler the French gen. Reynier were beaten by the Russians unler Winzingerode, 13 Feb. 1813.

Kalmucks. TARTARY.

Kamtschat'ka, a peninsula, east coast of Asia, disovered by Morosco, a Cossack chief, 1690; taken possession of y Russia in 1697; and proved to be a peninsula by Behring n 1728. In 1855 the country was incorporated with the martime province. It is over 800 miles long and about 300 miles vide at its widest part, and contains some 237,266 sq. miles.

Kane's arctic expeditions. FRANKLIN, EARCH FOR; UNITED STATES, 1850, '51, '53, '55.

kangaroos, marsupial animals indigenous to Australia first seen by capt. Cook, 22 June, 1770), bred at San Donato, he estate of prince Demidoff, in 1853, and since.

Kansas, Alaska excluded, is geographically the central tate of the United States, lying between lon. 94° 38′ and 102° W., and lat. 37° and 40° N. It is bounded by Nebraska on the north, Missouri on the east, Indian Territory on the south, and Colorado on the west. Area, 81,700 sq. miles. Pop. 1890, 1,427,096; 1900, 1,470,495. Capital, Topeka.

French explore the Missouri river as far as the mouth of the Kansas river...... 1705
M. Dutisne, a young French officer sent out by Bienville, *governor of Louisiana*, reaches the Pawnee country in Kansas, and erecting a cross of wood, takes formal possession in the name of the king of France........27 Sept. 1719
Spaniards from Santa Fé seeking to found a colony on the Missouri, are destroyed by the Missouri Indians near the present site of fort Leavenworth, only one settler, a Spanish priest, escaping and returning to Santa Fé................ 1720
Included in the Louisiana territory purchased of France (ANNEXATIONS, UNITED STATES).............................. 1803
Congress divides Louisiana into 2 unequal parts, the one, north of 33° N. lat., called the district of Louisiana, under the governor of Indiana territory..........................26 Mch. 1804
Lewis and Clarke leave St. Louis for the Pacific, under government authority, and find remains of an old French fort near the present site of Atchison..........................May, "
District of Louisiana made the territory of Louisiana...3 Mch. 1805
Territory of Louisiana admitted to the second grade of government as Missouri territory......................4 June, 1812
First steamboat, a stern-wheeler, called the *Western Engineer*, passes up the Missouri river, carrying maj. S. H. Long on an expedition up the Yellowstone............................ 1819
Section 8 of act for admission of Missouri into the Union provides that in all Louisiana, north of lat. 36° 30′. and not included in the state, slavery "shall be and is hereby forever prohibited," but runaway slaves may be lawfully reclaimed. Act passed (UNITED STATES)........................6 Mch. 1820
Major Sibley, appointed under act of Congress, surveys a wagonroad from Missouri through Kansas to Santa Fé........... 1825
By treaty with Osage Indians the tribe locate on a tract of 7,564,000 acres in S. Kansas, watered by the Arkansas, Verdigris, and Neosho rivers........................30 Dec. "
Fort Leavenworth, called a cantonment until 1832, established and U. S. troops stationed there............................ 1827
Treaty with the *Delaware Indians, locates them in the fork of* the Kansas and Missouri rivers....................24 Sept. 1829
Baptist Shawnee mission established 4 miles west of the Missouri line under rev. Isaac McCoy; also appointed agent for the government.. 1831
Indian tribes located in Kansas, including the Shawnees, Ottawas, and Wyandottes of Ohio, the Kickapoos, Kaskaskias, Peorias, Piankeshaws, and Weas..........................1831–32
First stock of goods landed below Kansas City, at Francis Chouteau's log warehouse.............................. 1834
First printing-press brought to Kansas by rev. Joseph Meeker, set up at the Baptist mission farm, 5 miles northeast of Ottawa... "
Congress makes all U. S. territory west of the Mississippi not in the states of Missouri and Louisiana or territory of Arkansas "Indian country"..........................30 June, "
Col. Henry Dodge, U.S.A., makes an expedition to the Rocky mountains, leaving fort Leavenworth 29 May, and returning along the line where the Atchison, Topeka and Santa Fé railroad now runs.. 1835
Fort Scott established on the Marminton river........30 May, 1842
Lieut. John C. Fremont, in his expedition west from St. Louis, reaches site of Lawrence, 12 June; Topeka, 14 June; and thence travels northwest to the Blue and Platte rivers...... "
Fremont passes up the Kansas river on a second expedition.. 1843
First emigrant train for California passes through Kansas, 50 wagons and 100 men.................................... 1844
Kansas Indians cede to the U. S. 2,000,000 acres in Kansas, 14 Jan. 1846
Gen. S. W. Kearny marches from fort Leavenworth to Santa Fé.. "
Mormons cross the plains for Utah, starting from near the site of Atchison.. "
Catholic Osage mission established in Neosho county...1 May, 1847
Military road built by the government from fort Leavenworth to fort Kearny.. 1850
Willard P. Hall of Missouri introduces a bill to organize the territory of Platte (Kansas and Nebraska)............13 Dec. 1852
Fort Riley, near junction of Republican and Kansas rivers, established.......................................17 May, 1853
Massachusetts Emigrant Aid Society, soon after incorporated as the New England Emigrant Aid Society, organized in Boston..Mch. 1854
Delawares, Shawnees, Iowas, and Kickapoos cede lands in Kansas to the U. S..................................May, "
Act of Congress passed organizing the territory of Kansas, to be admitted as a state with or without slavery......30 May, "
Thirty-two persons associate in Weston, Mo., to lay out Leavenworth, the first city in the territory.............13 June, "
Emigrants under Charles H. Branscomb of Massachusetts, sent out by Emigrant Aid Society to Kansas as an anti-slavery colony, settle at Lawrence and form a "squatter government," hon. John A. Wakefield chief-justice................30 July, "

First newspaper in Kansas, the *Leavenworth Herald*, pro-slavery, printed under an elm tree on the levee at Leavenworth, 15 Sept. 1854
Atchison laid out by an association from Platte county, Mo, and first sale of lots takes place 21 Sept. "
Rev S Y Lum, Congregational missionary, preaches at Lawrence on the 1st and organizes a church 15 Oct "
Andrew H Reeder of Pennsylvania appointed governor, arrives in the territory 7 Oct "
Secret societies called Blue Lodges begin in Weston, Mo, for extending slavery into Kansas Oct. "
Election as territorial delegate to Congress of J W Whitfield, pro slavery, by illegal votes 29 Nov "
Topeka founded 5 Dec. "
A Free state meeting at Lawrence 23 Dec "
Wyandotte Indians cede to the U S lands purchased by them from the Delawares in Kansas in 1843 31 Jan 1855
About 1000 Missourians enter Lawrence with arms, and vote for members of legislature 30 Mch "
Four sons of John Brown, abolitionist settle on the Pottawatomie river 8 miles from Ossawatomie "
William Phillips of Leavenworth protesting against election frauds, taken to Weston, Mo, tarred and feathered and ridden on a rail The outrage approved by the pro slavery party, 17 May, "
At a Free state convention at Lawrence it was "*Resolved*, That in reply to the threats of war so frequently made in our neighboring state our answer is, 'We are ready'" 8 June, "
Convention of national Democracy at Lawrence 27 June, "
State legislature meets at Pawnee, and at once drives out the Free state members 2 July, "
Legislature overriding gov Reeder's veto, removes the seat of government to the Shawnee Manual Labor school 6 July, "
Gov Reeder charged with irregularities in purchase of Indian lands by W L Marcy, secretary of state, 11 June is removed, and John L Dawson appointed, who declines to serve leaving Daniel Woodson as acting governor 31 July, "
Legislature selects Lecompton as permanent capital 8 Aug "
Delegates elected by a Free state convention at Lawrence 14 Aug, which repudiated the acts of the state legislature assemble at Big Springs They appoint delegates to a convention at Topeka, 19 Sept, to draw up a state constitution and seek admission to the Union 5 Sept. "
Wilson Shannon of Ohio, commissioned governor of Kansas, arrives and takes oath of office 7 Sept. "
Convention at Topeka to form Free state constitution 19 Sept "
Gen J W Whitfield, pro slavery elected to Congress 1 Oct "
Pro slavery party meet at Leavenworth, ask the "lovers of Law and order" to obey the laws of the first legislature, and declare it treason to oppose them 3 Oct. "
Free state party elect A H Reeder delegate to Congress, 9 Oct "
Free state convention meet at Topeka 23 Oct, complete their work 11 Nov "
Charles W Dow is killed by Franklin N Coleman a pro slavery man near Lawrence, on the 21st Free state men meet at the scene on the 22d, and sheriff Samuel J Jones arrests Jacob Branson, with whom Dow had lived for taking part At Blanton, Branson is released by Free state men A meeting is held at Lawrence, and Branson addresses the people Fearing a mob from Missouri, citizens are armed Nov "
Gov Shannon orders maj gen William P Richardson of the territorial militia to collect as large a force as possible and report to sheriff Jones 27 Nov "
About 800 Free state men enlist, among them John Brown and 4 sons, and about 1500 Missourians gather at Franklin near the mouth of the Wakarusa 29 Nov "
Gov Shannon makes a treaty with the Free state men, and orders the militia and sheriff to disband their forces 8 Dec "
Vote upon Topeka Free state constitution results in 1731 for and 46 against The pro slavery men carry off the ballot box at Leavenworth 15 Dec "
Office of the *Territorial Register* at Leavenworth entered by a mob, press and type thrown into the river 15 Dec "
Convention at Lawrence nominates state officers under the Topeka constitution The conservative Free state men bolt and nominate a "Free state, Anti abolition" ticket, 22 Dec "
Dr Charles Robinson elected governor under the Topeka constitution 15 Jan 1856
Pres Pierce in a special message recognizes "bogus" legislature and calls Topeka government revolutionary 24 Jan "
Whitfield takes his seat in Congress, and Reeder announces that he will contest it 4 Feb "
U S forces in Kansas, by order of secretary of war, are put under requisition of the governor 15 Feb "
Free state legislature meets at Topeka, gov Robinson delivers his message, and A H Reeder and J H Lane are elected senators 5 Mch "
Topeka constitution presented in U S Senate by Lewis Cass, 24 Mch, in the House by Daniel Mace of Indiana 7 Apr "
Maj Buford arrives in Kansas with a large body of pro slavery men from Georgia, Alabama and South Carolina Apr "
Sheriff Jones attempts to arrest S N Wood in Lawrence, charged with aiding in the rescue of Branson in Nov previous, but is prevented, shot at and wounded Col Sumner, U S A, arrives at Lawrence with his command 19-25 Apr "
Rev Pardee Butler for anti-slavery preaching is sent from Atchison adrift down the Missouri on a raft and on returning is stripped, tarred, and covered with cotton 30 Apr "
Grand jury of Douglas county indict Robinson, Reeder, and others for high treason in organizing a Free state government 5 May, "

KAN

Gov Reeder escapes arrest, going to Kansas City in disguise, and thence down the Missouri to St. Charles, and makes his way to Illinois 9 May, 1856
Gov Robinson is sent east but is arrested at Lexington, Mo, brought back, and imprisoned at Lecompton on charge of high treason 10 May, "
Marshal Donaldson calls upon all law-abiding citizens to aid him in serving writs at Lawrence, about 1000 men respond, and gov Shannon refuses to interpose between the people and the sheriff and marshal 11 May, "
Marshal Donaldson makes 2 arrests in Lawrence without opposition The Emigrant Aid Society hotel and the *Herald of Freedom* printing office are destroyed by sheriff Jones, and 2 pro slavery men are accidentally killed 21 May, "
Capt Pate, setting out to destroy "Old Brown" captures 2 of John Brown's sons, and driving them before his forces, encamps with 50 men on a stream called Black Jack (John Brown, jr, from inhuman treatment, becomes insane) Here they are overtaken by John Brown and capt Shore, who with 28 men give battle and compel Pate to surrender 2 June, "
Gov Shannon issues a proclamation commanding all military companies, not authorized by law, to disperse 4 June, "
Ossawatomie sacked by Pate and others 6 June, "
Civil war rages in the settled portion of Kansas, and the Missouri river is closed to Free state immigrants June, "
House of Representatives passes a bill to admit Kansas with the Topeka constitution but it fails to become a law 3 July, "
Kansas Free state legislature meeting at Topeka, dispersed by col Sumner and U S troops under orders from acting gov Woodson in gov Shannon's absence, and pres Pierce, 4 July, "
A substitute for House bill admitting Kansas passes Senate, but House refuses to recede and bill fails 8 July, "
Relief furnished the people of Kansas by the northern states, the Grand Kansas Aid Society, organized in Buffalo, N Y, raising $120 000 for this purpose "
House of Representatives excludes both Whitfield and Reeder as delegates 1 Aug "
Free state men seize the fort near Ossawatomie, driving out the Georgia forces. 5 Aug "
Free state men capture Franklin, attack col Titus's camp near Lecompton and take the party prisoners 12 Aug "
"Lane's Northern Army" advanced into Kansas via Iowa and Nebraska as follows 1 Aug there were congregated near Nebraska City 500 emigrants and 60 wagons Gen James H Lane and 6 others one week in advance of the emigrants enter Kansas 300 of the first emigrant train stop 3 miles south of the boundary of Kansas and found Plymouth, 75 proceed 15 miles farther, and locate at Lexington, and 30 more proceed 30 miles to what is now Holton, the remainder reaching Topeka. 13 Aug "
Gov Shannon makes a second treaty of peace, and Free state prisoners are exchanged 17 Aug "
John W Geary of Pennsylvania appointed governor, gov Shannon is removed and resigns on the same day 21 Aug "
Daniel Woodson acting governor, proclaims the territory in a state of open insurrection and rebellion 25 Aug "
David Atchison chosen commander of the pro slavery "Army of Law and Order in Kansas territory" 25 Aug "
Four hundred Missourians under J W Reed and rev Martin White attack and take Ossawatomie, John Brown's son Frederick losing his life 29 Aug "
Methodist Episcopal church in Kansas organized Sept "
Gov Robinson released on bail . 10 Sept. "
Gov Geary assumes office at Lecompton, delivers an inaugural address and issues a proclamation disbanding armed forces in the territory and directing enrolment of militia 11 Sept. "
Gen Lane's men under capts. Harvey and Whipple meet pro-slavery men under Lowe and Robertson at Hickory Point, Jefferson county, after 6 hours' fighting Lane's men surrender, and are taken to the U S camp at Lecompton 13 Sept. "
Gov Geary visits pro slavery camp at junction of Wakarusa and Kansas rivers, and orders the men to disband 15 Sept "
Election by pro slavery men for delegate to Congress, a legislature, and a call for a constitutional convention Free state men refuse to vote 6 Oct. "
About 20 of Lane's soldiers captured at Hickory Point are convicted and sentenced to 5 years in the penitentiary 13 Sept. "
Gov Geary announces that "Peace prevails throughout the territory of Kansas" 11 Nov "
Col William Phillips publishes his book "The Conquest of Kansas by Missouri and Her Allies" "
Free state legislature meets at Topeka, gov Robinson absent, judge Cato grants a writ, and 7 members of the legislature are arrested by the U S marshal 7 Jan 1857
Territorial legislature and a convention of Kansas National Democratic party meet at Lecompton 12 Jan "
Cities of Topeka Atchison, and Manhattan incorporated, 14 Feb. "
Gov Geary, resigned leaves Kansas secretly 10 Mch. "
Free state convention at Topeka resolves not to vote for delegates to the Lecompton constitutional convention 10 Mch "
Frederic P Stanton, acting governor, issues an address, 17 Apr "
Robert J Walker, appointed governor, arrives at Lecompton and reads his inaugural address 27 May, "
Gov Robinson's message to Topeka legislature 11 June, "
For the first time, the Free-state men elect city officers in Leavenworth 29 June, "
Gov Walker, with several companies of dragoons, encamps before Lawrence, intending to prevent action under the independent municipal charter, but soon withdraws 16 July, "
Under the Topeka constitution, Marcus J Parrott chosen to Congress, vote on the constitution, 7257 for, 34 against 9 Aug "

At a convention at Grasshopper falls, the Free state men agree to take part in territorial election 5 Oct 26 Aug 1857
At the Oct election the Free state party is successful 5 Oct "
Baker university established at Palmyra, now Baldwin City Oct "
Convention of delegates at Lecompton form a constitution and by ordinance assert the state's right to tax lands of the U S within it 7 Nov "
Free state convention at Lawrence rejects the Lecompton constitution and asks for a vote of the people to decide between it and the Topeka constitution 2 Dec "
Pres Buchanan, by message, urges admission of Kansas under Lecompton constitution 7 Dec "
J W Denver, acting governor in place of Robert J Walker, resigned 15 Dec "
State officers elected under Lecompton constitution 21 Dec "
Free state convention at Lawrence on 23 Dec, and a Democratic convention at Leavenworth, both in opposition to the Lecompton constitution 24 Dec "
Result of a people's vote on the Lecompton constitution was against, 10 226, for, with slavery, 138, for without slavery, 23 election held 4 Jan 1858
Last meeting of the Topeka legislature, no quorum 4 Mch "
Free state constitutional convention at Mineola 23 Mch, adjourned to Leavenworth 25 Mch, frames "The Leavenworth Constitution" 3 Apr "
Compromise bill known as the "English Swindle" and "Lecompton Junior" passed, admitting Kansas under Lecompton constitution amended, approved 4 May, "
Gov Denver takes oath of office 12 May, "
Leavenworth constitution adopted by the people 18 May, "
Attack on Free state men by a party of 25 under Charles A Hamilton, at Marais du Cygnes, 5 killed and 5 severely wounded 19 May, "
Twenty men leave Lawrence for Pike's Peak One of the first expeditions to the gold regions 21 May, "
First public school in Leavenworth opens 5 July, "
People's vote on the Lecompton constitution as modified, for, 1788, against, 11 300 2 Aug "
Gov Denver resigns, sec. Hugh S Walsh acting governor, 9 Oct "
Capt Montgomery, with 68 men, enters fort Scott and releases Benjamin Rice, a Free state prisoner 16 Dec "
Samuel Medary governor, arrives at Lecompton 17 Dec. "
John Brown and his men go into Missouri, liberate 14 slaves, and bring them to Kansas 20 Dec "
Democratic convention at Tecumseh 11 May, 1859
Republican party organized in Kansas, convention at Ossawatomie addressed by Horace Greeley 18 May, "
Beginning of a drought which lasted until Nov 1860 and caused the "Kansas famine" June, "
Convention at Wyandotte adopts a constitution 29 July, "
Vote for Wyandotte constitution, 10,421, against, 5530 4 Oct "
Abraham Lincoln speaks at Elwood 1 Dec. "
At election under Wyandotte constitution, Charles Robinson Republican, is chosen governor 6 Dec "
Legislature adjourns from Lecompton to Lawrence 21 Jan 1860
Track laying of first railroad in Kansas begun on the Elwood and Marysville railroad 20 Mch "
House of Representatives votes to admit Kansas under the Wyandotte constitution 11 Apr "
Last territorial legislature meets at Lecompton and adjourns to Lawrence 7 Jan 1861
George M Bebee, a Democrat appointed to succeed gov Medary, who resigns 10 Jan "
Act to admit Kansas under Wyandotte constitution passes Senate 21 Jan, House, 28 Jan, approved 29 Jan "
Gov Robinson assumes office 9 Feb "
Meeting of first legislature 26 Mch "
Steamboat *New Sam Gaty* arrives at Leavenworth from St Louis, under Confederate flag The captain is compelled by the people to substitute the stars and stripes 18 Apr "
First Confederate flag captured by Kansas troops at Iatan, Mo, brought into Leavenworth 3 June, "
First overland coach arrives, 17 days from San Francisco, 18 July, "
Battle with Confederates at Dry Wood. 2 Sept. "
First annual meeting of State Temperance Society at Topeka, 9 Oct. "
Vote for state capital stood Topeka, 7996, Lawrence, 5291, scattering, 1184 5 Nov "
State Agricultural Society formed 5 Mch 1862
Confederate guerilla chief Quantrell makes a raid into Johnson county burning Shawneetown 18 Oct. "
Legislature locates state university at Lawrence 20 Feb 1863
Establishes a state normal school at Emporia 3 Mch "
State insane asylum at Ossawatomie established "
State Agricultural college, in Riley county (late the Blue Mount Central college established 1858) founded 27 July, "
Quantrell with 300 men dashes into the streets of Lawrence at daylight and kills about 200 men 21 Aug "
Confederate gen Sterling Price advances with troops towards Kansas and enters Linn county 23 Oct. 1864
Battles near Mound City, Little Osage and Charlotte 25 Oct "
Kansas furnishes for the war a total of 23,000 men, a larger proportion of the population than any other state. 1861–65
Institution for deaf and dumb established at Olathe 1865
Colored men in convention at Topeka memorialize the legislature to strike the word "white" from the Constitution Jan 1866
Legislature authorizes sale of 500,000 acres of state land for the benefit of railroads. Jan "

KAN

Treaty made with many Indian tribes for removal to Indian territory 23 Feb 1867
Gens Hancock and Custer march against Indians in western Kansas 30 Apr "
Lucy Stone Susan B Anthony, Elizabeth Cady Stanton and George Francis Train, with the Hutchinson family of singers, advocate woman suffrage "
Vote upon amending Constitution For striking out the word "white," 10 483, against, 19,421 For striking out "male," 9070, against, 19 857 5 Nov "
Indian raids in Solomon valley and along the Republican and Saline rivers Aug 1868
Col George A Forsyth engages in an 8 days' fight with Indians on the north fork of the Republican river 17 Sept "
Woman suffrage convention at Topeka 4 Feb 1869
Indian raids on the Republican river 21 May, "
State convention of colored people at Topeka ask the legislature to memorialize Congress for negro suffrage 20 June, "
Legislature adjourns after ratifying the XVth Amendment to the Constitution of the U S 3 Mch 1870
Congress provides for removal of Osage Indians and the sale of their lands 15 July, "
Liberal Republican convention at Topeka organized to "rebuke the corruptions and usurpations which have characterized our state and national politics" 10 Apr 1872
Act of Congress for removal of the Kansas Indians 8 May, "
Session of farmers state convention at Topeka, constitution of the Farmers' Co operative association formed 26 Mch 1873
State temperance convention at Leavenworth nominates W K Marshall of Lawrence for governor, received at the November election about 3 per cent of the votes 10 Sept 1874
Mennonites buy 100,000 acres of railroad lands in the southern-central part of the state 14 Oct. "
Continued and severe drought throughout 1873-74
Legislature provides for issuing $95,000 state bonds to supply destitute citizens with grain and seed for the spring planting, 1875
Legislature abolishes all distinction of color in the laws 4 Mch 1876
Discovery of lead deposits in Cherokee county, Galena and Empire City spring into existence 1877
Monument to John Brown dedicated at Ossawatomie 30 Oct "
First refugees to Kansas, van guard of a great migration of colored people from slave states on the Mississippi arrive at Wyandotte Apr 1879
Kansas Pacific railroad seizes the telegraph along its line, a step in the American Union and Western Union telegraph war Feb 1880
Four drive well defence associations formed in southern Kansas to contest the Green drive well patent of 1868 "
Greenback Labor party in convention at Topeka nominates H B Vrooman for governor 4 Aug "
State election, vote upon adding to the constitution, "The manufacture and sale of intoxicating liquors shall be forever prohibited in the state except for medical scientific, and mechanical purposes" 92 302 votes for 84,304 against, and the decision was left to the Supreme court Nov "
Immigration of colored people continues through the year, at its close there were 40,000 colored immigrants in Kansas. "
Supreme court decides the prohibitory amendment valid, legislature attempts to strengthen it by another Feb 1881
Gov St John in his message pronounces the prohibition amendment "premature and indeed unfortunate," and suggests submitting to the people a proposition to repeal it 1882
George W Glick, Democrat, elected governor, remaining state officers and congressmen being Republican Nov "
Law creating a railroad commission and regulating passenger and freight charges 1883
Prohibition party organized in state convention at Lawrence, 2 Sept 1884
State Reformatory located at Hutchinson 1885
Kansas national guard fully organized under militia law of 1885 1886
Liquor law to suppress the so called "drug store saloons" 1887
Soldiers' Orphans home opened at Atchison 1 July, "
Legislature grants women in cities votes for school officers or for issuing bonds for school purposes "
Convention of 600 delegates at Abilene to begin a capitol-removal movement. 1888
Governor stations 2d regiment in Stevens county to preserve peace, sheriff John Cross having been murdered by an armed faction, result of a county seat contest July, "
National Farmers' congress and Farmers' Trust association at Topeka, delegates from all sections of the Union 4 Nov "
Convention of delegates from 15 states and territories at Topeka to devise means for securing a deep harbor on the coast of Texas 1 Oct. 1889
Legislature appropriates $13 000 for the establishment and maintenance of a silk station and to promote the culture of silk in the state "
State Re submission Republican league in convention at Wichita demand a re submission of the prohibitory amendment 15 Jan 1890
State convention of over 3000 delegates at Topeka to protest against the "Missouri whiskey invasion" and the "original package shops" 23 June, "
Wilson bill, overruling the "original package decision," passes Congress, receives the president's signature, and the "original package shops" are closed 8 Aug. "
People's party, an outgrowth of the Farmers' Alliance and State Grange, convenes at Topeka and nominates John F Willits for governor 13 Aug "

At state election the vote for governor stood: Humphrey, Republican, 115,025; Willits, 106,972 ....Nov. 1890
W. A. Peffer (Alliance) elected U. S. senator............28 Jan. 1891
William Ferrel, meteorologist, b. 1817, d. at Maywood, 18 Sept. "
U. S. senator Plumb dies at Washington, D. C., of apoplexy, 20 Dec. "
Bishop W. Perkins, appointed U. S. senator by the governor in place of Plumb, qualifies..............................5 Jan. 1892
Bob and Emmet Dalton, Joseph Evans, and "Texas Jack" shot and killed by a sheriff's posse while attempting to rob the First National and Coydon's banks in Coffeyville; 4 citizens are killed in the affray...................morning of 5 Oct. "
L. D. Lewelling elected governor by the Populists and Democrats..Nov. "
Republicans and Populists each claim the speakership in the House..10 Jan. 1893
[Separate organizations effected.]
Republicans take forcible possession of Representatives hall, Topeka..15 Feb. "
[Militia called out by the governor.]
A peace agreement signed............................17 Feb. "
Supreme court of Kansas decides that the Republican house was the legally constituted body.....................25 Feb. "

GOVERNORS OF THE TERRITORY.

Name.	Term.	Remarks.
Andrew H. Reeder, Pa.	1854 to 1855	Removed.
Wilson Shannon, O....	1855 " 1856	"
John W. Geary, Pa....	1856 " 1857	Resigns.
Robert J. Walker, Miss.	1857 " 1858	"
J. W. Denver..........	1858	"
Samuel Medary	1858 to 1861	"
George M. Bebee	1861	
	STATE.	
Charles Robinson......	1861 to 1862	
Thomas Carney	1862 " 1864	
S. J. Crawford.........	1864 " 1868	
James M. Harvey......	1868 " 1872	Afterwards U. S. senator.
Thomas A. Osborn.....	1873 " 1875	
George T. Anthony	1876 " 1878	Nominated by the Prohibition party for the presidency, 1884.
John P. St. John.......	1879 " 1883	
George W. Glick.......	1883 " 1885	
John A. Martin........	1885 " 1887	
Lyman U. Humphreys.	1887 " 1893	
L. D. Lewelling.......	1893 " 1895	
E. N. Morrill..........	1895 " 1897	

UNITED STATES SENATORS FROM THE STATE OF KANSAS.

Name.	No. of Congress.	Date.	Remarks.
James H. Lane..	37th to 39th	1861 to 1866	Committed suicide 11 July, 1866.
Samuel C. Pomeroy..................................	37th " 43d	1861 " 1873	
Edmund G. Ross.....................................	39th " 41st	1866 " 1871	Appointed in place of Lane.
Alexander Caldwell..................................	42d	1871 " 1873	Resigned 1873.
Robert Crozier.......................................	43d	1873 " 1874	Appointed in place of Caldwell.
James M. Harvey....................................	43d to 44th	1874 " 1877	Elected in place of Caldwell.
John J. Ingalls.......................................	43d " 51st	1873 " 1891	
Preston B. Plumb....................................	45th " 52d	1877 " 1891	Died 20 Dec. 1891.
William A. Peffer....................................	52d	1891	Term expires 1897.
Bishop W. Perkins...................................	52d	1892 to 1893	Appointed in place of Plumb.
John Martin..	53d	1893	Elected in place of Plumb. Term expires 1895.

Karaïtes or **Readers,** the Protestants of Judaism, a remnant of Sadducees, formed into a sect by Anan-ben-David in the 8th century. They accept the Scriptures alone, rejecting the Talmud and rabbinical traditions. They still exist in Turkey, Poland, Crimea, and other parts of the East. The name is of uncertain origin.

Kars, a town in Asiatic Turkey, captured by the Russians under Paskevitch, 15 July, 1828, after 3 days' conflict. In 1855 it was defended by gen. Fenwick Williams, with 15,000 men, and with 3 months' provisions and 3 days' ammunition, against the Russian gen. Mouravieff, with 40,000 infantry and 10,000 cavalry, from 18 June to 28 Nov. 1855. The garrison suffered much from cholera and want of food. The Russians made an assault 29 Sept., but were repulsed, losing above 6000 men, and the garrison were overcome by famine alone.—*Sandwith.* Kars was restored to Turkey, Aug. 1856; and the general was made a baronet, as sir William Fenwick Williams of Kars, and granted a pension.

Russians besieging Kars compelled to retire by Mukhtar Pacha, about 13 July, 1877
Under grand-duke Michael and Loris Melikoff, defeated 2, 4 Oct.; defeat Turks at ALADJA DAGH......................14, 15 Oct. "
Kars taken, after 12 hours' fighting, by surprise or treachery, 17, 18 Nov. "
[Killed and wounded: Russian, about 2500; Turkish, 5000, with loss of 10,000 prisoners, 100 guns, etc.]
Kars ceded to Russia by the Berlin treaty............13 July, 1878

Kashga'ria, a province of central Asia; subdued by China; annexed by Keen Lung, 1760; insurrections subdued, 1826 et seq. Mahomed Yakoob Beg, during an insurrection of the Tungani, made himself ruler of Kashgaria, 1866, and sent envoys to London, etc., 1867. He was at length attacked by the Chinese, totally defeated, and said to have been assassinated, 1 May, 1877. The capital, Kashgar, was taken; the country regained by China, Nov.; and the war closed, Dec. 1877.

Kashmir (*cash-meer'*), Vale of. This beautiful vale is an expansion of the valley of the upper Jhelum river, and is a plain about 75 miles long by 20 wide, where roses are cultivated. This valley is but a small part of the dominions of the maharajahs of Kashmir, and is in the Punjab province of India. It was subdued by the Mahometans under Akbar in 1586; by the Afghans, 1752; by the Sikh monarch of the Punjab in 1819. Ceded to the British by the treaty of Lahore, 9 Mch. 1846, who gave it to the maharajah Ghulab Singh.—The true Kashmir shawls were first taken to England in 1666.

Katzbach, Prussia. Near this river the Prussian gen. Blucher defeated the French under MacDonald and Ney, 26 Aug. 1813. He received the title of prince of Wahlstatt, a neighboring village.

Kearsarge (*keer'-sarj*) and **Alabama.** ALABAMA. (The *Kearsarge* was totally wrecked on Roncador reef in the Caribbean sea, 2 Feb. 1894; officers and crew saved).

Keble college, Oxford, Engl., founded in memory of the rev. John Keble, author of the "Christian Year," b. 25 Apr. 1792; d. 29 Mch. 1866. The first stone was laid by the archbishop of Canterbury, 25 Apr. 1868; the building was dedicated 23 June, 1870; the chapel, the gift of William Gibbs, was dedicated and the library opened 25 Apr. 1876. OXFORD.

Keely motor. About 1872, John W. Keely, of Philadelphia, Pa., began his experiments in that city to develop to practical results a machine worked by a power without cost, i. e., running itself. Nothing definite, however, has ever been given out concerning this motor except the name, Pneumatic-Pulsating-Vacuo-Engine, although it is supposed that he is still (1894) at work upon it. The criticisms regarding it from scientific men are in every case adverse to his idea, which includes that of perpetual motion, or an energy within the machine itself, causing its motion. Thus far, however, the energy that permeates nature has refused to yield itself to him or any one else without compensation.

keeper, lord, of the great seal of England differed only from the lord chancellor in that the latter had letters-patent, whereas the lord keeper had none. Richard, a chaplain, was the first keeper under Ranulph, in 1116. The 2 offices were made one by 5 Eliz. 1562.—*Cowell.* CHANCELLOR.—The office of lord keeper of the great seal of Scotland was established in 1708, after the union.

Kegs, Battle of the. In Jan. 1778, while the British occupied Philadelphia, the Americans sent kegs down the Delaware from Bordentown filled with powder and furnished with machinery (the invention of a Mr. Bushnell) which, coming in contact with any object, would explode; the intention being to destroy the British shipping at Philadelphia. The vessels that very day had been placed in dock for the winter, and thus escaped injury. Some of the kegs exploding near the city gave the alarm, whereupon the British opened fire upon every floating thing seen on the river for the rest of the day. This firing, called the "Battle of the Kegs," furnished Francis Hopkinson a subject for a facetious poem of 22 stanzas. The following is one of them:

"The cannons roar from shore to shore,
The small-arms loud did rattle.
Since wars began I'm sure no man
E'er saw so strange a battle."

Kem, ancient name of Egypt, signifying Black or Black Land, from the color of the earth.

KEN

Kenesaw mountain, Ga., Battle of. Here, on 27 June, 1864, Sherman assaulted the Confederate works, and was repulsed with an aggregate loss of 3000 men, including among the killed gens. Charles G. Harker and Dan. McCook. Confederate loss about 450. ATLANTA CAMPAIGN.

Kenilworth castle, Warwickshire, Engl., built about 1120, by Geoffrey de Clinton, whose grandson sold it to Henry III., was enlarged and fortified by Simon de Montfort, to whom Henry gave it as a marriage portion with his sister Eleanor. Queen Elizabeth conferred it on her favorite Dudley, earl of Leicester. His entertainment of the queen commenced 19 July, 1575, and cost the earl daily 1000*l*.

After the battle of Evesham and defeat and death of Simon de Montfort by prince Edward (afterwards Edward I. 1265, Montfort's younger son, Simon, shut himself up in Kenilworth castle, which sustained a siege for 6 months by the royal forces of Henry III., to whom it at length surrendered. Upon this occasion was issued the "Dictum de Kenilworth," or "ban of Kenilworth," enacting that all who had borne arms against the king should pay him the value of their lands for from 7 years to 6 months.—The name and scene of one of Scott's novels. LITERATURE.

Kent. BRITAIN, HOLY MAID. Odo, bishop of Bayeux, brother of William the Conqueror, was made earl of Kent, 1067; and Henry Grey was made duke of Kent in 1710; he died without male heirs in 1740. Edward, son of George III., created duke of Kent in 1799, was father of queen Victoria, and d. 23 Jan. 1820. ENGLAND.

Kentucky, a once noted hunting-ground of the American Indians, which, owing to frequent desperate encounters between them and the early white settlers, was named the "Dark and Bloody Ground." It is the 15th state in order of admission into the United States, and lies south of the Ohio river, which separates it from Ohio, Indiana, and Illinois, and east of the Mississippi, which divides it from Missouri. Lat. 36° 30′ N. marks almost the entire division line between it and Tennessee on the south, while 39° 6′ limits it on the north. On the east the Cumberland mountains and the Big Sandy river, which flows into the Ohio, separate it from Virginia and West Virginia. It is 300 miles in length from east to west, between 82° 3′ and 89° 26′ W. long., wedge-shaped, and averages 150 miles in breadth. Area, 40,400 sq. miles. Pop. 1890, 1,858,635; 1900, 2,147,174. Capital, Frankfort.

De Soto and his followers ascend the west bank of the Mississippi, opposite the lower portion of the state, during........ 1543
Kentucky included in the charter of Virginia................ 1584
Col. Wood, seeking trade with the Indians, explores Kentucky as far as the Mississippi.................................. 1654
Capt. Bolt, from Virginia, travels in Kentucky................ 1670
Jacques Marquette, a Jesuit missionary, Louis Joliet, and 5 other Frenchmen, spend several days at the mouth of the Ohio, July, 1673
Chevalier Robert de la Salle and his lieutenant, chevalier Henri de Touti, with others, pass from the Illinois river down the Mississippi, stop a few days at the mouth of the Ohio, and claim both sides of the Mississippi for France..........Feb. 1682
A vast tract, including Kentucky, deeded to the British by the Iroquois, by treaty at Albany, N. Y., concluded (NEW YORK), 1684
M. Longueil, from Canada, descends the Ohio, and discovers Big Bone Lick on a small creek which flows into the Ohio about 20 miles above the falls............................. 1739
Dr. Walker of Virginia discovers the Kentucky river (which he calls the Louisa), the Big Sandy, and others............ 1747
Christopher Gist, exploring for the Ohio Land company, reaches the Shawnee town, on both sides of the Ohio, just below the mouth of Scioto creek..........................29 Jan. 1751
James McBride, with others in a canoe, passes down the Ohio to the mouth of the Kentucky river........................ 1754
Capt. Harry Gordon, chief-engineer in the western department in North America, encamps "opposite to the Great Lick" in Lewis county, Ky..................................16 July, 1766
John Findlay and a few wandering white men from North Carolina visit Kentucky................................... 1767
By treaty at fort Stanwix, now Rome, N. Y., the Six Nations and the Delawares, Shawnees, and Mingoes of Ohio grant to the king of England territory south of the Ohio river including most of Kentucky..........................5 Nov. 1768
Daniel Boone reaches the Red river with 5 hunters from North Carolina..7 June, 1769
Out of 40 hunters from S.W. Virginia, 9, under col. James Knox, known as the Long Hunters (for the length of the hunting period), reach the Green and Cumberland rivers... 1770
Capt. Thomas Bullit, a surveyor, lays out the town of Louisville, 1773
Big Bone Lick, near Burlington, visited by James Douglas of Va., who finds on the ground bones of the mastodon....... "
First log cabin in Kentucky built by James Harrod at Harrodsburg... 1774
Treaty with Cherokees at Wataga, col. Richard Henderson, Nathaniel Hart, and others acquire, for 10,000*l*., the territory between the Ohio, Kentucky, and Cumberland rivers, 17 Mch. 1775
Fort begun on south side of Kentucky river called Boonesborough, and settlements started at Boiling Springs and St. Asaph's or fort Logan, in Lincoln county..............Apr. "
Under a call of col. Henderson, though his purchase was not recognized by Virginia, the people in convention at Boonesborough adopt a proprietary government for their new state of Transylvania and pass laws......................23 May, "
Simon Kenton and Thomas Williams land at the mouth of Limestone creek, now Maysville, and plant a corn crop, May, "
Daniel Boone and others bring wives and children into Kentucky..Sept. "
Representatives of Transylvania at Oxford, Greenville county, N.C., elect James Hogg delegate to the Continental Congress, but Virginia prevents seating him.......................Sept. "
Kentucky county formed by Virginia out of Fincastle county, 6 Dec. 1776
First siege of Harrodsburg by 47 Indians under Blackfish, 7 Mch. 1777
Indian attack on Boonesborough, Apr. 15, fails; a second unsuccessful attempt by 200...........................4 July, "
Daniel Boone, captured by the Indians, with 27 others, while making salt at the Blue Licks, 7 Feb. 1778, is carried to Chillicothe, O.; learning of a proposed attack of the Indians on Boonesborough, he escapes, and travelling 160 miles in 10 days, reaches Boonesborough......................20 June, 1778
Duquesne, with 11 French and 400 Indians, besieges Boonesborough for 13 days, till by treaty siege is raised.....7 Sept. "
Col. George Rogers Clarke, moving against British posts on the Wabash and Mississippi, leaves several families at the falls of the Ohio, who settle Louisville.........................Oct. "
Col. Robert Patterson begins a fort where Lexington now stands, and lays out the town..............................17 Apr. 1779
Legislature of Virginia passes land law for Kentucky. Each possessor of a warrant locating it at his will and surveying it. Many surveys overlapped; lawsuits followed, with confusion of titles, and many settlers lost their land.......... "
Governor of Virginia appoints William Fleming, Edmund Lyne, James Barbour, and Stephen Trigg, commissioners for Kentucky. At their first court at St. Asaph's, the first claim considered was that of Isaac Shelby's to settlement and pre-emption "for raising a crop of corn in the county in 1776," 13 Oct. "
In retaliation for col. Clarke's successes in Illinois, col. Byrd of the British army is sent against Ruddle's and Martin's stations in Kentucky, captures them, and retreats with plunder and prisoners to Detroit..........................22 June, 1780
County of Kentucky divided into Jefferson, Fayette, and Lincoln counties..1 Nov. "
Fort Jefferson, built on the Mississippi river, 5 miles below the mouth of the Ohio. Besieged by Chickasaw Indians, reinforced by gen. Clarke from Kaskaskia, and soon after abandoned as too remote to hold................................ "
Capt. Estill, in pursuit of Indians who had invested Estill's station, overtakes them near mount Sterling, and in the fight loses his life..................................22 Mch. 1782
Battle of BLUE LICKS..................................19 Aug. "
Gen. Clarke, with 1050 men, ends Indian invasions in Kentucky, Nov. "
A district court opened at Harrodsburg...................... 1783
Col. James Wilkinson opens a store in Lexington.........Feb. 1784
Convention at Danville, concerning proposed separation of Kentucky from Virginia...........................27 Dec. "
Second convention at Danville addresses assembly of Virginia and people of Kentucky in favor of separation......23 May, 1785
First act of Virginia favoring the separation of Kentucky on conditions...Jan. 1786
Second act of Virginia postpones separation until 1 Jan. 1789, Oct. "
Gen. James Wilkinson descends the Mississippi to New Orleans with a small cargo of tobacco and other products......June, 1787
First newspaper published in Kentucky, and the 1st west of the Alleghanies, the *Kentucky Gazette*, issued by John and Fielding Bradford at Lexington.........................Aug. "
Fifth convention at Danville, unanimously decides on separation on the terms offered by Virginia..............17 Sept. "
Eleven of the 14 Kentucky delegates in the Virginia convention vote against adopting the constitution of the U. S...28 June, 1788
Intrigues of the Spanish government in Kentucky, in which gen. Wilkinson, John Brown (one of the Virginia delegates to Congress), Benjamin Sebastian, and judge Innes are implicated. Spain seeks to separate the western states from the eastern, and Mr. Brown states that the Spanish minister, don Gardoqui, had authority to enter into an arrangement for the exportation of their produce to New Orleans on terms of mutual advantage, "if the people of Kentucky would erect themselves into an independent state"............... "
Fourth act of separation passed by Virginia, complying with the wishes of Kentucky............................18 Dec. 1789
Ninth convention of Kentucky accepts the terms of Virginia, and fixes 1 June, 1792, for independence............26 July, 1790
Local board of war for district of Kentucky, established by Congress for prosecution of war and defence against the Indians..Jan. 1791
Congress authorizes Kentucky to frame a constitution..4 Feb. "
First paper mill in Kentucky built at Georgetown by Craig, Parkers & Co.. 1792

State convention at Danville frames a constitution . 3 Apr 1792
Gen Isaac Shelby elected first governor May, "
Kentucky admitted into the Union 1 June, "
Legislature assembles at Lexington, 4 June, and Frankfort is selected as the capital 6 June, "
Gen Anthony Wayne's call for volunteers from Kentucky being unsuccessful gov Shelby orders a draft 28 Sept 1793
Lexington Democratic society resolves "that the rights of the people of the U S on waters of Mississippi ought to be peremptorily demanded of Spain by the government of the U S," Oct "
Legislature meets for the 1st time at Frankfort 1 Nov "
Four Frenchmen sent by minister Genet to Kentucky to instigate an expedition against the Spanish in Louisiana 1 Nov "
Citizens of Kentucky meet at Lexington and pass resolutions in reference to free navigation of the Mississippi 24 May, 1794
Thomas Powers sent by Carondelet, Spanish governor of Louisiana, to treat with the people of Kentucky for the navigation of the Mississippi July, 1795
Daniel Boone moves to the west of the Mississippi river "
Lexington public library established (400 vols.) "
First charter of Newport adopted 14 Dec "
Thomas Powers again sent by Carondelet to Kentucky with the outline of a provisional treaty and a letter to judge Sebastian to concert a separation of Kentucky from the Union, 12 July, 1797
Henry Clay removes from Virginia and opens a law office in Lexington Nov "
Endowment by the legislature of 5 educational academies in Kentucky, each with 6000 acres of land 10 Feb 1798
John Fitch, inventor of steamboat, d at Bardstown aged 55, June, "
"Kentucky resolutions of 1798," suggesting nullification of the alien and sedition laws, introduced by John Breckinridge, pass both houses of the legislature 16 Nov "
Transylvania university established at Lexington by union of Transylvania seminary (founded 1780) and Kentucky academy (founded 1796) 22 Dec "
Constitutional convention in Frankfort 17 Aug 1799
At Harpe's Head 3 miles from Dixon Webster county, highway man Micajah Harpe, *alias* Big Harpe, killed and head impaled, "
Boundary-line between Kentucky and Virginia defined 14 Oct. "
"Great revival" of religion begins in Kentucky, first great camp meeting held at Gaspar river July, 1800
Farmer's Library, first newspaper in Louisville 7 Jan 1801
Kentucky River company chartered to clear the river of obstructions 19 Dec. "
Kentucky Insurance company chartered at Lexington with banking powers 16 Dec 1802
John Breckinridge of Fayette county appointed attorney gen , 1805
Aaron Burr visits Lexington "
Trappist monks arrive in Kentucky "
Western World, a new weekly of Frankfort, describes intrigues with Spain, implicating Wilkinson, Brown, Innes, etc , 4 July, 1806
Aaron Burr again visits Kentucky "
Aaron Burr appears in court at Frankfort under process served by col Joseph Hamilton Daviess, U S attorney, to answer high misdemeanor in organizing within the U S a military expedition against Mexico Burr is acquitted 2 Dec. "
[A few days later his acquittal was celebrated by a ball at Frankfort]
Jefferson Davis born in Christian county 3 June, 1808
Abraham Lincoln born in Hardin (now Larue) county 12 Feb 1809
Dr Ephraim McDowell, the "father of ovariotomy," successfully performs the first in the world, at Danville "
MAMMOTH CAVE discovered "
Cumberland Presbyterian church organized 10 Feb 1810
Lottery authorized to raise $10 000 for the improvement of the navigation of the Kentucky river 10 Jan 1811
Henry Clay, Speaker of the House of Representatives 4 Nov "
Col Owen and Joseph H Daviess of Kentucky killed in action at the battle of Tippecanoe 7 Nov "
Six prominent citizens of Frankfort authorized to raise $4000 by lottery to complete an unsectarian house of worship on the public square 4 Feb 1812
Appropriation made by the legislature of $[illegible] for digging stumps out of the state house yard 8 Feb "
Brig gen Green Clay, with 3000 Kentuckians, reaches FORT MEIGS to reinforce gen Harrison, and with part of his force cuts his way through the enemy's lines into the fort 5 May, 1813
Two mummies found in Gothic avenue of the Mammoth cave, "
Col Richard M Johnson, authorized by Congress, raises a regiment of 1000 volunteers in Kentucky . "
Battle of the Thames, gov Shelby with 4000 Kentuckians, col Johnson, and others participate 5 Oct "
State house at Frankfort burned 25 Nov "
At the request of president Madison the legislature sets apart rooms in the penitentiary for British prisoners 8 Dec "
Congress grants Daniel Boone 1000 acres in upper La 10 Feb 1814
Several mummies discovered in a nitre cave near Glasgow "
Treaty of Ghent signed, Clay one of the commissioners 6 Aug "
Two thousand five hundred Kentucky militia, under maj gen John Thomas, reach New Orleans 4 Jan 1815
Town of Covington chartered by legislature 7 Feb "
Lexington and Maysville, and Lexington and Louisville Turnpike Road companies chartered 4 Feb. 1817
Corner stone of the lunatic asylum at Lexington laid It bears a brass plate inscribed, "The first erected west of the Appalachian mountains" 30 June, "
President James Monroe visits Louisville on his tour of inspection of arsenals, naval depots, and fortifications "
Forty six independent banks chartered in the state, aggregate capital $8,720 000, most of which fail during the year, 26 Jan. 1818
Ex gov Isaac Shelby, commissioner with gen Andrew Jackson, obtains by treaty with the Indians cession of the "Jackson Purchase" south and west of the Tennessee river 19 Oct. 1818
Centre college at Danville incorporated 19 Jan 1819
President Madison, gen Jackson, and others entertained at Louisville by the Freemasons 24 June, 1820
Legislature by resolutions requests president to negotiate with Great Britain for restoring fugitive slaves in Canada. Nov 1820
Owing to pressure of debt among the people the legislature extends the right of replevin from 3 to 12 months 11 Feb "
Bank of the Commonwealth at Franklin chartered, with branches in each judicial district and a capital of $2,000 000 (not required to redeem its notes, they are made receivable in public debts and taxes, and state lands were pledged for their redemption) 29 Nov "
Two political parties arise Relief party, composed of debtors and majority of voters and Anti relief, of merchants, farmers, etc and legality of the Replevin act is questioned. 1821
Augusta college (Methodist) founded 1822
Petition of Cleves Symmes of Newport presented in the U S Senate for aid in a voyage to the inside of the earth through the poles, which he claims are open 19 Nov "
Supreme court hold the Replevin act unconstitutional 1823
Institution for the deaf and dumb established at Danville "
Gen Joseph Desha elected governor by Relief party 7 Aug 1824
Capitol at Frankfort destroyed by fire 4 Nov "
Henry Clay candidate for the presidency (UNITED STATES) "
Legislature repeals court of appeals act and organizes a new court Anti relief party becomes Old Court party, and Relief party merged into New Court party 24 Dec "
Henry Clay appointed U S secretary of state 7 Mch 1825
Gen Lafayette visits Louisville 8 May, "
Old Court have a majority in the legislature, but senate remains New Court. "
Legislature restores the Old Court. 30 Dec 1827
Thomas Metcalf, National Republican, elected governor, 4 Aug 1828
Natural gas well discovered on Green river by Samuel White "
William T Barry of Lexington postmaster-general of U S 1829
American oil well near Burksville on the Cumberland river discovered in boring for salt, spouted 50 feet The oil, imagined to have healing qualities, was bottled and sold through the U S and Europe for medicine 1830
Pres Jackson vetoes a bill directing the secretary of the treasury to subscribe for 1500 shares of the Maysville, Washington and Lexington Turnpike Road company 27 May, "
First rail Lexington and Ohio railroad laid at Lexington 22 Oct. 1831
Henry Clay candidate for the presidency (UNITED STATES) 1832
Maysville incorporated as a city 31 Jan 1833
Kentucky Colonization society sends 102 freed negroes to Liberia Mch "
Lieut gov James T Morehead succeeds gov Breathitt, who d. 21 Feb 1834
Kentucky educational convention with delegates from 58 counties meets at Frankfort, 9 Jan 1834. Kentucky Common School society organized at Frankfort 28 Jan "
Covington incorporated as a city 24 Feb "
Amos Kendall of Frankfort postmaster general of U S. 1835
James Clark, Whig, elected governor 3 Aug 1836
Richard M Johnson of Kentucky elected vice president "
State Agricultural society organized 3 Feb. 1838
Felix Grundy of Nelson county attorney general of U S . "
Gov Clark d., lieut. gov C A Wickliffe takes oath of office, 5 Sept. 1839
Three hundred and fifty men from Bourbon and Harrison execute "Lynch law" at Williamstown, Grant county, on Smith May the and Lyman Crouch, who had cut the throat of Wm Utterback of Bourbon county He recovered, but lost speech, 10 July, 1841
Charles A. Wickliffe of Bardstown postmaster-general, John White, Speaker of the H. R , and John J Crittenden, attorney-general of the U S.—all from Kentucky "
Legislature passes anti state repudiation resolutions 14 Jan. 1842
Kentucky Institution for the Education of the Blind established at Louisville 5 Feb. "
Louisville Courier established . 13 Feb 1844
George M Bibb of Louisville secretary of U S treasury 15 June "
Raw silk produced in Somerset, 1842, and a manufactory established at Newport and silk spun and woven Oct. "
Henry Clay candidate for the presidency (ALABAMA LETTER, UNITED STATES) . . "
Miss Delia A Webster, for abducting slaves to Ohio, is sentenced to 2 years in penitentiary, 23 Dec 1844. By petition of jury and others she is pardoned by gov Owsley, and leaves for her home in Vermont . 25 Feb. 1845
Gov Bartley of Ohio refuses a requisition from gov Owsley for one Kissam, charged with kidnapping slaves 14 Mch. "
Gov Whitcomb of Indiana issues a warrant to an officer from Kentucky for the arrest of a free mulatto on charge of stealing several slaves from Harrodsburg . 25 Apr "
Methodist Episcopal church, South, organized Louisville May, "
Office of the *True American*, published at Lexington by Cassius M Clay, for its abolition utterances entered by 60 citizens, and Clay's effects shipped to Cincinnati .. .18 Aug "
Kentucky Military Institute at Farmdale, Franklin county, founded ... "
Reinterment of Daniel Boone and wife in the state cemetery at Frankfort . . . 13 Sept. "
Colony for "Kentucky in Liberia" leave Louisville under the auspices of the Kentucky Colonization society 7 Jan 1846
Burial of those Kentuckians who fell in the Mexican war in the state cemetery at Frankfort . . . . . 20 July, 1847
[It was at this burial that the poem, "Bivouac of the Dead," by Theodore O'Harra (1820-67), written to commemorate the event was read While the whole poem is excel-

ient, the first stanza may be reckoned as one of the gems of English literature:

"The muffled drum's sad roll has beat
The soldier's last tattoo,
No more on life's parade shall meet
That brave and fallen few;

On Fame's eternal camping-ground
Their silent tents are spread,
And glory guards with solemn round
The bivouac of the dead."]

Lines of telegraph erected from Maysville to Nashville and Cincinnati 1847

Bones of Kentuckians massacred by Indians at the river Raisin, 18 Jan. 1813, found while grading a street in Monroe, Mich., are reinterred in the state cemetery..........30 Sept. 1848

Emancipation meetings; the gradual emancipation of the slaves discussed at Maysville and Louisville......12, 13 Feb. 1849

Convention to remodel the constitution meets at Frankfort 1 Oct. "

Legislature requests the governor to place a block of Kentucky marble in the Washington monument at Washington, inscribed, "Under the auspices of Heaven and the precepts of Washington, Kentucky will be the last to give up the Union"..24 Jan. 1850

New constitution adopted..............................7 May "

John J. Crittenden of Kentucky appointed attorney-general of the U. S.; and John L. Helm becomes governor.....31 July, "

Battle monument erected in state cemetery, Frankfort 25 June, "

Lynn Boyd of Kentucky Speaker of the H. R...........1 Dec. 1851

Death at Washington, D. C., of Henry Clay...........29 June, 1852

U. S. Military Asylum located at Harrodsburg Springs..8 May, 1853

James Guthrie of Louisville secretary of the treasury, and Jefferson Davis of Christian county secretary of war....... "

Miss Delia A. Webster again appearing in Kentucky and assisting rev. Norris Day in transporting slaves to Ohio, is first requested and then compelled to leave the state........12 Mch. 1854

A jury having acquitted Matt. F. Ward of the murder of William H. G. Butler in Louisville (TRIALS), an indignation meeting is held in Louisville. A mob burns in effigy John J. Crittenden, of counsel for Ward and others, and is with difficulty subdued..29 Apr. "

Lunatic asylum at Hopkinsville opened..............18 Sept. "

State Temperance convention at Louisville nominates George W. Williams for governor..........................14 Dec. "

"Know-nothing" convention at Louisville nominates judge William V. Loring, Whig, for governor..............22 Feb. 1855

Riot on election day, "Bloody Monday," between Know-nothings and foreigners...............................6 Aug. "

Charles S. Morehead, American or Know-nothing candidate, elected governor.................................6 Aug. "

John C. Breckinridge elected vice-president of the U. S....... 1856

General assembly of Old School Presbyterian church at Lexington..21 May, 1857

Corner-stone of Henry Clay monument laid in the cemetery at Lexington with masonic ceremonies...................4 July, "

U. S. Agricultural exhibition opens at Louisville.......31 Aug. "

Kentucky university at Lexington organized.................. 1858

Methodist Episcopal Church, South, in conference at Hopkinsville, votes to expunge the general rule forbidding "the buying and selling of men, women, and children, with an intent to enslave them"...........................18 Oct. "

Death at Shippingport of James D. Porter, the Kentucky giant, height 7 feet, 9 inches................................24 Apr. 1859

Joseph Holt of Louisville appointed postmaster-general........ "

Destruction by a mob of the *True South*, an abolition paper pub. at Newport..................................28-29 Oct. "

Legislature adopts the boundary-line between Kentucky and Tennessee surveyed by Cox and Briggs, commissioners appointed in 1859..28 Feb. 1860

Gov. Magoffin, by circular, submits to the governors of slave states 6 propositions, among them: "To amend the U. S. Constitution to forbid nullifying the fugitive-slave law. That all territories north of 37° shall come in as free states, all south as slave states. To guarantee free navigation of the Mississippi forever to all states. To give the South protection in the U. S. Senate from unconstitutional or oppressive legislation upon slavery...........................9 Dec. "

Col. W. S. Featherstone as commissioner from Mississippi visits Frankfort to urge Kentucky to co-operate in "efficient measures for the common defence and safety".....25 Dec. "

Joseph Holt of Kentucky secretary of war...........31 Dec. "

Montgomery Blair of Frankfort postmaster-general.....7 Mch. 1861

Gov. Magoffin answers a war-department call for troops: "I say emphatically, Kentucky will furnish no troops for the wicked purpose of subduing her sister southern states".....15 Apr. "

Union meeting at Louisville declared that Kentucky would not take sides, but maintain a neutral position and remain loyal until the government became the aggressor.........18 Apr. "

Capt. Joseph Desha with a company of over 100 leaves Harrison county to join the confederates, with other companies from other counties...................................Apr. "

At an election of delegates to the Border State convention the vote was overwhelmingly in favor of the Union......4 May, "

Three union men and 3 Breckinridge men as arbitrators agree that Kentucky should not take part, but maintain armed neutrality.......................................11 May, "

House of Representatives resolves on state neutrality.16 May, "

Gov. Magoffin proclaims armed neutrality of state....20 May, "

Border State convention at Frankfort, with representatives from Kentucky and Missouri and one from Tennessee addresses Kentucky to remain neutral, and the U. S. to satisfy the slave states of the safety of slave property, 27 May-3 June, "

S. B. Buckner as commander of the state guards and adjutant-general orders 6 companies of state guards to Columbus, to preserve the neutrality of that district..............24 June, "

Brig.-gen. William Nelson establishes camp Dick Robinson in Garrard county, where companies of federal soldiers of Kentucky are formed into regiments.......................Aug. 1861

Confederate troops from Tennessee occupy Columbus...4 Sept. "

Gen. Grant with 2 regiments and 2 gunboats takes possession of Paducah and proclaims that he comes solely to defend the state from aggression..............................6 Sept. "

Legislature by resolution orders Confederate troops to leave the state, refusing to order both parties to leave........11 Sept. "

Legislature by resolution instructs the governor to call out the state troops to drive out the southern invaders, and resolves, "that Kentucky expects the confederates or Tennessee troops to be withdrawn from her soil unconditionally"....12 Sept. "

S. B. Buckner issues from Russellville an address to the people, calling on them to take up arms against the usurpation of Abraham Lincoln...................................12 Sept. "

Resolution passed over the governor's veto requesting gen. Robert Anderson, commander at fort Sumter, to take charge of the state troops, which he did...........................Sept. "

S. B. Buckner occupies Bowling Green with a Confederate force, 18 Sept. "

Sixth regiment, Indiana volunteers, reaches Louisville, 20 Sept. "

House passes a bill calling out 40,000 volunteers for 1 to 3 years to repel the invasion of Confederate forces..........24 Sept. "

Battle at camp Wildcat, the junction of 3 roads leading to Mount Vernon, London, and Richmond. Kentucky infantry under col. Theodore T. Garrard unsuccessfully attacked by confederates under brig.-gen. Felix K. Zollicoffer......4 Oct. "

Sovereignty convention in session at Russellville for 3 days. Over 200, representing 65 counties, adopt an ordinance of secession, choose col. George W. Johnson provisional governor, with Bowling Green the new seat of government....18 Nov. "

Confederate congress admits Kentucky as a state.......9 Dec. "

Self-styled legislative council of Kentucky assembles within the Confederate lines and elects 10 delegates to the Confederate congress at Richmond.............................14 Dec. "

At Middle creek, Floyd county, col. James A. Garfield routs the confederates under col. Humphrey Marshall..........10 Jan. 1862

Battle of Mill Springs, Pulaski county; maj.-gen. George B. Crittenden and brig.-gen. Zollicoffer attack the approaching federals under maj.-gen. George H. Thomas; gen. Zollicoffer is killed and the confederates routed...............19-20 Jan. "

Gen. Buckner evacuates Bowling Green................14 Feb. "

Confederates evacuate Columbus, 27 Feb.; federals take possession...3 Mch. "

Brig.-gen. John H. Morgan, with his Confederate cavalry or rangers (900 men), begins his first Kentucky raid in Monroe county...8 July, "

[In this raid he captured 17 towns.]

Prison for "rebel females" prepared at Newport, where they will be required to sew for the federal soldiers......28 July, "

Gov. Magoffin resigns; J. F. Robinson, speaker of state senate, succeeds him.......................................16 Aug. "

Gen. Bragg begins his march into Kentucky from Tennessee (BRAGG'S KENTUCKY CAMPAIGN)..........................24 Aug. "

Battle near Richmond, Madison county; confederates victorious...29-30 Aug. "

Col. Morgan's Confederate cavalry reach Lexington after 5 weeks, passing through the state on their second raid.4 Sept. "

Munfordville surrendered to the advancing army under gen. Bragg, 17 Sept.; again occupied by the federals.....21 Sept. "

Confederate state government organized at Frankfort, with Richard Hawes of Bourbon as governor, and 4 hours later leaves *Frankfort*, never to return...................4 Oct. "

Battle of Perryville fought on Chaplin hills in Boyle county (BRAGG'S KENTUCKY CAMPAIGN)..........................8 Oct. "

Nine Confederate soldiers captured and hung in Rockcastle county in retaliation for the hanging in Bell county, by some Confederate soldiers, of capt. H. King and 15 others as bushwhackers..6 Nov. "

Col. Cluke's Confederate cavalry take Mount Sterling..21 Mch. 1863

Battle of Dutton hill, Pulaski county; confederates retreat after 5 hours' engagement...............................30 Mch. "

Desperate engagement at Tebb's bend of Green river, Taylor county. 200 of 25th Michigan infantry, under col. Moore, in a strong natural fortification are attacked by 600 of Morgan's men. When summoned to surrender, col. Moore declined "because the 4th of July was not an appropriate day to surrender," and the confederates retreated after several ineffectual attempts to storm the intrenchments.....4 July, "

Gen. Burnside declares martial law in Kentucky......31 July, "

Capt. Edward Cahill having been sent into Kentucky in Dec. 1863 to recruit free colored men for the Union army, the legislature by resolution protests, and requests the president to remove all camps for negro soldiers, by which "our slaves are enticed to leave the service of their owners"....18 Feb. 1864

Meeting at Louisville of a Border State "Freedom" convention. 100 delegates from 4 states—Kentucky, Missouri, Tennessee, and Arkansas.....................................22-23 Feb. "

Brig.-gen. John H. Morgan enters the state from Virginia with 2400 men on his "June raid" (MORGAN'S RAID).....2 June, "

Parts of Morgan's forces demand the surrender of Lexington, which is refused, 9 June, and invest Frankfort, which is successfully defended.................................11 June, "

Gen. Burbridge overtakes Morgan's forces at Cynthiana and defeats them after an hour's desperate battle.......12 June, "

President Lincoln suspends writ of *habeas corpus* in Kentucky, and proclaims *martial law* in the state..............5 July, "

Many citizens arrested by gen. Burbridge, under gen. Sherman, as "Sons of Liberty," "American Knights," etc.............. "

A number of citizens of Paducah, Columbus, and vicinity banished to Canada..Aug. "

Commission sent by gen. Burbridge, to investigate the conduct of gen. Eleazer A. Paine, who had produced a 51 days' reign of terror at Paducah. Paine flees to Illinois..........Sept. 1864
James Speed of Louisville attorney-general U. S..........Nov. "
Law consolidating Transylvania and Kentucky universities, Feb. 1865
John C. Breckinridge appointed secretary of war, C. S. A....... "
Gen. Palmer relieves gen. Burbridge from command of the district of Kentucky..................................10 Feb. "
Agricultural college established......................22 Feb. "
By proclamation of the governor, business is suspended on the occasion of the funeral of Lincoln..................19 Apr. "
Old command of gen. Morgan surrenders to brig.-gen. E. H. Hobson at Mount Sterling...........................1 May, "
Pres. Johnson modifies pres. Lincoln's proclamation of 5 July, 1864, "in so far that martial law shall no longer be in force in Kentucky"....................................12 Oct. "
Mining begun in Fayette county, 7 miles from Lexington, for lead-ore...25 Nov. "
State Farmers' convention held at Frankfort. 40 counties represented... 11 Jan. 1866
"Ashland," the home of Henry Clay, near Lexington, purchased for the new Agricultural college of Kentucky, 15 Jan. "
Jesse Root Grant, father of gen. Grant, appointed postmaster at Covington..25 Feb. "
"Skaag's men," a band of over 100 armed and mounted outlaws, terrorize the colored population of Marion county..... "
Legislature rejects XIV.th Amendment to Constitution..10 Jan. 1867
Amnesty bill passed; no officer, soldier, or sailor of the U. S. or so-called Confederate States shall be held responsible, criminally or civilly, in courts of the state for any act done during the late rebellion, under military authority.....28 Feb. "
John L. Helm, elected governor 5 Aug., inaugurated while dangerously ill at his home in Elizabethtown, 3 Sept; d. 8 Sept., lieut.-gov. John W. Stevenson succeeds.............8 Sept. "
Gov. Stevenson authorizes 3 companies of volunteers against a band of "Regulators," and lynchers in Marion, Boyle, and adjoining counties.................................11 Oct. "
John W. Stevenson elected governor...................3 Aug. 1868
Legislature rejects XV.th Amendment to Constitution..13 Mch. 1869
A band of so-called "Ku-klux" attack Frank Bowen near Nicholasville, who in self-defence kills one..........16 Mch. "
State Temperance convention at Covington............4 May, "
Seven hundred colored delegates hold a State Educational convention near Louisville...........................14 July, "
Great Commercial convention at Louisville, ex-president Millard Fillmore presides; 520 delegates from 29 states, 13 Oct. "
Affray at Somerset, Pulaski county, from the whipping of one Cooper by Regulators; 40 men engaged, 3 killed.....20 Nov. "
Legislature establishes an insurance bureau..........20 May, 1870
An assault on a U. S. mail-agent (a negro, William H. Gibson), on the Lexington and Louisville railroad-train at North Benson depot, 26 Jan. 1871, occasions sending troops into Kentucky and stopping the mail-route for a month........Mch. 1871
Gov. Stevenson resigns, Preston H. Leslie, president of the Senate, acting lieutenant-governor, is inaugurated......13 Feb. "
Over 100 armed men enter Frankfort at dawn and free a white man charged with murdering a negro, though the jail was guarded by 4 militia men..........................25 Feb. "
Preston H. Leslie elected governor.......................7 Aug. "
National convention in Louisville of "Straight-out Democrats," who repudiate the action of the Baltimore convention nominating Horace Greeley for president, and nominate Charles O'Conor of New York for president, and John Quincy Adams for vice-president (POLITICAL PARTIES)......3-5 Sept. 1872
National Industrial Exposition opens at Louisville.....3 Sept. "
State House of Reform for Juvenile Delinquents opened by proclamation of the governor, at Anchorage, 12 miles east of Louisville......................................25 Sept. "
Colored Liberal Republican National convention at Louisville; delegates from 23 states; Greeley supported..........25 Sept. "
State Educational convention of colored men in session at Louisville......................................18-19 Feb. 1873
Kentucky Society for the Prevention of Cruelty to Animals, incorporated at Louisville..........................22 Mch. "
Gov. Leslie advertises in New York city and Louisville, that Kentucky is anxious to call in all her bonds, and is prepared to pay the principal and interest upon presentation..10 Sept. "
Ku-klux outrages in Shelby and Franklin counties........Oct. "
General law regulating the sale of intoxicating liquors........ 1874
Under authority of the legislatures of Kentucky and Indiana, the boundary above Evansville, Ind., deciding jurisdiction over Green island, is defined. This section had become the refuge of thieves, because of uncertain jurisdiction. The commissioners, governed by the U. S. survey of 1806, awarded Green island to Kentucky, the boundary running near the present bed of the Ohio river, on the Indiana side.......... 1875
Legislature establishes a Bureau of Agriculture, Horticulture, and Statistics, and reduces legal interest from 10 to 8 %..... 1876
Gen. Green Clay Smith of Kentucky nominated for president by the Prohibition party................................. "
Acts passed legislature making 6% the legal rate of interest in the state, and creating State Board of Health.............. 1878
Act of legislature appropriating $10,000 for a monument to the memory of John C. Breckinridge, who d. 17 May, 1875...... "
Bill to re-establish the whipping-post passes House, 63 to 21; lost in Senate by casting vote of lieutenant-governor........ "
Troops sent by governor to Jackson, Breathitt county, to quell an old feud revived by a mob attacking sheriff bringing a prisoner charged with murder to court, under 25 guards....29 Nov. "
Legislature incorporates the Kentucky College of Agriculture and Mechanics.. 1880
Legislature transfers to the U. S. the 5 locks and dams constructed by the state in the Kentucky river................ 1880
"Regulators," a vigilance association of large extent, disbands, 200 men giving themselves up to the civil authorities in Louisville, and furnishing names of 800 others.............. "
State Prohibition party organized at Louisville.........14 Oct. 1881
Legislature establishes a Board of Railroad Commissioners, and prohibits extortion and discrimination in transportation of freight and passengers.................................... 1882
McCoy of Pike county, Ky., kills Hatfield of Logan county, W. Va., in an election dispute. 4 McCoys arrested for this act are captured by a Hatfield mob, carried into West Virginia, and then secretly taken back to Kentucky and shot... "
One hundredth anniversary of the battle of Blue Licks celebrated on the battle-field..........................19 Aug. "
Convention of friends of popular education in Kentucky meets at Frankfort to organize against illiteracy............5 Apr. 1883
Southern exposition opens at Louisville................1 Aug. "
National convention of colored men at Louisville discusses and acts upon civil and political rights.................24 Sept. "
State colored normal school at Frankfort opened..........Apr. 1887
Disturbance in Rowan county arising from an old feud....... "
Gov. Buckner announces suspension of state treasurer Tate (state treasurer for 20 years) for defalcations which proved to amount to $229,009.21, and act passed creating office of state inspector and examiner.........................Mch. 1888
State troops stationed at Pikeville to prevent the rescue of 3 Hatfields who were captured by the sheriff of Pike county, in Logan county, W. Va., and lodged in Pike county jail, and 6 other Hatfields who were captured after burning the house of the elder McCoy, and killing his wife, daughter, and son.. "
Detachment of 70 troops sent to Perry county to protect the circuit court in the "French-Eversole" feud..........Nov. "
Stephen G. Sharp elected state treasurer in place of defaulter Tate..5 Aug. 1889
Perry and Knott counties "absolutely dominated and terrorized by savage and lawless bands," and the circuit court is suspended. The governor refuses to cause expense to the state by calling out troops.. "
State troops aid in defeat of the Howard faction in the so-called Howard-Turner feud in Harlan county.........21 Oct. "
Constitutional convention meets at Frankfort..........8 Sept. 1890
Tornado, leaving a path 400 yards wide and 3 miles long, passes through Louisville (STORMS). In Louisville 120 persons are killed; loss to the city, $2,500,000...................27 Mch. "
Sen. James B. Beck drops dead in a railway station in Washington, D. C...3 May, "
U. S. Supreme court decides in favor of the claim of Kentucky to the ownership of Green island in the Ohio river..19 May, "
John G. Carlisle elected U. S. senator qualifies.........26 May, "
Constitutional convention meets at the capitol..........8 Sept. "
Hatfield-McCoy feud ended by a marriage.............21 Mch. 1891
Constitutional convention adjourns to 2 Sept...........11 Apr. "
New constitution ratified, 213,950 for, 74,446 against...3 Aug. "
Constitutional convention reassembles 2 Sept., and after amending the constitution adopted by the people, signs and publishes the result.......................................28 Sept. "
Governor signs the Anti-lottery bill, which makes the dealing in lottery tickets a felony..........................15 Mch. 1892
One hundredth anniversary of the admission of Kentucky into the Union celebrated at Lexington.............1 June, "
Rush Morgan, the noted desperado who had killed 17 men, is shot and killed near Hubbard Springs...............31 Jan. 1893
John G. Carlisle resigns U. S. senatorship to become secretary of the treasury..Feb. "

GOVERNORS OF THE STATE.

Name.	Term.	Remarks.
Isaac Shelby............	1792 to 1796	
James Garrard..........	1796 " 1804	
Christopher Greenup.....	1804 " 1808	
Charles Scott...........	1808 " 1812	
Isaac Shelby............	1812 " 1816	
George Madison.........	1816	Dies in office.
Gabriel Slaughter........	1816 to 1820	Acting.
John Adair.............	1820 " 1824	
Joseph Desha...........	1824 " 1828	
Thomas Metcalfe........	1828 " 1832	
John Breathitt..........	1832 " 1834	Dies in office.
J. T. Morehead..........	1834 " 1836	Acting.
James Clark............	1836 " 1837	Dies in office.
C. A. Wickliffe..........	1837 " 1840	Acting.
Robert P. Letcher.......	1840 " 1844	
William Owsley.........	1844 " 1848	
John J. Crittenden.......	1848 " 1850	Appointed att'y-gen. U. S.
John L. Helm...........	1850 " 1851	Acting.
Lazarus W. Powell.......	1851 " 1855	
Charles S. Morehead.....	1855 " 1859	
Beriah Magoffin.........	1859 " 1861	
J. F. Robinson..........	1861 " 1863	
Thomas E. Bramlette....	1863 " 1867	
John L. Helm...........	1867	Dies in office.
John W. Stevenson......	1868 to 1871	
Preston H. Leslie........	1871 " 1875	
James B. McCreary.......	1875 " 1879	
Luke P. Blackburn.......	1879 " 1883	
J. Proctor Knott.........	1883 " 1887	
Simon B. Buckner.......	1887 " 1891	
J. Y. Brown............	1891 " 1895	

UNITED STATES SENATORS FROM THE STATE OF KENTUCKY.

Name.	No. of Congress.	Date.	Remarks.
John Brown	2d to 9th	1792 to 1805	President *pro tem.* 17 Oct. 1803.
John Edwards	2d " 4th	1792 " 1795	
Humphrey Marshall	4th " 7th	1795 " 1801	
John Breckinridge	7th " 9th	1801 " 1805	Resigned. Advocated the resolutions of 1798.
John Adair	9th	1805 " 1806	Elected in place of Breckinridge. Resigned 1806.
Henry Clay	9th	1806 " 1807	Elected in place of Adair 1806.
John B. Thurston	9th to 11th	1806 " 1809	Resigned 1809.
John Pope	10th " 13th	1807 " 1813	President *pro tem.* 23 Feb. 1811.
Henry Clay	11th	1810 " 1811	Elected in place of Thurston.
George M. Bibb	12th to 13th	1811 " 1814	Resigned 1814.
George Walker	13th	1814	Appointed in place of Bibb.
William T. Barry	13th to 14th	1815 to 1816	Elected in place of Bibb. Resigned 1816.
Jesse Bledsoe	13th " 14th	1813 " 1815	Resigned 1815.
Isham Talbot	14th " 19th	1815 " 1825	Elected in place of Bledsoe 1815.
Martin D. Hardin	14th	1816 " 1817	
John J. Crittenden	15th	1817 " 1819	Resigned 1819.
Richard M. Johnson	16th to 21st	1819 " 1829	
William Logan	16th	1819 " 1820	Resigned 1820.
John Rowan	19th	1825	
George M. Bibb	21st to 24th	1829 to 1835	
Henry Clay	22d " 27th	1831 " 1842	Resigned 1842.
John J. Crittenden	24th " 30th	1835 " 1848	Resigned 1848.
James T. Morehead	27th	1842	
Thomas Metcalfe	30th	1848 to 1849	Appointed in place of Crittenden.
Joseph R. Underwood	30th to 32d	1847 " 1852	
Henry Clay	31st " 32d	1849 " 1852	Died 29 June, 1852.
David Meriwether	32d	1852	Appointed in place of Clay.
Archibald Dixon	32d to 33d	1852 to 1855	Elected in place of Clay.
John B. Thompson	33d	1853	
John J. Crittenden	34th to 37th	1855 to 1861	Stanch supporter of the Union during the civil war.
Lazarus W. Powell	36th " 39th	1859 " 1865	
John C. Breckinridge	37th	1861	Expelled 1861.
Garrett Davis	37th to 42d	1861 to 1872	Died 1872.
James Guthrie	39th " 40th	1865 " 1868	Resigned.
Thomas C. McCreery	40th	1868 " 1871	Elected in place of Guthrie.
Willis B. Machen	42d	1872 " 1873	Appointed in place of Davis.
John W. Stevenson	42d to 45th	1871 " 1877	
Thomas C. McCreery	43d " 46th	1873 " 1879	Elected in place of Machen.
James B. Beck	45th " 51st	1877 " 1890	Died 3 May, 1890.
John S. Williams	46th " 49th	1879 " 1885	
Joseph C. S. Blackburn	49th ——	1885 ——	Term expires 1897.
John G. Carlisle	51st to 52d	1890 " 1893	Elected in place of Beck. Resigned 1893 to enter the cabinet.
William Lindsey	53d ——	1893 ——	Elected in place of Carlisle. Term expires 1895.

Kernstown or **Winchester.** Kernstown is a ittle village about 3 miles south of Winchester, Va., where ;en. Shields defeated Stonewall Jackson, 23 Mch. 1862. The onfederate forces consisted of Ashby's cavalry, about 300, and 200 infantry, with 27 pieces of artillery; while Shields had bout 6000 infantry, 750 cavalry, and 24 guns. The federal oss was 568, of which 103 were killed; the confederate loss vas 691. UNITED STATES.

Ket's rebellion, a revolt in July, 1549, instigated y William Ket, a tanner, of Wymondham, Norfolk, Engl. He emanded abolition of enclosures, and the dismissal of evil ounsellors. The insurgents, 20,000 men, were quickly defeated y the earl of Warwick. More than 2000 fell; Ket and others vere tried 26 Nov., and hanged soon after.

Kettle creek, Ga., Battle at, fought 14 Feb. 1779. 'atriots under Pickens routed Tories under Boyd.

Keystone state. PENNSYLVANIA.

Khartum' or **Khartoum',** a city of Soudan, at he confluence of the White and Blue Nile. Pop. 1882, about 0,000. SOUDAN.

Khedive' or **kederv',** king or lord, a title of the iceroy of Egypt, instead of vali or viceroy, 14 May, 1867.

Kher'son, a Russian city on the Dnieper, founded 1778. 'otemkin, favorite of Catherine, who died at Jassy in 1791, is uried here, and John Howard, the English philanthropist, vho died here, 20 Jan. 1790, is buried about 3 miles from the own, where an obelisk was erected to his memory by czar Alexander I. Pop. 62,000.

Khi'va, formerly **Carasmia,** an Uzbeck state in Tur- estan, Asia, founded on the ruins of Tamerlane's empire, dates rom the beginning of the 18th century; governed by a khan, Iuhammed Rachim. An expedition sent against it by the mperor Nicholas of Russia in 1839 perished through the igor of the climate in 1840. Russian influence is extending. Area, 22,320 sq. miles. Pop.: Uzbecks (Turk Tarters), 'adjiks, Persians, Nomads, and Turcomans estimated at 00,000.

'o redress outrages, a Russian expedition sent to Khiva..Feb. 1873
After defeats, the town surrendered unconditionally..10 June, "
Khan fled, but returned as vassal of the czar..........5 July, 1873
Insurrection against Russians repressed and punished....Aug. "
Part of Khiva annexed..............................15 Oct. "
Country disturbed by revolts..............................1873–74

Khokand', a khanate in central Asia, subject to China about 1760; rebelled and became tributary only, 1812. A rebellion in Sept. was suppressed Oct. 1874.

War with Russia; gen. Kaufmann defeats about 30,000 men, 4 Sept.; entered Khokand without resistance; khanate virtually subdued..............................16 Sept. 1875
He defeats 5000 more..............................21 Sept. "
People expel the new khan..............................21 Oct. "
Part of Khokand annexed by Russia..............................Oct. "
Massacre of Russian garrison by the people announced, 28 Nov. "
Rebels defeated at Assake (chiefs submit)..........30 Jan. 1876
Khokand formally annexed as Ferghana..............29 Feb. "

Khyber pass, the principal northern entrance into Afghanistan from India, 10 miles west of Peshawur, extends about 33 miles towards Jellalabad; lying between lofty slate cliffs, varying from 600 to 1000 ft. in height; held by Afreedees and other warlike tribes, to whom Dost Mahomed formerly paid subsidies, which were discontinued by his son Shere Ali, ameer of Afghanistan.

Pass forced by col. Wade, 26 July; and gen. sir John Keane retired through it after a victorious campaign.............. 1839
Forced by gen. (afterwards sir George) Pollock, on his way to chastise Cabul for massacres the previous winter..5-14 Apr. 1842
At Ali Musjid, a fort in the pass, further advance of sir Neville Chamberlain on a mission from the viceroy to the ameer was forbidden, with threats of violence..............22 Sept. 1878
Pass held by the British..............................till Mch. 1881
AFGHANISTAN.

Kickapoos. INDIANS.

Kidd, The Pirate. MASSACHUSETTS; NEW YORK, 1701.

Kilkenny, S.E. Ireland, an English settlement about 1170. The castle was built 1195 by Wm. Marshall, earl of Pembroke. At the parliament held here by Lionel, duke of Clarence, 1367, the statute of Kilkenny was passed. It enacted among other things, "that the alliance of the English by marriage with any Irish, the nurture of infantes, and gossipred with the Irish, be deemed high-treason." And again, "if anie man of English race use an Irish name, Irish apparell, or anie other guize or fashion of the Irish, his lands shall be seized, and his body imprisoned, till he shall conform to English modes and customs." Said never to have been enforced. After a siege, the town surrendered to Cromwell, 28 Mch 1650, on honorable terms

Killa'la, Sligo, Ireland an early see The author of the tripartite life of St Patrick says that "in 434 he came to a pleasant place where the river Muadas (Moy) empties itself into the ocean, and on the south banks of the said river he built a noble church called Kil-Aladh, of which he made one of his disciples, Murtdach, the first bishop" The see of Achonry was united to Killala in the 17th century, and both to Tuam in 1839 BISHOPS

Killiecrankie, a defile in Perthshire, Scotland Here the forces of William III, commanded by gen Mackay, were defeated by the adherents of James II under Graham of Claverhouse, viscount Dundee, who fell in the moment of victory, 17 or 27 July, 1689

Kilpatrick's raid. UNITED STATES, 1864

kinder-garten (children's garden), a system of education devised by Friedrich Wilhelm August Froebel (1782-1852), but carried out by Mr and Mrs Ronge, in Germany, in 1849, and in England in 1851 The system, founded mainly on self-tuition and enlivened by toys, games, and singing, is set forth in Ronge's "Kinder-garten," pub 1858, and has been partly adopted in English schools The Froebel society established 1874 In the United States up to 1870 only 5 kinder-garten schools were established and these little known The National Educational Association in 1872, meeting at Boston, Mass, appointed a committee to examine the kinder-garten system This committee reported a year later, recommending it. In the meantime, public attention was enlisted through the efforts of Miss Elizabeth Palmer Peabody, and before 1873 experimental kinder-gartens were established in Boston, Cleveland, and St. Louis Now most of the cities have the system in their public schools, and it is fast extending through the United States.

Kindred, Table of, in the "Book of Common Prayer," was set forth in 1563 (see Lev xviii, 1490 B.C)

kinematics (Gr κινέω, I move), the science of motion Reuleaux's "Kinematics of Machinery," translated by A B. W Kennedy, pub June, 1876 "Kinematism" is the treatment of disease by muscular movement. Prof Rankine's "Machinery and Millwork" first appeared 1809, new ed 1876 MOTION

king (Ger *König*, Lat. *rex*, Scythian, *reis*, Sp *rey*, It. *rè*, Fr *roy*, Heb *rosch*, chief or head) Nimrod was the first founder of a kingdom, 2245 B C.—*Dufresnoy* Mizraim built cities in Egypt, and was the first who assumed the title of king in that division of the earth, 2188 B.C The "manner of the king" is set forth in 1 Sam viii, 1112 B.C. Saul was the first king of Israel, 1095 B.C. Most of the Grecian states, as well as Rome, were originally governed by kings.

King of England —The style was used by Egbert 828, but the title *Rex gentis Anglorum*, king of the English nation, existed during the heptarchy BRITAIN

Plural phraseology, *we*, *us*, *our*, was first adopted among English kings by John 1199

Title "king of France" assumed, and the French arms quartered, by Edward III, in right of his mother . 1340

Pope Leo X. conferred the title "Defender of the Faith" on Henry VIII . 11 Oct. 1521

Henry VIII. changed "lord" of Ireland into "king" 1542

Style "Great Britain" adopted at the union of England and Scotland, 6 Anne 1707

That of the "United Kingdom of Great Britain and Ireland" at the union, when the royal style and title was appointed to run thus "*Georgius Tertius, Dei Gratia, Britanniarum Rex, Fidei Defensor*"—"George the Third, by the grace of God, of the United Kingdom of Great Britain and Ireland, king, Defender of the Faith" (France being omitted) 1 Jan 1801

Hanover omitted in the queen's style . 21 June, 1837

Queen Victoria was proclaimed in India, as "Victoria, by the grace of God, of the United Kingdom of Great Britain and Ireland and the colonies and dependencies thereof in Europe, Asia, Africa, America, and Australia, queen," etc 1 Nov 1858

National Assembly decreed that the title of Louis XVI "king of France," be changed to "king of the French" 16 Oct 1789

Royal title in France abolished. . .. 1792

Louis XVIII styled "by the grace of God king of France and Navarre" 1814

Louis Philippe I invited to be "king of the French" 9 Aug 1830

Emperors of Germany, that their eldest sons might be their successors, in their own lifetime politically obtained them the title of "king of the Romans" The first emperor so elected was Henry IV . 1053

Richard, brother of Henry III of England, was induced to go to Germany, where he disbursed vast sums under the promise of being next emperor, he was elected "king of the Romans" (but failed in succeeding to the imperial crown) 1256

Style "king of Rome" was revived by Napoleon I for his son, b 20 Mch 1811

Title "king of Italy" conferred on Victor Emmanuel II of Sardinia by Italian parliament 17 Mch 1861

King Philip's war. Philip, son of Massasoit, sachem of the Wampanoags and friend of the early settlers at Plymouth, New England, was induced by real and imaginary wrongs to attempt to exterminate the European settlers His home was at Mount Hope, R I. He struck his first blow at Swansea on 4 July, 1675 The white settlers sprang to arms Philip summoned other New England tribes, and until the summer of 1676 alarm and bloodshed filled the more remote New England settlements The Indians were finally subdued, Philip was chased from one hiding-place to another, and finally, in 1676, was shot in a swamp by a faithless Indian His head was carried in triumph to Plymouth, and his little son, the last survivor of his family, was sold for a slave in Bermuda INDIAN HISTORY, MASSACHUSETTS.

king-of-arms. Three for England—Garter, Clarencieux, and Norroy, Lyon king-at-arms for Scotland, and Ulster for Ireland These offices are very ancient Clarencieux is named from Lionel, third son of Edward III, founder of the order of the GARTER Lionel having by his wife the honor of Clare, was made duke of Clarence, the dukedom afterwards escheating to Edward IV, he revived the office of Clarence king-at-arms The office of Bath king-of-arms, created in 1725, was changed to Gloucester king-of-arms, 14 June, 1726. Ulster was substituted, it is said, in lieu of Ireland king-of-arms, by Edward VI, 1553, who named it as a new institution

King's Bench or **Queen's Bench,** Court of, in England, obtained its name from the king sometimes sitting here on a high bench, and the judges, to whom judicature belonged in his absence, on a low bench at his feet. This court in ancient times was called *Curia Domini Regis* The court of Queen's Bench sat for the last time July, 1875. SUPREME COURT Chief-justice Cockburn received the freedom of London, 9 Mch 1876, said to be the first case of the kind The Queen's Bench division of the High Court of Justice till 1881 consisted of the chief-justice of England and 4 judges. The chief-justice of the Queen's Bench division is now chief-justice of England, the Exchequer and Common-pleas division were abolished in 1881

CHIEF-JUSTICES IN ENGLAND FROM HENRY VIII.

1509 John Fineux
1526. John Fitz James
1539 Sir Edward Montagu
1546 Sir Richard Lyster
1552 Sir Roger Cholmely
1553 Sir Thomas Bromley
1554 Sir William Portman
1556. Sir Edward Saunders.
1559 Sir Robert Catlyn
1573. Sir Christopher Wray
1591 Sir John Popham
1607 Sir Thomas Fleming
1613 Sir Edward Coke
1616. Sir Henry Montagu
1620. Sir James Ley
1624 Sir Ranulph Crewe
1626. Sir Nicholas Hyde.
1631 Sir Thomas Richardson
1635 Sir John Brampston
1643 Sir Robert Heath
1648 Henry Rolle.
1655 John Glyn
1659 Sir Richard Newdigate
" Robert Nicholas.
1660. Sir Robert Foster
1663. Sir Robert Hyde
1665. Sir John Kelyng
1671 Sir Matthew Hale
1676. Sir Richard Raynesford.
1678. Sir William Scroggs
1681 Sir Francis Pemberton
1683 Sir Edmund Saunders.
" Sir George Jefferies, afterwards lord Jefferies and lord chancellor
1685 Sir Edward Herbert.
1687 Sir Robert Wright
1689 Sir John Holt
1709 Sir Thomas Parker, afterwards lord Parker earl of Macclesfield, and lord chancellor
1718. Sir John Pratt.
1725. Sir Robert Raymond, afterwards lord Raymond
1733 Sir Philip Yorke, afterwards lord Hardwicke and lord chancellor
1737 Sir William Lee.
1754. Sir Dudley Ryder
1756. Wm Murray, lord, afterwards earl of Mansfield
1788 Lloyd, lord Kenyon, 9 June
1802 Sir Edward Law, 12 Apr, aft. lord Ellenborough.
1818 Sir Charles Abbott, 4 Nov, aft. lord Tenterden
1832. Sir Thomas Denman, 7 Nov, afterwards lord Denman, resigned
1850 John, lord Campbell, Mch, aft. lord chancellor
1859 Sir Alexander Cockburn, June (d. 20 Nov 1880)
1880. John Duke, lord Coleridge, 26 Nov

King's Bench prison, Southwark, Engl., near the site of one of the oldest prisons of London, long used to confine debtors. Here, it is fabled that prince Henry (afterwards

Henry V.) was committed by justice Gascoigne. The prison was burned down by the London rioters, 7 June, 1780. GORDON'S "NO-POPERY" RIOTS. It was rebuilt in 1781, and contained about 230 rooms. Formerly, debtors were allowed to purchase liberties, to have houses or lodgings without the walls, or to purchase day-rules, to go out under certain regulations. The rules included St. George's Fields, etc. A consequence of the bankruptcy act, 1861, was the release of many insolvent debtors; and an act was passed in 1862 "for discontinuing the queen's prison and removal of the prisoners to Whitecross street prison." The buildings, used as a military prison, were pulled down and the site sold, 1879-80.

King's bridge, spanning Spuyten Duyvil creek, New York city, first erected in 1691, and called "the king's bridge." An unsuccessful attempt was made by Washington to cut off a force of the British here on the night of 2 July, 1781. NEW YORK, UNITED STATES.

King's college, now **Columbia.** NEW YORK, 1754, etc.

King's Daughters, a religious order of service starting in New York city, 18 Jan. 1886. It is Christian, but unsectarian, and deals with every topic by which women may be made helpful to humanity. It is loosely organized, but welcomes as members all women and girls who will make small regular contributions to Christian work. Its ranks are filled chiefly by correspondence, and its numbers fluctuate widely, but no statistics that can be trusted are published. Extends throughout the United States and Europe.

king's evil, scrofula, formerly supposed to be cured by the king's touch; first by Edward the Confessor, in 1058. In the reign of Charles II. 92,107 persons were touched; and, according to Wiseman, the king's physician, they were nearly all cured! Queen Anne officially announced in the *London Gazette*, 12 Mch. 1712, her intention to touch publicly. Samuel Johnson is said to have been touched by her for this disease in his third year, but in vain. The custom was dropped by George I., 1714.

King's Mountain, S. C., Battle of. Major Patrick Ferguson was sent by Cornwallis to embody the loyal militia west of the Broad river, in South Carolina. With 1500 of them, on his way to join the main army, on 7 Oct. 1780, while encamped upon a spur of King's mountain, about 1½ miles south of the North Carolina line, he was attacked by 1800 continental militia under several colonels, and totally defeated. Shelby, Cleveland, and Campbell were the chief leaders of the continentals. Ferguson was killed, and a small monument marks his grave. 300 of his men were killed or wounded, and about 800 made prisoners, with 1500 stand of arms. The Americans lost only 20 men.

king's speech. The first from the throne said to have been by Henry I., 1107.

Kingston, the shire town of Ulster county, N. Y., was settled by the Dutch and Huguenots. It is memorable in the United States as the place where the first constitution of New York was framed, in 1777, and the first legislature was convened under it; also as having been destroyed by a British marauding expedition up the Hudson in the autumn of the same year. NEW YORK.

Kingston trial. The duchess of Kingston was arraigned before the lords in Westminster hall for bigamy, having married first capt. Hervey, afterwards earl of Bristol, and next, during his lifetime, Evelyn Pierrepont, duke of Kingston, 15-22 Apr. 1776. She was found guilty, but, on pleading the privilege of peerage, the punishment of burning in the hand was remitted, and she was discharged on paying the fees.

kissing the hands of great men was a Grecian custom. Kissing was a mode of salutation among the Jews, 1 Sam. x. 1, etc. The "kiss of charity," or "holy kiss," commanded in the Scriptures (Rom. xvi. 16, etc.), was observed by the early Christians, and is still practised by the Greek church and some others. Kissing the pope's foot (or the cross on his slipper) began with Adrian I. or Leo III. about 800 A.D.

Kitchen Cabinet. CABINET, kitchen.

Kit-kat club, of above 30 noblemen and gentlemen, instituted in England in 1703, to promote the Protestant succession. The duke of Marlborough, sir Richard Walpole, Addison, Steele, and dr. Garth were members. It took its name from dining at the house of Christopher Kat, a pastry-cook in King street, Westminster.

Kittan'ning, Pa., Battle of. PENNSYLVANIA, 1756.

"Klad'deradatsch'," the German "Punch," first pub. in Berlin, by Albert Hoffmann.

Klondike. ALASKA.

kneeling. The knee was ordered bent at the name of Jesus (see Phil. ii. 10) about the year 1275 by the pope. The ceremony of a vassal kneeling to his lord is said to have begun in the 8th century.

knights and **knighthood.** The word knight is derived from the Saxon *cniht*, a servant (i. e. servant to the king, etc.). The institution of Roman knights (*equites* or horsemen, from *equus*, a horse) is ascribed to Romulus, about 750 B.C., when the curiæ elected 300. Knighthood was conferred in England by the priest at the altar, after confession and consecration of the sword, during the Saxon heptarchy. The first knight made by the sovereign with the sword of state was Athelstane, by Alfred, 900 A.D.—*Spelman.* The custom of ecclesiastics conferring knighthood was suppressed in a synod held at Westminster in 1100.—*Ashmole's Institutes.* All persons having 10*l.* yearly income were obliged to be knighted, or pay a fine, 38 Hen. III. 1254.—*Salmon.* On the decline of the empire of Charlemagne, all Europe being reduced to anarchy, the proprietor of every manor became a petty sovereign; his mansion fortified by a moat, and defended by a guard, and called a castle. Excursions were made by one petty lord against another, and women and treasure were carried off by the conqueror. At length the owners of rich fiefs associated to repress marauders, make property secure, and protect ladies, binding themselves to these duties by solemn vows and a religious ceremony. Cervantes' "Don Quixote," a satire on knighterrantry, was pub. 1605. BANNERET, CHIVALRY, HOLY SEPULCHRE, ROUND-TABLE, TOURNAMENTS.

PRINCIPAL MILITARY, RELIGIOUS, AND HONORARY ORDERS OF KNIGHTHOOD.

Albert, Saxony	1850
Albert the Bear, Anhalt	1836
Alcantara, instituted	about 1156
Alexander Nevskoi, St., Russia	1722
Amaranta, Sweden (female)	1645
Andrew, St., Russia	1698
Andrew, St., Scotland (THISTLE)	787, 1540, 1687
Angelic Knights, Greece	337, 1191
Anne, St., Holstein, now Russia	1735
Annonciada, Savoy	about 1360
Annunciada, Mantua	1618
Anthony, St., Bavaria	1382
Anthony, St., Hainault	"
Avis, Portugal	about 1162
Bath, England, 1399; revived (BATH)	1725
Bear, Switzerland	1213
Bee, France (female)	1703
Bento d'Avis, St., Portugal	1162
Black Eagle, Prussia	1701
Blaise, St., Armenia	12th century
Blood of Christ, Mantua	1608
Bridget, St., Sweden	1366
Broomflowers, France	1234
Brotherly (or Neighborly) Love, Austria (female)	1708
Calatrava, Castile, instituted by Sancho III	1158
Catherine, St., Palestine	1063
Catherine, St., Russia (female)	1714
Charles, St., Würtemberg	1759
Charles III. (or the Immaculate Conception), Spain	1771
Charles XIII., Sweden	1811
Chase, Würtemberg	1702
Christ, Livonia	1203
Christ, Portugal and Rome	1317
Christian Charity, France	1558
Cincinnati, America	1783
Compostello. ST. JAMES.	
Conception of the Virgin	1618
Concord, Prussia	1660
Constantine, St., Constantinople, about 313; by emperor Isaac, 1190; Parma, 1699; since removed to Naples.	
Crescent, Naples, 1268; revived	1464
Crescent, Turkey	1801
Cross of Christ	1217
Cross of the South, Brazil	1822
Crown, Prussia	1861
Crown, Würtemberg	1818

Crown of India (female) ... 31 Dec. 1877
Crown of Italy ... 1868
Crown of Oaks, Netherlands ... 1841
Crown Royal, France (Friesland) ... 802
Danebrog, Denmark, instituted by Waldemar II., 1219; revived by Christian V ... 1671
Death's Head (female), by the widow Louisa Elizabeth of Saxe-Masburg ... 1709
Denis, St., France ... 1267
Dog and Cock, France ... 500
Dove of Castile ... 1379
Dragon, Hungary ... 1439
Dragon Overthrown, German ... 1418
Ear of Corn and Ermine, Brittany ... about 1442
Elephant, Denmark (about 1190), by Christian I ... 1462
Elizabeth, St., Portugal and Brazil (female) ... 1801
Elizabeth Theresa, Austria (female) ... 1750
Empire of India ... 1877
Esprit, St., France ... 1579
Ferdinand, St., Naples ... 1800
Ferdinand, St., Spain ... 1811
Fidelity, Baden ... 1715
Fidelity, Denmark ... 1732
Fools, Cleves ... 1380
Francis I., Two Sicilies ... 1829
Francis Joseph, Austria ... 1849
Frederick, Würtemberg ... 1830
Friesland (or Crown Royal), France ... 802
GARTER, England ... 1349
Generosity, Brandenburg ... 1685
Genet, France ... 726
George, St., and the Reunion, Naples ... 1800 and 1819
George, St., Angelic Knights ... 1191
George, St., Austria ... 1470–94
George, St., Defender of the Immaculate Conception, Bavaria. 1279
George, St., England (GARTER) ... 1349
George, St., Genoa ... 1472
George, St., Hanover ... 1839
George, St., Ionian isles ... 1818
George, St., Rome ... 1492
George, St., Russia ... 1769
George, St., Spain ... 1317
George, St., Venice ... 1200
Gerion, St., Germany ... 1190
Glaive, Sweden ... 1522
Glory, Turkey ... 1831
Golden Angel (afterwards St. George) ... about 312
GOLDEN FLEECE, instituted at Bruges by Philip the Good, Austria and Spain ... 10 Jan. 1429
Golden Lion, Hesse-Cassel ... 1770
Golden Lion, Nassau and Holland ... 1858
Golden Shield and Thistle, France ... 1370
Golden Spur, by Pius IV ... 1559
Golden Stole, Venice ... before 737
Gregory, St., Rome ... 1831
Guelphic, Hanover ... 1815
Henry, St., Saxony ... 1736
Henry the Lion, Brunswick ... 1834
Hermengilde, St., Spain ... 1814
Hohenzollern, Prussia ... 1851
Holy Ghost, France ... 1579
Holy Sepulchre ... 1099, 1496
Holy Vial (St. Remi), France ... 499
Hospitallers, 1099; of Rhodes, 1308; of Malta ... 1512
Hubert, St., Germany (by the duke of Juliers and Cleves), Bavaria. 1444
Imtiaz, Turkey ... Nov. 1879
Iron Cross, Prussia ... 1813
Iron Crown, Lombardy, 1805; revived ... 1816
Iron Helmet, Hesse-Cassel ... 1814
Isabella, St., Spain, 1804; Portugal (female) ... 1801
Isabella the Catholic, Spain ... 1815
James, St., Holland ... 1290
James, St., Portugal ... 1310
James, St., of the Sword, Santiago, 1175; Spain and Portugal. 1177
[illegible]rius, St., Naples ... 1738
Jerusalem (MALTA) ... 1048
Jesus Christ, Rome, instituted by John XXII., 1320; reformed as Jesus and Mary by Paul V ... 1615
Joachim, St., Germany ... 1755
John of Acon, St ... after 1377
John of Jerusalem, St. (HOSPITALLERS), Rome ... 1048
John, St., Prussia ... 1812
Joseph, St., Tuscany ... 1807
Julian of Alcantara, St ... 1156
Katharine, St., England (female nurses) ... 1879
Knot, Naples ... 1352
La Calza, Venice ... about 737
Lamb of God, Sweden ... 1564
Lazarus, St., France, before 1154; united with that of St. Maurice, Savoy ... 1572
Legion of Honor, France ... 1802
Leopold, Austria ... 1808
Leopold, Belgium ... 1862
Lily of Aragon ... 1410
Lily of Navarre ... about 1043
Lion, Holland ... 1815
Lion (SUN) ... 1808
Lion of Zähringen, Baden ... 1812
Lioness, Naples ... about 1399
Loretto, Lady of ... 1587
Louis, Bavaria ... 1827

KNI

Louis, Hesse-Darmstadt ... 1807
Louis, St., France ... 1693
Louisa, Prussia (female) ... 1814
Malta (HOSPITALLERS).
Maria de Merced, St., Spain ... 1218
Maria Louisa, Spain (female) ... 1792
Maria Theresa, Austria ... 1757
Mark, St., Venice, about 828; renewed ... 1562
Martyrs, Palestine ... 1014
Maurice, St., Savoy ... 1434
Maximilian Joseph, Bavaria ... 1806
Medjidié, Turkey ... 1852
Merit, Bavaria ... 1808, 1866
Merit, Belgium ... 1867
Merit, Hesse-Cassel ... 1769
Merit, Military, Baden ... 1807
Merit, Oldenburg ... 1838
Merit, Prussia ... 1740
Merit, Saxony ... 1815
Merit, Würtemberg ... 1859
Mexican Eagle ... 1865
Michael, St., Bavaria ... 1693
Michael, St., France ... 1469
Michael, St., Germany ... 1618
Michael and George, Sts., 1818; reorganized ... Mch. 1869
Montjoie, Jerusalem ... before 1180
Neighborly Love, Austria (female) ... 1708
Nicholas, St. (Argonauts of), Naples ... 1382
Noble Passion, Saxony ... 1704
Oak of Navarre, Spain ... 722
Olaf, St., Sweden ... 1847
Osmanié, Turkey ... 1861
Our Lady of Montesa ... 1316
Our Lady of the Conception of Villa Viçosa ... 1818
Our Lady of the Lily, Navarre ... 1043
Palatine Lion ... 1768
Palm and Alligator, Africa, granted to gov. Campbell in ... 1837
Passion of Jesus Christ, France ... 1384
Patrick, St., Ireland ... 1783
Paul, St., Rome ... 1540
Pedro I., Brazil ... 1826
Peter, Frederick Lewis, Oldenburg ... 1838
Peter, St., Rome ... 1530
Philip, Hesse-Darmstadt ... 1840
Pius, founded by Pius IV ... 1559
Pius IX., Rome ... 1847
Polar Star, Sweden; revived ... 1748
Porcupine, France ... 1393
Reale, Naples ... about 1399
Red Eagle, Prussia, 1705, 1712, 1734; revived ... 1792
Redeemer (or Saviour), Greece ... 1833
Remi, St. (or Holy Vial) ... about 499
Rosary, Spain ... 1212
Rose, Brazil ... 1829
Round Table, England, by Alfred (GARTER) ... 516 or 528
Rue Crown, Saxony ... 1807
Rupert, St., Germany ... 1701
Saviour, Aragon ... 1118
Saviour, or Redeemer, Greece ... 1833
Saviour of the World, Sweden ... 1561
Savoy, Italy ... 1815
Scale, Castile ... about 1316
Scarf, Castile, 1330; revived ... 1700
Sepulchre, Holy, Palestine ... 1099
Seraphim, Sweden ... 1260 or 1265
Ship and Crescent, France ... 1269
Slaves of Virtue, Germany (female) ... 1662
Stanislas, St., Poland ... 1765
Star, France ... 1022
Star, Sicily ... 1351
Star of India, British ... 1861
Star of the Cross, Austria (female) ... 1668
Star of the North, Sweden ... 1748
Stephen, St., Hungary ... 1764
Stephen, St., Tuscany ... 1561
Sun and Lion, Persia ... 1808
Swan, Flanders ... about 500
Swan, Prussia (female) ... 1440, 1843
Sword (or Silence), Cyprus ... 1195
Sword, Sweden, 1525; revived ... 1748
TEMPLARS ... 1119
Teste Morte (Death's Head), Würtemberg (female) ... 1652
Teutonic, Austria, about 1190; abolished 1809; 1522; reorganized ... 1840, 1865
Thistle of Bourbon ... 1370
Thistle, Scotland, 809; revived ... 1540, 1687
Thomas of Acon, St ... after 1377
Toison d'Or (Golden Fleece) ... 1429
Tower and Sword, Portugal, 1459; revived ... 1808
Tusin, or Hungarian Knights ... about 1562
Two Sicilies ... 1808
Vasa, Sweden ... 1772
Vigilance, or White Falcon, Saxe-Weimar ... 1732
Virgin Mary, Italy ... 1233
Virgin of Mount Carmel, France ... 1607
Wends, Mecklenburg ... 1864
White Cross, Tuscany ... 1814
White Falcon, Saxe-Weimar ... 1732
Wilhelm, Holland ... 1815
Wing of St. Michael, Portugal ... 1172
Wladimir, St., Russia ... 1782

Knights of the Shire, or of Parliament. Summoned by the king's writ and chosen by the freeholders; first summoned by Simon de Montfort in 1258, and in a more formal manner, 20 Jan. 1265. There are writs extant as far back as 11 Edward I., 1283. The knights are still girded with a sword when elected, as the writ prescribes.

Knights of Labor, one of the largest labor organizations in the United States. A secret order was established in 1869 by Uriah S. Stevens, a clothing cutter at Philadelphia, for the protection of working-people and for the development of educated labor. Some time after a ritual was adopted and the society called the "Knights of Labor." In 1878 a general assembly of the national association was formed, with a supreme office of general master-workman. T. V. Powderly of Scranton, Pa., had filled that office since its formation until Nov. 1893, when James R. Sovereign was elected. Its membership reported at its annual convention at Toledo, O., Nov. 1891, was 200,000, but no exact figures were given; reported 1893 at 64,000. Its name was concealed until 1881.

Knights of the Golden Circle, a (supposed) organization in the southern United States for establishing a government recognizing slavery. This Golden Circle included territory reaching north to Mason and Dixon's line and south to the isthmus of Darien, embracing the West Indies, Mexico, etc., with a radius of about 16°. It was first known as the order of the LONE STAR, and was active in Texas and throughout the south. To this was due the filibustering movement in Central America and Cuba, 1850–57. FILIBUSTERS. The name was subsequently changed to "Knights of the Golden Circle." When secession began its members were active throughout the south and in some of the northern states, notably Ohio and Indiana. The organization was a dangerous element at the north throughout the civil war.

Knights of Pythias, founded by James H. Rathbone at Washington, D. C., 19 Feb. 1864. Objects, friendship, charity, and benevolence. From a membership of 78 in 1864, they numbered 456,450 in 1894, in 54 grand jurisdictions; number of subordinate lodges, 31 Dec. 1893, 6008. The chief officer is termed Supreme Chancellor. This order stands third in the list of fraternal and beneficiary organizations, being exceeded by the Freemasons and Odd-fellows only.

knives. In England, Hallamshire (the country around Sheffield) has been renowned for cutlery for 5 centuries. Chaucer speaks of the "Sheffield thwytel." Stow says that Richard Mathews, on the Fleet bridge, was the first Englishman who made *fine* knives, etc., and that he obtained a prohibition of foreign ones, 1563. Clasp or spring knives became common about 1650, coming originally from Flanders. FORKS.

Know-nothings, a society which arose in 1853 in the United States. They controlled several newspapers and had much political influence. Their principles were embodied in the following propositions (at New York, 1855):

1. Americans shall rule America.
2. The union of these states.
3. No North, no South, no East, no West.
4. The United States of America—as they are—one and inseparable.
5. No sectarian interferences in our legislation or in the administration of American law.
6. Hostility to the assumption of the pope, through the bishops, etc., in a republic sanctified by Protestant blood.
7. Thorough reform in the naturalization laws.
8. Free and liberal educational institutions for all sects and classes, with the Bible, God's holy word, as a universal text-book.

Known in politics as the "American party." UNITED STATES, 1856; POLITICAL PARTIES.

Knoxville, Tenn., Siege of. Gen. Burnside, with the army of the Ohio, occupied Knoxville 3 Sept. 1863. The Confederate gen. Buckner, upon his advance, evacuated E. Tennessee and joined Bragg at Chattanooga. Early in November, gen. Longstreet, with 16,000 men, advanced against Knoxville. On the 14th he crossed the Tennessee. Burnside repulsed him on the 16th at Campbell's station, gaining time to concentrate his army in Knoxville. Longstreet advanced, laid siege to the town, and assaulted it twice (18 and 29 Nov.), but was repulsed. Meantime Grant had defeated Bragg at Chattanooga, and Sherman, with 25,000 men, was on the way to relieve Knoxville. Longstreet, compelled to raise the siege, retired up the Holston river, but did not entirely abandon E. Tennessee until the next spring, when he again joined Lee in Virginia. CHATTANOOGA CAMPAIGN, FORT SANDERS.

Koh-i-noor, or "Mountain of Light," the India diamond. DIAMONDS.

Königgrätz (*ko'-neg-rēts*), a fortified town of Bohemia. Near here was fought the decisive battle between the Austrians under marshal Benedek, and the Prussians under king William I., 3 July, 1866. Prince Frederick Charles halted at Kamnitz on Monday, 2 July, his troops marched at midnight, and the first shot was fired about 7.30 A.M. 3 July. The attack began at Sadowa (after which the battle is also named) about 10 o'clock, the result appearing uncertain, till the army of the crown-prince of Prussia arrived about 12.30. When Chlum, which had been taken and lost 7 times by the Prussians, was taken for the 8th time, the fate of the day was decided; and the retreat of the Austrians, at first orderly, became a disastrous flight. About 400,000 men were engaged, one of the greatest battles of history. The Austrians are said to have lost 174 guns, about 40,000 killed and wounded, and 20,000 prisoners. The Prussians lost about 10,000 men. The victory made Prussia supreme in Germany, united North Germany, enabled Italy to obtain Venetia, and led to the legislative independence of Hungary.

Königsberg, capital of E. Prussia, founded by the Teutonic knights in 1255, became the residence of the grand-master in 1457. It joined the Hanseatic league in 1365. It was ceded to the elector of Brandenburg in 1657, and here Frederick III. was crowned first king of Prussia in 1701. It was held by the Russians 1758–64, and by the French in 1807. Here William I. and his queen were crowned, 18 Oct. 1861.

Königstein tun, Nassau, Germany, was built by Frederick Augustus, king of Poland, in 1725, to hold 233,667 gallons of wine; and on the top, which was railed in, was accommodation for 20 persons to regale themselves. The tun of St. Bernard's was said to hold 800 tons. HEIDELBERG.

Koran' or **Alcoran'** (*Al Kuran*, properly *Qurân*), the sacred book of the Mahometans, written about 610, by Mahomet (as revealed to him by the angel Gabriel in 23 years), was published by Abu-Bekr about 635. It sought to unite the professors of idolatry and the Jews and Christians in the worship of one God (whose unity was the chief point inculcated), under certain laws and ceremonies, exacting obedience to Mahomet as prophet. The leading article of faith combines an eternal truth and a necessary fiction—that there is only one God, and that Mahomet is his apostle.—*Gibbon.* The Koran was translated into Latin in 1143; into French, 1647; into English by Sale, 1734; and into other European languages, 1763 et seq. It is a rhapsody of 6000 verses, in 114 sections. MAHOMETANISM, etc.

Koreish, an Arab tribe which had charge of the Caaba, or sacred stone of Mecca, and strenuously opposed the pretensions of Mahomet. It was defeated by him and his adherents, 623–30.

Koszta affair. Martin Koszta, a Hungarian refugee, when in the United States in 1850, declared his intention to become a citizen. In 1853 he visited Smyrna, and on 21 June was seized by a boat's crew of the Austrian brig *Huzzar*. By direction of the American minister at Constantinople, capt. Ingraham, of the American sloop *St. Louis*, demanded his release; but, having heard that the prisoner was to be clandestinely transported to Trieste, he demanded his surrender by a certain time, and prepared to attack the Austrian vessel on 2 July; Koszta was then given up. On 1 Aug., the Austrian government protested against these proceedings in a circular addressed to the European courts, but eventually a compromise was effected, and Koszta returned to the U. S. UNITED STATES, 1854.

kraal (*krāl*), a Dutch name for a collection of huts within a stockade in S. Africa. ZULULAND.

kraken, a fabulous Scandinavian sea-monster of immense size.

> "Below the thunders of the upper deep—
> Far, far beneath, in the abysmal sea,
> His ancient, dreamless, uninvaded sleep
> The kraken sleepeth. . . .
> There hath he lain for ages and will lie
> . . . .
> Until the latter fire shall heat the deep;
> Then once by men and angels to be seen,
> In roaring he shall rise and on the surface die."
> —*Tennyson*, "The Kraken."

Kremlin, a palace at Moscow, built by Demetri, grand-duke of Russia, about 1376 It was burned down in Sept. 1812, during the city's occupancy by the French army, and rebuilt in 1816, partly burned about 23 July, 1879 Moscow

Krupp's cast-steel factory, Essen, Rhenish Prussia, established 1810 About 10,500 men employed, exclusive of about 5000 miners and others (1876)

Ku-klux-klan, a secret society in the southern United States, opposed to negro suffrage Early in 1868, this society issued lists of proscribed persons, who must quit the country or be liable to assassination Gen Grant endeavored to suppress this society in April Its repression by the militia in Arkansas was ordered, Nov. 1868, and it became the subject of legislation at Washington, June, 1871, under which many persons were tried and convicted for outrage and murder The Ku-klux outrages were generally committed at night, by masked men, with disguised horses The vigorous prosecution of Ku-klux offenders destroyed the organization.

Kunobitz'a, in the Balkan Here John Hunniades, the Hungarian, defeated the Turks, 24 Dec. 1443

Kurdistan' (the ancient Assyria), a country of W. Asia, subject partly to Turkey and Persia. In Oct. 1880 the Kurds, savage tribes, nominal Mahometans, ravaged Persia, and were subdued after fierce conflicts with their chief, Obeid-ullah, a Turkish sheik, Nov, Dec 1880. In June, 1881, he was said to have surrendered.

L

L. In Greek the form of this letter was generally Λ, but in the western Greek *L*, which appears in old Roman inscriptions, passing by degrees into the right angle of our alphabet. —*Encycl. Brit.* 9th ed

Labor, American Federation of, formed at Columbus, O, in Dec 1886, one of the largest labor organizations in the world, uniting the trades and occupations in the United States The total membership in 1890-91 was nearly 700 000 The trades represented by the largest membership are (1) the Brotherhood of Carpenters and Joiners of America, 65,000 to 70,000, (2) Association of Iron and Steel Workers, 60,000, (3) Iron-moulders' Union of America, 41,000 to 45,000, (4) Bricklayers and Stone-masons' Union, 35,000 to 40,000 (5) Brotherhood of Locomotive Engineers, 30,000 to 35,000, (6) International Typographical Union, 30,000, (7) Cigar-makers' International Union, 30,000, (8) Brotherhood of Locomotive Firemen, 25,000, (9) Coal Miners, 20,000, (10) Granite Cutters, 20,000, (11) Tailors, 17,000, (12) Bakers, 17,000, etc. KNIGHTS OF LABOR, STRIKES

LABOR MOVEMENT IN THE UNITED STATES

First trades-union in the U S, the tailors'	1806
Hatters organize a union	1819
Shipwrights and calkers organize a charitable association	1825-30
Agitation for less hours of labor, better wages, and protection of operatives in factories	1825
Appearance in local politics of the Workingmen's party	1828
Ebenezer Ford elected on this ticket to the legislature of New York	1829
Printers' first local union	1831
New England Association of Farmers, Mechanics, and Workingmen formed	"
Shipwrights and calkers of New England begin the 10 hour movement	1832
Convention of mechanics at Utica, N Y, protested against convict labor	1834
Pres. Van Buren establishes 10 hour system in navy yards	1840
"New England Workingmen's Association" organized in Boston	1845
New Hampshire makes 10 hours a legal day's work	1847
National and international trades unions organized from Maine to California	1850-60
International Typographical Union established	1852
Machinists and Blacksmiths' Union established	1859
Iron moulders' Association established	"
Cigar makers' International Union established	1864
Great revival in the labor movement	1866
An 8 hour bill introduced in Congress for the benefit of government employés, 1866, becomes a law	1868
"Knights of Labor" organize in Philadelphia	1869
Congress creates a national bureau of labor	1884
Erected into a department of labor	1888
Labor day, 1st Monday in Sept, made a national legal holiday	1894

Lab'rador, the most eastern portion of North America, extending from the entrance of Hudson's strait to the strait of Belle Isle, a distance of 740 miles on the Atlantic ocean, discovered by Sebastian Cabot, 1497, visited by Cortereal in 1500, made a Moravian missionary station in 1771. Since 1809 it has belonged to Newfoundland

labur'num (*Cytisus laburnum*), called also the golden chain, was brought to England from Hungary, Austria, etc., about 1576 —*Ashe.*

lab'yrinths. A structure with intricate passages rendering it difficult to find an exit 4 are mentioned, the first, said to have been built by Dædalus, in Crete, to secure the MINOTAUR, about 1210 B C, the second, of Arsinoe, in Egypt, near the lake of Mœris, by Psammeticus, king of that place, about 683 B C, the third, at Lemnos, remarkable for sumptuous pillars, which seems to have been a stalactite grotto, and the fourth, at Clusium, in Italy, erected by Porsenna, king of Etruria, about 520 B.C.—*Pliny* The labyrinth of Woodstock is connected with the story of fair ROSAMOND The maze at Hampton court was formed in the 16th century

lace. A fabric of fine thread of cotton, linen, or silk until recently made by hand, but now largely by machinery. It was made of very delicate texture in France and Flanders in 1320 Its importation into England was prohibited in 1483, but it was used in the court costume of Elizabeth's reign Dresden, Valenciennes, Mechlin, and Brussels are famous for fine lace. An ounce of Flanders thread has often sold for 4*l.* in London, and its value when manufactured has been increased to 40*l.*, 10 times the price of standard gold. A framework knitter of Nottingham, named Hammond, is said to have invented a mode of applying his stocking-frame to manufacture lace while studying the lace on his wife's cap, about 1768.—*MacCulloch.* So many improvements have been made in this manufacture, particularly by Heathcote (1809-1817, etc), Morley, and Leaver (1811, etc), that a piece of lace which about 1809 cost 17*l* may now be had for 7*s* (1853).—*Ure* The process of "gassing," which makes cotton lace said to equal fine linen lace, was invented by Samuel Hall of Basford, near Nottingham, Engl. He died in Nov. 1862. Seguin's "La Dentelle, Histoire," etc, pub 1874.

Lacedæ'mon or **Laco'nia** (*Tzakonia*) SPARTA

La Colle (*la koll'*) **Mills,** Attack on, in Lower Canada not far from Rouse's Point, by 3000 Americans of gen Wilkinson's division, on 30 Mch 1814 The mill was fortified and garrisoned by 200 British soldiers under maj Hancock. The Americans lost 16 killed and 122 wounded, the British loss was 10 killed and 46 wounded UNITED STATES

Laconia. NEW HAMPSHIRE, 1622

lacrosse. The national game of the dominion of Canada, made popular after 1860 First association in the United States, 1879 MICHIGAN, 1763

lacteals (absorbent vessels connected with digestion) were discovered in a dog by Jasper Asellius of Cremona, 1622, and their termination in the thoracic duct by Pecquet, 1651 LYMPHATICS.

Ladocе'a, in Arcadia Here Cleomenes III, king of Sparta, defeated the Achæan league, 226 B.C

Ladrone' isles, N Pacific, belonging to Spain, discovered by Magellan in 1520 He first touched at the island of Guam. Natives having stolen from him, he named the islands the *Ladrones*, or Thieves. In the 17th century they were named Marianna islands from the queen of Spain.

lady. Masters and mistresses of manor-houses, in former times, who served out bread to the poor weekly, were called *lafords* and *lefdays:* signifying bread-givers (from *hlaf*, a loaf); hence lords and ladies. Wedgewood derives the words from the Anglo-Saxon *laford*, lord, and *hlæfdig*, lady. —Lady-day (25 Mch.), a festival instituted in England about 350, according to some, and not before the 7th century according to others. ANNUNCIATION. The year, which previously began on this day, was ordered to begin on 1 Jan. in France in 1564; and in Scotland, by proclamation, on 17 Dec. 1599; but not in England till 3 Sept. 1752, when the style was altered.

Lafayette. FRENCH REVOLUTION. UNITED STATES, 1777–81–84, 1824–25.

Laffeldt, a village of Holland. Here marshal Saxe defeated the English, Dutch, and Austrians, 2 July, 1747.

Laffite (*la-fit'*), Jean, the "Pirate of the Gulf," born in France about 1780, coming to the United States, became a leader of pirates and smugglers at BARATARIA BAY. The British in the gulf of Mexico during the fall of 1814 urged him to join them with his forces, but instead he joined Jackson, and did valiant service at the battle of New Orleans. His subsequent career is obscure.

La'gos bay, Portugal. Here was fought a battle between adm. Boscawen and the French adm. de la Clue (who lost both legs and died next day), 17, 18 Aug. 1759. The *Centaur* and *Modeste* were taken, the *Redoutable* and *Océan* ran on shore and were burned; the scattered remains of the French fleet got into Cadiz.

La Hogue (*lä hōg*), N.W. France, Battle of, 19 May, 1692, when the English and Dutch fleets under adms. Russell and Rooke defeated the French fleet of adm. Tourville. The English burned 13 ships and destroyed 8 more, preventing a descent upon England.

Lahore', capital city of the Punjab, N.W. India, was taken by Baber about 1520, and was long the capital of the Mongol empire. It fell into the power of the Sikhs in 1798. It was occupied by sir Hugh Gough, 22 Feb. 1846, who in Mch. concluded a treaty of peace. Pop. 1891, 176,720. DURBAR.

lake Champlain, N. Y., a narrow body of water 120 miles long, lying between New York and Vermont. Area, 488 sq. miles. CROWN POINT and FORT TICONDEROGA; NAVAL BATTLES; NEW YORK, 1609, etc.; PLATTSBURG.

lake dwellings, dwellings built on piles or other support over the water of a lake. Name first applied to dwellings discovered at the bottom of lakes in Switzerland, and which contain relics of the stone, iron, and brass ages. Herodotus (about 450 B.C.) described the Pæonians as living on platforms in lake Prasias. In 1855 dr. Keller discovered remains of habitations which had been supported on piles in several Swiss lakes ages ago. His book was published in England in 1866. The artificial fortified islands termed "cranogues" in some Irish lakes are attributed to the 9th and 10th centuries. They have often been places of refuge.

lake Erie bounds part of New York, Pennsylvania, and Ohio on the north, and extends in a southwesterly direction from Buffalo, N. Y., to Toledo, O., 250 miles; breadth, 60 miles; average depth, 204 ft. Area, 10,000 sq. miles. NAVAL BATTLES, NEW YORK, 1679; OHIO, 1813; UNITED STATES.

lake George, and Battle of. First so called by the English in 1755; previously named by the French St. Sacrement, for the purity of its water. Extends northeast and southwest, mostly between Washington and Warren counties, New York. It is 33 miles in length, and from 1 to 4 miles wide. At the upper end, during colonial days, stood FORT WILLIAM HENRY, and at the lower end FORT TICONDEROGA. Near the upper end was fought the battle of Lake George, 8 Sept. 1755, in which gen. William Johnson, with a force variously estimated from 3000 to 5000 troops, mostly from Massachusetts, Connecticut, and New Hampshire, and a few Mohawk Indians under their chief Hendricks, defeated a mixed company of French regulars, Canadians, and Indians under baron Dieskau, numbering probably 2500. On the morning of the principal engagement Dieskau had ambuscaded and defeated an advanced detachment from Johnson's force of 1000 men, with the Indians under Hendricks, who was killed, as was col. Ephraim Williams, the commander. The French followed closely and reached the temporary defences of the main body as soon as the fugitives. After fighting for several hours, and losing heavily, the French retired, leaving Dieskau, wounded, a prisoner. NEW YORK. For this victory, Johnson, who, slightly wounded, retired early in the fight, received 5000*l.* and a baronetcy from the British government. The honor of the victory is usually awarded to gen. Phineas Lyman of Connecticut, who took command when Johnson was disabled. Among those engaged were Israel Putnam, John Stark, and Seth Pomeroy. It is said of col. Ephraim Williams, killed in the first engagement, that "while passing through Albany he made his will, leaving certain property to found a free school for western Massachusetts, since grown into Williams college."—*Hildreth's* "Hist. U. S." vol. ii. p. 463.

lake, Great Salt, Utah territory. Area, 1875 sq. miles.

lake Huron lies between Michigan and Canada; length, 270 miles; breadth, 105 miles; but from Bay City, at the extremity of Saginaw bay, across the lake and Georgian bay it is over 200 miles. Maximum depth, 1800 ft.; average depth between 300 to 500 ft. Area, 23,000 sq. miles.

lake Michigan, separating Wisconsin from Michigan, is the third in size of the great lakes, being 345 miles long, 84 miles wide. Area, 22,400 sq. miles. Its maximum depth 1000 ft.

lake Ontario, the most easterly of the 5 great lakes, extends from Hamilton, Ont., to Sackett's Harbor, N. Y., 190 miles; breadth 52 miles, and average depth 412 feet. NAVAL BATTLES; NEW YORK; UNITED STATES, 1812–14.

Lake poets, a term applied to Wordsworth (1770–1850), Coleridge (1772–1834), and Southey (1774–1843), who lived among the lakes of Wetsmoreland, Engl.

lake Regillus, Italy, where, tradition states, the Romans defeated the Latin auxiliaries of the expelled Tarquins, about 499 B.C.

lake Superior, the largest of the 5 great lakes. Michigan and Wisconsin lie on its south side, Minnesota and Canada on its north. Its length is 390 miles, breadth 160 miles, and average depth 900 feet. Area, 32,000 sq. miles.

Lamaism, the religion of Mongolia and Thibet (dating about 1357), is a corrupt form of BUDDHISM.

Lamian war, 323 B.C., of Athens and her allies (excited by Demosthenes), with Antipater, governor of Macedon. Antipater fled to Lamia, in Thessaly, and was there besieged. He escaped and defeated his adversaries at Cranon 322 B.C.

Lammas-day, 1 Aug., one of the English 4 cross quarter-days of the year. Whitsuntide was the 1st, Lammas the 2d, Martinmas the 3d, and Candlemas the last. This division of the year was once as common as that by Lady-day, Midsummer, Michaelmas, and Christmas. Rents are sometimes payable on these quarter days in England, and very generally in Scotland. Lammas probably comes from the Saxon *hlammæsse*, loaf mass, because formerly upon that day bread made of new wheat was offered. Anciently, tenants that held lands of the cathedral church of York were by tenure to bring a lamb alive into church at high-mass.

"It was upon a Lammas-night
When corn-rigs are bonnie."—*Burns.*

"Even or odd, of all days in the year,
Come Lammas-eve at night shall she be fourteen."
—*Shakespeare,* "Romeo and Juliet," act i. sc. iii.

lamps. The earthen lamp of Epictetus the philosopher sold after his death for 3000 drachmas. Lamps with horn sides said to be the invention of Alfred. London streets were first lighted with oil-lamps in 1681, and with gas-lamps in 1814. A lamp "constructed to produce neither smoke nor smell, and to give considerably more light than any lamp hitherto known," was patented by Aimé Argand in 1784, and was brought into general use in England early in the present century. On his principle are founded the lamp invented by Carcel about 1803, and since 1825 the moderator lamps of Levavasseur, Hadrot, and Neuburger. SAFETY-LAMP.

Lancasterian schools, on a system of education by mutual instruction, devised by Joseph Lancaster about 1796, were not much patronized till about 1808. The system led to the formation of the British and Foreign School Society in 1805, whose schools are unsectarian and use only the Bible in religious instruction. Lancaster was accidentally killed at New York in 1838.

Lancastrians. ROSES.

land. The first division of land was for tribal occupancy (Gen. x. 25-32). "The traditions of Roman law furnish the information that wealth consisted at first in cattle and the produce of the soil, and it was not until later that land came to be distributed among the burghess as their own special property."—*Mommsen,* "Hist. of Rome." The earliest measure of land personally owned by a Roman as "land of one's own" (*heredium*) consisted of 2 jugera, $1\frac{1}{4}$ acres, and should be distinguished from the *hide*, $12\frac{1}{2}$ acres, which while used was not owned. AGRARIAN LAW, LICINIAN LAW. During the mediæval period most of the land of Europe was subject to the conditions of Feudalism. FEUDAL LAWS. Great changes have marked the last hundred years, the tendency being to division and individual ownership. In France before the revolution land was owned by comparatively few; now there are over 2,000,000 owning 12 acres and over, 1,000,000 owning between 12 and 25 acres, while there are only 150,000 that possess 100 acres and over. Of the whole population more than 1,800,000 cultivate their own land, 850,000 are tenants, and only 55,000 cultivate by a steward or deputy. The land in Belgium, Switzerland, Denmark, Norway, Sweden, and a large part of Italy is now divided into small farms, and this is becoming the condition of Germany. In Great Britain the opposite appears; the land, estimated in 1890 at 77,695,246 acres, is in fewer hands than that of any other country in Europe. There are 1,173,794 owners, of whom 852,408 own less than an acre; 262,830 average about 70 acres; 51,000, 380 acres; 6200, 3150 acres, and 1200, 16,200 acres. As the population is 37,740,383, there are 36,566,489 without land. Of tenant farmers in Great Britain there are 561,000, and in Ireland 600,000; about 400,000 in Great Britain and 500,000 in Ireland hold less than 15 acres. All the land in the United States was originally claimed by the several rulers of Europe, by right of discovery, the Atlantic coast mostly by the British. Extensive grants were made by kings of England to individuals and companies, regardless of the rights of aborigines. While the Dutch held NEW YORK, grants were made several hundred square miles in extent to citizens of Holland, with feudal privileges, especially to the Van Rensselaers and afterwards to Robert Livingston (1686) from the English government. ANTI-RENTISM. In Virginia free settlers who emigrated at their own expense [illegible] they could cultivate, free from [illegible] 1615, 50 acres was granted in [illegible] province. In New England, not- [illegible] at first made only to com- [illegible] tations, but even here as early [illegible] a little land in fee. In 1777 [illegible] office for the sale of land lately [illegible] any man could enter 650 acres for [illegible] wife and each child, the whole [illegible] each 100 acres besides fees and [illegible] enacted many laws for the dis- [illegible] Of these there are 2 classes, [illegible] minimum price, and the other at [illegible] alternate sections reserved by [illegible] roads, etc. Title to these lands [illegible] ry or located under Homestead [illegible] laws. The Homestead law [illegible] land or 80 acres of the $2.50 to [illegible] ally settle on and cultivate the [illegible] years of occupancy on payment [illegible] sions. Under the Timber-culture [illegible] who had cultivated for 2 years as much as 5 acres in trees was entitled to 80 acres, or if 10 acres, to 160 acres; but this act was repealed 3 Mch. 1891. Under act, 29 Aug. 1890, no person can acquire more than 320 acres of public land. The estimated number of acres of vacant land in the U. S., 1893, was 571,013,595 acres, not including Alaska, military, Indian, or timber reservations.

Landen or **Neer'winden,** a town of Belgium. Near here the French under marshal Luxembourg defeated the allies, commanded by William III. of England, chiefly through the cowardice of the Dutch, 29 July, 1693. The duke of Berwick, illegitimate son of James II., fighting with the French, was taken.

landgrave (from *land*, and *graf*, a count), a German title, first given in 1130 to Louis III. of Thuringia. It became the title of the house of Hesse about 1263.

Landshut (*lawls'-hoot*), a town of Silesia, where the Prussians were defeated by the Austrians under marshal Laudohn, 23 June, 1760.

landslips are due to decay of rocks or excessive saturation of soil by rain.

Rossberg mountain behind the Rigi slipped down, burying villages and hamlets with above 800 inhabitants.......... 1806
Lyme Regis, Dorset, a strip of chalk cliff ¾ mile long, between 100 and 150 feet high, undermined by rain, slid forward on the beach, carrying fields, houses, and trees.....24-27 Dec. 1839
Naini or Nynee Tal, a sanitary hill station in the Himalayas, India, was destroyed by the descent of the mountain; about 30 British (including major Martin Morphy, col. Fred. Sherwood Taylor, and capts. F. T. Goodeve, H. S. F. Haynes, and A. Balderston) and 200 natives perished............18 Sept. 1880
Near Northwich, Cheshire, salt-works stopped...6 Dec. et seq. "

landwehr (*länt'vār*, Ger. for *land-defence*), the militia of Germany, especially of Prussia, which was effective in the wars with Austria in 1866, and with France in 1870. No rank is exempt from this service, and many persons in foreign countries returned to serve in 1870.

Langside, near Glasgow, S. Scotland, where the forces of the regent of Scotland, the earl of Murray, defeated the army of Mary queen of Scots, 13 May, 1568. Mary fled to England and crossed the Solway Frith, landing at Workington, in Cumberland, 16 May. Soon after she was imprisoned by Elizabeth.

language was regarded as a human invention by Horace, Lucretius, Cicero, and most of the Greek and Roman writers; as a gift of heaven by the Jews and Christians, and many modern philosophers. Some suppose Hebrew to have been spoken by Adam; others say that the Hebrew, Chaldee, and Arabic are only dialects of the original tongue. "And the whole earth was of one language and of one speech" (Gen. xi. 1). *Eminent linguists:* Anas Montanus, editor of the Antwerp Polyglot Bible (1527-98); sir William Jones (1746-94); cardinal Giuseppe Mezzofanti (1774-1849) is said to have known 114 languages or dialects, and 50 well; and Niebuhr (1776-1831) knew 20 languages in 1807, and more afterwards; Hans Conon von der Gabelentz knew many languages critically; he died 3 Sept. 1874, aged nearly 67.

Elihu Burritt, "the learned blacksmith" (1810-79), noted as having learned the principal ancient and modern languages while working as blacksmith.
Original European languages were 13, viz.: Greek, Latin, German, Slavonian, spoken in the east; Welsh; Biscayan, spoken in Spain; Irish; Albanian, in the mountains of Epirus; Tartarian; old Illyrian; Jazygian, remaining yet in Liburnia; Chancin, in the north of Hungary; and Finnic, in east Friesland.
From Latin sprang Italian, French, Spanish, and Portuguese.
Turkish is a mixed dialect of Tartarian.
From Teutonic sprang the present German, Danish, Swedish, Norwegian, English, Scotch, etc.
There are 3424 known languages, or rather dialects, in the world. Of these, 937 are Asiatic; 587 European; 276 African; and 1624 American languages and dialects.—*Adelung.*
In 1861 and 1862 prof. Max Müller lectured on the "Science of Language" at the Royal Institution, London. He divided languages into 3 families:
I. *Aryan* (in Sanskrit, *noble*).
Southern division.—India (Prakrit and Pali; Sanskrit; dialects of India; Gypsy).
Iranic (Parsi; Armenian, etc.).
Northern division.—Celtic (Cymric: Cornish, Welsh, Manx, Gaelic, Breton, etc.).
Italic (Oscan; Latin; Umbrian—Italian, Spanish, Portuguese, French, etc.).
Illyric (Albanian).
Hellenic (Greek and its dialects).
Wendic (Lettic: Old Prussian; *Slavonic dialects*—Bohemian, Russian, Polish, Lithuanian, etc.).

eutonic (*High*-German: Modern German; *Low*-German: Gothic, Anglo-Saxon, Dutch, Frisian, English; *Scandinavian;* Old Norse, Danish, Swedish, Norwegian, Icelandic).

II. *Semitic.*

outhern—Arabic (including Ethiopic and Amharic); *Middle*—Hebraic (Hebrew, Samaritan, Phœnician inscriptions); *Northern*—Aramaic (Chaldee, Syriac, Cuneiform inscriptions of Babylon and Nineveh).

III. *Turanian* (from *Tura*, swiftness).

orthern division.—Tungusic (Chinese, etc.), Mongolic, Turkic, Samoyedic, and Finnic.

outhern division.—Taic (Siamese, etc.), (Himalayas), Malayic (Polynesia, etc.), Gangetic, Lonitic (Burmese, etc.), Munda, Tamulic.

GROWTH OF THE PRINCIPAL EUROPEAN LANGUAGES.

(Estimated by Mulhall, 1891.)

Language.	In 1801 spoken by	In 1890 spoken by
nglish	20,520,000	111,100,000
rench	31,450,000	51,200,000
erman	30,320,000	75,200,000
talian	15,070,000	33,400,000
panish	26,190,000	42,800,000
ortuguese	7,480,000	13,000,000
ussia	30,770,000	75,000,000

Langue d'Oc (*lang-dok'*). TROUBADOURS.

Languedoc (*lang-dok'*), a province of S. France, ormed part of the Roman Gallia Narbonensis; was named othia, as having been held by the Visigoths 409, who were xpelled by the Saracens; in turn driven out by Charles Marel in the 8th century. In the dark ages the country was amed Septimania (probably from containing 7 important owns); afterwards Languedoc (from its dialect), about 1270, when annexed to the monarchy. It suffered during the perecutions of Albigenses and Huguenots.

Lansdown, an elevated tract of land near Bath, Somrsetshire, Engl. The parliamentary army under sir William Valler was here defeated, 5 July, 1643.

lanterns of scraped horn were invented in England, it s said, by Alfred; and it is supposed that horn was used for window lights also, as glass was not generally known, 872-901.—*Stow*. London was lighted by suspended lanterns with glass sides, 1415.

lan'thanum, a rare metal discovered in the oxide of erium by Mosander in 1839.

Laoc'oon, an exquisite work of Grecian art, in marble, modelled by Agesander, Athenodorus, and Polydorus, all of Rhodes, and other eminent statuaries (about 70 A.D.); it epresents the death of the Trojan hero Laocoön, priest of Neptune, and his 2 sons, as described by Virgil.—*Æneid*, i. 200. It was discovered in 1506 in the Sette Salle near Rome, and purchased by pope Julius II. It is now in the Vatcan.

Laodice'a. SEVEN CHURCHES.

lap'aro-elytrot'omy, an operation, marking an mportant advance in surgery, was devised and performed by Ir. T. G. Thomas of New York, in 1870. Dr. A. T. C. Skene of Brooklyn, N. Y., first successfully repeated the operation, Oct. 1875.

Lapland or **Sameland,** an extensive territory in N. Europe, nominally subject to Norway in the 13th century, and now to Sweden and Russia. Total area 153,200 sq. miles; pop. 30,000. Several Laplanders were exhibited at the Westminster aquarium, Nov. 1877, and at the World's Fair in Chicago, 1893.

Larenta'lia were festivals celebrated at Rome in honor of Acca Larentia, said to have been either the nurse of Romulus and Remus, or a rich dissolute woman who bequeathed her property to the Roman people. The festival commenced about 621 B.C., and was held on 30 Apr. and 23 Dec. FEASTS AND FESTIVALS.

La Rothière, France. Here the French, commanded by Napoleon, defeated the Prussian and Russian armies, with great loss, after a desperate engagement, 1 Feb. 1814. This was one of Napoleon's last victories.

laryn'goscope, an instrument consisting of a concave mirror, by which light is thrown upon a small plane mirror placed in the back part of the mouth for examining the vocal cords of the larynx, etc. It was invented by Manuel Garcia, and reported to the Royal Society, London, 24 May, 1855. One constructed by dr. Türck was greatly modified in 1857 by dr. Czermak, who exhibited it in London in 1862. A similar apparatus is said to have been constructed by John Avery, a surgeon in London, in 1846.

La Salle, born in France 1643, died in Texas 1687. INDIANA; ILLINOIS; LOUISIANA; MICHIGAN; MISSISSIPPI; NEW YORK; OHIO; TEXAS, 1669-82.

Lat'eran, a church at Rome, dedicated to St. John, "the mother of all churches," originally a palace of the Laterani, a Roman family, was given to the bishops of Rome by Constantine, and inhabited by them till their removal to the Vatican in 1377. 11 councils have been held there.

Latham house, Lancashire, Engl., was heroically defended for 3 months against parliamentarians by Charlotte, countess of Derby. She was relieved by prince Rupert, 27 May, 1644. The house was, however, surrendered 4 Dec. 1645, and dismantled.

lathe, a machine for working wood, metal, etc., by causing the substance to turn before a tool held at rest. The invention is ascribed to Talus, a grandson of Dædalus, about 1240 B.C. Pliny ascribes it to Theodore of Samos, about 600 B.C. Great improvements have been made in recent times.

Latin authors. LITERATURE.

Latin kingdom, empire, etc. EASTERN EMPIRE, 1204; JERUSALEM; LATIUM.

Latin language (founded on the Oscan, Etruscan, and Greek), one of the original languages of Europe, and from which sprang the Italian, French, and Spanish. LATIUM. A large part of the English language is derived from the Latin. It ceased to be spoken in Italy about 581; and was first taught in England by Adelmus, brother of Ina, in the 7th century. In law deeds in England Latin gave way to the common tongue about 1000; was revived in the reign of Henry II.; and again replaced by English in the reign of Henry III. It was finally discontinued in religious worship in 1558, and in conveyancing and in courts of law in 1731 (by 4 Geo. II. c. 25). A corrupt Latin is still spoken in Roumelia. The use of Latin in diplomacy died out towards the end of the 17th century. The foreign pronunciation of Latin (*a*, ah; *e*, a; *i*, e, etc.) was adopted in English universities and many schools about 18 1876.

Latin union, that of France, Italy, Belgium, a Switzerland, to maintain the use of the same coinage, fro 1865 to 1880. COIN AND COINAGE.

latitude. First determined by Hipparchus of Nice, about 162 B.C. It is the distance from the equator, measured in degrees north or south on a meridian. Maupertuis, in 1737, in latitude 66.20, measured a degree of latitude, and made it 69.493 miles. Swanberg, in 1803, made it 69.292. At the equator, in 1744, 4 astronomers made it 68.732; and Lambton, in latitude 12, made it 68.743. Mudge, in England, made it 69.148. Cassini, in France, in 1718 and 1740, made it 69.12; and Biot, 68.769; while a recent measurement in Spain makes it but 68.63—less than at the equator, which measurement, if correct, proves the earth to be a prolate spheroid (which was the opinion of Cassini, Bernoulli, Euler, and others), instead of an oblate spheroid. "Delicate operations in measurement have now been extended not only in Europe but in India, Cape Colony, United States, Peru, and Asiatic Russia. As a general result from these measurements it is found that a degree measures 68.7 English miles at the equator, and 69.4 in the neighborhood of the poles."—*Keith Johnston*, F.R.G.S. GLOBE, LONGITUDE, MAPS.

Latitudinarians, a name given to theologians who endeavored to reconcile the church and nonconformists in the 17th century—such as Hales, Chillingworth, Tillotson, and Burnet; and since often applied to those who welcome to church fellowship all worthy people regardless of creed.

Latium, now **Campania,** Italy; the country of Latinus, king of Janiculum, 1240 B.C. Laurentum was the capital in the reign of Latinus, Lavinium in that of Æneas, and Alba in that of Ascanius. Italy, Rome

	B C
Latins ally with Rome	about 520
Join Porsenna to restore Tarquin II	508
Defeated by Romans near lake Regillus	498 or 496
League with the Romans, 463, desert them in trouble, 388, union restored	359
Defeated, 340, 339, subdued and united with Rome	338
Obtain Roman citizenship	90

Latter-day Saints. Mormons

laurel was sacred to Apollo, god of poetry, and from earliest times poets and generals of conquering armies were crowned with laurel Petrarch was crowned with laurel, 8 Apr 1341 —The *Prunus laurocerasus* was taken to Britain from the Levant before 1629, the Portugal laurel, *Prunus lusitanica*, before 1648, the royal bay, *Laurus indica*, from Madeira, 1665, the Alexandrian laurel, *Ruscus racemosus*, from Spain, before 1713, the glaucous laurel, *Laurus aggregata*, from China, 1806 or 1821 Flowers and Plants

Lausanne (*lo-zann'*), capital of the canton of Vaud, Switzerland Here Gibbon completed his "Decline and Fall," 27 June, 1787 The International Workmen's Congress met here Sept 1867

Lavalette's escape. Count Lavalette, for joining Napoleon on his return in 1815, was condemned to death, but escaped from prison in his wife's clothes, 20 Dec 1815 Sir Robert Wilson, Michael Bruce, and capt J H Hutchinson, aiding the escape, were sentenced to 3 months' imprisonment in Paris, 24 Apr 1816 Lavalette was permitted to return to France in 1820, and died in retirement in 1830

La Vendée (*la von-da'*) a maritime department in W. France The French royalists of La Vendée took arms in Mch 1793, and were successful in some hard-fought battles with republicans, between 12 July, 1793, and 1 Jan 1794, when they were routed Their leader, Henri comte de la Rochejaquelein, was killed, 4 Mch. 1794 A short peace was made at La Jaunay, 17 Feb. 1795. The war was terminated by gen Hoche in 1796, and a treaty signed at Luçon, 17 Jan 1800 Chouans, Georges' conspiracy

lavender, *Lavandula spica*, taken to England from the south of Europe before 1568

law. Canons, Civil law, Codes, Common-law, Crime, Courts of the United States, Digest, Supreme Court The Jewish law was promulgated by Moses, 1491 B.C.

Laws of Phoroneus of Argos (1807 B C), the first Attic laws, were reduced to a system by Draco, for the Athenians, 623 B C, this code was superseded by Solon's, 594 B C
Spartan laws of Lycurgus, made about 844 B C, remained in force about 700 years, and moulded Spartan character
Roman laws of Servius Tullius, 566 B C, amended by the Twelve Tables, published in 449 B C, remained in force till Justinian, nearly 1000 years

BRITISH LAWS

	A D
Earliest British laws translated into the Saxon	590
Saxon laws of Ina published	about 690
Alfred's code, the foundation of the common law, is said to have been arranged	about 886
Edward the Confessor collected the laws	1050-65
Stephen's charter of general liberties	1136
Henry II 's confirmation of it	1154 and 1175
Maritime laws of Richard I (Oleron)	1195
Magna Charta, by king John, 1215, confirmed by Henry III., 1216 et seq, Magna Charta	
Lord Mansfield, lord chief justice of the king's bench, declared "that no fiction of law shall ever so far prevail against the real truth of the fact as to prevent the execution of justice,"	21 May, 1784
Many legal technicalities were got rid of by 14 and 15 Vict. c 100	
Act to improve the administration of criminal justice passed,	7 Aug 1851

LAWYERS

Pleaders or barristers, said to have been first appointed by Edward I	1291
"No man of the law" to sit in parliament, by stat. of 46 Edw III and 6 Hen IV	1372
This prohibition declared to be invalid by Coke and unconstitutional by Blackstone, discussed July, 1871, the statutes repealed	1871
Sergeants the highest members of the bar, alone could plead in the court of common pleas The first king's counsel not a sergeant was sir Francis Bacon	1604

International law

lawn-tennis. Introduced into England by major Wingfield under the name of "Sphairistikè," and played in a court shaped like an hour-glass (1874) The first important "tournament" of the game in America took place at Nahant, Mass, in 1875

Code of laws governing lawn tennis in England issued	1877
United States Lawn tennis Association organized	Jan 1881
Lawn tennis Association organized in England	26 Jan 1888
First professional lawn tennis match in the United States at Newport, between Thomas Pettitt, American champion, and George Kerr (English), Pettitt defeated	29 Aug 1889

Law's bubble. John Law of Edinburgh (b 1681) was made comptroller general of finances of France, on the strength of a scheme for a bank, and an East India and a Mississippi company, whose profits should pay the national debt Mississippi He first offered his plan to Victor Amadeus, king of Sardinia, who told him he was not powerful enough to ruin himself The French ministry accepted it, and in 1716 Law opened a bank in his own name, under protection of the duke of Orleans, regent of France, and the deluded rich subscribed for shares in both bank and companies In 1718 Law's was declared a royal bank, and the shares rose to upwards of twenty-fold the original value, so that in 1719 they were nominally worth more than eighty times all the current specie in France In 1720 this fabric of false credit fell, spreading ruin Law died in poverty at Venice in 1729 The South-sea bubble in England occurred in 1720 Arkansas, Louisiana, South sea.

"Layamon's Brut," or "Chronicle of Britain," a poetical semi Saxon paraphrase of the Brut of Wace, made about 1200-5, was published with a literal translation by sir Frederick Madden in 1847 Literature

Layer's conspiracy. Christopher Layer, a barrister, conspired with others to seize George I, the prince of Wales, lord Cadogan, and the principal officers of state, to seize the Tower, to plunder the Bank, and bring in the Pretender Layer was hanged, 17 May, 1723, being convicted of enlisting soldiers for the Pretender Bishop Atterbury was accused of complicity and attainted, but permitted to quit the country

lazzaro'ni (from *lazzaro*, Spanish for a pauper or leper), a term applied by Spanish viceroys to degraded beings in Naples, half-clothed and houseless No man was born a lazzaro, and he who turned to a trade ceased to be one The viceroy permitted lazzaroni to elect a chief, with whom he conferred respecting imposts on goods brought to market In 1647, Masaniello held the office, and led an insurrection. Naples In 1793, Ferdinand IV. enrolled thousands of lazzaroni as pikemen (spontoneers), who generally favored the court party, on 15 May, 1848, they were permitted, on the king's behalf, to ravage the ill-fated city.—*Colletta*

lead is found in various countries, chiefly Great Britain, Spain, and the United States, is abundant in various parts of Britain, and in some places richly mixed with silver ore. The famous Clydesdale mines were discovered in 1513 Pattinson's valuable method for extracting silver was made known in 1829 The lead-mines of Cumberland and Derbyshire yield about 15,000 tons per annum British mines yield on an average of 60,000 tons yearly The lead deposits of the U S. are found chiefly in the Mississippi valley and the Sierra Nevada mountains Elements

Leaden water pipes were brought into use	1236
Lead discovered in the Mississippi valley by Le Sueur	1700-1
First mining in America by Julien Dubuque, near the site of Dubuque, Ia.	1788
Mining leases issued by government under act of 1807	1822
Mining became general	1826-27
Mineral lands thrown open to purchase	1847
Production of lead in the U S 1829, 5000 tons, 1839, 10 000 tons, 1847, 25,000 tons, 1870, 52,293 tons, 1890, 161,754 tons.	

lead, black. Carbon, Graphite.

leagues. 4 kings combined to make war against 5, about 1913 B.C. (Gen xiv) The kings of Canaan combined against invasion of the Israelites, 1451 B C The more eminent Greek leagues were the Ætolian, powerful about 320 B C, which lasted till 189 B.C., and the Achæan, revived 280 B.C, broken by the conquest of Greece by Romans, 146 B.C The fall of these leagues was hastened by dissension.

Hanseatic league... 1140
Lombard leagues against the emperors (LOMBARDS)....1176 and 1226
CADDEE league.................................about 1400 et seq.
League of the Public Good formed Dec. 1464, by the dukes of Calabria, Brittany, and Bourbon, and other princes against Louis XI. of France, under pretext of reforming abuses; an indecisive battle fought at Montlhéry, 16 July; and a treaty signed..25 Oct. 1465
League of Cambray against Venice.......................... 1508
Holy league (the pope, Venice, etc.), against Louis XII.... 1510
League of Smalcald... 1530
League of the Beggars (GUEUX); the Protestants so called (though Roman Catholics joined the league), to oppose the institution of the Inquisition in Flanders................. 1566
Holy league, to prevent accession of Henry IV. of France, then of Reformed religion, formed at Peronne, lasted till Henry embraced Romanism.............................1576-93
League of Wurtzburg, by Catholics; of Halle, by Protestants.. 1610
League against emperor of Germany......................... 1626
Solemn league and covenant in Scotland, against the episcopal government of the church (COVENANTERS)................ 1638
League of Augsburg against France......................... 1686
Union league, United States, to assist the national cause in the war of the Rebellion...... 1863
League of St. Sebastian, to promote restoration of temporal dominions to the pope about 1870; held 9th annual meeting in London...20 Jan. 1879
League in aid of Christians in Turkey formed; earl of Shaftesbury chairman.....................................27 July, 1876
National Irish Land league ostensibly formed to buy farms for the tenants; supported by Mr. Parnell and others, 1879; by enforcing stringent rules against landlords and loyal tenants created a reign of terror; led to legislation (IRELAND)......1880-81
National Land league of Great Britain formed; Justin McCarthy president...............................26 Mch. 1881

leap-year or **bissextile,** devised by astronomers of Julius Cæsar, 45 B.C. Assuming the solar year, or the period from one vernal equinox to another, to be 365 days 6 hours, the 6 hours were set aside for 4 years, forming a day, and the 4th year was made to consist of 366 days. The added day was called intercalary, and was placed before 24 Feb., the 6th of the calends, which was reckoned *twice*, hence called *bissextile*, or *twice sixth*. This added day with us is 29 Feb. This Julian year is really nearly 3 minutes longer than the true astronomical year: to obviate this, 1700 and 1800 were not, and 1900 will not be, leap-years, but 2000 will be one. CALENDAR, YEAR.

learning and the arts flourished among the Greeks, especially under Pisistratus, 537 B.C., and under Pericles, 444 B.C.; and with the Romans under Augustus. The Greek refugees caused their revival in Italy, particularly after the Turks took Constantinople in 1453, and the invention of printing shortly before—the period of the *Renaissance*. Leo X. and his family (the *Medici*) promoted learning in Italy in the 16th century, when literature revived in France, Germany, and England. LITERATURE.

lease (from Fr. *laisser*, to let), a form of conveyance invented by sergeant Moore, soon after the statute of uses, 27 Henry VIII. 1535.

leather was early known in Egypt and Greece, and thongs of manufactured hides were used for ropes, harness, etc., by ancient nations. The Gordian knot was made of leather thongs, 330 B.C. A leather cannon was proved at Edinburgh, fired 3 times, and found to answer, 23 Oct. 1778.—*Phillips.* A plan for making artificial leather of cuttings, etc., was made known in 1860.—*Leather cloth* (invented by Messrs. J. R. & C. P. Crockett of Newark, N. J., and patented in 1849) is unbleached cotton coated with a mixture of boiled linseed-oil and turpentine, and colored.

Lebanon ("white mountain"). The mountain range between Syria and N. Palestine, assigned to Israel but never conquered, and long attached to Syria. In ancient times justly celebrated for its forests of cedar. Special ordinance for the reservation of the ancient cedar forest, Sept. 1881. Mountains and cedars frequently mentioned in the Bible, especially Kings, v. 6-15. The governor-general since 1861 has been [illegible]inted by Turkey, subject to the assent of the great powers. 2200 sq. miles; pop. 1890, 245,000.

"O, art thou sighing for Lebanon
In the long breeze that streams to thy delicious East,
Sighing for Lebanon,
Dark cedar, tho' thy limbs have here increased,
Upon a pastoral slope as fair."—*Tennyson*, "Maud."

Lech, a river of S. Germany, near which, at a village named Rain, the cruel imperialist gen. Tilly was defeated by the Swedes, under Gustavus Adolphus, 5 Apr. 1632, and died of his wounds.

Lecompton constitution. KANSAS, 1857-58; UNITED STATES, 1858.

lectures. Those on physic were instituted by dr. Thomas Linacre, of the College of Physicians (founded by Henry VIII.), about 1502. *Clinical* lectures at the bedside of patients in hospitals are said to have been given (by dr. John Rutherford) in Edinburgh about 1748; in Dublin about 1785; in London (by sir B. C. Brodie) 1813-17. G. Macilwain, about 1824, gave surgical clinical lectures in connection with a dispensary. BAMPTON LECTURES, BOYLE LECTURES, HIBBERT FUND, ROYAL INSTITUTION. The political lectures of Thelwall, commenced in Jan. 1795, were interdicted by act of Parliament. In the autumn of 1857 and since, many distinguished noblemen and gentlemen lectured at mechanics' institutes. An act passed in 1835 prohibited publication of lectures without consent of lecturers. Public lectures began to be popular in the United States about 1855. In 1860 more than 200 professional lecturers were enrolled. Since 1875 their popularity has gradually decreased.

Leeds, Yorkshire, the Saxon *Loidis*, once a Roman station, received a charter in 1627. Pop. 1861, 207,165; 1871, 259,212; 1881, 309,119; 1891, 367,506.

Leeds bridge built.. 1327
Shenfield's grammar school founded......................... 1552

leek, the Welsh emblem, by command of Dewi, or David, afterwards archbishop of St. David's in 519, who on the day that king Arthur routed the Saxons, is said to have ordered the soldiers to place a leek in their caps.

Pistol. "Tell him, I'll knock his leek about his pate,
Upon Saint Davy's day."
—*Shakespeare*, "Henry V.," act iv. sc. i.

Leeward isles, WEST INDIES: Antigua, Barbuda, Montserrat, St. Christopher's, Nevis, Anguilla, Virgin isles, and Dominica. Area of the whole group, 701 sq. miles; the largest, Dominica, 291 sq. miles; and the smallest, Montserrat, 32 sq. miles. Pop. 1891, 129,760.

legal holidays. There is no regular national holiday in the United States. Congress has at various times appointed special holidays. Thanksgiving day, designated by the president by proclamation, is a holiday in those states that so provide by law. The following are the principal days observed in most of the states as a holiday:

New-year's day, Jan. 1. Washington's Birth day, 22 Feb. Decoration day, 30 May in most states. Independence day, 4 July. General election day, 1st Tuesday after 1st Monday in Nov. Thanksgiving day, last Thursday in Nov. Christmas day, 25 Dec.
Labor day, 1st Monday in Sept., made national legal holiday 1894.
Arbor day is a legal holiday in some states, although the month and date of its observance vary. ARBOR DAY. Every Saturday after 12 o'clock noon is a legal holiday in New York, New Jersey, Pennsylvania and Maryland. Good Friday is observed in Alabama, Florida, Louisiana, Maryland, Pennsylvania, Minnesota, and Tennessee.

leg'ates (*legatus*). Roman ambassadors; also governors of provinces into which Augustus divided the empire, 27 B.C.; also ambassadors from the pope.

legations were the 20 administrative divisions in the States of the Church, governed by legates. They rebelled in 1859-60, and are now included in the kingdom of Italy. ROME.

legion, *legio*, a corps of soldiers in the Roman armies, first formed by Romulus, when it consisted of 3000 foot and 300 horse, about 720 B.C. When Hannibal was in Italy, 216 B.C., the legion consisted of 5200 soldiers; and under Marius, in 88 B.C., of 6200, besides 700 horse. There were 10, and sometimes as many as 18, legions kept at Rome. Augustus had a standing army of 45 legions, together with 25,000 horse and 37,000 light-armed troops, about 5 B.C.; and the peace establishment of Adrian was 30 legions. A legion contained 10 cohorts, and each cohort 6 centuries, with a *vexillum*, or standard, guarded by 10 men. The peace of Britain was protected by 3 legions. THUNDERING LEGION.

Legion of Honor, a French order embracing the army, civil officers, and other individuals distinguished for services to the state; instituted by Napoleon, when first consul, 19 May, 1802; confirmed by Louis XVIII. in 1815, and the constitution modified in 1816 and 1851. The honor of membership was conferred on many British subjects who distinguished themselves in the Russian war, 1854-56, and in the Paris exhibitions of 1855 and 1867. The palace and offices were burned by the communists, 23 May, 1871.—In the United States, a fraternal organization, founded 1878; number of members, 1891, 63,751.

Legitimists, a term (since 1814) applied to those who support the claims of the elder branch of the Bourbon family to the throne of France. Its last representative was Henry, duc de Bordeaux, comte de Chambord, born 29 Sept. 1820; died 24 Aug. 1883. They held a congress at Lucerne on 24-29 June, 1862, and agreed to continue a pacific policy. The party was active in Feb. 1871-75. Their efforts to recover power proved ineffectual. FRANCE.

Lein'ster, a kingdom in 1167, now one of 4 provinces of Ireland, divided into 4 archbishoprics by pope Eugenius III., represented by cardinal Paparo, at a national synod held at Kells, 9 Mch. 1151-52. The abduction of Devorgilla, wife of O'Ruarc, a lord of Connaught, by Dermot, king of Leinster, in 1152, is asserted to have led to the landing of the English and the subsequent conquest. The province of Leinster gave the title of duke to Schomberg's son in 1690. The title became extinct in 1719, and was conferred on the family of Fitzgerald in 1766.

Leipsic (*lip'-sic*), Saxony, an ancient city, famous for its university (founded 1409) and its fair (1458). At Breitenfeld, near here, Gustavus Adolphus, king of Sweden, defeated the imperialists under Tilly, 7 Sept. 1631; and the imperialists were again defeated here by the Swedes, under Torstensen, 23 Oct. 1642. Here took place, on 16, 18, 19 Oct. 1813, "the battle of the nations," between the French army and its allies, commanded by Napoleon (160,000), and the Austrian, Russian, and Prussian armies (240,000 strong). The French were beaten, 17 Saxon battalions, their allies, turning upon them in the heat of the engagement. 80,000 men perished on the field, of whom more than 40,000 were French, who also lost 65 pieces of artillery and many standards. The victory was followed by the capture of Leipsic, of the rear-guard of the French army, and of the king of Saxony and his family. The 50th anniversary was celebrated 18 Oct. 1863. The Leipsic book fair began 1545. The new supreme court for all Germany opened here 1 Sept. 1879. Pop. 1891, 293,525; 1901, 456,124.

Leisler's insurrection. NEW YORK, 1689, '91, '99.

Leleges, a Pelasgic tribe which inhabited Laconia about 1490 B.C., and after many contests merged into the Hellenes. "It is the almost universal opinion that the whole of the Ægean coast lands were occupied by homogeneous tribes of Aryan stock; on this view then the Leleges, i. e., as Strabo already maintained, the *mixed people*, represent one of the first stages of these original tribes in the path of civilization."—*Encycl. Brit.* 9th ed.

lemures (*lem'-u-rēz*). The ancients supposed that the soul, after death, wandered over the world and disturbed the peace of the living. The happy spirits were called *lares familiares*; and the unhappy, *lemures*. The Roman festival *Lemuralia*, kept on 9, 11, 13 May, is said to have been instituted by Romulus about 747 B.C., to propitiate the spirit of the slaughtered Remus.

Lenox Library. LIBRARIES; NEW YORK, 1870.

Lent (from the Sax. *lencten*, spring), the 40 days' fast observed in the Roman Catholic church from Ash-Wednesday to Easter-day, said to have been instituted by pope Telesphorus, 130. In early times Lent commenced on Sunday, now the first Sunday in Lent, and the 4 days beginning with Ash-Wednesday were added by pope Felix III. in 487, to make the fasting days 40. Lent was first observed in England by command of Ercombert, king of Kent, in 640 or 641. —*Baker's Chron.* Flesh was prohibited during Lent, but Henry VIII. permitted the use of white meats by a proclamation in 1543, which continued in force until, by proclamation of James I. in 1619 and 1625, and by Charles I. in 1627 and 1631, flesh was again wholly forbidden. ASH-WEDNESDAY, QUADRAGESIMA.

leonines, hexameter and pentameter verses, rhyming at the middle and the end, said to have been first made by Leoninus, a canon, about the middle of the 12th century, or by pope Leo II. about 682.

Lepanto (near Corinth), Battle of, 7 Oct. 1571, when the combined fleets of Spain, Venice, Genoa, Malta, and Pius V., commanded by don John of Austria, natural son of the emperor Charles V., defeated the maritime force of the Turks, and checked their progress. The Turks lost most of their fleet, 35,000 men slain or captured, while 15,000 Christian galley-slaves were released by the victors. Ranke calls it a decisive battle between the Turks and Christians.

leprosy, a skin disease described in Lev. xiii. (1490 B.C.), which prevailed in ancient times throughout Asia. It is almost unknown in modern Europe. It chiefly affected the lower classes, yet occasionally proved fatal to the highest personages. Robert Bruce of Scotland died of leprosy in 1329. A hospital for lepers was founded at Granada by queen Isabella of Castile about 1504, and a large number of leper-houses were founded in Britain. Lepers are still numerous in the Sandwich islands. Father Damien, who voluntarily took up his residence with the lepers of these islands, died of the disease after several years' association with them, 9 May, 1889. The disease is ascribed to a peculiar bacillus, and in 1893 Pasteur and other biologists undertook a scientific investigation of its treatment.

Ler'ida, the ancient ILERDA.

letters. ALPHABET, EPISTLES, LITERATURE, MARQUE, PRIVATEERS.

"Letters of a Pennsylvania Farmer," written by John Dickinson of Philadelphia, and published during the summer of 1767. They were powerful in strengthening the opposition to the oppressive measures of the British government. They were republished in England, and published in French at Paris.

lettres de cachet (*let'r de ka-shā'*), sealed letters issued by kings of France since about 1670, ordering persons thrown into prison or exiled. Under Louis XIV. and Louis XV. they became a monstrous evil, persons being imprisoned for life or for a long period on frivolous pretexts. During the contention of the Mirabeau family, 59 lettres de cachet were issued on the demand of one or other of the family. Dickens' "Tale of Two Cities" depicts their evils. The National Assembly decreed their abolition, 1 Nov. 1789.

lettuce, introduced into England from Flanders about 1520.

Leuctra, a small town in Bœotia, N. Greece, where Thebans under Epaminondas defeated the superior force of Cleombrotus, king of Sparta, 8 July, 371 B.C. 4000 Spartans, with their king, were slain. The Spartans gradually lost their preponderance in Greece.

Levant', from the French verb *lever*, to "rise" = the East, a term applied to Greece, Turkey, Asia Minor, etc.

levees', barriers built along rivers and sea-coasts to keep the water from overflow. Extensive levees line the Hoang-Ho or great Yellow river of China, the Ganges of India, the Euphrates, the Danube, the Po, Thames, and the sea-coasts of Holland. In the United States, along the banks of the Red, Arkansas, Yazoo rivers, and many of the bayous, but especially along the banks of the MISSISSIPPI RIVER.

Levellers, a fanatical party in Germany in the 16th century, headed by Münzer and Storck, who taught that distinctions of rank violate the rights of mankind. At the head of 40,000 men, Münzer commanded the sovereign princes of Germany and the magistrates of cities to resign, and his followers ravaged the country. The landgrave of Hesse at length defeated him at Frankenhausen 15 May, 1525, 7000 fanatics fell in the battle, and the rest fled, their leader was taken and beheaded at Mulhausen ANABAPTISTS The English "Levellers," powerful in Parliament in 1647, were put down by Cromwell in 1649, and their leader Lilburn imprisoned At the period of the French revolution some Levellers appeared in England A "Loyal Association" was formed against them by John Reeves, Nov. 1792

levels. The great level of the Fens, England, is a low-lying district of about 2000 sq miles in Lincolnshire, Huntingdonshire, Cambridgeshire, and Norfolk, said to have been overflowed by the sea during an earthquake, 368 It was long afterwards an inland sea in winter and a noxious swamp in summer, and was gradually drained by Romans, Saxons, and especially by monks during the reigns of Plantagenet kings One of the first works on a large scale was carried out by Morton, bishop of Ely, in the reign of Henry VII A General Drainage act was passed, by advice of lord Burghley, in 1601, but little work was done till James I, in 1621, invited the great Dutch engineer, Cornelius Vermuyden, to assist in the general drainage of the country After completing several great works, Vermuyden agreed (1629) to drain the "Great Level" He was at first prevented from proceeding by a popular outcry against foreigners, but eventually, aided by Francis, earl of Bedford, in spite of great opposition of the people, for whose benefit he was laboring, he declared his work complete in 1652 He also reclaimed much valuable land at Axholme, in Lincolnshire, 1626-30, and many Dutch and French Protestants settled here about 1634, and a few of their descendants still remain There are the Middle, Bedford, South, and North levels

Drainage of the Great level employed the talents of Rennie (about 1807), Telford (1822), and other eminent engineers
Middle Level commission cut through certain barrier banks, and replaced them by other works 1844
Reported unsound in Mch, and the outfall sluice at St Germains, near King's Lynn, gave way 4 May, 1862
High tides ensuing, about 6000 acres of fertile land were inundated, causing a loss of about 25,000*l*. After unwearied, and for a while unsuccessful, efforts, a new coffer dam constructed under Mr Hawkshaw, was reported sound July, "

Lewes, Sussex, Engl, where Henry III, king of England, was defeated by Montfort, earl of Leicester, and the barons, 14 May, 1264 —*Blaauw* The king, his brother Richard, king of the Romans, and his son Edward, afterwards Edward I, were taken prisoners One division of Montfort's army, a body of Londoners, gave way to the furious attack of prince Edward, who, pursuing the fugitives too far, lost the battle.—*Evesham*

Lewis and Clark's expedition. MISSOURI, 1806, OREGON, 1805, UNITED STATES, 1804

lexicon. DICTIONARY

Lexington, Mass., Battle of, fought 19 Apr 1775, the beginning of the American Revolution The British, 800 strong, marched to Lexington and Concord during the night of 18 Apr, to destroy stores of the patriots, 70 of whom they met at Lexington, fired upon, and dispersed The patriots round about speedily gathered under arms, and successfully opposed the British at Concord, compelling their retreat and severely harassing them on the march British loss, 273, American, 103. MASSACHUSETTS.

Lexington, Mo Here col James A Mulligan with 2780 men was besieged by the confederates under gen Price, with 25,000 men and 13 guns, from 11-20 Sept 1861, when he surrendered after a loss of 40 killed and 120 wounded

Leyden (*li'-den*), a town of Holland (*Lugdunum Batavorum*), important in the 13th century It endured 2 sieges by the armies of Spain between 31 Oct 1573 and 21 Mch. 1574, and 25 May and 3 Oct. 1574, when it was relieved, during which 6000 inhabitants died of famine and pestilence In commemoration the university was founded, 1575 In 1699 two thirds of the population perished by fever, aggravated, it was said, by improper treatment by prof. de la Boe The university was almost destroyed by a vessel laden with 10,000 pounds of gunpowder blowing up, and demolishing much of the town, and killing numbers of people, 12 Jan 1807.—The *Leyden jar* was invented about 1745 by Kleist, Muschenbroek, and others. ELECTRICITY.

Libby prison, an old tobacco warehouse on Main street, Richmond, Va, used by the confederates throughout the civil war as a place of confinement for federal prisoners Taken down in 1888 and carried to Chicago and re-erected as a museum of war-relics

libel. By the Roman laws of the Twelve Tables, libels injuring reputation were capital offences In the British law, whatever renders a man ridiculous, or lowers him in the opinion and esteem of the world, is deemed a libel "The greater the truth the greater the libel," sometimes cited as a maxim, is not law

Dispersing slanderous libels made felony 1545
William Prynne, a Puritan lawyer, fined 5000*l* pilloried his ears cut off, and imprisoned, for writing "Histriomastix" a condemnation of the stage, is a libel on the queen, who favored them 1633, he was tried and further punished for his satirical writings 1637

Liberal Republican party. POLITICAL PARTIES.

Liberals, a name given, since 1828, to the advanced Whigs and reformers in England, who held office under earl Grey, viscount Melbourne, earl Russell, viscount Palmerston, and W E Gladstone

Liberia, a republic of negroes on the coast of Upper Guinea, W Africa, founded in 1822 by the American Colonization Society, which was organized at Princeton N J, 1816, and formally constituted 1 Jan 1817, at Washington, D C, with Madison, Clay Randolph, and Bushrod Washington as leaders The independence of Liberia was proclaimed 24 Aug 1847, recognized by Europe in 1848, by the United States in 1861 The executive is vested in a president elected for 2 years, and the legislative power in a Senate and House of Representatives Area, 14,360 sq miles, pop 1,068,000, of whom 18,000 are Americo-Liberians, and the others native. Capital, Monrovia SLAVERY.

libertines (signifying freedmen and their sons) were a sect headed by Quintin and Corin, about 1525, who held monstrous opinions.

Liberty Enlightening the World. BARTHOLDI'S STATUE

libraries. Accadian or Chaldean libraries are said to have been formed 1700 B C The remains of those formed by Assyrian monarchs (744 et seq) at Nineveh, etc., consisting of tablets of baked clay, were discovered by Botta, Layard, and others, 1843 et seq, now mostly in the British museum NINEVEH Diodorus Siculus describes a library in the tomb of Osymandyas, king of Egypt 14 century B C. The first public library described in history was founded at Athens by Pisistratus, about 540 B.C The second of note, founded by Ptolemy Philadelphus, 284 B C, was partly destroyed when Julius Cæsar set fire to Alexandria, 47 B.C 400,000 valuable books in MS are said to have been destroyed by this catastrophe —*Blair*

B C
First private library was Aristotle's (*Strabo*) 334
First library at Rome brought from Macedonia 167
According to Plutarch the library at Pergamos contained 200,000 books. It fell to the Romans at the death of Attalus III, who bequeathed his kingdom to the Roman people, said to have been added to the splendid library in Alexandria 133
Library of Apellicon sent to Rome from Athens by Scylla 86
A D
Ulpian library of Trajan established in the Forum of Trajan 98
Library discovered at Herculaneum containing 1756 MSS. on shelves running round the room to the height of 6 feet
Library founded at Constantinople by Constantine about 355
Library of Pamphilus at Cæsarea increased by Eusebius, the historian of the church, to 30,000 volumes.
With the fall of the Western empire, 476, the ancient history of libraries may be said to end
An Alexandrian library said to have been burned by the caliph Omar I (ALEXANDRIA) .. 640

With regard to the libraries of ancient times, the tendency is to exaggerate the number and value of the books, etc A collection of books forming a library in the modern sense requires an advanced and elaborate civilization, so that stories of large and valuable collections of books, manuscript, and tablets in antiquity are not credible

EUROPEAN LIBRARIES OF 100,000 VOLUMES AND UPWARDS.

Name.	Founded.	Number of volumes.	
		Printed.	MSS.
Austria-Hungary:			
Buda-Pest	1802	400,000	18,000
[Matthias Corvinus, king of Hungary, collected a library of nearly 50,000 volumes at Buda, 1458–90. Destroyed by the Turks, 1527.]			
Buda-Pest university	1635, 1780	200,000	1,000
Cracow university	1364	210,000	5,000
Grätz university	1776	125,000	2,000
Martinsberg	....	100,000	
Prague	1818	130,000	3,000
[Exact sciences, Bohemian, and several others.]			
Vienna, Imperial library	1495	450,000 (6461 incunabula.)	20,000
[Most important collection in Europe.]			
Vienna university	1777	300,000	Few.
[Much used. Established by Maria Theresa.]			
[Besides the libraries mentioned above, there are many others in Austria ranging from a few thousand volumes to 80,000 and 90,000—more than 100 in Vienna alone. Many smaller libraries of Austria, rich in incunabula, date from the 6th to the 12th centuries—Salzburg, 6th century, Admont, 11th, Göttweih, 11th, St. Florian, 11th, Benedictine (Vienna), 12th.]			
Denmark:			
Copenhagen, Royal library	1670	500,000 (Incunabula and block books important.)	20,000
[Open to the public, 1793.]			
University	1482, 1728	275,000	5,000
France:			
Aix	1786, 1810	200,000	1,200
Besançon	1694	150,000	2,000
Bordeaux	1800	200,000	1,500
Caen	1809	100,000	Few.
[Succeeded the University library, founded 1431.]			
Douai	1789	110,000	1,300
Grenoble	1772	190,000	8,000
Lyons	1530	130,000	2,000
Marseilles	1796	100,000	1,600
Nantes	1588	200,000	Few.
Paris, Arsenal	1796	210,000	8,500
Institute	1759	120,000	
Mazarine. [Public since 1688.]	1643	175,000	6,000
Nationale	1595	2,500,000	80,000
[The most extensive in the world, with 450,000 volumes of French history, and more than 2,400,000 engravings. The annual grant for binding and purchases is $40,000.]			
Ste. Geneviève	1624	130,000	2,500
University (Sorbonne)	....	135,000	1,000
Rouen	1792	122,500	2,500
Troyes. [Jansenist collection.]	1691	100,000	3,000
[Besides collections of learned societies and educational institutions, etc., outside Paris, over 220 French provincial towns possess public libraries of from 3000 to 90,000 volumes, most of them founded near the first of this century.]			
Germany:			
Augsburg (mostly history)	1537	150,000	
Bamberg	1611	140,000	
Berlin	1661	800,000	16,000
" university	1831	250,000	
Bonn	1818	300,000	
Bremen	1660	125,000	
Breslau	1811	350,000	4,000
	1865	210,000	2,500
Carlsruhe	1766	140,000	
Cassel	1580	170,000	
Darmstadt	1817	550,000	3,000
Dresden	1590	350,000	6,500
Erlangen	1743	150,000	2,000
Frankfort-on-the-Main	1484	160,000	
Freiburg	1460	300,000	
Giessen	1612	165,000	
Gotha	1647	250,000	6,000
Göttingen	1737	425,000	5,000
Greifswald	1456	125,000	
Halle	1699	225,000	
Hamburg	1610	350,000	5,500
Hanover	1649	175,000	4,000
Heidelberg	1386	300,000	5,000
Jena	1502	190,000	
Kiel	1665	180,000	2,000
Königsberg	1534	190,000	
Leipsic	1409	550,000	4,500
Mainz (over 4000 incunabula)	1477	160,000	1,200
Marburg	1558	150,000	
Meiningen	1680	165,000	
Germany (continued):			
Munich	1500	1,000,000	26,000
" university	1472	330,000	1,800
Münster	1588	125,000	
Nuremberg	1852	100,000	
Oldenburg	1792	100,000	
Rostock	1419	150,000	
Strasburg	1871	525,000	
Stuttgart (Bible coll. 7200)	1765	430,000	4,000
Tübingen	1547	240,000	3,500
Weimar	17th cen.	200,000	2,000
Wolfenbüttel	1589	325,000	10,000
Würzburg	1582	300,000	2,000
[There are at least 1600 libraries in the German empire, distributed among 600 towns.]			
Great Britain and *Ireland:*			
Birmingham (free)	1860	110,000	
[partly burned, 1879.]			
Cambridge university	1475	220,000	5,723
Dublin (Trinity college)	1602	200,000	
Edinburgh	1680	275,000	3,000
" university	1580	150,000	2,000
Glasgow university	1473	130,000	
Leeds	1870	115,000	
Liverpool	1852	120,000	
British museum, London	1753	1,600,000	52,000, and 162,000 charters
Corporation library, London	1824	100,000	
University college, London	1828	110,000	
Manchester	1852	160,000	
Bodleian, Oxford	1602	450,000	31,000
St. Andrews university (Scotland)	1612	100,000	
[Besides these there are 400 libraries, ranging from 1000 to 80,000 vols.]			
Holland:			
Amsterdam	15th cen.	120,000	Few.
The Hague	1798	210,000	4,000
Leyden	1575	170,000	5,000
Utrecht	1582	160,000	1,000
Italy:			
Bologna	1712	170,000	6,000
	1801	130,000	
Ferrara	1753	110,000	
Florence	1752	140,000	3,800
" National	1714	425,000	16,000
Genoa	1773	120,000	1,400
Milan	1609	170,000	8,100
" National	1770	165,000	4,000
Modena	1598	100,000	3,000
Naples	1673	160,000	3,000
	1804	280,000	8,000
	1812	150,000	
Padua	1629	160,000	3,000
Palermo	1775	145,000	3,000
" National	1804	120,000	12,000
Parma	1779	225,000	4,500
Pavia	1772	190,000	
Pisa	1742	125,000	
Rome, Vatican	5th cen.	225,000	26,000
[MSS. and rarities; private library of pope.]			
Rome	1876	370,000	5,000
	1700	135,000	2,500
Turin	1723	240,000	3,400
" National	1720	180,000	
Venice	1362	270,000	10,000
Verona	1792	125,000	
Vicenza	1706	110,000	2,000
[Many libraries of Italy contain valuable MSS. dating from the 4th century.]			
Norway:			
Christiania	1811	240,000	1,200
Portugal:			
Lisbon	1796	210,000	10,000
Oporto	1833	100,000	
Russia:			
Dorpat	1801	145,000	
Helsingford	1828	140,000	
Kief	1833	115,000	
Moscow	1861	310,000	5,000
	1755	170,000	
St. Petersburg	1726	155,000	
" Imperial	1714	1,000,000	26,000
" Public	1824	440,000	
Spain:			
Madrid	1711	410,000	25,000
	....	100,000	
Sweden:			
Lund	1688	125,000	3,000
Stockholm	1585	260,000	8,000
Upsala	1620	225,000	10,000
Switzerland:			
Basel university	1460	120,000	4,000
Geneva	16th cen.	110,000	1,800
Lucerne	1832	100,000	
Zürich	1629	105,000	3,000

UNITED STATES LIBRARIES OF 50,000 VOLUMES AND UPWARDS.

State.	Location.	Name of Library.	When founded.	No. of volumes.	No. of pamphlets.
Arkansas	Little Rock	State	1846	51,000	
California	Sacramento	"	1852	85,000	
"	San Francisco	Free Public	1879	70,000	
"	"	Mechanics' Institute	1855	58,000	
"	"	Mercantile Library Association	1853	62,000	
"	"	Sutro	....	200,000	
Connecticut	Hartford	Case Memorial	....	55,000	
"	"	Hartford Theological	1834	55,000	
"	New Haven	Yale College	1701	185,000	100,000
District of Columbia	Georgetown	Riggs Memorial	1889	61,000	18,800
" "	Washington	Library of Congress	1800	660,000	210,000
" "	"	Department of State	1789	50,000	
" "	"	House of Representatives	1789	125,000	
" "	"	Scientific Library of Patent office	1836	50,000	
" "	"	Surgeon General, Medical	1865	104,500	
" "	"	United States Senate	1870	75,500	
Illinois	Chicago	Public	1872	175,874	25,293
"	"	University of Chicago	1890	380,000	
"	"	Newberry	1887	79,000	
Indiana	Indianapolis	Public	1873	50,000	
Kentucky	Frankfort	State	1821	80,000	
"	Louisville	Polytechnic Society	1870	50,000	
Maryland	Annapolis	State	1826	100,000	
"	Baltimore	Johns Hopkins University	1876	55,000	
"	"	Peabody Institute	1857	110,000	
"	Woodstock	Woodstock College	1869	75,000	
Massachusetts	Boston	Athenæum	1807	187,000	
"	"	Public	1852	557,000	
"	Cambridge	Harvard University	1638	292,000	278,000
"	New Bedford	Free Public	1852	60,000	
"	Salem	Essex Institute	1848	60,000	
"	Springfield	City Library Association	1857	80,000	
"	Worcester	American Antiquarian Society	1812	95,000	
"	"	Free Public	1859	86,000	
Michigan	Ann Arbor	University of Michigan General	1841	78,000	
"	Detroit	Public	1865	109,000	
"	Lansing	State	1828	55,000	
Minnesota	Minneapolis	Public	1889	50,000	
Mississippi	Jackson	State	1836	60,000	
Missouri	St. Louis	Mercantile Library Association	1846	78,500	
"	"	Public	1865	80,000	
New Hampshire	Hanover	Dartmouth College	1779	75,000	
New Jersey	Princeton	Theological Seminary	1812	54,000	
New York	Albany	State	1818	157,000	
"	Binghamton	Central High-school	....	64,241	
"	Brooklyn	Brooklyn	1857	113,251	
"	Buffalo	Buffalo	1836	67,000	8,000
"	"	Grosvenor Public	1859	50,000	
"	Ithaca	Cornell University	1868	111,000	25,000
"	New York city	Apprentice	1820	90,000	
"	"	Astor	1849	239,000	12,000
"	"	Columbia College	1754	135,000	
"	"	Lenox	1870	65,000	
"	"	Mercantile Library Association	1820	240,000	
"	"	Free Circulating	1880	58,000	
"	"	New York Historical Society	1804	75,000	
"	"	" Society	1754	90,000	
"	"	Union Theological Seminary	1836	68,000	40,000
Ohio	Cincinnati	Public	1867	157,000	18,000
"	"	Young Men's Mercantile Library Ass'n	1835	60,000	
"	Cleveland	Public	1868	67,000	
"	Columbus	State	1817	64,000	
Pennsylvania	Harrisburg	"	1790	60,000	
"	Philadelphia	Philosophical Library Company	1731	166,000	30,000
"	"	Mercantile Library Association	1821	166,000	10,000
"	"	University of Pennsylvania	1749	100,000	100,000
"	South Bethlehem	Lehigh University	1877	67,000	
Rhode Island	Providence	Providence Athenæum	1836	52,000	
"	"	Rhode Island Historical Society	1878	59,000	21,000
"	"	Brown University	1767	71,000	20,000
Virginia	Richmond	State	1823	50,000	
Wisconsin	Madison	State Historical Society	1851	72,000	75,000
"	Milwaukee	Public	1878	61,000	6,000

Public libraries in the United States in 1891 were 3804 of 1000 volumes and upwards. Number of bound volumes in these libraries 26,826,537; number of pamphlets 4,340,817. Average size of libraries 8194 volumes.

LIBRARIES OF CANADA.

Location.	Name of Library.	When founded.	No. of volumes.
Quebec	Laval University	1663	100,000
Toronto	Legislative Library of Ontario	1867	70,000
"	Public	1883	68,000
Ottawa	Library of Parliament	....	150,000

Library Association of the United Kingdom, founded at a conference of librarians at the London institution, 2 Oct. 1877, meets annually.

Library Association of the United States, organized 1876, meets annually.

Libya, in a general sense the ancient name for Africa; in a restricted sense the territory immediately west of Egypt. The Persians under Cambyses, about 525 B.C., unsuccessfully attempted its conquest. AFRICA.

Lichfield, Staffordshire, Engl. The see of Mercia (at Lichfield) was founded about 656; removed to Chester, 1075; to Coventry, 1102. In 1121 Robert Peche was consecrated bishop of Lichfield and Coventry. Here Samuel Johnson was born, 1709.

Lichfield cathedral was first built about 656; the present structure was founded by Roger de Clinton, the 37th bishop, in 1148. Walter de Langton (bishop in 1296) built the chapel of St. Mary, now taken into the choir, and under bishop Heyworth (1420) the cathedral was completed. It was despoiled at the Reformation, and scandalously injured in the Parliamentary war (monuments, fine sculptures, and beautiful windows being demolished). It was repaired at the Restoration, 1660; in 1788; and by Gilbert G. Scott, 1860-63.

In Lichfield castle, king Richard II. kept his Christmas festival, 1397, when 200 tuns of wine and 2000 oxen were consumed. A charter was granted to Lichfield as a city, by Edward VI., 1549.

Licin'ian laws. In 375 B.C., C. Licinius Stolo and L. Sextius, tribunes of the people, promulgated various *rogationes*, or laws, to weaken the patricians and benefit the plebs: one relieved plebeians from debts; another enacted that no person should possess more than 500 jugera of public land, or more than 100 head of large cattle or 500 of small, in the Roman states; a third, that one consul should be a plebeian. After much opposition these were carried, and L. Sextius became the first plebeian consul, 365. Another Licinian law, 56 B.C., imposed a severe penalty on party clubs, or societies for election purposes; and another, about 103 B.C. (proposed by P. Licinius Crassus), limited table expenses.

Lie'benau, a town of Bohemia. Here, in the first action of the Seven Weeks' war, 26 June, 1866, the Austrians were repulsed by the Prussians under gen. von Horn.

Liège (*le-aizh'*), Belgium, a bishopric, under the German empire, from the 8th century till 1795. Liège frequently revolted against its prince-bishops. In a severe contest, the citizens were beaten at Brusthem, 28 Oct. 1467, and Liège taken by Charles the Bold, duke of Burgundy, who treated them cruelly. In 1482 Liège fell into the power of De la Marck, the Boar of Ardennes, who killed the bishop, Louis of Bourbon, and was himself defeated and killed. Vivid description of this event in Scott's "Quentin Durward." Liège was taken by the duke of Marlborough, 23 Oct. 1702; and by the French and others at various times, till in 1796 it was annexed to France, in 1814 to the Netherlands, and in 1830 to Belgium. Iron-works established at Liège in the 16th century have been greatly enlarged by the Cockerills in the 19th.

lieutenants, lords, for counties, were instituted in England, 3 Edw. VI. 1549, and in Ireland in 1831. Their military jurisdiction abolished by Army Regulation act, 1871.

life-boat, a boat built very strong and buoyant for the purpose of saving the lives of crews and passengers of vessels wrecked near the shore.

Patent granted to Lionel Lukin for a life-boat ... 1785

Reward, offered by a committee in South Shields for a life-boat, 1788; obtained by Henry Greathead, of that town (he received 1200*l.* from Parliament), 1789; it first put to sea, 30 Jan. 1790

Another life-boat was invented by William Wouldhave. His name was inscribed on a memorial erected in honor of Henry Greathead on the pier at South Shields, uncovered..25 June, 1890

Thirty-one life-boats built, and 300 lives saved up to ... 1804

Duke of Northumberland offered a reward of 105*l.* for a life-boat, 1850; obtained by James Beeching of Yarmouth ... 1851

Tubular life-boat of H. Richardson, the *Challenger*, patented in Jan.; a cruise was made by him from Liverpool to London in it ... 1852

National Life-boat Institution, founded in 1824; its journal first published in 1852. In 1856 it received a bequest of 10,000*l.* from Hamilton Fitzgerald, and of 39,000*l.* from William Birks Rhodes, "the Hounslow miser," in 1878.

American life-raft, composed of cylinders lashed together, sailed from New York, 4 June, 1867, navigated by 3 men, capt. John Mikes and messrs. Miller and Mullane, and arrived at Southampton 25 July following.

Life-preserver, the apparatus of capt. Manby (brought into use in Feb. 1808), effects a communication with the distressed vessel by a rope, thrown by a shot from a mortar, with a line attached to it. For the night, a night-ball is provided with a hollow case of thick pasteboard, and a fuse and quick match, and charged with 50 balls and a sufficiency of powder to inflame them. The fuse is so graduated that the shell shall explode at the height of 300 yards. The balls spread a brilliant light for nearly a minute, and give a clear view of every surrounding object. In 20 years, 58 vessels and 410 of their crews and passengers had been saved. Capt. Manby d. 18 Nov. 1854, aged 89.

Boat-lowering apparatus, in consequence of many being lost when boats were lowered from the *Amazon* in 1852, invented by Charles Clifford of London in 1856, has been much approved of, and has been generally adopted in the English navy.

Capt. Kynaston's hooks were approved by adm. sir Baldwin Walker in 1862, and by a committee on the subject in ... 1872

Exhibition of life-boats, life-rafts, etc., at the London Tavern opened ... 15 Apr. 1873

Capt. Boyton's life-preserving dress (of india-rubber), with means for signalling at sea, tried by him on the Thames successfully, 23 Jan. and 6 Mch.; at Cowes, before queen Victoria (while in the water he fired rockets, caught fish, etc.), 5 Apr.; nearly crossed the Channel from Dover (paddled 2 miles an hour); stopped by the French pilot ... Apr. 1875

Capt. Boyton crossed the Channel from Grisnez to the South Foreland in 23½ hours ... 28–29 May, "

Christie's life-saving raft tried on the Thames; could not be sunk ... 17 Mch. "

Edmund Thompson's life-raft, partially successful off Poplar, 22 Apr. "

Rev. E. L. Berthon's collapsible life-boat taken out by the *Essequibo*, and proved to be successful ... Sept. 1882

Storm King patent life-boat, 30 feet long, with its inventor, capt. Joergensen and a man named Nelsen, left London 12 Sept. 1889; encountered heavy gales; arrived at Cape Town, 2 Mch. 1890

Duke of Northumberland, a new fast steel steam life-boat, with 15 water-tight compartments, designed by Messrs. R. and H. Green, to be stationed at Harwich, brought into service ... "

life-guard, Washington's. A corps, varying at different times from 60 to 250 men, was formed in the spring of 1776. The men, not less than 5 feet 9 inches nor more than 5 feet 10 inches in height, were selected from the Continental army for moral and personal perfections, to protect the person, baggage, and papers of the commander-in-chief. The last survivor, Uzal Knapp, of Orange county, N. Y., died in Jan. 1856, and was buried at the foot of the flag-staff in front of Washington's head-quarters at Newburg, on the Hudson. At the dedication of a freestone monument over his remains, 18 June, 1860, there was a large civic and military procession.

life-insurance. INSURANCE.

life-saving service in the United States. The first organized effort in the U. S. was made by the Massachusetts Humane Society in 1789; but its history may be said to have begun in 1846–47, when disasters on the New Jersey coast forced the federal government to consider the subject. In 1849, 8 stations were equipped between Montauk point and Coney island, but no great progress was made until the present effective system was adopted, 1871. The service, attached to the U. S. Treasury department, is divided into 12 districts, viz.:

1st district,		coasts of Maine and New Hampshire	12	stations.
2d	"	coast of Massachusetts	23	"
3d	"	coasts of Rhode Island and Long island	39	"
4th	"	coast of New Jersey (the most dangerous of all), called "the grave-yard of the sea"	41	"
5th	"	coasts of Delaware, Maryland, and Virginia	17	"
6th	"	coasts of S. Virginia and North Carolina	29	"
7th	"	coasts of South Carolina, Georgia, and E. Florida	12	"
8th	"	Gulf coast	8	"
9th	"	Lakes Erie and Ontario, and falls of the Ohio at Louisville, Ky	10	"
10th	"	Lakes Huron and Superior	15	"
11th	"	Lake Michigan	24	"
12th	"	Pacific coast	13	"
		Total	243	"

Owing to the extent of uninhabited coast, the service is obliged to erect houses of refuge at different points, provisioned, etc., so as to afford shelter and food to the shipwrecked crews frequently for several days. From 1871 to 30 June, 1891, there have been 5783 disasters, endangering property to the value of $96,247,559, of which $71,540,912 was saved. Of 49,530 lives imperilled, but 592 were lost. The cost of the service for the year ending 30 June, 1891, was $940,201. The total number of disasters for the year ending 30 June, 1892, was 507, endangering property to the amount of $8,352,335; amount of property saved $7,174,475; number of persons on board vessels, 2923; lives lost, 27. The cost of the service for the year ending 30 June, 1892, was $1,009,234. The total number of disasters for the year ending 30 June, 1893, was 427; value of property involved, $8,098,075; property saved, $6,442,505; number of persons involved, 3565; persons lost, 23; cost of service, $1,231,893. The chief appliances employed in saving life are the life-saving gun and projectile, the line-carrying rocket, the oil-distributing rocket, the breeches-buoy, an apparatus for conveying a person on a line from ship to shore, and the life and surf-boat. Under authority of the act of 20 June, 1874, 18 June, 1878, and 4 May, 1882, life-saving medals of honor have been awarded by the secretary of the treasury for rescuing a person from drowning. Total number awarded to 30 June, 1892, was 167 gold and 209 silver medals. Among the recipients were 7 women, viz.:

Name.	Residence.	Award.	Date.
Edith Morgan	Hamlin, Mich.	Silver	9 Nov. 1880
Ida Lewis-Wilson	Keeper Lime Rock light-house, R. I.	Gold	16 July, 1881
Edith Clarke	Oakland, Cal.	Silver	26 May, 1887
Marie D. Parsons	Fireplace Point, Long island, N. Y.	"	7 Feb. 1888

Name.	Residence.	Award.	Date.
Mary Whiteley	Charleston, S. C.	Silver	17 Nov. 1888
Mabel Mason	Mamajuda light station, Detroit river	"	15 Apr. 1891
Mrs. Edward White	Copalis, Wash.	Gold	18 Apr. 1892
Bertie O. Burr	Lincoln, Neb.	"	14 June, "

light. And God said, Let there be light: and there was light (Gen. i. 3). One of the phenomena attendant upon heat, and may be said to be its visible manifestation. It especially affects the eye, as sound does the ear, and together with the eye renders the outward world visible. Two theories have been advanced regarding the propagation of light—the older the corpuscular theory, and the later the undulatory. The advocates of the former were Newton, Laplace, Biot, and others, while more recent scientists support the undulatory theory; but neither of these theories explains satisfactorily all the phenomena, neither do they attempt to explain what is transferred or moved. The apparently incomparable velocity of light is said to have been computed with more or less accuracy by 4 distinct methods—(1) Römer's method, 1676; (2) Bradley's, 1728; (3) Fizeau's, 1849; (4) Foucault's, 1850—at from 186,000 to 187,000 miles a second. OPTICS, STARS, SUN.

light-house, a structure built on the coast or shore of navigable waters, and furnished for the purpose of indicating a point of danger or to serve as a guide, also called pharos (hence *phare*, Fr.; *faro*, It.), from one erected at Pharos, near Alexandria, Egypt, 550 feet high, said to have been visible 42 miles, about 285 B.C. There was one at Messina, at Rhodes, etc. COLOSSUS. These were lighted by fires. A coal-fire light was exhibited at Tynemouth castle, Northumberland, about 1638. The tower of Cordonan at the mouth of the Gironde, France, begun 1584. The first true light-house erected in England was the EDDYSTONE, finished 1859. Lights were exhibited in various places in England by the corporation of the Trinity-house early in the 16th century.

BRITISH LIGHT-HOUSES.

Besides the Eddystone light-house and that at BELL ROCK (Inch cape), the Skerryvore on the west coast of Scotland (1844), 158 ft. high, cost 83,126*l.* The Bishop Rock off Scilly islands (1853), 145 ft. high, cost 36,559*l.* Wolf Rock, Land's End (1870), Small's Rocks, entrance English channel, Harvis's Rock (1862), Island of Alderney, and others are important.

The usual source of light in British light-houses is oil; but in harbor lights gas has been successfully used. Glass reflectors were used in 1780, copper ones in 1807. A common coal-fire light was discontinued at St. Bees only in 1822. Fresnel's dioptric system, devised about 1819, was first adopted in England by messrs. Wilkins, at the direction of the corporation of the Trinity-house, 1 July, 1836.

A magneto-electric machine devised by prof. Holmes, producing a more brilliant artificial light than any then known, was first employed at the South Foreland light-house, near Dover, 8 Dec. 1858; and at Dengeness (or Dungeness) in 1862. It was shown with a similar one constructed by M. Serin, at the International Exhibition, London, 1862.

H. Wilde's apparatus, producing a powerful magneto-electric light, on trial in northern light-houses, Oct. 1866.

LIME-LIGHT employed at the South Foreland light-house in 1861.

Gas-light tried successfully at Howth Bailey light-house, Dublin bay, July, 1869.

Mr. Wigham's triform light; glass belt round the gas-light, prisms below the belt, and prisms forming a cupola; tried near Dublin; approved by dr. Tyndall, July, 1873.

C. William Siemens's magneto-electric light used at the Lizards, 29 Mch. 1878.

LIGHT-HOUSES IN THE UNITED STATES.

Since 1789 all light-houses on the U. S. coast have been maintained at the expense of the nation (no light-dues being charged upon commerce). The cost for the year ending 30 June, 1879, was $1,708,700, and for the year ending 30 June, 1894, $2,948,000.

Many light-houses in the U. S. are unsurpassed, and are of exceedingly difficult construction. The most noted is on Minot's Ledge, in Massachusetts bay, first erected in 1847. It was supported on iron piles 12 inches in diameter, firmly braced and tied with wrought-iron bands. It was finished in 1849, but in a terrible storm, Apr. 1851, the iron supports were twisted like straws, and the whole structure was swept away. In 1852 Congress appropriated money to rebuild the light. The design was a granite tower in the shape of the frustum of a cone; the base is 30 ft. in diameter, and the whole height 88 ft. The lower 40 ft. are solid. The difficulty of the work was such that, though every moment when the tide left the rock uncovered was taken advantage of, it was a year before the first layer of stones for the foundation was securely laid. It was first lighted in 1860. Cost $300,000.

Spectacle Reef light-house, north end of lake Huron, of the same type as Minot's Ledge, built 1871–74, 93 ft. high; cost $375,000. Tillamook Rock light-house, 20 miles south of the mouth of the Columbia river, Oregon, 1880–81; cost $123,492. Northwest Seal Rock light-house, California, commenced 1882. Petit Manon, off the coast of Maine, 125 ft. above sea level. "Mt. Desert Rock," coast of Maine. Matinicus Rock, coast of Maine, 1827; rebuilt 1846. Halfway Rock, coast of Maine, 1871. Boon island, coast of Maine, 1812. Cape Ann, on Thatheus island, 1790; rebuilt 1861. Boston Lights, on Little Brewster island, Boston harbor, the first on the coast; built 1715–16, rebuilt 1859; its first light-keeper, George Worthylake, was drowned with his wife and daughter, 3 Nov. 1718; Benjamin Franklin, then a boy, sold a ballad on the occasion in the streets of Boston. Fourteen Foot Bank light-house, Delaware bay, 1887; cost $123,811.

First coast-light in the U. S. 1673
First light-house built on Little Brewster island, Boston harbor, ... 1715–16
U. S. accepted cession of all light-houses .... 7 Aug. 1789
Control vested in commissioner of the revenue .... 8 May, 1792
Restored to secretary of treasury .... 6 Apr. 1802
Vested again in the commissioner .... 24 July, 1813
Vested in the 5th auditor of the treasury .... 1 July, 1820
Messrs. Blunt of New York brought charges against light-house management .... 30 Nov. 1837
Naval commission on light-houses appointed .... "
Congressional investigation of light-house management resulting in improvements 1838–43
Navy commission sent to inspect European systems 1845
Fresnel system authorized .... 3 Mch. 1851
First Light-house Board appointed .... 21 May, "
Fresnel system generally introduced 1852
Permanent Light-house Board authorized .... 31 Aug. "
Board organized .... 8 Oct. "
The U. S. maintains lights upon 9959 nautical miles of coast and river navigation, divided into 16 districts, as follows:

1st district,	Maine, New Hampshire, coasts, bays, inlets, and rivers.
2d "	from Hampton Harbor, N. H., to Warren Pt., R. I.
3d "	Long Island, Atlantic, and sound coasts, with New Jersey above the Highlands. Also lakes Champlain and Memphremagog, with bays and rivers.
4th "	New Jersey, Delaware, and Maryland coasts, bays, and rivers.
5th "	Virginia coast, including the Chesapeake bay, North Carolina coast and sounds.
6th "	South Carolina, Georgia, and Florida coasts to Jupiter's Inlet, Fla., with bays and rivers.
7th "	Florida coast, from Jupiter's Inlet to Perdido bay, Fla.
8th "	Gulf coast from Perdido bay to the Rio Grande, with lakes, rivers, and bays below New Orleans.
9th "	Lake Michigan, Green bay, strait of Mackinack, and tributary waters.
10th "	U. S. shore and waters of lakes Erie and Ontario, with the rivers Niagara, St. Lawrence, and the lower part of the Detroit river.
11th "	Upper Detroit river to the head of lake Superior.
12th "	800 miles Pacific coast, California.
13th "	Coast of Oregon and Washington, with Puget sound, Columbia river, and Alaskan waters.
14th "	The Ohio river from Pittsburg to the Mississippi, the Tennessee, Cumberland, and Great Kanawha, in all 1295 miles.
15th "	The Mississippi from the head of navigation to Cairo, Ill., with all navigable tributaries, in all 1582 miles.
16th "	The Mississippi, from Cairo, to New Orleans, with navigable tributaries, in all 1009 miles.

The following aids to navigation, operated by the Light-house Board, were in use 1 July, 1893:

Electric lights	4
First-order lights	56
Second-order lights	20
Third-order lights	52
Fourth-order lights	265
Fifth-order lights	148
Sixth-order lights	116
Lens lanterns	124
Range lenses	16
Reflectors	45
Tubular lanterns	1845
Light-ships	33
Electric buoys	20
Gas buoys	2
Total lighted aids	2746
Fog-signals by steam or hot air	114
" clockwork	189
Day beacons	419
Whistling buoys	64
Bell-buoys	90
Other buoys	4315
Total unlighted aids	5191
Total number of aids	7937

lighting cities. ELECTRICITY.

London first lighted at night by lanterns 1415
Glass lamps in streets 1694–1736
City generally lighted by gas 1814
Paris first lighted by gas 1819
New York generally lighted by gas 1825
Philadelphia generally lighted by gas .... "

lightning-conductors were first used to protect buildings by Franklin soon after 1752, when he drew electricity from a cloud. Prof. Richman of St. Petersburg was killed while repeating the experiment, Aug. 1753. First conductor in England set up at Payne's Hill, by dr. Watson. In 1766 one was placed on the tower of St. Mark's, at Venice, which has since escaped injury, although often struck by lightning previously.

Ligny (*leen-yee'*), a town near Fleurus, Belgium, where Napoleon defeated the Prussians under Blucher, 16 June, 1815. WATERLOO.

Ligu'rians, a Celtic tribe, N. Italy, invaded Roman territory, and were defeated 238 B.C., and subjugated 172 B.C. The Ligurian republic, founded in May, 1797, upon the ruins of the republic at Genoa, was incorporated with France in 1805, and then merged into the kingdom of Italy.

lilac-tree (*Syringa*). The Persian lilac from Persia was cultivated in England about 1638; the common lilac by John Gerard about 1597.

Lille. LISLE.

Lilybæ'um, a maritime fortress of Sicily, besieged by Pyrrhus, king of Epirus, 276 B.C.; relieved by the Carthaginians, 275 B.C. Its capture by the Romans, 241 B.C., after a siege of 9 years, ended the second Punic war.

Lima (*lee'ma*), Peru, South America. In 1534, Pizarro, marching through Peru, observing the beauty of the valley of Rimac, founded this city, calling it *Ciudad de los Reyes*, or city of the kings, 1535. Here he was assassinated, 26 June, 1541. Awful earthquakes occurred here, 1586, 1630, 1687, and 28 Oct. 1746. PERU.

lime or **linden tree** (the American basswood), probably introduced into England in the 16th century. The limes in St. James's park, London, are said to have been planted at the suggestion of Evelyn, who recommended multiplying odoriferous trees, in his "Fumifugium" (1661). A lime-tree planted in Switzerland in 1410 had in 1720 a trunk 36 feet in circumference. FLOWERS AND PLANTS.

lime-light, produced by burning hydrogen or carburetted hydrogen with oxygen on a surface of lime, evolving little heat and not vitiating the air. It is also called Drummond light, after lieut. Thomas Drummond, who successfully produced it in 1826, and employed it on the British Ordnance survey. It is said to have been seen 112 miles. It was tried at the South Foreland light-house in 1861. Lieut. Drummond was born 1797, died 15 Apr. 1840. To him is attributed the maxim that "property has its duties as well as its rights."

limitations, Statute of, in the United States. The following are the periods fixed by statute in the several states, after which, in all ordinary cases, the lapse of time, when pleaded against a claim, raises a conclusive presumption of payment:

PERIODS OF LIMITATION.

Judgments.		Notes and Contracts.		Open Accounts.	
State.	Time.	State.	Time.	State.	Time.
Ala.		Ky.	15 years.	Wyo.	8 years.
Fla.		O.		Col.	
Ill.		Ill.		Conn.	
Ia.		Ind.		Ind.	
Me.		Ia.	10 years.	Me.	
Mass.		Mo.		Mass.	
N. H.	20 years.	W. Va.		Mich.	
N. J.		Mont.	8 years.	Minn.	
N. Y.		Ala.		N. H.	
N. Dak.		Col.		N. J.	
R. I.		Conn.		N. Y.	
Wis.		Del.		N. Dak.	6 years.
Conn.	17 years.	Ga.		O.	
Ky.	15 years.	Me.		Ore.	
D. C.	12 years.	Mass.		Pa.	
Md.		Mich.		R. I.	
Ark.		Minn.		S. C.	
Del.		Miss.		S. Dak.	
Ind.		Nev.		Tenn.	
La.		N. H.		Vt.	
Mich.		N. J.	6 years.	Wis.	
Minn.		N. Mex.		Ill.	
Mo.		N. Y.		Ia.	
Mont.	10 years.	N. Dak.		Ky.	5 years.
N. C.		Or.		Mo.	
Or.		Pa.		Mont.	
S. C.		R. I.		W. Va.	
S. Dak.		S. C.		Ga.	
Tenn.		S. Dak.		Id.	
Tex.		Tenn.		Neb.	4 years.
Va.		Vt.		Nev.	
W. Va.		Wash.		N. Mex.	
Vt.	8 years.	Wis.		Ala.	3 years.

PERIODS OF LIMITATION.—(*Continued.*)

Judgments.		Notes and Contracts.		Open Accounts.	
State.	Time.	State.	Time.	State.	Time.
Ga.		Ark.		Ark.	
Miss.	7 years.	Ariz.		Ariz.	
N. Mex.		Fla.		Del.	
Col.		Id.		D. C.	
Id.		Kan.	5 years.	Kan.	
Nev.	6 years.	La.		La.	3 years.
Wash.		Neb.		Md.	
Ariz.		Va.		Miss.	
Cal.		Wyo.		N. C.	
Kan.		Cal.		Wash.	
Neb.		Tex.	4 years.	Cal.	
O.	5 years.	U. T.		Fla.	
Pa.		D. C.		Tex.	2 years.
U. T.		Md.	3 years.	U. T.	
Wyo.		N. C.		Va.	

Lincoln, the Roman *Lindum Colonia*, a city and county of England, at the Conquest was rich and populous. It was taken several times by Saxons and Danes. The castle was built by William I. in 1086. Without Newport gate upon Lincoln plain the partisans of the empress Maud, under the earl of Gloucester, defeated and captured king Stephen, 2 Feb. 1141. Discontented barons in the last year of king John invited Louis, dauphin of France, and acknowledged him as king of England here; but the nobility, summoned by the earl of Pembroke to Gloucester to crown Henry III., marched against them, and defeated them in a sanguinary fight (called the Fair of Lincoln), 20 May, 1217; and Louis withdrew.

Lincoln, Abraham, administration of. UNITED STATES, 1861-65.

Lincoln, Bishopric of. Sidnacester, or Lindisse and Dorchester, distinct sees in Mercia, were united about 1078, and the see was removed to Lincoln by bishop Remigius de Feschamp, who built a cathedral (1086), afterwards destroyed by fire, but rebuilt by bishop Alexander (1127) and bishop Hugh of Burgundy. The great bell of the cathedral, called Great Tom of Lincoln, weighs 4 tons, 8 pounds.

Lincoln tower, Westminster Bridge road, Engl., was erected by the united subscriptions of Britons and Americans, as a memorial of the abolition of slavery, and of Abraham Lincoln, president. The foundation was laid by gen. Schenck, then American minister, 9 July, 1874; and the head-stone was placed by Newman Hall, minister of Surrey chapel, 28 Sept. 1875. The tower, 220 feet high, cost about 7000*l.* The church, named Christ church (to replace Surrey chapel), and schools adjoining (costing about 60,000*l.*), were dedicated 4 July et seq. 1876. The rev. Rowland Hill's body was removed hither from Surrey chapel, 14 Apr. 1881.

Lincoln's inn, London, derives its name from Henry de Lacy, earl of Lincoln, who built a mansion here in the reign of Edward I., on the site of the bishop of Chichester's palace. It became an inn of court, 1310. The gardens of Lincoln's-inn fields, laid out by Inigo Jones about 1620, were erroneously said to occupy the same space as the largest pyramid of Egypt, which is 764 feet square; Lincoln's-inn square being 821 ft. by 625 ft. 6 in. William, lord Russell, was beheaded in Lincoln's-inn fields, 21 July, 1683. The square (formed in 1618) was enclosed with iron railings about 1737. The new hall and other buildings were opened 30 Oct. 1845, and the square planted. The theatre in Lincoln's-inn fields was built in 1695; rebuilt in 1714; made a barrack in 1756, and pulled down in 1848.

Lincoln's monument at Oak Ridge, Springfield, Ill., is a Quincy granite structure, 119 × 72 feet. At the height of 15 ft. 10 in. is the main platform, the apparent base of the shaft, and pedestals for the support of the statuary; from the centre rises the shaft, 12 ft. square at the base and 8 ft. at the top. The total height is 120 ft. Above the groups of statuary stands a bronze statue of Lincoln. Larkin G. Mead was the sculptor. The monument was dedicated 15 Oct. 1874; cost, $264,000.

Lindisfarne or **Holy island,** on the coast of Northumberland, became a bishop's see, 635. The Danes under Regnar Lodbrok ravaged it 793, and destroyed the monastery 875. The see was then removed to Chester-le-street, and to Durham in 995 (or 990).

linen. Pharaoh arrayed Joseph in vestures of fine linen, 1716 B.C. (Gen. xli. 42).

First manufactured in England by Flemish weavers, under protection of Henry III 1253
Company of linen-weavers established in London 1368
Art of staining linen known .... about 1579
Hemp, flax, linen, thread, and yarn, from Ireland, permitted to be exported duty free 1696
Scots in the reign of James I., and other Presbyterians who fled from persecution in succeeding reigns, settled in north-east Ireland, and established the linen manufacture; encouraged by lord deputy Wentworth in 1634; by William III 1698
Board of trustees to superintend Scotch linen manufacture established 1727
Irish linen board established in 1711; Linen hall, Dublin, opened 1728; board abolished 1828
Duty on linen taken off 1860
Dunfermline in Fifeshire, Dundee in Angusshire, and Barnsley in Yorkshire are chief seats of linen manufacture.

Linlith'gow bridge and **town,** about 17 miles from Edinburgh, near which the earl of Angus, with James V. in his power, defeated the earl of Lennox, who, after promise of quarter, was killed by sir James Hamilton, 1526. Mary queen of Scots was born in the palace of Linlithgow, 8 Dec. 1542; James V., her father, dying of a broken heart, 14 Dec.

Linnæ'an system of botany, arranged by Linné, or Linnæus, a Swede, 1725–30. He classed the plants according to the number and arrangement of the sexual parts, the flower and fruit marking his various genera. Linnæus lived from 1707 to 1778. His library and herbarium were purchased by sir James E. (then dr.) Smith, and given to the Linnæan Society in London, instituted in 1788, and incorporated 26 Mch. 1802. The system is now mostly superseded by the natural system.

lion. True lions belong to the Old World exclusively. They existed in Europe, Egypt, and Palestine, but have long disappeared from those countries; their present country being Africa. A lion named Pompey died in the Tower of London in 1760, after 70 years' confinement.

Gordon Cumming, the lion slayer, published his "Sporting Adventures in South Africa" 1850
Van Amburgh was successful in taming lions; but many have lost their lives in attempting it. The Lion-queen was killed at Chatham, 1850; and Massarti (John McCarthy) was killed by a lion .... 3 Jan. 1872
Lion sermon preached annually on 16 Oct. at St. Katherine Cree church, London, in memory of the escape of sir John Gayer from a lion in Arabia .... 16 Oct. 1630

lion and **unicorn,** the former English, the latter Scottish, became the supporters of the royal arms on the accession of James I. in 1603. The lions in Trafalgar square, designed by sir Edwin Landseer, were uncovered 31 Jan. 1867.

liquefaction. GAS.

Lis'bon (anciently *Olisippo* and *Felicitas Julia*) was taken by the Arabs about 716, and became important under the Moorish kings, from whom Alfonso I. of Portugal took it 1147. It was made capital of Portugal by Emanuel, 1506. Lisbon has suffered much by earthquakes, and was almost destroyed 1 Nov. 1755. EARTHQUAKE. The court fled to Brazil, 10 Nov. 1807; and on 30 Nov. the French, under Junot, entered Lisbon, and held it until at the battle of Vimeira, when they were defeated by British, under sir Arthur Wellesley, 21 Aug. 1808. Pop. 1878, 246,343.

Lisle (*leel*), now **Lille,** a town of N. France, with a strong citadel by Vauban, was besieged by the duke of Marlborough and allies; and, though deemed impregnable, taken after 3 months' siege in 1708. It was restored by the treaty of Utrecht in 1713, in consideration of the demolition of the fortifications of Dunkirk. Pop. 1891, 201,211. FORTIFICATIONS.

Lissa, an island and town in the Adriatic. Near here the Italian fleet, under Persano, was defeated with severe loss by the Austrian fleet, under Tegethoff, 20 July, 1866.

Italians had 23 vessels, 11 of them iron-clads; Austrians 23, only 7 iron-clads.
Admiral Persano tried for misconduct and dismissed the service (ITALY) .... 15 Apr. 1867

litanies (Gr. λιτανεία, supplication) first used in processions, it is said, about 469; others say about 400. Litanies to the Virgin Mary were first introduced by pope Gregory I. about 595. The first English litany was commanded to be used in Reformed churches by Henry VIII. in 1544.

Literary Club (at first called "The Club" and "Johnson's Club"), founded by dr. Johnson and sir Joshua Reynolds in 1764. Boswell, Burke, and Goldsmith were among the first members. The club's opinion of a new work was speedily known all over London, and had great influence. The club still exists. Hallam and Macaulay were members; dr. Milman, dean of St. Paul's, was in the chair at the centenary dinner on 7 June, 1864.

literature comprehends oratory, poetry, history, fiction, etc. The following names and works are the best known in literature:

GRECIAN LITERATURE AND AUTHORS (ANCIENT).

Authors.		Principal works.	
Name.	Time. (b. — d.)	Prose.	Poetry.
Homer	B.C. 962 — 927(?)	....	Iliad, Odyssey.
Hesiod	" 850	....	Works and Days, Theogony.
Æsop	" 572	Fables.	
Anacreon	" 559	....	Lyric
Æschylus	" 525 — 456	....	Dramas { Prometheus Bound, Seven Against Thebes, Agamemnon, etc.
Herodotus	" 443	History.	
Pindar	" 522 — 439	....	Odes.
Aristophanes	" 427	....	Comedy { The Clouds, The Birds, The Frogs, etc.
Euripides	" 480 — 406	....	Dramas, tragedy { Hecuba, Orestes, Medea, Iphigenia at Aulis, etc.
Sophocles	" 495 — 405	....	Dramas, tragedy { Electra, Œdipus, Antigone, Philoctetes, etc.
Thucydides	" 470 — 404	History of the war between Peloponnesus and Athens.	
Xenophon	" 443 — 359	Anabasis.	
Plato	" 429 — 347	Dialogues { Gorgias, Republic, Phædrus, Phœdon, etc.	
Isocrates	" 436 — 338	Orations—Areopagiticus, and many others.	
Aristotle	" 384 — 322	Philosophic—Organon.	
Demosthenes	" 382 — 322	Orations { Philippics, Concerning the Crown, etc.	
Æschines	" 389 — 314	Orations.	
Menander	" 342 — 292	....	Comedy.
Theophrastus	" 382 — 287	Philosophic.	
Theocritus	" 272	....	Idyls.
Epicurus	" 342 — 270	Philosophic.	
Archimedes of Syracuse	" 287 — 212	Philosophic and scientific.	
Polybius	" 207 — 122	General history—Second Punic War.	
Diodorus	" 50 A.D. 13	History.	
Strabo	" 54 " 10	Geography.	
Dionysius of Halicarnassus	" " 30	History and criticism.	
Plutarch	A.D. 49 — 120	Biography—Parallel Lives.	

GRECIAN LITERATURE AND AUTHORS (ANCIENT).—(*Continued.*)

Authors.		Principal Works.	
Name.	Time. b. — d.	Prose.	Poetry.
Epictetus	A.D. 118	Stoic philosophy.	
Appian	" 147	History.	
Arrian	" 148	History.	
Athenæus	" 194	Feast of the Learned, a fragment.	
Oppian	" 190(?)	....	On hunting, on fishing.
Lucian	" 120 — 200		
Herodian	" 240	History.	
Longinus	" 273	Criticisms, etc.	
Julian (emperor)	" 331 — 363	Satires, letters, etc.	

FATHERS OF THE CHURCH, PHILOSOPHY.

LATIN LITERATURE AND AUTHORS (ANCIENT).

Authors.		Principal Works.	
Name.	Time. b. — d.	Prose.	Poetry.
Plautus	B.C. 254 — 184	....	Dramas, comedy.
Ennius	" 239 — 169	....	Satires, etc.
Terence	" 193 — 159	....	Dramas, comedy.
Cato the Elder	" 232 — 147	On agriculture—Orations, etc.	
Lucilius	" 149 — 103	....	Satires, etc.
Lucretius	" 96 — 52	....	Philosophic.
Julius Cæsar	" 100 — 44	Commentaries.	
Cicero	" 107 — 43	Orations, Concerning Old Age, and other essays.	
Catullus	" 82 — 40	....	Lyric poems.
Sallust	" 86 — 34	Conspiracy of Catiline, Jugurthan War.	
Nepos	" 28(?)	Lives of eminent men.	
Vitruvius	" 27	On architecture.	
Propertius	" 51 — 16	....	Elegiac poetry.
Virgil	" 70 — 19	....	Georgics, Æneid.
Tibullus	" 18	....	Elegiac verse.
Horace	" 65 — 8	....	Odes, epodes, satires, epistles.
Celsus	A.D. 17	Medical works.	
Livy	" 59 — 17	History of Rome.	
Ovid	" 43 — 18	....	Metamorphoses, Art of Love, etc.
Paterculus	" 19 — 31	History.	
Seneca	" 5 — 65	Moralistic essays.	
Persius	A.D. 34 — 62	....	Satires.
Lucan	" 38 — 65	....	Pharsalia.
Pliny the Elder	" 23 — 79	Natural history.	
Quintilian	" 42 — 118	Rhetorics and critics.	
Flaccus, Valerius	" 88	....	Argonautics.
Pliny the Younger	" 61 — 115	Letters.	
Statius	" 61 — 96	....	Thebaid.
Tacitus	" 55 — 117(?)	Annals of Rome, etc.	
Silius Italicus	" 25 — 100	....	Poems.
Martial	" 40 — 104	....	Epigrammatic poet
Suetonius	" 72 — 140(?)	Lives of the Twelve Cæsars.	
Juvenal	" 40 — 120(?)	....	Satire.
Aulus Gellius	" 100 — 169(?)	Attic Nights.	
Apuleius	" 110 — 174(?)		
Ammianus Marcellinus	" 390	History.	
Claudian	" 365 — 408	....	Poems.
Macrobius	" 415	General topics.	
Boethius	" 470 — 525	Philosophic.	

FATHERS OF THE CHURCH.

ENGLISH LITERATURE AND AUTHORS.

Authors.		Principal works.		First appeared or published.
Name.	Time.	Prose.	Poetry and dramas.	
Unknown	....	....	Song of the Traveller	From the 5th to the 8th century.
"	....	....	The Fight at Fumesburg	
"	....	....	Beowulf	
Caedmon	7th century.	....	Paraphrase of the Scriptures	7th century.
Aldhelm	656-709	....	Translates Psalms into verse	8th century.
Bede, Venerable	672-735	Church Hist. of Engl. in Latin	....	731
Alcuin	735-804	Various prose works.		
Cynewulf	780	....	Two short poems.	
John Scotus, called (from his native land, Ireland) Erigena.	d. 877	Philosophic works (worthy of attention now). PHILOSOPHY.		
Alfred the Great	849-901	Translations for the people.		
Phegemund, archbishop of Canterbury, commenced them	891	Saxon Chronicles	....	From 55 B.C. continued until 1154 A.D.
Alfric, archbishop of Canterbury	d. 1006	Homilies, Latin grammar.		
William of Malmesbury	1095-1142	Hist. of Kings of Engl. (449-1120).		
Henry of Huntingdon	d. ab't 1154	Hist. of Kings of Engl. (55 B.C.-1154 A.D.).		
Geoffrey of Monmouth	d. 1154	Legendary Hist. of British Kings.		
Alfred of Rievaux	1109-66	Account of the Battle of the Standard, 1138.		
Richard Wace	1112-84	....	Brut of d'Angleterre and Romance of Rollo.	
Walter Mapes of Oxford	1150-96	Arthur's Legends.		
LAYAMON	1150-1210	....	Brut or Chronicles of Britain	1205
Orm	1187-1237	....	ORMULUM, paraphrase of Scripture	1215
Unknown	....	Ancren Riwle (the Rule of Female Anchorites, i. e., *nuns*)	....	1220
Roger Bacon	1214-94	Opus Majus (PHILOSOPHY)	....	1267
Matthew Paris	d. 1273	Historia Major.		
Unknown	....	Havelok the Dane, the Gest of King Horn, Bevis of Hampton, and Guy of Warwick	....	1280

F… LITERATURE AND AUTHORS.—(*Continued.*)

Authors.		Principal works.		First appeared or published.
Name.	Time.	Prose.	Poetry and dramas.	
Unknown	....		Willie Grice, The Owl and the Nightingale	1280
"	....		"Summer is y comen in"	13th century.
Michael of Kildare (?)	....		Land of Cockayne (Kitchen).	
Robert of Gloucester	1255–1307	Martyrdom of Thomas à Becket	Rhyming Chronicle of England	1297
Robert Manning	1273–1340		Metrical Chronicles of England	1303
Duns Scotus	1265–1308	Philosophic works.		
Richard Rolle	d. 1349		Pricke of Conscience.	
Lawrence Minot	....		War Poems of Edward III.'s time	1352
Sir John de Mandeville	1300–71	Travels		1356
William Langlande	1332–1400		Piers the Plowman	1362–78–80
John Barbour	1316–96		Bruce	1375–77
John Wycliffe	1324–84	Translation of the Bible.		
Geoffrey Chaucer ". . . The Morning Star of song who made His music heard below; Dan Chaucer, the first warbler, whose sweet breath Preluded those melodious bursts, that fill The spacious times of great Elizabeth With sounds that echo still." —*Tennyson.*	1328–1400		Canterbury Tales (25) Romaunt of the Rose The Flower and the Leaf Court of Love Cuckoo and the Nightingale Legend of Good Women. Troilus and Creseide. Assembly of Fowles, etc.	1384–98 Authorship doubtful.
John Gower	1325–1408		Speculum Meditantis. Vox Clamantis. Confessio Amantis	1483. Caxtons.
John Lydgate	1374–1460		Fall of Princes, from Boccaccio.	
James I. of Scotland	1394–1437		The King's Quair.	
Sir Thomas Malory	....	History of King Arthur		1470
Blind Harry, or "The Minstrel"	....		William Wallace	1470
Sir John Fortescue	1395–1483	On Monarchy.		
William Caxton	1412–92	Game and Play of Chesse		1474. First English printed book.
The Pastons	....	Paston Letters, correspondence		1422–1505
Stephen Hawes	1483–1512		Temple of Glass Pastime of Pleasure.	1500
Robert Henryson	d. 1500		Testament of Faire Creside. Robin and Makyne.	
Unknown	....		The Nut-Brown Maid	1500–10
William Dunbar	1460–1515		Dance of the Seven Deadly Sins.	
Gawyn Douglas	1474–1522		Palace of Honor Æneid, first translated into English verse	1501 1513
John Skelton	1460–1529		Booke of Colin Clout. Why Come Ye not to Court.	
Unknown	1450–75		Ballads: Sir Patrick Spens, Battle of Otterburne, Chevy Chase, Death of Douglas, etc.	
Sir Thomas More	1480–1535	Utopia, Life of Edward V.		
William Tyndale	1484–1536	Translation of the Bible		1525–30
Sir David Lindsay	1490–1557		The Dream The Complaint	1528 1536
Nicholas Udall	....		Ralph Royster Doyster, earliest comedy in English	1551
Hugh Latimer	1491–1555	Sermons.		
Sir Thomas Wyatt	1503–42		Sonnets and lyrics, first in England.	1557
Roger Ascham	1515–68	Toxophilus, The Schoolmaster		1544–70
Henry Howard, earl of Surrey	1516–47		Sonnets and lyrics	1557
Miles Coverdale	....	Translation of the Bible		1520–30
John Foxe	1517–87	Book of Martyrs		1563
John Jewel	1522–71	Apology.		
Ralph Holinshed	d. 1580	Chronicles		1578
John Still, bishop of Bath	1543–1607		Gammer Gurton's Needle.	
William Byrd	1543–1623		My Mind to Me a Kingdom is.	
Lord Berners	....	Translates Chronicles of Froissart.		
Thomas Wilson	d. 1581	Rhetoric and Logic		1553
Sir Walter Raleigh	1552–1618	History of the World		1614
Thomas Sackville	1536–1608		Gorboduc, first English tragedy Mirror for Magistrates.	1562
Edmund Spenser	1552–99		Faerie Queene The Shepard Calendar	1590–96 1579
Sir Philip Sidney	1554–86	Arcadia.	Astrophel and Stella, sonnets.	
Richard Hooker	1553–1600	Laws of Ecclesiastical Polity		1594–1600
John Lyly	1554–1606	Euphues		1579–80
Thomas Lodge	1556–1625		Rosalind, Euphues' Golden Legacy	1590
Francis Bacon	1561–1626	Essays Novum Organum (PHILOSOPHY)		1597–1624 1620
Samuel Daniel	1562–1619		Sonnets Complaint of Rosamond	1592 1594
Michael Drayton	1563–1631		Polyolbion, The Baron's Wars, Court of Fairy, etc.	
Sir John Davies	1570–1626		Nosce Teipsum	1599
George Peele	1552–98		Arraignment of Paris Love of King David and Fair Bethsabe.	1584
Robert Greene	1560–92		Looking-Glass for London and England.	
Christopher Marlowe	1564–93		Tamburlaine, Faustus, Jew of Malta, Edward II.	
William Shakespeare	1564–1616		Thirty-seven plays, etc. SHAKESPEARE AND HIS PLAYS.	
Thomas Nash	1567–1600		Summer's Last Will and Testament.	
George Chapman	1557–1634		Ovid's Banquet of Sense Translation of Homer.	1595
Thomas Middleton	1570–1627		The Witch and other plays.	

ENGLISH LITERATURE AND AUTHORS.—(*Continued.*)

Authors.		Principal works.		First appeared or published.
Name.	Time.	Prose.	Poetry and dramas.	
John Donne	1573–1631	Biathanatos	An Anatomy of the World	1625
Ben Jonson	1574–1637		Volpone the Fox	1605
			Every Man in his Humor	1595
			The Silent Woman	1609
			The Alchemist	1610
			Sad Shepherd, etc.	
Joseph Hall	1574–1656	Epistles, Contemplation	Satires	1597
Thomas Dekker	1576–1641			
John Fletcher	1576–1625		The Faithful Shepherdess, The Woman-hater.	
Robert Burton	1576–1640	Anatomy of Melancholy		1621
Philip Massinger	1584–1640		The Virgin Martyr	1622
			New Way to Pay Old Debts	1623
John Selden	1584–1654	Table-Talk, Titles of Honor		1614
John Marston	d. 1634		Satire (1593), The Malcontent	1604
William Drummond	1584–1649		The Flowers of Zion	1623
John Ford	1586–1639		The Lover's Melancholy	1629
			" Broken Heart	1633
			Perkin Warbeck	1634
Sir Henry Wotton	1568–1639		Farewell to the Vanities of the World.	
Francis Beaumont	1586–1616		The Maid's Tragedy	1609
			Philaster	1610
			Knight of the Burning Pestle	"
Thomas Heywood	d. 1648		A Woman Killed by Kindness	1617
John Webster	d. 1654		The White Devil	1612
			Duchess of Malfi	1623
			The Devil's Law-case, etc.	"
George Withers	1588–1667		Faire Virtue, etc.	1613
Thomas Carew	1589–1639		"He that loves a rosy cheek." "Sweetly breathing vernal air," etc.	
Thomas Hobbes	1588–1679	Leviathan, Philosophic (PHILOSOPHY)		1651
Robert Herrick	1591–1674		Hesperides and numerous other poems.	1648
Henry King, bishop of Chichester	1591–1669		Exequy on his wife.	
Francis Quarles	1592–1644		A Feast for Worms	1620
			Vanity of the World, etc.	
George Herbert	1593–1633		The Temple and other poems	1631
Izaak Walton	1593–1683	The Complete Angler		1653–55
James Shirley	1594–1666		The Traitor	1635
			The Lady of Pleasure	"
William Chillingworth	1602–44	The Religion of Protestants, a Safe Way to Salvation.		
Sir Thomas Browne	1605–82	Religio Medici		1643
		Hydriotaphia		1658
Sir William Davenant	1605–68		Gondibert	1651
Edmund Waller	1605–87		Go Lovely Rose, To Chloris, etc.	
Thomas Fuller	1608–61	Church History of England		1656
		Worthies of England		1662
JOHN MILTON	1608–74	Areopagitica	Comus (1634), Lycidas	1637
			Paradise Lost	1658–65
			Paradise Regained.	
			Samson Agonistes	1671
			L'Allegro and Il Penseroso, etc.	
Lord Clarendon	1608–74	History of the Rebellion		1702
Sir John Suckling	1609–41		The Bride.	
			Tell Me, ye Juster Duties.	
Jeremy Taylor	1613–67	Holy Living and Holy Dying.		
Sir John Denham	1615–68		Cooper Hill	1643
Sir Richard Lovelace	1618–58		To Althea from Prison	1649
Abraham Cowley	1618–67		Pindaric Odes	1656
			The Chronicle.	
George Fox	1624–90	Journal.		
Samuel Butler	1612–80		Hudibras	1663
Richard Baxter	1615–91	Saint's Everlasting Rest		1649
		A Call to the Unconverted		1659
Ralph Cudworth	1617–88	The True Intellectual System of the Universe		1678
Andrew Marvell	1620–78		Death of the White Fawn.	
John Evelyn	1620–1706	Diary.		
John Bunyan	1628–88	Pilgrim's Progress		1678
		Holy War.		
Sir William Temple	1628–98	Essays.		
John Tillotson	1630–94	Sermons.		
Isaac Barrow	1630–77	Sermons.		
John Dryden	1631–1700		Duke of Guise	1662
			Absalom and Achitophel	1681
			Hind and Panther	1687
			Virgil translated, St. Cecilia's Day, Alexander's Feast.	
Samuel Pepys	1632–1703	Diary		1660–69
John Locke	1632–1704	Essay on the Human Understanding (PHILOSOPHY)		1690
Sir Isaac Newton	1642–1727	Principia, etc.		1687
Gilbert Burnet	1643–1715	History of the Reformation		1679
		History of My Own Times.		
Sir George Etherege	1635–94		Man of Mode	1676
William Wycherly	1640–1715		Country Wife	1672
			Plain Dealer.	
Jeremy Collier	1650–1726	Sermons.		
Thomas Otway	1651–85		The Orphan.	
			Venice Preserved	1682
Sir John Vanbrugh	1666–1726		The Confederacy.	
			The Provoked Wife	1698
William Congreve	1670–1729		Love for Love	1695
			The Mourning Bride	1697
Nicholas Rowe	1673–1718		Jane Shore, The Fair Penitent.	
George Farquhar	1678–1708		The Recruiting Officer.	
			The Beaux' Stratagem	1707
Daniel Defoe	1661–1731	Robinson Crusoe		1719

ENGLISH LITERATURE AND AUTHORS.—(*Continued.*)

Authors. Name.	Time.	Principal works. Prose.	Poetry and dramas.	First appeared or published.
Daniel Defoe	1661–1731	Journal of the Plague		1722
Richard Bentley	1662–1742	Dissertations (2) upon the Epistles of Phalaris		1697–99
Matthew Prior	1664–1721		Alma.	
Jonathan Swift	1667–1745	Tale of a Tub		1704
		Gulliver's Travels		1726
		Journal to Stella.		
Bernard Mandeville	1670–1733	Fable of the Bees, Philosophic.		
Sir Richard Steele	1671–1729	Essays; establishes *The Tatler*		1709
Joseph Addison	1672–1719	Essays for the *Tatler*, *Spectator*, *Guardian*	Cato	1713
			Minor poems.	
Bishop Berkeley	1684–1753	Metaphysical and scientific. PHILOSOPHY.		
Edward Young	1684–1765		Night Thoughts	1742–46
Allan Ramsay	1686–1758		The Gentle Shepherd	1725
Samuel Richardson	1689–1761	Pamela		1741
		Clarissa Harlowe		1749
		Sir Charles Grandison		1753
John Gay	1688–1732		The Shepherd's Week	1714
			The Beggar's Opera	1726
			Fables, Songs.	
Alexander Pope	1688–1744		Essay on Criticism	1711
			Rape of the Lock	1712
			January and May, and transl. Homer	1715
			Dunciad	1728
			Essay on Man, etc.	1733
Lady Mary Montagu	1690–1762	Letters.		
Joseph Butler (bishop)	1692–1752	Analogy between Natural and Revealed Religion		1736
Henry Carey	1700–43		Sally in our Alley, etc.	
James Thomson	1700–48		The Seasons	1726–30
			Castle of Indolence	1748
William Hamilton	1704–54		Braes of Yarrow.	
Henry Fielding	1707–54	Joseph Andrews		1742
		History of Jonathan Wild		1743
		Tom Jones		1749
		Amelia.		
Samuel Johnson	1709–1784	Essays for the *Idler* and *Rambler*.		
			Vanity of Human Wishes	1749
		Dictionary of English Language		1755
		Rasselas		1759
		Lives of the Poets		1781
Thomas Reid	1710–96	Inquiry into the Human Mind, etc. (PHILOSOPHY)		1764
David Hume	1711–76	Philosophic. PHILOSOPHY.		
		History of England		1754–62
Laurence Sterne	1713–68	Tristram Shandy		1761
		Sentimental Journey.		
Thomas Gray	1716–71		Elegy in a Country Church-yard	1750
			Ode on a Distant Prospect of Eton College, etc.	1747
Gilbert White	1720–93	The Natural History of Selborne.		
Tobias George Smollett	1721–71	Roderick Random		1748
		Peregrine Pickle		1751
		Ferdinand Count Fathom		1753
		Humphry Clinker, etc.		
William Collins	1721–56		The Passions	1747
			How Sleep the Brave	″
			Ode to Evening, etc.	
Mark Akenside	1721–70		Pleasures of the Imagination	1744
William Robertson	1721–93	History of Scotland		1759
		″ ″ Reign of Charles V		1769
		″ ″ Discovery of America		1777
Adam Smith	1723–90	Wealth of Nations		1776
Oliver Goldsmith	1728–74		The Traveller	1764
		Vicar of Wakefield	The Hermit	1766
			Good-natured Man	1768
			Deserted Village	1770
			She Stoops to Conquer	1773
		Essays.		
Sir William Blackstone	1723–80	Commentaries on the Laws of England		1765
Jane Elliot	1727–1805		The Flowers of the Forest (a lament for Flodden).	
Bishop Percy	1728–1811		Ballads.	
			Reliques of Ancient Engl. Poetry.	1765
Edmund Burke	1730–97	Essay on the Sublime and Beautiful		1756
		Reflections on the French Revolution		1790
William Cowper	1731–1800		The Task	1785
			John Gilpin	″
			The Castaway.	
			On Receiving My Mother's Picture, etc.	
James Beattie	1735–1803		The Minstrel	1771
Edward Gibbon	1737–94	Decline and Fall of the Roman Empire		1776–88
James Macpherson	1738–96		Ossian: Fingal	1762
			Ossian: Temora	″
Augustus Montague Toplady	1740–78		"Rock of Ages," etc.	1776
James Boswell	1740–95	Biography of Samuel Johnson.		
Arthur Young	1741–1820	Travels in France		1792
William Paley	1743–1805	Evidences of Christianity		1794
		Natural Theology		1802
Hannah More	1745–1833		Percy	1777
			Sacred Dramas	1786
		Cœlebs in Search of a Wife		1809
		Moral Sketches		1818
Mrs. Anna Letitia Barbauld	1743–18[illegible]	Hymns in Prose	Miscellaneous Poems.	
			The Death of the Righteous.	

ENGLISH LITERATURE AND AUTHORS.—(*Continued.*)

Authors.		Principal works.		First appeared or published.
Name.	Time.	Prose.	Poetry and dramas.	
William Coxe	1747–1828	History of the House of Austria		1807
		Memoirs of the Kings of Spain of the House of Bourbon		1813
Jeremy Bentham	1748–1832	Philosophic, utilitarian.		
Thomas Chatterton	1752–70		Poems (antique).	
Richard Brinsley Sheridan	1751–1816	Speeches, SHERIDAN'S BEGUM SPEECH	The Rivals, School for Scandal, Duenna (opera), Critic, Songs.	
Frances Burney	1752–1840	Evelina		1778
Dugald Stewart	1753–1828	Metaphysician: Elements of the Philosophy of the Human Mind		1792
		Philosophical Essays		1810
George Crabbe	1754–1832		The Village	1783
			Tales in Verse	1812
			Tales of the Hall	1819
William Godwin	1756–1836	Caleb Williams		1794
		St. Leon		1799
William Blake	1757–1827		Songs of Innocence	1789
			Songs of Experience	1794
William Beckford	1759–1844	Vathek.		
Robert Burns	1759–96		Tam O'Shanter, Jolly Beggars.	
			The Twa Dogs	1786
			Halloween, Cotter's Saturday Night, Epistle to Davie, Highland Mary, Afton Water, To Mary in Heaven, etc.	
Joanna Baillie	1762–1851		Plays on the Passions	1798–1802
			Poems	1841
William Cobbett	1762–1835	English Grammar and Essays.		
Samuel Rogers	1763–1855		Pleasures of Memory	1792
			Human Life	1819
			Italy	1822
Ann Radcliffe	1764–1823	Romance of the Forest, Mysteries of Udolpho.		
Isaac D'Israeli	1766–1848	Curiosities of Literature		1791
		Amenities of Literature		1841
Maria Edgeworth	1767–1849	Castle Rackrent		1800
		Popular Tales		1804
		Fashionable Tales		1812
		Helen, etc.		
William Wordsworth	1770–1850		Lyrical Ballads	1798
			The Excursion	1814
			The White Doe of Rylstone	1815
			Peter Bell and The Waggoner	1819
			The Prelude, etc.	1850
James Hogg (Ettrick Shepherd)	1770–1835	The Shepherd's Calendar	The Queen's Wake	1813
		Winter Evening Tales	Kilmeny.	
James Montgomery	1771–1854		The Pelican Island	1827
			"There is a calm for those who weep."	
			"Make way for liberty," etc.	
Sir Walter Scott	1771–1832		Lay of the Last Minstrel	1805
			Marmion	1808
			Lady of the Lake	1810
			Rokeby	1813
			Bridal of Triermain, etc.	"
		Waverley (Chaps. i.–vii. were written and the whole work announced for publication as early as 1805.)		1814
		Guy Mannering		1815
		Antiquary, Black Dwarf, Old Mortality		1816
		Rob Roy, Heart of Midlothian		1818
		Bride of Lammermoor and Legend of Montrose		1819
		Ivanhoe, Monastery, and Abbot		1820
		Kenilworth		1821
		Pirate, Fortunes of Nigel		1822
		Peveril of the Peak, Quentin Durward		1823
		St. Ronan's Well, Redgauntlet		1824
		The Betrothed, Talisman		1825
		Woodstock		1826
		Two Drovers, Highland Widow, Surgeon's Daughter		1827
		Fair Maid of Perth		1828
		Anne of Geierstein		1829
		Count Robert of Paris, Castle Dangerous		1831
John Lingard	1771–1859	History of England		1819–30
Sidney Smith	1771–1845	Sermons and Essays.		
David Ricardo	1772–1823	Principles of Political Economy		1817
Samuel Taylor Coleridge	1772–1834	Essays, lectures, etc.	Christabel	1797
			Ancient Mariner	1798
			Youth and Age, etc.	1827
Robert Southey	1774–1843	Lives of Nelson, Wesley, etc.	Joan of Arc	1795
			Thalaba	1801
			Madoc	1805
			Curse of Kehama	1810
			Roderick, Last of the Goths	1814
Charles Lamb	1775–1834	Essays of Elia, etc.		1823
Walter Savage Landor	1775–1864	Imaginary Conversations		1824–29
Jane Austen	1775–1817	Sense and Sensibility		1811
		Pride and Prejudice		1813
		Mansfield Park		1814
		Emma		1816
Jane Porter	1776–1850	Thaddeus of Warsaw		1803
		Scottish Chiefs		1809

ENGLISH LITERATURE AND AUT .ORS.—(*Continued.*)

Authors.		Principal works.		First appeared or published.
Name.	Time.	Prose.	Poetry and dramas.	
Thomas Campbell	1777–1844		Pleasures of Hope	1799
			Gertrude of Wyoming	1809
			Lyrics: Battle of the Baltic, Hohenlinden, Ye Mariners of England, Lord Ullin's Daughter, Exile of Erin, Soldier's Dream, Lochiel's Warning, etc.	
Henry Hallam	1777–1859	Europe During the Middle Ages		1818
		Constitutional History of Engl.		1827
		Introduction to the Literature of Europe		1839
William Hazlitt	1778–1830	Character of Shakespeare's Plays		1817
		English Poets		1818
		Table Talk		1821
		Plain Speaker		1826
		Life of Napoleon, etc		1830
Thomas Moore	1779–1852		Irish Melodies	1813
			The Minstrel Boy, Those Evening Bells, Love's Young Dream, "Believe me, if all those endearing young charms," "Come, rest in this bosom," "Go where glory waits thee," "The harp that once through Tara's halls," "Oft in the stilly night," The Origin of the Harp, "'Tis the last rose of summer," The Meeting of the Waters, "She is far from the land," "I saw from the beach," etc.	
			Lalla Rookh	1817
		Life of Byron		1830
Horace Smith	1779–1849		Address to a Mummy.	
George Croly	1780–1860	Salathiel, etc.	Catiline	1827
Thomas De Quincey	1785–1859	Confessions of an English Opium Eater		1821; 1st edition of works, 1856–60
		Flight of a Tartar Tribe, Household Wreck, Klosterheim.		
		Three Memorable Murders.		
		Historical Essays, Narratives, etc.		
James Henry Leigh Hunt	1784–1859		Story of Rimini	1816
			Abou ben-Adhem and other poems.	
		Men, Women, and Books		1847
		Essays, etc.		
James Sheridan Knowles	1784–1862		Virginius	1820
			William Tell	1825
			The Hunchback, etc.	1832
Sir William Napier	1785–1860	Hist. of the War in the Peninsula		1828–40
John Wilson (Christopher North)	1785–1854	Lights and Shadows of Scottish Life	Isle of Palms	1812
			City of the Plague	1816
		Trials of Margaret Lindsay	Miscellaneous.	
		The Forresters, Noctes Ambrosianæ.		
Henry Kirke White	1785–1806		Clifton Grove	1803
			"I am pleased and yet I'm sad," To an Early Primrose, etc.	
George Gordon, Lord Byron	1788–1824		Hours of Idleness	1807
			Childe Harold's Pilgrimage	1812–17
			Giaour, Bride of Abydos	1813
			Corsair, Lara	1814
			Siege of Corinth, Parisina	1815
			Prisoner of Chillon	1817
			Mazeppa	1819
			Don Juan	1818–24
			Manfred	1817
			Marino Faliero; Sardanapalus; Two Foscari; Werner; Cain; The Deformed Transformed, etc.	1818–21
Sir William Hamilton	1788–1856	Philosophy of the Unconditioned (PHILOSOPHY)		1829
		Edition of Reid's Works		1846
		Discussions in Philosophy, Literature, and Education, etc.		1852–53
Richard Harris Barham (Thomas Ingoldsby)	1788–1845		The Ingoldsby Legends	1837–45
Mary Russell Mitford	1789–1855	Our Village		1824–32
			Rienzi	1828
Rev. Charles Wolfe	1791–1823		Burial of Sir John Moore	1817
Michael Scott	1789–1835	Tom Cringle's Log		1830
		The Cruise of the *Midge*		1834
Percy Bysshe Shelley	1792–1822		Queen Mab	1813
			Alastor, or the Spirit of Solitude.	1816
			Revolt of Islam	1817
			Witch of Atlas.	
			Prometheus Unbound	1819
			The Cenci	"
			Adonais	1821
			Rosalind and Helen.	
			Ode to a Skylark.	
			The Sensitive Plant, etc.	
Henry Hart Milman (dean)	1791–1868		The Italian Wife	1816
		History of Latin Christianity		1855
		Edits Gibbon's works.		
Charles Knight	1791–1873	History of England		1862

ENGLISH LITERATURE AND AUTHORS.—(*Continued.*)

Authors.		Principal works.		First appeared or published
Name.	Time.	Prose.	Poetry and dramas.	
Patrick Fraser Tytler	1791–1849	History of Scotland.		
Capt. Frederick Marryat	1792–1848	Peter Simple, Jacob Faithful, The Pacha of Many Tales, Japhet in Search of a Father, Midshipman Easy, Pirate and Three Cutters, Snarly-yow, or the Dog-Fiend, King's Own.		1830–39
		The Phantom Ship		1839
		Poor Jack		1840
		Masterman Ready, and others		1841
Sir Archibald Alison	1792–1867	History of Europe		1839–42 1852–57
Felicia Hemans	1793–1835		Lyrics: Treasures of the Deep, The Better Land, Homes of England, Landing of the Pilgrims, Casabianca, The Voice of Spring, The Traveller at the Source of the Nile, etc.	
George Grote	1794–1871	History of Greece		1845–56
Thomas Arnold	1795–1842	History of Rome, Sermons and Essays.		
Thomas Carlyle	1795–1881	Sartor Resartus		1834
		French Revolution		1837
		Heroes and Hero Worship		1840
		Cromwell		1845
		Frederick the Great		1865
		Essays, etc.		
John Keats	1796–1821		Endymion	1818
			Hyperion, Eve of St. Agnes, Lamia, Ode to a Nightingale, etc.	1820
Agnes Strickland	1796–1874	Lives of the Queens of England		1840–48
William Motherwell	1797–1835	Minstrelsy, ancient and modern	Poems	1827
Anna Jameson	1794–1860	Characteristics of Shakespeare's Women, etc.		1832
Samuel Lover	1797–1868	Rory O'More		1837
			Songs and Ballads	1839
		Handy Andy, etc.		1842
Robert Pollok	1799–1827		Course of Time	1827
Thomas Hood	1798–1845		Plea of the Midsummer Fairies, Hero and Leander, Miss Kilmansegg, Bridge of Sighs, Song of the Shirt, Eugene Aram, Tale of a Trumpet, etc.	
Thomas B. Macaulay	1800–59	Essays		1825–44
			Lays of Ancient Rome	1842
		History of England		1849–55
			Battle of Ivry, etc.	
George Payne Raynsford James	1801–60	Richelieu		1829
		Philip Augustus		1831
		Agincourt		1844
		Agnes Sorel		1853
		Lord Montagu's Page, etc.		1858
Hugh Miller	1802–56	Old Red Sandstone		1841
		Footprints of the Creator		1850
		My Schools and School-masters		1854
Harriet Martineau	1802–76	Illustrations of Political Economy		1831
		Society in America, Deerbrook.		
		The Hour and the Man		1844
		History of Thirty Years' Peace		1849
Francis Mahony (Father Prout)	1804–66		Bells of Shandon, etc.	
Sir Edward Bulwer Lytton	1805–73	Pelham		1828
		Paul Clifford		1830
		Last Days of Pompeii		1834
		Rienzi		1835
		Ernest Maltravers		1837
		Lady of Lyons, Richelieu, Money.		1838–40
		Zanoni		1842
		Last of the Barons	The New Timon	1843
				1846
		Caxtons		1848
		My Novel		1853
		What Will He Do With It?		1858
		A Strange Story		1862
		The Parisians		1873
Benjamin Disraeli (lord Beaconsfield)	1805–81	Vivian Grey		1827
		Contarini Fleming		1833
		Henrietta Temple		1836
		Coningsby		1844
		Sybil		1845
		Tancred		1847
		Lothair		1871
		Endymion		1880
John Stuart Mill	1806–73	System of Logic		1843
		Political Economy		1848
		Utilitarianism, etc.		1861
Charles Lever	1806–72	Harry Lorrequer		1837
		Charles O'Malley, Jack Hinton.		
		Tom Burke of "Ours"		1844
		The O'Donoghue, Knight of Gwynne, That Boy of Norcott's, Davenport Dunn.		
		Lord Kilgobbin		1872
		A Day's Ride, etc.		"
Samuel Warren	1807–77	Diary of a Physician		1830–31
		Ten Thousand a Year		1839–41

ENGLISH LITERATURE AND AUTHORS.—(*Continued.*)

Authors.		Principal works.		First appeared or published.
Name.	Time.	Prose.	Poetry and dramas.	
arles Darwin	1809–82	The Origin of Species		1859
		The Descent of Man		1871
izabeth Barrett Browning	1809–61		Aurora Leigh	1856
			Lady Geraldine's Courtship, Rime of the Duchess May, The Cry of the Children, Casa Guidi Windows, etc.	
fred Tennyson	1809–92		The Deserted House, Recollections of the Arabian Nights, Isabel, Mariana, Sea Fairies, and other poems	1830
			Dream of Fair Women, The Lotos-Eaters, The Miller's Daughter, Death of the Old Year, Lady Clara Vere de Vere, May Queen, Œnone, Lady of Shalott, and other poems	1832
			Morte d'Arthur, Dora, Edwin Morris, The Talking Oak, Ulysses, Locksley Hall, The Two Voices, Will Waterproof's Lyrical Monologue, St. Agnes, Lord of Burleigh, Vision of Sin, and other poems	1842
			The Princess	1847
			In Memoriam	1850
			Ode on Death of Wellington	1852
			Maud, and other poems	1855
			Idyls of the King	1859–72
			The Coming of Arthur, Gareth and Lynette, Geraint and Enid, Merlin and Vivien, Lancelot and Elaine, The Holy Grail, Pelleas and Ettarre, The Last Tournament, Guinevere, The Passing of Arthur.	
			Queen Mary (drama)	1875
			Harold (drama)	1877
			Becket (drama)	1884
			Demeter, and other poems, etc.	1890
ary Cowden-Clarke	1809–	A Concordance to Shakespeare		1845
exander William Kinglake	1811–90	Eōthen		1844
		History of the Crimean War		1863–87
illiam Makepeace Thackeray	1811–63	Vanity Fair		1846–48
		The History of Pendennis		1850
		The History of Henry Esmond, Esq		1852
		The English Humorists		1851
		The Newcomes		1855
		The Book of Snobs		1848
		The Virginians		1858
		Lovel the Widower		1860
		The Four Georges		"
		The Adventures of Philip		1862
		Denis Duval, etc		1864
artin Farquhar Tupper	1810–89		Ballads.	
			Proverbial Philosophy	1839–44
arles Dickens	1812–70	Sketches by Boz		1835
		Pickwick		1837
		Oliver Twist		1838
		Nicholas Nickleby		1839
		Master Humphrey's Clock		1840
		The Old Curiosity Shop		"
		Barnaby Rudge		"
		American Notes		1842
		Christmas Stories		1843
		Martin Chuzzlewit		1844
		The Chimes		"
		The Cricket on the Hearth		1845
		Dombey and Son		1848
		David Copperfield		1850
		Bleak House		1853
		Little Dorrit		1857
		A Tale of Two Cities		1859
		The Uncommercial Traveller		1860
		Great Expectations		1861
		Our Mutual Friend		1865
		The Mystery of Edwin Drood		1870
obert Browning	1812–89		Paracelsus	1835
			Pippa Passes	1841
			Dramatic Lyrics	1842
			Return of the Druses	1843
			A Blot in the 'Scutcheon	"
			Bells and Pomegranates	1846
			The Ring and the Book	1868–69
			Fifine, etc	1872
thur Helps	1813–75	Friends in Council		1847
		Life of Las Casas		1868
		" Columbus		1869
		" Pizarro		"
		" Cortez		1871
arles Reade	1814–84	Peg Woffington		1852
		It is Never Too Late to Mend		1856
		White Lies		1857
		The Cloister and the Hearth		1861
		Very Hard Cash		1863

ENGLISH LITERATURE AND AUTHORS.—(*Continued.*)

Authors. Name.	Time.	Principal works. Prose.	Poetry and dramas.	First appeared or published.
Charles Reade	1814–84	Griffith Gaunt		1866
		Put Yourself in His Place		1870
		A Terrible Temptation, etc.		1871
George Rawlinson	1815–	Five Great Monarchies, etc.		1862–67
Anthony Trollope	1815–82	The Warden		1855
		Barchester Towers		1857
		The Bertrams		1859
		Castle Richmond		1860
		Orley Farm		1861
		The Small House at Allington		1864
		Can You Forgive Her?		1865
		The Claverings		1867
		Phineas Finn		1869
		He Knew He Was Right		"
		The American Senator, and many others		1877
Samuel Smiles	1816–	Life of George Stephenson		1857
		Self-Help, etc.		1859
George Henry Lewes	1817–78	History of Philosophy		1845–67
		Problems of Life and Mind		1874–78
James Anthony Froude	1818–94	History of England from the Fall of Wolsey to the Armada		1856–70
		Cæsar, a Sketch		1879
		Thomas Carlyle, etc.		1882–84
Charles Kingsley	1819–75	Alton Locke		1849
		Yeast		"
		Hypatia		1853
		Westward Ho!		1855
		Two Years Ago		1857
			Andromeda, and other poems	1858
		Hereward the Wake		1866
		At Last. Sermons, etc.		
John Ruskin	1819–	Modern Painters		1843–60
		Stones of Venice		1850–53
		King of the Golden River		1851
		Unto this Last		1862
		Ethics of the Dust		1865
		Sesame and Lilies		"
		Crown of Wild Olive		1866
		Queen of the Air		"
		Munera Pulveris		1872
		Fiction Fair and Foul, etc.		1881
Herbert Spencer	1820–	A System of Philosophy. Programme issued		1860
		First Principles		1862
		Principles of Biology		1863
		" Psychology		1870–72
		" Sociology		1877
		" Morality		1879
		Essays, etc.		
George Eliot (Marian Evans Lewes)	1819–80	Adam Bede		1859
		Mill on the Floss		1860
		Silas Marner		1861
		Romola		1863
		Felix Holt		1866
			Spanish Gypsy	1868
		Middlemarch		1872
			Legend of Jubal	1874
		Daniel Deronda		1876
		Impressions of Theophrastus Such		1880
John Tyndall	1820–93	Heat as a Mode of Motion, and other scientific papers.		
Henry Thomas Buckle	1821–62	History of Civilization in England		1857–61
Matthew Arnold—poet, critic, essayist	1822–88		Alaric at Rome	1840
			Empedocles on Etna	1853
		Essays in Criticism		1865
		Culture and Anarchy		1869
		Literature and Dogma		1873
		God and the Bible, etc.		1875
Frederick Max Müller	1823–	Essays on Comparative Mythology		1858
		Science of Language		1861–64
		Chips from a German Workshop		1868–75
		Sacred Books of the East		1875–85
Edward A. Freeman	1823–92	History of the Norman Conquest		1867–79
		Ottoman Power in Europe		1877
		Reign of William Rufus		1882
		Historical Geog. of Europe, etc.		1881
Thomas Hughes	1823–	Tom Brown's School Days		1857
		Tom Brown at Oxford		1861
		Essays, etc.		
Wm. Wilkie Collins	1824–89	Queen of Hearts		1859
		Woman in White		1860
		No Name		1862
		The Moonstone		1868
		The New Magdalen, etc.		1873
Charlotte Brontë (Currer Bell)	1816–55	Jane Eyre		1847
		Shirley		1849
		Villette		1853
		Professor (the first written)		1856
Emily Brontë (Ellis Bell)	1818–48	Wuthering Heights		1847
Anna Brontë (Acton Bell)	1820–49	Tenant of Wildfell Hall		1848
George MacDonald	1824–	Phantastes		1858
		David Elginbrod		1862
		Alec Forbes of How Glen		1865
		Annals of a Quiet Neighborhood		1866
		Robert Falconer		1868
		Wilfred Cumbermede		1871

ENGLISH LITERATURE AND AUTHORS.—(*Continued.*)

Authors.		Principal works.		First appeared or published.
Name.	Time.	Prose.	Poetry and dramas.	
George MacDonald	1824–	Sir Gibbie, etc.		1879
Thomas Henry Huxley	1825–	Man's Place in Nature		1863
		Protoplasm the Basis of Life		1869
		Lay Sermons, etc.		1870
Richard D. Blackmore	1825–	Lorna Doone		1866
		The Maid of Sker		1872
		Alice Lorraine		1876
		Springhaven, etc.		1887
Dinah Maria Mulock (Mrs. Craik)	1826–87	John Halifax, Gentleman		1856
		A Life for a Life		1860
		A Noble Life, etc.		1861
Dante Gabriel Rossetti	1828–82		The Early Italian Poets	
			The Blessed Damozel, The White Ship, The King's Tragedy, Rose Mary, Troy Town, Sister Helen.	
			The House of Life	1870–81
Samuel R. Gardiner	1829–	The Thirty Years' War		1874
		History of England from James I. to the Civil War, etc.		1886
Justin McCarthy	1830–	My Enemy's Daughter		1869
		A Fair Saxon		1873
		Dear Lady Disdain		1875
		A History of Our Own Times, etc.		1880
Jean Ingelow	1830–		High Tide on the Coast of Lincolnshire, Divided, Songs of Seven, Songs of the Night Watches.	
			Story of Doom, and other poems	1867
			Winstanley, etc.	
		Off the Skelligs		1872
		Fated to be Free		1879
Edward Robert, lord Lytton (Owen Meredith)	1831–91		Lucile	1860
		Biography of his father, Bulwer-Lytton		1883
			Glenaveril	1885
Edmund H. Yates	1831–94	Running the Gauntlet		1865
		Kissing the Rod		1866
		Black Sheep, etc.		1867
Edwin Arnold	1832–		Light of Asia.	
			Potiphar's Wife, and other poems.	1892
John Robert Seeley	1834–	Ecce Homo		1866
		Life and Times of Stein		1879
		Natural Religion		1882
William Morris	1834–		Life and Death of Jason	1867
			Earthly Paradise	1868–70
			Story of Sigurd the Volsung and the Fall of the Niblung	1876
Philip G. Hamerton	1834–94	Etchings and Etchers		1868
		Intellectual Life, etc.		1873
George du Maurier	1834–	Peter Ibbetson		1892
		Trilby		1894
John Richard Green	1837–83	History of the English People		1875–80
		The Making of England, etc.		1881
Algernon Charles Swinburne	1837–		Atalanta in Calydon	1865
			Poems and Ballads	1866
		William Blake		1867
			Bothwell, a Tragedy	1874
			Songs of the Spring-tides	1880
			Mary Stuart	1881
			Tristram of Lyonesse, and other poems	1882
			Marino Faliero	1885
			Locrine	1887
James Bryce	1838–	The Holy Roman Empire		1864
		The American Commonwealth		1888
Walter Besant	1838–	Ready Money Mortiboy (with Jas. Rice)		1871
		My Little Girl		1873
		The Golden Butterfly, etc.		1876
		All Sorts and Conditions of Men		1882
		Dorothy Foster		1884
		The World Went Very Well Then		1887
		Fifty Years Ago		1888
		For Faith and Freedom, etc.		"
John Morley	1838–	Critical Miscellanies		1871
		Voltaire		"
		Rousseau		1873
		Burke		1879
		Cobden		1881
		Edits English Men of Letters.		
William E. H. Lecky	1838–	History of the Rise and Influence of Rationalism in Europe		1865
		History of European Morals from Augustus to Charlemagne		1875
		History of England in the 18th Century		1878–90
Thomas Hardy	1840–	Under the Greenwood Tree		1872
		A Pair of Blue Eyes		1873
		Far from the Madding Crowd		1874
		The Return of the Native		1878
		The Mayor of Casterbridge		1886
		Tess of the D'Urbervilles, etc.		1892
William Black	1841–	In Silk Attire		1869
		A Daughter of Heth		1871
		Strange Adventures of a Phaeton		1872
		A Princess of Thule		1873
		That Beautiful Wretch		1881

ENGLISH LITERATURE AND AUTHORS.—(*Continued.*)

Authors.		Principal works.		First appeared or published.
Name.	Time.	Prose.	Poetry and dramas.	
William Black	1841–	The Strange Adventures of a House-boat		1888
		In Far Lochaber, etc.		"
Robert William Buchanan	1841–		London Poems	1866
			Balder the Beautiful	1877
			Ballads of Life, Love, and Humor.	1882
		Alone in London		1885
		The Heir of Linne		1887
Robert Louis Balfour Stevenson	1850–95	The New Arabian Nights		1882
		The Strange Case of Dr. Jekyll and Mr. Hyde		1886
		Kidnapped		"
		The Merry Men		1887
		The Black Arrow		1888
		Master of Ballantrae, etc.		1889
Henry Rider Haggard	1856–	Dawn		1884
		The Witch's Head		"
		King Solomon's Mines		1885
		She		1887
		Maiwa's Revenge, etc.		1888
Rudyard Kipling	1865–	Plain Tales from the Hills		"
		Soldiers Three		1889
		Story of Gadsby		
		The Phantom Rickshaw, and Other Eerie Tales, etc.		"
			Ballads and Barrack-room Ballads	1892

ENGLISH (AMERICAN) LITERATURE AND AUTHORS.

Authors.		Principal works.		First appeared or published.
Name.	Time.	Prose.	Poetry and dramas.	
Jonathan Edwards	1703–58	Freedom of the Will		1754
		Original Sin		1757
		Sermons, etc.		
Benjamin Franklin	1706–90	Poor Richard's Almanac		1731
		Autobiography, essays, scientific papers, etc.		
Thomas Hutchinson	1711–80	History of the Province of Massachusetts		1764–67
Francis Hopkinson	1738–91		BATTLE OF THE KEGS	1778
Hugh Henry Brackenridge	1748–1816		Rising Glory of America	1774
		Modern Chivalry; or, The Adventures of Capt. Farrago, etc.		1796
John Trumbull	1750–1831		McFingal	1775–82
Phillis Wheatley (negress), b. Africa.	1753 (?)–94		Poems.	
Joel Barlow	1755–1812		The Vision of Columbus.	1787
			Hasty Pudding.	
			The Columbiad.	1807
Noah Webster	1758–1843	American Spelling Book		1783
		Dictionary of Engl. Language, 1st ed.		1828
		Same, 2d ed., etc.		1840
Susanna Rowson (b. Portsmouth, Engl.; d. Boston, Mass.)	1762–1824	Charlotte Temple, etc.		Eng. 1790 (?)
Alexander Wilson (b. Scotland; d. Phila.)	1766–1813	American Ornithology.		1808–16
		(Continued and finished by Charles Lucien Bonaparte).		1825–33
Joseph Hopkinson	1770–1842		HAIL, COLUMBIA!	1798
Charles Brockden Brown	1771–1810	Wieland		"
		Ormond		1799
		Arthur Mervyn		1800
		Edgar Huntly		"
		Clara Howard		1801
		Jane Talbot		1804
Robert Treat Paine	1773–1811		The Invention of Letters	1795
			The Ruling Passion.	
			Adams and Liberty	1798
			The Steeds of Apollo	1809
Clement Clarke Moore, LL.D.	1779–1863		The Visit of St. Nicholas.	
James Kirke Paulding	1779–1860	Salmagundi		1807
		The New Pilgrim's Progress		1828
		The Dutchman's Fireside		1831
		Westward Ho!		1832
		Life of Washington		1835
		The Old Continentals, etc.		1846
			The Backwoodsman	1818
Francis Scott Key	1779–1843		STAR-SPANGLED BANNER	1814
Washington Allston	1779–1843		Sylphs of the Season	1813
		Monaldi		1841
		Lectures on Art, and Poems		1850
John James Audubon	1780–1851	The Birds of America (87 parts, 448 plates)		1828
		The Quadrupeds of North America.		
Thomas Hart Benton	1782–1858	Thirty Years' View		1856
Washington Irving (Geoffrey Crayon)	1783–1859	Knickerbocker's Hist. New York.		1809
		Sketch Book		1819
		Bracebridge Hall		1822
		Tales of a Traveller		1824
		Life of Columbus		1828
		Conquest of Granada		1829
		Alhambra		1832
		Tour on the Prairie		1835
		Astoria		1836
		Adventures of Capt. Bonneville		1837
		Mahomet and His Successors		1849–50
		Oliver Goldsmith		1849

ENGLISH (AMERICAN) LITERATURE AND AUTHORS.—(*Continued.*)

Authors.		Principal works.		First appeared or published.
Name.	Time.	Prose.	Poetry and dramas.	
Washington Irving (Geoffrey Crayon)	1783–1859	Welfert's Roost		1855
		Life of Washington		1855–59
Joseph Emerson Worcester	1784–1865	Dictionary of the Engl. Language		1860
Samuel Woodworth	1785–1842	The Champions of Freedom		1816
		Edits the Parthenon		1827
			The Forest Rose (opera), The Old Oaken Bucket.	
John Pierpont	1785–1866		Airs from Palestine, and other poems	1816
			The Pilgrim Fathers, Passing Away.	
Richard Henry Dana	1787–1879	The Idle Man		1821
			The Buccaneers, and other poems.	1827
James Fenimore Cooper	1789–1851	The Spy		1821
		The Pioneers, The Pilot		1823
		Last of the Mohicans, The Prairie		1827
		The Pathfinder		1840
		The Deerslayer		1841
		Red Rover, Water Witch, Two Admirals, Wing-and-Wing, Bravo.		
Catharine Maria Sedgwick	1789–1867	New England Tales		1822
		Redwood		1824
		Hope Leslie		1828
		The Linwoods		1835
		The Poor Rich Man and the Rich Poor Man, etc		1836
James A. Hillhouse	1789–1841		Percy's Masque	1820
			Hadad	1825
Fitz-Greene Halleck	1790–1867		Twilight	1818
			Fanny	1819
			Joseph Rodman Drake	1820
			Alnwick Castle, Burns, Marco Bozzaris, Red Jacket	1827
			Young America	1864
Lydia Huntley Sigourney	1791–1865		Moral Pieces in Prose and Verse	1815
			Poems	1827
			Pocahontas, and other poems	1841
Charles Sprague	1791–1875		Ode on Shakespeare, Winged Worshippers, The Family Meeting.	
George Ticknor	1791–1871	History of Spanish Literature		1849
John Howard Payne	1792–1852		Home, Sweet Home [Song in Clari, or the Maid of Milan.]	1813
Samuel Griswold Goodrich (Peter Parley)	1793–1863	36 tales		1827–57
		History, geography, school-books, biography, and miscellanies.		
Henry Charles Carey	1793–1879	Principles of Political Economy		1837–40
		The Credit System		1838
		Principles of Social Science, etc		1858–59
William Cullen Bryant	1794–1878		Thanatopsis	1817
			To a Waterfowl	1818
			A Forest Hymn, June, Death of the Flowers, The Evening Wind, An Evening Reverie, Planting of the Apple-Tree, Robert of Lincoln, etc.	
			Translations of the Iliad and Odyssey, etc	1870–71
Joseph Rodman Drake	1795–1820		Culprit Fay, The American Flag, etc.	
James Gates Percival	1795–1856		Prometheus, and other poems	1821
			The Dream of Day, and other poems	1843
John P. Kennedy	1795–1870	Swallow Barn		1832
		Horse-shoe Robinson		1835
		Rob of the Bowl		1838
		Quod Libet		1840
		Memoirs of Wirt, etc		1849
John Gorham Palfrey	1796–1881	History of New England, 5 vols		1859–90
William H. Prescott	1796–1859	Ferdinand and Isabella		1838
		The Conquest of Mexico		1843
		The Conquest of Peru		1847
		Philip II. of Spain		1855–58
		Robertson's Charles V., etc		1856
Theophilus Parsons	1797–1882	Law of Business for Business Men		1857
		Deus Homo		1867
		Infinite and Finite		1872
		Religion and Philosophy of Swedenborg		1876
Thomas C. Haliburton	1797–1865	Sam Slick.		
George Bancroft	1800–91	History of the United States to 1789		1834–84
George P. Morris	1802–64		Lyrics: "Woodman, spare that tree," My Mother's Bible, "I'm with you once again, my friends," Near the Lake, Long Time Ago, "We were boys together," "When other friends are round thee," etc.	
Horace Bushnell	1802–76	Nature and the Supernatural		1858
		Moral Use of Dark Things.		
Ralph Waldo Emerson	1803–82	Essays, 1st series		1841
		" 2d "		1844
		Miscellanies, Nature, etc		1849

ENGLISH (AMERICAN) LITERATURE AND AUTHORS.—(*Continued.*)

Authors.		Principal works.		First appeared or published.
Name.	Time.	Prose.	Poetry and Drama.	
Ralph Waldo Emerson	1803–82	Representative Men		1850
		English Traits		1856
		Conduct of Life		1860
		Society and Solitude, etc.		1869
			May Day, The Humble-bee, The Titmouse, The Snow-storm, Brahma, Wood-notes, Monadnock, Two Rivers, Threnody, etc.	
Jacob Abbott	1803–79	Juveniles: Rollo Books, etc.		1838 et seq.
Nathaniel Hawthorne	1804–64	Twice-Told Tales		1837
		Mosses from an Old Manse		1846
		The Scarlet Letter		1850
		The House of the Seven Gables		1851
		The Blithedale Romance		1852
		The Wonder Book		1851
		Tanglewood Tales		1853
		The Marble Faun		1860
		Our Old Home, etc.		1863
John S. C. Abbott	1805–77	Life of Napoleon		1855
		French Revolution, Civil War in America, etc.		1859–66
William Gilmore Simms	1806–70		Poems and Early Lays	1827
			Vision of Cortez, and other poems	1829
		Guy Rivers		1834
		The Partisan		1835
		Yemassee		"
		Mellichampe		1836
			Southern Passages and Pictures	1839
		Border Beagles		1840
		The Scout		1841
		Confession		"
		Beauchampe		1842
		Count Julian		1845
		Southward Ho!		"
		Wigwam and Cabin		"
		The Huguenots		1850
		Katherine Walton		1851
		The Forayers		1855
		Eutaw		1856
		Charlemont, etc.		"
			Songs and Ballads of the South	1860
Henry W. Longfellow	1807–82	Outre Mer		1835
		Hyperion		1839
			Voices of the Night	"
			Skeleton in Armor, Wreck of the *Hesperus*, Village Blacksmith, Excelsior	1841
			Spanish Student	1843
			Evangeline	1847
		Kavanagh		1849
			Golden Legend	1851
			Hiawatha	1855
			Courtship of Miles Standish	1858
			Tales of a Wayside Inn, Birds of Passage	1863
			New England Tragedies	1868
			Hanging of the Crane, Morituri Salutamus	1875
			Keramos, and other poems, etc.	1878
Richard Hildreth	1807–65	History of the United States to 1821		1849–56
Nathaniel P. Willis	1807–67	Pencillings by the Way		1835
		Dashes at Life with a Free Pencil		1845
		People I Have Met		1850
		Life Here and There		"
		Famous Persons and Places		1854
		Paul Fane, etc.		1856
			Parrhasius, "The shadows lay along Broadway," Absalom, Jephthah's Daughter, The Leper, etc.	
John Greenleaf Whittier	1807–92		Mogg Megone	1836
			Voices of Freedom	1841
			Songs of Labor, and other poems. Ship-builders, Shoe-makers, Drovers, Fishermen, Huskers, Lumber-men.	1848
			Old Portraits. Barclay of Ury, Demon of the Study, etc.	1850
			Chapel of the Hermits, etc.	1852
			The Panorama. Burns, Tauler, The Barefoot Boy, etc.	1856
			Ballads. Mary Garvin, Maud Muller, The Ranger.	1858
			Home Ballads. The Witch's Daughter, Garrison of Cape Ann, Skipper Ireson's Ride, Telling the Bees, Swan Song of Parson Avery, etc.	1859
			In War Time. At Port Royal, Barbara Frietchie, etc.	1863

ENGLISH (AMERICAN) LITERATURE AND AUTHORS.—(*Continued.*)

Authors.		Principal works.		First appeared or published.
Name.	Time.	Prose.	Poetry and dramas.	
John Greenleaf Whittier	1807–92		Snow-Bound	1865
			Tent on the Beach	1867
			Among the Hills	1868
			Hazel Blossoms, etc.	1874
Samuel Francis Smith	1808–95		"My country, 'tis of Thee," "The morning light is breaking."	
Lucretia Maria Davidson	1808–25		Amir Khan, and other poems	1829
Oliver Wendell Holmes	1809–94		Earlier Poems	1830–36
			Old Ironsides, The Last Leaf, To an Insect, My Aunt, etc.	
			A Rhymed Lesson, and other poems	1837–48
			Agnes, and other poems	1849–56
			The Chambered Nautilus; Prologue; The One-Hoss Shay, etc	1858
		Autocrat of the Breakfast Table		"
		Professor at the Breakfast Table		1860
			Under the Violets	"
			De Sauty	"
		Elsie Venner		1861
		Soundings from the Atlantic		1863
		The Guardian Angel		1867
		Poet at the Breakfast Table		1872
			Bill and Joe, The Old Man's Dream, Mare Rubrum, The Boys, Dorothy Q., etc.	1851–77
		Our Hundred Days in Europe		1887
		Over the Tea Cups		1890
Edgar Allan Poe	1811–49		Al Aaraaf, Tamerlane, and other poems	1829
		Manuscript Found in a Bottle		1833
		A. Gordon Pym		1838
		Tales of the Grotesque and Arabesque		1840
		Gold Bug		1843
		Murders in the Rue Morgue		1844
		Fall of the House of Usher, etc.		"
			The Raven	1845
		Literati of New York		1846
			Ulalume, The Bells, The Haunted Palace, etc.	
		Eureka, etc.		1848
Henry James	1811–82	The Nature of Evil		1855
		Christianity the Logic of Creation		1857
		Substance and Shadow		1863
		The Secret of Swedenborg		1869
		Society the Redeemed Form of Man		1879
		Personal Reminiscences of Carlyle		1881
George Washington Greene	1811–83	Life of Nathaniel Greene		1867–71
		Short History of Rhode Island		1877
Alfred B. Street	1811–81		Frontenac	1849
			The Grey Forest Eagle, etc.	
John William Draper	1811–82	History of the Intellectual Development of Europe		1863
		History of the Civil War in America		1867–70
James McCosh	1811–94	Method of Divine Government		1850
		Intuitions of the Mind		1860
		The Supernatural in Relation to the Natural		1862
		Typical Forms and Special Ends in Creation		1869
		Scottish Philosophy, etc.		1874
Harriet Beecher Stowe	1812–	Uncle Tom's Cabin		1852
		Dred		1856
		The Minister's Wooing		1859
		Agnes of Sorrento		1862
		Pearl of Orr's Island		"
		Old Town Folks		1869
		True Story of Lady Byron's Life, etc.		"
George Ticknor Curtis	1812–94	History of the Constitution of the United States		1855–58
Benson J. Lossing	1813–91	Pictorial Field-book of the Revolution		1852
		Pictorial History of the Civil War		1866–69
		Pictorial Field-book of the War of 1812		1868
		Our Country		1873
		Harper's Cyclopædia of United States History		1876
		History of American Industries		1878
		Empire State, etc.		1887
John Romeyn Brodhead	1814–73	History of the State of New York, 1609–91		1853–71
John Lothrop Motley	1814–77	The Dutch Republic		1856
		The United Netherlands		1860–68
		Life and Death of John of Barneveld		1874
Richard Henry Dana, jr.	1815–82	Two Years Before the Mast		1839
John G. Saxe	1816–87		New Rape of the Lock	1848
			Progress	1849
			The Times	1852
			The Money King	1859
			Masquerade, etc.	1866

ENGLISH (AMERICAN) LITERATURE AND AUTHORS.—(*Continued.*)

Authors.		Principal works.		First appeared or published.
Name.	Time.	Prose.	Poetry and dramas.	
Samuel Austin Allibone	1816-89	A Critical Dictionary of English Literature and Authors		1859-91
Henry D. Thoreau	1817-62	A Week on the Concord River		1849
		Walden		1854
		Excursions		1863
		The Maine Woods		1864
		Cape Cod, etc.	Poems	1865
James Thomas Fields	1817-81		Poems	1849
		Yesterdays with Authors		1872
		Hawthorne		1876
John Bigelow	1817-	Life of Benjamin Franklin		1875
		Edits the Writings of Franklin (10 vols.), etc.		1888
Josiah Gilbert Holland (Timothy Titcomb)	1819-81	History Western Massachusetts		1855
		The Bay Path		1857
		Timothy Titcomb's Letters		1858
			Bitter Sweet	"
		Miss Gilbert's Career		1860
		Life of Lincoln		1866
			Kathrina	1867
		Arthur Bonnicastle, etc.		1873
			Mistress of the Manse	1874
Julia Ward Howe	1819-	Social and Philosophic Papers, etc.	Passion Flowers	1854
			Words for the Hour	1856
			Battle Hymn of the Republic	1861
			Later Lyrics	1866
James Russell Lowell	1819-91		Poems	1844
			Indian Summer Reveries	1848
			Vision of Sir Launfal and Biglow Papers	"
		Fireside Travels		1864
			Biglow Papers, 2d series	1867
			Under the Willows	1868
		Among My Books		1870
		My Study Windows		1871
			Heartsease and Rue, etc.	1888
Edwin Percy Whipple	1819-86	Essays and Reviews		1848
		Literature and Life		1849
		Characteristic Men		1866
		Literature of the Age of Elizabeth		1869
		American Literature		1887
		Recollections of Eminent Men.		
Walt Whitman	1819-92		Leaves of Grass	1855
			Drum Taps	1865
Richard Grant White	1822-85	Words and Their Uses		1880
		Every Day English		"
		England Without and Within		1882
		The Fate of Mansfield Humphreys		1884
		Studies in Shakespeare, etc.		1885
William Taylor Adams (Oliver Optic)	1822-	Juveniles: Boat Club Series, Woodville Series, Army and Navy Series, Riverdale Series, Young America Abroad, etc.		
Edward Everett Hale	1822-	His Level Best		1872
		My Double.		
		Philip Nolan's Friends		1876
		The Man Without a Country, etc.		1879
James Parton	1822-91	Life and Times of Aaron Burr		1857
		Life of Andrew Jackson		1860
		" Benjamin Franklin		1864
		" John Jacob Astor		1865
		" Thomas Jefferson		1874
		" Voltaire, etc.		1881
Donald G. Mitchell (Ik Marvel)	1822-	Reveries of a Bachelor		1850
		Dream Life		1851
		My Farm at Edgewood		1863
		Wet Days at Edgewood		1864
		Seven Stories		1865
		Doctor Johns, etc.		1866
Thomas Buchanan Read	1822-72		Lays and Ballads	1848
			The New Pastoral	1855
			The House by the Sea	1856
			The Wagoner of the Alleghanies	1862
			Sheridan's Ride, etc.	1864
Francis Parkman	1823-93	Oregon Trail		1849
		Conspiracy of Pontiac		1851
		Pioneers of France in the New World		1865
		Discovery of the Great West		1869
		Old Régime		1874
		Count Frontenac and New France		1877
		Montcalm and Wolfe, etc.		1884
Thomas Wentworth Higginson	1823-	Out Door Papers		1863
		Malbone, an Oldport Romance		1869
		Army Life in a Black Regiment		1870
		Short Studies of American Authors, etc.		1879
Adeline D. Whitney	1824-	Mother Goose for Grown Folks		1860
		Faith Gartney's Girlhood		1863
		The Gayworthys		1865
		Patience Strong's Outings		1868
		We Girls, etc.		1870
John Foster Kirk (b. Fredericton, N. B.)	1824-	History of Charles the Bold		1863-67
George H. Boker	1824-90		Calaynos, a Tragedy	1848
			Lessons of Life, and other poems	1847
			Anne Boleyn, a Tragedy	1850

ENGLISH (AMERICAN) LITERATURE AND AUTHORS.—(*Continued.*)

Authors.		Principal works.		First appeared or published.
Name.	Time.	Prose.	Poetry and dramas.	
George H. Boker	1824–90	....	Poems of the War: On Board the Cumberland, Dirge of a Soldier, Battle of Lookout Mountain, The Black Regiment, etc.	
			Street Lyrics	1865
			The Ivory Carver, The Podesta's Daughter, Song of Earth, etc.	
John Dawson Gilmary Shea	1824–92	The Catholic Church in America	....	1886
George William Curtis	1824–92	Nile Notes of a Howadji	....	1850
		Potiphar Papers	....	1853
		Prue and I	....	1856
		Trumps	....	1861
		Life of Wm. C. Bryant, etc	....	1879
Bayard Taylor	1825–78	Views Afoot	....	1846
		....	Rhymes of Travel, Ballads, and other poems	1848
		Eldorado	....	1850
		Central Africa	....	1854
		Land of the Saracen	....	"
		....	Poems of the Orient	1855
		Northern Travel	....	1857
		Greece and Russia	....	1859
		Hannah Thurston	....	1863
		John Godfrey's Fortunes	....	1864
		Story of Kennett	....	1866
		Joseph and His Friend, etc	....	1870
Henry Charles Lea	1825–	Superstition and Force	....	1866
		Historical Sketch of Sacerdotal Celibacy in the Christian Church	....	1867
		History of the Inquisition	....	1887–88
William Allen Butler	1825–	....	Nothing to Wear, Two Millions.	1857
Richard Henry Stoddard	1825–	....	Footprints	1849
		....	Castle by the Sea, and other poems	1852
		Loves and Heroines of the Poets.	....	1860
		....	The King's Bell	1862
		....	The Book of the East, and other poems	1871
Coates Kinney	1826–	....	Rain on the Roof.	
Stephen Collins Foster	1826–64	....	Songs: Old Uncle Ned, Oh Susannah! Nelly was a Lady, Old Folks at Home (for which he received $15,000), Come where my love lies dreaming, Old Dog Tray, etc.	
Rose Terry Cooke	1827–92	....	The Two Villages, Ellery Vane, etc.	
Lew. Wallace	1827–	The Fair God	....	1873
		Ben-Hur	....	1880
		The Prince of India	....	1893
Charles Dudley Warner	1829–	My Summer in a Garden	....	1870
		Backlog Studies	....	1872
		My Winter on the Nile	....	1876
		Washington Irving	....	1881
		Their Pilgrimage, etc	....	1886
		Studies in the South and West	....	1889
		A Little Journey in the World	....	"
		Southern California	....	1891
		As We Were Saying	....	"
		As We Go	....	1893
Paul Hamilton Hayne	1830–86	....	Sonnets and Other Poems	1857
			Legends and Lyrics, etc	1872
John Esten Cooke	1830–86	Last of the Foresters	....	1856
		Life of "Stonewall" Jackson	....	1863
		Wearing the Grey	....	1867
		Hammer and Rapier	....	1870
		Virginia—American Commonwealth, etc	....	1883
Mary Virginia Terhune (Marion Harland)	1830–	Alone	....	1854
		The Hidden Path	....	1855
		Moss Side	....	1857
		Helen Gardner's Wedding Day	....	1867
		Ruby's Husband	....	1868
		Common Sense in the Household, etc	....	1871
Justin Winsor	1831–	Reader's Hand Book of the Revolution	....	1880
		Edits Narrative and Critical History of America, etc	....	1884–89
Louisa May Alcott	1832–88	Little Women	....	1868
		An Old Fashioned Girl	....	1870
		Little Men	....	1871
		Aunt Jo's Scrap Bag, etc	....	1871–79
Edmund Clarence Stedman	1833–	....	The Diamond Wedding	1859
		....	Alice of Monmouth, and other poems	1864
		....	Pan in Wall Street.	
		Victorian Poets	....	1875
		Poets of America, etc	....	1885
Elisha Mulford	1833–	The Nation	....	1870
		Republic of God	....	1881
David R. Locke (Petroleum V. Nasby)	1833–88	Nasby Papers	....	1860–82
Frank R. Stockton	1834–	Rudder Grange	....	1879
		The Lady or the Tiger?	....	1884

ENGLISH (AMERICAN) LITERATURE AND AUTHORS.—(*Continued.*)

Authors.		Principal works.		First appeared or published.
Name.	Time.	Prose.	Poetry and dramas.	
Frank R. Stockton	1834–	The Casting Away of Mrs. Lecks and Mrs. Aleshine		1886
		The Late Mrs. Null		"
		The Hundredth Man		1887
		The Squirrel Inn		1891
		The Merry Chanter, etc.		1892
Moses Coit Tyler	1835–	History of American Literature		1878
Samuel L. Clemens (Mark Twain)	1835–	Innocents Abroad		1869
		Roughing It		1872
		The Gilded Age		1873
		Tom Sawyer		1876
		Prince and Pauper		1882
		Life on the Mississippi		1883
		Huckleberry Finn, etc.		1885
Harriet E. P. Spofford	1835–	Sir Rohan's Ghost		1859
		The Amber Gods, etc.		1863
Lyman Abbott	1835–	Various works explanatory of the Scriptures and its teachings, etc.		
		Life of Henry Ward Beecher		1883
Thomas Bailey Aldrich	1836–		Ballad of Babie Bell	1856
		Out of His Head		1864
		The Story of a Bad Boy		1869
		Marjorie Daw		1873
			Cloth of Gold, and other poems	1874
		Prudence Palfrey		"
		The Queen of Sheba		1877
		The Stillwater Tragedy		1880
			Mercedes, and Later Lyrics	1883
			The Sisters' Tragedy, and other poems	1891
William Dean Howells	1837–	Venetian Life		1866
		Italian Journey		1867
		Their Wedding Journey		1871
		A Chance Acquaintance		1874
		The Lady of the Aroostook		1879
		The Undiscovered Country		1880
		A Modern Instance		1882
		The Minister's Charge		1887
		The Rise of Silas Lapham		1885
		Modern Italian Poets		1887
		A Hazard of New Fortunes		1889
		The World of Chance		1893
		The Quality of Mercy		1892
Edward Eggleston	1837–	Mr. Blake's Walking Stick		1870
		The Hoosier School-master		1872
		The End of the World		"
		The Circuit Rider		1874
		Roxy		1878
		The Graysons		1887
		The Faith Doctor		1891
John Burroughs	1837–	Wakerobin		1871
		Winter Sunshine		1876
		Birds and Poets		1877
		Locusts and Wild Honey		1879
		Pepacton, etc.		1881
Mary Mapes Dodge	1838–	Irvington Stories		1864
		Hans Brinker		1876
		Theophilus, etc.		"
			Along the Way	1879
Henry Adams	1838–	Life of Gallatin		"
		Life of John Randolph		1882
		History of the United States		1891
Edward Payson Roe	1838–88	Barriers Burned Away		1872
		What Can She Do?		1873
		Opening of a Chestnut Burr		1874
		Manual of the Culture of Small Fruit		1876
		A Knight of the Nineteenth Century		1877
		His Sombre Rivals		1883
		An Original Belle		1885
		Miss Low, etc.		1888
Albion Winegar Tourgée	1838–	A Royal Gentleman		1874
		A Fool's Errand		1879
		Bricks Without Straw		1880
		Hot Plough-shares, essays, etc.		1883
Mary Abigail Dodge (Gail Hamilton)	1838–	Country Living and Country Thinking		1862
		Gala Days		1863
		Stumbling Blocks		1870
		Red-Letter Days		
		Divine Guidance, etc.		1881
Francis Bret Harte	1839–		The Heathen Chinee, and other poems	1870
		The Luck of Roaring Camp		"
		Tales of the Argonauts		1875
		Gabriel Conroy		1876
		Two Men of Sandy Bar, and other stories		1877
		The Crusade of the *Excelsior*		1887
		Col. Starbottle's Client, etc.		1892
James Schouler	1839–	History of the United States		1880–92
Cincinnatus Hiner Miller (Joaquin Miller)	1841–		Songs of the Sierras	1871
			Songs of the Sunland	1873
			Songs of Italy	1878
			Shadows of Shasta	1881
		The Danites, etc.		

ENGLISH (AMERICAN) LITERATURE AND AUTHORS.—(*Continued.*)

Authors.		Principal works.		First appeared or published.
Name.	Time.	Prose.	Poetry and dramas.	
ohn Fiske	1842-	Myths and Myth-makers		1872
		Outlines of Cosmic Philosophy		1875
		The Unseen World		1876
		The Idea of God as Affected by Modern Knowledge		1885
		Critical Period of American History, etc.		1888
idney Lanier	1842-81	Tiger Lilies		1867
			Poems	1876
		The Boys' Froissart		1878
		Science of English Verse		1880
ohn Habberton	1842-	Helen's Babies		1876
		The Barton Experiment		"
		Jericho Road		"
		Brueton's Bayou		1886
		A Lucky Lover		1892
lenry James	1843-	A Passionate Pilgrim		1875
		Roderick Hudson		"
		The American		1877
		Daisy Miller		1878
		Portrait of a Lady		1881
		The Bostonians		1886
		The Princess Casamassima		"
		The Tragic Muse, etc.		1890
eorge W. Cable	1844-	Old Creole Days		1879
		The Grandissimes		1880
		Doctor Sevier		1882
		The Silent South		1885
		Bonaventure, etc.		1888
lizabeth Stuart Phelps Ward	1844-	Gates Ajar		1868
		Hedged In		1870
		The Silent Partner		"
		The Story of Avis		1877
		My Cousin and I		1879
		Doctor Zay		1882
		Beyond the Gates, etc.		1883
Vill Carleton	1845-		Farm Ballads	1873
			Farm Legends	1875
			Farm Festivals	1881
			City Ballads	1885
			City Legends	1889
			City Festivals	1892
'rancis Marion Crawford	1845-	Mr. Isaacs		1882
		Tale of a Lonely Parish		1886
		Saracinesca		1887
		Paul Patoff		"
			Ballads	1890
		The Witch of Prague		1891
		Khaled		"
		Don Orsino		1892
ulian Hawthorne	1846-	Bressant		1873
		Idolatry		1874
		Garth		1877
		Archibald Malmaison		1879
		Beatrix Randolph		1883
		Miss Cadogna, etc.		1885
rthur S. Hardy	1847-	But Yet a Woman		1883
		The Wind of Destiny		1886
		Passé Rose, etc.		1889
Villiam Henry Bishop	1847-	Detmold		1879
		The House of a Merchant Prince		1883
		Choy Susan		1884
		The Golden Justice, etc.		1886
dgar Fawcett	1847-	A Gentleman of Leisure		1884
		Olivia Delaplaine		1886
		An Ambitious Woman		"
		The House at High Bridge		1887
			Romance and Revery	1888
			Songs of Doubt and Dreams	1891
		Women Must Weep		1892
		An Heir to Millions, etc.		"
ljalmar Hjorth Boyesen	1848-95	Gunnar		1874
		Falconberg		1879
		Queen Titania		1881
			Idyls of Norway, and other poems.	1882
		A Daughter of the Philistines, etc.		1883
oel Chandler Harris	1848-	Uncle Remus		1880
		Mingo		1884
		Free Joe		1888
		Balaam and His Master		1891
onstance Fenimore Woolson	1848-93	Castle Nowhere		1875
		Rodman the Keeper		1880
		Anne		1882
		For the Major		1883
		East Angels		1886
		Jupiter Lights		1889
		Horace Chase		1894
arah Orne Jewett	1849-	Deephaven		1877
		Old Friends and New		1879
		Country By-ways		1881
		The Mate of the *Daylight*		1883
		A Country Doctor		1884
		The King of Folly Island		1888
		A Native of Winby, etc.		1893
'rances Hodgson Burnett	1849-	That Lass o' Lowrie's		1877
		Pretty Polly Pemberton		1878

ENGLISH (AMERICAN) LITERATURE AND AUTHORS.—(*Continued.*)

Authors.		Principal works.		First appeared or published.
Name.	Time.	Prose.	Poetry and dramas.	
Frances Hodgson Burnett	1849–	Haworths	....	1879
		Louisiana	....	1880
		A Fair Barbarian	....	1881
		Through One Administration	....	1883
		Little Lord Fauntleroy, etc.	....	1886
Henry Cabot Lodge	1850–	Short History of the English Colonies in America	....	1881
		Life of Hamilton	....	1882
		Life of Webster, etc.	....	1883
Edward Bellamy	1850–	Looking Backward	....	1888
Mary Noailles Murfree (Charles Egbert Craddock)	1850–	In the Tennessee Mountains	....	1884
		Where the Battle was Fought	....	"
		Down the Ravine	....	1885
		The Prophet of the Great Smoky Mountains	....	"
		The Despot of Broomsedge Cove	....	1888
		In the "Stranger People's" Country, etc.	....	1891
George Parsons Lathrop	1851–	An Echo of Passion, etc.	....	1882
		....	Poems.	
John Bach McMaster	1852–	History of the People of the United States from the Revolution to the Civil War. Vols. I., II., III. pub.	....	1883–92
Thomas Nelson Page	1853–	Marse Chan	....	1884
		Collected Stories (In Virginia), etc.	....	1887
Amélie Rives Chanler	1863–	A Brother to Dragons	....	1888
		The Quick or the Dead?	....	"
		Virginia of Virginia	....	"
		Barbara Dering, etc.	....	1892

FRENCH LITERATURE AND AUTHORS.

Authors.		Principal works.		First appeared or published.
Name.	Time.	Prose.	Poetry and dramas.	
Unknown	....	....	Chanson de Roland	11th century.
Pierre Abélard	1079–1142	Epistles. PHILOSOPHY.		
Unknown	....	....	Roman d'Alexandre	12th century.
Robert Wace	1112–84?	....	Roman de Brut	" "
Unknown	....	....	Roman de la Rose	" "
Geoffroy de Villehardouin	1165–1213?	Historical.		
Jean Sire de Joinville	1224–1319?	Chronicles.		
Jean Froissart	1337–1410	Chronicles	....	1st ed. no date; 2d, 1505.
Enguerrand de Monstrelet	1390–1453	Chronicles.		
Philippe de Comines	1445–1509	Historical. The Memoirs	....	1524
François Rabelais	1495–1553	Philosophic and satirical	....	1st compl. ed. 1567.
Clement Marot	1495–1544	....	Poems	1514 et seq.
Théodore Beza	1519–1605	Theological.		
Pierre de Ronsard	1524–85	....	Poems—"Prince of Poets" of his time and country	1550 "
Michel E. de Montaigne	1533–92	Essays	....	1580–88
Théodore Agrippa d'Aubigné	1550–1630	Historical	Poems.	
François de Malherbe	1555–1628	....	"	1600 et seq.
Jacques Auguste de Thou	1553–1617	History of his own times	....	1604–20
René Descartes	1596–1650	Philosophic (PHILOSOPHY)	....	Col. works 1697.
Pierre Corneille	1606–84	....	Dramas—The Cid, and many others	1636 et seq.
Paul Scarron	1610–60	Comic. Plays, etc	....	1645 "
François de la Rochefoucauld	1613–80	Maxims	....	1665
		Memoirs	....	Complete ed. 1868–71.
Jean de la Fontaine	1621–95	....	Fables (241 in number), Contes	1666–78
Jean Baptiste Poquelin (Molière)	1622–73	....	Dramas (comedies)	1653 et seq.
Blaise Pascal	1623–62	Philosophic and mathematical	....	1st compl. ed. 1779.
Mme. de Sévigné	1626–96	Letters.		
Jacques Bénigne Bossuet	1627–1704	Sermons, etc.		
Louis Bourdaloue	1632–1704	Jesuit preacher.		
Esprit Fléchier	1632–1710	Pulpit orator.		
Nicolas Boileau Despreaux	1636–1711	....	Satirical poetry, criticisms.	
Nicolas Malebranche	1638–1715	Philosophic. PHILOSOPHY	....	1674 et seq.
Jean Racine	1639–99	....	Dramas	1st col. ed. 1675–76.
Claude Fleury	1640–1723	Ecclesiastical history	....	1691
Pierre Bayle	1647–1706	Philosophic.		
François de la Mothe Fénélon	1651–1715	Télémaque, etc	....	1st at Hague, 1699; 2d at Paris, 1717.
René A. de Vertot	1655–1735	Historical.		
Charles Rollin	1661–1741	Historical	....	1730–38
Jean Baptiste Massillon	1663–1742	Pulpit orations.		
Alain René le Sage	1668–1747	Gil Blas	....	1707
		Le Diable Boiteaux (The Devil on Two Sticks), etc.	....	1715
François Xavier, Bon de Saint-Hilaire	1678–1761	General literature.		
Charles de Montesquieu	1689–1755	Philosophic and judicial	....	1721 et seq.
François Marie Arouet (Voltaire)	1694–1778	Historical	Poems, dramas	1718 "
Georges Louis L. Comte de Buffon	1707–78	Natural history	....	1749–1804
Jean Jacques Rousseau	1712–78	Philosophic and general	....	1760–62 et seq.
Denis Diderot	1713–84	Philosophic, the principal encyclopædists	....	1751–72
Claude A. Helvetius	1715–71	Philosophic	....	1758
Étienne Bonnot de Condillac	1715–80	Metaphysical. PHILOSOPHY	....	Col. ed. 1798
Jean le Rond d'Alembert	1717–83	Mathematical.		
Jean François Marmontel	1723–99	Memoirs, etc.		
Pierre A. Caron de Beaumarchais	1732–99	....	Comic dramas—Le Barbier de Seville, Le Mariage de Figaro	1781
Jacques Henri B. de Saint-Pierre	1737–1814	Paul and Virginia.		

FRENCH LITERATURE AND AUTHORS.—(*Continued.*)

Authors.		Principal works.		First appeared or published.
Name.	Time.	Prose.	Poetry and dramas.	
ıcques Delille	1738-1813		Poems	1769 et seq.
ntoine L. Lavoisier	1743-94	Scientific.		
me. de Genlis	1746-1830	Novels.		
abriel Honore, Comte Mirabeau	1749-91	Orations, etc.		
onstantin F. C. de Volney	1757-1820	Ruins, etc.		1791
aude Joseph Rouget de l'Isle	1760-1836		Marseillaise	1792
me. de Staël	1766-1817	Delphine, Corinne, De l'Allemagne.		1802-8
oseph François Michaud	1767-1839	History of the Crusades, etc.		1811
rançois A. Chateaubriand	1768-1848	Genius of Christianity, Atala, René, etc.		1801 et seq.
eorges Leopold Baron de Cuvier.	1769-1832	Natural history		1817-30
rançois C. M. Fourier	1772-1837	Fourierism.		
ean Baptiste Biot	1774-1862	Philosophic and mathematical		1805 et seq.
erre Jean de Béranger	1780-1857		Lyric poems	1820-21 et seq.
ugues F. R., Abbé de Lamennais.	1782-1854	Religious and political.		
mable G. P. Barante	1782-1866	History and general literature		1824-61
rançois P. G. Guizot	1787-1874	Hist. of Civilization in Europe, Popular Hist. of France, etc.		1830 et seq.
iphonse M. L. de Lamartine	1790-1869	Historical, etc.		
bel François Villemain	1790-1870	Historical and educational		1826 et seq.
ugustin E. Scribe	1791-1861		Dramas	1811 “
ntoine E. Genoude	1792-1849	Historical.		
ictor Cousin	1792-1867	Philosophic and metaphysical. PHILOSOPHY		1834-59
ean F. C. Delavigne	1793-1843		Poems	1815-43
harles Paul de Kock	1794-1871	Novels.	Dramas.	
ıcques N. Augustin Thierry	1795-1856	His. Norman Conquest of Engl., etc.		1825
rançois A. M. Mignet	1796-1884	Historical.		
ouis Adolphe Thiers	1797-1877	French Revolution		1823-27
		History of the Empire, etc., finished		1862
médée S. D. Thierry	1797-1873	Historical.		
ippolyte N. J. Auger	1797-	Novels.		
ules Michelet	1798-1874	History of France, etc.		1830-67
oseph Xavier Boniface (Saintine).	1798-1865	Picciola, etc.		
uguste Comte	1798-1857	Positive Philosophy. PHILOSOPHY.		1830-42 et seq.
onoré de Balzac	1799-1850	Novels—Comedies of Human Life (central figure in French literature)		1825 et seq.
lfred Victor Vigny	1799-1864	Cinq-mars	Poems	1822 “
rédéric Bastiat	1801-50	Political economy		1845-50
ictor Hugo	1802-85		Poems, dramas	1828 et seq.
		Notre Dame		1831
		Les Misérables		1862
		Toilers of the Sea, etc.		1866
lexandre Dumas	1803-70	Novels—Monte Cristo, Three Musketeers, etc.	Dramas	1844 et seq.
rosper Mérimée	1803-70	Novels and histories		1825 “
dgar Quinet	1803-75	Historical, etc.		
ugène Suè	1804-57	Mysteries of Paris, Wandering Jew, etc.		1842 “
harles Augustin Sainte-Beuve	1804-69	Criticisms, etc.		1828 “
ules Janin	1804-74	Novels.		1829 “
me. Dudevant (Georges Sand)	1804-76	Indiana, Valentine, Consuelo, etc.		1831-52 et seq.
lexis Charles H. de Tocqueville	1805-59	Democracy in America		1835
lfred de Musset	1810-57	Novels	Poems, dramas	1829 et seq.
harles Forbes R. Montalembert	1810-70	Political orations.		
on Louis Henri Martin	1810-83	History of France		1838-79
héophile Gautier	1811-72	Novels and criticisms	Poems	1835 et seq.
eonard S. J. Sandeau	1811-83	Novels.		
ictor Duruy	1811-94	Histoire des Romains		1844
		Histoire des Temps Modernes, 1453-1789		1868
ctave Feuillet	1821-90	Novels	Dramas	1840 et seq.
ouis Blanc	1813-82	Political.		
lie Bertrand Berthet	1815-	Novels.		
aul H. C. Feval	1817-87	Novels—The Mysteries of London, etc.		1842 “
uillaume Louis Figuier	1819-94	Scientific.		
ustav Flaubert	1821-80	Novels.		
mile Erckmann	1822-	Novels (in connection with Chatrian)		1859 “
oseph Ernest Renan	1823-92	Vie de Jesus, etc.		1863
		Hist. Origin of Christianity		1883 “
lexandre Dumas, *fils*	1824-95	Novels.		
. Alexandre Chatrian	1826-90	Novels (in connection with Erckmann)		1859 “
harles Loyson, Père Hyacinthe	1827-	Pulpit orations.		
ippolyte A. Taine	1828-93	Historical and critical		1854 “
dmond François V. About	1828-85	Novels.		
ules Verne	1828-	Twenty Thousand Leagues Under the Sea, Around the World in Eighty Days, etc.		1860 “
dolphe Belot	1829-90	Novels	Dramas	1855 “
ictorien Sardou	1831-		“	1854 “
aul B. du Chaillu	1835-	Travels		1861-81
rnest Daudet	1837-	Novels.		
lphonse Daudet	1840-	“	Poems	1858 et seq.
mile Zola	1840-	“		186[illegible]
rançois Edouard J. Coppée	1842-		Poems, dramas	18[illegible]
ouis M. J. Viaud (Pierre Loti)	1850-	Novels		1[illegible]
enri René A. G. Maupassant	1850-93	“		1[illegible]

GERMAN LITERATURE AND AUTHORS.

Authors.		Principal works.		First appeared or published.
Name.	Time.	Prose.	Poetry and Dramas.	
Ulfilas	....	Gothic Bible		About 360 A.D.
Unknown	....		Hildebrandslied	Early 9th century.
Unknown	....		Ludwigslied	9th century.
Conrad	....		Rolandslied	12th century.
Heinrich von Veldeke	....		Eneit	1175-90 (?)
Wolfram von Eschenbach	....		Parzival	12th century.
Unknown	....		Nibelungenlied	" "
Unknown	....		Gudrun	" "
Unknown	....		Heldenbuch	" "
Hartmann von Auē	1170-1235		Der arme Heinrich. This poem furnished the subject for Longfellow's "Golden Legend" and Rossetti's "Henry the Leper."	
Meister Eckhart	d. 1329	Prose.		
	....	Limburg Chronicle		1336-98
	....	Alsace Chronicle		"
Sebastian Brandt	....		Das Narrenschiff	1494
Martin Luther	1483-1546	German Bible		1522-34
Ulrich von Hutten	1488-1523		Satirical verse.	
Hans Sachs	1494-1578		Poems.	
Johann Fischart	1545-90		Satires	1570-80
Johann Arndt	1555-1621	Four books on True Christianity.		
Jacob Boehme	1575-1624	Mysticism		1612-24 et seq.
Martin Opitz	1597-1639		Poems	1624
Paul Gerhardt	1606-75		Poems. Hymns	1st compl. ed. 1666-67
Paul Fleming	1609-40		Poems	Most brilliant Ger. poet of 17th cent'ry.
Gottfried Wilhelm Leibnitz	1646-1716	Philosophic and mathematical. PHILOSOPHY.		1st ed., not compl., 1768.
Christian Thomasius	1655-1728	Edits the first German periodical.		1681
Johann C. von Wolff	1679-1754	Philosophic.		
Johann C. Gottsched	1700-66	Critical, etc.		
Albrecht Haller	1708-77	Scientific.		
Christian F. Gellert	1715-69	Moralistic	Poems	Complete ed. 1769-74.
Johann J. Winckelmann	1717-68	History of Ancient Art.		
Johann W. L. Gleim	1719-1803		War Songs of a Grenadier	1748
Hieronymus K. F. baron von Münchhausen	1720-97	Fiction: stories. Originally 48		1785
Friedrich T. Klopstock	1724-1803		Dramas—Messiah.	
Immanuel Kant	1724-1804	Philosophic. PHILOSOPHY. The Critic of Pure Reason		1781 Col. ed. 1838.
C. G. Heyne	1729-1812	Critical and archæological.		
G. E. Lessing	1729-81	Laocoon, etc	Minna von Barnhelm, Emilia Galotti, Nathan the Wise	1754 et seq.
Ch. M. Wieland	1733-1813	Agathon	Oberon.	
J. G. von Herder	1744-1803	Philosophic	Voices of the People.	
G. A. Bürger	1748-94		Leonore, etc	1778-89
Johann Wolfgang Goethe	1749-1832	Werther, Götz von Berlichingen, Elective Affinities, Wilhelm Meister, etc	Faust, Iphigenia, Tasso, Egmont, Lyrics, etc	1774 et seq.
Johann H. Voss	1751-1826	Critical	Poems—Louise; translates Iliad.	
J. C. Friedrich von Schiller	1759-1805	Thirty Years' War	The Robbers, Wallenstein, Maria Stuart, The Maid of Orleans, William Tell, etc. Lyric—Song of the Bell.	1st col. ed 1812-15.
August von Kotzebue	1761-1819		Dramas.	
Johann Gottlieb Fichte	1762-1814	Philosophic. PHILOSOPHY		1790-1800
Christian A. Vulpius	1762-1827	Rinaldo Rinaldini		1799
Jean Paul F. Richter	1763-1825	The Year of Wild Oats, Titan, etc. Flower, Fruit, and Thorn Pieces The Campaner Thal		1802-5 1796 1797
Wilhelm von Humboldt	1767-1835	Philologic and critical.		
A. Wilhelm von Schlegel	1767-1845	Dramatic Art and Literature		1st col. ed 1846.
F. D. E. Schleiermacher	1768-1834	Philosophy		Col. works 1835-64.
Alexander von Humboldt	1769-1859	Scientific, travels—Cosmos		1845-58
Ernst M. Arndt	1769-1860		Poems.	
Georg W. F. Hegel	1770-1831	Philosophic. PHILOSOPHY		Col. works 1832.
Friedrich von Schlegel	1772-1829	History of Ancient and Modern Literature		1815 et seq.
Friedrich von Hardenberg (Novalis)	1772-1801	Fiction (mystical)	Poems.	
Ludwig Tieck	1773-1853	Novels	Poems	1794 "
Friedrich W. J. von Schelling	1775-1854	Philosophic. PHILOSOPHY		1st col. works 1856-61.
Berthold G. Niebuhr	1776-1831	Historical—History of Rome		1812 et seq.
F. C. Schlosser	1776-1861	Historical—Univ. History, History of the Eighteenth Century.		
Ernst T. W. Hoffmann	1776-1822	Imaginary Tales, The Golden Pot, Devil's Enchantments, Midnight Stories, etc		Selected ed. 1827-28.
Heinrich von Kleist	1776-1811	Novels	Poems.	
F. H. Karl de la Motte Fouqué	1777-1843	Undine, Sintram, etc		1814-15
Carl Ritter	1779-1859	Geography (the greatest geographer of modern times)		1817 et seq.
Johann Rudolph Wyss (Swiss)	1781-1830	Swiss Family Robinson		1813
F. C. Dahlmann	1785-1860	Historical		1840-75
Jakob L. Grimm	1785-1863	Philologic		1811 et seq.
Wilhelm K. Grimm	1786-1859	Philologic		" "
Andreas Justinus Kerner	1786-1862		Poems, lyrics, and ballads	Collected ed. 1826-59.
Ludwig Uhland	1787-1862		Lyrics.	
Arthur Schopenhauer	1788-1860	Philosophic—The World as Will and Idea, etc. PHILOSOPHY		1836 Compl. ed. 1874.

GERMAN LITERATURE AND AUTHORS.—(*Continued.*)

Authors.		Principal works.		First appeared or published.
Name.	Time.	Prose.	Poetry and dramas.	
. W. F. Freytag	1788–1861	Oriental scholar		1830–37
ohann A. W. Neander	1789–1850	Ecclesiastical history		1826–45
'riedrich Rückert	1789–1866	Oriental scholar	Poems	1816–38
Karl Theodor Körner	1791–1813		Poems	1812–13
Vilhelm Müller	1794–1827	Novels	Poems.	
.eopold Ranke	1795–1886	Historical.		
Ieinrich Heine	1797–1856		Poems.	
ohann J. J. Dollinger	1799–1890	Theological, historical.		
ohann P. Lange	1802–1884	Theological—Commentaries.		
ustus baron von Liebig	1803–73	Scientific, chemist.		
. G. Gervinus	1805–71	Historical and critical—Shakespeare, etc.		1849 et seq.
Ieinrich Laube	1806–1884	Novels	Poems.	
ohann G. Droysen	1808–1884	Historical.		
Berthold Auerbach	1812–1882	Village Tales On the Heights, etc.		1843 1865
.ouise Mühlbach (Mrs. Theodor Mundt)	1814–73	Novels.		
Ernst Curtius	1814–	Archæologistic and historical—History of Greece.		Engl. ed. 1868–74.
Edouard Zeller	1814–	Theologic and philosophic		1839 et seq.
Gustav Freytag	1816–	Novels	Poems, dramas	1845 "
'riedrich Gerstäcker	1816–72	Novels		1844 "
Rudolf H. Lotze	1817–81	Philosophic.		
Karl Vogt	1817–	Scientific.		
'heodor Mommsen	1817–	Historical—History of Rome		Engl. ed. 1862–63.
.udwig Hausser	1818–67	Historical.		
Albrecht Schwegler	1819–57	Historical—Rome.		
Ieinrich Schliemann	1822–92	Archæologistic—Ilios, the City and Country of the Trojans, Mycenae, etc.		
'riedrich Spielhagen	1829–	Problematical Characters, Hammer and Anvil, etc.		1861 et seq.
'aul Johann L. Heyse	1830–	Novels	Poems	1850 "
Geheimrath F. Dahn	1834–	Historical.		
Georg M. Ebers	1837–	Orientalistic and novels		1869 "
Edouard Hartmann	1842–	Philosophic. PHILOSOPHY		" "
Karl E. Franzos	1848–	Novels, travels		1876 "

ITALIAN LITERATURE AND AUTHORS.

It is now an established historical fact that there existed no writing in Italian before the 13th century.—*Encyclopædia Britannica*, vol. xiii., p. 499, 9th ed.

Authors.		Principal works.		First appeared or published.
Name.	Time.	Prose.	Poetry and dramas.	
Alighieri Dante	1265–1321		Divina Commedia.	
'rancesco Petrarch	1304–74		Poems	1st col. ed. 1581.
Giovanni Boccaccio	1313–75	Decameron		1353
.uigi Pulci	1431–87		Poems—Morgante Maggiore	At Venice 1481.
Niccolo Machiavelli	1469–1527	Historical—Political, The Prince, etc., MACHIAVELLIAN PRINCIPLES		1513
.udovico Ariosto	1474–1533		Orlando Furioso	1st compl. ed. 1532.
'rancesco Guicciardini	1482–1540	Historical, political.		
'rancesco Berni	1490–1536		Poems, burlesque	1541
'ietro Aretino	1492–1559	Satirical.		
'orquato Tasso	1544–95		Rinaldo, Aminta, Jerusalem Delivered	1573 et seq.
Galileo Galilei	1564–1642	Scientific.		
'ietro A. D. Metastasio	1698–1782		Musical dramas	1722 "
Carlo Goldoni	1707–95		Dramas, comedy.	
Giuseppe Parini	1729–99		Poems	1801–4
Girolamo Tiraboschi	1731–94	Historical—Italian Literature		1766–82
Alessandro Volta	1745–1827	Scientific.		
Vittorio Alfieri	1749–1803		Poems, dramas	1780 et seq.
Vincenzo Monti	1754–1828		Poems.	
Carlo G. Botta	1766–1837	Historical—Story of Italy, etc.		1789–1832
Jean Charles L. Sismondi	1773–1842	Historical—Literature of Southern Europe, etc.		1807 et seq.
Nicolo Ugo Foscolo	1777–1827	Miscellaneous	Poems	1797 "
Giovanni B. Niccolini	1782–1861		Dramas.	
Alessandro Manzoni	1784–1873	Novels—I Promessi Sposi, etc.	Dramas	1819 "
Cesare Balbo	1789–1853	Historical and political		1829–43
Giacomo Leopardi	1798–1837		Poems	1st compl. ed. 1845.
Vincenzo Gioberti	1801–52	Polemical		1838
Cesare Cantu	1804–81	History—Historical novels		1834 et seq.
Antonio C. N. Gallenga	1810–	Historical		1840 "
Paolo E. Giudici	1812–72	Historical—Italian Literature.		
Ruggiero Bonghi	1828–	Critical, etc.		1859 "

SCANDINAVIAN (DANISH) LITERATURE AND AUTHORS.

Authors.		Principal works.		First appeared or published.
Name.	Time.	Prose.	Poetry and dramas.	
Unknown	....	The Eddas		11th, 12th centuries.
Henrik Harpestrings	d. 1244	Medical.		
Unknown	....	Act of Union at Calmar		1397
Unknown	....		Danish ballads	1300–1500
Niels, monk of the monastery of Sorö (?)	....		History of Denmark. Rhymed Danish Verse. (First Danish book printed.)	1495
Mikkel, priest of St. Alban's church, Odense	....		Rose Garden of Maiden Mary, The Creation, Human Life	1514
Christian Pedersen	1480–1554	Karl Magnus, Ogier the Dane. Translates the Bible.		

SCANDINAVIAN (DANISH) LITERATURE AND AUTHORS.—(*Continued.*)

Authors.		Principal works.		First appeared or published.
Name.	Time.	Prose.	Poetry and dramas.	
A. G. Vedel	1542-1616	Saxon Grammar	Collects the Danish ballads	1591
Arild Hoitfeld	....	Chronicles of the Kingdom of Denmark		1595
Hieronymus Rauch	d. 1607		First original Danish dramas.	
Joost van den Voudel	1587-1679		Poems.	
Anders Arreboe	1587-1637		Father of Danish poetry.	
Thomas Kingo	1634-1703		Poems.	
Ludwig Holberg	1684-1754	Historical	Poems, dramas (comedy)	1719 et seq.
C. B. Tullin	1728-65		Poems.	
Johan Herman Wessel	1742-85		Poems.	
Johan Ewald	1743-81		Poems	1766-80
Niels Treschow	1751-1833	Philosophic.		
Christian H. Pram	1756-1821	Tales	Poems—Staerkodder, etc.	1824-29
Jens Immanuel Baggesen	1764-1826		Poems, comic and otherwise	1786 et seq.
Adolph Schack-Staffeldt	1769-1826		Lyric poems.	
Adam Gottlob Oehlenschläger	1779-1850		Poems, dramas—Harkon Jarl, etc.	1803 "
Steen Steensen Bilcher	1782-1848		Poems.	
Christian Molbech	1783-1857	Historical, critical, etc.		1811 "
Nikolai F. S. Grundtvig	1783-1872		Poems	Col. poems, 1869.
Rasmus C. Rask	1787-1832	Linguistical		1811 et seq.
Bernhard S. Ingemann	1789-1862	Novels	Poems	" "
Johan Ludvig Heiberg	1791-1860		Dramas, poems	1813-45
Niels M. Petersen	1791-1862	Historical, etc.		
Henrik Hertz	1798-1870		Poems, dramas	
Hans Christian Andersen	1805-75	Fairy Tales, Only a Player, etc.		
Frederik P. Müller	1809-76		Poems, dramas.	
Sören A. Kierkegaard	1813-55	Philosophic		1843 et seq.

SCANDINAVIAN (SWEDISH) LITERATURE AND AUTHORS.

Authors.		Principal works.		First appeared or published.
Name.	Time.	Prose.	Poetry and dramas.	
Snorri Sturluson (b. Iceland)	1178?		Collects the Sagas (The Heimskringla), and is supposed to have written the first part of the Snorri-edda.	
Clas Arrhenius	1627-95	Historical.		
Gustaf Adlerfeld	1675-1700	Historical.		
Eric Benzel	1675-1743	Moralistic.		
Emmanuel Swedenborg	1688-1772	Philosophic. PHILOSOPHY		1749-63
Olof Dalin	1708-63	History of Sweden	Poems	1733 et seq.
Jacob Henrik Mork	1714-63	Novels.		
Karl Mickel Bellman	1740-95		Lyrics	1760-80
Gudmund G. Adlerbeth	1751-1818		Poems.	
Thomas Thorild	1754-1808	Historical	Poems.	
Anna Maria Lengren	1754-1817		Poems.	
Franz Michael Franzen	1772-1847		Poems.	
Johan Olof Wallin	1779-1839		Hymns.	
Esaias Tegner	1782-1846		Poems (the greatest of Swedish poets)	1820 et seq.
Erik Gustaf Geijer (*yi-er*)	1783-1847	History		1825 "
Julia Christina Nyberg	1785-1865?		Poems	1821 "
Wilhelm F. Palmblad	1788-1852	Novels and biography.		
Peter Daniel A. Atterbom	1790-1855	Seers and Poets of Sweden	Poems	1818 "
Karl Johan Dahlgren	1791-1844		Poems	1825
Adolf Iwar Arwidsson	1791-1858	Pub. early Swedish ballads, poems.	Poems	1820 "
Erik Johan Stagnelius	1793-1828		Poems (the Swedish Wordsworth).	
Karl Jonas L. Almquist	1793-1866	Thorn-Rose, etc	Poems	1829
Anders Fryxell	1793-	Historical.		
Bernhard von Beskow	1796-1868		Dramas and poems	1818 "
Karl August Nicander	1799-1837		Poems.	
Fredrika Bremer	1801-65	Novels—The President's Daughter, The Neighbors, etc.		1828 "
Gustaf Henrik Mellin	1803-76	Historical novels.		
Karl Wilhelm Bottiger	1807-78		Poems.	
Henrik Arnold Wergeland	1808-45		Poems.	
Björnstjerne Björnson (*be-yorn-son*)	1832-	Novels and essays	Dramas	1854 "

SPANISH LITERATURE AND AUTHORS.

Authors.		Principal works.		First appeared or published.
Name.	Time.	Prose.	Poetry and dramas.	
Gonzalo de Berceo	1198-1268		Religious poems.	
Unknown			Early ballads	1200
Unknown	....		Poems of the Cid. [It was in the reign of Sancho the Great that D. Rodrigo Laynez was born (1026?), to whom the Spaniards gave the abbreviated title of Ruy Diaz, while the Moors called him *es sayd* or "my lord," whence the name Cid had its origin.—*Sismondi*, "Literature of Europe," vol. ii. p. 96.]	
Don Juan Manuel	1282-1349	Prose.		
Juan Ruiz de Hita	1300-60		Poems.	
Pedro Lopez de Ayala	1332-1407		Poems.	
Vasco de Labeira (?)	1390-1440?		Amadis de Gaula. [Original now lost. Supposed author a Portuguese attached to the court of John I. of Portugal. First printed in Spanish, 1519.—*Ticknor*, "Hist. of Spanish Literature," vol. i. p. 221.]	

SPANISH LITERATURE AND AUTHORS.—(*Continued.*)

Authors.		Principal works.		First appeared or published.
Name.	Time.	Prose.	Poetry and dramas.	
drigo Yanez	14th cen.		Rhymed Chronicles of Alfonso XI.	
Iñigo Lopez de Mendoza, marquis of Santillana	1398–1458		Sonnets.	
an de Mena	1411–56		Poems.	
an de la Euzina	1468–1534		Poems.	
s Casas	1474–1566	Historical.		
Vicente (Portuguese)	1485–1557		Dramas.	
an Boscan	1493–1543		Poems	1543
ristobal de Castillejo	1494–1556		Poems.	
rcilasso de la Vega	1503–36		Poems.	
ego de Mendoza	1503–75	Historical.	Poems	1520 et seq.
rge de Montemayor (Portuguese)	1520–62	Novels.		
iz de Camoens (Portuguese)	1524–79		LUSIAD, epic.	
onzo de Ercilla y Zunega	1533–95		La Araucana	1569
rnando Herrera	1534–97		Lyric poems	1582
an de Mariana	1536–1623	Historical.		
guel de Cervantes Saavedra	1547–1616	DON QUIXOTE, etc.	[To Don Quixote, Cervantes owes his immortality. No work of any language ever exhibited a more exquisite or a more sprightly satire or a happier vein of invention worked with more striking success.—*Sismondi*, "Literature of Europe."]	
cente Espinel	1551–1634	Esquire Marcos of Olregon (Spanish Gil Blas)	Poems	1618
is de Gongora y Argote	1561–1627		Poems.	
pe de Vega	1562–1635		Dramas.—Founder of the Spanish theatre.	
illén de Castro	1569–1631		Dramas	1621
ego Arduarte	1570–1637	Historical.		
ancesco Gomez de Quevedo y Villegas	1580–1647		Dramas and poems.	
briel Tellez (Tirso de Molina, Ecclesiastic)	1585–1648		Dramas.	
dro Calderon de la Barca	1600–81		The greatest of Spanish dramatists.	1st col. ed 1685.
eronimo de Contreras	1600?–48		Poems.	
an Ruiz de Alarçon y Mendoza (b. Mexico)	1598–1640		Dramas.	
tevan Manuel de Villegas	1596–1669		Lyrics.	
tonio de Solis	1610–86	Historical	Dramas	1684 et seq.
gustin Moreto y Cabana	1618–69		Dramas	1654
yjov y Montenegro	1676–1764	Essays and criticisms (the Spanish Addison).		
n Ignacio Luzan	1702–54		Poems.	
an de Yriarte	1750–98	Proverbs.		
mas José Gonzalas Carvahal	1753–1834		Poems.	
andro F. Moratin	1760–1828		Dramas and poems (the Spanish Molière)	1790 et seq.
an Bautista Arriaza	1770–1837		Poems.	
anuel Breton de los Herreros	1796–1873			
celia Böhl von Faber (Fernan Caballero)	1797–1877	Novels.		
n Patricio de la Escosura	1807–78	Novels	Poems and dramas	1830 et seq.
n José de Espronceda	1808–42		Poems	1st col. ed. 1840.
n Mariano Larra	1809–37	Novels.		
sé Zorilla y Moral	1818–		Dramas and poems (celebrated and popular).	
tonio Canovas del Castille	1830–	Historical.		
ñez de Arce Gaspes	1834?–		Poems, dramas (the Spanish Tennyson)	1860

literature, Forgeries of.

orks of Berosus, Mantheo, etc.—By Annius of Viterbo (b. 1432; d. 1502), contained in his "Antiquitatem Variorum Volumina XVII. cum Commentariis."

nnals of Tacitus.—By Bracciolini (Poggio) (1381–1459). An attempt has been made to prove that B. forged them, but without success. "There cannot be much doubt that the 'Annals' are genuine."—*Encycl. Brit.* 9th ed. article "Tacitus."

pistle of Barnabas.—This epistle is unanimously ascribed to Barnabas, the companion of St. Paul, by early Church writers. "The internal evidence is conclusive against its genuineness."—*Encycl. Brit.* 9th ed. vol. ii. p. 197. Probably written about 128 A.D. 5 parts were extant only in the Latin translation until Tischendorf discovered the entire Greek of the 1st part in "Codex Sinaiticus."

odex Sinaiticus.—Their genuineness impugned by Simonides (1863). He asserted it to be a MS. made by himself 4 years previously at Mount Athos. His statement has, however, been proved false. MANUSCRIPT.

lementines.—Not written by Clemens Romanus, to whom they have been ascribed.

pistles of St. Ignatius (martyred 107 A.D.).—Not settled as to the authenticity of all of them. Controversy arose through his defence and maintenance of the hierarchical system of the Church.

alse Decretals (Isadorian Decretals).—These decretals, collection of canons, etc. (820–36 A.D.), attributed to St. Isadore of Saville (570–636). "Said to have been forged for the maintenance of papal supremacy, and for 800 years formed the fundamental basis of the Canon law, the discipline of the Church, and even its faith."—*Disraeli*, "Curiosities of Literature."

pistles of Phalaris of Agrigentum (Sicily, 570 B.C.).—148 in number. Greek text first printed in Venice, 1498. First printed in English, Oxford, 1695. Edited by Charles Boyle. Richard Bentley proves them forgeries. LITERATURE.

Phœnician Stone.—Inscription dated 85th Olympiad, believed genuine for some time.

Is'iac Table.—Supposed Egyptian table, of brass, covered with emblems, etc.; first known in 1527. Now in Turin.

Early English MSS. of Rowley, etc.—The work of Thomas Chatterton. LITERATURE.

Ossian, etc.—The work of James Macpherson, at first believed genuine, but now no unbiased critic or scholar can be found to assert that the Ossianic poems as we have them are genuine. Macpherson never showed an original MS. LITERATURE.

Shakespeare.—One or two plays by William Ireland (1777–1835). IRELAND'S FORGERIES.

MS. Emendations of a Folio Shakespeare (2d edition).—In the possession of J. P. Collier. Emendations supposed to have been made about the time of printing, proved forgeries, but by whom made never made known. SHAKESPEARE AND HIS PLAYS.

An Historical and Geographical Description of the Island of Formosa: the Religion, Customs, and Manners of its People. By a Native of said Island.—Entirely made up by George Psalmanazar (1679–1763). Psalmanazar claimed to be a native of the island, pretended to speak and write the language, etc.—all invented by himself.

Ancient Classics of Various Times, both Greek and Latin.—Constantine L. Philip Simonides (1824–67), one of the ablest literary impostors ever known, succeeded in selling several of his MSS. in England, Germany, Greece, and Egypt. With some valuable MSS. he introduced forgeries. *Codex Sinaiticus, supra.*

Mormon Bible.—Written by Solomon Spaulding (1812) as "The Manuscript Found." Produced by Joseph Smith as the Mormon Bible. NEW YORK, OHIO.

Shelley's Letters.—Published by Moxon, 1852. 25 in number, and considered genuine for some time; discovered to be forgeries by mere accident. The perpetrator of the fraud not positively discovered.

[illegible]

lithium, [illegible]

lithofracteur or **stone-breaker**, [illegible]

lithography, [illegible]

lithotomy, [illegible]

lithotrity, [illegible]

Lithuania, [illegible]

liturgies [illegible]

Liverpool, [illegible]

[illegible]

Livingston Manor, N.Y. [illegible]

Livingstone, David. [illegible]

Livonia, a Russian province on the Baltic sea, [illegible]

loadstone. [illegible]

Loano, a village of Piedmont, N. Italy. Here the Austrians and Sardinians were defeated by the French, under [illegible]

loans [illegible]

lobby, [illegible]

members. "Lobbying" is practised in many forms, and often means no more than legitimate arguments addressed to representatives or committees; but in common use the word often suggests improper influences or even bribery. Professional lobbyists are in general disrepute. An attempt has recently been made in Massachusetts to remedy some of the evils of lobbying by the recognition of legislative counsel, and the regulation of their business by law.

local option, the relegation of the control of traffic in intoxicating drinks to the popular vote of each county or municipality. This principle has been tried in New York and several other states with varying success.

Lochlev´en castle, Kinross, Scotland, built on an isle in loch Leven, it is said by the Picts, was the royal residence of Alexander III. and his queen till taken to Stirling. It was besieged by the English in 1301, and in 1334. Patrick Graham, first archbishop of St. Andrews, imprisoned for attempting to reform the church, died here about 1478. The earl of Northumberland was confined in it, 1569; queen Mary in 1567, and she escaped from it Sunday, 2 May, 1568.

locks, early used by the Egyptians, Greeks, Romans, and the Chinese. Denon has engraved an Egyptian lock of wood. Du Cange mentions locks and padlocks as early as 1381.

Barron's locks (on the many tumbler principle) were patented in 1778, Bramah's in 1784, and Chubb's "detector" locks in 1818.

Loco-foco, a transient local (New York) term applied to the Democratic party. Originated in New York city, Oct. 1835, on account of the use of matches (loco-focos) by one of the Democratic factions (Anti-monopolists) to relight the lights extinguished at an evening meeting by the other faction for the purpose of breaking up the meeting. At once the Whig newspapers dubbed the Anti-monopolists, Loco-focos, and it soon became one of the names applied to the Democracy generally by the New York Whigs. LUCIFER MATCHES.

locomotives, NEW YORK, 1830; PENNSYLVANIA, 1829; UNITED STATES, 1829–31.

Locri, a people of N. Greece, resisted Philip of Macedon, were aided by Athenians and Thebans, and defeated by him at Chæronea, 7 Aug. 338 B.C.

locusts, one of the plagues of Egypt, 1491 B.C. (Exod. x.). Owing to the putrefaction of swarms in Egypt and Libya, 800,000 persons are said to have perished, 128 B.C. Palestine was infested with swarms that darkened the air; and, after devouring the fruits of the earth, died, and their stench caused a pestilential fever, 406 A.D. A similar catastrophe occurred in France in 873. A swarm of locusts settled upon the ground about London, and consumed the vegetables; great numbers fell in the streets; they resembled grasshoppers, but were 3 times the size, and their colors more variegated, 4 Aug. 1748. They infested Germany in 1749, Poland in 1750, and Warsaw in June, 1816. They are said to have been seen in London in 1857. Russia was infested by them in July, 1860; Algeria, severely, in 1866 and in 1874; Sardinia, in 1869; Kansas, Nebraska, and Minnesota, 1873–74. NEBRASKA, 1874–75.

Lo´di, a city of N. Italy. Napoleon Bonaparte, commanding the French, defeated the Austrians, under Beaulieu, after a bloody fight at the bridge of Lodi, 10 May, 1796. The republican flag floated in Milan a few days after.

log, an apparatus for measuring the speed of a ship, consisting of a log-chip, reel, and line, used in navigation about 1570; first mentioned by Bourne in 1577. The line was divided by knots into lengths of 50 feet, and the ship's speed was measured by a sand-glass, which bore the same proportion to an hour that 50 feet bears to a nautical mile. It has been superseded by a patent log, which has come into general use within the last 20 years. The record of the speed of a ship, its location (latitude and longitude), etc., is termed the log-book.

log´arithms, the indexes of the power of an assumed base, tabulated to facilitate arithmetical operations, were invented by baron Napier of Merchiston, who published his work in 1614. The device was improved by Henry Briggs at Oxford, who published tables, 1615–18. A method of computation by marked pieces of ivory discovered about the same time; they are called "Napier's bones."

log-cabin. The political canvas for president in 1840 is known as the log-cabin campaign. Gen. Wm. Henry Harrison, the Whig candidate, was represented as a plain farmer, who in early life had lived in a log cabin in Ohio; and such cabins, in every form, were adopted as the party symbol.

logic, "the science of reasoning." Eminent works on it are by Aristotle, Descartes; Bacon, "Novum Organon;" Locke, "On the Understanding;" and modern treatises by abp. Whately, sir William Hamilton, and John Stuart Mill.

Earl Stanhope's Demonstrator, or Logical Machine, invented in the latter part of the 18th century, was described by rev. Robert Harley to the British association, 19 Aug. 1878.

In his "Principles of Science," 1874, William Stanley Jevons describes his "logical abecedarium" and "Logical Slate."

G. Boole on "Laws of Thought," 1852.

J. Venn's "Symbolic Logic," July, 1881. METAPHYSICS, PHILOSOPHY.

log´ograph, apparatus invented by W. H. Barlow, about 1874, to record graphically the vibratory motions of air-waves of speech.

log´ograph´ic printing, in which each common word was cast in one piece, was patented by Henry Johnson and Mr. Walter of the London *Times* in 1783. Anderson's "History of Commerce," vol. iv., was printed by these types in 1789.

log-rolling, a common term in the United States for legislative combinations. The early settlers helped one another in clearing their land by combining to roll the logs away. When the supporters of 2 or more measures, in a legislature or in congress, joined forces and each set supported the measure of the other in exchange for similar aid, the union was called log-rolling. It is to prevent this that the constitutions of many states forbid any enactment which contains more than a single measure.

loi des suspects (*lwa day sus-pekts´*), enacted by the French convention, 17 Sept. 1793, during the Reign of Terror, filled the prisons of Paris. The Public Safety bill, of a similar character, was passed 18 Feb. 1858, after Orsini's attempt on the life of Napoleon III.

Lol´lards (by some derived from the German *lollen*, to sing in a low tone), the name given to the first reformers of the Roman Catholic religion in England, followers of Wycliffe. The sect is also said to have been founded in 1315 by Walter Lollard, who was burned for heresy at Cologne in 1322. The Lollards are said to have devoted themselves to acts of mercy. The first Lollard martyr in England was William Sawtree, parish priest of St. Osith, London, 12 Feb. 1401, when the Lollards were proscribed by Parliament, and numbers burned alive. Sir John Cobham, lord Oldcastle, a follower of Wycliffe, was accused of treason and condemned, Sept. 1413. He escaped to Wales, was captured, brought to London, and burned, 25 Dec. 1418. Lollards' Tower, part of the bishop's prison, was near St. Paul's, not Lambeth palace.—*Dr. Maitland.*

Lom´bard merchants, in England, were understood to be natives of the 4 republics: Genoa, Lucca, Florence, or Venice.—*Anderson.* Lombard usurers were sent to England by pope Gregory IX. to lend money to convents, communities, and persons who were not able to pay down the tenths collected throughout the kingdom with great rigor that year, 13 Hen. III. 1229. They had offices in the street named after them to this day. Their usurious transactions caused their expulsion from the kingdom in the reign of Elizabeth.

Lom´bardy, a province of N. Italy, derived its name from the Langobardi, a German tribe from Brandenburg, said (doubtfully) to have been invited into Italy by Justinian to serve against the Goths. Their chief, Alboin, established a kingdom which lasted from 568 to 774. The last king, Desiderius, was dethroned by Charlemagne. (For Lombard kings, ITALY.) About the end of the 9th century the chief towns of Lombardy fortified themselves, and became republics. The first Lombard league, consisting of Milan, Venice, Pavia, Modena, etc., was formed to restrain the German emperors, in 1167. On 29 May, 1176, they defeated Frederick Barbarossa at Legnano, and compelled him to sign the peace of Constance in 1183. In 1226 another league was formed against Frederick II.,

Ancient Ballads of Scotland.—By Robert Surtee (1779-1834). Imposed on sir Walter Scott and several others.

Squire's Letters.—Sent to Thomas Carlyle (1847) from an unknown source, correspondence pertaining to the time of Oliver Cromwell, and purporting to have been written by Samuel Squire.

Various Ancient Works, Modern Letters of Important Personages, etc.—Offered for sale by M. Chasles, member of the French Academy—all forgeries.

lithium, a metal, the lightest substance in nature except gases (specific gravity 0.59), is obtained from the alkali *lithia;* discovered by M. Arfwedson, a Swede, in 1817. ELEMENTS.

lithofracteur or **stone-breaker,** an explosive material, a modification of dynamite (composed chiefly of gun-cotton, nitro-glycerine, and constituents of gunpowder), invented by prof. Engels of Cologne, and made by Krebs in 1869. It was occasionally used by the Germans in the war of 1870-71, and was tried and well reported of for power and safety at Nant Mawy quarries, near Shrewsbury, Engl., 9, 10 May, 1871, and again on 20 Feb. 1872, before a British government commission on explosives.

lithog'raphy, drawing on stone. An invention ascribed to Alois Sennefelder, about 1796; and soon afterwards announced in Germany as polyautography. It became known in England in 1801, but its general introduction is referred to Mr. Ackermann of London, about 1817. Sennefelder died in 1841. Improvements have been made by Engelmann and others. PRINTING IN COLORS.

lithot'omy. The surgical operation of cutting for the stone, it is said, was performed by Ammonius, about 240 B.C. The "small apparatus," so called because few instruments were needed in the operation, was used by Celsus, about 17 A.D. The "high apparatus" was used (on a criminal at Paris) by Colot, 1475; by Franco, on a child, about 1566; and in England, by dr. Douglass, about 1519. The "lateral operation," invented by Franco, performed in Paris by Frère Jacques, in 1697, has been greatly improved. The "great apparatus," invented by John de Romanis, was described by his pupil Marianus Sanctus, 1524. SURGERY.

lithot'rity, stone-crushing. The apparatus produced by M. Leroy d'Etiolles in 1822 has since been improved.

Prizes of 6000 and 10,000 francs were awarded M. Jean Civiale for his method, 1827 and 1829.

Lithua'nia, formerly a grand-duchy, northeast of Prussia. The natives (Slavonic) long maintained independence against Russians and Poles. In 1386 their grand-duke, Jagellon, became king of Poland, and was baptized. Lithuania was incorporated with Poland 1501, when another duke, Casimir, became king. The countries were formally united in 1569. Most of Lithuania now belongs to Russia, the remainder to Prussia.

lit'urgies (Gr. λειτουργία, public service at private cost). The Greek and Roman church liturgies are ancient, having been committed to writing about the 4th and 5th centuries. The Roman church recognizes 4: the Roman or Georgian, the Ambrosian, the Gallican, and the Spanish or Mosarabic. The Greek church has 2 principal liturgies, St. Chrysostom's and St. Basil's, and several smaller ones. Parts of these are attributed to the Apostles, to St. Ignatius (250), to St. Ambrose (d. 397), and to St. Jerome (d. 420).

English liturgy was first composed, and was approved and confirmed by Parliament in 1547-48. The offices for morning and evening prayer then took nearly their present form.

At the solicitation of Calvin and others, the liturgy was reviewed and altered.......... 1551

It was first read in Ireland, in English, in 1550; in Scotland, exciting a tumult, in 1637, and was withdrawn.......... 1638

Liturgy revised by Whitehead, formerly chaplain to Anne Boleyn, and by bishops Parker, Grindall, Cox, and Pilkington, dean May, and secretary Smith.

John Knox is said to have used a liturgy for several years. Rev. Robert Lee of Edinburgh, introduced a form of prayer in public worship; discontinued it by order, May, 1859; soon after resumed it, and controversy ended at his death. 14 Mch. 1868

COMMON PRAYER, BOOK OF.

Liverpool, a borough of W. Lancashire, is supposed to be noticed in Domesday-book under the name *Esmedune* or *Smedune.* In other ancient records it is called *Litherpul* and *Lyrpul* (probably, in the ancient dialect, the lower pool, though some explain it as a pool frequented by an aquatic fowl, called the "liver," or from a sea-weed of that name; and others from a family of the name of Lever, whose antiquity is not sufficiently established). Soon after the Conquest, William granted the country between the rivers Mersey and Ribble to Roger of Poitiers, who, according to Camden, built a castle here about 1089. It afterwards was held by the earls of Chester and dukes of Lancaster. Pop. of the parliamentary borough in 1851, 375,995; 1861, 443,938; 1871, 493,405; 1881, 552,508; 1891, 517,951; 1901, 684,947.

Liverpool made a free borough by Henry III.......... 1229

Made an independent port.......... 1335

Liverpool "a paved town" (*Leland*).......... 1558

"The people of her majesty's decayed town of Liverpool" petition Elizabeth for relief from a subsidy.......... 1571

Town rated for ship-money in only 26*l.* by Charles I.......... 1634

Besieged and taken by prince Rupert..........26 June, 1644

Liverpool and Manchester railway opened..........15 Sept. 1830

[First grand work of the kind, about 31 miles long. At its opening the duke of Wellington and other illustrious persons were present; Mr. Huskisson, who alighted during a stoppage of the engines, was knocked down by one of them, which went over his thigh and caused his death, 15 Sept. 1830.]

Liverpool and Birmingham (Grand Junction) railway opened, 4 July, 1837

Railway to London (now the Northwestern) opened....17 Sept. 1838

Steamer *Liverpool*, 461 horse-power, sails for New York, 28 Oct. "

Tunnel under Mersey to Birkenhead begun..........Apr. 1872

Mersey tunnel opened..........13 Feb. 1885

Livingston Manor, N. Y. ANTI-RENTISM; NEW YORK, 1686.

Livingstone, David. AFRICA.

Livo'nia, a Russian province on the Baltic sea, first visited by Bremen merchants about 1158. After belonging successively to Denmark, Sweden, Poland, and Russia, it was ceded to Peter the Great in 1721. Area, 18,158 sq. miles; pop. 1889, 1,229,468.

loadstone. MAGNETISM.

Loa'no, a village of Piedmont, N. Italy. Here the Austrians and Sardinians were defeated by the French, under Massena, 23, 24 Nov. 1795.

loans for the public service were raised by Wolsey in 1522 and 1525. In 1559 Elizabeth borrowed 200,000*l.* of the city of Antwerp, to enable her to reform the coin, and sir Thomas Gresham and the city of London joined in the security.—*Rapin.* The amounts of some public loans of England and France at memorable periods were:

Seven Years' war	1755 to 1763....	52,100,000*l.*
American war	1776 " 1784....	75,500,000*l.*
French revolutionary war	1793 " 1802....	168,500,000*l.*
War with Bonaparte	1803 " 1814....	206,300,000*l.*
Two loans, 1813	21,000,000*l.* and	22,000,000*l.*
War with Russia	1855 to 1856....	16,000,000*l.*
For deficiency in revenue	1856....	10,000,000*l.*
[Last 2 taken by the Rothschilds alone.]		
By East India company	1858....	8,000,000*l.*

A subscription loan (18,000,000*l.*) for the war with France filled in London in 15 hours and 20 minutes, 5 Dec. 1796.

French loan, on 9 July, 1855, for war with Russia. French legislature authorized a loan of 750,000,000 francs (30,000,000*l.*). On the 30th the total subscribed in France amounted to 3,652,591,985 francs (about 146,103,679*l.*), nearly 5 times the amount required; 2,533,888,450 francs were from Paris; from the departments, 1,118,703,535 francs. The number of subscribers was 316,864, and 231,920,155 francs were in subscriptions of 50 francs and under. About 600,000,000 francs came from foreign countries. The English subscription of 150,000,000 francs was returned. France raised a loan of 20,000,000*l.* for the Italian war from its own people without difficulty, May, 1859.

Turkish loan in 1854 at 7½ per cent., recommended by lord Palmerston; a loan of 5,000,000*l.*, at 4 per cent., secured by England and France, taken by Rothschild, Aug. 1855, and rose to a small premium.

French loan for 17,600,000*l.* announced 29 Jan. 1868.

French loan for 2,000,000,000 francs (80,000,000*l.*); nearly twice the amount subscribed in France, 28 June, 1871; another (of 120,000,000*l.* at 6¼ per cent.), for payment of indemnity and evacuation of provinces held by Germans; announced 26 July, 1872; above twice the amount subscribed. FRANCE.

Foreign Loans committee appointed to inquire concerning loans to Honduras, Costa Rica, and Paraguay, report on the exaggerated statements respecting revenues and resources of the states in prospectuses, efforts of contractors to make fictitious markets, proceedings on the stock-exchange to maintain prestige, secrecy practised; "the best security against the recurrence of such evils will be found, not so much in legislative enactments as in enlightenment of the public as to their real nature and origin, thus rendering it more difficult for unscrupulous persons to carry out schemes . . . which have ended in so much discredit and disaster," July, 1875.

lobby, a general name for persons not members of a legislative body, who try to influence its action by appeals to

·mbers "Lobbying" is practised in many forms, and often ·ans no more than legitimate arguments addressed to repre·ntatives or committees, but in common use the word often ·ggests improper influences or even bribery Professional ·byists are in general disrepute An attempt has recently ·en made in Massachusetts to remedy some of the evils of ·bying by the recognition of legislative counsel, and the ·gulation of their business by law

local option, the relegation of the control of traffic intoxicating drinks to the popular vote of each county or ·nicipality This principle has been tried in New York ·d several other states with varying success

Lochlev'en castle, Kinross, Scotland, built on an ·e in loch Leven it is said by the Picts, was the royal resi·nce of Alexander III and his queen till taken to Stirling ·was besieged by the English in 1301, and in 1331 Patrick ·aham, first archbishop of St Andrews, imprisoned for at·mpting to reform the church, died here about 1478 The ·l of Northumberland was confined in it, 1569, queen Mary 1567, and she escaped from it Sunday, 2 May, 1568.

locks, early used by the Egyptians, Greeks, Romans, ·d the Chinese Denon has engraved an Egyptian lock of ·od Du Cange mentions locks and padlocks as early as 1381. ·rron's locks (on the many tumbler principle) were patented in ·778, Bramah's in 1788, and Chubb's "detector" locks in 1818.

Loco-foco, a transient local (New York) term applied the Democratic party Originated in New York city, Oct. ·35, on account of the use of matches (loco-foco) by one of ·e Democratic factions (Anti-monopolists) to relight the ·hts extinguished at an evening meeting by the other fac·n for the purpose of breaking up the meeting At once ·e Whig newspapers dubbed the Anti-monopolists, Loco·os, and it soon became one of the names applied to the ·mocracy generally by the New York Whigs. LUCIFER ·ATCHES.

locomotives. NEW YORK, 1830, PENNSYLVANIA, ·29, UNITED STATES, 1829-31

Locri, a people of N Greece, resisted Philip of Macedon, ·re aided by Athenians and Thebans, and defeated by him Chæronea, 7 Aug 338 B.C

locusts, one of the plagues of Egypt, 1491 B C (Exod ·) Owing to the putrefaction of swarms in Egypt and ·bya, 800,000 persons are said to have perished, 128 B.C. ·lestine was infested with swarms that darkened the air, ·d, after devouring the fruits of the earth, died, and their ·ench caused a pestilential fever, 406 A.D A similar catas·phe occurred in France in 873. A swarm of locusts settled ·on the ground about London, and consumed the vegetables, ·eat numbers fell in the streets, they resembled grasshoppers, ·t were 3 times the size, and their colors more variegated, 4 ·ug 1748 They infested Germany in 1749, Poland in 1750, ·d Warsaw in June, 1816 They are said to have been seen London in 1857 Russia was infested by them in July, ·60, Algeria, severely, in 1866 and in 1874, Sardinia, in ·68, Kansas, Nebraska, and Minnesota, 1873-74 NEBRAS·A, 1874-75.

Lo'di, a city of N Italy. Napoleon Bonaparte, command·g the French, defeated the Austrians, under Beaulieu, after ·bloody fight at the bridge of Lodi, 10 May, 1796 The re·blican flag floated in Milan a few days after.

log, an apparatus for measuring the speed of a ship, con·sting of a log-chip, reel, and line, used in navigation about ·70, first mentioned by Bourne in 1577. The line was di·ded by knots into lengths of 50 feet, and the ship's speed ·as measured by a sand-glass, which bore the same propor·on to an hour that 50 feet bears to a nautical mile. It has ·en superseded by a patent log, which has come into general ·e within the last 20 years. The record of the speed of a ·ip, its location (latitude and longitude), etc., is termed the ·g-book.

log'arithms, the indexes of the power of an assumed ·se, tabulated to facilitate arithmetical operations, were in·ented by baron Napier of Merchiston, who published his ·ork in 1614 The device was improved by Henry Briggs · Oxford, who published tables, 1616-18 A method of computation by marked pieces of ivory discovered about the same time, they are called "Napier's bones"

log-cabin. The political canvas for president in 1840 is known as the log-cabin campaign Gen Wm Henry Harrison, the Whig candidate, was represented as a plain farmer, who in early life had lived in a log cabin in Ohio, and such cabins, in every form, were adopted as the party symbol

logic, "the science of reasoning" Eminent works on it are by Aristotle, Descartes, Bacon, "Novum Organon," Locke, "On the Understanding," and modern treatises by abp Whately sir William Hamilton, and John Stuart Mill

Earl Stanhope's Demonstrator, or Logical Machine, invented in the latter part of the 18th century, was described by rev Robert Harley to the British Association, 19 Aug 1878

In his "Principles of Science" 1874 William Stanley Jevons describes his "Logical Abecedarium" and "Logical Slate"

G Boole on "Laws of Thought," 1852

J Venn's "Symbolic Logic," July, 1881 METAPHYSICS, PHILOSOPHY

log'ograph, apparatus invented by W H Barlow, about 1874, to record graphically the vibratory motions of air-waves of speech.

log'ograph'ic printing, in which each common word was cast in one piece, was patented by Henry Johnson and Mr Walter of the London *Times* in 1783 Anderson's "History of Commerce," vol iv, was printed by these types in 1789

log-rolling, a common term in the United States for legislative combinations The early settlers helped one another in clearing their land, by combining to roll the logs away When the supporters of 2 or more measures, in a legislature or in congress, joined forces, and each set supported the measure of the other in exchange for similar aid, the union was called log-rolling It is to prevent this that the constitutions of many states forbid any enactment which contains more than a single measure

loi des suspects (*loa des sus-pekts'*), enacted by the French convention, 17 Sept 1793, during the Reign of Terror, filled the prisons of Paris The Public Safety bill, of a similar character, was passed 18 Feb 1858, after Orsini's attempt on the life of Napoleon III.

Lol'lards (by some derived from the German *lollen*, to sing in a low tone), the name given to the first reformers of the Roman Catholic religion in England, followers of Wycliffe The sect is also said to have been founded in 1315 by Walter Lollard, who was burned for heresy at Cologne in 1322 The Lollards are said to have devoted themselves to acts of mercy The first Lollard martyr in England was William Sawtree, parish priest of St Osith, London, 12 Feb. 1401, when the Lollards were proscribed by Parliament, and numbers burned alive Sir John Cobham, lord Oldcastle, a follower of Wycliffe, was accused of treason and condemned, Sept 1413 He escaped to Wales, was captured, brought to London, and burned, 25 Dec 1418 Lollards' Tower, part of the bishop's prison, was near St Paul's, not Lambeth palace —*Dr Maitland*

Lom'bard merchants, in England, were understood to be natives of the 4 republics Genoa, Lucca, Florence, or Venice —*Anderson.* Lombard usurers were sent to England by pope Gregory IX to lend money to convents, communities, and persons who were not able to pay down the tenths collected throughout the kingdom with great rigor that year, 13 Hen III 1299 They had offices in the street named after them to this day Their usurious transactions caused their expulsion from the kingdom in the reign of Elizabeth

Lom'bardy, a province of N. Italy, derived its name from the Langobardi, a German tribe from Brandenburg, said (doubtfully) to have been invited into Italy by Justinian to serve against the Goths. Their chief, Alboin, established a kingdom which lasted from 568 to 774. The last king, Desiderius, was dethroned by Charlemagne (For Lombard kings, ITALY.) About the end of the 9th century the chief towns of Lombardy fortified themselves, and became republics. The first Lombard league, consisting of Milan, Venice, Pavia, Modena, etc, was formed to restrain the German emperors, in 1167 On 29 May, 1176, they defeated Frederick Barbarossa at Legnano, and compelled him to sign the peace of Constance in 1183. In 1226 another league was formed against Frederick II., which was also successful. *After this petty tyrants* rose in most of the cities, and foreign influence followed. The Guelph and Ghibelline factions distracted Lombardy, and from the 15th century it was contended for by German and French sovereigns. *Austria obtained it in 1748*, and held it till 1797, when it was conquered by the French, who incorporated it with the Cisalpine republic, and in 1805 with the kingdom of Italy. When the French empire fell, in 1815, the Lombardo-Venetian kingdom was established by the allied sovereigns and given to Austria, who had lost her Flemish possessions. Lombardy and Venice revolted, and joined the king of Sardinia in Mch. 1848; but did not support him well, and were again subjected to Austria after his defeat at Novara, 23 Mch. 1849. An amnesty for political offences was granted in 1856. Great jealousy of Sardinia was shown by Austria after 1849. In 1857 diplomatic relations were suspended; and in Apr. 1859 war broke out, the Austrians crossing the Ticino and entering Piedmont. The French emperor declared war against Austria, and sent troops into Italy. The Austrians were defeated at Montebello, 20 May; Palestro, 30, 31 May; Magenta, 4 June; and Solferino, 24 June. By the peace of Villafranca (11 July) most of Lombardy was ceded to Louis Napoleon, who transferred it to the king of Sardinia. It now forms part of the kingdom of Italy, to which Venetia was also surrendered by the treaty of Vienna, 3 Oct. 1867.

Lona'to, a town near the city of Brescia, N. Italy. Here Napoleon Bonaparte defeated Wurmser and the Austrians, 3 Aug. 1796.

London, the capital city of England, and the seat of government of the British empire. The fables of Geoffrey of Monmouth say that London was founded by Brute, a descendant of the Trojan Æneas, and called New Troy, or Troy novant, until the time of Lud, who surrounded it with walls, and gave it the name of Caer Lud, or Lud's town, etc.—*Leigh.* Lud was said to be a British king, buried where Ludgate formerly stood; but all this is fabulous; the name London is from *Llyndin*, the "town on the lake." Some assert that a city existed on the spot 1107 years before the birth of Christ, and 354 years before the foundation of Rome; that it was the capital of the Trinobantes, 54 B.C., and long previously. In 61 A.D. it was known to the Romans as Lundinium, or Colonia Augusta, chief residence of the merchants. The original walls of London said to have been the work of Theodosius, Roman governor of Britain, 379; but they are supposed to have been built about 306. There were originally 4 principal gates, but the number increased; and among others were the Prætorian way, Newgate, Dowgate, Cripplegate, Aldgate, Aldersgate, Ludgate, Bridegate, Moorgate, Bishopsgate, and the Postern on Tower hill. 8 gates were removed in 1760-61, and the last of the city boundaries, Temple Bar (rebuilt 1670-72), was removed early in Jan. 1878. London became the capital of the Saxon kingdom of Essex, and was called Lundenceaster. In 1860 London and the suburbs were estimated to cover 121 sq. miles (11 miles each way, being 3 times as large as in 1800); in 1880, 122 sq. miles. The metropolitan police district, 1891, extends over a radius of 15 miles from Charing Cross, exclusive of the city of London, 688.31 sq. miles. Total mileage of streets patrolled, 8360. The population of the metropolitan districts in 1851 was 2,362,236; in 1861, 2,808,862; county of London, 1891, 4,231,431; 1901, 4,536,541; metropolitan and city police districts, 1891, 5,633,332; 1901, 6,581,372. The population of the "city" in 1801, 156,859; in 1811, 120,909; in 1821, 125,434; in 1831, 125,574; in 1841, 125,008; in 1851, 122,440; in 1861, 112,063; in 1871, 74,897; in 1881, 50,526; in 1891, 37,694. Day census, 25-30 Apr. 1881, 260,670; 1891, 301,384. The London county council was constituted in common with county councils all over England and Wales under the Local Government act of 1888. It comprises a chairman, 19 aldermen, and 118 councillors. The term of office for an alderman is 6 years, but 10 or 9 retire every alternate 3 years. Councillors are elected for 3 years directly by the rate payers, and the councillors elect the aldermen. The positions of the aldermen and councillors are the same, except as to the term of office. The first meeting of the London county council was held 21 Mch. 1889.

Boadicea, queen of the ICENI, reduces London to ashes, and puts 70,000 Romans and strangers to the sword.......... 61

She is defeated by Suetonius, 80,000 Britons are massacred, and she takes poison.......... 61

Bishopric said to have been founded by Theanus.......... 179

London rebuilt and walled in by the Romans.......... 306

Eight hundred vessels said to be employed in the port of London for the export of corn.......... 359

St. Paul's church founded by Ethelbert..........about 597

Bishopric revived by St. Mellitus.......... 604

London pillaged by Danes.......... 839

Alfred repairs and strengthens London.......... 884

Easterlings settle in London..........before 978

Tower built by William I.......... 1078

First charter granted to the city by the same king.......... 1079

[It is still preserved in the city archives. It is written in beautiful Saxon characters, on a slip of parchment 6 inches long and 1 broad, and is in English as follows: "William the king *greeteth William the bishop, and Godfrey the portreve,* and all the burgesses within London, friendly. And I acquaint you that I will that ye be all there law-worthy as ye were in king Edward's days. And I will that every child be his father's heir, after his father's days. And I will not suffer that any man do you any wrong. God preserve you."]

Charter granted by Henry I.......... 1100

St. Bartholomew's priory founded by Rahere..........about "

London bridge built, 1014; burned.......... 1136

Charter granted by Henry II.......... 1154

Old London bridge begun.......... 1176

Henry Fitz-Alwyn, the first mayor (served 24 years).......... 1189

Massacre of Jews.......... "

First stone bridge finished.......... 1209

Charter of king John; mayor and common council to be elected annually.......... 1214

[Stowe incorrectly states this charter to have been given in 1209, but it bears date 19 May in the 16th year of John's reign, which began in 1199. It was acted on, many mayors holding office for several years (see below, Whittington, 1409).]

Modern times, alderman Wood, 1815-16; sir John Key, 1830-31; alderman Cubitt, 1861-62. The title of lord-mayor first bestowed by Edward III.......... 1354

Foreign merchants invited, settle here..........1199-1220

Charter of Henry III.......... 1233

Aldermen appointed..........about 1242

Watch in London, 38 Hen. III.......... 1253

Privileges granted to Hanse merchants.......... 1259

Tax called murage, to repair walls and ditches..........about 1282

Water brought from Tyburn to West Cheap.......... 1285

Expulsion of Jews by Edward I. (16,511).......... 1290

Livery companies incorporated.......... 1327

Charter granted by Edward III.......... 1328

Terrible pestilence, 50,000 (?) citizens perish.......... 1348

[It broke out in India, and spreading westward through every country, reached England. In London the common cemeteries were not sufficient, and land without the walls was assigned for burial. In the present precincts of the Charterhouse upwards of 50,000 bodies were deposited. The plague did not disappear till 1357.—*Leigh.*]

London sends 4 members to Parliament.......... 1355

William of Walworth lord mayor.......... 1380

Wat Tyler's rebellion (TYLER).......... 1381

Aldermen elected for life.......... 1394

Great plague; 30,000 (?) died.......... 1406

Whittington thrice lord mayor (in reality 4 times.—*Whitaker*), 1397, 1398, 1406, 1409

Jack Cade's rebellion (CADE'S INSURRECTION).......... 1450

First civic procession on the water; sir John Norman lord mayor.......... 1453

Falconbridge attempts the city.......... 1471

Printing-press set up by Caxton.......... "

Sweating sickness rages.......... 1485

Fleet ditch navigable.......... 1502

St. Paul's school founded by dean Colet.......... 1509

Fatal sweat, *Sudor Anglicus*.......... 1517

Evil May-day (so called from the riot of the populace in opposition to foreigners, especially to the French. The leader and 15 others were hanged, the others pardoned by king Henry VIII.)..........1 May, "

Streets first paved (*Viner's Stat.*).......... 1533

"Bills of mortality" ordered to be kept.......... 1538

Dissolution of religious houses.......... 1539

St. Bartholomew's monastery changed to a hospital.......... "

Forty taverns and public-houses allowed in the city, and 3 in Westminster, act 7 Edw. VI.......... 1553

Christ's hospital founded by king Edward VI.......... "

Russian Trading company established.......... "

Coaches introduced..........about 1563

Royal Exchange built (EXCHANGE).......... 1566

New buildings in London forbidden "where no former hath been known to have been," to prevent increase of size.......... 1580

[This decree *was dated Nonesuch, 7 July, 1580, forbidding* new buildings where none had existed in the memory of man. The extension of the metropolis was deemed to encourage the plague, create trouble in governing multitudes, a dearth of victuals, multiplying of beggars, and inability to relieve them; an increase of artisans more than could live together; impoverishing other cities for lack of inhabitants. The decree asserted that lack of air, lack of room to walk and shoot, etc., arose out of too crowded a city. A proclamation to the same effect was also issued by James I.]

Levant company established.......... 1581

Thames water brought into the city by leaden pipes..........1580-94

orden's map of London pub . . 1593
tow publishes his survey 1598
early all London yet built of wood 1600
ast India company incorporated "
n epidemic, the PLAGUE, 30,578 persons said to have died 1603
UNPOWDER PLOT 1605
homas Sutton founds Charterhouse school, etc 1611
ew river water brought to London 1613
irginia company established 1616
rincipal streets paved "
ackney coaches first plied 1625
uilding of the western parishes, St Giles's, etc begun 1640
ity held for the Parliament 1642
ondon fortified 1643
ews allowed to return to London by Cromwell 1650
anking begun by Francis Child about 1660
oyal Society of London chartered 1662
evastation of the PLAGUE, 68,596 persons said to have died 1665
xford afterwards *London Gazette*, pub 7 Nov "
reat fire of London (FIRES) 2-6 Sept. 1666
ct for a "new model of building" in the city "
udson's Bay company chartered 1670
ONUMENT erected by Wren 1671-77
t Paul's founded 21 June, 1675
ates's pretended popish plot 1678
ondon directory pub 1679
harter granted by Charles II 1680
enny post established 1683
ettlement of French Protestants 1685
harter declared forfeited, 1682, but restored 1689
ank of England established 1694
t Paul's opened 2 Dec 1697
acheverell's sermon and mob (RIOTS) 1709
outh Sea bubble begun, 1710, exploded (SOUTH SEA COMPANY), 1720
helsea water works formed 1722
ank of England built 1732-34
lass lamps in the street between 1694 and 1736
leet ditch covered, and Fleet market opened 1737
ondon hospital instituted 1740
ew MANSION HOUSE founded, 1739, completed 1753
ritish museum established "
ociety of Arts established "
ew road, 1755-56, City road projected about 1760
ight gates removed 1760-61
hop signs removed 1762
lackfriars bridge opened 19 Nov 1769
ord mayor (Brass Crosby) committed to the Tower by the House of Commons for breach of privilege 27 Mch 1771
ord George Gordon's No popery mob (GORDON'S RIOTS) June, 1780
uilding of Camden Town begun 1791
oyal Institution of Great Britain founded 1799
ondon docks opened 20 Jan "
ondon Institution founded 1805
lluminating gas first exhibited in Pall Mall 1807
int finished 1811
egent street begun 1813
ity generally lighted with gas 1814
aterloo bridge opened 18 June, 1817
outhwark bridge opened 24 Mch 1819
ank of England completed by sir John Soane 1821
abs introduced 1823
ondon Mechanics' Institution founded "
ondon university chartered 11 Feb 1826
ew post-office completed 1829
mnibuses introduced "
ew metropolitan police began 29 Sept "
ew London bridge opened 1 Aug 1831
ouses of Parliament burned . 16 Oct. 1834
ity of London school founded "
irst railway in the city (see below, Oct 6, 1864) opened to Birmingham, 17 Sept., to Greenwich 28 Dec 1838
enny postage begun 10 Jan 1840
ailway to Southampton opened 11 May, "
ood pavement tried, fails 1841
ondon library established "
ailway to Bristol opened 30 June, "
lackwall railway opened . 2 Aug "
ailway to Brighton opened . 21 Sept "
hames tunnel opened .. . 25 Mch 1843
LEET PRISON taken down .. 1845
enny steamboats begun . "
wopenny omnibuses begun 1846
hartist demonstration (CHARTISTS) 10 Apr 1848
oal exchange opened 30 Oct. 1849
ailway opened to Warrington, branch of Great Northern, Aug 1850
reat exhibition opened, 1 May, closed 11 Oct. 1851
uke of WELLINGTON d 14 Sept, funeral at St. Paul's. 18 Nov. 1852
Metropolitan Local Management act passed 14 Aug 1855
Metropolitan Board of Works, first meeting 22 Dec "
Royal British Bank stops payment 4 Sept. 1856
Metropolis divided into 10 postal districts 1 Jan 1858
Complaints of the state of the Thames, act for its purification passed. 2 Aug "
Metropolitan railway (underground) begun spring of . 1860
George Peabody, American merchant, gives 150,000*l* to ameliorate condition of poor of London 12 Mch 1862
International Exhibition opens. 1 May, "
Metropolitan railway opened . 10 Jan. 1863
Pneumatic Despatch company begins to convey post office bags 21 Feb "
Charing Cross railway opened ... 11 Jan. 1864
First block of Peabody's dwellings in Spitalfields opened 29 Feb 1864
First railway train enters the city of London near Blackfriars bridge 6 Oct "
Black Friday, commercial panic failure of Overend, Gurney & Co (limited) 10 May (BLACK FRIDAY) 11 May, 1866
Estimated population of the "city" by day, 283,520, by night, about 100,000 Dec "
Metropolitan Poor act passed 29 Mch 1867
Midland counties railway station opened 1 Oct 1868
Meeting to relieve sufferers by South American earthquake (11,000*l* collected) 13 Oct. "
Peabody gives another 100,000*l* for London poor 5 Dec "
London Association for Prevention of Poverty and Crime founded 17 Dec "
Tolls on commercial roads, London, E ceased 5 Aug 1871
National thanksgiving for recovery of prince of Wales, queen and prince go to St Paul's 27 Feb 1872
Forgery on Bank of England of 80,000*l* detected Mch 1873
First Hospital Sunday 15 June, "
First Hospital Saturday 17 Oct 1874
Freedom of city given to chief justice Cockburn (said to be the first case of the kind) 9 Mch 1876
Public meeting at Mansion house respecting atrocities in Bulgaria (TURKEY) 18 Sept "
Great Eastern street (Shoreditch to Old street) opened 12 Oct "
Temple Bar removed 2-14 Jan 1878
Great Eastern street completed and opened Aug "
Waterloo bridge opened toll free 5 Oct "
City and Guilds of London Institute for Advancement of Technical Education organized 11 Nov "
City Church and Churchyard Protection Society formed Feb 1879
New street, Shoreditch to Bethnal green opened (it completes direct road from Oxford street to Old ford) 29 Mch "
Temple Bar memorial uncovered (TEMPLE) 8 Nov 1880
City of London college, near Moorgate street, foundation laid, 31 Mch 1882
Attention to dwellings of "Outcast London" called by G R. Sims's "How the Poor Live," etc autumn, 1883
Meeting at Mansion house to raise 50,000*l* to aid the Beaumont legacy for an institution for instruction and recreation of people of East end 14 Dec "
Remains of Roman architecture, etc, discovered by excavations in Bevis Marks, E C Aug 1884
Common council authorize low level bridge between the Tower and Horsely down, with lifting sections for passage of ships, cost about 750,000*l* 24 Oct. "
Tower Bridge act passed 14 Aug 1885
Foundation stone of Tower bridge laid by prince of Wales, 21 June, 1886
New City of London court opened by the lord mayor 6 Dec 1888
Ball at the Mansion house to celebrate the 700th anniversary of the mayoralty 29 Oct 1889
Freedom of the city given to Henry M Stanley 13 May, 1890
Excavations for the post office, discoveries of Roman remains, the town ditch, etc Sept "
City and South London Electric railway opened by prince of Wales. 4 Nov "
Corporation medal commemorating foundation of mayoralty in 1189 finished by Messrs. Kirkwood of Edinburgh Nov "
Serious difficulty of Messrs Baring (liabilities 21,000,000*l*) promptly assisted by Bank of England and by Bank of France, panic averted 8-15 Nov "
Telephone system, London and Paris, inaugurated 18 Mch 1891
Stuart Knill, Roman Catholic, elected lord mayor of London, 29 Sept 1892

London, Bishopric of, is said to have been founded in the reign of Lucius, about 179, Theanus first archbishop. Augustin made Canterbury the metropolitan see of England. Mellitus was bishop in 604 The see has given to the church of Rome 5 saints, and to the British realm 16 lord chancellors and lord treasurers

London bridge. One is said to have existed 978 A bridge built of wood, 1014, was partly burned in 1136 The late old bridge was commenced about 1176 by Peter of Colechurch, and completed in 1209, with houses on each side, connected together by arches of timber which crossed the street At its gate-houses were exhibited the heads of traitors, etc, notably the head of sir William Wallace, 1305, Simon Frisel, 1306, 4 traitor knights, 1397, lord Bardolf, 1408, Bolingbroke, 1440, Jack Cade, 1451, Fisher, bishop of Rochester, 1535, sir Thomas More, 1535, and many others.

Fire at the Southwark end brought crowds on the bridge, houses at the north end caught fire and prevented escape, and 3000 persons were killed, burned, or drowned July, 1212
Bridge restored in 1300, again destroyed by fire in 1471, 13 Feb 1632, and Sept 1725
All houses pulled down . 1756
Water works begun, 1582, destroyed by fire 1774
Toll discontinued 27 Mch 1782
In 1822 the corporation advertised for designs for a new bridge, that by John Rennie was approved, and the work executed by his sons John and George The first pile was driven 200 feet west of the old bridge, 15 Mch. 1824, first stone laid by lord mayor, alderman Garratt 15 June, 1825
Bridge opened by William IV and his queen 1 Aug 1831

London company. VIRGINIA, 1606, 1609, 1612.

London stone. A stone said to have been placed by the Romans in Cannon street, then the centre of the city, 15 B.C. London stone was known before William I. It was removed from the opposite side of the way in 1742, and again to its present position in the wall of St. Swithin's church, 1798. Against this stone Jack Cade struck his sword, exclaiming, "Now is Mortimer lord of this city!" 1450.

Londonderry or **Derry,** N. Ireland, mentioned 546. An abbey here was burned by the Danes in 783. A charter was granted to the London companies in 1615. The town was surprised, and sir George Powlett, the governor, and the entire garrison were put to the sword by rebels, in 1606. It was besieged by O'Neill in 1641. A grant was made of Derry, with 210,000 acres of land, to various companies in London, in 1619, when it took its present name. The siege of Derry by James II.'s army commenced 20 Apr. 1689. The garrison and inhabitants were driven to the extremity of famine; but, under rev. George Walker, they defended it until the siege was raised by gen. Kirke, on 30 July. James's army, under the French general Rosen, retired with the loss of about 9000 men. Pop. 1891, 32,893.

Lone Star, a secret society formed in 1848, in Alabama, and other southern states, for the "extension of the institutions, power, influence, and commerce of the United States over the whole of the western hemisphere, and the islands of the Atlantic and Pacific oceans." The first acquisitions to be made by the order were Cuba and the Sandwich islands. KNIGHTS OF THE GOLDEN CIRCLE.

Long House, a name given to the confederate Five Nations extending from Albany, N. Y., to lake Erie. The Mohawks, the most eastern tribe, were called the "eastern door," and the Senecas, the most western, the "western door." The Great Council House (the Long House proper) and fire was in the territory of the Onondagas, where the whole confederacy would convene on business of importance.

Long Island, Battle of, 27 Aug. 1776, between the British troops under sir William Howe, and the Americans, who suffered defeat, after a well-fought action, losing 500 men killed and wounded and 1000 prisoners. Under a fog Washington crossed the East river before the British could take advantage of their victory. NEW YORK.

Long Parliament met 3 Nov. 1640; was forcibly dissolved by Cromwell 20 Apr. 1653.

longevity. Methuselah died aged 969, 3349 B.C. (Gen. v. 27). Golour M'Crain, of the isle of Jura, one of the Hebrides, is mythically said to have kept 180 Christmases in his own house, and died in the reign of Charles I.—*Greig.* "In 1014 died Johannes de Temporibus, who lived 361 years (!)." —*Stow.* Thomas Parr, a laboring man of Shropshire, was brought to London by the earl of Arundel in 1635, and said to be in his 153d year and in perfect health; he died 15 Nov. in the same year. Henry Jenkins, of Yorkshire, died in 1670, and was buried in Bolton churchyard, 6 Dec., aged 169 years (?). The researches of sir G. Cornewall Lewis, prof. Owen, Wm. J. Thoms (in his "Human Longevity," May, 1873), and others, have disproved many alleged cases of longevity; and few statements of lives extending beyond a century can be relied on. There were no records of baptism till the 16th century.

ALLEGED INSTANCES.

Died		Aged
1656.	James Bowles, Killingworth	152
1691.	Lady Eccleston, Ireland	143
1759.	James Sheil, Irish yeoman	136
1766.	Col. Thomas Winslow, Ireland	146
1772.	Mrs. Clum, Lichfield	138
1774.	William Beeby, Dungarvon (an ensign who served at the battles of the Boyne and Aughrim)	130
1780.	Robert MacBride, Herries	130
"	William Ellis, Liverpool	130
1785.	Cardinal de Solis	110
1797.	Charles Macklin, actor, London	107
1806.	Mr. Creeke, of Thurlow	125
"	Catherine Lopez, of Jamaica	134
1813.	Mrs. Meighan, Donoughmore	130
1814.	Mary Innes, isle of Skye	127
1816.	Jane Lewson, Coldbath fields, Clerkenwell	116
1840.	Martha Rorke, of Dromore, county of Kildare, 27 Aug.	133
1853.	Mary Power (aunt of rev. Lalor Sheil), Ursuline convent, Cork, 20 Mch.	[illegible]
1858.	James Nolan, Knockardrane, Carlow	116
1874.	Anthony Beresford (b. 8 Feb. 1772), d. at Alstonfield, 3 Mch. (authentic)	101
1875.	Count Jean Fred. Waldeck, painter; b. at Prague, 16 Mch. 1766; d. at Paris, 29 Apr.	109
"	Jacob Wm. Lüning, at Morden college	103
1876.	Madame Hulsenstein, said to have been maid of honor to the empress Maria Theresa	119
"	Elizabeth Abbott, Ipswich, said to be	105
1877.	Pleasance, widow of sir James E. Smith, botanist (b. 11 May, 1773; d. 3 Feb.)	103
"	Eunice Bagster, wife of Samuel, Bible bookseller, London, 22 Aug.	100
1878.	Thomas Budgen, Spitalfields, London, 4 Aug.	104
1879.	Jane Hooper, St. Pancras, London	102
"	Rev. Canon Beadon, Stoneham	102
"	Margaret Crook, Durham	112
1880.	Sarah Way, Bristol	104 and 9 months.
"	Johannette Polack (b. at Genth), Wiesbaden,	101 and 5 months.
1881.	Martha Gardner, Liverpool, 10 Mch.	104 and 5 months.
"	Fanny Bailey, Worthing, 6 Apr.	103 and 6 months.
1885.	Sir Moses Montefiore (b. 26 Oct. 1784)	100 and 9 months.

EXAMPLES FURNISHED BY DR. J. WEBSTER, F.R.S.

Died	Buried at	Aged
1652.	Dr. W. Meade, Ware, Herts, Engl.	148¾
1711.	Mrs. Scrimshaw, Rosemary lane, London	127
1739.	Margaret Patten, Christchurch, Westminster, London	136
1741.	John Rovin, Temesvar, Hungary	172
1757.	Alexander M'Cullough, Aberdeen, Scotland	132
1759.	Donald Cameron, Rannach, Aberdeenshire, Scotland	130
1763.	Mrs. Taylor, Piccadilly, London	131
1766.	John Mount, Langham, Dumfries, Scotland	136
"	John Hill, Leadhills, near Edinburgh, Scotland	130
1771.	Mr. Whalley, Rotherhithe, London	121
1775.	Widow Jones, Campbell	125
1780.	Mr. Evans, Spitalfields, London	139
1784.	Mary Cameron, Braemar, Aberdeen, Scotland	129
1791.	Archbd. Cameron, Keith, Aberdeenshire, Scotland	122
1851.	Jean Golembeski, Hôtel des Invalides, Paris	126

longevity in the United States. The census reports show the number of inhabitants 100 years of age and over as follows:

		Male.	Female.	
1850, pop. 23,191,876	White	357	430	
	Colored	720	1048	
	Total	1077	1478	=2555
1860, pop. 31,443,321	White	385	542	
	Colored	799	1141	
	Indians	49	37	
	Total	1233	1720	=2953
1870, pop. 38,558,371	Native white	259	383	
	Foreign born white	135	187	
	Colored	885	1652	
	Indians	7	14	
	Total	1286	2236	=3522
1880, pop. 50,155,783	Native white	237	355	
	Foreign born white	156	207	
	Colored	1016	2045	
	Total	1409	2607	=4016

[NOTE.—The Census Bureau not being ready to furnish the statistics on longevity for 1890 at the time of going to press, an approximate estimate is given of the total number of inhabitants 100 years of age and over for 1890 as between 4500 and 4600.]

Joseph Crele, said to have been born in Detroit, Mich., in 1725, died in Caledonia, Wis., 27 Jan. 1866, the oldest man known to have lived in America. The record of his baptism is shown in the French Catholic church at Detroit. He married his first wife in 1755, and was married twice afterwards. By his third wife he had a daughter born when he was 69 years of age.

RECENT CASES.

Died		Aged
1890.	Gabriel, the famous mission Indian, Salinas, Cal.	151 (?)
"	Mrs. Eva B. Hart, near Syracuse, N. Y.	113
1891.	Nancy Britt Kennedy, Augusta, Me., reported	118
"	Archibald Andrews, Hillsboro, N.C., oldest man in the state	107
"	Mary O'Connor, Elizabeth, N. J.	104
"	Mrs. Phœbe Campbell, Dexter, Me.	102
"	Col. Whitney, Franklin Grove, Ill. (one of the oldest members of the Masons in the world)	100
"	Nathan L. Fisk, St. Croix Falls, Wis. (school-mate of pres. Pierce)	100
"	Elizabeth M. Proctor, Salem, Mass.	100
1892.	John Reese, Bolivar, Pa. (the oldest iron-worker in the U. S.)	104
"	Keziah Randall, Mattaponsett, Mass.	103
"	Mrs. Sarah Shepard, Brazil, Ind.	104

longitude (Lat. *longitudino*, from *longus*, long, distance on the surface of the earth measured east or west from a certain meridian). To the ancient Greeks, confined between the cold north and the heat of the tropical south, the habitable earth seemed to extend limitlessly east and west. Hence they considered the earth as a plain extending in length east and west, and in breadth north and south; and the conception remains to us in the terms longitude and latitude. Longitude first determined by Hipparchus, at Nice, who fixed the first degree in the Canaries, 162 B.C. The lines of longitude are termed *meridians*, because every point along each of them has its midday *meridies* at the same moment. These imaginary lines, by crossing the equator and passing through both poles, divide the earth into an eastern and a western hemisphere, and the distances between them are measured by degrees, each $\frac{1}{360}$ part of the circumference. A degree of longitude at the equator is 69 statute miles, and narrows at the poles to 0. Each degree represents 4 minutes of time, so that difference in longitude is easily determined from difference in time. GLOBE, HARRISON'S TIMEPIECE, LATITUDE, MAPS.

Longobar'di. LOMBARDY.

Longwood, in St. Helena (S. Atlantic ocean), the residence of the emperor Napoleon from 10 Dec. 1815, till his death, 5 May, 1821.

Lookout Mountain, Battle of. CHATTANOOGA CAMPAIGN.

loom, a machine for weaving yarn or thread into fabric, was used by the early Egyptians and Greeks. Penelope, the wife of Ulysses, replies to her suitors:

"Young princes who are come to woo me since Ulysses is no more . . urge me not, I pray, to marriage till I finish in the loom . . . a funeral vesture for the hero-chief Laërtes."—*Odyssey.*

The weaver's, otherwise called the Dutch, loom was brought into use in London from Holland, about 1676. The first patent for a power-loom was taken out in England by the rev. Edmund Cartwright, in 1785. Later, Jacquard of Lyons, France, Roberts of Manchester, Engl., greatly improved the loom, while E. B. Bigelow invented and introduced at Lowell, Mass., the carpet power-loom; and William and George Crompton, father and son, at Worcester, Mass., invented and improved (patented 1837) the loom now bearing their name for weaving fancy woollens (making the first fancy cassimeres ever made by machinery); and later Lyall of New York invented the positive-motion loom, one of the greatest inventions for weaving yet produced.

Lopez (*lo'-pěs*) **expeditions.** FILIBUSTERS.

Lord (LADY). When printed in the English Bible in small capitals, LORD stands for Jehovah, the self-existing God, the name first revealed to Moses, 1491 B.C. (Exod. vi. 3). When Lord is in ordinary type, it represents *Adonai*, lord or master.

Lord's Day act, 29 Charles II. c. 7. SABBATH.

Lord's supper, instituted by Jesus Christ (Matt. xxvi. 17), 33. SACRAMENT, TRANSUBSTANTIATION.

lords. The nobility of England date their creation from 1066, when William Fitz-Osborn is said to have been made earl of Hereford by William I.; and afterwards Walter d'Evreux, earl of Salisbury; Copsi, earl of Northumberland; Henry de Ferrers, earl of Derby; and Gerodus (a Fleming), earl of Chester. 22 other peers were made in this sovereign's reign. The first peer created by patent was lord Beauchamp of Holt castle, by Richard II., in 1387. In Scotland, Gilchrist was created earl of Angus by Malcolm III., 1037. In Ireland, sir John de Courcy was created baron of Kinsale, etc., in 1181; the first peer after that kingdom was acquired by Henry II. Peers of England are free from arrests for debt, as being the king's hereditary counsellors; therefore a peer cannot be outlawed in a civil action, and no attachment lies against his person; but execution may be taken upon his lands and goods. For the same reason he is free from attendance at courts leet or sheriffs' turns; or, in case of riot, from attending the *posse comitatus*. He can act as justice of the peace in any part of the kingdom. BARON, EARL, etc.

Lords, House of. The peers of England were summoned *ad consulendum*, to consult, in early reigns, and by writ, 6 and 7 John, 1205; but the earliest writ extant is 49 Hen. III. 1265. The commons did not form a part of the great council of the nation until some ages after the Conquest. PARLIAMENT. The House of Lords includes the spiritual as well as temporal peers of Great Britain. The bishops are supposed to hold ancient baronies under the king, in right whereof they have seats in this house. Some temporal lords sit by descent, some by creation; others by election, since the union with Scotland in 1707, and with Ireland, 1801. Scotland elects 16 representative peers for each Parliament, and Ireland 28 temporal peers for life. The number of names on the "roll" was 401 in 1830, 457 in 1840, 448 in 1850, 458 in 1860, 503 in 1877, and 559 in 1891. About two thirds of these hereditary peerages were created in the present century. The 4 oldest existing peerages in the House of Lords, excluding royal and ecclesiastical, date from the 13th century, 5 from the 14th, 10 from the 15th. There are also 6 PEERESSES in their own right in the United Kingdom, and 3 Scotch peeresses, and 20 Scotch and 64 Irish peers who are not peers of Parliament. For dates of dignities see DUKE, EARL, MARQUIS.

King, barons, and clergy enact the constitutions of Clarendon. 1164
Obtain Magna Charta 1215
Held the government 1264-65
House of Lords abolished by commons .... 6 Feb. 1649
" " met again .... 25 Apr. "
With commons make William and Mary king and queen 1689
Reject the Reform bill, 7 Oct. 1831; pass it .... 4 June, 1832
Parliament house destroyed by fire .... 16 Oct. 1834
Take possession of new house .... 15 Apr. 1847
Oppose successfully creation of life peerages .... 7 Feb. 1856
Voting by proxy abolished by standing order .... 31 Mch. 1868
New regulations respecting committees .... 2 Apr. "
Six new peers gazetted .... 17 Apr. "
Bankrupt peers not to sit or vote, decided 10 Feb.; settled by act .... 13 July, 1871
That peers cannot vote for M.P.'s affirmed by court of common pleas on appeal .... 15 Nov. 1872
Two peers for life may be created by her majesty as lords of appeal in ordinary, to aid the House of Lords; as a court of ultimate appeal (SUPREME COURT).
Lords Blackburn and Gordon created peers for life ...... 5 Oct. 1876
Entitled to sit and vote in Parliament while appeal judges; first sitting .... 21 Nov. "
Lord Rayleigh (said to be) the first peer elected a professor of physics (at Cambridge) .... 12 Dec. 1879

Loretto, a city near Ancona, Italy. Here is the *Casa Santa*, or Holy House, said to have been the Virgin Mary's home at Nazareth, carried by angels into Dalmatia from Galilee in 1291, and brought here a few years after. The Lady of Loretto, gaudily dressed, stands upon an altar holding the infant Jesus in her arms, surrounded by gold lamps. Loretto was taken by the French in 1797; the holy image, carried to France, was brought back with pomp, 5 Jan. 1803.

L'Orient, a seaport town of W. France. Lord Bridport, off this port, defeated the French fleet, 23 June, 1795. The loss of the French was severe; that of the British inconsiderable.—The French flag-ship *L'Orient* blew up during the battle of the Nile, 1 Aug. 1798. Admiral Brueys and about 900 men perished. Mrs. Hemans has commemorated this event in her poem "Casabianca."

Lorraine (Lat. *Lotharingia*), formerly a French, now partly a German, province, became a kingdom under Lothaire (son of the emperor Lothaire I.) about 855; and was divided at his death, in 869, part of it being made a duchy. From the first hereditary duke, Gerard, nominated by the emperor Henry III. in 1048, descended the house of Lorraine, represented now by the emperor of Austria, whose ancestor, the empress Maria Theresa, married in 1736 Francis, formerly duke of Lorraine, then of Tuscany. Lorraine, given to the dethroned king of Poland, Stanislaus I., for life, was at his death, in 1766, united to France. NANCY. Lorraine was the seat of war in Aug. 1870, and about the 5th part, including Metz and Thionville, was annexed to Germany at the peace, 26 Feb. 1871.

lots. Casting lots, as an appeal to God, was sacred among the Jews, Prov. xvi. 33. It was employed in the division of the land of Canaan, about 1444 B.C., by Joshua (xiv.); in casting Jonah into the sea (Jonah i. 7); and in the election of Matthias the apostle, 33 A.D. (Acts i.). Lots for life or death have been frequently cast. For an instance, WALES, 1649.

lotteries originated in ancient Rome and gradually extended throughout Italy. The great cities of the Italian republics, Venice, Genoa, Pisa, Florence, etc., applied the lottery principle to encourage the sale of merchandise early in the 16th century. From Italy they were introduced into France and Germany. Were universal throughout the United States in its early history. They are now prohibited in most states and territories by the constitution and laws.

Legalized in France to help defray the expenses of the government early in.......... 1539

First mentioned in English history took place, day and night, at the western door of St. Paul's cathedral; it contained 40,000 "lots" at 10*s.* each lot; profits were for repairing the harbors; the prizes were pieces of plate, 11 Jan.-6 May, 1569

In great favor in France during reign of Louis XIII....1610 et seq.

Lottery, granted by James I. of England in favor of the colony of Virginia (prizes, pieces of plate), drawn near St. Paul's, 29 June-20 July, 1612

First lottery in England for sums of money took place........ 1630

Lotteries established in England (for more than 130 years yielded a large annual revenue to the crown................ 1693

Lotteries sanctioned by edicts, Louis XIV. of France......... 1700

[*This greatly increased private lotteries.*]

Lotteries prohibited by pope Benedict XIII............... 1724-30

Lotteries sanctioned by pope Clement XII................ 1730-40

Lottery for the British museum.......... 1753

Cox's museum, London, containing many rare specimens of art, disposed of by lottery.......... 1773

An act passed for the sale of the buildings of the Adelphi, London, by lottery..........16 June, "

[During this period lotteries became very popular in France, and gradually assumed an important place in the government finance; although protested against, they had the support of Mazarin and Pontchartrain, and thus raised the expenses of the war of the Spanish Succession. During this period there were lotteries for the benefit of religious communities and charity.]

To replace all private lotteries in France, the Royal lottery (Loterie Royale) was established by the famous decree of 30 June, 1776

French convention abolished lotteries...............12 Nov. 1793

Restored them in part.............................18 Apr. 1794

Restored them fully..................................1 Oct. 1797

Lottery for the Pigott diamond permitted in England, 2 Jan. 1801; it sold at Christie's auction for 9500 guineas, 10 May, 1802

For the collection of pictures of alderman Boydell, by act....1804-5

Lotteries abolished, 6 Geo. IV. c. 60, Oct.; last drawn...18 Oct. 1826

Act passed declaring that the then pending Glasgow lottery should be the last.......... 1834

Act passed imposing a penalty of 50*l.* for advertising lotteries in the newspapers.......... 1836

Lotteries partly suppressed in France, 1832; wholly so....... "

Lotteries for the assistance of charity and the fine arts, however, can be held in France under the law of........29 May, 1844

Mr. Dethiers's twelfth-cake lottery, Argyll-rooms, Hanover square, London, suppressed......................27 Dec. 1860

Twelve million national lottery tickets of one franc each, sold at Paris to pay for prizes to exhibitors, and expenses of working-men visitors, 1878; 1st prize worth 5000*l.*, 2d, 4000*l.*, 3d and 4th 2000*l.*; total 230,000 rewards; drawing began, 26 Jan. 1879

M. de Lesseps proposes a lottery loan for the purpose of raising funds for the Panama canal..........Jan. 1888

Panama Lottery Loan bill passed the French deputies, 28 Apr., the senate, 5 June; retarded and stopped.......July et seq. "

Louisiana State lottery was chartered in 1868 and established in New Orleans, to run 25 years from 1 Jan. 1869, and to pay $40,000 a year to charity. The ex-confederate gens. Beauregard and Early were paid $10,000 a year for the use of their names. After a protracted struggle against the moral sentiment of the country and the post-office, which refused in 1885 to deliver its mails, etc., it was finally driven from the city and state. Its prosperity was at its height from 1876-82. It is supposed to have collected from the people $300,000,000.

lotus, a prickly shrub or tree from 15 to 20 feet high (the jujube-tree), bearing a fruit of a sweet taste, mentioned by Herodotus. Extravagant tales were current among the Greeks of the marvellous power of the lotus; thus Ulysses narrates:

"Whoever tasted once of that sweet food
Wished not to see his native country more,
Nor give his friends the knowledge of his fate."
—*Homer*, "Odyssey," ix. 116-18 (Bryant's transl.).

And Tennyson:

"The mild-eyed, melancholy lotus-eaters came.
Branches they bore of that enchanted stem,
Laden with flower and fruit, whereof they gave
To each, but whoso did receive of them,
And taste, to him the gushing of the wave
Far far away did seem to mourn and rave
On alien shores."—"The Lotos-Eaters."

This must not be confounded with the Egyptian plant that grows in the Nile.

Louisburg, a French fortress on the island of cape Breton, gulf of St. Lawrence; built by the French, 1713; captured by the colonists, 1745-58. FRENCH IN AMERICA, MASSACHUSETTS.

louis-d'or, a French gold coin of 24 francs, first struck by Louis XIII. in 1640; it was not legal, 1795-1814; superseded by the napoleon, 1810.

Louisiana, the central gulf state of the United States, has for its southern boundary the gulf of Mexico, and south of 31° N. it extends from the Sabine river on the west to the Pearl river on the east, about 250 miles. North of 31° N. lat. its eastern boundary is the Mississippi river, which separates it from Mississippi, and the Sabine river and Texas form its western boundary. That portion of the state lying east of the Mississippi river is bounded on the north by the state of Mississippi, and that west of the Mississippi river by Arkansas. Its lat. is 28° 56′ to 33° N., and lon. 89° to 94° W. Area, 45,420 sq. miles, in 99 parishes; pop. 1890, 1,118,587; 1900, 1,381,625. Capital, Baton Rouge. It differs from the other states in that its jurisprudence is based on the Roman or civil law instead of the common law of England, and the counties are called parishes.

Robert Cavalier de la Salle descends the Mississippi to its mouth, names the country Louisiana, and takes possession in the name of the king of France..................9 Apr. 1682

Pierre Le Moyne d'Iberville enters the Mississippi.....2 Mch. 1699

D'Iberville, having settled Biloxi, sails for France, leaving his lieutenant, Sauvolle de la Villantry, in command....3 May, "

Jean Baptist Le Moyne Bienville (b. Montreal, 23 Feb. 1680), brother of D'Iberville, returning from an expedition north of lake Pontchartrain, finds an English ship at the mouth of the Mississippi, which sails away after being notified by Bienville that France had taken possession............15 Sept. "

Sauvolle appointed governor of Louisiana..............7 Dec. "

D'Iberville returns from France in company with Bienville, and establishes a fort on the Mississippi, where they are visited by the Chevalier de Tonti.......... ....17 Jan. 1700

Sauvolle dying, Bienville succeeds him...............22 Aug. 1701

De Muys, appointed governor-general of Louisiana, dies on his way from France, and Bienville continues in command.... 1707

King grants to sieur Antony Crozat exclusive trading rights in Louisiana for 15 years..........................14 Sept. 1712

Lamothe Cadillac arrives from France as governor, and appoints Bienville lieutenant.........................17 May, 1713

Bienville makes peace with the Choctaw Indians............ 1715

Gov. Cadillac, in search of silver, goes to the Illinois country and incurs the enmity of the Natchez Indians............ "

Bienville ascends the Mississippi to subject the Natchez, and establishes fort Rosalie in their country...............Apr. 1716

M. de l'Epinay arrives as governor from France.......9 Mch. 1717

Crozat surrenders his trading privilege to the king....23 Aug. "

Company of the West chartered to foster and preserve the colony..........6 Sept. "

Three French vessels arrive with 69 colonists and troops and Bienville's commission as governor of Louisiana.....9 Feb. 1718

Fort Naquitoches on the Red river established by M. Bienville, "

New Orleans founded by Bienville.......... "

Eighty girls from a house of correction in Paris arrive in charge of 3 Ursuline nuns..........Feb. 1721

Balize or buoy established at the mouth of the Mississippi.... 1722

Company of Germans, settlers on John Law's grant (LAW'S BUBBLE) on the Arkansas river, descend the river to near New Orleans and locate there.......... "

Seat of government removed to New Orleans.......... 1723

Black code for punishing slaves promulgated by Bienville.... 1724

Bienville recalled to France; Périer becomes commander-general..........9 Aug. 1726

Some Jesuits and Ursuline nuns arrive at New Orleans, and a nunnery is erected.......... 1727

Arrival of a cargo of girls sent from France by the company, each provided with a small casket of wearing apparel....... 1728

[*Known as "Filles à la Cassette" or casket girls.*]

Chevalier Loubois, with allied French and Choctaws, advances against Natchez Indians, who had massacred the garrison of fort Rosalie and occupied it; the Indians desert the fort and 200 prisoners in it..........Jan. 1730

M. Périer makes another expedition against the Natchez and secures their chief Great Sun and others...........24 Jan. 1731

[Great Sun died a prisoner, the others were sold as slaves to St. Domingo.]

Company of the West surrenders its charter to the king, 23 Jan. "

Superior Council of Louisiana reorganized by letters patent; Périer continued in office..........7 May, 1732

Settlement at Baton Rouge.......... 1733

Bienville reappointed governor.......... "

Bienville repulsed in an expedition against the Chickasaw Indians..........26 May, 1736

Second expedition of Bienville against the Chickasaws, who sue for peace.......... 1740

Marquis de Vaudreuil appointed governor; Bienville returns to France..........10 May, 1743

Marquis de Vaudreuil marches against the Chickasaws; unable to take their towns, he garrisons the fort on the Tombigbee erected by Bienville, and returns to New Orleans.......... 1753

Louis Billouart, Chevalier de Kerlerec, succeeds Vaudreuil, who was appointed governor of Canada.............9 Feb. 1754

First arrival of Acadians at New Orleans; they are sent to Attakapas and Opelousas (ACADIA)............................ 1756

M. Dubreuil erects a sugar mill in New Orleans (cane-growing having been started by the Jesuits in 1751)............... 1758

Garrison of fort Du Quesne flee towards New Orleans, evacuating and setting fire to the fort......................24 Nov. "

France cedes Louisiana to Spain, and to England all east of the Mississippi river except the island of New Orleans, and makes the Mississippi free to both nations.................3 Nov. 1762

Kerlerec succeeded by D'Abadie as director-general, who arrives at New Orleans.............................29 June, 1763

Delegates from all parts of the parish at New Orleans elect Jean Milhet to petition the king that the province be not severed from France.................................... "

English troops occupy Baton Rouge.....................Feb. 1764

Nyon de Villiers, who was in command, abandons the Illinois district and reaches New Orleans...................2 July, "

D'Abadie dies and is succeeded by Aubrey.............4 Feb. 1765

Large colony of Acadians from Maine arrive............Feb. 1766

Antonio d'Ulloa lands at New Orleans with civil officers and soldiers to take possession of the province...........5 Mch. "

Decree dictated by Ulloa and proclaimed by Aubrey, that all captains of vessels from France or St. Domingo report to Ulloa on arrival with bills of lading and passports, and that the agents for sale of cargo submit to competent examiners the prices they propose to sell at, subject to reduction by the examiners if too high.........................6 Sept. "

An address to the superior council signed by nearly 600 men claims freedom of commerce with the ports of France and America, and demands the expulsion of Ulloa; it was adopted by the council.................................25 Oct. 1768

Ulloa, enjoined to leave the city, flees to Havana. The French flag is displayed, Aubrey and Foucault (a leader in the revolution) are summoned to govern the colony as before, and the people institute a republic..................29 Oct. "

Don Alexander O'Reilly, captain-general, lands at the Balize, and demands the government in the name of Spain, 28 July, 1769

O'Reilly, with 24 Spanish vessels, appears before New Orleans, lands 2600 Spanish troops, and assumes possession of Louisiana...18 Aug. "

Nine leaders of the revolution arrested and brought before gen. O'Reilly; commissary Foucault sent to France and thrown into the Bastile..................................21 Aug. "

Six leaders of the revolution are imprisoned, and 6 sentenced to be hung are shot, no hangman being found.......25 Oct. "

O'Reilly abolishes by proclamation the superior council, and substitutes a cabildo of 6 perpetual regidors, 2 ordinary alcaldes, and an attorney-general syndic over which the governor presides....................................25 Nov. "

Black Code re-enacted by proclamation of O'Reilly.......... 1770

O'Reilly delivers up the government to don Luis de Unzaga, 29 Oct. "

Unzaga appointed captain-general of Caraccas, don Bernardo de Galvez assumes the government..................1 Feb. 1777

Galvez by proclamation grants privilege of trading with any part of the U. S.................................20 Apr. 1778

Settlement called New Iberia on the Bayou Teche by about 500 immigrants from Canary islands..................Jan. 1779

Galvez captures Baton Rouge from the British........21 Sept. "

Galvez moves against fort Charlotte on the Mobile river and captures it...14 Mch. 1780

John James Audubon born at New Orleans..................4 May, "

Galvez invests Pensacola, which capitulates............9 May, 1781

Father Cirilo, a Spanish Capuchin, made bishop of Louisiana.. "

Treaty of peace at Paris between Great Britain, Spain, and the U. S...3 Sept. 1783

Galvez succeeds his father in the vice-royalty of Mexico in 1785; don Estevan Miro acts in his place and receives his commission as governor................................2 June, 1786

Gen. James Wilkinson reaches New Orleans in June with a small cargo of tobacco and other goods. Perhaps to advance mercantile schemes he has interviews with gov. Miro and professes accord with him in seeking a rupture between the western and eastern U. S., and increase of Spanish power in America. He returns to Philadelphia.................Sept. 1787

Settlers from western North Carolina arrive, after failure to erect the state of FRANKLAND.........................Mch. 1789

French refugees from San Domingo reach New Orleans, and a few of them open the first regular theatre in the city... 1791

Don François Louis Hector, baron de Carondelet, succeeds Miro as governor and intendant of Louisiana...........Jan. 1792

Don Louis de Penalvert appointed bishop of Louisiana and Florida.. 1794

Publication of the first newspaper in Louisiana, *Le Moniteur de la Louisiane*.. "

Genet, the French ambassador to the U. S., plans an expedition against the Spanish dominions, and a society of French Jacobins in Philadelphia addresses an inflammatory circular to the French in Louisiana.................................. "

"Canal Carondelet," from New Orleans to lake Pontchartrain, projected, begun, and abandoned by gov. Perier in 1727; recommenced and completed.............................. 1795

Etienne de Boré succeeds in producing sugar from cane, beginning a new industry.................................... "

By treaty Spain grants the U. S. "the right to deposit their merchandise and effects at New Orleans for the space of 3 years, and at the end of that time to continue, or an equivalent establishment to be assigned at some other point on the Mississippi river"................................27 Oct. 1795

Spanish commissioner don Manuel Gayoso de Lemos, and U. S. commissioner Andrew Ellicot, meet at Natchez to define the boundary between Spanish and U. S. possessions, 24 Feb. 1797

Carondelet refuses to surrender the posts on the Mississippi, hoping for a separation of the western U. S. from the eastern.. "

Carondelet appointed governor of the Mexican provinces; don Manuel Gayoso de Lemos succeeds in Louisiana......1 Aug. "

Don Juan Ventura Morales, Spanish intendant, refuses a place of deposit to U. S. citizens in New Orleans................. 1799

On the death of Gayoso the marquis de Casa-Calvo succeeds as governor, and don Ramon de Lopez y Angullo as intendant of Louisiana.................................18 July, "

By a secret treaty at St. Ildefonso the king of Spain retrocedes Louisiana to France.................................1 Oct. 1800

Treaty at Madrid confirms treaty of St. Ildefonso......21 Mch. 1801

Right of deposit restored to the people of the U. S........... "

Don Juan Manuel de Salcedo arrives as governor of Louisiana and Florida, Morales succeeds Lopez as intendant, 15 June, "

By proclamation of Morales, citizens of U. S. are refused deposit in New Orleans, and importation in American bottoms is prohibited...Oct. 1802

Morales, fearing famine in the province, disregards his regulation and annuls the prohibition.......................... 1803

Laussat, the prefect appointed by Napoleon, arrives at New Orleans..26 Mch. "

By treaty at Paris, Napoleon cedes Louisiana to the U. S. for 60,000,000 francs..................................30 Apr. "

Casa-Calvo and Salcedo, Spanish commissioners, present the keys of New Orleans to citizen Laussat, who takes possession of Louisiana in the name of France................30 Nov. "

Gen. James Wilkinson encamps on the Mississippi near New Orleans, and the Spanish troops sail for Havana, 18 Dec. "

Citizen Laussat as commissioner for France delivers New Orleans to gen. Wilkinson and W. C. C. Claiborne as commissioners for the U. S., leaving left bank of lakes Borgne and Pontchartrain to the Spanish.......................20 Dec. "

Congress divides Louisiana into a southern territory of Orleans, and a northern district of Louisiana..........26 Mch. 1804

Territorial government in Orleans begins; William C. C. Claiborne governor......................................1 Oct. "

Vessel bringing nearly 200 French prisoners of the British government, who had captured the ship, gov. Claiborne refuses to allow it to ascend the river; the French desert the ship, which is seized by the U. S. marshal at request of British claimants.......................................3 Nov. "

New Orleans chartered as a city............................ "

Territorial government giving the people no power, the "merchants, planters, and other inhabitants of Louisiana" petition Congress, declaring its organization oppressive and degrading...4 Jan. 1805

Congress provides for a government of the territory of Orleans in all respects like that of Mississippi territory, except as to the descent and distribution of estates and the prohibition of slavery..2 Mch. "

Col. Aaron Burr arrives in New Orleans, to remain 10 or 12 days...26 June, "

Gov. Claiborne orders the marquis of Casa-Calvo and the intendant Morales out of the country, and a source of great anxiety is removed..................................July, 1806

Territorial legislature meets..........................24 Mch. "

Gen. Wilkinson, at St. Louis, receiving a confidential letter from Aaron Burr, denounces him in a message to Washington; 27 Nov. 1806, pres. Jefferson by proclamation makes known the traitorous enterprise; 29 Oct., Wilkinson by message to the Spanish commander-in-chief proposes the withdrawal of troops of both governments from advanced positions to Nacogdoches and Natchitoches respectively, which was agreed to; gen. Wilkinson reaches New Orleans, 25 Nov. "

Arrest in New Orleans of several men charged with abetting Burr's treason..Dec. "

Digest of civil law adopted, legislature adjourned......31 Mch. 1808

Gen. Wilkinson, ordered to New Orleans with troops, arrives 19 Apr. He is afterwards relieved by Wade Hampton...... 1809

Citizens of Baton Rouge territory attack the reduced garrison of the fort at Baton Rouge, and in the skirmish the Spanish governor Grandpré is shot, and the garrison capitulates, Sept. 1810

Convention of the people of Baton Rouge territory at St. Francisville frame a constitution, elect a governor, and establish the independent territory of West Florida..........29 Sept. "

Under proclamation of the president, gov. Claiborne takes possession of West Florida, and annexes it to the territory of Orleans...7 Dec. "

An insurrection of slaves in the parish of St. John is suppressed after 60 or more are killed. The heads of 16 who were captured and executed, were set on poles along the river as a warning.....................................Jan. 1811

Act to enable the people of Orleans to form a state government signed by pres. Madison............................20 Feb. "

Exclusive grant by legislature to Livingston and Fulton to build steamboats for 18 years from 1 Jan. 1812............. "

Arrival from Pittsburg of first steam-vessel on the Mississippi, 10 Jan. 1812

LOU

Constitutional convention at New Orleans adjourns....22 Jan. 1812

Congress admits Louisiana as a state..................8 Apr. "

Congress extends the limits of Louisiana to include all between the Mississippi and Pearl rivers south of 31° N. lat., 14 Apr. "

Gen. Wilkinson resumes command in Louisiana and arrives at New Orleans......................................8 June, "

First session of state legislature at New Orleans.........June, "

W. C. C. Claiborne elected governor..................19 Aug. "

Gen. Wilkinson superseded by gen. Flournoy...........June, 1813

Col. Nichols (British) by proclamation incites people of Louisiana and Kentucky to revolt.....................29 Aug. 1814

Citizens of New Orleans and vicinity meet, pass resolutions of loyalty, and address the people.................15 Sept. "

Barataria island occupied by pirates under Jean Lafitte; the British under sir William H. Percy invite them to hostility against the U. S.; Lafitte refuses (BARATARIA BAY), 30 Aug. "

Flotilla sails from New Orleans against the pirates, who prepare to resist, but abandon 9 ships to the Americans, 18 Sept. "

Gen. Jackson arrives at New Orleans.................2 Dec. "

British threaten New Orleans and capture gunboats under lieut. Thos. A. C. Jones (BORGNE LAKE)...............14 Dec. "

Battle at Villeré's plantation, 12 miles from New Orleans; the English advance repulsed by gen. Jackson...........23 Dec. "

Battle at Chalmette's plantation; British repulsed.....28 Dec. "

Battle at Rodriguez canal............................1 Jan. 1815

Battle of New Orleans (UNITED STATES)................ 8 Jan. "

Unsuccessful attack on fort St. Philip by the British, 9-18 Jan. "

British general Lambert abandons expedition against New Orleans...19 Jan. "

Gen. Jackson orders all French subjects having certificates of discharge to return to the interior, 28 Feb. Has Louallier arrested as a spy; Hall, as abetting a mutiny in granting a *habeas corpus* for Louallier; arrests Hollander; releases all three, and for high-handed methods is tried and fined $1000 (JACKSON IN NEW ORLEANS)........................... "

Frederic Tudor ships ice to New Orleans from Boston......... 1820

Thomas B. Robertson elected governor...................... "

Gov. Robertson resigning to become judge of U. S. District Court, pres. Thibodeaux of the senate acts as governor until inauguration of gov.-elect Henry Johnson.............Dec. 1824

Centenary college organized at Jackson, 32 miles north of Baton Rouge.. 1825

Visit of Lafayette; the legislature appropriates $15,000 for his entertainment.. "

Legislature grants $10,000 to Thomas Jefferson Randolph for the family of Thomas Jefferson, as a mark of gratitude from Louisiana....................................16 Mch. 1827

Seat of government removed from New Orleans to Donaldsonville.. 1829

Provision for running boundary-line between Louisiana and Arkansas territory under act of Congress.................. 1830

New Orleans again made the seat of government........8 Jan. 1831

Pontchartrain railroad, 4½ miles long, opened for traffic..Apr. "

Locomotive introduced on the Pontchartrain railroad.......... 1832

Branch mint at New Orleans receives first bullion......8 Mch. 1838

During this and the 2 previous years Louisiana furnished 1179 volunteers in the Florida war........................ "

New constitution adopted in convention.............14 May, 1845

State insane asylum established at Jackson.................. 1847

Legislature meets in new state-house at Baton Rouge..21 Jan. 1850

Death at Washington, D. C., of pres. Zachary Taylor....9 July, "

Steamer *Pampero*, with 500 men under Lopez, for expedition against Cuba, leaves New Orleans (FILIBUSTERS)...........3 Aug. 1851

Riot because of Cuban expedition in New Orleans; office of Spanish paper *La Patria* destroyed.....................21 Aug. "

State institution for deaf, dumb, and blind founded at Baton Rouge.. 1852

Convention to revise constitution meets at Baton Rouge, 5 July, "

University of Louisiana chartered.......................... 1853

Commercial convention of southern and southwestern states meets at New Orleans.............................8 Jan. 1855

William Walker, with his expedition, leaves New Orleans, ostensibly for Mobile, but really for Nicaragua, eluding the U. S. authorities (FILIBUSTERS)........................11 Nov. 1857

Walker surrenders to com. Hiram Paulding; indignation meetings at New Orleans, Mobile, and other southern cities, 8 Dec. "

Political disturbance in New Orleans; 500 men as a vigilance committee seize the court-house and state arsenal; Know-nothing party occupy Lafayette square..........4-5 June, 1858

Legislature in extra session provides for a state convention and votes $500,000 to organize military companies; Wirt Adams, commissioner from Mississippi, asks the legislature to join in secession.....................................Dec. 1860

Immense popular meeting in New Orleans on announcement of the secession of South Carolina.....................21 Dec. "

Mass-meeting held at New Orleans to ratify "Southern Rights" nominations for the convention.......................25 Dec. "

Seizure by confederates of forts St. Philip, Jackson, and Livingston, arsenal at Baton Rouge, and U. S. revenue cutter *Lewis Cass*..10-13 Jan. 1861

Ordinance of secession adopted in convention: yeas, 113; nays, 17.. 26 Jan. "

Mint and custom-house in New Orleans seized by confederates (COIN AND COINAGE)..................................31 Jan. "

Convention to join Southern Confederacy; state flag adopted, a red ground, crossed by bars of blue and white and bearing a single star of pale yellow..............................4 Feb. 1861

Louisiana ratifies the Confederate constitution..........22 Mch. "

Louisiana raises 3000 Confederate troops, and at call of gov. Moore, 3000 additional...............................24 Apr. "

First gun cast for Confederate navy at Phœnix iron works at Gretna, near New Orleans ....4 May, "

Port of New Orleans blockaded by U. S. sloop-of-war *Brooklyn*; Ship island occupied by Union troops........................ "

Banks of New Orleans suspend specie payments ......18 Sept. "

Confederate martial law instituted in New Orleans.....11 Oct. "

Federal steamship *Richmond*, under John Pope, while coaling near New Orleans, is struck by a Confederate ram....12 Oct. "

State casts its electoral vote for Jefferson Davis as president of the Confederate states..............................19 Feb. 1862

Adm. Farragut passes forts Jackson and Philip with his fleet morning..24 Apr. "

Surrender of New Orleans to adm. Farragut..........25 Apr. "

Capture of forts Jackson and Philip by the federals.....28 Apr. "

Confederate capital transferred to Opelousas.............Apr. "

Maj.-gen. Benjamin F. Butler takes possession of New Orleans, 1 May, "

Baton Rouge occupied by federals...................27 May, "

William B. Mumford, for taking down the U. S. flag from the U. S. mint after the surrender of the city to adm. Farragut, hanged at New Orleans by order of gen. Butler.....7 June, "

Federal troops in Baton Rouge, besieged by confederates, 5 Aug., evacuate by order from gen. Butler.........16 Aug. "

Brig.-gen. Geo. F. Shepley military governor of Louisiana, 21 Aug. "

Gen. Grover occupies Baton Rouge...................16 Dec. "

Maj.-gen. N. P. Banks relieves gen. Butler............ " "

Election held by order of pres. Lincoln; Messrs. Hahn and Flanders chosen to Congress; they take seats 9 Feb. 1863, and occupy them until......................................3 Mch. 1863

Henry W. Allen chosen governor by confederates; seat of government at Shreveport.. "

Michael Hahn chosen governor at Federal election in New Orleans and vicinity..................................22 Feb. 1864

Gov. Hahn appointed military governor by the president, 15 Mch. "

Convention at New Orleans to revise the constitution...6 Apr. "

Bureau of free labor, predecessor of the Freedmen's bureau, opened at New Orleans.. 1865

Gov. Hahn resigning, is succeeded by lieut.-gov. J. M. Wells, 4 Mch. "

Confederate gov. Allen resigns.........................2 June, "

Gov. Wells re-elected.....................................6 Nov. "

[This government, though never recognized by Congress, continued until Mch. 1867.]

Constitution of 1864 left the negroes still disfranchised; a convention, chiefly of blacks who wished to frame a new constitution, meets in New Orleans and results in a riot; several hundred negroes killed..............................30 July, 1866

Congress passes the Military Reconstruction act........2 Mch. 1867

Gen. Sheridan appointed commander of the 5th military district, Louisiana and Texas.............................19 Mch. "

Gen. Sheridan removes gov. Wells "for making himself an impediment to the faithful execution of the Reconstruction act," and substitutes Thomas J. Durant, who declines, and Benjamin F. Flanders is appointed.....................8 June, "

Sheridan relieved and gen. Hancock appointed........17 Aug. "

Constitutional convention at New Orleans adopts a constitution prohibiting slavery, declaring the ordinance of secession null, and wholly disfranchising ex-confederates......22 Nov. "

Gen. Hancock relieved by gen. Buchanan as commander of the 5th military district..................................18 Mch. 1868

State election; new constitution ratified, and Henry C. Warmouth elected governor...................................18 Apr. "

Congress readmits the southern states...............25 June, "

XIV.th Amendment adopted by the legislature............July, "

Numerous political and color riots occur in New Orleans, Opelousas, and other portions of the state during the year...... "

Passage of "Social Equality" bill, giving all persons, without regard to color or previous condition, equal privileges in public conveyances or places of public resort.............4 Jan. 1869

XV.th Amendment ratified by Senate, 27 Feb., and by House, 1 Mch. "

"Crescent City Live-Stock and Slaughter-house company," a monopoly in New Orleans which excited opposition, and was finally declared unconstitutional and restrained by perpetual injunction, was created by the legislature and went into operation...1 June, "

Legislature grants to the New Orleans, Mobile, and Chattanooga Railway company $3,000,000 in 8% state bonds, payable in 4 instalments.. 21 Feb. 1870

Legislature unites Jefferson City and Algiers with New Orleans under one charter.. "

George M. Wickliffe, state auditor, impeached and convicted of extortion and fraud...................................3 Mch. "

A political contest between two factions of the Republican party. The State Central committee—S. B. Packard, U. S. marshal at the head—call a convention to choose a state committee. The opposition, under lieut.-gov. Oscar J. Dunn (colored), meet in the custom-house. Gov. Warmouth and P. B. S. Pinchback (colored) are refused admission, and the Warmouthites meet in Turner's hall....................8 Aug. 1871

On the death of lieut.-gov. Dunn, the election of P. B. S. Pinchback by the Senate in extra session is claimed as unconstitutional by the opposition, led by George W. Carter, speaker of the House, and known as "Carterites"...........22 Nov. "

LOU

Warmouth legislature meets at Mechanics' Institute, the Carterites over the "Gem Saloon," on Royal street, 6 Jan. Col. Carter, by proclamation, proposes to seize the Mechanics' Institute building, and appears before it with several thousand men, but is prevented by gen. Emory 22 Jan 1872

In extra session the House, in the absence of col. Carter, declares the speaker's chair vacant, chooses O. H. Brewster speaker and approves the course of gov. Warmouth "

Act passed funding the indebtedness of the state 30 Apr "

Conventions of the two wings of the Republican party at Baton Rouge headed respectively by Packard and Pinchback. The Packard convention nominates William Pitt Kellogg for governor 19 June, "

Adjourned meeting of the Pinchback convention nominates P. B. S. Pinchback for governor 9 Aug "

Fusion of the two wings of the Republican party by the State Central committee nominates Kellogg for governor and Pinchback for congressman at large "

Judge Durell in December declares Kellogg elected governor at election held 4 Nov "

"Fusion legislature" in the city hall, New Orleans, impeaches and suspends gov. Warmouth 11 Dec "

Inauguration of Kellogg as governor, also of John McEnery, nominee of the Democratic reformers and liberals 14 Jan 1873

Members of McEnery legislature seized and marched to the guard house by armed police 6 Mch "

People submit to the Kellogg government "at the point of the bayonet" as many express it. People's convention at New Orleans 24 Nov "

"Crescent City White League" formed, "to assist in restoring an honest and intelligent government to the state of Louisiana" 1874

Six Republican officials arrested near Coushatta, in Red River parish while being taken to Shreveport, are shot 30 Aug "

People send a committee to demand the abdication of Kellogg, and the McEnery faction, 10,000 strong, led by D. B. Penn, lieutenant governor, appear before the state house. a conflict takes place between the insurgents and police the state house is captured, and members of the McEnery legislature installed 14 Sept "

McEnery and Penn surrender the state buildings without resistance to gen. Brooke 17 Sept. "

Gen. Brooke appointed military governor, and gov. Kellogg resumes his duties 19 Sept "

Legislature meets and U. S. troops are called in to quell disturbance, great excitement throughout the U. S. 8 Jan 1875

Claims of the several candidates are submitted to a congressional committee or board of arbitration in which William A. Wheeler is prominent, and the so called "Wheeler Adjustment" is agreed to 14 Apr "

Immigration convention held in the Chamber of Commerce, New Orleans comprising delegates from the southern and western states 1-2 Mch 1876

At election held this day both Republican and Democratic parties claim the victory 6 Nov "

S. B. Packard, Republican inaugurated governor at the state house, New Orleans. Francis T. Nicholls, Democrat, inaugurated at St. Patrick's hall, New Orleans, and both legislatures meet. 8 Jan 1877

Courts, police stations, and arsenal at New Orleans are peaceably surrendered to the Nicholls authorities 9 Jan "

Packard failing to receive aid from the U. S. government, and a commission appointed by pres. Hayes to investigate the political situation in Louisiana reporting public sentiment in favor of the Nicholls government, the Packard legislature is dispersed 21 Apr "

Nicholls government occupies state house 24 Apr "

Legislature, by concurrent resolution, directs senators and congressmen to use every effort to secure the passage of the Bland Silver bill and of the bill to repeal the so called Resumption act introduced in the Senate 19 Jan 1878

Political disturbance in Tensas and Concordia parishes, resulting in killing a man named Peck, and the wounding by his companions of 3 colored men, investigated by Congress "

By act of Congress, 3 Mch. 1875, a contract was made with capt. James Buchanan Eads for the construction of jetty work at the mouth of the South pass in the Mississippi river, to secure and maintain a navigable channel 200 feet wide and 20 feet deep. Capt. Eads's work has already resulted in a clear channel of the required width, and deeper than the 20 feet specified (MISSISSIPPI RIVER) "

Constitutional convention at New Orleans frames a constitution. Capital changed from New Orleans to Baton Rouge 21 Apr 1879

Louis A. Wiltz, Democrat, elected governor, and the new constitution ratified by the people 8 Dec "

"Debt Ordinance," fixing the interest on consolidated state bonds at 2½ per cent. for 5 years, 3 per cent. for 15 years, and 4 per cent. thereafter, and limit of state tax fixed at 6 mills, ratified by the people at the election 8 Dec. "

Bureau of Agriculture and Immigration created 14 Jan 1880

"Board of Liquidation" appointed in New Orleans, to retire all the valid debt of the city, a total of $17,736,508.96, exchanging it for 4 per cent. bonds payable in 50 years "

University for the higher education of colored boys opened "

Death of gov. Wiltz, lieut. gov. McEnery succeeds 17 Oct 1881

Suit begun against Louisiana by New York and New Hampshire on coupons on Louisiana state bonds transferred to these states by the holders thereof "

Two hundredth anniversary of the discovery of the mouths of the Mississippi by La Salle. . . 10 Apr 1882

Chief justice Waite renders his decision in the New York and New Hampshire suits against Louisiana, that "one state cannot create a controversy with another state within the meaning of that term as used in the judicial clauses of the Constitution, by assuming the prosecution of debts owing by other states to its citizens" 5 Mch 1883

Levee convention held at Baton Rouge recommending placing the entire convict force at work on the levees 19 June, "

World's Industrial and Cotton Centennial Exposition held at New Orleans 1885

First Prohibition convention ever held in Louisiana meets at Shreveport . 19 Aug "

North, Central, and South American Exposition opens 10 Nov "

Legislature grants relief to wounded and disabled Confederate soldiers of the state and to the widows of Confederate soldiers killed or wounded in the war 1886

Charter of the Louisiana State lottery expiring in 1894 the anti lottery people in convention at New Orleans, found an anti lottery league to oppose its renewal 28 Feb 1890

Louisiana Lottery company offers the state $1,000,000 per year, double its former offer, for the privilege of maintaining a lottery 13 May, "

House of Delegates passes a bill amending the state constitution by granting a re charter to the Louisiana State Lottery company for 25 years for $1,000,000 per annum 25 June, "

State legislature settles the lottery question conditionally by accepting $1,250,000 per year for the lottery privilege 1 July, "

Gov. Nicholls vetoes the lottery bill 7 July, "

Anti lottery league meets in New Orleans—500 delegates, 7 Aug "

Chief of police David C. Hennessy of New Orleans is waylaid and killed by Italian "Maffia" to whose band he had traced a number of crimes night of 15 Oct. "

Killing in the parish prison at New Orleans of 11 Italians (MASSACRES, UNITED STATES) 14 Mch 1891

Officers of the Louisiana lottery indicted by the grand jury in Sioux Falls, N. D. under U. S. laws 23 Oct "

John A. Morris, in a letter, withdraws his proposition for the renewal of the charter of the Louisiana lottery 4 Feb 1892

Convention of United Confederate Veterans meets in New Orleans 8 Apr "

Proposed constitutional amendment to continue the Louisiana State lottery for 25 years from 1 Jan. 1894, is rejected by vote at state election (LOTTERIES) 19 Apr "

Monument erected to David C. Hennessy (assassinated by Mafia in 1890) by the people of New Orleans, is unveiled at Metarie cemetery 30 May, "

Nicaragua Canal convention opens in New Orleans, delegates from every state and territory 30 Nov "

U. S. senator Randall L. Gibson d. at Hot Springs, Ark 15 Dec. "

Donaldson Caffrey appointed by gov. Foster U. S. senator to fill unexpired term 31 Dec "

Gen. P. G. T. Beauregard d. in New Orleans, aged 75 years, 20 Feb. 1893

Destructive cyclone along the gulf of Mexico, over 2000 lives lost 2 Oct "

U. S. senator Edward D. White appointed associate justice of the Supreme court of the U. S. 19 Feb 1894

Newton C. Blanchard member of Congress, appointed senator by gov. Foster to fill the unexpired term of White 7 Mch "

TERRITORIAL GOVERNOR.

Name	Term	Remarks
Wm C C Claiborne	1804 to 1812	

STATE GOVERNORS

Name	Term	Remarks
Wm C C Claiborne	1812 to 1816	
James Villeré	1816 " 1820	
Thos. B Robertson	1820 " 1824	Resigns
H S Thibodeaux	1824	Acting
Henry Johnson	1824 to 1828	
Pierre Derbigny	1828 " 1829	Dies in office
A Beauvais	1829 " 1830	Acting
Jacques Dupré	1830 " 1831	"
André B Roman	1831 " 1834	
Edward D White	1834 " 1838	
André B Roman	1838 " 1841	
Alexander Mouton	1841 " 1845	
Isaac Johnson	1845 " 1850	
Joseph Walker	1850 " 1854	
Paul O Hebert	1854 " 1858	
Robert C Wickliffe	1858 " 1860	
Thos O Moore	1860 " 1863	Confederate governor
Michael Hahn	1864	Governor of New Orleans and vicinity (Federal)
Henry F Allen	1864	Governor of Confederate portion
James M Wells	1864 to 1867	Not recognized by Congress.
B F Flanders.	1867 " 1868	Military governor appointed by gen Sheridan
Henry C Warmouth	1868 " 1872	
Wm Pitt Kellogg	1872 " 1877	*De facto*
John McEnery	1872 " 1877	Democratic claimant
Francis T Nicholls	1877 " 1880	See this record, 1877
Louis Alfred Wiltz	1880 " 1881	Dies in office
Samuel D McEnery	1881 " 1888	Acting. Elected 1884.
Francis T Nicholls	1888 " 1892	
Murphy J Foster	1892 " 1896	

UNITED STATES SENATORS FROM THE STATE OF LOUISIANA.

Name.	No. of Congress.	Date.	Remarks.
Thomas Posey	12th	1812	Appointed in place of John Noel Destrahan, who resigned in 1812, never having taken his seat.
James Brown	12th to 14th	1813 to 1817	Elected in place of Destrahan.
Allan B. Magruder	12th	1812	
Eligius Fromentin	13th to 15th	1813 to 1819	
Henry Johnson	15th " 18th	1818 " 1824	Resigned.
James Brown	16th " 18th	1819 " 1823	Resigned, being appointed minister to France.
Dominique Bouligny	18th " 20th	1824 " 1829	
Josiah S. Johnston	18th " 23d	1824 " 1833	Died, 1833.
Edward Livingston	21st " 22d	1829 " 1831	Resigned.
George A. Waggaman	22d	1832	Elected in place of Livingston.
Alexander Porter	23d to 24th	1834 to 1837	Elected in place of Johnston. Resigned 1837.
Alexander Mouton	24th " 27th	1837 " 1842	Elected in place of Porter. Resigned 1842.
Robert C. Nicholas	24th " 26th	1836 " 1841	
Charles M. Conrad	27th	1842 " 1843	Elected in place of Mouton.
Alexander Barrow	27th to 29th	1841 " 1846	Died 1846.
Alexander Porter	28th	1843 " 1844	Died 1844.
Henry Johnson	28th to 30th	1844 " 1849	
Pierre Soulé (*soo-lā'*)	29th	1847	Elected in place of Barrow.
Solomon W. Downs	30th to 32d	1847 to 1853	
Pierre Soulé	31st " 32d	1849 " 1853	Resigned, being appointed minister to Spain by pres. Pierce.
Judah P. Benjamin	33d " 36th	1853 " 1861	Retired from the senate.
John Slidell	33d " 36th	1853 " 1861	" " " "
....	36th " 40th	1861 " 1868	Vacant.
John S. Harris	40th	1868	Seated 17 July.
William Pitt Kellogg	40th to 42d	1868 to 1872	Seated 17 July. *Resigned for governorship.*
J. Rodman West	42d " 45th	1871 " 1877	The only senator from Louisiana from 1872 to 1877.
James B. Eustis	45th " 46th	1877 " 1879	
William Pitt Kellogg	45th " 48th	1877 " 1883	
Benjamin F. Jones	46th " 48th	1879 " 1885	
Randall L. Gibson	48th " 52d	1883 " 1892	Died 1892.
James B. Eustis	49th " 51st	1885 " 1891	
Edward D. White	52d " 53d	1891 " 1894	Appointed judge of the Supreme court of the U. S.
Donaldson Caffrey	52d ——	1893	Appointed in place of Gibson.
Newton C. Blanchard	53d ——	1894	Appointed in place of White.

Louvre (*loovr*), in Paris, is said to have been a royal residence in the reign of Dagobert, 628. It was a prison-tower constructed by Philip Augustus in 1204. It afterwards became a library, and Charles VI. made it his palace (about 1364). The new buildings, begun by Francis I. in 1528, were enlarged and adorned by successive kings, particularly Louis XIV. Napoleon I. turned it into a museum, the finest collection of paintings, statues, and treasures of art known in the world. The chief of those brought from Italy have since been restored. The magnificent buildings of the new Louvre, begun by Napoleon I. and completed by Napoleon III., were inaugurated by the latter, 14 Aug. 1857. The library was destroyed and other buildings injured by the communists, May, 1871.

Low Countries, the Pays Bas, now HOLLAND and BELGIUM.

Loyal Legion, military order of, organized 15 Apr. 1865, by officers and ex-officers of the army, navy, and marine corps of the United States who took part in the civil war of 1861–65. Membership descends to the eldest direct male lineal descendant. Men can become members who in civil life, during the war, rendered active and eminent service to the Union; the ratio not to exceed 1 to 33 of the first class. There are 20 commanderies, each representing a state, and one the District of Columbia. Total membership, Oct. 31, 1891, 9640.

Lubeck, a city in N. Germany, one of four republics of the German confederation, was founded in the 12th century, and was the originator of the Hanseatic league about 1240, which lasted till 1630. Lubeck was declared a free imperial city about 1226; but was frequently attacked by the Danes. The French took it by assault, 6 Nov. 1806, and Napoleon incorporated it with his empire in 1810. On his fall in 1814 it became once more a free imperial city. It joined the North German Confederation, 18 Aug. 1866. Pop. 1871, 52,158; 1875, 56,912; 1880, 63,571; 1890, 76,485. HANSE TOWNS.

Luca'nians, a warlike people of S. Italy, defeated Alexander of Epirus at Pandosia, 332 B.C.; were subdued by the Romans, 272; revolted after the battle of Cannæ, 216; were reduced by Scipio, 201; again revolted, 90; admitted as Roman citizens, 88.

Lucca, central Italy, a Roman colony, 177 B.C., a Lombard duchy, 1327 A.D.; a free city about 1370; was active in civil wars of Italian republics. It was united with Tuscany, and given as a principality to Eliza Bonaparte by her brother Napoleon I., 1805. Lucca, as a duchy, was given to Maria Louisa, widow of Louis, king of Etruria, in 1814. It was exchanged by her son Charles Louis for Parma and Placentia in 1847; annexed to Tuscany, and with it to the kingdom of Italy in 1860.

Lucerne, a canton of Switzerland, became independent in 1332, and joined the confederation. The city is said to derive its name from a light (*lucerna*) set up to guide travellers. It dates from the 8th century, and was subject to the abbots of Murbach, who surrendered it to the house of Hapsburg. It was taken by the French in Mch. 1798, and was for a short time capital of the Helvetic republic; which, as the focus of insurrection against the French, was suppressed Oct. 1802. As a Catholic canton, Lucerne was active on behalf of education by the Jesuits, 1844. SWITZERLAND.

Lu'cia, St., one of the British West India islands, first settled by the English, 1639; expelled by the natives; settled by French in 1650; taken by the British several times in subsequent wars. Insurrection of the French negroes, Apr. 1795. St. Lucia was restored to France at the peace of 1802; but was seized by England, 1803, and confirmed to her in 1814. Area, 245 sq. miles. Pop. 1871, 31,811—710 whites; 1876, 34,848—910 whites; 1891, 41,713.

lu'cifer-matches came into use about 1834. Friction matches were invented by Walker of Stockton-on-Tees, Engl., 1829. In Mch. 1842, Reuben Partridge patented machinery for manufacturing splints. In 1845, Schrötter of Vienna produced his amorphous phosphorus (by heating ordinary phosphorus in a gas which it cannot absorb), by the use of which lucifers are rendered less dangerous, and the manufacture less unhealthy. Φωσφόρος (Gr.) and *Lucifer* (Lat.) both signify *light-bearer*. In the United States termed for a while LOCO-FOCO, probably from the Latin *loco-foci*, instead *of fire*; but Bartlett says from a self-lighting cigar, an invention of John Marck, in New York, 1834. Matches first began to be used in the U. S. in 1831–32, when they were sold in boxes containing 25 for 25 cents. The first patent issued in the U. S. for their manufacture was to Alonzo D. Phillips of Springfield, Mass., 1836. It is estimated that over 6,000,000 gross of 14,400 matches each are used yearly in the U. S.

Lucknow, capital of Oude since 1675. Pop. 1891, 273,090. INDIA, 1857; OUDE.

Luddites. Large parties of men, so called from Ned Lud, an idiot, who once broke some frames in a passion, commenced depredations at Nottingham, breaking frames and machinery, Nov. 1811. Skirmish with the military there, 29 Jan. 1812. Serious riots occurred again in 1814, and bodies of unemployed artisans committed excesses in 1816 et seq. Several Luddites were tried and executed, 1813 and 1818. Derby.

lunatics. Insanity.

Lundy's Lane or **Bridgewater,** Battle of. New York, 1814.

Lu'neville, France, Peace of, between the French republic and the emperor of Germany, confirmed cessions made by the treaty of Campo Formio, stipulated that the Rhine, as far as the Dutch territories, should form the boundary of France, and recognized the Batavian, Helvetic, Ligurian, and Cisalpine republics, 9 Feb. 1801.

Luperca'lia, a yearly festival observed at Rome on 15 Feb. in honor of Pan, destroyer of wolves (*lupi*), instituted by the Romans, in memory of Romulus and Remus, according to Plutarch; but, according to Livy, brought by Evander into Italy. These feasts are said to have been abolished in 496, by pope Gelasius, on account of great disorders. Feasts.

"Lusiad," the great epic poem of the Portuguese, written in honor of their discoveries in India, by Luis de Camoens, and published by him at Lisbon, 1572. The English translations are by sir Richard Fanshawe, 1655; by William Julius Mickle, 1775, and others; the latest and best by J. J. Aubertin, 1878.

lustrum, an expiatory sacrifice made for the Roman people, at the end of every 5 years, after the census, 472 B.C. Every 5th year was called a *lustrum;* and 10, 15, or 20 years were commonly expressed by 2, 3, or 4 *lustra.* The number of Roman citizens was, in 293 B.C., 272,308; 179 B.C., 273,294; 70 B.C., 450,000; 28 B.C., 4,164,060; 48 A.D., 5,984,072. The last lustrum took place 74 A.D.

lute, an ancient instrument of Oriental origin (Arab. *al'ud*); said to have been brought to Mecca in the 6th century A.D., and thence to Europe. J. S. Bach and others composed for the western lute in the 18th century.

Lutherans, followers of Martin Luther, who was born at Eisleben, 10 Nov. 1483; studied at Erfurt, 1501; was professor of philosophy at Wittenberg, 1508; resisted the sale of indulgences, 1517; defended himself at Augsburg, 1518; at Worms, 1520; was excommunicated, 16 June, 1520; began his German Bible, 1521; married Katherine de Bora, 1525; published his German Bible complete, 1534; died 18 Feb. 1546. The majority of the people of the north of Germany, Prussia, Denmark, and Sweden are Lutherans. The doctrines are mainly embodied in Luther's catechisms, in the Augsburg Confession (Augsburg), and in the *Formula Concordiæ* of the Lutherans, pub. in 1580. Their first university was founded at Marburg in 1527, by Philip, landgrave of Hesse. The Luther memorial at Worms was unveiled in the presence of the king of Prussia and other sovereigns, 25 June, 1868. By the census of 1890 the number of Lutheran churches or organizations in the United States was 8427; value of church property $34,218,234, with 1,199,514 communicants.

Lutzen or **Lutzengen,** a town of N. Germany. Here Gustavus Adolphus, king of Sweden, defeated the imperialists under Wallenstein, 16 Nov. 1632, but was killed; and here the French army, commanded by Napoleon, defeated the armies of Russia and Prussia, under gen. Wittgenstein, 2 May, 1813. The battles of Bautzen and Wurschen immediately followed (19–21 May), both in favor of Napoleon. The allies were compelled to pass the Oder, and an armistice was agreed to, afterwards prolonged; but, unfortunately for the French emperor, this did not produce peace.

Luxembourg, Palace of, Paris, built 1615 for Marie de Medicis. Part is now occupied by a collection of paintings of contemporary artists, any of which, 10 years after the death of the painter, may be brought to the Louvre. Works of foreign artists are admitted upon equal terms with the French school, subject to 2 conditions, (1) merit, (2) artist willing to sell at price offered by the state. The Luxembourg gallery receives additions yearly from work of young painters. The picture that gains the Prix du Salon at the annual exhibition in the Palais de l'Industrie is usually bought by the state. Changes are constantly taking place in the collection as pictures are removed to the Louvre. It was made a national gallery in 1802.

Luxemburg, grand-duchy of, borders on the extreme southeast corner of Belgium. Luxemburg, the capital, once considered the strongest fortified city in the world, has been many times besieged and taken: by the French in 984, 1443, 1479, 1542–43; by the Spaniards in 1544; by the French in 1684; restored to Spain in 1697; taken by the French in 1701; given to the Dutch as a barrier town, but ceded to the emperor at the peace in 1713. It withstood several sieges in the last century. It surrendered to the French after a siege, from Nov. 1794 to July, 1795; and was retaken by the allies, May, 1814. Fortifications transformed to civil purposes, 1874. By the treaty of London, 1867, the grand-duchy was declared a neutral and independent state, with the crown hereditary in the Nassau family. The present reigning grand-duke since the death of the king of the Netherlands, William III., who was also grand-duke of Luxemburg, is Adolf, duke of Nassau. Area, 998 sq. miles; pop. 1867, 199,958; 1875, 205,158; 1890, 211,088; pop. of the city, 18,187.

Luxor or **El-Uksur,** Egypt. Thebes.

luxuries. "Give me the luxuries of life, and I can dispense with the necessaries," a famous paradox ascribed by dr. Holmes, in the "Autocrat of the Breakfast Table," to the historian Motley. But Plutarch quotes from Scopas of Thessaly the similar saying, "We who are rich find happiness in superfluities, not in necessaries," and the remark has been repeated in many forms.

Lyce'um (originally a temple of Apollo Lyceus, or a portico, or gallery, built by Lyceus, son of Apollo) was a spot near the Ilissus, in Attica, where Aristotle taught philosophy; and as he generally taught as he walked, his pupils were called *peripatetics,* "walkers-about," 342 B.C.—*Stanley.* Theatres.

Ly'cia, a country of Asia Minor, subject successively to Crœsus (about 560 B.C.), to the Persians (546 B.C.), to Alexander the Great (333 B.C.), and to his successors the Seleucidæ. The Romans gave Lycia to the Rhodians (188 B.C.). It became nominally free under the Romans, and was annexed to the empire by Claudius. The marbles brought from Lycia by sir Charles Fellows were deposited in the British museum, 1840–46.

Lyd'ia or **Mæo'nia,** an ancient kingdom in Asia Minor, under a long dynasty of kings, the last being Crœsus, "the richest of mankind." The coinage of gold and silver money, and other useful inventions, are ascribed to the Lydians. Æsop, the Phrygian fabulist, Alcman, the first Greek poet, Thales of Miletus, Anaximenes, Xenophanes, Anacreon of Teos, Heraclitus of Ephesus, etc., flourished in Lydia. The early history is mythical.

	B.C.
Agron, a descendant of Hercules, reigns in Lydia.—*Herod.* about	1223
Kingdom proper begins under Ardys I.—*Blair*	797
Alyattes I. reigns	761
Myrsus commences his rule	747
Reign of Candaules (or Myrsilus)	735
Gyges, first of the Mermnadæ, kills Candaules, marries his queen, usurps the throne, and makes great conquests, about	731
Ardys II. reigns, 678; the Cimbri besiege Sardis, capital of Lydia	635
Milesian war, commenced under Gyges, is continued by Sadyattes, who reigns	628
Reign of Alyattes II.	617
Battle upon the river Halys, between Lydians and Medes, interrupted by an almost total eclipse of the sun, predicted many years before by Thales of Miletus.—*Blair,* 28 May,	585
Crœsus, son of Alyattes, succeeds, conquers Asia Minor	560–50
Crœsus, dreading Cyrus, whose conquests had reached the borders of Lydia, crosses the Halys to attack the Medes, with 420,000 men and 60,000 horse	548
He is defeated, pursued, and besieged in his capital by Cyrus, who orders him burned alive; the pile is already on fire, when Crœsus calls aloud *Solon!* and Cyrus hearing him, spares his life. Lydia made a province of the Persian empire	546

Sardis burned by Ionians 499
Lydia conquered by Alexander 332
Becomes part of the kingdom of Pergamus 283
A D
Conquered by Turks 1326

Lygo'nia. MAINE, State of, 1630-40

lying-in hospitals. The first, established in Dublin by dr Bartholomew Mosse, a physician, amid strong opposition, was opened Mch 1745 HOSPITALS.

lymphat'ics, absorbent vessels connected with digestion, discovered about 1650 by Rudbek in Sweden, Bartholin in Denmark, and Jolyffe in England Asellius discovered the lacteals in 1622 In 1654 Glisson ascribed to these vessels the function of absorption, and their properties were studied by William and John Hunter, Monro, Hewson, and other great anatomists

lynch law, punishment inflicted by private individuals, without legal authority, said to derive its name from Charles Lynch, a planter of Virginia (1726-96), who undertook, with Robert Adams and Thomas Calloway, to protect society by punishing outlaws and traitors through the process of an informal or self-constituted court Its sentences, however, never went beyond flogging and banishment. Charles Lynch's brother John was the founder of Lynchburg, Va. Summary punishment is often inflicted by mobs in certain southern and western states 195 cases of lynching reported in 1891 CRIME

Lyons, S. France, the Roman Lugdunum, founded by M. Plancus, 43 B C The city was reduced to ashes in a night by lightning, 59 A D, and rebuilt in the reign of Nero It was a free city till its union with France in 1307 Pop 1891, 416,030

Battle near Lyons, Clodius Albinus defeated and slain by Septimius Severus 19 Feb 197
Two general councils held here (13th and 14th) 1245, 1274
Silk manufacture commenced 1515
Lyons taken by republicans after 70 days' siege, 9 Oct., awful pillage and slaughter follow, convention decreed demolition of city 12 Oct. 1793
Capitulated to Austrians Mch 1814
Railway to Paris opened 7 Apr 1839

lyre. Its invention is ascribed to the Grecian Hermes (the Roman Mercury), who, according to Homer, gave it to Apollo, the first that played it with method, and accompanied it with poetry The invention of the primitive lyre, with 3 strings, is ascribed to the first Egyptian Hermes. Terpander added several strings to the lyre, making 7, 673 B.C Phrynis of Mitylene added 2 more, making 9, 438 B C

M

M, the 13th letter of the English alphabet, the 12th of the Latin and Greek As an initial, M is used for master, meridiem medicine, mundi, member—as M.A, *Magister Artium* (master of arts), A M, *Ante Meridiem* (before noon), P M, *Post Meridiem* (after noon), A.M, *Anno Mundi* (year of the world), M D, *Medicinæ Doctor*, M C, member of Congress, M P, member of Parliament Also, as a symbol of numbers, M indicates 1000, $\bar{M}$ 1,000,000

macadam'izing, a system of road-making which John Loudon Macadam (b Scotland, 1756, d 1836) devised, and described in an essay in 1819, having practised it in Ayrshire, Scotland He used stones broken to 6 ounces' weight, recommending clean flints and granite clippings He received 10,000*l* from Parliament, and in 1827 was appointed surveyor-general of the metropolitan roads ROADS

McAllister, Fort FORT MCALLISTER

Maca'o, a seaport town of Quang-tong, S China, was ceded by China to Portugal as a commercial station in 1586 (in return for assistance against pirates), subject to an annual tribute, remitted in 1863 Here Camoens composed part of the "LUSIAD"

"Macaro'ni." A name given to a poem by Theophilus Folengo, 1509, and still applied to trifling performances, as buffoonery, puns, anagrams, "wit without wisdom, and humor without sense" The name was taken from a preparation of wheat, native to Italy, where it is an article of food of national importance. These poems, in Italy and France, gave rise to *Macaroni academies*, and in England to *Macaroni clubs* (about 1772), when everything ridiculous in dress and manners was called "Macaroni"

Mac'cabees, a name of the Asmonæans, whose career began during the persecution of Antiochus Epiphanes, 167 B.C Mattathias, a priest, resisted the tyrant, and his son, Judas Maccabæus, defeated the Syrians in 3 battles, 166, 165 B.C., but fell in an ambush, 161 B C. His brother Jonathan made a league with the Romans and Lacedæmonians, and after an able administration was treacherously killed at Ptolemais by Tryphon, 143 B.C His brother and successor, Simon, was murdered, 135 B.C John Hyrcanus, son of Simon, succeeded. His son Judas, called also Aristobulus, took the title of king, 107 B C The history of the Maccabees fills 5 books of that name, 2 of which are included in our Apocrypha 4 are accounted canonical by the Roman Catholic church, none by Protestant communions.

McCrea, Jane, Murder of NEW YORK, 1777

McDowell, Va. Here on 8 May, 1862, Stonewall Jackson attacked gen Schenck The federals retreated during the night, loss 256, confederates, 461

mace, a weapon anciently used by cavalry of most nations, originally a spiked club, usually of metal, hung at the saddle-bow —The mace, an ensign of authority, borne before officers of state, having an open crown at the top, commonly of silver gilt. The lord chancellor and speaker of the House of Commons have maces borne before them Edward III granted to London the privilege of having gold or silver maces carried before the lord mayor, sheriffs, aldermen, and corporation, 1354 It was with the mace usually carried before the lord mayor on state occasions that Walworth, lord mayor of London, is said to have knocked the rebel Wat Tyler off his horse, for rudely approaching Richard II, a courtier afterwards despatching him with his dagger, 15 June, 1381 When Cromwell came to disperse Parliament, he ordered a soldier to "take away that bawble," the mace, which was done, and the doors of the house locked, 20 Apr. 1653

Mac'edon or **Macedo'nia,** N Greece The first kingdom founded by Caranus, about 814 B.C., was successively under the protection of Athens, of Thebes, and of Sparta, until the reign of Philip, father of Alexander the Great, who by political wisdom and warlike exploits made it powerful, and paved the way for his son's greatness.

Reigns of Caranus, 814 B C, or 796, or 748, Perdiccas I, 729, Argæus I, 681, Philip I., 640 or 609 B C
Æropus conquers Illyrians 602
Reign of Amyntas, 540, of Alexander I 500
Macedon conquered by Persians, 513, delivered by victory of Platæa 479
Reign of Perdiccas II 454
Potidæa, revolting, 433, retaken by Athenians 429
Archelaus, natural son of Perdiccas, murders the legitimate heirs, seizes the throne, and improves the country 413, murdered by a favorite to whom he promised his daughter in marriage 399
Pausanias reigns 394
Reign of Amyntas II, after killing Pausanias 393
Illyrians enter Macedonia, expel Amyntas, and make Argæus, brother of Pausanias, king 392
Am[illegible]tas again recovers his kingdom 390
[illegible] of Alexander II, 369, assassinated 367
[illegible] of Perdiccas III, 364, killed in battle 360
[illegible] of Philip II, and institution of the Macedonian phalanx 359
[illegible]feats the Athenians and Illyrians 360, 359
[illegible] takes Amphipolis (ARCHERY) 358
[illegible] conquers Thrace, Illyria, and Thessaly 356-352
[illegible] of Alexander III, the Great 356
[illegible] the first sacred war 346
[illegible] overrun by the army of Philip 344
[illegible] made tributary to Macedon 343
[illegible]tle appointed tutor to Alexander "
[illegible]gainst the Athenians 341

Philip besieged Byzantium unsuccessfully		340
Battle of Chæronea, Philip victor		338
Philip assassinated by Pausanias at Ægæ during games at his daughter's nuptials Alexander III, the Great succeeds		336
Greeks appoint him general against the Persians		335
Thebans revolt, he destroys Thebes, house of Pindar alone left		"
He enters Asia and first defeats Darius at the Granicus 22 May,		334
Sardis surrenders, Halicarnassus taken, and cities in Asia Minor		"
Memnon ravages the Cyclades, Darius takes the field with 400,000 infantry and 100,000 cavalry		333
Darius defeated at Issus	Nov	"
Alexander, on his way to Egypt lays siege to Tyre, which is destroyed after 7 months		332
Damascus taken, Gaza surrenders		
Alexander enters Jerusalem, Egypt conquered, Alexandria founded		"
Persians defeated at Arbela	1 Oct	331
Alexander master of Asia enters Babylon		
Sits on the throne of Darius at Susa		330
Parthia Media, etc overrun by him		329
Thalestris, queen of the Amazons visits him		"
He puts his friend Parmenio to death on a charge of conspiracy supposed to be false		"
His expedition to India, Porus the king, defeated and taken, the country to the Ganges overrun		327
Callisthenes tortured for refusing divine homage to Alexander		328
Voyage of his admiral Nearchus from the Indus to the Euphrates		328-325
Returns to Babylon, 324, d		323
Philip III (Aridæus) king		"
Alexander's conquests divided among his generals 323, his remains taken to Alexandria, and buried by Ptolemy		322
Greeks defeated by Antipater and the Macedonians, near CRANNON		"
Cassander reigns, 316, rebuilds Thebes		315
Seleucus recovers Babylon		312
Cassander kills Roxana and her son (last of Alexander's family), and usurps the throne		311
Battle of Ipsus, Antigonus killed		301
New division of the empire		
Death of Cassander		298
Reign of his sons Alexander V and Antipater		"
Demetrius I, Poliorcetes son of Antigonus, murders Alexander, and seizes the crown of Macedon		294
Achæan league formed against Macedon		281-243
Governments of Pyrrhus, 287, Lysimachus, 286, Ptolemy Ceraunus		281
Irruption of the Gauls, Ptolemy killed		279
Sosthenes governs		278
Reign of Antigonus Gonatas, son of Demetrius		277
Pyrrhus invades Macedon, defeats Antigonus, and is proclaimed king		274
Pyrrhus slain, Antigonus restored		272
Antigonus takes Athens		268
Gauls again invade Macedon		"
Revolt of the Parthians		250
Reign of Demetrius II		239
Philip, his son, 232, set aside by Antigonus Doson		229
Philip V, 220, allies with Hannibal, 211, wars unsuccessfully against the Rhodians		202
Philip defeated by Romans at Cynoscephalæ		197
Reign of Perseus, his son, 178, war with Rome		171
Perseus defeated at Pydna, Macedon a Roman province		168
Perseus and his sons walk in chains before the chariot of Æmilius in his triumph over Macedon		167
Insurrection of Andriscus, calling himself Philip, son of Perseus, quelled		148
		A D
Macedonia plundered by Theodoric the Ostrogoth		482
Conquered by the Bulgarians		978
Recovered by emperor Basil		1001
Formed into the Latin kingdom of Thessalonica, by Boniface of Montferrat		1204
After various changes, conquered by Amurath II, and annexed to Turkey		1430

Macedo'nians, a religious sect, followers of Macedonius, made bishop of Constantinople about 341 His appointment was opposed and led to much bloodshed He was expelled by decree of a council held 360 He held that the Holy Ghost was not a distinct person of the Trinity, but a divine spirit or energy diffused through the universe —*Eadie* Also natives or inhabitants of Macedonia

"**McFingal,**" the title of a political satire by John Trumbull. LITERATURE, American

McHenry, Fort FORT MCHENRY.

Machiavel'ian principles, taught by Niccolo Machiavelli of Florence (b 1493, d 1527), in his "Practice of Politics" and "The Prince" By some they are styled "the most pernicious maxims of government, founded on the vilest policy," by others as "sound doctrines, notwithstanding the prejudice erroneously raised against them." The author said that if he taught princes to be tyrants he also taught the people to destroy tyrants "The Prince" appeared at Rome in 1532, and was translated into English in 1761

Macicowice (*mats-ya-o-veet'sa*), a town near Warsaw, Poland Here the Poles were defeated by the Russians, and their general, Kosciusko, taken prisoner 10 Oct 1794 after a murderous action He endeavored to prevent the junction of the Russian and Austrian armies The statement that he said "Finis Poloniæ" is contradicted

Mackinaw, Fort FORT MACKINAW

Madagas'car, southeast coast of Africa The third largest island in the world, not including Australia Distance from Africa, 230 miles, length, 975 miles, breadth, 358 miles, area, 228,500 sq miles pop estimated, 3,500,000 (no census ever taken) Said to have been discovered by Lorenzo Almeida, 1506

Portuguese settlement 1548 destroyed by the French one 1642 on arrival of a French governor		1669
French attempt to settle at Antongel bay		1774
Count Benyowski supreme Oct 1775, killed in an encounter with French	23 May	1786
Their establishment at fort Dauphin fell into the hands of the English with Bourbon and Mauritius		1810-11
Settlements ceded to king Radama on his giving up the slave trade		1818
Radama I king 1810 who favored Europeans and encouraged Christianity, d		1828
A reactionary policy under his energetic queen Ranavalona, 1828, English missionaries who came in 1820 expelled		1835
Amicable intercourse ceases, native Christians persecuted		1846 et seq
French defeated in an attack on the island	19 Oct	1855
Queen dies, her son Radama II a Christian succeeds	23 Aug	1861
Treaty with Great Britain and France signed	12 Sept	1862
Revolution, king and ministers assassinated, queen Rasohérina proclaimed sovereign	May,	1863
Treaty with Great Britain, Christians to be tolerated, etc, 27 June 1865, ratified	5 July,	1866
Queen died in Mch, her cousin, Ranavalona II succeeded as queen, 1 Apr 1868, baptized	Feb	1869
African slavery prohibited, 1873, solemnly	June,	1877
Queen Ranavalona II d	13 July,	1883
Succeeded by her niece Ranavalona III	July,	"
Treaty with France	12 Dec	1885
Protectorate of France recognized by Great Britain by Anglo French agreement of	5 Aug	1890

[Native government retains independence in domestic legislation]

madder, the root of the *Rubia tinctoria*, highly valued for dyeing properties. ALIZARINE

Madei'ra, an island, northwest coast of Africa, discovered, it is said, in 1344 by Macham, an Englishman, who fled from France for an illicit amour He was driven here by a storm, and his mistress, a French lady, dying, he made a canoe, and carried news of his discovery to Pedro, king of Aragon, hence the report that the island was discovered by a Portuguese, 1345 It is asserted that Portuguese did not visit this island until 1419 or 1420, nor colonize it until 1431 It was taken by British in July, 1801, and again by adm Hood and gen Beresford, 24 Dec 1807, and retained in trust for the royal family of Portugal, who had emigrated to the Brazils It was restored to the Portuguese in 1814 After 1852 the renowned vintages were almost ruined by the vine disease (oidium), but of late years the vineyards have recovered much of their former prosperity Area, 505 sq miles Pop 1872, 120,315, 1881, 132,223.

Madison, James, Administration of UNITED STATES, 1809-17

Madras', province and city of S E Hindostan, called by natives Chennapatam, colonized by the English, 1640 Area of province, 140,762 sq miles Pop 1891, 35,591,440, city, 449,950

Fort St. George built, 1641, made a presidency		1653
Bengal placed under Madras		1668
Calcutta, hitherto subordinate to Madras, made a presidency		1701
Madras taken by the French	14 Sept	1746
Restored to the English		1749
Vainly besieged by the French under Lally	12 Dec.	1758
Lord Pigot, governor, imprisoned by his own council, 24 Aug 1776, dies in confinement 17 Apr 1777, his enemies convicted and fined 1000*l* each	11 Feb	1780
Sir Eyre Coote arrives	5 Nov	"
He defeats Hyder	1 July,	1781
Lord Cornwallis arrives here	12 Dec	1790

Madras system of education introduced (MONITORIAL)... 1795
Gen. Harris, with Madras army, enters Mysore, 5 Mch.; reaches Seringapatam, 5 Apr., which is stormed by British under major-gen. Baird, and Tippoo Sahib killed... 4 May, 1799
Appointment of sir Thomas Strange, first judge of Madras under the charter... 26 Dec. 1800
Madras army, under gen. Arthur Wellesley (afterwards duke of Wellington), marches for Poonah (INDIA)... Mch. 1803

Madrid', capital of Spain, mentioned in history as Majerit, a Moorish castle. Pop. 1857, 271,254; 1870, 332,024; 1877, 397,690; 1887, 472,228. SPAIN.

Sacked by the Moors... 1190
Fortified by Henry III... about 1400
Humiliating treaty of Madrid between Charles V. and Francis I., his prisoner... 14 Jan. 1526
Made the seat of the Spanish court by Philip II... 1560

mad'rigal, an unaccompanied song for 3 or more voices; fine examples are by English composers. Madrigals, invented in the Netherlands, were adopted in Italy, where fine specimens were produced. Many were published by Morley, 1594; Weelkes, 1597; Wilbye, 1598; and Bennet, 1599. The Madrigal Society in London began in 1741. English Glee and Madrigal Union founded in 1851. Rimbault's "Bibliotheca Madrigalium" pub. 1847. The madrigal, "Summer is i cumen in," is attributed to the 13th or 14th century. MUSIC.

mæn'ades. ORGIES.

Maestricht (*mäs'-trikt*), Holland, the ancient *Trajectum ad Mosam*, the capital of Limburg. It revolted from Spain, and was taken by the prince of Parma in 1579, a massacre following. In 1632 the prince of Orange reduced it after a memorable siege, and it was confirmed to the Dutch in 1648; Louis XIV. took it in 1673; William, prince of Orange, invested it in vain in 1676; but in 1678 it was restored to the Dutch. In 1748 it was besieged by French, who obtained possession of the city on condition of its being restored at the peace then negotiating. In Feb. 1793, Maestricht was unsuccessfully attacked by the French, but they became masters of it Nov. 1794. In 1814, it was made part of the kingdom of the Netherlands, and now belongs to Holland. Pop. 1890, 32,225.

Mafi'a, a secret terrorist murderous society in Sicily, more powerful than the Camorra (ITALY, 1874), comprising persons of all classes; became prominent in 1860. Efforts for its suppression were made by the government in 1874–75. MASSACRES, 1890–91; UNITED STATES.

magazine rifle. FIRE-ARMS.

magazines and **reviews.** The earliest were literary miscellanies periodically published, but now there are special ones in every department of knowledge. The following table of the principal magazines and reviews in the United States since 1741 gives the dates of first and last publication, if known; those still in existence are marked with an obelisk (†).

AMERICAN MAGAZINES AND REVIEWS.

Magazines.	Reviews.	Commencement and continuance.
General Mag. and Hist. Chronicle (A. S. Bradford, pub.), Phila. [First pub. in the colonies.]	...	1741 [3 nos. pub.]
Boston Weekly	...	1743
Amer. Mag. and Hist. Chronicle (Daniel Fowle & G. Rogers, pub.), Boston	...	1743–46
N. Y. Independent Reflector	...	1752–54
New Engl. Mag. of Knowledge and Pleasure, Boston	...	1758
North American	...	1758–66
Royal American, Boston. [First illustrated.]	...	1774 [6 months.]
Pennsylvania (Thomas Paine, ed.), Phila	...	1775–76
The Columbian, Phila	...	1786–89
Amer. Museum (Cary's), Phila	...	1787–97
The Massachusetts, Boston	...	1789–96
The New York Mag. and Lit. Repository	...	1790–97
The Ladies', Phila	...	17[illegible]
Farmers' Museum	...	17[illegible]–99
The United States	...	17[illegible]
Theological Magazine	...	17[illegible]–98
The American Universal	...	17[illegible]
The Philadelphia	...	17[illegible]
	Amer. Monthly Review [First in the U. S.]	17[illegible]

AMERICAN MAGAZINES AND REVIEWS.—(*Continued.*)

Magazines.	Reviews.	Commencement and continuance.
The Portfolio (Joseph Dennie, 1st ed.), Phila. [Principal magazine during these years.]	...	1801–25
The Literary (Charles Brockden Brown, ed.), Phila	...	1803–8
The Monthly Anthology, Boston	...	1803–11
The Monthly Register (S. C. Carpenter, 1st ed.), Charleston, S. C. [First magazine south.]	...	1805
The Panoplist, Boston	...	1805
The Churchman (John H. Hobart, ed.)	...	1808
The Rambler, New York	...	1810
Literary Miscellany, New York	...	1811
	Amer. Review (Robt. Walsh, ed.) [Quarterly; first in the U. S.]	1811–13
Niles's Register, Baltimore	...	1811–49
Analectic (Washington Irving, 1st ed.), Phila	...	1813–20
	North American (William Tudor, 1st ed.)	1815 †
The Portico, Baltimore	...	1816–19
The Methodist (see quarterly, 1841)	...	1818–40
The Amer. Jour. of Science (Silliman's), New York	...	1818 †
The Lady's Companion	...	1820–44
The Casket, Phila. (see Graham's, 1841)	...	1821–39
The Atlantic. [Afterwards the N. Y. Rev.]	...	1824–25
	The N. Y. Rev. (William C. Bryant, ed.) [Succeeds The Atlantic.]	1825
	Franklin Institute Journal, Phila	1826 †
Biblical Repertory (see Princeton Review, 1871)	...	1825–28
The Boston Monthly	...	1825–26
The Parthenon (Sam'l Woodworth, ed.)	...	1827
	Amer. Quar. Rev., Phila.	1827–37
Ballou's, Boston	...	1827
	Southern, Charleston, S. C.	1828–32
Illinois Monthly (James Hall, 1st ed.), Vandalia. [First magazine in the west.]	...	1830–32
Godey's Lady's Book, Phila	...	1830 †
New England (Jos. T. Buckingham, ed.), Boston	...	1831–35
Western Monthly (Jas. Hall, ed.), Cincinnati, O. [Successor to the Illinois Monthly.]	...	1833–36
Knickerbocker (Chas. F. Hoffman, 1st ed.), New York. [This was the first definite American magazine.]	...	1833–65
American Monthly (H. W. Herbert, 1st ed.), New York	...	1833–38
Southern Literary Messenger, Richmond	...	1834–64
Southern Literary Journal, Charleston, S. C.	...	1835–37
Gentleman's Magazine (W. E. Burton, ed.), Phila	...	1837–40
	Democratic Review, Wash. and N. Y. [During this period it appeared under several names.]	1837–59
Hesperian, Columbus, O.	...	1838–39
	Boston Quarterly (see Brownson's, 1844)	1838–42
Merchants (Freeman Hunt, 1st ed.), New York	...	1839–70
The Dial (Sarah Margaret Fuller, 1st ed.), Boston. [Quarterly.]	...	1840–44
Arcturus, New York	...	1840–42
Graham's, Phila. (succeeds the Casket). [For a time the most popular magazine in the U. S., with a circulation of 35,000 copies.]	...	1841–58
Ladies' Repository (L. L. Hamline, 1st ed.), Cincinnati, O. [Continued as The National Repository.]	...	1841–77
	Methodist Quarterly (see Methodist Review, 1885)	1841–84

AMERICAN MAGAZINES AND REVIEWS.—(*Continued.*)

Magazines.	Reviews.	Commencement and continuance.
Magnolia, Charleston, S. C.	....	1842
Ladies' Garland and Dollar Magazine, Phila.	....	1842
The Pioneer (Jas. R. Lowell, ed.), Boston	....	1843 [3 nos. issued.]
	New Englander, New Haven	1843 †
Littell's Living Age, Boston. [Weekly.]	....	1844 †
Eclectic, New York	....	1844 †
	Brownson's Quarterly Rev. (see Boston Quarterly, 1838)	1844–75
	Whig Rev., New York.	1845–52
Bankers', New York	....	1846 †
	De Bow's Review, New Orleans	1846
	Massachusetts Quar.	1847–50
Literary World, New York	....	1847–53
New England Historical and Genealogical Register, Boston	....	1847 †
The Union, Phila.	....	1847
Sartains, Phila. [Formerly the Union.]	....	1849–53
International, New York	....	1850–52
Harper's Monthly, New York. [First of the illus. mags.]	....	1850 †
Putnam's Monthly, New York.	....	1853–57 1868–70
Atlantic Monthly (Phillips, Sampson & Co., 1st pub.; J. R. Lowell, 1st ed.), Boston.	....	1857 †
Hist. Mag. (Dawson's), Boston, and Morrisania, N. Y.	....	1857–75
	National Quar., N. Y.	1860–80
	Boston	1861–66
Catholic World, New York	....	1865 †
The Galaxy, New York	....	1866–78
	Baptist Quar., Phila.	1867–77
American Naturalist, Phila.	....	1867 †
Lippincott's, Phila.	....	1868 †
Overland Monthly (Francis Bret Harte, 1st ed.), San Francisco	....	1868–75 [1st series.] 1883 † [2d series.]
Lake Side Monthly, Chicago	....	1869–74
Eclectic English Mag. (Van Nostrand's), New York	....	1869–86
Old and New, Boston	....	1870–75
Literary World, Boston	....	1870 †
Scribner's Monthly (J. G. Holland, 1st ed.), New York. [See Century, 1881, and Scribner's Magazine, 1887.]	....	1870–81 [1st series.]
	Princeton Review. [See Biblical Repertory, 1825.]	1871–88
Pop. Science Monthly, N. Y.	....	1872 †
St. Nicholas, New York	....	1873 †
	International Rev., N.Y.	1874–83
Wide Awake, Boston	....	1876–93
Library Journal, New York	....	1876 †
	Amer. Catholic Quarterly, Phila.	1876 †
Mag. of Amer. Hist., New York.	....	1877–93
Magazine of Art, New York	....	1878
	Baptist Review, Cincinnati and N. Y.	1879 †
The Dial, Chicago	....	1880 †
The Chautauquan, Meadville, Pa.	....	1880 †
The Century, New York. [Succeeds the Scribner's Monthly.]	....	1881 †
The Critic, New York	....	1881 †
Outing, New York	....	1882 †
Continental, Baltimore	....	1883 †
Science, New York	....	1883 †
	Andover Rev., Boston.	1884 †
	Methodist Review (see Methodist Quarterly, 1841)	1885 †
New England, Boston	....	1886 †
Cosmopolitan, New York	....	1886 †
	The Forum, New York.	1886 †
Scribner's, New York. [See Scribner's Monthly, 1870.]	....	1887 †
Munsey's, New York	....	1889 †
The Arena, Boston	....	1889 †
	Review of Reviews, New York	1890 †
	Educational Rev., N. Y.	1891 †
	The World, Boston	1892 †
Peterson's, Philadelphia	....	1892 † [New series.]

MAG

ENGLISH MAGAZINES AND REVIEWS.

Magazines.	Reviews.	Commencement and continuance.
Gentleman's, London. [First mag. pub. in Engl.]	....	1731 †
London	....	1732
Scot's, Edinburgh	....	1739–1826
	Monthly Review, Lond.	1749–1845
	Critical, London	1759–1817
Royal	....	1759
Lady's	....	1772
Methodist (Wesleyan), London.	....	1778 †
European	....	1782
Monthly	....	1796
	Edinburgh, reprinted in the U. S.	1802 †
	Eclectic, London	1805–68
	Quarterly, Lond., reprinted in the U. S.	1809 †
Entertaining Magazine	....	1812
New Monthly, London	....	1814–83
Blackwood's, Edinburgh, reprinted in the U. S.	....	1817 †
	Westminster, London, reprinted in U. S.	1824 †
	Athenæum, London	1828 †
Fraser's, London	....	1830–82
Metropolitan, London	....	1831
Penny, London	....	1832–46
Tait's, Edinburgh	....	1832–61
	Dublin	1836 †
	North British, Edinb.	1844–71
	British Quar., London.	1845–86
	Saturday	1855 †
	National, London	1855–64 1883 †
Cornhill, London	....	1859 †
Macmillan's, London	....	1859 †
	Contemporary, Lond., reprinted in U. S.	1860 †
Good Words, London	....	1860 †
	The Spectator (a review from)	1861 †
The Argosy, London	....	1865 †
	Fortnightly, London, reprinted in U. S.	1865 †
Belgravia, London	....	1866 †
St. Paul, London	....	1867–74
	Academy, London	1869 †
	Nineteenth Century, reprinted in U. S.	1877 †
Cassell's Mag. of Art, London	....	1878 †
Antiquary, London	....	1880 †
Longman's, London	....	1882 †
	Scottish, reprinted in U. S.	1882 †
English Illustrated, London	....	1883 †
Murray's, London	....	1887–90
Strand, London	....	1891 †

Mag'dala. ABYSSINIA.

Magdalens and **Magdalenettes,** communities of nuns, chiefly penitent courtesans. The order of penitents of St. Magdalen was founded 1272, at Marseilles. The convent of Naples was endowed by queen Sancha, 1324. That at Metz was instituted in 1452. At Paris, 1492. The Magdalen at Rome was endowed by pope Leo X., in 1515, and favored by Clement VIII. in 1594. The Magdalen Hospital, London, was founded in 1758, under direction of dr. Dodd. The asylum in Dublin was opened in June, 1766.

Mag'deburg, a city of Prussia. The archbishopric was founded about 967. The city suffered much by the religious wars in Germany. It was besieged and taken by elector Maurice, Nov. 1550, and Nov. 1551; blockaded for 7 months by imperialists, under Wallenstein, 1629; and barbarously sacked by Tilly, 10 May, 1631. It was given to Brandenburg, 1648; taken by the French, 8 Nov. 1806; annexed to the kingdom of Westphalia, 9 July, 1807; restored to Prussia, May, 1813. Pop. 1890, 202,234.

In Magdeburg experiment, a hollow sphere, composed of 2 hemispheres, fitting air-tight, is exhausted by the air-pump. The hemispheres are held together by the pressure of the atmosphere, and require great force to separate them. The apparatus was suggested by Otto von Guericke, inventor of the air-pump. He died in 1686.—*Brande.*

Magellan, Strait of (connecting the Atlantic and Pacific oceans), and separating Patagonia from Terra del Fuego. AMERICA.

Magen'ta, a small town in Lombardy, near which the French and Sardinians defeated the Austrians, 4 June, 1859.

Napoleon III. commanded, and he and the king of Sardinia were in the thickest of the fight. It is said that 55,000 French and Sardinians and 75,000 Austrians were engaged; the former losing 4000 killed and wounded, and the Austrians 10,000, besides 7000 prisoners. The French generals Espinasse and Clerc were killed. The arrival of gen. MacMahon during a deadly struggle between the Austrians and the French greatly contributed to the victory. The contest near the bridge of Buffalora was very severe. The Austrians fought well, but were badly commanded. The emperor and king entered Milan on 8 June following; MacMahon and Regnault d'Angely were created marshals of France. A monument erected here in memory of the slain was solemnly inaugurated 4 June, 1872.—The red dye, rosaniline, obtained by chemists from gastar, is termed *magenta*. ANILINE.

ma'gi, or worshippers of fire. The Persians adored the invisible and incomprehensible God as the principle of all good, and paid homage to fire as the emblem of his power and purity. They built no altars nor temples; their sacred fires blazed in the open air, and their offerings were made on the earth. The magi, their priests, are said to have had skill in astronomy, etc.; hence all learned men were called magi, and even confounded with magicians. Zoroaster, king of Bactria, reformer of the sect of the Magi, flourished about 550 B.C. This religion was superseded in Persia by Mahometanism, 652 A.D., and the Parsees at Bombay are descendants of Guebres, or fire-worshippers.

magic. ALCHEMY, WITCHCRAFT, etc. See Godwin's "Lives of the Necromancers," 1834, and Ennemoser's "History of Magic," translated by W. Howitt, 1854. AUTOMATON FIGURES.

magic lantern. An optical instrument for projecting on a white background magnified representations of transparent pictures, painted or photographed on glass. Its invention is ascribed to Roger Bacon, about 1260, but more correctly to Athanasius Kircher, who died 1680.

Magna Charta (*mäg'na kär'ta*). Its fundamental parts were derived from Saxon charters, continued by Henry I. and his successors. On 20 Nov. 1214, the archbishop of Canterbury and the barons met at St. Edmondsbury. On 6 Jan. 1215 they presented demands to king John, who deferred his answer. On 19 May they were censured by the pope. On 24 May they marched to London, and the king had to yield. The charter was settled by John at Runnymede, near Windsor, 15 June, 1215, and often confirmed by Henry III. and his successors. The last grand charter was granted in 1224 by Edward I. FORESTS. The original MS. charter is lost. The finest MS. copy, which is at Lincoln, was reproduced by photographs in the "National MSS.," pub. by British government, 1865.

Magna Græcia, the independent states founded by Greek colonists in South Italy, Sicily, etc. Cumæ, in Campania, is said to have been founded in 1034 B.C., Pandosia and Metapontum in 774 B.C. These states ruined themselves by supporting Hannibal, 216 B.C.

	B.C.
Syracuse founded	about 734
Leontinum and Catana	730
Sybaris	721
Crotona	710
Tarentum	708
Locri Epizephyrii	673
Lipara	627
Agrigentum	582
Thurium	432

[See under separate articles.]

Magne'sia, Asia Minor. Here Antiochus the Great, king of Syria, was defeated by the Scipios, 190 B.C.—*Magnesia alba*, a white alkaline earth, used in medicine from about 1700, whose properties were explained by dr. Black in 1755.

magne'sium, a metal first obtained from magnesia by sir Humphry Davy in 1808, and since in larger quantities by Bussy, Deville, and especially by E. Sonstadt, in 1862-64. Its light when burned is very brilliant, and is so rich in chemical rays that it may be used in photography. Lamps for burning magnesium wire were employed in tunnelling Mount Cenis. By its light photographs of the interior of the Pyramids were taken in 1865. Larkin's magnesium lamp (burning the metal in powder) was exhibited at the Royal Institution on 1 June, 1866, and before the British Association at Nottingham in Aug. 1866. An improved magnesium-wire lamp is now used in the United States Geodetic survey. It has been seen and observed over lines 90 miles in length at night.

mag'netism. Magnes, a shepherd, is said to have been detained on Mount Ida by nails in his boots. The attractive power of the loadstone or magnet is referred to by Homer, Aristotle, and Pliny; it was also known to the Chinese and Arabians. The Greeks are said to have obtained the loadstone from Magnesia, in Asia, 1000 B.C. Roger Bacon is said to have been acquainted with its property of pointing to the north (1294). The science of magnetism made no real progress till the invention of the mariner's compass.—*Encyc. Brit.* 9 ed. vol. xv. p. 219. Georg Hartman of Nuremberg, first observed the dip of the needle about 1544. COMPASS, ELECTRICITY.

Robert Norman, of London, independently also, discovered the dip of the needle....about 1576
Gilbert's treatise "De Magnete" pub.... 1600
Halley's theory of magnetic variations pub.... 1683
Marcel observed that a suspended bar of iron becomes temporarily magnetic by position.... 1722
Artificial magnets made by dr. Gowan Knight.... 1746
Variation of the compass was discovered by Bond about 1668; the diurnal variation by Graham, 1722; on which latter Canton made 4000 observations previous to.... 1756
Coulomb constructed a torsion balance to investigate attraction and repulsion, 1786; similar researches by Michell, Euler, Lambert, Robison, and others....1750-1800
Deflection of the magnetic needle by the voltaic current discovered by Œrsted.... 1820
Mr. Abraham invents a magnetic guard to protect grinders of cutlery.... 1821
Magnetic effects of violet rays of light exhibited by Morichini, 1814; polarity of a sewing-needle so magnetized shown by Mrs. Somerville.... 1825
Mr. Christie proves that heat diminishes magnetic force, about "
Sir W. Snow Harris invents various forms of the compass.... 1831
Magnetic north pole discovered by commander (afterwards sir) James Clark Ross (during sir John Ross's second voyage)....1 June, "
Its position (vertical dip) was observed by him to be 70° 5′ N. lat. and 96° 43′ W. lon. In the southern hemisphere the magnetic pole was nearly attained by the same navigator in his voyage of....1839-43
[Its position is probably 73° 31′ S. lat. and 147° 30′ W. lon.]
Electricity produced by rotation of a magnet by Faraday, 1831; his researches on the action of the magnet on light, on magnetic properties of flame, air, and gases (pub. 1845), on diamagnetism (1845), on magno-crystallic action (1848), on atmospheric magnetism (1850), on magnetic force....1851-52
Magnetic observations instituted in British colonies under col. Edward Sabine....1840 et seq.
Prof. Tyndall proves dia-magnetic polarity.... 1856
Archibald Smith described investigations on deviation of the compass in iron ships at the Royal Institution....9 Feb. 1866
William Robinson patented a magnetic method of making wrought iron from cast iron; announced....July, 1867
Wilde's magneto-electric machine exhibited (ELECTRICITY).... "
Since 1800 knowledge of magnetism has been advanced by Arago, Ampère, Hansteen, Henry, Gauss, Weber, Poggendorff, Sabine, Lamont, Du Moncel, Archibald Smith, etc. (ANIMAL MAGNETISM).
In the Royal institution, London, is a magnet made by Logeman, of Haarlem, on the principles of dr. Elias, which weighs 100 lbs., and can sustain 430 lbs. Häcker, of Nuremberg, made one weighing 36 grains, and sustaining 146 times its own weight. This was exhibited in 1851, also at the Royal institution.

magneto-electricity, a discovery of Faraday; recently applied to telegraphic and to light-house purposes. The South Foreland light-house, near Dover, was illuminated by the magneto-electric light in the winter of 1858-59 and 1859-60 (the light removed to Dungeness in 1861); the Lizards, by dr. C. William Siemens's magneto-electric light, 1878. ELECTRICITY, FARADIZATION.

magno'lia, a genus of American and Asiatic trees with aromatic bark and large sweet-scented white or reddish flowers, named after Pierre Magnol, a French botanist of the 17th century. *Magnolia glauca*, North America. The laurel-leaved magnolia (*Magnolia grandiflora*), North America. The dwarf magnolia (*Magnolia pumila*), China, and (also China) the brown-stalked, the purple, and the slender. FLOWERS AND PLANTS.

Magua'ga, Mich., Battle of. Here on 9 Aug. 1812, lieut.-col. Miller defeated the British and Indians. American loss, 18 killed, 57 wounded. MICHIGAN, UNITED STATES.

Mag'yars. HUNGARY.

Mahdi (*mä'dē*), i. e. "he who is guided aright." The Mahometan "Messiah," who is one day to arise and fill the oppressed world with righteousness, etc. The sheik Mahomed

Ahmed of Dongola declared himself "Mahdi" in Soudan, 1881. SOUDAN.

mahog'any, the only species of the genus *Swietenia* of the order *Meliaceæ* is said to have been taken to England by Raleigh in 1595, but not to have come into general use till 1720. It is indigenous to Central America.

Mahometan year. The year consists of 12 lunar months, commencing with the approximate new moon, without any intercalation to keep them in the same seasons with respect to the sun, so that the months retrograde through the year in about 32½ years. ERAS.

TABLE SHOWING THE MONTHS OF THE MAHOMETAN YEAR, THEIR LENGTH, TIME OF THE BEGINNING OF EACH MONTH IN THE DATE OF OUR ERA, AND THE RETROGRESSION OF THE 1ST OF THE MAHOMETAN YEAR UP TO 1900.

Mahometan year 1311.	Name of month.	Length.	Date of beginning our era.
1st month	Muharran	30 days	15 July, 1893.
2d "	Saphar	29 "	14 Aug. "
3d "	Rabia I.	30 "	12 Sept. "
4th "	Rabia II	29 "	12 Oct. "
5th "	Jomada I	30 "	10 Nov. "
6th "	Jomada II	29 "	10 Dec. "
7th "	Rajab	30 "	8 Jan. 1894.
8th "	Shaaban	29 "	7 Feb. "
9th "	Ramadin	30 "	8 Mch. "
10th "	Shawall	29 "	7 Apr. "
11th "	Dulkaada	30 "	6 May, "
12th "	Dulheggia	29 "	5 June, "

RETROGRESSION OF DATE.

1312. 1st month Muharran....................begins 5 July, 1894
1313. " " " .... " 24 June, 1895
1314. " " " .... " 12 June, 1896
1315. " " " .... " 2 June, 1897
1316. " " " .... " 22 May, 1898
1317. " " " .... " 12 May, 1899
1318. " " " .... " 1 May, 1900

In 1344 Mahometan year, or 1926 of our era, the 1st of the year will be 12 July, having passed through the entire year.

Mahom'etanism, or **Moham'medanism,** embodied in the Koran, includes the unity of God, the immortality of the soul, predestination, a last judgment, and a sensual paradise. Mahomet asserted that the Koran was revealed to him by the angel Gabriel during 23 years. He enjoined on his disciples circumcision, prayer, alms, frequent ablution, and fasting, and permitted polygamy and concubinage.

Mahomet, or Mohammed, born at Mecca..................569 or 570
Announced himself as a prophet..........................about 611
Fled from his enemies to Medina (his flight is called the Hegira)..15 July, 622
Overcomes his enemies (the Koreish, Jews, etc.) in battle....623-25
Defeats the Christians at Muta.................................. 629
Is acknowledged as a sovereign.................................. 630
Dies, it is said, of slow poison, administered by a Jewess to test his divine character............................8 June, 632
Mahometans are divided into sects, the 2 chief being the *Sonnites*, or orthodox (who recognize as caliph Abubeker, father-in-law of Mahomet, in preference to Omar and Ali), and the *Shiites* (Sectaries), or *Fatimites*, the followers of Ali, who married Fatima, the prophet's daughter.
The former (also called Sunnites) recognize the "Sunna" (traditions) sayings of Mahomet (supplementary to the Koran), which the Shiites reject. Husan and other sons of Ali were murdered 680 A.D., and a miracle-play and a festival in their honor are still observed.
Ottoman empire is the chief seat of the Sonnites, the sultan being considered to represent the caliphs; Persia has been for centuries the stronghold of the Shiites.
Mahometans conquered Arabia, north Africa, and part of Asia, in the 7th century; in the 8th they invaded Europe, conquering Spain, where they founded the caliphate of Cordova, which lasted from 756 to 1031, when it was broken up into smaller governments, the last of which, the kingdom of Granada, endured till subjugated by Ferdinand in 1492; Mahometans finally expelled from Spain...................... 1609
Their progress in France was stopped by their defeat at Tours by Charles Martel (BATTLES).................................. 732
After a long contest the Turks under Mahomet II. took Constantinople; he made it his capital and the chief seat of his religion.. 1453
Though declining, Mahometanism is supposed to have 100,000,000 votaries.
Coomroodeen Tyabjee, a Mahometan, admitted as an attorney in England, taking the oaths upon the Koran..........Nov. 1858
Budroodeen Tyabjee, a Mahometan, admitted to practice law, 30 Apr. 1867

Mahrat'tas, a people of Hindostan, who originally dwelt northwest of the Deccan, which they overran about 1676. They endeavored to overcome the Mogul, but were restrained by the Afghans. They entered into alliance with the East India company in 1767, made war against it in 1774, again made peace in 1782, and were finally subdued in 1818. Their prince, Sindiah, is now a pensioner of the British government.

maid. HOLY MAID (Elizabeth Barton); JOAN OF ARC (Maid of Orleans).

maids of honor. Anne, daughter of Francis II., duke of Brittany, and queen successively of Charles VIII. and Louis XII. of France (1483-98), had young and beautiful ladies about her person, called maids of honor. The queen of Edward I. of England (1272-1307) is said to have had 4 maids of honor; queen Victoria has 8.

mail-coaches. STAGE-COACHES.

Main plot, a name given to a conspiracy to make Arabella Stuart sovereign of England in place of James I. in 1603. Lord Cobham, sir Walter Raleigh, and lord Gray were condemned to death for implication in it, but reprieved; others were executed. Raleigh was executed 29 Oct. 1618.

Maine, a province of N.W. France, seized by William I. of England in 1069. It acknowledged prince Arthur, 1199; was taken from John of England by Philip of France, 1204; was recovered by Edward III. in 1357; but given up, 1360. After various changes it was finally united to France by Louis XI. in 1481.

Maine. The extreme eastern point of the United States is West Quoddy Head, which is also the eastern extremity of the state of Maine. Maine is the largest of the eastern states, and, including islands, it has a south shore line of 2400 miles on the Atlantic. It is limited in latitude by 43° 4′ and 47° 31′ N., and in longitude by 66° and 71° W. Its extreme breadth is 210 miles, narrowing in the north to about half that distance. New Brunswick and the St. Croix river form the eastern and northern boundary; Quebec lies to the northwest, and New Hampshire to the west below lat. 45° 20′. Area, 33,040 sq. miles, in 16 counties. Pop. 1890, 661,086; 1900, 694,466. Capital, Augusta.

First Englishman known to have conducted an expedition to the shores of Maine, then "Norumbega," was John Walker, in the service of Sir Humphrey Gilbert, who reached the Penobscot river.. 1580
["Narrative and Critical History of America."]
Speedwell and *Discoverer*, from Bristol, Engl., commanded by Martin Pring, enter Penobscot bay and the mouth of a river, probably the Saco..................................7 June, 1603
Henry IV. of France grants to Pierre de Gast Sieur de Monts all the territory between 40° and 46° N. lat., and appoints him governor of the country, which is called Acadia, 8 Nov. "
De Monts, accompanied by M. de Poutrincourt, and Samuel Champlain, visits his patent, and discovers Passamaquoddy bay and the Schoodic or St. Croix river.................May, 1604
Later in the season De Monts erects a fort on St. Croix island and spends the winter there.................................. "
De Monts enters Penobscot bay, erects a cross at Kennebec, and takes possession in the name of the king. He also visits Casco bay, Saco river, and cape Cod................May, 1605
George Weymouth, sent out by the earl of Southampton, anchors at Monhegan island, 17 May, 1605; St. George's island, 19 May, and Penobscot bay, 12 June. After pleasant intercourse with natives, he seizes and carries away 5 of them... "
Colonies of Virginia and Plymouth incorporated with a grant of land between 34° and 45°, including all islands within 100 miles of the coast, and permission given the Plymouth colony to begin a plantation anywhere above lat. 38°...10 Apr. 1606
Lord John Popham, chief-justice of England, and sir Ferdinando Gorges, fit out 2 ships and 100 emigrants, under George Popham and Raleigh Gilbert, which land at Stage island, 11 Aug. 1607
Finding Stage island too small, they establish a colony and "Popham's fort" on the west bank of the Sagadahoc river. "
Discouraged by the death of George Popham, and the burning of their storehouse, they return to England in the spring of 1608
Two French Jesuits, Biard and Massé, with several families, settle on Mount Desert island.................................. 1609
Twenty-five French colonists land on Mount Desert island and found a settlement called St. Saviour..................Mch. 1613
[They were soon expelled by the English from Virginia under capt. Argal as trespassers on English territory.]
Capt. John Smith arrives at Monhegan from England. Building 7 boats, he explores the coast from Penobscot to cape Cod, and makes a map of it, to which prince Charles assigned the name of New England..............................Apr. 1614

MAI

War, famine, and pestilence depopulate the Indian territories in Maine during the years...1615–18

Plymouth company receives a new patent to lands between 40° and 48°, and in length "by the same breadth throughout the mainland from sea to sea"..................3 Nov. 1620

Gorges and capt. John Mason procure of the Plymouth council a patent of all the country between the Merrimac and Sagadahoc, from the Atlantic to the rivers Canada and Iroquois, which they called "The Province of Laconia"......10 Aug. 1622

Permanent settlement made at Monhegan.................. "

Permanent settlement at Saco............................... 1623

Gorges procures a patent from Plymouth council to 24,000 acres on each side of the Agamenticus (York) river, and plants a colony.. 1624

New Plymouth colony erects a trading-house at Penobscot; the first English establishment of the kind in these waters.. 1626

Abraham Shurte commissioned by Giles Elbridge and Robert Aldsworth to purchase Monhegan island; buys it for 50*l.* It is added to the Pemaquid plantation, over which Shurte acted as agent and chief magistrate for 30 years............ "

Eight patents granted by Plymouth council, covering the seaboard from the Piscataqua to the Penobscot, except the "territory of Sagadahoc" below the Damariscotta. Among these were the "Kennebec," "Lygonia" or Plough patent, with settlement on Casco bay, the "Waldo patent," and "Pemaquid," 1630–31

A French vessel visits the New Plymouth trading-house at Penobscot, and carries off booty valued at 500*l.*, and within 3 years the English abandon it to the French..........June, 1632

Crew of 16 Indian traders, under Dixy Bull, turn pirates, attack the fort at Pemaquid, and menace the coast until the next summer, when they are beaten off........................ "

Trading-house established by the English at Machias, which next year was seized by Claude de la Tour, the French commander at Port Royal.. 1633

Plymouth council surrender their charter, and sir Ferdinando Gorges appointed governor-general over the whole of New England..25 Apr. 1635

M. d'Aulney de Charnisy, from the Acadian country, takes possession of the trading-house at Biguyduce (Penobscot) for France, "

Gorges, empowered by the Plymouth council, 22 Apr. 1635, sends over his son William as governor of the territory between Piscataqua and Sagadahoc, called New Somersetshire, who organizes the first government and opens the first court within the present state of Maine...........................28 Mch. 1636

Gorges obtains from Charles I. a provincial charter to land between Piscataqua and Sagadahoc and Kennebec rivers, extending 120 miles north and south, which was incorporated and named "The Province and County of Maine"...3 Apr. 1639

Thomas Purchase, first settler at Pejepscot, on the Androscoggin, assigns to gov. Winthrop of Massachusetts "all the tract at Pejepscot, on both sides of the river, 4 miles square towards the sea"......................................22 Aug. "

Thomas Gorges appointed deputy-governor of the province of Maine...10 Mch. 1640

First general court under the charter opened at Saco.25 June, "

Gorges founds in Agamenticus a city of 21 square miles, which he calls Gorgeana....................................1 Mch. 1642

Alexander Rigby purchases the abandoned "Plough patent or Lygonia," and commissions George Cleaves deputy president, who opens a court at Saco styled "The General Assembly of the Province of Lygonia," which extended from cape Porpoise to Casco..Apr. 1643

Richard Vines elected deputy-governor of the province of Maine.. 1644

Commissioners appointed for the purpose decide that the province of Lygonia does not belong to the province of Maine, as the latter contended, and the Kennebec river is assigned as the boundary between the 2 provinces.....Mch. 1646

Court of province of Maine convenes at Wells, at mouth of the Kennebunk river, and Edward Godfrey elected governor of the province.. "

Massachusetts, in 1651, laying claim by her charter to all lands south of a line drawn eastward from a point 3 miles north of the source of the river Merrimac, found this point by survey to lie in lat. 43° 43′ 12″, with its eastern point on Upper Clapboard island, in Casco bay, and confirms it by assumption of jurisdiction...23 Oct. 1652

Isle of Shoals, and all territory north of Piscataqua belonging to Massachusetts, erected into county of Yorkshire............ "

Kittery, incorporated in 1647, and Agamenticus made into the town of York.. "

General Court of Elections at Boston admits for the first time 2 representatives from Maine: John Wincoln of Kittery and Edward Rishworth of York..........................May, 1653

Wells, Saco, and Cape Porpoise declared towns.............. "

English under major Sedgwick subdue Penobscot and Port Royal, 1654, and the whole Acadian province is confirmed to the English, who hold it for 13 years........................ 1655

Towns of Scarborough and Falmouth erected (see 1786)....... 1658

Quakers hold their first meeting in Maine, at Newichawannock or Piscataqua..Dec. 1662

Ferdinando Gorges, grandson of the original proprietor, obtains from the king an order to the governor and council of Massachusetts to restore his province in Maine..........11 Jan. 1664

A part of the grant of the king of England to the duke of York includes the territory between the St. Croix and Pemaquid and northward, variously called the "Sagadahoc Territory," "New Castle," and the "County of Cornwall"......12 Mch. "

King's commissioners establish a form of provisional government in the province of Maine.....................23 June, 1665

By the treaty of Breda the English surrender Nova Scotia to France, which also claims the province east of the Penobscot...31 July, 1667

Four commissioners from Massachusetts hold a convention in York, commanding the people of the province of Maine in his majesty's name to yield again all obedience to the colony, doing this at the request of prominent citizens in the province...July, 1668

New survey of the Massachusetts boundary to the north having been made by George Mountjoy, and the line fixed at lat. 43° 49′ 12″, its eastern terminus on White Head island in Penobscot bay, Massachusetts appoints 4 commissioners, who open a court at Pemaquid and proceed to organize the additional territory..May, 1674

Duke of York takes a new patent from the king, and commissions sir Edmund Andros governor of both New York and Sagadahoc...22 June, "

Indian depredations and massacres in KING PHILIP'S WAR begin, 12 Sept.; attack Saco, 18 Sept., and burn Scarborough, 20 Sept. 1675

King by council confirms the decision of a commission which had been appointed and reported that "the right of soil in New Hampshire and Maine probably belonged not to Massachusetts colony, but to the terre-tenants"................. 1676

For the second time (the first in 1674) the Dutch capture the French fortification at Penobscot, but are soon driven out by the English... "

Indians attack Casco, burn Arrowsick and Pemaquid, and attack Jewel's island...............................Aug.-Sept. "

Indians destroy the settlement at cape Neddock; 40 persons slain or captured...................................25 Sept. "

One hundred and twenty Indians capture the fort and part of its garrison, at Black Point........................14 Aug. "

Massachusetts employs John Usher, a Boston trader then in England, to negotiate the purchase of the province of Maine, who concluded a bargain, took an assignment, and gave Gorges 1250*l.*; original indenture bears date..........6 May, "

Indian hostilities continue throughout 1677; affair at Mare Point, 18 Feb.; Pemaquid, 26 Feb. Indians attack Wells several times; again attack Black Point, 16–18 May, and ambush a party of 90 men near that point, killing 60........29 June, 1677

Sir Edmund Andros, fearing French aggression in the duke's Sagadahoc province, sends a force from New York to Pemaquid to establish a fort and custom-house.............June, "

Peace made with the Indians upon the Androscoggin and Kennebec, at Casco, by a commission from the government of Massachusetts...12 Apr. 1678

Thomas Danforth chosen president of Maine by the governor and board of colony assistants of Massachusetts.............. 1680

Baptists make their first appearance in Maine in 1681; William Screven, their leader, organizes a church, but the members are obliged to remove to South Carolina to avoid persecution.. 1683

Charter of Massachusetts colony adjudged forfeited, and liberties of the colonies seized by the crown; col. Kirke appointed governor of Massachusetts, Plymouth, New Hampshire, and Maine; Charles II. dying before Kirke could embark, James II. did not reappoint him.........................18 June, 1684

Charter being vacated, various purchases were made from the Indians; the most important, known as the "Pejepscot Purchase," was made by Richard Wharton, and covered lands "lying between cape Small-point and Maquoit, thence northward on the west side of the Androscoggin, 4 miles in width to the 'Upper falls,' and 5 miles on the other side of the river down to Merry-meeting bay"..............7 July, "

Treaty made by Maine and New Hampshire with 4 tribes of Indians...8 Sept. 1685

Joseph Dudley, a native of Massachusetts, graduate of Harvard in 1665, made by James II. president of Maine........May, 1686

Sir Edmund Andros arrives at Boston to supersede Dudley as president of the colonies..........................20 Dec. "

Andros commissioned captain-general and vice-admiral over the whole of New England, New York, and the Jerseys..Mch. 1688

Andros seizes upon Penobscot, and sacks house and fort of baron de St. Castin, aiding to precipitate an Indian war, Apr. "

First outbreak of King William's war at the new settlement of North Yarmouth on Royals river. Indians surprise and break up the settlement, 13 Aug. They attack and burn New Dartmouth (Newcastle), and destroy the fort and break up the settlement on the Sheepscot river ....5–6 Sept. "

Gov. Andros using unwise measures in opposing Indians, arouses the people, who restore Danforth to the office of provincial president, appoint a council for the safety of the people, and resume the government according to charter rights..18 Apr. 1689

Garrison at Pemaquid attacked by Indians and forced to surrender..2 Aug. "

Maj. Benjamin Church, with 600 men raised by Massachusetts, proceeds to the Kennebec, and ranging along the coast, intimidates the Indians; leaving 60 soldiers at fort Loyal, he returns with the rest to Massachusetts.................... "

Newichawannock (now Salmon Falls), attacked by French and Indians under sieur Artel, and 54 settlers captured and the settlement burned..................................18 Mch. 1690

Five hundred French and Indians under Castin attack fort Loyal at Falmouth; the people abandon the village and retire to the garrison, 16 May, which capitulates on the 20th, when the French, after burning the town, retire to Quebec with 100 prisoners.......................................May, "

Sir William Phipps leaves Boston with 5 vessels for Nova Scotia. He captures Port Royal, and takes possession of the whole country and coast to Penobscot..........................May, "

Three hundred men under maj. Church are again sent from

MAI

Massachusetts 2 Sept., to reduce Indians in the province he attacks them at Pejepscot fort on the Androscoggin, freeing some English captives has an engagement with them at Purpooduck 21 Sept., and returns home leaving 100 men as garrison at Wells Sept 1690

Five months' truce signed at Sagadahoc by commissioners from Massachusetts and the Indians, who agree to surrender all prisoners and to make a lasting peace at Wells the following May 29 Nov "

Indians failing to meet pres Danforth as agreed at Wells on 1 May he returns to York and sends a reinforcement to Wells Shortly after their arrival they are attacked by 200 Indians whom they repulse 9 June 1691

Charter of William and Mary or the Provincial charter, passes the seals and receives royal sanction and the province of Maine is united with the royal province of Massachusetts bay 7 Oct. "

Two hundred Indians led by Canadian French assault York on the Agamenticus river The inhabitants find shelter in the garrisoned houses and repulse the enemy, who retire after burning the town and killing or capturing about half of the people 5 Feb 1692

Eight representatives from Maine appear in the Massachusetts House of Representatives at its first session 8 June, "

[For the governors of Maine up to its separation from Massachusetts in 1820 see the latter state.]

Five hundred French and Indians under Burneff attack Wells, defended by a small garrison and 2 sloops which had just arrived in the harbor bringing supplies and ammunition, repulsed after a siege of 48 hours 10 June "

Fort built at Pemaquid Aug "

Indians negotiate a treaty of peace with the English 11 Aug 1693

French and Indians under Iberville Villebon, and Castin capture the fort at Pemaquid 15 July 1696

Eastern Sagadahoc claimed by the French as part of Nova Scotia under the treaty of Ryswick 11 Sept 1697

Treaty of 11 Aug 1693 signed and ratified with additional articles at Mare Point (now in Brunswick) between the whites and Indians 7 Jan 1699

Indians under French leaders attack Wells Cape Porpoise, Saco, Scarborough, Casco, Spurwink and Purpooduck, the last 2 entirely destroyed Thus opened the 3d Indian war, known as Queen Anne's war 10 Aug 1703

Enemy destroy Black Point, attack York and Berwick, legislatures of Massachusetts and New Hampshire offer 20*l* for every Indian prisoner under 10 years of age, and 40*l* for every one older or for his scalp Sept-Oct "

Col Church leads an expedition against the enemy in the east, visits Penobscot bay, and proceeds as far as the bay of Fundy He returns having destroyed all the settlements in the vicinity of Port Royal and taken 106 prisoners and a large amount of plunder with the loss of only 6 men 1704

Francis Nicholson late lieut gov of Virginia, arrives at Boston 15 July, with his fleet He sails 18 Sept, reaches Port Royal 24 Sept., lands his forces, and opens 3 batteries 1 Oct., and Subercase the governor capitulates the next day, and Nicholson names the place Annapolis Royal 2 Oct 1710

By treaty of Utrecht all Nova Scotia Annapolis Royal, and all other things in these parts "belonging to France are ceded to Great Britain 30 Mch 1713

Berwick incorporated out of the northern settlements of Kittery 9 June, "

Fort George erected on the west side of the Androscoggin, opposite the lower falls 1715

Parker's island and Arrowsick made a town or municipal corporation by the name of Georgetown 13 June, 1716

Name of Saco changed to Biddeford 18 Nov 1718

First violence of the "Three Years' or Lovewell's war " the 4th Indian war was the taking of 9 families on Merry-meeting bay by 60 Indians in canoes 13 June, they attack the fort at St. George's river and burn Brunswick June, July, 1722

One thousand men raised by the General court to carry on the Indian war 8 Aug "

Capt Josiah Winslow and 16 men in 2 boats on the St George's river, ambushed and surrounded by about 100 Indians in 30 canoes, and all killed. 1 May, 1724

Father Sebastian Rasle, a Jesuit long located at the Indian village of Norridgewock on the Kennebec is suspected by the English settlers of instigating the Indians against them, a party under col Westbrook, sent to seize him in 1721, is unsuccessful, but a second party under capts. Moulton and Harmon, with 100 men each, succeed in putting him and about 30 Indian converts to death 12 Aug "

Capt John Lovewell with 34 men is surprised by Indians at Pegwacket, a desperate battle ensues, the Indians are repulsed, but with a loss to the English of 10 killed, including capt. Lovewell 14 wounded, and 1 missing 8 May, 1725

Treaty known as "Drummer's Treaty," signed by 4 Indian delegates at Boston 15 Dec "

David Dunbar, an Irishman, obtains royal sanction to settle and govern the province of Sagadahoc 1729

Owing to the arbitrary acts of Dunbar he is removed from his office, 4 Apr 1733, by royal instruction, and Massachusetts resumes jurisdiction of Sagadahoc territory 25 Aug. 1733

Brunswick incorporated 24 June, 1737

King in council fixes the line between Maine and New Hampshire to "pass through the entrance of Piscataqua harbor and the middle of the river to the farthermost head of Salmon Falls river, thence north 2°, west, true course, 120 miles," 5 Mch 1739

Rev George Whitefield visits Maine and preaches at York Wells, and Biddeford. 1741

First attack of Indians (the 5th Indian war) upon St George and Damariscotta (Newcastle) 19 July the provincial government declares war against all the eastern tribes and offers bounties for Indian captives or scalps 23 Aug 1745

Indian skirmishes and depredations throughout the Sagadahoc territory during 1746

By 1 May 1747, the whole frontier from Wells to Topsham is infested with Indians, who make an attack on Pemaquid 22 May, and unsuccessful attacks on forts Frederick and St George Sept 1747

Indian hostilities in Maine brought to an end by the treaty of Aix la Chapelle, signed 7 Oct. 1748

A treaty based on Drummer treaty of 1725 made with Indians at Falmouth by commission from Massachusetts 16 Oct 1749

Indians attack fort Richmond, on the Kennebec but hearing that the garrison had been reinforced they retire but attack Dresden Swan island, Wiscasset Sheepscot, and Georgetown and withdraw with 20 or 30 captives 11-25 Sept 1750

Commissioners meet the Indians at St George's fort 3 Aug., and proclaim a cessation of hostilities 3 Sept 1751

Newcastle incorporated the first of the towns in the territory of Sagadahoc 19 June, 1753

Fort Halifax, on the Kennebec river below the Ticonnet falls, fort Western at Augusta and fort Shirley or Frankfort in Dresden all built during the year 1754

In consequence of French and Indian depredations war is declared on all the Indian tribes east of Piscataqua and bounties offered for prisoners and scalps 11 June, 1755

Acadians or French Neutrals dwelling principally about Annapolis Grand Pré and vicinity are forcibly removed by order of lieut gov Lawrence and the provincial council and dispersed among the American colonies from Maine to Georgia (Acadia) Sept

Skirmishes with the Indians at Brunswick, New Gloucester, Windham where the Indian chief Poland is killed and at Georgetown and fort Halifax 1756

Possession is taken of the Penobscot country, and fort Pownal built and garrisoned with 100 men under Jedediah Preble 28 July 1759

Nauseag a precinct of Georgetown the birthplace of sir William Phipps first royal governor of the Massachusetts provinces, erected into a town by the name of Woolwich. 20 Oct "

Pownalborough embracing the present towns of Dresden Wiscasset Alna and Swan island is incorporated 13 Feb 1760

Peace made with the remnant of the Indian tribes in the vicinity of fort Pownal 29 Apr "

General court establishes the counties of Cumberland (that part of Maine between the Saco and Androscoggin) and Lincoln (that part east of the Androscoggin) 19 June, "

Mount Desert island granted to gov Barnard 1762

Town of Bristol, embracing the ancient Pemaquid, incorporated 18 June, 1765

Town of Hallowell embracing Cushnoc (Augusta), and Winslow, including Waterville incorporated 26 Apr 1771

Pepperellborough, afterwards Saco incorporated 9 June, 1772

Belfast incorporated, first town on the Penobscot 22 June, 1773

New Gloucester incorporated 8 Mch 1774

County convention 33 delegates from 9 towns in Cumberland county, held at Falmouth at which meeting sheriff William Tyng declared his avowal to obey the province law and not that of parliament and which advises "a firm and persevering opposition to every design, dark or open framed to abridge our English liberties" 21 Sept "

Capt Mowatt and 2 companions of the British sloop of war *Canseau* are made prisoners by 50 or 60 volunteers under lieut col Samuel Thompson while ashore at Falmouth The sailing master of the *Canseau* excites the people by threatening to burn the town if Mowatt is not restored, being released on parole, Mowatt weighs anchor, sails for Portsmouth 9 May, 1775

An English schooner, the *Margranetto* loading at Machias is seized by a party of volunteers under Benjamin Foster and Jeremiah O'Brien, after capturing this prize O'Brien sails into the bay of Fundy, and on his return captures a schooner and tender which were in search of the *Margranetto* June "

Col Benedict Arnold, with a force of about 1100 men passes up the Kennebec to attack Quebec Sept "

Capt. Mowatt arrives in Falmouth (now Portland) with 4 armed vessels 17 Oct., with orders from adm Graves to destroy the town, which he burns 18 Oct "

Warren incorporated, first town on St. George river 7 Nov 1776

Fryeburg, scene of Lovewell's fight in 1725 incorporated, 11 Jan 1777

Counties of York, Cumberland, and Lincoln, by vote of Congress erected into the "District of Maine" 1778

British general McLane and 900 troops take possession of the peninsula of Major Biguydure (now Castine), begin a fort, and station 3 sloops of war under capt. Mowatt 12 Jan 1779

Pittston, the fortieth and last town established by the general court under the royal charter incorporated 4 Feb "

Expedition of 19 armed vessels and 24 transports, under Gurdon Saltonstall, a Connecticut sea-captain, and 1500 men from Massachusetts under gen Lovell arrive at Penobscot 25 July, for the purpose of dislodging the British, they remain inactive, however, until the arrival of 5 British ships from New York, which force the Americans to burn their vessels and disperse 13 Aug "

Six hundred troops raised to protect the Eastern department, between Piscataqua and St Croix, and command given to gen. Peleg Wadsworth, with headquarters at Thomaston 1780

Bath incorporated, the first town established by the new government 17 Feb 1781

Gen Wadsworth captured at Thomaston and imprisoned at Castine, 18 Feb, escapes 18 June, "

Land office is opened at the seat of government, and state lands in the district of Maine are sold to soldiers and emigrants at $1 per acre on the navigable waters, elsewhere given, provided settlers clear 16 acres in 4 years 1784

First issue of the *Falmouth Gazette and Weekly Advertiser*, the earliest newspaper established in Maine 1 Jan 1785

Mount Desert, confiscated from gov Bernard is reconfirmed in part to his son John and to French claimants "

Convention to consider the separation of the district from Massachusetts meets at Falmouth 5 Oct. "

Convention appointed at the Oct meeting assembles at Falmouth and draws up a statement of particulars. 4 Jan 1786

Massachusetts lands, 1 107,396 acres between Penobscot and St Croix rivers disposed of by lottery, a large portion purchased by William Bingham of Philadelphia Mch "

Falmouth divided and the peninsula with several opposite islands incorporated and named Portland 4 July, "

Convention of 31 delegates meets at Portland and petitions the general court that the counties of York, Cumberland, and Lincoln be erected into a separate state, and suggests that the towns vote on the subject 6 Sept. "

[Convention reassembling 3 Jan 1787, finds votes cast on separation 994 618 being yeas, motion to present the petition to the legislature lost, but was presented the year following.]

General court sets off from Lincoln county the new counties of Hancock, from Penobscot bay to the head of Gouldsborough river, and Washington east of Hancock. 25 June, 1789

Bangor incorporated 25 Feb 1791

Last meeting of the Salem presbytery, marking the decline of the Presbyterian church founded at Londonderry, N H, in 1719, is held at Gray 14 Sept "

Charter granted by the general court for Bowdoin college in Brunswick 24 June, 1794

Augusta (the ancient Cushnoc) incorporated under the name of Harrington 20 Feb 1796, changed to Augusta 9 June, 1796

Seven families from Ireland associate at Newcastle to form a Catholic church 1798

At Providence, the commission appointed to determine and settle according to the Jay treaty, what river was the St. Croix made a report that the mouth of the river is in Passamaquoddy bay, in lat 45° 5′ 5″ N, and lon 67° 12′ 30″ W of London and 3° 54′ 15″ E of Harvard college, and that the boundary of Maine was up this river and the Cheputnatecook to a marked stake called "the Monument" 25 Oct. "

Kennebec county erected from north part of Lincoln 20 Feb 1799

Northern parts of York and Cumberland counties erected into the county of Oxford 4 Mch 1805

Henry Wadsworth Longfellow b in Portland 27 Feb 1807

County of Somerset established from the northerly part of Kennebec 1 Mch 1809

Three commissioners appointed by governor and council to act on land titles in Lincoln county 27 Feb 1811

Boxer, a British brig of 18 guns and 104 men, capt Blythe engages the American brig *Enterprise*, 16 guns and 102 men, capt Burrows off Portland. In 35 minutes the *Boxer* surrenders and is taken to Portland by her captor (both commanders killed) 5 Sept. 1813

"I remember the sea fight far away,
How it thundered o'er the tide!
And the dead captains, as they lay
In their graves, o'erlooking the tranquil bay
Where they in battle died "—*Longfellow*

Extent of "Pejepscot purchase" is declared according to the resolve of the general court, 8 Mch 1787, that "Twenty mile falls," 20 miles above Brunswick, are the "uppermost Great falls" in the Androscoggin river referred to in the deed to Wharton dated 7 July, 1684, matter settled 1814

Fort Sullivan in Eastport, under command of maj Perley Putnam, surrenders to a British force from Halifax 11 July, "

Fort at Castine destroyed by its garrison on the approach of a British fleet from Halifax 1 Sept "

[Part of the British fleet proceed up the Penobscot At Hampden lay the U S corvette *Adams* Her commander, capt Charles Morris, endeavors to defend the vessel, but, forsaken by the militia, burns the ship and retreats to Bangor, leaving Hampden to be pillaged by the British The British capture Bangor, and burn 14 vessels at anchor, return to Hampden, and from there proceed to Frankfort.]

Frankfort delaying surrender, the British denounce vengeance against the place and sail for Castine 1-7 Sept. "

British force under Sherwood and Griffiths land at Buck's harbor, about 3 miles below Machias, and march against the fort which the garrison desert and blow up 12 Sept "

British maj gen Gerard Gosselin appointed to govern the province between Brunswick and Penobscot "

British sloop from Halifax, with a cargo invoiced at $40 000, on her passage to Castine is captured and carried into Camden, Nov "

General court appoints a day of thanksgiving on news of peace and of the treaty of Ghent 24 Dec. 1814 22 Feb 1815

British troops evacuate Castine 25 Apr "

Between 10,000 and 15,000 inhabitants emigrate to Ohio 1815–16

County of Penobscot incorporated (the ninth and last prior to the separation) 15 Sept. 1815

Meetings held in all towns and plantations of the district of Maine and a vote taken on the question of separation from Massachusetts results in 10,393 yeas and 6501 nays 20 May, 1816

First separation law takes effect, directing voters to meet in their towns on the first Monday of Sept to vote on the question, and send delegates to Brunswick the last Monday of Sept who, if a majority of at least 5 to 4 favor separation, should form a constitution 20 June, 1816

Convention of 185 delegates convenes at Brunswick, vote shows 11,961 yeas to 10,347 nays, the attempt to seek admission as a state failing the convention was dissolved, Sept "

First meeting at St Andrews of joint commission, Thomas Barclay for Great Britain, Cornelius Van Ness for the U S, to determine the northeastern and northern boundary of Maine, no result 23 Sept. "

President Monroe visits Maine on his tour of inspection of fortifications, etc 1817

U S war ship *Alabama* 84 guns, 2633 tons commenced and left on the stocks at Kittery unfinished 1818

Agricultural Society of District of Maine incorporated 16 Feb "

Law of the U S making every state a district in which vessels must enter and clear, proving a stumbling block in the matter of the separation of Maine, is changed, and the eastern coast divided into 2 great districts. 2 Mch 1819

About 70 towns petition the legislature for separation, and bill passed granting it 19 June, "

Under separation act, after an election in July and the proclamation of the governor 24 Aug, a convention of 269 delegates at Portland, elects William King president, and appoints a committee of 33 to report a constitution 11 Oct "

Congress admits Maine into the Union, capital Portland, 3 Mch 1820

William King elected governor without opposition Apr "

Within 17 months gov King commissioner under the Spanish treaty, resigns his office to Mr Williamson, president of the Senate, who 6 months after, being elected to Congress, surrenders it to Mr Ames, speaker of the House The president of the next Senate was Mr Rose, who acted as governor one day, until gov Parris was inducted 1820–21

Waterville college (afterwards Colby university) established at Waterville 1820

Maine Historical Society incorporated 5 Feb 1822

Last meeting of commissioners to determine the northern and northeastern boundary of Maine held at New York (They disagree, and subsequently the matter is referred to William, king of the Netherlands) 13 Apr "

Building of the state prison at Thomaston begun 1823

Wild lands in Maine surveyed and divided between Maine and Massachusetts 1826

Boundary north and east of Maine referred to William, king of the Netherlands, for settlement. 12 Jan 1829

Corner stone of the state capitol at Augusta laid July, "

Cumberland and Oxford canal, from Portland to Sebago pond, completed "

Gov Lincoln dying, Nathan Cutler, president of the senate, succeeds him 8 Oct. "

Jonathan G Hunton inaugurated governor 1830

William king of the Netherlands recommends as the boundary of Maine, a line due north from the source of the St Croix to the river St. John, thence in the middle of that river through the St Francis to its source, and thence along the highlands southwesterly to "mile tree" and head of the Connecticut river 10 Jan 1831

Capital removed from Portland to Augusta, legislature meets, 4 Jan 1832

Bangor and Orono railroad, 10 miles in length, completed 1836

Rufus McIntire, land agent for Maine, and 2 others, sent to drive trespassers from timber on disputed territory in north of the state, are taken by an armed force as prisoners to Fredericton, but soon released by the governor of New Brunswick 11 Feb 1839

Lieutenant governor of New Brunswick issues a proclamation regarding as an invasion of her majesty's territory, the attempt of a force of 200 armed men from Maine to drive off persons cutting timber on disputed territory 13 Feb. "

Agreement made between the British government and the U S, to prevent immediate hostilities between the troops of Maine and New Brunswick, that armed men should be withdrawn from the territory, and the trespassers be kept off by the combined efforts of both governments 27 Feb. "

Act of Congress passed authorizing the president to resist any attempt of Great Britain to enforce exclusive jurisdiction over the disputed territory in the north of Maine 3 Mch "

Gen Winfield Scott, sent to command on the Maine frontier, arranges a truce and joint occupancy of the disputed territory by both governments (AROOSTOOK DISTURBANCE), 21 Mch "

State asylum for lunatics at Augusta completed 1840

Treaty concluded at Washington between Lord Ashburton for Great Britain, and Daniel Webster, secretary of state, for the U S, fixing the boundary of Maine on the north, freeing navigation of the St John's river, confirming land in disputed territory to those in possession, and allowing Maine and Massachusetts compensation for territory given up, to be paid by the U S 9 Aug 1842

Edward Kavanagh acting governor in the place of gov Fairfield, elected U S senator . . 3 Mch 1843

Act restricting sale of liquors Aug 1846

Law enacted establishing a state Board of Education "

Nathan Clifford appointed attorney general 23 Dec. "

Death at Hallowell of Nathan Read, inventor, the first man to apply for a patent before the patent law was enacted In 1798 he invented and patented a machine for cutting and heading nails and later invented a tubular boiler, d, 20 Jan 1849

State insane hospital at Augusta burned. 27 inmates and 1 assistant perish in the flames . , 4 Dec. 1850

"Maine Law," an act "to prohibit drinking-houses and tippling-shops," passed in May, approved by the governor 2 June, and enforced first at Bangor....................4 July, 1851
Act abolishing the state Board of Education, the governor to appoint a school commissioner for each county............. 1852
"Search and Seizure act" for the confiscation of liquors, passed.. 1853
James G. Blaine moves from Philadelphia to Augusta, and becomes editor of the *Kennebec Journal*.................... "
Maine purchases for $362,500 the share of Massachusetts in wild lands in the state.................................. "
Reform school for boys erected at Cape Elizabeth, and first inmate received..................................14 Nov. "
Act passed by legislature appointing a superintendent of common schools.................................17 Apr. 1854
Anson P. Morrill, Republican, inaugurated governor.......... 1855
Atlantic and St. Lawrence railroad leased to the Grand Trunk railway for 999 years.................................. "
Samuel Wells, candidate of the Whigs and Democrats, inaugurated governor.. 1856
Whole system of legislation on liquor repealed, and license law drafted by Phineas Barnes of Portland enacted......... "
Hannibal Hamlin, Republican, inaugurated governor......Jan. 1857
Joseph H. Williams, governor, to succeed Hannibal Hamlin, who was elected U. S. senator......................26 Feb. "
Nathan Clifford, justice of the Supreme court.........28 Jan. 1858
Maine liquor law in all its parts re-enacted................. "
Bill passed granting the proceeds of 1,000,000 acres of land and the claims of Maine on the government of the U. S., for the completion of the railroad from Portland to Halifax........ 1861
Hannibal Hamlin inaugurated vice-president U. S......4 Mch. "
Extra 3 days' session of the legislature, and provision made for 10 regiments of volunteers for the Federal army, and a coast-guard if necessary............................22 Apr. "
Office of the *Democrat*, a secession newspaper published in Bangor, entirely destroyed by a mob...............12 Aug. "
U. S. secretary of state Seward permits passage of British troops across the state from Portland to Canada........... 1862
Officers and crew of the Confederate privateer *Archer* enter the harbor of Portland, capture the revenue cutter *Caleb Cushing*, and put to sea; being pursued, they take to their boats and blow up their prize, and are themselves captured, 29 June, 1863
Bates college, located at Lewiston, founded; noted for having an endowed scholarship for a lady student................. "
Foreign Emigrant association of Maine incorporated, to which the state agrees to give $25 for every able-bodied foreign emigrant introduced into Maine by them................. 1864
William Pitt Fessenden, secretary of the treasury......1 July, "
A small party of Confederate raiders from St. John's, N. B., led by one Collins of Mississippi, attempt the robbery of a bank in Calais; but, the authorities being forewarned by the American consul at St. John's, the attempt fails..........18 July, "
Great fire in Portland, burning over an area 1½ miles long by ¼ of a mile wide; 1500 buildings burned; loss between $10,000,000 and $15,000,000.........................4 July, 1866
[The most destructive fire in the U. S. up to that time since the great fire in New York, 1835.]
National Home for Disabled Volunteers located at Togus springs, near Augusta, receives its first instalment of soldiers, 10 Nov. "
Legislature passes a stringent prohibitory liquor law, and appoints a state constable to enforce its provisions.......... 1867
State agricultural college established at Orono 1868
Constabulary law of 1867 repealed............................ "
James G. Blaine, speaker House of Representatives.......... 1869
State temperance convention assembles at Portland and nominates hon. N. C. Hitchborn for governor...........29 June, "
Gov. Chamberlain re-elected, the vote standing, Chamberlain, Republican, 51,439; Smith, Democrat, 39,033; and Hitchborn, 4783..13 Sept. "
A bill to increase the stringency of the prohibitory liquor laws passes both houses without opposition.................. 1870
Swedish colony founded in Aroostook county by 51 immigrants brought from Gothenburg by the board of commissioners of immigration, which arrive at "New Sweden"......23 July, "
Liquor law amended so as to bring cider and wine made from fruits grown in the state within the prohibition............ 1872
State convention for the formation of a woman's suffrage association assembles at Augusta..........................Feb. 1873
Act passed providing for a state board of immigration, consisting of the governor, secretary of state, and land agent...... "
Woman's suffrage convention at Augusta resolves: "That we pledge ourselves never to cease the agitation we have begun until all unjust discriminations against women are swept away"...28 Jan. 1874
Industrial school for girls opened at Hallowell............Jan. 1875
Compulsory Education act passed by the legislature.......... "
Death penalty in Maine abolished by law (see 1883–87)........ 1876
Senator Lot M. Morrill, secretary U. S. treasury.........June, "
At state election, Almon Gage, nominated for governor of the state by the "Greenback party," receives 520 votes. Gov. Connor is re-elected....................................Sept. "
Fifty-two Swedes in "New Sweden" are naturalized.......... "
Act passed relating to "tramps"............................ 1878
Marble statue of gen. William King, first governor of Maine, presented to the U. S. government and placed in Statuary hall, Washington...Jan. "
State Greenback convention held at Lewiston, 782 delegates; Joseph W. Smith nominated for governor...........5 June, "
September election: Selden Connor, Republican, 56,544; Joseph L. Smith, Greenback, 41,371; Alonzo Garcelon, Democrat, 28,218; no choice by people.....................9 Sept. 1878
Garcelon chosen governor by legislature................3 Jan. 1879
A convention of the surviving members of the Senate and House of 1851, who voted for the original Maine liquor law, meets at Augusta....................................2 June, "
Vote for governor: Daniel F. Davis, Republican, 68,766; Garcelon, Democrat, 21,688; Smith, National or Greenback, 47,590, 8 Sept. "
Republican press claims the Senate by 7 majority, the House by 28. In November great excitement is produced by the rumor that the governor and council would endeavor to count out the Republican majority and count in a Fusion (Democrat and National) majority. The sub-committee of the council make their report.......................26 Dec. "
Legislature convenes, and 78 Fusion members and 2 Republicans qualify. The Senate elects James D. Lamson (Fusion) president...7 Jan. 1880
Commanders of all military organizations in the state are required to report to maj.-gen. Chamberlain..........12 Jan. "
Republicans organize a legislature.................. " "
Gov. Garcelon's office being vacant after 7 Jan., president of Senate, Lamson, asks if maj.-gen. Chamberlain will recognize him as governor. Chamberlain refers the question to the Supreme court.................................12 Jan. "
Supreme court recognizes the Republican legislature. The Fusionists become demoralized, and Daniel Davis assumes the office of governor.............................16 Jan. "
Gen. Harris M. Plaisted, Greenback, elected governor..13 Sept. "
Act passed making women eligible to the office of supervisor of schools and superintending school committees........... 1881
U. S. senator James G. Blaine appointed secretary of state.... "
Meeting of the lawyers of Maine held at Augusta, and a state bar association formed..............................25 Apr. "
Act passed, restoring the death penalty for murder........... 1883
Vote on amending the constitution forever prohibiting the sale of intoxicating liquors, 70,783 for, 23,811 against......Sept. 1884
Convention of the "People's" party, held at Portland, nominate presidential electors favoring Benjamin F. Butler..Oct. "
Act establishing a state Board of Health..................... 1885
Acts abolishing capital punishment, and establishing "Arbor day".. 1887
First observance of Labor day in the state............5 Sept. "
Sebastian S. Marble, president of the Senate, succeeds gov. Bodwell, who d. ....15 Dec. "
Acts passed forbidding manufacturing "Trusts" and heating railroad cars by common stoves.......................... 1889
State convention of Union Labor party meets at Waterville, and nominates Isaac R. Clark of Bangor for governor, 20 May, 1890
Gov. Burleigh re-elected; Clark, candidate of the Union Labor party, receives 1296 votes...........................Sept. "
Legislature enacts an Australian ballot law...........24 Mch. 1891
First Monday in September (Labor day) made a legal holiday by legislature at session ending......................3 Apr. "
Ex-vice-pres. Hannibal Hamlin, b. 1809, d. at Bangor....4 July, "
James G. Blaine, secretary of state, resigned (UNITED STATES), 4 June, 1892
James G. Blaine d. at Washington, D. C., aged 63 years, 27 Jan. 1893

GOVERNORS.

(Prior to 1820 Maine was a part of Massachusetts.)

Name.	Term.	Remarks.
William King..........	1820 to 1821	Resigns.
William D. Williamson...	1821	Acting.
Albion K. Parris........	1822 to 1826	
Enoch Lincoln.........	1827 " 1829	Died in office, 1829.
Nathan Cutler..........	1829	Acting.
Jonathan G. Hutton......	1830 to 1831	
Samuel Emerson Smith..	1831 " 1833	
Robert P. Dunlap.......	1834 " 1837	
Edward Kent...........	1838 " 1839	
John Fairfield..........	1839 " 1840	
Edward Kent...........	1840 " 1841	
John Fairfield..........	1841 " 1843	Elected to the U. S. Senate
Edward Kavanagh......	1843 " 1844	Acting.
Hugh J. Anderson.......	1844 " 1847	
John W. Dana..........	1847 " 1850	
John Hubbard..........	1850 " 1853	
William G. Crosby......	1853 " 1855	
Anson P. Morrill........	1855 " 1856	Republican, the 1st.
Samuel Wells..........	1856 " 1857	
Hannibal Hamlin.......	1857	Elected U. S. senator.
Joseph H. Williams.....	1857 to 1858	Acting.
Lot M. Morrill..........	1858 " 1861	
Israel Washburn, jr.....	1861 " 1862	
Abner Coburn..........	1862 " 1864	
Samuel Corey..........	1864 " 1867	
Joshua L. Chamberlain..	1867 " 1870	
Sidney Perham.........	1871 " 1873	
Nelson Dingley, jr......	1874 " 1875	
Selden Connor.........	1876 " 1879	
Alonzo Garcelon........	1879 " 1880	
Daniel F. Davis........	1880 " 1881	
Harris M. Plaisted......	1881 " 1882	
Frederick Robie........	1883 " 1887	
Joseph R. Bodwell......	1887	Died in office, 1887
Sebastian S. Marble.....	1887 to 1888	
Edwin C. Burleigh......	1889 " 1892	
Henry B. Cleaves.......	1893 " 1895	Re-elected Sept. 1894

UNITED STATES SENATORS FROM THE STATE OF MAINE.

Name.	No. of Congress.	Date.	Remarks.
John Chandler	16th to 20th	1820 to 1829	Seated 13 Nov.
John Holmes	16th " 19th	1820 " 1827	" "
Albion K. Parris	20th	1828	Resigned.
John Holmes	20th to 22d	1829 to 1833	Elected in place of Parris.
Peleg Sprague	21st " 23d	1830 " 1835	Resigned.
John Ruggles	23d " 26th	1835 " 1841	Elected in place of Sprague.
Ether Shepley	23d " 24th	1835 " 1836	Resigned.
Judah Dana	24th	1836 " 1837	Appointed in place of Shepley.
Reuel Williams	25th to 28th	1837 " 1843	Elected in place of Shepley. Resigned 1843.
George Evans	27th " 29th	1841 " 1847	
John Fairfield	28th " 30th	1843 " 1847	Elected in place of Williams. Died 1847.
Wyman B. S. Moor	30th	1848	Appointed in place of Fairfield.
Hannibal Hamlin	30th	1848 to 1857	Elected in place of Fairfield. Resigned 1857. Elected governor.
James W. Bradbury	30th to 33d	1847 " 1853	
William Pitt Fessenden	33d " 41st	1854 " 1869	Died 1869.
Amos Nourse	34th	1857	Appointed in place of Hamlin.
Hannibal Hamlin	35th to 36th	1857 to 1861	Resigned. Elected vice-president of the U. S.
Lot M. Morrill	36th " 44th	1861 " 1876	Elected in place of Hamlin. Resigned 1876. Sec. of treasury.
Hannibal Hamlin	41st " 46th	1869 " 1881	
James G. Blaine	44th " 47th	1876 " 1881	Elected in place of Morrill. Resigned 1881. U. S. sec. of state.
William P. Frye	47th " ——	1881 " ——	Elected in place of Blaine. Term expires 1901.
Eugene Hale	47th " ——	1881 " ——	Term expires 1897.

Maine liquor law. MAINE, 1846, '51, '58, '72, '79, 1884.

maize or **Indian corn** (*Zea mays*). It is unknown in the wild state, but is probably indigenous to tropical America, although there is authority for saying that it had been cultivated in Asiatic islands under the equator, and had found its way into China before the discovery of America. Humboldt refers its origin to America, where the earliest colonists found it cultivated by the Indians all along the Atlantic coast. As food it has become one of the most important grains. AGRICULTURE.

majesty. The emperor and imperial family of Rome were thus addressed, also the popes and the emperors of Germany. The style was given to Louis XI. of France in 1461. —*Voltaire.* When Charles V. was chosen emperor of Germany in 1519, the kings of Spain took the style. Francis I. of France, at the interview with Henry VIII. of England, on the Field of the Cloth of Gold, addressed the latter as your majesty, 1520. James I. used the style "sacred," and "most excellent majesty."

majol'ica ware. POTTERY.

Major'ca. BALEARIC ISLANDS, MINORCA. Majorca opposed Philip V. of Spain in 1714; but submitted, 14 July, 1715. Its first railway, from Palma, capital of the Balearic isles, to Inca, 18 miles, opened 24 Feb. 1875.

Malabar', a district on the west coast of Hindostan. The Portuguese established factories here 1505, the English 1601.

Malac'ca, a district on the Malay peninsula, India, was made a Portuguese settlement in 1511. The Dutch factories were established in 1640. The Dutch government exchanged it for Bencoolen in Sumatra in 1824, when it was placed under the Bengal presidency. It is now part of the STRAIT SETTLEMENTS.

Mal'aga, S. Spain, a Phœnician town, taken by the Arabs, 714; retaken by the Spaniards, after a long siege, 1487. NAVAL BATTLES, 1704. An insurrection against the provisional government was put down with much slaughter, 31 Dec. 1868.

Malakhoff, a hill near Sebástopol, with an old tower, strongly fortified by the Russians during the Crimean war. The allied French and English attacked it on 17, 18 June, 1855, and, after a conflict of 48 hours, were repulsed; the English losing 175 killed and 1126 wounded; the French 3338 killed and wounded. On 8 Sept. the French again attacked the Malakhoff; at 8 o'clock the first mine was sprung, and at noon the French flag floated over the redoubt. SEBASTOPOL. In the Malakhoff and Redan were found 3000 pieces of cannon of every calibre, and 120,000 lbs. of gunpowder.

Malay archipelago. MOLUCCAS, PHILIPPINES, STRAITS.

Malden, now **Amherstburg,** a port of entry on the Canada shore of the Detroit river, 18 miles below Detroit, was a place of importance during the war of 1812–15. Most of the expeditions made by the British and Indians into Michigan and Ohio were from this point. Here the British fleet, defeated by Perry 10 Sept. 1813, was built.

Maldon, a borough of Essex county, Engl., built 28 B.C., is supposed to have been the first Roman colony in Britain. It was burned by queen Boädicéa, and rebuilt by the Romans; burned by the Danes, 991 A.D., and rebuilt by the Saxons. Maldon was incorporated by Philip and Mary. The custom of Borough-English prevails here, the youngest son, and not the eldest, succeeding to the burgage tenure on his father's death.

Ma'lo, St., N.W. France. This port, as a resort of privateers, sustained a tremendous bombardment by the English under adm. Benbow in 1693, and under lord Berkeley in July, 1695. In June, 1758, the British landed in considerable force in Cancalle bay, and went up to the harbor, where they burned upwards of a hundred ships, and did great damage to the town, making a number of prisoners. It is now defended by a strong castle, and the harbor is difficult of access.

Malplaquet (*mal-pla-kā'*), a village of N. France. Here the allies under the duke of Marlborough and prince Eugene defeated the French, commanded by marshal Villars, 11 Sept. 1709. Each army consisted of nearly 120,000 choice soldiers. There was great slaughter on both sides, the allies losing 18,000 men, a loss but ill repaid by the capture of Mons.

Malta, formerly **Mel'ita,** an island in the Mediterranean, held successively by Phœnicians, Carthaginians, and Romans, which last conquered it, 259 B.C. The apostle Paul was wrecked here, 62 A.D. (Acts xxvii., xxviii.). Malta was taken by the Vandals, 534; by the Arabs, 870; and by the Normans from Sicily, 1090. With Sicily it fell successively to the houses of Hohenstaufen, of Anjou (1266), and of Aragon (1260). In 1530 Charles V. gave it to the Knights Hospitallers, who defended it courageously and successfully, in 1551 and 1565, against the Turks, who were obliged to abandon the enterprise after the loss of 30,000 men. The island was taken by Bonaparte in the outset of his expedition to Egypt, 12 June, 1798. He found in it 1200 pieces of cannon, 200,000 lbs. of powder, 2 ships of the line, a frigate, 4 galleys, and 40,000 muskets, besides an immense treasure collected by superstition; and 4500 Turkish prisoners, whom he set at liberty. Malta surrendered to the British under Pigot, 5 Sept. 1800. At the peace of Amiens it was stipulated that it should be restored to the knights. The British, however, retained possession, and war recommenced; but, by the treaty of Paris, in 1814, the island was guaranteed to Great Britain. La Valetta, the capital, was founded in 1557 by the grandmaster La Valetta, and completed and occupied by the knights, 18 Aug. 1571. The Protestant college was founded in 1846. A grand new naval dry-dock was opened May, 1871. Area, 95 sq. miles, and with Gozo, 115 sq. miles. Pop. 1890, 165,662.

Malta, Knights of. A military religious order, called also Hospitallers of St. John of Jerusalem, Knights of St. John, and Knights of Rhodes. Some merchants of Malfi, trading to the Levant, obtained leave of the caliph of Egypt to build a house for pilgrims to Jerusalem, whom they received with zeal and charity, 1048. They afterwards founded a hospital for pilgrims, whence they were called Hospitallers (Lat. *hospes*, a guest). The military order was founded about

1099, confirmed by the pope, 1113 In 1119 the knights defeated the Turks at Antioch After the Christians had lost their interest in the East and Jerusalem was taken, the knights retired to Acre, which they defended valiantly in 1290 John, king of Cyprus gave them Limisso, where they stayed till 1310, when they took Rhodes under their grandmaster De Villaret, and the next year defended it under the duke of Savoy against Saracens The story that his successors have used F E R T (*Fortitudo ejus Rhodum tenuit*, or "His valor kept Rhodes") for their device is much doubted From this they were also called Knights of Rhodes, but Rhodes being taken by Solyman in 1522, they retired into Candia, thence into Sicily Pope Adrian VI granted them the city of Viterbo for their retreat, and in 1530 the emperor Charles V gave them the isle of Malta The order was suppressed in England in 1540, restored in 1557, and again suppressed in 1559 St John's Gate, Clerkenwell, preserves its name The emperor Paul of Russia declared himself grandmaster of the order in June 1799 After the death of the grandmaster, Tommasi di Contara, in 1805, the order was governed by a lieutenant and a college at Rome, till pope Leo XIII made count Ceschi a Santa Cisce (lieutenant since 14 Feb 1871) grandmaster, 28 Mch 1879 The knights sent a hospital establishment into Bohemia during the war in 1866, which afforded great relief to the wounded and sick

Mal'vern hill, Va A strong position selected by gen McClellan on the James river, about 20 miles south of Richmond for the concentration and final stand of the army of the Potomac at the close of the Peninsular campaign This position the confederates attempted to carry 1 July, 1862, but were repulsed with severe loss PENINSULAR CAMPAIGN

Mam'elon, a hill, one of the defences of Sebastopol, was captured by the French, 7 June, 1855

Mam'elukes, originally Turkish and Circassian slaves, established by the sultan of Egypt as a body-guard about 1240 They placed one of their own corps on the throne, May, 1250, and held it until Egypt became a Turkish province, in 1517, when the beys took them into pay, and filled their ranks with renegades from various countries On the conquest of Egypt by Bonaparte, in 1798, they retreated into Nubia, but, assisted by the Arnauts, reconquered Egypt from the Turks In 1804 Napoleon embodied some of them in his guard On 1 Mch 1811, they were decoyed into the power of the Turkish pacha, Mehemet Ali, and slain at Cairo

Mamerti'ni, sons of Mamers, or Mars, were Campanian soldiers of Agathocles. They seized Messina, in Sicily, in 281 B C, and when closely besieged by the Carthaginians and Hiero of Syracuse, in 264, they implored the help of the Romans, which led to the first Punic war

mammoth, an extinct species of elephant (*Elephas primigenius*) An entire mammoth, flesh and bones, was discovered in Siberia in 1799, and many tusks and bones since Remains of the animal were found at Harwich, Engl, in 1803, and since at places in Europe, Asia, and America "The mammoth belongs exclusively to the post-tertiary epoch of geologists, and it was undoubtedly contemporaneous with man in France and probably elsewhere"—*Encycl Brit* 9th ed

Mammoth cave, Edmondson county, Ky, discovered in 1809 by a Mr Hutchins while in pursuit of a bear Its extreme extent is less than 10 miles, and the combined length of all the accessible avenues is possibly 150 miles.

man, antiquity of In 1836 M. Boucher de Perthes found some rude flint implements, which he believed to be of human manufacture, mingled with bones of extinct animals, in the old alluvium near Abbeville, in Picardy, France, and also, in 1847, near Amiens Similar flints have since been found in Sicily by dr Falconer, at Brixham, Engl, by Mr Pengelly, and lately in various parts of the world Hence geologists infer that man has existed on the earth for many ages.

Some burned bricks found in the Nile are considered to be 20,000 years old, and some bones found in lacustrine deposits in Florida, 30,000 years old
"Engis skull" found by Schmerling in the valley of the Meuse about 1834
Fossil human remains found in extinct volcanoes of St Denis, near Puy en Velay 1844
Fragment of a human cranium found in auriferous gravel of Table mount, Cal, by C F Winslow, while sinking a shaft 1857
Human jaw said to have been found in the drift at Moulin Quignon, near Abbeville Mch 1863
Sir Charles Lyell's "Antiquity of Man" was pub in 1863 and sir John Lubbock's "Prehistoric Times" 1865
Skeleton of a man supposed a contemporary of the mammoth and cave bear found with polished flint implements by M Rivière in the Cavillon cavern, near Mentone, France 26 Mch 1872
[Regarded as one of the oldest human skeletons yet found —*Dana*, "Manual of Geology" p 575]
"The Ancient Stone Implements Weapons and Ornaments of Great Britain," by John Evans, F R S pub Feb "
"In our day quaternary man is a fact universally accepted but tertiary man is a problem under discussion"—*Virchow* 1877

Man, Isle of was subdued by Edwin, king of Northumberland, about 620, by Magnus of Norway, 1098, by Scots, 1266, occupied by Edward at the wish of inhabitants, 1290, recovered by Scots in 1313, but taken from them by Montacute, afterwards earl of Salisbury to whom Edward III gave the title of king of Man in 1343 It was afterwards subjected to the earl of Northumberland, on whose attainder Henry IV granted it in fee to sir John Stanley 1406 It was taken from this family by Elizabeth, but was restored in 1610 to the earl of Derby, through whom it fell by inheritance to the duke of Athol, 1735 He received 70 000*l* from Parliament for his rights in 1765, and the nation was charged with 132,944*l* more for the purchase of his remaining interest in the revenues of the island in Jan 1829 The countess of Derby held the isle against the parliamentary forces for a time in 1651 The bishopric is said to have been presided over by Amphibalus about 360 Some assert that St Patrick was the founder of the see, and that Germanus was the first bishop, about 447 It was united to Sodor in 1113 Area, 220 sq miles, being 33 miles long and 12 wide, pop 1891, 55,598 Chief town, Douglas, pop over 16 000

Manassas or **Second Bull Run,** Battle of POPE'S VIRGINIA CAMPAIGN

Manassas Junction, Va BULL RUN, Battle of

Manchester, Lancashire, Engl, in the time of the Druids, was one of their most popular stations, and had the privilege of sanctuary attached to its altar, in the British language *Meyne*, a stone It was a seat of the Brigantes who had a castle or stronghold, called *Mancenion*, or the place of tents, near the confluence of the rivers Medlock and Irwell The site of this, still called the "Castle Field," was, about 79, selected by the Romans as the station of the *Cohors Prima Frisiorum*, and called by them *Mancunium*, hence its Saxon name *Manceastre*, from which its modern appellation is derived —*Lewis* Pop 1891, 505,343, 1901, 543,968

Mancenion taken from the Britons 488
Captured by Edwin of Northumbria 620
Inhabitants become Christians about 627
Town taken by the Danes, 870, retaken 923
Charter (*Magna Charta* of Manchester) 14 May, 1301
"Manchester cottons" introduced 1352
Free grammar school founded 1516
Privilege of sanctuary moved to Chester about 1541
An aulnager (measurer) stationed here 1565
Sir Thomas Fairfax takes the town 1643
Walls and fortifications razed 1652
Prince Charles Edward the Young Pretender, makes it his quarters 28 Nov 1745
Cotton goods first exported 1760
Manchester navigation opened by Bridgewater canal 1761
Manufacture of muslin attempted here about 1780
Manchester reform meeting (called "Peterloo") of from 60,000 to 100 000 persons—men women, and children Mr Hunt, who took the chair, had spoken a few words when the meeting was suddenly assailed by cavalry, assisted by a Cheshire regiment of yeomanry, the outlets being occupied by other military detachments The unarmed multitude were driven together, many were ridden over or cut down The deaths were 11—men, women, and children—and the wounded about 600 16 Aug 1819
Manchester and Liverpool railway opened—Mr Huskisson killed (LIVERPOOL) 15 Sept 1830
Manchester made a parliamentary borough (2 members) by Reform act 7 June, 1832
Great free trade meetings here (CORN) 14 Nov 1843
Owens college opened 1851
Manchester declared a city 16 Apr 1853
Owens college made the nucleus of Victoria university July 1880

Manchester ship-canal, one of the important ship-canals of the world, from Manchester to Eastham, on the Mersey, thus connecting Manchester with the sea

First preliminary meeting held June, 1882
Manchester Ship canal act passed (with conditions). July, 1885

Company formed, proposed capital 8,000,000*l*. ....Oct. 1885
[To hold the property of the Bridgewater Navigation company, and to occupy 7500 sq. miles.]
Contract for work taken by Lucas & Aird for 5,750,000*l*. .July, 1886
First sod cut by lord Egerton (chairman of directors)..11 Nov. 1887
Work retarded by death of contractor, J. A. Walker, and by bursting of Mersey embankment at Stratham........7 Nov. 1890
Water admitted into the Eastham section.........18-19 June, 1891
Entire canal opened for ship navigation..................... 1893
[Length of canal 35½ miles from Manchester to Eastham, with 3 locks; the largest 600 ft. long, 80 ft. wide; 2d, 350 ft. long, 50 ft. wide; 3d, 150 ft. long, 30 ft. wide. Average depth of canal, 26 ft. Cost, 13,470,221*l*.]

ma'nes, the name applied by the ancients to the soul when separated from the body. The manes were reckoned among infernal deities, and were generally supposed to preside over burial-places and monuments of the dead. They were worshipped by the Romans and invoked by augurs; Virgil (22 B.C.) makes his hero sacrifice to the manes. The Romans superscribed their epitaphs with D. M., *Diis Manibus.*

manganese'. Black oxide of manganese, long used to decolorize glass, and called *Magnesia nigra*, was formerly included among ores of iron. Its distinctive character was proved by researches of Pott (1740), Kaim and Winterl (1770), and Scheele and Bergmann (1774); it was first eliminated by Gahn. Manganese combined with potassium is called mineral chameleon, from its rapid change of color under certain circumstances. Forchammer employed it as a test for the presence of organic matter in water; and dr. Angus Smith successfully applied this test to air in 1858. Manganese bronze, a new metal produced by P. M. Parsons, inventor of white brass, 1876.

Manhat'tan, island of. NEW YORK.

Maniche'ans, a sect founded by Manes, in Persia, about 261, spread into Egypt, Arabia, and Africa. A rich widow, whose servant Manes had been, leaving him much wealth, he assumed the title of apostle, or envoy of Jesus Christ, and claimed to be the paraclete, or comforter, that Christ had promised to send. He maintained 2 principles: the one, good, he called light; the other, bad, he called darkness. He rejected the Old Testament, and composed a system of doctrine from Christianity and dogmas of ancient fire-worshippers. Sapor, king of Persia, believed in him at one time, but afterwards banished him. He was burned alive by Bahram or Varanes, king of Persia, in 277. His followers dispersed, and several sects sprang from them.

Manil'la (built about 1578), capital of the Philippine isles, a great mart of Spanish commerce. Pop. 1903, 297,154. Manilla was taken by the English, 6 Oct. 1762, when the archbishop engaged to ransom it for about a million sterling; never wholly paid. Manilla has suffered greatly by earthquakes. EARTHQUAKE, 1852, '63, '80.

Manisees', Indian name for BLOCK ISLAND.

"Circled by waters that never freeze,
Beaten by billow and swept by breeze,
Lieth the island of Manisees.

. . . .

'No ghost, but solid turf and rock
Is the good island known as Block,'
The Reader said. 'For beauty and for ease
I chose its Indian name, soft-flowing Manisees.'"
—*Whittier*, "The Palatine."

Manitoba', one of the provinces of the dominion of Canada, admitted into the confederation 15 July, 1870. Area, 64,066 sq. miles; pop. 1891, 154,442. Capital, Winnipeg.

manom'eter (Gr. μανός, thin), an instrument for measuring the rarity of the atmosphere, gases, and vapors. One is said to have been made by Otto von Guericke about 1660, and the "statical barometer" of Robert Boyle was a simple manometer. Various forms were devised by Ramsden (about 1773), by Roy (1777), by Cazalet (1789), and by Bourdon and others. A manometer was constructed for investigations of the elasticity of steam conducted by Prony, Arago, Dulong, and Girard, 1830.

manors are as ancient as the Saxon times, and imply a territorial district with its jurisdiction, rights, and perquisites. They were formerly called baronies, and still are lordships. Each lord was empowered to hold a court called court-baron for redressing misdemeanors and settling disputes between tenants.—*Cabinet Lawyer.* ANTI-RENTISM.

Mansion house, London, residence of the lord-mayor.

Mansou'rah, a town of Lower Egypt. Here Louis IX. was defeated by the Saracens and taken prisoner, 5 Apr. 1250. He gave Damietta and 400,000 livres for his ransom.

Mantinea (*man-te-nee'a*), a village and ruined city of Arcadia, Greece. Here (1) Athenians and Argives were defeated by Agis II. of Sparta, 418 B.C. (2) Epaminondas and Thebans defeated the forces of Lacedæmon, Achaia, Elis, Athens, and Arcadia, 362 B.C. Epaminondas was killed, and Thebes lost its power in Greece. The emperor Adrian built a temple at Mantinea in honor of his favorite Alcinoüs. The town was also called Antigonia. Other battles were fought near it.

Man'tua, N. Italy, an Etruscan city, near which Virgil was born, 70 B.C. Mantua was ruled by the Gonzagas, lords of Mantua, from 1328 to 1708, when it was seized by the emperor Joseph I. It surrendered to the French, 2 Feb. 1797, after a siege of 8 months; retaken by the Austrians and Russians, 30 July, 1799, after a short siege. After the battle of Marengo (14 June, 1800), the French again obtained possession. It was included in the kingdom of Italy till 1814, then restored to the Austrians, who sold it to the Italians, 11 Oct. 1866, after peace.

manuscript, often written MS., in plural MSS., is derived directly from the Lat. *Codices manu scripti.* Until about 1440 every record was a written one. The first substance used to write upon was the bark or rind of the papyrus, a reed found in Egypt, which, when properly prepared, was a cheap material for writing. The PAPYRUS was prepared in long rolls, and not in the form of our books, some of these rolls being 150 feet long, with a right and wrong side for writing. The second substance for writing upon was PARCHMENT, and lastly, PAPER. The use of papyrus did not cease in Egypt until about the 10th century A.D., and the use of parchment continued until the advent of printing (about the middle of the 15th century), when it mostly ceased except for sumptuous editions and for legal and other records.

LIST OF A FEW OF THE MOST FAMOUS MSS. PRESERVED TO THE PRESENT TIME.

Kind.	Date of writing.	Remarks.
Inscription of Send	4000 B.C.	Egyptian hieroglyphics on the cornice over the door of a tomb. Supposed to have been written in the 2d dynasty of Egyptian rulers. Now in the Ashmolean museum at Oxford.
Papyrus Prisse	2500 or 3300 B.C.	18 pages in Egyptian hieratic writing—a treatise, "How to Behave Wisely." Now in the Louvre at Paris.
Papyrus	300 B.C.	Greek; the oldest (not an inscription) preserved to us. Its form a prayer. Preserved at Vienna.
Wax tablet	55 A.D.	Record of a payment made by a citizen of Pompeii, found at Pompeii, 1875. In the National museum at Naples.
Papyrus	79 A.D.	Pompeian.
The Cottonian Genesis	4th century	Text of Genesis in Greek; the oldest Septuagint MS. in existence; written in uncials, 165 quarto leaves, now mostly burned in the disastrous fire of 1731, which half destroyed the Cottonian collection.
The Codex Sinaiticus	4th century	The oldest of all existing New Testament codices (others call the Codex Vaticanus oldest). Found by Tischendorf in the convent of St. Catherine at the foot of mount Sinai, 1844-59. Now in St. Petersburg. Disputed as to authenticity. LITERATURE, FORGERIES OF.
Codex Argenteus	4th century	Gothic gospels, by Ulfilas, the apostle of the Goths, at Upsala, Sweden.

LIST OF A FEW OF THE MOST FAMOUS MSS. PRESERVED TO THE PRESENT TIME.—(*Continued.*)

Kind.	Date of writing.	Remarks.
Book of Kells	7th century	So called from the monastery of Kells, where it was written, or at least for a long time preserved. It contains the 4 gospels in Latin, ornamented with great richness, beauty, and freedom, and expressing the full maturity of the Irish style. Now in the possession of Trinity college, Dublin.
Lindisfarne Gospel	7th century	In the British museum.
Alcuin's Bible	9th century	In the British museum; bought 1836.
Caedmon (Kedmon)	7th century	Metrical paraphrase of Genesis, Exodus, and parts of Daniel; in the Bodleian library.
Beowulf	8th century	Earliest English epic; mostly destroyed in the Cottonian fire 1731. BEOWULF.
Old English Chronicles	9th and 12th centuries	There are 6 in all; a seventh was burned at the fire that destroyed part of the Cottonian library, 1731; 3 of these are in the British museum, 1 at Cambridge, 1 at the National library, and 1 at the Bodleian.
St. Margaret's Gospel Book	11th century	Belonging to queen Margaret of Scotland. In the Bodleian library.

BIBLE, BOOKS.

Ma'oris. NEW ZEALAND.

maple-tree. FLOWERS AND PLANTS.

maps. Anaximander, a pupil of Thales (about 560 B.C.), sketched the first map (γεωγραφικὸς πίναξ), in form a disk. Democritus of Abdera, about a hundred years after, with a wider range of knowledge, drew a new map, giving the world an oblong form, showing extension east and west rather than north and south. LONGITUDE. The first application of astronomy to geography was made by Phytheas of Marseilles (about 326 B.C.), he having made the first observation of latitude, and that for Marseilles. Dicæaschus of Messana, in Sicily (310 B.C.), made the first approach to a projection. Eratosthenes of Cyrene (276–196 B.C.) enlarged upon previous work by attempting a geodetic measurement of the size of the earth. Hipparchus of Nicæa (162 B.C.) first determined LATITUDE and LONGITUDE. Marinus of Tyre (about 150 B.C.) was the first to make use of Hipparchus's teachings in representing the countries of the world. Claudius Ptolemy of Pelusium, Egypt (about 162 A.D.) was in reality the first scientific map-maker; notwithstanding errors in locations and boundaries, the method was correct. The oldest MS. of Ptolemy, in the Vatopedi monastery of mount Athos, was first published in 1867. The Romans contributed nothing to map-making. No improvement was made in it from the time of Ptolemy until the 13th century, when the nautical (loxodormic or compass) map appeared in Italy, so called because constructed by the aid of the COMPASS. Gerhard Kramer, or Kauffman, usually called Mercator (1512–94), has the honorable name of reformer of cartography. There are extant his map of Palestine (1537), map of Flanders (1540), in 9 sheets, photographed 1882, a globe (1541) and the first critical map of Europe (1554), by which he laid the foundation of his fame. In 1569 appeared his famous map of the world, drawn, in the projection, with parallel meridians. It is the first map on which true rhumb lines could be drawn as straight lines. A series of important discoveries and inventions in mathematics, physics, and astronomy was followed by a like improvement in cartography. The telescope (1606); the discovery of Jupiter's moons by Galileo (1610); Cassini's calculation of their periods of rotation (1666); the first application of trigonometry to geodesy by Snellius (1615); Picard's measurement of a degree between Paris and Amiens (1669–70); the French measurement of a degree between Dunkirk and Perpignan by Cassini and Lahire (1683–1718); Hadley's mirror-sextant (1731); Mayer's improvements on the lunar tables (1753), and Harrison's chronometer (1761), with many later inventions and discoveries, have contributed to the accuracy of recent surveys and maps.

Mar'athon, a plain in Attica. Here, on 28 or 29 Sept. 490 B.C., the Greeks, only 11,000 strong, under Miltiades, Aristides, and Themistocles, defeated a Persian army of 110,000. Among the slain (about 6400) was Hippias, instigator of the war. The Persian army was forced to retreat to Asia. BATTLES, GREECE.

marble, a term applied to any limestone sufficiently close in texture to admit of polishing. Dipœnus and Scyllis, statuaries of Crete, were the first artists who sculptured marble and polished their works, all statues previously being of wood, about 568 B.C.—*Pliny.* The marble used by the Greek sculptors Phidias, Praxiteles, etc., was the famous Pentelic marble; its characteristics are seen in the Elgin marbles in the British museum. It was quarried from mount Pentelicus in Attica. Parian marble, also much used by the ancient Greek sculptors and architects, was quarried from mount Marpessa, on the isle of Paros. The Venus de Medici is a notable example of it. Carrara marble is used by the best sculptors of the present day. It is found in the Apuan Alps, and is largely worked in the vicinity of Carrara, whence its name. The finest work of Michael Angelo and Canova was executed in this marble. There are valuable deposits of marble in the eastern and middle states of the U. S., also in Tennessee and Georgia.

March, the first month of the year, until Numa added January and February, 713 B.C. Romulus, who divided the year into months, gave to this month the name of his supposed father, Mars; though Ovid observes that the people of Italy had the month of March before Romulus, but in a different place in the calendar. The year commenced 25 Mch. until 1753. YEAR.

march to the sea, Sherman's. SHERMAN'S GREAT MARCH.

marches. The old border lands between England and Wales, and England and Scotland. The lords marchers of the Welsh borders had vice-regal authority; the wardens of the Scotch marches were subordinate officers. These powers were abolished 1536 and 1689.

Marcionites (*mar'-shun-ites*), followers of Marcion, a heretic, about 150, who preceded the Manichees, and taught similar doctrines.—*Cave.*

Marcoman'ni, a people of S. Germany, expelled the Boii from Bohemia, and, united with other tribes, invaded Italy about 167, but were repelled by the emperors Antoninus and Verus. They were defeated by the legion called, from a fabled miracle, the Thundering legion, 179; and finally driven beyond the Danube by Aurelian, 271.

Mardi-Gras (*mar-de-grä'*; Fr. Fat Tuesday). Shrove Tuesday, the last day of the carnival—day before Ash-Wednesday, the first day of Lent. It is celebrated in New Orleans with revelry and elaborate display since 1827. In 1857 the "Mistick Krewe of Comus" added new life to the carnival, and in 1872 a "King of the Carnival" was appointed, whose authority is observed during the carnival.

Maren'go, a village of N. Italy. Here the French army, under Bonaparte, after crossing the Alps into Piedmont, attacked the Austrians, 14 June, 1800; the French were retreating, when the arrival of gen. Dessaix turned the fortunes of the day. By a treaty between the Austrian general Melas and Bonaparte, signed 15 June, the latter obtained 12 strong fortresses, and became master of Italy.

mareschals. MARSHALS.

Marigna'no, now **Melegnano** (*mä-len-yä'-no*), a town of N. Italy, 10 miles southeast of Milan. 3 battles have been fought near here. 1. Francis I. of France defeated the duke of Milan and the Swiss, 13, 14 Sept. 1515; above 20,000 men were slain. This conflict has been called the Battle of the Giants. 2. Near here was fought the battle of PAVIA, 24 Feb. 1525. 3. After the battle of Magenta, 4 June, 1859, the Austrians intrenched themselves at Melegnano. The emperor sent marshal Baraguay d'Hilliers with 16,000 men to dislodge them, which he did with a loss of about 850 killed and wounded, on 8 June. The Austrians are said to have lost 1400 killed and wounded, and 900 prisoners, out of 18,000 engaged.

marine turtle, a torpedo or infernal machine, invented by David Bushnell, to blow up the *Eagle*, a British

64-gun ship in New York harbor, Sept 1776 It failed, as the operator could not attach it to the bottom of the vessel, owing to the thickness of the copper An account of this machine is found in Silliman's *Journal* for 1820

mariner's compass. COMPASS, MAGNETISM

marines were first established in England as a nursery to man the fleet An order in council, dated 16 Oct 1664, authorized 1200 soldiers to be raised and formed into one regiment In 1684, the 3d regiment of the line was called the Marine regiment, but the system of having soldiers exclusively for sea service was not carried into effect until 1698, when 2 marine regiments were formed More regiments were embodied in subsequent years, and in 1741 the corps consisted of 10 regiments, each 1000 strong In 1759 they numbered 18,000 men In the latter years of the French war, ending in 1815, they amounted to 31,400, but there were frequently more than 3000 supernumeraries The *jollies*, as they are called, frequently distinguished themselves The "Royal Marine Forces" (so named 1 May, 1802) now comprise artillery and light infantry

Marines introduced into the U S army by Congress, directing 2 battalions to be organized 10 Nov 1775
Marine corps, liable to do duty either on board vessels of war or on land, organized by Congress 11 July, 1798
U S marine corps consisted of 86 officers and 1500 enlisted men 1880
Marine barracks near the navy yard Washington, D C, are the headquarters of the U S marine corps

mark, a silver coin of the northern nations, the name *mark-lubs* is still retained in Denmark In England "mark" means 13*s* 4*d*, and the name is retained in law courts. COIN AND COINAGE

Mark's, St., Venice The church was erected in 829, the piazza in 1592

Proposed restorations and changes in the façades and mosaic pavement created much excitement in England, and led to remonstrances which irritated the Italian people Nov, Dec 1879

Mar'onites, Christians in the east, followers of one Maron in the 5th century, they are said to have embraced errors of Jacobites, Nestorians, and Monothelites About 1180 they numbered 40,000, living near Mount Libanus, and were of service to the Christian kings of Jerusalem They were reconciled to the Church of Rome soon after For massacres of Maronites in 1860, DRUSES

maroons, a name given in Jamaica to runaway negroes. When the island was conquered from the Spaniards, a number of negroes fled to the hills and became very troublesome to the colonists After a war of 8 years, the maroons capitulated on being permitted to retain their free settlements, about 1730 In 1795 they again took arms, but were speedily put down and many were transported. —*Brande* Maroon, a brownish or dull red color.

mar-prelate tracts, virulently attacking episcopacy, were mostly written, it is believed, by Henry Penry, who was cruelly executed, 29 May, 1593, for seditious words against the queen (found on his person when seized) The tracts appeared about 1580 Some had very singular titles, such as "An Almand for a Parrat," "Hay any Worke for Cooper?" etc. They were collected and reprinted in 1843

marque, Letters of PRIVATEER

Marque'sas Islands, Polynesia, south Pacific ocean, 13 in number, were discovered in 1595 by Mendana, who named them after the viceroy of Peru, Marquesa de Mendoça. They were visited by Cook in 1774, and were taken possession of by the French admiral Dupetit Thouars, 1 May, 1842

marquess, a dignity, called by the Saxons markinreve, by the Germans Markgraf, takes its name from mark or march, a limit or bound (MARCHES), the office being to guard or govern the frontiers Marquess is next in honor in the British nobility to duke. The first Englishman to hold the title was the favorite of king Richard II, Robert de Vere, earl of Oxford, created marquess of Dublin, and placed in Parliament between the dukes and earls, 1385. James Stewart, second son of James III of Scotland, was made marquess of Ormond in 1476, without territories, afterwards earl of Ross

Marquette, Jacques (1637-75), Explorations of ILLINOIS, IOWA, MICHIGAN, MISSOURI, WISCONSIN, 1668-75.

marriage was instituted by God (Gen ii) and confirmed by Christ (Mark x), who performed a miracle at the celebration of one (John ii) Matrimonial ceremonies among the Greeks are ascribed to Cecrops, king of Athens, 1554 B.C AFFINITY, AGE

	B C
Law favoring marriage passed at Rome	18
	A D
Priests forbidden to marry after ordination	325
Marriage in Lent forbidden	366
Forbidden to bishops in 692, to priests in 1015, priests obliged to take the vow of celibacy	1073
Statute prohibiting marriages within prohibited degrees, 25 Hen VIII	1533-34
Marriage as a sacrament in churches ordained by pope Innocent III about 1199, affirmed by council of Trent	1547
Marriages by justices of the peace authorized by Parliament	1653
A tax laid on marriages viz marriage of a duke, 50*l*, of a common person, 2*s* 6*d*	1695
Irregular marriages prohibited (FLEET MARRIAGES)	1753
Marriages again taxed	1784
New Marriage act, 1822, partially repealed	1823
Acts prohibiting marriages by Roman Catholic priests in Scotland, or other ministers not of the church of Scotland, repealed	1834
Present Marriage act for England authorizing marriages without religious ceremony, by registrar's certificate, or in a dissenting chapel passed [Amended in 1837 and 1856]	1836
Marriage Registration act	1837
Amendment acts passed 1840 and	1856
Act to suppress irregular marriages in Scotland (GRETNA)	"
Court established for divorce and matrimonial causes, it may grant judicial separation for adultery, cruelty, or desertion without cause for 2 years and upwards (DIVORCE)	1857
Act to legitimate children of certain marriages within forbidden degrees (with deceased wife's sister), such marriages in future prohibited (Lyndhurst's act), (efforts made to legalize marriage with deceased wife's sister ever since)	1835
Civil marriages made legal in Austria (AUSTRIA)	1868
Marriage Law Reform association (to legalize marriage with a deceased wife's sister) 15 Jan 1851 Bill passed commons, 2 July, rejected by lords 23 July, 1858, again rejected, 1862, and again by the commons, 2 May, 1866, and 30 Apr 1870, rejected by lords (77-73), 19 May, 1870, passed by commons 9 Mch, rejected by lords (97-71), 27 Mch 1871, passed by commons in 1872 1873, and rejected by lords (49-74), 14 Mch 1873, rejected by commons (171-142), 17 Feb 1875, by lords (101-81, prince of Wales and duke of Edinburgh for it), 6 May, 1879, by lords (101-90) 25 June,	1880
These marriages made legal at Melbourne, Nov 1872, at Sydney, 1875, in Canada and New Zealand	"
Bill for recognition in Great Britain of such colonial marriages read a second time in the commons (192-141), 28 Feb 1877 (21 majority) 27 Feb	1878
Case of Brook *vs* Brook holds such a marriage celebrated in a foreign country not valid 17 Apr	1858
Decision confirmed on appeal to House of Lords 18 Mch	1861
Commission appointed to inquire into marriage laws of Scotland, 22 Mch 1865, reported in favor of changes to insure uniformity, simplicity, and certainty July,	1868
Consular Marriage act, enabling acting British consuls abroad to solemnize marriages, passed 16 July,	"
Married Women's Property act passed 9 Aug	1870
Marriage law of Ireland amended, 10 Aug 1870, again amended, July,	1871
MATRIMONIAL CAUSES ACT passed	1878
An act to encourage regular marriages in Scotland 8 Aug.	"

Royal Marriage act was passed in 1772, in consequence of the marriage of the duke of Gloucester, the king's brother, with the widow of the earl Waldegrave, and of the duke of Cumberland with the widow of col Horton and daughter of lord Irnham By this act, no descendant of George II, unless of foreign birth, can marry under age of 25, without consent of the king, at and after that age, consent of Parliament is necessary to render the marriage valid Marriage of duke of Sussex with the lady Augusta Murray, solemnized in 1793, was pronounced illegal, 1794, and the claims of their son, sir Augustus d'Este, declared invalid by the House of Lords, 9 July, 1844 He married lady Cecilia Underwood (afterwards duchess of Inverness), 1831

Princess Louise was married to the marquess of Lorne by queen Victoria's consent, 21 Mch 1871

Half marriage Semi matrimonium Among the Romans concubinage was a legitimate union, not merely tolerated, but authorized The concubine had the name of *semi conjux* Men might have either a wife or a concubine provided they had not both together Constantine the Great checked concubinage, but did not abolish it. This ancient custom of the Romans was preserved, not only among the Lombards, but by the French when they held dominion in that country Cujas assures us that the Gascons and other people bordering on the Pyrenean mountains had not relinquished this custom in his time, 1590. The women bore the name of "wives of the second order"—*Henault.* MORGANATIC MARRIAGES.

Double marriages There are a few instances of a husband with 2 wives in countries where polygamy was unlawful The first Lacedæmonian who had 2 wives was Anaxandrides, son of Leon, about 510 B C Dionysius of Syracuse married 2 wives, viz. Doris, daughter of Xenetus, and Aristomache, sister of Dion, 398 B C It is said that the count Gleichen, a German nobleman, was permitted, under peculiar circumstances, by Gregory IX 1237 A D, to have 2 wives MORMONS practised polygamy until Congress suppressed it

Forced marriages Stat 3 Henry VII 1487, made the principal and abettors in marriages with heiresses, etc, contrary to their will, equally guilty as felons By 39 Eliz 1596, such felons were denied benefit of clergy The offence was made punishable by transportation, 1 Geo IV 1820 Case of Miss Wharton heiress of the house of Wharton whom capt. Campbell married by force, occurred in William III's reign Sir John Johnston was hanged for seizing the young lady and the marriage was annulled by Parliament, 1690 Edward Gibbon Wakefield was tried at Lancaster and found guilty of the felonious abduction of Miss Turner, 24 Mch 1827, and his marriage with her was dissolved by act of Parliament

Marriages by sale Among the Babylonians at a certain time every year the marriageable females were assembled and disposed of to the best bidder This custom is said to have originated with Atossa daughter of Belochus, about 1433 B C

FLEET MARRIAGES

marriage in the United States Age at which minors may contract marriage lawfully varies in the different states, males from 14 to 18 years, females 12 to 16 years, and the age below which parental consent is required varies also males from 18 to 21 years, and females 15 to 21 years, mostly 18 years, but in Florida, Kentucky, Louisiana, Pennsylvania, and Rhode Island it is 21 years In all the states and territories except the Dakotas, Idaho, New Jersey, New Mexico, New York, South Carolina, and Wisconsin, a marriage license must be procured from some officer designated by law, for which fees are exacted The prohibited degrees of relationship vary also in the different states, extending in many to first cousins In many states marriages are void between white and colored persons, but not in Connecticut, Illinois, Iowa Kansas, Louisiana, Massachusetts, Michigan, Minnesota, New Jersey, New Mexico, New York, North Dakota, Ohio, Pennsylvania, Rhode Island, South Dakota, Vermont, Wisconsin, Wyoming DIVORCE, WIVES

Marrs murders. ENGLAND, 1886, RATCLIFFE HIGHWAY

Mar's insurrection. John, earl of Mar, proclaimed James III at Braemar, Aberdeenshire, 6 Sept 1715. He was defeated at Sheriffmuir, 13 Nov, and escaped from Montrose with the Pretender, 4 Feb 1716

Mars, a planet, next to the earth in order of distance from the sun, diameter, 4363 miles Its mass is about $\frac{1}{10}$ that of the earth Turns on its axis in $24\frac{1}{2}$ hours, mean distance from the sun, 139,311,000 miles. Its orbit is quite elliptical, the difference in its distance from the sun at perihelion and aphelion being 26,000,000 miles Its revolution round the sun is made in 687 of our days, its mean rate of motion being 16 miles a second The spots on its surface were first observed by Fontana, in 1636 2 satellites were discovered by prof Asaph Hall at Washington, D C, 11 Aug 1877. MYTHOLOGY.

"They have likewise discovered 2 lesser stars or satellites which revolve about Mars."—*Swift*, "Gulliver's Travels—Voyage to Laputa," about 1726

Marseillaise (*marsal-yāz'*) **hymn.** The words and music are ascribed to Rouget de Lille, or L'Isle, a French engineer officer, who, it is said, composed it by request, 1792, to cheer the conscripts at Strasburg It was named from troops of Marseilles who entered Paris in 1792 playing the tune This account is doubted (1879). The author was pensioned by Louis Philippe, 1830

Marseilles (*mar-sālz'*). The ancient Massilia, S France, a maritime city, founded by Phocæans about 600 B.C, an ally of Rome, 218 B.C Cicero styled it the Athens of Gaul, on account of its excellent schools.

	B C
Taken by Julius Cæsar after a long siege.	49
	A D
By Euric the Visigoth	470
Sacked by Saracens	839
Marseilles a republic	1214
Subjected to the counts of Provence	1251
United to crown of France	1482

marshals, or **mareschals,** of France, were originally the esquires of the king, who led the vanguard to observe the enemy and to choose places for encampment. Till the time of Francis I, in 1515, there were but 2 marshals, who had 500 livres per annum in war, but no stipend in peace. The number was afterwards increased The following were appointed by Napoleon I. during the French wars of 1804–14, all of whom were renowned for skill and courage

Arrighi (*ar ree gee*), duke of Padua, b 1778, d 21 Mch 1853
Augereau (*ōzh ro'*), duke of Castiglione, b 1757, d 12 June 1816.
Bernadotte, prince of Ponte Corvo, king of Sweden, 1818, b 1764, d 8 Mch 1844
Berthier (*bĕr te a*) prince of Neufchatel and Wagram, b 1753, killed or committed suicide at Bamberg, 1 June 1815
Bessières (*ba se ĕr*), duke of Istria, b. 1768, killed at Lützen 1 May, 1813
Brune, b 1763, murdered at Avignon 2 Aug 1815
Davoust (*da voo'*) prince of Eckmühl and duke of Auerstadt, b 1770, d 1 June 1823
Grouchy (*grou she*) b 1766, d 29 May 1847
Jourdan (*zhoor don'*), peer of France, b 1762, d 23 Nov 1833
Junot (*zon no*), duke of Abrantes, b 1771 suicide, 29 July, 1813
Kellermann duke of Valmy b 1735 d 12 Sept 1820
Lannes (*lan*), duke of Montebello, wounded at Aspern, b 1769, d. 31 May, 1809
Lefebvre (*leh faivr'*), duke of Dantzic, b 1755, d 14 Sept 1820
Macdonald, duke of Tarento, b 1765 d 24 Sept 1840
Marmont (*mar mon*) duke of Ragusa, b 1774, d 2 Mch 1852
Massena (*mas sa-nä*), prince of Essling and duke of Rivoli, b 1758, d 4 Apr 1817
Moncey (*mon sa'*), duke of Conegliano, b 1754, d 20 Apr 1842
Mortier (*mor te a*), duke of Treviso, b 1768, killed by Fieschi, 28 July, 1835
Murat (*mu ra*), king of Naples, b 1771 executed 13 Oct 1815
Ney, prince of Moskwa, b 1769, executed 7 Dec 1815
Oudinot (*oo de-no*) duke of Reggio, b 1767, d 13 Sept 1847
Perignon (*pa-ren yon'*) marquis de b 1754, d 25 Dec. 1818
Poniatowski (*po ne a tow' skee*), prince Josef Anton, b 1762, wounded at Leipsic and drowned, 19 Oct 1813
Soult (*soolt*), duke of Dalmatia, b 1769, d 26 Nov 1851
Suchet (*su-sha'*) duke of Albuera, b 1770, d 3 Jan 1826
Victor, duke of Belluno, b 1764, d 1 Mch 1841

Mar'shalsea court, a court formerly held before the steward and marshal of the king's house to administer justice between the king's domestic servants Its jurisdiction in the royal palace was very ancient, of high dignity, and coeval with the common-law. These courts were abolished by Parliament, and discontinued 31 Dec 1849 PRISONS

Mar'si, a brave people of S Italy, who, after several contests, yielded to Rome about 301 B C. During the civil wars they and their allies rebelled having demanded in vain Roman citizenship, 91 B C After many successes and reverses, they obtained peace and their rights, 87 B C The Marsi being *Socii* of the Romans, this was called the Social war.

Marston Moor, near York, Engl The Scots and parliamentary army were besieging York, when prince Rupert, joined by the marquess of Newcastle, determined to raise the siege Both sides drew up on Marston Moor on 2 July, 1644, the royalists 22 000 strong, while the parliamentary forces numbered 15 000 foot and 9000 horse, and the contest was long undecided Rupert, commanding the royalist right wing, was opposed by Cromwell, with troops disciplined by himself, "the Ironsides." Cromwell was victorious, he drove his opponents off the field, followed the vanquished, returned to a second engagement and a second victory The prince's artillery was taken, and the royalists never recovered from the blow

Martel'lo (or **Mortel'la**) **towers** were circular buildings erected in the beginning of the present century on the southern coast of England, and other parts of the empire, as defences against invasion The name was originally given to structures erected on the coast of Sicily and Sardinia for protection against pirates, in the time of Charles V of Spain they contained a bell with a hammer to give an alarm at their approach

martial law. MILITARY LAW

Martinique (*mar-te-neek'*), French West Indies, discovered in 1493 or 1502, settled by France, 1635 This and the adjacent isles of St Lucia and St Vincent, and the Grenadines, were taken by the British from the French in Feb 1762, but restored to France at the peace the next year. They were again taken, 16 Mch 1794, restored at the peace of Amiens in 1802, again captured 23 Feb 1809 A revolution in this island in favor of Napoleon was finally suppressed by the British, 1 June, 1815, and Martinique reverted to France. Severe earthquakes occurred here in 1767 and 1839. Area, 381 sq miles, pop 1888, 175,391.

Mar'tinmas, 11 Nov, the feast of St. Martin, bishop of Tours, in the 4th century, is quarter-day in parts of the north of England and in Scotland. The high-sheriffs of England and Wales are nominated on the morrow of St. Martin, 12 Nov.

martyrs. Stephen, the first Christian martyr, was stoned, 37. The festivals of the martyrs, of very ancient date, took their rise about the time of Polycarp, who suffered martyrdom about 169. St. Alban is the English protomartyr, 286. DIOCLETIAN ERA, PERSECUTIONS, PROTESTANTS. The Martyrs' Memorial, Smithfield, erected by the Protestant Alliance, was inaugurated 11 Mch. 1870. The Martyrs' Memorial church, St. John's street, Clerkenwell, Engl., was consecrated 2 June, 1871. John Foxe's "Book of Martyrs" was pub. 1563. LITERATURE.

Maryland, one of the United States, on the central Atlantic coast, lies wholly north of the Potomac river, which, forming the boundary-line that separates it from West Virginia and Virginia, gives the state a peculiar form. The state varies in width from about 5 miles near the West Virginia line to 120 along the Chesapeake bay, which cuts the state into 2 parts. On the east it is bounded by Delaware and the Atlantic ocean. It is limited in latitude by 37° 53′ to 39° 42′ N., the northern limit being the famous Mason and Dixon's line, marking its division from Pennsylvania. In longitude it is limited by 75° 2′ to 79° 30′ W. Area, 12,210 sq. miles. Pop. 1890, 1,042,390; 1900, 1,188,044. Capital, Annapolis.

Maryland is included in the grant of king James of England to the South Virginia colony........................10 Apr. 1606

Capt. John Smith leaves Jamestown to explore the Chesapeake bay, and discovers the mouths of the Susquehanna, North-east, Elk, and Sassafras rivers at its head.........July–Aug. 1608

Maryland included in the second charter to Virginia, which covered land from Point Comfort along the coast north for 200 miles, and south the same distance, and "from sea to sea" (Atlantic to the Pacific)......................23 May, 1609

Royal license given to William Clayborne, one of the council and secretary of state of the colony in Virginia, by king Charles to trade in all seas and lands in those parts of the English possessions in America for which there is not already a patent granted, and giving Clayborne power "to direct and govern" such of the king's subjects "as shall be under his command in his voyages and discoveries," 16 May, 1631

Sir George Calvert, lord Baltimore, obtains from king Charles the promise of a grant of land now Maryland, but dies before charter is executed...............................15 Apr. 1632

Cecilius Calvert, baron of Baltimore in the kingdom of Ireland, son of lord Baltimore, receives from king Charles a grant covering territory hitherto unsettled, having for its southern boundary the Potomac from its source to its mouth, the ocean on the east, and Delaware bay as far north as the 40th parallel, following that parallel to the meridian of the fountain of the Potomac.........20 June, "

Virginians objecting to the grant to lord Baltimore, the king refers their petition to the privy council, who decide "That the lord Baltimore should be left to his patent, and the other parties to the course of law"......................3 July, 1633

Colony sent out from Cowes in the isle of Wight by lord Baltimore, under his brother Leonard Calvert, to settle in Maryland, arrives off Point Comfort, Va.................24 Feb. 1634

At Point Comfort gov. Calvert has an interview with Clayborne, in which he intimates that certain settlements of the latter on the isle of Kent, in Chesapeake bay, would be considered as a part of the Maryland plantation. After the governor had explored the Potomac as far as Piscataway creek he returns to St. George's river, and sailing up about 12 miles to the Indian town of Yoamaco, makes a treaty with the tribe, and sends for the colonists, who arrive, take peaceable possession, and name the place St. Mary's, 27 Mch. "

Colony export a cargo of Indian corn to England............ 1635

First legislative assembly at St. Mary's...............26 Feb. "

Clayborne, having threatened the colony at St. Mary's, grants a warrant to Ratcliffe Warren to "seize and capture any vessel belonging to the colony." Warren fits out a pinnace, with which he attacks 2 armed pinnaces fitted out at St. Mary's and under the command of Thomas Cornwallis, and engages in a battle in the Pocomoke or Wighcomoc rivers, which results in the death of Warren and victory for the colony....................................Apr. or May, "

Lord Baltimore commissions gov. Calvert to call an assembly to signify to the colony his dissent to laws made by the assembly in 1635, and propounding others for their assent, 15 Apr. 1637

Governor commissions George Evelyn as commander of the isle of Kent now subjected to Maryland................30 Dec. 1637

Assembly, including representatives from the isle of Kent, considers laws offered by the lord proprietor. They reject them and frame others, which when sent to England lord Baltimore rejects. Assembly meets................25 Jan. 1638

By reference from the king and proclamation in Virginia, the claim of Clayborne to the isle of Kent and Palmer's island is rejected in favor of lord Baltimore...................4 Apr. "

Lord Baltimore finally gives assent to the right of the assembly to originate laws................................Aug. "

Assembly meets at St. Mary's and enacts laws for the government of the province..............................19 Mch. 1639

Order executed by the governor and council to equip an expedition against the Indians of the eastern shore and the Susquehannocks.......................................28 May, "

Nicholas Hervey commissioned to invade the territory of the Maquantequat Indians............................3 Jan. 1640

Petition of Clayborne to the governor and council to restore his property in the isle of Kent denied............21 Aug. "

Act regulating measures, and adopting the Winchester bushel as the standard.. 1641

Gov. Calvert, returning to England, appoints Giles Brent lieutenant-general, admiral, chief magistrate, and commander of Maryland in his absence..........................11 Apr. 1643

Gov. Brent issues a proclamation for arresting the person and seizing the ship of Richard Ingle, to answer the charge of treason in instigating a rebellion against the government in Maryland. Ingle arrested, but makes his escape...Jan. 1644

So-called "Ingle's and Clayborne's rebellion" occurs in Maryland. Of this rebellion little is known, except the destruction of the great seal of the province at St. Mary's in Feb. 1645, and the appointment of Edward Hill as governor in the absence of gov. Calvert, who fled from the parliamentary party, probably to Virginia. At the restoration of the authority of lord Baltimore, 1646, the insurrectionists carried away or destroyed most of the records and public papers of the province...1644–46

Gov. Calvert organizes a military force in Virginia and proceeds to St. Mary's, and regains that part of his province... 1646

First mention made in the legislative journal of the upper and lower houses of assembly................................ 1647

Recovering the isle of Kent, gov. Calvert pardons all the inhabitants, and appoints Robert Vaughan chief captain and commander of the militia and civil governor........18 Apr. "

Gov. Calvert nominates Thomas Greene as his successor, 9 June, "

Miss Margaret Brent, administratrix of gov. Calvert, asks from the assembly a vote in the House for herself, and another as attorney for lord Baltimore; refused...............Jan. 1648

New "great seal" for the province of Maryland sent over by lord Baltimore.................................12 Aug. "

Gov. Greene removed by lord Baltimore, and William Stone of Virginia, "a zealous Protestant, and generally knowne to have beene always zealously affected to the Parliament," appointed.. "

Tolerance act, the first securing religious liberty ever passed by an established legislature, provides that "no person professing to believe in Jesus Christ shall from henceforth be any waies troubled, molested, or discountenanced for, or in respect of, his or her religion, nor in the free exercise thereof within this province . . . nor any way compelled to the beleefe or exercise of any other religion against his or her consent"..Apr. 1649

Assembly grants lord Baltimore power to seize and dispose of any lands purchased of any Indian, unless the purchaser could show a lawful title thereto from his lordship under the great seal.. "

Mr. Durand, elder of a Puritan or Independent church founded in Virginia in 1642 (from Massachusetts), and which was broken up and driven out by that government, obtains permission of the lord proprietary's government to settle with his people at Providence or Anne Arundel, now Annapolis.. "

Commission granted by lord Baltimore to Robert Brooke, as commander of a county (Charles) "around about and next adjoining to the place which he should settle," on the south side of the Patuxent, with a colony he was transporting to Maryland..20 Sept. "

During the temporary absence of gov. Stone, Thomas Greene, the deputy governor, proclaims Charles II. king, and grants a general pardon....................................15 Nov. "

Settlement at Providence organized into a county called Anne Arundel...30 July, 1650

Act passed by the assembly punishing by death and confiscation of property any compliance with Clayborne in opposition to lord Baltimore's dominion over the province.. "

A rumor of the dissolution or resignation in England of lord Baltimore's patent leads the Puritans of Anne Arundel to refuse to send any burgesses or delegates to the general assembly at St. Mary's when summoned.................... 1651

Council of state in England appoints 3 officers of the navy, together with Richard Bennett and William Clayborne of Virginia, a commission to "use their best endeavors to reduce all the plantations upon the bay of Chesapeake to their due obedience to the Parliament and Commonwealth of England," 20 Sept. "

Numerous hostilities in the past having greatly reduced the

Indian tribes in Maryland, lord Baltimore grants a tract of land at the head of Wicomoco river, containing 8000 or 10 000 acres, to be known as Calverton manor, to be reserved for the Indians 1651

Commissioners proceed to Maryland and engage gov Stone and the rest of lord Baltimore's officers to "submit themselves to the government of the Commonwealth of England," thus taking the control from lord Baltimore, Mch 1652

By proclamation of the commissioners gov Stone is reinstated as governor of Maryland which he assumes "until the pleasure of the state of England be known," 28 June, "

Treaty with the Susquehannock Indians at the river of Severn, ceding their lands from the Patuxent river to Palmer's island on the west side of the Chesapeake bay, and from Choptank river to the northeast branch, northward of Elke river, on the eastern side of the bay 5 July, "

Lord Baltimore issues instructions to gov Stone for strictly enforcing the submission of all the inhabitants of the province of Maryland to his proprietary rights 7 Feb 1654

Gov Stone, by proclamation, declares that the province of Maryland is under the government of Oliver Cromwell lord protector of the Commonwealth of England, Scotland and Ireland etc 6 May, "

Robert Brooke, commander of Charles county having been discharged by lord Baltimore, gov Stone erects the county into the county of Calvert 3 July, "

Commissioners Bennett and Clayborne, hearing of the new orders and instructions from lord Baltimore, come to Maryland and make a second reducement of the province, appointing capt William Fuller and others commissioners for governing the affairs of Maryland 22 July, "

Capt Fuller and the other commissioners call an assembly at Patuxent, it passes an "act of recognition" 26 Oct "

Acts of the assembly, one concerning religion, declaring that "none who profess the popish religion can be protected in the province by the laws of England ... nor by the government of the Commonwealth of England etc, but to be restrained from the exercise thereof" One making void the declaration of gov Stone requiring the people to acknowledge lord Baltimore as absolute lord of the province Oct. "

Gov Stone, hearing from England that lord Baltimore still retained his patent, reassumes the government and organizes a military force in county of St. Mary's under Josias Fendall who seizes the provincial records, which had been deposited in the house of Mr Richard Preston, on the Patuxent, during the revolution in July, 1654, and also arms and ammunition which had been stored in the house Jan 1655

With 200 men and 12 vessels gov Stone proceeds by land and water against the Puritans of Anne Arundel 20 Mch "

People of Providence having prepared for an invasion a battle ensues between the Puritans and the "Marylanders," of which it is said "of the whole company of the Marylanders there escaped only 4 or 5", about 50 were slain or wounded Of the Puritans, 2 were killed and 2 died of wounds 25 Mch "

A few days after the battle, 4 of gov Stone's men were executed out of 10 who were court martialled and sentenced to be shot the others, including gov Stone, escaping sentence, but held as prisoners of war Mch "

Commission received from lord Baltimore appointing Josias Fendall governor of Maryland 10 July, 1656

In the matter of the proprietary rights of lord Baltimore in Maryland, at this time under consideration in England, the commissioners for trade report to Cromwell's council of state favorably to lord Baltimore 16 Sept "

Josias Fendall, arrested and imprisoned by the Puritans, takes an oath that he will neither "directly nor indirectly be any disturber to the government till there be a full determination ended in England of all the matters relating to the government," and is released 24 Sept. "

Lord Baltimore creates his brother Philip Calvert one of the councillors to the governor of Maryland and principal secretary of his province Nov "

Luke Barber appointed deputy governor in the absence of gov Fendall, who embarks for England 18 June, 1657

Puritan assembly meets at Patuxent 24 Sept. "

Report of the commissioners for trade made 16 Sept 1656, being favorable to the rights of lord Baltimore, the Puritan agents enter into a treaty with lord Baltimore to give up their power in the province and give due obedience to his lordship's government, he agreeing especially "that he will never give his assent to the repeal of the law established in Maryland, whereby all persons professing to believe in Jesus Christ have freedom of conscience there," 30 Nov "

First Quaker missionaries appear in Maryland "

Puritan party in Maryland surrender their power to the governor 24 Mch 1658

Governor of Maryland asserts lord Baltimore's title to the Dutch settlements on Delaware bay, and demands the submission of the settlement, which is refused 1659

Baltimore county founded "

Fendall, proving inimical to lord Baltimore, is removed, and succeeded by Philip Calvert, who is sworn in at the provincial council held at Patuxent Dec. 1660

Charles Calvert, eldest son of the lord proprietary, appointed governor . . 1661-62

MAR

At the request of the assembly, lord Baltimore coins in England (1661) a large quantity of shillings, sixpences, and pennies, which were put in circulation in the province by act of assembly passed 1662

On account of excessive production an act is passed prohibiting the planting of tobacco for 1 year 1666

First Naturalization act passed, admitting certain French and Bohemians to citizenship "

Boundary line between Maryland and Virginia from Chesapeake bay to the Atlantic ocean established, and the true location of Watkins Point on the bay, marking its beginning, settled by a commission, Philip Calvert of Maryland and Edmund Scarborough of Virginia appointed 25 June, 1668

Act to encourage importation of slaves 1671

George Fox visits the Friends in Maryland 1672

A number of outrages on the people of Maryland and Virginia by the Indians. 5 chiefs of the Susquehannocks, captured in a joint expedition are put to death by major Trueman, commanding the Maryland forces although they protested their innocence and blamed the Senecas for the outrages For this act major Trueman was impeached by the House of Delegates, but escaped punishment, 25 Sept. 1675

Cecilius Calvert dies and Charles Calvert third lord Baltimore, becomes proprietary 30 Nov "

Thomas Notley appointed governor to act as deputy in the name of his infant son Cecil Calvert 1676

Government land office erected in the province by the lord proprietary 1680

Charles, lord Baltimore reassumes personal government 1681

William Penn receives his grant to territory west of the Delaware and north of Maryland "

Ordinance promulgated by the proprietary limiting suffrage to freeholders or inhabitants of property Sept. "

In the contest between William Penn and lord Baltimore Penn claims 39° as the "beginning of the parallel of 40°," and the king and council decide that the Maryland charter only included "lands uncultivated and inhabited by savages" and that therefore the territory along the Delaware was not included, that the peninsula between the 2 bays be divided equally, all east of a line drawn from the latitude of cape Henlopen to the 40th degree to belong to Penn, Nov 1685

Council of 9 deputies with William Joseph as president, appointed by lord Baltimore, govern the province during his absence in England "

Deputies failing to proclaim William and Mary rulers in the province, a convention of Protestants (termed Associators), John Coode at the head, assembles for the defence of the Protestant religion and asserting the rights of king William and queen Mary to the province of Maryland and all English dominions Apr 1689

Associators move upon St Mary's, and the council abandons the state house and provincial records to them Pres Joseph and the council retiring to a fort upon the Patuxent, Coode marches upon them with several hundred men to whom they surrender, leaving the associators masters of the situation 25 July, "

King William approves the motives of the associators in taking up arms against lord Baltimore's government, and authorizes them to continue in power 1 Feb 1690

Sir Lionel Copley appointed royal governor of Maryland 1691

Immediately after gov Copley's arrival in Maryland he summons a general assembly at St Mary's, which passes an act of recognition of William and Mary, and then overthrows equal toleration in the province and establishes the church of England as the state church of Maryland May, 1692

On the death of gov Copley, sir Edmund Andros assumes the government until the arrival of his successor, Nicholson 1693

Capital removed by law to Providence, now Annapolis 1694

Public post established from the Potomac through Annapolis to Philadelphia, route to be covered 8 times in the year, and postman to receive a salary of 50*l.* sterling 1695

Annapolis incorporated by law, the government intrusted to 8 freeholders, called "commissioners and trustees" 1696

State house destroyed by fire, and many of the records of Anne Arundel county burned 1704

Royal charter of incorporation granted Annapolis by gov Seymour 16 Aug 1708

Benedict Leonard Calvert, 4th lord Baltimore being a Protestant, the province is surrendered to him shortly before his death, which occurred 16 Apr 1715

John Hart proprietary governor, representing Charles Calvert, 5th lord Baltimore, and infant heir of Benedict Leonard Calvert "

By resolution the lower house of assembly declare that "the people of Maryland are entitled to all the rights and immunities of free Englishmen, and are of necessity inheritors of the common law of England" 1722

Act passed for "the encouragement of learning, and erecting schools in the several counties of the province," under which law a public free school was established at Battle Creek, Calvert county 1723

"A Complete Collection of the Laws of Maryland," printed at Annapolis by William Parks 1727

First newspaper printed in Maryland, the *Maryland Gazette*, published at Annapolis by William Parks "

Baltimore laid out on lands belonging to Charles Carroll, by commissioners appointed by the legislature 1730

Agreement entered into that the boundary between Maryland and Delaware should be that fixed by the decree of 1685, and that between Maryland and Pennsylvania a line drawn due west 15 miles south of Philadelphia 1732
Baltimore increased by the addition of 10 acres of land east of the falls on the lands of Edward Fell "
Charles Carroll of Carrollton born at Annapolis 20 Sept. 1737
Legislature appropriates 7562l to meet the expense of raising and equipping 500 volunteers for the great expedition against the Spanish dominions 1740
Treaty concluded with the Six Nations by gov Bladen in connection with the representatives of Virginia and Pennsylvania, at Lancaster Pa whereby in consideration of the payment of 300l the Indians agree to relinquish all claims to territory within the boundary of Maryland 1744
Town of Frederick laid out by Patrick Dulany Sept. 1745
Assembly votes 4500l to raise a body of men for an expedition against Canada 26 June and an additional appropriation of 1100l Nov 1746
Nanticoke Indians emigrate from Maryland to Wyoming carrying the bones of their dead with them May 1748
Frederick Calvert becomes 6th lord Baltimore by the death of Charles Calvert 24 Apr 1751
Lord Baltimore directs gov Sharpe to investigate as to which branch of the Potomac is the source Virginia claiming the north branch and Maryland the south 1753
Maryland frontier being subjected to incursions of the French and Indians from fort Duquesne (Pittsburg Pa.) the General Assembly convenes at Annapolis and votes 6000l. to aid Virginia in the reduction of the fort. 11 July, 1754
Command of the forces engaged against the French on the Ohio given to gov Sharpe under royal commission "
Fort is erected at Cumberland and garrisoned with 2 companies as a resting place for expeditions against fort Duquesne "
Two companies under capt. Dagworthy and lieuts Bacon and Forty march from Annapolis to the western frontier "
General Assembly passes a law for the levying of troops, and providing a pension for those maimed in service, 24 Dec. "
After Braddock's defeat 9 July, 1755 the borders of Maryland and Pennsylvania became one extended field of battles, murder desolation and panic 1755
Acadians, consigned to the province at their expulsion, arrive (ACADIA) "
Act to raise 40,000l for erecting fort Frederick and other forts and block houses on the frontier and for a joint expedition against fort Duquesne. This sum was raised by bills of credit and taxation, on the list of 22 subjects of taxation between the duties on wines and liquors and the billiard table is a tax "on all bachelors of 25 years of age and upwards with 100l and less than 300l a duty of 5s per annum, and if worth over 300l 20s per annum," 22 Mch 1756
Gov Sharpe appoints a day of thanksgiving for the capture of fort Duquesne, and the assembly grants 1500l to the Maryland troops who took part in the expedition (PENNSYLVANIA), Nov 1758
Frederick lord Baltimore, agrees to the appointment of the commission messrs. Mason and Dixon, who surveyed the line known by their name, and set up mile stones, agreement made (PENNSYLVANIA 1682) 4 July 1760
Zachariah Hood, a merchant of Annapolis is appointed stamp distributer under the stamp act, arriving with his stamps, he is obliged to land clandestinely, his effigy is whipped, hanged and burned, and he seeks refuge in New York. The assembly prorogued from 1763, meets and protests against the Stamp act, and appoints col Edward Tilghman William Murdock, and Thomas Ringgold delegates to the congress of deputies from all the colonies . 1765
Frederick county court deciding the Stamp act unconstitutional a popular demonstration takes place the "Sons of Liberty" carry through the streets a coffin inscribed "The Stamp Act, expired of a mortal stab received from the Genius of Liberty in Frederick county court 23 Nov 1765, aged 22 days" 30 Nov "
Public officers in Annapolis, urged by the people, treat the Stamp act as a nullity . 3 Apr 1766
People of Maryland enter into articles for non importation of British superfluities and for the promotion of American manufactures 20 June. 1769
British bark *Good Intent*, arriving at Annapolis, a meeting of the associators is held, and it is resolved that the cargo of English goods should not be landed 1770
Assembly attempts to diminish the amount of fees collectible by the public officials and established clergy, but is prorogued by the governor, who issues a proclamation fixing the old rates, and requiring the officers to receive the amount in money if tendered . . 26 Nov "
Frederick, lord Baltimore dying without an heir, bequeaths his proprietary to Henry Harford, his natural son 1771
People aroused by the governor's proclamation, under the leadership of Charles Carroll, elect the popular candidates messrs. Paca and Hammond to the House, and bury the obnoxious proclamation in effigy . . . . 14 May, 1773
Convention meets at Annapolis, proposes an absolute cessation of intercourse with the mother country and nominates Samuel Chase, Robert Goldsborough, William Paca, Matthew Tilghman, and Thomas Johnson delegates to the first Continental Congress at Philadelphia. . . . . 22 June, 1774

MAR

Anthony Stewart the owner of the brig *Peggy Stewart*, having paid the duty on a few packages of tea included in the cargo the people are excited by his act and under advice of Charles Carroll of Carrollton Stewart burns his vessel, 14 Oct 1774
George Washington, present in Congress as a member from Virginia is nominated by Thomas Johnson of Maryland to be commander in chief of the American forces, and unanimously chosen.—*Hildreth*, "Hist of U S," vol iii, p 80 15 June, 1775
Convention of Maryland assembles and adopts the famous "Association of the Freemen of Maryland," which becomes the written constitution of Maryland for a year, 26 July, "
"Maryland Line," under col William Smallwood, engage in the battles of Long Island Harlem Heights White Plains, the storming of fort Washington battles of Trenton and Princeton, they begin the year 1444 strong, and are reduced to a mere handful at the close 1776
Batteries erected near Baltimore and Annapolis, and public records removed to Upper Marlborough for safety in preparation for an attack by the British under lord Dunsmore "
James Wilkinson repairs to the camp before Boston as a volunteer from Maryland. ARMY (List of gen off, U S) "
Convention assembles and unanimously orders the delegates to Congress to unite in declaring the colonies free and independent reserving to the state however complete internal sovereignty, Charles Carroll of Carrollton chief advocate of this resolution was on 4 July 1776, chosen a delegate convention met 28 June, "
Declaration of Independence publicly read at Baltimore, with acclamations for the prosperity of the U S 22 July, "
Convention for framing a state constitution assembles at Annapolis 14 Aug, and completes its labors (constitution never submitted to the people) . 11 Nov "
Continental Congress meets at Baltimore 20 Dec. "
Maryland Line under brig gen Smallwood, engage in the battles of Brandywine and Germantown, and are stationed at Wilmington during the winter to protect Delaware. 1777
First legislature under the new constitution assembles 5 Feb and elects Thomas Johnson governor 13 Feb "
Count Pulaski raises a legion in Maryland consisting of 68 horse and 200 foot. 1778

[To this legion was presented a banner by the Moravian Nuns, or Sisters of Bethlehem, Pa. Longfellow has commemorated this event in his "Hymn of the Moravian Nuns."]

Maryland Line active in battle of Monmouth. 28 June, "
Legislature votes officers of the Maryland Line who serve through the war, and their widows, half pay during life, to commence after seven years' pay voted by Congress. 1779
Maryland Line, under maj gen De Kalb, engage in the battles of Camden (where De Kalb was killed) Cowpens, Guilford Court house, Hobkirk's hill, assault of Ninety six, and Eutaw springs 1780–81
Bill to confiscate British property passes both houses Oct. 1780
Maryland, to secure rights to western lands delays signing the articles of confederation until, with other states, Virginia cedes lands northwest of the Ohio to the U S. in Jan 1781, Maryland delegates, John Hanson and Daniel Carroll, sign the articles 1 Mch 1781
Washington college, Chestertown, organized 1783
Officers of Maryland Line organize state "Society of the Cincinnati" at Annapolis, maj gen Smallwood president, 21 Nov "
U S Congress meets at Annapolis. . . 26 Nov "
Washington resigns his commission as commander in chief, at the state house in Annapolis . . . 23 Dec "
St. John's college Annapolis, organized 1784
Delegates from Virginia Pennsylvania Delaware, New Jersey, and New York assemble at Annapolis to consider the condition of the nation, and request all the states to send delegates to a convention at Philadelphia the following May, Sept. 1786
James McHenry, Daniel of St. Thomas Jenifer, and Daniel Carroll delegates from Maryland to the convention at Philadelphia, sign the Constitution of the U S. .. 17 Sept. 1787
Maryland adopts the Constitution. . 28 Apr 1788
Robert H. Harrison of Maryland nominated associate justice of the Supreme court . 26 Sept. 1789
John Carroll, D D., consecrated bishop of Baltimore with jurisdiction over all the Catholics in the U S., the first bishop consecrated in the U S. (CHURCH, ROMAN CATHOLIC) 1790
The state by law, 23 Dec. 1788, cedes to the U S such district 10 miles square Congress may select for the U S. capital, the District of Columbia selected . . "
Thomas Johnson of Maryland appointed associate justice of Supreme court . . . 5 Aug 1791
Publication of the *Baltimore American and Daily Advertiser* begun by Alexander Martin 14 May, 1799
Act extending the right of suffrage and substituting the ballot for viva voce voting passed. . . . . . 28 Dec 1801
Legislature presents a sword and belt to George Washington Mann of Maryland, one of 2 soldiers who planted the American flag on the walls of Derne, Tripoli 27 Apr 1805
Medical department of the University of Maryland established at Baltimore 1807
Several associations formed in Baltimore to encourage home manufacture and sale of domestic goods during the embargo against British vessels 1808

American Law Journal and Miscellaneous Repertory, edited by John E. Hall and pub. in Baltimore 1808
Baltimore Medical and Physical Recorder, edited by dr. Tobias Watkins 1809
First number of *Niles' Register* issued in Baltimore by Hezekiah Niles 7 Sept. 1811
Gabriel Duval of Maryland appointed associate justice of the supreme court of the U. S. 18 Nov. "
Printing office of the *Federal Republican*, an anti-war paper in Baltimore, destroyed by a mob 22 June 1812. They attack the house of the editor, A. C. Hanson, which was garrisoned; break into the jail whither some of the assailed had been taken, and in the riot gen. Lingan is killed and others left for dead (UNITED STATES) 28 July 1812
British adm. Cockburn with 4 ships of the line and 6 frigates plunders and burns Frenchtown, Havre de Grace, Fredericktown, and Georgetown Mch. 1813
Battle of BLADENSBURG, and capture of Washington by the British (UNITED STATES) 24 Aug. 1814
British advancing on Baltimore under gen. Ross are repulsed at North Point; gen. Ross is killed (UNITED STATES) 12 Sept. "
British fleet bombard FORT McHENRY 13 Sept. "
Francis S. Key, of Maryland, imprisoned on one of the British vessels, composes the "STAR SPANGLED BANNER" 13 Sept. "
Lancasterian school system introduced in Baltimore 1820
Act passed abolishing the old division into hundreds as fiscal, military, and election districts, and making an election district the jurisdiction of the constable 1824
Act passed for primary schools 28 Feb. 1826
Ground broken for the Chesapeake and Ohio canal by the president of the U. S. 4 July 1828
Ground broken by Charles Carroll and corner-stone set for the Baltimore and Ohio railroad, chartered 1827 4 July, "
Phœnix company erect their shot tower 234 feet high in Baltimore. Completed without scaffolding 25 Nov. "
First public school in Baltimore under law of 1827 opened 21 Sept. 1829
Mount St. Mary's college at Emmittsburg, established in 1809, is this year incorporated as a college 1830
House of Refuge for Juvenile Delinquents incorporated, 8 Feb. 1831
On death of gov. Martin George Howard, first named of the executive council succeeds to the office 10 July "
National anti-masonic convention assembles at Baltimore and nominates William Wirt for president of the U. S. 26 Sept. "
Roger Brooke Taney of Maryland appointed attorney-general of the U. S. 27 Dec. "
Taney appointed secretary of the treasury 24 Sept. 1833
Hospital for the insane at Spring grove, Baltimore county, opened 1834
Taney appointed chief-justice supreme court of the U. S. 15 Mch. 1836
Legislature passes the famous "Internal Improvement bill," subscribing $3,000,000 in state bonds to the Chesapeake and Ohio Canal company, $3,000,000 to the Baltimore and Ohio railroad, $500,000 to the Maryland Cross-cut canal, $500,000 to the Annapolis and Potomac canal, and $1,000,000 to the Eastern Shore railroad—in all $8,000,000 3 June, "
State convention irrespective of party meets in Baltimore and adopts resolutions for revising the constitution 6 June, "
Constitution revised; governor to be elected by the people, council abolished, Senate reorganized, one third to be elected by the people every 2 years "
Constitution providing "that the relation of master and slave in this state shall not be abolished unless a bill for that purpose shall be passed by a unanimous vote of both branches of the General Assembly, to be published 3 months before a new election and be unanimously confirmed by the succeeding legislature," ratified 1837
Convention of Whig young men, 15,000 to 20,000 delegates from every state in the Union, meets at Baltimore 4 May, 1840
Democratic National convention meets at Baltimore 5 May, "
Issue of state bonds reaches $16,050,000, deficit of treasury $756,357.38 1 Dec. "
State tax levied of 20 cts. on every $100, afterwards increased to 25 cts 1 Apr. 1841
College of St. James, Washington county, organized 1842
Maryland Historical Society founded Jan. 1844
Whig National convention in Baltimore, nominates Henry Clay for president . . 1 May, "
Morse magnetic telegraph from Washington to Baltimore completed . 20 May, "
Democratic National convention at Baltimore, nominates for president James K. Polk 27-29 May, "
Act waiving the state liens in favor of $1,700,000 bonds to be issued by the Chesapeake and Ohio Canal company at par, with a guarantee that for 5 years after completion not less than 195,000 tons would be transported annually upon it, and a contract is made for the completion of the canal to Cumberland .. . 10 Mch. 1845
United States Naval Academy established at Annapolis . "
Rev. Charles Turner Torrey dies in state prison under sentence for enticing slaves from the state . 9 May, 1846
State resumes the payment of interest on her debt at the Chesapeake bank, Baltimore . . 1 Jan. 1848
Democratic National convention at Baltimore nominates gen. Lewis Cass, U. S. senator from Michigan, for president, 22 May, "
Edgar Allan Poe, b. 26 Jan. 1809, d. in Washington University hospital, Baltimore; buried in Westminster graveyard 7 Oct. 1849

Election riots between Democrats and Know-Nothings 4 Nov. 1849
Convention to frame a new constitution meets at Annapolis, 4 Nov. 1850; completes its labors 13 May, 1851; the constitution ratified by the people 4 June 1851
Democratic National convention in Baltimore nominates gen. Franklin Pierce of New Hampshire for president 9 May 1852
Whig National convention at Baltimore nominates gen. Winfield Scott for president 16 June, "
Loyola college opened at Baltimore 15 Sept. "
State Institution for the Blind organized at Baltimore 1853
House of Refuge for Juvenile Delinquents near Baltimore opened 1855
Whig National convention at Baltimore adopts the nominees of the American party, Fillmore and Donelson, for president and vice-president (UNITED STATES) 17 Sept. 1856
George Peabody gives $300,000 to found Peabody institute, 12 Feb. 1857
Strike of the conductors and train-men on the Baltimore and Ohio railroad until a called out; amicably settled 29 Apr. "
Corner-stone of the Peabody institute in Baltimore laid, 16 Apr. 1859
Constitutional Union convention at Baltimore nominates John Bell of Tennessee for president 9 May, 1860
Democratic National convention meets by adjournment (from Charleston, S. C.) in Baltimore 18 June 1860. On the 23d a large number of delegates withdraw, and the remaining delegates nominate Stephen A. Douglas for president. The seceders nominate John C. Breckinridge of Kentucky (UNITED STATES) 23 June "
Philip Francis Thomas of Maryland appointed secretary of treasury 12 Dec. "
A. H. Handy, commissioner from Mississippi, addresses a meeting in Baltimore on the subject of secession 19 Dec. "
Secession flag raised and saluted with artillery on Federal hill, Baltimore, but on the third round the cannon are seized and the flag pulled down 18 Apr. 1861
Attack on Massachusetts troops in Baltimore by a mob; several soldiers and civilians killed and wounded (BALTIMORE) 19 Apr. "
House of Delegates rejects a secession ordinance by 53 to 13, 29 Apr. "
U. S. volunteers under gen. Butler take possession of the Relay house on the Baltimore and Ohio railroad 5 May, "
Gen. Butler at the head of 900 men occupies Baltimore without opposition 13 May, "
State legislature unable to organize, many members being arrested on suspicion of treason 17 Sept. "
Augustus W. Bradford, Union, elected governor 6 Nov. "
Gov. Hicks calls an extra session of the legislature "to consider and determine the steps necessary to be taken to enable the state of Maryland to take her place with the other loyal states in defence of the Constitution and Union." The legislature meets at Frederick 3 Dec. "
Confederates invade the state and occupy Frederick 8 Sept. 1862. Gen. Lee issues a proclamation to the people of Maryland promising protection and assistance in regaining their rights. On 10 Sept. the confederates evacuate the city, and it is occupied by the army of the Potomac 12 Sept. "
Battle of South Mountain 14 Sept. and Antietam (MARYLAND CAMPAIGN) 17 Sept. "
Gen. Robert C. Schenck proclaims martial law in the west-shore counties 30 June, 1863
Gen. Schenck arrests many persons suspected of treason, and suspends the "Maryland club" and similar societies . "
Issue at the state election is emancipation, and the Union party divides on the subject into the Union and Unconditional Union parties; the latter carries the election 4 Nov. "
Every Union master allowed $300 for each of his slaves enlisting by act of Congress 24 Feb. 1864
Gen. Lee detaches a force for the invasion of Maryland, which overpowers the federals under gen. Lew Wallace in a battle on the Monocacy river 9 July, "
Convention for framing a new constitution meets at Annapolis 27 Apr., completes its work, 6 Sept., ratified 12-13 Oct. "

[This constitution abolished slavery and disfranchised all who had aided or encouraged rebellion against the U. S. Home vote, 27,541 for, 29,536 against; soldiers, 2633 for, 263 against; majority for 375.]

Law for a state normal school at Baltimore . 1865
Maryland Agricultural college established in Prince George's county .. . . "
Legislature passes a very stringent Sunday law . . 1866
Fair held in Baltimore for the relief of the destitute in the southern states; net receipts, $164,569.97 Apr. "
Peabody institute formally inaugurated, George Peabody present 24 Oct. "
Johns Hopkins university incorporated 24 Aug. 1867
New constitution, framed by a convention which met at Annapolis 8 May 1867, which abolishes office of lieutenant-governor, ratified by the people 18 Sept. "

[Vote for, 27,152; against, 23,036.]

New School law passed giving control of educational matters in each county to a board of county commissioners, one for each election district, and state school tax fixed at 10 cents on each $100, the tax paid by colored people to be set aside for maintenance of colored schools 1 Apr. 1868
Institution for the education of the deaf and dumb established temporarily in barracks at Frederick . ... "
State election in Nov. 1869, the whole Democratic ticket elected, and a legislature unanimously Democratic meets . . 5 Jan. 1870

Legislature unanimously rejects the XV.th Amendment, and passes a school law vesting the supervision of schools in a state board, county boards, and school-district boards...... 1870

Celebration by the colored people of Baltimore of the passage of the XV.th Amendment..........................19 May, "

State convention of those favoring the extension of the right of suffrage to women held at Baltimore................29 Feb. 1872

Democratic National convention at Baltimore nominate Horace Greeley, by a vote made unanimous, for president, 9-10 July, "

State institution for colored blind and deaf mutes established in Baltimore.. "

Public Education act modified: Board of Education to consist of the governor, principal of normal school, and 4 persons appointed by the governor from presidents and examiners of the several county boards.............................. 1874

State Grange of the Patrons of Husbandry meets in Baltimore, and makes a declaration of policy and principle......7 Mch. "

James B. Groome elected governor by General Assembly, gov. Whyte being elected U. S. senator..................4 Mch. 1875

Foundation of the Johns Hopkins hospital, endowed with $4,500,000 by Johns Hopkins in 1873, is laid in Baltimore.... "

Daniel C. Gilman installed president of the Johns Hopkins University...22 Feb. 1876

Affray in the streets of Baltimore; the 6th regiment of militia being ordered out by gov. Carroll against strikers on the Baltimore and Ohio railroad at Cumberland; the soldiers are stoned, and fire on the mob, killing 9 and wounding 20 or 30; the mob sets fire to the railroad station, 20 July, 1877

Commissioners appointed by legislatures of 1874 and 1876 for boundary between Maryland and Virginia report....16 Jan. "

Congress appropriates $25,000 for surveying a route for a ship canal between the Chesapeake and Delaware bays to shorten the distance from Baltimore to the ocean by about 200 miles.. 1878

State convention of tax-payers held at Baltimore to redress grievances and secure relief from taxation..........12 Aug. 1879

Celebration of the 150th anniversary of the founding of Baltimore...10-15 Oct. 1880

Henry Lloyd, president of the Senate, succeeds gov. McLane, who is appointed U. S. minister to France..........27 Mch. 1885

Public library, established by gift of Enoch Pratt in 1882, formally opened in Baltimore..........................4 Jan. 1886

Legislature incorporates American College of the Roman Catholic Church of the U. S.................................... "

Sharp contest in Chester river between the state oyster steamer *McLane* and a fleet of illegal dredgers; 2 schooners are run down and sunk and others captured................10 Dec. 1888

State oyster steamer *Helen Baughman* fights with the schooner *Robert McAllister*, an unlicensed oyster boat..........2 Jan. 1889

Asylum for feeble-minded children opened in Baltimore..Jan. "

Chesapeake and Ohio canal wrecked by flood on the Potomac, which also swept away the historic building known as John Brown's Fort..June, "

In 1888, Virginia leased about 3200 acres of oyster ground on Hog island to one Lewis; Maryland claims a right to the ground, but the National Coast Survey rejects her claim; gov. Jackson proclaims the ground open to both states, and the Maryland schooner *Lawson* anchors on the Hog island grounds; the *Lawson* is attacked, run down, and sunk by the Virginia police-boat *Augustus*, 27 Nov.; harmony is restored between the states, Virginia withdrawing her exclusive claim...Dec. "

Australian ballot law passed by Maryland legislature, and a high-license law enacted for Baltimore...................... 1890

Decoration day made a legal holiday by act of legislature..... "

State-treasurer Stevenson Archer discovered to be a defaulter to the amount of $132,401.25, 27 Mch.; is arrested at his home in Belair, 10 Apr.; is tried, pleads guilty, and is sentenced to 5 years' imprisonment....................7 July, "

Rev. Robert Laird Collier, Unitarian minister, dies near Salisbury..27 July, "

Ex-gov. Philip Francis Thomas d. at Baltimore, aged 80, 2 Oct. "

U. S. senator Ephraim King Wilson d. in Washington, D. C., 24 Feb. 1891

Monument erected by the state to Leonard Calvert, first governor of the colony, at Old St. Mary's...............3 June, "

Charles H. Gibson qualifies as U. S. senator by executive appointment to fill place of senator Wilson, deceased....7 Dec. "

Ex-postmaster-gen. John A. J. Cresswell d. at Belair...23 Dec. "

Charles H. Gibson elected by the legislature as U. S. senator to fill unexpired term.............................21 Jan. 1892

Ex-gov. E. Louis Lowe d. in Brooklyn, N. Y., aged 70, 23 Aug. "

GOVERNORS UNDER THE BALTIMORES (Proprietary governors).

Name.	Term.	Remarks.
Leonard Calvert........	1637 to 1647	
Thomas Greene.........	1647 " 1648	Removed by Lord Baltimore.
William Stone..........	1648 " 1654	Conflicting governments, civil war.
......	1654 " 1658	
Josias Fendall..........	1658 " 1660	Removed by Lord Baltimore.
Philip Calvert..........	1660 " 1662	
Charles Calvert.........	1662 " 1676	Afterwards the third lord Baltimore and proprietary.
Thomas Notley.........	1677 " 1680	
Charles, Lord Baltimore.	1681 " 1689	His rights abrogated by William and Mary.

UNDER THE ENGLISH GOVERNMENT (Royal governors).

Name.	Term.	Remarks.
John Coode and the Protestant association....	1690 to 1692	
Sir Lionel Copley.......	1692 " 1693	Died in office.
Francis Nicholson......	1694 " 1695	
Nathaniel Blackstone...	1696 " 1702	
Thomas Trench.........	1703 " 1704	Acting.
John Seymour..........	1704 " 1708	
Edward Lloyd..........	1709 " 1713	Acting.
John Hart..............	1714 " 1715	

UNDER THE BALTIMORES RESTORED (Proprietary governors).

Name.	Term.	Remarks.
John Hart..............	1715 to 1719	
Charles Calvert.........	1720 " 1726	
Benedict L. Calvert.....	1727 " 1730	
Samuel Ogle...........	1731 " 1732	
Charles, Lord Baltimore.	1732 " 1733	
Samuel Ogle............	1734 " 1741	
Thomas Bladen.........	1742 " 1745	
Samuel Ogle............	1746 " 1751	
Benjamin Tasker.......	1752	Acting.
Horatio Sharpe.........	1753 to 1768	
Robert Eden............	1769 " 1774	

UNDER THE CONTINENTAL CONGRESS.

Name.	Term.	Remarks.
Thomas Johnson........	1777 to 1779	
Thomas Sim Lee........	1780 " 1782	
William Paca...........	1783 " 1784	Distinguished soldier in the revolution.
William Smallwood.....	1785 " 1788	

UNDER THE CONSTITUTION.

Name.	Term.	Remarks.
John E. Howard........	1789 to 1790	
George Plater...........	1791 " 1792	
Thomas Sim Lee........	1793 " 1794	
John H. Stone..........	1795 " 1797	
John Henry.............	1798	
Benjamin Ogle	1799 to 1801	
John F. Mercer.........	1802 " 1803	
Robert Bowie	1804 " 1805	
Robert Wright..........	1806 " 1808	
Edward Lloyd..........	1809 " 1810	
Robert Bowie...........	1811 " 1812	
Levin Winder	1813 " 1814	
Charles Ridgely.........	1815 " 1817	
Charles W. Goldsborough.	1818 " 1819	
Samuel Sprigg..........	1820 " 1822	
Samuel Stevens, Jr......	1823 " 1825	
Joseph Kent............	1826 " 1828	
Daniel Martin	1829	
Thomas K. Carroll	1830	
Daniel Martin	1831	Died in office.
George Howard.........	1831 to 1832	
James Thomas..........	1833 " 1835	
Thomas W. Veazey	1836 " 1838	
William Grayson	1839 " 1841	
Francis Thomas.........	1842 " 1844	
Thomas G. Pratt........	1845 " 1847	
Philip F. Thomas.......	1848 " 1850	
Enoch L. Lowe.........	1851 " 1865	
Thomas W. Ligon.......	1856 " 1857	
Thomas H. Hicks........	1858 " 1861	Opposes secession.
Augustus W. Bradford...	1862 " 1864	Republican or Unionist.
Thomas Swann.........	1865 " 1867	
Oden Bowie............	1868 " 1871	
W. P. Whyte...........	1872 " 1874	Elected U. S. senator.
James B. Groome.......	1875	
John Lee Carroll........	1876 to 1879	
William T. Hamilton....	1880 " 1883	
Robert M. McLane......	1884 " 1887	
Elihu E. Jackson	1888 " 1891	
Frank Brown...........	1892 —	Term expires 1896.

UNITED STATES SENATORS FROM THE STATE OF MARYLAND.

Name.	No. of Congress.	Date.	Remarks.
Charles Carroll....................	1st to 2d	1789 to 1793	Resigned.
John Henry.........................	1st " 5th	1789 " 1797	Resigned. Elected governor.
Richard Potts......................	2d " 4th	1793 " 1796	Elected in place of Carroll. Resigned.
John Eager Howard................	4th " 7th	1796 " 1803	Elected president *pro tem.* 21 Nov. 1800.
James Lloyd.......................	5th " 6th	1798 " 1800	Elected in place of Henry. Resigned.
William Hindman..................	6th " 7th	1800 " 1803	Elected in place of Lloyd.
Robert Wright.....................	7th " 9th	1801 " 1806	Resigned 1806.
Samuel Smith......................	8th " 13th	1803 " 1815	Elected president *pro tem.* 2 Dec. 1805, '6, '7, '8.
Philip Reed........................	9th " 12th	1806 " 1813	Elected in place of Wright.
Robert Henry Goldsborough........	13th " 15th	1813 " 1819	
Robert G. Harper..................	14th	1816	Resigned.

UNITED STATES SENATORS FROM THE STATE OF MARYLAND.—(*Continued.*)

Name.	No. of Congress.	Date.	Remarks.
Alexander C. Hanson	14th to 15th	1817 to 1819	Elected in place of Harper. Died 1819.
Edward Lloyd	16th " 19th	1819 " 1826	Resigned.
William Pinkney	16th " 17th	1820 " 1822	Elected in place of Hanson. Died 1822.
Samuel Smith	17th	1822	Elected in place of Pinkney. President *pro tem.* 1828, '29, '30.
Ezekiel F. Chambers	19th to 23d	1826 to 1834	Resigned 1834.
Joseph Kent	23d " 25th	1833 " 1837	Died 1837.
Robert Henry Goldsborough	23d " 24th	1835 " 1836	Died 1836.
John S. Spence	24th " 26th	1835 " 1840	Elected in place of Goldborough. Died 1840.
William D. Merrick	25th " 28th	1838 " 1845	Elected in place of Kent.
John L. Kerr	26th " 27th	1841 " 1843	Elected in place of Spence.
James A. Pearce	28th " 37th	1843 " 1862	Died 1862.
Reverdy Johnson	29th " 30th	1845 " 1849	Resigned.
David Stewart	31st	1849	Appointed *pro tem.* in place of Johnson.
Thomas G. Pratt	31st to 34th	1850 to 1857	Elected in place of Johnson.
Anthony Kennedy	35th " 38th	1857 " 1865	
Thomas H. Hicks	37th " 38th	1863 " 1865	Appointed in place of Pearce. Died 1865.
John A. J. Creswell	39th	1865 " 1867	
Reverdy Johnson	39th to 40th	1865 " 1868	Resigned.
William Pinckney Whyte	40th	1868 " 1869	Appointed in place of Johnson.
George Vickers	40th to 42d	1868 " 1873	
William T. Hamilton	41st " 43d	1869 " 1875	Elected in place of Johnson.
George R. Dennis	43d " 45th	1873 " 1879	
William Pinckney Whyte	44th " 46th	1875 " 1881	
James G. Groome	46th " 49th	1879 " 1885	
Arthur P. Gorman	47th	1881 ——	Term expires 1899.
Ephraim K. Wilson	49th to 52d	1885 " 1891	Died in office.
Charles H. Gibson	52d ——	1891 ——	Term expires 1897.

Maryland campaign. Immediately after Pope's defeat at Manassas, 30 Aug. 1862, McClellan was appointed (2 Sept.) to command the troops for the defence of the capital. The Confederate army (45,000 strong?) crossed the Potomac and occupied Frederick, Md., 6 Sept., where Lee issued a proclamation to "the people of Maryland," assuring them that the Confederate army had come to assist them in regaining rights of which they had been so unjustly despoiled, etc. Leaving Banks in command at Washington, McClellan crossed the Potomac river, and moved towards the Confederate army on 7 Sept., occupying Frederick on the 12th, with a force estimated at from 80,000 to 90,000 men. Here he had the good-fortune to secure a copy of Lee's general order of the 9th, explaining his movements, and pointing out as one of the objects of the expedition the capture of Harper's Ferry. In this order "Stonewall" Jackson, after passing Middletown, was to cross the Potomac at Sharpsburg and attack Harper's Ferry, while McLaws's and Anderson's divisions would come directly to his aid from Middletown.

Battles of South Mountain.—Gen. Lee meanwhile had passed "South Mountain," a continuation of the Blue Ridge north of the Potomac from Harper's Ferry. The road from Frederick to Boonsboro crosses South Mountain at Turner's Gap, while another road passes it at Crampton's Gap, about 6 miles to the south. Gen. Lee left D. H. Hill's division of 5 brigades to hold Turner's Gap, and Howell Cobb with 3 brigades at Crampton's Gap. The action at Turner's Gap began at 7 A.M., 14 Sept. The confederates at first had but 5000 or 6000 men in action, but Longstreet continued to reinforce Hill until they numbered at least 25,000, with Longstreet in command. The confederates held the gap through the day, and withdrew during the night. The Union forces lost in this engagement 1813, and the confederates about as many. Gen. Franklin, with the 6th corps, was attempting to force his way through Crampton's Gap, which he succeeded in doing before night, and bivouacked within 3 or 4 miles of Maryland Heights, overlooking Harper's Ferry. The Union loss at Crampton's Gap was 530 killed and wounded. These 2 battles of Turner's and Crampton's Gaps, having been fought on the same day and within about 6 miles of each other, are called Battles of South Mountain.

Surrender of Harper's Ferry.—Meanwhile Stonewall Jackson was rapidly concentrating his forces and surrounding Harper's Ferry, occupied by about 14,000 troops under col. D. S. Miles, who had won no enviable reputation at the first battle of Bull's Run. Jackson had recrossed the Potomac to the Virginia side at Williamsport, and, descending its right bank, appeared before Harper's Ferry on the morning of the 13th. Loudon Heights were immediately occupied by confederates without opposition, while Maryland Heights, the key to the position, were not occupied by them until the afternoon of the 14th, and then with scarcely any resistance. On the evening of the 14th, col. Davis, with 2000 U. S. cavalry, crossing the pontoon-bridge to the Maryland side, escaped between the Confederate forces. Jackson opened his batteries on the afternoon of the 14th on the cooped-up forces in Harper's Ferry; and on the morning of the 15th, after about one hour's cannonading, the place surrendered, with 12,520 men; other loss, killed and wounded, 217 (among them col. Miles, the commander, mortally wounded), and 47 pieces of artillery. The confederates sustained no loss. The head of gen. Franklin's corps of relief was within 3 or 4 miles at the time of surrender.

Battle of Antietam.—McClellan was so close upon the Confederate army that Lee was obliged to halt to protect Jackson's command at Harper's Ferry, and allow him to rejoin the main army. For this purpose he selected the west bank of Antietam creek, near Sharpsburg, Md. The position chosen by gen. Lee compensated somewhat for the numerical inferiority of his army. On the morning of the 16th the army of the Potomac was assembled on the border of the Antietam, except gen. Franklin's 2 divisions, while gen. Lee had not more than 25,000 men; but this was not known to McClellan at the time. Jackson arrived before noon of the 16th with 2 brigades badly broken up by a hard march from Harper's Ferry; while McLaws's, Anderson's, and D. H. Hill's divisions were still away towards the Potomac. At 2 P.M. McClellan advanced gen. Hooker's division across Antietam creek, but the engagement was soon ended by the darkness. At dawn on the 17th the battle was again opened by Hooker; with varying fortunes it continued through the day, until again ended by night. On the morning of the 18th McClellan had thoughts of resuming the offensive, but some of his ablest subordinates advised against it. During the day he was joined by the divisions of Couch and Humphreys, when, feeling assured of success, he ordered an attack on the morning of the 19th; but during the night of the 18th the enemy withdrew across the Potomac and retired towards Martinsburg. McClellan reoccupied Harper's Ferry a few days after. The Union loss at Antietam was, killed, 2108; wounded, 9549; missing, 753; total, 12,410; whole loss in the campaign, including Harper's Ferry and skirmishes, 27,940; Confederate loss during the whole campaign about 15,000. FREDERICKSBURG.

Masaniel'lo. NAPLES, 1647.

Auber's opera "La Muette de Portici," 1828, was produced in London, Engl., as "Masaniello," 4 May, 1829. MUSIC.

Masho'na, Mak'ala'kaland, and **Matabe'le lands,** territories in S. Africa, ruled by Lobengula, who entered into agreement with the British government, 11 Feb. 1888.

Successful progress of colonization, reported May, 1892.

Explorations of J. Theodore Bent; he discovers at Zimbabwe, an ancient fortress (probably Phœnician), a temple with ornamented walls, monoliths, specimens of good pottery, relics of gold-mining, etc., June–Aug. 1891. Mr. Bent gave an account of his exploration at a meeting of the Royal Geographical Society, London, 22 Feb. 1892.

masks. Poppæa, wife of Nero, is said to have invented the mask to guard her complexion from the sun; but theatrical masks were in use among the Greeks and Romans. Horace attributes them to Æschylus; yet Aristotle says the inventor and time of their introduction were unknown. Modern masks, muffs, fans, and false hair for women, were devised in Italy, and brought to England from France in 1572.—*Stow.* IRON MASK.

Mason and Dixon's line. PENNSYLVANIA, 1682.

Mason and Slidell affair. TRENT; UNITED STATES, 1861.

Masonry. FREEMASONRY.

Mas'orah (Heb. for *tradition*), a collection of conjectural readings (*keris*) of the Hebrew text of the Old Testament, with critical, grammatical, and exegetical notes by various Jewish doctors (written between the 6th and 10th centuries), who also furnished the *Masoretic vowel-points.*

First Rabbinical Hebrew Bible, containing the Masorah, Targums, and comments, was printed by Bomberg at Venice, 1518. The "Book of the Masorah, the Hedge of the Law," was first printed at Florence, 1750.

masques, precursors of the opera, introduced into England in the latter part of the 16th century; many were written by Ben Jonson; one at the Middle Temple on the marriage of princess Elizabeth, Feb. 1613. Milton's "Comus" was represented at Ludlow castle in 1634.

mass, in the Roman church, is the office of prayer used in the eucharist, in memory of the passion of Christ, to which every part of the service refers. Mass may be high or low; the former is sung by choristers, and celebrated with the assistance of a deacon and sub-deacon; in low mass the prayers are rehearsed without singing. Mass in Latin was first celebrated about 394; it was introduced into England in the 7th century. Prostration was enjoined at the elevation of the host in 1201. Dr. Daniel Rock, in "The Church of Our Fathers" (1849), describes an ancient MS. of "The Service of the Mass, called the Rite of Salisbury," compiled for that cathedral by St. Osmund and others in the 12th century. The English communion service was adopted in 1549. MISSAL, RITUALISM.

Massachusetts is the chief political division of New England and one of the original 13 United States. It lies for the most part between 40° and 42° 45′ N. lat., and 70° 30′ and 73° 30′ W. lon. The states of Vermont and New Hampshire lie immediately on the north; on the east lies the Atlantic ocean, giving it a sea frontage of about 250 miles; to the south lie the Atlantic ocean and the states of Rhode Island and Connecticut. Immediately on its west boundaries lie Rhode Island, New York, and New Hampshire. It extends east and west 190 miles, and 50 miles north and south, with a projection at the southeast, and a lesser one at the northeast, that increases the breadth to about 110 miles. Area 8315 sq. miles, in 14 counties. Pop. 1890, 2,238,943; 1900, 2,805,346. Capital, Boston.

Capt. Bartholomew Gosnold, sailing from Falmouth, Engl., after a passage of 49 days discovers land in lat. 43° 30′ N..14 May, 1602

He discovers a "mighty head-land," which from the quantity of codfish caught in the vicinity is called Cape Cod; the voyagers land; this is the first spot upon which the first known English discoverers of Massachusetts set foot. 15 May, “

Martin Pring in the *Speedwell*, of 60 tons, and William Browne in the *Discoverer*, of 26 tons, make discoveries along the New England coast.. 1603

Capt. George Weymouth with 28 men in the *Archangel* explores the coast of Massachusetts and Maine, also the Penobscot and Kennebec rivers.. 1605

Henry Hudson discovers the Hudson river.......................... 1609

Capt. John Smith explores the coast from the Penobscot river to Cape Cod, and names the country New England.......... 1614

Capt. John Smith publishes his "Description of New England" to invite permanent settlements there.......................... 1616

A disease among the Indians nearly depopulates the New England coast..1616–18

"Great Patent of New England" passes the seals......3 Nov. 1620

[This patent, which has scarcely a parallel in the history of the world, covered a territory extending from 40° to 48° of north latitude, and in length from the Atlantic to the Pacific ocean.]

Speedwell, of 60 tons, is purchased in Holland to take part of the English emigrants there to England, and thence across the Atlantic.. “

[These emigrants belonged to an English sect of Separatists who had sought an asylum in Holland to escape religious persecution in England. Their object in leaving Holland was to settle on the coast of North America where they could enjoy their religion without molestation.]

Speedwell leaves Delft, Holland, for Southampton, Engl. 22 July, “

Mayflower, of 180 tons, is chartered in England to accompany the *Speedwell*.. “

Speedwell is found to be unfitted for a voyage across the Atlantic and is dismissed..........................21 Aug. “

Mayflower sails from Plymouth harbor, having on board 101 passengers..6 Sept. “

After a stormy passage of 63 days sights the cliffs of Cape Cod and comes to anchor in Cape Cod harbor............9 Nov. “

Peregrine White born on board the *Mayflower* in Cape Cod harbor. The first white child born in New England....Nov. “

[He died at Marshfield, near Plymouth, 20 July, 1704.]

Mayflower sails from Cape Cod 15 Dec. and anchors at Plymouth, .16 Dec. “

[Four had died at Cape Cod, viz.: Edward Thompson, Jasper Carver, James Chilton, and Mrs. Dorothy Bradford, the latter being accidentally drowned.]

MAS

First death at Plymouth, Richard Butteridge..........21 Dec. 1620

Passengers leave the ship and land at Plymouth rock.. “ “

[This rock was raised from its bed in 1774, but in the act of raising it was broken. The upper part was removed to the public square. In 1834, on 4 July, it was again removed and placed in front of Pilgrim hall, where it rested, bearing the names of the 41 signers of the compact in the *Mayflower*, until 1880, when it was taken and reunited to the other portion. The honor of having first placed foot on this rock has been claimed for both John Alden and Mary Chilton. John Alden died at Roxbury, 12 Sept. 1686, aged 80, but the longest living of the first passengers of the *Mayflower* was Mary Allerton, daughter of Isaac Allerton, who died 1699, aged about 90.—"Narrative and Critical History of America." The company named their settlement Plymouth, because it had been so called by capt. John Smith, who had previously surveyed the harbor, and also after Plymouth, Engl., whose citizens had treated them kindly.]

Store-house erected at Plymouth, 20 feet square with a thatched roof..24–30 Dec. “

Colony begins to erect separate houses..................9 Jan. 1621

Store-house takes fire and nearly burns down...........14 Jan. “

Mrs. Rose Standish, the wife of Miles Standish, d.......29 Jan. “

Miles Standish made captain with military authority..17 Feb. “

William White d..21 Feb. “

Samoset the first Indian to visit the colony, saying, "Welcome, Englishmen!"..16 Mch. “

[Samoset visits them again a few days afterwards, accompanied by another Indian who was able to converse with the colonists. This Indian had been kidnapped in 1614 by one Thomas Hunt, master of one of capt. Smith's vessels, with some 26 others, and taken to Spain and sold into slavery. Liberated by some benevolent friars, he found his way to London, and in 1619 was restored to his own country, and now became an interpreter and friend of the English settlers. Known in early New England history as Squanto.]

Massasoit, the grand sachem of the Wampanoags, with about 60 of his warriors, visits the colony..................22 Mch. “

Treaty between the colony and Massasoit, which is faithfully observed for 55 years..22 Mch. “

John Carver unanimously confirmed as governor of the colony for the new civil year..23 Mch. “

Mayflower sails for England on her return voyage......5 Apr. “

Gov. Carver d.. “ “

[His wife survives him but 6 weeks.]

William Bradford elected governor, Isaac Allerton, deputy..... “

Forty-four deaths in the colony in 4 months to.........1 Apr. “

Susanna, the widow of William White, marries Edward Winslow, the first marriage in the colony................12 May, “

Twenty acres of corn and beans are planted and 6 acres of barley and pease by the colony in the spring of.............. “

[They obtain the corn or maize of the Indians, who teach them how to cultivate it, now first called *Indian corn*.]

First duel in New England was fought between Edward Dotey and Edward Leister, servants of Stephen Hopkins, with sword and dagger; they were sentenced to have their head and heels tied together, and thus remain for 24 hours without food or drink; after an hour's endurance they were relieved on promises and pleadings..........................18 June, “

First Thanksgiving in the colony..........................Sept. “

Village of Plymouth contains at this time 7 dwelling-houses, and 4 other buildings..Sept. “

Capt. Miles Standish with 9 Plymouth colonists and 3 Indians explores the country about Massachusetts bay..........Oct. “

Fortune, a vessel of 55 tons, bringing 35 passengers, arrives at Plymouth..11 Nov. “

[This ship also brings a patent granted 11 June by the president and council of New England. This patent did not fix territorial limits, but allowed 100 acres for each emigrant with 1500 acres for public buildings, and empowered the grantees to make laws and set up a government.]

Fortune laden with beaver and other skins and lumber, valued at $2400, the first remittance from New Plymouth, sails on her return voyage..3 Dec. “

John Alden marries Priscilla Mullens (the Puritan maiden), daughter of William Mullens.......................... “

Town surrounded by a palisade and a stockade built......Feb. 1622

Much suffering from lack of food........................spring of “

Canonicus, sachem of the Narragansetts, sends by way of defiance a bundle of arrows tied in a rattlesnake's skin to Plymouth; gov. Bradford sends back the skin stuffed with powder and balls; this intimidates the tribe.......................... “

Colonists plant 60 acres of corn.......................... “

Two ships, *Charity* and *Swan*, with about 60 passengers, sent over by a Mr. Weston, a dissatisfied member of the Plymouth company, to attempt a settlement, arrives...July, “

They attempt a settlement at a place called Wessagusset (now Weymouth) on Massachusetts bay during the year........ “

This colony, unable to support itself, breaks up, after nearly involving the Plymouth colony in a war with the Indians.. 1623

Great distress at Plymouth for want of food..........spring of “

[Tradition affirms that at one time there was but one pint of corn left, or 5 kernels for each person.]

Two ships, *Anne* and *Little James*, of 44 tons, the latter built for the colony, arrive at Plymouth, bringing 60 passengers..Aug. “

Harvest was abundant.. “

Capt. Robert Gorges, son of sir Ferdinando Gorges, with Mr. Morrell, an Episcopal minister, and many others, arrive and selects a site at Wessagusset for settlement...........Sept. “

Capt. Robert Gorges returns to England early in............ 1624

A few settlers remain at Wessagusset, some families come from Weymouth Engl and the name is changed to Weymouth 1624

Settlement commenced at Cape Ann with the intention of connecting the settlement with the fishing interests "

William Bradford again elected governor of Plymouth colony "

Ship *Charity*, bringing a supply of clothing and a bull and 3 heifers first neat cattle imported into New England 24 Mch "

[There come also a carpenter and a person to make salt, the carpenter builds 2 ketches a lighter, and 6 or 7 shallops]

John Lyford and John Oldham expelled from the colony "

Population of Plymouth colony 180 and number of dwelling houses 32, a substantial fort, a vessel of 44 tons with smaller boats, large tracts of land under cultivation and enclosures for the cattle, goats, swine and poultry spring, "

James I of England d 27 Mch 1625

Accession of Charles I "

Capt Wollaston and about 30 others commence a settlement at a place they call Mount Wollaston (now Quincy) "

Thomas Morton on the departure of Wollaston takes charge, and changes the name to Mare Mount 1626

Robert Conant removes from the settlement at Cape Ann to Naumkeag (now Salem) "

Plymouth colony establish an outpost on Buzzards bay, friendly commerce begins with the Dutch at New Amsterdam 1627

Partnership of merchants and colonists being unprofitable, and the community system failing 8 colonists of Plymouth buy of the London partners their interests for $9000, in 9 annual instalments, the community system is abandoned, a division made of movable property, and 20 acres of land near the town is assigned in fee to each colonist. Jan 1628

Rev John White, a Puritan minister of Dorchester Engl, enlists some gentlemen who obtain a patent conveying to them that part of New England lying between 3 miles to the north of the Merrimac river and 3 miles to the south of the Charles river, and every part thereof in Massachusetts bay and in length between the described breadth from the Atlantic ocean to the South sea 19 Mch "

[This grant from the throne does not pass the seals until 4 Mch 1629 —"Memorial History of Boston "]

Company appoint John Endicott governor of the colony "until themselves should come over" 30 May, "

Endicott, with wife and children and about 50 others, embarks in ship *Abigail* from England for Massachusetts 20 June, "

Plymouth people admonish Thomas Morton of "Merry Mount" twice, the third time they send capt Miles Standish "with some aid" Morton's followers are disarmed and dispersed without bloodshed, while he is conducted to Plymouth and from there sent to England (upon this incident Hawthorne writes "The Maypole at Merry Mount") June, "

A second and larger company, numbering 60 women and maids, 26 children, and 300 men, among whom is the rev Francis Higginson on several vessels, leave England for Salem, bringing food, arms tools, and 140 cattle May, 1629

[The *Mayflower* brought Francis Higginson, and was one of the fleet that brought Mr Winthrop and his colonists.]

Ralph Richard, and William Sprague with others commence a settlement at Mishawums, now Charlestown 24 June, "

A church established at Salem with Mr Skelton as ordained pastor and Mr Higginson as teacher Aug "

[This was the second church established in Massachusetts on the basis of Independent Congregationalism]

John and Samuel Browne, members of the colonial council and of the Massachusetts company, are sent back to England by gov Endicott for their opposition to the church and advocacy of Episcopacy "

Transfer of the Massachusetts colony's government from London to New England Aug "

John Winthrop chosen governor and Thomas Dudley lieut-governor of the Massachusetts colony 20 Aug "

Gov Winthrop, with Isaac Johnson and his wife, lady Arbella Johnson, daughter of the earl of Lincoln, sail from England in the *Arbella* for Massachusetts 8 Apr 1630

Vessel arrives at Salem 12 June, "

Lady Arbella Johnson d 30 Aug. "

Her husband, Isaac Johnson, d 30 Sept "

First general court met at Boston 19 Oct "

Seventeen ships bringing about 1500 emigrants, arrive in Massachusetts bay and at Plymouth during the year "

First church at Boston, third in order of time in the colony, gathered at Charlestown July, "

[In 1636 there were 9 churches in existence in the Massachusetts colony, and in 1650, 29]

Watertown settled by sir Richard Saltonstall "

Roxbury settled by William Pynchon "

Newtown (now Cambridge) settled by Mr Dudley, Mr Bradstreet, and others "

Dorchester and Boston settled "

[The Indian name of the peninsula of Boston was Shawmut, the inhabitants of Charlestown called it Trimountaine, or Tremont, and the general court, by order 17 Sept 1630, gave it the name of BOSTON In 1632 the same legislature declared it to be "the fittest place for public meetings of any on the bay," and thenceforth it was the capital of Massachusetts.—*Quincy*, "History of Boston "]

Lynn settled "

[The history of the Plymouth colony is the history of a people of very limited means, and without any support from the English government, having no charter from the crown Few, if any of them, had ever enjoyed the luxuries of life, neither had they ever enjoyed the opportunities for literary culture Unaccustomed to the ease and refinement of wealth, simple in their habits, inured to hardship and toil, and moderate in their desires, they were eminently fitted to establish a permanent colony on the bleak coast of New England —*Barry* "History of Massachusetts "]

[The Massachusetts Bay colonists were Puritans connected with the National church, though not fully conforming to its service and ritual Their ministers were men of standing, influence and education, of the laity, many were versed in public affairs, possessed fortunes lived in the enjoyment of wealth, and moved in high society, a few had titles of nobility Able to furnish both followers and funds they could easily equip a fleet and send many hundreds to the territory selected for their residence More fortunate than the pilgrims of Plymouth, their fortune and rank enabled them to obtain a charter from the crown which Plymouth never obtained Hence the history of the second colony though not destitute of incidents of hardship and suffering is of a stamp very different from the first It attains to such power and strength that its name becomes identified with the name of the state —*Barry*, History of Massachusetts. "]

Two hundred die before end of Dec 1630

Famine, Dec and Jan in the Massachusetts Bay colony 1630-31

A general fast appointed for 6 Feb, ship *Lyon* arrives laden with provisions and bringing 26 passengers, among them Roger Williams 5 Feb 1631

Roger Williams is appointed assistant to Mr Skelton in the ministry at Salem but asserting his views of religious toleration the independence of conscience, of the civil magistrates and the separation of church and state, he is obliged to withdraw to the Plymouth colony early in "

Second general court makes the Massachusetts colony a theocracy, which lasts for a half century 18 May, "

[No man was hereafter to be admitted a freeman that is, a citizen and a voter unless he were a member of some church of the colony, and admission to those churches was by no means an easy matter —*Hildreth*, "History U S" vol i p 189]

Rev John Eliot afterwards distinguished as "Apostle to the Indians," arrives at Massachusetts Bay and becomes first teacher of the church at Roxbury 2 Nov "

Gov Bradford of the Plymouth colony resigning, Edward Winslow is chosen governor 1632

Fort begun at Boston on Cornhill "

Gov Winthrop of Massachusetts visits Plymouth 25 Oct "

Gov Winthrop refuses to receive presents "

A vessel of 30 tons built at Mystic called *Blessing of the Bay* "

Plymouth colonists send capt. Holmes to erect a trading-house on the Connecticut river at Windsor above Hartford 1633

John Oldham and 4 others travel as far as the Dutch trading houses on the Connecticut river, and bring back flattering reports of that country "

Salary of the governor of Massachusetts Bay fixed at 150*l* "

Griffin brings 200 passengers, some of them eminent men as John Haynes, afterwards governor of Massachusetts, John Cotton, Thomas Hooker, and Samuel Stone "

Small pox destroys many of the Indians of Massachusetts "

Ipswich settled "

Scituate settled "

Roger Williams returns to Salem from Plymouth colony "

Thomas Dudley chosen governor and Robert Ludlow deputy governor of the Massachusetts colony 1634

John Endicott cuts from the flag the red cross at Salem as being a "relic of antichrist and a popish symbol" Jan "

Anne Hutchinson of Alford, Engl with her husband, William Hutchinson, arrives in the *Griffin* "

News of the creation of a colonial commission recall of the Massachusetts charter, and appointment of a general governor by the English government, received at Boston, 10 Apr "

Rev Samuel Skelton dies at Salem, the first minister who died in New England 2 Aug "

Elders of the church decide that if a governor general were sent over from England he ought not to be accepted 1635

Endicott reprimanded by the court for mutilating the colors at Salem "

First appointment of selectmen at Charlestown 10 Feb "

[This name presently extended throughout New England]

General court orders the fortifications repaired appoints a military commission with extraordinary powers to guard the rights and liberties of Massachusetts Mch "

[The disorders of the English government the unsuccessful attempt to launch a vessel intended to bring over the governor general, and the death of John Mason, the principal member and secretary of the council of New England, were the safeguards of the infant liberties of New England —*Palfrey*, "History of New England Under the Stuarts "]

Freemen choose John Haynes as governor of Massachusetts, selected by deputies from the towns, before the meeting of the court, the first instance of "caucus" on record (*Hildreth*, "History U S," vol i p 224) 6 May, "

Concord first settled "

Richard Dummer founds Newbury "

Roger Williams advocates the inviolable freedom of faith He appears before the magistrates to defend it Apr "

Rev John Avery drowned while on his way to Marblehead from Newbury, 14 Aug "

[The story is told of this shipwreck by Anthony Thacher, who escaped with his wife, and is further commemorated in Whittier's "Swan Song of Parson Avery "]

Roger Williams is sentenced to depart out of the jurisdiction of the colony within 6 weeks, but owing to clamor of a stanch minority is permitted to remain until spring Oct. 1635

John Winthrop the younger, Hugh Peters, and Henry Vane arrive at Boston 3 Oct. "

Capt Underhill is sent to apprehend Roger Williams, as he still continued "to preach," and carry him aboard a ship bound for England, but finds him gone Dec "

Roger Williams finds refuge with Massasoit, the sachem of the Wampanoags, and commences a settlement at Seekonk on the east side of Narragansett bay, but learning from Mr Winslow of Plymouth that he was within the patent of that colony, he and 5 others move to the other side of the bay, having obtained a grant of land from Canonicus, the head sachem of the Narragansetts He names this settlement Providence 1636

A law of the colony prohibits erecting a dwelling house more than half a mile from the meeting house "

Religious controversy with Mrs Anne Hutchinson begins "

[The controversy arose in this wise The clergy laid great stress upon the external evidences of sanctification or piety, gravity of deportment, precision of manner, formality of speech, peculiarity of dress, and other outward signs of holiness were held in such high estimate that all destitute of these signs, however irreproachable in life, were not considered worthy to be called the "children of God" Mrs. Hutchinson was the founder of the party in opposition to these notions She maintained that the outward signs of discipleship might be displayed by a hypocrite, and hence "sanctification" which embraced those signs, was not an infallible evidence of "justification" The clergy denied the unition of the Holy Ghost with the regenerate in any sense. Mrs Hutchinson maintained a personal union — *Hildreth*, "History U S," vol i pp 248-49 The difference is not very clear, and it would only be a waste of time to attempt to make it clearer The points of the controversy were not at all understood by many who took part Nevertheless a schism of the bitterest rent the New England church — *Hosmer*, "Young Sir Henry Vane "]

Sir Henry Vane chosen governor of Massachusetts "

Rev Thomas Hooker and friends remove from Newtown (Cambridge) to Connecticut and found Hartford June, "

John Oldham killed by the Indians near Block island July, "

[This event was one of the principal causes of the Pequot war The Pequots were a tribe of Indians occupying the eastern part of Connecticut, and ruled a part of Long island]

Expedition sent, under command of John Endicott, to punish the Indians of Block island for the murder of John Oldham "

Pequot war begins Aug "

General court of Massachusetts agrees to give 400*l* towards a school or college 28 Oct "

Roger Williams baffles the Pequots by an alliance with the Narragansett Indians, leaving the Pequots single handed against the English, visiting the sachem of the Narragansetts, Miantonomoh, near Newport, while the Pequot ambassadors were there in council Dec. "

John Winthrop chosen governor of Massachusetts 1637

Capt. John Mason, with some 60 men from the Connecticut colony, and capt John Underhill with 20 men from the Massachusetts colony, accompanied by 200 Narragansett warriors, attack the Pequot fort on the Mystic, capture and destroy it with all its occupants, numbering 600 and over 26 May, "

Gov Henry Vane returns to England 3 Aug "

Pequot war ends by total annihilation of the tribe (CONNECTICUT) Oct. "

Rev John Wheelwright, brother of Mrs Anne Hutchinson, disfranchised and banished for supporting her 2 Nov "

He journeys to New Hampshire and founds Exeter "

Mrs Anne Hutchinson under sentence of banishment, is committed to Joseph Welde of Roxbury for safe keeping, until the court shall dispose of her 2 Nov "

She is excommunicated, sent out of the jurisdiction, and retires to Narragansett bay, where her husband had gone, Mch 1638

[Remaining here until the death of her husband 1642, she removes to the New Netherland, and settles in Westchester county, where she and all her family, except one little grand daughter, are killed by Indians, 1643, in a war with the Dutch] NEW YORK.

John Harvard, a graduate of Emmanuel college, Cambridge, Engl, bequeaths his library and half of his estate which amounted to 700*l*, for a college 14 Sept. "

"Ancient and Honorable Artillery Company" organized as the "Military Company of Boston" Feb. "

[This company, with various changes of name and regulations, still continues ARTILLERY]

John Winthrop again chosen governor 2 May, "

Rev John Harvard dies at Charlestown. 14 Sept "

Mrs Dorothy Talbyre, for the murder of her child, 3 years old, hung "

Three thousand emigrants arrive from England during "

Printing press established at Cambridge by Stephen Daye, Mch. 1639

[The first printing done was the "Freeman's Oath," the second was an almanac for New England, made by capt. William Peirce, the third was the Psalms BOOKS, PRINTING]

College at Cambridge (then Newtown) the place fixed upon as the site of it, is named Harvard, after its founder (HARVARD COLLEGE). 13 Mch

Thomas Dudley elected governor "

Inhabitants from the town of Lynn settle on Long island "

First original publication from Massachusetts, a volume of poems by Mrs. Anne Bradstreet, wife of gov Bradstreet .

New England navigation and commerce date from

Cultivation of hemp and flax successfully undertaken, and the manufacture of linen, cotton, and woollen cloths are begun, particularly at Rowley a new town, where a colony of York shire clothiers settle, with Ezekiel Rogers, grandson of the famous martyr (John Rogers), for their minister 1640

Hugh Bewit is banished from the Massachusetts colony for maintaining that he was free from "original sin" By order of the court he was to be gone within 15 days upon pain of death, and if he returned he should be hanged (*Drake*, "History and Antiquities of Boston") 9 Dec "

Trouble of the Massachusetts and Plymouth colonies with Samuel Gorton begins 1641

Gov Bellingham of Massachusetts selects his bride, and performs the marriage ceremony himself "

A body of fundamental laws, being compiled from drafts submitted, is sent to every town within the jurisdiction of Massachusetts to be first considered by the magistrates and elders, and then to be published by the constables, "that if any man saw anything to be altered, he might communicate his thoughts to some of the deputies" Thus deliberately prepared, these laws, 98 in number, were formally adopted by the name of "Fundamentals" or "Body of Liberties" (*Hildreth* "History U S," vol i) Dec "

First commencement at HARVARD COLLEGE 1642

Elder William Brewster of Plymouth d 18 Apr 1643

[He leaves a library of 275 substantial volumes.]

Four of the New England colonies, Massachusetts, Connecticut, Plymouth and New Haven, unite as the "United Colonies of New England," for mutual protection and assistance Articles of union signed at Boston 19 May, "

Massachusetts divided into 4 counties, viz, Suffolk, Middlesex, Essex, and Norfolk "

Martha's Vineyard settled by some people from Watertown "

James Britton and Mary Latham put to death for adultery "

A thousand acres of land planted to orchards and gardens, 15 000 other acres under general tillage, the number of neat cattle estimated at 12,000, and sheep at 3000 Money scarce, and bullets for a time pass for farthings "

Samuel Gorton is banished for heresy and disrespect to the magistrates and purchases a tract of land called Shawomet of the Narragansetts, and begins a settlement there "

Gorton and his companions summoned to Boston, refusing, a detachment of 40 men is sent to arrest them, Gorton and his followers, after an unsuccessful attempt to defend themselves, are taken to Boston and tried Gorton and 7 others are found guilty They are sentenced to confinement in 7 different towns, and there to be kept at hard labor, in irons, under pain of death if they attempt to publish or maintain any of their blasphemous and abominable heresies Nov "

They are ordered, at the next court, to depart out of the jurisdiction within 14 days, and not to return to Massachusetts or Shawomet under pain of death . Mch 1644

Rev John Wheelwright's sentence of banishment revoked upon his acknowledging his error and asking pardon Mch "

[He was banished for his support of Mrs. Anne Hutchinson Shortly after his sentence had been revoked he sailed for England, where he enjoyed the special regard of Cromwell After the Restoration he returned to New England, where he lived to be the oldest minister in New England He d 15 Nov 1679, aged 85 years.]

Roger Williams proceeds to England and obtains a charter, including the shores and islands of Narragansett bay west of Plymouth and south of Massachusetts as far as the Pequot river and country, to be known as the Providence plantation, the inhabitants to rule themselves as they shall find most suitable He also brought a letter of commendation from influential members of Parliament, sufficient to procure him safe conduct through Massachusetts Sept "

Anabaptists banished from Massachusetts

Free schools established at Roxbury and other towns, to be supported by voluntary allowance or by tax upon such as refuse . 1645

Law passed against slave stealing "

Mrs Oliver, for reproaching the magistrates, is adjudged to be whipped, and a cleft stick placed upon her tongue for speaking ill of the elders 1646

Twenty graduates from Harvard college from its commencement to "

Plymouth and Boston visited by capt. Cromwell, who from a common sailor had come to command 3 ships, and amassed wealth as a buccaneer or "fighter of the Spaniard," he spends money freely in both places "

John Eliot preaches his first sermon to the Indians near Newtown Corners, afterwards called Nonantum or "place of rejoicing" . 28 Oct "

Thomas Morton of "Merry Mount" dies at Agamenticus, Me "

Law passed requiring every township which contained 50 householders to have a school house and employ a teacher, and each town containing 1000 freeholders a grammar school. 1647

Epidemic visits New England, which "took them like a cold and a light fever with it," it extended throughout the country among Indians, English, French, and Dutch, among those [illegible]died of it were Mr Thomas Hooker of Hartford [illegible] Winthrop, wife of the governor, and over 50 others [illegible]usetts 14 June, "

J[illegible] aches to the Indians in their own tongue regu[illegible] [illegible]tertown and on the southern borders of Dor[illegible] 1648

Sa[illegible], after the second banishment from Massachu[illegible] proceeds to England to obtain redress, this he [illegible], and returning again settles at Shawomet, which he now names Warwick, after the earl of Warwick, who had assisted him 1648

Margaret Jones of Charlestown indicted for a witch, found guilty, and executed 15 June, "

[This was the first trial and execution for witchcraft in Massachusetts.—*Barry* "History of Massachusetts."]

Charles I. of England executed 30 Jan 1649

Gov. John Winthrop, in the 10th term of his office as governor of Massachusetts, dies, aged 63, leaving a fourth wife; he also left a journal commencing with his departure from England and continued up to the time of his death 26 Mch "

[This journal is one of the most valuable records of early New England history extant.]

John Endicott chosen governor to fill the vacant office May, "

William Pynchon of Springfield, having published a book upon "Redemption and Justification," the general court orders it to be publicly burned in the market place as containing doctrines of a dangerous tendency "

Thomas Dudley chosen governor 1650

John Clarke, a minister from the Baptist church at Newport, R. I., and 2 others are arrested at Lynn as Baptists and sent to Boston, where Clarke is sentenced to pay a fine of 20*l*. or be whipped; the fine is paid and he is released with the injunction to leave the colony 1651

Obadiah Holmes one of Clarke's companions is fined 30*l*.; not paying it, he gets 30 strokes with a 3-corded whip and is sent out of the colony "

Hugh Parsons and his wife Mary tried for witchcraft; Mrs. Parsons dies in prison, Parsons is acquitted "

[*Drake*, "History and Antiquities of Boston."]

Oliver Cromwell invites people of Massachusetts to Ireland "

French of Canada appeal to the people of New England for aid against the Iroquois without success. "

Mint set up at Boston (by the General court) which coins shillings, sixpences, and a few smaller coin 1652

[The date (1652) was not changed for 30 years. John Hull was first mint master, and being allowed 15 pence out of every 20 shillings coined, he amassed a large fortune.]

Pres. Dunster of Harvard college is indicted for disturbing infant baptism in the Cambridge church; is convicted, sentenced to a public admonition on lecture day, laid under bonds for good behavior and compelled to resign and throw himself on the mercies of the general court Oct 1654

[*Quincy*, "History of Harvard University."]

Charles Chauncy accepts presidency of Harvard college Nov "

Edward Winslow, one of the *Mayflower's* first passengers and governor of Plymouth, dies, aged 60, on shipboard near Hispaniola and is buried at sea 8 May, 1655

Mrs. Anne Hibbins, sister of gov. Bellingham and widow of a magistrate, is condemned and executed as a witch. 1656

Two women, Mary Fisher and Ann Austin (Quakers), arrive from England and are landed at Boston July, "

Eight more arrive in the *Speedwell* 7 Aug "

These were all imprisoned and banished without ceremony, and the masters of the vessels which brought them were placed under bonds to take them away "

At the next session of the general court a penalty of 100*l*. was imposed upon the master of any ship bringing Quakers within the jurisdiction, and all brought in were to be sent to jail, given 20 stripes, and kept at work until transported 4 Oct "

Every male Quaker convicted was for the first offence to lose one ear and for the second the other ear; every female was to be whipped, and for the third offence male and female were to have their tongues bored with red-hot irons; and by a majority of a single vote, and at the instance as is said of a clergyman, John Norton, the penalty of death was denounced upon all returning to the jurisdiction after being banished (*Barry*, "History of Massachusetts") 1658

[John Norton was born in Hertfordshire, Engl. Educated at Cambridge. He came to Plymouth, Oct. 1635 and became one of the most zealous of the Massachusetts clergy. D. in Boston 1663.]

[Plymouth, Connecticut, and the Dutch at Manhattan (but not the government at Providence, R. I.) adopt similar laws.]

[In reviewing these early scenes it is very apparent that in general the pioneer sectaries rather courted than avoided persecution, and this should not be lost sight of when those branded as persecutors are held up to universal scorn.—*Drake*, "History and Antiquities of Boston."]

Death of Oliver Cromwell 3 Sept "

William Robinson and Marmaduke Stevenson hung as returned Quakers 27 Oct. 1659

Town of Hadley settled "

Mary Dyer was to be hung (as a Quaker) with Robinson and Stevenson, but through the pleadings of her son she was reprieved and again banished; returning again to Massachusetts she is hung 1 June, 1660

Charles II. restored 29 May, "

Edward Whalley and William Goffe, the regicides, arrive at Boston 27 July, "

[They remain a short time, but a warrant being issued for their arrest, seek concealment in various places, and are secreted in the house of the rev. John Russell at Hadley, from 1664 until their death, that of Whalley occurring about 1678.]

Hugh Peters executed in England "

General court forbids celebration of Christmas under a penalty of 5*s*. "

William Ledea is tried, convicted, and banished as a Quaker, but returning, he is tried and hanged 14 Mch 1661

Representations of the Quakers in England caused Charles II. to require the government to desist from proceedings against them; a ship was immediately chartered, and Samuel Shattock, who had been banished from Massachusetts, was appointed to convey the king's letter to gov. Endicott; soon after receiving it gov. Endicott orders the discharge of all Quakers in prison 9 Sept 1661

[There were 28 persons (Quakers) in jail at Boston, one, Wenlock Christison, under sentence of death.]

Eliot finishes translation of New Testament into Indian "

Charles II. proclaimed sovereign in Massachusetts 8 Aug "

Sir Henry Vane executed in England 1662

Children of respectable people not "professors" allowed to be baptized, called the "Half-way Covenant," adopted "

[Strong opposition to this in many churches of Massachusetts, so that it was not permitted in all parishes.]

Metacomet or Philip, youngest son of Massasoit, sachem of the Wampanoags and friend of the English, becomes sachem of the tribe on the death of his brother Alexander "

Four ships, *Guinea*, 36 guns, *Elias*, 30 guns, *Martin*, 16 guns, and *William and Nicholas*, 10 guns, with 450 soldiers, are sent from England against the Dutch at New Netherland. They bring 4 commissioners to arrange affairs in New England, viz.: col. Richard Nicolls, sir Robert Carr, col. Geo. Cartwright, and Samuel Maverick, who reach Boston 23 July, 1664

Gov. Endicott d. (aged 77) 3 May, 1665

Massachusetts ordered by the English government to send agents to England to answer for refusing the commissioners jurisdiction; she replies evasively 1666

Baptists form a church in Boston, first in Massachusetts 1664-68

Church of Massachusetts debates with Baptists at Boston, 14 Apr 1668

[But the Baptists remain obstinate.]

Title of "reverend" first applied to the clergy of New England, 1670

Two young married Quaker women walk naked through the towns of Newbury and Salem, in emulation of the prophet Ezekiel, as a sign of the nakedness of the land 1671

George Fox, founder and apostle of the Quakers, comes to Rhode Island, but does not venture into Massachusetts 1672

Gov. Bellingham d. in office 1673

Population of Massachusetts proper was over 22,000, that of the Plymouth colony was probably not far from 7000, while the Indian population was less than 8000 in both territories (*George Bancroft*, "History of the United States") 1675

Three Indians of the Wampanoags are seized, taken to Plymouth, tried, and executed for the murder of one Sausaman, an Indian of the Massachusetts tribe June "

[*This is the proximate cause of King Philip's war.*]

Indians attack Swanzey and kill several persons. 24 June, "

Wampanoags, under Philip, attacked by colonists, leave Narragansett bay, unite with the Nipmuks and attack Brookfield; the residents, in the principal building, defend themselves from 2 to 5 Aug., when maj. Willard with a troop of horse routs the Indians. "

Hadley attacked by Indians on a fast day while the inhabitants are at church 1 Sept "

[Tradition states that col. William Goffe, the regicide, appeared and led the successful defence; he was then concealed at the house of rev. John Russell at Hadley.—See this story as told by *Scott*, in "Peveril of the Peak."]

Capt. Beers and his party ambushed near Northfield, he with 20 of his men killed 4 Sept "

Capt. Lothrop of Beverly, having been sent with 90 picked men, the "flower of Essex," to bring in the harvest of the settlements, is surprised by a large body of Indians at a small stream, now Bloody Brook, and totally defeated 18 Sept "

[*This was the severest loss the colonists had sustained.*]

Deerfield and Northfield abandoned by the inhabitants and burned by the Indians Sept. "

Commissioners meet and agree that 1000 troops must be levied by the united colonies, Massachusetts to raise 527, Plymouth 158, and Connecticut 315 9 Sept. "

[Gov. Josiah Winslow of Plymouth to command the whole.]

Springfield attacked and about 50 buildings burned, but the Indians are driven off 5 Oct. "

Hatfield attacked 19 Oct. "

It was resolved to regard the Narragansetts as enemies, and to make a winter campaign against them 2 Nov "

Several bodies of troops from Massachusetts, Connecticut, and Plymouth, numbering about 1000, unite about 15 miles from the Narragansett fort. 18 Dec "

They spend the night in the open air, and after wading through the snow from daybreak until an hour after noon they reach the edge of the swamp and immediately commence the attack; the action was bloody and long, but the fort was carried and the Indians routed and the whole place burned; over a thousand Indians were killed and captured, the English lost about 200 killed and wounded and 6 captains killed; this "Swamp fight" occurred Sunday 19 Dec "

[The military strength of the formidable Narragansett tribe was irreparably broken in this conflict.—*Palfrey*, "History of New England."]

Indians attack Lancaster, and after killing all the men carry the women and children into captivity 5 Feb 1676

[The narrative of one of the captives, Mrs. Rowlandson, the wife of the minister, is still preserved.]

Six hundred additional troops ordered to be levied 8 Feb "

Medfield surprised and laid in ashes. 21 Feb "

Weymouth, within 18 miles of Boston, attacked and 7 buildings burned 24 Feb "

[This is as near as the war approached Boston.]

Groton attacked 3, 9, 13 Mch. "

Town of Plymouth assaulted and 12 persons killed.......Mch. 1676
Warwick burned and Providence partially destroyed..17 Mch. "
[The aged Roger Williams accepts a commission as captain for the defence of the town he had founded.—*Hildreth*, "History of the United States."]

Capt. Pierce of Scituate, with about 50 men and 20 Indians, routed near Seekonk; his entire party cut off.......26 Mch. "
Marlborough attacked and partially burned.......... " "
Seekonk laid in ashes.............................28 Mch. "
Canonchet, sachem of the Narragansetts, captured......9 Apr. "
Sudbury attacked and partially burned; capt. Wadsworth of Milton and his party surprised and totally defeated..21 Apr. "
[This is known as the Sudbury fight.]

Plymouth again attacked..........................11 May, "
Indians defeated at Turner's Falls, on the Connecticut, by capt. Turner, who is afterwards killed and his command partially defeated by the arrival of other Indians....18 May, "
Scituate threatened and partially destroyed..........20 May, "
Indians again attack Hadley, but are repulsed........12 June, "
King Philip's allies deserting him, he with a few of his own tribe moves back to Mount Hope in his own territory, July, "
Here, surrounded in a swamp by troops under capt. Church, he is shot by an Indian while attempting escape....12 Aug. "
[His little son sold into slavery.]
[Indians never recovered from this blow, but rapidly dispersed. Of the colonists, 600 were killed, almost every family losing a member; 13 towns wholly destroyed, and many others sustained much damage, over 600 houses being burned; expense of the war computed at $500,000.—*Barry*, "Hist. of Mass."]

Edward Randolph arrives at Boston as a special messenger from the English government to make minute inquiries into the condition of the country......................10 June, "
He sails for England, 30 July, and presents to the English government a description of New England, headed "An Answer to Several Heads of Inquiry concerning the Present State of New England" (see *Palfrey*, "History of New England," vol. iii. p. 296)...............................12 Oct. "
William Stoughton and Peter Bulkely sent to the king as agents by Massachusetts with an address...........30 Oct. "
Proceedings of England against Massachusetts charter....Jan. 1677
Massachusetts purchases the claims of Gorges to Maine for about $6000.......................................6 May, "
Gov. Leverett dies in office........................16 Mch. 1679
Simon Bradstreet made governor, then 76 years of age...May, "
Edward Randolph comes over as collector of customs at Boston, arrives at Boston...............................Dec. "
Stoughton and Bulkely return to Boston, unsuccessful in their efforts to conciliate the English government...........Dec. "
Massachusetts becomes the lord proprietary of Maine, and in obedience to an ordinance of the general court Massachusetts proceeds *to organize the government of Maine*........ 1680
Edward Randolph sends over a "Memorial" to the king, urging proceedings against the charter of Massachusetts........ 1683
Charter of Massachusetts Bay vacated in England....18 June, 1684
Charles II. dies..................................6 Feb. 1685
King James II. proclaimed in Boston.................20 Apr. "
Copy of the judgment of the forfeiture of the charter of Massachusetts received at Boston..........................2 July, "
[This charter had guided the colony for 55 years.]

Plymouth colony divided into 3 counties, viz.: Plymouth, Bristol, and Barnstable.. "
Election in Massachusetts..........................12 May, 1686
Provisional government constituted with Joseph Dudley as president..14 May, "
First Episcopal church organized in Boston.................. "
Sir Edmund Andros arrives at Boston in the *Kingfisher*, a 50-gun ship, bearing a commission for the government of all New England.......................................20 Dec. "
Charter government is publicly displaced by arbitrary commission, popular representation abolished, and the press subjected to censorship....................................... "
Legal consolidation of New England..................29 Dec. 1687
Gov. Andros's activity in oppressive legislation...........Jan. 1688
Increase Mather sent to England by the citizens of Massachusetts to lay before the king a petition of grievances; embarks, though opposed by government..............7 Apr. "
Extension of New England to Delaware bay; Andros made governor of all the territory; seat of government at Boston, the lieutenant-governor to reside at New York..........Apr. "
News of the landing of the prince of Orange (afterwards William III. of England) in England received in Boston, 4 Apr. 1689
People of Boston and vicinity overthrow the government and arrest gov. Andros and his adherents...............18 Apr. "
Provisional government established with Simon Bradstreet as governor, then in his 86th year......................20 Apr. "
William and Mary proclaimed.........................29 May, "
War with the French and Indians, known as King William's war, commences... "
Gov. Andros impeached and sent to England.........27 June, "
Edward Randolph a persistent disturber of the peace of Massachusetts in the interest of the government of England..1676–89
Fleet fitted out by Massachusetts against Port Royal sails from Boston under sir William Phipps......................28 Apr. 1690
[Phipps was born at Woolwich, Me., 1651. He was one of 26 children. Under patronage of the duke of Albemarle he was successful in recovering 300,000*l.* of wrecked treasure, of which he received about 17,000*l.* for his share. He was knighted and made high sheriff of New England.]

Attack on Port Royal is successful, and the fleet returns with spoils covering cost of the whole expedition.......30 May, 1690
Expedition against Canada—New England and New York unite. Gov. Winthrop of Connecticut commands the land forces, and sir William Phipps the fleet. The expedition is a total failure.. "
First paper money issued in Massachusetts to pay the troops in the Canada expedition.................................. "
John Eliot, "the apostle to the Indians," d. (aged 86)......... "
Second charter granted Massachusetts by England......7 Oct. 1691
New charter received.. 1692
[Under the new charter Massachusetts' jurisdiction was enlarged to include the Plymouth colony and Maine; the crown reserved the appointments of governor, lieutenant-governor, and secretary; the right of suffrage, limited under the old charter to church-members, now admitted all inhabitants possessing a freehold of the annual value of 40*s.*, or personal property to the amount of 40*l.*—*Hildreth*, "Hist. of the U. S.," vol. ii. p. 143.]

First appearance of the witchcraft delusion at Salem, at the house of the rev. Samuel Parris (WITCHCRAFT).........Mch. "
Sir William Phipps arrives at Boston as first governor of the new province......................................14 May, "
Post-office established in Boston.............................. 1693
Indians attack Haverhill..............................15 Mch. 1697
[Mrs. Hannah Dustin was captured with her nurse and young infant—her husband escaping with 7 of his children; she marched with the Indians over 150 miles, but with the nurse and a boy captive succeeded in killing and scalping all of the party, some 12 in charge, except one boy and an old woman, who escaped. They retraced their steps in safety. The general court granted them 50*l.* and they received valuable presents from others. This escape was famed throughout the country as one of the most remarkable on record.]

Gov. Bradstreet dies at Salem, aged 95..............27 Mch. "
Peace of Ryswick proclaimed at Boston..............10 Dec. "
Capt. Kidd seized in Boston as a pirate and sent to England (NEW YORK).. 1699
Earl of Bellamont supersedes William Stoughton as governor of Massachusetts, and arrives at Boston...........26 May, "
[Under the old charter the governors had received scarce 120*l.* per annum; and neither Phipps or Stoughton had been paid much more, but in 14 months the general court voted gov. Bellamont 2700*l.*, 1699–1700.—*Hildreth*, "Hist of U. S.," vol. ii. p. 201.]

Boston contains 1000 houses and 7000 people............... 1700
Joseph Dudley appointed governor.............................. 1702
French and Indians attack and burn Deerfield..........28 Feb. 1704
[There were about 40 killed and 100 taken prisoners. Among the captives was the rev. Mr. Williams and family; his wife was soon after killed by the Indians. The rest of the family were taken to Montreal, where they remained until Oct. 1706, when the survivors were sent to Boston. His daughter Eunice, 10 years of age, could not be ransomed from the Indians, and was left behind; she afterwards married an Indian. She visited her relatives after the war but would not remain, and returned to her Indian home. Eleazar Williams, "the 'Lost prince' of France," was a grandson of this union, if descendant at all.] WILLIAMS, ELEAZAR.

Boston *News-Letter*, the first newspaper in the British colonies, was published in Boston (John Campbell, editor)....24 Apr. "
[The first sheet of the first number was taken from the press by chief-justice Sewell, to show to pres. Williard of Harvard college as a curiosity in the colony. The paper lived 72 years. *The only complete file is with the N. Y. Hist. Soc.*]

Benjamin Franklin b. in Boston......................17 Jan. 1706
Haverhill again attacked by the French and Indians...29 Aug. 1708
Port Royal taken from the French by the English.......5 Oct. 1710
[Name changed from Port Royal to Annapolis, in honor of queen Anne.]

Expedition against Quebec and Canada leaves Boston..30 July, 1711
[The fleet, consisting of 15 ships of war and 40 transports, is under command of sir Hovenden Walker, and carries 7 regiments of veterans from Marlborough's army, and a battalion of marines. 8 vessels of this fleet are wrecked in the river St. Lawrence on the night of 22 Aug. 1711, and the remainder return, having accomplished nothing.]

Boundary between Massachusetts and Connecticut located.... 1713
Schooners invented and built at Cape Ann................... 1714
Queen Anne of England d...........................1 Aug. "
George I., elector of Hanover, succeeds her................... "
Elizabeth Goose marries Thomas Fleet of Boston............ 1715
[The mother of this Elizabeth Goose is said to have been the veritable "Mother Goose" of "Mother Goose Melodies for Children." See Hurd & Houghton's edition of the same, 1870; also *New England Historical and Genealogical Register*, Apr. 1873, pp. 144 and 311.]

Population of Massachusetts 94,000 and 2000 negroes.......... "
Samuel Shute arrives at Boston as governor...........4 Oct. 1716
Great snow-storm; snow from 10 to 20 feet deep...20–24 Feb 1717
Potatoes first introduced at Andover........................ 1719
Boston Gazette, the second newspaper started in Boston (William Brooker, publisher)..........................21 Dec. "
Small-pox breaks out in Massachusetts..................Apr. 1721
[Out of 5889 persons who were attacked in Boston, 844 died.—*Barry*, "History of Massachusetts."]

Great opposition to inoculation. Cotton Mather, one of the ministers of Boston, interests himself in urging inoculation, recently introduced into Europe. Dr. Boylston consents to the experiment upon his children and servants; he was one of the very few physicians of that time who encouraged or practised it, 100 inoculated during the year 1721

New England Courant started in Boston, with James Franklin, brother of Benjamin Franklin as editor 7 Aug "

Benjamin Franklin leaves Boston for Philadelphia Oct 1723

George I of England d 11 June, 1727

George II succeeds him " "

William Burnet arrives at Boston as governor July, 1728

Dispute between gov Burnet and the House regarding a fixed salary, the House refusing it 1728-29

Gov Burnet d 7 Sept 1729

Jonathan Belcher a native of Massachusetts, appointed governor, and arrives at Boston Aug 1730

Dispute concerning a fixed salary still continues 1730-31

Worcester county formed 1731

Massachusetts and New Hampshire boundary fixed "

England forbids the colonies to export hats 1732

First Freemason lodge in America established in Boston 1733

George Whitefield (WHITEFIELDITES) in Massachusetts "The Great Awakening" (religious) 1740

[*Palfrey* "History of New England" vol v chap viii]

Gov Belcher superseded by William Shirley as governor of Massachusetts 14 Aug 1741

[Gov Belcher was the last governor of the two provinces of Massachusetts and New Hampshire]

Gov Shirley renews the claim for a fixed salary, which is finally decided in favor of the House 1742

[This is a pronounced victory of the people]

Peter Faneuil builds "Faneuil Hall" and presents it to the town of Boston "

England at war with France commenced 31 Mch 1744

Expedition against Louisburg organized by gov Shirley, under command of William Pepperell 1745

[The fort at Louisburg had cost France 200,000*l*. It was a standing threat to New England seamen]

Troops—of which Massachusetts furnished 3250, Connecticut 600, and New Hampshire 300—rendezvous at Canseau, 1 Apr "

Commodore Warren joins them at Canseau with 5 ships of war and 6 frigates 23 Apr "

Combined forces land a short distance from the fort 29 Apr "

Louisburg capitulates 17 June, "

[Prizes and stores obtained by the English amounted to nearly 1 000,000*l*., 148 cannon 6 mortars and 76 large siege guns It was called the "Dunkirk" of America]

William Pepperell made a baronet and com Warren a vice admiral for their services "

French fleet of 40 ships of war, besides transports bearing a well appointed army of veterans for the purpose of recovering Louisburg come into the American waters Sept. 1746

[This expedition is a disastrous failure, through storms, sickness, death of commanders, and dissensions, and returns to France, having accomplished nothing]

Riot in Boston owing to impressment of citizens by com Knowles of the British navy, then in Boston harbor with his squadron, the rioters seized several officers of his command as hostages, gov Shirley took refuge in the castle 17 Nov 1747

[The officers were finally released, and most of the impressed men sent back —*Hildreth*, "U S History," vol ii p. 402]

Louisburg restored to France by the treaty of Aix la Chapelle, 7 Oct 1748

Gov Shirley goes to England on leave for 1 year Sept. 1749

Spencer Phipps acting governor in absence of Shirley "

Massachusetts extricates herself from the insolvency of more than 50 years, by appropriating to her debt 183,650*l*, received from England for her outlay in the expedition against Louisburg, this came over in solid coin, and 17 trucks laden with 217 chests full of Spanish dollars, and 10 trucks bearing 100 casks of coined copper were driven up King (now State) street (*Palfrey*, "History of New England," vol v) Sept "

Sir William Pepperell, Thomas Hutchinson, James Otis, and 2 others, as commissioners, meet delegates from the eastern Indian tribes at Falmouth (now Portland, Me), and renew the treaty made a quarter of a century before 16 Oct. "

Small pox again visits Boston 1752

[Of 2100 persons inoculated with it, only 31 died, of the 5550 taken without inocculation 514 died]

Gov Shirley, now past the age of 60, returns to Massachusetts, bringing with him a young French Catholic girl as his wife 1753

Expedition against the French in Nova Scotia sails from Boston under command of gen John Winslow 20 May, 1755

Acadians or "French Neutrals" at Grand Pre, on the northwestern coast of Nova Scotia, are stripped of everything, conveyed on board the English vessels, carried away, and scattered among the English colonists (ACADIA) Sept. "

Gov Shirley, being recalled, sails for England 25 Sept 1756

Thomas Pownall appointed governor . 3 Aug 1757

Sir William Pepperell commissioned lieut. gen. of the Massachusetts forces "

Louisburg again besieged and taken by the English, 2 June-26 July, 1758

Gov Pownall succeeded by Francis Bernard, who arrives at Boston . . 3 Aug. 1760

George II of England d 25 Oct. "

George III succeeds to the throne " "

Gov Bernard appoints Thomas Hutchinson chief justice of Massachusetts . Dec. "

James Otis's speech against the "Writs of Assistance" 1761

["American Independence was then and there born."—*Barry*, "History of Massachusetts."]

MAS

Dispute between gov Bernard and the House of Representatives on the right of originating taxes 1761

James Otis publishes a pamphlet entitled "A Vindication of the Conduct of the House of Representatives of the Province of Massachusetts Bay" 1762

[In this he lays down a series of political maxims, a part of which were 1 God made all men naturally equal, 2 The ideas of earthly superiority, pre eminence, and grandeur are educational, at least acquired, not innate, 3 Kings were, and plantation governors should be, made for the good of the people, and not the people for them, 4 No government has a right to make hobby horses asses, and slaves of the subject nature having made sufficient of the two former for all the lawful purposes of man, but none of the last, which infallibly proves them unnecessary, 5 Though most governments are *de facto* arbitrary and consequently the curse and scandal of human nature, yet none are *de jure* arbitrary —*Palfrey* "History of New England" vol v]

Parliament subjects various articles for the first time to duties on exportation from, or importation into the colonies passed, Apr 1764

Citizens of Boston assemble in town meeting on hearing of this act, instructions to their representatives in the general court are prepared by Samuel Adams May, "

Gov Bernard replies to the Lords of Trade Sept "

[After speaking of the trade, manufactures etc in Massachusetts, he says "It was an unfortunate error, in forming this government, to leave the council to be elected by the representatives of the people He would have the councillors appointed by the king for life, and some title as baron or baronet, annexed to the office The people in general he wrote, are as well inclined to his majesty s government and as well satisfied with their subordination to Great Britain, as any colony in America"—*Palfrey*, "History of New England"]

Duties laid by Parliament on foreign molasses imported into British colonies, called the Sugar or Molasses act "

Stamp act passed by Parliament Mch 1765

[This act which was to go into effect in the colonies 1 Nov 1765 levied in 63 sections on British subjects in America specific sums, for each of the common transactions of business Deeds, bonds, notes of hand, indentures insurance policies, leases, contracts of sale, were not to be enforced by courts unless written on stamped paper, bought of the officers of the crown Without stamped wills testamentary disposition would be void, without stamped receipts, debts could not be acquitted, vessels at sea without clearances written on stamped paper were liable to seizure and confiscation if they fell in with a king's ship Only stamped newspapers could be exposed for sale without stamped certificates marriages could not be lawfully contracted Unstamped writs and executions had no force or meaning In short, the American citizen must be daily paying money into the British treasury at its stamp office or in respect to much of the protection which society undertakes to afford, he was an outlaw —*Palfrey*, "History of New England," vol v p 289]

Andrew Oliver, secretary of Massachusetts, accepts the office of distributer of stamps for the province Aug "

Oliver hung in effigy on a tree ("Liberty Tree") corner of Orange and Essex streets, Boston, and in the evening his house was damaged by the mob 14 Aug "

Lieut. gov Hutchinson s house mobbed and everything destroyed in it, among other things many MSS relating to the history of the province, which he had been 30 years in collecting, and which could not be replaced, were lost, 26 Aug "

Vessel arrives at Boston with the stamps 25 Sept "

[These stamps were deposited at Castle William and remained there.]

Delegates from 9 Anglo American colonies meet at New York, 7 Oct "

[This congress was composed of 26 members. From New York, 4, Rhode Island and Delaware each 2, Massachusetts, Connecticut, New Jersey, Pennsylvania, Maryland, South Carolina, each 3. Thomas Ruggles of Massachusetts was chosen president of the congress The manifestoes brought out at this congress were "A Declaration of the Rights and Grievances of the Colonists of America," an address to the king, a memorial to the House of Lords, and a petition to the House of Commons The tone of all of these was loyal]

Stamp act goes into effect. 1 Nov "

[Under this act the courts were closed, business was suspended, and a universal stillness reigned Its provisions were stringent and as the people refused to use the stamps, nothing remained but to abide the consequences]

Andrew Oliver is compelled to resign his office 17 Dec "

Population of Massachusetts, 238,423 "

Dr Benjamin Franklin meets commons in committee of the whole, to consider petitions from America 3 Feb 1766

Repeal of the Stamp act 18 Mch "

[Repeal was carried in the commons by a vote of 275 against 167, and in the House of Lords 105 against 71]

News of the repeal received at Boston 16 May, "

[The news was brought over in the *Harrison*, capt Shubael Coffin, about 6 weeks from London —*Drake*, "History and Antiquities of Boston"]

News of the repeal celebrated in Boston 19 May, "

General court of Massachusetts sends a circular letter to all the American colonies. This letter asks the colonies to co operate in obtaining a redress of grievances 11 Feb. 1768

Massachusetts House of Representatives consists of upwards of 100 members, by far the most numerous assembly in America........ 1768

Seizure of the sloop *Liberty*, belonging to John Hancock, on charge of smuggling, occasions a great riot........*10 June*, "

Arrival of a squadron of 7 vessels from Halifax, with the 14th, 29th, and a part of the 59th regiments of British regulars. These troops, under the command of gen. Thomas Gage, are landed in Boston........28 Sept. "

Gov. Bernard recalled, and embarks for England, regretted by none........31 July, 1769

[He had been governor of the province for 9 years, and in that time had done more than all the other governors combined to inflame the jealousy of the ministry, to irritate the people over whom he ruled, and to strengthen the spirit of discord and disunion.—*Barry*, "History of Massachusetts."]

James Otis severely wounded in an affray at the British coffee-house on King st., now State st., in Boston........5 Sept. "

[These injuries ultimately led to his derangement.]

Gov. Bernard is succeeded by Thomas Hutchinson as governor, "

[He was b. at Boston, Sept. 9, 1711; d. near London, Engl., 3 June, 1780. He was descended through a line of reputable men from Anne Hutchinson.]

Affray in Richardson's house in Boston; the boy "Snider" is mortally wounded by a shot from the house—the first victim (*Barry*, "History of Massachusetts")........22 Feb. 1770

Affray at Gray's rope-walk in Boston between citizens and the British soldiers........2 Mch. "

BOSTON MASSACRE........5 Mch. "

[Three persons killed and 8 wounded. This day is memorable in the annals of the whole country.]

Graduates of Harvard college take degrees in "homespun"... "

David Everett, journalist, b. at Princeton, Mass........29 Mch. "

[Author of "You'd scarce expect one of my age
To speak in public on the stage," etc.

Written while teaching a grammar-school at Ipswich.]

Castle William, in Boston harbor, delivered into the hands of the king's troops by gov. Hutchinson........10 Sept. "

Population of the state, 262,680........ "

Gov. Hutchinson's salary, 2000*l.*, paid by the English government. He thus becomes independent of the province...... 1772

Ministry of England and the East India company secure an act relieving the company from paying duties on tea sent to America, thus encouraging its sale in the colonies. Aware of the danger of giving success to this insidious manœuvre and of permitting a precedent of taxation thus to be established, various methods were adopted by the colonists to elude the stroke (*Henry Sherman*, "Governmental History of the U. S.")........10 May, 1773

Arrival at Boston of the first of the tea-ships, with 114 chests of tea........28 Nov. "

Two others arrive early in........Dec. "

At the close of a spirited meeting of the citizens at Faneuil hall, between 50 and 60 men, disguised as Indians, take possession of the 3 tea-ships in the harbor, and empty 340 chests of tea into the bay during the evening of......16 Dec. "

New York and Massachusetts boundary established........ "

Passage of "Boston Port bill" by Parliament........7 Mch. 1774

[Under this bill nothing could be unloaded at this port but stores for his majesty's use, and fuel and food for Boston. This was to remain in force until the East India company had been indemnified for the loss of their tea, recently destroyed, and also reasonable satisfaction made to the officers of his majesty's revenue, and others who had suffered by riots and insurrections.—*Palfrey*, "History of New England."]

Failure to repeal the tax on tea in the British Parliament, Apr. "

Gen. Thomas Gage appointed governor........17 May, "

British Parliament passes 2 acts, virtually repealing the charter of Massachusetts. One, entitled "An act for the better regulating the government of Massachusetts Bay," and the other, an act for the more impartial administration of justice in said province. The first provided that the councillors, who were chosen by the representatives annually, should be appointed by the king, and should serve according to his majesty's pleasure; that the judges, sheriffs, and other civil officers should be appointed by the governor; that juries should be summoned by the sheriff, and that town-meetings, except the annual ones and other public meetings, should not be held without the permission of the governor. The other act provided that offenders against the laws might be carried to other colonies or to England for trial. Both bills pass Parliament and are approved........20 May, "

[It was the attempted execution of these laws that became the immediate occasion of the commencement of hostilities between the American colonists and England.—*Frothingham*, "History of the Siege of Boston."]

Port bill goes into effect........1 June, "

[The Port bill, in closing the harbor to navigation, struck a heavy blow at all the inhabitants of Boston. Business of all kinds came to a standstill; men of property received no rents, mechanics had no employment, laboring men could earn no wages. Stagnation soon brought actual want.—*Palfrey*, "History of New England," vol. v. p. 531.]

Gov. Thomas Hutchinson embarks for England, forever leaving the country which gave him birth........1 June, "

[He passed his last days a slighted and saddened man, longing for the native home which had closed against him, and as little sustained by the good-will of those to whom he had given his unsuccessful service as by any consciousness of upright endeavors in behalf of a righteous cause.—*Palfrey*, "History of New England."]

MAS

4th or "King's" regiment and the 49th of his majesty's forces land at Boston........14 June, 1774

5th and 38th arrive........5 July, "

59th arrives........6 Aug. "

First Continental Congress meets at Philadelphia......5 Sept. "

[Delegates from Massachusetts were: Thomas Cushing, James Bowdoin, Samuel Adams, John Adams, and Robert Treat Paine.]

Powder seized by British troops at Charlestown; about 13 tons, 1 Sept. "

Gov. Gage erects fortifications on the neck which commands the entrance to Boston........5 Sept. "

A provincial congress formed in Massachusetts, at Salem, adjourned to Concord, and chose John Hancock president, and Benjamin Lincoln, a farmer of Hingham and afterwards a major-general in the Revolutionary army, secretary, 1 Oct. "

[This congress constituted a permanent "Committee of Safety," with comprehensive military powers; it made a complete organization of the militia, embodied a force of minute-men, consisting of one quarter part of the force of the colony, and appointed to the chief command Jedediah Preble, Artemas Ward, and Seth Pomeroy; it proceeded to carry on the government; collectors of taxes were ordered to pay no more money to the late treasurer of the province, but to hand over all future collections to a treasurer appointed by the congress.]

Popular current in England sets strongly against America.... "

Josiah Tucker, dean of Gloucester, Engl., claims, after presenting different methods of meeting the difficulties between the colonists and England, that there remains but one wise solution, and that is to declare the North American colonies to be a free and independent people (*George Bancroft*, "History of the United States")........ "

Provincial congress of Massachusetts, consisting of upwards of 300 members, meet at Cambridge........1 Feb. 1775

Gov. Gage sends a detachment of soldiers to Salem to seize some cannon said to be deposited there; they are met by a party of militia, but no collision takes place........26 Feb. "

Gen. Gage has about 4000 British troops in Boston......1 Apr. "

British troops, about 800 strong, under lieut.-col. Smith, start towards Concord about 10 o'clock P.M........18 Apr. "

Paul Revere's ride to notify the country of the march of the British troops towards Concord, night of........18 Apr. "

Maj. Pitcairn with the advance at Lexington, about 12 miles northwest from Boston, is met by about 60 militia under capt. Parker; here the first collision takes place between British troops and Americans, early in the morning of, 19 Apr. "

[Here the Americans lose 8 killed and 10 wounded. The British troops proceed to Concord, and after destroying some property begin their march back to Boston. Near Lexington they are reinforced by about 1000 men and 2 field-pieces under lord Percy. The retreat is continued with constant fighting until they reach Charlestown and are protected by the guns of the ships of war. The Americans in this first battle lost 49 killed, 39 wounded, and 5 missing; the British 73 killed, 174 wounded, and 26 missing. This was the commencement of the war of the Revolution. See for the losses in this battle, *Frothingham*, "History of the Siege of Boston."]

George Washington appointed commander-in-chief of the American forces by the Continental Congress......15 June, "

Gen. Gage (lately reinforced) has at Boston about 10,000 men; gens. Clinton, Burgoyne, and Howe are also there......June, "

Massachusetts council of war decides to fortify Bunker hill, 16 June, "

[This is undertaken the same night by 1200 men under col. William Prescott, Thomas Knowlton, and capt. Samuel Gridley, the chief engineer; Breed's hill is, however, fortified instead.]

Observing these works, gen. Gage attempts to prevent their completion; the British troops, 3000 strong, under sir William Howe and gen. Robert Pigot, attack the Americans about 3 o'clock P.M........17 June, "

[Twice repulsed, the third time they succeed in driving the Americans (whose ammunition is exhausted) from their position about 5 o'clock P.M. The American troops slowly retire without pursuit across Charlestown Neck and occupy a position on Prospect hill, which they proceed to fortify. The loss of the Americans was 115 killed (among them dr. Joseph Warren, who had just been appointed major-general), 305 wounded, and 30 captured; British loss was 226 killed and 828 wounded. Maj. Pitcairn, who was with the British troops at Lexington, was mortally wounded here.]

[Result of this battle was the best possible end of the conflict.—*Carrington*, "Battles of the American Revolution."]

Charlestown burned by the British the same day; estimated loss, 118,000*l.*—*Frothingham*, "History of the Siege of Boston."

Gen. Washington reaches the army at Cambridge......2 July, "

Gen. Gage recalled; he sails for England........10 Oct. "

[Gen. Howe in command of the British forces in Boston.]

A heavy cannonade is opened upon Boston from all the American batteries, evening of........2 Mch. 1776

Americans occupy Dorchester Heights and throw up strong intrenchments, night of........4 Mch. "

British evacuate Boston........17 Mch. "

Seven thousand soldiers, 4000 seamen, and 1500 families of loyalists sail for Halifax 17 Mch 1776
Americans enter Boston 20 Mch "
Reading of the Declaration of Independence in Boston from the balcony of the state house 18 July, "
[At the same time the king's arms are removed]
Massachusetts quota of troops to serve for 3 years or during the war is 15 battalions 10 Sept "
Fourth of July, the anniversary of the Declaration of Independence, observed in Boston 1777
Massachusetts apportionment of the war debt, $820,000 Oct "
[Largest apportionment of any of the states]
Gen Gates supersedes gen Heath in command of the forces stationed in Massachusetts Nov 1778
State constitution framed by a convention met at Boston, 1 Sept 1779, labor completed 2 Mch 1780, submitted to the people and ratified 1780
Academy of Arts and Sciences incorporated at Boston, James Bowdoin president 4 May, "
"Dark day" Friday 19 May, "
[This darkness extended throughout most of New England, partial in New York and New Jersey, the cause of the darkness not well known]
John Hancock first governor "
Population of the state, 316 900 "
Phillips academy, Andover, founded, 21 Apr 1778, incorporated 4 Oct "
Definite treaty of peace with England signed 3 Sept. 1783
Population of Massachusetts Whites, 353 623, blacks, 4377 1784
First bank under the state constitution established, known as the Massachusetts bank "
Massachusetts mint established 1786
[Discontinued after adoption of Federal constitution]
First symptoms of "Shays's rebellion" at a convention in the county of Worcester 15 Aug "
[The dissatisfaction of the people originated in hardships at the close of the war, through the poverty of the country, they complained of much which they thought should be righted by the government Daniel Shays, who became leader of the insurgents, had been a captain in the army of the Revolution and had resigned]
This affair culminates at Springfield, when Shays attempts to capture the arsenal there 25 Jan 1787
[After this failure the insurgents rapidly disperse Shays and the other ringleaders at a subsequent date petition for pardon, which the state grants, Shays dies in Sparta N Y, 29 Sept 1825 aged 78, he received a pension from the U S government from 1820]
Massachusetts convention to ratify the Constitution of the U S convenes at Boston 9 Jan 1788
[Gov Hancock chosen president of the convention]
Constitution is ratified by a vote of 187-168 (CONSTITUTION OF THE UNITED STATES) 6 Feb "
[The small majority in favor of ratification is proof that the Constitution did not meet the approval of all —*Barry*, "History of Massachusetts"]
Slave trade prohibited in Massachusetts 26 Mch "
John Adams elected vice president of the U S. 1789
Pres Washington visits Boston 24 Oct. "
Williams college at Williamstown, Berkshire county, founded 1790
[Incorporated 22 June, 1793. Congregational]
John Hancock d at Quincy, aged 56 8 Oct 1793
Middlesex canal projected "
John Adams president of the U S 4 Mch 1797
Frigate *Constitution* "Old Ironsides," built at Boston (NAVY) 1799
Bradford academy (for women), Bradford, opened 1803
Andover Theological seminary (Congregational) opened 1808
State averse to war with England. The legislature in an address to the people, "declare themselves unable to find any satisfactory solution of it, but in an habitual and impolitic predilection for France" (*Hildreth*, "Hist U S") 2 Mch 1809
Massachusetts agrees to a Remonstrance, in which she denounces the perseverance in the war after the repeal of the British orders as impolitic and unjust 15 July, 1813
British land at Wareham and burn several vessels and a factory, they also land at Scituate, a few miles from Boston, and throw the whole coast into fresh alarm A million dollars is appropriated by the legislature for defence June, 1814
Gov Strong calls out 10,000 militia to defend the state "
A circular letter to the New England states against the continuance of the war, sent out by Massachusetts 17 Oct "
State sends 12 delegates to the HARTFORD CONVENTION 15 Dec. "
News of peace with Great Britain brought to New York by the British sloop of war *Favorite* 11 Feb 1815
[News conveyed to Boston in 32 hours, "thought to be a great effort of speed"]
Recorder, published by Nathaniel Willis or Sidney Edward Morse (disputed), No 76 State street, Boston 3 Jan 1816
[The first religious paper published in the world]
Maine separated from Massachusetts and erected into a state 1820
Constitution of the state revised "
Amherst college, Amherst, dedicated 18 Sept 1821
[Rev Zephaniah Swift Moore, D D, first president.]
Massachusetts Society organized to aid in the suppression of the slave trade 1822
Daniel Webster represents Boston in Congress 1823
Corner-stone of Bunker Hill monument laid 17 June, 1825
[Gen Lafayette present, Daniel Webster orator]
Journal of Education, afterwards the *Annals*, started in Boston, the first of its kind in the U S 1826

MAS

John Adams d at Quincy 4 July, 1826
Railroad (the first in the U S) 3 miles long from the granite quarries of Quincy to Neponset river, commenced "
Road finished 1827
Abbott academy (for women), Andover established 1829
Massachusetts obtains from the U S $430,748 26, for services of militia during the war of 1812-14 31 May, "
Lloyd Garrison first published the *Liberator* (anti slavery), Boston (SLAVERY IN THE U S) 1 Jan 1831
Burning of the St Ursula convent at Mount Benedict by a mob on the night of 11 Aug 1834
[This outrage was committed on the strength of a rumor that Mary St John Harrison, an inmate, had been abducted or secreted where she could not be found]
Alonzo D Phillips of Springfield obtains the first patent for the manufacture of matches in the U S 1836
Board of Education established and organized 29 June, 1837
Mount Holyoke college (for the education of women), South Hadley, opened "
Normal school at Framingham and Westfield opened 1839
Normal school at Bridgewater opened 1840
Arrest of George Latimer in Boston as a slave 1842
[Liberated on payment of $400 by citizens of Boston]
College of the Holy Cross founded at Worcester 1843
Completion and dedication of Bunker Hill monument with imposing ceremonies 17 June, "
[Pres Tyler present, Daniel Webster orator]
Samuel Hoar, sent by the state to Charleston, to test the constitutionality of the act of South Carolina, whereby any negro on any vessel entering her ports was to be lodged in jail Mr Hoar reaches Charleston 28 Nov 1844
[He is obliged to leave the city by force a few days afterwards —*Greeley*, "American Conflict"]
Gov Briggs sends to the legislature Mr Hoar's report It is referred to a committee who report on it 3 Feb 1845
[It is unanimously adopted and sent out to the country "This report sets forth clearly the whole case in issue, and justifies, by indisputable facts and impregnable arguments, the course Massachusetts had pursued"—*Wilson*, "Rise and Fall of the Slave Power in America"]
Capt. Henry Purkitt, the last survivor of the "Boston Mohawk Tea Party," d (aged 91) 3 Mch 1846
John Quincy Adams d at Washington, aged 80 23 Feb 1848
Water introduced in Boston through new water works, 25 Oct. "
Shadrach, colored waiter, arrested as a slave in Boston, 15 Feb 1851
[Rescued by colored persons and sent to Canada]
Thomas Sims, a fugitive slave, arrested in Boston and sent back into slavery 12 Apr "
[He is sold in New Orleans to a brick mason of Vicksburg, from whence he escapes in 1863 to the besieging army of gen Grant, who sent him north —*Wilson*, "Rise and Fall of the Slave Power in America."]
Senatorial contest in the state legislature between Charles Sumner (Free soil) and Robt C Winthrop Charles Sumner elected on the 26th ballot 24 Apr "
Daniel Webster dies at Marshfield, aged 70 24 Oct 1852
Boston Normal school, at Boston, opened "
Law fixing the hours of labor for a day, from 1 Oct 1853, to 1 Apr 1854, at 12 hours, from 1 Apr 1854, until 1 Oct 1854 at 11 hours, and after 1 Oct 1854 at 10 hours 17 May, 1853
New constitution framed by a convention met at Boston, 7 May, 1853, completed its work 1 Aug "
[Submitted to the people, but not ratified]
Massachusetts Emigrant Aid Society organized by Eli Thayer, and incorporated 20 Apr 1854
[This in the interest of the settlement of Kansas]
Anthony Burns seized as a slave at Boston 27 May, "
[He is remanded to slavery, and under a strong guard to prevent his release, is taken to the wharf and shipped south He was subsequently liberated by purchase, and settled in Canada The event created great excitement.]
A convention in Worcester declares in favor of a new political organization, to be called the "Republican" party, 20 July, "
State convention of the Republican party, held at Worcester, nominates Henry Wilson for governor and Increase Sumner for lieutenant governor 7 Sept "
Normal school at Salem opened "
Congress consents to the cession by Massachusetts to New York of Boston Corner, the southwesterly corner of Berkshire county 3 Jan 1855
Sumner's speech in the U S Senate on the admission of Kansas, known as the "Crime against Kansas" 20 May, 1856
[Great excitement among the southern members]
Senator Sumner assaulted and beaten down by Preston S. Brooks of South Carolina in the Senate chamber 22 May, "
[Brooks dies in Washington 27 July, 1857]
Adjutant general's report shows the state to have 147,682 men enrolled in the militia, and 5771 are in active service 1858
Pemberton mills at Lawrence fall by reason of defect in building, and afterwards take fire, 115 of the operatives perish and 165 more or less injured 10 Jan 1860
John A Andrews, "the war governor," elected 1861
Annual meeting of the Massachusetts Anti slavery Society at Tremont Temple, Boston, suppressed by the mayor 24 Jan. "
Seven commissioners to the Peace conference at Washington appointed by gov Andrews 5 Feb "
Legislature appropriates $25,000 for supplies for 2000 troops, 3 Apr "
6th regiment, mustered at Lowell, 16 Apr, leaves Boston for

Washington, 17th; attacked by a mob in BALTIMORE, 19 Apr.; 3 soldiers are killed, 23 wounded; arrives at Washington and is quartered in the Senate chamber.........5 P.M., 19 Apr. 1861

Legislature convenes in extra session 14 May, and passes an act for the maintenance of the Union and the Constitution, creating the "Union Fund," and authorizing the issue of $3,000,000 in scrip, supplemented afterwards by an act empowering the governor to issue scrip for $7,000,000 to be loaned to the U. S..............................May, "

Massachusetts 1st, the first 3-years regiment to reach Washington, leaves the state..........................15 June, "

San Jacinto arrives at Boston with Mason and Slidell, 19 Nov.; they are incarcerated in fort Warren................24 Nov. "

Maryland legislature appropriates $7000 to be transmitted to the governor of Massachusetts for distribution among the families of those of the Massachusetts regiment who were killed or wounded in the Baltimore riot...............Dec. "

New England Women's Auxiliary Association organized, with headquarters at Boston..............................Dec. "

Mason and Slidell released and sail for England (TRENT AFFAIR), 1 Jan. 1862

In response to a proclamation by gov. Andrews, calling for more troops, issued Sunday, 25 May, 3100 of the regular militia report at his headquarters on Boston Commons, 26 May, "

54th, colored regiment, the first formed in the free states, leaves Boston for Port Royal.......................28 May, 1863

[This regiment, in the unsuccessful assault on fort Wagner, 18 July, 1863, immediately on its arrival at the front, was almost annihilated. Its colonel, Robert G. Shaw, aged 25 years, was killed in this assault and buried by the confederates in the same pit with the dead of his regiment.]

Mob of non-Unionists, attempting to force the doors of the armory of the 11th Battery, Boston, fired upon and dispersed; several killed and many wounded...................14 July, "

Boston college, Boston, chartered and opened................ "

Work resumed on the Hoosac tunnel.....................Oct. "

Edward Everett d. in Boston........................16 Jan. 1865

Monument erected in Lowell to the first martyrs from Massachusetts in the civil war......................17 June, "

Commemoration day at Cambridge, in honor of the patriot heroes of Harvard college......................21 July, "

Massachusetts Institute of Technology, at Boston, chartered 1861; opened.. "

Massachusetts State Primary school at Palmer opened........ 1866

Legislature adopts the XIV.th Amendment to the Constitution of the U. S.....................................20 Mch. 1867

State Temperance convention organizes at Worcester..17 Sept. "

Clarke institute for deaf mutes at Northampton opened...... "

Massachusetts Agricultural college at Amherst, chartered 1863; opened.....................................Oct. "

State legislature adjourns after the longest session ever held in the state up to date, being 165 days............12 June, 1868

Worcester Polytechnic institute at Worcester, chartered 1865; opened.. "

Governor and council contract with Walter Shanly of Montreal and Francis Shanly of Toronto to complete the Hoosac tunnel before Mch. 1874, for $4,594,268.................24 Dec. "

Ebenezer R. Hoar appointed U. S. attorney-general.....5 Mch. 1869

Legislature adopts the XV.th Amendment to the Constitution of the U. S....................................9–12 Mch. "

George S. Boutwell appointed secretary of the treasury, 11 Mch. "

Great Peace jubilee in Boston (MUSIC)..............15 June, "

Legislature establishes a Bureau of Statistics, a state Board of Health, abolishes the district system of public schools, and adjourns after a session of 171 days...............25 June, "

Landing at Duxbury, 23 July, of the French Atlantic cable celebrated.....................................27 July, "

Labor Reform party organized at Worcester..........28 Sept. "

Horace Mann school for the deaf at Boston opened........... "

George Peabody buried at Peabody (South Danvers), Mass., 8 Feb. 1870

Wendell Phillips nominated for governor by the Prohibition party...17 Aug. "

Wendell Phillips nominated for governor by the Labor Reform party..8 Sept. "

Boston university, Boston, chartered 1869; opened.......... 1871

World's Peace jubilee and International Musical festival begins in Boston (MUSIC)...........................17 June, 1872

Great fire in Boston; 709 brick and stone and 67 wooden buildings burned, loss, $70,000,000; nearly 65 acres burned over; 14 lives lost.....................................9–10 Nov. "

Legislature meets in extra session to devise means of relief for Boston..19 Nov. "

William A. Richardson appointed secretary of the treasury, 17 Mch. 1873

Oakes Ames, M.C., father of the "Crédit Mobilier," d. (aged 69), 8 May, "

Massachusetts Normal Art school at Boston opened........... "

Charlestown, Brighton, and West Roxbury annexed to Boston by vote at election held..............................7 Oct. "

HOOSAC TUNNEL completed............................27 Nov. "

Prof. Louis J. R. Agassiz, scientist, b. 1807; d. at Cambridge, 14 Dec. "

U. S. senator Charles Sumner, b. in Boston, 1811, d. at Washington...11 Mch. 1874

Gov. Washburn, elected U. S. senator to [illegible] S[illegible]mner, resigns executive office to lieut.-gov. Thor[illegible] [illegible], 3[illegible] Apr. "

Bursting of a reservoir dam on Mill river, n[illegible] [illegible]burg, Hampshire co., nearly destroys Williamsb[illegible], Lee[illegible], Haydensville, and Skinnerville; 200 lives and $1,500,000 worth of property lost...................................16 May, 1874

State Normal school at Worcester opened..................... "

Prohibitory liquor law repealed........................5 Apr. 1875

Centennial celebration of the battles of Lexington and Concord...19 Apr. "

Centennial celebration of the battle of Bunker Hill....17 June, "

Celebration of the 100th anniversary of the day Washington assumed command of the army, at Cambridge........3 July, "

Smith college at Northampton, chartered 1871, opened....Sept. "

Wellesley college, Wellesley, chartered 1870, opened.......... "

Vice-pres. Henry Wilson dies suddenly at Washington..22 Nov. "

Marcella Street Home (reform school) at Boston opened....... 1877

State lunatic hospital at Worcester, state prison for women at Sherborn, state prison at Concord, state lunatic hospital at Danvers, and state asylum for the chronic insane at Worcester opened....................................... 1878

Public address in Faneuil hall, Boston, by Denis Kearney, the Sand-lot orator of San Francisco, Cal.................5 Aug. "

Act abolishing 9 separate state boards, and creating the Board of Health, Charity, and Lunacy, passed by legislature, which adjourns...30 Apr. 1879

French ocean cable landed at North Eastham, cape Cod, 15 Nov. "

Cape Cod ship canal from Buzzard bay to Barnstable bay begun.. 1880

Anti-screen Liquor Saloon law, enacted 1880, goes into effect... 1881

National Law and Order league organized at Boston....22 Feb. 1882

Henry W. Longfellow, b. 1807, d. at Cambridge........24 Mch. "

Ralph Waldo Emerson, b. 1803, d. at Concord..........27 Apr. "

Society for the Collegiate Instruction of Women, "Harvard Annex," organized 14 Jan. 1879, incorporated..........16 Aug. "

Celebration at Marshfield of the 100th anniversary of the birthday of Daniel Webster (postponed from 3 Oct.).......11 Oct. "

"Tom Thumb" (Charles H. Stratton), b. 1838, d. at Middleborough..15 July, 1883

Foreign exhibition opens in Boston, continuing until 12 Jan. 1884..3 Sept. "

Wendell Phillips, b. 1811, d. at Boston..................2 Feb. 1884

Charles O'Conor, b. 1804, d. at Nantucket.............12 May, "

Statue of John Harvard unveiled at Cambridge..........15 Oct. "

William C. Endicott appointed U. S. secretary of war...6 Mch. 1885

Elizur Wright, abolitionist, b. 1804, d. at Medford......22 Nov. "

Board of Health established separately....................... 1886

Charles Francis Adams, sen., b. 1807, d. at Boston.....21 Nov. "

State property in the Hoosac tunnel and Troy and Greenfield railroad sold to Fitchburg railroad company............... 1887

First Monday in Sept. (Labor day) made a legal holiday at session of legislature, which adjourned...............16 June, "

Spencer F. Baird, naturalist, b. 1823; d. at Wood's Holl, 19 Aug. "

Asa Gray, botanist, b. 1810, d. at Cambridge...........30 Jan. 1888

Ballot law modelled on the Australian system adopted by legislature at session ending............................29 May, "

Gen. P. H. Sheridan, b. 1831, d. at Nonquit.............5 Aug. "

Maria Mitchell, astronomer, b. 1818, d. at Lynn.......28 June, 1889

Maritime exhibition opens at Boston......................4 Nov. "

Great fire at Lynn; 296 buildings destroyed; 80 acres burned over; loss, $5,000,000..............................26 Nov. "

Haverhill celebrates its 250th anniversary...............2 July, 1890

Cyclone visits the suburbs of South Lawrence, the most severe ever recorded in the New England states; over $100,000 worth of property destroyed.........................26 July, "

John Boyle O'Reilly, Irish patriot, b. 1844, d. at Hull...10 Aug. "

First annual convention of the letter carriers of the U. S. held at Boston; 100 delegates...........................13 Aug. "

Accident on the Old Colony railroad near Quincy; 20 killed, 31 injured..19 Aug. "

Benjamin Penhallow Shillaber, the creator of "Mrs. Partington," b. 1814, d. at Chelsea........................25 Nov. "

Associate-justice Charles Devens, ex-attorney-general of the U. S., d. in Boston....................................7 Jan. 1891

James Russell Lowell, b. 1819, d. at Cambridge.........12 Aug. "

Phillips Brooks consecrated bishop of Massachusetts in Trinity church, Boston......................................14 Oct. "

James Parton, author, b. 1822, d. at Newburyport.......17 Oct. "

First world's convention of the Woman's Christian Temperance Union opens at Boston.........................10 Nov. "

Governor's salary raised from $5000 to $8000...........24 Mch. 1892

Also any town of 12,000 inhabitants may become incorporated as a city.. "

City of Quincy celebrates its centennial.................4 July, "

Ex-gov. Henry J. Gardner d. at Milton.................22 July, "

Lizzie Borden arrested at Fall River charged with the murder (Aug. 4) of her father and stepmother.................11 Aug. "

Celebration of the 250th anniversary of the founding of Gloucester opens....................................23 Aug. "

Poet Whittier dies at Hampton Falls, N. H., 7 Sept.; buried at Amesbury...10 Sept. "

Celebration of the 250th anniversary of the founding of Woburn begins..2 Oct. "

Lizzie Borden indicted by the grand jury at Taunton....2 Dec. "

Gen. Benj. F. Butler, b. 1818, d. at Washington, D.C., 11 Jan., buried at Lowell..................................16 Jan. 1893

Phillips Brooks, P. E. bishop of Massachusetts, d. at his home, Boston...23 Jan. "

Great fire in Boston, loss $5,000,000...................10 Mch. "

Lizzie Borden arraigned at New Bedford, pleads not guilty of the murder of her father and stepmother............8 May, "

Tried and acquitted...................................20 June, "

[Defended by ex.-gov. Robinson of Massachusetts.]

Statue of Wm. Lloyd Garrison unveiled at Newburyport, 4 July, "

Mrs. Lucy Stone, one of the earliest champions of women's rights, d. in Boston ... 18 Oct. 1893
Francis Parkman d. at Jamaica Plains, aged 70 years ... 8 Nov. "
Ex-gov. William Gaston d. in Boston, aged 74 ... 19 Jan. 1894
Miss Helen Shafer, president Wellesly college, b. 1840, d. 20 Jan. "
Fire in Boston, 137 buildings burned, loss $500,000 ... 15 May, "

GOVERNORS OF THE MASSACHUSETTS COLONIES.

PLYMOUTH COLONY, ELECTED.

Name.	Term.
John Carver	1620 to 1621
William Bradford	1621 " 1633
Edward Winslow	1633 " 1634
Thomas Prince	1634 " 1635
William Bradford	1635 " 1636
Edward Winslow	1636 " 1637
William Bradford	1637 " 1638
Thomas Prince	1638 " 1639
William Bradford	1639 " 1644
Edward Winslow	1644 " 1645
William Bradford	1645 " 1657
Thomas Prince	1657 " 1673
Josiah Winslow	1673 " 1681
Thomas Hinkley	1681 " 1686
Sir Edmund Andros, governor-general	1686 " 1689
Thomas Hinkley	1689 " 1692

MASSACHUSETTS BAY COLONY.

Name.	Term.
John Endicott (acting)	1629 to 1630
Mathew Cradock (did not serve)	
John Winthrop	1630 " 1634
Thomas Dudley	1634 " 1635
John Haynes	1635 " 1636
Henry Vane	1636 " 1637
John Winthrop	1637 " 1640
Thomas Dudley	1640 " 1641
Richard Bellingham	1641 " 1642
John Winthrop	1642 " 1644
John Endicott	1644 " 1645
Thomas Dudley	1645 " 1646
John Winthrop	1646 " 1649
John Endicott	1649 " 1650
Thomas Dudley	1650 " 1651
John Endicott	1651 " 1654
Richard Bellingham	1654 " 1655
John Endicott	1655 " 1665
Richard Bellingham	1665 " 1673
John Leverett	1673 " 1679
Simon Bradstreet	1679 " 1684
Joseph Dudley, president	1684 " 1686
Sir Edmund Andros, governor-general	1686 " 1689
Thomas Danforth (acting)	1689 " 1692

GOVERNORS OF MASSACHUSETTS APPOINTED BY THE KING UNDER THE SECOND CHARTER.

Name.	Term of office.	Remarks.
Sir William Phipps	1692 to 1694	Born in Maine; summoned to England, he dies there, 1695
William Stoughton	1694 " 1699	Lieutenant-governor and acting governor, one of the principals in the witchcraft delusion.
Richard Coote, earl of Bellamont	1699 " 1700	Goes to New York in 1700, and dies there, 1701.
William Stoughton	1700 " 1701	Acting.
The Council	1701 " 1702	
Joseph Dudley	1702 " 1715	Subservient to the English government.
The Council	Feb. to Mch. 1715	
Joseph Dudley	Mch. " Nov. "	
William Tailer	1715 to 1716	Lieutenant-governor and acting governor.
Samuel Shute	1716 " 1723	Controversy with the legislature as to a fixed salary.
William Dummer	1723 " 1728	Lieutenant-governor, acting as governor.
William Burnet	July, 1728 " Sept. 1729	Dies in office 7 Sept. 1729.
William Dummer	1729 to June, 1730	Acting.
William Tailer	June " Aug. "	Acting.
Jonathan Belcher	1730 to 1741	Recalled by the British court.
William Shirley	1741 " 1749	Visits England, 1749.
Spencer Phipps	1749 " 1753	Lieutenant governor, acting.
William Shirley	1753 " 1756	Recalled.
Spencer Phipps	1756 " 1757	Acting.
The Council	Apr. to Aug. 1757	
Thomas Pownall	1757 to 1760	Recalled. Enters Parliament and opposes the ministry on American measures.
Thomas Hutchinson	June to Aug. 1760	Lieutenant-governor, acting governor.
Sir Francis Bernard	1760 to 1769	Recalled, and made a baronet.
Thomas Hutchinson	1769 " 1771	Acting.
Thomas Hutchinson	1771 " 1774	The last of the royal governors.
The Council	1774 " 1780	Governing until the adoption of the state constitution.

GOVERNORS UNDER THE STATE CONSTITUTION.

Name.	Party.	Term.	Remarks.
John Hancock	......	1780 to 1785	The first signer of the Declaration of Independence.
James Bowdoin	......	1785 " 1787	Shays's rebellion occurs during this administration.
John Hancock	......	1787 to Oct. 1793	Dies in office, 8 Oct. 1793.
Samuel Adams	......	1793 to 1794	Lieutenant-governor acting. One of the foremost revolutionary patriots.
Samuel Adams	......	1794 " 1797	Governor. Dies in Boston, 2 Oct. 1803.
Increase Sumner	......	1797 to June, 1799	Dies in office, 7 June, 1799.
Moses Gill	......	1799 to 1800	Lieutenant-governor acting.
Caleb Strong	Federal.	1800 " 1807	A strong Federalist.
James Sullivan	Dem.-Rep.	1807 to Dec. 1808	A brother of gen. Sullivan. Dies in office, 10 Dec. 1808.
Levi Lincoln	"	1808 to 1809	Lieutenant-governor acting.
Christopher Gore	Federal.	1809 " 1810	
Elbridge Gerry	Dem.-Rep.	1810 " 1812	Vice-president of the U. S. 1813. Dies in office, 23 Nov. 1814.
Caleb Strong	Federal.	1812 " 1816	Opposes the war of 1812.
John Brooks	"	1816 " 1823	A revolutionary patriot and thorough soldier.
William Eustis	Dem.-Rep.	1823 to Feb. 1825	Dies in office, 6 Feb. 1825.
Marcus Morton	"	Feb. to July, 1825	Lieutenant-governor, acting.
Levi Lincoln	Democrat.	1825 to 1834	The first to exercise the veto power, the occasion being a bill for a bridge uniting Boston and Charlestown.
John Davis	Whig.	1834 to Mch. 1835	Elected to the U. S. Senate.
Samuel T. Armstrong	"	Mch. 1835 to 1836	Lieutenant-governor, acting.
Edward Everett	"	1836 to 1840	Scholar and orator.
Marcus Morton	Democrat.	1840 " 1841	
John Davis	Whig.	1841 " 1843	
Marcus Morton	Democrat.	1843 " 1844	
George N. Briggs	Whig.	1844 " 1851	
George S. Boutwell	Dem. and F. S.	1851 " 1853	Elected by coalition of Democrats and Free-soilers.
John H. Clifford	Whig.	1853 " 1854	
Emory Washburn	"	1854 " 1855	
Henry J. Gardner	Republican.	1855 " 1858	
Nathaniel P. Banks	"	1858 " 1861	
John A. Andrews	"	1861 " 1866	The "war governor" of Massachusetts.
Alexander H. Bullock	"	1866 " 1869	
William Claflin	"	1869 " 1872	
William B. Washburn	"	1872 to May, 1874	Elected to the U. S. Senate.
Thomas Talbot	"	May to Dec. 1874	
William Gaston	Democrat.	1875 to 1876	
Alexander H. Rice	Republican.	1876 " 1879	
Thomas Talbot	"	1879 " 1880	

GOVERNORS UNDER THE STATE CONSTITUTION.—(*Continued.*)

Name.	Party.	Term.	Remarks.
John D. Long	Republican.	1880 to 1883	
Benjamin F. Butler	Dem. and Ind.	1883 " 1884	
George D. Robinson	Republican.	1884 " 1887	
Oliver Ames	"	1887 " 1890	
John Q. A. Brackett	"	1890 " 1891	
William E. Russell	Democrat.	1891 " 1892	
William E. Russell	"	1892 " 1894	
Fred. T Greenhalge	Republican.	1894 " 1895	
Fred. T. Greenhalge	"	1895 " 1896	

UNITED STATES SENATORS FROM THE STATE OF MASSACHUSETTS.

Name.	No. of Congress.	Date.	Remarks.
Tristram Dalton	1st	1789 to 1791	Seated 14 Apr. 1789.
Caleb Strong	1st to 4th	1789 " 1796	Resigned.
George Cabot	2d " 4th	1791 " 1796	Resigned.
Benjamin Goodhue	4th " 6th	1796 " 1800	Elected in place of Cabot. Resigned.
Theodore Sedgwick	4th " 5th	1796 " 1798	Elected in place of Strong. Elected president *pro tem.* 27 June, 1798.
Samuel Dexter	6th	1799 " 1800	Resigned.
Dwight Foster	6th to 7th	1800 " 1803	Elected in place of Dexter. Resigned.
Jonathan Mason	6th " 7th	1800 " 1803	Elected in place of Goodhue.
John Quincy Adams	8th " 10th	1803 " 1808	Resigned.
Timothy Pickering	8th " 11th	1803 " 1811	Elected in place of Foster.
James Lloyd, jr	10th " 12th	1808 " 1813	Elected in place of Adams. Resigned.
Joseph B. Varnum	12th " 14th	1811 " 1817	Elected president *pro tem.*, and again 6 Dec. 1813.
Christopher Gore	13th " 14th	1813 " 1816	Appointed in place of Lloyd. Resigned.
Eli P. Ashmun	14th " 15th	1816 " 1818	Elected in place of Gore. Resigned.
Prentiss Mellen	15th " 16th	1818 " 1820	Elected in place of Ashmun. Resigned.
Harrison Gray Otis	15th " 17th	1817 " 1822	Resigned.
Elijah H. Mills	16th " 19th	1820 " 1827	Elected in place of Mellen.
James Lloyd	17th " 19th	1822 " 1826	Elected in place of Otis. Resigned.
Nathaniel Silsbee	19th " 23d	1826 " 1835	Elected in place of Lloyd.
Daniel Webster	20th " 26th	1827 " 1841	Webster's famous reply to Hayne of South Carolina, delivered in the Senate 26, 27 Jan. 1830. Resigned to become secretary of state.
John Davis	24th " 26th	1835 " 1840	Resigned.
Rufus Choate	26th " 28th	1841 " 1845	Elected in place of Webster.
Isaac C. Bates	26th " 28th	1841 " 1845	Died in office.
John Davis	29th " 32d	1845 " 1853	Elected in place of Bates.
Daniel Webster	29th " 31st	1845 " 1850	Resigned, became secretary of state; d. 24 Oct. 1852.
Robert C. Winthrop	31st	1850	Appointed *pro tem.* in place of Webster.
Robert Rantoul, jr	31st	1851	Elected in place of Webster.
Charles Sumner	32d to 43d	1851 to 1874	Struck down in the Senate chamber by Preston S. Brooks, 22 May, 1856. Owing to his injuries he did not take his seat during the 35th Congress. Died 11 Mch. 1874.
Edward Everett	33d	1853 " 1854	Resigned.
Julius Rockwell	33d	1854	Appointed *pro tem.* in place of Everett.
Henry Wilson	33d to 42d	1855 to 1873	Elected in place of Everett.
George S. Boutwell	43d " 44th	1873 " 1877	Elected in place of Wilson.
William B. Washburn	43d	1874	Elected in place of Sumner.
Henry L. Dawes	44th to 52d	1875 to 1893	
George F. Hoar	45th " —	1877 " —	Term expires 1901.
Henry Cabot Lodge	53d " —	1893 " —	Term expires 1899.

massacres. The indiscriminate killing of human beings incapable of defence; in war, the unnecessary slaughter of combatants surprised or after surrender. The following are among the most remarkable, but the accounts of many of them are exaggerated:

B.C.

All the Carthaginians in Sicily ... 397
Two thousand Tyrians crucified and 8000 put to the sword for not surrendering Tyre to Alexander ... 331
Two thousand Capuans, friends of Hannibal, by Gracchus ... 211
A slaughter of the Teutones and Ambrones, near Aix, by Marius, Roman general, 200,000 left dead ... 102
Romans throughout Asia, men, women, and children, in one day, by order of Mithridates, king of Pontus ... 88
Many Roman senators by Cinna, Marius, and Sertorius ... 87
Again, under Sulla and Catiline, his minister of vengeance ... 82
At Perusia, Octavianus Cæsar ordered 300 Roman senators and other eminent persons sacrificed to the manes of Julius Cæsar, 40

A.D.

At the destruction of Jerusalem, 1,100,000 Jews are said to have been put to the sword ... 70
Jews, headed by one Andræ, put to death many Greeks and Romans in and near Cyrene ... 115
Cassius, a Roman general under the emperor M. Aurelius, put to death 300,000 inhabitants of Seleucia ... 165
At Alexandria, many thousands of citizens were massacred by order of the Roman emperor Caracalla, for some insulting remarks while on his visit there ... 215
Emperor Probus said to have put to death 400,000 barbarian invaders of Gaul ... 277
Gothic hostages by Valens ... 378
Thessalonica, when 7000 persons invited into the circus were put to the sword by order of Theodosius ... 390
Circus factions at Constantinople ... 532
Latins at Constantinople by order of Andronicus ... 1184
Albigenses and Waldenses, commenced at Toulouse ... 1208
[Thousands perished by the sword and gibbet.]
French in Sicily (Sicilian Vespers) ... 1282
At Paris, of the Armagnacs, at the instance of John, duke of Burgundy ... 1418
Swedish nobility, at a feast, by order of Christian II ... 1520
Protestants at Vassy ... 1 Mch. 1562
Seventy thousand Huguenots, or French Protestants, in France (St. Bartholomew) ... 24 Aug. 1572
Christians in Croatia by Turks, 65,000 slain ... 1592
Pretender Demetrius, and his Polish adherents, at Moscow, 27 May, 1606
Protestants in the Valteline, N. Italy ... 19 July, 1620
Protestants at Thorn, under pretended legal sentence of the chancellor of Poland, for joining in a tumult occasioned by a Roman Catholic procession ... 1724
[All Protestant powers in Europe interceded in vain.]
At Batavia 12,000 Chinese were massacred by the natives, under pretext of intended insurrection ... Oct. 1740
At the taking of Ismail by the Russians, 30,000 old and young were slain (Ismail) ... Dec. 1790
French royalists (France, Septembrizers) ... 2 Sept. 1792
Poles at Praga ... 1794
In St. Domingo, Dessalines proclaims death to the whites, and thousands perish ... 29 Mch. 1804
Insurrection at Madrid, massacre of French ... 2 May, 1808
Mamelukes in the citadel of Cairo ... 1 Mch. 1811
Protestants at Nismes, by Catholics ... May, 1815
Massacre at Scio (Chios) ... 22 Apr. 1822
Janissaries at Constantinople, 14 June, 1826; at Cabul (Afghanistan) ... 1841
Six hundred Kabyles suffocated in a cave in Algeria (Dahra), 18 June, 1845
Massacre of Christians at Aleppo ... 16 Oct. 1850
Maronites, by Druses, in Lebanon, June, 1860; and of Christians by Mahometans at Damascus (Damascus, Druses), 9-11 July, 1860
French missionaries and others at Tien-tsin, 22 persons (China), 21 June, 1870
Foreigners, by native Gauchos, Tandel district, Buenos Ayres, South America ... 1 Jan. 1872
About 90 French colonists and others in New Caledonia by natives, during a revolt ... June, 1878
Mehemet Ali Pacha and others at Ipek, near Scutari, by Albanians ... 6 Sept. "
At Cabul (Afghanistan), 1879, and Turkey ... 1876

IN BRITISH HISTORY.

Three hundred British nobles, on Salisbury Plain, by Hengist. about 450

welve hundred monks of Bangor, by Ethelfrid, king of Bernicia 607 or 612
anes in southern counties of England, by order of Ethelred II night of 13 Nov 1002
[At London it was most bloody, the churches being no sanctuary Among the slain was Gunilda sister of Sweyn, king of Denmark left in hostage *for the performance of a* treaty newly concluded —*Baker*]
ews in England A few, pressing into Westminster hall at Richard I 's coronation, were killed by the mob, and on a false rumor that the king had ordered a general massacre of them, the people in many parts of England slew all they met In York 500, taking shelter in a castle, killed themselves to escape the multitude 1189
ristol colonists at Cullen's Wood Ireland (CULLEN'S WOOD) 1209
nglish factory at Amboyna to dispossess its members of the Spice islands Feb 1625
rotestants in Ireland in O Neill s rebellion, which began 23 Oct. 1641
[Upwards of 30 000 British were killed in the commencement of this rebellion —*Sir William Petty* In the first 3 or 4 days of it 40,000 or 50 000 Protestants were destroyed —*Lord Clarendon* During the rebellion 154,000 Protestants were massacred —*Sir W Temple*]
acdonalds of GLENCOE 13 Feb 1692
en women and children, numbering 184 chiefly Protestants, killed by insurgent Irish at the barn of Scullabogue, Ireland (*Musgrave*) 1798
uropeans at Meerut, Delhi, etc , by mutineers of the native Indian army (INDIA) May and June, 1857
hites at Kalangan south coast of Borneo 1 May, 1859
hites at Morant bay Jamaica by negroes (JAMAICA). 11, 12 Oct 1865
ieut Holcombe and surveying party (about 70) in Assam, on Naga hills about 24 Feb 1875
r Margary and servants (with col Browne s expedition into western China) at Manwyne by Chinese 21 Feb "
ommodore Goodenough of the *Pearl* and 2 seamen, by natives of Santa Cruz island, South Pacific ocean, attacked 12 Aug , d 20 Aug "
en Charles George (Chinese) Gordon and followers at Khartoum (SOUDAN) 26 Jan 1885

IN UNITED STATES HISTORY

rench Huguenots in Florida, by Spaniards under Menendez (FLORIDA) 19 Sept 1565
hites by Indians in VIRGINIA 22 Mch 1622
ndians at Pequot fort by New England colonists (CONNECTICUT), 26 May, 1637
ndians by the Dutch at Pavonia (NEW YORK) 25 Feb 1643
nne Hutchinson s family and others, near Westchester (NEW YORK) "
hites by Indians in VIRGINIA 18 Apr 1644
utch at Hoboken, Pavonia, and Staten Island (NEW YORK), 15-20 Sept 1655
hites in Massachusetts *Maine*, and New Hampshire, by Indians, 1675, '76, '77, by French and Indians, 1688, '90 '92, also in 1703-4, and again in 1722-25, 1744-48, 1754-60 MAINE, MASSACHUSETTS, NEW HAMPSHIRE
hites at Schenectady by French and Indians (NEW YORK), 8 Feb 1690
arrison at FORT WILLIAM HENRY after surrender 9 Aug 1757
arrison of fort Loudon, Tennessee, after surrender, by Cherokees 7 Aug 1760
oravian Indians at Conestoga, Pa , by the Paxton boys (PENNSYLVANIA) 27 Dec 1763
en Wayne s troop by British at PAOLI 20 Sept 1777
ettlers at WYOMING by Tories and Indians (PENNSYLVANIA) 2-4 July, 1778
ieut. col Baylor's command, by the British at Old Tappan (NEW YORK) 27 Sept "
ettlers at CHERRY VALLEY by Tories and Indians 11-12 Nov 1778
oravian Indians, by whites at Gnadenhutten, O (OHIO), 8 Mch 1782
arrison of fort Dearborn, Chicago, by Indians (FORT DEARBORN) 15 Aug 1812
merican troops at the river Raisin (MICHIGAN) 22 Jan 1813
hites by Indians at fort Mimms (ALABAMA) 30 Aug "
merican prisoners at DARTMOOR, England, by guards 6 Apr 1815
aj Dade's command by Seminoles (FLORIDA) 28 Dec 1835
exans at the ALAMO by Mexicans. 6 Mch 1836
migrants to California by Mormons at Mountain Meadow (UTAH, 1857-77) 11 Sept 1857
hite settlers at Spirit Lake, Iowa, by Sioux Mch "
hites in Minnesota by Sioux under Little Crow (MINNESOTA), Aug , Sept 1862
arrison at FORT PILLOW, Tenn , by confederates under Forrest, 12 Apr 1864
ndians by col Chivington's command at Sand Creek COLORADO 27 Nov "
en Canby and others by Modoc Indians (CALIFORNIA, UNITED STATES) 11 Apr 1873
en Custer and command by the Indians under Sitting Bull (MONTANA) 26 June, 1876
egroes at Hamburg, S. C , by armed citizens (SOUTH CAROLINA) 9 July, "
hites by Apache Indians at White River agency (COLORADO), 29 Sept. 1879
leven Italians (Maffia) at New Orleans, La , in prison as suspected murderers of David C. Hennessey, chief of police, by an organized body of citizens (LOUISIANA, UNITED STATES) 15 Mch 1891

Mas'sowah, a port on the Red sea, subject to Egypt Certain commercial rights secured to Abyssinia by treaty with England and Egypt, May, 1884
Italian flag hoisted beside the Egyptian 6 Feb 1885
Abyssinians under Ras Aloula severely defeat the Arabs at Kufeit near Amadib 23 Sept
Government of Massowah assumed by the Italians 2 Dec
Abyssinians attack Massowah and Italian outposts, but suffer loss and retire 18 Jan et seq 1887
About 500 Italians proceeding with supplies to Sahati cut off by Abyssinians under Ras Aloula at Dogoli, near Massowah, 25-26 Jan "
Negotiations with Ras Aloula with respect to release of *prisoners* 11 Mch "
Skirmishes between Italians and Dimer tribe 27-28 Mch "
Proclamation issued declaring a state of war in Massowah and its dependencies with blockade of ports 2 May, "
Major Savoiroux made *a prisoner*, still kept by the Abyssinians April released Sept "
Chief Kantibay submits to Italy 18 Oct "
Declared to be in a state of siege 10 Nov "
Italy notifies the powers that it has annexed Massowah July 1888
Protectorate proclaimed at Zulla 3 Aug "
Severe defeat of Italians at Saganeiti on the borders through native treachery , 4 Italian officers killed Aug "
Keren occupied and annexed by the Italians 2 June 1889
Gen Baldissera occupies Asmara 4 Aug
About 1000 dervishes repulsed after incursion into Italian protected country , captives and booty rescued, reported 29 June, 1890
Gen Gandolfi new *governor*, announces end of military rule in the Italian possessions on the Red sea 1 July, "

master of the rolls, an equity judge in England, so called because he has custody of all charters, patents commissions deeds and *recognizances entered upon rolls of* parchment, his decrees are appealable to the court of chancery The repository of *public papers called the rolls*, was in Chancery lane The rolls were formerly kept in a chapel founded for converted Jews, but after Jews were expelled the kingdom in 1290 they were placed in the office of the master of the rolls Here were kept all the records since the accession of Richard III, 1483, earlier ones being kept in the Tower of London RECORDS. The first recorded master of the rolls was either John de Langton, appointed 1286, or Adam de Osgodeby, appointed 1 Oct 1295, but the office clearly existed long before —*Hardy*

masters in chancery, chosen from the equity bar of England, were first appointed, it is said, to give instruction to sir Christopher Hatton (not informed in the duties of his office), lord chancellor of England, in 1587 The office was abolished in 1852

mas'todon. MAMMOTH

Mat'abe'le land. MASHONA

matches. LUCIFER-MATCHES

materialism, the doctrine that the soul is not a spiritual substance distinct from matter, but is the result of organization in the body The term is rather loosely applied to the systems of Epicurus, about 310 B.C , Hobbes, about 1642 A D , Priestley, about 1772, and of many eminent men in the present day. It is not necessarily identical with atheism. PHILOSOPHY

mathematics formerly signified all kinds of learning, but now includes the sciences of numbers and quantity. ARITHMETIC Among the most eminent mathematicians were Euclid, 300 B.C , Archimedes, 287 B.C , Descartes, died 1650 A D., Barrow, died 1677, Leibnitz, died 1716, sir Isaac Newton, died 1727, Euler, died 1783, Lagrange, died 1813, Laplace, died 1827 and dr Peacock, died 1858, sir G B Airy (astronomer royal), Bartholomew Price, J J Sylvester, and I. Todhunter are eminent mathematicians Mary Somerville, born 1790, author of the "Mechanism of the Heavens," died 1873 The London Mathematical Society was founded 16 Jan 1865, prof Aug De Morgan, president Zerah Colburn, a mathematical prodigy, Vermont, 1804-40

mat'ins, the service or prayers first performed in the morning or beginning of the day in the Roman Catholic church The French matins were the massacre of St Bartholomew, 24 Aug 1572 The matins of Moscow were the *massacre of prince Demetrius*, and the Poles his adherents, in the morning of 27 May, 1606.

matter exists in three states gaseous, liquid, and solid William Crookes considers that there is a fourth state, ' radiant matter," subtler than any of these, 1879-80 LIGHT According to Swedenborg, matter is the *ultimate* of divine order, and is related to spirit as an effect to its cause

Mat'terhorn, a peak of the main ridge of the Alps, about 14,836 feet high, S Switzerland After various fruitless attempts by prof Tyndall and other eminent climbers, in 1860, the summit was reached on 14 July, 1865, by Edward Whymper and others During their descent, 4 of the party were killed Mr Hadow fell, the connecting-rope broke, and he, lord Francis Douglas, the rev Mr Hudson, and Michael Croz, a guide, slipped, and fell from a precipice nearly 4000 feet high Miss Walker, with her father, ascended the Matterhorn, 22 July, 1871 3 gentlemen ascended without a guide, 21 July, 1876 Dr W O Moseley, an American, was killed here, 14 Aug 1879 3 persons attempting the ascent perished, 12 Sept 1890

Maumee' Rapids or **Fallen Timbers,** Battle of At the Maumee rapids, in northern Ohio, Wayne completely routed 2000 Indians, on 20 Aug 1794 The Americans lost 33 killed and 100 wounded This battle ended the Indian war in the Northwest OHIO

Maundy-Thursday (derived by Spelman from *maude*, a hand-basket, in which the king gave alms to the poor, by others from *dies mandati*, the day on which Christ gave his grand *mandate*, that we should love one another), the day before Good Friday —*Wheatley* The custom of the sovereigns of England or their almoners to give alms, food, and clothing to as many poor persons as they were years old on this day, was begun by Edward III., when fifty years of age, 1363, and is still continued

Maurita'nia, N Africa, with Numidia, became a Roman province, 45 B C, with Sallust for proconsul Augustus created (30 B.C.) a kingdom of Mauritania and part of Getulia, for Juba II, a descendant of ancient African princes Suetonius Paulinus suppressed a revolt here, 42 A D, when it was made a province, divided into parts The country was subjugated by Vandals and Greeks, and fell into the hands of Arabs, about 667 MOORS, MOROCCO

Mauritius (*maw-rish'e-us*) or **Isle of France,** in the Indian ocean, was discovered by the Portuguese, 1505, but the Dutch were the first settlers in 1598 They called it after prince Maurice, their stadtholder, but on acquiring the Cape of Good Hope deserted it, and it continued unsettled until the French landed, and named it for one of the finest provinces in France, 1715 The island was taken by the British, 2 Dec 1810, and confirmed to them by the treaty of Paris in 1814 Area, 705 sq miles, pop 1891, 377,986

mausole'um. Artemisia married her brother, Mausolus, king of Caria, Asia Minor, 377 B C After his death his body was burned, and she drank in liquor his ashes, and erected to his memory at Halicarnassus a monument, one of the 7 wonders of the world (350 B C), termed Mausoleum She invited all the literary men of her age, and proposed rewards for the best elegiac panegyric upon her husband The prize was adjudged to Theopompus, 357 B.C She died 352 B.C. The statue of Mausolus is among the antiquities brought from Halicarnassus by C T Newton in 1857, and placed in the British museum A mausoleum for the royal family of England was founded by queen Victoria at Frogmore, 15 Mch 1862

mauve (*mōv*, Fr for *malva*, mallow), a dye of a delicate purple color made by dr Stenhouse from lichens in 1848, now made from ANILINE.

maverick, a term used on the cattle-ranges of the West for a herd of cattle that bears no brand and is therefore regarded as ownerless It is said to have been the name of a Massachusetts man who settled in Texas, where he refused to follow the custom of branding his calves, because he trusted his neighbors, and, besides, was tender of his beasts.

Maxim gun. An automatic gun, the invention of Hiram S. Maxim, of London, Engl 1883. It consists of a single barrel mounted on a tripod and fires but a single shot at a time, but with such rapidity that the United States Ordnance Department, on a test experiment in rapidity, fired 2004 shots in 1 min 45 sec At the same time, in a test for accuracy, out of 334 shots fired at a target 12×26 ft at a distance of 300 yds, 268 hits were made The gun works itself after the first shot is fired until the cartridges in the belt or magazine are exhausted.

May, the 5th month of the year, named, some say, by Romulus, in respect to the senators and nobles of his city, who were denominated *majores*, others supposed it was so called from Maia, the mother of Mercury, to whom they offered sacrifices on the first day The ancient Romans used to go in procession to the grotto of Egeria on May-day

Mayflower. MASSACHUSETTS, 1620.

mayor of London. At the time of the Norman conquest, 1066, the chief officer of London was called *portgrave*, afterwards softened into *portreeve*, from Saxon words signifying chief governor of a harbor He was afterwards called provost, but in Henry II's reign the Norman title of *maire* (soon after *mayor*) was brought into use At first the mayor was chosen for life, but afterwards for irregular periods now he is chosen annually, but is eligible for re-election He must be an alderman and ex-sheriff His duties commence on 9 Nov The prefix "lord" is peculiar to the chief civic officer in London, Dublin, Edinburgh, and York LONDON, SALARY.

Lord Mayor's court is very ancient

First mayor of London, Henry Fitz Alwyn, held office for 24 years, appointed	1189
Prefix of lord granted by Edward III, with the style of right honorable	1354

mayors in the United States. BOSTON, CHICAGO, NEW YORK, etc.

mayors of the palace, high officers in France who had great influence during the later Merovingian kings, termed *faineants*, "do-nothings" Pepin the Old (or De Landen), 622 et seq , Pepin Heristal, 687-714, Charles Martel, despotic, 714-41, Pepin le Bref, 741, who shut Childeric III in a monastery, and took the kingdom, 752.

Mazarin' Bible. BOOKS

mazurka (*ma-zer'ka*), a Polish dance of the 16th century, introduced into England about 1845 Chopin's music for the mazurka is much admired

Meal-tub plot, a plot against the duke of York, afterwards James II, contrived by one Dangerfield, who secreted seditious letters in the lodgings of col Maunsell, and then advised the custom-house officers to search for smuggled goods, 23 Oct. 1679 After Dangerfield's apprehension, on suspicion of forging these letters, papers were found concealed in a meal-tub at the house of a woman with whom he cohabited, which contained the scheme to be sworn to, accusing the most eminent persons in the Protestant interest, who were against the duke of York's succession, of treason, particularly the earls of Shaftesbury, Essex, and Halifax When Dangerfield was whipped the last time, as part of his punishment, 1 June, 1685, one of his eyes was struck out by a barrister named Robert Francis This caused his death, for which his assailant was hanged.

measures. METRIC SYSTEM, MICROMETER, WEIGHTS —"Not men, but measures," a phrase used in Parliament by Brougham, 2 Nov 1830

Mecca, a city in Arabia, the birthplace of Mahomet, about 571, whence he was compelled to flee, 15 July, 622 (the Hegira) On one of the neighboring hills is a cave, where it is asserted he retired to perform his devotions, and where the greatest part of the Koran was brought to him by the angel Gabriel, 604 Mecca, after being vainly besieged by Hosein for the caliph Yezid, 682, was taken by Abdelmelek, 692 In 1803 it fell into the hands of the Wahabees, a Mahometan sect. They were expelled by the pacha of Egypt in 1818, who retired in 1841. It is said that 160,000 pilgrims visited Mecca in 1858, and only 50,000 in 1859 The grand shereef was assassinated by a fanatic, 21 Mch. 1880 Pilgrimage to Mecca still continues, annual average about 90,000

mechanics. The simple mechanical powers have been ascribed to heathen deities; the axe, wedge, wimble, etc., to Dædalus. MOTION, STEAM-ENGINE.

		B.C.
Aristotle writes on mechanics	about	320
Properties of the lever, etc., demonstrated by Archimedes, who d		212

[He laid the foundations of nearly all these inventions, the further prosecution of which is the boast of our age —*Wallis* (1695).]

Hand mill, or quern, was very early in use; the Romans found one in Yorkshire, Engl. B.C.
Cattle-mills, *molæ jumentariæ*, were also in use by the Romans.
Water-mill was probably invented in Asia; the first that was described was near one of the dwellings of Mithridates...... 70
Water-mill said to have been erected on the river Tiber, at Rome........ 50
A.D.
Pappus wrote on mechanics........about 350
Floating mills on the Tiber........ 536
Tide-mills were, many of them, in use in Venice........about 1078
Wind-mills were in very general use in the 12th century.
Saw-mills are said to have been in use at Augsburg........ 1332
Theory of the inclined plane investigated by Cardan.....about 1540
Work on statics, by Stevinus........ 1586
Galileo's "Scienza Mecanica"........ 1634
Theory of falling bodies, Galileo........ 1638
Laws of percussion, Huygens, Wallis, Wren........about 1660
Theory of oscillation, Huygens........ 1670
Epicycloidal form of the teeth of wheels, Roemer........ 1675
Percussion and animal mechanics, Borelli; he d........ 1679
Application of mechanics to astronomy, parallelism of forces, laws of motion, etc., Newton. Hooke, etc........1666-1700
Problem of the catenary with the analysis, dr. Gregory........ 1697
Spirit level (and many other inventions) by dr. Hooke, from 1660 to 1702
D'Alembert's researches on dynamics........about 1743
Lagrange's "Mécanique Analytique," pub........ 1788
Laplace's "Mécanique Céleste," pub........1799-1805
Borgnis's "Dictionnaire de Mécanique Appliquée aux Arts," 10 vols........1818-23
Edward H. Knight's excellent "Practical Dictionary of Mechanics," pub........1877-84

Mechanicsville, Va., Battle at, 26 June, 1862. PENINSULAR CAMPAIGN.

Mech'lin or **Malines** (*ma-leen'*), a city of Belgium, renowned for lace manufacture, was founded in the 6th century; destroyed by the Normans in 884; sacked by the Spaniards, 1572; taken by the prince of Orange, 1578, and by the English, 1580; and frequently captured in the 17th and 18th centuries, sharing the evil fortunes of the country. Pop. 1891, 50,962.

Meck'lenburg, N. Germany, formerly a principality in Lower Saxony, now independent as the 2 grand-duchies of Mecklenburg-Schwerin (area, 5135 sq. miles; pop. 1890, 578,446) and Mecklenburg-Strelitz (area, 1131 sq. miles; pop. 1890, 97,978). The house of Mecklenburg claims descent from Genseric the Vandal, who ravaged the western empire in the 5th century, and died 477. It is the only reigning family in western Europe of Slavonic origin. The genealogical table of the reigning grand-dukes begins with Niklot, who died 1160, and comprises 25 generations. During the Thirty Years' war Mecklenburg was conquered by Wallenstein, who became duke, 1628; it was restored to its own duke 1630. After several changes the government was settled in 1701 as it now exists in the 2 branches of Schwerin and Strelitz. In 1815 the dukes were made grand-dukes. The dukes joined the new North German Confederation by treaty, 21 Aug. 1866.

Mecklenburg Declaration of Independence. NORTH CAROLINA, 20 May, 1775.

medals. NUMISMATICS. The ancient medals resembled medallions. Modern medals began about 1453 in Germany. The English House of Commons resolved to grant rewards and medals to the fleet whose officers (Blake, Monk, Penn, and Lawson) and men defeated the Dutch fleet, off the Texel, in 1653. Blake's medal of 1653 was bought by William IV. for 150 guineas. An act of 1692 applied the tenth part of the proceeds of prizes for medals and other rewards for officers, seamen, and marines. After lord Howe's victory, 1 June, 1794, it was thought expedient to institute a naval medal. Medals were struck for the victory of Waterloo; a general war-medal (for the war 1793-1814) was ordered in 1847; and special medals were given after the Caffre and Chinese wars. Medals were presented by queen Victoria to persons distinguished in the war in the Crimea, 18 May, 1855. Medals were given to arctic voyagers of 1875-76, in 1877. A list of British military and naval medals is given in "Whitaker's Almanack" for 1888.

MEDALS AWARDED BY THE CONGRESS OF THE UNITED STATES.

Date of Resolution.	To whom presented.	For what service.	Metal.
Mch. 25, 1776	Gen. George Washington	Capture of Boston	Gold.
Nov. 4, 1777	Brig.-gen. Horatio Gates	Defeat of Burgoyne	"
July 26, 1779	Maj.-gen. Anthony Wayne	Storming of Stony Point	"
" "	Lieut.-col. De Fleury	" " "	Silver.
" "	Maj. John Stewart	" " "	"
Sept. 24, "	Maj. Henry Lee	Surprise of Paulus Hook	Gold.
Nov. 3, 1780	John Paulding	Capture of André	Silver.
" "	David Williams	" "	"
" "	Isaac Van Wart	" "	"
Mch. 9, 1781	Brig.-gen. Daniel Morgan	Victory of the Cowpens	Gold.
" "	Lieut.-col. William A. Washington	" " "	Silver.
" "	" John E. Howard	" " "	"
Oct. 29, "	Maj.-gen. Nathaniel Greene	Victory at Eutaw Springs	Gold.
Oct. 16, 1787	Capt. John Paul Jones	Capture of the *Serapis*, 1779	"
Mch. 29, 1800	" Thomas Truxton	Action with the *Vengeance* (French)	"
Mch. 3, 1805	Com. Edward Preble	Tripoli	"
Jan. 29, 1813	Capt. Isaac Hull	Capture of the *Guerrière*	"
" "	" Jacob Jones	" " *Frolic*	"
" "	" Stephen Decatur	" " *Macedonian*	"
Mch. 3, "	" William Bainbridge	" " *Java*	"
Jan. 6, 1814	Lieut. Edward R. McCall	" " *Boxer*	"
" "	Com. Oliver H. Perry	Victory on lake Erie	"
" "	Capt. Jesse D. Elliott	" " "	"
Jan. 11, "	" James Lawrence	Capture of the *Peacock*	"
Oct. 20, "	Com. Thomas Macdonough	Victory on lake Champlain	"
" "	Capt. Robert Henley	" " "	"
" "	Lieut. Stephen Cassin	" " "	"
Oct. 21, "	Capt. Lewis Warrington	Capture of the *Epervier*	"
Nov. 3, "	" Johnston Blakely (to the widow)	" " *Reindeer*	"
" "	Maj.-gen. Jacob Brown	Victory of Chippewa, etc.	"
" "	" Peter B. Porter	" "	"
" "	Brig.-gen. E. W. Ripley	" "	"
" "	" James Miller	" "	"
" "	Maj.-gen. Winfield Scott	" "	"
" "	" Edmund P. Gaines	" of Erie	"
" "	" Alexander Macomb	" " Plattsburg	"
Feb. 27, 1815	" Andrew Jackson	" " New Orleans	"
Feb. 22, 1816	Capt. Charles Stewart	Capture of the *Cyane* and *Levant*	"
" "	" James Biddle	" " *Penguin*	"
Apr. 4, 1818	Maj.-gen. William H. Harrison	Victory of the Thames	"
" "	Gov. Isaac Shelby	" " "	"
Feb. 13, 1835	Col. George Croghan—22 years after	Defence of fort Stephenson, 1813	"
July 16, 1846	Maj.-gen. Zachary Taylor	Victory on Rio Grande	"
Mch. 2, 1847	" " "	Capture of Monterey	"
Mch. 3, "	British, French, and Spanish officers and crews	Rescuing crew of the U. S. brig-of-war *Somers* before Vera Cruz, 7 Dec. 1846	Gold & silver.
Mch. 9, 1848	Maj.-gen. Winfield Scott	Mexican campaign	Gold.
May 9, "	" Zachary Taylor	Victory of Buena Vista	"
Aug. 4, 1854	Capt. Duncan N. Ingraham	Release of Martin Koszta	"

MEDALS AWARDED BY THE CONGRESS OF THE UNITED STATES.—(*Continued.*)

Date of Resolution.	To whom presented.	For what service.	Metal.
May 11, 1858	Dr. Frederick H. Rose, of the British navy..........	For humanity—care of yellow-fever patients from Jamaica to New York on the U. S. S. *Susquehanna*	Gold.
Dec. 21, 1861 July 16, 1862	Naval, to be bestowed upon petty officers, seamen, and marines distinguished for gallantry in action, etc.; 200 issued.		
July 12. " Mch. 3, 1863	Army, to non-commissioned officers and privates for gallantry in action, etc.; 2000 issued..............	At Gettysburg, 1 July, 1863, the 27th Maine volunteered to remain for the battle, although its term had expired. All its members received medals..	Bronze.
Dec. 17, "	Maj.-gen. Ulysses S. Grant..........................	Victories of fort Donelson, Vicksburg, Chattanooga....	Gold.
Jan. 28, 1864	Cornelius Vanderbilt..............................	Gift of ship *Vanderbilt*..............................	"
July 26, 1866	Capts. Creighton, Low, and Stouffler................	Rescuing 500 passengers from the S. S. *San Francisco*, 26 July, 1853. Creighton, of the *Three Bells*, Glasgow; Low, of the bark *Kelly*, of Boston, and Stouffler, of the ship *Antarctic*, Liverpool........	"
Mch. 2, 1867	Cyrus W. Field....................................	Laying the Atlantic cable............................	"
Mch. 16, "	George Peabody....................................	Promotion of education...............................	"
Mch. 1, 1871	George F. Robinson................................	Saving William H. Seward from assassination, 14 Apr. 1865. Besides the medal, $5000............	"
Feb. 24, 1873	Capt. Crandall and others, Long Island lighthouse keeper and crew..................................	Saving passengers from the *Metis*, of the N. Y. and Providence line, 31 Aug. 1872..................	"
June 16, 1874	Centennial medals.	There has been presented as awards for life-saving since the passage of the resolution 167 gold and 209 silver medals up to 1 July, 1892. LIFE-SAVING SERVICE..	Gold & silver.
June 20, "	Life-saving medals. 1st and 2d class.............		

J. F. Loubat's work on "The Medallic History of the United States" was pub.. 1878

Me'dia, a province of the Assyrian empire, revolted, 711 B.C. Its chronology is doubtful.

	B.C.
Revolt of the Medes..	711
Deioces, founder of Ecbatana, reigns.............................	709
Phraortes, or Arphaxad, reigns (he conquers Persia, Armenia, and other countries)..	656
Warlike reign of Cyaxares.......................................	632-594
War with the Lydians (HALYS)....................................	603
Astyages reigns...	594
Astyages deposed by Cyrus, 550; who established the empire of PERSIA..	560

medical science. The medical knowledge of the ancient Egyptians is presented to us in the Leipsic Papyrus, written in the 16th century B.C., and the Berlin Papyrus, 14th century B.C., supposed to be parts of the "Hermetic Books," the substance dating from 4000 B.C. From the Bible we learn much of the science of medicine among the Jews, 1500 B.C. India, in the 11th century B.C., possessed many branches of the science, though imperfectly, but in advance of the Egyptians and Jews. The healing art was studied among the Persians and Greeks about 500 B.C., and Pythagoras explained the philosophy of disease and the action of medicine about the same time. The science carried to Rome from the schools of Alexandria about 100 B.C. Hippocrates "the Great" of Cos, who died at Larissa in Thessaly 377 or 370 B.C., was "the creator of profane as distinguished from sacerdotal medicine, of public in place of secret practice," and the founder of prognosis. There were female doctors of the Roman school of Salerno, between the 12th and 14th centuries A.D., who wrote on all medical subjects, but particularly on gynecology. In Mayence a female physician practised as early as 1288, and another at Frankfort-on-the-Main in 1391. SURGERY.

DISCOVERIES AND GENERAL ADVANCE OF THE SCIENCE.

	B.C.
Praxagoras of Cos discovers the distinction between arteries and veins..	335
Herophilus of Chalcedon, founder of human dissection, discovers the chyliferous and lymphatic vessels.....................	335-280
	A.D.
Aulus Cornelius Celsus, a Roman author, compiles 8 books, "De Medicina"...	30 B.C. to 50
Electricity used in treatment of protracted headache by Scribonius Largus..	43
Rufus of Ephesus discovers the decussation of the optic nerve and the capsule of the crystalline lens..................about	50
Marinus, one of the greatest anatomists of antiquity, discovers the inferior laryngeal nerves and the intestinal glands, about	100
Claudius Galen of Pergamus, the greatest of the eclectics, and author of 83 medical works still extant, b. 131, d..........	201
"Presbyter" Ahrun, Alexandria, first describes the cause, symptoms, prognosis, and treatment of small-pox........	600-700
First public pharmacy erected by Al Mansur, the Arabian..	745
First Arabian Pharmacopœia pub. by Sabur ebn Sahel, president of the school at Jondisabur, who d...................	864
Avicenna, an Arabian, wrote a system of medicine......about	980
"Antidotarium," popular as a pharmacopœia, and a "Quid pro Quo," or list of equivalent drugs, pub. by Nicholas Præpositus, president of the school of Salerno......about	1240-50
Collége de St. Côme, an association of French surgeons organized by Jean Pitard..............................about	1254
Title of chirurgeon or surgeon first recognized by law in England (*Toner*)..	1299
Dissection of human subjects revived by Mondino de Luzzi (ANATOMY)..about	1300
Law for inspection of pharmacies promulgated in France.....	1336
Earliest mandate or warrant for the attendance of a physician at the English court is dated..............................	1454
"Barber-surgeons" in England incorporated under the title of "Masters or Governors of the Mystery or Commonalty of Barbers of London".............................24 Feb.	1461
Diseases of children made a distinct department of medicine by Paolo Magelardo of Fiume and Bartholomæus Metlinger,	1472-73
"Fasciculus Medicinæ" of Johannes de Ketham pub. at Venice, the first medical work illustrated by wood-cuts, pub..	1491
Dogmatic medicine prevailed till the Reformation, when it was attacked by Paracelsus, 1493-1541, and Vesalius..........	1514-64
First dissection at Strasburg.....................................	1517
College of physicians in London founded by Thomas Linacre..	1518
First law in England to aid the study of practical anatomy authorizes dissection of 4 executed felons each year by Masters of the Mystery of Barbers and Surgeons......................	1540
First English work on anatomy, "The Englishman's Treasure, or the True Anatomy of Man's Body," by Thomas Vicary..	1548
Caius college in Cambridge, Engl., established by John Kaye, about	1550
"Treatyse of Anatomie," with 39 copper plates, the first anatomical work so illustrated in England, pub. by Thomas Gemini..	1559
Matteo Realdo Colombo of Cremona, first to demonstrate experimentally that the blood passes from the lungs into the pulmonary veins, d..	"
Eustachian tube discovered by Bartolommeo Eustacchi, professor of anatomy at Rome....................................	1562
Ambrose Paré, father of modern surgery, b. 1510, d..........	1590
First London Pharmacopœia pub..................................	1618
William Harvey of Folkestone, Kent, explains the circulation of the blood in a book pub.......................................	1628
[This discovery made a revolution in physiology.]	
Wilhelm Fabriz, first surgeon to amputate the thigh, d.......	1634
First Pharmacopœia of Paris pub................................	1639
Medicinal use of cinchona or Peruvian bark introduced into Europe by Juan del Vego (CHINCHONA)..........................	1640
Discovery of the thoracic duct and its termination in the subclavian vein in the dog, made by Jean Pecquet of Dieppe in 1647, and in man by Jan van Horne, professor of anatomy in Leyden..	1652
Clinical lectures first held by Montanus, who died in Italy in 1552; clinics introduced in Utrecht by William van der Straten in 1636, and complete clinical method introduced at Leyden by Sylvius..	1658
Marcello Malpighi (1628-94) of Crevalcuore, near Bologna, discovers the capillary circulation in the lungs and mesentery of frogs (1661), and the blood corpuscles (1665); also the pigmentary layer of the skin.....................................about	1665
First transfusion of blood in man performed by Jean Baptiste Denis in France, 15 June, 1667, and by Edmund King in England...23 Nov.	1667
College of Physicians founded at Dublin, Irel..................	"
Anatomical plates of veins and nerves, purchased in Padua by John Evelyn, presented to the Royal Society of Great Britain, the first seen in England...............................31 Oct.	"
Tourniquet invented at the siege of Besançon by Morel.......	1674
Vienna acquires a skeleton in 1658; Strasburg a male skeleton in 1671 and a female in..	1678
"New London Dispensatory" pub. by William Salmon.........	"
College of Physicians founded at Edinburgh, Scotl............	1681
Frederich Hoffman, pioneer of the study of mineral waters, writes a work on the mineral springs of Herrnham.........	1684

"Pharmacopœia Bateana" pub in London by J Skipton 1688

Anatomical theatre first erected in Surgeon's hall Edinburgh 1697

Pierre Brisseau first demonstrates by dissection that the lens is clouded in cataract 1705

First university to create a chair of anatomy in Great Britain was the University of Edinburgh, with Robert Elliot as professor at 15*l* per year "

[Cambridge, 1707, Glasgow, 1718, Oxford, 1750, Dublin, 1785]

Theatricum Anatomicum founded in Berlin 1713

Inoculation for small pox, practised in China about 1000 B C, introduced into London by lady Mary Wortley Montagu 1721

"History of Physics" pub in London by John Freind 1725-26

Formation of artificial pupil by simple incision of the iris introduced by William Cheselden in London 1728

Science of otology founded by Joseph Guichard Duverney, professor of anatomy at Paris, who d 1730

Catheterization of the Eustachian tube from the mouth, attempted by postmaster Guyot of Versailles in 1724, and first performed through the nose by Archibald Cleland of England 1741

Thomas Dover inventor of "Dover's Powder" d "

First chair of clinical medicine in Great Britain established in Edinburgh John Rutherford incumbent "

Separation of surgeons from barbers in France effected by François Gigot de la Peyronie 1743

"Pharmacopœia Hippiatrica" (veterinary) issued by Mr Bartlett eminent Anglo French microscopist 1759

Leopold Auenbrugger, after 7 years' test in Spanish hospitals, publishes his new method for diagnosis of diseases of the chest by percussion 1761

Electricity first employed in treatment of paralysis by Christian Gottl Kratzenstein, who d in 1795, and electric baths introduced by Gottl Fried Rössler 1768

Excision of the elbow joint by Wainman of Shripton, Engl , in 1758, and of the shoulder joint by Charles White "

George Armstrong opens the first children's hospital in Europe, 1769

Existence of septic poisons proved by injection of putrefying matter into the veins of animals, by the great Albert von Haller of Berne, b 1708, d 1777

Foundation of modern public hygiene in a work of J Peter Frank on "System of Medical Police," pub at Mannheim 1779

Morgues instituted in France through Jos Jac de Gardanne (afterwards in Germany through Hufeland) 1781

London Hospital Medical school established 1785

Johann Ernst Wichmann of Hanover first designates the itch mite as the cause of contagion in itch 1786

John Hunter celebrated London physician b 1728, d 1793

First resort for sea bathing established in Germany at Dobberan, 1794

Vaccination or inoculation with cow pox performed in 1774 by farmer Benjamin Jesty of Gloucester, and in 1792 by schoolmaster Plett at Starkendorf in Holstein, but the discovery was completed and its practice advocated by dr Edward Jenner, of Berkeley, Gloucester who first made the discovery complete by the inoculation or vaccination of a boy, James Phipps 14 May, 1796

James Currie first makes extensive use of the thermometer in disease, and introduces the modern method of employing cold water in medical practice in England 1797

First aural hospital in London founded by sir John H Curtis 1816

Sir Charles Bell (1774-1842) of England discovers that the posterior roots of the spinal nerves preside over sensation, and the anterior over motion "

Rene Theodore Hyacinthe Laënnec of France invents the STETHESCOPE "

Modern germ theory first suggested in France by the discovery of the yeast plant by Cagniard Latour 1836

Pharmaceutical Society of Great Britain founded 1 June, 1841

Chloroform, discovered independently by Samuel Guthrie of Sackett's Harbor N Y (1831), and by Eugene Souberain in France, is studied by Liebig, and named by Dumas First employed as an anæsthetic by sir James Young Simpson of Edinburgh Nov 1847

Prof Hermann Ludwig Helmholtz invents the opthalmoscope, 1851

Artificial ear drums proposed by Marcus Banzer of Germany in 1640, by Autenreith in 1815, and by Joseph Toynbee of England 1853

Earliest dental clinic in Germany established by prof E Albrecht (ODONTOLOGY) 1855

Louis Pasteur demonstrates that fermentation and putrefaction are caused by the vital processes of lower organism 1857

Imperfect laryngoscope invented by Benjamin Guy Babington of Guy's hospital in 1829, and perfected by inventions of Czermak and Türck about 1858

Endoscope for the electrical illumination of the interior surface of the bladder invented by A J Desormeaux jr 1863

Miss Garrett (Mrs Anderson) licensed in London to practise medicine 1865

Antiseptic dressing of wounds with carbolic acid discovered by Runge in 1834, used by sir Joseph Lister of Glasgow, in Edinburgh 1869

School of Medicine for Women in London opened Oct. 1874

Hospital opened in Tien Tsin, China, at instance of dr Mackenzie of the London mission, by viceroy Li Hung Chang 1880

Pasteur first inoculates for HYDROPHOBIA 7-16 July, 1885

Dr Robert Koch announces, before the International Medical Congress at Berlin, his discovery of a lymph for checking the growth of tubercle bacillus in consumption, etc Aug 1890

IN THE UNITED STATES

The position of physician general of the colony of Virginia was held one year by dr Lawrence Bohun, who arrived 1610, and afterwards by dr John Pot the first permanent resident physician in the U S Dr Samuel Fuller, first physician of New England arrived in the *Mayflower* in 1620, and dr Johannes la Montagne, first permanent medical settler in New Amsterdam, arrived 1637 followed the next year by drs Gerrit Schult and Hans Kierstede while dr Abraham Staats settled at Albany prior to 1650 Lambert Wilson a "chirurgeon" or surgeon was sent to New England in 1629 to serve the colony 3 years and "to educate and instruct in his art one or more youths"

Anatomical lectures were delivered in Harvard college by dr Giles Firman before 1647

Earliest law to regulate practice of medicine in the colonies was passed in Massachusetts in 1649, adopted by New York 1665

Earliest recorded autopsy and verdict of a coroner's jury was made in Maryland on a negro supposed to have been murdered by his master surgeons received fees for "dissecting and viewing the corpse," 1 hogshead of tobacco 24 Sept. 1657

Treatise on small-pox and measles pub at Boston by dr Thomas Thacher, a sheet 15½×10¾ inches—the first medical work pub in America 1677

First Quarantine act passed by the General Assembly of Pennsylvania 1700

First general hospital chartered in the colonies—Pennsylvania hospital of Philadelphia—organized 1751 opened Dec 1756

Medical department University of Pennsylvania founded 1765

College of Physicians and Surgeons, medical department of King's college, N Y established 1767

First clinical instruction in America given by dr Thomas Bond in Pennsylvania hospital 1769

Term "doctor" first applied to medical practitioners or "physicians" in America (*Toner*) "

Medical department, Harvard university, founded 1783

Philadelphia dispensary for the gratuitous treatment of the sick poor, first in the U S established 1786

Earliest example of a special American Pharmacopœia is a 32 page work of dr William Brown, pub at Philadelphia and designed especially for the army 1788

"Doctors' mob" in NEW YORK "

New York dispensary organized 4 Jan 1791, incorporated 1795

Dr Elisha Perkins of Norwich, Conn , patents his "metallic tractors," afterwards known as "Perkinism" 1796

First original American medical journal, the *Medical Repository*, appears 1797

Medical department of Dartmouth college established 1798

First general Quarantine act passes Congress 23 Feb 1799

First vaccination in U S performed by dr Benjamin Waterhouse, professor in Harvard college, on his 4 children, July, 1800

First Vaccine institute in U S organized by dr James Smith in Baltimore, Md 1802

"American Dispensatory" pub by John Redman Coxe 1806

Ovariotomy performed incidentally by Robert Houston in Glasgow (1701) and by L'Aumonier, in Rouen (1781), is performed by dr Ephraim McDowell of Kentucky 1809

U S Vaccine agency established by Congress (discontinued in 1822) 1813

Work on "Therapeutics and Materia Medica," the first in the U S and best in the English language at that time, pub by Nathaniel Chapman 1817

John Syng Dorsey of Philadelphia, author of "Elements of Surgery" (1814) and first surgeon to tie the external iliac artery d (aged 35) 1818

New York Eye and Ear Infirmary, founded 1820

Pennsylvania Eye and Ear Infirmary, Philadelphia, founded 1822

Benjamin W Dudley, founder of the medical department University of Transylvania, Lexington, Ky , trephines the skull for epilepsy, probably the first instance in the U S 1828

Massachusetts Eye and Ear Infirmary, Boston, founded 1829

"Dispensatory of the United States of America" first pub by Franklin Bache and dr George B Wood 1833

Œsophagotomy first performed by John Watson of New York, case reported 1844

Water cures introduced into the U S by dr R T Trall, who opened a Hydropathic institute in New York in 1844, and dr Joel Shew at Lebanon Springs, N Y 1843

Left subclavian artery tied by J Kearney Rodgers 1846

Collodion first applied to surgical purposes by J Parker Maynard in Boston 1847

Elizabeth Blackwell graduated M D at the medical school of Geneva N Y (the first woman in the U S.) Jan 1849

First excision of the hip joint in the U S performed by Henry J Bigelow, professor in Harvard college 1852

Dr Elkanah Williams of Cincinnati, earliest specialist in ophthalmology, begins practice 1855

Arteria innominata tied for the first time by dr Valentine Mott of New York (1818), by dr R W Hall of Baltimore (1830), by dr E S Cooper of San Francisco (1859), and again, being the first case in which the patient's life was saved, by dr A W Smyth of New Orleans 1864

Dr Horace Green, said to have been the first specialist in diseases of the throat and lungs, d. 1866

Centennial international medical congress held in Philadelphia 1876

New York Polyclinic organized 1880-81, opened 1882

Dr Valentine Mott of New York reports 4 apparently successful inoculations for hydrophobia, performed by himself, Oct 1886

MEDICAL COLLEGES IN THE U. S., REGISTERING 100 STUDENTS AND UPWARDS (1890).

State.	Name.	Location.	Chartered.	Opened.
Alabama	Medical College of Alabama	Mobile	1859	1859
California	Cooper Medical College	San Francisco	1858	1858
Dist. Col.	National Medical College (Columbian University)	Washington	1821	1824
"	Howard University, Medical Department	"	1867	1867
Georgia	Medical College of Georgia (University of Georgia)	Augusta	1784	1829
"	Atlanta Medical College	Atlanta	1855	1856
"	Southern Medical College	"	1879	1879
Iowa	Medical Department, State University of Iowa	Iowa City	1847	1870
Illinois	Rush Medical College	Chicago	1837	1841
"	Hahnemann Medical College and Hospital	"	1851	1855
"	Chicago Medical College (Northwestern University)	"	1859	1859
"	Chicago Homœopathic Medical College	"	1876	1876
"	College of Physicians and Surgeons of Chicago	"	1881	1882
Kentucky	University of Louisville, Medical Department	Louisville	1837	1837
"	Kentucky School of Medicine	"	1850	1850
"	Louisville Medical College	"	1869	1869
"	Hospital College of Medicine (Central University)	"	1874	1874
Louisiana	Medical Department of Tulane University	New Orleans	....	1834
Mass.	Harvard University Medical School	Boston	1650	1783
Maryland	University of Maryland, School of Medicine	Baltimore	1807	1808
"	College of Physicians and Surgeons	"	1872	1872
Michigan	Department of Medicine and Surgery, University of Michigan	Ann Arbor	1837	1850
"	College of Physicians and Surgeons	Detroit	1885	1885
Minnesota	Medical Department of the University of Minnesota	Minneapolis	1851	1888
Missouri	Missouri Medical College	St. Louis	1845	1845
"	St. Louis College of Physicians and Surgeons	"	1879	1879
New York	College of Physicians and Surgeons (Columbia college)	New York	1754	1767
"	Albany Medical College	Albany	1839	1839
"	Medical Department, University of the City of New York	New York	1831	1841
"	Medical Department, University of Buffalo	Buffalo	1846	1846
"	Long Island College Hospital	Brooklyn	1858	1859
"	Bellevue Hospital Medical College	New York	1861	1861
"	New York Homœopathic Medical College	"	"	"
Ohio	Medical College of Ohio	Cincinnati	1819	1820
"	Western Reserve University, Medical Department	Cleveland	1843	1843
"	Eclectic Medical Institute	Cincinnati	1845	1845
"	Starling Medical College	Columbus	1847	1847
"	Homœopathic Hospital College	Cleveland	1849	1849
Oregon	Medical Department of Willamette University	Portland	1853	1866
Pa.	University of Pennsylvania, Medical Department	Philadelphia	1753	1765
"	Jefferson Medical College	"	1826	1826
"	Hahnemann Medical College and Hospital	"	1848	1848
"	Woman's Medical College of Pennsylvania	"	1850	1850
"	Medico-Chirurgical College of Philadelphia	"	"	1881
Tennessee	Medical Department of Vanderbilt University	Nashville	1873	1875
"	Medical Department of University of Tennessee	"	1794	1877
"	Memphis Hospital Medical College (Southwestern Baptist University)	Memphis	1878	1880
Vermont	Medical Department, University of Vermont	Burlington	1791	1823

COLLEGES OF PHARMACY IN THE UNITED STATES.

State.	Name.	Location.	Chartered.	Opened.
Illinois	Chicago College of Pharmacy	Chicago	1859	1859
"	Illinois College of Pharmacy (Northwestern University)	"	1851	1887
Mass	Massachusetts College of Pharmacy	Boston	1852	1867
Maryland	Maryland College of Pharmacy	Baltimore	1841	1841
Michigan	School of Pharmacy, University of Michigan	Ann Arbor	1837	1868
Missouri	St. Louis College of Pharmacy	St. Louis	1866	1866
New York	College of Pharmacy, city of New York	New York	1831	1829
Pa.	Philadelphia College of Pharmacy	Philadelphia	1822	1821

MEDICAL ASSOCIATIONS IN THE UNITED STATES.

	Organized.
American Medical Association	1847
" Pharmaceutical Association	1852
" Ophthalmological Society	1864
" Otological Society	1868
Association of American Medical Editors	1869
American Association for the Cure of Inebriates	1870
Association of Medical Superintendents of American Institutions for the Insane	"
American Public Health Association	1872
" Neurological Association	1875
" Gynecological Society	1876
Association of Medical Officers of American Institutions for Idiotic and Feeble-minded Persons	"
Association of American Medical Colleges	"
American Dermatological Association	"
" Academy of Medicine	"
" Laryngological Association	1878
" Surgical Association	1879
National Association for the Protection of the Insane and the Prevention of Insanity	1880
American Climatological Association	1883

PATHOLOGICAL LABORATORIES FOR THE STUDY OF BACTERIOLOGY.

Laboratory of the Alumni of the College of Physicians and Surgeons of New York	opened	1878
Carnegie Laboratory of New York	"	1885
Loomis Laboratory of New York	"	1886
Hoagland Laboratory of Brooklyn	"	1888
Laboratory of the Johns Hopkins University, Baltimore,	"	1889

SCHOOLS, SYSTEMS, AND THEORIES OF MEDICINE.

The ancient schools of philosophy more or less influenced the development of medicine down to the time of Hippocrates, the Great "creator of scientific medicine and of artistic practice." The previous practice of medicine was largely sacerdotal. The principal schools, systems, and theories, covering almost the entire field of medical treatment from his day, have been as follows:

School, system, or theory.	Founder.	Born. Died
		B.C.
Hippocratists	Hippocrates II. of Cos	460–about 370
Dogmatic school	Thessalus	380
	Draco	350
	Polybus	4th century.
Herophilists	Herophilus of Chalcedon	about 335–280
School of Erasistratus	Erasistratus of Iulius	about 340–280
School of empirics	Philimus of Cos	280
School of methodism	Asclepiades of Prusa	128–56
		A.D.
Pneumatic school	Athenæus of Attalia	about 90
Eclectics	Agathinus of Sparta	about 90
	Claudius Galen of Pergamus	131–201 or 210
Paracelsists	Theophrastus (Paracelsus) Bombast von Hohunheim	1493–1541
System of Joh. Bapt. van Helmont		1578–1644
Iatro-chemical system	François de le Boë	1614–1672
Iatro-mathematical system	Giovanni Alfonso Borelli	1608–1679
System of Sydenham	Thomas Sydenham, England	1624–1689
Eclectic system	Hermann Boerhaave	1668–1738
System of George Ernst Stahl		1660–1734
Mechanico-dynamic system	Friedrich Hoffmann	1660–1742
System of nervous pathology	William Cullen of Scotland	1712–1790
Old Vienna school	Gerhard van Swieten of Leyden	1700–1772

School, system, or theory	Founder	Born Died A D
Theory of Christopher Ludwig Hoffmann of Westphalia		1721-1807
Doctrine of infarctus	Johann Kampf	1726-1787
School of Montpellier (vitalism)	Theophile de Bordeu	1722-1776
Doctrine of vital force	John Christian Reil (elaborator)	1759-1813
System of Erastus Darwin		1731-1802
Theory of animal magnetism	Franz Anton Mesmer	1734-1815
Brunonian system	John Brown Scotland	1735-1788
Theory of realism	Philippe Pinel	1745-1826
Theory of excitement	Johann Andreas Roeschlaub	1768-1835
Theory of stimolo and contrastimolo	Giovanni Rasori of Milan	1762-1837
System of dr Rush	Benjamin Rush Philadelphia	1745-1813
Homœopathy	Samuel C F Hahnemann	1755-1843
Theory of physiological medicine	François Joseph Victor Broussais	1772-1838
French (Paris) school of pathological anatomy and diagnosis	Jean Nicolas Corvisart Desmarets	1755-1821
	René Théodore Hyacinthe Laënnec	1781-1826
English medical	Hostile to every eccentricity and to all schools —*Baas*	
Dublin school of pathological anatomy	Robert James Graves	1797-1853
	William Stokes	1804-1878
School of natural history	Johann Lukas Schönlein of Bamberg	1793-1864
School of natural philosophy	Lorenz Oken (Bavaria)	1779-1851
New Vienna school	Karl, baron von Rokitansky	1804-1878
	Joseph Skoda	1805-1881
	Johannes von Oppolzer	1808-1871
System of John Gottfried Rademacher		1772-1849
Rational medical	C Pfeufer of Bamberg	1806-1869
	Fr G Jac. Henle	1809-1885
Hydrotherapeutics	Vincenz Priessnitz	1772-1849
Cellular vitalism	Rudolph Virchow	1821-
Modern chemical system	Justus von Liebig	1803-1873
School of natural sciences	Hugo Wilhelm von Ziemssen	1829-
Seminal vitalism	Ernst Bouchet Paris	1818-
Phagocyte theory	Elias Metschnikoff	
Parasitic or germ theory	First complete theory brought forward by Karl Hueter professor of surgery in Greifswald	1873
	In the development of this theory the French and Germans are the most prominent workers, as Hallier Fries, Ehrenberg Pasteur, Koch, etc	

VETERINARY SCIENCE

Veterinary medicine was practised in ancient Egypt and India by specialists. The diseases and anatomy of animals are described by early Greek writers like Simon of Athens and Aristotle (384-322 B C) The Roman, Apsyrtus in the 4th century, described glanders, farcy, the strangles, founder etc	
Salaried Pferdeärtze mentioned as located in Ulm, 1388, and in Frankfort-on-the Main	1491
Thomas Fabyan appointed veterinary surgeon to king s horses (Henry VIII of England) salary 12*d* per day 4 Dec	1510
First general work on veterinary anatomy, "Bellerophon," pub by G S Winter von Adlersflügel	1668
Work on "The Anatomy of the Horse" written by Andrew Snape of London	1686
First special veterinary schools founded at Lyons (1762), and at Alfort, near Charenton by Claude Bourgelat	1763
Army veterinary schools opened in Vienna, 1777, Dresden, 1780, and Berlin	1790
London Veterinary college established by Charles Vial de St Bel,	1791
Edinburgh Veterinary college established	1823
Royal College of Veterinary Surgeons chartered	1844
Veterinary Department, Cornell university, established	1869
American Veterinary college, New York, chartered 1857, reorganized	1875

Medici (*med-e-chee*) **family,** the restorers of literature and the fine arts in Italy, were chiefs, or *signori*, of the republic of Florence from 1434, when Cosmo de' Medici, who had been banished from the republic, was recalled and made its chief, he ruled for thirty years Lorenzo de' Medici, styled "the Magnificent," and the "Father of Letters," ruled Florence from 1469 to 1492 Giovanni de' Medici (pope Leo X) was the son of Lorenzo.—*Roscoe.* From 1569 to 1737 the Medici family were hereditary grand-dukes of TUSCANY Catherine de' Medici became queen of France in 1547, and regent in 1550 She plotted with the duke of Alva to destroy the Protestants in 1565

Medina (*mā-dee'na*, Arabia Deserta) holds the tomb of Mahomet, in a large mosque, lighted by rich lamps. Medina was called City of the Prophet, because here Mahomet was protected when he fled from Mecca, 15 July, 622. HEGIRA Medina was taken by the Wahabees in 1804, retaken by the pacha of Egypt, 1818.

Medina, Bopora country, Africa, a kingdom annexed to Liberia by consent, Feb 1880 It is rich in African products and timber, with gold, iron, and other minerals

meg'aphone, a form of TELEPHONE, invented by T A Edison, for the use of the deaf, announced 1878

Meg'ara, a city of ancient Greece, was subdued by the Athenians in the 8th century B.C. Pericles suppressed a revolt, 445 B C The Megarians founded Byzantium 657 B C, and sent a second colony 628 B.C The Megarian (Eristic or disputatious) school of philosophy was founded by Euclid and Stilpo, natives of Megara

megathe'rium is the name given by Cuvier to a large extinct animal belonging to the order *Edentata* A nearly complete skeleton, found on the banks of the river Luxan, near Buenos Ayres, and sent to the Royal museum at Madrid in 1789, was for some time the only source of information regarding it In 1832 other bones were discovered near Rio Salado, and still another collection in 1837, now in the British museum From these prof Owen published a complete description of the skeleton in 1861 In size it exceeded any existing land animal except the elephant, and was inferior to it only in the shortness of its limbs, as in length and bulk its body was equal if not superior

Meigs (*mĕgz*), Fort. FORT MEIGS, OHIO, UNITED STATES, 1813

Meis'tersingers. MINNESINGERS

Melazzo (*me-lat'so*), a town of W Sicily Here Garibaldi, on 20, 21 July, 1860, defeated Neapolitans under gen Bosco, who lost about 600 men, Garibaldi's loss being 167 The latter entered Messina, and on 30 July a convention was signed, providing that the Neapolitan troops should quit Sicily They held the citadel of Messina till 13 March, 1861

Mel'bourne, Australia, capital of Victoria It was founded by J P. Fawkener, 29 Aug 1835, and laid out as a town by order of sir R Bourke, in April, 1837 The first land sale took place in June, and speculation continued till it caused wide-spread insolvency, in 1841-42 VICTORIA

Made a municipal corporation, 1842, a bishopric	1847
First legislative assembly of Victoria meets	1852
Gold found in abundance about 80 miles from Melbourne, autumn of 1851, and immense numbers of emigrants flocked in, causing enormous prices of provisions and clothing	"
Population 23,000 in 1851, about 100,000 end of 1852, 491,378 in	1891

mel'énite, a new explosive invented by M Turpin, a French chemist, approved by the French war minister, Dec. 1886 Several persons killed by an explosion of this material at Belfort The patent was bought by Messrs Armstrong & Co, of Elswick, named lyddite, and sold by them to the British government, announced Oct. 1888

melodrama, in which dialogue is interspersed with music, began in Germany in the 18th century, and was introduced in England by Thomas Holcroft

Melos, now **Milo,** one of the Cyclades in the Ægean sea, early colonized by the Spartans During the Peloponnesian war the Melians adhered to Sparta till the island was captured, after 7 months' siege, by the Athenians, who massacred all the men and sold the women and children as slaves, 416 B.C A statue of Venus, found here in 1820, was placed in the Louvre, 1834 SCULPTURE.

Memno'nium or **Ramesei'on,** Thebes, Egypt, the tomb of Osymandyas, according to Diodorus, now considered to be that of Rameses III, 1618 B C. Its ruins are regarded as the most ancient in THEBES

"And thou hast walked about (how strange a story)
In Thebes's streets three thousand years ago,
When the Memnonium was in all its glory"
—*Smith*, "Address to a Mummy"

Memphis, an ancient city of Egypt, is said to have been built by Menes, 3890 B.C, or by Misraim, 2188 B.C It was restored by Septimius Severus, 202 A D The invasion of Cambyses, 525 B.C., began the ruin of Memphis, and the founding of Alexandria, 332, completed it In the 7th century, under the Saracens, it fell into decay

Memphis, Tenn, on the Mississippi river Pop 1870, 40,226, 1880, 33,593, 1890, 64,495 TENNESSEE, 1803, '19, '49, 1862, '69, etc, YELLOW FEVER

Menai (*men'i*) **strait,** between the Welsh coast and the isle of Anglesey The foot-soldiers of Suetonius Paulinus, when he invaded Anglesey crossed in flat-bottomed boats, while the cavalry swam over and attacked the Druids in their last retreat Their horrid practice of sacrificing captives, and their opposition, so incensed the Roman general that he gave the Britons no quarter throwing all that escaped from that battle into fires which they had prepared for himself and his army, 61 The road from London to Holyhead has long been regarded as the highway to Dublin, Mr Telford was applied to by the government to perfect this route by the London and Holyhead mail-coach road which he did by erecting beautiful suspension bridges over the river Conway and the Menai strait—commenced in July, 1818, finished in July, 1825, opened 30 Jan 1826 The BRITANNIA tubular bridge over the Menai was constructed by Stephenson and Fairbairn in 1849–50 BRIDGES, Tubular

men'dicant friars. Several religious orders commenced alms-begging in the 13th century, in the pontificate of Innocent III They spread over Europe, and formed communities, but at length, by a general council held by Gregory X, at Lyons, in 1272, were reduced to 4 orders—Dominicans, Franciscans Carmelites and Augustines The Capuchins and others branched off FRANCISCANS, etc

Men'nonites, 4 sects of Dutch, Flemish, and German Baptists derive their name from Menno Simons (1492–1559), formerly a Catholic priest, who became a teacher and leader of the Anabaptists about 1537, and published his 'True Christian Belief' in 1556, subsequently divisions and changes ensued As early as 1683 German Mennonites settled in PENNSYLVANIA, and from time to time since When in 1871 Russia, which before had allowed them freedom from conscription imposed it upon them, they were given permission to leave the country A large number came to the United States and Canada, 1874, settling in Manitoba, and in Kansas, Nebraska, etc. As a religious body the different branches show as follows, according to the census of 1890 Churches, 550, church property, $643,800, communicants, 41,541.

mensuration. The properties of conic sections were discovered by Archimedes, to whom the leading principles of mensuration may be attributed He also determined the ratio of spheres, spheroids, etc, about 218 B C ARITHMETIC. The *mensurator*, a new machine for the solution of triangles, was explained by W Marsham Adams, at the British association meeting at Brighton, Aug 1872

Mentz or **Mayence** (*ma-yans'*), a city of Hesse, S W Germany, the Roman *Moguntiacum*, built about 13 B C The archbishopric was founded by Boniface, 745 Many diets have been held here, and here John Faust established a printing-press, about 1440 A festival in honor of John Gutenberg was celebrated here in 1837. PRINTING Mentz was given up to the Prussians, 26 Aug 1866

Menu, Institutes of, the ancient code of India Sir Wm Jones, who translated them into English (1794), dates them between Homer (about 962 B C) and the Roman Twelve Tables (about 419 B.C)

Merca'tor's charts. MAPS

Mercer, Fort. FORT MERCER

Merchant Adventurers' company, established by the duke of Brabant in 1296, was extended to England in Edward III's reign. "A company of merchant adventurers was incorporated for the discovery of unknown lands," 1555 —*Bancroft*, "Hist of the U. S.," vol i. p 79

Mercia. BRITAIN

Mercury, the planet nearest the sun, and the smallest known to the ancients Its distance varies from 42,669,000 miles to 28,115,000, difference over 15,000,000 miles Its light and heat is 7 times greater at its mean distance from the sun than the earth It turns on its axis in 24 hrs 5½ min Its year is 87⅞ days, density as compared with the earth as 112 to 100, diameter, 3000 miles The transit of Mercury over the sun's disk, and first observed by Gassendi, 1631, takes place at intervals, usually of 13, sometimes of 7 years The transits always occur in May or Nov, and may last 8 hrs. or very much less It was well observed 5 Nov 1868 The last transit took place 9 May, 1891 —The Greek god Hermes was the Roman Mercury CALOMEL, QUICKSILVER.

Mercy, Order of, in France, was established with the object of accomplishing the redemption of Christian captives among the Saracens, by John de Matha, in 1198.—*Hénault* Another order was formed by Pierre Nolasque in Spain, 1223

merino sheep. SHEEP

Mer'oe, an ancient city and country of Africa, an island formed by branches of the Nile, included in the present Soudan, lying east and south of the city of Khartoum, said to have flourished under sacerdotal government in the time of Herodotus, about 450 B C, and much earlier "The traditions of the Egyptian priesthood agree that Meroe in Ethiopia laid the foundation of the most ancient states"—*Anthon*

Merovingians, first race of French kings, 418–752 FRANCE, MAYORS

Merrimac. HAMPTON ROADS, UNITED STATES, 1862.

Merry-Andrew. A name said to have been first given to Andrew Borde, a physician in the reign of Henry VIII, and who, for his facetious manners, was sometimes received at court, 1547

Merry Mount. MASSACHUSETTS, 1626–30

Merton, Surrey, Engl At an abbey here, the barons under Henry III, 23 Jan 1236, held a parliament which enacted the Provisions or Statutes of Merton, the oldest body of laws save Magna Charta They were repealed in 1863 BASTARD

Merv or **Meru** (the ancient *Antiochia Margiana*), a town of independent Turkestan, central Asia It flourished under the Seljuk Turks, especially under sultan Alp Arslan, it was sacked by the Monguls in 1221, it became subject to Persia in 1510, to the emir of Bokhara in 1787, to the Turkomans in 1856, and to Russia 1883–84 RUSSIA, TURKESTAN

mesmerism. Frederick Anthony Mesmer (1733–1815), a German physician of Merseburg, taught in 1766, in a thesis on planetary influence, that the heavenly bodies diffuse through the universe a subtle fluid which acts on the nervous system Quitting Vienna for Paris, in 1778, he gained numerous proselytes and much money A committee of physicians and philosophers investigated his pretensions, among them Franklin, and Bailly, in a paper drawn up in 1784, exposed the futility of animal magnetism. In 1845 baron von Reichenbach excited considerable attention by announcing a so-called new "imponderable," or "influence," which he named ODYL. These phenomena are now usually classed under HYPNOTISM.

Messalians, a sect professing to adhere to the letter of the gospel, about 310, refused to work, quoting this passage, "Labor not for the food that perisheth"

Messe'nia, now **Maura-Matra,** in the Peloponnesus, a kingdom founded by Polycaon, 1499 B.C It had long sanguinary wars with Sparta, and once contained a hundred cities It was at first governed by kings, after regaining power in the Peloponnesus it formed an inferior republic, under the protection first of the Thebans and afterwards of the Macedonians

	B C
First Messenian war began 743 B C, occasioned by violence to some Spartan women in a temple common to both nations, the king of Sparta being killed in their defence. Eventually, Ithome was taken, and the Messenians enslaved.	724
Second war, to throw off the Spartan yoke, commenced about 685 ending in the defeat of the Messenians, who fled to Sicily,	668
Third war	466–55

Messiah, synonymous with Christ "the anointed," foretold by Dan ix 25, about 538 B.C. 'We have found the Messiah, which is, being interpreted, the Christ" (John i 41) —"The Messiah," Handel's greatest oratorio, composed by him in 23 days (22 Aug.–14 Sept 1741), was first performed at Dublin, 13 Apr 1742, in aid of the charities of that city

Messina (*mes-see'na*), Sicily, so named by the Samians who seized this city, then called Zancle, 671 B C It was seized by the MAMERTINI, about 281 B.C It belonged for many ages to the Roman empire, was taken by the Saracens, about 829 A D.—*Priestley* Roger the Norman took it from them by surprise, about 1072

metals, a class of elementary substances, characterized by fusibility, by opaqueness, by a peculiar lustre to the eye, and by certain chemical properties, and including many of the most useful forms of matter, as iron, copper, silver, gold, lead, tin, mercury, nickel, aluminium, etc. Tubal-Cain is mentioned as an "instructor of every artificer in brass and iron" (Gen. iv.). Moses and Homer speak of the 7 metals, and Virgil of melting steel. The Phœnicians had skill in working metals. Bunsen and Kirchhoff's method of chemical analysis by the spectrum has added cæsium, rubidium, thallium, indium, gallium, and others to known metals. ELEMENTS, MINES. See also the several metals.

metamor'phists, in the 15th century, affirmed that Christ's natural body, with which he ascended into heaven, was wholly deified.

metaphys'ics, the science of abstract reasoning, or that which contemplates existence without relation to matter. The term literally denoting "after physics" originated from these words having been put at the head of certain essays of Aristotle which follow his treatise on physics.—*Mackintosh.* Modern metaphysics arose in the 15th century—the period when an extraordinary impulse was given to the study of the human mind in Europe, commonly called the "revival of learning." LITERATURE, PHILOSOPHY.

Metau'rus, Battle of. Hasdrubal, brother of Hannibal, having crossed the Alps, had reached the Metaurus, in central Italy, while Hannibal was in the south. The Roman consuls (207 B.C.) were M. Livius and Claudius Nero. Livius opposed the advance of Hasdrubal, and Nero was appointed to watch Hannibal. The object of the Carthaginian generals was to unite, that of the Romans to prevent it. Nero, leaving the bulk of his army before Hannibal, marched with 10,000 of his best troops and joined Livius with secrecy and despatch, unknown to Hannibal, within 6 days. In the battle which immediately followed Hasdrubal was not only defeated but killed. Nero returned at once to his former position before Hannibal, whose first notification of the battle was the exhibition of the Carthaginian prisoners before his camp and the head of his brother thrown down before one of his outposts. This has been called one of the 7 decisive battles of the world. BATTLES, CARTHAGE.

metempsycho'sis, a doctrine attributed to Pythagoras, about 528 B.C., asserts the transmigration of the soul from one body to another. It is also ascribed to the Egyptians, who would eat no animal food lest they should devour the body into which the soul of a deceased friend had passed. They thought that so long as the body of the deceased was kept entire, the soul would not transmigrate, and therefore embalmed the dead. BUDDHISM.

meteor'ograph, an apparatus for which father Secchi of Rome received a prize at the Paris International Exhibition, July, 1867. It is self-acting, and registers the changes of the atmosphere in a diagram.

meteorol'ogy (Gr. μετέωρος, aerial), properly, is the scientific study of atmospheric phenomena and investigation of weather and climate. Aristotle composed a treatise called Μετεωρολογικά, in which he dealt with all which was then known of air, water, and earthquakes (cir. 300 B.C.). One of the earliest collections of prognostics is found in the Διοσημεῖα of Aratus, a Greek who flourished in Macedonia and Asia Minor about 270 B.C. The invention of the air thermometer by Sanctorio of Padua, 1590 A.D., improved by an Italian artist in 1655, who used alcohol, and by Römer who used mercury, and the barometer, invented by Torricelli in 1643, gave the first accurate means for instrumental observation of the temperature and pressure of the atmosphere. The publication of Dalton's "Meteorological Essays" in 1793 was the first instance of the principles of philosophy being brought to bear on the explanation of the complex phenomena of the atmosphere. Since then meteorology has gradually grown to be more and more nearly an exact science.

First attempt to explain the phenomenon of the rainbow by the reflection of light upon the interior of the drops was made by a German monk named Theodoric, and the second by an archbishop, A. de Dominis. . 1611
Weight of a column of atmosphere first ascertained by the Italian philosopher Torricelli about . 1643
M. Florin Perrier, brother in law of Pascal, takes Torricelli's column to summit of the Puy de Dome, France, 3500 feet high, and the mercury sinks from 30 to 27 inches 19 Sept. 1648
Daily readings of Torricelli column by Pascal at Paris, Perrier at Clermont, and Chanut and Descartes at Stockholm at the same time, the pioneers of synchronous observations 1649-50
Magdeburg hemispheres showing the equal pressure of the atmosphere in all directions, invented by Otto von Guericke of Magdeburg soon after his invention of the air pump 1650
English philosopher Robert Boyle, one of the first council of the Royal society, tests the compressibility of air; results pub. 1660
Pascal's treatise on the "Equilibrium of Fluids" and on the "Weight of Air" pub. 1663
Name barascope (afterwards changed to barometer) given to the Torricellian column by prof. G. Sinclair of Glasgow 1668-70
Contraction of air under pressure examined by Edme Mariotte, a Burgundian priest who died at Dijon 1684
Theorem that at altitudes in arithmetical progression the density of air is in geometrical progression proved by Halley 1685
Identity of lightning and electricity suspected by Wall 1708
Fahrenheit constructs thermometers, taking as fixed points in graduating them the melting point of ice and the boiling point of water 1714
Theory of the trade winds first propounded by George Hadley in the "Philosophical Transactions" (independently discovered by Dalton a half century later) 1735
First generalization of value in reference to the storms of the U. S. made by Lewis Evans, who remarks on his map, "All our great storms begin to leeward; thus a N. E. storm shall be a day sooner in Virginia than Boston" 1749
Benjamin Franklin by his kite experiment identifies lightning with electricity 15 June 1752
Lightning rods introduced by Franklin 1755
Experiments by dr. Heberden of London show that rain gauges on lofty buildings collect less than at the ground (now generally ascribed to the wind) 1766
Meteorological Society of the Palatinate established 1780
Patrick Wilson of Glasgow publishes his "Memoirs of Certain Great Frosts at Glasgow" about "
First self registering thermometer, which recorded maximum and minimum temperature, devised by James Six 1781
First scientific work on mirage by prof. Busch, who observed it on the Elbe near Hamburg and on the coasts of the Baltic sea 1783
Spectre of the Brocken witnessed and described by the traveller Haue 23 May 1797
Expansion of air by heat independently examined by the English philosopher Dalton and the French Gay Lussac 1801-2
Clouds classified as the cirrus, cumulus, stratus, cirro cumulus, cirro stratus, cumulo stratus, and cumulo cirro stratus, or nimbus, by Luke Howard 1803
Sir Francis Beaufort tabulates his scale of winds divided into 12 degrees of force . 1805
Theory of dew pub. by dr. W. C. Wells 1814
Humboldt publishes his treatise on "Isothermal Lines" 1817
First meeting of the Meteorological society of London 15 Oct. 1823
Daniell's "Meteorological Essays and Observations," discussing the hygrometry of the atmosphere, solar and terrestrial radiation, etc., pub.
Work entitled the "Law of Storms" pub. by sir W. Reed 1838
OZONE named by prof. Schönbein of Basle 1840
Lieut. Maury, of the Washington Observatory, makes researches as to the most favorable route for sailing vessels between the U. S. and Rio Janeiro; the ship *Wright*, capt. Jackson, from Baltimore, the first to steer by Maury's course, crossed the equator in 24 days from Baltimore, the usual time had been 41 days, the *Wright* leaves Baltimore 9 Feb. 1848
Hypothesis that the appearance of meteors or fire balls is often due to bodies of dusty consistency traversing space announced by M. Heiss in his work on shooting stars (METEORS), 1849
Conference at Brussels, the United States, France, England, Russia, Sweden, Norway, Denmark, Holland, Belgium, and Portugal agree upon a uniform plan of meteorological observations at sea (since adopted by other nations) 1853
Meteorological reports collected by telegraph and reports sent out daily by prof. Joseph Henry of the Smithsonian Institute, 1854
Dr. Andrews demonstrates by direct experiments, described in the "Philosophical Transactions of the Royal Society," that ozone is oxygen condensed to one half its volume 1856
Meteorological department of the Board of Trade (English) established 1855, under adm. Fitzroy, commences publication of reports 1857
Storm warnings first issued in Holland through M. Buys Ballot 1860
Storm warnings first sent to the coast of England by the Board of Trade, 6 Feb. 1861, and first pub. 31 July, 1861
Prof. Tyndall makes valuable experiments on radiant heat, showing that the vapor of water exerts extraordinary energy as a radiant and absorbent of heat 1862
Daily international bulletin of the Imperial Observatory at Paris, under direction of M. le Verrier, first pub. Nov. "
Rarefaction of the atmosphere in high regions investigated by sir James Glaisher, who ascended in a balloon with Mr. Coxwell, at Wolverhampton, Engl., 37,000 ft. 5 Sept. 1863
Storm warnings in England suspended 7 Dec. 1866
WEATHER BUREAU established in the U. S. . 1870
Kew Meteorological Observatory, given to the British Association Apr. 1860, purchased and presented to the Royal society by J. P. Gassiot 1871
Daily weather charts first issued by the Meteorological office of England. 11 Mch. 1872
International meteorological congress at Vienna. 2-16 Sept. 1873
Glycerine barometer 28 feet high, in which a change in the condition of the atmosphere equal to 1 inch in the mercury barometer caused the glycerine to rise or fall 10 inches, con-

structed by Mr Jordan for the Loan Exhibition of Scientific Instruments at South Kensington, Engl 13 May-30 Dec 1876

Meteorological department of Board of Trade (Engl) placed under a committee of the Royal society, R H Scott sec'y, July, 1877

International meteorological congress meets at Rome, 14-22 Apr 1879 and at Berne 9-12 Aug 1880

Plan for international simultaneous magnetic and meteorological observations in polar regions, proposed by lieut Carl Weyprecht, arctic explorer in Sept 1875 elaborated at an international polar congress at Hamburg Aug 1879, and at Berne, July 1880, and the "Polar Commission" organized by 10 delegates at St Petersburg Aug 1881

Important observations on solar radiation made by prof S. P Langley on mount Whitney, Cal, in July 1881, and results pub in "Professional Papers, No XV U S Signal service" 1881

Proof that a lightning flash diminishes electric tension in the atmosphere by experiments with the electrometer at the top of the Washington monument Washington D C 1886

Artificial rain making attempted by exploding dynamite bombs in the air, near Midland, Tex, by R G Dyrenforth and staff, 18-26 Aug 1891

William Ferrel, meteorologist, d at Maywood, Kan 18 Sept. "

METEOROLOGICAL PHENOMENA

Cyclones, hurricanes, tornadoes, hail storms, blizzards, etc are mentioned under STORMS, also RAIN and TEMPERATURE A few of the phenomena of meteorology are noted below

Extraordinary dry fog first remarked at Copenhagen, 9 May, 1783 extended over Europe and a part of Asia 1783

Complete solar halo observed by Lowitz at St Petersburg, 29 June, 1790

Frost every month in 1816 in the latitude of Philadelphia, and ice as thick as window glass formed in Pennsylvania, New York and throughout New England 5 July, 1816

Extensive deposit of red snow discovered by capt John Ross, R N near cape York, Greenland 1818

Dry fog in part of Europe, on the north coast of Africa, and in the United States Aug 1831

Barometer falls 2 59 inches in 3 hours in a hurricane near Calcutta 21 May, 1833, and 1 69 inches in 6 hours in a hurricane at St Thomas, W I 2 Aug 1837

Light shower of rain for 1 hour falls from a cloudless sky near Trinidad, observed by sir J C Ross 25 Dec. 1839

Ice forms at New Orleans, La, skating on the Mississippi, Dec. 1845

Barometer falls 1 47 inches in 6 hours in hurricane at Havana, Cuba 11 Oct 1846

Four luminous columns each about 15° long, like a cross with the sun in the centre seen from Paris sunset 22 Apr 1847

Barometer falls 1 05 inches in 2½ hours in a hurricane at Chittagong, Ind 13 May, 1849

Snow falls at Lynchburg, Va 11 June, 1857

Unexampled frost throughout the northern U S killing most of the wheat and other crops night 4 June 1859

Notable halos and paraselenæ at 8 P M in the departments of Indre et Loire and Loire et Cher, France 21 Feb 1864

Auroras seen over a large portion of the northern hemisphere (AURORA), 15 Apr 1869, and 24 Oct 1870

Wind storm in which the mean hourly velocity for 24 hours is 50 miles at Yankton, Dak 13 Apr 1873

Mercury falls 48° in 1 hour at Denver, Col 15 Jan 1875

Barometer reaches 31 21 inches at Barnaul, Siberia. 9 Jan 1877

Golden snow described in Klein's *Wochenschrift*, as observed by prof Weber in Peckeloh, Germany . 27 Feb "

Heavy shower lasting 5 minutes fell from an apparently clear sky at Vevay, Ind 30 June, "

Wind 186 miles per hour on mount Washington . Jan 1878

Wind 138 miles per hour during hurricane at cape Lookout, N C 17 Aug 1879

Extreme cloudiness at Unalaska, Aleutian islands, where cloudiness frequently ranges from 91 to 93 per cent per month, and where there was but 3 per cent of clear sky during Feb 1880

Dense fog in London Engl, for 3 months, the death rate from bronchitis rose to 431 per 100 per cent. and that from whooping cough to 331 per 100 per cent Nov 1879, to Feb. "

Barometer on the ship *Chateaubriand*, during a typhoon on the China sea, sank in 4 hours from 29 64 to 27 04 27 Sept. "

Remarkable solar halos observed in the U S in the Ohio, upper Mississippi, and lower Missouri valleys 29-31 Dec "

Dry fog from New Hampshire to North Carolina, largely obscuring the sun, at Salem, Mass., 6 Sept, it was the darkest since the "dark day" of 19 May, 1780 1-10 Sept 1881

Optical phenomenon of a mock sun, 120° from the true sun, seen by MM Barral and Bixio, 27 July, 1850, and by lieut A W Greely opposite Henrietta, Nesmith Glacier, Grinnell Land .. . 3 May, 1882

Remarkable red sunsets (SUN) Oct. to Dec 1883

Nearly three fourths of an inch of snow falls from a clear sky at Bloomington, Ill . 15 Mch 1885

Luminous cirrus like clouds appearing about 9 50 P M, cover the northwest and northern sky to a height of about 20° in 3 zones, the centre shining with a silver like light equal to the full moon at sunset, observed by O Jesse of Stegletz, 21 June, "
[The phenomenon lasted about an hour, was repeated several times within a few weeks, and again May, 1886]

Wind 144 miles per hour at cape Mendocino, Cal . . Jan 1886

Barometer 31 21 inches at fort Assiniboine. . . 6 Jan "

Wind storm on mount Washington, mean hourly velocity for 24 hours, 111 miles . ... 27 Feb "

Snow falls at Lynchburg, Va. . 12 June, 1887

Green clouds seen on the upper Yukon by William Ogilvie, 19, 29 Feb 1888

MET

Slight snow locally in Great Britain as far south as the Isle of Wight, 11 and 12 July, heavy snow on mount Washington, N H, nearly to the base of the mountain 12 July, 1888

meteors, luminous, include shooting-stars, fire-balls, and falling-stones or aerolites They were described by Halley, Wallis, and others early in the 17th century The periodicity of the star-showers about the 10th of August (termed in the middle ages St Lawrence's tears) was discovered separately by Quetelet, 1836, and by Herrick in 1837 The following are usual epochs for their annual return 2 Jan, 29 July, 3 and 9-12 Aug 8-14 Nov, 11 Dec —*R P Greg* ASTRONOMY, 1799 1833, '66, '67, '72, '85, '91

Star shower seen by Humboldt at Cumana (South America) 12 Nov 1799, and by dr D Olmsted, at New Haven (Conn) 13 Nov 1833 Magnificent continuous star shower of 14 Nov 1866, had been predicted by prof Newton A fine display occurred on the night of 13 Nov 1868 in the United States Others were observed in Britain and Europe, 27 Nov 1872, and in S and W Europe, 27 Nov 1885

Aerolites, falling-stones, accompanying meteors, are in many museums One weighing 1600 pounds is in the cabinet of Yale university They contain iron nickel and other minerals

Norman Lockyer announces his theory, based on spectrum experiments, that all self luminous bodies in the celestial spaces are composed of meteorites or masses of vapor produced by heat, brought about by condensation of meteor swarms due to gravity, Royal society, 17 Nov 1887

method (Gr μέθοδος, a way of transit), the organization of knowledge, the orderly use of the intellect in discovering truth S T Coleridge's treatise on the science of method is prefixed to the first volume of the "Encyclopædia Metropolitana," 1845

Most recent work on this subject is prof Stanley Jevons's "Principles of Science a Treatise on Logic and Scientific Method," 1874. "The powers of mind concerned in creation of science are discrimination, detection of identity, and retention"

Meth'odism. The name "Methodist" was applied to Charles Wesley by fellow-students, in ridicule, about 1729, but the expression had been previously used, as "Anabaptists and plain packstaff Methodists" were known 100 years before The term had been applied to non conformists in the days of Annesley, and a class of high Calvinistic divines in England bore the same title about the time of the Wesleys The first Methodist society was organized in London in 1739 According to its founder, John Wesley, Methodism received its earliest impulse at Oxford, Engl, Nov 1729, when, with his brother Charles, a Mr Morgan and Mr Kirkham, he founded the "Holy club," again at Savannah, Ga, where he spent a short time as a missionary and held meetings in his own house during 1736, and a third time at a meeting with 40 or 50 persons after his return, held in Fetter lane, London, 1 May, 1738 when they agreed to meet in conference every Wednesday evening.

Corner stone of first Methodist meeting house laid at Bristol, Engl 12 May, 1739

Cannon foundery in Moorfields, London, opened as a regular place of worship by Wesley . 11 Nov "

United society, first organized form of Methodism, established in connection with the foundery "

George Whitefield lays the corner stone of the Kingswood school, 1739, which is opened 1741

Methodist class meetings instituted at Bristol, Engl 1742

Wesley founds the Orphan house at Newcastle, Engl 20 Dec. "

First "conference" of 6 Methodist preachers at the invitation of Wesley at the foundery in London 25 June, 1744

Thomas Beard, Methodist evangelist, arrested during the persecution of the Methodists at Newcastle, dies in the hospital, "the proto martyr of Methodism" . . "

First list of circuits published in the minutes of the conference, 1746

Thomas Williams, a lay preacher from England, forms a Methodist society in Dublin Ireland 1747

Foundations of Calvinistic Methodism and the Lady Huntingdon Connection laid by the preaching of George Whitefield 1748

Conference orders quarterly meetings everywhere, and watch nights and love feasts monthly 1749

Corner stone of the City Road chapel, London, laid by John Wesley . . . 1 Apr 1777

Publication of the *Arminian Magazine* begun in England 1778

A "Deed of Declaration," constituting 100 preachers, named by Wesley the "Conference of the People called Methodists," recorded in the High court of Chancery 28 Feb 1784

Wesleyan Methodists establish a Sunday school in Bolton Le Moors, Engl Apr 1786

Methodism introduced into the West Indies . . "

Charles Wesley d in London. 29 Mch 1788

William Mahy ordained at Courseulles, Normandy, first Methodist ordination on the continent of Europe . 1790

John Wesley d in London 2 Mch 1791

New Methodist connection (Kilhamites) founded in England 1797

Plan for home missions in England adopted by conference 1806

First camp meeting in England held in Staffordshire by Lorenzo Dow. . .. 1807

"Primitive Methodists" or "Ranters" organized in England.. 1810
Methodism introduced into Africa.......................... 1811
Preachers' Auxiliary fund established; an outgrowth of the Preachers' fund begun in 1763.......................... 1813
British Wesleyan mission at Ceylon founded by associates of dr. Coke, who died on ship-board bound for India.....3 May. 1814
Bible Christian connection or "Bryanites" founded.......... 1815
Methodism introduced into Australia.......................... "
Contingent fund established by British conference............ "
Primitive Wesleyan Methodists or "Clonites" established in Ireland.......................... 1816
General Chapel fund instituted.......................... 1818
English Wesleyan Children's fund instituted, to provide for preachers' children.......................... 1819
Methodism introduced into Polynesia.......................... 1822
Methodist Episcopal mission in Liberia, Africa, established.... 1833
British Wesleyan Theological institution established by a committee of 20 preachers, who met in London..........23 Oct. "
Wesleyan Association Methodists or "Warrenites" organized under dr. Samuel Warren in England.......................... 1836
Centenary conference meets at Liverpool, Engl.......31 July, 1839
Methodist Episcopal mission in China begun by rev. Moses C. White and rev. J. D. Collins.......................... 1847
Methodist Episcopal mission established in India............. 1856
Martin's Mission institute (M.E.) founded at Frankfort, Germany.......................... 1858
Rev. Francis Burns (colored), a member of the Liberia conference, ordained bishop at Perry, N. Y................14 Oct. "
Bareilly Theological seminary (M.E.) at Bareilly, India, founded, 1871
Methodist Episcopal mission in Mexico established by dr. Butler, 1872
Foochow Biblical institute (M.E.) at Foochow, China, founded, "
Methodist Episcopal mission in Japan begun by dr. Maclay.... "
Mexican School of Theology (M.E.) at Puebla, founded........ 1874
Wesley monument in Westminster Abbey unveiled....29 Mch. 1876
Laity admitted to representation in conference of Wesleyan Methodist ministers at Bristol, Engl................25 July, 1877
City Road chapel, London, nearly destroyed by fire.....7 Dec. 1879
Japan Methodist Episcopal Theological school at Tokio, Japan, founded.......................... "
Œcumenical Methodist conference at City Road chapel, London (400 delegates, ministers and laymen, from all parts of the world) meets..........................7 Sept. 1881
Second Œcumenical Methodist conference in Washington, D.C., 7 Oct. 1891

METHODISM IN THE UNITED STATES.

So-called second rise of Methodism at Savannah, Ga., where 20 or 30 persons meet at the house of John Wesley........Apr. 1736
George Whitefield arrives in Philadelphia, Nov. 1739, and preaches throughout Pennsylvania, New Jersey, and New England..1739-40
First Methodist society in America organized in New York city by Philip Embury, influenced by Barbara Heck, "mother of American Methodism," and Robert Strowbridge preaches in Maryland.......................... 1766
Old John Street church, New York city, first Methodist meeting-house in America, dedicated..........................30 Oct. 1768
Francis Asbury, sent as a missionary to America by Mr. Wesley, arrives in Philadelphia..........................27 Oct. 1771
First annual conference of Methodist church in America held at Philadelphia..........................4 July, 1773
Thomas Coke ordained at Bristol, Engl., superintendent of the Methodist societies in America, 2 Sept., and Francis Asbury designated as general superintendent.......................... 1784
Christmas conference in the meeting-house in Lovely lane, Baltimore, unanimously agrees to form an independent church; the "Methodist Episcopal church" organized with 83 preachers and 15,000 members. Conference met..25 Dec. "
Francis Asbury, formally set apart by the imposition of hands as general superintendent (bishop) of the Methodist Episcopal church in America, at the Baltimore conference..27 Dec. "
Sunday-schools begun in the U. S. at the home of Thomas Crenshaw in Virginia.......................... 1786
General superintendent of the Methodist Episcopal church first called "bishop" in the minutes of the conference..... 1787
Methodist Book Concern organized at Philadelphia, with John Dickens as book steward; the *Arminian Magazine* begun... 1789
Title "presiding elder" first found in conference minutes..... "
First general conference M. E. church in Baltimore.....1 Nov. 1792
Cokesbury college, opened at Abingdon, Md., 6 Dec. 1787, burned 7 Dec. 1795; re-established in Baltimore, and burned, 1796
Miami circuit formed by John Kobler, missionary to the Northwestern territory.......................... 1798
Camp-meetings begun in Tennessee by 2 brothers M'Gee, one a Presbyterian, the other a Methodist.................. 1799
Methodism carried into Illinois by Benjamin Young, a missionary.......................... 1803
Methodist Book Concern removed to New York.............. 1804
First delegated general conference meets, New York...1 May, 1812
Union American M. E. church founded by rev. Peter Spencer at Wilmington, Del..........................June, 1813
Bishop Asbury dies in Spottsylvania, Va..............31 Mch. 1816
African M. E. church organized at Philadelphia by Richard Allen..........................Apr. "
Tract society organized in New York.......................... 1817
Methodist Magazine established (MAGAZINES).................. 1818
Missionary and Bible society of the M. E. church organized in the city of New York..........................5 Apr. 1819
Western Methodist Book Concern at Cincinnati established by the conference.......................... 1820
Christian Advocate, the first weekly publication under the patronage of the M. E. church, issued..................9 Sept. 1826
Sunday-school Union of the M. E. church organized....2 Apr. 1827

MET

Rev. John Lord, of the New England conference, introduces "4-days" or protracted meetings..........................Sept. 1827
Canada Annual conference and the Methodist Episcopal church in the U. S. separate by mutual consent.......................... 1828
Wesleyan university at Middletown, Conn., organized......... 1830
Mission to the Flathead Indians began.......................... 1833
Dickinson college at Carlisle, Pa., incorporated 1783, transferred to the M. E. church and opened..........................Sept. 1834
Methodist Book Concern destroyed by fire............18 Feb. 1836
Ohio Wesleyan university opened at Delaware, O............. 1844
Methodist Episcopal church, south, organized at Louisville, Ky., 1 May, 1845

[This separate organization due to slavery.]

Boston University School of Theology at Boston, Mass., founded, 1847
Congregational Methodist church organized in Monroe county, Ga.......................... 1852
First general conference in New England at Boston........... "
Northwestern university at Evanston, Ill., opened............ 1855
National Association of Local Preachers organized.......4 Oct. 1858
General Conference of the M. E. church organizes an annual conference in India, which meets at Lucknow........8 Dec. 1864
Board of Church Extension incorporated.............13 Mch. 1865
Centenary year of American Methodism celebrated. Church statistics show 7576 travelling preachers, 8602 local preachers, and 1,032,184 members.......................... 1866
Drew Theological seminary at Madison, N. J., founded........ "
Freedmen's Aid Society of the M. E. church organized in Cincinnati..........................7 Aug. "
Woman's Foreign Missionary Society organized at Boston, 22 Mch. 1869
Board of Education of the M. E. church incorporated......Apr. "
Colored M. E. church in America organized in a general conference which meets at Jackson, Tenn..............16 Dec. 1870
Second Sunday in June of each year designated as Children's day by M. E. conference which meets.......................... 1872
Centenary Biblical institute at Baltimore, Md., founded....... "
First Chautauqua assembly at Chautauqua lake, N. Y.....Aug. 1874
Woman's Home Missionary society organized at Cincinnati, O., 6 July, 1880
Gammon Theological School of Clark university, Atlanta, Ga., founded.......................... 1883
Methodist Episcopal General Hospital opened in Brooklyn, N. Y..........................15 Dec. 1887
Epworth League projected in Cleveland, O..............May, 1889

STATISTICS OF METHODISM PRESENTED AT THE ŒCUMENICAL CONFERENCE AT WASHINGTON, D. C., 7 OCT. 1891.

Name of society.	Organized.	Churches.	Ministers.	Members.
In America:				
Methodist Episcopal..........	1784	22,853	15,058	2,256,463
Methodist Episcopal, South....	1845	11,767	5,050	1,218,561
African Methodist Episcopal...	1816	4,069	4,150	475,565
African M. E., Zion..........	1820	3,500	3,650	425,000
Colored Methodist Episcopal...	1870	3,196	1,800	130,824
Methodist Protestant.........	1828	2,003	2,153	157,604
United Brethren in Christ.....	1815	2,779	2,017	197,123
Evangelical Association.......	1800	2,062	1,227	150,234
American Wesleyan..........	1842	600	650	19,525
Free Methodist..............	1860	952	1,050	20,998
Primitive Methodist..........	1810	77	64	5,620
Congregational Methodist.....	1852	50	50	5,525
Union American M. E.........	1813	50	112	3,500
African Union M. Protestant...		50	56	5,090
Independent Methodist........		35	8	2,500
United Methodist, Free........		29	8	3,785
Methodist Church of Canada...	1874	3,092	1,819	241,376
West India Methodist.........		279	101	58,575
British Wesleyan Conference Missions..................	....	22	19	5,226
Total American...........		57,465	39,042	5,383,994
In Europe..........................		15,584	4,488	915,986
In Asia..........................		311	588	35,313
In Africa..........................		571	365	77,234
Australasia, Polynesia, and South Sea Missions..........................		3,250	788	93,140
Total..........................		77,181	45,271	6,505,667

meth'yl, a colorless inodorous gas, a compound of hydrogen and carbon, first obtained free by Frankland and Kolbe separately, in 1849.

Meton'ic cycle, a period of 19 years, or 6940 days, at the end of which the changes of the moon fall on the same days. CALIPPIC PERIOD.

metric system, a uniform decimal system of weights and measures, originated in France with a committee of eminent scientists, named by the Academy of Sciences by order of the Constituent Assembly, 8 May, 1790. The basis of the system is the metre, which is 3.37 inches longer than the American "yard." This base, determined by Delambre and Méchain, is the $\frac{1}{40000000}$ part of the circumference of the earth on the meridian extending through France from Dunkirk to Barcelona. It was made the unit of length and the base of the system by law, 7 Apr 1795 A prototype metre was constructed in platinum by an international commission, representing the governments of France, Holland, Denmark, Sweden, Switzerland, Spain, Savoy, and the Roman, Cisalpine, and Ligurian republics, in 1799 This standard metre was deposited at the Palace of the Archives in Paris, 22 June, 1799, and declared to be the definitive base of the system forever The unit of weight is the *gramme*, the weight of a cubic centimetre of water at 4° centigrade (the temperature of greatest density) The unit of measure of surface is the *are*, which is the square of the decametre, or 10 metres The unit of measure of capacity is the *stere*, or cubic metre In the metric system the decimal increase is indicated by the prefix *deca*, ten, *hecto*, hundred, *kilo*, thousand, *myria*, ten thousand, and the decrease by *deci*, *centi*, and *milli* The system is now in use in the U S Marine Hospital service, in the foreign business of the post-office, in the U S Coast and Geodetic Survey, and to some extent in the mint, U S Signal service, and U S census

Decimal system of money adopted by the U S Congress, with the dollar as a unit 6 July, 1785
John Quincy Adams U S secretary of state, makes an elaborate report on the metric system to Congress 23 Feb 1821
Sir John Wrottesley brings the subject before British Parliament 25 Feb 1824
By legislation of 4 July 1837, the use of the system in France is enforced to take effect 1 Jan 1840
Decimal association formed in England to advocate the adoption of the system June, 1854
International Decimal association formed 1855
System enforced in Belgium 1856
Canada adopts the decimal currency used in U S 1 Jan 1858
System enforced in Spain 1859 in Italy 1863
Metric weight of 5 grammes (77 16 grains) and diameter of 2 centimetres given to the 5 cent copper nickel piece in the U S by act of Congress 16 May, 1866
Use in the U S. authorized by act of Congress, and table of equivalents approved 28 July, "
System enforced in Portugal, 1868, in the Netherlands and British India. 1870
Legalized in Germany, 1868, and made compulsory 1 Jan 1872
International Metric commission at Paris provides for duplicates of the standard metre at Paris for each nation using the system, to be made from one ingot, 90 per cent platinum and 10 per cent iridium 24 Sept "
Convention establishing an international bureau of weights and measures signed at Paris by representatives of Austria, Germany, Russia, Italy, Spain, Portugal Turkey, Switzerland, Belgium, Sweden, Denmark, United States, Argentine Republic, Brazil and Peru 20 May, 1875
System adopted by Austria. 1876
System legalized in Great Britain, 29 July, 1864, and law repealed by Weights and Measures act of 1878
International Congress on weights and measures meets at Paris 4 Sept. "
System adopted in Sweden, May, 1876, to take effect in 1889

METRIC SYSTEM

Unit of the measure of length

Metre = 39 37 inches.

Decametre	10 metres.	Myriametre	10,000 metres.
Hectometre	100 "	Decimetre	1 metre
Kilometre	1000 "	Centimetre	01 "

Millimetre 001 metre.

Unit of the measure of surface.

Centare = 1 sq metre = 1550 sq inches

Are	100 centares	Hectare	10,000 centares

Unit of the measure of capacity and solidity

Litre = cube of 1 metre (decimetre) = 61 022 cubic inches or 908 qt.

Decalitre	10 litres	Decilitre	1 litre
Hectolitre	100 "	Centilitre	01 "
Kilolitre or stere	1000 "	Millilitre	001 "

Unit of weight

Gramme = cube of 01 metre (centimetre) = 061022 cubic inch or 15 432 grs.

Decagramme	10 grammes	Millier or Tonneau	1,000,000 grammes.
Hectogramme	100 "	Decigramme	1 gramme
Kilogramme	1000 "	Centigramme	01 "
Myriagramme	10,000 "	Milligramme	001 "
Quintal	100,000 "		

met'ronome, to regulate time in music A metronome with double pendulum, invented by Winkel, was adopted by Maelzel, and patented by him in 1816

metropolis of Great Britain (Metropolitan districts) includes the cities of London and Westminster, and the boroughs of Southwark, Finsbury, Marylebone, Tower-Hamlets, Hackney, Lambeth, and Chelsea. LONDON

metropol'itan (from the Gr μητροπολιτης), a title given at the council of Nice, 325, to bishops who had jurisdiction over others in a province The dignity is said to have arisen in the 2d century, the dissentient bishops in a district referring to one bishop of superior intellect

Metropolitan Museum of Art, New York city PAINTING

Metropolitan railway, London (underground), at first between Paddington and Victoria street, near Holborn, was authorized by Parliament, 1853, begun in the spring of 1860, and opened for traffic 10 Jan 1863 Great difficulties were overcome by the engineer, John Fowler, and the contractors, Jay, Smith, and Knight In the first 6 months of 1865 there were 7,462,823 passengers. It has been continued to Moorgate street, and supplemented by the Metropolitan Districts railway

Metz, a fortified city in Lorraine, now in the department of the Moselle, N E France, was the Roman Divodurum or Metti, capital of the Mediomatrici, a powerful tribe of Gauls, and in the 6th century of the kingdom of Austrasia or Metz It was made a free imperial city, 985 Charles VII. of France besieged it for 7 months in 1444, it was ransomed for 100,000 florins, was captured by Henry II, 10 Apr. 1552, and successfully defended by the duke of Guise against the emperor Charles V with 100,000 men, 31 Oct 1552 to 15 Jan 1553 Metz was ceded to France by the peace of Westphalia, 24 Oct 1648, and was fortified by Vauban and Belleisle. On 28 July, 1870, the emperor Napoleon III. took command at Metz in person After the disastrous defeats at Woerth and Forbach, on 6 Aug, the whole French army (except the corps of MacMahon, De Failly, and Douay) was concentrated here, 10, 11 Aug, and hemmed in by the Germans. Marshal Bazaine assumed command, 8 Aug The emperor departed with the vanguard, which crossed the Moselle early on 14 Aug

1 Battle of Pange or Courcelles gained by the first army under Von Steinmetz, after several hours' fighting 14 Aug 1870
2 Battle of Vionville or Mars la Tour, gained by the 2d army under prince Frederick Charles, after 12 hours' fighting, 16 Aug "
[Twice as many Germans were killed as at Königgrätz, the killed and wounded being estimated at 17,000 The French loss was equally great]
Bazaine masses his troops for a decisive conflict 17 Aug "
3 Battle of Rézonville or Gravelotte, gained by the combined 1st and 2d armies, commanded by the king in person, after 12 hours' fighting 18 Aug "
[The most desperate struggle took place on the slopes over Gravelotte, which the Germans gained by nightfall, after repeated charges But the right of the French had been outflanked, they fell back and retired under cover of Metz The French are said to have lost 19,000, and the Germans 25,000]
Bazaine repulsed in a sortie at Courcelles, near Metz (he claimed a victory) 26 Aug "
His whole army defeated by gen Manteuffel, of the army of prince Frederick Charles, in a battle lasting from the morning of 31 Aug to noon 1 Sept. "
Von Steinmetz sent to govern Posen, prince Frederick Charles sole commander before Metz 21 Sept "
Three vigorous but ineffective sallies 23, 24, 27 Sept. "
Great sortie, the Germans surprised, about 40,000 French engaged, they are repulsed after a severe engagement from 3 P M till dark, loss about 2000 French and 600 Germans, 7 Oct "
Gen Boyer arrives at Versailles to treat for capitulation, 14 Oct. "
Metz surrenders with the army, including marshals Bazaine, Canrobert, and Le Bœuf, 66 generals, about 6000 officers, 173 000 men, including the imperial guard, 400 pieces of artillery, 100 mitrailleuses, and 53 eagles or standards 27 Oct "
Capitulation was signed at Frescati by gens Jarras (French) and Stiehle (German) 27 Oct. "
General order to the army issued by marshal Bazaine, saying that they were "conquered by famine" 27 Oct. "
Germans enter Metz 29 Oct. "
[One cause of the fall of Metz was the great army, it might have been successfully defended by 20,000 men]
Marshal Bazaine was tried and condemned to death for surrendering Metz and the army, 6 Oct –10 Dec, punishment commuted to 20 years' imprisonment, 12 Dec., he escaped from isle Ste Marguerite (FRANCE) 9 Aug 1874

Mexican war, a 2 years' war between the United States and Mexico, caused mainly by the persistence of Mexico in her claim to Texas which had declared its independence and been annexed to the U S TEXAS, 1844-46 Other causes were the disagreement as to the boundary between Texas and Mexico, the U S claiming the Rio Grande, and Mexico the Nueces river, also the violation on the part of Mexico of the treaty of 1831. Gen Mariano Paredes was president of Mexico when war was declared by the U. S., 13 May, 1846, and by Mexico, 23 May, 1846

MEX

exican general Mejia, in command at Matamoras, issues a proclamation of hostility to the U. S., and calls the people of the country to arms....................................18 Mch. 1846

n. Zachary Taylor, breaking camp at Corpus Christi, 8 Mch. 1846, appears on the Rio Grande opposite Matamoras, 28 Mch. "

n. Pedro de Ampudia arrives at Matamoras and assumes command of the Mexican forces....................11 Apr. "

npudia superseded by Mariano Arista, general-in-chief of the Mexican army of the north..........................24 Apr. "

oops under capt. Thornton, sent out by gen. Taylor to reconnoitre, are surprised and captured....................25 Apr. "

n. Taylor calls on the governors of Louisiana and Texas for an auxiliary force of 5000 volunteers................26 Apr. "

n. Taylor garrisons fort Brown, opposite Matamoras, and forces a march to Point Isabel, his depot of supplies. 1–2 May, "

rt Brown bombarded by Mexicans..................3–9 May, "

ista disputes Taylor's return to fort Brown, and is defeated at Palo Alto, 9 miles from Matamoras..................8 May, "

treating to Resaca de la Palma, 4 miles from Matamoras, he is routed and driven across the Rio Grande.........9 May, "

change of prisoners negotiated and Thornton's party released...11 May, "

es. Polk calls upon Congress to make provision for war with Mexico...11 May, "

ngress calls for volunteers, and officially recognizes the war, 13 May, "

ylor crosses the Rio Grande, and occupies Matamoras, evacuated by Arista...................................18 May, "

eut.-col. Garland, pursuing the Mexicans, disperses the rear guard, closing the campaign of the Rio Grande.......19 May, "

exican Congress declares war against the U. S.......23 May, "

n. S. W. Kearney directed by secretary of war to occupy New Mexico and Upper California, and establish civil governments therein (CALIFORNIA, 1846–48; NEW MEXICO, 1846–48), 3 June, "

n. Salas, chief of liberal party of Mexico, seizes the citadel in the city of Mexico and overthrows the government. 5 Aug. "

n. Taylor removes his headquarters from Matamoras to Camargo...8 Aug. "

rrison of Vera Cruz and San Juan d'Ulloa declare for Santa Aña, 31 July, 1846, who arrives at Vera Cruz from Havana, 16 Aug., his entrance being permitted by com. Conner, commanding the blockading squadron of the U. S., under instructions from his government, 13 May..................16 Aug. "

egular troops organized in 2 divisions under gens. Twiggs and Worth move against Monterey; Worth's first brigade marches to establish an entrepôt at Serralvo..............19 Aug. "

n. Santa Aña arrives at the city of Mexico, declines the presidency, and assumes military command........15 Sept. "

S. army concentrated on the banks of the San Juan, 3 miles from Marin, and the whole force, 425 officers and 6220 men, advances upon Monterey.............................18 Sept. "

onterey, defended by about 10,000 Mexicans under gen. Ampudia, is besieged by U. S. troops and surrenders, the Mexican forces retiring to Saltillo........................25–28 Sept. "

rms of capitulation of Monterey include an armistice of 8 weeks, during which gen. Taylor agrees not to advance beyond the line. Treaty concluded...................25 Sept. "

nta Aña arrives at San Luis de Potosi, and begins the organization of the Mexican army......................8 Oct. "

n. Ampudia, ordered to San Luis, evacuates Saltillo...18 Oct. "

m. Conner, by an expedition from Anton Lizardo, under Perry, up the Tabasco river, captures 5 merchant vessels, 23–25 Oct. "

ar department disapproves the armistice and orders its close, 13 Oct.; gen. Taylor announces the fact to Santa Aña, 6 Nov. "

mpico on the Panuco, abandoned by Santa Aña, is occupied by com. Conner...15 Nov. "

n. Taylor occupies Saltillo.............................16 Nov. "

n. Wool's forces at Monclova, march, 24 Nov., to Parras, and are merged into the army of occupation..............5 Dec. "

n. Santa Aña elected president of Mexico..............6 Dec. "

n. John A. Quitman's brigade of volunteers occupy Victoria, 29 Dec. 1846, where they are joined by gen. Taylor with Twiggs's and Patterson's divisions...................4 Jan. 1847

exican Congress orders sequestration of church property to raise funds for the war...................................7 Jan. "

nta Aña, with 23,000 men and 20 pieces of artillery, moves in the direction of Saltillo...........................27 Jan. "

aj.-gen. Scott arrives at Brazos San Jago, 1 Jan., and calls for a rendezvous of troops at the island of Lobos, 60 miles south of Tampico, for his expedition against Vera Cruz.......Jan. "

n. Taylor arrives at Saltillo, 2 Feb. 1847; at Agua Nueva, 5 Feb.; and at Buena Vista..............................21 Feb. "

attle of BUENA VISTA, the Mexicans retreat to Agua Nueva during the night of 23 Feb..............................22–23 Feb. "

l. Doniphan with 856 men marches from the Rio Grande to join gen. Wool, supposed to be marching against Chihuahua. He reaches El Paso 27 Dec., where he learns of Wool's change of plan, routs 4000 Mexicans at the pass of Sacramento, 28 Feb., and enters Chihuahua................1 Mch. "

ott's army sails from Lobos for Vera Cruz, lands 3 miles south of the city, 9 Mch., and begins the investment......10 Mch. "

the refusal of gen. Morales, commander at Vera Cruz, to surrender, the bombardment of the city and castle of San Juan d'Ulloa begins, 4 P.M. 22 Mch., and continues until Morales, under a flag of truce, proposes a surrender, 8 A.M. 26 Mch. "

exicans evacuate Vera Cruz and the castle of San Juan d'Ulloa...29 Mch. "

Santa Aña leaves the capital for the army near Vera Cruz, leaving don Pedro Añaya as "president substitute"..2 Apr. 1847

Gen. Scott, marching inland from Vera Cruz, defeats the Mexicans under Santa Aña at CERRO GORDO, 19 Apr., and Jalapa is constituted a depot for supplies.........................20 Apr. "

N. P. Trist, confidential agent of the U. S. to Mexico, arrives at Vera Cruz...May, "

Gen. Scott at Jalapa, by proclamation to the Mexican people, offers peace...11 May, "

Worth's command occupies Puebla, Santa Aña having retreated the day before..................................15 May, "

Com. Perry captures Tuspan.............................18 May, "

Doniphan's command arrives at Saltillo and proceeds to the Rio Grande the same day............................22 May, "

Com. Perry occupies Tabasco...........................15 June, "

Gen. Manuel Maria Lombardini, in command of the city of Mexico, expels residents of U. S............................June, "

Troops at Puebla, reinforced by the garrison, withdrawn from Jalapa, increase the force to 8000 men...............8 July, "

Gen. Franklin Pierce with about 2500 men leaves Vera Cruz 19 July, and arrives at Puebla..........................6 Aug. "

Scott advances upon the city of Mexico; Harney's cavalry brigade and Twiggs's division leave Puebla, 7 Aug.; Quitman's volunteers follow, 8 Aug.; Worth's, 9 Aug.; Pillow's, 10 Aug. Gen. Scott establishes headquarters at Ayotla, 9 miles from the Mexican fortified position of El Peñon..........10 Aug. "

Gen. Scott's headquarters at San Augustin.........17–18 Aug. "

He defeats Mexicans under gen. Valencia at Contreras, 19–20 Aug. "

Again at Churubusco; Santa Aña retreats to the capital, and gen. Scott returns to San Augustin.....................20 Aug. "

British embassy in Mexico meet gen. Scott at San Augustin, and represent that the moment is favorable for opening negotiations for peace................................20 Aug. "

Gen. Scott removes his headquarters to Tacubaya......21 Aug. "

Gen. Scott appoints gens. Quitman, P. F. Smith, and Pierce as commissioners to negotiate an armistice with gens. Mora y Villamil and Quijano, 22 Aug., and ratifies the terms, 23 Aug. "

Mr. Trist commences unsuccessful negotiations for peace, 25 Aug. "

Gen. Scott notifies Santa Aña that the armistice will end at 12 o'clock the following day..........................6 Sept. "

U. S. troops capture the castle of El Molino del Rey, 1 mile north of Tacubaya......................................8 Sept. "

Castle of Chapultepec taken by U. S. troops by storm..13 Sept. "

Mexican army leaves the capital, taking the northern road to Guadalupe Hidalgo, and U. S. troops occupy it...13–14 Sept. "

Santa Aña resigns at Guadalupe Hidalgo, and a new provisional government, organized under Señor Peña y Peña, president of the supreme council, is commenced at Toluca....27 Sept. "

Populace, reinforced by guerillas under gen. Rea, commence hostilities against U. S. garrison at Puebla under col. Childs, 14 Sept.; Santa Aña arrives at Puebla with a reinforcement for the besiegers, 22 Sept.; and the siege continues until the arrival of U. S. troops under gen. Joseph Lane from Vera Cruz, 12 Oct. "

By order of the new government Santa Aña gives up the command of his troops at Huamantla..................16 Oct. "

U. S. troops under Lane attack and disperse the Mexicans under Rea at Atlixco, temporary state capital..........19 Oct. "

Gen. Quitman, appointed by Scott military governor of the city of Mexico, is succeeded by gen. P. F. Smith............Oct. "

Gen. Añaya elected provisional president of Mexico, to serve until 8 Jan. 1848...................................11 Nov. "

Gen. Scott, in Order No. 376, announces his purpose to occupy the republic of Mexico until she sues for peace.......15 Dec. "

Peña y Peña again assumes the government of Mexico...8 Jan. 1848

Mr. Trist concludes the treaty of Guadalupe Hidalgo; Mexico cedes to the U. S. the territory now California, Nevada, Utah, New Mexico, western Colorado, and Arizona north of the Gila river...2 Feb. "

Gen. Lane occupies Orizaba, 25 Jan., Cordova, 28 Jan., and returns to Mexico....................................6 Feb. "

Gen. William O. Butler succeeds gen. Scott as commander of the troops in Mexico.................................18 Feb. "

Negotiations for an armistice begun in the city of Mexico 29 Feb., approved at the Mexican capital, Queretaro..5 Mch. "

Treaty received at Washington about 20 Feb. and ratified by the Senate: vote, 38 to 14; messrs. Sevier and Clifford appointed commissioners to exchange ratifications in the city of Mexico..10 Mch. "

Gen. Butler announces that the war is ended.........29 May, "

Treaty ratified by the Mexican Senate 24 May; ratifications exchanged at Queretaro..............................30 May, "

Under a salute from the Mexican batteries the U. S. flag on the palace in Mexico is replaced by the Mexican....12 June, "

Troops engaged throughout the war, 101,282; of these 27,506 were regulars. *Losses, 1049 killed and 3420 wounded.*

Mexico, a federal republic in North America, bounded on the north by the United States of America (California, Arizona, New Mexico, and Texas); the Pacific ocean forms its entire western and southern boundary, with the exception of Yucatan, giving it a Pacific coast line of nearly 6000 miles, while its eastern coast is washed by the waters of the Gulf of Mexico, with a coast line of 1600 miles. The word Mexico is related to or derived from the Aztec national war-god Mexitli. Prior to the coming of the Aztecs, who founded the city of Mexico, 1325, it was known as Anahuac (signifying "near the water"), or that portion of it now known as the valley of Mexico AMERICA It was discovered by the Spaniards, 1517–18, and conquered by Ferdinand Cortez, 1519–21 Visited and largely explored by Alexander von Humboldt, 1799–1804 It is limited in latitude between 15° and 32° 36′ N, and in longitude between 87° and 117° W, and extends about 2000 miles north-northwest and south-southeast, with a mean width, varying from 1000 miles on the 26° N to 130 miles at the Tehuantepec isthmus Area, 767,000 sq miles Pop 1874, 9,276,079, 1879, 9,686,777, 1890, 11,395,712, 1900 13,605,919 Capital, Mexico Pop 1890, 329,535, 1900, 344,721

Montezuma emperor 1503

Cortez lands, 1519, captures the city of Mexico 1521

Mexico constituted a kingdom, Cortez governor 1522

Mendoza, first viceroy of New Spain, 1530, establishes a mint, 1535

Unsuccessful insurrections of Miguel Hidalgo, 1810, of Morelos, 1815, of Mina 1817

Mexico independent by the treaty of Aquala 23 Aug 1821

Augustin Iturbide president of provisional junto, Feb, Mexico an empire, the crown declined by Spain, Iturbide emperor, May, 1822

Compelled to abdicate 26 Mch 1823

Mexican federal republic proclaimed 4 Oct "

Iturbide goes to England, returns and endeavors to recover power, shot 19 July, 1824

Federal constitution established Oct "

[First president D Felix Victoria]

Treaty of commerce with Great Britain Apr 1825

Expulsion of the Spaniards decreed Mch 1829

Spanish expedition against Mexico surrendered 26 Sept "

Revolution, president Guerrero deposed 23 Dec "

Santa Aña president, practically dictator 11 May, 1833

Loses her territory of TEXAS 1836

Independence recognized by Brazil, June, 1830, by Spain, 28 Dec "

Declaration of war against France 30 Nov 1838

This war terminated 9 Mch 1839

War with the United States (MEXICAN WAR) May, 1846

Pres Arista resigns, 6 Jan, and Santa Aña returns, Feb, dictator 16 Dec. 1853

He abdicates, Carera elected president Jan 1855

Who also abdicates, succeeded first by Alvarez, and afterwards by gen Comonfort Dec "

Property of clergy sequestrated 31 Mch 1856

New constitution established 5 Feb 1857

Beginning of Reformed church by Aguilar and others "

Comonfort chosen president July, "

Coup d'état, constitution annulled by church party, Comonfort compelled to retire, 11 Jan, gen Zuloaga takes the government 21–26 Jan 1858

Benito Juarez declared president at Vera Cruz 11 Feb "

Civil war Aug to Nov "

Gen Miguel Miramon nominated president at Mexico by the junta 6 Jan. 1859

Zuloaga abdicates 2 Feb "

Britain sends ships of war to Mexico to protect her subjects, Feb "

Miramon forces lines of liberal generals, enters capital, assumes office as governor and rules arbitrarily 10 Apr "

Juarez confiscates church property 13 July, "

Miramon and clericals defeat liberals under Colima 21 Dec "

Besieges Vera Cruz, 5 Mch, bombards it, compelled to raise the siege 21 Mch 1860

Zuloaga deposes Miramon, assumes presidency 1 May, "

Miramon arrests Zuloaga, 9 May, diplomatic bodies suspend official relations with former 10 May, "

Miramon defeated by Degollado 10 Aug "

He governs with tyranny, seizes 152,000*l.* of English bond holders, Sept., foreign ministers quit the city Oct. "

He is defeated, compelled to retire, Juarez enters Mexico 11 Jan, re elected president 19 Jan 1861

Juarez made dictator by congress 30 June, "

Mexican congress suspends payments to foreigners for 2 years, 17 July, "

Hence diplomatic relations broken with England and France, 27 July, "

England, France, and Spain, after vainly seeking redress and payment of interest by negotiations, sign a convention for joint hostilities against Mexico. 31 Oct "

Mexican congress dissolves, after conferring full powers on the president 15 Dec "

Spanish troops land at Vera Cruz 8 Dec., it surrenders 17 Dec "

British naval and French military expedition arrive 7, 8 Jan 1862

Mexicans resist, and invest Vera Cruz, taxes raised 25 per cent Jan "

Miramon arrives, but is sent back to Spain by the British admiral Feb "

Proposed Mexican monarchy for archduke Maximilian of Austria disapproved by Britain and Spain Feb "

Negotiation ensues between Spanish and Mexicans, convention between commissaries of allies and Mexican general Doblado at Soledad 19 Feb "

Gen Marquez arms against Juarez, and gen Almonte joins the French general Lorencez, Juarez demands a compulsory loan, and puts Mexico in a state of siege Mch "

Conference between plenipotentiaries of allies at Orizaba, English and Spanish declare for peace, the French dissent, 9 Apr, who declare war against Juarez 16 Apr "

MEX

Spanish and British retire, French government reinforces Lorencez May, 1862

French, induced by Marquez, enter interior, repulsed by Zaragoza at Fort Guadalupe, near Puebla 5 May, "

Juarez quits the capital 31 May, "

French defeat Mexicans at Cerro de Borgo, near Orizaba, 13, 14 June, "

Mexican liberals said to desire negotiation Aug "

Gen Forey and 2500 French soldiers land 28 Aug "

Napoleon III writes Lorencez, disclaims intention to impose a government on Mexico, announced Sept "

Death of Zaragoza a great loss to the Mexicans 8 Sept "

Gen Forey deprives Almonte of the presidency at Vera Cruz, and assumes civil and military power Oct "

Ortega takes command of the Mexicans 19 Oct. "

Mexican congress meets, protests against French invasion, 27 Oct "

French evacuate Tampico 13 Jan 1863

Forey marches towards Mexico 24 Feb "

Siege of Puebla, bravely defended, 29 Mch, assault, 31 Mch – 3 Apr, Ortega surrenders at discretion 18 May, "

Juarez removes his government to San Luis de Potosi 31 May, "

Mexico occupied by French under Bazaine, 5 June, Forey's army enters, 10 June, provisional government "

Assembly of notables at Mexico decide for a limited hereditary monarchy, with a Roman Catholic prince as emperor, and offer crown to archduke Maximilian of Austria, regency established 6–10 July, "

French reoccupy Tampico 11 Aug "

Marshal Forey resigns command to Bazaine and returns to France 1 Oct "

Archduke Maximilian will accept crown if it be the will of the people 3 Oct. "

Mexican gen Comonfort surprised and shot by partisans, 12 Nov "

Successful advance of imperialists, Juarez abandons San Luis de Potosi, 18 Dec, imperialists enter 24 Dec "

Ex president Santa Aña lands at Vera Cruz, professing adhesion to empire, 27 Feb., dismissed by Bazaine 12 Mch 1864

Juarez makes Monterey seat of government 3 Apr "

Archduke Maximilian accepts the crown from Mexican deputation at Miramar 10 Apr "

Emperor and empress land at Vera Cruz, 29 May, enter city of Mexico 12 June, "

Emperor visits the interior, grants a free press Aug "

Republicans defeat imperialists at San Pedro 27 Dec. "

Juarez, at Chihuahua exhorts the Mexicans to maintain independence 1 Jan 1865

Emperor institutes order of Mexican eagle "

Oaxaca surrenders to Bazaine 9 Feb. "

Constitution promulgated 10 Apr "

Ortega recruits at New York for republican army, May, discountenanced by the U S government. June, "

Anniversary of Mexican independence, descendants of Iturbide made princesses etc. 16 Sept "

Emperor proclaims the war ended and martial law against all armed bands, indignation excited 2 Oct "

Juarist generals taken prisoners, shot 16 Oct. "

U S protest against French occupation Nov–Dec "

Presidency of Juarez expires, he determines to continue to act, 30 Nov, he flees to Texas 20 Dec "

Bagdad, on the Rio Grande, seized by American Juarists, 4, 5 Jan, occupied by U S gen Weitzel, 5 Jan, his conduct disavowed, Bagdad reoccupied by imperialists 20 Jan 1866

Napoleon III agrees to withdraw all his soldiers from Mexico between Nov 1866 and Nov 1867 Apr "

Guerilla warfare, with varying success Mch–May, "

Matamoras captured by liberals under Escobedo 23, 24 June, "

Empress Charlotte departs for France, 13 July, conspiracy suppressed 15–17 July, "

Convention between Maximilian and the French, transfer of customs revenue to France 30 July, "

Juarez and party take Tampico 1 Aug. "

U S disallow Maximilian's blockade of Matamoras 17 Aug "

Dissension among liberals, 3 rival presidents—Juarez, Ortega, and Santa Aña Sept.–Oct "

Empress solicits help from France, Sept, she falls ill. Oct. "

Firm speech of emperor Maximilian 19 Sept "

Emperor leaves Mexico for Orizaba, giving authority to Bazaine Oct "

French evacuate several places. Nov "

Imperial council at Orizaba determine to maintain empire, 24 Nov "

Death of Augustin Iturbide. 11 Dec "

Maximilian with army, arrives at Queretaro 19 Feb 1867

Departure of French 13 Jan 5 Feb, 14 Mch "

Juarez, Diaz, and Ortega dispute the supremacy Apr "

Queretaro, after many conflicts, captured by treachery, Mendez shot 15 May, "

Emperor Maximilian, Miramon, and Mejia, after trial, shot, 19 June, "

Mexico city taken after 67 days' siege, republic re-established, 21 June, "

Surrender of Vera Cruz 25 June, "

Santa Aña captured, detained a prisoner July, "

Juarez enters Mexico, convokes assembly to elect president, 14, 15 July, "

Marquez and others said to be organizing against Juarez, Aug "

Porfirio Diaz nominated for presidency Sept. "

Santa Aña sentenced to 8 years' banishment Oct. "

Maximilian's body given to Austrian adm Tegethoff 26 Nov "

Mexican congress opened; Juarez provisional president; foreign consuls said to be leaving..8 Dec. 1867
Juarez re elected president..Dec. "
Juarez inaugurated..................................about 25 Dec. "
Maximilian's body buried at Vienna.....................18 Jan. 1868
Rebellion against Juarez in Yucatan and other provinces, Jan.-Feb. "
Mazatlan blockaded by capt. Bridge of British ship *Chanticleer* for an outrage, 20 June; relieved by adm. Hastings....July, "
Treaty with U. S...Dec. "
Insurrection at Puebla suppressed...............................Feb. 1869
Gen. Almonte d. at Paris..Mch. "
Encounter between Mexicans and U. S. troops pursuing Indian depredators; about 40 U. S. soldiers killed; reported. 12 Apr. 1871
Election for president: Diaz, 1982 votes; Juarez, 1963; Lerdo, 1366; Juarez retains power............................27 July, "
Insurrection headed by Negrete, Riveras, and others, suppressed with much slaughter..............................12 Oct. "
Juarez re-elected president.......................................Oct. "
Insurgents under Porfirio Diaz twice defeated; announced, Jan. 1872
Civil war going on with varying success...........Apr.-June, "
Benito Juarez d. (aged about 68) by apoplexy..........18 July, "
Country tranquil; Diaz accepts amnesty; announced..14 Aug. "
Lerdo de Tejado (of good character) elected president, Oct.; Diaz submits..Nov. "
Railway from Mexico to Vera Cruz completed; runs...23 Jan. 1873
Customs tariffs liberalized.......................................July, 1874
A senate voted by congress..Aug. "
Religious orders suppressed.......................................Dec. "
Insurrection by Diaz, Mch.; he takes Matamoras.......1 Apr. 1876
Progress of Reformed church; overtures for union with Episcopal church of U. S.................................about Apr. "
Insurgents defeated at Oaxaca, 29 May; at Queretaro....June, "
Death of Santa Aña, ex-president.......................20 June, "
Diaz defeats government troops at Tekoar, 12 Nov.; enters Mexico, assumes power as provisional president....20 Nov. "
Pres. Lerdo de Tejado retires; Iglesias takes arms as president, Dec. "
Diaz defeats Iglesias, who retreats; Diaz elected president, 18 Feb.; proclaimed...5 May, 1877
Insurrection of Negrete; Diaz marches against him...16 June, 1879
Manuel Gonzalez elected, 11 July; succeeds............1 Dec. 1880
Ancient city discovered in Sonora, near Magdalena, a great pyramid, rooms cut in a stony mountain, implements, etc., and hieroglyphic inscriptions...................................... 1883
Concession by Mexico to James B. Eads for 99 years for a railway for ships across the isthmus; estimated cost, 15,000,000*l.*; model exhibited at Long Acre, London.................Aug. 1884
Porfirio Diaz inaugurated president....................1 Dec. "
Cutting affair (UNITED STATES).........................July-Aug. 1886
Diaz re-elected president..................................11 July, 1892

EMPERORS.

1822. Aug. Augustin Iturbide, Feb.; abdicated 23 Mch. 1823; shot for attempting to recover his authority, 19 July, 1824.

1864. Maximilian (brother to the emperor of Austria), b. 6 July, 1832; accepted the crown, 10 Apr. 1864; married 27 July, 1857, to princess Charlotte, daughter of Leopold I., king of the Belgians; adopted Augustin Iturbide as his heir, Sept. 1865; shot (after a trial), 19 June, 1867.

Miamis. INDIANS.

Michaelmas, 29 Sept., feast of St. Michael, reputed guardian of the Roman Catholic church, under the title of "St. Michael and All Angels." Instituted, according to Butler, 487.

The custom in England of eating goose at Michaelmas has been explained by saying that queen Elizabeth heard of the destruction of the Spanish Armada while eating the bird at dinner on 29 Sept. 1588, at the house of sir Neville Umfreyville. The custom is much older, and extends to the other countries of Europe.—*Clavis Calendaria.*

Michigan, one of the north central states of the United States, consists of 2 peninsulas; the upper peninsula lies wholly south of lake Superior and north of Wisconsin, lakes Michigan and Huron, and is 318 miles long east and west. The lower peninsula extends north between lake Michigan on the west and lake Huron and the Detroit river on the east to the strait of Mackinaw, a distance of 280 miles. Canada lies to the east, lake Erie touches the southeastern corner, while Ohio and Indiana form the southern boundary. In latitude the whole state is limited by 41° 42′ to 48° 22′ N., and in longitude by 82° 86′ to 90° 30′ W. Area, 58,915 sq. m. Pop. 1890, 2,093,889; 1900, 2,420,982. Capital, Lansing.

Claude Dablon and Jacques Marquette establish a permanent mission at Sault Ste. Marie................................... 1668
Two Sulpician priests with 3 canoes and 7 men pass through the Detroit river and lake St. Clair.......................... 1670
French under M. de St. Lusson, permitted to occupy Sault Ste. Marie by the Indians, erect a cross at that place bearing the arms of France...May, 1671
Marquette commences fort Michilimackinac, starts a Huron settlement, and builds a chapel there........................ "
Marquette is buried near present site of Ludington....18 May, 1675
Robert La Salle, accompanied by father Louis Hennepin and Chevalier de Tonti, sails up lakes Erie and Huron in the *Griffon*, reaching Michilimackinac (NEW YORK).....28 Aug. 1679
Antoine de la Motte Cadillac, lord of Bouaget and Montdesert, under a commission from Louis XIV., leaving Montreal in June with 100 men and a Jesuit missionary, commences the settlement of Detroit..................................24 July, 1701
First grant of land (32 acres) made at Detroit by Cadillac to François Fafard Delorme.. 1707
Detroit attacked by the Fox Indians; after a 3 weeks' siege the French garrison of 20 soldiers under M. du Buisson drive the Indians back with severe loss.................May, 1712
Pontiac, with Ottawa Indians, assists in the defence of Detroit against the combined northern tribes under Mackinac...... 1746
Further emigration from France to Detroit.................... 1749
Maj. Robert Rogers is ordered by gen. Amherst, at Montreal, to take possession of the posts in Michigan and administer the oath of allegiance to the French subjects there..12 Sept. 1760
Pontiac makes peace with maj. Rogers, and attends the English to Detroit..7 Nov. "
Detroit capitulates, English flag raised on the fort.....29 Nov. "
British seize the forts at Mackinaw and Green Bay.....8 Sept. 1761
Indian tribes in the northwest, incited by Pontiac against the English, capture fort St. Joseph.........................25 May, 1763
Pontiac plans an attack on the fort at Detroit. He asks for a council in the fort, so that the Indians allowed in the fort, at a given signal, might begin a general massacre; his plan is disclosed by an Indian woman to the commandant, maj. Gladwin, who permits the council, but disposes the garrison so as to intimidate Pontiac.....................................9 May, "
[Pontiac immediately after begins the siege of Detroit.]
Twenty batteaux, with 97 men under lieut. Cuyler, sailing to reinforce the garrison at Detroit, are attacked by the Indians, taken, compelled to navigate the boats up the Detroit to Hog island, and there massacred..............................30 May, "
By the strategy of a game of "baggatiway," or lacrosse, played with bat and ball, Indians obtain entrance to the fort at Michilimackinac and massacre the garrison.......4 June, "
British garrison at Detroit, reinforced by a fleet of gunboats and a detachment of 300 regular troops under capt. Dalzell, send a force of about 274 men to make a night attack on Pontiac, who was encamped near Detroit. The Indians, hearing of the intended attack, form an ambush at Bloody Bridge, and compel the British to retreat after losing 20 killed, among them Dalzell, and 42 wounded........31 July, "
Pontiac remains before Detroit until forced to retire by the advance of col. Bradstreet...................................May, 1764
Charter granted in England to a company for working the copper mines of lake Superior. The miners blast 30 feet into the rock, and then abandon the mine............................ 1773
Parliament includes Michigan with Canada............22 Jan. 1774
Expedition from Detroit under gov. Hamilton against gen. Roger Clark at Vincennes, results in Hamilton's being captured and sent to Virginia; his troops allowed to return to Detroit...Mch. 1779
Formation of the Northwest company for fur trade........... 1783
Foundation of Frenchtown laid by a few Canadians who settle on the river Raisin.. 1784
Indians cede to the U. S. by treaty at fort McIntosh, a belt of land beginning at the river Raisin and extending to lake St. Clair, 6 miles wide, also a tract of land 12 miles square at Michilimackinac.. 1785
Congress includes Michigan in the Northwestern territory, formed by act of..13 July, 1787
First American settlement established on the river Raisin at Frenchtown, which becomes a depot for trade for the Northwestern Fur company.. 1793
Jay's treaty with Great Britain fixing the eastern boundary of the U. S., and calling for the surrender of Detroit and other western posts held by the British before 1 June, 1796, concluded..19 Nov. 1794
Robert Randall of Pennsylvania and Charles Whitney of Vermont enter into an agreement with 7 merchants of Detroit to endeavor to obtain from the U. S. government, by bribing members of Congress, a pre-emption right to nearly 20,000,000 acres of land in Michigan, but are exposed and receive a public reprimand... 1795
Forts Mackinac (Mackinaw) and Detroit evacuated by the British; Detroit garrisoned by a detachment of gen. Wayne's army, and capt. Porter first raises the U. S. flag upon the soil of Michigan...11 June, 1796
Thomas Powers, agent for the Spanish governor Carondelet, arrives at Detroit to endeavor to interest gen. Wilkinson in the Spanish intrigues in the west.....................24 Aug. 1797
Northwest territory assumes the second grade of territorial government; Michigan forms the single county of Wayne, and sends one representative to the General Assembly at Chillicothe. His election was the first held in Michigan under U. S. rule.. 1798
Act of Congress approved establishing Indiana territory, in which Michigan is partially included...................7 May, 1800

Article VI of the constitution of Ohio, confirmed by the U S government, specifies that the northern boundary should be a direct line from the southern extremity of lake Michigan to the most northerly cape of Miami bay " (Ohio) 1802
First U S land office opened in Detroit under act of Congress, 26 Mch 1804
Indiana territory divided, all north of a line east from the southerly extremity of lake Michigan to lake Erie and north through the lake to the northern boundary of the U S to be the territory of Michigan by act of 11 Jan 1805
William Hull appointed first governor of the territory 1 Mch "
Town of Detroit destroyed by fire 11 June, "
First code of laws for the territory adopted, called the "Woodward code" May, 1806
Congress authorizes the governor and judges of Michigan to lay out a town including old Detroit and 10,000 acres adjoining grants to be made of lots to sufferers by the fire "
Act of Congress passed granting a confirmation of claims of those who had been possessors of land in Michigan since 1796, 1807
Michigan Essay or Impartial Observer, the first paper printed in Detroit, issued 31 Aug 1809
Memorial presented to Congress setting forth the defenceless condition of Michigan, and praying for aid against the Indians 27 Dec. 1811
Gov Hull issues a proclamation from Sandwich, on the Detroit river, inviting people to come in under the American flag and promising protection, but extermination to those who joined the British and savages against the U S 12 July, 1812
Lieut Hanks, commandant at fort Mackinac, surrenders to the British 17 July, "
Battles of Brownstown 4 Aug, and Maguaga, 9 Aug "
Gen Hull surrenders Detroit to British under gen Brock 16 Aug "
[The forces for its defence were estimated at about 2000 men These with 2500 stands of arms 25 iron and 8 brass pieces of ordnance, 40 barrels of gunpowder, and a large quantity of other military stores, were delivered up to the British without even an attempt to defend them UNITED STATES, Jan and Mch 1814]
Sudden attack upon the U S troops under gen Winchester, at the river Raisin by the British and massacre of the panic stricken U S troops by the Indians 22 Jan 1813
Naval victory over British fleet of 6 vessels, under com Barclay, by U S squadron of 9 vessels under com Oliver Hazard Perry, off Sister islands, lake Erie, near Detroit (NAVAL BATTLES) 10 Sept "
Gen Harrison takes possession of Detroit 29 Sept. "
Col Lewis Cass appointed governor of the territory 29 Oct. "
Unsuccessful attempt of U S troops under col Croghan and com Sinclair, to reduce FORT MACKINAC 4 Aug 1814
Special commissioner arrives with the treaty of peace lately concluded at Ghent 17 Feb 1815
Detroit incorporated as a village "
President James Monroe visits Detroit 13 Aug 1817
By act of Congress Michigan territory is extended westward to the Mississippi, thus including the present state of Wisconsin, 1818
Remains of soldiers massacred at the Raisin river removed to Detroit, and buried with honors of war 8 Aug "
Steamboat *Walk in the water* arrives at Detroit, from Buffalo, N Y, on her first trip 27 Aug "
Congress provides for the election of a delegate to Congress by citizens of Michigan 16 Feb 1819
William Woodbridge elected territorial delegate 2 Sept. "
Treaty with Indians at Saginaw they cede lands, 60 miles wide, west of Detroit north to Thunder bay "
Walk in the water makes a trip to the island of Mackinac "
Expedition under gov Cass starts out in bark canoes to explore the northwestern lake coast of Michigan 24 May, 1820
Treaty with the Indians perfected through gov Cass, all country within the boundaries of Michigan south of Grand river not before ceded is granted to the U S 1821
Congress establishes a legislative council of 9 members, appointed by the president out of 18 elected by the people. 3 Mch 1823
Detroit incorporated as a city 1824
First legislative council at the council house in Detroit, 7 June, "
Congress grants the governor and council power to divide the territory into townships and incorporate the same, and increases the legislative council to 13 1825
Right of electing members of the legislative council granted to the electors of the territory . 29 Jan 1827
Pontiac and Detroit railroad chartered 31 July, 1830
Gov Cass resigns, appointed U S secretary of war 1 Aug 1831
George B Porter appointed governor 17 Sept. "
Troops raised in Michigan at the call of the U S government to engage in the Black Hawk war 22 May, 1832
Congress adds to Michigan the territory between the Mississippi river and the Missouri and White Earth rivers, thus including the whole of the present Minnesota, Iowa, and parts of North and South Dakota 28 June, 1834
Gov Porter dies, Stevens T Mason acting governor 6 July, "
Question of southern boundary being agitated, Ohio commissioners, running a line about 12 miles southwest of Adrian, are captured by Michigan troops after several shots 26 Apr 1835
Michigan having attained a population of over 60,000, a constitutional convention convenes at Detroit .. . 11 May, "
New constitution ratified by the people . 2 Nov "
Enabling act for Michigan approved. 15 June, 1836
Wisconsin territory formed comprising all of Michigan territory west of lake Michigan . "
Convention at Ann Arbor rejects the Enabling act, as giving Ohio 470 sq miles belonging to Michigan since 1787 (OHIO), 26 Sept "
New convention of delegates at Ann Arbor accepts the Enabling act 14 Dec 1836
After protracted discussion Congress admits Michigan, adding to the state in the upper peninsula 2500 sq miles, act approved 26 Jan 1837
Legislature passes an act to provide for the organization and support of primary schools 20 Mch "
Board of 7 Commissioners of Internal Improvement appointed by act of legislature Mch "
Meeting of citizens of Detroit friendly to the patriot cause is held, 1 Jan 1838. 5 Jan the schooner *Ann* is seized, loaded with 450 stands of arms stolen from the Detroit jail, and sails away with 132 men and provisions for the patriots Meeting of the public to preserve neutrality is held 8 Jan 1838
State prison at Jackson established "
William Woodbridge elected governor Nov 1839
Gov Woodbridge, elected U S senator, is succeeded by James W Gordon as acting governor 31 May, 1841
Gen Lewis Cass nominated for president of the U S. by the National Democratic convention at Baltimore 22 May, 1842
University of Michigan, planned by the governor and people in 1817, established by law, 18 Mch 1837, and located at Ann Arbor, is opened for reception of students 20 Sept "
State land office established at Marshall by law, to take charge of and dispose of 500,000 acres granted by Congress Apr 1843
James G Birney of Michigan nominated as Liberty candidate for president of the U S 1844
Copper mining in the upper peninsula of Michigan begun 1845
Seat of government permanently located at Lansing by act approved 16 Mch 1847
Michigan and Wisconsin troops enlisted for the Mexican war leave Detroit by boat for Vera Cruz 24 Apr "
Capital punishment, except for treason, abolished in the state, "
Epaphroditus Ransom elected governor Nov "
Constitution framed by a convention which met at Lansing 3 June, adopted by vote of the people 5 Nov 1850
Arrest of a band of desperadoes who for a year had terrorized Jackson county 21 Apr 1851
State Teachers' Association organized Mch 1852
Gov McClelland made U S secretary of the interior, lieut gov Andrew Parsons acting governor 6 Mch 1853
State Normal school at Ypsilanti, established by act of 28 Mch 1849, is opened for students Apr "
Maine liquor law passed "
State asylum for deaf, dumb, and blind, established by act of legislature in 1848, opens in rented rooms at Flint Feb 1854
Hillsdale college (Free will Baptist) established at Spring Arbor in 1844, chartered as Michigan Central college in 1845, is removed to Hillsdale and reorganized 1855
Kalamazoo college (Baptist), organized in 1833, is reorganized "
Ship canal around St Mary's falls opened "
Lands granted by Congress to aid in building a railroad from Ontonagon to the Wisconsin state line 1856
State Reform school at Lansing opened 2 Sept "
State Agricultural college at Lansing, established by act of legislature 12 Feb 1855 opened for students May, 1857
State confers the grant of Congress made in 1856 on the Ontonagon and State Line Railroad company "
Olivet college at Olivet, founded in 1844, reorganized and under Congregational and Presbyterian government 1859
State asylum for the insane at Kalamazoo opened for reception of patients "
Albion college, at Albion (Methodist Episcopal), organized in 1841 is reorganized. 1860
First Michigan regiment, ready and equipped 4 days after the president's call, leaves Detroit under orders of the war department 13 May, 1861
State receives from the federal government a grant of 5,891,598 acres of swamp land in Michigan 1868
All departments of Michigan university open to women 1870
Constitution amended, all distinction of civil and political rights based upon color abolished, ratified by the people, 8 Nov "
Two State Relief committees, with headquarters at Detroit and Grand Rapids, for the relief of sufferers by forest fires in northern Michigan disburse $462,106.30 in cash and about $250,000 in clothing and supplies from almost every state in the Union, Canada, and abroad Oct. 1871
Soldiers' monument at Detroit, erected by voluntary contributions from citizens of the state, the corner stone of which was laid 4 July, 1867, is unveiled 9 Apr 1872
Board of Fish Commissioners appointed to organize a state fish breeding establishment "
Corner stone of the new capitol at Lansing laid 2 Oct "
State Board of Health appointed 1873
Commission under legislative authority selects Ionia as the location for a state house of correction "
Constitutional commission of 18 members convenes at Lansing and draws up a constitution 27 Aug "
State public school for dependent children at Coldwater, organized 1871 is opened for reception of children 21 May, 1874
Battle Creek college chartered "
Revised state constitution ratified by people, a separate vote on woman suffrage stands 40,077 for and 135,957 against, 3 Nov "
Prohibitory liquor law repealed, and an annual tax imposed on dealers in and manufacturers of liquors 1875
Constitution amended, striking out *art iv sec 47*, which prohibits any act authorizing the license for selling intoxicating liquors . 1876
State house of correction and reformatory at Ionia opened for reception of prisoners . . 15 Aug 1877

ate insane asylum at Pontiac opened..................July, 1878
ew capitol at Lansing dedicated........................1 Jan. 1879
ate school for the blind opened in a leased building at Lansing..29 Sept. 1880
gislature, after heated discussion and opposition, confirms grant of 1857 to the Ontonagon and State Line Railroad company, although the road had not been constructed, and limitation of time had long expired........................... 1881
ichigan Reform school for girls at Adrian, opened......Aug. "
orest fires break out in Huron and Sanilac counties and burn over some 1800 square miles of territory, rendering 2900 families homeless and destroying 138 lives................Sept. "
te purchased for state insane asylum near Traverse City.... 1882
osiah W. Begole, union or fusion candidate of the Democratic and Greenback parties, elected governor..............Nov. "
ational Prison Association meets at Detroit...........17 Oct. 1885
ate asylum for insane criminals at Ionia completed........ "
ate Soldiers' Home near Grand Rapids dedicated.....30 Dec. 1886
ocal-option law passed by legislature......................... 1887
cts passed to incorporate the Women's Christian Temperance unions throughout the state.............................. "
en counties hold local-option elections, and in each case they resulted in prohibition.................................Dec. "
ecret ballot law, on the Australian ballot system, passed..... 1889
dwin B. Winans, Democrat, elected governor by 183,725 votes; the Prohibition candidate received 28,651 votes............. 1890
x-senator Thomas W. Palmer of Detroit appointed chairman of the National Commission of the World's Columbian Exposition...27 June, "
enry B. Brown commissioned associate justice of the U. S. Supreme court, 30 Dec. 1890; is sworn in............5 Jan. 1891
rof. Alex. Winchell, geologist, b. 1824, d. in Ann Arbor..19 Feb. "
egislature places all penal and reformatory institutions under a single board, extends the Australian ballot system, and requires presidential electors to be elected by congressional districts, instead of by general state ticket................. "
venty-fifth annual reunion of the Grand Army of the Republic opens at Detroit.................................4 Aug. "
Opening of the St. Clair River tunnel celebrated at Port Huron and Sarnia..19 Sept. 1891
Ex-gov. Henry C. Baldwin d. in Detroit................31 Dec. 1892

TERRITORIAL GOVERNORS.

Name.	Term of office.	Remarks.
William Hull........	1805 to 1813	
Lewis Cass..........	1814 " 1831	Resigns to become secretary of war.
George B. Porter......	1831 " 1834	Died in office.
Steven T. Mason......	1834 " 1836	Acting.

STATE GOVERNORS.

Name.	Term of office.	Remarks.
Steven T. Mason,.....	1836 to 1840	
William Woodbridge..	1840 " 1841	Elected U. S. senator.
James W. Gordon....	1841	Acting.
John S. Barry........	1842 to 1846	
Alpheus Felch........	1846 " 1847	Elected U. S. senator.
William L. Greenley..	1847	Acting.
Epaphroditus Ransom	1848 to 1850	
John S. Barry.........	1850 " 1852	
Robert McClelland....	1852 " 1853	Appointed U. S. secretary of the interior.
Andrew Parsons......	1853 " 1855	Acting.
Kinsley S. Bingham..	1855 " 1859	
Moses Wisner........	1859 " 1861	
Austin Blair..........	1861 " 1865	
Henry H. Crapo......	1865 " 1869	
Henry P. Baldwin....	1869 " 1873	
John J. Bagley.......	1873 " 1877	
Charles M. Crosswell..	1877 " 1881	
David H. Jerome......	1881 " 1883	
Josiah W. Begole.....	1883 " 1885	Elected by a fusion, Democrats and Greenbackers.
Russell A. Alger......	1885 " 1887	
Cyrus G. Luce........	1887 " 1891	
Edwin B. Winans....	1891 " 1893	
John T. Rich.........	1893 " 1895	Re-elected 1894.

UNITED STATES SENATORS FROM THE STATE OF MICHIGAN.

Name.	No. of Congress.	Date.	Remarks.
ucius Lyon....................	24th to 25th	1837 to 1839	Seated 26 Jan.
hn Norvell.....................	24th " 26th	1837 " 1841	" "
ugustus S. Porter...............	26th " 28th	1839 " 1845	
illiam Woodbridge..............	27th " 29th	1841 " 1847	
ewis Cass......................	29th " 30th	1845 " 1848	Resigned 1848. Nominated for president by the Democrats.
homas Fitzgerald...............	30th	1849	Appointed *pro tem.* in place of Cass.
pheus Felch....................	30th to 32d	1847 to 1853	
ewis Cass......................	31st " 34th	1851 " 1857	
harles E. Stuart................	33d " 35th	1853 " 1859	Elected president *pro tem.* 9 June, 1856.
chariah Chandler...............	35th " 43d	1857 " 1875	
insley S. Bingham..............	36th	1859 " 1861	Died 1861.
cob M. Howard..................	37th to 41st	1862 " 1871	Elected in place of Bingham.
homas W. Ferry.................	42d	1871	President *pro tem.* 9 Mch. 1875.
aac P. Christiancy..............	44th to 46th	1875 to 1879	Resigned.
chariah Chandler...............	46th	1879	Elected in place of Christiancy. Died 1879.
enry P. Baldwin................	46th	1879 to 1881	Appointed in place of Chandler.
mar D. Conger..................	47th to 50th	1881 " 1887	Elected in place of Chandler.
homas W. Palmer................	48th " 51st	1883 " 1889	
rancis B. Stockbridge...........	50th " 53d	1887 " 1894	Died in office 30 Apr. 1894.
ames McMillan..................	51st " ——	1889 " ——	Term expires 1895. Re-elected.
ohn Patton, jr..................	53d " ——	1894 " ——	Appointed to succeed Stockbridge 5 May, 1894.
ulius C. Burrows................	54th " ——	1895 " ——	

Micmacs. INDIANS.

microm'eter, an astronomical instrument to measure nall distances and minute objects in the heavens, such as the parent diameters of the planets, etc., was invented by William Gascoigne, who was killed at Marston Moor, 2 July, 1644. was improved by Huyghens about 1652. Sir Joseph Whitworth made a machine to measure the 1,000,000th of an inch out 1858; the measurement of the 30,000th of an inch is w common.

mi'crophone (Gr. μικρός, little; φώνη, sound), a me given by Wheatstone, in 1827, to an instrument for rendering weak sounds audible by solid rods. The name was so given to an arrangement invented (in Dec. 1877) by prof. E. Hughes (inventor of a printing telegraph), and shown the Royal society, 9 May, 1878.

n electric current is established between 2 imperfect conductors, in loose contact (such as pieces of charcoal, metallized by being plunged when heated into mercury), mounted on a piece of thin wood. Minute sounds produced on the wood disturb the electric conductivity at the place of contact, and may be heard by telephone. The sonorous and electric waves are thus rendered synchronous and convertible. The tread of a fly sounds like that of a large quadruped. TELEPHONE.

mi'croscopes, said to have been invented by Jansen Holland about 1590, by Fontana in Italy, and by Drebbel Holland, about 1621. They were made with double glasses hen the law of refraction was discovered, about 1624. Solar icroscopes were invented by Dr. Hooke. In England the icroscope was improved by Benjamin Martin (who invented and sold pocket microscopes about 1740), by Henry Baker, F.R.S., about 1763, and still more since 1800 by Wollaston, Ross, Jackson, Varley, Powell, and others. *Diamond microscopes* were made by Andrew Pritchard in 1824; and the use of "test objects," to prove the instruments, discovered by him and Goring in 1824-40. A *binocular microscope* (i. e. for two eyes) was constructed by prof. Riddell in 1851, and Wenham's improvements were made known in 1861. Treatises on the microscope by J. Quekett (1848), by dr. W. B. Carpenter (1856 et seq.), by dr. Lionel Beale (1858-64), and Griffith and Henfrey's "Micrographic Dictionary" (1856 and 1875), are valuable. The Microscopical Society of London was established 20 Dec. 1839, and the Quekett Microscopical Club, 1865. In 1865 H. Sorby exhibited his *spectrum microscope*, by which the 1,000,000th of a grain of blood was detected.

mi'cro-tasim'eter, an instrument invented by T. A. Edison, applying the principle of the carbon microphone to delicate barometers, thermometers, hygrometers, etc., in the measurement of infinitesimal pressure; announced July, 1878.

middle ages. DARK AGES.

Middle Creek, Ky., battle of, fought 10 Jan. 1862, in the valley of the Big Sandy. Gen. James A. Garfield, with about 1800 men, defeated gen. Humphrey Marshall, commanding 2500 confederates.

Midian, now **Arz Madian,** a country of N.W. Arabia; anciently held by descendants of Midian, a son of

Abraham. Having enticed the Israelites to idolatry, they were severely chastised, 1452 B.C. They invaded Canaan about 1249 B.C., and were defeated by Gideon.

Capt. Richard F. Burton explored ruined cities of Midian in 1877, and found remains of ancient mines, many relics, and gold. An expedition, under his command, equipped by the khedive of Egypt, started from Suez, 10 Dec. 1877, and returned 20 Apr. 1878; bringing 25 tons of geological specimens, samples of silver and copper ore, coins and other antiquities, and photographs of remains of ruined cities, etc.

Midland railway station, St. Pancras, N. London, with the largest known roof in the world (245 feet 6 inches wide, and 698 feet long), was opened for traffic 1 Oct. 1868. The engineer was H. W. Barlow.

midwifery. Women were the only practitioners among the Hebrews and Egyptians. Hippocrates, in Greece, 460 B.C., is styled father of midwifery as well as of physics. It advanced under Celsus, who flourished 37 A.D., and of Galen, who lived 131. In England midwifery became a science about the time when the college of physicians was founded, 10 Hen. VII. 1518. Dr. Harvey began the practice about 1603; Astruc affirms that madame de la Vallière, mistress of Louis XIV., in 1663, secretly employed Julian Clement, a surgeon.

Milan (*mil'an*) (Lat. *Mediolanum*), capital of the ancient Liguria, now Lombardy, is reputed to have been built by the Gauls, about 408 B.C. The cathedral, or *duomo*, was built about 1385. Pop. 1890, 414,551.

	B.C.
Conquered by the Roman consul Marcellus	222
	A.D.
Seat of government of the Western empire	286
Council of Milan	346
St. Ambrose, bishop of Milan	375
Milan plundered by Attila	452
Included in the Ostrogothic kingdom, 489; in the Lombard kingdom	569
Becomes an independent republic	1101
Emperor Frederic I. takes Milan, and appoints a podesta	1158
It rebels; is taken by Frederic and its fortifications destroyed,	1162
Rebuilt and fortified	1169
Milanese defeated by the emperor Frederic II	1237
Visconti become paramount in Milan	1277
John Galeazzo Visconti takes the title of duke	1395
Francesco Sforza, son-in-law of the last of the Visconti, subdues Milan and becomes duke	1450
Milan conquered by Louis XII. of France	1499
French expelled by the Spaniards	1525
Milan annexed to the crown of Spain	1540
Milan ceded to Austria	1714
Conquered by the French and Spaniards	1743
Reverts to Austria, Naples and Sicily being ceded to Spain	1748
Seized by the French 30 June,	1796
Retaken by the Austrians	1799
Regained by the French 31 May,	1800
Made capital of Italy, and Napoleon crowned with the Iron Crown here 26 May,	1805
Milan decree of Napoleon against all continental intercourse with England 17 Dec.	1807
Insurrection against the Austrians; flight of the viceroy, 18 Mch.	1848
Surrenders to the Austrians 5 Aug.	"
Treaty of peace between Austria and Sardinia 6 Aug.	1849
Peace of Villafranca; a large part of Lombardy transferred to Sardinia 12 July,	1859
Victor Emmanuel enters Milan as king 8 Aug.	1860

Milan decree. UNITED STATES, 1807.

Mile'tus, a Greek city of Ionia, Asia Minor, founded about 1043 B.C. The Milesians defended themselves successfully, 623–612 B.C. During the war with Persia it was taken, 494, but restored, 449. Here Paul delivered his charge to the elders of the church of Ephesus, 60 A.D. (Acts xx.).

military or **martial law** is built on no settled principle, but is arbitrary, and, in truth, no law; but sometimes indulged, rather than allowed, as law.—*Sir Matthew Hale.* It has been several times proclaimed in parts of Great Britain, and in 1798 was almost general in Ireland, where it was also proclaimed in 1803. HABEAS CORPUS, MILLIGAN CASE, UNITED STATES.

military departments of the United States. The U. S. form 8 military departments, viz.:

Department of the East, hd. qrs. Governor's island, N. Y.: New England states, Middle states, Maryland, Virginia, West Virginia, North Carolina, South Carolina, Georgia, Florida, Louisiana, Mississippi, Alabama, Kentucky, Tennessee, Ohio, and District of Columbia.

Department of the Missouri, hd. qrs. Chicago, Ill.: Michigan, Wisconsin, Indiana, Illinois, Missouri, Kansas, Arkansas, Indian and Oklahoma territories.

Department of California, hd. qrs. San Francisco, Cal.: California and Nevada.

Department of Dakota, hd. qrs. St. Paul, Minn.: Minnesota, North Dakota, part of South Dakota, Montana, and part of Wyoming.

Department of Texas, hd. qrs. San Antonio, Tex.: State of Texas.

Department of the Platte, hd. qrs. Omaha, Neb.: Iowa, Nebraska, part of Wyoming, Utah, part of Idaho, and part of South Dakota.

Department of Colorado, hd. qrs. Denver, Col.: Arizona, New Mexico, and Colorado.

Department of the Columbia, hd. qrs. Vancouver Barracks, Wash.: Oregon, Washington, part of Idaho, and Alaska.

Each under the supervision of a general officer of the army.

military districts. UNITED STATES, 1813.

military events in the United States. Besides special mention, STATE RECORDS, UNITED STATES.

militia, citizens of a state enrolled as soldiers for training and discipline, but called into active service only in emergencies, thus distinguished from the regular or constant soldier.

Act of Congress requiring every citizen between 18 and 45 years of age to be enrolled in the militia, and armed and equipped at his own cost 8 May,	1792
Act empowering the president, in case of invasion, to call out the militia of the states 28 Feb.	1795
Permanent appropriation of $200,000 a year to provide arms and equipments for militia, made by Congress 23 Apr.	1808
Board to consider changes in the militia laws is convened by secretary of war Barbour, with Winfield Scott as president. It reports a plan "that a select corps of militia be formed, to consist in each state of one brigade for every congressional representative, and that the officers assemble in camps of instruction ten days in each year;" that "the office of adjutant-general of militia be created, and that the U. S. furnish officers to instruct the camps"	1825
Congress enacts that whenever the president shall call out the militia, he may fix the period of service, not exceeding 9 months 17 July,	1862

Militia in the U. S. are officered and disciplined by state authority, but the Constitution makes the president commander-in-chief of the militia when in actual service of the U. S. In the constitutions of Massachusetts, Vermont, Oregon, and South Carolina, it is declared that every member of society is bound to yield his personal service or an equivalent to the state, for the defence of life, liberty, and property; but in most of the states the militia consists of all able-bodied male persons between 18 and 45, and a person conscientiously opposed to bearing arms is excused from service on paying an equivalent. The National Guard in the militia of the states in 1891 included:

Infantry	92,203
Cavalry	4,554
Artillery	5,224
Total enlisted	101,981
Total commissioned	9,311

Number of men available for military duty, not enrolled, 9,121,258.

The standing national force of England is traced to king Alfred, who made all his subjects soldiers, 872–901.

Commission of array to raise a militia	1122
Revived by Henry II	1176
Again revived	1557
Said to amount to 160,000 men	1623
Militia Reserve act passed	1862
141,488 in	1892

Milky Way (Galaxy, from Gr. γάλακτος, milk) in the heavens. Hera is said by Greek poets to have spilled her milk in the heavens after suckling Hermes or Heracles. Democritus (about 428 B.C.) taught that the *Via Lactea* consists of stars, and Galileo (1610–42) proved it by the telescope. "In the midst of this gigantic collection of stars lost in this vortex of worlds, our little solar system lies. The dimensions of the centre of this system—the sun which appears to us so great, but which in reality is that of a star of the second or third magnitude—are found to represent but an atom of the luminous sand of the Milky Way."—*Richard A. Proctor.*

Mill-boy of the Slashes, a term applied to Henry Clay (1777–1852), born Hanover county, Va. "Mill-boy," from his carrying grain to be ground at a mill in that vicinity, and "of the Slashes," from his boyhood residence, so called because the timber had been slashed or cut off.

Millena'rians. Some suppose that the world will end with the 7000th year from the creation; and that during 1000 years (millennium) Christ and the saints will reign upon the earth (Rev. xx.). The doctrine was inculcated in the 2d and 3d centuries by Papias, Justin Martyr, and others.

Millerites, followers of William Miller (1781–1849), who labored assiduously in the northern United States for 10 ears (1833–43), preaching and prophesying the end of the 'orld in 1843. His followers rapidly disappeared after the day of probation" passed. ADVENTISTS.

Milligan, Case of. On 5 Oct. 1864, Lambdin P. Milgan, while at home in Indiana, was arrested with others, for :easonable designs, by order of gen. Alvin P. Hovey, comıanding the military district of Indiana; on 21 Oct. brought efore a military commission convened at Indianapolis by gen. lovey, tried on certain charges and specifications, found guilty, nd sentenced to be hanged, Friday, 19 May, 1865. The proeedings of the military commission closed in Jan. 1865. When he Circuit court of the United States met at Indianapolis in an. 1865, the grand jury did not indict Milligan, who then etitioned the court to be brought before it and tried by jury r released. With the petition was filed the order appointing ıe commission, the charges, finding of the commission, with he order from the war department reciting that the sentence 'as approved by the president, and directing that the sentence e carried out without delay. The judges differed on 3 ques.ons: (1) Whether on the facts submitted a writ of habeas orpus should be issued; (2) Whether Milligan ought to be ischarged; (3) Whether the military commission had acted 'ithin its jurisdiction; and these were submitted to the Sureme court of the U. S. The first 2 questions were answered ı the affirmative, the third in the negative, justices Davis, irier, Nelson, Clifford, and Fields holding that Congress had ot the constitutional power to authorize such commission—hat the Constitution forbids it, and is the supreme law of the ınd, in war as in peace. Chief-justice Chase, supported by ustices Wayne, Swayne, and Miller, held that Congress has he power to authorize military commissions in time of war; ut all concurred in the answers given to the 3 questions subıitted, and Milligan was released. "This decision of the ourt overthrew the whole doctrine of military arrest and trial f private citizens in peaceful states."—*Lalor's* "Cyclopædia f Political Science," vol. ii. p. 433. HABEAS CORPUS.

Milliken's Bend, La., attacked by confederates :nder gen. H. McCulloch; repulsed 6 June, 1863, by Union orces (mostly colored), aided by the gunboats *Choctaw* and *exington.* Union loss, killed and wounded, 404.

Mill Spring, Ky., battle at. Gen. Zollicoffer, confederate, was here defeated by gen. George H. Thomas, with a oss of 300 men, 19 Jan. 1862. Gen. Zollicoffer was killed.

mills, anciently, any machine for grinding cereals for food; nodern meaning includes any machine or combination of ma:hinery used for any intended purpose, as cotton-mill, woollennill, grist-mill, saw-mill, cider-mill, etc. Moses forbade milltones to be taken in pawn, because it would be like taking a nan's life to pledge (Deut. xxiv. 6). The hand-mill was in ıse among Britons before the Roman conquest. The Romans ntroduced the water-mill. Cotton-mills moved by water were erected by sir Richard Arkwright at Cromford, Derbyhire, Engl., who died 1792. MECHANICS.

Milwau'kee, known as the "Cream city," the me:ropolis of Wisconsin, situated on the western shore of lake Michigan, was founded by Solomon Juneau, who arrived there 14 Sept. 1818. The place and name were known as early as 10 Nov. 1699, as John Buisson de St. Comes mentions being storm-bound at *Milwarck* on that date. The east side was first platted and named Milwaukee by Messrs. Juneau and Martin in 1835, the first sale of lots taking place in August of that year. In 1838 the population of Milwaukee was 700; 1840, 1700, and by decades since, 1850, 20,061; 1860, 45,246; 1870, 71,440; 1880, 115,587; 1890, 204,468; 1900, 285,315; by this census the 14th city in the U. S. in point of population. Lat 43° 5′ N., lon. 88° W.

Milwaukee visited by lieut. James Gorrell of the 80th Royal American regiment, stationed at Mackinaw.........21 Aug. 1762
Alexander Laframbois, trader from Mackinaw, establishes himself at Milwaukee, remaining 6 years.................. 1785
John Baptiste Mirandeau, a trader from Green Bay, settles at site of Milwaukee.. 1795
Solomon Juneau, founder of the city, arrives as clerk for his father-in-law, Jacques Vieux of Green Bay..........14 Sept. 1818
First invoice of goods landed at Milwaukee from a lake vessel, the *Chicago Packet*, a schooner of 30 tons, capt. Britton..... 1823
First frame building built for Solomon Juneau................ 1824
Col. George H. Walker, who erected the first dwelling-house on the south side, arrives...........................20 Mch. 1834
Byron Kilbourn, founder of Kilbourntown, now the west side, arrives...Nov. 1834
First ferry established at the mouth of the river by Horace Chase.. 1835
First Protestant meeting (Methodist)....................May, "
East side platted and named Milwaukee by Messrs. Juneau and Martin, and first recorded sale of lots................4 Aug. "
West side platted by Kilbourn; first recorded plat dated, 9 Oct. "
First election of town officers.........................19 Sept. "
Post-office established, with Solomon Juneau as postmaster... "
First white child, Milwaukee Smith, daughter of Uriel B. Smith, b..10 Oct. "
First tavern opened by J. and L. Childs, on northeast cor. Broadway and Wisconsin st.................................. "
Second tavern opened by Vieux, and known as the Cottage inn, "
[Destroyed by fire in 1845.]
First Episcopal service conducted by rev. Henry Gregory of Syracuse, N. Y.....................................10 Jan. 1836
Stage-coaches begin running weekly to Chicago..........Mch. "
First newspaper, *Milwaukee Advertiser*, pub..........14 July, "
First brick building erected on Jackson st. by William Sivyer, May, "
First vessel built near the intersection of North Water and Broadway, a schooner of 90 tons, the *Solomon Juneau*...... "
Steamer *Columbus*, first of regular line of lower lake steamers, arrives..Aug. "
First court-house built.. "
First school on the south side, kept at the cor. of Florida and Greenbush sts. by Eli Bates, jr., and another school on Third st. kept by Edward West.....................winter of 1836–37
First hotel, the Belle View, afterwards the Milwaukee house, cor. Broadway and Wisconsin st., begun by Juneau and Martin in 1835, and completed.......................... 1837
Milwaukee Sentinel first pub..................................... "
School held in the Methodist church, southeast cor. East Water and Huron sts.. "
First U. S. District court held...................................... "
Village of Milwaukee organized; Solomon Juneau elected president...14 Feb. "
Village of Kilbourntown organized; Byron Kilbourn president, "
First celebration of mass at the house of Solomon Juneau, Aug. "
First steamer, the *Badger*, 50 tons, built.................... "
First government light-house, on bluff at head of Wisconsin st., erected.. 1838
Ground broken for Kilbourn's famous Rock River canal, 4 July, "
Wisconsin Marine and Fire insurance company organized, May, 1839
St. Peter's church, on Market st. west of Jackson st., built.... "
Colony of 800 German immigrants land and camp on the lake shore near the foot of Huron st.................summer of "
First fire engine, "Neptune No. 1," purchased.............. "
Kilbourntown added to Milwaukee, and divisions of the town designated as the east and west wards, 1839; Elisha Starr elected president................................18 May, "
First brick block built, northwest cor. Third and Chestnut sts. 1840
[Held the first theatre in Milwaukee; razed in 1876.]
First brewery built at foot of Huron st. by Owens, Pawlet & Davis...spring, "
Old First Presbyterian church, cor. Milwaukee and Mason sts., begun 1839, completed.. "
First bridge built across the river, joining the east and west sides, between Chestnut and Division sts.................. "
First fire company organized at the Milwaukee house..14 Feb. "
First High school established in the old court-house by Charles Whipple...10 May, 1841
First cargo of wheat shipped...................................... "
Brewery erected by Herman Reidelschoefer, northeast cor. Hanover and Virginia sts....................................... "
Ordinance passed against hogs and cattle running at large.... 1842
First theatrical entertainment, "Shylock"............27 Sept. "
Philetus C. Hale opens the first book store, on East Water st., 2 Nov. "
First county buildings erected.................................. 1843
[Razed in 1870.]
Harbor improvements begun... "
Milwaukee lodge of Odd Fellows No. 2, the first in the town, instituted...Mch. "
Milwaukee lodge of Freemasons No. 22, organized......5 July, "
First German paper, the *Wisconsin Banner*, afterwards the *Banner and Volksfreund*, pub. by Moritz Schoeffler..7 Sept. 1844
First military organization, the Washington Guards (disbanded 1852), organized....................................8 Jan. 1845
Fire which destroys 2 entire squares.....................7 Apr. "
Young Men's Association founded.................................. "
First daily mail to Chicago..............................18 Nov. "
Milwaukee incorporated as a city; pop. 9660..........31 Jan. 1846
Solomon Juneau elected first mayor........................7 Apr. "
First meeting of the common council.....................10 Apr. "
Fire department organized... "
First Baptist church built at the southeast cor. Milwaukee and Wisconsin sts...1846–47
Female seminary opened by H. M. Lowe and John P. McGregor on southeast cor. Jackson and Oneida sts.....18 Jan. 1847
Evening Wisconsin first pub.............................8 June, "
First steam flouring mill erected by Goodrich & Easton on South Water st.; begins operation....................26 Sept. "
New jail built by William Sivyer................................. "
Corner-stone of St. John's cathedral laid...................5 Dec. "
First telegraph message sent from Milwaukee..........17 Jan. 1848
Milwaukee Collegiate institute established by prof. Amasa Buck, "
St. Rosa's Orphan asylum established.....................9 May, "
First steam grain elevator (Sweet's), erected at Walker's Point, "

Menomonee Locomotive works, where the first locomotive built in the state was constructed, established.............. 1849
Milwaukee Grammar school founded.......................... "
First Public school buildings erected; 5 brick structures...... "
Deaths from cholera, 104.........................July, Aug. "
Milwaukee orphan asylum, Protestant, on Marshall st. between Oneida and Biddle, established.......................4 Jan. 1850
First theatrical entertainment in German given........11 Feb. "
Failure of Hemenway's bank..........................12 Feb. "
Milwaukee Normal institute (afterwards the Milwaukee Female college) organized.................................... "
Ordinance to legalize the widening of Spring st. passed.5 May, "
Forest Home cemetery opened.......................3 Aug. "
Over 300 deaths from cholera.....................July-Sept. "
Milwaukee and Mississippi railroad opened to Waukesha, 25 Feb. 1851
City omnibus line established.......................20 Sept. "
First railroad passenger depot in the state erected at the foot of Second st.. 1852
City first lighted with gas...........................23 Nov. "
First express company established in Milwaukee........1 Feb. 1853
St. John's cathedral consecrated....................31 July, "
Fire begins at cor. Broadway and Huron st. and destroys 66 buildings, entailing a total loss of $400,000..........24 Aug. 1854
Cobble-stone pavements introduced.......................... "
Failure of the Germania bank.........................11 Jan. 1855
Light Guards (disbanded in 1876), organized............9 July, "
Night watch first established............................Sept. "
Board of Trade organized, Horatio Hill president......16 Jan. 1856
First shipment of wheat direct to Liverpool, 14,000 bush. on schooner *Dean Richmond*, leaves Milwaukee 19 July, arrives at Liverpool...29 Sept. "
Solomon Juneau d. at Shawano.......................14 Nov. "
Public funeral of Solomon Juneau held at Milwaukee..26 Nov. "
James H. Rogers's mansion, southwest cor. Fifteenth st. and Grand ave., completed..................................... 1857
Newhall house opened.................................25 Aug. "
Chamber of Commerce organized (L. J. Higby, president) in Apr., and formally opened at No. 1 Spring st. (now Grand ave.)...22 Nov. 1858
New post-office building, begun 1 May, 1856, opened....1 Jan. 1859
Municipal (police) court established..................18 Mch. "
Schooner *M. S. Scott* clears for Liverpool direct with 170,000 ft. of hardwood lumber (passage, 49 days).............31 May, "
St. Mary's hospital founded.................................... "
Ground broken for a street railroad from the foot of Wisconsin st. to Albion st., 28 Nov. 1859; first trip made.......30 May, 1860
Wreck of the *Lady Elgin*, capt. John Wilson; sunk after collision with schooner *Augusta*, on her return from Chicago with a party of about 400 excursionists; 225 citizens of Milwaukee drowned, besides 62 other passengers........8 Sept. "
Cross block burned; 5 lives lost; city records burned...30 Dec. "
Bank riot...24 June, 1861
Daily *Herald* established............................21 Sept. "
First steam fire-engine dates from...................10 Nov. "
Letter-carrier system introduced......................1 Jan. 1865
Academy of Music opened............................31 Jan. "
George H. Walker d..................................20 Sept. 1866
Plankington house begun, May, 1867; hotel opened......Sept. 1868
Old Settlers club organized...........................5 July, 1869
Board of Public Works created.................................. "
Fire-alarm telegraph introduced................................ "
Stock yards established.. 1870
Byron Kilbourn dies at Jacksonville, Fla.............16 Dec. "
Grand Opera House opened...........................17 Sept. 1871
City water works established...........................1872-73
Corner-stone of new court-house laid, 7 Sept. 1870; building completed at a cost of $650,000.....................22 Jan. 1873
City first supplied with water from tunnel under lake..14 Sept. 1874
Immanuel Presbyterian church on Astor st., corner-stone laid 25 Aug. 1873; cost $170,000; dedicated..............3 Jan. 1875
Wisconsin Industrial school for girls organized.........11 Feb. "
Milwaukee Free Public library opened.................8 July, 1878
National German-American Teachers' seminary opened....... "
Telephone exchange opened..................................... 1879
Milwaukee County Pioneer Association organized......13 Nov. "
Insane asylum opened................................26 Mch. 1880
New library building completed.......................1 May, "
New building for the Chamber of Commerce dedicated.18 Nov. "
Evening schools first established.....................22 Nov. "
Exposition building corner-stone laid, 14 May, 1881; opened, 6 Sept. 1881
Electric light introduced at Schlitz's park..................... "
Daily Journal established...........................16 Nov. 1882
Newhall house burned; 71 lives lost..................10 Jan. 1883
Public funerals of the victims of the Newhall-house fire held at the Exposition building and at St. John's cathedral.25 Jan. "
Milwaukee day school for the deaf opened...................... "
Milwaukee Club house opened.........................31 May, 1884
Failure of the Manufacturers' bank...................15 June, "
St. Paul's church, new edifice dedicated....................... "
State Normal school opened.................................... 1885
Old waterpower canal filled up................................ "
Semi-centennial of the first election of town officers...19 Sept. "
Statue of Washington by Parks, presented by Miss Elizabeth Plankington, unveiled on Grand ave....................7 Nov. "
Anarchist riot......................................5 May, 1886
Demolition of the old Kilbourn mansion, northwest cor. Fourth st. and Grand ave., begun.............................10 May, "
New Insurance building erected................................ "
Layton Art gallery opened............................5 Apr. 1888
Ex.-gov. Harrison Ludington d. (aged 78).............17 June, 1891
Fire destroys 300 buildings; loss, $5,000,000; 10 lives lost, 28 Oct. 1892
Davidson theatre (opened 1891) burned; 20 firemen thrown into the fire by the falling in of the roof; 9 lives lost, and the rest badly injured.................................9 Apr. 1894

MAYORS.

Solomon Juneau	1846	John J. Tallmadge	1865
Horatio N. Wells	1847	Edward O'Neill	1867
Byron Kilbourn	1848	Joseph Phillips	1870
Don A. J. Upham	1849	Harrison Ludington	1871
George H. Walker	1851	David G. Hooker	1872
Hans Crocker	1852	Harrison Ludington	1873
George H. Walker	1853	A. R. R. Butler	1876
Byron Kilbourn	1854	John Black	1878
James B. Cross	1855	Thomas H. Brown	1880
William A. Prentiss	1858	John M. Stowell	1882
Herman L. Page	1859	Emil Wallber	1884
William Pitt Lynde	1860	Thomas H. Brown	1888
James S. Brown	1861	George W. Peck	1890
Horace Chase	1862	Peter J. Somers	"
Edward O'Neill	1863	John C. Koch	1893
Abner Kirby	1864		

Minden, Prussia, battle of, 1 Aug. 1759, between the English, Hessians, and Hanoverians (under prince Ferdinand of Brunswick), and the French (under marshal de Contades), who were beaten and driven to the ramparts of Minden. Lord George Sackville (afterwards lord George Germaine), who commanded the British and Hanoverian horse, for disobedience of orders, dismissed by a court-martial on his return to England, 22 Apr. 1760. He was afterwards restored to favor, and became secretary of state, 1776.

mine explosion before Petersburg, Va. An attempt was made by the federals to break through the Confederate line before Petersburg in July, 1864, by blowing up a part of their works. The point selected was a fort in front of Burnside's corps, the 9th. On the suggestion of lieut.-col. Henry Pleasants, 48th Pennsylvania volunteers, to gen. Potter, and approved by gen. Burnside, the work was commenced under the supervision of col. Pleasants, 25 June. The main gallery was 511 feet in length, with lateral galleries extending under the Confederate works 37 and 38 feet to the right and left; it was finished 29 July, and 8000 pounds of powder placed in position for exploding. The mine was exploded successfully at 4.30 A.M., 30 July. The storming column, made up of troops from the 9th corps, was mismanaged and failed, with a total loss in killed and wounded and missing of about 4400 men. The success of the explosion was a surprise to the chief commanders of the army of the Potomac; in fact, they had given it no thought except to condemn it. The treatment of the subject by the chief officers of the army of the Potomac is shown by the following testimony of col. Pleasants before the committee on the conduct of the war: "Gen. Burnside told me that gen. Meade and maj. Duane, chief-engineer of the army of the Potomac, said that the thing could not be done, that it was all claptrap and nonsense; that such a length of mine had never been excavated in military operations and could not be," etc.—"Report of the Committee on the Conduct of the War on Battle of Petersburg," p. 2, 2d session, 38th Cong., 15 Dec. 1864, part I. 1864-65; also, "Report of Military Court of Inquiry (on Mine Explosion)," convened 5 Aug. 1864, in front of Petersburg; "War of the Rebellion," official record of Union and Confederate armies, series I. vol. xl. part I., reports, p. 42-129.

mineralogy, the science of minerals, is a branch of geology. CRYSTALLOGRAPHY, ELEMENTS, GEOLOGY, MINES. It was not much studied by the ancients. George Agricola in the 16th century made the first attempt to treat it scientifically. James D. Dana's "System of Mineralogy," 1st ed. 1837; 5th ed., 1883.

Minerva, an ancient Italian divinity, the same in general with the Pallas-Athene (Παλλὰς Ἀθήνη) of the Greeks, and to be considered therefore in common with her. The etymology of the word is doubtful.—*Anthon*, "Class. Dict." MYTHOLOGY.

mines. See different metals, coal, iron, etc., throughout the work.

Mingoes. The Algonquin name for the Indians of the Five Nations or Iroquois, especially of the Mohawk tribe.

Minié (*min-i-ā'*) **rifle**, invented at Vincennes, about 1833, by M. Minié (b. 1810). From a common soldier he rose to the rank of *chef d'escadron*. His rifle, considered to surpass all previous to it, was adopted by the French, and, with modifications, by the British, 1852. FIRE-ARMS.

Min'isink, Orange Co., N. Y. On the night of 19 July, 79, Brant, at the head of about 100 Tories and Indians, at-:ked and destroyed this little settlement. He was pursued xt day by a few (150) local militia; but on the second day rprised his pursuers, of whom only about 30 escaped.

Min'nesingers (Ger. *Minne*, love, and *Singer*, singer), ric German poets of the 12th and 13th centuries, who sang love and war to entertain knights and barons. They sang eir pieces to their own accompaniments on the viol, etc. ıe *Meistersingers*, their successors, an incorporated fraternity the 14th century, made satirical ballads to amuse citizens and wer-class people. Hans Sachs, a shoemaker (1494–1576), a et of the Reformation, was for a time their dean. His works ere published at Nuremberg, 1560. "Owleglass" and "Reyrd the Fox" are attributed to the Meistersingers.

Minneso'ta, one of the northern frontier states of the nion, containing lake Itasca, the source of the Mississippi river, is bounded north by Manitoba and Ontario, of the dominion of Canada; east by lake Superior and Wisconsin, south by Iowa, and west by North Dakota and South Dakota. It is limited in latitude from 43° 30′ to 49° N., and in longitude from 89° 29′ to 97° 5′ W. Area, 83,365 sq. miles. Pop. 1890, 1,301,826; 1900, 1,751,394. Capital, St. Paul.

Daniel Greysolon du Luth, a native of Lyons, builds a trading-post at the entrance of Pigeon river, on north shore of lake Superior (whence the name Duluth)................ 1678
.ther Louis Hennepin ascends the Mississippi from the mouth of the Illinois, passes through lake Pepin, and reaches the falls, which he names St. Anthony....................Oct. 1680
eur du Luth, with 4 Frenchmen and an Indian, in 2 canoes, from his trading-post reach a lake whose outlet enters the Mississippi, and on the river he meets father Hennepin..... "
cholas Perrot erects a fort on lake Pepin, and takes possession of the Minnesota country in the name of the king of France..8 May, 1689
: Seur builds a trading-post on an island in the Mississippi, just above lake Pepin.. 1695
eur le Seur, on a search for mines in Minnesota, builds fort L'Huillier on the St. Pierre, now the Minnesota.........Oct. 1700
nathan Carver, the first British explorer of Minnesota, arrives at Mackinaw from Massachusetts, Aug. 1766; Green Bay, Wis., 18 Sept.; at Prairie du Chien, 10 Oct.; falls of St. Anthony, 17 Nov.; and ascends the Minnesota river to the stream which now bears his name....................... 1766
orthwestern Fur company builds a stockade at Sandy Lake. 1794
eirs of Carver's American wife dispose of their interest in an alleged grant of land in Minnesota to Carver (made by the Naudowessies Indians, 1 May, 1767) to Edward Houghton of Vermont, in consideration of 50,000*l*.......................... "
.diana territory created, including part of present state of Minnesota..May, 1800
erritory of Upper Louisiana formed, including a large portion of Minnesota.....................................20 Mch. 1804
innesota east of the Mississippi a part of Michigan territory, 1805
eut. Z. M. Pike, ordered by gen. Wilkinson to visit Minnesota and expel the British traders, arrives at the site of fort Snelling, and in council with the Dakota Indians obtains a grant of land for the use of the U. S. 9 miles square on both sides of the river......................................23 Sept. "
ev. Samuel Peters alleges, in a petition to Congress, that he has purchased from the Carver American heirs their right to the grant made in 1767................................ 1806
innesota east of the Mississippi included in Illinois territory, 1809
art of Minnesota east of the Mississippi becomes a part of Michigan territory.. 1819
arracks erected at Mendota and occupied by a garrison which came from Green Bay, Wis., by the Wisconsin river........ "
orner-stone of fort Snelling laid; first called fort St. Anthony, 20 Sept. 1820
aree Mackinaw boats laden with seed wheat, oats, and pease, leave Prairie du Chien, 15 Apr. 1820, for the Scotch settlement at Pembina, where the crops were destroyed by grasshoppers the previous year. Proceeding entirely by water, except a portage from Big Stone lake to lake Traverse, 1½ miles, they arrive at Pembina.....................3 June, "
ov. Cass of Michigan, with an exploring party from Detroit under sanction of the U. S. government, reaching the Mississippi by Sandy lake, ascends to Cass lake........21 July, "
en. Leavenworth reports to the commissioners of the land office that the Indians do not recognize grant to Carver in 1767.. 1821
irst mill in Minnesota, erected under the supervision of the officers of fort Snelling on the site of Minneapolis.......... 1822
ommittee on public lands report to the Senate on rev. Samuel Peters's claim to the Carver grant of 1767; the original deed not being produced, and for other reasons, it is resolved that the petition be not granted...........................23 Jan. 1823
First steamboat to navigate the Mississippi from St. Louis to the Minnesota river, the *Virginia*, reaches fort Snelling, May, "
An expedition fitted out by government, in charge of maj. S. H. Long, discovers that Pembina, the fort of the Hudson Bay company on Red river, is within the U. S. Long erects an oak post on the line, raises the U. S. flag, and proclaims the territory a part of the U. S.............................5 Aug. "
A colony of Swiss from the Red River settlement establish themselves near fort Snelling.............................. 1827
Henry R. Schoolcraft, with an expedition for exploring the Mississippi, Crow Wing, and St. Croix rivers, reaches the Mississippi by lake Superior and Sandy lake, and reaches the source of the west fork in Itasca lake...............13 July, 1832
Rev. W. T. Boutwell establishes at Leech lake the first mission among the Indians in Minnesota west of the Mississippi, Oct. 1833
Jean N. Nicollet leaves fort Snelling to explore the sources of the rivulets that feed Itasca lake...................26 July, 1836
Gov. Dodge of Wisconsin territory meets the Ojibways at fort Snelling, and they cede to the U. S. the pine forests of the valley of the St. Croix and its tributaries...........29 July, 1837
Deputation of Dakotas conclude a treaty with the U. S. at Washington, ceding all lands east of the Mississippi....Sept. "
Minnesota is wholly included in Iowa, set off in 1838 from Wisconsin, which was set off from Michigan in 1836........ 1838
By order of secretary of war, troops from fort Snelling expel Swiss squatters on the military reservation east of the Mississippi, between St. Paul and the fort................6 May, 1840
A log chapel, erected by father Lucian Galtier and dedicated to St. Paul (whence the name of the city)...............1 Nov. 1841
Settlement begun at Stillwater by 4 proprietors, who erect a saw-mill..10 Oct. 1843
Capt. J. Allen, with a detachment of dragoons, ascends the Des Moines river and crosses to the St. Peter (Minnesota) and Big Sioux rivers.. 1844
First meeting in Minnesota on the subject of claiming territorial privileges for that part of Wisconsin territory not included in state constitution adopted 13 Mch. 1848, is held in Jackson's store, St. Paul...........................12 July, 1848
Convention at Stillwater to consider territorial government, 26 Aug. "
H. H. Sibley, of St. Peters, elected delegate to Congress from Wisconsin territory not included in the state.........30 Oct. "
Extract from the diary of Harriet E. Bishop, first school-teacher in St. Paul: "J. R. Clewett came into Mr. Irwine's house and said, 'My! how this town is growing! I counted the smoke of 18 chimneys this morning'"............winter of "
Congress establishes the territorial government of Minnesota; bounded on south by Iowa and Missouri river, west by the Missouri and White Earth rivers, north by the British possessions, and east by Wisconsin, with St. Paul as capital, 3 Mch. 1849
First number of the *Minnesota Pioneer* issued by James M. Goodhue..28 Apr. "
Alexander Ramsey, of Harrisburg, Pa., appointed governor of Minnesota territory, organizes the government at St. Paul, 1 June, "
Chronicle and Register issued at St. Paul..............25 Aug. "
First legislature, consisting of 9 councillors and 18 representatives, meets at the Central house in St. Paul.......3 Sept. "
Act passed to send the Washington Monument Association a slab of red pipe-stone from the Minnesota quarry........... "
St. Paul incorporated as a town.........................Nov. "
Minnesota Historical Society organized by law........15 Nov. "
Miss Frederika Bremer is the guest of gov. Ramsey........... 1850
Congress appropriates $20,000 for a territorial prison.......... 1851
Treaty at Traverse des Sioux, on Minnesota river, the Sioux cede all lands in Iowa and in Minnesota east of the Red River of the North, lake Traverse, and the Sioux river, 23 July, "
Dog train with explorers, under dr. Rae, after search for sir John Franklin, arrives at St. Paul from the north...14 Feb. 1852
Prohibitory Liquor law passed; ratified by the people, 5 Apr., but declared void by Supreme court....................... "
Joint resolution of Congress changing the name of the river St. Pierre, or St. Peter's, to the Minnesota..........19 June, "
College of St. Paul, chartered as the Baldwin school, dedicated, 29 Dec. 1853
City of St. Paul incorporated...........................4 Mch. 1854
Convention held at St. Anthony, and the Republican party of Minnesota formed..............................29 Mch. "
Hameline university at Red Wing chartered...........3 Apr. "
Duluth founded.. 1856
State Reform school at St. Paul opened......................... "
Bill to remove the government to St. Peter's passes the house; the council, Joseph Rolette, chairman of committee on enrolled bills, being absent, after continuous session of 5 days and nights, is dissolved without acting on the bill.......... 1857
Inkpadootah, a Dakota Indian, at the head of a band, massacres a settlement of whites at Springfield, capturing a number of women and children........................27 Mch. "
Congress grants to Minnesota 6 alternate sections of land per mile to aid in the construction of railroads.............Mch. "
St. John's university opened at Collegeville.................. "
Constitutional convention assembles at St. Paul 14 July, 1857. Republicans and Democrats organize separately, prepare drafts, but unite and submit one constitution to the people (ratified 36,240 to 700), St. Paul the capital.........29 Aug. "
State issues $2,275,000 in bonds, out of $5,000,000 authorized

by an amendment to the constitution, art. ix. sec. 10, called Minnesota State Railroad bonds, the credit of the state being pledged for interest and principal....................15 Apr. 1858
Minnesota admitted into the Union ....11 May, "
Macalester college opened at Macalester, Ramsey county...... "
State Normal school at Winona opened.......................... 1860
Railroads default in interest and the state forecloses.......... "
Amendment to constitution, art. ix. sec. 10, amended 1858, forbidding more bonds to aid railroads, and to sec. 2, providing that no tax or provision for interest or principal of bonds shall be in force until ratified by the people............Nov. "
First regiment of Minnesota volunteers leaves fort Snelling for Washington.................................22 June, 1861
Sioux Indians, under Little Crow, massacre the whites at Yellow Medicine agency, 18 Aug. 1862; at New Ulm, in Brown county, 21 Aug.; attack New Ulm and are repulsed, 23 Aug.; besiege fort Ridgely for 9 days; attack Cedar City, McLeod county, 3 Sept.; state troops under col. H. H. Sibley march against them, 26 Aug.; U. S. troops under maj.-gen. Pope are despatched to the seat of war, and after a sharp battle at Wood Lake the Indians are defeated, and 500 are taken prisoners, 300 of whom are sentenced to be hung.......22 Sept. 1862
Ninety-one captive white women and children surrendered by the Indians to col. Sibley near the Chippewa river..27 Sept. "
Thirty-eight of the 300 Indians sentenced are executed, 26 Dec. "
Little Crow killed by a settler in the neighborhood of Hutchinson, McLeod county..........................summer of 1863
Minnesota school for the deaf opened at Faribault............ "
Bennet seminary opened at Minneapolis.......................... 1865
Prof. Eames, state geologist, reports rich silver-bearing quartz near Vermilion lake, in the northeast part of the state...... "
State insane hospital at St. Peter opened...............6 Dec. 1866
Minnesota school for the blind opened at Faribault............ "
Carleton college opened at Northfield.......................... 1867
City of Minneapolis incorporated.................................. "
Amendment to art. vii. sec. 1 of the constitution, striking out the word "white," ratified by the people.............Nov. 1868
State Reform school at St. Paul opened.......................... "
Augsburg Theological seminary opened at Minneapolis.......... 1869
State university created by law, 1851; Congress grants it 46,000 acres of land, 1857, and same year the first building erected at St. Anthony; chartered 1868, opened.......................... "
State Normal school at Mankato opened.......................... "
State Normal school at St. Cloud opened.......................... "
Bill to remove seat of government from St. Paul to a place in Kandiyohi county passes both houses, but is vetoed........ "
Convention at St. Paul organizes a State Temperance Society, 6 Oct. "
Construction of the Northern Pacific railroad commenced at the Dalles of the St. Louis..........................15 Feb. 1870
Ship canal across Minnesota point at Duluth, begun............ "
Legislature ratifies the XV.th Amendment, establishes a Board of Immigration, and amends the liquor law so as to allow local option.. "
Minneapolis and St. Anthony incorporated as one city.......... 1872
Act passes legislature establishing a State Board of Health.... "
Act passed to create a fund for an inebriate asylum at Rochester, by tax upon saloon keepers.............................. 1873
State treasurer William Seeger impeached by the House of Representatives, 26 Feb.; pleads guilty, 22 May, "without any corrupt or wilful intent," and is removed from office... "
Amendment to the constitution ratified by popular vote, permitting women to vote for school officers or on school questions, and to be eligible to any office pertaining to schools, 2 Nov. 1875
Amendment adopted providing for biennial instead of annual sessions of the legislature................................Nov. 1877
Act passed, creating a public examiner to superintend the books and financial accounts of public educational, charitable, penal, and reformatory institutions of the state........ 1878
Minnesota Amber-cane Growers' Association organized at Minneapolis.. 1878
State insane asylum at Rochester, provided for by act of legislature in 1878, opened..............................1 Jan. 1879
Minnesota school for the feeble-minded opened at Faribault... "
Act of legislature creating Farmers' Board of Trade, to assume supervision over the agricultural interests of the state; one member appointed by the judge of each judicial district.. "
Alexander Ramsey appointed U. S. secretary of war....10 Dec. "
Second centenary of the discovery of the falls of St. Anthony celebrated at Minneapolis..........................4 July, 1880
North wing of asylum for the insane at St. Peter destroyed by fire; 30 lives lost...................................15 Nov. "
State capitol destroyed by fire..............................1 Mch. 1881
Supreme court decides that the amendment to art. ix. of the state constitution, ratified in 1860, is invalid, as impairing the obligation of contracts; the legislature provides for the settlement of state railroad bonds at 50 cents on the dollar.. "
William Windom secretary of the treasury...............5 Mch. "
State Normal school located by law at Moorhead............. 1885
State public school for dependent children at Owatonna founded.. "
State insane hospital located at Fergus Falls.................. 1886
Acts passed: For a State reformatory at St. Cloud; a municipal government for Duluth; a high-license law where local option does not prohibit, and to abolish the State Board of Immigration, created in 1878.............................. 1887
Soldiers' home opened at Minnehaha Falls...............Nov. "
State Normal school at Moorhead opened..............29 Aug. 1888
William Windom again secretary of treasury..................Mch 1889
Secret (Australian) ballot law, established in cities of over 10,000 inhabitants, by act of.............................. "
State reformatory at St. Cloud opened.....................Sept. "
Memorial day (30 May) made a legal holiday..................... "
Nearly 100 lives lost by a tornado on lake Pepin.......13 July, 1890
State insane hospital at Fergus Falls opened...........3 July, "
William Windom, secretary of treasury, dies suddenly after responding to a toast at a banquet given by the New York Board of Trade at Delmonico's............evening of 29 Jan. 1891
Gen. H. H. Sibley, first governor of Minnesota, d. in St. Paul (aged 80)..18 Feb. "
Whaleback steamer *Charles W. Wetmore* leaves Duluth with a cargo of grain for Liverpool...........................11 June, "
Washburn-Crosby Company of Minneapolis sends out 175 cars containing 22,000 barrels of flour, consigned to the Russian Relief Committee of Philadelphia.....................23 Mch. 1892
Republican National convention assembles at Minneapolis (UNITED STATES)....................................7 June, "
Fire in Minneapolis; loss, $2,000,000..................13 Aug. 1893

TERRITORIAL GOVERNORS.

Alexander Ramsey of Pennsylvania....appointed......2 Apr. 1849
Willis A. Gorman of Indiana............ " ......4 Mch. 1853
Samuel Medary........................... " 1857

STATE.

Henry H. Sibley..........................elected 1857
Alexander Ramsey......................... " ....Oct. 1859
Stephen Miller............................ " ....Oct. 1863
William R. Marshall, Republican...... " .... 7 Nov. 1865
Horace Austin, " ...... " ....Nov. 1869
Cushman K. Davis, " ...... " ....Nov. 1873
John S. Pillsbury, " ...... " ....2 Nov. 1875
Lucius F. Hubbard, " ...... " ....Nov. 1881
Andrew R. McGill, " ...... " ....2 Nov. 1886
William R. Merriam, " ...... " ....Nov. 1888
William R. Merriam, " ......term begins.........Jan. 1891
Knute Nelson, " ...... " " ....Jan. 1893
Knute Nelson, " ...... " " ....Jan. 1895

UNITED STATES SENATORS FROM THE STATE OF MINNESOTA.

Name.	No. of Congress.	Date.	Remarks.
James M. Rice	35th to 37th	1858 to 1863	Seated 12 May, 1858.
William W. Phelps	35th	1858 " 1859	Seated 22 May, 1858.
Morton S. Wilkinson	36th to 38th	1859 " 1865	
Alexander Ramsey	38th	1863	
Daniel S. Norton	39th to 41st	1865 to 1870	Died 13 July, 1870.
William Windom	41st " 45th	1870 " 1881	Appointed *pro tem.* in place of Norton; afterwards elected. Resigned. Secretary of treasury, Garfield's administration.
Ozora P. Stearns	41st " 43d	1871 " 1875	Elected in place of Norton.
Samuel J. R. McMillan	44th " 49th	1875 " 1887	
Dwight M. Sabin	47th " 49th	1881 " 1887	Elected in place of Windom.
Cushman K. Davis	50th " ——	1887 " ——	Term expires 1899.
William D. Washburn	51st " 54th	1889 " 1895	
Knute Nelson	54th " ——	1895 " ——	Elected gov. and after to the U. S. Senate.

Minor'ca, one of the BALEARIC ISLANDS. Port Mahon in Minorca was captured by lieut.-gen. Stanhope and sir John Leake in 1708, and was ceded to the British by the treaty of Utrecht in 1713. It was retaken by the Spanish and French in July, 1756, and adm. Byng fell a victim to public indignation for not relieving it. BYNG. It was restored to the British at the peace in 1763; taken 5 Feb. 1782; again captured by the British under gen. Stuart, without the loss of a man, 15 Nov. 1798; given up at the peace of Amiens, 25 Mch. 1802.

Mi'not's Ledge light-house. LIGHT-HOUSE.

Min'otaur, a mythological monster, half man and half bull, offspring of Pasiphaë, wife of Minos, king of Crete (1210 B.C.), and a bull. Dædalus built the labyrinth for it. LABYRINTHS. It fed on human flesh, which the Athenians were obliged to furnish in the persons of youths and maidens. Theseus slew it with the aid of Ariadne.

minster or **monasterium,** a home for monks. WESTMINSTER, YORK.

minstrels, originally pipers appointed by lords of manrs to divert copyholders at work, owed their origin to the Saxn *gleemen or harpers, and continued till about 1560. John of* launt erected a court of minstrels at Tutbury in 1380. So late s the reign of Henry VIII. they intruded without ceremony ito companies, even at noblemen's houses; but in Elizabeth's eign they were adjudged rogues and vagabonds (1597).

"The last of all the Bards was he
Who sung of Border chivalry;
A wandering harper, scorned and poor
He begged his bread from door to door,
And tuned, to please a peasant's ear,
The harp a king had loved to hear."
—*Scott*, "The Lay of the Last Minstrel."

mint, an office where money is coined by public auority. Athelstan made regulations to govern the mint bout 928. There were provincial mints under control of that f London. Henry I. is said to have instituted a mint at Winhester, 1125. Stow says the mint was kept by Italians, the nglish being ignorant of the art of coining, 7 Edw. I. 1278. he operators were incorporated by charter of king Edward II., including the warden, master, comptroller, assay-master, orkers, coiners, and subordinates. The first entry of gold rought to the mint for coinage occurs in 18 Edw. III. 1343. 'in was coined by Charles II. 1684; and gun-metal and pewter y his successor, James, after his abdication. While sir Isaac lewton was warden, 1699-1727, the debased coin was called 1, and new issued at the loss of the government.

mint of the United States was established at Philadelphia, 'a., by act of Congress in Apr. 1792, and began to coin money ie next year, but it was not until Jan. 1795 that it was put ito full operation. It was the only mint until 1835, when other iints were established at Charlotte, N. C., Dahlonega, Ga., and lew Orleans, La. In 1854 another was located at San Franisco, Cal., and in 1870 at Carson City, Nev., and shortly after t Denver, Col., although no minting has ever been done at the itter place, only assaying. The mints at Charlotte, N. C., and)ahlonega, Ga., were discontinued in 1861. ASSAY, COIN.

min'uet, a French dance, said to have been first danced y Louis XIV., 1653.

minus. PLUS.

minute-men. At a session of the Provincial Congress f Massachusetts, 23 Nov. 1774, it was voted to enroll 12,000 iinute-men—volunteers pledged to be ready for the field at minute's notice.

Min'yæ, a race celebrated in ancient epic poetry of ireece, but whose name almost disappears before history beins. The adventurers who sailed in the Argonautic expediion are called Minyans. Iolcos is said to have been founded y them. Their record is fabulous. ORCHOMENUS.

"In Thessaly, beside the tumbling sea,
Once dwelt a folk men called the Minyæ,
For coming from Orchomenus the old,
. . . . they built Iolcos."
—*William Morris*, "Jason."

miracle plays. DRAMA.

Miranda's expedition. UNITED STATES, 1809.

mirrors. Ancient mirrors were made of metal; those f the Jewish women of brass. Mirrors of silver were introuced by Praxiteles, 328 B.C. Mirrors or looking-glasses were nade at Venice, 1300 A.D.; and in England, at Lambeth, near ondon, in 1673. The improvements in manufacturing platelass of large size have cheapened looking-glasses very much. 'arious methods of coating glass by a solution of silver, avoidng the use of mercury, so injurious to health, have been made nown: by M. Petitjean in 1851; by M. Cimeg in 1861, and y Liebig and others.

Mischianza entertainment. UNITED TATES, 1778.

Misere're (Psalm li.), sung at Rome in the "*Tenebræ*," he service in Holy or Passion week, in a peculiarly effective nanner, to old music. One arrangement is by Costanzo Festa, ated 1517.

"Missal" or "Mass-book," the Romanist ritual ompiled by pope Gelasius I. 492-96; revised by Gregory I. 90-604. Various missals were in use till the Roman missal was adopted by the council of Trent, 1545-63. The "Missal" was superseded in England by the "Book of Common Prayer," 1549.

Missionary Ridge, Tenn., battle of, 25 Nov. 1863. CHATTANOOGA CAMPAIGN.

Mississippi, one of the Gulf states of the United States, is bounded north by Tennessee. The Tennessee river touches the state in the extreme northeast corner. On the west the Mississippi river separates it from Arkansas and Louisiana above lat. 31° N., which divides the state from Louisiana on the south, 110 miles east from the Mississippi river to the Pearl. That portion of the state east of the Pearl river extends south to the Gulf of Mexico, affording a coast line of about 80 miles. Alabama forms the entire eastern boundary. It is limited in latitude between 30° 13′ and 35° N., and in longitude between 88° 7′ and 91° 41′ W. Area, 46,340 sq. miles, in 75 counties. Pop. 1890, 1,289,600; 1900, 1,551,270. Capital, Jackson.

Fernando De Soto, on his expedition, enters the present state of Mississippi near the junction of the Tombigbee and Black Warrior rivers; crosses the Pearl in Leake county, and reaches the Indian village of Chickasaw.......Dec. 1540
Indians attack and burn Chickasaw, which De Soto had fortified and occupied as winter-quarters.......Feb. 1541
De Soto reaches the Mississippi, which he crosses, probably within 30 miles of Helena, in boats built for the purpose, Apr. "
Mississippi included in the proprietary charter of Carolina.... 1663
Louis Joliet and père Jacques Marquette descend the Mississippi as far as lat. 33°....... 1673
La Salle descends the Mississippi to its mouth....... 1682
Lemoine d'Iberville plants a colony on the bay of Biloxi, May, 1699
Iberville, Bienville, and chevalier de Tonti ascend the Mississippi to the present site of Natchez.......Feb. 1700
Fort Rosalie at Natchez erected by Bienville, governor of Louisiana, and completed.......3 Aug. 1716
"Mississippi company," under sanction of the regent of France, chartered with exclusive privilege of the commerce of Louisiana and New France, with authority to enforce its rights, and obligated to introduce within 25 years 6000 white persons and 3000 negro slaves.......Aug. 1717
Mississippi company grants land to various individuals and companies for settlements on the Yazoo, at Natchez, on the bay of St. Louis, and on Pascagoula bay....... 1718
Three hundred settlers locate at Natchez....... 1720
Three hundred emigrants, destined for the lands of Madame de Chaumonot, arrive at Pascagoula.......3 Jan. 1721
Seat of government of Louisiana removed from Biloxi to New Orleans....... 1723
Chopart, commander of fort Rosalie, demands that Great Sun, head of the Natchez tribe of Indians, should vacate White Apple village, about 6 miles from the fort, and surrender it to the French; a conspiracy of Indians and the massacre of the garrison follow on.......29 Nov. 1729
Destruction of the Natchez by the French and Choctaws, 28 Jan.-8 Feb. 1730
Mississippi company surrenders its charter; the king proclaims all Louisiana free to all his subjects....... 1732
Mississippi included in the proprietary charter of Georgia..... "
Unsuccessful expedition of Bienville against the Chickasaws in the northern part of the present state of Mississippi, May, 1736
Capt. George Johnstone appointed governor of west Florida, including portion of Mississippi south of 31st parallel acquired by treaty of Paris.......21 Nov. 1763
A second decree of the king in council extends the limits of west Florida north to the mouth of the Yazoo, to include the settlements on the Mississippi.......10 June, 1764
Scotch Highlanders from North Carolina and Scotland build "Scotia," a settlement on the upper branches of the Homochitto, about 30 miles eastward from Natchez.......1768-70
Richard and Samuel Swayze of New Jersey, the latter a Congregational minister, purchase land on the Homochitto, in Adams county, settle and establish a church.......1772-73
James Willing secures authority from Congress, assembled at Lancaster, Pa., to descend the Mississippi and secure the neutrality of the colonies at Natchez, Bayou Pierre, etc....... 1778
Fort Panmure, formerly the French fort Rosalie, garrisoned by a company of infantry under capt. Michael Jackson, by order of the governor of west Florida....... "
Gen. don Bernardo de Galvez, proposing to expel the English from Florida, storms fort Bute, 7 Sept. 1779, and captures Baton Rouge, commanded by lieut.-col. Dickinson, who surrenders all west Florida upon the Mississippi, including fort Panmure and the district of Natchez, to the Spanish, 21 Sept. 1779

Fort Panmure surrendered by the Spaniards to insurgents, under the British flag after a siege of a week 30 Apr 1781

Don Carlos de Grandpré, appointed civil and military commander of the district of Natchez, 29 July 1781, takes measures to punish insurgents who had not fled after the capture of Pensacola and imprisons 7, charged with promoting a general rebellion against government in the "district of Natchez" "

Definitive treaty of peace establishes the southern boundary of the U S at the 31st parallel N lat, from the Mississippi to the St Mary s river, but in ceding Florida to Spain no boundary on the north is mentioned, hence Spain claims north to the mouth of the Yazoo river, signed, 3 Sept 1782

County of Bourbon established by Georgia of all lands east of the Mississippi between lat 31° and the mouth of the Yazoo, to which Indian titles had been extinguished 7 Feb 1785

Act erecting Bourbon county repealed 1 Feb 1788

Four companies chartered by the Georgia legislature with control of more than 3,000,000 acres of land in Mississippi at the rate of 2½ cents per acre to be paid into the state treasury (YAZOO SPECULATIONS) 7 Jan 1795

Treaty at Madrid with Spain fixes the *southern boundary* of the U S at 31° N lat, the western boundary the middle of the Mississippi river, with free navigation 27 Oct. "

Georgia legislature rescinds grants to the Mississippi companies, 13 Feb. 1796

Spanish commissioner don Manuel Gayoso de Lemos meets the U S commissioner Andrew Ellicott at Natchez to carry out the provisions of the treaty regarding the boundary-line between the U S and Spain 24 Feb 1797

Col Ellicott, suspecting the fidelity of a committee of public safety, appointed by citizens impatient of delay in carrying out the provisions of the treaty, succeeds in dissolving the committee and securing the election of a permanent committee of public safety July, "

On 10 Jan 1798, col Ellicott receives notice from the governor general of New Orleans that orders had been received from the king to surrender the territory, but it was not until the Spanish had lost hope from intrigues in the west that on 23 Mch fort Nogales on Walnut hill was evacuated, and fort Panmure about midnight 29–30 Mch 1798

Act of Congress approved creating Mississippi territory with boundaries as follows Mississippi river on the west, the 31st parallel on the south, and a line drawn due east from the mouth of the Yazoo river to the Chattahoochee on the north, including the present state of ALABAMA 7 Apr "

Georgia constitution of this year defines definitely the boundaries claimed by the state, which include the Mississippi territory established by act of Congress "for the amicable settlement of limits with the state of Georgia and the establishment of a government in the Mississippi territory" "

Winthrop Sargent former secretary of the Northwest territory, appointed first territorial governor of Mississippi, and arrives at Natchez 6 Aug "

Gen Wilkinson reaches Natchez and fixes headquarters at Loftus Heights, afterwards fort Adams. 25 Aug "

Act of Congress supplemental regarding the government of the Mississippi territory, and providing that settlement shall be made with Georgia for claims on or before 10 Mch 1803 1800

Seat of government removed from Natchez to Washington, 6 miles east, by *act of assembly and council* 1 Feb. 1802

Articles of agreement and cession under the Compromise act, secures to the U S all territory south of Tennessee, north of the Spanish line of demarkation and eastward from the Mississippi to the Chattahoochee 24 Apr "

Outrages and murders by the bandit Mason and his gang along the great Natchez trace, the governor offers a reward for his head, which is brought to Washington by Little Harpe, who fled from *Kentucky* in 1799 and *joined Mason in his* depredations. Harpe and another of the band murder Mason for the reward, but are recognized, arrested, condemned, and executed at Greenville "

Weekly newspaper, the *Natchez Gazette*, pub by col Andrew Marschalk at Natchez .. "

Natchez incorporated as a city 10 Mch 1803

Jefferson college established at Washington by act of legislature "

"Mississippi Society for the Acquirement of Useful Knowledge" incorporated 8 Nov "

Natchez hospital for sick and distressed boatmen employed in the navigation of the Mississippi river and others, incorporated 1804

Whole of the territory ceded to the U S by Georgia, north of the Mississippi territory and south of Tennessee, is annexed to Mississippi territory by act of Congress 27 Mch. "

Aaron Burr, arrested at Natchez gives bonds to appear before the territorial court 3 Feb The court refusing release from his recognizance, 5 Feb, next morning it was ascertained that he had made his escape. 6 Feb. 1807

Judge Harry Toulmin's digest of the laws of Mississippi adopted by the legislature 10 Feb "

Congress to extend the right of suffrage in the territory permitting the people to elect delegates to Congress 9 Jan 1808

Bank of Mississippi chartered 23 Dec 1809

Mobile district, lying south of lat 31° and between the Pearl and Perdido rivers, is added to Mississippi by act of 14 May, 1812

Expedition under gen F L Claiborne attacks the holy city of the Creek Indians called Escanachaha, on the east side of the Alabama river, which they burn . 23 Dec. 1813

Enabling act for Mississippi passed by Congress, establishing the eastern boundary, "a line drawn direct from the mouth of Bear creek on the Tennessee river to the northwestern corner of Washington county on the Tombigbee, thence due south with western line of said county to the sea." and the territory of ALABAMA created 1 Mch 1817

Convention for framing a constitution meets at Washington, 7 July, 1817, and completes its labors 15 Aug "

First General assembly meets at Washington 6 Oct "

Mississippi admitted into the Union 10 Dec. "

Bank of Mississippi in Natchez authorized by law to establish branches, and the state becomes a stockholder 4 Feb 1818

By treaty with maj-gen Jackson of Tennessee, and maj gen Thomas Hinds of Mississippi, commissioners of the U S, the Choctaws relinquish nearly 5,500,000 acres of land, which formed the county of Hinds, known as the "New Purchase" treaty 18 Oct 1820

Legislature appoints a committee to locate the seat of government by act of 12 Feb 1821, and by a supplemental act styles the new capital Jackson. 28 Nov 1821

Board of Internal Improvement, consisting of the governor and 3 commissioners organized 1829

Planters' bank chartered 10 Feb 1830

Treaty of Dancing Rabbit creek, by which the Choctaws cede the rest of their lands in Mississippi to the U S 28 Sept. "

Treaty at Pontotoc creek, the Chickasaws cede their lands in Mississippi and agree to remove from the state 20 Oct. 1832

Convention for framing a new constitution meets at Jackson, 10 Sept. 1832, and completes its labors, 26 Oct Constitution ratified at the next general election "

Appropriation made for the erection of a state house and executive mansion at the capital 26 Feb 1833

Act approved incorporating the Mississippi Union bank and providing for $15,500 000 in state stock as capital as soon as a corresponding amount in private subscriptions should come in 21 Jan 1837

Supplementary act authorizes to an immediate issue of $[illegible] 000 000 of state stock which was sold at a heavy discount through the bank of the United States 15 Feb 1838

Legislature sanctions the sale of stock for the bank 1839

State penitentiary at Jackson opened 15 Apr 1840

Gov McNutt by message advises repudiating the Union bank bonds sold to the U S bank of Pennsylvania, an institution not authorized by its charter to buy or sell such bonds 1841

Legislature by resolution denies that the state is under any obligation, legal or moral, to redeem the Union bank bonds 1842

State treas Richard S Graves arrested for embezzlement of state funds to the amount of $44,838 46 He escapes from the house of the sheriff and flees to Canada 1843

Robert J Walker appointed secretary of U S treasury 6 Mch 1845

Law passed establishing common schools 4 Mch 1846

Mississippi regiment, under command of col Jefferson Davis, serves in the Mexican war "

University of Mississippi at Oxford, chartered in 1844, is opened 1848

Franklin female college at Holly Springs, opened in 1848, is chartered 1849

Mississippi institution for the education of the blind, at Jackson, opened "

Mississippi college at Clinton chartered and opened 1850

Gov Quitman, arrested by the U S. marshal for violation of the neutrality law of 1818 in abetting the expedition against Cuba, *resigns* as governor He is acquitted, renominated, but declines 1851

Chickasaw female college at Pontotoc chartered and opened 1852

Jefferson Davis of Mississippi appointed U S secretary of war by pres Pierce 5 Mch 1853

Mississippi institution for the deaf and dumb at Jackson opened, 1854

State lunatic asylum at Jackson opened 1855

Amendment to the constitution ratified, appointing the first *Monday in Oct as day for general election*, and making the term of office of the governor 2 years 2 Feb 1856

Jacob Thompson secretary of the interior 6 Mch 1857

Southern convention, delegates from 8 states assemble at Vicksburg and consider reopening the slave trade 11 May, 1859

Whitworth female college at Brookhaven opened and chartered "

By joint resolution the legislature directs the governor to appoint commissioners to the several slave-holding states asking their co operation in secession Legislature adjourned, 30 Nov 1860

State convention meets at Jackson, 7 Jan 1861, passes an ordinance of secession, 9 Jan, 84 to 15, and amends the state constitution by inserting "Confederate States" in the place of United States 15 Jan 1861

Confederates occupy the unfinished fort on Ship island, under construction since 1855 20 Jan "

State convention ratifies the constitution of the Confederate states 26 Mch "

Town of Biloxi captured by Federal naval force under capt Melancthon Smith 31 Dec "

Confederate government removes the state archives from Jackson to Columbus for safety 16 June, 1862

Chief military operations in Mississippi during 1862 were as follows Gen Beauregard evacuates Corinth, and Halleck takes possession, 29 May, U S. gunboat *Essex* bombards Natchez and the city surrenders, 10 Sept., Rosecrans defeats confederates under Price in a battle at Iuka, 19–20 Sept, unsuccessful attack on Corinth by the confederates under gen Van Dorn, 3–4 Oct, Grenada occupied by gen. Hovey's expedition, 20 000 strong, 2 Dec., Van Dorn defeats the Federal cavalry in battle of Coffeeville, 5 Dec., Holly Springs surrendered to the confederates, 20 Dec , unsuccessful attack of federals on Vicksburg 27-29 Dec 1862

Important military operations during 1863 Col Grierson with Federal troops makes a raid through the state from Tennessee to Louisiana, 17 Apr -5 May, naval battle of Grand Gulf 29 Apr , McClernand defeats the confederates at Port Gibson, 1 May, Raymond occupied by federals under gen McPherson 12 May, McPherson occupies Jackson, 14 May, Grant defeats Pemberton at Champion Hills, 16 May, and at Big Black river, 17 May, Vicksburg invested by forces under gen Grant 18 May, Vicksburg surrendered, 4 July, Jackson evacuated by gen Johnston who had occupied it after the advance of the federals on Vicksburg, and the city is occupied by gen Sherman 16 July, 1863

Sherman's Meridian expedition leaves Vicksburg 3 Feb 1864

Forrest, confederate defeats Sturgis at Guntown 10 June, "

Upon the surrender of gen Taylor to gen Canby gov Clarke by proclamation recalls the state officers with the archives, to Jackson and convenes the legislature He recommends a convention to repeal the ordinance of secession and remodel constitution 6 May, 1865

Judge William L Sharkey appointed provisional governor by pres Johnson the Federal government not recognizing gov Clarke and the legislature 13 June, "

Amendments to the constitution of 1832 and ordinances adopted by a convention called by the provisional governor, which met at Jackson, 14 Aug , and completed its labors 26 Aug "

Law conferring civil rights upon freedmen "

Gov Clarke arrested and imprisoned at fort Pulaski "

By Reconstruction act Mississippi is placed in the 4th military district under maj gen Ord 2 Mch 1867

By order of gen Ord W H McCardle, editor of the *Vicksburg Times*, is confined in a military prison on charge of obstructing the Reconstruction acts 13 Nov "

Maj gen Ord is directed by order of the president to turn over his command to gen A C Gillem 28 Dec "

Legislature unanimously rejects the XIV th Amendment Jan 1868

Convention of landowners from Mississippi Alabama Tennessee and Louisiana, at Jackson, to organize a "Freehold Land and Colonization Company" to encourage emigration in each of these states. 31 Mch "

Gen Irvin McDowell takes command of 4th military district, 4 June, "

Gov Humphreys reluctantly forced to vacate the executive mansion for maj gen Adelbert Ames, appointed provisional governor by gen McDowell 15 June, "

Constitution framed by a convention under the Reconstruction act which sits at Jackson, 7 Jan to 15 May, 1868, is rejected by the people by 56 231 for and 63 860 against 28 June, "

National Union Republican party of Mississippi in convention at Jackson nominate Louis Dent for governor, the majority of the Democrats concur 8 Sept. 1869

Rust university at Holly Springs chartered and opened "

Tougaloo university at Tougaloo established "

At state election the constitution of 15 May 1868, is ratified by 105,223 for and 954 against, the vote against disfranchising Confederate soldiers almost unanimous, 30 Nov -1 Dec "

Congress readmits Mississippi into the Union 17 Feb 1870

School law organizing a State Board of Education and providing for a superintendent of public education "

State Normal school at Holly Springs opened "

'Planters Manufacturers, and Mechanics' Association of the state of Mississippi" incorporated 1871

Alcorn university at Rodney, created by act of legislature 13 May, 1871, opened 7 Feb 1872

East Mississippi female college opened and chartered "

Starkville female institute, opened in 1869, chartered "

Any rate of interest agreed upon in writing made legal, 6 per cent the legal rate in the absence of any agreement 1873

At a mass meeting of taxpayers of Warren county at Vicksburg, 2 Dec 1874, a committee is sent to sheriff Peter Crosby and clerk of the Chancery court G W Davenport to demand their resignations, "satisfied that said officials of this county were stealing and plundering our substance" Crosby resigned and Davenport absconded Dec. 1874

Political strife between state officers and citizen taxpayers leads to a conflict of races Armed negroes approach Vicksburg from various directions, are met by citizens, and dispersed with considerable loss of life 7 Dec "

Legislature convened in extra session by gov Ames, 8 Dec 1874, calls upon the president "by military power to suppress domestic violence, to restore peace and order in this state, and to guarantee to all citizens the equal and impartial enjoyment of their constitutional and legal rights," 17 Dec. "

Pres. Grant by proclamation orders the people of Warren county to refrain from forcible resistance to the laws, and to submit peaceably to the authorities 21 Dec. "

People ratify the following amendment to art xii sec 5 of the constitution of 1868 "Nor shall the state assume, redeem, secure, or pay any indebtedness or pretended indebtedness claimed to be due by the state of Mississippi to any person, association, or corporation whatsoever, claiming the same as owners, holders, or assignees of any bond or bonds now generally known as Union bank bonds or Planters' bank bonds" 1875

Conflict between office holders and people still continuing, several riots occur, notably at Yazoo City, 1 Sept., and Clinton, 4 Sept. Gov Ames again appeals to the president for protection, which is refused and at the state election the Republican party is generally defeated Senator H R Revels colored, wrote to the president "My people are naturally Republicans, but as they grow older in freedom so do they in wisdom A great portion of them have learned that they were being used as mere tools, and as in the late election, not being able to correct the existing evil among themselves, they determined, by casting their ballots against these unprincipled adventurers, to overthrow them" Nov 1875

Lieut gov Alexander K Davis impeached and found guilty, 13 Mch , T W Cardoza, superintendent of public education, resigns 21 Mch , gov Ames, having been impeached 25 Feb , resigns his office 28 Mch 1876

Amendment to the constitution abolishing the office of lieutenant governor "

State Board of Health created by act of legislature 1877

Acts passed by legislature To establish and maintain in the state a system of public free schools, that Alcorn university be hereafter known as the Alcorn Agricultural and Mechanical college of the state of Mississippi, to establish the Agricultural and Mechanical college of the state of Mississippi, making the legislative sessions biennial 1878

Mississippi Valley Cotton Planters' Association organized at Vicksburg 1879

Mississippi Valley Labor convention meets at Vicksburg to consider the negro exodus question 5 May, "

Revised code of Mississippi laws made by hon J A P Campbell, adopted by the legislature 1880

Agricultural and Mechanical college of the state of Mississippi, for white students, opened at Starkville 6 Oct. "

Shuqualak female college opened at Shuqualak, 1880, chartered 1882

Southern Christian institute and industrial school at Edwards opened "

Law passed prohibiting the selling or giving away of intoxicating liquors within 5 miles of the University of Mississippi "

Interstate Levee convention assembles at Vicksburg 1 Oct. 1883

East Mississippi insane asylum, established at Meridian in 1884, opened 12 Jan 1885

Kavanaugh college, Holmesville, opened 1884, chartered "

Industrial institute and college for education of white girls of Mississippi chartered 1884, opened at Columbus 22 Oct. "

General Local Option law passed 1886

Extensive negro emigration from the hill country of Mississippi to the river bottoms along the Mississippi in the Yazoo section commences in Hinds and Rankin counties Nov "

Laying of the corner stone of the monument to the Confederate dead on the capitol grounds at Jackson 25 May, 1888

Legislature introduces the Australian ballot system of voting in all except congressional elections 1890

State treasurer Hemingway convicted of embezzling $315,-612 71 by the Supreme court 1 Dec "

Constitutional convention which meets at Jackson, 12 Aug 1890, adjourns 1 Nov , having promulgated a new constitution to take effect 1 Jan 1891

Monument to Confederate dead unveiled at Jackson 3 June, "

A fire started by an insane inmate, J D Brown consumes the main building of the State insane asylum at Jackson, the inmates, nearly 600, are saved except Brown 16 Feb 1892

TERRITORIAL GOVERNORS.

Winthrop Sargent	appointed	10 May,	1798
William C C Claiborne	"	10 July,	1801
Robert Williams	"		1804
David Holmes	appointed	Mch	1809

STATE GOVERNORS

David Holmes	term begins	Nov	1817
George Poindexter	"	"	1819
Walter Leake	"	"	1821
Lieut gov Gerard C Brandon	acting	"	1825
David Holmes	term begins	"	"
Gerard C Brandon	"	"	1827
Abram M Scott	"	"	1831
Lieut gov Fountain Winston	acting	"	1833
Hiram G Runnels	term begins	Jan	1834
Charles Lynch	"	"	1836
Alexander G McNutt, Democrat	"	"	1838
Tilgham M Tucker, "	"	"	1842
Albert G Brown, "	"	"	1844
Joseph W Matthews, "	"	"	1848
John A Quitman, "	"	"	1850
John Isaac Guion, president of the senate, acting		3 Feb	1851
James Whitefield, " " " "		25 Nov	"
Henry S Foote, Union	term begins	Jan	1852
John J McRae.	"	"	1854
William McWillie	"	16 Nov	1857
John J. Pettus, Democrat.	"	Jan.	1860
Jacob Thompson	"	"	1862
Charles Clarke	"	"	1864
W L. Sharkey, provisional	appointed	13 June,	1865
Benjamin G Humphreys	term begins	16 Oct.	"
Gen Adelbert Ames, provisional	appointed.	15 June,	1868
James L Alcorn, Republican	term begins	Jan	1870
R C Powers.	acting	Dec.	"
Adelbert Ames, Republican	term begins	Jan	1874
John M Stone	acting	29 Mch	1876
Robert Lowry	term begins	Jan	1882
John M Stone.	"	"	1890

UNITED STATES SENATORS FROM THE STATE OF MISSISSIPPI.

Name.	No. of Congress.	Date.	Remarks.
Walter Leake	15th to 16th	1817 to 1820	Seated 11 Dec. 1817. Resigned.
Thomas H. Williams	15th	1817	Seated 11 Dec. 1817.
David Holmes	16th to 18th	1820 to 1825	Elected in place of Leake. Resigned.
Powhatan Ellis	19th " 22d	1825 " 1832	Appointed *pro tem.* in place of Holmes. Resigned.
Thomas B. Reed	19th " 20th	1826 " 1829	Elected in place of Holmes. Died 1829.
Robert H. Adams	21st	1830	Elected in place of Reed. Died 1830.
George Poindexter	21st to 23d	1830 to 1836	Elected in place of Adams. Elected president *pro tem.* 25 June, 1834.
John Black	22d " 25th	1832 " 1838	Elected in place of Ellis. Resigned.
Robert J. Walker	24th " 29th	1836 " 1845	Resigned.
James F. Trotter	25th	1838	Elected in place of Black. Resigned.
Thomas H. Williams	25th	1838	Appointed in place of Trotter.
John Henderson	26th to 28th	1839 to 1845	
Joseph W. Chalmers	29th	1845	Elected in place of Walker.
Jesse Speight	29th to 30th	1845 to 1847	Died 1847.
Jefferson Davis	30th " 32d	1847 " 1851	Elected in place of Speight. Resigned 1851.
Henry S. Foote	30th " 32d	1847 " 1851	Resigned 1851.
John I. McRae	32d	1852	Appointed *pro tem.* in place of Davis.
Stephen Adams	32d to 34th	1852 to 1857	Elected in place of Davis.
Walter Brooke	32d	1852 " 1853	Elected in place of Foote.
Albert G. Brown	33d to 36th	1854 " 1861	Seat declared vacant 1861.
Jefferson Davis	35th " 36th	1857 " 1861	Seat declared vacant 1861.
[37th, 38th, 39th, 40th Congresses vacant.]			
Adelbert Ames	41st to 43d	1870 to 1874	Resigned.
Hiram R. Revels (colored)	41st	1870 " 1871	
James Lusk Alcorn	42d to 44th	1871 " 1877	
Henry R. Pease	43d	1874	Elected in place of Ames.
Blanche K. Bruce (colored)	44th to 46th	1875 to 1881	Appointed register of the treasury under Garfield.
Lucius Q. C. Lamar	45th " 48th	1877 " 1885	Secretary of the interior under pres. Cleveland.
James Z. George	47th " ——	1881 " ——	Term expires 1899.
Edward C. Walthall	49th " 53d	1885 " 1894	Resigned 18 Jan. Poor health.
A. J. McLaurin	53d " ——	1894 " ——	Elected in place of Walthall.

Mississippi river (Ind. *Miche-sepé*, "father of waters"), the largest river in North America, and in length of navigable tributaries and facilities afforded to commerce the greatest river in the world, being the recipient of all waters flowing east from the Rocky mountains and west from the Alleghanies. Lake Itasca, in the state of Minnesota, lat. 47° 15′ N., lon. 95° 54′ W., is considered the source of the Mississippi. The outlet of lake Itasca is about 12 feet wide and 15 to 18 inches deep; after flowing about 1330 miles, it unites with the Missouri (termed a tributary, but properly the main stream), which, rising in the remote Rocky mountains, flows 3000 miles before reaching the junction, after which their united waters enter the gulf of Mexico, 1286 miles below. Its width at mean water-mark is about 3500 ft. at St. Louis, 4000 ft. at Cairo, and 2500 ft. at New Orleans.

PRINCIPAL PRIMARY AND SECONDARY TRIBUTARIES OF THE MISSISSIPPI, THEIR LENGTH, AND AREA OF TERRITORY DRAINED.

Primary tributaries.	Secondary tributaries.	Length.	Area drained.
Missouri (length, 3000 miles)	Yellowstone	600 miles	518,000 sq. miles.
	Platte	900 "	
	Niobrara	450 "	
	Kansas	250 "	
	Osage	500 "	
	Big Sioux	300 "	
Ohio (length from Pittsburgh, 957 miles; from Coudersport, 1265 miles)	Tennessee	1100 "	214,000 "
	Cumberland	600 "	
	Kentucky	260 "	
	Licking	100 "	
	Great Kanawha	110 "	
	Big Sandy	120 "	
	Muskingum	110 "	
	Sciota	250 "	
	Green	300 "	
	Wabash	500 "	
Arkansas (length, 1500 miles)	Canadian	900 "	189,000 "
	Cimarron	600 "	
	Neosho	450 "	
Red (length, 1200 miles)	Ouachita	500 "	97,000 "

LESSER PRIMARY TRIBUTARIES ABOVE THE MISSOURI.

Tributary	Length	Area drained
Minnesota	length, 450 miles	169,000 "
St. Croix	" 200 "	
Wisconsin	" 500 "	
Rock	" 250 "	
Iowa	" 300 "	
Des Moines	" 450 "	
Illinois	" 400 "	

BELOW THE MISSOURI.

Tributary	Length	Area drained
Kaskaskia	length, 300 miles	57,000 "
St. Francis	" 450 "	
White	" 900 "	
Big Black	" 200 "	
Yazoo	" 500 "	
With many bayous.		

Mean annual discharge of the Mississippi into the gulf is computed at 20,000,000,000,000 of cubic ft., varying in dry seasons from 11,000,000,000,000 to 27,000,000,000,000 in wet. This amount being about ¼ of the rainfall on the area of its drainage.

Below the mouth of the Ohio the river traverses to the gulf rich alluvial bottom lands, often overflowed, with immense damage to property. The following notices mark the years of greatest recorded floods: Bienville, the French commander, had selected a place for a settlement on the Mississippi, but the high water prevented, 1718. Water so high that many levees were broken and great damage done, from Dec. 1735 to June, 1736. Severe again in 1770, '82, '85, '91, '96, '99, 1809; very severe, highest 4 May, 1811, '13, '15, '16, '23, '24, '28, '44; very disastrous Apr., May, June; 1849, '50, '51, '58, the worst up to this time; 1859–62, the highest at Memphis ever known; 1874, 1882, 1890 one of the worst ever known; 1892–93.

Levees.—To prevent these overflows the French began at once the erection of levees along the bank of the river in Louisiana, and when the engineer De la Tour laid out New Orleans in 1718, he directed that a levee be built on its river front. This was begun in 1720, and finished 1727, being 5400 ft. long, 4 ft. high, and 18 ft. wide at the top. During the year 1728 the work was extended above and below the city, the expense borne by each planter along his own front. In 1735 there were 12 miles of levees below the city and 30 above. After Louisiana came into possession of the U. S., 1803, the work was greatly extended, and by 1828 had reached the mouth of the Red river, and in 1844 extended to Napoleon, Ark. It was supposed that the immense swamp and bottom lands along the river above Louisiana acted as great reservoirs for retaining the surplus water in times of floods, and if the water was prevented from entering them the floods would be much worse below, therefore the action of the government in arranging for a general system of embankment of the river above Louisiana caused great alarm in that state, and in 1850 Congress ordered the necessary investigation and survey of the river. The work was placed in charge of capt. (later general) A. A. Humphrey and lieut. Abbott, U. S. A.; and their elaborate report, covering 10 years' labor and investigations, was pub. 1861. These investigations established that no diversion of tributaries was possible; that no reservoirs artificially constructed could keep back the spring freshets which caused the floods; that the making of cut-offs, sometimes advocated, would be in the highest degree injurious; and finally, that levees, properly constructed and judiciously placed, would afford protection to the entire alluvial region. By 1860 the levees had reached Cairo, Ill., and this system of protection was in good condition when the civil war put a stop to further improvement. It is estimated that up to this time the levees along the Mississippi and its tributaries had cost $24,000,000. During the war and for some time after no attempt was made to extend or keep in repair the levees already built.

After the great flood of 1874, Congress created a commission of 5 engineers to determine and report on the best system for permanent relief from floods. Their report, 1875, endorsed that of 1861, and advocated a general levee system. Another complaint was now heard, and that was low water; 43 places below Red river being reported at times less than 10 ft., and 13 places less than 5 ft. The aggregate length of such places being 150 miles. To devise relief, 5 commissioners were appointed, 1878, who recommended a narrowing of the wide places in the river to 3500 ft., whereby a depth of 10 ft. could be secured. Thereupon the Mississippi River Commission was constituted by act of Congress, 28 June, 1879, consisting of 7 members, to have in charge the improvement of the Mississippi river below the mouth of the Ohio to the head of the passes at its mouth; to supervise the deepening of its channel; to protect its banks; to improve and give safety to avigation; to prevent disastrous floods, and to promote and facilitate commerce. *The following is from* the report of the commission for 1893: "Below the junction of the Mississippi and the Ohio on the left bank, as far as Memphis, no general system of levees exists or is required. *On the right bank*, below Cairo, lies the St. Francis basin, extending from cape Girardeau, Mo., to Helena, Ark. This region is subject to overflow, but has never been protected; the local organizations and the general government are about to inaugurate a system of levees. On the left bank, a short distance below Memphis, and on the right bank at Helena, begin the existing levee systems—*that on the left bank* extending down to Vicksburg, and protects the Yazoo basin. It withstood the floods of 1892–93 without a break. On the right bank the levees extend from Helena to the mouth of the White river, intended to protect the White river basin; these are now being constructed. Below the Arkansas, on the right bank, a line of levees extend along the entire front of the Bayou basin to the Red river, 330 miles; not in good condition, crevasses of annual occurrence. On the right bank, below the Red river, the levees extend to about 70 miles below New Orleans. On the left bank, owing to the high bluff making them unnecessary, the levees only commence at Baton Rouge, and also extend 70 miles below New Orleans. Although the levees on both sides of the river have been much improved recently, no year passes without crevasses *on one side or the other of the river*; and much work is required to make them efficient."

tflow of the Mississippi into the gulf is through several channels termed passes; *the principal* are Pass à l'Outre, the Northeast, South, and Southwest. The bars formed at the entrance of these outlets greatly impeded navigation. After several appropriations by Congress, and repeated trials *of different methods* for deepening the channel permanently without success, Congress created a special board in 1874, which after visiting Europe and examining similar works of improvement there, reported in favor of constructing jetties, and selected the South pass for trial. A contract was therefore made with capt. James B. Eads (1820–87), who favored the jetty plan, to form and maintain for 20 years, in the South pass, a channel 30 ft. deep and 350 ft. wide. The South pass is 12½ miles long, 700 ft. mean width, and 34 ft. mean depth, and discharges about 10 per cent. of the outflow of the entire river; the crest of the bar is 2½ miles to seaward from the mouth of the pass, and the jetties extend 2¼ miles seaward. The work was begun 2 June, 1875, and finished 1879. Up to the present time the general result has proved entirely satisfactory, and of great benefit to the commerce of the river.

Mississippi scheme. LAW'S BUBBLE.

Missolon'ghi, a town in Greece, taken from the Turks, Nov. 1821, and heroically and successfully defended against the Turks by Marco Bozzaris, Oct. 1822–27 Jan. 1823. *It* was taken 22 Apr. 1826, after a long siege. Here lord Byron died, Apr. 1824. It was surrendered to the Greeks in 1829.

Missou'ri, one of the central United States, lies west of the Mississippi river, which separates it from Illinois, Kentucky, and Tennessee. Arkansas bounds it *on the* south. On the west, a line drawn south from Kansas City in about 94° 30′ lon. separates the state from the Indian Territory and Kansas, while the Missouri river marks the boundary of Kansas continued and Nebraska north of Kansas City. The state of Iowa *forms the northern* boundary. It is limited in latitude from 36° 40° 30′ N., and in longitude from 89° 2′ to 95° 44′ W. ea, 65,370 sq. miles, in 115 counties. Pop. 1890, 2,679,184; 00, 3,106,665. Capital, Jefferson City.

rnando De Soto ascends the west bank of the Mississippi river as far as the present site of New Madrid.............. 1541

is Joliet and père Jacques Marquette descend the Mississippi to lat. 33°.. 1673

bert Cavalier de La Salle descends Mississippi to its mouth. 1682

prospecting-party sent out by French governor of Louisiana ascends the Missouri river to the mouth of the Kansas..... 1705

souri included in a grant to Anthony Crozat for the exclusive privilege of the commerce of Louisiana for 15 years, made by Louis XIV..............................14 Sept. 1712

souri included in a grant to the Mississippi company on the resignation of Crozat ....Aug. 1717

d mining in St. Genevieve county by sieur Renault 1720

rre Ligueste Laclède, head of Louisiana Fur company, who in 1763 obtained from the director-general of Louisiana a monopoly of the fur trade with the Indians of Missouri, sends a party under Auguste Chouteau, who lays out St. Louis, 15 Feb. 1764

Ange de Belle Rive, the French commander of fort Chartres, about 15 miles above St. Genevieve, surrendering the fort to the British, removes with officers and troops to St. Louis and assumes command of upper Louisiana, 17 July, 1765

Spanish troops under capt. Rios reach St. Louis; Rios takes possession in the name of the king of Spain........11 Aug. 1768

Pontiac, chief of the Ottawas, who was murdered at Cahokia, is buried at St. Louis, where he was a guest of St. Ange....... 1769

Blanchette, surnamed "The Hunter," builds a log hut on hills now occupied by the city of St. Charles, and establishes a military post under the governor of upper Louisiana....... "

Lieut.-gov. don Pedro Piernas arrives at St. Louis to assume the Spanish authority over upper Louisiana................ 1770

Francisco Cruzat succeeds Piernas............................ 1775

Don Ferdinando Leyba appointed gov. to succeed Cruzat..... 1778

Massacre of whites near St. Louis by Indians who, led by British, intended a general attack on the settlement, but were repulsed.......................................26 May, 1780

Leyba removed and Francisco Cruzat *reinstated.* Under his government St. Louis was regularly fortified............... "

Old St. Genevieve, which tradition says was founded by settlers from Kaskaskia in 1735, is destroyed by a flood, the inhabitants remove from river bottoms to the present site........ 1785

New Madrid, settled as early as 1780, is laid out on an extensive scale by col. George Morgan of New Jersey, who had received a grant of over 12,000,000 acres of land from Spain.......... 1788

Cruzat succeeded by don Manuel Perez as commandant-general of the post of St. Louis.. "

Zenon Trudeau succeeds Perez.................................. 1793

Daniel Boone of Kentucky moves to what is now St. Charles county... 1795

Trudeau succeeded by Charles Dehault Delassus de Delusiere.. 1798

Delassus appoints Daniel Boone commandant or syndic of the Femme Osage district.. 1800

Maj. Amos Stoddard, agent of France for receiving upper Louisiana *from the Spanish*, arrives at St. Louis, and on 9 Mch. Delassus surrenders the territory to him, and next day it is transferred to the U. S., maj. Stoddard in command, 10 Mch. 1804

Missouri included in the district of Louisiana, set off from the territory of Louisiana, and placed under the government of Indiana territory by act of Congress.................26 Mch. "

Exploring expedition of Lewis and Clarke up the Missouri river leaves St. Louis (UNITED STATES)..............14 May, "

By act of Congress the district of Louisiana is *regularly* organized into the territory of Louisiana, and pres. Jefferson appoints gen. James Wilkinson as governor............3 Mch. 1805

Aaron Burr visits gen. Wilkinson at St. Louis...........Sept. "

Lewis and Clarke expedition return to St. Louis......23 Sept. 1806

Missouri Gazette established and published at St. Louis by Joseph Charless.. July, 1808

Treaty of fort Clark by which the Great and Little Osage tribes cede to the U. S. 33,173,383 acres of land in Missouri and 14,830,432 acres in Arkansas.........................10 Nov. "

Town of St. Louis incorporated........................9 Nov. 1809

Town of New Madrid destroyed by an earthquake......16 Dec. 1811

Act of Congress changing the name of the territory of Louisiana to the territory of Missouri approved............4 June, 1812

Edward Hempstead first delegate to Congress...........Nov. "

First General Assembly meets in the house of Joseph Robidoux, between Walnut and Elm sts., St. Louis........7 Dec. "

U. S. Congress *confirms to Daniel Boone* 1000 arpents (833 acres) of land in the Femme Osage district................10 Feb. 1814

Capt. James Callaway, with 15 men, returning to the settlement of Loutre island with some *horses* they had recovered from the Sac and Fox Indians, are attacked by the Indians in ambush and capt. Callaway and 3 of his men are killed..7 Mch. 1815

By act of Congress the election of the council in *Missouri* territory is by choice of the people......................29 Apr. 1816

Steamboat *General Pike* ascends the Mississippi to St. Louis, 2 Aug. 1817

Bill authorizing people of Missouri to frame a state constitution for admission into the Union introduced into Congress (UNITED STATES, 1819–1821)..........................13 Feb. 1819

By act of Congress, Arkansas territory is set off from Missouri, 2 Mch. "

Independence, a pioneer steamboat, ascends the Missouri river and arrives at Franklin, Howard county............28 May, "

Western Engineer, a steamboat constructed by col. S. H. Long for an expedition up the Missouri to the Yellowstone, leaves St. Louis..21 June, "

Act approved authorizing the people of Missouri territory to form a state constitution. Sec. 8 states: "That in all the territory ceded by France to the United States under the name of Louisiana north of 36° 30′ of lat. and not included within the limits of the state contemplated by this act, slavery shall be and is hereby forever prohibited, but runaway slaves may be *lawfully reclaimed*"............6 Mch. 1820

A constitutional convention meets at St. Louis, 12 June, completes its labors 19 July, and the constitution is ratified by the people at the ensuing *election*.......................... "

Art. iii. sec. 26 of state constitution requires the legislature "to pass such laws as may be necessary" to prevent free negroes and mulattoes *from coming to* and settling in the state .... "

General Assembly, elected 28 Aug., meets in the Missouri hotel at St. Louis and organizes a state government, 19 Sept. "

Daniel Boone dies at the residence of his son, on Femme Osage creek in St. Charles county.......................26 Sept. "

Missouri admitted into the Union with conditions that the legislature should pledge the faith of the state that the free-negro clause should never be executed...............2 Mch. 1821

Conditions of admission of Missouri into the Union being accepted, pres Monroe approves the bill (UNITED STATES). 10 Aug 1821

Thomas H Benton enters the U S senate and serves continuously until 1851 "

St Louis incorporated a city, pop 4800 9 Dec 1822

Public reception of Lafayette in St Louis 29 Apr 1825

Gov Frederick Bates d 1 Aug "

Seat of government removed from St Charles to Jefferson City, and legislature holds its first session there 20 Nov 1826

Joseph Smith, the Mormon leader having found a location for "Zion" at Independence Jackson county, in 1831 which he names "The New Jerusalem," arrives from Kirtland, O, with many followers 1832

St Louis university founded 1829, incorporated Dec "

Mormons in Missouri publish a paper the *Evening Star* the sentiments of which are obnoxious to the people who tar and feather the bishop and 2 others, and throw the presses into the river On 31 Oct. an encounter occurs in which 2 citizens and 1 Mormon are killed On 2 Nov the Mormons attack Independence but are routed and forced to promise to leave the county before 1 Jan 1834 (MORMONS), 2 Nov 1833

Congress adds the "Platte Purchase" a triangle north of the Missouri river, west of the western boundary of the state, and south of the northern boundary to Missouri, thus making it slave territory 7 June, 1836

Depredations and murders in Carroll county traced to a band of desperadoes composed principally of a family named Hetherly, old Mrs Hetherly being a sister of the Kentucky brigands Big and Little Harpe The band broken up by the arrest and imprisonment of some of its chief men, 17 July, "

State penitentiary at Jefferson City, created by act of the legislature in 1832, opened "

Bank of the state of Missouri established at St Louis, capital, $5,000,000, about four-fifths belonging to the state 1837

By proclamation of pres Van Buren, the law of 7 June 1836, regarding the Platte purchase, takes effect 28 Mch "

Col Richard Gentry s regiment (afterwards in battle at Okeechobee lake, Fla) leaves Columbia for the Seminole war, 6 Oct. "

State house burned with public papers and records 17 Nov "

Act of Congress to ascertain the true boundary-line of Missouri on the north, described in the act of admission as "the parallel of latitude which passes through the rapids of the river Des Moines, making the said line to correspond with the Indian boundary-line" 18 June, 1838

Numerous conflicts occurring between the Mormons and people lead gov Boggs to issue a proclamation to call out the militia and enforce the laws Skirmishes occur at Crooked River and Haughn s Mills, near Breckenridge, between the militia and Mormons under G W Hinkle, in the latter 18 Mormons were killed, some of them after surrender At Far West, Caldwell county, Joe Smith surrenders to the militia and agrees that the Mormons shall leave the state Oct. "

Corner stone of the University of the State of Missouri at Columbia laid 4 July, 1840

Suicide of gov Thomas Reynolds 9 Feb 1844

Remains of Daniel Boone and his wife are removed from the cemetery at Marthasville, Mo, to Frankfort, Ky 17 July, 1845

Full complement of troops to form the first regiment of Missouri troops for the Mexican war arrives at fort Leavenworth 18 June, 1846

State constitution completed, but rejected by the people "

Col. Doniphan, with 924 Missouri volunteers, defeats 4000 Mexicans under gen Heredia in the pass of Sacramento (MEXICAN WAR) 28 Feb 1847

First line of telegraph between East St. Louis and the east completed 20 Dec. "

Decision of the Supreme court of the U S upon the northern boundary, is confirmed by Congress, and the present boundary established by act 15 Feb 1848

Claiborne F Jackson, on 15 Jan 1849, introduces resolutions in the state senate, questioning the power of Congress to legislate on slavery in the territories, and asserting that "the right to prohibit slavery in any territory belongs exclusively to the people thereof" Passed by the senate, 26 Jan, and by the assembly 6 Mch. 1849

Fire in St Louis destroys 23 steamboats and their cargoes and a large section of the city 17 May, "

U S senator Thomas H Benton, in the hall of the House at Jefferson City, opposes the "Jackson Resolutions," as in the spirit of nullification and disunion, and appeals from the legislature to the people 26 May, "

Interstate convention at St Louis unanimously indorses a national Pacific railway across the continent. 16 Oct. "

Ground broken for the Pacific railroad by the mayor of St Louis 4 July, 1850

William Jewell college at Liberty, chartered in 1849 opened "

At a joint convention to choose a U S senator, Henry S. Geyer of St Louis Whig, defeats Thomas H Benton, 80 to 55 on the 40th ballot. 22 Jan 1851

Missouri school for the blind opened at St Louis "

State insane asylum at Fulton opened . . "

Missouri institution for the education of the deaf and dumb at Fulton opened 1852

Westminster college chartered and opened at Fulton. . 1853

House of Refuge at St. Louis opened . 1854

Destruction of the *Industrial Luminary*, a newspaper published at Parkville, by a pro-slavery faction 14 Apr 1855

College of the Christian Brothers at St. Louis, opened 1851, chartered 1855

Normal school at St. Louis opened 1857

Gov Trusten Polk resigns to become U S senator Mch "

Central college at Fayette chartered 1855, opened "

Dred Scott and family emancipated by Taylor Blow, under deed for that purpose from the family of Calvin C Chaffee, who inherited them (DRED SCOTT CASE) 26 May, "

First overland mail leaves St. Louis for San Francisco, 16 Sept. 1858

First overland mail from California arrives at St Louis 24 days 18½ hours from San Francisco 9 Oct "

Howard female college at Fayette, opened in 1855, chartered 1859

Washington university at St Louis, chartered 1853, opened "

Elizabeth Aull female seminary at Lexington chartered and opened "

Legislature calls a state convention, "that the will of the people may be ascertained and effectuated" but providing that no ordinance of secession should be valid unless ratified by the people 18 Jan 1861

Edward Bates of Missouri U S attorney general. 5 Mch "

State convention assembles in the court house at Jefferson City, 99 delegates Sterling Price chosen president, 28 Feb They adjourn to meet at St Louis on 4 Mch when a committee reports against secession 9 Mch "

In reply to pres Lincoln's call for troops gov Jackson writes, "Not one man will the state of Missouri furnish to carry on such an unholy crusade" 17 Apr "

U S arsenal at Liberty seized and garrisoned by state troops under order from gov Jackson 20 Apr "

Capt. Lyon at the head of the U S forces in St Louis, by a sudden move upon camp Jackson compels an unconditional surrender of the state militia there 10 May, "

Gen Harney, commandant at St Louis, addresses the people of Missouri denouncing a military act of the legislature as indirect secession and unconstitutional 14 May, "

Gov Jackson calls for 50,000 militia, "for the purpose of repelling invasion, and for the protection of the lives, liberty, and property of citizens of the state" 12 June, "

Gov Jackson, with the state troops proceeds to Booneville, leaving the capital to fall into the hands of Lyon 15 June, "

Gen Lyon defeats the state troops under col Marmaduke in battle at Booneville 17 June, "

An indecisive battle is fought at Carthage between state troops under gen Jackson and federals under gen Sigel, 5 July, "

State convention makes Robert Wilson president in place of Sterling Price, made major general in the Confederate army 22 July, "

State convention declares the office of governor, of lieutenant governor and of members of legislature vacant, and elects Hamilton R Gamble as provisional governor 31 July, "

Thomas C Reynolds ex lieutenant governor, proclaims from New Madrid that the forces of gen Pillow had come on the invitation of gov Jackson, "to aid in expelling the enemy," 31 July, "

Gov Gamble, by proclamation, promises protection to all citizens in arms who return peaceably to their homes, in which promise the U S war department concurs 3 Aug "

Gov Jackson, returning from Richmond, Va., to New Madrid, issues a "Declaration of Independence of the State of Missouri" 5 Aug "

Federals under gen Lyon defeat confederates under gen James Rains at Dug Springs, 2 Aug, and are defeated by gen Benj McCulloch at WILSON CREEK, gen Lyon killed, 10 Aug "

Missouri is placed under martial law by gen Fremont, at the head of the western department, and maj McKinstry, U S A, is created provost marshal general 30 Aug "

By proclamation 30 Aug, gen Fremont manumits 2 slaves of Thomas L Snead, a secessionist of St Louis 12 Sept "

Federals are defeated in battles at Blue Mills Landing, 17 Sept., LEXINGTON 20 Sept., and Papinsville 21 Sept. "

State convention at Jefferson City requires each civil officer within 60 days to subscribe an oath to support the constitution 16 Oct. "

Lexington reoccupied by the federals, 16 Oct, who are also victorious at Fredericktown, 22 Oct., and at Springfield, 26 Oct "

Gov Jackson issues (26 Sept 1861) a proclamation from Lexington, convening the legislature in extra session at Masonic Hall in Neosho, Newton county . 21 Oct "

Gen Fremont is relieved by gen David Hunter 2 Nov "

Legislature at Neosho passes an act of secession, 28 Oct., and resolution requesting all members to sign it 2 Nov "

Indecisive battle at BELMONT between gens. Grant and Polk, 7 Nov, Warsaw destroyed by confederates 19 Nov "

Maj gen Halleck, who succeeded gen Hunter, 7 Nov, declares martial law in St. Louis, 23 Dec, and, some men returning from gen Price's army having destroyed about 100 miles of the Missouri railroad, he extends the order to all the railroads in the state 25 Dec. "

Battles at Shawnee Mound and Milford, 18 Dec. 1861, and at Mount Zion 28 Dec. "

New Madrid captured by gen Pope 14 Mch 1862

Independence captured by the confederates 11 Aug "

Battle at Newtonia, confederates victorious 30 Sept. "

Andrew Allsman, an aged citizen of Palmyra, taken in a raid by col John C. Porter's band in Sept., and not heard of afterwards, gen McNeil hangs in retaliation 10 of Porter's raiders (ALLSMAN, CASE OF) .. . . 18 Oct "

MIS

ɔnfederate gen. John S. Marmaduke repulsed at Springfield, 8 Jan., and at Hartsville............................11 Jan. 1863

ɜn. John H. McNeil repulses gen. Marmaduke in a battle at Cape Girardeau.................................26 Apr. "

ˈdinance adopted by the state convention, ordaining that slavery should cease 4 July, 1870, subject to provisions with regard to age, etc......................................1 July, "

ɜath of gov. Gamble...................................31 Jan. 1864

ɔbbery and general massacre of citizens and Federal soldiers in Centralia by guerilla band under Bill Anderson, 27 Sept. "

ill Anderson killed in a fight near Albany, Ray county, 27 Oct. "

ɪntral Wesleyan college at Warrenton chartered and opened. "

ɜn. Price invades Missouri; defeats Curtis at Little Blue, 21 Oct., but is repulsed by federals at Big Blue, Little Osage, and Newtonia ....Oct. "

ɪnstitutional convention meets at St. Louis, 6 Jan. 1865, adopts an ordinance abolishing slavery..............11 Jan. 1865

ate Board of Immigration organized under act of legislature .... "

ate convention vacates on 1 May the offices of judges of the Supreme court, of all Circuit courts, and others.....17 Mch. "

ɜw constitution completed 10 Apr. Art. ii. sec. 9 provides that after 60 days "no person shall be permitted to practise as an attorney," "nor be competent as a bishop, priest, deacon, minister, elder, or other clergyman" to teach or preach or solemnize marriages unless he shall have taken, subscribed, and filed an oath of loyalty. Constitution ratified by the people, vote 43,670 for and 41,808 against, 6 June, "

ɪdges of the higher courts decline to yield to the new judges appointed by gov. Fletcher under ordinance of 17 Mch., as not in the power of the convention. By special order, gen. Coleman is directed to use such force as may be necessary to establish the new judges in office, which he accomplishes 14 June, "

ncoln Institute Normal school opened at Jefferson City...... 1866

ɛcitement in Lafayette from political strife and robbery and murder by desperadoes under Archie Clemmens, who is killed by troops sent to quell the disturbance............spring of 1867

ɜgislature makes prize-fighting for money punishable by imprisonment from 6 to 12 months, or a fine of $500 to $1000, 8 Feb. 1868

onument to Thomas H. Benton, raised for the state government on Lafayette square, St. Louis, is unveiled.....27 May, "

ɜople reject the amendment striking out the word "white" in the suffrage clause, by 74,053 to 55,236................. "

ɪginal seal of the state of Missouri, which had disappeared from the seat of government in 1861, is restored to gov. McClurg by ex-lieut.-gov. Thomas C. Reynolds......26 May, 1869

ɜgislature ratifies XV.th Amendment to the U. S. Constitution, 10 Jan. 1870

ate Agricultural college located at Columbia by law........ "

movement set on foot in 1866 by col. B. Gratz Brown, for universal amnesty, universal franchise, and revenue reform, divides the Republican party, at the state convention at Jefferson City, 31 Aug. 1870, into Radicals, and Liberals or "Bolters," headed by gen. Carl Schurz. The Liberal candidate B. Gratz Brown elected governor................8 Nov. "

ate Normal school at Warrensburg opened.................. 1871

ate Normal school at Kirksville opened..................... "

ɜt passes over gov. Brown's veto directing that 422 bonds of the state of Missouri, of $1000 each, issued in 1852 and falling due in 1872, "redeemable in gold or silver coin," be redeemed in legal-tender notes.........................8 Feb. 1872

ɜventy or 80 masked men stop a railroad train at Gun City, Cass county, and murder judge J. C. Stephenson, Thomas E. Detro, and James C. Cline, charged with complicity in the fraudulent issue of railroad bonds, which imposed a heavy burden upon the tax-payers in that county..........24 Apr. "

ulton Synodical female college, chartered in 1870, opened at Fulton.. "

ate Normal school opened at Cape Girardeau............... 1873

rury college at Springfield chartered and opened............ "

ailroad bridge over the Mississippi at St. Louis, designed by James B. Eads and constructed by the Illinois and St. Louis Bridge company, formally opened (BRIDGES).........4 July, 1874

ːate asylum for the insane established at St. Joseph......... "

ːate Railroad commission created by act of legislature, 27 Mch. 1875

rdinance passed by legislature to prevent the payment of 1918 bonds and coupons of $1000 each, executed by the Pacific railroad of Missouri under a law of 10 Dec. 1855, which had disappeared, but had not been cancelled or destroyed, 30 Oct. "

ew constitution framed by a state convention which sat at Jefferson City, 5 May, 1875, to 19 Aug., is submitted to the people and ratified by a vote of 90,600 to 14,362......30 Oct. "

ɔnvention of 869 delegates from 31 states and territories assembles at St. Louis to take action upon the construction of the Southern Pacific railroad....................23-24 Nov. "

arl Schurz of Missouri secretary of the interior......12 Mch. 1877

tate lunatic asylum at St. Joseph burned; the 218 inmates escape...25 Jan. 1879

Cottey law" passed, to take effect immediately, providing that county courts shall levy only 4 taxes: the state revenue tax, the state interest tax, tax for current county expenses, and school tax, unless ordered by the circuit court for the county or by the judge thereof in chambers, 8 Mch. "

Laws creating a State Fish commission, a Bureau of Labor statistics, and appropriating $3000 for a state hatchery...... 1879

Proposed amendment to the constitution, art. xiv., embodying the "Maine Liquor law," passes the house, and is rejected in the senate by 12 to 10..................................... "

Convention of representatives of the commercial and agricultural and other productive industries of the Mississippi valley meets at St. Louis.................................26 Oct. 1881

Missouri River Improvement convention meets at St. Joseph. 4 states and 2 territories are represented............29 Nov. "

"Downing High License law" passed, which fixes the maximum state and county tax on license for dram-shops at $1200 per annum, and requiring a petition signed by two-thirds of the tax-payers of cities, towns, and townships before it is mandatory on the county court to issue licenses... 1883

State Board of Health created by act of legislature............ "

Kansas City ladies' college at Independence opened in 1871, chartered.. 1884

Some 75 of the "Bald-knobber" organization of Christian county are arrested in Mch., some on the charge of murder, others for attending unlawful assemblies of "Regulators." All but the leaders are tried at Ozark and fined........Aug. 1887

Reform school for boys established by law at Booneville...... "

Fifty out of 78 elections under the "Wood Local-option law" result in favor of prohibition.............................. "

State insane asylum No. 3 at Nevada opened...........15 Oct. "

Gov. Marmaduke d....................................28 Dec. "

State institution for deaf and dumb at Fulton burned.....Feb. 1888

Bald-knobber leader David Walker and 3 accomplices tried, Mch. and Apr. 1888. Sentenced to be executed on 18 May; postponed. Their Bald-knobber friends, for revenge, seize and hang 5 of the witnesses........................14 Nov. "

State industrial school for girls opened at Chillicothe.....Jan. 1889

Norman J. Coleman appointed secretary of agriculture..12 Feb. "

Australian Ballot Reform act, applicable to cities and towns of 5000 or over, passed by the legislature..................... "

Act of legislature appointing the first Friday after the first Tuesday of Apr. to be observed as Arbor day............... "

David Walker, William Walker, and John Matthews, Bald-knobbers, sentenced Apr. 1888, finally executed at Ozark, 10 May, "

Interstate Wheat Growers' Association of Mississippi valley meets at St. Louis, N. J. Coleman presiding..........27 Oct. "

State treasurer E. T. Noland suspended from office for defalcation to the amount of $32,745.69....................4 Mch. 1890

Woman's temperance crusade in Lathrop, etc., from 10 Feb. "

Gov. Francis deposes state treasurer Noland for alleged shortage of about $33,000 in his accounts...................4 Mch. "

Semi-centennial of the laying of the corner-stone of the state university at Columbia celebrated..................4 July, "

Limited Kansas City express on the Mo. Pacific R. R. is "held up" by 7 highwaymen at Otterville, and express car robbed of $90,000...17 Aug. "

Representatives from the Union Labor, Prohibition, and Greenback parties meet at St. Louis, 3 Sept., and organize the National Reform party...............................5 Sept. "

Gen. W. T. Sherman died at New York city 14 Feb.; is buried at St. Louis...21 Feb. 1891

Legal rate of interest fixed at 8 per cent. by act of legislature, which adjourns...................................24 Mch. "

National industrial conference (over 650 delegates from Farmers' Alliance and mutual benefit associations) meets at St. Louis and decides to act with the People's party in the presidential campaign..................................22 Feb. 1892

National Nicaragua Canal convention, with delegates from 25 or more states, meets in St. Louis ....2 June, "

TERRITORIAL GOVERNOR.

William Clark	assumes duties	July,	1813

STATE GOVERNORS.

Alexander McNair	term begins	19 Sept.	1820
Frederick Bates	"	Nov.	1824
Abraham J. Williams	acting	1 Aug.	1825
Gen. John Miller	term begins	Nov.	"
Daniel Dunklin	"	"	1832
Lilburn W. Boggs	"	"	1836
Thomas Reynolds (Dem.)	"	"	1840
M. M. Marmaduke	acting	9 Feb.	1844
John C. Edwards (Dem.)	term begins	Nov.	"
Austin A. King (Dem.)	"	"	1848
Sterling Price (Dem.)	"	Dec.	1852
Trusten Polk (Dem.)	"	"	1856
Hancock Jackson	acting	Mch.	1857
Robert M. Stewart (Dem.)	term begins	Dec.	"
Claiborne F. Jackson (Dem.)	"	4 Jan.	1861
Hamilton R. Gamble (provisional)	elected	31 July,	"
Willard P. Hall	acting	31 Jan.	1864
Thomas C. Fletcher (Rep.)	term begins	"	1865
Joseph W. McClurg (Rep.)	"	"	1869
R. Gratz Brown (Lib.)	"	"	1871
Silas Woodson (Dem.)	"	"	1873
Charles H. Hardin (Dem.)	"	"	1875
John S. Phelps (Dem.)	"	"	1877
Thomas T. Crittenden (Dem.)	"	"	1881
John S. Marmaduke (Dem.)	"	"	1885
Albert G. Morehouse	acting	28 Dec.	1887
David R. Francis (Dem.)	term begins	Jan.	1889
William J. Stone (Dem.)	"	"	1893

UNITED STATES SENATORS FROM THE STATE OF MISSOURI.

Name.	No. of Congress.	Date.	Remarks.
David Barton	17th to 21st	1821 to 1831	
Thomas H. Benton	17th " 31st	1821 " 1851	Served 30 years as senator.
Alexander Buckner	22d	1831 " 1833	Died 1833.
Lewis F. Linn	23d to 27th	1833 " 1843	Elected in place of Buckner. Died 1843.
David R. Atchison	28th " 33d	1843 " 1856	Elected president *pro tem.* 8 Aug. 1846; and again, 20 Dec. 1852.
Henry S. Geyer	32d " 34th	1851 " 1857	Elected, defeating Benton.
James Stephen Green	34th " 36th	1857 " 1861	
Trusten Polk	35th " 37th	1857 " 1862	Expelled 10 Jan. 1862.
Waldo P. Johnson	37th	1861 " 1862	" " "
John B. Henderson	37th to 40th	1862 " 1869	Appointed in place of Polk.
Robert Wilson	37th	1862	Appointed in place of Johnson.
B. Gratz Brown	38th to 39th	1863 to 1867	Elected in place of Wilson.
Charles D. Drake	40th " 41st	1867 " 1870	Resigned.
Francis P. Blair, jr.	41st " 42d	1871 " 1873	Elected in place of Drake.
Carl Schurz	41st " 42d	1869 " 1875	Succeeds Henderson.
Lewis F. Bogy	43d " 45th	1873 " 1877	Elected to succeed Blair. Died 1877.
Francis M. Cockrell	44th " ——	1875 " ——	Term expires 1899.
David H. Armstrong	45th	1877 " 1879	Appointed in place of Bogy.
George G. Vest	46th " ——	1879 " ——	Term expires 1897.

Missouri compromise. UNITED STATES, 1819, '20, '21, '50, '54.

mith'ridate, a medical preparation in the form of an electuary, supposed to be an antidote to poison, and the oldest compound known, is said to have been invented by Mithridates, king of Pontus, about 70 B.C.

Mithrida'tic war, caused by the massacre of 80,000 Romans by Mithridates VI., king of PONTUS, 88 B.C., and remarkable for its duration, many sanguinary battles, and cruelties of its commanders. Mithridates having taken the consul Aquilius, made him ride on an ass through much of Asia, crying out, "I am Aquilius, consul of the Romans." He is said to have killed him by causing melted gold to be poured down his throat, in derision of his avarice, 85 B.C. Mithridates was defeated by Pompey, 66 B.C.; and committed suicide, 63 B.C.

Mitla, ancient ruins found in the Mexican state of Oxaca. The general character and design of the architecture and masonry is similar to that at PALENQUE, but the work seems to indicate a higher degree of art and science. AMERICA, COPAN.

mitrailleuse (*mē-trăl-yuz'*) or **mitrailleur** (*mē-tral-yer'*), a machine-gun combining 37 or more large-bored rifles with breech-action, so that a shower of bullets may be rapidly projected by one man. It was invented in Belgium, adopted by Napoleon III. soon after the Prusso-Austrian war in 1866, and much used in the Franco-Prussian war in 1870. When fired it has a peculiar dry, shrieking, terrible sound. Modifications of the mitrailleuse have been made by Montigny and others. The Fosbery mitrailleuse was tried and approved at Shoeburyness, 11 Aug. 1870. It is mentioned in *Grose's Military Antiquities* (1801) that in England, in 1625, a patent was granted to William Drummond for a machine composed of muskets joined together, by the help of which 2 soldiers can oppose 100, and named "thunder carriage," or, more usually, "fire carriage." An English mitrailleuse, a modification of the American Gatling, containing 50 cartridges, was tried at Woolwich, 18 Jan. 1872; 50 were ordered to be made by Armstrong.

mitre. The cleft cap or mitre was worn by the Jewish high-priest, 1491 B.C. It had on it a golden plate inscribed "Holiness to the Lord" (Exod. xxxix. 28). The most ancient mitre closely resembling the present one is upon the seal of the bishop of Laon, in the 10th century.—*Fosbroke.* Anciently the cardinals wore mitres; but the council of Lyons, in 1245, directed them to wear hats.

Mityle'ne or **Lesbos**, an island of the Ægean sea. Near here the Greeks defeated and nearly destroyed the Turkish fleet, 7 Oct. 1824.

mnemon'ics (from Mnemosyne, the goddess of memory and mother of the 9 muses), artificial memory, was introduced by Simonides the younger, 477 B.C.—*Arundelian Marbles.* A tractate, *De Arte Memorativa*, by Roger Bacon, exists in MS. at Oxford. Conrad Celtes, a German, published a work making use of the letters of the alphabet instead of places, 1492. Petrus de Ravenna's *Pheuix Artes Memoriæ*, pub. Venice, 1491, went through 9 editions. Lambert Schenkel, 1593; Winckelmann, 17th century; and Richard Grey, 1730, pub. works on mnemonics. Feinaigle's system appeared in Paris in 1806. Kothe's method, founded on the laws of association, has gone through several editions in Germany; and dr. Edwards Pick's work has a wide circulation. The fullest history of mnemonics is that given by J. C. von Aretin, 1810. In 1848, prof. Fauvel-Gourand of Paris visited the principal American cities, teaching to classes of many hundreds his improved system, called "Phreno-mnemotechny," which is still used by some students. "In certain cases mnemonical devices may be found of considerable service; but all systems which have aimed at completeness have been found rather to puzzle than aid the memory."—*Encycl. Brit.* 9th ed.

Mo'abites, descendants of Lot, a people living to the southeast of Judæa. They were often at war with the Israelites, and were subdued by Ehud about 1336, by David about 1040, and by Jehoshaphat, 895 B.C., but often harassed the Jews in the decay of their monarchy. The discovery of a stone, 1868, now in the Louvre, with inscription in Phœnician characters, said to relate to Mesha, king of Moab, referred to in 2 Kings iii., was announced in Jan. 1870, and impressions were exhibited soon after, which caused much discussion among Orientalists.

Mobile, Ala. The city is situated at the southwest corner of the state, at the mouth of Mobile river, and with a harbor on the Gulf. After the capture of Vicksburg in 1863 an attack on this city was contemplated, but was given up, the president preferring a Red river campaign. On 5 Aug. 1864, adm. Farragut attacked forts Morgan and Gaines; fort Powell was blown up; on the 8th fort Gaines was surrendered with its garrison, and fort Morgan was occupied on the 23d. After passing the forts on the 5th, Farragut captured the ram *Tennessee*. The result of his brief naval campaign was the possession of Mobile bay. After Hood's defeat at Nashville (Dec. 1864), military operations against Mobile were commenced. On 25 Mch. gen. Canby had the 13th and 16th corps (under Gordon Granger and A. J. Smith) at Danley's, on Fish river, east of Mobile. The siege of Spanish fort was commenced on the 27th. A week before this gen. Steele, having landed at Pensacola, marched northward against Montgomery, and, returning near 1 Apr., joined the army besieging Mobile. Spanish fort was evacuated by the confederates on 8 Apr., and occupied by the federal troops. The next day fort Blakely was assaulted and captured, and Mobile was evacuated (11, 12 Apr.). This was the last campaign of the civil war. Gen. Richard Taylor surrendered on 4 May. The population of Mobile decreased from 32,034 in 1870 to 31,205 in 1880, 31,076 in 1890.

Möck'ern, a town of Prussian Saxony. Here the French army under Eugène Beauharnais was defeated by the Prussians under Yorck, 5 Apr. 1813; and here Blücher defeated the French, 16 Oct. 1813.

models. The first were figures of living persons, and Dibutades, the Corinthian, is the reputed inventor of those in clay. His daughter, being about to be separated from her lover, traced his profile by his shadow on the wall; her father filled up the outline with clay, which he afterwards baked, and thus produced a figure of the object of her affection, giving rise to an art till then unknown, about 985 B.C. WAX-WORKS.

Mo'dena, formerly **Mu'tina,** capital of the late duchy in central Italy; was governed by the house of Este, from 1288 till 1796, when the last male of that house, the reigning duke Hercules III., was expelled by the French. By the treaty of Campo Formio the Modenese possessions were incorporated with the Cisalpine republic, 1797, and with the kingdom of Italy, 1805. The archduke Francis of Este, son of the archduke Ferdinand of Austria, and of Mary, the heiress of the last duke, was restored in 1814. Modena, in accordance with the voting by universal suffrage, was annexed to Sardinia on 18 Mch. 1860. Pop. of the city, 1881, 31,053; of the province, 1881, 279,254; 1889, 303,541.

GRAND DUKES.

1814. Francis IV. An invasion of his states by Murat was defeated, 11 Apr. 1815. He was expelled by his subjects in 1831, but was restored by the Austrians.

1846. Francis V. (b. 1 June, 1819) succeeded 21 Jan. His subjects rose against him soon after the Italian war broke out, in Apr. 1859. He fled to Verona, establishing a regency, 11 June; which was abolished, 13 June; Farina was appointed dictator, 27 July; a constituent assembly was immediately elected, which offered the duchy to the king of Sardinia, 15 Sept., who incorporated it with his dominions, 18 Mch. 1860. Francis d. 20 Nov. 1875.

Modoc Indians, a small tribe, originally part of the Klamath Indians dwelling in northern California. In 1864 they ceded their land to the United States, and were removed to the Klamath reservation in 1871. Not obtaining subsistence, a part returned to their old possessions, and their able leader, capt. Jack, defeated troops sent to expel them, 17 Jan. 1873. During negotiations for a peaceful settlement with the U. S. commissioners (11 Apr.) they massacred gen. Canby and commissioner Thomas. After fighting 15, 16 Apr., the Indians retreated to almost impregnable positions in the lava beds. The troops were fired on and suffered much loss, 27 Apr. The Indians were gradually surrounded. Jack and about 20 warriors held out desperately. Some surrendered, and he was captured 1 June, tried July, and executed 3 Oct. 1873. The remainder were placed on a reservation in the Indian Territory. CALIFORNIA, INDIANS.

Mœ'sia, now **Bosnia, Servia,** and **Bulgaria,** was finally subdued by Augustus, 29 B.C. It was successfully invaded by the GOTHS, 250 A.D., who eventually settled here.

Moguls. TARTARY.

Mohacz (*mo-hach'*), a town of Lower Hungary. Here Louis, king of Hungary, defeated by the Turks under Solyman II. with the loss of 22,000 men, was suffocated by the fall of his horse in a muddy brook, 29 Aug. 1526. Here also prince Charles of Lorraine defeated the Turks, 12 Aug. 1687.

Mohammedanism. MAHOMETANISM.

Mohawks. INDIANS, LONG HOUSE.

Mohe'gans. INDIANS.

Mohocks, ruffians who went about London at night wounding and disfiguring men and indecently exposing women. 100*l.* were offered by royal proclamation in 1712 for apprehending any of them.—*Northouck.*

Mokan'na (*Hakim ben-Allah*), "The Veiled" prophet, founder of a sect in Khorassan in the 8th century. He pretended to be an incarnation of God, and therefore veiled his face, but really to conceal the loss of an eye. He rebelled against the caliph Almahdi, was for a time successful, but was subdued in 780, when he and the remainder of his followers took poison. He is the subject of a poem by Thomas Moore, in "Lalla Rookh," 1817.

Moldavia. DANUBIAN PRINCIPALITIES.

Moli'nists, a Roman Catholic sect, followers of Louis Molina, a Jesuit, 1535-1600. He maintained the harmony of the doctrines of predestination and free-will, 1588. The Molinists subsequently passed into the Jansenist controversy. JANSENISTS.

Molly Maguires, Irish Ribbonmen who made forays disguised as women, named from Cornelius Maguire, baron of Inniskillen, who in 1641 took part with sir Phelim O'Neil in the Irish rebellion.—A secret society in the mining districts of Pennsylvania, 1870-80.

Moluc'cas, an archipelago in the Indian ocean (chief island Amboyna), discovered by Portuguese about 1511, and held by them secretly until the Spaniards arrived and claimed them. Charles V. yielded them to John III. of Portugal for a large sum of money, 1529. The Dutch conquered them in 1607, and have held them since—except from 1810 to 1814, when they were subject to the English.

Molwitz, a town in Prussian Silesia. Here the Prussians, commanded by Frederick II., obtained a victory over the Austrians, 10 Apr. 1741.

molyb'denum, a whitish, brittle, almost infusible metal. Scheele, in 1778, discovered molybdic acid in a mineral hitherto confounded with graphite. Hjelm, 1782, prepared the metal from molybdic acid; and in 1825 Berzelius described its chemical characters.—*Gmelin.*

mon'achism (from the Gr. μόνος, alone). Catholic writers refer to the prophet Elijah, and the Nazarites mentioned in Numb. vi., as early examples. The first Christian ascetics appear to be derived from the Jewish sect of the Essenes, whose life was austere, practising celibacy, etc. About the time of Constantine (306-22) numbers of ascetics withdrew into the deserts, and were called hermits, monks, and anchorets, of whom Paul, Anthony, and Pachomius were most celebrated. Simeon, the founder of the Stylitæ (or pillar saints), died 451. He is said to have lived on a pillar 20 years.

"Three years I lived upon a pillar, high
Six cubits, and three years on one of twelve;
And twice three years I crouch'd on one that rose
Twenty by measure; last of all, I grew,
Twice ten long weary, weary years to this,
That numbers forty cubits from the soil."
—*Tennyson,* "St. Simeon Stylites."

St. Benedict, the great reformer of western monachism, published his rules and established his monastery at Monte Casino, about 529. The Carthusians, Cistercians, etc., are varieties of Benedictines. In 964, by decree of king Edgar, all married priests were ineffectually ordered to be replaced by monks. Religious orders expelled from France, by decree, 29 Mch. 1880. The anchorites of the 12th, 13th, and 14th centuries must not be confounded with anachorets and anchorets, or hermits. The former were confined to cells; the latter free to go where they pleased. ABBEYS, BENEDICTINES.

Mon'aco, the smallest of the sovereign principalities of Europe, situated on the Mediterranean, 9 miles from Nice, held by the Genoese family Grimaldi since 968. By treaty on 2 Feb. 1861, the prince ceded the communes of Roquebrune and Mentone, the chief part of his dominions, to France for 4,000,000 francs. The present prince, Charles III., born 8 Dec. 1818, succeeded his father Florestan, 20 June, 1856. Heir: Albert, born 13 Nov. 1848. A commercial convention between the prince and France, signed 9 Nov. 1865, was regarded as looking to abolition of the French navigation laws. Petitions against Monte Carlo, the great gaming establishment, Dec. 1880. It has its own coinage and issues its own postage-stamps. Area, 8 sq. miles; pop. 1878, 7049; 1890, 12,000.

monarchy. Historians reckon various grand monarchies—those of ASSYRIA, BABYLONIA, CHALDÆA, EGYPT, GREECE, MEDIA, PARTHIA, PERSIA, and ROME.

monasteries. ABBEYS.

Moncontour', a town near Poitiers, France. Here adm. Coligny and French Protestants were defeated with great loss by the duke of Anjou (afterwards Henry III.), 3 Oct. 1569.

"Oh, weep for Moncontour! Oh, weep for the hour
When the children of darkness and evil had power,
When the horsemen of Valois triumphantly trod
On the bosoms that bled for their right and their God!"
—*Macaulay,* "The Battle of Moncontour."

monetary conferences, International, opened at Paris, 16 Aug. 1878, and 19 Apr. 1881; Cologne, 11-13 Oct. 1882; Paris, 21 July, 5 Aug. 1885; again at Paris, Sept. 1889.

money is mentioned as a medium of commerce in Gen. xxiii., 1860 B.C., when Abraham purchased a field as a sepulchre for Sarah. The coinage of money is ascribed to Lydians. Moneta was the name given to their silver by the Romans, as coined in the temple of Juno Moneta, 269 B.C. Money was made of different metals, and even of leather and other articles, both in ancient and modern times. It was made of pasteboard by the Hollanders so late as 1574. The czar Nicholas struck coins in platinum. COIN, CONTINENTAL MONEY, COPPER, GOLD, SILVER.

moneyers travelled with early English kings, and coined money as required. MINT.

Mongols. TARTARY.

Monitor and **Merrimac.** HAMPTON ROADS, Va., 1861; NAVAL BATTLES.

monitorial system in education, in which pupils are employed as teachers, was used by dr. Bell in the orphan asylum at Madras in 1795, and by Joseph Lancaster in London. EDUCATION.

monk. MONACHISM.

Monmouth, Battle of. Sir Henry Clinton left Philadelphia for New York on 18 June, 1778, with 11,000 British and an immense baggage and provision train. Washington pursued him, harassed him in New Jersey, and engaged him near Monmouth Court-house on Sunday, 28 June, 1778. The battle lasted all day. It was exceedingly sultry, and more than 50 American soldiers died of exhaustion. Night closed the conflict. Towards midnight Clinton silently withdrew to avoid another engagement in the morning, and escaped, leaving many sick and wounded behind. The Americans lost 228; less than 70 were killed. The British left about 300 dead on the field. It was in this battle that gen. Charles Lee, in command of the advance, received a reproof from gen. Washington, that finally led to Lee's dismissal.

Monmouth's rebellion. James, duke of Monmouth (b. at Rotterdam, 9 Apr. 1649), a natural son of Charles II. by Lucy Waters, was banished England for his connection with the Rye-house plot, in 1683. He invaded England at Lyme, 11 June, 1685; was proclaimed king at Taunton, 20 June; was defeated at Sedgmoor, near Bridgewater, 6 July; and beheaded on Tower hill, 15 July.

Monoc'acy, Md., Battle of. Here on 9 July, 1864, gen. Lew. Wallace with a force of about 5500 men successfully resisted for 8 hours a Confederate force of about 20,000 under gen. Early, and prevented his reaching Washington. Federal loss, 98 killed, 579 wounded, and 1282 missing.

mon'ochord, a box of thin wood, with a bridge, over which is stretched a wire or cord, said to have been invented by Pythagoras, about 600 B.C.

Monongahe'la, Battle of. PENNSYLVANIA, 1755.

monopolies (Gr. μονοπωλία, exclusive sale; the command of the market of anything for sale) were formerly so numerous in England that Parliament petitioned against them, and many were abolished, about 1601-2. Others were suppressed by 21 Jas. I. 1624. Sir Giles Mompesson and sir Francis Mitchell were punished for abuse of monopolies, 1621. In 1630, Charles I. established monopolies of soap, salt, leather, and other common things, to supply a revenue without Parliament. It was enacted that none should be in future created by royal patent, 16 Chas I. 1640. Monopolies established in France ruinous to that country prior to the revolution of 1789. In the United States monopolies are formed for controlling the market by means of enormous capital, sufficient to buy up any article for which there is a demand, holding it, and thus making a price for it, or in crowding out of business in various ways all competitors of less means, although equally capable of rendering the service of supplying the commodity. Monopolies thus constitute the most serious evils of modern times—evils that in time will require to be abolished by government.

Monoth'elites, heretics who affirmed that Jesus Christ had but one will; were favored by the emperor Heraclius, 630; they merged into the EUTYCHIANS.

Monroe, James, administration of. UNITED STATES, 1817-25.

Monroe doctrine. UNITED STATES, 2 Dec. 1823. The doctrine has been repeatedly reaffirmed as the settled policy of the people and government of the United States.

Monta'na, a northwestern frontier state of the United States, is included almost wholly between lat. 45° and 49° N., and lon. 104° and 116° W. It is bounded on the north by British America, east by North Dakota and South Dakota, south by Wyoming, the Yellowstone National park, and Idaho, and west by Idaho. Area, 146,080 sq. miles. Pop. 1890, 132,159; 1900, 243,329. Capital, Helena.

Sieur de la Verendrye and his sons, with a party of explorers, leave the Lake of the Woods, 29 Apr. 1742; they reach the upper Missouri and Yellowstone rivers and arrive at the Rocky mountains.............Jan. 1743
Lewis and Clarke's expedition cross Montana to the Pacific ocean. Returning, capt. Lewis descends the Missouri from the Great falls, and capt. Clarke the Yellowstone from Livingstone, and meet at the mouth of the Yellowstone........ 1805
Emanuel Lisa builds a trading-post on the Yellowstone....... 1809
Gen. William H. Ashley of St. Louis builds a trading-post on the Yellowstone.................................... 1822
American Fur company builds fort Union on the Missouri, 3 miles above the mouth of the Yellowstone................. 1829
Steamboat *Assiniboine*, built by the American Fur company, ascends the Missouri to fort Union in 1833; winters near the mouth of Poplar creek, 60 miles above the mouth of the Yellowstone.................................... 1835
Father Peter John de Smet visits the Flathead Indians in Gallatin valley.................................... 1840
De Smet establishes a mission on the St. Mary's river in the Bitter Root valley.... ....Sept. 1842
De Smet establishes St. Ignatius mission in the Flathead Lake valley.................................... 1845
American Fur company builds fort Benton.................. 1846
Steamboat *El Paso* reaches the mouth of Milk river.......... 1850
Francis Finlay, alias "Benetsee," a half-breed Scotch and Indian trader, settled in what is now Deer Lodge county on Gold creek, discovers gold, and takes a sample to Angus McDonald at the Hudson Bay company's post near St. Ignatius, 1852
Gov. Isaac I. Stevens explores a route for a Northern Pacific railroad from St. Paul across Montana to the Pacific ocean, under authority of Congress............................ 1853
Sir George Gore leaves St. Louis with 40 men, explores the headwaters of Powder river, and builds a fort on Tongue river, 8 miles from its junction with the Yellowstone....... 1855
[In this part of Montana lies the peculiar tract termed by the French Mauvaises Terres (Bad Lands), usually described as the Little Missouri Bad Lands, extending from that river west to the Little Big Horn, or from 104° lon. W. to 108° W.; watered by the Powder, Tongue, and Rosebud rivers. This labyrinth of ravines and singular and grotesque forms, devoid of vegetation, covers in the aggregate from 1600 to 2000 sq. miles. This singular formation is caused primarily by the subterranean fires of lignite coal veins or beds, and secondarily, by the action of water.]
John Silverthorn trades tobacco and supplies with "Benetsee" for gold-dust.................................... 1858
Stern-wheel steamboat, the *Chippewa*, reaches fort Bruló, 12 miles below fort Benton...........................17 July, 1859
Chippewa reaches fort Benton, the first steamboat to arrive there, but is followed the same day by the *Key West*, 2 July, 1860
Capt. James Fisk's first expedition, consisting of 100 men and 30 women and children from Minnesota, arrives at Gold creek, Deer Lodge county.......................26 Sept. 1862
Discovery of gold in the Alder gulch near present site of Virginia City, Madison county, by a party of prospectors consisting of William Fairweather and others...........22 May, 1863
Twenty-four outlaws, including the sheriff and 2 deputies, hung by a vigilance committee, and 8 banished. At their trial and by confession it was found that these outlaws had murdered 102 people in Montana................Dec. 1863-Feb. 1864
Law creating Montana territory out of a portion of Idaho approved by pres. Lincoln...............................26 May, "
Gold discovered in "Last Chance gulch," in Lewis and Clarke county, on present site of Helena.....................21 July, "
Montana Post, first newspaper in the territory, started at Virginia City.................................... "
Historical society of Montana incorporated..............2 Feb. 1865
First National bank of Helena, the first in Montana, organized, 1866
Helena Herald first issued.................................... "
Steamer *Key West* leaves Sioux City, 14 Apr. 1869, reaches the Yellowstone 6 May, and ascends that river to Powder river, a distance of 245 miles.................................... 1869
Congress sets apart a tract near the headwaters of the Yellowstone as a public park; a small portion lies in Montana, bordering on Wyoming...................................1 Mch. 1872
Expedition under Thomas P. Roberts explores the upper Missouri from the three forks down to fort Benton............ "
Seat of government removed from Virginia City to Helena.... 1875
Gen. Forsythe, under orders from gen. Sheridan, explores the Yellowstone, leaving Bismarck in the steamer *Josephine*, 15 June, ascending to Huntley, 418 miles............June, "
Sioux Indians under Sitting Bull, near the Little Big Horn

river, massacre gen. George A. Custer, with 5 companies (276 men) of the 7th cavalry, no man escaping.....25 June, 1876
Fort Assiniboine, near the Milk river, established......9 May, 1879
Uncalled *territorial bonds, amounting to $45,000, redeemed* and cancelled, thus extinguishing all registered indebtedness of the territory....................................1 Mch. 1883
Henry Villard, president of the Northern Pacific railroad, completes the work on that road, by driving the last spike opposite the entrance of Gold creek into Deer Lodge river, 8 Sept. "
Settlement in Deer Lodge and Gallatin counties of monogamic Mormons expelled from Utah for apostasy................ "
College of Montana at Deer Lodge, opened in 1883, chartered, 1884
Constitutional convention meets 14 Jan. 1884, and adjourns 9 Feb.; its constitution was ratified by the people, 4 Nov., and submitted to Congress, asking admission into the Union.... "
First steamboat to successfully navigate the Missouri river above Great falls is launched at Townsend................ 1886
Territorial legislature passes a local-option act, and provides for the observance of Arbor day......................... 1887
Coal-mining begun in Cascade county........................ 1888
Montana admitted to the Union by act of Congress....22 Feb. 1889
Legislature passes an Australian Ballot act................. "
Constitutional convention meets at Helena, 4 July, 1889; adopts a constitution and adjourns, 17 Aug. Constitution ratified by the people, 24,676 for and 2274 against............1 Oct. "
Proclamation of pres. Harrison, admitting Montana into the Union as a state...................................8 Nov. "
U. S. penitentiary at Deer Lodge becomes the property of the state of Montana upon its admission..................... "
Owing to a dispute concerning the election returns in Silver Bow county, a Democratic and Republican House, each claiming a quorum of 30 members, including those from the disputed county, convene. Gov. Toole, Democrat, sends a message to the Senate, comprised of 8 Republicans and 8 Democrats, and a Republican lieutenant-governor, and to the Democratic House also. The Republican Senate elects 2 U. S. senators, and the House and Senate in joint session elect 2 Democratic U. S. senators..............................Dec. "
To block legislation, the 8 Democratic senators flee the state, 6 going to the Pacific coast and 2 to St. Paul, until the session expires by constitutional limitation.............5 Feb. 1890
Three Indian chiefs of the Comanches, Cheyennes, and Arapahoes, meet near Crow agency to behold the Great Spirit on the rocks; beginning of the Messiah craze..........3 June, "
Rival houses of the legislature agree; the Republicans to have 28 members, the Democrats 27 and the speaker, subordinate offices, and control of committees..................29 Jan. 1891
Montana university opened at Helena; first graduation..June, "
September 1st made a legal holiday, as "Labor day"....... "
Legislature failing to elect a U. S. senator, the governor appoints Lee Mantle, *which appointee the senate refuses to seat*, 28 Aug. 1893

TERRITORIAL GOVERNORS.

Sydney Edgerton..........term begins...............22 June, 1864
Thomas Francis Meagher.. acting 1865
Green Clay Smith.........term begins...............13 July, 1866
James M. Ashley.......... " ....9 Apr. 1869
Benjamin F. Potts........ " ....13 July, 1870
John Schuyler Crosby..... " 1883
B. Platt Carpenter........ " 1884
Samuel T. Hauser......... " 1885
Preston H. Leslie.......... " 1887
Benjamin F. White........ " 1889

STATE GOVERNORS.

Joseph K. Toole...........term begins................8 Nov. 1889
John E. Rickards.......... " ....Jan. 1893

UNITED STATES SENATORS FROM THE STATE OF MONTANA.

Name.	No. of Congress.	Date.	Remarks.
Wilbur F. Sanders.	Fifty-first	1890 to 1893	Seated 16 Apr. 1890
Thomas C. Power..	"	*1890 " ——*	*Term expires, 1895*
Vacant............	Fifty-third		
Lee Mantle.......	Fifty-fourth	1895 to ——	
Thos. H. Carter....	"	1895 " ——	

Mon'tanists, followers of Montanus of Ardaba, in Mysia, about 171, who was reputed to have the gift of prophecy, and proclaimed himself the Comforter promised by Christ. He condemned second marriages, permitted dissolution of marriage, forbade avoiding martyrdom, and ordered a severe fast of 3 lents; he hanged himself with Maximilla, one of his female scholars, before the close of the 2d century.—*Cave.* The eloquent father Tertullian joined the sect, 204. The best work on the Montanistic movement in the early church is Ritschl's "Der Montanismus und die christliche Kirche des 2ten Jahrhunderts," Tübingen, 1841.

Mont Blanc (*mon blon'*), in the Swiss (Pennine) Alps, the highest mountain in Europe, is 15,781 feet above the sea level. The summit was first reached by Saussure, aided by a guide named Balma, on 2 Aug. 1787; again by dr. Hamel (when 3 guides perished) in 1820, and by many before and since. Accounts of the ascents of John Auldjo, Charles Fellows (1827), and prof. Tyndall (1857–58), have been published. 57 ascents reported in 1873. ALPS.

Mont Cenis (*mon su-ne'*). ALPS, TUNNELS.

MON

Montebel'lo, a village in Piedmont, where Lannes defeated the Austrians, 9 June, 1800, and acquired his title of duke of Montebello; and where after a contest of 6 hours, the French and Sardinians defeated the Austrians, who lost about 1000 killed and wounded, and 200 prisoners, 20 May, 1859. The French lost about 670 men, including gen. Beuret.

Mon'te Car'lo. MONACO.

Mon'te Casi'no, a mountain in central Italy. Here Benedict formed his first monastery, 529, and organized the order of the Benedictines. After affording a refuge for many eminent persons, its monastic character was abolished by the Italian government in 1866, care being taken of its historical and literary monuments.

monte di pietà (*mon'te de pe'a-ta*), charitable institutions for advancing money on pledges, first established at Perugia, Florence, Mantua, and other Italian cities, 1462 et seq. The Franciscans, in 1493, began to receive interest, which was permitted by the pope in 1515.—*Monts-de-piété*, established in France 1777, were suppressed by the Revolution, but restored 1804; regulated by law, 1851–52. PAWNBROKING.

Montenegro (*mŏn-ta-na'-gro*), an independent principality in European Turkey, was conquered by Solyman II. in 1526; rebelled early in the 18th century, and established an hereditary hierarchical government in the family of Petrovitsch Njegosch—permitted, but not recognized, by the Porte. Its independence was declared by the treaty of Berlin, 13 July, 1878. Area, 3630 sq. miles; pop. about 236,000. Capital, Céttinjé.

PRINCES.

1851. Daniel, b. 25 May, 1826; assassinated, 13 Aug. 1860.
1860. Nicolas, or Nikita (nephew), b. 7 Oct. 1841; married princess Milena, 8 Nov. 1860. Heir: Danilo, b. 29 June, 1871.

Montenot'te, a village in Piedmont, site of Bonaparte's first victory over the Austrians, 12 Apr. 1796.

Montereau (*mon-te-ro'*), a town near Paris. On the bridge of Montereau, at a meeting with the dauphin, John the Fearless, duke of Burgundy, was killed by Tanneguy de Châtel in 1419. This led to Henry V.'s conquest of France, the young duke Philip joining the English. Here the allied armies were defeated by the French, commanded by Napoleon, with great loss; but it was one of his last triumphs, 18 Feb. 1814.

Monterey', a city of Mexico, founded by the Spaniards, 1596. MEXICAN WAR.

Montferrat' (Lombardy), house of, celebrated in the history of the Crusades, began with Alderan, who was made marquess of Montferrat, by Otho, about 967. Conrad of Montferrat became lord of Tyre, and reigned from 1187 to 1191, when he was assassinated. William IV. died in a cage at Alexandria, having been thus imprisoned 19 months, 1292. Violante, daughter of John II., married Andronicus Palæologus, emperor of the east. Their descendants ruled in Italy amid perpetual contests till 1533, when John George Palæologus died without issue. His estates passed, after much contention, to Frederick II., Gonzaga, marquess of Mantua, in 1536, and next to the duke of Savoy.

Montgomery. ALABAMA; CONFEDERATE STATES; UNITED STATES, 1861.

Montgomery, Fort. FORT MONTGOMERY.

month (from *mona*, Anglo-Saxon *moon*), the 12th part of the calendar year. CALENDAR, FRENCH REVOLUTIONARY CALENDAR, JANUARY and other months, JEWISH ERA, MAHOMETAN YEAR, YEAR.

Lunar month.—The period of one revolution of the moon around the earth (synodical); mean length, 29 d. 12 h. 44 min. 2.87 sec.
Sidereal month.—Time of moon's revolution from a star to the same again, 27 d. 7 h. 43 min. 11.5 sec.
Solar month.—The time the sun passes through one sign of the zodiac, 30 d. 10 h. 29 min. 4.1 sec.
Information respecting the months of the Egyptians, Jews, Greeks, Romans, Persians, and other nations will be found in sir H. Nicolas's "Chronology of History."

Montiel, Spain, battle of, 14 Mch. 1369, between Peter the Cruel, king of Castile, and his brother, Henry of Trastamare, aided by the French warrior Bertrand du Guesclin. Peter was defeated, and afterwards treacherously slain.

Montlhery (*mon-la'-ree*), Seine-et-Oise, France, site of an indecisive battle between Louis XI. and a party of nobles, termed "The League of the Public Good," 16 July, 1465.

Montmar'tre, heights of, near Paris, taken by Blucher, 30 Mch 1814, fortified during the communist insurrection, Mch 1871, and retaken by the army of Versailles, 28 May

Montmirail (*mon-me-ril'*) a town of Marne, France. Here Napoleon defeated the allies, 11 Feb 1814

Montreal', the first city in Dominion of Canada built by the French, about 1642 Pop 1871, 107,225, 1891, 216 650 CANADA, FRENCH in America, NEW YORK, 1775

monument of London, built by sir Christopher Wren, 1671-77, in commemoration of the great fire Its pedestal is 40 feet high, and its total height 202 feet, the distance of its base from the spot where the fire commenced It cost about 14,500*l*. The staircase is of 345 black marble steps. Of the 4 original inscriptions, 3 were Latin, and the following in English—cut in 1681, obliterated by James II, recut in the reign of William III, and finally erased by order of the common council, 26 Jan 1831

THIS PILLAR WAS SET VP IN PERPETVAL REMEMBRANCE OF THAT MOST DREADFVL BVRNING OF THIS PROTESTANT CITY, BEGVN AND CARRYED ON BY Y^e TREACHERY AND MALICE OF Y^e POPISH FACTION, IN Y^e BEGINNING OF SEPTEM IN Y^e YEAR OF OVR LORD 1666, IN ORDER TO Y^e CARRYING ON THEIR HORRID PLOT FOR EXTIRPATING Y^e PROTESTANT RELIGION AND OLD ENGLISH LIBERTY, AND Y^e INTRODVCING POPERY AND SLAVERY

This provoked Pope's indignant lines

> "Where London's column, pointing at the skies,
> Like a tall bully, lifts the head and lies"

Several have lost their lives by falling from this monument accidentally or voluntarily Lyon Levy, a Jewish diamond-merchant, of considerable respectability, threw himself from it, 18 Jan 1810 an occurrence noted by Barham in the "Ingoldsby Legends" in 'Misadventures at Margate," viz

> "And now I'm here from this here pier it is my fixed intent
> To jump, as Mister Levi did from off the Monument' "

monuments. The principal monuments in the United States are BUNKER HILL, WASHINGTON'S, BARTHOLDI'S "LIBERTY ENLIGHTENING THE WORLD," LINCOLN'S, and GARFIELD'S Consult also BALTIMORE, BOSTON, CHICAGO, NEW YORK, OBELISK

moon, a satellite, and the only one of the earth Opacity of the moon, and the true causes of lunar eclipses, taught by Thales, 640 B C Hipparchus made observations on the moon at Rhodes, 127 B.C Posidonius accounted for the tides from the motion of the moon, and said that the moon borrows her light from the sun, 79 B.C —*Diog Laert* Its diameter is about 2162 miles, and it revolves around the earth in 27 d 7 h 43 min 11 461 sec at a mean distance of 237,300 miles, its distance varying between 253,000 and 221,600 miles, eccentricity of its orbit, mean, 0 05484, apparent diameter, 29′ 21″ and 33′ 31″, its mean diameter, 31 5″—nearly the same as the sun, 30′ Its surface is about 14,568,000 sq miles, and its volume near 5 200,000,000 cubic miles The moon's axis is nearly perpendicular to the plane of its orbit, deviating therefrom by an angle of only 1° 32′ 9″. There are therefore, properly speaking, no seasons on the moon. That the same hemisphere of the moon is constantly turned towards the earth is due to its rotation on its axis being equal to the time of its revolution in its orbit. As the moon has a slight oscillatory or balancing motion, called libration, we are enabled to see, according to Arago, $\frac{57}{100}$ of its surface, while $\frac{43}{100}$ remains always unseen When viewed with the naked eye the moon's disk shows parts much darker than others, for this conjectural causes have been given, one being the shadows cast by its immense mountain ranges, over 20,000 ft. high, and filled with volcanoes (supposed extinct) with craters large and very deep Many of these have been named, as Tycho, Kepler, Copernicus, Teneriffe, Archimedes, Pico, etc. It has no perceptible atmosphere, if any exists, it does not extend a mile above its surface It is probably without water, and therefore without animal or vegetable life Years of observations at various stations have proved that the moon has no discoverable influence on the weather Light of the moon if the whole sky was covered with full moons it would not give daylight The heat of the moon's rays is only observable by most delicate tests, and has been demonstrated by experiment within a few years, but the sun's heat at the surface of the moon, according to sir J. Herschel, is equal to 212° F, or the boiling-point of water The moon's centre of gravity does not coincide with its centre of figure, but is 33 miles farther from us according to Hansen, whose estimate is not accepted by all astronomers

Maps of the moon constructed by Hevelius, 1647, Cassini 1680
Beer and Mädler's map pub . 1834
Hansen's "Tables of the Moon," calculated at the expense of the British and Danish governments, pub by the latter 1857
Prof John Phillips invited the British Association to make arrangements to obtain a "systematic representation of the physical aspect of the moon" 1862
British Association "lunar committee" publish 2 sections of a map of the moon, on a scale of 200 inches to her diameter, July, 1867
Photographs of the moon taken by Draper at New York 1840, by Bond 1850, by Warren de la Rue, 1857, by Rutherford 1871
Earl of Rosse experiments on lunar radiation of heat 1868-73
Prof J F Julius Schmidt, of Athens, completed his map of the moon after 34 years work, diameter 2 metres 1874
Edmund Nelson pub. "The Moon, and the Conditions and Configurations of its Surface" July, 1876
Prof Schmidt's map pub at Berlin . 1878
James Nasmyth and J Carpenter pub the result of many years' observations in "The Moon," 1874, new edition 1885
Prof S P Langley, of Washington D C, published the results of experiments relative to the temperature of the moon, Nov 1887
C V Boys, of South Kensington, announced at the Royal Institution his demonstration of the heat of the moon by a very sensitive thermopile of quartz filaments, according to the anticipations of prof Piazzi Smyth 17 April et seq 1890

ECLIPSES

Moore's Creek Bridge, N C, battle at, between Americans, 1000 strong, and Tory Scotch settlers, numbering 1500, on 27 Feb. 1776 The Tories were beaten, losing 70, the Americans none

Moors, properly the natives of MAURITANIA, but Numidians and others, and now natives of Morocco and the neighborhood, are so called They often rebelled against the Roman emperors, and assisted Genseric and the Vandals in invading Africa 429 They resisted the Arab Mahometans, but were overcome in 707, and in 1019 by them introduced into Spain, where their arms were long victorious. In 1063 they were defeated in Sicily by Roger Guiscard The Moorish kingdom of Granada was set up in 1237, and lasted till 1492, when it fell before Ferdinand V of Castile, mainly owing to internal discord The expulsion of Moors from Spain was decreed by Charles V, but not fully carried out till 1609, when the bigotry of Philip III completed the work About 1518 the Moors established the piratical states of ALGIERS and TUNIS In the history of Spain, Arabs and Moors must not be confounded MOROCCO.

moral philosophy, the science of ethics, defined as knowledge of our duty, and the art of being virtuous and happy Socrates (about 430 B.C.) is regarded as father of ancient, and Grotius (about 1623) of modern ETHICS, PHILOSOPHY.

Morat', a town of Switzerland, where Charles the Bold of Burgundy was defeated by the Swiss, 22 June, 1476 A monument, made of the bones of the vanquished, was destroyed by French in 1798, and a stone column erected 400th anniversary kept, 1876

Mora'via, an Austrian province, occupied by Slavonians about 548, and conquered by Avars and Bohemians, who submitted to Charlemagne About 1000 it was subdued by Boleslas I of Poland, but recovered by Ulrich of Bohemia in 1030 After various changes, Moravia and Bohemia were united with Austria in 1526 Moravia was invaded by Prussians in 1866, who made headquarters at Brünn, the capital, 13 July The demand of the Moravians for home rule was resisted Oct 1871 Area, 8583 sq miles, pop 1890, 2,276,870

Moravians or **United Brethren,** said to have been part of the Hussites, who withdrew into Moravia in the 15th century, but the brethren refer their sect to the Greek church of the 9th century. In 1722 they formed a settlement called *Herrnhut*, "the watch of the Lord," on the estate of count Zinzendorf Their church consisted of 500 persons in 1727 They were introduced into England by count Zinzendorf about 1738, he died at Chelsea in June, 1760 In 1851 they had 32 chapels in England They are zealous missionaries, and founded settlements in foreign parts about 1732 London Association founded in 1817 In 1735 a number came over to GEORGIA, first Moravian settlement in the United States In 1738 most of these removed to Pennsylvania, owing to Georgia's trouble with Spaniards in Florida, and in 1741 founded on the Lehigh the town soon after named Bethlehem by count Zinzendorf, then for the first time in America Their labors among the Indians extended far and wide The first Indian congregation gathered by Moravians 'as at Pine Plains, Dutchess county, N. Y., at a place called he-kom-e-ko. Many Indian converts were killed by the 'hites, though not on account of their religion. OHIO, 1782; 'ENNSYLVANIA, 1763-64. According to the census of 1890, Ioravians have in the U. S. 94 churches; church property, 681,250; communicants, over 12,000.

More'a, a name given to the Peloponnesus in the 13th entury. GREECE.

Morey letter. During the presidential campaign f 1880 a letter on the Chinese question, purporting to have een written by the Republican nominee, gen. Garfield to H. L. Iorey of Lynn, Mass., was published. It asserted that indiiduals as well as companies have the right to buy labor where it is cheapest, etc. This letter appeared in New York, nd was circulated by Democratic journals. Garfield at once delared the letter a forgery. It had no influence in the election.

Morgan, William, fate of. In 1826 William Morgan nd a David C. Miller of Batavia, N. Y., announced an *exposé* f Freemasonry. Before the book was produced Morgan was rrested for a trifling debt and confined in Canandaigua jail, rom whence he was secretly taken on the night of 12 Sept. 1826, o fort Niagara, at the mouth of the Niagara river, and was ever heard of afterwards. Probably violence to a person so bscure never produced so much excitement; but the outrage vas cruel and wanton. An earnest attempt was made to discover the perpetrators, but without success. Such was the eeling against the order of Freemasons, that it created a poitical party antagonistic to it (Anti-masonic) which nomiated state and national tickets, 1829-31. See "Thurlow Veed's Autobiography," pp. 210-335.

Morgan's raid through Kentucky, Indiana, and Ohio.

ohn H. Morgan, confederate, starts from Sparta, Tenn., with between 3000 and 4000 cavalry and several guns....27 June, 1863
Captures the 20th Kentucky at Lebanon, Ky...........5 July, "
Crosses the Ohio at Brandenburg, about 40 miles below Louisville, and enters Indiana...........................7 July, "
At Salem, Ind., defeats "Home Guards"..............9 July, "
Crosses into Ohio at Harrison and passes north of Cincinnati, 13-14 July, "
Attempts to recross into Kentucky at Buffington island, near Parkersburg, but is prevented by gun-boats and cavalry; leaves his guns, wagons, and 600 prisoners.........19 July, "
At Belleville, Morgan again attempts to cross the river, and some 300 of his men succeed by swimming their horses; but are closely pursued, and more than 1000 of his force surrender; Morgan, with the remnant, pushes inland to Eastport; they are captured near New Lisbon, Columbiana county, by cavalry under gen. Shackelford.................26 July, "
Morgan and several officers are confined in the penitentiary at Columbus; he and 7 others escape by digging.....26 Nov. "
During this raid there were 4 skirmishes in Indiana, 12 in Ohio, and one engagement with a loss of 19 killed and 47 wounded of the U. S. troops; there were called out on this occasion 49,000 militia in Ohio, at a cost to the state of $212,318. The principal pursuers were brig.-gen. James M. Shackelford, brig.-gen. Henry M. Judah, and brig.-gen. Edward H. Hobson. TENNESSEE, 1864.

morganat'ic (said to be derived from *Morgengabe*, he gift of a husband of a limited part of his property to such bride on the morning after the marriage) **marriages,** when the left hand is given instead of the right, between a nan of superior and a woman of inferior rank, and it is stipuated that she and her children shall not enjoy the rank or nherit the possessions of the former. The children are legitmate. Such marriages are frequently contracted in Germany by royalty and the higher nobility. It has been asserted that George I. of England was thus married to the duchess of Kendal; the duke of Sussex to lady Cecilia Underwood, Frederic VI. of Denmark to the countess of Danner, 7 Aug. 1850; and several Austrian princes recently.

Morgar'ten, Switzerland. 1300 Swiss defeated 20,000 Austrians under duke Leopold, 15 Nov. 1315, on the heights of Morgarten, overlooking the defile through which the enemy was to enter their territory from Zug. SWITZERLAND.

morice-dance, an ancient dance peculiar to some country parts of England, and, it is said, also to Scotland; performed before James I. in Herefordshire.

Mormons (calling themselves the Church of Jesus Christ of Latter-day Saints), a sect founded by Joseph Smith, alled the Prophet, who announced in 1823, at Palmyra, N. Y., hat he had had a vision of the angel Moroni. In 1827 he aid that he found the Book of Mormon, written on gold plates in Egyptian characters. This book is said to have bee[n written] about 1812 by a clergyman named Solomon Spauldin[g] ... Martin Harris, who died Sept. 1875), as a religious roma[nce in] imitation of the Scripture style. NEW YORK, 1830; OHIO, ... It was published in America in 1830, in England in 1841. It fell into the hands of Rigdon and Smith, who determined to palm it off as a new revelation. The Mormons command payment of tithes, permit and enjoin polygamy, encourage labor, and believe in miracles wrought by their leaders. Missionaries have propagated these doctrines in Europe with much success.

Mormons organize a church at Manchester, N. Y.......6 Apr. 1830
Settle at Kirtland, O., where they number 1000 in............ 1831
They found Zion, in Jackson county, Mo..................1831-32
From 1833 to 1839 the sect endured persecution, driven from place to place, till the city Nauvoo, Ill., on the Mississippi, was laid out, 1837, and a temple built...................1840-41
Joseph Smith and his brother Hyrum, in prison on a charge of treason, shot by an infuriated mob, and Brigham Young chosen seer.......................................June, 1844
Much harassed by neighbors; departure from Nauvoo determined on.. 1845
Great Salt lake chosen "for an everlasting abode," and taken possession of (UTAH)...........................24 July, 1847

Morocco or **Marocco,** an empire in N. Africa, formerly MAURITANIA. In 1051 it was subdued for the Fatimite caliphs by the Almoravides, who eventually extended their dominion into Spain. These were succeeded by the Almohades (1121), the Merinites (1270), and in 1516 by the Scherifs, pretended descendants of Mahomet, the now reigning dynasty. The Moors have had frequent wars with Spaniards and Portuguese, due to piracy. Area, 219,000 sq. miles; pop. about 9,000,000.

Invasion of Sebastian of Portugal, who perishes with his army at the battle of Alcazar..............................4 Aug. 1578
TANGIERS acquired by England, 1662; given up.............. 1683
Moors attack the French in Algeria, instigated by Abd el Kader; prince de Joinville bombards Tangiers, 6 Aug., and Mogador, 16 Aug. 1844
Marshal Bugeaud defeats Moors at the river Isly, and acquires title of duke......................................14 Aug. "
Peace between France and Morocco.................10 Sept. "
Spaniards, who possess several places on the coast of Morocco (Ceuta, Peñon de Velez, Melilla, etc.), annoyed by Moorish pirates, declare war..............................22 Oct. 1859
Negotiations fruitless; Spaniards increasing demands as sultan yielded; Britain interfered in vain (SPAIN)..........1859-60
A Moorish ambassador (the first since Charles II.) in London (gave 200*l.* to lord mayor for London charities)...June-Aug. 1860
British government guarantee loan of 426,000*l.* to the sultan to meet engagements with Spain..........................24 Oct. 1861
Affray between Moors and Spanish cavalry of the fortress Melilla; several killed, 20 July; peace restored........25 July, 1890
Spanish garrison at Melilla attacked by Moors (Riffians).3 Oct. 1893
Garrison reinforced by troops from Spain...............7 Oct. "
Continued fighting about the town................Oct.-Nov. "
Spanish government rejects the sultan's terms for peace, 24 Nov. "
Spanish government requires guarantees for future peace; indemnity of 25,000,000 pesetas for loss of life and cost of war.8 Dec. "
Agreed to by the Moorish government................21 Dec. "
New treaty between Spain and Morocco provides for a neutral zone and the punishment of the Riffians who caused the trouble at Melilla...................................6 Mch. 1894
Sultan Muley-Hassan d. 7 June; succeeded by his youngest son, Abdul-Aziz.. "

[Succession not contested, as threatened by Muley-Ismail, brother of the late sultan.]

SULTANS.

Muley-Soliman.. 1794-1822
Muley-Abderahman..................................... 1822-1859
Sidi-Muley-Mohammed.................................. 1859-1873
Muley-Hassan... 1873-1894
Abdul-Aziz... 1894-

morphia, an alkaloid, discovered in opium by Sertürner in 1803.

Morrill tariff, so called from its author, Justin S. Morrill, M. C. from Vermont, who introduced the bill in Congress. TARIFF; UNITED STATES, 1860.

mortar, a short cannon with a large bore and short chamber for throwing bombs; said to have been used at Naples in 1435, and first made in England in 1543. On 19 Oct. 1857, a colossal mortar, constructed by Robert Mallet, was tried at Woolwich, Engl.; with a charge of 70 pounds it threw a shell weighing 2550 pounds $1\frac{1}{2}$ miles horizontally, and about $\frac{1}{4}$ mile in height.

Mortimer's Cross, Herefordshire, battle of. The earl of Pembroke and Lancastrians were here defeated by the young duke of York, afterwards Edward IV., 2 Feb. 1461. He assumed the throne in Mch. following.

cher, 30 Mch. Mch. 1871; Mont Here N

tmain acts (*mort main*, dead hand). When the ngland was surveyed by William I., 1085–86, the whole nd to amount to 62,215 knights' fees, of which the church ssed 28,015, besides later additions, till the 7th of Edward I. 1279, when the statute of mortmain was passed, from jealousy of the growing wealth of the church. It forbade gifts of estates to the church without the king's leave; and this prohibition was extended to all lay fraternities, or corporations, in the 15th of Richard II. 1391. The word "mortmain" is applied to such tenure of property as prevents alienation. Several statutes have been passed on the subject; legacies in mortmain were especially restricted by the 9 of Geo. II. c. 36 (1736).

mosaic-work (the Roman *opus tessellatum*) is of Asiatic origin, and is probably referred to in Esther i. 6, about 519 B.C. It had attained excellence in Greece in the time of Alexander and his successors, when Sosos of Pergamos, the most renowned mosaic artist of antiquity, flourished. He acquired fame by accurate representation of an "unswept floor after a feast." The Romans also excelled in mosaics, as evidenced by the innumerable specimens preserved. Byzantine *mosaics date from the 4th century* A.D. The art was revived in Italy by Tafi, Gaddi, Cimabue, and Giotto, who designed mosaics, and introduced a higher style in the 13th century. In the 16th century Titian and Veronese designed subjects for this art. Practice of copying paintings in mosaics came into vogue in the 17th century; and there is now a workshop in the Vatican where chemical science is employed in producing colors, and 20,000 different tints are kept. In 1861, dr. Salviati of Venice had established his manufacture of "enamel mosaics;" and in July, 1864, he fixed a large enamel mosaic picture in one of the spandrils under the dome of St. Paul's cathedral, London.

Moscow (*mos'kō*), the ancient capital of Russia, was founded, it is said, by Dolgorouki, about 1147. The occupation of the south of Russia by the Mongols in 1235 led to Moscow becoming the capital, and, beginning with Jaroslav II., 1238, its princes became the reigning dynasty. It is regarded as a holy city by the Russians. Pop. 1884, 753,469.

Cathedral of the Assumption built, 1326; of the Transfiguration, 1328
Kremlin founded 1367
Moscow plundered by Timour 1382
By the Tartars 1451, 1477
Massacre of Demetrius and his Polish adherents, the "Matins of Moscow" .... 27 May, 1606
Moscow ravaged by Ladislas of Poland 1611
University founded 1705
Entered by Napoleon I. and the French, 14 Sept.; the governor, Rostopchin, is said, doubtfully, to have ordered it set on fire (11,840 houses burned, besides palaces and churches), 15 Sept. 1812
French evacuate Moscow, and begin retreat .... 15 Oct. "

[Before the pursuit ceased in Dec., over 300,000 of the French army was lost as prisoners, killed, or died of cold and hunger.]

Mosquito Coast, Central America, lying east of the state of Nicaragua, with a coast line of about 250 miles on the Caribbean sea. The Indians of this coast were long under protection of the British, who held Belize and a group of islands in the bay of Honduras. The jealousy of the United States was aroused. In Apr. 1850, the 2 governments covenanted not "to occupy or fortify or colonize, or assume or exercise any dominion over, any part of Central America." In 1855 the U. S. charged the British government with infraction of the treaty; but the latter agreed to cede the disputed territory to Honduras, with some reservation. The matter was settled in 1859. NICARAGUA.

moss-troopers, desperate plunderers, and lawless soldiers secreting themselves in mosses on the borders of Scotland. In spite of severe laws they were not extirpated till the 18th century.

"A stark moss-trooping Scot was he,
As e'er couch'd border-lance by knee;
. . . .
Five times outlawed had he been
By England's king and Scotland's queen."—*Scott.*

motets, short pieces of church music, some of which are dated about the end of the 13th century. Good motets were written between 1430 and 1480; and very fine ones in the 16th and 17th centuries. The "Motet Society," for the publication of these, was founded in 1847, by William Dyce.

Mother Goose's melodies. MASSACHUSETTS, 1715.

motion, an expression of energy. HEAT. On 13 Nov. 1873, prof. Sylvester described to the London Mathematical Society a machine for converting spherical into rectilinear and other motions, and for producing perfectly parallel motion, the discovery of M. Peaucellier, a French engineer officer, about 1867. KINEMATICS.

motor, a source or originator of mechanical power. ELECTRICITY; KEELY MOTOR.

motto. A short sentence or phrase added to a device or to an essay or discourse, indicating its aim or describing some rule of conduct.

MOTTO OF THE UNITED STATES AND OF THE POLITICAL DIVISIONS OF THE UNION, WITH DATE OF ADOPTION OF SEAL.

State.	Adopted.	Motto.
United States	20 June, 1782	E pluribus unum. (Many in one.)
Alabama	29 Dec. 1868	Here we rest.
Alaska	....	None.
Arizona	1863	Ditat Deus. (God enriches.)
Arkansas	3 May, 1864	Regnant populi. (The people rule.)
California	....	Eureka. (I have found it.)
Colorado	1861	Nil sine numine. (Nothing without God.)
Connecticut	Oct. 1842	Sustinet qui transtulit. (He who transplanted still sustains.)
Delaware	....	Liberty and independence.
Dist. of Columbia,	....	Justitia omnibus. (Justice to all.)
Florida	1846	In God we trust.
Georgia	5 Dec. 1799	Wisdom, justice, moderation.
Idaho	5 Mch. 1866	Salve. (Welcome, or hail.)
Illinois	26 Aug. 1818	State sovereignty—National union.
Indiana	....	None.
Iowa	25 Feb. 1847	Our liberties we prize, and our rights we will maintain.
Kansas	29 Jan. 1861	Ad astra per aspera. (To the stars through difficulties.)
Kentucky	20 Dec. 1792	United we stand, divided we fall.
Louisiana	....	Union, justice, and confidence.
Maine	9 Jan. 1820	Dirigo. (I direct.)
Maryland	12 Aug. 1648	Fatti maschi parole femine. (Manly deeds and womanly words.) Scuto bonæ voluntatis tuæ coronasti nos. (With the shield of Thy good-will Thou hast covered us.)
Massachusetts	13 Dec. 1780	Ense petit placidam sub libertate quietem. (With the sword she seeks quiet peace under liberty.)
Michigan	1835	Si quæris peninsulam amœnam circumspice. (If thou seekest a beautiful peninsula, behold it here.)
Minnesota	1858	Etoile du nord. (The star of the north.)
Mississippi	....	None.
Missouri	11 Jan. 1822	Salus populi suprema lex esto. (The welfare of the people is the supreme law.)
Montana	24 May, 1864	Oro y plata. (Gold and silver.)
Nebraska	1 Mch. 1867	Equality before the law.
Nevada	24 Feb. 1866	All for our country.
New Hampshire ..	11 Feb. 1785	None.
New Jersey	3 Oct. 1776	Liberty and prosperity.
New Mexico	9 Sept. 1850	Crescit eundo. (It increases by going.)
New York	1809	Excelsior. (Higher, more elevated.)
North Carolina ...	1893	Esse quam videri. (To be rather than to seem.)
North Dakota	....	Liberty and union, one and inseparable, now and forever.
Ohio	6 Apr. 1866	Imperium in imperio. (A government within a government.)
Oregon	1857	The Union.
Pennsylvania	2 Mch. 1809	Virtue, liberty, and independence.
Rhode Island	1664	Hope.
South Carolina ...	....	Dum spiro, spero. (While I breathe I hope.)
South Dakota	....	Under God the people rule.
Tennessee	1796	Agriculture, commerce.
Texas	....	None.
Utah	....	"
Vermont	Sept. 1866	Freedom and unity.
Virginia	Oct. 1779	Sic semper tyrannis. (Thus always to tyrants.)
Washington	1853	Al-ki. (By and by.)
West Virginia	26 Sept. 1863	Montani semper liberi. (Mountaineers always freemen.)
Wisconsin	....	Forward.
Wyoming	1868	Cedant arma togæ. (Let arms yield to the gown.)

mottoes, Royal *Dieu et mon Droit*, first used by ichard I, 1198 *Ich dien*, "I serve," adopted by Edward the Black Prince at the battle of Cressy, 1346 *Honi soit qui mal pense*, the motto of the Garter, 1349 *Je maintiendrai*, "I vill maintain," adopted by William III, to which he added, n 1688, "the liberties of England and the Protestant relig-on" *Semper eadem* was assumed by queen Elizabeth, 1558, nd adopted by queen Anne, 1702

Mound Builders, a people who at an unknown eriod inhabited the country from the Great Lakes to the gulf f Mexico The only traces left by them are extensive mounds, hence the name The remains of these earthworks are nu-nerous north of the Ohio river, and especially in the state of Ohio, where there are supposed to be more than 10,000 mounds nd 2000 earth-enclosures, many of them extensive The most oted are found in Adams, Butler, Licking, Montgomery, Pike, Ross, and Washington counties This ancient race eems to have occupied nearly the whole basin of the Mis-issippi and its tributaries, as well as the fertile plains along he gulf There is great diversity of opinion as to their origin, ate, degree of civilization, etc, but decisive evidence on hese questions is lacking SERPENT MOUND

Mountain Meadow. MASSACRES, UTAH

mountains. The Himalaya (abode of snow) range, orth of India, are the loftiest mountains on the globe Mount verest—so named from sir Geo Everest—is supposed to be he highest point of the earth's surface, 29,002 feet, another eak, recently measured, reaches 28,278 ft, Kinchinjinga, 8,156 ft, Dhawalagiri, 26,826, and Naudadevi, 25,700 ft Iany other points have been measured exceeding 25,000 ft, nd the enumeration of all known peaks over 20,000 ft would e wearisome "It will not be surprising if peaks are event ally discovered in this range exceeding 30,000 ft. in height" —*Encycl Brit* 9th ed In North America an elevation of 0,000 feet is not reached east of 104° W lon The follow-g is a list of 10 of the highest peaks west of 104° of lon. 1) Mount St. Elias (Alaska), 19,500 ft, (2) mount Cook Alaska), 16,000 ft, (3) mount Crillon (Alaska), 15,900 ft., 4) mount Fairweather (Alaska), 15,500 ft, also mount Jeffer-on (Washington), same height, (5) mount Whitney, Cal, 4,898, (6) mount Harvard, Col, 14,452, (7) Fisherman's Peak, Cal., 14,448, (8) mount Rainier, Washington, 14,444, 9) mount Shasta, Cal., 14,412, (10) Uncompahgre, Col, 14,408 n all, there are 412 elevations of 10,000 ft and over in western Iorth America, of which the 10 mentioned above are the high-st.—"United States Geological Survey," compiled by Henry Gannett, 1884 ALPS, ANDES, APPALACHIAN, VOLCANOES.

mounts. BERNARD, CALVARY, ETNA, HECLA, MOUN-AINS, OLIVET, VESUVIUS, VOLCANOES

mourning for the dead. Israelites neither vashed nor anointed themselves during mourning, which for friend lasted 7 days, on extraordinary occasions a month Greeks and Romans fasted White was used in mourning for he imperial family at Constantinople, 323 The ordinary color or mourning in Europe is black, in China, white, in Turkey, iolet, in Ethiopia, brown; white in Spain until 1498 Anne f Brittany, queen of 2 successive kings of France, mourned in lack instead of white, then the custom, when her first hus-and, Charles VIII, died, 7 Apr 1498 —*Hénault*.

mousquetaires (*mous ke-tairs'*) or **musketeers,** orse-soldiers under the old French *régime*, raised by Louis III, 1622 This corps was considered a military school for he French nobility. It was disbanded in 1646, but was re-tored in 1657 A second company was created in 1660, and ormed cardinal Mazarin's guard —*Hénault*

Mozambique (*mo-zam-beek'*), chief of the Portu-uese territories, E Africa, was visited by Vasco de Gama, 498, conquered by Portuguese under Tristan da Cunha and lbuquerque, 1506, a settlement was established, 1508 By decree of 30 Sept 1891, the colony of Mozambique was onstituted as the free state of E Africa, and divided into 2 rovinces, Mozambique and Zambezi The area of this state 300,000 sq miles, and it extends along the coast from cape Delgado southward 1400 miles The city of Mozambique is n a small coral islet close to the mainland

Mud campaign. FREDERICKSBURG, Battle of.

"mud-sills." UNITED STATES, 1858, speech of Ham-mond of South Carolina

Muggleto'nians, a sect so called from Lodowic Mug-gleton, a tailor known about 1641, prominent about 1650, con-victed of blasphemy, Jan 1676. died 1697 He and John Reeve affirmed that God the Father, leaving the government of heaven to Elias, came down and suffered death in a human form They asserted that they were the two last witnesses of God who should appear before the end of the world, Rev xi 3 This sect existed 1850, the last member died in 1868.

Mugwump (Algonquin, *Mugquomp*), signifying, in Eliot's translation of the Bible into the Indian tongue (1661), chief, leader, or captain It was applied generally to Inde-pendent Republicans, especially to those who opposed Blaine in the national canvass of 1884 (probably used first in this sense in the New York *Sun*, 15 June, 1884) The word pleased the pop-ular fancy, and is often heard as a term of reproach for those who are supposed to fail in loyalty to party, sometimes as an hon-orable epithet of independent voters. POLITICAL PARTIES

Muhlberg, a town on the Elbe, Prussia Here Charles V, emperor, defeated the German Protestants, 24 Apr 1547, and captured John Frederick, elector of Saxony

Mühldorf, a town of Bavaria Near this place Fred-erick, duke of Austria, was defeated and taken prisoner by Louis of Bavaria, 28 Sept 1322

mulberry-trees (Gr μορον or μορέα), hence the bo-tanical name *Morus*, first introduced into England from Italy, about 1548 As the silk-worm thrives upon the leaves of the white mulberry, that variety is cultivated wherever the silk culture is carried on, notably in China and southern Europe. The fruit (berry) of the black and red species, the latter a na-tive of the United States, is agreeable to the taste Shake-speare planted a mulberry-tree with his own hands at Stratford-upon-Avon, and Garrick, Macklin, and others were entertained under it in 1742 Shakespeare's house was afterwards sold to Gastrel, a clergyman, who cut down the tree for fuel, 1765 A silversmith purchased it, and manufactured it into memorials. FLOWERS AND PLANTS.

mule, a hybrid animal generated between a jackass and a mare, if between a stallion and a she-ass it is called a *hinny*. With the mule, procreation ceases.—Also, a spinning-machine invented in 1779 by Samuel Crompton, born at Bolton, Lanca-shire, in 1753, so called from combining the advantages of Hargreaves' spinning-jenny and Arkwright's adaptation It is said that Crompton at the time knew nothing of the latter He did not patent his invention, but gave it up in 1780 It produced yarn treble the fineness and much softer than any before produced in England Parliament voted him 5000*l* in 1812, now considered a most inadequate compensation Mr. Roberts invented the *self-acting* mule in 1825

mummies (from Arab *mum*, wax) The process of mummification or embalming the dead as performed by the Egyptians, occupying from 70 to 72 days, was accompanied with ritualistic ceremonies, fully described on recently dis-covered papyri, now known as the "BOOK OF THE DEAD" It was formerly supposed that embalming was not practised in Egypt before 2000 B C, but recent explorations set back the art to 3800 or even to 4000 B C The most ancient mummies, or at least desiccated human remains, not prehistoric, which are now known are fragments of the body of Menkara, third king of Dynasty IV, and builder of the smallest of the 3 pyr-amids of Gizeh. They are now in the British museum, as-signed to about 4000 B C Next in antiquity comes the mummy of king Merenra, of Dynasty VI, now in the Bulak museum, date, 3800 B.C The most famous and interesting of all are the 36 royal mummies of Dynasties XVII, XVIII, XIX, and XXI, found in a vast tomb of the high-priests of Amen, at Dair al Bahari, on the left bank of the Nile opposite Karnak, July, 1881, more than 20 of them kings and queens; found with 4 royal papyri and other treasures, in all above 6000 objects They are now in the Bulak museum. Em-balming among the Egyptians ceased about 700 A.D

Mun'da, now **Monda,** a town of S. Spain Here Cneius Scipio defeated the Carthaginians, 216 B.C., and here Julius Cæsar defeated the sons of Pompey, 17 Mch 45 B.C., in a desperate action It is said that after the battle Cæsar told his friends that he had often fought for victory, but this was the first time he had fought for his life.

Mundane eras. That of Alexandria fixed the creation at 5502 B.C. This computation continued till 284 A.D., Alex. era 5786; but in 285 A.D. 10 years were subtracted, and 5787 became 5777. This coincided with the Mundane era of Antioch (which dated the creation 5492 B.C.).—*Nicholas.*

Mu'nich (Ger. *München*), capital of Bavaria, founded by duke Henry of Saxony, 962, was taken by Gustavus Adolphus of Sweden in 1632, by the Austrians in 1704, 1741, and 1743; and by the French under Moreau, 2 July, 1800. It abounds in schools, institutions, and manufactories. The university was founded by king Louis in 1826. Pop. 1871, 169,693; 1875, 198,829; 1890, 348,317.

murder, the highest offence against the law of God (Gen. ix. 6, 2348 B.C.). A court of Ephetæ was established by Demophoön of Athens for the trial of murder, 1179 B.C. The Persians did not punish the first offence. In England, during a period of the heptarchy, murder was punished by fines only. In the laws of Alfred is found the earliest recognition of the criminal consequences of homicide apart from the damage to be paid to the relatives of the deceased or compensation to the person whose peace had been broken. So late as Henry VIII.'s time the crime was compounded for in Wales. Murderers were allowed benefit of clergy in 1503. It was aggravated murder, or *petit treason* (a distinction now abolished), when a servant killed his master, a wife her husband, or an ecclesiastical person his superior (stat. 25 Edw. III. 1350). Under English law the unlawful killing of a human being is either murder or manslaughter; murder being unlawful homicide with malice aforethought, and manslaughter unlawful homicide without malice aforethought. In the United States the statutes seek to discriminate between the graver and less serious forms of the crime as 1st and 2d, etc., degrees of murder, and some states define degrees of manslaughter as well. ASSASSINS, CRIME, EXECUTIONS, TRIALS.

Muret (*moo-rä'*), a town of S. France. Here the Albigenses, under the count of Thoulouse, were defeated by Simon de Montfort, and their ally Peter of Aragon killed, 12 Sept. 1213.

Murfreesborough or **Stone River,** Tenn., Battle of. During Dec. 1862, the Federal army of 41,421 infantry, 3266 cavalry, and 2223 artillery, with 150 guns, under maj.-gen. Wm. S. Rosecrans (BRAGG'S KENTUCKY CAMPAIGN), lay at Nashville, Tenn., while between 35,000 and 40,000 confederates, under gen. Braxton Bragg, lay partly at Murfreesborough, about 30 miles southeast of Nashville, and partly at Triune, about 15 miles west of Murfreesborough. The federals advanced Friday, 26 Dec. On the evening of 30 Dec. both armies were in battle order, the confederates lying across a stream called Stone river, easily fordable, about 3 miles from Murfreesborough. Rosecrans's plan was to attack the Confederate right, early on the 31st, but before this movement accomplished anything Bragg anticipated it, attacked the Federal right under gen. McCook, and drove it from its position as early as 10 A.M. This disaster baffled Rosecrans's plan and endangered his whole army. By reinforcing the right from the left wing he re-established his line almost at a right angle with the left, and held the ground till night. But the condition of the federals was serious; they had lost much ground on the right and centre, though the left had repelled every attack; had lost 28 guns, 3000 prisoners, camp provisions, ammunition, etc., and their rear was threatened by the Confederate cavalry; several brigade and regimental commanders had fallen, and many regiments were weakened almost to dissolution. Rosecrans, however, held his position ready to meet the confederates again the next day. All day (1 Jan. 1863) both armies were inactive. On the 2d Rosecrans resumed his effort to turn the Confederate right; Bragg met the movement by pushing forward Breckinridge's division, which attacked at 4 P.M., at first successfully, compelling the federals to fall back across the river; but the success was transient, and the Confederate advance was driven back, with a loss of 1500 men and 4 pieces of artillery. The federals immediately reoccupied the ground and threw up temporary breastworks. Bragg, unable to dislodge Rosecrans, retired from his position 3 Jan. and occupied Murfreesborough, but evacuated it on 5 Jan., and fell back to the line of Duck river, leaving the field to the federals, who claimed a victory. The retreat was ordered by Bragg, according to his official report, under the impression that Rosecrans had received large reinforcements. Federal loss was 1533 killed, 7245 wounded, and 3000 prisoners; Confederate loss equal, if not greater, in killed and wounded. In the critical condition of affairs in the northern states at this time the moral effect of this battle was highly favorable to the Union cause. TULLAHOMA CAMPAIGN.

Muscat', now **Oman,** an Arab state on the gulf of Oman, was conquered by the Portuguese under Albuquerque in 1507, but recovered by the Arabs in 1648. Oman is practically on the footing of an independent Indian native state, and essentially under British protection. Area, 82,000 sq. miles; pop. 1,500,000. Capital, Muscat; pop. 60,000.

Ahmad bin Sa'id repelled a Persian invasion, and founded present dynasty 1741

muse'um (Gr. Μουσεῖον, the temple of the Muses; seat or haunt of the Muses; hence also a place of study, a school). The museum, a spot within the old walls of Athens where Musaeus, a Greek poet of the mythic age, son of Eumolpus and Selene of Athens, sang and was buried. Also a part of the palace of Alexandria, like the Prytaneum of Athens, where eminent learned men were maintained by the public. The foundation is attributed to Ptolemy Philadelphus, who here placed his library about 280 B.C. BRITISH MUSEUM.

music (Gr. μουσική) to the Greeks included all the arts and sciences presided over by the Muses, and in its most comprehensive sense denoted the entire mental training of a Greek youth. It is properly a language of the emotions or passions made manifest in harmonious sounds, and is developed by the science which treats of the properties and relations of sounds and the principles of harmony. St. Cecilia, a Christian martyr of the 2d century, said to have enticed an angel from the celestial regions by her melody, has long been considered the patron saint of music.

> "But bright Cecilia raised the wonder higher;
> When to her organ vocal breath was given
> An angel heard and straight appeared,
> Mistaking earth for heaven."
> —*Dryden*, "St. Cecilia's Day."

Jubal (3875 B.C., Gen. iv. 21) is called "the father of all such as handle the harp and organ." The flute and harmony, or concord in music, are said to have been invented by Hyagnis, 1506 B.C.—*Arund. Marbles.* Pythagoras (about 555 B.C.) maintained that the motions of the 12 spheres must produce delightful sounds, inaudible to mortal ears, which he called "the music of the spheres." Vocal choruses of men are first mentioned 556 B.C.—*Dufresnoy.*

Pope Sylvester institutes a singing-school at Rome......about 330

St. Ambrose, archbishop of Milan, arranges the 4 diatonic scales known as "authentic modes," and introduces CHANTING....350-70

Pope Gregory the Great adds to the authentic modes the "four plagal modes" (the 8 together are known as the "Gregorian modes") and adds tones to the Ambrosian chant..........590-604

Schools of church music established in France and Germany by trained teachers sent from Rome..........604-752

Organs introduced into churches by pope Vitalianus..........657-72

Troubadours appear in Provence, in south of France.......... 800

Hucbald, a Flemish monk, invents a system of scales, and publishes it in his "Enchiridion Musicæ".......... 930

Guido d'Arezzo, called "Inventor Musicæ," founds the system of musical notation upon which our present method is based, and invents the terms *ut, re, mi, fa, sol, la*.......990-1050

[Many fallacies are still entertained as to the dated organization of music in the church, and none greater than its ascription to St. Ambrose and pope Gregory, and the credit given Guido for the enunciation of its rules. From the end of the 10th century music in England was in advance of other nations, and remained so until its rise in Flanders in the 15th century, and even then the English kept abreast of their contemporaries.—*Encycl. Brit.*, "Music," 9th ed.]

Franco of Cologne invents "rests" in music and a system of musical measure of time by shape of the notes.......... 1220

Adam de la Halle and other troubadours flourish in England, Spain, and Italy, and minnesingers in Germany........1200-1300

Introduction of florid counterpoints ascribed to Jean de Muers, about 1330

Italy becomes the musical centre of Europe..........about 1400

Guillaume Dufay of the Belgian school, chapel-master at Rome, harmonizes melodies for 4 voices, and perfects the notes as now used (?)..........1380-1430

Organ pedal introduced by Bernhardt at Venice.......... 1490

Petrucci, an Italian, invents movable music types.......... 1502

Virginal, a small keyed instrument, comes into use.......... 1520

Claude Goudimel (c. 1510-72), a Fleming, opens the first school for musical tuition at Rome..........about 1540

Orlando di Lasso, last of the Belgian school, introduces the chromatic element into musical composition..........1520-94

"Chorale" introduced by Luther in Germany 1524

Conservatory at Naples founded 1535

Christopher Tye receives the degree of Doctor in Music from the University of Cambridge 1545

"*Old Hundred*" written 1551

Palestrina arranges his celebrated "Missa Papae Marcelli" for 6 voices—soprano, alto, 1st and 2d tenor, 1st and 2d bass—first sung in the Sixtine chapel June, 1556

Palestrina completes the divorce of secular airs from church music, and his 3 masses are accepted by a commission of cardinals appointed by the Council of Trent 1565

Violins introduced into England 1577

Society formed in Florence to revive the ancient Greek art of musical drama about 1580

First opera produced in Florence, entitled "Dafne," libretto by *Giulio Caccini*, music by Peri 1594

Ludovico Viadana, first composer to write harmony as distinguished from pure counterpoint, and to use "figured bass" 1560–1625

First oratorio of note, "l'Anima e Corpo," by Emilio del Cavalieri, performed at Rome 1600

[The oratorio dates its existence and name from the meetings held by San Filippo Neri in the oratory of his church in Rome for religious exercise and pious edification. 1540.]

Thorough bass invented by Peri about "

Renowned collection of madrigals, dedicated to queen Elizabeth by *Thomas Morley* and others and known as "The Triumphs of Oriana" pub 1601

Monteverde brings out at the court of Mantua his opera "Arianna" 1607

Harpsichords introduced into England about 1610

Giacomo Carissimi invents the "arioso," which later on develops into the "aria" 1660

Lully establishes the French grand opera 1672

First English opera produced, title "Psyche," author Matthew Lock 1673

Si, as a name for the 7th note of the modern scale, introduced about 1675

Publication of dr William Holder's "Treatise on Harmony" 1694

Double bass, said to have been invented by Salo, in 1580, introduced into the orchestra by Monteclair 1696

Equal tempered system of tuning introduced by Werckmeister and Bach about 1700

Handel's first opera, "Almira," produced at Hamburg 1705

Italian opera introduced into England, "Arsinoë" performed at Drury Lane 1706

Swell organ first introduced by *Jordan* 1712

Handel's first oratorio, "Esther," produced in England 1720

Gay's "Beggar's Opera" first performed at Lincoln's Inn theatre 1727

Royal Society of Musicians (charitable organization) founded in England 19 Apr 1738

Madrigal society, oldest vocal musical association in Europe, founded in England by John Immyns 1741

Gluck's first opera, "Artaxerxes" produced at Milan "

Emmanuel Bach first introduces a system of fingering for the harpsichord in which the thumb is used 1753

PIANOFORTE originating in ideas of Cristofali in 1711, and others coincidently, comes into popular favor 1760

Gluck's "*Orfeo*" produced, Vienna 1762

Mozart's opera, "Idomeneo," produced at Munich 1781

Double bassoon first introduced into the orchestra at the Handel Commemoration in Westminster abbey 1784

Mozart produces "Figaro," 1786, "Don Giovanni," 1787, "Magic Flute" (Zauberflöte) and "Requiem" 1791

Claude J Rouget de Lisle composes Marseillaise hymn 24 Apr 1792

Conservatoire de Musique established in Paris by the Convention Nationale 3 Aug 1795

Haydn's "Creation" composed 1796–98, first performed at Covent Garden, London 28 Mch 1800

Beethoven's "*Fidelo*" with the Leonoré overture produced at Vienna 1805

Royal Conservatorio of Milan opened 8 Sept 1808

Modern metronome invented by John Maelzel 1816

First performance of Spohr's "Faust" at Prague "

First musical journal in England, the *Quarterly Musical Magazine and Review*, pub 1818–28

Weber's "Der Freischütz" and "Preciosa" produced 1820

Royal Academy of Music founded at London 1822

Donizetti's "*Lucia di Lammermoor*" produced at Naples 1835

Meyerbeer's "Robert le Diable," 1831, and "Les Huguenots" produced 1836

Publication of the *Musical World* begun in England "

Wagner's "Rienzi" produced at Dresden 1842

Conservatory at Leipsic opened 1 Apr 1843

Tonic *sol-fa* system, in which the letters *d, r, m, f, s, l, t* (for *do, re, mi, fa, so, la, ti*, or *si*) are used instead of notes, was invented by Miss Glover of Norwich, and improved by rev John Curwen about 1844

Wagner's "Tannhäuser" produced at Dresden 1845

Mendelssohn produces "*Elijah*" 1846

Royal Irish Academy of Music founded 1848

Verdi produces "Il Trovator" at Rome, and "La Traviata" at Venice 1853

Conservatory at Stuttgart founded 1857

"Popular Monday concerts" at St James hall, London, founded by S A Chappell, commence with a "Mendelssohn night." 14 Feb 1859

Great Handel musical festival at Crystal palace, London, on the centenary of his death, commencing (HANDEL'S COMMEMORATIONS) 20 June, "

First public appearance of Miss Christine Nilsson in "La Traviata" 27 Oct. 1864

College of organists founded "

Wagner's "Tristan und Isolde" produced at Munich 1865

Wagner Society in London gave concerts to introduce Wagner's "Musik der Zukunft" (the due combination of music and poetry) Feb 1873

Musical Association for the Investigation and Discussion of Subjects connected with the Art and Science of Music founded by messrs Spottiswoode, Wheatstone, Tyndall, G A Macfarren, J Hullah, Sedley Taylor, Stone, Pole, Chappell, Barnby, and others in England 16 Apr 1874

An orchestra supplied with wind instruments made of terra cotta appeared in London "

Bizet's "Carmen" first produced at Paris 3 Mch 1875

Tonic Sol fa Association in England founded 1853, the college established 1862 by rev John Curwen, chartered

Wagner's "Lohengrin" performed at Covent Garden, 8 May, at Drury Lane, 14 June, 1875; "Tannhauser" performed at Covent Garden 29 Apr 1876

Three series of performances of Wagner's "Ring des Nibelungen," in 4 parts ("Rheingold," "Walküre," "Siegfried," and "Götterdämmerung"), at Bayreuth before the emperors of Germany and Brazil, king of Bavaria and other sovereigns and princes 13 Aug et seq "

Wagner festival, Royal Albert hall, London (Wagner present) 7–19 May, 1877

Sullivan's "Pinafore," London 1878

National training school for music building near the Albert hall London, *founded by the duke of Edinburgh* 18 Dec 1873, opened by him 17 May, 1876, first public concert 23 June, 1879

Wagner's "Parsifal" produced at Bayreuth "

Sullivan's "Pirates of Penzance," London 1880

Sullivan's "Patience" London 1881

First annual congress of National Society of Professional Musicians held in England 1881

Sullivan's "Mikado" 1885

Janko keyboard for the piano first publicly used by the inventor, Paul von Janko in Vienna 1886

Alfred Cellier's "Nell Gwynne" London, 1876, "Dorothy" "

New Leipsic Conservatory of Music dedicated 5 Dec 1887

Sullivan's "Yeoman of the Guard," London 1888

J Joachim celebrates the 50th anniversary of his début as a violinist (made at Pesth, 1839) at Cambridge, Engl 14 Mch 1889

MUSICAL PROGRESS IN THE UNITED STATES

First practical instruction book on singing, compiled by rev John Tufts pub in New England 1712

Organ presented to the Queen's chapel, Boston by Thomas Brattle, Esq Aug 1713

Singing societies established in different parts of New England 1720

"Beggar's Opera" written by *John Gay in 1727 (probably)* first produced in New York 3 Dec 1750

William *Billings* of Boston publishes a collection of his musical compositions entitled "The New England Psalm Singer, or American Chorister," in 4 and 5 parts 1770

Stoughton Mass, Musical Society organized 7 Nov 1786

Oliver Holden of Charlestown composer of "Coronation" publishes "The American Harmony" in 3 and 4 parts 1792

Mrs. Oldmixon *nee* George, makes her debut in America in "Inkle and Yarico" 5 Dec 1798

Euterpean Musical Society New York city 1800

Massachusetts Musical Society, Boston 1807

"Barber of Seville" sung by French artists in New Orleans 12 July 1810

Handel and Haydn Society organized in Boston, 20 Apr 1815, incorporated 9 Feb 1816

"Clari the Maid of Milan" libretto by John Howard Payne, containing the song "Home, Sweet Home," first produced in New York 12 Nov 1823

New York Sacred Music Society, organized 1823, gives its first concert 15 Mch 1824

New York Choral Society gives its first concert at St George's church Beekman st. 20 Apr "

Manuel Garcia, with his wife, his son Manuel daughter Marietta (Malibran) *appears in Italian opera* in New York city, 29 Nov 1825

Musical conventions in America originate in New Hampshire, where the Central Musical Society holds its first convention at Concord Sept. 1829

Thomas Hastings, invited by various churches, coming to New York, organizes church choirs, and regulates psalmody on a more religious basis 1832

Boston Academy of Music, founded for instruction in the Pestalozzian system with Lowell Mason at the head, opens 1833

Harvard Musical Association established 30 Aug 1837

Balfe's "Bohemian Girl" produced for the first time in America by the Seguin Opera company at the Park theatre, New York 25 Nov 1844

Louis Moreau Gottschalk makes his début at Paris, France 1845

Tour of the Hutchinson family temperance and anti slavery singers in the U S and England 1846–58

Concert tour of Edward Remenyi, violin virtuoso in the U S, 1848

Germania orchestra give their first concert in America at Astor Place Opera house, New York 5 Oct "

First public concert of the Mendelssohn Quintet club at Boston, 4 Dec. 1849

Jenny Lind sings in concert at Castle Garden, New York, 11 Sept. 1850

Chamber music introduced in New York, 1849, Theodore Eisfeld opens his quartet soirées at Hope chapel 18 Feb 1851

Henrietta Sontag who made her debut in England as Rosina, at the King's theatre, 19 Apr 1828, appears in the U S, Sept. 1852

Dwight's *Journal of Music* founded in Boston.................. 1852
Gottschalk's first concert in New York city.................. 1853
Cecilia Society of Cincinnati, O., organizes and gives its first concert..19 Sept. 1856
Peabody institute, Baltimore, Md., founded.................. 1857
Wagner's "Tannhäuser" produced for the first time in America, at the Stadt Theater, New York...........27 Aug. 1859
Adelina Patti makes her début in "Lucia" at the Academy of Music, New York..................................24 Nov. "
Clara Louise Kellogg makes her début in "Rigoletto" at the Academy of Music, New York.............................. 1860
Theodore Thomas begins his symphony soirées in New York, Dec. 1864
Oberlin Conservatory of Music founded.................. 1865
"Der Nordamerikanische Sängerbund" reorganized at Chicago, 1868
National Peace Jubilee held in Boston, Mass.; over 10,000 singers and 1000 musicians; P. S. Gilmore conductor, 15–20 June. 1869
New England Conservatory of Music established at Providence, R. I., 1859; removed to Boston, 1867; incorporated......... 1870
Beethoven's Conservatory of Music founded at St. Louis...... 1871
Fisk university "Jubilee Singers" make their "campaign for $20,000"..................................Oct. 1871–May, 1872
World's Peace Jubilee and International Musical Festival held in Boston..................................17 June–4 July, "
Beethoven Quintet Club organized in Boston.................. 1873
Music Teachers' National Association organized.............. 1876
New York College of Music incorporated.................. 1878
Cincinnati College of Music incorporated.................. "
Campanini's first appearance in the U. S.................. 1883
American College of Musicians incorporated.................. 1886
Opera "Erminie," by Jacobowski, first performed in the U. S. in New York.................................. "
Opera "The Lion Tamer," by Richard Stahl, first sung in the U. S. at the Broadway theatre, New York city.......30 Dec. 1891
"Montebanks," by W. S. Gilbert and Alfred Collier, first sung in the U. S. at Baldwin's theatre, San Francisco, Cal., 22 Sept. 1892
"Fencing Master," by Reginald De Koven (also composed "Robin Hood"), first performed in New York city at the Casino..26 Sept. "

PRINCIPAL MUSICAL SOCIETIES IN THE UNITED STATES.

		Organized
Baltimore, Md	Oratorio Society	1880
Boston, Mass	Handel and Haydn Society	1816
	Apollo Club	1871
	Boylston Club	1872
	The Cecilia	1876
	Boston Symphony Orchestra	1880
Brooklyn, N. Y.	Brooklyn Philharmonic Society	1857
	Apollo Club	1877
	Amphion Musical Society	1879
	Cæcilia Ladies' Vocal Society	1883
Buffalo, N. Y.	Liedertafel	1848
	Orpheus Singing Society	1869
Chicago, Ill	Apollo Musical Club	1871
Cincinnati, O	Apollo Club	1881
Cleveland, O.	Cleveland Vocal Society	1872
	Bach Society	1878
Milwaukee, Wis	Musik-Verein	1849
Minneapolis, Minn	Gounod Club	1883
Newark, N. J.	Schubert Vocal Society	1880
New York city	Philharmonic Society	1842
	Deutscher Liederkranz	1847
	Mendelssohn Glee Club	1865
	Oratorio Society	1873
	Symphony Society	1878
Philadelphia, Pa.	Orpheus Club	1871
	The Cecilian	1874
Pittsburg, Pa	The Mozart Club	1877
Rhode Island	Rhode Island Choral Association	1885
Salem, Mass	Salem Oratorio Society	1867
San Francisco, Cal	The Loring Club	1876
Springfield, Mass	Hampden County Musical Association	1887
St. Louis, Mo	St. Louis Choral Society	1879
Washington, D. C.	Choral Society	1883
Worcester, Mass	Worcester County Musical Association	1863

PRINCIPAL MUSICAL SOCIETIES IN ENGLAND.

Philharmonic Society, organized.................. 1813
Sacred Harmonic Society, organized.................. 1833
Musical Union, founded by John Ella.................. 1845
Glee Club existed from 1787 to.................. 1857
Catch Club, founded 1761, centenary kept................July, 1861
Cæcilian Society, founded by Z. W. Vincent and others in 1785, disbanded.................................. "

MUSICAL FESTIVALS.

First at Bologna, 1515, at a meeting of Francis I. of France and Pope Leo X. Several were held in Europe in the 18th century; for Haydn, at Vienna, 1808, 1811; others at Erfurt, 1811; Cologne, 1821; and often since. First in England at St. Paul's, London, about 1655, termed "Sons of the Clergy." Dr. Bysse, chancellor of Hereford, about 1724, proposed to the members of the choirs a collection at the cathedral door after morning service, when 40 guineas were collected and appropriated to charitable purposes. It was then agreed to hold festivals at Hereford, Gloucester, and Worcester, in rotation annually. Until 1753 the festival lasted only 2 days; it was then extended at Hereford to 3 evenings; and at Gloucester, in 1757, to 3 mornings, to introduce Handel's "Messiah," which was warmly received, and has been performed annually since. Musical festivals are now frequently held in the different cities of the U. S. HANDEL'S COMMEMORATIONS.

EMINENT MUSICAL COMPOSERS.

Abbreviations: Or. oratorio, Op. opera, Ms. mass, Md. madrigal, An. anthem, So. sonata, Sy. symphony, Gl. glee.

Date.	Name.	Compositions.
1500–60	Christopher Tye	An. "I will exalt Thee."
1514–94	Giovanni P. di Palestrina	Ms., Md., etc.
1523–85	Thomas Tallis	An. "I will call and cry."
1538–1623	William Byrde	*Non Nobis Domine;* An. "Bow down thine ear;" Md. "While the bright sun;" also, Ms.
1550–1600	Emilio del Cavaliere	Or. L'Anima e del Corpo.
1563–1604	Thomas Morley	Md. "My bonny lass she smileth."
1566–1651	Claudio Monteverde	Op. Orfeo, Arianna, etc.
1583–1625	Orlando Gibbons	An. "Hosanna to the son of David;" Md. "Oh that the learned poets."
1585–1672	Heinrich Schütz	Or. Passion, Resurrection, etc.; also, Op.
c. 1594	Jacopo Peri	Op. Dafne, 1594; Eurydice, 1600.
1604–74	Giacomo Carissimi	Or. Jonah, Jephtha, etc.
1620–77	Matthew Lock	Op. Psyche.
1633–87	Jean Baptiste Lully	Op. Tragédies Lyriques; also, So.
1658–95	Henry Purcell	An. "O give thanks;" Op. Dido and Æneas, King Arthur; also, So.
1659–1725	Alessandro Scarlatti	A fugue for two choirs; Tu es Petrus; Op. Carlo Re d'Almagna; also, Ms., So.
1673–1739	Reinhard Keiser	Or. Bleeding and Dying Jesus; also, Op.
1677–1727	William Croft	An. "God is gone up."
1683–1764	Jean Philippe Rameau	Op. Castor and Pollux.
1685–1750	J. Sebastian Bach	Or. Passion (St. Matthew and St. John); also, Ms., So.
1685–1759	George Frederick Handel	Or. Messiah, Israel in Egypt, Esther, Samson, Saul; Op. Almira, Rinaldo.
1694–1746	Leonardo Leo	Or. Death of Abel; Op. Olympiade; also, Ms.
1699–1783	Johann Adolph Hasse	Various Ms., Op., Sy.
1701–59	C. H. Graun	Or. Der Tod Jesu; also Ms., Op.
1710–78	Thomas A. Arne	Op. Artaxerxes; Or. Judith; also, Gl.
1710–79	William Boyce	An. "By the waters of Babylon;" Op. The Chaplet; also, So.
1714–87	Christopher W. R. Gluck	Op. Orfeo, Alceste, Iphigenia.
1722–95	Georg Benda	Op. Ariadne auf Naxos; Medea.
1728–1800	Nicola Piccinni	Op. Roland, Labuona Figliuola, Diden, Cecchina.
1728–1804	Johann Adam Hiller	Op. Liederspiele.
1732–1809	Joseph Haydn	Or. Creation, Seasons; Sy. London symphonies, Toy symphonies, etc.; also Ms., So.
1738–1801	Jonathan Battishill	An. for seven voices, "Call to remembrance;" also, Gl.
1740–1802	Samuel Arnold	An. "Who is this that cometh;" also, 40 English Op.
1740–1806	Luigi Boccherini	Orchestral music, Ms., Sy.
1741–1813	André Grétry	Op. Zemire et Azor; also, Sy.
1752–1832	Muzio Clementi	Gradus ad Parnassum; So., Sy.
1756–1791	Wolfgang Amadeus Mozart	Op. Don Giovanni, Figaro, Zauberflöte; Sy. Jupiter symphony; Requiem, So.
1757–1831	I. Pleyel	Pleyel's hymn, 29 symphonies; also, So.
1760–1842	Maria Luigi Cherubini	Op. Les Deux Journées, Requiem in C minor; also, Ms.
1767–1821	Andreas Romberg	Lay of the bell; Sy.
1767–1838	Thomas Attwood	An. "Come, Holy Ghost."
1770–1827	Ludwig von Beethoven	Or. Mount of Olives; Op. Fidelio; Sy. Pastorale, Eroica, Choral; also, Ms., So.
1778–1851	Gasparo L. P. Spontini	Op. La Vestale.

EMINENT MUSICAL COMPOSERS.—(*Continued.*)

Date.	Name.	Compositions.
1784-1859	Ludwig or Louis Spohr	Or. Des Heilands letzte Stunden (Calvary), Die letzten Dinge (Last Judgment); Op. Faust, Jessonda; Sy. Die Weihe der Töne.
1784-1871	Daniel F. E. Auber	Op. Fra Diavolo, La Muta de Portici (Masaniello), Zerline.
1786-1826	Carl Maria von Weber	Op. Der Freischütz, Preciosa, Euryanthe, Oberon.
1786-1855	Sir Henry R. Bishop	Op. Miller and his Men, Guy Mannering; Gl. "I gave my harp."
1791-1833	Louis J. F. Herold	Op. Zampa.
1792-1868	Gioacchino Antonio Rossini	Op. Guglielmo Tell, Tancredi, Otello, Barbiere di Siviglia, Semiramide, Mose in Egitto, Stabat Mater, etc.
1794-1864	Jacob Meyerbeer	Op. Les Huguenots, L'Africaine, Robert le Diable, L'Étoile du Nord.
1794-1870	Ignatz Moscheles	Various Sy., So.
1797-1828	Franz Schubert	Der Erlenkönig, Serenade; also, Ms., Op., So., Sy.
1797-1848	Gaetano Donizetti	Op. Lucrezia Borgia, Lucia, La Favorita.
1797-1870	Saverio Mercadante	Op. Elesa e Claudio, Il Giuramento.
1799-1868	J. E. Halévy	Op. La Juive, Les Mousquetaires.
1802-35	Vincenzo Bellini	Op. Norma, La Sonnambula, I Puritani.
1803-69	Hector Berlioz	Op. La Damnation de Faust, Benvenuto Cellini; Sy. Romeo et Juliette; also, Ms.
1804-49	Johann Strauss	Dance music, 251 pieces.
1804-85	Sir Jules Benedict	Op. Lily of Killarney, Gipsy's Warning, The Brides of Venice, The Crusaders; Or. St. Peter.
1808-70	Michael William Balfe	Op. Bohemian Girl, Talisman, Maid of Artois, Falstaff, etc.
1809-47	Felix Mendelssohn-Bartholdy	Or. Elijah, St. Paul; An. "Judge me, O God;" Op. Wedding of Camacho; also, Songs without Words, So., Sy.
1809-49	Francis Frederic Chopin	Nocturnes; So.; Waltzes.
1810-56	Robert Schumann	Op. Geneviève, Music to Faust, Sy. in C, B flat, etc.; So.
1810-76	Samuel Sebastian Wesley	An. The Wilderness.
1810-84	Sir Michael Costa	Or. Eli, Naaman; Op. Malvina, Don Carlos.
1811-86	Franz Liszt	Faust symphony, Tasso, etc.
1811-	Charles L. Ambroise Thomas	Op. Mignon, Hamlet.
1812-83	Friedrich Freiherr von Flotow	Op. Martha, Stradella.
1813-87	George A. Macfarren	Op. Robin Hood; Or. St. John the Baptist, The Resurrection; also, An.
1813-83	Richard Wagner	Op. Tannhäuser, Lohengrin, Niebelungen, Tristan und Isolde, Meistersänger, Rienzi, Der fliegende Holländer.
1813-	*Giuseppe Verdi*	*Op. Il Trovatore, Ernani, Rigoletto,* La Traviato, Aïda, Don Carlos.
1816-75	Sir William Sterndale Bennett	May Queen, The Woman of Samaria; also, Or., An., So., Sy.
1817-90	Niels W. Gade	Cantata, Erlking's daughter; Sy.
1818-93	Charles Gounod	Op. Faust, Romeo and Juliet.
1819-80	Jacques Offenbach	Op. La Grande Duchesse, Orphée aux Enfers, Barbe bleue, etc.
1822-82	Joseph Joachim Raff	Variations on an original theme; Sanges Frühling; Op., Sy.
1825-89	Rev. sir F. A. Gore Ouseley	Or. St. Polycarp, Hagar; An. "It came even to pass."
1829-94	Anton Gregor Rubinstein	Sy. Ocean symphony; also, Or., Op.
1832-	Charles Lecocq	Op. Giroflé-Girofla, La Princesse des Canaries, La Fille de Mme. Angot.
1833-	Johannes Brahms	Deutches requiem; Sy., etc.
1835-	Charles C. Saint-Saens	Op. Etienne Marcel.
1839-75	Leopold-Georges Bizet	Op. Carmen.
1840-93	Peter I. Tschaikowsky (*tschē-kow'-skē*)	Sy. Der Sturm, Francesca von Rimini; Op. Mazeppa.
1842-	Edmond Audran	Op. La Mascotte.
1842-	Arthur S. Sullivan	The Prodigal Son; The Light of the World; Op. H.M.S. Pinafore, Mikado, Patience, Iolanthe, *Pirates of Penzance, Yeoman of the Guard.*
1844-91	Alfred Cellier	Op. Nell Gwynne, Dorothy.
1852-	Charles V. Stanford	Op. The Veiled Prophet of Khoassan, The Canterbury Pilgrim; Sy., Or., So.

Other noted composers: Barnby, Boieldeau, Bruch, Buck, David, De Koven, Franz, Gossec, Hatton, Hiller, Hofmann, Jacobowski, Jensen, Lachner, Lawes, Moszkowski, Paisello, Porpora, Rheinberger, Scharwenka, Tausig, Talberg, Tours, Ulrich, Volkmann.

Noted singers: Albani, Alboni, Bordogni, Campanini, Catalini, Cummings, Formes, Girsta, Grisi, Hauck, Henschel, Kellogg, Lablache, La Grange, Lind, Lucca, Malibran, Mallinger, Mara, Mario, Materna, Maurel, Murska, Niemann, Nilsson, Novello, Parepa Rosa, Pasta, Phillips, Patti, Reeves, Reicherkniderman, Remmertz, Ronconi, Rubini, Rudersdorf, Santley, Scaria, Schroeder-Devient, Sontag, Stockhausen, Tamburini, Tichatscheck, Todi, Viardot Garcia, Whitney.

Noted pianists: Bendel, Brassin, D'Albert, Dreyschock, Dulcken, Dussek, Essipoff, Goddard, Gottschalk, Haberbier, Halle, Henselt, Herz, Hummel, Jaell, Joseffy, Kalkbrenner, Kousti, Krebs, Mayer, Mehlig, Mills, Paderewski, Reinecke, Ries, Rive-King, Salter, Schiller, Schoberlechner, Schulhoff, Sherwood, Von Bulow, Wolfsohn.

Noted organists: Blow, Buxtehude, Cooper, Couperin, Eddy, Eyken, Faisst, Fischer, Frescobaldi, Guilmant, Haupt, Hesse, Kittel, Kloss, Lefebre-Wely, Lemmens, Lux, Marpurg, Paine, Rinck, Reinken, Ritter, Reuter, Todt, Van den Cheyn.

Noted violinists: Camilla Urso, Corelli, Eichberg, Giardini, Joachim, Laub, Lauterbach, Le Clair, Leonhard, Lipinski, Listorman, Luestner, Nohr, Neruda, Ole Bull, Paganini, Rappoldi, Remenyi, Sarasate, Singer, Sivori, Taboronski, Tartini, Torelli, Viotti, Vieuxtemps, Wieniawsky, Wilhelmj.

Other virtuosos: Boehm, Drouet, Quantz (flute). Carcassi (guitar). Dragonetti (double bass). Godefroid, Oberthuer (harp). Piatti, Seligman, Servais (violoncello).

music, Cyclopædias and Dictionaries of: Rousseau's, pub. 1767; in "Encyclopédie Méthodique," 1791; Fétis, "Biographie Universelle des Musiciens," 1835–44; Mendell's "Conversations-Lexicon;" "Dictionary of Music and Musicians," 1450–1889, 11 vols., edited by sir George Grove, 1878–1890; "History of Music," by Emil Naumann, edited by sir F. A. Gore Ouseley, 1890.

musical pitch. The pitch of a note produced depends on the time in which the motion or vibration which gives rise to the sound takes place. Pitch then is defined by frequency of vibration and was settled for France by legislation in 1859, the middle A to be 870 simple or 435 double vibrations in a second; but through error of measurement the fork made gave (A) 439 double vibrations (C, 522). At a meeting on the subject, held at the Society of Arts, on 23 Nov. 1860, the concert pitch of C was recommended to be 528 vibrations in a second; but the fork made by J. H. Griesbach gives 539⅔ vibrations. Mr. Hullah adopted 512 vibrations. A lower pitch was adopted at concerts in London in Jan. 1869. 528 vibrations for C adopted for performances at the international exhibition of 1872, at a meeting 20 Jan. 1872. Handel's tuning-fork, 1740, was 495; the Philharmonic Society's, 1813–43, was 515. A. J. Ellis's elaborate "History of Musical Pitch" is pub. in *Journal of the Society of Arts*, 5 Mch. 1880, and separately.

muskets. FIRE-ARMS.

muslin, a fine cotton cloth, so called, it is said, from having a downy nap on its surface resembling moss (Fr. *mousse*); according to others, because it was first brought from Moussol, in India. Muslins were first worn in England in 1670.—*Anderson.* By means of the MULE, British much superseded India muslins.

mustang, a small, hardy wild horse of the southwest United States and Mexico, a descendant of the horse introduced into America by the Spaniards; also, the name of a variety of grape, south.

"Nor the red mustang
Whose clusters hang
O'er the waves of the Colorado."
—*Longfellow*, "Catawba Wine."

Muta, a village near Damascus, Syria. Here Mahomet defeated the Christians in his first conflict with them, 629.

mute. A prisoner arraigned for treason or felony is said to stand *mute* when he makes no answer, or one foreign to the purpose. Anciently a mute was subjected to torture.

Walter Calverly, esq, of Calverly in Yorkshire, having murdered 2 of his children, and stabbed his wife in a fit of jealousy, being arraigned for his crime at York assizes stood mute and was pressed to death in the castle by a large iron weight on his breast, 5 Aug 1605 —*Stow*
Major Strangeways suffered a similar death at Newgate for the murder of his brother in law, Mr Fussell 1657
Judgment was awarded against mutes, as if they were convicted or had confessed, by 12 Geo III 1772
A man refusing to plead was condemned and executed at the Old Bailey on a charge of murder, 1778, and another on a charge of burglary at Wells, 1792
An act directing the court to enter a plea of "not guilty" when the prisoner will not plead, 1827
Case of Giles Corey WITCHCRAFT, Salem, 17 Sept 1692.

Mu'tina, now **Modena,** a fortified city of N Italy Here Marc Antony, after defeating the consul Pansa, was himself beaten with great loss by Hirtius, the other consul, and fled to Gaul, 27 Apr 43 B.C

mutiny, a revolt against constituted authority, open resistance to officers in authority, especially in the army and navy The principal revolt or mutiny during the American Revolution was that of the Pennsylvania Line, 2000 strong, at Morristown, N J, 1 Jan 1781. The tardiness of Congress in supplying the wants of the army was the chief cause Unable to control the troops by his personal efforts, Gen Wayne appointed 2 officers, cols Stewart and Butler, to conduct them to Princeton, where they submitted to Congress, in writing, their demands. Meanwhile sir Henry Clinton sent 2 emissaries among them, making most liberal offers, if they would go over to the British These men they at once delivered up to the government Congress appointed commissioners to confer with the troops, and complied with most of their just demands Many were, however, disbanded during the winter, and their places filled in the spring with recruits A like action on the part of the New Jersey Line followed, 21-28 Jan 1781, but this was quickly subdued, and 2 ringleaders executed

Of the *Bounty* (BOUNTY MUTINY), 28 Apr 1789
Of sailors throughout the British fleet at Portsmouth, Apr 1797, and at the Nore at the mouth of the Thames, May–June, 1797, several executed
Of the *Danaë*, British frigate, the crew carried the ship into Brest harbor 27 Mch 1800
On board adm Mitchell's fleet at Bantry bay, Dec 1801, and Jan 1802 BANTRY BAY
At Malta, began 4 Apr 1807 and ended on the 12th, when the mutineers (chiefly Greeks and Corsicans) blew themselves up with a magazine of between 400 and 500 barrels of gunpowder
On board the U S ship *Somers*, 1842 SOMERS, UNITED STATES
Of the sepoys INDIA, 1857

Mycale (*myc'-a-le*) (Ionia, Asia Minor), Battle of, fought between the Greeks (under Leotychides, the king of Sparta, and Xantippus the Athenian) and the Persians, under Tigranes, 22 Sept 479 B.C, the day on which Mardonius was defeated and slain at Platæa by Pausanias The Persians (about 100,000 men) were completely defeated, thousands slaughtered, and their camp burned The Greeks returned to Samos with immense booty.

Myce'næ, a division of the kingdom of Argives, in the Peloponnesus, about 50 stadia from Argos, flourished till the invasion of the Heraclidæ Early history mythical.

	B.C
Perseus removes from Argos, founds Mycenæ	1431, 1313, or 1282
Reign of Eurystheus	1289, 1274 or 1258
[Towards the close of his reign is placed the story of the labors of Hercules]	
Ægisthus assassinates Atreus Agamemnon king of Sicyon, Corinth, and perhaps of Argos	1201
He is chosen generalissimo of Greece for the Trojan war, about	1193
Ægisthus, in the absence of Agamemnon, lives in adultery with queen Clytemnestra On the return of the king they assassinate him, and Ægisthus mounts the throne	1183
Orestes, son of Agamemnon, kills his mother and her paramour . .	1176
Orestes dies of the bite of a serpent. .	1106
Achaians are expelled	"
Invasion of the Heraclidæ, and the conquerors divide the dominions .	1103
Mycenæ destroyed by the Argives .	468
Discoveries at Mycenæ by dr Schliemann, reported,	A D
Mch 1874-Sept	1876
Visited by the emperor of Brazil . 15 Oct.	"
Discovery of tombs of Agamemnon and others, and many treasures, announced by dr Schliemann . 28 Nov	"
Dr Schliemann reports discoveries to Society of Antiquaries, London, 22 Mch., pub Mycenæ ... .. Dec.	1877

My'læ, a bay of Sicily where the Romans, under the consul Duilius, gained their first naval victory over the Carthaginians, and took 50 ships, 260 B.C Here Agrippa defeated the fleet of Sextus Pompeius, 36 B.C

myograph'ion, an apparatus for determining velocity of the nervous current, invented by H Helmholtz in 1850, and since improved by Dubois Raymond and others

Mys'ia, an ancient country of Asia Minor, lying to the north of Lydia and west of Bithynia It was the prevailing opinion of antiquity that the Mysians were not an indigenous people of Asia, but had migrated from the banks of the Danube Herodotus mentions that the Mysians were a numerous and powerful people before the Trojan war They became subject to the monarchs of Lydia, in the reign of Alyattes, father of Crœsus, and on the dissolution of the Lydian empire they passed under the Persian dominion and formed a part of the third satrapy in the division formed by Darius The ancient city of Troy was within its territory, as well as Pergamus and Abydos.

Mysore', S India, was made a flourishing kingdom by Hyder Ali, who dethroned the reigning sovereign in 1761, and by his son, Tippoo Sahib, who harassed the English Tippoo was chastised by them in 1792, and on 4 May, 1799, his capital, Seringapatam, was taken by assault, and himself slain The British established a prince of the old royal family as maharajah of part of Mysore in 1799 Being without an heir, he was permitted to adopt a child of 4 years of age, in Aug 1867, who succeeded him at his death, 27 Mch 1868, and assumed the government in May, 1881. Tippoo's last surviving son, Gholam Mahomet, a British pensioner, died at Calcutta, 11 Aug 1872

mysteries (from the Gr μυστήριον, a mystery or revealed secret) "The *Sacred* mysteries" is a term applied to the doctrines of Christianity, called the "mystery of godliness," 1 Tim iii 16, as opposed to the "mystery of iniquity," 2 Thess ii 7 The *Profane* mysteries were secret ceremonies performed by a select few in honor of some deity. From Egyptian mysteries of Isis and Osiris sprang those of Dionysus and Demeter among the Greeks. The Eleusinian mysteries were introduced at Athens by Eumolpus, 1356 B.C.

mystery plays. DRAMA

mystics, theologians who, in addition to the obvious meaning of Scripture, assert that other interpretations may be discovered by an emanation of the Divine Wisdom, by which the soul is enlightened and purified, and advocate seclusion for contemplation and asceticism

Mysticism taught at Alexandria by Clemens, Pantænus, Origen, and others, who mingled Christianity and Platonism, 2d and 3d centuries
Much promoted by the works of the Pseudo Dionysius ("The Mystic Theology," etc.), 6th century
Introduced into the Western empire, 9th century
Eminent mediæval mystics (opposed by schoolmen) Master Eckhart (1251-1329), John Tauler of Strasburg, where he acted heroically during the plague termed the "black death" (1290-1361), Henry Suso (1300-65) They aimed at a more spiritual religion than Romanism, but their followers were charged with immorality, pantheism, communism, and maintaining private inspiration
Jacob Böhme or Behmen, German mystic, pub his "Aurora" (alleged divine revelation), 1612, d 18 Nov 1624
[HUTCHINSONIANS, QUAKERS, QUIETISTS, SWEDENBORGIANS.]

mythol'ogy (Gr μυθολογια=μῦθος, fable, and λόγος, speech), fables or legends of cosmogony, of gods and of heroes of pagan peoples Of the earlier civilized nations, the Greeks had by far the most extensive and coherent mythology. The Egyptian, though older, is obscure, and her literature not fertile in myths. The principal Egyptian deities were Osiris, Horus, Typhon (Seth or Set), Isis, and Nephthys, Horus, the son of Osiris and Isis, and Nephthys, the sister of Isis. Osiris is essentially the good principle, as Typhon or Set, his brother, is his opponent. Scandinavian mythology is very prolific in gods, goddesses, and heroes, the principal gods and goddesses being

Odin or Woden, the all father, and his wife Frigga, Baldur (son of Odin) and his wife Nauna, Thor (son of Odin) and his wife Sif, Bragi (son of Odin) and his wife Idun, the latter the keeper for the gods of the Apples of Youth, Ty or Tyr (son of Odin), Njord and his wife Skadi, the Minerva of Scandinavian mythology, Frey (son of Njord) and his sister Freyia, Hiemdall, steward of the gods, Hod or Hödur, Vidar, Vali Uller, Loki, foster brother of Odin, and cause of all evil, Hela or Hel, goddess of the lower regions, Saga, goddess of history, Gefion and others, with the Norns, 3 sisters, corresponding to the Fates of the Greeks VALHALLA, YGGDRASIL.

PRINCIPAL GODS AND GODDESSES OF THE ROMANS AND GREEKS, WITH PARENTAGE AND PROVINCE.

Roman.	Greek.	Parentage.	Over what presiding.
Apollo	Apollon	Jupiter and Latona	Music, poetry, archery, prophecy.
Aurora	Eos	Hyperion and Theia	The dawn.
Æolus	Æolos	Hippotas and Melanippe	The winds.
Bacchus	Dionysus	Jupiter and Semele	The vine.
Bellona	Enyo	Phorcys and Ceto	War.
Ceres	Demeter	Saturn and Cybele	Agriculture.
Cupid	Eros	Venus	Love.
Cybele	Rhea	Uranus and Terra	Nature.
Diana	Artemis	Jupiter and Latona	Hunting and chastity.
Juno (sister and wife of Jupiter)	Hera	Saturn and Cybele	Marriage and domestic life.
Jupiter	Zeus	Saturn and Cybele	Over all, supreme god.
Mars	Ares	Jupiter and Juno	War.
Mercury	Hermes	Jupiter and Maia	Commerce and gain.
Minerva	Pallas-Athené	Jupiter	Wisdom.
Neptune	Poseidon	Saturn and Cybele	The sea.
Nox		Chaos	Night, death, sleep, ridicule. Mother of Charon, Fates, and the Furies, and sister of Erebus.
Pluto	Plouton or Hades	Saturn and Cybele	Lower world.
Saturn	Kronos	Uranus and Terra	Father of the gods and brother of the Titans.
Venus	Aphrodité	Jupiter and Diore	Love and pleasure.
Vesta	Hestia	Saturn and Cybele	Virginity.
Vulcan	Hephæstos	Jupiter and Juno	Fire.

See under separate articles.

N

N, the 14th letter and 11th consonant of the English alphabet. Its form and force is derived from the Greek letter N, thence from the Phœnician and Egyptian.

Nabonas'sar, Era of, named from a prince of Babylon, in whose reign astronomical studies were encouraged in Chaldæa. The years contain 365 days each, without intercalation. The first day of the era was Wednesday (erroneously made Thursday in "L'Art de Vérifier les Dates"), 26 Feb. 747 B.C.—3967 Julian period. To find the Julian year on which the year of Nabonassar begins, subtract the year, if before Christ, from 748; if after Christ, add to it 747.

Nag's Head story. Matthew Parker was consecrated archbishop of Canterbury at Lambeth, 17 Dec. 1559, by bishops Barlow, Coverdale, Scory, and Hodgkins. For forty-five years after, the Romish writers asserted that Parker and others had been ordained in an abnormal fashion by Scory at the Nag's Head tavern, Cheapside. This fiction was refuted by Burnet, and is rejected by Roman Catholic authorities, such as Lingard.

Na'hum, Festival of, Nahum, 7th of the 12 minor prophets, about 713 B.C.; the festival is 24 Dec.

nails of the earlier nations were of bronze. The nail used by Jael in killing Sisera (Judges iv. 21) was a wooden tent-pin. Up to the 19th century nails were mostly forged, the first cut-nails being made by Jeremiah Wilkinson, in Rhode Island, in 1775, followed by Ezekiel Reed, Mass., 1786. The Perkins cut-nail machine, patented 1795, made 200,000 nails in a day.

names. Adam and Eve named their sons (Gen. iv. 25, 26). A Roman citizen had generally 3 names; *prænomen*, denoting the individual; *nomen*, the gens or clan; *cognomen*, the family or branch of the clan; sometimes he had the *agnomen* (e. g. Publius Cornelius Scipio Africanus). The popes change names on assuming the pontificate, "a custom introduced by pope Sergius, whose name till then was Swine-snout," 687.—*Platina*. Onuphrius refers it to John XII., 956; stating that it was done in imitation of SS. Peter and Paul, who were first called Simon and Saul. In France the baptismal name was sometimes changed. The 2 sons of Henry II. of France were christened Alexander and Hercules; at confirmation they became Henry and Francis. Monks and nuns, entering monasteries, assume new names. SURNAMES. Miss Yonge's "History of Christian Names," pub. 1863 (new ed. 1884). M. A. Lower's "Patronymica Britannica," 1860.

Na'mur, in Belgium, was made a county, 932; taken by the French, 1 July, 1692; by William of England, 4 Aug. 1695; ceded to Austria by peace of Utrecht, 1713, and garrisoned by Dutch as a barrier town of the United Provinces in 1715. Taken by the French in 1746, but restored in 1749. In 1782, the emperor Joseph expelled the Dutch garrison. In 1792 it was again taken by the French, who were compelled to evacuate it in 1793; regained 1794; delivered to the allies, 1814; assigned to Belgium, 1831; fortifications destroyed, 1866.

Nancy (*nŏn-se'*), N.E. France, an ancient city, capital of Lorraine in the 13th century. After taking Nancy, 29 Nov. 1475, and losing it, 5 Oct. 1476, Charles the Bold of Burgundy was defeated beneath its walls, and slain by the duke of Lorraine and Swiss, 5 Jan. 1477. LORRAINE. Nancy was embellished by Stanislas, ex-king of Poland, who resided here, and died Feb. 1766; was captured by Blucher, Jan. 1814; and on the retreat of MacMahon's army, expecting the Germans, surrendered to 4 uhlans, 12 Aug. 1870. It was restored at the peace.

Nan'kin, said to have been made central capital of China, 420; was the court of the Ming dynasty from 1369 till Yung-lo removed to Pekin in 1410. On 4 Aug. 1842, British ships arrived at Nankin, and peace was made. The rebel Tae-pings took it on 19, 20 Mch. 1853. It was recaptured by imperialists, 19 July, 1864, and found desolate.

Nantes (*nănts*), W. France, formerly capital of the Namnetes. The edict in favor of Protestants issued here by Henry IV., 13 Apr. 1598, was revoked by Louis XIV., 22 Oct. 1685. Awful cruelties were committed here by the republican Carrier, Oct.–Nov. 1793. Pop. 1891, 122,750. DROWNING, FRENCH REVOLUTION.

Nantucket and **Martha's Vineyard,** islands off the south coast of Massachusetts, and belonging to that state, the former containing 60, the latter 120 sq. miles. First noted by capt. Gosnold, 1602, and first settled by some people under Thomas Mayhew from Watertown, Mass., 1643. Both islands in earlier days were famous for their skilled seamen and large business in whale-fishery.

naphtha, a clear, combustible rock oil, known to the Greeks, called "oil of Media," and thought to have been an ingredient in the Greek fire; also, an artificial, volatile, colorless liquid obtained from petroleum.

Napier's bones. A set of small square rods and rectangular pieces of bone, ivory, or other material, contrived by Baron John Napier, and first described by him in 1617, to facilitate multiplication and division. Nothing shows more clearly the rude state of arithmetical knowledge at the beginning of the 17th century than the universal satisfaction with which Napier's invention was welcomed by all classes and regarded as a real aid to calculation.—*Encyl. Brit.* 9 ed., Napier.

Naples, formerly the continental division and seat of government of the kingdom of the Two Sicilies, began with a

Walter Calverly, esq., of Calverly in Yorkshire, having murde[red] 2 of his children, and stabbed his wife in a fit of jealousy, be[ing] arraigned for his crime at York assizes stood mute, and w[as] pressed to death in the castle by a large iron weight on his bre[ast], 5 Aug. 1605.—*Stow.*

Major Strangeway suffered a similar death at Newgate, for the mu[r]der of his brother-in-law, Mr. Fussell, 1657.

Judgment was awarded against mutes, as if they were convicted [or] had confessed, by 12 Geo. III. 1772.

A man refusing to plead was condemned and executed at the [Old] Bailey on a charge of murder, 1778, and another on a charge [of] burglary at Wells, 1792.

An act directing the court to enter a plea of "not guilty" when [a] prisoner will not plead, 1827.

Case of Giles Corey. WITCHCRAFT, Salem, 17 Sept. 1692.

Mu'tina, now **Modena,** a fortified city of N. Ita[ly]. Here Marc Antony, after defeating the consul Pansa, was hi[m]self beaten with great loss by Hirtius, the other consul, a[nd] fled to Gaul, 27 Apr. 43 B.C.

mutiny, a revolt against constituted authority; op[en] resistance to officers in authority, especially in the arm[y] and navy. The principal revolt or mutiny during the Ame[ri]can Revolution was that of the Pennsylvania Line, 20[00] strong, at Morristown, N. J., 1 Jan. 1781. The tardiness [of] Congress in supplying the wants of the army was the ch[ief] cause. Unable to control the troops by his personal effo[rts], Gen. Wayne appointed 2 officers, cols. Stewart and Butler, [to] conduct them to Princeton, where they submitted to Co[n]gress, in writing, their demands. Meanwhile sir Henry Cli[n]ton sent 2 emissaries among them, making most liberal [of]fers, if they would go over to the British. These men th[ey] at once delivered up to the government. Congress appoint[ed] commissioners to confer with the troops, and complied w[ith] most of their just demands. Many were, however, disband[ed] during the winter, and their places filled in the spring w[ith] recruits. A like action on the part of the New Jersey Li[ne] followed, 21-28 Jan. 1781, but this was quickly subdued, a[nd] 2 ringleaders executed.

Of the *Bounty* (BOUNTY MUTINY), 28 Apr. 1789.

Of sailors throughout the British fleet at Portsmouth, Apr. 17[97], and at the Nore at the mouth of the Thames, May-June, 17[97]; several executed.

Of the *Danaë*, British frigate; the crew carried the ship into Br[est] harbor, 27 Mch. 1800.

On board adm. Mitchell's fleet at Bantry bay, Dec. 1801, and Ja[n.] 1802. BANTRY BAY.

At Malta, began 4 Apr. 1807, and ended on the 12th, when the m[u]tineers (chiefly Greeks and Corsicans) blew themselves up wit[h a] magazine of between 400 and 500 barrels of gunpowder.

On board the U. S. ship *Somers*, 1842. SOMERS, UNITED STATES.

Of the sepoys. INDIA, 1857.

Mycale (*myc'-a-le*) (Ionia, Asia Minor), Battle of, foug[ht] between the Greeks (under Leotychides, the king of Sparta, a[nd] Xantippus the Athenian) and the Persians, under Tigran[es], 22 Sept. 479 B.C.; the day on which Mardonius was defeat[ed] and slain at Platæa by Pausanias. The Persians (abo[ut] 100,000 men) were completely defeated, thousands slaughtere[d], and their camp burned. The Greeks returned to Samos w[ith] immense booty.

Myce'næ, a division of the kingdom of Argives, in t[he] Peloponnesus, about 50 stadia from Argos, flourished till t[he] invasion of the Heraclidæ. Early history mythical.

Perseus removes from Argos; founds Mycenæ...1431, 1313, or 1[...]

Reign of Eurystheus.............................1289, 1274, or 1[...]

[Towards the close of his reign is placed the story of the labors of Hercules.]

Ægisthus assassinates Atreus: Agamemnon king of Sicyon, Corinth, and perhaps of Argos.................................1[...]

He is chosen generalissimo of Greece for the Trojan war, about 11[...]

Ægisthus, in the absence of Agamemnon, lives in adultery with queen Clytemnestra. On the return of the king they assassinate him; and Ægisthus mounts the throne.................11[...]

Orestes, son of Agamemnon, kills his mother and her paramour..11[...]

Orestes dies of the bite of a serpent..............................11[...]

Achaians are expelled...

Invasion of the Heraclidæ, and the conquerors divide the dominions...

Mycenæ destroyed by the Argives.......................................4[...]

Discoveries at Mycenæ by dr. Schliemann; reported,

Mch. 1874-Sept. 18[...]

Visited by the emperor of Brazil.............................13 Oct.

Discovery of tombs of Agamemnon and others, and many treasures; announced by dr. Schliemann.................28 Nov.

Dr. Schliemann reports discoveries to Society of Antiquaries, London, 22 Mch.; pub. a *poem*............................Dec. 18[...]

My'læ, a bay of Sicily where the Romans, under the co[n]sul Duilius, gained their first naval victory over the Carth[a]ginians, and took 50 ships, 260 B.C. Here Agrippa defeated the fleet of Sextus Pompeius, 36 B.C.

myograph'ion, an apparatus for determining velocity of the nervous current, invented by H. Helmholtz in 1850, and since improved by Dubois Raymond and others.

Mys'ia, an ancient country of Asia Minor, lying to the north of Lydia and west of Bithynia. It was the prevailing opinion of antiquity that the Mysians were not an indigenous people of Asia, but had migrated from the banks of the Danube. Herodotus mentions that the Mysians were a numerous and powerful people before the Trojan war. They became subject to the monarchs of Lydia, in the reign of Alyattes, father of Crœsus, and on the dissolution of the Lydian empire they passed under the Persian dominion and formed a part of the third satrapy in the division formed by Darius. The ancient city of Troy was within its territory, as well as Pergamus and Abydos.

Mysore', S. India, was made a flourishing kingdom by Hyder Ali, who dethroned the reigning sovereign in 1761, and by his son, Tippoo Sahib, who harassed the English. Tippoo was chastised by them in 1792; and on 4 May, 1799, his capital, Seringapatam, was taken by assault, and himself slain. The British established a prince of the old royal family as maharajah of part of Mysore in 1799. Being without an heir, he was permitted to adopt a child of 4 years of age, in Aug. 1867; who succeeded him at his death, 27 Mch. 1868, and assumed the government in May, 1881. Tippoo's last surviving son, Gholam Mahomet, a British pensioner, died at Calcutta, 11 Aug. 1872.

mysteries (from the Gr. μυστήριον, a mystery or revealed secret). "The *Sacred* mysteries" is a term applied to the doctrines of Christianity, called the "mystery of godliness," 1 Tim. iii. 16, as opposed to the "mystery of iniquity," 2 Thess. ii. 7. The *Profane* mysteries were secret ceremonies performed by a select few in honor of some deity. From Egyptian mysteries of Isis and Osiris sprang those of Dionysus and Demeter among the Greeks. The Eleusinian mysteries were introduced at Athens by Eumolpus, 1356 B.C.

mystery plays. DRAMA.

mystics, theologians who, in addition to the obvious meaning of Scripture, assert that other interpretations may be discovered by an emanation of the Divine Wisdom, by which the soul is enlightened and purified; and advocate seclusion for contemplation and asceticism.

Mysticism taught at Alexandria by Clemens, Pantænus, Origen, and others, who mingled Christianity and Platonism, 2d and 3d centuries.

Much promoted by the works of the Pseudo-Dionysius ("The Mystic Theology," etc.), 6th century.

Introduced into the Western empire, 9th century.

Eminent mediæval mystics (opposed by schoolmen): Master Eckhart (1260-1329); John Tauler of Strasburg, where he acted heroically during the plague termed the "black death" (1290-1361); Henry Suso (1300-65). They aimed at a more spiritual religion than Romanism; but their followers were charged with immorality, pantheism, communism, and maintaining private inspiration.

Jacob Böhme or Behmen, German mystic, pub. his "Aurora" (alleged divine revelation), 1612; d. 18 Nov. 1624.

[HUTCHINSONIANS, QUAKERS, QUIETISTS, SWEDENBORGIANS.]

mythol'ogy (Gr. μυθολογία = μῦθος, fable, and λόγος, speech), fables or legends of cosmogony, of gods and of heroes of pagan peoples. Of the earlier civilized na[...] had by far the most extensive and coheren[...] Egyptian, though older, is obscure, and [...] tile in myths. The principal Egyp[...] Horus, Typhon (Seth or Set). [...] son of Osiris and Isis, and Nep[...] is essentially the good prin[...] is his opponent. Scandi[...] gods, goddesses, and [...] being:

Odin or Woden, [...]

PRINCIPAL GODS AND GODDESSES OF THE ROMANS AND GREEKS WITH PARENTAGE AND PROVINCE.

Roman.	Greek.	Parentage	Province
Apollo	Apollon	Jupiter and Latona	Music, poetry, archery, prophecy
Aurora	Eos	Hyper. and Thea	The dawn.
Æolus	Æolus	Hippo. and Melanippe	The winds.
Bacchus	Dionysus	Jupiter and Semele	The vine.
Bellona	Enyo	Phorcus and Ceto	War.
Ceres	Demeter	Saturn and Cybele	Agriculture.
Cupid	Eros	Venus	Love.
Cybele	Rhea	Uranus and Terra	Nature.
Diana	Artemis	Jupiter and Latona	Hunting and chastity.
Juno (sister and wife of Jupiter)	Hera	Saturn and Cybele	Marriage and domestic life.
Jupiter	Zeus	Saturn and Cybele	Over all, supreme god.
Mars	Ares	Jupiter and Juno	War.
Mercury	Hermes	Jupiter and Maia	Commerce and [illegible].
Minerva	Pallas-Athene	Jupiter	Wisdom.
Neptune	Poseidon	Saturn and Cybele	The sea.
Nox		Chaos	Night, death, sleep, ridicule. Mother of [illegible] Charon, Fates, and the Furies, and sister of Erebus.
Pluto	Plouton or Hades	Saturn and Cybele	Lower world.
Saturn	Kronos	Cœlus and Terra	Father of the gods and brother of the Titans.
Venus	Aphrodite	Jupiter and Dione	Love and pleasure.
Vesta	Hestia	Saturn and Cybele	Virginity.
Vulcan	Hephaestos	Jupiter and Juno	Fire.

See under separate articles.

N

N, the 14th letter and 11th consonant of the English alphabet. Its form and force is derived from the Greek letter N, thence from the Phœnician and Egyptian.

Nabonas'sar, Era of, named from a prince of Babylon, in whose reign astronomical studies were encouraged in Chaldæa. The years contain 365 days each, without intercalation. The first day of the era was Wednesday (erroneously made Thursday in "L'Art de Vérifier les Dates"), 26 Feb. 747 B.C.—3967 Julian period. To find the Julian year on which the year of Nabonassar begins, subtract the year, if before Christ, from 748; if after Christ, add to it 747.

Nag's Head story. Matthew Parker was consecrated archbishop of Canterbury at Lambeth, 17 Dec. 1559, by bishops Barlow, Coverdale, Scory, and Hodgkins. For forty-five years after, the Romish writers asserted that Parker and others had been ordained in an abnormal fashion by Scory at the Nag's Head tavern, Cheapside. This fiction was refuted by Burnet, and is rejected by Roman Catholic authorities, such as Lingard.

Na'hum, Festival of. Nahum, 7th of the 12 minor prophets, about 713 B.C.; the festival is 24 Dec.

nails of the earlier nations were of bronze. The nail used by Jael in killing Sisera (Judges iv. 21) was a wooden tent-pin. Up to the 19th century nails were mostly forged, the first cut-nails being made by Jeremiah Wilkinson, in Rhode Island, in 1775, followed by Ezekiel Reed, Mass., 1786. The Perkins cut-nail machine, patented 1795, made 200,000 nails in a day.

names. Adam and Eve named their sons (Gen. iv. 25, 26). A Roman citizen had generally 3 names; *prænomen*, denoting the individual; *nomen*, the gens or clan; *cognomen*, the family or branch of the clan; sometimes he had the *agnomen* (e. g. Publius Cornelius Scipio Africanus). The po[illegible] change names on assuming the pontificate, "a custom [illegible] duced by pope Sergius, whose name till then wa[illegible] snout," 687.—*Platina.* Onuphrius refers it to [illegible] stating that it was done in imitation of [illegible] who were first called Simon and Saul. [illegible] tismal name was sometimes changed [illegible] II. of France were christened Alex[illegible] confirmation they became Henri [illegible] nuns, entering monasteries, [illegible] Miss Yonge's "History of C[illegible] ed. 1884). M. A. Lowe[illegible]

Na'mur, [illegible] the French, [illegible] 1695; [illegible] tioned by [illegible]

[illegible] 15. Taken by the French in 1746, but restored in 1748. In [illegible] the emperor Joseph expelled the Dutch garrison. In 1792 [illegible] was again taken by the French, who were compelled to evacuate it in 1793; [illegible] 1794; delivered to the allies, 1814; [illegible] signed to [illegible] 1831; fortifications destroyed, 1866.

Nancy [illegible], N.E. France, an ancient city, capital of [L]orraine in the 15th century. After taking Nancy, 29 Nov. [1]475, and losing it, 5 Oct. 1476, Charles the Bold of Burgundy [w]as defeated beneath its walls, and slain by the duke of Lorraine and Swiss, 5 Jan. 1477. LORRAINE. Nancy was embellished by Stanislas, ex-king of Poland, who resided here, and [d]ied Feb. 1766; was captured by Blucher, Jan. 1814; and on [th]e retreat of MacMahon's army, expecting the Germans, surrendered to Uhlans, 12 Aug. 1870. It was restored at the peace.

Nan'kin, said to have been made central capital of [C]hina, 420; was the court of the Ming dynasty from 1369 till [Y]ung-lo removed to Pekin in 1410. On 4 Aug. 1842, British [s]hips arrived at Nankin, and peace was made. The rebel [T]ae-pings took it on 19, 20 Mch. 1853. It was recaptured by [i]mperialists, 19 July, 1864, and found desolate.

Nantes (*nänts*), W. France, formerly capital of the [N]amnetes. The edict in favor of Protestants issued here by [H]enry IV., 13 Apr. 1598, was revoked by Louis XIV., 22 Oct. [1]685. Awful cruelties were committed here by the republican [C]arrier, Oct.–Nov. 1793. Pop. 1891, 122,750. DROWNING, [F]RENCH REVOLUTION.

Nantucket and **Martha's Vineyard,** islands [o]f the south coast [illegible] and belonging to that [st]ate, the former [illegible] latter 120 sq. miles. First [illegible] settled by some people [illegible] Mass., 1643. Both [illegible] skilled seamen

[illegible] ...[illegible] ...umber of [illegible] upon the proposi[illegible] ...ce constituted [illegible] On the 20th [illegible] of the king; [illegible] ...aired to the *Jeu* [illegible] to dissolve until [illegible] ...ce. On the 22d they

Greek colony named Parthenope (about 1000 B C), afterwards divided into Palæopolis (the *old*) and Neapolis (the *new* city), the latter name became Naples. The colony was conquered by Romans in the Samnite war, 326 B.C. Naples, after resisting Lombards, Franks and Germans, was subjugated by Normans under Roger Guiscard, king of Sicily, A D 1131 Few countries have had so many political changes and despotic rulers, or suffered so much by convulsions of nature, such as earthquakes, volcanic eruptions, etc In 1856, the population of the kingdom of Naples was 6,886,030, of Sicily, 2,231,020, total, 9,117,050 It now forms part of the kingdom of Italy Pop of the city, 1881, 463,172

Naples conquered by Theodoric the Goth 493
City retaken by Belisarius 536
Taken again by Totila. 543
Retaken by Narses 552
Becomes a duchy nominally of the Eastern empire 568 or 572
Duchy of Naples greatly extended 593
Robert Guiscard the Norman, made duke of Apulia, founds the kingdom of Naples 1059
Naples conquered. kingdom of the Two Sicilies founded by Roger Guiscard II 1131
Imperial house of Hohenstaufen (GERMANY) obtains the kingdom by marriage and rules 1194–1266
Pope Clement IV appoints Charles of Anjou king, who defeats the regent Manfred (son of Frederick II of Germany) at Benevento (Manfred slain) 26 Feb 1266
Charles defeats Conradin (last of the Hohenstaufens invited to Naples by Ghibellines) at Tagliacozzo, 23 Aug, Conradin beheaded 29 Oct. 1268
Massacre called SICILIAN VESPERS 30 Mch 1282
Andrew of Hungary, husband of Joanna I murdered 18 Sept. 1345
His brother Louis, king of Hungary, invades Naples 1349
Queen Joanna put to death 22 May, 1382
Alphonso V of Aragon (called the Wise and Magnanimous), on the death of Joanna II, seizes Naples 1435
Naples conquered by Charles VIII of France 1494
And by Louis XII of France and Ferdinand of [illegible], who divide it 1501
Expulsion of the French 1504
Naples and Sicily united to Spain. "
Insurrection of Masaniello, occasioned by extortions of Spanish viceroys An impost was claimed on a basket of figs and refused by the owner, whom the populace joined, headed by Masaniello (Thomas Aniello), a fisherman, they obtained command of Naples, many nobles were slain and palaces burned, and the viceroy compelled to abolish the taxes and to restore privileges granted by Charles V to the city June, 1647
Masaniello, intoxicated by success, slain by his followers, 16 July, "
Another insurrection suppressed by don John of Austria Oct. "
Henry II, duke of Guise, landing is proclaimed king, in a few days taken prisoner by the Spaniards April, 1648
Naples conquered by prince Eugene of Savoy for the emperor 1706
Discovery of HERCULANEUM 1711
Spaniards by victory at Bitonto (26 May) having mastered both kingdoms, Charles (of Bourbon), son of the king of Spain, ascends the throne, with the ancient title of king of the Two Sicilies 1734
Order of St Januarius instituted 1738
Discovery of POMPEII 1748–50
Charles, becoming king of Spain, vacates the throne in favor of his third son, Ferdinand, agreeably to treaty 1759
Expulsion of the Jesuits 3 Nov 1767
Dreadful earthquake in Calabria 5 Feb 1783
Enrolment of the LAZZARONI as pikemen or spontoneers 1793
King flees on approach of French republicans, who establish the Parthenopean republic 14 Jan 1799
Nelson appears, Naples retaken, the restored king rules tyrannically June, "
Prince Caracciolo tried and executed by order of Nelson, 29 June, "
Neapolitans occupy Rome 30 Sept. "
Treaty of neutrality between France and Naples ratified 9 Oct 1805
Ferdinand, through perfidy, is compelled to flee to Sicily, 23 Jan, French enter Naples Joseph *Bonaparte made king* Feb 1806
French defeated at Maida. 4 July, "
Joseph Bonaparte after beginning many reforms, abdicates for the crown of Spain June, 1808
Joachim Murat made king (rules well) 15 July, "
His first quarrel with Napoleon 1811
His alliance with Austria Jan 1814
Death of queen Caroline 7 Sept. "
Murat declares war against Austria 15 Mch 1815
Defeated at Tolentino 3 May, "
He retires to France, 22 May, and Corsica, attempting to recover his throne lands at Pizzo, seized, tried, and shot, 13 Oct "
Ferdinand, re established, returns to tyrannical measures. June, "
Establishment of the society of the CARBONARI 1819
Successful insurrection of Carbonari under gen *Pépé*, the king compelled to swear to a new constitution 13 July, 1820
Austrians invade the kingdom at the king's instigation, gen Pépé defeated 7 Mch 1821
Fall of constitutional government 23 Mch "
Death of Ferdinand (reigned 66 years) 4 Jan 1825
Insurrection of the Carbonari suppressed Aug 1828
Accession of Ferdinand II, Bomba (faithless and tyrannical), 8 Nov 1830
Attilio and Emilio Bandiero, with 18 others, attempting an insurrection in Calabria, are shot 17 Jan 1844
Prospect of an insurrection in Naples, king grants a new constitution, with liberal ministry 29 Jan 1848
Fighting in Naples, liberals and national guard almost annihilated by royal troops aided by lazzaroni 15 May, "
Martial anarchy, the chiefs of liberal party arrested Dec 1849
Settembrini, Poerio Carafa and others, after a mock trial, condemned and consigned to dungeons for life June, 1850
After remonstrances with the king on his tyrannical government (May), the English and French ambassadors are withdrawn 28 Oct 1856
Attempted assassination of the king by Milano 8 Dec "
Cagliari, a Sardinian mail steamboat, sailed from Genoa for Tunis, 25 June 1857, with 33 passengers, who, after a few hours' sail, took forcible possession, and compelled the 2 English engineers (Watt and Park) to steer to Ponza, 25 June, 1857
[Here they landed released some prisoners, took them on board, and sailed to Sapri, where they again landed and restored the vessel to its commander and crew The latter steered for Naples, but on the way the vessel was boarded by a Neapolitan cruiser, and all the crew were landed and consigned to dungeons, where they remained nine months awaiting trial, under great privations and insults Excitement followed in England, and, after negotiation the crew were released, the vessel given to the British government, and 3000*l* paid as a compensation to the sufferers]
Poerio and 66 companions released and sent to North America, Jan, on their way they seize the vessel, sail to Cork, 7 Mch, and proceed to London 18 Mch 1859
Death of Ferdinand II 22 May, "
Garibaldi lands in Sicily, 11 May, defeats the Neapolitan army at Calatafimi 15 May, 1860
Francis II proclaims an amnesty, promises a liberal ministry, adopts a tricolor flag, etc 26 June "
A liberal ministry formed, destruction of the commissariat of the police in 12 districts, state of siege proclaimed at Naples, queen mother flees to Gaeta 28 June, "
Garibaldi defeats Neapolitans at Melazzo, 20 July, enters Messina, 21 July, Neapolitans agree to evacuate Sicily 30 July, "
King of Sardinia in vain negotiates with Francis II for alliance July, "
Francis [illegible] proclaims re establishment of constitution of 1848, 2 July, the army proclaim count de Trani king 10 July, "
Garibaldi lands at Melito, 18 Aug, takes Reggio 21 Aug "
Defection in army and navy, Francis II retires to Gaeta, 6 Sept., Garibaldi enters Naples without troops 7 Sept "
Garibaldi assumes dictatorship, 8 Sept., gives the Neapolitan fleet to the Sardinian admiral Persano, 11 Sept, expels Jesuits, establishes trial by jury, releases political prisoners Sept "
Repulses Neapolitans at Cajazzo, 19 Sept, defeats them at the Volturno 1 Oct. "
King of Sardinia enters the kingdom of Naples, and takes command of his army, which combines with Garibaldi's 11 Oct. "
Cialdini defeats the Neapolitans at Isernia, 17 Oct, at Venafro, 18 Oct "
Plébiscite at Naples, etc, vote for annexation to Piedmont (1 303,064 to 10,312) 21 Oct. "
Garibaldi meets Victor Emmanuel, and salutes him as king of Italy 26 Oct "
First English Protestant church built on ground given by Garibaldi, consecrated 11 Mch 1865
Great eruption of Vesuvius began 12 Nov 1867
Victor Emmanuel, prince of Naples (son of prince Humbert), born at Naples 11 Nov 1869
ITALY

SOVEREIGNS OF NAPLES AND SICILY

1131 Roger I (of Sicily, 1130), *Norman*
1154 William I the Bad, son
1166 William II the Good, son
1189 Tancred, natural son of Roger
1194 William III son, succeeded by Constance, married to Henry VI of Germany
1197 Frederick II of Germany (*Hohenstaufen*)
1250 Conrad, son
1254 Conradin, son, but his uncle,
1258. Manfred, natural son of Frederick II, seizes the government, killed at Benevento in 1266.
1266 Charles of Anjou, brother of St Louis, king of France. [Conradin beheaded, 29 Oct 1268]
1282 Insurrection in Sicily

(*Separation of the kingdoms in* 1282)

NAPLES.

1282 Charles I of Anjou
1285 Charles II, son
1309 Robert the Wise, brother
1343 Joanna (reigns with her husband, Andrew of Hungary), 1343–1345, with Louis of Tarento, 1349–62, Joanna put to death (22 May, 1382) by
1382 Charles III, grandson of Charles II, he becomes king of Hungary, assassinated there, 1386
" Louis I, titular, crowned
1385 Louis II, son of Louis I
1386 Ladislas of Hungary
1414 Joanna II, sister, dies in 1435, and bequeaths her dominions to Regnier of Anjou They are acquired by
1435 Alphonso I, thus king of Naples and Sicily

SICILY.

1282. Peter I. (III. of Aragon).
1285. James I. (II. of Aragon).
1295. Frederick II.
1337. Peter II.
1342. Louis.
1355. Frederick III.
1376. Maria and Martin (her husband).
1402. Martin I.
1409. Martin II.
1410. Ferdinand I.
1416. Alphonso I.

(*Separation of Naples and Sicily in* 1458.)

NAPLES.

1458. Ferdinand I.
1494. Alphonso II. abdicates.
1495. Ferdinand II.
1496. Frederick II.; expelled by the French, 1501.

SICILY.

1458. John of Aragon.
1479. Ferdinand the Catholic of Spain.

CROWNS UNITED.

1503. Ferdinand III. (king of Spain).
1516. Charles I. (V. of Germany).
1556. Philip I. (II. of Spain).
1598. Philip II. (III. of Spain).
1621. Philip III. (IV. of Spain).
1665. Charles II. (of Spain).
1700. Philip IV. (V. of Spain), Bourbons.
1707. Charles III. of Austria.

(*Separation in* 1713.)

NAPLES.

1713. Charles III. of Austria.

SICILY.

1713. Victor Amadeus of Savoy (exchanged Sicily for Sardinia, 1720).

THE TWO SICILIES.

(*Part of the Empire of Germany*, 1720–34.)

1735. Charles IV. (III. of Spain).
1759. Ferdinand IV. fled from Naples to Sicily, 1806.

(*Separation in* 1806.)

NAPLES.

1806. Joseph Napoleon Bonaparte.
1808. Joachim Murat; shot 13 Oct. 1815.

SICILY.

1806–15. Ferdinand IV.

THE TWO SICILIES.

1815. Ferdinand I., formerly Ferdinand IV., of Naples and Sicily.
1825. Francis I.
1830. Ferdinand II., Nov. 8 (termed king Bomba).
1859. Francis II., 22 May; b. 16 Jan. 1836; last king of Naples; deposed; fled 6 Sept. 1860; d. Dec. 1894.
1861. Victor Emmanuel II. of Sardinia, as king of Italy, Mch.; ITALY, end.

Narbonne (*nar-bonn'*), a city of S.E. France, the Roman Narbo Martius, founded 118 B.C., made capital of a Visigothic kingdom, 462; captured by Saracens, 720; retaken by Pepin le Bref, 759. Gaston de Foix, the last vicomte (killed at Ravenna, 11 Apr. 1512), resigned it to the king in exchange for duchy of Nemours. Many councils held here, 589–1374.

narceine (*när'-sē-in*) and **narcotine**, alkaloids obtained from OPIUM. Narceine was discovered by Pelletier in 1832; and *narcotine* by Derosne in 1803. Sometimes used as a substitute for morphine.

Narragansett Indians. INDIANS, MASSACHUSETTS.

Narva, a fortified town of Esthonia, Russia. Here Peter the Great of Russia was defeated by Charles XII. of Sweden, then in his 19th year, 30 Nov. 1700. Peter is said to have had 60,000 men, some Swedes affirm 100,000, while the Swedes were about 20,000. Charles attacked the enemy in his intrenchments, and slew 18,000; 30,000 surrendered. He had several horses shot under him. He said, "These people seem disposed to give me exercise." Narva was taken by Peter in 1704.

Naseby (*naz'bee*), a parish of Northamptonshire, Engl., the site of a decisive victory over Charles I. by the parliament army under Fairfax and Cromwell. The main royal army was commanded by lord Astley; prince Rupert led the right wing, sir Marmaduke Langdale the left, and the king himself the reserve. The king fled, losing his cannon, baggage, and nearly 5000 prisoners, 14 June, 1645.

Nashville, capital of TENNESSEE. Pop. 1900, 80,865.

Nashville, Tenn., Battle of. After the battle of FRANKLIN, gen. Schofield retreated to Nashville, 1 Dec. 1864, closely followed by Hood, who established his lines near that city, 4 Dec. From this time till 14 Dec. the armies fronted each other. Gen. Thomas was delayed in attacking Hood, although now superior in numbers; first, from want of horses, and second, owing to inclement weather, the ground from 9 to 14 Dec. being covered with ice, rendering it almost impossible to move horse or man. Gen. Grant becoming impatient of delay, signed an order suspending gen. Thomas, and placing gen. Schofield in command, 9 Dec., but fortunately it was not sent. On 15 Dec., the weather moderating, Thomas advanced against Hood and by skilful manœuvres succeeded in driving the confederates, before night, from every position held by them in the morning, capturing 16 guns and 1200 prisoners. During the night Hood fell back a short distance to a strong position at Overton's hill on the Franklin pike. Again the manœuvres on the Confederate left, with attacks on their front, broke their line at 4.30 P.M. on the 16th, and their retreat became a rout. The pursuit was kept up as rapidly as the weather and state of the roads would permit until Hood crossed the Tennessee with the remnant of his army, 28 Dec. The loss in killed and wounded on either side was not severe, but the Confederate prisoners captured numbered 5000, with 53 guns. The confederates in the campaign from 7 Sept. 1864, to 20 Jan. 1865, lost in prisoners 13,000 men, besides the killed and wounded, and 72 guns. The Federal loss was about 10,000 in all during the same time. Gen. Hood was relieved of command at his own request, 23 Jan. 1865, at Tupelo, Miss. Gen. Logan, under orders from gen. Grant, had reached Louisville, Ky., on his way from Washington to relieve Thomas, 15 Dec., but learning of the success of the Union troops, did not proceed farther.

Nassau, a German duchy, made a county by the emperor Frederick I. about 1180, for Wolfram, a descendant of Conrad I. of Germany; from whom are descended the royal house of Orange now reigning in Holland (HOLLAND, ORANGE), and the present duke of Nassau. Wiesbaden was made the capital in 1839. On 25 Apr. 1860, the Nassau chamber strongly opposed the conclusion of a concordat with the pope, and claimed liberty of faith and conscience. The duke adopted the Austrian motion at the German diet, 14 June, and after the war the duchy was annexed to Prussia by decree, 20 Sept., and possession taken 8 Oct. 1866. Pop. of the duchy in 1865, 468,311.

Natal, Cape of Good Hope. Vasco de Gama landed here on 25 Dec. 1497, and hence named it Terra Natalis. Area, 20,460 sq. miles; seaboard, 200 miles. Pop. 1876, 326,957 (20,490 whites); 1891, 543,913. (For the war, ZULULAND, 1879.)

Dutch attempted to colonize it about........................ 1721
Zulu power established about........................ 1812
Lieut. Farewell, with some emigrants, settled................ 1823
Capt. Allen Gardiner's treaty with the Zulus..........6 May, 1835
Dutch republic, Natalia, set up; put down by British. 12 May, 1842
Natal annexed to the British possessions..............8 Aug. 1843
Made a bishopric (dr. John Wm. Colenso, bishop), 1853; and an independent colony........................ 1856
Attempts to depose bishop Colenso for unsound doctrine failing, the rev. W. K. Macrorie was sent out as bishop of Maritzburg, to act with clergy opposed to the bishop......Dec. 1868
Railway to Orange Free State opened..................13 July, 1892

Nat'chez. INDIANS; MISSISSIPPI, 1729–30.

National Academy of Design, New York city, founded 1826. PAINTING.

National Academy of Science was incorporated by an act of Congress, 3 Mch. 1863; 1st meeting 22 Apr. 1863, Alexander D. Bach 1st president; duties consist in the investigation, examination, experimenting, and reporting on any subject of science and art. The actual cost of investigation, etc., to be paid for by the U. S. government; no other compensation to be received. At first the number of members was limited to 50; since 1870 to 100; a limited number of foreign members admitted.

National Assembly, French. Upon the proposition of abbé Sieyès, the States-general of France constituted themselves a *National Assembly*, 17 June, 1789. On the 20th the hall of this new assembly was shut by order of the king; upon which the deputies of the *tiers état* repaired to the *Jeu de Paume*, or Tennis-court, and swore not to dissolve until they had framed a constitution for France. On the 22d they met at the church of St Louis. They abolished the state religion, annulled monastic vows, divided France into departments, sold national domains, established a national bank, issued assignats, and dissolved 21 Sept 1792 NATIONAL CONVENTION OF FRANCE In 1848 the legislature was again termed National Assembly It met 4 May, and a new constitution was proclaimed, 12 Nov A new constitution was once more proclaimed by Louis Napoleon in Jan 1852, after dissolving the National Assembly, 2 Dec 1851

National Assembly, German GERMANY, 1848

national cemeteries. CEMETERIES

National Convention of France, constituted in the hall of the Tuileries 17 Sept., and formally opened 21 Sept. 1792, when M. Gregoire, at the head of the National Assembly, announced that that assembly had ceased its functions It was then decreed "That the citizens named by the French people to form the National Convention, being met to the number of 371, after having verified their powers, declare that the National Convention is constituted" On the first day it abolished royalty and declared France a republic 17 Jan 1793, it pronounced sentence of death on Louis XVI 5 Oct 1793, it declared all dates should be computed from the foundation of the republic, 22 Sept. 1792. 16 Oct 1793, it sentenced Marie Antoinette to the guillotine 21 Oct. 1793, it condemned to death 21 Girondists 5 Apr 1794, it sentenced to death Danton, Desmoulins, and many others of the CORDELIERS 27 July, 1794, it condemned to death Robespierre, and 26 Oct 1794, it dissolved, when a new constitution was organized, and the Executive Directory was installed at the Little Luxembourg, 1 Nov 1795 DIRECTORY, FRENCH REVOLUTION The CHARTISTS in England formed a national convention in 1839

national debt of the United States. The following statement shows the principal of the national debt of the U S on *1 Jan* of each year until 1843, and on 1 July in each year until 1890, and 1 June since

	1 Jan		*1 July*
1791	$75,463,476 52	1843	32,742,922 00
1792	77 227,924 66	1844	23,461 652 50
1793	80,352,634 04	1845	15,925,303 01
1794	78,427,404 77	1846	15,550 202 97
1795	80,747,587 39	1847	38,826 534 77
1796	83,762,172.07	1848	47,044 862 23
1797	82 064,479 33	1849	63,061,858 69
1798	79,228,529 12	1850	63,452,773 55
1799	78,408,669 77	1851	68,304,796 02
1800	82,976,294 35	1852	66,199 341 71
1801	83,038,050 80	1853	59,803,117 70
1802	80,712,632 25	1854	42,242 222 42
1803	77,054,686 30	1855	35,586,956 56
1804	86,427,120 88	1856	31,972,537 90
1805	82,312,150 50	1857	28 699 831 85
1806	75,723,270 66	1858	44,911 881 03
1807	69,218,398 64	1859	58,496,837 88
1808	65,196,317 97	1860	64,842 287 88
1809	57,023 192 09	1861	90,580,873 72
1810	53,173,217 52	1862	524,176,412 13
1811	48,005,587 76	1863	1,119,772 138 63
1812	45,209,737 90	1864	1,815 784, 370 57
1813	55,962,827 57	1865	2,680,647,869 74
1814	81,487,846 24	1866	2,773,236,173 69
1815	99,833,660 15	1867	2 678 126,103 87
1816	127,334,933.74	1868	2,611,687,851 19
1817	123,491,965 16	1869	2,588,452 213 94
1818	103,466,633 83	1870	2,480,672,427 81
1819	95,529,648 28	1871	2,353,211,332 32
1820	91,015,566 15	1872	2,253,251,328 78
1821	89,987,427 66	1873	2,234,482,993 20
1822	93,546,676 98	1874	2 251,690,468.43
1823	90,875,877 28	1875	2,232 284,531 95
1824	90,269 777 77	1876	2,180 395,067 15
1825	83,788,432 71	1877	2,205,301 392 10
1826	81,054,059 99	1878	2 256,205,892 53
1827	73,987,357 20	1879	2,349,567,482 04
1828	67 475,043 87	1880	2,120 415,370 63
1829	58,421,413 67	1881	2,069 013,569 58
1830	48,565,406.50	1882	1,918,312 994.03
1831	39,123,191 68	1883	1,884 171 728.07
1832	24,322,235 18	1884	1,830,528 923 57
1833	7,001,698 83	1885	1,863,964,873 14
1834	4,760 082 08	1886	1,775,063,013 78
1835	37,733 05	1887	1,657,602,592 63
1836	37,513 05	1888	1,692,858,984.58
1837	336,957 83	1889	1,619,052,922 23
1838	3,308,124 07	1890	1,552,140,204 73
1839	10,434,221 14		*1 June*
1840	3,573,343.82	1891	1,546,215 876 00
1841	5,250,875.54	1892	1,603,440,970 61
1842	$13,594,480 73	1893	1,556,281,905 63
1843	20,601,226 28	1894	1,638,045,005.18

NAT

The following is a statement of the various refunding operations of the national treasury

House of Representatives by resolution, 21 Sept 1789, directed Hamilton, secretary of the treasury to prepare a plan for supporting the public credit He responded in his first report, 9 Jan 1790

First Refunding act, embodying Hamilton's suggestions was approved 4 Aug 1790 Under it the state debts, and the foreign and domestic debt of the nation, were consolidated and refunded in 3 classes of bonds. The loans authorized being insufficient to refund the whole, a new loan was authorized by act approved 3 Mch 1795

Next effort to refund was in 1807 An act for conversion of various outstanding stocks into a new 6 per cent stock, was approved 13 Feb 1807 Holders of old bonds did not all respond, and the scheme partially failed

Next effort was in 1812, under an act for conversion of old 6 per cent and deferred stocks into new 6 per cent stock, approved 6 July 1812 About $3 000,000 was converted

Next effort in 1822, when an act approved 20 Apr, authorized a 5-per cent. stock in exchange for outstanding 6 and 7 per cent. stocks failed almost entirely

Next effort, in 1824, under act approved 26 May, authorizing a 4½ per cent bond, was in part successful, but a new attempt under act approved 3 Mch 1825, failed, the interest offered (4½ per cent) being too low

The debt matured and was paid during the next 10 years, being practically extinguished in 1836.

A new debt grew up and in 1861 amounted to $90,580,873 72 The civil war swelled it, until, on 31 Aug 1865, the interest bearing bonds amounted to $2,381,530,294 96, as follows

Four per cents	$618 127 98
Five per cents	69,175,727 65
Six per cents	1,281,736,439 33
Seven and three tenth per cents	830,000,000 00

Some of these were paid, others converted into five twenty consols of 1865, 1867 and 1868, at 6 per cent Refunding at lower rates was impossible until the credit of the government should be established more firmly the 6 per cent bonds being then below par

Improvement of credit may be said to have been begun by the act of 18 Mch 1869, pledging the faith of the government for payment of the debt in coin

First *post bellum* refunding act was approved 14 July, 1870, and an amendatory act 20 Jan 1871 Our 6 per cent. bonds were still at a discount in 1870, but the improvement was so rapid that the secretary of the treasury (Boutwell) gave notice on 28 Feb 1871, of subscriptions for a new 5 per cent loan under the refunding act. The books were opened on 6 Mch, and by 1 Aug the subscriptions received amounted to $65 775,550 Early in that month a "syndicate" or association of bankers was formed, which took the remainder of $200,000,000 offered, and the transaction was completed before 1 Apr 1872

Further sales of 5 per cent. bonds were made until the amount authorized by the act, $500,000,000, had been sold, and a like amount of 6 per cent bonds retired

On 24 Aug 1876 the secretary of the treasury (Morrill) contracted with bankers for the sale of $300.000,000 4½ per cent. bonds for refunding Of this sum was sold, before 4 Mch 1877, about $90,000,000 and that amount of 6 per cent bonds was retired On 6 Apr, his successor secretary Sherman, announced that the 4½ per cent. loan would be limited to $200,000,000 and before 1 July, 1877, this amount had been taken Of the proceeds, $15,000,000 was applied to resumption of specie payments, the remainder to retirement of old bonds.

On 9 June 1877, the first contract for sale of 4 per cent. bonds was made For 30 days this loan was open to the public, under agreement with the bankers contracting for it, and $75,496,550 was taken of which $25 000,000 were applied to resumption At the end of 1878 there had been sold for refunding $173,085,450 of 4 per cent. bonds

The fear that refunding operations would cause an outflow of gold to Europe in payment of called bonds led the secretary to make a contract. 21 Jan 1879, by which $5,000,000 of the 4 per cents was to be taken to England each month

An act approved 25 Jan 1879, authorized exchange of 4 per cent. consols of 1907 for equal amounts of 6 per cent. five twenty bonds, upon terms favorable to the holders Refunding certificates of $10 each, designed to popularize the loan, were authorized by act approved 26 Feb 1879

On 4 Apr 1879, subscriptions to the 4 per cent loan were received, amounting to more than $132,000,000. About half of these were rejected, and sales ceased

On 16 Apr 1879 $150,000,000 of 4 per cents, and $45,000,000 of refunding certificates were offered. the bonds at a premium of one half of 1 per cent., and 4-per cents also in exchange for ten forties Within 2 days the subscriptions exceeded the offering by nearly $35 000,000 A subscription for $40,000,000 of the certificates was declined, in order that the loans might be distributed widely, and restrictions were placed upon the sale of certificates, which was completed in June, 1879

All interest bearing obligations of the government, then subject to redemption, were thus refunded without loss to the government or disturbance of business saving $19 900,846 50 in yearly interest.

The interest bearing debt 1 Mch 1895, included

Funded loan of 1891, 4½ per ct, cont'd at 2 per ct.	$25,364,500
Funded loan of 1907, 4 per cent	559,623,900
Loan of 1904, 4 per cent., act of 14 Jan 1875	99 280,000
Loan of 1925, 4 per cent., act of 14 Jan 1875	62,400 000
Refunding certificates, 4 per cent	55,310
Total..	$746,723,710

national debt of Great Britain. The first mention ' parliamentary security for a debt of the nation occurs in ıe reign of Henry VI. The present national debt may be ıid to have commenced in the reign of William III., 1689. ı 1697 it amounted to about 5,000,000*l*., and was thought of ıarming magnitude. The sole cause of the increase has been ar. By act of 31 May, 1867, the conversion of 24,000,000*l*. ' the debt into terminable annuities was provided for. The ıw is consolidated by the National Debt act, passed 9 Aug. 870; amended by act passed 2 Aug. 1875. SINKING FUND.

	Debt.
389. William III	£664,263
'02. Anne	16,394,702
'14. George I	54,145,363
'63. George III. (end of Seven Years' war), nearly	138,865,430
'86. After American war	249,851,628
'93. Beginning of French war	244,440,306
302. Close of French war	571,000,000
315. At Peace of Paris	861,039,049
330.	840,184,022
354. Commencement of Crimean war	769,082,549
357. Close of Crimean war	808,108,722
360.	802,190,300
370.	748,286,181
380.	737,821,259
390.	618,212,157
91.	615,612,161

ıese figures do not include the terminable annuities which in 1891 were estimated at 68,458,798*l*.
r Stafford Northcote's act provides the annual charge of 28,000,-000*l*.; the surplus to reduce the debt—1876.
ıtal charge on management and interest, 31 Mch. 1891, was 25,207,000*l*.; whole debt about $3,350,000,000, or $88 per capita.

national debt of France. Following shows the ·owth of the French national debt from 1800 estimated in ıllars:

1800. First Republic	$143,000,000
1815. Napoleon I	254,500,000
1830. Louis XVIII. and Charles X	885,200,000
1848. Louis Philippe	1,182,600,000
1852. Second Republic	1,103,200,000
1871. Napoleon III	2,490,800,000
1889. Third Republic	4,250,200,000
1891. " "	6,400,000,000

Or over $160 per capita.

OTHER FOREIGN NATIONS, COMPILED FROM THE 11TH UNITED STATES CENSUS, 1890.

Countries.	Debt less sinking fund, 1890.	Debt per capita.
ıstro-Hungary	$2,866,339,539	$70
·azil	585,345,927	42
ıvaria	335,503,105	60
ussia	1,109,384,127	37
xony	143,897,747	41
urtemberg	107,735,500	52
pe of Good Hope	110,817,720	77
ınada	237,533,212	47
·w South Wales	233,289,245	214
·w Zealand	184,898,305	298
·eensland	129,204,750	333
uth Australia	102,177,500	321
ctoria	179,614,005	161
eece	107,306,518	49
ıly	2,324,826,329	76
ıxico	113,606,675	9
·therlands	430,589,858	95
ru	382,175,655	145
ıssia	3,491,018,074	30
·ain	1,251,453,696	73
rkey	821,000,000	37
·ypt	517,278,200	75

national gallery, London. PAINTING.

national guard of France was instituted by the ımmittee of Safety at Paris on 13 July, 1789 (the day be-·e destruction of the Bastile), to maintain order and defend e public liberty. Its first colors were blue and red, to which ıite was added, when its formation was approved by the ng. Its action was soon paralyzed by the Revolution, and ceased under the consulate and empire. It was revived by ıpoleon in 1814, and maintained by Louis XVIII., but broken by Charles X., after a tumultuous review in 1827. It was vived in 1830, and helped to place Louis Philippe on the rone. Its reconstitution and enlargement from 80,000 to 0,000 men led to the frightful conflict of June, 1848. Its nstitution was changed in Jan. 1852, when it was subjected tirely to the control of the government. Formerly it had ıny privileges, such as choosing officers, etc. In consequence of the defection of part of the national guard and the incompetency of the rest during the outbreak in Paris in 1871, its gradual abolition was decreed by the National Assembly at Versailles (488-154), 24 Aug. 1871. The peaceful disarmament began in Sept. National guards have been established in Spain, Naples, and other countries during the present century.

national guard, United States. ARMY, MILITIA.

National Republican party. POLITICAL PARTIES.

nationalism, the doctrine in the United States that the general government should exercise a larger control over affairs of national importance, as for instance: (1) control of telegraphs, telephones, and express companies; (2) nationalization of railroads; (3) ownership of mines, oil and gas wells; (4) control of heating, lighting, and street-car service of cities, all carried on in the interest of the general public and not for individuals or corporations; in other words, for use and not for profit; (5) children to be educated until 17 years of age; child labor prohibited, etc. Bellamy's novel, "Looking Backward," 1888, expresses these views.

nativity. The coming into life or into the world. 1. Especially the birth of Christ, 25 Dec. (CHRISTMAS); festival observed by all Christian nations. 2. That of the Virgin Mary, 8 Sept.; festival not observed by Protestants. Pope Sergius I., about 690, established it, but it was not generally received in France and Germany till about 1000; nor by eastern Christians till the 12th century. 3. That of St. John the Baptist, 24 June, midsummer-day, said to have been instituted in 488.

natural history was studied by Solomon, 1014 B.C. (1 Kings iv. 33); Aristotle (384-322 B.C.); by Theophrastus (394-297 B.C.); and by Pliny (23-79 A.D.). BOTANY, FLOWERS AND PLANTS, ZOOLOGY.

natural philosophy. PHILOSOPHY.

natural selection. SPECIES.

naturalism, a realistic style in literature, mainly introduced by Balzac, 1829 et seq.

Edmond and Jules de Goncourt published "Medical and Physiological Novels" ... 1846 et seq.
Émile Zola, in his "Rougon-Macquart" series, 1871 et seq., portrayed deformed and diseased rather than healthy characters. A dramatized form of his "Assommoir," entitled "Drink," was performed in London ... 1879

naturalization is defined to be the making a foreigner or alien a citizen of any nation or state, granting him the rights of a citizen or a subject that by birth he did not have.

First American naturalization law passed by the colonial legislature of Maryland ... 1666
Naturalization authorized by law in Virginia, 1671; in New York, 1683; in South Carolina, 1693; in Massachusetts ... 1731
General law in New York ... 1715
Act of British Parliament for colonial naturalization ... 1740
Uniform law passed by Congress (UNITED STATES, 1802), 26 Mch. 1790
Supreme court decided that legislation on this subject belongs exclusively to the nation ... 1817
Conditions and manner of naturalizing an alien are prescribed by secs. 2163-74 of the Revised Statutes of the United States. Naturalization of Chinamen is prohibited by sec. 14, chap. 126, laws of 1882. All naturalized citizens of the U. S. receive the same protection from that government when abroad as native-born citizens.

In England the first act of naturalization was passed in 1437; and similar enactments were made in later reigns; often special acts for individuals. An act for naturalization of Jews passed May, 1753; but was repealed in 1754, on the petition of all the cities in England. JEWS. The act naturalizing prince Albert passed, 3 Vict. 7 Feb. 1840. A committee to inquire into the naturalization laws, appointed May, 1868, earl of Clarendon chairman, met 25 Oct. 1868; reported about Feb. 1869; and new acts were passed 12 May, 1870, and 25 July, 1872, under which British subjects may renounce their allegiance. By convention signed 3 Feb. 1871, the nationality of British subjects is made dependent on choice and not on birth.

nature-printing consists in pressing objects, such as plants, mosses, feathers, etc., into plates of metal, causing them, as it were, to engrave themselves, and afterwards taking casts or copies for printing Kniphoff of Erfurt, between 1728 and 1757, produced his *Herbarium vivum* by pressing plants (previously inked) on paper, the impressions being afterwards colored by hand In 1833, Peter Kyhl, of Copenhagen, made use of steel rollers and lead plates In 1842 Mr Taylor printed lace In 1847 Mr Twining printed ferns, grasses, and plants, and in the same year dr Branson suggested electrotyping the impressions In 1849, prof Leydolt of Vienna, by assistance of Andrew Worring, obtained impressions of agates and fossils The first practical application of this process is in Von Heufler's work on the mosses of Arpasch, in Transylvania, the second (first in England) in "The Ferns of Great Britain and Ireland," edited by dr Lindley, with illustrations prepared under superintendence of Henry Bradbury in 1855-56, who also, in 1859-60, printed "The British Seaweeds," edited by W G Johnstone and Alex Croall The process was applied to butterflies by Joseph Merrin, of Gloucester, in 1864

naval battles. The first sea-fight on record is that between the Corinthians and Corcyreans, 664 B C—*Blair* The following are among the most celebrated naval engagements (see separate articles)

B C

Battle of Salamis, Greeks victorious over the Persians, most important naval battle of ancient times 20 Oct 480
Battle of Eurymedon, Cimon the Athenian defeats the Persians both by sea and land the same day 466
Athenian fleet under Phormio defeats the Peloponnesian fleet near Naupaktus 429
Battle of Cyzicus, Lacedæmonian fleet taken by Alcibiades the Athenian 410
Battle of Arginusæ 406
Battle of Ægospotamos (Spartans victors) 405
Persian fleet, under Conon the Athenian, defeats the Spartan at Cnidos, Pisander, the Spartan admiral, is killed, and the maritime power of Sparta destroyed 394
Battle of Mylæ (Romans defeat Carthaginians) 260
Roman fleet, off Drepanum, destroyed by the Carthaginians 249
Carthaginian fleet destroyed by the consul Lutatius 241
Battle of Actium 31

A D

Emperor Claudius II defeats the Goths and sinks 2000 of their ships 269
Battle of Lepanto (Turks defeated) 7 Oct 1571
Bay of Gibraltar, Dutch and Spaniards (a bloody and decisive victory for the Dutch) 25 Apr 1607
Austrians defeat Italians at Lissa 20 July, 1866

PRINCIPAL NAVAL ENGAGEMENTS IN BRITISH HISTORY.

[Hallam affirms that the naval glory of England can be traced "in a continuous track of light" from the period of the Commonwealth]

Alfred with 10 galleys, defeated 300 sail of Danish pirates on the Dorset and Hampshire coast —*Asser's* "Life of Alfred" 897
Edward III defeats the French near Sluys 24 June, 1340
Off Winchelsea, Edward III defeated the Spanish fleet of 40 large ships, and captured 26 29 Aug 1350
English and Flemings latter signally defeated 1371
Earl of Arundel defeats a Flemish fleet of 100 sail, and captures 80 24 Mch 1387
Near Milford Haven, English take 8 and destroy 15 French ships 1405
Off Harfleur, duke of Bedford takes or destroys nearly 500 French ships 15 Aug 1416
In the Downs, Spanish and Genoese fleet captured by earl of Warwick 1459
Bay of Biscay, English and French, indecisive 10 Aug 1512
Sir Edward Howard attacks French under Prior John, repulsed and killed 25 Apr 1513
SPANISH ARMADA destroyed 19 July 1588
Dover strait, Dutch adm Van Tromp defeated by adm Blake, 28 Sept Dutch surprise the English in the Downs, 80 sail engaging 40 English, take or destroy several, 28 Nov, Van Tromp sails the Channel with a broom at mast head, as having swept the English from the seas 29 Nov 1652
English adm Blake defeats Van Tromp off Portsmouth, taking and destroying 11 men of war and 30 merchantmen, 18-20 Feb 1653
Off the North Foreland, Dutch fleet under Van Tromp, English under Blake, Monk, and Deane nearly 100 men of war each, 6 Dutch ships taken, 11 sunk, the rest ran into Calais roads, 2 June, "
On the coast of Holland, Dutch lose 30 men of war, and adm Tromp was killed (7th and last battle) 31 July, "
Spanish fleet vanquished and burned in the harbor of Santa Cruz by Blake 20 Apr 1657
English and French, 130 of the Bordeaux fleet destroyed by the duke of York (afterwards James II) 4 Dec 1664
Duke of York defeats Dutch fleet off Harwich, Opdam, Dutch admiral, blown up with all his crew, 18 capital ships taken, 14 destroyed 3 June, 1665
Earl of Sandwich took 12 men of war and 2 India ships 4 Sept. "
Dutch and English fleets contend for 4 days, English lose 9, and the Dutch 15 ships. 1-4 June, 1666
Decisive victory at mouth of the Thames, Dutch lose 24 men-of-war, 4 admirals killed, and 4000 seamen 25, 26 July, 1666
Dutch adm De Ruyter sails up the Thames and destroys some ships. 11 June, 1667
Twelve Algerine ships of war destroyed by sir Edward Spragg, 10 May, 1671
Battle of Southwold bay (SOLEBAY) 28 May, 1672
Coast of Holland, by prince Rupert, 28 May, 4 June, and 11 Aug, sir E Spragg killed, D'Estrees and Ruyter defeated 1673
Off Beachy Head, English and Dutch defeated by French under Tourville 30 June, 1690
But defeat him near cape La Hogue 19 May, 1692
Off St. Vincent, English and Dutch squadrons, under adm Rooke, defeated by French 16 June, 1693
Off Carthagena, adm Benbow and French fleet under adm Du Casse 19 Aug 1702
[French retire For their conduct in this action the English capts. Kirby and Wade were shot at Plymouth]
Sir George Rooke defeats the French fleet off Vigo 12 Oct "
Spanish fleet of 29 sail totally defeated by sir George Byng in the Faro of Messina 31 July, 1718
Off cape Finisterre, the French fleet of 38 sail taken by adm Anson 3 May, 1747
Off Finisterre, when adm Hawke took 7 men of war of the French 14 Oct "
Adm Pocock defeats French fleet in the East Indies, in 2 actions 1758, and again 1759
Adm Boscawen defeats French under De la Clue, off cape Lagos 18 Aug "
Adm Hawke defeats French fleet under Conflans, in QUIBERON BAY, preventing a projected invasion of England 20 Nov "
Near cape St Vincent, adm RODNEY defeated Spanish fleet under adm don Langara 16 Jan 1780
Rodney defeated French going to attack Jamaica, took 5 ships of the line, and sent the French admiral, comte de Grasse, prisoner to England 12 Apr 1782
British totally defeated fleets of France and Spain in bay of Gibraltar 13 Sept "
Dutch fleet, under adm Lucas, in SALDANHA bay, surrenders to sir George Keith Elphinstone 17 Aug 1796
British victory off CAPE ST VINCENT 14 Feb 1797
Unsuccessful attempt on Santa Cruz, Nelson loses his right arm (NELSON'S VICTORIES) 24 July, "
Victory of CAMPERDOWN 11 Oct "
Of the NILE 1 Aug 1798
COPENHAGEN bombarded 2 Apr 1801
Victory off TRAFALGAR 21 Oct 1805
Adm Duckworth passes DARDANELLES. 19 Feb 1807
Copenhagen fleet captured 8 Sept "
Russian fleet in the Tagus surrenders to British 3 Sept. 1808
Bay of Rosas where lieut Tailour, by direction of capt Hallowell, takes or destroys 11 war and other vessels (ROSAS BAY), 1 Nov 1809
Off LISSA, victory gained over a Franco Venetian squadron by capt William Hoste 13 Mch 1811
ALGIERS bombarded by lord Exmouth 27 Aug 1816
NAVARINO 20 Oct 1827
Bombardment and capture of Acre, by British squadron under adm Stopford with trifling loss, the Egyptians lost 2000 killed and wounded, and 3000 prisoners (SYRIA) 3 Nov 1840

naval battles of the United States The navy, during the Revolution, was of little account. The principal exploits were performed by privateers In Dec 1775, a navy was established by Congress, and officers appointed Esek Hopkins was made commander-in-chief, and in the spring of 1776 went southward with a small squadron. NAVY, UNITED STATES

British armed schooner *Margaretta* captured off Machias, Me (first naval engagement of the Revolution). 11 May, 1775
Hopkins captures several British vessels Mch and Apr 1776
Two battles on lake Champlain, the Americans commanded by Benedict Arnold (NEW YORK) 11, 13 Oct. "
Paul Jones, in *Providence* privateer, takes 15 prizes in the autumn of "
John Manly and others make prizes on the northeast coast "
Paul Jones attacks Whitehaven on the English coast. Apr 1778
With the *Bonhomme Richard* and the *Pallas* he captures off the coast of Scotland the *Serapis*, 50 guns, and the *Countess of Scarborough*, 20 guns, after a desperate fight The battle began at 8 P M and continued until 10 30 P M, when the *Serapis* surrendered and the *Countess* 20 minutes after The *Richard* sank next day 23 Sept 1779
U S frigate *Constellation*, com Truxton, 36 guns, 309 men, captures the French frigate *L'Insurgente*, 40 guns, 409 men, off St. Kitts, after a contest of 1 h 15 min French loss, 70, U S 3 wounded 9 Feb 1799
U S frigate *Constellation*, com Truxton, engages *La Vengence*, a French frigate of 54 guns, 400 men, off Guadaloupe, after a sharp running fight from 8 P M until 1 A M a squall separates them, and the French frigate escapes 1 Feb 1800
Frigate *Philadelphia* taken by Tripolitans (UNITED STATES), Oct 1803
Philadelphia destroyed by Decatur (UNITED STATES) 16 Feb. 1804
Tripoli bombarded by com Preble. Aug "
U S. frigate *Chesapeake* fired upon by British frigate *Leopard* (UNITED STATES) 22 June, 1807
Contest between U S frigate *President* and British sloop *Little Belt* (UNITED STATES) 16 May, 1811

, S. frigate *Constitution*, off the New England coast, escapes from com. Broke's British squadron............17-20 July, 1812

. S. frigate *Constitution*, 44 guns, 468 men, capt. Isaac Hull, captures and destroys British frigate *Guerrière*, 38 guns, 253 men, capt. *Jas. R. Dacres*, in 30 minutes, off the coast of the U. S. American loss, 14; British, 85.........19 Aug. "

ieut. Jesse D. Elliott, U. S. navy, captures the brigs *Detroit* and *Caledonia* from under the guns of fort Erie, opposite Buffalo, N. Y., night of.............................8-9 Oct. "

[*Detroit*, becoming unmanageable, goes ashore on west side of Squaw island, and is burned by Americans. The *Caledonia* afterwards served in Perry's fleet on lake Erie.]

'asp, 18 guns. 135 men, capt. Jacob Jones, captures British brig *Frolic*, 20 guns, 108 men, capt. Whinyates, off the southern coast of the U. S., and immediately after is captured by British ship-of-war *Poictiers*, 74 guns................18 Oct. "

rigate *United States*, 44 guns, 478 men, capt. Decatur, captures British frigate *Macedonian*, 40 guns, 320 men, off Madeira. British loss, 104; American, 11. Contest 2 hours, 25 Oct. "

onstitution, capt. Wm. Bainbridge, captures off the coast of Brazil British frigate *Java*, 38 guns, 446 men, capt. Lambert. British loss, 161; American loss, 34.................29 Dec. "

oop-of-war *Hornet*, capt. Jas. Lawrence, 20 guns, 135 men, captures British brig *Peacock*, 20 guns, 136 men, capt. Peake, off the mouth of the Demerara river. Contest 15 minutes. British loss about 50 (9 of whom were drowned by the sinking of the vessel); American loss, 3.................24 Feb. 1813

. S. frigate *Chesapeake*, capt. Jas. Lawrence, rated at 36 guns, but carrying about 50, and 300 men, captured by British frigate *Shannon*, capt. Philip V. Broke, rated at 38 guns, but mounting 54, 335 men, off Boston harbor, Mass.......1 June, "

[*Chesapeake* lost 48 killed and 98 wounded, among them capt. Lawrence, mortally; the *Shannon* 26 killed and 58 wounded. As this was the only important naval capture by the British during the war, it excited great enthusiasm in England. The freedom of London and a sword were presented to Broke; he was knighted by the prince regent, and his native county Suffolk gave him a magnificent piece of plate. Lawrence has been charged with taking his crew into action while insubordinate and mutinous.]

loop-of-war *Argus*, 22 guns, capt. Wm. Henry Allen, captured by British sloop-of-war *Pelican*, 21 guns, capt. J. F. Maples, in the British channel. American loss, 23; British, 7, 14 Aug. "

[Capt. Allen, who was mortally wounded, was buried at Plymouth, Engl., with military honors, 21 Aug.]

. S. brig *Enterprise*, lieut. Wm. Burrows, 14 guns, captures British brig *Boxer*, 14 guns, capt. Sam'l Blyth, off the coast of Maine...4 Sept. "

[Burrows was mortally wounded and Blyth was instantly killed at the commencement of the action. Lieut. Ed. R. McCall of South Carolina succeeded Burrows in command.]

om. Oliver Hazard Perry, with 9 vessels, viz., *Lawrence* 20 guns, *Niagara* 20, *Caledonia* 3, *Scorpion* 2, *Ariel* 4, *Somers* 2, *Porcupine* 1, *Tigress* 1, *Trippe* 1, in all 54 guns and 2 swivels, with 490 men, captures the British fleet under R. H. Barclay, 6 vessels, viz., *Detroit* 19 guns, *Queen Charlotte* 17, *Lady Provost* 13, *Little Belt* 3, *Hunter* 10, *Chippewa* 1 and 2 swivels, in all 63 guns and 2 swivels, with about 500 men, off Put-in bay, lake Erie. The American loss was 27 killed, 96 wounded; British, 41 killed, 94 wounded.........................10 Sept. "

["We have met the enemy and they are ours."—*Perry to Harrison.*]

ruise and capture of the *Essex*. Com. David Porter in the *Essex*, 32 guns, but carrying 46, leaves the Delaware, 28 Oct. 1812; cruising off the coast of South America, just south of the equator, on 12 Dec. he captures British brig *Nocton*, and secures $55,000 in specie; passes cape Horn on 14 Feb. 1813, and cruises in the Pacific, doing much damage to the British whaling-service, till 3 Feb. 1814, when he enters the harbor of Valparaiso. Here the British frigates *Phœbe*, capt. Hillyar, carrying 52 guns, though rated at 36, with 320 men, and the *Cherub*, capt. Tucker, 28 guns, 108 men, soon appear; attack the *Essex*, already crippled by a squall in the attempt to get to sea, and capture her after a desperate conflict. The *Essex* loses 124 out of 225; British, 15...............28 Mch. 1814

loop-of-war *Peacock*, 18 guns, capt. Warrington, captures the British brig *Epervier*, 18 guns, capt. Wales, off coast of Florida. British loss, 22; American, 2 wounded. Contest, 40 minutes...29 Apr. "

[*Epervier* sold for $55,000, besides $118,000 in specie found on board.]

loop-of-war *Wasp*, 22 guns (2d of the name, built 1814; see 1812), capt. Johnston Blakeley, 173 men, captures the British brig *Reindeer*, capt. Wm. Manners, 118 men, in the British channel. Contest, 28 minutes......................28 June, "

[*Wasp* captures the British sloop *Avon*, 18 guns, 1 Sept., but is cut off from the prize by the approach of other British vessels. On 21 Sept., off the Azores, she took the British brig *Atlanta*. On 9 Oct. 1814, the *Wasp* was spoken by the Swedish bark *Adonis*. This was the last ever heard of her. UNITED STATES, 1816.]

'om. Thomas McDonough with 14 vessels—viz., *Saratoga* 26 guns, *Eagle* 20, *Ticonderoga* 17, *Preble* 7, and 10 gun-boats carrying in all 16 guns—86 guns, with 882 men—defeats the British fleet under George Downie, of 16 vessels—viz., *Confidence* 38 guns, *Linnet* 16, *Chub* 11, *Finch* 11, and 12 gun-boats carrying 20 guns—96 guns in all, with 1000 men—on lake Champlain, near Plattsburg. American loss, 52 killed and 58 wounded; British loss over 200; among the killed was Downie (NEW YORK)...............................11 Sept. "

Privateer *General Armstrong*, capt. Sam'l C. Reid, 7 guns and 90 men, destroyed by a British squadron in the harbor of Fayal, one of the Azores (Portuguese), a neutral port. After repulsing 3 attacks, capt. Reid scuttles the *Armstrong* and returns with his men to the shore. During the 10 hours of this assault the British lost over 300 in killed and wounded. The American loss was 2 killed and 7 wounded, 26 Sept. 1814

President, 44 guns, capt. Decatur, just out from New York, pursued and captured by the British frigates *Endymion* 40 guns, *Pomone* 38, *Tenedos* 38, and *Majestic*. A running fight was kept up from 3 P. M., principally with the *Endymion*, until 11 P. M., when Decatur surrendered his sword to capt. Hayes of the *Majestic*. American loss, 24 killed, 56 wounded; British, 11 killed, 14 wounded...........................15 Jan. 1815

Constitution, 52 guns, 470 men, capt. Stewart, off cape St. Vincent, captures the British frigate *Cyane*, 36 guns, 185 men, capt. Falcoln, and the brig *Levant*, 18 guns, capt. Douglass. American loss, 15; British, 77.....................20 Feb. "

Sloop-of-war *Hornet*, 18 guns, capt. Biddle, captures the British brig *Penguin*, 18 guns, capt. Dickenson, 132 men, off Brazil, 23 Feb. "

[This was the last regular naval battle in the war of 1812, although the U. S. sloop-of-war *Peacock* captured the British sloop *Nautilus* in the strait of Sunda, 30 June, 1815, long after peace was declared.]

Com. David Conner, with the U.S. fleet, bombards Vera Cruz, in conjunction with the land forces under gen. Scott..Mch. 1847

Capt. Duncan N. Ingraham of the U. S. sloop-of-war *St. Louis* rescues Koszta from the Austrian brig *Hussar* (KOSZTA AFFAIR; UNITED STATES, 1854)........................2 July, 1853

U. S. frigates *Congress* and *Cumberland* destroyed by the Confederate iron-clad *Merrimac* (HAMPTON ROADS; VIRGINIA, 1861-62)...8 Mch. 1862

Battle between the *Monitor* and *Merrimac* (HAMPTON ROADS), 9 Mch. "

Farragut passes forts Jackson and St. Philip, below New Orleans, 24 Apr. 1862, and anchors before the city.....25 Apr. "

Kearsarge destroys the *Alabama* (ALABAMA).........19 June, 1864

Farragut forces his way into Mobile bay, defeats the Confederate fleet, and captures the Confederate ram *Tennessee*. The Union loss 165 killed and 170 wounded..............5 Aug. "

Dewey destroys the Spanish fleet at Manila, P. I. (MANILLA), 1 May, 1898

Sampson and Schley destroy the Spanish fleet at Santiago, Cuba..3 July, "

naval reserve. NAVY, United States, 1891.

Navarino (*nä-vä-ree'-no*), a fortified seaport town of S.W. Greece, settled by the Arabs, 6th century; taken by the Turks, 1500; by Venetians, 1686; by Turks, 1718; by Greeks, 1821; by Turks, 1825. Near here, on 20 Oct. 1827, the combined fleets of England, France, and Russia, under adm. Codrington, nearly destroyed the Turkish and Egyptian fleet. More than 30 ships, many of them 4-deckers, were blown up or burned, chiefly by Turks, to prevent capture. This defeat of the Turks virtually secured the independence of Greece. The destruction of Turkish naval power was characterized by Wellington as an "untoward event."

Navarre (*na-var'*), now a province of Spain, was part of the Roman dominions, and was conquered from the Saracens by Charlemagne, 778. His descendants appointed governors, one of whom, Garcias Ximenes, took the title of king in 857. In 1076, king Sancho IV. was poisoned, and Sancho Ramorez of Aragon seized Navarre. In 1134, Navarre became again independent under Garcias Ramorez IV. In 1234, Thibault, count of Champagne, nephew of Sancho VII., became sovereign; and in 1284, by marriage of the heiress Jane with Philip IV. le Bel, Navarre fell to France.

SOVEREIGNS OF NAVARRE.

1274. Jane I. and (1284) Philip le Bel of France.
1305. Louis X., Hutin, of France.
1316. Philip V., the Long, of France.
1322. Charles I., the Fair, IV. of France.
1328. Jane II. (daughter of Jane I.), and her husband Philip d'Evreux.
1349. Charles II., the Bad.
1387. Charles III., the Noble.
1425. Blanche, his daughter, and her husband, John of Aragon.
1441. John II., alone, became king of Aragon in 1458. He endeavored to obtain the crown of Castile also.
1479. Eleanor de Foix, his daughter.
" Francis Phœbus de Foix, her son.
1483. Catharine (his sister) and her husband John d'Albret. Ferdinand of Aragon conquers and annexes all Navarre south of the Pyrenees, 1512.

NAVARRE ON THE NORTH (FRENCH) SIDE OF THE PYRENEES.

1516. Henry d'Albret.
1555. Jane d'Albret and her husband Anthony de Bourbon, who d. 1562.
1572. Henry III., who became in 1589 king of France (as Henry IV.) This kingdom formally united to France in 1609.

navigation (from Lat. *navis*, ship, and *agere*, to lead or direct), the science or art by which a mariner conducts a vessel from one port to another; it includes a thorough knowledge of mathematics, astronomy, geography, etc., and began with Egyptians and Phœnicians. The first navigation laws were those of the Rhodians, 916 B.C. The first account of a considerable voyage is that of Phœnicians round Africa, 604 B.C.—*Blair*.

Plane charts and mariner's compass used..............about 1420
Variation of compass observed by Columbus.......... 1492
That oblique rhomb lines are spiral, discovered by Nonius.... 1537
First treatise on navigation.......... 1545
Log first mentioned by Bourne.......... 1577
Mercator's chart.......... 1599
Davis's quadrant, or backstaff, for measuring angles.....about 1600
Logarithmic tables applied to navigation by Gunter.......... 1620
Middle-latitude sailing introduced.......... 1623
Mensuration of a degree, Norwood.......... 1631
Hedley's quadrant.......... 1731
Harrison's time-keeper used.......... 1764
"Nautical Almanac" first published.......... 1767
Barlow's theory of deviation of the compass.......... 1820
Quarterly Journal of Naval Science, edited by E. J. Reed, pub., April, 1872–75

COMPASS, LATITUDE, LONGITUDE, MAPS, STEAM.

navigators or **nav'vies.** Workmen building railways probably derived this name (about 1830) from working upon inland navigation in Lincolnshire, etc. They are doubtfully said to be descendants of the original Dutch canal laborers.

navy, the armed vessels and crew of a nation. The Phœnicians and the Greeks were the first to place much dependence on this method of warfare. Afterwards the Carthagenians, and later the Romans, maintained large navies. Since the invention of gunpowder and the steam-engine the construction of war-ships has been a subject of scientific study. The position of Great Britain has compelled her to depend on ships for defence or invasion, until she has become the greatest naval nation in the world. Other nations have followed her example, until now one of the principal branches of the national expenditure of every maritime country is the building and maintaining of its navy. NAVAL BATTLES.

navy of the United States. The present U. S. navy dates from an act of Congress 30 Apr. 1798, establishing a navy department. An act of 3 Mch. 1815 authorized a board of commissioners for the navy, but an act of 31 Aug. 1842 abolished it; reorganized the navy department with 5 bureaus, increased to 8 by act of 5 July, 1862: 1. Yards and docks; 2. Navigation; 3. Ordnance; 4. Provision and clothing; 5. Medicine and surgery; 6. Construction and repair; 7. Equipment and recruiting; 8. Steam engineering.

Law passed establishing a marine committee, consisting of John Adams, John Langdon, and Silas Dean..........13 Oct. 1775
Act of Congress for building 13 frigates: 5 of 32 guns, 5 of 28 guns, and 3 of 24 guns..........13 Dec. "
Congress appoints Esek Hopkins, commander-in-chief of the American fleet, consisting of the *Alfred*, 30 guns; *Columbus*, 28 guns; *Andrea Doria*, 16 guns; *Sebastian Cabot*, 14 guns; *Providence*, 12 guns..........22 Dec. "
Board of Admiralty established by resolution of Congress, 28 Oct. 1779
Secretary of marine created by resolution of Congress...7 Feb. 1781
First line-of-battle ship, *America*, built at Portsmouth, N. H., under act of 9 Nov. 1776, completed.......... "

SHIPS IN THE UNITED STATES NAVAL SERVICE DURING THE REVOLUTION, WITH THE FATE OF EACH.

Name.	No. of guns.	Fate.
Alliance	32	Sold after the war.
America	32	Presented to the French government, 1782.
Ariel	20	Borrowed from France and returned.
Alfred	30	Captured by the British, 1778.
Andrea Doria	16	Destroyed in the Delaware, 1777.
Bonhomme Richard	40	Sunk after action, 1779.
Boston	24	Captured at Charleston, 1780.
Confederacy	32	Captured off Virginia coast, 1781.
Congress	28	Destroyed in the Hudson, 1777.
Columbus	28	Destroyed in the Delaware, 1778.
Cabot	14	Driven ashore by the British, 1777.
Cerf	18	Left the service, 1779.
Deane (Hague)	32	Captured before getting to sea, 1778.
Delaware	24	Captured in the Delaware, 1777.
Diligent	14	Destroyed in the Penobscot, 1778.
Dolphin	10	Destroyed in the Delaware, 1777.
Effingham	28	Destroyed in the Delaware, 1777.

SHIPS IN THE UNITED STATES NAVAL SERVICE.—(*Continued.*)

Name.	No. of guns.	Fate.
Gates	42	Seized by the French, 1777.
Hancock	13	Captured by the British, 1777.
Hampden	14	Lost at sea, 1778.
Hornet	10	Seized by the French, 1777.
Independence	10	Destroyed in the Delaware, 1778.
Lexington	14	Captured in English channel, 1778.
Montgomery	24	Destroyed in the Hudson, 1777.
Pallas	32	Left the service, 1779.
Providence	12	Captured at Charleston, 1780.
Queen of France	28	Captured at Charleston, 1780.
Randolph	32	Destroyed in action with *Yarmouth*, 1778.
Raleigh	32	Captured, 1778.
Reprisal	16	Foundered at sea, 1778.
Ranger	18	Captured at Charleston, 1780.
Revenge	10	Sold, 1780.
Saratoga	16	Lost at sea, 1780.
Surprise	10	Seized by the French, 1777.
Sachem	10	Destroyed in the Delaware, 1778.
Trumbull	28	Captured, 1781.
Vengeance	12	Left the service, 1779.
Virginia	28	Captured before getting to sea, 1778.
Washington	32	Destroyed in the Delaware, 1778.
Warren	32	Destroyed in the Penobscot, 1779.
Wasp	8	Destroyed in the Delaware, 1778.

Secretary of war given control of naval affairs..........7 Aug. 1789
Act to provide for 6 ships, 27 Mch. 1794; 3 to be completed in. 1796
U. S. frigate *Constitution*, 44 guns, launched at Boston; *United States*, 44 guns, at Philadelphia; *Constellation*, 36 guns, at Baltimore.......... 1797
Act to establish a navy department, with Benjamin Stoddert, secretary of the navy (UNITED STATES)..........30 Apr. 1798
A marine corps raised by act of Congress..........11 July, "
Act appropriating the surplus of a fund for the relief of sick and disabled seamen to build marine hospitals.....16 July, "
Navy consists of 33 gun-ships, carrying 922 guns.......... 1799
Site for Norfolk navy-yard at Gosport, Va., on the Elizabeth river, purchased for $21,382; it contains 109 acres; defence, fort Monroe..........23 Jan. 1800
Site for a navy-yard at Washington purchased for $4000. Present area, 42 acres; defence, fort Washington........17 Mch. "
Rules and regulations for the navy adopted by Congress, to supersede act of 2 Mch. 1799..........23 Apr. "
Site for a navy-yard purchased at Kittery, Me., opposite Portsmouth, N. H., for $110,500; area, 164 acres; defences, forts McClary and Constitution..........13 June, "
Site for navy-yard purchased at Charlestown near Boston; area, 84 acres; cost, $163,000; defences, forts Warren and Independence..........30 Aug. "
Site purchased for a navy-yard at Brooklyn, N. Y.; price, $415,000; area, 193 acres..........18 May, 1801
Marine hospital established at New Orleans by act of Congress, 3 May, 1802
$200,000 appropriated annually for 3 years for timber for ship building and other naval purposes..........30 Mch. 1812
At the opening of the war with Great Britain the American navy consisted of:

FRIGATES.	Guns.	Commissioned.
Constitution	44	1798
United States	44	"
President	44	1799
Chesapeake	36	"
New York	36	"
Constellation	36	1798
Congress	36	1799
Boston	32	1798
Essex	32	1799
Adams	32	"
CORVETTE.		
John Adams	26	1799

BRIGS.	Guns.	SCHOONERS.	Guns.
Siren	16	Vixen	12
Argus	16	Nautilus	12
Oneida	16	Enterprise	12
		Viper	12
SLOOPS-OF-WAR.			
Wasp	18	BOMB KETCHES: Vengeance, Spitfire, Ætna, Vesuvius.	
Hornet	18	GUN-BOATS: 170.	

Most of the larger vessels carried more guns than the rating shown above. NAVAL BATTLES.

Robert Fulton builds a floating battery (BATTERIES).......... 1814
$1,000,000 annually for 8 years appropriated for gradual increase of the navy (repealed, 3 Mch. 1821)..........29 Apr. 1816
Public lands producing ship timber reserved from sale by act of Congress..........1 Mch. 1817
Act to employ the navy to suppress the slave-trade.....3 Mch. 1819
Site for the Pensacola navy-yard presented to the government, 10 Mch. 1828
Monument erected in Washington navy-yard in 1808 to officers who fell in the war with Tripoli, removed to Capitol square... 1832
Steamer-*Mississippi* launched at Philadelphia (armed with Paixhan guns).......... 1841
Princeton, first war screw-propeller, launched at Philadelphia (UNITED STATES, 1844).......... 1842

U. S. Naval academy at ANNAPOLIS opened.............10 Oct. 1845

The navy at the beginning of the Mexican war consisted of:

10 ships of the line	786 guns.	
13 frigates, first-class	682	"
2 frigates, second-class	72	"
23 sloops-of-war	438	"
8 brigs	80	"
9 schooners	17	"
11 steamers	20	"
4 store-ships	22	"
80	2017 guns....... 1846	

Publication of "American Nautical Almanac" for 1855 provided for by act of.................................3 Mch. 1849

Congress abolishes flogging in the navy and on board vessels of commerce.......................................28 Sept. 1850

Site of Mare Island navy-yard, 23 miles from San Francisco, Cal., purchased; area, 876 acres; price, $83,491; defences, fort Point and Alcatraces island.......................4 Jan. 1853

Sloop-of-war *Portsmouth* armed with 16 8-inch Dahlgren guns; first vessel in the navy carrying only shell-guns............ 1856

Naval monument removed from west front of Capitol to the grounds of the Naval academy at Annapolis................ 1860

The navy at the commencement of the civil war consisted of:

Available force.		In commission.
1 ship of the line	84 guns.	......
8 frigates	400 "	2..100 guns.
20 sloops	406 "	11..232 "
3 brigs	16 "	......
3 store-ships	7 "	3.. 7 "
6 steam-frigates	212 "	1.. 12 "
5 first-class steam-sloops	90 "	5.. 90 "
4 first-class side-wheel steamers	46 "	3.. 35 "
8 second-class steam-sloops	45 "	8.. 45 "
5 third-class screw steamers	28 "	5.. 28 "
4 sec'd-class side-wheel steamers	8 "	3.. 5 "
2 steam tenders	4 "	1.. 1 "
69	1346 guns.	42..555 guns.. 1861

Ericsson's battery, the *Monitor*, completed and delivered to the U. S. government for trial (HAMPTON ROADS)......5 Mch. 1862

Congress enacts "that from and after the first day of Sept. 1862, the spirit ration in the navy of the U. S. shall forever cease, and thereafter no distilled spirituous liquors shall be admitted on board of vessels-of-war, except as medical stores".......................................14 July, "

NAV

Officers of the navy divided into 9 grades.............16 July, 1862

New Ironsides, of wood, with 4-inch armor plate, built at Philadelphia, 4015 tons, 700 horse power, speed of 6 knots; armament, 20 11-inch smooth-bore guns.......................... "

Monitor sunk off North Carolina during a gale.........31 Dec. "

Rank of vice-admiral created by Congress and bestowed on David G. Farragut.................................21 Dec. 1864

Navy at the close of the civil war consisted of 671 vessels; combined tonnage, 510,396; mounting 4610 guns........... 1865

Rank of admiral created; bestowed on Farragut......25 July, 1866

[David D. Porter made vice-admiral same date.]

Site for navy-yard at League island, Delaware river, presented to the government by Philadelphia; area, 923 acres; defences, forts Delaware and Miflin.............................4 Aug. 1868

Torpedo school established at Newport, R. I.................... 1869

Adm. Farragut dies at Portsmouth, N. H...............14 Aug. 1870

Vice-adm. Porter made admiral.........................17 Oct. "

First advisory board appointed to consider need of appropriate vessels for the navy. June, 1881, report, that it should consist of 70 unarmored cruisers of steel................7 Nov. 1881

Frigate *Constitution* ("Old Ironsides") is formally put out of commission and consigned to "Rotten Row" in the Brooklyn navy-yard.......................................15 Dec. "

Trenton is the first man-of-war in the world to be lighted by electricity.. 1882

Congress prohibits repair of wooden ships at more than 20 per cent. of the cost of a new vessel.......................3 Mch. 1885

Contract for 6700 tons of steel armor plates and 1220 tons of gun forgings, awarded to the Bethlehem Iron Works company, at Bethlehem, Pa...............................May, 1887

Adm. David D. Porter d................................13 Feb. 1891

[Rank of admiral and vice-admiral became extinct. Highest rank is again rear-admiral.]

In 1888 W. C. Whitthorne, member of Congress from Tennessee, introduced a bill authorizing the maritime states to organize a naval force to constitute a naval reserve, to be trained and fitted for operating the coast and harbor defence vessels, etc., in time of war, thus liberating the regular naval force to man the heavy sea-going war-ships, etc. Massachusetts was the first state to act, and passed laws defining what should be done. New York followed, and now (1894) most of the maritime states have responded. Total number of men enrolled Jan. 1894 was 2456. On 2 Mch. 1891, Congress appropriated $25,000 for the equipment of the force and another appropriation of a like amount................ 1892

THE NEW UNITED STATES NAVY, 1895.

UNARMORED VESSELS.

Name, and act of Congress authorizing.	Where built and when launched	Class and displacement in tons.	Horse-power and maximum speed in knots.	Contract price.*	Number of guns and calibre.
Chicago, Aug. 1882	Chester, 1886	P. p. c.—4500	5,248—16.3	$889,000	4 8-in.; 8 6-in.; 2 5-in.
Boston, Aug. 1882	" 1885	P. p. c.—3189	4,030—16.6	619,000	2 8-in.; 6 6-in.
Atlanta, Aug. 1882	" 1885	P. p. c.—3189	4,000—16.4	617,000	2 8-in.; 6 6-in.
Dolphin, Mch. 1883	" 1884	Despatch boat—1485	2,240—15.3	315,000	2 4-in.
Charleston, Mch. 1885	San Francisco, 1888	P. c.—4040	6,943—18.8	1,017,500 (4 T. t.)	2 8-in.
Yorktown, Mch. 1885	Philadelphia, 1888	P. p. c.—1700	3,660—17.2	455,000 (6 T. t.)	6 6-in.
Petrel, Mch. 1885	Baltimore, 1888	P. p. (G. b.)—890	1,513—13.7	247,000	4 6-in.
Newark, Mch. 1885	Philadelphia, 1890	P. c.—4083	9,231—19.6	1,248,000 (6 T. t.)	12 6-in.
Baltimore, Aug. 1886	" 1888	P. c.—4400	10,725—20.6	1,325,000 (5 T. t.)	4 8-in.; 6 6-in.
Philadelphia, Mch. 1887	" 1889	P. c.—4325	8,815—19.7	1,350,000 (5 T. t.)	12 6-in.
San Francisco, Mch. 1887	San Francisco, 1889	P. c.—4083	10,400—20.2	1,428,000 (6 T. t.)	12 6-in.
Bennington, Mch. 1887	Chester, 1889	P. p. c. (G. b.)—1700	3,533—17.5	490,000 (6 T. t.)	6 6-in.
Concord, Mch. 1887	" 1889	P. p. c. (G. b.)—1700	3,513—17.1	490,000 (6 T. t.)	6 6-in.
Olympia, Sept. 1888	San Francisco, 1892	P. c.—5500	13,500—21.7	1,796,000 (6 T. t.)	4 8-in.; 10 5-in.
Cincinnati, Sept. 1888	New York, 1892	P. c.—3183	10,000—19	1,100,000 (6 T. t.)	1 6-in.; 10 5-in.
Bancroft, Sept. 1888	Elizabethport, 1892	G. b.—838	1,300—13	250,000 (2 T. t.)	4 4-in.
Raleigh, Sept. 1888	Norfolk, 1892	P. c.—3183	10,000—19	1,100,000 (6 T. t.)	1 6-in.; 10 5-in.
Montgomery, Sept. 1888	Baltimore, 1891	P. c.—2000	5,400—19	612,500 (6 T. t.)	2 6-in.; 8 5-in.
Detroit, Sept. 1888	" 1891	P. c.—2000	5,400—17	612,500 (6 T. t.)	2 6-in.; 8 5-in.
Marblehead, Sept. 1888	Boston, 1892	P. c.—2000	5,400—17	612,500 (6 T. t.)	2 6-in.; 8 5-in.
Machias, Mch. 1889	Bath, 1891	P. p. (G. b.)—1050	1,600—14	318,000 (1 T. t.)	8 4-in.
Castine, Mch. 1889	" 1892	P. p. (G. b.)—1050	1,600—14	318,000 (1 T. t.)	8 4-in.
Columbia, June, 1890	Philadelphia, 1892	P. c.—7400	21,000—22.8	2,725,000 (6 T. t.)	1 8-in.; 2 6-in.; 8 4-in.
Minneapolis, Mch. 1891	" 1893	P. c.—7400	21,000—28	2,690,000 (6 T. t.)	1 8-in.; 2 6-in.; 8 4-in.
ARMORED VESSELS.					
Puritan, Mch. 1885	Chester, 1888	B. s., 2 T.—6060	4,000—13	2,300,970	4 12-in.; 6 4-in.
Monadnock, Mch. 1885	Mare island, 1892	B. s., 2 T.—3990	3,000—14	1,592,849	4 10-in.; 2 4-in.
Amphitrite, Mch. 1885	Wilmington, 1892	B. s., 2 T.—3990	1,600—12	1,590,930	4 10-in.; 2 4-in.
Terror, Mch. 1885	Philadelphia, 1892	B. s., 2 T.—3990	1,600—12	1,891,077	4 10-in.
Miantonomoh, Mch. 1885	Chester, 1888	B. s., 2 T.—3990	1,600—12	1,637,110	4 10-in.
Maine, Aug. 1886	New York, 1890	Cruiser—6648	9,000—17	2,500,000 (6 T. t.)	4 10-in.; 6 6-in.
Texas, Aug. 1886	Norfolk, 1892	B. s., 2 T.—6300	8,600—17	2,500,000 (6 T. t.)	2 12-in.; 6 6-in.
Vesuvius, Aug. 1886	Philadelphia, 1888	D. c.—930	4,450—21.7	350,000	3 15-in. pneumatic.
Monterey, Mch. 1887	San Francisco, 1891	B. s.—4138	5,400—16	1,628,950	2 12-in.; 2 10-in.
Cushing, Mch. 1887	Bristol, 1890	T. b.—116	1,720—22.5	82,750 (3 T. t.)	....
New York, Sept. 1888	Philadelphia, 1891	Cruiser—8150	16,500—20	2,985,000 (6 T. t.)	6 8-in.; 12 4-in.
Alarm, Mch. 1889	Bath, 1892	Ram—2183	4,800—17	930,000	....
Ericsson, Jan. 1890	Dubuque, Ia., 1892	T. b.—120	1,800—24	113,500 (3 T. t.)	....
Massachusetts, June, 1890	Philadelphia, 1893	B. s., 2 T.—10,231	9,000—16.2	3,020,000 (6 T. t.)	4 13-in.; 8 8-in.; 4 6-in.
Brooklyn, 1890	Philadelphia, 1893	Cruiser—9250	16,900—21	2,986,000 (6 T. t.)	8 8-in.; 12 5-in.
Indiana, June, 1890	Philadelphia, 1893	B. s., 2 T.—10,231	9,000—16.2	3,020,000 (6 T. t.)	4 13-in.; 8 8-in.; 4 6-in.
Iowa, 1891	Philadelphia, 1893	B. s.—10,286	11,000—16.5	3,010,000 (6 T. t.)	4 12-in.; 8 8-in.
Oregon, June, 1890	San Francisco, 1893	B. s., 2 T.—10,231	9,000—16.2	3,180,000 (6 T. t.)	4 13-in.; 8 8-in.; 4 6-in.
Katahdin, 1889	Bath, Me., 1893	Ram—2050	4,800—17	930,000	

NOTE.—In above table, the abbreviations in column 3 signify: P. p. c., partly protected cruiser; P. c., protected cruiser; G. b., gun-boat; B. s., battle ship; D. c., dynamite cruiser; T. b., torpedo boat; T., torpedo; in column 5, T. t., torpedo tube. * Does not include total cost of construction, equipments, etc.

[The navy also includes about 75 iron and wood sailing and steam vessels, and 15 1-turret monitors.]

OFFICERS OF THE NAVY, WITH NUMBER IN EACH RANK, AND PAY.

No.	Rank		Rank with		Yearly pay at sea.
6.	Rear-admirals	to rank with	major-generals		$6000
10.	Commodores	"	brigadier-generals		5000
45.	Captains	"	colonels		4500
85.	Commanders	"	lieutenant-colonels		3500
74.	Lieutenant-commanders	"	majors	1st 4 years	2800
				after 4th year	3000
250.	Lieutenants	"	captains	1st 5 years	2400
				after 5th year	2600
75.	Masters or lieutenants (junior grade)	"	1st lieutenants	1st 5 years	1800
				after 5th year	2000
173.	Ensigns	"	2d lieutenants	1st 5 years	1200
				after 5th year	1400
300.	Midshipmen				500

For admiral and vice-admiral see this record, 1864, '66, '91.

navy of Great Britain. The British navy, originally governed by a lord high admiral, has, since the reign of queen Anne, been under a Board of Admiralty of 7 members—the first lord always a member of the cabinet and supreme in authority, and 6 assistant commissioners. The senior naval lord directs the movements of the fleet and is responsible for discipline. The second naval lord directs the manning and officering. The junior naval lord directs the food supply and transports. The parliamentary civil lord and the civil lord deal with the material and armament of the fleet. The parliamentary and financial secretary deals with all questions of expenditure.

Fleet of galleys built by Alfred.......... 897
Fleet for opposing the Danes, equipped by contributions of every town in England, gathers at Sandwich.......... 1007
Fleet collected by Edward the Confessor to resist Norwegians.......... 1042
Fleet collected by Harold to resist Normans..........1066
Richard I. collects a fleet and enacts naval laws.........about 1191
Royal Harry, a two-decker, built by Henry VII.; considered the beginning of the royal navy.......... 1488
Henri Grace à Dieu launched at Erith; 1000 tons, 141 guns, the heaviest 6000 lbs., first British vessel with port-holes for cannon (burned at Woolwich, 27 Aug. 1553)........13 June, 1514
Sovereign of the Seas, 1547 tons, 132 guns, the heaviest 6500 lbs.; launched at Woolwich.......... 1637
Victory, built 1737, lost in Channel with 1000 men......4 Oct. 1744
Naval uniforms first introduced.......... 1748
Royal George, 2041 tons, 100 guns, the heaviest 7250 lbs.; built at Woolwich, 1746; capsized at Spithead............29 Aug. 1782
Navy list first officially compiled and published monthly by John Finlaison, the actuary.......... 1814
Screw propeller introduced into the royal navy.......... 1840
Birkenhead, the 1st iron war-steamer in the British navy..... 1845
Duke of Wellington, 131 guns, the heaviest 10,000 lbs., is launched at Pembroke.......... 1852
Naval review by queen Victoria, at Spithead..........11 Aug. 1853
Review of the Baltic fleet at Spithead by queen Victoria, 23 Apr. 1856
Naval reserve force authorized by act of..............13 Aug. 1859
Warrior, the first English iron-plated steam-frigate, 6170 tons, costing about 400,000*l*., launched..................29 Dec. 1860
Twin screws for vessels of light draught introduced.......... 1863
Steam-ram *Valiant* launched..........14 Oct. "
Royal School of Naval Architecture established at South Kensington.......... 1864
Sir Robert Sepping's collection of naval models, from Henry VIII.'s time, deposited in South Kensington museum..Dec. "
Naval review before viceroy of Egypt, at Spithead....17 July, 1867
Unarmored iron frigate *Inconstant*, first iron hull sheathed with wood, the oldest of modern type, launched..........12 Nov. 1868
Monarch, first British armor-clad turret-ship, launched at Chatham..........25 May, "
Devastation, first British sea-going mastless ship, launched, Mch. 1869
Captain founders near Finisterre (WRECKS)...........7 Sept. 1870
Thunderer, ocean-going turret-ship, launched at Pembroke, 25 Mch. 1872
Naval review at Spithead, before the shah of Persia...23 June, 1873
Royal Naval Artillery Volunteer force, established by act, 5 Aug. "
Téméraire, carrying upper-deck armament in 2 fixed open-topped turrets, mounted on the disappearing plan, launched at Chatham..........9 May, 1876
Shannon, with broadside guns on open deck and without armor, built at Pembroke and commissioned.......... 1877
Grand naval review by queen Victoria, at Spithead....13 Aug. 1878
Boiler of the *Thunderer* explodes, 14 July, 1876; a gas explosion occurs in the coal-bunkers, 10 Dec. 1878, and one of her 2 38-ton guns bursts..........2 Jan. 1879
Great naval demonstration at Portsmouth; attack on forts; electric light used at night..........10 Aug. 1880
Polyphemus, double-screw, steam armor-plated ram and torpedo boat, 2610 tons, is launched at Chatham......15 June, 1881
Benbow, an armor-clad battle-ship, 2 of her guns of 111 tons each, the heaviest in any ship to the time; launched...... 1885
Naval Defence act, authorizing 10 first-class battle-ships each of 14,150 tons' displacement, and 9 first-class cruisers, 29 second-class cruisers, 4 third-class cruisers, 18 torpedo gunboats, passed..........31 May, 1889
Royal Naval Exhibition opened at Chelsea.............2 May, 1891
Victoria sunk off Tripoli, Syria (WRECKS)............22 June, 1893
According to the estimate for 1893-94, the approximate aggregate cost of the effective and non-effective (in building) of the British navy, under the Naval Defence act, amounts to 58,302,561*l*.
Under construction, by a more recent act, are the battle-ships *Renown*, *Majestic*, and *Magnificence*, and the first-class cruisers *Powerful* and *Terrible*, over 12,000 tons each.

CONDITION OF BRITISH NAVY AT VARIOUS INTERVALS SINCE 1603.

Year.	Vessels.	Tons.	Guns.	Men.
1603	42	17,000	....	....
1685	179	104,000	6,930	10,000
1760	325	321,000	10,600	51,000
1803	450	461,000	24,800	180,000
1850	585	570,000	17,200	48,000
1890	373	680,000	6,790	65,000

Strength of the British navy when the Naval Defence act is fully carried out will be as follows:

Ships.	Number.	Tons.	
Armored	77	618,500	1894
Protected	88	309,915	
Unprotected	336	198,634	
Total	501	1,127,049	

ARMOR-CLAD BATTLE-SHIPS OF 10,000 TONS AND OVER.

Name.	Launch.	Tons.	Horse-power.	Speed.	Heavy guns.
Minotaur (cruiser)	1863	10,690	6,700	13 2	17 12-ton.
Northumberland (cr.)	1866	10,780	6,560	14.1	17 12 "
Dreadnought	1875	10,820	8,210	14.2	4 38 "
Inflexible	1876	11,880	8,010	13.81	4 80 "
Rodney	1884	10,300	11,500	16.7	4 69 "
Howe	1885	10,300	11,500	16.7	4 67 "
Benbow	1885	10,600	11,500	17	2 111 "
Camperdown	1885	10,600	11,500	17	4 66 "
Agincourt (cruiser)	1885	10,690	6,870	14.8	17 12 "
Anson	1886	10,600	11,500	17.43	4 66 "
Sans Pareil	1887	10,470	14,000	16.75	2 111 "
Trafalgar	1887	11,940	10,500	16.5	4 67 "
Nile	1888	11,940	12,000	16.5	4 67 "
Hood	1891	14,150	13,000	17.5	4 67 "
Royal Sovereign	1891	14,150	13,312	18	4 67 "
Empress of India	1891	14,150	13,000	17.5	4 67 "
Repulse	1892	14,150	13,000	17.5	4 67 "
Royal Oak	1892	14,150	13,000	17.5	4 67 "
Ramillies	1892	14,150	13,000	17.5	4 67 "
Resolution	1892	14,150	13,000	17.5	4 67 "
Revenge	1892	14,150	13,000	17.5	4 67 "
Centurion	1892	10,500	13,000	18.2	2 29 "
Barfleur	1892	10,500	13,000	18.2	2 29 "

navy of France is first mentioned in history in 728, when, like the early navy of England, it consisted of galleys; in this year the French defeated the Frisian fleet. The French navy was in its splendor about 1781, but was reduced in the wars with England. It was much increased by the emperor Napoleon III., and in 1859 consisted of 51 ships of the line and 398 other vessels. Statistics of the reconstructed navy of France are given below.

French fleet almost annihilated by Edward III. at the battle of Sluys..........24 June, 1340
French fleet increased through Colbert, minister to Louis XIV., about 1697
Académie de Marines founded.......... 1752
First line-of-battle ship with screw propeller, the *Napoleon*, launched at Toulon..........16 May, 1850
Thirteen men-of-war launched, 9 of them ships of the line.... 1854
La Gloire, a wooden screw-steamer of 900 horse-power, armed with iron plates 4½ inches thick, launched.......... 1860
Programme for reconstructing navy drawn up by minister of marine, and adopted by National Assembly; 217 new armored ships proposed.......... 1872
Redoutable, first French war-ship in which steel was largely used, is launched at L'Orient..........Sept. 1876

VARYING STRENGTH OF THE FRENCH NAVY IN YEARS PAST.

Year.	Vessels.	Guns.	Men.
1780	266	13,300	78,000
1810	212	6,000	94,000
1840	146	7,600	24,500
1868	480	2,750	43,100
1889	348	1,450	54,000

Navy comprises: 58 sea-going armor-clads; 18 coast-defence armor-clads; 6 deck-protected cruisers; 146 torpedo-boats (steel); 185 unprotected vessels. Total, 413............Apr. 1891

ARMOR-CLAD BATTLE-SHIPS OF 10,000 TONS OR OVER.

Name.	Launch.	Tons.	Horse-power.	Speed.	Heavy guns.
Admiral Duperré.	1879	11,100	7,396	14.22	48 tons.
Dévastation......	1879	10,100	6,102	15.17	48 "
Admiral Baudin..	1883	11,380	8,500	15	75 "
Neptune.........	1885	10,581	6,000	15	48 "
Formidable......	1885	11,380	8,500	15	75 "
Hoche..........	1885	10,581	6,000	15	48 "
Marceau.........	1887	10,620	11,000	16	48 "
Magenta.........	1889	10,610	11,000	16.5	48 "
Brenus..........	1891	10,980	13.500	17.5	75 "
Massena.........	1892	11,730	11,000	18	50 "
Charles Martel...	1893	11,800	13,000	17.5	50 "
Jauregniberry....	1893	11,820	13,270	18	75 "
Bouvet..........	1893	12,205	11,000	18	75 "
Lazare Carnot....	1893	11,820	13,270	18	75 "
Henri Quatre.....	1893	10,780	14,000	18	75 "
Charlemagne.....	1893	10,780	14,000	18	75 "
St. Louis........	1893	10,780	14,000	18	75 "

navy of Italy. The navy of Italy has existed since 263 B.C., when the Romans built 100 "quinqueremes" and 20 "triremes," patterned after a Carthaginian vessel which was driven ashore on the coast of Italy.

OFFICIAL REPORT OF THE ITALIAN NAVY, 1 JAN. 1891.

	Iron.	Steel.	Wood.	Total.	No. of guns.	Men.
War-ships............	12	33	2	47	359	11,638
Transports...........	9	4	3	16	53	1,673
Other vessels..........	29	134	39	206	303	5,913
Totals......	50	171	44	269	715	19,224

REPRESENTATIVE ARMOR-CLAD BATTLE-SHIPS OF ITALY.

Ship.	Launch.	Tons.	Horse-power.	Speed.	Heaviest guns.
Duilio...................	1876	11,138	7,710	15	100 tons.
Dandolo..................	1878	11,202	7,500	15.5	100 "
Italia...................	1880	15,900	18,000	18	100 "
Lepanto..................	1882	15,900	16,150	18	100 "
Lauria...................	1884	11,000	10,000	16	105 "
Doria....................	1885	11,000	10,000	16	105 "
Morosini.................	1885	11,000	10,000	16	105 "
Umberto..................	1889	13,251	19,500	18	67 "
Sardegna.................	1890	13,251	22,800	19	105 "
Sicilia..................	1891	13,251	19,590	18	100 "

RELATIVE STRENGTH OF OTHER FOREIGN NAVIES.

	Armored ships.	Unarmored ships.	Torpedo catchers.	Torpedo boats.	Armored gun-boats.	Unarmored gun-boats.	Transports, tugs, etc.	Despatch boats.	Training-ships.
Germany.............	25	37	9	166	23	32	17	6	9
Russia..............	39	54	..	147	12	44	9	8	3
Austria.............	12	19	..	40	2	27	28	2	5
Netherlands.........	24	47	..	56	7	24	27	1	17
Spain...............	15	78	3	36	3	76	10	1	2
Sweden..............	5	8	3	29	11	18	3	..	..
Norway..............	5	6	..	5	..	13	10	..	..
Turkey..............	14	49	..	34	5	17	24	7	..
Denmark.............	11	25	..	23	5	3	..	..	..

China had 9 iron-clads and 121 other vessels of war in 1888.

Nazarene, a name given to Jesus Christ and his disciples; afterwards to a sect in the 1st century who rejected Christ's divinity. A sect named Nazarines, resembling the Society of Friends in Great Britain, became prominent in Hungary in 1867.

Nebraska, the 37th state of the Union in the order of admission, borders upon the Missouri river between lat. 40° and 43°, from which river it extends west from lon. 95° 23′ for a distance of about 420 miles to lon. 104°. It is bounded north by South Dakota, east by Iowa and Missouri, south by Kansas and Colorado, which cuts off a square from the southwestern part of the state, and on the west by Colorado and Wyoming. Area, 76,855 sq. miles. Pop. 1890, 1,058,910; 1900, 1,066,300. Capital, Lincoln.

Emanuel Lisa founds a trading post at Bellevue........... 1805
American Fur company founds a fort at Bellevue, 1810, where col. Peter A. Sarpy locates as their representative, 1824
Fort Kearney, on the Platte, established for the protection of the Oregon trail.... 1848
Most of the present Nebraska, and much more on the north, was acquired from France by treaty ceding Louisiana in 1803. It became a portion of the territory of Louisiana in 1805, and a part of the Indian country in 1834. That part west of 103° lon. was acquired from Mexico by the treaty of Guadalupe Hidalgo, proclaimed......4 July, "
Omaha founded.. 1854
Congress organizes the territory of Nebraska between lat. 40° and 49°, and between the Missouri river and Minnesota on the east and Utah territory on the west............30 May, "
Francis Burt, appointed governor, dies soon after reaching the territory; Thomas B. Cuming acting-governor......13 Oct. "
Legislature and delegates to Congress first elected....12 Dec. "
First legislature convenes at Omaha..................16 Jan. 1855
Capitol at Omaha completed..........................Jan. 1858
Gov. Black issues a proclamation calling out volunteers for the Federal army..................................1 May, 1861
Act to enable the people to form a state government..19 Apr. 1864
Constitution framed by convention, 9 Feb. 1866; ratified by the people, 3938 for and 3838 against..................21 June, 1866
Act to admit Nebraska as a state is passed over a veto, "upon the fundamental condition that within the state of Nebraska there should be no denial of the elective franchise or of any other right to any person by reason of race or color, except Indians not taxed"; the Nebraska legislature accepting these conditions...............................8–9 Feb. 1867
Act admitting Nebraska accepted by legislature......20 Feb. "
Nebraska admitted by proclamation of the president...1 Mch. "
A band of Indians wreck a freight train by placing obstructions on the track, and murder all the train hands. Gen. Augur sends a detachment of troops, who engage 500 Sioux Indians in battle at Plum creek, near Omaha.......16 Aug. "
Nebraska State Normal school opened at Peru.............. "
Seat of government removed from Omaha to a point in Lancaster county named Lincoln, in honor of pres. Lincoln..... "
Union Pacific railroad, chartered by act of Congress 1 July, 1862, is opened for traffic.........................10 May, 1869
Nebraska institute for the deaf and dumb opened at Omaha... "
State penitentiary located at Lincoln...................... "
Legislature ratifies the XV.th Amendment............17 Feb. 1870
State board of 3 commissioners of immigration provided for by act of legislature................................... "
Gov. David P. Butler impeached for corruption in office, in appropriating to his own use $17,000 of school fund, 2 June, 1871
Insane hospital at Lincoln opened....................... "
Omaha Daily Bee established by Edward Rosewater at Omaha. "
University of Nebraska at Lincoln, chartered 1869, opened... "
Doane college at Crete chartered and opened.............. 1872
Nebraska Relief and Aid Society, gen. E. O. C. Ord at the head, organized at request of the governor to relieve sufferers from famine caused by drought and locusts.............18 Sept. 1874
Legislature authorizes $50,000 in state bonds for relief of sufferers by locusts and famine............................ 1875
New constitution framed by a convention which met at Lincoln, 11 May, 1875, completing its labors 12 June, is ratified by the people...................................12 Oct. "
Institution for the blind at Nebraska City opened......13 Jan. 1876
Convention of governors from the western states and territories at Omaha to consider the grasshopper pest......Oct. "
Ponca chief Standing Bear and 25 followers on their way from the Indian territory, which they left in Jan. 1879, to their old home in Dakota are arrested on the Omaha reservation by brig.-gen. Crook, to be returned to the Indian territory. On 8 Apr. H. Tibbles, assist.-editor of the *Omaha Herald*, applies for a writ of habeas corpus on their behalf, to be served on gen. Crook. This writ was issued by judge Dundy of the U. S. district court of Nebraska, who decides that an Indian has a right to a habeas corpus in a Federal court. The secretary of war at Washington issues immediate orders for the release of Standing Bear and his followers......13 May, 1879
Creighton college at Omaha opened and chartered........... "
New school-law, repealing and remodelling the old system of public instruction, passed by legislature.................. 1881
State industrial school for juvenile offenders opened at Kearney..30 Nov. "
State Home for the Friendless located at Lincoln, founded by act of legislature in 1881, is opened..................1 Jan. 1882
Gates college at Neligh chartered in 1881; opened............ "

At state election E. P. Ingersoll, president of the State Farmers' Alliance and candidate of the Greenback and Anti-Monopoly parties, receives 16,991 votes, as against 28,562 for J. S. Morton, Dem., and 43,495 for James W. Dawes, Rep........Nov. 1882
Amendment to the constitution extending suffrage to women rejected: 25,756 for and 50,693 against.................Nov. "
Nebraska Central college at Central City chartered and opened, 1885
Nebraska institution for feeble-minded youth at Beatrice opened...May, 1887
Insane hospital at Norfolk opened......................... 1888
Soldiers and sailors' home at Grand Island opened.......July, "
First Monday in Sept. made a legal holiday; "Labor day".. 1889
Industrial home for women and girls at Milford opened, 1 May, "
Asylum for incurable insane at Hastings opened........1 Aug. "
Convention of 250 delegates representing Kansas, Iowa, North Dakota, South Dakota, and Nebraska, meets at Omaha to unite in a central prohibition organization................18 Dec. "
At state election the vote for governor stands as follows: James E. Boyd, Dem., 71,331; John H. Powers, People's Independent, 70,187; Lucius D. Richards, Rep., 68,878; B. L. Paine, Prohibition, 3676. A separate vote on adding a prohibitory liquor clause to the constitution stood: For the amendment, 82,292; against, 111,728..............................Nov. 1890
Candidates on the Independent ticket prepare to contest the election, and taking of testimony begins at Lincoln...5 Dec. "
The 3 candidates (Dem., Rep., and Ind.) claim the governorship...9 Jan. 1891
Gov. Thayer surrenders possession of the executive apartments to Boyd under protest.............................15 Jan. "
Supreme court of the state gives a decision ousting Boyd on ground that he is an alien and reinstating Thayer....5 May, "
Ex-gov. David Butler d. near Pawnee City............25 May, "
Eight-hour law goes into effect........................1 Aug. "
U. S. Supreme court declares James E. Boyd to be the rightful governor of the state.................................1 Feb. 1892
Public demonstration in honor of inauguration of gov. Boyd takes place at Lincoln...........................15 Feb. "
Silver anniversary of Nebraska celebrated at Lincoln..25 May, "
First national convention of People's party at Omaha, nominate Weaver and Field for president and vice-president, 4, 5 July, "
U. S. senator Allen makes the longest continuous speech (on the Silver-Purchase Repeal bill) ever delivered in the U. S. senate, speaking 14¾ hours..............................13 Oct. 1893
Interstate irrigation congress meets at Omaha........21 Mch. 1894

TERRITORIAL GOVERNORS.

Francis Burt................appointed........................ 1854
Thomas B. Cuming.......... acting ....13 Oct. "
Mark W. Izard..............appointed........................ "
William A. Richardson...... " 1857
J. Sterling Morton.......... acting 1858
Samuel Black..............appointed........................ 1859
Alvin Saunders............ " 1861

STATE GOVERNORS.

David Butler...............term began........................ 1867
William H. James.......... acting ....2 June, 1871
Robert W. Furnass.........term began..................9 Jan. 1873
Silas Garber............... " .... " 1875
Albinus Nance............. " .... " 1879
James W. Dawes............ " .... " 1883
John M. Thayer............ " .... " 1887
Lorenzo Crounse........... " .... " 1893
Silas A. Holcomb.......... " .... " 1895

UNITED STATES SENATORS FROM THE STATE OF NEBRASKA.

Name.	No. of Congress.	Date.	Remarks.
John M. Thayer......	40th to 42d	1867 to 1871	
Thomas W. Tipton....	40th " 44th	1867 " 1875	
Phineas W. Hitchcock,	42d " 45th	1871 " 1877	
Algernon S. Paddock..	44th " 47th	1875 " 1881	
Alvin Saunders......	45th " 48th	1877 " 1883	
Charles H. Van Wyck,	47th " 50th	1881 " 1888	
Charles F. Manderson,	48th " 54th	1883 " 1895	
Algernon S. Paddock..	50th " 53d	1888 " 1893	
William V. Allen.....	53d " ——	1893 " ——	Term expires 1899.
John M. Thurston....	54th " ——	1895 " ——	

nebular hypothesis, proposed by sir William Herschel, 1811, supposes that the universe was formed from shapeless masses of nebulous matter. It has been widely discussed. In Oct. 1860, Mr. Lassell strictly scrutinized the Dumbbell nebula, and stated that the brightest parts did not appear to be stars. In 1865, William Huggins reported that he had analyzed certain nebulæ by their spectra, and believed them to be entirely gaseous. In later years the spectroscope has proved beyond doubt the existence of many true nebulæ, or cloud-like aggregations of gaseous matter, in the heavens. ASTRONOMY.

nec'romancers. MAGIC.

needle-gun (*Zündnadelgewehr*), a musket invented by J. N. Dreyse, of Sömmerda, about 1827, made a breechloader in 1836, and adopted by the Prussian general Manteuffel about 1846. It was effective in war with Denmark in 1864, and with Austria in 1866. The charge is fired by pressing a fine steel rod or needle into the cartridge. The principle is claimed for James Whitley, of Dublin, 1823; Abraham Mosar, 1831; and John Hanson, of Huddersfield, 1843.

needles. "The making of Spanish needles was first taught in England by Elias Crowse, a German, about the 8th year of queen Elizabeth, and in queen Mary's time a negro made fine Spanish needles in Cheapside, but would teach his art to none."—*Stow.*

negro plot. NEW YORK, 1741.

negus (wine and water), said to be named after col. Francis Negus about 1714. The sovereign of Abyssinia is termed *negus*.

Nehemi'ah, a celebrated Jewish leader. In the 20th year of the reign of Artaxerxes, king of Persia 445 B.C., he obtained permission to return to Jerusalem and rebuild its walls. These walls said to have enclosed about 50 acres and contained about 15,000 Jews and 5000 slaves.

Nelson's victories, etc., see separate articles.

Horatio Nelson, born at Burnham Thorpe, Norfolk....29 Sept. 1758
Sailed with capt. Phipps to the North pole.................. 1773
Distinguished himself in West Indies........................ 1780
Lost an eye at the reduction of Calvi, Corsica.............. 1794
Captured Elba..9 Aug. 1796
With Jervis at victory off St. Vincent, 14 Feb.; knighted and made rear-admiral.................................20 Feb. 1797
Lost right arm at unsuccessful attack on Santa Cruz, 25, 26 July, "
Gained battle of the Nile, 1 Aug.; created baron Nelson of the Nile...6 Nov. 1798
Attacks Copenhagen, 2 Apr.; created viscount, 22 May; attacks Boulogne flotilla, destroys several ships...........15 Aug. 1801
Appointed to chief command in Mediterranean........20 May, 1803
Pursues French and Spanish fleets, Mch.-Aug.; returns to England, Aug.; reappears at Cadiz, defeats the fleets in Trafalgar bay, but is killed...........................21 Oct. 1805

Neme'an games, celebrated at Nemea, in Achaia, said to have been instituted by Argives in honor of Archemorus, who died by a serpent's bite; and revived by Hercules, 1226 B.C. The conqueror was rewarded with a crown of olives, afterwards of green parsley. They were celebrated every 3d year, or, according to others, on the 1st and 3d year of every Olympiad, 1226 B.C.—*Herodotus.* They were revived by the emperor Julian, 362 A.D., but ceased in 396.

Neo-Platonism or **New-Platonism.** PHILOSOPHY.

nepha'lia, sacrifices of sobriety among the Greeks, when they offered mead instead of wine to the sun and moon, to nymphs, to Aurora, and to Venus; and burned any wood but the vine, fig-tree, and mulberry-tree, esteemed symbols of drunkenness (613 B.C.).

neph'oscope (Gr. νέφος, a cloud). An apparatus for measuring velocity of clouds, invented by Karl Braun, reported to the Academy of Sciences, Paris, 27 July, 1868.

Neptune, a primary planet, the most distant of our system. Mean distance from the sun, 2,745,998,000 miles; revolves around the sun in 165 years; diameter, 37,000 miles. It was first observed on 23 Sept. 1846, by dr. Galle at Berlin, in consequence of a letter from M. Le Verrier, who had computed its position from the anomalous movements of Uranus. Calculations to the same effect had been previously made by J. Couch Adams, of Cambridge. A satellite of Neptune was discovered by Mr. Lassell on 10 Oct. following. Neptune is said to have been seen by Lalande, and thought to be a fixed star. The sun's light and heat Neptune receives are but $\frac{1}{1000}$ of that received by the earth.—The Greek god Poseidon became the Roman Neptune.

neptu'nium, a new metal discovered in tannalite, from Connecticut, by R. Herrmann in 1877; not admitted by chemists.

Ner'vii, a warlike tribe in Belgic Gaul, defeated by Julius Cæsar, 57, and subdued 53 B.C.

"You all do know this mantle; I remember
The first time ever Cæsar put it on:
'Twas on a summer's evening, in his tent
That day he overcame the Nervii."
—*Shakespeare,* "Julius Cæsar," act. iii. sc. ii.

Nestorians, followers of Nestorius, bishop of Constanople (428-31), regarded as a heretic for maintaining that, ough the virgin Mary was the mother of Jesus Christ as n, yet she was not the mother of God, since no human ature could impart to another what she had not herself; also held that God was united to Christ under one person, t remained as distinct in nature and essence as though he d never been united at all. He was opposed by Eutyches, d died 439. EUTYCHIANS. Nestorian Christians in the vant administer the sacrament with leavened bread in both ds, permit priests to marry, and use neither confirmation r auricular confession.—*Du Pin.* A Nestorian priest and acon were in London in July, 1862.

Netherlands. HOLLAND.

Neufchâtel (*nush-a-tel'*), a canton in Switzerland, formerly a lordship, afterwards a principality. The first known d was Ulric de Fenis, about 1032, whose descendants ruled l 1373, after which, by marriage, it frequently changed govors. On the death of the duchesse de Nemurs, the last of e Longuevilles, in 1707, there were many claimants, among em William III. of England. He and the allies gave it to ederick I. of Prussia, with the title of prince. In 1806 the incipality was ceded to France, and Napoleon bestowed it gen. Berthier, who held it till 1814, when the allies reored the king of Prussia, with the title of prince, with cern rights and privileges; but annexed it to the Swiss conleration.

ter an unsuccessful attempt in 1831, Neufchâtel repudiated allegiance to Prussia, and proclaimed itself a free and independent member of the Swiss confederation............... 1848
ng of Prussia protested; and a protocol of England, France, and Austria recognized his claims.......................... 1852
me of his adherents, headed by the count de Pourtalès, rose against the republican authorities, who quickly subdued and imprisoned them, to await trial......................Sept. 1856
ar threatened by Prussia, and great energy and determination manifested by the Swiss. On the intervention of Britain and France a treaty was signed, the king of Prussia virtually renouncing his claims for a pecuniary compensation, which he eventually gave up. He retains the title of prince of Neufchâtel, without political rights.............11 June, 1857
isoners of Sept. 1856 were released without trial.....18 Jan. "

Neustria, or **West France,** a kingdom allotted Clotaire by his father, Clovis, at his death, in 511. United France about 847, during the reign of Charles the Bald. It as conquered by the Northmen, and hence named NORANDY.

neutral ground extended along the eastern side the Hudson river northward from Spuyten Duyvil creek miles or more. This region, during the occupancy of New ork city by the British, 1776-83, suffered much from marauders, both American and British; the former were termed Skinners," and the latter "Cowboys." OKLAHOMA for "Neual Strip" or "No Man's Land."

neutral powers. By the treaty of Paris between reat Britain, France, Austria, Russia, Prussia, Turkey, and ardinia, 16 Apr. 1856, privateering was abolished; neutrals ight carry an enemy's goods not contraband of war; neutral ods not contraband were free even under an enemy's flag; ad blockades to be binding must be effective The United ates acceded to these provisions in 1861. INTERNATIONAL AW.

Nevada, one of the western states of the American nion, is bounded north by Oregon and Idaho, east by Utah and Arizona, south by Arizona and California, and west by California. It is limited in latitude by 35° to 42° N., and in longitude by 114° to 120° W.; and has an area of 110,-700 sq. miles in 14 counties. Pop. 1890, 45,761; 1900, 42,-335. Capital, Carson City.

Father Francisco Garcés sets out from Sonora for California, and passes through the southern portion of Nevada...... 1775
eter Skeen Ogden, of the Hudson Bay Fur company, discovers the Humboldt river.................................... 1825
edediah S. Smith crosses the southeast corner of Nevada on his way from Great Salt lake to Los Angeles, Cal., and on his return crosses the Sierra Nevada and the entire state of Nevada from west to east.............................. 1827
Joseph Walker and 35 or 40 men, trappers, pass through Nevada from Great Salt lake, by the Humboldt river into California..1832-33
A party under Elisha Stevens, sometimes called the Murphy company, pass through Nevada down the Humboldt in wagons on their way to California......... 1844
Gen. J. C. Fremont's expedition crosses Nevada from near Pilot Knob into California.. 1845
Nevada included in the territory ceded to the U. S. by the treaty of Guadalupe Hidalgo..........................2 Feb. 1848
H. S. Beatie takes possession of the present site of Genoa, erects a log-house, and opens a supply depot for emigrants.. 1849
Gold discovered in small quantities in Gold cañon, near Dayton, by Abner Blackburn..................................July, "
An immigrant named Hardin discovers silver in the Black Rock range 1½ miles from the place settled in 1866 as Hardinville... "
Nevada included in the territory of Utah by act of.....9 Sept. 1850
Trading-post erected on land where Carson City now stands... 1851
E. Allen, and Hosea B. Grosch discover silver ore in Gold cañon.. 1853
Carson City laid out in Eagle Valley by Abraham V. Z. Curry, who built a stone house there.......................... 1858
Chinese first introduced into Nevada to work on a mining-ditch at Gold cañon.................................... "
Territorial Enterprise started at Genoa by William L. Jernegan and A. James...............................18 Dec. "
Penrod Comstock & Co. discover the so-called Comstock lode in Six Mile cañon...............................11 June, 1859
First settlement on the site of Reno made by C. W. Fuller.... "
A constitution for the unorganized territory of Nevada, prepared in July, is adopted by the people............7 Sept. "
First Pony express reaches Carson Valley in 8½ days from St. Joseph, Mo. The news by it is telegraphed to San Francisco and published there in 9 days from New York.......12 Apr. 1860
First Catholic church in Nevada erected at Genoa by father Gallagher.. "
War between the settlers and the Pah Utes Indians opens by an attack on Williams station, 7 May. Battle at Pyramid lake fought 12 May, and at fort Storey 3 June, after which the Indians disperse....................................... "
Territory of Nevada organized by Congress.............2 Mch. 1861
Jesse L. Bennett, a Methodist preacher in Carson Valley during 1859, delivers the first sermon ever preached in Virginia City, then the capital..................................... "
Gov. Nye proclaims the territory organized...........11 July, "
Carson City declared the permanent seat of government by act of the legislature..............................25 Nov. "
Butler Ives, commissioner on the part of Nevada, and John F. Kidder of California, meet in Lake Valley to establish the boundary-line between California and Nevada.......22 May, 1863
Discovery of a salt basin 5 miles square, near the sink of the Carson river, containing pure rock salt to a depth of 14 feet, 1864
Under act of 21 Mch. 1864 a convention to form a state constitution meets at Carson City, 4 July; Nevada admitted by proclamation of.....................................31 Oct. "
State prison located at Warm Springs, Carson City........... "
Freemasonry established in the state in Feb. 1862, and the Grand Lodge of Nevada organized.....................Jan. 1865
Sutro Tunnel company chartered to build a tunnel some 4 miles long to intersect and drain the Comstock lode at a depth of 1600 feet....................................4 Feb. "
Eastern boundary of Nevada extended one degree by act of Congress...5 May, 1866
First railroad locomotive enters the state, running from the California side to Crystal Peak.......................... 1867
U. S. Supreme court declares unconstitutional an act of Nevada legislature levying a capitation tax of one dollar on every person leaving the state by any railroad, stage-coach, or other carrier of passengers............................ 1868
Legislature ratifies XV.th Amendment to the Constitution of the U. S...1 Mch. 1869
State orphans' home at Carson City erected.................. "
U. S. branch mint at Carson City, founded in 1866, begins operations..1 Nov. "
Corner-stone of the state capitol laid, 9 June, 1870, and building completed and occupied..............................Aug. 1871
Lieut.-gov. Denver refuses to surrender the state prison to his successor in office, P. C. Hyman, until compelled by militia and 60 armed men under gen. Van Bokkelen, with one piece of artillery.. 1873
Construction of new state prison at Reno begun.............. 1874
State University of Nevada, chartered in 1864, is opened at Elko... "
Bishop Whitaker's school for girls opened at Reno............ 1876
Legislature by joint resolution amends the constitution so as to exclude from the privilege of electors any bigamist or polygamist.. 1877
State Fish commission appointed by act of legislature, and a hatchery established at Carson City......................... 1878
Completion of the Sutro tunnel celebrated in the Carson Valley (TUNNELS)......................................30 June, 1879
State asylum for the insane at Reno opened...........1 July, 1882
Nickel mines discovered in Humboldt county................. "
U. S. branch mint at Carson City closed...................... 1885
State university removed from Elko to Reno and reopened, Mch. 1886
Acts of legislature passed providing for State Immigration bureau and for the observance of Arbor day in the state.... 1887

Fourteen constitutional amendments voted upon by the people, who reject one to authorize lotteries, and adopt one giving women the right to hold school offices. Election held, 11 Feb. 1889

Legislature appropriates $100,000 for a hydrographic survey of the state, and provides for State Board of Reclamation and Internal Improvement (IRRIGATION).................... "

Gov. Stevenson dies, and is succeeded by lieut.-gov. Frank Bell, acting..21 Sept. 1890

TERRITORIAL GOVERNOR.

James W. Nye..............commissioned...........22 Mch. 1861

STATE GOVERNORS.

James W. Nye....................acting...............31 Oct. 1864
Henry G. Blasdel..............assumes office...........5 Dec. "
Luther R. Bradley, Dem....... " " ....Jan. 1871
John H. Kinkead, Rep........ " " ....Jan. 1879
Jewett W. Adams, Dem......... " " ....Jan. 1883
Christopher C. Stevenson, Rep. " " ....Jan. 1887
Frank Bell.........................acting.............21 Sept. 1890
Roswell K. Colcord, Rep.......assumes office.............Jan. 1891
John E. Jones.................... " " ....Jan. 1895

UNITED STATES SENATORS FROM THE STATE OF NEVADA.

Name.	No. of Congress.	Date.	Remarks.
James W. Nye......	39th to 43d	1865 to 1873	
William M. Stewart.	39th " 44th	1865 " 1875	
John P. Jones......	43d " ——	1873 " ——	Term expires 1897.
William Sharon....	44th " 47th	1875 " 1881	
James G. Fair......	47th " 50th	1881 " 1888	
William M. Stewart.	50th " ——	1888 " ——	Term expires 1899.

Neville's Cross, or **Durham,** Battle of, between the Scots, under king David Bruce, and the English, it is said (probably incorrectly) under Philippa, consort of Edward III., and lord Percy, 12 or 17 Oct. 1346. More than 15,000 Scots were slain, and the king taken.

New Amsterdam. NEW YORK.

Newark, Canada. UNITED STATES, 1813.

Newbern, N. C. NORTH CAROLINA, 1862.

New Brunswick, *first settled by the French, 1604,* and called, with NOVA SCOTIA, ACADIA, was taken from Nova Scotia, and received its name as a separate colony in 1785. It was united with Canada for legislative purposes by an act passed 29 Mch. 1867. Area, 27,177 sq. miles. Population of New Brunswick in 1865, 272,780; in 1871, 285,594; 1881, 288,265.

Newburg address. UNITED STATES, 1783.

Newbury, a borough of Berkshire, Engl. Near here were fought 2 battles, (1) 20 Sept. 1643, when Charles I. obtained some advantage over the parliamentary forces under Essex. Among the slain was Lucius Cary, viscount Falkland. (2) A second battle of dubious result between royalists and parliamentarians under Waller, 27 Oct. 1644.

New Caledonia, an island in the Pacific ocean, discovered by Cook on 4 Sept. 1774, was seized by the French, 20 Sept. 1853, and made a penal colony. Area, 6000 sq. miles; pop. 1889, 62,752.

Newcastle-upon-Tyne, Northumberland, the Roman *Pons Ælia,* first coal port in the world, and commercial metropolis of the north of England. Coal mines were discovered here about 1234. The first charter granted townsmen for digging coal by Henry III. in 1239. In 1306 the use of coal for fuel was prohibited in London by royal proclamation, chiefly because it injured the sale of wood, which then abounded near the city; but the prohibition did not last long, and Newcastle coal has been exported for more than 500 years.

Castle built by Robert Courthose, son of William I............ 1080
Taken by William II.. 1095
St. Nicholas church built, about 1091; burned 1216; restored by Edward I., to whom John Balliol did homage here, 1292; rebuilt 1359
Newcastle surrenders to the Scotch.............................. 1640
Who here gave up Charles I. to the parliament........30 Jan. 1647
T. Bewick, the wood engraver, d................................. 1828
Strike of 9000 engineers for day of 9 hours......about 16 May, 1871
College of Physical Science in Durham university opened, Oct. "
Engineers' strike ends; terms, 9 hours a day, to begin on 1 Jan. 1872; men to work overtime when needed; wages unchanged; arranged by R. B. Philipson and Joseph Cowen, 6 Oct. "
New swing-bridge over the Tyne (281 feet long; weight, 1450 tons, lifted by a hydraulic crane); begun 1868; completed, June, 1876

New Church. SWEDENBORGIANS.

New England includes CONNECTICUT, MAINE, MASSACHUSETTS, NEW HAMPSHIRE, RHODE ISLAND, VERMONT.

New Forest, a royal forest and hundred of Hampshire, Engl., was made ("afforested") by William the Conqueror, 1079-85. It is said that the whole country for 30 miles was laid waste. William Rufus was killed here by an arrow shot by Walter Tyrrel, that accidentally glanced from a tree, 2 Aug. 1100, on whose site is now a triangular stone. The New Forest Deer Removal act was passed 14 and 15 Vict. c. 76, 7 Aug. 1851. Agitation for preservation of this forest, autumn, 1870. FORESTS.

Newfound'land, a large island at the entrance of the gulf of the St. Lawrence, discovered by Sebastian Cabot, who called it *Prima Vista,* 24 June, 1497, and formally taken possession of by sir Humphrey Gilbert, 1583. In Elizabeth's time other nations had the advantage of English in the fishery. In 1577 there were 100 fishing-vessels from Spain, 50 from Portugal, 150 from France, and only 15 (but larger) from England.—*Hakluyt.* But the English fishery by 1625 had increased so that Devonshire ports alone employed 150 ships, which sold fish in Spain, Portugal, and Italy. The sovereignty of England was recognized in 1713. Newfoundland obtained a colonial legislature in 1832. On 14 Jan. 1857, a convention between England and France confirmed to the French certain privileges of fishery in exchange for others. The English colonists were dissatisfied. Newfoundland refused to unite with the dominion of Canada, Mch. 1869. Area, 42,200 sq. miles; pop. 1874, 164,389; 1884, 193,124.

Fishery dispute.—At Fortune bay, U. S. fishers set nets on Sunday, 13 Jan. 1878, contrary to local regulations; they were forcibly removed; controversy ensued, Mr. Evarts for the U. S., sent despatch, 24 Aug.; correspondence, Sept., Oct.; marquis of Salisbury refused compensation; but earl Granville granted it; 15,000*l.* awarded by arbitration, 28 May, 1881

New France. CANADA, FRENCH IN AMERICA.

Newgate, London. The prison was named from the gate once part of it, and stood a little beyond the Sessions-house in the Old Bailey. It was used as a prison for persons of rank as early as 1218; but was rebuilt 2 centuries later by the executors of sir Richard Whittington, whose statue with a cat stood in the niche till destroyed by the great fire of 1666. It was then reconstructed; but, becoming an accumulation of misery and inconvenience, was pulled down and rebuilt between 1778 and 1780. During riots in 1780, the interior was destroyed by fire, but soon after restored. Newgate was disused as an ordinary prison 31 Dec. 1881.—*Griffiths* "Chronicles of Newgate" pub. Jan. 1884.

New Grana'da, a federal republic of South America, discovered by Ojeda in 1499, and settled by the Spaniards in 1536. It formed part of the republic of Bogota, established 1811; and with Caracas formed the republic of Colombia, 17 Dec. 1819. COLOMBIA.

New Guinea or **Papua,** Pacific ocean, between the equator and 11° S. lat., and 131° and 151° E. lon., the largest island in the world (excluding Australia). It is 1490 miles long and greatest width 430 miles; area, 306,000 sq. miles; discovered by the Portuguese after their settlement of the Moluccas, between 1512 and 1530. It was visited by Saavedra, a Spaniard, in 1528. It is said to have been named by Ortiz de Retes, a Portuguese, 1549. Torres strait, which divides New Guinea and Australia, discovered by Torres, a Spaniard, in 1606, was frequently visited by the Dutch in the 17th century. They established a colony with a fortress, named Dubus, on the S.W. coast, in 1828, but it failed and was removed in 1835. Inhabitants partly Malays, but the majority "Papuan negroes."

New Hampshire, one of the eastern states of the American Union, lies between Maine on the east and Vermont and Quebec on the west, from which it is separated by the Connecticut river. Quebec bounds it on the north and

Massachusetts on the south. The Atlantic, on the southeast corner, forms a coast-line of 18 miles, affording a good harbor at Portsmouth. Area, 9305 sq. miles, in 10 counties; pop. 1890, 376,530; 1900, 411,588. Capital, Concord.

New Hampshire formed a part of the grant to the colonies of Virginia and Plymouth, extending from lat. 34° to lat. 45° north, 10 Apr. 1606

Capt. John Smith, ranging the shore of New England, explores the harbor of Piscataqua.............. 1614

Ferdinando Gorges and capt. John Mason, members of the Plymouth council, obtain a joint grant of the province of Laconia, comprising all the land between the Merrimac river, the great lakes, and river of Canada..................10 Aug. 1622

Gorges and Mason establish a settlement at the mouth of the Piscataqua, calling the place Little Harbor, and another settlement, 8 miles farther up the river, Dover................ 1623

Mason, having agreed with Gorges to make the Piscataqua the divisional line, takes from the Plymouth council a patent of that portion lying between that river and the Merrimac, and calls it New Hampshire..............................7 Nov. 1629

Company of Laconia dividing their interests, Mason procures for himself a charter of Portsmouth........................ 1631

Towns of Portsmouth and Northam laid out.................. 1633

A number of families from England settle on Dover Neck and build a fortified church.. "

Mason's estate, after a few specific bequests, goes to a grandson Robert Tufton, who takes the surname of Mason..... 1635

George Burdet, a clergyman from Yarmouth, Engl., succeeds Wiggin as governor of the Dover plantations.............. 1636

Rev. John Wheelwright, banished from Boston as a result of the Antinomian controversy, and a few friends settle Exeter, and form a government with elections by the people....... 1638

Hampton, considered as belonging to the colony of Massachusetts, founded.. "

Burdet succeeded by capt. John Underhill........................ "

People of Portsmouth form a provisional government......... 1639

Provisional government established at Dover..........22 Oct. 1640

Four governments in New Hampshire subscribe to a union with Massachusetts, 14 Apr. 1641, which goes into effect, giving New Hampshire's representatives a vote in town affairs without regard to religious qualifications..............9 Oct. 1641

Colonies of Connecticut, New Haven, New Plymouth, and Massachusetts (including New Hampshire) form a confederacy.. 1642

White mountains explored by capt. Neal........................ "

Quakers William Robinson and Marmaduke Stevenson executed for returning to the province after banishment, 27 Oct. 1659

William Leddra hung for being a Quaker..............14 Mch. 1660

Warrant issued at Dover, directing 3 Quakeresses to be whipped out of the province. Stripped and tied to a cart, they are publicly whipped at Dover and Hampton, but freed at Salisbury through the agency of Walter Barefoot............Dec. 1662

Indians in King Philip's war ravage Somersworth and Durham, and between Exeter and Hampton..................Sept. 1675

Four hundred Indians captured by strategy at Dover. 7 or 8 are put to death, 200 discharged, and the balance sold in foreign parts as slaves...............................7 Sept. 1676

King's bench decided that Massachusetts had no jurisdiction over New Hampshire and Mason's heirs none within the territory they claimed. To establish Mason's title, the king makes New Hampshire a distinct province, with John Cutts of Portsmouth president..............................8 Sept. 1679

Royal commission declaring New Hampshire a royal province reaches Portsmouth ....1 Jan. 1680

President Cutts dies, and is succeeded by maj. Richard Waldron of Dover...5 Apr. 1681

Mason surrenders one-fifth of his quit rents from the province to Charles II., and thus secures the appointment of Edward Cranfield as lieutenant-governor with extraordinary powers, and devoted to his interests.........................25 Jan. 1682

Cranfield suspends Waldron and Richard Martyn, both popular leaders, from the council............................15 May, "

Edward Gove, voicing the popular feeling against gov. Cranfield, with a tumultuous body from Exeter and Hampton, declares for liberty and reform. Finding the people not yet ready for revolt, he surrenders, is convicted of high-treason and imprisoned in the tower of London 1683

People, called upon by the governor to take leases from Mason, refuse to acknowledge his claim..................14 Feb. "

Assembly refuse money for the Cranfield government.......... 1684

Cranfield, by authority of the governor and council, without the concurrence of the assembly, imposes taxes; but, unable to enforce payment, obtains a leave of absence and returns to England, Walter Barefoot, his deputy, succeeding as chief magistrate.......................................9 Jan. 1685

Indians attack Dover; surprise maj. Waldron in his own home, and massacre him and many other settlers, taking 29 captives, whom they sell as slaves to the French in Canada...27 Jan. 1689

People of New Hampshire effect a governmental union with Massachusetts....................................12 Mch. 1690

New Hampshire is purchased from the Mason heirs by Samuel Allen of London, who prevents its insertion in the charter of William and Mary, and becomes its governor, appointing his son-in-law, John Usher, as lieutenant-governor..1 Mch. 1692

Law passed requiring each town to provide a school-master, Dover excepted, it then being too much impoverished by Indian raids to do so.. 1693

Sieur de Villieu, and 250 Indians, approach Durham undiscovered, and, waiting in ambush during the night, at sunrise attack the place, destroy 5 houses, and carry away 100 captives..17 July, 1694

Richard Earl of Bellomont is installed governor of New York, Massachusetts, and New Hampshire; council and courts reorganized of opponents of the Mason claim..........31 July, 1699

Earl of Bellomont dies at New York, 5 Mch. 1701, and Joseph Dudley is appointed governor of Massachusetts and New Hampshire by queen Anne, his commission being published at Portsmouth....................................13 July, 1701

An attack of Indians on Durham is repulsed by a few women in disguise firing upon the Indians, who suppose the place well garrisoned...Apr. 1706

Indian hostilities cease on the arrival of news of the treaty of Utrecht, and a treaty ratified with them............11 July, 1713

George Vaughan made lieutenant-governor and Samuel Shute commander-in-chief of the province.................13 Oct. 1716

Vaughan superseded by John Wentworth, by commission signed by Joseph Addison, English secretary of state.7 Dec. 1717

Sixteen Scottish families settle at Londonderry, and the first Presbyterian church in New England is organized by rev. James McGregorie... 1719

Capt. John Lovewell makes his first excursion against the Indians in New Hampshire............................Dec. 1724

A grant of land made by New Hampshire to the survivors of the Lovewell defeat at Fryeburg, Me., overlaps a similar grant by Massachusetts in Bow county, which leads to a boundary litigation between New Hampshire and Massachusetts, which lasted 40 years. Grants made.......18-20 May, 1727

Duration of assembly limited to 3 years unless sooner dissolved by the governor ....21 Nov. "

David Dunbar appointed lieutenant-governor.........24 June, 1731

New Hampshire petitioning the crown in 1732 to decide the boundary question, obtains a royal order appointing commissioners, from the councillors of the neighboring provinces, to decide the question; board meets at Hampton.......Aug. 1737

Commissioners fix upon the present eastern boundary of New Hampshire. For the southern boundary an appeal is made to George III., who decides upon the present line, giving New Hampshire a territory 50 miles long by 14 broad in excess of her claim...................................5 Mch. 1740

Bennington Wentworth appointed governor and commander-in-chief of New Hampshire.................................. 1741

George Whitefield preaches in New Hampshire............... 1744

Indian depredations in the New Hampshire settlements; attacks on Keene, Number Four (Charlestown), Rochester, capture of fort Massachusetts at Hoosuck......Apr.-20 Aug. 1746

Three companies of rangers under Robert Rogers and the 2 brothers John and William Stark, formed from the New Hampshire troops by the express desire of lord Loudon..... 1756

First newspaper in New Hampshire and the oldest in New England, *New Hampshire Gazette*, published at Portsmouth, Aug. "

On application of New York, the king in council declares the western bank of the Connecticut river the boundary between New Hampshire and New York......................20 July, 1764

Concord, settled in 1727, is called Rumford in 1733, and takes the name of Concord (RUMFORD MEDAL)....................... 1765

George Meserve appointed stamp distributer for New Hampshire, resigns his office before landing at Boston, 9 Sept. 1765, compelled to make a formal resignation 18 Sept. It being suspected that he still intended to distribute the stamped paper, he is compelled to give up his commission, and is sent back to England..........................9 Jan. 1766

John Wentworth, appointed governor in place of his uncle, removed by the British ministry on charge of neglect of duty, 11 Aug. 1767

Dartmouth college at Hanover chartered..............30 Dec. 1769

Nathaniel Folsom and John Sullivan appointed delegates to Congress at Philadelphia by a convention of 85 deputies, which met at Exeter.............................14 July, 1774

By the request of a committee of the people, a cargo of tea consigned to a Mr. Parry of Portsmouth is reshipped to Halifax, 25 Jan. 1774. A second cargo consigned to Parry, arriving, the people attack his house, and quiet is only restored by sending of the vessel to Halifax............8 Sept. "

Town committee of Portsmouth, hearing of the order by king in council prohibiting exportation of gunpowder to America, seize the garrison at fort William and Mary, and carry off 100 barrels of gunpowder, 11 Dec.; next day they remove 15 cannon with small-arms and warlike stores........12 Dec. "

Armed men dismantle a battery at Jerry's Point on Great island and bring 8 pieces of cannon to Portsmouth ..26 May, 1775

Convention of the people assembles at Exeter...........June, "

New Hampshire troops in the battle of Bunker Hill...17 June, "

Gov. Wentworth convenes the assembly, 12 June, and recommends the conciliatory proposition of lord North, to which the house gives no heed. They expel 3 new royalist members, and the governor adjourns the assembly to 28 Sept., and sails for Boston. From the Isles of Shoals he adjourns the assembly until Apr. 1776, his last official act.......Sept. "

A constitution for New Hampshire is framed by a Congress styling itself the House of Representatives, which assembles at Exeter, 21 Dec. 1775, and completes its labors......5 Jan. 1776

Under the new form of government, Meshech Weare is appointed president of the council and of an executive committee chosen to sit during the recess of the council, as president of New Hampshire 1776

John Sullivan of New Hampshire appointed brigadier general by Congress "

Ship of war *Raleigh* built at Portsmouth by decree of Congress, "

A convention of both houses reports a declaration of independence which was adopted and sent forthwith to the delegates of New Hampshire in Congress 15 June, "

Declaration of Independence of the United States signed by Josiah Bartlett and William Whipple of New Hampshire, 2 Aug 1776 and by a third representative from the state, Matthew Thornton Nov "

New Hampshire troops engage in the battle of Bennington, under John Stark, who is made brigadier general by Congress . 18 Aug 1777

Articles of confederation ratified by New Hampshire, 4 Mch 1778, and signed by the state representatives at Philadelphia, Josiah Bartlett and John Wentworth 8 Aug 1778

Phillips academy at Exeter founded 1781

Daniel Webster b at Franklin, N H 18 Jan 1782

Sixteen towns on the eastern side of the Connecticut river refuse to send delegates to a constitutional convention in New Hampshire and desire to be admitted into the new state of Vermont. Vermont agrees to accept these additional towns, but Congress in its act of admission makes it an indispensable preliminary that the revolted towns shall be restored to New Hampshire The towns at last accept the situation and become part of New Hampshire "

A convention which meets at Concord, 10 June, 1778, frames a constitution which is rejected by the people A new convention meets at Exeter in 1781, and after 2 years a constitution is framed which goes into effect 2 June, 1784

John Langdon and Nicholas Gilman delegates from New Hampshire, sign the Constitution of the U S 17 Sept. 1787

Convention assembles at Exeter, 13 Feb, adjourns to Concord, and ratifies the Constitution of the U S, by a vote of 57 to 47 21 June, 1788

Pres Washington, on a tour of observation, arrives at Portsmouth 30 Oct 1789

Portsmouth Journal established at Portsmouth "

An academy, the second in the state, opened at New Ipswich, "

Publication of *Concord Herald* began by George Hough 5 Jan 1790

Academies incorporated at Atkinson and Amherst 1791

Four post routes appointed through the interior of the state "

New Hampshire Medical Society incorporated "

Bank established at Portsmouth 1792

Convention assembles at Concord, 7 Sept 1791, revises the state constitution changes the title of the chief magistrate from president to governor, and completes its labors 5 Sept "

Elder Jesse Lee, coming from Virginia, visits New Hampshire, founds the first Methodist society in the state "

A privateer ship, the *McClary* fitted out during the war at Portsmouth under the sanction of the legislature, captures an American merchant ship, the *Susanna*, bound for an enemy's port laden with supplies The matter is brought into court, and the U S Court of Appeals reverses the judgment of the State court and awards $32,721 36 damages to the owners of the *Susanna*. The legislature of New Hampshire, in special session, prepares a spirited remonstrance against this action as "a violation of state independence and an unwarrantable encroachment in the courts of the United States" . 1794

Bridge constructed over the Piscataqua near Portsmouth, from Newington to Durham nearly ½ mile in length "

Academy at Haverhill established "

Academy at Gilmanton incorporated . . 1795

First New Hampshire turnpike, extending from Concord to the Piscataqua bridge, chartered 1796

Medical department of Dartmouth college established 1798

Keene Sentinel established at Keene.. . Mch. 1799

New Hampshire Missionary Society, the earliest charitable society of a religious character in the state, incorporated 1801

Farmer's Cabinet published at Amherst 11 Nov 1802

First cotton factory in state erected at New Ipswich 1803

Piscataqua Evangelical Magazine pub at Portsmouth 1805

Law passed dividing towns into school districts "

From the preaching and teachings of Mr Murray in 1773, the Universalists are recognized as a religious sect in New Hampshire 13 June, "

From 1680 to 1775 the seat of government was at Portsmouth From 1775 to 1807 the legislature adjourned from town to town, assembling at Exeter, Concord, Hopkinton, Dover, Amherst, Charlestown, and Hanover The legislature of 1807 adjourns from Hopkinton to Concord for regular sessions . 1807

New Hampshire Iron Factory company, incorporated at Franconia in 1805, erects and puts in operation a blast-furnace. 1811

Horace Greeley b at Amherst. . 3 Feb. "

State prison at Concord established . . 1812

Kimball Union academy at Plainfield incorporated . 1813

New Hampshire troops under gen John McNiel take part in the battle of Chippewa, 5 July, 1814, and at Niagara, 25 July, 1814

Law passed giving to the state complete jurisdiction over Dartmouth college, the charter for which requires the trustees, professors, tutors, and officers to take the oath of allegiance to the British king . 27 June, 1816

Trustees and overseers of Dartmouth college, summoned by the governor to meet at Hanover, 26 Aug 1816, refuse to act under the law of 27 June, or to report to the governor as requested 28 Aug. "

Pres John Wheelock of Dartmouth college d . 4 Apr 1817

Pres James Monroe, on his tour of the Northern states, visits Portsmouth, Dover, Concord, and Hanover "

State house at Concord erected "

Gen Benjamin Pierce appointed sheriff of Hillsborough county by gov Plumer liberates 3 aged men confined for debt in Amherst jail, by paying their debts 20 Nov 1818

Toleration law making all religious sects on equal ground, and dependent on voluntary contributions . 1819

Control of Dartmouth college, after 2 years or more of litigation, awarded by the Supreme court of the U S to the trustees "

[Result chiefly due to the efforts of Daniel Webster]

Law of 29 June, 1821, imposing an annual tax of one half of one per cent on the capital stock of banks, for school purposes. The sum accrued is divided among the towns . 1829

Gov Matthew Harvey appointed judge of the U S. District court for New Hampshire, is succeeded by Joseph M Harper, acting governor Feb 1831

Levi Woodbury secretary of the navy May, "

Levi Woodbury secretary of the U S treasury 27 June, 1834

Nashua and Lowell railroad incorporated 1836

Act passed providing for a scientific, geological, and mineralogical survey of the state 3 July, 1839

New Hampshire asylum for the insane at Concord, founded Oct 1842

Office of state commissioner of common schools created 1846

Law authorizing towns to establish public libraries 1849

Office of school commissioner abolished, a Board of Education constituted of county school commissioners June, 1850

Democratic National convention at Baltimore, Md, nominates gen Franklin Pierce of New Hampshire for president, 9 May, 1852

New Hampshire Conference seminary and female college at Tilton, opened 1845, receives its charter "

Property qualification for state officers abolished "

Franklin Pierce inaugurated president 4 Mch 1853

Gold discovered at Plainfield, in the Connecticut valley 1854

State Teachers' Association incorporated "

House of Reformation for Juvenile and Female Offenders at Manchester dedicated 12 May, 1858

First regiment of Federal troops leaves Concord for the seat of war 25 May, 1861

Franklin Pierce's remarkable speech at Concord on the "war" 4 July, 1863

"Soldiers' Voting bill," passed 17 Aug, is returned 26 Aug with a veto, but becomes a law because retained in the governor's hands more than 5 days 17 Aug 1864

Law authorizing a commissioner to edit early provincial records, and rev dr Bouton of Concord chosen 1866

Office of superintendent of public instruction created 1867

Revision and codification of the laws, ordered by the legislature of 1865, completed "

New Hampshire College of Agriculture and the Mechanic Arts, at Hanover chartered 1866 opened 4 Sept 1868

Legislature ratifies the XV th Amendment to the U S Constitution 1 July, 1869

Robinson female seminary at Exeter, chartered 1867, opened. "

City training school, Manchester, opened . "

Ex pres Pierce dies at Concord 8 Oct. "

Labor Reform party holds its first state convention. 28 Jan 1870

Act passed creating a state Board of Agriculture "

James A Weston, Democrat, receives 34,700 votes for governor, and James Pike, Republican, 33,892. The legislature elect Weston by 326 to 159 June, 1871

State Normal school at Plymouth opened "

Orphans' Home and School of Industry on the ancestral Webster farm, near Franklin, opened "

Compulsory Attendance School law goes into effect "

Weston re elected by the legislature, no choice by the people, legislature meets 3 June, 1874

There being no choice for governor at the election, 9 Mch. 1875, Person C Cheney is chosen by the legislature 9 June, 1875

Thirteen amendments to the constitution, proposed by a convention at Concord, 6 to 16 Dec. 1876, are adopted except 2, one of which was "to strike out the word Protestant" in the Bill of Rights . . 1877

William E Chandler of New Hampshire appointed secretary of the navy . 1 Apr 1882

Prohibitionists in state convention at Nashua adopt a constitution for the State Temperance union. 7–8 June, "

Bronze statue of Daniel Webster, 8 feet in height, cast at Munich, and gift of Benjamin P Cheney, is erected in the State House park, Concord, and dedicated 17 June, 1886

For governor David H Goodell, Republican, 44,809 votes, Chas. H Amsden, Democrat, 44,093, Edgar L Carr, Prohibition, 1567 · the choice devolves upon the legislature Nov 1888

State Constitutional convention meets at Concord, 2 Jan. 1889, among the 7 amendments submitted to the people one favoring prohibition is lost .12 Mch 1889

Legislature elects Goodell governor by 168 to 114 . 5 June, "

Gov Goodell stricken with paralysis . 17 Mch 1890

Statue of gen John Stark, for which the legislature appropriated $12,000, unveiled in the state house yard, Concord, 23 Oct "

Vote for governor Hiram A Tuttle, Republican, 42,479, Charles H Amsden, Democrat, 42,386, Josiah M Fletcher, Prohibition, 1363, no choice Nov "

State Soldiers' home established at Tilton, 1889, dedicated, 3 Dec "

Hiram A Tuttle elected governor by legislature . . 7 Jan. 1891

J H Gallinger elected U S senator .. . 20 Jan "

egislature makes the first Monday in Sept. (Labor day) a legal holiday, directs removal of the New Hampshire College of Agriculture and the Mechanic Arts from Hanover to the farm of the late Benjamin Thompson of Durham, and passes a secret or Australian Ballot act at its session.....7 Jan.–11 Apr. 1891
t-gov. Samuel W. Hale d. at Brooklyn, aged 68........16 Oct. "
hn Greenleaf Whittier, b. 1807, d. at Hampton Falls..7 Sept. 1892
sane asylum at Dover burned; 45 lives lost..........9 Feb. 1893

GOVERNORS.

esbeck Weare	assumes office	1775
hn Langdon	"	1785
hn Sullivan	"	1786
hn Langdon	"	1788
hn Sullivan	"	1789
siah Bartlett	"	1790
hn Taylor Gilman	"	1794
hn Langdon	"	1805
remiah Smith	"	1809
hn Langdon	"	1810
illiam Plumer	"	1812
hn Taylor Gilman	"	1813
illiam Plumer	"	1816
muel Bell	"	1819
vi Woodbury	"	1823
vid L. Morrill	"	1824
njamin Pierce	"	1827
hn Bell	"	1828
njamin Pierce	"	1829
atthew Harvey	"	1830
seph M. Harper	acting	Feb. 1831
muel Dinsmoor	assumes office	June, 1831
William Badger	assumes office	1[illegible]
Isaac Hill	"	[illegible]
John Page	"	[illegible]
Henry Hubbard	"	[illegible]
John H. Steele	"	[illegible]
Anthony Colby	"	[illegible]
Jared W. Williams	"	[illegible]
Samuel Dinsmoor	"	[illegible]
Noah Martin	"	[illegible]
Nathaniel B. Baker	"	[illegible]
Ralph Metcalf	"	1855
William Haile	"	1857
Ichabod Goodwin	"	1859
Nathaniel S. Berry	"	1861
Joseph A. Gilmore	"	1863
Frederick Smyth	"	1865
Walter Harriman	"	1867
Onslow Stearns	"	1869
James A. Weston	"	1871
Ezekiel A. Straw	"	1872
James A. Weston	"	1874
Person C. Cheney	"	1875
Benjamin F. Prescott	"	1877
Nathaniel Head	"	1879
Charles H. Bell	"	1881
Samuel W. Hale	"	1883
Moody Currier	"	1885
Charles H. Sawyer	"	1887
David H. Goodell	"	1889
Hiram A. Tuttle	"	1891
John B. Smith	"	1893
Charles A. Busiel	"	1895

UNITED STATES SENATORS FROM THE STATE OF NEW HAMPSHIRE.

Name.	No. of Congress.	Date.	Remarks.
hn Langdon	1st	1789	Elected president of the senate [illegible] for the purpose of opening and counting the vot[illegible] president of the U. S. Elected preside[illegible]
ine Wingate	1st to 3d	1789 to 1793	
muel Livermore	3d " 6th	1793 " 1801	Elected president *pro tem.* 6 [illegible] 1801.
neon Olcott	7th " 9th	1801 " 1805	Elected in place of Samuel L[illegible]
mes Sheafe	7th	1801 " 1802	Resigned.
lliam Plumer	7th to 9th	1802 " 1807	Elected in place of James S[illegible]
cholas Gilman	9th " 13th	1805 " 1814	Died.
hum Parker	10th	1807 " 1810	Resigned.
arles Cutts	11th	1810	Elected in place of Parke[r]
remiah Mason	13th to 15th	1813 to 1817	Resigned.
omas W. Thompson	13th " 14th	1815 " 1817	Elected in place of Gilm[an]
vid L. Morrill	14th " 18th	1817 " 1823	
ement Storer	15th " 16th	1817 " 1819	Elected in place of Mason.
hn F. Parrott	16th " 19th	1819 " 1825	
muel Bell	18th " 24th	1823 " 1836	
vi Woodbury	19th " 22d	1825 " 1831	
aac Hill	22d " 24th	1831 " 1836	Resigned.
hn Page	24th	1836	Elected in place of Hill.
enry Hubbard	24th to 27th	1836 to 1842	
anklin Pierce	25th " 27th	1837 " 1842	Resigned.
onard Wilcox	27th	1842	Elected in place of Pierce.
vi Woodbury	27th to 29th	1842 to 1845	Resigned.
arles G. Atherton	28th " 31st	1843 " 1849	When he was a member of the House he introduced the famous resolution, 11 Dec. 1838, known as the ATHERTON GAG.
nning J. Jenness	29th	1845 " 1846	Appointed *pro tem.* in place of Woodbury.
seph Cilley	29th	1846 " 1847	Elected in place of Woodbury.
hn P. Hale	30th to 33d	1847 " 1853	
oses Norris, jr.	31st " 33d	1849 " 1855	Died 11 Jan. 1855.
arles G. Atherton	33d	1853	Died 1853.
hn S. Wells	"	1855	Appointed in place of Norris.
red W. Williams	"	1853	Appointed in place of Atherton.
mes Bell	34th	1855 to 1857	Died 1857.
hn P. Hale	34th to 38th	1855 " 1865	
niel Clark	35th " 39th	1857 " 1866	Elected in place of Bell. Elected president *pro tem.* 26 Apr. 1864, and 9 Feb. 1865. Resigned.
orge G. Fogg	39th	1866 " 1867	Appointed in place of Clark.
ron H. Cragin	39th to 44th	1866 " 1875	
mes W. Patterson	40th " 43d	1867 " 1873	
inbridge Wadleigh	43d " 46th	1873 " 1879	
lward H. Rollins	45th " 48th	1877 " 1883	
enry W. Blair	46th " 52d	1879 " 1891	
ustin F. Pike	48th " 49th	1883 " 1886	Died 1886.
rson C. Cheney	49th " 50th	1886 " 1888	Appointed in place of Pike.
illiam E. Chandler	50th " ——	1888 " ——	Term expires 1901
cob H. Gallinger	52d " ——	1891 " ——	To succeed Blair. Term expires 1897.

New Harmony. Robert Owen was the first social-[ist] to form a non-religious community in America. In 1824 [h]e purchased the town of Harmony (HARMONISTS), called it [N]ew Harmony, and organized a community which on 12 Jan. [18]26 adopted a constitution as "The New Harmony Commu[ni]ty of Equality." 4 July, 1826, at New Harmony, Owen de[liv]ered his Declaration of Mental Independence against the [tr]inity of man's oppressors, "Private Property, Irrational Re[lig]ion, and Marriage." SOCIALISM.

New Hebrides, a group of islands in S. Pacific [oc]ean, discovered by Quiros, who, believing them a continent, named them *Tierra Austral del Espiritu Santo*, in 1606. Bougainville in 1768 found them to be islands; and in 1774 Cook gave them their present name.

New Holland. AUSTRALIA, NEW SOUTH WALES.

New Ireland, an island in the Pacific, lat. 2° 3′ S., lon. 152° E.; 200 miles long, 25 miles average width. An attempt of the French marquis de Rays to colonize this island was reported a failure in Aug. 1880 and May, 1881.

New Jersey, one of the middle Atlantic states of the United States of America, lies between lat. 38° 56′ and 41° 21′

NEW

N., and lon. 73° 58′ 51″ and 75° 33′ W. It is bounded on the north by New York, east by New York and Atlantic ocean, south by Delaware bay, and west by Delaware and Pennsylvania, from which it is separated by the Delaware river. Area, 8715 sq. miles. Pop. 1890, 1,444,933; 1900, 1,883,669. Capital, Trenton.

Henry Hudson, in the ship *Half Moon*, enters Delaware bay, 28 Aug. 1609, and coasts the eastern shore of New Jersey on his way to Sandy Hook, where he anchors, 3 Sept. 1609
First Dutch settlement on the Delaware is made near Gloucester, N. J., where fort Nassau is built.......... 1623
Capt. Thomas Young, receiving a commission from Charles I., sails up the Delaware river until "stopped from further proceeding by a ledge of rock which crosseth the river" (Trenton falls)..........1 Sept. 1634
Number of English families settle on Salem creek, at a place called by the Indians Asamohaking.......... 1640
Dutch acquire by deed a large tract of land in the eastern part of New Jersey called Bergen..........30 Jan. 1658
Royal charter executed by Charles II., in favor of the duke of York, of the whole region between the Connecticut and Delaware rivers..........20 Mch. 1664
Present state of New Jersey granted by the duke of York to lord John Berkeley and sir George Carteret by deed of lease and release, to be called Nova Cæsaria or New Jersey, 23-24 June, "
By license from col. Nicholls, governor under the duke of York, a company, the "Elizabethtown Associates," purchase the site of Elizabethtown from Indians, and establish the first permanent settlement in New Jersey..........28 Oct. "
Philip Carteret, appointed first English governor of New Jersey, arrives at Elizabethtown with 30 settlers..........Aug. 1665
Newark settled by 30 families from Connecticut..........17 May, 1666
Grant of 276 acres issued for Hoboken..........12 May, 1668
Session of the first legislative assembly of New Jersey held at Elizabethtown..........26 May, "
Bergen chartered..........22 Sept. "
Settlers under grants from gov. Nicholls form an independent government whose deputies at Elizabethtown elect James Carteret governor..........14 May, 1672
Gov. Philip Carteret returns to England to lay the matter of the government of New Jersey before the proprietors.......... "
First Friends' meeting house built at Shrewsbury.......... "
Lord Berkeley sells his half interest in the province to 2 English Quakers, John Fenwick and Edward Byllinge...18 Mch. 1673
New Netherlands, including New Jersey, surrendered to the Dutch..........July, "
New Jersey again becomes an English province, under treaty of peace between England and Holland..........9 Feb. 1674
Edward Byllinge, becoming financially embarrassed, assigns his interest to William Penn and others..........10 Feb. "
Philip Carteret returns and resumes authority in New Jersey, meeting the General Assembly at Bergen..........6 Nov. "
Fenwick, sailing from London in the ship *Griffith*, arrives with a small company of Quakers and settles at Salem......June, 1675
"Concessions and Agreements" of the proprietors of the Fenwick and Byllinge purchase in New Jersey issued; Fenwick to have one-tenth interest, and the assignees of Byllinge nine-tenths, and a government established..........3 Mch. 1676
Quintipartite deed executed between William Penn and others, assignees of Byllinge, and sir George Carteret, for a division of New Jersey into east and west, by a line drawn from Little Egg harbor to the most northerly point or boundary on the Delaware, Carteret retaining East Jersey..........1 July, "
Richard Hartshore and Richard Guy of East Jersey, and James Wasse sent from England, authorized to establish a government for West Jersey, by the proprietors..........18 Aug. "
First recorded public action for the establishment of schools in Newark..........21 Nov. "
Nine executive commissioners appointed by the proprietors of West Jersey under a constitution promulgated 3 Mch. 1676, accompanied by a large number of settlers, arrive from England and purchase from the Indians a tract of land on the Delaware between Assunpink and Old Man's creek.....Aug. 1677
Burlington laid out by agents of the London Land company... "
Ship *Shields*, from Hull, the first ship to ascend the Delaware to Burlington, bringing settlers..........10 Dec. 1678
Sir George Carteret, proprietor of East Jersey, d.......... 1679
Asserting that the grant of the duke of York to Berkeley and Carteret did not convey the government, sir Edmund Andros claims the government of New Jersey, and appears before the General Assembly at Elizabethtown; which repudiates his authority..........2 June, 1680
Duke of York having submitted the claim of governmental power in New Jersey to a commission, which decides against Andros, he makes a second grant of West Jersey to the proprietors, 6 Aug., and of East Jersey..........6 Sept. "
Vicinity of Trenton settled by Phineas Pemberton.......... "
First yearly meeting of Friends for discipline in this country held at Burlington..........28 June, 1681
First assembly meets at Burlington and organizes a government, with Samuel Jennings as deputy governor....25 Nov. 1681
Carteret's heirs sell East Jersey to a company of proprietors, including William Penn and 11 others..........1-2 Feb. 1682
Penn company, now increased to 24 proprietors, secure a new conveyance of East Jersey from the duke of York, with full powers of government..........14 Mch. "
Robert Barclay appointed for life first governor of East Jersey under the new proprietary, with Thomas Rudyard as deputy, "
Revenues of Matenicunk island, in the Delaware opposite Burlington, set apart for education. This is believed to be the first school fund in America.......... 1683
Perth Amboy laid out into lots.......... "
First tavern or hotel in the province established at Woodbridge. "
Site of Camden occupied by messrs. Cooper, Runyon, and Morris.......... 1684
First Episcopal church in New Jersey, St. Peter's, founded at Perth Amboy.......... 1685
Byllinge dies, and dr. Samuel Coxe of London purchases his interest in West Jersey.......... 1687
First Baptist church in East Jersey built at Middletown.......... 1688
Gov. Barclay d..........3 Oct. 1690
Presbyterian churches established in Freehold and Woodbridge.......... 1692
First school law of the state enacted by the General Assembly of East New Jersey at Perth Amboy, to maintain a schoolmaster within the town..........12 Oct. 1693
Burlington incorporated.......... "
Salem incorporated.......... 1695
Government of New Jersey surrendered to the crown, and both provinces united..........17 Apr. 1702
Edward Hyde, lord Cornbury, appointed governor of New York and New Jersey by queen Anne..........16 Nov. "
General Assembly meets at Perth Amboy..........10 Nov. 1703
First association of Seventh-day Baptists formed in Piscataway..........Apr. 1707
Lord Cornbury, removed from office by queen Anne, is imprisoned for debt by his creditors.......... 1709
Paper money first issued in New Jersey.......... "
Assembly votes to aid the English expedition against the French in Canada..........16 July, 1711
Schuyler copper mines near Belleville discovered by Arent Schuyler.......... 1719
First freestone quarried in New Jersey.......... 1721
Law providing for triennial elections of deputies to assembly and triennial sessions alternately at Burlington and Amboy, 1727
Gov. Montgomery d..........1 July, 1731
Executive of New Jersey separated from New York, and Lewis Morris appointed governor.......... 1738
Weekly mail from Philadelphia to New York, carried by postboys through New Jersey, established.......... 1739
Rev. George Whitefield visits Elizabethtown.......... 1740
First iron run at furnace in Oxford, Warren county....9 Mch. 1743
Gov. Morris dies at Kingsbury, near Trenton..........21 May, 1746
College of New Jersey at Elizabethtown incorporated.......... "
College of New Jersey removed to Newark.......... 1748
Trenton public library founded.......... 1750
First printing-press in the province established at Woodbridge by James Parker.......... 1751
College of New Jersey finally located at Princeton, and Nassau hall erected.......... 1756
Stage line established from New York to Philadelphia by way of Perth Amboy and Trenton..........Nov. "
Gov. Jonathan Belcher d. aged 76..........31 Aug. 1757
New American Magazine, pub. at Woodbridge by James Parker, and edited by Samuel Nevil under the signature of "Sylvanus Americanus"..........Jan. 1758
Special conference with Indians at Easton, the governor, Francis Bernard, obtains from the chief of the united nations of the Minisinks, Wapings, and other tribes, for $1000, a release of the Indian title to every portion of New Jersey....18 Oct. "
Yearly meeting of the Society of Friends transferred from Burlington to Philadelphia.......... 1761
William Franklin, natural son of Benjamin Franklin, appointed governor (the last royal governor of New Jersey).......... 1763
William Coxe, appointed stamp distributer in New Jersey, voluntarily resigns his office..........Sept. 1765
Joseph Borden, Hendrick Fisher, and Robert Ogden, delegates to a convention of 9 colonies at New York, 7 Oct. 1765; it publishes a declaration of rights, and adjourns.......24 Oct. "
First medical society in the colonies organized in New Jersey, 23 July, 1766
First convention of Episcopal ministers of Connecticut, New York, New Jersey, and Philadelphia, is held at Elizabethtown..........Nov. "
Rutgers college at New Brunswick chartered under the name of Queen's college by George III.......... 1770
Isaac Collins, appointed public printer for New Jersey, begins the publication of an almanac which continues 20 years.... 1771
Stephen Crane, John de Hart, James Kinsey, William Livingston, and Richard Smith, chosen delegates to the Congress at Philadelphia by a convention at New Brunswick..21 July, 1774
Assembly of New Jersey unanimously approves the proceedings of Congress as reported by the delegates........11 Jan. 1775
Provincial congress of New Jersey at Trenton, elects Hendrick Fisher president, and assumes authority..........23 May, "
Provincial legislature, convened by gov. Franklin 16 Nov., is prorogued..........6 Dec. "
Gov. Franklin, sympathizing with the action of the British government, is arrested and sent to East Windsor, Conn., where (until exchanged in 1778) he is held as a prisoner..... 1776

rovincial congress convenes at Burlington, 10 June, 1776, appoints a committee to prepare a constitution, 24 June, who report, 26 June a constitution which is confirmed 2 July, 1776
rdinance passed denouncing the penalty of treason upon all who should levy war against and within the state, or be adherent to the king of Great Britain 18 July, "
braham Clark, John Hart, Francis Hopkins, Richard Stockton, and John Witherspoon, delegates from New Jersey, sign the "Declaration of Independence" 2 Aug "
egislature meets at Princeton 27 Aug, and in joint ballot chooses William Livingston governor of the state 31 Aug "
ort Washington being captured by the British, gen Greene abandons fort Lee, Bergen county 19 Nov "
ashington retreats through New Jersey Nov "
ashington crosses the Delaware into Pennsylvania 8 Dec "
attle of TRENTON 26 Dec. "
attle of PRINCETON 3 Jan 1777
rmy under Washington winters at Morristown "
en Maxwell captures Elizabethtown together with 100 British troops. 23 Jan "
ive vessels, part of a fleet bringing supplies for the British at New Brunswick, are sunk near Amboy 26 Feb. "
en Howe evacuates New Jersey for the purpose of approaching Philadelphia by water, crossing to Staten Island, 30 June, "
y act of assembly the word "state" is substituted for "colony" in the Constitution adopted in 1776 20 Sept. "
attle at FORT MERCER Col Greene repulses a force of Hessians under count Donop 22 Oct "
ew Jersey Gazette, the first newspaper in the state, is pub. at Burlington by Isaac Collins 3 Dec "
attle of MONMOUTH Court house 28 June, 1778
aac Collins prints 5000 copies of a family Bible at Trenton "
ssembly ratifies the "Articles of Confederation" 19 Nov "
ohn Witherspoon and Nathaniel Scudder, delegates from New Jersey, sign the "Articles of Confederation" 26 Nov "
ritish at PAULUS HOOK surprised by maj Henry Lee 19 Aug 1779
ew Jersey Journal established by Shepherd Kollock at Chatham "
merican army winters at Morristown Dec "
ve thousand troops under gen Clinton drive back the Americans under gen Greene at SPRINGFIELD, burn the town, and then retreat 23 June, 1780
lias Boudinot of New Jersey chosen president of the Continental Congress 4 Nov 1782
ontinental Congress meets at Princeton 30 June, 1783
ew Brunswick incorporated 1784
ontinental Congress meets at Trenton 1 Nov "
illiam Livingston, David Brearley, William Patterson, and Jonathan Dayton, delegates from New Jersey, sign the Constitution of the U S 17 Sept. 1787
onstitution of the U S adopted unanimously without amendments by the assembly of New Jersey 18 Dec. "
en Washington is received by a committee of Congress at Elizabethtown, 23 Apr, and escorted to New York, where he is inaugurated president of the U S 30 Apr 1789
ov Livingston dies at Elizabethtown 25 July, 1790
enton made the capital of the state 25 Nov "
enton incorporated 13 Nov 1792
irst factory at Paterson built, and calico goods printed, the first in New Jersey 1794
nterstate traffic in slaves forbidden by the legislature, 14 Mch 1798
omen vote at the Elizabethtown municipal election 1800
[The constitution of 1776 permitted women to vote]
orris turnpike, from Elizabethtown to the Delaware river, chartered 1 Mch 1801
ct for the gradual abolition of slavery, making free all persons born in the state after 4 July, 1804, passed. 15 Feb. 1804
ewark Bank and Insurance company chartered "
illiam Lewis Dayton born in Baskingridge 17 Feb 1807
ct confining suffrage to white male citizens 16 Nov "
ible Society organized 1809
rinceton Theological seminary established by the Presbyterian church 1812
ct passed creating a fund for free schools 12 Feb 1817
rsey City incorporated 28 Jan 1820
un L. Southard of New Jersey secretary of the navy, 16 Sept. 1823
orris canal from Newark to Phillipsburg on the Delaware, commenced 1825
amden and Amboy railroad incorporated 4 Feb 1830
oseph Bonaparte, brother of Napoleon, purchases an estate of 1100 acres at Bordentown, immediately after the downfall of his brother at Waterloo, where he resides until 1832
egislature appropriates $2000 to extinguish all Indian titles to land in the state "
oundary between New Jersey and New York settled by a board of joint commissioners, is confirmed by legislatures of both states in Feb, and by act of Congress 28 June, 1834
ahlon Dickerson appointed secretary of the navy under pres Jackson 30 June, "
. Mary's Hall, college for the superior instruction of women, chartered and opened at Burlington 1837
ate Educational convention held at Trenton to reorganize the school system 27-28 Jan 1838
ohn Stevens, engineer and inventor, petitions Congress for protection to inventors, which results in the patent laws of 10 Apr 1790 He builds a steamboat propelled by twin screws that navigates the Hudson river in 1804 Establishes a steam ferry from Hoboken to New York city, 11 Oct 1811, and at the age of 78, builds an experimental locomotive, which carries passengers at 12 miles an hour on his experimental track at Hoboken in 1826 He d in Hoboken, 6 Mch. "

NEW

At the state election for members of the House of Representatives the returns are contested, the Democratic candidates claiming a majority of about 100 votes in a poll of 57 000 The Whig candidates receive certificates of election under the "Broad" seal of the state 9-10 Oct 1838
Clerk of the House of Representatives, H A Garland of Virginia, refuses to call the names of the Whig delegates from New Jersey, on the ground that the seats were disputed, at the opening of Congress (as there were 5 contested seats, and as the House stood without New Jersey 118 Whig to 119 Democrats, success to either party in this controversy meant control of the House, hence the controversy) 2 Dec 1839
A speaker of the House was elected (Robert M T Hunter) by compromise but the 5 Democratic contestants are seated on the report of a committee declaring them elected by a vote of 111 to 81 16 July, 1839
[This governmental flurry is known as the "Broad Seal war"]
New Jersey Historical Society founded at Trenton 27 Feb 1840
Constitutional Convention assembles at Trenton 14 May, completes its labors 29 June and the constitution is ratified by the people 13 Aug 1844
Town superintendent of schools first authorized 7 Apr 1846
State lunatic asylum at Trenton opened 15 May, 1848
Bordentown female college at Bordentown, opened in 1851, receives its charter 1853
State Normal school established at Trenton 8 Oct 1856
State Union convention at Trenton resolves in favor of a compromise between the northern and southern states 11 Dec 1860
Committee on national affairs in the legislature report joint resolutions endorsing the Crittenden compromise, which were adopted 25 Jan 1861
Legislature appropriates $2,000,000, and an annual tax of $100,000 for military purposes 30 Apr "
In response to a proclamation by gov Olden, 17 Apr, 4 regiments of New Jersey Volunteers, under gen Runyon, are despatched to Annapolis 3 May, "
Soldiers' Children's home at Trenton incorporated 23 Mch 1865
Rutgers scientific school at New Brunswick opened Sept "
State Board of Education established 1866
Legislature ratifies the XIV th Amendment to the Constitution of the U S 11 Sept "
Home for disabled soldiers established at Mount Pleasant, Newark "
New Jersey State Reform school at Jamesburg opened 1867
Legislature by resolution, withdraws its ratification of the XIV th Amendment Apr 1868
George M Robeson of New Jersey secretary of the navy, 25 June, 1869
Camden and Amboy railroad and Delaware and Raritan canal surrender their reserved rights, after 40 years of monopoly, opening the carrying trade across the state "
Governor of New Jersey accepts the war vessel bequeathed to the state by Edwin A Stevens, known as the "Stevens battery," together with $1,000 000 for its completion, which is placed under the superintendence of gen. George B McClellan and gen. John Newton "
Legislature refuses to ratify the XV th Amendment to the Constitution of the U S 15 Feb 1870
Stevens Institute of Technology at Hoboken opened 1871
State industrial school for girls at Trenton opened "
Free school system inaugurated in New Jersey Apr "
Legislature passes a "general railroad law," providing that "no franchise heretofore granted to construct a railroad, or to build or establish bridges or ferries, or operate any line of travel, shall hereafter continue to be or be construed to remain exclusive" 1873
Compulsory Education law passed 1874
By act of legislature, 27 Mch 1874, the Stevens battery, in construction since 1843, which had cost over $2,500,000, still unfinished, is sold to U S government for $145,000 2 Nov "
Newark City Home reform school opened at Verona "
People ratify 28 amendments to the constitution, proposed by the legislatures of 1874 and 1875 7 Sept. 1875
State insane asylum at Morristown opened Aug 1876
Act passed creating a State Board of Health 1877
Soldiers' Children's home closed "
Centennial anniversary of the capture of Princeton celebrated by a mock fight of Newark and Pennsylvania militia 3 Jan "
Convention of colored men held at Princeton to consider the condition of their race, politically and socially 22 Aug "
Bureau of Labor and Statistics created by act of legislature 1878
Liberal League of New Jersey, the outgrowth of the Citizens' Protective Association of Newark, in state convention at Newark, demand remodelling of the Sunday laws Sept 1879
Thomas Alva Edison establishes a laboratory at Menlo park, 1876, exhibits his newly invented system of electric lighting by incandescent carbon vacuum lamps Dec "
Public Normal school at Newark opened "
St Benedict's college at Newark opened in 1868, chartered 1881
Frederick Theodore Frelinghuysen appointed secretary of state under pres Arthur 12 Dec "
Act passed to create a council of state charities and correction, to consist of 6 persons appointed by the governor 28 Mch 1883
Law enacted to abolish and prohibit the employment under contract of convicts and inmates of prisons, jails, penitentiaries, and all public reformatory institutions of the state 1884
New Jersey school for deaf-mutes at Chambersburg, near Trenton, opened 1885
Gen George B McClellan, b. 1826, d at Orange 29 Oct "
State Board of Agriculture established 1887

Acts of legislature passed making Labor day, the first Monday in September, a legal holiday, and giving women the right to vote at school-district meetings.......... 1887
New Jersey home for the education and care of feeble-minded children opened.......... 1888
Local-option and high-license law, passed in 1888, is repealed, and a high-license law enacted.......... 1889
Horatio Allen, the first locomotive engineer in the U. S., d. at Montrose, aged 88..........1 Jan. 1890
Governor's salary raised to $10,000 per year by law....15 Jan "
Australian ballot law adopted at session ending.......23 May, "
Strike of over 3000 employés in the Clark's thread mills at Newark and Kearney begins..........10 Dec. "
Saturday half-holiday established, and Rutgers scientific school awarded the funds granted by Congress in aid of colleges of agriculture and mechanic arts at session....13 Jan.–20 Mch. 1891
Spinners' strike in the Clark's thread mills declared off..18 Apr. "
Smokeless powder used for the first time in this country at Sandy Hook in an 8-inch rifled gun..........25 July, "
Walt Whitman, poet, b. 1819, d. at Camden..........26 Mch. 1892
U. S. practice cruiser *Bancroft*, the first war-ship built in the state, is launched at the yards of Samuel L. Moore & Sons Co. in Elizabeth..........30 Apr. "
City of Paterson celebrates the 100th anniversary of its founding..........4 July, "
Democrats and Republicans organize separate senates at Trenton—the governor recognizing the Democratic senate, 9 Jan. 1894
Republican senators force their way into the senate chamber, 10 Jan. "
Supreme court of New Jersey decides that the Republican senate is lawful..........21 Mch. "
Republican senate recognized as the legal senate......22 Mch. "

GOVERNORS.

Peter Minuit, gov. of New Netherlands......	assumes office....	1624
Wouter Van Twiller, "	"	1633
William Keift, "	"	1638
John Printz, gov. of New Sweden..........	"	1642
Peter Stuyvesant, gov. of New Netherlands..	"	1646
Philip Carteret, first Engl. governor......	"	1664
Edmund Andros, under duke of York.......	"	1674

East Jersey.		*West Jersey.*	
Philip Carteret..........	1676	Board of Commissioners..	1676
Robert Barclay..........	1682	Edward Byllinge..........	1679
Thomas Rudyard, deputy..	"	Samuel Jennings, deputy..	"
Gawen Lawrie, " ..	1683	Thomas Olive, " ..	1684
Lord Neill Campbell, " ..	1686	John Skeine, " ..	1685
Andrew Hamilton, " ..	1687	Daniel Coxe..........	1687
Edmund Andros..........	1688	Edward Hunloke, deputy..	1690
John Tatham..........	1690	West Jersey Proprietors...	1691
Col. Joseph Dudley........	1691	Andrew Hamilton..........	1692
Andrew Hamilton..........	1692	Jeremiah Basse..........	1697
Jeremiah Basse..........	1698	Andrew Hamilton..........	1699
Andrew Bowne, deputy....	1699		
Andrew Hamilton:........	"		

ROYAL GOVERNORS.

Edward Hyde, lord Cornbury..........	assumes office....	1702
Lord Lovelace..........	"	1708
Richard Ingoldsby, lieutenant-governor....	"	1709
Robert Hunter..........	"	1710
William Burnett..........	"	1720
John Montgomery..........	"	1728
Lewis Morris, president of council..........	"	1731
William Crosby..........	"	1732
John Anderson, president of council........	"	1736
John Hamilton, president of council........	"	"
Lewis Morris..........	"	1738
John Hamilton, president..........	"	1746
John Reading, president..........	"	"
Jonathan Belcher..........	"	1747
John Reading, president..........	"	1757
Francis Bernard..........	"	1758
Thomas Boone..........	"	1760
Josiah Hardy..........	"	1761
William Franklin..........	"	1763

STATE GOVERNORS.

William Livingston..........	assumes office....	1776
William Patterson..........	"	1790
Richard Howell..........	"	1794
Joseph Bloomfield..........	"	1801
John Lambert, acting..........	"	1802
Joseph Bloomfield..........	"	1803
Aaron Ogden..........	"	1812
William S. Pennington..........	"	1813
Mahlon Dickerson..........	"	1815
Isaac H. Williamson..........	"	1817
Peter D. Vroom..........	"	1829
Samuel Lewis Southard..........	"	1832
Elias P. Seeley..........	"	1833
Peter D. Vroom..........	"	"
Philemon Dickerson..........	"	1836
William Pennington..........	"	1837
Daniel Haines..........	"	1843
Charles C. Stratton..........	"	1844
Daniel Haines..........	"	1848
George F. Fort..........	"	1851
Rodman M. Price..........	"	1854
William A. Newall..........	"	1857
Charles S. Olden..........	"	1860
Joel Parker..........	"	1863
Marcus L. Ward..........	"	1866
Theodore F. Randolph..........	"	1869
Joel Parker..........	"	1872
Joseph D. Bedle..........	"	1875
George B. McClellan..........	"	1878
George C. Ludlow..........	"	1881
Leon Abbett..........	"	1884
Robert S. Green..........	"	1887
Leon Abbett..........	"	1890
George T. Werts..........	"	1893

UNITED STATES SENATORS FROM THE STATE OF NEW JERSEY.

Name.	No. of Congress.	Date.	Remarks.
Jonathan Elmer..........	1st to 2d	1789 to 1791	
William Patterson..........	1st	1789 " 1790	Resigned. Elected governor of New Jersey.
Philemon Dickenson..........	1st to 3d	1790 " 1791	Elected in place of Patterson.
John Rutherford..........	2d " 5th	1791 " 1798	Resigned.
Frederick Frelinghuysen..........	3d " 4th	1793 " 1796	Resigned.
Richard Stockton..........	4th " 6th	1796 " 1799	Elected in place of Frelinghuysen.
Franklin Davenport..........	5th " 6th	1798 " 1799	Appointed in place of Rutherford.
James Schureman..........	6th	1799 " 1801	Resigned.
Aaron Ogden..........	6th to 8th	1801 " 1803	Elected in place of Schureman.
Jonathan Dayton..........	6th " 9th	1799 " 1805	
John Condit..........	8th " 15th	1803 " 1817	
Aaron Kitchel..........	9th " 11th	1805 " 1809	Resigned.
John Lambert..........	11th " 14th	1809 " 1815	
James J. Wilson..........	14th " 16th	1815 " 1821	Resigned.
Mahlon Dickerson..........	15th " 23d	1817 " 1833	
Samuel L. Southard..........	16th " 18th	1821 " 1823	Elected in place of Wilson. Resigned.
Joseph McIlvaine..........	18th " 19th	1823 " 1826	Elected in place of Southard. Died 1826.
Ephraim Bateman..........	19th " 20th	1826 " 1829	Elected in place of McIlvaine. Resigned.
Theodore Frelinghuysen..........	21st " 23d	1829 " 1833	
Samuel L. Southard..........	23d " 27th	1833 " 1842	President *pro tem.* 11 Mch. 1841. Resigned May, 1842. Died June, 1842.
Garrett D. Wall..........	24th " 27th	1835 " 1842	
William L. Dayton..........	27th " 32d	1842 " 1851	Elected in place of Southard.
Jacob W. Miller..........	27th " 33d	1841 " 1853	
Robert F. Stockton..........	32d	1851 " 1853	Resigned.
John R. Thomson..........	33d to 37th	1853 " 1862	Died 1862.
William Wright..........	33d " 36th	1853 " 1859	
John C. Ten Eyck..........	36th	1859	
Richard S. Field..........	37th	1862	Appointed *pro tem.* in place of Thomson.
John W. Wall..........	"	1863	Elected in place of Thomson.
William Wright..........	38th to 39th	1863 to 1866	Died 1866.
Frederick T. Frelinghuysen..........	39th " 41st	1866 " 1869	Appointed in place of Wright.
John P. Stockton..........	39th	1865 " 1866	Unseated Mch. 26, 1866. See Blaine's "Twenty Years of Congress," vol. ii. pp. 154–159.
Alexander G. Cattell..........	39th to 42d	1866 " 1871	Elected in place of Stockton.
John P. Stockton..........	41st " 44th	1869 " 1875	
Frederick T. Frelinghuysen..........	42d " 45th	1871 " 1875	
Theodore F. Randolph..........	44th " 47th	1875 " 1881	
John R. McPherson..........	45th " 54th	1877 " 1895	
William J. Sewell..........	47th " 50th	1881 " 1887	
Rufus Blodgett..........	50th " 52d	1888 " 1893	
James Smith, jr..........	53d " ——	1893 " ——	Term expires 1899.
W. J. Sewell..........	54th " ——	1895 " ——	

New Jerusalem church. SWEDENBORGIANS.

New Lanark, a village of W. Scotland. Here Robert Owen endeavored to establish socialism in 1801; and here the first infant-school was set up, 1815. HARMONISTS.

New Market, Va. GRANT'S CAMPAIGN IN VIRGINIA, OPERATIONS IN THE SHENANDOAH VALLEY.

New Mexico, a territory of the United States, lying between lat. 31° 20′ and 37° N., and lon. 103° 2′ and 109° 2′ W. It is bounded on the north by Colorado, east by Texas, south by Texas and Mexico, and west by Arizona. Area, 122,580 sq. miles: pop. 1890, 153,593; 1900, 195,310. Capital, Santa Fé.

Francisco Vasquez de Coronado, with 400 Spaniards and 800 Indians, makes an expedition from Mexico to the Pueblo Indian villages near Santa Fé, which he conquers, and explores the surrounding region....July, 1540

Agustin Rodriguez, a Franciscan friar of San Bartolomé, Mexico, with 2 associates and an escort of 12 soldiers, ascends the Rio Grande, and 8 miles from the site of Albuquerque the party separate; the soldiers returning to Mexico, the 3 friars remaining..........Aug. 1581

Don Antonio Espejo, with a relief party, ascends the Rio Grande, and finding the missionaries located among the Pueblo Indians in 1581 had been killed, he returns to San Bartolomé by way of the Pecos river.......... 1582-83

Don Juan de Oñate, a wealthy citizen of Zacatecas, under authority from don Luis de Valasco, viceroy of New Spain, settles with a colony of 130 families, 10 friars, and a number of soldiers in the valley of the Chama river, just above its junction with the Rio Grande.......... 1598

Santa Fé founded under the title La Ciudad Real de la Santa Fé de San Francisco.......... 1605

Religious persecution of the Indians by the Spanish, who whip, imprison, and hang 40 natives who would not renounce their old faith, results in an unsuccessful revolt of Indians........ 1640

Native Indian tribes unite in a project to make a simultaneous attack on the Spanish settlements, but the plan is discovered and broken up by gov. Concha, who arrests and imprisons the leaders, hanging 9, and selling the others into slavery...... 1650

Four Indians are hung and 43 whipped and enslaved on conviction by a Spanish tribunal of bewitching the superior of the Franciscan monastery at San Yldefonso.......... 1675

Pueblo Indians under Popé, reduced to abject slavery by the Spanish, rise in rebellion. Their plan of a general massacre on 10 Aug. 1680, being discovered, they begin 2 days earlier a massacre of the Spanish, who are obliged to flee the country, the Pueblos taking possession of Santa Fé..........21 Aug. 1680

New Mexico reconquered by the Spanish under Diego de Vargas Zapata Lujan.......... 1692

Severe famine arising in the Spanish settlements, the Indians of 14 pueblos enter upon a desolating but unsuccessful war for the expulsion of the Spanish.......... 1696

Albuquerque founded during the administration of the duke of Albuquerque.......... 1701-10

Lieut.-col. Carrisco discovers the Santa Rita mines near Silver City.......... 1800

Baptiste Lalande, a Frenchman from Kaskaskia, reaches Santa Fé with a stock of merchandise, which he disposes of at a very large profit.......... 1804

James Pursley, a Kentuckian, leaves St. Louis in 1802, and after 3 years' wandering reaches Santa Fé.......... 1805

Lieut. Zebulon M. Pike, of the U. S. army, builds a fort on the Rio del Notre on Spanish soil, supposing it to be the Red river and American possessions, during the month of Feb. 1807. With his party he is taken to Santa Fé by a Spanish escort, where they arrive 3 Mch. From there he is sent to Chihuahua under escort, arriving 2 Apr., and has an audience with the commanding general don Nemecio Salcedo. After some detention he is sent forward, reaching San Antonio, Texas, 7 June, and Natchitoches..........1 July, 1807

Capts. Glenn, Becknell, and Stephen Cooper visit Santa Fé with small parties and a limited quantity of goods for trade... 1821-22

First wagon trains from Independence, Mo., to Santa Fé...... 1824

New Mexico made a territory of the republic of Mexico. 6 July, "

Santa Fé trail made an authorized road by act of Congress; the bill introduced by Thomas H. Benton, and passed.......Jan. 1825

Caravans being often attacked by Indians, U. S. government details 4 companies as escort on the Santa Fé road.......... 1828

Old Placer gold-mines discovered about 30 miles southwest of Santa Fé.......... "

Oxen first used on the Santa Fé trail.......... 1830

A Spanish newspaper, *El Crepusculo*, pub. at Taos.......... 1835

New Mexican constitution goes into effect, changing the territory into a department, centralizing power, and imposing extra taxes. The new system being obnoxious, the arrest and imprisonment of a local judicial officer on what the people considered a false charge, provokes a revolution, 1 Aug. 1837, which is central at Santa Cruz, but which is soon quelled by gen. Manuel Armijo.......... 1837

NEW

New Placer gold mines discovered.......... 1839

Expedition under gen. McLeod sets out from Austin, Tex., 18 June, 1841, to ascertain the feeling of the New Mexican people with respect to a union with Texas. When near San Miguel the force is met by Damacio Salazar and his Mexican troops, seized and imprisoned at San Miguel, from whence they are marched under guard to the city of Mexico..17 Oct. 1841

Pres. Santa Aña, by decree, closes the frontier custom-house at Taos, 7 Aug. 1843, but repeals the act..........31 Mch. 1844

Gen. Stephen W. Kearney, in command of a body of U. S. troops known as the "Army of the West," enters Santa Fé and takes formal possession..........18 Aug. 1846

Gen. Kearney establishes a government for the territory of New Mexico, with Santa Fé as capital, proclaiming himself provisional governor..........22 Aug. "

Fort Marcy established near Santa Fé..........23 Aug. "

Gen. Kearney promulgates the "Kearney Code of Laws," and proclaims Charles Bent governor of the territory....22 Sept. "

Donaciano Vigil becomes acting-governor in the room of gov. Charles Bent, who is assassinated at Taos..........19 Jan. 1847

Revolt against the U. S. government in New Mexico, planned by dons Diego Archuleta and Tomas Ortiz, breaks out at Taos, but is suppressed by American troops under col. Sterling Price, and gov. Montoya, prominent in the rebellion, is tried by court-martial and executed 7 Feb. 6 others, convicted of participating in the murder of gov. Bent, are executed, 3 Aug. "

Santa Fé Republican, the first newspaper printed in English, begins its career.......... "

By the treaty of Guadalupe Hidalgo, concluded 2 Feb. 1848, and proclaimed in Santa Fé in Aug. following, New Mexico becomes a part of the U. S..........Aug. 1848

People of New Mexico, in convention at Santa Fé, petition Congress for a territorial government, oppose the dismemberment of their territory in favor of Texas, and ask protection of Congress against the introduction of slavery..14 Oct. "

By proclamation of gov. Munroe, in Apr. 1850, a convention assembles at Santa Fé 15 May, and frames a constitution for the territory of New Mexico, 25 May, prohibiting slavery and fixing the east and west boundaries at 100° and 111°. This constitution was ratified by the people 20 June, by a vote of 8371 for to 39 against, and Henry Connelly was elected governor, but the movement was not recognized.......... 1850

Act of Congress establishing a territorial government for New Mexico approved..........9 Sept. "

First legislative assembly convenes at Santa Fé, and declares it the capital of the territory..........2 June, 1851

Santa Fé incorporated as a city.......... "

Gov. James S. Calhoun dies while on his way to the states, and John Greiner becomes acting-governor..........30 June, 1852

Academy of Our Lady of Light, in charge of the sisters of Loretto, organized at Santa Fé.......... "

Christopher or "Kit" Carson appointed Indian agent in New Mexico.......... 1853

Territory acquired from Mexico under the Gadsden purchase is incorporated with the territory of New Mexico.....4 Aug. 1854

School law passed requiring compulsory attendance, and the appointment of teachers by the justice of the peace in each precinct, who is entitled to collect the sum of 50 cents per month for each child attending..........23 Jan. 1860

Maj. Isaac Lynde, U. S. A., in command at fort Fillmore, surrenders the fort and his entire command of 700 to lieut.-col. John R. Baylor, confederate..........27 July, 1861

Confederates under gen. H. F. Sibley defeat the federals under col. Canby at Valverde, 10 miles below fort Craig....21 Feb. 1862

Battle at Apache cañon, near Santa Fé; col. Slough defeats the confederates under col. Scurry..........28 Mch. "

Santa Fé, in possession of the confederates since 11 Mch. 1862, is recovered by the federals..........21 Apr. "

Territory of Arizona formed from part of New Mexico, 24 Feb. 1863

Gov. Connelly dies; W. F. M. Arny acting-governor.......... 1865

Portion of New Mexico above 37° attached to Colorado........ 1867

By act of Congress peonage is abolished and forever prohibited in the territory of New Mexico..........2 Mch. "

Governor in his message announces telegraphic communication with the North.......... 1868

Archives of New Mexico, partly destroyed in 1680, are further depleted under the rule of gov. Pile, when they are sold for waste paper and only about one quarter of them recovered.. 1870

Legislature provides for common schools, under a board of supervisors and directors elected by each county.......... 1871

Serious election riot at La Mesilla..........2 Sept. "

Gov. Marsh Giddings dies, and is succeeded by William G. Ritch as acting-governor..........3 Jan. 1875

Ute Indians removed from New Mexico to the Colorado reservation..........Apr.-July, 1878

Locomotive on the new Atchison, Topeka, and Santa Fé railroad reaches Las Vegas..........4 July, 1879

New Mexico Historical Society, organized in 1859-60, is reorganized.......... 1880

Bureau of Immigration established by act of legislature...... "

University of New Mexico at Santa Fé chartered and opened.. 1881

Public-school law passed creating the office of county superintendent, and providing for the election by the people of 3 commissioners for each precinct.......... 1884

Act of assembly passed establishing an orphans' home and industrial school at Santa Fé.......... "

Destructive raids in the southwestern portion of the territory by Apache Indians from Arizona.......May, June, and Oct. 1885

Territorial prison at Santa Fé completed and opened.......... "

New Mexico school for the deaf and dumb at Santa Fé opened [illegible]
Ramona Indian school for girls located at Santa Fé [illegible]
New capitol building completed at Santa Fé, under act of [illegible] Feb. 1884, creating a capitol building commission [illegible]
Legislature passes over the governor's veto an act abolishing the office of attorney-general and substituting that of [illegible] general [illegible]
Acts of the legislature passed creating a state university at Albuquerque, an agricultural college at Las Cruces, and a school of mines at Socorro [illegible]
Insane asylum at Las Vegas created by act of legislature [illegible]
Territorial Board of Health provided for by act of legislature [illegible]
State convention [illegible] meets at Santa Fé 3 Sept., adopts a constitution for the proposed state of New Mexico, and prepares a memorial to present it to Congress [illegible]
Agricultural college at Las Cruces opened [illegible]
Constitution, amended by a convention which convened at Santa Fé 18 Aug., is rejected by the people by 16,180 [illegible] for and 7,943 against, at an election held [illegible]
Returns of Santa Fé county disappear mysteriously; the commissioners of Santa Fé refuse to canvass the returns [illegible], while Democratic commissioners [illegible] count [illegible] returns favoring Republicans. After [illegible] before justice Seeds of the District court, in Dec. [illegible] Benjamin M. Thomas, acting governor, swears in the Republican candidates [illegible]
Second Friday in Feb. designated as Arbor day, a territorial Board of Education created, and a high-license bill passed by the legislature, at session [illegible] 29 Dec. 1890, [illegible]
Ex-gov. Samuel B. Axtell d. at Morristown, N. J., aged 72 [illegible]
Forest preserve in New Mexico set apart by proclamation of pres. Harrison [illegible] 11 [illegible]
Territorial capitol building at Santa Fé burned [illegible] 12 [illegible]

GOVERNORS.

[A list of the governors ruling in New Mexico previous to 1846, with notes, may be found in "Historical Sketches of New Mexico," by L. Bradford Prince. A list of names only in "The Resources, Statistics and Economics," L. F. McCarty, [illegible]]

U. S. MILITARY GOVERNORS.

Gen. Stephen W. Kearney	assumes office	[illegible]
Charles Bent	appointed	[illegible]
Donaciano Vigil	acting	[illegible]
Lieut.-col. J. M. Washington	appointed	[illegible]
Maj. John Munroe	"	[illegible]

TERRITORIAL GOVERNORS.

James S. Calhoun	assumes office	[illegible]
Col. E. V. Sumner	acting	[illegible]
John Greiner	"	[illegible]
William Carr Lane	appointed	[illegible]
William S. Messervy	acting 2 months	[illegible]
David Meriwether	appointed	[illegible]
W. W. H. Davis	acting	[illegible]
Abraham Rencher	appointed	[illegible]
Henry Connelly	"	[illegible]
W. F. M. Arny	acting	[illegible]
Robert B. Mitchell	appointed	[illegible]
William A. Pile	"	[illegible]
Marsh Giddings	"	[illegible]
William G. Ritch	acting	[illegible]
Samuel B. Axtell	appointed	[illegible]
Lewis Wallace	"	[illegible]
Lionel A. Sheldon	"	[illegible]
Edmund G. Ross	"	[illegible]
L. Bradford Prince	"	[illegible]
William T. Thornton	"	[illegible]

New Netherland. New York, 1614.

New Orleans. The site of New Orleans, "the Crescent City," was selected by M. de Bienville, governor of Louisiana, as a location for the chief city of the colony in 1718, and settled by a detachment of 25 convicts, [illegible] carpenters, and some settlers from the Illinois country. The seat of government was established there in Aug. 1722, at which time the population numbered 300, and the town consisted of about 100 houses. New Orleans came under American rule 20 Dec. 1803, after the cession of Louisiana to the United States by France, and at this time had a population, including the suburbs, of about 10,000. In 1820 the pop. was [illegible], and by decades since: 1830, 29,737; 1840, 102,1[illegible]; 1850, 116,375; 1860, 168,675; 1870, 191,418; 1880, 216,0[illegible]; 1890, 242,039; 1900, 287,104. Area (U. S. census, 1890), [illegible] sq. miles. Lat. 29° 57' N., lon. 90° 3' W.

Bienville sends from Le Bayou de la Tour to the settlement [illegible] who surveys the town, works of secrets, and builds a [illegible] along the river front [illegible]
Seat of government of Louisiana removed to New Orleans [illegible] 1722
Storm destroys 30 houses, the church, and hospital [illegible] 11 Sept. [illegible]
Arrival of the Ursuline nuns [illegible] 1727
Arrival of the "filles à la cassette" or casket girls, sent from France in care of the Ursulines, to be disposed of in marriage [illegible] their discretion [illegible]
[illegible] convent erected on square bounded by the river, [illegible]

Chartres st., below Ursuline st. (occupied by them for 94 years) [illegible] 1730
Charity hospital founded by a sailor, Jean Louis [illegible] 1737
First sugar-cane grown in Louisiana introduced from St. Domingo, and planted by the Jesuits in the angle of Common and Tchoupitoulas sts. [illegible] 1751
First sugar mill erected by M. Dubreuil on his plantation, now part of the 3d district adjoining the 2d on the river [illegible] 1758
Spain takes formal possession of Louisiana [illegible] 1769

[From this time until 1803 New Orleans remained subject to the Spanish government. LOUISIANA.]

A cabildo established, composed of 6 perpetual regidors, 2 ordinary alcaldes, an attorney-general syndic, and clerk, 21 Nov. "

Special revenue assigned to the city of New Orleans: an annual tax of $40 on every tavern, billiard-table, and coffee-house, and $20 on every boarding-house; an impost of $1 on every barrel of brandy brought to the city, and a tax of $3 on the [illegible] of the place; an anchorage tax of $6 on every vessel of over 200 tons and $3 on smaller [illegible] 22 Feb. 1770
John James Audubon b. at New Orleans [illegible] 4 May, 1780
Charity hospital of St. Charles, a brick structure erected by don Andres Almonaster y Roxas at a cost of $114,000 on west side of Rampart, between Toulouse and St. Peter sts., on site of the charity hospital founded by Jean Louis and destroyed by a hurricane in 1779 [illegible] 1784–86
Fire breaks out in the rear of the government buildings and destroys 856 buildings, nearly half the town [illegible] 21 Mch. 1788
St. Louis cathedral, begun 1792, completed [illegible] 1794
Le Moniteur de la Louisiane, the first newspaper, published entirely in French, established [illegible] "
Second great fire destroys in 3 hours 212 houses [illegible] 8 Dec. "
Police department established, 1792, and 4 years after there were 13 night-watchmen in the town and 80 street lamps in operation [illegible] 1796
Carondelet canal, begun 1794, completed [illegible] "
Salcedo, in the hall of the cabildo, delivers to Laussat, the French colonial prefect, the keys of New Orleans [illegible] 30 Nov. 1803
Municipal government, composed of a mayor and council, established in place of the cabildo by Laussat [illegible] "
Laussat gives over the keys of the city to commissioners Claiborne and gen. Wilkinson of the U. S. [illegible] 20 Dec. "
Incorporated as a city under American charter with mayor, recorder, treasurer, and council of 14 aldermen [illegible] 17 Feb. 1805
Aaron Burr arrives in New Orleans [illegible] 26 June, "
Yellow fever; second and most serious outbreak occurring, 15 Sept. 1807
Christ's church, a small octagonal structure, erected on the [illegible] Bourbon and Canal sts. [illegible] 1809
First vessel propelled by steam, the Orleans from Pittsburg, arrives at New Orleans [illegible] 10 Jan. 1812
New Orleans college built and put into operation at cor. Bayou road and St. Claude st. [illegible] "
Gen. Jackson arrives at New Orleans (LOUISIANA) [illegible] 2 Dec. 1814
Battle of New Orleans fought (UNITED STATES) [illegible] 8 Jan. 1815
Portion of city flooded to the depth of 3 to 4 feet, the flood continuing nearly a month; cause, the breaking of the [illegible] levee [illegible] 1816
First cobble-stone pavement laid on Gravier st. [illegible] [illegible] and Magazine sts. [illegible]
One central and 3 primary schools established [illegible] [illegible]
Seat of government removed to Donaldsonville [illegible]
Parish prison on Orleans st., near Congo [illegible] of $200,000 [illegible]
[illegible]

St. Charles hotel burned (restored 1852-53)..........18 Feb. 1850
Telegraphic line to St. Louis completed.......... “
First granite block pavement laid.......... “
Three municipalities, together with the city of Lafayette, consolidated by a new charter..........12 Apr. 1852
Yellow-fever breaks out in June; reaches its maximum 22 Aug., on which day over 280 deaths were reported. The total interments in the cemeteries between 1 June and 1 Oct. were 11,000.......... 1853
Bronze equestrian statue of gen. Jackson erected in the Place d'Armes, now Jackson square.......... 1856
Banks suspend specie payment..........18 Sept. 1861
New Orleans surrendered to flag-officer Farragut, 25 Apr., and formal possession taken by land forces under gen. Butler (LOUISIANA)..........1 May, 1862
Times-Democrat established.......... 1863
Negro political riot; many negroes killed and wounded 30 July, 1866
Water-works purchased by the city.......... 1869
New charter, adopting the administrative system, and annexation of Jefferson City.......... 1870
Straight university, chartered 1869, opened.......... “
Exposition park, 180 acres, purchased by a commission appointed.......... 1871
New Orleans university chartered and opened.......... 1873
City of Carrollton annexed.......... 1874
New Orleans *City Item* established.......... 1877
City disposes of its water-works system to a private corporation—the New Orleans Water-works company..........10 Apr. “
Yellow-fever epidemic; about 4500 deaths; first case reported, 23 May, 1878
Auxiliary Sanitary Association of New Orleans organized, 24 Mch. 1879
The *States* established.......... 1880
Seat of government, which had been in New Orleans since the civil war, again removed to Baton Rouge.......... “
Southern university chartered and opened.......... “
New Orleans Drainage and Sewerage company, organized 17 Mch. 1880, and ordinance adopted by council providing for a contract with the company for drainage of the city..12 Apr. 1881
Southern Academic institute opened.......... “
New city charter adopted by the legislature..........June, 1882
Tulane University of Louisiana chartered and opened.......... 1884
World's Industrial Cotton Exposition opened by pres. Arthur setting the machinery in motion by telegraph from Washington, 16 Dec. 1884; continues until..........31 May, 1885
New Orleans Normal school established.......... “
New Orleans public school for deaf-mutes opened.......... 1886
Evening News established.......... 1889
New Orleans *New Delta* established.......... 1890
David C. Hennessy, chief of police, shot by Italians, supposed to be Mafia, near his home..........15 Oct. “
Eleven Italians, implicated in the killing of chief Hennessy, are massacred in the parish prison (UNITED STATES)..........14 Mch. 1891
Gen. Beauregard d. aged 75 years..........20 Feb. 1893
St. Charles hotel burned; loss $500,000..........28 Apr. 1894
U. S. court of appeals at New Orleans decided that the city is not liable for damages for the death of the Sicilians (Maffia) killed Mch. 1891..........30 May, “

MAYORS.

Joseph Mather..........	1807-12	Twelve mayors by U. S. military appointment.	1862-66
Nicolas Girod..........	1812-15	John T. Monroe..........	1866-68
Augustin Macarty..........	1815-20	John R. Conway..........	1868-70
Joseph Roufignac..........	1820-28	Benjamin F. Flanders..	1870-72
Denis Prieur..........	1828-40	Louis Alfred Wiltz..........	1872-74
[illegible] Freret..........	1840-43	Charles J. Leeds..........	1874-76
[illegible] Prieur..........	1843-44	[illegible]ard Pilsbury..........	1876-78
[illegible]		[illegible] W. Patton..........	1878-80
		[illegible] A. Shakspeare....	1880-82
		[illegible]han..........	1882-84
		[illegible]otte..........	1884-88
		[illegible]akspeare...	1888-92
		[illegible]rick..........	1892-96

[illegible] -place. RHODE [illegible] Berkeley, and [illegible] in America, [illegible] Narragansett [illegible] during the [illegible] British [illegible] also [illegible]

about miles from the head of Port Jackson, as a better situation for the capital. A new constitution was granted in 1855 (18 & 19 Vict. c. 54). Area, 310,700 sq. miles; pop. 1891, 1,134,207.

newspapers. Before the invention of printing, news was circulated by manuscript news-letters, the earliest of which was the ACTA DIURNA, said to have been issued at Rome [illegible]. As late as 1704 John Campbell published his news-letter in Boston, Mass., and [illegible] or more numbers are in the collection of the Massachusetts Historical society. The [illegible] printed from metal type with printing ink, began with the publication of the *Gazette* at Nuremberg, Bavaria, 1457. (Those marked with * in existence in 1891.) MAGAZINES.

Chronicle [illegible] by Cato Zell.......... 1439
[illegible] Venice.......... 1570
* *Diarium* [illegible], called the first daily paper [illegible], appeared at Frankfort, Germany.......... 1615
Nathaniel Butter [illegible] of *The Courant, or Weekly News from Foreign Parts*, sold in London streets by mercury women and hawkers.......... 1621
First [illegible] *Weekly News* published at London by Nicholas Bourne and Thomas Archer..........23 May, 1622
* *Gazette de France* established at Paris.......... 1631
* *Post [illegible]* established at Stockholm, Sweden.......... 1644
First newspaper advertisement [illegible] for 12 stolen horses in the London *Impartial Intelligencer*..........Feb. 1648
Mercurius Publicus issued in Leith, Scotland..........Oct. 1653
* *Oxford Gazette*, first official organ of the court, afterwards the *London Gazette*, the only authorized newspaper, contained little more than proclamations and advertisements, established..........Nov. 1665
First [illegible] newspaper, *Intelligence Newsletter*, established by John Ray.......... 1685
([illegible] at this time collected from the coffee-houses information which was printed weekly and sent into the country and called news-letters.)
Pue's Occurrences published in Dublin, Ireland.......... 1700
Daily Courant, first daily newspaper in English, published by Elizabeth Mallet, in London..........Mch. 1702
St. Petersburg Gazette published in Russia.......... 1703
* *Edinburgh Courant* established.......... 1705
Orion Postman, father of the penny press, established in England.......... 1706
To prevent abuse of liberty of the press, queen Anne imposes a tax on newspapers..........Jan. 1712
Journal de Paris, ou *Poste du Soir*, first daily paper in Paris, established.......... 1777
* *The Times* (daily) established in London..........1 Jan. 1788
* *Allgemeine Zeitung* established at Leipsic.......... 1798
First newspaper in Turkey, *The Spectator of the East*, started at Smyrna by M. Blacque.......... 1827
* London *Evening Standard* established.......... “
* *Spectator* (weekly) established at London.......... 1828
* *Athenæum* (literary and scientific weekly) established in London.......... “
La Caricature, a comic French paper established by Charles Philipon..........July, 1830
Copies of *The English Mercurie* (1588) in the British museum are proved to be forgeries (executed about 1766) by T. Watts, 1839
* *Punch* (comic weekly) established at London.......... 1841
* *Illustrated London News* (weekly) established.......... 1842
* *London Daily News* established..........21 Jan. 1846
Reuter's Telegram company founded in London.......... 1849
* *Notes and Queries* (literary and antiquarian weekly) established in London.......... “
Stamp duty on newspapers in England abolished.......15 June, 1855
* *Saturday Review* (literary weekly) established at London... “
* *London Daily Telegraph* established..........June, “
* *London Morning Standard* (daily) established......29 June, 1857
* *Pall Mall Gazette* established in London.......... 1865
London Press association founded.......... 1868
* *Academy* (literary weekly) established in London.......... 1869
Number of newspapers in the United Kingdom in 1891 was 2[illegible], of which 180 were daily, published as follows:

		Total.	Daily.
England..	London..........	470	142
	Provinces..........	1283	
Wales..........		90	6
Scotland..........		201	19
Ireland..........		157	15
Isles..........		22	1

[illegible]wspapers in the United States. The increase of newspaper literature in the U. S. is marvellous. In 1783 there [illegible] about 43 newspapers; in 1801 there were 200 weekly and 17 [illegible] journals. In 1830, with a population of 25,500,000, 852 [illegible]apers were published (50 dailies), issuing 68,117,796 cop[illegible]arly; in 1840, 1631 newspapers, with 195,838,673 copies [illegible] in 1850, 2526 newspapers with 426,409,978 copies year[illegible]60, 4051 newspapers, with an annual issue of 928,000,000 [illegible]ing an increase of 118 per cent. in 10 years. In 1870 [illegible]871 newspapers, with a circulation of 20,842,475 cop[illegible] there were 980 daily, 8718 weekly, and 1075 other

New Mexico school for the deaf and dumb at Santa Fé opened, 1885
Ramona Indian school for girls located at Santa Fe "
New capitol building completed at Santa Fé, under act of 28 Mch 1884, creating a capitol building committee 1886
Legislature passes over the governor's veto an act abolishing the office of attorney general and substituting that of solicitor general 15 Feb 1889
Acts of the legislature passed creating a state university at Albuquerque, an agricultural college at Las Cruces, and a school of mines at Socorro "
Insane asylum at Las Vegas created by act of legislature. "
Territorial Board of Health provided for by act of legislature "
Constitutional convention meets at Santa Fé 3 Sept., adopts a constitution for the proposed state of New Mexico, and appoints a committee to present it to Congress 21 Sept. "
Agricultural college at Las Cruces opened 21 Jan 1890
Constitution, amended by a convention which reconvened at Santa Fé 18 Aug, is rejected by the people by 16,180 votes for and 7943 against, at an election held 7 Oct. "
Ballot box in Santa Fé county disappears mysteriously, and the commissioners of Santa Fé refuse to canvass the vote in that precinct, while Democratic commissioners in Taos county throw out returns favoring Republicans. After litigation before justice Seeds of the District court, in Dec sec Benjamin M Thomas, acting governor, swears in the Republican candidates in both precincts Dec "
Second Friday in Mch designated as Arbor day, a territorial Board of Education created, and a high license bill passed by the legislature, at session 29 Dec 1890–26 Feb. 1891
Ex gov Samuel B. Axtell d at Morristown, N J, aged 72, 6 Aug "
Forest preserve in New Mexico set apart by proclamation of pres. Harrison 11 Jan 1892
Territorial capitol building at Santa Fé burned 12 May, "

GOVERNORS

[A list of the governors ruling in New Mexico previous to 1846, with notes, may be found in "Historical Sketches of New Mexico," by L. Bradford Prince A list of names only, in "The Annual Statistician and Economist," L. P McCarty, 1889, and elsewhere]

U S MILITARY GOVERNORS

Gen Stephen W Kearney	assumes office	22 Aug	1846
Charles Bent	appointed	22 Sept	"
Donaciano Vigil	acting	19 Jan	1847
Lieut col J M Washington	appointed		1848
Maj John Munroe	"		1849

TERRITORIAL GOVERNORS.

James S Calhoun	assumes office	3 Mch	1851
Col E V Sumner	acting		1852
John Greiner	"		"
William Carr Lane	appointed		"
William S Messervy	acting 4 months		1853
David Meriwether	appointed		"
W H H Davis.	acting		1857
Abraham Rencher	appointed		"
Henry Connelly	"		1861
W F M Arny	acting		1865
Robert B Mitchell	appointed		1866
William A Pile	"		1869
Marsh Giddings	"		1871
William G Ritch	acting		1875
Samuel B Axtell	appointed		"
Lewis Wallace	"		1878
Lionel A Sheldon	"		1881
Edmund G Ross	"		1885
L Bradford Prince.	"		1889
William T Thornton	"		1893

New Netherland. NEW YORK, 1614.

New Orleans. The site of New Orleans, "the Crescent City," was selected by M de Bienville, governor of Louisiana, as a location for the chief city of the colony in 1718, and settled by a detachment of 25 convicts, as many carpenters, and some settlers from the Illinois country The seat of government was established there in Aug 1722, at which time the population numbered 300, and the town consisted of about 100 houses. New Orleans came under American rule 20 Dec 1803, after the cession of Louisiana to the United States by France, and at this time had a population, including the suburbs, of about 10,000 In 1820 the pop was 27,176, and by decades since 1830, 29,737, 1840, 102,193, 1850, 116,375, 1860, 168,675; 1870, 191,418, 1880, 216,090; 1890, 242,039, 1900, 287,104 Area (U S census, 1890), 37 09 sq miles Lat. 30° N., lon 90° 5′ W

Bienville sends sieur Le Blond de la Tour to the settlement, who surveys the town, marks off streets, and builds a levee along the river front 1718–20
Seat of government of Louisiana removed to New Orleans, Aug 1722
Storm destroys 30 houses, the church, and hospital 11 Sept. "
Arrival of the Ursuline nuns 1727
Arrival of the "filles a la cassette" or casket girls, sent from France in care of the Ursulines, to be disposed of in marriage under their discretion 1727–28
Ursuline convent erected on square bounded by the river and Chartres st., below Ursuline st. (occupied by them for 94 years) 1730
Charity hospital founded by a sailor, Jean Louis 1737
First sugar cane grown in Louisiana introduced from St Domingo and planted by the Jesuits in the angle of Common and Tchoupitoulas sts. 1751
First sugar mill erected by M Debreuil on his plantation, now part of the 3d district (adjoining the 2d on the river) 1758
Spain takes formal possession of Louisiana 1769
[From this time until 1800 New Orleans remained subject to the Spanish government. LOUISIANA]
A cabildo established, composed of 6 perpetual regidors, 2 ordinary alcaldes, an attorney general syndic, and clerk, 21 Nov "
Special revenue assigned to the city of New Orleans an annual tax of $40 on every tavern, billiard table, and coffee house, and $20 on every boarding house, an impost of $1 on every barrel of brandy brought to the city and a tax of $375 on the butchers of the place an anchorage tax of $6 on every vessel of over 200 tons and $3 on smaller 22 Feb 1770
John James Audubon b at New Orleans 4 May, 1780
Charity hospital of St Charles, a brick structure erected by don Andres Almonaster y Roxas at a cost of $114,000 on west side of Rampart, between Toulouse and St. Peter sts, on site of the charity hospital founded by Jean Louis and destroyed by a hurricane in 1779 1784–86
Fire breaks out in the rear of the government buildings and destroys 856 buildings, nearly half the town 21 Mch 1788
St. Louis cathedral, begun 1792, completed 1794
Le Moniteur de la Louisiane, the first newspaper, published entirely in French, established "
Second great fire destroys in 3 hours 212 houses 8 Dec "
Police department established, 1792, and 4 years after there were 13 night watchmen in the town and 80 street lamps in operation 1796
Caroudelet canal, begun 1794, completed "
Salcedo, in the hall of the cabildo, delivers to Laussat, the French colonial prefect, the keys of New Orleans 30 Nov 1803
Municipal government, composed of a mayor and council, established in place of the cabildo by Laussat "
Laussat gives over the keys of the city to commissioners Claiborne and gen Wilkinson of the U S 20 Dec "
Incorporated as a city under American charter with mayor, recorder, treasurer, and council of 14 aldermen 17 Feb 1805
Aaron Burr arrives in New Orleans 26 June, "
Batture riots, second and most serious outbreak occurring, 15 Sept 1807
Christ's church, a small octagonal structure, erected on cor Bourbon and Canal sts 1809
First vessel propelled by steam, the *Orleans* from Pittsburg, arrives at New Orleans 10 Jan 1812
New Orleans college built and put into operation at cor Bayou road and St Claude st "
Gen Jackson arrives at New Orleans (LOUISIANA) 2 Dec 1814
Battle of New Orleans fought (UNITED STATES) 8 Jan 1815
Portion of city flooded to the depth of 3 to 4 feet, the flood continuing nearly a month, cause, the breaking of the Macarty levee 6 May, 1816
First cobble-stone pavement laid on Gravier st, between Tchoupitoulas and Magazine sts 1817
One central and 2 primary schools established by legislative act Mch 1826
Seat of government removed to Donaldsonville 1829
Parish prison on Orleans st, near Congo square, built at a cost of $200,000 1830
New Orleans again made the seat of government 8 Jan 1831
Cholera destroys ⅙ of the entire population, about 6000 deaths occurring in 20 days, it makes its appearance about 25 Oct 1832
Bank's Arcade, "a glass roofed mercantile court in the midst of the St. James's Hotel in Magazine st.," built 1833
First water works company chartered under the name of the Commercial Bank "
Charity hospital in Common st erected at a cost of $150,000, 1832–34
State house, formerly the Ursuline nunnery, occupied as the seat of the archbishop of Louisiana 1834
Streets lighted with gas. "
Jackson barracks built. 1834–35
St Charles theatre built at a cost of $350 000 1835
Branch U S mint of New Orleans founded "
New charter dividing the city into 3 distinct municipalities the old town, the Faubourg Ste. Marie, and the Faubourg Marigny, with a mayor and general council over the whole city 1836
Mississippi river water furnished through mains under the principal streets "
Merchants' Exchange on Royal st., below Canal, completed "
New Orleans *Picayune*, daily, established 1837
First St Charles hotel, called the Exchange hotel, begun 1835, completed at a cost of $600,000. 1838
State library of Louisiana founded. "
Modern system of free public schools established in the city of Lafayette 1841
Boys' House of Refuge opened 1843
Library of the New Orleans Law Association founded 1844
Public school and Lyceum library founded "
Over 2800 deaths from yellow fever during summer and fall of 1847
Large portion of the city overflowed by the breaking of the levee in front of Sauve's plantation above New Orleans, 3 May, 1849, 200 squares under water to a depth of from 4 to 6 feet, flood at its highest point. 30 May, 1849
Seat of government removed to Baton Rouge . . . 1850

St Charles hotel burned (restored 1852-53) 16 Feb 1850
Telegraphic line to St Louis completed "
First granite block pavement laid "
Three municipalities, together with the city of Lafayette, consolidated by a new charter 12 Apr 1852
Yellow fever breaks out in June, reaches its maximum 22 Aug, on which day over 283 deaths were reported The total interments in the cemeteries between 1 June and 1 Oct were 11,000 1853
Bronze equestrian statue of gen Jackson erected in the Place d Armes, now Jackson square 1855
Banks suspend specie payment 18 Sept 1861
New Orleans surrendered to flag officer Farragut, 26 Apr, and formal possession taken by land forces under gen Butler (LOUISIANA) 1 May, 1862
Times Democrat established 1863
Negro political riot, many negroes killed and wounded. 30 July, 1866
Water works purchased by the city 1869
New charter adopting the administrative system, and annexation of Jefferson City 1870
Straight university, chartered 1869 opened "
Exposition park, 250 acres, purchased by a commission appointed 1871
New Orleans university chartered and opened 1873
City of Carrolton annexed 1874
New Orleans *City Item* established 1877
City disposes of its water works system to a private corporation—the New Orleans Water works company 10 Apr "
Yellow fever epidemic, about 4500 deaths, first case reported, 23 May, 1878
Auxiliary Sanitary Association of New Orleans organized, 31 Mch 1879
The *States* established 1880
Seat of government, which had been in New Orleans since the civil war, again removed to Baton Rouge "
Southern university chartered and opened "
New Orleans Drainage and Sewerage company, organized 17 Mch 1880, and ordinance adopted by council providing for a contract with the company for drainage of the city 12 Apr 1881
Southern Academic institute opened "
New city charter adopted by the legislature June, 1882
Tulane University of Louisiana chartered and opened 1884
World's Industrial Cotton Exposition opened by pres Arthur setting the machinery in motion by telegraph from Washington, 16 Dec 1884, continues until 31 May, 1885
New Orleans Normal school established "
New Orleans public school for deaf mutes opened 1886
Evening News established 1889
New Orleans *New Delta* established 1890
David C Hennessy, chief of police, shot by Italians, supposed to be Mafia near his home 15 Oct. "
Eleven Italians, implicated in the killing of chief Hennessy, are massacred in the parish prison (UNITED STATES) 14 Mch 1891
Gen Beauregard d aged 75 years 20 Feb 1893
St. Charles hotel burned, loss $500,000 28 Apr 1894
U S. court of appeals at New Orleans decided that the city is not liable for damages for the death of the Sicilians (Mafia) killed Mch 1891 30 May, "

MAYORS.

Joseph Mather	1807-12	Twelve mayors by U S military appointment	1862-66
Nicolas Girod	1812-15	John T Monroe	1866-68
Augustin Macarty	1815-20	John R Conway	1868-70
Joseph Roufflgnac	1820-28	Benjamin F Flanders	1870-72
Denis Prieur	1828-40	Louis Alfred Wiltz	1872-74
William Freret	1840-43	Charles J Leeds	1874-76
Denis Prieur	1843-44	Edward Pilsbury	1876-78
Edgar Montegut	1844-46	Isaac W Patton	1878-80
A D Crossman	1846-54	Joseph A Shakspeare	1880-82
John Lewis	1854-56	W J Behan	1882-84
Charles M Waterman	1856-58	J V Guillotte	1884-88
Gerard Stith	1858-60	Joseph A Shakspeare	1888-92
John T Monroe	1860-62	John Fitzpatrick	1892-96

Newport, R I, a celebrated watering-place RHODE ISLAND, 1639, and throughout. Here bishop Berkeley, and Smybert, the earliest professional portrait-painter in America, resided for a while It is near the entrance of Narragansett bay, and was the scene of many stirring events during the American Revolution, being occupied alternately by British and American troops French, under Rochambeau, also landed in 1780.

New Rugby, Tenn, a colony of British farmers and others, founded on English principles by Thomas Hughes, formerly M P, author of "Tom Brown's School-days," etc, inaugurated 5 Oct. 1880

news-letters. NEWSPAPERS

New South Wales, the principal and oldest colony of Australia, on the eastern coast of New Holland, was explored, taken possession of, and named by capt. Cook in 1770. At his recommendation a convict colony was first formed here. Capt A. Phillip, first governor, arrived at Botany bay with 800 convicts, 20 Jan. 1788, but he subsequently preferred Sydney, about 7 miles from the head of Port Jackson, as a better situation for the capital A new constitution was granted in 1855 (18 and 19 Vict c 54) Area, 310,700 sq miles, pop 1891, 1,134,207

newspapers. Before the invention of printing, news was circulated by manuscript news-letters, the earliest of which was the ACTA DIURNA, said to have been issued at Rome 691 B.C As late as 1703 John Campbell published his news-letter in Boston, Mass, and 9 or more numbers are in the collection of the Massachusetts Historical society. The era of newspapers, printed from metal type with printing ink, began with the publication of the *Gazette* at Nuremburg, Bavaria, in 1457 (Those marked with * in existence in 1892) MAGAZINES

Chronicle printed at Cologne by Ulric Zell 1499
Gazetta printed in Venice 1570
* *Die Frankfurter Oberpostamts Zeitung* called the first daily paper in the world appeared in Frankfort, Germany 1615
Nathaniel Butters publishes 1 or 2 numbers of *The Courant or Weekly Newes from Forain Partes* sold in London streets by "mercury women" and "hawkers" 9 Oct 1621
First known issue of the *Weekly Newes* published at London by Nicholas Bourne and Thomas Archer 23 May, 1622
* *Gazette de France* established at Paris 1631
* *Postoch Inrikes Tidning* established at Stockholm Sweden 1644
First newspaper advertisement (a reward offered for 2 stolen horses), in the London *Impartial Intelligencer* Mch 1648
Mercurius Politicus issued in Leith, Scotland Oct 1653
* *Oxford Gazette*, first official organ of the court, afterwards the *London Gazette*, the only authorized newspaper, contained little more than proclamations and advertisements, established Nov 1665
First Irish newspaper, *Dublin News letter*, established by Joseph Ray 1685
[News writers at this time collected from the coffee houses information which was printed weekly and sent into the country and called news letters]
Pue's Occurrences published in Dublin, Ireland 1700
Daily Courant, first daily newspaper in English, published by Elizabeth Mallet, in London Mch 1702
St Petersburg Gazette published in Russia 1703
* *Edinburgh Courant* established 1705
Orange Postman, father of the penny press, established in England 1706
To prevent abuse of liberty of the press, queen Anne imposes a tax on newspapers June, 1712
Journal de Paris, ou Poste au Soir, first daily paper in Paris, established 1777
* *The Times* (daily) established in London 1 Jan 1788
* *Allgemeine Zeitung* established at Leipsic 1798
First newspaper in Turkey, *The Spectator of the East*, issued at Smyrna by M Blecque 1827
* London *Evening Standard* established "
* *Spectator* (weekly) established at London 1828
* *Athenæum* (literary and scientific weekly) established in London "
La Caricature, a comic French paper established by Charles Philipon July 1830
Copies of *The English Mercurie* (1588) in the British museum are proved to be forgeries (executed about 1766) by T Watts, 1839
* *Punch* (comic weekly) established at London 1841
* *Illustrated London News* (weekly) established 1842
* *London Daily News* established 21 Jan 1846
Reuter's Telegram company founded in London 1849
* *Notes and Queries* (literary and antiquarian weekly) established in London "
Stamp duty on newspapers in England abolished 15 June, 1855
* *Saturday Review* (literary weekly) established at London June, "
* London *Daily Telegraph* established June, "
* London *Morning Standard* (daily) established 29 June, 1857
* *Pall Mall Gazette* established in London 1865
London Press association founded 1868
* *Academy* (literary weekly) established in London 1869
Number of newspapers in the United Kingdom in 1891 was 2233, of which 183 were daily, published as follows

		Total	Daily
England	London	470	142
	Provinces	1293	
Wales		90	6
Scotland		201	19
Ireland		157	15
Isles		22	1

newspapers in the United States. The increase of newspaper literature in the U S is marvellous In 1783 there were but 43 newspapers, in 1801 there were 200 weekly and 17 daily journals In 1830, with a population of 23,500,000, 852 newspapers were published (50 dailies), issuing 68,117,796 copies yearly, in 1840, 1631 newspapers, with 195,838,673 copies yearly, in 1850, 2526 newspapers with 426,409,978 copies yearly, in 1860, 4051 newspapers, with an annual issue of 928,000,000 copies, being an increase of 118 per cent in 10 years. In 1870 there were 5871 newspapers, with a circulation of 20,842,475 copies In 1880 there were 980 daily, 8718 weekly, and 1075 other newspapers and periodicals. The circulation of daily newspapers was 3,637,424; that of weekly newspapers, 19,459,107 copies. The number of copies printed in 1880 was 2,077,659,675. (Those marked with * in existence in 1894.)

First and only issue of *Public Occurrences both Foreign and Domestick*, a proposed monthly at Boston, Mass.....25 Sept. 1690

Newspaper reporting begun by the *Boston News-Letter;* report of execution of 6 pirates published, with prayer, etc., "as near as it could be taken in writing in the great crowd"....30 June, 1704

John Peter Zenger, editor of the *New York Weekly Journal*, arrested; first prosecution for newspaper libel on this continent....17 Nov. 1734

"Carriers' addresses" originated by William Bradford of the *Pennsylvania Journal*....1 Jan. 1776

Isaiah Thomas, editor of *Massachusetts Spy*, advertises to pay 10 shillings per pound for paper rags....16 Nov. 1780

First daily newspaper in the U. S., *The American Daily Advertiser*, issued in Philadelphia.... 1784

National Intelligencer and Washington Advertiser, organ of the administration of Thomas Jefferson, established by Samuel Harrison Smith.... 1801

Enos Bronson, editor of the *United States Gazette* of Philadelphia, gives first full market-reports of prices current.... 1806

Niles's Weekly Register established in Baltimore by Hezekiah Niles....7 Sept. 1811

Nathan Hale, first to make editorial articles prominent, assumes editorship of the *Boston Daily Advertiser*....7 Apr. 1814

Boston Recorder, first religious newspaper in the U. S., published by Nathaniel Willis, Edward Morse, editor....3 Jan. 1816

**American Farmer*, pioneer agricultural paper in the U. S., established at Baltimore, Md., by John S. Skinner....2 Apr. 1818

First Sunday newspaper in the U. S., the *Sunday Courier*, established by Joseph C. Melcher in New York.... 1825

United States Telegraph becomes organ of gen. Jackson's administration at his accession....4 Mch. 1829

First regular news-boat, to intercept packet-ships for foreign intelligence, instituted by the New York *Journal of Commerce*.... 1830

United States Telegraph succeeded by the *Globe* as official organ of the administration....Dec. "

Garrison's *Liberator* (anti-slavery) founded at Boston....Jan. 1831

**Spirit of the Times*, first weekly sporting paper in the U. S., established in New York by William T. Porter.... "

New York *Journal of Commerce* establishes a pony express from Philadelphia to New York.... 1833

**Sun* begun as a one-cent paper in New York, by Benjamin H. Day....3 Sept. "

"Moon Hoax," by Richard Adams Locke, in New York *Sun*.. 1835

Shorthand reporters first employed on daily press in the U. S.... 1837

First report of religious anniversary meetings in New York *Herald* (disapproved by the clergy).... 1839

First reported sermons in New York *Herald* (Tuesday's).... 1844

Washington Union, edited by Thomas Ritchie and John P. Heiss, succeeds *Globe*, organ of Polk administration..1 May, 1845

New York Associated Press organized.... 1849

"Uncle Tom's Cabin," by Mrs. Stowe, appears as a serial in the *Washington National Era*, an organ of abolitionists....1851-52

"Blanket-sheets" in vogue; the New York *Journal of Commerce*, enlarged to 35×58¾ inches, announces itself "the largest daily paper in the world"....1 Mch. 1853

Origin of "interviewing"; New York *Herald* sends special reporter to Peterborough to interview Gerrit Smith on the John Brown raid.... 1859

Newspapers first stereotyped by the paper process.... "

James Gordon Bennett, founder and proprietor of the New York *Herald*, d. aged 77....1 June, 1872

Horace Greeley, founder of New York *Tribune*, d.....29 Nov. "

NUMBER OF NEWSPAPERS AND PERIODICALS PUBLISHED IN THE UNITED STATES AND BRITISH AMERICA IN 1894.

Issued.	United States.	Canada	Newfoundland.	Total.
Daily	1,841	106	3	1,950
Semi-weekly	242	20	2	264
Weekly	14,000	613	3	14,616
Bi-weekly	87	4	..	91
Tri weekly	34	2	..	36
Semi-monthly	352	22	..	374
Monthly	3,155	139	3	3,297
Bi-monthly	77	1	..	78
Quarterly	221	7	..	228
Total	20,009	914	11	20,934

NEWSPAPERS IN THE UNITED STATES FROM 1700 TO 1800.

Papers marked with * still published (1894). Established.

Boston News-Letter, John Campbell, publisher....24 Apr. 1709

Boston Gazette, William Brooker....21 Dec. 1714

American Weekly Mercury, Philadelphia, Andrew S. Bradford, 22 Dec. "

New England Courant, Boston, James Franklin....7 Aug. 1721

New York Gazette, William Bradford....Oct. 1725

New England Weekly Journal, Boston, Samuel Kneeland, 20 Mch. 1727

Maryland Gazette, Annapolis, William Parks. First in the state; suspended 1736; revived 1745; suspended 1839.... "

Estab'd.

Universal Instructor in all the Arts and Sciences, and Pennsylvania Gazette, Philadelphia, Benjamin Franklin. Called Pennsylvania Gazette after 28 Sept. 1729.... 1728

Weekly Rehearsal, Boston, Jeremy Gridley; became Boston Evening Post, 21 Aug. 1735; suspended 1775....27 Sept. 1731

South Carolina Gazette, Charleston, Thomas Whitemarsh, 8 Jan. "

Rhode Island Gazette, Newport, James Franklin. First in state; 12 numbers published....27 Sept. 1732

New York Weekly Journal, John Peter Zenger; suspended 1752....5 Nov. 1733

Boston Weekly Post-Boy, Ellis Huske.... 1734

Virginia Gazette, Williamsburg, William Parks (first in state), Aug. 1736

Pennsylvania Journal and Weekly Advertiser, Philadelphia, William Bradford.... 1742

New York Evening Post, Henry de Forrest (ran one year).... 1746

Independent Advertiser, Boston, Samuel Adams....4 Jan. 1748

New York Mercury, Hugh Gaine (called Gaine's New York Gazette and Mercury after 1767)....3 Aug. 1752

Boston Gazette or Weekly Advertiser, Samuel Kneeland; suspended Mch. 1755....3 Jan. 1753

Connecticut Gazette, New Haven, James Parker and John Holt, 1 Jan. 1755

Boston Gazette and Country Gentleman, Edes & Gill; suspended 1798....7 Apr. "

North Carolina Gazette, Newbern....Dec. "

* New Hampshire Gazette, Portsmouth, Daniel Fowle. Oldest paper in the U. S. Daily established 1852; weekly....7 Oct. 1756

Boston Weekly Advertiser, Green & Russell....22 Aug. 1757

South Carolina and American General Gazette, Charleston, Robert Wells.... 1758

* Newport Mercury, Rhode Island, James Franklin....12 June, "

New London Summary, New London, Conn., Timothy Green; suspended in 1763....8 Aug. "

New York Gazette, William Weyman....16 Feb. 1759

Wilmington Courant, Delaware, James Adams. Published for 6 months and the only paper in the state.... 1761

Providence Gazette and Country Journal, Rhode Island.... 1762

Rivington's Royal Gazette, New York, James Rivington. Changed to Rivington's New York Gazette and Universal Advertiser at close of the Revolution, and suspended in 1781.... "

Georgia Gazette, Savannah, James Johnston. Ran for 27 years, 17 Apr. 1763

New London Gazette. Name changed to Connecticut Gazette in 1773....1st Nov. "

Cape Fear Gazette and Wilmington Advertiser, Wilmington, N. C., Andrew Stewart; suspended in 1767.... "

* Connecticut Courant, Hartford, Thomas Green. First regular issue, 19 Nov. 1764....29 Oct. 1764

Portsmouth (N. H.), Mercury and Weekly Advertiser, Ezekiel Russell; suspended in 1768.... 1765

Gazette and Country Journal, Charleston, S. C., Charles Crouch, "

Constitutional Courant, Burlington, N. J., "Andrew Marvel" (William Goddard), publisher....21 Sept. "

Virginia Gazette, Williamsburg, William Rind....May, 1766

New York Journal or General Advertiser, John Holt..29 May, 1767

* Connecticut Journal and New Haven Post-Boy, Thomas and Samuel Green; now the Connecticut Herald and Journal. Oct. "

Boston Chronicle, Mein & Fleming....21 Dec. "

Pennsylvania Chronicle and Universal Advertiser, Philadelphia, William Goddard.... "

* Essex Gazette, Salem, Mass., Samuel Hall. Name changed to Salem Gazette in 1781....5 Aug. 1768

Cape Fear Mercury, Wilmington, N. C., Adam Boyd....13 Oct. 1769

* Massachusetts Spy, Isaiah Thomas & Zechariah Fowle, publishers, Boston, Mass. Removed to Worcester in 1775. Name changed to Thomas's Massachusetts Spy or Worcester Gazette in 1781; now styled, The Worcester Spy....July, 1770

Maryland Journal and Baltimore Advertiser, William Goddard, Aug. 1773

Norwich (Conn.) Packet....Oct. "

Essex Journal and Merrimack Packet, or the Massachusetts and New Hampshire General Advertiser, Newburyport, 4 Dec. "

Independent Chronicle and Universal Advertiser, Boston, Powers & Willis. United with Boston Patriot in 1819, and absorbed by Daily Advertiser, 1832.... 1776

New York Packet and American Advertiser, Samuel Loudon, Jan. "

Continental Journal and Weekly Advertiser, Boston, John Gill, 30 May, "

New Jersey Gazette, Isaac Collins. First regular newspaper issued in the state....3 Dec. 1777

New Jersey Journal, Chatham, N. J., David Franks.... 1778

Independent Ledger and American Advertiser, Boston, Draper & Folsom....15 June, "

American Herald, Boston, Edward E. Powars.... 1781

Vermont Gazette or Green Mountain Post-Boy, Westminster, Judah Paddock Spooner & Timothy Green.... "

Massachusetts Centinel and the Republican Journal (semi-weekly), Warden & Russell. Changed to Columbian Centinel, 16 June, 1790, and absorbed by Boston Daily Advertiser in 1840....24 Mch. 1784

American Daily Advertiser, Philadelphia, Benjamin Franklin Bache. The first American daily. Changed to Poulson's Advertiser in 1802, and absorbed by the North American, first issued 28 Oct. 1839.... "

Falmouth Gazette and Weekly Advertiser (Me.), Thomas B. Wait and Benjamin Titcomb. Called Cumberland Gazette in 1786....1 Jan. 1785

New York Daily Advertiser, Francis Childs & Co....1 Mch. "

	Estab'd
* Pittsburg (Pa) Gazette. First newspaper printed west of the Alleghany mountains 29 July,	1786
* Hampshire Gazette, Northampton, Mass, William Butler, 6 Sept	"
Independent Journal, New York, J & A. M Lean Changed to New York Gazette in 1788, and absorbed by the Journal of Commerce in 1840	1787
Herald of Freedom and Federal Advertiser, Boston, Freeman & Andrews 15 Sept	1788
United States Gazette, New York, John Fenno Removed to Philadelphia in 1790 --Special organ of Alexander Hamilton Absorbed by North American, 1847	1789
National Gazette, Philadelphia, Philip Freneau, suspended in 1793 Oct	1791
* Impartial Intelligencer, Greenfield, Mass, Thomas Dickman Changed to Greenfield Gazette the same year United with Courier in 1841 as Gazette and Courier 1 Feb	1792
State Gazette, Trenton, N J	"
Massachusetts Mercury (tri weekly), Boston Alexander Young & Samuel Etheridge New England Palladium added to the title in 1801 Absorbed by the Advertiser about 1830 1 Jan	1793
* Rutland (Vt) Herald "	"
* Centinel of the Northwestern Territory, now the Cincinnati Gazette, first newspaper and first printing office north of the Ohio, established by William Maxwell 9 Nov	"
* Minerva, New York Noah Webster, editor Name changed to Commercial Advertiser in 1794 Oldest daily in New York city 9 Dec	"
* Utica (N Y) Gazette, combined with the Herald, established 1847 as Morning Herald and Gazette	"
* Newburyport (Mass.) Herald (daily established 1832)	"
* Sciota Gazette Chillicothe O, Nathaniel Willis	1796
Western Spy and Hamilton Gazette, changed to National Republican and Ohio Political Register in 1823	1799

SELECTED LIST OF THE PRINCIPAL DAILY NEWSPAPERS IN THE UNITED STATES IN 1894 WITH A CIRCULATION OF 8000 AND UPWARDS

Name	Where published	Estab lished
North American	Philadelphia, Pa	1771
American	Baltimore, Md	1773
Commercial Gazette.	Pittsburg Pa	1786
Evening Post	New York	1801
News and Courier	Charleston, S C	1803
Commercial	Buffalo, N Y	1811
Advertiser	Boston, Mass	1813
Commercial Gazette	Cincinnati, O	1827
Advertiser	Montgomery Ala.	1828
Courier	Buffalo, N Y	"
Courrier des Etats-Unis	New York	"
Inquirer	Philadelphia, Pa.	1829
Evening Journal	Albany, N Y	1830
Post	Boston, Mass.	1831
Sun	New York	1833
New Yorker Staats Zeitung.	New York	1834
Herald	New York	1835
Free Press	Detroit, Mich	"
Republic	St. Louis, Mo	"
Public Ledger	Philadelphia, Pa	1836
Sun	Baltimore, Md	1837
Picayune	New Orleans, La	[illegible]
Hawk Eye	Burlington Ia	1839
Times	Hartford, Conn	1841
Tribune	New York	"
Enquirer	Cincinnati, O	1842
Plain Dealer	Cleveland O	"
Republican	Springfield, Mass	1844
Sentinel	Milwaukee, Wis	"
Herald	Boston, Mass.	1846
Tribune	Chicago, Ill	"
Express	Buffalo, N Y	"
Dispatch	Pittsburg, Pa	"
Blade	Toledo, O	1847
Evening Item	Philadelphia Pa	"
Dispatch	Richmond, Va	1850
Times	New York	1851
Globe Democrat	St Louis, Mo	1852
Evening Star	Washington, D C	"
Times	Chicago, Ill	1854
Pioneer Press	St. Paul, Minn	1855
Morning Call	San Francisco, Cal	1856
Press	Philadelphia, Pa	1857
Rocky Mountain News	Denver, Col	1859
World	New York	1860
Morning Oregonian	Portland, Or	1861
Evening Bulletin	Providence, R I	1863
Commercial	Louisville, Ky	"
Times-Democrat	New Orleans, La	"
Chronicle	San Francisco, Cal	1865
Examiner	San Francisco, Cal.	"
Republican	Denver, Col	1866
Tribune	Minneapolis, Minn	1867
News	New York	"
Courier Journal	Louisville, Ky	1868
Constitution	Atlanta, Ga.	"
News	Indianapolis, Ind	1869
Record	Philadelphia, Pa.	1870
Bee	Omaha, Neb	1871
Globe	Boston, Mass	1872
Inter Ocean.	Chicago, Ill	"
Evening News	Buffalo, N Y	1873

Name	Where published	Estab'd
News	Chicago, Ill	1875
Times	Philadelphia, Pa	"
Call	Philadelphia Pa	"
Times	Louisville Ky	1877
Journal	Minneapolis, Minn	1878
Press	Cleveland, O	"
News	New Haven Conn	1879
Capital	Topeka, Kan	"
Star	Kansas City, Mo	1880
Chronicle	St Louis, Mo	"
Post	Cincinnati, O	"
Times	Pittsburg, Pa	"
Herald	Chicago, Ill	1881
Morning Journal	New York	1882
Journal	Milwaukee, Wis	"
Evening News	Newark N J	1883
Press	Pittsburg, Pa	"
Times	Richmond Va	1886
Age Herald	Birmingham Ala	1887
Telegraph	Seattle Wash	1890
Recorder	New York	1891

Many of these publish also weekly or semi weekly and Sunday editions

SELECTED LIST OF PRINCIPAL WEEKLY PAPERS IN THE U S IN 1894 WITH A CIRC OF 40,000 AND UPW

Name	Where published	Estab-lished
Christian Advocate	New York	1826
Youth s Companion	Boston Mass	1827
Telegram	Harrisburg Pa	1828
Sunday Mercury	New York	1839
Yankee Blade	Boston, Mass	1841
Ledger	New York	1844
Scientific American	New York	1845
Street & Smith s N Y Weekly	New York	"
National Police Gazette	New York	1846
Ohio Practical Farmer	Cleveland, O	1848
Harper's Weekly	New York	1856
Sunday School Times	Philadelphia, Pa	1859
Fireside Companion	New York	1860
Saturday Night	Philadelphia Pa	1865
Harper s Bazar	New York	1867
Witness	New York	1871
Family Story Paper	New York	1873
Germania (semi weekly)	Milwaukee, Wis	"
Der Haus und Bauernfreund	Milwaukee Wis	"
Union Signal	Chicago, Ill	1874
Golden Rule	Boston Mass	1875
National Tribune	Washington, D C	1877
Puck	New York	"
National Stockman and Farmer	Pittsburg, Pa	"
Christian Herald and Signs of Our Times	New York	1878
Texas Siftings	New York and London	"
Graphic	Chicago, Ill	1879
Telegram	Elmira, N Y	"
Town Topics	New York	"
Farmer s Home	Dayton, O	1880
Sporting News.	St. Louis. Mo	"
Golden Days	Philadelphia, Pa.	"
Judge	New York	1881
Argosy	New York	1882
Saturday Globe	Utica, N Y	"
Pennsylvania Grit	Williamsport, Pa.	"
Voice	New York	1883
Sunday Telegram	Albany, N Y	1886
Catholic News	New York	"
National Economist	Washington, D C	1888
Saturday Blade	Chicago, Ill	"
Union Gospel News.	Cleveland, O	"
Good News	New York	1889

new style. Pope Gregory XIII, to rectify errors of the current calendar, published a new one, in which 10 days were omitted—5 Oct 1582 becoming 15 Oct. The "new style" was adopted in France, Italy, Spain, Denmark, Holland, Flanders, Portugal, in 1582, in Germany in 1584, in Switzerland in 1583 and 1584, in Hungary in 1587, and in Great Britain in 1752, when 11 days were dropped—3 Sept being reckoned as 14 Sept The difference between old and new style up to 1699 was 10 days, after 1700, 11 days, after 1800, 12 days In Russia, Greece, and the east, old style is retained. CALENDAR.

New Testament. BIBLE

Newtonian philosophy, doctrines respecting gravitation, etc, taught by sir Isaac Newton in his "Principia," pub in 1687 GRAVITATION. He was born 25 Dec. 1642, became master of the mint, 1699, president of the Royal society, 1703, and died 20 Mch. 1727.

New Year's day, etc. The beginning of the Jewish year was changed and the Passover instituted 1491 B.C. A feast is said to have been instituted by Numa and dedicated to Janus (who presided over the new year) 1 Jan 713 B C.

On this day the Romans sacrificed to Janus a cake of new-sifted meal, with salt, incense, and wine; mechanics began something in their art or trade; men of letters did the same, as to books, poems, etc.; and consuls, though chosen before, assumed their office. Nonius Marcellus refers the origin of New Year's gifts among the Romans to Titus Tatius, king of the Sabines, who accepted as of good omen a present of branches cut in a wood consecrated to Strenia, the goddess of strength, received on the first day of the new year, and sanctioned the custom, calling such gifts Strenæ, 747 B.C. YEAR.

New York, one of the original 13 states of the United States, lies between 40° 29′ 30″ and 45° 0′ 42″ N. lat., and between 71° 51′ and 79° 45′ 54″ W. lon. It is separated from Canada on the north by the eastern portion of lake Erie, lake Ontario, and the river St. Lawrence; on the east lie Vermont, Massachusetts, and Connecticut; on the south, the Atlantic ocean, New Jersey, and Pennsylvania; on the west, New Jersey, Pennsylvania, lakes Erie and Ontario, and the rivers Niagara and St. Lawrence. Its greatest length, north and south, is 312 miles, including Staten Island, while east and west it is 412 miles, including Long Island. It contains 49,170 sq. miles, in 60 counties. Pop. 1890, 5,997,853; 1900, 7,268,012. It is the "Empire state" of the Union in wealth and population. Capital, Albany.

Giovanni da Verazzano, a Florentine, under commission of Francis I. of France, with a single caravel, the *Dauphin*, enters the bay of New York....Apr. 1524

Half Moon, 80 tons, leaves Amsterdam; Henry Hudson, an Englishman, commander....4 Apr. 1609

Samuel de Champlain, coming from the north with a war party of Hurons, discovers lake Champlain....July, "

Defeats the Iroquois near Ticonderoga; hence dates the enmity between the French and Iroquois; fire-arms first seen by the Indians....30 July, "

Half Moon enters New York bay....11 Sept. "

Anchors for the night above the site of Yonkers....13 Sept. "

Anchors near West Point....14 Sept. "

Anchors near Catskill landing....15 Sept. "

Stops near the site of Hudson....17 Sept. "

Anchors just below Albany....19 Sept. "

Despatches a boat to sound the river farther up....22 Sept. "

Begins his voyage down the river....23 Sept. "

Sails out of the Narrows....4 Oct. "

[Fate of the *Half Moon:* wrecked on Mauritius island, 6 Mch. 1615.]

Hendrick Christiaensen and Adriaen Block sail 2 Amsterdam vessels, the *Fortune* and the *Tiger*, to Manhattan island.... 1611

Tiger accidentally burned at Manhattan.... 1613

Christiaensen builds "fort Nassau," a trading house, 36×26 feet in a stockade 58 feet square, with a moat 18 feet wide on Castle island (below Albany).... 1614

Block builds the *Onrust* (Restless) of 18 tons at Manhattan; launched near the Battery....spring of "

In the *Onrust* he passes Hell Gate and coasts along as far as Nahant bay.... "

States-general of Holland name the country about Manhattan "New Netherland," and grant its trade by charter to Amsterdam merchants....Oct. "

Christiaensen killed by Indians (first such recorded since Hudson's voyage).... 1615

Champlain, with 10 Frenchmen, joins a party of Hurons and allies moving against the Iroquois....1 Sept. "

Lands from lake Ontario near Henderson, Jefferson county, Oct. "

They attack the Iroquois castle at Onondaga lake, near Liverpool, Onondaga county, and are repulsed....10–16 Oct. "

A trading post fortified at the mouth of the Tawasentha (Noman's Kill) creek, near Albany, by Jacob Eelkins; first formal treaty between the Indians and the Dutch.... "

New Netherland charter expires; not renewed by the States-general....1 Jan. 1618

Fort Orange built (South Market st., Albany).... 1623

New Netherland a province under the Amsterdam chamber... "

New Amsterdam settled.... "

[NEW YORK CITY for further local history.]

New Netherland brings from the Texel 30 families, chiefly Walloons (French Protestant refugees)....Mch. "

Reaching the Hudson, some 8 families settle near fort Orange; the rest on Long Island at the Waal-bogt, Wahle-Bocht, or "Walloons' bay," now corrupted into Wallabout, May–June, "

Cornelis Jacobsen May, first director or governor of New Netherland under the Dutch West India company.... 1624

Sarah Rapelje the first known white child born in New Netherland....7 June, 1625

Peter Evertsen Hulft fits 3 vessels, each of some 250 tons, for New Amsterdam; lands at Nutten (Governor's island), July, "

William Verhulst succeeds May as director.... "

Peter Minuit, director, leaves Amsterdam in *Sea-Mew*...9 Jan. 1626

Arrives at Manhattan....4 May, "

Manhattan island, "rocky and full of trees," ceded by Indians to the Dutch West India company for 60 guilders ($23).... "

A block-house built, surrounded by a palisade of cedar posts, at the extreme southern end of the island and called fort Amsterdam.... "

Six farms or "boweries" laid out on the island, and specimens of the harvest sent to Holland to show the fertility of the soil.... "

Dutch in friendly relations with the Plymouth colony of New England.... 1627

Dutch inform Plymouth of the "Fresh" river (Connecticut).. "

Population at Manhattan estimated at 270.... 1628

Kiliaen Van Rensselaer, a merchant of Amsterdam, purchases land of the Indians around fort Orange through his agent, becoming patroon of the manor of Rensselaerwyck.... 1630

Michael Pauw purchases of the Indians the site of Jersey City (Pavonia) and Staten Island.... "

New Netherland (800 tons) built at Manhattan.... 1631

Mohawks receive fire-arms from the Dutch.... "

Peter Minuit, director, recalled....Mch. 1632

Ship *Eendragt* from Manhattan attached in Plymouth harbor, Engl., on a charge of illegally trading....3 Apr. "

British ministry claim New Netherland as English territory.. "

Eendragt released....27 May, "

Dutch occupy the west end of Long Island.... "

Wouter Van Twiller, clerk of the West India company, marries a niece of Kiliaen Van Rensselaer; made governor.... 1633

Friendly intercourse with the Virginians.... "

Jacob Eelkins (the same person who had previously established a trading-post up the Hudson) visits Manhattan in the *William*, a London vessel from New Plymouth, and sails up the Hudson to fort Orange in defiance of the governor (the first English vessel to ascend)....24 Apr. "

William brought down to Manhattan and forced to sea...May, "

A small trading-post, called the "House of Good Hope," built and fortified with 2 pieces of cannon by the Dutch, on or near the site of Hartford, Conn.... "

Wealthy colonists from Holland settle at fort Orange.... 1636

Jacob Van Corlaer purchased from the Indians a plat on Long Island, the first recorded grant in King's county....June, "

States-general notified of the inefficiency of the governor through Van Dincklagen....Aug. "

Gov. Van Twiller personally purchases from Indians the island Paggauck, south of fort Amsterdam; supposed to contain 160 acres; called by the Dutch Nooten or Nutten island (from its excellent nuts). Now "Governor's island".... 1637

Jonas Bronck purchases a tract in West Chester, opposite Haerlem....June, "

Pavonia and Staten Island purchased by the Amsterdam directors of Michael Pauw for 26,000 guilders ($10,000).... "

De Vries reiterates the charges of Van Dincklagen against gov. Van Twiller; Van Twiller recalled.... "

William Kieft director and commissioned....2 Sept. "

Arrives at New Amsterdam....28 Mch. 1638

Purchases of the Indians part of Long Island for the company, 1639

Thomas Belcher takes up a tract (in Brooklyn).... "

Lion Gardiner purchases Gardiner's island (the first permanent English settlement in the state)....10 Mch. 1640

Southampton, Long Island, settled by the English.... "

Rensselaerwyck rapidly increases in wealth and population... "

Indians near Manhattan alienated by the conduct of the Dutch, "

Expedition against the Raritan Indians (Delawares); several Indians killed and crops destroyed....16 July, "

Contributions levied on the Tappan Indians by gov. Kieft, but refused....Oct. "

Reformed Dutch church established.... "

Raritan Indians destroy De Vries's colony on Staten Island, June, 1641

Kieft sets a price on their beads....July, "

Kieft, anticipating an Indian war, consults the heads of families in New Amsterdam....23 Aug. "

These chose "12 select men" to act for them; the first representative assembly in the province....29 Aug. "

Ex-gov. Minuit dies at fort Christina.... "

"Select men" dissenting from the governor's warlike policy, he dissolves them....Feb. 1642

George Baxter, an exile from New England, English secretary; salary 250 guilders ($95).... "

Johannes Megapolensis the first clergyman in Rensselaerwyck, with a residence and 1000 guilders ($380).... "

Anne Hutchinson takes refuge near New Rochelle from religious persecution in Massachusetts.... "

Dutch at fort Orange seek in vain to ransom Jogues (a French missionary, prisoner of the Iroquois), but his life is spared.. "

Kieft rashly provokes an Indian war by sending soldiers to destroy the Indians at Pavonia and Corlaer Hook....25 Feb. 1643

Thus aroused, the Indians begin a war of retaliation.... "

They attack trading-vessels on the river....Aug. "

Capt. John Underhill, a hero of the Pequot war (CONNECTICUT, 1636–37) enters the Dutch service....Sept. "

Anne Hutchinson (MASSACHUSETTS, 1636, '37, '38) killed, the settlement destroyed, and her granddaughter, 8 years old, captured.... "

Throgmorton's settlement attacked and destroyed.... "

Gravesend, Long Island, attacked, but Indians repulsed.... "

Father Jogues escapes from the Indians at fort Orange; is brought to New Amsterdam and sails for Europe.... "

First church, 34 by 19 feet, built at fort Orange, with canopied pulpit.... "

NEW

English under Robert Fordham, from Stamford, settle Hempstead, Long Island, early in.... 1644
English and Dutch destroy an Indian village near Hempstead, "
Captain Underhill destroys an Indian village at Stamford, killing 600 Indians; 15 Dutch soldiers wounded....12 Mch. "
Kieft proclaims a public thanksgiving for the victory....Mch. "
Complaints against Kieft; his recall demanded.... "
Kiliaen Van Rensselaer dies at Amsterdam, Holland.... "
End of Indian war; treaty with some of the tribes....22 Apr. 1645
General treaty with the Indians after 5 years of disturbance, 30 Aug. "

[The treaty provides for the surrender of Anne Hutchinson's granddaughter. After nearly 4 years of captivity, she wished to remain with the Indians.]

Several Englishmen obtain a patent from gov. Kieft for about 16,000 acres about Flushing, Long Island, and settle..19 Oct. "
Adriaen Van der Donck buys of Indians land as far as "Spyt den Duyvel;" States-general confirm the title (the Dutch name, "de Jonkeers Landt," became Yonkers).... 1646
States-general, at the request of the company (July 13), ratify Stuyvesant's commission as governor....28 July, "
Patent issued to Cornelis Antonissen Van Slyck for a colony in Kaatskill....Aug. "
Father Jogues returns to Canada, revisits the Mohawks, and is put to death....18 Oct. "
Breuckelen (Brooklyn) obtains a municipal government, 26 Nov. "
Kieft protests against English encroachments on New Netherland.... "
Peter Stuyvesant lands at New Amsterdam....11 May, 1647
Kieft embarks for Holland in the *Princess*....16 Aug. "
Princess shipwrecked in Bristol channel; Kieft, dominie Bogardus, and about 80 others perish....22 Sept. "
Thomas Chambers, a farmer, with others from near the present city of Troy, coming to Esopus, now Kingston, are the first settlers of Ulster county.... 1652

[The name Esopus long continued in popular use after "Kingston" was legally adopted.]

Flatbush settled.... "
States-general recall Stuyvesant....27 Apr. "
His recall revoked....15 May, "
First public debt of New Amsterdam about 6000 guilders, 15 Mch. 1653
Dutch vessels excluded from New England harbors.... "
Landtdag (convention) at New Amsterdam....8 Dec. "
Convention organized. New Amsterdam had 3 representatives; Breuckelen, 3; Flushing, 2; Newtown, 2; Hempstead, 2; Flatlands, 3; Flatbush, 2; Gravesend, 2; 4 Dutch and 4 English towns sent 10 Dutch and 9 English delegates....10 Dec. "
Governor dissolves the convention....14 Dec. "
Pirates and robbers infest East river and plunder shores.... 1654
First church formed at Flatbush; Johannes Theodorus Polhemus, dominie.... "
News of a projected attack by the English received by gov. Stuyvesant....29 May, "
New Amsterdam put in a state of defence....June, "
Treaty of peace between England and Holland.... "
General Thanksgiving day appointed....12 Aug. "
Discovery of salt springs in central New York by father Le Moyne....Aug. "
English settle at Westchester under Thomas Pell....Nov. "
Seal and coat-of-arms of New Amsterdam received from Holland....8 Dec. "
Gov. Stuyvesant sails to West Indies to establish trade, 24 Dec. "
Indian invasion....15 Sept. 1655
Hoboken, Pavonia, and Staten Island laid waste, 100 killed, 150 made prisoners, $76,000 of property destroyed....15–20 Sept. "
Governor returns; prompt measures for defence....12 Oct. "
Prisoners ransomed from the Indians....26 Oct. "
Settlement of Jamaica, Long Island....Mch. 1656
Thirty-five thousand beaver and other skins exported from fort Orange.... "
New church at Beaverwyck (Albany)....June, "
French Jesuit missionaries among the Iroquois.... "
Proclamation against the Quakers.... 1657

[Any person entertaining a Quaker for a single night to be fined 50*l*., one-half to the informer, and vessels bringing any Quaker into the province to be confiscated.—*Brodheads*, "Hist. N. Y.," vol. i. p. 637.]

Village laid out at Esopus (Kingston)....31 May, 1658
French are obliged to abandon their colonizing efforts among the Iroquois after.... "
Massachusetts grants land to English colonists on the Hudson, 1659
Purchase of Schenectady Flats....27 July, 1661
Municipal charter granted to Esopus, now to be called "Wiltwyck" (Indian Village).... "
Curtius returns to Holland and is succeeded by dominie Algidius Luyck.... "

[The high-school gained such a reputation that pupils were sent to it from fort Orange, South River, and Virginia.]

John Browne arrested for harboring Quakers.... 1662
Village of Esopus attacked by Indians and partly burned, June, 1663
Browne banished. Goes to Amsterdam and appeals to the West India company. The directors rebuke Stuyvesant and enjoin moderation. Persecution ceases.... "
Severe earthquake throughout New Netherland, New England, and Canada.... "
Trouble with England and the English colony; a general provincial assembly called by the governor to consider the state of the province....19 Mch. 1664
Charles II. of England grants to the duke of York, his brother, territory including the New Netherland....22 Mch. "
Duke of York sends 4 ships against New Netherland: *Guinea*, 36 guns; *Elias*, 30 guns; *Martin*, 16 guns, and *William*, 10 guns, with 450 soldiers; col. Richard Nicolls in command, to be deputy-governor....Apr. 1664
Delegates meet at New Amsterdam; Jeremias Van Rensselaer of Rensselaerwyck chairman, as being from the oldest "colonie"....10 Apr. "
It is decided to be impossible to take active measures against the English, who were 6 times their number, and could bring overwhelming aid from Hartford....22 Apr. "
Mohegans devastate the east side of the Hudson....11 July, "
Population of New Amsterdam, 1500; of the province, 10,000.. "
English squadron at Nyack bay....28 Aug. "
Surrender of fort Amsterdam....8 Sept. "
Surrender of fort Orange....20 Sept. "
First treaty between the English and the Iroquois; this friendship continues for over a century....24 Sept. "
Name of New Amsterdam changed to New York and fort Orange to Albany.... "
Dutch government denounces the conquest of New Netherland and demands its restitution....6 Nov. "
West India company recall Stuyvesant....28 Nov. "
Principal Dutch residents, including gov. Stuyvesant and Van Rensselaer, swear allegiance to Charles II. and the duke of York.... "
Long Island adjudged to New York.... "
Stuyvesant returns to Holland with strong testimonials of approval....May, 1665
Negro slavery recognized.... "
Race-course at Hempstead, L. I., selected by gov. Nicolls and named "New Market"....May, "
Holland urgently demands the restoration of New Netherland, "
Ralph Hall and his wife Mary arrested for witchcraft and sorcery, but the jury (including Jacob Leisler, afterwards governor) "found nothing considerable against them".... "
Peter Stuyvesant returns to New York....Oct. 1667
Gov. Nicolls relieved at his own request.... "
Gov. Nicolls leaves New York....17 Aug. 1668
Col. Francis Lovelace governor....28 Aug. "
Staten Island adjudged to New York.... "
Twenty whales captured in New York harbor during spring of 1669
Name "Kingston" given to Esopus....25 Sept. "
La Salle, Dollier, and Galinée explore lakes Ontario and Erie; possession taken for France.... "
Staten Island purchased from the Indians for the duke of York, 13 Apr. 1670
Katherine Harrison, widow, banished from Weathersfield, Conn., for witchcraft, comes to Westchester. Citizens complain, but on inquiry the court of assizes finds nothing against her and directs her release. But the people of Westchester become "uneasy," and she is obliged to leave, July–Aug. "
George Fox, the Quaker, visits Long Island.... 1672
Monthly post between New York and Boston; first post messenger....22 Jan. 1673
Dutch fleet of 7 vessels, with 1600 men, arrives off Sandy Hook. The Dutch of New York welcome their countrymen..7 Aug. "
Dutch fire on fort James, which returns a shot. Fort James and New York surrender to the Dutch....9 Aug. "

[Province again named New Netherland, fort James called fort Willem Hendricks, and the city of New York, New Orange.]

Anthony Colve appointed governor....Aug. "
Albany and Esopus reduced.... " "
French build fort Frontenac on lake Ontario.... "
Peace between England and Holland; New Netherland restored to England....Feb. and Mch. 1674
New patent granted to the duke of York by Charles II., 29 June, "
Maj. Edmund Andros appointed governor....1 July, "
Formal delivery of New Netherland to the English....10 Nov. "
Capt. John Manning, who surrendered New York to the Dutch in 1673, court-martialled and sentenced to have his sword broken over his head, and forbidden to wear a sword or serve the crown....Feb. 1675
Philip of Pokanoket's or King Philip's war (MASSACHUSETTS).. "
New fort built by La Salle at Frontenac.... 1676
Andastes, a powerful tribe of Indians occupying western Pennsylvania and the southern shore of lake Erie, finally conquered by the Iroquois.... "
Gov. Andros asserts English sovereignty over the Iroquois.... "
Father Hennepin among the Mohawks.... 1677
France denies English sovereignty over the Iroquois.... "
Fresh discoveries in the interior of New York; a large tract purchased from the Indians by Louis du Bois, Jean Hasbrouck, and others. The governor confirms the grant extending along the Shawangunk mountains and along the Hudson river, now Ulster county....16 Sept. "
Prince William of Orange marries Mary, daughter of the duke of York, afterwards James II. of England....4 Nov. "
Gov. Andros allowed to return to England "to look after his own interests"....17 Nov. "
New York, as described in London by gov. Andros, contains 24 towns, villages, or parishes, in 6 precincts or courts of sessions; servants are much wanted; slaves, mostly from Barbadoes, are scarce, worth 30*l*. to 35*l*. A merchant with 500*l*. or 1000*l*., is thought substantial, and a planter worth half that in movables is accounted rich. The value of estates in the province is about 150,000*l*. 15 vessels, of 100 tons each, trade with the province each year from Old and New England. 5 small ships and a ketch belong to New York, of which 4 were built there. The exports are provisions, furs, tar,

and lumber. The imports of English manufactures amount to 50,000*l.* yearly. The customs, excises, and quit-rents do not nearly suffice for the public expenses. The chief trading places are New York and Southampton on Long Island for foreign commerce, and Albany for Indian traffic. There are about 2000 males able to bear arms, 140 of them horsemen. Fort James at New York is a square of stone with 4 bastions, mounting 46 guns; fort Albany at Albany is a small stockade with 4 bastions and mounting 12 guns, sufficient against the Indians. Ministers are scarce and religions many, so that there are no records of marriages or births in New York. There are about 20 churches in the province, mostly Presbyterians and Independents, with some Quakers, Anabaptists, and Jews, all supported by free gifts. The duke maintains an Episcopalian chaplain, which is all the "certain allowance" of the church of England. In New York there are no beggars, but all the poor are cared for........................ 1678

Gov. Andros knighted by the king in London.................. "

Gov. sir Edmund Andros lands in New York after a 9 weeks' voyage...8 Aug. "

Jacob Leisler, with other New-Yorkers, on the way to England, captured by a Turkish corsair; they are ransomed, Leisler for 2000 Spanish dollars.. "

French at Niagara; first mass by father Hennepin; a bark cabin built near Lewiston...........................19 Dec. "

La Salle builds fort Conty at the mouth of the Niagara river, "a habitation" with a palisade.........................Jan. 1679

La Salle begins building the *Griffin* (named in compliment to Frontenac, governor of Canada, whose armorial supporters were 2 griffins), of 60 tons' burden, above Niagara Falls at the mouth of Cayuga creek, near La Salle, Niagara county, 26 Jan. "

Griffin enters lake Erie (with La Salle, Tonti, and others on board. She proceeds to Green Bay, Wis. After leaving that place to return loaded with furs, she is never heard of), 7 Aug. "

Great comet seen in New York and New England; a day of fasting and humiliation appointed..........................1 Dec. 1680

Sir Edmund Andros recalled and leaves New York......11 Jan. 1681

Anthony Brockholls, by special commission, appointed provisional governor ....Jan. "

Col. Thomas Dongan, appointed governor, reaches New York, 25 Aug. 1683

First assembly under English rule........................17 Oct. "

Charter of liberty adopted. The assembly to meet once in 3 years at least; every free-holder an elector; entire freedom of conscience and religion guaranteed; no tax levied without the consent of the representatives....................30 Oct. "

New York divided into 10 counties. The county of New York, Manhattan island. Westchester county containing all the land eastward of Manhattan as far as the government extends, and northward along the Hudson to the Highlands. Dutchess county extended from Westchester northward to Albany county, and from the Hudson river eastward to Massachusetts and Connecticut. Albany county included all the territory on the east of the Hudson, north of Dutchess, and on the west side to Saratoga. Ulster county, which was named after the duke of York's Irish earldom, embraced all the territory from the Highlands to the southern boundary of Albany county, near Saugerties. Orange included the region on the west side of the Hudson from the New Jersey boundary northward to Ulster and west to the Delaware river. Richmond, all Staten Island. Kings, the western portion of Long Island; Queens, the central, and Suffolk the eastern portion...1 Nov. "

A high-sheriff commissioned for each county........................ "

Agreement as to the boundary between New York and Connecticut..28 Nov. "

Gov. Dongan commissions James Graham first recorder of New York city ....16 Jan. 1684

Francis, Lord Howard, governor of Virginia, visits New York and is made "freeman" of the metropolis. First British peer thus honored..29 June, "

Iroquois submit to the king of England................30 July, "

Death of Charles II..6 Feb. 1685

James, duke of York, becomes king as James II........ " "

Colonial post-office established by New York...........2 Mch. "

New York charter not confirmed by James II..................... "

[No colonial assemblies under James II.]

City of Albany incorporated; Peter Schuyler first mayor, 22 July, 1686

Albany charter published...................................26 July, "

Robert Livingston secures the Indian title to the territory on the Hudson opposite Catskill to a point opposite Saugerties, and eastward to Massachusetts. Gov. Dongan confirms his title by patent with manorial privileges. This territory embraced 160,240 acres (ANTI-RENTISM). ....July, "

Charters of liberties repealed (adopted 1683).......................... "

Population of the province about 18,000.............................. "

Governor's salary fixed at 600*l.* sterling, to be paid out of the provincial revenues... "

French invade and occupy the Seneca country in New York, destroy many thousand bushels of corn and many hogs; then fall back and build a palisaded fort at the mouth of the Niagara river, on the east side.............................. 1687

Francis Stepney, a dancing-master, being forced to leave Boston, comes to New York, but is forbidden to teach...3 June, "

Iroquois appeal to the governor for protection against the French. He supplies them with arms and ammunition, Aug. "

French continue to assert their sovereignty over the Iroquois, "

French governor of Canada makes peace with the Iroquois... 1688

Gov. Dongan required to surrender the government of New York to Andros...22 Apr. "

NEW

French fort at Niagara demolished..........................6 July, 1688

Gov.-gen. Andros reaches New York.......................11 Aug. "

Francis Nicholson lieutenant-governor of New York.......... "

Revolution in England; James II. flees to France; William, prince of Orange, arrives in England..........................Dec. "

William and Mary proclaimed king and queen.........13 Feb. 1689

War declared between England and France..............May, "

Frontenac reappointed governor of Canada...........21 May, "

Jacob Leisler seizes fort James...........................3 June, "

Leisler assumes command of New York.............12 June, "

William and Mary proclaimed in New York..........22 June, "

Lieut.-gov. Nicholson leaves New York for England...24 June, "

Leisler summons a convention..................................June, "

Iroquois ravage the country about Montreal...........5 Aug. "

Leisler commissioned commander-in-chief by the assembly, pending instructions from England..................16 Aug. "

Henry Sloughter appointed governor of New York.....2 Sept. "

Frontenac returns to Quebec from France..................Sept. "

Leisler assumes the title of lieutenant-governor........10 Dec. "

Frontenac organizes 3 expeditions against the English: one against New York, the second against New England, and the third to ravage Maine...............................Jan. 1690

Party of 210, including 80 Indians, advance towards Schenectady and Albany......................................Jan.-Feb. "

They surprise and burn Schenectady, about 16 miles from Albany, then the western frontier post of New York, containing upwards of 40 well-built houses surrounded by a palisade, kill 60 or more people, and carry away many captives; some escape to Albany..8-9 Feb. "

French retreat, and are pursued by the Iroquois.................. "

Colonial congress called at New York by Leisler........2 Apr. "

Expedition against Canada fails.. "

Gov. Sloughter sails for New York..............................1 Dec. "

Leisler refuses to give up the fort at New York to Richard Ingoldsby, gov. Sloughter's deputy............................Jan. 1691

Arrival of gov. Sloughter....................................19 Mch. "

Leisler imprisoned..20 Mch. "

Leisler, Milborne, and others indicted for treason and murder, Apr. "

Eight of the prisoners convicted.............................. " "

Petition for Leisler's pardon. Others demand his execution. Gov. Sloughter signs the death-warrant of Leisler and Milborne ....14 May, "

Leisler and Milborne executed................................16 May, "

Gov. Sloughter d...23 July, "

Richard Ingoldsby acting-governor.............................. " "

Gov. Sloughter succeeded by Benjamin Fletcher.......29 Aug. 1692

Frontenac sends an expedition against the Mohawks...15 Jan. 1693

Peter Schuyler of Albany pursues the French with English and Iroquois; they escape across the upper Hudson on floating cakes of ice...Feb. "

Fort Frontenac rebuilt by the French.................................. 1694

Frontenac prepares a great expedition against the Iroquois; but only destroys 3 villages and some corn.................. 1696

William Kidd, with the *Adventure*, of 30 guns, sails from New York with a crew of 155 men, commissioned as a privateer against the French, and pirates in the Indian ocean...6 Sept. "

[This was something of a "private enterprise." Some noblemen of the English ministry invested 6000*l.* in the undertaking. Kidd and Robert Livingston of New York were to have one fifth of the proceeds.]

Richard Coote, earl of Bellomont, appointed to succeed gov. Fletcher in 1695; not commissioned until 1697, and only reached New York..2 Apr. 1698

John Nanfan, a kinsman of gov. Bellomont, appointed lieutenant-governor.. "

Louis de Buade, count de Frontenac, governor of Canada, d. aged 78..22 Nov. "

Remains of Jacob Leisler and Milborne disinterred by friends and honorably buried in the Dutch church, Garden street... 1699

Gov. Bellomont dies at New York (is buried there)......5 Mch. 1701

Kidd is denounced as a pirate, and returning to New York, and thence to Boston, is there arrested and ultimately sent to England, where he is tried, convicted, and hanged, with 9 accomplices, at Execution dock, London.................24 May, "

William III. of England d.....................................8 Mch. 1702

Queen Anne succeeds.. " "

Lieut.-gov. John Nanfan acts as governor until the arrival of Edward Hyde, lord Cornbury (son of the 2d earl of Clarendon)..3 May, "

Yellow-fever in New York. General assembly at Jamaica, L. I., "

Lord Cornbury prohibits Presbyterians from preaching without his license.. 1707

Lord Cornbury removed; succeeded by lord Lovelace, who arrives at New York..18 Dec. 1708

Slave market established at the foot of Wall street, New York, 1709

Lord Lovelace d...12 May, "

Lieut.-gov. Ingoldsby, acting-governor................................ "

Expedition fitted out against Montreal; failure...................... "

Peter Schuyler takes to England 5 distinguished chiefs of the Iroquois to visit the queen.. 1710

Richard Ingoldsby displaced; Gerardus Beekman acting-governor from...10 Apr. "

Robert Hunter, governor, arrives at New York with 3000 German Lutherans, refugees from the PALATINATE of the Rhine, 14 June, "

Preparations to invade Canada. Nicholson leaves Albany with 4000 men, and a fleet under sir Hovenden Walker sails from Boston with 7000 men and a fine train of artillery, against Quebec and Montreal...30 July, 1711

Fleet loses 8 transports and more than 1000 men on the rocks.

NEW

at the mouth of the St Lawrence and sails for England, the army disbands 17[illegible]

Tuscaroras, a branch of the Iroquois leave North Carolina and join their brethren in New York, near Oneida lake, thus forming the Six Nations 1712

Pretended discovery of a negro insurrection in New York, 19 negroes hung "

Schoharie Flats settled by Germans from the PALATINATE 1713

Peace of Utrecht between England and France 11 Apr "

Queen Anne d, succeeded by George I (elector of Hanover), 1 Aug 1714

Court of Chancery established and confirmed Lewis Morris appointed chief justice of the province 1715

Gov Hunter resigns, Peter Schuyler acting-governor 19 July, 1719

William Burnet, son of bishop Burnet, governor arrives at New York 17 Sept 1720

English establish a trading post at Oswego 1722

William Bradford issues the *New York Gazette*, the first newspaper in the province Oct 1725

Fort Niagara built by the French 1726

George I of England d, George II his son, king 11 June, 1727

Gov Burnet succeeded by John Montgomery 15 Apr 1728

Boundary with Connecticut established May, 1731

Gov Montgomery d 1 July, "

Rip Van Dam acting governor "

Population in the province of New York 50 289 }
" " city " " 8,632 } "
Total number of negroes 7 231 }

William Cosby, governor of New York, arrives 1 Aug 1732

First stage runs between New York and Boston, round trip 28 days. "

John Peter Zenger establishes the *New York Weekly Journal* in the interests of the people 5 Nov 1733

Zenger arrested for libel and imprisoned 35 weeks Nov 1734

Andrew Hamilton of Philadelphia successfully defends Zenger "The magistrates of New York present him with a gold box as a token of their esteem for his noble advocacy of popular rights" July, 1735

Gov Cosby d 10 Mch 1736

George Clarke governor "

Law disfranchising Jews in New York 1738

Capt Norris, of the ship *Tartar* lying in the harbor of New York, applies to the mayor for authority to impress 30 seamen The governor and council order the mayor to assent, but he refuses, and the matter is passed by "

Supposed negro plot to burn New York 13 negroes burned, 20 hung and 70 transported to the West Indies (all probably innocent victims to groundless fear) Mch 1741

Sir George Clinton governor 20 Sept 1743

"War of the AUSTRIAN SUCCESSION" between England and France 1744

French and Indians destroy the village of Saratoga and carry away captive over 100 men, women, and children 28 Nov 1745

Peace between England and France Oct 1748

Theatre established in New York city 1750

First house on the present site of Troy 1752

Gov Clinton resigns 7 Sept 1753

Sir Danvers Osborne governor "

Gov Osborne commits suicide by hanging 12 Sept "

James De Lancey acting-governor "

Convention representing New Hampshire, Massachusetts, Rhode Island, Connecticut, New York, Pennsylvania, and Maryland, at Albany to consider a colonial confederacy 19 June, 1754

[Articles of union drawn by Benjamin Franklin, PENNSYLVANIA.]

King's college (now Columbia), New York city, founded, with rev William Samuel Johnson, D D, first president "

Sir Charles Hardy governor 1755

Fort Edward and fort William Henry built "

Battle of LAKE GEORGE Defeat of the French, and capture of their leader, baron Dieskau 8 Sept. "

[He was severely wounded, not mortally, as often asserted He was exchanged in 1763, and, returning to France, was pensioned.]

Fort Oswego, with 1600 men, 120 cannon, 14 mortars, 2 sloops, and 200 boats and bateaux, surrenders to Montcalm 14 Aug 1756

Montcalm, governor of Canada, besieges fort William Henry at the head of lake George with about 8000 French and 2000 Indians 2 Aug 1757

Col Monroe surrenders with the garrison of nearly 3000 (FORT WILLIAM HENRY) 9 Aug "

James de Lancey governor, sir Charles Hardy goes to England, "

Gen Abercrombie attacks FORT TICONDEROGA and is repulsed, 8 July, 1758

Fort Frontenac surrenders to the English under col John Bradstreet 27 Aug "

Fort Stanwix built (FORT SCHUYLER) "

English under gen. John Prideaux besiege fort Niagara, gen Prideaux killed 20 July, 1759

French surrender the fort 25 July, "

Battle of Quebec, gen Wolfe killed 13 Sept. "

Surrender of Quebec. 18 Sept "

Gov De Lancey d. 30 July, 1760

Cadwallader Colden acting governor " "

Capitulation of M de Vaudreuil at Montreal and the entire reduction of Canada 8 Sept. "

Death of George II, George III succeeds 25 Oct. "

Robert Monckton governor Nov 1761

Takes command of an expedition against Martinique, and leaves the government to Cadwallader Colden. "

New York claims jurisdiction over the present state of Vermont, hence a controversy with New Hampshire 1762

Sir Henry Moore, governor, arrives 1765

Sons of Liberty organized in New York "

Colonial convention in New York to consider the Stamp act 7 Oct "

[Colonies represented were Massachusetts, Rhode Island, Connecticut, New York New Jersey, Pennsylvania Delaware, Maryland, and South Carolina Virginia, North Carolina, and Georgia were prevented from sending delegates by their governors]

Stamp act to go into operation, causes great disturbance in New York 1 Nov "

Repeal of the Stamp act 18 Mch 1766

English treaty with the Iroquois Delawares, Shawnees, and Mingoes at fort Stanwix (KENTUCKY, PENNSYLVANIA) 5 Nov 1768

Sir Henry Moore dies, Cadwallader Colden again acting governor 1 Sept 1769

Boundary settled between New York and New Jersey "

Liberty pole in New York city cut down by British soldiers, 13 Jan 1770

John, lord Dunmore governor "

Gov Dunmore transferred to Virginia, William Tryon last royal governor of New York 1771

Line of jurisdiction between New York and Massachusetts settled 1773

Gov Tryon gives 10,000 acres of land to King's college, and founds a chair of law 1774

New York publishes a Declaration of Rights 23 May, "

Sir William Johnson dies at Albany, aged 60 11 July, "

Delegates chosen to 1st CONTINENTAL CONGRESS 25 July, "

Provincial convention in New York, delegates to the Continental Congress appointed 22 Apr 1775

FORT TICONDEROGA surprised and taken by Ethan Allen and Benedict Arnold with 80 men 10 May, "

CROWN POINT surrenders 12 May, "

Benedict Arnold captures St Johns, Canada 16 May, "

First Provincial congress in New York, Nathaniel Woodhull, president appoints a Committee of Safety 22 May "

[Gen Woodhull was wounded and captured at the battle of Long Island 30 Aug 1776 and died a few days afterwards]

Gen Tryon retires to the *Asia*, an armed English ship in the harbor of New York "

City and county of New York ask advice from Congress how to deal with the British troops expected in the city, and the military stores captured at Ticonderoga May, "

Richard Montgomery commissioned brigadier general by Congress 22 June, "

Congress orders capt. Lamb to remove the cannon from the fort at New York to the highlands, 24 pieces secured, 23 Aug "

[English ship *Asia*, lying in the harbor, attempted in vain to prevent this Alexander Hamilton, then a student in King's (Columbia) college assisted in securing the cannon]

Col Ethan Allen taken prisoner with 38 men by the British near Montreal 25 Sept "

Montreal captured by gen Richard Montgomery 13 Nov "

Gen Montgomery attempts the capture of Quebec, he is killed and the Americans repulsed 31 Dec. "

On the news of the Declaration of Independence, the leaden statue of the King of England in New York is made into 42 000 bullets 6 July, 1776

Northern army falls back from Crown Point to Ticonderoga, 7 July, "

New York Provincial congress at White Plains sanctions the Declaration of Independence, making the 13 colonies unanimous (DECLARATION OF INDEPENDENCE) 9 July, "

[This congress meets 4 times up to 9 July, 1776 when it takes the name Convention of the Representatives of the state of New York, meeting at Kingston]

One sloop, 3 schooners, and 5 smaller boats, carrying 58 guns and 86 swivels built at Whitehall by the Americans to control lake Champlain, manned by about 400 men 22 Aug "

Lord Howe lands 10,000 men and 40 guns near Gravesend, L. I, 22 Aug "

Americans under gen Sullivan defeated by gen Howe and gens. Sullivan and Sterling taken prisoners, battle of Long Island 27 Aug "

[Gen Howe was decorated with the order of the Bath for this success by the British government]

Gen Washington withdraws his forces to the city of New York from Long Island night of 29th and morning of 30 Aug "

British use condemned hulks moored in Wallabout bay as prison ships, it is estimated that 11,400 American prisoners died in them during 8 years beginning "

New York city evacuated, occupied by the British 14 Sept. "

Battle of Harlem Heights, British repulsed 16 Sept. "

Nathan Hale executed as a spy at New York by command of gen Howe (HALE) 22 Sept. "

Fleet on lake Champlain under Benedict Arnold meets a vastly superior British armament under capt. Pringle, and is defeated with a loss of about 90 men 11-13 Oct. "

Battle of White Plains, Americans driven back 28 Oct. "

Washington crosses the Hudson 12 Nov "

Fort Washington on the Hudson captured by the British, with 2000 prisoners and artillery 16 Nov "

Fort Lee, opposite fort Washington on the Hudson, evacuated by the Americans under gen Greene 18 Nov "

New York convention adopts a constitution 6 Mch -13 May, 1777

[It made the governor elective and remained in force 45 years.]

Gen Burgoyne with 7173 British and German troops, besides

NEW

several thousand Canadians and Indians, appears before Ticonderoga..1 July, 1777

George Clinton elected governor......................3 July, "

John Jay appointed chief-justice and Robert R. Livingston chancellor.. "

Garrison under gen. St. Clair abandon Ticonderoga, and retreat through Vermont (HUBBARDTON)....................6 July, "

Murder of Jane McCrea by the Indians near fort Edward (see Lossing's "Field Book of the Revolution," vol. i. pp. 98, 99), 27 July, "

Gen. St. Clair joins gen. Schuyler at fort Edward, which is abandoned, and the Americans retire across the Hudson to Saratoga, and thence to Stillwater; Burgoyne reaches the Hudson...29 July, "

St. Leger, co-operating with Burgoyne, advances from Montreal with a large force of Canadians and Indians; invests fort Stanwix (Schuyler)..............................3 Aug. "

Gen. Herkimer, with about 800 men, advances to the relief of fort Stanwix; when within 6 miles of the fort, falls into an ambuscade at Oriskany, is mortally wounded, but repulses the enemy with aid from the fort under col. Willett..6 Aug. "

Two detachments of British and Indians from Burgoyne's army, numbering about 500 men each, under cols. Baume and Breyman, defeated by gen. John Stark near Hoosick, N. Y., 5 miles from BENNINGTON...................16 Aug. "

Gen. Philip Schuyler superseded in command of the northern army by gen. Horatio Gates......................22 Aug. "

A detachment of Americans under gen. Sullivan lands on Staten Island, surprises 2 regiments of Tories, and captures many prisoners..22 Aug. "

St. Leger retreats from fort Stanwix to Montreal, losing most of his baggage and stores, before gen. Arnold, sent with 3 regiments by gen. Schuyler to relieve fort Stanwix..22 Aug. "

Gen. Gates encamps at Stillwater.........................8 Sept. "

Gen. Burgoyne encamps at Saratoga...................14 Sept. "

Battle of Stillwater; both armies claim the victory, but the Americans had greatly the advantage (BEMIS'S HEIGHTS), 19 Sept. "

Forts Clinton and Montgomery, on the Hudson, taken by sir Henry Clinton (CLINTON and MONTGOMERY FORTS).....6 Oct. "

Battle of Saratoga; British defeated (BEMIS'S HEIGHTS)..7 Oct. "

Surrender of the army under gen. Burgoyne...........17 Oct. "

[Total number surrendered, 5642 (CONVENTION TROOPS); previous losses about 4000.]

Lieut.-col. Baylor's troop of horse (unarmed) surprised and mostly killed and wounded (67 out of 104) by a party of British under Grey, near old Tappan, on the night of 27 Sept. 1778

Schoharie ravaged by Indians and Tories..............16 Oct. "

CHERRY VALLEY ravaged by Indians and Tories....11-12 Nov. "

Settlement at Elmira.. "

Sir Henry Clinton captures Verplanck's and Stony Point, June, 1779

STONY POINT surprised and captured, with 500 prisoners, by gen. Anthony Wayne.............................16 July, "

Gen. Sullivan leaves the Wyoming valley with a force of 3000 men, 31 July, on an expedition against the Six Nations. He is joined at Tioga Point, 22 Aug., by gen. James Clinton, with 1600 men. They attack and disperse a body of Indians and Tories at Chemung (now Elmira)....................29 Aug. "

[In the course of 3 weeks the troops destroy 40 Indian villages and extensive fields of grain.]

Verplanck's and Stony Point evacuated by the British....Oct. "

Command in the Highlands of the Hudson, with the works at West Point, is given to gen. Benedict Arnold........3 Aug. 1780

Major John André, adjutant-general of the British army, lands from the British sloop of war *Vulture*, a little below Stony Point, and meets gen. Arnold on the night of........21 Sept. "

Attempting to return to New York, he is captured by 3 soldiers, John Paulding, David Williams, and Isaac Van Wart, near Tarrytown...................................23 Sept. "

Arnold, hearing of the capture of André, escapes to the *Vulture*..24 Sept. "

[Arnold received from the British government 10,000*l.* and commission of brigadier-general.]

A military board, gen. Nathaniel Greene president, convict André as a spy.................................29 Sept. "

Gen. Washington approves the finding of the board...30 Sept. "

Major André hung at Tappan at 12 o'clock noon, and buried there..2 Oct. "

[André's remains were disinterred Aug. 10, 1821, and taken to England and placed in a vault in Westminster abbey, 28 Nov. 1821. See 1879 of this record for monument.]

Ann Lee, founder of the Shakers, coming from England, settles with a body of that sect near Albany, 1774, and establishes a community of them at New Lebanon (SHAKERS)............ "

William Alexander (lord STIRLING), major-general in the American army, dies at Albany, aged 57..................15 Jan. 1783

Order of the Cincinnati founded by the officers of the army encamped on the Hudson (CINCINNATI, ORDER OF)......13 May, "

Treaty of peace with Great Britain signed at Paris.....3 Sept. "

British evacuate New York city........................25 Nov. "

Long Island and Staten Island evacuated by the British, who embark...4 Dec. "

Gen. Washington bids farewell to his officers at Fraunce's tavern, New York...4 Dec. "

University of the State of New York is established by an act of the legislature...................................1 May, 1784

[Governing body of the university is a board of regents, chosen by the legislature and holding office, without pay, for life, under certain restrictions. An annual meeting of the board is held the second Thursday of Jan.; the semi-annual meeting is held on the first Tuesday of July.]

Town of Hudson settled by Seth and Thomas Jenkins, from Providence, R. I.. 1784

Hugh White, from Middletown, Conn., the first settler at Whitestown, Oneida county.. "

Continental Congress meets in New York..............11 Jan. 1785

Population of the state, 238,897.............................. 1786

Dispute between Massachusetts and New York about lands, settled by commissioners appointed by the 2 states......... 1787

[A pre-emption title to certain territory in New York was claimed by Massachusetts under its colonial charter, which extended to the Pacific. The charter of New York interfering with this claim, the differences were settled by commissioners: New York retained the sovereignty and jurisdiction of the territory in dispute, and Massachusetts the property of the soil. See 1773.]

Samuel Prevost, rector of Trinity church, consecrated bishop at Lambeth palace, Engl., for the state.................... "

Columbia college incorporated.................................. "

Oliver Phelps, of Granville, Mass., explores the wilderness from the German Flats to the present site of Canandaigua....... "

Binghamton settled by William Bingham from Philadelphia.. "

Syracuse settled.. "

New York accepts the Constitution of the U. S., with amendments..25 July, "

First number of the *Federalist* appears in New York...27 Oct. "

"Doctors' mob," caused by the discovery of human remains for dissection in the hospital in New York city...13-14 Apr. 1788

Oliver Phelps and Nathaniel Gorham purchase of the Six Nations 2,500,000 acres—part of the land already granted them by Massachusetts—in western New York (see 1787). The leading chiefs were Farmer's Brother and Red Jacket...... "

Ebenezer Allen erects a mill where Rochester now stands.... "

First house built in Canandaigua.............................. "

New York ratifies the Constitution of the U. S........26 July, "

Congress meets in New York, in the old City Hall, corner of Wall and Nassau streets, opposite Broad; only 8 senators and 13 representatives present.......................4 Mch. 1789

House obtains quorum and organizes...................30 Mch. "

[Frederic A. Muhlenburg speaker.]

Senate having a quorum, organizes.....................6 Apr. "

[John Langdon, N. H., chosen to preside at the counting of votes for president. All the 69 votes were cast for Washington, and 34 for John Adams, who became vice-president.]

John Adams takes the chair of the Senate...............21 Apr. "

Washington arrives at Elizabeth Point, and is escorted to New York by a committee from both houses in a barge rowed by 13 pilots dressed in white..........................23 Apr. "

[His progress from Mount Vernon had been a continuous triumphal procession.]

Oath of office taken by Washington....................30 Apr. "

[Oath was administered by chancellor Livingston in the balcony of the City Hall.]

First recorded party contest in New York state; votes polled, 12,453.. "

Oliver Phelps opens in Canandaigua the first private land office in America, for the sale of forest land to settlers (LAND).... "

U. S. buys of Stephen Moore the site of West Point........... 1790

[It purchased the tract adjoining in 1824, and in 1826 New York ceded jurisdiction over it to the U. S.]

Population of the state...............340,120 }
Rank among the states......................5th } .... "
Population to the sq. mile.....................7.1 }

11th, 12th, 13th, and 14th sessions of the Continental Congress met in New York city—that is, from 11 Jan. 1785 to 21 Oct. 1788. Also the 1st and 2d sessions of the first Congress under the Constitution.................4 Mch. 1789-12 Aug. "

Phelps & Gorham sell to Robert Morris 1,204,000 acres of their Massachusetts purchase in western New York for 8*d.* an acre, "

Boundary between New York and Vermont established....... "

Geneseo settled by William and James Wadsworth from Connecticut.. "

Congress leaves New York city and meets in Philadelphia, Dec. "

Part of Vermont formed Cumberland and Gloucester counties in New York till.. 1791

Society for the promotion of agriculture, arts, and manufactures established at New York................................. "

Hamilton Oneida academy established......................... 1793

Auburn first settled by col. Hardenbergh....................... "

Paper mill erected at Troy, which makes from 4 to 5 reams of paper daily.. "

French privateer fitted out in New York is seized by militia by order of gov. Clinton...............................14 June, "

Frederick William Augustus, baron Steuben, major-general in the Revolutionary army, d. at Steubenville, Oneida county, 28 Nov. 1794

Union college incorporated at Schenectady.................... 1795

George Clinton, after 18 years' service, declines re-election as governor, and is succeeded by John Jay...................... "

Legislature appropriates $50,000 for public schools........... "

Sloop *Detroit* the first American vessel on lake Erie........ 1796

Massachusetts deeds to Robert Morris of Philadelphia nearly 3,300,000 acres of land in western New York (see 1787), 11 May, "

[Robert Morris, b. Engl. 1733, d. Philadelphia, 1806, was a delegate to the Continental Congress, 1776-78, and signer of Declaration of Independence. He greatly assisted the government financially during the Revolution, but in his old age embarked in vast land speculations which proved ruinous to his fortunes. He passed his latter days in prison for debt.—*Drake*, "Dict. of Amer. Biog."]

He extinguishes the Indian title, sells several tracts from the

east side along the Genesee river, and mortgages the residue to Wilhelm Willink and others of Amsterdam, Holland, called the Holland Land company 1796
[By this purchase the Holland Land company acquired the present counties of Niagara, Erie Chautauqua, Cattaraugus, Wyoming, except some small reservations and most of the counties of Alleghany, Genesee, and Orleans]
State road from Whitestown to Geneva built "
Forts Oswegatchie (now Ogdensburg) Oswego, and Niagara evacuated by the British "
John Fitch moves a small boat on Collect pond in New York city by a small steam engine and a "worm screw" projecting from the stern of the boat "
Albany becomes the permanent capital of the state at the 20th session of the legislature 1797
Shakers at Watervliet begin the manufacture of brooms, sold at 50 cts each 1798
Legislature grants to chancellor Livingston an exclusive right to navigate the inland waters of the state by vessels propelled by fire or steam "
New York appropriates $1,200,000 to defend her harbor against France "
Washington nominates Alexander Hamilton as first in rank of major generals in the Provisional army "
Road cut from the Genesee to Buffalo and Lewiston "
Legislature enacts the gradual abolition of slavery Apr 1799

Population of the state	589,051	1800
Rank among the states	3d	
Population to the sq mile	12 4	
Per cent of increase	73 1	

George Clinton again elected governor 1801
Democrats predominant, led by col Aaron Burr, the Clintons, and Livingstons "
Buffalo laid out by the Holland Land company, who open an office at Batavia Joseph Ellicott agent, for the sale of land "
Academy of fine arts founded at New York city "
Duel between col John Swartwout and De Witt Clinton 5 shots exchanged, Swartwout slightly wounded 1802
Military academy established at West Point by Congress "
Gen Joseph G Swift first graduate. 12 Oct. "
Burr's Democratic friends resolve to support him for governor against any regular nominee He is formally nominated at Albany, a meeting held at New York city ratifies it 1804
Morgan Lewis elected as the regular Democratic candidate "
Burr proposed as Federalist candidate in coalition with his faction, the plan defeated by Alexander Hamilton "
This opposition of Hamilton to Burr culminates in a duel at Hoboken in which Burr kills Hamilton 11 July, "
New York Historical Society founded "
Philip Schuyler dies at Albany, aged 73 18 Nov "
Legislature appropriates the proceeds of the remaining state lands, over a million acres, for the school fund 1805
Corner stone of the old state capitol laid at Albany 23 Apr 1806
Robert Fulton's steamboat, the *Clermont*, makes first trip, New York to Albany, average speed, 5 miles an hour 7 Aug 1807
Daniel D Tompkins elected governor
First carding and cloth dressing establishment erected on the Holland purchase at Batavia by William H Bush 1808
James Geddes of Onondaga surveys a route for a canal from lake Erie to the Hudson river, and reports it practicable 1808-9
First house built in Rochester 1810

Population of the state	959,049	"
Rank among the states	2d	
Population to the sq mile	20 1	
Per cent of increase	62 8	

A commission appointed to inquire into the practicability of a canal from lake Erie to the Hudson explores the whole route, "
It reports in favor of the canal, estimated cost, $5,000,000 1811
West Point reorganized and made efficient 1812
Hamilton college, at Clinton, Oneida county, established "
"Detached militia" of New York arranged by the War department in 2 divisions and 8 brigades 21 Apr "
War declared against Great Britain by the U S 20 June, "
[British forts near the state were Fort Erie, opposite Buffalo, with a small garrison, a small stockade at Chippewa, a little above Niagara falls, and a small earthwork, fort George, near the mouth of the Niagara river, while at York (now Toronto) there was an old fort and block house, and near Kingston, formerly fort Frontenac, was a small battery]
Stephen Van Rensselaer (the patroon) of Albany commissioned major general and assigned to the 1st division, and Benjamin Mooers of Plattsburg to the 2d "
British attack Sackett's Harbor and are repulsed 29 July, "
Lieut J D Elliott captures the *Caledonia* and *Detroit*, British vessels anchored near fort Erie, opposite Buffalo 8 Oct "
[Congress votes lieut. Elliott a sword for this exploit]
Battle of Queenstown, Upper Canada, and death of sir Isaac Brock, governor of Upper Canada 12-13 Oct. "
[The Americans, at first successful, are finally beaten]
Albany *Argus* started in Albany, Jesse Buel editor 13 Jan 1813
Ogdensburg attacked and captured by the British 22 Feb "
York (now Toronto) taken by the Americans, gen. Pike killed, 27 Apr "
Fort George, Canada, at the mouth of the Niagara river, evacuated by the British 27 May, "
Fort Erie captured by the Americans 28 May, "
British repulsed at Sackett's Harbor 29 May, "
Perry's victory on lake Erie (Naval battles) 10 Sept "
Burning of the village of Newark, Canada, near fort George, by the Americans under gen McClure, who was severely censured, and fort George evacuated 10 Dec "

British capture fort Niagara 19 Dec. 1813
They burn Buffalo and Black Rock (Buffalo) 30 Dec "
Fort Ontario at Oswego captured by the British (Fort Ontario) 5-6 May, 1814
Fort Erie occupied by the Americans 3 July, "
Battle of Chippewa Canada Americans victorious 5 July, "
Battle of Bridgewater, or Lundy's Lane, Canada one of the most destructive of the war The Americans 2600 strong lose 858 men killed and wounded, and the British (4500) lose about 20 more, fought from 8 P M to midnight 25 July, "
[Here gen Winfield Scott greatly distinguished himself]
Fort Erie besieged by the British 4 Aug "
Col Drummond assaults the works and is repulsed 15 Aug "
Com McDonough defeats British fleet on lake Champlain at Plattsburg, under com Downie (Naval battles) 11 Sept "
Gen Macomb with about 6000 men, defeats 12,000 British under sir George Provost, at Plattsburg 11 Sept "
Americans make a successful sortie at fort Erie and destroy the British works 17 Sept "
British raise the siege after 50 days 21 Sept "
Americans, under gen Izard, abandon fort Erie and blow it up, 5 Nov "
Treaty of peace ratified and promulgated 17 Feb 1815
Robert Fulton dies in New York city 24 Feb "
General disappearance of the Federal party 1815-17
[The 2 political parties of the nation up to this period were the Federal and Republican, afterwards called Democratic Virtually but one party remained after the collapse of the Federalists until the Whig party was formed Political parties]
De Witt Clinton elected governor to succeed gov Tompkins, chosen vice president of the U S 1817
Legislature abolishes slavery from 4 July, 1827 Apr "
Erie canal begun at Rome Oneida county 4 July, "
State grants $20 000 to county agricultural societies to promote agriculture and family domestic manufactures "
First paper mill west of the Genesee river built by William H Bush at Batavia "
State library founded at Albany 21 Apr 1818
[It is open daily for the use of the public]
First steamboat, *Walk in the water*, on lake Erie "
[360 tons, built at Black Rock, a suburb of Buffalo Her engine and boiler were made in New York She was lost in a gale in 1821]
Hamilton Theological seminary, Madison county, incorporated, 1819
[The oldest American Baptist divinity school]
Steamship *Savannah*, 380 tons, capt Moses Rodgers, sails from New York, where she was built, for Savannah, Ga 10 Apr "
[Arriving there 17 Apr she sails from that port 24 May for St Petersburg, Russia, *via* Liverpool, reaches L. 20 June, sails for St P 23 July, return to Savannah 50 days from St P Dec 1819, first Amer steamship to cross the Atlantic]

Population of the state	1,372,111	1820
Rank among the states	1st	
Population to the sq mile.	28 8	
Per cent. of increase	43	

[From this time the state has been styled the "Empire State"]
Lockport, Niagara county, settled 1821
Revised state constitution adopted and ratified Feb. 1822
Joseph C Yates governor "
Champlain canal begun 1816, finished 1823
De Witt Clinton elected governor 1824
Lafayette lands in New York city (United States) 15 Aug "
New State prison commenced at Sing Sing 1825
Geneva college, Geneva, Ontario county, incorporated "
[Name changed to Hobart college, 27 Mch 1860]
Daniel D Tompkins, b 1774, d on Staten Island 11 June, "
[Governor 1807-17, vice president 1817-25]
Erie canal completed 26 Oct "
[Tidings of the opening conveyed from Buffalo to New York in 80 minutes by firing relays of cannon]
First boat, *Seneca Chief*, conveying the governor and others, passes from lake Erie to the Hudson, and reaches New York city Grand celebration 4 Nov "
[The Erie canal was 8 years in building As originally built, it was 40 ft wide at the top, 28 ft. wide at the bottom, and 4 ft deep, and 352 miles in length, cost, $9,027,456. The legislature, in 1835, ordered its enlargement to 70 ft wide at the top, 42 ft wide at the bottom, and 7 ft. deep, at a cost of about $25,000,000 Canals]
Delaware and Hudson canal commenced 1826
Abduction of William Morgan from Canandaigua (Morgan, William) 12 Sept "
Thurlow Weed edits the *Anti Masonic Enquirer*, at Rochester, N Y 1826-27
Owing to Morgan's abduction, a county convention at Le Roy, Genesee county, begins the anti-Masonic movement 1827
Journal of Commerce started in New York city "
Gov De Witt Clinton d suddenly at Albany, aged 59 11 Feb 1828
Nathaniel Pitcher acting governor "
Oswego canal finished "
Martin Van Buren elected governor, resigns 12 Mch 1829
Enos T Throop acting governor "
Manufacture of brick by machinery successfully begun in New York "
John Jay dies at Bedford, Westchester county 17 May, "
[No one of the great men of the Revolution approached so near Washington in lofty disinterestedness as John Jay — *Hildreth*]
Sam Patch jumps from the Genesee falls at Rochester and is killed "

Albany *Evening Journal* started, edited by Thurlow Weed 1830
First omnibus built and used in New York city "
Book of Mormon first published by E B Grandin at Palmyra (MORMONS) "
[Real author was rev Solomon Spaulding Ohio]
Population of the state 1 918,608 }
Rank among the states 1st }
Population to the square mile 40 3 } "
Per cent of increase 39 8 }
University of the City of New York opened "
First locomotive engine, "The Best Friend," built in the U S, finished at West Point foundery, New York city, and tested, 9 Dec "
[For the South Carolina railroad.]
Albany and Schenectady railroad opened 16 miles 1831
[Second locomotive built in the U S was for this road, the "De Witt Clinton" built in New York city]
Chloroform first obtained by Samuel Guthrie of Sackett's Harbor, "
[About the same time made by Liebig in Germany and Souberein in France First used as an anæsthetic, 1844]
Imprisonment for contract debt, except for fraud, abolished "
Whig party formed 1832
[Name suggested by James Watson Webb of the New York *Courier and Enquirer* — 'Empire State," *Lossing*]
Cholera in New York city, 27 June until 19 Oct, 4000 die "
Buffalo and Utica incorporated as cities "
First horse street railroad in the world opened in Fourth ave, New York city "
Red Jacket, the Indian chief dies near Buffalo, aged 78, 20 Jan "
Anti slavery society of New York organized 2 Oct 1833
William L Marcy governor "
Riot in New York against the abolitionists 1834
A geological survey of the state ordered 1836
Union Theological seminary in New York city founded "
Schenectady and Utica railroad opened "
Aaron Burr dies in New York aged 80 14 Sept. "
Legislature appropriates $200,000 a year for 3 years to form township and district libraries (one of the best appropriations ever made of public funds for educational purposes, aside from public schools) 1837
American and Foreign Bible Society established in New York, "
Patriot war—Canada. "
Navy island in Niagara river occupied by the "Patriots," Dec. "
Steamer *Caroline*, at Schlosser's landing, on the American side of Niagara river, is fired and sent over the falls by Canadian soldiers under col. McNab night of 29 Dec. "
Auburn and Syracuse railroad opened .. "
William H Seward, Whig, elected governor over William L Marcy, Democrat 1838
Rutgers female institute, New York city, opened. 11 Apr "
[Name changed to college, 1867]
Free banking law passed "
Steamboat *Lexington* burned in Long Island sound 13 Jan 1840
First state prison library in the U S started at Sing Sing "
Population of the state 2,428,921 }
Rank among the states 1st }
Population to the square mile 51 } "
Per cent of increase 26 5 }
Railroad completed from Boston to Albany 1841
Steam packet *President* sails for Liverpool (never heard from), 11 Mch. "
First Washington Temperance meeting in New York 24 Mch. "
Steamboat *Erie* burned on lake Erie, 180 perish 9 Aug. "
Auburn and Rochester railroad opened "
Croton aqueduct finished, 5 years in construction, cost, $12,500,000, length, 40½ miles (CROTON AQUEDUCT) 1842
Attica and Buffalo railroad opened. "
William C. Bouck governor .. . 1843
Armed resistance begun by anti renters in Albany, Delaware, and Rensselaer counties 1844
[Tenants of the patroon refuse to pay rent. ANTI-RENTISM.]
State Normal school established at Albany . "
Silas Wright, jr, governor . . 1 Jan 1845
Steamer *Swallow* capt Squires, from New York to Albany, strikes a rock near Athens, many passengers drowned, 7 Apr "
Gov Silas Wright proclaims Delaware county in a state of insurrection on account of anti-rentism 27 Aug. "
Packer Collegiate Institute, Brooklyn, L. I., opened . "
Madison university at Hamilton, Madison county, chartered, 26 May, 1846
[Hamilton Literary and Theological seminary, at the same place, established in 1819, is included in this charter]
State constitution revised and adopted . Nov "
ONEIDA COMMUNITY established .. 1847
Meeting at Seneca Falls to advocate political equality of women . . 1848
Hamilton Fish elected governor by the Whigs. . . "
"Spirit rappings" phenomena begun in the house of John D Fox, Hydersville, and afterwards in Rochester on his removal there the same year (SPIRITUALISM) . . .. "
Continuous railroad, Boston to New York opened.. . 1 Jan. 1849
Population of the state. 3,097,394 }
Rank among the states . 1st }
Population to the sq mile.. . 65 } . 1850
Per cent of increase. . . 27 5 }
University of Rochester, at Rochester, chartered . . 8 May, "
Arctic expedition in search of sir John Franklin sails from New York under lieut. De Haven and dr Elisha Kent Kane, 24 May, "
Collins line of steamships begin between New York and Liverpool—an American line .. .. "
Washington Hunt elected governor by the Whigs, with a majority of 262 over Horatio Seymour, Democrat. . 1850
Erie railroad complete, Piermont on the Hudson to lake Erie. A train goes over the road with the directors 28–29 Apr 1851
Hudson River railroad opened "
James Fenimore Cooper, b 1789, d at Cooperstown, N Y, 14 Sept "
Whig party disappears from state and national politics after 1852
Second Arctic expedition in search of sir John Franklin sails from New York under dr Kane. Funds mostly furnished by Henry Grinnell, of New York, and George Peabody Grinnell land discovered 30 May, 1853
New York Clearing house established. . "
District libraries of the state have 1,604,210 volumes "
[This number was reduced more than one-half through carelessness and loss up to 1890]
New York Central railroad formed by consolidating the local railroads . "
Continuous line of railway opened, New York to Chicago "
First train over a uniform gauge from Buffalo to Erie and Chicago 1 Feb 1854
Office of the State Superintendent of Public Instruction created by a law of 30 Mch "
First kerosene oil factory in the U S established on Newtown creek, Long Island. June, "
[Name kerosene originated by Abraham Gesner, who made oil from coal on Prince Edward isle in 1846]
Brooklyn Collegiate and Polytechnic institute, non sectarian, chartered . "
Railway suspension bridge at Niagara falls completed 1855
Charter of the Elmira female college "
[First charter granted by the state for a female college.]
Last survivor of Washington's Life guard, sergeant Uzel Knapp, dies aged 97, at New Windsor, Orange county (LIFE GUARD, Washington's) 11 Jan 1856
St Lawrence university, Canton, St Lawrence county, incorporated 3 Apr "
Dudley observatory built at Albany "
Alfred university, at Alfred, opened . 1857
Ingham university, at Le Roy, Genesee county, incorporated, 3 Apr "
Failure of the Ohio Life and Trust company in New York, a commercial panic spreads throughout the U S 24 Aug "
First telegraphic despatch received in New York from London by the Atlantic telegraph (ELECTRICITY, submarine) 5 Aug 1858
[First messages were the only intelligible ones received]
Edwin D Morgan, Republican elected governor "
M Blondin (Émile Gravelet) crosses the Niagara river, just below the falls, for the first time on a tight-rope 30 June, 1859
Washington Irving, b. New York city, 1783, d at Tarrytown, N Y . . 28 Nov "
Population of the state . 3,880,735 }
Rank among the states 1st }
Population to the square mile 81 3 } . 1860
Per cent. of increase 25 2 }
William H Seward before the Republican convention at Chicago as a candidate for the presidency . .. . "
St. Stephen's college, Annandale, Dutchess county, Prot.-Epis.; date of charter . . . "
Erie canal enlargement completed, entire cost, $52 491,915.74. 1862
Manhattan college at Manhattanville, New York city, incorporated by the regents . .. . 2 Apr 1863
"Peace Meeting" held in New York city, called by leading Democrats to devise means for ending the civil war, 3 June, "
Clement C Moore, b. in New York, 1779, d. at Newport, R. I., 10 July, "
[Author of the ballad, "'Twas the night before Christmas."]
DRAFT RIOTS in New York city . 13-16 July, "
[About 1000 killed Claims for damages amounting to $1,500,000 presented]
Normal school at Oswego established . "
Number of troops furnished by the state in the civil war in all branches of the service reduced to a 3 years' standard was 392 270, about 12 per cent of the population . .. 1865
Eliphalet Nott, b 1773, d. at Schenectady . 29 Jan 1866
[Made president of Union college in 1804 Over 3700 students graduated during his presidency]
Fenian raid into Canada, about 1200 men cross Niagara river near Buffalo, camping near old fort Erie . . .. . 31 May, "
Slight conflict takes place near Ridgeway . . . 2 June, "
[Force withdraws the next evening.]
Vassar female college at Poughkeepsie incorporated, 11 Jan 1861, name changed by legislature to Vassar college .1 Feb. 1867
[Founded by Matthew Vassar]
Normal school at Brockport established .. . . "
Public schools made entirely free . . . . 1 Oct. "
State Board of Charities organized . .. . "
Memorial or Decoration day made a legal holiday, date of first celebration. .. . .30 May, 1868
Wells college, Aurora, N Y, founded.. .... "
Normal school at Fredonia established .. . . "
Commission of Fisheries created by an act passed .... "
Cornell university at Ithaca opened to students . Oct. "
[Founded by Ezra Cornell in 1865]
Normal school at Potsdam, St Lawrence county, established. 1869
Normal school at Cortland opened .... "
Henry Jarvis Raymond, journalist, b. Lima, Livingston county, N Y, 24 Jan. 1820, d. in New York city.. .. 18 June, "
[He started the New York *Times* in 1851]
Financial panic in New York city culminates in "Black Friday," the price of gold reaches 162½ .... 24 Sept. "

[During the excitement it is estimated that contracts were made for the sale of $500 000 000 of gold The crisis ruined thousands, and disarranged the business of the country]

Cardiff giant discovered on the farm of Wm C. Newell, near Cardiff, Onondaga county 16 Oct. 1869

[The originator of this successful hoax was George Hull of Binghamton, who, after maturing his plan, went to Iowa in 1868 and quarried near fort Dodge, the block of gypsum out of which at Chicago the giant was made Securely boxed it was shipped to Binghamton by rail and thence to Cardiff and secretly buried, 9 Nov 1868, on the farm of Newell at the bottom of a partly dug well, here it was found by some workmen employed a year later to finish the well When found it had cost Hull $2600 It gave rise to much controversy, and proved a financial success to its owners]

Population of the state	4 382,759	1870
Rank among the states	1st	
Population to the sq mile	92	
Per cent of increase	12 9	

Lenox Public library, New York city incorporated 20 June, "

[Endowed by James Lenox with his private library, which in American history and certain other departments is unrivalled Library of George Bancroft, consisting of 15,000 bound volumes and 5000 pamphlets, purchased Apr 1893, for $80,000]

Corner stone of the new capitol at Albany laid 24 June, 1871

Syracuse university (Meth Epis) founded at Syracuse "

Capt Hall sails from New York in the U S ship *Polaris*, on an Arctic exploring expedition (NORTHEAST AND NORTHWEST PASSAGES) 29 June, "

Normal school opened at Geneseo "

Normal school opened at Buffalo "

William M Tweed arrested in New York city 27 Oct. "

[His bail bond was fixed at $2,000,000]

Legislature establishes a commission of state parks 23 May, 1872

Topographical survey of the Adirondack wilderness begun by the state under the supervision of Verplanck Colvin "

Susan B Anthony and some other women vote at Rochester (WOMEN, ADVANCEMENT OF) 5 Nov "

Horace Greeley d 29 Nov "

One hundred and nine short horn cattle sold at a public sale at New York Mills, N Y , for about $382,000 10 Sept 1873

[Highest price paid was for a cow, $4600, and $2700 for a calf 5 months old]

Commercial panic beginning in the Stock exchange of New York spreads throughout the country 19 Sept "

International Railway Bridge crossing Niagara river at Black Rock (Buffalo) to Canada, built under authority of Congress and the British Parliament and the state and province governments at a cost of over $1,500 000 Total length 3651½ ft , over the river proper 1967½ ft Began 1870, opened 31 Oct "

Tweed sentenced to 12 years in the penitentiary 22 Nov "

[He is discharged, but is rearrested, and escapes 4 Dec. 1875 He goes to Spain, is there arrested at Vigo, and brought back, 24 Nov 1876 He dies in prison, 12 Apr 1878.]

Compulsory educational law passed 15 Apr 1874

Term of the governor changed from 2 years to 3 "

New York State Soldier s Home incorporated at Bath 15 May, 1876

Hallett's Point reef, "Hell Gate," successfully blown up, work directed by gen John Newton, U S army, from the beginning, 1869 The excavations were completed in 1875, but for want of an appropriation the reef was not destroyed until 24 Sept. "

Cornelius Vanderbilt d at New York 4 Jan 1877

Rock salt first discovered in the state by Charles B Everest, 4 miles from Warsaw, Wyoming county, while boring for oil at a depth of 1279 feet, strata of salt 70 feet thick 20 June, 1878

William Cullen Bryant, b 1794, d New York city "

[Editor of the *Evening Post*, 1826]

Cyrus W Field erects a monument in memory of maj John André on the site of his grave at Tappan 1879

[This monument was badly damaged by attempts to blow it up on the nights of 31 Mch and 1 Apr 1882]

Alonzo B Cornell, Rep., elected governor "

New capitol at Albany opened 12 Feb. "

State Board of Health authorized by law 18 May, 1880

Commission for the protection of game and fish established by law 26 June, "

New York and Connecticut joint boundary commission award to New York a small strip, 4 68 sq miles in area, called the "oblong tract," east of the straight line boundary which runs north and south 20 miles east of the Hudson river, as agreed upon, 1685 It was given to New York by a faulty survey, 1787, and came into dispute in 1856 This commission also established the southern boundary of Connecticut through the middle of Long Island sound. . "

Population of the state	5,082,871	"
Rank among the states	1st	
Population to the sq mile.	106 7	
Per cent. of increase	15 97	

New York agricultural experiment station instituted by law, 26 June, "

Egyptian obelisk erected in Central park. 22 Jan 1881

[Brought from Alexandria, Egypt, to New York by the steamer *Dessoug*, commander Henry H. Gorringe, U S navy, which sailed from Alexandria, 12 June, reaching New York, 20 July, 1880 Total height, 90 ft., height of shaft, 69 ft., weight of shaft in pounds, 443,000 Total expense of removal and erection, $103,732, paid by William H Vanderbilt. This obelisk is supposed to have been made 1591-1565 B C at Heliopolis, removed to Alexandria 22 B C OBELISKS.]

Alfred B. Street, poet, b. at Poughkeepsie, 1811, d at Albany, "

NEW

U S senators Conkling and Platt resign 16 May, 1881

Warner Miller and Elbridge G Lapham elected 17 July "

William G Fargo, pres of the American Express company, b 1818 d at Buffalo 3 Aug "

Thurlow Weed, politician and journalist, d. in New York city, aged 85 22 Nov 1882

Grover Cleveland Dem , elected governor Nov "

Edwin D Morgan, b 1811, d in New York city 14 Feb 1883

Commission of statistics of labor established by law 4 May, "

East River suspension bridge, connecting New York and Brooklyn opened (BRIDGES) 24 May, "

Civil service commission created by law 24 May, "

[Three commissioners, to be appointed by the governor with the advice and consent of the senate]

Centennial of the disbanding of the army of the Revolution celebrated at Newburg 18 Oct "

New railroad (cantilever) bridge across the Niagara below the falls opened 20 Dec "

New York state dairy commission established by law 24 Apr 1884

Gov Cleveland nominated for president of the U S at the Democratic National convention in Chicago 8 July, "

Susan Warner, b in New York city, 1818 d there 18 Mch 1885

[Author of "Wide, Wide World," and other novels]

Richard Grant White critic, philosopher, and Shakespearian scholar, b 1822, d in New York city 8 Apr "

Common schools cost the state $13,466 367 97 "

Legislature authorizes the governor, with the advice and consent of the senate to appoint 3 forest commissioners, 15 May, "

[To control and superintend the forest preserve, being lands owned or to be acquired by the state within Essex, Franklin Fulton Hamilton, Herkimer Lewis, Saratoga St Lawrence, Warren, Washington, Greene, Ulster, Sullivan, Oneida and Clinton counties, except the towns of Altona and Dannemora, to be kept forever as wild forest lands, not to be sold or leased The commissioners also superintend forest and tree planting throughout the state]

Niagara Falls reservation made a state park 16 July, "

[State park extends along the river front from the upper suspension bridge to a point nearly a mile above the falls It includes what was formerly known as Prospect park, at the edge of the American falls, and Goat island, with the group of smaller islands The total area is 115 acres]

Gen Ulysses S Grant, b 1822, d. at Mt McGregor, near Saratoga. 23 July "

David B Hill, Dem , elected governor "

Commission created to report the most humane and practical method of executing the death sentence 13 May, 1886

[It consisted of Elbridge T Gerry, dr Alfred P Southwick, and Matthew Hale. Their report of Jan 1888, recommended the use of electricity]

State Board of Arbitration created by law 18 May, "

[To consist of 3 members]

Office of factory inspector established for the state "

Arthur Quartley, artist, d in New York city 19 May, "

Normal school at New Paltz, Ulster county, opened. "

John Kelly, Dem politician, d. in New York 1 June, "

Orson S Fowler, phrenologist, b 1809, d at Sharon Station, N Y 18 Aug 1887

Total cost of new capitol at Albany, $17,914,875 02, to 30 Sept "

William Dorsheimer, b at Lyons, N Y , 1832, d at Savannah, Ga 26 Mch 1888

[Elected lieut gov by the Democrats, 1874 and 1876]

Cornelius R Agnew, surgeon, b 1830, d in New York, 18 Apr "

John T Hoffman, b. 1828, d in Germany . . . 10 June, "

[Elected governor by the Democrats, 1868 and 1870.]

E P Roe, b 1838, d in New York city 19 July, "

[Author of "Barriers Burned Away" and other novels.]

Centennial of the first inauguration of George Washington celebrated in New York 29, 30 Apr -1 May, 1889

State Normal school at Oneonta, Otsego county, opened. "

Population of the state	5,997,853	1890
Rank among the states	1st	
Population to the sq mile	121 98	
Per cent of increase	18	

Henry R Pierson, chancellor of the University of the state of New York, d at Albany 1 Jan "

Miss Pink E Corkran, "Nellie Bly," of the New York *World*, finishes a trip around the world eastward, in 72 days 6 hr 11 min 25 Jan "

George William Curtis elected chancellor of the Board of Regents of the state of New York 30 Jan. "

Schenectady commemorates the 200th anniversary of the massacre by French and Indians 9 Feb "

John Jacob Astor, b. 1822, d in New York 22 Feb "

Gov Hill signs the Adirondack State Park bill appropriating $25 000 for park purposes 11 Mch "

Charles T Saxton introduced in 1888 the first bill embodying the Australian ballot system presented to any legislature in the U S., passes the assembly by 72 to 51, 13 Mch , but is vetoed by gov Hill 31 Mch. "

Gov Hill approves the Corrupt Practices act for preventing bribery and intimidation at elections . 4 Apr "

Compromise Election bill allowing a "paster ballot" and a series of tickets, instead of a "blanket ballot," is approved by the governor . 2 May, "

Gen Clinton B Fisk, b 1828, d in New York 9 July, "

Maj gen John C. Fremont, b 1813, d in New York 13 July, "

Dr C. H F Peters, astronomer, the discoverer of 50 asteroids, b 1813, d. 18 July, "

First execution in the world by electricity, William Kemmler (murderer) at Auburn prison . ... 6 Aug. "

Strike of 3000 trainmen owing to discharge of certain Knights of Labor on the New York Central railroad..........8 Aug. 1890
Boundary-line with Pennsylvania agreed upon by commissioners from each state, 26 Mch. 1886, and confirmed by the legislatures, approved by the Congress..................19 Aug. "
Single-tax convention meets in New York city, 2 Sept., and adopts a platform..................................3 Sept. "
Strike on the New York Central railroad declared off..17 Sept. "
Gov. Hill is elected U. S. senator from New York, receiving 81 votes on joint ballot, to 79 for Evarts................21 Jan. 1891
Secretary of the treasury, William Windom, b. 1827, dies suddenly at a banquet at Delmonico's, New York........29 Jan. "
James Redpath, journalist, b. 1833, d. in New York city, 10 Feb. "
Board of Regents of the University adopt a plan for university extension under a University Extension council of 5 representatives of colleges to be appointed annually.......11 Feb. "
Gen. William T. Sherman, b. 1820, d. at New York.....14 Feb. "
Ex-governor Lucius Robinson d. in Elmira, aged 81....23 Mch. "
Legislature appropriates $10,000 for university extension, 16 Apr. "
Ground broken for Grant monument in New York......27 Apr. "
Charles Pratt, philanthropist, b. 1830, d. at New York..4 May, "
School children of the state choose the rose as state flower by a vote of: rose, 294,816; golden-rod, 206,402; majority, 88,414..8 May, "
Benson John Lossing, historian, b. 1813, d. at Chestnut Ridge, Dutchess county...............................3 June, "
Chauncey Vibbard, called "the father of the American railway," d. at Macon, Ga..............................5 June, "
Statue of Henry Ward Beecher unveiled at Brooklyn..24 June, "
Four murderers, Slocum, Smiler, Wood, and Jugiro, executed by electricity at Sing Sing..........................7 July, "
A train on the New York Central railroad runs from New York to East Buffalo, 436 miles in 426 minutes, running time. Of this, 37 miles was at a rate averaging 70.78 miles per hour, and 151 miles at a rate of from 65 to 70 miles........14 Sept. "
First regular Empire State Express makes the run from New York to Buffalo in 8 hrs. 42 min.....................26 Oct. "
Field, Lindley, Wiechers & Co., stock-brokers of New York city, make an assignment, liabilities $2,000,000; and E. M. Field said to be insane....................................27 Nov. "
A lunatic enters the office of Russell Sage, in New York; being refused his demand for $1,250,000, he drops a hand-bag containing explosives, killing himself, a bystander, bruising Sage and others, and wrecking the building...............4 Dec. "
Martin D. Loppy, the wife-murderer, executed by electricity at Sing Sing...7 Dec. "
Randolph Rogers, American sculptor, b. 1825, d. at Rome, N. Y..14 Jan. 1892
Dr. Wesley Newcomb, one of the leading conchologists of the world, d. at Ithaca, N. Y., aged 84 years............27 Jan. "
"Greater New York" bill fails in Assembly...........15 Mch. 1892
Legislature appropriates $300,000 for the Columbian Exposition...22 Mch. "
Charles Kendall Adams resigns the presidency of Cornell university..5 May, "
Prof. Jacob Gould Schurman elected in his place......18 May, "
Cyrus W. Field, b. 1819, d. at Ardsley, N. Y..........12 July, "
Switchmen's strike at Buffalo, on the Erie railroad, begins; strikers burning freight trains and destroying about $1,000,000 worth of property........................14 Aug. "
65th and 74th regiments of national guards are ordered out at Buffalo by gen. Doyle..............................15 Aug. "
National guards from New York, Brooklyn, and elsewhere, about 8000 men, ordered to Buffalo by gov. Flower, on appeal from the sheriff and mayor at Buffalo..............17 Aug. "
Ex-gov. Myron H. Clark dies at Canandaigua, aged 86, 23 Aug. "
Switchmen's strike at Buffalo declared off by grand-master Sweeney...24 Aug. "
George William Curtis, b. 1824, d. at West Brighton, Staten Island...31 Aug. "
Ex-U. S. senator Francis Kernan, b. 1816, d. at Utica...7 Sept. "
Opening in New York city of the Continental Congress of the Salvation Army of the U. S..........................21 Nov. "
Act authorizing the purchase of Fire island for quarantine purposes signed.......................................11 Mch. 1893
Naval review and parade at New York city.........27–28 Apr. "
[10 nations participate.]
"Viking ship" arrives at New York city.............17 June, "
State monument to its fallen soldiers dedicated on the battle-field of Gettysburg.................................2 July, "
Hamilton Fish, ex-governor and ex-secretary of state, b. 1808, d. at Garrison's, N. Y..................................7 Sept. "
State Normal school building burned at Oneonta, loss $200,000, 15 Feb. 1894
John Y. McKane of Gravesend, L. I., found guilty of election frauds and intimidation, and sentenced at Brooklyn to 6 years in Sing Sing prison...............................19 Feb. "
Joseph Keppler, founder of *Puck*, d. in New York city, 20 Feb. "
"Greater New York" bill, after repeated defeats, passes the Assembly, 8 Feb., Senate, 27 Feb., and is signed by the governor (New York city)...........................28 Feb. "
David Dudley Field, b. 1805, d. at Gramercy Park, New York city..13 Apr. "
Gen. Henry W. Slocum, b. 1827, d. in Brooklyn........14 Apr. "
Constitutional convention meets at Albany............8 May, "
Richard Croker, leader of "The Tammany Hall Society," resigns the position.......................................10 May, "
Brooklyn Tabernacle (dr. Talmage's) and adjoining buildings burned...13 May, "

GOVERNORS OF NEW YORK.

Name.	Term of office.	Remarks.
	UNDER THE DUTCH.	
Cornelis Jacobsen May	1624	
William Verhulst	1625	
Peter Minuit	4 May, 1626 to 1633	Recalled.
Wouter Van Twiller	Apr. 1633 " 1638	
William Kieft	28 Mch. 1638 " 1647	
Peter Stuyvesant	11 May, 1647 " 1664	Surrendered to the English.
	UNDER THE ENGLISH.	
Richard Nicolls	8 Sept. 1664 to 1668	Resigned.
Francis Lovelace	17 Aug. 1668 " 1673	Surrendered to the Dutch.
	DUTCH RESUMED.	
Anthony Colve	1673 to 1674	
	ENGLISH RESUMED.	
Edmund Andros	10 Nov. 1674 to 1683	
Thomas Dongan	27 Aug. 1683 " 1688	
Francis Nicholson	1688 " 1689	Lieutenant-governor.
Jacob Leisler	3 June, 1689 " 1691	
Henry Sloughter	19 Mch. 1691	Dies in office.
Richard Ingoldsby	26 July, 1691 " 1692	Deputy-governor.
Benjamin Fletcher	30 Aug. 1692 " 1698	
Richard, earl Bellomont	1698 " 1701	Dies in office.
John Nanfan	1701 " 1702	Acting-governor.
Lord Cornbury	3 May, 1702 " 1708	Commission revoked.
John, lord Lovelace	18 Dec. 1708 " 1709	Dies in office.
Richard Ingoldsby	9 May, 1709 " 1710	Lieutenant-governor.
Gerardus Beekman	10 Apr. 1710	President of the council.
Robert Hunter	14 June, 1710 " 1719	
Peter Schuyler	21 July, 1719 " 1720	President of the council.
William Burnet	17 Sept. 1720 " 1728	Transferred to Massachusetts government.
John Montgomery	15 Apr. 1728 " 1731	Dies in office.
Rip Van Dam	1731 " 1732	President of the council.
William Cosby	1 Aug. 1732 " 1736	Dies in office.
George Clarke	1736 " 1743	President of the council. Lieutenant-governor.
George Clinton	2 Sept. 1743 " 1753	Resigned.
Sir Danvers Osborne	10 Oct. 1753	Commits suicide 5 days after his arrival.
James De Lancey	12 Oct. 1753 " 1755	Lieutenant-governor.
Sir Charles Hardy	3 Sept. 1755 " 1757	
James De Lancey	3 June, 1757 " 1760	Dies in office.
Cadwallader Colden	4 Aug. 1760 " 1761	President of the council. Lieutenant-governor.
Robert Monckton	26 Oct. 1761	Sails at the head of an expedition against Martinique.
Cadwallader Colden	18 Nov. 1761 " 1765	
Sir Henry Moore	18 Nov. 1765 " 1769	Dies in office.
Cadwallader Colden	12 Sept. 1769 " 1770	
John, lord Dunmore	19 Oct. 1770 " 1771	Appointed governor of Virginia.
William Tryon	9 July, 1771 " 1777	Last royal governor of New York.

GOVERNORS OF THE STATE OF NEW YORK.

Name.	Party.	When elected.	Opponents.	Party.	Remar
George Clinton		1777 1780 1783 1786 1789 1792	 Robert Yates John Jay.		First opposing candidate.
John Jay		1795 1798	Robert Yates Robert R. Livingston.	Dem.-Rep.	
George Clinton		1801	Stephen Van Rensselaer		
Morgan Lewis	Dem.-Rep.	1804	Aaron Burr.		
Daniel D. Tompkins	"	1807 1810 1813 1816	Morgan Lewis. Jonas Platt. Stephen Van Rensselaer. Rufus King		Tompkins elected vice-pres.
John Taylor		1817			Lieutenant-governor. Acting.
De Witt Clinton		1817 1820	Peter B. Porter. Daniel D. Tompkins.		
Joseph C. Yates		1822	Solomon Southwick.		
De Witt Clinton		1824 1826	Samuel Young. William B. Rochester		Clinton dies in office.
Nathaniel Pitcher					Lieutenant-governor. Acting.
Martin Van Buren	Democrat	1828	Smith Thompson Solomon Southwick	 Anti-masonic.	Resigned. Appointed secretary of state by Jackson.
Enos T. Throop	"	1829 1830	 Francis Granger Ezekiel Williams.	 Anti-masonic.	Lieutenant-governor. Acting.
William L. Marcy	"	1832 1834 1836	Francis Granger William H. Seward Jesse Buel. Isaac S. Smith.	Anti-masonic. Whig.	
William H. Seward	Whig	1838 1840	William L. Marcy William C. Bouck Gerrit Smith.	Democrat. "	
William C. Bouck	Democrat	1842	Luther Bradish. Alvan Stewart.		
Silas Wright, jr.	"	1844	Millard Fillmore Alvan Stewart.	Whig.	
John Young	Whig	1846	Silas Wright, jr Ogden Edwards. Henry Bradley.	Democrat.	
Hamilton Fish	"	1848	John A. Dix Reuben H. Walworth. William Goodell.	"	
Washington Hunt	"	1850	Horatio Seymour	"	
Horatio Seymour	Democrat	1852	Washington Hunt Minthorne Tompkins.	Whig.	
Myron H. Clark	Whig	1854	Horatio Seymour Daniel Ullman. Green C. Bronson.	Democrat.	
John A. King	Republican	1856	Amasa J. Parker Erastus Brooks.	Democrat.	
Edwin D. Morgan	"	1858 1860	Amasa J. Parker Lorenzo Burrows. Gerrit Smith. William Kelly. James T. Brady.	Democrat.	
Horatio Seymour	Democrat	1862	James S. Wadsworth	Republican.	
Reuben E. Fenton	Republican	1864 1866	Horatio Seymour John T. Hoffman	Democrat. "	
John T. Hoffman	Democrat	1868 1870	John A. Griswold Stewart L. Woodford	Republican. "	
John A. Dix	Republican	1872	Francis Kernan	Democrat.	
Samuel J. Tilden	Democrat	1874	John A. Dix	Republican.	
Lucius Robinson	"	1876	Edwin D. Morgan	"	
Alonzo B. Cornell	Republican	1879	Lucius Robinson John Kelly Harris Lewis. John W. Mears.	Democrat. Tam.-Dem.	
Grover Cleveland	Democrat	1882	Charles J. Folger Alphonso A. Hopkins Epenetus Howe	Republican. Prohibition. Greenback.	Cleveland resigns, 1884. Elected president.
David B. Hill	"	1884 1885 1888	 Ira Davenport H. Clay Bascom Warner Miller W. Martin Jones.	 Republican. Prohibition. Republican. Prohibition.	Lieutenant-governor. Acting.
Roswell P. Flower	"	1891	J. Sloat Fassett John W. Bruce Daniel De Leon	Republican. Prohibition. Socialist.	
Levi P. Morton	Republican	1894	David B. Hill Everett P. Wheeler F. E. Baldwin Charles B. Matthews	Democrat. " Prohibition. Socialist.	

The first governors of the state entered office on 1 July following election, but since 1823 the date has been 1 Jan. The term of office was, up to 1823, 3 years; then until 1876, 2 years; from 1876 until 1895, 3 years; from 1895, 2 years. The governor and lieutenant-governor must be 30 years of age, a citizen of the U. S., and 5 years a resident of the state.

UNITED STATES SENATORS FROM THE STATE OF NEW YORK.

Name.	No. of Congress.	Date.	Remarks.
Philip Schuyler	1st	1789 to 1791	
Rufus King	1st to 4th	1789 " 1796	Resigned. Appointed minister to Great Britain by Washington.
Aaron Burr	2d " 5th	1791 " 1797	Vice-president of the U. S., 1801-5.
John Lawrence	4th " 6th	1796 " 1800	Resigned. Elected president *pro tem.* 6 Dec. 1798.
Philip Schuyler	5th	1797 " 1798	Resigned.
John Sloss Hobart	5th	1798	Elected in place of Schuyler. Resigned 1798.
William North	5th	1798	Appointed in place of Hobart.
James Watson	5th to 6th	1799 to 1800	Elected in place of Hobart. Resigned.
Gouverneur Morris	6th " 7th	1800 " 1803	Elected in place of Watson.
John Armstrong	6th " 8th	1801 " 1804	Elected in place of Lawrence. Resigned 1802. Appointed in place of De Witt Clinton. Resigned.
De Witt Clinton	7th " 8th	1802 " 1803	Resigned.
Theodore Bailey	8th	1803 " 1804	Resigned.
Samuel L. Mitchell	8th to 11th	1804 " 1809	Elected in place of Armstrong.
John Smith	8th " 13th	1803 " 1813	Elected in place of De Witt Clinton.
Obadiah German	11th " 14th	1809 " 1815	
Rufus King	13th " 19th	1813 " 1825	Appointed minister to Great Britain by pres. John Q. Adams, 1825.
Nathan Sanford	14th " 17th	1815 " 1821	
Martin Van Buren	18th " 20th	1823 " 1828	Resigned. Elected governor of the state.
Nathan Sanford	19th " 22d	1826 " 1831	
Charles E. Dudley	20th " 23d	1828 " 1833	Elected in place of Van Buren.
William L. Marcy	22d	1831 " 1832	Resigned.
Silas Wright, jr.	22d to 28th	1832 " 1844	Elected in place of Marcy. Resigned.
Nathaniel P. Tallmadge	23d " 28th	1833 " 1844	Resigned.
Henry A. Foster	28th	1844	Appointed *pro tem.* in place of Wright.
John A. Dix	28th to 31st	1845 to 1849	Elected in place of Wright.
Daniel S. Dickinson	28th " 32d	1845 " 1851	Elected in place of Tallmadge.
William H. Seward	31st " 37th	1849 " 1861	Resigned to enter the cabinet of pres. Lincoln.
Hamilton Fish	32d " 35th	1851 " 1857	
Preston King	35th " 38th	1857 " 1863	Committed suicide, New York city, 13 Nov. 1865.
Ira Harris	37th " 40th	1861 " 1867	
Edwin D. Morgan	38th " 41st	1863 " 1869	
Roscoe Conkling	40th " 47th	1867 " 1881	Resigned 16 May.
Reuben E. Fenton	41st " 44th	1869 " 1875	
Francis Kernan	44th " 47th	1875 " 1881	The first Democratic senator from New York since 1851.
Thomas C. Platt	47th	1881	Resigned 16 May.
Elbridge G. Lapham	47th to 49th	1881 to 1885	Elected in place of Conkling.
Warner Miller	47th " 50th	1881 " 1887	Elected in place of Platt.
William M. Evarts	49th " 52d	1885 " 1891	
Frank Hiscock	50th " 53d	1887 " 1893	
David B. Hill	52d " ——	1891 " ——	Term expires 1897.
Edward Murphy, jr.	53d " ——	1893 " ——	Term expires 1899.

New York city, the metropolis of the United States, covers an area of 41½ sq. miles, comprising Manhattan island, Ward's, Randall's, and Blackwell's islands in the East river, and Governor's island in New York bay, also the portion north of Manhattan island annexed in 1874. ("Greater New York," see this record, 1894.) Lat. 40° 44′ N.; lon. 74° W. First settled by the Dutch, it was known as New Amsterdam, and in 1656 had 17 streets and about 1000 inhabitants, including negro slaves; 8 years later it was surrendered to the English, and received its present name. In 1712 the population was 5840; in 1731, 8632; in 1774, 22,750. Since 1790 the population according to the U. S. census has been:

Year	Population	Year	Population
1790	33,131	1850	515,507
1800	60,489	1860	805,651
1810	96,373	1870	942,292
1820	123,706	1880	1,206,299
1830	202,589	1890	1,515,301
1840	312,710	1900	3,437,202

Manhattan island ceded to the Dutch by the Indians for about $23, 6 May, and fort Amsterdam and a stone warehouse built, 1626
Everardus Bogardus, first clergyman, and Adam Rolandsen, school-master, arrive at Manhattan....Apr. 1633
First church built on Broad street.... "
Gov. Kieft builds a stone hotel on northeast corner Pearl street and Coenties slip, fronting the North river (afterwards the Stadt-Huys).... 1642
Stone church built, 72×50 ft., and 15 ft. high (cost $950), within the fort.... "
First recorded sale of city lots: one of 30 ft. front, by 110 ft. deep, on Bridge street, sold for $9.60.... "
School, taught at first by dr. La Montagne, opened in a room in the Stadt-Huys....Apr. 1652
Proclamation of the governor naming first officials of New Amsterdam....2 Feb. 1653
Seal and coat-of-arms received from Holland....8 Dec. 1654
New Amsterdam has about 1000 people, including negro slaves, 1656
First street paved; Dehoogh, now Stone street, between Broad and Whitehall sts.... 1657
A "rattle-watch" from 9 P.M. until morning drum-beat established, 1658; and 250 leather fire-buckets, also hooks and ladders, ordered from Holland, arrive....12 Aug. 1658
Alexander Carolus Curtius, the first Latin school-master, arrives....4 July, 1659
He returns to Holland, dominie Aigidius Luyck succeeds.... 1661
["The high-school gains such a reputation that pupils come from 'Fort Orange,' 'South River,' and even Virginia."]
Fort Amsterdam surrendered to the English (name of New Amsterdam changed to New York)....8 Sept. 1664
Capt. Thomas Willett of Plymouth, Engl., first mayor; Thomas Delavall, Oloff Stevenson Van Cortlandt, Johannes Van Brugh, Cornelis Van Ruyven, and John Lawrence, aldermen; Allaid Anthony, sheriff....15 June, 1665
Peter Stuyvesant dies at his "Bouwery," aged 80....Feb. 1672
[A pear-tree, brought from Holland and planted by him, stood at corner of Third ave. and Thirteenth st. until 1867.]
Monthly post established between New York and Boston. 22 Jan. 1673
New York surrendered to the Dutch, who name it New Orange, 9 Aug. "
Peace declared between England and Holland, Feb.-Mch. 1674, and New Netherland formally delivered to English..10 Nov. 1674
New docks to meet increase of commerce built by city tax, Nov. 1676
City divided into 6 wards, each with one alderman, as follows: South ward, Nicholas Bayard; Dock ward, John Inians; East ward, William Pinhorne; North ward, Gulian Verplanck; West ward, John Robinson; Outer ward, William Cox. 8 Dec. 1683
James Graham commissioned first recorder....16 Jan. 1684
New charter, known as the Dongan charter, granted by James II., issued....27 Apr. 1686
Old South or Garden Street Dutch Reformed church erected (rebuilt, 1766).... 1693
William Bradford sets up the first printing press in New York, 12 Apr. "
Nassau street opened....June, 1696
Streets first lighted with lanterns.... 1697
Trinity church, begun 1696, opened for service....13 Mch. 1698
New city hall built on Wall street, facing Broad; corner-stone laid 1699, completed.... 1700
Nicholas Bayard convicted of high-treason, 9 Mch., and sentenced to death; on confession is pardoned....30 Mch. 1702
Yellow-fever visitation.... "
Act passed to establish a public grammar-school.... 1703
Corner-stone of French Huguenot church laid on north side of Pine street (then King st.), near Nassau....8 July, 1704
City charter granting ferry privileges issued.... 1708
Jewish synagogue erected on Mill street.... 1709
Slave-market established at the foot of Wall street.... "
Pretended discovery of a negro insurrection in the city, 6 Apr. The result, says gov. Hunter, was "27 condemned, whereof 21 were executed; some were burned, others hanged, 1 broken on the wheel, and 1 hung alive in chains".... 1712
First Presbyterian church, a stone structure, built on Wall street, between Nassau and Broadway (rebuilt 1748, and stood until 1844).... 1719
New York *Gazette* (weekly), the first newspaper in New York, published by William Bradford; first issued....16 Oct. 1725
Library of rev. John Millington of England, 1600 volumes, donated to New York, Sept. 1728, and added to that of rev. John Sharp (1700), and placed in the city hall for public use.... 1729
First smelting-furnace built near corner of Centre and Reade sts.... 1730
New charter, under seal of George III., formally presented to the city....11 Feb. 1731
First fire-engines received from England.... "

New Dutch church erected on east side Nassau street, corner stone laid 1727, opened 1729, completed (rebuilt 1764) 1731

Plot at the lower end of Broadway laid out for a bowling green by the corporation 1732

Monthly stage route opened between New York and Boston "

New York *Weekly Journal* established by John Peter Zenger, 5 Nov 1733

First poor house built on the common (City Hall park) 1734

Zenger imprisoned for libel, 17 Nov 1734, defended by Andrew Hamilton and acquitted July, 1735

Alleged conspiracy to burn the city, 154 negroes and 21 whites arrested, of whom 14 negroes were burned at the stake, 18 hanged and 71 transported, and Hughson (a white man), his wife and maid and John Ury, a nonjuring Episcopalian clergyman, hanged, all probably innocent Mch et seq 1741

A play enacted at a theatre in Nassau st 5 Mch 1750

Merchants exchange or Royal exchange at foot of Broad street, built upon arches, completed 1752

First regular theatre opened in Nassau street by Lewis Hallam's company performing "The Conscious Lover" 17 Sept 1753

New York Society library founded 1754

King's (now Columbia) college founded, rev William Samuel Johnson, D D first president "

Ferry to Staten Island established 1755

Stage route to Philadelphia, "three days through only," established 1756

Corner stone of Columbia college laid 23 Aug "

First British packet boat carrying the mail between New York and Falmouth, established "

St Andrew's society organized, Philip Livingston first president "

Beekman Street theatre opened with the tragedy "Fair Penitent" 18 Nov 1761

[Destroyed by a mob 1766]

Lamp posts erected and streets lighted at public cost 1762

Light house at Sandy Hook completed and first lighted June, 1763

Rhinelander sugar house, used during the Revolution as a British prison, erected by Bernart R Cuyler "

First sermon in English, in the Middle Dutch church 15 Apr 1764

Sons of Liberty organized . 1765

Stamp Act congress meets in New York 7 Oct "

Non importation agreements signed by more than 200 merchants at a meeting held 31 Oct. "

St. Paul's church, cor Broadway and Vesey sts, completed except the spire 1766

Old Brick church, cor Nassau and Beekman sts, erected 1767

John Street theatre opened 7 Dec. "

Wesley chapel, on site of St John's M E church, dedicated, [Rebuilt, 1817 and 1841] 30 Oct 1768

Attempts by British soldiers to cut down the Liberty pole, on evenings of 13, 14 and 15 Jan They succeed 16 Jan 1770

Collision between Sons of Liberty and British soldiers, 1 citizen killed and 3 wounded 18 Jan "

New York Chamber of Commerce, founded 5 Apr 1768, incorporated by royal charter 13 Mch "

Statue of William Pitt erected at junction of Wall and William sts 7 Sept "

First Provincial Congress at New York appoints a committee of safety 22 May, 1775

First regiment organized in New York city under col Alexander McDougal, and company of artillery under John Lamb, 28 June, "

Gilded leaden statue of George III, erected in the Bowling Green 16 Aug 1770, torn down by the people 9 July, 1776

[Most of it was melted into 42 000 bullets in Connecticut]

Water works for supply of the city through wooden pipes, in course of construction "

City evacuated by Americans, occupied by British 14 Sept "

Fire destroys 493 houses, burns Trinity church, and "consumes the fourth part of the city," begins near Whitehall slip . 21 Sept. "

Capt. Nathan Hale executed as a spy by the British in the Rutger's orchard on East Broadway 22 Sept. "

City records, carried off by gov Tryon, 1775, restored Oct. 1781

British evacuate the city ... 25 Nov 1783

First American post office opened at 38 Smith st 28 Nov "

Gen Washington bids farewell to his officers at Fraunce's tavern New York . 4 Dec. "

First American city government established, James Duane appointed mayor by the governor . 7 Feb 1784

First meeting of the common council 10 Feb. "

Empress of China, capt. Green, bound for Canton with merchandise, leaves port . . . 22 Feb. "

Bank of New York established . . . "

[Chartered 21 Mch 1791]

Chamber of Commerce reincorporated by law 13 Apr "

Custom house established at the port of New York by act of legislature . 18 Nov "

Continental Congress assembles in the city 11 Jan 1785

Society for the manumission of slaves, organized 1785, holds its first quarterly meeting at the Coffee house . 12 May, "

Theatres reopened in the city "

Charter for King's college altered, changing the name to Columbia college, 1 May, 1784, first commencement 11 Apr 1786

Bunker's Mansion-house erected at 39 Broadway as a residence by gen. Alexander Macomb "

First Catholic church built . .. "

First city directory published . "

Charter of Columbia college amended . 1787

First number of the Federalist papers printed in the *Independent Journal or Weekly Advertiser* .. 27 Oct. "

NEW

Doctors' mob caused by the discovery of human remains for dissection in the hospital 13, 14 Apr 1788

City hall erected 1700, remodelled for U S government use, and called "New Federal Hall" "

"The Power of Sympathy, or, the Triumph of Nature," pub by Robert Hodges, advertised as "first American novel," 4 Feb 1789

Oath of office as president of the U S administered to gen Washington by chancellor Livingston on the balcony of the City hall 30 Apr "

TAMMANY SOCIETY or Columbian Order organized 12 May, "

"President's March" composed by one Fayles, German, leader of the John Street theatre orchestra First played on the president and Mrs Washington entering the theatre box (HAIL! COLUMBIA) 24 Nov "

Corner stone of new Trinity church laid 21 Aug 1788, and church consecrated 25 Mch 1790

Fort at the Battery taken down and ground levelled "

New York Dispensary established "

General Society of Mechanics and Tradesmen of the City of New York, organized 17 Nov 1785 chartered 14 Mch 1792

[Apprentices' Library instituted by it, 1820]

Third centenary of the discovery of America celebrated, 12 Oct. "

Minerva, edited by Noah Webster soon after and still called the *Commercial Advertiser*, first issued 9 Dec 1793

Yellow fever scourge, 525 deaths 6 Oct 1794-19 July, 1795

System of underground sewers first established "

New York Missionary Society founded 1796

Park theatre, on Park row near Ann st, opened 29 Jan 1798

Yellow fever, 329 deaths during Aug, 924 during Sept, total in the city, 1524 Aug –Nov "

Charles Brockden Brown, "America's earliest romance writer," publishes his first novel, "Wieland, or, the Transformation" "

Vauxhall garden, east of Broadway between Fourth st and Astor place, founded (remained until 1826) 1799

New York *Evening Post* first issued 16 Nov 1801

New York Historical Society founded 20 Nov 1804

New York orphan asylum organized 15 Mch 1806

Free School Society incorporated, De Witt Clinton president, 1805, and first free school opened 19 May, "

First issue of the *Salmagundi* 24 Jan 1807

Clermont, Fulton's steamboat, leaves the city for Albany on her first trip, going 150 miles in 32 hours 11 Aug "

College of Physicians and Surgeons organized "

American Academy of Fine Arts, organized 1802, incorporated, 13 Feb. 1808

"Knickerbocker's History of New York" pub 1809

Brick school-house erected on Chatham st., dedicated 11 Dec "

Fire which destroys from 80 to 100 large buildings begins in Chatham st, near Duane 19 May, 1811

City hall—corner stone laid by Edward Livingston, 30 Sept 1803—completed 1812

First steam ferry from New York to Jersey City established "

First steam ferry boat between New York and Brooklyn, the *Nassau*, begins running 10 May, 1814

Collect pond on the site of the Tombs, filled up 1817

First steamship to cross the Atlantic, the *Savannah*, sails from New York where she was built, for Savannah, Ga 10 Apr 1819

New York *Observer* first issued 1820

Old Park theatre burned 25 May, "

Yellow fever in New York 1822

U S government cedes Castle Garden to the city "

Assay office in Wall st erected 1823

Gen Lafayette lands in New York 15 Aug 1824

First gas pipes laid, and residence of Samuel Leggett, 7 Cherry st, the first house lighted with gas 1825

Foundation of the Merchants' exchange laid "

First opera troupe appears in New York (MUSIC) "

Gov Clinton and party arrive at New York on the first boat, the *Seneca Chief*, from Lake Erie by Erie canal 4 Nov "

National Academy of the Arts of Design organized, Samuel F B Morse, president. 18 Jan 1826

New York theatre, on present site of Bowery theatre, and then the largest in U S (seating capacity 3000), opened 22 Oct "

[In it appeared Forrest, Booth, Charlotte Cushman, and others It was burned 1828, 1836, and 1838]

Bellevue hospital established Nov "

Journal of Commerce started 1827

Superior court of the city established 1828

Fire destroys more than $600,000 worth of property "

Manufacture of bricks by machinery successfully begun in New York 1829

Mercantile Library founded, 1820, building on Astor place erected . 1830

Stage line from Bowling Green to Bleecker st. opened "

Spirit of the Times, first sporting paper in the U S., started in New York 1831

Four thousand deaths from cholera 27 June to 19 Oct 1832

First horse railroad in the world opened in Fourth ave "

John Stephenson's first street car, the *John Mason*, makes its initial trip between Prince and Fourteenth sts. 26 Nov "

Sun, the first one cent daily paper, started 1833

Anti slavery Society of New York organized 2 Oct "

Riot against the abolitionists, mob dispersed by the National Guard 11 July, 1834

New York *Herald*, James Gordon Bennett, editor, first issued, 6 May, 1835

Convention of more than 100 delegates from the state at large meet in the City hall, Oct. 1830, and found the University of the City of New York, which opens . "

Fire destroys 693 buildings including the marble Exchange in Wall st. and South Dutch church in Garden st., loss esti-

mated $20 000,000 (fire breaks out on the evening of the 16th, thermometer at zero, a gale blowing) 16-17 Dec 1835
"Shakespeare Tavern," cor Fulton and Nassau sts., demolished 1836
Astor House opened 31 May, "
[At the time the finest hotel in the U S]
Union Theological seminary (Presbyterian) founded "
Union club organized Aug "
Bread riot 10 Feb 1837
New York banks suspend 10 May, "
American and Foreign Bible Society established "
Fourth avenue tunnel opened 26 Oct. "
Tombs building finished 1838
Express line to Boston opened by W F Harnden 4 Mch 1839
New York *Tribune*, Horace Greeley, editor, first issued 10 Apr 1841
Property qualification for city voters abolished 1842
Celebration of the completion of the CROTON AQUEDUCT 14 Oct "
Mayor Harper institutes a uniformed police corps of 200 men under city ordinance enacted 1844
Fire destroys 345 buildings, it begins in New st, and an explosion of saltpetre wrecks several buildings and puts the fire beyond control 19 July, 1845
Telegraph line between New York and Philadelphia opened 1846
Present Trinity church begun 1839, consecrated "
German Liederkranz founded 9 Jan 1847
College of St Francis Xavier (Roman Catholic) opened "
[Incorporated by the regents 10 Jan 1861]
First steam grain elevator in the port of New York erected by col Daniel Richards 1846-47
Park theatre burned 16 Dec. 1848
College of the City of New York established as the New York Free academy 1847, and opened (incorporated 1866) Jan 1849
Astor place riot against Macready an English actor, 141 soldiers wounded, 34 of the mob killed, and many wounded, 10 May, "
Cholera begins in the Five Points, number of deaths estimated, 3000 14 May et seq "
Amended city charter passed 2 Apr, takes effect 1 June, "
Taylor's machine shop fire, 63 lives lost 4 Feb 1850
American Bible Union organized 10 June, "
Jenny Lind's first concert in U S in Castle Garden 11 Sept. "
Erie railway opened from Piermont to Goshen, 23 Sept. 1841, and to Dunkirk 22 Apr 1851
New York *Times*, Henry J Raymond, editor, first issued, 18 Sept "
Hudson River railroad opened to East Albany 3 Oct. "
New York *Ledger* first issued "
Young Men's Christian Association organized (building in Twenty third st. erected 1869 at total cost of $500,000) June, 1852
American Bible Society organized, 8 May, 1816, and Bible House erected at cost of $300,000 "
Five Points' Mission founded 1850, corner stone of mission building laid, 27 Jan 1853, building dedicated 18 June, 1853
Crystal palace opened for a universal industrial exhibition, 14 July, "
Clearing house established 11 Oct "
Children's Aid Society organized (incorporated 1856) "
Harper & Brothers' publishing house burned, loss $1,250,000, 10 Dec "
Astor Library, incorporated 13 Jan 1849, opened 9 Jan 1854
American Geographical Society, founded 1852, chartered "
Academy of Music formally opened, Giulia Grisi and signor Mario in "Norma" 2 Oct. "
Castle Garden becomes an emigrant depot. 1855
Five Points' House of Industry established 1850, and building erected 1856
Harper's Weekly begun, Theodore Sedgwick, editor 13 Jan 1857
St Vincent's hospital (Roman Catholic), Eleventh st., founded 1849, incorporated 13 Apr "
Ohio Life and Trust company fails, and a commercial panic spreads throughout the U S 24 Aug "
Fulton Street prayer meeting organized Sept "
Metropolitan Police act passed "
St Luke's hospital incorporated 1850, building commenced 1854, and opened. May, 1858
Cooper Institute opened to the public. "
First message from London by Atlantic telegraph. 5 Aug "
Crystal palace burned 5 Oct. "
Great fire in Elm st., 50 lives lost 2 Feb 1860
Central park, work begun 1856, opened to the public "
New York *World* first issued June, "
Mass convention in Union square, more than 100,000 persons present. 20 Apr 1861
Produce exchange organized (new building on Bowling Green opened 1884) "
Manhattan college at Manhattanville incorporated 2 Apr 1863
DRAFT RIOTS, about 1000 persons killed. 13-16 July, "
Corner-stone of National Academy of Design laid Oct. "
Metropolitan fair in aid of the sanitary commission, main building on Fourteenth st. opened 4 Apr 1864
Journal of Commerce and the *World* suppressed by order of pres. Lincoln 18 May, "
Mr Seward telegraphs the mayor of New York of a conspiracy to burn the principal cities of the north 2 Nov "
Maj gen B F Butler takes command in the city of New York 4 Nov "
Attempt made to fire hotels in New York city 25 Nov "
[Robert Kennedy arrested and subsequently hung]
Union League club instituted Feb 1863, incorporated Feb. 1865
Volunteer Fire Department and hand fire engines replaced by paid department and steam 2 May, "
Manhattan club founded 1865
Board of Health established 26 Feb 1866
American Society for the Prevention of Cruelty to Animals, Henry Bergh, president, organized Apr "
National Academy of the Arts of Design erected and completed at a cost for site and building of $237,000 "
County Court house, building begun 1861, and occupied 1867
Single track elevated railroad operated by a cable, opened from Battery place to Thirtieth st 2 July, "
Barnum's Museum burned, 13 July, 1865, and again 2 Mch 1868
Financial panic culminates in "Black Friday," gold 162½, 24 Sept 1869
Tweed Frear city charter, consolidating county and city, etc., becomes a law 5 Apr 1870
Riot between Orangemen and Irish Catholics 12 July, 1871
[The occasion was an Orange parade on the anniversary of the battle of Aghrim, Ireland, when William III of England overthrew the cause of James II]
Grand Central station at Forty second st. opened 9 Oct "
William M Tweed arrested (NEW YORK, 1871 et seq) 27 Oct. "
Horace Greeley d 29 Nov 1872
City charter amended 1873
Young Women's Christian Association founded 1870, incorporated "
Society for the Suppression of Vice incorporated "
Commercial panic which spreads throughout the country begins on the Stock exchange 19 Sept "
Morrisania, West Farms, and Kingsbridge annexed by act 23 May, 1873, taking effect 1 Jan 1874
Society for the Prevention of Cruelty to Children organized 1874, incorporated 1875
North Dutch church, erected 1769, cor Fulton and William sts., demolished "
Railroad approach in Fourth ave leading to Grand Central station, tunnels, etc, completed "
New post office first occupied 1 Sept "
Society for the Prevention of Crime, rev dr Howard Crosby, president, founded 1876
Hallett's Point reef blown up (NEW YORK) 24 Sept "
Cornelius Vanderbilt dies in New York 4 Jan 1877
Lenox Library incorporated 20 June, 1870, opened to the public (NEW YORK) 4 Jan "
New building of New York Hospital in Fifteenth st opened, 16 Mch "
[This hospital was organized 1770, chartered by king George III, 13 June, 1771, corner stone of building laid, 27 July, 1773, burned, 28 Feb 1775, rebuilt and opened, 3 Jan 1791, and abandoned, 19 Feb 1870]
Bronze statue of Fitz Greene Halleck unveiled in Central Park 16 May, "
Burning of Greenfield candy works, 50 to 60 lives lost 20 Dec "
First building of American Museum of Natural History—corner stone laid by pres Grant, 2 June, 1874—opened. 22 Dec "
Metropolitan elevated railroad opened from Rector st. to the park 5 June, 1878
University club chartered 1865, reorganized May, 1879
St. Patrick's Cathedral (Roman Catholic), corner-stone laid, 15 Aug 1858, dedicated by cardinal McCloskey 25 May, "
Metropolitan Museum of Art formally opened by the president of the U S 30 Mch 1880
Broadway, for about a mile, lighted with electricity 20 Dec "
Egyptian obelisk erected in Central park (NEW YORK, OBELISKS) 22 Jan 1881
Old Walton house, erected 1754, on Pearl st, opposite Harper & Brothers' publishing house, torn down "
Elephant "Jumbo" arrives in New York. 9 Apr 1882
Thurlow Weed, politician and journalist, dies in New York, aged 85 22 Nov "
East River or Brooklyn Bridge opened (BRIDGES) 24 May, 1883
Metropolitan Opera house opened Oct "
Centennial of the final evacuation of New York by the British celebrated. 25 Nov "
Failure of the Marine Bank and of Grant & Ward. 6-7 May, 1884
Panic in Wall st. 14 May, "
Corner stone of the pedestal of the Bartholdi statue laid on Bedlow's island 5 Aug "
Collapse of 8 partly finished buildings, 12 injured 12 Apr 1885
Gen Grant's body buried at Riverside park 8 Aug "
Flood rock blown up (UNITED STATES) 10 Oct. "
General tie up of street railroads by Knights of Labor 5 June, 1886
"Boodle" aldermen arraigned for BRIBERY 19 Oct "
BARTHOLDI'S STATUE of Liberty Enlightening the World unveiled 28 Oct "
Ex pres Chester A Arthur d in New York 18 Nov "
Fire in horse car barns, 1200 horses suffocated 27 May, 1887
Henry Bergh b. 1823, d in New York 12 Mch 1888
[Founder of the American Society for the Prevention of Cruelty to Animals, 1866]
Great blizzard in New York and vicinity 12-13 Mch. "
Roscoe Conkling, b at Albany, 1829, d in New York. 18 Apr "
Mary Louise Booth, b 1831, d in New York. 5 Mch 1889
[Author "History of the City of New York" and editor of *Harper's Bazar*]
Centennial of first inauguration of Washington, 29 Apr-1 May "
Corner-stone of Washington Memorial Arch in Washington square laid 30 May, 1890
New CROTON AQUEDUCT first used 15 July, "
Bronze statue of Horace Greeley by John Q A Ward unveiled in front of the *Tribune* building 20 Sept "
Corner-stone of Criminal Courts building, north of the Tombs, laid 25 Oct. "

One hundred and twenty fourth anniversary of the Old John Street Methodist church celebrated 26 Oct 1890
[Oldest Methodist church in America]

Manhattan Athletic club, "Cherry Diamonds," organized 1877, club house opened 29 Nov "

Castle Garden formally surrendered to the city by the State Commission of Immigration, and immigrant depot removed to Ellis island 31 Dec "

First Sunday opening of the Metropolitan museum, 10 000 visitors 31 May, 1891

More than 60 persons killed by the collapse of a building on Park place 22 Aug "

"Greater New York" bill killed in the assembly 15 Mch 1892

Corner stone of Grant monument in Riverside park laid by pres Harrison 27 Apr "

Hamburg American steamship *Moravia* arrives at New York, bringing the first case of cholera (UNITED STATES) 30 Aug "

Columbus celebration 10-12 Oct "

Jay Gould, b 1836, d in New York 2 Dec "

Corner stone of Cathedral of St John the Divine laid 27 Dec "

United Charities building, the gift of John S Kennedy to the 4 leading charity organizations of New York, formally dedicated 6 Mch 1893

Two hundredth anniversary of the introduction of printing into the city celebrated 12 Apr "

International review of war ships in New York harbor and Hudson river by pres Cleveland passing between the 2 lines, 3 miles long, in the DOLPHIN 27 Apr "

Infanta Eulalia arrives at New York 18 May, "

Edwin Booth d 7 June, "

Madison Square bank closes its doors 9 Aug "

Statue erected by the Sons of the Revolution to the memory of Nathan Hale in the City Hall park unveiled 25 Nov "

Bronze statue of Roscoe Conkling unveiled on southeast corner Madison square 3 Dec "
[Placed here as the point where he was overcome by the great blizzard of 12 Mch 1888]

Greater New York bill passed Assembly 8 Feb , Senate, 27 Feb , signed 28 Feb 1894
[Greater New York will include the city of New York, Brooklyn Long Island City, Flatbush, Flushing, New Utrecht, Gravesend, etc., with adjacent territory, increasing the area to over 300 sq miles, with a population of nearly 3,000,000, next to London the largest city in the world]

MAYORS

Thomas Willett	1665	Richard Varick	1789
Thomas Delavall	1667	Edward Livingston	1801
Cornelius Steenwyck	1668	De Witt Clinton	1803
Thomas Delavall	1671	Marinus Willett	1807
Matthias Nicoll	1672	De Witt Clinton	1808
John Lawrence	1673	Jacob Radcliff	1810
Johannes De Peyster* }		De Witt Clinton	1811
Johannes Pietersen Van Brugh* }	1674	John Ferguson	1815
		Jacob Radcliff	"
William Dervall	1675	Cadwallader D Colden	1818
Nicholas De Meyer	1676	Stephen Allen	1821
Stephen Van Cortlandt	1677	William Paulding	1824
Thomas Delavall	1678	Philip Hone	1826
François Rombouts	1679	William Paulding	1827
William Dyre	1680	Walter Bowne	1829
Cornelius Steenwyck	1682	Gideon Lee.	1833
Gabriel Minville	1684	Cornelius W Lawrence	1834
Nicholas Bayard	1685	Aaron Clark	1837
Stephen Van Cortlandt	1686	Isaac L Varian	1839
Peter Delanoy	1688	Robert H Morris	1841
John Lawrence.	1691	James Harper	1844
Abraham De Peyster	1692	William V Brady	1847
Charles Lodowick	1694	William F Havemeyer	1848
William Merritt	1695	Caleb S. Woodhull	1849
Johannes De Peyster	1698	Ambrose C Kingsland	1851
David Provost	1699	Jacob A Westervelt	1853
Isaac De Riemer	1700	Fernando Wood	1855
Thomas Noell	1701	Daniel F Tieman	1858
Philip French	1702	Fernando Wood	1860
William Peartree	1703	George Opdyke	1862
Ebenezer Wilson	1707	C. Godfrey Gunther	1864
Jacobus Van Cortlandt	1710	John T Hoffman	1866
Caleb Heathcote	1711	Thomas Coman (acting)	1868
John Johnston	1714	A Oakey Hall	1869
Robert Walters.	1720	William F Havemeyer	1873
Johannes Jansen	1725	William H Wickham	1875
Robert Lurting	1726	Smith Ely	1877
Paul Richard	1735	Edward Cooper	1879
John Cruger, sr	1739	William R Grace	1881
Stephen Bayard	1744	Franklin Edson	1883
Edward Holland	1747	William R Grace	1885
John Cruger, jr	1757	Abram S Hewitt	1887
Whitehead Hicks	1766	Hugh J Grant	1889
David Matthews.	1776	Thomas F Gilroy	1893
James Duane	1784	William L. Strong	1895

* Burgomasters under the Dutch

New Zealand (in the Pacific), discovered by Tasman in 1642 It consists of 2 islands, separated by Cook strait The North island contains 44,000 sq miles, and South island 58,000 sq miles. They were supposed to be part of a southern continent, till circumnavigated by capt Cook, 1769–70. In 1773 he planted European garden-seeds here and in 1777 found fine potatoes The natives are called Maoris, a Polynesian race The right of Great Britain to New Zealand wa[s recog]nized at the peace of 1814. Pop 1858, European, 59,41[3] 256,260, 1881, 489,933, 1891, 626,830, and 41,523 M[aoris], total, 668,353

New Zealand company established and Wellington founded 1839
First governor, capt Hobson 1840
Auckland founded "
Nelson and New Plymouth founded 1841
Otago founded 1848
Canterbury founded 1850
Present form of government established 1852

Ney's execution. Michel Ney, b 1769, duke of Elchingen, prince of the Moskwa, a marshal of France, who at the battle of Friedland was characterized by Napoleon as "le brave des braves," was shot as a traitor, 7 Dec 1815. On 7 Dec 1853, his statue was erected where he fell

After the abdication of Napoleon I 5 Apr 1814, Ney swore allegiance to Louis XVIII On Napoleon's return to France from Elba Ney marched against him, but his troops deserting, he regarded the Bourbon cause as lost, and opened the invader's way to Paris, Mch 1815 Ney led the French charge at Waterloo, where his clothes were pierced with bullets, and 5 horses shot under him, night and defeat obliged him to flee Though included in the decree of 24 July, 1815 which guaranteed the safety of all Frenchmen, he was arrested on 5 Aug at the castle of a friend at Urillac, and brought to trial before the Chamber of Peers, 4 Dec The 12th article of the capitulation of Paris, fixing a general amnesty, was quoted in his favor in vain

Nez Percés (Pierced Noses), a tribe of Indians belonging to the Sahaptin nation and inhabiting parts of Idaho, Oregon, and Washington early in this century In 1877, under chief Joseph, they attempted to defend their possessions against the whites, but in vain INDIANS

Niagara river and falls. The Niagara river, the "Thunderer of Waters," is 36 miles in length, 22 from lake Erie to the falls, and 14 from the falls to lake Ontario. In its course it descends 336 feet, 216 of it in the falls and rapids above Goat island, containing 61 acres, at the verge of the cliff, divides the American falls, 1100 feet wide and 164 feet high, from the Horseshoe or Canadian falls, 2000 feet wide and varying in height from less than 150 feet near the centre to 159 feet at the outer edges The New York state engineer reports that comparisons of surveys show the mean total recession of the American fall has been $30\frac{75}{100}$ feet, and of the Horseshoe falls $104\frac{51}{100}$ feet in 48 years The boundary-line between the United States and Canada is the deepest channel of the Horseshoe falls. CAVE OF THE WINDS.

Father Hennepin publishes a description of the falls 1678

La Salle launches his ship the *Griffin*, at Cayuga creek, about 5 miles above the falls (NEW YORK) 1679

A mass 40 feet wide and 160 long breaks off from Table rock on the Canada side just below the falls July, 1818

Niagara river, obstructed by ice at lake Erie, runs nearly dry above the falls for one day 29 Mch 1848

Niagara gorge below the falls is crossed in an iron basket hung on a wire cable suspended across the channel by Charles Ellet, foreshadowing the suspension bridge "

Portions of Table rock fall, 9 Dec 1828 and in 1829, and the remainder 200 feet long by 60 feet wide, falls 29 June, 1850

Suspension railroad bridge across Niagara gorge, 2 miles below the falls, first locomotive crosses (BRIDGES) Mch 1855

M Blondin (Émile Gravelet) crosses the gorge just below the falls on a tight rope 30 June, 1859

Steamer *Maid of the Mist* safely passes the rapids below the falls 15 June, 1861

Suspension bridge at Queenston Heights, built 1856, is wrecked by floating ice and a tornado 1866

Suspension bridge, ¼ of a mile below the falls, completed (for pedestrians and carriages) (BRIDGES) 1869

Visited by prof Tyndall Nov 1872

Terrapin Tower, at the Goat Island end of Horseshoe falls, built in 1833, being considered unsafe, is blown up 1873

International railway bridge crossing the river at Black Rock (Buffalo) opened (NEW YORK) "

Capt. Matthew Webb, famous English swimmer, drowned in an attempt to swim through the whirlpool rapids at Niagara, 24 July, 1883

New *Maid of the Mist* passes the lower rapids and whirlpool in safety 6 Sept. "

Cantilever bridge across the gorge, about 300 feet above the Roebling suspension bridge, completed and opened (BRIDGES), 20 Dec. "

State Reservation at Niagara falls opened as a park (NEW YORK) 16 July, 1885

Niagara Power company, to construct a tunnel for the use of falls as a water power, incorporated 11 Mch 1886

C D Graham passes in safety through the Whirlpool rapids in an oak barrel constructed by him for the purpose 11 July, "

Queen Victoria Niagara Falls park, on the Canadian side, opened to the public 24 May, 1888

Charles A Percy passes safely through the Whirlpool rapids, 16 Sept 1888
Walter S Campbell swims the Whirlpool rapids in a cork jacket, 15 Sept 1889
Water let into the great tunnel and turbine wheels started, 25 Jan. 1894

Niagara, Fort FORT NIAGARA.

Nibelungenôt or **Nibelungen-Lied,** a popular German epic of the 12th century, composed of ancient mythical poems, termed sagas, which, according to William Morris, should be to our race what Homer was to the Greeks. There are 28 manuscripts of this epic, some complete, others in fragments, dating from the 12th to the 16th century

First critical edition, by K Lachmann appeared 1826 and 1846. The best translation in modern German, by Simrock, 1827, a useful edition with translation and glossary, by L. Braunfels, 1846, in English by W N Lettsom 2d ed 1874
Richard Wagner s musical dramas, "The Ring of the Nibelungen," are founded on this poem the persons are the great northern gods and goddesses, the giants, the dwarfs, and the daughters of the Rhine (MUSIC)

Nicæ'a, or **Nice,** a town in Bithynia, Asia Minor, N W. Antigonus gave it the name Antigoneia, which Lysimachus changed to Nicæa, the name of his wife. It became the residence of the kings of Bithynia about 208 B.C At the battle of Nicæa, 194 A D, the emperor Severus defeated his rival, Pescennius Niger, and again at Issus, and soon after captured and put him to death The first general council was held here 19 June-25 Aug 325, which adopted the Nicene Creed and condemned the Arians. It was attended by 318 bishops, who settled the doctrine of the Trinity and the time for observing Easter An addition to the creed was made, 381, was rejected, 431 (when it was decreed unlawful to make further additions), but accepted, 451 When the crusaders took Constantinople, and established a Latin empire there in 1204, the Greek emperors removed to Nicæa, and reigned there till they returned to Constantinople, 1261. EASTERN EMPIRE. It was taken by the Ottoman Turks in 1330.

Nicara'gua, a state of CENTRAL AMERICA, joined the federal union of 5 Central American states in 1823, which lasted until 1839 At the commencement of 1855 it was disturbed by 2 political parties—that of pres. Chamoro, who held Grenada, the capital, and that of the democratic chief, Castellon, who held Leon The latter invited Walker, the filibuster, to his assistance, who soon became sole dictator By the united efforts of the confederated states the filibusters were all expelled in May, 1857. FILIBUSTERS The present constitution was adopted 19 Aug 1858 Great Britain, by the Clayton-Bulwer treaty of 1850, resigned all claims to the Mosquito Coast, and by the treaty of Managua, in 1860, ceded the protectorate to Nicaragua.

Revolt against pres Sacasa began 30 Apr 1893
Revolutionists successful 5 May, "
Revolutionists institute a provisional government with Morales president 7 May, "
Revolutionists in possession of the Nicaragua canal. 11 May, "
Government troops defeated 19 May, "
Pres Sacasa resigns, provisional government takes control, 31 May, "
Provisional government formed under pres Machado. 2 June, "
Revolt against the provisional government 13 July, "
Gen Zelaya, leader of the later revolutionists, made president, 5 Aug "
Nicaragua seizes the MOSQUITO country 18 Feb. 1894
A British force lands at Bluefields to protect the autonomy of Mosquito 2 Mch "
U S cruiser *San Francisco* at Bluefields 15 Apr "

Nicaragua canal. In Mch 1887, Nicaragua conceded to a New York association exclusive right of way through Nicaragua for a ship canal between the Atlantic and Pacific oceans The route surveyed begins at Greytown, on the Atlantic coast, following the San Juan river 72½ miles, and lake Nicaragua 56½ miles, thence to Brito, on the Pacific coast, total length, 169$\frac{8}{10}$ miles. Only 28$\frac{9}{10}$ miles require excavation The summit level of the canal and lake is 110 feet above the sea, and extends 153¼ miles without locks. Estimated cost from $75,000,000 to $100,000,000

Gil Gonzales Divala explores Nicaragua and sends his lieutenant Cordova to circumnavigate the great lake . 1522
Portuguese navigator, Antonio Galvao, proposes 4 routes for a canal across the isthmus, one by lake Nicaragua and the San Juan river 1550
Route for a canal surveyed for Spanish government, by don Manuel Galisteo 1781
Route for a canal surveyed for the government of Central America by John Baily 1838
Col O W Childs makes surveys between lake Nicaragua and the Pacific, and locates a route for a canal through the divide from the mouth of the river Lajas to Port Brito on the Pacific, 1850
U S government makes a survey for a canal route. 1872-73
Maritime Ship canal company incorporated . 20 Feb 1889
First expedition for construction leaves New York, 25 May, 1889, lands at Greytown . 3 June, "
Maritime Ship canal company goes into the hands of a receiver 30 Aug 1893
[Application made by Louis Chable of New York city Judge Benedict of the U S. Circuit Court names Thomas B Atkins, secretary of the Maritime Ship canal company, as receiver]
Several bills presented in Congress, both in the House and Senate, for the purpose of obtaining assistance from the U S government in building the canal 1893-94
Senator Morgan of Alabama introduces a bill fixing the stock of the company at $100 000,000, and the company to issue bonds to the amount of $70,000 000, to be guaranteed by the U S, etc 22 Jan 1894

Nice (*nees*), a city of S France, originally a Roman colony from Massilia, now Marseilles In the middle ages it was subject to Genoa, and suffered from frequent wars, being taken and retaken by the imperialists and French It was seized and annexed to France, 1792, taken by Austrians under Melas, 1800, restored to Sardinia in 1814, again annexed to France under treaty of 24 Mch 1860, the people voting nearly unanimously for this change French troops entered 1 Apr, and took definite possession 14 June. Garibaldi, a native, protested against this annexation.

Nic'ias, Peace of, between Athens and Sparta for 50 years, 421 B.C., negotiated by that unfortunate Athenian general, who, with his colleague Demosthenes, was put to death after the failure of the expedition against Syracuse, 413 B.C.

nickel, a white, ductile, malleable, magnetic metal, employed in the manufacture of German silver. Cronstadt, in 1751, discovered nickel in the mineral copper-nickel. Lancaster county, Pa, furnishes nearly all the nickel for American coinage ELEMENTS

Nicobar' Isles, 20 in number, Indian ocean, south of bay of Bengal, given up by Denmark and occupied by Great Britain to suppress piracy, announced June, 1869 Largest, "Great Nicobar," 30 miles long, 14 wide.

Nic'ojack cave, in the Raccoon mountains, Ga., about 4 miles in extent.

Nicola'itanes, a sect mentioned in Rev ii 6, 15, ascribed to Nicolas, one of the first 7 deacons (Acts vi), said to have advocated community of wives, and denied the divinity of Christ.

Nicome'dia, the metropolis of Bithynia, N W Asia Minor, founded by king Nicomedes I, 264 B.C., on the remains of Astacus, destroyed by an earthquake, 115 A D, and restored by the emperor Adrian, 124 Roman emperors often resided here during eastern wars. Here Diocletian abdicated, 305, and Constantine died at his villa near by, 337 It surrendered to Seljukian Turks, 1078, and to Orchan and Ottoman Turks in 1338.

Nicop'olis, a town of Bulgaria, on the Danube, founded by Trajan Here the allied Christian powers under Sigismund, king of Hungary, afterwards emperor, fought the Turks under Bajazet. In this, called the first battle between Turks and Christians, the latter were defeated, losing 20,000 slain and as many wounded and prisoners, 28 Sept. 1396. Nicopolis was taken by Russians after a severe conflict (2 pachas, about 6000 men, 2 monitors, and 40 guns were captured), 15, 16 July, 1877 —A city in Pontus, Asia Minor, near here was fought the last battle between Romans under Pompey and Mithridates, in which the latter was defeated, 66 B.C.

nicotine, a volatile liquid alkaloid, constituting the active principle of the tobacco plant. In a pure state it is intensely poisonous. Vauquelin in 1809 ascertained that the acrid principle of tobacco was volatile and capable of separation from its compounds by means of a fixed alkali. Posselt and Reimann in 1828 succeeded in obtaining it in a state of comparative purity from the leaves of the tobacco plant. TOBACCO.

niello-work, believed to have been produced by rubbing a mixture of silver, lead, copper, sulphur, and borax into engravings on silver, etc., an art known to the ancients, and practised in the middle ages, which is said to have suggested to Maso Finiguerra the idea of engraving upon copper, about 1460

Niemen (*nee'men*) or **Memel,** a river flowing into the Baltic, and separating Prussia from Russia On a raft on this river the emperor Napoleon met Alexander of Russia, 22 June 1807, and made peace with him and Prussia He crossed the Niemen to invade Russia, 24 June, 1812, and recrossed with the remnant of his army, 28 Dec Near it the Poles defeated the Russians, 27 May, 1831

Niger (*ni'jer*), the great river of western Africa, as the Nile is of eastern Africa First definite knowledge obtained through Mungo Park, and later Richard and John Lander, 1830 It rises on the inner side of Mt Loma, one of the summits of the Kong mountains, flows northeast to Timbuktoo lat 17° 30' N thence turning to the southeast empties into the gulf of Guinea, about lat 5° N Total length, 3000 miles Its delta extends along the coast 120 miles and inland 150 miles, forming an extensive swampy region AFRICA, 1811, PARK

Nihilism, a popular name for a school of philosophy which believes nothing without physical evidence, renounces divine revelation and all faith in the supernatural

Nihilists, a body or school of radicals in Russia said to aim at the overthrow of all existing forms of government, and the reconstruction of society on a communistic basis The name was first given by the novelist Turguenieff in 1862 to the socialists who denounced the institution of marriage, but has come, especially since 1892, to be generally applied to all the many agitators and conspirators who secretly strive to break down imperialism in Russia, to make way for some form of democracy The assassination of czar Alexander II in 1881 was doubtless one of the efforts of the Nihilists to terrorize the government

Nika contests. FACTIONS

Nile, Egypt. This great river flows in greater part from lake Victoria Nyanza, an enormous body of water in CENTRAL AFRICA, and in a known course of 1250 miles receives no tributary streams. Total length, 3370 miles. The travels of Bruce were undertaken to discover the source of the Nile. He set out from England in June, 1768, on 14 Nov 1770 discovered the source of the Blue Nile, lake Tana, Abyssinia, and returned home in 1773, considering the Blue Nile the main branch, and so claiming for himself the honor of discovering *Caput Nili*. This river overflows regularly every year, from about 15 June to 17 Sept., when, having fertilized the land, it begins to decrease It must rise 16 cubits to irrigate the average amount of land cultivated The first nilometer (a pillar) was set up by Solyman the caliph, 715 At Thebes the average rise is 40 feet, at Cairo, 27 feet, but in 1829 the inundation was so excessive that 30,000 people were drowned and an immense amount of property destroyed AFRICA. A bridge over the Nile (over 1300 feet long) at Cairo was completed by a French company, Aug 1872.

Nile, Battle of the (or Aboukir), 1 Aug 1798, near Rosetta, between the French fleet under Brueys and the British under sir Horatio Nelson 9 French line-of-battle ships were taken, 2 burned, and 2 escaped The French ship L'ORIENT, with Brueys and 1000 men on board, blew up, and only 70 or 80 escaped Nelson's exclamation upon entering battle was "Victory or Westminster Abbey!"

Ninety-six, Siege of. FORT NINETY-SIX.

Nin'eveh, capital of the Assyrian empire (ASSYRIA), founded by Ashur about 2245 B.C. Ninus reigned in Assyria, and named this city Nineveh, 2069 B.C —*Abbe Lenglet.* Jonah preached against Nineveh (about 862 B.C) It was taken by Nebuchadnezzar, 606 B C. Layard and others since 1839 have made immense excavations near Mosul, at Koyunjik and other places, revealing the ruins of a city which for centuries had been almost forgotten. Botta began explorations at Khorsabad in 1843, and pub "Monuments de Ninive," 1849-1850. In 1848 Mr. Layard pub "Nineveh and its Remains," and in 1853 "Discoveries," made on his second visit in 1849-1850. Hormusd Rassam, in 1854, discovered an ancient palace George Smith described his excavations and their rest 1873-74, in "Assyrian Discoveries," 1875 He died at Aleppo, 19 Aug 1876 ASSYRIA Mr Rassam, appointed his successor, among other valuable discoveries at Balawât, 9 miles northeast of Nimroud, and at Koyunjik, etc found a bronze monument with inscriptions recording the names title, genealogy, and exploits of king Assur-nazir pal (885-860 B C), builder of the palaces and temples of Kalakh, capital of the middle Assyrian empire

The forms, features costume, religion, modes of warfare, and ceremonial customs of its inhabitants stand before us as distinct as those of a living people, and the sculptures and cuneiform inscriptions reveal much of Assyrian history Among sculptures that enrich the British museum may be mentioned the winged bull and lion, numerous hunting and battle pieces and a bas relief of an eagle headed human figure, probably representing the Assyrian god Nisroch (from *Nisr*, "an eagle or hawk"), whom Sennacherib was worshipping when assassinated by his 2 sons, about 710 B C (2 Kings xix 37)

Ni'obe, in Greek mythology, the daughter of Tantalus, king of Lydia, and wife of Amphion, by whom she had 7 sons and 7 daughters Through her pride in her children she incurred the envy and hatred of Latona, who thereupon incited her children, Apollo and Artemis, to slay the children of Niobe, which they did with their arrows Through excessive grief for her children, Niobe was changed into a statue of stone This legend has furnished numerous subjects for art—especially sculpture

> "The Niobe of nations! there she stands
> Childless and crownless in her voiceless woe"
> —*Byron*, "Childe Harold"

nio'bium, a rare metal discovered by Hatchett in the black earth columbite, and named columbium, 1801 It was pronounced to be identical with tantalum by Wollaston, but was rediscovered by H Rose in 1846, and named niobium

Nirvana, a term of Hindu philosophy, indicating annihilation of selfhood, or absorption of the individual in the universal BUDDHISM

ni'si pri'us ("unless before"), words in a writ summoning a person to be tried at Westminster, Engl, unless the judges should come to hold their assizes in the place where he is Judges sit in Middlesex, Engl, by virtue of 18 Eliz c 12 (1576)

Nismes or **Nimes,** S. France, was the flourishing Roman colony Nemausus. The inhabitants embraced Protestantism, and suffered persecution in consequence The treaty termed Pacification of Nismes (14 July, 1629) gave religious toleration for a time to the Huguenots.

nitre. SALTPETRE

nitric acid, a compound of nitrogen and oxygen, formerly called *aqua fortis*, first obtained in a separate state by Raymond Lully, an alchemist, about 1287 Cavendish demonstrated its nature in 1785 *Nitrous acid* was discovered by Scheele about 1774 Nitrous gas was discovered by Hales. *Nitrous oxide gas* (laughing-gas) was discovered by Priestley in 1776 Its use as an anæsthetic began in America in 1864, at Paris, 1866, in London, 31 Mch. 1868.

ni'trogen or **azote,** an irrespirable elementary gas discovered by Rutherford about 1772 Before 1777, Scheele separated oxygen of air from nitrogen, and almost simultaneously with Lavoisier discovered that the atmosphere is a mixture of these

nitro-glycerine, an intensely explosive amber like fluid, discovered by Sobrero in 1847, produced by adding glycerine to a mixture of nitric acid and sulphuric acid Alfred Nobel, a Swede, first employed it as an explosive in 1864.

Nobel bequest. Dr. Alfred Nobel, a Swede (d 1896), left a large sum, of which the interest was to be awarded annually by a board of control at Stockholm in prizes each of the value of about $40,000 to those who in the previous year should have rendered the greatest service to mankind in inventions or discoveries in physical sciences, chemistry, physiology, or medicine, literary work, and the cause of international brotherhood, in the suppression or reduction of standing armies, or the founding of peace congresses

nobility. The Goths, after seizing part of Europe, rewarded heroes with titles of honor to distinguish them from common people The right of peerage seems to have been at first territorial. Patents to persons of no estate were first granted by Philip the Fair of France, 1095. George Neville, duke of Bedford (son of John, marquess of Montague), ennobled in 1470, was degraded from the peerage by Parliament for want of property, 19 Edw IV 1478 Noblemen's privileges were restrained in June, 1773 LORDS See names of various orders of the nobility

In 1845 a statistical writer said that there were 500,000 nobles in Russia, 239 000 in Austria, in Spain (in 1780), 470,000, in France (before 1790), 360 000 (of whom 4120 were of the *ancienne noblesse*), in the United Kingdom, 1631 with transmissible titles (dukes to baronets)

nobility of France preceded that of England On 18 June, 1790, the National Assembly decreed that hereditary nobility could not exist in a free state, that the titles of dukes, counts, marquises, knights, barons, excellencies, abbots, and others be abolished, that all citizens take their family names, liveries and armorial bearings also to be abolished The records of the nobility, 600 volumes, were burned at the foot of the statue of Louis XIV, 25 June, 1792 A new nobility was created by the emperor Napoleon I, 1808. The hereditary peerage was abolished 27 Dec 1831, reinstituted by Napoleon III, 1852

nobility, order of Proposed and rejected in Massachusetts, 1636 —*Bancroft*, vol. i. p 385

noble, an English gold coin (value 6*s*. 8*d*), first struck in the reign of Edward III, 1343 or 1344, said to have derived its name from the excellence of its metal.

nocturne, a name given by John Field (d. 1837) to a new musical composition. He was followed by Chopin, who died 1849 The term was adopted by Mr Whistler, the artist, for night pieces, in which he began with line, form, and color, 1877–78

"nolumus leges Angliae mutari." BASTARDS, MERTON

No Man's Land. NEUTRAL GROUND

Nominalists or **Conceptualists,** a scholastic sect, opposed to Realists, maintain that general ideas have no existence save in the names we give them The founder of the sect, Jean Roscellin, a canon of Compiègne, was condemned by a council at Soissons, 1092, but the controversy was revived in the 12th century Among the Nominalists are reckoned Abélard, St Thomas Aquinas (partially), Occam, Hobbes, Locke, Berkeley, and Dugald Stewart. The Realists assert that general ideas are realities. PHILOSOPHY.

nominating conventions. UNITED STATES.

noms de plume. LITERATURE.

non-conformists. Protestants in England are divided into conformists and non-conformists, or churchmen and dissenters. The first place of meeting of the latter in England was at Wandsworth, near London, 20 Nov 1572 The name "non-conformists" was taken by Puritans when the act of Uniformity took effect, 24 Aug 1662 (termed "Black Bartholomew's day"), when 2000 ministers of the established religion resigned, not choosing to conform to the statute passed "for the uniformity of public prayers and administration of the sacraments" DISSENTERS, PURITANS The laws against them were relaxed by the Toleration act, 24 May, 1689 —The *Non-conformist* (edited by Edward Miall, since M P) first appeared 14 Apr 1841.

nones, in the Roman calendar, the 5th day of each month, except March, May, July, and October, when the nones fell on the 7th

non-intercourse with France. UNITED STATES, 1798. With England, UNITED STATES, 1807, '09, '10, 1812.

nonjurors thought James II. unjustly deposed, and refused to swear allegiance to William III. in 1689. Among them were Sancroft, archbishop of Canterbury, Ken, bishop of Bath and Wells, and the bishops of Ely, Gloucester, Norwich, and Peterborough, and many of the clergy, who were deprived 1 Feb. 1691 Nonjurors were subjected to double taxation, and obliged to register their estates, May, 1723 They formed a separate communion, which existed till about 1800.

"Non nobis, Domine!" ("Not unto us, O Lord" etc., Psa cxv 1), a musical canon, sung as a grace at public feasts, was composed by W Birde in 1618

non-resistance oath (declaring it unlawful to take arms against the king upon any pretence), enforced by the Corporation act, 1661, was repealed in 1719

Nootka sound, Vancouver's island, discovered by capt Cook in 1778 Here a few British merchants of the East Indies formed a settlement in 1786 to supply the Chinese market with furs, but the Spaniards, in 1789, captured 2 English vessels and took possession The British ministry demanded reparation, the affair was amicably terminated by a convention, and a free commerce confirmed to England in 1790 WASHINGTON

"No Popery riots." GORDON'S "NO POPERY" RIOTS

Nördlingen, a town of Bavaria. Here Swedes under count Horn were defeated by Austrians, 27 Aug 1634, and Austrians and allies by Turenne in 1645.

Nor'folk (*nor'fok*), Va. VIRGINIA, 1776, 1861, '62

Norfolk island, Pacific ocean, discovered in 1774 by capt. Cook, then inhabited only by birds, area, 10 sq miles The settlement was made by a detachment from Port Jackson under governor Phillip, in 1788, in Sydney bay, on the south side of the island. This was at one time the most dreaded penal colony of Great Britain The island was abandoned in 1809, but reoccupied as a penal settlement in 1825 Some of the descendants of the mutineers of the *Bounty* were removed to it in June, 1856, from PITCAIRN'S ISLAND

normal schools (from *norma*, a rule), schools for the instruction of teachers. One established at Paris by law, 30 Oct 1794, opened 20 Jan 1795, under the direction of La Place, La Harpe, Haüy, and other eminent men, was soon closed Another, established by Napoleon in 1808, was closed in 1822 The plan was revived in 1826, and has been carried out extensively in England and other countries For the United States, see each state separately EDUCATION

First in New York at Albany 1844

Nor'mandy, N France, part of Neustria, a kingdom founded by Clovis in 511 for his son Clotaire, which, after various changes, was united to France by Charles the Bald in 847 From about 800 it was devastated by Scandinavians, termed Northmen or Normans, and to purchase repose Charles the Simple of France ceded the duchy to their leader Rollo, 911, who held it as a fief of the crown of France, as did his successors until William, the 7th duke, acquired England, in 1066 It remained a province of England till the reign of John, 1204, when it was reunited to France. It was reconquered by Henry V, 1418, and held by England partially till 1450 The English still possess the islands on the coast, of which Jersey and Guernsey are the principal.

DUKES

912 Rollo (or Raoul), baptized as Robert
927 William I, Longsword
943 Richard I the Fearless.
996 Richard II the Good
1027 Richard III
1028 Robert I the Devil
1035 William II (I of England)
1087 Robert II, Courthose (his son), after a contest despoiled by his brother
1106 Henry I (king of England)
1135 Stephen (king of England)
1144 Matilda and Geoffrey Plantagenet
1151 Henry II (king of England in 1154)
1189 Richard IV (I of England)
1199–1204 Arthur and John of England

Norridgewock, Me MAINE, 1724.

Norsemen in America. AMERICA

Northallerton, a borough of Yorkshire Near here was fought the "Battle of the Standard," where the English defeated the Scotch, 22 Aug. 1138. The archbishop of York brought forth a consecrated standard on a carriage when they were hotly pressed by the invaders, headed by king David.

North America. AMERICA, CANADA, INDIANS, UNITED STATES.

North America, Bank of. BANKS in the United States.

"North American." NEWSPAPERS, 1771.

North Anna, Crossing of. GRANT'S VIRGINIA CAMPAIGN.

North Carolina, one of the Atlantic states of the United States, is bounded north by Virginia, east by the Atlantic ocean, with a coast line of over 400 miles, southeast by the Atlantic ocean, south by South Carolina and Georgia, west by South Carolina and Tennessee. It lies between 33° 50′ and 36° 33′ N. lat., and between 75° 27′ and 84° 20′ W. lon. Area, 52,250 sq. miles in 96 counties; pop. 1890, 1,617,947; 1900, 1,893,810. Capital, Raleigh. For first exploration of coast, VIRGINIA, 1584.

John Porey, secretary of the colony of Virginia, explores the country to the Chowan river, 1622

Charles I. grants a patent for all the territory between 36° and 31° N. latitude to sir Robert Heath....1629-30

[If no immediate colonization ensued, if the plans formed in England by sir Robert Heath or by lord Maltravers, Heath's assign, were never realized, the desire to extend the settlements to the south still prevailed in Virginia.—*Bancroft*, "Hist. of the U. S.," vol. ii.]

Roger Green, with colonists from Virginia, settles on the Roanoke and the Chowan rivers....July, 1653

Chief of the Yeopim Indians grants to George Durant land in Perquimans county.... 1662

Charles II. grants to the earl of Clarendon and 7 others, viz.: Monk, duke of Albemarle, lord Craven, lord Ashley Cooper (earl of Shaftesbury), sir John Colleton, lord John Berkeley, sir William Berkeley, his brother, and sir George Carteret, territory extending westward from the Atlantic ocean between lat. 31° and 36°, which they call Carolina, 20 Mch. 1663

Berkeley, governor of Virginia, visits Carolina, organizes a government for the northern part, calling it Albemarle county, and appoints William Drummond governor.... "

Several hundred persons, under sir John Yeamans, land at the junction of Cape Fear river and Old Town creek, and lay out a village called Charlestown, near the present site of Wilmington....29 May, 1665

Grant of 20 Mch. 1663, enlarged and extended south to lat. 29°, 30 June, "

[This enlarged grant comprised all North and South Carolina, Georgia, Tennessee, Alabama, Mississippi, Louisiana, Arkansas, part of Florida and Missouri, nearly all of Texas, and a large portion of northern Mexico.]

Gov. Drummond dying, succeeded by Samuel Stephens.... 1667

Form of government for Carolina, known as *Fundamental Constitutions*, framed by John Locke, and amended by the earl of Shaftesbury, partly put into operation, the first set bearing date....21 July, 1669

William Edmundson, a Quaker, sent out from Maryland by George Fox, preaches at the narrows of Perquimans river, where Hertford was afterwards built.... 1672

Gov. Stephens dies and George Cartwright, speaker of the assembly of Albemarle, succeeds in 1673, but resigns and is succeeded by gov. Eastchurch, represented by a secretary, one Miller, whom he appoints president of the council and acting governor....July, 1673

People, tried by the extortion and tyranny of Miller, revolt under John Culpepper, imprison the president and 6 members of the council, call a legislature and assume control....Dec. 1677

Culpepper goes to England to explain to the lords proprietors, and John Harvey, president of the council, takes charge of the government, John Jenkins, being appointed governor by the proprietors, succeeding him....June, 1680

Gov. Jenkins dies and is succeeded by Henry Wilkinson..Dec. 1681

Seth Sothel, who had purchased the rights of lord Clarendon, arrives as governor of Albemarle.... 1683

Fundamental Constitutions, framed in 1669, are abrogated by the lords proprietors....Apr. 1693

Law passed by the General Assembly disfranchising all Dissenters from any office of trust, honor, or profit.... 1704

First church in North Carolina built in Chowan county.... 1705

Lords proprietors grant to Christopher, baron de Graaffenreidt, 10,000 acres of land on the Neuse and Cape Fear rivers in 1709. About 15,000 Swiss and a large number of Palatines follow the baron and settle at the confluence of the Trent and Neuse, calling the town New-Berne....Dec. 1710

One hundred and twelve persons, principally settlers on the Roanoke and Chowan, are massacred by the Tuscaroras and other allied Indian tribes....22 Sept. 1711

Militia of North and South Carolina and friendly Indians attack the Tuscaroras on the banks of the Neuse, in the present county of Craven, and more than 300 savages are killed and 100 made prisoners....28 Jan. 1712

Troops under col. James Moore of South Carolina capture fort Nahucke, a stronghold of the Tuscaroras in Greene county, with 800 prisoners....Mch. 1713

Bills of credit for 800*l.* issued by the colony to pay Indian war debt. First issue of paper money in North Carolina.... "

Edenton, on the Chowan river, founded.... 1715

Tuscarora Indians enter into a treaty, and a tract of land on the Roanoke, in the present county of Bertie, is ceded to them by gov. Eden....5 June, 1718

Pirate Edward Teach, commonly called Black Beard, long a terror to North Carolina, is attacked by lieut. Maynard near Ocracoke, with 2 small coasters; he is killed, and Maynard carries off his head hung to the bowsprit (VIRGINIA), 21 Nov. "

Boundary-line between North and South Carolina established.. 1727

Last assembly under proprietary government at Edenton; issues 40,000*l.* more in paper money....27 Nov. 1728

Lords proprietors surrender the government to king George II. except one-eighth interest retained by lord Granville.... 1729

Carolina, on becoming the property of the crown, is divided into 2 provinces, and George Burrington is appointed governor of North Carolina....30 Apr. 1730

Commissioners run the boundary-line between North and South Carolina. Beginning at the mouth of Little river, they run northwest to what they suppose to be 35°, when by mutual consent they run west to the Peedee.... 1738

One-eighth interest in the proprietary charter retained by John, lord Carteret, heir of lord Granville, is laid off for him, being bounded on the north by the Virginia line, south by lat. 35° 34′, and extending from the Atlantic to the Pacific.. 1743

War having been declared by England against France, fort Johnston on the south bank of Cape Fear is built.... 1745

Large accession to the settlement near Cross creek is made by Scotch Highlanders who had been supporters of prince Charles Edward and exiled to America.... 1747

James Davis sets up a printing-press at New-Berne and issues the first newspaper in the state, the North Carolina *Gazette*, 1749

Moravians purchase from lord Granville 100,000 acres between the Dan and Yadkin, which they name Wachovia. The land is conveyed to James Hutton in trust for the brethren.... 1750

First edition of the laws of North Carolina by Samuel Swann, published by James Davis at New-Berne, and from the yellow leather used in binding becomes known as "Yellow Jacket" 1752

Act passed to erect a school-house at New-Berne.... 1764

A sloop-of-war, the *Diligence*, arrives in the Cape Fear river with stamped paper for use in the colony, 28 Sept. 1765. *Cols. Ashe and Waddell, with an armed force, so terrify the* captain that no attempt is made to land the paper, and seizing James Houston, stamp distributer, they compel him to take an oath not to distribute the stamped paper.... 1765

British ship-of-war *Viper*, Jacob Lobb captain, lying at anchor off Brunswick, seizes 2 merchant vessels, the *Dobbs* and *Patience*, from Philadelphia, showing clearance papers without stamps. 580 men under col. Hugh Waddell, having secured the clearance papers from the collector of the port, proceed from Wilmington to Brunswick, and compel the release of the 2 vessels....21 Feb. 1766

George A. Selwyn obtains from the crown large grants of land in Mecklenburg county, but the people prevent their survey, "

Rev. Daniel Caldwell opens a classical school in Guilford county, 1767

People of Orange county, oppressed by the unjust acts of Edmund Fanning, clerk of the court of Orange, form an association, headed by Herman Husbands and William Hunter, for regulating public grievances and abuse of power.... 1768

James Hunter and Rednap Howell sent by the Regulators to the governor with a statement of grievances....21 May, "

*Governor and council decide that the grievances of the Regu*lators do not warrant their course, which tends to high-treason....June, "

Regulators assembling, 11 July, the governor raises troops and marches from Salisbury to Hillsborough, swearing the people to allegiance to the king and requiring the Regulators to disperse. At the September term of the Hillsborough Superior court Husbands is indicted for a riot, but acquitted. Hunter and others are imprisoned. Fanning, indicted, pleads guilty, and is fined sixpence....Sept. "

Regulators present a petition for redress to the governor, 15 May, which is rejected, and in the battle of Alamance the Regulators are dispersed by the troops....16 May, 1771

Regulators taken prisoners in the battle of Alamance are executed, Herman Husbands escaping....19 June, "

Settlements at Cross Creek increased by the addition of 300 families of Scotch Highlanders, among them Flora McDonald (famous for aiding Charles Edward, the young pretender, to escape after his defeat at CULLODEN) and her husband, who settle near the present site of Fayetteville.... 1773

Col. John Harvey, *former speaker of the assembly*, calls a convention to form a provincial congress, which meets at New-Berne; Harvey is chosen speaker....25 Aug. 1774

The Provincial congress decides that after 1 Sept. 1774, all use of East India tea should be prohibited; that after 1 Nov. 1774, importation of African slaves should cease; and that after 1 Jan. 1775, no East India or British goods should be imported, Aug. "

Richard Caswell, Joseph Hewes, and William Hooper delegates to the Continental Congress at Philadelphia....5 Sept. "

Committee of Safety orders the return of a cargo of tea which had been shipped to William Hill; committee appointed, 23 Nov. "

Gov. Martin by proclamation denounces the Provincial Congress as "tending to introduce disorder and anarchy"....1 Mch. 1775

Gov. Martin dissolves the assembly after a session of 4 days, ending the royal rule in the state....8 Apr. "

NOR

Delegates from Mecklenburg county meet at Charlotte to take into consideration the existing *state of affairs*; sign and forward to the Continental Congress at Philadelphia a declaration of independence, one clause reading as follows: "We do hereby declare ourselves a free and independent people, under the control of no power other than that of our God and the general government of the Congress"...........20 May, 1775

Col. John Harvey dies at his home at Harvey's Neck, Perquimans county.......................................June, "

Articles of agreement to "resist force by force" in the support of the country, and to "go forth and be ready to sacrifice our lives and fortunes to secure *her freedom and safety*," *adopted* by the Cumberland association at Wilmington......19 June, "

Fort Johnston burned by militia under col. Ashe......18 July, "

Gov. Martin issues a proclamation from the British ship-of-war *Cruiser*, denouncing the Mecklenburg declaration of independence...8 Aug. "

One hundred and eighty-four delegates meet at Hillsborough, 21 Aug. 1775; choose Samuel Johnston president; declare that the people of North Carolina would pay their due proportion of expenses in forming a Continental army, and establish a state government, vested in a *provincial council*, a district committee of safety for each district, and county and town committees.................................24 Aug. "

First meeting of the provincial council at the court-house in Johnston county...................................18 Oct. "

Donald McDonald, a Scottish Highlander, commissioned by gov. Martin, raises a force of about 1500 loyalists, who, under col. Donald McLeod, attack the Continental troops, 1000 strong, under cols. James Moore, Caswell, and Lillington, but are routed, and gen. McDonald taken prisoner ....27 Feb. 1776

Provincial congress assembles at Halifax, 4 Apr. 1776; *resolves* "that the delegates from this colony in congress be empowered to concur with the delegates from the other colonies in declaring independence and forming foreign alliances, reserving to this colony the sole and exclusive right of forming a constitution and laws for this colony"...........12 Apr. "

Ninehundred British, under lord Cornwallis, land on gen. Howe's plantation in Brunswick, ravage and plunder it, 12 May, and after burning some mills in the vicinity embark, having gov. Martin on board, and sail for Charleston............29 May, "

Declaration of Independence of the U. S. read before the court-house in Halifax by Cornelius Harnett...............1 Aug. "

Joseph Hewes, William Hooper, and John Penn, for North Carolina, sign the Declaration of Independence........2 Aug. "

A congress chosen by election assembles at Halifax, 12 Nov. 1776, frames a constitution for North Carolina not submitted to the people, elects Richard Caswell governor by ordinance, and completes its labors...............................18 Dec. "

Articles of confederation ratified by North Carolina.....5 Apr. 1778

John Penn, Cornelius Harnett, and John Williams sign the articles of confederation on the part of North Carolina, 21 July, "

Four hundred North Carolina Whigs under col. Francis Locke attack a camp of Tories under lieut.-col. John Moore, and rout them at Ramsour's mill, near Lincolnton...........20 June, 1780

Battle of Charlotte...................................26 Sept. "

Gen. Greene successfully conducts his retreat across North Carolina from Cowpens to the river Dan, a distance of 230 miles, pursued by British under lord Cornwallis (United States), Feb. 1781

Cornwallis issues at Hillsborough a proclamation, *inviting all* loyal citizens to join him.............................20 Feb. "

Battle at Guilford Court-house; the British under Cornwallis defeat the Americans under gen. Greene............15 Mch. "

General Assembly meets at the court-house of Wake, where now stands the city of Raleigh.........................June, "

Tories under col. Hector McNeill, numbering 600 men, in the early morning march into Hillsborough and capture gov. Burke and his suite and plunder the town..........13 Sept. "

David Fanning, a freebooter, appointed lieutenant-colonel of the royal militia in June, 1781, captures 44 persons at Chatham Court-house, while a court-martial is in progress, 16 July; besieges the garrisoned house of col. Philip Alston, of Chatham, 8 Aug.; captures 44 Whigs under col. Wade, and disperses his troops at McFalls Mills, 1 Sept., and fights the Whigs at Lundley's Mill, Chatham county, 14 Sept. "

Maj. James H. Craig, who had occupied Wilmington with British troops since 29 June, whence he directed raids into the surrounding country, receiving news of the surrender of Cornwallis at Yorktown, evacuates the place........18 Nov. "

Legislature grants maj.-gen. Nathaniel Greene 25,000 acres of state land, afterwards located on Duck river, and 640 acres to each private, with larger grants to officers in the Continental army, North Carolina troops.......................... 1782

Thomas Hart Benton, statesman, son of Jesse Benton, private secretary of gov. Tryon, born near Hillsborough, Orange county...14 Mch. "

General Assembly at Hillsborough, among acts for relief of the general government, cedes her western lands and authorizes her delegates to execute a deed provided Congress would accept the offer within 2 years ....Apr. 1784

Convention at Jonesborough appoints John Sevier president, and resolves that a person be despatched to Congress to press the acceptance of the offer of North Carolina........23 Aug. "

General Assembly meets at New-Berne, and repeals the act of 23 Apr. regarding the cession of western lands.......22 Oct. "

Convention of 5 delegates from each county meets at Jonesborough, chooses John Sevier president, and forms a constitution for the state of Frankland...................14 Dec. "

Constitution for the new state of Frankland accepted by a convention of the people, which meets at Greenville and chooses John Sevier to be governor of the state........Nov. 1785

Gov. Caswell of North Carolina by proclamation denounces the revolt of Frankland as usurpation, and warns all to return to their allegiance to North Carolina................14 Apr. 1786

State of Frankland continues to exist under difficulties for about 2 years, courts being held by both governments, military officers appointed, and taxes levied which people pay to neither, until the legislature of Frankland at Greenville authorizes the election of 2 representatives to the legislature of North Carolina, members of assembly are elected by the people, and the new state is reabsorbed...............Sept. 1787

William Blount, Richard Dobbs, Spaight, and Hugh Williamson sign the Constitution of the U. S. as representatives from North Carolina.............................17 Sept. "

State convention fixes the seat of government at Wake Court-house, now Raleigh.. 1788

North Carolina ratifies the Constitution of the U. S. by a vote of 193 to 75......................................21 Nov. 1789

Dismal Swamp canal, uniting the waters of Pasquotank and Elizabeth rivers, incorporated............................ 1790

As authorized by act of the General Assembly of 1789, Samuel Johnston and Benjamin Hawkins, senators from North Carolina, execute a deed to the U. S. in the words of the Cession act of 1784, 25 Feb. 1790; Congress accepts it.........2 Apr. "

General Assembly meets at the new city of Raleigh....30 Dec. 1794

University of North Carolina at Chapel Hill, chartered in 1789, opened...13 Feb. 1795

Col. James Glasgow, secretary of state, tried and convicted for abetting issue of fraudulent land grants, and locating them in fraud of the Continental soldiers.......................... 1798

Joseph Gates establishes the Raleigh *Register* at Raleigh...... 1799

Great revival of religion began in Kentucky in 1801; spreads through Tennessee and North Carolina.................... 1802

Bank of Cape Fear, with branches incorporated, the mother bank at Wilmington...................................... 1804

Gold discovered on Meadow creek, in Cabarrus county, during the year 1801 or 1802. The first considerable amount sent to the U. S. mint was $11,000 during the year............ 1814

State geological and mineralogical survey conducted by prof. Denison Olmstead of the university of North Carolina....... 1817

Reception to Lafayette at Murfreesborough............26 Feb. 1825

Fund for public schools established by law.................. "

State Board of Internal Improvements established........... "

First toll-gate on the Buncombe turnpike from the Saluda gap *via* Asheville to the Tennessee line, erected............Oct. 1827

John Branch of North Carolina secretary of the navy...9 Mch. 1829

State-house, containing the statue of Washington by Canova, destroyed by fire.................................21 June, 1831

Railroad from Cape Fear to Weldon, 162 miles in length, to connect with a short road begun in 1832, is commenced...... 1833

Wake Forest college at Wake Forest chartered and opened.... 1834

Convention meets at Raleigh, 4 June, 1835, frames amendments to the constitution of 1776 (ratified by the people by 26,771 to 21,606) and adjourns..............................11 July, 1835

Edward B. Dudley, first governor elected by the people, inaugurated..1 Jan. 1837

U. S. branch mint at Charlotte begins operations.........Dec. "

Davidson college, in Mecklenburg county, chartered and opened, 1838

Raleigh and Gaston railroad, incorporated in 1835, is completed..4 July, 1839

Raleigh and Wilmington railroad, incorporated in 1833, completed and opened..Mch. 1840

George E. Badger of North Carolina secretary of the navy, 5 Mch. 1841

St. Mary's school for young ladies established at Raleigh by rev. Albert Smedes..................................... 1842

Gold discovered on the lands of Andrew Troutman in Rowan county, afterwards known as Gold hill.................... "

Greensborough female college at Greensborough, chartered in 1838, opened.. 1846

North Carolina institution for the deaf and dumb and the blind, at Raleigh, opened................................ 1847

William A. Graham of North Carolina secretary of the navy, 22 July, 1850

Trinity college chartered and opened at Trinity College....... 1852

Wesleyan *female college* at Murfreesborough, chartered 1851, opened.. "

James C. Dobbin secretary of the navy ....7 Mch. 1853

State hospital for the insane on Dix hill, Raleigh, opened...... 1856

Charlotte female institute at Charlotte opened................ 1857

Thomasville female college at Thomasville, opened in 1849, receives its charter..................................... "

Forts Caswell and Johnston, occupied by state troops unauthorized, 8 Jan. 1861, are ordered restored to the proper authorities by gov. Ellis...........................12 Jan. 1861

Resolutions passed in the House, unanimously, declaring that in case reconciliation between north and south fails, North Carolina goes with the slave-states.................4 Feb. "

Gov. John W. Ellis, in a telegram replying to the request for troops from the U. S. secretary of war, says: "You can get no troops from North Carolina"..................15 Apr. "

Forts Caswell and Johnston seized by confederates.....16 Apr. "

U. S. branch mint at Charlotte seized by state.........20 Apr. "

Arsenal at Fayetteville surrendered to the confederates, 22 Apr. "

Blockade of *ports of* Virginia and North Carolina proclaimed, 27 Apr. "

State convention passes secession ordinance, revises state constitution, and ratifies the constitution of the Confederate States..20 May, "

Battle of Hatteras inlet, forts Hatteras and Clark taken by federals under gen Butler and com Stringham 29 Aug. 1861

Union movement, soon after suppressed, begun by a convention in Hyde county which declares independence of the state government 12 Oct. A convention is called, which elects M N Taylor provisional governor, after declaring vacant all state offices 18 Nov "

Joint naval and military expedition against North Carolina under flag officer L M Goldsborough and gen Burnside sails from Hampton Roads Jan 1862, engages in the battle of Roanoke island, 8 Feb, and occupies Elizabeth City 11 Feb 1862

Gen. Burnside defeats confederate gen Branch, and occupies New Berne Federal loss 100 killed, 500 wounded 14 Mch "

Fort Macon surrendered to the federals. 26 Apr "

Edward Stanley, commissioned by pres. Lincoln temporary governor of that part of North Carolina still under Federal control, arrives at New Berne 26 May, "

Battles at Kingston, 14 Dec, White Hall, 16 Dec., and Goldsborough 17 Dec. "

Plymouth surrendered by gen Wessels to the confederates under gen Hoke 20 Apr 1864

Naval battle of Albemarle sound, the *Sassacus* defeats the Confederate ram *Albemarle* 5 May, "

Confederate ram *Albemarle* blown up by lieut Cushing at Plymouth 27 Oct "

Plymouth recaptured by com Macomb 31 Oct "

FORT FISHER bombarded by adm Porter, 24 Dec. and an attack by gen Butler and adm Porter successfully repulsed, 25 Dec "

Fort Fisher captured by adm Porter and gen Terry 15 Jan 1865

Federals under gen Cox capture fort Anderson 18 Feb "

Wilmington captured by gen Schofield 22 Feb "

Battles at Wise's Forks, 8 Mch, at Fayetteville and at Kingston, 10 Mch "

Gen Sherman occupies Fayetteville, 12 Mch, and destroys the arsenal 14 Mch "

Sherman crosses the Cape Fear river, 15 Mch, federals under gen Slocum defeat confederates under Hardee in the battle of AVERASBORO, 16 Mch, Sherman defeats Johnston at BENTONVILLE, 19 Mch, the armies of Sherman, Terry, and Schofield join at Goldsborough, 23 Mch, Boone, N C, is captured by Stoneman 28 Mch "

Stoneman defeats confederates under Pemberton at Grant's creek, 12 Apr, and captures Salisbury . 12 Apr "

Raleigh occupied by gen Sherman 13 Apr "

Sherman and Johnston meet at Durham station, 17 Apr, they sign an agreement for peace, 18 Apr, it is rejected at Washington, 21 Apr, gen Grant arrives at Raleigh 24 Apr "

Gen J E Johnston surrenders to Sherman, agreement signed at Bennett's house, near Durham station 26 Apr "

Maj gen J M Schofield appointed to command the department of North Carolina, makes his headquarters at Raleigh Apr "

William W Holden proclaimed provisional governor of the state by pres. Johnson 29 May, "

Maj gen Thomas H Ruger succeeds Schofield in command of the department of North Carolina June, "

Convention called by prov gov Holden meets at Raleigh, 2 Oct., repeals the ordinance of secession, adopts an ordinance prohibiting slavery 9 Oct, and adjourns 19 Oct "

People ratify the repeal of the ordinance of secession by 20,506 to 2002, and the ordinance prohibiting slavery by 19 039 to 3039 7 Nov "

Gov Holden is relieved of his trust by pres. Johnson, and gov Worth assumes office 23 Dec "

Convention of colored delegates meets at Raleigh to promote the mental and political elevation of their race 1 Oct 1866

Legislature passes an act "granting a general amnesty and pardon to all officers and soldiers of the state of North Carolina, or of the late Confederate States armies, or of the United States, for offences committed against the criminal laws of North Carolina" 22 Dec "

Gen. D E Sickles assigned by the president to command the Second Military district, North and South Carolina, with headquarters at Columbia 11 Mch 1867

Gen Sickles removed, and gen Edward R S Canby appointed to the command 26 Aug "

Conservative mass meeting at Raleigh, define their aim "to ward off the dangers which threaten us from the success of the ultra-Republicans or Radical party in the state," 27 Sept. "

Convention called under the Reconstruction acts of Congress by gen Canby assembles at Raleigh, 14 Jan, frames a constitution and adjourns, 16 Mch Constitution is ratified by a popular vote of 93,118 to 74,009 Apr 1868

North Carolina readmitted into the Union 25 June, "

XIV th Amendment to the Constitution of the U S rejected by North Carolina, 4 Dec 1866, is ratified by legislature 4 July, "

Legislature ratifies the XV th Amendment 5 Mch 1869

Acts of violence by secret organizations in Lenoir, Jones, Orange, and Chatham counties lead gov Holden to issue a proclamation of admonition and warning 20 Oct. "

Owing to alleged outrages of the "Ku Klux," gov Holden proclaims Alamance county in a state of insurrection, 7 Mch 1870, and Caswell county, 8 July, and sends militia into the disturbed counties under col Kirk July, 1870

Col Kirk arrests persons implicated in deeds of violence, writs of *habeas corpus* are issued by chief justice Pearson, but col. Kirk refuses to produce 4 of his prisoners, 16 July, during proceedings in the state and U S courts gov Holden orders col Kirk to obey the writs 19 Aug "

New state penitentiary at Raleigh occupied "

Gov Holden impeached of malfeasance in office, 14 Dec 1870, convicted and removed from office 22 Mch 1871

NOR

Office of the State Commissioner of Immigration established 1871

Rutherford college at Rutherford opened "

Corner stone of the Tileston normal school building at Wilmington laid 30 Nov "

State Educational Association established 11 July, 1873

Eight amendments to the constitution ratified by the people, one for biennial meetings of the legislature 7 Aug "

Act passed for amnesty and pardon to members of secret or other organizations known as Heroes of America, Loyal Union League, Red Strings, Constitutional Union Guards, Whitebrother, Invisible Empire, Ku Klux Klan, North Carolina State troops North Carolina militia, and Jayhawkers "

Chang and Eng the Siamese twins, b at Bangesau, Siam 15 Apr 1811, d at their home, near Mount Airy 17 Jan 1874

Local Option law passed "

Gov Tod R Caldwell d at Hillsborough, and is succeeded by lieut gov Curtis H Brogden 17 July, "

Shaw university at Raleigh chartered 1875

Act changing the day for state elections to the Tuesday after the first Monday in November passed "

Bureau of Agriculture, Immigration, and Statistics established, "

Constitutional convention meets at Raleigh 6 Sept, adjourns 12 Oct Constitution ratified at the state election by 122,912 to 108 829 "

Biddle university at Charlotte chartered 1877

State Colored Normal school at Fayetteville opened "

State Industrial Association organized by colored people 1879

State insane asylum for colored people opened at Goldsborough 1880

State Colored Normal school at Salisbury opened 1881

Plymouth State Normal school at Plymouth opened "

Prohibition bill, passed to take effect 1 Oct 1881, if ratified by people, is lost by 48,370 votes to 166,325 1 Aug. "

State hospital for the insane at Morganton, known as the Western, opened 1883

Survey of state oyster beds, covering 1,307,000 acres, by department of agriculture aided by Federal government. 1886

State Colored Normal school at Goldsborough opened 1887

Convention representing nearly all southern states east of the Mississippi at Hot Springs under the auspices of the southern railroad and steamship companies, to promote immigration, resolve to establish Southern Immigration Association headquarters in New York 25 Apr 1888

Annual meeting of the Interstate Farmers' Association held at Raleigh 21 Aug "

State Agricultural college at Raleigh opened Oct. 1889

School law revised requiring school books recommended by the State Board of Education, and giving funds hitherto devoted to normal schools for white teachers, for county teachers' institutes "

Confederate pension laws of 1885 amended, increasing the pension funds, and excluding persons worth $500 and widows not indigent from relief "

Negro exodus, fostered by emigration agents from western states, depopulates North Carolina nearly 50,000 "

Laws creating a railroad commission and regulating railroad charges and management, locating a school for white deaf and dumb children at Morganton, establishing a normal and industrial school for girls at Greensborough, declaring the birthday of Robert E Lee (19 Jan) a legal holiday, establishing a normal school for the colored race at Elizabeth City, and incorporating a Soldiers' Home for needy Confederate soldiers at camp Russell, near Raleigh Session begins 8 Jan and closes 9 Mch 1891

Gov Daniel G Fowle dies suddenly of apoplexy, in Raleigh, 7 Apr, and lieut gov Thomas Holt is sworn in 8 Apr "

Southern Inter state exposition opens at Raleigh 1 Oct. "

Ex gov William Worth Holden d at Raleigh, aged 74, 1 Mch 1892

Col L L Polk, president of the National Farmers' Alliance, dies in Washington, D C 11 June, "

New state seal ordered 1893

Zebulon B Vance, U S senator, d at Washington, aged 64, 14 Apr 1894

PROPRIETARY GOVERNORS

COLONY OF ALBEMARLE

William Drummond	appointed.		1663
Samuel Stephens .	"	Oct	1667
George Cartwright .. .	president of council		1674
——— Miller .	" "	July,	1677
John Culpepper	usurps the government	Dec	"
John Harvey . .	president of council		1680
John Jenkins .	appointed governor	June,	"
Henry Wilkinson.	" "	Feb	1681
Seth Sothel . .	" "		1683
Philip Ludwell .	" "		1689
Alexander Lillington .	" deputy governor		1693
Thomas Harvey . .	" " "	.	1695

NORTH CAROLINA

Henderson Walker ...	president of council		1699
Robert Daniel. .	appointed deputy governor		1704
Thomas Carey .	" " "		1705
William Glover .	president of council	May,	1709
Edward Hyde	" "	Aug	1710
Edward Hyde	appointed governor	24 Jan	1712
Thomas Pollock .	president of council. .	12 Sept	"
Charles Eden	assumes office as governor	28 May,	1714
Thomas Pollock. .	president of council	30 Mch	1722
William Reed	" "	7 Sept.	"
George Burrington	assumes office as governor	15 Jan.	1724
Sir Richard Everard....	" " "	17 July,	1725

ROYAL GOVERNORS.

George Burrington	assumes office	25 Feb. 1731
Nathaniel Rice	president of council	17 Apr. 1734
Gabriel Johnston	assumes office	2 Nov. "
Nathaniel Rice	president of council	1752
Matthew Rowan	" "	1 Feb. 1753
Arthur Dobbs	assumes office	1 Nov. 1754
William Tryon	" "	27 Oct. 1764
James Hasell	president of council	1 July, 1771
Josiah Martin	assumes office	Aug. "

STATE GOVERNORS (elected by the Assembly).

Name	Elected.	Name	Elected.
Richard Caswell	Dec. 1776	Nathaniel Alexander	1805
Abner Nash	" 1779	Benjamin Williams	1807
Thomas Burke	July, 1781	David Stone	1808
Alexander Martin	1782	Benjamin Smith	1810
Richard Caswell	1784	William Hawkins	1811
Samuel Johnston	1787	William Miller	1814
Alexander Martin	1789	John Branch	1817
Richard Dobbs Spaight	1792	Jesse Franklin	1820
Samuel Ashe	1795	Gabriel Holmes	1821
William R. Davie	1798	Hutchings G. Burton	1824
Benjamin Williams	1799	James Iredell	1827
James Turner	1802	John Owen	1828
Montford Stokes	1830	Richard Dobbs Spaight	1835
David L. Swain	1832		

STATE GOVERNORS (elected by the people).

Edward B. Dudley	assumes office	1 Jan. 1837
John M. Morehead	" "	" 1841
William A. Graham	" "	1845
Charles Manly	" "	1849
David S. Reid	" "	1851
Thomas Bragg	" "	1855
John W. Ellis	" "	1859
Henry T. Clarke	acting	1861
Zebulon B. Vance	assumes office	17 Nov. 1862
William W. Holden	provisional governor	12 June, 1865
Jonathan Worth	assumes office	15 Dec. "
William W. Holden	" "	4 July, 1868
Tod R. Caldwell	" "	1872
Curtis H. Brogden	acting	17 July, 1874
Z. B. Vance	assumes office	1877
Thomas J. Jarvis	" "	18 Jan. 1881
Alfred M. Scales	" "	" 1885
Daniel G. Fowle	" "	" 1889
Thomas M. Holt	" "	" 1891
Elias Carr	" "	" 1893

UNITED STATES SENATORS FROM THE STATE OF NORTH CAROLINA.

Name.	No. of Congress.	Date.	Remarks.
Benjamin Hawkins	1st to 3d	1789 to 1795	
Samuel Johnston	1st " 2d	1789 " 1793	
Alexander Martin	3d " 6th	1793 " 1799	
Timothy Bloodworth	4th " 7th	1795 " 1801	
Jesse Franklin	6th " 9th	1799 " 1805	Elected president *pro tem.* 10 Mch. 1804.
David Stone	7th " 9th	1801 " 1807	Resigned.
James Turner	9th " 14th	1805 " 1816	Resigned.
Jesse Franklin	10th " 13th	1807 " 1813	
David Stone	13th " 14th	1813 " 1815	
Nathaniel Macon	14th " 20th	1815 " 1828	Elected president *pro tem.* 20 Mch. 1826, and 2 Mch. 1827. Resigned.
Montford Stokes	14th " 18th	1816 " 1823	Elected in place of Turner.
John Branch	18th " 21st	1823 " 1829	Resigned.
James Iredell	20th " 22d	1828 " 1831	Elected in place of Macon.
Bedford Brown	21st " 26th	1829 " 1840	Elected in place of Branch. Resigned.
Willie P. Mangum	22d " 24th	1831 " 1836	Resigned.
Robert Strange	24th " 26th	1836 " 1840	Elected in place of Mangum. Resigned.
William A. Graham	26th " 28th	1840 " 1843	Elected in place of Strange.
Willie P. Mangum	26th " 33d	1840 " 1854	Elected in place of Brown. Elected president *pro tem.* 31 May, 1842.
William H. Haywood	28th " 29th	1843 " 1846	Resigned.
George E. Badger	29th " 34th	1846 " 1855	Elected in place of Haywood.
David S. Reid	33d " 36th	1854 " 1859	
Asa Biggs	34th " 35th	1855 " 1858	Resigned.
Thomas L. Clingman	35th " 36th	1858 " 1861	Elected in place of Biggs. Withdrew 21 Jan. 1861.
Thomas Bragg	36th	1859 " 1861	Withdrew, 1861.
	37th, 38th, and 39th Congresses vacant.		
Joseph C. Abbott	40th to 42d	1868 to 1872	
John Pool	40th " 43d	1868 " 1873	
Matt. W. Ransom	42d " 54th	1872 " 1895	
Augustus S. Merrimon	43d " 46th	1873 " 1879	
Zebulon B. Vance	46th " 53d	1879 " 1894	Died in office, 14 Apr. 1894.
Thomas J. Jarvis	53d " 54th	1894 " 1895	Appointed in place of Vance.
J. C. Pritchard	54th " ——	1895 " ——	
Marion Butler	54th " ——	1895 " ——	

North Dakota, a northern frontier state, formed by the division of Dakota territory into 2 states in 1889, is bounded on the north by the Canadian provinces of Assiniboia and Manitoba, east by Minnesota, south by South Dakota, and west by Montana. It is limited in lat. by 46° to 49° N., and in lon. by 96° 30′ to 104° 5′ W. Area, 70,795 sq. miles. Pop. 1890, 182,719; 1900, 319,146. Capital, Bismarck.

French trader settles at Pembina 1780

U. S. government expedition under Lewis and Clarke ascend the Missouri river on their way to the Columbia river, 1804, and descend it on their return from the Pacific 1806

Scottish colony, planted under a grant from the Hudson Bay company, settles at Pembina 1812

Maj. S. H. Long, on a U. S. government expedition, reaches Pembina, and finding it to be within the U. S., takes possession and raises the stars and stripes .... 8 Aug. 1823

Yellowstone, a side-wheel steamboat built by the American Fur company at Pittsburg, Pa., ascends the Missouri river as far as fort Union, near the mouth of the Yellowstone 1832

Steamboat *Assiniboine*, built by the American Fur company, returning to St. Louis from the Yellowstone, is burned with her cargo of furs, at the mouth of the Heart river 1836

By the organization of Nebraska territory, 30 May, 1854, and the state of Minnesota, 11 May, 1858, the rest of the present Dakota is left without legal name or existence, 11 May. 1858

Territory of Dakota, comprising the present states of North Dakota and South Dakota, organized by act of .... 2 Mch. 1861

Capital located at Yankton 1862

Sioux Indians make 2 unsuccessful assaults on fort Abercrombie .... Sept. "

First ground in Dakota broken for the Northern Pacific railroad at Grand Forks .... 2 Jan. 1872

Settlement begun at Bismarck .... "

Military reconnoitring expedition to the Black Hills under gen. Custer, accompanied by a scientific exploring party, leaves fort Abraham Lincoln .... 2 July, 1874

Senate bill to form territory of Pembina, from the northern part of Dakota, is amended, changing the name to Huron, and passes the Senate 20 Dec. 1876. Referred in House to committee on territories .... 4 Jan. 1877

Seat of government of Dakota territory removed to Bismarck 1883

Delegates from North Dakota at Fargo protest against the state constitution framed by a convention at Sioux Falls, 4 Sept. 1883, for Dakota, with the 46th parallel for northern boundary, 12 Sept. "

Act for admission of state of Dakota passes the U. S. senate, the remainder of the territory to be called Lincoln 1884

North Dakota university at Grand Forks, chartered in 1883, opened .... "

Jamestown Insane hospital opened .... 30 Apr. 1885

Prisoners transferred from Sioux Falls to the penitentiary at Bismarck .... 31 July, "

North Dakota university partially destroyed by a storm .. June, 1887

Majority in territory vote for separation of South Dakota; North Dakota voting against it .... Nov. "

Legislature of Dakota territory passes a Local Option law .... "

Fargo college at Fargo chartered and opened .... "

Convention at Watertown favors the division, the northern portion to form the state of North Dakota .... 5 Dec. 1888

Admission act, for a convention at Bismarck, 4 July, 1889, to form a constitution and to divide with South Dakota the institutions, debts, records, etc., of the territory, signed, 22 Feb. 1889

Seventy-five delegates elected 14 May, 1889, under proclamation of the governor in Apr.; convention meets at Bismarck 4 July, adopts a constitution, provides for a division of the territorial indebtedness and property, and locates the capital of North Dakota permanently at Bismarck............July, 1889
Constitution ratified by 27,441 to 8107. The article prohibiting the manufacture and sale of intoxicating liquors is adopted by 18,552 to 17,393, and the Republican state ticket elected..1 Oct. "
Pres. Harrison proclaims North Dakota admitted.......2 Nov. "
First legislative session of the state meets at Bismarck, 19 Nov. "
Agricultural college established at Fargo by act of legislature.. 1890
School for the deaf and dumb established at Devil's Lake..... "
State normal schools established at Valley City and Mayville.. "
Acts requiring the U. S. flag to be displayed throughout each day on all public state institutions, and making 7 per cent. the legal rate of interest; legislature adjourns.......18 Mch. "
Tatonka Otanka, "Sitting Bull," b. in Dakota in 1837, is killed near Grand river, 40 miles from Standing Rock agency, in an attempt by Indians to rescue him after his arrest for refusing to peaceably disperse his band and break up the "ghost dances"..15 Dec. "
Congressman Henry C. Hansborough, Republican, elected U. S. senator..23 Jan. 1891
Australian Ballot law; laws giving Fargo Agricultural college the congressional land donation; locating the blind asylum in Pembina county; and directing that the Scandinavian language be taught in the state university at Grand Forks, are passed at session..........................Jan.–Mch. "
Proclamation of the president opening up 1,600,000 acres of the Indian reservation to settlers at fort Berthold....21 May, "
Officers of the Louisiana lottery indicted under U. S. laws by the grand jury in Sioux Falls..........................23 Oct. "
Business portion of Fargo destroyed by fire; loss estimated over $3,000,000..8 June, 1893

TERRITORIAL GOVERNORS.

William Jayne.............appointed........................ 1861
Newton Edmunds........... " 1863
Andrew J. Faulk........... " 1866
John A. Burbank........... " 1869
John L. Pennington........ " 1874
William A. Howard......... " 1878
N. G. Ordway.............. " 1880
Gilbert A. Pierce......... " 1884
Louis K. Church........... " 1887
Arthur C. Mellette........ " 1889

STATE GOVERNORS.

John Miller..................elected........................ 1889
A. H. Burke.................. " 1891
E. Shortridge...............term began.................Jan. 1893
Roger Allin.................. " ....Jan. 1895

UNITED STATES SENATORS FROM THE STATE OF NORTH DAKOTA.

Name.	No. of Congress.	Date.	Remarks.
Gilbert A. Pierce......	51st	1889 to 1891	
Lyman R. Casey......	51st to 53d	1889 " 1893	
Henry C. Hansborough	52d " ——	1891 " ——	Term expires 1897.
William N. Roach.....	53d " ——	1893 " ——	Term expires 1899.

northeast and northwest passages and Polar expeditions. The attempt to discover a northwest passage was made by a Portuguese named Corte Real, about 1500. In 1585, a company was formed in London called the "Fellowship for the Discovery of the Northwest Passage." From 1743 to 1818 British Parliament offered 20,000*l.* for this discovery. In 1818 the reward was modified by proposing that 5000*l.* should be paid when either 110°, 120°, or 130° W. lon. should be passed; one payment was made to sir E. Parry. For the voyages enumerated in the list below, Parry, Franklin, Ross, Back, and Richardson were knighted.

Sebastian Cabot's voyages to the Arctic regions..........1498, 1517
Sir Hugh Willoughby and Richard Chancellor's expedition to find a *northeast* passage to China, in the *Edward Bonaventura*, *Bona Esperanza*, and *Bona Confidentia*, sailed from the Thames (NOVA ZEMBLA)..............................20 May, 1553
Richard Chancellor, in the *Edward*, reached Archangel and Moscow; the rest perished off Lapland....................about 1554
Sir Martin Frobisher seeks a northwest passage to China...... 1576
Capt. Davis's expeditions to find a northwest passage..1585, '86, '87
Barentz's Dutch expeditions (by N.E.)........................1594–96
Waymouth and Knight's expedition................................ 1602
Hudson's voyages (HUDSON'S BAY).............................1607–10
Sir Thomas Button's.. 1612
Baffin's (BAFFIN'S BAY).. 1616
Foxe's expedition... 1631
[Many others, from various countries, followed.]
Behring's voyages...............................1728, 1729, 1741
Middleton's expedition.. 1742
Moore's and Smith's.. 1746
Hearne's land expedition.. 1769
Capt. Phipps, afterwards lord Mulgrave, his expedition........ 1773
Capt. Cook, in the *Resolution* and *Discovery*..............July, 1776
Mackenzie's expedition.. 1789
Capt. Duncan's voyage.. 1790
Discovery, capt. Vancouver, returned from surveys and discoveries on the northwest coast of America............Sept. 1795
Lieut. Kotzebue's expedition.................................Oct. 1815
Capt. Ross and lieut. Parry in the *Isabella* and *Alexander*..... 1818
Capt. Buchan and lieut. Franklin's expedition in the *Dorothea* and *Trent*.. "
Franklin's second expedition...................................1819–22
Lieuts. Parry and Liddon, in the *Hecla* and *Griper*.....4 May, 1819
They return to Leith...3 Nov. 1820
Capts. Parry and Lyon in *Fury* and *Hecla*..........8 May, 1821–23
Parry's third expedition with the *Hecla*...............8 May, 1824
Capts. Franklin and Lyon, after having attempted a land expedition, again sail from Liverpool................ 16 Feb. 1825
Capt. Parry, again in the *Hecla*, sails from Deptford, reaches a spot 435 miles from the North pole, 22 June; returns..6 Oct. 1827
Capt. Ross arrived at Hull, on return from Arctic expedition, after 4 years, and when nearly despaired of.........18 Oct. 1833
[He discovered Boothia Felix, 1830, and on 1 June, 1831, his nephew, James C. Ross, discovered the magnetic North pole in 70° 5′ 17″ N. lat., and 96° 46′ 45″ W. lon.]
Capt. Back and companions arrived at Liverpool from their Arctic land expedition (1833), after following Great Fish river to the Polar seas..8 Sept. 1835
Capt. Back sailed from Chatham in British ship *Terror*, on an exploring adventure to Wager river................21 June, 1836
[The Geographical Society awarded the king's annual premium to capt. Back for his Polar discoveries and enterprise, Dec. 1835.]
Sir John Franklin, and capts. Crozier and Fitzjames, in the ships *Erebus* and *Terror*, leave England (FRANKLIN)..24 May, 1845
[The northwest passage was discovered by sir John Franklin and his companions, who sailed down Peel and Victoria strait, now Franklin strait. The monument in Waterloo place is inscribed: "*To Franklin and his brave companions, who sacrificed their lives in completing the discovery of the northwest passage*, A.D. 1847–48." Lady Franklin received a medal from the Royal Geographical Society.]
Capt. M'Clure sailed in the *Investigator* with com. Collinson in the *Enterprise* in search of sir John Franklin........20 Jan. 1850
[On 6 Sept. he discovered high land, which he named Baring's land; on the 9th, other land, which he named after prince Albert; on the 30th the ship was frozen in. Convinced that the waters in which they lay communicated with Barrow's strait, he set out on 21 Oct., with a few men in a sledge, to test his views. On 26 Oct. he reached Point Russell (73° 31′ N. lat., 114° 14′ W. lon.), where from an elevation of 600 feet he saw Parry or Melville sound beneath them. The strait connecting the Atlantic and Pacific oceans he named after the prince of Wales. The *Investigator* was the first ship which traversed the Polar sea from Behring's strait to Behring island. Intelligence of the discovery was brought to England by com. Inglefield, and the Admiralty chart was published 14 Oct. 1853. Capt. M'Clure returned to England, Sept. 1854. In 1855, 5000*l.* were paid to capt. (afterwards sir Robert) M'Clure, and 5000*l.* were distributed among the officers and crew. On 30 Jan. 1855, the Admiralty promised the Arctic medal to all persons engaged in the expeditions from 1818 to 1855.]
German Arctic expedition (the *Germania* and the *Hansa*) sailed 15 June; arrived at Pendulum bay, Greenland, 18 July, 1869; the vessels parted; the *Germania* arrived at Bremen 11 Sept. 1870; the *Hansa* was frozen and sank, Oct. 1869; the crew escaped with provisions, and reached Copenhagen..1 Sept. 1870
Norwegian Arctic expedition sailed in the spring............ 1872
Swedish expedition under prof. Nordenskjöld sailed from Tromso, 21 July, 1872; unsuccessful; returned in summer of 1873
Capt. Hall sailed from New York in U. S. ship *Polaris*, 29 June, 1871; frozen in Sept.; d. 8 Nov. After much suffering, the crew (about half of them having floated 6 months on an ice-field) are rescued (UNITED STATES)................Apr.–June, "
B. Leigh Smith sailed to lat. 81° 24′, and discovered land northeast of Spitzbergen, 1871; in other voyages he discovered undercurrents of warm water flowing into the polar basin; he relieved the Swedish expedition..............1872–73
An Austro-Hungarian expedition in the *Admiral Tegethoff*, and the *Isbjörnen*, under Weyprecht and Payer, sailed from Tromso, in Norway, 14 July, 1872; the ships parted company, and the *Tegethoff* sailed northward and discovered Franz-Joseph land, 31 Aug. 1873; frozen in, abandoned ship, May, 1874; reached Vardoe, Norway, by sledges, 3 Sept.; arrived at Vienna.....................................25 Sept. 1874
Mr. Disraeli consents to a new British Arctic expedition, 17 Nov. 1874; 38,620*l.* voted for the expedition.........5 Mch. 1875
Capt. G. S. Nares, of the *Challenger*, appointed to command the *Alert*, and capt. H. F. Stephenson to command the *Discovery*. The ships sailed from Portsmouth.........................29 May, "
Alert (on return) arrived at Valentia, 27 Oct.; the *Discovery* at Queenstown, 29 Oct.; at Portsmouth..............2 Nov. 1876
[*Results.* Sledges reached 83° 20′ 26″, 12 May, 1876; passage to the Pole declared impracticable; no signs of open polar sea; ships wintered 82° 27′ lat.; sun absent 142 days; no Esquimaux beyond 81° 52′. Out of 120 persons 4 deaths (1 frost-bitten, 3 scurvy); greatest cold 72° below zero; extreme northern point reached by Markham named cape Columbia. Cost of the expedition 120,000*l.*]

Expedition of capt. Allen Young in the *Pandora* (aided by lady Franklin), sailed 25 June; returned 19 Oct. 1875; sailed again 2 June; returned....................................31 Oct. 1876

Dutch expedition sailed from Holland....................Apr. 1878

"Voyage," pub. by capt. Nares.............................. "

James Gordon Bennett's expedition; lieut. G. W. De Long sailed in yacht *Jeannette* (420 tons) from San Francisco, Cal.; 2d officer, C. W. Chipp; 3d officer, John W. Danenhower; engineer, G. W. Melville...........................8 July, 1879

[*Jeannette* crushed by ice 23 June, 1881; 2 of her 3 boats arrive at mouth of Lena river, Siberia, 19 Sept. 1881. First news received 21 Dec. 1881. Search for crew of missing boat (commanded by lieut.-commander De Long, chief of expedition) was begun at once, under orders from U. S. and Russian governments. Tidings received, 2 Feb. 1882; the missing party traced to a forest in Siberia on west bank of Lena river. After a prolonged search, engineer Melville found the bodies of De Long and his party, 24 Mch. 1882.]

Dutch exploring expedition in the *Willem Barentz*, sailed for Arctic ocean, 6 May; successful; returned to Hammerfest, Norway.......................................24 Sept. "

Another expedition in *Vega*, under prof. Nordenskjöld, started 4 July, 1878; at Port Dickson on the Yenisei, 6 Aug.; at mouth of Lena, 27 Aug.; at Yakutsk, 22 Sept.; ice-bound near Tschutshe settlement, 28 Sept. 1878–18 July, 1879; passed East cape, Behring's strait; entered St. Lawrence bay, in Pacific ocean, 20 July; reached Yokohama........2 Sept. "

Northeast passage from the Atlantic to the Pacific is thus accomplished, chiefly at the expense of Oscar Dickson, a merchant of Gothenburg.................................1878–79

B. Leigh Smith's successful expedition to the North pole, in his yacht *Eira*, from and to Peterhead......22 June–12 Oct. 1880

[Charts of latest discoveries in Petermann's "Mittheilungen der Geographie."]

Ship *Corwin* sailed from San Francisco in search of the *Jeannette* and missing whalers..........................4 May, 1881

Ship *Rodgers* sailed from same port on a like mission, 16 June, "

[Lieut. Berry of the *Rodgers* the first to land on Wrangel's Land; found to be an island; desolate; coal found.]

Rodgers burned at sea (crew escaped in boats).........3 Nov. "

Expedition by U. S. government to explore, and if possible to reach, the North pole, lieut. A. W. Greely, 5th U. S. cavalry, 1st in command, lieut. F. F. Kislingbury, 2d, and lieut. Jas. B. Lockwood, 3d, with 22 others; sail in the *Proteus*......June, "

Another expedition by B. Leigh Smith, in the *Eira*, 14 June; *Eira* seen in strait of Nova Zembla.................8 July, "

[*Eira* injured by ice; at cape Flora sank in deep water, 21 Aug.; stores saved, tent and house erected; the party live on seals, walrus, etc., during winter, 1881–82; return voyage began (boats hauled, etc.), 21 June; fell in with Dutch vessel, *Willem Barentz*, and soon after with the *Hope* (capt. sir Allen Young, sent in search of the *Eira*, 22 June, 1882), near Matotchkin strait, Nova Zembla, 3 Aug.; sail for home, 6 Aug.; arrive at Aberdeen, 20 Aug. 1882.]

Corwin returned to Sitka..............................3 June, 1882

Neptune sent to relieve Greely exploration party; lieut. Beebe deposits stores at Littleton island and other places, and returns.. "

German Arctic expedition; *Germania* sailed, summer, returned..23 Oct. "

British circumpolar expedition started..............11 May, "

Austrian Polar expedition; *Polar* started, 2 Apr. 1882; returned to Drontheim, 11 Aug.; to Vienna..........22 Aug. 1883

Proteus, with lieut. E. A. Garlington, 7th U. S. cavalry, sent to give relief to the Greely expedition........................ "

[Efforts not successful; lead to a court of inquiry.]

Thetis and *Bear*, under commander Winfield S. Schley, start in search of lieut. Greely.............................10 May, 1884

Discover the survivors at Baird's inlet................22 June, "

Of the party (25) only lieut. Greely and 6 others were alive, 1 of whom (Ellison) died shortly after. These arrived at Portsmouth, N. H. (Abstinence)..........................1 Aug. "

Lieut. R. E. Peary's expedition to ascertain the northern extension of Greenland......................June, 1891–Sept. 1892

Extreme limit reached by the expedition, 81° 37′ N. lat., at Independence bay......................................4 July, "

North coast of Greenland not yet fully developed............ 1894

Dr. Fridtjof Nansen's polar expedition.......................... "

Mr. F. G. Jackson arrives at Hull after spending some months within the Arctic circle...................................4 Feb. "

Bjorling and Kalstennius, young Swedish naturalists, leave St. John's in the *Ripple* for Smith's sound, 24 June, 1892; reach Disco island, Greenland, insufficiently equipped, 31 July; they crossed Baffin's bay, and arrived at Carey island, 16 Aug.; the vessel is driven on shore, 17 Aug.; in a desperate condition with shortness of provisions, embark for Cape Faraday, Ellesmere Land, in a small boat, 12 Oct.; not since heard of; reported, Dec. 1893; traces of them found on Carey island; reported..19 Oct. "

The *Falcon* wrecked off S. Greenland, Oct.; all perish; reported...27 Nov. "

The Jackson-Harmsworth expedition (33 persons) in the *Windward*, Mr. A. C. Harmsworth defraying all expenses, about 25,000*l.* starts for Franz-Josef Land, London, 12 July; left Archangel, 5 Aug.; reached Franz-Josef Land, Sept. 1894, frozen in; exploration by Mr. Jackson; he and his party remain; the *Windward* leaves 3 July, and arrives at Gravesend...22 Oct. 1895

Dr. Fridtjof Nansen starts from Christiania in the *Fram* for Arctic regions, 24 June, 1893; dr. Nansen with lieut. Johansen, left the *Fram* in charge of capt. Sverdrup and lieut. Scott-Hansen, 14 Mch. 1895, after having touched a point 4° farther north than any previous explorer. In their journey over the ice they reached 86° 14′ lat., 8 Apr.; and arrived at Franz-Josef Land, 14 Aug., and there wintered; dr. Nansen met Mr. Jackson there, 17 June, 1896; and they returned in the *Windward* to Vardöe, 3 Aug.; arrival of the *Fram* at Skjervöe, after reaching 85° 57′ N. lat., 20 Aug.; dr. Nansen and his companions received by the king at Christiania, 9 Sept.; arrived in London, 3 Feb.; farewell lecture at St. James's Hall, 24 Mch.; Paris, 25 Mch.; Berlin, received by the emperor, and granted medals, 3 Apr., received by the king at Copenhagen.......................................7 Apr. 1897

"Farthest North," by dr. Nansen and lieut. Johansen, published...Feb. "

The Norwegian parliament grants sums of money to the members of the expedition......................................Mch. "

Peary relief expedition in the *Falcon* leaves St. John's, 7 July, 1894; returns there with the members of the expedition, including Mrs. Peary all well, 15 Sept.; lieut. Peary, Mr. Hugh Lee, and Henson, a servant, remain in Greenland to continue their explorations, Peary relief expedition in the *Kite* leaves St. John's for Bowdoin bay, Inglefield gulf, July, returns with lieut. Peary, Mr Lee, and Henson, who were nearly starved, 21 Sept. 1895, lieut. Peary returns to Cape Breton with scientific collections, 26 Sept 1896; returns to St. John's with the Cape York meteorite (45 tons)..............20 Sept. "

Herr Andrée and M. Eckholm leave Trömso in the *Virgo* for a balloon expedition to the N pole, 15 June, 1896; prevented, and return, 24 Aug.; he ascends in the *Eagle* with drs. Strindberg and Fraenkel from Danes island (617 miles from the N. pole) 2.30 p.m. 11 July, relief expedition in the *Victoria* returns to Trömso without news..........21 Nov. "

Capt. Robertson, of the Dundee whaler *Balæna*, discovers several islands on the S. coast of Franz-Josef Land; reported, 3 Sept. "

Arctic relief expedition to rescue whalers; arrived at Cape Vancouver..16 Dec. "

Herr Theodor Lerner's N. polar expedition in the German steamship *Helgoland* leaves Berlin..................30 May, 1898

Capt. Sverdrup's polar expedition in the *Fram* leaves Christiania...24 June, "

The Swedish expedition in the *Antarctic*, under herr. Nathorst, successfully explores King Charles Land, W. Spitzbergen, and Northeast Land; returns to Trömso....................7 Sept. "

"Northward over the 'Great Ice,' 1886 and 1886–97," by lieut. R. Peary, 2 vols; published..........................autumn, "

Mr. Wellman's expedition to Franz-Josef Land; established an outpost, Fort McKinley, 81° lat., autumn, 1898; Mr. Wellman pushed northward, mid. Feb.; unknown regions explored, and good scientific results reported; they return to Trömso...17 Aug. 1899

Andrée search expedition, under dr. Nathorst, discovers new inlets E. of Greenland, and arrives at Malmö.......12 Sept. "

Mr. Walter Wellman's American N. polar expedition in the *Frithyof* leaves Trömso..........................27 June, 1900

Andrée's buoy No. 4 found at Skjervöe, containing message: N. 45° E., in excellent spirits, 11 July; M. Andrée reported by some to have been killed by natives.................31 Aug. "

The duke of Abruzzi's expedition in the *Stella Polare* to Franz-Josef Land; left Christiania, 12 June, 1899; wintered on Rudolf Land; capt. Cagni's party (the duke too severely frostbitten to go) started for the N. pole, 11 Mch.; reached 86° 33′ 49″ N., 25 Apr.; returned............................Sept. "

Baron Toll's expedition left Cape Wyssoki for Bennett Land, 13 July, 1902

The Baldwin-Ziegler expedition left Dundee, 28 June, 1901; visited Rudolf Land, Nansen's hut, Greely island; returned with new charts, etc., to Norway..................31 July, "

Lieut. Peary advanced to extremity of Greenland, 83° 50′, spring, 1900; was stopped by the ice opening; again he started from Cape Hecla, Grinnell Land, and reached 83° 15′, but had to fall back, spring, 1901; he started again, 1 Apr. 1902, with Henson and 4 Eskimos, etc., but failed to reach the pole; all returned in the *Windward* to Sydney, Cape Breton island......................................18 Sept. "

Capt. Sverdrup, in the *Fram*, was blocked in the ice about 79° N. near Cape Sabine, Aug. 1898; in Aug. 1899 he rounded S. end of Ellesmere Land, through Jones sound and Cardigan Strait; explored new lands, with important scientific results, to 81° 37′; returned to Norway..................19 Sept. "

[Charts of the latest discoveries are published in Petermann's "Mittheilungen der Geographie."]

Scientific expedition to the region of the N. pole, subsidized by the French Academy of Sciences. The expedition will include scientific investigations in Iceland, Spitzbergen, and Nova Zembla, with special reference to the biology of the codfish and the N. currents of the gulf stream; reported, Jan. 1903

Third Ziegler expedition in the *America*, capt. Fiala, leaves Trondhjem for Franz-Josef Land.......................23 June, "

Canadian Arctic expedition in the *Neptune* leaves Halifax for Hudson bay and the Arctic seas................................Aug. "

Mr. Champ, in charge of the Ziegler relief expedition ship *Frithiof*, made 2 attempts to reach Franz-Josef Land, without result; returned to Norway.................................... 1904

Nothing has been heard from baron von Toll, the Russian, who disappeared 2 years ago while exploring near the New Siberian islands, off the coast of Siberia, and it is believed he has perished.. "

Capt. Amundsen, the Norwegian who attempted to locate the N. magnetic pole, using a small sailing sloop instead of a

steamer, and as to whose fate great anxiety was felt last year, is now known to be safe. But he has accomplished little or nothing of the work which he set out to do........ 1904
Peary's new Arctic steamer, *Roosevelt*, launched......23 Mch. 1905
Death of William Ziegler at Stamford, Conn., of apoplexy, aged 62 years....................................24 May, "
The duke of Orleans in planning an Arctic expedition tries to buy the *Fram*.

RECORD OF THE HIGHEST NORTH.

The following is a record of the highest north made in Arctic exploration during the past 300 years, in the eastern and western hemispheres, and by both land and sea:

EASTERN HEMISPHERE.

Commander.	Date.	N. Lat.		Locality.
William Barents..	July, 1594	77°	20'	Nova Zembla.
Ryp Heemskerck.	June, 1596	79	49	Spitzbergen Sea.
Henry Hudson.....	July, 1607	80	23	Spitzbergen Sea.
William Scoresby..	May, 1806	81	30	Spitzbergen Sea.
W. E. Parry.......	July, 1827	82	45	Spitzbergen Sea.
Nordenskiold......	Sept. 1868	81	42	Spitzbergen Sea.
Julius Payer......	Apr. 1874	82	05	Franz Josef Land.
Fridtjof Nansen...	Apr. 1896	86	14	N. of Franz-Josef Land.
Frederick Jackson.	May, 1896	81	20	Franz-Josef Land.
Walter Wellman...	Mch. 1899	82	00	Franz Josef Land.
Duke of Abruzzi...	Apr. 1900	86	34	N. of Franz-Josef Land.

WESTERN HEMISPHERE.

Commander.	Date.	N. Lat.		Locality.
John Davis.......	June, 1587	72°	12'	West Greenland.
Henry Hudson....	June, 1607	73	00	Op. East Greenland.
William Baffin....	July, 1616	77	45	Smith Sound.
E. K. Kane.......	June, 1854	80	10	Smith Sound.
C. F. Hall.........	Aug. 1870	82	11	Greenland waters.
G. S. Nares.......	May, 1876	83	20	Grinnell Land.
A. W. Greely......	May, 1882	83	24	North Greenland.
Robert E. Peary...	Apr. 1902	84	17	North of Grinnell Land.

Antarctic Expeditions—The De Gerlache expedition in the *Belgica* leaves Antwerp 16 Aug. 1897; explored the S. Shetlands, 21 Jan. 1898; discovered strait Belgica, land to the east, named Danco Land, 23 Jan.; ice-bound, 23 Feb.; continual night, 17 May–21 July; lieut. Danco died, 5 June; Punta Arenas, Patagonia, reached; good scientific results; 71° 36' was the farthest south reached............28 Mch. 1899
Mr. C. E. Borchgrevink, a Norwegian explorer, first to land at Cape Adair, on the S. continent, 23 Feb. 1895; a scientific expedition under him, equipped by sir Geo. Newnes, left London in the *Southern Cross* (capt. B. Jensen) for S. Victoria Land, 22 Aug. 1898; reached Cape Adair, 17 Feb. 1899; which they ascend to 3670 ft., 12 Mch.; valuable collection made at Duke of York island and Geike land; Mr. N. Hansen died, 5 Oct.; magnetic position of the S. pole fixed at about 73° 20' S. lat., and 146° E.; farthest point S. ever reached up to that time, 78° 50', 17 Mch.; they returned to Stewart island..4 Apr. 1900
British expedition fund started by a donation of 25,000*l*. from Ll. W. Longstaff received a treasury grant of 45,000*l*. The *Discovery*, capt. Scott, left Port Chalmers..........24 Dec. 1901
German expedition. The *Gauss*, capt. Hans Ruser, left Hamburg, 11 Aug. 1901; Reached Kerguelen island.......2 Jan. 1902
[A magnetic station founded there. Found bottom at 3950 fathoms, 18° 15' W. 0° 11' S.]
The *Morning*, relief ship, left London..................2 Aug. "
Found letters from capt. Scott at Cape Crozier........18 Jan. 1903
Penetrated ice-pack to within 10 miles of the *Discovery*; transferred coal, stores, etc., and left the *Discovery* snugly berthed, her men blasting the ice to force a passage..........2 Mch. "
Swedish expedition in the *Antarctic* under dr. O. Nordenskjold sailed 16 Oct. 1901, crushed and sunk by the ice in Erebus and Terror bay.....................................8 Nov. "
[The crew rescued by the Argentine relief ship *Uruguay*.]
Relief ship *Terra Nova* left Portland for Hobart, Tasmania, to be joined there by the *Morning*, from Lyttleton, N. Zealand, 24 Aug.; left Hobart..................................4 Dec. "
The *Scotia* of the Scottish Antarctic expedition reached latitude 70° 25', and returned to Buenos Ayres.........16 Dec. "
The *Discovery*, capt. Scott, returned to England, having reached the farthest south in 1902, 80° 17' by sledging.............. "
The Charcot exploring expedition is reported as having arrived at Puerto Madria, Argentina.................4 Mch. 1905
FRANKLIN, Search for.

Northmen or **Norsemen.** AMERICA, NORMANDY, SCANDINAVIA.

North Point, Md., Battle of. An indecisive engagement between the United States troops under gen. Stricker, and the British under Ross and Cockburn, in which Ross was killed, 12 Sept. 1814. MARYLAND, UNITED STATES.

North pole. NORTHEAST AND NORTHWEST PASSAGES.

Northwestern territory. UNITED STATES, 1787.

Norway, until the 7th century, was governed by petty rulers. About 630, Olaf Trætelia, of the race of Odin termed Ynglings, or youths, expelled from Sweden, established a colony in Vermeland, the nucleus of a monarchy, founded by his descendant, Halfdan III. the Black, a great warrior and legislator, whose memory was long revered. Area, 124,495 sq. miles; pop. 1875, 1,807,555; 1891, 1,999,176.

Olaf Trætelia, 630; slain by his subjects........................ 640
Halfdan I., 640; Eystein I., 700; Halfdan II., 730; Gudrod, 784; Olaf Geirstade and Halfdan III.............................. 824
Halfdan recovers his inheritance from his brother, whom he subdues, with neighboring chiefs, 840; accidentally drowned. 863
Chiefs regain their power during the youth of his son, Harold Harfager, or fair-haired, who vows neither to cut nor comb his hair till he recovers his dominion..................... 865
He defeats his enemies at Hafsfiord, 872; d.................. 934
Eric I. (the bloody axe), his son, a tyrant, expelled, and succeeded by
Hako (the Good), 940; he endeavors in vain to establish Christianity; d.. 963
Harold II., Graafeld, son of Eric, succeeds........................ "
Killed in battle with Harold of Denmark........................ 977
Hako Jarl, made governor of several provinces; becomes king, 977; his licentiousness leads to his ruin; deposed by Olaf I., Trygvæson; and slain by his slave........................ 995
Olaf I., 995; establishes Christianity by force and cruelty..... 998
Defeated and slain, during an expedition against Pomerania, by the kings of Denmark and Sweden, who share Norway.. 1000
Olaf II., the Saint (his son), lands in Norway.................. 1012
Defeats his enemies and becomes king........................ 1015
Fiercely zealous in the diffusion of Christianity............1018–21
Successful invasion of Canute, who becomes king............1028–29
Olaf expelled; returns and is killed in battle.................. 1030
Sweyn, at death of Canute, succeeds as king, but is expelled for Magnus I., bastard son of Olaf II........................ 1035
Magnus becomes king of Denmark, 1036; d..................... 1047
Harold Hardrada, king of Norway................................ "
Invades England; defeated and slain by Harold II. at Stamford bridge...25 Sept. 1066
Olaf III. and Magnus II. (sons), kings, 25 Sept. 1066; Olaf alone (pacific)...1069–93
Olaf III. founds Bergen.. 1070
Magnus III. (Barefoot), son of Olaf............................ 1093
Invades the Orkneys and Scotland............................ 1096
Killed in Ireland... 1103
Sigurd I., Eystein II., and Olaf IV. (sons)........................ "
Sigurd visits the Holy Land as a warrior pilgrim............1107–10
Becomes sole king, 1122; d.................................... 1130
Magnus IV. (his son) and Harold IV............................ "
Magnus dethroned.. 1134
Harold IV. murdered; succeeded by his sons, Sigurd II., etc.; civil war rages.. 1136
Nicolas Breakspear (afterwards pope Adrian IV.), the papal legate, arrives, reconciles the brothers, and founds archbishopric of Trondheim.. 1152
Numerous competitors for the crown; civil war; Inge I., Eystein III., Hako III., Magnus V...........................1136–62
Magnus V. alone.. 1162
Rise of Swerro, an able adventurer, who becomes king; Magnus defeated; drowned...................................... 1186
Swerro rules vigorously; d..................................... 1202
Hako, his son, king, 1202; Guthrum, 1204; Inge II............ 1205
Hako IV., bastard son of Swerro................................ 1207
Unsuccessfully invades Scotland, where he d.................. 1263
Magnus VI., his son (the legislator), d.......................... 1280
Eric II., the priest-hater, marries Margaret of Scotland; their daughter, the Maid of Norway, becomes heiress to the crown of Scotland.. 1286
Hako V., his brother, king....................................1299–1319
[Decline of Norwegian prosperity.]
Magnus VII. (III. of Sweden), king...........................1319–43
Hako VI...1343–80
Olaf V. of Norway (II. of Denmark)..........................1380–87
Norway united with Denmark and Sweden under Margaret.... 1389
At assembly at Calmar the 3 states are formally united........ 1397
Sweden and Norway separated from Denmark, 1448; reunited. 1450
Denmark and Norway separated from Sweden.................. 1523
Christiania, the modern capital, built by Christian IV.......... 1624
Norway given to Sweden by the treaty of Kiel; Pomerania and Rugen annexed to Denmark..........................14 Jan. 1814
Norwegians declare independence........................17 May, "
Swedish troops enter Norway...........................16 July, "
Charles Frederic, duke of Holstein, elected king; abdicates, 10 Oct. "
Charles XIII. of Sweden proclaimed king by National Diet (Storthing) at Christiania; accepted constitution which declares Norway a free, independent, indivisible, and inalienable state, united to Sweden...........................4 Nov. "
Nobility abolished... 1821
National order of St. Olaf instituted by king Oscar I.......... 1847
Millennial of foundation of kingdom celebrated.......18 July, 1872
King Oscar II. crowned at Drontheim...................17 July, 1873
Statue of Charles John XIV. unveiled at Christiania....7 Sept. 1875
DENMARK, SWEDEN.

notables, French assemblies of nobles, bishops, knights, and lawyers. An assembly of notables was convened by the duke of Guise, 20 Aug. 1560, and later by other statesmen Calonne, minister of Louis XVI, summoned one which met on 22 Feb 1787, on account of the king's disordered finances, and again in 1788, when he opened his plan, but reforms interfered with private interests Calonne was dismissed, and soon retired to England Louis having lost his confidential minister, De Vergennes, by death, called De Brienne, an ecclesiastic, to his councils The notables reassembled on 6 Nov 1788 In the end, the States-general were convoked 5 Dec, and hence the NATIONAL ASSEMBLY The notables were dismissed by the king, 12 Dec 1788.—The Spanish notables assembled and met Napoleon in obedience to a decree issued by him at Bayonne, 25 May, 1808

notaries public, said to have been appointed by the primitive fathers of the Christian church, to collect the acts or memoirs of the martyrs of the first century —*Du Fresnoy* The name was afterwards given to a legal office to attest deeds and writings, and establish their authenticity everywhere A statute to regulate public notaries was passed in 1801, and others since

Notre Dame (*nō-tr dam'*), the cathedral at Paris, was founded in 1163 It narrowly escaped destruction by communists, May, 1871 It has been beautifully and judiciously restored, at a cost of about $1,250,000, under the superintendence of Viollet-le-Duc, 1866 et seq

Nova Scotia, one of the provinces of the dominion of Canada, is a peninsula lying southeast of New Brunswick, and nearly separated from it by the bay of Fundy It was discovered by Cabot, 1497, visited by Verazzano, 1524 French settled at Port Royal, 1605-7, and named the country ACADIA Partial settlement made in 1622 by Scotch under sir William Alexander, in the reign of James I of England, and named Nova Scotia Since its first settlement it has more than once changed proprietors Ceded to France by the treaty of Breda, 1667, to England by treaty of Utrecht, 1713, disputed possession for a number of years until confirmed to England in 1763 Nova Scotia was divided into 2 provinces in 1784, and was made a bishopric in Aug 1787 King's college, Windsor, was founded in 1788 BARONETS Gold was found in Nova Scotia in 1861 By act of 29 Mch 1867, Nova Scotia and New Brunswick were united with Canada for legislative purposes On the agitation for secession John Bright presented a petition in the commons, 15 May, his motion for a royal commission of inquiry negatived, 16 June, 1868 The agitation soon subsided Area, 20,550 sq miles Pop 1881, 440,572, 1891, 450,523, 1901, 459,474 FRENCH IN AMERICA

Novatians, a sect which denied restoration to the church to those who relapsed during persecution, began with Novatian, a Roman presbyter, in 250. CATHARI

Nova Zembla ("New Land"), a large island in the Arctic ocean, about 600 miles in length, north and south, from 70° to 77° N lat Area about 40,000 sq miles First known geographically when sighted by sir Hugh Willoughby, 1553. Russia, to which it belongs, established a permanent station here for scientific observations

Novels (Novellæ), a part of Justinian's Code, published 535 LITERATURE, ROMANCES

November (*novem*, nine), anciently the 9th month of the year. When Numa added January and February, in 713 B C, it became the 11th as now The Roman senators wished to name this month in which Tiberius was born by his name, in imitation of Julius Cæsar and Augustus, but the emperor refused, saying, "What will you do, conscript fathers, if you have *thirteen* Cæsars?"

Nov'gorod, a city of central Russia, made the seat of his government by Ruric, a Varangian chief, in 862, at the foundation of the Russian empire Novgorod became a republic about 1150 In 1475 Ivan III entered and abolished its charters, and a century later Ivan the Terrible destroyed the last vestige of its independence In the beginning of the 17th century the Swedes occupied Novgorod for 7 years The city is supposed to have had a population of at least 400,000 in the 15th century, now about 17,000. A national monument was placed here, 20 Sept 1862, by the czar in memory of the origin of the Russian empire.

Novi, a town of N. Italy. Here the French under Joubert were defeated by the Russians under Suwarrow with immense loss, 15 Aug 1799 Among the French slain were their leader, Joubert, and other distinguished officers

"No'vum Or'ganum," the great work of lord Bacon, containing his system of philosophy, was pub 1620

Nu'bia, the ancient Æthiopia *supra* Ægyptum, said to have been the seat of the kingdom of the Meroë, received its name from a tribe named Nubes or Nubates The Christian kingdom, with Dongola, the capital, lasted till the 14th century, when it was broken up into Mahometan principalities. It was subject to the viceroy of Egypt, having been conquered by Ibrahim Pacha in 1822, until the revolt of the Mahdi in 1882, when all of this region passed out of the hands of the Egyptians SOUDAN.

nucleus theory in chemistry. COMPOUND RADICAL

Nullification ordinance of South Carolina. SOUTH CAROLINA, UNITED STATES, 1832-33

Numantine war. The war between Romans and Celtiberians (Celts who possessed the country near the Iber, now the Ebro) began 143 B C, the latter having given refuge to their allies the Sigidians, who had been defeated by the Romans Numantia, an unprotected city, withstood a long siege, in which the army of Scipio Africanus, 60,000 men, was opposed by no more than 4000 men able to bear arms The Numantines fed upon horse-flesh, and their own dead, and then drew lots to kill one another At length they set fire to their houses, and destroyed themselves, so that not one remained to adorn the triumph of the conqueror, 133 B.C. (Nothing in the annals of ancient Rome exhibits its remorseless and vindictive spirit more than this war)

numerals. The use of visible signs to denote numbers can be traced to remote times, but our present decimal system in its complete form with the zero is of Indian or Hindu origin From the Hindus it passed to the Arabians, probably about 750 A D In Europe the complete system was derived from the Arabs in the 12th century. The use of numerals in India can be traced back to the Náná Ghat inscriptions supposed to date from the early part of the 3d century B C The earliest known example of a date written on the modern system is of 738 A D ABACUS, ARITHMETIC.

Numid'ia, a country of N Africa, the seat of the war of the Romans with Jugurtha, which began 111 B.C., and ended with his subjugation and captivity, 106 The last king, Juba, joined Cato, and was killed at the battle of Thapsus, 46 B.C., when Numidia became a Roman province. MAURITANIA.

numismat'ics, the science of coins and medals, an important aid to the study of history In England Evelyn (1697), Addison (1726), and Pinkerton (1789), published works on medals. Pellerin's "Recueil des Médailles," 9 vols. 4to (1762) Ruding's "Annals" is the great work on British coinage (new edition, 1840) The Numismatic Society in London was founded by Dr John Lee in 1836 It publishes the *Numismatic Chronicle*. Yonge Akerman's "Numismatic Manual" (1840) is a useful introduction to the science Foreign works are numerous. COIN, MEDALS.

nun'cio, an envoy from the pope to Catholic states. The pope deputed a nuncio to the Irish rebels in 1645 The arrival in London of a nuncio, and his admission to audience by James II, July, 1687, hastened the English Revolution.

nunnery. The first founded is said to have been that to which the sister of St. Anthony retired at the close of the 3d century The first founded in France, near Poictiers, by St. Marcellina, sister to St. Martin, 360 —*Du Fresnoy*. The first in England was at Folkestone, in Kent, by Eadbald, or Edbald, king of Kent, 630.—*Dugdale*. ABBEYS, FRENCH IN AMERICA, 1639, MONACHISM The nuns were expelled from convents in Germany, in July, 1785, in France, in Jan 1790 In Feb. 1861, monastic establishments were abolished in Naples, with compensation to inmates For memorable instances of fortitude of nuns, ACRE, COLDINGHAM.

Nu'remberg, a mediæval city of Germany dating from the 11th century, and a free imperial city from 1219. From this city Charles IV. of Germany issued his famous

Golden bull, 1355, and here Albert Durer was born, 1471 In 1522, the diet here demanded ecclesiastical reforms and a general council, and in 1532 secured religious liberty to the Protestants It was annexed to Bavaria in 1805 Now noted for having maintained its mediæval aspect substantially unimpaired, so that it is virtually in its architecture a city of the middle ages Pop 1890, 142,403

"In the valley of the Pegnitz, where across broad meadow lands
Rise the blue Franconian mountains, Nuremberg the ancient stands"
—*Longfellow*, "Nuremberg"

Nutten island. New York, 1637

Nystadt, a seaport town of S W Finland By treaty, signed here 30 Aug 1721, Sweden ceded Livonia, Esthonia, and other territories to Russia

O

O, the 15th letter and 4th vowel of the English alphabet, is the ὂ μικρον, little or short *o* of the Greek. Traced to the Phœnician, but as yet no evidence of the letter found in the Egyptian In Irish or Gaelic surnames it signifies son of, as O Brien, son of Brien, etc

oak (Ang-Sax *āc* The name common to the Teutonic tongue Lat. *Quercus*, a tree belonging to the order *Cupuliferæ*), styled the monarch of the woods, and an emblem of strength, virtue, constancy, and long life That produced in England is considered to be the best for ship building, except the live-oak of the United States. Flowers and plants In June, 403, the "Synod of the Oak" was held at Chalcedon The constellation Robur Caroli (the oak of Charles), was named by Dr Halley in 1676, in memory of the oak in which Charles II saved himself from his pursuers, after the battle of Worcester, 3 Sept 1651 Boscobel, Races

Charter oak (Connecticut) 1687-1856
Herne's oak, Windsor park, mentioned in "Merry Wives of Windsor" destroyed by wind (Herne's oak) 31 Aug 1863
Existing oaks, 1879 Cowthorpe, Yorkshire, girth at the ground, 55 feet 6 inches Newland, Gloucester (mentioned in Domesday Book), 46 feet.
"Talking Oak," poem by Tennyson Literature

Oates's plot. Titus Oates, at one time chaplain in the British navy, was dismissed for immoral conduct, and became a lecturer in London In conjunction with Dr Tongue, he invented a plot of the Roman Catholics, who he asserted had conspired to assassinate Charles II and extirpate the Protestant religion He made it known, 12 Aug 1678, and about 18 Roman Catholics were accused, and, upon false testimony, convicted and executed, among them the aged viscount Stafford, 29 Dec. 1680 Oates was afterwards tried for perjury (in the reign of James II), and, being found guilty, was fined put in the pillory, publicly whipped from Newgate to Tyburn, and sentenced to imprisonment for life, May, 1685 On the accession of William and Mary he was pardoned, and a pension of 3*l* a week granted to him, 1689

oaths, solemn appeals to God for the truth of an affirmation There are 2 classes of oaths (1) assertatory, when made as to a fact, etc., (2) promissory, oaths of allegiance, of office, etc. Taken by Abraham, 1892 B C (Gen xxi 24), and authorized 1491 B C. (Exod xxii 11) The administration of an oath in judicial proceedings was introduced by the Saxons into England, 600 —*Rapin* That administered to a judge was settled 1344

Icelandic oath "Name I to witness that I take oath by the ring, law oath so help me Frey and Niörd, and almighty Thor, as I shall this suit follow or defend, or witness bear or verdict or doom, as I wit rightest and soothe stand most lawfully," etc about 925
Of supremacy, first administered to British subjects, and ratified by Parliament, 26 Henry VIII (*Stow's Chron*) 1535
Oaths were taken on the Gospels so early as 528, and the words "So help me God and all saints" concluded an oath until 1550
Ancient oath of allegiance in England, "to be true and faithful to the king and his heirs, and truth and faith to bear of life and limb and terrene honor, and not to know or hear of any ill or damage intended him without defending him therefrom," to which James I added a declaration against the pope's authority 1603
It was again altered 1689
Affirmation of a Quaker authorized instead of an oath, by statute, in 1696 et seq
Of abjuration, being an obligation to maintain the government of king, lords, and commons, the church of England, and toleration of Protestant dissenters, and abjuring all Roman Catholic pretenders to the crown, 13 Will. III 1701
Affirmation, instead of oath, was permitted to Quakers and other dissenters by acts passed in 1833, 1837, 1838, and 1863 (Affirmation)
In 1858 and 1860 Jews elected members of Parliament were relieved from part of the oath of allegiance (Jews)
By 24 and 25 Vict c 66, a solemn declaration may be substituted for an oath by persons conscientiously objecting to be sworn in criminal prosecutions 1861
A bill for modifying the oath taken by Roman Catholics (passed by the commons) was rejected by the lords 26 June, 1865
Oath to be taken by members of Parliament was modified and made uniform by an act passed 30 Apr 1866
New oath of allegiance by 31 and 32 Vict c 72 (1868) for members of the new Parliament "I do swear that I will be faithful and bear true allegiance to her majesty queen Victoria, her heirs and successors, according to law, so help me God" (Bradlaugh case, Parliament, 1880)
New Parliamentary Oaths bill brought in, discharged 5 July, 1881
Following is the form of the oath of allegiance Washington was directed by Congress to administer to the officers of the army before leaving Valley Forge "I [name and office] in the armies of the United States of America, do acknowledge the United States of America to be free independent and sovereign states, and declare that the people thereof owe no allegiance or obedience to George III, king of Great Britain, and I renounce, refuse, and abjure any allegiance or obedience to him, and I do —— that I will to the utmost of my power support, maintain, and defend the said United States against the said king George III, his heirs and successors, and his or their abettors, assistants, and adherents and will serve the said United States in the office of —— which I now hold with fidelity according to the best of my skill and understanding" June, 1778
[By act of Congress, 3 Aug 1861, the oath of allegiance for the cadets at West Point was amended so as to abjure all allegiance, sovereignty, or fealty to any state county, or country whatsoever, and to require unqualified support of the Constitution and the national government]
Oaths of allegiance, as a condition of pardon, required of persons who had participated in the rebellion 1865
[The oath required of persons appointed to office from the southern U S, declaring that they had in no way aided or abetted the rebellion, was called the "iron clad oath" Its terms were modified as soon as all apprehension of further difficulty at the South had passed away]
Affirmations ordered to be accepted for oaths in France, 2 Feb, in Spain April, 1883

ob'elisk (Gr ὀβελός, a spit, μονόλιθος, a single stone), a column of rectangular shape, slightly tapering from the bottom to near the top, which draws sharply to a point in the form of a pyramid The Egyptian symbol of the supreme god The first mentioned in history was that of Rameses, king of Egypt, about 1485 B C. The Arabians called them Pharaoh's needles, and the Egyptian priests the fingers of the sun Several were erected at Rome, one by the emperor Augustus in the Campus Martius, on the pavement of which was a horizontal dial that marked the hour, about 14 B.C Of the obelisks brought to Rome by the emperors, several have been restored and set up by various popes One was excavated and set up in the piazza of St. John Lateran, Rome, by Sixtus V 1588

In London are 3 English obelisks first in Fleet st, at the top of Bridge st., erected to John Wilkes, lord mayor of London in 1775, and immediately opposite to it at the south end of Farringdon st., stands another of granite to the memory of Robert Waithman lord mayor in 1824, erected 25 June, 1833, the third, at the south end of the Blackfriars road, marks the distance of one mile and a fraction from Fleet st.
Egyptian obelisks 42 are known, some broken 12 at Rome, 1, from Luxor, set up in the Place de la Concorde, Paris, Oct 1836, 5 in England (2 British Museum, 1 Alnwick, 1 Soughton hall, 1 on Thames embankment), 1 in New York
Obelisks improperly named "Cleopatra's Needles" were erected by Thothmes III at On (Heliopolis), about 1500 B C One was removed to Alexandria by Augustus, about 23 B.C After being long imbedded in the shore, it was acquired for Great Britain by sir Ralph Abercromby in 1801, but not removed It was offered to the British government by Mehemet Ali, and again by the Khedive, 15 Mch 1877
Erasmus Wilson having offered to pay all expenses, John Dixon, the engineer, undertook to convey it to England The vessel *Cleopatra*, containing it, sailed with the *Olga*, 21 Sept. During a violent gale the vessels were separated, 14, 15 Oct., 6 lives

were lost in a fruitless attempt to recover it. The *Cleopatra*, which was abandoned, was found by the *Fitzmaurice* (capt. Carter), and towed to Ferrol, whence it was towed by the *Anglia*, and arrived in London, 20 Jan. 1878.

Salvage awarded was 2000*l.*, 6 Apr. 1878.

After much discussion, the Thames embankment (between Charing Cross and Waterloo bridges) was selected for its site, where, by much engineering skill, it was placed, 12 Sept. 1878.

Obelisk weighs 186 tons, 7 cwt., 2 stones, 11 lbs. Height, from base to point, 68 feet 5½ inches.

It was placed under the care of the metropolitan board of works by act passed 22 July, 1878.

Fellow of the obelisk of London (reared at Heliopolis about 1500 B.C. by Thothmes III., and removed to Alexandria about 23 B.C.) was offered to the U. S. in 1877.

Offer was confirmed, May, 1879. The work of lowering the shaft begun by lieut.-com. Gorringe, 6 Dec. 1879. NEW YORK, Jan. 1881.

Ober-Ammergau passion-play. DRAMA.

Oberlin college, at Oberlin, Lorain county, O., founded in 1833 by the rev. John J. Shipherd and Philo P. Stewart, and so named in honor of J. F. Oberlin (1740–1826), a Protestant pastor of Waldbach, Alsace. COLLEGES.

Oblong tract, The. A tract of land claimed by Connecticut, 580 rods in width, containing 61,440 acres, and called from its form "The Oblong." This was ceded to New York as an equivalent for lands near Long Island sound, now including the towns of Greenwich, Stamford, New Canaan, and Darien, surrendered to Connecticut, by agreement of the commissioners of New York and Connecticut, 1731. But the dividing line of "The Oblong" was not run correctly, and this gave rise to a vexatious controversy which was not settled until 1880. NEW YORK, 1880.

observatory, a building with apparatus for observing natural, especially astronomical, phenomena. The first is said to have been the top of the temple of Belus, at Babylon. On the tomb of Ozimandyas, in Egypt, was another, with a golden circle 200 feet in diameter; that at Benares was at least as ancient as these. The first in authentic history was at Alexandria, about 300 B.C., erected by Ptolemy Soter. The first observatory in Europe was erected at Nuremberg, 1472, by Walthers. The 2 most celebrated of the 16th century were the one erected by landgrave William IV. at Cassel, 1561, and Tycho Brahe's at Uranienburg, 1567. The first attempt in the United States was at the University of North Carolina, 1824; and the first permanent one at Williams college, 1836.

PRINCIPAL ASTRONOMICAL OBSERVATORIES, ARRANGED ACCORDING TO THE SIZE OF REFRACTOR.

Name.	Place.	Size of refractor.	Maker and date furnished.
Lick	Hamilton, Cal.	36 inches	A. Clark & Sons, 1887.
Pulkowa	Russia	30 "	A. Clark & Sons, 1884.
Nice	South France	29.9 "	Henry Bros., 1886.
Paris	France	28.9 "	Martin, 1885.
Vienna	Austria	27 "	Grubb, 1882.
Washington	Washington, D. C.	26 "	A. Clark, 1873.
McCormick's	Virginia, U. S.	26 "	A. Clark, 1883.
Newall's	Gateshead, Engl.	25 "	Cooke, 1870.
Princeton	Princeton, N. J.	23 "	A. Clark & Sons, 1883.
Mt. Etna	Sicily	21.8 "	Merz, 1880.
Strasburg	Germany	19.1 "	Merz, 1879.
Milan	Italy	19.1 "	Merz, 1879.
Chicago	Chicago, Ill.	18.5 "	A. Clark, 1864.
Warner	Rochester, N. Y.	16 "	A. Clark & Sons, 1880.
Washburn	Madison, Wis.	15.5 "	A. Clark & Sons, 1879.
Edinburgh	Scotland	15.1 "	Grubb, 1875.
Brussels	Belgium	15 "	Merz & Son, 1877.
Madrid	Spain	15 "	Merz.
Rio Janeiro	Brazil	15 "	
Paris	France	15 "	Lerebours & Brûnner, 1854.
Huggins	Tulse Hill, London, Engl.	15 "	Grubb, 1882.
Paris	France	15 "	Henry.
Tacubaya	Mexico	15 "	Cauchoix, 1882.
Bordeaux	France	14.9 "	Merz & Son.
Nice	South France	14.9 "	Henry.
Pulkowa	Russia	14.9 "	Merz & Mahler, 1840.
Harvard	Cambridge, Mass.	14.9 "	Merz, 1843.
Lisbon	Portugal	14.6 "	Merz, 1863.
Litchfield	Hamilton college, Clinton, N. Y.	13.5 "	Spencer & Eaton, 1856.
Coopers	Markree, Sligo, Ireland	13.3 "	Cauchoix, 1834.
Cadiz	San Fernando, Portugal	13 "	Brunner.
Rutherfurd's	Columbia college, N. Y.	13 "	Rutherfurd & Fitz.
Allegheny	Pennsylvania, U. S.	13 "	Fitz, remounted by Clark, 1874.
Dudley	Albany, N. Y.	13 "	Fitz, 1856.
Greenwich	England	12.8 "	Merz.
Lyons	France	12.7 "	Henry.
Algiers	Africa	12.5 "	Henry.
Ann Arbor	Ann Arbor, Mich.	12.5 "	Fitz.
Vassar	New York	12.3 "	A. Clark, 1855.
Glasgow	Missouri, U. S.	12.3 "	A. Clark, 1876.
Oxford university	England	12.3 "	Grubb.
Paris	France	12.2 "	Secretan.
Lick	Hamilton, Cal.	12 "	A. Clark & Sons, 1881.
Vienna	Austria	12 "	A. Clark & Sons, 1882.
Middletown university	Middletown, Conn.	12 "	A. Clark.
White's	Brooklyn, N. Y.	12 "	A. Clark.
Dresden	Saxony	12 "	Grubb, 1880.
Sunderlin	England	12 "	Cooke.
Dublin	Ireland	11.9 "	Cauchoix, 1868.
Cambridge university	England	11.5 "	Cauchoix, 1840.
Potsdam	Germany	11.5 "	Schröder, 1874.
Mt. Lookout	Cincinnati, O.	11.3 "	Merz, 1846. [Obs. 1886–87.
Hastings	New York	11 "	Clark, removed to Harvard College

[There are many others, both in Europe and the U. S., with refractors ranging from 10 in. downwards.]

occult sciences (from *occultus*, concealed). ALCHEMY, ASTROLOGY, MAGIC, etc.

ocean areas and depth. The *Challenger's* expedition states the areas and depth as follows:

	Area.	Greatest depth.
Atlantic	24,536,000 sq. miles	27,366 feet.
Pacific	50,309,000 "	30,000 "
Indian	17,084,000 "	18,582 "
Arctic	4,781,000 "	9,000 "
Antarctic	30,592,000 "	25,200 "

DEEP-SEA SOUNDINGS.

oc'tarch, the chief of the kings of the heptarchy, was called *Rex gentis Anglorum.* Hengist was the first octarch, 455, and Egbert the last, 800. BRITAIN. Some authors call the English heptarchy the *octarchy.*

Octo'ber, the 8th month in the year of Romulus, as its name imports, and the 10th in the year of Numa, 713 B.C. October still retained its first name, although the senate ordered it to be called *Faustinus*, in honor of Faustina, wife of Antoninus the emperor; and Commodus called it *Invictus* and *Domitianus.* October was sacred to Mars.

octrois (*oc-trwa'*; from Latin *auctorium*, authority), a term applied to concessions from sovereigns, and to taxes levied at the gates of towns in France on articles of food entering the city. These octrois, of ancient origin, were suppressed in 1791; re-established, 1797; and reorganized in 1816, 1842, and 1852. In 1859 the octrois of Paris produced above 54,000,000 francs. The Belgian government became very popular in July, 1860, by abolishing the octrois.

Odd-fellows, a name adopted by members of a social institution having signs of recognition, initiatory rites and ceremonies, grades of dignity and honor; object purely social and benevolent, confined to members. Mention is made by Defoe of the society of "Odd-fellows," but the oldest lodge, the name of which has been handed down, is the "Royal Aristarchus" No. 9, which met 1745 in London. Independent order of Odd-fellows formed, Manchester, Engl., 1813. Odd-fellowship was introduced into the United States from Manchester, 1819; and the Grand Lodge of Maryland and the U. S. was constituted 22 Feb. 1821. In 1842 the society severed its connection with the Manchester unity. In 1843 it issued a dispensation for opening the Prince of Wales Lodge No. 1, at Montreal, Canada. The American society, including the U. S. and Canada, has its headquarters at Baltimore. In 1882 its membership was 500,000; income, $6,000,000; disbursements for relief of members, $2,000,000. In 1891 its membership was 647,471; total relief paid, over $3,000,000, of which $175,000 went to the education of orphans.

ode (Gr. ᾠδή or ἀοιδή, a song, a short poem or song), among the Greeks originally extempore songs in honor of the gods. Anacreon's odes were composed about 532; Pindar's, 498 or 446; and Horace's from 24 to 13, all B.C. An ancient ode consisted of strophe, antistrophe, and epode. LITERATURE.

odom'eter (from the Gr. ὁδός, way, and μέτρον, measure). PEDOMETER.

odontol'ogy (from the Gr. ὀδόντες, teeth), the science of the teeth, may be said to have begun with the researches of prof. Richard Owen, who in 1839 made the first definite announcement of the organic connection between the vascular and vital soft parts of the frame and the hard substance of a tooth. His comprehensive work "Odontography" (illustrated with beautiful plates) was published 1840-45. The Odontological Society was established 1856. DENTISTRY.

Od'rysæ, a people of Thrace. Their king, Teres, retained his independence of the Persians, 508 B.C. Sitalces, his son, enlarged his dominions, and in 429 aided Amyntas against Perdiccas II. of Macedon with an army of 150,000 men. Sitalces, killed in battle with the Triballi, 424, was succeeded by Seuthes, who reigned prosperously. Cotys, another king (382-353), disputed the possession of the Thracian Chersonesus with Athens. After 9 or 10 years' warfare, Philip II. of Macedon reduced the Odrysæ to tributaries, and founded Philippopolis and other colonies, 343. The Romans, after their conquest of Macedon, favored the Odrysæ, and in 42 their king, Sadales, bequeathed his territories to the Romans. The Odrysæ, turbulent subjects, and often chastised, were finally incorporated into the empire by Vespasian, about 70 A.D.

od'yl, od, or **odic,** the name given in 1845 by baron von Reichenbach to a so-called new "imponderable, or influence," said to be developed by magnets, crystals, the human body, heat, electricity, chemical action, and the whole material universe. The odylic force is said to give rise to luminous phenomena, visible to certain sensitive persons only. The baron's "Researches on Magnetism, etc., in Relation to the Vital Force," translated by dr. Gregory, was pub. 1850. MESMERISM.

> "That od-force of German Reichenbach
> Which still from female finger-tips burnt blue."
> —*E. B. Browning*, "Aurora Leigh," bk. vii.

œcumen'ical bishop (Gr. οἰκουμένη, the habitable, *globe* understood), "universal bishop," a title assumed by John, bishop of Constantinople, 587. COUNCILS OF THE CHURCH.

Œnoph'yta, a city of Bœotia, N. Greece. Here Myronides and the Athenians defeated the Bœotians, 456 B.C.

Offa's dyke, the intrenchment from the Wye to the Dee, made by Offa, king of Mercia, to defend his country from the incursions of the Welsh, 779.

Og'densburg, a town of New York, captured by the British, 22 Feb. 1813. NEW YORK.

Ogul'nian law, carried by the tribunes Q. and Cn. Ogulnius, increased the number of pontiffs and augurs, and made plebeians eligible to those offices, 300 B.C.

Og'yges, Deluge of (which laid Attica waste for more than 200 years, and until the arrival of Cecrops), is stated to have occurred 1764 B.C. DELUGE.

Ohio, one of the central northern states of the United States, is situated between 38° 27′ and 41° 57′ N. lat., and between 80° 34′ and 84° 49′ W. lon. The Ohio river separates it from Kentucky on the south and from West Virginia south and east. Pennsylvania bounds it in part on the east, Indiana on the west, and lake Erie on the north. Its greatest length from east to west is about 225 miles; greatest breadth from north to south is about 210 miles. Area, 39,964 sq. miles in 88 counties. The surface consists of an undulating plain, most of it arable without excessive outlay. Pop. 1890, 3,672,316; 1900, 4,157,545. It ranks 4th in point of wealth and population among the states. Capital, Columbus. CINCINNATI, CLEVELAND.

Letters patent issued by James I. of England, under which England claimed Ohio afterwards..................10 Apr. 1606
Charter of the London company granted by James I. embracing the lands west of the Alleghanies and northwest of the Ohio river 1609
Eries, inhabiting the southern and eastern shores of lake Erie, are conquered by the Iroquois.......... 1656
La Salle enters the Ohio valley from the Niagara region, discovers the Ohio river, and explores it as far as the rapids at Louisville ....Aug. 1669
[It is now generally held that La Salle discovered the Ohio, descending to the falls at Louisville. This conclusion, while no doubt sound, is reached by cautious criticism of fragmentary documents.—*B. A. Hinsdale*, "The Old Northwest," p. 31.]
France takes formal possession of the northwest "from the mouth of the great river on the eastern side, otherwise called the Ohio".......... 1671
Joliet indicates the Ohio country on his map of the northwest.......... 1674
La Salle launches the *Griffin* on lake Erie and coasts along the northern frontier of Ohio (NEW YORK)..........Aug. 1679
Iroquois convey certain of their western lands east of the Illinois to the English by treaty.......... 1684
Nicholas Perrot with 20 Frenchmen marches into the Miami country; French establish a post near the Ohio boundary... 1686
English traders crossing the Ohio country are arrested by the French.......... 1687
Treaty of Ryswick, by which France claims the valley of the Ohio..........Sept. 1697
French erect a trading-post near the mouth of the Maumee... 1705
Gov. Spotwood of Virginia urges the English government to occupy the valley of the Ohio.......... 1709
Vaudreuil, governor of Canada, opens a trading route to the Mississippi by lake Erie, the Maumee and Ohio rivers....... 1720
Treaty of Lancaster, Pa.: territory "beyond the mountains" ceded by the Iroquois to the English..........June, 1744
Virginia colonists form the "Ohio company" for occupation and settlement of the Ohio valley.......... 1748
Céleron de Bienville's expedition to, and down the Ohio river to the mouth of the great Miami; he buries at various points leaden plates bearing record of the French claims.......... 1749
England grants the Ohio company 600,000 acres of land....... "
Gist and Croghan lead a party of English explorers into the Ohio country.......... "
Charles Townshend of the English ministry urges the forcible seizure of the Ohio region.......... 1752
French and Indians attack the English trading-post of Pickawillany (Pickaway or Piqua), capture and destroy it....June, "
Duquesne, governor of Canada, sends a French expedition of occupation into the Ohio valley.......... 1753
Dinwiddie, governor of Virginia, determines upon the forcible occupation of the Ohio country.......... "
Expedition of Washington to St. Pierre at Le Bœuf; sent by gov. Dinwiddie of Virginia (PENNSYLVANIA).......... "
Frederick Post, the first Moravian missionary in Ohio, settles on the Muskingum.......... 1761
Treaty of Paris: France cedes to England all Canada and the French possessions from the Alleghanies to the Mississippi, 10 Feb. 1763

OHI

First general conspiracy of the northwestern Indians under Pontiac 1763

Bouquet's expedition into the Ohio country, treaty with the Indians Indians return captives 1764

[Col Henry Bouquet was one of the most efficient officers on the frontier during the PONTIAC WAR (b Switzerland, 1719, d Pensacola, Fla 1766) He entered the British service 1756 His relief of fort Pitt (now Pittsburg Pa) was one of the best conducted campaigns in Indian warfare PENNSYLVANIA, 1763 In 1764 he commanded an expedition against the Ohio Indians, then very hostile towards the whites, having been engaged in the Pontiac war This expedition of 1500 men with baggage cattle, etc, left fort Pitt 3 Oct, marched in the best order and with strict discipline, as near as possible the troops moved in a square with baggage in the centre, protected against surprise by flankers, and at night the vigilance was thorough At the 16th encampment 25 Oct, on the Muskingum at a point now Tuscarawas, the Indians, without an attempt to resist met Bouquet in council for treaty It provided that the Indians should deliver to him all white persons held by them, and he took from them 81 males, 125 females and children, afterwards 100 more sent to fort Pitt, hostages being held meanwhile His object having been accomplished, Bouquet returned to fort Pitt without the loss of a man]

Ohio country made part of Canada by act of Parliament 1765

Indian and Moravian village of Schönbrunn (beautiful spring) built on the Tuscarawas under David Zeisberger 1772

Lord Dunmore's expedition against the Indian towns on the Scioto 1774

Battle of Point Pleasant on the Ohio (VIRGINIA) 10 Oct "

Two block houses built on the site of Cincinnati 1780

Birth of Mary Heckewelder, daughter of John Heckewelder the Moravian missionary, first white child known to have been born in Ohio 16 Apr 1781

English establish a fort at Sandusky 1782

Massacre of the Moravian Indians at Gnadenhütten on the Tuscarawas by a company of men from western Pennsylvania and Virginia under command of col Williamson 8 Mch "

Expedition under col William Crawford against the Ohio Indians on the Muskingum 500 volunteers from Pennsylvania and Virginia, mounted, assemble at a deserted Mingo village on the west bank of the Ohio, about 75 miles below Pittsburg 20 May, "

March commences from Mingo Bottom in what is now Steubenville township, Jefferson county 25 May, "

They are attacked and defeated by the Indians near upper Sandusky, Wyandot county . 5-6 June, "

Col Crawford, being captured by the Indians, is put to death with barbarity 11 June "

Territory east of the Mississippi, north of the Ohio and west of Pennsylvania, belonging to the province of Quebec before the Revolution is claimed by Virginia Her legislature authorizes her delegates in Congress to convey it to the U S, *on condition that it be formed into states.* 20 Dec. 1783

Virginia deed of cession dated 1 Mch 1784

New Ohio company formed in Boston, Mass. " 1786

Rufus Putnam, Samuel Parsons, and Manasseh Cutler made directors of the Ohio company Mch 1787

Northwest territorial government established 13 July, "

Gen Samuel H Parsons appointed judge in and over the territory of the U S, northwest of the Ohio river "

Mayflower leaves Sumrill's Ferry on the Youghiogheny with pioneers from Danvers, Mass, and Hartford, Conn, to form a permanent settlement in Ohio 2 Apr 1788

They land at Marietta 7 Apr "

First meeting of the agents and directors of the Ohio company west of the Alleghanies, they name the place Marietta, after Marie Antoinette, queen of France 2 July, "

Gen Arthur St. Clair arrives at fort Harmar as governor of the Northwestern territory 9 July, "

Washington county formed 12 July, "

Gov St Clair establishes civil government in the northwest. 15 July, "

Losantville, afterwards Cincinnati, laid out Aug "

First court held in Ohio at Marietta 2 Sept. "

Act confirming the territorial government of the Northwest territory passed first session, 1st Congress 1789

Gen James M Varnum, pioneer of the state and a judge of the Northwestern territory, dies at Marietta "

Hamilton county formed 2 Jan 1790

Fort Washington erected at Cincinnati "

First Masonic lodge of the west established at Marietta. "

Whites at Big Bottom, Morgan county, massacred by Indians "

Gen Joseph Harmar's expedition against the Miami Indians. 30 Sept "

Partially defeated near the Miami villages, the expedition fails, 22 Oct. "

Expedition of gen St Clair against the Indians, surprised and defeated near Miami villages (now in Darke county) 4 Nov 1791

[Except Braddock's, the worst defeat ever experienced in Indian warfare, of about 1800 men he lost 800]

Benj Tupper, one of the chief promoters of the settlement of Marietta, dies there 1792

First newspaper of the Northwest, the *Sentinel*, editor William Maxwell, appears at Cincinnati 1793

After the defeat of St Clair, gen Wayne was appointed to command against the Indians Marching into the Indian country late in the autumn of 1793 he built a stockade near the scene of St. Clair's defeat, naming it fort Recovery, here he remained until the spring of 1794, when he proceeded through the wilderness to the Maumee Before meeting the Indians in battle Wayne offered to treat, but on their refusal advanced with his usual dash and vigor, with about 2000 men (the Indians numbering about the same), and defeated them at Fallen Timbers, or Maumee Rapids (now in Lucas county) 20 Aug 1794

Gen Wayne's treaty with the Indians at Greenville, Darke county 3 Aug 1795

Town of Dayton laid out 4 Nov "

First settlement on the Western Reserve begun at Conneaut, "the Plymouth of the Reserve" 4 July, 1796

Town of Chillicothe laid out "

Settlement started at Cleveland Sept "

[Named after gen Moses Cleveland of Conn]

William Henry Harrison appointed secretary of the Northwestern territory 1798

Steubenville settled Sept "

Gov St Clair directs an election of delegates for a territorial assembly 29 Oct "

First territorial assembly meets at Cincinnati 22 Jan 1799

First weekly newspaper in the Northwest, the *Western Spy and Hamilton Gazette*, Joseph Carpenter, editor, appears at Cincinnati 28 May, "

William Henry Harrison elected delegate to Congress 3 Oct. "

Zanesville settled "

Territory divided into (1) territory northwest of the Ohio river (now Ohio) and (2) territory of Indiana 7 May, 1800

Chillicothe made the seat of government for Ohio "

St. Clair reappointed governor "

Four land-offices established in Ohio territory to sell public lands at Steubenville, Marietta, Cincinnati, and Chillicothe, 10 May, "

First state house erected at Chillicothe 1801

Abraham Whipple takes the first ship, 100 tons, built at Marietta, down the Ohio and Mississippi to Havana, and thence to Philadelphia "

By authority from Congress, a convention meets at Chillicothe, 3 Nov which signs and ratifies for the people the first constitution of Ohio 29 Nov 1802

Ohio is admitted into the Union as the 4th under the Constitution of the U S, and the 17th in the roll of states. 29 Nov "

[Except in the case of Ohio, Congress has passed a distinct act of admission for each new state or has provided for admission on proclamation by the president. The people of Ohio elected delegates to a convention by whom a constitution was formed, 29 Nov 1802, which in Jan 1803, was submitted to Congress for ratification, and on 19 Feb 1803, the president approved the first act which recognized the new state The U S. census gives date of admission 29 Nov 1802 Boundaries of the state when admitted into the Union East, the Pennsylvania line, south the Ohio river, west, the meridian of the mouth of the Miami river, north, the parallel of the southern extreme of lakes Michigan and Erie See this record, 1836]

St Clair deposed as governor by Jefferson .. Dec "

State legislature meets at Chillicothe, the capital 1 Mch 1803

Ohio university (non-sectarian) opened at Athens 1804

[This university was founded in 1802 by the territorial legislature and endowed by Congress with 2 townships, or 46,000 acres of land In 1804 the act was confirmed by the state legislature In 1810 a grammar school was opened, and in 1821 a college was organized]

Aaron Burr's expedition to the Southwestern territory (BLENNERHASSETT'S ISLAND, BURR'S CONSPIRACY) 1805

Ebenezer Sproat, a pioneer of the state, dies at Marietta Feb "

Portsmouth, Scioto county, settled "

Indians cede to the U S the tract known as the Connecticut Reserve, treaty concluded at fort Industry 4 July, "

Canton settled 1806

State legislature orders the seizure of the boats building on the Muskingum for the "Aaron Burr expedition" 2 Dec. "

Mansfield settled 1807

Cleveland made a county seat 1809

State capital removed from Chillicothe to Zanesville, Muskingum county 1810

Population of the state, 230,760, rank among the states, 13th, population to the sq mile, 5 6 "

Matthew Simpson, bishop M E church, b Cadiz 21 June, "

First steamboat on the Ohio, the *New Orleans*, 400 tons, built at Pittsburg, descends the Ohio in the autumn of 1811

[She had a stern wheel, and made the passage from Pittsburg to New Orleans in 14 days]

War with England declared, 3 regiments raised in Ohio 1812

Columbus laid out "

Col Israel Putnam, one of the pioneers of the state, and a son of gen Israel Putnam, dies at Belpre "

Solomon Spaulding writes a work of fiction, "The Manuscript Found," at Salem, which afterwards furnishes the basis of the Mormon Bible (MORMONS, NEW YORK) "

Gen Harrison builds fort Meigs (so called after gov Meigs), Wood county . Feb 1813

Gen Harrison defends this fort against the combined attack of 2800 British and Indians under gen Proctor and the Indian chief Tecumseh (FORT MEIGS) 1-8 May, "

Fort Meigs again besieged by about 4000 British and Indians under the same commanders without success 21 July, "

Fort Stephenson held by maj George Croghan with 150 men against 1300 British and Indians (FORT STEPHENSON) 2 Aug "

Judge John C Symms, one of the first settlers of Cincinnati, dies there . 26 Feb 1814

Edwin McMasters Stanton, secretary of war, 1862-68, b. Steubenville . . 19 Dec. "

Great financial distress.... 1815
Columbus made the capital of the state.... 1816
First steamboat built at Cincinnati.... "
United States bank opened at Cincinnati....28 Jan. 1817
German community established at Zoar, Joseph M. Bimeler, leader.... "
United States bank opened at Chillicothe....Oct. "
Sandusky settled.... "
Don Carlos Buell born at Marietta....23 Mch. 1818
Indians of Ohio cede all their remaining lands in that state, about 4,000,000 acres, to the state....27 Sept. "
Irwin McDowell, major-general, born at Columbus......15 Oct. "
Medical college opened at Cincinnati.... 1819
First steamboat on lake Erie.... "
Wm. S. Rosecrans born at Kingston....6 Dec. "
Wm. Tecumseh Sherman born at Mansfield....8 Feb. 1820
Population: 581,295, 14.1 to the sq. mile; 5th state in population.... "
Ulysses S. Grant born at Point Pleasant....27 Apr. 1822
Rutherford B. Hayes born at Delaware....4 Oct. "
John Sherman born at Lancaster....10 May, 1823
Gen. Rufus Putnam, one of the first settlers of Marietta, dies at that place....4 May, 1824
Quincy A. Gillmore, major-general of volunteers, born at Black River, Lorain county....28 Feb. 1825
County tax of ½ mill levied for the support of common schools, "
Return Jonathan Meigs, jr., one of the first settlers of Marietta, and governor of the state, 1810-14, dies at Marietta..29 Mch. "
Great tornado, "the Burlington storm," passes through Licking county....18 May, "
Ohio and Lake Erie canal begun, gov. Clinton of New York removing the first shoveful of earth....4 July, "
Maumee canal begun.... "
Lafayette visits Ohio; received with great honor.... "
Akron settled.... "
Franklin college (United Presbyterian) founded at New Athens, "
Kenyon college (Protestant Episcopal) opened at Gambier..... "
Western Reserve college (now Adelbert college, Cleveland) opened at Hudson (see 1882).... 1826
David S. Stanley, brigadier-general U. S., born at Cedar Valley, Wayne county....1 June, 1828
George Crook, major-general U. S., born at Dayton.....8 Sept. "
Ohio Mechanics' institute established at Cincinnati.... "
County school tax increased to ¾ mill.... 1829
Population: 937,903, 22.7 to sq. mile; 4th state in population.. 1830
College of Teachers organized at Cincinnati.... 1831
St. Xavier college (Roman Catholic) opened at Cincinnati...... "
James A. Garfield born at Orange, Cuyahoga county...19 Nov. "
Dennison university (Baptist) established at Granville.... "
Great floods throughout Ohio.... 1832
Lane Theological seminary (Presbyterian) opened at Cincinnati, "
Charter granted to the Cincinnati, Sandusky, and Cleveland railroad....5 June, "
Mormons, under Joseph Smith, settled at Kirtland, Lake county, "
Ohio and Lake Erie canal, from Portsmouth on the Ohio to Cleveland on lake Erie, 307 miles, cost $5,000,000, finished, "
Law school opened at Cincinnati college.... 1833
Oberlin college (Congregational) opened at Oberlin.... "
School tax increased to 1 mill.... 1834
Maumee canal, Cincinnati to Defiance, 178 miles, where it meets the Wabash and Erie; whole distance to lake Erie, 265 miles, cost $3,750.000, finished.... "
County school tax increased to 1½ mills.... 1835
Charter granted to the Sandusky, Mansfield, and Newark railroad....11 Mch. "
Charter granted to the Cleveland, Columbus, and Cincinnati railroad, capital $3,000,000....16 Mch. "
Marietta college (Presbyterian) established.... "
Mad River and Lake Erie railroad, from Dayton to Sandusky, 153 miles, commenced (first in the state)....Sept. "
City charter granted Cleveland.... 1836
Northern boundary of the state changed from parallel of the most southern point of lake Michigan to a direct line running from this point to the most northern cape of Maumee bay, giving the state its present boundary (see this record, 1802).... "
Prof. W. W. Mather makes the first geological survey of the state.... 1837
Muskingum college (non-sectarian) opened at New Concord... "
A portion of the Mad River and Lake Erie railroad opened; first in the state.... 1838
Gen. George A. Custer born at New Rumley, Harrison co., 5 Dec. 1839
Population: 1,519,467, 37.3 to sq. mile, 3d state in population.. 1840
First railroad completed; Cincinnati to Springfield.... 1842
Cleveland Medical college opened.... "
Cincinnati Wesleyan university for women (Methodist Episcopal) opened.... "
Corner-stone of the Cincinnati observatory laid.... 1843
Cincinnati Historical Society organized.... 1844
Ohio Wesleyan university (Methodist Episcopal) opened at Delaware.... "
Wittenberg college (Evangelist Lutheran) opened at Springfield.... 1845
Richmond college (non-sectarian) opened at Richmond.... "
Farmers college (non-sectarian) opened at College Hill.... 1846
Five volunteer regiments raised for the Mexican war.... "
Otterbein university (United Brethren) opened at Westerville, 1847
Philip H. Sheridan, general U. S. army, born at Albany, N. Y., 1831, appointed to West Point from Ohio.... 1848
Homœopathic hospital opened at Columbus.... 1849

OHI

No railroads of importance constructed in Ohio prior to...... 1849
Columbus and Xenia railroad opened to Cincinnati.... 1850
Xenia college (Methodist Episcopal) opened at Xenia.... "
Capital university (Evangelist Lutheran) opened at Columbus, "
Population: 1,980,329, 48.6 to sq. mile, 3d state in population.. "
Urbana university (New Church—Swedenborgian) opened at Urbana.... 1851
Railroad opened from Cleveland to Columbus, 135 miles.... "
Heidelberg college (Reformed German) opened at Tiffin.... "
Second constitution of the state: Convention met at Columbus 6 May, 1850; adjourned 7 July on account of the cholera; reassembled at Cincinnati 2 Dec.; completed its labors, 10 Mch. "
Ratified by the people 126,663 to 109,699.... 1852
Governor's term of office 2 years from....1 Jan. "
Cleveland and Pittsburg railroad opened.... "
Laws reorganizing common schools, creating state school commissioner, Board of Education, abolishing rate bills, state tax of ½ mill yearly in place of county tax....14 Mch. 1853
Antioch college (Unitarian) opened at Yellow Springs.... "
Cleveland and Toledo railroad opened.... "
Railroad opened from Wheeling, Va., to Columbus, 137 miles.. 1854
Ohio Central college (United Presbyterian) opened at Iberia... "
Baldwin university (Methodist Episcopal) opened at Berea.... 1856
[Previously known as Baldwin institute.]
Ohio State and Union Law school opened at Cleveland.... "
It is made a penitentiary offence to claim or hold slaves in the state, or to attempt to carry from the state as a slave any person of color.... 1857
Arrest and confinement in the county jail at Cleveland of prof. Henry E. Peck of Oberlin college and others under the Fugitive-slave law for rescuing at Wellington the negro "Little John," taken from Oberlin as a slave by a U. S. deputy marshal....13 Sept. 1858
Indicted in the U. S. court....Dec. "
Bushnell, one of the rescuers, is found guilty in the Federal court at Cleveland....15 Apr. 1859
Supreme court of Ohio refuse Bushnell's application for a *habeas corpus*, the proceeding against him in the Federal court not being terminated....28 Apr. "
Severe frosts throughout the state destroy most of the wheat, 5 June, "
Gov. Dennison, on the requisition of gov. Letcher, refuses to arrest Owen Brown and Francis Merriam, indicted in Virginia for acts at Harper's ferry....8 Mch. 1860
Tornado on the Ohio river from Louisville, Ky., to Marietta; 150 lives lost and property destroyed to the amount of $1,000,000. Great damage done in Cincinnati......21 May, "
Population: 2,339,511; 57.4 to sq. mile; 3d state in population, "
U. S. calls for 13 regiments from Ohio....15 Apr. 1861
Law authorizing the acceptance of 10 regiments beyond required number, and providing $500,000 to support them.... "
Two regiments organized at Columbus and sent forward without arms or uniforms to Washington....18 Apr. "
$1,000,000 appropriated to prepare the state for war... " "
Law declaring the property of volunteers free from execution for debt during term of service.... "
Adjutant-general of the state reports that the following troops have been raised: infantry, 67,546; cavalry, 7270; artillery, 3028; total for 3 years' service, 77,844, up to....31 Dec. "
Under the "3 months' call" the state had furnished 22,000 infantry, 180 cavalry, and 200 artillerymen.... "
Gen. Kirby Smith threatens Cincinnati....6, 7 Sept. 1862
Ohio State university founded.... "
Clement L. Vallandigham, a resolute, persistent, and dangerous opponent of the North in the civil war, arrested by gen. Burnside (UNITED STATES)....5 May, 1863
Democratic convention nominates Clement L. Vallandigham for governor....11 June, "
Confederate gen. John H. Morgan, with cavalry, crosses the Ohio on a raid through Indiana and Ohio....3 July, "
Captured with most of his command at New Lisbon..26 July, "
Confined in Ohio penitentiary, he escapes (MORGAN'S RAID), Nov. "
Wilberforce university (Methodist Episcopal, African) founded near Xenia....
Soldiers' monument erected at Cincinnati.... 1864
German Wallace college (Methodist Episcopal) established at Berea.... "
Number of men, reduced to a 3-years' standard, furnished by Ohio for the civil war, 240,514, from 15 Apr. 1861, to..9 Apr. 1865
Willoughby college (Methodist Episcopal) established at Willoughby.... "
University of Wooster (Presbyterian) established at Wooster... 1866
One Study college (Methodist Episcopal) established at Scio, Newmarket station, Harrison county.... "
Cincinnati suspension bridge opened to the public.... 1867
Hiram college (Disciple) opened at Hiram.... "
Storrs township, Mount Auburn, and Corryville annexed to Cincinnati.... 1870
Ohio Agricultural and Mechanical college, state control, opened at Columbus.... "
Cincinnati university (non-sectarian) opened at Cincinnati.... "
Population: 2,665,260; 65.3 to sq. mile; 3d state in population, "
Vallandigham accidentally kills himself with a revolver while illustrating in court a case of homicide....18 June, 1871
Buchtel college (Universalist) opened at Akron.... "
Completion of the canal around Louisville.... 1872
McCorkle college (Presbyterian) opened at Bloomfield.... 1873
Revised constitution rejected by the people.... "
Wilmington college (Friends) opened at Wilmington.... 1875
Ashland college (Brethren) opened at Ashland.... 1878
Population: 3,198,062; 78.5 to sq. mile; 3d state in population, 1880

OHI

Train leaves Washington for Cleveland, bearing the remains of pres. Garfield ....23 Sept. 1881
Arrives at Cleveland....................24 Sept. "
His remains lie in state....................24–25 Sept. "
Western Reserve college at Hudson removed to Cleveland and renamed Adelbert, after a son of Amasa Stone, who gave the college $500,000.................... 1882
Great flood in the Ohio, submerging parts of Cincinnati and Louisville; at Cincinnati the river rose 66 ft......10–15 Feb. 1883
Ninety-fifth anniversary of the settlement of Ohio celebrated at Marietta .... "
Great flood of the Ohio; thousands rendered homeless. Congress appropriates $500,000 for relief..............12–15 Feb. 1884
Riots at Cincinnati, because of failure to punish criminals by law; 42 killed and 120 wounded....................28–30 Mch. "
"Dow law" passed, taxing the liquor traffic.................... 1885
State Board of Health established.................... "
After a long struggle in the legislature, John Sherman is re-elected U. S. senator over Allen G. Thurman, 84 to 61, 12 Feb. 1886
Waterspout at Xenia destroys 25 persons, 100 houses...19 May, "
Charles Whittlesey, geologist and scholar, b. 1808, d. in Cleveland....................18 Oct. "
Centennial celebration of the first settlement in Ohio at Marietta....................7 Apr. 1888
Sunday liquor law passed.................... "
Ohio Valley and Central States Centennial exhibition opens at Cincinnati....................4 July, "
Organization of "White Caps" disband on promise from authorities not to proceed against them; last outbreak, the whipping of Adam Berkes in Sardinia, Brown county, accused of immoral conduct....................17 Nov. "
Wife of ex-pres. Hayes, b. 1831, d. at Fremont........25 June, 1889
Population: 3,672,316; 92.1 to sq. mile; 4th state in population.................... 1890
Calvin S. Brice elected U. S. senator....................14 Jan. "
Woman's Christian Temperance League organized at Cleveland....................23 Jan. "
Lieut.-gov. Lampson, Republican, unseated by Democratic majority in the Senate....................30 Jan. "
First Monday in Sept. (Labor day) made a legal holiday by legislature, which adjourns....................28 Apr. "
Garfield memorial at Lakeview cemetery, Cleveland, dedicated (GARFIELD MONUMENT)....................30 May, "
Ex-gov. Edward F. Noyes dies at Cincinnati, aged 58...7 Sept. "
Legislature meets in extraordinary session, 14 Oct., passes a bill suggested by gov. Campbell, abolishing 2 public boards of Cincinnati, and creating a non-partisian Board of Improvement, appointed by the mayor, and adjourns, 24 Oct. "
Charles Foster, secretary of the U. S. treasury.........25 Feb. 1891
Modified Australian Ballot act passed at an adjourned session of the legislature....................6 Jan.–4 May, "
People's party organized at the National Union Conference, held at Cincinnati, 1418 delegates from 32 states, 19 May, "
City of Hamilton celebrates its centennial............19 Sept. "
William McKinley, jr., inaugurated governor..........11 Jan. 1892
National Prohibition convention meets in Cincinnati, 29 June, "
Gen. John Pope, b. 1823, d. at Sandusky..............23 Sept. "
Ex-pres. Hayes, b. 1822, d. at his home at Fremont....17 Jan. 1893
Gen. J. S. Coxey's army of the Commonweal, numbering 75 men, organizes at Massilon, moves from that place to Canton, 8 miles (UNITED STATES)....................26 Mch. 1894

TERRITORIAL GOVERNORS.

Name.	Term began.	Term expired.	Politics.	Remarks.
Arthur St. Clair	1788	1802	....	Deposed by pres. Jefferson.
Charles W. Byrd	1802	1803	....	Acting.

STATE GOVERNORS.

Name.	Term began.	Term expired.	Politics.	Remarks.
Edward Tiffin	1803	1807	....	Resigned to take seat in U. S. senate.
Thomas Kirker	1807	1808	....	Acting.
Samuel Huntington	1808	1810		
Return Jonathan Meigs	1810	1814	....	Resigned to become postmaster-general.
Othniel Looker	1814	1814	....	Acting.
Thomas Worthington	1814	1818		
Ethan Allen Brown	1818	1822	....	Resigned to take seat in U. S. senate.
Allen Trimble	1822	1822	....	Acting.
Jeremiah Morrow	1822	1826		
Allen Trimble	1826	1830		
Duncan McArthur	1830	1832		
Robert Lucas	1832	1836	Democrat.	
Joseph Vance	1836	1838	Whig.	
Wilson Shannon	1838	1840	Democrat.	
Thomas Corwin	1840	1842	Whig.	
Wilson Shannon	1842	1844	Democrat.	Resigned; appointed minister to Mexico.
Thomas W. Bartley	1844	1844	....	Acting.
Mordecai Bartley	1844	1846	Whig.	
William Bebb	1846	1849	"	
Seabury Ford	1849	1850	"	
Reuben Wood	1850	1853	Democrat.	Resigned; appointed U. S. consul at Valparaiso.
William Medill	1853	1854	"	Acting.
" "	1854	1856	"	
Salmon P. Chase	1856	1860	Republican.	
William Dennison	1860	1862	"	
David Tod	1862	1864	"	
John Brough	1864	1865	"	Died in Cleveland, 29 Aug. 1865.
Charles Anderson	1865	1866	"	Acting.
Jacob Dolson Cox	1866	1868	"	
Rutherford B. Hayes	1868	1872	"	
Edward F. Noyes	1872	1874	"	
William Allen	1874	1876	Democrat.	
Rutherford B. Hayes	1876	1878	Republican.	
Richard M. Bishop	1878	1880	Democrat.	
Charles Foster	1880	1884	Republican.	
George Hoadley	1884	1886	Democrat.	
Joseph B. Foraker	1886	1890	Republican.	
James E. Campbell	1890	1892	Democrat.	
William McKinley, jr.	1892	1894	Republican.	Re-elected 1894.

UNITED STATES SENATORS FROM THE STATE OF OHIO.

Name.	No. of Congress.	Date.	Remarks.
John Smith	8th to 10th	1803 to 1808	Seated 25 Oct. 1803. Tried by the senate for complicity with Aaron Burr, but resolution of expulsion negatived, 9 Apr. 1808. Resigned 25 Apr. 1808.
Thomas Worthington	8th " 10th	1803 " 1807	Seated 17 Oct. 1803.
Return Jonathan Meigs	10th " 11th	1809 " 1810	Elected in place of Smith. Resigned. Elected governor.
Edward Tiffin	10th " 11th	1807 " 1809	Resigned.
Stanley Griswold	11th	1809	Appointed in place of Tiffin.
Alexander Campbell	11th to 13th	1810 to 1813	Elected in place of Tiffin.
Thomas Worthington	11th " 13th	1811 " 1814	Elected in place of Meigs. Resigned. Elected governor.
Joseph Kerr	13th " 14th	1814 " 1815	Elected in place of Worthington.
Jeremiah Morrow	13th " 16th	1813 " 1819	
Benjamin Ruggles	14th " 23d	1815 " 1833	
William A. Trimble	16th " 17th	1819 " 1821	Died 13 Dec. 1821.
Ethan Allen Brown	17th " 19th	1822 " 1825	
William Henry Harrison	19th " 20th	1825 " 1828	Resigned.
Jacob Burnett	20th " 23d	1828 " 1831	Elected in place of Harrison.
Thomas Ewing	22d " 25th	1831 " 1837	

UNITED STATES SENATORS FROM THE STATE OF OHIO.—(*Continued.*)

Name.	No. of Congress.	Date.	Remarks.
Thomas Morris....................	23d to 26th	1833 to 1839	
William Allen....................	25th " 31st	1837 " 1849	
Benjamin Tappan..................	26th " 29th	1839 " 1845	
Thomas Corwin....................	29th " 31st	1845 " 1850	Resigned. Appointed secretary of treasury.
Thomas Ewing.....................	31st	1850	Appointed in place of Corwin.
Salmon P. Chase..................	31st to 34th	1849 to 1855	Free-soil party. Governor of the state, 1856.
Benjamin F. Wade.................	32d " 41st	1851 " 1869	Free-soil, then a Republican. President *pro tem.* 2 Mch. 1867.
George E. Pugh...................	34th " 37th	1855 " 1861	Democrat.
Salmon P. Chase..................	37th	1861	Republican. Resigned 6 Mch. 1861, to become secretary of treasury.
John Sherman.....................	37th to 45th	1861 to 1877	Elected in place of Chase. Republican. Resigned. Appointed secretary of treasury, 1877.
Allen G. Thurman.................	41st " 47th	1869 " 1880	Democrat. President *pro tem.* 15 Apr. 1879.
Stanley Matthews.................	45th " 46th	1877 " 1879	Republican. Elected in place of Sherman.
George H. Pendleton..............	46th " 49th	1879 " 1885	Democrat.
James A. Garfield................	47th	1880	Resigned to accept the presidency of the U. S., Nov. 1880.
John Sherman.....................	47th to ——	1881 to ——	Elected in place of Garfield. President *pro tem.* 7 Dec. 1885. Term expires 1899.
Henry B. Payne...................	49th " 52d	1885 " 1891	Democrat.
Calvin C. Brice..................	52d " ——	1891 " ——	Democrat. Term expires 1897.

Ohio company. OHIO, 1748-87.

Ohm's law, for determining the quantity of the electro-motive force of the voltaic battery, was published in 1827. It is in conformity with the discovery that the earth may be employed as a conductor, thus saving the return wire in electric telegraphy. ELECTRICITY.

oil. The term oil is a generic expression, under which are included several extensive series of bodies of diverse chemical character and physical properties, however having in common these characteristics: that they are compounds consisting principally, in some cases exclusively, of carbon and hydrogen, are mostly insoluble in water, and are all readily inflammable. It was used for burning in lamps as early as the epoch of Abraham, about 1921 B.C. The fact that oil, if passed through red-hot iron pipes, will yield a combustible gas, was long known to chemists; and after lighting by coal-gas began, messrs. Taylor and Martineau contrived apparatus for producing oil-gas on a large scale, 1815. The idea of using oil to calm the waves originated with Benjamin Franklin, and was tried successfully by him.—*Sparks*, "Works of Franklin," vol. vi. pp. 253 and 357. It is commonly practised in heavy storms at sea; and guns are used in throwing oil-shells so as to extend the area of oil surface. The principal oils of commerce are: from vegetable sources, almond, cotton-seed, rape-seed, linseed, hemp-seed, castor, cocoanut, croton, from animal (fats), butter, lard, tallow; from fish, cod, sperm, whale; insect, beeswax; mineral, coal-oil (PETROLEUM).

Okeecho'bee Swamp, Battle of. FLORIDA, 1837.

Oklaho'ma is a territory of the United States of America, formed in 1890 from the western part of the Indian territory and the Public Land strip or No Man's Land, a strip 167½ miles long and 34½ miles wide, lying north of Texas and west of 100° lon. Oklahoma is bounded on the north by Kansas and Colorado, east by the Indian territory, south by Texas, and west by Texas and New Mexico. Area, 39,030 sq. miles. Pop. 1890, 61,834; 1900, 398,331. Capital, Guthrie.

No Man's Land ceded to the U. S. by Texas............25 Nov. 1850

Extensive scheme organized to take possession of the portion of Oklahoma not occupied by Indians, and parties from Missouri and Texas enter the territory, but are ordered removed by proclamation of pres. Hayes.......................26 Apr. 1879

Second proclamation to prevent settlement in Oklahoma, 12 Feb. 1880

Expedition under David L. Payne—who had organized in Kansas the Oklahoma Town company and the Southwest colony—with 25 men, enter the territory and begin the settlement of the town of Ewing, but within 3 weeks they are arrested by U. S. troops and imprisoned.............................. "

Payne enters Oklahoma with a colony of 600 men, women, and children, and founds the town of Rock Falls.......May, 1884

Under proclamation by pres. Arthur, 1 July, the settlement at Rock Falls is broken up by U. S. troops................Aug. "

Many armed men under W. L. Couch encamp at Stillwater on the Cimmaron river and defy the military.............Dec. "

Couch and his forces surrender to the U. S. troops, and are marched across the Kansas line and arrested under Federal warrants..27 Jan. 1885

Inhabitants of No Man's Land organize the territory of Cimmaron, not recognized by Congress.......................... 1886

Delegates of Creek nation meet in Washington 19 Jan., and cede the western half of their domain for $2,280,857.10; ratified by the Creek council 31 Jan., by Congress.......1 Mch. 1889

Seminoles execute a release and conveyance of their lands ceded by treaty in 1866..............................16 Mch. "

Oklahoma opened for settlement by proclamation of pres. Harrison, 27 Mch., to take effect at noon, 22 Apr. During the afternoon of this day 50,000 or more settlers, encamped on the borders of the territory, enter and locate........22 Apr. 1889

First bank in Guthrie opened in a tent with a capital of $50,000, 22 Apr. "

An attempt to form a provisional government for Oklahoma fails. Convention meets at Guthrie...............22 May, "

Proclamation of the president against the occupation of the Cherokee strip......................................17 Feb. 1890

Many "boomers" invade the Cherokee strip.... .....23 Mch. "

Pres. Harrison signs act creating territory of Oklahoma, 2 May, "

George W. Steele appointed first governor................May, "

First election held for representative-at-large..........5 Aug. "

Congress appropriates $47,000 for the relief of destitute persons in the territory......................................8 Aug. "

Milton W. Reynolds, Republican, elected representative-at-large, dies from over-exertion during the canvass.....9 Aug. "

First meeting of the legislature at Guthrie.............27 Aug. "

Santa Fé and Rock Island railroad companies bring into the territory and loan to the needy farmers, without interest, 25,000 bush. seed wheat.................................... "

Agricultural college founded in Payne county; a normal school located at Edmond if the people give it $5000 and 40 acres of land; a territorial university located at Norman, Cleveland county; public schools established; Australian ballot system introduced; legislature adjourns.....................24 Dec. "

Cherokee strip closed to whites by order of president..13 Aug. 1891

New Indian lands in Oklahoma (about 300,000 acres) opened for settlement...................................22 Sept. "

Resignation of gov. Steele accepted by pres. Harrison...18 Oct. "

Statehood convention meets at Oklahoma City........15 Dec. "

State Agricultural college at Stillwater opened......... " "

Proclamation of the president, 12 Apr., opens to settlement Cheyenne and Arapahoe Indian lands from..........19 Apr. 1892

Cherokee outlet or strip, about 9409 sq. miles, was ceded to the U. S. by the Cherokees, 19 May, 1893; the U. S. paying $8,300,000 in 5 annual instalments, beginning 4 Mch. 1875, interest 4 per cent. on deferred payments, besides paying $300,000 to the Cherokees at once, and $110,000 to other tribes, making in all about $8,710,000. By proclamation of the president, Aug. 23, the strip was opened at noon....16 Sept. 1893

[It is estimated that 100,000 people had gathered on the boundary-line awaiting the opening.]

TERRITORIAL GOVERNORS.

George W Steele............	resigns......................	1891
Abraham J Seay............	Republican..................	1891-1894
William C. Renfrow	Democrat....................	1893 ——

Old Bailey Sessions court is held in England for the trial of criminals, and its jurisdiction comprehends the county of Middlesex as well as the city of London. It is held 8 times in the year by the royal commission of oyer and terminer. The judges are the lord mayor, those aldermen who have passed the chair, the recorder, and the common sergeant, who are attended by both the sheriffs and one or more of the national judges. The court-house was built in 1773, and enlarged in 1808.

Old Catholics, the name assumed by German Roman Catholics rejecting the dogma of papal infallibility, headed by prof. Döllinger of Munich. After 3 days' conference at Munich, Sept. 1871, they decided on independent worship, first meeting in a church given by the town council of Munich. The abbé Michaud began a similar movement in Paris in Feb. 1872. Dr. Döllinger advocated union with the Church of England, Mch. 1872. Père Hyacinthe (Charles Loyson), president of the party at Rome, issued a programme respecting the Vatican decrees, recognizing ecclesiastical authorities, demanding reform, yet opposing schism, about 5 May, 1872.

The bishops of Lincoln (Wordsworth) and Ely (Browne), and the dean of Westminster (dr. Stanley), by invitation attended the conference at Cologne, and delivered addresses, 20–22 Sept. 1872. The Old Catholics elected their first bishop, dr. Joseph Reinkens, 1 June, 1873, who was recognized by the emperor and other powers.

First synod held in Germany at Bonn, opened ....27 May, 1874
Congress of Old Catholics held at Constance, 18 Sept. 1873; at Freiburg..6 Sept. "
Dr. Döllinger received delegates from eastern and western churches at Bonn, with a view to union with the Old Catholics, only preliminaries were agreed on............14 Sept. "
First Old Catholic church in Berlin opened...............30 Nov. "
In Prussia about 20,000 Old Catholics (about 8,000,000 Romanists), 1875
Congress at Bonn; bishop of Winchester, canon Liddon, and several Oriental clergy present, 12 Aug.; agreement respecting the FILIOQUE clause..............................16 Aug. "
Old Catholics at Bonn ask by circular for a church (they reject the Vatican decrees of 18 July, 1870; do not secede from the Catholic church, but desire Catholicism free from debasing doctrines; repudiate papal infallibility and supremacy; sanction reading of the Bible, worship in the vulgar tongue, and marriage of priests)..................................Dec. "
Congress at Bonn; strong opposition to celibacy of clergy; question deferred..............................early in June, 1876

Old Dominion. Virginia is so called because it was sometimes recognized as a separate dominion, as Spenser dedicates his "Faërie Queene," 1590, to Elizabeth, queen of England, France, Ireland, and *Virginia.* When James VI. of Scotland (I. of England) came to the English throne, Scotland was added and Virginia was called in compliment the 5th kingdom. And as Virginia stood firm for Charles II. after the execution of his father (VIRGINIA, 1644–52), Charles, in gratitude, caused the arms of Virginia to be quartered with those of England, Scotland, and Ireland, as an independent member of the kingdom.

Old Ironsides, a name given to the frigate *Constitution.* NAVY; UNITED STATES, 1797–1812, etc.

Old Man of the Mountain, in the Franconia mountains, New Hampshire. "The Great Stone Face then was a work of Nature in her mood of majestic playfulness, formed on the perpendicular side of a mountain by some immense rocks, which had been thrown together in such a position as, when viewed at a proper distance, precisely to resemble the features of the human countenance. It seemed as if an enormous giant or a Titan had sculptured his own likeness on the precipice."—*Hawthorne*, "The Great Stone Face."

Old Probabilities. WEATHER BUREAU.

Old style. NEW STYLE.

Oldenburg, a grand-duchy in North Germany, was annexed to Denmark in 1448; in 1773 Christian VII. ceded the country to Russia in exchange for Holstein Gottorp, and soon after the present dignity was established. The duke joined the North German confederation 18 Aug. 1866, and obtained a slight increase of territory from Holstein, 27 Sept. following. Area, 2479 sq. miles; pop. 1864, 301,812; 1871, 314,591; Dec. 1875, 319,314; 1880, 337,478; 1890, 354,968.

olef'iant gas, a combination of hydrogen and carbon which burns with much brilliancy. In 1862 Berthelot formed it artificially by means of alcohol.

Oléron, Laws of, relating to sea affairs, are said to have been enacted by Richard I. of England, when at the island of Oléron, France, 1194, which is now doubted.

olives, the fruit of a tree belonging to the order *Oleaceæ.* They are named in the earliest accounts of Egypt and Greece; and at Athens their cultivation was taught by Cecrops, 1556 B.C. They were first planted in Italy about 562 B.C. The olive has been cultivated in England since 1648 A.D.; the Cape olive since 1730. Its introduction into California by the Spanish monks, and recently the introduction of the best varieties from France and Italy, together with adaptability of climate and soil near the Pacific coast, have made its cultivation exceedingly remunerative, and placed California among the great olive-producing countries of the world.

Olmstead, Case of. During the American Revolution capt. Gideon Olmstead, with some other Connecticut men, was captured at sea by a British vessel and taken to Jamaica, where the captain and 3 others of the prisoners were compelled or persuaded to enter as sailors on the British sloop *Active*, then about to sail for New York with stores for the British there. When off the coast of Delaware the captain and the other 3 Americans contrived to secure the rest of the crew and officers (14 in number) below the hatches. They then took possession of the vessel and made for Little Egg harbor. A short time after, the *Active* was boarded by the sloop *Convention* of Philadelphia, and, with the privateer *Girard*, cruising with her, was taken to Philadelphia. The prize was there libelled in the state court of admiralty. Here the 2 vessels claimed an equal share in the prize, and the court decreed ¼ to the crew of the *Convention*, ¼ to the state of Pennsylvania as owner of the *Convention*, ¼ to the *Girard*, and the remaining ¼ only to Olmstead and his 3 companions. Olmstead appealed to Congress, and the committee of appeals decided in his favor. The Pennsylvania court refused to yield, and directed the prize sold and the money paid into court to await its further order. This contest continued until 1809, when the authorities of Pennsylvania offered armed resistance to the U. S. marshal at Philadelphia, upon which he called to his assistance a *posse comitatus* of 2000 men. The matter was, however, adjusted without an actual collision, and the money, amounting to $18,000, paid to the U. S. marshal.

Olmütz, the ancient capital of Moravia. Gen. Lafayette was confined here by the Austrians from 1792 until 25 Aug. 1797. FRENCH REVOLUTION, Lafayette. Here the emperor Ferdinand abdicated on behalf of his nephew, Francis Joseph, 2 Dec. 1848; and here the latter promulgated a new constitution, 4 Mch. 1849. A conference was held here 29 Nov. 1850, under the czar Nicholas, when the difficulties between Austria and Prussia respecting the affairs of Hesse-Cassel were arranged.

Olus'tee, Fla., Battle of, 20 Feb. 1864. Gen. Truman Seymour was defeated by the confederates under gen. Finnegan. The federals, 5000 strong, lost about 2000 killed, wounded, and prisoners. The expedition was a total failure, and returned to Hilton Head.

Olym'piads, the era of the Greeks, dating from 1 July, 776 B.C., the year in which Chorœbus was successful at the Olympic games. This era was reckoned by periods of 4 years, each period being called an Olympiad, and in marking a date the year and Olympiad were both mentioned. The computation of Olympiads ceased with the 305th, 440 A.D.

Olympic games, most famous of the Greek festivals, said to have been instituted in honor of Zeus by the Idæi Dactyli, 1453 B.C., or by Pelops, 1307 B.C., revived by Iphitus, 884 B.C., were held at the beginning of every 4th year, on the banks of the Alpheus, near Olympia, in the Peloponnesus (now the Morea), to exercise the youth in 5 kinds of combats, the conquerors being highly honored. The prize contended for was a crown made of a kind of wild olive, appropriated to this use. The festival was abolished by Theodosius, 393 A.D., the first year of the 294th OLYMPIAD. In 1858 M. Zappas, a wealthy Peloponnesian, gave funds to re-establish these games, under the auspices of the queen of Greece.

Olympie'ium, near Peloponnesus, the great temple of Zeus erected by Libon of Elis, at the charge of the Eleans, after their conquest of the country, 572–472 B.C. For this temple Phidias made the colossal statue of the god, in gold and ivory, 437–433 B.C.

German explorations by Hirschfeld and Bötticher, planned by prof. Ernst Curtius, the historian, began in Oct. 1875, aided by the German government. Torsos and other relics were found. Above 904 objects in marble, many coins, bronzes, inscriptions, etc., found, 1875–78. Explorations closed, Nov. 1880. These excavations have determined the exact position of the principal buildings, the plan of the Altis, with the main local conditions of the festival.

Olyn'thus, a city of N. Greece, subdued in war by Sparta, 382–379 B.C. It resisted Philip of Macedon, 350 B.C., by whom it was destroyed, 347. Demosthenes delivered 3 orations on its behalf, 349.

Omahas. INDIANS.

omens. AUGUR. Amphictyon was the first who is recorded as having drawn prognostications from omens, 1497 B.C. Alexander the Great and Mithridates the Great are said to have studied omens. At the birth of the latter, 131 B.C., there were seen for 70 days together 2 splendid comets; and this omen, we are told, directed all the actions of Mithridates throughout his life.—*Justin.*

Ommi'ades, a dynasty of Mahometan caliphs, beginning with Moawiyah, of whom 14 reigned in Arabia, 661-750; and 18 at Cordova, in Spain, 755-1031.

omnibus (Lat. *omnibus*, for all), including all or a great number. Covering or designing to cover many cases or things. —A long-bodied 4-wheeled vehicle for passengers. The idea of such conveyances is ascribed to Pascal, about 1662, when similar carriages were started, but soon discontinued. They were revived in Paris about 11 Apr. 1828; and introduced into London by a coach-proprietor named Shillibeer. The first omnibus started from Paddington to the Bank of England on Saturday, 4 July, 1829.

Omnibus bill. UNITED STATES, Jan., May, etc., 1850.

omnim'eter, a new surveying apparatus (combining the theodolite and level, and comprising a telescope and microscope), invented by Eckhold, a German engineer, to supersede chain measuring; announced Sept. 1869.

Onei'da community was founded by John H. Noyes, of New Haven, Conn., who in 1834 joined the Perfectionists, a new sect who professed the belief that every being is either wholly sinful or wholly righteous, similar to the English sect of Princites. In 1847 he established the Oneida community at Oneida creek, N. Y., where both sexes lived in a "Unitary Home," and where was practised a community of wives as well as goods. Branches were established at Wallingford, Conn., and Willow Place, near Oneida. The community are also known as "Free Lovers" and "Bible Communists." Opposition to this community, under the lead of prof. Mears, of Hamilton college, and others, resulted in its dissolution in 1879. Since 1881 it has maintained simply the standing of a business corporation.

Oneidas. INDIANS.

Ononda'gas. INDIANS, LONG HOUSE.

Ontario, Province of, formerly Canada West or Upper Canada; capital, Toronto. Area, 219,650 sq. miles; pop. 1861, 1,396,091; 1871, 1,620,851; 1881, 1,923,228; 1891, 2,112,989.

operas. Adam de la Hale, a Trouvère, surnamed "le Bossu d'Arras," born in 1240, is, as far as has yet been ascertained, the composer of the first comic opera, "Li Gieus (Le Jeu) de Robin et de Marion." The Italian opera began with the "Il Satiro" of Cavaliere, and the "Dafne" of Rinuccini, with music by Peri, about 1590. Their "Eurydice" was presented at Florence, 1600, on the marriage of Marie de Médicis with Henry IV. of France. "L'Orfeo, Favola in Musica," composed by Monteverde, was performed in 1607, and is supposed to have been the first opera that was ever published. About 1669 the abbot Perrin obtained a grant from Louis XIV. to set up an opera in Paris, where, in 1672, was acted "Pomona." For list of operas and composers, MUSIC.

oph'icleide (ὄφις, serpent, and κλεῖδες, keys), the keyed bassoon, said to have been invented by Frichot, a Frenchman, in London, between 1791 and 1800; but owing its origin to a wind instrument called the "serpent," the invention of which is generally attributed to Edme Guillaume, canon of Auxerre, about 1590.

ophthal'moscope, an apparatus for inspecting the interior of the eye, invented by prof. H. Helmholtz, and described by him in 1851.

opium, the juice of the white poppy (*Papaver somniferum*), was known to the ancients, its cultivation being mentioned by Homer, and its medicinal use by Hippocrates. It is largely cultivated in British India, and was imported into China by English merchants, which led eventually to the war of 1839, the importation being forbidden by the Chinese government. Laudanum, a preparation of opium, was employed early in the 17th century. A number of alkaloids have been discovered in opium: narcotine by Derosne, and morphia by Sertürner, in 1803. The cultivation of opium is possible in all countries where there is not an excessive rainfall and the climate is temperate or subtropical; but, owing to its limited yield, it is not profitable. In 1865 its cultivation was attempted in Virginia, and a product was obtained which yielded 4 per cent. of morphia. In 1867 opium was grown in Tennessee which yielded 10 per cent. of morphia; and in California, in 1873, it yielded 7¾ per cent.

Opor'to, W. Portugal, the ancient *Calle*, one of the most impregnable cities in Europe, and the mart of Portuguese wine known as "Port." The French, under marshal Soult, were surprised here by lord Wellington, and defeated in an action fought 12 May, 1809. The Miguelites besieged Oporto, and were repulsed by the Pedroites, with considerable loss, 19 Sept. 1832.

optic nerves are said to have been discovered by N. Varole, a surgeon and physician of Bologna, about 1538.—*Nouv. Dict.*

optics, the science of light and vision; studied by the Greeks; and by the Arabians about the 12th century. LIGHT.

	B.C.
Burning lenses known at Athens	424
A treatise on optics doubtfully attributed to Euclid......about	300
Magnifying power of convex glasses and concave mirrors, and the prismatic colors produced by angular glass, mentioned by Seneca......about	A.D. 50
Treatise on optics by Ptolemy......about	120
Two of the leading principles known to the Platonists	300
Greatly improved by Alhazen, who d.	1038
Hints for spectacles and telescopes by Roger Bacon......about	1280
Spectacles said to have been invented by Salvinus Armatus of Pisa......before	1300
Camera-obscura said to have been invented by Baptista Porta,	1560
Telescopes invented by Leonard Digges......about	1571
Kepler publishes his "Dioptrice"	1611
Microscopes, according to Huyghens, invented by Drebbel, about	1621
Law of refraction discovered by Snellius......about	1624
Telescope made by Jansen (said also to have invented the microscope) about 1609, and independently by Galileo....about	1630
Inflection of light discovered, and the undulatory theory suggested by Grimaldi......about	1665
Reflecting telescope, James Gregory, 1663; Newton	1666
Velocity of light determined by Roemer, and after him by Cassini	1667
[Its velocity, 190,000,000 miles in 16 minutes.]	
Double refraction explained by Bartholinus	1669
Cassegrainian reflector	1672
Newton's discoveries in colors, etc.	1674
Telescopes with a single lens by Tschirnhausen......about	1690
Polarization of light and undulatory theory discovered by Huyghens......about	1692
Structure of the eye explained by Petit......about	1700
Aberration of light discovered by Bradley	1727
Achromatic telescope constructed by Mr. Hall (but not made public) in	1733
Constructed by Dollond, most likely without knowledge of Hall's telescope	1757
Herschel's great reflecting telescope erected at Slough	1789
Dr. T. Young's discoveries (undulatory theory, etc.)	1800-3
Camera-lucida (dr. Wollaston)	1807
Malus (polarization of light by reflection)......about	1808
Fraunhofer maps 590 lines in the solar spectrum	1815
Fresnel's researches on double reflection, etc.	1817
Optical discoveries of Wheatstone	1838 et seq.
Large telescope constructed by lord Rosse	1845
Arago (colors of polarized light, etc.)	1811-53
Sir D. Brewster, optical researches (KALEIDOSCOPE, PHOTOGRAPHY)	1814-57
Dr. Tyndall's lectures on light first illustrated by Duboscq's electric lamp at the Royal Institution, London	1856
Spectroscope constructed and used by Kirchhoff and Bunsen..	1861
Researches of Wm. Spottiswoode on polarized light	1871-73

op'timism (from *optimus*, the best), the doctrine that everything which happens is for the best, in opposition to pessimism (from *pessimus*, the worst). The germ of optimism is to be found in Plato, and in St. Augustin and other fathers; it was supported by Malebranche and Leibnitz, and adopted by Pope, Bolingbroke, Rousseau, and others. Optimism, as expressed in the term "the best of all possible worlds," is ridiculed by Voltaire (1694-1778) in his "Candide." The term *meliorism* (from *melior*, better) has been lately introduced. PESSIMISM.

oracles, supposed revelations by divine beings. They were given to the Jews at the Mercy-seat in the tabernacle; see Exod. xxv. 18-22. The Holy Scriptures are the Christian "oracles," Rom. iii. 2; 1 Pet. iv. 11. King Ahaziah sent to consult the oracle of Baal-zebub at Ekron about 896 B.C. The Greeks consulted especially the oracles of Zeus and Apollon (DELPHI, DODONA); and the Italians those of Faunus, Fortune, and Mars.

O'ran, Algeria, N. Africa, a Moorish city several times captured by the Spaniards; definitively occupied by the French in 1831, who have since added docks, etc.

Orange, a principality in S.E. France, formerly a lordship in the 9th or 10th century. It has been ruled by 4 houses successively: that of Giraud Adhemar, to 1174; of Baux, 1182–1393; of Châlons, to 1530; and of Nassau, 1530–1713; NASSAU. Philibert the Great, prince of Orange, the last of the house of Châlons, having been wronged by Francis I. of France, entered the service of the emperor Charles V., to whom he rendered great services by his military talents. He was killed at the siege of Florence, 3 Aug. 1530. He was succeeded by his nephew-in-law, René of Nassau. PRINCES OF ORANGE, under HOLLAND. The eldest son of the king of Holland is styled the prince of Orange, although the principality was ceded to France in 1713. ARAUSIO.

Orange Free State, a state of Dutch Boers in S. Africa, founded by them in 1836. The British government proclaimed its authority over this territory on 3 Feb. 1848. Its independence was declared 23 Feb. 1854, and a constitution proclaimed 10 Apr. 1854; revised 1866 and 1879. The executive is vested in a president chosen for 5 years by universal suffrage. The legislative authority is vested in a popular assembly, the Volksraad, elected by suffrage of the burghers for 4 years. Area, 41,500 sq. miles; pop. 1877, about 50,000 (half whites); 1890, 207,503, of which 77,716 were white.

Orangemen, an association of Irish Protestants originating and chiefly flourishing in Ulster, but found in other parts of the United Kingdom, British colonies, and in the United States. Orangemen derive their name from William III., prince of Orange. The "Battle of the Diamond," 21 Sept. 1795, and the treachery experienced by the Protestants on that occasion, convinced them they would become an easy prey to the Roman Catholics, from their small numbers, unless they associated for their defence, and the first Orange lodge was formed in Armagh. An Orange lodge was formed in Dublin; the members published a declaration of their principles (the maintenance of church and state) in Jan. 1798. After 1813 Orangeism declined, but revived again in 1827, when the duke of Cumberland became grandmaster. After a parliamentary inquiry, Orange clubs were broken up in conformity with resolutions of the House of Commons, but were revived in 1845. In Oct. 1857, the lord chancellor of Ireland ordered that justices of the peace should not belong to Orange clubs. The Orangemen's parade in New York, 12 July, 1871, led to a riot, in which 60 lives were lost. The 1st and 12th July are celebrated by them as anniversaries of the battles of the BOYNE and AUGHRIM.

oranges, the fruit of the *Citrus aurantium* (sweet orange-tree). To this family also belong the citron, lemon, and lime. The sweet orange was first brought into Europe from the East by the Portuguese in 1547. Orange-trees were first brought to England and planted, with little success, in 1595; they are said to have been grown at Beddington park, near Croydon, Surrey. The culture of oranges in California and Florida has rapidly grown into a great industry since 1865.

orato'rio, a kind of musical sacred drama, the subject of it being generally taken from the Scriptures. The origin of English oratorios (so named from having been first performed in an oratory) is ascribed to St. Philip Neri, about 1550. The first true oratorio—Emilio del Cavaliere's "Rappresentazione"—was performed at Rome in 1600. He was followed by Giovanni Carissimi, Alessandro Scarlatti, etc. The first oratorio in London was performed in Lincoln's Inn theatre, in Portugal street, in 1732. Handel's oratorio of "Israel in Egypt" was produced in 1738, and the "Messiah" in 1741; Haydn's "Creation" in 1798; Beethoven's "Mount of Olives," 1803; Spohr's "Last Judgment" (properly "Die letzten Dinge"), 1825; Mendelssohn's "St. Paul" in 1836, and "Elijah" in 1846; "Naaman," 1864; Costa's "Eli," 1865; S. Bennett's "Woman of Samaria," 1867; Benedict's "St. Peter," 1870; Macfarren's "John the Baptist," 1873; "Resurrection," 1876; and "Joseph," 1877; Dr. P. Armes's "Hezekiah," 1878. MUSIC.

or'chids. FLOWERS AND PLANTS.

Orchom'enus, a small Greek state and city in Bœotia, was destroyed by the Thebans, 368 B.C.; restored by Philip II. of Macedon, 354; and given up by him to Thebes, 346. It was the capital of the MINYÆ. The most remarkable relic of the early city is the so-called "treasury," said to be the oldest in Greece. It was larger than the building of similar style at MYCENÆ, and its beauty, spoken of by Pausanias, has been brought to light by Schliemann's excavations.

ordeal, a form of trial, consisted of testing the effect of fire, poison, water, etc., upon the person of the accused. It was known among the Greeks and Jews (Numb. v. 12–28). It was introduced into England by the Saxons. In principle, and often in the forms used, it belongs to ancient tradition, extending throughout all nations and peoples until its force dies out before modern civilization. Trial by ordeal was abolished in England in 1218, before which a prisoner who pleaded not guilty might choose whether he would put himself for trial upon God and his country, by 12 men, as at this day, or upon God only. APPEAL, GODWIN'S OATH, etc.

orders in council. UNITED STATES, 1793, 1806, 1807, 1809; BRITISH ORDERS IN COUNCIL.

ordination of ministers in the Christian church began with Christ and his apostles; see Mark iii. 14, and Acts vi. and xiv. 23. In England, in 1549, a new form of ordination of ministers was ordered to be prepared by a committee of 6 prelates and 6 divines.

Ordnance office. Before the invention of guns, this office was supplied by officers in England under the following names: the bowyer, the crossbowyer, the galeater, or purveyor of helmets, the armorer, and the keeper of the tents. Henry VIII. placed it under the management of a master-general, a lieutenant, surveyor, etc. The master-general was chosen from among the first generals in the service of the sovereign. The appointment was formerly for life; but since the Restoration was held *durante bene placito*, and not unfrequently by a cabinet minister.—*Beatson*. The letters-patent for this office were revoked 25 May, 1855, and its duties vested in the minister of war, lord Panmure. The last master-general was lord Fitzroy-Somerset, afterwards lord Raglan. In the United States, the Ordnance department of the U. S. army has charge of the arsenals and armories, and furnishes all ordnance and ordnance stores for military service, including all cannon and artillery carriages and equipments; apparatus for the service of artillery, small-arms and accoutrements, ammunition, tools, and materials for the ordnance service, horse medicines, material for shoeing, and all horse equipments whatever. The department is under charge of a chief of ordnance, at present (1894) brig.-gen. D. W. Flagler; salary $5500.

Ordnance survey. The trigonometrical survey of England was commenced by gen. Roy in 1783, continued by col. Colby, and completed by col. (afterwards sir Henry) James in 1856. The publication of the maps commenced in 1819, under the direction of col. Mudge, and was completed in 1862; a large part of these maps have been colored geologically. The survey of Ireland has been completed and published; that of Scotland completed 1882. COAST SURVEY.

ordonnances (*or-don-nans'*), the laws enacted by the Capetan kings of France previous to 1789. They began with "In the name of the king," and ended with "Such is our good pleasure." The first in French is dated 1287 (Philip V.). The publication of these "ordonnances," ordered by Louis XIV., 1706, is still in progress. The "ordonnances" of Charles X., promulgated 26 July, 1830, led to the revolution.

Or'egon, one of the Pacific coast states of the American Union, has a coast line of 300 miles, extending from lat. 42° N., which marks the boundary between the state and California and Nevada, to the Columbia river, which separates the state from Washington on the north in lat. 46° 15′ N. Idaho lies to the east, the Snake river forming about half of the eastern boundary. It is limited in longitude between 116° 45′ to 124° 30′ W. Area, 96,030 sq. miles, in 31 counties. Pop. 1890, 313,767; 1900, 413,536. Capital, Salem.

A Spanish expedition, sent out under Bruno Heceta in the *Santiago*, discovers the mouth of the Columbia river....... 1775

Captain Robert Gray enters the Columbia river in the American ship *Columbia* from Boston 7 May, 1792

Lieut Broughton of the British navy ascends the Columbia river, about 100 miles to the region of the cascades, Oct -Nov "

By purchase, the U S acquires the claims of France to Oregon 30 Apr 1803

Lewis and Clarke U S government expedition descends the Columbia to its mouth where it arrives 5 Nov 1805

Capt Nathaniel Winship a New-Englander builds the first house in Oregon at Oak Point on the Columbia 4 June, 1810

Pacific Fur company, of which John Jacob Astor was a leading member, establishes a trading post at the mouth of the Columbia river which it calls Astoria 1811

D McKenzie explores the Willamette river 1812

Convention between U S and Great Britain for joint occupation of Oregon concluded in London 20 Oct 1818, ratified 19 Jan 1819

Convention between the U S and Russia regulating fishery and trading on the Pacific coast and fixing 51° 40 as the northern boundary claimed by the U S, concluded at St Petersburg 5-7 Apr 1824 and ratified 12 Jan 1825

Convention between the U S and Great Britain the articles of 1819 are indefinitely extended with proviso that either party might annul the agreement on 12 months notice, 6 Aug 1827

Capt Nathaniel J Wyeth of Wenham, Mass establishes a fishery on Sauvies island, at the mouth of the Willamette 1832

John McLeod and Michael la Framboise erect fort Umpqua a post for the Hudson Bay company on the Umpqua river "

Jason and Daniel Lee, Methodist missionaries reach Oregon in capt Wyeth's second overland expedition which left Independence 28 Apr 1834, and establish a mission on the banks of the Willamette, 60 miles from its mouth 6 Oct 1834

Methodist mission station established on Clatsop plains, near Young bay 10 Feb 1841

First meeting of settlers at the Methodist mission to make a code of laws for the settlements south of the Columbia river 17-18 Feb "

Star of Oregon, the first American vessel constructed of Oregon timber, is launched from Oak island in the Willamette, and sails for San Francisco "

A provisional government and organic laws for Oregon are adopted by the people met at Champoeg, and Oregon City fixed as the seat of government 5 July, 1843

First house in Portland erected by A L Lovejoy and F W Pettygrove 1845

Publication of the *Oregon Spectator* begun at Oregon City 1846

Resolutions pass the House of Representatives giving notice to Great Britain that the convention of 1818 and 1827 for joint occupation of Oregon should be terminated at the expiration of 12 months from the notice 9 Feb. "

Articles of the Oregon convention between U S and Great Britain held 15 June, 1846, are ratified in London, 17 July, and proclaimed (UNITED STATES) 5 Aug "

First sale of town lots for Salem 10 Sept "

First mail contract in Oregon let to Hugh Burns in the spring of 1846, and first regular mail service in the territory is established by the U S government 1847

Congress enacts a territorial government for Oregon 14 Aug 1848

Gen Joseph Lane, first territorial governor, arrives, and proclaims the territorial government 3 Mch 1849

About $50,000, in 5 and 10 dollar gold pieces, coined and put into circulation by the Oregon Exchange company This is known as "beaver money" "

First territorial legislature meets at Oregon City 16 July, "

Gens. Smith and Vinton arrive in Oregon to examine the country with reference to the location of military posts, 28 Sept "

Hudson Bay company conveys to U S the rights of the company under its charter and the treaty with Great Britain "

Seat of government located at Salem by legislature, the penitentiary at Portland, and the university at Corvallis 1850

Five of the Cayuse Indians, principals in the massacre of dr M Whitman and other missionaries at Waiilatpu, 29 Nov 1847, are delivered to the Oregon authorities, tried at Oregon City, condemned, and executed 18 June, "

Schooner *Samuel Roberts*, with an exploring party formed in San Francisco to discover the mouth of the Klamath river, enters the Umpqua river 6 Aug "

Oregon Donation act, Congress grants each missionary station then occupied 640 acres of land, with the improvements To each white settler, 640 acres To each emigrant settling in Oregon between 1 Dec 1850 and 1 Dec 1853, 160 acres, 27 Sept "

Troops under maj Philip Kearny engage the Indians in the battle of Rogue river 23 June, 1851

A party of 23, under T'Vault, set out to explore the interior, 24 Aug 1851 1 Sept, all but 9 turn back, at the Rogue river, about 50 miles from the ocean These reach the headwaters of the Coquille 9 Sept, descend it, are attacked, and 5 of the 9 killed by Indians 14 Sept "

Yam Hill River bridge, the first in the country, constructed at Lafayette "

Gold discovered by some half breeds in the sand of the old sea beach at the mouth of a creek near the Coquille 1852

Willamette university at Salem, opened 1844, chartered 1853

War with the Indians of Rogue river, begun in June, ended by a treaty signed by Joel Palmer, superintendent of Indian affairs, and Samuel H Culver, Indian agent By this treaty the Indians sell their lands, comprising the whole Rogue River valley to the U S for $60,000 8 Sept. 1853

Town of Roseburg laid out 1854

Pacific university and Tualatin academy, at Forest Grove, opened in 1848, is chartered "

T J Dryer and party ascend mount Hood, and ascertain that it is an expiring volcano still emitting smoke and ashes, Aug "

Gov Davis resigns Aug 1854, Geo. Law Curry appointed, Nov "

Volunteer company under J A Lupton attack an Indian camp at the mouth of Butte Creek killing 23 and wounding many, early in the morning Daylight showed that the dead were mostly old men women, and children 8 Oct. 1855

In retaliation, the Indians plunder and massacre settlers in the upper Rogue River valley 9 Oct. "

Astoria chartered "

Gov Curry issues a proclamation calling for 5 companies of volunteers, 15 Oct, and orders all companies not duly enrolled by virtue of said proclamation to disband 20 Oct "

Convention of Free soilers meets at Albany 27 June, and drafts a platform for the anti-slavery party to be reported at an adjourned meeting appointed at Corvallis for 30 Oct "

Volunteer force organized 12 Oct, by col J E Ross engages the Indians at Rogue river near Galice creek, 17 Oct, and at Bloody Springs or Grave Creek hills 30 Oct "

New state house at Salem burned, with the library and furniture, the work of an incendiary 30 Dec "

Indians murder 13 out of 15 of the garrison at Whaleshead on Rogue river, during the absence of the rest (22 Feb) at a dancing party, murder many farmers near the fort and burn their houses and barns, 130 who escaped the massacre and fled to the fort are besieged 31 days until relieved by 2 companies under col Buchanan Mch 1856

Troops under capt A J Smith attacked at the Meadows, on the Rogue river, where the Indians had agreed to meet and give up their arms, by Indians under chief John, 27 May, they are rescued by capt Augur 28 May, "

Chief John surrenders 29 June, "

Willamette woollen mills at Salem erected "

Convention assembles at Albany, and organizes the Free state Republican party of Oregon 11 Feb 1857

Oregon Constitutional convention assembles at Salem, 17 Aug, completes its labors 18 Sept constitution ratified by the people, majority in favor of adoption, 3980, against slavery, 5082, against free negroes 7559 9 Nov "

Stage line opened from Portland to Salem "

Coal discovered at Coos Bay, near Empire City 1853, and mines discovered by James Aiken at Newport and Eastport, opened, 1858

State legislature meets, 5 July, and gov Whiteaker is inaugurated 8 July, "

Act admitting Oregon signed by the president 14 Feb 1859

Gov Whiteaker convenes the legislature, and completes the organization of the State government 16 May, "

Joseph Lane, ex governor of Oregon, nominated for vice president of the U S on the Breckinridge ticket 23 June, 1860

McMinnville college at McMinnville chartered in 1859, opened, "

Fort Stevens, at the mouth of the Columbia, completed 1864

First National bank of Portland, the oldest west of the Rocky mountains, is established July, 1865

Mount Hood, not previously in eruption since the settlement of California, continues for a month or more to emit smoke and flames followed by the earthquake of 8-9 Oct "

Oregon ratifies XIII th Amendment to Constitution 11 Dec "

Oregon ratifies the XIV th Amendment by 1 majority and this act is disputed, as secured by the votes of 2 Republican members of the House afterwards expelled 19 Sept 1866

Cincinnatus H Miller (Joaquin Miller) appointed judge of Grant county "

Cargo of wheat shipped from Oregon direct to Australia by the bark *Whistler* 1867

Grading for Oregon Central railroad begun at Portland, 14 Apr, of the rival Oregon and California railroad 16 Apr 1868

First full cargo of wheat exported from Oregon direct to Europe, sent by Joseph Watt to Liverpool by the *Sallie Brown* "

State Agricultural college at Corvallis opened "

St Helen's hall, Portland, chartered and opened 1869

Legislature rejects the XV th Amendment to the Constitution of the U S, and protests against the treaty with China 1870

Oregon school for deaf mutes at Salem opened "

Reform school at Portland established by act of legislature 1872

Legislature rescinds the resolution of 1870, rejecting the XIV th and XV th Amendments "

Capt Jackson, commissioned to remove the Modocs to a reservation, fights them on Lost river, near Tule lake. 29 Nov "

First convention of the Oregon State Woman's Suffrage Association held at Portland Feb 1873

Oregon institute for the blind at Salem opened "

Congress grants public lands in Oregon to construct a military road across the state. 2 July, 1864, the legislature grants 1920 acres of this for each mile to be built by the Oregon Central Military Road company, which builds to the summit of the Cascade mountains in 1867, the company sells its lands to the Pacific Land company of San Francisco "

Oregon Pioneer Association organized 18 Oct. "

State Board of Immigration created by law 28 Oct. 1874

Oregon and Washington Fish Propagating company incorporated, hatching establishment near Oregon City Apr 1875

University of Oregon at Eugene City, chartered in 1872, is opened 18 Oct. 1876

Constitutional amendment, that "the elective franchise in this state shall not hereafter be prohibited to any citizen on account of sex," passed and approved by the governor........ 1880
State asylum for the insane at Salem completed.............. 1883
Amendment conferring the suffrage on women is lost; 28,176 votes against to 11,223 in favor......................2 June, 1884
Local Option bill passed by the legislature.................... 1885
State Normal school at Drain created by law.................. "
Bill passed creating a State Board of Agriculture............. "
First Saturday in June made a legal holiday, "Labor day"... 1887
State reform school for juvenile offenders established by law.. 1889
State convention at Salem forms an amalgamated party, including Prohibitionists, Grangers, Free-traders, Greenbackers, American Party men, Knights of Labor, Union Labor, and Woman Suffragists, under the title "Union Party," to oppose the Republicans and Democrats...14 Sept. "
Australian ballot law enacted, and State Board of Charities and Correction established at the session......12 Jan. to 20 Feb. 1891
Women over 21 years of age and citizens of the U. S. and of the state made eligible to all educational offices............ 1893

TERRITORIAL GOVERNORS.

George Abernethy..............appointed.................. 1845
Joseph Lane.................. " 1849
J. P. Gaines.................. " .... "
Joseph Lane.................. " 1853
George L. Curry.................. " .... "
John W. Davis.................. " .... "
George L. Curry.................. " 1854

STATE GOVERNORS.

John Whiteaker................asumes office.............. 1859
Addison C. Gibbs.............. " " 1862
George L. Woods.............. " " 1866
Lafayette Grover.............. " " 1870
S. F. Chadwick.....................acting...........1 Feb. 1877
W. W. Thayer.................assumes office.............. 1878
Zenas Ferry Moody.............. " " 1882
Sylvester Pennoyer, Dem........ " " ....1 Jan. 1887
William Paine Lord.............. " " 1895

UNITED STATES SENATORS FROM THE STATE OF OREGON.

Name.	No. of Congress.	Date.	Remarks.
Delazon Smith....................	35th	1859 to 1860	Seated 14 Feb.
Joseph Lane....................	35th to 37th	1859 " 1861	Seated 15 Feb.
Edward D. Baker....................	36th	1860 " 1861	Seated 5 Dec. B. London, Engl., 1811; killed at battle of Ball's Bluff, Va., 21 Oct. 1861.
Benjamin Stark....................	37th	1862	*Appointed in place of Baker.*
Benjamin F. Harding....................	37th to 39th	1862 to 1865	Elected in place of Baker.
James W. Nesmith....................	37th " 40th	1861 " 1867	
George H. Williams....................	39th " 42d	1865 " 1871	
Henry W. Corbett....................	40th " 43d	1867 " 1873	
James K. Kelly....................	42d " 45th	1871 " 1877	
John H. Mitchell....................	43d " 46th	1873 " 1879	
Lafayette F. Grover....................	45th " 47th	1877 " 1883	
James H. Slater....................	46th " 49th	1879 " 1885	
Joseph N. Dolph....................	47th " 54th	1883 " 1895	
John H. Mitchell....................	48th " ——	1885 " ——	Term expires 1897.
George W. McBride....................	54th " ——	1895 " ——	Term expires 1901.

organ, a development of the pandean-pipes; the "organ" in Gen. iv. 21 should be translated *pipe.* The invention is attributed to Archimedes, about 220 B.C.; and to Ctesibius, a barber of Alexandria, about 250 B.C. The organ was brought to Europe from the Greek empire, and was applied to religious devotions in churches about A.D. 657.—*Bellarmin.* Organs were used in the Western churches by pope Vitalianus 658.—*Ammonius.* It is affirmed that the organ was known in France in the time of Louis I., 815, when one was constructed by an Italian priest. The organ at Haarlem is one of the largest in Europe; it has 60 stops and 8000 pipes. At Seville is one with 110 stops and 5300 pipes. The organ at Amsterdam has a set of pipes that imitate a chorus of human voices. Of the organs in England, that at St. George's hall, Liverpool, by Mr. Willis, was the *largest;* next *in* order, that at York minster, and that in the Music-hall, Birmingham. In London, the largest was, perhaps, that of Spitalfields church; and that in Christ church was nearly as extensive. The erection of the famous Temple organ was competed for by Schmidt and Harris; after long disputes, the question was referred to vote, and Mr. Jefferies, afterwards chief-justice, gave the casting-vote in favor of Schmidt (called father Smith), about 1682. A monster organ was erected in the Crystal palace, Sydenham, in June, 1857. The organ by Willis, at the Royal Albert hall, is now said to be the largest in the world, 1871. The largest organ ever in America was in the Music-hall, Boston. It was built by Walker, and had 4 manuals, 89 stops, and 4000 pipes. Other organs in the United States having from 2500 to 4000 pipes are those in Trinity and St. George's churches, New York; Plymouth church, Brooklyn; Holy Trinity and Temple Emanuel, New York. These are all the work of American builders. MUSIC.

organic chemistry. CHEMISTRY.

orgies (Gr. *Ὀργία*), secret rites of worship practised by the initiated alone, especially in the worship of Dionysus (Bacchus.) These rites, celebrated by women clad in fawn-skins with hair dishevelled, swinging the thyrsus and beating the cymbal, prevailed in almost all parts of ancient Greece. The celebrants were called Mænads or Bacchæ. Their ecstatic enthusiasm was accompanied with coarse and frantic revels, often of an immoral character.

Oriel college, Oxford, founded in 1326, by Adam de Brome, archdeacon of Stow, and almoner to king Edward II. This college derives its name from a tenement called *l'Oriole,* on the site of which the building stands.

Or'igenists pretended to draw their opinions from the writings of Origen (185-253), one of the most distinguished and influential theologians of the early church. They maintained that Christ was the son of God only by adoption and grace; that souls were created before the bodies; that the sun, moon, stars, and the waters that are under the firmament have souls; that the torments of the damned shall have an end; and that the fallen angels shall, after a time, be restored to their first condition. They were condemned by councils, and the reading of Origen's work was forbidden.—*Burke.* These doctrines were condemned by the council of Constantinople in 553.

"Origin of Species," Darwin's. LITERATURE.

Ori'on, in Greek mythology a giant and hunter noted for his beauty and prowess, son of Hyrieus of Hyria in Bœotia. After his death he was placed with his hounds among the stars, hence the name of one of the most beautiful constellations in the heavens; mentioned in Job ix. 9, xxxviii. 31; Amos v. 8; also by Homer and Hesiod.

> "Many a night from yonder ivied casement, ere I went to rest,
> Did I look on great Orion sloping slowly to the west."
> *Tennyson,* "Locksley Hall."

Oris'kany, N. Y., Battle of. NEW YORK, 6 Aug. 1777.

Orkney and **Shetland isles,** north of Scotland, were conquered by Magnus III. of Norway, 1099, and were ceded to James III. as the dowry of his wife Margaret, in 1469. The Orkneys were the ancient Orcades; united with Shetland, they now form one of the Scotch counties. Area, 957 sq. miles; pop. 1891, Orkney, 30,438; Shetland, 28,711. The bishopric of Orkney, founded by St. Servanus early in the 5th century—some affirm by St. Colm—ended with the abolition of episcopacy in Scotland, about 1689. BISHOPS IN SCOTLAND.

Orleans (*or-la-on'*), a city in central France, formerly *Aurelianum:* gave title to a kingdom, 491, and afterwards to a duchy, usually held by one of the royal family. Attila the Hun, besieging it, was defeated by Aetius and his allies, 451. It was besieged by the English under earls of Salisbury and Suffolk, 12 Oct. 1428; bravely defended by Gaucour (as its fall would have ruined the cause of Charles VI., king of France), and relieved by the heroism of Joan of Arc, afterwards surnamed the Maid of Orleans, 29 Apr. 1429, and the siege was raised 18 May. JOAN OF ARC. (The 439th anniversary was celebrated 10 May, 1868). During the siege of Orleans, Feb. 1563, the duke of Guise was assassinated. Pop. 1891, 63,705. FRANCO-PRUSSIAN WAR, 11 Oct., 10 Nov., 4-5 Dec. 1870.

DUKES OF ORLEANS

Louis contended for the regency with John the Fearless duke of Burgundy, by whose instigation he was assassinated 1407
Charles, taken prisoner at Agincourt, 1415 released, 1440, d 1465
Louis became Louis XII of France, when the duchy merged in the crown 1498
Bourbon branch —Philip, youngest son of Louis XIII, b 1640, d 1701
Philip II, son b 1673, regent, 1715, d 1723
Louis, son b 1703 d 1752
Louis Philippe, son b 1725, d 1785
Louis Philippe Joseph, son, b 1747, opposed the court in the French revolution, took the name *Egalité* 11 Sept 1792, voted for the death of Louis XVI, was guillotined (FRENCH REVOLUTION) 6 Nov 1793
Louis Philippe, son b 6 Nov 1773, chosen king of the French, 9 Aug 1830, abdicated 24 Feb 1848, d 26 Aug 1850
[His queen, Marie Amélie d 24 Mch 1866 (FRANCE)]
Ferdinand Philippe, son, duke of Orleans, b 3 Sept 1810, d through a fall 13 July, 1842
Louis Philippe son, count of Paris b 24 Aug 1838, married Maria Isabella, daughter of the duke of Montpensier, 30 May, 1864
[A daughter, Maria Amelia, b 28 Sept. 1865]
Demand of the Orleans princes to return to France, 19 June, refused by the legislative assembly after discussion 2 July, 1870
Their request to serve in the army after the fall of the empire declined Sept. "
[The duc de Chartres served *incognito*]
After discussion the duc d'Aumale and the prince de Joinville permitted to sit in the national assembly 19 Dec. "
After much discussion, the comte de Paris at a personal interview recognized the comte de Chambord as the legitimate head of the Bourbon family and king of France 5 Aug 1873
[For consequent proceedings, FRANCE, 1873 et seq]
Bodies of king Louis Philippe and others of his family removed from England to the mausoleum at Dreux 9 June, 1876

or'mulum, a metrical version of the Gospels and Acts, in early English, made by Orm, an ecclesiastic, in the 12th century, printed at Oxford in 1852, from a MS. in the Bodleian library. LITERATURE

ornithol'ogy. BIRDS

ornithorhyn'chus, the duck-billed platypus, or water-mole, a singular compound of the mammal and the bird, a native of Australia, was first described by dr Shaw in 1819

orphan-houses. The emperor Trajan first formed establishments for this purpose Pliny relates in his panegyric that he had caused 5000 free-born children to be sought out and educated, about 105 A D Orphan-houses properly so called are mentioned for the first time in the laws of the emperor Justinian At the court of Byzantium the office of inspector of orphans *orphanotrophos*, was so honorable that it was held by the brother of the emperor Michael IV. in the 11th century. FOUNDLING HOSPITALS

Orphanotropheon at Halle, established by August Francke 1698-99
Orphan working asylum for 20 boys was established at Hoxton in 1758 It is now situated at Haverstock hill, and contains 350 boys and girls
Asylum for female orphans Lambeth, removed to Beddington, near Croydon, instituted 1758
London orphan asylum, founded 1813, removed to Clapton, 1823, new building at Watford, founded by the prince of Wales, 13 July, 1869, opened 20 July, 1871
First orphan asylum in U S, called "Bethesda" founded about 9 miles from Savannah Ga, by George Whitefield 1740
Second was the Charleston orphan asylum, Charleston, S C 1792
Orphan Asylum Society of New York, and St Stephen's female orphan asylum of Philadelphia, Pa, chartered 1807
Next founded was at Annapolis, Md 1828
They have rapidly increased (see the states separately) since 1840

or'rery, a planetary machine to illustrate and explain the motions of the heavenly bodies, appears to have been coeval with the CLEPSYDRA Ptolemy devised the circles and epicycles that distinguish his system about 130 The planetary clock of Finee was begun 1553. The planetarium of De Rheita was formed about 1650 The planetarium, now termed the orrery, it is said, was constructed by Rowley, after a pattern devised by the clock-maker George Graham, at the expense of Charles Boyle, earl of Orrery, about 1715 A large planetarium was constructed by the rev. William Pearson, for the Royal Institution, London, about 1803. An excellent planetarium, constructed in London by signor N. Perini, was exhibited in Dec 1879

Orsini's plot against the emperor Napoleon III. FRANCE, Jan. 1858.

Osceo'la, chief of the Seminoles FLORIDA, UNITED STATES, 1835

os'mium, one of the heaviest-known metals, discovered in platinum ore by Tennant in 1803 ELEMENTS

Ostend manifesto. For the purpose of promoting negotiations with Spain for the purchase of Cuba by the United States, Soulé, the American minister to Spain (empowered to negotiate for the purchase of Cuba), Mason, minister to France, and Buchanan, to England, met at Ostend, Belgium 9 Oct 1854, and after 3 days' session adjourned to Aix-la-Chapelle, and thence wrote to the U S government, 18 Oct 1854, their views of the policy of the U S. That, as Spanish oppression in Cuba was such that Cuba would speedily resort to arms to free herself, (1) the U S should offer Spain for Cuba a sum not to exceed $120,000,000, and (2) in event of Spain's refusal to sell, the U S would be justified in taking possession of Cuba by force This proposition passed unrebuked by the government at Washington, but pres Pierce did not think it prudent to act upon the advice, and Soulé, disgusted, soon after resigned and returned home

os'tracism (Gr ὄστρακον, a potsherd or shell) a mode of proscription at Athens, is said to have been first introduced by the tyrant Hippias, others ascribe it to Cleisthenes about 510 B.C The people wrote the names of those whom they most suspected upon small shells, these they put in an urn or box and presented to the senate Upon a scrutiny, he whose name was oftenest written was sentenced by the council to be banished from his altar and hearth 6000 votes were required Aristides, noted for his justice, and Miltiades, for his victories, were thus ostracized The custom was abolished by ironically proscribing Hyperbolus, a mean person, about 338 B.C.

ostrich, a very large bird of the genus *Struthio* (its ancient name), a native of Africa (see Job xxxix 13) Ostriches were hatched and reared at San Donato, near Florence, 1859-60, and at Tresco abbey, the seat of Augustus Smith in the Scilly isles, 1866 There are several ostrich ranches in California where ostriches are reared with success

Os'trogoths or **Eastern Goths,** were distinguished from the Visigoths (Western Goths) about 330 After ravaging eastern Europe, Thrace, etc, their great leader, Theodoric, established a kingdom in Italy, which lasted from 493 to 553 ITALY

Ostrolen'ka, a town of Poland Near here the French defeated the Prussians, 16 Feb 1807 In another battle here, between the Poles and Russians, the slaughter was immense, but the Poles remained masters of the field, 26 May, 1831

Oswe'go, a city of New York, southeastern shore of lake Ontario Pop 1891, 21,812. FORT ONTARIO, NEW YORK, 1722, 1756, 1814.

Otahei'te or **Tahiti** (*ta-hee'-tee*), one of the group of the Society islands in the south Pacific ocean, seen by Byron in 1765, and visited in 1767 by capt Wallis, who called it George III island Capt Cook came here in 1768 to observe the transit of Venus, sailed around the island in a boat, and stayed 3 months, he visited it twice afterwards COOK Omai, a native of this island was brought to England by Cook, and carried back in his last voyage In 1799 king Pomare ceded the district of Matavai to some English missionaries Queen Pomare was compelled to put herself under the protection of France, 9 Sept. 1843 She retracted, and Otaheite and the neighboring islands were taken possession of by adm Dupetit-Thouars in the name of the French king, Nov. 1843 The island was formally annexed to France 29 June, 1880 Area, 412 sq miles, pop 11,200

o'theoscope (Gr ὠθέω, I propel), apparatus invented by W. Crookes for studying molecular motion, the effects of radiation, described by him Apr 1877.

Ot'tawa, formerly **Bytown,** a city of Ontario, on the river Ottawa, was appointed to be the capital of Canada by queen Victoria in Aug 1858 The executive council met here 22 Nov 1865, and the Canadian parliament was, for the first time, opened here by the gov.-gen lord Monck, on 8 June, 1866 Pop. 1871, 21,545, 1890, 44,150

Ottawas. INDIANS, PONTIAC'S WAR

Otterburn, a township of Northumberland In 1388 the

Scotch besieged Newcastle, and were driven off by Henry Percy (Hotspur), son of the earl of Northumberland Percy pursued them to Otterburn, where a battle was fought on 10 Aug, in which the earl of Douglas was killed and Percy taken prisoner On this battle the ballad of "Chevy Chace" is founded

Ottoman empire. TURKEY

Oude (*owd*) or **Oudh,** N India, formerly a viceroyalty held by the vizier of the great mogul About 1760 it was seized by the vizier Sujah-ud-Dowlah, ancestor of the late king Area, 24 216 sq miles, pop 1891, 12,652 730

Battle of Buxar, Sujah and his ally, Meer Cossim, are defeated, and the British control Oude 23 Oct 1764
Reign of Asoph ud Dowlah, who cedes Benares, etc, to the East India company who place troops in Oude (CULNAR) 1775-81
In consequence (by virtue of the treaty of 1801), Oude is annexed to the British territories by decree, proclaimed 7 Feb 1856

Oudenarde', a town of Belgium Here the English and allies, under the duke of Marlborough and prince Eugene, thoroughly defeated the French besiegers, 11 July, 1708

ounce (from *uncia*), the 16th part of the pound avoirdupois and 12th of the pound troy Its precise weight was fixed by Henry III, who decreed that an English ounce should be 640 dry grains of wheat, that 12 of these ounces should be a pound, and that 8 pounds should be a gallon of wine, 1233 METRIC SYSTEM

Ourique (*oo-reek'*), a town of Portugal, where Alfonso, count or duke of Portugal, is said to have encountered 5 Saracen kings and a great army of Moors, 25 July, 1139, and signally defeated them, and then to have been hailed the first king Lisbon, the capital, was taken, and he soon after was crowned.

ovariot'omy. This important surgical operation of removing the ovaries was devised and first performed by dr E McDowell, of Kentucky, 1809 His cases amounted to 13, with 8 recoveries.—*Dr D H Agnew's* "Principles and Practice of Surgery," vol ii p 803 SURGERY

ovation, public ceremonies held to honor an individual. In Roman antiquity, when a victory had been gained with little difficulty or the like, a lesser triumph was granted called *ovatio*, in which the general entered the city on foot or on horseback crowned with myrtle and not with laurel, and sacrificed a sheep (*ovis*, whence the name), instead of a bullock Publius Posthumius Tubertus was the first who was decreed an ovation, 503 B.C.

overland mail. CALIFORNIA, MISSOURI, 1858, UNITED STATES

Owhy'hee. HAWAII

oxal'ic acid, which exists in several plants, especially in sorrel is now abundantly obtained for use in the arts from sawdust acted upon by caustic potash or soda, according to dr Dale's process, patented in 1862

Oxford, an ancient city of England, restored by king Alfred, who resided here and established a mint, etc, about 879

Canute held a national council here 1018
Stormed by William I 1067
Charter by Henry II, the city granted to burgesses by John 1199
Henry III holds the "mad" parliament here . 1258
Bishops Ridley and Latimer burned here, 16 Oct. 1555, and archbishop Cranmer 21 Mch 1556
Fatal (or Black) Oxford assizes, the high sheriff and 300 others died of a jail fever caught from prisoners. . 1557
Charles I took Oxford, 1642, and held a parliament here 1644
Taken by the parliament 24 June, 1646
Charles II held parliaments here 1665 and 1681

Oxford marbles. ARUNDELIAN MARBLES

Oxford university. An academy here is described as ancient by pope Martin II in a deed, 802 Alfred founded "the schools" about 879

Charter granted by Henry III . 1248
Charter of Edward III, 1355, of Henry VIII 1510
University incorporated by Elizabeth 1570
Empowered to send 2 members to Parliament 1604
Bodleian library opened, 8 Nov 1602, building completed 1613
Botanic garden, etc., established by the earl of Danby 1622
Radcliffe library opened, 13 Apr 1749, the Radcliffe observatory completed. 1786
A commission appointed (31 Aug 1850) to inquire into its "state, studies discipline, and revenues," reported 27 Apr 1852
Acts making alterations passed 1854, 1856
University museum opened . . . July, 1860
Examination statutes passed 1801, 1807, 1850, 1862
Extension of the university proposed at a meeting held 16 Nov 1865
University tests abolished by act passed 16 June, 1871
Royal commission to inquire respecting university property, etc appointed 6 Jan 1872
Income in 1871 reported to be—university, 47,589*l* 0*s* 3*d*, colleges and halls, 366 253*l* 16*s* 3*d*, total, 413,842*l*. 16*s* 6*d*, Oct 1874
Hebdomadal board reported that about 100,000*l* was needed for education in science June, 1875
Lord Ilchester's bequest to promote the study of Slavonian literature, especially Polish, first lectures given May, "
New commission appointed (lords Selborne and Redesdale, Montague Bernard, sir M W Ridley, dean Burgon, and justice Grove), announced 27 Mch 1876
Oxford University bill withdrawn, July, 1876, the Universities act passed 10 Aug 1877
Commission publish a new scheme for professors, etc., very restrictive 2 Nov 1880
Statute admitting women to examination passed 29 Apr 1884

COLLEGES

University said to have been founded by king Alfred, 872, founded by William, archdeacon of Durham about 1232
Balliol founded by John Baliol, knight (father to Baliol, king of the Scots), and Deborah his wife . 1263
Merton college, by Walter de Merton, bishop of Rochester 1264
Exeter, by Walter Stapleton bishop of Exeter 1314
Oriel college, by king Edward II, Adam de Brome, archdeacon of Stowe 1326
Queen's college, by Robert de Eglesfield, clerk, confessor to queen Philippa, consort of Edward III 1340
New college, by William of Wykeham bishop of Winchester, first called St. Mary of Winchester, founded 1379, occupied 1386 (500th anniversary celebrated 14 Oct. 1879)
All Souls' college, by Henry Chichely, archbishop of Canterbury 1437
Magdalen, by William of Waynflete, bishop of Winchester 1456
Lincoln college, by Richard Fleming, 1427, finished by Rotherham, bishop of Lincoln 1479
Brazenose, by William Smyth, bishop of Lincoln, and sir Richard Sutton 1509
Corpus Christi by Richard Fox, bishop of Winchester 1516
Christ church, by cardinal Wolsey, 1525, and afterwards by Henry VIII 1532
Trinity by sir Thomas Pope, on the basis of a previous institution called Durham college 1554
St John's, by sir Thomas White lord mayor of London 1555
Jesus college, by dr Hugh Price and queen Elizabeth 1571
Wadham by Nicholas Wadham, and Dorothy, his wife 1613
Pembroke, by Thomas Teesdale and Richard Wightwick, clerk, 1624
Worcester, by sir Thomas Coke, of Bentley, in Worcestershire, it was originally called Gloucester college 1714
Keble college, first stone laid by archbishop of Canterbury, 25 Apr 1868, consecrated 23 June, 1870
Hertford college, 1312, dissolved in 1805, and a Hertford scholarship appointed, revived, and Magdalen hall incorporated with it . 1874
Indian institute founded 1879

HALLS (not incorporated)

St Edmund's 1269
St Mary's 1333
New Inn hall 1392
St Mary Magdalen (incorporated with Hertford college, 1874) 1487
St Alban's 1547
First professorships —Divinity (Margaret), 1502, Divinity, Law, Medicine, Hebrew, Greek, 1540, etc

Number of undergraduates, 1893	3,197
Members of the convocation, 1893	6,087
" on the book, 1893.	12,165
Matriculated, 1865 .	524
" 1875	718
" 1891 .	802

DEGREES CONFERRED.

	M A	B.A	D.D.	D C L	M.D	B M.	B.D	B.C.L	B M	B.Mus.
1865.	343	297	5	15	1	4	7	4	3	6
1875.	294	394	2	11	2	2		2	5	11
1891	392	521	12	10	6	2	9	12	14	11

—*Oxford University Calendar*, 1893

Oxford's assault on queen Victoria. Edward Oxford, a youth who had been a servant in a publichouse, discharged 2 pistols at queen Victoria and prince Albert, as they were proceeding up Constitution hill in an open phaeton from Buckingham palace, 10 June, 1840. He stood within a few yards of the carriage, but no one was injured. Oxford was tried at the Old Bailey (10 July), was adjudged insane, and sent first to Bethlehem hospital, next to Broadmoor, and set at liberty in 1863, on condition of going abroad.

Ox'us (the Persian and Turkish Djihoun; local name, Amou Darya), a river of central Asia, supposed to have changed its course before 1000 A.D., and to have resumed its ancient bed in 1878.

ox'ygen, a gas (named from the Gr. ὀξύς, sharp, and the root γεν-, produce, as it was long supposed to be the essential element of acids), is the most abundant of all substances, constituting about one-third of the solid earth, and forming about nine-tenths of water and one-fifth of the atmosphere It was first separated from red oxide of mercury by Priestley, 1 Aug 1774, and by Scheele, who was ignorant of Priestley's discovery, in 1775 It is a supporter of animal life (in respiration) and of combustion An oxygen-gas company was announced in Dec 1864, its object being the cheap manufacture of oxygen for its application to the production of perfect combustion in lamps, stoves, furnaces, etc. Oxygen was liquefied by Raoul Pictet at Geneva (pressure, 320 atmospheres, temp —140 C), 22 Dec 1877 AIR, GAS, OZONE, WATER, etc

A statue of Joseph Priestley 1733-1804, at Birmingham, was unveiled by prof T H Huxley 1 Aug 1874, the centenary of the discovery of oxygen This was also celebrated at Northumberland, Pa , where he was buried, Feb 1804, having left England 1794 and settled at Northumberland

A method of obtaining oxygen from air devised and patented by M Margis, of Paris The principle is that of dialysis, or diffusion under pressure (GAS liquefaction) Sept 1882

Prof Dewar obtained 2 cubic centimetres (one tenth of a fluid oz) of liquid oxygen by means of liquid ethylene (the illuminating part of coal gas) temp —140 C (by Wroblewski and Olzewski s method) at the Royal institution, London. 26 June, 1884

He first exhibited solid oxygen in the form of snow (temperature —200 C) produced by placing liquid oxygen in a partial vacuum, at the Royal institution 27 May 1886

Prof Dewar exhibited between 300 to 400 centimetres liquid oxygen at the Faraday centenary 26 June, 1891 The feeble magnetism of oxygen demonstrated by Faraday was shown by prof Dewar to be greatly increased when reduced to the liquid state by a temperature of —180 C , announced 10 Dec 1891 Some liquid oxygen placed in the magnetic field sprang to the poles and adhered to them till evaporated , this was publicly shown by the professor at the Royal institution, 10 June, 1892 Several pints of liquid oxygen and liquid air were then produced in the presence of the audience

oyster (the Lat *Ostrea edulis*) British oysters are celebrated by the Roman satirist Juvenal (*Sat* iv 140), about 100

ozok'erit, a mineral hydro-carbon found in Moldavia and Wallachia From it is distilled a substance suitable for making candles, introduced in the autumn of 1871

o'zone (from Gr ὄζειν, to yield an odor) was discovered by Schonbein of Basel in 1840, when experimenting with the then newly invented battery of sir William Grove, and was recognized by him successively as a minute constituent of the oxygen gas resulting from the electrolysis of water effected by a current of high tension, of air or oxygen, through which electric discharges have taken place, and of air in which moist phosphorus has been undergoing slow oxidation

Marignac determined the action of ozone on various substances to be due to oxidation 1845

Ozonometers constructed 1858

M Schönbein announced his discovery of another modification of oxygen, which he termed *antozone*, hitherto found only in the compound state (in peroxides of sodium potassium etc), 1859

French Academy of sciences appointed a committee to inquire into the nature and relations of ozone 4 Dec 1865

Andrews and Tait demonstrated ozone to be a condensed form of oxygen 1860, "

This further established by Soret and Brodie by quantitative reactions. (Odling suggested and Brodie proved ozone to be 3 molecules of oxygen in the space of 2) 1872

Ozone generated by a current produced by Wilde s magneto electric machine, employed to bleach sugar, by Edward Beane's patent Aug 1868

Liquefied by Hautefeuille and Chappuis Oct 1880

P

P, the 16th letter and 12th consonant of the English alphabet, known to the Greeks, Phœnicians, and Egyptians

Pacific ocean. AMERICA, Balboa, Magellan, OCEAN

Pacific railroads.

Senate committee reports favorably Asa Whitney s bill for northern railway to the Pacific (Whitney was a merchant of New York city, zealous for such a road), senator Benton speaks against it, tabled by the Senate, 27 to 21 1848

Again agitated by Whitney without success 1849

Benton introduces a Pacific railroad bill into Congress "

Act providing for surveys passed Mch 1853

UNION PACIFIC AND CENTRAL PACIFIC

Bill passes the House, 6 May, 1862, 79 to 49, Senate, 20 June, 35 to 5, approved 2 July, granting as subsidies 6 per cent gold bonds, to the Union Pacific, $16,000 per mile for the great plain west from Omaha, $48 000 per mile for 150 miles over the Rocky mountains, $32,000 per mile for the remainder, in all 1034 miles, $27,236,512 For the Central Pacific, $16 000. $48,000, and $32 000 per mile in all 883 miles, $27,855,562 Each company also received 12,800 acres land per mile of road, in all 25,000,000 acres, by a subsequent act, 2 July, 1864 The companies were allowed to issue an equal amount of their own bonds, which were to be a first lien on the road, the government bonds the second Time fixed for opening, 1 July, 1876, opened 10 May, 1869 General direction nearly east and west on 40th degree of latitude

Miles built by the Union Pacific	1865	40	
	1866	265	
	1867	245	
	1868	350	
	1869	134	
	Total	1034	miles
Miles built by the Central Pacific	1865	56	
	1866	38	
	1867	44	
	1868	362	
	1869	243	
	Total	743	"
Sacramento to San Francisco		140	"
	Grand total	1917	"

NORTHERN PACIFIC.

Charter granted, 2 July, 1864, and subsidies, from lake Superior to Puget sound, 1800 miles, and thence to the Columbia river, 200 miles, land granted to this railroad was 47,000,000 acres or 73,000 sq miles. Road to be finished 4 July, 1879, commenced July, 1870, company became embarrassed in 1873, ceased work, reorganized 1875, time extended, finished 9 Sept. 1883, last spike driven by Henry Villard on the Pacific slope, 60 miles west of Helena, Mon

Great Northern extension, from Pacific Junction, Montana, to Lowell, on Puget sound (the 5th transcontinental line) completed 6 Jan 1893

ATLANTIC AND PACIFIC

Chartered 27 July, 1866. From Springfield Mo , to the Pacific, nearly on 35th degree of latitude, in all a distance of nearly 2000 miles The land granted to this road was 12,800 acres per mile in the states and 25,000 acres per mile in the territories, in all 42,000,000 acres.

SOUTHERN PACIFIC

Chartered 3 Mch 1871, extending from Marshall, Tex , to El Paso thence through New Mexico, Arizona, to Los Angeles Cal , along 32d degree of latitude The land grant the same per mile as the others

Pacification, Edicts of, a name given to edicts of toleration granted by the French kings to the Protestants GHENT

First edict, by Charles IX., permitting the reformed religion near all the cities and towns in the realm Jan 1562

Reformed worship permitted in the houses of lords justiciaries, and certain other persons Mch 1563

These edicts revoked, and all Protestant ministers ordered to quit France in 15 days 1568

Edict allowing lords and others to have service in their houses, and granting public service in certain towns 1570

[In Aug 1572, the same monarch authorized the massacre of St. Bartholomew (BARTHOLOMEW)]

Edict of Pacification by Henry III , Apr , revoked, Dec 1576, renewed for 6 years Oct. 1577

[Several edicts were published against the Protestants after the 6 years expired.]

Edict of Henry IV , renewing that of Oct 1577 1591

EDICT OF NANTES by Henry IV 13 Apr 1598

Pacification of NISMES 14 July, 1629

padlock, a portable lock that, with hasp and staple, fastens a door, gate, etc , said to have been invented by Beecher at Nuremberg, 1540, but mentioned much earlier

Pad'ua, the Roman *Patavium*, in Venetia, N Italy, a city said to have been founded by Antenor soon after the fall of Troy, 1183 B.C It flourished under the Romans. Patavian Latin was considered inelegant, and is traced by some critics in Livy, a native of Padua. After being an independent republic, and a member of the Lombard league, Padua was ruled by the Carrara family from 1318, with a short interruption, till 1405, when it was seized by the Venetians. The university was founded about 1220. It was closed through disturbances,

1848-50. Pop. 1881, 47,334. Scene of Shakespeare's "The Taming of the Shrew."

> "*Hortensio.* What happy gale
> Blows you to Padua here, from old Verona?"
> —Act i. sc. ii.

pagans (Lat. *paganus*, belonging to a district or canton), a name given by the early Christian church to all not accepting its doctrine; so called because the villagers and countrymen long remained unconverted. The word now means the heathen, worshippers of idols in general. Constantine ordered the pagan temples to be destroyed throughout the Roman empire, 331; his nephew, Julian, *attempted their restoration*, 361; but paganism was renounced by the Roman senate in 388, and finally overthrown in the reign of Theodosius the younger, about 391.

painting. *The art of laying on, or reproducing objects by, colors.* Osymandyas (in Egypt) caused his exploits to be represented in painting, 2100 B.C.—*Usher.*

	B.C.
Polygnotus of Athens paints in outline in 4 unshaded colors on a colored ground....about	460
Zeuxis of Heraclea and Parrhasius of Ephesus flourish...about	400
Pausias of Sicyon invents the process of encaustics...about	360-330
Apelles, most celebrated for his painting of Venus, "Aphrodite Emerging from the Waves," flourishes....about	332
Antiphilus, an Egyptian, reputed inventor of the grotesque (*Pliny*)....	"
Art introduced at Rome from Etruria by Quintus Fabius, styled Pictor (*Livy*)....	291
	A.D.
Painting on canvas said to have been known at Rome....	66
Council of Constantinople replaces the lamb, former symbol of our Lord in painting, by the man Christ....	692
"Achirotapeton" or "picture made without hands," held authentic by the Romish church, placed in the chapel of the Sancta Sanctorum....	752
Art of miniature painting, imperfect among the Greeks, is applied to Christian uses in the 4th century, and practised extensively by the Byzantine school....*about*	800
Painting on glass practised in France and Germany.... about	1100
Guido of Sienna, first recognized Italian painter, paints the "Enthroned Madonna" in church of San Domenico....	1221
Period of the "Renaissance," culminating with Michael Angelo and Raphael, begins....about	1400
Jan van Eyck of Flanders, by mixing colors in oil and resin, supersedes drying in the sun....about	1415
Masaccio (Tommaso Guidi), pioneer of realists, and leader in the study of the nude, flourishes....about	1425
Andrea Mantegna, the first artist who engraved his own works, *born near Padua*....	1431
"The Last Supper" (known by Raphael Morghen's engraving), on the refectory wall of the old convent of Santa Maria della Grazie, Milan, completed by *Leonardo da Vinci*....	1498
"The Assumption of the Virgin" in the Academy of Fine Arts, Venice, was painted by Titian for an altar-piece in the church of Santa Maria de Frari....	1516
"The Transfiguration," now in the Vatican, was left by Raphael unfinished at his death....	1520
"The Nativity" or "Santa Notte," in the Dresden gallery, was painted for Alberto Pratonieri by Correggio and finished....	1527
"The Last Judgment," a fresco by Michael Angelo over the altar of the Sistine chapel at Rome, completed....	1541
"The Descent from the Cross," in the church of San Trinità de Monti at Rome, by Daniel da Volterra, who lived....	1509-66
Jacopa da Ponte, the first Italian genre-painter, d....	1592
"The Last Communion of St. Jerome," in the Vatican, made for the monks of Ara Cœli by Domenichino, who lived,	1581-1641
"The Aurora," one of the best-preserved frescos in Italy, on *ceiling of the* Rospigliosi palace, Rome, by Guido Reni; finished....about	1610
"The Portrait of Beatrice Cenci," in the Barberini collection at Rome, *ascribed to* Guido Reni....*about*	1600-10
"The Descent from the Cross," in the Antwerp cathedral, the *chef-d'œuvre* of Flemish art, was painted by Rubens, about	1610-15
"The Immaculate Conception," in the Salon Carré of the Louvre, was painted by Murillo....	1678
Robert Feke, the earliest native colonial painter in America, executes several portraits in Philadelphia, Pa....	1746
"The Sistine Madonna," originally an altar-piece by Raphael for the cloister of San Sisto in Piacenza, Italy, purchased by king Augustus III. of Saxony and removed to Dresden....	1753
Charles Wilson Peale executes the first portrait of George Washington as a Virginia colonel....	1772
Benjamin West succeeds sir Joshua Reynolds as president of the ROYAL ACADEMY, England....	1792
Pope Pius VII. purchases for the Vatican the "Nozze Aldobrandini," one of the finest ancient paintings in Rome, representing in 10 figures a Greek marriage....	1818
National gallery, London, Engl., established....	1824
[Began by purchase of the Angerstein collection of 38 pictures for 57,000*l.* by *the government*; since increased by gifts and purchases to over 1100 paintings.]	
First exhibition of paintings ever held in Egypt in modern times opened in Cairo....20 Feb.	1891

EMINENT PAINTERS.

	Born. Died.		Born. Died.
Florentine.			
Giovanni Cimabue....	1240-1302	Fra Bartolommeo (Baccio della Porta)....	1475-1517
Giotto di Bordone....	1276-1336	Michael Angelo Buonarotti....	1475-1564
Fra Angelico (Il Beato)....	1387-1455	Andrea del Sarto (Andrea d'Agnolo)....	1487-1531
Andrea Mantegna....	1431-1506	Daniele da Volterra...	1509-1566
Domenico Ghirlandajo.	1449-1494	Carlo Dolci....	1616-1686
Leonardo da Vinci....	1452-1519		
Filippino Lippi....	1460-1504		
Umbrian.			
Il Perugino (Pietro Vanucci)....			1446-1524
Bolognese.			
Il Francia (Francesco Raibolini)....	1450-1517	Domenichino (Domenico Zampieri)....	1581-1641
Annibale Carraci....	1560-1609	Guercino (Francesco Barbieri)....	1590-1666
Guido Reni....	1575-1642		
Francesco Albani....	1578-1660		
Lombardian.			
Bernardino Luini, about	1460-1530	Correggio (Antonio Allegri)....	1494-1534
Benvenuto Tisio Garofalo....	1481-1559	Il Parmagiano (Francesco Mazzuola)....	1503-1540
Roman.			
Raphael Sanzio....	1483-1520	Giulio Romano....	1498-1546
Neapolitan.			
Josef de Ribera (Lo Spagnoletto)....	1588-1656	Salvator Rosa....	1615-1673
Venetian.			
Giovanni Bellini....	1426-1516	Sebastian del Piombo....	1485-1547
Cima da Conegliano, about	1460-1518	Paris Bordone....	1500-1571
Giorgione (Giorgio Barbarelli)....	1477-1511	Il Tintoretto (Jacopo Robusti)....	1512-1594
Titian (Tiziano Vecellio)....	1477-1576	Paul Veronese (Cagliari)....	1528-1588
Palma Vecchio....	1480-1528	Antonio Canale....	1697-1768
Flemish.			
Hubert and Jan van Eyck....about	1366-1440	Franz Snyders....	1579-1657
Hans Memling....	—— 1495	Franz Hals....	1584-1666
Quintin Matsys..about	1460-1531	Jacob Jordaens....	1593-1678
Antoni Moro....	1512-1581	Anton Vandyck....	1599-1641
Jan Breughel....	1568-1625	David Teniers (the younger)....	1610-1694
Peter Paul Rubens...	1577-1640		
German.			
Albrecht Dürer....	1471-1528	Johann Friedrich Overbeck....	1789-1869
Lucas Cranach....	1472-1553	Wilhelm von Kaulbach.	1805-1874
Hans Holbein (the younger)....	1497-1543	Karl Friedrich Lessing....	1808-1880
Peter Lely....	1617-1680	Adolphe Schreyer....	1828 ——
Godfrey Kneller....	1648-1723	Hans Makart....	1840-1884
Peter von Cornelius...	1783-1867		
Dutch.			
Gerard Honthorst....	1592-1666	Jacob Ruysdael....	1625-1681
Adriaen Brouwer....	1605-1638	Jan Steen....	1626-1679
Albert Cuyp....	1605-1691	Jan ver Meer....	1632-1696
Rembrandt van Ryn..	1606-1669	Pieter de Hooch....	1632-1681
Gerard Terburg....	1608-1681	William van de Velde.	1633-1707
Jan Both....	1610-1656	Frans van Mieris....	1635-1681
Adrian van Ostade....	1610-1685	Mindert Hobbema, about	1635-1700
Ferdinand Bol....	1611-1681	Caspar Netscher....	1639-1684
Bartholomew van der Helst....	1612-1670	Adrian van de Velde..	1639-1672
Gerard Dow....	1613-1680	Adrian van der Werff.	1659-1722
Philip Wouvermans..	1620-1668	Jan van Huysum....	1682-1749
Isaac Jansz van Ostade.	1621-1649	Jean Auguste Henri Leys....	1815-1869
Nicolas Berchem....	1624-1683	L. Alma-Tadema....	1836 ——
Paul Potter....	1625-1654		
Spanish.			
Juan de Juanes....	1506-1579	Bartolomeo Esteban Murillo....	1618-1682
Francisco Zurbaran...	1598-1662	Mariano Fortuny....	1838-1874
Diego Velasquez....	1599-1660		
Alonzo Cano....	1601-1667		
French.			
Nicolas Poussin....	1594-1665	Jean Baptiste Camille Corot....	1796-1875
Claude Lorraine (Claude Gelée)....	1600-1682	Paul Delaroche....	1797-1856
Eustache Lesueur....	1616-1655	Eugène Delacroix....	1799-1863
Charles le Brun....	1619-1690	Narcisse Virgile Diaz.	1807-1876
Hyacinthe Rigaud....	1659-1743	Constant Troyon....	1810-1865
Antoine Watteau....	1684-1721	*Jules Dupré*....	1811 ——
Claud Joseph Vernet..	1714-1789	Pierre E. T. Rousseau.	1812-1867
Louis Jacques David..	1748-1825	Charles Emile Jacque.	1813 ——
Elizabeth Louise Vigée Lebrun....	1755-1842	Jean Francois Millet..	1814-1875
Pierre Prud'hon....	1758-1823	Thomas Couture....	1815-1879
Carle (A. C. H.) Vernet.	1758-1836	Jean Louis Ernest Meissonier....	1815-1891
Antoine Jean Gros...	1771-1835	Henri-Felix-E. Philippoteaux....	1815-1884
Jean Dominique Augustin Ingres....	1780-1867	Charles François Daubigny....	1817-1878
Horace Vernet....	1789-1863	Gustave Courbet....	1819-1877
Ary Scheffer....	1795-1858		

French.—(Continued.)

	Born. Died.		Born. Died.
ıgène Fromentin...	1820–1876	Jehan Georges Vibert.	1840 ——
ırie Rosa Bonheur..	1822 ——	Alexander G. H. Regnault...	1843–1871
exander Cabanel....	1823 ——	Jean-Joseph-Benjamin Constant..........	1845 ——
ın Leon Gérôme....	1824 ——	Jules Bastien Lepage.	1848–1884
lolphe-Williams Bouguereau...........	1825 ——	Edouard-Jean-B. Detaille..............	1848 ——
on J. F. Bonnat.....	1833 ——	Pascal-Adolph-J. Dagnan-Bouveret......	1852 ——
ul Gustave Doré...	1833–1883	Gustave-Claude-E. Courtois...........	1852 ——
les J. Lefebvre.....	1836 ——		
nile-Auguste-Carolus Duran..............	1838 ——		
stave Achille Guillaumet..............	1840 ——		

English.

nuel Cooper.......	1609–1672	Richard Redgrave....	1804–1888
lliam Dobson......	1610–1646	P. F. Poole..........	1806–1879
Thornhill.........	1676–1732	John R. Herbert.....	1810–1890
lliam Hogarth.....	1679–1764	Thomas Creswick....	1811–1869
hard Wilson.......	1713–1782	Daniel Maclise.......	1811–1870
shua Reynolds.....	1723–1792	E. W. Cooke..........	1811–1880
orge Stubbs........	1724–1806	C. W. Cope...........	1811–1890
ul Sandby..........	1725–1809	Augustus Egg........	1816–1863
omas Gainsborough,	1727–1788	E. M. Ward..........	1816–1879
orge Romney.......	1734–1802	J. C. Horsley.........	1817–1890
Mortimer..........	1741–1779	J. Gilbert............	1817 ——
nes Barry.........	1741–1806	Edward Armitage....	1817 ——
nry Fuseli.........	1741–1825	William P. Frith.....	1819 ——
nes Northcote.....	1746–1831	J. C. Hook...........	1819 ——
lliam Beechey.....	1753–1839	George Frederick Watts.............	1820 ——
omas Stothard.....	1755–1834	Carl Haag...........	1820 ——
nry Raeburn......	1756–1823	James Sant..........	1820 ——
ın Opie...........	1761–1807	Frederick [illegible]	1822 ——
orge Morland......	1763–1804	Birket [illegible]	[illegible]25 ——
omas Lawrence....	1769–1830	Thom[illegible]	[illegible]26 ——
seph Mallord William Turner........	1775–1851	William [illegible]	[illegible]27 ——
hn Constable.......	1776–1837	Dante Ga[illegible]	1828–1882
vid Wilkie.........	1785–1841	William [illegible]glas..	1829–1891
lliam Hilton.......	1786–1839	John Ever[illegible]illais..	1829 ——
njamin Robert Haydon...............	1786–1846	H. S. Ma[illegible].......	1829 ——
lliam Mulready....	1786–1863	Frederick Leighton...	1830 ——
F. Witherington...	1786–1865	Vicat Cole...........	1833 ——
lliam Etty.........	1787–1849	Edward Burne-Jones..	1833 ——
raham Cooper.....	1787–1868	Phil. Calderon.......	1833 ——
lliam Collins......	1788–1847	J. A. M. Whistler....	1835 ——
n Martin..........	1789–1854	G. D. Leslie.........	1835 ——
arles Hayter.......	1792–1871	W. Q. Orchardson....	1835 ——
arles Eastlake.....	1793–1865	E. J. Poynter.........	1836 ——
arles Robert Leslie.	1794–1859	John Pettie..........	1839–1894
vid Roberts........	1796–1864	Marcus Stone........	1839 ——
rkson Stanfield....	1798–1867	Elizabeth Thompson (lady Butler).......	1844 ——
omas Webster......	1800–1886	Walter W. Ouless....	1848 ——
win Landseer......	1802–1873	Hubert Herkomer....	1849 ——
ancis Grant.......	1803–1878		

American.

hn Copley.........	1737–1815	Richard M. Staigg....	1817–1881
njamin West......	1738–1820	John F. Kensett......	1818–1872
arles Wilson Peale..	1741–1826	William Hart.........	1822 ——
lbert Charles Stuart,	1756–1828	Sanford R. Gifford....	1823–1880
hn Trumbull......	1756–1843	Jasper Francis Cropsey	1823 ——
hn Vanderlyn......	1776–1852	William Morris Hunt.	1824–1879
ward G. Malbone...	1777–1807	Edward H. May......	1824–1887
mbrandt Peale.....	1778–1860	Eastman Johnson....	1824 ——
ashington Allston...	1779–1843	James W. Glass......	1825–1857
omas Sully........	1783–1872	Richard Caton Woodville..............	1825–1855
nry Inman........	1801–1846	William H. Beard....	1825 ——
omas Cole.........	1801–1848	George Inness........	1825–1894
bert W. Weir......	1803–1889	Frederick E. Church..	1826 ——
mes E. Freeman...	1808–1884	William Bradford.....	1827 ——
hn Gadsby Chapman...............	1808–1889	M. Wight.............	1827 ——
lliam Page.........	1811–1885	Jervis McEntee.......	1828–1891
arles Loring Elliott,	1812–1868	James M. Hart........	1828 ——
mpkins Matteson...	1813–1884	Albert Bierstadt......	1828 ——
orge L. Brown.....	1814–1889	Edward Moran.......	1829 ——
mes H. Beard......	1814–1893	George H. Boughton..	1833 ——
manuel Leutze....	1816–1868	Thomas Moran.......	1837 ——
niel Huntington....	1816 ——	Arthur Quartley......	1839–1886

PRINCIPAL ART GALLERIES OF EUROPE.

ademia delle Belle Arts, Florence.	Dresden Gallery.
llery of the Uffizi, Florence.	The Royal Pinakothek at Munich.
e Pitti Gallery, Florence.	The Berlin Museum.
e Vatican, Rome.	The Hermitage, St. Petersburg.
llery of the Capitol, Rome.	Brera Gallery, Milan.
rghese Gallery, Rome.	National Gallery, London.
rsini Palace, Rome.	South Kensington Museum.
ria, Rome.	Hampton Court.
ademy of Fine Arts, Venice.	Bridgewater, London.
yal Museum, Madrid.	Dulwich, England.
llery of the Louvre, Paris.	Belvedere, Vienna.
LUXEMBOURG.	Cassel, Germany.

UNITED STATES.

w York Historical Society, established........................ 1804
Pennsylvania Academy of Fine Arts, Philadelphia, incorporated...28 Mch. 1806
Wadsworth Gallery, Hartford, Conn., founded.................... 1842
Buffalo (N.Y.) Fine Arts Academy, incorporated.........4 Dec. 1862
Yale School of Fine Arts, New Haven, Conn., opened......... 1866
Metropolitan Museum of Art, Central Park, New York, chartered...13 Apr. 1870
[Contains the largest collection of art in the U. S. Here are the Cesnola art works from Cyprus, the Summerville gems, noted collections of statuary, and many valuable paintings.]
Museum of Fine Arts, Boston, incorporated.................. "
Corcoran Gallery of Art, Washington, D. C., chartered..24 May, "
Powers Art Gallery, Rochester, N. Y., established............ 1875
Lenox Library Art Gallery, New York, opened.............. 1877
Chicago Art Institute, incorporated........................24 May, 1879
Peabody Institute Art Gallery, Baltimore, Md., opened..2 May, 1881
Museum of Fine Arts, St. Louis, established..........10 May, "
Milwaukee Museum of Fine Arts, incorporated.........1 July, 1882

Paixhan gun, so called from col. Paixhan, of the French army, who invented it in 1822. It was intended for war-ships and fortresses. The original Paixhan was 9½ feet long, bore 8½ inches, weight 7400 lbs., and was charged with from 10 to 18 lbs. of powder, and carried a ball of about 80 lbs.

palaces. BUCKINGHAM, ESCURIAL, PARLIAMENT, ST. CLOUD, ST. JAMES'S, TUILERIES, VERSAILLES, etc.

palæog'raphy, ancient writing. DIPLOMATICS, WRITING.

Palæol'ogi, a family which reigned as emperors of the East from 1260 to 1453. George Palæologus raised Alexius Comnenus to the throne in 1081, and thereby founded his own family. Andrew, the last Palæologus, son of Thomas, ruler of the Morea, after the overthrow of his father, became a Mahometan at Constantinople about 1533. A person who called himself John Anthony Palæologus Lascaris died at Turin, Sept. 1874. His claims were doubted.

palæontol'ogy (from Gr. παλαιός, ancient, and ὄντα, beings), treats of the evidences of organic beings in the earth's strata. *It is a branch of* GEOLOGY. Cuvier, Mantell, Agassiz, Owen, Edward Forbes, and Blainville—all of the present century—may be reckoned as fathers of this science. The Palæontographical Society, which publishes elaborate monographs of British organic remains, was founded in 1847. The journal *Palæontographica* (German) began 1851. Prof. Owen's "Palæontology" was published in 1860. "Nearly 40,000 species of animals and plants have been added to the 'Systema Naturæ' by palæontological research."—*Huxley*. MAN.

Palat'inate of the Rhine, one of the 7 ancient electorates of Germany. It was long united to Bavaria, but was separated in 1294.—Frederick V., the elector palatine in 1610, married in 1613 Elizabeth, the daughter of James I. of England, and thus was an ancestor of queen Victoria. HANOVER. In 1619 he was elected king of Bohemia, but lost all by his defeat by the Austrians at Prague in 1620. The Palatinate was ravaged by Tilly in 1622, and by the French in 1688. England received many fugitives, of whom thousands were sent to America by the British government and people. These settled mostly in New York along the Hudson and Mohawk rivers, and in Berks county, Pennsylvania. NEW YORK, 1713. *The elector palatine* Charles Theodore inherited Bavaria in 1778; since when the 2 electorates have been united. BAVARIA.

Pale, the name given to the part of Ireland colonized by the English, viz., parts of the counties of Louth, Dublin, Meath, and Kildare. Anglo-Irish rulers were termed lords of the Pale. Their arbitrary exactions led to a royal commission of inquiry in 1537. The defection of the lords of the Pale in 1641 was followed by a general insurrection, and the royal cause was ruined in 1647. In 1652 Ireland was committed to the rule of 4 commissioners.

Palenque (*pä-lenk'ä*), a name given to extensive ruins in the northern part of the Mexican state of Chiapas bordering on Central America, whose history is conjectural. They were discovered about 1750. Capt. Del Rio visited them in 1787, and others have visited them since. They indicate a higher civilization than do any other ancient relics found on the continent. AMERICA, COPAN.

Paler'mo, a city of N.W. Sicily, the ancient *Panormus*.

It was held by the Carthaginians, 415 B.C.; taken by the Romans, 254 B.C.; by the Saracens, 832 A.D.; and by the Normans, 1072. Here Roger II. was crowned king of Sicily, 1130. Palermo was the scene of the SICILIAN VESPERS, 30 Mch. 1282. It suffered from earthquake in 1726 and 1740. The king Ferdinand resided at Palermo from 1806 to 1815, while Naples was ruled by Joseph Bonaparte and Joachim Murat. It revolted against the tyranny of Ferdinand II. 12 Jan. 1848. It was attacked by gen. Filangieri, 29 Mch. 1849, and surrendered on 14 May. It was taken by Garibaldi, 6 June, 1860. An insurrection against the abolition of the monastic establishments broke out in Palermo on 13 Sept. 1866, and was suppressed by the royal troops with much bloodshed; order was restored by 22 Sept. University was founded 1447. Pop. 1881, 205,712; 1890, 267,416.

Pal'estine, the country formerly inhabited by the JEWS. It was united to the Ottoman empire by Selim I. in 1516. Area of Palestine proper about 12,000 sq. miles. CRUSADES, HOLY PLACES, JERUSALEM, JUDÆA, SAMARIA, etc.

"Palestine Exploration Fund" was founded by many eminent persons as a society "for the investigation of the archæology, topography, geology, and manners and customs of the Holy Land;" at the first meeting the archbishop of York was in the chair.........22 June, 1865

[By its means capt. Wilson and a party left England for Palestine in Nov. 1865; they arrived at Damascus, 20 Dec.; and in the following spring explored Jezreel, Nazareth, and many other parts of the Holy Land.]

Excavations in Jerusalem carried on by capt. Warren...... 1867-70
Moabite stone discovered............ 1868
Systematic trigonometrical survey of Palestine carried on by capt. Stewart, R.E., lieuts. Conder and Kitchener, R.E., 1872-77
A similar fund established in New York............ 1871
Ordnance survey of Sinai by capts. Wilson and Palmer pub... 1872
Surveying party attacked by natives, rescued by soldiers, after much suffering............10 July, 1875
Survey of Western Palestine completed; announced.......Oct. 1877
Publication of map (1 inch to the mile) in 26 sheets......May, 1870
Map and Memoirs of the Survey of Western Palestine pub. 1880-81
Survey of Eastern Palestine begun by lieuts. Conder and Kitchener............ 1881
"Twenty-one Years' Work" in the Holy Land pub......June, 1886
Capt. Conder discovers a key to HITTITE inscriptions...26 Feb. 1887

pal'impsest (from Gr. πάλιν, again; and ψάω, I efface), parchments written on after previous writing had been partially effaced. Cardinal Mai, by removing the second writing in some MSS., recovered the original. This was the case with Cicero's "De Republica," pub. by Mai in 1821. It had been covered by a treatise of Lactantius.

pall, pal'lium, in the Roman church an ensign of dignity conferred by the pope upon archbishops. By a decretal of pope Gregory XI. (about 1370), no archbishop could call a council, bless the chrism, consecrate churches, ordain a clerk, or consecrate a bishop till he had received his pall from the see of Rome. The pall was first worn by an Irish archbishop in 1152, when Gelasius was recognized as primate of all Ireland.

Pal'ladium, the statue of Pallas (Minerva), said to have fallen from heaven near the tent of Ilus, as he was building Ilium, which the oracle of Apollo declared should never be taken so long as the Palladium was found within its walls. The Greeks are said to have obtained it during the siege of Troy, being stolen by Ulysses and Diomede, 1184 B.C., but some writers assert another statue was taken, and that the real Palladium was conveyed from Troy to Italy by Æneas, 1183 B.C., and preserved by the Romans with the greatest secrecy in the temple of Vesta.—*Palladium* is a rare metal discovered in platinum ore by dr. Wollaston in 1803.

Pall Mall (*pell mell*), a street near St. James palace, London, is named from a French game at ball (*paille-maille*, being a wooden mallet), resembling the modern croquet, having been played there about 1621.

Palm Sunday, Sunday before Easter. When Christ made his entry into Jerusalem, multitudes of the people who were come to the feast of the Passover took branches of the palm-tree, and went forth to meet him, 33.

Palmy'ra, a ruined city of Syria, was supposed to have been the Tadmor in the wilderness built by Solomon, but was manifestly Grecian. The brilliant part of the history of Palmyra was under Odenatus and his queen, Zenobia. At the death of Odenatus, Zenobia assumed the title of queen of the East in 267. Aurelian defeated her at Emesa in 272, and made her captive, 273, and killed Longinus, the philosopher, her friend. Palmyra is now inhabited by a few Arab families. The ruins were visited in 1751 by Mr. Wood, who published an account of them in 1753. Others have visited them since.

Palo Alto, Battle of. Gen. Taylor, in command of the army of occupation in Texas, marched from Point Isabel on the evening of 7 May, 1846, to the relief of fort Brown, opposite Matamoras. FORT BROWN. At noon next day he discovered a Mexican army, under gen. Arista, full 6000 strong, drawn up in battle order upon a beautiful prairie called Palo Alto. Taylor, with little more than 2000 men, attacked him. The contest lasted 5 hours. At twilight the Mexicans gave way and fled. The Americans lost, in killed and wounded, 53; Mexican loss was about 600. MEXICAN WAR.

Pam'irs, a lofty mountain ridge in Turkestan, central Asia.

Col. Gromtchevski's Russian exploring expedition stopped by Afghan and British outposts............ 1889
Capt. Yonoff, with a military force, excludes capt. Younghusband and lieut. Davison, travellers, from the little Pamir, on the frontiers of Afghanistan, etc. Russians afterwards retire on the advance of a party of Goorkhas..............Aug. 1891
Russian government declares the action of capt. Yonoff to be illegal, and apologizes.............Feb. 1892

[illegible] n mythology the god of shepherds [illegible] ented as both man and beast; [illegible] lean pipe; inspirer of sudden [illegible] ing rise to panics.

[illegible] which joins the 2 Americas. [illegible], New Granada, was divided [illegible] h is named Panama. A rev- [illegible] n 9 Mch. 1865; the government [illegible] Colunje became president; succeeded by Vincent Olarte, 1 Oct. 1866. Panama is now subject to COLOMBIA. The government overthrown by Colombian troops without bloodshed, about 12 Oct. 1875. Across the isthmus a ship-canal was proposed by the BULWER-CLAYTON TREATY, 19 Apr. 1850. A treaty for the construction of a ship-canal through the isthmus by the United States was signed with Colombia, 26 Jan. 1870.

First exploration for canal route between Chagres and Panama by H. de la Serna............1527-28
Canal proposed by Lopez de Gomarfa............ 1551
Canal or road from Caledonia bay proposed by William Patterson............ 1698
Gogonche, a Biscayan pilot, laid his scheme for a canal before the Spanish government............ 1799
Humboldt proposed a canal............ 1803
First formal exploration made by Lloyd and Falmark......1827-29
Garella's survey............ 1843
Canal scheme of Michel Chevalier proposed............ 1844
Macadamized road from Panama to Portobello proposed by W. B. Liot, R.N............ 1845
Survey for Panama railroad by col. G. W. Hughes, U. S. A..... 1849
Panama railroad begun............Jan. 1850
Exploration of capt. Fitzroy, R. N............ "
" dr. Cullen............ "
" J. C. Trautwine............ 1852
" capt. Prevost, R. N............ 1853
" Lionel Gisborne............ 1854
" lieut. Strain, U. S. N............ "
" capt. Kennish............ 1855
First train from ocean to ocean............28 Jan. "
Exploration of lieut. Michler, U. S. A............ 1858
" Frederick N. Kelley............ 1864
" M. de la Charne............ 1865
De Paydt announces discovery of a favorable route............ "
Exploration of Gonzorga............ 1866
" com. T. O. Selfridge, U. S. N............ 1870
" com. Tull, U. S. N............ 1875
Gen. Türr and a committee propose a canal............Oct. 1876
Lieut. L. A. B. Wyse's survey (1875) published........autumn, 1877
Explorations of Reclus and Sosa............ 1878
International canal congress convened in Paris........15 May, 1879
Seven schemes proposed; canal from gulf of Limon to bay of Panama recommended (by 74-8)............29 May, "
De Lesseps arrives at the isthmus............31 Dec. "
Scheme suspended for want of funds............ "
Canal through Nicaragua proposed by Americans; favored by gen. Grant............Sept. "
Lesseps's scheme opposed by the U. S. government.......Mch. 1880
Lesseps, at Liverpool, describes his plan; canal to be 46 miles long............31 May, "
Engineers leave Paris 3 Jan.; at work........24 Feb. 1881
Work commenced on ship-canal............ "
Number of men said to be employed, 11,000............ 1883
Company had expended 1,400,000,000 francs up to............ 1888

French government authorizes a lottery for the work...8 June, 1888
[Subscriptions very disappointing.]

Company suspends payment..........................11 Dec. "

Tribunal of the Seine appoints judicial liquidation.....early in 1889

Report of inquiry commission states that 900,000,000 francs will be required to finish the work..................5 May, 1890

Total collapse of scheme; legal investigation demanded..Sept. 1891

Committee appointed by the French Chamber of Deputies begun the investigation of the Panama work........25 Nov. 1892

M. Charles de Lesseps, Fontane, and Sans-Leroy arrested for alleged complicity with the Panama frauds..........16 Dec. "

Trial of C. de Lesseps, Fontane, Cotter, and Eiffel begins, 9 Jan. 1893

Ex-ministers Rouvier and Paul Deves, senators Albert Grevy and Leon Renault accused, but accusation withdrawn, while ex-minister Provost and senator Beral are committed for trial..7 Feb. "

De Baihaut, Blondin, Cotter, and others arraigned on an indictment charging corruption in the matter of the Panama Lottery Bond bill (LOTTERIES)..............................Feb. "

M. Ferdinand and Charles de Lesseps, Fontane, Cotter, and Eiffel sentenced in the French Court of Appeals to imprisonment and fine..9 Feb. "

Congressional committee begin to investigate Panama frauds in America..12 Feb. "

M. Le Guay and Provost convicted of complicity, and sentenced to fine and imprisonment....................15 Feb. "

Conviction of Charles de Lesseps, M. Baihaut, and Blondin; prisoners sentenced to 1, 2, and 5 years' imprisonment, 21 Mch. "

French Court of Cassation quash the sentence of Charles de Lesseps and other Panama defendants, and all are released except Charles de Lesseps..........................15 June, "

Sentence of Charles de Lesseps set aside under statute of limitations.................. [illegible]

Plant and works gone to ut [illegible]

Proposed formation of a ne [illegible] by M. Eiffel, M. Bartisso [illegible] made with the old compa [illegible]

At a meeting of the sharel [illegible] syndicate of 5 persons to f [illegible] tal to be 20,000,000 franc [illegible]

M. Ferdinand de Lesseps; b [illegible]

Meeting of the new Panama [illegible] Tournerie appointed chair [illegible] 21 Dec. 1895; 2d annual me[illegible] 1896; other meetings in 1897; steady work reported on the canal, 3500 laborers employed; reported..............................10 Jan. 1898

Dr. Cornelius Herz arrested at Bournemouth, 19 Jan. 1893; ill; extradition not effected; in default, sentenced to 5 years' imprisonment with a fine of 3000 francs, 3 Aug. 1894; his appeal to the court at Paris, 15 May, disallowed, 2 Aug. 1895; sentence of imprisonment confirmed, 4 Nov.; legal proceedings begun against him at Bournemouth, 27 Apr. 1896; the charge dismissed at Bow street, 2 May; another committee of inquiry appointed in 1897; he died 6 July, "

A company formed in New Jersey to purchase the canal; French interests acquired, 27 Dec.; the French directors resign; reported......................................30 Dec. 1899

Panama canal bill (property of the Panama canal co., purchased for 8,000,000*l.*), etc., signed by pres. Roosevelt, 28 June, 1902; the new company meets, Paris; report adopted 30 Dec. 1902

Panama canal treaty, between the U. S. and Colombia, signed at Washington, 22 Jan.; ratified....................17 Mch. 1903

Treaty rejected by the Colombian senate; reported....17 Sept. "
[Under the terms of the Spooner act the president is directed to proceed at once to negotiate with Nicaragua and Costa Rica, and then take the necessary steps for the construction of a canal by the Nicaraguan route.]

Revolution in Panama; independence of the isthmus proclaimed; Colombian officials made prisoners, and Colombian warships captured..........................3 Nov. "

Junta, pending the constitution of a republic, consisting of J. A. Arango, Fred'k Boyd, and Tomas Arias; reported 4 Nov. "

Colombian troops abandon Colon.......................5 Nov. "

Panama formally recognized as a republic by the U. S..13 Nov. "

Concessions by Colombia rejected; reported..........20 Nov. "

Canal (neutral) treaty; by its terms Panama to receive $250,000 annually, and $10,000,000 on ratification of the treaty signed at Washington, 18 Nov.; ratified by Panama..2 Dec. "

Colombian troops landed at the mouth of the Altrato; subsequently withdrawn; reported....................9, 11 Dec. "

Great Britain recognizes the new republic...........24 Dec. "

Manuel Amador inaugurated as president of Panama..20 Feb. 1904

Treaty of 18 Nov. ratified at Washington.............23 Feb. "

Canal transferred to the U. S......................22 Apr. "

Canal zone government act approved by pres. Roosevelt, 28 Apr. "

Panama receives $10,000,000 from the U. S...........9 May, "

Canal company receives $40,000,000 from the U. S.....9 May, "

The president extends civil-service rules to Panama canal service...15 Nov. "

Col. Frank J. Hecker resigns from the canal commission, 17 Nov. "

Secretary Taft inspects the canal and visits Panama as representative of the president........................27 Nov. "

Congressional committee which inspected the canal favors construction at the sea-level..........................10 Dec. "

U. S. attorney-general decides that the U. S. laws do not apply to the Panama zone..............................27 Dec. 1904

Secretary Taft decides to use laborers from Porto Rico on the canal..31 Dec.

18 yellow fever cases reported in Panama zone during 5 months..2 Feb. 1905

Engineers report that a sea-level canal can be completed in 10 years..4 Feb. "

Isthmian canal commission claim authorization by the president in accepting fees as directors of the Panama railroad, 18 Feb. "

Engineering committee recommend a sea-level canal, to be completed in 10 years, at cost of $230,000,000.......26 Feb. "

Dr. C. A. L. Reed's charges against the canal commission regarding sanitation are denied in Washington........19 Mch. "

The president notifies sec. Taft that the canal commission should be reorganized............................21 Mch. "

U. S. purchases the Panama railroad..................29 Mch. "
[Five shares only could not be purchased.]

The original commission appointed by the president (adm. Walker, chairman); resigned (29 Mch.) and a new commission is appointed (Theodore P. Shonts, chairman)....3 Apr. "
[The other members are John F. Wallace, chief-engineer; Charles E. Magoon, governor of the zone; rear-adm. M. T. Endicott; brig.-gen. P. C. Hains; col. O. M. Ernst; Benjamin M. Harrod.]

The president invites Germany, England, and France to each appoint one eminent engineer to serve on the canal commission in an advisory capacity......................5 Apr. "

The Panama railroad is reorganized..................17 Apr. "

Some clerks and other officials who resigned from fear of yellow fever return via New York........................May, 1905

The Panama canal. The treaty between the U. S. and the republic of Panama, signed by the secretary of state and the minister from Panama, 18 Nov. 1903, by which Panama ceded to the U. S. in perpetuity "the use, occupation, and control of the zone of land and land under water, for the construction, maintenance, operation, sanitation, and protection of said canal, of the width of 10 miles, extending to the distance of 5 miles on each side of the centre line of the route of the canal to be constructed," etc., was ratified by the U. S. Senate, 23 Feb. 1904, by a vote of 66 to 14.

The treaty went into effect 26 Feb. with the exchange of ratifications between the representatives of the two countries and the proclamation of the president of the U. S.

THE ISTHMIAN CANAL COMMISSION.

Following the ratification of the treaty, the president appointed as members of the Isthmian canal commission, to take charge of the construction of the canal and the government of the canal zone, the following persons: rear-adm. John G. Walker, U.S.N. (retired), chairman; maj.-gen. Geo. W. Davis, U.S.N. (retired); William Barclay Parsons, New York; William H. Burr, New York; Benjamin M. Harrod, Louisiana; Carl Ewald Crunsky, California, and Frank J. Hecker, Michigan. Messrs. Parsons, Burr, Harrod, and Crunsky are engineers, and Mr. Hecker was director of transportation for the government during the Spanish-American war. Mr. John F. Wallace, general manager of the Illinois railroad system, was appointed chief-engineer of the canal, and resigned his connection with the railroad to accept this position.

Congress passed the following act, approved 28 Apr. 1904, "to provide for the temporary government of the canal zone at Panama, the protection of the canal works, and for other purposes":

"Be it enacted by the Senate and House of Representatives of the U. S. of America in Congress assembled, that the president is hereby authorized, upon the acquisition of the property of the new Panama canal company, and the payment to the republic of Panama of the $10,000,000 provided by article 14 of the treaty between the U. S. and the republic of Panama, the ratifications of which were exchanged 26 Feb. 1904, to be paid to the latter government to take possession of and occupy on behalf of the U. S. the zone of land and land under water of the width of 10 miles, extending to the distance of 5 miles on each side of the centre line of the route of the canal to be constructed thereon, which said zone begins in the Caribbean sea 3 marine miles from mean low-water mark and extends to and across the isthmus of Panama into the Pacific ocean to the distance of 3 marine miles from mean low-water mark, and also of all islands within said zone, and in addition thereto the group of islands in the bay of Panama named Perico, Naos, Culebra, and Flamenco, and, from time to time, of any lands and waters outside of said zone which may be necessary and convenient for the construction, maintenance, operation, sanitation, and protection of the said canal, or of any auxiliary canals or other works necessary and convenient for the construction, maintenance, operation, sanitation, and protection of said enterprise, the use, occupation, and control whereof were granted to the U. S. by article 2 of said treaty. The said zone is hereinafter referred to as 'the canal zone.' The payment of the $10,000,000 provided by article 14 of said treaty shall be made in lieu of the indefinite appropriation made in the third section of the act of 28 June, 1902, and is hereby appropriated for said purpose.

"Section 2. That until the expiration of the 58th Congress, unless provision for the temporary government of the canal zone be sooner made by Congress, all the military, civil, and judicial powers, as well as the power to make all rules and regulations necessary for the government of the canal zone, and all the rights, powers, and authority granted by the terms of said treaty to the U. S. shall be vested in such person or persons, and shall be exercised in such manner as the president shall direct for the government of said zone, and maintaining and protecting the inhabitants thereof in the free enjoyment of their liberty, property, and religion."

THE PROGRAMME OF CONSTRUCTION.

The work of constructing the Panama canal will naturally be separated into 3 grand divisions, considered from the engineering and purely constructive stand-point. First is the comparatively simple matter of completing the excavation along the level stretches, and including the famous Culebra cut, which, though a big operation, is not at all complicated or difficult. Second is the building of the Bahia dam, which is to create the interior fresh-water lake. This calls for engineering skill of the highest order, and it is possible that the commission may decide to do this part of the work itself instead of letting it out to contractors. It is well known that this is the only phase of the project which gives the engineers any anxiety, for they realize its difficulty and delicacy. The third division will be the construction of the locks and the piers at the ocean ends of the channel.

Panama, Congress at. UNITED STATES, 1826.

Pan-American Congress. UNITED STATES, 1889–90.

pan'dean pipes (said to be the Greek syrinx, and the *ugab* or organ of the Bible, Gen. iv. 21 and Psa. cl.), usually 7 tubes, popular in Britain early in the 19th century. A "Preceptor" for Davies's "new invented syrynx" was published in 1807.

Pandects, a digest of the civil law, made by order of Justinian, 533. It is stated that a copy of these Pandects was discovered in the ruins of Amalfi, 1137; removed from Pisa in 1415, and preserved in the library of the Medici at Florence as the *Pandectæ Florentinæ*.

Pando'sia, a city of Bruttium, S. Italy. Here Alexander, king of Epirus, was defeated and slain by the Bruttians, 326 B.C. Lævinus, the Roman consul, was defeated at Pandosia, in Lucania, by Pyrrhus, king of Epirus, 280 B.C.

Pan'eas or **Pa'nius,** an ancient town of Syria. Here Antiochus the Great defeated Scopas, the Egyptian general, and his Greek allies, 198 B.C.

panics, commercial. CRISIS; PAN.

Panno'nia, part of Illyria, now Hungary. Was finally subdued by Tiberius, 8 A.D.

panoram'a, invented by Robert Barker, consists of bird's-eye views painted around the wall of a circular building. In 1788 he exhibited at Edinburgh a view of that city, the first picture of the kind. He then commenced similar exhibitions in London in 1789, having adopted the name "Panorama," and was ultimately enabled to build commodious premises in Leicester square for that purpose. (He d. Apr. 1806.) J. P. Loutherbourg, a painter, termed the panoramist, invented the "Eidophusikon," consisting of natural phenomena represented by moving pictures, exhibited at Lisle street, Leicester square, London, 3 Apr. 1781.—Cyclorama, a species of panorama recently introduced, is, as its name indicates, a painting representing some important scene, as a battle or view from nature, so placed that every part of the picture is at about the same distance from the spectator. The finest of those exhibited in the United States are the battle of Gettysburg, by the French painter Philippoteaux, and the battle of Chattanooga. Philippoteaux also painted a view of Niagara Falls, which was exhibited with great success in London, 1890.

pan'tagraph (from the Gr. πάντα, all things, and γραφειν, to write, and incorrectly termed pentagraph), an instrument for copying, reducing, or enlarging plans, etc., invented by Christopher Scheiner, about 1603; improved by prof. Wallace, and called "Eidograph," about 1821.

pan'theism, the formula of which is "everything is God, and God is one," was especially taught by Xenophanes, who died 500 B.C. The doctrine is attributed to Spinoza, Kant, Fichte, and other modern philosophers. Amalric of Chartres, censured for holding the doctrine, recanted, 13th century. He is said to have asserted that "all is God, and God is all." Pantheism, as well as atheism, is a troublesome element in philosophic thought. According to Swedenborg, all things are created from God, but only spiritually; nature is not the sphere of creation, but simply of regeneration. He thus eliminates materialism from the problem of creation.

Pan'theon, at Rome, a circular temple built by Agrippa, the son-in-law of Augustus, 27 B.C. It had niches in the wall, where the image or representation of a particular god was set up; the gates brass, the beams covered with gilt brass, and the roof covered with silver. Pope Boniface III. dedicated it to the Virgin Mary and all the saints by the name of S. Maria della Rotunda, or "ad Martyres," 608 A.D. Victor Emmanuel, first king of united Italy, was buried here, 17 Jan. 1878. Pantheon at Paris founded by Louis XV., built by Soufflot, 1757–90. Victor Hugo buried here, 1 June, 1885.

pan'togen. ATOMIC THEORY.

pan'tomimes were representations by gestures and attitudes among the Greeks, and were introduced on the Roman stage by Pylades and Bathyllus, 22 B.C. Comic masks were introduced into England from Italy about 1700. The first regular English pantomime is said to have been "Harlequin Execut[illegible] [illegible]roduced by John Rich at the Lincoln's-inn-fields the[illegible]7. Joseph Grimaldi (1779–1837) was the most [illegible]

Pao'li, [illegible]at. On the night of 20 Sept. 1777, a corps of 1500 Am[illegible]s, under gen. Wayne, were attacked in their camp, nea[illegible] tavern, in Pennsylvania, by a party of British and Hessians under gen. Greig, and about 300 of them were killed or mortally wounded in the gloom. 53 of them found upon the ground the next morning were buried in one grave. A marble monument marks the spot.

papal infallibility. This dogma, maintained by one party in the Roman church, tolerated by another, and utterly rejected by a third, was adopted and promulgated at the general council at Rome, 18 July, 1870, a great many bishops having withdrawn. The doctrine was inculcated by the false decretals of Isidore and others, but not adopted by the council of Trent. COUNCILS OF THE CHURCH, XXI. Prof. Döllinger, the historian, was excommunicated at Munich for rejecting this dogma, 18 Apr. 1871; he was made a D.C.L. at Oxford about 16 June following. OLD CATHOLICS. The doctrine was strenuously attacked by W. E. Gladstone in his pamphlet, "The Vatican Decrees," Nov. 1874.

Papal States. POPES, ROME.

paper, thin sheets or leaves of fibrous material, to receive writing or printing, or for wrappers. PAPYRUS. Paper was probably made in Egypt centuries before the Christian era. It was made of cotton about 600 A.D., and of rags about 1300. Joseph Hunter (in the *Archæologia*, xxxvii.) states that the earliest paper he had seen was a MS. account-book, dated 1302, probably of Bordeaux manufacture. He gives engravings of manufacturers' marks, French and English, dated from 1330 to 1431. He also gives an extract from a work by Bartholus, about 1350, mentioning a paper manufactory in the Marches of Ancona. At the end of Wynkin de Worde's edition of Bartholomæus, "De Proprietatibus Rerum," 1494, its thin paper, made by John Tate in England, is commended. White coarse paper was made by sir John Speilman, a German, at Dartford, Engl., 33 Eliz. 1580; and here paper-mills were erected.—*Stow.* Paper for writing and printing manufactured in England, and an act passed to encourage it, 2 Will. III. 1690; before this time England paid for these articles to France and Holland 100,000*l.* annually. The French refugees taught the English people, who had made coarse brown paper almost exclusively until the French came among them; white paper first made in England in 1690.—*Anderson.* Paper-making by a machine was suggested by Louis Robert, who sold his model to Didot, the great printer, who took it to England, and, conjointly with Fourdrinier, perfected the machinery. The latter obtained a patent for paper-making machinery in 1801, and for manufacturing paper of an indefinite ngth in 1807. The machinery was improved by Bryan onkin. Esparto, a Spanish grass, first imported into England in 1857, has been largely employed in the paper manufacture since 1864.

irst paper-mill in America was built by William Rittinghuysen and William Bradford, near Philadelphia, 1690. A second was built in Germantown in 1710; and Ivy mill, Delaware county, by Thomas Willcox, 1727. First in New Jersey, 1728.

irst in Massachusetts at Milton, 1730, by Daniel Henchman. Dalton mill founded in 1801. One at Troy, N. Y., noted for making from 4 to 5 reams in a day, 1793.

1890 there were between 1100 and 1200 paper and pulp mills, with a capital investment of $100,000,000, producing about 10,000,000 pounds daily.

ethod of grinding wood as raw material for paper was introduced in the U. S. in 1869-70. Olcott paper mill of Vermont, one of the largest wood-pulp mills for paper in the U. S., produces 80 tons of printing-paper daily. PARCHMENT.

paper money. First issued in the American colonies by Massachusetts, 1690. Continental paper money issued during the American Revolution, first issued 1775. Depreciation: value of $100 in specie in Continental money, in. 1777, $105; 1778, $325; 1779, $742; 1780, $2934; 1781, 7400. ASSIGNATS, BANKS, CONFEDERATE STATES, GREENBACKS.

papier-maché (*pap'-yă-ma-sha'*). This manufacture (of paper-pulp combined with gum and sometimes with china clay) has existed for above a century. Martin, a German snuffbox-maker, is said to have learned the art from one Lefevre about 1740. In 1745 it was taken up by Baskerville, the printer at Birmingham, and soon spread over that district. Papier-maché is now largely employed in ornamenting the interior of buildings, etc.

papy'rus, the reed from which was made the paper of Egypt and India, used for writings until the discovery of parchment, about 190 B.C. Ptolemy prohibited the exportation of it from Egypt, lest Eumenes of Pergamus should make a library equal to that of Alexandria, 263 B.C. Many papyri were discovered at Herculaneum in 1754 (LIBRARIES); and many were collected by the French in Egypt, 1798. A manuscript of the "Antiquities" of Josephus on papyrus, among the treasures seized by Bonaparte in Italy, and sent to the National Library at Paris, was restored in 1815.

ac-similes of the largest known papyrus, found in 1855, behind Shedinat Habu, on the Nile, and now in the British museum, were published with translations by the trustees in 1876.

par'able. FABLES.

par'achute. BALLOONS, 1785, 1802, 1837, 1874, 1887.

Par'aclete (Gr. for comforter), a name given by ABÉLARD to the convent which he founded in Champagne in 1122, of which Héloïse became the first abbess. Montanus (MONTANISTS) in the 2d century, Manes (MANICHEANS) in the 3d, and Mahomet in the 7th, claimed to be the promised Paraclete, whom none of the 3 however identified with the Holy Ghost.

par'adox (Gr. παρά, beyond, and δόξα, opinion), something contrary to common opinion. Prof. De Morgan's "Budget of Paradoxes" (of all kinds) was published in 1872. John Paget's "Paradoxes and Puzzles, Historical, Judicial, and Literary," pub. 1874.

par'affine (from *parum affinis*, from its having little affinity with anything), also called photogen, a solid substance, somewhat like spermaceti, produced by distillation of coal, and first obtained by Reichenbach in 1830, and by dr. Christison about the same time. It was procured from mineral oil by James Young about 1848 at Alfreton, in Derbyshire. Soon after it was largely obtained from Boghead coal. It is also obtained from Irish peat. It makes excellent candles. Much litigation ensued through interference with Mr. Young's patent-right.

paragraph Bibles. BIBLES.

Par'aguay, a republic in South America, discovered by Sebastian Cabot in 1526; conquered by Alvarez Nuñez in 1535, and civilized by the Jesuits, who in 1608 commenced their missions there and held it till their expulsion in 1768. Paraguay rose against the Spanish yoke in 1811. In 1814 José G. R. Francia was elected dictator; he ruled vigorously, but tyrannically; he was succeeded, on his death in 1840, by Vibal. From 1814 to 1844 the country was rigidly closed against foreigners. The president, C. A. Lopez, elected in 1844, was succeeded by his son, Francis S. Lopez, Sept. 1862. Paraguay was recognized as an independent state by the Argentine Confederation, 14 July, 1852, and by Great Britain in 1853. Area, 98,000 sq. miles; pop. 1857, 1,337,431; 1873, 221,079; 1876, 293,844; 1887, 329,645.

Hostilities between Paraguay and Brazil; a Brazilian steamer captured as an intruder on the Paraguay............11 Nov. 1864
Brazil invaded..Dec. "
Lopez invades the Argentine republic, which immediately makes alliance with Brazil...........................14 Apr. 1865
Army of Lopez defeated..................................Sept. "
Allies capture Uruguyana and a Paraguayan army....18 Sept. "
[For details of the war, BRAZIL, 1865-69.]
A provisional government installed; Lopez defeated; proclaimed an outlaw.................................17 Aug. 1869
Lopez killed near the Aquidaban........................1 Mch. 1870
Peace signed with Brazil and the Argentine republic..20 June, "
Pres. Salvador Jovellanos elected for 3 years..........12 Dec. 1871
Pres. Juan Bautista Gill................................25 Nov. 1874
President and his brother assassinated; announced, Apr.; Higinio Uriarte president...............................12 Apr. 1877
President, Candido Bareiro (for 4 years)..............25 Nov. 1878
Don Juan G. Gonzales elected president..................1890

parasols were used by the ancient Egyptians. Came into general use in the United States about 1820.

parchment (Gr. περγαμήνη, parchment; lit. paper of Pergamum), the skin of animals prepared for writing. First used for books by Eumenes (some say by Attalus) of Pergamus, the founder of the celebrated library at Pergamus, formed on the model of the Alexandrian, about 190 B.C. From being first written on in this library, parchment was called "*Pergamenæ chartæ*," but it was not invented at Pergamus. Ptolemy of Egypt, to check if possible the growth of the Pergamenean library, forbade the exportation of papyrus from Egypt, thus forcing Eumenes to use parchment instead of papyrus for books.—*Anthon*, "Class. Dict." Parchment books from this time became those most used, and the most valuable as well as oldest in the world are written on the skins of goats. The Persians and others are said to have written all their records on skins long before Eumenes' time.

Parchment paper (or vegetable parchment) was invented and patented in 1857 by W. E. Gaine, C.E., who discovered that when paper is drawn through a mixture of 2 parts of concentrated sulphuric acid and 1 part of water, it is converted into a strong, tough, skin-like material. It must be instantly washed with water. Its great strength points out many applications, e. g., maps, school and account books, and drawing-paper. In 1859 it appeared that a similar invention had been made in Paris by Figuier and Poumarède in 1846.

pardon, an act of grace remitting punishment for a crime. General pardons were proclaimed at coronations, first by Edward III. in 1327. The king's power of pardoning is said to be derived *a lege suæ dignitatis;* and no other person has power to remit treason or felonies, stat. 27 Hen. VIII. 1535.—*Blackstone.* A pardon cannot follow an impeachment of the House of Commons: stat. Will. III. 1700. In the United States the president has power to grant reprieves and pardons for offences against the government except in cases of impeachment; as has the governor in many states *within his jurisdiction He can also commute a sentence.*

Parian marbles. PAROS.

Paris (formerly *Lutetia Parisiorum*), the capital of France, situated *on the river Seine, which cuts it into 2 unequal parts, the larger being towards the north. It includes 3 isles: *la ville* (the city), the *ile St. Louis* and the *ile Louviers*. In the time of Julius Cæsar, Lutetia comprised the city only. It was greatly improved by the emperor Julian, who made it his residence while he governed Gaul, 355-361. It became successively the capital of the kingdoms of Paris, Soissons, and Neustria, and eventually of all the kingdom. Many ecclesiastical councils were held at Paris, 360-1528. The representative of the house of Orleans is styled count of Paris. Population of Paris in 1856, 1,178,262; in 1872, estimated population, 1,851,792; in 1876, 1,988,806; 1891, 2,447,957; 1901, 2,714,068.

Clovis makes Paris his residence..........................about 508
St. Denis founded...613
Hôtel-Dieu hospital founded by bishop Landry.........about 656
Paris ravaged by the Normans (or Danes), 845, 855, 861; suffered from famine..845-940
Defended against Danes by count Eudes and bishop Goslin.... 885

University founded....................................about 1200
Rebuilt.. 1231
Church of Notre Dame built.......................1160–1270
Parliament established.............................. 1302
Suffers by factions of Armagnacs and Burgundians.........1411–18
Taken by the English................................. 1420
Retaken by the French............................... 1436
Pont Notre Dame built............................... 1499
Louvre commenced (LOUVRE)......................... 1522
Hôtel de Ville founded.............................. 1533
Boulevards commenced............................... 1536
Fountain of the Innocents erected................. 1551
Tuileries begun (TUILERIES)....................... 1564
Massacre of St. Bartholomew's..................24 Aug. 1572
Pont Neuf begun...................................... 1578
Vainly besieged by Henry IV.........................1589–90
Entered by him.......................................Mch. 1594
Hospital des Invalides............................... 1595
Place Royale begun.................................. 1604
Hôtel Dieu founded.................................. 1606
Jardin des Plantes formed.......................... 1610
LUXEMBOURG, by Mary de' Medici..................... 1615
Palais Royal built.................................... 1629
Val-de-Grâce... 1645
Conflicts of the Fronde..............................1648–53
Royal palace at Versailles built; the court removed there..1661–72
Academy of Sciences founded........................ 1666
Observatory established.............................. 1667
Champs Élysées planted............................... 1670
Arch of St. Denis erected............................ 1672
Palace d'Élysée Bourbon built....................... 1718
Palace of the Deputies............................... 1722
Military school.. 1751
Pantheon, Ste. Geneviève, founded.................. 1764
FRENCH REVOLUTION breaks out; the Bastile taken....14 July, 1789
Pont de Louis XIV. finished.......................... 1790
Cemetery of Père La Chaise consecrated.............. 1804
Pont des Invalides, etc., erected.................... 1806
Paris surrenders to the allies....................30 Mch. 1814
Paris lit with gas..................................... 1819
Fortifications of Paris (for which 140,000,000 of francs were voted, 1833) commenced 15 Dec. 1840; completed......Mch. 1846
Paris much improved by Louis Napoleon (probable cost 320,000,000 francs)..................................1853–62
Industrial Exhibition opened by emperor and empress, 15 May; visited by Victoria and prince Albert (first English sovereign in Paris since 1422), 24 Aug.; closes..............15 Nov. 1855
Bois de Boulogne opened as a garden of acclimatation...6 Oct. 1860
Decree for an international exhibition of agriculture, industry, and fine arts at Paris in 1867; commissioners appointed, 21 Feb. 1864
International Exhibition on the Champ de Mars (with a new park, comprising more than 100 acres); the oblong building designed by Leplay (enclosing 35 acres), 1245 feet wide, 1500 feet long, consisting of circles within circles; the external corridor was a belt of iron, 85 feet high and 115 feet wide; opened by the emperor and empress................1 Apr. 1867
Visits by prince of Wales; kings of Greece, Belgium, Prussia, and Sweden; czar of Russia, viceroy of Egypt, sultan of Turkey, emperor of Austria, and other sovereigns, May–Nov. "
Exhibition closed (instead of on 31 Oct.) Sunday, 3 Nov.; gross receipts, 9,830,309 francs.
International Exhibition: site, 2 unequal parts divided by the Seine. The main building in the Champ de Mars covers 263,593 square yards (765 by 360 yards); the TROCADERO palace is a stone structure, with a rotunda supported by columns, crowned by a dome, flanked by 2 lofty towers, the exterior gallery ornamented with statues.
Exhibition opened by the president, marshal MacMahon ("in the name of the republic"), in presence of the prince of Wales, the duc d'Aosta, etc...........................1 May, 1878
111,955 persons visited exhibition (a fête day).........15 Aug. "
Closed Sunday..10 Nov. "
Total admissions, 16,032,725; daily average, 82,000; gross receipts, 12,653,746 francs.
Universal exhibition of arts, manufactures, etc., opened by pres. Carnot...6 May, 1889
Officially closed..6 Nov. "
[Greatest exhibition hitherto. Chief building, the EIFFEL TOWER, 985 feet high, mostly of iron. Total visitors, 28,149,353; 402,065 admitted 13 Oct. (the largest number for any one day).]
Receipts, 41,000,000 francs; surplus, 4,000,000 francs. EXHIBITIONS.
Telephone between London and Paris opened.........18 Mch. 1891
Behring sea court of arbitration meets in Paris (BEHRING SEA). 23 Mch. 1893
Marie François Sadi Carnot, 4th president of France, b. 1837, assassinated at Lyons by Cesare Santo, an anarchist, on Sunday, 24 June. State funeral at Paris............1 July, 1894
FRANCE, FRANCO-GERMAN WAR.

IMPORTANT TREATIES OF PARIS.

Between England, France, Spain, and Portugal; cession of Canada to Great Britain by France, and Florida by Spain, 10 Feb. 1763
Between France and Sardinia; the latter ceding Savoy, etc., 15 May, 1796
Between France and Sweden, Swedish Pomerania and the island of Rügen given up to the Swedes, who adopt the French prohibitory system against Great Britain......6 Jan. 1810
Capitulation of Paris: Napoleon abdicates.............11 Apr. 1814
Convention of Paris, between France and the allied powers; boundaries of France as on 1 Jan. 1792...............23 Apr. "
Peace of Paris ratified by France and all the allies....14 May, "
Convention of St. Cloud, between marshal Davoust and Wellington and Blucher, for the surrender of Paris.......3 July, 1815
[The allies entered it on the 6th.]
Treaty of Paris, between Great Britain, Austria, Russia, and Prussia, styling Napoleon the prisoner of those powers, and confiding his safeguard to England....................2 Aug. "
Establishing boundaries of France; certain fortresses to be occupied by foreign troops for 3 years.................20 Nov. "
Treaty of Paris, confirming the treaties of Chaumont and Vienna, same day..20 Nov. "
Treaty of Paris, confirming the congress of Vienna....10 June, 1817
Treaty of Paris between Russia and Turkey, England, France, and Sardinia (revised 13 Mch. 1871; RUSSIA).........30 Mch. 1856
Declaration of Paris, signed by European powers, not by U. S., Mch. 1856: 1. Privateering abolished. 2. Neutral flags to protect enemy's goods, except contraband of war. 3. Neutral goods under an enemy's flag exempt. 4. Blockade to be binding must be effective. This declaration was censured in Parliament in 1871. Assented to by U. S. 1861.
Treaty of Paris between England and Persia...........4 Mch. 1857
Treaty of Paris between the European powers, Prussia, and Switzerland, respecting Neufchâtel..................26 May, "
Commercial treaty between France and England.......23 Jan. 1860
Convention between France and Italy for withdrawal of French troops from Rome.................................15 Sept. 1864

parishes (Gr. πάροικος, dwelling beside or near), territory of an ecclesiastical society. Their boundaries in England were first fixed by Honorius, archbishop of Canterbury, 636. They were enlarged, and the number of parishes was consequently reduced in the 15th century, when there were 10,000. Parish registers were commenced in 1538. The state divisions of Louisiana are termed parishes instead of counties.

park, Central, New York. In the centre of New York city is the Central park, open to everybody. It extends from Fifty-ninth street to One Hundred and Tenth street, 13,507 feet. Its breadth, from Fifth to Eighth avenue, is 2718 feet; its area 862 acres. There are 9 miles of roads, 5¼ of bridle paths, 28½ of walks. It contains the great Croton reservoir for the use of New-Yorkers, with a surface of 96 acres and a depth, when full, of about 38 feet; its capacity more than 1,000,000,000 gallons. The cost of the reservoir was nearly $600,000. The park was laid out in 1858. It contains the American Museum of Natural History, and the Metropolitan Museum of Art and Archæology; of which the Cesnola collection of Cypriote antiquities is a chief feature. Frederick L. Olmsted and Calvert Vaux were the landscape architects.

parkesine (*park'-seen*). A new substance, obtained from various vegetable bodies and oil, the same as xylotile. It can be formed with the properties of ivory, tortoise-shell, wood, india-rubber, gutta-percha, etc. It is named after Alexander Parkes of Birmingham, its inventor, and was shown by him at the exhibition in 1862. In Dec. 1865, at the Society of Arts, parkesine was proved to be an excellent electric insulator, and therefore likely to be suitable for telegraphic purposes.

parks. The Romans attached parks to their villas. Fluvius Lupinus, Pompey, and Hortensius had large parks. In England the first great park of which particular mention is made was that of Woodstock, formed by Henry I. in 1125. Among the noted parks in Europe are those in and near Paris: Fontainebleau, 41,000 acres; St. Cloud, 1000 acres; Bois de Boulogne 2500 acres, and the Bois de Vincennes, 2225 acres; the last 2 acquired by the municipality of Paris in 1854. Vienna has its "Prater park," 2300 acres, and Munich its Royal park, 1300 acres. Phœnix park, in Dublin, Ireland, contains 1752 acres. The civic parks of England, Scotland, and Ireland are numerous, acts for their establishment in England and Ireland passed 12 July, 1869, and in Scotland, 18 Mch. 1878. The most noted parks of London and vicinity are as follows:

Green park, 70 acres, near Buckingham palace, enclosed by Henry VIII.. 1530
St. James, 90 acres, laid out by [illegible] Henry VIII.................. "
Hyde park, 390 acres, which [illegible] became crown property.......... 1535
Richmond park, 225[illegible] acres, enclosed by Charles I...........1625–50
Greenwich par[illegible] acres, laid out................................1660–80
Regent's par[illegible] 180 acres, laid out............................ 1812
Kensing[illegible] 470 acres, laid out..
Kensington Gardens, 210 acres, connected with Hyde park by a [illegible] bridge, opened.. 1826
Victoria park, 290 acres, opened to the public.......................... 1845
Battersea park, 180 acres, opened..................................Apr. 1858
Herne's oak in Windsor park blown down............................ 1863

uthwark park, 62 acres, laid out at a cost of 100 000*l.* and opened to the public 19 June, 1869
nsbury park 115 acres, opened 7 Aug "
ping Forest, 5600 acres, preserved by act of Parliament, is dedicated to the people 6 May, 1882
rnham Beeches purchased by the city of London for a public park in 1879 and dedicated 3 Oct 1883

parks in the United States The development of the rk system, national, state, and civic, in the U S, is recent, ough Boston had its "Common" part of a purchase for a w pasture in 1634, and since 1878 protected from encroachment by law Interest in public parks was created by the pers of A J Downing in 1849, and led to the establishment Central park (862 acres) in the city of New York in 1857 ie national parks or reservations in the U S are

semite park and Mariposa grove on the Merced river in Mariposa county, Cal, discovered in 1851 and established by ongress 1864
llowstone National park, 3575 sq miles, nearly all in north western Wyoming established by act of Congress 1 May, 1872
[Canada has also reserved 260 sq miles in the Rocky mountain region, reached by the Canadian Pacific railroad at Banff as a public park and on 24 May 1888, the reservation at Niagara falls Canada side, was opened]
1885 a forestry commission (NEW YORK) was appointed by New York state for the preservation of the Adirondack forest State reservation at Niagara Falls opened to the public, 15 July, 1885

IMPORTANT CIVIC PARKS IN THE UNITED STATES.

irmount park, Philadelphia, 2740 acres, acquired by purchase and gift 1844-67
ospect park, Brooklyn, 530 acres established 1859
uid Hill park, Baltimore, 693 acres acquired by the city 1860
icago park system comprises 2 south parks 372 and 593 acres, Jackson park, 600 acres, Douglas park, 171 acres, Garfield park, 185 acres, Humboldt park, 194 acres, and Lincoln park, 310 acres, a total, including 37½ miles of boulevards, of 2530 acres, cost about $10 000,000 1869
ffalo park system, 638 acres and 17 miles park driveways, work begun 1871
rks of Cincinnati are Eden park, 207 acres, and Burnett Wood 168 acres, established 1872-73
ston, Back Bay park system comprising Charles River embankment, 69 acres, Back Bay park, 106 acres, Muddy river, 110 acres, Jamaica park, 120 acres, Arnold Arboretum, 167 acres, West Roxbury, 485 acres, in all, including park ways, 1059 acres, established 1877
troit has Belle Isle, containing about 700 acres, bought 1880
lden Gate park, extending to and along the ocean at San Francisco, contains 1043 acres.
Louis has 2 parks, Tower Grove, 276 acres, and Forest park, 1370 acres.
rks of New York are under the control of a board of 4 commissioners who hold office for 5 years Besides Central park, mentioned above, there are Bowling Green (the cradle of New York), Battery, with Castle Garden, Bryant park so named in 1884, once the site of Crystal palace, City Hall park, East River park, Mount Morris park Morningside park, Riverside park 178 acres, the burial place of gen U S Grant, Pelham Bay park, 1700 acres, established in 1888, Van Cortland park, 1069 acres, established in 1888, Bronx park, 653 acres, on both sides of the Bronx river, and several others, as Gramercy, Jeanette, Claremont, Crotona, Audubon and St. Mary's

Park's travels. Mungo Park set sail on his first yage to Africa under the patronage of the African Society, trace the source of the river Niger, 22 May, 1795, and returned 22 Dec 1797, after having fruitlessly encountered great nger He sailed from Portsmouth on his second voyage, 30 n 1804, sent by British government, but never returned is murder at Broussa on the Niger, Nov 1805, was well authenticated His "Travels in Africa" pub. in 1799

Parliament (from the French *parlement*, discourse) rives its origin from the Saxon general assemblies, called *itenagemotes* The name was applied to the assemblies of e state under Louis VII of France, about the middle of the th century, but, it is said, not in English law till the statute of Westminster I, 3 Edw I 1272, and yet Coke declared his "Institutes," and when speaker (1592), that this name is used in the time of Edward the Confessor, 1041. The st clear account we have of representatives of the people rming a House of Commons is in 43d Hen III 1258, the atutes of Oxford, directing that 12 persons be chosen to represent the commons in 3 parliaments, which, by the 6th statute, were to be held yearly —*Burton's Annals* The general presentation by knights, citizens, and burgesses took place, Hen. III 1265.—*Dugdale's Summons to Parliament*, edit. 85. The power and jurisdiction of Parliament are absolute d cannot be confined, either for causes or persons, within any bounds It hath sovereign and uncontrollable authority in making and repealing laws. It can regulate or new-model the succession to the crown (as was done in the reigns of Henry VIII and William III) It can alter and establish the religion of the country, as was done in the reigns of Henry VIII, Edward VI, Mary, and Elizabeth —*Sir Edward Coke* The 4th edition of May's "Practical Treatise on Parliament" was pub in 1859 SEPTENNIAL, TRIENNIAL. Return of the names of members of Parliament from the earliest period to the present time ordered by the House of Commons, 4 May, 1876, and 9 Mch 1877 Part I (1213-1702) pub 1879 COMMONS, LORDS

First summons of barons by writ directed to the bishop of Salisbury by John 1205
Parliament of Merton 1236
An assembly of knights and burgesses (the *Mad* Parliament), 11 June, 1258
First assembly of the commons as a confirmed representation (*Dugdale*) 20 Jan 1265
First regular Parliament (according to many historians) 22 Edw I 1294
First a deliberative assembly, it becomes a legislative power, whose assent is essential to constitute a law 1308
Commons elect their first speaker, Peter de la Mare 1377
Parliament of only 1 day (Richard II deposed) 29 Sept 1399
"*Parliamentum Indoctum*" at Coventry (lawyers excluded), 6 Oct 1404
Members obliged to reside at the places they represented 1413
Forty shilling freeholders only to elect knights 1430
"*Parliamentum Diabolicum*" at Coventry, attainted the Yorkists 1459
Journals of the Lords commenced 1509
"Acts of Parliament" printed in 1501, and consecutively from "
Members protected from arrest (FERRARS'S ARREST) 1542
Journals of the Commons begun 1547
Francis Russell, son of the earl of Bedford was the first peer's eldest son who sat in the House of Commons 1549
Addled Parliament, remonstrated with James I respecting benevolences, dissolved by him in anger 5 Apr 1614
Parliament in which were first formed the Court and Country parties, 1614, disputes with James I June, 1620
Charles I dissolves Parliament, no meeting for 11 years 1629
Long Parliament (which voted the House of Lords as useless) first assembled 3 Nov 1640
Bishops excluded from voting on temporal matters "
Rump Parliament, it voted the trial of Charles I Jan 1649
House of Peers abolished 6 Feb "
Peer sat as a member of the Commons "
Cromwell roughly dissolves the Long Parliament 20 Apr 1653
Convention Parliament (CONVENTION PARLIAMENTS) 1660
Roman Catholics excluded from Parliament 1678
Commons committed a secretary of state to the Tower Nov "
Speaker of the Commons refused by the king 1679
Convention Parliament (CONVENTION PARLIAMENTS) 1689
James II convenes the Irish Parliament at Dublin, which attaints 3000 Protestants "
Act for triennial Parliament (TRIENNIAL) 1694
First Parliament of Great Britain met 23 Oct. 1707
Member of House of Commons accepting any office of profit vacates his seat by statute, 6 Anne, cap 7 "
Triennial act repealed, and Septennial act voted (SEPTENNIAL PARLIAMENT) 7 May, 1716
Journals ordered to be printed 1752
Privilege of freedom from arrest for servants relinquished by Commons 1770
Lord mayor of London (Oliver) and alderman Crosby committed to the Tower by the Commons in Wilkes's affair 1771
Reporting the debates permitted about "
First Parliament of the United Kingdom meets 2 Feb 1801
Clergymen prohibited from becoming M P 's "
Sir F Burdett committed to the Tower 6 April, 1810
Murder of Spencer Perceval by Bellingham at the House of Commons 11 May, 1812
Return for Clare county, Ireland, of Mr O'Connell, first Roman Catholic elected since English revolution 5 July, 1828
Duke of Norfolk took his seat in the Lords, the first Roman Catholic peer under the Relief bill (ROMAN CATHOLICS) 28 Apr 1829
Reformed Parliament meet 7 Aug 1832
Joseph Pease, the first Quaker, admitted M P on his affirmation 15 Feb 1833
Houses of Parliament destroyed by fire 16 Oct. 1834
Privilege of franking letters relinquished by members of commons and House of Lords (FRANKING) 10 Jan 1840
New houses of Parliament commenced "

[Termed the 'Palace of Westminster' The first contract for the embankment of the river was taken in 1837 by messrs. Lee, this embankment faced with granite, is 886 feet in length, and projected into the river in a line with the inner side of the third pier of old Westminster bridge Sir Charles Barry (b 1795, d 1860) was the architect of the sumptuous pile of buildings raised since 1840 The whole stands on a bed of concrete 12 feet thick, to the east it has a front of about 1000 feet, and covers an area of 9 statute acres. It contains 1100 apartments, 100 staircases, and 2 miles of passages or corridors. The great Victoria tower at the southwest extremity is 340 feet in height, and towers of less magnitude crown other portions of the building]

Peers took possession of their house..................15 Apr. 1847
Commons assemble in their new house..............4 Nov. 1852
Two houses began to communicate by letter.......... 1855
Baron L. Rothschild the first Jew admitted..........26 July, 1858
Henry Fawcett (blind) elected M.P.....................July, 1865
Parliamentary oaths modified and made uniform......30 Apr. 1866
Arthur M. Kavanagh (without arms and legs) elected.....Nov. "
House of Lords abolish proxies by standing order......31 Mch. 1868
Death of earl of Onslow, father of House of Lords, aged 93, 24 Oct. 1870
Mr. Fawcett alone in the lobby (350-1 on grant of 30,000*l.* to princess Louise on her marriage)...................16 Feb. 1871
Ballot act passed...18 July, 1872
Commons, obstructed by Irish members (principally messrs. Parnell, Biggar, O'Donnell, Power, Gray, Kirk, and Nolan), sat from 3.45 P.M. 2 July to 7.15 A.M. 3 July; from about 4 P.M. 31 July to 6.10 P.M..1 Aug. 1877
Temporary resolution to check obstruction (by motions of adjournment) passed (282-32).......................27 July, "
Charles Bradlaugh, M.P. for Northampton (not believing in God), objects to take oath of allegiance; his affirmation refused, 3 May; his offer to take oath not permitted..........21 May, 1880
Committee appointed; recommends that he be allowed to affirm, 16 June; much discussion ensues; resolution of Mr. Labouchere, M.P. for Northampton, that Mr. Bradlaugh be permitted to affirm, negatived (275-230)............22 June, "
Mr. Bradlaugh's claim to take the oath or affirm denied by house; he refuses to withdraw, and is imprisoned in clock-tower (vote 326-38), 23 June; released by vote......24 June, "
Resolution of Mr. Gladstone permitting affirmation instead of oath in certain cases; opposed by sir Stafford Northcote as rescinding vote of 22 June; passed (303-249), 1, 2 July; Mr. Bradlaugh affirms, is admitted, and votes..........2 July, "
Commons sat 21 hours (devoted to Irish affairs)....26-27 Aug. "
On first reading of Mr. Forster's Coercion bill, debate summarily closed by H. Brand, the speaker (termed *coup d'état*), 4 P.M. 31 Jan. to 9.30 P.M..................................2 Feb. 1881
Thirty-six Irish members, Mr. Parnell, Justin McCarthy, and others, suspended for the sitting for disorderly conduct; Mr. Gladstone's resolutions; speaker invested with all the powers of the house to regulate business when voted urgent by three-fourths of the members (at least 200) (234-150)...3 Feb. "
Mr. Bradlaugh re-elected for Northampton.............9 Apr. "
His offer to take the oath opposed (208-175); he is forcibly removed, 26 Apr.; again ejected.....................10 May, "
Mr. Bradlaugh's attempt to enter the House of Commons forcibly resisted by the police. Mr. Labouchere's motion to rescind the resolution of 10 May, 1881, negatived (191-7), 3 Aug. "
Mr. Bradlaugh not permitted to sit; government motion negatived (286-228)..7 Feb. 1882
New rules of procedure, including clôture (closing a debate) and delegation of business, proposed by Mr. Gladstone, 13 Feb. "
Proposal for writ for Northampton negatived (307-18); Mr. Bradlaugh repeats oath and takes a seat; withdraws when directed; 21 Feb., expelled (291-83); new writ to be issued, 22 Feb. "
Michael Davitt, convict, elected M.P. for county Meath, " "
Mr. Bradlaugh re-elected for Northampton............2 Mch. "
Resolution of 7 Feb. reaffirmed (286-228)..............6 Mch. "
Mr. Gibbons's amendment (the clôture to be carried by two-thirds instead of bare majority) negatived (322-238), 1-2 Nov. "
Clôture adopted (304-260)..........................10-11 Nov. "
New rules made standing orders...............27 Nov.-1 Dec. "
Affirmation bill introduced in commons (184-53)....19-20 Feb. 1883
Affirmation bill rejected (292-289)...................3-4 May, "
Mr. Bradlaugh not permitted to take the oath..........4 May, "
His exclusion voted (232-65)..............................9 July, "
Arrested by Mr. Gossett, the sergeant-at-arms, for attempting to enter the house, 3 Aug.; brings an action against the sergeant, 7 Dec.; verdict for defendant.................9 Feb. 1884
Mr. Bradlaugh administers the oath to himself, sits, and votes; excluded by vote (228-120), 11 Feb.; re-elected for Northampton (4032-3664), 19 Feb.; re-excluded (226-173)......21 Feb. "
Queen *v.* Bradlaugh for voting without taking the oath, Queen's Bench..13 June, "
Verdict for the crown.......................................30 June, "
Explosion (dynamite) on the stair above the crypt in the House of Commons; much damage done; 2 police constables, Wm. Cole and Thos. Cox, and Mr. Green, seriously hurt. [Cole picked up a blazing parcel, carried it out, and saved the building; he and Cox commended by the queen, and rewarded for steady courage. Cole received the Albert medal, in Westminster hall, 26 Mch.] Westminster hall much injured by another explosion a few minutes past 2 P.M., 24 Jan. 1885
Mr. Bradlaugh's appeal disallowed by the lords justices, 28 Jan. "
New rules, clôture first applied; Mr. O'Brien expelled..24 Feb. "
Mr. Bradlaugh takes the oath; intervention stopped by the speaker...13 Jan. 1886
Mr. Gladstone introduces his bill, "to make better provision for the future government of Ireland"..................8 Apr. "
New procedure with more rigid clôture, etc., introduced 21 Feb.; first and principal rule adopted (222-120)......16 Mch. 1887
House of Commons sat above 21 hours...............21-22 Mch. "
C. Graham and E. Harrington suspended for speaking disrespectfully of the House of Lords.........................13 Sept. "
New rules introduced: rule (1) limiting the sittings of the commons on ordinary days from 3 P.M. to 1 A.M. passed 24 Feb.; rule (2) giving clôture to a majority in a house of 100; rules (3-8) for repressing disorder and waste of time, passed 28 Feb.; (9-12) passed 29 Feb.; rule (13) reviving grand committee, etc. ....7 Mch. 1888
Commons sat from 3 P.M. to 7 A.M.; obstruction to Irish light railways bill..14-15 Aug. 1890
Resolution against Mr. Bradlaugh, 22 June, 1880, ordered expunged from the journals, 27 Jan. He d.............30 Jan. 1891
Geo. W. Hastings, M.P. for E. Worcestershire, sentenced to 5 years' penal servitude for fraud as a trustee, 11 Mch.; expelled from the house...................................21 Mch. 1892
Mr. Fenwick's resolution for the payment of members of Parliament rejected by the commons (227-162)..........25 Mch. "
Directors of the Cambrian railway admonished by the speaker, by direction of the House, for breach of privilege in dismissing John Hood, a station-master, for evidence before the committee on hours of railway servants..........7 Apr. "

NUMBER AND DURATION OF PARLIAMENTS, FROM 27 EDW. I. 1299 TO 59 VICT. 1895.

	Parliaments		Years' reign	
Edward I.	8	parliaments in	8	years' reign.
Edward II.	15	"	20	"
Edward III.	37	"	50	"
Richard II.	26	"	22	"
Henry IV.	10	"	14	"
Henry V.	11	"	9	"
Henry VI.	22	"	39	"
Edward IV.	5	"	22	"
Richard III.	1	"	2	"
Henry VII.	8	"	24	"

Reign.	Day of meeting.	When dissolved.
Henry VIII.	21 Jan. 1510	23 Feb. 1510
	4 Feb. 1511	4 Mch. 1513
	5 Feb. 1514	22 Dec. 1515
	15 Apr. 1523	13 Aug. 1523
	3 Nov. 1529	4 Apr. 1536
	8 June 1536	18 July "
	28 Apr. 1539	24 July 1540
	16 Jan. 1541	28 Mch. 1544
	30 Jan. 1545	Uncertain.
	23 Nov. "	31 Jan. 1547
Edward VI.	4 Nov. 1547	15 Apr. 1552
	1 Mch. 1553	31 Mch. 1553
Mary	5 Oct. "	5 Dec. "
	2 Apr. 1554	5 May 1554
	12 Nov. "	16 Jan. 1555
	21 Oct. 1555	9 Dec. "
	20 Jan. 1558	17 Nov. 1558
Elizabeth	23 Jan. 1559	8 May 1559
	11 Jan. 1563	2 Jan. 1567
	2 Apr. 1571	29 May 1571
	8 May 1572	19 Apr. 1583
	23 Nov. 1584	14 Sept. 1585
	29 Oct. 1586	23 Mch. 1587
	12 Nov. 1588	29 Mch. 1589
	19 Feb. 1593	10 Apr. 1593
	24 Oct. 1597	9 Feb. 1598
	27 Oct. 1601	19 Dec. 1601
James I.	19 Mch. 1604	9 Feb. 1611
	5 Apr. 1614	7 June 1614
	16, 23, 30 Jan. 1621	8 Feb. 1622
	12 Feb. 1624	27 Mch 1625
Charles I.	17 May 1625	12 Aug. "
	6 Feb. 1626	15 June 1626
	17 Mch. 1628	10 Mch. 1629
	13 Apr. 1640	5 May 1640
LONG PARLIAMENT	3 Nov. "	20 Apr. 1653
COMMONWEALTH	3 Sept. 1654	22 Jan. 1655
	17 Sept. 1656	4 Feb. 1658
	27 Jan. 1659	22 Apr. 1659
	7 May "	16 Mch. 1660
Charles II.	25 Apr. 1660	29 Dec. "
PENSIONARY PART.	8 May 1661	24 Jan. 1679
	6 Mch. 1679	12 July "
SEVEN PROROGATIONS	17 Oct. "	18 Jan. 1681
James II.	21 Mch. 1681	28 Mch. "
CONVENTION	19 May 1685	2 July 1687
William III.	22 Jan. 1689	6 Feb. 1690
	20 Mch. 1690	11 Oct. 1695
	22 Nov. 1695	7 July 1698
	24 Aug. 1698	19 Dec. 1700
Anne	6 Feb. 1701	11 Nov. 1701
	30 Dec. "	2 July 1702
	20 Aug. 1702	5 Apr. 1705
	25 Oct. 1705	11 Apr. 1708
	18 Nov. 1708	28 Sept. 1710
	25 Nov. 1710	8 Aug. 1713
George I.	11 Nov. 1713	15 Jan. 1715
	21 Mch. 1715	10 Mch. 1722
George II.	9 Oct. 1722	7 Aug. 1727
	28 Jan. 1728	18 Apr. 1734
	14 Jan. 1735	28 Apr. 1741
	4 Dec. 1741	18 June 1747
	10 Nov. 1747	8 Apr. 1754
George III.	14 Nov. 1754	21 Mch. 1761
	3 Nov. 1761	12 Mch. 1768
	10 May 1768	30 Sept. 1774
	29 Nov. 1774	1 Sept. 1780
	31 Oct. 1780	25 Mch. 1784
	18 May 1784	12 June 1790
	2[illegible] 1790	20 May 1796

OF THE UNITED KINGDOM.

‹st Parliament after the union with Ireland.........22 Jan. 1801

Reign.	Day of meeting.	When dissolved.
	27 Sept....... 1796	29 June...... 1802
	16 Nov....... 1802	24 Oct....... 1806
orge III............	15 Dec....... 1806	29 Apr....... 1807
	22 June...... 1807	24 Sept...... 1812
	24 Nov....... 1812	10 June...... 1818
	14 Jan....... 1819	29 Feb....... 1820
orge IV............	23 Apr....... 1820	2 June...... 1826
	14 Nov....... 1826	24 July...... 1830
	26 Oct....... 1830	22 Apr....... 1831
illiam IV............	14 June...... 1831	3 Dec....... 1832
	29 June...... 1833	30 Dec....... 1834
	19 Feb....... 1835	17 July...... 1837
	15 Nov....... 1837	23 June...... 1841
	19 Aug....... 1841	23 July...... 1847
	18 Nov....... 1847	1 July...... 1852
	4 Nov....... 1852	21 Mch....... 1857
	1 Apr....... 1857	23 Apr....... 1859
	31 May....... 1859	6 July...... 1865
ctoria...............	1 Feb....... 1866	11 Nov....... 1868
	10 Dec....... 1868	26 Jan....... 1874
	5 Mch....... 1874	23 Mch....... 1880
	29 Apr....... 1880	18 Nov....... 1885
	12 Jan....... 1886	26 June...... 1886
	5 Aug....... "	28 June...... 1892
	4 Aug....... 1892	8 July...... 1895

Parliament of Ireland, it is said, began with nferences of the English settlers on the hill of Tara, in 1173. rits for knights of the shire were issued in 1295. The Irish ırliament met last on 2 Aug. 1800, the bill for the union ving passed.

Parliament of Paris was made the chief court justice in France by Philip IV.; at his suggestion it re- ked a bull of pope Boniface VIII., 1302. It was suppressed Louis XV., 1771; restored by Louis XVI., 1774; demand- a meeting of the States-general in 1787; and was suspended the National Assembly, 3 Nov. 1789. COMMUNES.

Parliament of Religions held at the World's ir in Chicago in 1893. The objects proposed were: (1) To ing together in conference the leading representatives of fferent religions; (2) to define and expound the important uths they hold and teach in common; (3) to promote and epen human brotherhood; (4) to strengthen the foundations theism and the faith in immortality; (5) to hear from holars, Brahman, Buddist, Confucian, Parsee, Mahometan, wish, and other faiths, and from all sects and denominations the Christian church, accounts of the influence of each belief literature, art, science, commerce, government, social life, c.; (6) to record the present condition and outlook of the va- ous religions of the world. In June, 1891, the committee ap- inted for that purpose sent from Chicago a general address all governments and to the chief representatives of the dif- rent religions asking for approval. The result was that the ırliament of Religions was opened at Chicago 11 Sept. 1893 and osed 27 Sept. The large attendance expressed the great and neral interest in such an assemblage. "Parliament of Relig- ns," by rev. John Barrows, D.D., 2 vols., pub. Chicago, 1893.

Parliament of Scotland consisted of barons, elates, and abbots, and occasionally of burgesses. A great ıtional council was held at Scone by John Baliol, 9 Feb. 1292, d by Robert Bruce at Cambuskenneth in 1326. A house commons was never formed in Scotland. The Parliament Scotland sanctioned the act of union on 16 Jan. 1707, and et for the last time on 22 Apr. same year.

Parma, a city and country of N. Italy, founded by the ıcient Etrurians. It took part with the Lombard league in ıe wars with the German emperors. It was made a duchy vith Placentia), 1545. Pop. 1892, 51,500.

ıited to Spain by Philip V.'s marriage with Elizabeth Far- nese.. 1714
ıke of Parma made king of Etruria....................Feb. 1801
ırma united to France: with Placentia and Guastalla con- ferred on Maria Louisa, ex-empress, by treaty of Fontaine- bleau......................................5 Apr. 1814
ıke Charles II. abdicates in favor of his son Charles III., 14 Mch. 1849
ıarles III. stabbed by Antonio Carra, 26 Mch., d.....27 Mch. 1854
[Carra did this in revenge of a private injury, and on be- half of the *Giovane Italiane.* He was acquitted through a flaw in the evidence, and died in Philadelphia, 1887.]
ırma is now part of the province of Æmilia in Italy, to which it was annexed by decree after a plebiscite..........18 Mch. 1860

Parnell and Parnellites. Charles Stewart Parnell, the principal leader of the more energetic section of the Home-rule party (Parnellites), 1880 et seq., was born 28 June, 1846, at Avondale, county Wicklow, Ireland. He was grandson of com. Charles Stewart, U.S.N., his father, John Henry Parnell, having married Delia Tudor Stewart, daughter of the commodore. Elected M.P. for county Meath, 1875-80; for Cork, 1880-91. Became Irish parliamentary leader with great influence, which he lost greatly Nov. 1890. He died suddenly near Brighton, 6 Oct. 1891; funeral at Dublin, 11 Oct. 1891. HOME-RULE; IRELAND, 1879 et seq.

Times articles headed "Parnellism and Crime," 7, 10, 14 Mch. et seq. 1887
Third series, pub. June, 1887, related to the Clan-na-Gael, based upon statements in *United Ireland* (Dublin), *Irish World* (New York), and other papers. The *Times* published the fac-simile of a letter alleged to be signed by Parnell (dated 15 May, 1882), in which he is made to say, "though I regret the accident of lord Cavendish's death, I cannot refuse to admit that Burke got no more than his deserts"..........18 Apr. "
This letter Parnell in Parliament termed an anonymous fabrication....................................1 A.M., 19 Apr. "
F. H. O'Donnell *v.* John Walter and others (for libel in the *Times*, "Parnellism and Crime"); damages claimed, 50,000*l.*, Queen's Bench division, no case, verdict for defendants, 2-5 July, 1888
Court of Sessions, Edinburgh, dismisses Parnell's action against the *Times*.........................23 Oct. 1888 and 5 Feb. 1889
Parnell moves for a trial in exchequer division, Dublin; afterwards stopped..11 Feb. "
Parnell's action against the *Times* in London deferred till Michaelmas week....................................18 June, "

PARNELLITE COMMISSION.

Sir James Hannen, president; commission constituted by act passed 13 Aug. 1888. Sir Charles Russell, Mr. Asquith, and others counsel for Parnell and other M.P.'s; attorney-general sir Richard Webster, W. Graham, and others for the *Times.* Proceedings begin, 22 Oct. 1888. Examination of Parnell's alleged letters, 14 Feb. 1889. Richard Pigott, Irish journalist, who had sold the letters to Mr. Houston, on cross-examination, grossly prevaricated.....................20-22 Feb. "
Pigott fled to Paris; his confession of forging alleged letters, and of perjury read in the court, 27 Feb. (57th sitting); the attorney-general, on behalf of the *Times*, accepted the confession and expressed deep regret for the publication, 27 Feb.; confirmed by the *Times*.....................28 Feb. "
Pigott commits suicide at Madrid.......................1 Mch. "
Sir Charles Russell's address ends...................12 Apr. "
Patrick Malloy sentenced to 6 months' hard labor for perjury before the commission..............................15 Apr. "
Commission continued until the128th sitting; sir Henry James's address for the *Times*, occupying from....31 Oct. to 22 Nov. "
Report of the commissioners was laid before Parliament 13 Feb. 1890. The following is an abridgment of their conclusions: I. That the respondent members of Parliament collectively were not guilty of conspiring for the absolute independence of Ireland as a separate nation, but that some of them (messrs. M. Harris, Dillon, W. O'Brien, W. Redmond, O'Connor, J. Condon, and J. J. O'Kelly), together with Mr. Davitt, established the Land League mainly for that purpose. II. That the respondents [44] did conspire to promote agrarian agitation, the non-payment of rents, and the expulsion of the landlords (styled the English garrison). III. They acquitted Mr. Parnell and others of insincerity in denouncing the Phœnix Park murders, and found the fac-simile letter a forgery. IV. They found that the respondents did disseminate the *Irish World* and other newspapers, intending to incite to sedition and other crimes. V. That the charges of incitement to crime, except by intimidation, and of payments for that purpose, were not proved. VI. They found that the respondents did not denounce the system of intimidation, though they knew its effects. VII. That they defended persons charged with agrarian crime, and supported their families, but it was not proved that they subscribed for testimonials for, or were intimately associated with, notorious criminals, or aided their escape by payments. VIII. They found that the respondents made payments to compensate persons injured in the commission of crime. IX. That the respondents did invite and obtain the assurance and co-operation of the Physical Force party in America, including the Clan-na-Gael, and did not repudiate the action of that party.
[Other allegations against Mr. Parnell not proven.]
Report adopted with thanks, by the Commons, after 7 days' debate, 3-11 Mch.; by the Lords (without a division), 21 Mch. 1890. Mr. Gladstone's amendment rejected by 339 to 268.
Parnell *v.* Walter and another, for libel, Queen's Bench division, justices Denman and Wills; damages claimed, 100,000*l.*; 40*s.* paid into court, 11 Jan. Verdict for the plaintiff, by consent, 5000*l.* damages.......................................3 Feb. 1890
[Publication voted not a breach of privilege by the Commons (260-212), 11 Feb. 1890.]

After the divorce suit, capt. O'Shea, Mrs. O'Shea, and C. S. Parnell, 15-17 Nov. 1890, Mr. Parnell was requested by W. E. Gladstone and other English liberals to retire as chairman of the Irish party He declined, and in a manifesto to the people of Ireland reported private conferences with Mr Gladstone and John Morley, 29 Nov Irish Roman Catholic bishops demanded Mr Parnell's retirement 3 Dec After a week's angry discussion in the commons' committee room No 15, the Irish party divided, Justin McCarthy, the vice chairman, was elected chairman by 44 members, Mr Parnell continuing chairman with 26 followers, 6 Dec Manifestoes of the 2 parties issued 9, 10 Dec. 1890

Collapse of negotiations (chiefly at Boulogne) of Mr Parnell, with messrs Wm O'Brien, Dillon, Justin McCarthy, Sexton, and others, Mr Parnell refuses to resign the leadership, 11 Feb, counter manifestoes issued 12 Feb et seq 1891

Dispute between Mr Parnell and Mr McCarthy respecting the disposal of the league funds (in Paris) Feb, Mch "

Mr Parnell in his campaign visits Roscommon, 22 Feb, Drogheda, and other places 1 Mch et seq "

NATIONAL FEDERATION established by Anti Parnellites, 10 Mch "

Nine Parnellites, 72 Anti Parnellites, elected M P July, 1892

Par'os, now **Paro,** one of the Cyclades After the battle of Marathon it was besieged 26 days by Miltiades without success and thus proved the cause of his disgrace It was on this island that the marble (Parian Chronicle) was discovered ARUNDELIAN MARBLES, MARBLE

Parsees, or **Guebres,** the followers of Zerdusht, dwelt in Persia till 638, when, at the battle of Kadseah, their army was decimated by the Arabs, and the monarchy annihilated at the battle of Náhárand in 641 Many submitted to the conquerors, but others fled to India, and their descendants still reside at Bombay (where they are termed Parsees), and where they numbered 114,698 in 1849 Sir Jamsetjee Jejeebhoy, the 3d baronet, was elected president of the community there, July, 1877 Dadabhai Naoroji, a Parsee merchant, was for several years professor of *Gujerati at University college, London* BOMBAY.

Par'thenon (from Gr παρθένος, virgin), a temple at Athens dedicated to Pallas, erected about 442 B.C In beauty and grandeur it surpassed all other buildings of its kind, and was built entirely of Pentelic MARBLE The expense of its erection was estimated at 6000 talents The architects were Ictinus and Callistratus In it Phidias placed his renowned statue of that goddess, 438 B.C This temple had resisted all the outrages of war and time, had been a Christian church and later a Turkish mosque, and still remained entire until the Venetians under gen. Konigsberg besieged the Turks in the citadel of Athens in 1687, when a Venetian bomb, exploding near the temple, fired the powder which the Turks kept within, and entirely destroyed its roof and most of the walls. ACROPOLIS, ELGIN MARBLES.

Par'thia, a country of Asia, to the south of the Caspian sea The Parthians were originally a tribe of Scythians who, being exiled, as their name implies, from their own country, settled near Hyrcania Arsaces laid the foundation of an empire which ultimately extended over a large part of Asia, 250 B C At the battle of Carrhæ, they utterly defeated the Romans under Crassus, whom they put to death, 53 B.C, and though afterwards sometimes defeated by the Romans, they were never wholly subdued by them The last king, Artabanus V, was killed 226 A.D, and his territories were annexed to the new kingdom of Persia founded by Artaxerxes, who had revolted against Parthia

parties. POLITICAL PARTIES

partition treaties. The first treaty between England and Holland for regulating the Spanish succession (declaring the elector of Bavaria next heir, and ceding provinces to France) was signed 19 Aug 1698, and the second (between France, England, and Holland, declaring the archduke Charles presumptive heir of the Spanish monarch, Joseph Ferdinand having died in 1699), 13 Mch 1700 Treaties for the partition of Poland beginning with a secret convention between Russia and Prussia, 17 Feb. 1772, and consummated between the same powers and Austria, 5 Aug same year, the second between Russia and Prussia, 1793, third and final between Austria, Prussia, and Russia, 24 Oct 1795 POLAND

pasig'raphy (from Gr πᾶσι, for all), a system which professes to teach people to communicate with each other by means of numbers which convey the same ideas in all languages A society for this purpose was established at Munich, and the president, Anton Bachmaier, published a dictionary and grammar for German, French, and English, 1868–1871, 4334 mental conceptions may be thus communicated

pasquinades'. Small satirical poems obtained this name about 1533

At the stall of a cobbler named Pasquin, at Rome, idle persons used to assemble to listen to his sallies, to relate anecdotes, and rail at the passers by After the cobbler's death, his name was given to a statue to which lampoons were affixed

Passar'owitz treaty, concluded 21 July, 1718, between Germany, Venice, and the Turks, by which Austria ceded certain commercial rights, and obtained from Turkey the Temeswar, Belgrade, and part of Bosnia, Servia, and Wallachia The Turks gained the Morea

Passau (a city of Germany), Treaty of, whereby religious freedom was established, was ratified between the emperor Charles V. and the Protestant princes of Germany, 31 July, 1552 In 1662 the cathedral and great part of Passau were consumed by fire

Passion-play (Passion of Christ). DRAMA

Passion-week, the name given since the Reformation to the week preceding Easter, was formerly applied to the fortnight. Archbishop Laud says the 2 weeks were so called "for a thousand years together," and refers to an epistle by Ignatius, in the first century, in which the practice is said to have been 'observed by all" The week preceding Easter is now by some termed "Holy-week," the previous week 'Passion-week"

Passion Music Gregory Nazianzen (330-90 A D) is said to have first set forth the history of the Passion in a dramatic form

Guidetti in 1586 published music for this subject, which has been treated since by many composers

J S Bach's great "Passion Musik," first performed on Good Friday, 1729 has been revived with great success in England, beginning with that "according to St Matthew," 6 Apr 1854.

Pass'over, the most solemn festival of the Jews, instituted 1491 B C. (Exod. xii) in commemoration of their coming out of Egypt, because the night before their departure the destroying angel, who put to death the first-born of the Egyptians, *passed over* the houses of the Hebrews without entering them, the door-posts being marked with the blood of the Paschal lamb killed the evening before. The Passover was celebrated in the new temple, 18 Apr 515 B.C.—*Usher*

passport, a document permitting the bearer to pass the barriers of an army or government, usually containing a description of his person Passports are still required upon the frontiers of some countries of Europe, from all foreigners entering them, notably in Russia, and it is customary in Germany, and even in Italy, to ask them from suspicious persons They are issued to citizens by the government, on application, for a small fee, now $2 in the United States, and only 6*d*. in Great Britain. Passports were abolished in Norway in 1859, in Sweden in 1860, and (with regard to British subjects) in France, 16 Dec 1860, in Italy, 26 June, 1862, in Portugal, 23 Jan 1863, and are falling into disuse in most countries. The passport system, revived in France on account of the war, 1 Aug 1870, was abolished by M. Thiers, 10 Apr. 1872, in compliance with the wish of the British government.

pastel, a roll of paste made of different colors ground with gum water, used as a crayon Pastel painting has been recently much practised. The Society of British Pastellists first exhibited in London, 18 Oct 1890. Its members included Mr Watts, Orchardson, and other eminent artists.

Paston letters, the correspondence of a Norfolk family, 1422–83, giving a picture of social life in England, were edited by sir John Fenn, and published in 5 volumes, quarto, 1787–1823. Their authenticity was questioned, Sept. 1865, but was satisfactorily vindicated by a committee of the Society of Antiquaries in May, 1866 Part of the MS was soon after purchased by the trustees of the British museum. The publication of a new edition, by James Gairdner, with additional letters, 1872–75 The MS of the second series, with other letters, was found in 1875, by Mr Frere of Roydon hall, near Diss, Norfolk The MS. of the first series, long lost from the Royal library, found in the library of col. Geo. Tomline, at Orwell park, London, who died 1889, announced Apr. 1890.

Patago'nia, all [illegible] of South America lying south of the river Rio N[illegible]rth of the strait of Ma-an, by whom it was discovered, 1520, and so named on account of the "big feet" of the natives By a treaty between li and the Argentine Republic in 1881, all that part of Patnia to the east of the Andes was placed under the jurisdiction of the Republic Area of Patagonia and Terra del Fuego mated at 375,000 sq miles

Patay', a city of France, where Joan of Arc, the Maid of ans, was present when earl of Richemonte signally defeated English, 18 June, 1429 Talbot was taken prisoner, and the ant Fastolfe was forced to flee In consequence, Charles of France entered Rheims in triumph, and was crowned 17 , following year, Joan of Arc assisting in the ceremony in armor, and holding the sword of state JOAN OF ARC

patents or **letters-patent,** properly, open letters m *pateo,* I lie open) in England, licenses and authorities ted by the king Patents granted for titles of nobility e first made 1344, by Edward III They were first grantfor the exclusive privilege of printing books in 1591 property and right of inventors in arts and manufactures were secured by letters-patent by an act passed in 1623 t commissioners of patents were appointed 1852, viz., lord chancellor the master of the rolls, the attorneyeral for England and Ireland, the lord advocate, and the itors general for England, Scotland, and Ireland In 1853, urnal was published under their authority, and indexes of nts from Mch 1617 to the present time

patents in the United States First patent law aped, 10 Apr 1790 Only 3 patents were granted the first r (the first being to Samuel Hopkins for making potash and rlash, 31 July, 1790), 33 the second, and 11 the third In 6 the patent-office was burned with most of the records, reupon Congress revised the whole system that year all vious acts being substantially repealed and the present tem substituted with a new record. The patent-office is Washington, D C, and occupies one of the finest buildings the country, and is under the supervision of a commisner of patents, with a salary of $5000 a year, who, appointby the president, makes a yearly report to the secretary the interior, to whose department he belongs A larger nber of patents are granted than in any other country

NUMBER OF PATENTS ISSUED FROM 1836.

1836–46	5,019
1846–56	12,578
1856–66	44 334
1866–76	125,155
1876–86	169,478
1886–94	156,453
Total	513,017
Number issued prior to 1836	9,957
Grand total	522,974

[This enumeration does not include designs, re issues, rade marks, or labels Registration of labels practically eased 27 May, 1891 under decision of the U S supreme ourt, in the case of Higgins *vs* Keuffel]

Receipts from patents in 1837	$29,289 08
" " " " 1892	1,288,809 13
Total receipts from 1837–93	29,209,915 13

icial gazette of the patent office, published monthly, gives a description and illustration of every patent issued)

pa'triarch, properly, a ruler by virtue of fatherhood, head of a family or tribe (a name given to Abraham, ac, Jacob, and his sons). The ecclesiastical historian Soces gives this title to the chiefs of Christian dioceses, about) It was first conferred on the 5 grand sees of Rome, Conntinople, Alexandria, Antioch, and Jerusalem. The Latin urch had no patriarchs till the 6th century The first inders or heads of religious orders are called patriarchs.

ctarius, bishop of Constantinople, as *ex officio* chief of the east rn bishops, was nominated patriarch of Constantinople at the econd general council of Constantinople, 9 July, 381 This led he way to the schism between the Eastern and Western churches.

patri'cians, the senators of Rome, their authority ben with the city itself. ROME

patroon', a title given to early Dutch settlers of New rk or New Netherlands, who, having bought lands of the dians, had such title confirmed by the Dutch government e first who made such purchases were Kilian Van Rensseer, Samuel Godyn, Samuel Bloemart, and Michael Pauw, 30. Godyn and Bloemart purchased on the Delaware ver; Pauw in New Jersey, from Hoboken to the Kills; Van Rensselaer on the upper Hudson, a tract 42 miles east and west and 24 miles north and south, with Albany its centre, Livingston, Phillipse, Van Cortland, and others came afterwards ANTI-RENTISM, NEW YORK, 1630, 1686.

Paulian'ists or **Paulin'ians,** followers of Paul bishop of Samosata, afterwards patriarch of Antioch, 260 who is said to have denied Christ's divinity and the trinity, he was excommunicated (269) by a council at Antioch

Pauli'cians, a sect of Christian reformers, arose about 652 Although they were severely persecuted, they spread over Asia Minor in the 9th century, and finally settled at Montford, in Italy, where they were attacked by the bishop of Milan in 1028 Severe decrees against them were made in 1163, and they gradually dispersed, very probably sowing the seeds of the great reformation of the 16th century

Paul's, St., cathedral, London

First church built on the site of a temple to Diana supposed to have been destroyed during the Diocletian persecution (302) rebuilt in the reign of Constantine	323–337
Demolished by the pagan Saxons, and restored by Ethelbert and Sebert	about 597–610
Destroyed by the great fire, 1086, Mauritius bishop of London, commenced a magnificent edifice, with the highest spire in the world, about 1087, completed	1240
It was destroyed by the fire of Sept	1666
First stone of the present edifice laid 21 June,	1675
Choir opened for divine worship 2 Dec	1697
Whole edifice completed under sir Christopher Wren (except some decorations, finished 1723) [Total cost 1 511 202*l*.]	1710
Ball and cross restored by Mr Cockerell	1822
Peal of 12 bells (by Taylor, of Loughborough) given by the corporation and some of the companies, dedicated 1 Nov	1878
Reconciliation service after desecration of the cathedral by suicide of Edward Easton on 28 Sept 13 Oct	1890

DIMENSIONS

	Feet
Length of St Paul s from the grand portico to east end	510
Breadth north to south portico	282
Height from ground to top of cross	404
Circumference of dome	420
Entire circumference of the building	2292
Diameter of ball	6

Paul's cross, St., London, near the cathedral, a pulpit or speaking-place used not only for preaching but for political speaking as well. Here the most eminent divines were appointed to preach every Sunday in the forenoon, and to this place the court, the mayor, aldermen, and principal citizens used to resort It was used as early as 1259, but was demolished in 1643 by order of Parliament.

Paul's school, St., London, was endowed in 1512 by John Colet, dean of St Paul's, for 153 boys, "of every nation, country, and class," in memory of the number of fishes taken by Peter (John xxi 11) The first school-house was burned in 1666, the second, by Wren, was taken down in 1824, and the present building erected by George Smith William Lilly was the first master, and his grammar was till recently used by the school —*Timbs*

Paulus's Hook, Capture of The British had a small garrison (500 men under maj Sutherland) at Paulus's Hook (now Jersey City), opposite the city of New York, in the summer of 1779. The post was attacked at 3 o'clock in the morning of 19 Aug by maj Henry Lee with 300 picked men 30 of the garrison were killed and 160 made prisoners, the remainder retreated to a strong circular redoubt, too strong to be captured, and Lee fell back with his prisoners to camp Congress rewarded Lee with thanks and a gold medal.

pavements. The Carthaginians are said to have been the first who paved their towns, the Romans in the time of Augustus had pavements in many of their streets, the Appian Way, a paved road, was constructed 312 B C. Pavements of blocks of lava, worn into ruts by wheels, are met with in Herculaneum and Pompeii Roads built of heavy flags of freestone, of unknown age, exist in Peru, 1500 to 2000 miles in extent In Mexico, among the ruins of Palenque, are found pavements of large square blocks of stone Modern pavements are, wood, vitrified bricks, or stone blocks set in cement, or asphalt laid in sheets. Of the last, the city of Buffalo, N Y, had within its limits in 1894 180 linear miles, or more than any other city in the world

Cordova in Spain paved by Abderrahman II	850
Streets in Paris first paved by Philip Augustus	1184

London streets first paved . 1553
Stone tramway, parallel wheel tracks of blocks of granite, built from West India docks to Whitechapel, London 1820
Part of Broadway, New York city, between Chambers and Warren sts, paved with hexagonal wooden blocks 1835
Experimental pavement of asphalt laid at the entrance of the Place de la Concorde, Paris 1837
Artificial asphalt from gas works used in England about 1838
Wood pavement of hexagonal blocks bedded in gravel introduced in England "
Pavement of granite blocks 3 in broad and 9 in deep on a bed of concrete 1 ft thick the first of modern set pavements, laid on Blackfriars bridge, London 1840
Nicolson pavement, wooden blocks on end on a foundation of hemlock boards, introduced in Boston, Mass 1848
Asphalt first used extensively for pavement in Paris 1854
Claridge's patent asphalt laid in Trafalgar square, London, Jan 1864
Wood pavement of concrete foundation laid in London 1872
Pavement of vitrified brick laid in Charleston, W Va 1873
Fifth ave, New York city, from 26th to 27th sts, laid with Neufchatel asphalt. July, 1879

Pa'via, a city of N Italy, the ancient *Ticinum* or *Papia* Its university, ascribed to Charlemagne (really founded in the 14th century), is said to be the oldest in Europe Pavia was built by the Gauls, who were driven out by the Romans, and these by the Goths In 568 it was taken by the Lombards, and became their capital In the 12th century it was erected into a republic, but soon after was subjected to Milan, and followed its fortunes On 24 Feb 1525, in a battle near here, the imperialists defeated the French, whose king, Francis I, after killing 7 men with his own hand, was at last obliged to surrender It was long asserted that Francis wrote to his mother, Louisa of Savoy, regent of the kingdom during his absence, saying, *Tout est perdu, madame, fors l'honneur* (All is lost, madam, except honor) The words are now said to have been, *L'honneur et la vie qui est saulvé* PRISONERS

Pavo'nia, territory now occupied by Jersey City and Hoboken, so called by the Dutch when first settled by them, 1630 NEW YORK.

pawnbroking. The Roman emperors lent money upon land The origin of borrowing money on pledges is referred to Perugia, in Italy, about 1462 The institutions were termed MONTE DI PIETÀ Soon afterwards, it is said that the bishop of Winchester established a system of lending on pledges, but without interest. The business of pawnbrokers was regulated in England in 1756, and licenses issued in 1783 The rate of interest on pledges was fixed in 1800 In 1860 an act was passed enabling pawnbrokers to charge a halfpenny for every ticket describing things pledged for a sum under 5*s* Number of pawnbrokers in Great Britain in 1871, 3540, it increases faster than the population In the United States this business is confined to the large cities, and is carried on without that watchful care bestowed upon it by the government in other countries, especially in Great Britain.

Pawnees. INDIANS.

pax, a small tablet, generally silver, termed *tabula pacis* or *osculatorium*, kissed by the Roman Catholic priests and laity, substituted for the primeval kiss of peace in the early church. The pax is said to date from the 12th century.

Paxton boys, Massacre of the Indians PENNSYLVANIA, 1763

Peabody fund. George Peabody, an American merchant (b S. Danvers, Mass., 18 Feb 1795, d. London, Engl., 4 Nov. 1869), who had made his fortune in London, gave, on 12 Mch 1862, 150,000*l*, on 21 Jan 1866, 100,000*l*, on 5 Dec 1868, 100,000*l*, and by his will directed his trustees to pay 150,000*l*.—in all 500,000*l*, to ameliorate the condition of the London poor

An autograph letter, promising her portrait in miniature, was sent him by queen Victoria 28 Mch. 1866
[Inscription on the miniature sent "V R. Presented by the queen to G Peabody, Esq, the benefactor of the poor of London "]
First block of buildings for working classes, termed "Peabody dwellings," in Commercial st., Spitalfields, was opened 29 Feb. 1864, and others since, in Spitalfields, Islington, Shadwell, Westminster, Chelsea, Bermondsey, etc., they have been found to be self supporting, 1878. In 1879, net gain, 24 786*l*.]
Mr Peabody's statue, at the east end of the Royal Exchange, was inaugurated by the prince of Wales . 23 July, 1869
Funeral service at Westminster Abbey 12 Nov "
Funeral at Portland, Me, prince Arthur present 8 Feb 1870
[He also gave large sums for educational purposes in the U S, as follows]
$30,000 to found Peabody institute at South Danvers, Mass . 1852
$150,000 to same institute soon after
$50,000 to similar institute at North Danvers "
$300,000, afterwards increased to $1,000,000, to found Peabody institute at Baltimore, Md 1857
$300 000 to scientific departments of Harvard and Yale colleges 1866
$2,100,000, afterwards increased to $3,500,000 to promote education in the Southern states "
$200,000 to other objects "
$315,000 to various educational institutions 1869

peace. A temple was dedicated to Peace by Vespasian, 75 The gates of the Roman temple Janus Quirinus were always shut in time of peace, they were closed only once between the time of Numa and Augustus, viz, at the close of the first Punic war

Peace of religion (between Catholics and Protestants) signed at Augsburg 15 Sept 1555
Benj Franklin, John Adams, and Edward Rutledge, appointed by Congress, meet lord and adm Howe on Staten Island in a peace conference without result. 11 Sept. 1776
Earl of Carlisle, George Johnstone and William Eden, commissioners of Great Britain, arrive at Philadelphia 4 June, 1778
[As they had no power to acknowledge the independence of the colonies, Congress declined to appoint commissioners to meet them]
Motion in House of Commons by gen Conway for a cessation of hostilities, lost by a majority of one 22 Feb 1782
Conway again moves, "That the house would consider as enemies to his majesty and the country all those who should advise or by any means attempt the further prosecution of offensive war on the continent of North America," carried without a division the same day 4 Mch "
Peace treaty of 1814 UNITED STATES
Peace conference at Washington, D C., a vain attempt to prevent the civil war (UNITED STATES) 4 Feb 1861
Horace Greeley, sent by pres Lincoln, confers in the interest of peace with confederates, among them Clement C Clay of Alabama, and James P Holcombe of Virginia, at the Clifton house, Niagara falls, without result July, 1864
Rev col James F Jaques, 73d Illinois, and J R Gillmore visit Richmond, confer with pres Davis on peace, without result, June–July, "
Peace conference at Hampton Roads brought about by Francis P Blair, sr, Confederate commissioners Alexander H Stephens, John A Campbell, and R. M T Hunter, meet pres. Lincoln and sec Seward on steamer in Hampton Roads, without result . 3 Feb 1865
Stormy international arbitration and peace congress at Geneva, Garibaldi present . . 9-12 Sept. 1867
A peace congress met at Berne, Switzerland 24 Sept. 1868
At the peace congress held at Lausanne, the violence of the communists at Paris in May was warmly reprobated 25 Sept 1871
Congress at Lugano, 23 Sept 1872, at the Hague, 25 Sept. 1873, at Paris, 6 Sept 1875, at Geneva, Oct. 1877, at Paris, 25 Sept 1878, at Brussels, 17 Oct 1882, at Berne 4-9 Aug 1884
The principle of arbitration in place of war was adopted by the Pan American congress at Washington, treaty signed for several states 28 Apr 1890
The international arbitration society meets at Frankfort, 17 Sept. 1890, at Westminster, 1 July, 1891, 30 May, 1892, 30 June, 1893, 4 July (annual meetings) 1894
The British and foreign arbitration association vote an address to the government respecting the Chinese and Japanese war 15 Nov "
International peace demonstration in Hyde park, delegates from 19 countries. 26 July, 1896
Meeting at Crystal palace, near London, 22 July, 1885, another meeting, 16 July, 1886, at Geneva, 9 Sept. 1887, at Paris, 23 June, 1889, in London, 14 July, 1890, Rome, 11 Nov 1891, Berne, Aug. 1892, Antwerp, Aug 1894, Budapest . .. 21 Sept. "
"Peace day" celebrated throughout Europe and America, 22 Feb. 1898
International peace congress meets at Turin . 26 Sept "
Meeting at St. James's hall, in support of a peace conference, Aug -Sept "
An international peace crusade favored by lord Salisbury and others 18 Dec "
The bishop of London chairman of executive committee, 27 Dec. "
International peace conference (26 states represented) meets at the Hague, M de Staal Russian ambassador in London, elected president, M de Beaufort (Netherlands foreign minister) delivers an address to the czar, the initiator of the conference, Aug 1898, work divided into 3 sections disarmament, laws of war, and arbitration, presidents and vice presidents elected, sub committee of 8, to discuss independent projects, 20-26 May, the Russian proposals for the limitation of armaments outvoted, 30 June, arbitration scheme (60 articles), permanent arbitration court, discussed, 7 July, Great Britain and U S left in a minority concerning the prohibition of asphyxiating gases and expanding bullets of the "dum-dum" type, 23 July, signed by 16 powers, codification of the rules of war and the extension of the Geneva convention to naval warfare, signed by 15 powers, the disarmament proposals left unsettled, protocol signed by all the 26 states represented . 29 July, 1899

ıtional convention at St Martin's town hall, lord Aberdeen and others present 21 Mch 1899
ternational peace bureau meets at Berne May, 1900
e acts ratifying the treaties and declarations signed at the conference placed in the foreign office at the Hague, and a message sent to the czar 4 Sept "
ternational peace congress in Paris 2 Oct "
rmanent court of arbitration established at the Hague, Dec 1900-mid Apr 1901
er appeal for arbitration signed by dr Leyds, messrs Fisher and Wolmarans, 10 Sept 1901, rejected 20 Nov "
Carnegie gives $1,500,000 for a palace of peace, reported 25 Apr 1903
peace society, founded 1816, for the promotion of universal peace, holds annual meetings, proposed amalgamation with the international arbitration and peace association (founded by Mr Lewis Appleton in 1880), Dec 1884 the association divided in May 1886, when the British arbitration association was founded by Mr Appleton, a congress of the friends of peace from all parts of the world commenced its sittings at Paris, 22 Aug 1849, it met in London in Exeter hall, 30 Oct. following, and at Frankfort, in St Paul's church, 22 Aug 1850, at Birmingham, 28 Nov 1850, and in Exeter hall, 22 July, 1851, a meeting was held at Manchester, 27 Jan 1853, and at Edinburgh, 12 Oct. 1853, Glasgow 10 Sept 1901, London, 20 May, 1902, and 20 May, "
ernational peace congress meets at the hotel de Ville, Rouen, about 100 French and foreign delegates present, M Arnaud, of Paris, appointed president, addresses by the prince of Monaco, Mme Severine, and others, resolutions carried exhorting the powers to stop the cruelties in Macedonia 22-24 Sept. "
ace society meets in Queen's hall, London 27 Oct "
er parliamentary conferences on international arbitration members of different legislatures), first meeting at Paris, M Jules Simon, president, June, 1889, London, lord Herschel, president, 22 July, 1890, Rome, 3-7 Nov 1891, at Berne, 29-31 Aug 1892, Brussels 10 Oct 1893, the Hague, Sept 1894, Brussels, 13 Aug 1895, Brussels, 7 Aug 1897, Christiania, 2 Aug 1899, Paris, 31 July, 1900, Monaco, 2 Apr 1902, St Louis 1904
ernational arbitration society organized at Chicago 6 Feb "
the St Louis meeting a unanimous request was sent to pres. Roosevelt to call a peace conference, presented 24 Sept "
's Roosevelt's call for a peace conference 30 Oct "
[Favorable responses from Germany, France, Japan and other powers Russian reply was cordial, but suggested the conference be postponed until after the war with Japan]

PRES ROOSEVELT'S CALL FOR A PEACE CONFERENCE.

On 30 Oct 1904, the secretary of state, under the instructions of the president, sent a note to the representatives of the S accredited to the governments signatories to the acts of Hague conference of 1899, reciting the great work accomplished by that council of the nations, the questions affecting rights and duties of neutrals, the inviolability of private property in naval warfare, and the bombardment of ports and towns by a naval force, then left for discussion by a second conference, and the unanimous request addressed to the president by the Inter-parliamentary Union, held at St Louis in connection with the World's Fair, in Sept 1904, that he should invite all the nations to send delegates to such a conference. The continuation of sec Hay's note was as follows

On 24 Sept. 1904, these resolutions were presented to the president by a numerous deputation of the Inter-parliamentary Union. The president accepted the charge offered to him, feeling it to be most appropriate that the executive of the nation which had welcomed the conference to its hospitality should give voice to its impressive utterances in a cause which the American government and people hold dear He announced that he would at an early day invite the other nations, parties to the Hague conventions, to reassemble, with a view to pushing forward towards completion the work already begun at the Hague, by considering the questions which the first conference had left unsettled with the express provision that there should be a second conference

At this time it would seem premature to couple the tentative invitation thus extended with a categorical programme of subjects of discussion It is only by comparison of views that a general accord can be reached as to the matters to be considered by the new conference It is desirable that in the formulation of a programme the distinction should be kept clear between the matters which belong to the province of international law and those which are conventional as between individual governments The final act of the Hague conference, dated 29 July, 1899, kept this distinction clearly in sight. Among the broader general questions affecting the right and justice of the relation of sovereign states which were then relegated to a future conference were the rights and duties of neutrals, the inviolability of private property in naval warfare, and the bombardment of ports, towns, and villages by a naval force The other matters mentioned in the final act take the form of suggestions for consideration by interested governments

The three points mentioned cover a large field The first, especially, touching the rights and duties of neutrals, is of universal importance Its rightful disposition affects the interests and well-being of all the world The neutral is something more than an onlooker His acts of omission or commission may have an influence—indirect, but tangible—on a war actually in progress, while, on the other hand, he may suffer from the exigencies of the belligerents It is this phase of warfare which deeply concerns the world at large Efforts have been made time and again to formulate rules of action applicable to its more material aspects, as in the Declaration of Paris As recently as 28 Apr 1904, the Congress of the U S adopted a resolution reading thus

Resolved by the Senate and House of Representatives of the U S of America, in Congress assembled That it is the sense of the Congress of the U S that it is desirable, in the interest of uniformity of action by the maritime states of the world in time of war, that the president endeavor to bring about an understanding among the principal maritime powers with a view of incorporating into the permanent law of civilized nations the principle of the exemption of all private property at sea, not contraband of war, from capture or destruction by belligerents

Other matters closely affecting the rights of neutrals are the distinction to be made between absolute and conditional contraband of war and the inviolability of the official and private correspondence of neutrals As for the duties of neutrals towards the belligerent, the field is scarcely less broad. One aspect deserves mention from the prominence it has acquired during recent times—namely, the treatment due to refugee belligerent ships in neutral ports It may also be desirable to consider and adopt a procedure by which states non signatory to the original acts of the Hague conference may become adhering parties

You will explain to his excellency the minister of foreign affairs that the present overture for a second conference to complete the postponed work of the first conference is not designed to supersede other calls for the consideration of special topics, such as the proposition of the government of the Netherlands, recently issued, to assemble for the purpose of amending the provisions of the existing Hague convention with respect to hospital ships JOHN HAY.

peaches (fruit of a small tree, *Persica vulgaris*, of the order *Rosaceæ*) are said to have been introduced into England from Persia about 1562 FLOWERS AND PLANTS

Peach-tree Creek, Ga., Battle of ATLANTA CAMPAIGN, 20 July, 1864

Pea Ridge, Battle of ARKANSAS, 1862

pearls, mentioned Job xxviii. 18 M Réaumur, in 1717, alleged that pearls are formed like other stones in animals. An ancient pearl was valued by Pliny at 80,000*l* One which was brought, in 1574, to Philip II, of the size of a pigeon's egg, was valued at 14,400 ducats. A pearl named the *Incomparable*, spoken of by De Boote, weighed 30 carats, equal to 5 pennyweights, and was about the size of a muscadine pear. The pearl mentioned by Tavernier as being in possession of the emperor of Persia was purchased of an Arab in 1633, and is valued at a sum equal to 110,400*l*

Peasants' war. JACQUERIE

"Peculiar People," a small sect in Essex and other parts of England, formed about 1845 2 members, Thomas and Maryanne Wagstaffe, were tried and acquitted of manslaughter, 29 Jan. 1868 They had neglected getting medical assistance for their sick child, and depended on the efficacy of their elders' prayers and anointing it with oil (James v 14) The child died On 8 May, 1872, a father was convicted for neglecting to get medical advice for his child who died of small-pox; and the sect agreed to modify their practice. Establishments for healing diseases by prayer exist in Germany This sect is known in the United States under the name of "Faith Healers," and also as "Christian Scientists"

pedestrianism (Lat. *pes*, the foot; *pedes*, one that moves on foot. The act or practice of walking). It is said that Euchidas, a citizen of Platæa, went thence to Delphi, and returned with the sacred fire the same day before sunset, having travelled 125 miles. He fell dead from the exertion. Authentic records of pedestrian feats begin about the close of the 18th century, when Foster Powell, in 1773, walked on a wager of 100 guineas from Hicks hall, London, to York, and return, a distance of 394 miles, in 6 days less about 6 hours. From this time records of professional and amateur walking and running matches are numerous. The greatest distance hitherto walked by an American without rest is 121 miles 385 yards, by C. A. Harriman, Truckee, Cal., 6-7 Apr. 1883. In England, Peter Crossland, Manchester, covered 120 miles 1560 yards without resting, 11-12 Sept. 1876.

Foster Powell walks from Falstaff inn, Canterbury, to London bridge and back, 112 miles, in 23 h. 50 min.; the best record up to that time....... 1787
Powell, on a wager of 20 guineas to 13, walks from London to York and return in 5 days, 16 h. 10 min.......Aug. 1790
Daniel Crisp walks 1 mile in 7 min. 50 sec....... 1802
Capt. Barclay Allardice of Ury runs a mile in 4 min. 50 sec., outpacing John Ireland, a noted swift runner....... 1804
Capt. Barclay Allardice walks 1 mile each hour for 1000 successive hours on Newmarket Heath for a wager of 1000 guineas.......12 P.M. 1 June-4 P.M. 12 July, 1809
Thomas Standen of Salehurst, aged 60, walks 1100 miles in 1100 hours (1 mile in each hour), finished.......July, 1811
Richard Manks of Warwickshire walks 1000 miles in 1000 hours at Sheffield.......17 June-29 July, 1850
Charles Westhall, at Slough, walks 7½ miles in 58 min. 25 sec. in 1857; and at Newmarket, 21 miles in 59 seconds less than 3 hours.......Feb. 1858
L. Bennett (Deerfoot) runs 11 miles, 970 yards in 1 hour, London, Engl.......3 Apr. 1863
Miss Richards walks 1000 miles in 1000 hours, 18 May-29 June, 1874
Edward Payson Weston, at Newark, N. J., walks 500 miles in 5 days, 23 h. 34 min.......21-26 Dec. "
Bella St. Clair walks 1000 miles in 950 hours....25 July et seq. 1876
William Gale, aged 45, walks 1500 miles in 1000 consecutive hours, at Lillie Bridge, London, 26 Aug.-6 Oct., and 4000 quarter miles in 4000 consecutive 10 minutes, at Agricultural hall, London, completed.......17 Nov. 1877
Match of 17 pedestrians at Agricultural hall, London, won by O'Leary, who walked 520 miles in 6 days.......18-23 Mch. 1878
Six days' walking-match for championship, at Agricultural hall, won by W. Corkey; 16 competitors; 521 miles, 28 Oct.-2 Nov. "
Weston walks 550 miles in 6 days at Agricultural hall, and wins the Sir John Astley belt.......16-21 June, 1879
Blower Brown walks 553 miles in 6 days; champion of England.......16-21 Feb. 1880
John Meagher walks 8 miles, 302 yards in 1 hour, New York city.......29 Nov. 1882
Weston walks 5000 miles in 100 days, abstaining from alcohol.. 1883
Zoe Gayton, an actress, walks from San Francisco to New York, 3395 miles, in 6 months, 26 days, receiving $1300; arrives at New York.......27 Mch. 1891

PROFESSIONAL AND AMATEUR WALKING RECORD.

Miles.		Nationality.	Time. Hours.	Min.	Sec.	Name.	Place.	Date.
1	Professional....	English.......	..	6	23	W. Perkins.......	London.......	1 June, 1874
	Amateur.......	American.......	..	6	29.6	F. P. Murray.......	New York.......	27 Oct. 1883
2	Professional....	English.......	..	13	14	J. W. Raby.......	London.......	20 Aug. "
	Amateur.......	American.......	..	13	48.6	F. P. Murray.......	Brooklyn, N. Y.......	30 May, 1884
3	Professional....	English.......	..	20	21.5	J. W. Raby.......	London.......	20 Aug. 1883
	Amateur.......	American.......	..	21	9.2	F. P. Murray.......	New York.......	6 Nov. "
4	Professional....	English.......	..	27	38	J. W. Raby.......	London.......	20 Aug. "
	Amateur.......	".......	..	29	10	W. H. Meek.......	".......	12 July, 1884
5	Professional....	".......	..	35	10	J. W. Raby.......	".......	20 Aug. 1883
	Amateur.......	".......	..	37	17	H. Curtis.......	Birmingham, Engl.......	12 July, 1890
6	Professional....	".......	..	43	1	J. W. Raby.......	London.......	20 Aug. 1883
	Amateur.......	".......	..	44	57	H. Curtis.......	Birmingham, Engl.......	12 July, 1890
7	Professional....	".......	..	51	4	J. W. Raby.......	London.......	20 Aug. 1883
	Amateur.......	".......	..	52	28.4	H. Curtis.......	Birmingham, Engl.......	12 July, 1890
8	Professional....	American.......	..	58	37	John Meagher.......	New York.......	29 Nov. 1882
	Amateur.......	".......	1	2	8.5	J. B. Clark.......	".......	8 Sept. 1880
9	Professional....	English.......	1	7	14	J. W. Raby.......	London.......	3 Dec. 1883
	Amateur.......	American.......	1	10	8	E. E. Merrill.......	Boston, Mass.......	5 Oct. 1880
10	Professional....	English.......	1	14	45	J. W. Raby.......	London.......	3 Dec. 1883
	Amateur.......	American.......	1	17	40.75	E. E. Merrill.......	Boston, Mass.......	5 Oct. 1880
20	Professional....	English.......	2	39	57	W. Perkins.......	London.......	1 July, 1877
	Amateur.......	".......	2	47	52	Thomas Griffiths.......	".......	3 Dec. 1870
50	Professional....	".......	7	54	16	J. Hibberd.......	".......	14 May, 1888
	Amateur.......	".......	8	25	25.5	A. W. Sinclair.......	".......	14 Nov. 1879
100	Professional....	".......	18	8	15	William Howes.......	".......	15 May, 1880
	Amateur.......	".......	19	41	50	A. W. Sinclair.......	".......	26 " 1881
200..	Professional....	".......	40	46	30	George Littlewood.......	Sheffield, Engl.......	7-11 Mch. 1882
300..	".....	".......	66	30	—	".......	" ".......	"
400..	".....	".......	96	51	3	".......	" ".......	"
500..	".....	".......	130	34	50	".......	" ".......	"
531..	".....	".......	138	49	8	".......	" ".......	"

RECORD OF GREATEST DISTANCE COVERED IN 6 DAYS' 'GO-AS-YOU-PLEASE" WALKING MATCHES (72 HOURS—12 HOURS DAILY.)

Hours.	Distance. Miles.	Yards.	Name.	Nationality.	Place.	Date.
12	89	880	G. Littlewood.......	English.......	London.......	24 Nov. 1884.
	78	1280	John Dobler.......	American.......	Buffalo, N. Y.......	9 Aug. 1880.
24	162	704	G. Littlewood.......	English.......	London.......	25 Nov. 1884.
	150	800	John Dobler.......	American.......	Buffalo, N. Y.......	9-10 Aug. 1880.
36	229	1408	G. Littlewood.......	English.......	London.......	24-26 Nov. 1884.
	216	1280	John Dobler.......	American.......	Buffalo, N. Y.......	9-11 Aug. 1880.
48	296	1056	G. Littlewood.......	English.......	London.......	24-27 Nov. 1884.
	282	320	John Dobler.......	American.......	Buffalo, N. Y.......	9-12 Aug. 1880.
60	362	528	C. Rowell.......	English.......	London.......	27 Apr.-1 May, 1885.
	349	1120	John Dobler.......	American.......	Buffalo, N. Y.......	9-13 Aug. 1880.
72	430	..	C. Rowell.......	English.......	London.......	27 Apr.-2 May, 1885.
	416	602	Gus. Guerrero.......	American.......	Boston, Mass.......	13-18 Apr. 1891.

PROFESSIONAL AND AMATEUR RUNNING RECORD.

Yards.		Nationality.	Time. Hours.	Min.	Sec.	Name.	Place.	Date.
50	Professional....	American.......	..	..	5.25	H. M. Johnson.......	New York.......	22 Nov. 1884
	Amateur.......	".......	..	..	5.5	L. E. Meyers.......	".......	12 Dec. "
100	Professional....	".......	..	..	9.8	H. M. Johnson.......	Cleveland, O.......	31 July, 1886
	".......	".......	..	..	9.8	Harry Bethune.......	Oakland, Cal.......	22 Feb. 1888
	Amateur.......	".......	..	..	9.8	John Owen, jr.......	Washington, D. C.......	11 Oct. 1890
500	Professional....	".......	..	..	59	John Powers.......	Boston, Mass.......	5 Sept. 1881
	Amateur.......	".......	..	..	58	L. E. Meyers.......	Staten Island.......	29 May, 1880

PROFESSIONAL AND AMATEUR RUNNING RECORD.—(*Continued.*)

ards.		Nationality.	Time.			Name.	Place.	Date.
			Hours.	Min.	Sec.			
00	Professional....	English........	..	2	17	W. Cummings..............	Preston, Engl............	30 Apr. 1881
	Amateur.......	American.....	..	2	13	L. E. Meyers..............	New York................	8 Oct. "
iles.								
1	Professional....	English........	..	4	12.75	W. G. George..............	London, Engl............	23 Aug. 1886
	Amateur.......	American.....	..	4	17.8	T. P. Conneff..............	Cambridge, Mass.........	26 " 1893
2	Professional....	English........	..	9	11.5	William Lang..............	Manchester..............	1 " 1863
	Amateur.......	"	..	9	17.4	W. G. George..............	London, Engl............	26 Apr. 1884
3	Professional....	Scotch........	..	14	19.5	P. Cannon..............	Govan, Scotland.........	14 May, 1888
	Amateur.......	English........	..	14	24	S. Thomas..............	London, Engl............	3 June, 1893
4	Professional....	Scotch........	..	19	25.4	P. Cannon..............	Glasgow................	8 Nov. 1888
	Amateur.......	English........	..	19	33.8	E. C. Willers..............	London, Engl............	10 June, 1893
5	Professional....	"	..	24	40	J. White..............	" "	11 May, 1863
	Amateur.......	"	..	24	53.6	S. Thomas..............	" "	24 Sept. 1892
6	Professional....	"	..	29	50	J. White..............	" "	11 May, 1863
	Amateur.......	"	..	30	17.8	S. Thomas..............	" "	22 Oct. 1892
7	Professional....	"	..	34	45	J. White..............	" "	11 May, 1863
	Amateur.......	"	..	35	37	W. G. George..............	" "	28 July, 1884
8	Professional....	"	..	40	20	J. Howitt..............	" "	1 June, 1852
	Amateur.......	"	..	40	57.4	W. G. George..............	" "	28 July, 1884
9	Professional....	"	..	45	21	J. Howitt..............	" "	1 June. 1852
	Amateur.......	"	..	46	12	W. G. George..............	" "	7 Apr. 1884
10	Professional....	"	..	51	6.6	W. Cummings..............	" "	18 Sept. 1885
	Amateur.......	"	..	51	20	W. G. George..............	" "	7 Apr. 1884
20	Professional....	American.....	1	54	..	Patrick Byrnes..............	Halifax, N. S............	4 Oct. 1879
	Amateur.......	English........	1	52	51.2	W. H. Morton..............	London................	22 Mch. 1890
50	Professional....	"	5	55	4.5	George Cartwright..........	"	21 Feb. 1887
	Amateur.......	"	6	18	26.2	J. E. Dixon..............	"	11 Apr. 1885
00..	Professional....	"	13	26	30	Charles Rowell..............	New York................	27 Feb. 1882
" ..	Amateur.......	American.....	17	36	14	J. Saunders..............	"	22 " "
00..	Professional....	English........	35	9	28	Charles Rowell..............	"	27 " "
00..	"	"	58	17	6	" "	"	2 Mch. "
00..	"	"	84	31	18	Jas. Albert..............	"	6-11 Feb. 1888
00..	"	"	109	18	20	P. Fitzgerald..............	"	5 May, 1884
00..	"	"	135	..	..	G. Littlewood..............	"	1 Dec. 1888
23..	"	"	141	40	30	"	"	" "

Pedo-Baptists (Gr. παίς παίδος, child, and Βαπτης, ıe who dips), a term (not a sect) implying a belief in infant ıptism.

pedometer and **odometer,** apparatu. r measuring the distance traversed by a walker or carriage.

lometers, or road-measurers, are said to have been known in the 15th century; improved in England by Butterfield about 1678; and by Meynier, in France....................about 1724
ılph Gouts's pedometer, for indicating the number of steps taken by a walker, was patented....................4 Nov. 1799
illiam Payne's pedometer for the waistcoat pocket, patented, 15 Feb. 1831
illiam Grayson's odometer, or road-measurer, to be attached to carriages, was patented..........................1 Dec. 1851

peeresses of the United Kingdom (*in their* ɔn *right*). 6 in 1891: baronesses Berkeley, Berners, Bolver, Burdett-Coutts, Macdonald of Earnscliff, viscountess ambleden.

peers. LORDS.

Pegu (*pe-goo'*), a province of the Burmese empire, disıvered by the Portuguese, 1520. This province was annexed · the British Indian possessions by proclamation, 20 Dec. 1852. ı Feb. 1862, it was united with Arracan and Tenassarim as ritish Burmah.

Peking' was made the capital of China about 1260. ere was held the court of the Mongol or Yuen dynasty, 280-1368. Marco Polo visited it in 1271. In 1369 Hungu, of the Ming dynasty, removed to Nankin, which was the ıpital till Yung-lo removed his court to Peking in 1410; and y him and his successors the city was enlarged, fortified, and eautified. It was visited by lord Macartney, Sept. 1793; ırrendered to the allied English and French armies, 12 Oct. 360; and evacuated by them 5 Nov., after peace was signed, 4 Oct. It was described as desolate, and the inhabitants scatered and indigent. About 8 miles northwest lies the imperial ark, with the famous Summer palace; it was sacked by the rench and English troops in 1860 and left a heap of ruins, ıd so remains. The population in 1864 was estimated at 600,000. English and French representatives were settled t Peking, Mch. 1861.

Pela'gians, followers of Pelagius, a Briton, appeared t Rome about 400. Their doctrines were condemned by ouncils at Jerusalem, Carthage, and other places, 415, 530. hey maintained:

That Adam was by nature mortal, and, whether he had sinned or not, would certainly have died. 2. That the consequences of Adam's sin were confined to his own person. 3. That new-born infants are in the same condition as Adam before the fall. 4. That the law qualified men for the kingdom of heaven, and was founded upon equal promises with the Gospel. 5. That the general resurrection of the dead does not follow in virtue of Christ's resurrection.

Pelas'gi, the primitive inhabitants of Greece and Italy, appear to have belonged to the Indo-Germanic race. They were in Greece about 1900 B.C., and in Italy about 1600 B.C. "The Greek traditions represent the Pelasgic race as spread widely over most of Greece and the islands of the Aegean. The whole of Hellas, according to Herodotus, was originally called Pelasgia."—*Anthon*, "Class. Dict." There is little doubt but that the Pelasgian and the Hellenic peoples united to form the Greek as known to us.

Pelew' islands, N. Pacific ocean, discovered by the Spaniards in 1543, and still belonging to Spain. Area, 170 sq. miles. The East India company's packet *Antelope*, capt. Wilson, was wrecked here in 1783. The king, Abba Thulle, allowed capt. Wilson to bring prince Le Boo, his son, to England, where he arrived in 1784, and died of small-pox soon after. The East India company erected a monument over his grave in Rotherhithe church-yard.

Peloponne'sus, the island of Pelops, S. Greece, termed Morea in the 13th century, said to have been settled by Pelops about 1283 B.C. Peloponnesian war continued for 27 years between the Athenians and the people of the Peloponnesus, with their respective allies, and is the most famous of the wars of Greece. It began by an attempt of the Bœotians to surprise Platæa, 431 B.C., on 7 May, and ended 404 by the taking of Athens by the Lacedæmonians.

Pelu'sium, now **Tineh,** formerly Sin, the key of Egypt. Here, in 525 B.C., Psammeticus III. was defeated by Cambyses, the Persian, who thereby obtained possession of the kingdom. Pelusium surrendered to Alexander, 333; was taken by the Persians, 309; by Antiochus, 173; by Augustus, 30 B.C.; and after a protracted resistance by Amrou, the Saracen, 638 A.D.

penance, a sacrament in the Roman church, arose out of the practice of AURICULAR CONFESSION. The council of Trent, in its 14th session (1551), decreed that every one is accursed who shall affirm that this sacrament was not instituted by Christ.

pen'dulums. The isochronous property of the pendulum is said to have been applied to clocks by Galileo about

1639, and by Richard Harris about 1641. Christian Huyghens claimed this discovery, 1658. CLOCK. George Graham invented the compensating pendulum, 1715. Experiments were made to determine the density of the earth by pendulums by G. B. Airy (afterwards astronomer royal) and others, in a mine in Cornwall, in 1826 and 1828, and at Horton colliery in 1854. In 1851, M. Foucault demonstrated the rotation of the earth by the motion of a pendulum.

Peninsular campaign of maj.-gen. Geo. B. McClellan. Immediately after the battle of BULL RUN, McClellan, then in command of the department of the Ohio, was called 27 July, 1861, to take command of all troops in and around Washington. To him belongs the credit of organizing the "Potomac army." ARMY, U. S. In this work he was occupied from the time of his first taking command until Mch. 1862, at which time all troops under his immediate command, that is, in northern Virginia, were 172,000 infantry, 23,000 cavalry, 62 batteries volunteers, 30 batteries regulars, amounting to 520 guns and 15,000 men. He had assumed command of all troops of the Northern states on the retirement of gen. Scott, 1 Nov. 1861. On 13 Jan. 1862, Edwin M. Stanton of Ohio was appointed secretary of war; not for his military knowledge, but for his energy and zeal. The president issued an order, 27 Jan. 1862, commanding a general advance upon the Confederate lines from every quarter on 22 Feb.; and on 31 Jan. one to McClellan, requiring him to move with the army of the Potomac upon Manassas Junction, which the confederates had held from the battle of Bull Run, 21 July, 1861. McClellan objected, and urged that the advance should be made from Urbana, near the mouth of the Rappahannock. The president assented, in an order 8 Mch. 1862. This plan assumed that the confederates would continue to occupy Manassas Junction. As they abandoned it 8 Mch., the federals occupying it on the 10th, the Urbana plan was dropped. McClellan now presented the peninsular plan, from fortress Monroe as a base, to move upon Richmond by Yorktown and West Point. This was agreed to 13 Mch. 1862, provided McClellan should (1) leave force enough at Manassas Junction to protect it; (2) leave Washington amply guarded; (3) move the remainder of the army at once by *some* route in pursuit of the enemy. On 11 Mch. McClellan's command was restricted to the army of the Potomac. The peninsula of Virginia, from which this campaign receives its name, lies between the James and York rivers, which empty into Chesapeake bay. Fortress Monroe occupies the extremity of the peninsula, and is connected with the main portio[illegible] only by a narrow sand-beach. The extreme length is abo[illegible] miles; the average breadth about 12. At Yorktown, 20 [illegible] up, it is narrowed to 8, which width it preserves 10 mile[illegible] Williamsburg; then the rivers begin to diverge. The shores of the lower portion of the peninsula are deeply indented with creeks, some of which extend half way across. The land is flat and low, covered with swampy forests, through which sluggish streams flow lazily, expanding after every rain into miry ponds.

Heintzelman's corps embarks for fortress Monroe.....17 Mch. 1862

Headquarters of the army of the Potomac transferred to vicinity of fortress Monroe..... ....1 Apr. "

McDowell's corps detached from the army.............4 Apr. "

Yorktown and its line of defence, about 13 miles in length, occupied by 11,000 confederates under Magruder, is attacked by the federals; repulsed.............................4 Apr. "

Siege, so-called, of Yorktown..................4 Apr.-5 May, "

McClellan prepares to open on the defences at Yorktown with his siege guns when the confederates evacuate.......5 May, "

Battle of Williamsburg .... " "

[Gen. Hooker attacked the confederates with his division alone until reinforced by Kearney's division about 4 P.M. The confederates retired towards Richmond during the night. The Federal loss in killed, wounded, and missing, 2228.]

Gen. Franklin's division lands at West Point..........6 May, "

Norfolk evacuated by the confederates...............10 May, "

Iron-clad *Merrimac* blown up by the confederates.....11 May, "

Com. John Rodgers moving up the James to within 8 miles of Richmond with his fleet, retires after an unequal contest with batteries on Drewry's Bluff or fort Darling, 15 May, "

McClellan's headquarters established at the "White House" (belonging to Mrs. Robt. E. Lee) on the Pamunkey..16 May, "

McDowell with a corps of 40,000 men and 100 pieces of artillery instructed to co-operate with the army of the Potomac advancing on Richmond..............................17 May, "

To frustrate this union "Stonewall" Jackson assumes the offensive by threatening Washington. The Federal forces in northern Virginia at this time were: Banks, 20,000, Milroy and Schenck, 6000, Fremont, 10,000, and McDowell's corps at Fredericksburg, 40,000. Jackson succeeds, and McDowell is retained to defend Washington by an order issued, 24 May, 1862

[This order saved the Confederate capital.]

Jackson drives Banks out of Winchester..............25 May, "

[Appears before Harper's Ferry, 28 May; commences his retrograde movement 31 May, pursued by Banks, Fremont, and McDowell; fights the battle of CROSS KEYS with Fremont, 8 June; battle of Port Republic with a part of McDowell's command, 9 June; and then retires to reinforce the confederates before Richmond, having succeeded in completely paralyzing all the forces in northern Virginia.]

Hanover Court-house................................27 May, "

[Fitz-John Porter, with a corps of 12,000 men, is ordered by McClellan to destroy the bridges over the South Anna, as instructed to do from Washington; opposed by the confederates under Branch at Hanover Court-house, he defeats them.]

Porter returns to his former position at Gaines's Mills. 29 May, "

[Position of the army of the Potomac invites attack. Its left, composed of the corps of Keyes and Heintzelman, occupies the right bank of the Chickahominy from Bottom Bridge to Seven Pines, about 7 miles from Richmond at the nearest point; the rest of the army is on the left bank of the river; Porter in the vicinity of Gaines's Mills and Mechanicsville. The object of this division was to cover the base of supplies at the "White House," and to keep up communication with McDowell, whom McClellan still expected.]

Battle of Fair Oaks or Seven Pines............31 May-1 June, "

[The confederates, hoping to crush the left wing of the army of the Potomac, combined their whole force about Richmond. The attack was to be made early in the day, but the excessive rains of May 30 delayed it until 1 P.M. The federals were outnumbered and gradually forced back until reinforced at 6 P.M. by Sumner's corps, who, from the right wing, crossed the swollen Chickahominy just in time to save the left. The confederates withdrew after dark. On the next day, 1 June, the federals reoccupied most of the lost ground. The Confederate loss was 4500, and the Federal 5727. Gen. Joseph E. Johnston, Confederate commander, severely wounded. Gen. O. O. Howard lost his right arm, June 1.]

Robt. E. Lee assumes command of the confederates....3 June, "

Gen. J. E. B. Stuart with a small cavalry division passes around the army of the Potomac...............12-13 June, "

Battle of Mechanicsville..............................26 June, "

[Corps of Fitz-John Porter, 27,000 men, attacked at 3 P.M. by the corps or divisions of A. P. Hill, D. H. Hill, and Longstreet. Jackson, though expected, did not arrive in time. Though continued until after dark it signally failed.]

Battle of Gaines's Mills..............................27 June, "

[McClellan orders Fitz-John Porter to leave Mechanicsville for a position near Gaines's Mills. By noon of the 27th he is there awaiting attack, which A. P. Hill's corps begins about 1 P.M. Till 5 P.M., Lee, although reinforced by Jackson, failed to break the line; but Porter's entire force was in action. On Porter's call for reinforcements McClellan sent Slocum's division, which arrived at 3.30 P.M. Towards 6 o'clock the general attack was renewed so successfully that but for the approach of night and the timely arrival of 2 brigades Porter would have been crushed. He lost 20 guns, but held the approaches to the bridge, over which he withdrew unmolested during the night, having lost 8000 men out of 35,000. [illegible]he Confederate forces were estimated at 60,000.]

[illegible]iege of Richmond abandoned; Keyes's corps ordered to [illegible]mes on the evening of.........................27 June, "

[illegible] failing to comprehend McClellan's plans, loses the [illegible] June in false movements.]

Ba[illegible]'s Station...................................29 June, "

[Sumner repulses Magruder.]

Entire a[illegible] Potomac safely across "White Oak swamp" on the m[illegible] ....30 June, "

Battle of Wh[illegible] or "Frazer Farm"...... " "

[Gen. Fran[illegible] White Oak swamp, with 9 brigades and 8 batteries, ho[illegible]k Jackson, who with 4 divisions and 20 batteries [illegible] cross.]

Battle of Glendale.......... ....30 June, "

[This was Lee's m[illegible]ined effort to break the Federal line of retreat. But J[illegible]n was stopped by Franklin at White Oak swamp. The [illegible] was indecisive, but assured the federals safe retreat

Army of the Potomac wi[illegible]mense trains concentrated on and around Malvern [illegible] the morning of......1 July, "

Battle of Malvern Hill.......... .... " "

[In this attack upon a s[illegible]osition the confederates fail, after persistent effort fro[illegible] until 9 P.M. Though successful, McClellan continu[illegible] retreat to Harrison's Landing during the night of 1 [illegible] 2 July, unmolested by the enemy. Federal loss, 26 J[illegible]-2 July, 1734 killed, 8062 wounded, 6053 missing; tot[illegible]49. Confederate loss, estimated, 20,771.]

President visits McClellan at H[illegible]'s Landing.......7 July, "

Hooker reoccupies Malvern H[illegible]......................4 Aug. "

McClellan ordered to withdraw [illegible] Aquia creek........... " "

Harrison's Landing entirely v[illegible]......................16 Aug. "

McClellan reaches Aquia creek [illegible].....................24 Aug. "

Reports at Alexandria (POPE'S V[illegible]IA CAMPAIGN)....26 Aug. "

Peninsular war, [illegible]ng which the French were driven out of Spain by W[illegible]n. SPAIN, 1807-14.

Napier's "Hist. of the War i[illegible] Peninsula," pub..........1828-40

penitentiaries. [illegible]SONS.

Pennsylvania, one of the original "Middle" States, being the 7th in geographical order of the "Thirteen," is known as the "Keystone state." It lies between 39° 43′ and 42° N. lat.—except a small portion in the northwest corner, which extends north to 42° 15′, and thus borders on lake Erie—and between 74° 40′ and 80° 36′ W. lon. New York and a small portion of lake Erie lie on the north, Delaware river separates it from New Jersey on the east, the states of Delaware, Maryland, and West Virginia bound it on the south, while West Virginia and Ohio are on the west. Area, 45,215 sq. miles, in 67 counties. Pop. 1890, 5,258,014; 1900, 6,302,115. Capital, Harrisburg.

Henry Hudson enters Delaware bay, examines its currents and soundings, but leaves without landing.................Aug. 1609
Delaware bay visited by lord de la Warr....................... 1610
Cornelius Hendricksen, in the interest of the Dutch, explores Delaware bay and river as far as mouth of the Schuylkill... 1616
Cornelius Mey ascends the Delaware river (then called by the Dutch "South river," to distinguish it from the North or Hudson river), and builds fort Nassau, on the east side, nearly opposite the present Philadelphia..................... 1623
[This first occupation by the Dutch is soon abandoned.]
Swedish government sends out 2 vessels, the *Key of Calmar* and the *Griffin*, with a few Swedes; entering the Delaware, they erect a fort near the mouth of Christiana creek, called fort Christiana in honor of the then queen of Sweden....... 1638
Swedish gov. Printz fixes his residence on Tinicum island, a few miles below Philadelphia, and builds a fort for defence.. 1643
[First European settlement in Pennsylvania.]
Swedes settle Upland (now Chester), first town settled in Pennsylvania... "
Dutch from New York capture the Swedish forts on the Delaware, and take possession of the country...........25 Sept. 1655
This territory surrendered to the English...............Sept. 1664
Dutch recover possession for a few months, 1673, but the "Peace of Westminster" restores it to the English..........19 Feb. 1674
William Penn receives from Charles II., in payment of 16,000*l.* due his father from the English government, a charter for lands north of Maryland and west of the Delaware....4 Mch. 1681
[To the name "Sylvania," intended for the province by the proprietary, the king prefixes "Penn," in honor of the grantee and of adm. Penn, his father.]
Penn issues an address to his subjects in Pennsylvania concerning the grant......................................8 Apr. "
Penn appoints William Markham deputy-governor, who sails in May, and arrives in Pennsylvania...................June, "
Penn contracts to sell an association, "Company of Free Traders," 20,000 acres for 400*l.*, subject to a quit-rent of 2½ mills per acre....................................11 July, "
Court held at Upham by the deputy-governor.........13 Sept. "
Three vessels sail with emigrants, and 3 commissioners with plans for the proposed city of Philadelphia.............Oct. "
Penn publishes "frame of government:" council of 72 persons elected for 3 years, ⅓ to go out annually; governor or deputy to preside with triple vote; laws proposed to be submitted to the people, afterwards to delegates. 40 "fundamental laws" agreed upon by Penn and the intended emigrants, were added, 25 Apr. 1682
Pennsylvania, though not included in duke of York's charter, had been claimed by governors of New York; to perfect his title, Penn obtains from the duke a quit-claim to Pennsylvania, also 2 deeds of feoffment, of town of New Castle with a circle of 12 miles round, and of district thence to cape Henlopen, 21 Aug. "
Penn, now 38 years of age, accompanied by 100 colonists, sails in the *Welcome*, 1 Sept., and lands at New Castle.....27 Oct. "
[Twenty-three ships arrive in the Delaware this year with colonists for Pennsylvania.]
Penn reaches Upland and calls it Chester..............29 Oct. "
Spacious brick residence built at a cost of 7000*l.* for Penn on "Pennsbury Manor," opposite Burlington, about 20 miles above Philadelphia.. "
Penn visits New Jersey, New York, and Long Island, and returns to Chester.................................... 4 Dec. "
[Penn's famous treaty with the Indians under the elms at Shackamaxon, at the northern limits of Philadelphia, occurs about this time, according to Hildreth, Bancroft, and Lossing; the "Narrative and Critical History of America" gives the date, 23 June, 1683. It is the subject of a picture by Benjamin West. The whole story of this treaty has been doubted. Hildreth calls it "the famous traditionary treaty."—Hist. U. S., vol. ii. p. 72. Bancroft says: "It is to be regretted that no original record of the meeting has been preserved."—Hist. U.S., vol. ii. p. 381, 9th ed. Lossing says: "There is no written record of the treaty extant; it seemed a tradition among both races."—"Harper's Cyclop. U. S. Hist.," vol. ii. p. 1073.]
First assembly of the province meets at Chester in 3 days' session..4 Dec. "
[This meeting made changes in the "frame of government," tending to strengthen the power of the proprietary. The territories (Delaware) were enfranchised by a joint act, and united with Pennsylvania on the basis of equal rights, and a code called the "Great Law," furnishing a complete system for the provinces, was enacted; all laws ordered to be printed and taught in the schools.]
Counties of Bucks, Chester, and Philadelphia organized...Dec. 1682
Penn attends to the completion of laying out Philadelphia, Dec. "
Penn meets lord Baltimore at New Castle to adjust boundary claims between Pennsylvania and Maryland............Dec. "
[Dispute not settled until 1760, when it was referred to 2 English mathematicians, Charles Mason and Jeremiah Dixon, who ran the boundary-line due west 244 miles (1763–67) in lat. 39° 43′ 26″; stones erected every mile up to 132, every 5th stone bearing the arms of the Baltimore and Penn families. Resurveyed, 1849. While debating in Congress the "Missouri compromise," in 1820, John Randolph introduced the phrase "Mason and Dixon's line," as separating freedom from slavery, or the north from the south; the phrase became at once exceedingly popular.]
Penn summons the assembly to Philadelphia, where changes are made in the "frame of government" and new laws enacted; and to settle disputes and prevent law-suits 3 "peace-makers" are appointed for each county....10 Mch. 1683
Weekly post established (letters carried from Philadelphia to Chester 2*d.*, to New Castle 4*d.*, to Maryland 6*d.*).......July, "
First mill built at Chester.. "
Frankfort Land company of Germany purchase 25,000 acres of land around Germantown, and begin a settlement, consisting of 20 families under Francis D. Pastorius............24 Oct. "
A woman tried as a witch; acquitted, but bound to keep the peace; Penn presides; first and only case of such trial in Pennsylvania ....27 Feb. 1684
Penn, establishing a provincial court of 5 judges, Nicholas Moore, chief-justice, and leaving the executive to the council, Thomas Lloyd, president, sails for England..........12 Aug. "
[Province has 20 settled townships and 7000 inhabitants.]
William Bradford establishes the first printing-press in Philadelphia (the third in the colonies); first publication, an almanac, the "Kalendarium Pennsilvaniense" (PRINTING in the U. S.), 1685
Several members of the settlement at Germantown send a written protest against slavery to a Friends' meeting....... 1688
[First anti-slavery effort in America.]
"William Penn charter" school established in Philadelphia.. 1689
First paper mill in America built by William Rittenhouse and William Bradford on a branch of the Wissahickon............ 1690
Penn sanctions the separation of the lower counties (Delaware) as a separate government under William Markham..11 Apr. 1691
Government of Pennsylvania taken from Penn.........31 Oct. 1692
Pennsylvania placed under gov. Fletcher of New York........ 1693
[On account of Penn's personal regard for James II. he was not favored by William III. He was accused of disaffection to the new government and was constantly under surveillance; he was several times arrested and once imprisoned.]
Penn's chartered rights restored.......................30 Aug. 1694
First Episcopal place of worship built in Philadelphia, rev. Mr. Clayton, minister.. 1695
Penn returns to Pennsylvania after absence of 15 years, 1 Dec. 1699
[The government prevented him from coming sooner.]
Yellow-fever in Philadelphia.. "
Discontent of the inhabitants leads Penn to summon an assembly to prepare a new frame of government..........16 Sept. 1701
New charter or "charter of privileges" adopted........28 Oct. "
[It gave the Delaware counties option of a separate administration, of which they availed themselves soon after, though under the same governor and council as Pennsylvania until 1776.]
Philadelphia incorporated as a city....................28 Oct. "
Anticipating that the British ministry were about to abolish the proprietary governments in America, Penn, to oppose this, sails for England and never visits America again, 1 Nov. "
Thomas Rutter establishes the first iron works in Pennsylvania, near Pottstown, 30 miles from Philadelphia................ 1716
Penn dies at Rushcombe, Buckinghamshire, Engl., aged 74 years...30 July, 1718
Andrew S. Bradford establishes the *American Weekly Mercury* at Philadelphia.....................................22 Dec. 1719
[First newspaper in America outside of Boston.]
Pennsylvania puts in practice the "paper-money loan system" by the issue of 15,000*l.* in 1722, followed by an additional issue of 30,000*l.*...Mch. 1723
Franklin, 17 years old, arrives in Philadelphia............Oct. "
Pennsylvania Gazette started by Franklin............28 Sept. 1729
Franklin founds the library of Philadelphia, 40 persons subscribing "40 shillings" each and agreeing to pay "10 shillings" annually...................................8 Nov. 1731
Franklin commences the publication of "Poor Richard's Almanack".. 1732
To secure their friendship against the overtures of the French, a treaty is made with the Six Nations..................... 1733
Masonic lodge formed in Philadelphia, the second in America.. 1734
A Catholic church built and mass celebrated in Philadelphia.. "
[The only Catholic church allowed previous to the Revolution in any Anglo-American colony.—*Hildreth's* "Hist. U. S.," vol. ii. p. 343. Consult *Shea's* "The Catholic Church in Colonial Days," vol. i. p. 389.]
County of Lancaster organized.................................. 1737
George Whitefield, the celebrated Calvinistic-Methodist preacher, arrives at Philadelphia from England..............Nov. 1739
[Second voyage to America.]
American Philosophical society established in Philadelphia by Benj. Franklin (PHILADELPHIA)................................. 1743
Hostilities with the Six Nations, after a bloody collision between

tween them and the backwoods-men of Virginia, are averted by a treaty at Lancaster between Virginia, Pennsylvania, and Maryland and the Six Nations, the Indians ceding the whole valley of the Ohio for 400*l*..........................July, 1744

War of England with France, termed "King George's war"... "

For the reduction of Louisburg (MASSACHUSETTS) Pennsylvania furnishes 4000*l*. in provisions.......................... 1745

Thomas and Richard Penn, the sole proprietors of Pennsylvania, Thomas holding three-quarters of the whole by bequest from his brother John who d. this year...................... 1746

Over 5000 immigrants, mostly Germans, arrive in Pennsylvania, 1750

Franklin identifies lightning and electricity...........5 June, 1752

French build a fort at Presque Isle, now Erie................. 1753

One at Le Bœuf, on French creek........................ "

Another at Venango.. "

George Washington sent by the governor of Virginia to meet the French commander at fort Le Bœuf and learn his reasons for invading British dominions (VIRGINIA, 1753)........Nov. "

Thirty-three men of the Ohio company begin a fortification at the junction of the Alleghany and Monongahela, now Pittsburg, but on the approach of the French capitulate ..17 Apr. 1754

French occupy and finish the fort, calling it Duquesne, in honor of the governor of Canada........................ "

Washington sent with about 150 men by gov. Dinwiddie of Virginia to the Great Meadows (VIRGINIA).............Apr. "

Congress of commissioners of the colonies at Albany, N. Y., 19 June, "

[Held to concert measures of defence against the French, to renew the treaty with the Six Nations and allies, and to secure a closer union of the colonies. Franklin, one of the commissioners, submitted a plan for a systematic and closer union of the colonies, which was rejected. Had this plan been successful, "the subsequent pretence for taxing America would not have been furnished, and the bloody contest it occasioned might have been avoided."—*Bigelow*.]

Gen. Edward Braddock, commander-in-chief of the British in America, arrives in the Chesapeake with 2 British regiments, the 44th, sir Peter Halket, and the 48th, col. Dunbar....Feb. 1755

Gen. Braddock meets Shirley, governor of Massachusetts, Delancey of New York, Morris of Pennsylvania, Sharpe of Maryland, and Dinwiddie of Virginia, in a congress at Alexandria, Va.......................................14 Apr. "

[Object of the meeting was the establishing of a colonial revenue, and the advice to the British government, in which all concurred, was taxation by act of Parliament.—*Bancroft*.]

Assembly appropriates 30,000*l*. for carrying on the war...Apr. "

Gen. Braddock is 27 days on the march from Alexandria to fort Cumberland, and arrives with 2150 men........10 May, "

[Here he remains for want of transportation until Franklin, assuming the responsibility, obtains wagons and horses from the Pennsylvania farmers, 150 wagons with 4 horses each and 1500 pack-horses. Owing to the loss arising from the defeat the expense amounts to 30,000*l*., and as only 10,000*l*. was paid, it left claims against Franklin of 20,000*l*., which were not settled by the government until after much delay and trouble.]

Braddock advances from fort Cumberland for fort Duquesne, distance, 130 miles..............................10 June, "

Braddock leaves col. Dunbar to bring up the heavy baggage, and pushes on with 1200 chosen men.............19 June, "

Battle of Monongahela..............................9 July, "

[When within 5 or 6 miles of fort Duquesne and 40 miles in advance of col. Dunbar, after fording the Monongahela the second time, about 1 P.M., Braddock's advance was attacked by 637 Indians and 230 French and Canadians concealed in the woods and undergrowth. After fighting for over 2 hours, the British gave way, leaving baggage and artillery. Out of 86 officers 26 were killed and 37 wounded; among them Braddock, who died on the 13th. Of the privates 710 were killed or wounded, while the French and Indians lost not above 70. There was no pursuit.]

Col. Dunbar burns public stores and heavy baggage worth 100,000*l*., destroys the remaining artillery and retreats, 13 July, "

[Fort Cumberland is evacuated, leaving the frontier of Pennsylvania without a post of defence.]

Assembly levy a tax of 55,000*l*., from which the proprietary estates are exempted..................................Nov. "

Quakers cease to act with the government on its declaring war against the Delawares and Shawanese.............Nov. "

Estimated annual value of rents, etc., to the proprietary estates 30,000*l*.; not subject to taxation...................... "

Franklin undertakes the military command and defence of the frontier with the rank of colonel.......................Jan. 1756

There were active hostilities between the English and the French along the entire frontier of the colonies from the spring of 1753, but war was not declared until......18 May, "

Indian village at Kittanning, on the Alleghany, 45 miles to the north of Pittsburg, headquarters of the Delaware Indians, is surprised and destroyed by col. John Armstrong with 300 Pennsylvanians..................................7 Sept. "

[The county in which this occurred now bears his name.]

Franklin sent to England in support of the Assembly's petition against the proprietaries Thomas and Richard Penn, who oppose taxing their vast estate, and controlled the deputy-governor. He arrives in London..............27 July, 1757

[Succeeds in securing the assessment of taxes on the surveyed lands at the usual rate to others.]

Gen. John Forbes begins the advance against fort Duquesne with some 7000 troops..............................July, 1758

[Pennsylvania furnished 2700 under col. John Armstrong; among them Benj. West, afterwards the painter, and Anthony Wayne, a lad of 13 years; Virginia 1900, with Washington as leader. The Virginia troops rendezvous at fort Cumberland, Md., and the Pennsylvania and other troops at Raystown, now Bedford, Pa. Washington advised the Braddock route for the advance, while cols. Bouquet and Armstrong recommended a more central one, which was adopted. Col. Bouquet is pushed forward with 2500 men; reaches Loyal Hanna, now Ligonier, Westmoreland county, and from here detaches maj. Grant with 800 men to attempt the surprise of fort Duquesne; they are themselves attacked when near the fort and driven back with severe loss, 15 Sept. On 12 Oct. the French and Indians attack Bouquet in his camp, but are repulsed. Gen. Forbes with the main body joins Bouquet, 8 Nov., 50 miles from the fort. It is now proposed to abandon the campaign owing to the lateness of the season, but on 12 Nov. some prisoners are taken who expose the weakness of the fort. 2500 men are now sent forward, the advance under Washington. The garrison, only 500 strong, burn and leave the fort on the 24th; on 25 Nov. the English occupy it, and name the place Pittsburg, in honor of William Pitt, the prime-minister. On the 28th Forbes sends a detachment to the scene of Braddock's defeat, who gather the scattered remains of those who had there fallen more than 3 years before, and bury them in one grave.]

Extensive emigration to the western part of Pennsylvania..1759–62

Beginning of the "PONTIAC WAR"............................ 1763

Treaty of peace between England and France, termed the treaty of Paris....................................10 Feb. "

Attack made by the Indians along the frontier of Pennsylvania and Virginia...................................May, "

Fort Le Bœuf burned by Indians; garrison escapes...18 June, "

Fort Venango destroyed, garrison and all........... " "

Presque Isle, now Erie, garrison of 24 men, surrenders, 22 June, "

Fort Pitt, with a garrison of 330 men, and 200 women and children, besieged by the Indians...............June–July, "

Col. Bouquet, at the head of 500 British troops, advances from Carlisle to the relief of fort Pitt......................July, "

When within a half-mile of "Busby Run," and about 25 miles from fort Pitt, he is attacked by the Indians early in the afternoon with unusual audacity....................5 Aug. "

Battle continues during the day, and begins again at early dawn. After several hours' fighting, Bouquet feigns a retreat, bringing the Indians within the circle of his troops and defeating them. His loss was 8 officers and 115 privates. He reaches and relieves fort Pitt..................10 Aug. "

[The battle of Bushy Run was one of the best-contested actions ever fought between white men and Indians. The Indians displayed throughout a fierceness and impetuosity matched only by the steady valor with which it was met. —*Parkman*, "The Conspiracy of Pontiac," vol. ii. p. 70.]

Connecticut colony in the Wyoming valley driven out by the Indians (SUSQUEHANNA SETTLERS)..................15 Oct. "

Surveyors Mason and Dixon begin running the southern boundary line (see this record, 1682).......................9 Dec. "

Barbarities of Indians at this time disposed the frontiersmen to destroy every Indian—enemy or not. A remnant of a friendly tribe at Conestoga, under guidance of Moravian missionaries, is massacred by frontiersmen termed "Paxton Boys," from Paxton township; a few escape and flee to Lancaster for refuge, but are followed and killed. The pursuers hearing of friendly Indians in Philadelphia, march towards them, but are met by Franklin, who, after a long negotiation, persuades them to dispere....27 Dec. 1763–Jan. 1764

Col. Bouquet's expedition against the Ohio Indians from fort Pitt (OHIO)......................................30 Oct. "

Dr. Shippen begins in Philadelphia the first course of lectures upon anatomy ever delivered in America................ "

Franklin, having returned from England in 1762, is sent again by the Assembly to petition for a change of government from proprietary to royal authority; sails..........7 Nov. "

[The petition, however, was dropped owing to other matters of more weight. See this record, 1779.]

Pittsburg was first occupied by peaceful settlers in 1760, but the settlement was destroyed by Indians during the Pontiac war, 1763. A permanent settlement was begun............ 1765

Franklin examined before the English House of Commons on the effect of the passage of the Stamp act...........13 Feb. 1766

First appearance of the *Pennsylvania Chronicle and Universal Advertiser*, William Goddard publisher, Philadelphia........ 1767

Treaty with the Six Nations at fort Stanwix, N. Y......5 Nov. 1768

[This treaty extinguished the Indian claim to the whole region of the Alleghanies from New York to Virginia, so that Thomas and Richard Penn were proprietaries of more than 25,000,000 acres, 250,000 inhabitants, and one of the largest cities in America.]

First course of instruction in chemistry attempted in America by dr. Benjamin Rush at the college of Philadelphia........ 1769

American Philosophical Society instituted at Philadelphia.... "

[Not incorporated until 1780. PHILADELPHIA.]

Philadelphia calls a public meeting, condemns the duty on tea and taxation by Parliament, and requests the tea agents to resign, which they readily do..........................2 Oct. 1773

Tea ship sent back to England before it reaches Philadelphia, 25 Dec. "

First Continental Congress assembles at Philadelphia (UNITED STATES).......................................5 Sept. 1774

Assembly of Pennsylvania approves the doings of Congress, and appoints delegates to the new one...............15 Dec. "

Franklin returns to Philadelphia from England, giving up hope of reconciliation, after an absence of 10 years...........Apr. 1775

Second Continental Congress meets at Philadelphia....10 May, "

Committee of Safety appointed, Franklin president...30 June, "

nnsylvania instructs her delegates to the Continental Congress to dissent from and reject any proposition looking to a separation from England Nov 1775
Common Sense,' a pamphlet by Thomas Paine, pub in Philadelphia Jan 1776
[This had a wide circulation throughout the colonies, and gave a powerful impulse to the cause of independence'—*Hildreth*]
ssembly of Pennsylvania, under pressure of public opinion, rescind the instructions to delegates in Congress 24 June, "
Declaration of Independence' adopted by Congress, and announced in Philadelphia 4 July, "
[The signers from Pennsylvania were, Robert Morris, b in England, Benj Rush, b near Philadelphia, Benj Franklin, b in Boston, Mass, George Clymer b in Philadelphia, James Smith b in Ireland, George Taylor b in Ireland, James Wilson, b in Scotland, George Ross, b in Delaware. At a grand demonstration in Philadelphia on 8 July, John Nixon read the Declaration to a vast concourse]
ate convention assembles at Philadelphia and assumes the government of Pennsylvania 15 July, "
ranklin one of the 3 commissioners sent to France, sails for that country (UNITED STATES) Oct. "
ornwallis pursues Washington through New Jersey into Pennsylvania Dec "
ndangered by the approach of the British, Congress, at Philadelphia adjourns to meet again at Baltimore 12 Dec "
The Crisis," a patriotic pamphlet by Thomas Paine, appears in Philadelphia ("CRISIS") 19 Dec "
ate government organized, with Thomas Wharton, jr as president (see this record, 1779) 4 Mch 1777
ritish fleet enters Delaware bay July, "
ashington and Lafayette first meet in Philadelphia Aug "
attle of BRANDYWINE 11 Sept "
ongress adjourns to Lancaster 18 Sept. "
assacre of Wayne's troops at PAOL 21 Sept. "
ate government removes to Lancaster 24 Sept "
owe with the British army occupies Philadelphia. 27 Sept "
attle of GERMANTOWN 4 Oct "
uccessful defence of FORTS MIFFLIN and MERCER 22-23 Oct. "
ritish in possession of the defences of the Delaware 20 Nov "
merican army go into winter quarters at Valley Forge, on the Schuylkill 19 Dec "
[Out of 11,000 troops in camp here, 3000 were unfit for duty for want of clothing Until the soldiers had cabins erected, Washington occupied his tent]
Battle of the KEGS' 5 Jan 1778
ffair at BARREN HILL 20 May, "
[Lafayette, in command of a division is sent by Washington to occupy Barren Hill, between Valley Forge and Philadelphia, the British try to cut him off without success He retreats skilfully across the Schuylkill]
ritish evacuate Philadelphia and retire across the Delaware through New Jersey towards New York 18 June, "
ashington crosses the Delaware pursuing the British, leaving gen Benedict Arnold in command at Philadelphia June, "
assacre in the Wyoming valley (WYOMING) 2-4 July, "
ohn Roberts and Abram Carlisle, wealthy citizens of Philadelphia, executed as Tories 22 Nov "
[23 others tried but acquitted]
y act of Assembly the proprietary claims of the Penn family to ungranted lands or quit rents were vested in the state, leaving the late proprietaries all private property including manors, etc The Assembly also granted to the Penns, in remembrance of the founder of Pennsylvania, the sum of 130,000*l* =$524,000, payable in instalments, to commence one year after the peace, 1779
[Besides this, which was faithfully paid, the British government settled 4000*l*. on the head of the Penn family]
ct for the gradual emancipation of slaves passed 1 Mch 1780
ank of North America established at Philadelphia, capital $400,000 (BANKS, U S) 31 Dec 1781
irst manufacture of "fustians and jeans' in the U S begins in Philadelphia 1782
ickinson college at Carlisle incorporated 1783
merican Daily Advertiser, afterwards the *Aurora*, the first daily newspaper in America, issued in Philadelphia 1784
[Pub by Benjamin Franklin Bache]
irst city directory of Philadelphia, and first in the U S, pub 1785
eneral convention of the Protestant Episcopal church, the first in America, meets at Philadelphia 27 Sept. "
ittsburg Gazette, first paper published west of the Alleghanies issued 29 July, 1786
oundary line between Pennsylvania and Virginia, continuation of Mason and Dixon's line, extended to a point 5 degrees west from the Delaware, completed "
onvention of the states to frame a Federal constitution meets at Philadelphia 14 May, 1787
tate convention ratifies the Federal Constitution 12 Dec. "
[The ratification of the Federal Constitution by Pennsylvania procured for her, in allusion to her geographical position the title of the "Keystone state"]
homas Mifflin first governor under the Federal Constitution. 1788
ranklin dies in Philadelphia, aged 84 years 17 Apr 1790
ew state constitution goes into effect 2 Sept. "
stock company formed in Philadelphia to run a steamboat, invented by John Fitch between Philadelphia and Trenton, making regular trips, company soon fails "
S government removed from New York to Philadelphia, 6 Dec "
irst bank of the U S. established at Philadelphia Feb 1791
nthracite coal discovered in Carbon county The Lehigh Coal company organized in Philadelphia, but fail to find a market, "

Purchase of the triangle bordering on lake Erie, and containing Erie harbor completed Mch 1792
[In 1785 D Rittenhouse was appointed by Pennsylvania, and Samuel Holland by New York to ascertain the boundaries between the states from the Delaware river to the western boundaries Point fixed 42° N lat, line running due west 259 miles, marked by stones every mile survey completed 1787, confirmed by the Assembly 1789 The state discovers that it will have no harbor on lake Erie, proposes to buy the triangle of Phelps and Gorham of New York, but finds that the land does not belong to New York, the Indian title having never been extinguished The U S purchase it of the Indians, paying 1200*l* or $4000, in 1789 Pennsylvania authorizes her governor to purchase of the U S, amount paid $151 640 25 in Continental certificates of various descriptions (worthless) The triangle contains 202,187 acres and Erie harbor]
U S mint established in Philadelphia (the only one in the U S until 1835) "
Yellow fever rages in Philadelphia (YELLOW FEVER) July, 1793
WHISKEY INSURRECTION 1794
First turnpike road in the U S completed from Philadelphia to Lancaster 62 miles "
Four daily stages run between Philadelphia and New York, and one between Philadelphia and Baltimore 1796
Resistance to the Federal "House tax," known as the "Hot water war" suppressed 1798
Capital of the state removed to Lancaster (Philadelphia had been the capital 117 years) 3 Apr 1799
U S government removed from Philadelphia to Washington July 1800
Prof Robert Hare of Philadelphia invents the compound blowpipe 1801
Philadelphia first supplied with water from the Schuylkill through pipes laid in the streets 1 Jan "
Coach route established from Philadelphia to Pittsburg Aug 1804
Commission house opened in Philadelphia for the sale of cotton yarns and thread made at Providence R I, the first in the U S 1805
Steamboat *Phenix* arrives at Philadelphia from New York, the first steamboat navigating the ocean 1808
Bible Society founded at Philadelphia, the first in the U S "
State resists with an armed force attempt of the U S to serve a writ in the "OLMSTEAD case" at Philadelphia for 26 days 1809
Sunday-school organized in Philadelphia the first in the U S marking the transfer from secular instruction to religious, from the control of individuals to the churches "
Famous "traditionary" elm tree of the "Penn Indian treaty" blown down 3 Mch 1810
First steamboat, the *New Orleans* on the Ohio, leaves Pittsburg for New Orleans 29 Oct 1811
Capital removed from Lancaster to Harrisburg 1812
[Harrisburg so named from John Harris, who settled there in 1726, town laid out in 1785]
In anticipation of the war with England gov Snyder calls for 14,000 troops 12 May, "
Another unsuccessful attempt to use anthracite coal as fuel "
[Most of the coal brought to Philadelphia was given away, while the cry of "fraud' was raised by those buying, as they were unable to burn the "stone"]
British blockade the Delaware, which seriously interferes with the commerce of Philadelphia Mch 1813
Com Perry builds his fleet at Erie during the spring and early summer of "
[The *Lawrence* is launched on 25 June and the *Niagara* on 4 July]
First rolling mill erected at Pittsburg "
Banks in Philadelphia suspend specie payment 1814
Fairmount water works Philadelphia, completed 7 Sept. 1815
Schuylkill Navigation company build a canal from Philadelphia to Mauch Chunk, 108 miles, cost $3,000,000, completed "
Second U S bank established in Philadelphia chartered by Congress, capital stock, $3,500,000, of which the U S takes one fifth 10 Apr 1816
Theatre in Philadelphia lighted by gas, the first place of amusement so lighted in the U S 25 Nov "
Anthracite coal begins to come into use, 365 tons shipped to Philadelphia are disposed of with difficulty 1820
State institution for the deaf and dumb opened "
Number of tons of anthracite coal received in Philadelphia 1073 in 1821, 2440 tons in 1822
Lafayette visits the U S, received at Philadelphia with distinguished honors Sept. 1824
American Sunday school Union founded at Philadelphia "
Monument erected on the site of the "treaty elm," to commemorate Penn's treaty with the Indians 1827
Store for the sale of American hardware opened in Philadelphia by Amos Goodyear & Sons, the first in the U S "
Paper from straw first manufactured in the U S at Meadville, 1828
First locomotive used in the U S run on the Carbondale and Honesdale road (see U S record, 1829) Aug 1829
Delaware and Hudson canal from Honesdale to Rondout on the Hudson 108 miles, completed "
The *Cent*, Christopher C Cornwell pub, the first one cent daily paper issued in the U S, starts in Philadelphia 1830
Internal improvements connecting Philadelphia with Pittsburg completed at a cost to the state of over $18,000 000 1831
[They consisted of 292 miles canal and 125 miles railroad]
First cases of CHOLERA in Philadelphia 5 July, 1832
State institution for the blind opened 1833
State provides for educating all persons between 6 and 21 1834
Philadelphia and Trenton railroad completed. 1 Nov "
Philadelphia first lighted by gas 8 Feb. 1836

New charter obtained from the state under the name of the U.S. Bank of Pennsylvania........................18 Feb. 1837
Public Ledger of Philadelphia founded, price one cent, 25 Mch. "
Charter of Second U. S. bank expires (see U. S. record, 1832-34), "
U. S. Bank of Pennsylvania and all other banks of the state suspend specie payment during the commercial panic of.... "
State constitution amended........................20 Feb. 1838
[Previous to this, county officers were appointed instead of elected.]
Pennsylvania hall in Philadelphia, dedicated as an abolition hall on the 14th, is burned by a mob..............17 May, "
Buckshot war....................................Nov.-Dec. "
[In a close election between Whigs and Democrats for control of the legislature, which was to choose a U. S. senator, both parties charged fraud, especially in certain districts in Philadelphia. The disturbance became so violent at the capital that gov. Ritner (Whig) called on the U. S. government (7 Dec.) for troops to aid in suppressing it, but the president (Van Buren) refused, as it was a disturbance growing out of politics, etc. The Whigs ultimately receded from their position, leaving the Democrats in power. A remark made during the height of the excitement that the mob would feel the effect of "ball and buckshot before night" gave this episode the name of "Buckshot war."]
Iron successfully made with anthracite coal at Mauch Chunk, 12 Jan. 1839
U. S. Bank of Pennsylvania again suspends specie payment... "
It finally closes its doors, its capital being lost..........4 Sept. 1841
Use of wire rope as cables introduced on the inclined planes of the Alleghany and Portage railroad by John A. Roebling.... 1842
Philadelphia and Reading railroad completed.............. "
Riots between the native Americans and Irish in Philadelphia suppressed by the military....................Apr., May, 1844
Petroleum is obtained while boring for salt on the Alleghany, a few miles above Pittsburg............................ 1845
[It had been previously known to Indians and early settlers as "Seneca oil," "Rock oil," and "Genesee oil."]
Pittsburg nearly destroyed by fire; loss $10,000,000...10 Apr "
Telegraphic communication between Philadelphia and fort Lee, opposite New York, completed.................20 Jan. 1846
Philadelphia and Pittsburg connected by telegraph.....26 Dec. "
State forbids the use of jails to hold fugitive slaves.....3 May, 1848
Re-survey of Mason and Dixon's line completed.......19 Nov. 1849
Judiciary made elective.................................... 1850
Manufacture of galvanized iron begun in Philadelphia........ 1852
Railroad track torn up, ties and culvert bridges burned, and railroad grade reduced to former level at Harbor creek, near Erie, by the opposition to the railroad..............9 Dec. 1853
Pennsylvania State Agricultural college organized in Centre county...13 Apr. 1854
Zinc works at Bethlehem go into operation............12 Oct. "
Entire traffic-line of state improvements from Philadelphia to Pittsburg, completed by the state in 1831, sold to the Pennsylvania railroad company for $7,500,000...........31 July, 1857
State divided into 12 (afterwards 13) normal-school districts.. "
Banks suspend specie payment.............................. "
First Normal school in the state opened at Millersville........ 1859
First oil-well drilled in the U. S. by E. L. Drake, near Titusville; depth, 71 feet; yield, 1000 gallons per day.....29 Aug. "
[Mr. Drake failing to take advantage of the "occasion," and afterwards becoming destitute, the legislature in 1873 grants him a pension of $1500.]
Gov. Curtin's inaugural pledges the state to the national cause against secession..................................15 Jan. 1861
Five companies of state troops (530 men) reach Washington, D. C., the first troops to arrive there for its defence, on the evening of...18 Apr. "
Camp Curtin established near Harrisburg............. " "
[This camp remained the main point of transportation, of supplies, and school of instruction throughout the war.]
Gov. Curtin calls an extra session of the legislature for 30 Apr. "
In anticipation of invasion, gen. Lee having crossed the Potomac into Maryland, gov. Curtin calls 50,000 volunteer militia to Harrisburg (ANTIETAM CAMPAIGN)................11 Sept. 1862
Confederate gen. Stuart raids Chambersburg with about 2000 cavalry......................................12-14 Oct. "
Confederate advance enters Pennsylvania.............22 June, 1863
Carlisle occupied by the advance of the Confederate forces under Ewell; Kingston, 13 miles from Harrisburg, entered on the 27th; and a skirmish takes place within 4 miles of the capital on.......................................28 June, "
Confederate advance called back by gen. Lee to concentrate at Gettysburg.......................................28 June, "
Battle of GETTYSBURG...................................1-3 July, "
National cemetery at Gettysburg consecrated (CEMETERIES), 19 Nov. "
[During the civil war the state furnished 269,645 troops (3-years standard); among them 8612 were colored. Answering the first call of the president for troops, the state furnished 20,979 3-months troops.]
Chambersburg again raided and mostly burned by McCausland's Confederate cavalry (GRANT'S VIRGINIA CAMPAIGN)...30 July, 1864
Citizens of the counties bordering on Maryland reimbursed by the state for damages sustained during the civil war..9 Apr. 1868
All the miners in the Avondale coal mine (108) suffocated by the burning of the main and only shaft..............6 Sept. 1869
[A searching investigation ensues, which results in effecting needed reform in working the coal mines of the state.]
Bureau of Labor Statistics established by the state....26 July, 1873
New state constitution goes into effect..................1 Jan. 1874
"Centennial Exposition," at Fairmount park, Philadelphia, commemorating the hundredth anniversary of the Declaration of American Independence, opens (EXHIBITIONS, PHILADELPHIA).......................................10 May, 1876
"Great strike" of railroad employés, rapidly extending over most of the lines of the northern U. S., inaugurated, 19 July, 1877
[In the different conflicts throughout the state 50 rioters and 5 soldiers were killed and 100 wounded. The state expended for transportation of troops, pay, subsistence, etc., $700,000, while several millions of property was destroyed. The strike was not entirely quieted until November.]
Natural gas used as fuel in western counties.................. 1884
State industrial reformatory at Huntingdon opened....15 Feb. 1889
JOHNSTOWN FLOOD......................................1 June, "
William D. Kelley, b. 1814, the oldest member of the House of Representatives, d. in Washington, D. C..............9 Jan. 1890
Proposal of Mr. Carnegie to expend $1,000,000 for a public library in Pittsburg accepted.......................10 Feb. "
Cyclone at Wilkesbarre and other towns, killing 14, injuring 180, and damaging property to $1,000,000..........19 Aug. "
Boundary between Pennsylvania and New York agreed upon by commissioners, 26 Mch. 1886, and confirmed by both legislatures, is approved by Congress...................19 Aug. "
International Brotherhood of Locomotive Engineers is organized at Pittsburg...................................15 Oct. "
Over 100 miners killed by an explosion of fire-damp in the shaft of Frick & Co.'s coke works, near Mt. Pleasant......27 Jan. 1891
Strike in Connellsville coke regions begins; 10,000 miners involved...9 Feb. "
Eleven strikers killed and 40 wounded in an attack on the Morewood coke works in Connellsville region........2 Apr. "
Gov. Pattison vetoes the Compulsory Education bill..18 June, "
Governor signs the Baker Ballot Reform bill..........19 June, "
Gov. Pattison calls an extra session of the Senate, to meet 13 Oct., to investigate charges against the state's financial officers..26 Sept. "
Human Freedom League organized at Independence hall, Philadelphia..12 Oct. "
David Hayes Agnew, surgeon, b. 1818, d. at Philadelphia, 22 Mch. 1892
"High-water Mark" monument, indicating the point reached by the Confederate advance in the assault of 3 July, at Gettysburg, dedicated......................................2 June, "
Dam at Spartansburg bursts, and gasoline, from tanks broken by the rushing waters, ignites on the surface of Oil creek, between Titusville and Oil City; over 100 lives lost.....5 June, "
Rev Father Mollinger, famous for reputed cures on St. Anthony's day, d. at Pittsburg, aged 70 years..........15 June, "
Lockout of strikers at mills of the Carnegie Steel company, Homestead, begins (UNITED STATES)..................1 July, "
Gov. Pattison orders the entire division of National guard to Homestead..10 July, "
Chairman Crawford, Hugh O'Donnell, John McLuckie, and 30 others, members of the advisory committee of the Amalgamated Association, are arrested on charge of treason against the commonwealth of Pennsylvania (the first such charge in any state growing out of labor troubles)............30 Sept. "
Strike at Carnegie steel mills, Homestead, declared off, 20 Nov. "
Ex-gov. Henry M. Hoyt d. at Wilkesbarre..............1 Dec. "
Second annual conference on university extension opens in Philadelphia.......................................28 Dec. "
First summer meeting for University extension students opens at Philadelphia under the auspices of the American society, 5 July, 1893
Hon. Charles O'Neill of Philadelphia, b. 1821, who had been a member of the U. S. House of Representatives for 30 years, styled "Father of the House," d.......................25 Nov. "
Agitation regarding the desecration of the battle-field of Gettysburg by electric cars for carrying sight-seers........... "
Coxey army, moving on Washington, reach Pittsburg 2 Apr., and leave on the 5th and enter Maryland from Pennsylvania near Cumberland.................................13 Apr. 1894

GOVERNORS OF PENNSYLVANIA.

[Under the proprietary government, when there was no deputy-governor the president of the council acted as such.]

Name	Office	Year
William Penn	Proprietor and governor	1682
Thomas Lloyd	President	1684
John Blackwell	Deputy-governor	1688
Benjamin Fletcher	Governor	1693
William Markham	"	"
William Penn	"	"
Andrew Hamilton	Deputy-governor	1701
Edward Shippen	President	1703
John Evans	Deputy-governor	1704
Charles Gookin	" "	1709
Sir William Keith	" "	1717
Patrick Gordon	" "	1726
James Logan	President	1736
George Thomas	Deputy-governor	1738
Anthony Palmer	President	1747
James Hamilton	Deputy-governor	1748
Robert H. Morris	" "	1754
William Denny	" "	1756
James Hamilton	" "	1759
John Penn	Governor	1763
James Hamilton	President	1771
Richard Penn	Governor	"
John Penn	"	1773

[Proprietary government ended by the Constitution of 1776. The representatives of the Penn family were paid for the surrender of their rights, and a government by the people established. (See this record, 1779).]

STATE GOVERNORS.

Name	Office	Year
Thomas Wharton	President (died in office 1778).	1777
George Bryan	Acting.	
Joseph Reed	President	1778
William Moore	"	1781
John Dickinson	"	1782
Benjamin Franklin	"	1785
Thomas Mifflin	Governor*	1788
Thomas McKean		1799
Simon Snyder		1808
William Findley		1817
Joseph Hiester		1820
J. Andrew Shulze		1823
George Wolf		1829
Joseph Ritner		1837
David R. Porter		1839
Francis R. Shunk	Resigned, 1848	1845
William F. Johnson	Acting	1849
William Bigler		1852
James Pollock		1855
William F. Packer		1858
Andrew G. Curtin		1861
John W. Geary		1867
John F. Hartranft		1873
Henry M. Hoyt		1879
Robert E. Pattison		1883
James A. Beaver		1887
Robert E. Pattison		1891–95
Daniel H. Hastings		1895–99

* From 1790, under the new state constitution, the head of the executive has been termed governor instead of president.

UNITED STATES SENATORS FROM THE STATE OF PENNSYLVANIA.

Name.	No. of Congress.	Date.	Remarks.
William Maclay	1st to 2d	1789 to 1791	
Robert Morris	1st " 4th	1789 " 1795	
Albert Gallatin	3d	1793 " ——	Election declared void, 25 Feb. 1794; being foreign born, residence in the United States too short to make him eligible.
James Ross	3d to 8th	1794 " 1803	
William Bingham	4th " 7th	1795 " 1799	Elected president *pro tem.* 16 Feb. 1797.
John Peter G. Muhlenberg	7th	1801 " 1802	Resigned.
George Logan	7th to 9th	1801 " 1805	Elected in place of Muhlenberg; seated 7 Dec. 1801.
Samuel Maclay	8th " 10th	1803 " 1808	Resigned.
Andrew Gregg	10th " 13th	1807 " 1813	Elected president *pro tem.* 26 June, 1809.
Michael Leib	10th " 13th	1809 " 1814	Elected in place of Maclay. Resigned.
Jonathan Roberts	13th " 17th	1814 " 1821	Elected in place of Leib.
Abner Lacock	13th " 16th	1813 " 1819	
Walter Lowrie	16th " 19th	1819 " 1825	
William Findley	17th " 20th	1821 " 1827	
William Marks	19th " 22d	1825 " 1831	
Isaac D. Barnard	20th " 22d	1827 " 1831	Resigned.
George M. Dallas	22d " 23d	1831 " 1833	Elected in place of Barnard.
William Wilkins	22d " 23d	1831 " 1834	Resigned.
James Buchanan	23d " 29th	1834 " 1845	Elected in place of Wilkins; resigned; appointed secretary of state by president Polk.
Samuel McKean	23d " 26th	1833 " 1839	
Daniel Sturgeon	26th " 32d	1839 " 1851	
Simon Cameron	29th " 31st	1845 " 1849	Elected in place of Buchanan.
James Cooper	31st " 34th	1849 " 1855	
Richard Brodhead	32d " 35th	1851 " 1857	
William Bigler	34th " 37th	1855 " 1861	
Simon Cameron	35th " 37th	1857 " 1861	Resigned; appointed secretary of war by president Lincoln.
Edgar Cowan	37th " 40th	1861 " 1867	
David Wilmot	37th " 38th	1861 " 1863	Elected in place of Cameron; sat in House of Representatives, 1845-51, introducing, 1846, the WILMOT PROVISO.
Charles R. Buckalew	38th " 41st	1863 " 1869	
Simon Cameron	40th " 45th	1867 " 1877	Resigned.
John Scott	41st " 44th	1869 " 1875	
William A. Wallace	44th " 47th	1875 " 1881	
James Donald Cameron	45th " ——	1877 " ——	Elected in place of Simon Cameron. Term expires 1897.
John I. Mitchell	47th " 50th	1881 " 1887	
Matthew S. Quay	50th " ——	1887 " ——	Term expires 1899.

penny. The ancient silver penny was the first silver coin struck in England, and the only one current among the Anglo-Saxons. The penny until the reign of Edward I. was struck with a cross, so deeply indented that it might be easily parted into 2 for half-pence, and into 4 for farthings, and hence these names. COIN.

The value of the Roman *penny* (mentioned Matt. xx. 2), or *denarius*, was estimated at 7½*d.* of English money, or 14 cents.

Pennymites, a term first applied to the inhabitants of Pennsylvania by the SUSQUEHANNA SETTLERS.

Penob'scot. MAINE throughout.

Penruddock's rebellion, on behalf of Charles II., was suppressed, and col. John Penruddock himself executed, 16 May, 1655.

Pensacola. FLORIDA, UNITED STATES.

pension system. In several countries pensions are granted to servants of the crown and public, and in England a committee, appointed in 1834, designated those entitled to pensions "who by their useful discoveries in science, and attainments in literature and the arts, have merited the gracious consideration of their sovereign and the gratitude of their country." Under this regulation there was expended by the British government during the year ending 31 Mch. 1891, in pensions,

For naval and military service	£29,720
For political and civil service	13,841
For judicial service	43,977
Miscellaneous	4,067
Total	£91,605

In the United States, pensions have been granted for meritorious service from time to time since 1790, when baron Frederick William Steuben was granted by act of Congress an annuity of $2500 during life for "sacrifices and eminent services made and rendered to the U. S. during the late war." Pensions of $5000 are now paid to the widows of gens. Grant and Garfield, and there are on the pension rolls 22 widows of prominent officers in the army and navy who receive pensions of from $1200 to $2500, the latter being granted to the widow of adm. David D. Porter. There were on the pension rolls of the U. S. 30 June, 1893, 966,012 pensioners, classified as follows:

Widows and daughters of Revolutionary soldiers	17
Army invalid pensioners	360,658
Army widows, minor children, etc.	107,627
Navy invalid pensioners	4,782
Navy widows, minor children, etc.	2,578
Survivors of the war of 1812	86
Widows of soldiers in war of 1812	5,425
Survivors of Mexican war	14,149
Widows of soldiers in Mexican war	7,369
Indian wars (1832–42), survivors	2,544
" " " widows	1,338
Under act of Congress, 27 June, 1890:	
Army invalid pensioners	365,084
Army widows, minor children, etc.	77,838
Navy invalid pensioners	12,119
Navy widows, minor children, etc.	4,114
Under act of Congress, 5 Aug. 1892:	
Nurses	284
Total	966,012

Of these, 961,917 are in the U. S., 2002 in Canada, 740 in Great Britain, 590 in Germany, 239 unknown, and the remainder scattered throughout other foreign countries.

Continental Congress passes a resolution to provide for disabled soldiers of the Revolution by pension.........26 Aug. 1776

Continental Congress recommends to the states to provide for invalid soldiers.........7 June, 1785

Pensions heretofore granted by the several states to be paid by the U. S. government by act of Congress.........29 Sept. 1789

Pension to be paid, not to exceed one half monthly pay, to soldiers enlisting under act of this date and wounded or disabled in service.........30 Apr. 1790

Act directing arrears of pensions now due to be discharged by

certificate, and widows and orphans of those killed or who died in service to be entitled to the benefits of this act....11 Aug. 1790
Officers and seamen in the navy wounded or disabled to be placed on the pension lists by act of................1 July, 1797
Money accruing from prizes constitutes a fund for payment of naval pensions by act of.........2 Mch. 1799, and 23 Apr. 1800
Law enacted providing pensions for widows and children of officers dying in the service of wounds received in actual battle, at rate of one half monthly pay for 5 years...16 Mch. 1802
All persons on list of states for disabilities incurred in the Revolution are made U. S. pensioners by act of......25 Apr. 1808
Special pension granted to Robert White of Reading, Vt., who lost both arms at fort Erie, $40 per month; to J. Wrighter, Trenton, N. J., who lost his right arm and leg at Little York, Can., $30 per month; to John Young of Boston, Mass., who lost both arms at French creek, $40; and to J. Crampersey, Beverly, Mass., who lost both arms, $40; by act of Congress...22 Feb. 1816
Militia disabled in service to be placed on pension rolls in same manner as if of the regular army, and special pension granted William Monday of Baltimore, who lost both arms in battle at Leonard's creek, $20; by act of Congress, 16 Apr. "
Pensions heretofore or hereafter granted to be: for highest rate of disability, first lieutenant, $17 per month; second lieutenant, $15 per month; third lieutenant, $14; ensigns, $13; non-commissioned and privates, $8 per month..24 Apr. "
Young King, a Seneca Indian, for meritorious service, granted a pension of $200 per annum, by act of Congress.....26 Apr. "
Act of Congress passed placing on pension list all revolutionary officers at $20 per month, and soldiers and seamen at $8 per month who had served 9 months in the war..18 Mch. 1818
[27,948 persons applied for the benefit of this act; 18,000 were admitted; the expenditure for the first year was $1,847,900, and for the second, $2,766,440.]
Pension Bureau established with a commissioner of pensions (hitherto under the secretary of war); J. L. Edwards first commissioner.......................................2 Mch. 1833
Pension business of the navy department transferred to the commissioner of pensions, by act of................4 Mch. 1840
Pension office becomes a bureau of the newly created department of the interior...............................3 Mch. 1849
Samuel Downing of Saratoga county, N. Y., the last revolutionary pensioner under general acts, dies, aged 101, 18 Feb. 1867
John Gray, Noble county, O., a revolutionary pensioner by special act of 22 Feb. 1857, dies, aged 105...........28 Mch. 1869
Daniel F. Bakeman of Cattaraugus county, N. Y., a revolutionary pensioner under same act, dies, aged 109.....5 Apr. "
Surviving veterans and widows of deceased soldiers of the war of 1812 who served 60 days, allowed a service pension of $8 per month by act of Congress.................14 Feb. 1871
Total disability rates for pensioners raised: lieutenant-colonel and higher in the army, captains, commanders, etc., in the navy, to receive $30 per month; majors in army and lieutenants in navy, $25; captains, $20; first lieutenants, $17; second lieutenants, $15; cadet midshipmen, etc., $10; enlisted men, $8; by act of Congress.....................3 Mch. 1873
Act passed to place colored persons, now prohibited from receiving pensions on account of being borne on the rolls of their regiments as "slaves," on the same footing as other soldiers..3 Mch. "
Fifty-eight pension agencies in the U. S. consolidated; 18 now (1894) perform the business.............................. 1877
Soldiers and widows of soldiers who served 14 days in the war of 1812, granted a pension of $8 per month by act of Congress, 9 Mch. 1878
Arrears of pension act passed, dating all pensions granted under general laws, from the death or discharge from service of claimant.......................................25 Jan. 1879
Pensions under acts of 14 Feb. 1871, and 9 Mch. 1878, $8 per month increased to $12, by act of Congress.........19 Mch. 1886
Surviving officers and enlisted men of the military and naval services of the U. S. who served 60 days with the army or navy in the Mexican war, over 62 years of age or disabled, to receive a pension of $8 per month, by act of......29 Jan. 1887
Act granting pensions of $6 and $12 per month to all persons who served 90 days or more in the army, and who are suffering from permanent mental or physical disability, which incapacitates them for manual labor, and to their widows..27 June, 1890
Act of Congress granting pensions to army nurses......5 Aug. 1892
Of the 86 survivors of the war of 1812 the oldest is 106 years, the youngest 87.. 1893

INCREASE OF PENSION ROLL SINCE 1861.

Year.	Total number of applications.	Total number of claims allowed.	Number of pensioners. Invalids.	Widows, etc.	Total.	Disbursements.
1861	....	....	4,337	4,299	8,636	$1,072,461.55
1862	2,487	462	4,341	3,818	8,159	790,384.76
1863	49,332	7,884	7,821	6,970	14,791	1,025,139.91
1864	53,599	39,487	23,479	27,656	51,135	4,504,616.92
1865	72,684	40,171	35,880	50,106	85,986	8,525,153.11
1866	65,256	50,177	55,652	71,070	126,722	13,459,996.43
1867	36,753	36,482	67,565	83,618	153,183	18,619,956.46
1868	20,768	28,921	75,957	93,686	169,643	24,010,981.99
1869	26,066	23,196	82,859	105,104	187,963	28,422,884.08
1870	24,851	18,221	87,521	111,165	198,686	27,780,811.81
1871	43,969	16,562	93,394	114,101	207,495	33,077,383.63
1872	26,391	34,333	113,954	118,275	232,229	30,169,341.00
1873	18,303	16,052	119,500	118,911	238,411	29,185,289.62
1874	16,734	10,462	121,628	114,613	236,241	30,593,749.56
1875	18,704	11,152	122,989	111,832	234,821	29,683,116.63
1876	23,523	9,977	124,239	107,898	232,137	28,351,599.69
1877	22,715	11,326	128,723	103,381	232,104	28,580,157.04
1878	44,587	11,962	131,649	92,349	223,998	26,844,415.18
1879	57,118	31,346	138,615	104,140	242,755	33,784,526.19
1880	141,466	19,545	145,410	105,392	250,802	57,240,540.14
1881	31,116	27,394	164,110	104,720	268,830	50,626,538.51
1882	40,939	27,664	182,633	103,064	285,697	54,296,280.54
1883	48,776	38,162	206,042	97,616	303,658	60,431,972.85
1884	41,785	34,192	225,470	97,286	323,756	57,273,536.74
1885	40,918	35,767	247,146	97,979	345,125	65,693,706.72
1886	49,895	40,857	270,346	95,437	365,783	64,584,270.45
1887	72,465	55,194	306,298	99,709	406,007	74,815,486.85
1888	75,726	60,252	343,701	108,856	452,557	79,646,146.37
1889	81,220	51,921	373,699	116,026	489,725	89,131,968.44
1890	105,044	66,637	415,654	122,290	537,944	106,493,890.19
1891	363,799	156,486	536,821	139,339	676,160	118,548,959.71
1892	198,345	224,047	703,242	172,826	876,068	141,086,948.84
1893	110,361	121,630	759,706	206,306	966,012	158,155,342.51
	2,034,695	1,357,921				$1,576,503,554.42
Total amount paid prior to 1861 (1789–1860)......						$79,713,465.20
Grand total............						$1,656,217,019.62

INCREASE OF HIGHEST RATES FOR DISABILITY AS ESTABLISHED BY ACTS OF CONGRESS SINCE 1864.

Disability.	Monthly pension by Act of Congress.					
	4 July, 1864.	8 June, 1872.	18 June, 1874.	17 June, 1878.	12 Feb. 1889.	Rate for 1892.
Loss of both hands	$25.00	$31.25	$50.00	$72.00	$100.00	$100.00
" " feet	20.00	31.25	50.00	72.00	....	72.00
" " eyes	25.00	31.25	50.00	72.00	....	72.00
	3 Mch. 1865.	8 June, 1872.	28 Feb. 1877.	3 Mch. 1883.	4 Aug. 1886.	
Loss of 1 hand and 1 foot	20.00	24.00	36.00	....	....	36.00
" 1 hand or 1 foot	....	18.00	....	24.00	30.00	30.00
" 1 arm above elbow or 1 leg above knee	....	....	....	30.00	36.00	36.00
" 1 arm at shoulder or 1 leg at hip	....	....	....	....	45.00	45.00
Incapacity for performing manual labor	....	....	....	30.00	....	30.00
Totally deaf, 3 Mch. 1873, $13.00; 27 Aug. 1888, $30.00						30.00
Permanent helplessness, 4 Mch. 1890, $72.00						72.00
Totally helpless, 18 June, 1874, $50.00; 16 June, 1880, $72.00, dating from 17 June, 1878						72.00

AMOUNT DISBURSED AT THE DIFFERENT PENSION AGENCIES FOR THE YEAR ENDING 30 JUNE, 1893.

Location of agency.	Amount.
1. Augusta, Me	$3,096,877.58
2. Boston, Mass.	8,626,953.39
3. Buffalo, N. Y.	7,619,080.82
4. Chicago, Ill.	12,048,088.22
5. Columbus, O.	16,556,521.35
6. Concord, N. H.	3,424,287.91
7. Des Moines, Ia.	9,246,332.92
8. Detroit, Mich.	7,782,720.72
9. Indianapolis, Ind.	11,919,097.35
10. Knoxville, Tenn.	8,824,548.00
11. Louisville, Ky.	4,879,388.08
12. Milwaukee, Wis.	7,819,024.89
13. New York city	8,338,523.17
14. Philadelphia, Pa.	8,994,666.70
15. Pittsburg, Pa.	7,499,455.99
16. San Francisco, Cal.	3,134,832.88
17. Topeka, Kan.	16,456,194.76
18. Washington, D. C.	12,278,263.71
Paid by treasury settlements	110,484.07
Total	$158,155,342.51

[Total amount appropriated for the year ending 30 June, 1893, by the U. S. government, including the Deficiency Appropriation act of 3 Mch. 1893, amounting to $13,844,437.35, $160,581,787.35.]

pentam'eter verse (5 feet), first used about the 7th century B.C.; Pope's "Essay on Man" an example. ELEGY.

Penta'teuch, the 5 books of Moses, probably written about 1452 B.C. BIBLE.

Pen'tecost signifies the 50th, and is the solemn fesl of the Jews, called also "the feast of weeks," because it celebrated 50 days, or 7 weeks, after the feast of the Pass-r, 1491 B C (Lev. xxiii 15, Exod xxxiv 22) WHIT-RIDE.

Pentland hills, near Edinburgh Here the Scotch sbyterians, since called CAMERONIANS, who had risen inst the government on account of the establishment of copacy, were defeated by the royal troops, 28 Nov. 1666

Penzance, Cornwall The town was burned by the niards July 1595 It was taken by Fairfax in 1646 e sir Humphry Davy was born, 17 Dec 1778, and here inaugurated his memorial statue, 17 Oct. 1872

pepsin, a peculiar organic substance found by Schwamm he gastric juice, and named by him from πέψις, digestion vas experimented on by M Blondlot in 1843, and has e been prescribed as a medicine

Pepys's (*pēp'-is* or *pēps*) **"Diary."** Samuel Pepys born 23 Feb 1632, became secretary to the English ad-alty about 1664; president of the Royal Society, 1684, 26 May, 1703 His "Diary," as published, begins 1 Jan)-60, ends 31 May, 1669

MS at Magdalen college, Cambridge, was deciphered by e rev John Smith The first edition (with a selection om his correspondence) by Richard lord Braybrooke, ap ared in 1825 The new edition, "deciphered with addi-onal notes, by the rev Mynors Bright," began in 1875

Pequots. CONNECTICUT, 1636-37, INDIANS

"Percy's Reliques." The earliest ballads of the glish language that had been preserved in manuscript or ted in the rudest manner, collected, systematized, and ex-ned by dr Percy, bishop of Dromore, and so named after LITERATURE

Per'ekop, an isthmus, 5 miles broad, connecting the nea with the mainland It was called by the Tartars apou, "gate of the isthmus," which the Russians changed s present name, which signifies a barren ditch The lines ss the isthmus were forced by the Russian marshal Munich, , 1736, and the fortress was taken by Lacy, July 1738 was again strongly fortified by the khan, but was again en by the Russians in 1771, who have since retained it.

perfumery, the art or practice of making perfumes the gratification of the sense of smell In Exod xxx)0 B C) directions are given for making incense

Per'gamos. SEVEN CHURCHES, 3

Peri (Persian), an imaginary female being like the elf or y, represented in Persian mythology as a descendant of en angels, excluded from Paradise until their penance is omplished

> "Farewell—farewell to thee Araby's daughter
> (Thus warbled a Peri beneath the dark sea)"
> —*Moore's "Lallah Rookh,"* song Araby's Daughter

periodical literature. NEWSPAPERS, MAGA-ES, REVIEWS

"Periplus." The voyage of Hanno, the Carthaginian igator probably in the 6th century B.C His account of his els, *written in* the Punic language, was translated into Greek, English translation edited by Falconer, London, in 1797.

perjury, the formal and wilful attestation by oath of a ehood The early Romans threw the offender headlong from Tarpeian precipice, and the Greeks set a mark of infamy n him After the empire became Christian, any one who re falsely upon the Gospels was to have his tongue cut out canons of the primitive church enjoined 11 years' penance, in some countries the false swearer became liable to any ishment to which his testimony has exposed an innocent son In England perjury was punished with the pillory, , and imprisonment, 1562 Perhaps the most notorious jurer of modern times was Titus Oates OATES

Peronne (*pe-ron'*), a town of N France Louis XI. France, having placed himself in the power of the duke of gundy, here was forced to sign a treaty, confirming those of as and Conflans, and recognizing the duke's independence, Oct 1468. The notables declared the treaty invalid and duke a traitor, Nov 1470

perpetual motion. For this purpose machines e been constructed by the marquess of Worcester and many others, although the impossibility of attaining it was demonstrated by sir Isaac Newton and De la Hire and affirmed by the Academy of Sciences at Paris, 1775 It is still an object of experiment with many fanatics KEELY MOTOR

Perry's victory. NAVAL BATTLES

Perryville, Ky BRAGG'S KENTUCKY CAMPAIGN

persecutions. Historians usually reckon 10 general persecutions of the Christians BARTHOLOMEW, ST, HERETICS, HUGUENOTS, INQUISITION, JEWS, MASSACRES, PROTESTANTS, etc

I Under Nero, who, having set fire to Rome threw the odium upon the Christians, multitudes were massacred, wrapped up in the skins of wild beasts, and torn and devoured by dogs, crucified, burned alive, etc	64-68
II Under Domitian	95
III Under Trajan	106
IV Under Marcus Aurelius	166-77
V Under Septimus Severus	199-204
VI Under Maximus.	235-38
VII Under Decius more bloody than any preceding	250-52
VIII Under Valerian	258-60
IX Under Aurelian	275
X Under Diocletian who prohibited divine worship, houses filled with Christians were set on fire and many of them were bound together with ropes and cast into the sea.	303-13

Persep'olis, the ancient splendid capital of Persia Ruins of this city still exist Alexander is accused of setting fire to the palace of the Persian kings here, 331 B C, "at the royal feast for Persia won," while under the influence of wine and instigated also by Thais as a penalty for the cruelties inflicted by the Persians upon the Greek prisoners Dryden makes this act of Alexander due to music by Timotheus

> "And the king seized a flambeau with zeal to destroy,
> Thaïs led the way
> To light him to his prey,
> And like another Helen fired another Troy"
> —"Alexander's Feast"

Persia or **Iran,** in the Bible called **Elam,** a country of Asia, is said *to have received its appellation from Perseus*, the son of Perseus and Andromeda, who settled here, and established a petty sovereignty The name is more probably of Indian origin Persia was included in the first Assyrian monarchy, 900 B C When that empire was dismembered by Arbaces, etc, it appertained to Media Area about 628 000 sq miles—a large portion desert, pop of the present kingdom about 9,000,000

	B C
Zoroaster, king of Bactria, founder of the Magi	2115
Zoroaster II, Persian philosopher, generally confounded with the king of Bactria	1082
Cyrus, king of Persia, 559, overthrows the Medo Babylonian monarchy about 557, conquers Asia Minor about 548, master of the East, 536, killed in war with the Massagetæ	529
Cambyses his son, king 529, conquers EGYPT	525
False Smerdis killed, Darius Hystaspis king, 521, conquers Babylon	517
Conquest of Ionia, Miletus destroyed	498
Darius equips 600 sail, with an army of 300 000 to invade the Peloponnesus which is defeated at MARATHON	490
Xerxes king 485, recovers Egypt, 484, enters Greece in the spring at head of an immense force, battle of Thermopylæ	480
Xerxes enters Athens, after having lost 200,000 of his troops, and is defeated in a naval engagement off Salamis	480
Persians defeated at Mycale and Platæa 22 Sept	479
Cimon, son of Miltiades with a fleet of 250 vessels takes several cities from the Persians, and destroys their navy, consisting of about 340 sail, near Cyprus	470
Xerxes is murdered in his bed by Artabanus	465
Artaxerxes I (Longimanus) king, 464, marries Esther	458
Xerxes II. king, slain by Sogdianus, 425, who is deposed by Darius II (Nothus)	424
Artaxerxes II (Mnemon) king, 405, battle of Cunaxa, Cyrus the younger killed	401
Retreat of the 10,000 Greeks (RETREAT)	"
War with Greece, 399, invasion of Persia	396
Peace of ANTALCIDAS	387
Artaxerxes III (Ochus) kills all his relations at his accession	359
He is killed by his minister Bagoas and his son, Arses, made king,	338
Bagoas kills him and sets up Darius III (Codomanus), by whom he himself is killed	336
Alexander the Great enters Asia, defeats the Persians at the river Granicus, 334, near Issus, 333, at Arbela	331
Darius III treacherously killed by Bessus	"
Persia partly reconquered from the Greeks, subjugated by the Parthians.	250
	A D.
Artaxerxes I founds the Sassanides dynasty, restores kingdom of Persia	226
Religion of Zoroaster restored and Christianity persecuted	227
Artaxerxes murdered, succeeded by Sapor I, Armenia becomes independent under Chosroes.	240
Sapor conquers Mesopotamia, 258, repels the Romans and slays the emperor Valerian.	260

[illegible]

peruke, periwig, or **wig,** [illegible]

[illegible]

Peruvian bark. [illegible]

pessimism [illegible]

[illegible]

Pestalozzian [illegible] **system** [illegible]

[illegible]

petard or **petar,** [illegible]

[illegible]

Peter the wild boy, a savage creature [illegible]

[illegible]

Peterborough, [illegible]

[illegible]

Peterloo. [illegible]

Petersburg. [illegible]

Petersburg, St., the modern capital of Russia, [illegible]

[illegible]

Peter's church, St., [illegible]

[illegible]

Peter's pence, [illegible]

[illegible]

Peterwardein, [illegible]

[illegible]

petitions. [illegible]

[illegible]

Petra, [illegible]

[illegible]

Petrarch and **Laura,** [illegible]

[illegible]

petroleum [illegible]

[illegible]

Sapor assassinated; succeeded by Hormisdas I., who favors the Manichees.... 272
Varanes I. (Baharam) persecutes them and the Christians.... 273
Varanes II. defeated by the emperor Probus; makes peace... 277
Persia invaded by the emperor Carus, who conquers Seleucia and Ctesiphon.... 283
Varanes III. king, 293; Narses.... 294
Emperor Galerius conquers Mesopotamia, etc.... 298
Peace with Diocletian.... "
Hormisdas II. king.... 301 or 303
Ormuz built....about "
Sapor II. king, 309; proscribes Christianity, 326; makes war successfully with Rome for the lost provinces.... 337–60
Emperor Julian invades Persia; slain near the Tigris, 26 June; his successor Jovian purchases his retreat by surrendering provinces.... 363
Sapor annexes Armenia, 365; and Iberia, 366; makes peace with Rome.... 372
Artaxerxes II. king, 380; Sapor III.... 385
Armenia and Iberia independent.... 386
Varanes IV., 390; Yezdejird I., 404; conquers Armenia.... 412
Varanes V., 420, persecutes Christians; conquers Arabia Felix, 421; makes peace with the Eastern Empire for 100 years... 422
Armenia again united to Persia.... 428
Wars with Huns, Turks, etc.....430–32
Yezdejird II. king, 440; Hormisdas III., 457; civil war, 458–86; *Feroze king, 458; Pallas, 484; Kobad, 486; Jamaspes, 497;* Kobad again.... 497
His son Chosroes I. king; long wars with Justinian and his successors, with various fortune....531–79
Successful campaigns of Belisarius....541–42
Hormisdas IV. continues the war; degrades his general, Baharam, who deposes him; but is eventually defeated.... 590
Chosroes II., 591; renews the war with success, 603; Egypt and Asia Minor subdued....614–16
Chosroes totally defeated by the emperor Heraclius, who advances on Persia.... 627
Chosroes put to death by his son Siroes, 628; Artaxerxes III. king, 629; Purandokt, daughter of Chosroes, reigns, 630; Shenendeh, her lover, 631; Arzemdokt, her sister, 631; Kesra, 631; Ferokhdad, 632; Yezdejird III.... 632
Persia invaded by the Arabs; the king flees, 651; is betrayed to them and is put to death, and his army exterminated... 652
Persia becomes the seat of the Shiite or Fatimite Mahometans. 661
Taherite dynasty established, 813; Sofferide, 872; Samanide. 902
Persia subdued by Togrul Beg and the Seljukian Turks, 1038; who are expelled, 1194; subdued by Genghis Khan and the Mongols, 1223
Bagdad made the capital.... 1345
Poet Hafiz died about.... 1388
Persia invaded by Timour, 1380; ravaged by him.... 1399
Poet Jami born.... 1414
Persia conquered by the Turcomans.... 1468
Who are expelled by the Shiites, who establish the Sophi dynasty under Ismail I.... 1501
Ispahan made the capital.... 1590
Turks take Bagdad; great massacre.... 1638
Georgia revolts to Russia.... 1783
Teheran made the capital.... 1796
War with Russia....1826–29
Rupture with England through the Persians taking Herat, 25 Oct.; war declared....1 Nov. 1856
Persians defeated; Bushire taken....8–10 Dec. "
Gen. Outram defeats the Persians at Kooshab, 8 Feb.; and at Mohammerah....26 Mch. 1857
Peace ratified at Teheran....14 Apr. "
Commercial treaty with France, etc....June, "
Herat given up by the Persians....July, "
Shah reorganizes the government....9 Sept. 1858
Railways in process of formation.... 1865
Electric telegraph introduced.... 1867
Great sufferings *from 3 years' drought, with fever and cholera;* about 16,000 persons perished at Ispahan, etc....July–Oct. 1871
Concession to baron Julius de Reuter to make railways, waterworks, etc., for 70 years, with great power....25 July, 1872
Prosperity restored through a good harvest....Mch. 1873
Shah visits Europe summer of.... "
Postal service established....Jan. 1877
Shah visits Europe in summer; returns to Teheran....9 Aug. 1878
Rebellious incursions of the Kurds suppressed after much bloodshed (Kurdistan)....Oct.–Dec. 1880
First railway in Persia, from Teheran to Azim, opened..25 June, 1888
River Karun decreed open to all nations....9 Sept. "
Shah visits Europe.... 1889
Imperial bank of Persia established....23 Oct. "

A.D. SHAHS.

1502. Ismail, or Ishmael; conquers Georgia, 1519.
1523. Tamasp, or Thamas, I.
1576. Ismail II. Meerza.
1577. Mahommed Meerza.
1582. Abbas I. the Great; makes a treaty with English, 1612; d. 1628.
1628. Shah Sophi.
1641. Abbas II.
1666. Shah Sophi II.
1694. Hussein; deposed.
1722. Mahmoud, chief of the Afghans.
1725. Ashraff the usurper; slain in battle.
1730. Tamasp, or Thamas, II.; recovers the throne of his ancestors from the preceding.
[Thamas-Kouli-Khan, his general, obtains great successes in this and the subsequent reigns.]
1732. Abbas III., infant son of Tamasp, under the regency of Kouli-Khan, who afterwards proclaims himself king as
1736. Nadir Shah (the victorious king); conquers India, 1739; assassinated at Khorassan by his nephew,
1747. Shah Rokh.
1751. [Interregnum.]
1759. Kureem Khan.
1779. Many competitors for the throne, and assassinations till
1795. Aga Mahommed Khan obtains the power, and founds the reigning (Turcoman) dynasty; assassinated, 1797.
1798. Futteh Ali Shah.
1834. Mahommed Shah, grandson of Futteh; d. 10 Sept. 1848.
1848. Nasr-ed-din, son; b. 18 July, 1831; the present shah of Persia. *Heir:* son, Muzaffer-ed-din, b. 25 Mch. 1853.

perspective, in drawing, is the art of representing objects on a plane surface in the proportions due to their relative distances from the eye. Observed by the Van Eycks (1426–46), and treated scientifically by Michael Angelo, Leonardo da Vinci, and Albert Dürer, early in the 16th century. Guido Ubaldo published a treatise in 1608; Dubreuil's treatise (the "Jesuits' perspective") appeared in 1642, and the mathematical theory was demonstrated by Brook Taylor in 1731.

Perth, the old capital of Scotland, said to have been founded by Agricola about 70 A.D. It was besieged by the regent Robert, 1339. On 20 Feb. 1437, James I. was murdered at the Black Friars' monastery here, by Robert Graham and the earl of Athol, for which they suffered condign punishment. This murder is powerfully delineated in Rossetti's poem, "The King's Tragedy." Gowrie's conspiracy occurred here, 6 Aug. 1600. Perth was taken from the French garrison by the reformers, 26 June, 1559. The "Articles of Perth," relating to religious ceremonies, were agreed to by the General Assembly of Scotland, 25 Aug. 1618. Perth was taken by Cromwell in 1651, and by the earl of Mar after the battle of Dunblane, in 1715. Pop. 1891, 30,760. Scene of Scott's "Fair Maid of Perth." Literature.

Peru', a country of South America, was long governed by incas, said to be descended from Manco Capac, who ruled in the 11th century. Area, 463,747 sq. miles; pop. 2,621,844, and about 350,000 uncivilized Indians.

Peru explored and conquered by Francisco Pizarro and Almagro.... 1524–33
Last inca, Atahualpa, put to death....29 Aug. 1533
Pizarro assassinated at Lima....26 June, 1541
Fruitless insurrection of the Peruvians under Tapac Amaru, an inca.... 1780
San Martin proclaims the independence of Peru....28 July, 1821
War against Spain....14 Jan. 1824
Bolivar made dictator....Feb. "
Mariano Prado president....28 Nov. "
Spaniards defeated at Ayacucho, and freedom of Peru and Chili achieved....9 Dec. "
New Peruvian constitution signed by the president of the republic....21 Mch. 1828
War with Colombia; treaty of peace....28 Feb. 1829
After a succession of fierce party conflicts, gen. Ramon Castilla becomes president; firm and politic.... 1845
New constitution, 1856; modified.... 1860
Spanish admiral Pinzon took possession of the Chincha isles (valuable for guano) belonging to Peru, stating that he would occupy them till the claims of his government on Peru were satisfied....14 Apr. 1864
American congress at Lima; plenipotentiaries from Chili and other states meet to concert measures for defence against European powers....Nov. "
Negotiations followed by peace with Spain, 28 Jan.; Chincha islands restored....3 Feb. 1865
Peru joins Chili, and declares war against Spain....Feb. 1866
Spanish admiral Nuñez, in his attempt to bombard Callao, repulsed and wounded....2 May, "
Spaniards quit Peruvian waters....10 May, "
Several towns in Peru suffered by great earthquakes (Earthquakes)....13–15 Aug 1868
Gold mines discovered at Huacho....Oct. 1871
Military insurrection at Lima; Tomas Gutierrez, minister of war, makes himself dictator, and imprisons pres. Balta...22 July, 1872
Unsupported by the people, and not recognized by diplomatic representatives, he orders Balta to be shot; is himself compelled to fly; caught; killed by the people, and hanged to a lamp-post; col. Zavallos, vice-president, assumes the government; order restored; about 200 lives were lost during the *coup d'état*....26 July, "
Manuel Pardo, elected president by the people, assumes office, 2 Aug. "
Talisman sailed from Cardiff for South America; consigned to Peruvian rebels; seized and condemned as a prize, and English sailors imprisoned, Nov. 1874–Nov. 1875; report on ill-usage; English government promises inquiry....Mch. 1876
Pres. Mariano I. Prado....2 Aug. "
Reported insurrection of Nicolas de Pierolas, with about 6000 men, to establish a southern confederacy....6–10 Oct. "
He sails away with the iron-clad *Huascar*, 29 May; is at-

tacked by adm. De Horsey, with the British war-vessels *Shah* ınd *Amethyst*, as piratical, for attacking mail-ships; is compelled to run into Lima and surrender; the Peruvians resent British interference and threaten reprisals...........June, 1877
ru and Bolivia declare war against Chili, announced..2 Apr. 1879
[For the events of the war, CHILI, 1879-81.]
ma occupied by the Chilians.........................17 Jan. 1881
forts made by the United States to promote the restoration of peace, leads to some misunderstanding in Chili.......... "
es. Iglesias forms a ministry about 12 Sept.; he signs peace with Chili at Ancon................................20 Oct. 1883
ma evacuated by the Chilians......................23 Oct. "
equipa surrendered to the Chilians..................26 Oct. "
n. Iglesias's government confirmed by elections, about 29 Jan. 1884
eaty with Chili ratified by the notables, Mch.; partial evacuation of Peruvian territory...........................May, "
ternal disturbances continue through.......................1884-85
volutionary attempt of Pierola's supporters near Lima defeated...2 Dec. 1890

peruke, periwig, or **wig,** an artificial cap or vering of hair for the head. The ancients used false hair, t the present peruke was first worn in France and Italy out 1620; introduced into England about 1660, and preiled more or less till about 1810.

is said that either bishop *Blomfield (of London) or Tomline (of* ıncoln) obtained permission for the bishops to discontinue wearng wigs in Parliament, *of which they gradually availed themselves.*
On account of the heat, sir J. P. Wilde, and other judges and several counsel, appear in court without wigs, 22, 23 July, 1868.

Peruvian bark. CINCHONA.

pessimism (from *pessimus*, the worst), the opposite docne to OPTIMISM. James Sully's "Pessimism, a History and Criticism," was published in 1877. Arthur Schopenhauer 788-1860), an eminent pessimist, says, "All life is effort; all ort is painful; the pains of life must predominate." PHISOPHY. Pessimism is a form of atheism, a disbelief in the ınitude of good or its power to use evil to express itself.

"Let Love clasp Grief lest both be drown'd."
ADES. —*Tennyson*, "In Memoriam."

Pestalozzian (*pes-tä-lot'-se-an*) **system** of eduᴄion was devised by John Henry Pestalozzi, born at Zurich Switzerland, in 1746, died 17 Feb. 1827. In 1775 he turned farm into a school for educating poor children in reading, iting, and working; but he did not succeed. In 1798 he ablished an orphan school, where he began with the mutualıtruction or monitorial system, since adopted by Lancaster; t his school was soon after turned into a hospital for the ıstrian army. In 1802, in conjunction with Fellenberg, he ablished his school at Hofwyl, which at first was successful, t eventually declined through mismanagement.

petard' or **petar,** an invention ascribed to the Huenots in 1579. Petards of metal, nearly in the shape of a t, were employed to blow up gates or other barriers, and o in countermines to break through into the enemy's galies. Cahors was taken by Henry IV. by means of petards, 1580, when it is said they were first used.

"Hoist with his own petar."
—*Shakespeare*, "Hamlet," act iii. sc. iv.

Peter the wild boy, a savage creature found in forest of Hertswald, electorate of Hanover, when George I. d his friends were hunting. He was found walking on his nds and feet, climbing trees like a squirrel, and feeding on grass d moss, Nov. 1725. At this time he was supposed to be 13 ars old. He died, while under the care of an English farmer, b. 1785. He preferred wild plants, leaves, and the bark of es to any other kind of food. No efforts could greatly change savage habits or cause him to utter one distinct syllable. rd Monboddo represented him to be a proof of the hypoths that "man in a state of nature is a mere animal."

Peterborough, anciently **Medeshamstede,** ity of Northamptonshire, Engl.; obtained its present name m a king of Mercia founding an abbey and dedicating it St. Peter, about 655. The church, destroyed by the Danes, ıs rebuilt with great beauty. First bishop was John Chamrs, the last abbot of Peterborough, 1541.

Peterloo. MANCHESTER, 16 Aug. 1819.

Petersburg. GRANT'S VIRGINIA CAMPAIGN, MINE PLOSION, VIRGINIA.

Petersburg, St., the modern capital of Russia, ınded by Peter the Great, 27 May, 1703. He built a small t for himself, and some wooden hovels. In 1710, the count olovkin built the first house of brick; and the next year the emperor, with his own hands, laid the foundation of a house of the same material. The *seat of empire* was transferred from Moscow to this place in 1711. RUSSIA. Pop. 1890, winter 1,003,315, summer 849,315.

Peace of St. Petersburg, between Russia and Prussia, the former restoring all her conquests to the latter, signed..5 May, 1762
Treaty of St. Petersburg for the partition of Poland (PARTITION TREATIES)..5 Aug. 1772
Great fire, 11,000 houses burned.................................. 1780
Treaty of St. Petersburg leads to a coalition against France, 8 Sept. 1805
Treaty of Alliance, signed at St. Petersburg, between Bernadotte, prince royal of Sweden, and the emperor Alexander; the former agreeing to join in the campaign against France, in return for which Sweden was to receive Norway. 24 Mch. 1812
Winter palace burned.................................29 Dec. 1837
Railway to Moscow finished.. 1851
" " Berlin opened....................................5 May, 1862
Grand new Alexander II. bridge over the Neva opened, 12 Oct. 1879

Peter's church, St., Rome, originally erected by Constantine, 306. About 1450, pope Nicholas V. commenced a new church. The present magnificent pile was designed by Bramante; the first stone laid by pope Julius II. in 1506. In 1514 Leo X. employed Raphael and two others to superintend the building. Paul III. committed the work to Michael Angelo, who devised the dome, in the construction of which 30,000 lbs. of iron were used. The church was consecrated 18 Nov. 1626. The front is 400 feet broad, rising to a height of 180 feet, and the majestic dome ascends from the centre of the church to a height of 324 feet; the length of the interior is 600 feet, forming one of the most spacious halls ever constructed. The length of the exterior is 669 feet; its greatest breadth within is 442 feet; and the entire height from the ground 432 feet.

Peter's pence, presented by Ina, king of the West Saxons, to the pope at Rome, for the endowment of an English college there, about 725; so called because agreed to be paid on Peter mass, 1 Aug. The tax was levied on all families possessed of 30 pence yearly rent in land, out of which they paid 1 penny. It was confirmed by Offa, 777, and was afterwards claimed by the popes as a tribute from England, and regularly collected, till suppressed by Henry VIII., 1534.—*Camden.* A public collection (on behalf of the pope) was forbidden in France in 1860.

Peterwardein, a fortress in Slavonia, Austria, was taken by the Turks, July, 1526. Here prince Eugene of Savoy gained a great victory over the Turks, 5 Aug. 1716.

petitions. The right of petitioning the crown and Parliament for redress of grievances is a fundamental principle of the British constitution. Petitions are extant of the date of Edward I. In the reign of Henry IV. petitions began to be addressed to the House of Commons in considerable numbers. The right of petition is secured by the Constitution of the United States; but in Jan. 1800, great excitement and rancorous debate were induced in Congress by the presentation of a petition from free negroes. John Quincy Adams, who was a champion of the right of petition, presented a petition in Congress purporting to come from slaves—the first of the kind ever offered—Feb. 1837. ATHERTON GAG; UNITED STATES, 1838.

Pe'tra, the ancient **Sela,** in Mount Seir, near Mount Hor, in the land of Edom. In the 4th century B.C. it was held by the Nabathæans, who successfully resisted Antigonus. About 70 A.D. it was the residence of the Arab princes named Aretas. It was conquered by Cornelius Palma, and annexed to the empire under Trajan, 105, to which period its remarkable monuments are ascribed. It was an important station for commercial traffic with Rome. Its ruins were discovered by Burckhardt in 1812, and described by him and others since.

Petrarch and **Laura,** celebrated for the refined passion of the former for the latter, begun in 1327, and the chief subject of his sonnets. He was born 1304; crowned with laurel, as a poet and writer, on Easter-day, 8 Apr. 1341; and died at Arqua, near Padua, 18 July, 1374. Laura died 6 Apr. 1348. A commemoration of his death at Avignon and other places, 18 July, 1874. LITERATURE.

petroleum (Gr. πέτρα, rock; ἔλαιον, oil). An oily substance of great economic importance as a source of light. It is obtained chiefly from coal strata. Its distribution is extensive, reaching every continent. In Alsace, Germany, it was discovered in 1735, permeating sandstone, which is mined like coal, and the petroleum afterwards extracted. The oil-lands of Peru were developed by American capital in 1864, but Russia and the United States furnish most of the world's supply. In 1872 oil from the Baku wells, Russia, was used as fuel for the production of steam. Baku, which is a port on the western coast of the Caspian sea, was a resort for the Persian fire-worshippers, 600 B.C., and petroleum is known to have existed in that vicinity for 2500 years. Marco Polo, in his journal written in the 13th century, said that at Baku was "a fountain of oil in great abundance . . . not good to use with food, but good to burn, and is also used to anoint camels that have the mange." This use of petroleum or rock-oil as a medicine obtained among the Indians of America before its discovery in central New York by French missionaries in 1627; and in the early part of the present century it was collected from the surface of oil-springs by the whites, by spreading woollen blankets thereon and wringing out the adhering scum, its principal use being as a medicine under the name of Seneca oil.

In a map of the countries about lakes Ontario and Erie, prepared by messrs. Dollier and Galinée, missionaries of the order of St. Sulpice, appears a "Fontaine de bitumen" near the present site of Cuba, Alleghany county, N. Y. 1670
In a map of the Middle Colonies, published by Mr. Evans, appears "Petroleum," marked near the mouth of Oil creek, on the Alleghany river, Pa. 1755
Petroleum, as found in oil springs on the Alleghany river, described by David Zeisberger, missionary of the Moravian church 1767
Highest annual yield of petroleum along Oil creek estimated by gen. Samuel Hays at 16 barrels, worth $1 per gallon in Pittsburg, 1803
Petroleum observed and described in salt wells in Washington county, Ohio 1814
S. M. Kier, of Pittsburg, Pa., bottles and sells as medicine, at 50 cts. per pint, petroleum or rock-oil 1849
Petroleum first refined at Pittsburg, Pa. 1854
Pennsylvania Rock Oil company, the first oil company in the U. S., organized with a capital of $500,000 .... "
William Smith and sons, in the employ of the Pennsylvania Rock Oil company, boring for oil on Oil creek, "strike oil" at a depth of 69½ feet (PENNSYLVANIA) .... 28 Aug. 1859
Highest price for petroleum reached in the U. S., $19.25 per barrel of 42 gallons 1860
Price of petroleum in the U. S. reaches its lowest mark, crude oil being quoted at 10 cts. per barrel .... Jan. 1862
First flowing oil well on Black creek, Canada, begins...11 Jan. "
"Shooting" oil wells, by explosion of nitro-glycerine to increase their production, first suggested and put into practical operation by col. E. A. L. Roberts .... "
Crude petroleum quoted at $12.12½ per barrel .... July, 1864
Tank cars first used for railroad transportation of oil 1865
First successful pipe-line, 4 miles in length, laid by Samuel Van Syckel at Pithole, Pa. .... "
Combination of oil-refiners in the U. S., under the name of Standard Oil company 1872
United Pipe Line, first known as the Fairview Pipe Line, incorporated .... 29 Apr. 1874
Construction of long-distance pipe-lines begun by the United Pipe Lines company 1880
Standard Oil Trust organized 1881
A well on Thorn creek, Butler county, Pa., flows for a few hours at the rate of 9000 to 10,000 barrels per day. Well shot .... 27 Oct. 1884

PRODUCTION OF PETROLEUM IN THE UNITED STATES AT VARIOUS PERIODS SINCE 1871.

Year ending June.	Barrels of 42 gallons.	Gallons.	Exported gallons.	Value.
1871	5,558,775	233,468,550	149,892,691	$36,894,810
1875	10,083,828	423,520,776	221,955,308	30,078,568
1880	22,382,509	940,065,378	423,964,699	36,218,625
1885	21,750,619	913,525,998	574,668,180	50,257,947
1890	21,486,406	902,429,052	664,068,170	51,403,089

pews in churches. "In a London will we read of *sedile vocatum pew*" (a seat called pew), 1453. Pews were censured by Latimer and Bradford, 1553.—*Walcot.* The church of Geddington St. Mary, Northamptonshire, long contained a pew dated 1602. The rev. W. M. H. Church (vicar 1844–46) restored and reseated the church, and preserved the panel with the date in the door of the surplice press. Another pew in the chancel was dated 1604.

pha'lanx. The Greek phalanx consisted of 8000 men in a square battalion, with shields joined, and spears crossing each other. The battalion of Philip of Macedon, called the Macedonian phalanx, was formed by him about 360 B.C. In the battles of Cynoscephalæ and Pydna the Grecian phalanx competed with the Roman legion for supremacy, and the victory secured to the legion in both battles would seem to prove its superiority. ARMY, PIKE.

Phar'isees, a sect among the Jews; so called from *pharash*, a Hebrew word for separated, because they pretended to a greater degree of holiness than the rest of the Jews (Luke xviii. 9-12). The Talmud enumerates 7 classes of Pharisees. The word also indicates a giver without charity:

> "A long row of alms-houses amply endowed
> By a well-esteemed Pharisee, busy and proud."
> —*Jane Taylor*, "The Philosopher's Scales."

pharmacopœ'ia. MEDICAL SCIENCE.

phar'macy. MEDICAL SCIENCE.

Pha'ros, of Ptolemy Philadelphus of Alexandria, was esteemed as one of the wonders of the world. It was a tower built of white marble, completed about 283 B.C. On the top fires were constantly kept to direct sailors in the bay. The building cost 800 talents, which are equivalent to $850,000, if Attic; or, if Alexandrian, double that sum. It is said that there was this inscription upon it—"King Ptolemy to the gods, the saviours, for the benefit of sailors;" but Sostratus the architect, wishing to claim all the glory, engraved his own name upon the stones, and afterwards filled the hollow with mortar, and wrote the above inscription. When the mortar had decayed, Ptolemy's name disappeared, and the following inscription became visible: "Sostratus the Cnidian, son of Dexiphanes, to the gods, the saviours, for the benefit of sailors." LIGHT-HOUSES.

Pharsa'lia, a strong city in Thessaly, N. Greece. Near it Julius Cæsar defeated his rival Pompey, 9 Aug. 48 B.C., and became virtually master of the known world. Pompey fled to Egypt, where he was treacherously slain, by order of Ptolemy the younger, then a minor, and his body left naked on the strand, till burned by a faithful freedman, Philip.

phenol or **phenic acid,** names for carbolic acid.

phenophthal'moscope, an apparatus for investigating the movements of the eyeball; invented by Donders of Utrecht, and announced in 1870.

Phiga'lian marbles, in the British museum, were purchased for it by the prince regent in 1815. They consist of portions of the frieze taken from the temple of Apollo Epicurus at Phigaleia in Arcadia, and are reputed to be works of the earlier school of Phidias, who died 432 B.C. The bas-reliefs represent the conflicts of the Greeks and Amazons, and of the Centaurs and Lapithæ.

Philadel'phia, the third city in the United States in population, and the metropolis of Pennsylvania, was laid out in 1682 at the narrowest part of the peninsula formed by the confluence of the Schuylkill and Delaware rivers, now included between Vine and South streets. The following year the place contained about 80 houses and 500 people. A charter, evidently genuine, found in the possession of col. Alexander Biddle in 1887, and dated "Third Month, 20th, 1691," shows incorporation as a city by William Penn 10 years earlier than the date usually given, when the first recorded mayor, Edward Shippen, was appointed. On 2 Feb. 1854, the city was enlarged to include the county of Philadelphia, taking in 9 districts: Southwark, Northern Liberties, Kensington, Spring Garden, Moyamensing, Penn, Richmond, West Philadelphia, and Belmont; also 6 boroughs and 13 townships. Present area 128⅛ sq. miles; lat. 40° N., lon. 75° W.; population at various dates:

1700	4,500	1840	258,037
1749	12,500	1850	408,762
1760	18,756	1860	565,529
1783	37,000	1870	674,022
1800	70,287	1880	847,170
1810	110,210	1890	1,046,964
1820	137,097	1900	1,293,697
1830	188,797	1910	

One of the earliest surveys of city lots recorded .... 10 July, 1682
Blue Anchor Inn, northwest cor. Front and Dock sts., afterwards called the "Boatman and Call," built by George Guest, "
Laying out of Philadelphia completed under the personal supervision of William Penn .... Dec. "
First meeting of the governor and council held in Philadelphia 10 Mch., and of the General Assembly .... 12 Mch. 1683
Brick Quaker meeting-house built on Centre square 1684
William Bradford establishes the first printing-press in Philadelphia, and prints his "Kalendarium Pennsylvaniense, or America's Messenger;" an almanac edited by Samuel Atkins, and the first work printed in Philadelphia 1685
First regular jail built in the middle of Market st., near Second, 1687
"William Penn Charter" school, on Fourth st., below Chestnut, established in charge of George Keith 1689
Christ church (Episcopal) built (enlarged 1711 and 1727) 1695
"Slate Roof House" (removed in 1867 to make way for the

Chamber of Commerce) erected about 1698, and the largest at that time in Philadelphia, occupied by William Penn, Jan. 1700

loria Dei church (Swedish) on Swanson st., dedicated..2 July, "

irst watchman "to go round ye town with a small bell in ye night time" appointed....13 July, "

harter as a borough city granted Philadelphia by William Penn, and Edward Shippen appointed mayor....25 Oct. 1701

nthony Morris elected mayor by the common council..5 Oct. 1703

irst Presbyterian church, called "Buttonwood church," built on south side Market st., between Second and Third......1704-5

hiladelphia Baptist Association organized, and church built at Pennepek or Lower Dublin.... 1707

ourt-house built on arches, used as a town-hall and seat of municipal council and legislature until 1735, erected on High st., between Second and Third.... 1710

irst almshouse established by the Friends in a house on south side of Walnut st., between Third and Fourth.... 1713

erry to Gloucester established.... 1715

ire-engine purchased by the council from Abraham Bickley for 50*l*....8 Dec. 1718

rdinance passed for paving the streets with stone, and footways with brick....Apr. 1719

merican Weekly Mercury, the first newspaper in America outside of Boston, established by Andrew S. Bradford...22 Dec. "

enjamin Franklin, aged 17, arrives in Philadelphia......Oct. 1723

arpenters' Guild established.... 1724

unto, or club for mutual improvement, organized by Franklin (the basis of the American Philosophical Society)....... 1727

riends' almshouse erected on site of one established 1713 (stood until 1841).... 1729

ranklin begins the *Pennsylvania Gazette*....28 Sept. "

hree fire-engines, total value about 100*l*., and 200 leather fire-buckets ordered from England, arrive....Jan. 1731

ranklin founds the Library of Philadelphia, sustained by subscription....8 Nov. "

atholic chapel of St. Joseph, on Walnut st., erected and mass celebrated by *father Greaton*....26 Feb. 1732

State in Schuylkill" (Schuylkill Fishing company) organized....1 May, "

irst stage route from Philadelphia to New York established.. "

ranklin's first "Poor Richard" almanac for 1733........Dec. "

tate-house, south side of Chestnut, between Fifth and Sixth sts., building begun 1732; first occupied by legislature..Oct. 1735

nion Fire company established....7 Dec. 1736

ranklin stove invented by Benj. Franklin.... 1742

ranklin establishes the American Philosophical Society..... 1743

[Society died out 10 years later, to be revived in 1769.]

econd Market-house, on Second st., south of Pine, established, 1745

itizens associate for military defence at a meeting....21 Nov. 1747

irst theatrical company appears in Philadelphia.... 1749

t. Andrew's Society formed.... "

treets lighted with lamps....Sept. 1751

allam's company give their first theatrical performance in a brick warehouse in *King or Water st.*, between Pine and Lombard sts.; play, "The Fair Penitent"....25 Apr. 1754

hime of 8 bells hung in Christ church.... "

ennsylvania general hospital, projected by dr. Thomas Bond; chartered 1751; opened Feb. 1752; corner-stone of building, on Pine st., between Eighth and Ninth, laid 28 May, 1755, and eastern wing opened....Dec. 1756

irst commencement at the college, on *Fourth st. below Arch*; chartered 16 June, 1755, and afterwards developed into the University of Pennsylvania....17 May, 1757

ct for "regulating, pitching, paving, and cleansing the streets, lanes, and alleys, etc., within the settled parts of Philadelphia," passed.... 1762

irst medical college in Philadelphia organized by dr. William Shippen, jr....Nov. "

irst fish market established between King and Front sts., Apr. 1764

on-importation agreement subscribed to by merchants and *traders of Philadelphia*....25 Oct. 1765

irst issue of the *Pennsylvania Chronicle* and *Universal Advertiser* by William Goddard....6 Jan. 1766

ld Southwark theatre, corner South and Apollo sts., opened (burned 9 May, 1821)....12 Nov. "

ransit of Venus successfully observed by the Am. Phil. Soc. at temporary observatory in the State-house yard....3 June, 1769

ethodist service held in an unfinished church bought and presented to the society, and named St. George's.......Nov. "

arpenters' hall built on south side Chestnut, between Third and Fourth sts.... 1770

ailors' mob; dr. Shippen's house damaged by rioters; the outcome of an excitement caused by supposed removal of dead bodies from the city burying-grounds for dissection in the medical college.... "

ammany Society started....1 May, 1772

irst Continental Congress assembles at Philadelphia...5 Sept. 1774

hiladelphia troop of light horse associated....17 Nov. "

piano, probably the first built in this country, made by John Behrent in Third st., below Brown. "Made of mahogany, being of the nature of a harpsichord, with hammers and several changes".... 1775

ew jail on Walnut st. completed and occupied....Jan. 1776

hiladelphia Society for Assisting Distressed Prisoners established (see 1787).... "

igning of the Declaration of Independence celebrated by a grand demonstration....8 July, "

mall-pox and camp-fever cause 2500 deaths.... 1776-77

hiladelphia occupied by the British under gen. Howe, 27 Sept. 1777

eschianza, on occasion of gen. Howe's farewell, held at the Wharton mansion and grounds at Walnut grove (junction of Fifth and Wharton sts.)....18 May, 1778

British evacuate Philadelphia....18 June, "

American Philosophical Society revived by union of 2 scientific societies, 1769; incorporated....15 Mch. 1780

Bank of North America incorporated....18 Dec. 1781

First English Bible printed in the U. S., published by R. Aitken, Market st.... 1782

First manufacture of fustians and jeans in the U. S. begins in Philadelphia.... "

Hot-air balloon ascension attempted from the prison-yard by Mr. Carnes of Baltimore, who was thrown out by basket striking prison-wall; balloon takes fire in mid-air...17 July, 1784

American Daily Advertiser, afterwards the *Aurora*, the first daily newspaper issued in America; Benjamin Franklin Bache, editor....21 Dec. "

Two city directories issued; *one by John Macpherson in Oct.* and one by Francis White.... 1785

Skiff-steamboat built by John Fitch and navigated at Philadelphia....26 July, 1786

"Society for Alleviating the Miseries of Public Prisons," an outgrowth of the society of 1776, established, with rt. rev. William White, D.D., president....May, 1787

Gen. Washington's birthday first celebrated officially by public salute of artillery....22 Feb. 1788

Celebration of the new Union by a federal procession...4 July, "

Levi and *Abraham* Doane, brothers, outlaws, hung on the commons....24 Sept. "

[They were of the noted Tory family of 6 brothers, the terror of Bucks county. The legislature set a price on their heads, 8 Apr. 1783. Joseph was shot and killed in Bucks county, 1783; Moses captured and executed, 1783; the hanging of Levi and Abraham left 2, Mahlon and Eleazar, under ban.]

City incorporated by act....11 Mch. 1789

Samuel Powel, first of the mayors elected by the council under new charter....13 Apr. "

Steamboat, 60 ft. in length, runs from Philadelphia to Burlington....Dec. "

Franklin d. in Philadelphia, aged 84....17 Apr. 1790

U. S. government removed from New York to Philadelphia, and Congress holds its session in the *county court-house*, erected and completed in Mch. 1789....6 Dec. "

Bank of North America begins keeping accounts in dollars and cents.... 1791

"Trustees of the University of Pennsylvania" incorporated... "

Bank of the United States, chartered 25 Feb.; subscription for stock opened, 4 July, and bank commences business in Carpenters' hall....Dec. "

[Branch banks established in Boston, New York, Baltimore, Washington, Norfolk, and Savannah.]

U. S. mint established *by act*, 2 Apr. 1792; mint erected on east side Seventh st., above Filbert, and coining begun..Oct. 1792

Blanchard, the French aeronaut, makes a balloon ascension from the prison-yard; witnessed by gen. Washington; he lands near Cooper's Ferry, N. J....9 Jan. 1793

Bank of Pennsylvania chartered....30 Mch. "

Yellow-fever epidemic; about 5000 deaths......1 Aug.-9 Nov. "

New theatre on Chestnut st., above Sixth, opened (*burned* 2 Apr. 1820; rebuilt and opened 2 Dec. 1822)....17 Feb. 1794

First turnpike road in the U. S. completed from Philadelphia to Lancaster, Pa., 62 miles.... "

White Fish, a small schooner, 23 ft. long, 6 ft. beam, arrives at Market st. wharf, after a voyage of nearly 1000 miles (29 covered by 5 portages), from Presque Isle on lake Erie, crossing New York state, and descending the Hudson to New York; boat in charge of John Thomson and David Lummis, 10 Nov. 1795

Select council, consisting of 12 citizens to serve 3 years, created by act of *legislature*....4 Apr. 1796

David Rittenhouse, astronomer, dies at his home, corner Arch and Seventh sts....26 June, "

First gas-light in America, exhibited by Ambroise & Co., manufacturers of fire-works, at their amphitheatre in Arch st., above Eighth....Aug. "

Yellow-fever epidemic; 1292 deaths....17 Aug.-Nov. 1797

Act passed allowing chains to be placed across the *streets in front* of churches during service to prevent passage of wagons, 4 Apr. 1798

Yellow-fever epidemic, 3645 deaths.... "

Bill to *remove* the seat of state government to Lancaster after Nov. 1799, signed by the governor....3 Apr. 1799

U. S. government removed from Philadelphia to Washington, July, 1800

Ground broken for water-works in Chestnut st., 12 Mch. 1799, and city first supplied with water from the Schuylkill through street mains....1 Jan. 1801

The *Portfolio*, by "Oliver Oldschool" (Joseph Dennie), first issued....3 Jan. "

Philadelphia Society for the Free Instruction of Indigent Boys opens a night school, 1800, and is incorporated.... "

Charles Wilson Peale opens his museum in the upper part of the state-house....spring of 1802

[In his collection were the Ulster county, N. Y., mastodon skeletons. *Museum removed to the Arcade building*, 1828.]

Republication of the "Encyclopædia Britannica" begun, 1790, by Thomas Dobson at the Stone-house in Second st., near Chestnut, and completed.... 1803

Philadelphia hose company organized....15 Dec. "

Bank of Philadelphia incorporated....5 Mch. 1804

Coach route established from Philadelphia to Pittsburg...Aug. "

Corner-stone of permanent bridge across the Schuylkill *laid*, 18 Oct. 1800; bridge opened to the public....1 Jan. 1805

"Orukter Amphiboles, or Amphibious Digger," a heavy mud

PHI

flat, with machinery for cleaning docks, run by a steam engine, invented by Oliver Evans designed for land or water, is exhibited on wheels on Centre square July, 1805

Commission house for sale of cotton yarns and thread made at Providence, R I (the first in the U S) opened "

Pennsylvania Academy of Fine Arts incorporated 17 Mch 1806, and building erected the same year in Chestnut st. between Eleventh and Twelfth sts 1806

Farmers and Mechanics' National bank organized 17 Jan 1807

Adelphi school or "Hollow School," on Pegg's Run, in the Northern Liberties, opened under auspices of Philadelphia Association for the Instruction of Poor Children 11 Jan 1808

New building of Bank of Philadelphia, northwest cor Fourth and Chestnut sts., completed (stood until 1836) "

Steamboat *Phœnix* arrives at Philadelphia from New York, the first steamboat navigating the ocean June, "

Philadelphia's first fountain, a carved wooden figure of Leda and the swan, by Rush, erected on Centre square 1809

New prison in Arch st opened (abandoned 1836) "

First Sunday school, under the control of the churches and confined to religious instruction, organized "

Experimental railroad set up in the Bull's Head tavern yard by Thomas Leiper, on which, with a grade of 1½ inches in a yard, a single horse "hauled up a 4 wheeled carriage loaded with the enormous weight of 1696 pounds" Sept "

First steam ferry between Philadelphia and Camden 1810

George Frederick Cooke, English tragedian, makes his first appearance at Chestnut street theatre as *Richard III*, receipts the first night, $1,348 50 25 Mch 1811

Academy of Natural Sciences founded 21 Mch 1812

Spring Garden st bridge built by the Upper Ferry Bridge company over the Schuylkill and opened Jan 1813

[Burned 1 Sept 1838 and replaced by a wire suspension bridge built by Charles Ellet and completed 2 Jan 1842 This was replaced in 1875 by bridge built by Keystone Bridge company]

Religious Remembrancer, first religious weekly newspaper in the U S, established 4 Sept "

Athenæum of Philadelphia founded, 1814, incorporated 5 Apr 1815

Fairmount water works pumping station completed 7 Sept "

[Dam completed, 1822]

Second United States bank established 10 Apr 1816

State house property purchased by city from the state "

White & Hazard erect a wire suspension foot bridge at the falls of Schuylkill "

Gas lights exhibited in Peale's museum, Apr 1816, and theatre lighted by gas, the first place of amusement in the U S. so lighted 25 Nov "

Philadelphia Sunday and Adults' School Union formed, Alexander Henry president 1817

First U S custom house erected on Second st. below Dock, and opened 12 July, 1819

Musical Fund Society established 1820

Apprentices' Library incorporated and Philadelphia Law Library established 1821

Saturday Evening Post established "

Pennsylvania institution for the deaf and dumb opened "

Mercantile Library Association organized, 17 Nov, and constitution adopted 1 Dec "

First lodge of Odd Fellows in the state (Pennsylvania No 1) organized in Philadelphia 26 Dec "

American edition of "Rees' Cyclopædia," in 47 vols., completed 1822

Franklin Institute organized . 5 Feb. 1824

Reception tendered gen Lafayette 28 Sept. "

American Sunday school Union founded in Philadelphia . "

Historical Society of Pennsylvania organized 2 Dec. "

Musical Fund hall, Locust st west of Eighth st, opened, 24 Dec. "

Jefferson Medical college incorporated 7 Apr 1826

United States hotel, Chestnut st, between Fourth and Fifth sts, north side, opened "

Store for the sale of American hardware, the first in the U S, opened by Amos Goodyear & Sons. 1827

Penn Treaty monument erected on Beach st, Kensington. "

Corner stone of the Philadelphia arcade, Chestnut and Carpenter sts, laid 3 May, 1826, building completed Sept. "

[Torn down, 1863]

Pennsylvania Horticultural Society founded, 78 members, 21 Dec. "

[Incorporated 24 Mch 1831, Horticultural hall, adjoining Academy of Music, opened, 29 May, 1867, destroyed by fire, 31 Jan 1881, and rebuilt]

Arch street theatre, on Arch st, west of Sixth st. opened, 1 Oct. 1828

[Theatre rebuilt, 1863]

House of Refuge erected on Ridge road and Fairmount ave, corner stone laid, 21 June, 1827, formally opened. 29 Nov "

Name of Centre square changed to Penn square 19 May, 1829

Philadelphia Inquirer first issued as the *Pennsylvania Inquirer* . 29 June, "

A series of riots between whites and blacks begin 22 Nov "

William Cramp establishes his ship yard at Kensington 1830

Christopher C Conwell issues the *Cent*, the first one cent daily paper issued in the U S . "

Godey's Lady's Book established . July, "

Stephen Girard d at his home on Water st., above Market, 26 Dec "

Corner stone of the Philadelphia Exchange laid. 22 Feb 1832

Corner stone of Philadelphia county prison laid at Moyamensing . 2 Apr "

Girard National bank incorporated Apr "

Cholera epidemic, 2314 cases reported. 935 deaths, 5 July–4 Oct "

Railroad to Germantown opened, 6 June, 1832, and locomotive engine first used. .. .. 23 Nov "

Corner stone of an intended monument to Washington laid in Washington square 22 Feb 1833

First triennial parade of the Fire Department 27 Mch "

John Randolph of Roanoke, Va, d. at the City hotel 24 May, "

Philadelphia club organized "

First omnibus line, navy yard to Kensington "

Pennsylvania institution for the instruction of the blind opened, "

Riot between whites and blacks, colored people's church destroyed 12-13 Aug "

Board of Trade organized 15 Oct. "

Merchants' Exchange organized, 19 May, 1831, and building occupied 1834

Epiphany church, Fifteenth and Chestnut sts, consecrated, 1 Oct. "

Streets first lighted with gas 8 Feb 1836

Public Ledger established 25 Mch "

Laurel Hill Cemetery company incorporated 9 Feb 1837

Last public execution in Philadelphia takes place at present intersection of Seventeenth and Green sts., James Moran, convicted 27 Apr for murder on the high seas, 22 Nov 1836, of capt Smith of the schooner *William Wirt*, hung 19 May, "

Pennsylvania hall, cor Sixth and Haines st, dedicated as an Abolitionist hall on 14 May is burned by a mob 17 May, 1838

High school on Juniper st, east of Penn square, opened 21 Oct. "

[Building sold to Pennsylvania Railroad company in 1853.]

Fire breaks out on Chestnut st wharf, and burns about 40 buildings, 2 firemen killed and 7 injured by falling walls 4 Oct. 1839

City purchases the gas works. 1841

John Morin Scott, first mayor elected by the people 12 Oct "

Riots between native Americans and Irish suppressed by the military Apr–May, 1844

Telegraphic communication between Philadelphia and Fort Lee, opposite New York, completed 20 Jan 1846

Philadelphia and Pittsburg connected by telegraph 26 Dec. "

Philadelphia *Evening Bulletin* established 12 Apr 1847

North American and *United States Gazette* consolidated, 1 July, "

Evening Item established "

Girard college corner stone laid 4 July, 1833, transferred to the directors, 13 Nov 1847, and opened 1 Jan 1848

St Mark's church, Locust st, near Sixteenth, corner stone laid 25 Apr 1848, consecrated 21 May, 1849

Cholera epidemic, whole number of deaths in city and county, 1012, epidemic at its height 13 July (32 deaths), 30 May–8 Sept. "

Race riot, whites burn the California House, cor Sixth and St Mary's sts., the proprietor being a mulatto and his wife a white woman 9 Oct. "

Woman's Medical college of Pennsylvania, oldest regular college for female physicians incorporated 11 Mch. 1850

Act to establish the marshal's police passed 3 May, "

[Repealed, 1856]

Fire breaks out on North Water st below Vine, 367 buildings destroyed, an explosion kills 28 and injures 58 persons, 9 July, "

Freshet on the Schuylkill, water at Fairmount dam about 11 feet above ordinary level, portions of the city flooded, including the gas works, and city left in darkness 3 Sept. "

Reception to Louis Kossuth 24 Dec 1851

Girard House opened 1852

Manufacture of galvanized iron begun in Philadelphia. "

Lafayette hotel opened (enlarged, 1883) Oct 1853

Consolidation act extending the city so as to include Philadelphia county, passed 2 Feb 1854

Young Men's Christian Association instituted June, "

High school, Broad and Green sts., dedicated 28 June, "

Line of passenger cars drawn by horses, from Willow st. along Front, etc, to Cohocksink depot, about 1½ miles, established by the North Pennsylvania Railway company 3 Jan 1855

Wagner Free Institute of Science opened by gov Pollock, 21 May, "

Fairmount Park improvement begun by purchase of the Lemon Hill estate, 24 July, 1844, and Lemon Hill park dedicated, 18 Sept "

[Sedgely acquired, 1856, Lansdown, 1866]

Masonic hall, on Chestnut st. above Seventh, dedicated 27 Sept. "

[The winter of 1855–56 was very severe, the Delaware froze from bank to bank as far down as the "Horseshoe channel" On 15 Mch 1856, the Philadelphia and Camden ferry boat *New Jersey* caught in a mass of ice, and taking fire burned, over 30 out of 100 passengers lost their lives.]

Police and fire alarm telegraph goes into operation 19 Apr 1856

Office of chief of police created by act 13 May, "

Collision of a Sunday school excursion train from Kensington, carrying 600 children and young people, with a passenger-train at Camp Hill, over 50 killed and 100 injured 17 July, "

Corner stone of the Pennsylvania Hospital for the Insane laid, 1 Oct "

United States agricultural exhibition opened 7 Oct "

Streets first swept by revolving machine-brooms. .. "

Opera house or American Academy of Music, corner stone laid 26 July, 1855, opened with a ball 26 Jan 1857, and with the first operatic performance, "Il Trovatore" . 25 Feb. 1857

The *Press* established 1 Aug "

Bank of Pennsylvania closes its doors 25 Sept "

Cathedral of Sts Peter and Paul, corner stone laid 16 Sept 1846, dedicated .. 13 Dec "

Fifth and Sixth sts railroad, first car run 8 Jan, and opened to the public 20 Jan 1858

First steam fire engine, the "Miles Greenwood," from Cincinnati, exhibited 12 Feb 1855, and first engine purchased by the city, arrives 20 Jan "

Church of the Holy Trinity built "

St. Clement's church, Twentieth and Cherry sts., erected 1858–59

Sunday School Times established 1859

Continental hotel opened to the public (ARTESIAN WELLS), 13 Feb 1860
Japanese embassy, guests of the city, arrive 9 June, "
First artillery regiment, Pennsylvania volunteers, col Francis E Patterson, leaves the city for the South 8 May, 1861
First regiment National Guards, Penn vols and Philadelphia Light Guards regiment and First regiment Pennsylvania volunteers leave for the South 14 May, "
Cooper shop volunteer refreshment saloon which catered to more than 600 000 soldiers passing the city during the war, opened on Otsego st, near Washington ave May, "
St Paul's Catholic church built 1843 et seq, burned 25 Nov "
Christ church hospital, begun 1856, entirely completed 14 Dec "
Union League club organized 15 Nov 1862
New Chestnut st theatre opened, Edwin Forrest as "Virginius" and McCullough as "Icilius" 26 Jan 1863
First National bank, the first organized under the National Banking act, incorporated 10 Jan 1863, and opened 11 July, "
Evening Telegraph first issued 4 Jan 1864
Philadelphia Sanitary fair opens 7 June, "
Philadelphia and Erie railroad formally opened 4 Oct "
Fire in Ninth st and Washington ave, 50 buildings burned, fire begins in a coal oil establishment 8 Feb 1865
New Municipal hospital opened 27 Apr "
Coldest day on record, thermometer at Merchants' Exchange 18° below zero 7 Jan 1866
Great fire in North Third st, loss, $800 000, begins in Roberts's hardware store 26 Feb "
Evening Star first issued 2 Apr "
Public Ledger building opened 20 June, "
Chestnut-st bridge, begun 19 Sept 1861, opened 23 June, "
Reception of flags returned to the state, held on Independence square 4 July, "
New court house begun 2 Nov 1866, opened. 1867
Americus club organized 30 Apr "
Explosion at Geasy & Ward's saw mill, Samson st., 22 killed, 7 injured 6 June, "
American (formerly Continental) theatre, on Walnut st, burned, 10 lives lost by falling walls 19 June, "
Lippincott's Magazine established 1868
Monument to Washington and Lafayette, Monument cemetery, dedicated 29 May, 1869
Washington monument in front of the state house dedicated, 5 July, "
Mercantile Library company remove to the Franklin Market house (erected 1860), Tenth st., above Chestnut 15 July, "
Record first issued as the *Public Record* 14 May, 1870
St James's church erected "
Chamber of Commerce dedicated 1 Mch 1869, burned 7 Dec 1869, rebuilt and opened 27 Dec. "
Volunteer fire department abolished 1870, and paid department goes into operation 15 Mch 1871
Fire destroys a planing mill in Marshall st. and about 40 other buildings 5 June, "
Lincoln monument in Fairmount park unveiled 22 Sept "
Public building of Philadelphia commenced "
[When completed its estimated cost will be over $10,000,000, it will cover over 4 acres, its tower will be 537½ ft. high, surmounted by a bronze statue of William Penn 36 ft high, to be completed 1895]
Small pox epidemic, 4464 deaths 1871-72
Corner stone of the new building for the Pennsylvania Academy of Fine Arts, southwest corner Broad and Cherry sts, laid 7 Dec 1872
Banking houses of Jay Cooke & Co and E W Clarke & Co close their doors. 18 Sept 1873
New Masonic temple, Broad and Filbert sts, dedicated, 25 Sept. "
Produce Exchange organized 25 Apr 1874
Hospital of the University of Pennsylvania, main building completed and dedicated 4 June, "
Little Charley Ross, son of Christian K Ross, abducted from his home 1 July, "
New bridge over the Schuylkill at Girard ave opened 4 July, "
Corner stone of the new public buildings on Penn square laid, 4 July, "
Centennial celebration of the formation of the first city troop, 15-17 Nov "
The *Times*, daily, established 13 Mch 1875
Penn club organized 18 Mch "
The *Call* daily, established "
Religious revival, Moody and Sankey, evangelists, hold their first service in the old freight depot, southwest corner Thirteenth and Market sts 21 Nov "
Market st. bridge destroyed by fire, 20 Nov 1875, rebuilt in 21 days by the Pennsylvania Railway company "
Academy of Natural Sciences building, corner stone laid 30 Oct 1872, occupied 11 Jan and opened to the public 2 May, 1876
Centennial exhibition at Fairmount park opens 10 May, "
Normal school, northeast corner Seventeenth and Spring Garden sts, dedicated 30 Oct "
Ex pres. Grant sails from Philadelphia for his trip around the world 15 May, 1877
Aldine hotel opened "
Jefferson Medical College hospital formally opened. 17 Sept "
First telephone exchange established 1878
Oil refinery fire caused by lightning, which destroys several refineries and 5 vessels loading at the docks, and burns for 2 days, begins. 11 June, 1879
News established "
First electric lighting, the store and warerooms of John Wanamaker, at Thirteenth and Market sts . Dec. "
Committee of 100 organized. Dec 1880
Randolph cotton and woollen mills Randolph st., burned, 9 employees killed, 13 seriously injured 12 Oct 1881
Chestnut st lighted by 47 electric lights, first electric street lights in the city 3 Dec "
Two hundredth anniversary of the settlement of Philadelphia celebrated. 22-27 Oct 1882
Enterprise cotton and woollen mills, Main st burned, 2 killed 16 injured 12 Dec "
William Penn's cottage (the Letitia house), built in Market st, between Front and Second sts, about 1683, the first brick house in Philadelphia, rebuilt in Fairmount park 1883
Ladies' Home Journal established "
Nineteen out of 26 buildings in the block bounded by Knox, Brown Kessler, and Parrish sts destroyed by fire, loss, $1,500 000 28 Feb 1884
New post office building opened for business Mch "
Fire destroys 9 large business houses, loss $3,000,000 19 Feb 1885
John McCullough d at his home, aged 48 8 Nov "
Temple theatre burned, 2 firemen killed, loss $100,000 27 Dec 1886
Reform charter or the "Bullett act," for the better government of cities, passed 1 June, 1886 takes effect 1 Apr 1887
Constitutional centennial celebration 15-17 Sept "
First electric street railroad opened Nov 1892
George W Childs, philanthropist and proprietor of the *Public Ledger*, d. 3 Feb 1894

MAYORS

Edward Shippen	1701	Thomas Lawrence	1764
Anthony Morris	1703	John Lawrence	1765
Griffith Jones	1704	Isaac Jones	1767
Joseph Wilcox	1705	Samuel Shoemaker	1769
Nathan Stanbury	1706	John Gibson	1771
Thomas Masters	1707	William Fisher	1773
Richard Hill	1709	Samuel Rhoads	1774
William Carter	1710	Samuel Powel	1775
Samuel Preston	1711	(Office vacant, 1776-89)	
Jonathan Dickinson	1712	Samuel Powel	1789
George Roche	1713	Samuel Miles	1790
Richard Hill	1714	John Barclay	1791
Jonathan Dickinson	1717	Matthew Clarkson	1792
William Fishbourne	1719	Hilary Baker	1796
James Logan	1722	Robert Wharton	1798
Clement Plumsted	1723	John Inskeep	1800
Isaac Norris	1724	Matthew Lawler	1801
William Hudson	1725	John Inskeep	1804
Charles Read	1726	Robert Wharton	1806
Thomas Lawrence	1728	John Baker	1808
Thomas Griffitts.	1729	Robert Wharton	1810
Samuel Hasell	1731	Michael Keppele	1811
Thomas Griffitts	1733	John Baker	1812
Thomas Lawrence	1734	John Geyer	1813
William Allen	1735	Robert Wharton	1814
Clement Plumsted	1736	James Nelson Barker	1819
Thomas Griffitts	1737	Robert Wharton	1820
Anthony Morris	1738	Joseph Watson	1824
Edward Roberts	1739	George Mifflin Dallas	1828
Samuel Hasell	1740	Benjamin W Richards	1829
Clement Plumsted	1741	William Milnor	1829
William Till	1742	Benjamin W Richards	1830
Benjamin Shoemaker	1743	John Swift	1832
Edward Shippen	1744	Isaac Roach	1838
James Hamilton	1745	John Swift	1839
William Attwood	1746	John Morin Scott	1841
Charles Willing	1748	Peter McCall	1844
Thomas Lawrence	1749	John Swift.	1845
William Plumsted	1750	Joel Jones	1849
Robert Strettell	1751	Charles Gilpin	1850
Benjamin Shoemaker	1752	Robert Taylor Conrad	1854
Thomas Lawrence	1753	Richard Vaux	1856
Charles Willing	1754	Alexander Henry	1858
William Plumsted	1754	Morton McMichael	1866
Attwood Shute	1756	Daniel Miller Fox	1869
Thomas Lawrence	1758	William Strumburg Stokley	1872
John Stamper	1759	Samuel George King	1881
Benjamin Shoemaker	1760	William Burns Smith	1884
Jacob Duché	1761	Edwin H Fitler	1888
Henry Harrison	1762	Edwin S Stuart	1891
Thomas William	1763	Charles F Warwick	1895

Philadelphia, a city in Asia Minor SEVEN CHURCHES

Philip'haugh, near Selkirk, S Scotland, where the marquess of Montrose and the royalists were defeated by David Leslie and the Scotch Covenanters, 13 Sept. 1645

Philip'pi, a city of Macedonia, so named by Philip II of Macedon. Here Octavius Cæsar and Marc Antony, in 2 battles, defeated the republican forces of Cassius and Brutus, who both committed suicide, Oct 42 B C Paul preached here, 48 A.D, and wrote an epistle to the converts, 64

Philip'pics, originally the orations of Demosthenes against Philip II of Macedon, 352-341 B.C The name was given also to the orations of Cicero against Marc Antony, because of the vigor of invective in them (one of which, called divine by Juvenal, cost Cicero his life), 44-43 B.C, and has since been often used to describe any oratorical attack upon persons in power.

Phil'ippine islands, in the Malay archipelago, discovered by Magellan, in Mch 1521, who here lost his life in a skirmish They were taken possession of in 1565 by a fleet from Mexico, which first stopped at the island of Zeba, and subdued it In 1570 a settlement was effected at the mouth of the Manila river, and Manila became the capital of the Spanish possessions in the Philippines The Philippine group numbers about 2000 islands, great and small The actual land area is about 140,000 miles The 6 New England states, New York, and New Jersey have about an equivalent area The island of Luzon, on which the capital city (Manila) is situated, is the largest member of the group, being about the size of the state of New York Mindanao is nearly as large, but its population is very much smaller The latest estimates of areas of the largest islands are as follows Luzon, 41,400, Mindanao, 34,000, Samar, 4800, Panay, 4700, Mindoro, 4000, Leyte, 3800, Negros, 3300, Cebu, 2400 A census of the Philippines was taken by the U S government, under the auspices of the Census Bureau, in 1902-3, the estimate of population is about 8,000,000, of whom about 7,000,000 are civilized and the remainder savages Racially the inhabitants are principally Malays The country had been in the possession of Spain since 1565, and the religion introduced by the proprietors has long been that of the natives. The church has been a strong ruling power and the priesthood numerous There are 30 different races, all speaking different dialects The climate is one of the best in the tropics The islands extend from 5° to 21° N lat, and Manila is in 14° 35′ The thermometer during July and August rarely goes below 79° or above 85° The extreme ranges in a year are said to be 61° and 97°. There are 3 well marked seasons temperate and dry from Nov to Feb, hot and dry from Mch to May, and temperate and wet from June to Oct. The rainy season reaches its maximum in July and Aug The total rainfall has been as high as 114 inches in 1 year Although agriculture is the chief occupation of the Filipinos, yet only one-ninth of the surface is under cultivation The soil is very fertile, and it is probable that the area of cultivation can be very largely extended, and that the islands can support a population of 50,000,000 The chief products are rice, corn, hemp, sugar, tobacco, cocoanuts, and cacao. Coffee and cotton were formerly produced in large quantities—the former for export and the latter for home consumption, but the coffee-plant has been almost exterminated by insects, and the home-made cotton cloths have been driven out by the competition of those imported from England The rice and corn are principally produced in Luzon and Mindoro, and are consumed in the islands The cacao is raised in the southern islands, the best quality of it at Mindanao. The sugar cane is raised in the Visayas. The hemp is produced in S. Luzon, Mindoro, the Visayas, and Mindanao It is nearly all exported in bales Tobacco is raised in all the islands, but the best quality and greatest amount in Luzon A large amount is consumed in the islands, smoking being universal among women as well as the men, but the best quality is exported In the fiscal year ending June 30, 1904, the exports from the U S to the Philippines were $1,832,900, and the total imports from the Philippines for the same period were $12,066,934 The imports from foreign countries, year ending June 30, 1903, were $32,971,882, and the exports were $33,121,780 The principal foreign countries trading with the Philippines are Great Britain, the United States, China, and Spain On July 1, 1902, Congress passed "An act temporarily to provide for the administration of the affairs of civil government in the Philippine islands, and for other purposes" Under this act military rule was terminated. EARTHQUAKE, MANILA.

MILITARY GOVERNORS

Gen Wesley Merritt . . . 11 May, 1898
Gen Elwell S Otis . . 29 Aug "
Gen Adna R Chaffee .. . . 4 July, 1900

CIVIL GOVERNORS

William H Taft ... . 5 June, 1901
Luke E Wright . . .. 25 Aug 1903

Manila has suffered greatly by earthquakes. It is stated that nearly 3000 persons perished by one in. . . . 1645
Manila was taken by the English, when the archbishop engaged to ransom it for about a million sterling, never wholly paid. . . .. 6 Oct 1762
The city nearly destroyed . . Sept 1852
And about 1000 lives were lost in the earthquake of 3 July, 1863

Destructive typhoon . 20, 21 Oct. 1882
Great fire 4000 houses burned, many deaths . 1 Apr 1893
Conflicts with the natives, reported Mch *et seq*, the natives defeated 24 July, 1894
Severe fighting in Mindanao, the Malay Mohammedans defeated, their sultan killed . 10 Mch. 1895
Great fire, 30,000 persons homeless, reported 5 Apr 1896
Insurrection near Manila, state of siege proclaimed, rebels repulsed 30 Aug. "
Help from Hong Kong requested Sept "
Rebels defeated in 2 engagements, many ringleaders killed and others captured and shot Sept "
Insurgents suffer heavy losses in 10 engagements near Manila, a plot discovered and 100 conspirators arrested Sept "
The insurgents masters of all the towns in Cavité, convents sacked, Spanish monks (40) murdered in the island of Luzon 19, 20 Sept. "
Mutiny of native soldiers in Mindanao officers killed Oct "
Gen Polavieja succeeds gen Blanco as governor general Dec. "
Revolt of some of the troops at Mindanao Dec "
Insurgents defeated at Bulacan Dec "
Dr Rizal shot for fomenting the rebellion . 28 Dec "
Insurgents surprised and routed at Agony, Alimansas, and Novelcta . Jan 1897
13 persons, charged with conspiracy, shot . 4 Jan "
Señ Rojas and 11 other insurgents shot, as instigators of the rebellion . 11 Jan "
Signal victory by the Spaniards, Silang stronghold captured, much slaughter Feb "
Native rising in Manila city, suppressed with bloodshed, 25 Feb "
Salitran captured by the Spaniards, gen Zaballa, 5 officers, 10 men and 76 insurgents killed . . Mch "
Gen Primo de Rivera appointed captain general Mch "
Imus and Cavité captured by the Spaniards, Mch, Naic, 500 rebels killed and 200 prisoners . May, "
Rebels repulsed with loss at San Rafael Aug "
Fire, public buildings destroyed, several deaths, 28 Sept "
Disastrous cyclone at Leyte .. 12 Oct. "
Complete submission of rebels in return for pardon, 25 Nov *et seq* "
Aguinaldo, rebel chief, exiled to Hong Kong 27 Dec. "
Great Fire, 200 houses burned, reported 7 Feb 1898
Gen Augustin appointed governor general 26 Feb "
A Spanish detachment surprised and 40 killed at Bolinao, Mch "
Battle of Manila Bay (SPANISH-AMERICAN WAR), adm Dewey destroys the Spanish fleet . 30 Apr-May, "
Rebel town in Panay island captured by the Spaniards and destroyed, great slaughter, 672 rebels killed, reported, 8 May, "
Assembly of 15 members of natives and others, instituted by the governor general, señ Paterno, president 13 May, "
Aguinaldo returns from Hong Kong supplied with arms, etc., captures Cavité province after 3 days' fighting, the whole archipelago in revolt except Visayas isles, 31 May-2 June, concessions offered to the natives by gen. Augustin, he appeals to Madrid for help 8 June, "
Aguinaldo allies himself with the insurgents in the north, insurgent conquest of Luzon, 9000 Spanish prisoners, 9 Sept., the insurgents evacuate Manila, 14 Sept, the Filipino republic constituted at Malolos, gen Aguinaldo president Nov "
The Spaniards, under gen Rios, evacuate Iloilo 24 Dec "
The government of the islands taken over by the U S, proclamation issued 5 Jan 1899
Spanish governor and officers murdered by natives at Port Royal, reported 23 Jan "
The U S flag raised by the natives on Negros island Feb "
The Filipinos under Aguinaldo attack the American defences at Manila. The Americans assume the offensive the next day, and in the fighting which ensued for several days the American loss is 57 killed and 215 wounded. 500 Filipinos are killed, 1000 wounded, and 500 captured 4 Feb "
Battle of Caloocan . .. 10 Feb "
Iloilo and Jaro captured by gen Miller 11, 12 Feb "
Aguinaldo issues a manifesto calling on the Filipinos to declare their independence, 8 Jan, again . . 22 Feb "
Sharp fighting in and around Manila, incendiary fires, insurgents driven out with heavy loss 21-24 Feb "
Gen Wheaton attacked and occupied Pasig 13-19 Mch "
Gen MacArthur advances towards and captures Malolos, 21-30 Mch "
Insurgents repulsed with great loss at Caloocan 25 Mch "
Col Egbert and prince Loewenstein killed near Polo 26 Mch "
Aguinaldo's main army routed near Malolos . 27 Mch "

[Military operations were partially suspended during the rainy season Meanwhile the southern islands were occupied by the American forces, Iloilo by gen Miller, 11 Feb, Cebu by the navy, 27 Mch, and Negros, Mindanao, and the smaller islands subsequently A treaty was concluded with the sultan of Sulu, in which his rights were guaranteed and he acknowledged the supremacy of the U S With the advance of the dry season military operations on a much larger scale than heretofore were begun, the army of occupation having been reinforced by 30,000 men]

The commission issue a proclamation promising "the amplest liberty of self government reconcilable with just, stable, effective, and economical administration and compatible with the sovereign rights and obligations of the U S" 4 Apr "
Yorktown U S warship, rescues 85 Spaniards at Balar Luzon, lieut. Gillmore and 14 men captured . 12 Apr "
Rebel intrenchments carried by gens. MacArthur and Hale's brigades, 75 rebels killed . ... 24 Apr. "

Calumpit captured, the Rio Grande river crossed by U S troops under gen Wheaton, Americans advance to Apalit, 26, 27 Apr 1899

Gen Lawton leads an expedition to San Isidro 22 Apr -17 May, "

Gen MacArthur captures Calumpit and San Fernando, 25 Apr -5 May, "

U S civil commissioners receive Aguinaldo's peace commissioners, negotiations fail 22 May, "

Enemy repulsed near San Fernando, 50 killed and 28 captured, 24 May, "

Gen Luna, insurgent officer assassinated at Cabanatuan 6 June, "

Gen Lawton defeats the rebels on the Zapote river 13 June, "

Insurgent attack on San Fernando repulsed 16 June, "

Gens Lawton and Wheaton advance south to Imus, 10-19 June, "

Gen Hall takes Calamba 26 June "

Gen MacArthur drives the rebels north from San Fernando, 9 Aug "

Chinese exclusion law applied to the islands by gen Otis Aug "

Gen MacArthur captures Angeles 16 Aug "

Col Snyder defeats the rebels near Cebu 22-23 Sept. "

Gen MacArthur, after several days' fighting, occupies Porac, 28 Sept "

Gen Schwan's column operates in the southern part of Luzon and captures Rosario and Malabon 1-10 Oct "

Cabal occupied 31 Oct "

The Philippine commission, appointed by the president, consisting of J G Schurman, prof Dean Worcester, Charles Denby, adm Dewey, and gen Otis which began its labors at Manila, 20 Mch, and returned to the U S in Sept, submits its preliminary report to the president 2 Nov "

A military expedition on board transports, under gen Wheaton, captures Dagupan 7 Nov "

Col Bell captures Tarlac, the Filipino government seat, 12 Nov "

Insurgents routed near San Jacinto 12 Nov "

3000 Spanish prisoners released during Nov "

Col March destroys Aguinaldo's body guard, and liberates 575 Spaniards, reported 13 Dec "

Gen Lawton killed while leading the attack on San Mateo, reported 19 Dec "

Gen S B M Young appointed military governor of north-western Luzon 25 Dec "

The Filipino gen Santo Ana, with a force of insurgents attacks the garrison at Subig, the Americans successfully repelled the attack 26 Dec "

Col Lockett, with a force of 2500 men, attacks a force of insurgents near Montalban, many Filipinos killed 27 Dec "

General advance of the American troops in S Luzon, Cabuyac, on Laguna de Bay, taken by 2 battalions of the 39th infantry, 2 Americans killed and 4 wounded 1 Jan 1900

Lieut Gillmore and the party of Americans held as prisoners by the Filipinos arrive at Manila 7 Jan "

A troop of the 3d cavalry defeats the insurgents near San Fernando de la Union, the Americans lose 2 killed and 3 wounded, gen Otis reports all of Cavite province as occupied by gen Wheaton 12 Jan "

Lieut McRae, with a company of the 3d infantry, defeats an insurgent force under gen Hizon, and captures rifles and ammunition near Mabalacat 17 Jan "

Gen Schwan captures San Diego, insurgents routed, 67 killed, 21 Jan "

5000 Filipino insurgents attack American garrison at Duroga and are repulsed 6 Feb "

Expedition under gens. Bates and Bell leave Manila to crush rebellion in Camarines 16 Feb "

Civil commission appointed by pres McKinley (Wm H Taft, Dean C Worcester, Luke E Wright, Henry C Ide, Bernard Moses), they reach the Philippines in April Mch "

Gen Otis relieved, succeeded by gen MacArthur 7 Apr "

Gen. Pantelon Garcia, the chief Filipino insurgent in central Luzon, is captured . 5 May, "

Insurgents capture San Miguel de Mayomo, 5 Americans killed, 7 wounded, and capt Charles D Reports made a prisoner, 29 May, "

Gen Pio del Pilar is captured at San Pedro Macati 8 June, "

Gen MacArthur issues a proclamation of amnesty 21 June, "

U S military stations, 53, 1 Nov 1899, 413 1 Sept, "

Fresh outbreaks, desperate fight at Mavitac, American loss heavy . mid Sept "

3227 insurgents killed, 694 wounded, 2684 captured, 1 Nov 1899-1 Sept. "

[Total American loss, 357 killed or mortally wounded, 1085 died from disease, 1899-1900]

Brisk fighting near San Jacinto, maj John A. Logan killed, 14 Nov "

Gen Otis announces to the war department that the whole of central Luzon is in the hands of the U S authorities, that the president of the Filipino congress, the Filipino secretary of state, and treasurer are captured, and that only small bands of the enemy are in arms, retreating in different directions, while Aguinaldo, a fugitive with a small escort, is being pursued towards the mountains 24 Nov "

Bautista, president of the Filipino congress, surrenders to gen MacArthur . . . 24 Nov "

The navy captures Vigan, on the coast 26 Nov, "

At Pavia, island of Panay, the 18th and 19th regiments drive the Filipinos out of their trenches, a captain and 1 private killed . . 26 Nov "

Col. Bell disperses the insurgents in the Dagupan valley, Bayombong, in the province of Nueva Viscaya, defended by 800 armed Filipinos, surrenders to lieut. Monroe and 50 men of the 4th cavalry ... . 28 Nov "

Gen Gregorio del Pilar, one of the Filipino insurgent leaders, is killed in a fight near Cervantes 3 Dec 1900

Vigan, held by American troops under lieut col Parker, attacked by 800 Filipinos, they are driven off, leaving 40 killed and 32 prisoners, the Americans lose 8 men 4 Dec "

Gen Tierona, the Filipino insurgent commander in Cagayan, surrenders the entire province to capt McCalla. 11 Dec "

The president directs gen Otis to open the ports of the Philippines to commerce 11 Dec "

Deportation of insurgent generals and others to Guam Jan 1901

Treaty with Spain for the purchase of the island of Cibutu and Cagayan for $100,000 ratified by U S senate 22 Jan "

Petition from Filipino federal party praying for civil government presented to the senate 28 Jan "

21 officers and 120 bolomen surrender 1 Mch "

Gen Trias, 9 officers, and 199 men surrender, reported 16 Mch "

Aguinaldo captured by gen Funston 23 Mch "

Aguinaldo takes oath of allegiance . 2 Apr "

The Americans release 1000 prisoners 19 Apr "

Gen Tinio surrenders 20 Apr "

U S Philippine commission appoints Arellano, chief justice, and 6 other supreme court judges 15 June, "

Total American expenditure on the war, $170,326,586, reported, 20 June, "

Promulgation of pres McKinley's order establishing civil government, William H Taft the first governor 21 June, "

Gen MacArthur is succeeded by gen Chaffee 23 June "

American authority accepted, pacification complete, except in the Moro country, Aguinaldo and other political prisoners pardoned, general amnesty proclaimed 1-4 July, "

Civil government established 4 July, "

Gen Bellarmino and 1000 men surrender 6 July, "

Gen Zimbano, with 547 men, surrenders at Zabayas 24 July, "

Maj Alhambra and the remnants of Aguinaldo's followers captured at Casiguran, reported 22 Sept "

Massacre of 48 Americans at Balangiga Samar 29 Sept "

Insurrection prevails in Samar, San Jose, in Batangas, burned by the insurgents 24 Oct "

Severe act against treason and sedition drafted by U S commission 1 Nov "

Maj Waller captures Sojotan, 26 insurgents killed 9 Nov "

Fighting at Dapday, Samar, rebels repulsed with loss. 27 Dec "

22 officers and 245 men surrender to the U S 14 Jan 1902

Malvar, rebel leader, surrenders 25 Apr "

Gen Davis captures the chief fort of the Dattos 4 May, "

Cholera throughout Luzon, about 40 deaths per day June, "

Despite fresh outbreaks the rebellion is dying out, and the number of U S troops is being gradually reduced July, "

Amnesty by pres. Roosevelt of all political prisoners 4 July, "

U S customs steamer lost in a typhoon, 19 men drowned, 15 July, "

Another typhoon cleanses the cholera districts 31 July, "

Gov Taft returns from conferences at Washington and Rome, 22 Aug "

Cholera epidemic, 19,640 deaths, agricultural depression, reported . . 30 Aug "

Rios, a fanatical leader, routed in Tayabas 3 Sept "

Gen Chaffee leaves, succeeded by gen Davis about 1 Oct "

The main Moros routed, 40 forts destroyed, reported 4 Oct "

Brigandage suppressed in Leyte and Bilaran, reported, 27 Nov "

Insurgents defeated near Mariquira . 8 Feb 1903

Further fighting at Cus and Surigao in Mch, insurgents routed with loss near Mariquira, reported 27 Mch "

A stronghold captured, 100 natives killed, reported 10 Apr "

Gen Miles's report, confirming some American cruelties during the war, published . 27 Apr "

Capture of 10 forts, heavy loss of the enemy, reported, 7 May, "

Defeat of insurgents in Jolo, 75 killed 20 Nov "

Friars agree to sell their lands for $7,250,000 16 Dec "

The Philippine commission appropriates $75,000 to send 50 educated Filipinos to spend 3 months in the U S 22 Dec "

Ex gov Taft sails for the U S ... . 24 Dec "

Condition of the archipelago more favorable than at any period of its history, record crop of hemp, 1,000,000 bales, produced in 1903, sugar and tobacco showed an increase over 1902, 24 Dec "

Mexican silver importation prohibited 14 Jan 1904

New Philippine currency ordered 27 Jan "

[Insurrection of the Moros, many small skirmishes and fights Throughout the southern islands the ladrones attack small detachments of the U S soldiers, 1904-5]

Luke E Wright inaugurated as civil governor 1 Feb "

Sixto Lopez sentenced to deportation for not taking the oath of allegiance . . .. 5 Feb "

17 Filipino members of the constabulary start a revolt 9 Feb "

Lieut McRae and 6 privates killed by bolomen in Samar, 19 Feb "

Lieut West and 6 privates killed in battle with Datto Moros in Jolo . 29 Feb "

The Bates treaty of 1899 with the sultan of Sulu abrogated by order of the president ... 2 Mch "

Gen Wood reports the capture of 51 cannon from the sultan of Sulu, who was defying the antislavery law 16 Mch "

The sultan of Sulu accepts the abrogation of the Bates treaty, 22 Mch "

The so called president of the Filipino republic and 15 followers killed, the remainder captured 23 Mch "

5 torpedo boat destroyers and the cruiser *Buffalo* arrive at Cavite from Hampton Roads (18,051 miles) . 14 Apr "

2 U S. officers and 15 men of the 7th U S I killed in an ambuscade in Mindanao . . ..9 May, "

53 Filipinos killed by Moros near Malabang ....23 May, "

Maj.-gen. Corbin appointed to succeed gen. Wade (to take effect Oct. 1904)....16 June, 1904
Archbishop Guidi dies in Manila....26 June, "
Several hundred lives lost in a flood near Manila....13 July, "
4 companies of 100 men each ordered to Mindanao to overthrow the Datto Ali....23 Aug. "
First payment of $2,000,000 for friars' lands....20 Sept. "
The outlaw Oyamo and 50 of his followers killed in Samar, 18 Oct. "
Lieut. Hoyt and 37 scouts ambushed and killed in Samar, 23 Dec. "
Outlaws capture the family of gov. Trias in Cavité (the outlaws demand a ransom of $10,000)....24 Jan. 1905
Outlaws defeated in Silang....26 Jan. "

philip'pium, a metal of the yttrium series, found in Samarskite earth (in Russia, North Carolina, etc.) by Marc Delafontaine by means of the spectroscope; announced Oct. 1878. Also said to have been found by Lawrence Smith, and named mosandrium, July, 1878.

Philis'tines, a people of Palestine, conquered Israel, 1156 B.C., and ruled it 40 years. They were defeated by Samuel, 1116, at Mizpah; and by Saul and Jonathan, 1087, at Michmash. They again invaded Israel, about 1063, when David slew their champion, Goliath. They defeated Saul and Jonathan at Mt. Gilboa, 1055, where both were slain. After David became king he thoroughly subdued them, 1040. In common with Syria, their country was subjugated by the Romans. under Pompey, about 63.—In Germany, about 1830, Heine and the liberal party applied the term "Philistines" to the opponents of progress, or conservative party. In England the term has been applied to opponents of "culture" and refinement, and especially by Matthew Arnold and others to the dull advocates of traditional views and institutions.

philol'ogy, the science of language, much studied during the present century.

John Horne-Tooke's "Diversions of Purley" pub.... 1786
Philological Society of London established....18 May, 1842
Lorenz Diefenbach's "Lexicon Comparativum"....1846-51
Thirty-second congress of German philologists meet at Wiesbaden, prof. Curtius president....26-29 Sept. 1877
DICTIONARY, GRAMMARIANS, LANGUAGE.

philos'ophy (love of wisdom), the knowledge of the reason of things (distinguished from history, the knowledge of facts, and from mathematics, the knowledge of the quantity of things); the hypothesis or system upon which natural effects are explained.—*Locke.* Pythagoras first adopted the name of philosopher (such men having been previously called sages) about 528 B.C.

ANCIENT GREEK AND MODERN PHILOSOPHERS AND PHILOSOPHY.

The early Greeks had no predecessors from whom to learn.—*Lewes*, "History of Philosophy."

Name.	Time. b. d. B.C.	Teachings.
Thales of Miletus (father of Greek speculation)	636..546	He made the first attempt to establish a physical beginning, teaching that the principle of all things was water. Said to have been the founder of physics, geometry, and astronomy.
Anaximander of Miletus	610..547	That infinity is the first principle in all things; that all things are produced from infinity and terminate in it.
Anaximenes of Miletus	(?) 556.. —	That the principle of all things is air, diffused through all nature and perpetually active.
Pythagoras of Samos (representative of the second epoch of Ionian philosophy)	(?) 580..500(?)	Numbers the principle or first of things; pantheistic; taught metempsychosis. He formed the first true conception of the solar system, and taught vaguely the orbital revolution of the earth, and its daily revolution on its axis, afterwards systematized by Copernicus. Geometry; demonstrated the square of the hypotheneuse, etc.
Xenophanes of Colophon (founder of the Eleatic school of philosophy, so called from Elea in Sicily).	556..456	Taught that if there ever had been a time when nothing existed, nothing must ever exist. That whatever is always has been, that nature is one and without limit, that God is one incorporeal eternal being of the same nature with the universe, comprehending all things within himself, pervades all things intelligently, but bears no resemblance to human nature either in body or mind.
Heraclitus of Ephesus	(?) 500 fl. —	The principle which is eternal, ever-living unity and pervades and is in all phenomena he called fire or heat. The rational principle which governs the whole moral and physical world is also the law of the individual.
Empedocles of Agrigentum	(?) 500.. —	Love the primal force that binds like to like, and its contrary that tends to separation. No real destruction of anything, but only change of combinations. Rejected the evidence of the senses; pure intellect alone can arrive at truth. Believed in metempsychosis.
Anaxagoras of Clazomenæ	(?) 490.. —	Conjectured the right explanation of the moon's light and of solar and lunar eclipses.
Democritus of Abdera	404 fl. —	Expanded the atomic theory of Leucippus. From the infinity of atoms have resulted all the worlds with all the properties belonging to them. ABDERA, ATOMS.
Protagoras of Abdera (pupil of Democritus)	(?) 480..411(?)	Sophist and skeptic.
Socrates	469..399	Belief in one supreme being, and the divine authority of moral law. Known chiefly through the writings of Plato. "To Socrates we are indebted for the moral entities, the absolute good and beautiful; the god of reason; final causes, and providence; in fact, the sum total of metaphysics."—*André Lefèvre*, "Philosophy, Historical and Critical."
Plato (the most celebrated of philosophers, ancient or modern)	428..347	True source of knowledge the reason. We come to consciousness through innate ideas developed by contact with the outer world through the senses. Separated between empirical knowledge and reason. Divided philosophy into logic, metaphysics, and morals. Philosophy indebted to him *quoad formam*. The first to attempt the construction of philosophic language; to develop an abstract idea of knowledge and science; to state logically the properties of matter, form, substance, accident, cause and effect, reality and appearance; to describe the divinity as a being essentially good, and his moral attributes. He taught that matter is an eternal and infinite principle; that God is the supreme intelligence, incorporeal, without beginning, end, or change; the immortality of the soul, etc. ACADEMIES.
Aristotle of Stagira, hence termed the Stagirite	384..322	Pupil of Plato and preceptor of Alexander the Great. He was the most voluminous of ancient philosophic writers, and many of his works are preserved. Rejected the doctrine of ideas, made all knowledge the fruit of experience gathered from externals. Makes logic the instrument by which all general knowledge is obtained. Enlarged the limits of philosophy, to include all sciences except history. He taught that nature is a machine, active through deity or a first cause. The history of his school, "the Peripatetic" (LYCEUM) may be divided into 4 periods: 1st, from the death of Aristotle, 322 B.C., to Cicero, of gradual decline; 2d, from Cicero to 600 A.D., almost unknown; 3d, from 600 to 1000 A.D., revived but corrupted; 4th, from the 11th century until set aside by Bacon and Descartes.

ANCIENT GREEK AND MODERN PHILOSOPHERS AND PHILOSOPHY.—(*Continued.*)

Name.	Time.	Teachings.
	b. d. B.C.	
Epicurus of Samos	341..270	A follower of Democritus in his atomic theory. Taught that there was no over-ruling providence, that if there was a god or gods they had no power or care over man. That happiness or pleasure should be the chief end of man. His memory and his teachings have been much reproached, because his system has often been a pretext for refined sensuality.
Pyrrho of Elea	(?)340..270(?)	Taught that all human knowledge is involved in uncertainty, so that it is impossible ever to arrive at certainty. He is known as the sceptic.
Zeno (founder of the Stoic school of philosophy)	362..264	The universe, though one, contains 2 principles distinct from elements, one passive, the other active. The passive is pure matter; the active is reason or God. Providence only another name for necessity or fate, and while teaching a resurrected life, it was a life forgetful of any former life. Wisdom consists in distinguishing good from evil. Good is that which produces happiness according to man's nature, and virtue, which is seated in the mind, is alone sufficient for happiness; external things contribute nothing towards happiness, therefore are not in themselves good. The sum of man's duty is to subdue his joy and sorrow, hope and fear, and even pity.
Arcesilaus (founder of the *Middle Academy*)	316.. (?)	Conceived himself to be a follower and a teacher of the Platonic doctrine.
Carneades (founder of the *New Academy*)	215..130	Maintained that all the knowledge the human mind is capable of attaining is not science, but opinion.
Philo of Alexandria	A.D. 20 fl.	Attempts the union of Platonic philosophy with the Jewish scripture.
Ammonius Saccas	—..245	Founder of Neo-Platonism.
Plotinus (Neo-Platonist)	205.. 70	This world a shadowy copy of a truly real world. The instinctive certainty that there is a supreme good beyond empirical experience, and yet not an intellectual good, and the conviction of the utter vanity of all earthly things, were produced and sustained by Neo-Platonism.
Porphyry of Tyre (Neo Platonist)	233..304	God without limit, form, or definition.
Proclus (Neo-Platonist)	411.. 85	He brought the Neo-Platonic philosophy to that form in which it was transferred to Christianity and Mahometanism in the middle ages.—*Encyc. Brit.*, 9th ed. 44 years after the death of Proclus the school of Athens was closed by Justinian (529 A.D.).

MEDIÆVAL SCHOLASTIC PHILOSOPHY.

Name.	Time.	Teachings.
John Scotus Erigena (precursor of modern philosophy). LITERATURE	b. d. A.D. —.. 877	God alone has true being, all-containing and incomprehensible. He is above goodness, wisdom, and truth. No finite predicate can be applied to him. His mode of being cannot be determined by any category. The world a revelation of God; we recognize his being in all things, his wisdom in their orderly arrangement, his life in their constant activity. God is a trinity in substance, form, and spirit, or what we see in individuality. This trinity is most perfectly reflected in man because he is the highest of created things, but as God is incarnate in all things, this trinity is not expressed in man alone, but in all things there is a *trine.* Things are only *real* as they are *good;* being, without well-being, is naught. Ideas manifest themselves in their effects, i.e., the individual created thing. God manifests himself in the world, and is not without the world. As causes are eternal and timeless, so creation is eternal and timeless. The Mosaic account merely expresses a mode, is altogether allegorical, and needs interpretation. Paradise and the Fall have no local or temporal being. As God is true being, i. e., good, sin can have no substantive existence—cannot really be; sin results from the will representing something as good which is not so; punished by finding its pursuits turn out vanity and emptiness. Hell has no local existence, but is a state of unreality, insanity, a result that admits of redemption, as the object of destruction is not the will, but its disease or misdirection. The ultimate goal of the soul is to arrive to a full knowledge of God, in which being and knowing are one.
William of Champeaux (realism)	1070..1121	He held that the essence of all individuals of a genus is the universal, and that is an existence independent of the individual, i. e., a self-subsistent nature, distinct from the mind conceiving it and the individuals conforming to it; both antecedent and superior to these individuals.
Roscelin, Jean (nominalism)	1106 (?)	He maintained that general ideas are not endowed with reality, that the universal or genus exists only in name and has no existence apart from the individual.
Abélard (conceptualism)	1079..1142	Along with Aristotle and the nominalists generally, he ascribed full reality only to the particular concretes, while in opposition he declared the universal to be no mere word, but to consist (or better) to be produced in the fact of predication born as a conception of the mind. For this he has been classed as a conceptualist.
Averroes (Arabian)	1126..1198	Maintained that the eternity of the world finds its true expression in the eternity of God. The ceaseless movement of growth and change which matter ever undergoes in an ascending series is a continual search after a finality or end, which in time and movement cannot be reached. This movement is only its aspect to the senses. In the eye of reason the full fruition of this desired finality is already and always attained. This end, invisible to the senses, is that which the world of nature is forever seeking, but as this end is infinite and eternal—God—nature, in this ascending, never-ending change or series, develops eternal life.

MODERN.

Name.	Time.	Teachings.
	b. d. A.D.	
Bacon, Roger	1214..1294	His fame rests on scientific and mechanical discoveries.
Bacon, Francis (inductive or rational)	1561..1626	Into metaphysics, Bacon can hardly be said to have entered, but a long line of thinkers have drawn inspiration from the practical or positive spirit of his system. Experience and observation are the only safeguards against prejudice and error. The rules laid down by Bacon were averse to hypothesis, and still progress is chiefly made in scientific discovery by the use of hypothesis. The inductive formation of axioms by a gradual ascending scale is a route which no science has ever followed, and by which no science could ever make progress. The work upon which his philosophic reputation rests is the "Novum Organum."

ANCIENT GREEK AND MODERN PHILOSOPHERS AND PHILOSOPHY.—(*Continued.*)

Name.	Time.	Teachings.
	b. d. A.D.	
Descartes, René (Cartesian)	1596..1650	According to Descartes, God is the unity of thought and being; man a mean between God and nothing, between being and not-being; connected on the one hand with the infinite and on the other with the finite. Man has in him an idea of the infinite or God, superior to his own consciousness, or how could he doubt or desire, how could he be conscious of anything as a want, how could he know he was not altogether perfect, if he had not within him the idea or consciousness of a being more perfect than himself, by comparison with whom he recognizes the defects of his own existence? The existence of self he makes dependent on thought: *cogito, ergo sum.* In science, to account for the movement and origin of the planets and all physical phenomena, he conceived the hypothesis of vortices.
Hobbes, Thomas (common-sense)	1588..1679	Follower of Baconian rationalism. Nothing exists except bodies and their accidents. Philosophy dwells within us, all its elements being supplied by sensation, memory, and experience, put in order by reflection. Ratiocination and philosophizing are the same, operating on signs and terms representing ideas, images—the residuums of sensation. Without definition there can be no satisfactory demonstration.
Spinoza (the philosopher of intuitions)	1632..1677	Perfect being is substance. Nothing exists except infinite substance accompanied by infinite attributes which constitute it. Each in its own degree manifests the supreme reality, which is God. He is the unity of diversity; he is the infinite expansion and the divided expansion. Body and soul are two modes of the substance, one the attribute of expansion, the other of thought. The human soul is the *idea* of the body. Thought is represented by its object. Free will is an illusion; would disappear if it were possible to trace back the line of causes.
Malebranche, Nicolas	1638..1715	Evidence is the criterion of truth. Believe what *seems* so evidently true that to withhold our assent occasions the reproaches of reason. The incarnation, the union of creator and creature, is the necessary condition of creation. Reason is supreme and infallible; it is wisdom, the word, Christ! Faith is the mirror of revelation, God's expression to us of his being. God is infinite and eternal goodness. Evil is the necessary result of the laws established for the general welfare. Divides the universe into matter and spirit. The understanding comprises 3 faculties: sensibility, imagination, and reason, which alone thinks, knows, and acquires truth. Will is the natural divine impulse.
Leibnitz, Gottfried W. (elective)	1646..1716	The ultimate reason of all motion or action is the *force* originally communicated to the universe, a force everywhere present, but diversely restrained and limited in different bodies; this force is inherent in all substance, natural and spiritual. Every spirit is a world in itself, self-sufficient, embracing the infinite, expressing the universe, as lasting and absolute as the universe itself, which it represents from its point of view and by its own virtue. The ultimate elements of the universe are individual centres of force, or *monads.*
Locke, John (perceptive)	1632..1704	The eternal existence of God is only another way of expressing the principle of causality and sufficient reason in its universality as suggested by our conviction that our own personal existence had a beginning. Each person knows that he now exists and is convinced that he once had a beginning; with not less intuitive certainty he knows that *nothing* cannot produce any real thing. The rational conclusion is that there must be eternally a most powerful and most knowing being, in which, as the origin of all, must be contained all perfection, and out of which can come only what it has in itself, so that as the adequate cause it must involve mind. Have no knowledge of the real existence of anything other than our own individual existence, that of universal reason, and of particular objects of sense, and they only while they are present to our senses. Locke deals with the understanding and not with the affections.
Berkeley, George, bishop of Cloyne (immaterialism)	1685..1753	Spirit which is immaterial alone exists, and the representation of sensible things is but a mode of its activity. The objects of knowledge are ideas and nothing more. We are forced by the laws of our nature to invest objects with the forms in which we perceive them.
Swedenborg, Emmanuel	1688..1772	Makes the Scriptures the foundation of his philosophy, and asserts that no philosophy worthy of the name can rest on any other foundation. Claims that nature reveals spirit or the reality of things by correspondence and not directly; that no one, however intelligent or wise, can without divine assistance interpret spiritual things by natural. He therefore claimed to have had the spiritual faculties of his mind vivified or opened by the Lord to the true nature and science of correspondence revealing the reality of things. Makes nature the ultimate of divine order, that is, the boundary of things understood by form; has no being or existence in itself aside from the substance (spirit) it seeks to reveal. It expresses in itself that sphere of utter destitution and want which belongs to creatureship, being "without form and void" of life and everything in itself. Characterizes consciousness as composite and not simple, made up of object and subject, the former element dominating the latter, although the latter renders the former known to itself or alive in consciousness. He makes the objective element the sphere of nature, and the subjective the sphere of the mind or spirit. These are united in consciousness or a valid creation. A misapprehension of his system, with a determination to reduce it to a form of ecclesiasticism, has hindered a favorable reception of his philosophic views, so that with one or two exceptions no men of scientific reputation have given his writings the notice they deserve.
Hutcheson, Francis	1694..1747	Devoted his efforts to the exposition of the philosophy of morals.

ANCIENT GREEK AND MODERN PHILOSOPHERS AND PHILOSOPHY.—(*Continued.*)

Name.	Time. b. d. A.D.	Teachings.
Hume, David (skepticism)	1711..1776	Hume's philosophy leads to scepticism. All ideas proceed from sensation. The outward world merely the *unknown* object of our sensations, and cause is the relation between facts constantly succeeding each other, while nothing but an inveterate illusion lurks under the terms efficient and final causes. He says, "Do you follow the instinct and propensities of nature in assenting to the veracity of the senses? But these lead you to believe that the very perception or sensible image is in the external object. Do you disclaim this principle in order to embrace a more rational opinion that the perceptions are only representations of something external? You here depart from your natural propensities and more obvious sentiments, and yet are not able to satisfy your reason, which can never find any convincing argument from experience to prove that the perceptions are connected with external objects."
Reid, Thomas (common-sense)	1710..1795	Opposed to Hume and the idealism of Berkeley—a protest against scepticism. Believed in the reality of the outward world.
Condillac, Etienne de, B.	1715..1780	Opposes the innate idea of Descartes, the mental faculties of Malebranche, and the monadology of Leibnitz. He maintained that the mind is not a congeries of faculties, but is one and indivisible, and appears in all its activity in the simplest state of consciousness. His definition of personality is, a collection of sensations plus the power to *say me*. He divides philosophical systems into 3 classes: (1) Abstract systems, resting only on abstract principles; (2) hypotheses, or systems grounded on mere suppositions; (3) one true system, that of Locke, which is evolved from facts of experience—the true method of philosophy.
Kant, Immanuel (transcendental)	1724..1804	His "Critique of Pure Reason" brought out to oppose the scepticism of Hume. By pure reason is understood reason independent of experience. This "critique" subjects the pure speculative reason to a critical scrutiny. His philosophy termed transcendental owing to his recognition of a *noumenal* world or a world of things-in-themselves; these are unknowable for man. They are related neither to space nor time; all co-existence and succession are only in phenomenal objects and consequently only in the perceiving subject. The forms of thought are the 12 categories or original conceptions of the understanding on which all the forms of our judgments are conditioned. They are: Unity, plurality, totality; reality, negation, limitation; substantiality, causality, reciprocal action; possibility, existence, necessity. The categories have to do only with phenomenal objects within our consciousness. Things-in-themselves have none of these, and therefore do not come within the sphere of consciousness.
Fichte, Johann Gottlieb (subjective idealism)	1762..1814	Substance is nothing but the synthesis of accident. It is a mental synthesis. The basis of idealism is consciousness. God is to be believed in, not inferred—we cannot attribute to him intelligence or personality. He is infinite, therefore beyond the reach of science, which can only embrace the finite—but not beyond faith, which has nothing to do with science. The knowledge and love of God is the end of life; for in God alone have we a permanent, enduring object of desire. The infinite God is the all; the world of independent objects is the result of reflection or self-consciousness, by which the infinite unity is broken up. God is thus over and above the distinction of subject and object; our knowledge is but a reflex or picture of the infinite essence. Being is not thought. The ego important; the tree and the image of the tree are but one thing. *I* alone exist; the tree is but a modification of my mind.
Schelling, W. J. Friedrich von (objective idealism)	1775..1854	Makes the ego absolute and infinite, the all, corresponding to the substance of Spinoza. This absolute manifests itself in two forms, the ego and the non-ego, as nature and mind or spirit; nature being spirit visible and spirit invisible nature. Subject and object are identical in a third which is absolute. This absolute is neither real nor ideal, neither nature nor mind, but both. This absolute is God. He is all in all, the eternal source of all existence. He realizes himself under one form as in objectivity, and under another as subjectivity. He becomes conscious himself in man through reason. Knowledge and being are identical. To know the infinite we must be in the infinite, i. e., lose ourselves in the universal. The tree and the ego are equally real or ideal, but they are nothing else in their union but manifestation of the absolute.
Hegel, Georg Wilhelm Friedrich (absolute idealism)	1770..1831	Being and non-being the same. Being absolute, that is, unconditioned, apart from any individual thing, is the same as nothing; existence does not exclude non-existence; everything is contradictory in itself; contradiction forms its essence; existence is therefore identical with negation. Light without color or shade is unapproachable. Must be united with darkness to be known. The same with being and non-being, subject and object, force and weakness, etc. The only thing existing is the idea, the relative; the ego and the object the terms of the relation, and these terms owe their being to such relation. God is ever active. Creation without beginning or end, or infinite.
Schopenhauer, Arthur	1788..1860	Space, time, and the categories of Kant have purely a subjective origin, and are only valid for phenomena, which are merely subjective representations in consciousness. The absolutely real cannot be a transcendental object, for no object is without a corresponding subject, and all objects are representations in the subject and hence phenomena. The will includes not only conscious desire, but unconscious instinct as well, and all forces which manifest themselves in inorganic nature. Consciousness first becomes manifest in life in the objectification of the will. Views pessimistic; this world not the best, but the worst of all possible worlds. To will without motive, to suffer and struggle incessantly, and then to die, and so on forever, until all life disappears from the earth. Happiness, if any, comes through the destruction of the will or desires—Nirvana. "For not to desire or admire, if a man could learn it, were more Than to walk all day like the sultan of old in a garden of spice." —*Tennyson's "Maud."*

ANCIENT GREEK AND MODERN PHILOSOPHERS AND PHILOSOPHY.—(*Continued.*)

Name.	Time. b. d. A.D.	Teachings.
Cousin, Victor (eclectic)	1792..1867	All science referred to ideas, which must contain the explanation of all things. There are 3 fundamental ideas: The infinite, the finite, and the relation they sustain to each other. These 3 ideas are met with everywhere and in everything, a trinity inseparable. A God without a world as incomprehensible as a world without a God. Creation a necessity. History the development of ideas; a nation, a century, a great man, each the manifestation of an idea. His work on "The True, the Beautiful, and the Good," pub. 1853. Philosophy without method or precision.
Comte, Auguste (positivism)	1798..1857	The beginning and the end of things are unknowable for us. It is only what lies between that can come within the sphere of our knowledge. Repudiates all metaphysical hypotheses, neither atheist nor theist, rejects Pantheism. History and science the 2 ideas or terms of positivism. 6 fundamental sciences: Mathematics, astronomy, physics, chemistry, biology, and sociology. History justifies this order. His great work, "Cours de Philosophie Positive," pub. 1830–42.
Hamilton, sir William (conditional)	1788..1856	"Philosophy of the Unconditioned," pub. 1829, treats consciousness under 3 chief aspects: (1) As it is in itself; (2) as realized under actual conditions; (3) as a source of truth. (1) Consciousness in itself is immediate or intuitive knowledge; this involves the existence of both subject and object; it is the affirmation by the subject implicitly of its own existence, explicitly of that of the object; (2) as realized under actual conditions includes all particular forms of knowledge, and yet its development into a whole is the effect of the agencies which make up its contents; (3) as a source of truth consciousness is embodied in the *conditioned*, and common sense; the *conditioned* being the only possible object of knowledge and of thought. Quality realized under the twofold aspect of substance and phenomenon; quantity under time, space, and degree; knowledge essentially relative; self cannot be known except with and through not-self; natural realism a corollary of the general principle of the relativity of knowledge; perception and sensation differently related to the ego as space to thought and sense, the reason supreme; freedom and necessity alike inconceivable; pleasure the reflex in consciousness of the spontaneous and unimpeded exercise of power or energy; pain the consciousness of overstrained or repressed exertion.
Spencer, Herbert (evolution)	1820..	After Kant and Hamilton recognizes an unknowable power. Knowable likenesses and differences among the manifestations of that power, resulting in subject and object, space, time, matter, and motion. Force persistent, never disappears—it is only transformed. The law of evolution applies equally to all orders of phenomena, astronomic, geologic, biologic, psychologic, sociologic, etc. The genesis of religion he traces to ancestor worship. The notion of another life from shadows, reflections, echoes, etc., as doubles or the other self.
Hartman, Eduard von (philosophy of the unconscious)	1840..	Presents the will of Schopenhauer and the absolute idea of Hegel as necessary to a true philosophy of the world, both being attributes of the workings of the unconscious. The unconscious is will, wisdom, activity, creation continuous, and foreseeing intelligence. Without thought it is the essence of thought, the reality of consciousness, and so above consciousness. It explains everything that lies within the range of creation, i.e., nature. "Philosophy of the Unconscious" pub. 1869.

Phipps's expedition. Capt. Phipps (afterwards lord Mulgrave) sailed from England in command of the *Seahorse* and *Carcase* to make discoveries as near as possible to the North Pole. In Aug. 1773, he was for 9 days environed with ice in the Frozen ocean, north of Spitzbergen, 80° 48′ N. lat. All progress or retreat seemed impossible; but a brisk wind in 2 or 3 days accomplished their deliverance. They returned to England without having made any discoveries, 20 Sept. 1773. Horatio Nelson was coxswain to the second in command. NORTHEAST AND NORTHWEST PASSAGES.

phlogis'ton, a term employed by Stahl to designate the matter or principle of fire; the "inflammable principle" of bishop Watson, near the close of the 17th century. The chemical theory based upon it, refuted by Lavoisier, 1790, has been thought to have some resemblance to recent theories of atomic matter.

Phocis, a state in N. Greece. The Phocians seized Delphi 357 B.C., and commenced the second Sacred war. They were opposed by Thebes and other states, and were utterly subdued by Philip II. of Macedon in 346.

Phœni'cia, on the sea-coast of Syria. The natives were the most eminent navigators and traders of antiquity, their cities or allied states being Tyre, Sidon, Berytus, Tripoli, Byblos, and Ptolemais, or Acre. From the 19th to the 13th century before Christ they established colonies on the shores or isles of the Mediterranean—Carthage, Hippo, Utica, Gades, Panormus (now Palermo)—and are said to have visited the British isles. Phœnicia was conquered by Cyrus, 537 B.C.; by Alexander, 332; by the Romans, 47; and, after partaking of the fortunes of Palestine, was added to the Ottoman empire, 1516 A.D.

phœ'nix, a fabulous bird of Egypt and Arabia, said to live 500 years, when from its ashes a young phœnix arose. An account given of it by *Herodotus*.

Phœnix Park murders. IRELAND, 1882–83.

phonau'tograph. ACOUSTICS.

phoneid'oscope, an instrument for observing the color-figures of liquid films under the action of sonorous vibrations, being a visible demonstration of the vibratory and molecular motion of a telephone plate, invented by Sedley Taylor, 1877; manufactured by S. C. Tisley & Co., London, 1878.

pho'nograph, a machine proposed to be attached to pianofortes and other keyed instruments, so that the playing of any music upon them will automatically print the notes of it on blank paper. It was patented by Mr. Fenby, 13 June, 1863. The motive-power is electro-magnetism. Machines with a similar object were projected by Creed in 1747, J. F. Unger in 1774, and by Carreyre in 1827.

A new phonograph by Thomas Alva Edison, electrician, of New Jersey, was announced .... Dec. 1877
[Linear indentations are made by a pin pressed by the voice in speaking or singing in a sheet of tin-foil, fixed on a revolving cylinder, and from these casts may be taken. When these are placed upon another cylinder revolving before a telephone, the sounds may be reproduced.]
Improved by Shelford Bidwell (TELEPHONE) 1879
Prof. Graham Bell's *graphophone*, a modification of the phonograph, announced .... Nov. 1887
Emile Berliner of Washington announces his *gramophone*, a modification of Scott's *phonautograph* .... Nov. "
Improved instrument by Mr. Edison for postal communication; announced 21 Nov. 1887; successful experiment.....12 May, 1888
Edison greatly improves the phonograph. Considered perfect

in the record, reproduction, and preservation of sounds of all kinds (wax used instead of tin foil) Nov 1888

Edison adapts his phonograph to a water motor as well as to electricity Sept 1890

phonog'raphy (from Gr φωνη, sound, and γράφω, to write), suggested by Franklin, 1768 The Phonetic Society, whose object was to render writing and printing more consonant to sound, was established 1 Mch 1843, sir W C Trevelyan president, and Isaac Pitman secretary, the latter being the inventor of the system, which was made known in 1837 Among other works published by the promoters of the system was the "Phonetic News," in 1849 VISIBLE SPEECH

"Pickwick Papers in Shorthand," first of a series pub by Pitman 1 May, 1883

"Solfa System of Shorthand," first pub 5 Feb 1887

pho'noscope, an apparatus for testing the quality of musical strings, invented by M Koenig, and exhibited at the International Exhibition in 1862

Mr Edmunds's phonoscope, exhibited to the British Association, Aug 1878, is an instrument for producing figures and light from the vibrations of sound

phosphate, a salt of phosphoric acid In chemistry a generic term for salts formed by the union of the acid-anhydride $P_2 O_5$ with a basis, or water or both Phosphorite is a name given to many impure forms of amorphous apatite, modified more or less by disintegration The South Carolina and Florida phosphates belong to this category —*Encyc Brit*, 9th ed, sub phosphates As phosphoric acid is one of the most important elements of plant-food, no soil can be productive which is destitute of it, as the plant in its growth draws this important element from the soil, it must be restored to replace the outlay. PHOSPHORUS The ancient cultivators of the soil recognized this necessity and the Romans used the excrements from their pigeon-houses, while Edrisi relates that the Arabians as early as 1154 used guano (bird deposits) found along the Arabian coast for agricultural purposes. GUANO It was not, however, until the early part of this century, when Liebig and others showed the importance of phosphoric acid in vegetable life, that artificial manures came into use, and it is only in the last 20 years that the mining of natural phosphates with their conversion into super-phosphates has assumed its present great importance The importance of this fertilizer is shown by the following statistics World's consumption of phosphates for 1891 was 1 587,133 tons, of which the United States produced 757,133 tons, mostly mined from South Carolina and Florida.

phosphor-bronze, an alloy of copper, tin, and phosphorus, invented by messrs Montefiore-Levi and Kunzel, of Belgium, in 1867 It is very hard, ductile, and elastic, with a color resembling gold

phosphores'cence is properly the glow of a substance which has absorbed light, when removed into darkness, and is so called from the faint luminosity shown by phosphorus when rubbed in the dark. Observed by the ancients, especially noticed by Vincenzo Cascariolo (1602), Boyle, Canton, Wilson, and others, and especially studied by Edmond Becquerel and Balmain. The phosphorescence of decayed wood is due to the presence of mycelium of *Agaricus melleus*, a species of fungi. This property is also possessed by certain plants, and in the animal kingdom several infusoria, polyps, fishes, etc, and in the insect world the glowworm and fire-fly are notable examples.

phos'phorus was discovered in 1667 by Brandt, of Hamburg, who procured it from urine. The discovery was prosecuted by John Kunckel, a Saxon chemist, about 1670, and by the hon R Boyle about the same time —*Nouv Dict* Phosphoric acid is first mentioned in 1743, but is said to have been known earlier Gahn pointed out its existence in bones in 1769, and Scheele devised a process for extracting it. Canton's phosphorus is so called from its discoverer, 1768. It is one of the most universally distributed elements, being found in all animal and vegetable matter, as well as in eruptive and sedimentary rocks Phosphoric acid composes over 40 per cent. of the ashes of bones, and in the vegetable kingdom it is especially abundant in seeds The ash of wheat contains over 49 per cent. of phosphoric acid Phosphuretted hydrogen was discovered by Gengembre in 1812 The consumption of phosphorus has immensely increased since the invention of lucifer matches. In 1845, Schrötter, of Vienna, discovered allotropic or amorphous phosphorus, which ignites more slowly and is less unwholesome in working than ordinary phosphorus.

photog'raphy. A lens, now in the British museum, was found in the ruins of Nineveh The CAMERA-OBSCURA provided with a lens was described by Giovanni Baptiste Porta in 1589 As early as 1556, Fabricius published a book on metals He was acquainted with the fact that horn silver (a compound of silver and chlorine) turned black on exposure to the sunlight J. H Schulze, in 1727, obtained copies from writing by transmitted sunlight on a surface prepared with a mixture of chalk and silver nitrate, the writing appearing white Scheele of Stralsund, in 1777, proved that light decomposes chloride of silver Thomas Wedgwood, assisted by Humphry Davy, obtained prints on paper and white leather made sensitive to light by a coating of silver nitrate and placed underneath paintings on glass and exposed to sunlight Davy published an account of the experiment in the *Journal of the Royal Institute* for 1802 The advance in the science of photography may be seen in the following table

Process	Time required		Discovered
Heliography	6 hours' exposure		1816
Daguerrotype	30 minutes'	"	1839
Calotype or talbotype	3 "	"	1841
Collodion	10 seconds'	"	1851
Collodion emulsion (dry plate)	15 "	"	1864
Gelatine emulsion	1 second	"	1878

Joseph Nicéphore Niépce of Châlons (1765-1833), the inventor of photolithography, discovers the bitumen process in photography about 1813, and produces the first permanent photograph by aid of the camera . about 1816

Niepce forms a partnership with Louis Jacques Mandé Daguerre, who began investigations in photography about 1824 1829

Henry Fox Talbot (1800-77) obtains a "photogenic drawing" of his residence, Lacock Abbey, on prepared paper exposed in the camera-obscura about an hour 1835

On condition that he publish his process in France without patenting, the French government settles on Daguerre a life pension of 6000 francs per annum, and on his partner, Isidore Niepce 4000 francs per annum (1838) Daguerre takes out a patent in England 1839

Hyposulphite of soda, discovered by Chaussier in 1799, and its solvent power on haloid salts of silver, demonstrated by sir John Herschel as early as 1819, is suggested by him and adopted for fixing daguerrotypes "

Herschel suggests the use of glass plates in photography "

First attempt at portraiture by photography made by John W Draper, professor of chemistry in the University of New York, by dusting the sitter's face with flour, successful portraits made independently by S F B Morse in Oct "

First photograph of the moon is presented to the Lyceum of Natural History in New York by prof Draper Mch 1840

Talbot discovers that sensitive paper brushed with a mixture of gallic acid and nitrate of silver and exposed wet in the camera, produces a picture in 2 or 3 minutes, from which copies can be taken by transmitted light on sensitive paper (Sept. 1840) His discovery (disputed by rev J B Reade) he calls the calotype process and patents. Feb 1841

Sir John Herschel invents "blue prints," and first applies the term "negative" to photography 1840-42

First issue of "The Pencil of Nature," a book illustrated by calotype prints by Fox Talbot appears 1844

Albumen process on glass published by Niepce de St Victor 1848

Colored photographs, evanescent however, produced by Robert Hunt of England, in 1843, and by Edmond Becquerel of France, "

Humphrey's *Journal of Photography and the Allied Arts and Sciences*, the first of its kind in the U S, begins publication, 1850

Collodion process in photography, suggested by Gustave Le Gray in 1849 and by Robert J Bingham in 1850, is developed by Frederick Scott Archer of England, and described in the London *Chemist* Mch 1851

Instantaneous views made by Mr Cady and Alexander Beckers in New York . "

Talbot produces instantaneous pictures by a flash light from Leyden jars lasting the 0001 part of a second "

First public exhibition of photography, held under the auspices of the Society of Arts in the Adelphi, London 22 Dec 1852

Photographic Society of London, since 1876 styled the Photographic Society of Great Britain, established 30 Jan 1853

Process of "vignetting," or shading of portrait backgrounds, described by Latimer Clark Dec "

Albumen paper introduced by Talbot about 1854

Collodion albumen dry plates, the first practical dry plate process, published by dr J M Taupenot, French scientist 1855

CARTES DE VISITE portraits taken by M Ferrier at Nice 1857

Photographic composition, or combination printing, introduced in 1855, and Oscar G Rejlander of Wolverhampton sends to the Manchester exhibition a large photograph, called "The Two Ways of Life," which he printed from 30 negatives "

Toning process, introduced by the French scientist Fizeau in 1841, is perfected by Maxwell Lyte 1858

Prof O N Rood of Troy, N Y, describes his process of micro-photography in *American Journal of Science* (No 82) . 1861

Mr Thompson of Weymouth photographs the bottom of the sea "

Ammonia first used in developing pictures by Anthony and Broda in the U S. 1862
Magnesium light employed for photography by Mr Brothers of Manchester 1864
"Magic photographs," on process known to Herschel in 1840, produced upon blank paper by a blotting pad saturated with hyposulphite of soda, obtain widespread popularity about 1866
Fogging of collodion plates prevented by use of aqua regia, recommended by Carey Lea of Philadelphia Apr 1870
Photographs of the first page of the *Times*, 1½ inches long by 1 inch wide, sent from Bordeaux to Paris by balloons Jan 1871
Spectra of the stars, showing the fixed lines photographed for the first time by dr Draper, with telescopic apparatus constructed by himself 1872
W Willis, jr., inventor of the platinotype process, takes out a patent in England June, 1873
"Albumen beer dry plate process," devised by capt Abney, and used by expeditions to study the transit of Venus 1874
"Beechey dry plates" described by rev canon Beechey of England Oct. 1875
Ferrous oxalate used as a developer by Carey Lea in America and Willis in England 1877
H Van der Weyde an American artist, succeeds in making electric light very effectual in photography 1876–78
Use of gelatine emulsion with bromide of silver, imperfectly known as early as 1850 by Gustave Le Gray, displaces the collodion process 1878
Dr Draper photographs the nebulæ in Orion 1880–81
Bust of Daguerre (1787-1851), the contribution of photographers of all civilized nations, unveiled at Cormeilles, near Paris 1883
Roller slide, invented by A J Melhuish in England in 1854, and M Leon Warnerker, a Hungarian engineer in 1871 practically applied in photography by Eastman, Walker & Co of Rochester N Y 1885
Gelatino bromide paper for negatives introduced in U S and England by Eastman Co "
Complete photographic map of the heavens begun by the International Photographic Congress of Astronomers of the World organized in Paris, charts of the whole heavens expected in 10 years 1887
W E Woodbury's "Encyclopædia of Photography" pub 1890
M Marey's chrono photograph for animal motions applied by M G Demeny to the movement of the lips in speech, the result being readable by deaf mutes Aug 1891
F E Ives at the Royal Institution London, 10, 17 May, 1892, exhibited his patented method of photographing colors
Photoheliograph, an apparatus for registering the position of the sun's spots by means of clockwork and photography, erected at the suggestion of sir John Herschel at Kew observatory about 1857 It was used by Warren de la Rue to photograph the disc of the sun during the eclipse of 18 July, 1860
Photogalvanography the art of producing engravings by the action of light and electricity The earliest specimens were produced by Nicéphore Niépce, and presented by him in 1827 to the great botanist, Robert Brown Great advances have since been made in this art by Niépce de St. Victor (who published a treatise on it in 1856), Vitry, W R. Grove, H Fox Talbot, etc In 1852 Paul Pretsch patented a process which he called "Photogalvanography"
Photoglyphy and *Photogravure* (a process by which light etches a picture on a plate that may be printed from) was patented by Mr Fox Talbot in 1858, and is described and exemplified in the *Photographic News*, 9 and 16 Sept 1859
Photozincography (a process by which photographs are transferred to zinc plates which may be printed from) was devised by sir Henry James, chief of the ordnance survey and made known in 1860 By it maps, charts, and engravings may be printed at small cost
Photo sculpture M Villeme's employment of photographs in the formation of sculpture was announced in 1863

photom'eter (light-measurer); one was constructed by dr W Ritchie in 1825 Many improvements have been made recently in connection with photography.

Stellar photometry, the measurement of the light of the stars, much studied by Herschel, Argelander, Pritchard, and others W J Dibdin describes his application of terrestrial photometry to stellar light, in his "Guide to the Measurement of Light" pub 1889

pho'tophone. In this apparatus, constructed by prof Graham Bell and Sumner Tainter of Washington, in 1880, a thin plane mirror is thrown into vibration by the voice a beam of light is reflected from this mirror and received at a distance by a cell of the metal selenium, when, by arrangement, this is connected with a telephone, the sounds are reproduced

pho'tosphere. SUN.

phrenol'ogy, the study of the form, texture, dimensions and distribution of parts of the brain as the organ of mental powers and moral qualities. Dr Gall, the propounder, was a German physician, born Mch 1758, and his first observations were among his school-fellows Observing that in these an "ox-eye," a full, protuberant eye-ball, was always associated with fluency in language, and that an eye sunk below the cheek-bone was found only in those slow and unready of speech, he inferred that the part of the brain just behind the eye is the organ of language Afterwards he studied the heads of criminals and others, and eventually reduced his ideas to a system, describing the brain as composed of some 40 or more distinct organs, some estimate of the comparative and even of the actual power of which he believed could be formed from an examination of the skull His first lecture was given at Vienna in 1796, but in 1802 the Austrian government prohibited his teaching In 1800 he was joined by dr Spurzheim, and in 1810-12 they published at Paris their work on the "Anatomy and Physiology of the Nervous System, and of the Brain in particular" Gall died in 1828 The researches of Gall and Spurzheim led to increased study of the brain. Combe's "Phrenology," first pub in 1819, is the popular English work on this subject Phrenological societies were formed early in London and Edinburgh

Introduced into the United States by dr Charles Caldwell of North Carolina, about 1825. Among the most active of its teachers were O S Fowler and S R Wells They established the *Phrenological Journal*, 1863
The system of Gall was opposed by lord Jeffrey in the *Edinburgh Review* in 1826, and more recently by dr W B Carpenter Prof. Ferrier reported the results of researches tending to prove localization of certain faculties in the brain to the British Association, Sept 1873.

Phryg'ia, now **Karama'nia,** a province in Asia Minor, became part of the Persian empire in 537 B.C, and partook of its changes It became a Roman province in 47 B C, and a Turkish one 1392 A D

Phrygian cap, the red cap of Liberty, worn by the leaders of the French Revolution, 1792, in shape, the same as that of the ancient Phrygians In Roman history a badge denoting emancipation from slavery, worn by emancipated slaves, and probably selected by the French leaders for this reason, as denoting manumission from the thraldom of tyrants.

physicians. MEDICAL SCIENCE.

physics and **physicists.** ACOUSTICS, ASTRONOMY, CHEMISTRY, ELECTRICITY, OPTICS, PHILOSOPHY, etc.

physiog'nomy, a science which affirms that the dispositions of mankind may be discovered from the features of the face. The origin of the term is referred to Aristotle, and Cicero was attached to the science It became a fashionable study from the beginning of the 16th century, and in the last century, the essays of Le Cat and Pernethy led to the modern system Lavater's researches arose from observing the singular countenance of a soldier who passed under a window at which he and Zimmerman were standing, his "Fragment" on this subject appeared in 1776

physiology is that part of physics which treats of the inner constitution of animals and plants, and the several functions and operations of all their organs and tissues. The works of Muller, Milne-Edwards, Huxley, Foster, and Carpenter are much celebrated, and Todd's "Cyclopædia of Physiology" (1836-1859) is a library in itself MEDICAL SCIENCE.

pianoforte (*pē-ăn'o-fōr'-tē*) The nucleus of the instrument was a little box over which were stretched strings; such was the citole, the dulcimer, and the psaltery. The clavitherium had keys; the clavichord (about 1500) had dampers; successive improvements were the virginals (on which queen Elizabeth played), the spinet (about 1700), and the harpsichord (with 2 rows of keys), said to have been used in the 15th century, for which Bach and Handel composed in the 17th century A collection of harpsichords (one dated 1555) is in the South Kensington museum The invention of the piano is attributed to Cristofalli (or Cristofori), an Italian, J. C. Schröter, a German and Marius, a Frenchman, early in the 18th century The strings are struck by small hammers, and not by quills as in harpsichords. Schroter is said to have presented a model of his invention to the court of Saxony in 1717, and G. Silberman manufactured pianofortes with considerable success in 1772. Pianofortes were made in London by M. Zumpie, a German, 1766, and have been since greatly improved by Clementi, Broadwood, Collord, Kirkman, Erard, Pleyel, Chickering & Sons of Boston, Mass., Steinway & Co. of New York, and others

Upright pianos, first made in England, were suggested by Isaac Hawkins in 1800, and Thomas Lond in 1802 William Southwell patented "cabinet pianos" in 1807, superseded, from about 1840, by the cottage, piccolo, and other pianos.
A keyed instrument at Modena was named "piano e forte," 1598.
A "stone pianoforte," formed of a series of flints and other stones of various sizes, collected in France, and arranged by M Baudre, was played on by him at the Royal Institution on 16 Mch 1866.

A double pianoforte (with 2 keyboards reversed), giving remarkable effects (patented by M M Mengeot), played on at Covent Garden theatre, 21 Oct 1878

See Grove's "Dictionary of Music," article *Pianoforte*

Pic'ardy, a province of N France, was conquered by the English in 1346, and by the duke of Burgundy in 1417, to whom it was ceded by the treaty of Arras, 21 Sept 1435, and annexed to France by Louis XI, 1463

Pic'cadilly, a fine street in W London The name, of uncertain origin, was Pickadilla and Pigudello, about 1660, when a house of entertainment existed near the Haymarket, termed Pickadilly hall, after which buildings were gradually extended westwards

pic'colo, a small flute an octave higher than the ordinary flute, introduced by Robert Wornum in 1829

Picen'tines, a Sabine tribe, subdued by the Romans, and their capital, Asculum, taken, 268 B C They began the Social war in 90, and were conquered in 89 B.C

piquet (*pĕ kā'*), a game with cards, invented, it is said, by Joquemin for the amusement of Charles VI of France, then in feeble health, 1390 —*Mezeray*

Picts (from *picti* painted), Scythians, who landed in Scotland just about the time that the Scots began to seize upon the Hebrides, or Western Isles (Ebudes) They afterwards lived as 2 distinct nations—the Scots in the highlands and isles, and the Picts in that part now called the lowlands Between 838 and 842, the Scots under Kenneth II totally subdued the Picts, and seized all their kingdom Their incursions in England led to the Saxon invasion HADRIAN'S WALL.

Piedmont (Lat *Pedemontium*, foot of the mountain), region in N Italy, formerly the seat of government of the kingdom of SARDINIA SAVOY

Pierce, Franklin, administration of UNITED STATES, 1853-57

Pietists, a Lutheran sect, instituted in Leipsic by Philip James Spener, a professor of theology, about 1680, with the view of reforming the popular religion He established "colleges of Pietists," with preachers resembling those of the Society of Friends and the Methodists in Britain, about 1760 A body resembling the Pietists, named Chasidim, arose among the Jews in the Ukraine, and spread through Poland and European Turkey

piezam'eter (Gr. πιέζω, I compress), an apparatus for measuring the compressibility of liquids, invented by Œrsted (d 1851), improved by Despretz and Saigey

pigeons were employed as carriers by the ancients Hirtius and Brutus corresponded by means of pigeons at the siege of Modena The pigeons of Aleppo served as couriers at Alexandretta and Bagdad 32 pigeons liberated in London at 7 o'clock in the morning of 22 Nov 1819, at noon one of them arrived at Antwerp, a quarter of an hour afterwards a second arrived, the remainder on the following day.—*Phillips* At a pigeon race, 25 July, 1872, from Spalding to London, the time allowed was 90 seconds a mile. Tournament flying was inaugurated in the United States in 1886 Competition open throughout the entire year. In 1889 the best record stood 1476 yards per minute, same year best long distance 25 miles in 11 hrs. 25 min, average 1349 yards per minute, 1891, 100 miles, average 1374 yards per minute, same year 325 miles, average 1733 yards per minute POST-OFFICE, 1870

pike, a weapon of war Before the introduction of the BAYONET, infantry—that is, heavy-armed footmen—were from the earliest times armed with the pike or spear, consisting of a stout pole, 10 to 14 feet long, tipped with a flat-pointed iron head, sometimes with cutting sides, from 6 to 18 inches long The Macedonian pike was 24 feet long PHALANX As a defence against cavalry the pike was of great value, till guns and gunpowder superseded it

Pilgrimage of Grace, name given to an insurrection commencing in Lincolnshire, Engl, in Sept. 1536, caused by the dissolution of the monasteries by Henry VIII., such suppression being very unpopular among the people. The Lincolnshire movement was easily suppressed, but it was soon revived in Yorkshire, Durham, and Lancaster, where, under the leadership of one Aske, and several other men, the force was raised to 40,000, with banners on which were depicted a crucifix, a chalice, and the five wounds of Christ. Their object was the restoration of the monasteries and suppression of heresy They took Hull, York and Pomfret castle. The duke of Norfolk proceeded against them with a force of about 5000 men Numerous negotiations followed, while no general engagement ensued, owing to severe storms, until after several months the insurrection came to an end on promise of general pardon, etc A number of executions of gentlemen, knights, and nobility followed

pilgrimages began with the pilgrimage of the empress Helena to Jerusalem, 326 They became very frequent at the close of the 10th century Robert II of France made several pilgrimages, among others one to Rome about the year 1016, perhaps in 1020, when he refused the imperial dignity and the kingdom of Italy The pilgrimage to Canterbury is described by Chaucer in his "Canterbury Tales" about 1383. The pilgrimage of Mahometans to Mecca, the birthplace of the prophet, is commanded in the Koran Pilgrimages to shrines of the Virgin Mary in France revived in 1873 and since, in consequence of miracles alleged to have taken place at La Salette in 1846, and at Lourdes, 11 Feb 1858, those of La Salette discredited by pope Leo X, 1879 SACRED HEART. For children's pilgrimages, CRUSADES

American pilgrims received by the pope ... 9 June, 1874
English Roman Catholic pilgrimage to shrine of St Edmund, archbishop of Canterbury, at Pontigny ... Sept. "
English pilgrimage to Lourdes directed by the "Catholic Union of Great Britain," start proposed, given up ... Aug 1880
BOULOGNE

Pilgrim fathers, first settlers of New England. MASSACHUSETTS, 1620

"Pilgrim's Progress from this World to that which is to Come," written by John Bunyan, in Bedford jail, where he was imprisoned 12 years, 1660-72 The first part pub in 1678. A Hebrew version appeared in 1851 BEDFORD

pillar saints. MONACHISM

pil'lory, a scaffold for persons to stand on, to render them publicly infamous This punishment was inflicted in England on persons convicted of forgery, perjury, libelling, etc In some cases the head was put through a hole, the hands through 2 others the nose slit, the face branded with one or more letters, and one or both ears were cut off There is a statute of the pillory, 41 Hen III 1256 Many persons died in the pillory by being struck with stones by the mob, and pelted with rotten eggs and putrid offal It was abolished as a punishment except for perjury, 1815, and totally abolished in 1837 The last who suffered at the Old Bailey was Peter James Bossy, for perjury, 24 June, 1830

pinchbeck, an alloy of 25 percent of zinc and 75 copper, used for watch-cases, etc., named after Christopher Pinchbeck, a toy-seller in Cockburn street, London, who died Mch. 1873.

pine. FLOWERS AND PLANTS

pine-tree flag, a flag with a pine-tree in a white centre, used by New England at the commencement of the Revolution

Pinkie, near Edinburgh Here the English totally defeated the Scots, 10 Sept. 1547

pins have been found in British barrows (*Fosbroke*), and are mentioned in a statute of England of 1483 Brass pins were brought from France in 1540, and first used in England by Catherine Howard, wife of Henry VIII. Pins were made in England in 1543 —*Stowe* They were first manufactured by machinery in England in 1824, under a patent procured there by Lemuel Wellman Wright, an American Among the earlier inventors of machinery for pin-making in the United States was John J. Howe, 1836, and Samuel Slocum, 1838, the latter also invented a pin-sticking machine, 1840 Great improvements have since been made The annual production of pins in the U. S. has a value of over $1,000,000

piracy, properly the business of cruising on the high seas for plunder, forcible robbery at sea It was practised from the earliest days of navigation, and the Romans in the time of Julius Cæsar made great national exertions to suppress the pirates. By the laws of all civilized nations, piracy is punishable by death Pompey destroyed the Cilician pirates, 67 B.C. BUCCANEERS, BARATARIA BAY, KIDD, the pirate, RHODE ISLAND, 1728 The slave trade was made piracy by the statute law of Great Britain and the United States.—The publication of a copyrighted book without license from the owner is often improperly termed piracy

Piræus, the port of Athens, was united to the city by 2 long walls, one erected by Themistocles and the other by Pericles, 456 B.C., which were destroyed by Lysander, 404 B.C These walls, about 4½ miles long and 60 feet high, were of stone, and wide enough at the top to allow 2 wagons to pass each other It was fortified by Conon, 393 B.C. The Piræus was able to contain 400 Greek vessels It was occupied by the French during the Russian war in 1854

Pisa (*pee'sa*) an ancient city in Tuscany, was founded about 6 centuries before Christ, and was favored by the early Roman emperors as a flourishing republic. The citizens took an active part in the Italian wars of the middle ages, but became subject to Florence, after a long siege, 1405-6 In 1494 Pisa became independent under the protection of Charles VIII. of France, but was retaken by the Florentines in 1509. The university was founded in 1343, and revived by the Medici in 1472 and 1542 The rival popes, Benedict XIII and Gregory XII, were deposed at a council held at Pisa in 1409, and Alexander V elected in their place The Campanile or leaning tower was built about 1154, to contain bells, and stands in a square close to the cathedral It is built entirely of white marble, and is a cylinder of 8 stories, each adorned with a round of columns. It inclines so far that a plummet dropped from the top, which is 188 feet in height, falls 16 feet from the base Some have imagined that the inclination was designed by the architect, but it is certainly due to a gradual subsidence of the foundation during its construction The efforts of the builders to counteract this by making the colonnade higher in upper stories on the side that was depressed are easily seen From this tower Galileo made his observation on gravitation (about 1635)

pistols, the smallest fire-arms, said to have been invented at Pistoia in Italy, were first used by the cavalry of England about 1544 Of late years they have been made with a revolving cylindrical breech, in which are formed several chambers for receiving cartridges, and bringing them in succession into a line with the barrel ready for firing The earliest model of this kind of arm is to be found in the museum of the United Service Institution, and is supposed to date from the reign of Charles I An 8-chambered matchlock revolver of the 16th century is placed in the Royal Artillery museum, Woolwich The manufacture of pistols by machinery was first introduced into England from the United States, in the year 1853, by col. Colt, who invented the Colt revolving pistol, 1851 This system induced the British government to establish the Enfield armory, in 1855. FIRE-ARMS.

Pitcairn's island, in the Pacific ocean, said to have been discovered by Pitcairn in 1768, seen by Cook in 1773, and since colonized by 10 mutineers from the ship *Bounty*, capt Bligh, in 1789 BOUNTY MUTINY

The mutineers remained unknown to England until discovered accidentally in 1814 A ship nearing the island was hailed in the English language by a swarthy youth, when it appeared that the mutineers, soon after settling there, had married some black women from a neighboring island, and had become a well conducted community under the care of Adams, the principal mutineer He died in 1829, when Nobbs, an Englishman, who arrived a few years before, became chief In Aug 1852 adm Moresby spent a few days on the island By his means Nobbs was sent to England and obtained ordination As their numbers increased, the island proved incapable of their support, its area being but 3 sq miles The English government removed some of them, with their property, in the ship *Moravshire*, on 3 May, 1856, and landed them, after a boisterous passage, on Norfolk island, prepared previously for their reception, 8 June. The government stocked Norfolk island with 2000 sheep, 450 head of cattle, and 20 horses, and gave them stores to last 12 months, their numbers were 96 males and 102 females

Pitcairn's island, visited by British ship *Petrel*, was found to be prosperous, Dec 1875, 86 inhabitants, 2 Mch 1878, 93, 15 Aug 1879, in 1890, 126

Pittsburg, known as "The Smoky City" or "The Iron City" from its extensive iron industries and manufactures, covers an area of 29¾ square miles, lying between the Alleghany and Monongahela rivers at their confluence with the Ohio in western Pennsylvania It takes its name from fort Pitt, erected at that point in 1759 Washington visited fort Pitt in Oct. 1770, and says of the town, distant about 300 yards from the fort "The houses, which are built of logs and ranged in streets, are on the Monongahela, and I suppose may be about twenty in number and inhabited by Indian traders." A census of the borough, published in the Pittsburg *Gazette*, 9 Jan 1796, gives the population as 1395, in 1800 Pittsburg contained 1565 inhabitants, and by decades since the population has been, 1810, 4768, 1820 7248, 1830, 12,568, 1840, 21,115, 1850, 46,601, 1860, 49,221, 1870, 86,076, 1880, 156,389, 1890, 238,617, 1900, 321,616 Lat 40° 33′ N, lon 80° W

Leaden plate deposited at forks of the Ohio by Celeron de Bienville, despatched by governor general of New France to take possession of the country, bore date 3 Aug 1749
Washington, standing on the site of Pittsburg, pronounces it "extremely well situated for a fort, as it has absolute command of both rivers" 24 Nov 1753
Stockade erected by capt Trent, who arrives 17 Feb 1754
Unfinished stockade, commanded by ensign Ward with 40 men, is surrendered to the French under capt. Contrecouer, who brings 60 batteaux 300 canoes 18 pieces of cannon, and 1000 men 17 Apr, and begins erection of fort Duquesne Apr "
Fort Duquesne burned and evacuated by the French, 24 Nov, is occupied by British under gen Forbes (PENNSYLVANIA), 25 Nov 1758
Fort Pitt erected on site of fort Duquesne by gen Stanwix, Sept 1759, completed in spring 1760
Redoubt, between Penn st and Duquesne way, erected by col Bouquet (PENNSYLVANIA) 1764
Col John Campbell lays out 4 squares of village lots near the fort, between Water and Second and Ferry and Market sts "
First shingle roofed house, a 2 story, double hewn log, erected on corner Water and Ferry sts by col George Morgan, about "
Survey of the "manor of Pittsburg" completed and returned, embracing 5766 acres 19 May, 1769
Fort Pitt abandoned by British under orders of gen Gage, Oct 1772
Fort Pitt occupied by Virginia troops under capt. John Neville, 11 Sept. 1775
First sale of lots made by John Penn, jr, to Isaac Craig and Stephen Bayard, comprising about 3 acres of ground between fort Pitt and the Alleghany river Jan 1784
Laying out of the town completed by Thomas Vickroy, June, 1784, and approved by attorney of the proprietors. 30 Sept "
First number of the Pittsburg *Gazette*, issued by John Scull and Joseph Hall 29 July, 1786
Post ordered by the government between Philadelphia and Pittsburg Sept "
Mayflower, the first boat with New England emigrants bound for the mouth of the Muskingum, passes Pittsburg 3 Apr 1788
Alleghany laid out 1789
Small blast furnace (abandoned after 3 years), known as Anschutz's, is erected at what is now Shady Point, 3 miles from the Union depot, on the Pennsylvania railroad 1792
Meeting of "sundry inhabitants of the western counties of Pennsylvania" to consider legal means against the law taxing spirits, at Pittsburg (WHISKEY INSURRECTION). 21 Aug "
Pittsburg incorporated as a borough 22 Apr 1794
Line of keel boats established between Cincinnati and Pittsburg, "
Whiskey insurgents assemble at Braddocks for the purpose of attacking Pittsburg, they march into the place, are treated to refreshments, and most of them march out again July, "
Army of 1500 men under gen Lee arrive at Pittsburg to protect the place and suppress the insurgents. Nov "
Manufacture of glass, begun in 1795, is extended by gen James O'Hara and maj Isaac Craig, who establish a glass house with 8 pots, with capacity of 3 boxes at a blowing 1796
President Adams, first of 2 armed galleys and first sea going vessel built on the Ohio, launched at Pittsburg 19 May, 1798
First paper mill built "
Schooner *Amity*, 120 tons, and ship *Pittsburg*, 250 tons sea going vessels, built by a company at the head of which was Louis Anastasius Tarascon, launched at Pittsburg 1801
Branch of the Bank of Pennsylvania established on east side of Second st, near Ferry st Jan 1804
First iron foundery in Pittsburg erected by Joseph McClurg "
First stage line from Pittsburg to Chambersburg opened May, 1805
Steam flouring mill erected at corner Water st. and Redoubt alley by Oliver and Owen Evans 1809
First steamboat built in Pittsburg, the *New Orleans*, about 400 tons, 138 feet keel, launched (snagged and lost near Baton Rouge, La, in 1814) Mch 1811
Rolling mill erected by Christopher Cowan on corner Penn st. and Cecil's alley 1812
Steel furnace erected by Tuper and McKowan 1813
United States arsenal built 1814
Bank of Pittsburg incorporated and organized 22 Nov "
Pittsburg incorporated as a city under the style of the "mayor, aldermen and citizens of Pittsburg" by act 18 Mch 1816
Bridge over the Monongahela and over the Alleghany at St Clair st built 1819
Water works established, taking supply from the Alleghany river about 1 mile from its mouth 1824
Second rolling mill in the city, the first to puddle and to roll bar iron, was the Union mill erected in 1819 on the Monongahela, and accidentally blown up and dismantled in. 1829
First boat on Pennsylvania canal arrives at Pittsburg 10 Nov "
Great freshet on the Ohio Feb 1832
Manufacture of blister steel begun by G and H Shoenberger about 1833
First boat built of iron that navigated the western waters was the *Valley Forge*, 180 feet long, the frame of angle iron, beams of T iron, and outside of ⅜ inch Juniata boiler plate, launched at Pittsburg during summer of 1839

Chronicle Telegraph established.... 1841
Daily Post established.... 1842
Improvement of Monongahela river by locks and dams, begun 1843, and opened to National road at Brownsville...13 Nov. 1844
Fire destroys 982 buildings, covering 56 acres, along the Monongahela river front nearly a mile; loss $3,479,950..10 Apr. 1845
Alleghany cemetery established.... "
Iron war-vessel *George M. Bibb* built and launched; dimensions 210 ft. keel, 21 ft. beam, 17 ft. depth of hold.... "
Daily Dispatch established.... 1846
Mercy hospital chartered.... 1848
Board of Health created by act of Assembly approved..8 Apr. 1851
Pennsylvania and Ohio railroad opened to New Brighton, 28 miles....July, "
Library association founded.... "
Western Pennsylvania hospital organized, 9 Mch. 1847; chartered 18 Mch. 1848, and hospital building opened....Jan. 1853
Crucible cast-steel, of the best quality, made as a regular product by Hussey, Wells & Co.... 1859
Clinton blast furnace of Graff, Bennett & Co. blown in....Oct. "
Order from secretary of war, John B. Floyd, to ship to New Orleans 150 pieces of cannon lying at the Alleghany arsenal; the people determine to resist, but the order is countermanded within 3 days....26 Dec. 1860
Turner Rifles leave for Harrisburg....17 Apr. 1861
12th and 13th regiments leave for Harrisburg....24 Apr. "
Pittsburg fortified by earthworks, and prepared for a siege, 14 June et seq. 1863
Sanitary fair opens; receipts $361,516.17....1 June, 1864
Commercial Gazette established.... "
Homœopathic hospital chartered.... 1866
City's area increased to include the land between the 2 rivers from 7 miles above their junction.... 1867
Alleghany County Law library founded.... "
Pittsburg *Leader* established.... 1870
Eleven boroughs on the South side, with a population of 35,723, consolidated with Pittsburg by act of assembly 29 Mch., approved by the governor....2 Apr. 1872
Town of Wilkins incorporated with Pittsburg.... 1874
Strike declared by the conductors and brakemen on the Pennsylvania railroad at Pittsburg....19 July, 1877
Strikers attack the 6th division of the Pennsylvania state guards who tried to clear the Twenty-third st. crossing; the beginning of the riot of (STRIKES)....21-22 July, "
Daily Times established.... 1879
County court-house destroyed by fire....May, 1882
Holy Ghost college opened 1878; chartered.... "
Daily Press established.... 1883
Exposition society's buildings burned with all the exhibits; loss $1,000,000....3 Oct. "
Natural gas as fuel introduced in the city.... 1884
St. Peter's church burned....12 Nov. 1886
First cable street-railroad opened—Fifth ave. line....12 Sept. 1888
Centennial of Alleghany county celebrated and new county court-house dedicated....24 Sept. "

MAYORS.

Name.	Term of office.	Remarks.
Ebenezer Denny....	1816-17	
John Darragh....	1817-25	
John M. Snowden....	1825-27	
Magnus M. Murray....	1828-29	
Matthew B. Lowry....	1830	In 1834 the mayor was first elected by the people. Prior to this appointed by city councils; and he was one of the aldermen.
Magnus M. Murray....	1831	
Samuel Pettigrew....	1832-35	
Jonas R. McClintock....	1836-38	
William Little....	1839	
William W. Irwin....	1840	
James Thompson....	1841	
Alexander Hay....	1842-44	
William J. Howard....	1845	
William Kerr....	1846	
Gabriel Adams....	1847-48	
John Herron....	1849	
Joseph Barker....	1850	
John B. Guthrie....	1851-52	
Robert M. Riddle....	1853	
Ferdinand E. Volz....	1854-55	
William Bingham....	1856	
Henry A. Weaver....	1857-59	Jan., 1858, the mayor was elected for 2 years.
George Wilson....	1860-61	
B. C. Sawyer....	1862-63	
James Lowry....	1864-65	
W. C. McCarthy....	1866-67	
James Blackmore....	1868	The mayor was elected for 3 years under act of 1868.
Jared M. Brush....	1869-71	
James Blackmore....	1872-74	
William C. McCarthy....	1875-77	
Robert Liddell....	1878-80	
Robert W. Lyon....	1881-83	
Andrew Fulton....	1884-86	
William McCallum....	1887-89	
H. I. Gourley....	1890-92	
Bernard McKenna....	1893-96	

Pittsburg Landing, or **Shiloh,** Battle of. Shortly after the capture of fort Donelson, gen. Grant moved his army to Pittsburg Landing, on the Tennessee river, about 8 miles above Savannah, and 20 miles from Corinth, Miss. This position was occupied during the latter part of Mch. 1862. The army, numbering about 40,000 men, was in 6 divisions, viz., Sherman's, Hurlbut's, W. H. L. Wallace's, McClernand's, Prentis's, and Lew. Wallace's; the latter, however, being at Crump's Landing, some 6 or 7 miles below. The confederates also concentrated at Corinth, with Albert Sidney Johnston in chief command, and Beauregard as second, with 4 corps commanders, Polk, Bragg, Hardee, and Breckinridge; in numbers the army fully equalled the federals. On 1 Apr. 1862, both were expecting reinforcements. Grant expected Buell with about 40,000 men, and Johnston expected Van Dorn with 30,000. Johnston, however, concluding to attack Grant before joined by Buell, moved his army out from Corinth on the morning of the 3d, but, owing to the heavy rains of the 4th, he could not attack until early dawn of Sunday the 6th, when, by persistent and continuous fighting, he succeeded in forcing the federals back during the day from the vicinity of Shiloh church nearly to the river, over 3 miles. At the close of the day's fighting Nelson's division of Buell's command arrived in part (Ammen's brigade) on the battlefield, and helped repulse the last charge of the victorious confederates. The day's fighting was favorable to them, although Johnston fell about 2 P.M. while leading a charge. The battle of the 7th was opened at early light by Buell on the left, who had reinforced Grant during the night to the extent of 20,000 men. He was further strengthened by the addition of Lew. Wallace's division, whose absence from the field the preceding day was owing to a misunderstanding of orders; this brought the Federal forces up to about their original numbers. But while the confederates were thus outnumbered, their success of the previous day had so emboldened them that the battle of the 7th was quite as severe as that of the 6th; in fact, it was not until nearly noon that the Federal successes warranted them any assurance of victory. As early as 2 P.M. Beauregard, now in command, ordered a retreat, having already sent back his trains towards Corinth, and by 4 o'clock had enveloped his retiring columns with his rearguards, and the second day's battle ended without pursuit by the federals. The losses in this battle, the most severe that had as yet occurred, were: Confederates, killed, 1728; wounded, 8012; prisoners, 959; total, 10,699. Federals, killed, 1735; wounded, 7882; prisoners, 3956; total, 13,573. CORINTH.

pituri̇ne, a new narcotic, said to have been discovered in 1882 in Australia. It resembles a mixture of opium and tobacco. It is extracted from the dried leaves of the *Duboisia pituri.*

Placen'tia, now **Piacen'za,** a city of N. Italy, founded by the Romans about 220 B.C. It suffered in all the convulsions attending the fall of the empire and the wars of the middle ages. In 1254 it fell under the rule of the family of the Scotti. In 1302 Alberto Scotto was overcome, and Placentia was united to Milan, then ruled by the Visconti. On their extinction in 1447, Placentia revolted, but was taken by Sforza, duke of Milan, and treated very cruelly. In 1513 it was given to pope Leo X. In 1545, Paul III. gave it with Parma as a duchy to his son Peter Louis Farnese. The French and Spaniards were defeated by the Austrians and Sardinians near Placentia, 16 June, 1746. PARMA.

Placil'la, Chili. The site of the decisive victory of the Congressists over pres. Balmaceda, 28 Aug. 1891.

plague (Gr. πληγή, a blow), a malignant fever of the most aggravated kind. The plagues of Egypt (1491 B.C.) are described in Exod. ix., etc. The first recorded plague general in all parts of the world occurred 767 B.C.—*Petavius.* At Carthage a plague was so terrible that people sacrificed their children to appease the gods, 534 B.C.—*Baronius.* At Rome a desolating plague prevailed, 453 B.C. The devastating plague at Athens, which spread into Egypt and Ethiopia, 430 B.C., is admirably described by Thucydides. Another which raged in the Greek islands, Egypt, and Syria, destroyed 2000 persons every day, 187 B.C.—*Pliny.* CATTLE.

In Italy a most awful plague; 10,000 persons perished daily, 80 A.D.
Again ravaged the Roman empire, 167, 169, 189.
Another in the Roman empire. For some time 500 persons died daily at Rome, many towns depopulated, 250-65. It has been assumed that this plague was the small-pox or the bubo-plague.
In Britain, a plague swept away such multitudes that the living were scarcely sufficient to bury the dead, 446.
Long-continued dreadful one began in Europe in 558, extending all over Asia and Africa.

At Constantinople, when 200,000 of its inhabitants perished, and in Calabria, Sicily, and Greece, 746-49.
In London, 962.
At Chichester, in England, an epidemic disease carried off 34,000 persons, 772.—*Will. Malmes.*
In Scotland, 40,000 persons perished, 954.
In London, great mortality, 1094; in Ireland, 1095.
Again in London; it extended to cattle, fowl, and other domestic animals, 1111.—*Holinshed.*
In Ireland; after Christmas this year, Henry II. was forced to quit the country, 1172.
Again in Ireland, when a prodigious number perished, 1204.
"Black Death" in Italy and throughout Europe, 1347-50. Britain and Ireland suffered grievously. In London alone 200 persons were buried daily in the Charter-house yards, 1348-49. (That at Florence described by Boccaccio.) This was probably the worst epidemic ever visited on man; it is estimated that in Asia 23,-000,000 perished by it, and 25,000,000 in Europe.
In London and Paris a dreadful mortality prevailed in 1361-62, 1367, 1369, and in Ireland in 1370.
Great pestilence in Ireland, called the *Fourth*, destroyed a great number of the people, 1383.
30,000 persons perished of a dreadful pestilence in London, 1407.
Again in Ireland, superinduced by a famine; great numbers died, 1466; and Dublin was wasted by a plague, 1470.
An awful pestilence at Oxford, 1471; and throughout England; destroyed more people than the continual wars for the 15 preceding years, 1478.—*Rapin; Salmon.*
Sudor Anglicus, or sweating sickness, very fatal in London, 1485. —*Delaune.*
Plague in London so dreadful that Henry VII. and his court removed to Calais, 1499-1500.—*Stow.*
Sweating sickness (mortal in 3 hours) in London, 1506, and in 1517. In most of the capital towns in England half the inhabitants died, and Oxford was depopulated, 9 Henry VIII.—*Stow.*
Limerick was visited by a plague; many thousands perished, 1522.
Sweating sickness again in England, 1528; and in North Germany in 1529; and for the fifth time in England in 1551.
30,578 persons perished of the plague in London alone, 1603-4. It was also fatal in Ireland.
200,000 perished of a pestilence at Constantinople in 1611.
In London, great mortality, 35,417 persons perished, 1625.
In Italy, 1630: in Florence, 12,000 died; in Mantua, 25,000; in Bologna, 30,000; in Milan, 180,000. In Milan the barber Mord and the health commissioner Piazza, convicted of rubbing "plague salve" upon house walls, after all kinds of tortures had their hands cut off, were broken on the wheel, and then burned.—*Baas*, "Hist. of Medicine."
In France a general mortality; at Lyons, 60,000 persons died, 1632.
Plague brought from Sardinia to Naples (by a transport with soldiers on board) carried off 400,000 of the inhabitants in 6 months, 1656.
Great plague of London began Dec. 1664, which carried off 68,596 persons; some say 100,000. Fires were kept up night and day to purify the air for 3 days; and it was thought the infection was not totally destroyed till the great conflagration of Sept. 1666.
[Graphically described by De Foe in his partly imaginative "History of the Plague."]
60,000 persons perished of the plague at Marseilles and neighborhood, brought in ship from the Levant, 1720.
Awful plague in Syria, 1760.—*Abbé Mariti.*
In Persia, a fatal pestilence, which carried off 80,000 of the inhabitants of Bassora, 1773.
In Egypt, about 800,000 persons died of plague, 1792.
In Barbary, 3000 died daily, and at Fez 247,000 perished, 1799; in the east, 1800, 1840, 1873; many deaths in Bagdad, etc., Apr.-May, 1876.
In Spain and at Gibraltar immense numbers were carried off by a pestilent disease in 1804 and 1805.
Again at Gibraltar, an epidemic fever much resembling the plague caused great mortality, 1828.
Asiatic cholera made its first appearance in England at Sunderland, 26 Oct. 1831; in Scotland, at Haddington, 23 Dec. same year; in Ireland, at Belfast, 14 Mch. 1832, and in the U. S. the same year.
Cholera again visited England, etc., 1848 and 1849.
Cholera raged at Smyrna and Constantinople, and appeared in Paris, Marseilles, Naples, July-Dec. 1865.
Great cattle-plague in England, resembling typhus, near London, begins June, 1865.
New disease appeared in Dublin; many persons died a few hours after the seizure, Mch. et seq. 1866.
Plague in Astrakhan, Jan.-Apr. 1879. CHOLERA, YELLOW-FEVER, etc.
The statistics here given are not exaggerated, but rather underestimated. The plagues and pestilences both of antiquity, mediæval, and later times arose from various causes: (1) Ignorance of the laws of health; (2) restless migrations of the people; (3) insecurity of property, giving rise to idleness and imperfect cultivation of the land, and the consequent failure of crops; (4) total lack of commercial facilities to supply the wants of any destitute community—the first post-road in Europe being opened in 1497; (5) uncleanliness; (6) improper food; (7) want of proper and sufficient clothing; (8) dense crowding in the very circumscribed areas of the walled towns; (9) their total lack of drainage, unpaved and filthy streets poisoning the water of the wells, etc.; (10) gross and barbarous immorality; (11) constant wars and disputes, with religious fanaticism, tended to keep up an over-tension of the mind, giving rise to manias, etc.; (12) want of sympathy for the sick and diseased.

planeta'rium, an astronomical machine representing the motion and orbits of the planets. David Rittenhouse, the eminent mechanic and mathematician of Philadelphia, Pa., constructed a planetarium in 1768 which has elicited the highest praise. It was superior to anything that had been previously constructed, and was purchased by the college of New Jersey, at Princeton, where it remains. Upon it is this inscription: "*Invented by David Rittenhouse*, A.D. 1768; *repaired and extended by Henry Voight*, 1806; *both of Philadelphia.*" It is said that when Cornwallis took possession of Princeton, after Washington left it on the morning of 3 Jan. 1777, he intended to carry off this planetarium and send it as a trophy to England; but the Americans kept him too busy to allow him to plunder. ORRERY.

planets, celestial bodies which revolve about the sun in a fixed orbit with a moderated degree of eccentricity. We now know 9 primary planets, termed major—MERCURY, VENUS, the EARTH, MARS, JUPITER, SATURN, URANUS, NEPTUNE, and VULCAN (doubtful), and 384 (1893) secondary or minor planets, termed asteroids, situated between the orbits of Mars and Jupiter. The first 4 were discovered as follows, viz.:

Ceres, discovered by Piazzi (visible to the naked eye)...1 Jan. 1801
Pallas, discovered at Bremen by Olbers..............28 Mch. 1802
Juno, discovered by Harding..........................1 Sept. 1804
Vesta, by Olbers.......................................29 Mch. 1807
The fifth, *Astræa*, by K. C. Hencke, 8 Dec. 1845, since which time many others have been discovered. So far as known, *Pallas*, with a diameter of 600 miles, is the largest of them.

planim'eter, a machine for measuring the area of any figure by the passage of a tracer round about its perimeter. Amsler's planimeter (in use for several years) was described at the British Association meeting at Brighton, Aug. 1872.

planing-machine, a machine for trimming up and facing wood, and iron also. One for wood was constructed by Bramah, about 1802, and one for iron by Joseph Clement, 1825.

Plantag'enet, House of, to which belonged 14 English kings, from Henry II., 1154, to Richard III., killed at the battle of Bosworth, 1485. Fulke Martel, earl of Anjou, having contrived the death of his nephew, the earl of Brittany, in order to succeed to the earldom, his confessor sent him, in atonement for the murder, to Jerusalem, attended by only 2 servants, one of whom was to lead him by a halter to the Holy Sepulchre, the other to strip and whip him there, like a common malefactor. Broom, in French *genet*, in Latin *genista*, being the only tough, pliant shrub in Palestine, the noble criminal was smartly scourged with it, and from this instrument of his chastisement he was called *Planta-genista*, or Plantagenet. Other accounts are given.—*Skinner* and *Mézeray*. ENGLAND, KING.

plantations, charters granted to. RHODE ISLAND, 1643-63.

Plas'sey, formerly a village of Bengal, India, the site of a battle fought between the British under Clive and the Hindus under Surajah Dowlah, 23 June, 1757. The nabob, although at the head of about 68,000 men, was vanquished by 1000 British and about 2000 sepoys. The victory laid the foundation of the British empire of India. The village and fortifications have been destroyed by the river Hoogly. INDIA.

plaster of Paris. Gypsum, sulphate of lime, used for moulds, statuary, etc., first found at Montmartre, near Paris, whence its name. The method of taking likenesses by its use was first discovered by Andrea del Verrochio, about 1466.

Platæ'a, a ruined city of Bœotia, N. Greece, site of the battle between Mardonius, commander of the army of Xerxes of Persia, and Pausanias, commander of the Lacedæmonians and Athenians, 22 Sept. 479 B.C.; the same day as the battle of Mycale. Of 300,000 Persians, scarce 3000 escaped with their lives.

"There had the Persian thousands stood,
There had the glad earth drunk their blood,
On old Platæa's day."
—*Halleck*, "Marco Bozzaris."

The Grecian army, about 110,000, lost but few men. The Greeks obtained immense plunder, and were henceforth delivered from the fear of Persian invasions. Platæa, as an ally of Athens, was destroyed by the Thebans, 372, and rebuilt by Philip II. after his victory at Chæronea, 338.

plat'inum, the heaviest of all the metals except iridium. The name originated with the Spaniards on account of its silvery color; *plata* signifying silver. It was found in the auriferous sand of the river Pinto, in South America, nd was unknown in Europe until 1741, when don Antonio Jlloa announced its existence in the narrative of his voyage o Peru —*Greg* In its ore have been found the metals palladium, rhodium, osmium, iridium, and ruthenium ELEMENTS. In 1859, M H Ste-Claire Deville made known a new nethod of obtaining platinum from its ore, in great abundance nd purity, and at the international exhibition of 1862 was hown a mass worth 3840*l*, weighing 266½ lbs., of a metal litherto considered infusible, obtained by his process, employng the oxy-hydrogen flame

Dode s process for coating iron with platinum to prevent rust, shown at Johnson & Matthey s, London 11 Jan 1870

Platon'ic philosophy, the most popular of all systems. Plato's dialogues have been termed "Philosophy backed by example" He was a disciple of Socrates, 409 B.C, nd died 347 The leading feature of his mind was comprehensiveness PHILOSOPHY

Platonic year, the period of time which the equinoxes take to finish their revolution, at the end of which the tars and constellations have the same place with regard to he equinoxes that they had at first Tycho Brahe says that his year or period requires 25,816 common years to complete t, Riccioli computes it at 25,920, and Cassini at 24,800, at the end of which time some imagined that there would be a otal and natural renovation of the whole creation EQUINOX

Plattsburg. UNITED STATES, 1814

plays. DRAMA, SHAKESPEARE, THEATRES

pleadings. Clothaire held a kind of movable parliament called *placita*, whence came the word pleas, 616 A D —*Henault* In the early courts of judicature in England, pleadngs were made in the Saxon language in 786, and in Norman-French from the period of the Conquest in 1066 until 1362 Pleadings were ordered to be in English by 36 Edward III 1362, and Cromwell extended the rule to all legal proceedings, 1650 In English law the proceedings are the mutual statements of the plaintiff's cause of action and the defendant s ground of defence

Pleasant Grove and **Pleasant Hill,** Battles of. RED RIVER CAMPAIGN

plebe'ians, plebes, the citizens of Rome, as distinguished from the patricians ROME, 494-366 B C

plebisci'tum, a term given to a law passed by the *comitia tributa*, an assembly of the Roman people in their tribes, first established in 491 B.C The term has been recently revived in France and Italy, and applied to universal suffrage

Ple'iades, a notable group of stars in the constellation Taurus, commonly known as the "7 stars," although but 6 are visible to the naked eye, viz Alcyon of the third magnitude, Electra and Atlas of the fourth, and Merope, Maïa, and Taygete of the fifth The name is possibly derived from the Gr πλεῖν, to navigate (mentioned in Job xxxviii 31) According to recent calculation the sun is moving towards a point in he constellation Hercules, and possibly the movement is orbital, the centre of which is the Pleiades

'Many a night I saw the Pleiads, rising thro' the mellow shade,
Glitter like a swarm of fire flies, tangled in a silver braid"
—*Tennyson*, "Locksley Hall"

plethys'mograph, an apparatus for detecting the state of the mind by observing the relations of the circulation of the blood from the heart to the brain, invented by M Mosol of Turin, 1882

Plevna, Bulgaria RUSSO-TURKISH WARS, 1877

plots. CONSPIRACIES, REBELLIONS

plough. "Thou shalt not plough with an ox and an ass together" (Deut xxii 10, 1451 B.C) The Roman plough s minutely described by Virgil, about 31 B C Engines to plough grounds, whether inland or upland, were patented by David Ramsay and Thomas Wildgoose, Engl, in 1618 AGRICULTURE in the United States, STEAM-PLOUGHS.

plum. FLOWERS AND PLANTS. Formerly damsons, apricots, and peaches went by this name, as raisins do to this day.

plural number. WE

plus (+) and **minus (−)** Prof De Morgan attributes these signs to either Christopher Rudolf, who published a book on algebra about 1522, or Michael Stifelius, about 1544

Plymouth. MASSACHUSETTS, 1620, etc

Plymouth Brethren. A sect calling themselves simply "Brethren," and also known as Darbyites, from one of their founders John W Darby They originated in Dublin, Plymouth, and Bristol, Engl, about 1829 They receive into communion all who confess Christ and acknowledge the Holy Ghost as his vicar They recognize no order of ministers In 1838 Darby removed to Switzerland, from whence the society spread into France and Italy It also has a considerable following in the United States Their strength cannot be satisfactorily estimated, since they have no formal organization

pneumatics (*nū-mat'iks*), the science which treats of the mechanical properties of air and gases AIR, ATMOSPHERIC RAILWAYS

Pocahon'tas. VIRGINIA, 1607, '12, '13, '16

podestà (from *potestas*, power) an Italian governor, afterwards a judge, one with supreme authority was appointed at Milan by the emperor Frederick I, when he took the city in 1158

poet-laureate. Selden could not trace the precise origin of this office

Warton, in his "History of English Poetry," states that in the reign of Henry III there was a *Versificator Regis*, to whom an annual stipend was first paid of 100s

Chaucer, on his return from abroad assumed the title of poet laureate, and in the twelfth year of Richard II, 1389, he obtained a grant of an annual allowance of wine

In the reign of Edward IV, John Kay was laureate, Andrew Bernard was laureate, *temp* Henry VII, and John Skelton, *temp* Henry VIII

James I, in 1615, granted to his laureate a yearly pension of 100 marks, and in 1630 this stipend was augmented by letters patent of Charles I to 100*l*. per annum with an additional grant of 1 tierce of Canary Spanish wine to be taken out of the king's store of wine yearly It is believed that on Southey s appointment the tierce of Canary wine was commuted for 27*l*.

Laurence Eusden commenced a series of Birthday and New year's Odes which continued till the death of Pye, in 1813

On the death of Warton, its abolition was recommended by Gibbon whose elegant compliment on the occasion still more forcibly applied on Wordsworth s death, in 1850 "This is the best time for not filling up the office, when the prince is a man of virtue, and the poet just departed was a man of genius."

POETS-LAUREATE

Edmund Spenser, d 1599
Samuel Daniel, d 1619
Ben Jonson (b 1574), d 1637
Sir William Davenant, 1637, d 1668
John Dryden 1670, deposed at the revolution, 1688.
Thomas Shadwell, 1688, d 1692
Nahum Tate, 1692, d 1715.
Nicholas Rowe d 1718.
Rev Laurence Eusden, 1718, d. 1730
Colley Cibber 1730, d 1757
William Whitehead (on the refusal of Gray), 1757, d 1785
Rev dr Thomas Warton (on the refusal of Mason), 1785, d 1790
Henry James Pye 1790, d 1813
Dr Robert Southey (on the refusal of Scott), 1813, d 21 Mch 1843.
William Wordsworth, 1843, d 23 Apr 1850.
Alfred Tennyson (b 1809), installed 1850, d 6 Oct 1892
The office is now vacant, 1895

poetry. Technically, composition in verse, but "poetry is the blossom and the fragrance of all human knowledge, human thoughts, human passions, emotions, and language"—*Coleridge* The song of Moses on the deliverance of the Israelites, and their passage through the Red sea, 1491 B.C (Exod xv.), is the most ancient poetry extant. Orpheus of Thrace is deemed the inventor of poetry (at least in the western part of the world) about 1397 B.C BALLADS, COMEDY, EPIC POEMS, HYMNS, LITERATURE, ODES, SATIRE, SONNETS, TRAGEDY, and VERSE

Point Pleasant, Battle of VIRGINIA, 1774

Poitiers (*pwa-tyā'*), a town of W. France, near which was fought the battle between Edward the Black Prince, and John, king of France, in which the English arms triumphed, 19 Sept 1356 The standard of France was overthrown, many of her nobility slain, and her king was taken prisoner, and brought to London. PRISONERS, TOURS, VOUGLE

Poland, N.E Europe, part of ancient Sarmatia. It is

said to have become a duchy under Lechus or Lesko I., 550; and a kingdom under Boleslas, about 992; the natives belong to the great Slavonic family. The word Pole is not older than the 10th century. This kingdom in its best days embraced a territory of about 284,000 sq. miles, and extended 713 miles north and south and 693 east and west. Its destruction as a separate nationality and the absorption of its territory by Austria, Prussia, and Russia, commencing in 1772 (when it embraced an area of about 282,000 sq. miles, with a population of not far from 12,000,000) and finished in 1795, could not have been accomplished without the aid of Poland herself, and while sympathy is aroused at the needless destruction of a nation, still it was due (1) to the inveterate jealousy and feuds of the Polish nobility among themselves; (2) the absence of a middle or national class, which the nobles made impossible; (3) the intolerance of the Jesuitical Romish party; (4) total incapacity of its later rulers; (5) no natural frontier boundaries. Its history as a nation ceased 1795 with Stanislas II.

Piastus, a peasant, is elected to the ducal dignity........about 842

[Piastus is said to have lived to the age of 120, reigning so prosperously that succeeding native sovereigns were called Piasts.]

Introduction of Christianity..............about 992

Boleslas II. murders St. Stanislas, the bishop of Cracow, with his own hands, 1079; his kingdom laid under an interdict by the pope, and his subjects absolved of their allegiance...... 1080

He flies to Hungary for shelter; but is refused it by order of Gregory VII., and at length kills himself or dies in a monastery.. 1081

Tartar invasion.............. 1241

Premislas assassinated.............. 1296

Louis of Hungary elected king.............. 1370

Ladislas VI. defeated and slain by the Turks.............. 1444

War against the Teutonic knights..............1410, 1447

Wallachian invaders carry off 100,000 Poles, and sell them to the Turks as slaves.............. 1498

Wallachians defeated.............. 1531

Splendid reign of Sigismund II.............. 1548

Lithuania incorporated with Poland.............. 1569

Stephen forms a militia composed of Cossacks, on whom he bestows the Ukraine.............. 1575

Poland conquered by the Swedes.............. 1655

Recovered its independence.............. 1660

Abdication of John Casimir.............. 1668

Victories of John Sobieski over the Turks at Vienna.......... 1683

Many Protestants killed after an affray at Thorn.............. 1724

Stanislas abolishes torture.............. 1770

Awful pestilence destroys 250,000 persons.............. "

Civil war so weakened the kingdom that it fell an easy prey to Russia, Austria, and Prussia.............. 1772

First partition convention, secret between Russia and Prussia, 17 Feb. "

Public partition treaty between Austria, Prussia, and Russia, 5 Aug.; acted on..............18 Sept. "

[In this partition Russia obtains 42,000 sq. miles; Prussia, 13,500; and Austria, 27,000.]

Kosciusko joins American army (and serves throughout the Revolution).............. 1776

New constitution granted by the king..............3 May, 1791

Russians, etc., on various pretexts enter Poland.............. 1792

Second partition treaty signed between Russia and Prussia.... 1793

[At this time Russia takes 96,000 sq. miles and Prussia 22,000.]

Insurrection under Kosciusko..............Mch. 1794

After many successes he is defeated by the Russians at Maciejovice and taken prisoner..............10 Oct. "

Praga sacked and Warsaw taken by Suwarrow.......... Nov. "

Courland is annexed to Russia.............. 1795

Stanislas resigns his crown at Grodno; third and final partition of the kingdom..............25 Nov. "

[Russia takes 43,000 sq. miles; Prussia, 21,000; and Austria, 18,000.]

Kosciusko set at liberty by emperor Paul..............25 Dec. 1796

He arrives in London..............30 May, 1797

Poles enter the French army and greatly help France to gain her victories..............1797 et seq.

Stanislas dies at St. Petersburg..............12 Feb. 1798

Napoleon I. enters Warsaw; his army wintered in Poland...1806–7

Poles neglected by the treaty of Tilsit..............7 July, 1807

General diet at Warsaw..............June, 1812

Central provinces (the duchy at Warsaw, between 1807 and 1813) made the kingdom of Poland under Alexander of Russia..............30 Apr. 1815

New constitution granted, Cracow a free republic......27 Nov. "

Kosciusko dies in Switzerland, aged 81..............16 Oct. 1817

Polish diet opened..............Sept. 1820

A revolution at Warsaw; the army declare in favor of the people..............29 Nov. 1830

Diet declares the throne vacant..............25 Jan. 1831

Battle of Grochow, near Praga; the Russians lose 7000 men; the Poles, who keep the field, 2000..............19, 20 Feb. "

Battle of Wawz..............31 Mch. "

Insurrection in Wilna and Volhynia..............3 Apr. "

Russians defeated at Zelicho, 6 Apr.; Seidlece, 10 Apr.; at Ostrolenka..............26 May, "

Russian general Diebitsch d..............10 June, 1831

Battle of Wilna; Poles defeated..............19 June, "

Grand-duke Constantine d..............27 June, "

Battle of Minsk..............14 July, "

Warsaw taken by Russians..............8 Sept. "

Insurrection suppressed..............5 Oct. "

Ukase by the emperor Nicholas, the kingdom of Poland henceforth an integral part of the Russian empire........26 Feb. 1832

Attempted revolution in Austrian Poland..........22-27 Feb. 1846

Courts of Austria, Russia, and Prussia revoke the treaty of 1815, which constituted Cracow a free republic, and it is declared Austrian territory..............16 Nov. "

[This annexation was protested against by England, France, Sweden, and Turkey.]

Kingdom of Poland declared a Russian province.........May, 1847

[From this time up to 1868 several attempts were made by the Poles to achieve their independence without success.]

Poland designated the "Vistula province" in a ukase.....Jan. 1868

Its separate internal government abolished, and complete union with the empire effected..............29 Feb. "

Distinct financial departments of Poland abolished.......Apr. "

Polish language interdicted in public places.............July, "

Polish language prohibited in courts of law and public offices in Russian Poland..............June, 1876

About 35,000 Poles expelled from Prussia...........Oct.-Nov. 1885

Movement for denationalizing Poland..............Feb. 1886

Centenary of the Polish constitution of 1791 celebrated in Austrian Poland..............3 May, 1891

Emperor William of Germany appoints a Polish archbishop of Posen, 1891, and otherwise favors the Poles.............. 1892

CRACOW, RUSSIA, WARSAW.

DUKES AND KINGS OF POLAND.

842. Piastus, duke.
861. Ziemovitus, his son.
892. Lesko or Leskus IV.
913. Ziemomislas, son of Lesko.
964. Miecislas I. becomes Christian.
992. Boleslas I., surnamed the Lion-hearted; obtained the title of king from the emperor Otho III.
Miecislas II.
1034. Richense or Richsa, his consort, regent; driven from the government.
1037. [Anarchy.]
1041. Casimir I., her son, surnamed the Pacific; he had retired to a monastery, but was invited to the throne.
1058. Boleslas II., styled the Intrepid.
1081. Ladislas I., called the Careless.
1102. Boleslas III., surnamed Wry-mouth.
1138. Ladislas, son of the preceding.
1146. Boleslas IV., the Curled.
1173. Miecislas III., the Old; deposed.
1177. Casimir II., surnamed the Just.
1194. Lesko V., the White; abdicated.
1200. Miecislas III.; restored.
1202. Ladislas III.; retired.
1206. Lesko V.; restored; assassinated; succeeded by his son, an infant.
1227. Boleslas V., surnamed the Chaste.
1279. Lesko VI., surnamed the Black.
1289. [Horrid anarchy.]
1295. Premislas, styled king of Poland, governs wisely; assassinated.
1296. Ladislas I. (IV.), the Short; deposed.
1300. Wenceslas, king of Bohemia, abandons Poland.
1304. Ladislas IV., the Short.
1333. Casimir III., the Great; encourages the arts and amends the law; killed by a fall from his horse.
1370. Louis, king of Hungary.
1382. Maria; and 1384 Hedwige (daughters of Louis), and her consort, Jagello, duke of Lithuania, by the style of Ladislas V.
1399. Ladislas II. (V.), alone; annexed Lithuania.
1434. Ladislas III. (VI.), son; succeeded as king of Hungary, 1440.
1445. [Interregnum.]
" Casimir IV.
1492. John (Albert) I., son.
1501. Alexander, prince of Livonia, his brother.
1506. Sigismund I., brother; obtained the surname of the Great.
1548. Sigismund II., Augustus, son (last of the Jagellon dynasty); a splendid reign; added Livonia to his kingdom; d. 1572.
Interregnum.

ELECTED MONARCHS.

1573. Henry de Valois, duke of Anjou, brother to the king of France; he afterwards succeeded to the French throne.
1575. Stephen Bathori, prince of Transylvania; established the Cossacks as a militia.
1586. [Interregnum.]
1587. Sigismund III., son of the king of Sweden, to the exclusion of Maximilian of Austria, elected by the nobles.
1632. Ladislas IV. (VII.), Vasa, son of Sigismund III.; succeeded by his brother.
1648. John II., or Casimir V.; abdicated 1668, and retired to France, where he died a monk in 1672.
1668. [Interregnum.]
1669. Michael-Koributh-Wiesnowiski; in this reign the Cossacks join the Turks and ravage Poland.
1674. John III., Sobieski; the last independent king; illustrious for victories over the Cossacks, Turks, and Tartars.
1697. [Interregnum.]
" Frederick Augustus I., son of John George, elector of Saxony; and elector in 1694; deprived of his crown.

04. Stanislas I. (Lezinski); forced to retire from his kingdom in 1709.
09. Frederick Augustus I. again.
33. Frederick Augustus II., son of the preceding sovereign.
63. [Interregnum.]
64. Stanislas II. Augustus Poniatowski, resigned his sovereignty, 25 Nov. 1795; d. at Petersburg, a state prisoner, 12 Feb. 1798.

polar clock, an optical apparatus invented by prof. 'heatstone (about 1849), whereby the hour of the day is and by means of the polarization of light.

polar regions. NORTHEAST AND NORTHWEST ASSAGES, SOUTH POLE.

polariza'tion of light. OPTICS.

pole-star, or **polar star, Pola'ris,** a star of e second magnitude, the last in the tail of the constellation Jrsa Minor," or "Little Bear." 2 other stars in this con-ellation are known as the "Guardians of the Pole." 2 stars *)ubhe* and *Merak*) in the constellation "Ursa Major," or Great Bear," are called *pointers* to the pole-star. The discov-y of the pole-star is ascribed by the Chinese to their emperor ong-ti, the grandson (they say) of Noah, who reigned and urished 1970 B.C.—*Univ. Hist.* EQUINOX, STARS.

police. The police system, being almost entirely mu-cipal in its character, has gradually developed with the owth of cities. In London, Engl., a night-watch was ap-inted in 1253 to proclaim the hour with a bell before the troduction of clocks. The old watch system was discon-ued, and a new police on duty day and night commenced Sept. 1829. In 1881 the maintenance of police in London st $5,200,000; Paris, $1,160,000; Vienna, $1,900,000. In the nited States there were 24 cities in 1890 whose annual ex-nditure for their police department exceeded $100,000, viz.:

City.	No. police.	Annual cost.
·w York, N. Y.	3421	$4,391,766
iladelphia, Pa.	1717	1,000,000
icago, Ill.	1625	979,894
ooklyn, N. Y.	1157	859,184
oston, Mass	916	963,355
ltimore, Md.	782	677,914
Louis, Mo.	613	475,408
ncinnati, O.	433	330,000
ashington, D. C.	408	399,060
n Francisco, Cal.	406	545,500
etroit, Mich.	368	222,509
uffalo, N. Y.	342	297,994
eveland, O.	319	250,000
ttsburg, Pa.	308	339,899
·w Orleans, La.	266	170,000
ovidence, R. I.	218	274,000
ewark, N. J.	214	170,000
uisville, Ky.	213	180,000
inneapolis, Minn.	199	151,337
ilwaukee, Wis.	196	122,488
vannah, Ga.	125	100,000
olumbus, O.	114	120,072
·w Haven, Conn.	112	102,481
lanta, Ga.	106	108,918

political economy, the science of improving the ndition of mankind, and promoting civilization, wealth, and appiness. It began with Adam Smith's "Wealth of Na-ons," 1776. The principal writers on this subject have been althus, Lauderdale, Ricardo, Mill, McCulloch, and Fawcett, nglish; Say and Sismondi, French; with Carey, Perry, 'alker, Sumner, Thompson, Americans. A professorship of litical economy was established at Oxford by Henry Drum-ond, M.P., 1825; and at Cambridge, first by G. Pryme, in 28, but regularly established by the university in 1863, enry Fawcett (blind) being the first professor.

rchbishop Whately endowed a professorship at Trinity college, Dublin, Isaac Butt first professor........................ 1832
H. Inglis Palgrave's "Dictionary of Political Economy," 1st part pub. 1891. Only 6 parts have appeared, A to E, up to.. 1895
naginary systems: Plato's "Republic;" Sir Thomas More's "Utopia," 1548; Sir Philip Sidney's "Arcadia," 1590; James Harrington's "Oceana," 1656; E. Bellamy's "Looking Backward," 1888; Wm. Morris's "News from Nowhere," 1891.

political parties in the United States. Before e Revolution the 2 political parties in America were the 'higs and Tories. The latter favored royalty, and the former, cluding Sons of Liberty, Liberty Men, and Patriots, advo-ated independence. At the close of the Revolution the Whig rty divided into Particularists, favoring state sovereignty d advocating confederation; and Strong Government, favor-ing a constitution. In 1787 the Particularists became Anti-Federalists and the Strong Government party Federalists. Since this, the history of the various political parties in the U. S. has been as follows:

PRINCIPAL PARTIES.

Federal, 1787-1816.—Formed from the Strong Government or Constitutional party. Elected 2 presidents: Washington, 2 terms, and Adams, 1 term. Advocated a tariff; internal revenue; funding the public debt; a U. S. bank; a militia; assumption of state debt by the government; favored England as against France; opposed a war with England and a protective tariff. Washington, John Adams, Hamilton, Madison, and Jay were among its principal supporters.

Democratic-Republican, 1793-1828.—Formed from the Anti-Federal (1787-93), the Republican or Jeffersonian party (1791-93), and Democrats or sympathizers with the French revolutionists (1791-93). Elected 3 presidents: Jefferson, 2 terms; Madison, 2 terms; Monroe, 2 terms. Favored state-rights; enlarged freedom; France as against England; war with England; internal improvement; purchase of Louisiana; purchase of Florida; Missouri compromise, 1820; Monroe doctrine; Free-trade in 1800 and a protective tariff in 1828. Jefferson its founder and leader.

Democratic, 1828.—The Democratic-Republican party divided into 4 parts in the presidential campaign of 1824 and never reappeared again in a national contest. The Democratic (and Whig) party was constructed out of its ruins. Has elected 6 presidents: Jackson, 2 terms; Van Buren, Polk, Pierce, Buchanan, 1 term; Cleveland, 2 terms. Favored internal improvements; state banks; removal of deposits; sub-treasury; state rights; free-trade; tariff for revenue only; annexation of Texas; Mexican war; compromise of 1850; Monroe doctrine; Dred Scott decision; Fugitive-slave law; acquisition of Cuba; frugal public expense. Opposed agitation of the slavery question in any form or place; coercion of the seceded states; the amelioration of the condition of the freed negroes; Freedman's bureau; Chinese immigration; strong government; opposes in general the policy of the other party in power. This party has had but one leader, Jackson.

Whig, 1834-54.—Formed from a union of the National Republicans and disrupted Democratic-Republicans. Elected 2 presidents: Harrison and Taylor. Favored non-extension of slavery; slavery agitation, i.e., right of petition and free circulation of anti-slavery documents; a U. S. bank; protective tariff; vigorous internal improvements; compromise of 1850. Opposed the Seminole war; annexation of Texas; Mexican war; state-rights; Democratic policy towards slavery. Principal leaders of this party, Webster and Clay. UNITED STATES, 1834-54.

Republican, 1854.—Formed from other parties, principally from the Whig party, on the issues of the slavery question. Has elected 5 presidents: Lincoln, 2 terms; Grant, 2 terms; Hayes, Garfield, and Harrison, 1 term. Favored the suppression of slavery; suppression of the rebellion; all constitutional means to accomplish it, financial and otherwise; emancipation of slaves; prohibition of slavery throughout the U. S.; full citizenship to the emancipated slaves; Monroe doctrine; full payment of the national debt; protective tariff; free ballot; generous pension legislation; decided increase of the navy and coast defence. Opposed the general policy of the Democrats. This party, while showing many able men, has never had a leader. It has maintained its national position through the principles it has advocated. Remark: Both the Democratic and Republican, as the chief parties, recognize and assume to legislate on all questions of national importance, viz.: Civil-service reform; woman's suffrage; free ballot; justice to the laboring classes; private interests as against monopolies; the general finances of the country; temperance, etc.

MINOR PARTIES.

Anti-Federalist.—A continuation of the Particularists. See *Democratic-Republican* above.

Peace party, 1812-15.—Composed of Democratic-Republicans and Federalists, mostly in New England. Opposed the war of 1812. HARTFORD CONVENTION.

Clintonians, 1812.—An offshoot of the Democratic-Republican party who opposed long terms of office, caucus nominations, a Virginia president, and an official regency. United with the Federalists. Nominated De Witt Clinton of New York for president. UNITED STATES, Feb. 1813.

People's party, 1824.—An offshoot of the Democratic-Republicans in New York, who favored the choosing of electors by the people instead of state legislatures. Supported William H. Crawford for president. UNITED STATES, 9 Nov. 1824-Feb. 1825.

Coalition, 1825.—So called from the union of the supporters of Clay with those of John Q. Adams in the House, thus giving the presidency to Adams. UNITED STATES, Nov. 1824 and Feb. 1825.

Anti-Masonic, 1827-34.—Consisted of those who believed the members of the Masonic fraternity held their civil obligations subordinate to their fraternal, hence unworthy to hold office. MORGAN; UNITED STATES, 1830-31, Feb. 1833.

National-Republican, 1828-34.—The broad-construction wing of the Democratic-Republican party. For internal improvements, protection, and a U. S. bank; for dividing proceeds of land sales among states. Opposed to the spoils system. United to form the Whig party, 1834. Supported John Q. Adams, 1828, and Henry Clay, 1832. UNITED STATES.

Nullification, 1831-33.—A South Carolina party organized by Calhoun. SOUTH CAROLINA; UNITED STATES, 1832.

Liberty party, 1840-48.—Founded at a national convention of abolitionists at Albany, N Y, deriving additional strength from Whigs and Democrats For the immediate abolition of slavery and equal rights Against the fugitive slave clause of the constitution Nominated James G Birney for president, 1839 and again in 1843 Withdrew their candidates and joined the Free soil party in 1848

Free soil party 1848-54 —Formed from the Liberty party, Democrats, and Whigs Chief cause of its appearance, opposition to slavery Merged into the Republican party Nominated Martin Van Buren for president, 1848, and John P Hale, 1852 UNITED STATES

American, 1852-60 —Generally known as the "Know Nothing party" Formed from members of other parties dissatisfied with the influx and power of the foreign element Favored more stringent naturalization laws, reserved rights of states Opposed foreign immigration, suffrage and office holding by foreign born citizens, efforts to reject the Bible from the public schools, etc Nominated Millard Fillmore for president in 1856 Merged into the Constitutional Union party in 1860. KNOW NOTHINGS, UNITED STATES, 1856.

Douglas Democrats, 1860 —Northern Democrats, supporters of Stephen A Douglas in the disruption of the Democratic party in 1860 UNITED STATES, 1860.

Breckinridge Democrats, 1860.—Southern Democrats, supporters of Breckinridge in 1860 UNITED STATES, 1860

Constitutional Union party, 1860 —Democrats, for the Union, the Constitution, and the enforcement of law, supporters of Bell and Everett. UNITED STATES, 1860

Liberal Republicans 1872 —Formed by dissatisfied Republicans, formerly mostly War Democrats Favored greater leniency towards the confederates Nominated Horace Greeley for president, 1872 UNITED STATES

"*Straight out*" *Democrats*, 1872 —The "Tap root" Democrats, displeased by the nomination of Greeley by the Regular Democrats nominated Charles O'Conor for president, declined, but received about 30,000 popular votes

Temperance 1872 —A national combination of local temperance organizations, became

Prohibition, 1876 —For legal prohibition, female suffrage, direct presidential vote, currency convertible into coin Nominated James Black from Pennsylvania for president, 1872, Green Clay Smith, 1876, Neal Dow 1880, John P St John, 1884, C B Fisk, 1888, John Bidwell 1892

Greenback 1874, became *National Greenback*, 1878, became *Union Labor* 1887 —Unlimited coinage of gold and silver, substitution of greenbacks for national bank notes, suffrage without regard to sex, legislation in the interest of the laboring classes, etc. Nominated Peter Cooper for president, 1876, James B Weaver, 1880, Benj F Butler, 1884, Alson J Streeter, 1888 These various elements, uniting with the "Farmers' Alliance," form the

People's or *Populists' party*, 1891 —A meeting was held at St. Louis, Dec 1889, of the "Farmers and Laborers' Union of America," for the purpose of consolidating the various bodies of organized farmers in the U S, which had at different times and places formed since 1867, and known under the general term of "Granger movement" GRANGE This meeting was a success, and the consolidated body was called the "Farmers' Alliance and Industrial Union" 2 Dec 1890, a national convention was held at Ocala, Fla, 35 states and territories were represented by 163 delegates, at this convention independent political action was decided upon, and a platform adopted embracing the following principles (1) The abolition of the national banks, establishment of sub treasuries to loan money to the people at 2 per cent., increase of circulation to $50 per capita, (2) laws to suppress gambling in agricultural products, (3) unlimited coinage of silver, (4) laws prohibiting alien ownership of land, and to permit the ownership of land in actual use only, (5) restricting tariff, (6) government to control railroads, telegraphs, etc, (7) direct vote of the people for president, vice president, and U S senators. Second convention held at Cincinnati, 19 May, 1891, 30 states and territories represented with 1418 delegates, at this convention the platform of Ocala, Fla., 1890, was heartily endorsed and the party given the name of "People's party" Third national meeting at St Louis, 22 Feb 1892. National convention for the nominating of president and vice president held at Omaha, 4 July, 1892, James B Weaver of Iowa nominated for president and James G Field of Virginia for vice-president

Socialist Labor —First national convention held in New York city, 28 Aug 1892, and nominated Simon Wing of Mass, for president, and Charles H Matchett, of Brooklyn, N Y, for vice president

LOCAL PARTIES AND POLITICAL NAMES

Abolitionists —ABOLITIONISTS

Anti Renters —ANTI RENTISM

Anti Nebraska.—Opposers of the Kansas Nebraska bill, 1854

Barnburners —BARNBURNERS.

Doughfaces —DOUGHFACES.

Half breeds —A term of contempt bestowed by the Stalwarts upon those who supported the administration of pres Hayes and opposed the nomination of Grant for a third term, etc

Hunkers —BARNBURNERS, HUNKER

Independent Republicans —Started in 1879 in opposition to senator Conkling's leadership of the party and still maintain an independent attitude MUGWUMP

Ku-klux klan —KU KLUX KLAN

Loco focos.—LOCO FOCOS.

Mugwumps —MUGWUMP

Re Adjusters, 1878 —A division of the Democratic party in Virginia advocating the funding of the state debt at 3 per cent, under the leadership of gen Mahone

Stalwarts —A branch of the Republican party followers of Conkling, Cameron and Logan, opposed to the reconciling course of pres. Hayes towards the south Favored the nomination of Grant for a third term Opposers of Blaine, etc.

Silver Grays —SILVER GRAYS

Tammany —TAMMANY

politicians. A politician is described as a man well versed in policy or the well regulating and governing of a state or kingdom, a wise and cunning man. A man of artifice, one of deep contrivance —*South* Never rising to the height of statesmanship. The term was first used in France about 1569

Polk, James K, administration of UNITED STATES, 1845

polka, a dance said to have been invented between 1830 and 1834 in Bohemia, and to have obtained its name in Prague in 1835 It became very popular, and was introduced into England about 1844, and into the United States shortly after.

Pollen'tia, a town of Piedmont, N Italy, the site of a great victory of Stilicho, the imperial general, over Alaric the Goth, 29 Mch 403

poll-tax or **capitation-tax** existed among the ancient Romans It was first levied in England in 1380, and occasioned the rebellion of Wat Tyler (TYLER), 1381 It was again levied in 1513 By 18 Charles II every subject was assessed by the head, viz a duke, 100*l*, a marquess, 80*l*, a baronet, 30*l*, a knight, 20*l*, an esquire, 10*l*, and every single private person, 12*d.*, 1667 This grievous impost was abolished by William III 1689

polo. The Byzantine princes played a game which differed but little from the modern polo It is recorded that the emperor Manuel Comnenus (1143-80) was injured by his horse falling while engaged in this sport. The game of ball termed hockey, played on horseback, became popular in England in 1872, having been introduced into India a few years previously. Games were played by lancers and life-guards at Woolwich, 16, 19 July, 1872 A polo club was formed and international contests held, at Brighton, one opened 3 Aug, 1878

Westchester, N Y, Polo club, the pioneer club in America, organized Mch 1876

First game in the U S played at Jerome park, New York, 11 May, "

polyg'amy (Gr πολύς, many, and γαμέω, to marry) The condition of a person with more than 1 wife or husband living Some writers strictly limit the word to the cases in which there are more than 2 consorts, calling the double relation bigamy. A plurality of wives was permitted among the early nations, and is now by Mahometans In Media it was a reproach to a man to have less than 7 wives. Among the Romans, Marc Antony is mentioned as the first who took 2 wives The practice was forbidden by Arcadius, 393 The emperor Charles V punished polygamy with death In England, by stat 1 James I 1603, it was made felony, with benefit of clergy It was formerly punished with tranportation, but now by imprisonment or penal servitude MARRIAGE. Polygamy was practised by the MORMONS until 1892 Polyandry (where one woman has several husbands) is permitted in some eastern countries, the children having equal rights.

pol'yglot (Gr πολύς, many, and γλῶττα, tongue), is chiefly applied to editions of the Bible in several languages

Hexapla of Origen

Giustiniani published a polyglot psalter, 1576

1 The Complutensian Polyglot, in 6 vols folio, was printed at Alcala (Complutensis), in Spain, 1502-14 the first edition pub 1522, at the expense of the celebrated cardinal Ximenes, costing 250,000 ducats 600 copies of it were printed, 3 on vellum Count MacCarthy of Toulouse paid 483*l* for one of these copies at the Pinelli sale

2 The Polyglot, printed at Antwerp by Montanus, 8 vols. folio, in 1559-69, at the expense of Philip II of Spain

3 Printed at Paris by Le Jay, in 10 vols. folio 1628-45.

4 Edited by Bryan Walton, in 6 vols. folio 1654-57 [Copies of all 4 are in the library of the British and Foreign Bible Society]

5 Edited by dr Samuel Lee, published by S [illegible] 1 vol folio, 1831.

Hexaglot Bible, begun by Henry Cohn, completed by the rev Edward R De Levante and others, 6 vols 4to, 1874

Polyne'sia (Gr. πολύς, many, and νῆσος, island), a me given to the numerous groups of islands throughout e Pacific ocean, but specifically to the various groups ly- g between 125° and 170° lon W, north and south of the uator, including the Sandwich, Samoan, Society, Friendly, :

pol'ypes or **pol'yps**, also named hydræ (many-footed imals), on account of their property of reproducing themves when cut in pieces, every part soon becoming a perfect imal, first discovered by Leeuwenhoek, and described by m in the "Philosophical Trans" 1703 The polypes are of e order zoophytes, and partake of the animal and vegetable ture

polytech'nic school (Gr πολύτεχνος, skilled in iny arts), first established in Paris, 1794, by the National Connition as a school of public works, particularly devoted to in- ucting recruits for the corps of civil and military engineers

pom'egranate-tree (*Punica granatum*) was ken to England from Spain before 1584

Pomera'nia, a Prussian province, N Germany, was ld by the Poles, 980, and by Denmark, 1210, made an in- pendent duchy, 1479, and divided between Sweden and andenburg, 1648 The Swedish part, awarded to Denmark 1814, was given up to Prussia for Lauenburg, 1815 DEN- RK, WRECKS, 1878

Pom'fret or **Ponte'fract,** a town and ruined cas- ot S York, Engl At the castle (built 1069), Richard II s confined and murdered, 10 Feb 1399 Henry IV, by om he was deposed, wishing for his death, sir Piers Exton, ended by 8 followers, rushed into the king's apartment The ter wrested a pole-axe from one of his assailants, and laid f their number dead at his feet, but was at length overpow- d and slain This account is doubted by many historians, t that he here met his death by violence or starvation is e Some writers assert that Richard escaped and died in otland In this castle, also, the earl Rivers, lord Grey, sir omas Vaughan, and sir Richard Haut or Hause, were put death by order of the duke of Gloucester, then protector England (afterwards Richard III), about 26 June, 1483 tle, even of its ruins, now remain The first parliament- election by ballot took place here, 15 Aug 1872, very ietly

Pompeii (*pom-pā'-yē*) S Italy, an ancient city of mpania, was partly demolished by an earthquake in 63 A D was afterwards rebuilt, but was overwhelmed by an eruption Vesuvius on the night of 24 Aug 79 The ashes buried the ole city to a depth of 90 to 125 feet In 1713, a country- n, while excavating for a well, descended upon the theatre Hercules and Cleopatra, and this discovery led to further rch, which brought numerous other objects to light, and at gth the city was partly uncovered The part first cleared s supposed to be the main street, 1750 The kings of ples greatly aided in exhuming Pompeii, and the present lian government resumed the work in 1863

commemorative meeting of antiquaries and philosophers t Pompeii	25 Sept 1879
rther discoveries made	1882 et seq
mains of a 5 story house were uncovered	July, 1890

Pompey's pillar stands about three quarters of a le from Alexandria, between the city and the lake Mareotis e shaft is fluted, and the capital ornamented with palm- ves, the whole, which is highly polished, composed of pieces, and of the Corinthian order The column meas- es, according to some, 94 feet; to others, 141, and even) feet, but of its origin, name, use, and age, nothing is cer- n

s generally believed that the column has no reference to Pompey, o whom a mark of honor was, nevertheless, set up somewhere n this vicinity One supposes that the pillar was dedicated to Vespasian, another to Severus, and Mr Clarke, from a half effaced nscription on the base, considers that Hadrian is the person hon ored, while many assert, from the same inscription, that it is ledicated "to Diocletian Augustus, most adorable emperor, tutelar leity of Alexandria."

Pondicherry (*pon-de-sher'-ree*), S.E India, the capital of French India, and first settled by the French in 1674. It was taken from them by the Dutch in 1693, restored 1697, besieged by the English, 1748, taken by them, Jan 1761, restored, 1765, again taken, Oct 1778, restored in 1783, taken 23 Aug 1793, and in 1803, restored, 1815

Pontiac's war. Pontiac, a chief of the Ottawas (b about 1710), shortly after the surrender of the French possessions to the English, 1760, conceived the idea of retarding, if not completely restraining, the advance of the English settlements west of Pittsburg For this purpose he attempted to confederate the Indian tribes throughout the west and south against the English In this he was so successful that in the spring of 1763 the conspiracy was ripe for action, and so secretly and suddenly was the attack made along the whole western frontier that most of the advanced posts fell into the hands of the Indians, with the exception of Detroit and Pittsburg, and these were saved with the greatest difficulty This war lasted throughout the year, when the Indians were subdued, but Pontiac, unconquered, was killed by a Peoria Indian near St Louis in 1769, bribed, it is said, by an English trader INDIAN HISTORY, 1763, MICHIGAN, PENNSYLVANIA

pontiffs (Lat *pontifices*) the highest Roman sacerdotal order, established by Numa The college first consisted of 4 patricians, with a chief (Pontifex Maximus), to these 4 plebeians were added by the Ogulnian law, 300 B C. Sulla increased the number to 15 (8 *majores*, 7 *minores*), and Julius Cæsar to 16 T Coruncanius, a plebeian, obtained this office, 254 B C

pontoons, boat-shaped vessels used in military operations for supporting a temporary bridge Used by Darius and Xerxes in their invasion of Greece in passing from Asia to Europe Two of the most essential qualities of such vessels are strength and lightness

Pontus, Asia Minor, seems to have been a portion of Cappadocia, and received its name from its vicinity to the *Pontus Euxinus* Artabazus was made king of Pontus by Darius Hystaspis, 487 B C His successors were mere satraps of the kings of Persia

	B C
Reign of Mithridates I	383
Ariobarzanes invades Pontus	363
Mithridates II recovers it	336
Mithridates III reigns	301
Ariobarzanes II reigns	266
Mithridates IV is besieged in his capital by the Gauls etc	252
Mithridates attacks Sinope, and is obliged to raise the siege by the Rhodians.	219
Reign of Pharnaces, 190, he takes Sinope, and makes it the capital of his kingdom	183
Reign of Mithridates V	157
He is murdered in the midst of his court	123
Mithridates VI, surnamed the Great, or Eupator, receives the diadem at 12 years of age	"
Marries Laodice, his own sister	115
She attempts to poison him, he puts her and accomplices to death	112
Mithridates conquers Scythia, Bosporus, Colchis, and other countries	111
He enters Cappadocia	97
His war with Rome	89
Tigranes ravages Cappadocia	86
Mithridates enters Bithynia and makes himself master of many Roman provinces, and puts 80,000 Romans to death	"
Archelaus defeated by Sylla, at Chæronea, 100,000 Cappadocians slain	"
Victories and conquests of Mithridates up to this time	74
Fleet of Mithridates defeats that under Lucullus in 2 battles	73
Mithridates defeated by Lucullus	69
Mithridates defeats Fabius	68
But is defeated by Pompey	66
Mithridates stabs himself, and dies	63
Reign of Pharnaces	"
Battle of ZELA, Pharnaces defeated by Cæsar	47
Darius [illegible]	39
Polemon, son of Zeno, reigns	36
	A D
Polemon II succeeds his father	33
Mithridates VII reigns	40
Pontus afterwards became a Roman province.	
Alexis Comnenus founded a new empire of the Greeks at Trebizond, in this country, 1204, which continued till the Turks destroyed it in 1459	

poor. The poor of England, till the time of Henry VIII, subsisted, as did the poor of Ireland until 1838, entirely upon private benevolence. By statute 23 Edw III 1349, it was enacted that none should give alms to a beggar able to work. By the common-law, the poor were to be sustained by "parsons, rectors of the church, and parishioners, so that none should die for default of sustenance;" and by 15 Rich. II. impropriators were obliged to distribute a yearly sum to the poor; but no compulsory law was enacted till 27 Hen. VIII. 1535. The origin of the present poor-law is referred to 43 Elizabeth, 1601, by which overseers were appointed for parishes.

PAUPERS RECEIVING RELIEF (NOT VAGRANTS) IN THE UNITED KINGDOM.

Country.	1849	1858	1870	1883	1890
England and Wales..	934,410	968,186	1,079,391	799,296	787,545
Scotland.......about	82,357	69,217	126,187	92,618	88,606
Ireland..............	620,747	50,582	73,921	115,684	107,774
Total...	1,637,523	1,087,985	1,279,499	1,007,598	983,925

AMOUNT EXPENDED IN RELIEF OF THE POOR IN THE UNITED KINGDOM IN THE FOLLOWING YEARS:

Country.	1886	1887	1888	1889	1890
England and Wales..................................	£8,296,230	£8,176,768	£8,440,821	£8,366,477	£8,434,345
Scotland...	894,077	899,135	887,867	882,836	874,389
Ireland..	1,289,024	1,376,010	1,390,994	1,446,171	1,409,280
Total..............	£10,479,331	£10,451,913	£10,719,682	£10,695,484	£10,7[illegible],014

poor in the United States. State Boards of Charity were established in Massachusetts in 1863; Ohio and New York in 1867; Illinois, North Carolina, Pennsylvania, and Rhode Island in 1869; and in other states of the Union subsequently. The New York State Charities Aid Association was founded in 1872, as an aid to the State Board of Charities. Under the influence of CHARITY ORGANIZATION pauperism in Elberfeld, Germany, was reduced 78 per cent. in 15 years; in London, England, 30 per cent. in 10 years; and in Buffalo, N. Y., where the system was inaugurated by rev. S. H. Gurteen in 1877, 37 per cent. in 10 years. For 5 years ending with 1888, the average of burials in the Potter's Field of New York city was 10.03 per cent. of all deaths in the city.

NUMBER OF PAUPERS IN ALMSHOUSES IN THE UNITED STATES AT VARIOUS DATES.

	1850	1860	1870	1880	1890
Male....................	....	....	....	35,564	40,741
Female..................	....	....	....	30,639	32,304
Native..................	36,916	50,483	53,939	43,236	43,123
Foreign born............	13,437	32,459	22,798	22,967	29,922
White..................	....	....	67,337	60,486	66,578
Colored................	....	....	9,400	5,717	6,467
Total......	50,353	82,942	76,737	66,203	73,045

RATIO OF PAUPERS TO EACH MILLION OF POPULATION.

	1850	1860	1870	1880	1890
Male....................	....	....	....	1394	1270
Female..................	....	....	....	1244	1057
Native..................	1765	1849	1635	944	808
Foreign born............	5986	7843	4095	3438	3239
White..................	....	....	2005	1394	1210
Colored................	....	....	1928	847	846
General average..	2171	2638	1990	1320	1166

Out-door paupers, i. e., not in almshouses........1880........21,590
" " " " ....1890........24,225

pope (from Gr. *πάππας* and *πάπα*, a father or grandfather), considered by Romanists to be the visible chief of the church, the vicar of Jesus Christ, and the successor of St. Peter. He styles himself "servant of the servants of God." The title pope was formerly given to all bishops, and is regularly applied to presbyters in charge in the Russian church. It was first adopted by Hyginus, 139; and pope Boniface III. induced Phocas, emperor of the East, to confine it to the prelates of Rome, 606. By the connivance of Phocas also, the pope's supremacy over the Christian church was established. ITALY, REFORMATION; ROME, Modern.

Wilfrid, abp. of York, expelled from his diocese, appeals to the pope.. 679
Custom of kissing the pope's toe introduced................. 708
Adrian I. caused money to be coined with his name.......... 780
Indulgences for sin granted by pope Leo III............about 800
Sergius II. the first pope who changed his name on his election, 844; some contend that it was Sergius I. 687, and others John XII.. 956
John XVIII., a layman, made pope.............................. 1024
First pope who kept an army, Leo IX........................... 1054
Gregory VII. (Hildebrand) obliges Henry IV., emperor of Germany, to stand 3 days, in the depth of winter, barefooted at the gate of the castle of Canossa, to implore his pardon.... 1077
Pope's authority fixed in England.............................. 1079
Appeals from English tribunals to the pope introduced (*Viner*), 19 Stephen.. 1154
Henry II. of England holds the stirrup for pope Alexander III. to mount his horse... 1161
Celestine III. kicked the emperor Henry VI.'s crown off his head while kneeling, to show his prerogative of making and unmaking kings.. 1191
John, king of England, did homage to the pope's legate for his dominions, and bound himself and his successors to an annual payment to the pope..........................15 May, 1213
Pope collected the tenths of the whole kingdom of England... 1226
Papal seat removed for 70 years to Avignon in France....... 1308
Pope's demands on England refused by Parliament............ 1363
Great schism at which time 2 rival popes claimed supremacy, one at Rome and the other at Geneva..................1378-1417
After the discovery of America, pope Alexander VI. granted to the Portuguese all the countries to the east, and to the Spanish all the countries to the west, of cape Non, Africa, they might conquer...................................... 1493
Pope Leo X. published the sale of general indulgences throughout Europe.. 1517
Appeals to Rome from England abolished (*Viner*)............... 1533
Words "lord pope" struck out of all English books.......... 1541
Kissing the pope's toe and other ceremonies abolished by Clement XIV... 1773
Pope's political influence greatly diminished by the French revolution...1789-1814
His temporal power lost (ROME)...........................Dec. 1870
PIUS IX. under POPES.

BISHOPS AND POPES OF ROME.

(*Names in italics were antipopes.*)

42. St. Peter (said to have been the first bishop of Rome, and to have been crucified, head downwards, in 66).
** St. Clement (Clemens Romanus); according to Tertullian.
66. St. Linus: martyred? cir. 78.
* [St. Linus is frequently called immediate successor of St. Peter; but Tertullian maintains that it was St. Clement. In the first century neither the dates nor order of succession of bishops can be fixed with certainty. Some assert *that there were 2 or 3 bishops of Rome at the same time.*]
78. St. Cletus, or Anacletus? martyred?
91. St. Clement II.: abdicated?
100. St. Evaristus: martyred; multiplied churches.
109. St. Alexander: martyred.
119. St. Sixtus I.: martyred?
127. St. Telesphorus: martyred.
139. St. Hyginus: condemns Gnostics; called himself *pope*.
142. St. Pius: martyred.
157. St. Anicetus.
168. St. Soterus: martyred under Marcus Antoninus.
177. St. Eleutherius: opposed the Valentinians.
193. St. Victor I.: martyred under Severus.
202. St. Zephyrinus: claimed to be Peter's successor.
219. St. Calixtus: martyred.
222. [The chair vacant.]
223. St. Urban I.: beheaded.
230. St. Pontianus: banished by the emperor Maximin.
235. St. Anterus: martyred.
236. St. Fabian: martyred under Decius, 250.
250. [The chair vacant.]
251. St. Cornelius: died.
252. St. Lucius: martyred 252. *Novatianus* (denied restoration to the repentant lapsed).
253. St. Stephen I.: martyred in the persecution of Valerian.
257. St. Sixtus II. (his coadjutor): martyred 3 days before his disciple St. Laurence, in the persecution of Valerian, 258.
258. [The chair vacant.]
259. St. Dionysius: opposed the heresy of Sabellius.
269. St. Felix I.: died in prison.
275. St. Eutychianus.
283. St. Caius: *a relative of the emperor Diocletian.*
296. St. Marcellinus: said to have lapsed under a severe persecution? canonized.
304. [The chair vacant.]
308. St. Marcellus: banished from Rome by the emperor Maxentius.
310. St. Eusebius: died the same year.
311. St. Miltiades or Melchiades: coadjutor to Eusebius.
314. St. Silvester: commencement of temporal power by gifts of Constantine.
336. St. Marcus: died the next year.
337. St. Julius I.: of great piety and learning; maintained the cause of St. Athanasius.
352. Liberius: banished.
355. *Felix II.*: placed in the chair by Constans, during the exile of Liberius, on whose return he was driven from it with ignominy. [The emperor would have the 2 popes reign together; but the people cried out, "*One God, one Christ, and one bishop!*"]
358. Liberius again: abdicated.

in the afternoon. The federals are at first successful, although largely outnumbered, and after relinquishing the ground gained, maintain their original position. Federal losses, 314 killed, 1445 wounded, 620 missing; Confederate loss, 229 killed, 1047 wounded.]

ckson retires to the Rapidan, 11 Aug.; Pope follows on the 12th. Pope reinforced by 2 divisions of Burnside's corps, Reno's and Stevens's..............................14 Aug. 1862

pe retires from the Rapidan to the Rappahannock, taking positions at Kelly's ford and Rappahannock station, 18–19 Aug. "

[Pope is now directed by Halleck to hold the line at the Rappahannock, promising him immediate reinforcements from the army of the Potomac.]

aj.-gen. Jas. E. B. Stuart assigned to the command of all the cavalry of the Confederate army of northern Virginia, 17 Aug. "

uart's cavalry raid on Catlett's station, and destruction of Pope's headquarters.............................22 Aug. "

ynolds's division, by way of Fredericksburg, reinforces Pope, 23 Aug. "

gagement at Great Run.......................... " "

earney's and Hooker's divisions of Heintzelman's corps, by the way of Alexandria, reinforce Pope.............24 Aug. "

Stonewall" Jackson with Stuart's cavalry, after a forced march of 50 miles in 36 hours, pass Thoroughfare gap, attack Bristow and Manassas stations, and destroy Pope's supplies and munitions of war..............................26 Aug. "

pe further reinforced by Fitz-John Porter's corps, the 5th, Morell's and Sykes's divisions, and Platt's brigade...26 Aug. "

pe falls back from the Rappahannock towards Gainesville and Manassas Junction.............................27 Aug. "

ckson occupies the former battle-field of Bull Run.. " "

ngstreet advances through Thoroughfare gap and joins Jackson...29 Aug. "

ttle of Groveton.................................. " "

[Results favorable to the confederates, owing to the union of Longstreet's troops with those of Jackson's. It was for his conduct in this battle that charges were preferred against Fitz-John Porter by Pope. PORTER, FITZ-JOHN.]

ttle of Manassas or Second Bull Run...............30 Aug. "

[This was a continuation of the battle of *Groveton*. In this battle the confederates are well united, and force Pope to retire across Bull Run to Centreville.]

ttle of Chantilly..................................1 Sept. "

[While the federals are strongly posted in and around Centreville and still further reinforced by Franklin's and Sumner's corps, Lee pushes Jackson on the right flank of the federals towards Washington. This movement brings on the battle of Chantilly, in which the troops under McDowell, Hooker, and Kearney repulse Jackson, but with the loss of gens. Kearney and Stevens.]

pe retires within the defences of Washington, and is relieved at his own request of the command of the army of Virginia, and appointed to a command in the northwest.......2 Sept. "

n. McClellan appointed to command the army and the defences of Washington ....2 Sept. "

[From this date the army of Virginia is merged into the army of the Potomac. MARYLAND CAMPAIGN.]

CASUALITIES IN THE FEDERAL FORCES UNDER MAJ.-GEN. JOHN POPE FROM 16 AUG.–2 SEPT.

	Killed.	Wounded.	Captured or missing.	Aggregate.
icers.............	132	461	106	699
listed men.......	1615	7991	4157	13,763
Total...........	1747	8407	4263	14,462

[No separate report made for the several battles of the campaign.]

poplar-trees. FLOWERS AND PLANTS.

poplin or **tabinet,** an elegant rich fabric, composed silk and worsted, introduced into England by the Huguet refugees from France about 1693; first manufactured in ublin. Irish poplins are still deservedly esteemed.

popular or **"squatter" sovereignty** (the rm "squatter" being applied to it by Calhoun in derision) s expressed in the doctrine advanced by Lewis Cass in 47, and may be stated in general terms as the right of every rritory to legislate for itself. "Popular sovereignty in the rritories is and always has been a privilege, and not a right, d the privilege is always to be exercised in strict conform- to the terms of the grant."—*Lalor,* "Cycl. of Political ience."

popular vote for president. Previous to 1824 no urns were preserved of the popular vote for president, for e reason that in the earlier elections the legislatures of the ferent states chose the presidential electors. Even as late 1824 6 states, viz., Delaware, Georgia, Louisiana, New York, uth Carolina, and Vermont, thus voted, and one state, South rolina, so continued to vote until 1868. For the electoral te, UNITED STATES.

POPULAR VOTE FOR THE PRINCIPAL PRESIDENTIAL CANDIDATES FROM 1828 to 1892.

Party.	1828.	1832.	1836.	1840.	1844.	1848.	1852.	1856.	1860.			1864.	1868.	1872.	1876.	1880.	1884.	1888.	1892.
Democratic	Jackson. 647,231	Jackson. 687,502	Van Buren. 761,549	Van Buren. 1,128,702	Polk. 1,337,243	Cass. 1,220,544	Pierce. 1,601,474	Buchanan. 1,838,169	Douglas. 1,375,157	Breckinridge. 845,763	Bell. 589,581	McClellan. 1,808,725	Seymour. 2,759,315	Greeley. 2,834,079	Tilden. 4,284,885	Hancock. 4,442,035	Cleveland. 4,911,017	Cleveland. 5,538,233	Cleveland. 5,556,533
National Republican	Adams. 509,097	Clay. 530,189																	
Anti-Masonic	....	Wirt. 33,108																	
Whig........	....	....	W. H. Harrison. 736,656	Harrison. 1,275,017	Clay. 1,299,068	Taylor. 1,360,101	Scott. 1,380,578												
Liberty......	....	....	....	Birney. 7059	Birney. 62,300														
Free-Soil....	....	....	....	....	....	Van Buren. 291,263	Hale. 156,149												
Republican..	....	....	....	....	....	....	...	Fremont. 1,341,264	Lincoln. 1,866,352			Lincoln. 2,216,067	Grant. 3,015,071	Grant. 3,597,070	Hayes. 4,033,950	Garfield. 4,449,053	Blaine. 4,848,334	B. Harrison. 5,440,216	Harrison. 5,175,577
American....	....	....	....	....	....	....	....	Fillmore. 874,538											
Temperance or Prohibition	....	....	....	....	....	....	....	....	....			....	....	Black. 5608	Smith. 9522	Dow. 10,305	St. John. 151,809	Fisk. 249,907	Bidwell. 279,191
Greenback or United Labor or People's Party	....	....	....	....	....	....	....	....	....			....	....	....	Cooper. 81,740	Weaver. 307,306	Butler. 133,825	Streeter. 148,105	Weaver. 1,122,045
Socialistic Labor	....	....	....	....	....	....	....	....	....			....	....	....	....	....	....	....	Wing. 21,191

POLITICAL PARTIES.

POPULAR VOTE FOR PRESIDENTIAL CANDIDATES IN 1896, 1900, AND 1904

(For the vote from 1828 to 1892 inclusive, see preceding page.)

Year of election	Candidates for President.	States	Political party	Popular vote	Plurality	Elect'l vote	Candidates for Vice President	States	Political party	Elect'l vote
1896	William McKinley	Ohio	Rep	7 104,779	601,854	271	Garret A Hobart.	N J	Rep	271
	William J Bryan	Neb	Dem }	6,502,925		176	Arthur Sewall	Me	Dem	149
	William J Bryan	Neb	Peop }				Thomas E Watson	Ga.	Peop	27
	Joshua Levering	Md	Pro	132,007			Hale Johnson	Ill	Pro	
	John M Palmer	Ill	N Dem	133,148			Simon B Buckner	Ky	N Dem	
	Charles H Matchett	N Y	Soc L	36,274			Matthew Maguire	N J	Soc L	
	Charles E Bentley	Neb	Nat	13,969			James H Southgate	N C	Nat	
1900	William McKinley	Ohio	Rep	7,207,923	849,790	292	Theodore Roosevelt	N Y	Rep	292
	William J Bryan	Neb	Dem - P	6,358,133		155	Adlai E Stevenson	Ill	Dem - P	155
	John G Woolley	Ill	Pro	208,914			Henry B Metcalf	Ohio	Pro	
	Wharton Barker	Pa	M P	50,373			Ignatius Donnelly	Minn	M P	
	Eugene V Debs	Ind	Soc.	87 814			Job Harriman	Cal	Soc	
	Jos F Malloney	Mass	Soc L	39,739			Valentine Remmel	Pa	Soc L	
	J F R Leonard	Iowa	U C	1,059			John G Woolley	Ill	U C	
	Seth H Ellis	Ohio	U R	5 698			Samuel T Nicholson	Pa	U R	
1904	Theodore Roosevelt	N Y	Rep	7 624,489	2,541,735	336	Charles W Fairbanks	Ind	Rep	336
	Alton B Parker	N Y	Dem	5,082,754		140	Henry G Davis	W Va	Dem	140
	Eugene V Debs	Ind	Soc	402,286			Benjamin Hanford	N Y	Soc	
	Silas C Swallow	Pa	Pro	258,787			George W Carroll	Tex	Pro	
	Charles H Corrigan	N Y	Soc L.	32 088			William W Cox	Ill	Soc L	
	Thomas E Watson	Ga	Peop	117 935			Thomas H Tibbles	Neb	Peop	

COMPARATIVE RANK OF STATES AND TERRITORIES IN 1900

(Exclusive of Porto Rico and the Philippines.)

State	Population at first census	Rank 1890	Rank 1900	Population 1900.
Alabama	127,901	17	18	1,828,697
Alaska			51	63,592
Arizona	9,658	48	49	122,931
Arkansas	14,273	24	25	1,311,564
California	92,597	22	21	1,485,053
Colorado	34,277	31	31	539,700
Connecticut	237,946	29	29	908,420
Delaware	59 096	42	46	184,735
District of Columbia	14 093	39	42	278,718
Florida	34 730	32	32	528,542
Georgia	82,548	12	11	2,216,331
Hawaii			48	154,001
Idaho	14,999	45	47	161,772
Illinois	12,282	3	3	4,821,550
Indiana	5,641	8	8	2,516,462
Indian Territory			39	392,060
Iowa	43,112	10	10	2,231,853
Kansas	107,206	19	22	1,470,495
Kentucky	73,677	11	12	2,147,174
Louisiana	76 556	25	23	1,381,625
Maine	96,540	30	30	694,466
Maryland	319,728	27	26	1,188,044
Massachusetts	378 787	6	7	2,805,346
Michigan	4,762	9	9	2,420,982
Minnesota	6,077	20	19	1,751,394
Mississippi	8,850	21	20	1,551,270
Missouri	20,845	5	5	3,106,665
Montana	20,595	44	44	243,329
Nebraska	28,841	26	27	1,066,300
Nevada	6,857	49	52	42,335
New Hampshire	141,885	33	36	411,588
New Jersey	184,139	18	16	1,883,669
New Mexico	61,547	43	45	195,310
New York	340,120	1	1	7,268,012
North Carolina	393,751	16	15	1,893,810
North Dakota }	4,837	41	41	319,146
South Dakota }		37	37	401,570
Ohio	45 365	4	4	4,157,545
Oklahoma		46	38	398,331
Oregon	13,294	38	35	413,536
Pennsylvania	434,373	2	2	6,302,115
Rhode Island	68,825	35	34	428,556
South Carolina	249,073	23	24	1,340,316
Tennessee	35,691	13	14	2,020,616
Texas	212,592	7	6	3,048,710
Utah	11,380	40	43	276,749
Vermont	85,425	36	40	343,641
Virginia	747,610	15	17	1,854,184
Washington	11,594	34	33	518,103
West Virginia	442,014	28	28	958,800
Wisconsin	30,945	14	13	2,069,042
Wyoming	9,118	47	50	92,531

LARGEST CITIES OF THE U S

City	Population 1900	Population 1890	Increase since 1890
New York, N Y	3,437,202	2,492,591	944 611
Chicago, Ill	1,698,575	1,099,850	598,725
Philadelphia, Pa	1,293,697	1,046,964	246,733
St Louis, Mo.	575,238	451,770	123 468
Boston, Mass	560,892	448,477	112,415
Baltimore, Md	508,957	434,439	74,518
Cleveland, O	381,768	261,353	120,415

LARGEST CITIES OF THE U S (Continued)

City	Population 1900	Population 1890	Increase since 1890
Buffalo, N Y	352,387	255,664	96,723
San Francisco, Cal	342,782	298,997	43,785
Cincinnati, O	325,902	296,908	28,994
Pittsburg, Pa	321,616	238,617	82,999
New Orleans, La	287,104	242,039	45,065
Detroit, Mich	285,704	205,876	78,828
Milwaukee, Wis.	285,315	204,468	80,847
Washington, D C	278,718	230,392	48,326
Newark, N J	246,070	181,830	64,240
Jersey City, N J	206,433	163,003	43,430
Louisville, Ky	204,731	161,129	43,602
Minneapolis, Minn	202,718	164,738	37,980
Providence, R I	175,597	132,146	43,451
Indianapolis, Ind	169,164	105,436	63,728
Kansas City, Mo	163,752	132,716	31,036
St Paul, Minn	163,065	133,156	29,909
Rochester, N Y	162,608	133,896	28,712
Denver, Col.	133,859	106,713	27,146
Toledo, O	131,822	81,434	50,388
Allegheny, Pa.	129,896	105,287	24,609
Columbus, O	125,560	88,150	37,410
Worcester, Mass	118,421	84,655	33,766
Syracuse, N Y	108,374	88,143	20,231
New Haven, Conn	108,027	81,298	26,729
Paterson, N J	105,171	78,347	26,824
Fall River, Mass.	104,863	74,398	30,465
St Joseph, Mo	102,979	52,324	50,655
Omaha, Neb	102,555	140,452	*37,897
Los Angeles, Cal	102,479	50,395	52,084
Memphis, Tenn	102,320	64,495	37 825
Scranton, Pa	102,026	75,215	26,811
Lowell, Mass.	94,969	77,696	17,273
Albany, N Y	94,151	94,923	*772
Cambridge, Mass	91,886	70,028	21,858
Portland, Ore	90,426	46,385	44,041
Atlanta, Ga	89,872	65,533	24,339
Grand Rapids, Mich	87,565	60,278	27,287
Dayton, O	85,333	61,220	24,113
Richmond, Va	85,050	81,388	3,662
Nashville, Tenn	80,865	76,168	4,697
Seattle, Wash	80,671	42,837	37,834
Hartford, Conn	79,850	53,230	26,620
Reading, Pa	78,961	58,661	20,300
Wilmington, Del	76,508	61,431	15,077
Camden, N J	75,935	58,313	17,622
Trenton, N J	73,307	57,458	15,849
Bridgeport, Conn	70,996	48,866	22,130
Lynn, Mass	68,513	55,727	12,786
Oakland, Cal	66,960	48,682	18,278
Lawrence, Mass	62,559	44,654	17,905
New Bedford, Mass.	62,442	40,733	21,709
Des Moines, Ia	62,139	50,093	12,046
Springfield, Mass	62,059	44,179	17,880
Somerville, Mass	61,643	40,152	21 491
Troy, N Y	60,651	60,956	*305
Hoboken, N J	59,364	43,648	15,716
Evansville, Ind	59,007	50,756	8,251
Manchester, N H	56,987	44,126	12,861
Utica, N Y	56,383	44,007	12,376
Peoria, Ill	56,100	41,024	15,076
Charleston, S C	55,807	54,955	852
Savannah, Ga	54,244	43,189	11,055
Salt Lake City, Utah	53,531	44,843	8,688
San Antonio, Tex	53,321	37,673	15,648
Duluth, Minn	52,969	33,115	19,854

* Decrease.

population of the United States in its various phases is best seen in tabulated form. Early census estimates give the population of the U. S. in 1688, 200,000; 1714, 434,600; 1750, 1,260,000; 1760, 1,695,000; 1770, 2,312,000; 1780, 2,945,000.

POPULATION AND RANK OF STATES AND TERRITORIES.

State.	Population at first census.	Rank each decade. 1790	1800	1810	1820	1830	1840	1850	1860	1870	1880	1890	Population 1890.
Alabama	127,901	..	..	..	19	15	12	12	13	16	17	17	1,513,917
Arizona Terr.	9,658	..	..	..	..	..	..	..	..	46	44	48	59,620
Arkansas	14,273	..	..	..	26	28	25	26	25	26	25	24	1,128,179
California	92,597	..	..	..	..	..	..	29	26	24	24	22	1,208,130
Colorado	34,277	..	..	..	..	..	..	..	38	41	35	31	419,198
Connecticut	237,946	8	8	9	14	16	20	21	24	25	28	29	746,258
Delaware	59,096	16	17	19	22	24	26	30	32	35	38	42	168,493
District Columbia	14,093	..	19	22	25	25	28	33	35	34	36	39	230,392
Florida	34,730	..	..	..	..	26	27	31	31	33	34	32	391,422
Georgia	82,548	13	12	11	11	10	9	9	11	12	13	12	1,837,353
Idaho	14,999	..	..	..	..	..	..	..	..	44	46	45	84,385
Illinois	12,282	..	..	24	24	20	14	11	4	4	4	3	3,826,351
Indiana	5,641	..	21	21	18	13	10	7	6	6	6	8	2,192,404
Iowa	43,112	..	..	..	..	..	29	27	20	11	10	10	1,911,896
Kansas	107,206	..	..	..	..	..	..	..	33	29	20	19	1,427,096
Kentucky	73,677	14	9	7	6	6	6	8	9	8	8	11	1,858,635
Louisiana	76,556	..	..	18	17	19	19	18	17	21	22	25	1,118,587
Maine	96,540	11	14	14	12	12	13	16	22	23	27	30	661,086
Maryland	319,728	6	7	8	10	11	15	17	19	20	23	27	1,042,390
Massachusetts	378,787	4	5	5	7	8	8	6	7	7	7	6	2,238,943
Michigan	4,762	..	..	25	27	27	23	20	16	13	9	9	2,090,889
Minnesota	6,077	..	..	..	..	..	..	36	30	28	26	20	1,301,826
Mississippi	8,850	..	20	20	21	22	17	15	14	18	18	21	1,289,600
Missouri	20,845	..	..	23	23	21	16	13	8	5	5	5	2,679,184
Montana	20,595	..	..	..	..	..	..	..	..	43	45	44	132,159
Nebraska	28,841	..	..	..	..	..	..	..	39	36	30	26	1,058,910
Nevada	6,857	..	..	..	..	..	..	..	41	40	43	49	45,761
New Hampshire	141,885	10	11	16	15	18	22	22	27	31	31	33	376,530
New Jersey	184,139	9	10	12	13	14	18	19	21	17	19	18	1,444,933
New Mexico Terr.	61,547	..	..	..	..	..	..	32	34	37	41	43	153,593
New York	340,120	5	3	2	1	1	1	1	1	1	1	1	5,997,853
North Carolina	393,751	3	4	4	4	5	7	10	12	14	15	16	1,617,947
North Dakota / South Dakota	4,837	..	..	..	..	..	..	..	42	45	40	41 / 37	182,719 / 328,808
Ohio	45,365	..	18	13	5	4	3	3	3	3	3	4	3,672,316
Oklahoma Terr.	....	..	..	..	..	..	..	..	..	..	..	46	61,834
Oregon	13,294	..	..	..	..	..	..	34	36	38	37	38	313,767
Pennsylvania	434,373	2	2	3	3	2	2	2	2	2	2	2	5,258,014
Rhode Island	68,825	15	16	17	20	23	24	28	29	32	33	35	345,506
South Carolina	249,073	7	6	6	8	9	11	14	18	22	21	23	1,151,149
Tennessee	35,691	17	15	10	9	7	5	5	10	9	12	13	1,767,518
Texas	212,592	..	..	..	..	..	..	25	23	19	11	7	2,235,523
Utah Territory	11,380	..	..	..	..	..	..	35	37	39	39	40	207,905
Vermont	85,425	12	13	15	16	17	21	23	28	30	32	36	332,422
Virginia	747,610	1	1	1	2	3	4	4	5	10	14	15	1,655,980
Washington	11,594	..	..	..	..	..	..	..	40	42	42	34	349,390
West Virginia	442,014	..	..	..	..	..	..	..	..	27	29	28	762,794
Wisconsin	30,945	..	..	..	..	..	30	24	15	15	16	14	1,686,880
Wyoming	9,118	..	..	..	..	..	..	..	..	47	47	47	60,705

LARGEST CITIES OF THE EARTH.

POPULATION ACCORDING TO THE LATEST OFFICIAL CENSUSES.

Cities.	Population.	Cities.	Population.
London	4,536,541	Melbourne	496,079
New York	3,437,202	Milan	491,460
Paris	2,714,068	Marseilles	491,161
Berlin	1,888,848	Sydney	481,830
Chicago	1,698,575	Copenhagen	476,806
Vienna	1,674,957	Rome	462,783
Canton	1,600,000	Lyons	459,099
Tokio, Japan	1,440,121	Leipzig	456,124
Philadelphia	1,293,697	Hyderabad	448,466
St. Petersburg	1,267,023	Leeds	428,953
Calcutta	1,125,400	Breslau	422,709
Constantinople	1,125,000	Odessa	405,041
Peking	1,000,000	Dresden	396,146
Moscow	988,614	Cleveland	381,768
Buenos Ayres	865,490	Sheffield	380,717
Osaka	821,235	Shanghai	380,000
Bombay	776,006	Cologne	372,529
Rio de Janeiro	750,000	Lisbon	356,009
Glasgow	735,906	Kioto	353,139
Buda-Pesth	732,322	Buffalo	352,387
Hamburg	705,738	Belfast	349,180
Liverpool	684,947	Rotterdam	348,474
Warsaw	638,209	Mexico City	344,721
Bangkok	600,000	San Francisco	342,782
St. Louis	575,238	Turin	335,656
Cairo, Egypt	570,062	Bristol, Eng.	328,842
Naples	563,541	Cincinnati	325,902
Brussels	562,893	Pittsburg	321,616
Boston	560,892	Alexandria	319,766
Manchester, Eng.	543,969	Edinburg	316,479
Madrid	539,835	Lodz	315,209
Amsterdam	538,815	Palermo	309,694
Barcelona	533,090	Stockholm	305,819
Birmingham, Eng.	522,182	Manila	297,154
Madras	509,346	Santiago, Chile	296,695
Baltimore	508,957	Dublin	290,638
Munich	499,932	Frankfort-on-Main	288,989

population in general.

ESTIMATED POPULATION OF THE WORLD.

(IN MILLIONS.)

Year.	Author.	World.	Europe.	America.	Asia.	Africa.	Australia.
1810	Gotha	682	180	21	380	99	2
1828	Balbi	847	214	40	481	109	3
1845	Michelot	1009	245	50	620	90	4
1874	Behm-Wagner.	1391	301	85	798	203	4
1886	Levasseur.	1483	347	112	822	197	5

[Estimates vary widely; that of Wagner and Supan in the "Bevölkerung der Erde," for 1891, is 1,479,000,000—less than that of Levasseur in 1886.]

TOTAL AND URBAN POPULATION OF THE UNITED STATES FOR EACH DECADE SINCE 1790; WITH PER CENT. OF INCREASE, BALANCE OF SEXES, POPULATION TO EACH SQUARE MILE, AND THE CENTRE OF POPULATION.

Date.	Total population.	Per cent. of increase.	Population to every sq. mile.	Sexes per 1000 population. Male.	Female.	Urban population.	Per cent. of city population to total.	Centre of population. N. lat.	W. lon.	Location described.	Westward movement
1790	3,929,214	....	4.75	509	491	131,472	3.35	39° 16.5′	76° 11.2′	23 miles E. of Baltimore, Md.	
1800	5,308,483	35.11	6.41	512	488	210,873	3.97	39° 16.1′	76° 56.5′	18 " W. of Baltimore, Md.	41 miles
1810	7,239,881	36.40	3.62	510	490	356,920	4.93	39° 11.5′	77° 37.2′	40 " N.W. by W. of Washington, D. C	36 "
1820	9,633,822	33.06	4.82	508	492	475,135	4.93	39° 5.7′	78° 33′	16 " N. of Woodstock, Va.	50 "
1830	12,866,020	33.55	6.25	508	492	864,509	6.72	38° 57.9′	79° 16.9′	19 " W.S.W. of Moorefield, W. Va.	39 "
1840	17,069,453	32.67	8.29	509	491	1,453,994	8.52	39° 2′	80° 18′	16 " S. of Clarksburg, W. Va.	55 "
1850	23,191,876	35.86	7.78	511	489	2,897,586	12.49	38° 59′	81° 19′	23 " S.E. of Parkersburg, W. Va.	55 "
1860	31,443,321	35.58	10.39	511	489	5,072,256	16.13	39° 0.4′	82° 48.8′	20 " S. of Chillicothe, O.	81 "
1870	38,558,371	22.63	10.70	507	493	8,071,875	20.93	39° 12′	83° 35.7′	48 " E. by N. of Cincinnati, O.	42 "
1880	50,155,783	30.08	13.92	510	490	11,318,547	22.57	39° 4.1′	84° 39.7′	8 " W. by S. of Cincinnati, O.	58 "
1890	62,622,250	24.85	20.78	511	489	18,235,670	29.12	39° 11.9′	85° 32.9′	20 " E. of Columbus, Ind.	48 "
1900	76,303,387	21.00	25.60	512	488	25,031,505	32.90	39° 9.6′	85° 48.9′	6 " S. E. of Columbus, Ind.	26 "

The population of the U. S. has increased largely by immigration. The total number of immigrants from 1654 to 1701 was 134,000; from 1702 to 1800, 492,000; from 1801 to 1820, 178,000; from 1821 to 1890, about 15,426,000, making a grand total of 16,230,000. IMMIGRATION.

PROPORTION OF FOREIGN TO AMERICAN POPULATION IN THE U. S. IN EACH 1000 PERSONS BETWEEN 15 AND 60 YEARS.

Nativity.	1830.	1840.	1850.	1860.	1870.	1880.
American	960	928	866	821	807	817
Foreign	40	72	134	179	193	183

POPULATION OF ROMAN EMPIRE 14 B.C., ESTIMATED BY BODIE.

Italy 6,000,000
Spain 6,000,00
Greece .... 3.
Gaul ....
Other countries ....

Europe ....
Asia ....
Africa ....

POPULATION AND AREA OF ANCIENT CITIES (Dr. Beloch).

City.	Date.	Population.	Area, acres.	Population per acre.
Athens	350 B.C.	150,000	145	103
Thebes	335 B.C.	50,000	500	100
Tyre	332 B.C.	40,000	185	210
Palermo	254 B.C.	27,000	115	230
Alexandria	60 B.C.	500,000	230	218
Rome	14 A.D.	900,000	2950	306

DENSITY OF POPULATION IN NOTED CITIES (1881).

City.	Population.	Acres.	Population per acre.
London	3,893,000	75,000	52
Paris	2,240,000	14,500	154
Berlin	1,193,000	4,500	264
Vienna	724,000	2,800	258
Rome	273,000	800	341

CITIES OF THE WORLD HAVING A POPULATION OF 500,000 AND MORE.

London	1891	4,231,431	Calcutta	1891	840,130
Paris	1886	2,344,550	Brooklyn	1890	806,343
New York	1892	1,801,739	Bombay	1891	804,470
Canton	(estimated)	1,600,000	Moscow	1885	753,469
Berlin	1890	1,579,244	Glasgow	1891	565,714
Tokio	1890	1,389,684	Buenos Ayres	1891	546,986
Vienna	1890	1,364,548	Naples	1890	530,872
Chicago	1890	1,099,850	Liverpool	1891	517,951
Philadelphia	1890	1,046,964	Buda-Pesth	1890	506,384
St. Petersburg	1890	956,226	Manchester	1891	505,343
Constantinople	1885	873,565	Pekin	(estimated)	500,000

GROWTH IN POPULATION OF EUROPEAN POWERS IN 310 YEARS.—*Mulhall.*

Country.	1580.	1680.	1780.	1880.	1890.
France	14,300,000	18,800,000	25,100,000	37,400,000	38,800,000
Austria	16,500,000	14,000,000	20,200,000	37,830,000	40,100,000
Italy	10,400,000	11,500,000	12,800,000	28,910,000	30,300,000
Spain	8,150,000	9,200,000	9,960,000	16,290,000	17,600,000
England	4,600,000	5,532,000	9,561,000	35,004,000	38,200,000
Prussia, including Germany since 1871.	1,000,000	1,400,000	5,460,000	45,260,000	48,600,000
Russia (European)	4,300,000	12,600,000	26,800,000	84,440,000	92,000,000

RATIO OF FOREIGNERS TO 1000 POPULATION IN VARIOUS COUNTRIES.

United States	133	Holland	17
Switzerland	74	Austria	16
Denmark	32	Hungary	15
France	29	Germany	6
Belgium	26	Great Britain	4
Servia	21	Sweden	4
Norway	20	Spain	3
Greece	19	Italy	2

INHABITANTS PER SQ. MILE IN THE FOLLOWING COUNTRIES IN 1820 AND 1890.—*Mulhall.*

Country.	1820.	1890.	Country.	1820.	1890.
Austria	99	166	Norway	8	16
Belgium	287	530	Portugal	92	136
Denmark	71	133	Russia	20	42
France	172	329	Sweden	15	28
Germany	124	233	Switzerland	127	190
Greece	40	88	Engl. (United Kingd.)	148	184
Holland	195	350	United States	3	20
Italy	138	260	Europe	54	90

porcelain. Pottery.

porphyrogen'itus, "born in the purple," a term applied to emperors of the East born while their fathers were reigning.

"Round about a throne where sitting
(Porphyrogene)
In state his glory well befitting,
The ruler of the realm was seen."
—*Poe,* "The Haunted Palace."

Port Gibson. Vicksburg campaign.

Port Hudson, a post-village of Louisiana, on the Mississippi river, at the terminus of the Clinton and Port Hudson railroad, 25 miles above Baton Rouge. This post, which [illegible]d by the confederates, Aug. 1862, lay within [illegible]ment of the Gulf, of which maj.-gen. [illegible] 14 Dec. 1862. In Mch. 1863, Banks [illegible] against it as a diversion in favor of adm. Farragut, who then ran the Port Hudson batteries. After a victorious campaign in Louisiana, in which gen. Richard Taylor was driven to Shreveport, leaving Alexandria an easy prey to Porter's fleet (6 May), Banks again moved against Port Hudson, then commanded by gen. Gardiner. On 25 May Port Hudson was invested by Banks's army, 12,000 strong. An unsuccessful assault was made on the 27th, which involved a national loss of over 2000 men. A second assault (14 June) was also repulsed, but resulted in a nearer approach to the Confederate lines. On the surrender of Vicksburg, Port Hudson was also surrendered, 9 July, with over 6000 prisoners and 51 guns.

Port Republic, Battle of. Peninsular campaign, Virginia.

Port Royal, capital of the French colony Acadia, Nova Scotia. After having been taken and restored several times, it was finally acquired by the British in 1710, and named Annapolis. French in America.

Port Royal expedition. This expedition (29 Oct.–7 Nov. 1861) was under the joint command of gen. Thomas West Sherman and com. Dupont. The fleet consisted of 50 vessels. Fort Walker, on Hilton Head, S. C., and on the opposite side of Broad river fort Beauregard, were reduced, 7 Nov. 43 guns were captured, and possession was taken of Hilton Head, which became, subsequently, an important centre of naval operations.

Porte, or **Sublime Porte,** official name of the court of the sultan of Turkey. Mostasem, the last of the Abbasside caliphs (1243–58), fixed in the threshold of the principal entrance to his palace at Bagdad a piece of the black stone adored at Mecca, and thus this entrance became the "porte" by eminence, and the title of his court. The sultans, successors of the caliphs, assumed the title.—*Bouillet.*

Porteous mob. Capt. Porteous, at Edinburgh, on 15 Apr. 1736, commanded the guard at the execution of Wilson, a smuggler, who had saved the life of a fellow-criminal by springing upon the soldiers around them, and by main force keeping them back while his companion fled. This excited great commiseration, and the spectators pelted the guard with stones. Fearing a rescue, Porteous ordered his men to fire upon the mob, and 17 persons were killed or wounded. He was found guilty of murder, 22 June, 1736; but the queen granted him a reprieve (the king being then in Hanover). The people, at night, broke open the prison, took out Porteous, and hanged him on a dyer's signpost in the Grassmarket, 7 Sept. 1736. None of the rioters were ever detected.

Porter, maj.-gen. Fitz-John, Case of. Fitz-John Porter, in command of the 5th corps of the army of the Potomac, was with his corps temporarily attached to the army of Virginia. For conduct on the battle-field of Groveton (Pope's Virginia campaign), maj.-gen. Pope formally preferred charges against him, and he was deprived of his command. At the request of maj.-gen. McClellan he was restored, and served throughout the Maryland campaign. In Nov. 1862, he was ordered to Washington for trial by court-martial, court consisting of maj.-gen. David Hunter, president, maj.-gen. Hitchcock, brig.-gens. R. King, Prentiss, Ricketts, Casey, Garfield, Buford, Slough, and col. J. Holt, judge-ad.-gen., and after a trial of 45 days he was, on 21 Jan. 1863, found guilty and sentenced to be cashiered and to be forever disqualified from holding any office of trust or profit under the government. This sentence was approved by the president. In 1870 he appealed to the president for a reversal of this sentence. On 12 Apr. 1878, a military board, consisting of maj.-gens. Schofield, Terry, and Getty, was appointed for a rehearing of the case. This board made a report, 19 Mch. 1879, exonerating Porter entirely. They were unable to find anything in his conduct subject to criticism, much less deserving of censure or condemnation, and recommended that the findings and sentence of the court-martial be set aside, and that Porter be restored to the powers of which the sentence deprived him. Pres. Arthur, on 4 May, 1882, remitted so much of the sentence of the court-martial remaining unexecuted as "forever disqualified the said Porter from holding any office of trust or profit under the government." A bill for the relief of Porter came up in the Senate, 28 Dec. 1882, and passed, 33 to 27, but the nsideration of the measure was strongly objected to in the louse, 17 Jan. 1883. On 18 Jan. 1884, gen. Henry W. Slocum New York brought a bill before the House for the relief of orter, which passed by a vote of 184 to 77, 1 Feb., and in e Senate with some changes, 36 to 25, 13 Mch. The House d the Senate agreed, 18 June, and on 2 July it was returned ith the president's veto. On 21 Dec. 1885, Wheeler of Alaama brought before the House another bill, which passed the louse, 171 to 113, 19 Feb. 1886, and the Senate, 30 to 17, 25 une, and was approved by the president 1 July. This bill as as follows: "The president to nominate and by and with e consent of the Senate appoint *Fitz-John Porter*, late maj.-en. of the U. S. volunteers and brevet brig.-gen. and col. in . S. army, to same grade and rank held by him at the time his dismissal from the army, promulgated 27 Jan. 1863, and the discretion of the president to be placed on the retired st; *provided* he receive no pay, compensation, or allowance hatsoever prior to his appointment under this act."

Portland cement, so named from its resemblance Portland stone, made from chalk and fine mud, now used xtensively in the United States, is first mentioned in a patent ranted to Joseph Aspden, a bricklayer of Leeds, Engl., 1824. lis son made the true cement at Northfleet. Its value as a uilding material was established by John Grant's tests, 1859 1871. Portland cement concrete was used by E. A. Bernay 1867.

Portland isle (off Dorset), the English Gibraltar. ortified before 1142. Portland castle was built by Henry III. about 1536. Off this peninsula a naval engagement ommenced between English and Dutch, 18 Feb. 1653, which ontinued for 3 days. The English destroyed 11 Dutch men-f-war and 30 merchantmen. Van Tromp was admiral the Dutch and Blake of the English. Here is found the oted freestone used for building the finest edifices. The ortland lights were erected 1716 and 1789. The pier, with early half a mile square of land, was washed into the sea in eb. 1792. Prince Albert laid the first stone of the Portland reakwater, 25 July, 1849, and the last stone was laid by the rince of Wales, 10 Aug. 1872. James Rendel, the first chief-ngineer, was succeeded, on his death in 1856, by (aft. sir) ohn Coode. The breakwater and other harbor works cost 035,000*l.*, exclusive of convict labor.

Portland or **Barberini vase.** This beautiful ecimen of Greek art (composed of a glass-like substance, ith figures and devices raised on it on white enamel; height inches; diameter in the broadest part, 7; with a handle on ach side) was discovered about the middle of the 16th cenry in a marble sarcophagus in a sepulchre at Monte del Grano, out 2½ miles from Rome, supposed to have been that of the oman emperor Alexander Severus (222-235) and his mother lammæa, and the vase was probably the cinerary urn of one the two. It was placed in the palace of the Barberini family Rome, where it remained till 1770, when it was purchased y sir William Hamilton, from whose possession it passed to at of the duchess of Portland, 1787; at the sale of her effects, is said to have been bought by the then duke of Portland, ho, in 1810, deposited it (on loan) in the British museum. n 7 Feb. 1845, this vase was maliciously broken in many ieces with a stone; it has been skilfully repaired, and is now own to the public in a special room. Josiah Wedgwood ade a mould of it, and took a number of casts.

Porto Bello, a town on the north side of the isthmus Darien, not far from Aspinwall, in the department of Panaa, of the republic of Colombia. Harbor discovered by Coumbus, 2 Nov. 1502. Settled by the Spaniards, 1584. Was ken by Morgan, the buccaneer, in 1668; by the British under dm. Vernon, from the Spaniards, 21 Nov. 1739, and the fortications destroyed. Before the abolition of trade by the galons, in 1748, it was the great mart for the gold and silver Peru and Chili.

Porto Novo, a French settlement on the coast of ahomey; captured by the French in Apr. 1900. It was beeged by the Dahomeyans in 1902, but the French overrew the natives, inflicting great loss, May-Dec. 1902.

Porto Novo, a maritime town of S. India. Here sir yre Coote, with about 9500 men and 55 light field-pieces, skilfully defeated Hyder Ali, ruler of the Carnatic, with 80,000 men and some heavy cannon, 1 July, 1781. Hyder lost about 10,000, the British 587 killed and wounded.

Port Philip. The original name of the colony of Victoria in Australia.

Porto Rico. The island of Porto Rico, over which the flag of the U. S. was raised in token of formal possession on 18 Oct. 1898, is the most eastern of the Greater Antilles in the West Indies, and is separated on the east from the Danish island of St. Thomas by a distance of about 50 miles, and from Hayti on the west by the Mona passage, 70 miles wide. Distances from San Juan, the capital, to important points are as follows: New York, 1411 miles; Charleston, S. C., 1200 miles; Key West, Fla., 1050 miles; Havana, 1000 miles. The island is a parallelogram in general outline, 108 miles from the east to the west, and from 37 to 43 miles across, the area being about 3600 sq. miles, or somewhat less than half that of the state of New Jersey (Delaware has 2050 sq. miles and Connecticut 4990 sq. miles). The pop., according to an enumeration made by the U. S. government in 1900, showed a population of 953,243, of whom 589,426 are white and 363,817 are colored. The density was 264 to the sq. mile; 83.2 per cent. of the pop. cannot read. Porto Rico is unusually fertile, and its dominant industries are agriculture and lumbering. In elevated regions the vegetation of the temperate zone is not unknown. There are more than 500 varieties of trees found in the forests, and the plains are full of palm, orange, and other trees. The principal crops are sugar, coffee, tobacco, cotton, and maize, but bananas, rice, pineapples, and many other fruits are important products. The largest article of export from Porto Rico is coffee, which is over 63 per cent. of the whole. The next largest is sugar, 28 per cent. The other exports in order of amount are tobacco, honey, molasses, cattle, timber, and hides. The principal minerals found in Porto Rico are gold, carbonates, and sulphides of copper and magnetic oxide of iron in large quantities. Lignite is found in Utuado and Moca, and also yellow amber. A large variety of marbles, limestones, and other building-stones are deposited on the island, but these resources are very undeveloped. There are salt works at Guanica and Salinac on the south coast, and at Cape Rojo on the west, and these constitute the principal mineral industry of Porto Rico. The principal cities are Mayaguez, with 15,187, Ponce, 27,952 inhabitants, and San Juan, the capital, with 32,048. The shipments of domestic merchandise from the U. S. to Porto Rico, year ending 30 June, 1904, were $10,727,015. The exports of domestic merchandise to the U. S. were $11,576,912. The foreign trade, year ending 30 June, 1903, was: imports, $2,326,957; exports, $3,957,497. An official statement covering recent calendar years shows that Porto Rico's imports have grown from $10,955,813 in 1901, to $14,135,061 in 1904, and her exports, in the same period, from $10,472,270 to $17,043,932. Since 1898 her imports from the U. S. have increased from $1,404,000 to $11,934,000, and her exports to the States from $2,382,000 to $12,963,483. Since 1901 trade with the States (imports and exports) shows an increase of about $9,000,000. The bulk of Porto Rico's sales to us consists of sugar and cigars; in the list of products bought from us by the islanders the most prominent are cotton goods, iron and steel manufactures, flour, pork, lard, ham, and lumber. An act providing for a civil government for Porto Rico was passed by the 56th Congress, and received the assent of the president 12 Apr. 1900. Under this act a civil government was established, which went into effect 1 May, 1900. There are 2 legislative chambers—the executive council, or "upper house," composed of the government secretary, attorney-general, treasurer, auditor, commissioner of the interior, and commissioner of education, and 5 citizens appointed by the president; and the house of delegates, or "lower house," consisting of 35 members elected by the people. The island is represented in the Congress of the U. S. by a resident commissioner.

MILITARY GOVERNORS.

Gen. John R. Brooke....................18 Oct. 1898
Gen. Guy V. Henry....................6 Dec. 1898
Gen. George M. Davis....................9 May, 1899

CIVIL GOVERNORS.

Charles H Allen 12 Apr 1900
William H Hunt 30 Aug 1901
Beekman Winthrop 23 Apr 1904

Columbus discovered Porto Rico 1493
Ponce de Leon took possession of the island 1508
Capaira (now known as Pueblo Viejo) first town 1510
Towns of Aguada and San German begun 1511
[Estimated Indian population at this time 600,000, all of whom are destroyed within a hundred years]
Sebastian Cabot and sir Thomas Pert attacked Aybonito and Guaynia 1519
French privateers destroved the town of San German 1529
Francis Drake plundered San Juan 1595
San Juan and Morro castle captured by the earl of Cumberland, but abandoned on account of an epidemic 1598
The Dutch, under gen Henry, invaded the island, but were driven away with considerable loss 1625
The French attempted a landing but were repulsed 1626
Pirates and filibusters plundered the settlements continually between 1625–1650
British attacked San Juan, but lost most of their fleet by a storm which drove the vessels ashore 1678
British fleet repelled 1702
Population of the island estimated at 80,000 1778
Sir Ralph Abercromby, with 10,000 men, besieged San Juan and Aguadilla unsuccessfully 1797
Taxes on Mexico, which had been applied to pay Spanish officials in Porto Rico, discontinued 1810
Royal decree to foster emigration by donation of lands 1815
Don Miguel de la Torre appointed governor general 1825
[He makes the island self supporting for the first time]
During the period between the deposition of queen Isabella II, in 1868 and accession of Alfonso, in 1874, Porto Rico is governed by the Moret law, vesting civil rights in the municipalities 1874
Elduayen law, centralizing power in the hands of the governor general 1875
"Court of Military Justice" established Jan 1891
[Used to determine cases and alleged insults by civilians to individuals in the army, navy, or civil guard, and to suppress free speech and the press]
Commission of citizens sent to Madrid to ask for autonomy and home rule 1896
[Their report to the people led to the organization of the two parties—Liberals and Puros]
The Canovas reform scheme, granting autonomy, displaced the Elduayen law . Nov 1897
Commission to arrange and superintend the evacuation of the island by the Spaniards, under Art. IV of the peace protocol consisted of maj gen John R Brooke, rear-adm Winfield S Schley, brig gen W W Gordon, for the U S, and maj gen Ortego y Diaz, com Vallarino y Carrasco, and judge adv Aguila y Leon, for Spain 1898
Liberals and Puros coalesced and formed the Union party (this date thereafter known as "Glory day") 11 Feb "
The U S army, 3415 men, under gen Miles, made a landing at Guanico, near Ponce . 25 July, "
The Americans advanced to Yauco . . 26 July, "
A second detachment of troops landed at Ponce . 29 July, "
Spanish forces on the island were 8223 regulars, 9107 volunteers . . Aug "
A third detachment debarked at Arroyo 2 Aug "
167 Spanish soldiers captured by gen Ernst in a skirmish at Coamo 9 Aug "
Gen Miles, with 17,000 men, started across the island, meeting with no resistance until the Spanish troops at Hormigueros were defeated 10 Aug "
Spanish troops at Rio Canas driven off 13 Aug "
Armistice proclaimed 14 Aug "
Raising of U S flag in token of formal possession 18 Oct "
Disastrous hurricane, converting a large portion of the interior of the island into a temporarily unproductive country 8 Aug 1899
Qualifications of a voter established 21 Sept. "
[He must be a bona fide male resident of the municipality, and a taxpayer of record, or able to read and write, with qualifications as to time of residence, etc.]
Civil government established . 1 May, 1900
Porto Rico made a collection district 22 June, "
In Insular case, the U S Supreme Court declared duties collected prior to passage of the Porto Rican tariff bill illegal, 27 May, 1901
Proclamation by pres. McKinley of civil government in Porto Rico and free trade with the U S 25 July, "
Gov Hunt's message to the legislature reported marked prosperity . 4 Jan 1902
Second session of the first Porto Rican legislature ended 4 Mch "
Att. gen Knox decided that the public lands of Porto Rico are the property of the U S. government 25 Mch "
Porto Rico out of debt and $500,000 in the treasury Apr 1903
University of Porto Rico opened at San Juan 29 Sept "
The U S Supreme Court decided that Porto Ricans are not aliens of the U S., though they are not necessarily citizens, 4 Jan 1904
The Porto Rican assembly, by a vote of 60 to 15, demanded statehood or independence .. . 20 Feb. "
Charles Hartzell, secretary of Porto Rico, resigned office so as to represent the insular government in property cases representing a value of $3,000,000 claimed by the Roman Catholic church, the property included churches, schools, and hospitals 27 July, 1904
Annual report showed that there are accommodations for only one fifth of the children of school age. . 22 Jan 1905

portreeve (derived from Saxon words signifying the governor of a port or harbor) The chief magistrate of London was originally so styled, but Richard I appointed 2 bailiffs, and afterwards London had mayors —*Camden.* MAYOR OF LONDON

Portsmouth, Hampshire, the most considerable haven for men of-war, and most strongly fortified place in England The dock, arsenal, and storehouses were established in the reign of Henry VIII Pop in 1851, 72,096, in 1861, 94,799, in 1871, 112,954

French under D'Annebaut attempted to destroy Portsmouth, but were defeated by viscount Lisle, in the then finest warship in the world, the *Great Harry* 1545
Here George Villiers, duke of Buckingham, was assassinated by Felton 23 Aug 1628
Adm Byng (BYNG) on a very dubious sentence was shot at Portsmouth 14 Mch 1757
Royal George sunk 29 Aug 1782

Portugal, ancient **Lusita'nia.** The present name is derived from Porto Callo, the original appellation of Oporto. After a 9 years' struggle under Viriathes, a brave, able leader, the Lusitanians submitted to the Roman arms about 137 B.C. Portugal underwent the same changes as Spain on the fall of the Roman empire There are in Portugal 2 universities—that of Coimbra, founded in 1308, and the smaller one of Evora, founded in 1533 Lisbon has also its royal academy, and the small town of Thomar has an academy of sciences, but, in general, literature is at a low ebb in Portugal. The poet Camoens, called the Virgil of his country, and author of the "LUSIAD" (1569), translated into English by Mickle, was a native of Lisbon Area, 34,038 sq miles Pop. of the kingdom and colonies, 31 Dec. 1863, 8,037,194, 1872, kingdom on the continent with Madeira and Azores, 4,390,589, colonies, 3,258,140, 1881, 4,708,178, colonies, 12,650,540, mostly in Africa. The constitution granted in 1826 was revised in 1852.

Settlement of the Alains and Visigoths here 472
Conquered by the Moors 713
Kings of Asturias subdue some Saracen chiefs, and Alfonso III establishes bishops 900
Moors, conquered by Alfonso VI, the Valiant, of Castile, assisted by many other princes and volunteers, Henry of Besançon (a relative of the duke of Burgundy and king of France) very eminent, Alfonso bestowed upon him Theresa, his natural daughter, and Portugal as her marriage portion, which he was to hold of him as count 1095
Alfonso Henriquez defeats 5 Moorish kings, and proclaimed king (OURIQUE) 25 July, 1139
Assisted by a fleet of crusaders on their way to the Holy Land, he takes Lisbon from the Moors 25 Oct 1147
Part of Algarve taken from the Moors by Sancho I 1189
Reign of Dionysius I, or Denis, father of his country, who builds 44 cities or towns in Portugal 1279
University of Coimbra founded 1308
Military orders of Christ and St James instituted 1279 and 1325
Inez de Castro murdered 1355
John I surnamed the Great, carries his arms into Africa. 1415
Maritime discoveries . 1419–30
Madeira and the Canaries seized 1420
Code of laws digested 1425
Lisbon made the capital about 1433
Passage to the East Indies by the cape of Good Hope discovered by Vasco de Gama . 20 Nov 1497
Discovery of the Brazils 1499
Brazil discovered by Cabral Apr 1500
Camoens, author of the "Lusiad," b about 1520
Inquisition established . 1526
University of Evora founded . 1451 or 1533
African expedition, king Sebastian defeated and slain in the battle of Alcazar 4 Aug 1578
Kingdom seized by Philip II of Spain 1580
Dutch seize the Portuguese settlements in India 1602–20
Portuguese throw off the yoke, and place John, duke of Braganza, on the throne Dec 1640
Portuguese defeat the Spaniards at Villa Viciosa. 1665
Great earthquake destroys Lisbon 1 Nov 1755
Joseph I narrowly escapes death by assassins. . 1758
[Some of the first families were tortured to death, their very names being forbidden to be mentioned, the innocence of many was soon after made manifest, the Jesuits were also expelled]
Joseph, having no son obtains a dispensation from the pope to enable his daughter and brother to intermarry, which took place. 6 June, 1760
Spaniards and French invade Portugal, which is saved by the English . .. 1762 and 1763
John, prince of Brazil, marries his aunt, Maria Francesca 1777
Regency of John (afterwards king), owing to the lunacy of queen Maria 1792

'ar with Spain, 3 Mch. ; peace.........................6 June, 1801
reaty between France and Spain for the partition of Portugal, Oct. ; French invasion; Junot arrives at Lisbon, 27 Nov. ; the court sail for Brazil..........................29 Nov. 1807
lise of the Portuguese ; several times defeated, June and July ; arrival of Wellington at Oporto, July; he defeats Junot at Vimeira, 21 Aug. ; convention of Cintra confirmed...30 Aug. 1808
porto taken by Soult..............................29 Mch. 1809
lmeida taken by Massena..........................27 Aug. 1810
lassena defeated at Busaco........................27 Sept. "
'ellington secures the lines of Torres Vedras............Oct. "
lassena defeated at Fuentes de Onoro; retreats........5 May, 1811
ritish Parliament grants the sufferers by war in Portugal 100,000*l*.. "
ortugal cedes Guiana to France.............................. 1814
'nion of Portugal and Brazil.................................. 1815
evolution begins in Oporto.........................29 Aug. 1820
onstitutional Junta established.......................1 Oct. "
eturn of the court.................................4 July, 1821
ıdependence of Brazil; the prince regent made emperor (Brazil)..12 Oct. 1822
ing modifies the constitution........................5 June, 1823
isturbances at Lisbon; Miguel departs..............1-9 May, 1824
reaty with Brazil...................................29 Aug. 1825
eath of John VI......................................10 Mch. 1826
om Pedro grants a constitutional charter, and confirms the regency..26 Apr. "
le relinquishes the throne in favor of his daughter, donna *Maria da Gloria*......................................2 May, "
larquess of Chaves's insurrection at Lisbon in favor of dom Miguel, brother of dom Pedro............................6 Oct. "
om Miguel and donna Maria betrothed...................29 Oct. "
ortugal solicits the assistance of Great Britain, 3 Dec. ; the first British auxiliary troops start for Portugal.......17 Dec. "
om Miguel made regent; takes the oath at Lisbon....22 Feb. 1828
ritish armament quits Portugal........................28 Apr. "
om Miguel assumes the title of king....................4 July, "
le dissolves the 3 estates.............................12 July, "
lis troops take Madeira................................24 Aug. "
uke of Palmella appointed regent..........................Mch. 1830
om Pedro arrives in England........................16 June, 1831
lis expedition sails from Belle isle, 9 Feb. ; at *Terceira* proclaims himself regent, 2 Apr. ; takes Oporto ....8 July, 1832
liguelites attack Oporto and are defeated.............19 Sept. "
dm. Napier takes dom Miguel's squadron off cape St. Vincent, 5 July, 1833
isbon evacuated by the duke of Cadaval; queen proclaimed, 24 July; enter Lisbon................................22 Sept. "
fter various conflicts dom Miguel capitulates to the Pedroites, and Santarem surrenders, 26 May; dom Miguel embarks at Evora for Genoa...31 May, 1834
om Pedro d...24 Sept. "
ueen marries Ferdinand of Saxe-Coburg..................9 Apr. 1836
ction at Evora; queen's troops defeat insurgents......31 Oct. 1846
ritish squadron under adm. Parker arrives in the Tagus, at the queen's request..31 Oct. "
ondon conference; England, France, and Spain determine to assist the queen to terminate the civil war..........21 May, 1847
paniards enter Oporto, and the Junto capitulates.....26 June, "
n American squadron in the Tagus to enforce claims against the Portuguese.......................................22 June, 1850
evision of the charter by the Cortes sanctioned by the queen; the prince royal takes the oath to the constitution, 18 July, 1852
eath of the queen, Maria II..........................15 Nov. 1853
laves on royal domains freed.........................30 Dec. 1854
naugaration of the king..............................16 Sept. 1855
irst Portuguese railway (Lisbon to Santarem) opened..26 Oct. 1856
'rench emigrant ship for negroes, *Charles-et-Georges*, seized, 29 Nov. 1857
'rance sends ultimatum, 13 Oct. ; and ships of war to the Tagus; vessel restored (Charles-et-Georges)........25 Oct. 1858
edro V. dies; his brother, the duke of Oporto, succeeds, 11 Nov. 1861
aw of succession altered in favor of the king's sisters ..3 Jan. 1862
'ree-trade measures introduced........................1 June, 1864
. S. vessels *Niagara* and *Sacramento* in the Tagus fired on, suspected of sailing after the confederate vessel *Stonewall*, 27 Mch. ; difficulty with the U. S. arranged............7 Apr. 1865
onstitutional privileges granted to the colonies...........May, "
en. Prim enters Portugal, 20 Jan. ; ordered to depart, 17 Feb. 1866
'rench republic recognized..............................Sept. 1870
elebration in honor of Camoens and Vasco de Gama at Lisbon...June, 1880
ircular affirming Portuguese rights over the Congo issued, Oct. 1883
eath of king Luis I...................................19 Oct. 1889
ing Carlos inaugurated................................28 Dec. "
ritish government demands the immediate recall of the Portuguese forces from British sphere in Africa..........5 Jan. 1890
ritish government insisting, the Junta of Portugal accedes to all the British demands under protest...........11-12 Jan. "
laj. Serpa Pinto, African explorer, arrives at Lisbon...20 Apr. "
nglo-Portuguese agreement respecting Africa settled in London...20 Aug. "
50th anniversary of the restored monarchy............1 Dec. "

[For the disputes with the South African company respecting the Manica company, Zambesi, Sept.-Dec. 1890.]

ew Anglo-Portuguese convention signed (afterwards ratified), 11 June, 1891

SOVEREIGNS OF PORTUGAL.

I. HOUSE OF BURGUNDY.

1095. Henry, count or earl of Portugal.
1112. Alfonso, his son, and Theresa.
1128. Alfonso, count of Portugal, alone.
1139. *Alfonso I. declared king, having obtained a signal victory over a prodigious army of Moors on the plains of Ourique.*
1185. Sancho I., son of Alfonso.
1212. Alfonso II., surnamed Crassus, or the Fat.
1223. Sancho II., or the Idle; deposed.
1248. Alfonso III.
1279. Denis, or Dionysius, the father of his country.
1325. Alfonso IV., the Brave.
1357. Peter the Severe.
1367. Ferdinand I., son.

II. HOUSE OF AVIS.

1385. John I., the Bastard and the Great; natural brother; married Philippa, daughter of *John of Gaunt, duke of Lancaster.*
1433. Edward, or Duarte.
1438. Alfonso V., the African.
1481. *John II., the Great and the Perfect.*
1495. Emmanuel the Fortunate; cousin.
1521. John III., son; admitted the Inquisition.
1557. Sebastian; drowned after the great battle of Alcazarquivir, in Africa, 4 Aug. 1578.
1578. Henry, the cardinal, son of Emmanuel; great-uncle.
1580. Anthony, prior of Crato, son of Emmanuel; deposed by Philip II. of Spain, who united Portugal to his other dominions.

III. INTERVAL OF SUBMISSION TO SPAIN.

1580. Philip II. }
1598. Philip III. } kings of Spain.
1621. Philip IV. }

IV. HOUSE OF BRAGANZA.

1640. John IV., duke of Braganza; dispossessed the Spaniards in a bloodless revolution, and was proclaimed king, 1 Dec.
1656. Alfonso VI.; deposed in 1667, and his brother Peter made regent.
1683. Peter II., brother.
1706. John V., son.
1750. Joseph Emmanuel, son. The daughter and successor of this prince married his brother, by dispensation from the pope, and they ascended the throne as
Maria I. and Peter III. jointly.
Maria I. alone; this princess afterwards fell into a state of melancholy and derangement; d. 1816.
1792. Regency—John, son (afterwards king); declared regent 1791.
1816. John VI., *previously regent. He had withdrawn in 1807,* owing to the French invasion of Portugal, to his Brazilian dominions; but the discontent of his subjects obliged him *to return in* 1821; d. 1826.
1826. Peter IV. (dom Pedro), son; making his election of the empire of Brazil, abdicated the throne of Portugal in favor of
" Maria II. (da Gloria), daughter; 7 years of age.
1828. Dom Miguel, brother to Peter IV., usurped the crown, which he retained, amid civil contentions, until 1833.
1833. Maria II. restored; declared in Sept. 1834 to be of age; d. 15 Nov. 1853.

V. HOUSE OF BRAGANZA-COBURG.

1853. Peter V. (*dom Pedro*), *son*; b. 16 Sept. 1837; d. 11 Nov. 1861.
1861. Luis I., brother; b. 31 Oct. 1838; married Maria Pia, daughter of Victor Emmanuel, king of Italy (b. 16 Oct. 1847), 6 Oct. 1862; d. 19 Oct. 1889.
1889. Carlos I., b. 28 Sept. 1863; married Marie Amalie, daughter comte de Paris, 22 May, 1886. Heir: Luis Felippe, b. 21 Mch. 1887.

Posen, a Polish province, annexed to Prussia 1772 and 1793; made part of the duchy of Warsaw, 1807; restored to Prussia, 1815. An insurrection here quelled, May, 1848.

positive philosophy, set forth by Auguste Comte, an eminent mathematician, born about 1798; died at Paris, 1857. M. P. Émile Littré, the great French philologist, ardently embraced the system, and published "De la Philosophie Positive," in 1845.

Comte's "Cours de Philosophie Positive," pub. 1830-42; Système de Politique Positive, ou Traité de Sociologie, instituant la Religion de l'Humanité (l'amour pour principe, l'ordre pour base, et le progrès pour but)," 1851-54.

It professes to base itself wholly on positive facts or observed phenomena, and rejects all metaphysical conceptions, which it considers negatives, having nothing real or true in them; and dispenses with the science of mind. *It sets aside theology and metaphysics as two merely preliminary stages in life,* abandons all search after causes and essences of things, and restricts itself to the *observation and classification of phenomena and the discovery of their laws.* Comte asserted that Europe had now arrived at the third stage of its progress. The Society of Positivists in London professes to promote the perfection of man by means of education in its widest sense, aiming at the attaining of universal brotherhood independently of all professed religious sects. Positivism does not recognize the supernatural or the future state. "The Church of Humanity" is a modified form of positivism, described by Richard Congreve (*Pall Mall Gazette*, 17 Jan. 1884).

Postal International convention. POSTAL SERVICE, 1863-91.

postal service. Among the ancients, news was conveyed by runners (2 Sam. xviii. 19-33) or by mounted posts (Esther viii. 10). The first mention of carrier pigeons was by Ovid, who, in his "Metamorphoses," tells us that Taurosthenes, by a pigeon stained with purple, gave notice of his being victor at the Olympic games, on the very same day, to his father at Ægina. The first letter-post in Europe was established in the Hanse towns in the early part of the 13th century. Post-paid envelopes were in use in France in the time of Louis XIV. According to Pelisson, they originated in 1653 with M. de Velayer, who established, under royal authority, a private penny-post in Paris, and placed boxes to receive letters enclosed in these envelopes at the corners of the principal streets.

B.C.
First recorded riding post established in Persia by Cyrus...... 599
Postal service introduced among the Romans by Augustus.... 31

A.D.
Postal service established by the emperor Charlemagne....... 807
Louis XI. establishes post-houses in France, the first of the kind in Europe (*Hénault*)................................ 1470
In England in the reign of Edward IV., riders on post-horses bore by 20-mile stages news of the war with the Scots...... 1481
Regular line of posts established in the Tyrol, connecting Germany and Italy, by Roger, count of Thurn-und-Taxis....... 1516
In Peru the Spanish invaders establish a system of posts by runners on the great highway from Quito to Cuzco............ 1527
Carrier pigeons employed at the siege of Leyden............. 1575
Postage-stamps adopted at Zurich, Switzerland (first on the continent).. 1843
Postal treaty between U. S. and Great Britain............Dec. 1848
Postal convention between U. S. and France...........2 Mch. 1857
First International Postal congress convenes at Paris, John A. Kasson representing the U. S.......................11 May, 1863
Pneumatic tube system introduced in Berlin, 1865; in Paris.. 1866
Pigeon post between London and Tours during the siege of Paris (48 day mails and 1180 night mails sent), 18 Nov. 1870 to 28 Jan. 1871
General Postal union concluded at Berne, international letter postage reduced generally to 5 cents per half-ounce, 9 Oct. 1874
Convention for a Universal Postal Union signed at Paris by James N. Tyner and Joseph H. Blackfan for the U. S., 1 June, 1878
Fourth Postal congress meets at Lisbon and adopts a convention, 4 Feb. 1885; rate, 5 cents per half-ounce, if prepaid; postal-cards 2 cents. Convention takes effect........1 Apr. 1886
International Postal congress held at Vienna..........20 May, 1891

COMPARATIVE TABLE OF POST-OFFICE BUSINESS (Pieces mailed).

Country.	Year.	Letters.	Postal-cards.	Newspapers.	Misc. printed.	Merchandise.	Total.
United States.............	1888	1,769,800,000	372,200,000	1,063,100,000	......	372,900,000	3,578,000,000
Great Britain.............	1888	1,512,200,000	188,800,000	152,300,000	389,500,000	36,732,000	2,279,532,000
France	1886	591,451,811	35,923,379	92,957,793	713,962,439	28,953,858	1,463,249,280
Germany..................	1886	720,497,240	245,282,540	523,873,340	210,108,220	116,305,050	1,816,066,390

postal system in England. Thomas Randolph received the title of chief-postmaster of England in 1581. Previous to this the postal service was in charge of sir Brian Tuke, designated *Magister Nunciorum Cursorum sive Postarum*, who was succeeded by sir William Paget and John Mason, jointly in 1545, and they by Thomas Randolph under same title in 1567. The office of postmaster-general of England for foreign parts was created by letters patent of James I., who appointed Matthew de Quester in 1619. The first regular system of internal post was established by proclamation of Charles I. in 1635, commanding his postmaster of England for foreign parts "to settle a running post or two, to run night and day between Edinburgh and London, to go thither and come back again in 6 days."

Franking privilege, characterized by sir Heneage Finch as "a real poor-mendicant proviso," is granted to knights, etc., chosen to represent the commons in Parliament............ 1660
Penny-post first established in London and its suburbs by Robert Murray, who assigned his interest in the undertaking to Mr. Dockwra 2 years later.............................. 1681
Penny-post annexed to the revenue of the crown.............. 1690
General post established throughout the British colonies...... 1710
Cross posts established by Ralph Allen, deputy-postmaster of Bath, whom Fielding has immortalized as Mr. Allworthy, in "Tom Jones," and of whom Pope writes:
"Let humble Allen, with an awkward shame,
Do good by stealth and blush to find it fame"......... 1720
First mail-coaches started by John Palmer, theatre manager of Bath, leaving London 8 A.M., arriving at Bristol 11 P.M., 24 Aug. 1784
[These coaches were attended by an armed guard to prevent robbery of the mail, then very common.]
Money-order system in England founded by 3 post-office officials as a private speculation (incorporated into the general system in 1838); established.. 1792
Mails sent in steamers first by British post-office............ 1821
First contract made by postmaster-general of England with the Mona Isle Steam company to run mail-steamers twice a week between Liverpool and Douglas.............................. 1833
First travelling post-carriage used on the Grand Junction railway between Liverpool and Birmingham............1 July, 1837
Rowland Hill's plan of penny postage adopted................ 1839
Stamped postage covers come into use................6 May, 1840
Sir James Graham exercises his power of opening letters under warrant; contents of letters of the Italian patriot Mazzini disclosed to the Austrian government......................... 1844
Stamp perforating machine invented by Henry Archer and purchased by the British government for 4000*l*............. 1852
Street letter-boxes erected in London...................Mch. 1855
Post-office savings-banks established by Parliament.......... 1861
Pneumatic-tube system, originating with Dennis Papin in 1667, put into use in post-office business in London............. 1863
Half-penny stamped postal-cards issued................1 Oct. 1870
System of telegraph money-orders inaugurated........2 Sept. 1889
Number of street letter-boxes in London 21,857.............. 1891
Number of post-offices in the United Kingdom 40,643......... "

postal system in the United States. The first organized system of post-offices in the U. S. was established by the English Parliament in 1710, when a general letter-office was opened in London, another in New York, and others in each colony. Postage on a single letter from London to New York was 1*s.*, and thence for 60 miles or less, 4*d.* additional. From 75 post-offices and 1875 miles of mail routes in 1790, the number has increased to 64,329 post-offices and 439,027 miles of mail route on 30 June, 1891.

Post-office established in Boston at the house of Richard Fairbanks for "all letters which are brought from beyond the seas, or are to be sent thither"............................ 1639
Act passed by Virginia assembly for the immediate transmission of official letters from plantation to plantation on penalty of 1 hogshead of tobacco for each default.......13 Mch. 1657
Government of New York establishes a monthly mail to Boston, 1672
Colonial court establishes a post-office in Boston, appointing John Heyward postmaster.................................. 1676
Office of deputy postmaster-general for America created by authority of Great Britain..................................... 1692
Public post established from the Potomac, through Annapolis to Philadelphia, 8 times a year, postmaster's salary 50*l*.... 1695
Col. J. Hamilton of New Jersey devises a post-office scheme for British America in 1700, for which he obtains a patent and the profits accruing. He afterwards sold it to the crown, and a general system is established in America............ 1710
Mail route established, carrying letters from Boston, Mass., to Williamsburg, Va., in 4 weeks.............................. 1717
Benjamin Franklin appointed deputy-postmaster in America.. 1737
Benjamin Franklin and col. William Hunter appointed postmaster-generals in America; Franklin on a tour of inspection visits every post-office except Charleston.............. 1753
Mails carried between Philadelphia and New York by stage... 1756
Franklin summarily dismissed from office by the king, 30 Jan. 1774
Independent post-office established in New York, and John Holt appointed postmaster; operations begin.......11 May, 1775
Post-office department created, with headquarters at Philadelphia, and Benjamin Franklin elected postmaster-general for 1 year by Continental Congress.....................26 July, "
Richard Bache succeeds Franklin as postmaster-general, 7 Nov. 1776
Inspector of dead letters appointed under resolution of Continental Congress......................................17 Oct. 1777
Ebenezer Hazard appointed postmaster-general........28 Jan. 1782
Rate of postage fixed by Continental Congress as follows:
Single letters, under 60 miles.................. 7.4 cts.
60 to 100 miles........................11.1 cts.
100 to 200 miles.....................14.8 cts.
And 3.4 cts. additional for each 100 miles..........18 Oct. "
Temporary establishment of post-offices by act of Congress, 22 Sept. 1789
Revenue for one year of the 10 principal post-offices in the U. S.:

Philadelphia, Pa..	$7087.06	Petersburg, Va..	$1472.18
New York, N.Y...	3788.04	Alexandria, Va..	1234.00
Baltimore, Md....	3034.64	Fredericksburg, Va..........	1059.08
Boston, Mass.....	2883.67	Norfolk, Va.....	1016.00
Richmond, Va....	2777.07	Charleston, S. C.	810.00...1790-91

Laws of 18 Oct. 1782 and 23 Oct. 1786, which gave authority to commander-in-chief of the army, the president of Congress, governors of states, and secretary of foreign affairs, to open or authorize the opening of letters in the mails, are repealed, 1792
Act to organize the post-office system; franking privilege extended to members of Congress, etc.................20 Feb. "
Letter-carriers are to be employed at such post-offices as the postmaster-general may direct, for delivery of letters, who

may collect on each letter 2 cents, unless persons lodge in the post-office a request that their letters be not delivered (repealed 1872), act of Congress......................8 May, 1794
All letters to *George Washington* to be received and conveyed by post during his life free of charge..................3 Mch. 1797
Privilege of franking given John *Adams*.................. " 1801
Mail between Petersburg, Va., and Louisville, Ga., to go in mail-coaches instead of on horseback, by act of............3 Mch. 1802
A general post-office established at Washington........30 Apr. 1810
Postage rates of 1799 increased 50 per cent. by act of...23 Dec. 1814
Act of 23 Dec. 1814 repealed and old rates restored......1 Feb. 1816
Franking privilege granted to Charles Carroll of Carrollton, only surviving signer of the *Declaration of Independence*, by resolution of Congress..............................23 May, 1828
Postmaster-general made a cabinet officer (CABINET COUNCIL, UNITED STATES)...................................... 1829
Mails first transported by railroad.................................. 1834
Franking privilege extended to Dolly P. Madison during life. 2 July, 1836
Postmaster-general *authorized* to contract for carrying mails on navigable canals, and to establish an "express mail" for slips from newspapers or letters at *triple the ordinary* rates of postage...2 July, "
Every railroad declared to be a post-route by Congress .7 July, 1838
Envelopes first used for letters...................................... 1839
Franking privilege granted to the widow of president Wm. H. Harrison..9 Sept. 1841
Issue of postage-stamps first authorized..................3 Mch. 1847
Post-offices established at *Astoria*, 1847; at San Diego, Monterey, and San Francisco, with postage rate from any place on the Atlantic coast, 40 cents..................................14 Aug. 1848
Letter postage reduced to 3 cents per half-ounce for distance under 3000 miles, postage prepaid.....................3 Mch. 1851
Stamped envelopes provided for by act of Congress....31 Aug. 1852
System of registered letters introduced...................3 Mch. 1855
Compulsory prepayment of postage *on all transient* printed matter required by act of..............................2 Jan. 1857
Iron boxes placed in the city of *Boston for prepaid letters*, to be collected by postmen; beginning.......................2 Aug. 1858
First overland mail from St. Louis to San Francisco.....Sept. "
Letters not called for to be returned to the address of writer on the envelope, by act of...............................6 Apr. 1860
Merchandise first admitted *to the mails*, and postmaster-general authorized to furnish stamped letter sheets (combining sheet and envelope), by act of.........................27 Feb. 1861
Delivery of letters and newspapers by carriers throughout a circuit of 9 miles from the city hall in New York city, daily or semi-daily, authorized by act of.....................27 Feb. "
Pillar-boxes or other receiving boxes authorized ....3 Mch. 1863
Trial trip of the first railroad post-office from Chicago to Clinton, on system of col. George B. Armstrong.........28 Aug. 1864
Money-order system established by act of 17 May; goes into operation..1 Nov. "
Franking privilege extended to Mary Lincoln, wife of Abraham Lincoln, during life, by act of..........................10 Feb. 1866
Letters and circulars concerning lotteries or gift concerts to be excluded from the mails by act of.....................27 July, "
Uniforms, as prescribed by the postmaster-general, to be worn by letter-carriers, *by act of*..............................27 July, 1868
Free delivery by letter-carriers, in cities of 50,000 population and upward, established by act of.....................8 June, 1872
Franking privilege after 1 July, 1873, abolished by act of Congress...31 Jan. 1873

[*Exceptions*: (1) Public documents printed by Congress, *Congressional Record* sent by member of Congress, secretary of state, or clerk of *House*; (2) seeds sent from the Department of Agriculture by member of Congress, or through the secretary; (3) letters and packages *relating exclusively* to the business of the government, sent by officers of the same; (4) matter sent to the librarian of Congress under provisions of the Copyright law; (5) matter pertaining to the Smithsonian institution.]

One-cent postal-cards provided for by act of 8 June, 1872; first sold..May, "
Postal-notes limited to $4.99 authorized by act of......3 Mch. 1883
Postage on first-class mail-matter reduced from 3 to 2 cents per half-ounce, by act of......................................3 Mch. "
Special-delivery system authorized, and postage on first-class mail-matter reduced to 2 cents per ounce, by act of...3 Mch. 1885
First issue of *stamped* letter-sheet envelopes.............Aug. 1886
Free-delivery system extended to places of 10,000 population, by act of..3 Jan. 1887

RATES OF LETTER POSTAGE AS ESTABLISHED BY ACTS OF CONGRESS.

Rate.	Miles of transit for a single sheet at rate named.			
	20 Feb. 1792.	2 Mch. 1799.	9 Apr. 1816.	3 Mch. 1845.
5 cents.	over 450	over 500	over 400	....
2 "	350–450	....	....	....
0 "	250–350	300–500	....	....
8½ "	....	....	150–400	....
7 "	200–250	150–300	....	....
5 "	150–200	....	....	....
2½ "	....	90–150	80–150	....
2 "	100–150	....	....	....
0 "	60–100	40–90	30–80	over 300
8 "	30–60	under 40	....	....
6 "	under 30	....	under 30	....
5 "	....	....	....	under 300

RATES OF LETTER POSTAGE AS ESTABLISHED BY ACTS OF CONGRESS.—(*Continued.*)

Rate.	Miles of transit per half-ounce at rate named.			
	3 Mch. 1851.	3 Mch. 1855.	3 Mch. 1863.	3 Mch. 1883.
10 cents.	over 3000 unpaid.	over 3000	....	....
6 "	over 3000 prepaid.	....	....	....
5 "	under 3000 unpaid.	....	....	....
3 "	under 3000 prepaid.	under 3000	Everywhere in U. S.	....
2 "	....	....	....	Everywhere in U. S.

Two cents per ounce to any point in the U. S..........3 Mch. 1885

GROWTH OF POSTAL SYSTEM (1790–1893).

Year.	Number of post-offices.	Miles of mail-routes.	Revenue.	Expenditures.
1790	75	1,875	$37,935	$32,140
1800	903	20,817	280,804	213,994
1810	2,300	36,406	552,366	495,969
1820	4,500	72,492	1,111,927	1,160,926
1830	8,450	115,176	1,850,583	1,932,708
1840	13,468	155,739	4,543,522	4,718,236
1850	18,417	178,672	5,499,985	5,212,953
1860	28,498	240,594	8,518,067	19,170,610
1870	28,492	231,232	19,772,221	23,998,838
1880	42,989	343,888	33,315,479	36,542,804
1890	62,401	427,990	60,882,097	65,930,717
1893	68,403	453,833	75,896,933	81,074,104

potas'sium, a remarkable metal, discovered by Humphry Davy, who first succeeded in separating it from its oxide, potash, by means of a powerful voltaic battery, in the laboratory of the Royal institution, London, about 19 Oct. 1807; and also the metals sodium from soda, and calcium from lime, etc. The alkalies and earths had been previously regarded as simple substances. Potassium ignites on contact with moisture.

pota'to (*Solanum tuberosum*), native of Chili and Peru, generally considered to have been taken to England from America by sir John Hawkins, 1565. Others ascribe its introduction to sir Francis Drake in 1586; its *general introduction*, 1592. *Its first culture* in Ireland is referred to sir Walter Raleigh, who had large estates in that country, about Youghal, in the county of Cork. Although it now constitutes so large a portion of the food of man, it was scarcely known prior to the 17th century, and was not greatly cultivated until the middle of the 18th, its culture not becoming general even in England, until after 1765. AGRICULTURE.

potato, Sweet. FLOWERS AND PLANTS.

Potawat'omies. INDIANS.

Potidæ'a, a town in Macedonia, a tributary of Athens, against which it revolted, 432 B.C., but submitted in 429. It was taken from the Athenians, after 3 years' siege, by Philip II. of Macedon in 358 B.C.

Poto'mac. ARMY, PENINSULAR CAMPAIGN.

Poto'si, a city of Bolivia, Peru. Silver mines here were discovered by the Spaniards in 1545; they are situated in the Cerro de Potosi, a conical mountain 18 miles in circumference.

Potsdam, a city near Berlin, the Versailles of Prussia. It was made an arsenal in 1721. Here is situated the palace of Sans-souci (built 1660–73), embellished by Frederick II., and occupied by Napoleon I. in Oct. 1806; and the new palace, the residence of late emperor Frederick William and his wife, the princess royal of England.

pottery and **porcelain.** The potter's art is coeval with civilization. Bricks, burned thoroughly, were used in building the tower of Babel (Gen. xi. 3). Bricks with true glaze were used in Babylon 2122 B.C. The manufacture of earthenware (the ceramic art) existed among the Jews as an honorable occupation (1 Chron. iv. 23); and the power of the potter over the clay, as a symbol of the power of God, is described by Jeremiah 605 B.C. (Jer. xviii.). Earthenware was made by the ancient Egyptians, Assyrians, Greeks, Etruscans, Romans, and prehistoric inhabitants of America. Tiles and vessels of lead-glazed ware were made in England as early as the 14th century.

B. C.
College or guild of potters instituted by Numa.............. 715
Chinese authorities date the invention of porcelain or translucent pottery.. 185
A. D.
Samian ware, a fine, glossy, red enamel, made by the Romans. 150

Moorish tiles introduced into Italy at the conquest of Majorca by the Pisans 1115
James I of Arragon grants a special charter to the Saracens of Xativa, now San Felipe, Spain, for making pottery, which mentions vases, domestic pottery and wall tiles 1239
Delft ware manufactured in Holland 1310

> "What land is this? Yon pretty town
> Is Delft, with all its wares displayed
> The pride, the market place, the crown
> And centre of the Potter's trade"
> —*Longfellow*, "Kéramos"

Oldest known Chinese work treating of the ceramic art, entitled "Feou leang thien tchi" issued 1325
[This work passed through 21 editions It begins in the Wou te period of the Thang dynasty, about 621 A D, when the government first directed its attention to the industry]
Lucca della Robbia said to have first used stanniferous enamel in Florence, Italy, on majolica ware, introduced into that country after the conquest of Majorca by the Pisans in 1115 (?) 1425

> "A nobler title to renown
> Is thine, O pleasant Tuscan town,
> Seated beside the Arno's stream,
> For Lucca della Robbia there
> Created forms so wondrous fair,
> They made thy sovereignty supreme"
> —*Longfellow*, "Kéramos"

Famous porcelain tower at Nankin, 330 feet high, designed by the emperor Yung lo to commemorate his mother, and destroyed by Tae ping rebels in Mch 1853, was completed. 1431

> "And yonder by Nankin, behold!
> The Tower of Porcelain, strange and old,
> Uplifting to the astonished skies
> Its ninefold painted balconies"—*Longfellow*, "Kéramos"

Antuonio, an alchemist, succeeds in making and firing translucent porcelain, at San Simone, near Venice 1470
Oriental porcelain first introduced into Europe by Portuguese. 1518
Faience d'Orion, made of fine pipe clay, decorated with inlaid work by lady Hélène de Hangest Genlis, and fired by her private potter, she died at her château near Thouars, France 1537
Bernard Palissy discovers hard enamel at Saintes, France .. 1550

> "Who is it in the suburbs here
> This Potter, working with such cheer,
>
> This madman, as the people say,
> Who breaks his tables and his chairs
> To feed his furnace fires!
> O Palissy! within thy breast
> Burned the hot fever of unrest,
> Thine was the prophet's vision "
> —*Longfellow*, "Kéramos"

Manufacture of true porcelain carried on at Florence under the patronage of grand duke Francis I (*Dr Foresi*) 1580–90
Finely crackled ware of Satsuma, Japan, first produced about 1592

> "The leaves that rustle, the reeds that make
> A whisper by each stream and lake,
> The saffron dawn, the sunset red,
> Are painted on these lovely jars"
> —*Longfellow*, "Kéramos"

Thomas Roos and Abraham Cullyn receive a patent for the making of stone pots and jugs of Cologne ware in England. 1626
Decorated wares made at Rouen, France 1640
Art of glazing pottery with salt accidentally discovered at Stanley farm, near Bagnall, Engl, by a servant of J Yale, about 1680
John Philip Elers and his brother David establish the first pottery of importance in art history in England, at Bradwell, about 1690
Porcelain manufactured at St Cloud, France, by the Chicanneau family 1693
John Frederic Böttcher makes a red stone ware which he calls red porcelain, from clay found near Meissen, on the Elbe, 12 miles from Dresden, about 1705. Encouraged by Augustus II he experiments and produces hard paste porcelain by using kaolin found in the mining district of the Erzgebirge, about 1710 First sale of Dresden or Meissen porcelain at the Leipsic fair 1715
English fine earthenware made with pounded flint, sand, and pipe clay, and colored with oxide of manganese and copper, called agate ware 1725
First soft paste porcelain factory in England established at Stratford le Bow about 1730
American clay used at Bow potteries 1744
Hard paste porcelain factory established at St. Petersburg by empress Elizabeth "
Chelsea works (England) founded about 1745
Worcester Porcelain company organized in England by dr Wall and others (becomes Royal Porcelain works in 1788) 1751
Discovery of kaolin in Cornwall, Engl, by Wm Cookworthy 1755
John Sadler invents printing on pottery and porcelain in England 1756
Porcelain works, started at Vincennes, France, in 1745, and removed to Sèvres in 1753, are purchased by Louis XV, who, by decree, prohibits gilding or making other than white porcelain painted in blue, in Chinese patterns, elsewhere "
Cream ware changed in name to "queen's ware" when Josiah Wedgwood manufactures a complete table service by order of queen Charlotte of England 1762
Kaolin discovered in France by Guettard 1765
China works erected at Philadelphia, Pa. 1769
First hard-paste porcelain produced at the Royal factory at Sèvres "
Pebble wares invented by Josiah Wedgwood, 1763, and Jasper ware 1774
Jewelled porcelain first produced in France 1777
Service of 744 pieces, costing nearly $200,000, executed at Sèvres for empress Catherine II of Russia. 1778
[160 pieces were stolen and sold in England, they were mostly restored to emperor Nicholas about 1852 1 plate sold at baron Thibon's sale, Feb 1875, for 2400 francs]
Thomas Turner of England introduces the willow pattern 1780
King Louis XV presents to the comtesse du Nord a toilet table and mirror in porcelain which cost 75,000 livres 1782
Enoch Wood, called the "father of pottery," begins business at Burslem, Engl 1784
Hamilton's returns of exports of the U S from Aug 1789 to Sept. 1790 gives for earthen and glass ware $1990 1790
Pottery established at Norwich, Conn 1796
Alexander Brongniart becomes director of the Sèvres factory 1800
Ceramic museum founded at Sèvres by Brongniart. 1805
PORTLAND VASE placed in the British museum 1810
Exports of coarse earthenware from the U S exceeded imports in "
Hard paste porcelain made in Jersey City, N J, 1816, business continued by American Pottery company, organized 1829
Tile factory of the Mintons at Stoke upon Trent, Engl, founded, 1840
Parian or Carrara ware introduced into England 1845
Factory established at Bennington, Vt, by Lyman & Fenton, where bisque or Parian wares and soft paste porcelain decorated were produced 1847
Manufacture of English majolica begun by messrs. Minton 1850
Imperial Mosaic works, established at Rome in 1846, transferred to St Petersburg Russia 1856
Principle of compressing paste in moulds of large objects by means of air pressure, first used at Sèvres 1861
"Kéramos," a poem of the ceramic art, written by Longfellow, 1878
Potter's wheel has greatly superseded moulding as producing more original work 1898

pound (from Lat *pondus*) The value of the Roman *pondo* is not precisely known, though some suppose it was equivalent to an Attic *mina*, or 3*l.* 4*s* 7*d* The pound sterling was in Saxon times, about 671, a pound troy of silver, and a shilling was its twentieth part, consequently the latter was 3 times as large as it is at present —*Peacham* —The English avoirdupois pound weight came from the French, and contains 16 ounces, it is in proportion to the troy weight as 17 to 14 COIN, STANDARD.

Powhatans. INDIANS, VIRGINIA

præmuni're, Law of This law (which obtained its name from the first 2 words *præmoneri*, or *præmunire facias*, "cause to be forewarned," which is applied to any offence in the way of contempt of the sovereign or his government), derived its origin from the aggressive power of the pope in England The offence introduced a foreign power into the land, and created an *imperium in imperio* The first statute of præmunire was enacted 35 Edward I 1306.—*Coke* The pope bestowed most of the bishoprics, abbeys, etc, before they were void, upon favorites, on pretence of providing the church with better-qualified successors before the vacancies occurred To stop these encroachments, Edward III enacted a statute in 1353. The statute commonly referred to as the statute of præmunire is 16 Richard II. 1392 Several similar enactments followed. The assertion that Parliament is independent of the sovereign was declared a *præmunire*, 1661

prætorian guards, a body of soldiers instituted by the emperor Augustus (13 B.C), their numbers enlarged by Tiberius, until under Vitellius they numbered 16,000. Their term of service was at first 12 years, afterwards increased to 16 They received double pay, the private ranking with the centurion of the legionary, and at retirement received 20,000 sesterces (about $800). At first supporters of the imperial tyrants, they eventually became their masters, actually putting up the diadem for sale (as in Mch 193 A D, when it was bought by Didius Julianus). They were greatly reduced by Servius, and finally disbanded by Constantine in 312

prætors, Roman magistrates In 365 B.C one prætor was appointed, a second appointed in 252 B.C The *prætor urbanus* administered justice to the citizens, and the *prætor peregrinus* acted in causes relating to foreigners. In 227 B.C. 2 more prætors were created to assist the consul in the government of Sicily and Sardinia, lately conquered, and 2 more when Spain was made a Roman province, 197 B.C Sulla, the dictator, added 2, and Julius Cæsar increased the number to 10, which afterwards became 16. After this their number fluctuated, being sometimes 18, 16, or 12, till, in the decline of the empire, their dignity decreased, and their numbers were reduced to 3

pragmat'ic sanction, an ordinance relating to

church and state affairs The ordinances of the kings of France are thus called, in one the rights of the Gallican church were asserted against the usurpation of the pope in the choice of bishops by Charles VII in 1438 The pragmatic sanction for settling the empire of Germany in the house of Austria, 1439 The emperor Charles VI published the pragmatic sanction, whereby, in default of male issue, his daughters should succeed in preference to the daughters of his brother Joseph I, 19 Apr 1713, and he settled his dominions on his daughter Maria Theresa, in conformity thereto, 1723 She succeeded in Oct 1740, but it gave rise to a war in which most of the powers of Europe were engaged, and which lasted till 1748 AUSTRIAN SUCCESSION

Prague (*prāg*), the capital of Bohemia The old city was founded about 759, the new city rebuilt in 1348 by the emperor Charles IV, who made it his capital and erected a university Prague has suffered much by war

Victory of the Hussites under Ziska 14 July, 1420
Frederick, the king totally defeated by the Austrians near Prague 8 Nov 1620
Prague taken by the Swedes in 1648, and by the French in 1741, they left it 1742
Taken by the king of Prussia, obliged to abandon it 1744
Great battle of Prague (the Austrians defeated by prince Henry of Prussia, and their whole camp taken, their commander, gen Braun mortally wounded, and the Prussian marshal Schwerin killed) 6 May, 1757

Prairie Grove, Battle of ARKANSAS, 1862

Praise-God Barebone's parliament. BAREBONE'S PARLIAMENT

prayer, First, in Congress UNITED STATES, 1774

prayers. "Then began men to call upon the name of the Lord" (Gen iv 26), 3875 B C The mode of praying with the face to the east was instituted by pope Boniface II 532. Prayers for the dead, first introduced into the Christian church about 190, are now advocated by ministers of the English church, 1872 Prayers addressed to the Virgin Mary and to saints are said to have been introduced by pope Gregory, 593 LITURGIES.

Pre-Adamites, a sect which arose about the middle of the 16th century, holding for its principal tenet that there must have been men before Adam

preb'endary, a clergyman attached to a cathedral or collegiate church, who receives an income termed *prebenda* for officiating at stated times The office slightly differs from that of a canon

prece'dence was established in very early ages, and was among the laws of Justinian. In England the order of precedence was regulated chiefly by 2 statutes, 31 Hen. VIII 1539, and 1 Geo I 1714.

predestination (Lat *prædestino*, to determine beforehand, to foreordain), commonly applied to the doctrine that all events are ordained beforehand from all eternity by the Supreme Being, a belief regarded by Calvinists as a necessary logical inference from his omniscience and omnipotence (Eph i) It is defined in the 17th article of the Church of England (Eph i and Rom ix) It was maintained by St Augustin, and opposed by Pelagius, in the early part of the 5th century In later times it has been maintained by the Augustinians, Jansenists, and Calvinists), and opposed by the Dominicans, Jesuits, Arminians, especially the Methodists

prehistoric archæol'ogy began in Sweden, and was first systematized by Mr Nillson Daniel Wilson's "Archæology and Prehistoric Annals of Scotland," pub 1851. An international congress for treating prehistorical subjects met at Neufchâtel in 1866, and at Paris in 1867. At the third meeting at Norwich, Aug 1858, it assumed the name of "International Congress for Prehistoric Archæology," and published its transactions in 1869 A meeting was held at Stockholm 7-14 Aug 1874. ANTIQUARIES, BARROWS, MAN

Sir John Lubbock divides prehistoric archæology into 4 great epochs 1 The Drift or Palæolithic or old stone age, 2 The Neolithic or polished stone age, 3 The Bronze age, 4 The Iron age, when bronze was superseded.—(1880)

Pre-Raphaelite school, a name given about 1850 to J E Millais, Wm Holman Hunt, D G. Rossetti, and other artists, who opposed the routine conventionality of academic teaching, and resolved to study nature as it appeared to them, and not as it appeared in the antique For a short time they published "The Germ, or Art and Poetry," beginning in 1850 Their works have been much criticised, but their influence has been beneficial Their principles are defended in substance by the great art-critic, John Ruskin

prerog'ative royal. In England the sovereign is the supreme magistrate, the head of the established church, of the army and navy, and the fountain of office, honor, and privilege, but is subject to the laws, unless exempted by name The royal prerogatives were greatly exceeded by several despotic sovereigns, such as Elizabeth, James I, and Charles I, as it was a maxim that the sovereign could do no wrong Elizabeth used the phrase, "We, of our royal prerogative, which we will not have argued or brought in question" (1591) James I told his parliament 'that is it was blasphemy to question what the Almighty could do of his power, so it was sedition to inquire what a king could do by virtue of his prerogative" These extreme doctrines were nullified by the revolution of 1688, and the exercise of the prerogative is now virtually subject to Parliament LORDS

Pres'burg, the ancient capital of Hungary, where the diets were held and the kings crowned On 26 Dec 1805, a treaty was signed here between France and Austria, by which the ancient states of Venice were ceded to Italy, the principality of Eichstadt, part of the bishopric of Passau, the city of Augsburg the Tyrol, all the possessions of Austria in Suabia, in Brisgau, and Ortenau, were transferred to the elector of Bavaria and the duke of Wurtemberg, who, as well as the duke of Baden, were then created kings by Napoleon The independence of the Helvetic republic was also stipulated A new iron and stone railway and passenger bridge over the Danube was inaugurated by the emperor, 30 Dec. 1890 Pop 1890, 52,411.

Presbyte'rians are so called from their maintaining that the government of the church appointed in the New Testament was by presbyteries, or associations of ministers and ruling elders, equal in power, office, and in order. "The elders (Gr πρεσβυτέρους) I exhort, who am also an elder (συμπρεσβυτερος)" (1 Pet v 1) Presbyterianism was accepted by Parliament in place of episcopacy in England in 1648, but set aside at the Restoration in 1660 It became the established form of church government in Scotland in 1696 Its tenets were embodied in the formulary of faith said to have been composed by John Knox in 1560, which was approved by Parliament and ratified, 1567, and finally settled by an act of the Scottish senate, 1690, and afterwards secured by the treaty of union with England in 1707 The first Presbyterian meeting-house in England was established at Wandsworth, Surrey, 20 Nov 1572.

A Pan Presbyterian congress held in London Representatives of about 50 bodies, British American, and foreign, form an "Alliance of Presbyterian churches" 19-22 July, 1875
Presbyterian church of England reconstituted at Liverpool (in union with the United Presbyterian church of Scotland), 13 June, 1876
General council of the "Alliance of Reformed churches throughout the world holding the Presbyterian system," has its first meeting at Edinburgh 3 July, 1877
Second meeting of Presbyterian Alliance at Philadelphia, Pa., 23 Sept 1880
Third meeting of Presbyterian Alliance at Belfast, Ireland, 24 June, 1884
Fourth meeting of Presbyterian Alliance at London, Engl, 3 July, 1888
Fifth meeting of Presbyterian Alliance at Toronto, Ont 1892
CAMERONIANS, CHURCH OF SCOTLAND, CONGREGATIONALISTS, GLASITES

Presbyterians in the United States The earliest Presbyterian emigrants were French Huguenots led by Ribault, who came to the Carolinas in 1562 A Puritan Presbyterian church was established on Long Island about 1641, and in New York city, 1643 Dutch Presbyterianism was planted in New Amsterdam in 1628 In 1790 the strength of the Presbyterian church in the U S. was represented by 4 synods, 16 presbyteries, 431 churches, 177 ministers, and 18,000 communicants In 1890 there were 30 synods, 213 presbyteries, 6894 churches, 6158 ministers, and 775,903 communicants. Or, if all the different bodies are estimated, as the Cumberland Presbyterians, United Presbyterians, etc., they number 12,462 churches and 1,278,815 members, value of church property, $94,876,233

Francis Makemie, licentiate of the Presbytery of Laggan in 1681, establishes the first organized Presbyterian church in America, at Snow Hill, Maryland.......... 1684

Church under Presbyterian government established at Jamaica, L. I., John Hubbard, pastor, but suppressed by gov. Cornbury the same year.......... 1702

Makemie visits England and returns to Maryland with John Hampton and George Macnish, sent out by the London union of Presbyterian and Independent ministers..........1703-4

First presbytery in the U. S., probably formed at a meeting held at Freehold, N. J., of 7 ministers: Francis Makemie, John Hampton, George Macnish, Samuel Davis, John Wilson, Jedediah Andrews, and Nathaniel Taylor..........1705 or 1706

Synod organized consisting of 19 ministers..........19 Apr. 1717

Celebrated "Adopting act" of the synod, accepting for the Presbyterian church in U. S. the Confession of Faith and Larger and Shorter Catechism of the Assembly of Divines at Westminster.......... 1729

Synod divided on questions of church polity, into the Old Side, and New Brunswick party or New Side.......... 1741

Morris's reading-house erected in Hanover county, Va., about 1743

New Brunswick party and New York presbytery meet at Elizabethtown, N. J., and form the synod of New York....Sept. 1745

College of New Jersey, chartered and opened at Elizabethtown, N. J., 1746, is removed to Newark after the death of pres. Jonathan Dickinson (7 Oct. 1747), and Aaron Burr appointed president under a new charter, 1748. College removed to Princeton, 1755

Reunion of Old and New Side synods at Philadelphia, the "Synod of New York and Philadelphia," with 94 ministers and 14 elders, Gilbert Tennent moderator..........29 May, 1758

Rev. James Waddel (blind), whose eloquence is described by William Wirt in the *British Spy*, is licensed by the old presbytery of Hanover, Va.......... Apr. 1761

Plan of missionary collections in all of the churches of each presbytery adopted by synod.......... 1767

Provision made for circulation by committees appointed in Philadelphia and New York, of Bibles and religious books in the frontier settlements.......... 1773

Presbytery of 4 seceding ministers, Presbyterian in form, but Congregational in fact, known as the Associated Presbytery of Morris county, is formed at Hanover, Va..........3 May, 1780

Washington college in Rockbridge, Va., opened in 1774 as Augusta academy, is incorporated as Liberty hall.......... 1782

Synod recommends the final abolition of slavery.......... 1787

Constitution for the Presbyterian church in the U. S. ratified and adopted by synod..........16 May, 1788

First general assembly of the church meets at Philadelphia... 1789

Robert Marshall and Carey H. Allen, the first missionaries sent out under the general assembly, enter Kentucky.......... 1790

Associated presbytery of Westchester county, N. Y., organized, Jan. 1792

Northern associated presbytery in state of New York organized at New Canaan..........12 Nov. 1793

First theological department in connection with a college in America, added to Liberty hall under the patronage of the synod of Virginia.......... Jan. 1794

Convention of Correspondence, to meet annually, organized by Associated presbyteries at Poughkeepsie..........10 Apr. "

General assembly meets at Carlisle..........1792 and 1795

Union college at Schenectady founded.......... "

New York missionary society formed..........1 Nov. 1796

General assembly meets at Winchester, Va.......... 1799

Great revival in Kentucky, Tennessee, New York, and New England.......... 1799-1800

Rev. James Hall, licensed by the presbytery of Orange in 1776, begins mission work at Natchez, Miss.......... "

"A Plan of Union" between Presbyterians and Congregationalists is proposed to the general assembly by the general association of Connecticut, and adopted.......... 1801

A permanent missionary fund of $12,359.92½, the interest only to be used, is established by the assembly.......... "

Synod of the Reformed Presbyterian church in America, or Covenanters, organized at Philadelphia..........24 May, 1809

Schism, originating in licensing laymen as exhorters during the revival of 1801; Cumberland presbytery withdraws and organizes the Cumberland Presbyterian church.......... 1811

Standing committee of missions appointed 1802, and title changed to Board of Missions in.......... 1816

United Foreign Missionary Society organized to succeed the New York Missionary Society..........28 July, 1817

Elias Cornelius and Sylvester Larned, missionaries, organize a church in New Orleans. Corner-stone laid..........8 Jan. 1819

Board of Education established.......... "

United Domestic Missionary Society of New York established, 1822

United Foreign Missionary Society amalgamates with the American Board of Commissioners for Foreign Missions.... 1826

American and Presbyterian education societies united.......... 1827

Steps taken in 1819 providing an authorized psalmody for the church results in the publication adopted.......... 1830

Western Foreign Missionary Society of the U. S. organized by the synod of Pittsburg.......... 1831

"Western Memorial," signed by 18 ministers and 99 elders, charging "a widely spread principle of evil operating in the Presbyterian church, to the general change of its form of government and the character of its creed," is refused a record in the assembly of 1834, by vote of 56 to 42. The memorialists meet and draw up a paper styled "The Acts and Testimony," re-echoing the statements of the memorial.... 1834

"Acts and Testimony convention" at Pittsburg, 41 presbyteries and 13 minorities of presbyteries represented, draw up a list of grievances for the assembly..........May, 1835

General assembly meets at Pittsburg, Pa.......... 1835

Presbytery and synod of Cincinnati, try and acquit dr. Lyman Beecher, charged by dr. Wilson of Cincinnati with teaching Pelagian and Arminian doctrines..........9 June et seq. "

Assembly acquit dr. Albert Barnes, charged with teaching "dangerous errors or heresies" in his *Notes on Romans*, and suspended by the synod of Philadelphia.......... 1836

"Plan of union" of 1801 abrogated by vote 143 to 110 in the general assembly at Philadelphia, as unnatural and unconstitutional..........22 May, 1837

Assembly resolve "that, by the operation of the abrogation of the plan of union of 1801, the synod of the Western Reserve is and is hereby declared to be no longer a part of the Presbyterian church of America," by 132 to 105..........30 May, "

Assembly direct that the so-called American Home Missionary Society and American Education Society cease to operate with any Presbyterian church, 124 to 86, 2 June, 1837, and exscind the synods of Utica, Genesee, and Geneva, by 115 to 88, 3 June, "

Presbytery of Philadelphia, of which Albert Barnes was a member, is dissolved by vote of general assembly..........7 June, "

Board of Foreign Missions established by assembly......June, "

Convention of exscinded synods at Auburn, N. Y., propose to retain their organization..........17 Aug. "

In accordance with the exscinding act of 1837, the general assembly organizes at the Seventh Presbyterian church, Philadelphia, 17 May, 1838. Representatives from the exscinded synods being refused recognition, John P. Cleaveland, of the presbytery of Detroit, moves to organize, which is rapidly done, and dr. S. Fisher chosen moderator. This organization adjourns to the First Presbyterian church (Mr. Barnes's), where it rescinds the obnoxious acts of the assembly of 1837, 1838

Assembly at the First Presbyterian church (New School assembly) is declared the true general assembly of the Presbyterian church in the U. S., by the Supreme court..........4 Mch. 1839

Board of Church Erection established.......... 1844

First Presbyterian church on the whole Pacific coast organized at Astoria..........19 Sept. 1846

Standing Committee on Publication appointed.......... 1852

Permanent Committee on Ministerial Education established.. 1854

Board of Ministerial Relief established.......... 1855

United Presbyterian church formed by union of Associate Presbyterian and Associate Reformed Presbyterian church.. 1858

Southern general assembly formed with title "The Presbyterian Church in the United States".......... 1861

Reunion of the Old and New Schools at Pittsburg, Pa., 12 Nov. 1869

Presbyterian hospital, Philadelphia, chartered..........Apr. 1871

Presbyterian hospital opened in New York city..........10 Oct. 1872

Presbyterian eye, ear, and throat hospital at Baltimore, Md., opened..........1 Dec. 1877

Board of Aid for colleges established.......... 1883

Centenary of the general assembly celebrated by the northern and southern assemblies, at Philadelphia..........24 May, 1888

Committee on the revision of the Westminster Confession meets at Alleghany, Pa..........7 Sept. 1890

Trial of dr. Briggs.......... 1892

PRESBYTERIAN THEOLOGICAL SEMINARIES IN THE U. S.

	Estab.	Chart.
United Presbyterian Theological Seminary of Xenia, Xenia, O.	1877—	1794
Theological Seminary of the Presbyterian Church, Princeton, N. J.	1822—	1812
Auburn Theological Seminary, Auburn, N. Y.	1820—	1821
Union Theological Seminary, Hampden Sidney, Va.	1867—	1824
Theological Seminary of the United Presbyterian Church, Alleghany, Pa.	1830—	1825
Western Theological Seminary of the Presbyterian Church, Alleghany, Pa.	1844—	1827
Theological Seminary of the General Assembly of the Presbyterian Church, Columbia, S. C.		1828
Lane Theological Seminary, Cincinnati, O.	1829—	1831
Union Theological Seminary, New York	1839—	1836
Associate Reformed Theological Seminary, Due West, S. C.		1839
German Presbyterian Theological School of the Northwest, Dubuque, Ia.		1852
Danville Theological Seminary, Danville, Ky.	1854—	1853
Theological School of Cumberland University, Lebanon, Tenn.	1842—	"
Theological Seminary of the Reformed Presbyterian Church, Alleghany, Pa.		1858
McCormick Theological Seminary of the Presbyterian Church, Chicago, Ill.	1859—	1859
Theological Department of Biddle University, Charlotte, N. C.	1877—	1868
German Theological School of Newark, Bloomfield, N. J.		1869
San Francisco Theological Seminary, San Francisco, Cal.		1871
Institute for training colored ministers, Tuscaloosa, Ala.		1876

President and **Endymion.** NAVAL BATTLES.

President and **Little Belt.** UNITED STATES, 1811.

President of the United States. To be eligible, must be 35 years old; a natural-born citizen of the U. S., and a resident for 14 years. Elected by electors chosen by the different states, for a term of 4 years. Powers: To approve and negative bills; to grant reprieves and pardons for offences against the U. S., except in case of impeachment; to make treaties, and to nominate ambassadors and other public ministers, consuls, judges of the supreme court, etc., and by and with the consent of the Senate appoint such officers; to fill vacancies that may occur during the recess of the Senate by granting commissions, but which shall expire at the end of the next session; to convene Congress, one or both houses; to adjourn Congress to such a time as he may think proper, in case it cannot agree upon an adjournment. The president is also commander-in-chief of the army and navy, and of the militia of the several states when called into the service of the U. S. Duties: To give information to Congress from time to time regarding the state of the Union, and to recommend to its consideration such measures as he shall judge necessary and expedient; to receive ambassadors and other public ministers; to see that the laws are faithfully executed, etc.

PRESIDENTS OF THE UNITED STATES AND THEIR WIVES, BIRTHS, MARRIAGES, DEATHS, ETC.

Name.	Born.	Married.	Died.	Buried.	Family.
1. George Washington..	22 Feb. 1732, nr. Fredericksburg, Va.	17 Jan. 1759...	14 Dec. 1799	Mt. Vernon, Va....	None.
Mrs. Martha Custis...	— May, 1732, Kent county, Va....		28 May, 1802		
2. John Adams........	30 Oct. 1735, Braintree, Mass......	25 Oct. 1764...	4 July, 1826	Quincy, Mass.......	3 boys, 2 girls.
Abigail Smith........	22 Nov. 1744, Weymouth, Mass....		28 Oct. 1818		
3. Thomas Jefferson....	13 Apr. 1743, Shadwell, Va.........	1 Jan. 1772...	4 July, 1826	Monticello, Va......	6 girls.
Mrs. Martha Skelton.	19 Oct. 1748, Charles City co., Va...		5 Sept. 1782		
4. James Madison......	16 Mch. 1751, Port Conway, Va....	— Oct. 1794...	28 June, 1836	Montpelier, Vt......	None.
Mrs. Dorothy Todd...	20 May, 1772, North Carolina......		12 July, 1849		
5. James Monroe.......	28 Apr. 1758, Westmoreland co., Va.	23 Feb. 1786...	4 July, 1831	First N.Y.; transferred 1858 to Richmond, Va.	2 girls.
Eliza Kortwright....	—— 17—, New York city......		23 Sept. 1830	Oak Hill, Va......	
6. John Q. Adams......	11 July, 1767, Quincy, Mass.........	26 July, 1797...	23 Feb. 1848	Quincy, Mass.......	3 boys, 1 girl.
Louisa C. Johnson....	11 Feb. 1775, London, Engl........		15 May, 1852		
7. Andrew Jackson.....	15 Mch. 1767, Mecklenburg co., N.C.	— Jan. 1791...	8 June, 1845	Hermitage, Tenn....	3 boys.
Mrs. Rachel Robards.	—— 1767........................		22 Dec. 1828		
8. Martin Van Buren...	5 Dec. 1782, Kinderhook, N. Y....	— Feb. 1807...	24 July, 1862	Kinderhook, N.Y....	4 boys.
Hannah Goes........	8 Mch. 1783, " "		5 Feb. 1819		
9. William H. Harrison..	9 Feb. 1773, Berkeley, Va.........	22 Nov. 1795...	4 Apr. 1841	North Bend, O......	6 boys, 4 girls.
Anna Symmes........	25 July, 1775, Morristown, N. J....		25 Feb. 1864		
10. John Tyler..........	29 Mch. 1790, Charles City co., Va..	29 Mch. 1813...	17 Jan. 1862	Richmond, Va....	3 boys, 4 girls.
Letitia Christian.....	12 Nov. 1790, Cedar Grove, Va.....		10 Sept. 1842	Cedar Grove, Va..	
Julia Gardiner.......	—— 1820, East Hampton, N. Y..	26 June, 1844...	10 July, 1889	Richmond, Va....	4 boys, 2 girls.
11. James K. Polk.......	2 Nov. 1795, Mecklenburg, N. C...	1 Jan. 1824...	15 June, 1849	Nashville, Tenn.....	None.
Sarah Childress......	4 Sept. 1803, Murfreesboro, Tenn..		14 Aug. 1891		
12. Zachary Taylor......	24 Nov. 1784, Orange county, Va...	— ——, 1810...	9 July, 1850	Near Louisville, Ky..	1 boy, 3 girls.
Margaret Smith......	—— 1790, Calvert county, Md....		18 Aug. 1862		
13. Millard Fillmore.....	7 Jan. 1800, Summer Hill, N. Y...	5 Feb. 1826...	9 Mch. 1874	Buffalo, N. Y.....	1 boy, 1 girl.
Abigail Power........	13 Mch. 1798, Stillwater, N. Y......		30 Mch. 1853		
Mrs. Caroline McIntosh	21 Oct. 1813......................	18 Feb. 1858...	11 Aug. 1881	....	None.
14. Franklin Pierce......	23 Nov. 1804, Hillsborough, N. H...	19 Nov. 1834...	8 Oct. 1869	Concord, N. H......	3 boys.
Jane M. Appleton.....	12 Mch. 1806, Hampton, N. H......		2 Dec. 1863		
15. James Buchanan.....	23 Apr. 1791, Stony Batter, Pa.......	Unmarried......	1 June, 1868	Wheatland, Pa.	
16. Abraham Lincoln....	12 Feb. 1809, La Rue county, Ky...	4 Nov. 1842...	15 Apr. 1865	Springfield, Ill......	4 boys.
Mary Todd..........	12 Dec. 1818, Lexington, Ky.......		16 July, 1882		
17. Andrew Johnson.....	29 Dec. 1808, Raleigh, N. C.........	17 May, 1827...	31 July, 1875	Greenville, Tenn....	3 boys, 2 girls.
Eliza McCardle......	4 Oct. 1810, Leesburg, Tenn.......		15 Jan. 1876		
18. Ulysses S. Grant......	27 Apr. 1822, Point Pleasant, O.....	22 Aug. 1848...	23 July, 1885	Riverside, New York city.....	3 boys, 1 girl.
Julia Dent..........	26 Jan. 1826, St. Louis, Mo.........		....	....	
19. Rutherford B. Hayes.	4 Oct. 1822, Delaware, O..........	30 Dec. 1852...	17 Jan. 1893	Fremont, O.......	7 boys, 1 girl.
Lucy Ware Webb.....	28 Aug. 1831, Chillicothe, O........		25 June, 1889		
20. James A. Garfield....	19 Nov. 1831, Orange township, O..	11 Nov. 1858..	19 Sept. 1881	Cleveland, O......	4 boys, 1 girl.
Lucretia Randolph...	19 Apr. 1832, Hiram, O...........		....	....	
21. Chester A. Arthur....	5 Oct. 1830, Fairfield, Vt..........	29 Oct. 1859...	18 Nov. 1886	Albany, N. Y.......	1 boy, 1 girl.
Ellen L. Herndon.....	30 Aug. 1837, Culpeper C. H., Va...		12 Jan. 1880		
22. Grover Cleveland....	18 Mch. 1837, Caldwell, N. J........	2 June, 1886.....	....	....	3 girls.
Frances Folsom......	21 July, 1864, Buffalo, N. Y........				
23. Benjamin Harrison...	20 Aug. 1833, North Bend, O........	20 Oct. 1853...	....	....	1 boy, 1 girl.
Caroline L. Scott.....	1 Oct. 1832, Oxford, O............		25 Oct. 1892	Indianapolis, Ind.	

presidents, Administrations of. UNITED STATES.

presidents, Continental Congress. UNITED STATES.

press, Liberty of the. The *imprimatur* ("let it be printed") was much used on the title-pages of books printed in the 16th and 17th centuries. The liberty of the press was severely restrained, and the number of master-printers in London and Westminster limited by the star-chamber, 13 Charles I. 1 July, 1637.

"Disorders in printing" were repressed by Parliament in 1643 and 1649, and by Charles II.. 1662
Censorship of the press (by a license established in 1655 and 1693) abandoned.. 1695
Zenger of the New York *Weekly Journal* arrested (NEW YORK), 1734
The toast, "The liberty of the press: it is like the air we breathe—if we have it not, we die," was first given at the Crown and Anchor tavern, London, at a Whig dinner....... 1795
Presses licensed, and the printer's name required on the first and last pages of a book in Great Britain..................July, 1799
Affair of the *Federal Republican* at Baltimore, Md. (MARYLAND, UNITED STATES).. 1812
Case of the *Observer* (ALTON RIOT, UNITED STATES).............. 1837
Bill greatly freeing the press in France introduced into the Chamber...24 Jan. 1881

pressing to death. MUTE, TORTURE.

Prester John. The first mention of this traditionary oriental ruler occurs in the chronicles of Otho or Otto, bishop of Freisingen, 1145; also mentioned by Marco Polo. "The history of Prester John is that of a phantom taking many forms." —*Encyc. Brit.*, 9 ed., subject "Prester John." ABYSSINIA.

Preston, a city of Lancashire, Engl. Near here Cromwell totally defeated the royalists under sir Marmaduke Langdale, 17 Aug. 1648. Preston was taken in 1715 by the Scotch insurgents under Forster, who proclaimed king James VII. They were defeated on 12, 13 Nov. by gens. Willes and Carpenter.

Prestonpans, near Edinburgh, the scene of a battle between the young Pretender, prince Charles Stuart, and his Scotch adherents, and the royal army under sir John Cope, 21 Sept. 1745. The latter was defeated with the loss of 500 men, and fled.

Pretenders. A name given to the son and grandsons of James II. of England.

Old Pretender, James Francis Edward Stuart, chevalier de St. George, b. 10 June, 1688, was acknowledged by Louis XIV. as James III. of England.. 1701
Proclaimed, and his standard set up, at Braemar and Castletown, in Scotland...3 Sept. 1715
Landed at Peterhead, in Aberdeenshire, from France, to encourage the rebellion that the earl of Mar and his other adherents had prompted.......................................25 Dec. "
This rebellion having been suppressed, the Pretender escaped to Montrose (thence to Gravelines).........................4 Feb. 1716
Died at Rome...30 Dec. 1765
Young Pretender, Charles Edward, b.................................. 1720
Landed in Scotland, and proclaimed his father king...25 July, 1745
Gained the battle of Prestonpans, 21 Sept. 1745; and of Falkirk..17 Jan. 1746
Defeated at Culloden, and sought safety by flight.......16 Apr. "
He wandered among the wilds of Scotland for nearly 6 months; and as 30,000*l.* was offered for him, was constantly pursued, often hemmed round by his enemies, but still rescued by some lucky accident, and escaped from the isle of Uist to Morlaix in Sept. He d...............................31 Jan. 1788

[NORTH CAROLINA, 1747 and 1771.]

His natural daughter assumed the title of the duchess of Albany, d 1789
His brother, the cardinal York calling himself Henry IX of England, b Mch 1725, d at Rome Aug 1807
His alleged grandson, Charles Edward Stuart, comte d'Albanie, d 24 Dec 1880
FRANCE Sovereigns, Louis XVII, IMPOSTORS, BONAPARTE FAMILY, BOURBON

prices. BREAD, CORN, PROVISIONS

Pride's purge. On 6 Dec 1648, col Pride, with 2 regiments, surrounded the House of Parliament, and seizing in the passage 41 members of the Presbyterian party, sent them to a low room then called *hell* Above 160 other members were excluded, and none admitted but the most furious of the Independents The privileged members were named the *Rump Parliament*, which was dismissed by Cromwell, 20 Apr 1653

Prie'ne, one of the 12 cities of the Ionian league in Asia Minor The temple of Minerva Polias, founded here by Alexander the Great, and the work of Pythios, was excavated by R. P Pullan, for the Dilettanti Society, in 1868-69

priest (from Gr πρεσβύτερος, elder), in the English church the minister who presides over the public worship In Gen xiv 18, Melchizedek, king of Salem, is termed "priest of the most high God" (1913 B.C, see Hebrews vii) The Greek ιερεύς, like the Jewish priest, had a sacrificial character, which idea of the priesthood is still maintained by the Romanists and those who favor their views Among the Jews the priests assumed their office at the age of 30 years The dignity of high or chief priest was fixed in Aaron's family, 1491 B.C After the captivity of Babylon, the civil government and the crown were superadded to the high-priesthood, it was the peculiar privilege of the high-priest that he could be prosecuted in no court but that of the great Sanhedrim The heathens had their arch-flamen, or high-priest, resembling the Christian archbishop

prim'er (Lat *primus*, first), a book so named from the Romish book of devotions, and formerly set forth or published by authority, as the first book children should publicly learn or read in schools, containing prayers or portions of the Scripture Primers were printed 1535, 1539 Henry VIII issued a prayer-book called a "primer" in 1546 The 3 were published by dr Burton in 1834, also an elementary work for teaching children, as the "New England Primer" EDUCATION

primogen'iture, Right of, a usage brought down from the earliest times The first-born, in the patriarchal ages, had a superiority over his brethren, and in the absence of his father was priest to the family In some parts of England, by the ancient customs of gavel-kind and borough-English, primogeniture was superseded It came in with the feudal law, 3 Will I 1068 The rights of primogeniture abolished in France, 1790

Prince Edward island, a province of Canada, in the gulf of St Lawrence, North America, was discovered by Cabot in 1597, was finally taken from the French by the British in 1758, united with Cape Breton as a colony in 1763, but separated in 1768 Joined to Canadian Confederacy, 1 July, 1873 Area, 2000 sq miles, pop. 1891, 109,088.

Princeton, N J, Battle of On 2 Jan 1777, Washington, with a force of about 5000 men, half of them militia, was encamped at Trenton, N J Cornwallis, in command of the British troops at Princeton, leaving 3 regiments at that place, moved to attack the Americans The British encamped for the night, 2 Jan, a short distance from the American camp Washington, fully realizing the extreme peril of either fighting or retreating, conceived the bold movement of passing to the rear of the enemy during the night and attacking the force at Princeton, thus saving his army, and at the same time inflicting a severe blow on his adversary This was successfully accomplished, and early on the morning of 3 Jan Washington surprised and defeated the British at Princeton before Cornwallis was fully aware that the Americans had moved The British loss was 450 in all, while the American's was about 100, but among them gen Mercer The Americans then went into winter quarters at Morristown. TRENTON.

printing. The art of impressing letters, characters, or figures on any fitting material. Block-printing was invented by the Chinese about 593 A D, movable types made in the 10th century The invention of copper types is attributed to the Coreans in the beginning of the 15th century The honor of first printing with single types in Europe has been appropriated by Mentz, Strasburg, Haarlem, Venice, Rome, Florence, Basle and Augsburg The earliest dated wood-cut known is the St. Christopher of 1423, preserved in the library of lord Spencer at Althorp (now—1891—in possession of Mrs Rylands of Manchester). "When we consider that printing of a rudimentary kind had existed for so many centuries, and that during the whole of the early part of the 15th century examples with words or even whole lines of inscription were produced, we can only wonder that the discovery of printing from movable types should have been so late It has been said inventions will always be made when the need for them has arisen, and this is the real reason, perhaps, why the discovery of printing was delayed We may say, therefore, that the intellectual activity of the 15th century not only called printing into existence, but furnished it with the noblest models. The scribes of Italy, at this epoch, had revived the Caroline minuscules, as used in the 11th and 12th centuries, and it was this beautiful hand which has given us the 'Roman' type in which our books are still printed."—*E G Duff*, "Early Printed Books"

Lourens Janszoon Coster of Haarlem "printed with blocks a book of images and letters, 'Speculum Humanæ Salvationis,' and compounded an ink more viscous and tenacious than common ink" (*Adrian Junius*, BOOKS) about 1438
["On no subject connected with printing has more been written and to less purpose than on the Haarlem invention of printing by Lourens Janszoon Coster During the 15th century much had been said about the invention, accrediting it always to Germany, and it was not till 1499 that a reference was made to an earlier Dutch discovery"—*Duff*, "Early Printed Books," London, 1893]
John Faust establishes a printing office at Mentz (Mayence), and prints the "Tractatus Petri Hispani" 1442
Earliest specimen of printing from movable type known to exist was the famous indulgence of Nicholas V to such as should contribute money to aid the king of Cyprus against the Turks, printed at Mainz 1454
[Of the "Biblia Pauperum" there are 3 dated editions known, one of 1470, and 2 of 1471]
John Guttenberg of Mentz (Mayence) invents cut metal type, used in printing the earliest edition of the Latin (Mazarine) Bible (42 lines to the page) (BOOKS) 1455
First book with a printed date, "Psalmorum Codex," printed by Schöffer 1457
"Durandi Rationale," the first work printed with cast metal types, is issued by Faust & Schöffer at Mentz. 1459
First Latin Bible with a date completed at Mentz by Faust & Schöffer 1462
Sack of Mentz by Adolphus of Nassau in Oct. 1462, leads to the dispersion of the printers in that city, and a consequent wide spread knowledge of the art of printing "
Roman type first used at Strasburg, Germany, by John Mentelin about 1461-64
Greek type first seen in "Cicero de Officiis," printed at Mentz by Faust & Schöffer 1465
First printing at Cologne by Ulric Zee 1465-66
Roman characters first used at Rome instead of the semi Gothic Here first appeared the long ſ introduced by Sweynheym & Pannartz, printers 1467
First printing at Augsburg by Gunther Zainer, first dated book, "Meditationes Vitæ Domini nostri Jesu Christi" Mch. 1468
First printing press set up in Paris by 3 Germans, Martin Crantz Ulrich Gering, and Michael Friburger First book they issued was "Gasparini Pergamensis Epistolarum Opus," 1470
[Among the books printed by them during the next 3 years were, "Florus and Sallust," "Terence," Virgil's "Eclogues and Georgics," "Juvenal and Persius," Cicero's "Tusculan Disputations," and "Valerius Maximus."]
First printing in Nuremberg "
First book printed in the English language was a translation of "Le Recueil des Histoires de Troyes," translated by William Caxton at Cologne, and probably printed by him there 1471
Music printed from wooden blocks by Hans Froschauer of Augsburg 1473
Caxton erects his press in the almonry at Westminster, where he prints the "Dictes or Sayengis of the Philosopers," the first book printed in England, "Game and Playe of the Chesse," 1474
[Second edition, without date or place, is the first book printed in English with wood cuts]
Salomon Jarchi's "Commentary on the Pentateuch," printed in Hebrew type at Reggio, Italy 1475
"Æsop's Fables," printed by Caxton, is supposed to be the first book with its leaves numbered 1484
Theobaldus Manutius (Aldus) moves to Venice in 1488, and begins the printing of the celebrated Aldine editions there 1494
Earliest specimen of music type appears in Hegden's "Polychronicon," printed by Wynkyn de Worde, at Westminster 1495
Total number of places where printing was practised in Germany was at least 50 as early as. 1500
Aldus of Venice introduces italic types, which he first used in the "Virgil" of 1501

rinting introduced into Scotland by Andrew Myllar in the Southgate at Edinburgh....... 1508
Manual de Adultos," printed by Juan Cromberger, in Mexico, 1540
Liturgy," the first book printed in Ireland, is issued from the press of Humphrey Powell....... 1550
)octrina Christiana," printed at Lima, Peru, by Antonio Ricardo, 1584
irst patent granted for printing....... 1591
unic type first used at Stockholm in a Runic and Swedish "Alphabetarium"....... 1611
'illiam Jansen Blaeuw of Amsterdam invents the so-called "Nine Muses" printing-press....... 1620
irst printing-press in the U. S. set up in the house of Henry Dunster, president of Harvard college at Cambridge, and the *Freeman's Oath* and an almanac printed by Stephen Daye.. 1639
irst Bible printed in America, Eliot's Indian translation, issued from the Cambridge press (BIBLE)....... 1663
overnment of Massachusetts appoints licensers of the press (1662), and passes laws that "no printing should be allowed in any town within the jurisdiction, except in Cambridge".... 1664
dlico-printing, introduced from India into Europe, was commenced in London, Engl....... 1676
r John Harrington's translation of "Orlando Furioso," the first English work with copper-plates used, printed....... 1690
rst printing in New York was gov. Fletcher's proclamation, from the press of William Bradford, and dated......25 Aug. 1693
illiam Caslon establishes a type-foundry in London, Engl.... 1716
ereotype printing practised by William Ged, a goldsmith of Edinburgh, who made *plaster-of-Paris moulds*.........about 1730
hristopher Sower, or Sauer, prints at Germantown, Pa., the first German almanac printed in America, 1738, and an edition of the Bible, the second *Bible* printed in North America.... 1743
oel Buell of Killingworth, Conn., presents a memorial to the General Assembly, setting forth his discoveries in the art of type-founding, printed with type of his own casting.....*Oct.* 1769
rst regular type-foundry in America established in Germantown, Pa., by Christopher Sower, jr....... 1772
enjamin Mecom, nephew of dr. Franklin, makes an unsuccessful attempt to stereotype portions of the New Testament, 1775
'esent mode of stereotyping invented by Mr. Tilloch...about 1779
ogotypes, or words and syllables cast in one piece, invented in England....... 1783
rst successful effort to introduce printing in raised characters for the blind made by abbé Valentin Hauy, at Paris.... 1784
achine-printing first suggested by William Nicholson, editor of the *Philosophical Journal* of England....... 1790
rst printing in the U. S. west of the Mississippi river by Jacob Húnkle at St. Louis....... 1808
atent granted in England to Frederick König for a power printing-press.......29 Mch. 1810
rst work by a power-press was sheet "H" of the *Annual Register* for 1810, at the rate of 800 impressions per hour, Apr. 1811
ereotyping introduced into the U. S. from England by David Bruce, 1812. The "Larger Catechism of the Westminster Assembly" printed by J. Watt & Co. of New York, claims on its title-page to be the first work stereotyped in America..June, 1813
omposition roller, an invention claimed by several persons, comes into use.......about "
önig constructs the first successful power-machine (capacity 1800 sheets per hour on one side), from which was printed the London *Times* of.......28 Nov. 1814
eorge Clymer of Philadelphia invents the Columbian press, 1817, which he introduces in London, Engl....... 1818
'illiam Church of England patents a type-setting machine.... 1822
ed and platen press invented by Isaac Adams of Boston...... 1830
red. Rosenberg in the U. S. patents a type-setting machine... 1840
nastatic printing from zinc plates invented by Baldermus of Berlin.......about 1841
arly specimens of printing from electrotype plates are the *London Journal* for Apr. 1840, and *Mapes's Magazine* in the U. S.; plates for the latter were produced by Joseph A. Adams, a wood-engraver....... "
. M. Hoe of New York invents the "type-revolving printing-machine," or lightning-press, first used by the *Public Ledger* of Philadelphia....... 1846
oe rotary press introduced into Paris, France....... 1848
apier-maché stereotyping first used in Paris for books....... "
ullock's web-perfecting press, which prints on both sides from a continuous roll or web of paper, self-feeding, patented by William Bullock of Pittsburg, Pa.......14 Apr. 1863
he linotype, a type-casting machine, operated by a lettered key-board, the invention of Ottmar Mergenthaler of Baltimore, Md., and covered by numerous patents, is perfected.. 1888

[This machine sets up the type matrices, justifies each line, makes metal casts for printing, and distributes the matrices at the rate of from 3600 to 6000 ems per hour.]

Printing was introduced into the 13 *original states* of the U. S. y the following named persons at the time and place noted:

assachusetts.......Cambridge.......Stephen Daye.......1639
irginia.......Williamsburg......John Buckner......1680–82
ennsylvania.......near Philadelphia..William Bradford......1685
ew York.......New York city....William Bradford......1693
onnecticut.......New London......Thomas Short.......1709
aryland.......Annapolis.......William Parks.......1726
outh Carolina......Charleston.......Eleazer Phillips......1730
hode Island.......Newport.......James Franklin.......1732
ew Jersey.......Woodbridge......James Parker.......1751
orth Carolina......New-Berne.......James Davis.......1749
ew Hampshire.....Portsmouth.......Daniel Fowle.......1756
elaware.......Wilmington.......James Adams.......1761
eorgia.......Savannah.......James Johnston......1762

printing in colors was first done with blocks to imitate the initial vari-colored letters of MSS., as in Coster's "Speculum Humanæ Salvationis" of 1438, and the Mentz "Psalter" of Faust, 1455. *Stenochromy, or printing* in several colors at one impression, and chromo-lithography, printing from a number of separate stones, one for each color, are the processes of color-printing in general use. The latter has reached high perfection. Prang, in the famous chromo, "Family Scene in Pompeii," used 43 separate stones.

"Hints on Color-printing," illustrated by printed imitations of chiaroscuro and of *colored drawings, giving details of the* process, written and published by William Savage....... 1819–22
Parisian named Lacroix exhibits at the Paris industrial fair specimens of female heads printed in *tints of different colors*, by a process which he calls lithochromy....... 1826
George Baxter issues a "Pictorial Album," using as many as 20 different blocks for a single picture....... 1836
Sterch and Kramer of Berlin successfully reproduce oil-paintings by chromo-lithography.......1840–50
Adams poly-chromatic press, producing a number of colors at 1 impression by separate inking fountains, invented....... 1844
Chromo-lithography introduced into Philadelphia, where are produced chromos of Washington and Lafayette....... 1849
G. C. Leighton begins color-printing by machinery....... 1851
Large colored prints of the *Illustrated London News* first issued.......Dec. 1856
Rubber stamps. Hand-stamps, made of vulcanized india-rubber, by John Leighton, F.S.A., about 1862, and patented....... 1864
BIBLE and BOOKS for early records.

priories, religious houses next in dignity below abbeys, and at first were dependent on them, are mentioned in 722 in England. ABBEYS. Alien priories were seized by the king (Edward I.) in 1285, and in succeeding reigns on the breaking out of war with France; but were usually restored on the conclusion of peace. These priories were dissolved, and their estates vested in the crown, 3 Hen. V. 1414.—*Rymer's Fœdera.*

Priscillianists, disciples of Priscillian, a Spanish bishop who was accused of teaching gnosticism and manichæism, 372. When condemned he appealed from the pope to the emperor, but was beheaded at Treves, 385.

prisoners, Rulers of nations as noted:

Harold, afterwards II. of England, wrecked on the coast of France, 1063(?); imprisoned by count Guy of Ponthieu, who at the request of William, duke of Normandy, afterwards William I. of England, gave Harold to him. Harold, to gain his liberty, swore on holy relics to support William's claim to the crown. HASTINGS.
Richard I. of England, returning from the crusade *incognito*, taken prisoner by Leopold V., duke of Austria, 1192, and sold to Henry VI. of Germany. England paid 300,000*l.* for his release, 1194.
David II. of Scotland captured at the battle of Durham, 1346, and detained a prisoner for 11 years by Edward III. of England.
John II. king of France, taken prisoner by the Black Prince at the battle of Poitiers, 1356; gained his liberty, 1360; his son, left as hostage, having fled, John returned voluntarily to captivity, and died in London, 1364.
James I. of Scotland, captured on his way to France, when 11 years old, by Henry IV. of England, 1405, and remained a captive until 1424, when liberated by Henry V., the Scots paying 40,000*l.* as the cost of his maintenance while a prisoner.
Francis I. of France, prisoner to Charles V. of Spain, captured at the battle of Pavia, 1525, only regains his liberty by ceding to Charles Burgundy and Milan, 21 Feb. 1526.
Mary, queen of Scots, passing voluntarily into England, 1568, imprisoned 19 years, and executed by order of Elizabeth, 8 Feb. 1587.
Napoleon I. of France, surrendering to the English, 1815, imprisoned by them on the island of St. Helena, where he d. 1821.

prisoners of war, among the ancient nations, when spared, were usually enslaved. About the 13th century, civilized nations began to exchange their prisoners.

Spanish, French, and American prisoners of war in England were 12,000 in number.......30 Sept. 1779
Number exchanged by cartel with France, from the commencement of the then war, was 44,000.......June, 1781
English prisoners in France estimated at 6000, and the French in England 27,000.......Sept. 1798
English in France amounted to 10,300, and the French, etc., in England to 47,600....... 1811
Great numbers made by the Germans in the war.......1870–71

AMERICAN CIVIL WAR.

No official record of the number of prisoners captured or exchanged during the civil war has at this writing (1894) been compiled. Complete figures are promised in series 2 of the official records of the war department, now being published. Early in 1864 the secretary of war reported the number of captures during the war as follows: 1 lieutenant-general, 5 major-generals, 25 brigadier-generals, 186 colonels, 146 lieutenant-colonels, 244 majors, 2497 captains, 5811 lieutenants, 16,563 non-commissioned officers, 121,156 privates, and 5800 citizens, a total of 152,434. There had been exchanged up to that time 121,937 confederates, against 110,866 Union soldiers returned. On 14 June, 1862, a conference was held on the banks of the Chickahominy, between col. Thomas

M. Key and gen. Howell Cobb, regarding the exchange of prisoners of war. A cartel was signed by maj.-gen. John A. Dix, U. S. A., and maj.-gen. D. H. Hill, C. S. A., at Haxall's Landing, on the James river, Va., 22 July, and announced in public order 25 Sept. The value of prisoners was to be rank for rank, or 60 privates for a commanding general in-chief, 40 for a major general, 20 for a brigadier-general, 15 for a colonel, 10 for a lieutenant-colonel, etc. An act of the Confederate Congress, 1 May, 1863, to punish by death or otherwise, commanders of negro troops captured in battle, stopped exchanges except by agreement between generals in the field. The matter was placed in charge of lieut.-gen. Grant, 18 Oct. 1864, and negotiations renewed for exchange of all prisoners. Between 1 Jan. and 20 Oct. 1865, there were in the custody of the U. S. 98,802 prisoners of war; of these 1955 enlisted in the service of the U. S., 63,442 were released after cessation of hostilities, and 33,127 were exchanged; besides these, 174,223 prisoners surrendered in the Confederate armies, and were released on parole.

prisons and **penitentiaries.** Prison reform in England began with the efforts of John Howard (1726-90), who was appointed sheriff of Bedford in 1773, and made a personal investigation of English prisons. Between 1775 and 1783 Howard travelled on the Continent, finding the prisons there on the whole superior to those of England. At Augsburg he found instruments of torture and dungeons for people convicted of witchcraft. In Russia he saw the different instruments of death and torture: the axe and block, a machine for breaking arms and legs, a knife for slitting noses, the cat, knout, etc. Of the prison at Venice, the best he could say was, "Mercifully there were no irons, happily there was no fever." Holland was in advance in reform, and Howard writes, "I know not which to admire most: the neatness and cleanliness appearing in the prisons, the industry and regular conduct of the prisoners, or the humanity and attention of the magistrates and governors." Howard died at Kherson, southern Russia, on his way to Constantinople. Of English prisons at this period, Joseph Kingsmill, chaplain of the Pentonville prison, says: "The state of prisons in England when the illustrious Howard began his work of inspection was in the highest degree disgraceful to the nation. A comm to prison was, in fact, equivalent in many cases to a of death by some frightful disease; and in all, to th extremes of hunger and cold. One of these diseas ated by the want of proper ventilation, warmth, clean food, became known as the jail-fever. It swept away every year, and sent out others on their liberation enfeebled. The keeper cared for none of these th highest duty was to keep his prisoners safe, and h aspiration the fees squeezed out of their miserable re

English Parliament enacts laws abolishing prison fees, an improving the sanitary condition of jails..............

Prison built at Horsham, on Howard's plan, by duke of R mond ....

First of John Howard's works on prisons, "The Stat Prisons in England and Wales," pub..............

Gloucester jail, England, on the solitary plan, completed .

Elizabeth Fry begins her mission to the female prisoner Newgate..............at

Prison Discipline Society of England, for the amelioration jails, the classification and employment of prisoners, and prevention of crime, instituted..............

Royal Prison Society of France organized..............

Penitentiary at Millbank, on plan of Jeremy Bentham in h "Panopticon; or, the Inspection House," completed.......

Ticket of leave legalized by statute in England..............

Separate system of imprisonment first tried in the prisons of Ghent..............

Juvenile prison at Parkhurst, in the isle of Wight, opened....

Cellular prison at Pentonville, England, opened..............

First prison congress, proposed by Ducpetiaux, inspector general of prisons in Belgium, meets at Frankfort on the Main,

International prison congress at Brussels.............. 1

New system of imprisonment in England, under which convicts pass through the prisons of Pentonville, Millbank, and Portsmouth before being conditionally released, is adopted.. 18

Irish convict, or Crofton system, attributed to Alexander Maconochie in 1840, introduced by sir Walter Crofton into Ireland.............. 18

International prison congress at Frankfort on the Main....... 18

Howard Association in England instituted.............. 18

Parole system adopted in the German empire.............. 1

First International prison congress meets in London...3 July, 1

Parole system adopted in Japan ....

Control of jails in England vested in a body of prison commissioners appointed by the home secretary, by act of......

International prison congress meets at Stockholm..............

Prisoners' aid society, ... act passed by British Parliament..............

Parole system adopted in ....

International prison congress meets at Rome..............

Centenary of the death of John Howard celebrated.....20

...ernational prison congress at St. Petersburg, 19 June et seq. 1890

...iving-house for discharged prisoners was opened by gen. ...th at 30 Argyle square, London.............. 1891

prisons and **penitentiaries** in the United States. ...e first prison-reform association in the world, called the "Philadelphia Society for Assisting Distressed Prisoners," ...s formed in Philadelphia, Pa., 2 Feb. 1776, but owing to the ...volution dissolved the following year; was reorganized 8 ...y, 1787, and is still in existence. The next oldest existing ...ison association is that of New York state, founded in 1846. ...was through the efforts of its secretary, rev. dr. E. C. Wines, ...spired by count Sollohub of Russia, tha... ...ational ...ison congress now existing was organi... ...at Middle Temple, London, 3 July, ...

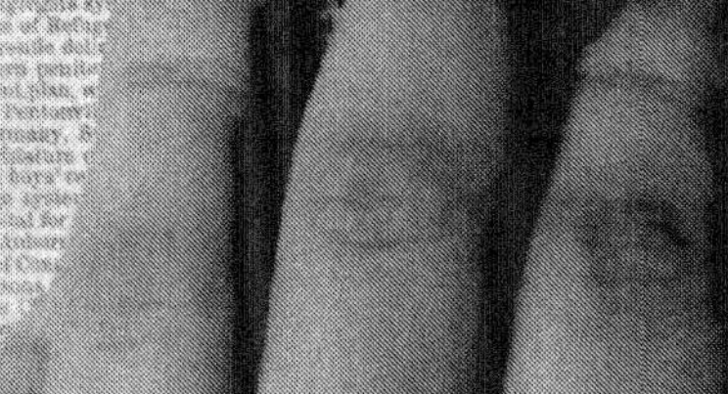

Apr. 1862; the *Jeff. Davis* escaped from Charleston, July, 1861, wrecked in Aug.; the *Nashville* escaped from Charleston, Oct. 1861, destroyed by the *Montauk*, 1 Mch. 1863; the *Florida*, built at Birkenhead, near Liverpool, received her armament at sea, entered Mobile harbor, Aug. 1862, escaped from that port, Jan. 1863, captured by the *Wachusett*, Oct. 1864, and afterwards sunk by collision in Hampton Roads; the *Alabama*, built at Liverpool, escaped 29 July, 1862, destroyed by the *Kearsarge*, 19 June, 1864. It is estimated that during the war 80 vessels of all description were employed by the confederates. ALABAMA CLAIMS. By the treaty of Washington privateering was prohibited.

privy council of England. A council was instituted [y] Alfred, 895. The number of the council was about 12 when [...] discharged the functions of state, now confined to the mem[...] of the cabinet; but it had become unwieldy in number [...]e 1679, when it was remodelled upon sir William Temple's [...] and reduced to 30 members, Anthony Ashley, earl of [...]sbury, being president. The number is now unlimited.

[p]**rivy seal,** the lord, the 5th great officer of the British [...], has the custody of the privy seal, which he must not [...]ny grant without good warrant under the sovereign's [...] This seal is used by the sovereign to all charters, [...]d pardons signed before they come to the great seal.

[...]**fighting.** BOXING.

[...]**money,** arising from captures made from the [...]red by the English government to be divided [...], and distributed by order of ranks, 17 Apr. [...]ution of army prize-money is regulated by [...]2. Naval prize-money is now regulated [...]; the last, 19 May, 1866. In the United [...]ed in 1812 that in the distribution of [...]m the captures by national vessels, one [...]vernment, and the other half, divided [...]d be distributed by order of rank.

[...]ory of (termed by Butler, "the guide [...] sense reduced to calculation"), was [...]ken up by Fermat, in their corre-

[...]of the number of ways in which an [...]der that we may judge whether [...]ailing are greater."—*Jevons.* [...] eminent mathematicians—viz., [...]bert, Euler, Lagrange, Laplace,

[...]f Probability," pub. 1865.

[...]l, whose tenure of office was [...]), Publilius was the first pro- [...]thenope war, 327 B.C. The [...]e governors of provinces.

[...]thical robber of Attica, killed [...]ng all travellers captured to [...]ff their limbs if too long, or [...]ated the word procrustean, [...]onformity to a law, measure, [...]y deforming force.

[...], an office in English ecclesi- [...]at of an attorney or solicitor [...]s abolished by the Judicature [...] to represent the clergy in con- [...] The university proctors enforce

[...]ofile taken, as recorded, was that [...]ut one eye, his likeness was so [...]ntil the end of the 3d century [...]peror with a full face; they were [...] in profile, which gives us the view [...]e manner."—*Addison.* OLD MA[...]

[...]**heory** supposes that species of [...]ot originally created, but were grad[...] [...]simple form. EVOLUTION, SPECIES.

[...]**rty.** POLITICAL PARTIES.

[...]**to** (in Spain or South America), [...]nouncement of policy, usually by [...]ANCE, SPAIN.

[P]**ropaganda fide,** Congregatio de (congregation for [th]e propagation of the faith of the Roman Catholic church), was instituted at Rome by Gregory XV. in 1622; the college in '27.

[P]**rophets.** JEWS.

[P]**roprietaries.** PENNSYLVANIA, 1746, '55, '68, '73.

[P]**rose writers.** LITERATURE.

[P]**rotectionists.** POLITICAL PARTIES; TARIFF; UNITED STATES, 1789, and throughout.

[P]**rotectorates** in England. That of the earl of Pembroke, 19 Oct. 1216, ended by his death, 1218. Of Humphry, duke of Gloucester, began 31 Aug. 1422; he was seized 11 Feb. 1447, and found dead a few days after. Of Richard, duke of Gloucester, began May, 1483, and ended by his assuming the royal dignity, 26 June, the same year. Of Somerset, began 28 Jan. 1547, and ended by his resignation in 1549. Of Oliver Cromwell, began 16 Dec. 1653, and ended by his death, 3 Sept. 1658. Of Richard Cromwell, began 3 Sept. 1658, [...] by his resignation, 25 May, 1659. ENGLAND.

[P]**ro'teine** (from Gr. πρωτεῖον, principal), a chemical [...] introduced by Mulder about 1841 for the basis of albu[men], fibrine, and caseine.

[P]**rotestant Episcopal church.** CHURCH.

[P]**rotestants.** The emperor Charles V. called a diet [at Sp]ires in 1529 to request aid from the German princes [ag]ainst the Turks, and to devise means for allaying the relig[iou]s disputes which then raged owing to Luther's opposition [to] the Roman Catholic clergy. Against a decree of this diet, [to] support the doctrines of the church of Rome, 6 Lutheran [prin]ces, with the deputies of 13 imperial towns, formally and [sol]emnly *protested*, 19 Apr. 1529. Hence the term Protestants [wa]s given to the followers of Luther; it afterwards included Cal[vin]ists, and other sects separated from the see of Rome. The 6 [pro]testing princes were: John, elector of Saxony; George, mar[gra]ve of Brandenburg; Ernest and Francis, the dukes of Lunen[bur]g; the landgrave of Hesse; and the prince of Anhalt. These [we]re joined by the citizens of Strasburg, Nuremberg, Ulm, Con[st]ance, Heilbron, and 7 other cities. CALVINISTS, CHURCH OF [E]NGLAND, GERMANY, HUGUENOTS, LUTHERANS, etc.

[Pr]otestants persecuted in Scotland and Germany 1546
[Ed]ward VI. established Protestantism in England 1548
[M]ary re-establishes Romanism, and persecutes the Protestants; above 280 put to death 1553-58
[R]idley, bishop of London, and Latimer, bishop of Worcester, were burned at Oxford, 16 Oct. 1555; and Cranmer, archbishop of Canterbury ..... 21 Mch. 1556
[During 3 years of Mary's reign, 277 persons were brought to the stake, besides those punished by imprisonment, fines, and confiscations. Among those who suffered death by fire were 5 bishops, 21 clergymen, 8 lay gentlemen, 84 tradesmen, 100 husbandmen, servants, and laborers, 55 women, and 4 children. The principal agents of the queen were the bishops Gardiner and Bonner.]
[E]lizabeth restores Protestantism 1558
[P]rotestant settlements formed in Ulster, N. Ireland 1608-11
[P]rotestant union of princes in Germany, 4 May, 1608; met last, May, 1621
[T]HIRTY YEARS' WAR between Romanists and Protestants in Germany 1618-48
Protestants persecuted at Thorn, in Poland 1724
Protestant Association (GORDON'S "NO POPERY" riots) 1780
Pan-Protestant conference held at Worms (about 1000 delegates) ..... 31 May, 1869
Meeting of a general synod of the Reformed church of France (M. Guizot present) to propose return to early doctrine and discipline, held at Paris ..... 7 June, 1872

pro'toplasm, the material of the minute ultimate particles of all animal and vegetable tissues, termed "the physical basis of life" by Huxley (1868). The protamoeba, the lowest form of life, is a structureless mass of protoplasm; the amoeba, a similar mass, contains a nucleus. Protoplasm is composed of carbonic acid, water, and ammonia.

Provence (*pro-vonss'*) (the Roman *Provincia*), a province of S.E. France, now included mostly in the departments of Alpes Maritimes, Bouches-du-Rhone, and the Var, was made a kingdom by the emperor Lothaire for his son Charles. It afterwards became part of the kingdom of Arles as a feudal fief, and was reunited to the German empire in 1032 by Conrad II. On the fall of the Hohenstaufens it was acquired by Charles of Anjou, who married the heiress of the count in 1245, and became king of Naples in 1268; and was held by his successors till its an-

M Key and gen Howell Cobb, regarding the exchange of prisoners of war A cartel was signed by maj gen John A Dix, U S A, and maj gen D H Hill, C S A at Haxall's Landing, on the James river, Va., 22 July and announced in public order 25 Sept The value of prisoners was to be rank for rank or 60 privates for a commanding general in-chief, 40 for a major general 20 for a brigadier-general 15 for a colonel 10 for a lieutenant colonel etc An act of the Confederate Congress, 1 May 1863, to punish by death or otherwise commanders of negro troops captured in battle stopped exchanges except by agreement between generals in the field The matter was placed in charge of lieut gen Grant, 15 Oct 1864, and negotiations renewed for exchange of all prisoners Between 1 Jan and 20 Oct 1865 there were in the custody of the U S 98 802 prisoners of war, of these 1955 enlisted in the service of the U S, 63,442 were released after cessation of hostilities, and 33 127 were exchanged, besides these, 174,223 prisoners surrendered in the Confederate armies, and were released on parole

prisons and **penitentiaries.** Prison reform in England began with the efforts of John Howard (1726-90), who was appointed sheriff of Bedford in 1773, and made a personal investigation of English prisons. Between 1775 and 1783 Howard travelled on the Continent, finding the prisons there on the whole superior to those of England At Augsburg he found instruments of torture and dungeons for people convicted of witchcraft In Russia he saw the different instruments of death and torture the axe and block, a machine for breaking arms and legs a knife for slitting noses, the cat, knout, etc Of the prison at Venice, the best he could say was, "Mercifully there were no irons, happily there was no fever" Holland was in advance in reform, and Howard writes, "I know not which to admire most the neatness and cleanliness appearing in the prisons, the industry and regular conduct of the prisoners, or the humanity and attention of the magistrates and governors" Howard died at Kherson, southern Russia, on his way to Constantinople Of English prisons at this period, Joseph Kingsmill, chaplain of the Pentonville prison, says "The state of prisons in England when the illustrious Howard began his work of inspection was in the highest degree disgraceful to the nation A committal to prison was, in fact, equivalent in many cases to a sentence of death by some frightful disease, and in all to the utmost extremes of hunger and cold One of these diseases, generated by the want of proper ventilation, warmth, cleanliness, and food, became known as the jail-fever It swept away hundreds every year, and sent out others on their liberation miserably enfeebled The keeper cared for none of these things, his highest duty was to keep his prisoners safe, and his highest aspiration the fees squeezed out of their miserable relatives"

English Parliament enacts laws abolishing prison fees, and for improving the sanitary condition of jails 1774
Prison built at Horsham, on Howard's plan, by duke of Richmond 1776
First of John Howard's works on prisons, 'The State of Prisons in England and Wales," pub 1777
Gloucester jail, England on the solitary plan, completed 1792
Elizabeth Fry begins her mission to the female prisoners in Newgate about 1813
Prison Discipline Society of England, for the amelioration of jails, the classification and employment of prisoners, and the prevention of crime instituted 1816
Royal Prison Society of France organized 1819
Penitentiary at Millbank on plan of Jeremy Bentham in his 'Panopticon, or, the Inspection House,' completed 1821
Ticket of leave legalized by statute in England 1834
Separate system of imprisonment first tried in the prisons of Ghent 1835
Juvenile prison at Parkhurst, in the isle of Wight, opened 1838
Cellular prison at Pentonville, England, opened 1842
First prison congress, proposed by Ducpétiaux, inspector general of prisons in Belgium, meets at Frankfort on the Main, 1845
International prison congress at Brussels 1846
New system of imprisonment in England, under which convicts pass through the prisons of Pentonville, Millbank, and Portsmouth before being conditionally released, is adopted 1847
Irish convict, or Crofton system, attributed to Alexander Maconochie in 1840, introduced by sir Walter Crofton into Ireland 1854
International prison congress at Frankfort on the Main 1857
Howard Association in England instituted 1866
Parole system adopted in the German empire 1871
First International prison congress meets in London 3 July, 1872
Parole system adopted in Japan "
Control of jails in England vested in a body of prison commissioners appointed by the home secretary, by act of 1877
International prison congress meets at Stockholm 1878
Prisoners' aid societies, Prison Charities act passed by British Parliament . 1882
Parole system adopted in France ... 1885
International prison congress meets at Rome . . "
Centenary of the death of John Howard celebrated. 20 Jan. 1890
International prison congress at St. Petersburg, 19 June et seq 1890
Receiving house for discharged prisoners was opened by gen Booth at 30 Argyle square, London 1891

prisons and **penitentiaries** in the United States. The first prison-reform association in the world, called the "Philadelphia Society for Assisting Distressed Prisoners," was formed in Philadelphia, Pa, 2 Feb 1776, but owing to the Revolution dissolved the following year, was reorganized 8 May, 1787, and is still in existence The next oldest existing prison association is that of New York state, founded in 1846 It was through the efforts of its secretary, rev dr E C Wines, inspired by count Sollohub of Russia, that the international prison congress now existing was organized, the first meeting held at Middle Temple, London, 3 July, 1872

Congress recommends to the several states to make it the duty of keepers of jails to receive prisoners committed under authority of the U S 23 Sept 1789
Law passed by legislature of Pennsylvania to try the system of solitary confinement of prisoners at hard labor . 1790
Society for the improvement of prison discipline and for the reformation of juvenile offenders organized in Boston 1815
Construction of Auburn (N Y) prison begun, 1816, and the congregate system established there by capt Elam Lynde 1824
House of Refuge on Blackwell's island the first institution for juvenile delinquents in the U S opened 1825
Eastern penitentiary in Philadelphia, on the solitary confinement plan which was taken as a model for the English prison at Pentonville, and of prisons in Paris Belgium, Holland, Germany, Sweden Norway, Denmark, etc., authorized by legislature of 1821, and opened 25 Oct. 1829
First boys' reformatory in the U S, upon the family or cottage system established at Lancaster O 1858
Hospital for insane criminals, the first in the U S, established at Auburn, N Y "
Act of Congress passed directing marshals to be appointed and prisons to be established for American prisoners, 1 in Japan, 4 in China, 1 in Turkey and 1 in Siam 22 June, 1860
Contract system of leasing prisoners in southern prisons to private parties, begins with the Mississippi penitentiary, 21 Feb 1867
National Prison Association organized at Cincinnati, O, Rutherford B Hayes presiding 12 Oct 1870
Territorial penitentiaries placed under control of the U S marshal, and U S attorney-general authorized to prescribe rules for their government by act of Congress 10 Jan 1871
U S military prison established at fort Leavenworth, Kan, by act of Congress 21 May, 1874
U S jail located at Fort Smith Ark, by act of 16 Mch 1886
Contract labor in prisons of New York state abolished July, 1888
Congress authorizes 3 U S prisons 1 north and 1 south of 39° N lat and east of the Rocky mountains, the other west of the Rocky mountains 3 Mch 1891

U S PRISON STATISTICS.

Year	No of prisoners	Ratio to population
1850	6 737	1 out of 3422
1860	19,086	1 " " 1647
1870	32,901	1 " " 1171
1880	58 609	1 " " 855
1890	. 79,621	. 1 " " 786 5

["It is estimated by the best authorities that not over one third of the criminals are in prison at any one time"—*Boies*, Prisons and Paupers, p 87]

privateer, an armed ship of private owners, licensed (letter of marque) by a government at war to seize and plunder the ships of the enemy The practice, said to have been adopted by Edward I against the Portuguese in 1295, was general during the war between Spain and the Netherlands in the 17th century, and during the last Anglo-French war During the war of 1812-15 between the United States and Great Britain the American privateers did great damage to British commerce, having taken, burned, and destroyed about 1780 British merchantmen of all classes, while the British captured about 500 of the American merchantmen The American privateers numbered 250, 46 of which were letters of marque Privateering was abolished by the great sovereigns of Europe by treaty, 30 Mch. 1856 The U S government refused to agree unless the right of blockade was also given up. The British government declined this, asserting "that the system of commercial blockade was essential to its naval supremacy" On 17 Apr 1861, Jefferson Davis, president of the Southern Confederacy, announced his intention of issuing letters of marque, and on the 19th pres. Lincoln proclaimed that all southern privateers should be treated as pirates This decree was not carried out. All the great powers forbade privateering during the American civil war Among the principal Confederate privateers were the following. The *Savannah* ran the blockade at Charleston, S. C., 2 June, 1861, captured 4 June, the *Sumter* ran the blockade at New Orleans, La, July, 1861, sold

Apr. 1862; the *Jeff. Davis* escaped from Charleston, July, 1861, wrecked in Aug.; the *Nashville* escaped from Charleston, Oct. 1861, destroyed by the *Montauk*, 1 Mch. 1863; the *Florida*, built at Birkenhead, near Liverpool, received her armament at sea, entered Mobile harbor, Aug. 1862, escaped from that port, Jan. 1863, captured by the *Wachusett*, Oct. 1864, and afterwards sunk by collision in Hampton Roads: the *Alabama*, built at Liverpool, escaped 29 July, 1862, destroyed by the *Kearsarge*, 19 June, 1864. It is estimated that during the war 10 vessels of all description were employed by the confederates. ALABAMA CLAIMS. By the treaty of Washington privateering was prohibited.

privy council of England. A council was instituted by Alfred, 895. The number of the council was about 12 when it discharged the functions of state, now confined to the members of the cabinet; but it had become unwieldy in number before 1679, when it was remodelled upon sir William Temple's plan, and reduced to 30 members, Anthony Ashley, earl of Shaftesbury, being president. The number is now unlimited.

privy seal, the lord, the 5th great officer of the British empire, has the custody of the privy seal, which he must not put to any grant without good warrant under the sovereign's signet. This seal is used by the sovereign to all charters, grants, and pardons signed before they come to the great seal.

prize-fighting. BOXING.

prize-money, arising from captures made from the enemy, was decreed by the English government to be divided into 8 equal parts, and distributed by order of ranks, 17 Apr. 1708. The distribution of army prize-money is regulated by an act passed in 1832. Naval prize-money is now regulated by royal proclamation; the last, 19 May, 1866. In the United States Congress decreed in 1812 that in the distribution of prize-money arising from the captures by national vessels, one half should go to the government, and the other half, divided into 20 equal parts, should be distributed by order of rank.

probability, Theory of (termed by Butler, "the guide of life;" by Laplace, "good sense reduced to calculation"), was originated by Pascal, and taken up by Fermat, in their correspondence in 1654.

Its object is "the determination of the number of ways in which an event may happen or fail, in order that we may judge whether the chances of its happening or failing are greater."—*Jevons.*
It has been treated upon by the most eminent mathematicians—viz., the Bernouillis, De Moivre, D'Alembert, Euler, Lagrange, Laplace, and Quetelet.
Isaac Todhunter's copious "History of Probability," pub. 1865.

proconsul, a Roman consul, whose tenure of office was extended beyond his legal term. Q. Publilius was the first proconsul appointed during the Parthenope war, 327 B.C. The name was afterwards given to the governors of provinces.

Procrustes, a famous mythical robber of Attica, killed by Theseus. His method of bringing all travellers captured to the length of his bed, by cutting off their limbs if too long, or stretching them if too short, originated the word procrustean, or reducing by violence to strict conformity to a law, measure, or model; producing uniformity by deforming force.

proctor (from *procurator*), an office in English ecclesiastical courts, corresponding to that of an attorney or solicitor in courts of common-law. It was abolished by the Judicature Act, 1873. The persons chosen to represent the clergy in convocation are termed proctors. The university proctors enforce discipline.

profiles. The first profile taken, as recorded, was that of Antigonus, who, having but one eye, his likeness was so taken, 330 B.C.—*Ashe.* "Until the end of the 3d century I have not seen a Roman emperor with a full face; they were always painted or appeared in profile, which gives us the view of a head in a very majestic manner."—*Addison.* OLD MAN OF THE MOUNTAIN.

progressionist theory supposes that species of animals and plants were not originally created, but were gradually developed from one simple form. EVOLUTION, SPECIES.

Prohibition party. POLITICAL PARTIES.

pronunciamen'to (in Spain or South America), a proclamation or formal announcement of policy, usually by a revolutionary leader. FRANCE, SPAIN.

Propaganda fide, Congregatio de (congregation for the propagation of the faith of the Roman Catholic church), was constituted at Rome by Gregory XV. in 1622; the college in 1627.

prophets. JEWS.

proprietaries. PENNSYLVANIA, 1746, '55, '68, '79.

prose writers. LITERATURE.

Protectionists. POLITICAL PARTIES; TARIFF; UNITED STATES, 1790, and throughout.

protectorates in England. That of the earl of Pembroke, 19 Oct. 1216, ended by his death, 1218. Of Humphrey, duke of Gloucester, began 31 Aug. 1422; he was seized 11 Feb. 1447, and found dead a few days after. Of Richard, duke of Gloucester, began May, 1483, and ended by his assuming the royal dignity, 26 June, the same year. Of Somerset, began 28 Jan. 1547, and ended by his resignation in 1549. Of Oliver Cromwell, began 16 Dec. 1653, and ended by his death, 3 Sept. 1658. Of Richard Cromwell, began 3 Sept. 1658, and ended by his resignation, 25 May, 1659. ENGLAND.

pro'teine (from Gr. πρωτεῖον, principal), a chemical term introduced by Mulder about 1844 for the basis of albumen, fibrine, and caseine.

Protestant Episcopal church. CHURCH.

Protestants. The emperor Charles V. called a diet at Spires in 1529 to request aid from the German princes against the Turks, and to devise means for allaying the religious disputes which then raged owing to Luther's opposition to the Roman Catholic clergy. Against a decree of this diet, to support the doctrines of the church of Rome, 6 Lutheran princes, with the deputies of 13 imperial towns, formally and solemnly *protested,* 19 Apr. 1529. Hence the term Protestants was given to the followers of Luther; it afterwards included Calvinists, and other sects separated from the see of Rome. The 6 protesting princes were: John, elector of Saxony; George, margrave of Brandenburg; Ernest and Francis, the dukes of Lunenburg; the landgrave of Hesse; and the prince of Anhalt. These were joined by the citizens of Strasburg, Nuremberg, Ulm, Constance, Heilbron, and 7 other cities. CALVINISTS, CHURCH OF ENGLAND, GERMANY, HUGUENOTS, LUTHERANS, etc.

Protestants persecuted in Scotland and Germany.............. 1546
Edward VI. established Protestantism in England.............. 1548
Mary re-establishes Romanism, and persecutes the Protestants: above 300 put to death.............................. 1553–58
Ridley, bishop of London, and Latimer, bishop of Worcester, were burned at Oxford, 16 Oct. 1555; and Cranmer, archbishop of Canterbury.......................... 21 Mch. 1556
[During 3 years of Mary's reign, 277 persons were brought to the stake; besides those punished by imprisonment, fines, and confiscations. Among those who suffered death by fire were 5 bishops, 21 clergymen, 8 lay gentlemen, 84 tradesmen, 100 husbandmen, servants, and laborers, 55 women, and 4 children. The principal agents of the queen were the bishops Gardiner and Bonner.]
Elizabeth restores Protestantism.............................. 1558
Protestant settlements formed in Ulster, N. Ireland...... 1608–11
Protestant union of princes in Germany, 4 May, 1608; met last, May, 1621
THIRTY YEARS' WAR between Romanists and Protestants in Germany.. 1618–48
Protestants persecuted at Thorn, in Poland.................. 1724
Protestant Association (GORDON'S "NO POPERY" RIOTS)....... 1780
Pan-Protestant conference held at Worms (about 1000 delegates)... 31 May, 1869
Meeting of a general synod of the Reformed church of France (M. Guizot present) to propose return to early doctrine and discipline, held at Paris.......................... 7 June, 1872

pro'toplasm, the material of the minute ultimate particles of all animal and vegetable tissues, termed "the physical basis of life" by Huxley (1868). The protamœba, the lowest form of life, is a structureless mass of protoplasm; the amœba, a similar mass, contains a nucleus. Protoplasm is composed of carbonic acid, water, and ammonia.

Provence (*pro-vonss'*) (the Roman *Provincia*), a province of S.E. France, now included mostly in the departments of Alpes Maritimes, Bouches-du-Rhone, and the Var, was made a kingdom by the emperor Lothaire for his son Charles. It afterwards became part of the kingdom of Arles as a feudal fief, and was reunited to the German empire in 1032 by Conrad II. On the fall of the Hohenstaufens it was acquired by Charles of Anjou, who married the heiress of the count in 1245, and became king of Naples in 1268; and was held by his successors till its annexation to France by Charles VIII in 1487 In this region in the 11th century Provençal literature first made its appearance It took a poetic form and gave rise to the Troubadour poetry and music which lasted until the 14th century TROUBADOUR

proverbs. The book of Proverbs by Solomon is dated about 1000 B C The latter part was collected by order of Hezekiah about 700 B.C Ray's collection of English proverbs appeared in 1672 and Bohn's general collection in 1857 Alfred Henderson's Latin Proverbs," 1869

provincial assemblies, congresses and conventions. NEW YORK, PENNSYLVANIA, etc, 1760-89

provisional army. The course of the French government (Directory) towards the government of the United States became so aggressive and insolent during the years 1797-98 that the U S decided to take measures for defence and retaliation To this end, therefore, an addition to the army of 10,000 men was ordered by Congress in 1798, and officers commissioned, with Washington as lieutenant-general and commander-in-chief Although commissions were issued to the officers the men were never called out and no money disbursed This provisional army was held in readiness until the summer of 1800, when it was disbanded See list of general officers under army NAVY, UNITED STATES, 1798

provisions, prices of, in England, remarkable statements concerning them The high value of money and the non-existence of produce and stock exchanges at the time must be borne in mind

Sale of Food and Drugs act passed 11 Aug 1875

Wheat for food for 100 men for 1 day worth only 1*s*, and a sheep for 4*d*, Henry I about 1130 The price of wine raised to 6*d* per quart for red and 8*d* for white, that the sellers might be enabled to live by it, 2 John, 1200 —*Burton's Annals*

When wheat was at 6*s* per quarter the farthing loaf was to be equal in weight to 24 ounces (made of the whole grain) and to 16 the white When wheat was 1*s* 6*d* per quarter, the farthing white loaf was to weigh 64 ounces and the whole grain (the same as standard now) 96, by the first assize, 1202 —*Mat. Paris*

A remarkable plenty in all Europe, 1280 —*Dufresnoy*

Wheat 1*s* per quarter, 14 Edw I 1286 —*Stow*

Price of provisions fixed by the common council of London as follows 2 pullets, 3 halfpence, a partridge or 2 woodcocks, 3 halfpence, a fat lamb, 6*d*. from Christmas to Shrovetide, the rest of the year 4*d*, 29 Edw I 1299 —*Stow*

Price of provisions fixed by Parliament at the rate of 2*l* 8*s* of our money for a fat ox, if fed with corn, 3*l* 12*s*, a shorn sheep, 6*s*, 2 dozen of eggs, 3*d*, other articles nearly the same as fixed by the common council above recited, 7 Edw II 1313 —*Rot. Parl.*

Wine, the best sold for 20*s* per tun 10 Rich II 1387

Wheat at 1*s* 1*d* the bushel in 1390, was deemed so high that it is called a dearth of corn by the historians of that era.

Beef and pork settled at a halfpenny the pound, and veal 3 farthings, by act of Parliament, 24 Hen VIII 1533 —*Anderson.*

Document from a "Book of the Joint Diet, Dinner and Supper, and the Charge thereof, for Cranmer, Latimer, and Ridley," kept by the bailiffs of Oxford, while they were in their custody

1 Oct 1554 DINNER.

Bread and ale	2*d*
Oysters	1*d*.
Butter	2*d*.
Eggs	2*d*
Lyng	8*d*.
A piece of fresh salmon	10*d*.
Wine	3*d*
Cheese and pears	2*d*.
The 3 dinners	2*s* 6*d*.

Milk sold 3 pints ale measure for 1 halfpenny, 2 Eliz 1560 —*Stow's Chronicle*

provisions, prices of, in the United States TARIFF, WAGES

Prussia, a kingdom of central Europe. The country was anciently possessed by the Veneti, about 320 B.C They were conquered by the Borussi, who inhabited the Riphæan mountains, and from these the country was called Borussia Some historians derive the name from *Po*, signifying near, and *Russia* The Porussi afterwards intermixed with the followers of the Teutonic knights, and latterly with the Poles HOHENZOLLERN The constitution, established 31 Jan 1850, was modified 30 Apr. 1851, 21 May, 5 June, 1852, 7 and 24 May, 1853, 10 June, 1854, 30 May, 1855, 15 May, 1857, 17 May, 1867; 27 Mch 1872, 5 Apr 1873, 18 June, 1875, 19 Feb 1879, and 27 May, 1888. Area, 1713, 43,400 sq. miles, pop 1,731,000, 1797, 118,000 sq miles, pop. 8,700,000, 1816, 106,820 sq miles, pop 10,349,031, 1867, 134,463 sq miles, pop. 23,971,337, 1890, pop 29,955,281, 1900, 34,472,509

St Adalbert arrives in Prussia to preach Christianity, and is slain about 997
Boleslaus of Poland revenges his death by dreadful ravages 1018
Berlin built by a colony from the Netherlands, in the reign of Albert the Bear 1163
Teutonic knights returning from the holy wars, undertake the conquest and conversion of Prussia 1225
Thorn founded by them 1231
Königsberg, lately built, made the capital 1286
[Largely repeopled by German colonists 12th-13th century]
Frederick IV of Nuremberg (the founder of the reigning family) obtains by purchase from Sigismund, emperor of Germany, the margraviate of Brandenburg 1415
Casimir IV of Poland assists the natives against the oppression of the Teutonic knights 1446
Albert of Brandenburg, grand master of the Teutonic order, seizes its territories renounces the Roman Catholic religion, embraces Lutheranism, and is acknowledged duke of East Prussia, to be held as a fief of Poland 1525
University of Königsberg founded by duke Albert 1544
John Sigismund created elector of Brandenburg and duke of Prussia. 1608
Principality of Halberstadt and the bishopric of Minden transferred to the house of Brandenburg 1648
Poland obliged to acknowledge Prussia as an independent state, under Frederick William, surnamed the Great Elector 1657
Order of Concord instituted by Christian Ernest elector of Brandenburg and duke of Prussia, to commemorate the part he had taken in restoring peace to Europe 1660
Frederick III, in an assembly of the states crowns his own head and his consort's, is proclaimed king of Prussia as Frederick I, and institutes Order of the Black Eagle 18 Jan 1701
Gueldres taken from the Dutch 1702
Frederick I seizes Neufchâtel or Neuburg, and purchases Tecklenburg 1707
Principality of Meurs added to Prussia 1712
Frederick II the Great, king, who made the Prussian monarchy rank among the first powers of Europe . 1740
Breslau ceded to Prussia 1741
Silesia, Glatz, etc, ceded 1742
Seven Years' war (BATTLES) 1756–63
Frederick II victor at Prague, 6 May, defeated at Kolin, 18 June, victor at Rossbach 5 Nov 1757
Gen Lacy with an Austrian and Russian army, marches to Berlin, city is laid under contribution, etc, magazines destroyed Oct 1760
Peace of Hubertsburg ends Seven Years' war, part of Silesia gained by Prussia 15 Feb 1763
Shares in the first partition of Poland 1772
Frederick the Great d. 17 Aug 1786
Frederick William II invades France 1792
Joins the coalition against France 1793
Shares in the second and third partition of Poland 1793-95
Prussians seize Hanover 1801 and 1806
Prussia joins the allies of England against France 6 Oct. "
Fatal battles of Jena and Auerstadt 14 Oct "
[Nearly all the monarchy subdued by France]
Berlin decree promulgated 20 Nov "
Peace of TILSIT 9 July, 1807
Formation of the TUGENDBUND, a patriotic society (promoted by Von Stein) "
Convention of Berlin 5 Nov 1808
Scharnhorst secretly restores the army by the system of reserves, forming a nation of soldiers 1809-13
People rise to expel the French from Germany at the king's appeal and form the "landwehr" or militia 17 Mch 1813
Treaty of Paris 11 Apr 1814
Congress of Carlsbad 1 Aug 1819
Blücher d in Silesia, aged 77 12 Sept "
[From this time Prussia pursued a peaceful and undisturbed policy until 1848]
Government disputes with Roman Catholic clergy begin, through ultramontanism of the Radziwill family since 1830 1840
Serious attempt made on the life of the king by an assassin named Tesch, who fired 2 shots at him 26 July, 1844
Insurrection in Berlin 18 Mch 1848
Berlin declared in a state of siege 12 Nov "
Constituent assembly dissolved, the king issues a new constitution 5 Dec "
German National Assembly elect the king of Prussia "hereditary emperor of the Germans" 28 Mch 1849
King declines the imperial crown . . 29 Apr "
Kingdom put under martial law . 10 May, "
Bavaria declares for an imperial constitution with the king of Prussia at its head 8 Sept. "
Austria protests against the alliance of Prussia with the minor states of Germany 12 Nov "
New constitution, 31 Jan, the king takes the oath required by it 6 Feb 1850
Hanover withdraws from the Prussian alliance 25 Feb "
Treaty signed at Munich between Austria, Bavaria, Saxony, and Würtemberg to maintain the German union 27 Feb "
Würtemberg denounces the insidious ambition of the king of Prussia, and announces a league with Bavaria, and Saxony, under the sanction of Austria 15 Mch "
Hesse Darmstadt withdraws from the Prussian league, 30 June, "
Convention of Olmütz for the pacification of Germany, 29 Nov "
150th anniversary of the Prussian monarchy celebrated. 18 Jan 1851
King revives the council of state as it existed before the revolution of 1848 . 12 Jan 1852
Agrees to a protocol for preservation of the integrity of Turkey, which is signed at Vienna. ... . 7 Apr 1854

eclares neutrality in the war 6 Sept and Oct 1854

xcluded from the conferences at Vienna Feb 1855

sputes with Switzerland (NEUFCHATEL) Nov 1856, to May, 1857

ental illness of the king, the prince of Prussia appointed regent 23 Oct "

ince of Prussia permanent regent 7 Oct 1858

alian war—Prussia declares its neutrality, but arms to protect Germany May and June, 1859

gent announces that "the Prussian army will be in future the Prussian nation in arms" 12 Jan 1860

egent and several German sovereigns meet the emperor of the French at BADEN 15-17 June, "

eath of Frederick William IV Accession of William I, 2 Jan 1861

tempted assassination of the king by Becker, a Leipsic student, 14 July, who is sentenced to 20 years' imprisonment, 23 Sept "

ng and queen crowned at Königsberg, he declares that he will reign by the "grace of God 18 Oct "

ll for making the ministry responsible passed 6 Mch 1862

amber of Representatives opposes the government as to length of military service, 6 Mch, and resolves to discuss items of the budget, ministry resigns, king will not accept the resignation, but dissolves the chambers 11 Mch "

nistry (liberal) resigns, and a reactionary cabinet formed under Van der Heydt 18 Mch -12 Apr "

ections go against the government, only one minister elected May, "

n der Heydt resigns, succeeded as premier by the count Bismarck Schönhausen 23 Sept, who informs the chamber that the budget is deferred till 1863, the chamber protests against this as unconstitutional 30 Sept "

amber of Peers passes the budget without the amendments of the Chamber of Representatives, which (by 237 against 2) resolves that the act is unconstitutional 11 Oct "

ng closes the session (65th) saying "The budget for the year 1862 as decreed by the Chamber of Representatives, having been rejected by the Chamber of Peers as insufficient, the government is under the necessity of controlling the public affairs outside the constitution" 13 Oct "

itation in favor of the constitution proceeding, passive resistance adopted, several liberal papers suppressed Nov "

ambers reassemble, *unconciliatory address from the king*, 14 Jan, bold reply of the deputies, adopted 23 Jan 1863

ey recommend neutrality in the Polish insurrection, 28 Feb "

olent dissension between the deputies and the ministry, May, "

amber of Deputies address the king on their relation with the ministry and the state of the country, 22 May, the king replies that his ministers possess his confidence, and adjourns the session 27 May, "

ng resolves to govern without a parliament "

ess severely restricted, 1 June, the crown prince in a speech disavows participation in the recent acts of the ministry, 5 June and censures them in a letter to the king 6 July, reconciled to the king 8 Sept. "

tion in favor of the rights of the duchies of Schleswig and Holstein, carried 2 Dec, but the chamber refuses to assent or to defray the expenses of war Dec "

ambers dissolved Jan 1864

[For the events of the war, DENMARK]

ace with Denmark signed 30 Oct "

ening of the chambers, 14 Jan, revival of the constitution and agitation for control over the army budget 16 Jan 1865

puties having rejected the budget, the bills for reorganizing the army and increasing the fleet, and meeting the expense of the war with Denmark, the chamber is prorogued, the government *will rule without it* 17 June, "

ng at Carlsbad issues a despotic decree appropriating and disposing of the revenue 5 July, "

litical dinner of the Liberal deputies prohibited at Cologne, and forcibly prevented at Overlahnstein, in Nassau 24 July, "

nvention at Gastein signed 14 Aug "

ng takes possession of Lauenburg, purchased from Austria with his own money 15 Sept. "

cree asserting Prussian jurisdiction over Holstein 11 Mch 1866

ussian circular asking German states whether they will support Austria or Prussia (they profess neutrality) 24 Mch "

ussia prepares for war 27 Mch "

ench government professes neutrality Apr "

stria demands the demobilization of the Prussian army, 7 Apr, Bismarck proposes a German parliament 9 Apr "

eat meeting at Berlin in favor of peace 15 Apr "

nd's attempt to assassinate Bismarck fails 7 May, "

criminatory correspondence between Mendsdorff (Austrian) and Bismarck, calling for disarmament April-May, "

iance with Italy May, "

ussians enter Holstein, Austrians retire 7 June, "

eting of the Federal diet at Frankfort, the demobilization of the Prussian army proposed by Austria, voted for by Bavaria, Saxony, Hanover, Hesse Cassel, Nassau, and others, Prussia declares the Germanic confederation to be dissolved, 14 June, "

nce Alexander of Hesse appointed to command the Federal army June, "

ussians declare war against Hanover and Saxony 15 June, "

stificatory manifestoes issued by Austria and Prussia, 17 June, "

ussia declares war, *royal manifesto to the people* 18 June, "

ussians occupy Hanover and Hesse Cassel, Saxony and Nassau 16-20 June, "

strian northern army enters Silesia, 18 June, joined by the Saxons about 19 June, "

arly all the northern states join *Prussia* about 23 June, "

nce Frederick Charles and the first army, and the army of the Elbe, enter Bohemia, 23 June, victorious in severe engagements at Liebenau, Türnau, and Podoll, 26 June, Hühnerwasser, 27 June, Munchengrätz, 28 June, Gitschin, 29 June, 1866

Crown prince and the second army (of Silesia) enter Bohemia, 22 June, repulsed at Trautenau, 27 June, victorious at Soor and Trautenau, 28 June, Königinhof 29 June, "

Left column of the crown prince's army defeat the Austrians at Nachod, 27 June, Skalicz, 28 June, Schweinschadel 29 June, "

Fruitless victory of the Hanoverians at Langensalza, 27 June, they capitulate to the Prussians 29 June, "

Communications opened between the 2 armies 30 June, "

Command assumed by the king 1 July, "

Battle of Königgrätz, or Sadowa, total defeat of the Austrians under Benedek 3 July, "

Benedek superseded by the archduke Albrecht 8 July, "

Campaign of the army under Vogel von Falkenstein against the army of the confederation, under princes Charles of Bavaria and Alexander of Hesse, Prussian victories at Wiesenthal and Dermbach 4 July, Hammelburg and Kissingen 10 July, "

Advance of the united armies under the king, cavalry skirmish at Saar, Austrians retire 10 July, "

Prince Frederick Charles enters Brünn, capital of Moravia, 12 July, "

Campaign on the Main Prussian victories at Laufach, 13 July, and Aschaffenburg 14 July, "

Members of German diet retire from Frankfort on the Main to Augsburg 13 July, "

Austrians defeated at Tobitschau 15 July, "

Frankfort occupied by Falkenstein 16 July, "

Fight at Blumenau stopped by news of an armistice 22 July, "

Preliminaries of peace signed at Nikolsburg 26 July, "

Prussians occupy Wiesbaden 18 July, victorious at Tauberbischofsheim, Hochhausen, Werbach, 24 July, Neubrunn, Helmstadt, Germersheim, 25 July, Würzburg, 28 July, armistice granted 30 July, "

Army reviewed by the king 15 miles from Vienna, 31 July, begin their return home 1 Aug "

Franconia occupied by the Prussian reserve under grand duke of Mecklenburg Schwerin, 23 July-1 Aug, armistice 1-3 Aug "

Diet at Augsburg recognized the dissolution of the Germanic confederation 4 Aug "

Bohemia and Moravia cleared by 18 Aug "

Treaty of peace signed at Prague 23 Aug "

Meeting of special committee of the Chamber of Deputies, cost of the war stated, $88,000,000 29 Aug "

Peace with Wurtemberg concluded 13 Aug, with Baden, 17 Aug, with *Bavaria*, 23 *Aug*, with Hesse Darmstadt (*ceding* Hesse-Cassel, Hesse Homburg, etc) 3 Sept "

Formation of the North German confederation (GERMANY) Aug "

Entry of the army into Berlin, enthusiastic reception 20 Sept "

Decree for the annexation of Hanover, Electoral Hesse, Nassau, and Frankfort 20 Sept. "

Possession taken of Hanover, 6 Oct, of Hesse, Nassau and Frankfort 8 Oct "

Treaty of peace with Saxony 21 Oct. "

Electoral law for new German parliament promulgated at Berlin 23 Oct "

Schleswig and Holstein incorporated with Prussia by decree, promulgated 24 Jan 1867

North German parliament meet at Berlin, 24 Feb, adopt a federal constitution, closed 17 Apr "

Prussian chambers opened by the king 29 Apr "

They accept the North German constitution (sacrificing Prussian civil rights to German unity) 8 May, "

Luxemburg question settled by a conference at London (LUXEMBURG) 7-11 May, "

Prussian chambers approve North German constitution, closed by the king 24 June, "

Treaty with the U S respecting naturalization of aliens signed at Berlin 22 Feb 1868

Much of the king of Hanover's property sequestrated, on account of his maintaining a Hanoverian legion, etc Mch "

All property of king of Hanover sequestrated 15 Feb 1869

Prince Leopold of Hohenzollern Sigmaringen consents to become candidate for the throne of Spain about 5 July, 1870

In consequence of opposition by France, he, with the king's consent, relinquishes the candidature 12 July, "

French government requiring guarantees from the king against the future, the king repulses and declines to receive the French minister, Benedetti, 13 July, and issues a circular to his representatives at foreign courts 15 July, "

Emperor of the French declares for war " "

North German parliament meet, and vote to support Prussia, 19 July, "

Proclamation of the king, granting "amnesty for political offences," and "accepting the battle for the defence of the fatherland," 31 July, and to the army, undertaking the command of the whole army 3 Aug "

[For the events of the war, FRANCO PRUSSIAN WAR]

Order of the "Iron Cross" (distributed in the war of 1813) revived, given to the crown prince for his victory at Wissembourg on 4 Aug "

Prussian bishops protest against infallibility of the pope, end of Aug "

Berlin, etc, rejoice at the surrender of Napoleon 3 Sept. "

Munich, Stuttgart, and other southern cities demand union with North Germany 6 Sept "

King proclaimed emperor of Germany at Versailles 18 Jan 1871

Emperor arrives at Berlin 17 Mch "

Bismarck created a prince 22 Mch "

Triumphal entry of the German army into Berlin, inauguration of the statue of Frederick William III 16 June, "

Bishop of Ermeland excommunicates dr Wollner for denying the pope's infallibility, 5 July, similar acts disapproved by the government. July, 1871
Law for expulsion of the Jesuits pub 5 July, 1872
Government disputes with the Roman Catholic clergy supporting papal infallibility the bishop of Ermeland s salary ordered to be suspended from 1 Oct "
Subjection of the church to the state affirmed by the legislature 12 Mch 1873
Laws introduced by M Falk, minister of public worship, establishing a royal tribunal of ecclesiastical affairs, in opposition to the authority of the pope, 9 Jan, passed 11 May, "
Emperor recognizes the "Old Catholic" bishop Reinkens, about Aug "
Letter from the pope to the emperor complaining of the ecclesiastical prosecutions and asserting his authority over all baptized persons, 7 Aug, the emperor replies justifying them, and asserting that there is no mediator between God and man but Jesus Christ 3 Sept "
Archbishop Ledochowski of Posen fined for threatening to excommunicate a professor, and archbishop Melchers fined for instituting priests without government permission Oct "
Pope (by letter) encourages archbishop Ledochowski to resist, 3 Nov "
New oath of implicit obedience to the state proposed for the clergy, the Civil Marriage bill passed Dec "
Arrest of count Harry Arnim and confinement in Berlin for retaining documents sent him as ambassador, 4 Oct, for illness released on bail, 28 Oct., again arrested 12 Nov 1874
Arnim s trial 9 Dec, convicted of making away with ecclesio political documents, acquitted of other charges, sentence 3 months' imprisonment 19 Dec. "
Civil marriage adopted by the parliament 25 Jan 1875
Encyclical of the pope to the bishops encouraging firmness, the Roman Catholic deputies of parliament protest 5 Feb "
Count Arnim s new trial, 15 June, sentence confirmed 20 Oct "
Letter from count Arnim rebutting accusations in the *Times* of 19 Nov "
He is to be prosecuted for treason in a pamphlet entitled "Pro Nihilo," published at Zurich Nov "
Berlin conference on Eastern question (emperor of Russia, prince Gortschakoff, and count Andrassy, BERLIN), 11-12 May, 1877
Count Arnim publishes "Quid faciamus nos?" Jan 1879
Marriage of princess Louise Margaret of Prussia to the duke of Connaught 13 Mch "
Discussion on the social movement against the Jews through jealousy, no vote 20-22 Nov 1880
Anti Semitic league very active, much opposed by the prince imperial and others Jan 1881
Death of count Arnim at Nice 19 May, "
For continuation, GERMANY

MARGRAVES, ELECTORS, DUKES, AND KINGS

MARGRAVES OR ELECTORS OF BRANDENBURG

1134 Albert I, the Bear, first elector of Brandenburg.
1170 Otho I
1184 Otho II
1206 Albert II
1221 John I and Otho III
1266 John II
1282 Otho IV
1309 Waldemar
1319 Henry I, the Young
1320 [Interregnum]
1323 Louis I of Bavaria
1352 Louis II, the Roman
1365. Otho V, the Sluggard
1373 Wenceslas of Luxemburg
1378 Sigismund of Luxemburg
1388 Jossus, the Bearded
1411 Sigismund again emperor
1415 Frederick I of Nuremberg (of the house of Hohenzollern)
1440 Frederick II, surnamed Ironside
1470 Albert III, surnamed the German Achilles.
1476. John III, his son, as margrave, styled the Cicero of Germany.
1486 John III, as elector
1499 Joachim I, son of John
1535 Joachim II, poisoned by a Jew
1571 John George
1598 Joachim Frederick.
1608 John Sigismund.

DUKES OF PRUSSIA.

1618. John Sigismund
1619 George William
1640 Frederick William, his son, the "Great Elector"
1688 Frederick III, son of the preceding, crowned king, 18 Jan 1701.

KINGS OF PRUSSIA.

1701 Frederick I, king, b 1657, d 27 Feb 1713.
1713 Frederick William I, son of Frederick I, b 1688, d. 31 May, 1740
1740 Frederick II (or Frederick III, styled the Great), son, made Prussia a military power, b 24 Jan 1712, d 17 Aug 1786
1786 Frederick William II, nephew of the preceding, b 1744, d. 16 Nov 1797
1797 Frederick William III (he had to contend against the might of Napoleon, and, after extraordinary vicissitudes, he aided England in his overthrow), b 3 Aug 1770, d 7 June, 1840
1840. Frederick William IV, son, b 15 Oct. 1795, d 2 Jan. 1861

1861. William I, brother (b 22 Mch 1797) proclaimed emperor of Germany at Versailles, 18 Jan 1871, married princess Augusta of Saxe Weimar, 11 June, 1829, golden wedding kept, 11 June 1879, d 9 Mch 1888, queen d 7 Jan 1890
1888. Frederick III (William) son, b 18 Oct 1831 (married Victoria, princess royal of England, 25 Jan 1858), d 15 June, 1888.
" William II, son, b 27 Jan 1859, married princess Augusta Victoria of Schleswig Holstein, 27 Feb 1881.
Heir William, b 6 May, 1882 GERMANY

prussic acid (sym HCN or HCy) (hydrocyanic acid), accidentally discovered by Diesbach, a German chemist, in 1709, and first obtained in a separate state by Scheele about 1782 It is colorless, smells like peach flowers, freezes at 5° Fahrenheit, is very volatile, and turns vegetable blues into red Simple water distilled from the leaves of the *lauro-cerasus* first ascertained to be a most deadly poison by dr. Madden of Dublin BLUE, CYANOGEN

psalms of David were collected by Solomon, 1000 B.C others added, 580 and 515 B C The church of England Old Version in metre by Sternhold and Hopkins was published in 1562, the New Version by Tate and Brady in 1698

The version of Francis Rous provost of Eton, first pub 1641, was ordered to be used by Parliament in 1646 It is the basis of the Scotch version which appeared in 1650 "Bay State Psalm Book," pub 1640 BOOKS Many other versions published

pseu'doscope (from Gr ψευδος, false), a name given by prof Wheatstone (1852) to the stereoscope, when employed to produce "conversions of relief," i e, the reverse of the stereoscope, a terrestrial globe appears like a hollow hemisphere

Psychical Research, Society for SPIRITUALISM.

psychol'ogy, the science of the soul and its phenomena, studied by Aristotle, Plato, Descartes, Leibnitz, Locke, Hume, James Mill, J S Mill, Spencer, sir William Hamilton, Alexander Bain, and others

Society for Psychological Research founded 1882
International Congress of Experimental Psychology, Paris, 1889, London 1 Aug 1892
Prof William James s "Principles of Psychology" "

psychrom'eter (from Gr. ψυχρός, cold), an apparatus for measuring the amount of elastic vapor in the atmosphere, invented by Gay-Lussac (d 1850), and modified by Regnault (about 1848) An electric psychrometer was described by Edmond Becquerel, 4 Feb 1867.

Ptolema'ic system. Claudius Ptolemy of Pelusium, in Egypt (about 140 A D), supposed that the earth was fixed in the centre of the universe, and that the sun, moon, and stars moved around it once in 24 hours The system (long the official doctrine of the church of Rome) was universally taught till that of Pythagoras (500 B.C) was revived by Copernicus, 1530 A D, and demonstrated by Kepler (1619) and Newton (1687) ASTRONOMY, COPERNICAN SYSTEM

public land. LAND, REVENUE

public-land strip. NEUTRAL GROUND

Public Safety, Committee of, was established at Paris during the French revolution on 6 Apr. 1793, with absolute power, in consequence of the coalition against France The severe government of this committee is termed the "Reign of Terror," which ended with the execution of Robespierre and his associates, 28 July, 1794 A similar committee was established at Paris by communists, Mch -May, 1871

pub'licans, farmers of the state revenues of Rome. Soon after the battle of Cannæ they were so wealthy as to be able to advance large sums to the government, payable at the end of the war No magistrate was permitted to be a publican

publishers. BOOKS, MAGAZINES, NEWSPAPERS

pugilism. BOXING.

Pulaski's banner. Count Casimir Pulaski, a Pole, came to the United States in 1777, and fought under Washington at the battle of Brandywine, and soon after was appointed brigadier-general in the Continental army In 1778 he organized an independent legion in Maryland, and when about to take the field in the south the "Moravian nuns," or single women at Bethlehem, Pa, sent him a banner wrought by them, which he received with grateful acknowledgments, and which he bore until he fell at Savannah in 1779 This event is commemorated in Longfellow's "Hymn of the Moran Nuns" This banner is now in possession of the Mary-l Historical Society MARYLAND, 1778

Pulaski, Fort FORT PULASKI

pulley, a wheel with a broad or grooved rim for carry-a rope or other line or belt for the purpose of transmitting er, said to have been invented by Archytas of Tarentum, ut 400 B.C, or by Archimedes, 287-212 A single fixed ey gives no increase of power, but in a single movable ley the power is doubled, but what is gained in power is in time, in a continued combination the power is equal he number of pulleys, less one, doubled

Pullman cars. RAILWAYS

Pultowa, a country and city of Russia, where Charles of Sweden was entirely defeated by Peter the Great of sia 8 July, 1709 He fled to Bender, in Turkey

Pultusk, a town of Poland, where a battle was fought ween the Saxons, under their king Augustus, and the des under Charles XII, in which the former were sig-y defeated 1 May, 1703 Here also the French, under oleon, fought the Russian and Prussian armies, both sides med the victory, but it inclined in favor of the French, 26 1806

pump, an apparatus for lifting a fluid Ctesibius of xandria is said to have invented pumps (with other hy-ulic instruments), about 224 B C, although the invention is ibed to Danaus, at Lindus, 1485 B.C. Pumps were in gen-use in England, 1425 A D An inscription on the pump in t of the late Royal Exchange, London, stated that the well sunk in 1282 The air-pump was invented by Otto Gue-ke in 1654, and improved by Boyle in 1657 AIR, WELLS

Pumpkinvine Creek, Battle of ATLANTA IPAIGN

Punch, the puppet-show, borrowed from the Italian ichinello, is descended from a character well known in the atres of ancient Rome —*Fosbroke*—The satirical weekly lication, *Punch*, or the London *Charivari* was established Henry Mayhew, Mark Lemon, Douglas Jerrold, Gilbert a' kett, and others, first pub 17 July, 1841 Mark Lemon, first editor, died 23 May, 1870, 2d, Shirley Brooks, died 23 1874, 3d, Tom Taylor died July, 1880, 4th, Francis Cow-Burnand CARICATURES, "CHARIVARI"

punctuation. The ancients do not appear to have l any system The *period* (.) is the most ancient, the on (:) was introduced about 1485, the comma (,) was first n about 1521, and the semicolon (;) about 1570 In Sir ilip Sidney's "Arcadia" (1587) they all appear as well as note of interrogation (?) asterisk (*), and parentheses ()

Punic (Lat *Punicus*, from *Puni* or *Pœni*, Carthaginian) **ars.** CARTHAGE, ROME, 264 B C

punishment (Gr ποινη—strictly, quit-money or fine blood spilled), any penalty inflicted on a person for a crime offence committed "Cruel and unusual punishments ll not be inflicted," Art VIII, Amendments to the United tes Constitution BEHEADING, BLINDING, BOILING TO ATH, BURNING ALIVE, BURYING ALIVE, DROWNING, FLOG-NG, ROASTING, STARVING, TORTURE

Punjab, a province forming N W Hindostan, was trav-ed by Alexander the Great, 327 B C, by Tamerlane, 1398 , by Mahmoud of Ghizni, about 1000 It was an inde-ident state under Runjeet Sing, 1791-1839 English wars th the Sikhs began here, 14 Dec 1845, and were closed on Mch 1849, when the Punjab was annexed INDIA The njab has since greatly flourished, and on 1 Jan 1859, was de a distinct presidency (to include the Sutlej states and e Delhi territory) Area, 150,315 sq miles, pop 1891, ,063,690

puppets (Ital *puppi*, Fr *marionnettes*), of which the es, arms, etc., were moved by strings, were used by the cients, and are mentioned by Xenophon, Horace, and others. ilful theatrical performances with puppets have been sev-l times given in London (at the Adelaide gallery, 1852). performance with puppets as large as life began at St. mes's hall, July, 1872 Ch Magnin published a "Histoire s Marionnettes," 1852

Purâ'na (Sanskrit=old, ancient, from *pura*, old, past), the last great division of Hindu sacred literature 18 princi-pal Puranas are mentioned, but none are dated, and do not ap-pear older than the 9th century A D The most celebrated are the Vishnû and the Bhâgavat Puranas They are full of legends relating to holy places and ceremonials, with mi-nute fragments of history Modern Hinduism is largely founded on these compositions There are other Puranas of less importance

purchase system of commissions in the British army The payment of a present or gratuity for a commission was prohibited by William III, 1693, but in 1702 purchase was legally recognized In 1711 the sale of com-missions was forbidden without the royal permission, in 1719-20 regulations were issued, and a fixed scale of prices was adopted in consequence of a commission in 1765 Large over-regulation payments continued to be made Commissions of inquiry were held frequently since 1858, and in 1871 the system was abolished, with compensation, by royal warrant, 20 July, 1871 the bill for the purpose having been rejected by the House of Lords.

purgatives of the mild species (aperients), particularly cassia, manna, and senna, are ascribed to Actuarius, a Greek physician of Constantinople, 1215

pur'gatory, the supposed middle place between heaven and hell, where, it is believed by the Roman Catholics, the soul passes through the fire of purification before it enters the king-dom of God The doctrine was known about 250 A D, was introduced into the Roman church in the 6th century, and made a religious dogma by Gregory I, 590-604 It was first set forth by a council at Florence, 1439, enforced by the coun-cil of Trent, Dec 1563 HADES, INDULGENCES

purification, after childbirth, was ordained by the Jewish law, 1490 B C (Lev xii) The feast of the purifica-tion was instituted 542, in honor of the Virgin Mary's going to the temple (Luke ii) Pope Sergius I ordered the pro-cession with wax tapers, whence Candlemas-day

Pu'ritans, the name first given, it is said, about 1564, to persons who aimed at greater purity of doctrine, holiness of living and stricter discipline than others They withdrew from the established church, professing to follow the word of God alone, and maintaining that the church retained many human inventions and popish superstitions CATHARI, CON-GREGATIONALISTS, NON-CONFORMISTS, PRESBYTERIANS

purple, a mixed tinge of scarlet and blue discovered at Tyre. It is said to have been found by a dog's having by chance eaten a shell-fish, called *murex*, or *purpura*, upon re-turning, his master, Hercules Tyrius, observed his lips tinged, and made use of the discovery Purple was anciently used by the princes and great men for their garments It was restricted to the emperor by Justinian I 532, and PORPHYROGENITUS, attached to the names of some emperors, signifies "born to the purple"

purveyance, an ancient prerogative of the sovereigns of England of purchasing provisions, etc, without the consent of the owners, led to much oppression It was regulated by Magna Charta, 1215, and other statutes, and was only surren-dered by Charles II, in 1660, for a compensation

Puseyism, a name attached to the views of certain clergymen and lay members of the church of England, who proposed to restore practices in the church of England which they believed to be required by her liturgy and rubrics, but which were considered by their opponents to be of a Romish tendency The term was derived from the name of the pro-fessor of Hebrew at Oxford, Dr Pusey The heads of houses of the university of Oxford passed resolutions, 15 Mch 1841, censuring dr Pusey's attempts to renew practices which are now obsolete, and his celebrated sermon was condemned by the same body, 30 May, 1843 Dr Pusey died 16 Sept. 1882, aged 82 years RITUALISM, TRACTARIANS

Pyd'na, a city of Macedon, where Perseus, the last king of Macedon, was defeated and made prisoner by the Romans, commanded by Æmilius Paulus, 22 June, 168 B C PHALANX.

pyr'amids of Egypt. The 3 principal are situated on a rock, at the foot of some high mountains which bound the Nile The first building commenced, it is supposed, about 1500 B.C. The greatest is said to have been erected by Cheops, 1082 B.C., but earlier dates are assigned The largest, near Gizeh, is 461 feet in perpendicular height, with a platform on the top 32 feet square, and the length of the base is 746 feet It occupies about 12 acres of ground, and is constructed of stupendous blocks of stone There are many other smaller pyramids to the south of these They have been visited and described by Belzoni, 1815, Vyse, 1836, C Piazzi Smyth, and others Some 11 pyramids at Sakkara have been explored by M Maspero, 1880 et seq The Battles of the Pyramids, when Bonaparte defeated the Mamelukes and thus subdued Lower Egypt, took place 13 and 21 July, 1798 C Piazzi Smyth's "Life and Work at the Great Pyramid," with full description of the facts, 3 vols., Edinburgh, 1867 —"Our Inheritances in the Great Pyramids," C Piazzi Smyth, London, 1880 EGYPT.

Pyrenees (*pir'-ĕ-nēz*), a lofty mountain-chain, forming the boundary between France and Spain After the battle of Vittoria (fought 21 June, 1813), Napoleon sent Soult to supersede Jourdan, with instructions to drive the allies across the Ebro, Soult retreated into France with a loss of more than 20,000 men, having been defeated by Wellington in a series of engagements from 25 July to 2 Aug, one at the Pyrenees on 28 July. A railway through the Pyrenees (from Bilbao to Miranda) was opened 21 Aug 1862 The Peace of the Pyrenees was concluded between France and Spain, by cardinal Mazarin for the French king, and don Louis de Haro on the part of Spain, in the island of Pheasants, on the Bidassoa By this treaty Spain yielded Roussillon, Artois, and her right to Alsace, and France ceded her conquests in Catalonia, Italy, etc, and engaged not to assist Portugal, 7 Nov 1659.

pyrol'eter, a mechanical and chemical apparatus for extinguishing fires, especially in ships, invented by dr Paton, tried at Greenhithe, and reported successful, 1 June, 1875

pyrom'eter ("fire-measurer"), an apparatus employed to ascertain the temperature of furnaces, etc, where thermometers cannot be employed, Muschenbrock's pyrometer (a metallic bar) was described by him in 1731 Improvements were made by Ellicott and others. Wedgwood employed clay cylinders, 1782-86 In 1830 prof Daniell received the Rumford medal for an excellent pyrometer made in 1821 Mr Ericsson's pyrometer appeared in the great exhibition of 1851 —*Eng Cyc.* C W Siemens employed electric resistance in his pyrometers, exhibited in 1871.

py'rophone (Gr πῦρ, fire, φωνή, voice), a musical instrument, invented by Frédéric Kastner of Paris. It consists of glass tubes of various lengths, the tones being produced by what are termed "singing flames." It is based upon the "chemical harmonicon" Keys are attached for playing, as in the piano The invention was reported to the French Academy of Sciences, 17 Mch 1873, exhibited at Vienna, same year, and at the Society of Arts, London, 17 Feb 1875.

pyrox'ylin, the chemical name of gun-cotton.

pyrrhic dance (Gr πυρρίχη), a warlike dance said to have been introduced by Pyrrhus, son of Achilles, to grace his father's funeral Probably described by Homer in his description of the shield of Achilles·

> "And the illustrious Vulcan also wrought
> A dance—a maze like that which Daedalus,
> In the broad realm of Gnossus once contrived
> For fair haired Ariadne."
> —*Bryant's* "Trans Homer," bk. xviii line 731, etc.

> "You have the Pyrrhic dance as yet
> Where is the Pyrrhic phalanx gone?"
> —*Byron's* "Don Juan" canto iii stanza lxxxvi song

pyrrho'nism. SCEPTICS, PHILOSOPHY

Pythago'rean philosophy. PHILOSOPHY.

Pyth'ian games (so named from Gr Πυθώ, that part of Phocis in which Delphi lay), one of the 4 great national festivals of ancient Greece, celebrated every 5th year in honor of Apollo, near the temple of Delphi, asserted to have been instituted by himself, in commemoration of his victory over the serpent, Python Also said to have been established by Agamemnon, or Diomedes, or Amphictyon, or, lastly, by the council of the Amphictyons, 1263 B C They lasted till 394 A D.

pyx, the casket in which Catholic priests keep the consecrated wafer. In the ancient chapel of the pyx, at Westminster abbey, are deposited the standard pieces of gold and silver, under the joint custody of the lords of the treasury and the comptroller-general The "trial of the pyx" signifies the verification by a jury of goldsmiths of the coins deposited in the pyx or chest by the master of the mint, this took place on 17 July, 1861, at the exchequer office, Old Palace yard, London, in the presence of 12 privy-councillors, 12 goldsmiths, and others, and on 15 Feb 1870. This trial is said to have been ordered in the reign of Henry II 1154–89, king James was present at one in 1611 The first annual trial of the pyx, appointed by the Coinage act of 1870, took place 18 July, 1871.

Q

Q, the 17th letter of our alphabet, from the Egyptian, Phœnician, and Greek, lost for a time to the Greek, where it is often represented by κ, it reappeared in the Latin alphabet. The latter is absent from the Anglo-Saxon, the same being expressed by cw, as cwen, queen, and cwic for quick, etc. It made its full appearance about 1160, at first used only in Latin and French words, as quarter and quarrel By the close of the 13th century it was adopted in English words In English it is always followed by u

Quadrages'ima Sunday, first Sunday in Lent and 40th day before Good Friday LENT, QUINQUAGESIMA

quadrant, a mathematical instrument for measuring altitudes, in the form of a quarter of a circle, whose arch is divided into degrees and minutes The solar quadrant was introduced about 290 B C The Arabian astronomers under the caliphs, in 995, had a quadrant of 21 feet 8 inches radius, and a sextant 59 feet 9 inches radius. Davis's quadrant for measuring angles was produced about 1600, Hadley's quadrant about 1731 NAVIGATION.

quadrature of the circle. CIRCLE.

quadrilat'eral or **quadran'gle**, terms applied to 4 strong fortresses in N Italy, long held by the Austrians, but surrendered to the Italians Oct 1866 Peschiera, on an island in the Mincio, Mantua, on the Mincio, Verona and Legnago, both on the Adige. FORTIFICATIONS.

Turkish quadrilateral was Shumla, Varna, Rustchuk, and Silistria, lost to the sultan by the treaty of Berlin, which established the autonomy of Bulgaria.

quadrille (*kwa-dril'*), a dance (originally *quadrille de contre danse*, introduced into French ballets about 1745), in its present form became popular in France about 1804 It was introduced into England about 1808 (*Miss Berry*), and promoted by the duke of Devonshire and others in 1813.—*Raikes.*

quadriv'ium. ARTS

quadruple alliance. That between Great Britain, France, and Austria (signed at London, 22 July, 1718), was so called after Holland joined it, 8 Feb. 1719 It guaranteed the succession to the thrones of Great Britain and France, settled the partition of the Spanish possessions, and led to war.

quadruple treaty, concluded in London, 22 Apr. 1834, between Great Britain, France, Spain, and Portugal, guaranteed her throne to Isabella II, the young queen of Spain

quadruplex telegraphy. ELECTRICITY

quæstor, in ancient Rome, was the public treasurer, appointed about 484 B.C. It was the first office thrown open to the common people, and gave a seat in the senate. At first there were 2 quæstors, afterwards 8. 2 were added in 409 B.C. Sulla raised the number to 20, Julius Cæsar to 40. 2 were called peregrini, 2 (for the city) urbani.

Quaker Hill, Battle of At Quaker Hill, near the

north end of Rhode Island, on 29 Aug 1778, the Americans under gen Sullivan, invading the island, drove back the British (then occupying it) under gen Pigot, but Sullivan thought it prudent to withdraw The Americans lost in the expedition about 200 men, the British about 220

Quakers or **Society of Friends**, originally called Seekers (of the truth), and afterwards Friends (John 14) Justice Bennet, of Derby, called them Quakers in 1650, because George Fox admonished people to quake at the word of the Lord This sect was founded in England about 1646 by George Fox (then aged 22), who was joined by George Keith, William Penn, and Robert Barclay, of Ury, and others Fox rejected all religious ordinances, explained away the commands relative to baptism, etc, discarded the ordinary names of days and months, and used *thee* and *thou* for *you*, as more consonant with truth He published a book of instructions for teachers and professors, visited America in 1672, and died in London, 13 Jan 1691 The first meeting-house in London was in White Hart Court, Gracechurch street PENNSYLVANIA

It was asserted in Parliament that 2000 Friends had endured sufferings and imprisonment in Newgate, and 164 Friends offered, by name, to be imprisoned in lieu of an equal number in danger (from confinement) of death		1659
Fifty five (out of 120 sentenced) were transported to America by an order of council		1664
[For treatment of Quakers by the early colonists, MASSACHUSETTS NEW YORK, etc, 1656-63]		
First meeting of Quakers in Ireland, in Dublin, in 1658, first meeting house opened in Eustace street		1692
Quakers permitted by law to affirm in England in courts where oaths are required from others (AFFIRMATION)		1696
John Archdale, a Quaker elected M P for Chipping Wycombe, refused to take the oaths and his election was declared void,		1699
At Philadelphia the society in the U S. separated into 2 bodies, the Liberal or Hicksite, named from their leader, Elias Hicks, and the Orthodox		1827
Joseph Pease a Quaker, was admitted to Parliament on his affirmation	15 Feb.	1833
Yearly meeting recommends that mixed marriages be permitted, and that many peculiarities in speech and costume be no longer insisted on	2 Nov	1858
Act authorizing Quaker marriages when one party is a Quaker,	May,	1860
In the U S they numbered 995 meetings, with a membership of 107,208 including the 4 branches, Orthodox, Hicksites, Wilburites, and Primitive		1890

quarantine (*kwor-an-teen'*, Fr *quarantaine*, a period of 40 days), a custom at Venice as early as 1127, whereby all merchants and others from the Levant must remain in the house of St Lazarus, or the Lazaretto, 40 days before entering the city Various cities of southern Europe have now lazarettos, that of Venice is built in the water In times of plague, all nations impose a quarantine on vessels and persons from infected places for a longer or shorter time In Sept 1892, the president of the United States proclaimed a quarantine of 20 days, on account of cholera, for ships entering New York from infected ports

quarter sessions were established 25 Edw III 1350-51 The days of sitting were appointed 2 Hen V 1413 Various changes since.

"Quarterly Review," organ of the Tory party in England, first appeared in Feb. 1809, with William Gifford, translator of Juvenal, as editor. He died 31 Dec 1826 MAGAZINES and REVIEWS.

quasi modo, a name given to *Low Sunday* (the first Sunday after Easter) from the first words of a hymn sung on that day

quater'nions, a mathematical method or calculus, invented by sir William Rowan Hamilton, about 1843 It is based upon the separation of multiplication from addition, and its fundamental conception is the representation of motion, in extent and direction, by lines called vectors. He attributed to addition motion from a point, to multiplication motion about a point. 4 numbers are generally involved, hence the name quaternion Hamilton's "Lectures on Quaternions" was pub. 1853, his "Elements," 1866 Other works by profs. Kelland and Tait pub since. Also 4 parts, series, etc., applied to the elements considered as 4, air, earth, fire, and water.

> "Air and ye elements, the eldest birth
> Of Nature s womb, that in quaternion run "
> —*Milton*, "Paradise Lost," bk v lines 180-1

Quatre Bras (*kat'r brar'*), a village of Belgium Here on 16 June, 1815, 2 days before the battle of Waterloo, the British and allied armies under the duke of Brunswick, the prince of Orange, and sir Thomas Picton, fought the French under marshal Ney The British fought intrepidly, though outnumbered and fatigued by marching all night The 42d regiment (Royal Highlanders) suffered severely while pursuing a French division from cuirassiers in ambush behind growing corn The duke of Brunswick was killed

Quebec', one of the provinces of the dominion of Canada Area 227,500 sq miles, pop 1891, 1,488,586 —City of, pop 1890, 70,000 For history of city and province, CANADA, FRENCH IN AMERICA, NEW YORK.

queen (Sax *cwen*, Ger *Konigin*) The first woman with sovereign authority was Semiramis, queen of Assyria, 2017 B.C. An act of England of 1554 declares "that the regall power of this realme is in the quenes majestie [Mary] as fully and absolutely as ever it was in any of her moste noble progenitours kinges of this realme" The Hungarians called a queen-regnant king HUNGARY, SALIC LAW

Queen Anne's farthings. The popular stories of the value of this coin in England are fabulous, though those of a few dates have been purchased at high prices. The current farthing with the broad brim, in fine preservation, is worth 1*l* The common patterns of 1713 and 1714 are worth 1*l* The 2 patterns with Britannia under a canopy, and Peace on a car, R R R, are worth 2*l* 2*s* each The pattern with Peace in a car is more valuable and rare, and worth 5*l* —*Pinkerton* (d 1826)

Queen Anne's war, 1702-13 In this war, known in Europe as the war of the "SPANISH SUCCESSION," the New England colonies suffered from frequent inroads of French and Indians from Canada, while the New York colony was protected by the barrier of the Five Nations, then at peace with the English MAINE, MASSACHUSETTS, NEW HAMPSHIRE, NEW YORK

queen Caroline's trial, etc

Caroline Amelia Elizabeth second daughter of Charles William Ferdinand, duke of Brunswick, b 17 May, 1768, married to George, prince of Wales	8 Apr	1795
Their daughter, princess Charlotte, b	7 Jan	1796
"DELICATE INVESTIGATION"	22 May,	1806
Charges against her again disproved		1813
Princess embarks for the continent	Aug	1814
Becomes queen, 20 Jan, arrives in England	6 June,	1820
A secret committee of lords appointed to examine papers on charges of incontinence.	8 June,	"
Bill of pains and penalties introduced by lord Liverpool,	5 July,	"
Queen removes to Brandenburg House	3 Aug	"
Receives an address from the married ladies of the metropolis (many others afterwards)	16 Aug	"
Her trial commences	19 Aug	"
Last debate on the bill of pains and penalties, report approved by 108 against 99, the majority of 9 being the ministers themselves Lord Liverpool moves that the bill be reconsidered that day 6 months	10 Nov	"
Great public exultation, illuminations for 3 nights in London,	10, 11, 12 Nov	"
Queen goes to St Paul s in state	29 Nov	"
She protests against her exclusion from the coronation, 19 July, taken ill at Drury-lane theatre, 30 July, dies at Hammersmith	7 Aug	1821
Her remains en route to Brunswick, alarming riot, affray with guards, 2 persons killed	14 Aug	"

queen of England, title of Her majesty Victoria, by the grace of God, of the United Kingdom of Great Britain and Ireland queen, defender of the faith, empress of India (in India, *Kaisar-i-Hind*).

Queen's college, now RUTGERS

queens of England. ENGLAND.

Queensland, Moreton Bay, a British colony, comprising all northeastern Australia, was separated from New South Wales as a distinct colony, in 1859, when Brisbane, the first settlement and capital, founded by Oxley, 1823, was made a bishopric Chinese immigrants are virtually excluded. Area estimated at 668,497 sq miles, pop. 1891, 393,718, pop. Brisbane, 50,000.

Queenstown, a seaport town of Ireland, formerly "Cove of Cork," received its present name on the visit of queen Victoria in 1849 It is a calling station for American mail steamers

Queenstown or **Queenston Heights,** Battle of Gen Van Rensselaer, with about 3000 regulars and 2500 militia, stationed along the Niagara frontier from Buffalo to fort Niagara, attempted to invade Canada by crossing the river at Lewiston, opposite Queenston Without waiting to concentrate his forces he pushed a few hundred men across the river early on 13 Oct 1812 The British were at first driven from the heights with the loss of their commander, maj-gen sir Isaac Brock, but being reinforced they again advanced Van Rensselaer meanwhile hastened to the American side to forward troops but the militia refused to cross, being required to serve only in the state The Americans who had crossed were compelled to surrender, loss, 190 killed and wounded, and 900 prisoners The British loss was 130 in all Among the captured Americans was col Winfield Scott, while capt Wool, afterwards gen Wool, was among the wounded On these heights a monument was erected to mark the spot of Brock's fall and burial In 1840 it was maliciously destroyed by one Lett, since, another has been built, 185 feet high surmounted by a dome of 9 feet

Quentin (*ken-tan'*) **St.,** a village of N France The duke of Savoy, with the army of Philip II of Spain, assisted by the English, defeated the French under the constable De Montmorency, at St Quentin, 10 Aug 1557 In fulfilment of a vow made before the victory, the king built the monastery, palace, etc, the ESCURIAL, considered by the Spaniards the eighth wonder of the world The French army of the north, under Faidherbe, was defeated here by the Germans after 7 hours' fighting, on 19 Jan 1871, total loss about 15,000, German loss about 3100

Queretaro (*kay-ray' ta-ro*), capital of Queretaro, Mexico, was besieged and, through the treachery of Lopez, forced to surrender to the Liberal general Escobedo, 15 May, 1867 The emperor Maximilian and his generals Miramon and Mejia were taken prisoners and, after trial, were shot, 19 June following

quern or **handmill** for grinding grain is of Roman, or, as some say, of Irish invention, so-called Roman querns have been found in Yorkshire

Quesnoy (*kay-nwa'*), a town of N France, was taken by the Austrians, 11 Sept 1793 but was recovered by the French, 16 Aug 1794 It surrendered to prince Frederick of the Netherlands, 29 June, 1815, after the battle of Waterloo. Here cannon were first used (called bombards) —*Henault*

Quiberon (*keeb-ron'*) **bay,** W France A British force landed here, Sept 1746, but was repulsed In the bay adm Hawke routed the French adm Conflans, preventing the invasion of Great Britain, 20 Nov 1759 Quiberon was taken by some French regiments in the pay of England, 3 July, 1795 but on 21 July, through treachery, French republicans, under Hoche, retook it by surprise, and many emigrants were executed About 900 troops, and nearly 1500 royalist inhabitants who had joined the regiments in the pay of Great Britain, escaped by the ships

quicksilver, a metal, also called mercury, which has a bright metallic lustre, and retains the liquid state at ordinary temperatures. Its use in refining silver was discovered 1540 There are mines of it in various countries, the most famous are at Almaden, in Spain, and at Idria, in Illyria, the latter, discovered by accident in 1497, for several years yielded 1200 tons a year A mine was discovered at Ceylon in 1797, and at New Almaden and other places in California Quicksilver was congealed in winter at St Petersburg, in 1759 It was congealed in England by a chemical process, without snow or ice, by Mr Walker, in 1787 Corrosive sublimate, a deadly poison, is a combination of mercury and chlorine. CALOMEL.

Qui'etists, followers of Miguel Molinos, a Spaniard (1627-96), whose work, the "Spiritual Guide," pub 1675, was the foundation of the sect in France He held that religion consisted in an internal silent meditation on the merits of Christ and the mercies of God Madame de la Mothe Guyon a Quietist, was imprisoned in the Bastile for visions and prophecies, but released through the interest of Fenélon, archbishop of Cambray, between whom and Bossuet, bishop of Meaux, arose a controversy, 1697 Quietism was finally condemned by pope Innocent XII in 1699

quills are said to have been first used for pens in 553, some say not before 635

quince, the *Pyrus cydonia*, taken to England from Austria before 1573 The Japan quince, or *Pyrus japonica*, taken there from Japan, 1796

quindecem'viri, 15 men chosen to keep the Sibylline books The number, originally 2 (duumviri) about 520 B C, was increased to 10 in 365 B.C, and afterwards (probably by Sulla) to 15, about 82 B.C Julius Cæsar added 1, but the precedent was not followed

quinine (*ke-neen'* or *qui -nine*) or **quinia,** an alkaloid (much used in medicine), discovered in 1820 by Pelletier and Caventou Its manufacture was begun at Philadelphia by John Farr in 1820 There never were more than 4 manufacturers of it in the United States, and after the removal of the duty in 1879 the business ceased to be remunerative Its price has been decreasing ever since 1823, when it sold for $20 an ounce, while it is now quoted at 50c. It is a probable constituent of all genuine chinchona barks, especially of the yellow bark CHINCHONA Artificial quinine was prepared (synthetically) by W L Scott, Oct 1865 FLUORESCENCE.

Quinquages'ima Sunday. The observation is said to have been appointed by Gregory the Great (pope, 590-604) The first Sunday in Lent having been termed *Quadragesima*, and the 3 weeks preceding having been appropriated to the gradual introduction of the Lent fast, the 3 Sundays of these weeks were called by names significant of their position in the calendar, and, reckoning by decades (10ths), the Sunday preceding Quadragesima received its present name, *Quinquagesima*, the second *Sexagesima*, and the third *Septuagesima*

Quintil'ians, heretics in the 2d century, the disciples of Montanus, who took their name from Quintilia, a lady deceived by his pretended sanctity, whom they regarded as a prophetess They made the eucharist of bread and cheese, and allowed women to be priests and bishops.—*Pardon*

Quiri'nus, a Sabine god, afterwards identified with Romulus. L. Papirius Cursor, general in the Roman army, first erected a sundial in the temple of Quirinus, from which time the days began to be divided into hours, 293 B C —*Aspin.* The sundial was sometimes called the Quirinus, from the original place in which it was set up —*Ashe.*

Quiri'tes, a name given to the Sabines who united with the Romans, and extended in time indifferently to all citizens of Rome ROME, 747 B.C.

Quito (*kee'-to*), capital of Ecuador, South America, situated on a plateau about 10,000 feet above the sea-level, celebrated as the scene of the measurement of a degree of the meridian, by French and Spanish mathematicians, 1736-42 40,000 persons perished by an earthquake in the city of Quito, 4 Feb 1797 Since then less violent shocks occurred, by one, on 22 Mch 1859, about 5000 persons were killed Pop. 1894 about 80 000 EARTHQUAKE, ECUADOR.

Quo Warran'to act, passed in England in 1289 By it a writ may be directed to any person to inquire by what authority he assumes to hold any office or franchise Charles II directed a writ against the corporation of London in 1683, and the court of King's Bench declared their charter forfeited The decision was reversed in 1690 On the accession of James II he planned to procure a surrender of the patents of the New England colonies and to form northern America into 12 provinces with a governor-general over all. Writs of *quo warranto* were issued July, 1685, requiring the several colonies to appear by representatives before the council to show by what right they exercised certain powers and privileges. Notwithstanding petitions and remonstrances the charters were annulled, and sir Edmund Andros appointed governor-general CONNECTICUT, 1687

quoits, a game said to have originated with the Greeks, and to have been first played at the Olympic games, by the Idæi Dactyli, 50 years after the deluge of Deucalion, 1453 B.C.

Perseus, the grandson of Acrisius by Danae, having inadvertently slain his grandfather, when throwing a quoit, exchanged the kingdom of Argos, to which he was heir, for that of Tirynthus, and founded the kingdom of Mycenæ, about 1313 B.C.

"And there a town within a while he built
Men called Mycenæ."
—*William Morris*, "The Doom of King Acrisius."

quotations. Athenæus's "Deipnosophistæ" or "Banquet of the Learned" (compiled about 228), and Burton's "Anatomy of Melancholy" (1621), contain masses of extracts. Henry Ainsworth's (d. 1622) "Communion of Saints" is a mosaic of Scripture quotations.

Macdonnel's "Dictionary of Quotations," 1796; Moore's...... 1831
Riley's "Dictionary of Latin Quotations," with a Selection of Greek, published by H. Bohn.......................... 1856
Collections of English quotations are now numerous:
Adams's "Cyclopædia of Poetical Quotations"............ 1853
Friswell's "Familiar Words," 2d ed...................... 1866
Bartlett's "Familiar Quotations"........................ 1869

R

R, the 18th letter of our alphabet, from the Egyptian, Phœnician, and the P of the Greeks, being the 17th letter of that alphabet. When beginning a Greek word it was sounded as *rho* (aspirated). It was called by the ancients the "dog letter," from some fancied resemblance in its pronunciation to the snarling of a dog. It is the last letter that most children learn to pronounce, using *w* instead—as *vewy* for very, and *Wobert* for Robert, etc. The Chinese invariably use l in the place of r, which they cannot pronounce.

Ra, one of the primary Egyptian divinities, worshipped as the sun; second only to Osiris in importance. Usually represented as a hawk-headed man.

rabies. HYDROPHOBIA.

races of mankind. ETHNOLOGY.

racing was one of the ancient sports of Greece. CHARIOTS. Horse-races were early known in England, being mentioned in the days of Henry II. (1154–89). James I. purchased the first Arab sire ever imported into England, a small bay, known as the "Markham" Arabian. During his reign Croydon in the south and Garterly in the north were celebrated courses. Near York there were races and the prize was a little golden bell, 1607. In the end of Charles I.'s reign races were performed at Hyde park. Charles II. patronized them, and, instead of bells, gave a silver cup valued at 100 guineas. William III. founded a riding academy.

Racing established at Newmarket by Charles II.............. 1667
[*Darley Arabian*, imported from the East during the reign of Queen Anne.]
Races at Ascot, begun by the duke of Cumberland, uncle to George III., mentioned.................................... 1727
First racing calendar said to have been pub.................. "
Races begun at Epsom, Surrey, about 1711, by Mr. Parkhurst, and held annually since................................... 1730
Flying Childers, bred in 1715 by the duke of Devonshire, and who ran 4 miles under saddle in 6 minutes 48 seconds, at Newmarket, d. aged 26 years.............................. 1741
Jockey club founded.. 1750
"Tattersall's," the great exchange, which existed nearly 100 years, established by Richard Tattersall, near Hyde Park corner, for the sale of horses............................. 1766
St. Leger stakes founded, and races established on Doncaster Town Moor in 1776, and so named in honor of lieut.-gen. Anthony St. Leger of Park Hill, 1778; first won by lord Rockingham's *Sampson*....................................... 1776
[Distance now, 1 mile, 6 furlongs, 132 yards. Usually run on second Wednesday in Sept.]
The Oaks (named from Lambert's oaks, parish of Woodmansterne, near Epsom), a race run on Friday of the Epsom meeting, begun by the 12th earl of Derby, and first won by his *Bridget*.. 1779
One mile Derby race at Epsom, first run and won by sir Charles Banbury's *Diomed*.........................4 May, 1780
Derby race increased to 1½ miles, weight 115 lbs. for colts and 112 for fillies.. 1784
Eclipse, race-horse never beaten, d. aged 25 years........Feb. 1789
Races begun by the duke of Richmond in his park at Goodwood... 1802
New horse-market at Brompton opened...............10 Apr. 1865
John Scott, eminent trainer, d. aged 77...................Oct. 1871
Present course first used for Derby races, and weight increased to 126 lbs. for colts and 121 for fillies...................... 1872
Lieut. Lubowitz, Hungarian, riding from Vienna reaches Paris on his horse *Caradoc* in 15 days, winning a wager....9 Nov. 1874
Metropolitan Race-course act, to check gate-meetings (races held in fields by publicans and others) passed........3 July, 1879
C. H. Anderson rode 1304 miles in 90 hours, 15 hours daily, changing mustangs at will, at Bay District Track, San Francisco, Cal.....................................15–21 May, 1880
Count Stahrenberg, Austrian officer, rode 1 horse from Vienna to Berlin, Ger., 400 miles, 71 hours, 34 minutes, 2–5 Oct. 1892

BEST DERBY RECORDS SINCE 1850.—DERBY-DAY.

Time. m.	s.	Horse.	
2	50	..Lord Zetland's Voltigeur	1850
2	45	..W. I'Anson's Blink Bonny	1857
2	43	..Col. Towneley's Kettledrum	1861
2	43	..Mr. Abington's Merry Hampon	1887
2	40.8.	.W. C. Whitney's Vlodyovski	1901

THE OAKS, BEST RECORD SINCE 1850.

Time. m.	s.	Winning horse.	
2	56	..Mr. Hobson's Rhedycina	1850
2	52	..Lord Stanley's Iris	1851
2	50	..W. I'Anson's Blink Bonny	1857
2	44	..J. Saxon's Brown Duchess	1861
2	43.4.	.Lord Cadogan's Lonely	1885
2	42.8.	.Lord Calthorpe's Seabreeze	1888
2	40.8.	.Duke of Portland's Memoir	1890

THE ST. LEGER, BEST RECORD SINCE 1850.

Time. m.	s.	Winning horse.	
3	24.	.Lord Zetland's Voltigeur	1850
3	20.	.A. Nichol's Newminster	1851
3	14.	.W. I'Anson's Caller On	1861
3	10.	.Mr. Launde's Apology	1874

Trotting, the favorite form of horse-racing in the United States, belongs to the present century, the first recorded public trotting race taking place in 1818 at Boston, when *Boston Blue* trotted a mile within 3 minutes. No regular turf register was kept until 1829.

Selima mare sired by *Godolphin Arabian*, imported into Maryland by col. Tasker.. 1750
Fearnaught, foaled in 1755, imported into Virginia from England by col. John Baylor.................................... 1764
Wildair and *Lath*, imported into the colonies by col. Delancy of Kingsbridge, N. Y....................................1764–65
A 4-mile running race for purse of 100 guineas at Philadelphia, Pa., in 1767; *Selim* ran the first heat in 8 min. 2 sec.; recorded in the Maryland *Gazelle*.......................22 Oct. 1767
Messenger, foaled in 1780, imported from England by Mr. Benger of Philadelphia... 1788
[It is conceded that this horse was the most valuable one ever brought to the U. S. In him the blood of the best Arabs and Barbs mingled with the best race-stock in England. His direct sire was *Mambrino*, 2d *Engineer*, 3d *Sampson*, 4th *Blaze*, 5th *Flying Childers*, 6th *Darley Arabian*.]
Justin Morgan, progenitor of the Morgans, foaled at Springfield, Mass.. 1793
Diomed, winner of the first Derby race in England, is imported.. 1799
First racing club to hold regular meetings at the Newmarket course in Suffolk county, N. Y., organized................ 1804
Duroc, sired by *Diomed*, and bred by Wade Mosby of Powhatan county, Va., foaled............................4 June, 1806
Grand Bashaw, progenitor of the Clay and Bashaw families, imported from Tripoli....................................... 1820
Trotting-horse *Bellfounder*, imported from England by James Boott of Boston, arrives...............................11 July, 1822
New York Trotting club organized in 1825, and first races held at the club's course..................................16 May, 1826
Hunting Park association, for encouragement of the breeding of trotters, organized at Philadelphia.....................8 Feb. 1828
First sporting paper in America, the *American Turf Register*, begins publication......................................1 Sept. 1829
Pilot, the Canadian pacer, bought by D. Heinshon of Louisville, Ky...about 1832
Stallion *St. Lawrence*, bred near Montreal, is bought by Joseph Hall of Rochester, N. Y..................................... 1848
Lady Suffolk, purchased from a farmer in Suffolk, L. I., for $90 in 1836, trots a mile under saddle in 2.26 on the Cambridge course...14 June, 1849
Flora Temple, foaled near Utica in 1845, and sold at 4 years old for $13, trots her first race on the old Red House track.. 1850
Flora Temple sold to Mr. McDonald of Baltimore for $8000 (d. near Philadelphia, Pa., 21 Dec. 1877)......................... 1858
Robert Bonner drives *Lady Palmer* and *Flatbush Maid* 2 miles in 5 min. 1½ sec., on Fashion course, L. I...........29 May, 1862

Young Pocahontas sold to Mr. Bonner for $25,000............ 1866
Hiram W. Woodruff, trainer, and author of "The Trotting Horse of America," d. at Jamaica Plains, L. I..............15 Mch. 1867
Dexter sold to Robert Bonner for $33,000 (d. 1888)............ "
Hambletonian (Rysdyk's), sired by *Abdallah*, foaled 1849, Orange Co., N. Y., d.................................... 1876
Rarus purchased by Robert Bonner for $36,000.............. 1879
Maud S. purchased from William H. Vanderbilt by Robert Bonner for $40,000.. 1885
Kite-shaped track at Stockton, Cal., opened.................. 1891
Pneumatic tire sulkies come into use.......................... 1892

BEST 1 MILE TROTTING RECORD TO 1850.

Time.	Horse.	Place.	How trotted.	Year.
m. s.				
3	Boston Blue....	Boston, Mass...	In harness..	1818
2 40 ..	Albany Pony...	Long Island....	To saddle...	1824
2 31½..	Edwin Forrest..	Long Island....	" ...	1834
2 28 ..	Dutchman	Beacon course..	" ...	1839
2 27 ..	Highland Maid..	Long Island....	In harness..	1847
2 26 ..	Lady Suffolk....	Cambridge	To saddle...	1849

BEST TROTTING RECORDS, 1850–1894.

1 MILE IN HARNESS.

Time.	Horse.	Place.	Date.
m. s.			
2 25½	Lady Mac.......	New Orleans, La..........	19 Nov. 1850
2 19¾	Flora Temple....	Kalamazoo, Mich..........	15 Oct. 1859
2 17¼	Dexter..........	Buffalo, N. Y.............	14 Aug. 1867
2 16¾	Occident........	Sacramento, Cal..........	17 Sept. 1873
2 14	Goldsmith Maid..	Mystic park, Boston......	2 Sept. 1874
2 13¼	Rarus...........	Buffalo, N. Y.............	3 Aug. 1878
2 8¾	Maud S.........	Cleveland, O.............	30 July, 1885
2 8¼	Sunol...........	Stockton, Cal. (kite track).	20 Oct. 1891
2 4	Nancy Hanks....	Terre Haute, Ind.........	28 Sept. 1892
2 3¾	Alix............	Galesburg, Ill............	19 Sept. 1894
		1 MILE TO SADDLE.	
2 25½	Tacony	Philadelphia, Pa..........	2 June, 1853
2 22¼	Rockingham	Fashion course, L. I......	31 Oct. 1862
2 21	General Butler...	Fashion course, L. I......	24 June, 1863
2 18	Dexter..........	Buffalo, N. Y.............	18 Aug. 1866
2 15¾	Great Eastern ...	Fleetwood park, N. Y.....	22 Sept. 1877
		1 MILE TO WAGON.	
2 24½	Flora Temple....	Union course, L. I........	2 Sept. 1856
2 24	Dexter..........	Fashion course, L. I......	7 June, 1867
2 16¾	Alfred S.........	Philadelphia, Pa..........	4 Sept. 1890
2 15	Allerton	Independence, Ia.........	25 Sept. 1891
2 14¼	Greenlander.....	Terre Haute, Ind..........	10 Nov. 1893
		5 MILES IN HARNESS.	
13 16	Fillmore	San Francisco, Cal........	18 Apr. 1863
13 11	Morrissey........	Detroit, Mich.............	26 Aug. 1868
13 ..	Lady Mac	San Francisco, Cal........	2 Apr. 1874
12 30¾	Bishop Hero.....	Oakland, Cal..............	14 Oct. 1893
		10 MILES IN HARNESS.	
28 8½	Prince	Union course, L. I........	11 Nov. 1853
28 2½	John Stewart....	Riverside, Boston.........	30 June, 1868
27 23¼	Controller.......	San Francisco, Cal........	23 Nov. 1878
26 15	Pascal...........	New York city............	2 Nov. 1893
		20 MILES IN HARNESS.	
58 25	Captain McGowan	Riverside, Boston.........	18 Oct. 1865

MISCELLANEOUS TROTTING RECORDS TO 1895.

50 MILES IN HARNESS.

Time.	Horse.	Place.	Date.
h. m. s.			
3 00 57	Black Joke......	Providence, R. I...........	July, 1835
		100 MILES IN HARNESS.	
9 38 34	Fanny Jenks....	Albany, N. Y..............	5 May, 1845
8 55 53	Conqueror.......	Centreville, L. I...........	12 Nov. 1853

DOUBLE HARNESS, 1 MILE.

Time.	Team.	Place.	Date.
m. s.			
2 32	Jessie Wales and Ben Franklin...	Boston.........	20 Sept. 1867
2 29¾	Jessie Wales and Honest Allen....	Boston.........	30 Sept. 1869
2 29	Kirkwood and Idol..	Brooklyn........	31 May, 1870
2 28	George Wilkes and Honest Allen....	Boston.........	4 July, 1871
2 26½	Joe Clark and Mollie Morris	Boston.........	3 Sept. 1874
2 15½	Maud S. and Aldine..	New York.......	15 June, 1883
2 13	Belle Hamlin and Justina	Independence, Ia.	24 Oct. 1890
2 12	Belle Hamlin and Globe	Kirkwood, Del...	4 July, 1892
	WITH RUNNING MATE, 1 MILE.		
2 3½	Ayres P. and Telephone..........	Kirkwood, Del...	4 July, 1893

BEST PACING RECORDS TO 1894.

One mile in harness :
Direct at Nashville, Tenn.; time, 2:05½..............8 Nov. 1892
Mascot at Terre Haute, Ind.; time, 2:04............29 Sept. "
Hal Pointer at Chicago (pneumatic sulky); time, 2:05¼, 17 Aug. "
Flying Jib at Chicago, Ill., fastest consecutive heats on record; time, 2:04, 2:05¾, 2:06¾, 2:08½, 2:08¼, 15 Sept. 1893
Robert J. at Terre Haute, Ind.; time, 2:01½........14 Sept. 1894
Three miles in harness :
James K. Polk at Centreville, L. I.; time, 7:44.....13 Sept. 1847
Joe Jefferson at Knoxville, Ia.; time, 7:33¼.........6 Nov. 1891
One mile to wagon :
Roy Wilkes at Independence, Ia.; time, 2:13........30 Oct. "
Three miles to wagon :
Longfellow at Sacramento, Cal.; time, 7:53..........7 Sept. 1869
Five miles to wagon:
Lady St. Clair at San Francisco, Cal.; time, 12:54¾, 11 Dec. 1874
One mile to saddle :
Johnston at Cleveland, O.; time, 2:13................3 Aug. 1888
Three miles to saddle :
Oneida Chief at Hoboken, N. J.; time, 7:44.........15 Aug. 1843
One mile in double harness :
Daisy D. and *Silver Tail* at East Saginaw, Mich.; time, 2:18½, 15 July, 1887
With running mate:
Westmont at Chicago, Ill.; time, 2:01¾.............10 July, 1884

TROTTING RECORDS, 1895–1905.

1 MILE.

Time.	Horse.		Place.	Date.
m. s.				
2 02¼	Cresceus*.........	Stallion.	Columbus.......	2 Aug. 1901
2 03¼	Cresceus..........	Stallion.	New York	15 Aug. 1901
1 59¾	Major Delmar*....	Gelding.	Memphis †......	22 Oct. 1903
1 58½	Lou Dillon*.......	Mare...	Memphis †......	24 Oct. 1903
1 58¼	Lou Dillon*.......	5-y-old..	Memphis †......	24 Oct. 1903
1 58½	Lou Dillon*.......	Mare...	Memphis †......	24 Oct. 1903
2 07	Major Delmar*....	Sulky ..	Memphis........	26 Oct. 1904
2 01	Lou Dillon*.......	6-y-old..	Memphis........	11 Nov. 1904
		2 MILES.		
4 17	Cresceus*........	Stallion.	Memphis †.....	22 Oct. 1902
		TO WAGON—1 MILE.		
2 04¾	Lou Dillon........	Mare....	Memphis	21 Oct. 1903
2 00	Lou Dillon *......	Mare....	Memphis †......	28 Oct. 1903
		BY TEAMS—1 MILE.		
2 07¾	The Monk* ..... Equity*	....	Memphis	21 Oct. 1904

* Against time. † Paced by runner to sulky carrying a wind or a dust shield, runner preceding trotter.

PACING RECORDS, 1895–1905.

1 MILE.

Time.	Horse.		Place.	Date.
m. s.				
2 05½	Klatawah.........	3-y-old..	Louisville......	28 Sept. 1898
2 10½	Ecstasy..........	2-y-old..	Lexington	15 Oct. 1898
1 57	Prince Alert*	Gelding.	New York †.....	23 Sept. 1903
2 00¼	Dariel	Mare ...	Memphis	24 Oct. 1903
2 04¾	Dan Patch*	Sulky...	Macon †	30 Nov. 1903
2 20¾	Paul D. Kelley*...	Yearl'g.	Syracuse........	8 Sept. 1904
1 56	Dan Patch*	Stallion.	Memphis †......	26 Oct. 1904
2 03	Dan Patch	Stallion.	Oklahoma	17 Nov. 1904
		½ MILE.		
0 56	Dan Patch*	Stallion.	Memphis †.....	27 Oct. 1903
		2 MILES.		
4 17	Dan Patch*......	Stallion.	Macon †.......	30 Nov. 1903
		TO WAGON—1 MILE.		
1 57½	Dan Patch*.......	Stallion.	Memphis*......	27 Oct. 1903
2 04½	Angus Pointer....	....	Memphis.......	20 Oct. 1904
		2 MILES.		
4 58½	Young America..	....	....	....
		BY A TEAM—1 MILE.		
2 05½	Direct Hal*... Prince Direct.	....	Memphis	26 Oct. 1902

* Against time. † Paced by runner to sulky carrying a wind or a dust shield, runner preceding pacer.

RECORD OF BEST AMERICAN PERFORMANCES ON THE RUNNING TURF.

(Revised to 1 Dec. 1904.)

Time.	Horse.	Distance.	Place.	Date.
m. s.				
4 58½	Hubbard	2½ miles.	Saratoga	9 Aug. 1873
4 58½	Ten Broeck	2⅝ miles.	Lexington	16 Sept. 1876
5 24	Drake Carter	3 miles.	Sheepshead Bay.	6 Sept. 1884
0 46	Geraldine	½ mile..	Morris Park	30 Aug. 1889
1 23½	Bella B.	⅞ mile..	Monmouth	8 July, 1890
0 21½	Bob Wade	¼ mile..	Butte	20 Aug. 1890
1 35½	Salvator	1 mile..	Monmouth	28 Aug. 1890
0 34	Fashion	⅜ mile..	Lampasas	15 Aug. 1891
7 16¾	Bachelor	4 miles.	Oakland	22 Feb. 1893
3 42	Joe Murphy	2¼ miles.	Chicago	30 Aug. 1894
0 56¾	Maid Marian	⅝ mile..	Morris Park	9 Oct. 1894
0 34	Red S.	⅜ mile..	Butte	23 July, 1896
7 11	Lucrezia Borgia	4 miles.	Oakland	20 May, 1897
0 52	Handpress	4½ furl..	Morris Park	26 May, 1897
3 26½	Judge Denny	2 miles.	Oakland	12 Feb. 1898
2 30½	Goodrich	1½ miles.	Chicago	16 July, 1898
0 46½	Bessie Macklin	½ mile..	Dallas, Tex.	3 Oct. 1899
4 24½	Kyrat	2¼ miles.	Newport	18 Nov. 1899
3 19	Julius Cæsar	1¾ miles.	New Orleans	27 Feb. 1900
3 49 1-5	Ethelbert	2¼ miles.	Brighton Beach	4 Aug. 1900
0 58	Lady Uncas	⅝ mile..	Morris Park	3 Oct. 1900
1 08½	Endurance	¾ mile..	Coney Island	28 Sept. 1901
0 40½	Judge Thomas	3½ furl..	Butte	14 July, 1902
1 51	Bonnibert	1⅛ miles.	Brighton Beach.	30 July, 1902
1 25	Musketeer	⅞ mile..	Saratoga	18 Aug. 1902
1 02½	Plater	5½ furl..	Morris Park	21 Oct. 1902
1 32 1-5	Rag Tag	7½ furl..	Chicago	1 July, 1903
2 45 1-5	Africander	1⅝ miles.	Sheepshead Bay.	7 July, 1903
2 03 1-5	Waterboy	1¼ miles.	Brighton Beach.	8 July, 1903
1 37 2-5	Dick Welles	1 mile..	Chicago	14 Aug. 1903
1 05 1-5	McGee	5½ furl..	Chicago	1 Oct. 1903
2 57	Major Daingerfield.	1¾ miles.	Morris Park	3 Oct. 1903
0 51 3-5	Tanya	4½ furl..	Morris Park	12 May, 1904
2 17 3-5	Irish Lad	1⅜ miles.	Sheepshead Bay.	25 June, 1904
1 18 2-5	Mineola	6½ furl..	Coney Island	5 July, 1904
2 02 4-5	Broomstick	1¼ miles.	Brighton Beach.	9 July, 1904
1 18 2-5	Martinmas	6½ furl..	Coney Island	7 Sept. 1904
1 08	Artful	¾ mile..	Morris Park	15 Oct. 1904
1 38	Orthodox	1 mile..	Aqueduct, N. Y..	4 Nov. 1904

GREAT AMERICAN RACES, 1904.

The American Derby. 1½ miles, Chicago. Highball, 2 m. 33 s. $26,325
The Futurity. 6 furlongs, Sheepshead Bay. Artful, 1 m. 11 4-5 s. 42,880
Brighton Handicap. 1¼ miles, Brighton Beach. Broomstick, 2 m. 2 4-5 s. 21,750
Suburban Handicap. 1¼ miles, Sheepshead Bay. Hermis, 2 m. 5 s. 16,800

rack. TORTURE.

radiom'eter (termed a *light-mill*), an instrument constructed by William Crookes, F.R.S., 1873-76. Two little disk-arms, mounted on a pivot placed in an exhausted glass bulb, revolve when placed in bright light. The motion has been variously explained as due to the impact of rays of light, or to heat-absorption, but is now ascribed to residual molecules of air, set in vibration by the irregularly warmed bulb.

radium. This new and extremely rare metal is found in combination with chlorine and bromine, as radium chloride and radium bromide. It is obtained in very minute quantities from pitchblende, after the metal uranium has been extracted. The principle of radio-activity was discovered by M. Becquerel, in Paris, in 1896, from the study of uranium, and Mme. Sklodowska Curie's investigation of this metal, when taking up the subject of radio-activity as the thesis for her doctorate degree, led to the discovery of radium, Mme. Curie being assisted in her experiments by M. Curie. The discovery of the new metal was communicated by M. Curie to the Academy of Sciences, Paris, in Mch. 1903, and on 19 June of the same year M. Curie gave a demonstration of this new substance at the Royal Institution, London. Investigations of the properties and phenomena exhibited by radium have also been carried on by M. Becquerel, prof. Rutherford, sir Wm. Ramsay, Mr. Soddy, prof. J. J. Thompson, sir Wm. Crookes, and others.

Radium possesses the extraordinary property of continually producing heat without combustion, and spontaneously producing electricity, and maintains its own temperature, 1.5° Cent. or 2.7° Fahr. above its surroundings. It gives off an emanation or gas which shines by its own light, resembling in appearance that of the glowworm. This emanation under the cold of liquid air, condenses and leaves behind a rare gas—helium—an element existing in the sun, and, next to hydrogen, the lightest matter known, the atomic weight, of radium being 225 (on the scale hydrogen = 1). It is supposed that radium is an element breaking up, and in its dissolution giving out energy.

Three kinds of rays are continually in a state of radiation, and are known as the alpha, beta, and gamma rays. The *alpha* rays consist of atoms of matter, each 1 per cent. of the weight of a radium atom, projected with an enormous velocity, but can be stopped by a thin sheet of metal; these are the projectiles which are rendered visible on a chemical screen, as the zinc-sulphide screen in sir Wm. Crookes's ingenious spinthariscope. The *beta* rays consist of flying or escaped electrons, atoms of atoms, a thousand times smaller than anything else known, and possess the power of penetrating most metals. The *gamma* rays, also very penetrating, are probably a variety of the X-rays.

Radium has been detected in the deposit of the hot mineral waters of Bath and Buxton, pointing to its existence in considerable quantities in the interior of the earth. As a therapeutic agent, radium rays are being used in cases of cancer, lupus, and other skin diseases, and also appear to have a bactericidal action in certain cases. Experiments made by M. Danysz in Feb. 1903 *et seq.*, at the Pasteur institute, on the action of radium on larvæ, demonstrated the power of the rays to suspend or modify functional developments. Experiments on various low forms of life have also been made by M. Bohn, at the biological laboratories of the Sorbonne, with remarkable results. M. and Mme. Curie have been the recipients of various honors in recognition of their eminent services to scientific research.

Radstadt, a village of Salzburg, Austria. Here the French under gen. Moreau defeated the Austrians, 5 July, 1796.

Raid of Ruthven. RUTHVEN.

raids. MORGAN'S RAID; UNITED STATES, 1862-64.

railways. The length of the world's railways in 1835 was 1600 miles; in 1845 it had increased to 10,000 miles; in 1855 to 41,000; in 1865 to 90,000; in 1875 to 185,000, and in 1890 there were over 354,000 miles.

railways, English and foreign. Of TRAM-ROADS, laid in and about Newcastle, Engl., by Mr. Beaumont as early as 1602, Roger North wrote in 1676 as follows: "The manner of the carriage is by laying rails of timber from the colliery to the river exactly straight and parallel; and bulky carts are made with 4 rollers fitting those rails, whereby the carriage is so easy that 1 horse will draw down 4 or 5 chaldron of coals, and is an immense benefit to the coal merchants."

An iron railway built near Sheffield, by John Curr (destroyed by the colliers) 1776
First iron railway sanctioned by Parliament was the Surrey, from the Thames at Wandsworth to Croydon, operated by horses 1801
William Hedley of Wylam colliery makes the first travelling engine or locomotive; substituted for horses in a colliery 1813
First locomotive, by George Stephenson, travels 6 miles per hour 1814
Stockton and Darlington railway, built by Edward Pease and George Stephenson, first opened for passengers, 27 Sept. 1825
Daily passenger coach, called the "Experiment," carrying 6 passengers, put on Stockton and Darlington railway, 10 Oct. "
Liverpool and Manchester railway (4 ft. 8½ in. gauge) begun, Oct. 1826
Stephenson's locomotive, the "Rocket," weighing 4 tons 5 cwt., attains a speed of 29½ miles per hour at the Rainhill trial, and secures the prize of 500*l.* offered by the directors of the Liverpool and Manchester railway company, 6 Oct. 1829
Liverpool and Manchester railway opened (accident occurs, see below) .... 15 Sept. 1830
First railroad in Russia, from St. Petersburg to Charsko Selo, opened 1837
Railway mania and panic year; 272 railway acts pass in England 1846
George Stephenson d. .... 12 Aug. 1848
Panama railroad opened .... 28 Jan. 1855
System of interlocking switches, begun in England in 1846, perfected 1856

First railway in Egypt, from Alexandria to Cairo, opened...... 1856

First steel rails made at the Ebwy-Vale Iron company's works in South Wales........ 1857

Underground railway in London opened.................... 1862

Welsh railway train, about to start, is seized for debt, 27 Nov. 1866

350 men strike on London and Brighton railway...25-27 Mch. 1867

Strike of 500 men on Northeastern railway, 11 Apr.; overcome by the company..........................25 Apr. "

Locomotives for mountain climbing, by a central rail, first tried on High Peak railway, Sept. 1863. A climbing locomotive ascended mount Cenis in 1865; Mount Cenis railway opened for traffic.............................15 June, 1868

Midland railway station opened.........................1 Oct. "

Mr. Fairlie builds a locomotive called "Little Wonder," to run on a horse tram-way of 2-foot gauge, in Wales, since called the Festiniog railway; first of modern narrow-gauge railways.. 1869

Railway association of directors and shareholders to watch legislation established in England....................July, 1870

Rigi Mountain railway (up to 4000 feet above sea-level) opened, 23 May, 1871

George Hudson of England, since 1844 styled "the railway king," d. aged 71..............................14 Dec. "

First railway in Japan opened......................12 June, 1872

Thomas Brassey of England, who built 6600 miles of railway, d.. "

One-rail railway built at Paris by M. Larmenjat..........Aug. "

First railway in Persia begun at Resht...............11 Sept. 1873

Pullman palace cars introduced into England on Midland railway.......................................21 Mch. 1874

Railway Travellers' Protection Society organized in England, duke of Manchester president....................23 July, "

Trial of continuous railway brakes on Midland railway, Engl.; Westinghouse automatic brake considered the best, June, 1875

Jubilee of Stockton and Darlington railway celebrated, and statue of Joseph Pease unveiled at Darlington.......27 Sept. "

Communication between passenger carriages on English trains by bell-cords first comes into general use............about 1877

First railway in China, constructed by Europeans, from Shanghai to Oussoon (11 miles), at first opposed, opened 30 June, 1876. Operation stopped and plant taken to Formosa...1877-78

Unsuccessful strike of goods-guards on Midland railway of England.......................................3-20 Jan. 1879

First electric railway, constructed by Siemens and Halse of Berlin, at the exhibition in that city..................... "

Electric railway at Berlin opened to the public........16 May, 1881

Centenary of George Stephenson's birth celebrated throughout England...9 June, "

International railway congress for unification of rolling-stock opens at Berne.................................16 Oct. 1882

Strike on Caledonian railway at Glasgow, etc., compromised, 15-21 Jan. 1883

First railroad train from Buenos Ayres crosses the Andes in Chili..15 Feb. 1884

M. Lartigue's balance railway (single rail) reported successful in Normandy, June, 1884; and experimental line built in London..Sept. 1886

Zone railway system, or Regional passenger tariff, introduced in Hungary, 1 Aug. 1889, and in Austria.............1 June, 1890

Brienzer Rothhornbahn, Alpine railway, ascending 5606 feet, the highest in Europe, is opened.......................... 1891

Czarowitz drives the first spike for the great Siberian railway at Vladivostok on the Japan sea.....................24 May, "

[Total length to the Ural mountains over 5000 miles.]

railways, United States. First tram-road was built from the granite quarries at Quincy, Mass., to the Neponset river in 1826. The following year a gravity road for the *transportation of* coal was constructed at Mauch Chunk, Pa. The first road built expressly for transporting freight and passengers was the Baltimore and Ohio, commenced in 1828, and for a time run as a horse-railroad.

INCREASE IN RAILROAD MILEAGE.

Year.	Total mileage.	Yearly increase.	Year.	Total Mileage.	Average yearly increase.
1830........	23	..	1850........	9,021	620
1831........	95	72	1860........	30,626	2160
1832........	229	134	1870........	52,922	2229
1833........	380	151	1880........	93,296	4037
1834........	633	253	1890........	166,817	7352
1835........	1098	465	1893........	171,804	1663
1836........	1273	175	[The U. S. has more than 6 times the mileage of any other country.]		
1837........	1497	224			
1838........	1913	416			
1839........	2302	389			
1840........	2818	516			

Experimental trip of the first locomotive used in the U. S., "The Stourbridge Lion," built in England, and run by Horatio Allen on the Honesdale and Carbondale railroad, built by the Delaware and Hudson canal company in 1827. It was found too heavy for the tracks (weight 6 tons), 9 Aug. 1829

First 14 miles of Baltimore and Ohio railroad opened..24 May, 1830

Peter Cooper of New York builds a locomotive, and on a trial trip on the Baltimore and Ohio beats a horse-car, 28 Aug. 1830

Locomotive called "The Best Friend," built at the West Point foundry (weight 4½ tons) for the South Carolina railroad, which was opened...............................2 Nov. "

Swivelling truck for locomotives first suggested by Horatio Allen for the South Carolina railroad in 1831, and put in practical use on the Mohawk and Hudson railroad.. 1831

South Carolina railroad from Charleston to Hamburg, opposite Augusta, Ga., 135 miles, then the longest continuous line in the world, completed.......................... 1833

Bogie cars, or cars with trucks and aisles through the centre, first put in general use on Baltimore and Ohio railroad, about 1835

Cars with "monitors," or raised roofs with ventilators, used on Philadelphia and Germantown railroad.................... 1836

Car fitted with berths, and in use until 1848, is put on the Cumberland Valley railroad of Pennsylvania between Harrisburg and Chambersburg.............................1836-37

Fish-plates for joining rails (now universal) first tried at Newcastle, Del.. 1843

First state railroad commission established in New Hampshire..1844

Continuous railroad connects Boston and New York....1 Jan. 1849

Hodge hand-brakes introduced.............................. "

Stevens's brake introduced............................... 1851

The Cleveland and Toledo railroad completes a continuous line of 1000 miles between Boston and Chicago................ 1853

Chicago and Rock Island railroad, connecting Chicago with the Mississippi river, completed.....................Feb. 1854

Wagner's sleepers introduced, 4 in operation................ 1858

Railway system reaches the Missouri river by completion of the Hannibal and St. Joseph railroad...................... 1859

Cars with seats that could be turned into beds used in 1845; sleeping-cars with 3 tiers of bunks used on the Baltimore and Ohio railroad in 1850; patent granted George W. Pullman for sleeping-cars...................................... "

Miller car-coupler and buffer patented....................... 1863

Railroad built up mount Washington, N. H.................1866-69

Wagner's Palace-car company incorporated.................. 1867

[Pullman sleepers mostly used west and southwest; Wagner's, east and south.]

Pullman sleeper, the "Pioneer," built at a cost of $18,000, put on the Chicago and Alton railroad in 1865, and Pullman Car company organized...................................... "

First hotel-car, the "President," put on the Great Western railway of Canada...................................... "

First dining-car, the "Delmonico," begins running on the Chicago and Alton railroad................................. 1868

Dr. Thomas Durant and gov. Leland Stanford drive the last spikes connecting the Union and Central Pacific railroads at Promontory Point, Utah, completing line across the continent (PACIFIC RAILROADS).........................10 May, 1869

First narrow-gauge locomotive built in the U. S., shipped from the works of M. Baird & Co., Philadelphia, to the Denver and Rio Grande railroad (3 ft. gauge)...............13 July, 1871

First narrow-gauge railroad in the U. S., the Denver and Rio Grande, opened to Pueblo, 118 miles..................June, 1872

Westinghouse air-brakes first applied to passenger trains (1868), and triple valve attachment introduced..................... "

Trial trip on the Metropolitan (first called Gilbert) elevated railroad in New York city..........................30 Apr. 1878

System of competitive examinations, prizes awarded to supervisors and foremen for best kept division, devised and put in operation on the Pennsylvania railroad by Frank Thomson, general manager..................................... 1879

Locomotives with speed of 70 miles per hour built in the U. S... 1882

Northern Pacific railroad completed (last spike driven at Independence Gulch, Montana)...........................8 Sept. 1883

Unsuccessful railroad strike on the Missouri Pacific railroad and connections..........................6 Mch.-3 May, 1886

First vestibuled train on the Pennsylvania railroad......June, "

Special newspaper train on New York Central runs from Syracuse to Buffalo, 148.77 miles, at average speed of 65.6 miles per hour; 10 miles run at 75 miles per hour, 18 Aug. "

Train on the Canada Southern railroad runs from St. Clair junction to Windsor, Ont., 107 miles, in 97 minutes, including 2 or 3 stops. Average speed about 69 miles per hour, 16 Nov. "

Brake trials at Burlington before Master Car-builders' Association...1886-87

Westinghouse, by modifying his triple valve and train-pipe, succeeds in applying the brakes throughout a 50-car train in 2 seconds. Exhibition trip (3000 miles) made with special train throughout the country.......................Oct.-Nov. 1887

Train on the New York Central runs from New York to East Buffalo, 436.5 miles, in 7 h. 19 m. 30 sec. including 3 stops, or 7 h. 5 m. 15 sec. in motion, averaging 61.56 miles per hour, the fastest time for so long a distance, 14 Sept. 1891

Last spike in construction of the Great Northern's extension to the Pacific, the 5th transcontinental line, driven, in the Cascade mountains.................................6 Jan. 1893

Fastest time on record made by the Empire State express on New York Central, locomotive 999, engineer Charles Hogan, being 1 mile in 32 sec. from Crittenden, west, or at the rate of 112.5 miles an hour.............................11 May, "

PRINCIPAL RAILROAD SYSTEMS, TERRITORY, AND NUMBER OF MILES IN EACH ROAD IN UNITED STATES AND CANADA

Name.	General location of main line and branches.	Number of miles of main line and branches.
Atchison, Topeka, and Santa Fé	Illinois, Iowa, Missouri, Kansas, Nebraska, Arkansas, Oklahoma, Indian Territory, Texas, Colorado, Arizona, New Mexico, California	9346
Atlantic Coast Line	Virginia, North Carolina, South Carolina	1280
Baltimore and Ohio	New Jersey, Pennsylvania, Delaware, Maryland, District of Columbia, Virginia, West Virginia, Ohio, Indiana, Illinois	2097
Boston and Albany	New York and Massachusetts	388
Boston and Maine	Massachusetts, Vermont, New Hampshire, Maine, Quebec	1239
Burlington, Cedar Rapids, and Northern	Iowa, Minnesota, South Dakota	1134
Canadian Pacific	New Brunswick, Maine, Vermont, Quebec, Ontario, Michigan, Manitoba, Assiniboia, Saskatchewan, Alberta, B.C. (steamer to China, Japan, Australia)	7008
Central of Georgia	Georgia and Alabama	1384
Central of New Jersey	New York, New Jersey, Pennsylvania	628
Central of Vermont	Connecticut, Massachusetts, Vermont, New York, Quebec	882
Chesapeake and Ohio	Virginia, West Virginia, Kentucky, Ohio	1365
Chicago and Alton	Illinois and Missouri	843
Chicago and Northwestern (including the Northwestern line)	Michigan, Illinois, Iowa, Wisconsin, Minnesota, North Dakota, South Dakota, Nebraska, Wyoming	7952
Chicago, Burlington, and Quincy ("Burlington Route," including the Burlington and Missouri River in Nebraska)	Illinois, Wisconsin, Iowa, Missouri, Nebraska, Kansas, Colorado, Wyoming, South Dakota	5604
Chicago, Milwaukee, and St. Paul	Illinois, Wisconsin, Michigan, Minnesota, Iowa, Missouri, North Dakota, South Dakota	6076
Chicago Great Western	Illinois, Iowa, Minnesota, Missouri	904
Chicago, Rock Island, and Pacific	Illinois, Iowa, Missouri, Minnesota, South Dakota, Nebraska, Kansas, Oklahoma, Indian Territory, Colorado	3572
Cleveland, Cincinnati, Chicago, and St. Louis ("Big Four" route)	Ohio, Indiana, Michigan, Illinois	2290
Delaware and Hudson	Pennsylvania, New York, Vermont	757
Delaware, Lackawanna, and Western	New York, New Jersey, Pennsylvania	916
Denver and Rio Grande	Colorado and New Mexico	1687
Duluth, South Shore, and Atlantic	Minnesota, Wisconsin, Michigan	594
East Tennessee, Virginia, and Georgia	North Carolina, Georgia, Alabama, Mississippi, Tennessee, Kentucky, Louisiana	2943
Evansville Route	Indiana and Illinois	876
Florida Central and Peninsular	South Carolina, Georgia, Florida	920
Grand Rapids and Indiana	Michigan and Indiana	585
Grand Trunk of Canada	Maine, New Hampshire, Quebec, Ontario, Michigan	3510
Great Northern	Minnesota, North Dakota, South Dakota, Montana, Idaho, Washington	4413
Illinois Central	Illinois, Wisconsin, Iowa, South Dakota, Tennessee, Mississippi, Louisiana	3808
Intercolonial of Canada	Nova Scotia, New Brunswick, Quebec	1114
International and Great Northern	Texas	825
Kansas City, Fort Scott, and Memphis	Alabama, Mississippi, Tennessee, Arkansas, Missouri, Kansas	1179
Lake Shore and Michigan Southern	New York, Pennsylvania, Ohio, Indiana, Illinois, Michigan	1608
Lake Erie and Western	Ohio, Indiana, Illinois	725
Lehigh Valley	New York, New Jersey, Pennsylvania	1039
Long Island	Long Island, N. Y	367
Louisville and Nashville	Kentucky, Indiana, Illinois, Tennessee, Alabama, Florida, Louisiana, Mississippi	3164
Maine Central	Maine, New Hampshire, Vermont, Quebec	804
Michigan Central	New York, Ontario, Michigan, Indiana, Illinois	1662
Missouri, Kansas, and Texas	Missouri, Kansas, Indian Territory, Texas	2023
Missouri Pacific	Missouri, Kansas, Nebraska, Colorado, Arkansas, Louisiana, Indian Territory	5415
Mobile and Ohio	Alabama, Mississippi, Tennessee, Illinois	688
Nashville, Chattanooga, and St. Louis ("The Lookout Mountain Route")	Georgia, Alabama, Tennessee	1016
New York and New England	Massachusetts, Rhode Island, Connecticut, New York	566
New York Central and Hudson River	New York and Pennsylvania	†2627
New York, Chicago, and St. Louis ("Nickel Plate" line)	New York, Pennsylvania, Ohio, Indiana, Illinois	523
New York, Lake Erie, and Western	New York, New Jersey, Pennsylvania, Ohio, Indiana, Illinois	2063
New York, New Haven, and Hartford	Massachusetts, Rhode Island, Connecticut, New York	1630
Norfolk and Western	Maryland, West Virginia, Virginia, North Carolina, Ohio	1477
Northern Pacific	Minnesota, North Dakota, Montana, Idaho, Washington, Oregon, Manitoba (steamer from Tacoma, Wash., to China and Japan)	4495
Pennsylvania	New York, New Jersey, Pennsylvania, Delaware, Maryland, District of Columbia, Ohio, Indiana, Illinois, Michigan	7916
Philadelphia and Reading	New Jersey and Pennsylvania	891
Plant System (including several railroads, the principal being Savannah, Florida, and Western)	South Carolina, Georgia, Alabama, Florida	1492
Queen and Cresent System	Ohio, Kentucky, Tennessee, Alabama, Mississippi, Louisiana, Texas	1272
Richmond and Dansville	Virginia, North Carolina, South Carolina, Georgia, Alabama, Mississippi	2446
Rome, Watertown, and Ogden	New York	685
Seaboard Air Line	Virginia, North Carolina, South Carolina, Georgia	926
Southern Pacific	Louisiana, Texas, New Mexico, Arizona, California, Nevada, Oregon, Utah	6586
St. Louis Southwestern ("Cotton Belt" route)	Missouri, Arkansas, Louisiana, Texas	1226
Terre Haute and Indianapolis	Indiana, Illinois, Michigan	675
Texas and Pacific	Louisiana and Texas	1490
Union Pacific (the Overland route)	Kansas, Nebraska, Texas, New Mexico, Colorado, Wyoming, Utah, Idaho, Montana, Oregon, Washington	8034
Wabash	Ohio, Indiana, Michigan, Illinois, Missouri, Iowa	2124
Western New York and Pennsylvania	New York and Pennsylvania	655
Wisconsin Central	Illinois, Wisconsin, Minnesota	765
Yazoo and Mississippi Valley (Illinois complete system)	Louisiana, Mississippi, Tennessee	807

† With West Shore, etc.

MEMORABLE RAILROAD ACCIDENTS IN THE U. S. AND CANADA.

"In proportion to the whole number carried, the accidents to passengers in 'the good old days of stage-coaches' were, as compared to the present time (1879), about as 60 to 1. In Massachusetts, between 1871 and 1879, 303,000,000 passenger journeys of 13 miles each were made. The average distance travelled by all before death happened to any one was about 80,000,000 miles."—*Charles Francis Adams, Jr.*

Express train from New York runs into an open draw at Norwalk, Conn.; 46 killed, 30 injured....6 May, 1853

Collision between passenger and gravel train on the Great Western railway of Canada, between Chatham and Detroit; 47 killed, 80 injured....25 Oct. 1854

Bridge over Gasconade on Pacific railroad of Missouri gives way under an excursion train; 22 killed, 50 injured..1 Nov. 1855

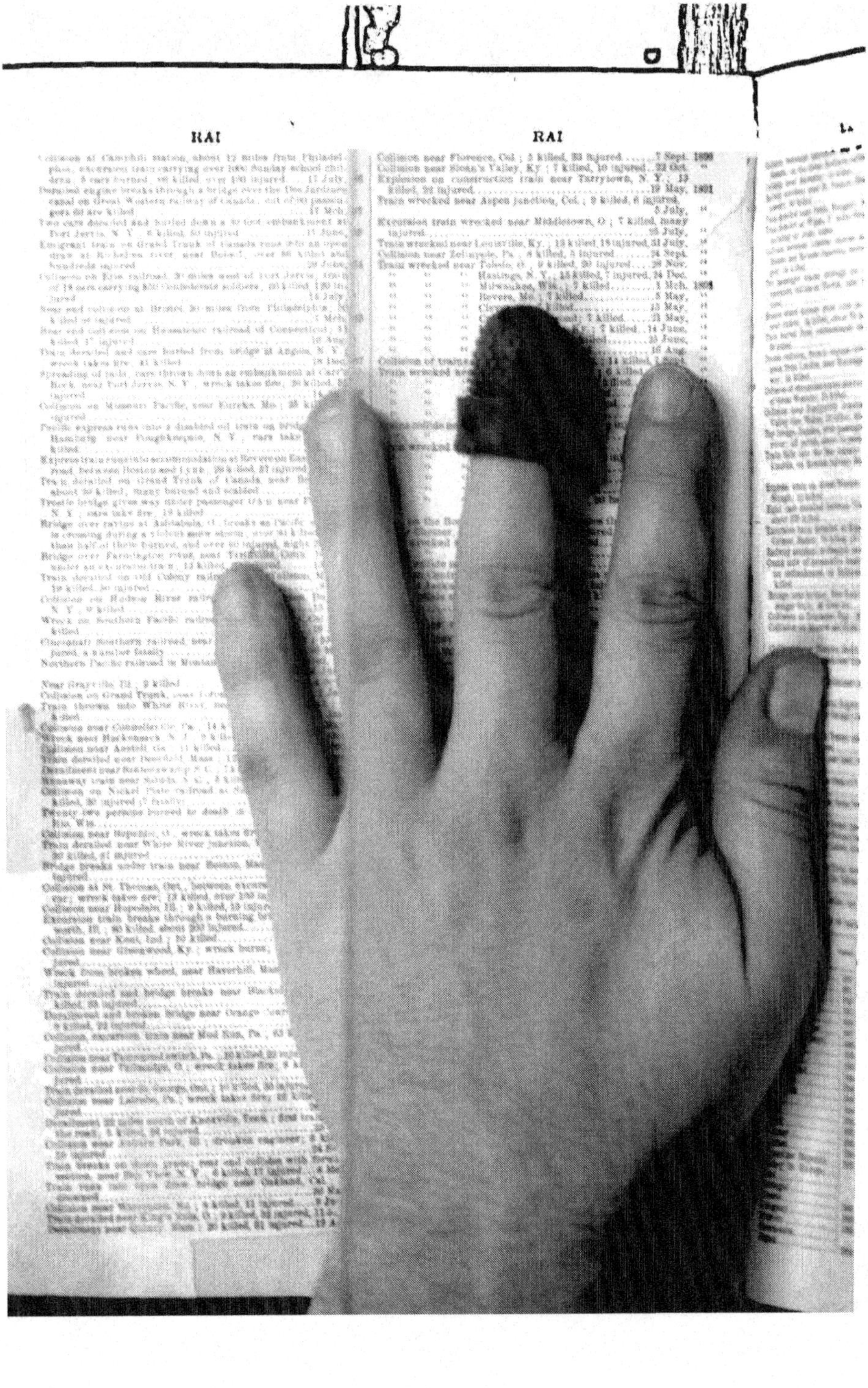

RAI

RAI

Collision between excursion train and derailed freight near Newark, on the Great Northern railway; 19 killed..21 June, 187[illegible]
Collision near Barnsley; 14 killed..........12 Dec. "
Railway accident near St. Nazaire, France; explosion of gunpowder; 60 killed..........25 Feb. 187[illegible]
Train derailed near Pesth, Hungary; 21 killed..........May, 187[illegible]
Train derailed at Wigan, 17 miles from Manchester; 13 killed, including sir John Anson..........23 Aug. "
Collision between London express and a mineral train near Manuel and Bo'ness Junction, between Edinburgh and Glasgow; 16 killed..........27 Jan. 187[illegible]
Two passenger trains, through the carelessness of telegraph operators, collide at Thorpe, near Norwich; 26 killed, 30 injured..........10 Sept. "
Broken wheel throws train over an embankment at Shipton, near Oxford; 44 killed, about 70 injured..........24 Dec. "
Train hurled from embankment near Odessa, Russia; about 68 killed..........8 Jan. 187[illegible]
Double collision, Scotch express with coal train, and Leeds express from London, near Huntingdon on Great Northern railway; 14 killed..........21 Jan. "
Collision of excursion trains about 4 miles from Bath, on branch of Great Western; 14 killed..........7 Aug. "
[illegible]ollision near Pontypridd Junction, Rhondda branch of Taff Valley line, Wales; 13 killed, about 40 injured..........19 Oct. 187[illegible]
[illegible]y bridge, Dundee, with passenger train on it, blown into the river; all perish, about 74 passengers..........28 Dec. 187[illegible]
[illegible]ain falls into the San Antonio river through a bridge near Cuartla, on Morelos railway, Mexico; about 200 lives lost, night of 24 June, 188[illegible]
[illegible]xpress train on Great Western railway runs into freight at [illegible]lough; 12 killed..........24 Dec. "
[illegible]ht cars derailed between Tcherny and Bastigeur, Russia; [illegible]bout 178 killed..........13 July, 188[illegible]
[illegible]ursion train derailed at Hugstetten, between Freiburg and [illegible]lmar, Basles; 70 killed, 150 injured..........7 Sept. "
[illegible]way accident at Steglitz, near Berlin; 40 killed..........9 Sept. 188[illegible]
[illegible]k axle of locomotive breaks, throwing express train over [illegible] embankment at Bullhouse bridge, near Penistone; 24 [illegible]d..........16 July, 188[illegible]
[illegible] near Sydney, New South Wales, gives way under a pas[illegible]er train; 40 lives lost..........30 Jan. 188[illegible]
[illegible]n at Doncaster, Engl.; 28 killed, 70 injured..........16 Sept. 188[illegible]
[illegible]n on Moscow and Kursk railway, in Russia; 11 killed, 15 May, 188[illegible]
[illegible]n near [illegible], Mexico; 18 killed, 41 injured..4 June, "
[illegible] bri[illegible] near Groenandael, Belgium; 14 killed, 3 Feb. 188[illegible]
[illegible]d near Armagh, Ireland; 76 killed, 12 June, "
[illegible], Bulgaria; 15 killed..........9 July, "
[illegible]uttgart, Germany; 10 killed, 50 injured, 2 Oct. "
[illegible]estern railway near Norton Fitzwarren; [illegible]..........11 Nov. 1890
[illegible]r Basel, Switzerland; 100 killed, 150 in[illegible]..........14 June, 1891
[illegible]ins at St. Mandé, near Paris; 50 killed, [illegible]..........26 July, "
[illegible]rne, Switzerland; 14 killed, many in[illegible]..........17 Aug. "
[illegible]os, Spain; 14 killed, 24 injured. 24 Sept. "
[illegible]ans, France; 16 killed, 50 injured, 26 Oct. "
[illegible]re, India; 30 killed, many injured, 7 Nov. "
[illegible]k, Scotland; 10 killed..........2 Nov. 1892
[illegible]affvale line, Wales; 12 killed, 60 in[illegible]..........12 Aug. 1893
[illegible] Italy; 13 killed, 23 injured..28 Nov. "

[illegible]AILROADS IN THE WORLD.

[illegible]d.	Miles of road completed.					
	1840.	1850.	1860.	1870.	1880.	188[illegible].
[illegible]	1857	6621	10,433	15,537	17,933	19,940
[illegible]	2818	9021	30,626	52,922	93,296	160,544
[illegible]	..	1714	5,700	11,142	16,275	21,899
[illegible]	341	3637	6,979	11,729	20,693	24,845
[illegible]5	207	554	1,074	1,799	2,399	2,778
[illegible]7	..	817	1,813	3,790	7,088	9,345
[illegible]38	..	210	988	7,098	14,026	17,534
[illegible]839	13	265	1,117	3,825	5,340	7,830
[illegible]839	10	110	208	874	1,143	1,632
1844	..	15	653	885	1,596	1,859
1846	..	137	1,004	2,157	4,421	6,731
1847	..	20	69	470	975	1,217
1848	..	17	1,190	3,400	4,550	5,931
1851	..	..	126	452	1,100	1,801
1851	..	..	134	564	2,174	5,546
1854	..	..	42	692	970	976
1856	..	..	375	1,080	3,654	4,896
1857	..	..	..	697	1,536	4,506
[illegible]	..	..	41	392	727	1,021
[illegible]	..	..	47	247	1,179	1,836
[illegible]	..	..	42	444	710	1,188
[illegible]869	..	..	..	6	7	416
[illegible]869	..	..	..	61	268	399
[illegible]868	..	..	..	215	855	5,012
[illegible]	..	..	..	152	850	1,537
[illegible]74	..	..	..	..	75	642

rain. The exact manner in which rain forms is unknown. Blanford advanced the general law that "however vapor-laden may be any current of air, however saturated, it does not bring rainfall so long as it preserves a horizontal movement." "Either increased elevation or eddies from increase of friction, or the convection around borders of a barometric depression causes formation of clouds and rain."—*Greely.* Places having a great annual fall of rain are: Cherrapunjee, Hindostan, 592 in.; Matouba, Guadeloupe, 292 in.; Maranhao, Brazil, 280 in.; Uttray Mullay, Hindostan, 267 in.; and Mahabaleshwar, Hindostan, 251 in. Lima (Peru), Thebes (Egypt), Tatta (south Africa) are said to be rainless; other places having a small annual rainfall are: Cairo, Egypt, 1.31 in.; Karachi, India, 1.5 in.; Camp Mohave, Arizona, 1.85 in.; Mammoth Tank, San Diego co., Cal., 1.88 in.; Bishop Creek, Inyo co., Cal., 2.02 in., and Yuma, Ariz., 2.81 in. From observations made by Charles Pierce, resident of Portsmouth, N. H., 1763, and of Philadelphia, Pa., from 1813, the smallest rainfall in any one year in Philadelphia from 1737 to 1846, was 20.25 in. in 1815, and the greatest, 65.5 in. in 1813. Records at Central Park observatory, New York city, show a rainfall in 1889 of 55 in., the largest recorded in 21 years. In New England, from 11 to 13 Feb. 1886, 5 in. of rain fell over nearly 5000 sq. miles of territory, and one of the most remarkable rainfalls recorded in the U. S. occurred at Alexandria, La., 15–16 June, 1886, when 21.4 in. fell in 24 hours. Numerous authenticated instances of red rain, or "showers of blood," have been collected by M. Grellois, beginning with one which occurred in and around Paris, referred to by Gregory of Tours, 582 A.D. Some of the most celebrated instances are: in France and Germany, 1181; at Genoa, 1744; at Naples, 14 Mch. 1813; at Beauvais, 1 May, 1863; near Rome, 13 Feb. 1870, etc. Yellow rains, owing to pollen of pine-trees floating in the air, have been observed in the U. S.; a noticeable instance occurred at Lynchburg, Va., 21 Mch. 1879. The absolute range of barometric readings in the U. S. varies from 1.014 in. at San Diego, Cal., and 1.176 in. at Key West, Fla., to 2.201 in. at New York, and 2.523 in. at Eastport, Me. STORMS, Cloudbursts and Rainfalls.

rainbow (mentioned Gen. ix. 13–16), a luminous bow or arch formed by the prismatic dispersion of rays of sunlight passing through falling rain-drops. It exhibits the 7 prismatic colors in the order of the spectrum. Its theory was developed by Kepler in 1611, and by René Descartes in 1629. SPECTRUM.

Raleigh's settlements on the Atlantic coast. VIRGINIA, 1585.

Ramadan, the Mahometan month of fasting, in 1865, 28 Jan. to 27 Feb.; and from 27 Dec. 1867 to 30 Jan. 1868 inclusive. It is followed by the festival of BAIRAM. MAHOMETAN YEAR.

Rambouillet (*ram-boo-ee-yea'*), a royal château, about 25 miles from Paris. Here Francis I. died, 31 Mch. 1547; and here Charles X. abdicated, 2 Aug. 1830. After belonging to the count of Thoulouse and the duc de Penthièvre, it was bought by Louis XVI. 1778. Rambouillet decree, UNITED STATES, 1810.

ramie, a Javanese name now adopted in the United States for the Chinese grass, a plant of the order *Urticaceæ* or nettle. The fibre can be manufactured into a fabric resembling silk. The climate of the southern U. S. is favorable to its cultivation.

Ramillies (*ram'-e-leez*), a village of Belgium, the site of one of the battles and victories in the war of the SPANISH SUCCESSION, gained by the duke of Marlborough over the French, commanded by the elector of Bavaria and marshal de Villeroy, on Whitsunday, 23 May, 1706. The French were seized with a panic and routed; about 4000 of the allies were slain. This accelerated the fall of Louvain, Brussels, etc.

Ramona. INDIAN EDUCATION; NEW MEXICO, 1885.

Rangoon', maritime capital of the Burmese empire, on the Irrawaddy, built by Alompra, 1753, was taken by a British force under sir A. Campbell on 11 May, 1824. In Dec. 1826, it was ceded to the Burmese on condition of payment of a sum of money, the reception of a British resident at Ava, and freedom of commerce. Oppression of the British merchants led to the second Burmese war, 1852. Rangoon was

Collision at Camphill station, about 12 miles from Philadelphia; excursion train carrying over 1000 Sunday-school children; 5 cars burned; 66 killed, over 100 injured....17 July, 1856

Derailed engine breaks through a bridge over the Des Jardines canal on Great Western railway of Canada; out of 90 passengers 60 are killed..17 Mch. 1857

Two cars derailed and hurled down a 30-foot embankment at Port Jervis, N. Y.; 6 killed, 50 injured.............17 June, 1858

Emigrant train on Grand Trunk of Canada runs into an open draw at Richelieu river, near Belœil; over 86 killed and hundreds injured..................................29 June, 1864

Collision on Erie railroad, 20 miles west of Port Jervis; train of 18 cars carrying 850 Confederate soldiers; 60 killed, 120 injured..15 July, "

Rear-end collision at Bristol, 30 miles from Philadelphia; 50 killed or injured..7 Mch. 1865

Rear-end collision on Housatonic railroad of Connecticut; 11 killed, 17 injured..16 Aug. "

Train derailed and cars hurled from bridge at Angola, N. Y.; wreck takes fire; 41 killed..........................18 Dec. 1867

Spreading of rails; cars thrown down an embankment at Carr's Rock, near Port Jervis, N. Y.; wreck takes fire; 26 killed, 52 injured..14 Apr. 1868

Collision on Missouri Pacific, near Eureka, Mo.; 25 killed, 41 injured..12 May, 1870

Pacific express runs into a disabled oil train on bridge at New Hamburg, near Poughkeepsie, N. Y.; cars take fire; 21 killed..6 Feb. 1871

Express train runs into accommodation at Revere on Eastern railroad, between Boston and Lynn; 29 killed, 57 injured, 26 Aug. "

Train derailed on Grand Trunk of Canada, near Belleville; about 30 killed; many burned and scalded..........22 June, 1872

Trestle bridge gives way under passenger train near Prospect, N. Y.; cars take fire; 19 killed...........................24 Dec. "

Bridge over ravine at Ashtabula, O., breaks as Pacific express is crossing during a violent snow-storm; over 80 killed, more than half of them burned, and over 60 injured, night 29 Dec. 1876

Bridge over Farmington river, near Tariffville, Conn., breaks under an excursion train; 13 killed, 33 injured.......15 Jan. 1878

Train derailed on Old Colony railroad, near Wollston, Mass.; 19 killed, 50 injured.......................................8 Oct. "

Collision on Hudson River railroad, near Spuyten Duyvil, N. Y.; 9 killed..13 Jan. 1882

Wreck on Southern Pacific railroad, near Tehichipa, Cal.; 15 killed..19 Jan. 1883

Cincinnati Southern railroad, near Mason's Station, O.; 53 injured, a number fatally.................................30 Mch. "

Northern Pacific railroad in Montana; 18 Chinamen killed, 26 June, "

Near Grayville, Ill.; 9 killed.......................................4 Sept. "

Collision on Grand Trunk, near Toronto, Ont.; 25 killed, 2 Jan. 1884

Train thrown into White River, near Indianapolis, Ind.; 6 killed..31 Jan. "

Collision near Connellsville, Pa.; 14 killed............14 May, "

Wreck near Hackensack, N. J.; 9 killed.................18 Oct. 1885

Collision near Austell, Ga.; 11 killed..................15 Dec. "

Train derailed near Deerfield, Mass.; 12 killed..............7 Apr. 1886

Derailment near Santee swamp, S. C.; 7 killed, 13 injured, 7 June, "

Runaway train near Saluda, N. C.; 5 killed, 8 injured..25 Aug. "

Collision on Nickel Plate railroad at Silver Creek, N. Y.; 13 killed, 20 injured (7 fatally)..........................14 Sept. "

Twenty-two persons burned to death in railway wreck near Rio, Wis..28 Oct. "

Collision near Republic, O.; wreck takes fire; 13 killed..4 Jan. 1887

Train derailed near White River junction, Vt.; cars take fire; 30 killed, 37 injured......................................5 Feb. "

Bridge breaks under train near Boston, Mass.; 24 killed, 115 injured..14 Mch. "

Collision at St. Thomas, Ont., between excursion train and oil car; wreck takes fire; 13 killed, over 100 injured....15 July, "

Collision near Hopedale, Ill.; 9 killed, 15 injured......27 July, "

Excursion train breaks through a burning bridge near Chatsworth, Ill.; 80 killed, about 200 injured..................10 Aug. "

Collision near Kout, Ind.; 10 killed.....................10 Oct. "

Collision near Greenwood, Ky.; wreck burns; 6 killed, 21 injured..31 Dec. "

Wreck from broken wheel, near Haverhill, Mass.; 9 killed, 13 injured..10 Jan. 1888

Train derailed and bridge breaks near Blackshear, Ga.; 27 killed, 35 injured......................................17 Mch. "

Derailment and broken bridge near Orange Court-house, Va.; 9 killed, 22 injured......................................12 July, "

Collision, excursion train near Mud Run, Pa.; 63 killed, 23 injured..10 Oct. "

Collision near Tamanend switch, Pa.; 10 killed, 23 injured, 16 Oct. "

Collision near Tallmadge, O.; wreck takes fire; 8 killed, 6 injured..14 Jan. 1889

Train derailed near St. George, Ont.; 10 killed, 30 injured, 27 Feb. "

Collision near Latrobe, Pa.; wreck takes fire; 12 killed, 6 injured..26 June, "

Derailment 22 miles south of Knoxville, Tenn.; first train over the road; 5 killed, 26 injured.............................23 Aug. "

Collision near Auburn Park, Ill.; drunken engineer; 6 killed, 10 injured..24 Sept. "

Train breaks on down grade; rear end collides with forward section, near Bay View, N. Y.; 6 killed, 17 injured...6 Mch. 1890

Train runs into open draw-bridge near Oakland, Cal.; [illegible] drowned..30 May, "

Collision near Warrenton, Mo.; 8 killed, 11 injured.....9 June, "

Train derailed near King's Mills, O.; 9 killed, 32 injured, 11 July, "

Derailment near Quincy, Mass.; 20 killed, 31 injured...19 Aug. "

RAI

Collision near Florence, Col.; 5 killed, 33 injured.......7 Sept. 1890

Collision near Sloan's Valley, Ky.; 7 killed, 10 injured..22 Oct. "

Explosion on construction train near Tarrytown, N. Y.; 13 killed, 22 injured...19 May, 1891

Train wrecked near Aspen junction, Col.; 9 killed, 6 injured, 5 July, "

Excursion train wrecked near Middletown, O.; 7 killed, many injured..25 July, "

Train wrecked near Louisville, Ky.; 13 killed, 18 injured, 31 July, "

Collision near Zelinpole, Pa.; 8 killed, 5 injured.......24 Sept. "

Train wrecked near Toledo, O.; 9 killed, 20 injured....28 Nov. "

" " " Hastings, N. Y.; 15 killed, 7 injured, 24 Dec. "

" " " Milwaukee, Wis.; 7 killed.........1 Mch. 1892

" " " Revere, Mo.; 7 killed..............5 May, "

" " " Cleves, O.; 7 killed...............15 May, "

" " " Cotton Belt railroad; 7 killed......21 May, "

" " " Lonesome Hollow, Ky.; 7 killed..14 June, "

" " " Harrisburg, Pa.; 12 killed........25 June, "

" " " Cochocton, O.; 6 killed............16 Aug. "

Collision of trains near Eckenrode Mills, Pa.; 14 killed, 7 Sept. "

Train wrecked near West Cambridge, Mass.; 6 killed, 11 Sept. "

" " " West Manchester, Pa.; 7 killed.....24 Oct. "

" " " Phillipsburg, Mo.; 6 killed..........25 Oct. "

" " " Grand Island, Neb.; 7 killed.........1 Nov. "

" " " Nelson, Minn.; 8 killed..............18 Dec. "

Trains collide near Alton, Ill.; 9 killed, 12 fatally injured, 21 Jan. 1893

" " " Somerset, Pa.; 5 killed.............25 Apr. "

Train wrecked near Lafayette, Ind.; 10 killed......... 7 May, "

" " " Parkville, L. I.; 8 killed, 29 injured, 20 June, "

" " " Patterson, N. J.; 5 killed.........24 June, "

" " " Newburg, N. Y.; 5 killed..........13 July, "

" " " Melton, Va.; 7 killed..............16 Aug. "

" " " Berlin, L. I.; 16 killed, 50 badly injured, 26 Aug. "

Train on the Boston and Albany railroad goes through a bridge near Chester, Mass.; 15 killed and 15 injured........31 Aug. "

Train wrecked near Colehour, Ill.; 11 killed...........7 Sept. "

" " " Manteno, Ill.; 8 killed............19 Sept. "

Trains collide near Wabash, Ind.; 11 killed........... 22 Sept. "

Michigan Central excursion train, 2d section runs into 1st section at Jackson, Mich.; 13 killed and 40 injured......13 Oct. "

Trains collide near Battle Creek, Mich.; 26 killed, many fatally hurt...20 Oct. "

NUMBER OF PERSONS KILLED IN TRAIN ACCIDENTS ON THE DIFFERENT RAILROADS IN THE U. S. FOR THE YEARS 1891, '92, '93.

Year.	Passengers.	Trespassers.	Employees.	Total.
1891....................	177	63	550	790
1892....................	121	61	490	672
1893....................	178	89	424	691
Total...........	476	213	1464	2153

Average for the past 14 years (1880 to 1893 inclusive) is 573.4.

MEMORABLE RAILROAD ACCIDENTS, ENGLISH AND FOREIGN.

In 1846, in England, was passed the Campbell act, to compel railway companies to make compensation for injuries by culpable accidents (9 and 10 Vict. c. 93). The statistics of railway accidents in Great Britain for one year (1889) show—Killed: passengers, 183; employés, 435; trespassers, 351; various, 170; total, 1139. Injured: passengers, 1829; employés, 2769; trespassers, 122; various, 53; total, 4773; total killed and injured, 5912.

W. Huskisson, M. P., killed at the opening of the Liverpool and Manchester railway..................................15 Sept. 1830

Derailment of engine at Sonninghill cut, near Reading; 8 killed, 24 Dec. 1841

Railway train takes fire at Versailles, France; passengers locked in. Over 50 lives lost, including adm. d'Urville; over 40 injured...8 May, 1842

Collision on Great Southern and Western near Straffan, Ireland; 13 killed...5 Oct. 1853

Collision near Moret in Seine-et-Marne, France, 16 killed, 23 Oct. 1855

Collision at Kirby, between Liverpool and Blackpool; 200 injured, none killed................................27 June, 1857

Collision at Lewisham, near London; 11 killed........28 June, "

Wreck near Mons, Belgium; 21 killed..................June, 1858

Collision of excursion train about 10 miles from Birmingham, near Round Oak station.............................23 Aug. "

Collision, excursion train at Helmshore, near Manchester; 11 killed..4 Sept. 1860

Collision of mail and cattle train on Northwestern railway at Atherstone; 11 killed..................................16 Nov. "

Collision in Clayton tunnel, on London and Brighton railway; 23 killed, 176 injured................................25 Aug. 1861

Wreck at Kentish Town, near London; 16 killed, 320 injured, 2 Sept. "

Collision near Winchburgh, on Edinburgh and Glasgow railway; 15 killed, 100 injured...............................13 Oct. 1862

Train derailed near Rednall on branch of Great Western railway; 13 killed, about 40 injured.......................7 June, 1865

Derailment near Staplehurst, on Southeastern railway; 10 killed, about 50 injured.....................................9 June, "

Collision between Irish mail train and freight, Abergele, N. Wales. Barrels of petroleum ignite; 33 burned to death.....20 Aug. 1868

Derailment on Great Indian Peninsular railway, near Khandalla, Bombay; about 18 killed.........................26 Jan. 1869

Collision between excursion train and derailed freight near Newark, on the Great Northern railway; 19 killed..21 June, 1870
Collision near Barnsley; 14 killed....................12 Dec. "
Railway accident near St. Nazaire, France; explosion of gunpowder; 60 killed....................25 Feb. 1871
Train derailed near Pesth, Hungary; 21 killed...........May, 1873
Train derailed at Wigan, 17 miles from Manchester; 13 killed, including sir John Anson....................23 Aug. "
Collision between London express and a mineral train near Manuel and Bo'ness Junction, between Edinburgh and Glasgow; 16 killed....................27 Jan. 1874
Two passenger trains, through the carelessness of telegraph operators, collide at Thorpe, near Norwich; 26 killed, 50 injured....................10 Sept. "
Broken wheel throws train over an embankment at Shipton, near Oxford; 34 killed, about 70 injured............24 Dec. "
Train hurled from embankment near Odessa, Russia; about 68 killed....................8 Jan. 1876
Double collision, Scotch express with coal train, and Leeds express from London, near Huntingdon on Great Northern railway; 14 killed....................21 Jan. "
Collision of excursion trains about 4 miles from Bath, on branch of Great Western; 14 killed....................7 Aug. "
Collision near Pontypridd Junction, Rhondda branch of Taff Valley line, Wales; 13 killed, about 40 injured.......19 Oct. 1878
Tay bridge, Dundee, with passenger train on it, blown into the river; all perish, about 74 passengers..............28 Dec. 1879
Train falls into the San Antonio river through a bridge near Cuartla, on Morelos railway, Mexico; about 200 lives lost, night of 24 June, 1881
Express train on Great Western railway runs into freight at Slough; 12 killed....................24 Dec. "
Eight cars derailed between Tcherny and Bastigeur, Russia; about 178 killed....................13 July, 1882
Excursion train derailed at Hugstetten, between Freiburg and Colmar, Baden; 70 killed, 150 injured..........7 Sept. "
Railway accident at Steglitz, near Berlin; 40 killed.....2 Sept. 1883
Crank axle of locomotive breaks, throwing express train over an embankment at Bullhouse bridge, near Penistone; 24 killed....................16 July, 1884
Bridge near Sydney, New South Wales, gives way under a passenger train; 40 lives lost....................30 Jan. 1885
Collision at Doncaster, Engl.; 28 killed, 70 injured.....16 Sept. 1887
Collision on Moscow and Kursk railway, in Russia; 11 killed, 15 May, 1888
Collision near Tampico, Mexico; 18 killed, 41 injured..4 June, "
Railway bridge breaks near Groenandael, Belgium; 14 killed, 3 Feb. 1889
Excursion train wrecked near Armagh, *Ireland*; 76 killed, 12 June, "
Collision near Ciulnita, Bulgaria; 15 killed............9 July, "
Train derailed near Stuttgart, Germany; 10 killed, 50 injured, 2 Oct. "
Collision on Great Western railway near Norton Fitzwarren; 10 killed, 8 injured....................11 Nov. 1890
Railway accident near Basel, Switzerland; 100 killed, 150 injured....................14 June, 1891
Collision of express trains at St. Maudé, near Paris; 50 killed, over 100 injured....................25 July, "
Train wrecked near Berne, Switzerland; 14 killed, many injured....................17 Aug. "
Train collision near Burgos, Spain; 14 killed, 24 injured, 24 Sept. "
Train wrecked near Moirans, France; 15 killed, 50 injured, 26 Oct. "
Trains collide near Lahore, India; 30 killed, many injured, 7 Nov. "
Trains collide near Thirsk, Scotland; 10 killed.........2 Nov. 1892
Train wrecked on the Taffvale line, Wales; 12 killed, 60 injured....................12 Aug. 1893
Trains collide near Milan, Italy; 13 killed, 22 injured..28 Nov. "

GROWTH OF RAILROADS IN THE WORLD.

Country.	Opened.	Miles of road completed.					
		1840.	1850.	1860.	1870.	1880.	1889.
Great Britain	1825	1857	6621	10,433	15,537	17,933	19,943
United States	1827	2818	9021	30,626	52,922	93,296	160,544
France	1828	..	1714	5,700	11,142	16,275	21,899
Germany	1835	341	3637	6,979	11,729	20,693	24,845
Belgium	1835	207	554	1,074	1,799	2,399	2,776
Austria (proper)	1837	..	817	1,813	3,790	7,083	9,345
Russia in Europe	1838	..	310	988	7,098	14,026	17,534
Italy	1839	13	265	1,117	3,825	5,340	7,830
Holland	1839	10	110	208	874	1,143	1,632
Switzerland	1844	..	15	653	885	1,596	1,869
Hungary	1846	..	137	1,004	2,157	4,421	6,751
Denmark	1847	..	20	69	470	975	1,217
Spain	1848	..	17	1,190	3,400	4,550	5,951
Chili	1851	..	..	120	452	1,100	1,801
Brazil	1851	..	..	134	504	2,174	5,546
Norway	1854	..	..	42	692	970	970
Sweden	1856	..	..	375	1,089	3,654	4,899
Argentine Republic	1857	..	..	..	637	1,536	4,506
Turkey in Europe	..	..	..	41	392	727	1,024
Peru	..	..	..	47	247	1,179	1,836
Portugal	..	..	..	42	444	710	1,188
Greece	1869	..	..	..	6	7	416
Uruguay	1869	..	..	..	61	268	399
Mexico	1868	..	..	..	215	655	5,012
Roumania	..	..	..	..	152	859	1,537
Japan	1874	..	..	..	..	75	542

rain. The exact manner in which rain forms is unknown. Blanford advanced the general law that "however vapor-laden may be any current of air, however saturated, it does not bring rainfall so long as it preserves a horizontal movement." "Either increased elevation or eddies from increase of friction, or the convection around borders of a barometric depression causes formation of clouds and rain."—*Greely.* Places having a great annual fall of rain are: Cherapoonjee, Hindostan, 592 in.; Matouba, Guadeloupe, 292 in.; Maranhao, Brazil, 280 in.; Uttray Mullay, Hindostan, 267 in.; and Mahabalishwar, Hindostan, 254 in. Lima (Peru), Thebes (Egypt), Tatta (north Africa) are said to be rainless; other places having a small annual rainfall are: Cairo, Egypt, 1.31 in.; Karachi, India, 1.5 in.; Camp Mohave, Arizona, 1.85 in.; Mammoth Tank, San Diego co., Cal., 1.88 in.; Bishop Creek, Inyo co., Cal., 2.02 in.; and Yuma, Ariz., 2.81 in. From observations made by Charles Pierce, resident of Portsmouth, N. H., 1793, and of Philadelphia, Pa., from 1813, the smallest rainfall in any one year in Philadelphia from 1797 to 1846, was 23.25 in. in 1819, and the greatest, 55.5 in. in 1841. Records at Central Park observatory, New York city, show a rainfall in 1889 of 55 in., the largest recorded in 21 years. In New England, from 11 to 13 Feb. 1886, 5 in. of rain fell over nearly 5000 sq. miles of territory, and one of the most remarkable rainfalls recorded in the U. S. occurred at Alexandria, La., 15-16 June, 1886, when 21.4 in. fell in 24 hours. Numerous authenticated instances of red rain, or "showers of blood," have been collected by M. Grellois, beginning with one which occurred in and around Paris, referred to by Gregory of Tours, 582 A.D. Some of the most celebrated instances are: in France and Germany, 1181; at Genoa, 1744; at Naples, 14 Mch. 1813; at Beauvais, 1 May, 1863; near Rome, 13 Feb. 1870, etc. Yellow rains, owing to pollen of pine-trees floating in the air, have been observed in the U. S.; a noticeable instance occurred at Lynchburg, Va., 21 Mch. 1879. The absolute range of barometric readings in the U. S. varies from 1.014 in. at San Diego, Cal., and 1.176 in. at Key West, Fla., to 2.201 in. at New York, and 2.523 in. at Eastport, Me. STORMS, Cloudbursts and Rainfalls.

rainbow (mentioned Gen. ix. 13-16), a luminous bow or arch formed by the prismatic dispersion of rays of sunlight passing through falling rain-drops. It exhibits the 7 prismatic colors in the order of the spectrum. Its theory was developed by Kepler in 1611, and by René Descartes in 1629. SPECTRUM.

Raleigh's settlements on the Atlantic coast. VIRGINIA, 1585.

Ramadan, the Mahometan month of fasting, in 1865, 28 Jan. to 27 Feb.; and from 27 Dec. 1867 to 30 Jan. 1868 inclusive. It is followed by the festival of BAIRAM. MAHOMETAN YEAR.

Rambouillet (*ram-boo-ee-yea'*), a royal château, about 25 miles from Paris. Here Francis I. died, 31 Mch. 1547; and here Charles X. abdicated, 2 Aug. 1830. After belonging to the count of Thoulouse and the duc de Penthièvre, it was bought by Louis XVI. 1778. Rambouillet decree, UNITED STATES, 1810.

ramie, a Javanese name now adopted in the United States for the Chinese grass, a plant of the order *Urticaceæ* or nettle. The fibre can be manufactured into a fabric resembling silk. The climate of the southern U. S. is favorable to its cultivation.

Ramillies (*ram'-e-leez*), a village of Belgium, the site of one of the battles and victories in the war of the SPANISH SUCCESSION, gained by the duke of Marlborough over the French, commanded by the elector of Bavaria and marshal de Villeroy, on Whitsunday, 23 May, 1706. The French were seized with a panic and routed; about 4000 of the allies were slain. This accelerated the fall of Louvain, Brussels, etc.

Ramona. INDIAN EDUCATION; NEW MEXICO, 1885.

Rangoon', maritime capital of the Burmese empire, on the Irrawaddy, built by Alompra, 1753, was taken by a British force under sir A. Campbell on 11 May, 1824. In Dec. 1826, it was ceded to the Burmese on condition of payment of a sum of money, the reception of a British resident at Ava, and freedom of commerce. Oppression of the British merchants led to the second Burmese war, 1852. Rangoon was taken by storm by gen. Godwin, 14 Apr., and annexed to the British dominions in Dec. An English bishopric founded, 1877. Pop. 1890, 182,000. BURMAH.

Ransome's artificial stone, invented by Fred. Ransome, 1848, is made by dissolving flint (silica) in heated caustic alkali, adding fine sand. The mixture is pressed into moulds and heated to redness.

rape was punished with death by Jews, Romans, and Goths; by mutilation and loss of eyes in William I.'s reign. This was mitigated by the statute of Westminster 1, 3 Edw. I. 1274. Made felony by stat. Westminster 2, 12 Edw. III. 1338; and without benefit of clergy, 18 Eliz. 1575. Rape made punishable by transportation in 1841; by penal servitude for life, or a less period, 1861. In the United States the punishment differs according to the laws of the several states; but in most of them the sentence may be for 10 to 20 years of imprisonment at hard labor.

Raphia, a port of Palestine. Here Antiochus III. of Syria was defeated by Ptolemy Philopator, king of Egypt, 217 B.C.

Rappahannock, a river in Virginia, about half way between Washington and Richmond, along the line of which, or near it, were fought some of the great battles of the civil war, as Chancellorsville, Fredericksburg, and the Wilderness; while several severe minor engagements, namely, Kelly's Ford, Beverly Ford, Rappahannock Station, etc., might well entitle it to the name of "Bloody River." UNITED STATES, 1863.

raspberry. FLOWERS AND PLANTS.

Ratcliffe highway (now St. George's street), East London. Mr. Marr, a shopkeeper here, with his wife, child, and boy, were murdered in a few minutes, 7 Dec. 1811. In the same neighborhood, on 11 Dec., Mr. and Mrs. Williamson, their child and servant, were also murdered. A man named Williams, arrested on suspicion, committed suicide, 15 Dec. Graphically depicted by De Quincey in "Three Memorable Murders." ENGLAND, 1886.

ra'tionalism, the doctrine which rejects divine revelation and admits no way to truth but experience and reason. The leading writers are Reimarus of Hamburg (d. 1768), Paulus of Heidelberg (1761-1851), Eichhorn, Reinhard, Strauss, Frederick Henry Jacobi, and Schleiermacher. W. Lecky's "History of Rationalism in Europe" appeared July, 1865; and dr. J. Hurst's, Apr. 1867. PHILOSOPHY.

Ratisbon or **Regensburg,** in Bavaria, was made a free imperial city about 1200. Several diets have been held here. A peace was concluded here between France and the emperor of Germany ending the war for the Mantuan succession, 13 Oct. 1630. In a diet held here, the German princes seceded from the Germanic empire, to accept the protection of the emperor Napoleon, 1 Aug. 1806. Ratisbon was made an archbishopric in 1806; secularized in 1810; ceded to Bavaria in 1815; became again an archbishopric in 1817.

Raucoux (*rō-coo'*), a village of Belgium. Here the French army under marshal Saxe totally defeated the allies under prince Charles of Lorraine, 11 Oct. 1746.

Ravaillac's (*rā-văl-yăc'*) **murder** of Henry IV. of France, 14 May, 1610. The execution of the assassin on 27 May was accompanied by horrible tortures. TORTURE.

Raven'na, on the Adriatic, a city of the Papal States, founded by Greek colonists, fell under Roman power about 234 B.C. It was favored and embellished by the emperors, and Honorius made it capital of the Western Empire about 404 A.D. In 568 it became capital of an exarchate. It was subdued by the Lombards in 752, and their king, Astolphus, in 754 surrendered it to Pepin, king of France, who gave it to pope Stephen, founding the temporal power of the Holy See. On 11 Apr. 1512, a battle was fought between French, under Gaston de Foix (duke of Nemours and nephew of Louis XII.), and Spanish and papal armies. De Foix perished in the moment of victory, and his death closed the good-fortune of the French in Italy. Ravenna became part of the kingdom of Italy in 1860.

Raymond, Miss., Battle of. VICKSBURG CAMPAIGN.

readers, a new order of ministrants in the church of England, received the assent of the archbishops and bishops in July, 1866. They were not to be ordained or addressed as reverend.

Reading (*rĕd'ing*), a borough of Berkshire, Engl. Here Alfred defeated the Danes, 871. The abbey was founded in 1121 by Henry I. The last abbot was hanged in 1539 for denying the king's supremacy. The palace prison was erected 1850.

Real Presence. TRANSUBSTANTIATION.

Realists. NOMINALISTS, PHILOSOPHY.

Reams's Station, Affair at. GRANT'S CAMPAIGN IN VIRGINIA.

reaping-machines. The gathering of grain with a sickle is as old as history. Cradles, or scythes with a gathering frame of 4 or 5 wooden fingers above the blade and parallel to it are still in use, and as late as 1848, at a trial of reaping-machines held at the state fair at Buffalo, N. Y., the decision was in favor of cradles. A heading-machine, which caught the heads of grain by sharp teeth set on the edge of a receiving box pushed against the grain by an ox in harness, was used in Gaul as early as 60 A.D. This principle of pushing was followed out in modern reapers up to 1820; in only one case, a machine invented in 1806, were the horses attached in front.

Reaper with rows of combs or ripples on a cylinder, which tore off the heads and discharged them into a box, was invented by Pitt in England 1786
First reaper patented was by Boyce of England, and had a vertical shaft with 6 rotating scythes 1799
Gladstone of England patents a side-cutting reaper with revolving knife, finger gathering bar, and front draft 1806
Bailey's American mowing-machine, the first patented in the U. S., made with a horizontal rotary circular blade 1822
Ogle of England invents a reaper with front draft, side cut, grain platform, and gathering reel .... "
Reaper invented by rev. Patrick Bell, and tried near Forfar, Scotland, had a reel and travelling-apron to deliver the cut grain at the side, and was pushed by horses 1828
Obed Hussey, then of Cincinnati, O., patents a mower and reaper with front draft, side cut, triangular sectional knife, and guards 1833
Cyrus H. McCormick of Virginia patents his reaping-machine. 1834
Public trial of Hussey's reaper before the Maryland Agricultural Society .... 12 July, 1837
[During the season this machine cut 180 acres of oats on a farm in Maryland.]
First reaping-machine with a platform to receive the gavels and carry the binder invented by Mr. Lamb, in the U. S. 1840
Header invented by Jonathan Haines of Illinois 1849
W. H. Seymour of New York invents a self-raking attachment for reapers 1851
Watson's automatic binder patented .... "
At trial of American reapers on farm of Mr. Mechi, 45 miles from London, the McCormick reaper receives a prize medal..July, "
Trial of reaping-machines held at Buffalo, N. Y. 1848; trial of 9 competing reaping-machines held at Geneva, N. Y. 1852
American reapers receive the prize at trial made on the farm of M. Dailley, postmaster-general of France, at La Trappe... 1855
Owen Dorsey of Maryland invents a combined reel and rake for reapers 1856
Automatic self-binding harvesters come into use in the U. S... 1871
McCormick's self-binding harvester takes gold medal at Royal Agricultural Society's competition at Bristol, Engl....6 Aug. 1878

reason was decreed to be worshipped as a goddess by the French republicans, 10 Nov. 1793, and was personified by an actress, madame Maillard.—Thomas Paine's "Age of Reason" was published in 1794-95; Immanuel Kant's "Critique of Pure Reason" ("Kritik der reinen Vernunft"), 1781. LITERATURE, PHILOSOPHY.

Rebecca, Lady (Pocahontas). VIRGINIA, 1613.

rebeck, the English name of a 3-stringed musical instrument of Arabian or Persian invention. This instrument gradually assumed the form of the viol, of which it was the origin.

"When the merry bells ring round
And the jocund rebecks sound."
—*Milton*, "L'Allegro."

rebellions or **insurrections in British history.** Details of many are given in separate articles. CONSPIRACIES.

Against William the Conqueror, in favor of Edgar Atheling, aided by the Scots and Danes, 1069.
Odo of Bayeux and others, against William II., in favor of his brother Robert, 1088; suppressed, 1090.
In favor of the empress Maude, 1139; ended, 1153.
Of prince Richard against his father Henry II., 1189.
Of the barons, Apr. 1215. Compromised by the grant of Magna Charta, 15 June following.

Of the Barons, 1261-67.
Of lords spiritual and temporal against Edward II. on account of his favorites, the Gavestons, 1312. Again, on account of the Spencers, 1321.
Of Walter the Tyler, of Deptford, vulgarly called Wat Tyler; occasioned by the brutal rudeness of a poll-tax collector to his daughter. He killed the collector in his rage, and raised a party to oppose the tax, 1381. TYLER.
In Ireland, when Roger, earl of March, the viceroy and heir presumptive to the crown, was slain, 1398.
Of Henry, duke of Lancaster, who caused Richard II. to be deposed, 1399.
Against king Henry IV. by a number of confederated lords, 1402-3.
Against Henry V. by earl of Cambridge and other lords, 1415.
Of Jack Cade, against Henry VI., 1450. CADE'S INSURRECTION.
In favor of the house of York, 1452, ending in imprisonment of Henry VI. and seating Edward IV. of York on the throne, 1461.
Under Warwick and Clarence, 1470, ending in expulsion of Edward IV. and restoration of Henry VI. the same year.
Under Edward IV., 1471, ending with death of Henry VI.
Earl of Richmond, against Richard III., 1485, which ended with the death of Richard.
Under Lambert Simnel, 1486, who pretended to be Richard III.'s nephew, Edward Plantagenet, earl of Warwick; his army was defeated, leaders slain, and he was discovered to be a baker's son; he was pardoned, and employed by the king as a menial.
Under Perkin Warbeck, 1492; defeated; executed 1499.
Under Thomas Flammock and Michael Joseph, in Cornwall, against taxes levied to pay the Scottish war expenses. They marched towards London, and lord Audley took the command at Wells. They were defeated at Blackheath, 22 June, and the 3 leaders were executed, 28 June, 1497.
"Pilgrimage of Grace," against Henry VIII., 1536-37.
Of the English in the west, to restore the ancient liturgy, etc., 1549; suppressed same year.
In Norfolk, headed by Ket the tanner, but soon suppressed, Aug. 1549.
For lady Jane Grey, against queen Mary. Lady Jane was proclaimed queen on the death of Edward VI., 10 July, 1553; but resigned the crown to Mary after a few days, and beheaded for high-treason, in the Tower, 12 Feb. 1554, aged 17.
Sir Thomas Wyatt, son of the poet, and others, against queen Mary's marriage with Philip of Spain, etc.; fails; he is beheaded, 11 Apr. 1554.
Of the Roman Catholic earls of Northumberland and Westmoreland against queen Elizabeth, Nov. and Dec. 1567. The former fled to Scotland, but was given up by the regent Morton and executed.
Irish under the earl of Tyrone, 1599; suppressed 1601.
Earl of Essex, against queen Elizabeth, 1600; he d. 1601.
Of the Irish under Roger More, sir Phelim O'Neil, etc., against the English in Ireland, 1641-45.
"Great Rebellion," 1641-60.
Rebellion of the Scots Covenanters, 1666; soon put down.
Under the duke of Monmouth, 1685; executed 15 July.
Of Scots for the Old Pretender, 1715; quelled 1716.
Of the Scots under the Young Pretender, 1745; suppressed in 1746; lords Lovat, Balmerino, and Kilmarnock beheaded.
Of the Americans on account of taxation, 1774. This rebellion lost to England her chief North American colonies, which became the United States, 1782.
In Ireland, the "Great Rebellion," great numbers taking arms, began 24 May, 1798; suppressed next year.
Again in Ireland, under Robert Emmett, a gifted enthusiast, 23 July, 1803, when lord Kilwarden was killed, with several others, by the insurgents.
Canadian insurrection, Dec. 1837 to Nov. 1838. CANADA.
Of CHARTISTS at Newport, Engl., 4 Nov. 1839.
Smith O'Brien's rebellion; ended by defeat and dispersion of his followers, by sub-inspector Trant and about 60 police constables, on Boulagh common, Ballingary, county Tipperary, 29 July, 1848. IRELAND.
Sepoy mutiny in INDIA, 1857-58.
Of FENIANS in IRELAND, 1865-67.

For the United States, DORR'S, SHAYS'S, and WHISKEY REBELLION, and for the Southern states, UNITED STATES, 1860-1866.

Rech'abites, Independent Order of, a temperance society introduced into the United States in 1842 from England, where it had existed since 1835. The order takes its name from the Rechabites of Scripture (Jer. xxxv.), and at one time had over 100,000 members. 50th anniversary of the order held at Washington, D. C., 2 Aug. 1892.

recitative, a species of singing differing little from ordinary speaking, and used for narratives in operas, is said to have been first employed at Rome by Emilio del Cavaliere, who disputed the claim of Rinuccini to the introduction of the opera, 1600. OPERAS.

Reconstruction period embraced the administrations of Johnson and Grant. UNITED STATES, 1865-77.

records, Public, in England, first regularly preserved in 1100 by order of Henry I. The repositories of ancient materials most interesting to historians were the Chapter-house of Westminster Abbey, the Tower of London, the Rolls Chapel, and the Queen's Remembrancer's offices of the exchequer. The early records of Scotland, going from London, were lost by shipwreck in 1298. In Ireland, the council-chamber and most of the records were burned, 1711. Public Records act, 2 Vict. c. 94 (10 Aug. 1838). F. Thomas's valuable "Handbook to the Public Records" was pub. in 1853; Mr. Ewald's "Our Public Records" in 1873.

Recovery, fort, Defence of. Gen. Wayne succeeded St. Clair in command of the troops in the Northwest, and on the site of the latter's defeat (OHIO, 1791) he erected a fort, and called it Recovery. In June, 1794, the garrison, under maj. William M'Mahon, were attacked by many Indians. M'Mahon and 22 others were killed, and 30 were wounded. The Indians were repulsed. On 20 Aug. the Indians were defeated by Wayne at the MAUMEE RAPIDS.

recu'sants, persons in England who refuse to attend church, 1 Eliz. c. 2, 1559; dissenters relieved from this act, 1689; it was repealed, 1844.

Red Bank, the site of fort Mercer, on the New Jersey shore of the Delaware river. FORT MERCER.

red crag, deposits of fossil remains on the coast of Essex and Suffolk, England, so called by Edward Charlesworth about 1835; used in the manufacture of fertilizer.

Red Cross. The Red Cross is "a confederation of societies in different countries for the amelioration of the condition of wounded soldiers in the armies, in campaigns on land or sea." It carries on its work under the sign of a red cross on a white ground used as a flag, always with the national flag or as an arm badge. By article 7 of the Geneva convention this sign protects its wearers as neutral. The society originated with Henri Dunant (Swiss) after the battle of Solferino, 1859, ably seconded by dr. Louis Appia and Gustave Moynier of Geneva. The latter, president of the "Society of Public Utility of Switzerland," called a meeting "to consider the formation of permanent societies for the relief of wounded soldiers," which was held 9 Feb. 1863, and resulted in an international meeting 26 Oct. following, and a treaty between 12 European governments, assuring neutrality and protection to all working under the Red Cross. This treaty is known as the Geneva Convention, and was concluded at Geneva, 22 Aug. 1864. It was adopted by Great Britain, 18 Feb. 1865; Prussia, 22 June, 1865; Turkey, 5 July, 1865; and Russia, 22 May, 1867. The United States Senate acceded to it, 16 Mch. 1882, and it was proclaimed by pres. Arthur, 26 July, 1882. The treaty is now generally adopted by civilized governments of the world. The American (National) Association of the Red Cross was organized at Washington, D.C., 21 May, 1881, and was incorporated for 20 years, 1 July, 1881. Miss Clara Barton was elected first president. Associate societies in the various states have done noble work in aiding sufferers by calamity from forest fires, floods, fevers, etc.

Red River campaign of 1864. After the capture of Port Hudson, gen. Halleck urged upon Banks (6 Aug.) the necessity, for diplomatic reasons, of occupying Texas. There was some difference, Halleck preferring an advance upon Shreveport, and Banks a descent upon the coast and thence into the interior. An expedition against SABINE PASS started from New Orleans 5 Sept. 1863, but failed. Brazos Santiago, at the mouth of the Rio Grande, was occupied 2 Nov. During that month nearly the entire Texan coast was occupied by Banks's forces. He was about to attack Galveston, when Halleck recalled him to the original plan for an advance up the Red river to Shreveport, La. On 25 Mch. 1864, his army was concentrated at Alexandria; it advanced to Natchitoches (2, 3 Apr.) and to Pleasant Hill (7 Apr.). On 8 Apr. was fought the battle of Sabine Cross-roads, in which Banks's advance was forced to retire by Kirby Smith and Dick Taylor with about 20,000 men. Banks fell back 3 miles to Pleasant Grove, where the confederates were checked by Emory's division of the 19th corps until nightfall, when the retreat was continued 15 miles to a strong position at Pleasant Hill. Here the federals, about 15,000 men, were joined by A. J. Smith's corps, 10,000 strong. The confederates attacked about 4 P.M. on the 9th, in full force, but were repulsed. On the 10th Banks continued his retreat to Grand Ecore unassailed. The fleet under adm. Porter, which had followed the army with difficulty from Alexandria to Grand Ecore, found it still more difficult to return, the river constantly falling. Most of the fleet reached Alexandria, but here could not pass the rapids until lieut.-col. Joseph Bailey, of the 4th Wisconsin infantry, succeeded in damming the river, a brilliant feat of engineering. The rapids were over a mile long and from 100 to 1000 ft. wide, with a current 13 miles an hour. The work began 30 Apr., and by 12 May the entire fleet had passed safely through the chute to the waters below the rapids. Over 3000 men were engaged day and night on the work. The expedition from first to last was mismanaged; and even if, with Porter's co-operating fleet, it had reached Shreveport, that position could not have been maintained, and the fleet would have been captured or destroyed. Gen. Steele, who marched a cooperative column from Little Rock against Kirby Smith, encountered great difficulties in his movements; and before he could be of any assistance Banks had already retreated. The Federal losses during the whole expedition were between 5000 and 6000 men, of whom 1000 were lost during the battles of 8 and 9 Apr.

Red River settlements, a name given to part of the Hudson Bay settlements, now MANITOBA.

Red sea, an extensive inland sea, over 1300 miles in length, and greatest width 205 miles. It is connected with the Mediterranean sea by the SUEZ CANAL, which passes through the isthmus of Suez, and it communicates with the Indian ocean by the strait of Bab-el-Mandeb, 15 miles in width. In 1826, Ehrenberg discovered that the color was due to marine plants, the *Trichodesmium erythræum*. EGYPT.

redowa, a Bohemian dance in ¾ time, introduced in 1846 or 1847 at Paris, and soon after in London.

Reformation, The. Generally applied to the time and labors of Martin Luther, although other efforts for the reformation of the church may be traced to the reign of Charlemagne, when Paulinus, bishop of Aquileia, employed his voice and pen to accomplish it; to Wickliffe, Huss, Jerome of Prague, Savonarola, Erasmus, Zwinglius, Tyndal, Calvin, Melanchthon, Cranmer, Latimer, Knox, and Browne. Luther thus characterized himself and his fellow-reformers: "Res et non Verba—*Luther*." "Verba non Res—*Erasmus*." "Res et Verba—*Melanchthon*." "Nec Verba nec Res—*Carlstadt*." CALVINISTS, LUTHERANS, PRESBYTERIANS, PROTESTANTS, WICKLIFFITES, etc.

ERAS OF THE REFORMATION.

In France (*Albigenses*) ... about	1170
In England (*Wickliffe*)	1380
In Bohemia (*Huss*)	1405
In Italy (*Savonarola*)	1498
In France (*Farel*) ... before	1512
In Germany (*Luther*)	1517
In Switzerland (*Zwinglius*)	1519
In Denmark (*Andreas Bodenstein*)	1521
In Prussia	1527
In France (*Calvin*)	1529
Protestants first so called	"
In Sweden (*Petri*)	1530
In England (*Henry VIII.*)	1534
In Ireland (archbishop *George Browne*)	1535
In England, completed (*Cranmer, Bucer, Fagius*, etc.) 1547; annulled by Mary, 1553, restored by Elizabeth	1558
In Scotland (*Knox*), established	1560
In the Netherlands, established	1562

reformatories. Pope Clement XI. founded at Rome (1704) the first reformatory institution established by a government—the prison of St. Michael, for boys and young men. On its wall was inscribed: "It is of little use to restrain criminals by punishment, unless you reform them by education."

Reformatory prison founded at Ghent under Viscount Vilain XIV.	
First English Reform school founded by the Philanthropic Society near London	
First permanently successful reformatory for criminal youth in the world, established by John Falk at Weimar, Germany.	
First Reform school, with farm and out door labor for training inmates, opened in Warwickshire, Engl.	
Rauhe Haus, near Hamburg, Germany, a reform school with family groups and agricultural labor, established by dr. Wichern	
Act passed in England for a separate prison at Parkhurst, Isle of Wight, for offenders under 18, with discipline educational and reformatory	

Agricultural colony reformatory at Mettray, France, established by MM. de Metz and de Bretignères	1839
Foundation of Reformatory school, Redhill, Surrey, laid 30 Apr.	1849
Act passed in England for committing juvenile offenders to reformatories	1854
First conference of National Reformatory Union of Great Britain ... Aug.	1856
International exhibition of works of Reform schools, held at Agricultural Hall, Islington, near London	1865

[In 1890, there were in England 46 Reformatory schools with 4183 inmates under 16, and 133 industrial schools with 16,130 inmates.]

reformatories in the United States. The House of Refuge on Randall's island, the oldest reformatory in the U. S., was the first founded and controlled by legislation. It was conceived by Edward Livingston, authorized by law 29 Mch. 1824, and opened 1825. Juvenile reformatories were made public penal institutions in Massachusetts in 1848.

PRINCIPAL REFORM SCHOOLS.

Name.	Location.	Opened.
House of Refuge (Randall's island)	Harlem, N. Y.	1825
House of Refuge	Philadelphia, Pa.	1828
Boys' House of Refuge	New Orleans, La.	1843
Lyman School for Boys	Westborough, Mass.	1848
State Industrial School	Rochester, N. Y.	1849
Sockanosset School for Boys	Howard, R. I.	1850
Cincinnati House of Refuge	Cincinnati, O.	"
New York Juvenile Asylum	New York city	1851
Lowell Reform School	Lowell, Mass.	"
State Reform School	Portland, Me.	1853
State Reform School	Meriden, Conn.	"
Pennsylvania Reform School	Morganza, Pa.	1854
House of Refuge	St. Louis, Mo.	"
Cambridge Truant School	North Cambridge, Mass.	"
Reform School	Lansing, Mich.	1855
State Industrial School for Girls	Lancaster, Mass.	1856
Brooklyn Truant Home	Brooklyn, N. Y.	"
Boys' Industrial School	Lancaster, O.	1857
State Industrial School	Manchester, N. H.	"
Industrial School	San Francisco, Cal.	1859
Wisconsin Industrial School for Boys	Milwaukee, Wis.	1860
Detroit House of Correction	Detroit, Mich.	
Worcester Truant School	Worcester, Mass.	
New York Catholic Protectory	Westchester, N. Y.	
Vermont Reform School	[illegible]ennes, Vt.	
St. Mary's Industrial Sc[illegible] Boys	[illegible], Md.	
Massachusetts State Pri[illegible]	[illegible]	
Convent of the Good Sh[illegible]	[illegible]	
New Jersey State Refo[illegible] for Boys	[illegible]	
Minnesota State Refor[illegible]	[illegible]	
Indiana Reform Schoo[illegible]	[illegible]	
Truant School	[illegible]	
Plummer Farm Schoo[illegible]	[illegible]	
Reform School [illegible]	[illegible]	
State Indu[illegible]	[illegible]	
Reform [illegible] Women	[illegible]	
Iowa Ind[illegible] part[illegible]	[illegible]	
[illegible]	[illegible]	

Christian Intelligencer, organ of the Reformed Dutch church, established in New York city........ 1826
Reformed churches established in the western states and strengthened by colonists from the Netherlands........about 1835
Hope college, Holland, Mich., established........ 1865
Word "Dutch" dropped from the corporate name at general synod held at Geneva, N. Y........ 20 Nov. 1867
Present strength of Reformed church of America: 570 churches, 582 ministers, 94,323 members........ June, 1891

Reformed church in the United States, formerly known as the German Reformed church, was formed principally of peasants of the PALATINATE, driven from their homes, and sent to America by charity of queen Anne, 1683-1687. They settled mostly in Pennsylvania and New York, and the first *coetus*, or ministerial conference, of the church was held at Philadelphia in 1746.

First synod at Lancaster, Pa........ 1793
Classes or presbyteries introduced........ 1820
First theological seminary opened at Carlisle, Pa........ 1825
Marshall college founded at Mercersburg, Pa........ 1836
Rev. dr. Philip Schaff of Berlin installed professor of church history and biblical literature in Marshall college........ 1844
Marshall college united with Franklin college at Lancaster, Pa. 1853
Word "German" erased from church title........ 1869
Theological seminary at Mercersburg removed to Lancaster, Pa. 1871
Society numbered 8 synods, 55 classes, 835 ministers, 1554 congregations, 200,500 members in........ 1890

Reformed Episcopal church, founded in the United States in 1873; introduced into England 1877.

Dr. Cummins, assistant bishop of Kentucky, after revising the prayer book, consecrated Gregg, Cheney, and others, as bishops........ 1873
Dr. Gregg and others ordained presbyters and formed churches here, July, 1877; said to have 10,000 members........April, 1878
Another bishop consecrated by dr. Gregg at Southend...5 Nov. "
"Book of Common Prayer" modified, issued by dr. Gregg early in........ 1879

regalia. CROWN.

Regency, Albany (first so called by Thurlow Weed), a strong political Democratic combination, which largely con[illegible] not only the nominating conventions and other ma[illegible] of that party in the state of New York from 1820 to [illegible] was almost as potential in national politics as well. [illegible] members were Martin Van Buren, William L. [illegible]el L. Talcott, John A. Dix, A. C. Flagg, Silas [illegible] others, with the Albany *Argus* to enforce its [illegible]

[illegible] **bills** of the English government. One [illegible] One was proposed to Parliament in con[illegible] mental illness of George III., and debated 10 [illegible] relinquished on his recovery, 26 Feb. 1789. [illegible] malady led to the prince of Wales (after [illegible] being sworn in before the privy council as [illegible] 5 Feb. 1811. The Regency bill pro[illegible] of the government, should the [illegible] Victoria while under 18 years of [illegible] A Regency bill appoint[illegible] of the demise of the [illegible] be under age, passed 4 [illegible]

[illegible] *caedere*, to kill, the [illegible] put a king to death. [illegible] appointed to try king [illegible] the death-warrant, [illegible] executed: Harri[illegible] Peters, 16 Oct., [illegible] Axtell and Hac[illegible] Okey arrested at [illegible] 1662. 3 of them, [illegible] England colo[illegible] arrest. MASSA[illegible] More than 20 [illegible] Cromwell, Ireton, [illegible]

[illegible] 20 Feb. 1437
[illegible] 11 June, 1488
[illegible] 2 Aug. 1589
[illegible] 14 May, 1610
[illegible] 21 Jan. 1793
[illegible] 29 Mch. 1792
[illegible] 24 Mch. 1801
[illegible] 14 Mch. 1881

regiments of infantry, bodies of foot-soldiers commanded by a colonel, now usually divided into 10 companies, were formed in France about 1558. INFANTRY. The following are the approximate dates of the establishment of several British regiments:

CAVALRY.

Oxford Blues, erroneously ascribed to the reign of Henry VIII.; named from their colonel, the earl of Oxford........ 1661
Three life regiments (1st, 2d, and 3d) raised........ Aug. "
Dragoon Guards, the Royal Irish, and the Scots Greys were formed, James II........about 1684-86
Several regiments of Light Dragoons were armed with lances and termed "Lancers"........ Sept. 1816

INFANTRY.

1st Royal [illegible] 1633; the old title [illegible] 1821
Coldstream [illegible] 1660
3d Buffs, [illegible]
2d Queen's [illegible] 1661
4th King's Own [illegible] 1680
5th Northumberland Fusiliers [illegible]
26th Cameronians [illegible]
100th Cameron [illegible]
101st to 109 [illegible] 1861
Highland [illegible]
For the Unit[illegible] States ARMY.

regium donum ("royal gift"), an allowance from the sovereign for the maintenance of the Presbyterian ministers in Ireland, commenced by Charles II. in 1672, and revived by William III. in 1690, was commuted by the Irish Church act passed Ju[illegible], 1871. The allowance to certain Protestant dissenting ministers in Ireland was given up by them in 1857, in deference to the wishes of English dissenters.

Regulators. NORTH CAROLINA, 1768-71.

Reichenbach (*rīk'en-bahk*), a town in Prussian Silesia. Here Duroc, Napoleon's chief of staff, was killed during the conflicts between the French and the allies, 22 May, 1813. BAUTZEN. Here was signed a subsidy treaty between Russia, Prussia, and England, whereby the last engaged to provide means for carrying on the war against Napoleon I. on certain conditions, 14-15 June, 1813. Austria joined the alliance soon after.

Reichsrath (*rīks'rāt*), the representative council of the empire of Austria, several times changed; reconstituted by decree 5 Mar., met on 31 May, 1860. In May, 1861, the upper house consisted of 17 spiritual, 56 hereditary, and 39 peers. The lower house consisted of 136 elected deputies. No representatives came from Hungary, Transylvania, Venetia, the Banat, Slavonia, Croatia, and Istria. The Reichsrath was abolished by a rescript, 21 Sept. 1865, with the view of restoring autonomy to Hungary and other provinces. It again met 20 May, 1867. Now constituted (1894) of 2 houses, upper and lower. The upper house consists of members of the royal family over 19 years of age, of the nobility, of church dignitaries (archbishops and bishops), of distinguished scientists nominated by the emperor; in all, 113 members. Lower house, elected by the people for 6 years, numbers 353 members. The emperor nominates president and vice-president of the upper house; the lower house elects its own officers. Bills to become laws must pass both houses and receive the sanction of the head of the state.

Reichstag (*rīk'stag*), diet or parliament of the German empire, is composed of 397 deputies elected by universal suffrage for the term of 5 years.

reign of terror. Maximilien Robespierre headed the populace in the Champ de Mars, in Paris, demanding the dethronement of the king, 17 July, 1791. He was triumphant in 1793, and numbers of eminent men and citizens were sacrificed during his sanguinary administration. Billaud Varennes denounced the tyranny of Robespierre in the tribune, 27 July, 1794. The next day Robespierre suffered death, with many of his companions. FRENCH REVOLUTION. This has been termed the Red Terror. The reaction after the restoration of the Bourbons, 1815, disgraced by many atrocious acts of wanton cruelty, has been termed the White Terror. The Jesuits were conspicuous in the destruction of their enemies.

reigning families of Europe. Nations separately.

reign of sovereigns. The average duration, according to Newton, is 19 years; according to Hales, 22½ years;

army with difficulty from Alexandria to Grand Ecore, found it still more difficult to return, the river constantly falling. Most of the fleet reached Alexandria, but here could not pass the rapids until lieut.-col Joseph Bailey, of the 4th Wisconsin infantry, succeeded in damming the river, a brilliant feat of engineering. The rapids were over a mile long and from 700 to 1000 ft wide, with a current 10 miles an hour. The work began 30 Apr, and by 12 May the entire fleet had passed safely through the chute to the waters below the rapids. Over 3000 men were engaged day and night on the work. The expedition from first to last was mismanaged, and even if, with Porter's co-operating fleet, it had reached Shreveport, that position could not have been maintained, and the fleet would have been captured or destroyed. Gen Steele, who marched a co-operative column from Little Rock against Kirby Smith encountered great difficulties in his movement, and before he could be of any assistance Banks had already retreated. The Federal losses during the whole expedition were between 5000 and 6000 men, of whom 4000 were lost during the battles of 8 and 9 Apr

Red River settlements, a name given to part of the Hudson Bay settlements, now MANITOBA.

Red sea, an extensive inland sea, over 1300 miles in length, and greatest width 205 miles. It is connected with the Mediterranean sea by the SUEZ CANAL, which passes through the isthmus of Suez, and it communicates with the Indian ocean by the strait of Bab-el-Mandeb, 13½ miles in width. In 1826, Ehrenberg discovered that the color was due to marine plants, the *Trichodesmium erythræum*. EGYPT

red'owa, a Bohemian dance in ¾ time, introduced in 1846 or 1847 at Paris, and soon after in London

Reformation, The. Generally applied to the time and labors of Martin Luther, although other efforts for the reformation of the church may be traced to the reign of Charlemagne, when Paulinus, bishop of Aquileia, employed his voice and pen to accomplish it, to Wickliffe, Huss, Jerome of Prague, Savonarola, Erasmus, Zuinglius, Tyndal, Calvin, Melanchthon, Cranmer, Latimer, Knox, and Browne. Luther thus characterized himself and his fellow-reformers: "Res non Verba—*Luther*." "Verba non Res—*Erasmus*." "Res et Verba—*Melanchthon*." "Nec Verba nec Res—*Carlstadt*." CALVINISTS, LUTHERANS, PRESBYTERIANS, PROTESTANTS, WICKLIFFITES, etc

ERAS OF THE REFORMATION

In France (*Albigenses*)	about 1177
In England (*Wickliffe*)	1360
In Bohemia (*Huss*)	1405
In Italy (*Savonarola*)	1498
In France (*Farel*)	before 1512
In Germany (*Luther*)	1517
In Switzerland (*Zuinglius*)	1519
In Denmark (*Andreas Bodenstein*)	1521
In Prussia	1527
In France (*Calvin*)	1529
Protestants first so called	"
In Sweden (*Petri*)	1530
In England (*Henry VIII*)	1534
In Ireland (archbishop *George Browne*)	1535
In England completed (*Cranmer, Bucer, Fagius*, etc.) 1547, annulled by Mary, 1553, restored by Elizabeth	1558
In Scotland (*Knox*), established	1560
In the Netherlands, established	1562

reformatories. Pope Clement XI founded at Rome (1704) the first reformatory institution established by a government—the prison of St Michael, for boys and young men. On its wall was inscribed "It is of little use to restrain criminals by punishment, unless you reform them by education."

Reformatory prison founded at Ghent under Viscount Vilain XIV	1775
First English Reform school founded by the Philanthropic Society near London	1788
First permanently successful reformatory for criminal youth in the world, established by John Falk at Weimar, Germany,	1813
First Reform school, with farm and out door labor for training inmates, opened in Warwickshire, Engl	1818
Rauhe Haus, near Hamburg, Germany, a reform school with family groups and agricultural labor, established by dr Wichern	1833
Act passed in England for a separate prison at Parkhurst, Isle of Wight, for offenders under 16, with discipline educational and reformatory	1838
Agricultural colony reformatory at Mettray, France, established by MM de Metz and de Bretignères	1839
Foundation of Reformatory school, Redhill Surrey laid, 30 Apr	1849
Act passed in England for committing juvenile offenders to reformatories	1854
First conference of National Reformatory Union of Great Britain Aug	1856
International exhibition of works of Reform schools, held at Agricultural Hall, Islington, near London	1865

[In 1890 there were in England 40 Reformatory schools with 4183 inmates under 16, and 133 Industrial schools with 16,156 inmates.]

reformatories in the United States. The House of Refuge on Randall's island, the oldest reformatory in the U S, was the first founded and controlled by legislation. It was conceived by Edward Livingston, authorized by law 29 Mch 1824, and opened 1825. Juvenile reformatories were made public penal institutions in Massachusetts in 1848

PRINCIPAL REFORM SCHOOLS

Name	Location	Opened
House of Refuge (Randall's island)	Harlem N Y	1825
House of Refuge	Philadelphia, Pa	1828
Boys' House of Refuge	New Orleans, La	1843
Lyman School for Boys	Westborough, Mass	1848
State Industrial School	Rochester, N Y	1849
Sockanosset School for Boys	Howard, R I	1850
Cincinnati House of Refuge	Cincinnati, O	"
New York Juvenile Asylum	New York city	1851
Lowell Reform School	Lowell, Mass	"
State Reform School	Portland, Me	1853
State Reform School	Meriden, Conn	"
Pennsylvania Reform School	Morganza, Pa	1854
House of Refuge	St Louis, Mo	"
Cambridge Truant School	North Cambridge, Mass	"
Reform School	Lansing, Mich	1855
State Industrial School for Girls	Lancaster, Mass	1856
Brooklyn Truant Home	Brooklyn, N Y	"
Boys' Industrial School	Lancaster, O	1857
State Industrial School	Manchester, N H	"
Industrial School	San Francisco Cal	1859
Wisconsin Industrial School for Boys	Milwaukee, Wis	1860
Detroit House of Correction	Detroit, Mich	1862
Worcester Truant School	Worcester, Mass	1863
New York Catholic Protectory	Westchester, N Y	"
Vermont Reform School	Vergennes, Vt	1865
St Mary's Industrial School for Boys	Carroll, Md	1866
Massachusetts State Primary School	Palmer, Mass	"
Convent of the Good Shepherd	Newport, Ky	"
New Jersey State Reform School for Boys	Jamesburg, N J	1867
Minnesota State Reform School	St Paul Minn	1868
Indiana Reform School for Boys.	Plainfield Ind	"
Truant School	Boston, Mass	1869
Plummer Farm School	Salem, Mass	1870
Reform School Dist of Columbia	Washington, D C	"
State Industrial School for Girls	Trenton, N J	1871
Reform School for Girls and Woman's Prison	Indianapolis, Ind	1873
Iowa Industrial School, Girls' Department	Mitchellville, Ia	1874
Lawrence Industrial School	Lawrence, Mass	"
Newark City Home	Verona, N J	"
Wisconsin Industrial School for Girls	Milwaukee, Wis	1875
New York State Reformatory	Elmira, N Y	1876
State House of Correction and Reformatory	Ionia, Mich	1877
Marcella Street Home	Boston, Mass	"
Illinois Industrial School for Girls	South Evanston, Ill	1878
New Bedford Truant School	New Bedford, Mass	1879
State Industrial Home for Girls	Adrian, Mich	"
State Industrial School	Golden, Col	1880
Kansas State Reform School	Topeka, Kan	1881
State Industrial School for Juvenile Offenders	Kearney, Neb	"
Massachusetts Reformatory	Concord, Mass	1884
Pennsylvania Reformatory	Huntington, Penn	1885
Burnham Industrial Farm	Canaan Four Corners, N Y	1887
Dakota Reform School	Plankinton, S Dak	1889

Reformed church in America. The Reformed Protestant Dutch church arose in the Netherlands early in the 16th century. "The Belgic Confession," published in 1561 by Guido de Bres, was adopted by the first synod at Wesel on the Rhine, in 1568. The Reformed church in America was organized on Manhattan island by rev. Jonas Michaelius, with about 50 members, in 1628

Michaelius succeeded by rev Everardus Bogardus, and a small church erected in Broad street, New York city	1633
Second church erected within the walls of Fort Amsterdam	1642
English language introduced in the church service	1763
Rutger's college, near New Brunswick, N J, established	1770
Reformed Dutch church in America adopts a constitution embracing the church orders of the synod of Dort.	1794

Christian Intelligencer, organ of the Reformed Dutch church, established in New York city 1828
Reformed church established in the western states, and strengthened by colonists from the Netherlands about 1835
Hope college Holland, Mich established 1865
Word "Dutch" dropped from the corporate name at general synod held at Geneva, N Y 20 Nov 1867
Present strength of Reformed church of America 570 churches, 582 ministers, 94,323 members June, 1891

Reformed church in the United States formerly known as the German Reformed church, was formed principally of peasants of the PALATINATE, driven from their homes, and sent to America by charity of queen Anne 1689-1697 They settled mostly in Pennsylvania and New York, and the first *coetus*, or ministerial conference, of the church was held at Philadelphia in 1746

First synod at Lancaster Pa 1793
Classes or presbyteries introduced 1820
First theological seminary opened at Carlisle, Pa 1825
Marshall college founded at Mercersburg Pa 1835
Rev dr Philip Schaff of Berlin installed professor of church history and biblical literature in Marshall college 1844
Marshall college united with Franklin college at Lancaster, Pa 1853
Word "German" erased from church title 1869
Theological seminary at Mercersburg removed to Lancaster Pa 1871
Society numbered 8 synods, 55 classes 835 ministers, 1554 congregations, 200,500 members in 1890

Reformed Episcopal church, founded in the United States in 1873, introduced into England 1877.

Dr Cummins, assistant bishop of Kentucky, after revising the prayer book, consecrated Cridge, Gregg, Cheney, and others, as bishops 1873
Dr Gregg and others ordained presbyters and formed churches here July, 1877, said to have 10 000 members April, 1878
Another bishop consecrated by dr Gregg at Southend 5 Nov "
"Book of Common Prayer" modified issued by dr Gregg early in 1879

regalia. CROWNS.

Regency, Albany (first so called by Thurlow Weed), a strong political Democratic combination which largely controlled not only the nominating conventions and other machinery of that party in the state of New York from 1820 to 1850, but it was almost as potential in national politics as well. Among its members were Martin Van Buren, William L Marcy, Samuel L Talcott, John A Dix, A C Flagg, Silas Wright, and others, with the Albany *Argus* to enforce its views.

Regency bills of the English government. One was passed 1751 One was proposed to Parliament in consequence of the mental illness of George III, and debated 10 Dec 1788 It was relinquished on his recovery, 26 Feb 1789 The return of the malady led to the prince of Wales (afterwards George IV) being sworn in before the privy council as regent of the kingdom, 5 Feb 1811 The Regency bill providing for the administration of the government, should the crown descend to the princess Victoria while under 18 years of age, passed 1 Will IV 23 Dec 1830 A Regency bill appointing prince Albert regent in the event of the demise of the queen, should her next lineal successor be under age, passed 4 Aug 1840

reg'icides (Lat *rex*, a king, and *caedere*, to kill, the killing or murder of a king), those who put a king to death In English history, 150 commissioners appointed to try king Charles I, of whom 70 acted, and 59 signed the death-warrant, Jan. 1649 Of these 29 were tried, and 13 executed Harrison, 13 Oct., Carew, 15 Oct, Cook and Peters, 16 Oct, Scott, Scroop, Clement, and Jones, 17 Oct, Axtell and Hacker, 19 Oct 1660 Barkstead, Corbet, and Okey arrested at the Hague, Holland, and executed 19 Apr 1662 3 of them, Goffe, Whalley, and Dixwell, came to the New England colonies, and were successfully concealed from arrest. MASSACHUSETTS, 1660-75. Others were imprisoned More than 20 who were dead were tried, and 3 of them, Cromwell, Ireton, and Bradshaw, were exhumed and hung at Tyburn.

OTHER REGICIDES

James I of Scotland, by nobles 20 Feb 1437
James III " " 11 June, 1488
Henry III of France, by Clement, 1 Aug, d 2 Aug 1589
Henry IV " by Ravaillac 14 May, 1610
Louis XVI " by convention 21 Jan 1793
Gustavus III of Sweden, by Ankarstrom, 16 Mch, d 29 Mch 1792
Paul of Russia, by nobles 24 Mch 1801
Alexander II of Russia, by nihilists 13 Mch 1881

regiments of infantry bodies of foot-soldiers commanded by a colonel, now usually divided into 10 companies, were formed in France about 1588 INFANTRY The following are the approximate dates of the establishment of several British regiments

CAVALRY

Oxford Blues are erroneously ascribed to the reign of Henry VIII, named for their colonel the earl of Oxford, in 1661
Three Hindu regiments (19th, 20th and 21st) added Aug "
Dragoon Guards, the Royal Irish and the Scots Greys were formed by James II about 1684-86
Several regiments of Light Dragoons were armed with lances and termed "Lancers" Sept 1816

INFANTRY

1st Royal or Royal Scots regiment, 1633, the old title resumed Dec 1871
Coldstream Guards, established by Monk in 1660
3d Buffs, represent London train bands, and have special privileges
2d Queen's Royal 1661
4th King's Own 1685
5th Northumberland Fusiliers
26th Cameronian 1689
100th Canadian 1858
101st to 109th (Hindu) added Aug 1861
Highland regiments are the 42d, 71st, 72d 78th, 79th, 92d, and 93d
For the United States, ARMY

regium donum ("royal gift"), an allowance from the sovereign for the maintenance of the Presbyterian ministers in Ireland, commenced by Charles II in 1672, and revived by William III in 1690, was commuted by the Irish Church act passed June, 1871. The allowance to certain Protestant dissenting ministers in Ireland was given up by them in 1857, in deference to the wishes of English dissenters

Regulators. NORTH CAROLINA, 1768-71

Reichenbach (*ri'ken-bak*) a town in Prussian Silesia Here Duroc, Napoleon's chief of staff was killed during the conflicts between the French and the allies, 22 May, 1813 BAUTZEN Here was signed a subsidy *treaty between Russia*, Prussia, and England, whereby the last engaged to provide means for carrying on the war against Napoleon I on certain conditions, 14-15 June, 1813 Austria joined the alliance soon after

Reichsrath (*riks'rat*), the representative council of the empire of Austria, several times changed reconstituted by decree 5 Mch, met on 31 May, 1860 In May, 1861, the upper house consisted of 17 spiritual, 55 hereditary, and 39 peers The lower house consisted of 136 elected deputies. No representatives came from Hungary, Transylvania, Venetia, the Banat, Slavonia, Croatia, and Istria The Reichsrath was abolished by a rescript, 21 Sept 1865, with the view of restoring autonomy to Hungary and other provinces It again met 20 May, 1867 Now constituted (1894) of 2 houses, upper and lower The upper house consists of members of the royal family over 19 years of age, of the nobility, of church dignitaries (archbishops and bishops), of distinguished scientists nominated by the emperor, in all, 113 members Lower house, elected by the people for 6 years, numbers 353 members The emperor nominates president and vice-president of the upper house, the lower house elects its own officers Bills to become laws must pass both houses, and receive the sanction of the head of the state

Reichstag (*rik'stag*), diet or parliament of the German empire, is composed of 397 deputies elected by universal suffrage for the term of 5 years

reign of terror. Maximilien Robespierre headed the populace in the Champ de Mars, in Paris, demanding the dethronement of the king, 17 July, 1791. He was triumphant in 1793, and numbers of eminent men and citizens were sacrificed during his sanguinary administration. Billaud Varennes denounced the tyranny of Robespierre in the tribune, 27 July, 1794 The next day Robespierre suffered death, with many of his companions FRENCH REVOLUTION This has been termed the Red Terror The reaction after the restoration of the Bourbons, 1815, disgraced by many atrocious acts of wanton cruelty, has been termed the White Terror The Jesuits were conspicuous in the destruction of their enemies

reigning families of Europe Nations separately

reigns of sovereigns. The average duration, according to Newton, is 19 years, according to Hales, $22\frac{1}{2}$ years;

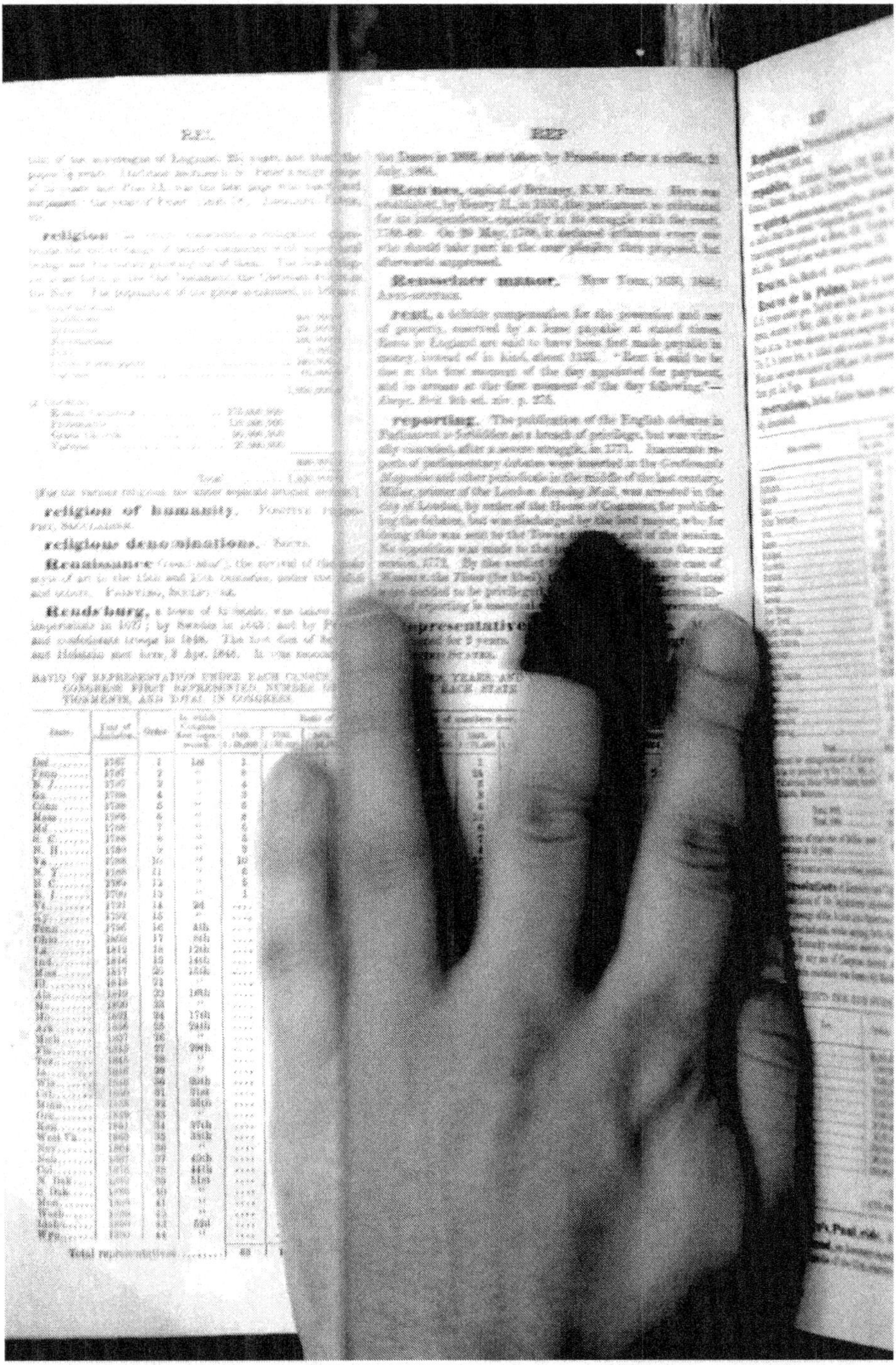

[illegible]

religion of humanity. POSITIVE PHILOSOPHY, SAINT-SIMONISM.

religious denominations. SECTS.

Renaissance (French, *new birth*), the revival of the classic style of art in the 15th and 16th centuries, under [illegible] and others. PAINTING, SCULPTURE, etc.

Rendsburg, a town of Schleswig, was taken [illegible] imperialists in 1627; by Swedes in 1643; and by P[illegible] and confederate troops in 1848. The first diet of S[illegible] and Holstein met here, 3 Apr. 1848. It was [illegible]

RATIO OF REPRESENTATION UNDER EACH CENSUS [illegible] CONGRESS FIRST REPRESENTED, NUMBER [illegible] TIONMENTS, AND TOTAL IN CONGRESS.

[illegible]

[illegible] July, 1866.

Rennes, capital of Brittany, N.W. France. Here was established, by Henry II., in 1553, the parliament so celebrated for its independence, especially in its struggle with the court, 1788-89. On 20 May, 1788, it declared infamous every one who should take part in the cour plénière then proposed, but afterwards suppressed.

Rensselaer manor. New York, 1630, 1845; ANTI-RENTERS.

rent, a definite compensation for the possession and use of property, reserved by a lease payable at stated times. Rents in England are said to have been first made payable in money, instead of in kind, about 1135. "Rent is said to be due at the first moment of the day appointed for payment, and in arrears at the first moment of the day following."—*Encyc. Brit.* 9th ed. xiv. p. 375.

reporting. The publication of the English debates in Parliament is forbidden as a breach of privilege, but was virtually conceded, after a severe struggle, in 1771. Inaccurate reports of parliamentary debates were inserted in the *Gentleman's Magazine* and other periodicals in the middle of the last century. Miller, printer of the London *Evening Post*, was arrested in the city of London, by order of the House of Commons, for publishing the debates, but was discharged by the lord mayor, who for doing this was sent to the Tower [illegible] of the session. No opposition was made to the [illegible] the next session, 1772. By the verdict [illegible] the case of Wason v. the *Times* (the libel [illegible] debates [illegible] entitled to be privileg[illegible] reporting is essential [illegible]

representative [illegible]

Republicans. POLITICAL PARTIES; POPULAR VOTE; UNITED STATES, 1856, etc.

republics. ATHENS; FRANCE, 1792, 1848, 1870; GENOA; ROME; SPAIN, 1873; UNITED STATES; VENICE.

re'quiem, a solemn mass, sung on 2 Nov., All-Souls' Day, so called from the introit "Requiem Æternam," etc. Palestrina's requiem was printed at Rome, 1591; Vittoria's at Madrid, 1605. Mozart's last work was a requiem, 1791.

Resa'ca, Ga., Battle of. ATLANTA CAMPAIGN.

Resa'ca de la Palma, Battle of, between the U. S. troops under gen. Taylor and the Mexicans under gen. Arista, occurred 9 May, 1846, the day after the conflict at PALO ALTO. It was shorter, but more sanguinary than that. The U. S. forces lost, in killed and wounded, 110 men. The Mexican loss was estimated at 1000, and 100 prisoners; among them gen. La Vega. MEXICAN WAR.

reservations, Indian, United States (area being rapidly diminished).

State or territory.	Area.	
	Sq. miles.	Acres.
Arizona	10,317	6,603,191
California	772	494,045
Colorado	1,710	1,094,400
Idaho	3,552	2,273,421
Indian Territory	40,411	25,863,372
Iowa	2	1,258
Kansas	159	102,026
Michigan	42	27,319
Minnesota	3,523	2,254,781
Montana	16,349	10,591,360
Nebraska	214	136,947
Nevada	1,400	954,135
[illegible]ew Mexico	15,630	10,002,528
[illegible]w York	137	87,677
[illegible]th Carolina	102	65,211
[illegible]th Dakota	9,158	5,861,120
[illegible]homa	20,779	13,292,668
[illegible]	3,242	2,075,240
[illegible] Dakota	18,221	11,661,360
[illegible]	......	....
[illegible]	6,207	3,972,480
[illegible]ngton	6,321	4,045,284
[illegible]nsin	800	512,120
[illegible]ing	2,560	2,342,400
Total	162,988	104,314,349
[illegible] by extinguishment of Indian [illegible] purchase by the U. S., 1891, in [illegible]ma, Idaho, North Dakota, South [illegible] Montana	12,757	8,164,786
Total, 1892	150,231	96,149,563
Total, 1880	241,800	154,741,349
[illegible] total area of Indian reser-[illegible] 12 years	91,569	58,591,766

[illegible]on of Indian tribes, population, etc., INDIANS.]

[illegible]**tions** of Kentucky and Virginia of 1798. These [illegible] the legislatures expressed dissatisfaction with [illegible] the ALIEN AND SEDITION LAWS, declaring them [illegible]nal, while setting forth the state-rights theory. [illegible] resolutions asserted the right of any state to [illegible] of Congress deemed unconstitutional. The [illegible]tion was drawn by Madison, the Kentucky resolution by Jefferson, with the understanding that his name was not to be divulged.

res'onnor, a small apparatus placed in the mouth to increase the tone of the voice in singing, invented by signor Alberto Bach, who exhibited it at the Royal Academy of Music, 29 June, 80.

restoraon, The, of king Charles II. to the crown of England, after an interregnum of 11 years and 4 months, between 30 Jn. 1649, when Charles I. was beheaded, and 29 May, 1660, when Charles II. entered London amid acclamations. The annual form of prayer, with thanksgiving, then appointed, was abolished by 22 Vict. c. 2, 25 Mch. 1859. FRANCE, 1814.

retreat of the French from Moscow (1812), the most disastrous known to history. BEREZINA, FRANCE, MOSCOW, RUSSIA.

retreat of the ten thousand Greeks, who had joined the younger Cyrus in revolt against his brother, Artaxerxes Mnemon. The Greeks were victors, but Cyrus was defeated and slain at the battle of CUNAXA, 401 B.C. Artaxerxes having enticed the Greek leaders into his power and killed them, Xenophon was called to command. Under continual alarms from sudden attacks, he led them across rapid rivers, through deserts, over mountains, to the sea. The march of 1155 parasangs or leagues (3465 miles) was performed in 215 days. This retreat has been immortalized by Xenophon's account, the "Anabasis Cyri" (Expedition of Cyrus).

Revelsion. APOCALYPSE.

revenue, In this connection, the annual income of a state derived from taxation, customs and other sources, to be appropriated to governmental expenditures. In England, the revenue collected for the civil list and the other charges of government, ordinary and extraordinary, was 1,200,000*l.* per annum in 1660, the first after the restoration of Charles II. In 1690 it was 6,000,000*l.*, every branch of the revenue being anticipated; this was the origin of the funds and the national debt, 2 William and Mary.—*Salmon.* The revenue laws were amended in 1861, and frequently since.

TOTAL PUBLIC YEARLY REVENUE OF ENGLAND UP TO THE UNION IN THE REIGNS SHOWN, AND OF THE UNITED KINGDOM OF GREAT BRITAIN FOR THE YEARS GIVEN.

William I.	£400,000	George IV., 1825	£62,871,300
Henry VI.	64,976	William IV., 1835	50,494,732
Elizabeth	500,000	Victoria, 1845	53,060,354
Charles I.	900,000	" 1855	63,364,605
Commonwealth	1,517,247	" 1865	70,313,437
William III.	4,000,000	" 1875	74,921,873
Anne at the union	5,600,000	" 1882	85,100,000
George III., 1788	15,572,971	" 1887	89,860,000
George III., 1800	38,000,000	" 1891	87,610,000
George IV., 1820, United Kingdom	65,599,570		

revenue of the United States. The principal sources of revenue of the U. S. are, customs, internal revenue, sale of public lands and miscellaneous receipts; premiums on bonds sold were also counted as revenue from 1864 to 1873. EXPENDITURE, INCOME-TAX, TARIFF and TAX.

[illegible] FROM EACH SOURCE IN EACH OF THE YEARS NAMED; ALSO GROWTH OF REVENUE FROM 1789.

	Customs.	Internal revenue.	Sale of public lands.	Prizes.	Miscellaneous.	Others. Direct tax, interest, dividends.	Total revenue.
[illegible]	$4,399,473	......	......	....	$10,478	......	$4,409,951
[illegible]	9,080,933	$809,397	$444	....	152,712	$805,264	10,848,749
[illegible]	8,583,309	7,431	696,549	....	84,477	12,449	9,384,214
[illegible]	15,005,612	106,261	1,635,872	[illegible],000	61,338	1,031,587	17,840,670
[illegible]	21,922,391	12,161	2,329,356	....	73,228	506,981	24,844,117
[illegible]	13,499,502	1,682	3,411,819	....	2,567,112	......	19,480,115
[illegible]	39,668,686	......	1,859,894	[illegible],350	2,064,308	......	48,592,839
[illegible]	53,187,512	......	1,778,558	[illegible],008	1,088,530	......	56,064,008
[illegible]	194,538,374	184,899,756	3,350,482	[illegible],644	12,942,118	229,103	411,255,478
[illegible]	186,522,065	124,009,375	1,016,507	110	21,978,525	31	333,526,611
[illegible]	229,668,585	142,606,706	6,358,273	...	24,447,420	......	403,080,983
REVENUE RECEIPTS FROM 1789 TO [illegible] INCLUSIVE.							
	6,751,088,381	4,111,760,798	280,505,641	[illegible]9,221	670,565,471	38,337,830	12,065,416,863

[illegible]**l, ride.** MASSACHUSETTS, Apr. 1775.

[illegible]norary appellation given to the clergy [illegible] 17th century.

In Tamwor[illegible] parish register the minister is first styled "reverend" [illegible]57, occasionally afterwards; regularly after 1727.

It first appears in the registry of All-Hallows, Barking 1732

Prefix on a [illegible]ly tombstone was refused to Mr. Keet, a Wes-

that of the sovereigns of England, 23½ years, and that of the popes 7½ years. Tradition ascribes to St. Peter a reign as pope of 25 years, and Pius IX. was the first pope who reached and surpassed "the years of Peter" (1846–78). ENGLAND, FRANCE, etc.

religion (Lat. *religio*, conscientious obligation) comprehends the entire range of beliefs connected with supernatural beings, and the duties growing out of them. The Jewish religion is set forth in the Old Testament, the Christian religion in the New. The population of the globe is claimed, in 1890, as:

(1) Non-Christian:		
Buddhists		400,000,000
Brahmins		250,000,000
Mahometans		180,000,000
Jews		8,000,000
Fetish worshippers		150,000,000
Various		62,000,000
		1,050,000,000
(2) Christian:		
Roman Catholics	175,000,000	
Protestants	110,000,000	
Greek Church	90,000,000	
Various	25,000,000	
		400,000,000
Total		1,450,000,000

[For the various religions, see under separate articles, sects, etc.]

religion of humanity. POSITIVE PHILOSOPHY, SECULARISM.

religious denominations. SECTS.

Renaissance (*re-nā-säns'*), the revival of the classic style of art in the 15th and 16th centuries, under the Medici and others. PAINTING, SCULPTURE.

Rends'burg, a town of Holstein, was taken by the imperialists in 1627; by Swedes in 1643; and by Prussians and confederate troops in 1848. The first diet of Schleswig and Holstein met here, 3 Apr. 1848. It was reoccupied by the Danes in 1852, and taken by Prussians after a conflict, 21 July, 1864.

Ren'nes, capital of Brittany, N.W. France. Here was established, by Henry II., in 1553, the parliament so celebrated for its independence, especially in its struggle with the court, 1788–89. On 20 May, 1788, it declared infamous every one who should take part in the *cour plenière* then proposed, but afterwards suppressed.

Rensselaer manor. NEW YORK, 1630, 1844; ANTI-RENTISM.

rent, a definite compensation for the possession and use of property, reserved by a lease payable at stated times. Rents in England are said to have been first made payable in money, instead of in kind, about 1135. "Rent is said to be due at the first moment of the day appointed for payment, and in arrears at the first moment of the day following."—*Encyc. Brit.* 9th ed. xiv. p. 275.

reporting. The publication of the English debates in Parliament is forbidden as a breach of privilege, but was virtually conceded, after a severe struggle, in 1771. Inaccurate reports of parliamentary debates were inserted in the *Gentleman's Magazine* and other periodicals in the middle of the last century. Miller, printer of the London *Evening Mail*, was arrested in the city of London, by order of the House of Commons, for publishing the debates, but was discharged by the lord mayor, who for doing this was sent to the Tower until the end of the session. No opposition was made to the publication of debates the next session, 1772. By the verdict for the defendant in the case of Wason *v.* the *Times* (for libel), reports of parliamentary debates were decided to be privileged, Nov. 1868. The unfettered liberty of reporting is essential to freedom and good government.

Representatives, House of, United States. Members elected for 2 years. For speakers, see each Congress under UNITED STATES.

RATIO OF REPRESENTATION UNDER EACH CENSUS, NUMBER OF STATES, YEARS, AND ORDER OF ADMISSION, IN WHICH CONGRESS FIRST REPRESENTED, NUMBER OF MEMBERS FROM EACH STATE UNDER THE DIFFERENT APPORTIONMENTS, AND TOTAL IN CONGRESS.

State.	Year of admission.	Order.	In which Congress first represented.	Ratio of representation, and number of members from each state under each census.											
				1789. 1:30,000	1793. 1:33,000	1803. 1:33,000	1813. 1:35,000	1823. 1:40,000	1833. 1:47,700	1843. 1:70,680	1853. 1:93,423	1863. 1:127,381	1873. 1:131,425	1883. 1:151,911	1893. 1:173,901
Del.	1787	1	1st	1	1	1	2	1	1	1	1	1	1	1	1
Penn.	1787	2	"	8	13	18	23	26	28	24	25	24	27	28	30
N. J.	1787	3	"	4	5	6	6	6	6	5	5	5	7	7	8
Ga.	1788	4	"	3	2	4	6	7	9	8	8	7	9	10	11
Conn.	1788	5	"	5	7	7	7	6	6	4	4	4	4	4	4
Mass.	1788	6	"	8	14	17	20	13	12	10	11	10	11	12	13
Md.	1788	7	"	6	8	9	9	9	8	6	6	5	6	6	6
S. C.	1788	8	"	5	6	8	9	9	9	7	6	4	5	7	7
N. H.	1788	9	"	3	4	5	6	6	5	4	3	3	3	2	2
Va.	1788	10	"	10	19	22	23	22	21	15	13	11	9	10	10
N. Y.	1788	11	"	6	10	17	27	34	40	34	33	31	33	34	34
N. C.	1789	12	"	5	10	12	13	13	13	9	8	7	8	9	9
R. I.	1790	13	"	1	2	2	2	2	2	2	2	2	2	2	2
Vt.	1791	14	2d	....	2	4	6	5	5	4	3	3	3	2	2
Ky.	1792	15	"	....	2	6	10	12	13	10	10	9	10	11	11
Tenn.	1796	16	4th	....	....	3	6	9	13	11	10	8	10	10	10
Ohio.	1803	17	8th	....	....	....	6	14	19	21	21	19	20	21	21
La.	1812	18	12th	....	....	....	....	3	3	4	4	5	6	6	6
Ind.	1816	19	14th	....	....	....	....	3	7	10	11	11	13	13	13
Miss.	1817	20	15th	....	....	....	....	1	2	4	5	5	6	7	7
Ill.	1818	21	"	....	....	....	....	1	3	7	9	14	19	20	22
Ala.	1819	22	16th	....	....	....	....	3	5	7	7	6	8	8	9
Me.	1820	23	"	....	....	....	....	7	8	7	6	5	5	4	4
Mo.	1821	24	17th	....	....	....	....	1	2	5	7	9	13	14	15
Ark.	1836	25	24th	....	....	....	....	....	....	1	2	3	4	5	6
Mich.	1837	26	"	....	....	....	....	....	....	3	4	6	9	11	12
Fla.	1845	27	29th	....	....	....	....	....	....	....	1	1	2	2	2
Tex.	1845	28	"	....	....	....	....	....	....	....	2	4	6	11	13
Ia.	1846	29	"	....	....	....	....	....	....	....	2	6	9	11	11
Wis.	1848	30	30th	....	....	....	....	....	....	....	3	6	8	9	10
Cal.	1850	31	31st	....	....	....	....	....	....	....	2	3	4	6	7
Minn.	1858	32	35th	....	....	....	....	....	....	....	2	2	3	5	7
Ore.	1859	33	"	....	....	....	....	....	....	....	1	1	1	1	2
Kan.	1861	34	37th	....	....	....	....	....	....	....	....	1	3	7	8
West Va.	1863	35	38th	....	....	....	....	....	....	....	....	....	3	4	4
Nev.	1864	36	"	....	....	....	....	....	....	....	....	1		1	1
Neb.	1867	37	40th	....	....	....	....	....	....	....	....	1	1	3	6
Col.	1876	38	44th	....	....	....	....	....	....	....	....	..	1	1	2
N. Dak.	1889	39	51st	....	....	....	....	....	....	....	....	....	....	....	1
S. Dak.	1889	40	"	....	....	....	....	....	....	....	....	....	....	....	2
Mon.	1889	41	"	....	....	....	....	....	....	....	....	....	....	....	1
Wash.	1889	42	"	....	....	....	....	....	....	....	....	....	....	....	2
Idaho.	1890	43	52d	....	....	....	....	....	....	....	....	....	....	....	1
Wyo.	1890	44	"	....	....	....	....	....	....	....	....	....	....	....	1
Total representatives				65	105	141	181	213	240	223	237	243	293	325	356

Republicans. Political parties; Popular vote; ited States, 1856, etc.

'epublics. Athens; France, 1792, 1848, 1870; noa; Rome; Spain, 1873; United States; Venice.

'e'quiem, a solemn mass, sung on 2 Nov., All-Souls' Day, called from the introit "Requiem Æternam," etc. Palesıa's requiem was printed at Rome, 1591; Vittoria's at Ma-1, 1605. Mozart's last work was a requiem, 1791.

Resa'ca, Ga., Battle of. Atlanta campaign.

Resa'ca de la Palma, Battle of, between the S. troops under gen. Taylor and the Mexicans under gen. sta, occurred 9 May, 1846, the day after the conflict at lo Alto. It was shorter, but more sanguinary than that. e U. S. forces lost, in killed and wounded, 110 men. The xican loss was estimated at 1000, and 100 prisoners; among m gen. La Vega. Mexican war.

reservations, Indian, United States (area being rap-ʏ diminished).

State or territory.	Area.	
	Sq. miles.	Acres.
zona	10,317	6,603,191
ifornia	772	494,045
orado	1,710	1,094,400
ho	3,552	2,273,421
ian Territory	40,411	25,863,372
'a	2	1,258
nsas	159	102,026
chigan	42	27,319
inesota	3,523	2,254,781
ntana	16,549	10,591,360
oraska	214	136,947
vada	1,490	954,135
w Mexico	15,629	10,002,525
w York	137	87,677
rth Carolina	102	65,211
rth Dakota	9,158	5,861,120
lahoma	20,770	13,292,668
gon	3,242	2,075,240
ith Dakota	18,221	11,661,360
xas	.....	....
ıh	6,207	3,972,480
shington	6,321	4,045,284
sconsin	800	512,129
'oming	3,660	2,342,400
Total	162,988	104,314,349
duced by extinguishment of Indian title by purchase by the U. S., 1891, in Oklahoma, Idaho, North Dakota, South Dakota, Montana	12,757	8,164,766
Total, 1892	150,231	96,149,583
Total, 1880	241,800	154,741,349
duction of total area of Indian reservations in 12 years	91,569	58,591,766

(For location of Indian tribes, population, etc., Indians.)

resolutions of Kentucky and Virginia of 1798. These olutions of the legislatures expressed dissatisfaction with e passage of the Alien and Sedition laws, declaring them constitutional, while setting forth the state-rights theory. e Kentucky resolutions asserted the right of any state to llify any act of Congress deemed unconstitutional. The rginia resolution was drawn by Madison, the Kentucky resolution by Jefferson, with the understanding that his name was not to be divulged.

res'onator, a small apparatus, placed in the mouth to increase the volume of the voice in singing, invented by signor Alberto Bach, who exhibited it at the Royal Academy of Music, 29 June, 1880.

restoration, The, of king Charles II. to the crown of England, after an interregnum of 11 years and 4 months, between 30 Jan. 1649, when Charles I. was beheaded, and 29 May, 1660, when Charles II. entered London amid acclamations. The annual form of prayer, with thanksgiving, then appointed, was abolished by 22 Vict. c. 2, 25 Mch. 1849. France, 1814-15.

retreat of the French from Moscow (1812), the most disastrous known to history. Beresina, France, Moscow, Russia.

retreat of the ten thousand Greeks, who had joined the younger Cyrus in revolt against his brother, Artaxerxes Mnemon. The Greeks were victors, but Cyrus was defeated and slain at the battle of Cunaxa, 401 b.c. Artaxerxes having enticed the Greek leaders into his power and killed them, Xenophon was called to command. Under continual alarms from sudden attacks, he led them across rapid rivers, through deserts, over mountains, to the sea. The march of 1155 parasangs or leagues (3465 miles) was performed in 215 days. This retreat has been immortalized by Xenophon's account, the "Anabasis Cyri" (Expedition of Cyrus).

Revelation. Apocalypse.

revenue, in this connection, the annual income of a state derived from taxation, customs, and other sources, to be appropriated to governmental expenditures. In England, the revenue collected for the civil list and the other charges of government, ordinary and extraordinary, was 1,200,000*l.* per annum in 1660, the first after the restoration of Charles II. In 1690 it was 6,000,000*l.*, every branch of the revenue being anticipated; this was the origin of the funds and the national debt, 2 William and Mary.—*Salmon.* The revenue laws were amended in 1861, and frequently since.

TOTAL PUBLIC YEARLY REVENUE OF ENGLAND UP TO THE UNION FOR THE REIGNS SHOWN, AND OF THE UNITED KINGDOM OF GREAT BRITAIN FOR THE YEARS GIVEN.

William I.	£400,000	George IV., 1825	£62,871,300
Henry VI.	64,976	William IV., 1835	50,494,732
Elizabeth	500,000	Victoria, 1845	53,060,354
Charles I.	900,000	" 1855	63,364,605
Commonwealth	1,517,247	" 1865	70,313,437
William III.	4,000,000	" 1875	74,921,873
Anne at the Union	6,000,000	" 1882	85,190,000
George III., 1788	15,572,971	" 1887	89,869,000
George III., 1800	38,000,000	" 1891	87,610,000
George IV., 1820, United Kingdom	65,599,570		

revenue of the United States. The principal sources of revenue in the U. S. are, customs, internal revenue, sale of public lands, and miscellaneous receipts; premiums on bonds sold were also counted as revenue from 1864 to 1873. Expenditures, Income-tax, Tariff and Tax.

RECEIPTS FROM EACH SOURCE IN EACH OF THE YEARS NAMED. ALSO GROWTH OF REVENUE FROM 1789.

Year.	Customs.	Internal revenue.	Sale of public lands.	Premiums.	Miscellaneous.	Others. Direct tax, interest, dividends.	Total revenue.
1789	$4,399,473	......	......	......	$10,478	......	$4,409,951
1800	9,080,933	$809,397	$444	......	152,712	$805,264	10,848,749
1810	8,583,309	7,431	696,549	......	84,477	12,449	9,384,214
1820	15,005,612	106,261	1,635,872	$40,000	61,338	1,031,587	17,840,670
1830	21,922,391	12,161	2,329,356	......	73,228	506,981	24,844,117
1840	13,499,502	1,682	3,411,819	......	2,567,112		19,480,115
1850	39,668,686	......	1,859,894	10,550	2,064,308	......	43,592,889
1860	53,187,512	......	1,778,558	10,008	1,088,530	......	56,064,008
1870	194,538,374	184,899,756	3,350,482	15,295,644	12,942,118	229,103	411,255,478
1880	186,522,065	124,009,375	1,016,507	110	21,978,525	31	333,526,611
1890	229,668,585	142,606,706	6,358,273	......	24,447,420	......	403,080,983
REVENUE RECEIPTS FROM 1789 TO 1891 INCLUSIVE.							
....	6,751,088,381	4,111,760,798	280,505,641	204,259,221	679,565,471	38,337,350	12,065,416,863

Revere's, Paul, ride. Massachusetts, Apr. 1775.

reverend, an honorary appellation given to the clergy ıce the middle of the 17th century.

In Tamworth parish register the minister is first styled "reverend" in 1657, occasionally afterwards; regularly after 1727.
It first appears in the registry of All-Hallows, Barking...... 1732
Prefix on a family tombstone was refused to Mr. Keet, a Wes-

leyan preacher, by the bishop of Lincoln, but permitted by the archbishop of Canterbury....1874
On trial, Walter G. F. Phillimore, the chancellor of Lincoln, decided against Mr. Keet, who gave notice of appeal, 3 June. Sir R. Phillimore gave a similar decision in the Court of Arches....31 July, 1875
On appeal to the privy council, it was decided that there is no law or usage restricting the epithet to ministers of the Church of England; it is merely complimentary.....21 Jan. 1876

reviews, periodicals established for the purpose of critically examining new publications, or topics of science, art, etc. The *Journal des Sçavans*, published on 5 Jan. 1665, by Denis de Salo, under the name of Hédouville, was the parent of critical journals. It was imitated throughout Europe, was translated into various languages, and is still published. The *Bibliothèque Anglaise* came out 1716-27. CRITICS, MAGAZINES AND REVIEWS.

revivals of religion, a sudden increase of spiritual activity in the Protestant church of English-speaking people. In Scotland, 1625, '30, '42; Wesley and Whitefield, 1738-42; Massachusetts, 1734; the "Great Awakening" throughout the American colonies, 1740; and again in 1797-1808, principally in New England; and a third throughout the United States, 1857-58; a fourth, national revival under the leadership of Moody and Sankey, 1875-76.

Revolution, American. CONNECTICUT; MASSACHUSETTS; NEW YORK, etc.; UNITED STATES, 1775-82.

Revolution, American, Last survivors of:

Lemuel Cook, b. Plymouth, Litchfield county, Conn., 1764; d. Clarendon, Orleans county, N. Y., 1866.
William Hutchings, b. York, Me., 1764; d. York, Me., 1866.
Samuel Downing, b. 1766; d. Saratoga county, N. Y., 1867.
John Gray, b. 1764; d. Noble county, O., 1869.
Daniel F. Bakeman, b. 1760; d. Cattaraugus county, N. Y., 1869.

revolutionary calendar. CALENDAR, FRENCH REVOLUTION.

revolutionary tribunal, established at Paris, Aug. 1792.

By 27 July, 1794, when Robespierre was deposed, it had put to death 2774 persons, including queen Marie Antoinette, the princess Elizabeth, and a large number of nobility and gentry, male and female. The oldest victim was counsellor Dupin, aged 97; the youngest, Charles Dubost, aged 14. From 27 July to 15 Dec. 1794, only Robespierre and his accomplices (about 100) suffered by it.

revolutions, armed, concentrated, and successful resistance against existing government, producing a radical change in governmental conditions.

	B.C.
Assyrian empire destroyed, and that of the Medes and Persians founded by Cyrus the Great....	536
Macedonian empire founded on the destruction of the Persian of Darius Codomannus by Alexander the Great....	331
Roman empire established on the ruins of the republic by Julius Cæsar....	47
	A.D.
Empire of the western Franks begun under Charlemagne.....	800
In Portugal....	1640
In England....	1649 and 1688
In Russia....	1730 and 1762
In North America (REVOLUTION, AMERICAN)....	1775
In Venice....	1797
In Sweden....	1772 and 1809
In Holland, 1795; counter-revolution....	1813
In Poland....	1704, 1795, and 1830
In the Netherlands....	"
In Brunswick....	"
In Brazil....	1831, 1889
In Hungary....	1848
In Rome....	1798 and 1848
In France....	1789, 1830, 1848, 1851, 1870, and 1871
In Italy....	1859 and 1860
In Danubian principalities....	1866
In Papal States, suppressed....	Oct. 1867
In Spain....	Sept. 1868 and Dec. 1874

[See each country.]

revolvers. PISTOLS.

"Revue des Deux Mondes," a French literary and historical periodical published on the 1st and 15th of each month, first appeared in 1831. Its contributors are the most eminent writers in France.

Reynard the Fox, "Reineke Fuchs," a satirical epic in Low German, in which beasts are actors and speakers, was first printed as "Reineke Vos," at Lubeck, in 1498, and professes to be written by Hinreck van Alkmer. It has been frequently translated. Goethe's version in High (or literary) German hexameters appeared in 1794. Jacob Grimm has shown that the subject-matter of this "Thier-sage" or "beast-fable" is ancient, many incidents being found in Pilpay and other Oriental writers. The early French had a "Roman de Renart," and "Renart le Nouvel." A poem entitled "Der Reinaert," in Flemish, was known in the 11th century; Caxton's translation in English prose was printed 1481; a poetic English translation of Goethe's version, by T. J. Arnold, in 1855.

Rhæ'tia or **Ræ'tia,** an ancient Alpine country, comprising the modern Grisons, Tyrol, and part of Lombardy, inhabited by a wild, rapacious people. After a long struggle it was conquered by Drusus and Tiberius, 15 B.C.

Rhea. MYTHOLOGY.

Rhe'gium, now Reggio, S. Italy, a Greek colony, flourished in the 5th century B.C. It was held by the Campanian legion, 281-271, afterwards punished for rebellion. Reggio was taken by Garibaldi, Aug. 1860.

Rheims (*reemz*), or **Reims** (*răns*), a city of N. France. The principal church here, built before 406, rebuilt in the 12th century, is very beautiful. The corpse of St. Remy, the archbishop, is behind the high-altar, in a magnificent shrine. The kings of France were crowned at Rheims—probably because Clovis, founder of the French monarchy, when converted from paganism, was baptized in the cathedral in 496. Several ecclesiastical councils have been held here. The city was taken and retaken several times in the last months of the Napoleonic war, 1814. University founded by cardinal Lorraine, 1547, suppressed about 1790.

rhetoric (Gr. ῥητοριχή, from ῥέω, to flow, to speak fluently; hence ῥήτωρ, a speaker, orator, etc.). The art of constructing and applying discourse. Rhetorical points and accents were invented by Aristophanes of Byzantium, 200 B.C. Rhetoric was first taught in Latin at Rome by Plotius Gallus, about 87 B.C. He taught Cicero, who said, "We are first to consider what is to be said; secondly, how; thirdly, in what words; and lastly, how it is to be ornamented." A regius professor of rhetoric was appointed in Edinburgh, 20 Apr. 1762, dr. Blair being first professor.

Rhine (Lat. *Rhenus*, Ger. *Rhein*, Fr. *Rhin*), a river, about 760 miles long, rising in Switzerland, receiving the Moselle, Marne, Neckar, and other rivers, branching into many arms in Holland, and falling into the German ocean. On its banks are Constance, Basel, Strasburg, Spires, Mannheim, Cologne, Düsseldorf, Utrecht, and Leyden. The banks of the Rhine have been the cause of many wars, and it has been crossed by French armies more than 20 times in a century. In the beginning of the French revolution, Custine invaded Germany by crossing it in 1792; and at the close of the war in 1815 France retained the left bank, but lost it by the FRANCO-PRUSSIAN WAR, 1870-71. A navigation treaty with other powers was signed by France, 17 Oct. 1868. A central committee for navigation consists of members for Alsace, Lorraine, Baden, Bavaria, Hesse, Holland, and Prussia.

Becker's German song, "They shall not have it, the free German Rhine," and Alfred de Musset's reply, in French, "We have had it, your German Rhine," appeared in 1841. Max Schneckenburger, author of "The Watch on the Rhine," d. 1851. All were popular during the war, 1870-71.

rhine-stone, an imitation stone made of paste, invented at Strasburg in 1680, extensively used in the latter part of the 18th century.

Rhode Island, one of the 13 original states of the Union, and the smallest of the United States, is bounded on the north and east by Massachusetts, on the west by Connecticut, and on the south by the Atlantic ocean. Block island, about 9 miles from the mainland, is a portion of the state's territory. Area, 1250 sq. miles, in 5 counties; pop. 1890, 345,506; 1900, 428,556; Capital, Providence.

Roger Williams, banished from Plymouth colony, with 5 companions settles at a spot which he calls Providence....June, 1636
Aquedneck island settled by 18 proprietors at Portsmouth, now New Town, first called Pocasset....1637

ıuonicus and his nephew Miantunomo, sachems of the Narragansetts, deed to Roger Williams all lands between the Pawtucket and Pawtuxet rivers........................24 Mch. 1638

oger Williams and gov. Winthrop make a joint purchase of Prudence island..10 Nov. “

irst general training or militia muster in Rhode Island held at Portsmouth..12 Nov. “

irst Baptist church in America founded in Providence....... 1639

ɔhn Clarke and several proprietors of Aquedneck remove to the southern part of the island and found Newport......... “

ırst Baptist church in Newport founded.................... “

quedneck purchased from the Indians by “William Coddington and his friends”..............................23 Nov. “

ɔrm of government, 12 articles of agreement, framed and adopted by the inhabitants of Providence..........27 July, 1640

ev. Robert Lenthel called by vote to open a public school in Newport.. “

eneral Assembly asserts Rhode Island to be a democracy, *saving only the right of the king*, and grants freedom of religious opinions...Mch. 1641

our land-holders, 3 of them original proprietors, at Pawtuxet dissatisfied with the opposition of one Samuel Gorton and his partisans to the government, offer themselves and their lands to Massachusetts, and are received by the general court, 8 Sept. 1642

ımuel Gorton and his companions remove to Shawomet, where they had purchased lands from the Indians, and commence the settlement of Warwick (MASSACHUSETTS, 1643–48), 12 Jan. 1643

oger Williams is sent to England as agent for Providence, Aquedneck, and Warwick, to secure a charter from the king, “

ıtent granted by Robert, earl of Warwick, governor-in-chief and lord-high admiral, and commissioners, to planters of the towns of Providence, Portsmouth, and Newport, for incorporation of Providence plantations in Narragansett bay, 14 Mch. “

eneral court changes the name of Aquedneck to the “Isles of Rhodes” or Rhode Island..........................13 Mch. 1644

ant to John Smith to establish a grist-mill above Mill bridge in Providence, the first in Rhode Island.................... 1646

ommittees from Providence, Portsmouth, Newport, and Warwick at Portsmouth, adopt the charter of 1643, choose John Coggeshall president of the colony, and give a tax of 100*l.* to Roger Williams for obtaining the charter........19–21 May, 1647

ıonicus, sachem of the Narragansetts, d..............4 June, “

illiam Coddington receives from the council of state in England a commission, signed by John Bradshaw, to govern Rhode Island and Connecticut during his life, with a council of 6, to be named by the people and approved by himself. Authority procured 3 Apr. 1651, and asserted..........Aug. 1651

oger Williams sent as agent of Providence to obtain a confirmation of their charter, and dr. John Clarke, agent of Portsmouth and Newport, to obtain a repeal of Coddington's commission, sail for England..................................Oct. “

land towns submit to Coddington, but the mainland towns, in legislative session, elect John Smith president, and appoint other officers. They enact that no man, negro or white, shall be held to service more than 10 years after coming into the colony..May, 1652

eneral Assembly in Providence passes a libel law, also an alien law; no foreigner to be received as a freeman or to trade with Indians but by consent of assembly..........Oct. “

illiam Dyer, secretary of the province, and husband of Mary Dyer (afterwards executed in Boston as a Quaker), arrives from England with news of the repeal of Coddington's power, 18 Feb. 1653

ssembly of island towns, Portsmouth and Newport, restore code of 1647, and elect John Sandford as president, 17–18 May, “

ovidence and Warwick with Portsmouth and Newport in one general assembly re-establish code of 1647, forbid sale of liquors to Indians, and prohibit French and Dutch trade with them..31 Aug. 1654

ıwtuxet men withdraw allegiance to Massachusetts, given in 1642, and transfer it to Rhode Island..................26 May, 1658

ock island is granted for public services to gov. Endicott and 3 others, 19 Oct. 1658, who sell it to Simon Ray and 8 associates in 1660; they begin a settlement........................ 1661

ettlement of Misquamicut, now Westerly, begun............. “

ıarter of Rhode Island and Providence Plantations obtained from Charles II. by John Clarke, agent for the colony, 8 July, 1663

[This charter continued in force till 1843—180 years.]

ɔhn Clarke presented with 100*l.* and payment of his expenses attendant upon the procuring of the charter.........24 Nov. “

oundary dispute between Rhode Island, Massachusetts, and Connecticut settled by a royal commission.................. 1664

'esterly incorporated as a town...........................May, 1669

eventh-Day Baptist church established at Newport.......... 1671

eorge Fox, Quaker, preaches in Newport, 1672, and Roger Williams, 73 years old, holds a controversy with 3 disciples of Fox at the Quaker meeting house at Newport, 9–12 Aug. 1672

lock island incorporated by the General Assembly, and at the request of the inhabitants named New Shoreham.....6 Nov. “

ing Philip's war opens by an Indian massacre at Swanzey, Mass..24 June, 1675

roops repulsed by king Philip, intrenched in a swamp at Pocasset, and he withdraws into Massachusetts........18 July, “

irst event of King Philip's war in Rhode Island is the massacre of 15 persons at Bull's garrisoned house in South Kingston about 15 Dec. 1675. *Troops under gov. Winslow attack* the fort of the Narragansetts in a swamp in South Kingston, and after about 3 hours' fighting enter in the rear and fire the fort and wigwams (MASSACHUSETTS)....................19 Dec. 1675

Warwick destroyed by Indians, except one stone house, 16 Mch. 1676

Canonchet, chief of the Narragansetts, captured, refuses to ransom his life by making peace, is turned over for execution to friendly Indians, who send his head “as a token of love and loyalty” to the commissioners at Hartford...........4 Apr. “

Massacre in a cedar swamp near Warwick of 171 Indians by a party of English who did not lose a man...............3 July, “

King Philip shot through the heart by an Indian while attempting to escape from a swamp near mount Hope, 12 Aug. “

Gov. Benedict Arnold d. 20 June, 1678, and is succeeded by William Coddington..................................28 Aug. 1678

Gov. Coddington d. 1 Nov. 1678, and is succeeded by deputy-gov. John Cranston...................................15 Nov. “

Maj. Peleg Sandford succeeds Cranston as governor, who d., 12 Mch. 1680

Custom-house established at Newport to enforce the navigation acts published by the beat of drums.....................1 Apr. 1681

Assembly first meets at Providence under new charter, 26 Oct. “

Roger Williams æt. 84th and is buried in Portsmouth......... 1683

Royal government established in Narragansett, with a court of records, civil and military officers, and Connecticut and Rhode Island excluded from jurisdiction...............June, 1686

The “Atherton claim” to land purchased near Warwick from the Indians by Humphrey Atherton, John Winthrop, and others in 1659, is thrown out by gov. Andros; but other lands are granted the company by the royal council............. 1687

Gov. sir Edmund Andros, stopping at Newport for the charter of Rhode Island, is foiled by gov. Clarke, who sends the charter to his brother to be hidden. Andros destroys the seal of the colony and departs.................................Nov. “

Learning of the accession of William and Mary, Rhode Island resumes the charter government.....................1 May, 1689

Sir Edmund Andros, who had fled to Rhode Island from Boston, is captured by maj. Sandford at Newport, sent back, and is again imprisoned......................................3 Aug. “

Seven French privateers capture Nantucket, Martha's Vineyard, and Block island, but part of the fleet entering the harbor of Newport by night, fails in its surprise........14 July, 1690

Capt. Thomas Paine, from Newport, attacks 5 French privateers near Block island, who withdraw after several hours' fighting, 21 July, “

Admiralty act passed, conferring power of admiralty court on the general council of Rhode Island......................7 Jan. 1695

Law dividing the legislature into an upper house, the council, and a lower of delegates from the people..............May, 1696

Yearly meeting of Friends established at Newport........... 1700

Boundary with Connecticut established from the head of the Paweatuck to the southwest corner of the Warwick purchase, and thence due north to Massachusetts.............12 May, 1703

Two sloops manned by 120 men, captain John Wanton, capture a French privateer with its prize, a sloop loaded with provisions captured the day before near Block island...June, 1706

Colony of Rhode Island first issues paper money (5000*l.*) to defray the expenses of war..............................16 Aug. 1710

Latin school in Newport opened by Mr. Galloway............. 1711

First Quarantine act, against small-pox..................... “

First edition of the laws of Rhode Island printed in Boston.... 1719

Thirty-six pirates, captured by capt. Solgard of British ship *Greyhound*, off the southeast coast of Long island, are brought to Newport, tried, and 26 sentenced and hung on Gravelly Point, opposite the town............................12 July, 1723

First almshouse in Rhode Island erected at Newport.......... “

Property qualification for suffrage established, requiring a freehold of value of 100*l.* or an annual income of 2*l.*......18 Feb. 1724

Mainland towns empowered by Assembly to build a house of correction for vagrants and “to keep mad persons in.” 15 June, 1725

Boundary-line with Connecticut run by a joint commission, and final agreement signed at Westerly.............27 Sept. 1728

George Berkely, dean of Derry, afterwards bishop of Cloyne, arrives in Rhode Island and purchases a farm in Middletown near New York......................................23 Jan. 1730

[After 2½ years he returned to England, giving his farm and a collection of books to Yale college.—*Hildreth's* “Hist. U. S.,” vol. ii. p. 349.]

Assembly passes an act for the relief of poor sailors; 6*d.* a month to be deducted for the purpose from the wages of every Rhode Island seaman...............................May, “

Rhode Island Gazette published by James Franklin, brother of Benjamin, for 7 months at Newport; first in the state; first issue..27 Sept. 1732

A private company petitions the legislature to sanction a lottery; it suppresses by statute under a penalty of 500*l.*, and 10*l.* for any one who takes a ticket......................23 Jan. 1733

Sloop *Pelican*, the first regularly equipped whaling vessel from Rhode Island, arrives at Newport with 114 bbls. of oil and 200 lbs. of whalebone..................................June, “

Assembly meets at Greenwich for the first time........18 Feb. 1734

Newport artillery incorporated by act of Assembly......1 Feb. 1742

Gen. Nathaniel Greene born at Potowamet in township of Warwick...22 May, “

Legislature resolves to raise 150 men and to fit out the colony ship *Tartar* for the siege of Louisburg...............May, 1745

Two large privateers, with 400 men, sail from Newport into a

RHO

northeast snow storm, are lost, and nearly 200 women in Newport are made widows 24 Dec 1745

Eastern boundary of Rhode Island, disputed by Massachusetts and settled by a royal commission in 1741, is confirmed by royal decree received 11 Nov 1746

Company of the Redwood Library, formed in 1735 at Newport, receives a charter from the colony Aug 1747

Providence Library Association chartered by the General Assembly 25 Feb 1754

Newport Mercury first published by James Franklin 1758

Masonic society in Newport incorporated as "The Master Wardens and Society of Free and Accepted Masons" 11 June, 1759

A lottery for raising $2400 is granted to erect a Masonic hall, and the first public celebration of the order ever held in Rhode Island takes place this year "

Property qualification for right of suffrage modified to $134 freehold or $7.50 annual rent 1762

Providence Gazette and Country Journal published in Providence by William Goddard, first issue 20 Oct. "

Jewish synagogue, erected in Newport the year previous, is dedicated 1763

Brown university chartered in 1764 as the college of Rhode Island, is opened at Warren 1765

Maidstone, a British vessel, impresses seamen in Newport harbor; 500 sailors and boys seize one of her boats, drag it to the Commons, and burn it 4 June, "

Augustus Johnston, Martin Howard jr., and dr Moffat, who had advocated the Stamp act, are hung and burned in effigy at Newport 27 Aug "

Samuel Ward of Rhode Island, alone of royal governors, refuses the oath to sustain the Stamp act taking effect 1 Nov "

Society "The Daughters of Liberty" organized by 18 young ladies at dr. Ephraim Bowen's house in Providence 4 Mch. 1766

British armed sloop *Liberty*, fitted out to enforce the revenue laws in Newport harbor, making an unprovoked assault on a Connecticut brig which had been seized and brought into Newport, the people of Newport dismantle and scuttle the *Liberty* and set her adrift 17 July, 1769

College of Rhode Island (Brown university) removed to Providence . 1771

British schooner *Gaspee*, of 8 guns, capt William Duddington, stationed at Newport, destroyed by a body of armed men (GASPEE, Affair of) night of 9 June, 1772

County jail built at Newport . . "

Rev. Samuel Hopkins and rev. Ezra Stiles of Newport issue a circular inviting subscriptions to colonize free negroes on the western shores of Africa. This was the inception of the American Colonization Society Aug 1773

People of Newport in town meeting resolve that any one aiding or abetting the unloading, receiving, or vending of tea sent by the East India company or others while subject to duty in America, is an enemy to his country 12 Jan 1774

General Assembly at Newport elects Stephen Hopkins and Samuel Ward delegates to Continental Congress. 15 June, "

Act of 22 May, 1744, creating the "Artillery Company of the County of Providence," amended by changing the name to "The Cadet Company of the County of Providence." June, "

Three hundred pounds of tea publicly burned in Market square at Providence, with copies of ministerial documents and other obnoxious papers 2 Mch 1775

Gov Joseph Wanton suspended from office, to which he had just been elected for the 7th time, for upholding the action of the British government 3 May, "

Adm Wallace, commanding British fleet in Rhode Island, bombards Bristol, plunders the people, and burns gov Bradford's house and 17 others, together with 2 churches 7 Oct. "

Charles Dudley, the king's collector of customs for Rhode Island, flees for refuge on board a ship of war . 15 Nov "

British troops, 250, landed at Providence are driven to their ships by troops from Warren and Bristol 13 Dec "

A false alarm brings troops under gens. Greene, Sullivan, and Washington to Providence, Washington returning to New York. 7 Apr 1776

Last Colonial Assembly of Rhode Island at Providence, 1 May, 1776, abjures allegiance to the British crown, substituting the words "The governor and company of the English colony of Rhode Island and Providence Plantations," in place of the name and authority of the king May, "

Declaration of Independence celebrated in Rhode Island, which the Assembly names "The State of Rhode Island and Providence Plantations" July, "

William Ellery and Stephen Hopkins, representing Rhode Island, sign the Declaration of Independence "

Eight thousand British troops land and take possession of Rhode Island . 28 Nov "

Gen John Sullivan, appointed by Washington to succeed gen Joseph Spencer in command in Rhode Island, arrives at Providence . . 17 Apr 1777

Col William Barton of Providence, with 40 men, guided by a negro, Quako Honeyman, captures gen Richard Prescott at his quarters, about 5 miles from Newport, and brings him to the American camp, on the night of . 10 July, "

[Prescott is afterwards (May, 1778) exchanged for gen. Charles Lee, captured by the British in New Jersey, Dec. 1776.]

Articles of Confederation adopted by Rhode Island ... 9 Feb. 1778

British commander at Newport sends out 500 men, who destroy some 70 flat bottomed boats and property on the *Kickemuit river*, and burn the church and a number of houses at Warren . . . . 25 May, "

William Ellery, Henry Marchant, and John Collins sign the Articles of Confederation 9 July, 1778

French fleet of 11 sail of line ships, under count d'Estaing, appearing off Brenton's reef, 6 British war vessels attempt to leave the harbor. They are pursued, and are run ashore and set on fire by their crews 5 Aug "

While the French fleet, dispersed by storms, refits at Boston, occurs the battle of Rhode Island. The British forces from Quaker hill attack the Americans on Butts hill, the Americans lose 211 men, the British somewhat more 29 Aug "

Americans under gen. Sullivan retreat from Rhode Island to Tiverton 30 Aug 1778 and the British fleet with the army of sir Henry Clinton arrives at Newport 31 Aug "

Maj Silas Talbot with the sloop *Hawk*, captures the *Pigot*, a British galley which blockaded the eastern passage 28 Oct "

General Assembly grants 600*l* for distressed inhabitants of Newport besides contributions from adjoining states Jan 1779

British embark for New York 11-25 Oct "

French army lands at Newport (UNITED STATES) 10 July, 1780

Public reception given to gen. Washington in Newport, 6 Mch 1781

General Assembly authorizes manumission of slaves, makes free negroes or mulattoes born in the state after 1 Mch 1784, and repeals slavery act of 1774 23 Feb 1784

Marine Society instituted in 1754 under the name of "The Fellowship Club," is chartered by act of legislature June, 1785

Stephen Hopkins dies near Providence 13 July, "

First spinning jenny in the U. S. made and put in operation by Daniel Jackson of Providence 1786

Act passed for emitting 100,000*l* in bills of credit, and making the same a legal tender at par . "

Newport, incorporated as a city, 1 June, 1784, resumes its old form of town government . 27 Mch. 1787

African slave trade forbidden, with penalties of 100*l* for each person imported from Africa, and 1000*l* for the vessel 29 Oct "

Motion made in the General Assembly for the appointment of delegates to the general convention of the colonies at Philadelphia is lost by a majority of 23 votes "

Providence Association of Mechanics and Manufacturers incorporated Mch 1789

Congress subjects to duty all goods from Rhode Island not of her own production May, "

Assembly addresses the president and Congress of the 11 states, assigning reasons for opposing the Constitution, setting forth its attachment to its democratic charter, and the fear that it would be limited by the new Federal system Sept. "

Act passed repealing the Legal Tender act of 1786, and promising to redeem the paper at the rate of 15 to 1 12 Oct. "

After long and bitter opposition the convention assembled at Newport, first in the state house and adjourned to the Second Baptist church, adopts the Federal Constitution and Bill of Rights by 34 to 32, 5 P.M. Saturday 29 May, 1790

Providence bank, the oldest in the state, goes into operation 1791

First known copyright granted under the U. S. law is made to rev. William Patten of Newport for a book entitled "Christianity the True Theology" . 9 May, 1795

Marine corps of artillery chartered at Providence . 1801

College of Rhode Island changed to Brown university in honor of Nicholas Brown . . 1804

British occupy Block island . . 1813

Com Oliver H. Perry leaves Newport with a detachment of seamen from the gunboats in the harbor, to take command of the American squadron on lake Erie . . "

Friends' school at Portsmouth established in 1784 but discontinued after 4 years, is revived and established at Providence, 1814

Pres James Monroe visits Rhode Island, arriving at Providence 30 June, 1817

Newport asylum for the poor on Coaster's Harbor island completed and occupied 1822

Rhode Island Historical Society incorporated. . "

Reception given gen Lafayette at Providence .23 Aug. 1824

Com Perry died aged 34, of yellow-fever on the U. S. schooner *Nonesuch* in the harbor of Port Spain, island of Trinidad; buried with military honors at Newport 4 Dec 1826

General Assembly of Rhode Island passes an act establishing public schools throughout the state ... . Jan 1828

Dexter asylum for the poor erected at Providence with funds devised by Ebenezer Knight Dexter, who d. 10 Aug 1824, asylum opened . . . . "

Race riot in Providence begins between sailors and negroes, military aid is called in and the Riot act read 21-24 Sept. 1831

City of Providence incorporated . . . .22 Nov 1832

Company incorporated to construct a railroad from Providence to Stonington in 1832, and railroad building commenced. . 1835

State prison at Providence completed ... 1838

Fort Adams in Newport harbor, begun in 1824, is completed 1839

Convention of delegates elected by friends of extension of suffrage, without regard to the law regulating the right of voting, at Providence, 4 Oct. 1841, forms a "people's constitution," and declares it adopted by a vote of the people, 27-29 Dec. 1841

Thomas W. Dorr elected governor under the people's constitution . . . . 18 Apr 1842

Dorr government attempts to organize, 3 May, 1842, but is resisted by legal state government (DORR'S REBELLION). . 3 May, "

Constitution to supersede the charter of 1663 is framed by a convention which meets at Newport, 12 Sept. 1842, adjourns to East Greenwich, and completes its labors 5 Nov ; constitution ratified by vote of the people, 7032 to 59...21-23 Nov "

Franklin lyceum, formed in 1831, is incorporated at Providence, 1843
Dorr sentenced to imprisonment for life..............25 June, 1844
Butler hospital for the insane on the Seekonk river in Providence opened.. 1847
Sockanosset school for boys at Howard (a reform school) is opened..1 Nov. 1850
T. W. Dorr, released from prison under an act of general amnesty in 1847, is restored to civil and political rights........ 1851
Rhode Island adopts the Maine liquor law..............7 May, 1852
Newport incorporated as a city.......................20 May, 1853
Statue of Franklin, the first public statue in Rhode Island, is unveiled at Providence............................19 Nov. 1858
Legislature repeals the Personal Liberty bill.............Jan. 1861
On news of the fall of fort Sumter, the governor tenders the U. S. government 1000 infantry and a battalion of artillery. He convenes the legislature in extra session, 17 Apr., and the Rhode Island Marine Artillery pass through New York on their way to Washington.........................20 Apr. "
Legislature ratifies the XIII.th Amendment to the Constitution.. 1865
Legislature ratifies the XIV.th Amendment.............7 Feb. 1867
Board of State Charities and Correction established.......... 1869
State farm, 421 acres in town of Cranston, afterwards site of State house of correction, State work-house, State asylum for incurable insane, and State alms-house, is purchased....... "
Rhode Island Woman Suffrage Association holds a convention at Providence.......................................Oct. "
State Teachers' Institute held at East Greenwich, which expresses the need of State Normal schools.........22-23 Oct. "
XV.th Amendment to the Constitution of the U. S. is ratified, 18 Jan. 1870
Cove lands ceded to the towns by the colony, 28 May, 1707, are conveyed to the city of Providence by the state on payment of $200,000... "
Legislature, by 56 to 2, abolishes imprisonment for debt...... "
Marble statue of Roger Williams, executed for the state by Franklin Simmons in Italy, is received and presented to the Federal government to be placed in the capitol........Mch. 1871
Free public library, art gallery, and museum for the city of Providence chartered under the combined auspices of the Providence Franklin Society, the Association of Mechanics and Manufacturers, the Franklin Lyceum, and the Rhode Island Horticultural Society and Society for the Encouragement of Domestic Industry................................ "
Rhode Island State Normal school at Providence opened. 6 Sept. "
Prohibition party in the state adopt the Republican candidate for governor, Henry Howard............................... 1873
State convention of the Prohibition party at the state-house in Providence nominates "a distinct, separate, teetotal prohibition ticket for state officers," with Henry Howard for governor, 26 Feb. 1874. The Republican party adopt Howard by acclamation, 11 Mch. The Democratic convention at Providence, 23 Mch., adjourns without platform or ticket, 23 Mch. 1874
Stringent prohibition law is passed, and a constabulary act providing for the appointment by the governor of a state constable with 7 deputies for enforcing it................May, "
Vote for governor at election 7 Apr. 1875; Rowland Hazard, of the National Union Republican and Prohibition parties, 8724; Henry Lippitt, Republican, 8368; Charles B. Cutler, Democrat, 5166. There being no choice, the legislature elects Lippitt by 70, to 36 for Hazard ....25 May, 1875
Constabulary act repealed, and an act "to regulate and restrain the sale of intoxicating liquors" passed in its place .... "
Corliss engine of 1400 horse-power, and weighing 700 tons, designed to furnish power in Machinery hall, by George H. Corliss of Providence, is set in motion at the opening of the Centennial exhibition in Philadelphia by pres. U. S. Grant and dom Pedro II., emperor of Brazil...............10 May, 1876
There being no choice for governor at the April election, Henry Lippitt, Republican, is chosen by the legislature.....30 May, "
First Board of Harbor Commissioners appointed by the governor..14 June, "
State school for the deaf at Providence opened..........2 Apr. 1877
Prisoners removed from the old state prison to the new building at Cranston... 1878
State Board of Health established.......................... "
Legislature elects Alfred H. Littlefield, Republican, governor, there being no choice at the election in April........25 May, 1880
Act passed abolishing the tribal authority and relation of the Narragansett Indians.................................... "
Congress awards the first-class gold medal to Mrs. Ida Lewis Wilson, keeper of Lime Rock lighthouse, who, since 1859, had saved 13 lives at the risk of her own................... 1881
Ambrose E. Burnside, b. Liberty, Ind., 1824, gov. of Rhode Island, 1866-69, and U. S. senator at the time of his death (FREDERICKSBURG)..................................3 Sept. "
Colored voters of Rhode Island, in convention at Newport, resolve hereafter to act independently of the Republican party, 18 Oct. 1882
State home and school for neglected and dependent children opened at Providence....................................Apr. 1885
Amendment to the state constitution prohibiting the manufacture and sale of intoxicating liquors as a beverage, goes into effect...1 July, 1886
Compulsory Education act passed requiring at least 12 weeks of school attendance, 6 of them consecutive, by all children between 7 and 15 years of age............................ 1887
Arbor day established as a legal holiday .... "
City of Woonsocket incorporated............................ 1888
Bourn amendment to the state constitution, abolishing property qualification for electors, proclaimed by governor..Nov. "

RHO

State agricultural school established by act of legislature... . 1888
Vote at April election for governor: John W. Davis, Democrat, 21,289; H. W. Ladd, Republican, 16,870; James H. Chace, Law Enforcement party, 3597; H. H. Richardson, Prohibition, 1346. There being no choice, the legislature chose H. W. Ladd, 28 May, 1889
Prohibitory amendment rescinded at a special election, 20 June, 1889, and a high-license law passed....................1 Aug. "
Australian ballot-reform law passed......................... "
First state convention of the Union Reform party held, and Arnold B. Chace nominated for governor............25 Feb. "
Australian ballot system introduced at state election....2 Apr. "
John W. Davis elected governor by the legislature, there being no choice by the people..............................May, 1890
Celebration of the centennial of the introduction of cotton spinning into America begins at Providence........29 Sept. "
Monument to Samuel Smith Collyer dedicated at Pawtucket at close of Cotton Centennial celebration..............4 Oct. "
Vote for governor: Davis, Democrat, 22,249; Ladd, Republican, 20,995; Larry, Prohibition, 1829; Burton, National, 384.1 Apr. 1891
Soldiers' home at Bristol dedicated...................21 May, "
Herbert W. Ladd, Republican, elected governor by the legislature...26 May, "
Ex-gov. Henry Lippitt dies at Newport, aged 73........5 June, "
D. Russell Brown reelected governor.......................Apr. 1894

GOVERNORS.

PORTSMOUTH.	NEWPORT.
Wm. Coddington....7 Mch. 1638	William Coddington, 28 Apr. 1639-47
Wm. Hutchinson... 30 Apr. 1639	
Wm. Coddington...12 Mch. 1640	

PRESIDENTS UNDER THE PATENT.

PROVIDENCE, WARWICK, PORTSMOUTH, AND NEWPORT.

John Coggeshall......May, 1647	John Smith.......... May, 1649
Wm. Coddington......May, 1648	Nicholas Easton......May, 1650

PROVIDENCE AND WARWICK.	PORTSMOUTH AND NEWPORT.
Samuel Gorton.........Oct. 1651	John Sandford, sr.....May, 1653
John Smith ....May, 1652	
Gregory Dexter.......May, 1653	

4 TOWNS UNITED.

Nicholas Easton ......May, 1654	William Brenton......May, 1660
Roger Williams.......Sept. "	Benedict Arnold......May, 1662
Benedict Arnold......May, 1657	

GOVERNORS UNDER ROYAL CHARTER.

Benedict Arnold......Nov. 1663	Gideon Wanton.......May, 1747
William Brenton......May, 1666	William Greene...... " 1748
Benedict Arnold...... " 1669	Stephen Hopkins..... " 1755
Nicholas Easton...... " 1672	William Greene...... " 1757
William Coddington... " 1674	Stephen Hopkins...14 Mch. 1758
Walter Clarke. ...... " 1676	Samuel Ward.........May, 1762
Benedict Arnold...... " 1677	Stephen Hopkins..... " 1763
Wm. Coddington... 28 Aug. 1678	Samuel Ward......... " 1765
John Cranston........Nov. "	Stephen Hopkins ..... " 1767
Peleg Sandford.....16 Mch. 1680	Josias Lyndon........ " 1768
Wm. Coddington, jr. ..May, 1683	Joseph Wanton....... " 1769
Henry Bull........... " 1685	Nicholas Cooke.......Nov. 1775
Walter Clarke........ " 1686	William Greene......May, 1778
Henry Bull.........27 Feb. 1690	John Collins.......... " 1786
John Easton..........May, "	Arthur Fenner........ " 1790
Caleb Carr........... " 1695	James Fenner........ " 1807
Walter Clarke.........Jan. 1696	William Jones........ " 1811
Samuel Cranston..... May, 1698	Nehemiah R. Knight.. " 1817
Joseph Jenckes....... " 1727	William C. Gibbs..... " 1821
William Wanton...... " 1732	James Fenner........ " 1824
John Wanton......... " 1734	Lemuel H. Arnold.... 1831
Richard Ward......15 July, 1740	John Brown Francis.. 1833
William Greene.......May, 1743	William Sprague...... 1838
Gideon Wanton....... " 1745	Samuel Ward King ... 1840
William Greene....... " 1746	

GOVERNORS UNDER THE STATE CONSTITUTION.

James Fenner.. 1843
Charles Jackson... 1845
Byron Diman... 1846
Elisha Harris 1847
Henry B. Anthony 1849
Philip Allen.... 1851
William Warner Hoppin....................................... 1854
Elisha Dyer.. 1857
Thomas G. Turner.. 1859
William Sprague 1860
William C. Cozzens.............................3 Mch. 1863
James Y. Smith.. "
Ambrose E. Burnside... 1866
Seth Padelford 1869
Henry Howard.. 1873
Henry Lippitt 1875
Charles C. Van Zandt (Republican) ....29 May, 1877
Alfred H. Littlefield (Republican)......................25 May, 1880
Augustus O. Bourn (Republican).........................29 May, 1883
George P. Wetmore (Republican)..........................May, 1885
John W. Davis (Democrat)................................ " 1887
Royal C. Taft (Republican)............................... " 1888
H. W. Ladd (Republican) .... " 1889
John W. Davis (Democrat)................................. " 1890
H. W. Ladd (Republican).................................. " 1891
D. Russell Brown (Republican; re-elected 1893-94)....... " 1892

UNITED STATES SENATORS FROM THE STATE OF RHODE ISLAND.

Name.	No. of Congress.	Date.	Remarks.
Theodore Foster	1st to 8th	1789 to 1803	
Joseph Stanton	1st " 3d	1789 " 1793	
William Bradford	3d " 5th	1793 " 1797	Elected president *pro tem.* 6 July, 1797. Resigned.
Ray Greene	5th " 7th	1797 " 1801	Elected in place of Bradford. Resigned.
Christopher Ellery	7th " 9th	1801 " 1805	Elected in place of Greene.
Samuel J. Potter	8th	1803 " 1804	Died.
Benjamin Howland	8th to 11th	1804 " 1809	Elected in place of Potter.
James Fenner	9th " 10th	1805 " 1807	Elected governor.
Elisha Matthewson	10th " 12th	1807 " 1811	Elected in place of Fenner.
Francis Malbone	11th	1809	Died 4 June, 1809.
Christopher G. Champlain	11th to 12th	1810 to 1811	Resigned.
William Hunter	12th " 17th	1811 " 1821	
Jeremiah B. Howell	12th " 15th	1811 " 1817	
James Burrell, jr.	15th " 16th	1817 " 1820	Died 25 Dec. 1820.
Nehemiah R. Knight	16th " 27th	1820 " 1841	Elected in place of Burrell.
James D'Wolf	17th " 20th	1821 " 1825	Resigned.
Asher Robbins	20th " 26th	1825 " 1839	Elected in place of D'Wolf.
Nathan F. Dixon	26th " 27th	1839 " 1842	Died 29 Jan. 1842.
William Sprague	27th " 28th	1842 " 1844	Elected in place of Dixon. Resigned.
James F. Simmons	27th " 30th	1841 " 1847	
John B. Francis	28th	1844 " 1845	Elected in place of Sprague.
Albert C. Greene	29th to 33d	1845 " 1851	
John H. Clark	30th " 33d	1847 " 1853	
Charles T. James	32d " 35th	1851 " 1857	
Philip Allen	33d " 36th	1853 " 1859	
James F. Simmons	35th " 37th	1857 " 1862	Resigned.
Henry B. Anthony	36th " 48th	1859 " 1884	Elected president *pro tem.* 23 Mch. 1869; 10 Mch. 1871. Died 2 Sept. 1884.
Samuel G. Arnold	37th	1862 " 1863	Elected in place of Simmons.
William Sprague	38th to 44th	1863 " 1875	
Ambrose E. Burnside	44th " 47th	1875 " 1881	Died 3 Sept. 1881.
Nelson W. Aldrich	47th " ——	1881 " ——	Elected in place of Burnside. Term expires 1899.
William P. Sheffield	48th " ——	1884 " 1885	Appointed in place of Anthony.
Jonathan Chace	49th " 51st	1885 " 1889	Resigned.
Nathan F. Dixon	51st " 54th	1889 " 1895	Elected in place of Chace.
George P. Wetmore	54th " ——	1895 " ——	Term expires 1901.

Rhodes, an island on the coast of Asia Minor, is said to have been peopled from Crete, as early as 916 B.C. The Rhodians were great navigators, and institutors of a maritime code afterwards adopted by the Romans. The city was built about 432, and flourished 300–200 B.C. COLOSSUS OF RHODES. Rhodes, long an ally of the Romans, was taken by the emperor Vespasian, 71 A.D. It was held by Knights Hospitallers from 1309 to 1522, when it was conquered by Turks, who still retain it. The knights retired to MALTA. Rhodes suffered by an earthquake on 22 Apr. 1863.

rho'dium, a rare metal, discovered in platinum ore by dr. Wollaston in 1804, has been used for points of metallic pens.

rhu'barb. This plant was first cultivated for its stalks as food by Mr. Myall, of Deptford, Engl., about 1820, and soon after came into general use. FLOWERS AND PLANTS.

Rial'to. BRIDGES.

Ribbonism, the principles of a secret society in Ireland, organized about 1820, to retaliate on landlords who injured tenants. To the ribbonmen are attributed many agrarian murders, 1858–71–79. An act was passed to repress them, 16 June, 1871.

rice, the *Oryza sativa* of botanists, in husk termed paddy; largely grown in intertropical regions, occupying the same place as wheat in warmer parts of Europe. It was brought to South Carolina from the island of Madagascar in 1695, and its cultivation greatly increased.

Rich Mountain, West Virginia, Battle of. Here gen. Rosecrans defeated the confederates, 11 July, 1861, capturing 600 men. The strategic operations of which this battle was the culmination deprived the confederates of all hope of holding or drawing strength from WEST VIRGINIA.

Richmond, a town of Surrey, anciently **Sheen** (i. e., in Saxon, *resplendent*). Here stood a palace in which Edward I. and II. resided, and Edward III. died, 1377. Here also died Anne, queen of Richard II., 1394. The palace was repaired by Henry V., who founded 3 religious houses near it. In 1497 it was burned, but Henry VII. rebuilt it, and called the village Richmond, from his title, earl of Richmond (Yorkshire) before he obtained the crown; and here he died in 1509. Queen Elizabeth was prisoner in this palace for a short time during Mary's reign. When she became queen it was one of her favorite places of residence; and here she died, 24 Mch. 1603. It was afterwards the residence of Henry, prince of Wales. The beautiful park and gardens were enclosed by Charles I. The observatory was built by sir W. Chambers in 1769. In Richmond, Thomson "sang the Seasons and their change;" and died 27 Aug. 1748.

Richmond, Va. VIRGINIA, 1679, 1742, '79, 1811, 1861, '65, '75. Pop. 1890, 81,388.

Richmond, Ky., Battle of. Here Kirby Smith defeated the federals under gen. Manson, 30 Aug. 1862. Federal loss about 5000; confederate, about the same. BRAGG'S KENTUCKY CAMPAIGN.

rifles, FIRE-ARMS.

rights, Bill of. To the petition of rights, preferred 17 Mch. 1627–28, Charles I. answered, "I will that right be done according to the laws and customs of the realm." Both houses addressed the king for a fuller answer to the petition of rights, whereupon he gave them an answer less evasive, "*Soit droit fait comme il est désiré,*" 7 June, 1628. The petition thus became a statute, 13 Car. I. c. 1. An important declaration was made by the lords and commons of England to the prince and princess of Orange on 13 Feb. 1689, in an act "declaring the rights and liberties of the subject, and settling the succession of the crown." BILL OF RIGHTS.

Rig Veda. VEDAS.

Rimnik, a town near Martinesti, Wallachia. Here the Austrians and Russians, under prince Coburg and gen. Suwarrow, crushed the Turks, 22 Sept. 1789.

Ring der Nibelungen (*nē-bel-oong'en*). NIBELUNGENÔT.

rings anciently held an engraved seal or signet, to seal writings, and they are so used to this day. In Gen. xli. 42 it is said that Pharaoh gave Joseph his ring. A ring is now put upon a woman's third finger at marriage; but the Jews used them at the espousal before marriage.

Rio Janeiro (*ree-ō' ja-nee'ro*), a city and seaport of Brazil, South America, on a bay of the same name, one of the finest harbors in the world, discovered by De Sousa, 1 Jan. 1531. Made the capital of BRAZIL 1807. Pop. 1892, 800,000.

Disturbance between 2 rival factions in the government of Brazil; one party headed by adm. Custodio de Mello and later by adm. de Gama, the other by pres. Peixoto, representing the regular government, begins active warfare in Rio Grande do Sul.....June–July, 1893

Adm. de Mello, with a fleet, in the harbor of Rio Janeiro..Aug. "

Foreign admirals decide to prevent bombardment of city, 8 Sept. "

Bombardment of forts in the harbor and bay of Rio Janeiro commences.....14 Sept. "

[This is kept up at intervals during the occupancy of the harbor, 14 Sept. 1893–14 Mch. 1894.]

Com. Oscar F. Stanton, commanding the South Atlantic squadron, arrives in the harbor of Rio Janeiro and salutes both the flag of the Brazilian government and that of the rebels; recalled by the U. S. government.....Oct. "

[Rear-adm. Benham succeeds.]

U S cruiser *San Francisco*, with rear adm Benham, arrives in the harbor 12 Jan 1894
Rebel fleet attempt to prevent the unloading the cargo of an American merchantman U S war ship *Detroit* is ordered by adm Benham to support the merchantman, rebels desist, cargo unloaded 30 Jan "
Rebellion fails, officers of insurgent fleet escape from the harbor 14 Mch "
U S cruiser *San Francisco* with rear adm Benham, sail from Rio Janeiro for Bluefields, Nicaragua 18 Mch "

riots in the United States

BOSTON MASSACRE 1770
"Doctor's mob" NEW YORK 1788
At Baltimore Md (UNITED STATES) 1812-61
ALTON Ill 1837
PHILADELPHIA 1844
Astor Place riots in New York growing out of rivalry between the actors Forrest and Macready (NEW YORK CITY) 10 May, 1849
Draft riot in New York, mob in possession of the city (NEW YORK) 13-17 July, 1863
Orange riot in New York between Catholic and Protestant Irish 60 persons killed (ORANGEMEN) 12 July 1871
Anarchists in Chicago Ill (ILLINOIS) 4 May, 1886
For railroad riots or strikes, STRIKES

Most important of the many riots in England were

GORDON'S "NO POPERY" riots 10 May-9 June, 1780
"Field of Peterloo" at MANCHESTER 16 Aug 1819

Ritualists, a name given in 1866 to a party in the church of England, largely resembling the PUSEYITES, and seeking to give a more imposing character to public worship, by colored vestments, lighted candles, incense, etc, professing to go back to the practices of the church in the time of Edward VI An exhibition of these things was held during the church congress at York in Oct 1866, but was not officially connected with it The practices of Ritualists (said by Mr Disraeli to be symbolical of doctrines they were bound to renounce) were censured in Episcopal charges in Dec 1866, in 2 reports of the Ritualistic commission, 19 Aug 1867 and Apr 1868, and by the judicial committee of the privy council on appeal, 23 Dec 1868 At a convocation of the American Episcopal church at Philadelphia, 27, 28 Oct 1868, a warm discussion on Ritualism was held, and renewed at the convocation 10 Oct 1874, and the Ritualists were beaten by the Evangelical party, a stringent canon on ceremonies being passed 27 Oct The Public Worship Regulation act was passed 7 Aug 1874, for the repression of Ritualism in England

River and Harbor bills. The first bill for harbor improvements in the United States was passed 3 Mch 1823 Polk in 1846 and Pierce in 1854 vetoed such bills In 1870 a $2,000 000 appropriation was made, the largest amount up to that time In 1882 pres Arthur vetoed a $19,000,000 appropriation bill which was ultimately passed over his veto

River Raisin, Mich , is remarkable in history as the place of a massacre on 23 Jan 1813 Gen Winchester, with about 800 Americans, was encamped on that river, and at dawn, on 22 Jan , gen Proctor, with 1500 British and Indians, fell upon them After a severe action Winchester surrendered, under promise of protection from the Indians But Proctor marched off, leaving no guard for the Americans His Indians returned, and killed and scalped a large number of them The American loss was over 300 killed (mostly after the fight), and the rest were made prisoners The British lost 24 killed and 158 wounded MICHIGAN, 1818.

Rivoli (*ree'vo lee*), a village near Verona, N Italy. Near here the Austrians defeated the French, 17 Nov 1796, and were defeated by Bonaparte, 14, 15 Jan 1797. Massena was made duke of Rivoli for his share in the actions

roads. The ancient Egyptians must have had substantial paved roads Highways mentioned in Judges v 6 The Persians, Greeks, and Carthaginians were excellent road makers, but to the Romans belongs the honor of being the greatest and best road-builders of ancient times At the zenith of her greatness there centred at Rome 29 superior roads, some of them extending into Spain, Gaul, Illyria, and Thrace Thence road-making passed into Asia Minor, Pontus, the East, Egypt, Africa, and Britain The empire was divided into 11 districts and 113 provinces, united by 372 great roads According to the survey of Antoninus Pius, 138-161 A D, their entire distance covered 52,964 Roman miles. The principal Roman roads in Italy were (1) Via Appia, the Appian way, called *Regina Viarum*, the first of Roman roads in time and celebrity It was commenced by Appius Claudius Cæcus, 312 B.C , and extended to Capua 120 miles from Rome, completed to Brundisium, 320 miles, 30 B C Its centre, 16 feet wide, was intended for infantry , its side tracks, 8 feet each, for horsemen and carriages , in all from 32 to 36 feet in width (2) Via Numicia traversed the northern part of Samnium, communicated with the Appian way, and united with the Via Aquilia in Lucania (3) Via Flaminia, constructed by C Flaminius when censor, 533 A U C (221 B C), extended from Rome to Ariminum (4) Via Aurelia extending along the coast of Etruria (5) Via Cassia, extending to Modena (6) Via Æmilia Lepida, built by M Æmilius Lepidus when consul, 187 B C , a continuation of the Via Flaminia through Cisalpine Gaul (7) Via Latina, from Rome to Brundisium The smaller roads were Via Prænestina, Via Tiburtina to Tivoli, Via Ostiensis to Ostia, Via Laurentina, Via Salaria, etc ROMAN ROADS IN ENGLAND The empire of Peru at the time of the Spanish conquest was traversed by excellent roads The Moguls in India built several extended and excellent roads Highways first made public in Britain by the Romans Greatly improved by Edward I Tolls granted on one in London, 1346 Parishes made answerable for their condition in 1553 During the reign of Charles II turnpike roads established in various parts of England Toll gates erected in 1663 Roads were commenced through the highlands of Scotland by gen Wade in 1726, afterwards continued by Mr Telford, who also built an excellent road from Glasgow to Carlisle, and from Holyhead to Shrewsbury SIMPLON road built, 1801-7 Road-making in the United States has never received the attention it deserves either by the local, state or U S government, and probably no nation with the intelligence, wealth, etc , of the U S has so poor public roads CUMBERLAND ROAD commenced 1806 MACADAMIZING

Roanoke island, N C, discovered by sir Walter Raleigh, 1584, and settled by him, 1585, without success. Other settlers also failed VIRGINIA During the civil war Roanoke island was early occupied by the confederates under gen Wise with 2500 men. On the north shore were 3 forts—Barton, Huger, and Blanchard A federal expedition against the island left Hampton Roads, 11 Jan 1862—a fleet of 20 vessels, 50 guns, under flag-officer L M Goldsborough, and nearly 15,000 men under gen A. E Burnside The forts were bombarded 7 Feb , and under cover of this bombardment the troops were landed On the 8th, after a short conflict, Wise's command surrendered The Federal loss amounted to 260 On the Confederate side a son of gen Wise was killed

roasting to death. An early instance is that of Bocchoris, king of Egypt, by order of Sabacon of Ethiopia, 737 B C.—*Lenglet* Sir John Oldcastle, lord Cobham, was thus put to death in 1418, and Michael Servetus for heresy, at Geneva, 27 Oct 1553 BURNING, MARTYRS.

robbers and **highwaymen** were punished with death by Edmund I's laws, which directed that the eldest robber should be hanged Remarkable robbers in England were ROBIN HOOD, 1189, and Claud Du Val, "executed at Tyburn," says an historian, quaintly, "to the great grief of the women," Jan 1670 In Ireland, MacCabe was hanged at Naas, 19 Aug 1691 Galloping Hogan, the rapparee, flourished at this period Jack Sheppard hanged at Tyburn, 16 Nov. 1724, and Dick Turpin at York, 10 Apr 1749 Freney, the highwayman, surrendered himself, 10 May, 1749 Barrington was transported, 22 Sept 1790. TRIALS

Robin Good-fellow, the brownie of Scotland, the kobold of Germany, Puck, etc

> "Either I mistake your shape and making quite,
> Or else you are that shrewd and knavish sprite,
> Call'd Robin Good fellow,
> Those that Hobgoblin call you, and sweet Puck,
> You do their work " etc
> —*Shakespeare*, "Midsummer-Night's Dream," act ii sc i

Robin Hood, captain of a band of about 100 robbers, in Sherwood forest, Nottinghamshire, robbing the rich and protecting the poor, traditionally said to have been the earl of Huntingdon, disgraced and banished the court by Richard I. at his accession (1189) Robin Hood, Little John, Will Scarlet, Friar Tuck, and Maid Marian were the famous characters of the band in the ballads of that day. The band is •

said to have continued its depredations till 1247, when Robin died.—*Stow.*

"Robinson Crusoe," by Daniel De Foe; the first part appeared in 1719. JUAN FERNANDEZ. Three old ladies, Mary Ann, Jane Amelia, and Sarah Frances De Foe, lineally descended from De Foe, pensioned by queen Victoria, May, 1877.

"Robinson, Swiss Family," by Johann Rudolph Wyss, pub. 1813.

Rochefort (*rosh-fōr'*), W. France, a seaport on the Charente, made by Louis XIV. in 1666. In Aix-roads or Basque-roads, near Rochefort, capt. lord Cochrane attacked the French fleet and destroyed 4 ships, 11, 12 April, 1809. Near Rochefort, Napoleon surrendered himself to capt. Maitland of the *Bellerophon*, 15 July, 1815.

Rochelle (*ro-shel'*), W. France, a seaport on the Atlantic, long English, but surrendered to the French leader, Du Guesclin, in 1372. As a stronghold of Calvinists, it was vainly besieged by the duke of Anjou in 1573; and taken after a siege of 13 months by cardinal Richelieu in 1628. The duke of Buckingham was sent with fleet and army to relieve it; but the citizens declined to admit him. He attacked the Isle of Rhé, near Rochelle, and failed, 22 July, 1627. He was repulsed 8 Nov. following.

rockets, an invention of sir William Congreve about 1803, are of 2 kinds—*signal* or *sky* rockets and *war* rockets. The case of the former is generally made of paper with a stick attached to its side, with one large vent in the centre of the case. This case contains combustibles, the bur[illegible] which produces gases so rapidly that their expansion drives the case upward with swiftness to a great height, where it usually explodes. In the war rocket the stick is in the centre of the barrel or case, and the vents, of which there are several, are near the edge. For military purposes the rocket has never been considered a success. Rockets are now largely used in the Life-saving service for line-carrying and oil-distributing. The rocket was greatly improved by Hales in 1846.

"Rock of Ages," a celebrated hymn, by Augustus Montague Toplady, 1740-78, pub. 1776.

Rock of Chickamauga, a term applied to gen. Geo. H. Thomas for his conduct in that battle. CHICKAMAUGA.

Rocky Mount, S. C. Here gen. Sumter attacked a British post, 30 July, 1780, and was repulsed with small loss.

Rocroy (*ro-krwa'*), N. France. Here, 19 May, 1643, the Spaniards were defeated by the French, commanded by the great Condé.

Rodman gun, so named from the inventor of this method of casting the gun, gen. Thomas J. Rodman. The first gun cast (15 inch) was at the Fort Pitt foundry, Pittsburg. A second one of 20 inches was successfully cast at the same place in 1863, and many since. CANNON.

Rodney's victories. Adm. Rodney fought, near Cape St. Vincent, the Spanish adm. don Langara, whom he defeated and captured, with 6 ships, 1 of which blew up, 16, 17 Jan. 1780. On 12 Apr. 1782, he met a French fleet in the West Indies, under count de Grasse, took 5 ships of the line, and sent the French admiral prisoner to England. Rodney was raised to the peerage, June, 1782.

Roga'tion week. Rogation Sunday, the Sunday before Ascension Day, named from the Monday, Tuesday, and Wednesday following it, called Rogation days (from Lat. *rogare*, to beseech). Extraordinary prayers and supplications for these 3 days are said to have been appointed in the 3d century, as preparation for celebrating our Saviour's ascension on the next day, Holy Thursday or Ascension Day. The whole week is styled Rogation week, and sometimes Crop week, Grass week, or Procession week. The perambulations of parishes have usually been made in this week.

Rohan, an illustrious family, descended from ancient sovereigns of Brittany. Henri de Rohan, son-in-law of the great Sully, after the death of Henry IV. (14 May, 1610), became head of the Protestant party, fought 3 wars against Louis XIII., but later entered the service of the duke of Saxe-Weimar, and died of wounds received in battle in 1638. Of this family was the cardinal de Rohan. DIAMONDS.

Rohilcund', a tract of N.E. India, was conquered by the Rohillas, an Afghan tribe, who settled here about 1747. After aiding the sovereign of Oude to overcome the Mahrattas, they were treated treacherously by him and nearly exterminated. Rohilcund was ceded to the British in 1801. After the great mutiny, Rohilcund was tranquillized in July, 1858.

rolling-mills, in the metal manufactories, were in use in England in the 17th century, and in 1784 Mr. Cort patented his improvements.

Romagna (*ro-măn'ya*), a province of the former Papal States, comprised in the legations of Forli and Ravenna. It was conquered by the Lombards; but taken from them by Pepin, and given to the pope, 753. Cæsar Borgia held it as a duchy in 1501, but lost it in 1503. In 1859 the Romagna threw off the temporal authority of the pope, and declared itself subject to the king of Sardinia, who accepted it in Mch. 1860. It now forms part of the province of Æmilia, in the new kingdom of Italy. ROME, 1859.

Romainville' and **Belleville,** heights near Paris, where Joseph Bonaparte, Mortier, and Marmont were defeated by the allies after a vigorous resistance, 30 Mch. 1814. The next day Paris capitulated.

Roman Catholicism, Development of.

Prayer for the dead began	200
Paul the first hermit	251
Constantine makes Sunday the Christian Sabbath	321
First general council at Nicea in Bithynia	325
Celibacy of the clergy recommended	"
Scriptures called the Bible by Jerome	340
Adoration of saints, martyrs, and angels	360
Christmas day a religious festival	375
Bells used in church	390
Nicene creed introduced	391
[Except the words "dead" and "communion of saints."]	
Mary called the mother of God	431
Sprinkling of ashes in Lent (Felix III.)	487
Canon of Scriptures completed	494
Priests began to wear a distinctive dress	500
Stone altars enjoined	506
Extreme unction introduced by Felix IV.	525
Lenten fast extended to 40 days, by council of Orleans	547
Prayers addressed to the Virgin Mary	593
Title of pope and papal supremacy first assumed by Boniface III.,	606
All-saints' day introduced	625
Athanasian creed introduced	670
Holy water introduced	682
Kissing the pope's toe introduced (abolished in 1773)	708
Veneration of images imposed	788
Tithes exacted	789
Rogation days established by Leo III.	801
Assumption festival introduced	813
Cardinals created	817
Filioque dogma introduced	821
Baptism of bells introduced	965
Canonization of saints (pope John XVI.)	993
All-souls' day appointed	998
Advent Sunday appointed	1000
Celibacy of priests made obligatory	"
Prayer for souls in purgatory introduced	"
Indulgences first bestowed by Ponce, bishop of Arles	1002
Interdicts introduced	1073
Infallibility of the Roman church taught	"
Excommunication introduced by Gregory VII.	1077
Sale of indulgences sanctioned	1087
Plenary indulgences in this life and in the life to come authorized by the council of Clermont	1095
Transubstantiation made a church dogma	1215
Auricular confession officially imposed	"
Adoration of the Host enjoined	1218
Inquisition established	1229
Cup withheld from the laity	1263
"Angelus" announced by a bell	1316
Dogma of purgatory officially recognized	1439
Holy oil in chrism first used	1540
Veneration of relics enjoined by council of Trent	1563
Marriage made a sacrament	"
Confirmation made a sacrament	"
Immaculate conception proclaimed	1854
Papal infallibility proclaimed	1870

CHURCH; POPES.

Roman Catholics in England and the British empire. Their religion was established in Britain until the Reformation; when first introduced is conjectural. Bede says, Lucius Verus, king of Britain, was made a Christian at his own request by Eleutherius, 156 A.D., and the Britons received the faith unto the time of Diocletian.—"Ecclesiastical History," chap. v. The church of England is always put on an equality with the church of Spain and Gaul, and at the council of Arles, 314, the names of 3 British bishops are met with —*Lingard* Pope Celestine I sent missionaries to Ireland, 422(?) "A band of Roman missionaries carried Christianity to distant England, and in England first was founded a church which owed its existence to the zeal of the Roman bishop" (pope Gregory I, 590–604) —*Creighton* From 1558 the power of the Romish church over the English government was lost, and severe laws were made against Roman Catholics, since repealed As early as 1602, they were excluded from corporate offices and from Parliament forbidden to marry Protestants, to possess arms, to go beyond 5 miles from their homes without a permit, etc In England, from 1623 to 1850 the Roman Catholics were under bishops, as vicars-apostolic, with first 1 and then 4, and afterwards 8 vicariates, in 1850. the hierarchy was restored, now including 1 archiepiscopal and 14 episcopal sees In Scotland, the hierarchy was restored in 1878, including 2 archiepiscopal and 4 episcopal sees In Ireland, the hierarchy has been uninterrupted, with 4 archiepiscopal and 23 episcopal sees Besides the United Kingdom, there are hierarchies in Canada, India, Australia, and Africa—in all numbering 28 archiepiscopal and 97 episcopal sees, and 23 vicariates and 10 prefectures apostolic.

Persecutions of Diocletian, St Albans put to death 304

Germanus of Auxerre visits Britain once 429 and again 446

Augustin lands in the isle of Thanet 596

Ethelbert, king of Kent baptized 597

Dunstan promotes monachism and the celibacy of the clergy, 952

Canute makes a pilgrimage to Rome 1028

Edward the Confessor a devotee to the church of Rome 1042–66

Pope Alexander II approves of William duke of Normandy's claim on England, and sends a consecrated banner 1066

Stigand, the last Anglo Saxon bishop, deposed by Rome 1050–69

Rome deposes the English prelates, and appoints Norman Lanfranc archbishop of Canterbury 1070

Nicholas Brakespeare, Adrian IV, pope 1154–59

CONSTITUTIONS OF CLARENDON enacted 1164

Annulled by the pope 1174

England under the interdict of Rome 1208

King John excommunicated 1209

" deposed by the pope 1213

" swears fealty to the pope 13 Nov "

Charter annulled by pope Innocent III 1215

First statute of PRÆMUNIRE enacted by Edward I 1306

Abolition of the order of the Templars—inquisition introduced, 1308

["Thus for once the papal inquisition found a foothold in England "—*Lea's* 'History of the Inquisition']

Irish memorial to the pope 1317

Second statue of præmunire enacted by Edward III 1353

Attempted reformation of Wickliffe 1380–1414

Wickliffe dies 1384

Sir John Oldcastle (lord Cobham) leader of the Lollards roasted to death 1418

Henry VIII wins, as the defender of Roman doctrines against Luther, the title of "Defender of the Faith" 1521

Henry VIII declared head of the English church by Parliament, 3 Nov 1534

Excommunicated by the pope 30 Aug 1535

Bishop Fisher, sir Thomas More, and others executed for denying the king's supremacy "

Catholics absolved from allegiance to the king by Paul III "

Suppression of the monasteries (PILGRIMAGE OF GRACE) 1536–38

Queen Mary marries Philip II of Spain July, 1554

Accession of Elizabeth (England becomes Protestant) 1558

ARMADA 1588

GUNPOWDER PLOT 1605

Catholics suffer by Oates's fictitious popish plot 1678

They are excluded from the throne 1689

Henry Stuart created cardinal. 1747

[The first cardinal since the reign of queen Mary CARDINALS]

They suffer by the GORDON RIOTS June, 1780

Various disabilities removed in 1780 and 1791

Mr Pitt proposes further relief, but gives it up 1801–4

Roman Catholic association organized in Ireland, to agitate against political and civil disabilities 1824

Bills to remove these often introduced from 1813 to 1828

Act passed to suppress the Catholic association (it had voted to dissolve, 12 Feb) 5 Mch 1829

Duke of Wellington and sir Robert Peel carry Catholic emancipation bill (10 Geo. IV c. 7) in commons, 30 Mch, in lords, 10 Apr, approved 13 Apr "

Duke of Norfolk and lords Dormer and Clifford, the first Catholic peers, take their seats 28 Apr "

First English Catholic member returned, the earl of Surrey, for Horsham 4 May, "

Mr O'Connell elected for Clare 1828, takes his seat (first Roman Catholic M P since 1689) Aug "

Alexander Raphael first Catholic sheriff of London 28 Sept. 1834

Sir Michael O'Loghlen, the first Catholic judge (as Master of the Rolls in Ireland), appointed 30 Oct. 1836

St. George's cathedral, Southwark, erected by A W Pugin, founded. 1840

Tablet newspaper established "

Mr O'Connell elected first Catholic lord mayor of Dublin 1841

"Catholic Poor School Committee" established 1847

Cardinal Nicholas Wiseman appointed archbishop of Westminster 30 Sept 1850

Catholic university, Dublin originated 5 May, 1851

Universe newspaper established 1860

Agitation in favor of the pope 1860–62

Missionary college founded at Drumcondra Ireland 20 July, 1862

Catholic chaplains permitted for jails, by Prison Ministers act, July, 1863

Sergeant William Shee made a justice of the Queen's Bench, first Catholic judge since the Reformation (d 19 Feb 1868), 15 Dec "

Death of cardinal Wiseman aged 63, 6th English cardinal since the reign of queen Mary 15 Feb 1865

Henry Manning (formerly archdeacon in the English church) consecrated archbishop of Westminster 8 June, "

Conference of Catholic bishops at Dublin, by resolution decline state help (under papal injunctions 1801 and 1805) and condemn mixed education and secret societies 17 Oct. 1867

In Great Britain 1639 Catholic priests, 1283 chapels and churches, 227 convents for women (principally educational), 21 colleges and large schools Dec "

Derby government proposes to endow a Catholic university for Ireland Oct. 1867, fails because Catholic bishops claim entire practical control 31 Mch 1868

Justice Thomas (afterwards lord) O'Hagan appointed lord chancellor of Ireland the first Catholic in that office since the revolution of 1688–89 Dec "

A Roman Catholic made M A at Oxford, after abolition of the test 22 June 1871

Catholics opposing the dogma of papal infallibility term themselves "OLD CATHOLICS" "

Ecclesiastical Titles act repealed 24 July, "

Pastoral issued by the Catholic bishops in Ireland claiming endowment for colleges, etc under their sole control Oct "

"Catholic Education Crisis Fund" established "

Two Roman Catholic bishops consecrated at Salford 28 Oct 1872

"Catholic Union," Dublin reorganized to obtain education under ecclesiastical control about 4 Dec 1873

Roman Catholic university senate meet 21 May, 1874

Archbishop Manning made a cardinal 1875

Catholic congress at Venice met 12 June, "

Marquess of Ripon becomes a Catholic 7 Sept "

Catholic university college, Kensington monsignor Capel principal, opened 15 Oct "

Several English clergymen secede to Rome Oct "

New Catholic club opened in London by duke of Norfolk lords Denbigh and Petre, and others 27 Nov "

Mr Gladstone's pamphlet, "The Vatican Decrees," occasions declarations from archbishop Manning M Capel, the Catholic union and others, for papal infallibility, from lords Acton, Camoys, and sir George Bowyer against it Nov "

Roman Catholic hierarchy re established in Scotland by pope Leo XIII 4 Mch 1878

[For dissension between church and state respecting papal infallibility, GERMANY, PRUSSIA]

Lord Petre a Roman Catholic priest, takes his seat in the house of lords 3 Nov 1884

Stuart Knill, Roman Catholic, elected lord mayor of London 1891

Roman law. CODES.

Roman literature. LITERATURE, LATIN LANGUAGE.

Roman roads in England. "The Romans," says Isidore, "made roads almost all over the world, to march in straight lines and to employ the people," and criminals were frequently condemned to work at such roads as we learn from Suetonius, in his 'Life of Caligula" They were commenced and completed at various periods, between the 2d and 4th centuries, and the Roman soldiery were employed on them that inactivity might not be opportunity for disturbances.—*Bede* The 4 principal great roads built in England by the Romans were

1st. Watling street, so named from Vitellianus, who is supposed to have directed it, the Britons calling him in their language *Guetalin* (from Kent to Cardigan bay)

2d, Ikenild or Ikenild street from its beginning among the *Iceni* (from St. David's to Tynemouth)

3d. Fosse or Fosse Way, probably from its being defended by a fosse on both sides (from Cornwall to Lincoln)

4th Ermin street, from *Irmunsul* a German name under which the German ancestors worshipped Mercury (from St David's to Southampton) ROADS.

Roman walls in England One was erected by Agricola (79 to 85) to defend Britain from incursions of Picts and Scots. The first wall extended from the Tyne to the Solway Firth (80 miles), the second from the Firth of Forth, near Edinburgh, to the Firth of Clyde, near Dumbarton (36 miles) The former was renewed and strengthened by the emperor Hadrian (121), and by Septimus Severus (208) It commenced at Bowness, near Carlisle, and ended at Wallsend, near Newcastle It had battlements and towers to contain soldiers. HADRIAN'S WALL. The more northern wall was renewed by Lollius Urbicus, in the reign of Antoninus Pius, about 140 Many remains of these walls still exist, particularly of the southern one.—*Bruce*, "Roman Wall" pub. 1853–68

 ROM

romance, originally a composition in the Romance or Provençal idiom The term in the middle ages was extended to narrative poetry in general Heliodorus, a bishop of Tricca, in Thessaly, about 398, was the author of "Æthiopica" (relating to the loves of Theagenes and Chariclea), the first work of this kind The first part of the "Roman de la Rose" was written by Guillaume de Lorres (1226-70), the second, a separate poem, by Jean de Meung (1285-1314), the "Decameron" of Boccaccio was pub 1358, "Don Quixote," by Cervantes, 1605, "Gil Blas," by Le Sage, 1715 Dunlop's "History of Fiction" pub 1814 "Story of Sancha," an Egyptian romance discovered in a tomb near Thebes, 1886, by M Maspero, and translated by him, is said to be many centuries older than the time of Moses LITERATURE, English, French, German, etc

Romantic School of Germany, 1800-10 Founders Schlegel, Novalis (Friedrich von Hardenberg), Ludwig Tieck, Hoffmann, De la Motte-Fouqué, and Chamisso, author of "Peter Schlemil, the Shadowless Man" LITERATURE, German.

Rome, the most celebrated city in the world, the capital of Italy, stands upon the river Tiber, about 14 miles from its mouth The origin of the name is unknown, in the oldest form known to us the inhabitants are not called Romans, but Rammans (*Ramnes*), possibly meaning 'foresters" or "bushmen" Long before a city was built the 3 tribes, Rammans, Tities, and Luceres probably had habitations on the 7 hills, the Aventine, Capitoline, Cœlian, Esquiline, Palatine, Quirinal, and Viminal From these settlements the later Rome originated —*Mommsen*, "Hist of Rome," bk i chap iv Legend ascribes the foundation of the city to Romulus, and, according to Varro, it was laid on the 20 Apr, in the year 3961 of the Julian period (3251 years after the creation of the world, 753 years before the birth of Christ, 431 years after the Trojan war, and in the 4th year of the 6th Olympiad Other dates given Cato, 751, Polybius, 750, Fabius Pictor, 747, Cincius, 728 B.C) Rome in her best days politically (reign of Trajan, 98-117 A D) dominated the known world From Italy west to the Atlantic, east to the Caspian sea and Euphrates river, south to the waters of the Mediterranean and the entire northern coast of Africa, including Egypt to Ethiopia, north to the Firth of Forth or Edinburgh, thence to the mouth of the Rhine, which may be termed its eastern, and the Danube its northern boundaries in Europe, although her Dacian possessions extended to the northern shores of the Euxine sea To the question why Rome so early attained supremacy, first in Italy and then in the world, the answer may be because the Roman had such complete control over himself When, where, or how this Roman characteristic began, history does not reveal, but it was conspicuous from the first from the traditionary Romulus suckled by the wolf, to the Cato of the later republic And, further, no nation before or since has exhibited such courage and resolution under reverses, such stern, unyielding determination to uphold the laws, however destructive to individual feeling or interests, such heroic patriotism, as the deed of Marcus Curtius, 362 B.C, and that of Publius Decius at the battle of Sentinum, 295 B.C., and many other instances, witness These characteristics suffice to explain how the Roman dominated and controlled the ancient world Rome has long since lost its republican simplicity, imperial splendor, and national name, and is again but a city, of less significance in the world of politics and war than it was before Cæsar began his conquests Pop 1872, about 240,000, 1877, 250,000, 1881, 273,268, 1890, 423,217, 1900, 462,783 Chiefly through the exertions of J H. Parker, the Roman exploration fund was established, for preserving ancient architectural remains. His "Archæology of Rome" (with many photographs) pub 1874-78. The Italian government votes $6000 a year for a similar purpose.

	B C
Foundation of the city by Romulus	753
Romans seize on the Sabine women at a public spectacle, and detain them for wives	750
Cæninians defeated, and first triumphal procession	748
Rome taken by the Sabines, the Sabines incorporated with the Romans as one nation	747
Romulus sole king of the Romans and Sabines	742
CIRCENSIAN games established by him	732
Romulus murdered by senators	716
Numa Pompilius elected king, 715, institutes the priesthood, the augurs and vestals	710
Roman CALENDAR of 10 months reformed and made 12 (DECEMBER)	"

	B C.
Romans and Albans agree to choose 3 champions each to decide their contest The *Horatii*, Roman knights, overcome the *Curiatii*, Albans, and unite Alba to Rome	about 669
War with the Fidenates, the city of ALBA LONGA destroyed	665
Ostia at the mouth of the Tiber, built	627
Capital founded	615
First census of the Roman state taken	566
Political institutions of Servius Tullius	550
Rape of Lucretia by Sextus son of Tarquin	510
Royalty abolished the patricians establish an aristocratical commonwealth	509
Junius Brutus and Tarquinius Collatinus first consuls, first alliance of the Romans with Carthage	508
CAPITOL dedicated to *Jupiter Capitolinus*	507
First dictator Titus Lartius	501
Latins and the Tarquins declare war against the republic, 501, defeated at lake Regillus	498 or 496
Secession of plebeians to the sacred mount, establishment of tribunes of plebeians	494
C Martius Coriolanus banished	491
He (with the Volsci) besieges Rome, but withdraws at the suit of his wife and mother	488
Contests between patricians and plebeians on AGRARIAN laws	486
Spurius Cassius, advocate of the law put to death by patricians,	485
Quæstors appointed	about 484
FABII slain	477
Cincinnatus, dictator defeats the Æqui	458
Secular games first celebrated	456
DECEMVIRI created	451
Virginius kills his daughter, Virginia, to save her from the decemvir Appius Claudius (Appius kills himself in prison, decemviral government abolished)	449
Canuleian law permitting patricians to marry plebeians	445
Military tribunes first created	444
Office of censor instituted	443
Famine in Rome, many drown themselves in the Tiber	440
Veientes defeated, and their king Tolumnius slain	437
War with the Tuscans	434
Temple dedicated to Apollo on account of a pestilence	431
Æqui and Volsci defeated by Tubertus, dictator	"
Two more quæstors appointed	421
Another famine at Rome	411
Three quæstors first chosen from plebeians	409
Lectisternian festival instituted on account of a pestilence	399
Veii taken by Camillus after 10 years' siege (ETRURIA)	396
Banishment of Camillus.	391
GAULS, under Brennus, besiege Clusium	390
They are expelled by Camillus.	389
Rome burned by the Gauls, who besiege the capital	387
Rebuilt, Capitoline games instituted (CAPITOL)	"
M Manlius Capitoline thrown from the Tarpeian rock on a charge of aiming at sovereign power	384
First appointment of curule magistrates	371
Lucius Sextus the first plebeian consul (LICINIAN LAWS)	366
Marcus Curtius leaps into a gulf opened in the forum	362
Gauls defeated in Italy	360
Treaty with Carthage to repress Greek piracy	348
War with the Samnites (with intermissions) 51 years	343
Latin war	340-38
Embassy to Alexander the Great	324
Defeat at the CAUDINE FORKS	321
Appian way began (ROADS)	312
Etruscans defeated at lake Vadimonis	310
Priests first elected from the plebeians.	300
Etruscans and Samnites defeated at Sentinum by Fabius	295
End of 3d Samnite war	290
HORTENSIAN LAW passed	286
Gauls invade Roman territory, siege of Arezzo	284
Etruscans again defeated at lake Vadimonis	283
Pyrrhus of Epirus invades Italy, 281, defeats Romans at Pandosia, 280, and at Asculum, 279, defeated at Benevento.	275
All Italy subdued by Rome	266
First Punic war commenced (CARTHAGE)	264
First Roman fleet built	260
Attilius Regulus put to a cruel death by the Carthaginians	255
End of first Punic war, Sicily annexed	241
Temple of Janus closed	235
Corsica and Sardinia annexed	231
First Roman embassy to Greece	228
Invasion of the Gauls, beaten by the consuls	225
Second Punic war breaks out	218
Hannibal enters Italy over the Alps.	"
Romans are defeated at Thrasymene, 217, Cannæ 2 Aug	216
Hannibal occupies CAPUA during the winter of	216-15
Syracuse taken by Marcellus	212
Marcellus slain by Hannibal's scouts, near Venusia.	208
Battle of METAURUS	207
Hannibal, recalled to Carthage, leaves Italy	203
Scipio defeats Hannibal at Zama, in Africa	202
Macedonian wars with Philip begin, 213 and 200, his defeat at Cynoscephalæ	197
Death of Scipio Africanus the elder	185
Third Macedonian war begins, 171, Perseus beaten at Pydna, Macedon annexed	168
First public library erected at Rome	167
Philosophers and rhetoricians banished from Rome	161
Third Punic war begins	149
CORINTH and CARTHAGE destroyed by the Romans	146
Celtiberian and NUMANTINE war in Spain	153-33
Attalus III of Pergamus bequeaths his kingdom and riches to the Romans	133

Servile war in Sicily B.C. 132

Two plebeian consuls chosen "

Agrarian disturbances, Gracchus slain 121

JUGURTHINE WAR 112-106

MITHRIDATIC WAR 108-63

Ambrones defeated by Marius 102

Social war 90-88

Rome besieged by 4 armies (viz., those of Marius, Cinna, Carbo, and Sertorius) and taken 87

Sulla defeats Marius, becomes dictator, sanguinary proscriptions, 82, abdicates 79

Bithynia bequeathed to the Romans by king Nicomedes 74

Revolt of SPARTACUS and the slaves 73-71

Syria conquered by Pompey 65

CATILINE CONSPIRACY suppressed by Cicero 63

First triumvirate Cæsar, Pompey, and Crassus 60

Cæsar's campaigns in Gaul, 58, in Britain 55

Romans defeated at Carrhæ by the Parthians, Crassus killed 53

Gaul conquered and made a province by Julius Cæsar 51

War between Cæsar and the Senatorial party 50

Pompey defeated at PHARSALIA 48

Cæsar defeats Pharnaces at Zela, and writes home "Veni, vidi, vici" 47

Cato kills himself at Utica, Cæsar dictator for 10 years 46

Cæsar assassinated in the senate house 15 Mch 44

Second triumvirate Octavius, Antony, and Lepidus 43

Cicero proscribed by Antony, killed "

Battle of PHILIPPI, Brutus and Cassius defeated 42

Lepidus ejected from triumvirate, 36, war of Octavius and Antony, 32, Antony defeated at ACTIUM 2 Sept 31

Octavius emperor, as Augustus Cæsar 27

Empire at peace with the world, temple of Janus shut 4 Apr 5

Jesus Christ born (JEWS) A.D.

Varus defeated by the Germans under Arminius 9

Ovid banished to Tomi "

Death of Ovid and Livy 18

Tiberius retires to CAPREÆ, tyranny of Sejanus 26

Census taken by Claudius emperor and censor, Rome said to have 6,944,000 people (probably less than 1,000,000 within the walls) 48

Caractacus brought from Britain in chains to Rome 50

St Paul arrives in bonds at Rome 62

Christians charged with the crime of burning Rome by Nero 64

Seneca, Lucan, etc., put to death by Nero 65

Peter and Paul said to be put to death 67

Jerusalem levelled to the ground by Titus 8 Sept 70

COLISEUM founded by Vespasian 75

Dacian war begins (continues 15 years) 86

Pliny jr., proconsul in Bithynia, sends Trajan his celebrated account of the Christians 102

Trajan's expedition into the East against the Parthians, etc., subdues DACIA 106

Trajan's column erected at Rome 114

Hadrian resides in Britain, and builds the wall 121

Byzantium taken, its walls razed 196

Goths take tribute 222

[The Goths, Vandals, Alani, Suevi, and other northern nations attack the empire.]

Pompey's amphitheatre burned 248

Invasion of the Goths. 250

Pestilence throughout the empire 252

Great victory over the Goths by Claudius II., 300,000 slain 269

Dacia relinquished to the Goths 270

Palmyra taken by Aurelian, queen Zenobia carried to Rome, and Longinus put to death 273

Era of martyrs, or of Diocletian 284

Franks settle in Gaul (*Frerel*) 287

Constantius dies at York 306

Four emperors reign at one time 308

Constantine the Great, it is said, in consequence of a vision, places the cross on his banners and favors Christians 312

Constantine defeats Licinius at Chrysopolis, and reigns alone, 18 Sept 323

He tolerates the Christian faith "

Puts his son Crispus to death 324

Constantine convokes the first general council of Christians at Nicea 325

Seat of empire removed from Rome to BYZANTIUM, 321, dedicated by Constantine 330

Constantine orders the heathen temples to be destroyed "

Revolt of 300,000 Sarmatian slaves suppressed 334

Death of Constantine soon after being baptized 337

Army under Julian proclaims him emperor 360

Julian, educated for the priesthood, after often officiating, abjures Christianity and reopens heathen temples. 361

Julian killed in battle in Persia, Christianity restored by Jovian 363

Empire divided into Eastern and Western by Valentinian and Valens, brothers, the former has the western portion, or Rome 364

Final division of the empire (ITALY, EASTERN and WESTERN EMPIRES) 395

Rome placed under the exarchate of Ravenna. 404

Taken by ALARIC 24 Aug 410

Taken and pillaged by Genseric 15 July, 455

Odoacer, king of the HERULI, takes Rome, and becomes king of Italy 476

Theodoric, king of the East Goths, receives commission from the Greek emperor Zeno, at Constantinople, to assume control of Italy 488

Rome recovered for Justinian by Belisarius 536

Retaken by Totila the Goth, 546, recovered by Belisarius, 547, seized by Totila. 549

Recovered by Narses, annexed to Eastern empire, senate abolished 553

Rome at her lowest state about 600

Rome independent under the popes about 728

Pepin of France compels Astolphus king of the Lombards, to cede Ravenna, etc., to the church 755

Confirmed and added to by Charlemagne 774

Charlemagne crowned emperor of the West by the pope at Rome 25 Dec 800

Rome taken by Arnulf and the Germans 896

Otho I. crowned at Rome 2 Feb 962

Emperor Henry IV. takes Rome Mch 1084

Arnold of Brescia seeking to reform church and state and to establish a senate is slain as a heretic 1155

Pope removes to Avignon 1309

Nicola di Rienzi tribune of the people, establishes a republic, 20 May, compelled to abdicate 15 Dec 1347

Returns, made senator, 1 Aug., assassinated 8 Oct 1354

Papal court returns to Rome 1377

Rise of the families Colonna, Orsini, etc about "

Pope Julius II. conquers Romagna, Bologna, and Perugia. 1503-13

Rome greatly embellished by pope Leo X 1513-21

Captured by constable de Bourbon who is slain 6 May, 1527

Ferrara annexed 1597

Execution of the Cenci Beatrice and others, whereby the Romish Church secured all the property of that family, and for which purpose they were put to death 1599

St. Peter's dedicated 18 Nov 1626

Expulsion of the Jesuits 16 Aug 1773

[Harassed by French, German, and Spanish factions from the 16th to the 18th century.]

French invasion, the Legations incorporated with the Cisalpine republic 1796

French proclaim the Roman republic 20 Mch 1798

Recovered for the pope by the Neapolitans Nov 1799

Retaken by the French 1800, restored to Pius VII July, 1801

Annexed by Napoleon to the kingdom of Italy, and declared second city of the empire May, 1808

Restored to the pope, who returns 23 Jan 1814

He re establishes the Inquisition and the Jesuits 7 Aug "

Papal government seeks to annul innovations provoking much opposition, CARBONARI increase in numbers 1815-17

Political assassinations in the Romagna 1817

"Young Italy" party established by Joseph Mazzini, insurrections at Bologna suppressed by Austrian aid 1831

Election of Pius IX 16 June, 1846

He proclaims amnesty, authorizes a national guard and municipal institutions 1847

Romans desire to join the king of Sardinia against the Austrians, the pope hesitates, the Antonelli ministry retires, the Mamiani ministry formed 1848

Count Rossi, papal minister of justice, assassinated on the staircase of the Chamber of Deputies at Rome 15 Nov "

Insurrection at Rome the populace demand a democratic ministry and proclamation of Italian nationality, the pope (Pius IX.) hesitates, Romans surround the palace, and a conflict ensues Pope accepts a popular ministry (cardinal Palma, the pope's secretary, shot in the conflict) 16 Nov "

A free constitution published 20 Nov "

Pope escapes in disguise from Rome to Gaeta 24 Nov "

Roman National Assembly divests the pope of temporal power, and adopts republican government 8 Feb 1849

Pope appeals to Catholic powers 18 Feb "

Civita Vecchia occupied by French under marshal Oudinot, 26 Apr "

French under marshal Oudinot attack Rome 3 June, "

Romans capitulate to the French army 30 June, "

Re establishment of the pope's authority proclaimed at Rome, 15 July, "

Oudinot by general order states that the pope (or his representative) now repossesses the administration, but that public security in his dominions remains under the special guarantee of the French army 3 Aug "

Pope's bull establishing a Roman Catholic hierarchy in England 24 Sept 1850

Important concordat with Austria 18 Aug 1855

Pope appeals to Europe against Sardinia 12 July, 1859

Assembly at Bologna vote annexation to Piedmont, 7 Sept., the king engages to support them before the great powers, 15 Sept., the pope annuls the acts of the assembly at Bologna, proclaims punishment of those who attack the holy see, 26 Sept., and dismisses the Sardinian chargé d'affaires at Rome, 1 Oct. "

Romagna, Modena, and Parma formed into a province, to be called Æmilia (ITALY, 1859-60) 24 Dec "

Sardinian government annul the Tuscan and Lombard concordats 27 Jan., 20 Mch 1860

Pope excommunicates all rebels in his states. 26 Mch "

Insurrection in the Marches, 8 Sept., Fossembrone subdued by papal troops, the people appeal to the Sardinian government, whose troops, under Cialdini and Fanti, enter the Papal States. 11 Sept. "

Allocution of the pope against France and Sardinia, he appeals to Europe for help 28 Sept "

Subscriptions for the pope in various countries, forbidden in France and Belgium, permitted in England Nov "

Monastic establishments suppressed in legations, monks pensioned, educational institutions founded Dec. "

Publication of *Rome et les Evêques*, 6 Jan., and of *La France, Rome et l'Italie*, 15 Feb., earnest advocacy of pope's temporal government (attacked by prince Napoleon) in French chambers....................Mch. 1861

Cavour claims Rome as capital of Italy...............27 Mch. "

Emperor of France declines union with Austria and Spain to support pope's temporal power........................June, "

CANONIZATION of 27 Japanese martyrs...................8 June, "

Pope issues an allocution against the Italians..........9 June, "

Garibaldi calls for volunteers, taking as his watchword "Rome or death!"....................................19 July, 1862

Railway between Rome and Naples completed; its opening opposed by papal government.........................Nov. "

Earl Russell's offer to the pope of a residence at Malta, 25 Oct.; declined....................................11 Nov. "

Encyclical letter of the pope, publishing a "syllabus," censuring 80 errors in religion, philosophy, and politics (causes much dissatisfaction, *forbidden to be read in churches in* France and other countries)..........................8 Dec. 1864

Jews persecuted at Rome.............................Dec. "

Pope's allocution against secret societies (Freemasons, Fenians, etc.)..25 Sept. 1865

Merode, papal minister of war, dismissed..............20 Oct. "

Part of the French troops leave the papal dominions.....Nov. "

Pope invites all Catholic bishops to Rome to celebrate the 18th centenary of the martyrdom of Peter and Paul.......8 Dec. 1866

Pope's blessing given to French troops, 6 Dec., who all quit Rome...2-12 Dec. "

Law prohibiting Protestant worship in Rome, except at embassies, enforced..31 Dec. "

Five hundred and ninety-nine bishops and thousands of priests present at the pope's allocution, 26 June; and canonization of 25 martyrs.....................................29 June, 1867

Attempt at insurrection in Rome suppressed, 22 Oct.; siege proclaimed; Garibaldi within 20 miles of Rome, 24 Oct.; takes Monte Rotondo..............................26 Oct. "

French brigades enter Rome..........................30 Oct. "

Italian troops cross the frontier, 30 Oct.; occupy several posts, 1 Nov. "

Garibaldians defeated by papal and French troops at Mentana, 3 Nov. "

Italian troops retire from Papal States..................Nov. "

Pope's short allocution (thanking and blessing the French government)......................................19 Dec. "

New cardinals made; Lucien Bonaparte one..........13 Mch. 1868

Pope, in an allocution, censures the Austrian new civil-marriage law...22 June, "

Encyclical letter of the pope, summoning an œcumenical council at Rome on 8 Dec. 1869, and inviting ministers of the Greek and other churches.......................13 Sept. "

Patriarch of the Greek church declined to attend..about 3 Oct. "

Pope asserts in a letter to archbishop Manning that no disputed points can be discussed at the council.........4 Sept. 1869

Council XXI. opened (COUNCILS OF THE CHURCH)........8 Dec. "

British and American bishops protest against discussing the dogma of papal infallibility in the council, 11 Apr.; the discussion begins.......................................14 May, 1870

Count Arnim, for North German confederation, protests against the dogma.................................May, "

Papal infallibility approved by the council and promulgated (533 for, 2 against; many retire); the council adjourns to 11 Nov...18 July, "

Rome evacuated by French because of war; 8 mortars and 15,000 shells said to be ceded to the pope, 8 Aug.; the troops sent from Civita Vecchia...........................21 Aug. "

Pope refuses terms offered by king of Italy (sovereignty of Leonine city and retention of his income)..........11 Sept. "

Gen. Cadorna crosses Tiber at Casale; sends flags of truce to gen. Kanzler, commanding the Zouaves, who refuses to surrender; baron Arnim in vain negotiates............17 Sept. "

Italians occupy Civita Vecchia without resistance, about 15 Sept. "

Letter from pope to gen. Kanzler directing merely formal defence at Rome, to avoid bloodshed.................19 Sept. "

After brief resistance from foreign papal troops, stopped by the pope, Italian troops under Cadorna make a breach and enter Rome amid acclamations...................20 Sept. "

[Reported Italian loss, about 22 killed, 117 wounded; papal troops, 55 killed and wounded.]

Papal troops surrender arms; about 8500 foreigners march out with honors of war............................22 Sept. "

About 10,000 persons meet in the Coliseum; choose 44 men for a provisional government (*giunta*)..............22 Sept. "

Protest of pope.......................................26 Sept. "

Castle of St. Angelo occupied by Italian troops at pope's request..28 Sept. "

Circular letter from pope to cardinals complaining of invasion, loss of liberty, and interference with private mail...29 Sept. "

Giunta of 14 (duke Gaetani chief) selected from the 44 names chosen; approved by Cadorna.......................30 Sept. "

Gen. Masi in command of Rome and the provinces; S.P.Q.R. appears on proclamations...........................30 Sept. "

Plébiscite: only 167,548 vote; 133,681 for union with the kingdom of Italy, 1507 against.........................2 Oct. "

Pope said to have accepted 50,000 crowns (his monthly civil list) from Italian government.........................4 Oct. "

Result of the plébiscite sent to the king, 8 Oct.; Rome and provinces incorporated with kingdom by royal decree, 9 Oct. "

Gen. La Marmora enters Rome as viceroy; guarantees pope his sovereign powers as head of the church..........11 Oct. "

Roman provinces united into one by decree...........19 Oct. "

Pope issues encyclical letter adjourning the council....20 Oct. "

Bill introduced into the Italian parliament for transfer of government to Rome in about 6 months, preserving spiritual and *temporal sovereignty of the pope.................about* 12 Dec. 1870

Law guaranteeing pope personal liberty and honors, a revenue of 3,225,000 livres, etc., 13 May; rejected by pope in allocution...15 May, 1871

Pope celebrates a jubilee on 25th anniversary of his election, 16 June, "

Italian government removes to Rome..............2, 3 July, "

King opens parliament, saying, "The work to which we have consecrated our life is completed"................27 Nov. "

Commission appointed to dredge the Tiber for antiquities, Dec. "

American Protestant church dedicated to St. Paul; founded, 25 Jan. 1873

First Anglican church within the walls opened.........25 Oct. 1874

Reinterment on the Janiculum of remains of Angelo Brunetti (*termed Ciceruacchio*) *and other unarmed Italian patriots* (shot by Austrians, 10 Aug. 1849)..............12 Oct. 1879

2634th anniversary of the foundation of Rome kept....21 Apr. 1880

Sale of part of Castellani collection, 21 days, about $240,000 realized..Apr. "

ITALY, POPES.

KINGS OF ROME.

B.C.

735. Romulus; murdered by the senators.
[Tatius, king of the Sabines, had removed to Rome in 747, and ruled jointly with Romulus 6 years.]

716. [Interregnum.]

715. Numa Pompilius, son-in-law of Tatius the Sabine, elected; died at the age of 82.

673. Tullus Hostilius; murdered by his successor, who set his palace on fire; his family burned.

640. Ancus Martius, grandson of Numa.

616. Tarquinius Priscus, son of Demaratus, a Corinthian emigrant, chosen king.

578. Servius Tullius, a manumitted slave; married the king's daughter, and succeeded by united suffrages of army and people.

534. Tarquinius Superbus, grandson of Tarquinius Priscus; assassinates his father-in-law, and usurps the throne.

510. [Rape of Lucretia, by Sextus, son of Tarquin, and consequent insurrection, causing abolition of royalty and establishment of consulate.]

REPUBLIC.

510-82. *First period.* From the expulsion of Tarquin to the dictatorship of Sulla.

82-27. *Second period.* From Sulla to Augustus.

48. Caius Julius Cæsar perpetual dictator; assassinated, 15 Mch. 44 B.C.

31. Octavianus Cæsar.

EMPERORS.

27. Augustus Imperator; d. 19 Aug. 14 A.D.

A.D.

14. Tiberius (Claudius Nero).

37. Caius Caligula; murdered by a tribune.

41. Claudius I. (Tiberius Drusus); poisoned by his wife, Agrippina, to make way for

54. Claudius Nero; deposed; kills himself, 68.

68. Servius Sulpicius Galba; slain by the prætorians.

69. M. Salvius Otho; stabbed himself.

" Aulus Vitellius; deposed by Vespasian, and put to death.

" Titus Flavius Vespasian.

79. Titus (Vespasian), his son.

81. Titus Flavius Domitian, brother of Titus; last of the *twelve* Cæsars; assassinated. CÆSARS, THE TWELVE.

96. Cocceius Nerva.

98. Trajan (M. Ulpius Crinitus).

117. Adrian, or Hadrian (Publius Ælius).

138. Antoninus Titus, surnamed Pius.

161. Marcus Aurelius (a philosopher) and Lucius Verus, his son-in-law; the latter died in 169.

180. Commodus (L. Aurelius Antoninus), son of Marcus Aurelius; poisoned by his favorite mistress, Martia.

193. Publius Helvius Pertinax; killed by prætorian band.
[4 emperors start up: Didianus Julianus, at Rome; Pescennius Niger, in Syria; Lucius Septimius Severus, in Pannonia; and Clodius Albinus, in Britain.]

" Lucius Septimius Severus; died at York, in Britain, in 211; succeeded by his sons,

211. M. Aurelius Caracalla and Septimius Geta. Caracalla murders Geta, 212; is slain by his successor,

217. M. Opilius Macrinus, prefect of the guards; beheaded in a mutiny.

218. Heliogabalus (M. Aurelius Antoninus), a youth; put to death for enormities.

222. Alexander Severus; assassinated by soldiers corrupted by Maximinus.

235. Caius Julius Verus Maximinus; assassinated in his tent before the walls of Aquileia.

237. M. Antonius Gordianus and his son; the latter falling in battle with partisans of Maximinus, the father strangled himself in despair, at Carthage, in his 80th year.

238. Balbinus and Pupienus; put to death.

" Gordian III., grandson of the elder Gordian, in his 16th year assassinated by guards, instigated by

244. Philip the Arabian; assassinated by his soldiers; his son Philip murdered at the same time, in his mother's arms.

249. Metius Decius; he perished with 2 sons and their army, in battle with Goths.

251. Gallus Hostilius, and his son Volusianus; both slain by soldiers.

253. Æmilianus; put to death after reign of 4 months.

" Valerianus, and his son Gallienus; the first was taken prisoner by Sapor, king of Persia, and flayed alive.

260 Gallienus alone
[About this time 30 pretenders to imperial power arose in different parts of the empire, of these Cyriades was the first, but he was slain]
268 Claudius II (Gallienus having been assassinated by the officers of the guard) succeeds, dies of the plague
270 Quintillus, his brother, elected at Rome by the senate and troops, Aurelian by the army in Illyricum Quintillus, despairing of success, his rival marching against him, opened his veins and bled to death
" Aurelianus, assassinated by soldiers on march against Persia, in Jan 275
275 [Interregnum of about 9 months]
" Tacitus, elected 25 Oct., died at Tarsus in Cilicia, 13 Apr 276
276 Florianus, his brother not recognized by senate
" M Aurelius Probus, assassinated by troops at Sirmium
282 M Aurelius Carus, killed at Ctesiphon by lightning, succeeded by his sons,
283 Carinus and Numerianus, both assassinated
284 Diocletian, who took as his colleague
286 Maximianus Hercules, the two resign in favor of
305 Constantius I Chlorus and Galerius Maximianus, the first died at York, in Britain in 306, and the troops saluted as emperor his son,
306 Constantine afterwards styled the Great, while at Rome, the prætorian band proclaimed
" Maxentius son of Maximianus Hercules Besides these were
" Maximianus Hercules, who endeavored to recover his abdicated power,
" Flavius Valerius Severus, murdered by the last named pretender, and
307 Flavius Valerianus Licinius, the brother in law of Constantine
[Of these, Maximianus Hercules was strangled in Gaul in 310, Galerius Maximianus died wretchedly in 311, Maxentius was drowned in the Tiber in 312, and Licinius was put to death by order of Constantine in 324]
323 Constantine the Great alone died on Whitsunday, 22 May, 337
337 {Constantine II, Constans, Constantius II} Sons of Constantine, divided the empire, the first was slain in 340, the second murdered in 350, when the third became sole emperor
360 Julian the Apostate, who abjured Christianity, though educated for the priesthood, mortally wounded in battle with Persians 363
363 Jovian, reigned 8 months, found dead in his bed, supposed from fumes of charcoal
364 Valentinian and Valens
375 Valens with Gratian and Valentinian II
379 Theodosius I, etc
392 Theodosius alone
395 The Roman empire divided EASTERN EMPIRE, ITALY, POPES, WESTERN EMPIRE

Roncesval'les, a frontier village of Spain, in the Pyrenees, where, it is said, Charlemagne's paladin, Roland or Orlando, was surprised, defeated, and slain by the Gascons, 778.

Rontgen rays. Prof W C. Rontgen, while experimenting with a Crookes's vacuum tube, electrically excited and enveloped in a black covering, observed that some rays proceeding from the tube passed through the black paper and affected a fluorescent screen, 8 Oct. 1895 RADIUM

roof. The largest in the world was said to cover a riding-school at Moscow, erected in 1791, 235 ft in span. That of the London station of the Midland railway, Euston road, London, N W, is 240 ft wide, 690 ft long, 125 ft high, and covers about 165,000 sq ft WORLD'S FAIR.

Rorke's Drift, boundary of British territory of Natal, in South Africa and Zululand Behind extemporized trenches, a handful of British soldiers here successfully resisted a large Zulu army, and probably saved the colony, 22 Jan 1879 ZULULAND

Rosamond's Bower. Rosamond was daughter of lord Walter Clifford of Hertfordshire, mistress of Henry II, and mother of William Longsword The story of Henry's keeping her in a labyrinth at Woodstock, where his queen, Eleanor, it is said, discovered her apartments by the clew of a silk thread and poisoned her, is probably a mere invention of romance, as she retired to the convent of Godestow, near Oxford, where she died, and from whence Hugh, bishop of Lincoln, had her ashes removed, 1191

rosary. BEADS

A brief of pope Pius IX 30 Sept. 1852 asserted that 40 repetitions on a rosary of 40 beads of "Sweet heart of Mary, be my salvation!" will obtain many days of indulgence for souls in purgatory (23,300 days calculated)

Ro'sas, Bay of, N E. Spain, where a naval action was fought by the boats of the *Tigre, Cumberland, Volontaire, Apollo, Topaze, Philomel, Scout* and *Tuscan*, led by lieut. John Tailour of the *Tigre*, which ended in the capture or destruction of 11 armed vessels, 1 Nov. 1809. Lord Collingwood had organized the expedition commanded by capt Hallowell for this purpose Rosas was gallantly defended by lord Cochrane, 27 Nov., but surrendered, 4 Dec 1809

Ros'bach or **Rosbec'qu,** a village of Flanders (Belgium) Here Charles VI of France subdued the Flemings, who had revolted against their count, 27 Nov. 1382

Roscius (*rosh'i-us*) **Infant,** Wm Henry West Betty, born 13 Sept 1791 So called after an illustrious Roman actor in the time of Cicero. After acting at Belfast, 16 Aug 1803, and at other places, with much applause, he appeared at Covent Garden, 1 Dec 1803, as Selim, in "Barbarossa," and is said to have gained in his first season 17,210*l*

After several years' retirement, he reappeared but soon left the stage, not being successful He retired on the fortune he had amassed and died Aug 1874 His portrait may be seen at the Garrick club, London

rose. The rose, a symbol of silence, gave rise to the phrase *sub rosâ*, "under the rose," as Italian writers say, because the pope gave consecrated roses, which were placed over the confessionals at Rome, to denote secrecy, 1526 The pope sent a golden rose to the queen of Spain, which was given to her with much solemnity, 8 Feb 1868 A 'national rose society" opened its first annual show, St James's hall, London, 4 July, 1877 FLOWERS AND PLANTS

Roses, Wars of the, between the Lancastrians (who chose the red rose as their emblem) and the Yorkists (who chose the white rose), 1455-85 It is asserted that in the Wars of the Roses 12 princes of the blood, 200 nobles, and 100,000 gentry and common people perished The union of the houses was effected by the marriage of Henry VII to the princess Elizabeth, daughter of Edward IV, 1486

Richard II, who succeeded his grandfather Edward III in 1377, was deposed and succeeded in 1399 by his cousin Henry IV (son of John of Gaunt duke of Lancaster, the fourth son of Edward III), in prejudice to the right of Roger Mortimer (grandson of Lionel, duke of Clarence, Edward's *third* son), declared presumptive heir to the throne in 1385
Roger's grandson, Richard, duke of York, first openly claimed the crown in 1449
Attempts at compromise failed, war begun in 1455
Lancastrians defeated at St. Alban's, protector Somerset slain, truce made, Richard declared successor to Henry VI 23 May, "
War renewed, Lancastrians defeated at Blore-heath 23 Sept 1459
Yorkists eventually dispersed, the duke was attainted
He defeated his opponents at Northampton, took Henry prisoner and was declared heir to the crown, but was killed in an ambuscade near Wakefield 31 Dec 1460
His son (Edward) continued the struggle, was installed as king 4 Mch 1461
Defeated Lancastrians at Towton 29 Mch "
Was deposed by Warwick, who restored Henry VI Sept 1470
Edward defeated Lancastrians at Barnet, 14 Apr, finally at Tewkesbury 4 May. 1471
Richard III overthrown and killed at Bosworth 22 Aug 1485

Rosetta (*ro-zet'ta*), a town of Lower Egypt, taken by the French in 1798, and by the British and Turks, 19 Apr 1801 The Turks repulsed the British here, 22 Apr 1807 Near Rosetta was fought the battle of the Nile, 1 Aug 1798 NILE Mehemet Ali rendered great service to his country by constructing a canal between Rosetta and Alexandria.—The Rosetta stone, discovered by the French in 1799, was brought from Rosetta in a French vessel, from whence it was taken by Wir R Hamilton, who deposited it in the British museum In 1841, Mr Letronne published the text and a translation of the Greek inscription It is a piece of black basalt, about 3 ft long and 2½ ft wide, with an inscription in 3 languages—viz hieroglyphics, modified hieroglyphics (enchorial), and Greek, setting forth the praises of Ptolemy Epiphanes (about 196 B.C) It has been studied by dr T Young and Champollion

Rosicru'cians, a sect of mystical philosophers who appeared in Germany, alleged to have been founded by a German noble, Christian Rosenkreuz, 1388 They pretended to be able to transmute metals, prolong life, and to know what was passing in distant places They died out in the 18th century and their secret with them The "Confessio Roseæ Crucis," 1615, is attributed to Valentine Andreas It is also affirmed that the ancient philosophers of Egypt, the Chaldæans, Magi of Persia, and Gymnosophists of the Indies taught the same doctrine This society has given rise to much controversy, some asserting that it never existed It was also known as the *Brothers of the Rosy Cross*, it being supposed that the term *Rosicrucian* was derived from *crux*, cross, and *rosa*, rose.

Ross'bach, a village of Prussia. Here a battle was fought between the Prussians, under Frederick the Great, and the combined French and Austrians, and the latter were defeated, 5 Nov. 1757.

Rothschild (Germ. pronounced *roth'sheeld*, but in England called *ros'child*) **family.** Meyer Amschel, or Anselm, a Jew, was born at No. 148 Judengasse (Jew lane), Frankfort-on-the-Main, in 1743. In 1772 he began business as a money-lender and dealer in old coins, in the same house, over which he placed the sign of the red shield (in German, Roth Schild). He had dealings with the landgrave of Hesse, who intrusted him with his treasure (said to have been 250,000*l*.) in 1806, when the French held his country. With this capital Anselm traded and made a large fortune, and restored the 250,000*l*. to the landgrave in 1815. At his death his sons continued the business as money-lenders. His son Nathan began at Manchester in 1798, removed to London in 1803, and died immensely rich, 28 July, 1836. The baron, James, head of the family, died at Paris, 15 Nov. 1868.

Rot'terdam, the second city in Holland. Its importance dates from the 13th century. The commerce of Antwerp was transferred to it in 1509. In 1572 Rotterdam was taken by the Spaniards by stratagem, and cruelly treated. It suffered much from French revolutionary wars, and from inundations in 1775 and 1825. Desiderius Erasmus was born here in 1467. The museum and picture-gallery were destroyed at the fire of the Schieland palace, 16 Feb. 1864.

Rouen (*roo-an'*), N. France, an archbishopric, 260, became the capital of Normandy in the 10th century. It was held by the English kings till 1204, and was retaken by Henry V., 19 Jan. 1419. Joan of Arc, the Maid of Orleans, was burned here, 30 May, 1431. It was taken by Charles VII. of France in 1449, and by the duke of Guise from the Huguenots, Oct. 1562 and 1591. Rouen, after slight resistance, 4, 5 Dec. 1870, surrendered to gen. von Goben, 6 Dec. It was ordered to pay a contribution of 17,000,000 francs.

Rouma'nia, the name assumed by the DANUBIAN PRINCIPALITIES on 23 Dec. 1861, when their union was proclaimed at Bucharest and Jassy. Area, 48,307 sq. miles; pop. 1887, 5,500,000. The language is a Latin dialect introduced by the Roman colonists, who settled in Dacia in the time of Trajan.

M. Catargi, president of council of ministers, assassinated while leaving Chamber of Deputies ... 20 June, 1862
United chambers of the 2 principalities meet at Bucharest, 5 Feb. "
Coup d'état of prince Couza against aristocrats; plébiscite for a new constitution, 2 May; adopted ... 28 May, 1864
Law passed enabling peasants to hold land ... Aug. "
Revolt at Bucharest suppressed, 15 Aug.; amnesty ... 11 Sept. 1865
Revolution at Bucharest, forced abdication of prince Couza, provisional government established ... 22 Feb. 1866
Offered crown declined by count of Flanders, Feb.; prince Charles of Hohenzollern-Sigmaringen elected hospodar by plebiscite, 20 Apr.; welcomed at Bucharest, 22 May; swears to the constitution ... 12 July, "
Recognized hereditary hospodar by sultan; received at Constantinople ... 24 Oct. "
Roumania unsettled; "nationality" projects ... Nov. 1867
Legislature repudiates just claims of German shareholders in Roumanian railways; prince assents reluctantly; Bismarck appeals to the Porte, which declines to interfere ... July–Aug. 1871
Peace between prince and chambers ... Nov. "
Austria, Germany, and Russia assert the right to conclude separate treaties with Roumania; sultan objects ... Oct. 1874
Convention with Russia, giving permission to cross Roumania, signed 16 Apr.; Russians enter Moldavia ... 24 Apr. 1877
Senate declares independence and war with Turkey ... 21 May, "
Roumanians actively engaged before Plevna (RUSSO-TURKISH WARS) ... "
Roumania declared independent by treaties of San Stefano (3 Mch.) and of Berlin (exchanging part of Bessarabia acquired in 1856 for the Dobrudscha) ... 13 July, 1878
Independence recognized by England, France, and Germany, 20 Feb. 1880
Prince and princess crowned king and queen ... 23 May, 1881
Constitution modified ... 1884

PRINCES AND KING OF ROUMANIA.

1859. Alexander Couza, abdicated 1866.
1866. Charles I. (of Hohenzollern-Sigmaringen), b. 20 Apr. 1839, elected 20 Apr. 1866, married Elizabeth, daughter of prince Hermann von Wied, 15 Nov. 1869, nominated king, 26 Mch. 1881, crowned with the queen, 23 May, 1881.

Roume'lia or Roma'nia, Turkey, part of THRACE. The Roumelian railway opened 17 June, 1873.

By treaty of Berlin, the province of Eastern Roumelia constituted partly autonomous, with a Christian governor, nominated by sultan ... 13 July, 1878
Sir H. D. Wolff appointed H. M.'s European commissioner for organization of the province ... 10 Aug. "
Russian prince Dondoukoff Khorsakoff rules here ... July–Nov. "
Scheme for government of province approved by sultan and allied commissioners ... Nov. "
Russian evacuation begins ... 5 May, 1879
Aleko Pacha (prince Alexander Vogorides, a Bulgarian) installed as governor at Philippopolis ... 30 May, "
Great prosperity reported ... 1883
M. Crestovitch appointed gov.-gen. by the Porte ... May, 1884

Roundheads. In the civil war which began in 1642, the adherents of Charles I. were called Cavaliers and the friends of the parliament Roundheads. The term, it is said, arose from the practice of putting a round bowl or dish on the head and cutting the hair to the edge of the bowl. CAVALIERS.

round table, according to romance, a circular table around which were wont to sit king Arthur of Britain and his knights, hence called "knights of the round table." It was fitted to seat 13 in memory of the 13 disciples, but 12 seats were occupied, that of Judas being vacant. The most famous of the knights were Sirs Bedivere, Bors, Gaheris, Galahad, Gareth, Gawain, Geraint, Kay, Launcelot, Launfal, Meliadus, Modred, Pelleas, Percivale, and Tristram. Most of these are often mentioned in Tennyson's "Idylls of the King."

rowing. BOAT-RACES.

Rowley (*row'ly*), Thomas, a priest of Bristol, Engl., during the time of Edward III., a creation of Chatterton's, to whom he ascribed the authorship of the poems which he had written himself, and which he endeavored to pass off as productions of Rowley in the 15th century. The MSS. were said to have been found in the church of St. Mary Redcliffe at Bristol. These poems have variety and merit, and, though crude as forgeries of an earlier age, their brilliancy and numbers deceived many scholars at that day. LITERATURE, Forgeries of.

Royal Academy. A society of artists met in St. Peter's court, St. Martin's lane, London, about 1739, which Hogarth formed into the Society of Incorporated Artists, who held their first exhibition at the Society of Arts, Adelphi, 21 Apr. 1760. From this sprang the Royal Academy, in consequence of a dispute between the directors and the fellows. On 10 Dec. 1768, the institution of the present Royal Academy was completed under patronage of George III., and sir Joshua Reynolds, knighted on the occasion, was appointed first president.—*Leigh.* The first exhibition of academicians (at Pall Mall) was on 26 Apr. 1769, when 136 works appeared. In 1771 the king granted them apartments in old Somerset House, and afterwards, in 1780, in new Somerset House, where they remained till 1838, when they removed to the National gallery. From the honorary members, professors of ancient literature and ancient history are appointed. Among them have been Johnson, Gibbon, Goldsmith, Scott, Macaulay, and Hallam. Turner, the painter, gave 20,000*l*. to the academy at his death, 1851. A commission of inquiry into the affairs of the academy, appointed in 1862, recommended changes in July, 1863, which were carried into effect. The hundredth anniversary of its foundation was celebrated 10 Dec. 1868. The Royal Academy held its first exhibition in the new building, 3 May, 1869. An annual exhibition of pictures by the old masters, with some British, began 3 Jan. 1870. The money received has been used to endow a professorship of chemistry, a laboratory, etc. In 1874 the exhibition included many of Landseer's pictures.

PRESIDENTS.

1768. Sir Joshua Reynolds.
1792. Benjamin West.
1805. James Wyatt.
1806. Benjamin West.
1820. Sir Thomas Lawrence.
1830. Sir Martin A. Shee.
1850. Sir Charles Eastlake, d. 23 Dec. 1865.
1866. Sir Edwin Landseer elected, declines, 24 Jan.
" Sir Francis Grant, 1 Feb., d. 5 Oct. 1878.
1878. Sir Frederick Leighton, 13 Nov.

Royal exchange (*Cambium Regis*), London. The foundation of the original edifice was laid by sir Thomas Gresham, 7 June, 1566, on the site of the ancient Tun prison. Queen Elizabeth opened it on 23 Jan. 1571, and her herald named it the Royal exchange.—*Hume.* It was destroyed by the great fire, Sept. 1666. Charles II. laid the foundation-stone of the next edifice, 23 Oct. 1667, which was completed by Mr Hawkesmore, a pupil of sir Christopher Wren, in about 3 years, it was repaired and beautified in 1769 This also was burned, 10 Jan 1838 New Royal exchange, erected under the direction of Mr Tite opened by queen Victoria 28 Oct 1844

Royal exchange, Dublin, commenced 1769, opened 1779

Royal George. Wrecks, 1782

Royal Institution of Great Britain, the earliest of the kind in London, was founded 9 Mch 1799, by count Rumford, sir Joseph Banks, earls Spencer and Morton, and other noblemen and gentlemen It was favored by George III, and incorporated 13 Jan 1800, by royal charter, as "The Royal Institution of Great Britain, for the diffusing knowledge and facilitating the general introduction of useful mechanical inventions and improvements, and for teaching, by courses of philosophical lectures and experiments, the application of science to the common purposes of life" It was enlarged and extended by act of Parliament in 1810, the original plan, as drawn up by count Rumford in 1799, having been modified The members are elected by ballot, and pay 10 guineas on admission and 5 guineas annually, or a composition of 60 guineas Members, July, 1881, 1054 "The Royal Institution, Its Founder, and Its First Professors" by dr. Bence Jones, hon secretary, pub 1871

House (in Albemarle street, Piccadilly) was purchased in June, 1799, and the present front was added by subscription in 1838 The lecture theatre was erected in 1803, under the superintendence of T Webster

Laboratory established in 1800, was rebuilt, with the modern improvements, 1872

Library was commenced in 1803, by munificent subscriptions of proprietors of the institution In 1881 it comprised about 42 000 volumes Classified catalogues (by W Harris) were published in 1809 and 1821, new ones (by B Vincent) in 1857 and 1881

Museum contains original philosophical apparatus of Young Cavendish, Davy and Faraday

First *lecture* was delivered 4 Mch 1801 by dr Garnett, the first professor of natural philosophy and chemistry

Succeeded in 1802 by dr Thomas Young celebrated for researches in optics showing the interference of light and proving the undulatory theory His "Lectures on Natural Philosophy and the Mechanical Arts" first published in 1807 are still a text book of physical science His antiquarian works (hieroglyphic inscriptions, etc) are also esteemed

In Feb 1801 Mr (afterwards sir Humphry) Davy was engaged as assistant lecturer and director of the laboratory, and on 31 May, 1802, was appointed professor of chemistry His lectures were successful and his discoveries in chemistry and electricity have honored the institution He discovered the alkaloids potassium and sodium in 1807, the nature of chlorine in 1810, and invented the safety lamp in 1815

William Thomas Brande succeeded sir Humphry as professor of chemistry in 1813, and resigned in 1852, continuing to be honorary professor till his death (Feb 1866) From 1816 to 1850 he delivered, in the laboratory of this institution chemical lectures to students

In 1813 Michael Faraday (b 22 Sept 1791), on the recommendation of sir H Davy, was engaged as assistant in the laboratory, and in 1825 as director, in 1827 he became a permanent lecturer In 1820 he commenced researches in electricity and magnetism which form an era in science In 1823-24 he discovered the condensability of chlorine and other gases, in 1831 he obtained electricity from the magnet, in 1845 he exhibited the twofold magnetism of matter, comprehending all known substances the magnetism of gases, flame, etc , in 1850 he published researches on atmospheric magnetism, d 25 Aug 1867

John Tyndall, F R S, professor of natural philosophy, first elected in July, 1853, eminent for researches on magnetism, heat, glaciers, etc , d 4 Dec 1893

Edward Frankland F R.S, professor of chemistry, 1863-68, eminent for his discoveries in organic chemistry

"Fund for the Promotion of Experimental Researches" was founded, 6 July, 1863, by sir Henry Holland, prof Faraday, sir R I Murchison dr Bence Jones and others

The first officers were sir Joseph Banks, president, till the charter was granted, afterwards the earl of Winchelsea, Mr (afterwards sir Thomas) Bernard treasurer, rev dr Samuel Glasse, secretary Algernon, duke of Northumberland, K G , elected president, 1842, succeeded by sir Henry Holland in 1865 (d 27 Oct 1873), by Algernon George, duke of Northumberland, 1873 W Pole, esq , treasurer, elected 1849, succeeded by Wm Spottiswoode, esq , in 1865, by George Busk, esq , 1873 Rev John Barlow, secretary, elected 1842, succeeded by Henry Bence Jones, M D , 1860, by Wm Spottiswoode, 1873, by Warren de la Rue, 1879 Librarians Wm Harris, 1803-23, S Weller Singer, 1826-35, Wm Mason, 1835-1848, Benjamin Vincent, 1849

Royal Society, London In 1645 several learned men met in London to discuss philosophical questions and report experiments, the "Novum Organum" of Bacon pub in 1620, having stimulated such pursuits Some of them (drs. Wilkins, Wallis, etc), about 1648-49, removed to Oxford, and with dr. (afterwards bishop) Seth Ward, the hon Robert Boyle, dr (afterwards sir) W Petty, and several doctors of divinity and physic often met in the apartments of dr Wilkins, in Wadham college, Oxford They formed what has been called the Philosophical Society of Oxford, which only lasted till 1690 The members were, about 1658, called to various parts of the kingdom by professional duties, and the majority coming to London, constantly attended lectures at Gresham college, and met occasionally till the death of Oliver Cromwell, 3 Sept 1658 Societies

Society was organized in 1660 and constituted by Charles II a body politic and corporate, as "The President Council and Fellowship of the Royal Society of London for Improving Natural Knowledge," 22 Apr 1662

Evelyn records the first anniversary meeting, St Andrew s day, 30 Nov 1663

Philosophical Transactions begin 6 Mch 1664-65

In 1668 Newton invented his reflecting telescope (now owned by the society), and on 28 Apr 1686 presented the society in MS his "Principia" which the council ordered printed This was done under the superintendence and at the expense of Halley the astronomer then clerk to the society

Society met for some years at Gresham college and afterwards at Arundel house (1666), where it came into possession of a valuable library, presented by Mr Howard grandson of its collector, the earl of Arundel After various changes the fellows returned to Gresham college, where they remained till their removal to Crane court, in a house purchased by themselves 8 Nov 1710

Bakerian lecture was established by Henry Baker, 1774

First Copley medal was awarded to Stephen Gray in 1731, the royal medal to John Dalton, 1826, the Rumford medal (instituted in 1797) to count Rumford himself in 1800

Society removed to apartments granted in Somerset house, 1780, to apartments in Burlington house, Piccadilly, 1857

Parliament votes annually 1000*l* to the Royal Society for scientific purposes

Regulations by which 15 fellows are annually elected who pay 10*l* on admission, and 4*l*. annually, or a composition of 60*l*., Mch 1847 In consequence, the number of fellows was reduced from 839 in 1847, to 626 in 1866, to 567 in 1875, to 552 in 1877 Entrance fee abolished, and the annual payment reduced to 3*l*, Nov 1878.

PRESIDENTS

1660	Sir Robert Moray	1772	James Burrow
1663	Lord Brouncker	"	Sir John Pringle
1677	Sir Joseph Williamson	1778	Sir Joseph Banks
1680	Sir Christopher Wren	1820	Dr W H Wollaston
1682	Sir John Hoskyns	"	Sir Humphry Davy
1683	Sir Cyril Wyche	1827	Davies Gilbert
1684	Samuel Pepys	1830	Duke of Sussex
1686.	John, earl of Carbery	1838	Marquess of Northampton.
1689	Thomas, earl of Pembroke	1848	Earl of Rosse
1690	Sir Robert Southwell	1854	Lord Wrottesley
1695	Charles Montague (afterwards earl of Halifax)	1858.	Sir Benjamin C Brodie
1698	John, lord Somers.	1861	Maj gen sir Edward Sabine
1703	Sir Isaac Newton	1871	Sir G B Airy
1727	Sir Hans Sloane	1873.	Dr (afterwards sir) Joseph Dalton Hooker
1741	Martin Folkes	1878	William Spottiswoode
1752	George, earl of Macclesfield	1883	T H Huxley
1761	James, earl of Morton.	1885.	Sir Geo G Stokes.
1768	James Burrow	1890	Sir Wm Thomson
"	James West.		

Ru'bicon, a small river flowing into the Adriatic sea, separated Cisalpine Gaul from Italy proper Roman generals were forbidden to pass this river at the head of an army Julius Cæsar did so Jan 49 B C, beginning the civil war

rubid'ium, an alkaline metal, discovered by Bunsen by spectrum analysis made known in 1861.

ru'brics, directions in church offices, often printed in red New ones for the English service agreed to by convocation, 4 July, 1879.

ruffles became fashionable about 1520, and went out about 1790

Rugby school, Warwickshire, was founded in 1567 by Lawrence Sheriff, a London tradesman, its arrangements were affected by the Public Schools act, 1868 Dr Thomas Arnold, the historian, took charge as head-master in Aug. 1828, and under him the school prospered He died 12 June, 1842 New Room. "Tom Brown's School Days at Rugby," by Thomas Hughes, pub 1857

"Rule, Britannia." Nearly all the words are by James Thomson, the music, ascribed to dr Arne, is said by Schœlcher (in his life of Handel) to have been taken from an air in Handel's "Occasional Oratorio," composed 1746

rule of the road. Seas

ruler. The emperor, king, governor, or sovereign of a country.

RULERS AND SOVEREIGNS OF THE PRINCIPAL EUROPEAN NATIONS FROM THE 11TH CENTURY, ARRANGED BY CENTURIES.

Nation.	11th century.	12th century.	13th century.	14th century.	15th century.	16th century.	17th century.	18th century.	19th century.
England.	1066. William I. 1087. William II.	1100. Henry I. 1135. Stephen. 1154. Henry II. 1189. Richard I. 1199. John.	1216. Henry III. 1272. Edward I.	1307. Edward II. 1327. Edward III. 1377. Richard II. 1399. Henry IV.	1413. Henry V. 1422. Henry VI. 1461. Edward IV. 1483. Edward V. 1483. Richard III. 1485. Henry VII.	1509. Henry VIII. 1547. Edward VI. 1553. Mary. 1558. Elizabeth.			
Great Britain.							1603. James I. (VI. of Scotland). 1625. Charles I. 1649. Commonwealth. 1660. Charles II. 1685. James II. 1689. William and Mary 1694. William III.	1702. Anne. 1714. George I. 1727. George II. 1760. George III.	1811. George, prince of Wales, *regent.* 1820. George IV. 1830. William IV. 1837. Victoria.
Scotland.	1057. Malcolm III. 1093. Donald. 1094. Duncan. 1094. Donald again. 1098. Edgar.	1107. Alexander I. 1124. David I. 1153. Malcolm IV. 1165. William.	1214. Alexander II. 1249. Alexander III. 1292. John Baliol.	1306. Robert Bruce I. 1329. David II. 1332. Edward Baliol. 1342. David II. again. 1371. Robert II. 1391. Robert III.	1406. James I. 1437. James II. 1460. James III. 1488. James IV.	1513. James V. 1542. Mary. 1567. James VI. (I. of Great Britain).			
France.	1060. Philip I.	1108. Louis VI. 1137. Louis VII. 1180. Philip II.	1223. Louis VIII. 1226. Louis IX. 1270. Philip III. 1285. Philip IV.	1314. Louis X. 1316. John I. 1316. Philip V. 1321. Charles IV. 1328. Philip VI. 1350. John II. 1364. Charles V. 1380. Charles VI.	1422. Charles VII. 1461. Louis XI. 1483. Charles VIII. 1498. Louis XII.	1515. Francis I. 1547. Henry II. 1559. Francis II. 1560. Charles IX. 1574. Henry III. 1589. Henry IV.	1610. Louis XIII. 1643. Louis XIV.	1715. Louis XV. 1774. Louis XVI. 1793. Louis XVII. 1793. *Republic* (1).	1802. Consulate. 1804. Napoleon I. 1814. Louis XVIII. 1824. Charles X. 1830. Louis-Philippe. 1848. *Republic* (2). 1852. Napoleon III. 1870. *Republic* (3). 1871. Thiers, presid't. 1873. MacMahon, president. 1879. Grévy, presid't. 1887. Carnot, " 1894. Casimir-Perier, president. 1895. Faure, presid't.
Prussia. (A duchy from 1618 to 1701, and a kingdom from 1701.)					1415. House of Hohenzollern, established as the ruling house under Frederick of Nuremberg, as margravate of Brandenburg.		1618. John Sigismund, first duke of Prussia.	1701. Frederick I. 1713. Fred. Will. I. 1740. Frederick II. the Great. 1786. Fred. Will. II. 1797. Fred. Will. III.	1840. Fred. Will. IV., king of Prussia only. 1860. William I., king of Prussia, and from 1871 emperor of Germany.
Germany. (Emperors elected.)	1024. Conrad II. of the house of Franconia. 1039. Henry III. 1056. Henry IV. the Great.	1106. Henry V 1125. Lothaire II., duke of Saxony 1138. Conrad III., duke of Suabia, and first Hohenstaufen. 1152. Frederick I. (Barbarossa). 1190. Henry VI. 1197. Philip.	1208. Otho IV. of Brunswick. 1215. Frederick II. 1250. Conrad IV. 1254. William. 1256. Richard of Cornwall (never ruled). 1273. Rudolph I., count of Hapsburg and duke of Austria from 1276–78. 1292. Adolf of Warsaw. 1298. Albert I., duke of Austria.	1308. Henry VII. of Luxemburg. 1314. Louis V. of Bavaria. 1347. Charles IV. of Luxemburg. 1378. Wenceslaus of Bohemia.	1400. Rupert. 1410. Sigismund, margrave of Brandenburg and king of Hungary. 1438. Albert II., duke of Austria. 1440. Frederick III., archduke of Austria. 1493. Maximilian I., archduke of Austria.	1519. Charles V., archduke of Austria, etc. 1558. Ferdinand I. of Austria. 1564. Maximilian II. of Austria. 1576. Rudolph II. of Austria.	1612. Matthias of Austria. 1619. Ferdinand II. of Austria. 1637. Ferdinand III. of Austria. 1658. Leopold I. of Austria.	1705. Joseph I. of Austria. 1711. Charles V of Austria. 1740. Maria Theresa, archduchess of Austria. 1745. Francis I. of Austria. 1765. Joseph II. of Austria. 1790. Leopold II. of Austria. 1792. Francis II. of Austria, who resigns as emperor 1806. Germany without an emperor until 1871.	1888. Frederick III., king of Prussia and emperor of Germany. 1888. William II., king of Prussia and emperor of Germany.

RUL

Austria. (A margravate until 1156; then a dukedom until 1453; then an archduchy until 1804, when Francis II., emperor of Germany, declared himself Francis I., emperor of Austria.)			1278. Rudolph I., duke of Austria and emperor of Germany. 1282. Albert I. and Rudolph II., dukes of Austria. Albert, emperor of Germany, 1298.	1308. Frederick I. and Leopold I., dukes of Austria. Frederick contested with Louis V. of Bavaria for the sovereignty of Germany. 1330. Albert II. and Otho. 1358. Rudolph III. 1365. Albert III. and Leopold II. Leopold killed in battle with the Swiss at Sempach, 1386. 1390. Albert IV., William, and others.	1411. Albert V., emperor of Germany as Albert II., 1438. Also king of Hesse and Bohemia. 1439. Ladislaus. 1457. Albert VI.; right contested by Frederick, his brother, emperor of Germany, 1440. On death of Albert, 1463, Frederick obtained the archduchy. With Frederick originated, *Austri est imperare orbi universo;* i. e., A. E. I. O. U. 1493. Maximilian I.				1804. Francis I. of Austria, emperor of Austria and king of Hungary; resigned as emperor of Germany, 1806. 1835. Ferdinand, emperor of Austria and king of Hungary. 1848. Francis Joseph.
Hungary.	1061. Bela I. 1064. Salamon. 1075. Geisa I. 1077. Ladislas I. 1095. Coloman.	1114. Stephen II. 1131. Bela II. 1141. Geisa II. 1161. Stephen III. 1173. Bela III. 1196. Emeric.	1204. Ladislas II. 1205. Andrew II. 1235. Bela IV. 1270. Stephen IV. 1272. Ladislas III. 1290. Andrew III.	1301. Wenceslaus. 1305. Otho of Bavaria. 1309. Charles Robert of Anjou. 1342. Louis I. the Great. 1382. Mary. 1385. Charles II. 1386. Mary and Sigismund. 1392. Sigismund. Also king of Bohemia and emperor of Germany, 1410.	1437. Albert V. of Austria, emperor of Germany. 1439. Elizabeth, widow of Albert. 1442. Ladislaus IV. 1445. John Hunniades, *regent.* 1458. Ladislaus V. 1458. Matthias Corvinus. 1490. Ladislaus VI.	1516. Louis II. 1526. Ferdinand I. of Austria. From this date the rulers of Austria have been kings of Hungary, and until 1806 emperors of Germany.			
Denmark.	1047. Sweyn II. 1076. Harold. 1080. Canute IV. 1086. Olaus IV. 1095. Eric I.	1105. Eric II. 1137. Eric III. 1147. Sweyn III. 1147. Canute V. 1157. Waldemar I. 1182. Canute VI.	1202. Waldemar II. 1241. Eric IV. 1250. Abel. 1252. Christopher. 1259. Eric V.	1320. Christopher II. 1340. Waldemar III. 1376. Olaus V. 1387. Margaret.	1440. Christian I. 1481. John.	1513. Christian II. 1523. Frederick I. (also of Norway). 1534. Christian III. (also of Norway). 1559. Frederick II. (also of Norway). 1588. Christian IV.	1648. Frederick III. 1670. Christian V. 1699. Frederick IV.	1730. Christian VI. 1746. Frederick V. 1766. Christian VII. 1784. Prince Frederick, *regent.*	1808. Frederick VI. 1839. Christian VIII. 1848. Frederick VII. 1863. Christian IX.
Norway.	1069. Olaf. 1093. Magnus.	1103. Sigurd I. and others. 1122. Sigurd again. 1130. Magnus IV. and others. 1186. Swerro.	1202. Hako III. and others. 1207. Hako IV. 1263. Magnus VI. 1280. Eric. 1299. Hako.	1319. United to Sweden. 1389. United to Denmark under Margaret. Formally united at CALMAR, 1397.	United to Denmark.	United to Denmark.	United to Denmark.	United to Denmark.	1814. Annexed to Sweden.
Sweden.	1066. Halstan. 1090. Ingo.	1112. Philip. 1118. Ingo II. 1129. Swerker. 1155. Eric. 1161. Charles VII. 1167. Canute. 1199. Swerker II.	1210. Eric II. 1216. John I. 1222. Eric III. 1250. Birger Jarl. 1266. Waldemar. 1275. Magnus I. 1290. Birger II.	1319. Magnus II. 1350. Eric XII. 1359. Magnus II. restored. 1363. Albert. 1389. United to Denmark under Margaret. Formally united at CALMAR, 1397.	United to Denmark.	1523. Gustavus I. (Vasa). 1560. Eric XIV. 1568. John III. 1592. Sigismund.	1604. Charles IX. 1611. Gus. Adolphus. 1633. Christina. 1654. Charles X. 1660. Charles XI. 1697. Charles XII.	1719. Ulrica and Frederick I. 1741. Frederick I. 1751. Adolphus Frederick. 1771. Gustavus III. 1792. Gustavus IV.	1809. Charles XIII. 1818. Charles XIV. (Bernadotte). 1844. Oscar I. 1859. Charles XV. 1872. Oscar II.

RUL

RULERS AND SOVEREIGNS OF THE PRINCIPAL EUROPEAN NATIONS FROM THE 11TH CENTURY, ARRANGED BY CENTURIES.—(*Continued*).

Nation.	11th century.	12th century.	13th century.	14th century.	15th century.	16th century.	17th century.	18th century.	19th century.
Portugal.	1065. Sancho of Castile. 1072. Alfonso VI. 1093. Henry, *count.*	1112. Alfonso, *count.* 1139. Alfonso I., *king.* 1185. Sancho I.	1212. Alfonso II. 1223. Sancho II. 1248. Alfonso III. 1279. Dionysius.	1325. Alfonso IV. 1357. Peter. 1367. Ferdinand. 1383. John I.	1433. Edward. 1438. Alfonso V. 1481. John II. 1495. Emanuel.	1521. John III. 1557. Sebastian. 1578. Henry. 1580. Annexed to Spain.	Kingdom restored. 1640. John of Braganza. 1656. Alfonso VI. 1667. Peter, *regent.* 1683. Peter II.	1706. John V. 1750. Joseph. 1777. Maria and Peter. 1786. Maria, alone. 1791. John, *regent.*	1816. John VI. 1826. Peter IV. 1826. Maria II. 1828. Miguel. 1833. Maria II. 1853. Peter V. 1861. Luis I. 1889. Carlos I.
Castile and Leon. (Spain.)	1066. Sancho II. 1072. Alfonso VI.	1109. Urraca and Alfonso VII. 1126. Alfonso VII. 1157. Sancho III. 1158. Alfonso VIII. 1188. Alfonso IX.	1214. Henry I. 1217. Ferdinand III. (Castile). 1230. (Leon). 1252. Alfonso X. 1284. Sancho IV. 1295. Ferdinand IV.	1312. Alfonso XI. 1350. Peter. 1369. Henry. 1379. John I. 1390. Henry II.	1406. John II. 1454. Henry IV. 1474. Isabella. 1479. United with Aragon. Joanna and Philip I. for a short time.	1512. Ferdinand V. of Castile, II. of Aragon, conquers Navarre and Grenada; unites all Spain. 1516. Charles V. of Germany, I. of Spain. 1556. Philip II. 1598. Philip III.	1621. Philip IV. 1665. Charles II. 1700. Philip V.	1724. Philip V. (*abdicated*). 1724. Louis. 1724. Philip V. again. 1746. Ferdinand VI. 1759. Charles III. 1788. Charles IV. (*abdicated* 1808).	1808. Ferdinand VII. (*dethroned*). 1808. Joseph Bonaparte. 1814. Ferdinand VII. (*restored*). 1833. Isabella II. 1868. *Dethroned.* 1870. Amadeus. 1873. *Abdicated.* 1873. *Republic.* 1874. Alfonso XII. 1886. Alfonso XIII.
Arragon. (Spain.)	1065. Sancho. 1094. Peter.	1104. Alfonso I. 1134. Ramiro. 1137. Petronella and Raymond. 1163. Alfonso II. 1196. Peter II.	1213. James I. 1276. Peter III. 1285. Alfonso III. 1291. James II.	1327. Alfonso IV. 1336. Peter IV. 1387. John I. 1395. Martin.	1410. *Interregnum.* 1412. Ferdinand of Sicily. 1416. Alfonso V. 1458. John II. 1479. Ferdinand (united with Castile and Leon).				
Poland.	1058. Boleslas II. 1082. Ladislas I.	1102. Boleslas III. 1138. Ladislas II. 1145. Boleslas IV. 1173. Miecislas III. 1178. Casimir II. 1194. Lesko V.	1200. Miecislas III. (*restored*). 1202. Ladislas III. 1227. Boleslas V. 1279. Lesko VI. 1290. Premislas. 1296. Ladislas IV.	1300. Wenceslas. 1333. Casimir III. 1370. Louis. 1382. Mary. 1384. Hedwige. 1396. Ladislas V. (*Lithuania annexed*).	1434. Ladislas VI. 1445. Casimir IV. 1492. Albert.	1501. Alexander. 1506. Sigismund I. 1548. Sigismund II. 1573. Henry. 1575. Stephen. 1587. Sigismund III.	1632. Ladislas VII. 1648. John Casimir. 1669. Michael. 1674. John Sobieski. 1697. Fred. Aug. I.	[illegible] [illegible] [illegible] I. 1764. Stanislas II. 1795. Partition. Disappears as a power.	
Russia.					1462. Ivan III. Took the title of czar of Muscovy, 1482.	1505. Basil V. 1533. Ivan IV. (the Terrible). 1584. Feodor I. 1598. Boris.	1605. Feodor II. 1606. Basil. 1613. Michael (Romanoff). 1645. Alexis. 1676. Feodor III. 1682. Ivan V. and Peter I. 1689. Peter (the Great), alone.	1725. Catherine I. 1727. Peter II. 1730. Anne. 1740. Ivan VI. 1741. Elizabeth. 1762. Peter III. 1762. Catherine II. 1796. Paul.	1801. Alexander I. 1825. Nicholas I. 1855. Alexander II. 1881. Alexander III. 1894. Nicholas II.
Holland or Netherlands.						1579. William, prince of Orange, stadtholder. 1587. Maurice.	1625. Fred. Henry. 1647. William II. 1650–72. No stadtholder. 1672. William Henry (William III. of England).	1702–47. No stadtholder. 1747. William Henry. 1757. William IV.	1806. Louis Bonaparte. 1814. William Frederick. 1840. William II. 1849. William III. 1890. Wilhelmina.

RUL

Belgium.									1831. Leopold I. 1865. Leopold II.
Greece.									1832. Otho I. 1863. George I.
Italy.									1861. Victor Emmanuel. 1878. Humbert.
Turkey.			1299. Othman or Ottoman, founder of the empire.	1326. Orchan, first sultan. 1360. Amurath I. 1389. Bajazet I., defeated and imprisoned by Tamerlane.	1403. Solyman. 1410. Musa-Chelebi. 1413. Mahomet I. 1421. Amurath II. 1451. Mahomet II., took Constantinople 1453. 1481. Bajazet II.	1512. Selim I. 1520. Solyman II. 1566. Selim II. 1574. Amurath III. 1595. Mahomet III.	1603. Achmet I. 1617. Mustapha I. 1618. Osman II. 1622. Mustapha II. again. 1623. Amurath IV. 1640. Ibrahim. 1648. Mahomet IV. 1687. Solyman III. 1691. Achmet II. 1695. Mustapha II.	1703. Achmet III. 1730. Mahomet V. 1754. Osman III. 1757. Mustapha III. 1774. Abdul Hamid I. 1789. Selim III.	1807. Mustapha IV. 1808. Mahmud VI. 1839. Abdul Medjid. 1861. Abdul Aziz. 1876. Amurath V. 1876. Abdul Hamid II.

ruling-machines for ruling paper with faint lines, for merchants' account-books, etc., were invented by a Dutchman, resident in London, in 1782, and much improved by Woodmason, Payne, Brown, and others. They were improved in Scotland in 1803. A recent invention numbers the pages of account-books with type, instead of a pen, so that a page cannot be torn out from one without discovery.

rum (Fr. *rhum*), ardent spirit distilled from sugar lees and molasses, deriving its flavor from a volatile oil. Rum is principally made in the West Indies.

Rumford, Count. Benjamin Thompson (count Rumford) was born at Woburn, Mass., 1753. In 1772 he taught an academy at Rumford (now Concord), N. H. While sharing the feelings of the colonists towards England, his sympathies were not strong. In 1775 he joined the British army and remained in its service until the close of the war, when, on his return to England, he was knighted. In 1784 he entered the service of the Elector of Bavaria, by whom he was made a count, taking the name of Rumford from his old New Hampshire residence. He died at Auteuil, France, 1814. His contributions to science were numerous and important. The Rumford medal instituted by the Royal Society of London, 1797. ROYAL INSTITUTION and ROYAL SOCIETY.

Rump parliament. PRIDE'S PURGE.

Run'nymede (council-mead), a meadow near Egham, Surrey. Here king John granted Magna Charta, 15 June, 1215.

Rupert's Land, North America, or Red River Settlement, formerly territory of the Hudson's Bay company, was made a bishopric, 1849. CANADA, HUDSON'S SEA, MANITOBA.

Russell trial. William, lord Russell's trial for complicity in the Rye-house plot was marked by a most touching scene. When he requested to have some one near him to take notes to help his memory, he was answered that any of his attendants might assist him, upon which he said, "My wife is here, and will do it for me." He was beheaded in Lincoln's-inn fields, 21 July, 1683. Lady Russell survived him 40 years, dying 29 Sept. 1723, in her 87th year. His attainder was reversed, 1 Will. III. 1689.

Russia (*rush'a*), formerly called **Muscovy,** the largest country in the world, comprising the whole of N. Europe and Asia between lat. 38° 20′ and 78° N., and extending 172° 20′ east from lon. 17° 40′ E. The name is generally derived from the Roxolani, a Slavonic tribe. Ruric, a Varangian chief, appears to have been the first to establish a government, 862. His descendants ruled amid many vicissitudes till 1598. The rapid progress of Russian power under Peter the Great and Catherine II. is unequalled. The established religion of Russia is the Greek church, with toleration of other sects, even Mahometans. The points in which the Græco-Russian church differs from the Roman Catholic faith are its denial of the spiritual supremacy of the pope, its not enforcing the celibacy of the clergy, and its authorizing all to read and study the Scriptures in the vernacular. The emperor is head of the church, although he has never claimed to decide theological and dogmatic questions. The government of Russia is an absolute hereditary monarchy. The whole legislative, executive, and judicial power is united in the emperor, whose will alone is law. Succession to the throne is by regular descent with right of primogeniture, with preference of male over female heirs. Every sovereign of Russia, with his consort and children, must be a member of the Orthodox Greek church. The princes and princesses of the imperial house must obtain consent of the emperor to marriage, or their issue cannot inherit the throne. By an imperial ukase in 1802, 6 universities were established, viz., at St. Petersburg, Moscow, Wilna, Dorpat (in Livonia), Charcov, and Kasan, and 3 have since been added, besides one in Finland. Literature made little progress till the present century, the native publications being few, and the best books being translations. In 1889 8699 books, with an aggregate of 24,780,423 copies, were published, and periodicals to the number of 694 were published in 1890. The Russian language, though not devoid of elegance, is, to a foreigner, difficult of pronunciation; the number of letters and diphthongs is 42. The area of the empire, including its internal waters, is 8,660,282 sq. miles. In 1722 its population was 14,000,000; 1815, 45,000,000; 1859,

74,000,000, 1867, 81,696 965, 1872, 86,151,413, 1882, 102,970,831, 1887, 113,354,649; 1890, 117,568,874, 1893, 126,000,000, estimated Of this last number about 96 000 000 are inhabitants of European Russia, 1903, 129 400,514 Revenue in 1891, 2,202,708,141 rubles, expenditures, 2,107,868,816 rubles. For defence, ARMY, NAVY

A D

Russia invaded by the Huns 376

Ruric the Norman or Varangian, arrives at Novgorod (or New City) and becomes grand duke (anniversary kept 20 Sept 1862) 862

Oleg successfully invades the Greek empire 907

Baptism of Olga widow of duke Igor, at Constantinople, about 955

Vladimir the Great marries Anne sister of the emperor Basil II and is baptized 988

Golden Horde of Tartars conquer a large part of Russia about 1223

Grand-duke Iurie killed in battle 1237

Alexander Newski defeats the invading Danes 1241

Tartars establish the empire of the khan of Kaptschak, and exercise great influence in Russia 1242

He is made grand duke of Russia by the Tartars 1252

Moscow made the capital 1300

Tartar war, 1380, Moscow burned 1383

Tamerlane invades Russia, but retires 1395

Accession of Ivan III the Great, able and despotic, founds the present monarchy 1462

Ivan introduces fire arms and cannon into Russia 1475

Great invasion of the Tartars, consternation of Ivan 1479

His general Svenigorod, annihilates their power 1481

War with Poland 1506-23

English "Russian company" established 1553

Richard Chancellor sent to open the trade 1554

Discovery of Siberia "

Royal body guard (the Strelitz) established 1568

Ivan solicits the hand of queen Elizabeth of England 1579

Murder of Feodor I last of the race of Ruric, which had governed Russia for 700 years 1598

Imposition of Demetrius (IMPOSTORS), Matins of Moscow, 29 May, 1606

Michael Fedorovitz of the house of Romanoff, ascends the throne 1613

Finland ceded to Sweden 1617

Russian victories in Poland 1654

Subjugation of the Cossacks 1671

Reign of Ivan and Peter I or the Great 1682

Peter sole sovereign 1689

He visits Holland and England, and works in the dock yard at Deptford 1697

Recalled by a conspiracy of the Strelitz, which he cruelly suppresses, 2000 tortured and slain, he beheads many with his own hand 1698

Russians begin their new year from 1 Jan (but retain the old style) 1700

War with Sweden, Peter totally defeated by Charles XII at Narva 30 Nov "

Peter founds St. Petersburg as a new capital 27 May, 1703

Strelitz abolished 1704

Charles XII totally defeated by Peter at Pultowa, and flees to Turkey 8 July, 1709

Fourteen thousand Swedish prisoners sent to Siberia "

War with Turkey, Peter and army cross the Pruth, are surrounded by Turks, and escape by energy of empress Catherine, who obtains a truce , June, 1711

Esthonia, Livonia, and a large part of Finland added to the empire . 1715

Peter visits Germany, Holland, and France "

Jesuits expelled 1718

Conspiracy and mysterious death of prince Alexis 7 July, "

Peter II (last of the Romanoffs) deposed, and the crown given to Anne of Courland 1730

Elizabeth, daughter of Peter I. reigns, in prejudice of Ivan VI., an infant, who is imprisoned for life 1741

Peter III, dethroned and murdered, succeeded by Catherine, his wife 1762

Ivan VI, rightful heir, till now immured, put to death 1764

Treaty of Kutschouc Kainardji, independence of the Crimea and freedom of the Black sea July, 1774

Rebellion of the Cossacks, 1774, suppressed 1775

Successful invasions of the Crimea 1769-84

Dismemberment of POLAND, commenced by Catherine, 1772, completed. . . 1795

Catherine gives her subjects a new code of laws, abolishes torture in punishing criminals d 1796

Unsuccessful war with Persia "

Russian treaty with Austria and England 1798

Suwarrow, with an army joins the Austrians, and checks the French in Italy 1799

Mental derangement of Paul 1800, murdered. 24 Mch 1801

Alexander I makes peace with England . May, "

He joins the coalition against France 11 Apr 1805

Allies defeated at Austerlitz 2 Dec. "

Treaty of Tilsit with France. 7 July, 1807

Russians defeated by the Turks, near Silistria . 26 Sept 1809

War with France . .. June, 1812

Russians defeated at Smolensko, 17 Aug, and at the Borodino, 7 Sept "

Moscow burned by the Russians, 14 Sept., retreat of the French begins. 15 Oct. "

Alexander present at the battle of Leipsic, Oct. 1813, enters Paris Mch 1814

RUS

He visits England June, 1814

Forms the Holy Alliance 1815

Grand duke Constantine renounces the succession 26 Jan 1822

Death of Alexander, 1 Dec, Pestal's conspiracy against Nicholas I., insurrection of troops at Moscow, suppressed, 26-29 Dec. 1825

Nicholas crowned at Moscow 3 Sept 1826

War against Persia 28 Sept. "

Nicholas visits England, receives the order of the Garter, 9 July, 1827

Peace between Russia and Persia 22 Feb 1828

War between Russia and the Ottoman Porte declared (BATTLES, TURKEY) 26 Apr "

Peace of Adrianople 14 Sept 1829

War for the independence of POLAND against Russia 29 Nov 1830

Failure of expedition against Khiva Jan 1840

Treaty of London (SYRIA) 15 July, "

Grand duke Constantine arrives at Portsmouth in the *Ingermanland* of 74 guns 9 June, 1846

[For Russia in the Hungarian war of 1848-49, HUNGARY]

Russia demands the expulsion of the Hungarian and Polish refugees from TURKEY 5 Nov 1849

They are sent to Konieh in Asia Minor Jan 1850

Harbor of Sebastopol completed . Feb "

Emperor decrees enrolment of 7 men in each thousand in western Russia, total increase 180,000 soldiers Aug "

St Petersburg and Moscow railway begun 1851

Czar concentrates forces on frontiers of Turkey Feb 1853

Origin of the RUSSO TURKISH WAR (HOLY PLACES) Mch "

Czar issues a manifesto to his subjects, he will combat only for the faith and Christianity 23 Apr 1854

Death of czar Nicholas, accession of Alexander II, no change of policy 2 Mch 1855

Treaty of peace at Paris 30 Mch 1856

Amnesty granted to the Poles, 27 May, 5 political offenders, etc, Alexander II crowned at Moscow 7 Sept "

St Petersburg and Warsaw railway begun by government, 1851, ceded to Great Russian Railway company (about 335 miles, the half completed) "

Partial emancipation of serfs on imperial domains 2 July, 1858

Russian naval station established at Villa Franca, on the Mediterranean, creates political excitement Aug "

Czar protests against the recognition of the sovereignty of peoples 13 Feb 1860

Treaty with China for enlargement of commerce 1 Jan 1861

Decree for the total emancipation of serfs (23,000,000) throughout the empire in 2 years (19 Feb) 3 Mch "

Demonstrations and repression in POLAND Feb-Apr "

Disturbances in S Russia, caused by an impostor claiming to be a descendant of Peter III, many peasants shot or flogged, May and June, "

Nobles sign a petition for a political constitution Nov "

Increased privileges granted to the Jews 26 Jan 1862

Russia recognizes the kingdom of Italy 10 July, "

1000th anniversary of the foundation of the Russian monarchy at Novgorod celebrated 20 Sept. "

Reorganization of the departments of justice decreed, juries to be employed in trials, etc 14 Oct. "

Insurrection in Poland 22-24 Jan 1863

[For events, POLAND]

Termination of serfdom 3 Mch "

Provincial institutions established throughout Russia 13 Jan 1864

Great victory over the Oubykhs in the Caucasus, 31 Mch, emigration of the Caucasian tribes into Turkey, Apr, submission of the Abgas, the war declared at an end 2 June, "

Czarowitz betrothed to princess Dagmar of Denmark 28 Sept "

Serfdom abolished in the Transcaucasian provinces, new judicial system promulgated Dec "

Russian nobles request emperor to establish 2 houses of representatives (declined) 24 Jan 1865

New province, "Turkestan," in central Asia, created, 14 Feb. "

Czarowitz Nicholas d at Nice 24 Apr "

Rupture with the pope on account of Russian severity to Polish clergy Jan. and Feb 1866

Inauguration of trial by jury in Russia 8 Aug "

Karakozow attempts to assassinate the czar, 16 Apr, after long investigation he is executed 15 Sept "

War with Bokhara, conflicts with varying results, Russians advance in May et seq, ended Nov "

Marriage of prince Alexander, heir to the crown, to princess Dagmar of Denmark 9 Nov "

Emancipation of many state serfs in Poland 11 Nov "

Three decrees, abolishing remains of Polish nationality 1 Jan. 1867

Congress of Slavonian deputies at Moscow 5 May, "

Russian America sold to U S for $7,200,000, by treaty, 13 Mch, ratified 15 May, "

Amnesty in favor of the Poles 29 May, "

Czar escapes assassination by Berezowski, a Pole 6 June, "

Decree for Russian language in Baltic provinces 7 July, "

A Romanist college to replace the authority of the pope, established at St. Petersburg 2 Aug "

Separate interior government in Poland suppressed 29 Feb 1868

Samarcand taken by Kaufmann .. 26 May, "

Polish language interdicted in public places in Poland July, "

Government Messenger, official journal, published at St. Petersburg . 13 Jan. 1869

Socialist secret conspiracy of students, headed by Sergius Netschajew, detected, informer assassinated. Jan 1870

Burlingame, Chinese envoy, arrives 2 Feb. "

Dies at St. Petersburg 22 Feb "

Schamyl, the Circassian chief, d. .. about Apr 1871

ectric telegraph between St. Petersburg and Nagasaki, Japan, completed....Nov. 1871

0th anniversary of the birth of Peter the Great, 30 May, 1672 (o.s.), celebrated by court and nation....11 June, 1872

ıssian encyclopædia undertaken by prof. Beresina..autumn, "

econnoitring expedition to Khiva; defeat of gen. Markosoff announced....Dec. "

cpeditions against Khiva start....Mch. 1873

ıiva surrenders, 10 June; a rebellion suppressed....July, "

muden Turcomans defeated at Tschandyr....25, 27 July, "

ew treaty with Bokhara published....Dec. "

rand-duchess Marie marries duke of Edinburgh....23 Jan. 1874

ar with KHOKAND....4 Sept.-Oct. 1875

ıltic provinces (formerly a provincial federation with a governor) incorporated with empire under the ministry of the interior, on death of governor Bagration....29 Jan. 1876

hokand formally annexed (as Ferghana)....29 Feb. "

ersecution of the sect "White Doves" (Skoptzi)....Apr. "

any Russian volunteers in Servian army....July-Sept. "

epression through Servian defeats....Oct. "

nthusiasm for Bulgarians; partial mobilization of the army ordered....about 14 Nov. "

reat enthusiasm for Bulgarians; war declared and begun (TURKEY and RUSSO-TURKISH WARS, 1877)....24 Apr. 1877

reat trial of Nihilists for revolutionary propagandism begun, about 31 Oct. "

ıssian loan of 15,000,000*l.* at 5 per cent. announced..12 Nov. "

hilist trial ended; about 160 sentenced to hard labor; about 90 acquitted....about 9 Feb. 1878

eaty of peace with Turkey signed at San Stefano; Europe dissatisfied....3 Mch. "

era Zasulitch (or Sassulitch), a young woman who acknowledged firing at gen. Trepoff, prefect of St. Petersburg (5 Feb.), for severity to prisoners, acquitted by jury....12 Apr. "

eported spread of Nihilism in Kief, Moscow, etc....Apr. "

ıblic depression: feeling against Bulgarians; desire to get quit of the Eastern question....May-June, "

onference at BERLIN meets 13 June; treaty signed, 13 July, "

en. Kaufmann's advance on the Oxus to occupy Balkh reported....Aug. "

hilists tried and condemned at Odessa; riots ensued..5 Aug. "

eneral disaffection to the government; gen. de Mesentzoff, chief of police, assassinated in the street in St. Petersburg, 16 Aug. "

ew 5-per-cent loan (300,000,000 rubles) issued, 29, 30, 31 Aug. "

kase, state offences to be punished by military law, end of Aug. "

en. Drentelen made chief of police....6 Oct. "

ince *Demetrius Krapotkine*, governor, assassinated returning from a ball at Kharkoff....21 or 22 Feb. 1879

tempted assassination of Drentelen, 25 Mch.; and of czar by Alexander Solovieff, a school-master, with a revolver, 14 Apr. "

ll-tax abolished by ukase....Apr. "

kase, martial law ordained in provinces of St. Petersburg, Moscow, Kief, Odessa, and Warsaw....17 Apr. "

ınd and Liberty, a Nihilist newspaper, freely yet surreptitiously circulated....Apr. "

lovieff condemned, 7 June; executed....9 June, "

ials, convictions, and executions of Nihilists at Kief and Odessa....May-Aug. "

en. Lazareff, commander of expedition against the Tekké Turcomans, d. at Tchat....about 13 Aug. "

en. Lomakine succeeds in command; severe battle at Geok Tepé or Dengli Tepé; Russians said to be victorious, yet retreat with heavy loss....9 Sept. "

ergukasoff succeeds Lomakine in command....25 Sept. "

eon Mirsky condemned to death for attempted assassination of gen. Drentelen, chief of police....27, 28 Nov. "

tempted assassination of czar by undermining railway train near Moscow; none hurt; baggage carriages destroyed, 1 Dec. "

oclamation of the executive revolutionary committee justifying the attempted assassination on 1 Dec....4 Dec. "

ot to blow up the Winter palace, St. Petersburg, discovered, 12 Dec. "

'ill of the People, revolutionary paper, freely circulated, Nov., Dec. "

xplosion in a guard-room filled with dynamite and gun-cotton under the dining-room of the Winter palace, St. Petersburg; czar and family escape, being late for dinner; 11 soldiers killed, 47 wounded; between 6 and 7 P.M....17 Feb. 1880

artmann, owner of a house near the explosion, arrested at Paris....about 20 Feb. "

ınic at St. Petersburg; ukase issued, appointing supreme executive commission, gen. Loris Melikoff president, with extensive powers; virtual dictator....24 Feb. "

xtradition of Hartmann requested by Russia; declined..Mch. "

venty-fifth anniversary of the czar's accession celebrated at St. Petersburg....2 Mch. "

ippolyte Molodzoff (Mladetsky, or Wladitsky, or Mlodecki), a converted Jew, fires at gen. Loris Melikoff, 4 Mch.; hanged, 5 Mch. "

artmann expelled from France; goes to England; prince Orloff, ambassador, quits France....about 6 Mch. "

ihilist trials at St. Petersburg; sentences to death and imprisonment (dr. Weimar and others); commuted....May, "

eath of the empress after a long illness....3 June, "

venty-one extreme Nihilists convicted at Kief (capital sentences remitted)....about 7 Aug. "

kase of 24 Feb. superseded; Melikoff, who had governed well, appointed minister of the interior, with charge of the police, 18 Aug. "

Melikoff's scheme for administrative reform sanctioned by the czar; announced 3 Oct.; put into action....25 Oct. et seq. 1880

Russia, new national daily paper, published....Oct. "

Nihilists tried at St. Petersburg for assassinations, explosion at Winter palace, etc.; Kviatolski and 4 others condemned to death; 8 men and 3 women to imprisonment....10 Nov. "

Kviatofski and Priessnakoff hanged....16 Nov. "

Gen. Skobeleff's expedition into central Asia....24 Dec. "

Severe conflicts with the Tekké Turcomans....14 Jan. 1881

Geok Tepé besieged; taken....24 Jan. "

Assassination of the czar Alexander II. by explosion of a bomb; assassin himself killed; Risakoff seized....2 P.M. 13 Mch. "

Mine for explosion discovered in the middle of St. Petersburg, about 15 Mch. "

Circular of the new czar Alexander III. to foreign powers; he will aim at moral and material development of Russia, and a pacific foreign policy....16 Mch. "

Manifesto from the Nihilist executive committee to the czar offering peace, for amnesty with a legislative assembly elected by universal suffrage, free press, etc....22 Mch. "

Trial of Risakoff, Sophie Peroffskaja, Jelaboff, Jessie or Hessie Heljmann, Kibaichick, and Michailoff (4 men and 2 women), all condemned to death....8, 9 Apr. "

Tekkés submit; maraudings cease; object of Skobeleff's expedition accomplished; announced....9 Apr. "

Risakoff and others hanged; Heljmann (*enceinte*) reprieved, 15 Apr. "

Changes in ministerial offices; tendency to reduce autocracy of the czar announced....about 4 May, "

Ukase supplementary to that of 19 Feb. 1861, for emancipating serfs, remitting payments to many peasant proprietors, announced....early May, "

Reactionary proclamations in favor of autocracy (29 Apr.), 11 May; resignation of count Loris Melikoff and other liberal ministers soon after....about 13 May, "

Gen. Ignatieff, chief minister, issues manifesto declaring for suppression of rebellion, and promising reforms; manifesto from Nihilists offering peace if reforms be granted...23 May, "

Nihilist trials at St. Petersburg; 10 sentenced to death, 28 Feb.; sentence commuted to penal servitude (except as to Suchanoff, who is to be shot)....Mch. 1882

Gen. Strelnikoff, public prosecutor, assassinated at Odessa by 2 students, 30 Mch.; students executed....3 Apr. "

Retirement of Gortschakoff, succeeded by De Giers as chancellor and foreign minister....about 9 Apr. "

Mine discovered under Moscow cathedral; 80 workmen arrested....about 15 Apr. "

Decree for the gradual abolition of the poll-tax (imposed by Peter the Great)....beginning June, "

Ignatieff resigns, succeeded by count Tolstoi....*about* 12 *June*, "

Death of gen. Skobeleff, the hero of Plevna, aged 39....7 July, "

Death of prince Gortschakoff, aged 85....11 Mch. 1883

Trial of Nihilists at St. Petersburg; some sentenced to death (remitted), others to imprisonment....19 Apr. "

Emperor and empress crowned at Moscow....27 May, "

Poll-tax abolished for the poorest, reduced for others (1 Jan. 1884) on....8 June, "

Foundation of memorial church at the place where Alexander II. was assassinated at St. Petersburg, laid by the czar, 16 Oct. "

Sixty-three Nihilists sentenced to Siberia....19 Oct. "

Lieut. Sudeikin, chief of secret police, and his nephew, M. Sadovsky, assassinated at St. Petersburg; attributed to Nihilists aided by Jablonsky, a subordinate, whose life Sudeikin had saved....night of 28-29 Dec. "

Thirty-seven students at Moscow arrested; announced..9 Jan. 1884

Loyal address of the nobles to the czar, advocating union of nobles and peasantry....25 Jan. "

Surrender of Merv to Russia, effected by gen. Komaroff, announced....14 Feb. "

Convention with Persia for cession of Sarakhs (threatening to Afghanistan) reported....6 May, "

Majority of the czarowitz (aged 16) declared....18 May, "

Death of gen. Todleben, born 1818....1 July, "

Maria Wassilieona Kalouchnaia, at Odessa, sentenced to 20 years' hard labor for attempt to shoot col. Katensky, about 11 Sept. "

Letters of "Stepniak" and others expose cruel, dishonest, and unscrupulous conduct of government officials in prohibiting diffusion of knowledge and literature; proposed united opposition of nobility and peasantry....Sept.-Oct. "

Circulation of many religious books prohibited.... "

Fourteen Nihilists (including 6 officers and 3 women, one, *Mary F. Figner*) convicted by secret court-martial; 8 sentenced to death at St. Petersburg, 11 Oct.; 2 men executed, 18 Oct. "

Nihilist journal, *Narodnaia Volia*, reappears....about 27 Oct. "

Mission of M. Lessar, engineer-diplomatist, to London respecting central Asian boundaries....Feb. 1885

Ship-canal from St. Petersburg to Cronstadt completed.... " "

Russians advance to about 90 miles from Herat, and hold Zulfikar pass....Feb. "

Three courses before them: to retire; to remain and negotiate; to make war....1 Mch. "

Agreement, no farther advance on "debated or debatable ground" by Russians or Afghans (since termed a "solemn covenant")....16 or 17 Mch. "

Gen. Komaroff attacks the Afghans at Ak-tepe, on the river Kushk, alleging provocation; hundreds of Afghans killed, others perish from exposure, and the rest retire from their camp; 53 Russians killed and wounded, 30 Mch.; his statements controverted by sir Peter Lumsden....14 Apr. "

Russian gen Komaroff, near the Kushk and Murghab rivers, commands Afghans to retire, on refusal, defeats them at Ak tapa (or Ak tepe or Pul i khus khusti), near Penjdeh and captures artillery and stores, many Afghans perish in retreat through exposure, 30 Mch, sir Peter Lumsden reports the attack unprovoked about 21 Apr 1885

British government announces agreement to arbitration (by Denmark) 4 May, et seq "

Britain prepares for war with energy, strongly supported by the colonies and Indian princes May, "

British government statement, new agreement with Russia, arbitration respecting fight on 30 Mch accepted 4 May, Denmark accepts work of arbitration May, "

Agreement on delimitation settled by earl Granville and earl of Kimberley, with MM de Staal and Lessar, approval reported 30 May, "

Tchesme ironclad launched by the czar at Sebastopol (other vessels constructing) 18 May, 1886

Russia violates treaty of Berlin by declaring Batoum not to be a free port July, "

Russian interference in BULGARIA Sept -Dec. "

Plot against the czar, students with dynamite and other explosives detected, 13 Mch, 200 arrested Mch 1887

Three plotters executed, 31 Mch, 7 political offenders sentenced to death, the rest to various terms of imprisonment, 1 May, more arrests about 18 May, 5 executed 16 May, "

Prince Nicholas the czarowitz made chief ataman (hetman) of all the Cossacks at Novo Tcherkask 18 May, "

Baron Hirsch's present of 2,000,000*l* for primary Jewish schools in Russia accepted by the czar, to be paid into the bank of England, trustees, barons Rothschild and Henry de Worms announced Nov, said to be premature Dec "

Stringent restrictions on studies of universities, insubordination among students, and severe punishment, universities of Moscow St Petersburg, Odessa, and many other academical institutions closed, nearly all undergraduates in rebellion Nov -Dec "

Highest courts of law reject the claim of prince Hohenlohe to inherit the Wittgenstein estates in Lithuania, as a foreigner (in accordance with the ukase, 14 Mch 1887) Mch 1888

Central Asian (or Transcaspian) railway opened, promoted by gen Annenkoff May, "

Ninth centenary of the introduction of Christianity celebrated at Kieff 27 July, "

Grand council disapproves administrative changes proposed by count Tolstoï substituting centralization for local self government, which the czar had approved (1888), the *Zemtvo*, established about 1864, being virtually abolished Feb 1889

Death of count Tolstoï, minister of the interior 7 May, "

Czarowitz, aged 21, appointed to military and political office, 18 May, "

Marriage of the grand duke Paul and the princess Alexandra of Greece 17 June, "

Count Tolstoï s administrative changes effected, with increased Russification of the German provinces and Finland Feb 1890

Man chosen to assassinate the czar, by lot, commits suicide, leaving a letter incriminating associates 31 Mch "

Czar threatened by a letter from Maria Tshebrikova, a popular writer on education, for continuing to suppress liberty, 5 Mch, she is arrested and transported to the Caucasus, Apr "

Revival of severe edicts against the JEWS July, "

Great protest against persecution of Jews, headed by count Leon Tolstoï, publication forbidden by government Nov "

Decree for the revision of all foreign titles of nobility 15 Dec "

New law for the legitimatizing of bastards promulgated Apr 1891

Rescript from the czar placing the Siberian railway under the direction of the czarowitz (RAILROADS) 24 May, "

Count Tolstoï s administrative changes relative to the peasantry effected at St Petersburg and other provinces .. July, "

Czarowitz returns to Moscow after a tour . 16 Aug "

[He visited Vienna, 6 Nov, at Athens, 12 Nov, at Cairo, 23 Nov, at Bombay, 23 Dec. 1890, received by the viceroy at Calcutta, 26–28 Jan 1891, at Madras, 6 Feb, Ceylon, 13 Feb, Bangkok, Siam, 26 Mch, travels in China, Japan, Apr, May, at Otsu, in Japan, he is wounded by a fanatical officer in a theatre, 11 May, traverses Siberia, June, July, 1891]

Disputes with Great Britain respecting the Pamir ridge Aug "

Great distress through famine in certain districts of the Volga and other places about 2 Sept. et seq "

Ivan Alexandrovitch Gontcharoff, popular novelist, aged 80, d., 27 Sept "

In order to relieve famine, the czar forbids all state balls and festivities, great economy adopted by all classes Oct. "

Famine very severe in the central and eastern provinces Oct. "

Decree issued prohibiting the exportation of wheat and all its products 22 Nov "

Czarowitz president of a committee to deal with the famine by private charity, the ministry, the holy synod and others, 5 Dec, public relief works established Dec "

Grand-duke Constantine (brother of Alexander II), learned, able, and liberal, sometime viceroy of Poland, removed on suspicion of favoring the Poles, 1886, dies, aged 64, 24 Jan 1892

Count Tolstoï (novelist) relieves distressed people early Mch "

Russian Jewish emigrants excluded from Germany 25 Mch. "

Large supplies of American wheat, flour, and provisions, transmitted for the relief of the famine by the citizens of Philadelphia, in the *Indiana*, from Minnesota, in the *Missouri*, arrive at Libau, Courland, Mch, Apr, transmitted to the distressed districts . 4 Apr "

About 125,370,500 rubles expended in relief of the sufferers by famine, Dec. 1891–May, 1892, reported .. .13 June, "

RUS

Trial of 154 rioters against cholera regulations (at Saratoff, etc., 10 July), hundreds sentenced to death and imprisonment, Nov -Dec. 1892

Rescript of the czar for expediting the construction of the Siberian railway about 1 Feb 1893

New internal loan, 100,000,000 rubles at 4½ per cent. for 81 years 10 Mch "

Ukase expelling the Jews from the Asiatic provinces 19 May, "

Tariff war, duties on German imports raised Aug "

German reprisals, mutual injury Aug "

A Russian squadron (5 vessels) under adm Avellan arrives at Toulon 13 Oct. "

Death of M Tschaikowsky, musical composer .. 9 Nov "

Religious persecution in Lithuania, reported 3 Jan 1894

Commercial treaty with Germany for 10 years, signed 10 Feb "

M Jablochkoff, inventor of the electric candle, d 6 Apr "

Conspiracy of nihilists and anarchists suspected, many political arrests at St Petersburg and other places. April-May, "

Death of the czar Alexander III, at Livadia (aged 49) 1 Nov "

Nicholas II proclaimed czar 2 Nov "

Decree of the czar depriving his ministers and other officials of the power of appointing or dismissing their subordinates, and re establishing imperial committee of control 13 Nov "

Death of Anton Rubinstein (aged 65), at Peterhof 20 Nov "

Marriage of the czar to princess Alix (Alexandra) of Hesse, at St Petersburg 26 Nov "

New loan of 100 000,000 rubles at 3½ per cent 13 Dec "

Death of M de Giers (aged 74), minister of foreign affairs, at St. Petersburg .26 Jan 1895

The czar declares his intention to maintain the principle of autocracy 29, 30 Jan. "

Delimitation of the Russo Persian frontier, settled by commission Feb "

Agreement with Great Britain respecting the Pamirs Mch "

Russia guarantees a loan of 16,000,000*l* for China June, "

[See CHINO JAPANESE WAR]

A Russian mission to Abyssinia returns with an embassy and presents to the czar from the Negus . 29 June, "

The czar crowned at Moscow 26 May, 1896

M Witte appointed secretary of state 27 May, "

At a fête held on the Khodinsky plain, Moscow, 1429 persons were crushed to death and 644 injured 30 May, "

Pan Russian exhibition opened at Nijni Novgorod 9 June, "

The czar and czarina enter St Petersburg in state 4 July, "

Prince Khilkoff, minister of railways, etc, returns from his tour in the U S, etc 30 Oct "

The czar and czarina start on a foreign tour, 25 Aug, return to St Petersburg 31 Oct "

Imperial edict issued sanctioning the formation of the eastern Chinese railway company, shareholders to be exclusively Russians and Chinese, line to be completed, 1280 miles, in 6 years 23 Dec. "

Currency reform, resumption of specie payments Jan 1897

Pres. Faure arrives at St Petersburg 24 Aug "

Railway from Moscow to Archangel, completed . 30 Sept "

The sale of spirituous liquors made a state monopoly Jan 1898

Russia demands from China 99 years' lease over Port Arthur and Ta lien wan, 3 Mch, 25 years' lease of these ports granted, railway concessions, 23 Mch, China to retain sovereign rights, agreement signed, Chinese garrisons withdrawn, Russian troops landed 28 Mch "

Ta lien wan declared open to commerce . . Apr "

Russo Japanese convention respecting Korea, signed 25 Apr "

Circular of count Muravieff on behalf of the czar, proposing a conference of the powers for the preservation of general peace by disarmament. PEACE 24 Aug "

Russification of Finland Feb et seq 1899

Severe famine in the central and S E provinces Jan -May, "

The czarowitz, grand duke George (b. 9 May, 1871), d suddenly at Abbas Tuman, in the Caucasus 10 July, "

Measure passed imposing (1 to 3 years) military service on rebellious students, reported .. . . Aug "

Educational system for the aristocracy, largely at government expense, established .. Aug "

Trial of 43 officers in the Russian navy for bribery and corruption, at Sebastopol, 17 Feb, 16 acquitted, 26 found guilty . 3 Apr 1900

Count Muravieff, foreign minister (b 1845), d suddenly, 21 June, "

Ukase, largely abolishing banishment to Siberia .. 3 July, "

Import duties of the common tariff increased from 50 to 100 per cent . . . . 4 Aug "

Gen Gourko, distinguished commander, d (aged 73) 29 Jan 1901

Famine, due to failure of crops, population of 24,000,000 affected, government relief organized . Feb et seq "

M Bogoliepoff, minister of public instruction, mortally wounded by Peter Karpovich (sentenced to 20 years' imprisonment, 30 Mch), in St Petersburg 27 Feb "

Students' demonstration in St. Petersburg ends in serious rioting in Kazan square, 700 arrests . 17 Mch "

Riots in Kieff, quelled by troops . 24 Mch "

Count Tolstoï excommunicated . 19 Mch and 9 Apr "

Epidemic of scurvy in the famine stricken S districts May, "

Strike riots in St Petersburg and elsewhere, 20 May, troops called out . . 14 June, "

State of siege in the province of Moscow continued 23 Aug. "

Student disorders, university at Kharkoff closed 11-14 Dec "

About 20 cities and towns placed under state of siege mid Dec. "

Death of M de Bloch, state councillor (aged 66) 7 Jan 1902

American note protests against Russian aggression in Manchuria . . 1 Feb "

University of St. Petersburg closed, owing to disorders, 20

Feb -11 Mch , riots and disorders in Moscow 22 Feb and 2 Mch , 567 students and others, convicted of riot and political disaffection imprisoned (95 banished to Siberia), announced 25 Mch 1902

ncreasing distress and poverty due to bad harvests and oppressive taxation, great economic and agricultural depression over the country Apr "

ioting in Poltava and Kharkoff, many estates plundered (compensation granted by decree, 27 May) mid Apr "

[illegible] Sipiaguine, minister of the interior, reactionist, assassinated at St Petersburg 15 Apr "

[illegible] de Plehve appointed minister of the interior 17 Apr "

he zemstvos, local institutions forbidden to collect rural statistics in S Russia spring, "

artial law proclaimed in Poltava 5 May, "

evolutionary outbreak at Saratoff 18 May, "

res Loubet visits the czar 20 May, "

rave disturbances in Ekaterinoslaff June, "

rince Obolenski, the governor, wounded by a peasant (death sentence commuted, Nov), at Kharkoff 11 Aug "

he students imprisoned at Smolensk freed by the czar's orders early Aug "

abor troubles in the S , conflict with troops, 4 deaths, 102 arrests, 24, 30 Nov , great distress Dec "

lanifesto from the czar, favoring religious freedom reform of peasant taxation 11 Mch 1903

ishineff atrocities 45 Jews killed 84 seriously wounded 500 crippled and injured, 10,000 rendered destitute 19, 20 Apr "

en Bogdanovitch, the governor, assassinated at Ufa 19 May, "

gitation and unrest all over the empire May et seq , general strikes in the S , riots at Baku, Odessa, Kieff, and elsewhere, conflicts with the troops July-Aug "

mperial viceroyalty appointed in the far East 12 Aug "

linisterial changes M Witte appointed president of the committee of ministers and members of the imperial council, M Pleske, minister of finance 29 Aug "

ew law of expulsion of foreigners, issued Oct "

ussian substituted for Swedish at the opening of the Finnish senate. 22 Oct. "

evolutionary disturbances throughout Russia Oct -mid Nov "

ishineff massacres (19, 20 Apr), trial began, 19 Nov , Gretschin and Marosjuk sentenced to 7 and 5 years penal servitude, 22 others to periods of 1 to 2 years 21 Dec "

erious disturbances among the students of the universities of Tomsk, Kazan, and Kieff Nov -end Dec "

trained relations with Japan, negotiations continued, war preparations proceeding Dec 1903-Jan 1904

apan severs her diplomatic relations with Russia 6 Feb "

dm Togo attacks the Russian fleet at Port Arthur 8 Feb "

ar against Japan declared 10 Feb "

[For the events of the war see Russo Japanese war]

en Bobrikoff, governor of Finland, assassinated at Helsingfors 16 June, "

linister Plehve assassinated at St Petersburg July 28, "

irth of an heir to the throne 12 Aug "

ussia protests against the Anglo Thibetan treaty 20 Sept "

he contraband commission at St. Petersburg declare coal, cotton, and iron contraband of war 22 Sept. "

he Baltic fleet attacks a British fishing fleet in the North sea, 22 Oct "

ussia and England agree to arbitrate the North sea difficulty, 28 Oct "

irst zemstvos assembly meets at St Petersburg 19 Nov "

he petition of the zemstvoists presented to the czar 24 Nov "

early 100,000 men on strike, they demand shorter hours, more pay, universal suffrage, cessation of war 18 Jan 1905

ttempt to assassinate the czar on the Neva 19 Jan "

he strikers, headed by father Gapon, try to present their petition to the czar, troops fire upon the unarmed men, women, and children, official report, 96 killed, 333 wounded 22 Jan "

he czar addressed a deputation of 32 working men, assuring them that their wrongs would be redressed 1 Feb "

rince Sviatopolk-Mirsky resigns, 11 Jan , Bouligan succeeds, 2 Feb "

ommittee appointed by the czar draw up an extensive programme of reforms, the czar approves the report 2 Feb "

oinien, procurator general of Finland, assassinated 7 Feb "

rand duke Sergius assassinated at Moscow 17 Feb "

rofessors and students of St Petersburg university vote to close the institution, and demand a constitution 20 Feb "

orth sea commission finds that there were no hostile vessels, but justifies Rojestvensky's attack on account of his fears, 25 Feb. "

he czar announces his intention to convene a representative assembly which will have no real power 3 Mch "

ithuania demands civil rights and the use of the Lithuanian language 20 Mch "

he city of Yalta set on fire, police stations wrecked and prisoners liberated 27 Mch "

inland agrees to pay $2,000,000 war contribution yearly, recruiting to be stopped in Finland, and the judges to be made irremovable 29 Mch "

Unrest and riot among the peasants throughout Russia, many mansions are sacked and burned, the peasants demand a division of the land in their favor . Mch -Apr "

The holy synod requests the election of a patriarch 3 Apr "

A medical congress, numbering over 1300 doctors from all parts of Russia, demand civil rights and reforms 5 Apr "

The czar's Easter ukase cancels the peasant's indebtedness to the government, opens altars to adherents of the Old Faith, and provides that converts from the orthodox church shall not be punished, and that non Christian subjects excepting Jews shall have equal rights 29 Apr 1905

[Similar action has been taken by various organizations of professional men throughout the empire May-June 1905]

Ukase providing for a parliamentary body with legislative powers 20 May, "

Zemstvo congress at Moscow demands a constitution May-June "

Russia and Japan reply favorably to President's Roosevelt's peace suggestion 12 June "

SOVEREIGNS OF RUSSIA.

DUKES OF KIEF

850 ? Ruric
879 Oleg
913 Igor I
945 Olga widow, regent
955 Swiatoslaw I , the Victorious.
973 Jaropalk I
980 Vladimir, or Wladimir, the Great
1015 Swiatopalk
1018 Jaraslaw, or Jaroslaf, I
1054 Isiaslaw I
1073 Swiatoslaw II
1078 Wsewolod I
1093 Swiatopalk II
1113 Vladimir II
1125 Mitislaw
1132 Jaropalk II
1138 { Wiatschelaw
1139 { Wsewolod II
1146 { Isiaslaw II and Igor II
1153 { Rostislaw
1149. Jurie, or George, I , the city of Moscow was built by this duke

GRAND-DUKES OF WLADIMIR.

1157 { Andrew I until 1175, first grand duke
1175 { Michael I
1177 Wsewolod III
1213 { Jurie, or George, II
1217-18 { Constantine
1238 Jaraslaw II , succeeded by his son
1245 Alexander Nevski, or Newski, the Saint.
1263 Jaraslaw III
1270 Vasali, or Basil, I
1275 Dmitri, or Demetrius, I
1281 Andrew II
1294 Daniel Alexandrovitz
1303. Jurie, or George, III , deposed.
1305 Michael III
1320 Vasali, or Basil II
1325 Jurie, or George, III , restored.
1327 Alexander II

[The dates are doubtful, owing to the difficulty that occurs at every step in early Russian annals]

GRAND-DUKES OF MOSCOW

1328 Ivan, or John, I
1340 Simeon the Proud.
1353 Ivan, or John, II
1359 Demetrius II , prince of Susdal
1362 Demetrius III Donskoi
1389 Vasali, or Basil, III Temnoi
1425 Vasali, or Basil, IV

CZARS OF MUSCOVY.

1462 Ivan (Basilovitz) or John, III , took the title of czar, 1482
1505 Vasali, or Basil, V obtained the title of emperor from Maximilian I
1533 Ivan IV the Terrible, a tyrant
1584 Feodor, or Theodor, I , and his son, Demetrius, murdered by his successor,
1598. Boris Godonof, who usurped the throne.
1605 Feodor II , murdered
1606. Demetrius the Impostor, a young Polish monk, pretended to be the murdered prince Demetrius, put to death
" Vasali Chouiski, or Zouinski
1610 Ladislaus of Poland, retired 1613.
1613 Michael Feodorovitz, of the house of Romanoff, descended from the czar Ivan Basilovitz
1645 Alexis, son , styled the father of his country
1676 Feodor, or Theodor, II
1682 { Ivan V and Peter I , brothers of the preceding

EMPERORS AND EMPRESSES.

1689 Peter I the Great, alone, took the title of emperor 22 Oct. 1721, founded St Petersburg
1725 Catherine I , his widow, at first the wife of a Swedish dragoon said to have been killed on the day of marriage.
1727 Peter II , son of Alexis Petrovitz, and grandson of Peter the Great, deposed
1730 Anne, duchess of Courland, daughter of the czar Ivan
1740 Ivan VI , an infant, grand nephew to Peter the Great, immured in a dungeon for 18 years, murdered in 1764
1741 Elizabeth, daughter of Peter the Great, reigned during Ivan's captivity
1762 Peter III , son of Anne and of Charles Frederick, duke of Holstein-Gottorp, deposed, and died soon after, supposed to have been murdered
" Catherine II , his consort, a great sovereign, extended the Russian territories on all sides, d 17 Nov 1796.

1796. Paul, her son; murdered 24 Mch. 1801.
1810. Alexander I., son; b. 28 Dec. 1777; d. 1 Dec. 1825.
1825. Nicholas I., brother; b. 25 June, 1796; d. 2 Mch. 1855.
1855. Alexander II., son; b. 29 Apr. 1818; married 28 Apr. 1841, Mary, princess of Hesse (d. 3 June, 1880); said to have married (morganatic) princess Dolgourouki, 19 (31) July; marriage announced, Oct. 1880; assassinated at St. Petersburg, 2 P.M., 13 Mch. 1881.
1881. Alexander III., b. 10 Mch. 1845; d. 1 Nov. 1894; married Mary (formerly Dagmar), princess of Denmark, 9 Nov. 1866.
1894. Nicholas II., son; b. 18 May, 1868; married princess Alix of Hesse-Darmstadt, 26 Nov. 1894.

Russo-Japanese war. The causes of the war declared by Japan against Russia lie in the feeling of outraged national pride following the Russian occupation of Port Arthur after Japan had been forced to let go this important prize of its war with China. Russia hastened after the treaty of peace between Japan and China to establish a practical occupation of Manchuria, her political and naval interests demanding a naval base on the Yellow Sea, free of ice. Russia extended its Trans-Siberian railroad system to Port Arthur, and, without annexing Manchuria in fact, gave so many evident signs of intent to make her control there permanent that Japan took alarm. Between Manchuria and Japan lies Korea, which, Japanese statesmen hold, must be under Japanese control for the safety of Japan itself. Russia in Manchuria meant Russian intrigue in Korea, and the prevention of the expansion of Japan. And expansion is imperative for Japan by reason of her growing population. The Boxer troubles in China strengthened the Russian position in Manchuria, and, when these disturbances ceased, Japan began a diplomatic campaign to force Russia back. This continued until the presentation of an ultimatum by Japan in Jan. The contents of the Russian reply, sent to Tokio on 6 Feb., was known to the mikado's ministers before it could be presented, and was of so unsatisfactory a character that the Japanese minister at St. Petersburg, count Kurino, was summarily recalled. The Russian minister, baron de Rosen, was recalled on the same day. Subsequent events have proved that Japan's military and naval progress in the previous 10 years had been governed by the realization that sooner or later war with Russia was inevitable. The Russians, on the other hand, had counted on being able to prevent a war, or, at least, to postpone it for some years to come. At the outbreak of hostilities Russia was unprepared, both as regards her army in Manchuria and her naval establishment at Port Arthur and Vladivostok, to cope with the Japanese. The story of the war is of an almost unchecked Japanese advance and of a brilliantly executed Russian retreat. In some respects the movement of the Japanese armies can be compared, for machine-like precision, to that of the Prussian armies directed by von Moltke against those of the emperor Napoleon III. The Japanese army began to be moved into Korea on 18 Feb., 11 days after the first shot of the war had been fired. In 10 days more they had occupied Ping Yang, without having met anything like resistance in force. Gen. Kuropatkin, on taking command of the Russian forces, had not more than 100,000 troops in eastern Siberia, and these, for a large part, were stationed at points where they were needed to guard the railway, the only military communication with Russia. The problem before Kuropatkin was to retard his enemy's advance until he could collect a force to match him. Collecting such a force meant the transportation of men, horses, supplies, and guns over a single-track railroad. The summary of the land campaign in Manchuria which follows is based largely upon the military criticism written for *The World* by lieut.-gen. Nelson A. Miles.

First Russia reinforced gen. Stoessel, in command of the Port Arthur garrison, foreseeing that one of the first moves of Japan would be to invest this stronghold by land and sea. Stoessel was left with 25,000 effectives, including the crews of the fleet and the soldiery of the naval yards. A force under gen. Zassulitch was posted at the Yalu river to resist invaders into Manchuria. Zassulitch had about 18,000 infantry, 5000 cavalry, and 72 guns. Kuroki had 42,000 infantry, 5000 cavalry, and 124 guns. Kuroki, on 26 Apr., seized the Kiurito and Osenkito islands in the Yalu, encountering feeble resistance. By well-contrived strategy Kuroki so managed that Zassulitch concentrated his heaviest forces at a great distance from the point he had selected for the delivery of his principal attack on 1 May, and Kuroki's 3 divisions were thrown across the river, the twelfth crossing a bridge built at Suikauchen on 30 Apr. From Kiuluto the Japanese artillery silenced the Russian guns on Conical Hill, and batteries north of Wiju disposed of the Russian artillery force opposed at that point. The second division was manœuvred so as to take the Russians in flank. On the morning of 1 May the Japanese forces had been so disposed that the order to advance was given for the first important land battle of the war. By a brilliant charge made across the Aiko river, in an exposed position, the Japanese overcame what at first appeared to be a Russian advantage of position, and by mid-afternoon their enemy was in full retreat. The Russians lost 2600 killed and wounded in this affair; the Japanese about 1000. The victors captured 600 prisoners, 21 field pieces, 1000 rifles, 350,000 rounds of ammunition, and a great quantity of supplies. Zassulitch had disobeyed orders, and was outgeneralled and outfought, with losses that his chief, gen. Kuropatkin, could ill afford. Zassulitch moved his force slowly to the northwest, abandoning Fengwangcheng without resistance. Kuroki's advance was slow, while he awaited the development of the other prearranged movements of his country's forces. The Japanese second army, under gen. Oku, had by 23 May cut off the Port Arthur garrison's communication with gen. Kuropatkin, and made itself master of the neck of the Liao-Tung peninsula. The third Japanese army, under gen. Nodzu, moved up from Takushan to Siuyen, in touch with Kuroki, by 8 June. Operations began on 23 May, by gen. Nodzu's third army, against gen. Stoessel's advanced positions in the Liao-Tung peninsula. These operations culminated in the battle of Nanshan. It was a complete but hard-won victory for Japan. In this battle, lasting until 26 May, the Japanese first exhibited that apparent recklessness in sacrifice of lives in order to attain a desired object which has distinguished their method of warfare throughout the campaign. The Japanese fleet in Kinchau bay enabled the army at length, after many desperate charges, to carry the positions held by the Russian gen. Fock, and force the latter's retreat southward. The Russians left 600 dead and 50 pieces of artillery behind. The Japanese loss was about 4300 in killed and wounded. The Russians began to concentrate a large force at Telissu, on the line of the railroad to Port Arthur, under gen. Stakelberg, whose purpose was a movement southward to the relief of the Port Arthur garrison. Gen. Oku moved 50,000 men near Port Adams and advanced northward in 3 columns. On 14 June his force came into collision with Stakelberg's. The strategy of Oku enabled him within 3 days to catch the Russians, already in retreat, in an ambush. The Russians lost 4300 to the Japanese 1163 in this battle. The Russians fell back to Kaiping, from which position they were driven on 8 July, fighting only a rear-guard action to protect their retreat, which was accomplished without noteworthy loss. Gen. Nodzu had gained a junction with gen. Kuroki, and on 27 June had flanked the Russians, enabling him to advance to Sunuchen after 2 days of fighting. Kuroki advanced towards Motien pass and along the valley of the Patao river, occupying Fengshailing pass on 29 June. Gen. Meschenko's cossacks were raiding to the north and east of this position, and provision was made against an attack from that quarter. On 8 July he gained other important positions at Hanchen and Sidoguir. This closed the first stage of the Japanese advance. Four armies had now been landed. Kuroki's was advancing on three roads towards Liaoyang, having gained the principal passes which lead from the mountains westward into the Manchurian plains. Oku had moved up the railroad to Tashichiao, and Nodzu was beyond the Fenschui pass on the road to Haicheng. The fourth army, under gen. Nogi, had taken up the task of driving Stoessel's forces back into Port Arthur. In the middle of July the Japanese operations, heretofore directed by the general staff, were intrusted to field-marshal Oyama. The imminent danger to the Russian position now was a movement by the enemy with the object of seizing the railroad between Liaoyang and Mukden. Gen. Keller was sent on 17 July, with 20,000 men and 24 guns, to attack the Japanese at Fengshui pass. His expedition failed. He lost 1200 men without dislodging the enemy, and he retired to a strong position in the Yantze pass, where he could protect the retreat in case of need. Oku marched ahead, and on 23 July attacked gen. Zaronbaieff's position before Tashichiao. After an all-day artillery attack, he moved at night against the Russian left, accomplishing a turning movement which compelled the Russians to abandon Tashichiao and Yinkow. The success of this movement deprived Russia of its last base on the Chinese sea-coast, and cut off supplies theretofore received by the Peking railroad. Kuroki engaged Keller again on 31 July at Yantze pass and Yushulin, and after 2 days' fighting Keller retired towards Liaoyang. At the same time Oku and Nodzu made a combined attack on the Russian right, 15 miles below Haicheng, and turned their enemy northward. The Russians abandoned Haicheng on 2 Aug. Kuroki had lost 2400 men, but the point gained was that the operations had forced the enemy to a concentrated area. The fighting hitherto had been in mountainous country. The future operations were to be conducted in the rich agricultural plain wherein the Manchu conquerors of China had their origin. The Russians were now extended along a front of 25 miles between Anping and the railroad at Anshanchan. The rainy season now enforced a comparative truce, which endured through the greater part of Aug. This was to the advantage of the Russians, who had made most of the summer to bring up reinforcements and supplies to depots at Harbin and Mukden. On the morning of 26 Aug. the Japanese renewed the attack. The Russian position extended along a semicircle of hills 12 miles from Liaoyang, and the force available consisted of about 148,000 men with 400 guns, so disposed as to guard all the 3 roads which centre upon Liaoyang. The Japanese right consisted of Kuroki's first army, with Nodzu's army in the centre and Oku's on the left. These combined armies consisted of about 200,000 men with 520 guns. With this superior force, marshal Oyama ordered a general advance. Kuroki turned the Russian left at the Taitse river, and Oku broke through the Russian right near Anshanchan. Kuropatkin was compelled to move back to a position only 5 miles distant from Liaoyang. The Russian retreat was accomplished in good order, and without severe losses. Kuropatkin threw a corps across the Taitse river on 29 Aug. to protect his left. Kuroki crossed the Taitse to destroy this force, while the other Japanese armies pressed the Russian left centre. Kuropatkin discovered the dangerous character of Kuroki's move in time, and he ordered a strong force to envelop Kuroki. This failed, and the

Russians were obliged to evacuate Liaoyang, the retreat beginning on 3 Sept. Kuropatkin was in a tight place, but he managed, nevertheless, to make his escape with his whole army. The rear guard's heroism saved the day. The army had retired upon Mukden on 7 Sept. Again there was a long cessation of severe operations, owing to the heavy rains. At last on 5 Oct. what was intended to be the decisive battle of the war was joined. Kuropatkin, with a force estimated at 300,000 men, and with a superior force of artillery to Oyama's, moved forward against the Japanese position. Gen. Kuropatkin, previous to this advance, had inspired his troops with a proclamation in which he declared in effect that now Russia was prepared to drive the enemy back and to begin a campaign whose intent was to crush Japan. The Russian change of policy was in part a failure and in part a success. For a week the armies, estimated as of about equal strength in men, engaged in a struggle called the battle of the Sha river. Men fought without sleep, even without rest, day after day. The crucial moment of this battle was the occupation by the Russians of an eminence called Lone Tree Hill. It was essential to the Russians that this should be taken from their enemy. After repeated failures a charge, led by an officer named Putiloff, captured the position with severe loss. So brilliant was the achievement that the place was named Putiloff Hill in official orders. Its importance was demonstrated afterwards by successive Japanese attacks, all of which failed. When gen. Stoessel was shut up in Port Arthur he announced his intention to hold this fortress to the last limit of his endurance. From May to Dec. a number of assaults, each conducted with disregard of its cost in lives, were made by the Japanese. The Japanese, after many failures and great loss of life, succeeded on 29 and 30 Nov. in capturing an eminence known as 203 Metre Hill, which commands the harbor of Port Arthur. Siege guns placed there destroyed or damaged almost all the vessels in the harbor. This made it impossible for the fleet to attempt a final sortie. During Dec. the Japanese continued to harass the garrison of Port Arthur by the fire of their 11 inch howitzers and by constant pushing forward of their intrenchments, and frequent attacks on the more or less isolated forts. The N. side of the Ehrlung fort was blown up by dynamite on 26 Nov., after the Japanese had tunnelled hundreds of feet up the mountain. On 18 Dec. the Kikwan fort was blown up, on the 28th the Rihlung mountain fort was stormed, and on 1 Jan. 1905 the Paulung fort was captured. Negotiations were opened between gen. Stoessel and gen. Nogi, which resulted in the surrender of Port Arthur on 2 Jan. Before surrendering the Russians torpedoed their own ships in the harbor. The garrison consisted of about 10,000 sick and wounded and about 5,000 effective men. Japan proceeded at once to rebuild the fortifications and to store several years' supplies of munitions and provisions. On 19 Feb. the Japanese attacked Tsinkehchin, held by gen. Rennenkampff with 40,000 men, forcing the Russians to retreat. The Russians made a counter attack on 26 Feb., but were unsuccessful, as they were flanked by Japanese reinforcements. Two days later the Japanese captured the very important Da pass, Kuroki attacked the Russian left, Nodzu the centre, and Oku the right. The Russians were driven back to Mukden, when Nogi, with his Port Arthur army, suddenly appeared west and north of Mukden. For 3 weeks the series of battles proceeded, ending with the retreat of Kuropatkin's entire army on to Tieling, which had been strongly fortified and was the Russian base of supplies. Nearly 50,000 Russians were taken prisoners, and Tieling could not be held. The Japanese captured Tieling on 15 Mch., the Russians retreating to Harbin. Kuropatkin resigned his command, which was given to Linevitch. From April to June both armies were recuperating. While attacks and counter attacks were made daily, no general movement was attempted by either army. Pres. Roosevelt, believing the time opportune, addressed an identical note to Japan and Russia, suggesting direct negotiations between themselves for peace, and offering his friendly offices to facilitate bringing the two nations together. No armistice was arranged, as Japan was not willing to make any changes in the prosecution of the campaign until after the exchange of credentials between properly and fully empowered plenipotentiaries.

The Story of the Navy.—The supreme command of the Russian forces in the East at the outbreak of the war was vested in vice-adm. Alexieff. In the development of Russia's advance on Manchuria he had displayed marked administrative ability, but when the test of war came he was shown to be lacking in the qualities of a competent commander. His only offensive move against the enemy appears to have been a sortie of the Vladivostok squadron of 4 cruisers, which raided the W. coast of Japan and sank several merchant ships. On 20 Feb. he moved his headquarters from Port Arthur to Harbin. The appointment of vice adm. Makharoff to command the Port Arthur fleet, and of gen. Kuropatkin, minister of war, to command the armies in the East, followed within 3 days. Two days after the severance of diplomatic relations the first blow was struck. The main fleet of Japan, consisting of 6 modern battleships, several cruisers, and a large flotilla of torpedo boats and destroyers, under adm. Togo, suddenly attacked the Russian naval force at Port Arthur. The attack was a complete surprise. The precautions which one would have expected to be taken by any civilized power, even in a period of merely "strained relations," were neglected by the Russians. This attack damaged 2 battle ships and a first class cruiser. On the following day a second attack was made, resulting in further damage to the Russian squadron; thereafter the Port Arthur squadron was not strong enough to risk a battle with its enemy. On the same day a cruiser squadron with torpedo boats compelled the modern Russian cruisers *Variag* and *Corietz* to leave the harbor of Chemulpo, Korea, and fight. The Russian vessels were destroyed, with a loss of more than 500 men killed and wounded. This settled the question of Japan's naval supremacy in the Pacific, and made it a simple matter for Japan to carry out a scheme of land operations, prepared long in advance, whose effect was twofold: the capture of Port Arthur and the expulsion of Russian armies from Manchuria, involving the seizure of the railway at Harbin, which would also cut off Vladivostok, Russia's more northern port and garrison on the Pacific coast. Secretary Hay's proposals resulted in an agreement of the belligerent powers to restrict their operations to Manchuria, and that other Chinese territory should be respected. Neutrality was proclaimed by the U. S. on 11 Feb., the day after Russia's declaration of war and the day of Japan's declaration. Before the siege proper of Port Arthur can be said to have begun, Togo's navy made several attempts to block the harbor entrance with old steamships, much as Hobson had done in the blockade of Santiago in the war of America with Spain. These were not successful. On 13 Apr. adm. Makharoff attempted a sortie. The battle-ship *Petropavlovsk* was sunk just outside the harbor. Makharoff perished, with the famous Russian artist Vasili Vereschagin. Several general bombardments of Port Arthur by Togo's fleet failed of their purpose. On 15 May the Japanese battle ship *Hatsuse* was destroyed by a mine, and the Japanese cruiser *Yoshino* was accidentally rammed and sunk by the cruiser *Kasuga* of the same fleet. The Russian Vladivostok squadron made a second raid in June and sank 3 Japanese transports. Adm. Wittshaeft attempted another dash out of Port Arthur with the Russian fleet on 22 June, but was driven back with heavy loss. Again, 10 Aug., the Russian fleet attempted to effect a junction with the Vladivostok squadron. Two cruisers were compelled to seek neutral ports and dismantle. The Vladivostok squadron was disabled in a September sortie, and compelled to return to that port. It was not until October that official admission was made by Japan that the battle ship *Yashima*, one of the best of Togo's fleet, had been destroyed months before. This left Togo with only 4 modern battle ships, the *Asahi*, *Fuji*, *Mikasa*, and *Shikishima*. In the early summer the Russians sent out the torpedo boat destroyer *Ryeshitelni*, which made Shanghai. Her commander, under neutrality laws, agreed to dismantle her. Nevertheless Japanese torpedo boats attacked her at her pier, and after a hand to hand fight the Russian commander and his men jumped overboard. The uncertain position in which this left other belligerent vessels in Chinese ports caused the commander of the torpedo boat *Rastoropny*, which ran the blockade and made Chefoo on 13 Nov. with important despatches from Stoessel to St. Petersburg, to blow up his vessel rather than allow her to fall into the enemy's hands. The *Smolensk* and *St. Petersburg*, two vessels of the Russian volunteer fleet, passed the Dardanelles in July, and later appeared in the Red sea, holding up and capturing British and German vessels. Representations by the governments concerned led Russia to restore these vessels' prizes and to undertake that they would confine their attention to ships undoubtedly containing contraband of war. On 22 July the steamer *Arabia*, German, but chartered by an American company, was seized in the Pacific by the Vladivostok squadron. This was the subject of remonstrance by the U. S. state department. Two days later the Vladivostok vessels sank the British steamer *Knight Commander* with an American cargo. This also called out a protest from secretary Hay. In view of the non-effectiveness of her Pacific fleet, Russia hastened preparations to send the most formidable vessels of her Baltic fleet to the Pacific. Its first division, proceeding through the North sea on the way to the Mediterranean to take the Suez canal route, attacked by night a peaceful fleet of British steam trawlers, killing 2 men. The incident created, for some days, an apprehension of war with Great Britain. The Russian admiral, Rojestvensky, declared that he had been attacked by torpedo boats. Russia acceded to the British demands, and a commission, consisting of 4 high naval officers, British, American, French, and Russian, sat at Paris to determine the facts, 25 Feb. 1905. The court decided that Rojestvensky was not justified in firing on the fleet, but did not impugn either his valor or humanity. Russia was condemned to pay $325,000 as an indemnity. On 7 Dec. the czar ordered a third squadron to sail in Mch. 1905, under adm. Nebogatoff. The first two squadrons remained in French waters at Madagascar for several months, and then went to Cochin China, where they were met by the third squadron early in May. Adm. Rojestvensky left the supply ships and transports behind while he, with the entire fighting force of the fleet, endeavored to reach Vladivostok by way of the straits of Korea. There, on the morning of 27 May, he was met by adm. Togo with his fleet, which had been lying in ambush nearly 2 months. The Japanese fire was accurate and deadly, the Russian weak and uncertain. In this, the greatest naval battle of modern times, the Russian fleet was utterly destroyed, with practically no loss on the part of the Japanese. Nearly 10,000 Russians were drowned, over 3,000 captured, including adms. Rojestvensky and Nebogatoff, while adm. Voelkersham was killed, and adm. Enquist escaped to Manila with the cruisers *Oleg*, *Aurora*, and *Jemchug*, which were interned. The cruiser *Almaz* and 3 torpedo boats reached Vladivostok. The battle ships *Orel* and *Nicolas I.*, the coast defence ships *Apraxin* and *Seniavin* and the torpedo boat *Biedovy* were captured and taken to Sasebo, Japan. The battle ships *Kniaz Suvaroff*, *Alexander III.*, *Oslabya*, *Navarin*, *Sissoi Veliki* and *Borodino*, the armored cruisers *Dmitri Donskoi*, *Admiral Nakhimoff*, *Vladimir Monomach*, and *Admiral Oushakoff*, together with a number of other fighting vessels, were sunk. The ships in neutral harbors were interned until the end of the war.

Peace Negotiations.—The Russian and Japanese envoys met the President on board the *Mayflower* at Oyster Bay, on 5 Aug., and met formally at Portsmouth, N. H., on 9 Aug., and negotiations continued until 5 Sept., when the treaty was signed, the important terms of which were: 1. Recognition of Japan's paramount interests in Korea; 2. The transfer of the lease of Port Arthur and the Liao Tung peninsula to Japan; 3. Restoration of the Chinese administration in Manchuria, and its evacuation by Russians and Chinese within eighteen months; 4. The transfer to Japan of the railroad between Port Arthur and Chang chun fu and all its branches and rights to coal mines, &c.; 5. The cession to Japan of Saghalien south of the 50th degree of north latitude; 6. The cession to Japan

RUS

of fishing rights along the coasts of the Russian possessions 7 The mutual right of Japan and Russia to maintain railway guards in Manchuria, limited to fifteen men per kilometer, 8 Russia and Japan to pay each other the costs of maintenance and return of all prisoners of war, 9 The ratification of the treaty to be completed within fifty days from 5 Sept. The conclusion of peace led to some rioting in Japan which was quickly suppressed (England and Japan signed a treaty of alliance 27 Sept, 1905) In Russia the dissatisfaction with the government assumed a revolutionary aspect, initiated by general strikes On 30 Oct the Czar issued a manifesto assuring freedom of the press, civil liberty, and consent of the douma in legislation

Russo-Turkish (Crimean) **war—1853-56.** In 1844 czar Nicholas in England conversed with the duke of Wellington and lord Aberdeen (whom he had known many years) respecting dissolution of the Turkish empire, and on return embodied his views in a memorandum drawn up by count Nesselrode, which was transmitted to London, but kept secret till Mch 1854. In Jan and Feb of that year the czar had several conversations on the subject with the British envoy at St. Petersburg, sir G H Seymour, in one of which (14 Jan) he compared Turkey to a "sick man" in a state of decrepitude, on the point of death, and made proposals to the British government for the disposal of his property He stated frankly that he would not permit the British to establish themselves at Constantinople, but said, in another conversation, he would not object to their possessing Egypt The purport of these conversations was conveyed in despatches to lord John Russell, who replied that the British government declined to make any provision for the contingency of the fall of Turkey The czar made similar proposals to the French government, with the same result. The Russian and French governments having each taken a side in the dispute between the Greek and Latin churches as to the exclusive possession of the HOLY PLACES in Palestine, the Porte advised a mixed commission, which decided in favor of the Greeks, and a firman was promulgated accordingly, 9 Mch 1853 To this decision the French acceded, although dissatisfied.

Russians make further claims, and prince Menschikoff (who arrived at Constantinople 28 Feb 1853) by various notes (between 22 Mch and 18 May) demands that the sultan sign a convention granting the czar such a protectorate over the Greek Christians in Turkey as the sultan considered inimical to his own authority 22 Mch -18 May, 1853
Demand rejected, Menschikoff quits Constantinople 21 May, "
Sultan issues a hatti scherif confirming rights and privileges of Greek Christians, and appeals to his allies 6 June, "
English and French fleets anchor in Besika bay . 13 June, "
Russians, under gen Luders, cross the Pruth and enter Moldavia 2 July, "
Circular of count Nesselrode in justification, 2 July, lord Clarendon's reply . . 16 July, "
Representatives of England, France, Austria, and Prussia meet at Vienna, agree to a note, 31 July, accepted by czar, 10 Aug, sultan requires modifications, 19 Aug, which the czar rejects 7 Sept. "
Two English and 2 French ships enter Dardanelles 14 Sept "
Sultan (with consent of a great national council) declares war against Russia .. 5 Oct. "
Turkish fortress at Issaktocha fires on a Russian flotilla (the first act of war) .. . 23 Oct. "
Turks cross the Danube at Widdin and occupy Kalafat, 28 Oct.-3 Nov "
Russia declares war against Turkey . .. .1 Nov "
English and French fleets enter Bosporus ... . . 2 Nov "
Russians defeated at Oltenitza .. 4 Nov "
Turks (in Asia) defeated at Bayandur, Atskur, and Achaltzik, 14, 18, 26 Nov "
Turkish fleet destroyed at Sinope 30 Nov "
Collective note from the 4 powers, demanding on what terms the Porte will negotiate for peace 5 Dec "
Contests at Kalafat 31 Dec 1853 to 9 Jan 1854
At the request of Porte (5 Dec), allied fleets enter the Black sea. . . 4 Jan "
Russians defeated at Citate 6 Jan "
Reply of Porte to note of 5 Dec proposes 4 points as bases of negotiation—viz 1 Prompt evacuation of the principalities 2 Revision of the treaties 3. Maintenance of religious privileges to communities of all confessions 4 A definitive settlement of the convention respecting Holy Places (dated 31 Dec), approved by the 4 powers 13 Jan "
Vienna conferences close 16 Jan. "
Kalafat invested by the Russians 28-31 Jan "
Proposal in a letter from the emperor of the French to the czar (29 Jan) declined 9 Feb. "
Turkish flotilla at Rustchuk destroyed by the Russians under Schilders. . . 15 Feb. "
Ultimatum of England and France sent to St Petersburg, 27 Feb "
Czar "did not judge it suitable to give an answer" 19 Mch. "
Baltic fleet sails, under sir C Napier 11 Mch "
Treaty between England, France, and Turkey 12 Mch "
Russians under Gortschakoff pass the Danube and occupy the Dobrudscha, conflicts, the Turks retire 23, 24 Mch. 1854
France and England declare war against Russia. 27, 28 Mch "
Rupture between Turkey and Greece 28 Mch "
Gen Canrobert and French troops arrive at Gallipoli, soon after followed by the English 31 Mch "
English vessel *Furious*, with a flag of truce, fired on at Odessa, 8 Apr "
Austria, England, France, and Prussia sign a protocol at Vienna guaranteeing the integrity of Turkey and civil and religious rights of her Christian subjects 10 Apr "
Russians defeated at Kostelli by Mustapha Pacha " "
Offensive and defensive alliance between England and France, 10 Apr "
Treaty between Austria and Prussia 20 Apr "
Bombardment of Odessa by allied fleet 22 Apr "
Russians under gen Schilders, assault Kalafat, repulsed, the blockade raised 19-21 Apr "
Steamer *Tiger* run aground near Odessa, captured by the Russians 12 May, "
Russians defeated at Turtukai 13 May, "
Siege of Silistria begun 17 May, "
Allied armies disembark at Varna . 29 May, "
Russians defeated by the Turks at Karakai 30 May, "
Mouths of the Danube blockaded by allied fleets. 1 June, "
Russians repulsed at Silistria, Paskiewitsch and many officers wounded 5 June, "
Turks defeated at Ozurgheti (in Asia) 16 June, "
Severe conflict before Silistria, the siege raised 18-26 June, "
Batteries at the Sulina mouths destroyed . 26, 27 June, "
Russians defeated at Giurgevo 7 July, "
French troops (10 000) embark at Boulogne for the Baltic, 15 July, "
Turks defeated at Bayazid in Armenia, 29, 30 July, and near Kars . 5 Aug "
Surrender of BOMARSUND 16 Aug "
[In July and August the allies suffered severely from cholera]
Russians defeated by Schamyl in Georgia about 28 Aug "
They evacuate the principalities Aug -20 Sept "
By virtue of a treaty with Turkey (June 14) the Austrians, under count Coronini, enter Bucharest 6 Sept "
Allies sail from Varna, 3 Sept, and land at Old Fort, near Eupatoria . 14 Sept "
Skirmish at the Bulganac . . 19 Sept "
Battle of the ALMA 20 Sept. "
Russians sink part of their fleet at Sebastopol. . 23 Sept "
Allies occupy Balaklava 26 Sept. "
Death of marshal St Arnaud 29 Sept "
Gen Canrobert his successor 24 Nov "
Siege of Sebastopol begins, grand attack unsuccessful 17 Oct. "
Battle of BALAKLAVA, charge of the light cavalry, with severe loss 25 Oct "
Sortie from Sebastopol repulsed by gens Evans and Bosquet 26 Oct "
Russian attack at Inkerman, defeated . 5 Nov "
Miss Nightingale and nurses arrive at Scutari . 6 Nov "
Great tempest in the Black sea, loss of the *Prince* and store vessels . . 14-16 Nov "
Treaty of alliance between England, France, Austria, and Prussia, a commission to meet at Vienna, signed . 2 Dec. "
Russian sortie . 20 Dec. "
Omar Pacha arrives in the Crimea (followed by the Turkish army from Varna) . . . 5 Jan 1855
Sardinia joins England and France . 26 Jan "
Great sufferings in the camp from cold and sickness Jan -Feb "
Russians defeated by the Turks at Eupatoria 17 Feb "
Death of emperor Nicholas, accession of Alexander II (no change of policy) 2 Mch "
Sortie from the Malakhoff tower .. . 22 Mch "
Capture of Russian rifle-pits 19 Apr "
Arrival of Sardinian contingent .. . 8 May "
Resignation of gen Canrobert, succeeded by gen Pelissier, 16 May, "
Desperate night combats. . .. 22-24 May, "
Expedition into sea of Azof (under sir E Lyons and sir G Brown), destruction of Kertch and large amount of stores, 24 May-3 June, "
Taganrog bombarded . . . . . 3 June, "
Massacre of an English boat's crew with flag of truce at Hango, 5 June, "
Russians evacuate Anapa . . .. " "
White Works and Mamelon Vert taken . 6, 7 June, "
Unsuccessful attack on Malakhoff tower and Redan 18 June, "
Death of lord Raglan, succeeded by gen Simpson 28 June, "
Russians invest KARS in Armenia, defended by gen. Williams, 15 July. "
Bombardment of Sweaborg . 9 Aug "
Defeat of the Russians at the Tchernaya 16 Aug "
Ambuscade on the glacis of the Malakhoff taken, Russian sortie repulsed . 18 Aug. "
French take the MALAKHOFF by assault, English assault the Redan without success, Russians retire from Sebastopol to the North Forts, and the allies enter the city, Russians destroy or sink the remainder of their fleet. 8 Sept. et seq "
Tanan and Fanagoria captured . . ... 24 Sept. "
Russians assaulting Kars are defeated .. . . 29 Sept "
Kinburn taken . . . 17 Oct. "
Russians blow up Oczakoff .. 18 Oct. "
Defeat of the Russians, and passage of the Ingour by the Turks, under Omar Pacha. . . .. . 6 Nov "
Czar visits his army near Sebastopol . . 10 Nov "
Sir Wm Codrington relieves gen. Simpson ... 14 Nov "

Explosion of 100,000 lbs of powder in the French siege-train at Inkerman, great loss of life 15 Nov 1855
Sweden joins the allies by a treaty 21 Nov "
Capitulation of Kars to gen Mouravieff after a gallant defence by gen Williams 26 Nov "
Russian attack on the French posts at Baidar repulsed 8 Dec "
Proposals of peace from Austria, with the consent of the allies, sent to St Petersburg 12 Dec "
Centre dock at Sebastopol blown up by the English 2 Jan 1856
Council of war at Paris 11 Jan "
Protocol signed accepting Austrian propositions as basis of negotiation 1 Feb "
Destruction of Sebastopol docks " "
Report of sir John M'Neill and col Tulloch on state of the army before Sebastopol, pub 5 Feb "
Peace conferences open at Paris, an armistice till 31 Mch agreed on 25 Feb "
Suspension of hostilities 29 Feb "
Treaty of peace concluded at Paris 30 Mch "
Proclamation of peace in Crimea, 2 Apr, in London 29 Apr "
Crimea evacuated 9 July, "
The English lost killed in action and died of wounds about 3500, died of cholera, 4244, of other diseases, nearly 16,000, total loss, nearly 24 000 (including 270 officers), 2873 were disabled The war added to the national debt 41 041 000*l*. The French lost about 63,500 men, the Russians about half a million The army suffered greatly by sickness

Russo-Turkish War, 1877. For the insurrections, Servian war, and the negotiations, TURKEY

Czar addresses the army near Kischeneff, saying that "he has done everything in his power to avoid war, and patience is exhausted," Russian embassy quits Constantinople 23 Apr 1877
War declared, czar's manifesto says that he is compelled, by the haughty obstinacy of the Porte, to proceed to decisive acts, a justificatory circular to foreign powers sent out by prince Gortschakoff, Russians enter Turkish dominions in Roumania and Armenia 24 Apr "
Sultan's circular protests against the war and refers to his reforms and the treaty of Paris 25 Apr "
[Russian general in chief in Bulgaria grand duke Nicholas, in Armenia, grand duke Michael Turkish generals Abdul Kerim in Europe, Mukhtar Pacha in Asia Minor]
Russians defeated at Tchuruk Sou, near Batoum 26 Apr "
Russians, under grand duke Michael and Loris Melikoff advance into Armenia, defeat Turks, and occupy Bayazid (deserted) 29, 30 Apr "
Earl of Derby replies to Russian circular, he refers to the treaty of 1856 as broken, does not consider that the war will benefit Christians and asserts that Russia has separated herself from European concert, the British government gives neither concurrence nor approval to the war 1 May, "
Turks stop the passage of the Danube, and blockade the Black sea 3 May, "
Kalafat occupied by Roumanians " "
Russians defeated in attacking Batoum 4 May, "
Turkish monitor *Lufti Djelil*, with 300 men, blown up near Ibraila, or Braila, on the Danube (said to be by Russian shells) 11 May, "
Sukhum Khaleh, Russian fortress in the Caucasus, captured by Turks 14 May, "
Ardahan, near Kars, Armenia, stormed by Melikoff 17 May, "
Insurrection in Caucasus supported by the sultan 18 May et seq "
Explosion of Turkish monitor *Dai Matoun*, by lieuts 1 Daubassoff and Sheshlakoff, with torpedoes 26 May, "
Neutrality of Suez canal assured, correspondence May June, "
Kars invested by Russians 3 June, "
Czar arrives at Plojesto (Ployesto) in Roumania 6 June, "
Turks defeated at Tahir, or Taghir, Armenia 16 June, "
Turks victors at Zewin Dooz, Esbek Khalian, Delibaba, and other places, Russians retreating 20 June, "
Turks successful in Montenegro, country reported subdued, 12-20 June, "
Russians cross Lower Danube by bridges at Galatz and Braila, 6 hours' conflict ensues, Turks retire, 22 June, Russians occupy Matchin, 23 June, and Hirsova 25, 26 June, "
Grand duke Nicholas crosses the Danube at Simnitza by 208 pontoons, and enters Bulgaria, Turks retire after severe conflicts, 289 Russians said to be killed 27 June, "
Czar in proclamation to Bulgarians, encourages Christians and warns Mahometans 28 June, "
Simnitza bridge destroyed by a storm or by Turks, about 30 June, "
British fleet arrives at Besika bay 3 July, "
Biela, Bulgaria, taken by Russians about 5 July, "
Plevna, Bulgaria, occupied by Russians 6 July, "
Tirnova, ancient capital of Bulgaria, captured by Russians under gen Gourko 6, 7 July, "
Bayazid reoccupied by Turks 12 July, "
Russians forced from Kars by Mukhtar Pacha 13 July, "
Invasion of Armenia considered a failure July, "
Gourko crosses the Balkans and enters Roumelia, 13 July (this movement censured), several skirmishes 14, 15, 20 July, "
Nicopolis (Nikopol) surrenders (after severe conflicts, 12-14 July), capture of 2 pachas, 6000 men, 2 monitors, and 40 guns ... 15, 16 July, "
Turkish commander, Abdul Kerim replaced by Mehemet Ali (Jules Détroit, of French extraction), Russians retreating, July, "

RUS

Suleiman Pacha brought from Montenegro to the Schipka passes about 21 July, 1877
Aziz Pacha (able and popular) killed in a rash conflict at Eski-Djuma, near Rasgrad 26 or 28 July, "
Russians severely defeated, Plevna retaken by Osman Pacha, 19, 20 July, Russians again defeated 30, 31 July, "
Hostilities revived in Montenegro, the Turkish fortress Niksich besieged July, "
Severe conflicts between Russians and Suleiman Pacha, the Turks eventually victors Eski Saghra and Yeni Sagra, July, Kezanlik and Kalofer 30 July et seq "
Roumanian army joins the Russians 9 Aug "
Russians under Gourko expelled from Roumelia, retreat to Schipka passes about 11 Aug "
Russians in the Schipka passes relieved by Radetzky 21 Aug "
Russians defeated at Kara Silar near Osman Bazar 14 Aug, in the valley of the Lom by Mehemet Ali about 22-24 Aug "
Russians defeated by Mukhtar Pacha at Kurukdara or Kizil Tepé, between Kars and Alexandropol 24, 25 Aug "
Desperate fruitless attempts of Suleiman Pacha to gain the Schipka pass held by Gourko and Radetzky 20, 27 Aug "
Severe 12 hours' battle in the valley of the Lom, near Szedina, Karahassankoi taken and retaken 6 times, Russians (under the czarowitz) retire in good order 30 Aug "
Prince Charles with Roumanians crosses the Danube, about 31 Aug "
Lovatz or Luftcha captured by prince Imeritinsky and Russians after a sharp conflict 3 Sept "
Further successes of Mehemet Ali on the Lom at Katzelevo, Ablava, etc 4 Sept "
Niksich (left by Turks) captured by Montenegrins 7 Sept "
Sanguinary conflicts at Plevna, greatly strengthened by Osman Pacha, artillery duel 7-10 Sept "
Fierce assault by Russians and Roumanians, they gain the strong Gravitza redoubt (with others, which are retaken), the czar present, Russian loss about 20 000 11, 12 Sept "
Fort St Nicholas in Schipka pass taken by Suleiman Pacha and quickly lost, much bloodshed 17 Sept "
Russian losses, killed, wounded, and missing, 47,400 reported up to 20 Sept "
Mehemet Ali repulsed in his attack on positions at Tchercovina, 15 miles from Biela 21 Sept "
Siege of Plevna, Chefket Pacha enters with reinforcements after several skirmishes 22 Sept "
Montenegrin successes continued Sept "
Mehemet Ali retires to Kara Lom about 25 Sept. "
Gen Todleben made chief of staff before Plevna 28 Sept "
Battles of the Yagni, severe conflicts, Russians repulsed near Ardahan Asia about 27, 30 Sept "
Mehemet Ali replaced by Suleiman Pacha, Raouf Pacha sent to Schipka 2, 3 Oct "
Battles near Kars, army of grand duke Michael attacks Turks under Mukhtar Pacha, severely defeated 2-4 Oct "
Turkish monitor in the Danube exploded by torpedoes, 8 Oct "
Relief and supplies received by Turks at Plevna about 9 Oct "
Battle of Aladja Dagh before Kars, Russians, under grand duke Michael and gens. Loris Melikoff, Lazareff, and Heimann, defeat Ahmed Mukhtar, taking 10,000 prisoners 14, 15 Oct "
Gravitza battery, near Plevna, captured by Roumanians, is quickly retaken 19 20 Oct "
Battle at Gorny Dubnik, near Plevna, losses about equal (2500), 24 Oct "
Battle of Sofia Road, near Plevna, Turkish position at Telische captured 28 Oct "
Mukhtar Pacha defeated by Heimann and Tergukasoff at Deve Boyun, Armenia, after 9 hours' conflict 4 Nov "
Russians defeated at Azizi, before Erzeroum, by Mukhtar Pacha 9 Nov "
Change in Turkish generals, Suleiman ordered to command the army of Roumelia replaced by Azli Pacha, Mehemet Ali organizes army to relieve Plevna early in Nov "
Russian attack on Plevna repulsed 12 Nov "
Turks thrice repulsed near Plevna 15 Nov "
Plevna thoroughly invested (30 miles round, with 120,000 men), Nov "
Osman Pacha refuses to surrender Plevna about 16 Nov "
Kars taken by storm, Russians climb steep rocks, struggle from 8 P M to 8 A M, 300 guns and 10,000 prisoners taken, about 5000 Turks killed and wounded, Russian loss about 2500, grand duke Michael present . 17, 18 Nov "
Rahova on the Danube taken by Roumanians 21 Nov "
Entrepol (fortified) near Plevna taken by Russians 24 Nov "
Indecisive fighting in the valley of the Lom between the czarowitz and Mehemet Ali 30 Nov "
Turks capture Elena with guns and prisoners, after sharp conflict 4 Dec "
Skirmishing on the Lom 4-6 Dec. "
Osman Pacha endeavors to break out of Plevna, about 7 P M 9 Dec., 6 hours' fierce conflict, surrounded, unconditional surrender, said to be 30,000 prisoners, 128 officers, 100 guns, great slaughter both sides 10 Dec. "
Turkish circular note to the great powers requesting mediation, 12 Dec., acknowledged action declined about 12 Dec. "
Servians declare war against Turkey, 12 Dec, cross the frontier and capture villages 15 Dec et seq "
Montenegrins successful Dec. "
Suleiman made general of the army of Roumelia, and Todleben of that of Rustchuk about 19 Dec "
Suleiman retires on the quadrilateral, visits Constantinople, armies concentrating near Adrianople about 20 Dec. "

Erzeroum, Armenia, nearly invested, brave resistance by Mukhtar Pacha about 24 Dec 1877
Many Turkish wounded prisoners perish from cold during removal Dec. "
Alleged Russian losses, 80,435 men, Turkish many more, and 80,000 prisoners Dec "
Mukhtar Pacha recalled to Constantinople about 29 Dec. "
Sultan requests mediation of England, the British government only convey to Russia the sultan's desire to make peace, Russia declines mediation 26-31 Dec "
Gourko crosses the Balkans, advances on Sofia about 31 Dec "
Col Baker gallantly protects the retreating Turkish army, defeating the Russians 1 Jan 1878
Sofia taken by Russians after an engagement 3 Jan "
Servians defeated, Kurschumli reoccupied by Turks 6, 7 Jan "
Nisch taken by the Servians, Antivari by the Montenegrins, about 10 Jan "
Gen Radetzky crosses the Balkans, the Trojan pass taken about 9 Jan, Turkish army (about 32 000) and cannon taken by Skobeleff and Radetzky, after conflicts, 8, 9, 10 Jan (SENOVA), Gourko advances towards Adrianople 11 Jan "
Russians advance successfully, Turkish envoys proceed to treat for peace about 16-18 Jan "
Gourko advances towards Philippopolis, totally defeats Suleiman Pacha who retreats to the sea, losing prisoners and cannon 16, 17 Jan "
Adrianople abandoned, occupied by Russians 19,20 Jan "
Suleiman with remains of his army at Karala on the Ægean transporting his troops about 21 Jan "
Servians occupy nearly all Old Servia 29 Jan "
Russian attack on Batoum defeated 30 Jan. "
An armistice signed at Adrianople 31 Jan. "
Russian losses announced—89,879 men Feb. "
Continued advance of Russians towards Constantinople, panic of Turks, great sufferings Jan -Feb "
Part of British fleet ordered to Constantinople to protect British life and property, 8 Feb, enters Dardanelles without permission of Porte 13 Feb "
Erzeroum evacuated by Turks 17-21 Feb "
Rustchuk occupied by Russians 20 Feb "
War lasted 322 days. 12 Apr 1877 to 3 Mch "
Treaty of peace signed at San Stefano, 3 Mch, ratified at St. Petersburg 17 Mch. "
Long negotiation respecting a European congress Mch -May, "
Grand duke Nicholas in Roumelia replaced by gen Todleben, who assumes command 30 Apr "
Conference at BERLIN, meets 13 June, treaty signed 13 July, ratified (RUSTCHUK) 3 Aug "
Grand review of 80,000 Russians near Constantinople, 17 Aug "
Forty thousand Russians sail for home 12 Sept. "
Definitive treaty of peace with Turkey signed at Constantinople 8 Feb 1879
Estimated cost of the war to Russia, 120,000,000*l*

Rústchuk', a Turkish town on the Danube, one of the QUADRILATERAL fortresses lost to Turkey with Bulgaria by treaty of Berlin, 13 July, 1878

Rutgers college, New Brunswick, N. J, was chartered in 1766 as Queen's college, and was first opened in 1771 under the auspices of the Reformed Dutch church The buildings were burned by the British during the Revolution Its first president was rev dr J R. Hardenburg It received the name of Rutgers college in 1825, when col Henry Rutgers gave it $5000 In 1865 the State College of Agriculture and the Mechanic Arts was opened as a department of this college with $116 000 from the U S land-grant. It numbered about 26 teachers and 222 students in 1890.

ruthe'nium, a rare metal, discovered in the ore of platinum by M Claus in 1845

Ruthven, Raid of, a term applied to the seizure of the person of James VI of Scotland by William Ruthven, earl of Gowrie, and other nobles, in 1582, to compel the king to dismiss his favorites, Arran and Lennox Ostensibly for this, Gowrie was judicially put to death by his 2 opponents in 1584.

rye, a grain of the order *Gramineæ*, botanical name *Secale* (from Celtic *sega*, a sickle) *cereale*—native country unknown It comes nearer to wheat in bread-making qualities than any other grain, although very inferior to it. It is the principal bread-grain of Northern and Central Europe AGRICULTURE.

Rye-house plot, a plot (some think pretended) to secure the succession of the duke of Monmouth to the British throne in preference to the duke of York (afterwards James II), a Roman Catholic Some of the conspirators are said to have projected the assassination of the king, Charles II., and his brother This design is said to have been frustrated by a fire in the king's house at Newmarket, which hastened the royal party away 8 days before the plot was to take effect, 22 Mch 1683 The plot was discovered 12 June following Lord William Russell on 21 July, and Algernon Sidney on 7 Dec following, suffered death as conspirators The name was derived from the conspirators' place of meeting, the Rye-house at Broxbourne, Hertfordshire.

Ryswick (*riz'wik*), a village of Holland, where the celebrated peace was concluded between England, France, Spain, and Holland, signed by their representatives, 20 Sept., and by the emperor of Germany, 30 Oct 1697. The war which this treaty ended was begun in 1689 by Louis XIV. of France to restore James II. of England.

S

S, the nineteenth letter and fifteenth consonant of the English alphabet, the Greek *sigma* (Σ), known to the Phœnicians and Egyptians.

Saar'brück, the Roman *Augusti Muri*, or *Saræ pons*, an open town on the left bank of the Saar, in Rhenish Prussia, founded in the 10th century, long subject to the bishops of Metz, afterwards ruled by counts (about 1237), and by the house of Nassau about 1380 It was captured by the French and retaken by the Germans 1676, reunited to France 1794-1814, and ceded to Prussia 1815 On 2 Aug 1870, it was bombarded by the French under Frossard (between 11 and 1 in the day time), the few Prussians were dislodged, and the town occupied by the French general Bataille. The mitrailleuses were said to be very effective The emperor Napoleon, who was present with his son said in a telegram to the empress, "Louis has gone through his baptism of fire He has not been in the least startled We stood in the foremost rank, and the rifle-balls were dropping at our feet, and Louis picked up one that fell near him His bearing was such as to draw tears from the soldiers' eyes." On 6 Aug the Prussian generals Goeben and Von Steinmetz, with the first army, recaptured Saarbruck, after a sanguinary conflict at the village of Spicheren The heights taken by the French on the 2d are in Germany, those taken by the Germans on the 6th are in France, and both battles were fought between Saarbrück and the town of Forbach, which was captured, and has given a name to the second conflict. The loss was great on both sides, and the French 2d corps under Frossard nearly destroyed. The French retreated to Metz FRANCO-PRUSSIAN WAR.

Sabbata'rians. Traces exist of Sabbatarii, or Sabbathaires, among the sects of the 16th century on the European continent. Upon the publication of the "Book of Sports" in 1618, a violent controversy arose among English divines on 2 points first, whether the 4th commandment is in force among Christians, and, secondly, whether, and on what ground, the first day of the week ought to be distinguished and observed as "the Sabbath" In 1628, Theophilus Brabourne, a clergyman, published the first defence of the 7th day, or Saturday, as the Christian Sabbath He and others were persecuted for this doctrine, but after the Restoration 3 or 4 congregations in London kept Saturday as their holy day, and 7 or 8 in the country parts of England In 1851 there were 3 Sabbatarian or Seventh-day Baptist congregations in England, but in America (especially in the New England states) they are more numerous Joseph Davis suffered imprisonment in 1670. He and his son bequeathed property to maintain the sect, and litigation respecting its disposal was settled by vice-chancellor Stuart in conformity with their intentions in June, 1870. Very few Sabbatarians then remained.

Sabbath, the 7th day of the week, a sacred day of rest ordained by God, Gen ii, Exod. xx. 8, Isa lviii 13 Jews observe the 7th day in commemoration of the creation of the world, and of their redemption from the bondage of the

Egyptians, Christians observe the first day of the week in commemoration of the resurrection of Christ from the dead and the redemption of men SUNDAY

Sabbath-schools. SUNDAY SCHOOLS

Sabbat'ical year, a Jewish institution, 1491 B.C, Exod xxiii During every 7th year the very ground had rest, and was not tilled, and every 49th year all debts were forgiven, slaves set at liberty, and estates, etc, that were before sold or mortgaged, returned to their original families, etc

Sabe'ism, worship of sun, moon, and stars, so called from the Sabeans, a people of Arabia Felix, now Yemen

Sabel'lianism, from Sabellius (of Ptolemais, Egypt), who flourished in the 3d century, and who taught that there was but *one* person in the Godhead, whose 3 names were the Trinity This doctrine was condemned at a council at Rome, 260

Sabine Cross-roads, La, Battle of RED RIVER CAMPAIGN

Sabine Pass, Texas Here a small body of confederates repulsed a naval force and prevented a further advance of a land force under maj-gen Franklin, Sept 8, 1863

Sabines, an indigenous tribe of Italy, northeast of Rome, from whom, according to tradition, the Romans, under Romulus, took their daughters by force, having invited them to public sports or shows for the purpose When the Sabines sought revenge, the women mediated for their husbands, the Romans, and secured a lasting peace, 750 B C After many conflicts the Sabines became a part of the Roman people, about 266 B.C One of the ecclesiastical provinces is still called Terra Sabina, chief town, Magliano

saccharim'eter, an instrument for determining the amount of sugar in solution Soleil, an optician of Paris, in 1847 made use of rotary polarized light for this purpose in a saccharimeter, since improved by Dubosc

Sackett's Harbor, British repulsed NEW YORK, 1812 and 1813

sac'rament (from *sacramentum*, an oath, obligation, also mystery) The Christian sacraments are baptism and the Lord's supper The council of Trent, in 1547, following the schoolmen, recognized 7 sacraments baptism, the Lord's supper, confirmation, penance, holy orders, matrimony, and extreme unction The name was given to the Lord's supper by the Latin fathers The wine was laid aside, and communion by the laity under one form alone, that of bread, took its rise in the West, under pope Urban II, 1096 —*M de Marca* Communion in one kind was authoritatively sanctioned by the council of Constance in 1414.—*Dr Hook* Henry VII of Germany was poisoned by a priest in the consecrated wafer, 24 Aug 1313 The sacramental wine was poisoned by the grave-digger of the church at Zurich, by which sacrilegious deed a number of persons lost their lives, 4 Sept. 1776 In 1614 members of both houses of Parliament were ordered to take the sacrament, as a guard against the introduction of Roman Catholics In 1673 the Test act was passed repealed in 1828 TRANSUBSTANTIATION

Sacramento Pass, Battle of MEXICAN WAR, 1847

Sacra Via (holy street), a celebrated street of Rome, fabled scene of a treaty of peace and alliance between Romulus and Tatius It led from the amphitheatre to the capitol, and was the principal street for triumphal processions.

Sacred Band. THEBES

sacred books of the East. The publication of translations of the sacred books of the religion of the Brahmins, Buddhists, and Mahometans, and of the followers of Khung-fu-tze and Lao-tze, edited by prof Max Muller, began in 1879 45 volumes have been published, Feb 1895

Sacred Heart of Jesus, a form of devotion said to have been instituted in England in the 17th century, and much promoted by Marguerite Marie Alacoque, an enthusiastic French nun, who asserted that Christ had appeared to her, and taken out her heart, placed it in his own, glowing in flame, and then returned it She died in 1690

Her book, 'Dévotion au Cœur de Jésus' published in 1698, much advocated by father Joseph Gallifet about 1726, and introduced into France by request 1765
A pilgrimage from England, blessed by the pope and headed by the duke of Norfolk, to the shrine of Marguerite at Paray-le Monial . . 1-6 Sept. 1873
R C diocese of Salford dedicated to the Sacred Heart, 4 Sept 1873, and a church at Montmartre, near Paris, founded for the same purpose 16 June, 1875
Pope dedicated the universal church to "the Sacred Heart," 15 June, "

sacred standard, the, of green silk, unfolded by the Mahometans in time of imminent danger This standard went to the Osmanlis in 1517, when Selim I conquered Egypt, displayed in 1597 in the war with Hungary It was confided to the care of 300 emirs, again displayed in 1828 by the sultan of Turkey, at war with Russia

sacred wars. (1) Declared by the Amphictyons against Cirrha, near Delphi, for robbery and outrage to the visitors to the oracle 595 B.C Cirrha was razed to the ground, 586 (2) Between the Phocians and Delphians for the possession of the temple at Delphi, 448, 447 (3) The Phocians, on being fined for cultivating the sacred lands seized the temple, 357 They were conquered by Philip of Macedon, and their cities depopulated, 346 CRUSADES

sac'rifice, an offering to God or to any supposed deity or divinity as an atonement for sin, or to procure favor or express thankfulness. Sacrifice was offered to God by Abel, 3875 B C Sacrifices to the gods were introduced into Greece by Phoroneus, king of Argos, 1773 B.C Human sacrifices seem to have originated with the Chaldæans, from whom the custom passed to many other Eastern nations All sacrifices to the true God were to cease with the sacrifice of Christ, 33 A D (Heb x 12-14) Pagan sacrifices were forbidden by the emperor Constantius II 341

sac'rilege, the crime of violating or profaning sacred things. In 1835, the punishment (formerly death) in Great Britain was made transportation for life By 23 and 24 Vict. c 96, s 50 (1861), breaking into a place of worship and stealing therefrom was made punishable with penal servitude for life

Sacripor'tus, a place in Latium, Italy Here Sulla defeated the younger Marius and Papirus Carbo with great slaughter, 82 B C, and became dictator, 81

Sacs and **Foxes.** INDIANS

saddles. In the earlier ages the Romans used neither saddles nor stirrups. Saddles were in use in the 3d century, and are mentioned as made of leather in 304, and were known in England about 600 Stirrups were not known before the 5th century and not in general use before the 12th Side-saddles for ladies were introduced by Anne, queen of Richard II, c. 1388 —*Stow*

Sad'ducees, a Jewish sect, said to have been founded by Sadoc a scholar of Antigonus, about 200 B.C., who, misinterpreting his master's doctrine, taught that there was neither heaven nor hell, angel nor spirit, that the soul was mortal, and that there was no resurrection of the body The Sadducees rejected the oral law, maintained by the Pharisees, see Matt. xxii 23, Acts xxiii. 8.

Sado'wa. KÖNIGGRATZ

safety-lamp. That invented in 1815 by sir Humphry Davy, to prevent accidents in coal and other mines, is founded on the principle that flame, in passing through iron wire meshes, loses heat, and will not ignite inflammable gases The father of all safety-lamps was dr Reid Clanny, of Sunderland, whose invention and improvements are authenticated in the Transactions of the Society of Arts for 1817 The "Geordy," constructed by George Stephenson the engineer, in 1815, is said to be the safest A miner's electric light, by MM Dumas and Benoit, was exhibited in Paris on 8 Sept 1862 On 14 Aug 1867, safety lamps were rigidly tested by several mining engineers, and serious doubts thrown upon their complete efficacy. Col Shakespeare's safety-lamp (light extinguished by opening) exhibited at Royal institution, London, etc, May, 1879

saffron (Fr *saffran*, It *zaffrano*), the flower of crocus, was first taken to England in the reign of Edward III by a pilgrim, about 1339, probably from Arabia, as the word is from the Arabic *saphar* —*Miller* It was cultivated in England in 1582

sagas (Icel *saga*, a tale, Anglo-Sax. *sagu*, a saying), poetical compositions by scalds or Scandinavian bards, composed or collected from the 11th to the 16th centuries Subjects mythological and historical traditions of Norway, Sweden, Denmark, and Iceland The most remarkable are those of Lodbrok, Hervara, Vilkina, Völsunga, Blomsturvalla, Ynglinga, Olaf Tryggva-Sonar, Jomsvikingia, and of Knythinga (which contains the legendary history of Iceland), the Heims-kringla, and New Edda of Snorri Sturluson. EDDAS, LITERATURE, Scandinavian. NIBELUNGENÔT.

sage (Fr *sauge*: Lat. *salvia*), a wholesome herb, comfortable to the brain and nerves.—*Mortimer.* A species of this garden plant grew early in England, and some varieties were imported. The Mexican sage, *Salvia mexicana*, was brought from Mexico, 1724. The blue African sage, *Salvia africana*, and the golden African sage, *Salvia aurea*, were taken to England from the Cape of Good Hope in 1731. FLOWERS AND PLANTS.

Sagun'tum or **Zacyn'thus**, now **Murviedro** (*moor-ve-a'dro*), a fortified town of Valentia, E. Spain, renowned for the dreadful siege it sustained, 219 B.C., against the Carthaginians under Hannibal. The citizens, allies of Rome and under her protection, after performing incredible acts of valor for 8 months, chose, rather than surrender, to burn themselves, with their houses, and the conqueror became master of a pile of ashes, 218 B.C.

Saha'ra, the immense region in Africa lying between the Nile valley and the Atlantic ocean and from the inner slope of the Barbary plateau south on an average of 1200 miles. Area, 2,500,000 sq. miles. The term Sahara is modified from the Arabic *Sara* or *Zaharah*, meaning desert. The interior of this desert consists in great part of table-lands called *hammada*, with here and there a few green habitable spots termed "oases." Hot winds, blowing outward, occur during the year: in Egypt from April until June, called *Khamsin*; in Algeria and South Italy, July, the *Sirocco*; in Morocco, the *Shume*; and along the Atlantic and Guinea coast, the *Harmattan*. This region, with its thinly scattered inhabitants, has, since 1890, come within the influence of France and somewhat under her protection. A project for making an inland sea here was entertained in 1883, and the construction of a railway from Algeria south was proposed Oct. 1890. A large natural reservoir of water was discovered at El Golea in the desert in 1891. AFRICA.

sailing, a vessel moving on the water by the use of sails, as well as the art of navigating it. William of Orange (about 1570) was a yachtsman; and a small sail-boat was maintained on the Thames by Charles II. Sailing as a sport was greatly stimulated in the United States by the winning of the "Royal Yacht Squadron Cup" by the *America* in a race round the Isle of Wight, at Cowes regatta, open to all comers. The *America* was built by George Steers in 1851; sold in England after her victory, and used as a blockade-runner during the civil war. She was sunk by a U. S. cruiser in Savannah river; raised, and used as a practice-boat for the U. S. Naval academy, and purchased by gen. B. F. Butler in 1867. The sailing of ice-boats is a modern sport in the U. S., most popular on the Hudson river and in Canada. "The Hudson River Club" is the largest ice-yacht association in the world, owning about 50 boats.

Cornwall Yacht club established at Falmouth, Eng........... 1720
Royal Yacht Squadron, at Cowes, Eng., organized........... 1815
Hoboken Model Yacht club, the first in America, organized.... 1840
Royal London Yacht club, established as Arundel Yacht club in 1838, assumes its present name........................ 1849
America's cup, won in 1851, presented by the owners to the New York yacht club as a perpetual international challenge cup..8 July, 1857
Ice-boats, fitted up with long blades of iron, like skates, and sails, "tacking and beating to windward as if they were in the water," are mentioned as in use on Boston harbor, then frozen over, at the time the Atlantic mail-steamer *Britannia* was released by cutting a channel 7 miles long and 100 feet wide through ice over 2 feet thick......................Feb. 1844
Ice-yacht *Dreadnought* sails 1 mile in 1 min. 10 sec. at Red Bank, N. J...23 Jan. 1884
Ice-yacht race for championship of America, sailed at Orange lake over a 20-mile course, and won by the *Scud*, of the Shrewsbury Ice Yacht club..........................16 Jan. 1891

WINNERS OF TRANSATLANTIC YACHT RACES.

Henrietta, J. G. Bennett, owner, in race with the *Fleetwing* and *Vesta*, crosses the ocean in 13 days, 21 h. 55 min., sailing 3106 miles (the quickest voyage ever made in a sailing-vessel), Dec. 1866
Cambria, James Ashbury, owner, in race with the *Dauntless*, crosses the ocean in 23 days, 5 h. 17 min., sailing 2881 miles, 1870
Coronet, R. T. Bush, owner, in race with the *Dauntless*, crosses the ocean in 14 days, 23 h. 30 min., sailing 2949 miles...... 1887

RACES FOR *AMERICA'S* CUP.

Winners (all American).	Losers.	Waters.	Date.
America....	Aurora, England........	English....	22 Aug. 1851
Magic......	Cambria, "	American..	8 Aug. 1870
Columbia...	Livonia, "	" ..	16 Oct. 1871
Sappho.....	" "	" ..	21 Oct. "
Madeline...	Countess of Dufferin, } Canada....	" ..	11 Aug. 1876
Mischief....	Atalanta, Canada........	" ..	9 Nov. 1881
Puritan.....	Genesta, England........	" ..	14 Sept. 1885
Mayflower..	Galatea, "	" ..	7 Sept. 1886
Volunteer...	Thistle, Scotland.........	" ..	27 Sept. 1887
Vigilant....	Valkyrie II., England ...	" ..	7 Oct. 1893
Defender...	Valkyrie III., "	" ..	7 Sept. 1895
Columbia...	Shamrock I., "	" ..	16 Oct. 1899
Columbia...	Shamrock II., "	" ..	28 Sept. 1901
Reliance....	Shamrock III., "	" ..	22 Aug. 1903

Sailor's Creek, Va., Affair at. GRANT'S CAMPAIGN IN VIRGINIA.

Saint. See the names themselves throughout the book.

St. Clair's defeat. OHIO, 1791.

St. Louis, known as the "Mound City," covers 61.35 sq. miles (1890) on the west bank of the Mississippi river, about 15 miles below the mouth of the Missouri. Lat. 38° 38′ N.; lon. 90° 21′ W. When St. Louis came into the possession of the United States, 10 Mch. 1804, there were only 2 American families in the place, and 925 inhabitants in all. There were about 150 houses and 3 streets: La Rue Principale (Main st.), La Rue de L'Eglise (Second st.), and La Rue des Granges (Third st.); the whole encircled by fortifications. Pop. by the U. S. census: 1810, 1400; 1820, 4598; 1830, 6694; 1840, 16,469; 1850, 77,860; 1860, 160,773; 1870, 310,864; 1880, 350,518; 1890, 451,770; 1900, 575,238.

Pierre Ligueste Laclede establishes the chief post of the Louisiana Fur company, and names it St. Louis...........15 Feb. 1764
St. Ange de Bellerive, French commandant at fort De Chartres, arrives, and is invested with civil and military power...Oct. 1765
Spanish troops under capt. Rios take possession in the name of the king of Spain, 11 Aug. 1768, but exercise no civil functions, and retire...17 July, 1769
Pontiac, visiting St. Louis as a friend of St. Ange, is murdered at a feast, near Cahokia, and buried near Walnut and Fourth sts., "
Don Pedro Piernas, Spanish, made lieutenant-governor and military commandant of upper Louisiana, with headquarters at St. Louis, takes possession.........................20 May, 1770
Log church erected by Piernas on west side of Second, between Market and Walnut sts., and dedicated............24 June, "
St. Ange dies, and is buried near Pontiac's grave........Sept. 1774
Francis Cruzat succeeds Piernas as governor............May, 1775
Cruzat succeeded by don Ferdinando Leyba.................. 1778
Laclede dies; buried near the mouth of the Arkansas, 20 June, "
Wall of brush and clay 5 ft. high built around the town, and a small fort called La Tour built on Fourth st., near Walnut... 1779
About 1500 savages, led by British regulars from fort Michilimackinac, surprise a number of people outside the stockade, and kill 15 or 20; the town successfully defended....26 May, 1780
Leyba commits suicide, and is succeeded by Cruzat.......... "
Great flood; the year called "L'Anne des Grandes Eaux," June, 1785
Cruzat succeeded by Manuel Perez as commander of the post.. 1788
Perez succeeded by Zenon Trudeau........................ 1793
Trudeau succeeded by Charles Dehault Delassus de Delusière.. 1798
Delassus, at St. Louis, transfers Louisiana to Amos Stoddard, representing France, 9 Mch., and Stoddard transfers it to the U. S...10 Mch. 1804
First session of Court of Common Pleas held in the old fort (cor. Fourth and Walnut sts.); Supreme court organized and postmaster appointed...................................... "
First English school established............................. "
Aaron Burr visits St. Louis..............................July, 1805
First newspaper printed west of the Mississippi, the *Missouri Gazette*, issued by Joseph Charless at St. Louis......12 July, 1808
Young man hung for murder; the first execution of a white man in the territory of Louisiana...................16 Sept. "
St. Louis incorporated as a town.......................9 Nov. 1809
First market built on Centre square, between Market and Walnut sts., Main st., and the river (the town contained 12 stores, 2 schools, and a printing-office)..................Jan. 1811
First Territorial General Assembly meets at the house of Joseph Robidoux, between Walnut and Elm sts.............7 Dec. 1812
First brick house built..................................... 1814
Bank of St. Louis chartered..........................21 Aug. 1816
General Pike, the first steamboat to ascend from the Ohio, lands near the foot of Market st......................2 Aug. 1817
Bank of Missouri chartered.................................. "
Duel in which Thomas H. Benton kills Charles Lucas..27 Sept. "
First paving with stone on edge done by Wm. Deckers on Market, between Main and Water sts........................ 1818
Log church torn down and a brick cathedral erected.......... "
Baptist society begins a church at cor. Market and Third sts.. "
Harriet, capt. Armitage, the first steamboat, arrives from New Orleans in 27 days.................................2 June, 1819

stern Engineer, a steamboat constructed for Long's expedition o the mouth of Yellowstone river, leaves St. Louis, 21 June, 1819

st legislature under the Constitution meets in the Missouri otel, cor. Main and Morgan sts....................19 Sept. 1820

st brick-paved sidewalk laid on Second st................ 1821

st Methodist church erected.............................. "

st directory pub... "

st fire-engine purchased................................. 1822

Louis incorporated as a city; area, 385 acres............. "

in st. graded and paved.................................. 1823

st Presbyterian church built at cor. Fourth and St. Charles sts., 1824

st Episcopal church erected at cor. Third and Chestnut sts. 1825

n. Lafayette visits St. Louis, arriving...............29 Apr. "

l brick court-house built................................ 1827

l market building erected................................ "

anch of the U. S. mint established at St. Louis............ 1829

st water-works built, 1830, and water supplied............ 1832

ntral Fire company, a volunteer organization, founded...... "

olera appears, destroying about 4 per cent. of the population within a month...............................25 Sept. "

Louis university opened, 1829; chartered.............Dec. "

st school-board elected under the new charter............ 1833

st daily paper, the *Herald*, pub. by Treadway & Albright... 1834

w city charter...................................26 Feb. 1835

finished brick cathedral and other buildings, including about 0 residences, destroyed by fire.........................Apr. "

ily Republic established................................ "

l St. Louis theatre, on cor. Third and Olive sts., afterwards occupied by the custom-house, erected at a cost of $60,000.. 1836

st daily mail to and from the East....................Sept. "

niel Webster visits St. Louis, and a "barbecue" is tendered him, in a grove west of Ninth st., near where Lucas market afterwards stood.. 1837

w city charter...................................11 Feb. 1839

ea of the city increased to 2630 acres by act........15 Feb. 1841

storic mansion, occupied by Laclede and col. Auguste Chouteau, pulled down, and grounds divided into city lots; afterwards the site of Barnum's hotel........................Oct. "

st steamboat built entirely in St. Louis launched......Apr. 1842

st despatch established.................................. "

alth department, harbor-master, street-commissioner, and nspectors created... 1843

fayette park, 29.94 acres, acquired by the city............ 1844

st omnibuses run from Market st. to Upper ferry, the arsenal, and the Camp spring................................. "

ver flood began about 8 June, and drove 400 or 500 persons from their homes, rising 7 ft. 7 in. above the city directrix, 24 June, "

st public-school building erected and opened.............. 1846

Louis Mercantile library founded.......................... "

rk-packing business established.......................... "

s company incorporated 1841; city first lighted with gas, 4 Nov. 1847

y hospital opened.. "

st line of telegraph from the East reaches E. St. Louis, 20 Dec. "

ot-tower completed and shot manufactured by Kennett, Simonds & Co... 1848

e breaks out on the steamboat *White Cloud*, near the foot of Cherry st.; 23 steamboats, 3 barges, 1 canal-boat burned, and spreading to the city, 400 buildings destroyed; loss estimated at $2,750,000.........................night of 17 May, 1849

er 4000 deaths by cholera occur between 30 Apr. and 16 Aug., the mortality reaching 160 per day...............July, "

llefontaine cemetery incorporated 1849; dedicated..15 May, 1850

st underground sewer built................................ "

ound broken for the Pacific railway at St. Louis by hon. Luther M. Kennett, mayor, on south bank of Chouteau's pond, west of Fifteenth st.............................4 July, "

ssouri school for the blind opened........................ 1851

iler of steamer *Glencoe* explodes at the landing, foot of Chestnut st.; steamer burns; many lives lost.............3 Apr. 1852

obe-Democrat established................................ "

Marble building," cor. Fourth and Olive sts., then the finest n St. Louis, built.. 1853

st division of the Pacific railroad opened to Franklin, 38 miles..July, "

rcantile Library hall, cor. Fifth and Locust sts., erected.... "

llege of Christian Brothers, opened 1851; chartered......... 1855

cursion train, on the opening of the Pacific railroad to Jefferson City, breaks a temporary bridge over the Gasconade river: 22 killed, 50 injured; many from St. Louis, 1 Nov. "

orary of the Academy of Science founded.................... 1856

rchants' Exchange building on Main, between Market and Walnut sts., erected...................................1856–57

Louis Normal school opened................................ 1857

id fire department established............................ "

rst overland mail for California leaves St. Louis.....16 Sept. 1858

st overland mail from California, 24 days, 18½ hours from San Francisco, arrives at St. Louis......................9 Oct. "

re-alarm telegraph put in operation........................ "

Louis and Iron Mountain railroad opened to Pilot Knob, 85 miles... "

ashington university chartered, 1853; opened.............. 1859

ree street-railway lines opened in the city................ "

etropolitan police force established by act of legislature..... 1861

mp Jackson, at Lindell's grove, in the western suburbs of the city, organized 3 May, 1861, and captured...........10 May, "

artial law proclaimed, and citizens forbidden to leave the limits without a pass, by provost-marshal gen. J. McKinstry...30 Aug. "

urt-house, on block bounded by Chestnut, Market, Fourth, and Fifth sts., begun 1839, finished (cost about $1,200,000) July, 1862

ssouri Historical Society established...................... 1865

St. Louis public library founded............................ 1865

Lindell hotel, opened 19 Oct. 1863, burned............31 Mch. 1867

New water-works, begun 1865, completed 1872, come under control of Water-works commissioners.........................May, "

Legislative act passed, incorporating Carondelet with St. Louis, "

Foundation of eastern pier of Eads's Mississippi river bridge laid..27 Oct. "

Monument to Thomas H. Benton in Lafayette square, raised at instance of the state government and at public expense, unveiled..27 May, 1868

Tower Grove park, 276.76 acres, donated to the city.......... 1869

St. Louis made a port of entry under act of.................. 1870

New city charter, obtained in 1867, bringing Carondelet into St. Louis, goes into effect..............................Apr. 1871

Headquarters of the U. S. army established at St. Louis....... 1874

Eads's tubular steel bridge across the Mississippi completed and opened (BRIDGES).....................................4 July, "

New constitution divides city from county of St. Louis, and extends city to include nearly 40,000 acres, bordering on the river 17 miles.. 1875

Carondelet park (180 acres), Forest park (1371.94 acres), and O'Fallon park (158.32 acres) acquired by the city........... "

Court of Appeals decides the new separate charter for St. Louis (1875) adopted...5 Mch. 1877

Burning of the Southern hotel; 11 lives lost..........11 Apr. "

St. Louis day-school for the deaf opened...................... 1878

St. Louis Manual Training-school established................. 1879

Daily Chronicle established................................. 1880

Evening Star Sayings established............................ 1883

Maria Consilia Institute for the Deaf opened.................. 1885

Planters' House burned; 4 lives lost....................3 Apr. 1886

Railroad strike; sheriff's officers at East St. Louis fire into a crowd of supposed strikers, killing 6 persons, including 1 woman...9 Apr. "

Merchants' bridge across the Mississippi, commenced 24 June, 1889 (2420 ft. long; cost $6,000,000), completed.......3 May, 1890

Street-railway mail car, the first in the world, begins collecting, sorting, and distributing mail in transit here........11 Dec. 1892

CHAIRMEN OF BOARD OF TRUSTEES.

Auguste Chouteau.........	1810	Thomas F. Riddick........	1818
Charles Gratiot...........	1811	Peter Ferguson............	1819
Clement B. Penrose.......	1814	Pierre Chouteau, sen......	1820
Elijah Beebe..............	1815	Thomas McKnight........	1822

MAYORS.

William Carr Lane........	1823	Washington King.........	1855
Daniel D. Page............	1829	John How..................	1856
John W. Johnson..........	1834	John M. Wimer............	1857
John F. Darby.............	1835	Oliver D. Filley...........	1858
William Carr Lane.........	1838	Daniel G. Taylor..........	1861
John F. Darby.............	1840	Chauncey I. Filley.........	1863
John D. Daggett...........	1841	James S. Thomas.........	1864
George Maguire............	1842	Nathan Cole...............	1869
John M. Wimer............	1843	Joseph Brown.............	1871
Bernard Pratte............	1844	Arthur B. Barret...........	1875
Peter G. Camden..........	1846	Henry Overstoltz..........	1876
Byran Mullanphy..........	1847	William L. Ewing.........	1881
John M. Krum.............	1848	D. R. Francis..............	1885
James G. Barry............	1849	E. A. Noonan..............	1889
Luther M. Kennett.........	1850	C. P. Walbridge............	1893
John How..................	1853		

St. Philip, Fort. FORT ST. PHILIP.

Sakya Muni. BUDDHISM.

salads are stated to have been used in the middle ages. Lettuces are said to have been introduced into England from the Low Countries, 1520–47.

Salaman'ca, a city of W. Spain, taken from the Saracens 861. The university was founded 1240, and the cathedral built 1513. Here a council, mostly of ecclesiastics, called (1487) to confer with Columbus, examine his design, and hear his arguments for reaching the Indias by sailing west, decided that the project was vain and impracticable. Near here the British and allies, commanded by lord Wellington, totally defeated the French army under marshal Marmont, 22 July, 1812. The loss of the victors was most severe, amounting in killed, wounded, and missing to nearly 6000 men. Marmont left in the victors' hands 7141 prisoners, 11 pieces of cannon, 6 stands of colors, and 2 eagles. This victory was followed by the capture of Madrid.

Sal'amis, an island near Athens. In a great sea-fight here, 20 Oct. 480 B.C., Themistocles and Eurybiades, the Greek commanders, with only 366 sail, defeated the fleet of Xerxes, king of Persia, which consisted of 2000 sail. Near Salamis, in Cyprus, the Greeks defeated the Persian fleet, 449 B.C.; and Demetrius Poliorcetes defeated the fleet of Ptolemy and his allies, 306 B.C.

salary (Lat. *salarium;* from *sal*, salt, originally salt-money—money given the Roman soldiers for salt, which was part of their pay), stipulated amount paid to a person for services or for the duties of an office. Fixed salaries belong almost exclusively to the more enlightened nations and those of stable governments; in earlier times, or among the less civilized nations, the emoluments of a public office depend on the caprice of rulers.

SUMMARY OF SALARIES PAID TO THE PRINCIPAL GOVERNMENT OFFICIALS IN THE UNITED STATES.

UNITED STATES GOVERNMENT.

	Per annum.		Per annum.
President	$50,000	Vice-president	$8000

State Department.

Secretary of state	$8000	Chief clerk	$2500
Assistant secretaries	3500	Chief of the bureaus	2100

Treasury Department.

Secretary of treasury	$8000	Comptroller of currency	$5000
Assistant secretaries	4500	Solicitor of treasury	4500
First and second comptrollers	5000	Superintendent life-saving service	4000
Six auditors	3600	Chief of bureau of engraving	4500
Director of the mint	4500	Chief of light-house board	5000
Treasurer of the U. S.	6000	Supervising architect	4500
Superintendent coast survey	6000	Commissioner of internal revenue	6000
Register	4000	Sup't of immigration	4000

War Department.

Secretary of war	$8000	Chief clerk	$2700
Assistant secretaries	4500		

[As the different branches of the department are under U. S. army officers ranking as brigadier-generals, see ARMY for salaries.]

Navy Department.

Secretary of navy	$8000	Chiefs of the different branches	$5000
Assistant secretaries	4500		

Post-office Department.

Postmaster-general	$8000	Assistant postmaster-generals	$4000

Department of Interior.

Secretary of interior	$8000	Commissioner of railroads	$4500
First assistant secretary	4500	" " Indian affairs	4000
Assistant secretaries	4000	Commissioner of education	3000
Commissioner of pensions	5000	" " land office	5000
" " patents	5000	Chief architect of U. S. capitol	4500
Superintendent of census	6000		
Director of geological survey	6000		

Department of Agriculture.

Secretary of agriculture	$8000	Chief of weather bureau	$4500
Assistant secretaries	4500		

Department of Justice.

Attorney-general	$8000	Assistant attorney-generals	$5000
Solicitor-general	7000		

Judiciary.

COURTS OF THE UNITED STATES.

Miscellaneous.

Commissioners of interstate commerce	$7500	Commissioner of civil service	$3500
Commissioner of labor	5000	Government printer	4500
" " fish and fisheries	5000	Librarian of Congress	4000

UNITED STATES AMBASSADORS, ENVOYS EXTRAORDINARY, ETC., TO THE PRINCIPAL NATIONS.

		Per annum.
France,	ambassador-extraordinary and plenipotentiary	$17,500
Great Britain,	" " " "	
Germany,	" " " "	
Italy,	" " " "	
Russia,	envoy-extraordinary and minister-plenipotentiary	12,000
Mexico,	" " "	
Austria-Hungary	" " "	
Brazil,	" " "	
China,	" " "	
Japan,	" " "	
Spain,	" " "	
Argentine Republic	" " "	10,000
Chili,	" " "	
Colombia,	" " "	
Costa Rica,	" " "	
Guatemala,	" " "	
Honduras,	" " "	
Nicaragua,	" " "	
Peru,	" " "	
Salvador,	" " "	
Turkey,	" " "	
Belgium,	" " "	7,500
Denmark,	" " "	
Hawaii,	" " "	
Netherlands,	" " "	
Paraguay and Uruguay	" " "	
Sweden and Norway	" " "	
Venezuela,	" " "	

CONGRESS.

	Per annum.		Per annum.
Members of the Senate	$5000	Speaker of the House	$8000
" " House	5000		

GOVERNORS OF THE STATES.

New York	$10,000	Texas	$4,000
New Jersey		Washington	
Pennsylvania		Arkansas	3,500
Massachusetts	8,000	Florida	
Ohio		South Carolina	
California	6,000	Alabama	3,000
Illinois		Georgia	
Colorado	5,000	Idaho	
Indiana		Iowa	
Kentucky		Kansas	
Minnesota		North Carolina	
Missouri		North Dakota	
Montana		Rhode Island	
Nevada		West Virginia	2,700
Virginia		Nebraska	2,500
Wisconsin		South Dakota	
Maryland	4,500	Wyoming	
Connecticut	4,000	Delaware	2,000
Louisiana		Maine	
Michigan		New Hampshire	
Mississippi		Oregon	1,500
Tennessee		Vermont	

TERRITORIES.

Alaska	$3000	Oklahoma	$2,600
Arizona	3500	Utah	
New Mexico	2600		

MEMBERS OF THE STATE LEGISLATURES.

Alabama	$4 per diem.	Montana	$6 per diem.
Arkansas	6 "	Nebraska	5 "
California	8 "	Nevada	8 "
Colorado	6 "	New Hampshire	200 per annum.
Connecticut	300 per annum.	New Jersey	500 "
Delaware	3 per diem.	New York	1500 "
Florida	6 "	North Carolina	4 per diem.
Georgia	4 "	North Dakota	5 "
Idaho	5 "	Ohio	600 per annum.
Illinois	5 "	Oregon	3 per diem.
Indiana	6 "	Pennsylvania	1500 per annum.
Iowa	500 per annum.	Rhode Island	1 per diem.
Kansas	3 per diem.	South Carolina	5 "
Kentucky	5 "	South Dakota	5 "
Louisiana	4 "	Tennessee	4 "
Maine	150 per annum.	Texas	5 "
Maryland	5 per diem.	Vermont	3 "
Massachusetts	750 per annum.	Virginia	360 per annum.
Michigan	3 per diem.	Washington	5 per diem.
Minnesota	5 "	West Virginia	4 "
Mississippi	300 per annum.	Wisconsin	500 per annum.
Missouri	5 per diem.	Wyoming	5 per diem.

SALARIES OF THE PRINCIPAL OFFICES OF GREAT BRITAIN, IRELAND, AND COLONIES.

(No office under a salary of £2000 given.)

Lord high chancellor	£10,000	$50,000
Attorney-general	7,000	35,000
and fees usually about	5,000	25,000
Solicitor-general	6,000	30,000
" " "	3,000	15,000
First lord of the treasury and lord of the privy seal	5,000	25,000
Lord president of the privy council	"	"
Home secretary	"	"
Foreign secretary	"	"
Colonial secretary	"	"
War secretary	"	"
Chancellor of the exchequer	"	"
First lord of the admiralty	4,500	22,500
Postmaster-general	2,500	12,500
President of the Board of Trade	2,000	10,000
President of the Local Government Board	"	"
Chancellor of the Duchy of Lancaster	"	"
President of the Council of Education	"	"
First commissioner of public works	"	"
Chief charity commissioner of England and Wales	"	"
President Board of Agriculture	"	"
Surveyor-general of prisons	"	"

Law.

Lord high chancellor, see above.

Lords of appeal in ordinary (4), each	6,000	30,000

Supreme Court of Judicature (Court of Appeal).

Master of the rolls	6,000	30,000
Lords justices (5), each	5,000	25,000

High Court of Justice (Chancery division).

Justices (5), each	5,000	25,000

Queen's Bench.

Lord chief-justice of England	8,000	40,000
Justices (14), each	5,000	25,000

Probate, Divorce, and Admiralty.

Justices (2), each	5,000	25,000

Court of Arches.

One judge	5,000	25,000

IRELAND.	Per annum.	
ord-lieutenant	£20,000	$100,000
ord chancellor	8,000	40,000
ord vice-chancellor	4,000	20,000
hief-justice. Queen's Bench	5,000	25,000
ttorney-general	"	"
hief-secretary and keeper privy seal	4,425	22,125
laster of the rolls	4,000	20,000
nder-secretary	2,500	12,500
ther judges of the High Court of Justice	3,500	17,500

LONDON.		
ord-mayor	£10,000	$50,000
ecorder	3,500	17,500
own-clerk	"	"
udge of the city	3,200	16,000
hamberlain	2,500	12,500
ergeant	2,250	11,250
emembrancer	2,000	10,000
olicitor	"	"

GOVERNORS OF BRITISH COLONIES.		
ov.-general of India....£25,000, and £12,000 additional		$185,000
" " Canada	£10,000	50,000
overnor of Victoria, Australia	"	"
" " Cape of Good Hope	9,000	45,000
" " Ceylon	8,000	40,000
" " New South Wales, Australia	7,000	35,000
" " Hong-Kong, China	6,500	32,500
" " Jamaica	6,000	30,000
" " Gibraltar	5,000	25,000
" " Malta	"	"
" " British Guiana	"	"
" " Trinidad	"	"
" " New Zealand	"	"
" " Queensland, Australia	"	"
" " South Australia	"	"
" " Tasmania	"	"
" " Cyprus	4,000	20,000
" " Natal, S. Africa	"	"
" " Barbadoes	3,600	18,000
" " Bermuda	3,000	15,000
" " Leeward Islands	"	"
" " Western Australia	"	"
" " Newfoundland	2,500	12,500
" " Windward Isles	"	"
" " Honduras	2,400	12,000
" " Bahamas	2,000	10,000

BRITISH AMBASSADORS, ENVOYS, ETC., TO THE FOLLOWING NATIONS:

ustria-Hungary	ambassador	£8000	$40,000
razil	minister	4500	22,500
hili	"	2000	10,000
hina	"	5500	27,500
enmark	"	3000	15,000
gypt	consul-general, etc.	6000	30,000
rance	ambassador	9000	45,000
ermany	"	7500	37,500
old Coast	minister	3500	17,500
reece	"	"	"
taly	ambassador	7000	35,000
apan	minister	4000	20,000
exico	"	3750	18,750
etherlands	"	4000	20,000
ersia	"	5000	25,000
eru	"	2300	11,500
ortugal	"	3750	18,750
ussia	ambassador	7800	39,000
pain	"	5500	27,500
weden	minister	3400	17,000
urkey	ambassador	8000	40,000
nited States	"	6000	30,000
	consul-general, N.Y.	3660	18,300

ALARIES OF THE PRESIDENTS, ETC., OF THE PRINCIPAL REPUBLICS.

rgentine Republic	President	$36,000
	Vice-president	18,000
	Cabinet members....each	12,000
	Senate and House... "	8,400
olivia	President	24,000
	1st vice-president	6,000
	2d " "	5,000
	Cabinet.....each	5,000
hili	President	18,000
rance	" ....600,000 fr. and allowed an additional 600,000 fr.	240,000
ayti	President	24,000
exico	"	30,000
	Cabinet.....each	8,000
	Senate and House.... "	3,000
witzerland	President	3,000
	Vice-president and members of the council, each	2,400

Salem. MASSACHUSETTS, 1626, '29, '31, '34, '71, '92.

Saler'no, anciently **Saler'num,** S. Italy, an ancient Roman colony. Its university, with a celebrated school of medicine, reputed to be the oldest in Europe, was founded by Robert Guiscard the Norman, who seized Salerno in 1077. Salerno suffered much in the wars of the middle ages.

Salique (*sa-leek'*) or **Salic law,** by which females were excluded from inheriting the crown of France, is said to have been instituted by Pharamond, 424, and ratified in a council of state by Clovis I., the real founder of the French monarchy, in 511.—*Hénault.* This law, introduced into Spain by the Bourbons, 1700, was formally abolished by decree, 29 Mch. 1830; and on the death of Ferdinand VII. his daughter succeeded as Isabella II., 29 Sept. 1833. BOURBONS, SPAIN. By this law also Hanover was separated from England, when queen Victoria ascended the English throne, 1837.

Salisbury (*sawlz'ber-e*), a city of Wilts, Engl., founded in the beginning of the 13th century, on the removal of the cathedral hither from Old Sarum. National councils or parliaments were repeatedly held at Salisbury, particularly in 1296, by Edward I.; in 1328, by Edward III.; and in 1384. Henry Stafford, duke of Buckingham, was executed here, by order of Richard III., in 1483. On Salisbury plain is STONEHENGE. This plain was estimated at 500,000 acres. On it were many cross-roads, and few houses to take directions from, so Thomas, earl of Pembroke, planted a tree at each mile-stone from Salisbury to Shaftesbury as a traveller's guide. The cathedral was begun, 28 Apr. 1220, and completed in 1258. It is one of England's finest ecclesiastical edifices. Its spire, the loftiest in the kingdom (404 ft.), was considered in danger in Apr. 1864, and subscriptions were begun for its immediate repair. The choir was reopened, after restoration by sir G. G. Scott, 1 Nov. 1876.

Sallenti'ni, allies of the Samnites, the only Italian tribe not subject to Rome, were overcome in war in 267 and 266 B.C. and Brundisium, their port, taken.

salmon fisheries. A salmon-fishery congress opened at South Kensington, Engl., 7 June, 1867. Salmon eggs sent to New Zealand, Jan. 1878. Salmon were very abundant in all the New England rivers at the time of the first settlement of the country, but the many dams built upon some of these rivers—notably the Merrimac—have excluded the fish. A large supply for American markets comes now from the Kennebec river in Maine, and from Canadian streams. Considerable attention has been given to the restocking of American streams with salmon by the United States Fish Commission. In Nov. 1871, the Russian method of artificial propagation was tried in the Penobscot region with success. The hatching of eggs and stocking rivers with salmon has since been steadily prosecuted with good results. The lower Columbia river, Oregon, is one of the most important salmon fisheries in the world, over 600,000 cases being put up annually. To keep up the supply the U. S. government hatchery puts 5,000,000 young salmon in the river every year.

salt (chloride of sodium, a compound of the gas chlorine and the metal sodium) is procured from salt-rocks, from salt-springs, and from sea-water. The famous salt-mines of Wieliczka, near Cracow in Galicia, have been worked 600 years. The salt-works in Cheshire, called the Wiches (Nantwich, Northwich, and Middlewich), were important during the Saxon heptarchy. The salt-mines of Staffordshire were discovered about 1670. Salt-duties were first exacted in England in 1702; they were renewed in 1732; reduced in 1823, and in that year were ordered to cease in 1825. During the French war the duty reached to 30*l.* per ton. For the salt-tax in France, GABELLE. The government salt monopoly in India was abolished in May, 1863, by sir C. Trevelyan. Since 1810, 23 states of the United States have produced salt for market. Virginia salt-works were in operation before 1620. Salt was made in South Carolina in 1689, and acts to encourage the manufacture were passed in 1725. The Onondaga salt-springs, in New York, were worked by the Indians. First discovered in central New York by father Le Moyne, 1654. Salt was first made near Syracuse by white men in 1788. The state of New York owns the salines, and, until 1846, charged a royalty of 6 cents a bushel for salt made from the water. In that year the royalty was reduced to 1 cent a bushel. Rock salt first discovered in New York state, 4 miles from Warsaw, Wyoming county, 1878. NEW YORK. Salt was first made in Ohio in

1798; in Michigan about 1859. Since 1797 salt has been largely employed in the manufacture of chloride of sodium or bleaching powder (by obtaining its chlorine) and soap (by obtaining its soda). For these purposes the chemical works of Cheshire, Lancashire, and other places are operated. ALKALIES.

Saltaire. ALPACA.

Salt Lake. GREAT SALT LAKE.

Salt Lake City. UTAH.

saltpetre (from *sal petrae*, salt of the rocks), or **nitre,** is a compound of nitric acid and potash (nitrogen, oxygen, and potassium), properly called nitrate of potash. It is the explosive ingredient in gunpowder, many detonating powders, and lucifer-matches. Boyle, in the 17th century, demonstrated that saltpetre is composed of aquafortis (nitric acid) and potash; the discoveries of Lavoisier (1777) and Davy (1807) showed its real composition. Its manufacture in England began about 1625. During the French Revolution the manufacture was greatly increased by the researches of Berthollet.

salute at sea. It is a received maxim at sea that he who returns the salute always fires fewer guns than he receives, even between ships of princes of equal dignity; but the Swedes and Danes return the compliment without regard to the number of guns fired to them. The English claim the right to be saluted first in all places, as sovereigns of the seas; the Venetians claimed this honor within their gulf, etc. The English admiralty issued a code of rules for salutes, Dec. 1876. FLAG, NAVAL SALUTE.

Sal'vador, San, one of the Bahamas and the first point of land discovered in the West Indies or America by Columbus. It was previously called Guanahani, or Cat's isle; but Columbus (in acknowledgment to God for deliverance) named it San Salvador, 11 Oct. 1492. The capital, San Salvador, was destroyed by an earthquake, 16 Apr. 1854, and is now abandoned.

Sal'vador, San, a republic of Central America, independent since 1853, with a constitution proclaimed 24 Jan. 1859. Gen. Barrios, elected president 1 Feb. 1860, was compelled to flee in Oct. 1863, when Francis Dueñas became provisional president; his formal election took place Apr. 1865. The ex-president, Gerard Barrios, was surrendered by Nicaragua, tried, and shot, Aug. 1876. A re-attempted revolution failed, 1872. The capital, San Salvador, founded 1528, was nearly destroyed by an earthquake, 19 Mch. 1873; about 50 persons perished; suffered again severely, 1879. Area, 7225 sq. miles; pop. 1891, about 777,900.

Salvation army, a quasi-military organization for mission work, using, as special means, a uniform, out-door processions, with banners and music, and religious talks in the streets, public halls, theatres, etc. The army is an outgrowth of the East London Christian Revival Society, or, as afterwards called, the "Christian Mission," established in London by rev. Wm. Booth in 1865. Its aims are: 1st, to go to the people with the message of salvation; 2d, to attract the people; 3d, to save the people; 4th, to employ the people in salvation work. Their motto is "Blood and Fire." The army is now established in 32 countries, with about 10,780 officers, and holds about 13,000,000 religious meetings every year. It publishes 33 weekly newspapers and 15 monthly magazines, with a total annual circulation of 43,826,000 copies. They support 40 Rescue-homes for fallen women and 58 "slum-posts."

William Booth holds his first open-air meeting at the Mile End Waste, London, from which his bearers "procession" to a large tent near Baker's Row, Whitechapel.........5 July, 1865
Work of the Christian Mission first introduced temporarily in the United States, at Cleveland, O., by a London cabinet-maker.......... 1872
First 2 hallelujah lasses (women evangelists) leave King's Cross, Engl., for Felling-on-Tyne..........30 Mch. 1878
First "war congress" held, and "Salvation army" formally organized, with 50 stations under 88 evangelists....... Aug. "
War Cry, a weekly newspaper, first issued.......... 1879
Salvation Army corps established in Philadelphia by the family of Mr. Shirley, from Coventry, Engl.......... "
Meeting held in Castle Garden, New York, and at "Harry Hill's," by commissioner Railton and 7 hallelujah lasses sent over from England (the first uniformed corps sent out), spring, 1880
First American headquarters opened in Philadelphia......... "
Expedition to Australia under capt. Sutherland, commonly called Glory Tom.......... 1881
Miss Booth, eldest daughter of gen. William Booth, with Miss Soper and 2 others, land in France..........Mch. "
First Training-home for Women opened at Gore road, Hackney, Engl..........Nov. "
Devonshire House Training-home for Salvation lads, opened... 1882
Salvation army established in Gothenburg, Sweden, by Miss Ouchterloney.......... "
Three officers despatched to Toronto to commence an attack on Canada..........July, "
Col. Tucker leaves England for India, with his wife and a few English officers..........23 Aug. "
Maj. Simmonds, his wife and lieut. Teager, sail from the Thames to establish the army in Cape Colony, Africa........30 Jan. 1883
Miss Booth and other army leaders, expelled from Geneva, Switzerland, set out for Neufchâtel..........12 Feb. "
Miss Booth and other leaders arrested while holding a meeting in the Jura forest, 5 miles from Neufchâtel, but released under bail, 9 Sept. 1883. They are tried at Boudy and acquitted, 29 Sept., but forced by the people to leave the canton.....11 Oct. "
Battle between the Salvation army and the "Skeleton army," organized to oppose their work, at Gravesend, Engl...15 Oct. "
First Rescue-home in England begun under the direction of Bramwell Booth.......... 1884
Lyons, France, invaded.......... 1885
Death of Mrs. Catharine Booth, wife of gen. Booth, at Clacton-on-Sea..........4 Oct. 1890
Gen. Booth publishes his book, "In Darkest England, and the Way Out"..........Oct. "
Mrs. David Bell bequeaths about $300,000 to gen. Booth in support of his work..........May, 1892
Continental congress of Salvation army of the U. S. begins its session in New York city..........21 Nov. "
Through a syndicate the Salvation army purchase 200,000 acres in Chiapa, South Mexico, for settlement under direction of the army..........22 Feb. 1894

Salz'bach, a town of Baden. Here the French general Turenne was killed, at the opening of a battle, 27 July, 1675.

Samaj (*sa-mi'*) or **Somaj.** BRAHMO SOMAJ.

Samarcand', a city of Tartary, was conquered by the Mahometans, 707; by Genghis Khan, 1220; and by Timur, or Tamerlane, who ruled here in great splendor. Samarcand was occupied by the Russians under Kaufmann, 26 May, 1868, after a conflict on the previous day. The garrison resisted a fierce siege till relieved by Kaufmann, 13–20 June, 1868.

Samar'itans. Samaria was built by Omri, 925 B.C.; and became the capital of the kingdom of Israel. On the breaking-up of that kingdom (721 B.C.), the conqueror Shalmaneser placed natives of other countries at Samaria. The descendants of these mixed races were abominable to the Jews, and especially so because of the rival temple built on Mount Gerizim by Sanballat the Samaritan, 332 B.C., which was destroyed by John Hyrcanus, 130 B.C. (see John iv. and viii. 48, and Luke x. 33). The Samaritan Pentateuch (of uncertain origin) was published in his Polyglot by Morinus, 1632.

Sam'nites, a warlike people of S. Italy, who strenuously resisted the Roman power, and were only subjugated after 3 sanguinary wars, from 343 to 292 B.C. Their brave leader, Caius Pontius, who spared the Romans at Caudium, 320, having been taken prisoner, was basely put to death, 292. They did not acquire citizenship till 88 B.C. CAUDINE FORKS.

Samo'an or **Navigator's isles** (nine inhabited), near the Fiji islands; christianized by rev. John Williams, 1830. King Malietoa succeeded, 8 Nov. 1880. The isles have a political constitution. At a Samoan conference at Berlin, 1889, between Great Britain, Germany, and the United States, an act was signed 14 June, guaranteeing the neutrality of the islands, in which the 3 nations have equal rights of residence, trade, and protection. The independence of the Samoan government was also recognized, with Malietoa as king. Area, 1701 sq. miles; pop. about 36,000. Apia, in the island of Upola, is the capital.

King Malietoa deposed by the Germans and replaced by Tamatese..........8 Sept. 1887
Mataafa's insurrection and victory over Tamatese...Oct.–Nov. 1888
Germans interfere in favor of Tamatese, and are beaten; 16 killed..........18 Dec. "
Conflicting interests arise between the German, British, and United States governments..........Jan. 1889
Germans oppose Mataafa.......... " "
Bismarck yields to the claims of the U. S..........Feb. "
Three U. S. war-vessels, *Nipsic*, *Vandalia*, and *Trenton*, and 3 German, driven ashore at Apia, on the island of Upola, and destroyed, in a great storm..........15–16 Mch. "
[50 lives were lost from the U. S. ships and 96 from the

German The British war ship *Calliope* escaped by steaming out of the harbor For his skill and seamanship in accomplishing this the captain of the *Calliope* was thanked by the British admiralty]

Conference on Samoan affairs at Berlin, plenipotentiaries England, sir Edward Malet, Germany, count H Bismarck, United States, Mr John Kasson first met 29 Apr, closing conference, agreement signed subject to legislative ratification 11 June, 1889

[The convention declares the Samoan isles to be independent neutral territory, the 3 powers to have equal rights, Malietoa recognized as king, a supreme court created to which were to be referred all civil suits concerning real property situated in Samoa all civil suits between natives and foreigners or between foreigners of different nationalities, all crimes committed by natives against foreigners, or committed by such foreigners as are not subject to consular jurisdiction, with other provisions]

Mataafa supports Malietoa, who is warmly received on his return to Apia 11 Aug "

He resigns kingship to Mataafa "

Mataafa elected king and Malietoa vice-king, announced, 14 Oct "

Malietoa reinstated as king, with the assent of foreign powers, 10 Dec "

Death of Tamasese, reported 28 Apr 1891

The powers promise the king needed help Aug 1892

Threatened war averted by intervention Dec "

A German white book, containing the diplomatic correspondence from spring, 1890 to 6 Dec 1892 (supporting the statements of Mr Robert L Stevenson and describing the troubles attributed to the misconduct of baron Senfft von Pilsach, adviser to the king, and herr von Cederkrantz, chief justice), issued at Berlin 16 Jan 1893

Herr von Senfft Pilsach and herr von Cederkrantz dismissed, reported 11 May, "

Disputes between the king and Mataafa, fighting began, 7 July, "

Stopped by foreign war ships 19 July, "

Mataafa subdued and transported to Kukaofo island, reported, 1 Sept "

Mr Henry Ide, an American citizen, appointed chief justice, Sept "

A rebellion against king Malietoa suppressed, reported, 30 Jan 1894

Civil war, caused by the repressive measures of the chief justice, Mr Henry Ide, 35 men killed, many wounded 10 Mch *et seq* "

New Zealand proposes to exercise a protectorate over the group Apr "

Cessation of war through foreign influence, reported 25 Apr "

Insurrection in Atua, reported 1 June *et seq* "

Intervention of British and German war-ships, the rebel stronghold bombarded 10 Aug "

The rebels surrender 15 Aug "

End of war 6 Sept, "

Death of Mr Robert Louis Stevenson, at Apia, aged 44 years, 4 Dec. "

Much beloved by the Samoans, and buried by them on the top of Vaea mountain, 1300 feet above sea level 5 Dec "

Pago Pago harbor ceded to the U S in 1872 (confirmed by treaty 1878) is a coaling and naval supply station, with freedom of trade and extra consular jurisdiction, accepted, 1898

[*Very little work was done on this project until after the treaty of 1899, by which exclusive sovereignty was assumed by the U S*]

Death of king Malietoa. 22 Aug "

Combined demonstration of British and German war ships against Mulinuu, reported 24 Nov "

Dispute over the election of a king, chief justice Chambers decides in favor of Tanu, son of Malietoa, and against Mataafa (according to international compact, 14 June, 1889), 31 Dec "

Negotiations between the British, American, and German governments Jan 1899

Mataafa, encouraged by the Germans, rebels, fighting ensues, houses looted and burned in Apia, capt Sturdee lands with British marines, Tanu, Mr Chambers, and others take refuge on H M S *Porpoise* 1 Jan "

Foreign consuls acknowledge Mataafa *de facto* king 4 Jan "

Provisional government formed, dr Raffel, president of the municipal court, proclaims himself acting chief-justice, British and U S consuls protest, capt Sturdee, of H M S *Porpoise*, threatens to open fire if any resistance is offered to chief justice Chambers, who resumes his court under escort 7 Jan "

Germans oppose chief justice Chambers 9 Jan "

Mr Robert Louis Stevenson's house looted by the rebels Feb "

Dr Raffel is recalled to Berlin, leaves Apia Feb "

Adm Kautz, U S. *Philadelphia*, arrives 6 Mch "

A proclamation issued, denouncing Mataafa s government as illegal under the Berlin treaty 12 Mch "

A counter proclamation issued by herr Rose, German consul, 13 Mch "

Apia surrounded by rebels 14 Mch "

British and American blue jackets landed under capt. Sturdee, the Tivoli hotel attacked by the rebels, 3 British marines killed, the war ships open fire 15 Mch "

Rebels repulsed at the British consulate by blue-jackets under gen Cutliffe 17 Mch "

Malietoa crowned king in presence of the foreign consuls (Germans excepted). 23 Mch "

Much friction and anarchy, 4 British marines, 1 private, and 1 American guarding the consulates killed, German consul issues an aggressive proclamation, villages shelled by British and U S war ships, brisk fighting 30 Mch 1899

An Anglo American force ambuscaded while reconnoitring at Vailele, British lieut Freeman and 2 men U S lieut Philip Lansdale ensign John Monaghan, and 2 marines killed, 100 rebels killed and wounded 1 Apr "

Rebel posts at Valima and elsewhere captured by lieut Gaunt s brigade 12-17 Apr "

Much skirmishing, ultimatum, Mataafa and chiefs agree to keep outside boundary 25 Apr "

And surrender arms May, "

International commission Mr Bartlett Tripp (U S), president, Mr Eliot and baron Sternburg arrive at Apia 13 May, "

Mr Chambers s decision concerning the kingship confirmed, Tanu voluntarily abdicates 10-13 June, "

Further fighting, 3 chiefs arrested 4 July, "

Chief justice Chambers resigns, and leaves Apia 14 July, "

Rival parties sign an agreement abolishing the kingship, an administrator, with a council of 3, to be nominated by Great Britain, U S and Germany, a native assembly and high court of justice to be appointed, Mr Osborne, U S consul, to act as chief justice 17 July, "

The commissioners leave 18 July, "

Government in the hands of dr Solf the municipal president, and 3 consuls Aug "

Their report issued 13 Oct "

Convention signed by England, U S, and Germany, referring compensation claims to the arbitration of the king of Sweden 7 Nov "

Samoa treaty Anglo German convention, Samoa ceded to Germany, the Tonga Savage, and Solomon isles, etc, to Great Britain, Tutuila and adjacent isles to U S, Gold Coast and Togoland (Hinterland) frontiers settled, signed, 14 Nov "

Ratified 16 Feb 1900

German flag hoisted dr Solf, governor 1 Mch "

Great Britain and U S pronounced liable for losses to foreigners incurred during the fighting, award signed 14 Oct 1902

The German claims for indemnity in the Samoan islands, $160,000, were refused by Great Britain and the U S as being exorbitant It was agreed to refer the matter to the arbitration of the king of Sweden and Norway, in accordance with the treaty of 14 Oct 1902 29 Mch 1904

The Manua islands were ceded to the U S by the king of the group, population about 1500 8 Aug "

Tutuila, the Samoan island which, with its attendant islets of Tau, Olesinga, and Ofu, became a possession of the U. S. by virtue of the tri-partite treaty with Great Britain and Germany in 1899, covers, according to the bureau of statistics of the treasury department, 54 square miles, and has 5800 inhabitants. It possesses the most valuable island harbor, Pago-Pago, in the S Pacific, and perhaps in the entire Pacific ocean Commercially the island is unimportant at present, but is extremely valuable in its relations to the commerce of any nation desiring to cultivate transpacific commerce Ex chief-justice Chambers, of Samoa, says of Pago-Pago that "The harbor could hold the entire naval force of the United States, and is so perfectly *arranged* that only 2 vessels can enter at the same time. The coaling station, being surrounded by high bluffs, cannot be reached by shells from outside" The government is increasing the capacity to 10,000 tons The Samoan islands in the S Pacific are 14 in number, and lie in a direct line drawn from San Francisco to Auckland, New Zealand They are 4000 miles from San Francisco, 2200 miles from Hawaii, 1900 miles from Auckland, 2000 miles from Sydney, and 4200 miles from Manila Germany governs all the group except the part owned by the United States The 2 largest islands, Savaii and Upolu, contain the bulk of the population, which is estimated at 33,000 The port of Apia is in Upolu. The exports are in value about $350,000, the imports about $750,000 annually The inhabitants are native Polynesians and Christians of different denominations.

Samos, an island on the west coast of Asia Minor Colonized by Ionians about 1043 B C The city was founded about 986 Polycrates, ruler of Samos (532-522 B.C), was one of the most able, fortunate, and treacherous of the Greek tyrants, and possessed a powerful fleet. He patronized Pythagoras (born here) and Anacreon. Samos was taken by the Athenians, 440, and, with Greece, became subject to Rome, 146 It was taken by the Venetians, 1125 A.D., who here made velvet (*samet*), and became subject to the Turks about 1459 It is now a principality under the sovereignty of Turkey, guaranteed by France, Great Britain, and Russia from 1832 Area, 180 sq miles, pop, 1890, 44,661

New autonomous constitution granted 1850
Prince Constantine Adossides, b 23 Feb 1822, appointed, 4 Mch 1879
Alexander Karatheodory, b 20 July, 1833, appointed 1885
Geoighi Pasha Berovitch, appointed Jan 1895
Succeeded by Stephanaky Musurus Bey about 28 June, 1896
Costaki Valgan's Efendi . Mch 1899
Mihailaki Georgiadis . Aug. 1900
Alexander Mavrogeuo Mch 1902

Samoset. MASSACHUSETTS, 1621

Sampford Courtenay (Devon) Here John, lord Russell, defeated the Cornish and Devonshire Catholic rebels, the middle of Aug 1549

san. For names with this prefix, see the names themselves throughout the book

sanatorium, see TUBERCULOSIS

sanction, see PRAGMATIC AUSTRIAN SUCCESSION

sanctuaries. The privilege of refuge for offenders was granted in ancient Greece and Rome, but especially among the Jews. These places were generally (particularly in Greece and Rome) some temple, sacred grove, or place sacred to some deity Under Constantine the Great, all Christian churches were sanctuaries, and later in France and Spain it was favored, but in Germany the custom was never very effective It is said to have been granted by Lucius, king of the Britons, to churches and their precincts St John's of Beverley was thus privileged in the time of the Saxons. St Burian's, in Cornwall, was privileged by Athelstan, 935, Westminster, by Edward the Confessor, St Martin's-le-Grand, 1529 Being much abused, the privilege of sanctuary was limited by the pope in 1503 (at the request of Henry VII), and much more in 1540 In London, persons were secure from arrest in certain localities these were the Minories, Salisbury court, Whitefriars, Fulwood's rents, Mitre court, Baldwin's gardens, the Savoy, Clink, Deadman's place, Montague close, and the Mint. This security was legally abolished 1696, but lasted in some degree till the reign of George II. (1727) ASYLUMS, CITIES OF REFUGE.

sand-blast. Gen B C Tilghman, of Philadelphia, invented a method of cutting stone or hard metal by a jet of quartz sand impelled by compressed air or steam A hole of 1½ inches diameter and 1½ inches deep was bored through a block of corundum, nearly as hard as diamond, in 25 minutes The invention was submitted to the Franklin Institute, Philadelphia, 15 Feb 1871. It is now employed in the arts for decorating and etching glass, etc

Sandema'nians. GLASITES

Sander's Creek, Battle of CAMDEN.

Sander's fort. FORT SANDERS

Sandusky. Expedition against the Indians there OHIO, 1782.

Sandwich Islands. HAWAII

Sandy Creek, near Sackett's harbor, lake Ontario, Battle at. Here a British force of 160 men attacked 120 Americans with a few Indian allies, 30 May, 1814. 70 of the British were killed, the rest captured.

San Francisco, commercial metropolis of California. On 17 June, 1776, two friars, Francisco Palou and Benito Cambon, left Monterey with 7 civilians and 17 dragoons and their families, reaching 27 June the place where they established the Spanish mission of San Francisco, 8 Oct 1776 The settlement by Americans dates from 1836, when Jacob P Leese, an American residing in Los Angeles, obtained from gov Chico a grant of land in Yerba Buena, and built a small frame house on present south side of Clay street west of Dupont, celebrating its completion by raising the American flag, 4 July, 1836 In 1840 there were 4 Americans, 4 Englishmen, and 6 other Europeans in Yerba Buena. In Jan 1847 the name was changed to San Francisco. In Aug. 1847 the population was 459, and increased to 36,154 in 1852, owing to the discovery of gold In 1870, 149,473; 1880, 233,959, 1890, 298,997, 1900, 342,782 It is the 9th city in the U S in population. In 1890 the city covered 41⅞ sq miles, lat 37° 36′ N., lon. 122° 26′ W

William A. Richardson, an Englishman who settled in California in 1822 moves to Yerba Buena and, in a tent on what is now Dupont street, begins dealing in hides and tallow 1835
Jacob P Leese arrives at the mission June, 1836
First house at Yerba Buena completed by Mr Leese 4 July, "
First child born in Yerba Buena, a daughter to Mr and Mrs. Leese Apr 1838
First survey made by Jean Vioget 1839
Messrs Spear and Hinckley, Americans, build a saw mill in Yerba Buena 1841
Capt Montgomery, of the war sloop *Portsmouth*, hoists the American flag on what is now Portsmouth square 8 July, 1846
Ship *Brooklyn*, from New York, with 200 Mormon immigrants, arrives at Yerba Buena July, "
California Star first issued as a weekly 9 Jan 1847
Name Yerba Buena changed to San Francisco by decree of the alcalde Jan. "
Private school opened by a Mr Marston on Dupont st, between Broadway and Pacific Apr "
City hotel, the first in San Francisco, a story and a half adobe building on southwest cor Clay and Kearny sts, opened "
New survey of the town made by Jasper O Farrell "
Committee appointed to establish a public school 24 Sept "
Public Institute built on Portsmouth square, and school opened by Thomas Douglas 3 Apr 1848
First steamer of the Pacific Mail company, the *California*, arrives 28 Feb 1849
Oregon brings John W Geary, first postmaster at San Francisco, and the first U S mail to the Pacific coast 31 Mch "
St Francis hotel opened, a 3 story wooden structure on south west cor Clay and Dupont sts. "
First Presbyterian church in San Francisco organized by Albert Williams, services in a tent on Dupont st 20 May, "
First Baptist church organized by O C Wheeler 24 June, "
First Congregational church organized, rev T D Hunt, pastor, July, "
First steamboat to make regular trips between San Francisco and Sacramento, the *McKim*, arrives 3 Oct. "
Upon the discovery of gold the population of California increases 6 to 8 fold, at one time there are 400 ships in the harbor deserted by their crews . "
First great fire occurs 21 Dec "
Daily Alta California first issued 22 Jan 1850
Jenny Lind theatre opened "
San Francisco incorporated as a city, and John W Geary elected first mayor 1 May, "
Second great fire, burning over 3 blocks, 4 May, and third, which burns every thing between Clay, California, and Kearny sts. and the water front . 14 June, "
Society of California pioneers organized Aug "
Steamboat *Sagamore* explodes, 80 persons killed and wounded, Oct. "
San Francisco Protestant orphan asylum organized 31 Jan. 1851
Fourth, called *the great* fire, burns 16 blocks, more than 1500 houses, the burned district being ¾ mile long, ¼ mile wide, 4 May, "
Vigilance committee organized June, "
Fifth large fire, entailing a loss of $2,000,000, begins on Pacific st near Powell, burning 8 blocks 22 June, "
James Stuart, professional murderer and robber, hung by the Vigilance committee on Market Street wharf 11 July, "
Samuel Whittaker and Robert McKenzie hung by Vigilance committee on Battery st, between Pine and California, 24 Aug "
City divided into 7 school districts and free schools under the school law provided for in each district 25 Sept. "
Chamber of Commerce organized 1 May, 1850, incorporated 3 Nov "
Jenny Lind theatre bought for a city hall and court house for $200,000 1852
Yerba Buena cemetery opened ... "
Pacific club organized . "
Streets first lighted with 90 oil lamps "
First Unitarian church on Stockton st., between Clay and Sacramento, and First Congregational church and St. Mary's cathedral, on opposite sides of Dupont and California sts., completed. . . . 1853
Evening Post established .. . . "
Mercantile library founded . . "
First telegraph line to Marysville opened . . 24 Oct "
Streets lighted with gas . . . . Feb 1854
U S. Branch Mint opened 3 Apr "
Failure of Henry Meigs for $800,000, after forging city warrants, promissory notes, and shares in a lumber company to the amount of $200,000, he flees to Chili 6 Oct. "
Montgomery and Washington sts. partly paved with cobblestones . "
Lone Mountain cemetery opened .. . . "
Failure of Adams & Co 's bank . . 23 Feb 1855
[A financial crisis followed, with 197 failures during the year, with liabilities of over $8 300,000]
Mechanics' Institute library founded. . "
Evening Bulletin first issued . . 8 Oct. "
Vigilance committee organizes 15 May, 1856
James King of William, editor of the *Bulletin*, shot by James P Casey, whom King had accused of election frauds, 14 May, d. . . 20 May, "
Casey and Charles Cora, the latter murderer of U S marshal Richardson, hung by the Vigilance committee . . 22 May, "
Morning Call founded . Dec "
First savings bank opened 1857
San Francisco Water-works company organized . ... . "

irst Industrial Fair of the Mechanics' Institute held on site of the Lick house ... 1857
pring Valley Water-works company organized ... June, 1858
irst overland mail from St. Louis arrives ... Sept. "
t. Ignatius college opened, 1855; chartered ... 1859
ndustrial school opened ... "
ancroft Pacific library founded ... "
uel between David S. Terry and David C. Broderick in San Mateo county, 10 miles from San Francisco, 13 Sept. 1859; Broderick dies from a pistol shot in the left lung ... 18 Sept. "
irst pony-express arrives, 9 days *en route* from St. Joseph, Mo., 1 A.M. 14 Apr. 1860
team railroad constructed on Market and Valencia sts. to the Mission and Hayes valley ... July, "
an Francisco connected with New York by telegraph, 23 Oct. "
amous oration on the rights of freedom, etc., by Edward D. Baker at the American theatre ... 29 Oct. "
Examiner established ... 1862
ars of the Omnibus street railroad begin running ... "
ass. Lick, and Occidental hotels opened ... "
an Francisco Stock and Exchange Board organized .. 12 Sept. "
ailroad to San José opened ... 1863
nion club established ... 1864
ong bridge across Mission cove, on line of Fourth and Kentucky sts., completed ... "
Daily Examiner established ... 1865
Chronicle first issued as an advertising sheet for the theatre .. "
an Francisco Law library founded ... "
Mountain View cemetery established ... "
lectric fire-alarm telegraph introduced ... "
evere earthquake ... 8 Oct. "
earny street widened on the west side, from Market st. to Broadway, at a cost of $579,000 ... 1866
aid Fire department established, and hand-engines replaced by steam ... "
olunteer Fire department abolished ... Dec. "
ank of California and Merchants' Exchange completed ... 1867
orse cars substituted for steam on Market st. ... "
lms-house completed ... "
rinity church completed ... "
everest earthquake yet recorded ... 8 A.M. 21 Oct. 1868
rand hotel completed ... 1869
t. Patrick's church completed ... 1870
mprovement of Golden Gate park commenced ... "
lossom Rock, ¾ of a mile from North Point, blown up, 23 May, "
Evening Post established ... 1871
orner-stone of city-hall laid ... Feb. 1872
lay st. cable railway, the pioneer cable road of the world, put in operation ... Sept. 1873
ew U. S. mint on Fifth st. opened ... 1874
ork begun on Palace hotel, 1874; building completed ... 1875
Montgomery avenue opened ... "
acific Stock Exchange holds its first meeting ... 7 June, "
ank of California fails, and pres. Ralston dies the same day; verdict, congestion of the lungs and brain, caused by a bath in the bay at North Beach ... 26 Aug. "
ew Pacific Stock Exchange on Leidesdorff st. opened, 15 May, 1876
ormal department of Girls' High-school established ... "
entennial celebration of the establishment of the mission at San Francisco ... 8 Oct. "
aldwin hotel completed ... 1877
nti-Chinese riot breaks out; subdued by the Vigilance committee of 1856, reorganized ... 23 July, "
uilding of San Francisco Stock and Exchange Board on Pine st. completed and occupied ... "
upont st. widened ... "
all of Records in new city-hall opened ... "
elephone introduced ... "
an Francisco free public library founded ... 1879
large number of poor people settled on a tract called the Mussel Slough district (Sand-lots); this district came into possession of the Southern Pacific railroad 1867-77. The settlers refusing to vacate, the dispute was carried to the U. S. court. The decision of the court being against the settlers, efforts were made to dispossess them, which led to a conflict in which several were killed ... 1880
ennis Kearney, a leader of the Labor or Sand-lot party, arrested and found guilty of misdemeanor and sentenced to 6 months' imprisonment and a fine of $1000, 16 Mch.; decision and sentence reversed by State Supreme court ... 27 May, "
evere gale; extensive damage ... 19 Jan. 1886
elebration of Arbor day inaugurated; school children set out 40,000 young trees, supplied by Adolph Sutro, 27 Nov. "
anic in the Stock Exchange, and failure of 14 leading stock brokers ... 2 Dec. "
Monument to Francis Scott Key unveiled in Golden Gate park, 4 July, 1888
ogswell Polytechnic college opened ... "
Metropolitan electric railroad opened; first in the city ... May, 1892
rain carrying $20,000,000 in gold leaves the city for New York, 5 Aug. "
Midwinter Exposition opened ... 27 Jan. 1894
ol. Jonathan D. Stevenson, a pioneer of '49, d ... 14 Feb. "

MAYORS.

ohn W. Geary	1850	S. B. Webb	1854
harles J. Brenham	1851	James Van Ness	1855
tephen R. Harris	1852	E. W. Burr	1856
harles J. Brenham	"	Henry F. Teschemacher	1860
. K. Garrison	1853	H. P. Coon	1864
Frank McCoppin	1868	Maurice C. Blake (11 months),	1882
Thomas H. Selby	1870		
William Alvord	1872	Washington Bartlett	1883
James Otis	1874	E. B. Pond	1887
George Hewston	1875	George H. Sanderson	1891
Andrew J. Bryant	1876	L. R. Ellert	1893
Isaac S. Kalloch	1880	Adolph Sutro	1895

San Gabriel, *Battle of.* CALIFORNIA, 1847.

San'hedrim. An ancient Jewish council of the highest jurisdiction, of 70, or, as some say, 73 members, usually considered to be that established by Moses (Numb. xi. 16), 1490 B.C. It was yet in existence at the time of Jesus Christ (John xviii. 31). A Jewish Sanhedrim was summoned by the emperor Napoleon I., 23 July, 1806. The Jewish deputies met 18 Sept., and the Sanhedrim 9 Mch. 1807.

Sanitary Commission of the United States. On 15 Apr. 1861, a woman of Bridgeport, Conn., organized a society to relieve and comfort volunteers. On the same day Miss Almena Bates, of Charlestown, Mass., established another. The city of Lowell followed, and other cities rapidly. This was the origin of the commission. On 9 June the secretary of war appointed Henry W. Bellows, prof. A. D. Bache, of the coast survey, Jeffries Wyman, M.D., W. H. Van Buren, M.D., R. C. Wood, surg.-gen. U.S.A., gen. G. W. Cullum, and Alex. Shiras, U.S.A., a commission of inquiry and advice in respect to the sanitary interests of the U. S. forces. Board organized 13 June and named "U. S. Sanitary Commission." The object of the commission was to supplement government deficiencies. An appeal was made to the people with gratifying results. This commission followed the army throughout the war with supplies for alleviating the sufferings of the soldiers. It is estimated that in money and supplies no less than $25,000,000 was contributed during the war. The archives of the commission, containing a full record of its work, were deposited in the Astor Library in 1878 as a gift. The principal branches of the U. S. sanitary commission were:

New England Woman's Auxiliary Association, organized ... 1861
Soldiers' Aid Society of Northern Ohio, organized ... 20 Apr. "
Woman's Central Association of Relief, New York, organized, 29 Apr. "
General Aid Society of Buffalo, N. Y., organized ... Dec. "
Cincinnati Branch, organized ... "
Woman's Relief Association of City of Brooklyn, organized ... 1862
Northwestern Branch, Chicago ... "
Philadelphia Branch, organized ... 1863
Pittsburg Branch ... "
Pioneer Sanitary Fair opened at Chicago ... 27 Oct. "
European Branch, organized at Paris ... 30 Nov. "
Auxiliary Society, organized in London by Americans .. 5 Mch. 1864
Auxiliary Relief Corps in the U. S., organized ... May, "

sanitary science. Strict cleanliness is enjoined in the Mosaic law, 1490 B.C. In London, Engl., a law was passed to keep the streets clean in 1297, and the casting of filth from houses into the streets was made punishable in 1309. In America a quarantine law was passed by the colony of Massachusetts Bay for yellow-fever in 1648. Similar laws were passed in South Carolina, 1698; Pennsylvania, 1699; Rhode Island, 1711; New Hampshire, 1714; and New York, 1755. Great attention has been paid to the public health in France since 1802. Tardieu published his "Dictionnaire de Hygiène," 1852-54. To dr. Southwood Smith is ascribed the first agitation on the subject of public health in England about 1832, his "Philosophy of Health" having excited much attention.

Venice establishes its first lazaretto (1423) and creates a permanent health-magistracy ... 1485
First English quarantine law passed ... 1664
Quarantine act passed by Congress of United States ... 1799
Board of Health established in London ... 20 June, 1831
Public vaccination begun in London ... 1840
City Sewers' act, with provision for the sanitary interests of London, passed ... 1848
International Sanitary conference held at Paris ... 1850
Smoke Nuisance Abatement act passed in England ... 1853
Crimean Sanitary Commission, drs. Sutherland, Milroy, and Mr. Rawlinson, established by British government ... Apr. 1855
After the British Sanitary Commission was formed in the Crimea, sickness in the army was reduced to less than $\frac{1}{6}$, and mortality to less than $\frac{1}{47}$ of the former rate ... 1855-56
First Quarantine and Sanitary convention in the U. S., held at Philadelphia ... 13 May, 1857
Efficacy of steam as a purifier and preventive of contagion first suggested at the meeting of the Quarantine and Sanitary convention at Boston, Mass. ... 14-16 June, 1860
SANITARY COMMISSION, U. S., established ... 13 June, 1861
Medical act passed by Congress of U. S., appointing a special corps of 8 sanitary inspectors ... 16 Apr. 1862

Sanitary Police company, not to exceed 10 persons, appointed for the District of Columbia by act of Congress 16 July, 1862

International Sanitary conference convenes at Geneva 26 Oct 1863

Metropolitan Health Board established in New York 1866

New Sanitary act for England passed Aug "

American Public Health Association organized 1872

National Health Society founded in England 1873

International Sanitary congress in Vienna closed 1 Aug 1874

New Consolidated Public Health act for England passed 1875

"An act to prevent the introduction of contagious or infectious diseases in the United States" becomes a law 29 Apr 1878

Parkes's "Museum of Hygiene" begun at University college, London "

National Board of Health (U S) of 7 members, to be appointed by the president not more than one from a state and one medical officer from the army navy, marine hospital, and department of justice, authorized by act of Congress 3 Mch 1879

Sanitary Assurance Association of England formed by sir Joseph Fayrer drs Andrew Clark, Corfield, Tyndall and others constituted 14 Dec 1880

International Sanitary conference assembles at Washington on invitation of the government of U S to the maritime powers of the world 5 Jan 1881

London Sanitary Protection Association founded by sir William W Gull, prof Huxley, and others "

International Sanitary exhibition held at Royal Albert Hall, Kensington Engl 16 July-13 Aug "

International Sanitary congress at Geneva. 1882

National Health Society's exhibition opened in England 2 June 1883

International Health exhibition held in England 8 May-30 Oct. 1884

Fifth International Sanitary conference at The Hague, 21 Aug "

International Sanitary conference at Rome (28 states represented) 20 May-13 June, 1885

National quarantine stations established in the U S, at Chandeleur island Gulf of Mexico, near Key West, coast of Georgia, at entrance to Chesapeake bay, mouth of Delaware bay, San Diego Cal, San Francisco, and Port Townsend, Wash 1 Aug 1888

State Boards of Health have been established in the U S as follows Massachusetts, 1869, California, Virginia, District of Columbia, 1871, Minnesota, 1872, Louisiana Michigan, 1873, Alabama, Georgia, Maryland, 1875, Colorado, New Jersey Wisconsin, 1876, Illinois, Mississippi, Tennessee, 1877, Connecticut Kentucky, Rhode Island, South Carolina, 1878, Delaware, North Carolina 1879, Iowa, New York 1880 Arkansas Indiana, New Hampshire, West Virginia 1881, Texas, 1882 Missouri 1883, Kansas, Maine, Pennsylvania, 1885, Ohio, 1886, Vermont "

Congress of Hygiene met at Paris 4 Aug 1889

san'itas ("health"), a new antiseptic and disinfectant, invented by C. T Kingzett, about 1875

Having discovered that the salubrity of the air surrounding certain trees, such as the *Eucalyptus globulus* and pines is due to volatile oils producing peroxide of hydrogen and camphoric acid, he devised a method for procuring these reagents by the decomposition of common turpentine, and in 1877 they were manufactured and sold as "sanitas"

San Jacin'to, Tex, Battle of TEXAS, 1836.

San Juan island. JUAN

San Mari'no, a republic in Italy, is one of the oldest states in Europe Its origin is ascribed to St. Marinus, a hermit who resided here in the 5th century Its independence was lost for a short time to Cæsar Borgia, 1503, and to the pope, 1739, was confirmed by pope Pius VII in 1817, in 1872 it concluded a treaty of protective friendship with the kingdom of Italy. Area, 32 sq miles, pop. 1891, about 8000

San Salvador'. SALVADOR.

San'scrit, the language of the Brahmins of India, at least as ancient as the time of Solomon, has been much studied of late years. Sir Wm Jones, who published a translation of the poem "Sakuntala" in 1783, discovered that a complete literature had been preserved in India, comprising sacred books (the Vedas), history and philosophy, lyric and dramatic poetry Texts and translations of many works have been published by the aid of the East India company, the Oriental Translation fund, and private liberality The professorship of Sanscrit at Oxford was founded by col Boden. The first professor, H H Wilson, appointed in 1832, translated part of the "Rig-Veda Sanhitá," the sacred hymns of the Brahmins, several poems, etc. Prof Monier Williams (elected 1860) published an English and Sanscrit dictionary, 1851, and a Sanscrit grammar Prof Max Muller published his "History of Sanscrit Literature" in 1859, has edited the original text of the Vedas, and the more important works of Indian literature, under the title, "THE SACRED BOOKS OF THE EAST," of which about 40 8vo volumes have appeared (1894) Prof. William D Whitney, of Johns Hopkins university, issued a very valuable Sanscrit grammar The Sanscrit belongs to the Indo-European or Aryan group of languages, which includes also the Persian, Greek, Latin, Teutonic, Slavonian, Celtic, and Scandinavian languages

Sans-culottes (*sang-cu-lot*), a term of reproach applied to the leaders of the French republicans about 1790, on account of their negligence in dress, and afterwards assumed by them with pride The complementary days of their new calendar were named by the Mountain party *Sans-culottides*

San Stef'ano. STEFANO

Santa Cruz de Teneriffe', the capital city and chief commercial port of the Canaries Here adm Blake, with daring bravery, entirely destroyed 16 Spanish ships, secured with great nautical skill, and protected by the castle and forts on the shore, 20 Apr 1657 —*Clarendon* In an unsuccessful attack made upon Santa Cruz by Nelson, several officers and 141 men were killed, and the admiral lost his right arm, 24 July, 1797 VIRGIN ISLES

Santa Fé. NEW MEXICO, 1605, etc

Santa Marie. AMERICA, 1492

Santiago (*san-tee-ah'gō*), the capital of Chili, South America, founded by Valdiña in 1541, has suffered much by earthquakes, especially in 1822 and 1829 Pop 1885, 237,000

About 7 o'clock in the evening of 8 Dec 1863, the feast of the Immaculate Conception of the Virgin Mary, and the last day of a series of religious celebrations in the "month of Mary," the church of the Campania, when brilliantly illuminated, was burned down, the fire beginning amid the combustible ornaments, and more than 2000 persons, principally women, perished, the means of egress being utterly insufficient.

On 20 Dec the government ordered the church to be razed to the ground, and much public indignation was excited against the fanatical priesthood

Santiago de Compostel'la, a town of N W Spain, was sacked by the Moors, 995, and held by them till it was taken by Ferdinand III, 1235 The order of Santiago, or St. James, was founded about 1170 to protect pilgrims to the shrine of St James, said to be buried in the cathedral. The town was taken by the French, 1809, and held till 1814.

Sapphic (*saf'ik*) **verse,** invented by Sappho, the lyric poetess of Mitylene She was celebrated for her poetry, beauty, and a hopeless passion for Phaon, a youth of her native country, on whose account it is said she threw herself into the sea from mount Leucas, and was drowned, about 590 B C The Lesbians, after her death, paid her divine honors, and called her the 10th muse Some consider the story fabulous.

sapphire (*saf'ir*), a precious stone, azure in color, and transparent, in hardness it exceeds the ruby, and is next to the diamond One was placed in the Jewish high-priest's breastplate, 1491 AARON'S BREASTPLATE Thamas Kouli Khan is said to have possessed a sapphire valued at 300,000*l.*, 1733 They are found in Burmah, British India, Ceylon, Australia, North Carolina, and Montana Artificial sapphires were made in 1857 by M Gaudin Equal parts of alum and sulphate of potash were heated in a crucible.

Sar'acens (Arab. *Sharkin*, the eastern people, from *Sharq*, the East), a term applied to the first followers of Mahomet, who within forty years after his death (632) had subdued a part of Asia and Africa They conquered Spain in 711 et seq, but were defeated at Tours, France, by Charles Martel, 732, and (under Abderahman) established the caliphate of Cordova in 755, which gave way to the Moors in 1237 The empire of the Saracens closed by Bagdad being taken by the Tartars, 1258

Saragos'sa, a city of N E. Spain, anciently Cæsarea Augusta, founded 27 B.C, was taken by the Goths, 470, by the Arabs, 712, by Alfonso of Spain, 1118 Here Philip V was defeated by the archduke Charles, 20 Aug 1710 On 17 Dec. 1778, 400 of the inhabitants perished in a fire at the theatre. Saragossa, after successfully resisting the French in 1808, was taken by them after a most heroic defence by gen Palafox, 20 Feb. 1809 The inhabitants, of both sexes, resisted until worn out by fighting, famine, and pestilence

Sarato'ga, Battle of BEMIS'S HEIGHTS, NEW YORK, UNITED STATES, 1777.

Sardin'ia, an island in the Mediterranean, successively

possessed by the Phœnicians, Greeks, Carthaginians (about 500 B.C.), Romans (238), Vandals (456 A.D.), Saracens (720–40), Genoese (1022), Pisans (1165), Aragonese (1352), and Spaniards. From settlers belonging to these various nations the present inhabitants derive their origin. Victor Amadeus, duke of Savoy, acquired Sardinia in 1720, with the title of king. SAVOY. Area, 9399 sq. miles. Pop. of Sardinia, 1875, 654,432; 1890, estimated, 726,522. The king of Sardinia was recognized as king of Italy by his parliament in Feb. 1861. ITALY.

Conquered by English naval forces, under sir John Leake and gen Stanhope ... 1708
Ceded to the emperor Charles VI ... 1714
Recovered by the Spaniards ... 22 Aug. 1717
Ceded to the duke of Savoy with the title of *king*, as an equivalent for Sicily ... 1720
Victor Amadeus abdicates in favor of his son ... 1730
Attempting to recover his throne, he is taken, and dies in prison ... 1732
Court kept at Turin, till Piedmont is overrun by the French .. 1792
Charles Emmanuel yields the throne to his brother, the duke of Aosta ... 4 June, 1802
Piedmont annexed to Italy ... 26 May, 1805
King resides in Sardinia ... 1798–1814
Piedmont restored to its king. Genoa added ... Dec. "
King Charles Albert promulgates a new code ... 1837
Cavour establishes the newspaper *Il Risorgimento* ("the Revival") ... 1847
King grants a constitution, and openly espouses Italian regeneration against Austria ... 23 Mch. 1848
Defeats the Austrians at Goito; and takes Peschiera ... 30 May, "
Incorporation of Lombardy with Sardinia, 28 June, and Venice, 4 July, "
Sardinian army defeated by Radetzky ... 26 July, "
Sardinians at Milan capitulate to Radetzky ... 5 Aug. "
Defeat of the Sardinians by Austrians at Novara ... 23 Mch. 1849
Charles Albert abdicates in favor of his son, Victor Emmanuel, 23 Mch. "
Death of Charles Albert at Oporto ... 28 July, "
Treaty of Milan between Austria and Sardinia ... 6 Aug. "
Adoption of the Siccardi law, which abolishes ecclesiastical jurisdictions ... 9 Apr. 1850
Cavour minister of foreign affairs ... 1851
Act to suppress convents and support clergy by the state, 2 Mch. 1855
Convention with England and France; 15,000 troops to be supplied against Russia ... 10 Apr. "
Ten thousand troops under gen. La Marmora arrive in the Crimea ... 8 May, "
Distinguished in the battle of the Tchernaya ... 16 Aug. "
King visits London, etc ... 30 Nov. et seq. "
Important note on Italy from Cavour to England ... 16 Apr. 1856
Rupture with Austria; subsequent war. AUSTRIA, 1857 et seq.
Cavour declares in favor of free-trade ... June, 1857
Prince Jerome Napoleon marries princess Clotilde (ITALY), 30 Jan. 1859
Preliminaries of peace signed at Villa Franca, 11 July; Cavour resigns, 13 July; Rattazzi administration formed ... 19 July, "
Emperor Napoleon's letter to Victor Emmanuel advocating an Italian confederation: the latter declares it impracticable, and maintains his engagements with the Italians ... 20 Oct. "
Treaty of peace signed at Zurich ... Nov. "
Garibaldi retires to private life ... 17 Nov. "
Count Cavour returns to office ... 16 Jan. 1860
Sardinian government refers the annexation of Tuscany, etc., to the vote of the people ... 29 Feb. "
Annexation of Savoy and Nice proposed by France; Sardinia refers it to the people ... 25 Feb. "
Annexation to Sardinia voted almost unanimously by Æmilia, 14 Mch; by Tuscany, 16 Mch.; accepted by Victor Emmanuel ... 18–20 Mch. "
Treaty ceding Savoy and Nice to France, signed ... 24 Mch. "
Prussia protests against Italian annexations ... 27 Mch. "
New Sardinian parliament opens ... 2 Apr. "
Annexation to France almost unanimously voted for by Nice, 15 Apr.; by Savoy ... 22 Apr. "
Government disapproves Garibaldi's expedition to SICILY, 18 May, "
Chambers ratify cession of Savoy and Nice ... 29 May, "
Sardinian troops enter papal territories (ITALY, ROME), 11 Sept. "
Victor Emmanuel enters the kingdom of Naples ... 15 Oct. "
Naples and Sicily vote for annexation to Sardinia ... 21 Oct. "
Railway from Sassari to the sea opened ... 9 Apr. 1872

[For the disputes and war with Austria, and the events of 1859–61, 1866, AUSTRIA, FRANCE, NAPLES, ROME, SICILY. For later history, ITALY.]

KINGS OF SARDINIA. (SAVOY.)

1720. Victor Amadeus I. king (as duke II.); resigned, in 1730, in favor of his son; d. 1732.
1730. Charles Emmanuel I. (III. of Savoy), son.
1773. Victor Amadeus II., son.
1796. Charles Emmanuel II., son; resigned his crown in favor of his brother.
1802. Victor Emmanuel I., brother; 4 June.
1805. [Sardinia merged into Italy; Napoleon crowned king, 26 May, 1805.]
1814. Victor Emmanuel restored; resigned in Mch. 1821; and d. 1824.
1821. Charles Felix.
1831. Charles Albert; abdicated in favor of his son, 23 Mch. 1849. Died at Oporto, 28 July, 1849.
1849. Victor Emmanuel II., son; born 14 Mch. 1820; d. 9 Jan. 1878. ITALY.

Sardis. SEVEN CHURCHES.

Sarma'tia, the ancient name for the country in Asia and Europe between the Caspian sea and the Vistula, including Russia and Poland. The Sarmatæ, or Sauromatæ, troubled the early Roman empire by incursions. After subduing the Scythians, they were subjugated by the Goths, in the 3d and 4th centuries. They joined the Huns and other barbarians in invading Western Europe in the 5th century.

Sarum, Old, Wiltshire, an ancient British town, the origin of SALISBURY. Although completely decayed, it returned 2 members to Parliament till 1832.

Sassan'ides, descendants of Artaxerxes, or Ardishir, whose father, Babek, was the son of Sassan. He revolted against Artabanus, the king of Parthia; defeated him on the plain of Hormuz, 226; and re-established the Persian monarchy. This dynasty was expelled by the Mahometans, 652. PERSIA.

Satan, the spirit of evil, the prince of devils. According to Swedenborg pertaining more to the understanding than the will. Mentioned in the Old Testament 1 Chron. xxi. 1; Job i. 6, ii. 1-2; Ps. cix. 6; and more frequently in the New Testament. Graphically described in Milton's "Paradise Lost," of which he is the central figure: book i. lines 285–300; book ii. lines 1–5, 706–710; book vi. lines 245–255.

Satellites. JUPITER, MARS, MOON, NEPTUNE, PLANETS, SATURN.

satire. About a century after the introduction of comedy, satire made its appearance at Rome in the writings of Lucilius, called the inventor of it, 116 B.C.—*Livy.* The Satires of Horace (35 B.C.), Juvenal (about 100 A.D.), and Persius (about 60 A.D.) are the most celebrated in ancient times, and those of Churchill (1761) and Pope (1729) in modern times. Butler's "Hudibras," satirizing the Presbyterians, first appeared in 1663. "Satire Ménippée," a celebrated satirical pamphlet, partly in verse and partly in prose, attacking the policy of the court of Spain and the league, written in the style of the biting satires of the cynic philosopher Menippus. The first part, "Catholicon d'Espagne," by Leroy, appeared in 1593; the second, "Abrégé des États de la Ligue," by Gillot, Pithou, Rapin, and Passerat, appeared in 1594.—*Bouillet.*

sat'rapies, divisions of the Persian empire, formed by Darius Hystaspis about 516 B.C.

Saturday, the last or 7th day of the week; the Jewish Sabbath; SABBATH. It was so called from an idol worshipped on this day by the Saxons; and, according to Verstegan, was named by them Saterne's day.—*Pardon.* It is more probably from Saturn, *dies Saturni.*

Sat'urn, a planet, taking its name from the father of the gods in the Roman mythology, about 900 millions of miles distant from the sun, with mean diameter about 70,230 miles; difference between its polar and equatorial diameters is 7000 miles. Its time of rotation on its axis is 10 hrs. 29 min. 17 sec. Its revolution around the sun 24,630 of its days or 10,760 of ours, or 29 years 167 days. Its volume as compared with our globe is as 744 to 1, but its mass only as 90 to 1, its density being something less than water. The sun's light and heat at this planet are but $\frac{1}{91}$ as intense as at the earth. It is accompanied by 8 satellites, discovered in the following order:

Name.	Discoverer.	Date.
Titan	Huyghens	1655
Japetus	Cassini	1671
Rhea	"	1672
Dione	"	1684
Tethys	"	"
Enceladus	Herschel	1787
Mimas	"	1789
Hyperion	Bond	1848

Of these satellites Mimas is nearest to Saturn, being 79,000 miles away, while Japetus, the most distant, about 2,150,000 miles. The largest of these satellites is Titan, whose diameter is over 4000 miles. Compared with our moon the moons of Saturn give but very little light; all full together they would give but $\frac{1}{16}$ part of the light of our full moon —*R A Proctor* The ring was observed by Galileo about 1610, its annular form determined by Huyghens about 1655, and discovered to be twofold by messrs Ball, 13 Oct 1665, an inner ring was detected in 1850 by Bond in the United States (15 Nov) and by Dawes in England (29 Nov) The exterior diameter of the outer ring is 166,920 miles, and its inner diameter 147,670 miles, its breadth nearly 10,000 miles The dimensions of the middle ring 144,300, 109,100, and 17,600 miles The dark ring's breadth is nearly 8700 miles, making the entire breadth of the ring system over 36,000 miles Its thickness is probably about 100 miles The rings are now known not to be continuous, but to consist of innumerable small aggregations of more or less solid matter, so that the rings as a whole are constantly changing shape Their equilibrium seems to be far less stable than that of any other bodies of the solar system, except comets ASTRONOMY

Saturn (called by the Greeks Κρονος), a son of Uranus and Terra, and the father of Jupiter, Neptune, and Pluto. MYTHOLOGY

Saturna'lia, festivals in honor of Saturn, father of the gods, were instituted long before the foundation of Rome, in commemoration of the freedom and equality which prevailed in his golden reign Some, however, suppose that the Saturnalia were first observed at Rome in the reign of Tullus Hostilius (673-640 B.C), after a victory obtained over the Sabines, while others suppose that Janus first instituted them in gratitude to Saturn, from whom he had learned agriculture Others assert that they were first celebrated after a victory obtained over the Latins by the dictator Posthumius, when he dedicated a temple to Saturn, 497 B.C During these festivals no business was allowed, amusements were encouraged, and distinctions ceased —*Lenglet*

Savage's Station, Va, Battle of Here gen Sumner, with the divisions of gens Sedgwick, Richardson, Heintzelman, and Smith, repulsed an attack of the confederates under gen Magruder, 29 June, 1862 PENINSULAR CAMPAIGN

Savan'nah, Ga. GEORGIA

savings-banks. The first was instituted at Berne, in Switzerland, in 1787, by the name of *caisse de domestiques*, intended for servants only, another in Basel in 1792, open to all depositors. The rev Joseph Smith of Wendover began a benevolent institution in 1799, and in 1803-4 a "charitable bank" was instituted at Tottenham by miss Priscilla Wakefield The rev Henry Duncan established a parish bank at Ruthwell in 1810 One was opened at Edinburgh in 1814 The benefit clubs among artisans having accumulated money for their progressive purposes, a plan was adopted to identify these funds with the public debt of the country, and an extra rate of interest was held out as an inducement, hence were formed savings-banks to receive small sums, returnable with interest on demand. Rt.-hon. George Rose developed the system, and brought it under parliamentary control, 1816.

savings-banks in the United States. The first savings-bank established in the U S was the Philadelphia Saving-fund Society, organized 1816. It still exists in a prosperous condition. The second was established at Boston in 1816, and the third at New York in 1819 The system now extends to all parts of the country For statistics, BANKS, table 6.

Savo'na, a manufacturing town of N. Italy, long held by the Genoese, was captured by the king of Sardinia in 1746, by the French in 1809, and annexed, restored to Sardinia at the peace Pope Pius VII. was kept here by Napoleon I, 1809-12 Soap is said to have been invented here, and hence its French name, *savon.*

Savoy', the ancient *Sapaudia* or *Sabaudia*, formerly a province in N Italy, east of Piedmont. It became a Roman province about 118 B.C The Alemanni seized it in 395 A.D, and the Franks in 490 It shared the revolutions of Switzerland till about 1048, when Conrad, emperor of Germany, gave it to Humbert, with the title of count. Count Thomas acquired Piedmont in the 13th century Amadeus, count of Savoy, having entered his dominions, solicited Sigismund to erect them into a duchy, which he did at Cambray, 19 Feb 1416 Victor Amadeus, duke of Savoy, obtained the kingdom of Sicily from Spain by a treaty in 1713, but afterwards exchanged it with the emperor for the island of Sardinia, with the title of king, 1720 The French subdued Savoy in 1792, and made it a department of France under the name of Mont Blanc, in 1800 It was restored to the king of Sardinia in 1814, but with Nice annexed to France in 1860, in accordance with a vote by universal suffrage, 23 Apr 1860

DUKES OF SAVOY.

1391 Count Amadeus VIII is made duke in 1416, he was named pope, as Felix V He abdicated as duke of Savoy, 1439, renounced the tiara, 1449, d 1451
1439 Louis
1465. Amadeus IX
1472 Philibert I
1482 Charles I
1489 Charles II
1496 Philip II
1497 Philibert II
1504 Charles III
1553 Emmanuel Philibert
1580 Charles Emmanuel I
1630 Victor Amadeus I
1637 Francis Hyacinthe
1638 Charles Emmanuel II
1675 Victor Amadeus II became king of Sicily, 1713, exchanged for SARDINIA in 1720

saw. Invented by Dædalus.—*Pliny* Invented by Talus. —*Apollodorus* Talus, it is said, used the jawbone of a snake to cut through a piece of wood, and then formed an instrument of iron like it In use in Egypt long before it was in Greece Saw-mills driven by water at Augsburg 1322, and, according to a 13th-century MS, saw-mills had then been erected at Paris. Saw-mills erected in Madeira in 1420, at Breslau in 1427. Norway had the first saw-mill in 1530. The bishop of Ely, ambassador from Mary of England to the court of Rome, describes a saw-mill there, 1555. The attempts to introduce saw-mills in England were violently opposed, and one erected by a Dutchman in 1663 had to be abandoned. Saw-mills were erected near London about 1770. The excellent saw machinery in Woolwich dockyard is based upon the invention of the elder Brunel, 1806-13. Powis and James's band-saw was patented in 1858

Saxe-Coburg-Go'tha, a duchy of Central Germany, capitals Coburg and Gotha. The reigning family is descended from John Ernest (son of Ernest the Pious, duke of Saxony), who died in 1729 Pop 1875, 182,599, 1890, 206,513.

DUKES.

1826 Ernest I, duke of Saxe Saalfeld Coburg, b 2 Jan 1784, married Louisa, heiress of Augustus, duke of Saxe-Gotha, and became by convention duke of Saxe Coburg Gotha, 12 Nov 1826, d 29 Jan. 1844
[His brother Leopold married the princess Charlotte of England, 2 May, 1816, became king of the Belgians, 12 July, 1831, and Ferdinand, the son of his brother Ferdinand, married Maria da Gloria, queen of Portugal, 9 Apr 1836.]
1844 Ernest II, son of Ernest I and brother of Albert, prince consort of Great Britain, b 21 June, 1818, married Alexandrina, duchess of Baden 3 May, 1842, no issue He entered into alliance with Prussia, 18 Aug 1866, d 23 Aug 1893.
1893 Prince Alfred of England, duke of Edinburgh, b 6 Aug 1844 (in whose favor the prince of Wales resigned his rights, 19 Apr 1863)

Saxe-Mei'ningen, a duchy in central Germany. The dukes are descended from Ernest the Pious, duke of Saxony. The first duke, Bernard (1680), died in 1706 Bernard (duke, 24 Dec. 1803) abdicated in favor of his son, George II., 20 Sept. 1866, who professed his adhesion to the Prussian policy; he was born 2 Apr 1826. Pop Dec 1875, 194,494; 1890, 223,832.

Saxe-Wei'mar-Ei'senach, a grand-duchy of Central Germany The grand-dukes are descended from John Frederic, the Protestant elector of Saxony, who was deposed by the emperor Charles V in 1548. SAXONY The houses of Saxe-Coburg-Gotha, Saxe-Gotha, Hilberghausen, and Saxe-Meiningen also sprang from him. They are all termed the senior or *Ernestine* branch of the old family Saxe-Weimar became a grand-duchy in 1815 The dukes have greatly favored literature, and their capital, Weimar, has been called the Athens of Germany. Goethe resided here from 1775 Pop of the duchy, 1875, 292,933, 1890, 326,091.

sax-horn, a musical instrument of the trumpet kind, invented by Adolphe Sax, a Frenchman, about 1840

Sax'ony, a kingdom in N Germany. The Saxons were a fierce, warlike race, frequently attacked France, and conquered Britain. They were completely subdued by Charlemagne, who instituted many fiefs and bishoprics in their country. Witikind, their great leader, who claimed descent from Woden, professed Christianity about 785. From him descended the first and the present ruling family (the houses of Supplinburg, Guelf, and Ascania intervened from 1106 to 1421); thus the royal house of Saxony counts among the oldest reigning families in Europe. Saxony became a duchy 880, an electorate 1180, and a kingdom 1806. It was the seat of war, 1813, the king being on the side of Napoleon. In the conflict of 1866 the king took the side of Austria, and his army fought in the battle of Königgrätz, 3 July. The Prussians entered Saxony 18 June. Peace between Prussia and Saxony was signed 21 Oct. (subjecting the Saxon army to Prussia), and the king returned to Dresden 3 Nov. Area, 5787 sq. miles; pop. 1890, 3,500,513.

ELECTORS.

1423. Frederic I., first elector of the house of Misnia.
1428. Frederic II.
[His sons Ernest and Albert divide the states.]

1464. Ernest.	1464. Albert.
1486. Frederic III.	1500. George.
1525. John.	1539. Henry.
	1541. Maurice.

1532. John Frederic; deposed by the emperor Charles V.; succeeded by
1548. Maurice (of the Albertine line).
1553. *Augustus.*
1586. Christian I.
1591. Christian II.
1611. John George I.
1656. John George II.
1680. John George III.
1691. John George IV.
1694. Frederic Augustus I., king of Poland, 1697.
1733. Frederic Augustus II., king of Poland.
1763. Frederic Augustus III., becomes king 1806.

KINGS.

1806. Frederic Augustus I.; increased his territories by alliance with France, 1806-9; suffered by peace of 1814.
1827. Anthony Clement.
1836. Frederic Augustus II., nephew (regent, 1830); d. 9 Aug. 1854.
1854. John, brother; b. 12 Dec. 1801; celebrated his golden wedding (50 years), 10 Nov. 1872; d. 29 Oct. 1873.
1873. Albert; b. 23 Apr. 1828; married, 18 June, 1853, Caroline of Wasa.
Heir: George, his brother; b. 8 Aug. 1832.

scan'dalum magna'tum, a special statute in England relating to any wrong done to high personages, such as peers, judges, ministers of the crown, officers in the state, and other great public functionaries, by the circulation, orally or in writing, of scandalous statements, false news, or defaming messages, by which any debate or discord between them and the commons, or any scandal to their persons, might arise.—*Chambers.* This law was first enacted 2 Rich. II. 1378.

Scandina'via, ancient name of Sweden, Norway, and great part of Denmark, whence proceeded the Northmen or Normans, who conquered Normandy (about 900), and eventually England (1066). They were also called Sea-kings, or Vikings. They settled Iceland and Greenland, and, it is thought, visited the northern regions of AMERICA, about the 9th century. A "National Scandinavian Society" has been formed at Stockholm. LITERATURE.

scarlet, or kermes dye, was known in the East in the earliest ages; cochineal dye, 1518. Kepler, a Fleming, established the first dye-house for scarlet in England, at Bow, 1643. The art of dyeing red was improved by Brewer, 1667.—*Beckmann.*

Sceptics, the sect of philosophers founded by Pyrrho, about 334 B.C. He gave 10 reasons for continual suspense of judgment; he doubted everything, never drew conclusions, and, when he had carefully examined a subject, and investigated all its parts, he concluded by still doubting. He advocated apathy and unchangeable repose. Similar doctrines were held by Bayle (d. 1706). PHILOSOPHY.

sceptre, a more ancient emblem of royalty than the crown. In the earlier ages the sceptres of kings were long walking-staves; afterwards carved and made shorter. Tarquin the elder was the first who assumed the sceptre among the Romans, about 468 B.C. The French sceptre of the first race of kings was a golden rod, 481 A.D.—*Le Gendre.*

Schaff'hausen, N. Switzerland, a fishing village in the 8th century, became an imperial city in the 13th; was subjected to Austria, 1330; independent, 1415; became a Swiss canton, 1501.

Schehal'lion, a mountain in Perthshire, Scotland, where dr. Neville Maskelyne, the astronomer-royal, made observations with a plumb-line, 24 Oct. 1774, from which Hutton calculated that the density of the earth is five times that of water.

Scheldt tolls were imposed by the treaty of Münster (or Westphalia), 1648. The tolls were abolished for a compensation, 1867. The House of Commons voted 175,000*l.* for the British portion on 9 Mch. 1864. The Scheldt was declared free on 3 Aug. with much rejoicing at Antwerp and Brussels.

Schenec'tady, Indian massacre at. NEW YORK, 1690.

Schipka passes, on the Balkans, Turkey. Through these the Russian general Gourko entered Roumelia, 1877. After his retreat, they were fortified, and desperately, but on the whole unsuccessfully, assailed by the Turks under Suleiman Pacha, with great slaughter on both sides, 20-27 Aug. He took and lost fort St. Nicholas, 17 Sept. 1877. The Russians re-entered Roumelia, Jan. 1878.

schism (*sizm*). HERESY, POPES.

Schles'wig. DENMARK, GASTEIN, HOLSTEIN.

School board. EDUCATION.

schoolmen or **scholastic philosophy** began in the schools founded by Charlemagne, 800-14; and prevailed in Europe from the 9th to the 15th century. DOCTORS, PHILOSOPHY.

schools. EDUCATION, MEDICAL SCIENCE, PAINTING, PHILOSOPHY.

schooner Pearl. In 1848 capt. Drayton and his mate Sayles attempted to carry away to freedom, from the vicinity of Washington, D. C., 77 fugitive slaves concealed in this schooner; as the schooner neared the mouth of the Potomac river, she was overtaken and obliged to return. These fugitive slaves, men, women, and children, were immediately sold to the cotton planters of the Gulf states; while Drayton and Sayles, with difficulty saved from death by mob-violence, were brought to trial in Washington. The aggregate bail required amounted to $228,000. They were convicted and in prison until 1852, when, through the influence and efforts of Charles Sumner, pres. Fillmore granted them an unconditional pardon; but, notwithstanding this, they were immediately hurried out of the city and sent to the north to save them from violence and re-arrest.

Schweiz, a Swiss canton, which with Uri and Unterwalden renounced subjection to Austria, 7 Nov. 1307. The name Switzerland, for all the country, dates from about 1440.

scientific surveying expedition. DEEP SEA SOUNDINGS, EXPEDITIONS.

Scilly isles, the Cassiterides or Tin islands, southwest of Land's End, Engl., consist of 140 islets and many rocks. They held commerce with the Phœnicians, and are mentioned by Strabo. They were conquered by Athelstan, 936, and given to the monks. They were granted by Elizabeth to the Godolphin family, who fortified them; the works were strengthened in 1649 by the royalists, from whom Blake wrested them, 1651. Augustus Smith, the owner, termed king of these isles, after a long paternal rule, died in Aug. 1872. Area, 5770 acres; pop., 1880, 2090.

A British squadron under sir Cloudesley Shovel was wrecked here, returning from an expedition against Toulon; he mistook the rocks for land. His ship, the *Association*, in which were persons of rank, and 800 brave men, went instantly to the bottom. The *Eagle*, capt. Hancock, and the *Romney* and *Firebrand*, were also lost; the rest of the fleet escaped, 22 Oct. 1707. Sir Cloudesley's body was buried in Westminster Abbey, where a monument stands to his memory.

Scinde. SINDE.

Scio massacre, 11 Apr. 1822. CHIOS.

Scone, near Perth, was of early historical importance. It received the title of the "Royal city of Scone" as early as 906 or 909 A.D. The Scotch coronation chair was brought from Scone to Westminster Abbey by Edward I. in 1296. Here Charles II. was crowned, 1 Jan. 1651.

"He is already nam'd; and gone to Scone, to be invested."
—*Shakespeare*, Macbeth, act ii. sc. iv.

Scoti, prehistoric invaders of Ireland, from whom the island took the name Scotia and retained it exclusively from the 4th to the 11th century. The Scoti were probably a branch of the Teutons or Scandinavians. The famous Milesians were Scoti. It was not until invaded by Henry II. that the island was known as Ireland.—*Brewster.*

Sco'tists, those who adopted the doctrines of John Duns Scotus (d. 8 Nov. 1308) respecting the birth of the Virgin Mary, etc., strongly opposed by the Thomists, disciples of St. Thomas Aquinas, who died 7 Mch. 1274.

Scotland, the N. division of the island of Great Britain, separated from England on the southeast by the Tweed, southwest by the Solway Firth, and south partly by the Cheviot hills. At the death of queen Elizabeth, 24 Mch. 1603, James VI. of Scotland, as the most immediate heir, was called to the throne of England, and proclaimed king of Great Britain, 24 Oct. 1604. Each country had a separate parliament till 1707, when the kingdoms were united. Area, 30,417 sq. miles in 33 counties including 186 islands. Pop. 1891, 4,033,103; 1901, 4,472,103. ALBANY, CALEDONIA, ENGLAND.

Camelon, capital of the Picts, taken by Kenneth II. and every living creature put to the sword or destroyed — 843
Norwegians occupy Caithness, 9th century
Scotland ravaged by Athelstan — 933
Feudal system established by Malcolm II. — 1004
Invaded by Canute — 1031
Divided into baronies. — 1032
Danes driven out of Scotland — 1040
Duncan I. is murdered by his kinsman Macbeth, by whom the crown is seized — "
Malcolm III., aided by Edward the Confessor, defeats Macbeth at Dunsinane, 1054; Macduff kills Macbeth — 1056 or 1057
Saxon English language introduced into Scotland by fugitives from the Normans in England — 1080
Siege of Alnwick, Malcolm III. killed — 1093
Reign of David I., a legislator — 1124–53
Scotland invaded by Haco, king of Norway, with 160 ships and 20,000 men; invaders are defeated by Alexander III., who now recovers the Western isles — 1263
Margaret of Norway, heiress to the throne, d. — 7 Oct. 1290
John Baliol and Robert Bruce claim the throne, 1291; Edward I. of England, as umpire, decides in favor of John — Nov. 1292
John Baliol, king of Scotland, appears in his own defence in Westminster hall against the earl of Fife — 1293
Edward, wishing to annex Scotland to England, dethrones John, ravages the country, destroys the muniments of Scottish history, and seizes the prophetic stone (CORONATION) — 1296
William Wallace defeats the English at Cambus Kenneth, and expels them, 1297; is defeated at Falkirk, 22 July, 1298; taken by the English and executed at Smithfield — 23 Aug. 1305
Robert Bruce crowned, 1306; he defeats the English, 1307, and takes Inverness, 1313; defeats the English at Bannockburn, — 24 June, 1314
Edward Baliol gains the throne for a little time by victories at Dupplin, 11 Aug. 1332, and at Halidon hill — 19 July, 1333
David II. taken prisoner by the English at the battle of Durham (and detained in captivity 11 years) — 1346
Battle of Chevy Chase between Hotspur Percy and earl Douglas (OTTERBURN) — 10 Aug. 1388
Murder of duke of Rothesay, heir of Robert III., by starvation, — 3 Apr. 1401
Scots defeated at Homildon Hill — 14 Sept. 1402
James I. captured by the English near Flamborough head on his passage to France — 30 Mch. 1406
St. Andrews university founded by bishop William Turnbull — 1451
University of Aberdeen founded — 1494
James IV. invades England, slain at FLODDEN FIELD, and his army cut to pieces — 9 Sept. 1513
James V. banishes the Douglases — 1528
He establishes the court of session — 1532
Order of St. Andrew, or the Thistle, is revived — 1540
Mary, queen of Scots, b. 7 Dec., succeeds her father, James V., who d. — 14 Dec. "
Regent, cardinal Beaton, persecutes the reformers, 1539, 1546; he is assassinated at St. Andrews — 29 May, 1546
Scots defeated at Pinkie — 10 Sept. 1547
Mary marries the dauphin of France — Apr. 1558
Parliament abolishes the jurisdiction of the pope in Scotland, — 24 Aug. 1560
Francis II. dies, leaving Mary a widow — Dec. "
Reformation in Scotland, by John Knox and others, during the minority of Mary — between 1550 and "
Mary, after an absence of 13 years, arrives at Leith from France — 21 Aug. 1561
Upon an inquisition, which was officially taken, by order of queen Elizabeth only 58 Scotsmen were found in London (*Stow*) — 1562
Mary marries her cousin, Henry Stuart, lord Darnley — 29 July, 1565
David Rizzio, her confidential secretary, murdered by Darnley in her presence — 9 Mch. 1566
Lord Darnley blown up by gunpowder in his house (Mary accused of conniving at his death) — 10 Feb. 1567
James Hepburn, earl of Bothwell, carries off the queen, who marries him . . . . 15 May, "
Mary made prisoner at Carberry hill by her nobles — 15 June, 1567
Resigns her crown to her infant son, James VI.; earl of Murray appointed regent — 22 July, "
Mary escapes, and collects a large army; is defeated by regent Murray at Langside, 13 May; enters England — 16 May, 1568
Regent Murray murdered — 23 Jan. 1570
Earl of Lennox appointed regent — 12 July, "
Earl of Lennox murdered, 4 Sept.; earl of Mar regent — Sept. 1571
Death of the reformer John Knox — 24 Nov. 1572

[His funeral in Edinburgh is attended by most of the nobility and by the regent Morton, who exclaims, "There lies he who never feared the face of man!"]

University of Edinburgh founded — 1582
Raid of RUTHVEN — "
Mary takes refuge in England, 16 May, 1568; is, after a long captivity, beheaded at FOTHERINGAY castle — 8 Feb. 1587
Gowrie's conspiracy fails — 5 Aug. 1600
Crowns of Scotland and England united in James VI. — 24 Mch. 1603
James proclaimed "king of Great Britain, France, and Ireland" — 24 Oct. 1604
Charles I. attempts in vain to introduce the English liturgy; tumult at Edinburgh — 23 July, 1637
Solemn league and covenant subscribed (COVENANTERS), 1 Mch. 1638
A Scotch army enters England — 1640
Charles joins the Scotch army, 1646; betrayed into the hands of the English parliament — 30 Jan. 1647
Marquis of Montrose defeated at Philiphaugh, 13 Sept. 1645; executed at Edinburgh — 21 May, 1650
Charles II. crowned at SCONE, 1 Jan.; defeated at Worcester, — 22 Aug. 1651
Scotland united to the English Commonwealth by Oliver Cromwell — Sept. "
Charles II. revives episcopacy in Scotland — 1661
Argyll beheaded — 27 May, "
Scottish hospital, London, incorporated — 1665
Covenanters defeated on the Pentland hills — 1666
Archbishop Sharpe murdered near St. Andrews by John Balfour of Burley and others — 3 May, 1679
Covenanters defeat Claverhouse at Drumclog, 1 June; are routed at Bothwell bridge — 22 June, "
Richard Cameron's declaration for religious liberty — 22 June 1680
Earl of Argyll beheaded — 30 June 1685
Resolution of a convention in favor of William III.; re-establishment of presbytery — 14 Mch. 1689
Insurrection of Claverhouse, killed at Killiecrankie — 27 July, "
Massacre of the Macdonalds at Glencoe — 13 Feb. 1692
Legislative union of Scotland with England — 1 May, 1707
Insurrection under the earl of Mar in favor of the son of James II. (PRETENDER) — 1715
Rebels defeated at Preston, 12 Nov., and at Dumblane (or Sheriffmuir) — 13 Nov. "
Capt. PORTEOUS killed by a mob in Edinburgh — 7 Sept. 1736
Prince Charles Edward proclaimed at Perth, 4 Sept.; at Edinburgh, 16 Sept.; with the Highlanders defeats sir John Cope at Prestonpans, 21 Sept.; takes Carlisle, 15 Nov.; arrives at Manchester, 28 Nov.; at Derby, 4 Dec.; retreats to Glasgow, — 25 Dec. 1745
Defeats gen. Hawley at Falkirk, 17 Jan.; is totally defeated at Culloden — 16 Apr. 1746
Highland dress prohibited by parliament — 12 Aug. "
Lords Kilmarnock and Balmerino executed for high treason on Tower hill — 18 Aug. "
Simon Fraser, lord Lovat, aged 80, executed . — 9 Apr. 1747
Heritable jurisdictions abolished by parliament — "
Thomson, the poet, d. — 27 Aug. 1748
Old Pretender, "Chevalier de St. George," d. at Rome, — 30 Dec. 1765
Prince Charles Edward Louis Casimir, the Young Pretender, d. at Rome . — 31 Jan. 1788
Death of Robert Burns . — 21 July, 1796
Scott's "Lay of the Last Minstrel" pub. . — 1806
Cardinal Henry, duke of York (last of the Stuarts), d. — 31 Aug. 1807
Royal Caledonian asylum, London, founded — 1813
Scott's "Waverley" pub. (LITERATURE) . — 1814
Establishment of a jury court under a lord chief commissioner, 1815
Visit of George IV. to Scotland — Aug. 1822
Sir Walter Scott d. — 21 Sept. 1832
Seven ministers of the presbytery of Strathbogie are deposed by the General Assembly of the church of Scotland for obeying the civil in preference to the ecclesiastical law. (Their deposition was formally protested against by the minority of ministers and elders, headed by dr. Cook) — 28 May, 1841
General Assembly condemn patronage as a grievance to the cause of true religion that ought to be abolished — 23 May, 1842
Secession of the non-intrusion ministers of the church of Scotland (about 400) at the General Assembly — 18 May, 1843
Death of Francis (lord) Jeffrey, principally known as one of the founders of and contributors to the EDINBURGH REVIEW, and its editor for 26 years — 26 Jan. 1850
National association for vindication of Scottish rights formed, — Nov. 1853
Salmon Fisheries act passed — July, 1864
Scotch Reform bill introduced into the commons, 17 Feb., passed . — 13 July, 1868
Scotch Reform act passed — " " "
Land Registers and Titles to Land act passed . — July, "
Robert Chambers, author and publisher, d., aged 69 — 17 Mch. 1871
Scott centenary celebrated in Edinburgh, etc. (Scott b. 15 Aug. 1771) — 9 Aug. "
Return of owners of land and heritages, 1872–73 (a kind of Domesday book), published by government — Apr. 1874

Patronage in the established church (see 1842) abolished by act passed....7 Aug. 1874
Scottish Church Disestablishment Association; first annual meeting....8 Mch. 1875
Romanist hierarchy revived by the pope; archbishop of Glasgow, bishopric of Dunkeld, etc., 2 Mch.; the Scotch Protestant bishops protest against this....13 Apr. 1878
Movement for home rule begun....4 Apr. 1882
Secretary of Scotland act passed....14 Aug. 1885
Local government bill for Scotland passed....26 Aug. 1889
Great railroad bridge over the river FORTH opened....4 Mch. 1890

KINGS OF SCOTLAND.

BEFORE CHRIST.

[The early accounts of the kings are fabulous. The series is carried as far back as Alexander the Great.]

330. Fergus I.; ruled 25 years; lost in the Irish sea.
[Fergus, a brave prince, came from Ireland with an army of Scots, and was chosen king. Having defeated the Britons and slain their king Coilus, the kingdom of the Scots was entailed upon his posterity forever. He went to Ireland, and, having settled his affairs there, was drowned on his return, launching from the shore, near the harbor, called *Carrickfergus* to this day.—*Anderson.*]

AFTER CHRIST.

357. Eugenius I., son of Fincormachus; slain in battle by Maximus, the Roman general, and the Picts.
*** With this battle ended the kingdom of the Scots, after having existed from the coronation of Fergus I., a period of 706 years; the royal family fled to Denmark.—*Boece, Buchanan.*
[Interregnum of 27 years.]
404. Fergus II. (I.), great-grandson of Eugenius, and 40th king; slain in battle with the Romans.
420. Eugenius II. or Evenus; reigned 31 years.
451. Dongardus or Domangard, brother; defeated and drowned.
457. Constantine I., brother; assassinated.
479. Congallus I., nephew; just and prudent.
501. Goranus, brother; murdered.—*Boece.* Died while Donald of Athol was conspiring to take his life.
535. Eugenius III., nephew; "none excelled him in justice."
558. Congallus II., brother.
569. Kinnatellus, brother; resigned for
570. Aidanus or Aidan, son of Goranus.
605. Kenneth, son of Congallus II.
606. Eugenius IV., son of Aidanus.
621. Ferchard or Ferquhard I., son; confined for misdeeds to his palace, where he slew himself.—*Scott.*
632. Donald IV., brother; drowned in Loch Tay.
646. Ferchard II., son of Ferchard I.; "most execrable."
664. Malduinus, son of Donald IV.; strangled by his wife for supposed infidelity; she was immediately burned.
684. Eugenius V., brother.
688. Eugenius VI., son of Ferchard II.
698. Amberkeletus, nephew; fell by an arrow from an unknown hand.
699. Eugenius VII., brother; ruffians designing the king's murder, entered his chamber, and, in his absence, stabbed his queen, Spontana, to death.—*Scott.*
715. Mordachus, son of Amberkeletus.
730. Etfinus, son of Eugenius VII.
761. Eugenius VIII., son of Mordachus; sensual and tyrannous; put to death by his nobles.
764. Fergus III., son of Etfinus; killed by his jealous queen, who afterwards stabbed herself to escape a death of torture.
767. Solvathius, son of Eugenius VIII.
787. Achaius; just and wise.
819. Congallus III.; a peaceful reign.
824. Dongal or Dougal, son of Solvathius; drowned.
831. Alpine, son of Achaius; beheaded by the Picts.
834. Kenneth II., son; surnamed Mac Alpine; defeated the Picts, slew their king, united them with the Scots as first sole monarch of all Scotland, 843.
854. Donald V., brother; dethroned; committed suicide.
858. Constantine II., son of Kenneth II.; taken in battle by the Danes and beheaded.
874. Eth or Ethus, surnamed Lightfoot; died of grief in prison; confined for sensuality and crime.
876. Gregory the Great; brave and just.
893. Donald VI., son of Constantine II.; excellent.
904. Constantine III., son of Ethus; became a monk, and resigned in favor of
944. Malcolm I., son of Donald VI.; murdered.
953. Indulfus or Indulphus; killed by the Danes in an ambuscade.
961. Duff or Duffus, son of Malcolm; murdered by Donald, the governor of Forres castle.
965. Cullen or Culenus, son of Indulphus; avenged the murder of his predecessor; assassinated.
970. Kenneth III., brother of Duffus; murdered by Fenella, the lady of Fettercairn.
994. Constantine IV., son of Cullen; slain.
995. Kenneth IV. or Grimus, the Grim, son of Duffus; routed and slain in battle by Malcolm, the rightful heir to the crown, who succeeded.
1003. Malcolm II., son of Kenneth III.; assassinated on his way to Glamis; the assassins in their flight crossing a frozen lake were drowned.
1033. Duncan I., grandson; assassinated by his cousin.
1039. Macbeth, usurper; slain by Macduff, the thane of Fife.
*** Historians so differ up to this reign in the number of kings, dates of succession, and circumstances narrated, that no account can be trusted.
1057. Malcolm III. (Canmore), son of Duncan; killed while besieging Alnwick castle.
1093. Donald VII. (Donald Bane), brother; usurper; fled to the Hebrides.
1094. Duncan II., natural son of Malcolm; murdered.
" Donald VII. again; deposed.
1098. Edgar, son of Malcolm (Henry I. of England married his sister Maud).
1107. Alexander I., the Fierce, brother.
1124. David I., brother; married Matilda, daughter of Waltheof, earl of Northumberland.
1153. Malcolm IV.; grandson.
1165. William the Lion; brother.
1214. Alexander II., son; married Joan, daughter of John, king of England.
1249. Alexander III., married Margaret, daughter of Henry III. of England; dislocated his neck when hunting near Kinghorn.
1285. Margaret, the "Maiden of Norway," granddaughter of Alexander. "recognized by the states of Scotland, though a female, an infant, and a foreigner"; died on her passage to Scotland.
A competition for the vacant throne; Edward I. of England decides in favor of
1292. John Baliol, who afterwards surrendered his crown, and died in exile.
[Interregnum.]
1306. Robert (Bruce) I.; a great prince.
1329. David (Bruce) II., son; Edward Baliol disputed the throne with him.
1332. David II. again; a prisoner in England, 1346–57 (Edward Baliol king, 1332–34).
1371. Robert (Stuart) II., nephew; d. 19 Apr.
1390. Robert (John Stuart) III.; son; d. 4 Apr.
1406. James I., second son; imprisoned 18 years in England; set at liberty in 1423; conspired against, and murdered at Perth, 21 Feb.
1437. James II., son; killed at the siege of Roxburgh castle by a cannon bursting, 3 Aug.
1460. James III., son; killed in a revolt of his subjects at Bannockburn field, 11 June.
1488. James IV., son; married Margaret Tudor, daughter of Henry VII. of England; killed at the battle of Flodden, 9 Sept.
1513. James V., son; succeeded when little more than a year old; a sovereign possessing many virtues; d. 14 Dec.
1542. Mary, daughter; b. 7 Dec. 1542; succeeded 14 Dec. (see Annals above).
1567. James VI., son; succeeded to the throne of England, and the kingdoms were united, 1603.
ENGLAND.

Scott centenary celebrated in London and throughout Scotland, 9 Aug. 1871. Sir Walter Scott was born 15 Aug. 1771. LITERATURE.

"Scouring of the White Horse." ASHDOWN.

screw, a cylinder surmounted by a spiral ridge or groove, every part of which forms an equal angle with the axis of the cylinder; one of the 6 mechanical powers known to the Greeks, but probably not to the Egyptians. The pumping-screw of Archimedes, or screw-cylinder for raising water, invented about 236 B.C., is still in use. It is asserted that with the screw one man can press down or raise as much as 150 men without it.

screw-propeller consists of two or more twisted blades, like the vanes of a windmill, set on an axis running parallel with the keel of a vessel, and revolving beneath the water at the stern. It is driven by a steam-engine. The principle was shown by Hooke in 1681, and since by Du Quet, Bernouilli, and others. Patents for propellers were taken out by Joseph Bramah in 1784; by Wm. Lyttelton in 1794; and by Edward Shorter in 1799. But these led to no useful result. In 1836 patents were obtained by Francis Pettit Smith, a farmer of Romney, Engl. (knighted July, 1871; d. 12 Feb. 1874) and capt. John Ericsson, and to them the successful application of the screw-propeller must be attributed. The first vessels with the screw were the *Archimedes*, built on the Thames in 1838 by H. Wimshurst, and the *Rattler*, built in the United States (1844), and tried in England in 1845. Double screw-propellers are now employed. A new form of screw-propeller, invented by col. W. H. Mallory, of the U. S. army, was tried on the Thames and reported successful, Aug. 1878. STEAM NAVIGATION.

Scrible'rus club, a literary club, founded by Swift in 1714, included among its members Bolingbroke, Pope, Gay, and Arbuthnot.

scrof'ula. KING'S EVIL.

scrutin (French for ballot). In *scrutin de liste* the voter writes on his paper as many names as there are persons to be elected; for instance, for the whole department. In *scrutin d'arrondissement*, the members are elected separately. These modes were much discussed in France in 1875. The conservatives prefer the latter, the radicals the former. FRANCE, Nov. 1875. The *scrutin de liste* was adopted in the elections of 1848, 1849, 1871, and 1875.

M. Bardoux's bill for *scrutin de liste* (warmly advocated by M. Gambetta) passed by the Chamber of Deputies (243-235), 18 May, 1881; rejected by the senate (148-114).........9 June, 1881
M. Welbeck Rousseau's bill for the *scrutin de liste* passed by the French deputies (412-99).......................24 Mch. 1885
Scrutin de liste adopted by the Italian chamber........14 Feb. 1882

sculpture is much older than history, rude figures of men and animals carved in stone having been found among the relics of the stone age; but the first artistic sculpture is referred to the Egyptians. Bezaleel and Aholiab built the tabernacle in the wilderness, and made all the vessels and ornaments, 1491 B.C., and their skill is recorded as the gift of God (Exod. xxxi. 3). Dipœnus and Scyllis, statuaries at Crete, established a school at Sicyon. Pliny speaks of them as being the first who sculptured marble and polished it, all statues before their time being of wood, 568 B.C. Phidias, whose statue of Jupiter passed for one of the wonders of the world, was the greatest statuary among the ancients. His statue of Minerva in the Parthenon, made of ivory and gold, was 39 feet in height. Lysippus invented the art of taking likenesses in plaster moulds, from which he afterwards cast models in wax. Alexander the Great gave him the sole right of making his statues, 326 B.C. He left no less than 600 pieces, some of which were so highly valued in the age of Augustus that they sold for their weight in gold. Sculpture did not flourish among the Romans, and in the middle ages, with few exceptions, was generally degraded. With the revival of painting, it revived also; and Donato di Bardi, born at Florence 1383 A.D., was the earliest professor among the moderns, while Michael Angelo was the greatest artist. Two statues of Rameses II. and one of his queen (about 1322 B.C.) were discovered at Aboukir by Daninos Pacha, Oct. 1891.

EMINENT GREEK (ANCIENT) SCULPTORS.

Name.	Flourished.	Best works.	Present location.
Agesander	450 B.C. ? or 70 A.D.	Laocoön	Vatican, Rome.
	B.C.		
Agasias	400	Fighting Gladiator	Louvre, Paris.
Alcamenes	440	Venus of Melos	" "
Apollonius	300	Torso of Hercules	Vatican, Rome.
Apollonius and Tauriscus	200	Torso Farnese	Museum, Naples.
Calamis	480	Apollo Belvedere Head of Apollo	Vatican, Rome. Museum, Basle.
Chares	288	Colossus of Rhodes	Destroyed.
Cleomenes	370	Venus de' Medici	Uffizi, Florence.
Cresilas	445	Wounded Amazon Bust of Pericles Dying Gaul	Capitol, Rome. Glyptothek, Munich. Capitol, Rome.
Glycon	...	Farnese Hercules	Museum, Naples.
Lysippus	328	Apoxyomenos Ludovisi Mars Æsop	Vatican, Rome. Villa Ludovisi, Rome. Villa Albani, Rome.
Myron	430	Discobolus (Disk thrower)	Palazza Massini.
Phidias	440	Sculptures of the Parthenon	British museum.
Polycletus	420	Amazon Head of Juno	Museum, Berlin. Museum, Naples.
Praxiteles	364	Cnidian Venus. Thespian Cupid Faun Niobe group	 Vatican, Rome. Capitol, Rome. Uffizi, Florence.

RENAISSANCE AND MODERN SCULPTORS.

AMERICAN.

Name.	Flourished.	Best works.	Present location.
Bailly, Joseph A	1825–83	Statue of Washington Statue of gen. John A. Rawlins	Philadelphia, Pa. Washington, D. C.
Ball, Thomas	1819–	Equestrian statue of Washington Emancipation monument Statue of Daniel Webster	Boston, Mass. Washington, D. C. Central park, N. Y. city.
Bartholomew, Edward Sheffield	1822–58	Repentant Eve Shepherd Boy Sappho	Wadsworth athenæum, Hartford, Conn. Wadsworth athenæum, Hartford, Conn.
Brown, Henry K	1814–86	Equestrian statue of Washington Statue of Lincoln Statue of gen. Greene Equestrian statue of gen. Scott Angel of the Resurrection	Union square, N. Y. city. Statuary hall, Washington, D. C. Washington, D. C. Greenwood cemetery, Brooklyn, N. Y.
Calverley, Charles	1833–	Bust of Horace Greeley " " John Brown	" " " " Union League club, N. Y. city.
Crawford, Thomas	1814–57	Orpheus Hebe and Ganymede Equestrian statue of Washington Statue of Liberty Indian chief	Athenæum, Boston, Mass. Museum of Fine Arts, Boston, Mass. Capitol at Richmond, Va. Capitol at Washington, D. C. Historical Society, N. Y. city.
Frazee, John	1790–1852	Bust of judge Marshall " " John Jay	Academy Fine Arts, Philadelphia, Pa. U. S. Supreme court, Washington, D. C.
French, Daniel C.	1850–	Minute Men of the Revolution Statue of John Howard. " " Thomas Star King	Concord, N. H. San Francisco, Cal.
Foley, Margaret E.	(?) –1877	Bust of Theodore Parker, bust of Charles Sumner, Excelsior, etc.	
Gould, Thomas R.	1818–81	West wind, Cleopatra, Timon of Athens. Bust of gov. Andrew, Mass	 Hingham cemetery, Mass.
Greenough, Horatio	1805–52	Statue of Washington The Rescue	Capitol at Washington, D. C.
Greenough, Richard S.	1819–	Statue of Franklin Boy and Eagle Statue of gov. Winthrop	Boston, Mass. Washington, D. C.
Hart, Joel T.	1810–77	Statues of Henry Clay	Louisville, Ky. New Orleans, La.
Hosmer, Harriet G.	1830–	Will-o'-the-Wisp Zenobia Beatrice Cenci Statue of col. Benton	Museum of Fine Arts, Boston, Mass. Collection of A. W. Griswold, N. Y. city. Mercantile library, St. Louis, Mo. Lafayette park, St. Louis, Mo.

RENAISSANCE AND MODERN SCULPTORS.—(*Continued.*)

AMERICAN.

Name.	Flourished.	Best works.	Present location.
acDonald, James W. A.	1824–	Head of Washington Irving	Prospect park, Brooklyn, N. Y.
		Statue of Fitz-Greene Halleck	Central park, N. Y. city.
		" " gen. Nathaniel Lyon.	
ead, Larkin G.	1835–	Statue of Lincoln	Lincoln monument, Springfield, Ill.
		" " Ethan Allen	National Art gallery, Washington, D. C.
		" " Vermont	State house, Montpelier, Vt.
		" " Columbus	Capitol, Sacramento, Cal.
ilmore, Martin	1843–83	Soldiers' monument	Boston Common.
		" "	Roxbury, Mass.
		Statue of America	Fitchburg, Mass.
		Soldiers' memorial	Colby university, Waterville, Me.
ills, Clark	1815–83	Equestrian statue of Jackson	Lafayette square, Washington, D. C.
		" " " Washington	Washington circle, " "
		Statue of Freedom	On dome of capitol, " "
ozier, Joseph	1812–	Esther, Peri, Pocahontas, Silence and Truth, Prodigal Son, Jephtha's Daughter.	
lmer, Erastus D.	1817–	The Infant Ceres, Indian Girl, The Sleeping Peri, etc.	
rry, John D.	1845–	Bust of Horace Greeley, Beggar Maid, Christmas Morning, etc.	
assmann, Ernest	1823–77	Statue of Franklin	Printing House square, N. Y. city.
		Statue of Vanderbilt	Freight depot, Hudson square, N. Y. city
wers, Hiram	1805–73	Statue of Eve	Collection of A. T. Stewart, N. Y. city.
		Greek Slave	Corcoran gallery, Washington, D. C.
		Ginevra	Corcoran gallery, Washington, D. C.
		California	Metropolitan museum, N. Y. city.
		Statue of Webster	State house, Boston, Mass.
		Statue of Jefferson	Capitol at Washington, D. C.
		La Penserosa	Lenox library, N. Y. city.
		Calhoun.	
am, Vinnie (Mrs. Hoxie)	1850–	Statue of Lincoln	Capitol at Washington, D. C.
		" " adm. Farragut	Washington, D. C.
		Spirit of the Carnival, The West, etc.	
mmer, William	1821–	Statue of Alexander Hamilton	Boston, Mass.
		Falling Gladiator, Head of St. Stephen.	
ineliart, William H.	1825–74	Clytie	Peabody institute, Baltimore, Md.
		Endymion	Corcoran gallery, Washington, D. C.
		Sleeping Children	Corcoran gallery, Washington, D. C.
		Statue of chief-justice Taney	Annapolis, Md.
berts, Howard	1843–	Hester Prynne, Première Rose, etc.	
gers, Randolph	1825–92	Statue of John Adams	Mount Auburn, near Boston, Mass.
		" " William H. Seward	Madison square, N. Y. city.
		Soldiers' monument	Providence, R. I.
		Angel of the Resurrection	Hartford, Conn.
gers, John	1829–	Slave Auction, The Picket Guard, School Days, One More Shot, John Alden, etc.—small plaster groups.	
int-Gaudens, Augustus	1848–	Statue of adm. Farragut	New York city.
		" " Lincoln	Lincoln park, Chicago.
		" " The Puritan	Springfield, Mass.
nmons, Franklin	1842–	Statue of Roger Williams	National Statuary hall, Washington, D.C.
		" " Oliver P. Morton	Indianapolis, Ind.
		" " Longfellow	Portland, Me.
		Naval monument	Front of national capitol, " "
bbins, Emma	1815–82	Angel of the Waters	Central park, N. Y. city.
		Statue of Columbus	Central park, N. Y. city.
ne, Horatio	1810–75	Statue of Alexander Hamilton	National Statuary hall, Washington, D.C.
ry, William W.	1819–95	Beethoven	Boston, Mass.
		Statue of George Peabody	London, Engl.
		Statue of Philip Barton Key	San Francisco, Cal.
		" " Edward Everett	Boston, Mass.
		Cleopatra and Semiramis	Metropolitan Museum of Art, N. Y. city.
ompson, Launt	1833–94	Bust of William Cullen Bryant	Central park, N. Y. city.
		Statue of gen. Scott	Soldiers' Home, Washington, D. C.
		" " Napoleon	Mr. Pinchot, Milford, Pa.
		Bust of Rocky Mountain Trapper.	
		Equestrian statue of gen. Burnside	Providence, R. I.
rner, William Green	1833–	Transition	Philadelphia Academy of Fine Arts.
		Fisherman's Daughter	Collection of Mr. Wolverton, Philadelphia, Pa.
		Rhoda, etc.	
ard, John Q. A.	1830–	Statue of com. O. H. Perry	Newport, R. I.
		Statue of Washington	U. S. Sub-treasury building, N. Y. city
		The Indian Hunter	Central park, N. Y. city.
		Statue of Shakespeare	Central park, N. Y. city.
		Freedman	Capitol at Washington, D. C.
		Equestrian statue of gen. G. H. Thomas	Washington, D. C.
		Statue of com. Perry	Newport, R. I.
		Bronze statue of Horace Greeley (sitting)	Front of *Tribune* building, N. Y. city.
rner, Olin L.	1844–	Statue of gov. Buckingham.	
		" " William Lloyd Garrison.	

DANISH.

Name.	Flourished.	Best works.	Present location.
orwaldsen, Bertel	1770–1844	Jason	Thorwaldsen museum, Copenhagen, Denmark.
		Cupid and Psyche	Thorwaldsen museum, Copenhagen, Denmark.
		Night and Morning	Thorwaldsen museum, Copenhagen, Denmark.
		Ganymede and the Eagle	Thorwaldsen museum, Copenhagen, Denmark.
		Dying Lion	Lucerne, Switzerland.
		Schiller monument	Stuttgart, Germany.
		The Last Supper	Copenhagen, Denmark.
		Equestrian statue of Maximilian	Munich, Germany.

ENGLISH.

Name.	Flourished.	Best works.	Present location.
con, John	1740–99	Monument of earl of Chatham	Westminster abbey
		" " John Howard	St. Paul's, London.
		" " dr. Samuel Johnson	St. Paul's, London.
		Statue of Blackstone	All-Souls' college, Oxford.

RENAISSANCE AND MODERN SCULPTORS.—(*Continued.*)

ENGLISH.

Name.	Flourished.	Best works.	Present location.
Banks, Thomas	1738–1805	Cupid catching a Butterfly	Russia.
		Caractacus before Claudius	Stowe, Engl.
		Monument of sir Eyre Coote	Westminster abbey.
Behnes, William	1801–64	Statue of Havelock	Trafalgar square, London.
		" " dr. Bell	Westminster abbey.
Campbell, Thomas	1790–1858	Statue of Mrs. Siddons	" "
		" " lord Bentinck	Cavendish square, London.
Chantrey, Sir Francis	1782–1841	Statue of George III	London.
		Two Sleeping Children	Lichfield chapel.
		Statue of James Watt	Westminster abbey.
		" " bishop Heber	St. Paul's, London.
		" " Washington	State house, Boston, Mass.
Cibber, Caius G	1630–1700	Figures of Raving and Melancholy Madness	South Kensington museum, London.
		" " Faith and Hope	Chapel, Chatsworth.
Damer, Anne Seymour	1748–1828	Statue (colossal) of George III	Register's office, Edinburgh.
		Bust of Nelson	Guildhall, London.
		Bust of Bacchus	University gallery, Oxford.
Flaxman, John	1755–1826	Statue of Pitt	Glasgow, Scotland.
		" " sir John Moore	Glasgow, Scotland.
		" " Robert Burns	Edinburgh.
		Archangel Michael and Satan.	
Foley, John Henry	1818–74	Statue of Hampden	Parliament house.
		" " father Mathew	Cork.
		" " John Stuart Mill.	
		" " Burke and of Goldsmith	Glasgow, Scotland.
		" " Stonewall Jackson	Richmond, Va.
		Figure of Prince Consort	Albert memorial, London.
Gibbons, Grinling	1650–1721	Decorations in Wood-carving	Chatsworth, Engl.
Gibson, John	1791–1866	Mars and Cupid	Collection of duke Devonshire.
		Psyche borne by Zephyrs	" " sir George Beamont.
		Statue of queen Victoria	Buckingham palace.
Nollekens, Joseph	1737–1823	Officers' monument	Westminster abbey.
		Medallion of Goldsmith	Westminster abbey.
		Tomb of bishop Thomas	Westminster abbey.
Rossi, John Charles F	1762–1839	Monument of lord Cornwallis	St. Paul's, London.
		" " lord Rodney	St. Paul's, London.
Stevens, Alfred G	1817–75	Monument of duke of Wellington	St. Paul's, London.
Westmacott, Sir Richard	1775–1856	Monument of Fox	Westminster abbey.
		" " gens. Pakenham and Gibbs	St. Paul's, London.
		Statue of duke of Wellington	Hyde park, London.
Westmacott, Richard	1799–1872	Wycliffe preaching (bas-relief)	Church, Lutterworth.
		David with head of Goliath, Guardian Angel, Resignation.	
Wilton, Joseph	1722–1803	Monument to gen. Wolfe	Westminster abbey.
Woolner, Thomas	1825–92	Statue of Macaulay	Cambridge, Engl.
		" " lord Bacon	Oxford, Engl.
		Busts of Darwin, Tennyson, Cobden, Gladstone, Dickens, Carlyle, Kingsley	Westminster abbey.
		Death of Boadicea, etc.	
Wyatt, Matthew Cotes	1778–1862	Equestrian statue of Wellington	Green park arch, London.
		Statue of George III	Pall Mall.
		Monument to lord Nelson	Liverpool.

FRENCH.

Name.	Flourished.	Best works.	Present location.
Auguier, François	1604–69	Monument of duc de Rohan	Louvre, Paris.
		Marble Crucifix	Church of the Sorbonne, Paris.
Auguier, Michel	1612–86	Nativity	Church of Val de Grace.
		Bust of Colbert	Louvre, Paris.
		Christ on the Cross	St. Roche, Paris.
		Statues of Pluto, Ceres, Neptune, and Amphitrite.	
Bartholdi, Frédéric Auguste	1834–	Lion	Belfort.
		Malediction of Alsace	Paris.
		Statue of Lafayette.	
		Liberty Enlightening the World	New York harbor.
Barye, Antoine L	1795–1875	Combat of the Centaurs.	
		Lion	Colonnade Juillet, Paris.
		Jaguar devouring a Hare	Luxembourg gallery, Paris.
		Lion and Boa	Tuileries.
		Tiger fighting a Crocodile.	
		Collection of sculptures (114 pieces)	Corcoran gallery, Washington, D. C.
Bosio, François Joseph	1769–1845	Reliefs	Colonne Vendôme.
		Marble group	Chapelle Expiatoire, Paris.
Bouchardon, Edme	1698–1762	Statues of the Apostles	St. Sulpice, Paris.
		Cupid and Psyche	Louvre, Paris.
		Girl with a Stag	Louvre, Paris.
Chaudet, Antoine D	1763–1810	Shepherd of Polybus carrying away Œdipus	" "
		Statue of Napoleon	Old museum, Berlin.
Colomb, Michael	1431–1514	Bas-relief of St. George and the Dragon	Louvre, Paris.
Cortot, Jean Pierre	1787–1843	Marble group	Chapelle Expiatoire, Paris.
		Crowning of Napoleon	Arc de l'Étoile.
Coysevox, Charles A	1640–1715	Bust of Richelieu	Louvre, Paris.
		Fame and Mercury	Garden of Tuileries.
Dalou, Jules	1838–	Allegorical group—The Triumph of the Republic	Paris.
		États-Généraux	"
David, Pierre Jean	1789–1856	Statue of Jefferson	Hall of Statuary, Washington, D. C.
		" " Gutenberg	Strasburg, Germany.
Duquesnoy, François	1594–1646	Groups of Children	St. Peter's, Rome.
		Statue of St. Andrew	St. Peter's, Rome.
Fremin, Réné	1673–1745	Saint Sylvie, Bas-relief of Notre Dame, Hercules, Minerva, etc.	
Girardon, François	1628–1715	Rape of Proserpine	Gardens, Versailles.
		Monument of Richelieu	Church of the Sorbonne, Paris.
Goujon, Jean	1515–72	Fountain of the Innocents	Paris.
		Statue of Diana	Louvre, Paris.
		Four Evangelists	Louvre, Paris.

RENAISSANCE AND MODERN SCULPTORS.—(*Continued.*)

FRENCH.

Name.	Flourished.	Best works.	Present location.
illain, Simon	1581–1658	Bronze statue of Louis XIII	Louvre, Paris.
illaume, Jean Baptiste	1822–	Theseus.	
udon, Jean Antoine	1741–1828	Statue of Voltaire	Théâtre Français, Paris.
		" " Washington	State house, Richmond, Va.
		Bust of Lafayette	
		" " Washington	Collection of Hamilton Fish, N. Y. city.
ste, Jean	–1534	Monument of Louis XIII. and Anne of Bretagne	Abbey church, St. Denis.
maire, Philippe H	1798–1880	Last Judgment	Pediment of the Madeleine, Paris.
		Sculptures	Gallery of the Luxembourg, Paris.
Mot, François F	1773–1827	Bas-reliefs	Façade of Louvre, Paris.
galle, Jean Baptiste	1714–85	Monument of marshal Saxe	Strasburg, Germany.
		Statue of Voltaire	Institute of France, Paris.
		Venus	Sans Souci, *Potsdam.*
lon, Germain	1520–90	Monument of Henry II. and Catherine de' Medici	Abbey church, St. Denis.
adier, *Jacques*	1790–1852	Niobe group	Luxembourg gallery, Paris.
		Psyche	
		Marriage of the Virgin	Madeleine, Paris.
get, Pierre	1622–94	Milo of Crotona	Louvre, Paris.
		Perseus liberating Andromeda	
		Alexander and *Diogenes*	
din, Auguste	1840–	Statue of Dante	Paris.
		Decorates the entrance of the Palace of Arts, etc.	
ubiliac, Louis F	1695–1762	Statue of sir Isaac Newton	Trinity college, Cambridge, Engl.
		Monument to Handel	Westminster abbey.
		Mrs. Nightingale	
de, François	1784–1855	Statue of Joan of Arc	Garden of the Luxembourg, Paris.
		" " marshal Ney	

GERMAN, FLEMISH, AND DUTCH.

Name.	Flourished.	Best works.	Present location.
gas, Rheinhold	1831–	Monument to Schiller	Berlin, Germany.
		Rape of the Sabines.	
nnecker, John Henry	1758–1841	Statue of Christ	St. Petersburg, Russia.
		Bust of Schiller	Museum, Stuttgart, Germany.
		Bacchus	New Palace, Stuttgart, Germany.
		Venus	
ake, Friedrich	1805–82	Equestrian statue of William of Prussia	Cologne, Germany.
		Allegorical figure of Prussian Provinces	Palace, Berlin, Germany.
		Statue of Melancthon	Wittenberg, Germany.
		Dying Warrior	Aix-la-Chapelle, Germany.
afft, Adam	1430–1507	Seven Stages	Nuremberg, Germany.
		Entombment	Cemetery, Nuremberg, Germany.
ss, Augustus	1802–65	Equestrian statue of Frederick the Great	Breslau, Germany.
		Model of equestrian statue of Frederick the Great	Pennsylvania Academy of Fine Arts, Philadelphia, Pa.
uch, Christian D	1777–1857	Statue of Frederick William III	Potsdam, Germany.
		Statue of queen Louise	Sans Souci, Potsdam, Germany.
		Monument of Frederick the Great	Unter den Linden, Berlin, Germany.
		Statue of Albert Dürer	Nuremberg, Germany.
		" " Blücher	Berlin, Germany.
		Victories	Walhalla, Ratisbon, Germany.
		Moses	Potsdam, Germany.
etschel, Ernst	1804–61	Statues of Goethe and Schiller	Weimar, "
		Madonna and the Dead Christ	Potsdam, "
		Statue of Lessing	Brunswick, "
		Luther monument	Worms, "
		Quadriga	Portal of the Palace, Brunswick.
		Reliefs	Hall of University, Leipsic.
		Morning, Noon, Evening, and Night	Dresden, private collection.
hadow, John Gottfried	1764–1850	Statue of Frederick the Great	Stettin, Germany.
		" " Blücher	Rostock, "
		" " Luther	Wittenberg, Germany.
hievelbein, Herman	1817–67	Pegasus and the Horæ	Old museum, Berlin.
		Destruction of Pompeii	New museum, "
hwanthaler, Ludwig M.	1802–48	Statue of Bavaria	Hall of Fame, Munich.
		" " Mozart	Salzburg, Austria.
		" " Jean Paul Friedrich Richter	Baireuth, Germany.
		" " Goethe	Frankfort-on-the-Main.
		" " Christ and Evangelists	Munich, Germany.
		Shield of Hercules	Frankfort-on-the-Main.
		Pediment group	Walhalla, Ratisbon, Germany.
oss, Veit	1438–1533	High altar	St. Mary's, Cracow, Austria.
		Monument of Casimir the Great	Cracow, Austria.
		Panel of roses	Nuremberg, Germany.
eck, Christian F	1776–1851	Sculptures	Theatre, Berlin, Germany.
scher, Peter	1460–1529	Tomb of S. Sebald	Nuremberg, Germany.
		Monument of bishop Ernst	Magdeburg, "
		Statue of Apollo	Nuremberg, "

ITALIAN.

Name.	Flourished.	Best works.	Present location.
gardi, Alessandro	1598–1654	Flight of Attila	St. Peter's, Rome.
		God of Sleep	Villa Borghese, Rome.
nadeo, Giovanni A	1400–74	Monument of Colleoni	Chapel, Bergamo.
		Sculptures	Certosa, Pavia.
nmanati, Bartolommeo	1511–89	Statues of the Four Seasons	Florence, Italy.
ndinelli, Baccio	1487–1559	Hercules and Cacus	Palazzo Vecchio, Florence, Italy.
		Adam and Eve	
rnini, Giovanni L	1598–1680	Apollo and Daphne	Villa Borghese, Rome.
		Tomb of Urban VIII	St. Peter's, Rome.
		" " Alexander VII	
		Rape of Proserpine	Villa Ludovisi, Rome.
logna, Jean de	1524–1608	Flying Mercury	Uffizi gallery, Florence.
		Equestrian statue of Cosmo I	Florence.
		Rape of the Sabines	Loggia de' Lanzi.
		Crucifixion	Cathedral, Pisa.
		Bronze doors	

RENAISSANCE AND MODERN SCULPTORS.—(*Continued.*)

Name.	Flourished.	Best works.	Present location.
		ITALIAN.	
Buonarotti, Michael Angelo	1475–1564	Head of Faun	Uffizi gallery, Florence.
		Battle of Hercules and Centaurs	Casa Buonarotti, Florence.
		Kneeling Cupid	South Kensington museum, London.
		Statue of David	Academy of Fine Arts, Florence.
		" " Christ	Rome.
		Tombs of the Medici	Florence.
		Madonna and Child	
		Captives	Louvre, Paris.
		Madonna of Bruges	Cathedral, Bruges.
Canova, Antonio	1757–1822	Tomb of the archduchess Christina of Austria	Church of the Augustines, Vienna.
		Dædalus and Icarus	Pisani palace, Venice.
		Theseus conquering the Minotaur	Vienna.
		Perseus	Vatican, Rome.
		Venus Victrix	Borghese gallery, Rome.
		Hebe	Museum, Berlin.
		Psyche	Royal palace, Munich.
		Statue of Napoleon	Apsley house, London.
		" " Washington	State house, Raleigh, N. C.
		Venus at the Bath	Pitti palace, Florence.
		Cupid and Psyche	Villa Carlotta, Como.
		Monument of Alfieri	S. Croce, Florence.
		Busts of eminent Italians	Palace Conservatori, Rome.
		Head	Corcoran gallery, Washington, D. C.
Donatello (Donato di Betto Bardi)	1386–1468	Relief in marble, Dancing Children	Uffizi gallery, Florence.
		Bronze David	
		" Judith	Loggia de' Lanzi.
		Equestrian statue of Francesco Gattamalota	Padua, Italy.
Fiesole, Mino da	1400–86	Sculptures	Badia, Florence.
		Monument of pope Paul II	St. Peter's, Rome.
		Marble pulpit	Cathedral, Prato.
		Ciborium	Baptistery, Volterra.
Ghiberti, Lorenzo	1381–1455	Bronze doors	" Florence.
		Statue of John the Baptist	San Michele, "
		" " St. Matthew	
		" " St. Stephen	
Leopardo, Alessandro	1450–1510	Statue of Colleoni	San Marco, Venice.
		Pedestals of the Pillars of S. Marco	
		Altar in Zeno chapel	
Lombardi, Alfonso	1488–1537	Reliefs	Cathedral, Cesena.
		Hercules and Hydra	Palazzo Publico, Bologna.
Majano, Benedetto da	1444–98	Tomb of Filippo Strozzi	Florence.
		Marble pulpit	
Pisano, Niccolá	1207–78	" "	Baptistery, Pisa.
		" "	Cathedral, Siena.
		Fountain	Perugia, Italy.
Pisano, Giovanni	1240–1320	Statue of Madonna	Cathedral, Florence.
		Marble pulpit	" Pistoja.
		" "	" Pisa.
Porta, Fra Guglielmo della	1512–77	Monument of pope Paul III	St. Peter's, Rome.
		Statues of Peace and Plenty	Farnese palace, Rome.
Robbia, Luca della	1400–81	Reliefs	Campanile, Florence.
		Bronze door of sacristy	Cathedral, "
		Altar in terra-cotta	S. Apostili, "
		Works of Luca and his school	Museum Bargello, Florence.
Rossellino, Antonio	1427–90	Monument of Mary of Aragon	Monte Oliveto, Naples.
		Reliefs upon Pulpit	
		Reliefs	Uffizi gallery, Florence.
Rossellino, Bernardo	1409–70	Monument of Leonardi Bruni	S. Croce, Florence.
		" " Beato Villani	S. M. Novella, Florence.
		Bust of St. John	Uffizi gallery, "
Sansovino, Andrea	1460–1529	Baptism of Christ	Baptistery, "
		Virgin Child and St. Anna	S. Agostino, "
		Statues and reliefs	Casa Santa, Loreto.
Sansovino, Jacopo Tatti	1477–1570	Bronze reliefs	S. Marco, Venice.
		Bronze gates of the sacristy	
		Four Evangelists	
		Statue of St. John	Font S. M. die Frari, Venice.
Vela, Vincenzo	1822–91	Sparticus and The Dying Napoleon.	
Verrocchio, Andrea del	1432–88	Bronze David	Museum Bargello, Florence.
		Equestrian statue of Colleoni, St. Thomas, and Christ	Venice, and San Michele, Florence.
		RUSSIAN.	
Martos, Ivan Petrovitch	1760–1835	Statues of Minin and Pozharski	Moscow, Russia.
		Monument of prince Potemkin	Cherson, "
		" " emperor Alexander	Taganrog, "
		SPANISH.	
Alvarez, Don José	1768–1827	Statue of Ganymede	Academy of San Fernando, Madrid
Berruguete, Alonzo	1480–1561	Reliefs	Cathedral, Toledo.
		Monument of cardinal Tavera	Hospital of San Juan.
Cano, Alonzo	1601–67		
Hernandez, Gregorio	1566–1636	Bas-relief, Baptism of Christ	Museum of Valladolid.
Montañes, Juan M.	–1650	Conception	Cathedral, Seville.
		Sculptures	Museum, "
Roldan, Pedro	1624–1700	The Entombment of Christ	Seville, Spain.

scu'tage or **es'cuage.** The service of the shield (scutum) in England is either uncertain or certain. Escuage uncertain is where the tenant by his tenure is bound to follow his lord; and is called castleward, where the tenant is bound to defend a castle. Escuage certain is where the tenant is set at a certain sum of money to be paid in lieu of such uncertain services. The first tax levied in England to pay an army, 5 Hen. II. 1159.—*Cowel.*

Scu'tari, a city of Asiatic Turkey, opposite Constantinople, of which it is a suburb. It was anciently called *Chrysopolis,* golden city, in consequence, it is said, of the Persians having established a treasury here when they attempted the nquest of Greece. Near here Constantine finally defeated cinius, 323.

Scyth'ia, a country situate in the most northern parts Europe and Asia. The boundaries were unknown to the cients. The Scythians made several irruptions upon the ›re southern provinces of Asia, especially 624 B.C., when ey remained in possession of Asia Minor for 28 years, and different periods extended their conquests in Europe, pen-ating as far as Egypt. TARTARY.

sea. Lieut. Maury, U. S. N., first published his "Physical ography of the Sea" in 1854, and other important works ce; he died Feb. 1873. DEEP-SEA SOUNDINGS.

seals or **signets.** Engraved gems were used as such the Egyptians, Jews, Assyrians, and Greeks; see Exod. viii. 14. Ahab's seal was used by Jezebel, 899 B.C. (1 Kings i. 8). The Romans in the time of the Tarquins (about 600 .) had gemmed rings. They sealed rooms, granaries, bags money, etc. The German emperor, Frederick I. (1152 A.D.) d seals of gold, silver, and tin. Impressions of the seals of xon kings are extant; and the English great seal is attrib-ed to Edward the Confessor (1041-66). "A seal with armo-l bearings before the 11th century is certainly false."—*sbroke.* The most ancient English seal with arms on it is d to be that of Richard I. or John. White or colored wax s used. The present sealing-wax, containing shellac, did t come into general use in Germany and England until about 56. Red wafers for seals came into use about 1624, but were t used for public seals till the 18th century. GREAT SEAL.

seas, Sovereignty of the. The claim of England to rule British seas is of very ancient date. Arthur is said to ve assumed it, and Alfred afterwards supported this right. was maintained by Selden, and measures were taken by English government in consequence, 8 Caro I. 1633. The tch, after the death of Charles I., made some attempts to ain it, but were roughly treated by Blake and other ad-rals. Russia and other powers of the north armed to avoid rch, 1780; again, 1800. ARMED NEUTRALITY, FLAG. The ernational rule of the road at sea was settled in 1862; yet r Great Britain alone there have been 13,000 collisions in years. Wm. Stirling Lacon proposes to reduce the rules m 749 words to 144, for simplicity and security. His form l been 9 times before Parliament, 1873.

Sebastian, St., a town of N. Spain, was taken by French, under the duke of Berwick, in 1719. It was be-ged by the allied army under Wellington. After a heavy nbardment, by which the whole town was laid nearly in ns, it was stormed by gen. Graham (afterwards lord Lyne-h), and taken 31 Aug. 1813. On 5 May, 1836, the fortified rks were carried by the English under gen. Evans. The itish naval squadron, off St. Sebastian, under lord John Hay, ed the victors in this contest. An assault was made on the es of gen. De Lacy Evans, at St. Sebastian, by the Carlists, Oct. 1836. The Carlists were repulsed. The loss of the glo-Spanish force was 376 men and 37 officers, killed and unded. LEAGUES.

Sebas'topol or **Sevas'topol,** a town and once a val arsenal, at southwest point of the Crimea, formerly the le village of Aktiar. The buildings were commenced in 84, by Catherine II., after conquering the country. The vn is in the shape of an amphitheatre, on the rise of a large l flattened on its summit, according to a plan laid down be-e 1794, which has been since adhered to. The fortifications l harbor were constructed by an English engineer, col. ton, and his sons, since 1830. The population in 1834 was 000. This place underwent 11 months' siege by the Eng-h and French in 1854 and 1855. Immediately after the bat-of the Alma, 20 Sept. 1854, the allied army marched to Se-stopol, occupied the plateau between it and Balaklava, and attack and bombardment commenced 17 Oct. 1854, with-t success. After many sanguinary encounters by day and ght, and repeated bombardments, a grand assault was made 8 Sept. 1855, upon the Malakhoff tower and the Redans, most important fortifications to the south of the town. e French succeeded in capturing and retaining the Mala-off, but the attacks of the English on the great Redan and the French upon the little Redan were repulsed after a desperate struggle. The French lost 1646 killed, of whom 5 were generals, 24 superior and 116 inferior officers, 4500 wounded, and 1400 missing. The English lost 385 killed (29 being commissioned and 42 non-commissioned officers), 1886 wounded, and 176 missing. In the night the Russians abandoned the southern and principal part of the town and fortifications, after destroying as much as possible, and crossed to the northern forts. They also sank or burned the remainder of their fleet. The allies found abundant stores when they entered the place, 9 Sept. The works were utterly destroyed in Apr. 1856, and the town was restored to the Russians in July. RUSSO-TURKISH WARS.

secession ordinances of the Confederate States. CONFEDERATE STATES; UNITED STATES, 1861.

secret societies. ASSASSINS, FENIANS, RIBBONISM, ROSICRUCIANS, VEHMIC TRIBUNAL, etc.

secretaries of state. The earliest authentic record of a secretary of state is in the reign of Henry III., when John Maunsell is described as "*Secretarius Noster,*" 1253.—*Rymer.* Towards the close of Henry VIII.'s reign, 2 secretaries were appointed; and upon the union with Scotland, Anne added a third as secretary for Scotch affairs; this appointment was afterwards laid aside; but in the reign of George III. the number was again increased to 3, 1 for the American department. In 1782 this last was abolished by act of Parliament; and secretaries were appointed for home, foreign, and colonial affairs. When there were but 2 secretaries, 1 held the *portefeuille* of the northern department, comprising the Low Countries, Germany, Denmark, Sweden, Poland, Russia, etc.; the other, of the southern department, including France, Switzerland, Italy, Spain, Portugal, and Turkey; the affairs of Ireland belonging to the elder secretary; both secretaries then equally directed the home affairs.—*Beatson.* The British government now has 5 secretaries—home, foreign, colonial, war, and (in 1858) India, all in the cabinet. ADMINISTRATION. For the United States, CABINET; UNITED STATES throughout.

sects in religion are the various bodies separated from each other by doctrinal belief. They may be classified as Christian, Jewish, Mahometan, and Heathen. More or less extended summaries of the various sects in the list here given may be found under their respective titles.

EARLY CHRISTIAN (1st to 7th century A.D.).

Abelians.
Acacians.
Adamites.
Ærians.
Agnoitæ.
Apollonarists.
Aquarians.
Arians.
Armenians.
Audiani.
Cataphrygians.
Cathari.
Cyrenaic sect.
Docetæ.
Donatists.
Ebionites.
Encratites (AQUARIANS).
Eutychians.
Greek church.
Jacobites.
Manicheans.
Marcionites.
Maronites.
Messalians.
Millenarians.
Monothelites.
Montanists.
Nazarenes.
Nestorians.
Novatians.
Origenists.
Paulianists.
Pelagians.
Priscillianists.
Sabellians.
Simonians.
Water Drinkers (AQUARIANS).
Zanzaleens.

MEDIÆVAL CHRISTIAN.

Abrahamites.
Adamites.
Albigenses.
Apostolici.
Berengarians.
Bohemian Brethren.
Calixtins.
Lollards.
Mystics.
Paulicians.
Scotists.
Waldenses.
Wickliffites.

MODERN CHRISTIAN (Reformation and subsequent).

Adventists.
Anabaptists.
Arminians.
Baptists.
Broad church.
Burghers.
Calvinists.
Cameronians.
Camisards.
Campbellites.
Christian Connection.
Christian Endeavor Society.
Congregationalists.
Cumberland Presbyterian (PRESBYTERIAN).
Disciples of Christ.
Dutch Reformed (REFORMED CHURCH IN AMERICA).
Episcopalians (CHURCH).
Evangelical Association.
Free-will Baptists.
Friends (QUAKERS).
German Reformed (REFORMED CHURCH IN THE UNITED STATES).
Glasites.
Gospellers.
Greek.
Illuminati.
Independents.
Irvingites.

Jansenists.
Lutherans (17 synods and bodies).
Mennonites (12 divisions, generally communistic).
Methodist Episcopal.
Millerites.
Molinists.
Moravians.
Mormons or Latter-day Saints, reorganized.
Muggletonians.
Nonjurors.
Old Catholics.
Plymouth Brethren.
Pietists.
Pre-Adamites.
Presbyterians.
Puseyites.
Quakers { Orthodox. Hicksites. Wilburites. Primitive.
Quietists.
Reformed Church in America.
" " in the United States.
Reformed Episcopal.
Ritualists.
ROMAN CATHOLICS (CHURCH).
Sabbatarians.
Sandemanians (GLASITES).
Separatists (CONGREGATIONALISTS).
Seventh-day Baptists (SABBATARIANS).
Shakers.
Socinians.
Southcotters.
Spiritualists.
Supralapsarians.
Swedenborgians.
Tunkers.
Ubiquitarians.
Unitarians.
United Brethern.
United Presbyterians.
Universalists.
Wesleyan Methodists.
Whitefieldites.
Zoarites.
Zwinglians.

JEWISH.

Essenes.
Karaites.
Nazarenes.
Pharisees.
Sadducees.

MAHOMETAN.

Ali.
Almohades.
Almoravides.
Babi-ists.
Carmathians.
Fatamists (ALI).
Shiites.
Sonnites.
Wahabees or Wahabites.

For heathen religions and sects, BRAHMO SOMAJ, BRAHMINS, BUDDHISTS, GUEBRES, JAINS, MAGI OF FIRE-WORSHIPPERS, PARSEES, and YEZIDEES OF DEVIL-WORSHIPPERS.
For the various schools of thought, ATHEISM, DEISM, HUMANITARIANS, HUTCHINSONIANS, MATERIALISM, PANTHEISM, PHILOSOPHY, POSITIVISM, RATIONALISM, and SECULARISM.
For doctrines and church parties, ANTINOMIANS, ANTITRINITARIANS, DISSENTERS, LATITUDINARIANS, NONCONFORMISTS, PURITANS, SOLIFIDIANS, TRINITARIANS, and ULTRAMONTISTS.

secular games (*ludi sæculares*), very ancient Roman games, celebrated on important occasions. Horace wrote his "Carmen Sæculare" for their celebration in the reign of the emperor Augustus (17). They took place again in the reign of Claudius (47), of Domitian (88), and, for the last time, in that of Philip (248), when it was claimed that 2000 years had elapsed since the foundation of the city.

secularism, a name given to the principles advocated by G. J. and Austin Holyoake, about 1846, and since by Mr. Bradlaugh. Its central idea is free, not lawless, thought, and it considers scepticism to be scrutiny. It advocates liberty of action without injury to others. It is not against Christianity, but independent of it. Its standard is utilitarian; it is the religion of the present life only; teaching men to seek morality in nature, and happiness in duty. Austin Holyoake and other secularists repudiated atheism; Mr. Bradlaugh and others profess it.

Sedan', an ancient fortified city in the valley of the Meuse, N.E. of France, the seat of a principality long held by the dukes of Bouillon. On 6 July, 1641, a victory was gained at La Marfée, near Sedan, by the count of Soissons and the troops of Bouillon and other French princes, over the royal army supporting Richelieu; but the count was slain on 23 June, 1642. The duke was arrested in the midst of his army, and was made to cede Sedan to the crown. The Protestant university was abolished after the revocation of the edict of Nantes, 22 Oct. 1685. Around this place a series of desperate conflicts on 29, 30, and 31 Aug., between the French army of the north, under marshal MacMahon (about 150,000 men), and the greater part of the 3 German armies under the king and crown-prince of Prussia, and the crown-prince of Saxony (about 250,000 men), was brought to a close on 1 Sept. 1870.

The battle began with attacks on the French right and left about 5 A.M., and was very severe at 2 P.M. At 4 P.M. the Germans remained masters of the field, and the crown-prince of Prussia announced a complete victory, the chief part of the French army retreating into Sedan. The emperor Napoleon was present during the battle. The Germans contracted their circle close round Sedan; their artillery held all the heights, from which they could destroy the town and the army. At first gen. De Wimpffen (called to the command when MacMahon was wounded) rejected the terms offered by the victor, and the emperor had a fruitless interview with count Bismarck to endeavor to mitigate them. On 2 Sept. the emperor wrote in autograph to the king of Prussia, "Mon frère, n'ayant pu mourir à la tête de mes troupes, je dépose mon épée au pied de votre majesté.—Napoleon." A capitulation of Sedan and the whole army therein was signed by generals Von Moltke and De Wimpffen at the château of Bellevue, near Frenois, at 11.30 A.M., 2 Sept. About 25,000 French prisoners were taken in the battle, and 83,000 surrendered, together with 70 mitrailleuses, 400 field-pieces, and 150 fortress guns. The French emperor and his suite arrived at Wilhelmshöhe, a castle near Cassel appointed for his residence (formerly inhabited by his uncle Jerome, when king of Westphalia), on the evening of 5 Sept. In a letter dated 12 May, 1872, the emperor Napoleon took upon himself the whole responsibility of the surrender of Sedan.

Sedan' chairs (so called from Sedan) were first seen in England in 1581. One used in the reign of James I., by the duke of Buckingham, excited indignation, the people declaring that he was employing fellow-creatures to do the service of beasts. Sedan chairs came into London in 1634, when sir Francis Duncomb obtained the sole privilege to use, let, and hire a number of them for 14 years. They came into general use in 1649.

Sedgemoor, a wild country of Somersetshire, Engl., where the duke of Monmouth (natural son of Charles II. by Lucy Waters), who had risen in rebellion on the accession of James II., was completely defeated by the royal army, 6 July, 1685. The duke, in the disguise of a peasant, at the bottom of a ditch, overcome with hunger and fatigue, was made a prisoner. He was tried and beheaded on 15 July following. BLOODY ASSIZES.

sedition. Sedition acts were passed in England in the reign of George III. The proclamation against seditious writings was published May, 1792. The celebrated Sedition bill passed Dec. 1795. Seditious societies were suppressed by act, June, 1797. The Seditious Meetings and Assemblies bill passed 31 Mch. 1817. In Ireland, during the Roman Catholic and Repeal agitation, acts or proclamations against sedition and seditious meetings were published from time to time until 1848. ALIEN AND SEDITION LAWS.

Seekers. QUAKERS.

Segedin (*seg-ed-in'*) or **Szegedin,** a town of Hungary. Here was concluded a treaty between Ladislaus IV. and Amurath II., 12 July, 1444. It was treacherously annulled at the instigation of cardinal Julian, who with Ladislaus perished in the fatal battle of Varna, 10 Nov. 1444. VARNA.

seismom'eter (from σεισμός, Greek for earthquake), an apparatus for measuring earthquake shocks, in violence, duration, and amplitude of movement. One is described by Robert Mallet in his work on earthquakes, pub. 1858.

selection, natural. SPECIES.

selectmen, the earliest officers of the townships formed by the first colonists of New England, 1635. MASSACHUSETTS, 1635.

sele'nium, a grayish-white elementary substance (chemically resembling sulphur), discovered in the stone riolite by Berzelius in 1817.

The variation in its resistance to the electric current when subjected to light was observed by Willoughby Smith in 1873, and utilized in the PHOTOPHONE. Dr. C. William Siemens constructed a "selenium eye."

Seleu'cia, Syria, made the capital of the Syrian monarchy by its builder, Seleucus Nicator, 312 B.C. On the fall of the Seleucidæ, it became a republic, 65 B.C. It was taken by Trajan, 116 A.D.; several times given up and retaken; subjugated by the Saracens, and united with Ctesiphon, 636.

Seleu'cidæ, Era of the, dates from the reign of Seleucus Nicator. It was used in Syria for many years, and frequently by the Jews until the 15th century, and by some Arabians. Opinions vary as to its commencement. To reduce it to our era (supposing it to begin 1 Sept. 312 B.C.), subtract 311 years 4 months.

self-denying ordinance, that no member of Parliament should hold any civil or military office or command conferred by either or both of the houses, or by authority derived from them, was passed after much discussion, 3 Apr. 1645, by the influence of Cromwell, who thus removed the earl of Essex and other Presbyterians out of his way. A somewhat similar ordinance was adopted by the parliament at Melbourne in Australia, in 1858. The name was given to

ı arrangement made respecting British naval promotions ıd retirements in 1870.

Sella'sia, a town of Laconia. Here the Spartans, un- ꝛr Cleomenes, were defeated by Antigonus Doson and the chæans, 221 B.C.

Semina'ra, a town of Naples. Near here Gonsalvo ꝫ Cordova, the great captain, was defeated by the French, ꜞ 1495; but defeated them, 21 Apr. 1503.

Semi'nole war. FLORIDA, 1833-42; UNITED STATES.

Semit'ic, a sub-division of the Caucasian race, so called ꜞ indicating descendants of Shem, a son of Noah. ALPHABET, THNOLOGY, LANGUAGE.

Sempach *(sem'pak)*, a town of Switzerland. Here the ꞩiss gained a great victory over Leopold, duke of Austria, July, 1386. The duke was slain, and the liberty of their ountry established. The day is still commemorated.

semper ea'dem ("always the same"), one of the ottoes of queen Elizabeth, was adopted by queen Anne, 13 ee. 1702. Many suspected this motto to denote her Jacotism, and it ceased to be used after her reign.

senate (Lat. *senatus*). In the ancient republics the government was divided between the *senatus* (from *senis*, old; in r. *γερουσία*, from *γέρων*, old), an assembly of the elders, ıd the popular assembly (*comitia*, Lat.; *ἐκκλησία*, Gr.), the ng being merely the executive. The Roman senate, said have had originally 100 members, was increased to 300 ꝛ Tarquinius Priscus; to about 600 by Sulla, about 81 B.C.; ıd to 900 by Julius Cæsar. It was reformed and reduced to 0 by Augustus; and gradually lost its power and dignity ıder the emperors. The mere form existed in the reign of ıstinian. A second senate, formed at Constantinople by onstantine, retained its office till the 9th century. S.P.Q.R. ı the Roman standard stood for "Senatus Populusque Romanus," "the senate and people of Rome." A *senatus consultum* was a law enacted by the senate. The French senate as created by the constitution of the year 8 of the Republic, omulgated 24 Dec. 1799, to watch over the administration of e laws. The number of senators was raised gradually from ꜞ to 137. The senate was replaced by the chamber of peers 1814; re-established by Napoleon III., 14 Jan. 1852; and olished, 5 Sept. 1870. The senate as now constituted by act 22 Feb. 1875, consists of 300 members, 225 elected by the departments for 9 years, one third retiring every 3 years; 75 for 'e, elected by the National Assembly. By the Senate bill of 384 it was enacted that vacancies arising among life-senators ould be filled by nine-year senators.

Senate of the United States. The constitution of the U. S. provides that Congress shall consist of a senate ıd a house of representatives. In the Senate, representation by states, without regard to population, each state having senators (chosen by their state legislatures for 6 years), one ird retiring every 2 years. The executive of any state has ıe power to make a temporary appointment of a senator if a ıcancy should occur in that state during the recess of its leglature. Senators must be at least 30 years of age, and be for years citizens of the U. S. The vice-president of the U. S. president of the Senate, without a vote on questions unless ıually divided. Besides its legislative capacity the Senate tifies or rejects all treaties made by the president with foreign ›wers, a two-thirds majority of senators present is required r ratification. The consent of the Senate is necessary to all ›pointments made by the president, and its members constitute high court of impeachment. The Senate also elects the vice-ꞩesident of the U. S. in case the electors fail to do so. For list members consult each state record; UNITED STATES, 1868.

Sen'ecas. INDIANS, LONG HOUSE.

Seneffe *(se-nef')*, a village of Belgium. Near here was ught a severe but indecisive battle between the Dutch, unꝛr the prince of Orange (afterwards William III. of England), and the French, led by the great Condé, 11 Aug. 1674.

Sen'egal, French colonies on the river of that name Senegambia, W. Africa, settled about 1626; several times ken by the British, but recovered by the French, to whom ıey were finally restored in 1814. Native tribes revolted, 1885; continued war of the French with the natives, 1890-1892. Area of Senegal proper about 54,000 sq. miles, with a pop. of 1,100,000, 1891. Chief town, St. Louis; pop. 20,000.

sen'eschal (from Goth. *sins*, old, and *skalks*, a servant, a high-steward). In the reign of Philip I. of France, 1059, the office was esteemed the highest place of trust in the royal household.

Senlac. HASTINGS.

Sen'ones, a people of Gallia, defeated by Camillus, 367 B.C. They defeated Metellus, the consul at Arretium, 284, but were almost exterminated by Dolabella, 283. They invaded Greece in 279; were defeated by Antigonus Gonatas, 278; and sued for peace. GAULS.

Sen'ova, near Schipka, in the Balkans. Here Suleiman Pacha and the Turks were defeated by the Russian general Skobeleff, 9 Jan. 1878. This victory virtually closed the war, and opened the road to Adrianople. About 26,000 Turks and 283 officers were made prisoners, with 40 Krupp guns. About 8000 Turks and 2000 Russians were killed or wounded.

Senti'num, central Italy. The site of a great victory of the Romans over the Samnites and Gauls, whose general, Gellius Egnatius, was slain, 295 B.C.

Separatists. CONGREGATIONALISTS.

Sephardim', the name given to the descendants of the highly civilized Jews of Spain and Portugal, who fled from the persecutions of the Inquisition, 1492-1505. The Jews interpret Sepharad, in Obadiah 20, as Spain.

sepoys (a corruption of *sipáhi*, Hindostanee for a soldier), the term applied to the native troops in India. Under able generals, they greatly aided in establishing British rule in India. INDIA, 1857; MUTINIES.

September, the 7th Roman month, reckoned from Mch. (from *septimus*, seventh). It became the 9th month when January and February were added to the year by Numa, 713 B.C. The Roman senate would have given this month the name of Tiberius, but the emperor opposed it; the emperor Domitian gave it his own name, Germanicus; the senate under Antoninus Pius gave it that of Antoninus; Commodus gave it his surname, Herculeus; and the emperor Tacitus his own name, Tacitus. "Sept. 4 government," FRANCE, Sept. 1870.

Septembriz'ers. In the French revolution, a dreadful massacre took place in Paris, 2-5 Sept. 1792. The prisons, especially the ABBAYE, were broken open, and the prisoners butchered, among them an ex-bishop, and nearly 100 non-juring priests. Some accounts put the number of persons slain at 1200, others at 4000. The agents in this slaughter were named Septembrizers.

septennial parliaments (English). Edward I. held but one parliament every 2 years. In 4 Edward III. it was enacted "that a parliament should be holden every year once." This continued to be law till the act of 16 Charles I., 1641, requiring a parliament once in three years at least; repealed in 1664. The Triennial act was re-enacted in 1694. Triennial parliaments thence continued till 2 Geo. I., 1716, when, in consequence of the allegation that "a popish faction were designing to renew the rebellion in this kingdom, and the report of an invasion from abroad," it was enacted that "the then parliament should continue for 7 years." This *Septennial act*, entitled "An Act for Enlarging the Continuance of Parliaments" (1715 in the statutes, 4to, given as 1 Geo. I. stat. 2, c. 38), was passed 7 May, 1716. PARLIAMENTS. Several unsuccessful motions have been made for its repeal; one in May, 1837.

Septuages'ima Sunday, 13 Feb. 1881; 5 Feb. 1882. *Septuagesima* is the season between Epiphany and Lent. QUADRAGESIMA SUNDAY and WEEK.

Sept'uagint Version of the Old Testament, made from Hebrew into Greek by order and during the reign of Ptolemy Philadelphus, king of Egypt (283-247 B.C.). King Ptolemy to Eleazer, the high-priest . . . "I have determined to procure an interpretation of your law and to have it translated out of Hebrew into Greek, and to be deposited in my library. Thou wilt therefore do well to choose out and send to me men of a good character who are now elders in age and 6 in number from every tribe to make accurate interpretations of them." . . .—Eleazer, the high-priest, to king Ptolemy . . . "We have also chosen 6 elders out of every tribe, whom we have sent, and the law with them." . . . "The labor of interpretation came to its conclusion in 72 days."—*Josephus*, "Antiquity of the Jews," bk. xii. chap. ii. Whiston's translation. This request of king Ptolemy was accompanied by an immense treasure as a present.

Ser'apis, a celebrated Egyptian deity, introduced into Greek worship, and temples were erected by the Romans to Jupiter-Serapis. A temple erected to him at Pozzuoli, near Naples, Italy, had its roof supported by 46 columns 42 ft. high and 5 ft. in diameter; 3 of these columns are now standing, and bear evidence of having been at some time submerged to half their height (12 ft.) in mud, and 9 ft. above this in water. The submerging and rising of this temple were thoroughly investigated by Lyell, being a subject of great geological interest.

seras'kier, the Turkish minister of war.

serfs. RUSSIA, 1861, 1863; SLAVERY, serfdom.

sergeants-at-law, in the English courts, are pleaders from among whom the judges are ordinarily chosen, and who are called sergeants of the coif. The judges call them brothers. COIF. Their exclusive rights of addressing court of Common Pleas suspended, 1834; restored, 1840; abolished, 1846. By the Supreme Court of Judicature act, judges on their appointment need not be made sergeants, 1873. INNS OF COURT.

Seringapatam', S. India, the capital of Hyder Ali, sovereign of MYSORE. The battle of Seringapatam, called also the battle of Arikera, in which the British defeated Tippoo Sahib, was fought 15 May, 1791. The redoubts were stormed, and Tippoo was reduced by lord Cornwallis, 6 Feb. 1792. After this capture, preliminaries of peace were signed, and Tippoo agreed to cede one half of Mysore, and to pay 33,000,000 rupees (about 3,300,000*l.*) to England, and to give up to lord Cornwallis his 2 eldest sons as hostages. In a new war, the Madras army, under gen. Harris, arrived before Seringapatam, 5 Apr. 1799; it was joined by the Bombay army, 14 Apr.; and the place was stormed and carried by maj.-gen. Baird, 4 May, same year. In this engagement Tippoo was killed.

serpent, an ancient wind instrument, parent of the cornet family. A "contra serpent" in the London exhibition, 1851, made by Jordan of Liverpool. The "serpentcleid" was produced by Beacham in Jullien's orchestra about 1840.

Serpent mound. An embankment in the form of a serpent many rods in length, in Adams county, Ohio, attributed to the mound-builders. This mound, with the surrounding land, belongs to Harvard university.

Ser'via, an hereditary principality south of Hungary, nominally subject to Turkey until 1878. The Servians are of Slavonic origin. They embraced Christianity about 640. The emperor Manuel subjugated them in 1150; but they recovered their independence in 1180, and were ruled by princes, generally named Stephen, till their country was finally subdued by the sultan Mahomet II., in 1459. Area, 18,855 sq. miles; pop. in 1854, 985,000; 1873, 1,338,505; 1876, 1,366,923; 1891, 2,162,759.

An empire founded by king Duschaw, 1340; Lazar, emperor, defeated, 15 June, 1389, by the Turks under Amurath I. in the plains of Cossova.

Servia subdued by Mahomet II. 1459
Ceded to Austria 1718
Regained by Turkey 1739
Servians aid Austria by free companies 1788-90
Again rebel, and capture Belgrade 1806
Kara George chosen leader, 1801; aided by the Russians, establishes a government 1807-11
Turks break a treaty, and Kara George flees 1814
Their governor, Milosch, rebels .... Mch. 1815
Kara George, returning, is executed 1816
Alexander Milosch I. (Obrenovitch) recognized as hereditary prince by the sultan .... 15 Aug. 1829
Milosch, becoming despotic, made to abdicate, and a new constitution established .... 13 June, 1839
His son and successor, Milan, dies, his brother Michael retires; Alexander, son of Kara George, chosen prince .... 14 Sept. 1842
Alexander, becoming unpopular, made to abdicate by the national party; Alexander Milosch re-elected .... 23 Dec. 1858
Plot against Milosch frustrated, 11 July; the Servian assembly meets .... 13 July, 1860
Milosch dies; succeeded by his son, Michael Obrenovitch (b. 4 Sept. 1825) .... 26 Sept. "
Movement for independence against Turkey .... Mch. 1861
Servians and the Turkish garrison at Belgrade quarrel, leading to bloodshed; the city bombarded, 15 June; submits, 17 June; the Turkish pacha dismissed .... 19 June, 1862
Representatives of the great powers meet at Constantinople, Aug.; the Porte agrees to liberal concessions to the Servians, which their prince accepts .... 7 Oct. "
Servians demand withdrawal of Turkish garrisons from Belgrade and other fortresses .... 5 Oct. 1866
Which are evacuated, Mch.; prince Michael, at Constantinople, thanks the sultan .... 30 Mch. 1867
Prince Michael assassinated in Belgrade .... 10 June, 1868
Milan IV., grand-nephew of prince Michael, chosen successor, 22 June; 14 murderers executed .... 28 July, "
Constitution affirming the hereditary rights of the Obrenovitch family 1869
Prince Karageorgevitch accused of complicity with murder; imprisoned at Pesth, Jan.; acquitted .... May, 1871
Regents surrender the government to prince Milan at Belgrade .... 22 Aug. 1872
Insurrection in Herzegovina; new ministry, hostile to Turkey, formed, about 31 Aug.; resign; announced, 4 Oct.; peace ministry formed .... 9 Oct. 1875
Marriage of the prince to Natalie Keschko, daughter of col. Keschko of the Russian Imperial guard .... 17 Oct. "
Ristics, premier, opposed to Turkey .... July, 1876
TURKEY for the war declared .... 1 July, "
Milan proclaimed king by Tchernayeff and the army at Deligrad; not approved .... 16 Sept. "
Peace with Turkey ratified .... 4 Mch. 1877
[Servian losses in the war, about 8000 killed, 20,000 wounded.]
Servians again declare war and enter Turkey (RUSSO-TURKISH WARS) .... 14, 15 Dec. "
Sultan deposes prince Milan .... 22 Dec. "
Servia declared independent, with new frontiers, by treaty of San Stefano, 3 Mch., and of Berlin .... 13 July, 1878
Execution of Markovitch and other rioters .... end of May, "
Proclamation of peace and national independence at Belgrade, 22 Aug. "
Ministry remodelled by Ristics .... about 15 Oct. "
Resignation of Ristics (virtual dictator) announced .... 25 Oct. 1880
Milan proclaimed king by the assembly .... 6 Mch. 1882
Declares war against BULGARIA .... 13 Nov. 1885
Success followed by disaster and retreat .... 14-24 Nov. "
Peace signed 3 Mch.; ratified by the sultan .... 13 Mch. 1886
Milan divorced from Natalie .... 24 Oct. 1888
[He favors Austria, she Russia.]
Queen protests against the divorce, 20 Aug. and 30 Oct.; the divorce decreed by the metropolitan Theodosius, abp. of Belgrade (authority questioned) .... Oct. "
Royal commission recommends universal suffrage; all electors eligible to the skuptschina; independence of the church; all religions free and protected; liberty of the press, etc., 24 Oct. "
Elections annulled by the king .... 26 Oct. "
New elections give majority to the radicals .... 16 Dec. "
Skuptschina opened .... 30 Dec. "
New constitution passed (494-73) .... 2 Jan. 1889
Milan abdicates, proclaiming his son Alexander (b. 14 Aug. 1876) king, under a regency until his majority (18 years) .... 6 Mch. "
Elections; great radical majority .... 1 Oct. "
Queen Natalie agitates to annul her isolation from her son; her petition to the parliament dismissed .... 8 Dec. et seq. 1890
King Milan agrees to live out of Servia till his son's majority, on receipt of a sum of money and a pension .... 14 Apr. 1891
Queen, requested by the government to leave the country, refuses; attempted expulsion met by riots and resistance; the queen forcibly conveyed to Semlin in Hungary .... 19 May, "
King Milan resigns all his military and political rights .... Nov. "
King Alexander arrests his regents and ministers and assumes the government .... 14 Apr. 1893
Ex-king Milan returns to Servia .... 21 Jan. 1894

HEREDITARY PRINCES.

1829. Milosch (Obrenovitch) I., recognized by Turkey, 15 Aug. 1833; abdicates, 13 June, 1839.
1839. Michael II., son; d. 1840.
1840. Michael III., brother; abdicates, 1842.
1842. Alexander (Karageorgevitch), son of Kara George; chosen, 14 Sept.; deposed, 23 Dec. 1858.
1858. Milosch (Obrenovitch) re-elected, 23 Dec.; d. 1860.
1860. Michael III., son; succeeds, 26 Sept.; assassinated, 10 June, 1868.
1868. Milan (Obrenovitch) IV., grand-nephew; again proclaimed, 2 July, 1868; marries Natalie Keschko (b. 1859), 17 Oct. 1875; abdicates, 6 Mch. 1889.
1889. Alexander I., son; b. 14 Aug. 1876.

servile wars, insurrections of slaves against their masters. 2 were quelled in Sicily, after much slaughter, 132, 99 B.C. SPARTACUS.

session courts in England were appointed to be held quarterly in 1413, and the times for holding them regulated in 1831. COURT OF SESSION, QUARTER SESSIONS. The *kirk session* in Scotland consists of the minister and eld-

of each parish. They superintend religious worship and cipline, dispense money collected for the poor, etc.

Sestos, on the Thracian Chersonesus. Near Sestos was western end of Xerxes' bridge across the Hellespont, 480 . Sestos was retaken from the Persians by the Athenians, , and held by them till 404, giving them the command of trade of the Euxine. HELLESPONT.

Settlement, Act of, for the succession to the British one, excluding Roman Catholics, was passed in 1689. This ne is also given to the statute by which the crown, after demise of William III. and queen Anne, without issue, s limited to Sophia, electress of Hanover, granddaughter of nes I., and her heirs, being Protestants, 1702. The Irish : of Settlement, passed in 1662, was repealed in 1689. HANER.

settlements in America. AMERICA, FRENCH IN ERICA, and each state of the United States separately.

seven brothers: Januarius, Felix, Philip, Silvanus, exander, Vitalis, and Martial, martyrs at Rome, under Aninus; their feast is kept 10 July.

seven champions of Christendom: St. orge, the patron saint of England, St. Denis of France, St. nes of Spain, St. Anthony of Italy, St. Andrew of Scotd, St. Patrick of Ireland, and St. David of Wales.

seven churches of Asia, to the angels (*minis*s) *of which the apostle* John was commanded to write the stles contained in the second and third chapters of his Revion — viz., Ephesus, Smyrna, Pergamos, Thyatira, Sardis, iladelphia, and Laodicea, 96.

EPH'ESUS. Paul founded the church here, 57. In 59, he was in reat danger from a *tumult created* by Demetrius; to the elders f this church he delivered his warning address, 60 (Acts xix. xx.). phesus was in a *ruinous state* even in the time of Justinian 27), and still remains so.

Smyrna. An *ancient* Greek city, claiming to be the birthplace f Homer; was destroyed by the Lydians; about 627 B.C. rebuilt y Antigonus and Lysimachus. Its first bishop, Polycarp, was artyred here about 169. It has been frequently captured. It as sacked by *Tamerlane in* 1402; and finally taken by the Turks, 424. It is now the chief city of Asia Minor, and the seat of the evant trade. Earthquake (above 2000 perish), 12 May, 1875. op. 1885, 186,510.

Per'gamos. Capital of the kingdom of the same name, founded y Philetærus, whom Lysimachus, one of Alexander's generals, ad made *governor*, 283 B.C. He was succeeded by Eumenes I., 33; Attalus (who took the title of king), 241; Eumenes II. (who ollected a great library), 197. LIBRARIES. Attalus II., 159; Attalus III., 138. He bequeathed his kingdom to the Romans, 133. revolted, was subdued, and made the Roman province, Asia. ergamos is still an important place, called Bergamo. PARCHENT is said to have been invented here.

Thyati'ra. Now a mean town of 2000 houses, called Akhissar, White Castle."

Sardis. Formerly the capital of Lydia, the kingdom of Crœsus 60 B.C.); taken by *Cyrus*, 548; burned by the Greeks, 499; it ourished under the Roman empire; was taken by the Turks, d destroyed by Tamerlane about 1462; it is now a miserable illage named Sart.

Philadel'phia was built by Attalus (III.) Philadelphus, king of ergamos (159–138 B.C.); was taken by Bajazet I., 1390 A.D. It now called Allah Shehr, "The City of God," and is a miserable own of 3000 houses.

Laodice'a. In Phrygia, near *Lydia*; has suffered much from arthquakes. It is now a deserted place, called Eskehissar, "The ld Castle."

Seven Days' battles around Richmond, Va. A es of severe conflicts between the confederates under , and the Federal army under McClellan, lasting from 25 ie to 1 July, 1862. PENINSULAR CAMPAIGN, UNITED ATES.

Seven Pines or **Fair Oaks,** Va., Battle of. PENULAR CAMPAIGN.

seven sages. GREECE, 590 B.C.

seven sleepers. According to an early legend, 7 ths, in 251, commanded to worship a statue set up in Ephs by the emperor Decius, refused, and fled to a cavern in mountain, where they were enclosed, and slept, accordto Durandus, for 300 years. *Other writers give shorter* iods, and various accounts of the awakening. A festival their honor is kept in the Roman Catholic church on 27 y.

Seven Weeks' war. PRUSSIA, 1866.

seven wonders. WONDERS.

Seven Years' war, the conflict maintained by Frederick II. of Prussia against Austria, Russia, and France, from 1756 to 1763. He gained part of Silesia. BATTLES, PRUSSIA.

Seventh-Day Baptists. SABBATARIANS.

Sev'ille, S.W. Spain, the *Hispalis* of the Phœnicians and the *Julia* of the Romans, *was the capital until* Philip II. finally established his court at Madrid, 1563. It opened its gates to the Saracens in 712, and was taken from them by the Christians in 1247, *after an obstinate siege.* The peace of Seville between England, France, and Spain, and also a defensive alliance to which Holland acceded, signed 9 Nov. 1729. In the *Peninsular war* Seville *surrendered* to the French, 1 Feb. 1810; and was taken by assault by the British and Spaniards, after the battle of Salamanca, 27 Aug. 1812. It was besieged but *not* taken by Espartero, July, 1843. Pop. 1887, 143,182.

Sèvres (*sāvr*). POTTERY.

sewers and **sewage.** Sir A. H. Layard's explorations in Nineveh disclose an elaborate system of drainage in connection with the older palace of Nimrod, consisting of a square brick sewer, with pipe drains leading from almost every chamber of the palace. Excavations of ancient Jerusalem show a complex and perfect system of reservoirs and drains. Agrigentum was provided with sewers, marvels of workmanship, named from Phæx, the city architect, who built them in the 5th century B.C. The CLOACA MAXIMA at Rome still exists; probably referred to by Strabo *as one of the sewers* "along which a hay cart might be driven," and an elaborate system of sewers connected with the Colosseum has been discovered. Modern sewers are *constructed on the separate* or the combined system, in the latter case being large enough to carry off the surface or storm water. The utilization of disinfected sewage as manure is *now much* advocated, and in many places in the United States and England sewage is disposed of by sub-surface irrigation, and systems for drying or *cremating much waste* matter, which would otherwise find its way into the sewers, are in operation in many cities.

First *legislative enactment* providing for drainage of London.. 1225
Hugues Aubriot covered an open sewer in Paris during the reign of Charles VI., originating the Paris sewer system, 1380–1422
Sewer commissions appointed in England in the reign of Henry VI.......1428–30
Act for *commissioners of sewers* in all parts of England...... 1532
Sewer in Paris, now called the *grand égout de ceinture*, walled and covered.......... 1740
Covered sewers of Paris extended by Napoleon..............1805–6
Earthenware pipes *for* refuse drainage tried in London under royal commissioners.......... 1842
Act *passed requiring* the London house sewers to empty into public sewers.......... 1847
Enlargement of sewer system of London, discharging into the Thames, completed.......... 1855
Present system of Parisian sewers on plan of M. Belgrand, dates from.......... 1857
New sewer system for London, consisting of three intercepting sewers on each side of the Thames, running parallel with it, and discharging into gigantic reservoirs below Barking creek and Erith marshes, completed..........4 Apr. 1865
Commission on the contamination of the Thames by London sewage advise a change, combining chemical precipitation with filtration through earth..........Dec. 1884
William Webster's method of decomposing London sewage by *electricity, set up* at Crossness, reported successful on inspection..........Mch. 1889
H. Wollheim's *process*, the "amines," or ammonia compounds, reported successful at Wimbledon sewage farm.....18 Sept. "

sewing-machine. It is said that Thomas Saint patented *one for boots* and shoes in 1790. Similar inventions are ascribed to Duncan (1804), Adams and Dodge (American, 1818), Thimonnier (French, 1830); Walter Hunt of New York invented one that made a lock-stitch, 1834, but did not apply for a patent until 1854, when his invention was essentially covered by a patent obtained by Elias Howe of Cambridge, Mass., 8 years before (Sept. 1846), the first really practical sewing-machine; since then many improvements have been made by American inventors.

Sexages'ima Sunday. QUADRAGESIMA SUNDAY, WEEK.

sextant, an instrument used like a quadrant, containing 60 degrees, or the sixth part of a circle, invented by Tycho Brahe, at Augsburg, in 1550 Arabian astronomers are said to have had a sextant of 59 feet 9 inches radius, about 995.

Seychelles (*sa-shel'*) **isles,** Indian ocean, settled by the French about 1768, captured by the British, 1794, ceded to them, 1815 Pop 1890, 16,162

Shakers, an English sect, now chiefly found in the U S, arose in the time of Charles I, and derived its name from voluntary convulsions. It soon disappeared, but was revived by James Wardley in 1747, and more successfully by Ann Lee (or Standless), expelled Quakers, about 1757 The sect emigrated to America, May, 1772, and settled near Albany, N Y, 1774 NEW YORK, 1774-80 They have several communities in the United States, they hold all goods in common, live uprightly, and are noted for frugality, industry, integrity, and thrift They denounce marriage as sinful, regard celibacy as holy, oppose war, disown baptism and the Lord's supper, and use a sort of dancing as part of worship —*Marsden* They are also called Bible Christians and Girlingites, from Mrs. Girling, a leader among them

Shakespeare and his plays. William Shakespeare was born at Stratford-upon Avon, Warwickshire, 23 Apr 1564, and died on his birthday, 1616 In 1582 he married Anne Hathaway issue, Susanna, baptized 26 May, 1583, Hamnet and Judith, twins, baptized 2 Feb 1585 Hamnet died 11 Aug 1596 Susanna married dr John Hall, 5 June, 1607, and Judith married Thomas Quiney, vintner, Feb. 1616. Lineage of Shakespeare expired with Elizabeth Hall, granddaughter, who died 1670 The first collected edition of his works is dated 1623 (fac-simile pub 1862-65), the second, 1632 (In 1849, J P Collier, editor of Shakespeare, purchased a copy of this folio, on which were written in pencil corrections, supposed to have been made soon after the time of publication At first he thought little of these marks, but in 1853 he was induced to publish "Notes and Emendations," derived from this volume Much controversy ensued as to the authenticity of these corrections, and in 1859 it was generally agreed that they were of modern date, and of little value, messrs Knight, Halliwell, and Dyce supporting this estimate) The third in 1664, the fourth 1685, all in folio. Rowe's editions appeared in 1709, 1714, Pope's, 1725-28, Theobald's, 1733-40, Hanmer's, 1740, Warburton's, 1747, Johnson's, 1775, Capell's, 1768, Malone's, 1790, Boydell's, with numerous plates, was published in 9 vols fol, 1802 Since then many others, notably, Alexander Dyce's, Knight's, Staunton's, White's, Irving's, Furness's Variorum edition, 1890, Wright's, Rolfe's, Hudson's, Appleton Morgan's Bankside edition, 1888-94, etc Ayscough's "Index to Shakespeare" was published in 1790, Twiss's Index, in 1805, Mary Cowden Clarke's Concordance, 1847 "Shakespeareana Genealogica," compiled by Geo Russell French, 1869. "Shakespeare's Commentaries," prof G G Gervinus, Heidelberg, Ger, 1875. Mrs Horace H Furness, "Concordance to Shakespeare's Poems," 1875. Alex Schmidt's "Shakespeare Lexicon," Berlin, 1876 Halliwell-Phillipps's "Outlines of the Life of Shakespeare," 1883 Charles Cowden-Clarke's "Key to Shakespeare," 1879 John Bartlett's "Shakespeare Concordance," pub in Boston, Mass, 1881, new edition, 4to, including "Concordance to Poems," New York and London, 1894 Appleton Morgan's "Shakespeare in Fact and Criticism," 1888 F J Furnivall's "Introduction to the Leopold Shakespeare," 1889 Mr Bartlett has also issued a "Shakespeare Phrase-Book" Prof Wendell's "Shakespeare—a Study," 1894.

SHAKESPEARE'S PLAYS ARRANGED CHRONOLOGICALLY AS PRODUCED AND PRINTED, ACCORDING TO REV HENRY P STOKES

Plays	Written	Published
Titus Andronicus	*cir* 1590	1600
1 King Henry VI	*cir* 1592	1623
2 King Henry VI	*cir* 1592	1594
3 King Henry VI	*cir* 1592	1595
Two Gentlemen of Verona	*cir* 1591	1623
Comedy of Errors	1591	"
Romeo and Juliet	1591	1597
Love's Labor's Lost	1591-92	1598
King Richard III	1593-94.	"
Taming of the Shrew	*before* 1594	1594
King Richard II	1594.	1597

SHAKESPEARE'S PLAYS.—(*Continued.*)

Plays	Written	Published
King John	1593-94	1623
Midsummer Night's Dream	1595	1600
Merchant of Venice	1597-98	"
1 King Henry IV	1597	"
2 King Henry IV	1598-99	"
Troilus and Cressida	*cir* 1599, *cir* 1602	1603
Merry Wives of Windsor	1598-99	1601-2
As You Like It	1599	1623
Much Ado About Nothing	1599-1600	1600
Hamlet	1599-1600	1603
King Henry V	1599	1600
Julius Cæsar	1599-1600	1623
Twelfth Night, or, What You Will	1601	"
Measure for Measure	1603-4	"
All's Well that Ends Well	*cir* 1592, *cir* 1604	"
Othello	1604.	1622
King Lear	1605	1607
Macbeth	1606	1623
Timon of Athens	1607	"
Pericles	1607-8	1609
Antony and Cleopatra	1608.	1623
Coriolanus	1610	"
Cymbeline.	1610	"
Tempest	1610-11	"
Winter's Tale	1610-11	"
King Henry VIII	(1611?) 1613	"
POEMS		
Venus and Adonis		1593
Lucrece		1594
Passionate Pilgrim		1599
Sonnets		1609

"An essay (The Harness essay, 1877) on the 'Chronological Order of Shakespeare's Plays,' by the rev Henry P Stokes, pub London, 1878, is one of the best that has yet appeared"—*Halliwell-Phillipps*

PLAYS THAT APPEARED IN THE FIRST EDITION OF 1623.

COMEDIES (order of publication)

1 Tempest.	9 Merchant of Venice
2 Two Gentlemen of Verona	10 As You Like It
3 Merry Wives of Windsor	11 Taming of the Shrew
4 Measure for Measure.	12 All's Well that Ends Well
5 Comedy of Errors.	13. Twelfth Night, or, What You Will
6 Much Ado About Nothing	14. Winter's Tale.
7 Love's Labor's Lost	
8 Midsummer Night's Dream	

HISTORIES.

15. King John	20 King Henry VI, Part I
16 " Richard II	21 " " " " II
17 " Henry IV, Part I	22 " " " " III
18 " " " " II	23 " Richard III
19 " " V	24. " Henry VIII

TRAGEDIES.

25 Troilus and Cressida.	31 Macbeth
26 Coriolanus	32 Hamlet.
27 Titus Andronicus	33 King Lear
28 Romeo and Juliet	34 Othello
29 Timon of Athens	35 Antony and Cleopatra.
30 Julius Cæsar	36 Cymbeline

Pericles was not added to Shakespeare's collected works until 1664, in the 3d folio edition

Shakespeare-Bacon controversy. The obscurity resting upon the early life of Shakespeare and the wonderful intelligence and culture shown by his works, in contrast with his education and social relations as far as known, have puzzled all students The first attempt to refer the plays to another author was by miss Delia Bacon (b. Tallmadge, O, 1811, d 1859) She asserted that lord Bacon was the author, and devoted much time and labor to prove it. Wm H Smith (English) disputes with miss Bacon the origin of the Baconian theory Nathaniel Holmes, in his "Authorship of Shakespeare," follows the same line of thought. Mrs. Henry Pott attempted to show, in a work pub 1883, the identity of expression in the "Promus" of Bacon with the plays of Shakespeare In 1888 appeared Ignatius Donnelly's work, "The Great Cryptogram," published simultaneously in Chicago, New York, and London, a volume of nearly 1000 pages, an attempt to prove that Bacon's authorship is avowed under a cipher in the text of the plays in the folio of 1623 No Shakespearian scholar has accepted the Baconian theory.

Shakespeare forgeries. LITERATURE, Forgeries of

Shakespeare fund, established in Oct. 1861, to purchase Shakespeare's garden, birthplace estate, and to erect and endow a public library and museum at Stratford-upon-Avon The catalogue of the library and museum was pub. Feb. 1868.

Shakespeare gallery. Boydell.

Shakespeare's Globe theatre, London. ıeatres.

Shakespeare's house. In 1847, a number of ɛrsons of distinction interested themselves for the preserva- ɔn of the house in which Shakespeare was born, then actu- ly for sale. They held a meeting at the Thatched-house vern, London, 26 Aug. in that year, and promoted a sub- ription set on foot by the Shakespearian club at Stratford- ɔon-Avon; and a committee was appointed to carry out their ɔject. In the end, Shakespeare's house was sold at the auc- ɔn mart in London, where it was "knocked down" to the nited Committee of London and Stratford for 3000*l.*, 16 Sept. 347. In 1856, a learned Oriental scholar, John Shakespeare ıo relation of the poet), gave 2500*l.* to purchase the adjoin- g house, that it might be pulled down in order to insure the ɔet's house from the risk of fire. An act to incorporate the ustees and guardians of Shakespeare's birthplace was passed ; Mch. 1891.

Shakespeare society issued 20 volumes, 1841–53.

Shakespeare society, New, issues works, 1874 seq.

ıakespeare Society of New York pub. the "Bankside" edi- tion...1888–94
O. Halliwell-Phillipps, Shakespearian scholar, d.......4 Jan. 1889
is "Shakespearian Rarities" (portraits, personal relics, books, etc.) offered for sale.................................Jan. 1890

shamrock. It is said that the shamrock used by the ish as a national emblem was adopted by Patrick M'Alpine, nce called St. Patrick, as a simile of the Trinity, about 432.

Shang-Haï, incorrectly **Shanghae,** a seaport city ıd foreign settlement of China, captured by the British, 19 ıne, 1842; by the Tae-Ping rebels, 7 Sept. 1853; retaken by e imperialists, 1855. The rebels were defeated near Shang- aï by the English and French, allies of the emperor, 1 Mch. 362. China.

shawls, of Oriental origin, were introduced into Paris ter the return of Napoleon Bonaparte from Egypt, 1801. he manufacture was introduced by Barrow and Watson in '84, at Norwich. It began at Paisley and Edinburgh about 305.—*Ure.*

Shawmut. Massachusetts, 1630.

Shawnees. Indians.

Shays's rebellion. At the end of the Revolution, ıe United States were burdened with a heavy foreign and do- estic debt. They were impoverished by the long war, and ıuld not meet the arrears of pay due the soldiers of the Rev- ution. On the recommendation of Congress, each state en- ɛavored to raise its quota by a direct tax. Much excitement llowed in some states, and in 1787 some people of Massachu- tts openly rebelled. Daniel Shays, who had been a captain the Continental army, marched at the head of a thousand en, took possession of Worcester, and prevented a session of ıe Supreme court. He repeated his performance at Spring- ɛld; and the insurrection became so formidable that the gov- nor was compelled to call out several thousand militia under ɛn. Lincoln to suppress it. This was speedily accomplished. hough some of the insurgents were sentenced to death, none ere executed. A free pardon was finally given to all. Mas- ıchusetts, 1787.

sheep. Abel was a keeper of sheep (Gen. iv. 2). The ıtriarch Job had 14,000 sheep, and Solomon at the dedication ' the temple, about 1000 B.C., offered a sacrifice of 120,000 ıeep. America has no indigenous domestic sheep, the first ı the English colonies having been brought by colonists to ımestown, Va., 1607–10, and to all the colonies when settled, though few sheep were raised until after 1800. In 1810 ıe estimated number of sheep in the U. S. was 7,000,000. f the English domestic breeds the Leicesters, Cotswolds, ɔuthdowns, Shropshires, Dorsets, and Cheviots are the most ɔted.

A.D.
ɔlumella introduces the Tarentine breed, noted for fine fleece (probable progenitors of the Merino), into Spain from Italy... 41
dward IV. of England sends a present of Cotswold rams to Henry of Castile (1464) and to John of Aragon.............. 1468
ɛrinos from Spain introduced into Sweden by Mr. Alstroe- mer.. 1723
Two hundred Merinos, bought in Spain by the Elector of Sax- ony, shipped from Cadiz..............................May, 1765
Empress Maria Theresa of Hungary imports several hundred Merinos from Spain.. 1775
French government buys 376 Merino ewes and lambs in Spain, and sends them to Rambouillet, near Paris.................. 1786
Frederick II. of Prussia imports 300 Merinos from Spain...... "
A few Spanish Merinos imported into England by George III. and placed on his farm at Kew.............................. 1787
Otter sheep, with a long body and short, crooked legs, origi- nated in Massachusetts from a malformed twin ram. Efforts were made to preserve this sporadic variety on account of its inability to run and jump, and thus escape from an enclosure. In the eastern states it promised to become a distinct species, but it has disappeared. Imagining that the ewe had been frightened by an otter (then occasionally seen in the vicinity), people called it the Otter sheep.............................. 1791
First authentic introduction of Merino sheep into the U. S. was a ram, sole survivor of 2 pair imported from the celebrated Rambouillet flock by Mr. Delessert, a French banker, and placed on his farm near Kingston, N. Y....................... 1801
Flock of about 200 Merinos, imported from Spain by gen. David Humphreys of Connecticut.. "
Chancellor Livingston of New York, minister to France, sends from the Rambouillet flock 4 Merinos to New York......... 1802
Four of the best flocks of Merinos in Spain confiscated by the Junta, and sold at Badajos to buyers from the U. S. and England chiefly, after the second invasion of the French, Dec. 1808
Hon. William Jarvis ships to the U. S. 1400 Paulars, 1700 Aqueirres, 200 Escurials, 100 Negrettis, and about 200 Montar- cos, which he purchases from the Junta of Spain, 1808.....1809–10
Merino society organized in England; sir John Banks at the head and 54 vice-presidents.................................. 1811
First large importation of Saxon Merinos into the U. S., made by G. & T. Searle of Boston.................................... 1824
Twenty ewes and 2 rams, selected from the celebrated Ram- bouillet flock, imported into the U. S. by D. C. Collins of Hartford, Conn.. 1840
Leicesters introduced into the U. S.......................about 1825
Merinos introduced into Texas.................................. 1852

NUMBER AND VALUE OF SHEEP IN THE UNITED STATES.

Year.	Number.	Value.
1850	21,723,220	....
1860	22,471,275	....
1870	40,853,000	$93,364,433
1880	40,765,900	90,230,537
1890	44,336,072	100,659,761
1892	44,938,365	116,121,290
1893	47,273,553	125,999,264

Prior to 1880 more sheep were raised east of the Missis- sippi river than west, but in 1890 the number west compared to the number east was as 3 to 2. According to the U. S. Commissioner of Agriculture there were about 467,500,000 sheep in the world in 1888. Of these there were:

In United States	43,544,755	In France	22,688,230
" South America	99,928,607	" Germany	19,189,715
" Australasia	86,245,520	" Spain	16,939,288
" Russia in Europe	46,724,736	" Great Britain and Ireland	29,401,750
" British India	30,453,724		
" South Africa	23,746,179	Scattered	47,500,000

Wool.

Sheffield, a town on the river Sheaf, West Riding, Yorkshire, Engl., renowned for cutlery, plated goods, etc. Sheffield thwytles are mentioned by Chaucer, in the time of Edward III. Sheffield in the time of the Conqueror was obtained by Roger de Buisli, and has since been held by the Lovetots, Nevils, Talbots, and Howards. Pop. 1891, 324,243.

Sheffield Scientific school. Yale college.

shells. Bombs.

Shenando'ah valley, Operations in. Grant's campaign in Virginia.

Sheridan's Begum speech. This speech, made by Richard Brinsley Sheridan during the impeachment trial of Warren Hastings, 1788, and said by Macaulay to have produced an impression such as has never been equalled, was on the charge of the "spoliation of the Begums." The excite- ment of the house was so great at its close that no other speaker could obtain a hearing, and the debate was adjourned. It is said of Sheridan that he wrote the best comedy, "The School for Scandal," made the best speech—as above—and composed the best convivial song, "Here's to the Maiden of Bashful Fifteen," in the English language.

Sheridan's raids. Grant's campaign in Virginia, 1864.

sheriff, or *shire-reve*, governor of a shire or county. London had its sheriffs prior to William I.'s reign, but some say that sheriffs were first nominated for every county in England by William in 1079. According to other historians, Henry Cornhill and Richard Reynere were the first sheriffs of London, 1 Rich. I., 1189. The nomination of sheriffs, according to the present mode, took place in 1461.—*Stow.* Anciently sheriffs were hereditary in Scotland, and in some English counties, as Westmoreland. The sheriffs of Dublin (first called bailiffs) were appointed in 1308, and obtained the name of sheriff by an incorporation of Edward VI., 1548. 35 sheriffs were fined, and 11 excused, in one year, rather than serve the office for London, 1734. BAILIFFS. The high-sheriffs of the counties of England and Wales, except Middlesex and Lancaster, are nominated on the morrow of St. Martin, Nov. 12.

Sheriffmuir. DUMBLANE.

Sherman's great march. This designates the bold and important movement of Sherman's army from Atlanta to Savannah, and thence through the Carolinas to Goldsborough, 16 Nov. 1864 to 22 Mch. 1865. When Hood, after the loss of Atlanta, moved against Sherman's communications, the latter followed him with nearly his entire army, to protect the railroad until it should have served his purpose. After the Confederate reverse at ALLATOONA PASS, Hood evaded a battle, and Sherman gave up the chase, left the department of the Mississippi virtually in Thomas's hands (FRANKLIN, Battle of), and, on 16 Nov., having destroyed Atlanta and made a wreck of the railroad back to Dalton, marched eastward for the Atlantic coast with the 14th, 15th, 17th, and 20th corps, numbering 60,000 infantry and artillery, and about 6000 cavalry. Gen. O. O. Howard commanded the right wing, comprising the 15th corps, gen. P. J. Osterhaus, and the 17th, gen. Frank P. Blair; the left, under gen. H. W. Slocum, formed by the 14th corps, gen. Jeff. C. Davis, and the 20th, gen. A. S. Williams, and the cavalry under gen. Judson Kilpatrick. He destroyed the railroad as he moved, threatened both Macon and Augusta, thus forcing the confederates to divide their forces, then passed both, and moved down the peninsula between the Ogeechee and Savannah rivers. About the middle of Dec., Sherman stood before Savannah, then held by the Confederate general Hardee, almost completely invested the city, and captured fort M'Allister (13 Dec.), thus gaining access to Dahlgren's fleet. Hardee evacuated Savannah 20 Dec., and the next day Sherman's army entered that city. Over 200 guns were captured with Savannah, and 35,000 bales of cotton were seized as a legitimate prize of war. Sherman transferred the forts and city to gen. Foster (18 Jan. 1865), and began his march through the Carolinas. He threatened at once Augusta and Charleston, and passed both. On 12 Feb., Charleston, evacuated by Hardee, was occupied by the national forces. While Sherman was approaching Goldsborough, Hardee's forces, with the remnants of Hood's old army and detachments from other sources, were gathered together in North Carolina and placed under gen. Johnston. A portion of this force, under Hardee, contested Sherman's approach to Goldsborough (16 Mch.) at Averysborough, and was defeated. Johnston's entire army was encountered at Bentonville (18 Mch.), but Slocum held his ground until the right wing came to his support, and Johnston retreated on the 22d. Terry and Schofield in the meantime joined Sherman. After Lee's surrender (9 Apr.), Johnston and Sherman entered into negotiations for surrender, which were disproved by the government. UNITED STATES. Johnston's army was surrendered on 26 Apr.

Shetland isles. ORKNEYS.

shib'boleth, the word by which the followers of Jephthah tested their opponents the Ephraimites, on passing the Jordan, about 1143 B.C. (Judg. xii.). The term is now applied to any party watchword or dogma.

Shi'ites, the Mahometan sect predominating in Persia. MAHOMETANISM.

shilling. The value of the ancient Saxon coin of this name was fivepence, but it was reduced to fourpence about a century before the Conquest. After the Conquest the French *solidus* of 12 pence, in use among the Normans, was called *shilling*. The true English shilling was first coined, some say, in small numbers, by Henry VII., 1504.—*Ruding.* A peculiar shilling, value 9 pence, but to be current at 12, was struck in Ireland, 1560; and a large but very base coinage in England for the service of Ireland, 1598. Milled shillings were coined 13 Chas. II. 1662. COINS.

Shi'loh, Battle of. PITTSBURG LANDING.

ship-building. The first ship (probably a galley) was brought from Egypt to Greece by Danaus, 1485 B.C.—*Blair.* The first double-decked ship was built by the Tyrians, 786 B.C.—*Lenglet.* The Romans built their first fleet of boats by copying a Carthaginian vessel wrecked on their coast 260 B.C. The first double-decked one built in England was of 1000 tons' burden, by order of Henry VII.; was called the *Great Harry*, and cost 14,000*l.*—*Stow.* Portholes and other improvements were invented by Descharges, a French builder at Brest, in the reign of Louis XII., about 1500. Ship-building was first treated as a science by Hoste, 1696.

First vessel built in New York harbor.......................... 1614
First in Massachusetts, at Plymouth (small)....................... 1624
First vessel on lake Erie.. 1679
First ship down the Ohio to the ocean.............................. 1801
A prehistoric ship, cut out of solid oak, 48 ft. long, 4 ft. 4 in. wide, and 2 ft. deep, was found while excavating in Lincolnshire, Engl.......................................Apr. 1885
France, a sailing-ship, built on the Clyde by messrs. Henderson, 5 masts, 360 ft. long, 48 ft. wide, bowsprit 50 ft. long, tonnage over 6000 tons.......................................Sept. 1890
CARRACK, NAVY, SHIPPING, STATES mentioned, STEAM NAVIGATION, etc.

ship-money was first levied in England about 1007, to form a navy to oppose the Danes. This impost, levied by Charles I. in 1634–36, was much opposed, and led to the revolution. He assessed London in 7 ships of 4000 tons, and 1560 men; Yorkshire in 2 ships of 600 tons, or 12,000*l.*; Bristol in 1 ship of 100 tons; Lancashire in 1 ship of 400 tons. Among others, John Hampden refused to pay the tax; he was tried in the exchequer in 1636. The judges declared the tax legal, 12 June, 1637. Ship-money was one of the grievances complained of in 1641. The 5 judges who had sustained it were imprisoned. Hampden received a wound in a skirmish with prince Rupert, at Chalgrove, 18 June, and died 24 June, 1643.

"Ship of Fools" or "Narrenschiff." An allegorical satire in verse, by Sebastian Brandt of Strasburg; pub. 1494; very popular at the time. LITERATURE.

shipping, American. The following tables show the various statistics regarding the vessels and tonnage of American shipping for the several years named:

TONNAGE OF SAIL AND STEAM VESSELS OF THE MERCHANT MARINE OF THE U. S. EMPLOYED IN FOREIGN AND COASTWISE TRADE AND IN FISHERIES.

Year.	Foreign trade.	Coastwise.	Whale fisheries.	Other fisheries.	Sail.	Steam.	Total.	Per cent. of increase or decrease.
	tons.	tons.	tons.	tons.	tons.	tons.	tons.	
1789..........	123,893	68,607	....	9,062	201,562	....	201,562	....
1790..........	346,254	103,775	....	28,348	478,377	....	478,377	137.33
1800..........	667,107	272,492	3,466	29,427	972,492	....	972,492	3.52
1810..........	981,019	405,347	3,589	34,828	1,424,783	....	1,424,783	5.51
1823..........	600,003	617,805	40,503	78,255	1,311,687	24,879	1,336,566	.89
1840..........	762,838	1,176,694	136,927	104,305	1,978,425	202,339	2,180,764	4.02
1850..........	1,439,694	1,797,825	146,017	151,918	3,009,507	525,947	3,535,454	6.64
1860..........	2,379,396	2,644,867	166,841	162,764	4,485,931	867,937	5,353,868	4.06
1870..........	1,448,846	2,638,247	67,954	91,460	3,171,412	1,075,095	4,246,507	2.41
1880..........	1,314,402	2,637,686	38,408	77,538	2,856,476	1,211,558	4,068,034	—2.42
1890..........	928,062	3,409,435	18,633	68,367	2,565,409	1,859,088	4,424,497	2.71

In 1861 the foreign trade tonnage reached its maximum of 2,643,628 tons, including the whale fisheries. In 1858, 73 per cent. of the exports and imports was carried in American ships; in 1891, less than 13 per cent.

CLASS, NUMBER, AND TONNAGE OF VESSELS BUILT IN THE U. S. FROM 1820 FOR THE YEARS GIVEN.

Year.	Ships and barks.	Brigs.	Schooners.	Sloops, canal-boats, and barges.	Total.	Tons.	Steam.	Tons.	Total vessels.	Total tons.
1820.....	22	60	301	152	535	47,784	22	3,610	557	51,394
1830.....	25	56	403	116	600	51,491	48	7,068	648	58,560
1840.....	97	109	378	224	808	106,518	87	14,685	895	121,203
1850.....	247	117	554	307	1225	227,907	197	51,258	1422	279,255
1860.....	110	36	373	289	807	145,427	275	69,370	1082	214,797
1870.....	73	27	519	709	1328	206,332	290	70,620	1618	276,953
1880.....	23	2	286	243	554	78,556	348	78,853	902	157,409
1890.....	10	..	347	284	641	135,077	410	159,045	1051	294,122

NUMBER AND TONNAGE OF VESSELS BUILT IN THE DIFFERENT DISTRICTS AND YEARS GIVEN.

Year.	New England coast.		Entire seaboard.		Mississippi and tributaries.		Great lakes.		Total vessels.	Total tons.
	No.	Tons.	No.	Tons.	No.	Tons.	No.	Tons.		
1857....	412	183,625	1008	285,453	244	41,854	182	51,498	1434	378,805
1867....	451	135,189	998	230,810	225	35,106	296	39,679	1519	305,595
1877....	233	90,992	708	132,996	232	34,693	89	8,903	1029	176,592
1890....	208	78,577	756	169,091	104	16,506	191	108,526	1051	294,123

Largest number of ships and barks built in any year since 1789 (1855), 381; brigs (1815), 224; schooners (1816), 781; canal-boats and barges (1873), 1221; steam-vessels (1864), 520.

NUMBER OF VESSELS IN THE U. S. MERCHANT MARINE, 1891.

Engaged in foreign trade.	Number.	Tons.
Steamers	263	236,070
Sail-vessels	1,246	749,968
Canal-boats	....	....
Barges	7	2,680
Total	1,516	988,718
Engaged in home trade.		
Steamers	5,945	1,776,269
Sail-vessels	12,407	1,339,530
Canal-boats	1,146	121,000
Barges	1,331	373,077
Total	20,829	3,609,876
Total foreign and home	22,345	4,598,594

shipping, British. Shipping was first registered in the river Thames in 1786; and throughout the empire in 1787. In the middle of the 18th century, the shipping of England was but 500,000 tons—less than that of London now. In 1830, the number of ships in the British empire was 22,785.

NUMBER OF REGISTERED SAILING AND STEAM VESSELS OF THE UNITED KINGDOM ENGAGED IN HOME AND FOREIGN TRADE FOR THE YEARS GIVEN.

Vessels.		Number.	Tons.
1861..	Sail	19,288	3,918,511
	Steam	997	441,184
	Total	20,285	4,359,695
1871..	Sail	19,650	4,343,558
	Steam	2,557	1,290,003
	Total	22,207	5,633,561
1877..	Sail	17,101	4,138,149
	Steam	3,218	1,977,489
	Total	20,319	6,115,638
1888..	Sail	12,292	3,054,059
	Steam	5,202	4,297,829
	Total	17,494	7,351,888
1890..	Sail	11,570	2,893,372
	Steam	5,855	5,021,764
	Total	17,425	7,915,136

In 1889 the total tonnage of the British merchant marine was 9,472,060, of which 7,641,157 tons were of the United Kingdom; for the same year the U. S. had 4,307,475 tons.

NUMBER OF VESSELS BUILT FOR THE UNITED KINGDOM MERCHANT MARINE FOR THE YEARS HERE GIVEN.

Vessels.		Number.	Tons
1888..	Sail	269	75,[illegible]
	Steam	465	407,446
	Total	734	483,1[illegible]
1889..	Sail	277	117,48[illegible]
	Steam	582	554,024
	Total	859	671,505
1890..	Sail	277	123,224
	Steam	581	528,789
	Total	858	652,013

shipwrecks. WRECKS.

shirts are said to have been first generally worn in the west of Europe early in the 8th century.—*Du Fresnoy.* Woollen shirts were commonly worn in England until about 1253, when coarse linen (fine coming at this period from abroad) was first manufactured in England by Flemish artisans.—*Stow.*

shoddy, woollen goods, manufactured from old woollen rags, or refuse, to which new wool is added, is stated to have been first manufactured about 1813, at Batley, near Dewsbury, Yorkshire. Manufactured and sold extensively in the United States, 1863-73.

shoes among the Jews were made of leather, linen, rush, or wood. Moons were worn as ornaments in their shoes by Jewish women (Isa. iii. 18). Pythagoras would have his disciples wear shoes of the bark of trees, probably to avoid the use of the skins of animals, as they refrained from taking life. The Romans wore an ivory crescent on shoes; and Caligula enriched his with precious stones. In England, about 1462, the people wore the beaks or points of their shoes so long as to encumber them in walking, and were forced to tie them up to their knees; the fine gentlemen fastened theirs with chains of silver or silver gilt, others with laces. This was prohibited, on the forfeiture of 20*s.* and on pain of being cursed by the clergy, 7 Edw. IV. 1467. DRESS. Shoes, as at present worn, were introduced about 1633. The buckle was not used till 1668.—*Stow; Mortimer.* Pieter Camper, an eminent Dutch surgeon, published a treatise on the best form of the shoe, 1782. The buckle-makers petitioned against the use of *shoe-strings* in 1791.

shooting-stars. METEORITES.

short-hand. STENOGRAPHY.

"short-lived" administration—that of William Pulteney, earl of Bath, lord Carlisle, lord Winchelsea, and lord Granville—existed from 10 Feb. to 12 Feb. 1746.

Shoshones (*sho-sho'nes*) or **Snake** INDIANS.

shot. In early times various missiles were shot from cannon. Bolts are mentioned in 1413; and in 1418 Henry V. ordered his clerk of ordnance to get 7000 stone shot made at the quarries at Maidstone. Since then chain, grape, and canister shot have been invented, as well as shells; all are described in Scoffern's "Projectile Weapons of War, and Explosive Compounds," 1858. BOMBS, CANNON.

Shrewsbury, a town of Shropshire, Engl., arose after the ruin of the Roman town Uriconium (WROXETER), and became one of the chief cities of the kingdom, having a mint till the reign of Henry III. Here Richard II. held a parliament in 1397.—On 23 July, 1403, was fought a sanguinary battle at Hately field, near Shrewsbury, between the army of Henry IV. and that of the nobles, led by Percy (surnamed Hotspur), son of the earl of Northumberland, who had conspired to dethrone Henry. Henry was seen in the thickest of the fight, with his son, afterwards Henry V. The death of Hotspur by an unknown hand gave the victory to the king.—*Hume.*

Prince Henry. Why, Percy I killed myself, and saw thee dead.
Falstaff. Didst thou?—Lord, lord, how this world is given to lying! I grant you, I was down, and out of breath; and so was he: but we rose both in an instant, and fought a long hour by Shrewsbury clock. —*Shakespeare,* "Henry IV." pt. i. act v. sc. iv.

Shrop'shire (corrupted from *Salop-shire*), Battle of, in which the Britons were subjugated, and Caractacus, king of the Silures, became, through the treachery of the queen of the Brigantes, a prisoner to the Romans, 50.

Shrove Tuesday, the day before Ash-Wednesday, the first day of the Lent fast. CARNIVAL.

Siam', a kingdom in India, bordering on the Burmese empire. Siam was rediscovered by the Portuguese in 1511, and a trade established, in which the Dutch joined about 1604. A British ship arrived about 1613. In 1683 a Cephalonian Greek, Constantine Phaulcon, became foreign minister of Siam, and opened a communication with France; Louis XIV. sent an embassy in 1685 to convert the king, without effect. After several attempts, sir John Bowring succeeded in obtaining a treaty of friendship and commerce between England and Siam, which was signed 30 Apr. 1855, and ratified 5 Apr. 1856. 2 ambassadors from Siam arrived in England in Oct. 1857, and had an audience with queen Victoria; they brought with them magnificent presents, which they delivered crawling, on 16 Nov. They visited Paris in June, 1861. By a treaty with France, the French protectorate over Cambodia was recognized; signed 15 July, ratified 24 Oct. 1867. The king, Khoulalonkorn, born 21 Sept. 1853, has reigned from 1 Oct. 1868; the king was entertained at Calcutta, 7-12 Jan. 1872; a political constitution was decreed, 8 May, 1874. Queen Victoria received the order of the White Elephant from the Siamese minister at Windsor, 2 July, 1880. Area, 250,000 sq. miles. Population of Siam (1891) about 9,000,000.

King Khoulalonkorn (b. 21 Sept. 1853); succeeded his father, Mongkout....1 Oct. 1868
Changes and political reforms were begun by the king, 16 Nov. 1873
On 9 Oct. 1874, he invited astronomers to Bangkok to view the eclipse of....5 Apr. 1875
Telegraphic communication with France opened....14 July, 1883
Gradual abolition of slavery nearly completed.... 1886
Bangkok-Pankam railroad commenced....16 July, 1891
Prince Damrong, half-brother of the king, on a mission, travels through Europe....1891-92
French troops occupy Khone island in the Mekong river; Siamese withdraw without resistance....9 Apr. 1893
French begin active hostilities; gun-boats fire on the Pakim forts, Bangkok (FRANCE, 1893).... "

Siamese twins. 2 persons born about 1811, with all the faculties of distinct individuals, though united by a short cartilaginous band at the pit of the stomach. They were named Chang and Eng, and were discovered on the banks of the Siam river by an American, Robert Hunter, who took them to New York, where they were exhibited. Capt. Coffin brought them to England. After several years in Britain, they went to America, where they settled on a farm, and married two sisters. In 1865 they were in North Carolina in declining health. Their exhibition in London began again, 8 Feb. 1869. They died in America, within 2 hours of each other, 16, 17 Jan. 1874.

Sibe'ria, a country of N. Asia. In 1580 the conquest was begun by the Cossacks under Jermak Timofejew. In 1710 Peter the Great began to send prisoners thither. An insurrection broke out among the Poles in Siberia in June, 1866, and was soon suppressed. Area, 4,833,496 sq. miles. Pop. 4,484,-549. RUSSIA.

sib'yls (Lat. *sibyllæ*), women believed to be inspired. Plato speaks of 1, others of 2, Pliny of 3, Ælian of 4, and Varro of 10, as follows: The *Persian, Libyan, Delphian, Cumæan, Erythræan, Samian, Cyma, Hellespontine, Phrygian, Tiburtine.* An Erythræan sibyl is said to have offered to Tarquin II. 9 books containing the Roman destinies, demanding for them 300 pieces of gold. He denied her, whereupon the sibyl threw 3 into the fire, and asked the same price for the other 6, which being denied, she burned 3 more, and again demanded the same sum for the rest; when Tarquin, conferring with the pontiffs, was advised to buy them. Two magistrates were created to consult them on all occasions, 531 B.C. QUINDECEMVIRS.

Sicil'ian Vespers, the term given to the massacre of the French (who had conquered Sicily, 1266) which began at Palermo, 30 Mch. 1282.

On Easter Monday conspirators assembled at Palermo, and while the French were engaged in festivities a Sicilian bride passed with her train. One Drochet, a Frenchman, used her rudely, under pretence of searching for arms. A young Sicilian stabbed him with his own sword; and, a tumult ensuing, 200 French were instantly murdered. The populace ran through the city, crying out, "Let the French die!" and, without distinction of rank, age, or sex, slaughtered all of that nation they could find, to the number of about 8000. Even the churches proved no sanctuary, and the massacre became general throughout the island.

Sic'ily (anciently *Trinacria*, three-cornered), the largest island in the Mediterranean, on which mount Ætna is situated. The early inhabitants were the Sicani, who probably came from Italy about 1294 B.C. Afterwards the Siculi, according to Niebuhr, of Pelasgian origin, dwelling in Latium about the Tiber, crossed to the island, and from them it received its name. The Phœnicians and Greeks settled some colonies here (735-582), and it was made a Roman province 212 B.C. In the production of wheat the Romans considered the island one of their best granaries. It is supposed that Sicily was separated from Italy by an earthquake, and that the strait of Messina was thus formed. Its government has frequently been united with and separated from that of NAPLES. It now forms part of the kingdom of Italy. Area, 11,289 sq. miles. Pop. in 1856, 2,231,020; 1871, 2,565,323; 1875, 2,698,-672; 1881, 2,927,901; 1890, estimated 3,285,472.

B.C.
SYRACUSE founded (*Eusebius*)....about 732
Gela founded (*Thucydides*)....680 or 713
AGRIGENTUM founded.... 582
Phalaris, tyrant of Agrigentum, put to death (BRAZEN BULL).... 549
Law of Petalism instituted.... 460
Athenian expedition fails.... 413
War with Carthage.... 409
Dionysius becomes master of Syracuse, makes peace with the Carthaginians, and reigns....406-367
Dionysius II. sells Plato for a slave, who is ransomed by his friends.... 360
Dionysius expelled by Timoleon.... 343
Who governs well; and dies.... 337
Agathocles usurps power at Syracuse, 317; defeated at Himera by Carthaginians, 310; poisoned.... 289
Pyrrhus, king of Epirus, invades Sicily; expels most of the Carthaginians; returns to Italy....278-277
Hiero II. defeated by the Romans.... 265
Becomes their ally.... 264
Romans enter Sicily (PUNIC WARS).... "
Agrigentum taken by the Romans.... 262
Palermo besieged by the Romans.... 254
Archimedes flourishes....about 236
Hiero II. dies, over 90 years of age.... 216
Romans take Syracuse, and make Sicily a province; Archimedes slain.... 212
Carthaginians lose half their possessions, 241; the remainder.... "
Servile wars; much slaughter....135, 134, 132
Tyrannical government of Verres (for which he was accused by Cicero)....73-71
Sicily held by Sextus Pompeius, son of the great Pompey, 42; defeated; expelled.... 36
Invaded by the Vandals, 440 A.D.; by the Goths, 493; taken for the Greek emperors by Belisarius.... A.D. 535
Conquered by the Saracens....832-78
Greeks and Arabs driven out by a Norman prince, Roger I., son of Tancred, 1058; who takes the title of count of Sicily....1061-90
Roger II., son of the above-named, unites Sicily with Naples, and is crowned king of the Two Sicilies.... 1131
Charles of Anjou, brother of St. Louis, king of France, conquers Naples and Sicily, deposes the Norman princes, and makes himself king.... 1266
French massacred (SICILIAN VESPERS).... 1282
Sicily seized by a fleet sent by the king of Aragon; Naples remains to the house of Anjou.... "
Alphonso, king of Aragon, takes possession of Naples.... 1435
Kingdom of Naples and Sicily united to the Spanish monarchy under Ferdinand the Catholic.... 1501
Victor, duke of Savoy, by the treaty of Utrecht made king of Sicily.... 1713
Which he gives up to the emperor Charles VI., and becomes king of Sardinia.... 1720
Charles, son of the king of Spain, becomes king of the Two Sicilies.... 1735
Throne of Spain becoming vacant, Charles, who is heir, vacates the throne of the Two Sicilies in favor of his third son Ferdinand, agreeably to treaty.... 1759
Dreadful earthquake at Messina, in Sicily, which destroys 40,000 persons.... 1783
French conquer NAPLES; Ferdinand IV. retires to Sicily.... 1806
Political disturbances.... 1810
New constitution granted, under British auspices.... 1812
French expelled; kingdom of Two Sicilies re-established; Ferdinand returns to Naples; abolishes the constitution.... 1815
Revolution at Palermo suppressed.... 1820
Great towns in Sicily rise and demand the constitution; a provisional government proclaimed....12 Jan. 1848
King nominates his brother, the count of Aquila, viceroy, 17 Jan.; promises a new constitution....29 Jan. "
Sicilian parliament decrees the exclusion of the Bourbon family, 13 Apr.; and invites the duke of Genoa to the throne, 11 July, "

Messina bombarded, taken by the Neapolitans. 7 Sept 1848
Catania taken by assault, 6 Apr, Syracuse surrenders, 23 Apr, and Palermo 15 May, 1849
Insurrections suppressed at Palermo, Messina, and Catania, 4 Apr et seq, the rebels retire into the interior, 21 Apr et seq 1860
Garibaldi and 2200 men embark at Genoa 5 May, land at Marsala, 11 May, he abandons his ships and assumes dictatorship in the name of the king of Sardinia 14 May, "
He defeats the royal troops at Calatafimi, 15 May, storms Palermo, 27 May, which is bombarded by the royal fleet, 28 May, armistice 31 May, "
A provisional government formed at Palermo, 3 June, which is evacuated by the Neapolitans 6 June, "
Garibaldi defeats the Neapolitans at Melazzo 20, 21 July, "
Convention signed the Neapolitans to evacuate Sicily (retaining the citadel of Messina) 30 July, "
New Sicilian constitution proclaimed 3 Aug "
Garibaldi embarks for Calabria (NAPLES) 19 Aug "
Prof Saffi (late of Oxford) a short time dictator Sept. "
Sicilians by universal suffrage vote for annexation to Sardinia (432,054 against 667) 21 Oct. "
Victor Emmanuel visits Sicily 1 Dec "
Citadel of Messina blockaded, 28 Feb, surrenders to gen Cialdini 13 Mch 1861
King Victor Emmanuel warmly received at Messina May, 1862
ITALY, NAPLES

"sick man," an epithet applied to Turkey, by the czar Nicholas, 14 Jan 1854 RUSSO-TURKISH WARS

Sic'yon, an ancient Grecian kingdom in the Peloponnesus, founded, it is said, about 2080 B C Its people took part in the wars in Greece, usually supporting Sparta In 252 it became a republic and joined the Achæan league formed by Aratus It was the country of the sculptors Polycletes (436) and Lysippus (328 B C)

side'real time. The time in which the earth rotates on its axis, the sidereal day, is the interval between 2 consecutive passages of a star across the meridian This day is divided into 24 equal parts, called sidereal hours, the hour into 60 sidereal minutes, etc This time is practically invariable The interval of time from the moment the sun leaves a fixed star until it returns to it constitutes a sidereal year, and measured by solar time is 365 days 6 hrs 9 min 9 6 sec., being longer than the solar year The solar year is the interval between 2 successive passages of the sun through the same EQUINOX, if the equinoxes were fixed points the solar and sidereal year would be identical, but the equinoxes recede from east to west 50 27" annually, thus the sun reaches the equinox sooner every year by 50 27" of arc, or by 20 min. 22 9 sec of time, and the mean solar year is 20 min 22 9 sec shorter than the sidereal year, or 365 days 5 hrs 48 min 46.7 sec

sider'ostat (from *sidus*, Lat for a star), an apparatus constructed by M. Leon Foucault, shortly before his death, 11 Feb. 1868, for observing the light of stars just as that of the sun is studied in the camera-obscura It consists of a mirror moved by clockwork, and a fixed objective glass for concentrating the rays into a focus

Si'don or **Zi'don,** Syria, a city of Phœnicia, to the north of Tyre. It was conquered by Cyrus about 537 B C, and surrendered to Alexander, 332 B C PHŒNICIA. The town was taken from the pacha of Egypt by the troops of the sultan and of his allies, assisted by some ships of the British squadron, under commodore Charles Napier, 27 Sept. 1840. SYRIA

Siedlce (*sēd'l-ce*), a village of Poland, where a battle was fought 10 Apr 1831, between the Poles and Russians The Poles obtained the victory after a bloody conflict, taking 4000 prisoners and several pieces of cannon, but this success was soon followed by fatal reverses

siege. Azotus or Ashdod, which was besieged by the Egyptian monarch Psammetichus the Powerful, held out 19 years—*Usher* For 29 years.—*Herodotus* This was the longest siege of antiquity The siege of Troy, the most celebrated, lasted 10 years, 1184 B C But the siege of Jerusalem by Titus, 70 A D (surrendered 8 Sept), was the most dreadful ever recorded Following are the principal sieges since the 12th century, for details of most, see separate articles

Acre, 1192, 1799, 1832, 1840.
Algesiras, 1341
Algiers, 1681 (bomb vessels first used by French engineer named Renau), 1816
Alkmaer, 1573
Almeida, 27 Aug 1810
Amiens, 1597
Ancona, 1174, 1799, 1860
Antwerp, 1576, 1583, 1585, 1746, 1832
Arras, 1640
Atlanta, U S, 1864
Azof, 1736
Badajoz, 11 Mch 1811, 6 Apr 1812
Bagdad, 1258
Barcelona, 1697, 1714
Basing House, Hampshire, Engl, one of the most gallant defences made by the royalists during the civil war, Cromwell carried it by assault 14 Oct 1645, after repeated trials by others and a desultory siege of 2 years. The Plundering of Basing House" is one of Landseer's most popular paintings
Belgrade, 1439, 1456, 1521, 1688, 1717, 1739, 1789
Belle Isle, 1761
Bergen op Zoom, 1622, 1747, 1814
Berwick, 1333, 1481
Bethune, 1710.
Bilbao, by Carlists, 1874
Bois le Duc, 1603, 1794
Bologna, 1512, 1796, 1799
Bommel (the invention of the covered way), 1794
Bonn, 1672, 1689, 1703
Boston, U S, 1775.
Bouchain, 1711
Boulogne, 1544
Breda, 1625
Brescia, 1238, 1512, 1849
Breslau, 1807
Brisac, 1638, 1704
Brussels, 1695, 1746.
Bomarsund, 1854.
Buda, 1541, 1686
Burgos, 1812, 1813.
Cadiz, 1812
Calais, 1347 (British historians affirm that cannon were used at Cressy, 1346, and here in 1347 First used here in 1388 —*Rymer's Fœd*), 1558, 1596
Calvi 1794
Candia (the largest cannon then known in Europe used here by the Turks), 1667
Carthagena, 1706-7, 1740, 1873-74.
Cawnpore, 1857
Chalus, 1199
Charleroi, 1693
Charleston, U S, 1864-65
Chartres, 1568
Cherbourg, 1758.
Ciudad Rodrigo, 1810, 1812
Colchester, 1648.
Comorn, 1849
Compiègue (Joan of Arc), 1430
Condé, 1676, 1793, 1794
Coni, 1691, 1744
Constantinople, 1453
Copenhagen, 1658, 1801, 1807
Corfu, 1716
Courtray 1646.
Cracow, 1702
Cremona, 1702
Dantzic, 1734, 1793, 1807, 1813, 1814
Delhi, 1857
Douay, 1710
Dresden, 1756, 1813.
Drogheda, 1649.
Dublin, 1500
Dunkirk, 1646, 1793.
Flushing, 15 Aug 1809
Fredericksbald (Charles XII killed), 1718
Gaeta, 1435, 1734. 1860-61
Genoa, 1747, 1800
Gerona, 1809
Ghent, 1708
Gibraltar, 1734, 1779, 1782-83
Glätz, 1742, 1807
Göttingen, 1760
Graves 1674
Grenada, 1491, 1492
Groningen, 1594.
Haerlem, 1572, 1573
Harfleur, 1415
Heidelberg, 1688
Herat, 1838
Humaitá, 1868
Ismail, 1790
Kars, 1855
Kehl 1733, 1796
Landau, 1702 et seq, 1792
Landrecy, 1712, 1794
Laon 988 991
Leipsic, 1757 et seq, 1813
Lerida, 1647, 1707 1810
Leyden, 1574
Liege, 1408, 1688, 1702
Lille, 1708, 1792
Limerick, 1651, 1691
Londonderry, 1689
Lucknow 1857
Louisburg 1758
Luxemburg, 1795
Lyons 1793
Maestricht, 1579, 1673 (Vauban first came into notice), 1676, 1748
Magdala, 1868
Magdeburg 1631, 1806
Malaga, 1487
Malta, 1565, 1798 1800
Mantua, 1797 1799
Marseilles, 1524
Menin, 1706
Mentz, 1689, 1793
Messina 1282, 1719, 1848, 1861
Metz 1552-53 1870
Mons, 1691, 1709, 1792
Montargis, 1426.
Montauban, 1621
Montevideo, Jan 1807
Mothe (the French, taught by a Mr Muller, first practised the art of throwing shells), 1634
Namur, 1692, 1746, 1794
Naples 1435, 1504, 1557, 1792, 1799, 1806
Nice, 1706
Nieuport, 1600.
Olivenza, 1801, 1811
Olmütz, 1758
Orleans, 1428, 1563
Ostend, 1601, 1798
Oudenarde, 1706
Padua, 1509
Pampeluna, 1813
Paris, 1420, 1594, 1870, 1871
Parma, 1248
Pavia, 1524, 1655
Perpignan, 1542, 1642
Phalsbourg, 1814, 1815, 1870
Philipsburg, 1644, 1676, 1688 (first experiment of firing artillery *a ricochet*, 1734, 1799)
Plevna, 1877
Pondicherry, 1748, 1793
Prague 1741-44
Quesnoy, 1793-94
Rheims, 1359
Rhodes, 1521
Richmond U S, 1864-65
Riga, 1700 1710
Rochelle, 1573, 1627
Rome, 1527, 1798, 1849
Romorantin (artillery first used in sieges—*Voltaire*), 1356
Rouen, 1419, 1449, 1591
Roxburgh, 1460
St. Sebastian, 1813
Saragossa, 1710, 1808, 1809 (the 2 last dreadful)
Sebastopol, 1854-5.
Schweidnitz (first experiment to reduce a fortress by springing globes of compression), 1757-1762
Scio (GREECE), 1822
Seringapatam, 1799
Seville, 1247-48
Silistria, 1854
Smolensko, 1632, 1812.
Stralsund (the method of throwing red hot balls first practised with certainty), 1715
Strasburg, 1870
Tarragona, 1811
Temeswar, 1716
Thionville, 1792
Thorn, 1703
Tortosa, 1811
Toulon, 1707, 1793
Toulouse, 1217
Tournay, 1340, 1513, 1583, 1667, 1709 (this was the best defence ever drawn from counter mines), 1792
Trèves, 1635, 1673, 1675
Tunis, 1270, 1535.

Turin, 1640 1706
Valencia, 1705, 1707, 1712
Valenciennes, 1677, 1793, 1794
Vannes, 1342.
Venloo, 1702
Verdun, 1792
Vicksburg U S 1863
Vienna, 1529, 1683
Wakefield, 1460
Warsaw, 1831
Xativa, 1246.
Xeres 1262
Yorktown, 1781
Ypres 1648
Zurich, 1544
Zutphen, 1586

Siena (*se-a'na*) (formerly *Sena Julia*, Italy), in the middle ages a powerful republic rivalling Florence and Pisa, weakened through intestine quarrels, was subjugated by the emperor Charles V, and given to his son in 1555, who ceded it to Cosmo of Tuscany, 1557 It was incorporated with France, 1808 14

Sierra Leone (*se-er'ra le-o'ne*), a colonial settlement of W Africa, discovered in 1460 In 1786, London swarmed with free negroes in idleness and want, and 400 of them, with 60 whites, mostly women of bad character and in ill-health, were sent out to Sierra Leone at the charge of government to form a settlement, 9 Dec 1786 In 1807 the settlement was given up to the crown It extends from the Scarcies river on the north to Liberia on the south, 180 miles By agreement with the French government, 10 Aug 1889 a commission was appointed for the delimitation of the British and French possessions in W Africa, Oct 1890 Commissioners met Dec 1891 Area, 15,000 sq miles, pop 180,000

signals are alluded to by Polybius Elizabeth had instructions drawn up for the admiral and general of the expedition to Cadiz, to be announced to the fleet in a certain latitude, this is said to have been the first set of signals given to commanders of the English fleet A system for the navy was invented by the duke of York, afterwards James II, 1665 —*Guthrie* A regular code of day and night signals was arranged by adms. Howe and Kempenfelt of the British navy, about 1790, and in 1812 capt Rodgers, of the United States navy, arranged an admirable signal system A code of signals was adopted by the U S navy department in 1857 Another board in 1859 tested and approved a system of night-signals invented by B F Coston of the U S navy, and in Oct 1861 they were adopted in the U S army A new system was invented by gen Albert J Myer, which was used in both branches of the service by night and day during the civil war In 1870 the signal-service of the army was partly formed into a meteorological bureau to study the scientific law and to notice the advance of storms In 1891 this branch of the service was transferred from the war department to the department of agriculture, and the WEATHER BUREAU was organized For fog signals, etc, ACOUSTICS

signboards were used by the Greeks and Romans. A "History of Signboards," by Jacob Larwood and John Hotten, was pub in 1866

signers of the Declaration of Independence and Constitution CONSTITUTION, DECLARATION

Sikhs (*sēks*), a people of N India, invaded the Mogul empire, 1703-8. INDIA, 1849, PUNJAB.

Sil'chester, county Hants, Engl Here are the remains of the Roman town Calleva (built on the site of the British Caer Segeint or Segont), including walls of excellent masonry, a basilica and forum, private dwellings, etc Many discoveries have been made during excavations carried on under the patronage of the duke of Wellington, since 1863 Coins of Claudius I and later emperors have been found A systematic investigation of these remains was begun by the Society of Antiquaries, London, 23 June, 1890

Many vases, tools, etc., discovered — 1890
Remains of a presumed Romano-British church, probable date 4th century, uncovered — June 1892

Sile'sia, formerly a province of Poland, was invaded by John of Bohemia, 1325, and ceded to him, 1355 It was taken by the king of Hungary, 1478, and added to the Austrian dominion, 1526 It was conquered and lost several times during the Seven Years' war by Frederick of Prussia but a part was retained by him at the peace in 1763 In 1587 the duke of Leignitz made an agreement with the elector of Brandenburg that if either died without issue the survivor should have both realms The duke died without issue, but Leopold I. claimed the dukedom as a forfeited fief. At the death of Charles VI. the elector of Brandenburg, then Frederick II. (the Great), claimed Silesia as his right, based upon the above agreement; and as Maria Theresa of Austria refused to give it up, the Silesian wars followed, 1741-63

sil'icon or **silicium** (*se-lish'e-um*) (from *silex*, flint), a non-metallic element, next to oxygen the most abundant substance in the earth, as it enters into many earths, metallic oxides, and a great number of minerals The mode of procuring pure silicon was discovered by Berzelius in 1823.—*Gmelin.* RANSOME'S STONE, WATER-GLASS

Silis'tria, a strong military town in Bulgaria, European Turkey It was taken by the Russians, 30 June, 1829, and held some years by them as a pledge for the payment of a large sum by the Porte, but was eventually restored In 1854 it was again besieged by the Russians, 30 000 strong, under prince Paskiewitch and many assaults were made. RUSSO-TURKISH WARS, 1854.

silk. Wrought silk was brought from Persia to Greece, 324 B C Known at Rome in Tiberius's time, when the senate prohibited the use of plate of massive gold, and forbade men to debase themselves by wearing silk, fit only for women Heliogabalus first wore a garment of silk, 220 A D Silk was at first of the same value with gold, weight for weight, and was thought to grow like cotton on trees Silk-worms were brought from India to Europe in the 6th century Charlemagne sent Offa, king of Mercia, a present of two silken vests, 780 The manufacture was encouraged by Roger, king of Sicily, at Palermo, 1146, when the Sicilians not only bred the silk-worms, but spun and wove the silk The manufacture spread into Italy and Spain, and also into the south of France, a little before the reign of Francis I about 1510, and Henry IV propagated mulberry-trees and silk-worms throughout the kingdom about 1600 In England, silk mantles were worn by some noblemen's ladies at a ball at Kenilworth castle, 1286 Silk was worn by the English clergy in 1534. Cultivated in England in 1604, and broad silk woven from raw silk in 1620 Brought to perfection by the French refugees in London at Spitalfields, 1688 A silk-throwing mill was made in England, and fixed up at Derby, by sir Thomas Lombe, merchant of London modelled from the original mill then in the king of Sardinia's dominions, about 1714. He obtained a patent in 1718, and died 3 Jan 1739 6 new species of silk-worm were rearing in France, 1861 In 1858, M Guerin-Meneville introduced into France a Chinese worm termed the *Cynthia bombyx*, which feeds on the *Ailanthus glandulosa*, a hardy tree of the oak kind The cynthia yields a silk-like substance termed *Ailantine* It was brought to Turin by Fantoni in 1856

silk in the United States James I of England, seeking to introduce silk culture into the American colonies, forwarded eggs to Virginia, and offered bounties on silk cultivation, but the superior profit of tobacco culture brought the experiment to naught Silk culture was introduced in Louisiana in 1718, and government encouragement was given to the industry in Georgia Artisans were sent to Georgia to carry on silk industries in 1732 The first export of raw silk (8 pounds) was made in 1734 In 1749 the production at Ebenezer, on the Savannah river, amounted to 1000 lbs A public filature or reel for drawing off silk from cocoons was set up in Savannah in 1751 From 1751 to 1754 the exports amounted to $8880, and for the next eighteen years there was an annual export averaging 546 lbs. In 1760, 15,000 lbs of cocoons were delivered at the filature The production rapidly declined under British taxation, and was destroyed entirely by the Revolutionary war The history of silk culture in South Carolina was almost identical with that in Georgia. In Connecticut 200 lbs of raw silk were made in 1789 In 1790, 50 families in New Haven and 30 in Norfolk were engaged in the business In 1839 the product of Mansfield, Conn, was about 5 tons A filature was established in Philadelphia in 1770 With a climate every way adapted to the production of silk, California bids fair to become a great silk-producing state Thousands of mulberry-trees have been imported to afford food for the silk-worms. In 1875, one cocoonery in San José had 1,000,000 silk-worms There are now over 200 silk-factories in the U. S., and the cultivation of native silk seems to be reviving. The Women's Silk-culture Association held an exhibition in Philadelphia, 1881-82. For early culture, CONNECTICUT, 1747; GEORGIA, 1735; SOUTH CAROLINA, 1755.

silot'vaar, a new explosive, invented by a Russian engineer, M. Rouckteshell, in 1886; said to be 10 times more powerful than gunpowder.

Sil'ures, a British tribe, occupying the counties of Monmouth and Hereford, was subdued by the Roman general Ostorius Scapula, 50. SHROPSHIRE. From this tribe is derived the geological term "Silurian strata," among the lowest of the palæozoic, or primary series, from their occurrence in the above-mentioned counties. Murchison's "Siluria" was pub. 1849.

silver exists in most parts of the world, and is found mixed with other ores in various mines in Great Britain. The silver-mines of South America are by far the richest, especially those of Peru and Bolivia, there having been mined over $650,000,000 from the mines of POTOSI, Bolivia, since their discovery. In 1749, one mass of silver weighing 370 lbs. was sent to Spain. From a mine in Norway a piece of silver was dug, and sent to the Royal museum at Copenhagen, weighing 560 lbs., and worth 1680*l*. In England silver plate and vessels were first used by Wilfrid, a Northumbrian bishop, 709.—*Tyrrell*. According to the estimate of Mulhall, Mexico has produced more silver since 1523 than any other country within the last 500 years, amounting to over $3,050,000,000; next in order is Peru, with nearly $3,000,000,000; followed by the United States, with $1,000,000,000 from 1849. The amount of silver produced in the U. S. in 1890 was $70,465,000, the largest output in the world, followed by Mexico with $50,000,000. The states depositing the most silver at the U. S. mints up to 1891 were, 1st, Nevada, amount $100,279,775; 2d, Colorado, $24,467,565; 3d, Utah territory, $19,576,538; 4th, Montana, $16,556,225; 5th, Arizona territory, $13,857,358, etc., down to New Hampshire with $1.74. The ratio of the value of silver to that of gold varies, viz.: 1000 B.C., 12 to 1; 500 B.C., 13 to 1; commencement Christian era, 9 to 1; 500 A.D., 18 to 1; 1100, 8 to 1; 1400, 11 to 1; 1554, 6 to 1; 1561, 2 to 1; 1600, 10 to 1; 1727, 13 to 1; 1800, 15.5 to 1. This ratio was maintained until 1872, when it began to rise. The following shows the range of silver quotations in London, the chief market of the world, and the dollar value and the ratio of silver to gold for the years given:

RATIO OF SILVER TO GOLD.

	Average price per oz., London.	Ratio of silver to gold.
1845-49	59⅝*d*. = $1.30+	15.8+
1850-72	61*d*. = 1.33+	15.4+
1874	59*d*. = 1.28	16.17
1876	52+*d*. = 1.15+	17.88
1879	51+*d*. = 1.12+	18.40
1883	50+*d*. = 1.11	18.64
1886	45+*d*. = 1.00+	20.78
1888	42+*d*. = 0.94	21.99
1889	42+*d*. = 0.93+	22.09
1890	47+*d*. = 1.04+	19.76
1891	45+*d*. = 0.98+	20.92
1892	39+*d*. = 0.87+	23.72
1893	36+*d*. = 0.80+	25.77

[During Feb. 1894, the price of silver in the London market fell as low as 29¼*d*., about 65 cts., or ½ part of the price of gold, the lowest price on record up to that time.]

BLAND SILVER BILL, COIN AND COINAGE, GOLD.

Silver Grays, a term applied to the Whigs of New York who supported the administration of president Fillmore, and regarded the slavery question settled by the compromise of 1850. A convention of the administration was held at Syracuse, 27 Sept. 1850, to secure a vindication of the president's policy, etc. The convention resulted in an emphatic majority against the administration; whereupon the chairman, Mr. Granger, and several other administration men, left the convention; as they were elderly men, they, with their following, were immediately dubbed "Silver Grays."

Siman'cas, a town of Castile, Spain. Near it Ramirez II. of Leon and Ferdinand of Castile gained a great victory over Abderahman, the Moorish king of Cordova, 6 Aug. 938.

Sim'nel conspiracy. REBELLIONS, 1486.

Simo'nians, a sect named from the founder, Simon Magus, the first heretic, about 41. A sect of social reformers called "St. Simonians" sprang up in France in 1819, and attracted considerable attention; the doctrines were advocated in England, particularly by dr. Prati, who lectured upon them in London, 24 Jan. 1834. St. Simon died in 1825, and his follower, Père Enfantin, died 1 Sept. 1864.

si'mony (trading in church offices) derives its name from Simon desiring to purchase the gift of the Holy Spirit (Acts viii. 18, 19).

Sim'plon, a mountain road leading from Switzerland into Italy, constructed by Napoleon in 1801-7. It winds up passes, crosses cataracts, passes by galleries through solid rock, and has 8 principal bridges. The number of workmen employed varied from 30,000 to 40,000.

Sinai (*si'na-i*), **Mount,** north of the Red sea, between Suez and Akabah gulfs. Here, as is supposed, the 10 commandments were promulgated, 1491 B.C. (Exod. xx.). After much investigation and discussion by many persons, dr. Beke, in Feb. 1874, confidently identified Sinai with a peak in 28° 30′ N. lat. 34° E. lon.

Sinde, a province of N.W. India, was traversed by the Greeks under Alexander, about 326 B.C.; conquered by the Persian Mahometans in the 8th century A.D.; tributary to the Ghaznevide dynasty in the 11th century; conquered by Nadir Shah, 1739; reverted to the empire of Delhi after his death, 1747; after various changes of rulers, Sinde was conquered by the English, and annexed, Mch. 1843. Napier announced its conquest to his government by the single Latin word *peccavi*, i. e. "I have sinned."

singing. HYMNS, MUSIC.

Sino'pe, an important Greek colony on the Euxine, after resisting several attacks was conquered by Mithridates IV., king of Pontus, and made his capital. It was the birthplace of Diogenes, the cynic philosopher. On 30 Nov. 1853, a Turkish fleet of 7 frigates, 3 corvettes, and 2 smaller vessels was attacked by a Russian fleet of 6 sail of the line, 2 sailing-vessels, and 3 steamers, under adm. Nachimoff, and totally destroyed, except 1 vessel, which conveyed the tidings to Constantinople. 4000 lives were lost by fire or drowning, and Osman Pacha, the Turkish admiral, died at Sebastopol of his wounds. In consequence of this act (considered treacherous) the Anglo-French fleet entered the Black sea, 3 Jan. 1854.

Sioux (*soo*). INDIANS.

sirene (*si-reen'*), an instrument for determining the velocity of aerial vibrations corresponding to the different pitches of musical sounds, was invented by baron Cagniard de la Tour of Paris in 1819. The principle was shown in an apparatus exhibited by Robert Hooke before the Royal Society of England, 27 July, 1681. ACOUSTICS.

sisterhoods in the English church were begun by Lydia Priscilla Sellon about 1846, in Devonshire; she died Nov. 1876.

Sisters of Charity, an order for the service of the sick poor, was founded by Vincent de Paul, in 1634. Their establishment in London began in 1854.

Siva (*see'va*), known in Hindu mythology as the Avenger or Destroyer. BRAHMINS.

Six Nations. NEW YORK, 1712.

skating (on bones, etc.) is said to have been practised in prehistoric times by northern nations.

Mentioned by the Danish historian Saxo-Grammaticus..about 1134
William Fitz-Stephens speaks of it in London..........about 1180
Figures of skates in Olaus Magnus's history..........printed 1555
Blade-skates, probably from Holland, about 1660, were seen in St. James's park by Evelyn and Pepys..............1 Dec. 1662
An Edinburgh club established.............................. 1744
Robert Jones's "Art of Skating" pub........................ 1772
London Skating club, 1830; Oxford club..................... 1838
Roller-skates invented by James L. Plimpton of New York.... 1869
National Skating Association organized in England.......... 1879
Frank Delmont skates 1 mile on roller-skates in 2 min. 50.4 sec., at Olympia, Engl..............................27 Aug. 1890
J. F. Donoghue, of Newburg, N. Y., wins the 1½-mile international race at Lingay Fen, near Cambridge, Engl., in 4 min. 46 sec. (1890), and the International races at Amsterdam.6-7 Jan. 1891

BEST SKATING RECORDS.

Distance.	Time.			Skater.	Place.	Date.
	hour.	min.	sec.			
.5 mile.	..	1	05.4	J. F. Donoghue, straightaway with strong wind..	Newburg, N. Y..................	27 Jan. 1892
.5 "	..	1	22	J. S. Johnson..............................	Minneapolis, Minn..............	25 Feb. 1893
1 "	..	2	12.6	J. F. Donoghue, straightaway with strong wind..	Newburg, N. Y..................	1 " 1887
1 "	..	2	45.6	J. S. Johnson..............................	Minneapolis, Minn..............	21 Jan. 1893
1 "	..	2	49	Harald Hagen...............................	Hamar, Norway..................	2 " 1892
2 miles.	..	5	43.8	" "	Christiania, Norway............	28 Feb. "
2 "	..	6	01	J. S. Johnson..............................	Minneapolis, Minn..............	26 " 1893
3 "	..	8	46.4	Harald Hagen...............................	Hamar, Norway..................	3 Jan. 1892
3 "	..	8	56.2	P. Oestlund	" "	26 Feb. 1893
4 "	..	13	16.4	J. F. Donoghue.............................	Orange Lake, N. Y..............	8 Mch. 1890
5 "	..	15	11	Harald Hagen...............................	Hamar, Norway..................	27 Dec. 1891
5 "	..	15	36.4	J. F. Donoghue	Newburg, N. Y..................	7 Feb. "
10 "	..	32	38.7	A. D. Norseng..............................	Hamar, Norway..................	——— 1893
10 "	..	33	26	Harald Hagen...............................	Christiania Fiord, Norway.......	21 Feb. 1892
15 "	..	55	00	A. Paulsen.................................	Brooklyn, N. Y.................	2 " 1884
20 "	1	13	08	J. F. Donoghue.............................	Cove Pond, near Stamford, Conn..	26 Jan. 1893
25 "	1	31	29	" "	" " "	" "
50 "	3	15	59.4	" "	" " "	" "
100 "	7	11	38.2	" "	" " "	" "

"Sketch Book," Irving's. The first number was deposited for copyright 15 May, 1819. It contained 93 pages, and consisted of the "Prospectus," "The Author's Account of Himself," "The Voyage," "Roscoe," "The Wife," and "Rip Van Winkle."

Skinners. NEUTRAL GROUND.

Skrae'lings (signifying dwarfs), a name given to the natives (Esquimaux) found on the New England coast by the Northmen at the time of their supposed discovery. AMERICA.

slavery and **slave-trade.** The traffic in men introduced from Chaldæa into Egypt and Arabia, and spread over the East. In Greece, in the time of Homer, all prisoners of war were treated as slaves. The Lacedæmonian youths, trained in the practice of deceiving and butchering slaves, were from time to time let loose upon them to show their proficiency; and once, for amusement only, murdered, it is said, 3000 in one night. HELOTS. Alexander, when he razed Thebes, sold the whole people for slaves, 335 B.C. There were 400,000 slaves in Attica, 317 B.C. In Rome slaves were often chained to the gate of a great man's house, to give admittance to the guests invited to the feast. By one of the laws of the XII. Tables, creditors could seize their insolvent debtors, and keep them in their houses, till by their services or labor they had discharged the sum they owed. C. Pollio threw such slaves as gave him offence into his fish-ponds, to fatten his lampreys, 42 B.C. Cæcilius Isidorus left to his heir 4116 slaves, 12 B.C. The first Janissaries were Christian slaves, 1329. The slave-trade from Congo and Angola was begun by the Portuguese in 1481. The commerce in man has brutalized a tract 15 degrees on each side of the equator, and forty degrees wide, or of 4,000,000 sq. miles; and men and women have been bred for sale to the Christian nations during the last 250 years, and war carried on to make prisoners for the Christian market. The Abbé Raynal computed (1777) that, at the time of his writing, 9,000,000 of slaves had been consumed by the Europeans. The slave-trade is now approaching extinction.

In 1768 the slaves taken from Africa amounted to 104,100. In 1786 the annual number was about 100,000.

In 1807 it was shown by documents, produced by the English government, that since 1792 upwards of 3,500,000 Africans had been torn from their country, and had either perished on the passage or been sold in the West Indies.

Slave-trade abolished by Austria in 1782; by the French convention in.. 1794

Allies at Vienna declare against it.......................Feb. 1815

Napoleon, in the Hundred Days, abolishes the trade....29 Mch. "

Treaty for its repression with Spain, 1817; with the Netherlands, May, 1818; with Brazil.......................Nov. 1826

French government gives permission to M. Regis to convey free negroes from Africa to Guadeloupe and Martinique, French colonies.....................................June, 1857

Abuses being disclosed, the license is revoked...........Jan. 1859

It is said that about 40,000 slaves were landed at Cuba in...... 1860

Serfdom abolished by Frederick I. of Prussia in 1702; by Christian VII. of Denmark in 1766; by Joseph II., emperor of Germany, in his hereditary states, in 1781; by Nicholas I. of Russia, in the imperial domains, in 1842; and by his successor, Alexander II., throughout his empire...........3 Mch. 1861

Slavery ceases in the Dutch West Indies..............1 July, 1863

Spanish government denounces the slave-trade as piracy, Nov. 1865

By decree of 1867, all children thereafter born in Brazil were free, and all slaves to be free in 20 years. In Nov. slaves of the state became free when made soldiers. Slavery to be abolished gradually by law of......................27 Sept. 1871

Species of slave-trade having risen in the South seas, the natives being enticed on board certain British vessels and shipped to Queensland, Australia, and the Fiji isles; the subject was brought before Parliament.........................1871–72

Ship *Carl* (owner, dr. James P. Murray; master, Joseph Armstrong) leaves Melbourne for South Sea isles; anchors off Malokolo, Solomon's, and Bougainville isles, and kidnaps many natives as laborers for the Fiji isles; while about 20 miles from land, the prisoners rise and attempt to set fire to the ship; are fired on; about 50 killed and 20 wounded are cast into the sea. At Melbourne, Murray gives evidence, and Armstrong is committed for trial, 16 Aug.; the master and mate sentenced to death......................Nov. 1872

Sir Bartle Frere goes to Zanzibar on a mission to suppress the East African slave-trade (ZANZIBAR)..................... 1872–73

Slavery abolished in Porto Rico.......................23 Mch. 1873

Act of Parliament, for consolidating with amendments the acts for carrying into effect treaties for suppression of the slave-trade (36 and 37 Vict. c. 88), passed.................5 Aug. "

Sir Samuel Baker heads an expedition to put down slave-trading on the Nile (EGYPT), Jan. 1870; reported to be partially successful, 30 June, 1873. He published "Ismailia," a history of the expedition, 1874. He estimates that at least 50,000 are annually captured and sold as slaves..............Nov. 1874

Several African kings and chiefs, at Cape Coast Castle, agree to give up slave-trade, at an interview with gov. Strahan.3 Nov. "

Slave-trade on the Gold Coast abolished by proclamation of gov. Strahan.....................................17 Dec. "

Immediate suppression of slavery in the colonies of St. Thomas, etc., by Portugal, announced...........................Feb. 1876

Convention with Egypt forbidding the traffic, 4 Aug. 1877; col. Gordon's efforts in the Soudan reported successful.......... 1879

Slavery to be abolished in Egypt.................end of July, 1881

Gradual emancipation in Cuba; bill passes in Spanish senate, 24 Dec. 1879; by deputies, 21 Jan.; promulgated, 18 Feb. 1880; slavery totally abolished..................................... 1886

Abolition of slavery in BRAZIL.................................. 1867–88

Abolished in ZANZIBAR...................................Oct. 1889–90

Anti-slavery conference at Brussels meets, 18 Nov. 1889; delegates from 17 states; conferences: 19 Nov.–Dec. 1889, Jan.–May, 1890; general act for regulating the immediate suppression of the slave-trade agreed to and ratified by all, 2 Apr. 1892

slavery and **slave-trade** in England. Laws respecting the sale of slaves were made by Alfred. The English peasantry were commonly sold for slaves in Saxon and Norman times; children were sold in Bristol market like cattle for exportation. Many were sent to Ireland and to Scotland. Under the Normans, the vassals (termed villeins, of and pertaining to the *vill*) were devisable as chattels during the feudal times.

Severe statutes were passed in the reign of Richard II., 1377 and 1385; the rebellion of Wat Tyler arose partly out of the evils of serfdom.. 1381

By law of Edward VI., a runaway, or any one who lived idly for 3 days, to be brought before 2 justices, branded V on the breast, and sold as a slave for 2 years. The master must give him bread, water or small drink, and refuse meat, and cause him to work by beating, chaining, or otherwise; and if he absented himself 14 days, he was to be branded on the forehead or cheek with an S, and be his master's slave forever; second desertion was made felony. It was lawful to put a ring of iron round his neck, arm, or leg. A child might be put apprentice, and, on running away, became a slave to his master.. 1547

Queen Elizabeth orders her bondsmen in the western counties to be made free at easy rates..................................... 1574

[Serfdom finally extinguished in 1660, when tenures *in capite*, knights' service, etc., were abolished.]

Slave-trade begun by sir John Hawkins; his first expedition, with the object of procuring negroes on the coast of Africa,

and conveying them for sale at the West Indies, takes place (ASSIENTO GUINEA) Oct 1562
Slave named Somerset, brought to England, is, because of his ill state, turned adrift by his master By the charity of Granville Sharp he is restored to health, when his master again claims him but lord Mansfield, of the Court of King's Bench, decides that slavery cannot exist in Great Britain 22 June, 1772
Thomas Clarkson, of Wadesmill, Hertford, devotes his life to the abolition of the slave trade June, 1785
England employs 130 ships and carries off 42 000 slaves 1786
"Society for the Suppression of the Slave trade," founded by Clarkson, Wilberforce, and Dillwyn 1787
Slave trade question is debated in Parliament "
Debate for its abolition, 2 days Apr 1791
Mr Wilberforce's motion lost by a majority of 88 to 83 3 Apr 1798
Question introduced under the auspices of lord Grenville and Mr Fox, then ministers 31 Mch 1806
Trade abolished by Parliament 25 Mch 1807
Act to abolish slavery throughout the British colonies to promote industry among the manumitted slaves and for compensation to owners, by the grant of 20,000 000*l* 28 Aug 1833
Slavery terminates in the British possessions, 770,280 slaves become free 1 Aug 1834
Slavery abolished in the East Indies 1 Aug 1838
Thomas Clarkson d aged 85 Sept. 1846
In 1853, John Anderson a runaway slave, kills Septimus Digges, a planter of Missouri who attempts to arrest him, and escapes to Canada The American government claims him as a murderer The Canadian judges deciding that the law requires his surrender, Edwin James Q C (15 Jan) obtains a writ of habeas corpus from the Court of Queen's Bench Anderson is discharged on technical grounds 16 Feb 1861
Circular from the Admiralty concerning the surrender of fugitive slaves on British ships to their owners, dated 31 July, censured by the public, Sept, Oct withdrawn Nov 1875
Revised circular issued near end of Dec 1875, meets with much adverse criticism Jan 1876
Government commission appointed (the duke of Somerset, chief justice Cockburn sir Henry S Maine, and others), Feb, report unfavorable to the circulars, pub 13 June "
New admiralty instructions fugitive slaves to be received and not given up, action left to captain's discretion, breach of international faith and comity to be avoided, issues, 10 Aug "
An obelisk, as a memorial to Thomas Clarkson erected by Arthur Giles Puller, at Wadesmill, inaugurated 9 Oct 1879

slavery in the United States Before the War of Independence all the states contained slaves In 1783, the statement in the Massachusetts Bill of Rights, "All men are born free and equal," was declared in the Supreme court at Boston to bar slaveholding in that state Slavery was begun within the domain of the U S in 1619, when 20 negroes were sold by a Dutch trading vessel to settlers of Virginia It was recognized by law in Virginia in 1620, in Massachusetts, 1641, in Connecticut and Rhode Island, about 1650, in New York, 1656, in Maryland, 1663, in New Jersey, 1665, in the Carolinas from the time of their settlement, and in Georgia, 1749 There were also a few slaves in PENNSYLVANIA as early as 1688, but mostly in Philadelphia.

Severe laws against slaves in South Carolina 1712
Decisions in Maryland and elsewhere that conversion and baptism do not confer freedom 1715
Importation of slaves into Virginia (1000 annually) 1724
Georgia prohibits slavery 1735
Strong public opinion in Georgia in favor of slavery, supported by Whitefield and Habersham 1737-49
Slavery legalized in Georgia 1749
Laws of great severity against slaves enacted in South Carolina, 1750
Authority for dismemberment of slaves general throughout the South "
Little effort made to convert slaves anywhere before or after "
Slave code quite severe in Massachusetts "
Slave population in Connecticut greater than in Massachusetts, and in Rhode Island than in either "
Very few slaves in Pennsylvania before or after "
Controversy in Massachusetts on slavery 1766-73
Virginia prohibits the introduction of slaves 1778
Virginia repeals the old colonial statute forbidding the emancipation of slaves except for meritorious service 1782
After this, for a period of 23 years, private emancipations were numerous, and, but for subsequent re enactments, the colored free population would have exceeded the slave
In the reorganization of the army (Revolution), 1778, except for local defence, no troops were asked of South Carolina and Georgia in consideration of their larger slave population —*Hildreth's* "Hist U S," vol. iii p 244

About the time of the Revolution, societies of prominent men were formed for the purpose of ameliorating the condition of the slaves Pennsylvania was the first state to organize such a society, 1787, with Franklin as president. New York followed, with John Jay as its first president, and Alexander Hamilton as its second Immediately after, Rhode Island, Maryland in 1789, with such members as Samuel Chase and Luther Martin, Delaware, with James A. Bayard and C A Rodney, Connecticut, 1790, Virginia, 1791, New Jersey, 1792 The most that was accomplished by this agitation was the suppression of the slave-trade from 1808 Pennsylvania abolished slavery by gradual emancipation, 1780, Massachusetts by a Bill of Rights prefixed to the constitution, 1780, New Hampshire by her constitution, 1784, Connecticut and Rhode Island, 1784, Vermont by her constitution, New York by gradual abolition, 1799, further legislation in 1817 decreed total abolition after 4 July, 1827, when about 10,000 slaves were liberated, New Jersey, gradual abolition, 1804

SLAVE POPULATION IN THE UNITED STATES ACCORDING TO THE CENSUS OF 1790

North		South	
New Hampshire	158	Delaware	8 887
Vermont	17	Maryland	103 036
Rhode Island	952	Virginia	293 427
Connecticut	2 759	North Carolina	100 572
Massachusetts	none	South Carolina	107 094
New York	21,324	Georgia	29 264
New Jersey	11,423	Kentucky	11 830
Pennsylvania	3,737	Tennessee	3 417
Total	40,370	Total	657,527

In 1810 1,191 364, in 1820, 2 009 031, in 1850, 3 204.313, in 1860, 4,002 996 In 1870, 4,880,193 free colored persons, in 1880, 6 577,-151, in 1890, 7,638,360

Congress passes unanimously the celebrated ordinance for the government of the territory to the N W of the Ohio," which contained an "*unalterable*" article, forbidding slavery or involuntary servitude in the said territory 13 July, 1787
Debate in Congress on the power of that body over slavery 1790
Slavery opposed by the Presbyterian and Methodist churches "
Right of petition to Congress on the subject of slavery debated, 1792
Slave laws introduced into Kentucky "
Quakers present a memorial to Congress praying for the abolition of slavery 1794
Slavery legalized in Tennessee 1796
Georgia forbids the emancipation of slaves 1798
Free colored men petition Congress for protection against being enslaved 1800
Louisiana purchased, thus increasing the slave territory 1803
Memorial to Congress of the people of Indiana to suspend the ordinance prohibiting slavery north of the Ohio river 1804
["Had this decision rested with them both Indiana and Illinois would have come into the Union as slave states"—*Hildreth*, vol v p 497]
Great debate in Congress on the abolition of the slave trade 1806
[Enormous increase in the growth of cotton in the southern states, owing to the invention of the cotton gin in 1792, which greatly increases the demand for slave labor]

A National Colonization Society organized at Washington 23 Dec 1816, to encourage and aid emigration to Africa Its indirect object was to rid the south of its free colored population Henry Clay, John Randolph, Bushrod Washington, and other slave-holders took a leading part in its formation. The only result was the establishment of LIBERIA Clay, Charles Carroll, Madison, King of Alabama, W H Harrison, dr W E Channing, Benj Lundy, Birney, Gerrit Smith, and the Tappan brothers were all interested members of this organization Following are some of the principal events occurring in the United States relating to slavery

Missouri Compromise (UNITED STATES) 1817-21
Anti slavery societies organize in New York city and Philadelphia 1833
Prudence Crandall's school for colored children (girls) broken up (CONNECTICUT) "
Incendiary literature (regarding slavery) noticed in Jackson's message (UNITED STATES, Aug and Dec.) 1835
Murder of rev Elijah P Lovejoy (ALTON RIOTS) 1836
AMISTAD CASE THE 1839
Creole case, the (UNITED STATES) 1841
Samuel Hoar in Charleston, S C (MASSACHUSETTS, UNITED STATES) 1844-45
SCHOONER PEARL 1848
Fugitive Slave law and other compromise measures pass (UNITED STATES) 1850
Slave trade suppressed in the District of Columbia "
Negro Sims seized at Boston under the Fugitive Slave law (MASSACHUSETTS) 1851
Negro Shadrach seized at Boston under the Fugitive Slave law (MASSACHUSETTS) "
"Uncle Tom's Cabin" pub 1852
Repeal of the Missouri Compromise by Kansas and Nebraska bill (UNITED STATES) 1854
Republican party formed (POLITICAL PARTIES) "
Seizure of the negro Burns at Boston (MASSACHUSETTS, UNITED STATES) "
Kansas war (KANSAS) 1854 et seq
DRED SCOTT decision 1857
Seizure of the negro Littlejohn at Oberlin, O, under the Fugitive Slave law (OHIO) 1859
JOHN BROWN'S INSURRECTION "
Abraham Lincoln, Republican, elected president. 4 Nov 1860

SLA

SOA

tale was 1 in 10. For attempts to alleviate this scourge, INOCULATION, introduced into England in 1722, and VACCINATION, announced by dr. Jenner in 1798. Small-pox raged in parts of London, and thousands died, 1870-71. The Anti-vaccination Society has been active, and many parents have been fined in England for opposing the vaccination of their children, 1870-78. In Sept. and Oct. 1862, a great many sheep died of small-pox in the west of England, till successful preventive measures were resorted to. MASSACHUSETTS, 1721.

Smectym'nuus, a name made up of the initials of certain nonconformists, who composed a treatise in common against episcopacy ... century.—Stephen Marshall, Edmund C... Matthew Newcomen, William Spurstow ... by bishop Hall in his "Divine Ri...

Smithfie...

Slavo'nia or **Sclavo'nia,** a province ... derives its name from the Slavs, a Sarmatian ... placed the Avars in Pannonia early in the ... 864, Cyril and Methodius, Greek missionaries, ... and adapted the Greek alphabet to the Slavo... the letters of which have since been a little ... country, after having been held at times by the ... and Hungarians, and the cause of sanguinary ... ceded finally to Hungary in 1699, at the peace ... Deputies from the Slavonian provinces of Austria ... tained at Moscow and St. Petersburg, May, 1867. ... tian-Slavonian diet at Agram was dissolved, May, ... protested against incorporation ... family of languages includes ... man, Bulgarian, Wendic, Slo... number of Slavs in Europe is ... Ruthenians, 66,129,590; Serbo... 5,123,952; Slovenes, 1,260,000; ... 4,815,154; Poles, 9,492,162.

sling, an instrument ... stones, consisting of a piece of lea... a string attached to each end, ... letting one string loose the stone ... ity. In Judg. xx. 16 is mentioned ... slingers (about 1406 B.C.), and with ... liath, 1063 B.C. (1 Sam. xvii.). ... isles (Majorca, Minorca, and Iviça) ... as mercenaries in the Carthaginian ... are said to have been used by the Hu... of Sancerre, in 1672, to economize their po...

Sloane, Sir Hans. Collection, ... MUSEUM.

Sluys, a town of Holland, near which Ed... a signal naval victory over the French. The ... wind of the enemy, and the sun at their backs, ... sanguinary action. 230 French ships were take... of Frenchmen were killed, with 2 of their admi... of the English was inconsiderable; 24 June, 1340.

Smalcald (Hesse), Treaty of, entered into ... elector of Brandenburg and the other princes of ... favor of Protestantism, 31 Dec. 1530. The empe... hensive that the kings of France and England would ... league, signed the treaty of Passau, 31 July, 1552, ... liberty of conscience. PROTESTANTS.

small-pox, *variola* (diminutive of *varus*, a pi... highly contagious disease, supposed to have been intr... into Europe from the East by the Saracens. Rhazes, a... bian, described it accurately about 900. From Europe it ... carried to America, soon after its discovery, and raged ... with great severity, destroying the Indians by thousands. ... 1694, queen Mary of England died of small-pox, as did in ... Joseph I., emperor of Germany, and the dauphin of Fra... and in 1712 his son, in 1730 the emperor of Russia, in ... the queen of Sweden, and in 1774 Louis XV. of France. ... is stated that in the middle of the last century 2,0... perished by it in Russia. In London, in 1726, 1 out ... deaths was caused by small-pox, and in France, in 17...

mans used fuller's earth. *Savon*, the French word for soap, is ascribed to its having been manufactured at Savona, near Genoa. The manufacture of soap in London began in 1524, before which it was supplied by Bristol at one penny per pound.

Sobraon', a town of N. W. India. The British army, 35,000 strong, under sir Hugh (afterwards viscount) Gough, attacked the Sikh force on the Sutlej, 10 Feb. 1846. The enemy was dislodged after a dreadful contest, and all their batteries taken: and in attempting the passage of the river by a floating bridge in their rear, the weight of the crowds upon it broke it down, and thousands of Sikhs were killed, wounded, or drowned. The British loss was 2383 men.

social wars. ATHENS, MARSI.

socialism is defined as "a plan for the reorganization of society on the basis of social or state ownership of all instruments of production, and the determination by state enactment of the price to be paid for labor and the products of labor." "Socialism is the genus, of which communism is a species; every communist is a socialist, but all socialists are not communists." The Disciples of Christ at Jerusalem were [illegible]rst communists (Acts ii. 44), 33 A.D. The Taborites or [illegible]ites in Bohemia, Anabaptists in Germany, Levellers in [illegible]d, and Tunkers in the United States, were early examples of communists. The most advanced schools of socialism [illegible] are German.

[illegible]s More publishes his "Utopia" 1516
[illegible] socialism, "Civitas Solis," by Campanella appears 1623
[illegible]n their first complete community at Mt. Lebanon. .... 17[illegible]
[illegible] Babœuf, leader of the French communists in 1796, at Paris, is guillotined .... 28 May, 17[illegible]
[illegible]le in Pennsylvania .... 1[illegible]
[illegible] French (1772–1837), publishes his work, "The Four Movements and the General Destinies" 1808
[illegible] Ohio .... 1[illegible]
[illegible] [illegible] community before the [illegible] committee on the poor law .... [illegible]
[illegible] Simon, founder of French socialism [illegible] "Christianisme," and other [illegible] .... 18[illegible]
[illegible] Community of Equality." .... 22 Jan. 18[illegible]
[illegible] made on an estate near [illegible] [illegible] of Fourier 1832
[illegible] publishes his "Organization of [illegible]"
[illegible] his work, "What is Property [illegible]" and "Property [illegible]"
[illegible] Social Destiny of Man" .... [illegible]

Karl Rodbertus, German (1805–75), publishes his book "Our Economic Condition" 1842
Christian Metz establishes a community at Ebenezer, N. Y. (Amana [illegible]) .... [illegible]
A column in the New York *Tribune* purchased for expounding the principles of the Advocates of Association, and edited by Albert Brisbane, the apostle of Fourierism
Brisbane establishes in New York an independent paper called the *Phalanx*, organ of Fourierism .... 5 Oct. 1843
Convention of Associationists at Clinton hall, N. Y. .... 4 Apr. 1844
"Brook Farm," originally the West Roxbury community, established in 1842, adopts the principles of Fourierism
The *Phalanx* succeeded by the *Harbinger*, and published at Brook Farm .... 14 June 1845
[illegible] Janson forms a Swedish colony of [illegible] and [illegible] at Bishop Hill, Ill. (incorporated 1853) 1846
[illegible] of Fourierism in the U. S. [illegible] by the [illegible] controversy .... 20 Nov. 1846–20 May, 1847
[illegible] community established
Christian socialism, under Charles Kingsley, Frederick D. Maurice, Thomas Hughes, etc., arises in England .... about 1850
Ferdinand Lassalle begins agitation in behalf of the working classes, founding the German Social Democratic party 1862
Universal German Laborers' union, under the leadership of Lassalle, formed at Leipsic .... 23 May, 1863
Delegates of all nations, in St. Martin's hall, London, form the International Working-men's association .... 28 Sept. 1864
[illegible] of [illegible] of Lassalle organized in New York 1865
Universal congress for all concurrent and complete emancipation of the working classes at Geneva, Switzerland .... 3 Sept. 1866
Carl Marx, German [illegible], publishes his work, "Das Kapital," called the Bible of the Social Democrats 1867
[illegible] community founded by rev. Thomas Lake Harris at [illegible], N. Y. .... [illegible]
[illegible] socialism in Germany organized 1869
International congress at the Hague, 5 delegates from America [illegible] in the formation of a new international association on anarchist principles under leadership of [illegible] and removal of seat of general council of the old association, which soon after ceased to exist, to New York. Congress held .... 2–7 Sept. 1872
Union for Social Politics formed by German professors [illegible] at Eisenach .... [illegible]
Universal socialistic congress opens at Ghent .... 9 Sept. 1877
[illegible] organized a party in the U. S. [illegible] "The Socialist Labor party" .... [illegible] 1878
Henry George publishes his work entitled "Progress and Poverty" 1879
Social Democratic federation [illegible] in England, favoring [illegible] communism, [illegible], republicanism, and [illegible] 1881
Leading principles of state socialism of Germany announced in an imperial message to the German Reichstag .... [illegible]
[illegible] mass-meeting held in Cooper Union, New York, [illegible] to honor the memory of Karl Marx, d. 14 Mch. 1883 .... [illegible] 1883
[illegible] Morris, poet, author of the "Earthly Paradise," H. M. Hyndman, H. H. Champion, and John Burns, become leaders of the "Socialist league," formed 1884
Bellamy's "Looking Backward" pub. 1888

[illegible] OF PRINCIPAL [illegible] COMMUNITIES IN THE UNITED STATES

Name.	Location.	Members.	Acres.	Ended.	Duration.
[illegible]	[illegible]	[illegible]	[illegible]	[illegible]	[illegible]
[illegible]	Ravenna, [illegible]	[illegible]	[illegible]	–	2 months
[illegible]	Northampton, Mass.	[illegible]	[illegible]	[illegible]	4 years
[illegible]	Bear [illegible]	[illegible]	[illegible]	–	[illegible]
[illegible]	[illegible], Pa.	[illegible]	2,[illegible]	–	[illegible] months
[illegible]	[illegible]	[illegible]	[illegible]	[illegible]	Few months
[illegible]	Hilltown, Pa.	[illegible]	[illegible]	[illegible]	[illegible] years
[illegible]	[illegible] county, [illegible]	[illegible]	2,[illegible]	[illegible]	2 yrs. 3 mo.
[illegible]	Jefferson county, N. Y.	[illegible]	1,2[illegible]	–	Few months
[illegible]	[illegible]	[illegible]	1,[illegible]	–	6 years
[illegible]	Hamilton county, N. Y.	–	[illegible]	–	Few months
[illegible]	[illegible] county, N. Y.	[illegible]	[illegible]	–	[illegible] years
[illegible]	[illegible] county, Pa.	–	[illegible]	–	1 year
[illegible]	Warren county, Pa.	–	[illegible]	–	–
[illegible]	[illegible], N. Y.	[illegible]	[illegible]	–	[illegible] years
[illegible]	[illegible], Pa.	[illegible]	2,[illegible]	–	2 years
[illegible]	[illegible], N. Y.	[illegible]	[illegible]	[illegible]	1 year
[illegible]	[illegible] county, N. Y.	[illegible]	1,[illegible]	–	[illegible] months
[illegible]	[illegible] county, [illegible]	[illegible]	[illegible]	–	2 years
[illegible]	[illegible] county, Pa.	[illegible]	[illegible]	–	4 months
[illegible]	[illegible] county, [illegible]	[illegible]	1,[illegible]	–	[illegible]
[illegible]	[illegible], N. Y.	[illegible]	[illegible]	–	1 year
[illegible]	[illegible]	[illegible]	[illegible]	–	–
[illegible]	[illegible], N. Y.	[illegible]	[illegible]	–	Few months
[illegible]	[illegible] county, [illegible]	[illegible]	1,[illegible]	–	[illegible] years
[illegible]	Green Lake, Wis.	[illegible]	2,[illegible]	–	[illegible]
[illegible] Association	[illegible] county, Ill.	[illegible] fam.	[illegible]	[illegible]	[illegible] months
[illegible]	[illegible] county, Wis.	[illegible] fam.	[illegible]	[illegible]	[illegible] years
[illegible]	[illegible], N. Y.	–	–	[illegible]	[illegible]

[illegible]lations. Many of these are found in this work in the various state records and under [illegible]tive titles, and others may [illegible] general titles as: ARBITRATION, [illegible], LABOR, [illegible]

Secession of South Carolina (SOUTH CAROLINA, CONFEDERATE STATES, UNITED STATES)	Dec 1860
Slavery abolished in the District of Columbia	16 Apr 1862
President Lincoln proclaims the abolition of slavery in all states in rebellion 1 Jan 1863	22 Sept "
Slavery practically abolished by the submission of the southern armies	Apr 1865
Total abolition of slavery in the United States officially announced	18 Dec "

CONSTITUTION OF THE UNITED STATES Amendments of

PRINCIPAL ANTI SLAVERY PUBLICATIONS

Genius of Universal Emancipation	Mt Pleasant O, 1821; Baltimore Md, 1824	Benjamin Lundy
Journal of the Times	Bennington, Vt 1828	Lloyd Garrison
The Liberator	Boston, Mass, 1831-65	" "
The Observer	St. Louis, Mo, 1832; Alton, Ill 1836	Rev Elijah P Lovejoy
The Emancipator	New York N Y, 1833	R J Williams
The African Observer	Philadelphia Pa, 1835	Enoch Lewis
The Philanthropist	Cincinnati O 1836	James G. Birney
National Inquirer	Philadelphia, Pa. "	Benjamin Lundy
Pennsylvania Freeman	" 1838-40	John G Whittier
The Abolitionist	Boston, Mass 1839	Elizur Wright, jr

Slavo'nia or **Sclavo'nia,** a province of Austria, derives its name from the Slavs, a Sarmatian people who replaced the Avars in Pannonia early in the 9th century In 864. Cyril and Methodius, Greek missionaries, preached here, and adapted the Greek alphabet to the Slavonian language, the letters of which have since been a little altered The country after having been held at times by the Greeks, Turks, and Hungarians, and the cause of sanguinary conflicts, was ceded finally to Hungary in 1699, at the peace of Carlowitz Deputies from the Slavonian provinces of Austria were entertained at Moscow and St Petersburg May, 1867 The Croatian-Slavonian diet at Agram was dissolved, May, 1867 It protested against incorporation with Hungary The Slavonian family of languages includes Russian, Polish, Servian, Bohemian, Bulgarian, Wendic, Slovak, and Polabic Estimated number of Slavs in Europe in 1875, 90,365,633, Russians and Ruthenians, 66,129 590, Serbo-Croats, 5,940 539, Bulgarians, 5,123 952, Slovenes, 1,260,000, Slovaks, 2,223,830, Czechs, 4,815,154, Poles, 9,492,162

sling, an instrument of great antiquity for throwing stones, consisting of a piece of leather to hold the stone, with a string attached to each end, when by whirling rapidly and letting one string loose the stone is thrown with great velocity In Judg xx 16 is mentioned the skill of the Benjamite slingers (about 1406 B.C), and with a sling David slew Goliath, 1063 B.C (1 Sam xvii) The natives of the Balearic isles (Majorca, Minorca, and Iviça), celebrated slingers, served as mercenaries in the Carthaginian and Roman armies Slings are said to have been used by the Huguenots at the siege of Sancerre in 1672, to economize their powder

Sloane, Sir Hans. Collection, books, etc BRITISH MUSEUM

Sluys, a town of Holland, near which Edward III gained a signal naval victory over the French The English had the wind of the enemy and the sun at their backs, and began this sanguinary action 230 French ships were taken, thousands of Frenchmen were killed, with 2 of their admirals, the loss of the English was inconsiderable, 24 June, 1340

Smalcald (Hesse), Treaty of, entered into between the elector of Brandenburg and the other princes of Germany in favor of Protestantism, 31 Dec 1530. The emperor, apprehensive that the kings of France and England would join this league, signed the treaty of Passau, 31 July 1532, allowing liberty of conscience PROTESTANTS

small-pox, *variola* (diminutive of *varus*, a pimple), a highly contagious disease, supposed to have been introduced into Europe from the East by the Saracens Rhazes, an Arabian, described it accurately about 900 From Europe it was carried to America, soon after its discovery, and raged there with great severity, destroying the Indians by thousands. In 1694, queen Mary of England died of small-pox, as did in 1711 Joseph I emperor of Germany, and the dauphin of France, and in 1712 his son, in 1730 the emperor of Russia, in 1741 the queen of Sweden, and in 1774 Louis XV of France It is stated that in the middle of the last century 2,000,000 perished by it in Russia In London, in 1723 1 out of 14 deaths was caused by small-pox, and in France, in 1754, the rate was 1 in 10. For attempts to alleviate this scourge, INOCULATION, introduced into England in 1722, and VACCINATION, announced by dr. Jenner in 1798 Small-pox raged in parts of London, and thousands died, 1870-71 The Anti-vaccination Society has been active, and many parents have been fined in England for opposing the vaccination of their children, 1870-76 In Sept and Oct 1862, a great many sheep died of small-pox in the west of England, till successful preventive measures were resorted to MASSACHUSETTS, 1721

Smectym'nuus, a name made up of the initials of certain nonconformist writers who composed a treatise in common against episcopacy in the 17th century—Stephen Marshall, Edmund Calamy, Thomas Young, Matthew Newcomen, William Spurston They were answered by bishop Hall in his "Divine Right of Episcopacy," 1640

Smithfield, West, in the heart of London, was once a favorite walk of the London citizens, outside the city walls Sir W Wallace was executed here, 23 Aug 1305 On 15 June, 1381, Wat Tyler was met by Richard II at this place, and was stabbed by Walworth the mayor Many tournaments were also held here In the reign of Mary (1553-58) many persons were burned at the stake, the first being rev John Rogers, 4 Feb 1555 Bartholomew Leggatt, an Arian, was burned here, 18 Mch 1612 Bartholomew fair was held here till 1853 This place is mentioned as the site of a cattle market as far back as 1150 It was used for this purpose the last time, 11 June, 1855

Smithsonian Institution, "for the increase and diffusion of knowledge among men," a handsome building at Washington, D C., was founded in 1846 by means of a legacy, total amount of original bequest being $541,379, bequeathed for the purpose to the U S government by James Smithson, illegitimate son of sir Hugh Smithson, who became duke of Northumberland in 1766 James Smithson died in Italy, 1829 It publishes and freely distributes scientific memoirs and reports. The library was burned on 25 Jan 1865 Prof Joseph Henry, the first secretary, died 13 May, 1878, succeeded by prof S F Baird Present secretary, prof S P Langley The total permanent Smithsonian fund is now about $900,000 It is governed by a board of regents, consisting of the vice-president and chief-justice of the U S., 3 senators, 3 members of the House, 4 citizens from different states, and 2 citizens of Washington

Smolen'sko, a town of Russia The French in sanguinary engagements here were 3 times repulsed, but ultimately succeeded in entering Smolensko, and found the city, which had been bombarded, burning and partly in ruins, 16, 17 Aug 1812 Barclay de Tolly, the Russian commander-in-chief, incurred the displeasure of the emperor Alexander because he retreated after the battle, and Kutusoff succeeded to the command.

Smyrna. SEVEN CHURCHES

sneezing. The custom of saying "God bless you" to the sneezer originated, according to Strada, among the ancients, who, fearing danger from it, after sneezing made a short prayer to the gods, as "Jupiter, help me" The custom is mentioned by Homer, the Jewish rabbis, and others Polydore Virgil says it took its rise at the time of the plague, 558, when the infected fell dead, sneezing, though seemingly in good health

> "Shall not Love to me,
> As in a Latin song I learnt at school,
> Sneeze out a full God bless you right and left?"
> —*Tennyson*, "Edwin Morris or the Lake"

snuff-taking took its rise in England from the captures made of vast quantities of snuff by sir George Rooke's expedition to Vigo in 1702, and the practice soon became general.

soap is a salt, a compound of a fatty acid with an alkali, soda or potash The Hebrew *bôrith*, translated soap, is merely a general term for cleansing substances (Job ix 30, Jer ii 22). Pliny declares soap an invention of the Gauls, though he prefers the German to the Gallic soap Nausicaa and her attendants, Homer tells us, washed clothes by treading them with their feet in pits of water —*Odyssey*, book vi The Romans used fuller's earth. *Savon*, the French word for soap, is ascribed to its having been manufactured at Savona, near Genoa. The manufacture of soap in London began in 1524, before which it was supplied by Bristol at one penny per pound.

Sobraon', a town of N. W. India. The British army, 35,000 strong, under sir Hugh (afterwards viscount) Gough, attacked the Sikh force on the Sutlej, 10 Feb. 1846. The enemy was dislodged after a dreadful contest, and all their batteries taken; and in attempting the passage of the river by a floating bridge in their rear, the weight of the crowds upon it broke it down, and thousands of Sikhs were killed, wounded, or drowned. The British loss was 2338 men.

social wars. ATHENS, MARSI.

socialism is defined as "a plan for the reorganization of society on the basis of social or state ownership of all instruments of production, and the determination by state enactment of the price to be paid for labor and the products of labor." "Socialism is the genus, of which communism is a species; every communist is a socialist, but all socialists are not communists." The Disciples of Christ at Jerusalem were at first communists (Acts ii. 44), 33 A.D. The Taborites or Hussites in Bohemia, Anabaptists in Germany, Levellers in England, and Tunkers in the United States, were early examples of communists. The most advanced schools of socialism of to-day are German.

Sir Thomas More publishes his "Utopia" 1516
A work on socialism, "Civitas Solis," by Campanella, appears, 1623
SHAKERS form their first complete community at Mt. Lebanon, N. Y. 1787
François Noël Babœuf, leader of the French communistic insurrection of 1796, at Paris, is guillotined ....24 May, 1797
HARMONISTS settle in Pennsylvania 1804
Charles Fourier, French (1772-1837), publishes his work, "The Theory of the Four Movements and the General Destinies". 1808
ZOARITES settle in Ohio 1817
Robert Owen advocates a socialistic community before the English House of Commons' committee on the poor-law.... "
Count Claude Henry de Saint-Simon, founder of French socialism and author of "Nouveau Christianisme," and other socialistic works, b. 1760, d. 1825
Constitution for the "NEW HARMONY Community of Equality," signed ....12 Jan. 1826
Unsuccessful trial of Fourierism made on an estate near Versailles; only one during the lifetime of Fourier.......... 1832
Louis Blanc, French (1813-82), publishes his "Organization of Labor" in the *Revue du Progrès* 1840
Pierre Joseph Proudhon publishes his work, "What is Property?" affirming, "Property is theft" and "Property-holders are thieves" .... "
Albert Brisbane publishes his "Social Destiny of Man" ...... "
Karl Rodbertus, German (1805-75), publishes his book, "Our Economic Condition" 1842
Christian Metz establishes a community at Ebenezer, N. Y. (AMANA INSPIRATIONISTS) .... "
A column in the New York *Tribune* purchased, for expounding the principles of the Advocates of Association, and edited by Albert Brisbane, the apostle of Fourierism.......... "
Brisbane establishes in New York an independent paper called the *Phalanx*, organ of FOURIERISM ....5 Oct. 1843
Convention of Associationists at Clinton hall, N. Y......4 Apr. 1844
"BROOK FARM," originally the West Roxbury community, established in 1842, adopts the principles of Fourierism....... "
The *Phalanx* succeeded by the *Harbinger*, and published at Brook Farm ....14 June, 1845
Erick Janson forms a Swedish colony of Pietists and Separatists at Bishop Hill, Ill. (incorporated 1853).......... 1846
Decline of Fourierism in the U. S. marked by the Greeley-Raymond controversy..........20 Nov. 1846-20 May, 1847
ONEIDA COMMUNITY established .... "
Christian socialism, under Charles Kingsley, Frederick D. Maurice, Thomas Hughes, etc., arises in England..... about 1850
Ferdinand Lassalle begins agitation in behalf of the laboring classes, founding the German Social Democratic party...... 1862
Universal German Laborers' union, under the leadership of Lassalle, formed at Leipsic.................... .23 May, 1863
Delegates of all nations in St. Martin's hall, London, form the International Workingmen's association............28 Sept. 1864
Band of disciples of Lassalle organized in New York 1865
Universal congress, for advancement and complete emancipation of the working classes, at Geneva, Switzerland, 3 Sept. 1866
Karl Marx, German (1818-83), publishes his work, "Das Kapital," called the Bible of the Social Democrats............... 1867
Brocton community founded by rev. Thomas Lake Harris at Brocton, N. Y. ....Oct. "
Catholic socialism in Germany organized.................... 1868
International congress at the Hague (6 delegates from America) results in the formation of a new international association on anarchistic principles under leadership of Michael Bakounine, and removal of seat of general council of the old association, which soon after ceased to exist, to New York. Congress held....................2-7 Sept. 1872
"Union for Social Politics" formed by German professorial socialists at Eisenach ....Oct. "
Universal Socialistic congress opens at Ghent..........9 Sept. 1877
Workingmen's party in the U. S. reorganized as "The Socialistic Labor party" ....Jan. 1878
Henry George publishes his work entitled "Progress and Poverty" 1879
Social Democratic federation organized in England, favoring "Co-operative communism, international republicanism, and atheistic humanism" 1881
Leading principles of state socialism of Bismarck announced in an imperial message to the German Reichstag.......Nov. "
Great mass-meeting held in Cooper Union, New York city, to honor the memory of Karl Marx (d. 14 Mch. 1883), 19 Mch. 1883
William Morris, poet, author of the "Earthly Paradise," H. M. Hyndman, H. H. Champion, and John Burns, become leaders of the "Socialist league," formed 1886
Bellamy's "Looking Backward" pub.................... 1888

STATISTICS OF PRINCIPAL SOCIALISTIC COMMUNITIES IN THE UNITED STATES.

Name.	Location.	Members.	Acres.	Estab.	Duration.
New Harmony	Harmony, Ind.	900	30,000	1825	3 years.
Nashoba, founded by Francis Wright for negroes	Shelby county, Tenn.	15	2,000	"	"
Yellow Springs Community	Greene county, O.	400	..	"	3 months.
Kendal Community	Stark county, O.	200	200	1826	2 years.
Haverstraw Community	Haverstraw, N. Y.	80	120	"	5 months.
Northampton Association	Northampton, Mass.	130	500	1842	4 years.
Brook Farm	Near Boston, Mass.	115	200	"	5 "
Social Reform Unity	Pike county, Pa.	20	2,000	"	10 months.
Goose Pond Community (successor)	" " "	60	..	1843	Few months.
Hopedale	Milford, Mass.	200	500	1842	18 years.
Alphadelphia Phalanx	Kalamazoo county, Mich.	500	2,814	1843	2 yrs. 9 mo.
Jefferson County Industrial Association	Jefferson county, N. Y.	400	1,200	"	Few months.
Lagrange Phalanx	Springfield, Ind.	150	1,045	"	4 years.
Moorhouse Union	Hamilton county, N. Y.	..	120	"	Few months.
North American Phalanx	Monmouth county, N. J.	112	673	"	12 years.
One-mention Community	Monroe county, Pa.	..	800	"	1 year.
Peace Union Settlement	Warren county, Pa.	..	10,000	"	"
Skaneateles Community	Skaneateles, N. Y.	150	354	"	2½ years.
Sylvania Association	Lackawaxen, Pa.	145	2,394	"	2 years.
Bloomfield Association	Honeoye Falls, N. Y.	150	500	1844	1 year.
Clarkson Industrial Association	Monroe county, N. Y.	420	2,000	"	9 months.
Clermont Phalanx	Clermont county, O.	120	900	"	2 years.
Leraysville Phalanx	Bradford county, Pa.	40	300	"	8 months.
American Phalanx	Belmont county, O.	100	2,200	"	10 "
Ontario Union	Hopewell, N. Y.	150	280	"	1 year.
Prairie Home Community	Logan county, O.	130	500	"	"
Sodus Bay Phalanx	Sodus Bay, N. Y.	300	1,400	"	Few months.
Trumbull Phalanx	Trumbull county, O.	200	1,500	"	3 years.
Wisconsin Phalanx	Green Lake, Wis.	180	1,800	"	6 "
Integral Phalanx and Sangamon Association	Sangamon county, Ill	30 fam.	508	1845	17 months.
Spring Farm Association	Sheboygan county, Wis	10 fam.	30	1846	3 years.
Oneida Community	Oneida Creek, N. Y.	..	..	1847	34 "

societies and associations. Many of these are mentioned under their respective titles, and others may be found in this work in the various state records and under general titles as: ANTIQUARIAN, ARCHITECTURE, ARTS, CHAR-

ITY, ENGINEERING, LABOR, MEDICINE, MUSIC, PAINTING, SOCIALISM, etc.

Society islands, in the Pacific ocean, discovered by De Quiros in 1606; rediscovered by capt. Wallis, 1767, who gave Otaheite or Tahiti the name of King George's island. Capt. Cook, who visited them in 1769 and 1777, named them Society islands in honour of the Royal Society. These now belong to France. OTAHEITE.

Socin'ians, who accept the opinions of Faustus Socinus (d. 1562) and his nephew Lælius (d. 1604), Siennese noblemen. They held, 1. That the Eternal Father is the one only God, and that Jesus Christ is no otherwise God than by his superiority to all other creatures; 2. That Christ is not a mediator; 3. That hell will endure for a time, after which the soul and body will be destroyed; 4. That it is unlawful for princes to make war.—*Hook.* The Socinians established a church at Rakow, in Poland, and made proselytes in Transylvania, 1563. They were expelled from Poland in 1658. The Rakovian catechism was established in 1574. UNITARIANS.

Soco'tra (*Dioscoridis insula*), an island in the Indian ocean, 120 miles east of cape Guardafui, E. Africa. In the summer of 1878, it was given up to the British by the sultan, and formally annexed in 1886. Area, 1382 sq. miles; pop. 10,000.

so'dium, a metal remarkable for its lightness (specific gravity about .97), and for its strong affinity for oxygen, with which it combines spontaneously when exposed to water or moist air. It was first obtained in 1807 by sir Humphry Davy from soda (which was formerly confounded with potash, but proved to be a distinct substance by Duhamel in 1736). This metal, like potassium, was obtained by the agency of the electric battery. Common salt (chloride of sodium) is a compound of sodium and chlorine. ALKALIES.

Sod'om and **Gomor'rah,** 2 cities of Palestine, with their inhabitants, supposed to have been destroyed by fire from heaven 1898 B.C. (Gen. xix.).

So'dor, said to be derived from Sodor-eys, or South isles (the Æbrides or Hebrides), in distinction from Orkneys, the North isles. The southern or western isles were made an episcopal diocese by Magnus, king of Norway, 1098, and joined to the Isle of Man about 1113. MAN.

Soffar'ides dynasty reigned in Persia, 872-902.

Softas, Mahometan students devoted to the Koran only. TURKEY, May, 1876.

Soissons (*swas-son'*), France, capital of the Gallic Suessiones, was subdued by Julius Cæsar, 57 B.C. It was held by Syagrius, after his father Ægidius, till his defeat by Clovis, 486 A.D. Several councils have been held at Soissons (744, 1082, 1122). Its academy was established in 1674. During the Franco-Prussian war, Soissons, after 3 weeks' investment and 4 days' bombardment, surrendered to the Germans under the grand-duke of Mecklenburg, 16 Oct. 1870. 99 officers, 4633 men, 128 guns, etc., were said to be taken. The Germans thus obtained a second line of railway from Châlons to Paris.

Soko'to, Empire of, is the largest and most populous in the whole of the Soudan. It is attached by treaty to the Royal Niger company (British), chartered 10 July, 1886. Area, 219,500 sq. miles; pop. 15,000,000.

solar system, nearly as now accepted, is said to have been taught by Pythagoras of Samos, about 529 B.C. He placed the sun in the centre and all the planets moving in elliptical orbits round it—a doctrine superseded by the PTOLEMAIC SYSTEM. The system of Pythagoras, revived by Copernicus (1543), is called the Copernican system. Its truth was demonstrated by sir Isaac Newton in 1687. PLANETS, SUN.

solar time. SIDEREAL TIME, YEAR.

soldiers. ARMY, MILITIA.

soldiers' homes. Homes have been established, both national and state, for all disabled soldiers and sailors of the United States who served in the civil or Mexican war. The first institution of this character established by the U. S. government was founded by act of Congress, 3 Mch. 1851, for the aged and invalid soldiers of the regular army. This home is situated a short distance from the city of Washington. Besides this, there are national and state homes for disabled volunteer soldiers. The first branch of the former was established at Tagus, Me., 10 Nov. 1866.

BRANCHES OF THE NATIONAL HOME.

Branches.	Location.
Eastern	Togus, Me.
Central	Dayton, O.
Southern	Hampton, Va.
Western	Leavenworth, Kan.
Marion	Marion, Ind.
Northwestern	Milwaukee, Wis.
Pacific	Santa Monica, Cal.

STATE HOMES.

State.	Location.	Incorporated or opened.
California	Yountville	1882
Colorado	Monte Vista	1889
Connecticut	Noroton	1863
Illinois	Quincy	1885
Iowa	Marshalltown	1884
Kansas	Dodge City	"
Massachusetts	Chelsea	1877
Michigan	Grand Rapids	1885
Minnesota	Minnehaha	1887
Nebraska	Grand Island	1888
New Hampshire	Tilton	1889
New Jersey	Kearney	1866
New York	Bath	1876
Ohio	Sandusky	1886
Pennsylvania	Erie	1886
Rhode Island	Bristol	1891
South Dakota	Hot Springs	1889
Vermont	Bennington	1887
Washington	Orting	1890
Wisconsin	Waupaca	1887

There are 5 homes for disabled confederate soldiers in the south: Richmond, Va., New Orleans, La., Austin, Tex., Pikesville, Md., and Nashville, Tenn.

Sole'bay or **Southwold bay,** Suffolk, Engl., where a fierce naval battle was fought between the fleets of England and France on one side, and the Dutch on the other; the former commanded by the duke of York, afterwards James II., 28 May, 1672. The English lost 4 ships, and the Dutch 3; but the enemy fled, and were pursued to their coasts.

sol-fa system. MUSIC.

Solferi'no, a village in Lombardy, the site of the chief struggle of the great battle of 24 June, 1859, between the allied French and Sardinian army, commanded by their respective sovereigns, and the Austrians under gen. Hess, the emperor being present. The Austrians, after defeat at Magenta, gradually retreated across the Mincio, took up a position in the celebrated quadrilateral, and were expected there to await the attack. But the advance of Garibaldi on one side, and of prince Napoleon and the Tuscans on the other, induced them to recross the Mincio and take the offensive on 23 June. The conflict began early on the 24th, and lasted fifteen hours. At first the Austrians had the advantage; but the successful attack of the French on Cavriana and Solferino changed the fortune of the day, and the Austrians, after desperate encounters, were compelled to retreat. The French attribute the victory to the skill and bravery of their emperor and the generals MacMahon and Neil; the Austrians, to the destruction of their reserve by the rifled cannon of their adversaries. The Sardinians maintained a fearful contest of 15 hours at San Martino, it is said against double their number. Loss of the Austrians, 630 officers and 19,311 soldiers; of the allies, 8 generals, 936 officers, and 17,305 soldiers killed and wounded. This battle closed the war, preliminaries of peace being signed at Villafranca, 12 July. On 24 June, 1870, on the site of the battle, 3 ossuaries, containing the bones of thousands of the slain, were solemnly consecrated in the presence of representatives of Austria, France, and Italy.

Solfid'ians (from *solus*, only, and *fides*, faith), a name given to the ANTINOMIANS.

Solomon islands. A group of islands to the east of Papua or New Guinea, discovered by Alvaro Mendana de Neyra, 1568, and so named by him in anticipation of their riches. Aggregate area, about 9000 sq. miles; pop. 80,000. Germany established a protectorate over these islands in 1884.

Solomon's temple. TEMPLE.

Solway Moss, a swamp or bog-lands in Cumberland,

Engl, bordering on Scotland, 7 square miles in extent On 13 Nov 1771, it swelled, owing to heavy rains Upwards of 400 acres rose to such a height above the level of the ground that at last it rolled forward like a torrent above a mile, sweeping along with it houses, trees, and covering 600 acres at Netherby, and destroying about 30 hamlets It is now partially drained Near Solway Moss the Scots were defeated by the English, 25 Nov 1542

Somaj. BRAHMO SOMAJ, DEISM

Sombre'ro, an islet of the British West Indies. On this desert isle Robert Jeffery, a British man-of-war's man, was put ashore by his commander, capt W Lake, for having tapped a barrel of beer when the ship was on short allowance After sustaining life for eight days on a few limpets and rain-water, he was saved by an American vessel, 13 Dec 1807, and returned to England Sir Francis Burdett advocated his cause in Parliament, and he received 600*l* as a compensation from capt Lake, who was tried by a court-martial, and dismissed the service, 10 Feb 1810

Somerset, Case of SLAVERY IN ENGLAND

Somers's isles. BERMUDAS

Somers, U. S. brig-of-war, Mutiny on This brig of 266 tons' burden, and fitted to carry 14 guns, but carrying 10, with a crew of officers, men, and boys of 120, under command of Alexander Slidell McKenzie, cruising along the coast of Africa, left Liberia on 11 Nov 1842, for the U S *via* St Thomas. On 25 Nov McKenzie received information through lieut Gansevoort of a conspiracy on board to seize the brig and convert her into a pirate, etc The leaders in this movement were reported to be midshipman Philip Spencer, son of John C Spencer, then secretary of war, and Samuel Cromwell, the boatswain's mate, and a seaman, Elisha Small Spencer was arrested on 27 Nov, and the other 2 on the 28th, and put in irons These 3 were convicted by a court on board, and sentenced to be hung at the yard-arm, which was done on 1 Dec, 525 miles from St. Thomas The *Somers* arrived at New York 14 Dec, with several of the boys in confinement A naval court of inquiry, convened on 28 Dec., consisting of commodores Charles Stewart, Jacob Jones, Alexander J Dallas, and Ogden Hoffman, judge advocate, sat until Jan 19, 1843, and decided that com McKenzie had simply performed his duty, etc. This court and verdict did not satisfy public opinion, and for a further vindication McKenzie called for a regular court-martial, which was held at the Brooklyn navy-yard, and by a vote of 9 to 3 also acquitted him An attempt was now made to bring the case before the Circuit court of the U S, but judge Betts, although no overt act had been committed, and the hanging had been done on mere suspicion, dismissed the case for want of jurisdiction. This case at the time created great excitement, many approving the course of McKenzie, and many considering him guilty of a great crime McKenzie died at Tarrytown, N. Y, 13 Sept. 1848 The brig *Somers* was lost in the harbor of Vera Cruz while blockading it, 8 Dec 1846 MEDALS.

Somnath gates, the gates of an ancient Hindu temple at Guzerat, destroyed by Mahmoud of Ghuznee in 1025 The priests wished to preserve the idol, but Mahmoud broke it, and found it filled with diamonds, etc. He carried the gates to Ghuznee When that city was taken by gen. Nott, 6 Sept. 1812, lord Ellenborough ordered the gates restored, after an exile of 800 years, and issued a proclamation much censured at the time The gates are of sandal-wood, and are described and figured in the "Archæologia" of the Society of Antiquaries, vol. xxx.

sona'ta (Ital, Engl. "sound-piece"), the highest form of instrumental music, consisting of 3 or 4 movements intending to express diverse feelings It was developed from the *suite*, varied dance music (Tartini, 1824, and others) The form fixed by Corelli (1653–1713) was adopted and modified by Scarlatti, the Bachs, Handel, Mozart, Haydn, and culminated in the masterpieces of Beethoven (1770-1827) Fine sonatas have been composed by Dussek, M Clementi, Weber, Schubert, Mendelssohn, Schumann, Wm Sterndale Bennett, Chopin, Liszt, and Rubinstein.

songs of the Civil War, Popular. The most familiar only are mentioned A few of them as the "Battle Flag of the Republic," "Battle Hymn of the Republic," "The Blue and the Gray," and "Maryland, my Maryland," have a place in standard literature, others, which will be recognized by all who remember the years 1861-65, though with less literary merit, became favorites as expressions of patriotic sentiment

Battle Cry of Freedom —*Geo F Root*
"Yes, we ll rally round the flag boys "

Battle Flag of the Republic —*O W Holmes*
"Flag of the heroes who left us their glory "

Battle Hymn of the Republic —*Julia Ward Howe.*
"Mine eyes have seen the glory of the coming of the Lord "

The Blue and the Gray —*Francis M Finch.*
"By the flow of the inland river "

Brave Boys are They —*Henry C Work*
"Brave boys are they gone at their country's call "

Dixie (Southern) —*Albert Pike*
"Southrons hear your country call you "

Dixie (Northern) —*T M Cooley*
"Away down South where grows the cotton "

John Brown s body—
"John Brown's body lies a mould ring in the grave "

Just before the Battle, Mother —*Geo F Root*
"Just before the battle, mother, I am thinking most of you "

Marching through Georgia —*Henry C Work*
"Bring the good old bugle boys, we ll sing another song "

Maryland, my Maryland (Southern) —*Jas R Randall*
"The despot's heel is on thy shore, Maryland "

O wrap the flag around me boys —*R Stewart Taylor*

Tramp, Tramp, Tramp —*Geo. F Root*
"In the prison cell I sit "

When Johnny comes Marching Home —*Louis Lambert.*

When this Cruel War is Over —*Charles C Sawyer*
"Dearest love, do you remember "

sonnet, a poem of 14 lines, with rhymes, formally arranged according to precise rules, was invented, it is said, by Guido d'Arezzo about 1024 Many celebrated sonnets are by Petrarch (about 1327), Shakespeare (1609), Milton (about 1650), and Wordsworth (1820). LITERATURE.

Sonn'ites or **Sunn'ites,** the orthodox Mahometans, who now possess the Turkish empire MAHOMETANISM

Sophia, St., principal mosque in Constantinople The first church was dedicated to St Sophia (holy wisdom) by Constantius II, 360, this having been destroyed, the second, the present edifice, was founded by Justinian, 531, and dedicated 537. Since the Mahometan conquest, in 1453, it has been used as an imperial mosque Height 182 feet, length 269 feet, and breadth 243 feet 6 of its pillars are of green jasper, from the temple of Diana at Ephesus, and of porphyry, from the temple of the Sun at Rome 4 minarets were added by Selim II, who reigned in 1566. The interior of the dome is ornamented with mosaics.

Sophists, rhetoricians and teachers of youth in Athens, censured by Socrates, and instrumental in causing his judicial murder, 399 B.C. The controversy against them was carried on by Plato and his disciples PHILOSOPHY.

Sorbonne (*sor-bon'*), a society of ecclesiastics at Paris, founded by Robert de Sorbonne in 1252 The members lived in common, and devoted themselves to study and gratuitous teaching They soon attained a European reputation as a faculty of theology, their judgment being frequently appealed to, from the 14th to the 17th century The influence of the Sorbonne was declining when the society was broken up in 1789 The buildings are now devoted to education ACADEMY.

sorcerers and **magicians.** A law was enacted against their seductions, 33 Hen VIII 1541, and another statute, equally severe, was passed, 5 Eliz 1563 The pretension to sorcery was made capital, 1 James I 1603. WITCHCRAFT

sorghum, Chinese sugar-cane, introduced into France in 1851, and into the United States about 1854 In 1857 there were also imported from Natal, South Africa, several varieties of sorghum, known also as African millet and imphee In its general appearance, sorghum resembles maize or Indian corn or more nearly broom corn, which belongs to the same genus, and flourishes in the same soils, doing best in the south and southwestern states For securing and manufacturing its juice into syrup it is treated like sugar-cane SUGAR

sortes Biblicæ, introduced during the reign of Charlemagne, was a method of telling fortunes by opening the Bible at the 4 evangelists or the Psalms, at random, and the finger falling upon a passage, it was received as prophetic

> "Then desperately seized the holy Book,
> Suddenly set it wide to find a sign
> Suddenly put her finger on the text"
> —*Tennyson*, "Enoch Arden"

soudan' or **soujah** (*sou'yah*), the title of the lieutenant generals of the caliphs, which they bore in their provinces and armies The officers afterwards made themselves sovereigns Saladin, general of the forces of Noureddin king of Damascus, was the first that took upon him this title in Egypt, 1165, after having killed the caliph Caym

Soudan' or **Nigritia** (*ne grish'e a*), a region of Central Africa partly subject to the khedive of Egypt until 1882 It was well governed by col Gordon till 1879 Before the revolt of the mahdi in 1882, the khedival possessions beyond Egypt proper extended from the frontier of Upper Egypt for a distance of nearly 1400 miles southward to lake Albert Nyanza (3° to 23° N), with a total area of about 1,000,000 sq miles, and with a probable population of from 10,000,000 to 12,000,000 It includes the region of Darfur, reduced to Egyptian rule in 1874, Kordofan in 1821, Upper Nubia and Senaar in 1822, the Zeriba lands of the White Nile basin, organized and administered by the Egyptian government 1870-82, and since held partly by Emin Pacha until relieved by Stanley in 1889 This territory was placed under a governor-general, with residence at Khartoum (pop about 70 000, 1882), at the confluence of the White and Blue Nile Since the mahdi's revolt, Suakim, Berber, and Zeilah have been occupied by the English, Massawah by the Italians, and Lower Dongola by the Egyptians

Insurrection headed by sheik Mahomed Ahmed of Dongola, declaring himself a prophet (mahdi or muhdi, foretold by Moslem prophets) July, 1881

Defeated, retires up the Blue Nile, crosses White Nile with increased army winter, "

Defeats the Egyptians Nov "

Surrounds and massacres 6000 Egyptians under Yussuf pacha, 14 June, occupies Shela, July, defeated at Bara, 19 Aug , at Duem, 28 Aug , repulsed at Obeid 8, 14 Sept , defeats the Egyptians, 15 Sept -24 Oct , rebels defeated at Bara, 4 Nov , col Stewart at Khartoum 16 Dec 1882

Mahdi captures Bara and Obeid, 5 Jan , repulsed 23-26 Feb 1883

Col Hicks pacha with an army starts for the Kordofan, arrives at Berber, 1 Mch , routs the mahdi 29 Apr "

Mahdi defeated at Khartoum about 14 May, "

Sennaar chiefs submit, announced 25 June, "

Hicks marches up the Nile, 9 Sept , arrives at Duem 20 Sept. "

Surprise and defeat of Egyptian detachment at Tokar, near Suakim, about 150 killed including the British consul, 6 Nov "

Battle of El Obeid, or Kashgal, col Hicks decoyed into a defile, about 11 000 men attacked by overwhelming multitudes, form squares and resist till nearly all are killed, including cols Hicks and Farquhar, of European officers, only 2 escape, reported desertion of some of Hicks's troops, the mahdi gains cannon and ammunition 3-5 Nov "

Egyptian force concentrates at Khartoum under col Coetlogon, Nov "

General rising, the British government sends gunboats to defend Suakim and Red Sea ports, about 23 Nov , attack on Suakim forts, 26 Nov -1 Dec , about 720 Egyptians surrounded and 682 killed (asserted) 2 Dec. "

V Baker pacha sent to Suakim with plenary powers, about 18 Dec "

Khartoum garrison strengthened about 26 Dec "

Osman Digma, a ruined slave dealer, commander for the mahdi, Dec "

Gen (Chinese) Gordon sent to the Soudan (to report), 18 Jan , starts 19 Jan , appointed governor general of the Soudan by the khedive 25 Jan 1884

Sinkat closely besieged Nov 1883-Jan "

Tokar besieged by rebels, surrenders, 21 Feb , Baker pacha with 3500 men defeated near Tokar loses about 2250 men, with remnant retreats to Trinkitat, 4 Feb , received by British ship *Ranger*, 5, 6 Feb , reinforcements ordered to adm Hewett at Suakim, 6 Feb , Baker pacha recalled, remains, Suakim in a state of siege, adm Hewett in full command 7-9 Feb , sortie of the garrison, headed by Tewfik bey, from Sinkat all killed, women and children prisoners, town taken 8 Feb "

Reinforcements sent to Suakim 11, 12 Feb "

Gen Gordon arrives at Berber, 11 Feb , welcomed as a deliverer at Khartoum, proclaims the mahdi sultan of Kordofan, remission of half the taxes, and non interference with the slave trade, releases prisoners, remits debts. 18 Feb, "

Restoration of the former sultanate of Darfour proposed, Kassala besieged by Osman Digma Feb "

Black troops at Suakim mutiny and disperse, announced, 25 Feb "

Battle of El Teb, near where Baker pacha was defeated, 4 Feb After fruitless attempts at negotiation, gen Gerald Graham, with about 4000 men (10th and 19th Hussars, Gordon Highlanders, the Black Watch, Lancashire and Yorkshire battalions, and marines), at 11 A M advance on about 12,000 rebels who, after a desperate resistance, are defeated with loss of about 2000 men at 2 30 P M , the British loss was major M M Slade, lieuts F H Probyn, F A Freeman, and Frank Royds, quartermaster James Wilkins, and 24 men killed, and 112 wounded 29 Feb 1884

Tokar surrenders, rebel garrison flees 1 Mch "

Battle of Tamanieb British advance against Osman Digma's camp at Tamasi, near El Teb, 7 20 A M , massed in oblong squares, one square broken by an ambush of Arabs, who creep under and capture the Gatling and other guns, col Wood with 700 cavalry charges the Arabs in flank and drives them back, the infantry rally and recover the guns, the other square successful, camp taken 12 30 P M The British loss killed, capts H G V Ford, Walker, and Aitken, lieuts Montresor, Almack and Houston Stewart, and 86 men, 111 wounded, and 19 missing, 2000 of the 10 000 rebels killed The Black Watch and naval brigade suffered much 13 Mch "

Osman Digma's camp (with stores captured 4 Feb) burned, 14 Mch "

Gordon defeats rebels and brings off garrison of Halfyeh about 15 Mch

Through cowardice and treachery Gordon's troops (1500) defeated by about 60 rebels with great slaughter 16 Mch "

£1000 offered for Osman Digma alive or dead, 15 Mch , countermanded from England 17 Mch "

Troops march to Handoub wells 18 Mch "

Hassan and Said pachas, Turko Egyptian generals tried and shot 23 Mch "

Gen Graham advances on Tamanieb, slight skirmish, Arabs flee, Osman Digma's villages burned 27 Mch "

March to Berber reported safe 29 Mch "

Gordon contending with the rebels, Kassala closely besieged, 30 Mch "

Khartoum said to be closely invested, the rebels frequently defeated Apr "

Gen Gordon col Stewart and Mr Power, the *Times* correspondent the only British there 8 Apr "

Egyptian troops arrive at Suakim 10 Apr "

Shendy closely besieged 19 Apr "

Berber closely invested 20 Apr "

Evacuation of Berber, troops withdrawn to Korosko 26 Apr "

Whole country in insurrection, Egyptian troops joining the mahdi Apr "

[British government declining to send help Gordon writes to sir Evelyn Baring "I shall hold on here as long as I can, and if I can suppress the rebellion, I will do so. If I cannot, I shall retire to the equator "]

Col Stewart and Mr Power decide to remain with him May, "

Subscriptions proposed to support Gordon " "

Adm Hewett well received by the king of Abyssinia at Adowa, treaty signed about 26 May, "

Fruitless attacks on Suakim checked by marines, 27, 28, 31 May, 2, 4, 10 June, "

Highly successful sally from Khartoum, maj Chermside made governor of Suakim 28 May, "

Advance of Egyptian troops May, "

Fall of Berber announced 10 June, "

Assouan fortified June, "

Rebels defeated at Debbeh 29, 30 June, "

Assouan occupied by the British 12 July, "

More troops sent to Alexandria from Malta July, "

Gordon successful at Khartoum, reported 22 July, "

Gen Gordon repulses severe attack, 10 Aug , defeats rebels, 12 Aug "

Osman Digma, near Suakim defeated Aug "

Expedition prepared to relieve Khartoum, gen Earle commander, British troops arrive at Wady Halfa 23 Aug et seq "

Expedition to ascend the Nile in about 800 flat bottomed boats, navigated by Canadian Indians (*voyageurs*), Sarras Sept -Oct. "

Defeat of the mahdi's troops by the mudir of Dongola at Ambikol 8 Sept "

Gen Earle to be at Wady Halfa, col Stewart and lord Airlie at Dongola, col Maurice at Assiout Sept. "

Telegrams from Gordon requiring assistance " "

Friendly tribes defeat rebels and relieve Suakim, about 17 Sept. "

Victories of Gordon on 24 July and 30 Aug and raising of the siege of Khartoum, reported 20 Sept "

British army in Egypt, 13,559 about 22 Sept. "

Lord John Hay arrives with the fleet at Alexandria 24 Sept. "

Several camel corps start from Woolwich for the Soudan, about 25 Sept. "

Mr Power's journal of the siege of Khartoum, April to 31 July, published in London *Times* 29 Sept "

Lord Wolseley arrives at Wady Halfa 5 Oct "

Shendy taken 6 Oct. "

Col J D Stewart, with Mr Power and M Herbin, and about 40 men in a steamer wrecked near Wady Garna, 5th cataract, land, massacred by Arabs offering guidance, announced, about 6 Oct. "

Gordon defeats rebels, returns to Khartoum, announced, 1 Nov "

Lord Wolseley arrives at Dongola 3 Nov "

Attacks on Suakim repulsed 3, 4 Nov "

Gordon reports all well at Khartoum 4 Nov "

Two steamers disabled by rebels near Khartoum, announced, 18 Nov "

Lord Wolseley's proclamation to soldiers and sailors 1 Dec "

Two hours' attack of the rebels on Suakim without effect, 3 Dec , rebels defeated with loss 8 Dec. "

Lord Wolseley arrives at Korti 15 Dec "

Successful sally of the garrison of Kassala. 26 Dec "

Forward movement of the army 28 Dec 1884
Rapid marches of gen sir Herbert Stewart Dec "
Successful march in the desert Jan 1885
Gen Earle ascending Nile, and gen Stewart crossing desert towards Metammeh Jan "
Near Abu Klea wells about 120 miles from Khartoum gen Stewart with 1500 men defeats about 10,000 Arabs who leave about 800 dead British lose 9 officers (col Fred Gus Burnaby, majors Atherton Carmichael and Gough, capts Law and Darley, lieuts Pigott, Delisle and Wolfe) and 65 men killed 85 wounded 17 Jan "
Gen Stewart, marching towards Metammeh severely wounded by sharpshooters, 12 killed including correspondents of the *Morning Post* and *Standard* Thos St Leger Herbert, and John A Cameron sir Charles Wilson takes command 18 Jan "
At Gubat, near Metammeh, fierce Arab onset on British square repulsed with heavy loss 19 Jan "
Message from gen Gordon received dated 29 Dec "Khartoum is all right could hold out for a year" about 19 Jan "
Communications opened with Khartoum 21 Jan "
Gen Earle with army marches to Handoub for Berber " "
Successful skirmishes of gen Earle Jan "
Gen Stewart succeeded by sir Redvers Buller "
Surrender of Khartoum by treachery of Faragh pacha, *Gordon and followers killed* early 26 Jan "
Sir Charles Wilson sails up the Nile 28 Jan "
Reconnoissances of gen Fremantle, heavy Arab loss about 30 Jan, Handoub captured and burned by a party which is intercepted by Arabs, and lose 12 men 2 Feb "
Italian flag hoisted beside Egyptian at Massowah 6 Feb "
Sir Charles Wilson and party, within 800 yards of Khartoum, fired upon, retreat, his steamer wrecked by treachery of Arab pilots, lands on an island, is rescued from peril by lord Charles Beresford in face of batteries, arrives at Korti 9 Feb. "
Victory at Kirbekan, Arabs on a ridge, surrounded by gen Earle's column (the Black Watch and Staffordshire regiments), many killed, gen Earle lieut cols Eyre and Coveney and nine others killed, gen Brackenbury takes command, 10 Feb "
Gen Buller retreats from Gubat to Abu Klea wells 13 15 Feb "
Death of sir H Stewart at Gakdul 16 Feb "
Railway ordered between Suakim and Berber Feb "
Second Italian expedition reaches Port Said 17 Feb "
Near Abu Klea, maj Wardrop takes the heights after much skirmishing, Arabs flee 17 Feb "
Sir Evelyn Wood arrives at Gakdul " "
Gen Gerald Graham with Coldstream and Grenadier Guards and others, start for Soudan, farewell by the queen and prince of Wales 19-21 Feb "
Osman Digma massing his forces near Suakim about 21 Feb "
Rebels' attack on Kassala garrison defeated with great loss announced 22 Feb "
Gen Brackenbury's column reaches Gakdul 26 Feb "
Gen Buller's column marches to Korti 1 Mch "
Gen Graham's staff and 15th Sikhs regiment arrive at Suakim, 4 Mch "
Queen's address of thanks read to the army at Korti by Lord Wolseley 7 Mch "
17th Bengal Infantry and the Royal Engineers balloon corps arrive at Suakim 7 Mch "
Gen Graham calls on Osman Digma to surrender, to avoid bloodshed about 16 Mch "
Battle of Hasheen Graham, with part of his army, starts at daybreak, several of Osman Digma's positions on hills taken after conflicts, about 21 British killed 20 Mch "
Gen McNeil's brigade attacked by about 4500 Arabs, about 6 miles from Suakim, they are repulsed with heavy loss (about 1500), British loss about 100 killed including lieuts Swinton, Seymour, and Newman, capt Romilly and others 22 Mch "
Manifesto of the mahdi claiming the caliphate, pub. Mch "
Korti evacuated by the army about 23 Mch "
Zebehr pacha arrested at request of lord Wolseley, 14 Mch, sent to Gibraltar 29 Mch "
Lord Wolseley arrives at Suakim . 2 May, "
Proposed armed defence of line from Assouan to Wady Halfa, announced 11 May, "
Dongola evacuated 15 June, "
Death of the madhi by small pox June, "
Country south of Wady Halfa abandoned by Egyptians. Apr 1886
British evacuation of Suakim completed 16 May, "
Osman Digma's forces dispersed and all his military stores captured 7 Oct. "
Emin Bey (Austrian physician), an associate of gen. Gordon, holds Wadelai as governor of equatorial Africa since 1878 with black troops, news brought by dr Junker Nov "
Expedition of Henry M Stanley for the Emin Pacha committee with a small armament and able volunteer officers, leaves London (AFRICA) 21 Jan 1887
Suakim on the Red sea declared open to commerce 20 Feb 1889
Battle of Toski, dervishes defeated by gen. sir Francis Grenfell 11 Aug "
Osman Digma defeated at Tokar by the Egyptians under col H Smith . 19 Feb 1891
Red sea Littoral reported clear of rebels 23 Feb "
Father Ohrwalder and 2 Roman Catholic sisters, prisoners in the madhi's camp at Khartoum, escape to Cairo 21 Dec. "

sound and **sound-shadow.** ACOUSTICS

Sound duties. Till 1857 no merchant ship was allowed to pass the Sound (a narrow channel separating Zealand from Sweden) without clearing at Elsinore and paying toll. These duties had their origin in an agreement between the king of Denmark and the Hanse towns (1348), by which the former undertook to maintain light-houses, etc, along the Cattegat, and the latter to pay duty for the same The first treaty with England in relation to this was in 1450, other countries followed In 1855 the United States determined to pay the dues no more, and in the same year the Danish government proposed that these dues should be capitalized, which was eventually agreed to the sum being 30,476,325 rix-dollars In Aug 1857 the British government paid 10,126,855 rix-dollars (1,125,206*l*.) to the Danes as their proportion The passage of the sound was effected in defiance of strong fortresses, by sir Hyde Parker and lord Nelson, 31 Mch 1801 BALTIC EXPEDITION

soundings at sea. Capt Ross of British steamship *Erebus*, in 1840, took extraordinary soundings at sea One taken 900 miles west of St Helena was said to reach a depth of 5000 fathoms In lat 33° S and lon 9° W, about 300 miles from the cape of Good Hope 2266 fathoms were sounded, the weight employed amounted to 450 pounds On 13 July, 1857, lieut Joseph Dayman, in the North Atlantic ocean, lat 51° 9′ N, lon 40° 2′ W, in sounding, found a bottom at 2424 fathoms. The deepest sounding accurately known (3875 fathoms) was taken by the *Challenger*, capt Nares, 24 Mch 1873, in the North Atlantic, north of St Thomas DEEP-SEA SOUNDINGS, OCEAN AREAS AND DEPTH

South African Republic, name assumed by the Boers in the TRANSVAAL in 1880 81

South African war. The long-continued antagonism between the English government and the Boers in the Transvaal and the Orange Free State broke out into war in 1899, ending in the extinction of the Dutch republics TRANSVAAL, ORANGE FREE STATE.

A conference between sir Alfred Milner, governor of Cape Colony and the presidents of the Dutch republics was held at Bloemfontein, in which terms for the adjustment of the claims of the Outlanders were discussed, but no agreement was reached 31 May, 1899
Negotiations proceeded between the governments of Great Britain and the Transvaal, the Orange Free State announced its determination to support the Transvaal in case of hostilities 1 June-10 Oct "
The Transvaal sent the following ultimatum to the British government 10 Oct. "
First—that all points of mutual difference be regulated by arbitration, second—that all troops on the borders of this republic shall be instantly withdrawn, third—that all reinforcements of troops which have arrived in South Africa since 1 June, 1899, shall be removed from South Africa within a reasonable time, fourth—that her majesty's troops which are now on the high seas shall not be landed in any part of South Africa.
The British reply being unsatisfactory, the Transvaal Boers invaded Natal . 12 Oct "
The British evacuated Newcastle and fell back on Ladysmith, where there was a strong British force 13 Oct "
The siege of Kimberley by the Boers began 20 Oct. "
Battle of Dundee in Natal, in which the British repulsed the Boers, British loss 215 in killed and wounded 20 Oct "
Battle of Elandslaagte, gen French captured the Boers' position, British loss in killed and wounded, 257 21 Oct "
Gen White repulsed a Free State force at Reitfontein near Ladysmith 24 Oct "
The siege of Ladysmith by the Boers began 29 Oct "
In a sortie near Ladysmith the British were entrapped and defeated, and the Boers captured 870 prisoners 30 Oct. "
The British evacuated Colenso in Natal 3 Nov "
The Boers shelled Mafeking and an attack on the British position was repulsed 6 Nov "
A British armored train near Eastcourt, Natal, was wrecked by Boers, and 56 prisoners, including Winston Churchill, were captured 16 Nov "
Near Gras Pan, lord Methuen attacked the Boers and drove them from their position 23 Nov "
Battle of Modder river, a sanguinary British victory 28 Nov "
The British, under gen Gatacre, were led into a Boer ambuscade near Stormberg junction, and lost 1000 men, including 672 captured 10 Dec "
Lord Methuen failed to take the Boer positions at Spytfontein after desperate fighting, and lost heavily, gen Wauchope being killed 10, 11 Dec. "
Gen Buller was severely defeated while attempting to force the Tugela river, near Colenso, his loss was over 1000 men and 11 guns, British losses to date in killed, wounded, and missing 7630 15 Dec "
Field marshal lord Roberts was ordered to South Africa to take command of military operations, with lord Kitchener as chief of staff, and a reinforcement of 100,000 men 18 Dec. "
Gen French captured Colesburg 1 Jan 1900

Lords Roberts and Kitchener arrived in South Africa...6 Jan. 1900
A British storming party, under gen. Warren, captured Spion Kop, but after heavy losses withdrew............23-25 Jan. "
Buller's third attempt to relieve Ladysmith failed.....9 Feb. "
Invasion of the Orange Free State began..............12 Feb. "
Gen. French relieved Kimberley.......................15 Feb. "
Severe fighting between Roberts and Cronje, terminating in the capitulation of the latter, with 4000 men and 6 guns, 22-27 Feb. "
Lord Dundonald entered Ladysmith...................28 Feb. "
Gen. Gatacre occupied Stormberg......................5 Mch. "
Lord Roberts turned the Boer position near Modder river and advanced on Bloemfontein..... ....7 Mch. "
Bloemfontein surrendered............................13 Mch. "
The Boer commander-in-chief, gen. Joubert, died.....27 Mch. "
Col. de Villebois Mareuil, French officer with the Boers, was killed in a skirmish.................................5 Apr. "
Gen. Cronje and other Boer prisoners arrived at St. Helena, 14 Apr. "
The U. S. Senate voted down Mr. Pettigrew's resolution of sympathy with the Boers, 29 to 20...................20 Apr. "
Lord Roberts began his advance on Pretoria...........3 May, "
The U. S. government received from consul Hay, at Pretoria, a telegram stating that he was officially requested by the governments of the republics to urge intervention by the U. S. with a view to the cessation of hostilities.....10 May, "
The British crossed the Zand river and occupied Kroonstadt, 10 May, "
Gen. Buller occupied Dundee.........................15 May, "
The Boer envoys to the U. S. reached New York.......16 May, "
Mafeking was relieved after a siege of 217 days.......16 May, "
Sec. Hay informed Boer delegates that U. S. could not intervene in the war.....................................21 May, "
Pres. McKinley received the Boer envoys unofficially..22 May,
The annexation of the Orange Free State proclaimed..28 May, "
The British entered Johannesburg; pres. Krüger retired from Pretoria..30 May, "
Pretoria surrendered to the British army.............5 June, "
Gen. Prinsloo and 3348 Boers surrendered at Naauwpoort, 29 July, "
Harrismith surrendered to gen. Macdonald.............4 Aug. "
Machadodorp, Krüger's new capital, was occupied by gen. Buller..28 Aug. "
The Transvaal was proclaimed a part of the British empire by lord Roberts..1 Sept. "
The Boer generals, De Wet and Botha, continued to harass the British by sporadic raids.......................1 Sept. "
Ex-pres. Krüger abandoned the Transvaal and began his journey to Europe....................................12 Sept. "
Ex-pres. Krüger arrived at Marseilles and had an ovation from the French people during his journey to Paris; resolutions of sympathy adopted by the national assembly......22 Nov. "
The supreme military command in South Africa was turned over to lord Kitchener by lord Roberts, who departed for home...30 Nov. "
The German government intimated to Mr. Krüger that a visit to Berlin would be inopportune......................1 Dec.
The British met with a severe reverse at Nooitgedacht; col. Legge was killed..................................13 Dec. "
Sir Alfred Milner was appointed administrator of the Orange River and Transvaal colonies.......................14 Dec. "
Queen Wilhelmina, of the Netherlands, gave a dinner to Mr. Krüger...15 Dec. "
40 British officers and men were killed or wounded at Lindley, Orange River Colony..........................6 Jan. 1901
The Boers attacked a British column under gen. Colville north of Standerton and were driven back..............17 Jan. "
800 Boers were routed by New Zealand troops and bushmen under col. Gray near Ventersburg..................18 Jan. "
Bloemfontein-Ladybrand line was crossed by De Wet near Israel's Poort..30 Jan. "
The British post at Modderfontein (in the Transvaal) was captured by the Boers.................................3 Feb. "
Gen. Smith-Dorrein was attacked by Louis Botha with 2000 men at Orange Camp, but repulsed him.............6 Feb. "
De Wet crossed the railway at Bartman's siding and was engaged by Crabbe and an armored train..............16 Feb. "
The Boers, 5000 strong, were defeated by gen. French, at Piet Retief..22 Feb. "
De Wet's force scattered at Disselfontein, Orange river..23 Feb. "
Gen. French captured 300 Boers at Middleburg....... 26 Feb. "
Lord Kitchener drove De Wet north of the Orange river with a loss of 280 men captured.........................1 Mch. "
Lord Kitchener granted gen. Botha a seven days' armistice to make communication with other Boer leaders.......8 Mch. "
The Boers were defeated near Vryheid by gen. French..25 Mch. "
Fourie's commando and Bruce Hamilton's command held a running fight for 20 miles.......................27 Mch. "
Commandants Prinsloo and Engelbrecht surrendered to the British...30 Mch. "
The British reoccupied Pietersburg....................9 Apr. "
The Boers captured 75 men of the 5th Infantry and Imperial Yeomanry............ ....9 Apr. "
Negotiations for peace were renewed by gen. Botha...10 Apr. "
Sir Alfred Milner, returning home from South Africa, was received by the king and created a peer..............24 May, "
The Boers captured a British post of 41 men near Maraisburg, 27 May, "
Gen. Dixon's brigade of the 7th Yeomanry were attacked by Delarey, near Vlakfontein, and lost heavily.........29 May, "
An attack of 700 Boers under Scheeper upon Willowmore, Cape Colony, was repulsed after a 9 hours' fight.....3 June, 1901
The British and Boers lost heavily in an engagement between Elliot and De Wet near Reitz.......................6 June, "
200 Victorian Mounted Rifles captured by Boers at Steenkoolspruit..12 June, "
The Midland Mounted Rifles overpowered at Waterkloof, 20 June, "
Presidents Schalk-Berger of the South African Republic and Steyn of Orange Free State issued a proclamation for "no peace without independence"...........................20 June, "
Lord Kitchener issued a proclamation of banishment against all Boers not surrendering by 15 Sept..................7 Aug. "
50 of gen. French's scouts captured in Cape Colony....16 Aug. "
Treason trials of Boer-British subjects held at Bergersdorp, 21 Aug. "
The Boers captured 3 officers and 65 men north of Ladybrand, 21 Aug. "
The British troops captured Lotter's commando south of Pietersburg..16 Sept. "
3 companies of British mounted infantry captured near Scheeper's Nek...17 Sept. "
Boers defeated at Witkranz...........................12 Dec. "
Col. Damant defeated by the Boers under Wessels at Tafelkop, 20 Dec. "
Col. Firman's camp at Tweefontein crushed by De Wet..25 Dec. "
Gen. Viljoen captured at Lydenburg....................25 Jan. 1902
Boer proposals for peace declined by the British.......29 Jan. "
The Scots Greys captured at Klipdam.................18 Feb. "
Lord Methuen, defeated by Delarey at Klip Drift, is captured, but afterwards released.............................7 Mch. "
Peace negotiations begun.............................22 Mch. "
British terms accepted...............................30 May, "
[Total Boer force during the war about 75,000; total British force sent to South Africa from 1 Aug. 1899 to 31 May, 1902, 396,000; cost of the war to England over $1,000,000,000.]

South America. AMERICA.

South Australia was visited by capt. Sturt in 1830, and explored shortly after by capt. Parker and Mr. Kent, the former of whom was killed by the natives. The boundaries of the province were fixed by 4 and 5 Will. IV. c. 95 (1834); and it was occupied 26 Dec. 1836, by capt. Hindmarsh, the first governor. It was colonized according to E. Gibbon Wakefield's scheme, which was carried out by the South Australian Colonization association. The colony for several years underwent severe trials through the great influx of emigrants, land-jobbing, building speculations, etc., which produced almost universal bankruptcy in 1839. In 5 years after, the energy of the colonists had overcome their difficulties, and the prosperity of the colony appeared fully established. In 1842 the highly productive Burra-Burra copper-mines were discovered, and large fortunes were suddenly realized; but in 1851 the discovery of gold in New South Wales and Victoria almost paralyzed this province by drawing off a large part of the laboring population. Very little gold was found in South Australia; but a reaction took place in favor of the copper-mines, agriculture, etc. Before the discovery of gold, little trade existed between Adelaide (the capital of South Australia) and Melbourne; but in 1852 gold was transmitted from the latter to the former to the amount of 2,215,167*l*., principally for breadstuffs, farm produce, etc. Area, 903,690 sq. miles. Pop. in 1855, 85,821; 1865, 156,605; 1871, 185,626; 1877, 225,677; 1891, 315,048.

South Carolina, one of the original southern states of the United States, is bounded eastward by North Carolina and the Atlantic ocean, with a coast-line of 200 miles; Georgia lies to the west, and North Carolina bounds it on the north. It is triangular in form, with the apex south. Area, 30,570 sq. miles. Pop. 1890, 1,151,149; 1900, 1,340,316. Capital, Columbia.

Velasquez de Ayllon, with 2 ships sailing northward from St. Domingo to procure Indians as slaves, anchors at the mouth of the Combahee river. The natives crowding on the vessels are carried to St. Domingo... 1520
Velasquez de Ayllon again sails from Hispaniola with 3 ships, 1 of which is lost at the mouth of the Combahee, and 200 of the men are massacred by the natives; but few escape... 1525
Expedition fitted out by adm. Coligny, under Jean Ribault of Dieppe, explores St. Helena sound and Port Royal, and builds Charles fort, near Beaufort.................................. 1562

Charles II conveys by charter territory lying between lat 31° and 36° N, to the earl of Clarendon and 7 others, who form a proprietary and call the country Carolina (NORTH CAROLINA) 20 Mch 1663

Grant of land to the earl of Clarendon and others enlarged and extended to lat 29° N 30 June, 1665

Capt William Sayle explores the coast under the direction of the proprietors 1667

Settlement near Port Royal by a few English colonists sent out by the proprietors with William Sayle as governor 1670

Settlers at Port Royal remove to the western bank of the Ashley river and found Old Charleston 1671

Settlement at Charleston increased by a small colony from Barbadoes under sir John Yeamans, who had a large grant of land from the proprietors. With this colony came the first slaves in South Carolina "

Freemen of Carolina meet at Charleston and elect representatives for the civil government of the colony 1674

Fundamental constitutions framed by John Locke, and amended by the earl of Shaftesbury in 1669, are put into operation in South Carolina "

By invitation a colony of Dutch from New York settle on the southwest side of the Ashley river "

Settlers remove from Old Charleston to Oyster Point, at the confluence of the Ashley and Cooper rivers, and found Charleston 1680

Baptists from Maine under Mr Screven settle on Cooper river, 1683

Scotch settlement on Port Royal is broken up and dispersed by Spaniards from St Augustine 1686

Gov James Colleton, in endeavors to exact arrears of quit rents, proclaims martial law The Assembly meet and banish him thereupon Seth Sothel, claiming to be a proprietor, usurps the government 1690

Sothel is compelled to relinquish the government on charge of malfeasance and Philip Ludwell is appointed governor 1692

Fundamental constitutions abrogated by the lords proprietors, Apr 1693

Act making all alien inhabitants freemen on petitioning the governor and swearing allegiance to the king, with liberty of conscience to all Christians except Papists 1696

Small colony of Congregationalists from Dorchester, Mass, with their pastor rev Joseph Lord, settle near the head of Ashley river about 22 miles from Charleston "

Combined naval and land expedition from Carolina, under gov Moore and col Daniel, besiege St Augustine. 2 Spanish vessels appearing in the harbor, gov Moore raises the siege after burning the town Sept 1702

First issue of paper money in America made by Carolina to meet 6000*l*., expenses of the expedition against Florida, Sept "

Carolina troops, under gov Moore, make an expedition against the Indian towns of northern Florida Jan 1703

Combined expedition of French, under mons Le Feboure, and the Spanish, made upon Charleston proves fruitless Aug 1706

South Carolina troops attack and defeat the Tuscaroras on the Neuse, with a loss to the Indians of more than 300 killed and 100 captured 28 Jan 1712

An incipient civil war breaks out in Carolina in 1710, between col Broughton one of 3 deputies of the lords proprietors, and Robert Gibbes, the proclaimed governor The controversy being referred to the proprietors, they appoint Charles Craven governor "

Fort Nabucke, Greene county, N C, garrisoned by 800 Tuscarora Indians, captured by col James Moore of South Carolina 20 Mch 1713

Yamassee Indians, incited by the Spaniards, massacre 90 colonists at Pocotaligo 15 Apr 1715

Gov Craven defeats the Indians on the Salkehatchie In this war 400 South Carolinians are massacred "

King in council so advising, proprietors repeal the duty of 10 per cent on all goods of British manufacture, and also the act regulating elections and that enabling the Assembly to nominate a public receiver . 1717

Governor and council impeach the administration of chief justice Trott, and present the case to the proprietors The proprietors uphold Trott, and order the governor to publish at once the repeal of the late popular acts of the legislature, and to convene a new council and a new assembly 1718

Steed Bonnett and Richard Worley, pirates, and 40 followers, captured, convicted, and hung "

Gov Johnson, by letter of Alexander Skene, George Logan and William Blakeway, asked to accept the government from the people under the king 28 Nov 1719

Gov Johnson declining the office of governor, the People's Association proclaim James Moore governor, and elect 12 councillors, choose Richard Allein chief justice, and appoint col John Barnwell agent for the province "

Lords of the regency appoint Francis Nicholson provisional governor, having decided that the proprietors had forfeited their charter 1720

Gov Nicholson arrives, summons a new assembly, which elects the late popular governor, James Moore speaker of the house, 1721

Lords proprietors surrender the charter and government to the king except lord Granville's one eighth 1729

Sir Alexander Cumming, sent out by Great Britain makes a treaty with the Cherokees at Nequassee, who proclaim allegiance to the king 3 Apr 1730

On assuming the government, the crown divides Carolina, and appoints Robert Johnson governor of South Carolina 30 Apr "

First newspaper in South Carolina published at Charleston, Thomas Whitmarsh, editor 8 Jan 1732

Forty thousand acres of land on the Savannah is given to John Peter Pury and his colony of some 370 Swiss, Purysburg is settled 1732-33

Williamsburg township formed by Irish settlers 1734

Boundary line between North and South Carolina partly established 1738

Negro insurrection at Stono suppressed, and its leader, Cato, and principals hung 1740

Ship building begun 5 ship yards established, 4 in the vicinity of Charleston and 1 at Beaufort "

Fire consumes nearly one half of Charleston 18 Nov "

Col Clark, with emigrants from Virginia and Pennsylvania, settles on the Pacolet and on the forks of the Tyger river 1750-55

Cotton in small quantities exported 1754

Mrs Pinckney, who 10 years previously cultivated the first indigo, manufactures near Charleston silk for 3 dress patterns, one she presents to the princess dowager of Wales, one to lord Chesterfield and one to her daughter 1755

Gov Glen erects fort Prince George on the Savannah about 300 miles from Charleston "

Patrick Calhoun and 4 families settle in Abbeville district 1756

Treaty of peace concluded with the Cherokees at fort Prince George 17 Dec 1759

Two ships reach Charleston with several hundred poor German emigrants from England, deserted there by their leader Stumpel Apr 1764

Two hundred and twelve French settlers in charge of rev Mr Gilbert, arrive at Charleston in Apr and are assigned lands, which they settle under the name of New Bordeaux Oct "

Christopher Gadsden, Thomas Lynch and John Rutledge appointed delegates to the second Colonial Congress (UNITED STATES) 7 Oct. 1765

Stamped paper stored in fort Johnson on James island, by order of gov Bull 150 volunteers compel the captain of the ship which brought the paper to reload it and sail immediately for Europe Oct "

An association of regulators formed in the inland settlements to suppress horse stealing, etc, leads to a Circuit Court law establishing courts of justice at Ninety Six (now Cambridge), Orangeburg and Camden 1769

Cargoes of tea sent to South Carolina are stored, and consignees constrained from exposing it for sale 1773

Christopher Gadsden, Thomas Lynch, Henry Middleton, Edward Rutledge and John Rutledge appointed deputies to the first Continental Congress at Philadelphia 6 July, 1774

Henry Middleton chosen president of the Continental Congress 22 Oct "

First Provincial Congress of 184 members, including the 49 members of the Constitutional Assembly, meet and approve proceedings of Continental Congress 11 Jan 1775

Letters from England to public officials in America intercepted at Charleston furnish abundant evidence of the determination of England to coerce America by force 19 Apr "

On receiving news of the battle of Lexington the arms are removed from the arsenal at Charleston and distributed among the enlisted men Apr "

Ship *Betsey*, from London surprised by a Carolina privateer, and 111 barrels of powder captured Aug "

Fort Johnson garrisoned by capt Heyward and 35 of the Charleston artillery Sept "

Gov Campbell, last royal governor, dissolves the Assembly and retires to the sloop of war *Tamar* 15 Sept "

Hostilities in South Carolina begun by the British vessels *Tamar* and *Cherokee* making a night attack on the schooner *Defence*, capt Tufts, while blocking Hog Island channel by sinking hulks. Shots are exchanged, but at sunrise the British vessels retire 12 Nov "

Col Moultrie authorized by the Council of Safety, takes possession of Haddrell's Point, and with artillery drives the British vessels from Charleston harbor Dec "

Constitution framed by the Provincial Congress of South Carolina adopted, 26 Mch 1776, and courts of justice under its sanction opened 23 Apr 1776

British fleet under sir Peter Parker unsuccessfully attacks fort Moultrie, Sullivan's island (FORT MOULTRIE) 28 June, "

Thomas Heyward, jr, James Lynch, jr, Arthur Middleton, and Edward Rutledge sign the Declaration of Independence "

Col Williamson with 2000 men marches against the Cherokees, 13 Sept, and lays waste all their settlements east of the Appalachian mountains Sept "

Cherokee Indians by treaty cede to South Carolina all their land eastward of the Unaka mountains 20 May, 1777

Henry Laurens of South Carolina chosen president of the Continental Congress. 1 Nov "

Constitution passed by the General Assembly as an act, 19 Mch 1778, goes into effect Nov 1778

State Supreme court declares the constitutions of 1776 and 1778 acts of General Assembly, which it could repeal or amend 1779

Maj gen Benjamin Lincoln takes command of all the forces to the southward, establishes his first post at Purysburg on the Savannah river "

President Lowndes lays a general embargo, and prohibits the sailing of vessels from any port of the state "

British under maj Gardiner driven from Port Royal island by gen Moultrie 3 Feb "

Americans repulsed at Stono ferry 20 June, "

British fleet from New York against Charleston lands forces under sir Heny Clinton 30 miles from the city 11 Feb 1780

Royal fleet commanded by adm Arbuthnot anchors near fort Johnson on James island 9 Apr "

Gov Rutledge retires from Charleston northward 12 Apr "

American cavalry surprised by British under cols. Tarleton and Webster, and routed at Monk's Corner 14 Apr 1780

Fort Moultrie, weakened reinforcing Charleston, surrenders to capt Hudson of the British navy 6 May, "

Charleston capitulates 12 May, "

British forces under col Tarleton surprise the Americans under col Buford at Waxhaw on the North Carolina border, the Americans lose 117 killed and 200 taken prisoners, while the British lose but 5 men killed and 12 wounded 29 May, "

Sir Henry Clinton and adm Arbuthnot as peace commissioners by proclamation offer the inhabitants, with a few exceptions, pardon and reinstatement in their rights 1 June, "

All paroles to prisoners not taken by capitulation and not in confinement at the surrender of Charleston are declared null and void after 20 June and holders required actively to aid military operations or be treated as rebels 3 June, "

Affair at ROCKY MOUNT 30 July, "

Battle of HANGING ROCK 6 Aug "

Battle of Camden, Americans under gen Gates attack the British under Cornwallis and are repulsed 16 Aug "

Americans under col Williams defeat the British at Musgrove's Mills on the Enoree 18 Aug "

Sixty distinguished citizens of South Carolina are seized by the British and transported to St Augustine as prisoners, 27 Aug "

Battle of KING'S MOUNTAIN 7 Oct. "

Col Thomas Sumter extends his campaign into South Carolina, he captures a British supply train 15 Aug, is surprised by Tarleton and defeated at Fishing creek 18 Aug, defeats maj James Wemyss in a night attack on Broad river, 8 Nov, and defeats col Tarleton at Blackstock Hill 20 Nov "

Battle of COWPENS, near Broad river, Americans under Morgan defeat the British under Tarleton, Andrew Jackson, then a boy of 14 years, takes part in the engagement 17 Jan 1781

Francis Marion, appointed brigadier-general by gov Rutledge in July, 1780, after numerous successful sorties on the British and Tories from camp on Snow island during the winter of 1780-81, joins gen Greene on his return to the state, Apr "

Battle of Hobkirk's Hill, Americans under gen Greene retreat before an attack of the British under lord Francis Rawdon (HOBKIRK'S HILL) 25 Apr "

British evacuate fort Ninety Six 21 June, "

Indecisive battle between gen Greene and col Stuart at Eutaw Springs *each claiming a victory* (EUTAW SPRINGS) 8 Sept. "

Gov Rutledge issues a proclamation offering pardon to the Tories in South Carolina 27 Sept "

General Assembly convenes at Jacksonborough on the Edisto river, Jan elects John Mathews governor, and passes laws for confiscating the estates of Tories Feb 1782

British evacuate Charleston 14 Dec "

Charleston (hitherto Charlestown) incorporated 1784

South Carolina relinquishes to Georgia her claim to a tract of land lying between the Altamaha and St Mary's rivers 1787

South Carolina cedes to the U S government her claim to a strip of land 12 miles wide west of a line from the head of the Tugaloo river to the North Carolina border 9 Aug "

Constitution of the U S ratified by the state 23 May, 1788

Convention at Columbia completes state constitution 3 June, 1790

Orphan house asylum established at Charleston 1792

Medical Society of South Carolina, formed 1789, incorporated 1794

Santee canal, connecting Charleston harbor with the Santee, 22 miles long, begun 1792, completed 1802

Severe hurricane at Charleston Sept 1804

College of the University of South Carolina, chartered 1801, opened at Columbia 1805

Owing to the peculiar distribution of the slave population, which gave the upper counties the power to tax, while the lower counties held most of the property taxed, a compromise is made in the constitution, making the members of the lower House 124, 62 from each section 1808

Madison appoints Paul Hamilton secretary of the navy 7 Mch. 1809

Legislature creates a Free school fund, its use to be confined to the poor if not enough for all 1811

State bank of South Carolina incorporated 1812

Literary and Philosophical Society of South Carolina incorporated 1813

Decatur capt. Diron, a privateer from Charleston, captures the British ship *Dominica* of 15 guns and crew of 80 men, and shortly after the *London Trader* with a valuable cargo Aug. "

Cherokees cede territory lying within the chartered limits of South Carolina, by treaty at Washington, 22 Mch 1816, ratified by the legislature of South Carolina 19 Dec 1816

Monroe appoints John C Calhoun secretary of war 8 Oct. 1817

Territory ceded by the Cherokees in 1816, annexed to the election district of Pendleton 1820

College of Charleston, commenced in Charleston in 1785, reorganized and opened 1 Jan 1824

Legislature denounces the U S. tariff as encroaching on state rights 12 Dec 1827

South Carolina gold mines yield $3500 in . "

State lunatic asylum at Columbia opened 1828

Public meeting on states rights held at Columbia 20 Sept. 1830

Gov Hamilton recommends to legislature a nullification act "

Legislature calls a convention at Columbia, 19 Nov 1832, to consider the protective tariff 25 Oct 1832

President instructs the collector at Charleston to seize and hold every vessel entering that port until the duties be paid, and "to retain and defend the custody of said vessels against any forcible attempt." Gen Scott and a naval force are also sent to the state 6 Nov "

State convention meets 19 Nov 1832, and passes an ordinance of nullification, declaring (1) the tariff acts of 1828 and 1832 to be null, void, and no law, nor binding upon the state, its officers or citizens, (2) prohibiting the payment of duties under either act within the state after 1 Feb 1833, (3) making any appeal to the Supreme court of the U S as to the validity of the ordinance a contempt of the State court from which the appeal was taken, punishable at the discretion of the latter, (4) ordering every office holder and juror to be sworn to support the ordinance, (5) giving warning that if the federal government should attempt to enforce the tariff by use of army or navy, or by closing the ports of the state, or should in any way harass or obstruct the state's foreign commerce, South Carolina would no longer consider herself a member of the Union 24 Nov 1832

President Andrew Jackson proclaims nullification to be "*incompatible* with the existence of the Union and destructive of the great object for which it was formed" 11 Dec. "

Calhoun resigns the office of vice president 28 Dec. "

Gov Hayne issues a proclamation in answer to that of the president's, in which he warns the people not to be seduced from their primary allegiance to the state 31 Dec "

A bill to enforce the tariff, nicknamed the "Bloody bill" and "Force bill," becomes a law of the U S 2 Mch 18 3

Henry Clay introduces a compromise tariff bill, 12 Feb 1833, which is signed by the president and becomes a law, 2 Mch "

A state convention passes 2 ordinances 1st repealing the Nullification act of 24 Nov 1832, 2d, an ordinance to nullify the act of Congress, 2 Mch 1833, commonly called the "Enforcing bill" 16 Mch "

Van Buren appoints Joel R. Poinsett secretary of war 7 Mch 1837

During this and the 2 previous years, 2265 volunteers furnished for the Florida war 1838

Death of gov Noble, Benjamin K. Henuegan, lieutenant governor succeeds him in office 7 Apr 1840

Hugh S Legaré attorney general of U S 13 Sept. 1841

Tyler appoints Calhoun secretary of war 6 Mch 1844

South Carolina *Institution for the Education of the Deaf, Dumb,* and Blind at Cedar Springs opened 1849

Calhoun dies at Washington 31 Mch 1850

Furman university at Greenville, chartered 1850, opened 1851

Convention of Southern Rights' associations of the state resolve that "with or without co operation they are for dissolution of the Union" 8 May, "

State convention declares the right of the state to secede 1852

Greenville female college at Greenville, chartered 1854, opened, 1855

Gov Adams in his annual message recommends the revival of the slave trade 24 Nov 1856

Columbia female college at Columbia chartered 1854, opened 1857

U S steamship *Niagara* sails from Charleston for Liberia with Africans captured from the *Echo*, a slave ship sailing under American colors, 21 Aug, and brought to Charleston, where the 300 or more slaves are placed in charge of the U S. marshal (UNITED STATES) 20 Sept. 1858

Grand jury at Columbia returns "no bill" on all 3 indictments against the crew of the slaver *Echo* 30 Nov "

Grand jury at Charleston refuses to indict capt. Corrie of the *Wanderer*, a slave ship seized in New York harbor 16 May, 1859

Resolution offered in the House, that "South Carolina is ready to enter, *with other slave holding states, into the formation* of a Southern confederacy" 30 Nov "

Due West female college at Due West, chartered 1859, opened 1860

Democratic National convention meets at Charleston, and adjourns to Baltimore after delegates from southern states had withdrawn (UNITED STATES) 23 Apr "

Seceding Southern delegates to the Democratic convention organize a Southern convention, electing senator Bayard of Delaware president, but adjourn to meet at Richmond without making any nominations (UNITED STATES) 1 May, "

A convention called by the legislature, 7 Nov, assembles at Columbia, 17 Dec. but adjourns to Charleston, 18 Dec., where they pass an ordinance of secession and declare South Carolina an independent commonwealth 20 Dec "

Maj Anderson evacuates fort Moultrie and retires to fort Sumter, on night of 26 Dec. "

Fort Pinckney, in Charleston harbor, seized by state troops, 27 Dec "

State troops seize the arsenal at Charleston, lower the Federal flag after a salute of 32 guns, and run up the Palmetto flag with a salute of 1 gun for South Carolina. 31 Dec "

Fort Johnson, in Charleston harbor, occupied by state troops, 2 Jan 1861

Star of the West, with a small force of troops and supplies for fort Sumter, being fired upon by batteries on Morris island and fort Moultrie, retires 9 Jan "

Charles G Memminger appointed Confederate secretary of the treasury 21 Feb "

State convention called by the legislature, 17 Dec 1860, revises the state constitution which goes into effect without being submitted to the people for ratification 8 Apr "

Gov Pickens's demand for the surrender of fort Sumter being refused by maj Anderson, 11 Jan, and also by the secretary of war, 6 Feb, the civil war is opened by a shell fired from the howitzer battery on James island at 4 30 A M Friday (UNITED STATES) . . 12 Apr "

Fort Sumter evacuated by maj Anderson (FORT SUMTER), 14 Apr "

U S steam frigate *Niagara* begins the blockade of Charleston harbor, 11 May, captures the English ship *General Parkhill*, 13 May, "

Gov Pickens proclaims that all persons remitting money to pay debts due in the North are guilty of treason 6 June, "

James M Mason of Virginia and John Slidell of Louisiana leave Charleston on the Confederate steamer *Theodora* for Europe

via Havana, to represent the Confederate government at the courts of Great Britain and France (TRENT AFFAIR)...12 Oct. 1861
'wenty five vessels of the great Southern expedition anchor off Port Royal..........4 Nov. "
'ederals capture *forts Walker and Beauregard, Port Royal*, 7 Nov. "
'onfederate privateer *Isabel* runs the blockade at Charleston, avoiding 11 U. S. vessels..........27 Dec. "
ien. David Hunter declares free the slaves in Georgia, Florida, and South Carolina (UNITED STATES)..........9 May, 1862
lattle of Secessionville (James island), in which col. T. G. Lamar defeats the federals under gen. Henry W. Benham...16 June, "
ien. P. G. T. Beauregard assumes command of the department of South Carolina and Georgia..........24 Sept. "
ien. J. M. Brannan defeats the confederates under gen. Walker in the battle of Pocotaligo..........22 Oct. "
'om. Samuel F. Dupont's squadron is repulsed in the battle of Charleston harbor..........7 Apr. 1863
'ol. Montgomery, with U. S. troops, makes a raid from Beaufort up the Combahee river, securing 800 slaves and a quantity of provisions and horses..........June, "
'ederals victorious in the battles of Morris Island, 10 July; FORT WAGNER, 11 July; James Island..........16 July, "
'ort Wagner bombarded by gen. Q. A. Gillmore..........18 July, "
'harleston bombarded by the "SWAMP ANGEL," which bursts, 24 Aug. "
'ort Wagner bombarded by Gillmore..........5 Sept. "
ieorge A. Trenholm appointed Confederate secretary of the treasury.......... 1864
'onfederates defeat gen. John P. Hatch at Honey Hill..30 Nov. "
'onfederates repulsed in battles of Pocotaligo, 14 Jan.; Salkhatchie, 3 Feb.; Williston Station, 8 Feb.; Orangeburg, 12 Feb.; *Congaree Creek*..........15 Feb. 1865
'olumbia surrendered to gen. Sherman..........17 Feb. "
'harleston, burned and evacuated by gen. Hardee the day previous, is occupied by Federal troops..........18 Feb. "
ien. O. O. Howard *defeats the confederates* at Cheraw..3 Mch. "
ienjamin F. Perry appointed provisional governor of South Carolina by pres. Johnson..........30 June, "
. convention called by gov. Perry assembles in Baptist church at Columbia, 13 Sept., *repeals the ordinance of secession*, 19 Sept., and completes an amended constitution, which takes effect without being submitted to the people..........27 Sept. "
egislature ratifies the amendment of the Constitution of the U. S. abolishing slavery..........13 Nov. "
egislature rejects the XIV.th Amendment of the Constitution of the U. S..........Dec. 1866
ien. D. E. Sickles assigned by the president of the U. S. to the command of Second Military district, embracing North and South Carolina, with headquarters at Columbia..........11 Mch. 1867
ien. Sickles superseded by gen. E. R. S. Canby..........26 Aug. "
. constitution, framed by a convention called under the Reconstruction acts of Congress, which assembles at Charleston, 14 Jan., and completes its labors, 17 Mch., ratified by the people, 70,558 to 27,288..........14–16 Apr. 1868
outh Carolina readmitted into the Union..........25 June, "
tate penitentiary at Columbia opened.......... "
. K. Jillson elected the first state superintendent of public instruction in South Carolina.......... "
egislature ratifies the XV.th Amendment of the Constitution of the U. S..........16 Mch. 1869
tate Labor convention held at Columbia..........Nov. "
'nion Reform party organized and holds its first state convention at Charleston..........16 June, 1870
'ree Common-school system established.......... "
'ax-payers' convention held at the state capitol in Columbia "to devise means for the redemption of the state from her financial embarrassments"..........May, 1871
)wing to murder and outrage in the upper country, by the Ku-klux, pres. Grant, by proclamation, 12 Oct., suspends the habeas corpus in the counties of Spartansburg, York, Union, Chester, Laurens, Newberry, Fairfield, Lancaster, and Chesterfield, and commands secret organizations to disband within 5 days. Many troops are stationed in the state and about 600 arrests made.......... "
.ct establishing the validity of bonds of the state, issued between 26 Aug. 1868 and 26 Mch. 1869.......... 1872
'laflin university and South Carolina Agricultural college and Mechanical institute, organized at Orangeburg in 1869, is reopened and chartered.......... "
Valhalla female college at Walhalla, chartered and opened.... "
'ax-payers' convention at Columbia by resolution asking for amendments, simplifying and abridging the tax laws, 17 Feb. 1874
iov. Moses is indicted personally for official acts; indictment is quashed on the ground that he should have been impeached..........8 June, "
'onvention of Independent Republicans at Charleston nominates candidates for governor, etc., who are supported by the Conservative party..........2 Oct. "
tate Normal school opened at Columbia.......... "
)rphan House asylum removed from Charleston to Columbia. 1875
.lleged blocking of a highway at Hamburg, 4 July, by a colored militia company; armed citizens attack them; 5 negroes killed and others wounded..........9 July, 1876
iov. Chamberlain, by proclamation, orders all organizations, except the militia of the state, to disband within 3 days, 7 Oct.; a similar proclamation by pres. Grant..........17 Oct. "
Vhile the result of the state election is pending in the Supreme court, the State Board of Canvassers, holding that their powers were limited by statute to 10 days, on the last day issue certificates to the Republican presidential electors and state officers, refusing certificates to members of the legislature

from Edgefield and Laurens counties for irregularities in elections..........22 Nov. 1876
On the assembling of the legislature, 64 Democratic members, including those from Edgefield and Laurens counties, withdraw to Carolina hall and organize separately with William H. Wallace as speaker..........28 Nov. "
Senate and Republican house canvass the votes for governor and lieutenant-governor, and declare D. H. Chamberlain *elected governor*, 5 Dec.; sworn into office..........7 Dec. "
Speaker Wallace, having a certificate from the secretary of state of the votes cast for governor and lieutenant governor, proceeds to canvass the votes and declares Wade Hampton and *William D. Simpson, Democrats, elected; oath of office* is administered by trial-judge Mackay..........12 Dec. "
Both governors, being invited to Washington, hold a private conference with pres. Hayes, which results in a proclamation by gov. Chamberlain *withdrawing his claim*..........11 *Apr.* 1877
F. L. Cardoza, state treasurer under gov. Chamberlain, is arrested for fraud upon the state government, 21 July, and sentenced to 2 years in the county jail and \$4000 fine, 8 Nov. "
Legislature by joint resolution provides that "*all the unfunded* debts and liabilities of the state, including the bills of the bank of the state, and so much of the funded debt as is known as the Little Bonanza, be settled at the rate of 50 per cent," Mch. 1878
Wade Hampton, elected U. S. senator, resigns as governor, and is succeeded by W. D. Simpson, who is installed.....26 Feb. 1879
Department of agriculture established.......... "
Act to settle state debt in accordance with decision of state Supreme court; James C. Colt named a special commissioner.. "
Gov. Simpson, resigning his office to take the chief-justiceship, is succeeded by lieut.-gov. T. B. Jeter..........1 Sept. 1880
Centennial anniversary of the battle of Cowpens, 17 Jan. 1781, commemorated at Spartansburg by the unveiling of a statue of gen. Daniel H. Morgan..........11 May, 1881
Exodus of 5000 colored people from Edgefield county, bound for Arkansas and Beaufort county..........24–31 Dec. "
State Military academy at Charleston reopened..........1 Oct. 1882
Constitution amended, forbidding counties to contract a debt greater than 8 per cent. of the taxable valuation.......... 1884
Earthquake destroys \$5,000,000 worth of property; first shock felt at Charleston, 9:51 P.M. (EARTHQUAKES)..........31 Aug. 1886
Winthrop training-school for teachers at Columbia, opened... "
Act passed providing a pension of \$5 per month for disabled *Confederate soldiers* and the widows of those killed in the Confederate service.......... 1887
Legislature accepts a devise of 814 acres in Oconee county by Thomas G. Clemson, on condition that the state erect and maintain an *agricultural and mechanical college*.......... 1888
First colored state fair ever held in the state opens at Columbia..........1 Jan. 1890
Act passed creating a Board of Phosphate commissioners..... "
Department *of Agriculture and office of Commissioner of Agriculture* abolished, and powers bestowed on trustees of the Clemson Agricultural college at session.....25 Nov.–24 Dec. "
Col. Samuel B. Pickens dies at Charleston..........17 Sept. 1891
Nathaniel Duncan Ingraham, formerly of the U. S. navy (KOSZTA AFFAIR), afterwards in the Confederate service, dies at Charleston..........16 Oct. "
Maj. George Washington Earle of Darlington, noted mathematician and civil engineer, d..........5 May, 1892
Evans liquor law goes into effect, by which the state assumes control of the sale of intoxicants..........1 July, 1893
First state dispensary in Charleston opened; 1st day's sales, \$50..........22 Aug. "
Three counties in rebellion against state authority on account of the state dispensary law; militia called out, 31 Mch.–1 Apr. 1894
Gov. Tillman assumes control of the police and marshals in all cities and incorporated towns..........3 Apr. "
Supreme court of the state decides that prohibition is in force in the state..........8 May, "
Gov. Tillman issues a proclamation to open 1 Aug. the state liquor dispensaries..........23 July, "

PROPRIETARY GOVERNORS.

William Sayle	appointed	26 July,	1669
Joseph West	"	28 Aug.	1671
Sir John Yeamans	"	26 Dec.	"
Joseph West	"	13 Aug.	1674
Joseph Morton	"	26 Sept.	1682
Joseph West	"	6 Sept.	1684
Richard Kirk			"
Robert Quarry			"
Joseph Morton			1685
James Colleton			1686
Seth Sothel			1690
Philip Ludwell			1692
Thomas Smith			1693
Joseph Blake			1694
John Archdale			1695
Joseph Blake			1696
James Moore			1700
Sir Nathaniel Johnson			1703
Edward Tynte			1709
Robert Gibbes			1710
Charles Craven			1712
Robert Daniel			1716
Robert Johnson			1717
James Moore			1719

TEMPORARY REPUBLIC.

Arthur Middleton.......... 1719

ROYAL GOVERNORS.

Francis Nicholson........ 1721
Arthur Middleton.......... 1725
Robert Johnson........... 1730
Thomas Broughton........ 1735
William Bull............. 1737
James Glen.............. 1743
William H. Littleton....... 1756
William Bull............. 1760
Thomas Boone............ 1762
William Bull............. 1763
Charles Montague.......... 1766
William Bull............. 1769
William Campbell......... 1775

GOVERNORS UNDER THE CONSTITUTION.

John Rutledge.................. 1775
Rawlin Lowndes.................. 1778
John Rutledge.................. 1779
John Matthews.................. 1782
Benjamin Guerard.................. 1783
William Moultrie.................. 1785
Thomas Pinckney.................. 1787
Arnoldus Vanderhorst.................. 1792
William Moultrie.................. 1794
Charles Pinckney.................. 1796
Edward Rutledge.................. 1798
John Drayton..........acting.......... 1800
James B. Richardson.................. 1802
Paul Hamilton.................. 1804
Charles Pinckney.................. 1806
John Drayton.................. 1808
Henry Middleton.................. 1810
Joseph Alston.................. 1812
David R. Williams.................. 1814
Andrew J. Pickens.................. 1816
John Geddes.................. 1818
Thomas Bennet.................. 1820
John L. Wilson.................. 1822
Richard J. Manning.................. 1824
John Taylor.................. 1826
Stephen D. Miller.................. 1828
James Hamilton.................. 1830
Robert Y. Hayne.................. 1832
George McDuffie.................. 1834
Pierce M. Butler.................. 1836
Patrick Noble.................. 1838
B. K. Hennegan..........acting.......... 1840
J. P. Richardson.................. "
James H. Hammond.................. 1842
William Aiken.................. 1844
David Johnson.................. 1846
W. B. Seabrook.................. 1848
John H. Means.................. 1850
John L. Manning.................. 1852
James H. Adams.................. 1854
R. F. W. Alston.................. 1856
William H. Gist.................. 1858
Francis W. Pickens.................. 1860
M. L. Bonham.................. 1862
A. G. Magrath..........inaugurated..........19 Dec. 1864
Benjamin F. Perry, provisional, appointed..........30 June, 1865
James L. Orr..........inaugurated..........29 Nov. "
Robert K. Scott.......... " ....9 July, 1868
F. J. Moses, jr.................. 1873
Daniel H. Chamberlain.................. 1875
Wade Hampton.................. 1877
William D. Simpson.......assumes office..........26 Feb. 1879
T. B. Jeter.......... " " ....1 Sept. 1880
Johnson Hagood..........inaugurated..........30 Nov. "
Hugh S. Thompson.................. 1882
John P. Richardson.................. 1886
Benjamin R. Tillman.......inaugurated..........4 Dec. 1890
John Gary Evans..................1 Dec. 1894

UNITED STATES SENATORS FROM THE STATE OF SOUTH CAROLINA.

Name.	No. of Congress.	Date.	Remarks.
Pierce Butler	1st to 4th	1789 to 1796	Resigned.
Ralph Izard	1st " 4th	1789 " 1795	Elected president *pro tem.* 31 May, 1794.
John Hunter	4th " 5th	1796 " 1798	Elected in place of Butler. Resigned.
Jacob Read	4th " 7th	1795 " 1801	Elected president *pro tem.* 22 Nov. 1797.
Charles Pinckney	5th " 7th	1798 " 1801	Resigned.
Thomas Sumter	7th " 11th	1801 " 1810	Elected in place of Pinckney. Resigned.
John Ewing Calhoun	7th	1801 " 1802	Died in office.
Pierce Butler	8th	1803 " 1804	Elected in place of Calhoun. Resigned.
John Gailard	8th to 20th	1805 " 1826	Elected in place of Butler. Elected president *pro tem.* 28 Feb. and 17 Apr. 1810; 18 Apr. and 25 Nov. 1814; 2 Dec. 1816; 1 Dec. 1817; 20 Dec. 1820; 1 Feb. 1822; 21 May, 1824; 9 Mch. 1825. Died 26 Feb. 1826.
John Taylor	11th " 14th	1810 " 1816	Elected in place of Sumter. Resigned.
William Smith	14th " 18th	1817 " 1823	Elected in place of Taylor.
Robert Y. Hayne	18th " 22d	1823 " 1832	Great speech in the Senate on the Foote resolution, 25 Jan. 1830. Resigned. Elected governor.
William Harper	19th	1826	Appointed *pro tem.* in place of Gailard.
William Smith	20th to 22d	1826 to 1831	Elected in place of Gailard.
John C. Calhoun	22d " 28th	1833 " 1843	Elected in place of Hayne. Resigned.
Stephen D. Miller	22d	1831 " 1833	Resigned.
William C. Preston	23d to 27th	1833 " 1842	"
George McDuffie	27th	1843 " 1846	Elected in place of Preston. Resigned.
Daniel E. Huger	28th	1843 " 1845	Resigned.
Andrew P. Butler	29th to 35th	1846 " 1857	Elected in place of McDuffie. Died in office.
John C. Calhoun	29th " 31st	1845 " 1850	Died 31 Mch. 1850.
Franklin H. Elmore	31st	1850	Appointed in place of Calhoun. Died 6 May, 1850.
Robert W. Barnwell	31st	"	Appointed in place of Elmore.
R. Barnwell Rhett	31st to 32d	1851 to 1852	Elected in place of Calhoun. Resigned.
William F. De Saussure	32d	1852	Appointed in place of Rhett.
Josiah J. Evans	33d to 35th	1853 to 1858	Died in office.
Arthur P. Hayne	35th	1858	Appointed in place of Evans.
James Chestnut	35th to 36th	1859 to 1860	Elected in place of Evans. Resigned 10 Nov. 1860, and expelled 11 July, 1861.
James H. Hammond	35th to 36th	1857 " 1860	Retired from the Senate, 11 Nov. 1860.
37th, 38th, 39th Congresses vacant.			
Thomas J. Robertson	40th to 45th	1868 to 1877	
Frederick A. Sawyer	40th " 43d	1868 " 1873	
John J. Patterson	43d " 46th	1873 " 1879	
Matthew C. Butler	45th " 54th	1877 " 1895	
Wade Hampton	46th " 52d	1879 " 1891	
John L. M. Irby	52d " ——	1891 " ——	Term expires 1897.
B. R. Tillman	54th " ——	1895 " ——	Term expires 1901.

South Dakota, one of the United States, was formed by the division of Dakota territory into 2 states in 1889. It is bounded on the north by North Dakota, east by Minnesota and Iowa, south by Nebraska, and west by Wyoming and Montana. In latitude it lies between 43° and 46° N., and in longitude between 96° 20′ and 104° W.; area, 77,650 sq. miles, in 51 counties; pop. 1890, 328,808, 1900, 401,570. Captial, Pierre.

Lewis and Clarke ascend the Missouri river on their way to the Pacific, leaving the mouth of the river, 14 May, 1804, reaching the mouth of the Columbia river, 7 Nov. 1805; and returning by the Missouri, arrive at St. Louis..........23 Sept. 1806
Fort Pierre established.................. 1829
First steamboat to navigate the Upper Missouri, the *Yellowstone*, built by the American Fur company at Pittsburg, ascends the river as far as fort Pierre.................. 1831
Treaty of Traverse des Sioux signed by the Indians, ceding to the U. S. the territory east of the Big Sioux river.................. 1851
Gen. W. S. Harney, with 1200 men, marches from the Platte river to fort Pierre, where they encamp for the winter...... 1855
First settlement established at Sioux Falls by the Western Town-lot company of Dubuque, Ia.................. 1857
By organizing Nebraska territory, 30 May, 1854, and Minnesota state, 11 May, 1858, the remainder of Dakota is left without legal name or existence.................. 1858
Territory of Dakota organized with an area of 150,932 sq. miles, by act of Congress..........2 Mch. 1861
Seat of government for Dakota territory located at Yankton.................. 1862
Sioux Falls destroyed by the Sioux Indians, and settlers flee to Yankton.................. "

Fort Dakota built on reservation at Sioux Falls 1865
Line of the Chicago, Milwaukee, and St. Paul railroad built from Sioux City, Ia., to Yankton, completed..................... 1873
Military and Scientific Exploring Expedition, under gen. G. A. Custer, arrives at the Black Hills, July, 1874, from fort Abraham Lincoln. Specimens of gold are washed from the soil near Harney's Peak, where it was known to exist in 1867, but emigration thither was stopped by gen. Sherman on account of Indian troubles. This visit causes great excitement among the Sioux Indians.................................. 1874
Gold discovered in Deadwood and Whitewood gulches......... 1875
Indians relinquish their titles to lands in the Black Hills and western counties of southern Dakota...................... 1876
Town of Deadwood laid out................................. "
Dakota School for Deaf-mutes at Sioux Falls opened.......... 1880
Yankton college, chartered in 1881, opened at Yankton....... 1882
Tin, detected as a black sand accompanying gold from the Black Hills, by prof. Pearce of Argo, is practically discovered by maj. Andrew J. Simmons of Rapid City................ 1883
Seat of government for Dakota territory removed from Yankton to Bismarck...............................11 Sept. "
A convention called by some 400 delegates who met at Huron, 19 June, convenes at Sioux Falls, 4 Sept., and frames a constitution for the state of Dakota to comprise the southern half of the territory..............................19 Sept. "
University of South Dakota at Vermilion opened............ "
Pierre university at East Pierre chartered and opened........ "
Sioux Falls university opened.............................. "
Yankton Insane hospital established........................ "
Normal schools established at Spearfish and Madison......... "
Dakota penitentiary established at Sioux Falls................ "
U. S. Senate passes a bill for the admission as a state of the southern half of Dakota territory; that portion north of the 46th parallel to be called the Territory of Lincoln.. 1884
Agricultural college at Brookings opened .... "
Dakota University at Mitchell opened...................Sept. 1885
Constitutional convention called by the legislature at Sioux Falls frames a constitution for South Dakota....... 25 Sept. "
Legislature of Dakota territory passes a Local Option law..... 1887
School of Mines at Rapid City, established by act of legislature in 1885, is opened... "
A majority vote for the division of Dakota territory into 2 states, North and South Dakota, at an election held....Nov. "
Act admitting South Dakota signed, a constitutional convention to meet at Sioux Falls, 4 July, 1889.............22 Feb. 1889
Election held by proclamation of territorial governor, A. C. Mellette, 15 Apr. 1889, for delegates to a constitutional convention to meet 4 July, and the Sioux Falls constitution of 1885 favored by 37,710 votes to 3414................14 May, "
Sioux Falls constitution amended and adopted by a convention at Sioux Falls, 4 July, which adjourns...........5 Aug. "
Charles A. Foster of Ohio, William Warner of Missouri, and gen. George A. Cook, a committee appointed by the president, arrive at the Sioux reservation early in June, and secure the consent of three fourths of the Indians to open for settlement 26,751,105 acres of their land in the northwestern part of South Dakota......................................Aug. "
Arthur C. Mellette, Republican, elected governor of South Dakota, the Sioux Falls constitution adopted by 70,131 to 3267; the article prohibiting the manufacture and sale of intoxicating liquors adopted by 40,234 to 34,510, and Pierre chosen as the temporary capital..............................1 Oct. "
First state legislature convenes at Pierre..............15 Oct. "
South Dakota admitted into the Union with the northern boundary the 7th standard parallel..................2 Nov. "
Dakota Reform school in Plankinton opened.................. "
Proclamation by pres. Harrison opening up the Sioux reservation, 9,000,000 acres, and a rush of immigrants who had assembled on the east bank of the Missouri...........10 Feb. 1890
Large amount of seed grain supplied to the famine-stricken farmers, chiefly in the central portion of the state, by appropriation by the legislature and from outside the state.. "
Legislature creates a State Board of Charities and Correction, a Board of Regents of Education, a State Board of Equalization, a Board of Pardons, a Bureau of Labor Statistics, the office of state engineer of irrigation, a State Meteorological Bureau, a state inspector of mines, and a State Board of Pharmaceutical Examiners.................................. "
Pierre selected as the permanent capital of the state.......... "
Farmers' Alliance and Knights of Labor parties meet in state convention at Huron, report in favor of woman suffrage, prohibition, and tariff for revenue only, and unite under the name of the Independent party.......................6 June, "
Dakota Soldiers' Home, established at Hot Springs, Fall River county, in 1889, is opened..........................27 Nov. "
Battle with Big Foot's Indian band on Wounded Knee creek; some 250 Indians killed, including 44 squaws and 18 papooses. Loss to U. S. troops, 32 killed, 39 wounded, 29 Dec. "
Gen. Miles, after the Indians at Pine Ridge agency surrender, 15 Jan., declares the Indian outbreak at an end, 19 Jan. 1891
James H. Kyle elected U. S. senator..................16 Feb. "
Australian ballot law enacted at session of.......6 Jan.–7 Mch. "
Dr. Chas. O. Merica chosen to succeed Howard B. Grose, president of state university at Vermilion, resigns..........Sept. "
Sisseton Indian reservation opened to settlers............15 Apr. 1892
Catholic Sioux congress opens at Cheyenne agency; 6000 Sioux Indians present....................................3 July, "

GOVERNORS—TERRITORIAL.

William Jayne.............appointed...................... 1861
Newton Edmunds........... " 1863
Andrew J. Faulk........... " 1866
John A. Burbank .... " 1869
John A. Pennington........ " 1874
William A. Howard......... " 1878
N. G. Ordway.............. " 1880
Gilbert A. Pierce.......... " 1884
Louis K. Church........... " 1889
Arthur C. Mellette .... " .... "

GOVERNORS—STATE.

Arthur C. Mellette...........elected 1889
Charles H. Sheldon.......... " 1893–97

U. S. SENATORS FROM THE STATE OF SOUTH DAKOTA.

Name.	No. of Congress.	Date.	Remarks.
Gideon C. Moody......	51st to 52d	1889 to 1891	
Richard F. Pettigrew..	51st " —	1889 " ——	Term expires, 1901
James H. Kyle........	52d " —	1891 " ——	Term expires, 1897

South Mountain, Maryland, Battles of, fought 14 Sept. 1862, 3 days before the battle of Antietam. South mountain is a prolongation of a range of the Blue Ridge north of the Potomac from Harper's Ferry. Turner's gap affords a passage from Frederick City to Williamsport; Crampton's gap, 6 miles south, gives a similar opening towards Harper's Ferry. Lee, after crossing the Potomac, divided his forces, sending "Stonewall" Jackson to capture Harper's Ferry. To relieve Harper's Ferry, McClellan ordered gen. Franklin through Crampton's gap. The remainder of the army was to move by Turner's gap upon Lee's main column. The Confederate gen. D. H. Hill succeeded in reaching Turner's gap, as did M'Laws Crampton's gap, before the federals. The battles of the 14th were fought to wrest these positions from the confederates. As gen. Lee's object in occupying and holding these gaps was to delay the Federal advance until the surrender of Harper's Ferry and the concentration of his forces, they were held tenaciously. D. H. Hill, reinforced by Longstreet's corps and other troops until the confederates numbered at least 25,000, succeeded in holding Turner's gap until night, when he retired. Gen. Franklin forced Crampton's gap late in the afternoon, but not soon enough to relieve Harper's Ferry. Lee succeeded in capturing Harper's Ferry, and in uniting his forces for the battle of Antietam. MARYLAND CAMPAIGN.

southern continent. The southern ocean was first traversed by Magellan in 1520, and explored by Wallis and Carteret in 1766, and by Cook in 1773 and 1774. Of the southern continent little is known but that it is icebound and contains active volcanoes. It was discovered by capt. John Biscoe, on 27 Feb. 1831, in lat. 65° 57′ S., lon. 47° 20′ E., extending east and west 200 miles—this he named Enderby land, after the gentleman who had equipped the voyage. Capt. Biscoe also discovered Graham's land on 15 Feb. 1832, situated in lat. 67° 1′ S., lon. 71° 48′ W. The messrs. Enderby equipped 3 other expeditions in search of the southern continent, the last (in connection with others) in 1838, when capt. Balleny had command, who, on 9 Feb. 1839, discovered the Balleny islands, lat. 67° S., lon. 165° E., and in Mch. 1839, Sabrina land, lat. 65° 10′ S., lon. 118° 30′ E. In 1838 the United States fitted out an expedition under lieut. Charles Wilkes, which returned in 1842. UNITED STATES, 1838, '42. A French expedition was despatched under adm. d'Urville in 1840. An English expedition, in 1839, under the command of capt. sir James Clark Ross, discovered Victoria Land in 1841 and subsequently penetrated as far south as 78° 11′. (A history of the later Antarctic expeditions will be found under NORTHEAST AND NORTHWEST PASSAGES.)

Mr. C. E. Borchgrevink, a Norwegian explorer, in the *Southern Cross* (capt. B. Jensen), reached Cape Adair, 17 Feb. 1899, ascended this to 3670 ft., 12 Mch.; magnetic position of the S. pole fixed at about lat. 73° 20′ S. and 146° E.; farthest point south 78° 50′, 17 Mch. 1900; returned to Stewart island, 4 Apr. 1900.

British Expedition Fund—the *Discovery*, capt. Scott, left Port Chalmers 24 Dec. 1901. The *Morning*, relief ship, left London 2 Aug. 1902, found letters from capt. Scott at cape Crozier, 18 Jan. 1903. By sledging capt. Scott reached 80° 17′ S., lat. 163° W., in 1902.

German expedition—the *Gauss*, capt. Ruser, left Hamburg 11 Aug. 1901, reached Kerguelen island 2 Jan. 1902; a magnetic station founded there. Found bottom at 3950 fathoms, 18° 15′ W., 0° 11′ S.

South-sea bubble commenced with the establishment of the South-sea company in London in 1710, for the purpose of carrying on a monopoly of trade with the Spanish coasts of South America, which was at first unwisely and afterwards dishonestly managed It failed in 1720, ruining thousands of families, and the directors' estates, to the value of 2,014,000*l*, were seized in 1721 and sold Mr Knight, the cashier, absconded with 100,000*l*, but he compounded the fraud for 10 000*l*., and returned to England in 1743 Almost all the wealthy persons in the kingdom had become speculators in the legion of projects for money-making, the artifices of the directors having raised the shares, originally 100*l*, to the price of 1000*l* A parliamentary inquiry took place in Nov 1720, and Aislabie, chancellor of the exchequer, and several members of Parliament were expelled the house in 1721. LAW'S BUBBLE

southwark bridge, one of the London bridges over the Thames, was designed by John Rennie, and built by a company, 1815-19, at an expense of $4,000,000 It consists of 3 great cast-iron arches, resting on massive stone piers and abutments, the distance between the abutments is 708 feet, the centre arch is 240 feet span, the 2 others 210 feet each, and the total weight of iron 5308 tons The bridge was freed from toll on 8 Nov 1864, the company receiving a compensation from the city An act for the payment of dividends to share-holders was passed in 1872

southwestern territory. NORTH CAROLINA, 1784-90, SOUTH CAROLINA, 1787, TENNESSEE, 1790

sovereign, an ancient and modern British gold coin In 1489 22½ pieces, in value 20*s* each, "to be called the sovereign" were ordered to be coined out of a pound of gold.—*Ruding* In 1542 sovereigns were coined in value 20*s*, which afterwards, in 1550 and 1552 (4 and 6 Edw VI), passed for 24*s* and 30*s* "Sovereigns" of the new coinage were directed to pass for 20*s*, 1 July, and half-sovereigns for 10*s*, 10 Oct 1817. COIN, GOLD By the Coinage act, 1870, the weight of the sovereign is fixed at 123 27447 grains troy, specific gravity, 17 57 (916 67, gold being 1000), half-sovereigns, 61 63723 grains The *dragon* sovereigns were reissued in 1871

Spain (the ancient *Iberia* and *Hispania*), a kingdom in southern Europe The first settlers are supposed to have been the progeny of Tubal, 5th son of Japhet. The Phœnicians and Carthaginians (360 B C) successively planted colonies on the coasts, and the Romans conquered the whole country, 206 B C The present constitution, drawn up by the government and laid before a Cortes, elected for its ratification, 27 Mch 1876, was proclaimed 30 June, 1876 Under this Spain was made a constitutional monarchy, the executive resting in the king, and the power to make laws "in the Cortes with the king" The Cortes is composed of a senate and congress equal in authority The senators are in 3 classes (1) senators by their own right, (2) 100 life-senators nominated by the crown, these 2 classes not to exceed 180, (3) 180 senators elected by the corporations of the state, half of these are elected every 5 years, and all of them whenever the monarch dissolves this part of the Cortes The congress is formed by deputies one to every 50,000 of the population By the law of 26 June, 1890, all male Spaniards, 25 years old, who enjoy full civil rights and have been citizens of a municipality for at least 2 years, are voters. The island of Cuba, from 8 Aug 1878, sends deputies to the Cortes, one to every 40,000 free inhabitants, paying in taxes 125 pesetas annually. Area of continental Spain, 191,100 sq miles Pop. 1789, 10,061,480, estimated, 1820, 11,000,000, 1846, 12,168 774, 1860, 15 658,531, 1887, 17,550,246, 1900 (latest census), 18,618,086 There are about 440,000 Basques in the north, some 60,000 Morescoes in the south, and 50,000 gypsies Madrid, the capital and largest city, had a population of 539,835 in 1900 Revenue, 1904, 1,000,066,839 pesetas.

	B C
Carthaginians, enriched by the mines of Spain (480 B C et seq), form settlements	360
New Carthage (Carthagena) founded by Hasdrubal	242
Hamilcar extends their dominions in Spain	238-233
At his death, Hannibal, his son, takes the command, 221, prepares for war, 220, takes Saguntum, 219, crosses the Alps, and enters Italy	218
Romans carry the war into Spain, 2 Scipios defeated and slain by Hasdrubal	212
Pub Cornelius Scipio Africanus takes New Carthage, 210 drives the Carthaginians out of Spain, 207, and annexes it. . . .	205
Celtiberian and Numantine war . . .	153-133
Viriathus, general of the Celtiberians and Lusitanians, subdues all west Spain, 145, makes peace with the consul Fabius Servilianus 142, assassinated by order of the Romans	140
Insurrection of Sertorius, 78, subdued by Pompey, and assassinated	72
Julius Cæsar quells an insurrection in Spain	67
Pompey governs Spain	60-50
Revolt through the rapacity of Crassus	48-47
Era of Spain, conquest by Augustus begun . . . 1 Jan	38
	A D
Vandals, Alani and Suevi wrest Spain from the Romans	409
Adolphus founds the kingdom of the Visigoths.	414
Vandals pass over to Africa	427
Theodoric I vanquishes the Suevi	452
Assassinated by his brother Euric who becomes master of all Spain	466
Recared I expels the Franks	587
He abjures Arianism, and rules ably till	601
Wamba's wise administration, he prepares a fleet for defence against the Saracens.	672-77
Saracens invited into Spain against king Roderic by count Julien,	709
Gabel al Tarik lands at Calpe . . . 30 Apr	711
Roderic's defeat and death at Xeres	"
Establishment of the Saracens at Cordova	"
Victorious progress of Musa and Tarik	712-13
Emirs rule at Cordova, Pelayo of Gothic blood, rules in Asturias and Leon	718
Saracens defeated at Tours by Charles Martel	732 or 733
Abderahman the first king at Cordova	755
Invasion of Charlemagne	777-78
Sancho Iñigo, count of Navarre, etc	873
Sancho of Navarre becomes king of Castile	1026
Kingdom of Aragon commenced under Ramirez I	1035
Leon and Asturias united to Castile	1037
Portugal taken from the Saracens by Henry of Besançon (PORTUGAL)	1095
Saracens, beset on all sides by Christians, call in Moors from Africa, who seize their dominions, and subdue the Saracens,	1091 et seq
Exploits of the Cid Rodrigo, d	about 1099
Dynasty of the Almoravides at Cordova	1094-1144
Moors defeated in several battles by Alfonso of Leon	1144
Dynasty of the Almohades at Cordova	1144-1225
Cordova, Toledo, Seville, etc., taken by Ferdinand of Castile and Leon	1233-48
Kingdom of Granada begun by the Moors, last refuge from the power of the Christians	1238
Crown of Navarre passes to king of France	1274
Two hundred thousand Moors arrive to assist the king of Granada	1327
They are defeated at Tarifa by Alfonso XI of Castile with great slaughter	1340
Reign of Pedro the Cruel	1350
His alliance with Edward the Black Prince	1363
Defeated at Montiel and treacherously slain .	1369
Ferdinand II of Aragon marries Isabella of Castile, 18 Oct 1469, and nearly the whole Christian dominions of Spain are united in one monarchy	1479
Establishment of the Inquisition	1480-84
Persecution of the Jews	1492-98
Granada taken after a 2 years' siege, and the power of the Moors is finally extirpated by Ferdinand	1492
Jews expelled	"
Contract with Columbus to explore the western ocean, 17 Apr	"
Columbus sails on his first voyage from Palos (AMERICA), 3 Aug	"
Mahometans persecuted and expelled	1499-1502
Death of queen Isabella . . . 26 Nov	1504
Death of Columbus . . . 20 May,	1506
Ferdinand conquers great part of Navarre	1512
Accession of the house of Austria to the throne of Spain, Charles V of Germany I of Spain	1516
Able administration of Ximenes, ungratefully used, 1516, his death	1517
Charles elected emperor of Germany .	1519
Insurrection in Castile	1520-21
Philip of Spain marries Mary of England . 25 July,	1554
Charles abdicates and retires from the world	1556
War with France, victory at St. Quentin . 10 Aug	1557
Charles dies, aged 58 years . 21 Sept.	1558
Philip II commences his bloody persecution of the Protestants,	1561
Escurial begun . .	1563
Revolt of the Moriscoes, 1567, suppressed	1570
Naval victory of Lepanto over the Turks . 7 Oct.	1571
Revolt of William prince of Orange (HOLLAND) . .	1572
Portugal united to Spain by conquest . .	1580
The Netherlands declare their independence.	"
Spanish Armada destroyed (ARMADA) .	1588
Philip III banishes the Moors (900 000).	1598-1610
Ministry of the duke of Lerma	1598-1618
Ministry of Olivarez .	1621-43
Philip IV loses Portugal	1640
Death of Charles II, last of the house of Austria, accession of Philip V of the house of Bourbon . .	1700
War of the Succession . .	1702-13
Gibraltar taken by the English	1704
Siege of Barcelona.	1713
Cardinal Alberoni re-establishes the authority of the king reforms many abuses, and raises Spain to the rank of a first power, 1715-20, ordered to quit Spain . . .	1720
Charles, son of Philip V, conquers Naples	1735

SPA

Charles III, king of the Two Sicilies, succeeds to the crown of Spain 1759

War with England 1762-63 and 1796

Battle of Cape St Vincent 14 Feb 1797

Spanish treasure ships, valued at $3 000,000 seized by the English Oct 1804

Battle of TRAFALGAR 21 Oct. 1805

Sway of Godoy, Prince of Peace 1806

French enter Spain, a Spanish army sent to the Baltic 1807

Prince of Asturias conspires against his father 25 July "

Treaty of Fontainebleau 27 Oct "

French take Madrid Mch 1808

Prince of Peace dismissed 18 Mch "

Abdication of Charles IV in favor of Ferdinand, 19 Mch, and at Bayonne on Ferdinand s refusal in favor of his "friend and ally," Napoleon 1 May, "

Revolution, French massacred at Madrid 2 May,

Province of Asturias rises *en masse* 3 May, "

Napoleon assembles the notables at Bayonne 25 May, "

Joseph Bonaparte enters Madrid as king of Spain, 12 July, retires 29 July, "

Battle of Vimiera, French defeated 21 Aug "

Supreme Junta installed Sept "

Madrid taken by the French, and Joseph restored 2 Dec "

Napoleon enters Madrid 4 Dec "

Royal family of Spain imprisoned in the palace of Chambery, in Savoy 5 Dec "

French defeated at Corunna, 16 Jan, take Ferrol, 27 Jan, Saragossa, 21 Feb, Oporto, 29 Feb, Cordova and Seville, Nov, Gerona 12 Dec 1809

Ney takes Ciudad Rodrigo 10 July, 1810

Spanish Cortes meets 24 Sept "

Wellington defeats Massena at Fuentes de Onoro 5 May, 1811

Soult defeated at Albuera 16 May, "

Constitution of the Cortes (democratic) 8 May, 1812

Wellington takes Ciudad Rodrigo 19 Jan, storms Badajos, 6 Apr, defeats Marmont at Salamanca 22 July, "

He occupies Madrid, and defeats the French at Vittoria, 21 June, defeats Soult in the Pyrenees, 28 July, takes St. Sebastian 31 Aug, and enters France 8 Oct. 1813

Ferdinand VII restored (constitution set aside) 14 May, 1814

Slave trade abolished for a compensation 1817

Insurrection at Valencia repressed 1819

Spanish revolution begun by Riego Jan. 1820

Ferdinand swears to the constitution of the Cortes 8 Mch "

French enter Spain 7 Apr, and invest Cadiz 25 June 1823

Battle of the Trocadero 31 Aug "

French evacuate Cadiz 21 Sept 1828

Salique law abolished, 29 Mch, Carlist and Christina parties formed 1830

Don Carlos declares himself legitimate successor to the king, 29 Apr 1833

Death of Ferdinand VII, his queen assumes power until Isabella II, her infant daughter attains majority 29 Sept. "

Constitution termed "Estatuto Real" granted by advice of Martinez de la Rosa "

Queen Christina marries Ferdinand Muños (afterwards duke of Rianzarés) 28 Dec. "

Quadruple treaty establishes the right of Isabella to the throne, 22 Apr 1834

Don Carlos appears in Spain 10 July, "

Peers vote his exclusion 30 Aug "

Mendizabal prime minister, Mina and Espartero command the royalists, the rebel leader, Zumalacarregui, killed near Bilbao June, 1835

Sir De Lacy Evans and others raise a British legion for the queen of Spain "

They defeat the Carlists at St Sebastian 1 Oct 1836

Espartero gains the battle of Bilbao 25 Dec "

Gen Evans takes Irun 17 May, 1837

Constituent Cortes proclaimed "

Dissolution of the monasteries "

Carlists under Maroto desert don Carlos and make peace with Espartero, at Vergara 31 Aug 1839

Don Carlos seeks refuge in France 13 Sept. "

Surrender of Morello 28 May, 1840

Queen regent appoints a ministry, nominated by Espartero, 5 Oct, she abdicates and leaves Spain, visits France and Sicily, returns to France 12 Oct. "

Espartero, duke of Vittoria, expels the papal nuncio 29 Dec "

Spanish Cortes declares Espartero regent during the queen's minority 12 Apr 1841

Queen Christina s protest 19 July, "

Insurrection in favor of Christina commenced at Pampeluna by gen O'Donnell and Concha 2 Oct "

Don Diego Leon attacks the palace at Madrid, his followers repulsed, and numbers slain by the queen s guards, 7 Oct., he is shot at Madrid 15 Oct "

Zurbano captures Bilbao 21 Oct. "

Rodil constitutional general, enters Vittoria " "

Montes de Oca shot " "

Gen. O'Donnell takes refuge in French territory " "

Espartero suspends queen Christina's pension 26 Oct. "

Fueros of the Basque provinces abolished 29 Oct "

Borio and Gobernado, implicated in the Christina plot put to death at Madrid 9 Nov "

Espartero enters Madrid 23 Nov "

General pardon of persons not yet tried concerned in the events of October 13 Dec. "

Effective army fixed at 130,000 men 28 June, 1842

Insurrection at Barcelona, national guard joins the populace, 13 Nov, street battle between national guard and troops, the latter lose 500 killed and wounded and retreat to the citadel 15 Nov 1842

Barcelona blockaded, 26 Nov, Espartero arrives before it, 29 Nov, its bombardment and surrender 3, 4 Dec "

Disturbances at Malaga 25 May, 1843

Revolutionary junta re established at Barcelona 11 June, "

[Corunna, Seville, Burgos Santiago and other towns "pronounce" against the regent Espartero]

Arrival of gen Narvaez at Madrid, which surrenders 15 July, "

Espartero bombards Seville 21 July "

Siege is raised 27 July, "

[Revolution is successful and Espartero flees to Cadiz and embarks on British ship *Malabar*]

New government deprives Espartero of his titles and rank, 16 Aug, he arrives in London 23 Aug "

Reaction suppressed at Madrid Aug "

Isabella II, 13 years old is declared by the Cortes of age, Narvaez (friend of the queen mother), lieutenant general, 8 Nov "

Queen mother returns to Spain 23 Mch 1844

Zurbano s insurrection 12 Nov 1844, he is shot 21 Jan 1845

Don Carlos relinquishes his right to the crown in favor of his son 18 May, "

Reactionary constitution "

Narvaez and his ministry resign, 12 Feb, return to power 17 Mch, again resign 28 Mch 1846

Escape of don Carlos from France 14 Sept "

Queen married to her cousin Francisco d Assisi duke of Cadiz, and the infanta Louisa to the duc de Montpensier 10 Oct "

[The Spanish marriages disturb the friendly relations of the French and English governments]

Espartero restored 3 Sept 1847

Sir Henry Lytton Bulwer, British envoy, ordered to quit Spain in 48 hours 17 May 1848

Diplomatic relations with England restored 18 Apr 1850

American expedition under Lopez against CUBA (UNITED STATES) 1850 1851

Madrid Araujuez railway opened 9 Feb "

Law respecting the public debt (Spain since excluded from European money markets) 1 Aug "

Death of Godoy prince of peace 4 Oct. "

Queen pardons the prisoners taken in the attempt upon Cuba, 11 Dec "

Movement headed by Espartero, Barcelona and Madrid pronounce against the government, barricades in Madrid, 1–17 July, 1854

Triumph of the insurrection, resignation of the ministry, the queen sends for Espartero 19 July, "

Espartero forms an administration 31 July, "

Queen mother impeached she quits Spain 28 Aug "

New constitution of the Cortes 13 Jan 1855

Cortes votes that power proceeds from the people, it permits liberty of belief, but not of worship Feb "

Don Carlos d 10 Mch "

Birth of the prince royal 28 Nov 1857

Joint French and Spanish expedition against Cochin China announced 1 Dec 1858

War with MOROCCO Nov -Dec 1859

O Donnell commands the army in Africa, indecisive conflicts reported battle at Castillejos; a Spanish "Balaklava" charge 1 Jan 1860

Moors defeated near Tetuan, which surrenders 4 Feb "

An ineffectual truce 16-23 Feb. "

Moors defeated at Guad el ras 23 Mch "

Treaty of peace signed, 400 000 000 reals to be paid by Moors, and Tetuan to be held till paid 26 Mch "

Gen Ortega governor of the Balearic isles lands near Tortosa, in Valencia with 3000 men and proclaims the comte de Montemolin king as Charles VI his troops resist and he is compelled to flee, with the comte and others, 3 Apr, Ortega shot 19 Apr "

Comte de Montemolin and his brother Ferdinand arrested at Tortosa, 21 Apr, renounce their claim to the throne, 23 Apr "

Napoleon III 's proposal to admit Spain as a first class power is opposed by England and given up Aug "

Annexation of St Domingo to Spain ratified, slavery not to be re established 19 May, 1861

Intervention in MEXICO 8 Dec "

José Albama and Manuel Matamoras Protestant propagandists, sentenced to 10 years' imprisonment 14 Oct. 1862

Don Juan de Bourbon renounces the throne 8 Jan 1863

Insurrection in St. Domingo, war ensues (DOMINGO) 1 Sept "

Rupture with PERU Apr 1864

Gen Prim exiled for conspiracy 13 Aug "

Peace with Peru, which has to pay a heavy indemnity, 27 Jan 1865

Queen orders sale of crown lands, giving three fourths to the nation 20 Feb "

Decree relinquishing St Domingo 5 May, "

Suppression of a conspiracy at Valencia to reunite Spain and Portugal 10 June, "

Kingdom of Italy recognized by Spain 26 June "

Dispute with Chili, M Tavira's settlement (20 May) disavowed by the government 25 July, "

Adm Pareja, at Valparaiso, insults the Chilian government, 18 Sept, which declares war, 25 Sept, Pareja declares a blockade Oct "

Chilian capt Williams captures the Spanish vessel *Covadonga* (Pareja commits suicide) 26 Nov "

Queen Victoria, British sloop, seized by a guardacosta, 15 Jan 1866

Adm Mendez bombards Valparaiso, destroying property, 31 Mch, repulsed at Callao with loss 2 May, "

Queen declares Pacific campaign ended 15 June 1866

British screw steamer *Tornado*, com E Collier, seized by Spaniards (charged with aiding Chili), and carried to Cadiz, 21, 22 Aug "

Public instruction placed under the clergy Oct "

Reform of the municipal institutions decreed on account of revolutionary proceedings Oct "

Crew of *Tornado* detained as prisoners, 31 Oct, the case referred to law Nov "

Queen dismisses the Cortes (and imprisons many eminent deputies for petitioning against it) 30 Dec "

Decision in *Tornado* case—the ship a prize and the crew prisoners of war, 18 Dec. 1866, lord Stanley protests against the proceedings 8 Feb 1867

Decree making secret publication of journals and pamphlets penal 16 Feb "

Tornado prisoners released Feb "

Sloop *Queen Victoria* declared by Spain wrongfully seized, reparation to be made 21 Apr "

Law abolishing normal schools and subjecting education to the priests 2 June, 1868

Insurrection begins in the fleet, 18 Sept, joined by the garrison and city of Cadiz, 19 Sept, by nearly all Spain, 19–30 Sept "

Prim arrives at Cadiz, 17 Sept., announces a provisional government. 19 Sept. "

Ministers resign, 19 20 Sept, José Concha becomes president of the council, 22 Sept, Bravo Murillo and his colleagues flee to Bayonne 23 Sept. "

[Royalist leaders José Concha, marques de Havaña, Manuel Concha, marques de Duero, at Madrid, the marques de Pezuela at Barcelona, Eusebio de Calonge in the north, Pavia y Lacy, marques de Novaliches in Andalusia.]

Novaliches the royalist general, defeated at Alcolea, by Serrano, 27 Sept, surrenders 28 Sept "

Queen flies to Bayonne and Pau, and protests 29, 30 Sept "

Deposition of the queen declared at Madrid 29 Sept. "

National guard organized 30 Sept. "

Don Juan, son of don Carlos, renounces his hereditary rights in favor of his son, Carlos 3 Oct "

Serrano enters Madrid, 3 Oct., Serrano, Prim, and Olozaga constitute a provisional government 5 Oct "

Education law of 2 June annulled, Jesuits and other religious orders suppressed, laws expelling Jews abrogated, freedom of worship decreed about 12, 13 Oct. "

Local juntas dissolved by manifesto of the provisional government 20 Oct. "

Provisional government recognized by the U S, 13 Oct., by England France, and Prussia, 25 Oct., by Austria, Sweden, and Belgium about 31 Oct "

Manifesto of the government for universal suffrage, and free press and education . 26 Oct "

Prim created marshal . about 6 Nov "

Queen arrives at Paris 6 Nov "

Joint electoral committee at Madrid declare in favor of a limited monarchy 14 Nov "

Peaceful elections for constituent Cortes. 19, 20 Dec "

Election of members for the Cortes 17 Jan 1869

Spanish envoy at Rome not received 23 Jan "

Cortes meets, 11 Feb, Rivero elected president 13 Feb "

Provisional government resigns, Serrano reappointed head of the government with same ministry 25, 26 Feb "

Spanish Protestant religious service at Madrid 28 Mch "

Cortes votes for a monarchy (214 to 71) 21 May, "

New constitution promulgated 6 June, "

Marshal Serrano elected regent by the Cortes, 15 June, sworn. 18 June, "

New ministry under Prim about 18 June, "

U S overtures respecting Cuba indignantly rejected, about 18 Sept "

Candidature of the duke of Genoa discussed Sept -Oct. "

Republican speech of Castelar in the Cortes. about 18 Dec "

Resignation of Prim and ministry on the Italian government opposing the nomination of the duke of Genoa as king of Spain 4 Jan 1870

Prim resumes office with Topete and Rivero 10 Jan "

Majority in the assembly for Prim against the combined unionists and liberals 3 Apr "

Duc de Montpensier, after great provocation, kills don Enrique de Bourbon, brother of the ex king, in a duel, 12 Mch, tried, condemned, and fined 12 Apr "

Crown declined by Espartero May, "

Bill for gradual abolition of slavery in the colonies presented to the Cortes 28 May, "

Rojo Arias carries a resolution requiring an absolute majority in the Cortes for any proposed sovereign (179 out of 356), this excludes all present candidates June, "

Isabella II abdicates in favor of her son, Alfonso 25 June, "

Prince Leopold of Hohenzollern-Sigmaringen nominated king, accepted by the regent and ministry, 6 July, this justified by the government in a circular, 7 July, on opposition of France he resigns 12 July, "

Neutrality in Franco Prussian war announced 27 July, "

Renewed agitation for a republic about 9 Aug "

Amnesty for political offences since 29 Sept. 1868, published, 10 Aug "

French republic warmly recognized Sept "

Amadeus, duke of Aosta (b 30 May, 1845) accepts the candidature for the crown 20 Oct. "

Elected by the Cortes by 191 votes (63 for a republic, 27 for the duc de Montpensier) 16 Nov "

SPA

Proclaimed king 17 Nov 1870

Ex queen, on behalf of her son Alfonso, protests against the election 21 Nov "

Duke accepts the crown from a deputation of the Cortes at Florence, and says that his honesty should rise above the struggle of parties, and that he has no other object than the peace and prosperity of the nation 4 Dec "

Stormy session in the Cortes on arrangements for the new king, 19 Dec, Rivero, president, resigns 25 Dec "

Prim fired at and wounded in his carriage by 6 men, who escape, indignation at Madrid, 27 Dec, Topete rejoins the ministry, vote of confidence 28 Dec "

Prim dies in the evening (aged 56), the king received by Topete at Cartagena. 30 Dec "

Funeral of Prim 31 Dec "

King enters Madrid, and takes the oath 2 Jan 1871

New ministry under Serrano 5 Jan "

New Cortes opened, king's speech applauded 3 Apr "

Del Castillo and other Alfonsists recognize the king Apr "

Olozaga elected president of the Cortes. 4 Apr "

Tornado difficulty settled (Aug -Nov 1866), compensation to be paid by the Spanish government. May, "

King visits the provinces, warmly received, 1 Sept et seq, welcomed by Espartero at Logroño 30 Sept. "

Espartero, duke of Vittoria, made prince of Vergara Jan 1872

New Cortes opened, king says, "I will never impose myself on the Spanish people but neither will I allow myself to be accused of deserting the post which I occupy by their will," 24 Apr "

Navarre, etc, in state of siege 25 Apr "

Marshal Serrano enters Navarre, don Carlos calling himself Carlos VII crosses the frontier near Véra, and takes the command, Rada retiring, 2 May, totally defeated at Oroquieta 4 May, "

Letter of the duc de Montpensier advocating the rights of prince Alfonso, 17 Apr published June, "

Attempted assassination of king and queen by about 15 men, 1 assassin killed, 2 taken, after midnight of 18, 19 July, "

Don Carlos calls on Catalonia Aragon and Valencia to rise, promising their ancient liberties 16 July, "

King's popular visit to the provinces, travelling nearly 2000 miles. 26 July-24 Aug "

Cortes opened by the king with a fine speech 15 Sept "

Bill for abolition of slavery in Porto Rico, for compensation, brought into congress 24 Dec "

King Amadeus abdicates in a message, saying that he sees Spain in a continual struggle the era of peace more distant, he sought remedies within the law, and did not find them, his efforts were sterile, the 2 chambers combine as the sovereign Cortes of Spain, and vote for a republic (126–32), 11 Feb 1873

Reported success of Carlists, agitation for the duc de Montpensier among Orleanists in France 12 Feb "

Irruption of Carlists, they hold part of Catalonia, demonstrations in favor of a federal republic 22, 23 Feb "

Circular to European powers from Castelar, foreign minister, 27 Feb "

Permanent committee of the Cortes appointed 22 Mch "

Slavery in Porto Rico abolished 23 Mch "

Carlists beaten in several encounters, don Alfonso de Bourbon re enters France 23 Apr "

Old "monarchical volunteers" occupy the bull ring at Madrid, are disarmed and dispersed by government troops, the "permanent committee" dissolved by the government, which assumes supreme power 26 Apr "

Elections for the Cortes commence, monarchists abstain from voting 10 May, "

Mr Bradlaugh, the English republican, entertained at Madrid, 24 May, "

Intransigentes, or Irreconcilables (extreme republicans) very powerful . June, "

New Cortes opened, a speech by Figueras 1 June, "

Carlists besiege Irun . 7 June, "

Federal republic voted by the Cortes (210–2), and proclaimed, 8 June, Pi y Margall, president of a new ministry, rejected, Figueras and his ministry resume office 9 June, "

Ministerial crisis renewed, 10 June, Pi y Margall becomes minister, Figueras quits Spain . 11 June, "

Carlists defeat Castañon near Murieta 26 June, "

Intransigentes withdraw from the Cortes 1 July, "

Defeat and death of Calvinety by Carlists, insurrection at Alcoy, promoted by Internationalists, mayor and others killed, announced. 11 July, "

Don Carlos (as Carlos VII) enters Spain, "to save the country," 13 July, "

Desperate fighting at Igualada, Catalonia 17, 18 July, "

[Four prevailing parties (1) Government, highly democratic, (2) Intransigentes or Irreconcilables, extremely democratic, (3) International or Communists, (4) Legitimists, Carlists.]

Murcia and Valencia proclaim themselves federal cantons, 18 July, "

Pi y Margall compelled to resign, Salmeron forms a ministry opposed to the Intransigentes 18 July, "

Igualada taken by Carlists under don Alfonso. 19 July, "

Don Carlos enters Biscay 31 July, "

Carlists hold chief of N Spain Aug

Insurgents repulsed in attack on Almeria, beaten in fights at Seville, 28–30 July, gen Pavia warmly received 31 July

Troops attack Valencia, 26 July, it surrenders. . 8 A

New constitution printed, 27 July, discussed 1720

[118 articles, includes separation of church and stat . 1735 religious worship, nobility abolished, 15 states in and near peninsula, 2 in the Antilles, Cortes (senate and congress) to have legislative power, one deputy to 50,000 inhabitants, Cortes to be renewed in 2 years, members to be paid, executive, president and ministry, president elected for 4 years.]

Bombardment of Malaga stopped by the British and German admirals 1 Aug 1873

Cadiz surrenders to gen. Pavia 4 Aug "

Reported total defeat of the insurgents at Chinchilla, while marching on Madrid 10 Aug "

Cartagena held by Intransigentes, besieged 22 Aug "

Deerhound, English yacht, conveying stores to Carlists, seized by the Spaniards 11½ miles off Biarritz, crew imprisoned and captain sent to Ferrol 13 Aug "

Carlists defeat republicans at Arrichulegui, near Renteria, 21 Aug "

They take Estella after a conflict at Dicastillo 25 Aug "

Castelar elected president of the Cortes 26 Aug "

Capt. Werner of German ship *Friedrich Carl*, captures *Almanza* and *Vittoria* Spanish iron clads, held by rebels, gives them up to adm. Yelverton, who prepares for action against Intransigentes claiming them, and sends them to Gibraltar unmolested 1 Sept "

Ministry propose abolition of capital punishment in the army, defeated in the Cortes, resign 5 Sept. "

Castelar heads a ministry, proposes calling out 150,000 men, to end the war 7, 8 Sept "

Salmeron elected president of the Cortes 9 Sept "

Castelar virtual dictator 15 Sept "

Deerhound and crew given up, announced about 18 Sept "

Speech of Castelar, Cortes to be closed 2 Jan. 1874 18 Sept "

Combination of parties to support Castelar about 6 Oct. "

Indecisive battle at Maneru, near Puenta de la Reyna, in Navarre, between republicans under Moriones, and Carlists under Ollo, advantage with Carlists 6 Oct. "

Battle of Escombrera bay, Intransigentes' ships attempt to break blockade of Cartagena, repulsed by adm. Lobo, 11 Oct "

Lobo declines to fight, and retires, pursued by the Intransigentes 13 Oct., justifies himself at Madrid 22 Oct. "

Death of Rios Rosas, statesman 3 Nov "

Murillo captured, condemned to be sold by the British Court of Admiralty Nov "

Pronunciamento. Meeting of the Cortes, speech of Castelar, vote of confidence lost by 20, he resigns, Salmeron attempts to form a ministry, 2-3 Jan., Pavia, capt. gen. of Madrid, forcibly dissolves the Cortes 3 Jan 1874

Marshal Serrano president of a new ministry, including Topete, national guard of Madrid disarming 4 Jan "

New government issue a moderate manifesto 9, 10 Jan "

Cartagena captured by Lopez Dominguez 12 Jan "

Numancia, iron clad, with Intransigentes leaders and convicts, escapes, they land at Mers el Kebir, near Oran, on the African coast, are returned by the French 12 Jan "

Blockade of the coast of Spain announced 31 Jan "

Carlists besiege Bilbao, Moriones defeated at Somorrostro, 25 Feb "

Marshal Serrano resigns presidency of the ministry, and becomes chief of the executive, succeeded by Zabala, Serrano proceeds to Bilbao 28 Feb. et seq "

Serrano assumes command about 8 Mch "

Blockade of the coast (31 Jan.) raised 2 Mch "

Three days' conflict at Somorrostro, near Bilbao, Carlists defeated but retain their positions (about 2000 killed and wounded on both sides) 25-27 Mch "

Armistice for 3 days 28 Mch "

Gen. Manuel da Concha joins Serrano at Santander, about 8 Apr "

Great national effort to relieve Bilbao, union of parties, hostilities resumed 20 Apr "

After several days' conflict, Carlists retreat, marshal Concha enters Bilbao, which is much injured by long bombardment, 2 May, "

A battle at Prats de Llusanés indecisive 6 May, "

Carlists repulsed in attack at Ramales about 20 May, "

Carlists defeated at Gondesa about 6 June, "

Republicans repulsed before Estella. 25-27 June, "

Concha killed (succeeded by Zabala) 27 June, "

Carlists hold Navarre, Guipuscoa, Biscay, and Alara July, "

Carlists capture Cuenca (about 80 miles from Madrid) 13 July, "

Don Carlos's manifesto, promising constitutional government, 16 July, "

All Spain placed under martial law, levy of 125,000 men, about 18 July, "

Government appeals to France respecting French assistance to Carlists, justificatory reply 3 Aug "

British Mediterranean squadron, under adm. Drummond, sails from Malta for Barcelona 4 Aug "

Don Carlos appeals to the chief powers not to intervene, justifies Dorregaray's severities, and the execution of Schmidt, 6 Aug "

Moriones's alleged defeat of Mendiri and Carlists at Oteiza, 12 Aug "

Serrano's government recognized by Great Britain, Germany, France, and other powers (not by Russia) about 14 Aug "

Letter of sympathy and encouragement from the Comte de Chambord to don Carlos Aug "

[illegible]cerda vigorously besieged by Carlists Aug.-Sept "

[illegible]ts fire on German gun boats *Nautilus* and *Albatross*, near [illegible] Sebastian, Germans fire shells into the town, about 5 Sept "

[illegible]feated by Lopez Pinto near Mora, about 9 Sept., by [illegible] Barasoam near Tafalla about 25 Sept. "

SPA

Note to French government, complaining of neglect respecting the Carlists on the frontiers early in Oct 1874

Prince Alfonso in a manifesto replies to address, declaring himself "a true Spaniard, Catholic, and liberal" 1 Dec "

Army at Murviedro pronounces for Alfonso, he is proclaimed king by gen. Martinez Campos, 29 Dec., recognized by the other armies and the navy, 30 Dec., proclaimed by gen. Primo da Rivera at Madrid, Antonio Canovas del Castillo, head of a royal ministry 31 Dec "

Pres. Serrano withdraws to France 1 Jan 1875

Proclamation of Carlos against Alfonso 6 Jan "

Alfonso XII recognized throughout Spain, well received at Barcelona, 9 Jan., enters Madrid 14 Jan "

Order of knighthood re-established, payments to clergy to be renewed Jan "

Alfonso reviews 30,000 troops near Tafalla, 22 Jan., issues proclamation to northern provinces promising amnesty and respect to local rights 22 Jan "

Serrano returns to Madrid Feb "

Carlists retreat from Pampeluna, entered by the king, 6 Feb., he exchanges decorations with Espartero at Logrono 9 Feb "

Resignation of gens. Moriones, Loma, and Blanco, Concha sent for from Cuba Feb "

Serrano received by the king 8 Mch "

Cabrera, an old Carlist general (see 1840), publishes an address, declaring for Alfonso XII 11 Mch "

Papal nuncio received by the king 3 May, "

Vigorous action of government troops, Carlists expelled from Castile, sympathizers suppressed July, "

Carlists defeated at Quesada and others 31 July, "

Citadel at Urgel surrendered by Carlists to Campos 26 Aug "

Resignation of "conciliation ministry," 11 Sept., liberal cabinet headed by gen. Jovellar 12 Sept "

Circular of papal nuncio against toleration about 13 Sept "

Don Carlos declares his mission "to quell the revolution, and that it will die" Sept. "

Bombardment of San Sebastian, 28 Sept.-2 Oct., resumed, 11 Oct "

Government declare the civil war at an end, and purpose summoning the Cortes to assist the king in reorganizing the country early in Oct "

Don Carlos proposes to the king a truce, and offers help if war occurs with the U. S. (no answer) 9 Nov "

New constitutional party under Sagasta formed Nov "

Cortes elected, 364 ministerialists out of 400 Jan 1876

Cortes opened by the king 15 Feb "

Carlists defeated at Estella, Vera, and Tolosa by Quesada and Moriones Feb "

King assumes command, Estella surrenders to Primo da Rivera, severe loss 18 Feb "

Reported letter from the pope recommending Carlos to retire from the contest 22 Feb "

Don Carlos, with gen. Lizarraga and 5 battalions, surrender to the governor of Bayonne at St. Jean Pied de Port, 27 Feb., he, with some officers, lands at Folkestone and proceeds to London 4 Mch "

Triumphal entry of Alfonso XII into Madrid 20 Mch "

Draft of new constitution submitted to the Cortes 28 Mch "

Pope opposes moderate religious toleration in article 11 of the constitution Apr "

Jews (expelled in 1492) petition for readmission " "

Long debate in Cortes, confidence in ministry voted (211 to 26), constitution passed, adjourn about 21 July, "

Queen Isabella received by king at Santander, declares "her share in public affairs is at an end" 31 July, "

Public worship of Protestants repressed by authority Sept "

Amnesty to Carlists and others surrendering Apr 1877

Meeting of the new Cortes 25 Apr "

Cortes suddenly closed 11 July, "

New tariff passed, customs duties raised in respect to Great Britain, France, and U. S. 17 July, "

Ex queen, after visiting her son, disapproves of proposed marriage, and associates with don Carlos in Paris who is privately forbidden to remain, and goes to England, she is forbidden to return to Spain, her pension stopped end of Dec "

King married to his cousin Mercedes, daughter of the duc de Montpensier 23 Jan 1878

End of the insurrection in Cuba announced 21 Feb "

Death of queen Mercedes, deeply lamented 26 June "

Death of queen dowager Christina 21 Aug "

King fired at (not injured) by Juan Oliva Moncasi, a member of the International society, aged 23 25 Oct "

Moncasi executed 4 Jan 1879

Espartero, duque de Vittoria, d. 8 Jan "

Cortes dissolved, 16 Mch., to meet 1 June, "

King married to archduchess Maria Christina of Austria, 29 Nov "

Attempted assassination of king and queen by Francisco Otero y Gonzalez by shooting 30 Dec "

Law gradually abolishing slavery in Cuba promulgated, 18 Feb 1880

Manifesto from 279 senators and deputies claiming liberty of religion, the press, etc., and education, universal suffrage, etc 6 Apr "

Otero executed 14 Apr "

Permission said to be given to about 60,000 Russian Jews to come to Spain June, 1881

Don Carlos expelled from France for expressing sympathy with legitimists (goes to London) 17 July, "

Consolidation of the national debt (60,000,000*l.*) proposed, Sept., law published 10 Dec. "

King invested with the order of the Garter ....7 Oct. "

SPA

Queen declares Pacific campaign ended 15 June 1866

British screw steamer *Tornado*, com F. Collier, seized by Spaniards (charged with aiding Chili), and carried to Cadiz, 21, 22 Aug "

Public instruction placed under the clergy Oct "

Reform of the municipal institutions decreed on account of revolutionary proceedings Oct "

Crew of *Tornado* detained as prisoners, 31 Oct, the case referred to law Nov "

Queen dismisses the Cortes (and imprisons many eminent deputies for petitioning against it) 30 Dec "

Decision in *Tornado* case—the ship a prize and the crew prisoners of war, 18 Dec 1866, lord Stanley protests against the proceedings 8 Feb 1867

Decree making secret publication of journals and pamphlets penal 16 Feb. "

Tornado prisoners released Feb "

Sloop *Queen Victoria* declared by Spain wrongfully seized, reparation to be made 21 Apr "

Law abolishing normal schools and subjecting education to the priests 2 June 1868

Insurrection begins in the fleet, 18 Sept, joined by the garrison and city of Cadiz, 19 Sept., by nearly all Spain, 19–30 Sept. "

Prim arrives at Cadiz, 17 Sept, announces a provisional government 19 Sept. "

Ministers resign, 19, 20 Sept, Jose Concha becomes president of the council 22 Sept, Bravo Murillo and his colleagues flee to Bayonne 24 Sept "

[Royalist leaders José Concha, marques de Havaña, Manuel Concha, marques de Duero, at Madrid, the marquis de Pezuela at Barcelona, Eusebio de Calonge in the north, Pavia y Lacy, marques de Novaliches in Andalusia.]

Novaliches the royalist general, defeated at Alcolea, by Serrano, 27 Sept, surrenders 28 Sept "

Queen flies to Bayonne and Pau and protests 29, 30 Sept "

Deposition of the queen declared at Madrid 29 Sept. "

National guard organized 30 Sept. "

Don Juan, son of don Carlos, renounces his hereditary rights in favor of his son, Carlos 3 Oct "

Serrano enters Madrid, 3 Oct, Serrano, Prim, and Olozaga constitute a provisional government 5 Oct "

Education law of 2 June annulled, Jesuits and other religious orders suppressed, laws expelling Jews abrogated, freedom of worship decreed about 12, 13 Oct. "

Local juntas dissolved by manifesto of the provisional government 20 Oct. "

Provisional government recognized by the U S, 13 Oct., by England France, and Prussia, 25 Oct., by Austria, Sweden, and Belgium about 31 Oct. "

Manifesto of the government for universal suffrage, and free press and education 26 Oct "

Prim created marshal about 6 Nov "

Queen arrives at Paris 6 Nov "

Joint electoral committee at Madrid declare in favor of a limited monarchy 14 Nov "

Peaceful elections for constituent Cortes. 19, 20 Dec "

Election of members for the Cortes 17 Jan 1869

Spanish envoy at Rome not received 23 Jan "

Cortes meets, 11 Feb, Rivero elected president 13 Feb "

Provisional government resigns, Serrano reappointed head of the government with same ministry 25, 26 Feb "

Spanish Protestant religious service at Madrid 28 Mch "

Cortes votes for a monarchy (214 to 71) 21 May, "

New constitution promulgated 6 June, "

Marshal Serrano elected regent by the Cortes, 15 June, sworn 18 June, "

New ministry under Prim about 18 June, "

U S overtures respecting Cuba indignantly rejected, about 18 Sept. "

Candidature of the duke of Genoa discussed Sept.-Oct "

Republican speech of Castelar in the Cortes about 18 Dec "

Resignation of Prim and ministry on the Italian government opposing the nomination of the duke of Genoa as king of Spain 4 Jan 1870

Prim resumes office with Topete and Rivero 10 Jan "

Majority in the assembly for Prim against the combined unionists and liberals 3 Apr "

Duc de Montpensier, after great provocation, kills don Enrique de Bourbon, brother of the ex king, in a duel, 12 Mch, tried, condemned and fined. 12 Apr "

Crown declined by Espartero May, "

Bill for gradual abolition of slavery in the colonies presented to the Cortes. 28 May, "

Rojo Arias carries a resolution requiring an absolute majority in the Cortes for any proposed sovereign (179 out of 356), this excludes all present candidates June, "

Isabella II abdicates in favor of her son, Alfonso 25 June, "

Prince Leopold of Hohenzollern-Sigmaringen nominated king, accepted by the regent and ministry, 6 July, this justified by the government in a circular, 7 July, on opposition of France he resigns 12 July, "

Neutrality in Franco Prussian war announced 27 July, "

Renewed agitation for a republic about 9 Aug "

Amnesty for political offences since 29 Sept. 1868, published, 10 Aug "

French republic warmly recognized Sept. "

Amadeus, duke of Aosta (b 30 May, 1845) accepts the candidature for the crown 20 Oct "

Elected by the Cortes by 191 votes (63 for a republic, 27 for the duc de Montpensier) 16 Nov "

Proclaimed king 17 Nov 1870

Ex queen, on behalf of her son Alfonso, protests against the election 21 Nov "

Duke accepts the crown from a deputation of the Cortes at Florence, and says that his honesty should rise above the struggle of parties, and that he has no other object than the peace and prosperity of the nation 4 Dec "

Stormy session in the Cortes on arrangements for the new king 19 Dec, Rivero, president, resigns 25 Dec "

Prim fired at and wounded in his carriage by 6 men, who escape, indignation at Madrid, 27 Dec, Topete rejoins the ministry vote of confidence 28 Dec "

Prim dies in the evening (aged 56), the king received by Topete at Cartagena. 30 Dec "

Funeral of Prim 31 Dec "

King enters Madrid, and takes the oath 2 Jan 1871

New ministry under Serrano 5 Jan "

New Cortes opened, king's speech applauded 3 Apr "

Del Castillo and other Alfonsists recognize the king Apr "

Olozaga elected president of the Cortes. 4 Apr "

Tornado difficulty settled (Aug-Nov 1866), compensation to be paid by the Spanish government May, "

King visits the provinces warmly received, 1 Sept et seq, welcomed by Espartero at Logroño 30 Sept "

Espartero, duke of Vittoria made prince of Vergara Jan 1872

New Cortes opened, king says, "I will never impose myself on the Spanish people but neither will I allow myself to be accused of deserting the post which I occupy by their will," 24 Apr "

Navarre, etc, in state of siege 25 Apr "

Marshal Serrano enters Navarre, don Carlos calling himself Carlos VII, crosses the frontier near Vera, and takes the command, Rada retiring, 2 May, totally defeated at Oroquieta 4 May, "

Letter of the duc de Montpensier advocating the rights of prince Alfonso, 17 Apr published June, "

Attempted assassination of king and queen by about 15 men, 1 assassin killed, 2 taken, after midnight of 18, 19 July, "

Don Carlos calls on Catalonia, Aragon, and Valencia to rise, promising their ancient liberties 16 July, "

King's popular visit to the provinces, travelling nearly 2000 miles 26 July–24 Aug "

Cortes opened by the king with a fine speech 15 Sept. "

Bill for abolition of slavery in Porto Rico, for compensation, brought into congress 24 Dec. "

King Amadeus abdicates in a message, saying that he sees Spain in a continual struggle the era of peace more distant, he sought remedies within the law and did not find them, his efforts were sterile, the 2 chambers combine as the sovereign Cortes of Spain, and vote for a republic (126–32), 11 Feb 1873

Reported success of Carlists, agitation for the duc de Montpensier among Orleanists in France 12 Feb "

Irruption of Carlists, they hold part of Catalonia, demonstrations in favor of a federal republic 22, 23 Feb. "

Circular to European powers from Castelar, foreign minister, 27 Feb "

Permanent committee of the Cortes appointed 22 Mch "

Slavery in Porto Rico abolished 23 Mch "

Carlists beaten in several encounters, don Alfonso de Bourbon re enters France. 23 Apr "

Old "monarchical volunteers" occupy the bull ring at Madrid, are disarmed and dispersed by government troops, the "permanent committee" dissolved by the government, which assumes supreme power 26 Apr "

Elections for the Cortes commence, monarchists abstain from voting 10 May, "

Mr Bradlaugh, the English republican, entertained at Madrid, 24 May, "

Intransigentes, or Irreconcilables (extreme republicans) very powerful June, "

New Cortes opened, a speech by Figueras. 1 June, "

Carlists besiege Irun 7 June, "

Federal republic voted by the Cortes (210–2), and proclaimed, 8 June, Pi y Margall, president of a new ministry, rejected, Figueras and his ministry resume office 9 June, "

Ministerial crisis renewed, 10 June, Pi y Margall becomes minister, Figueras quits Spain 11 June, "

Carlists defeat Castañon near Murieta 26 June, "

Intransigentes withdraw from the Cortes 1 July, "

Defeat and death of Calvinety by Carlists, insurrection at Alcoy, promoted by Internationalists, mayor and others killed, announced 11 July, "

Don Carlos (as Carlos VII) enters Spain, "to save the country," 13 July, "

Desperate fighting at Igualada, Catalonia 17, 18 July, "

[Four prevailing parties (1) Government, highly democratic, (2) Intransigentes or Irreconcilables, extremely democratic, (3) International or Communists, (4) Legitimists, Carlists.]

Murcia and Valencia proclaim themselves federal cantons, 18 July, "

Pi y Margall compelled to resign, Salmeron forms a ministry opposed to the Intransigentes 18 July, "

Igualada taken by Carlists under don Alfonso. 19 July, "

Don Carlos enters Biscay 31 July, "

Carlists hold chief of N Spain Aug "

Insurgents repulsed in attack on Almeria, beaten in fights [illegible] Seville, 28–30 July, gen Pavia warmly received 31 J[illegible] "

Troops attack Valencia, 26 July, it surrenders 8 [illegible] "

New constitution printed, 27 July, discussed Aug "

[118 articles, includes separation of church and st[illegible]e, free religious worship, nobility abolished, 15 states in and near peninsula, 2 in the Antilles, Cortes (senate and congress) to have legislative power, one deputy to 50,000 inhabitants, Cortes to be renewed in 2 years, members to be paid, executive, president and ministry, president elected for 4 years]

ombardment of Malaga stopped by the British and German admirals 1 Aug 1873

idiz surrenders to gen Pavia 4 Aug "

eported total defeat of the insurgents at Chinchilla, while marching on Madrid 10 Aug "

artagena held by Intransigentes, besieged 22 Aug "

eerhound English yacht, conveying stores to Carlists, seized by the Spaniards 11½ miles off Biarritz, crew imprisoned and captain sent to Ferrol 13 Aug "

arlists defeat republicans at Artichulegui, near Renteria, 21 Aug "

ney take Estella after a conflict at Dicastillo 25 Aug "

astelar elected president of the Cortes. 26 Aug "

apt Werner, of German ship *Friedrich Carl*, captures *Almanza* and *Vittoria* Spanish iron clads, held by rebels, gives them up to adm Yelverton, who prepares for action against Intransigentes claiming them, and sends them to Gibraltar unmolested 1 Sept. "

inistry propose abolition of capital punishment in the army, defeated in the Cortes, resign 5 Sept "

astelar heads a ministry, proposes calling out 150,000 men to end the war 7, 8 Sept "

almeron elected president of the Cortes 9 Sept "

astelar virtual dictator 15 Sept "

eerhound and crew given up, announced about 18 Sept. "

peech of Castelar, Cortes to be closed 2 Jan 1874 18 Sept. "

ombination of parties to support Castelar about 6 Oct "

ndecisive battle at Maneru, near Puenta de la Reyna, in Navarre, between republicans under Moriones, and Carlists under Ollo, advantage with Carlists 6 Oct. "

attle of Escombrera bay, Intransigentes' ships attempt to break blockade of Cartagena, repulsed by adm Lobo, 11 Oct "

obo declines to fight, and retires, pursued by the Intransigentes 13 Oct, justifies himself at Madrid 22 Oct "

eath of Rios Rosas, statesman 3 Nov "

'urillo captured, condemned to be sold by the British Court of Admiralty Nov "

ronunciamento Meeting of the Cortes, speech of Castelar, vote of confidence lost by 20, he resigns, Salmeron attempts to form a ministry, 2 3 Jan, Pavia, capt gen of Madrid, forcibly dissolves the Cortes 3 Jan 1874

arshal Serrano president of a new ministry, including Topete, national guard of Madrid disarming 4 Jan "

ew government issue a moderate manifesto 9, 10 Jan "

artagena captured by Lopez Dominguez 12 Jan "

'umancia, iron clad with Intransigentes leaders and convicts, escapes, they land at Mers el Kebir, near Oran, on the African coast, are returned by the French 12 Jan "

lockade of the coast of Spain announced 31 Jan. "

arlists besiege Bilbao, Moriones defeated at Somorrostro, 25 Feb "

arshal Serrano resigns presidency of the ministry, and becomes chief of the executive, succeeded by Zabala, Serrano proceeds to Bilbao 28 Feb et seq "

errano assumes command about 8 Mch "

lockade of the coast (31 Jan) raised 2 Mch "

hree days' conflict at Somorrostro, near Bilbao, Carlists defeated but retain their positions (about 2000 killed and wounded on both sides) 25–27 Mch "

rmistice for 3 days 28 Mch "

en Manuel da Concha joins Serrano at Santander, about 8 Apr "

reat national effort to relieve Bilbao, union of parties, hostilities resumed 20 Apr "

fter several days' conflict, Carlists retreat, marshal Concha enters Bilbao, which is much injured by long bombardment, 2 May, "

battle at Prats de Llusanes, indecisive 6 May, "

arlists repulsed in attack at Ramales about 20 May, "

arlists defeated at Gondesa about 6 June, "

epublicans repulsed before Estella. 25-27 June, "

oncha killed (succeeded by Zabala) 27 June, "

arlists hold Navarre, Guipuscoa, Biscay, and Alara July, "

arlists capture Cuenca (about 80 miles from Madrid) 13 July, "

on Carlos's manifesto, promising constitutional government, 16 July, "

ll Spain placed under martial law, levy of 125,000 men, about 18 July, "

overnment appeals to France respecting French assistance to Carlists, justificatory reply 3 Aug "

ritish Mediterranean squadron, under adm Drummond, sails from Malta for Barcelona 4 Aug "

on Carlos appeals to the chief powers not to intervene, justifies Dorregaray's severities, and the execution of Schmidt 6 Aug "

loriones's alleged defeat of Mendiri and Carlists at Oteiza, 12 Aug "

errano's government recognized by Great Britain, Germany, France, and other powers (not by Russia) about 14 Aug "

etter of sympathy and encouragement from the Comte de Chambord to don Carlos Aug "

uycerda vigorously besieged by Carlists Aug–Sept. "

arlists fire on German gun boats *Nautilus* and *Albatross*, near San Sebastian, Germans fire shells into the town, about 5 Sept. "

arlists defeated by Lopez Pinto near Mora, about 9 Sept, by Moriones at Barasoam near Tafalla. about 25 Sept "

SPA

Note to French government, complaining of neglect respecting the Carlists on the frontiers early in Oct. 1874

Prince Alfonso in a manifesto replies to address, declaring himself "a true Spaniard, Catholic, and liberal" 1 Dec. "

Army at Murviedro pronounces for Alfonso, he is proclaimed king by gen Martinez Campos, 29 Dec, recognized by the other armies and the navy, 30 Dec, proclaimed by gen Primo da Rivera at Madrid, Antonio Canovas del Castillo, head of a royal ministry 31 Dec. "

Pres Serrano withdraws to France 1 Jan 1875

Proclamation of Carlos against Alfonso 6 Jan "

Alfonso XII recognized throughout Spain, well received at Barcelona, 9 Jan, enters Madrid 14 Jan "

Order of knighthood re established, payments to clergy to be renewed Jan "

Alfonso reviews 30 000 troops near Tafalla, 22 Jan, issues proclamation to northern provinces, promising amnesty and respect to local rights 22 Jan "

Serrano returns to Madrid Feb "

Carlists retreat from Pampeluna, entered by the king, 6 Feb, he exchanges decorations with Espartero at Logroño 9 Feb "

Resignation of gens Moriones, Loma, and Blanco, Concha sent for from Cuba Feb "

Serrano received by the king 8 Mch "

Cabrera an old Carlist general (see 1840) publishes an address, declaring for Alfonso XII 11 Mch "

Papal nuncio received by the king 3 May, "

Vigorous action of government troops, Carlists expelled from Castile, sympathizers suppressed July, "

Carlists defeated at Quesada and others 31 July, "

Citadel at Urgel surrendered by Carlists to Campos 26 Aug "

Resignation of "conciliation ministry," 11 Sept, liberal cabinet headed by gen Jovellar 12 Sept "

Circular of papal nuncio against toleration about 13 Sept. "

Don Carlos declares his mission "to quell the revolution, and that it will die" Sept. "

Bombardment of San Sebastian, 28 Sept–2 Oct, resumed, 11 Oct "

Government declare the civil war at an end, and purpose summoning the Cortes to assist the king in reorganizing the country early in Oct. "

Don Carlos proposes to the king a truce, and offers help if war occurs with the U S (no answer) 9 Nov "

New constitutional party under Sagasta formed Nov "

Cortes elected, 364 ministerial sts out of 406 Jan 1876

Cortes opened by the king 15 Feb "

Carlists defeated at Estella, Vera, and Tolosa by Quesada and Moriones Feb "

King assumes command, Estella surrenders to Primo da Rivera, severe loss 18 Feb "

Reported letter from the pope recommending Carlos to retire from the contest 22 Feb "

Don Carlos, with gen Lizarraga and 5 battalions, surrender to the governor of Bayonne at St. Jean Pied de Port, 27 Feb., he, with some officers, lands at Folkestone and proceeds to London 4 Mch "

Triumphal entry of Alfonso XII into Madrid 20 Mch "

Draft of new constitution submitted to the Cortes 28 Mch "

Pope opposes moderate religious toleration in article 11 of the constitution Apr "

Jews (expelled in 1492) petition for readmission " "

Long debate in Cortes, confidence in ministry voted (211 to 26), constitution passed, adjourn about 21 July, "

Queen Isabella received by king at Santander, declares "her share in public affairs is at an end" 31 July, "

Public worship of Protestants repressed by authority Sept. "

Amnesty to Carlists and others surrendering Apr 1877

Meeting of the new Cortes 25 Apr "

Cortes suddenly closed 11 July, "

New tariff passed, customs duties raised in respect to Great Britain, France, and U S 17 July, "

Ex queen, after visiting her son, disapproves of proposed marriage, and associates with don Carlos in Paris who is privately forbidden to remain, and goes to England, she is forbidden to return to Spain, her pension stopped end of Dec "

King married to his cousin Mercedes, daughter of the duc de Montpensier 23 Jan 1878

End of the insurrection in Cuba announced 21 Feb. "

Death of queen Mercedes, deeply lamented 26 June, "

Death of queen dowager Christina 21 Aug "

King fired at (not injured) by Juan Oliva Moncasi, a member of the International society, aged 23 25 Oct. "

Moncasi executed . 4 Jan 1879

Espartero, duque de Vittoria, d 8 Jan "

Cortes dissolved, 16 Mch, to meet 1 June, "

King married to archduchess Maria Christina of Austria, 29 Nov "

Attempted assassination of king and queen by Francisco Otero y Gonzalez by shooting 30 Dec. "

Law gradually abolishing slavery in Cuba promulgated, 18 Feb. 1880

Manifesto from 279 senators and deputies claiming liberty of religion, the press, etc., and education, universal suffrage, etc 6 Apr "

Otero executed 14 Apr "

Permission said to be given to about 60,000 Russian Jews to come to Spain June, 1881

Don Carlos expelled from France for expressing sympathy with legitimists (goes to London) 17 July, "

Consolidation of the national debt (60,000,000*l.*) proposed, Sept., law published . 10 Dec. "

King invested with the order of the Garter .. ....7 Oct. "

Kings of Spain and Portugal open a new railway between Madrid and Lisbon — 8 Oct. 1881

"Dynastic Left," a new party formed by marshal Serrano and others, constituted (dividing the liberals) — 27 Oct. 1882

Gen. Maceo and 5 Cuban insurgent leaders surrendered at Gibraltar to Spaniards (they had escaped from Cadiz, 20 Aug.), petition queen Victoria to ask their release, application made for inquiry, gen. Baynes, colonial secretary at Gibraltar, and Mr. Blair, chief inspector of police, dismissed for exceeding authority, announced — 4 Dec. "

"Dynastic Left" in Cortes pronounce in favor of advanced liberalism — 15 Dec. "

King visits Vienna 10 Sept., Berlin, Homberg and Brussels, — 27 Sept. 1883

King honorably received by pres. Grevy, hissed and reviled by the Paris mob (having been made a colonel of Uhlans by emperor William), behaved with dignity — 29, 30 Sept., 1 Oct. "

Last section of the great Asturian railway opened by the king — 15 Aug. 1884

Much suffering by EARTHQUAKES — 25-31 Dec. "

Protocol restoring Great Britain to position of most "favored nation" in regard to commerce (lost since 1845) wine duties modified, signed at Madrid, 21 Dec. 1884, gazetted — 6 Feb. "

King d. — 25 Nov. "

Alfonso XIII. son b. — 17 May, 1886

Don Carlos protests against the recognition of Alfonso XIII., — 20 May, "

Attempted revolution at Madrid — 19 Sept. "

Ministers of Germany, Austria, Italy, and England, to the court of Spain, raised to the rank of ambassadors by their respective governments, thus placing Spain among the first-class powers — 1887

Opening of the Cortes, infant king enthroned — 1 Dec. "

Trial by jury introduced by the senate — 27 Feb. 1888

Trial by jury first put in force at Madrid — 29 May, 1889

Duke of Aosta, formerly king of Spain as Amadeo I., d. at Turin, aged 45 — 18 Jan. 1890

Inundations throughout the central and southern parts of Spain, over 100,000 persons rendered homeless — Sept. 1891

Anarchist disturbances, several executed — Mch.-Apr. 1892

Widespread rioting excited by the OCTROIS duties — 17 July, "

Celebration in honor of the discovery of America by Columbus formally begun in Cadiz — 31 July, "

War in Morocco begun — Oct. 1893

Cargo of dynamite explodes in the harbor of Santander, killing about 1000 people and wrecks part of the town — 4 Nov. "

Explosion of dynamite bomb thrown by anarchists in a theatre at Barcelona kills 30 and injures 80 persons — 7 Nov. "

Second explosion of dynamite from the submerged hulk of the steamer blown up in the harbor of Santander Nov. 1893 and 30 persons killed — 22 Mch. 1894

Six anarchists guilty of complicity in an attempt to assassinate capt. gen. Campos executed at Barcelona — 21 May, 1894

SOVEREIGNS OF SPAIN

GOTHIC SOVEREIGNS.

411 Ataulfo, murdered by his soldiers
415 Sigerico, reigned a few days only
" Valia, or Wallia
420 Theodoric I., killed in a battle which he had gained against Attila
451 Thorismund, or Torrismund, assassinated
452 Theodoric II., assassinated by
466 Euric, the first monarch of all Spain
483 Alaric II., killed in battle
506 Gesalric, his bastard son
511 Amalric, or Amalaric, legitimate son of Alaric
531 Theudis, or Theodat, assassinated by a madman
548 Theudisela, or Theodisele, murdered
549 Agila, taken prisoner and put to death.
554 Atanagildo
567 Liuva, or Levua I.
568 Leuvigildo, associated on the throne with Liuva in 568, and sole king in 572
586 Recaredo I.
601 Liuva II., assassinated.
603 Vitericus, also murdered
610 Gundemar
612 Sisibut, or Sisebuth, or Sisebert.
621 Recaredo II.
" Suintila, dethroned
631 Sisenando
636 Chintella
640 Tulga, or Tulca.
642 Cindasuinto, d. in 652
649 Recesuinto, associated, in 653 became sole king
672 Vamba or Wamba, dethroned, and died in a monastery
680 Ervigius, or Ervigio
687 Egica, or Egiza.
698 Vitiza or Witiza, associated, in 701 sole king
711 Rodrigo or Roderic, *slain in battle.*

Six independent Suevic kings reigned 409-69, and two Vandalic kings: Gunderic, 409-25, his successor, Genseric, with his whole nation, passed over to Africa

MAHOMETAN SPAIN

CORDOVA

Emirs: The first, Abdelasis, the last, Yussuf-el Tehri, A.D. 714-55
Kings: The first, Abderahman I., the last, Abu Ali, 755-1238

GRANADA

Kings: The first, Mohammed I., the last, Abdalla, 1238-1492

CHRISTIAN SPAIN

KINGS OF ASTURIAS AND LEON

718 Pelagius, or Pelayo, overthrew the Moors, and checked their conquests
737 Favila, killed in hunting
739 Alfonso the Catholic
757 Froila, murdered his brother Samaran, in revenge for which he was murdered by his brother and successor
768 Aurelius, or Aurelio
774 Mauregato the Usurper
788 Veremundo (Bermuda) I.
791 Alfonso II. the Chaste
842 Ramiro I., he put 70,000 Saracens to the sword in one battle —*Rabbe*
850 Ordoño I.
866 Alfonso III. surnamed the Great, relinquished his crown to his son
910 Garcias.
914 Ordoño II.
923 Froila II.
925 Alfonso IV. the Monk, abdicated.
930 Ramiro II., killed in battle
950 Ordoño III.
955 Ordoño IV.
956 Sancho I., the Fat, poisoned with an apple
967 Ramiro III.
983 Veremundo *II.* (Bermuda), the Gouty
999 Alfonso V., killed in a siege
1027 Veremundo III. (Bermuda), killed

KINGS OF NAVARRE

873 Sancho Iñigo, *count*
885 Garcia I. king
905 Sancho Garcias, a renowned warrior
924 Garcias II., surnamed the Trembler
970 Sancho II., surnamed the Great (king of Castile through his wife)
1035 Garcias III.
1054 Sancho III.
1076 Sancho IV., Ramirez, king of Aragon
1094 Peter of Aragon
1104 Alfonso I. of Aragon
1134 Garcias IV., Ramirez
1150 Sancho V., surnamed the Wise
1194 Sancho VI., surnamed the Infirm
1234 Theobald I., count of Champagne.
1253. Theobald II.
1270 Henry Crassus
1274 Joanna, married to Philip the Fair of France, 1285
1305 Louis Hutin of France
1316 John, lived but a few days
" Philip V., the Long, of France
1322 Charles I., the IV. of France
1328 Joanna II., and Philip, count d'Evreux.
1343 Joanna alone
1349 Charles II., or the Bad
1387 Charles III., or the Noble
1425 Blanche and her husband, John II., *afterwards king of Aragon.*
1479 Eleanor
" Francis Phœbus de Foix
1483 Catherine and John d'Albret.
1512 Navarre conquered by Ferdinand the Catholic, and united with Castile

KINGS OF LEON AND CASTILE.

1035. Ferdinand the Great.
1065 Sancho II. the Strong, son of Ferdinand, Alfonso in Leon and Asturias, and Garcias in Galicia
1072 Alfonso VI., the Valiant, king of Leon
1109 Uraca and Alfonso VII.
1126 Alfonso VII., Raymond
1157 Sancho III., surnamed the Beloved
1158 Alfonso VIII., the Noble
[*Leon is separated from* Castile *under* Ferdinand II., 1157-88.]
1188 Alfonso IX. of Leon
1214 Henry I.
1217 Ferdinand III., the Saint and the Holy. By him Leon and Castile were permanently united
1252 Alfonso X. the Wise (the Alphonsine Tables were drawn up under his direction)
1284. Sancho IV. the Great and the Brave
1295 Ferdinand IV.
1312. Alfonso XI.
1350 Peter the Cruel, deposed, reinstated by Edward the Black Prince of England, slain by his natural brother and successor
1369 Henry II., the Gracious, poisoned by a monk
1379 John I., he united Biscay to Castile
1390 Henry III., the Sickly
1406 John II., son of Henry
1454 Henry IV., the Impotent
1474. Isabella, sister (had married Ferdinand of Aragon 18 Oct. 1469)
1504 Joanna (daughter of Ferdinand and Isabella), and Philip I. of Austria. On her mother's death Joanna succeeded, jointly with her husband Philip, but Philip dying in 1506, and Joanna becoming imbecile, her father Ferdinand continued the reign, and thus perpetuated the union of Castile with Aragon

KINGS OF ARAGON

1035 Ramiro I
1065 Sancho Ramirez (IV of Navarre)
1094 Peter of Navarre
1104 Alfonso I, the Warrior king of Navarre
1134 Ramiro II, the Monk
1137 Petronilla and Raymond, count of Barcelona.
1163 Alfonso II
1196 Peter II
1213 James I, succeeded by his son
1276 Peter III, conquered Sicily in 1282
1285 Alfonso III, the Beneficent
1291 James II, surnamed the Just
1327 Alfonso IV
1336 Peter IV, the Ceremonious.
1387 John I
1395 Martin
1410 [Interregnum.]
1412 Ferdinand the Just, king of Sicily
1416 Alfonso V, the Wise
1458 John II, king of Navarre, brother of Alfonso, d. 1479
1479 Ferdinand II, the Catholic, the next heir, by marriage with Isabella of Castile (styled the Catholic kings), the kingdoms were united.

SPAIN

HOUSE OF ARAGON

1512 Ferdinand V (Castile) II (Aragon) having conquered Granada and Navarre, becomes king of all Spain

HOUSE OF HAPSBURG.

1516 Charles I, grandson son of Joanna of Castile and Philip of Austria (emperor of Germany, as Charles V, in 1519), resigned both crowns and retired to a monastery
1556 Philip II, son, king of Naples and Sicily, a merciless bigot married Mary, queen regnant of England, died covered with ulcers
1598 Philip III, son drove the Moors from Granada and the adjacent provinces
1621 Philip IV, son, wars with the Dutch and French, lost Portugal in 1640
1665 Charles II, son, last of the Austrian line, nominated by will his successor

HOUSE OF BOURBON

1700 Philip V, duke of Anjou, grandson of Louis XIV of France, hence arose the "War of the Succession," terminated by the treaty of Utrecht in 1713, resigned
1724 Louis I, son, reigned only a few months
" Philip V again
1746 Ferdinand VI, the Wise, son, liberal and beneficent
1759 Charles III, brother, king of the Two Sicilies, which he gave to his third son, Ferdinand
1788 Charles IV, son, the influence of Godoy, Prince of Peace, reached to almost royal authority in this reign, Charles abdicated in favor of his son in 1808, and d. in 1819
1808 Ferdinand VII, whom Napoleon also forced to abdicate

HOUSE OF BONAPARTE.

1808 Joseph Bonaparte, brother of Napoleon, forced to abdicate

HOUSE OF BOURBON RESTORED

1813. Ferdinand VII restored, married Maria Christina of Naples, 11 Dec. 1829, d. 29 Dec. 1833, succeeded by
1833. Isabella II, daughter (b. 10 Oct. 1830), declared of age, 8 Nov 1843, married her cousin don Francis d'Assisi, 10 Oct 1846, deposed 30 Sept 1868, separated from her husband Mch 1870, and abdicated 25 June, 1870, in favor of her son, Alfonso, prince of Asturias (b. 28 Nov 1857)

HOUSE OF SAVOY.

1870 Amadeo I (duke of Aosta, son of Victor Emmanuel II, king of Italy), b. 30 May, 1845, married Maria Victoria of Pozzo della Cisterna, 30 May, 1867, accepted the crown offered him by the Cortes, 4 Dec. 1870, abdicated, 11 Feb 1873, d. at Turin, aged 45, 18 Jan 1890

REPUBLIC

1873 Executive of the Cortes.
" Estanislao Figueras
" Nicolas Salmeron
1871 Pi y Margall
" Emilio Castelar

HOUSE OF BOURBON

1874 Alfonso XII, son of Isabella II (b. 28 Nov 1857), proclaimed 30 Dec 1874, married, 1st, his cousin Mercedes, daughter of the duc de Montpensier (b. 24 June 1860) 23 Jan 1878, she d. 26 June, 1878; 2d, archduchess Maria Christina of Austria (b. 21 July, 1858), 29 Nov 1879, d. 25 Nov 1885
1886 Alfonso XIII, b. 17 May, 1886.

CARLIST LEGITIMATE PRETENDERS.

(See above 1833 et seq.)

Carlos V, brother of Ferdinand VII, b. 29 Mch 1788, d. 10 Mch. 1855
Carlos VI, his son (conde de Montemolin), d. 14 Jan 1861
Carlos VII (son of don Juan, brother of Carlos VI, who renounced his right, 8 Jan 1863), b. 30 Mch 1848, see above 1873-76

Spala'tro or **Spala'to,** a seaport city of Dalmatia, the ancient Spalatum, and Salona. At his palace here, Diocletian spent his last 9 years, and died July, 313. R. Adam published the "Antiquities of Diocletian's Palace." 1764

Spanish-American war. The geographical position of Cuba has made the ownership of the island, and its social and political conditions, at all times a matter of intense interest to the U. S. As early as 1762 an expedition, under lord Albemarle, consisting largely of American colonists, among whom were gen. Israel Putnam, Lawrence Washington (brother of George Washington), General Lyman, and others, captured Havana, but the island was restored to Cuba at the peace of Paris in 1763. The declaration of the Monroe doctrine, 2 Dec. 1823, was the first official notice of our interest. Henry Clay, while secretary of state, 1825, stated to the French government that the U. S. could not see with indifference the passing of Cuba from Spain to any other European power, and that for ourselves no change was desired in their present political and commercial condition. John C. Calhoun, in a speech in the U. S. Senate, 15 May, 1848, made the following statement:

"So long as Cuba remains in the hands of Spain—a friendly power, a power of which we have no dread—it should continue to be, as it has been, the policy of all administrations to let Cuba remain there, but with a fixed determination, which I hope will never be relinquished, that if Cuba pass from her it shall not be into any other hands but ours."

Pres. Polk, in 1848, directed the U. S. minister at Madrid to ascertain the terms upon which Spain would be willing to transfer Cuba to the U. S. The unofficial reply of Spain was that, sooner than see the island transferred to any power, they would prefer seeing it sunk into the ocean. In 1852 Great Britain and France proposed to the U. S. that they should enter into a tripartite arrangement relative to Cuba, the essential point of which was that the contracting parties declared "severally and collectively that they will not obtain or maintain for themselves, or for any one of themselves, any exclusive control over the said island, nor assume nor exercise any dominion over the same." The U. S. declined to enter into any such arrangement on the ground that while equal in terms it would be unequal in substance. Mr. Everett in his reply said:

"The island of Cuba lies at our doors. It commands the approach to the Gulf of Mexico, which washes the shores of five of our states. It bars the entrance of that great river which drains half the North American continent, and forms the largest system of internal water communication in the world. It keeps watch at the doorway of our intercourse with California by the Isthmus route."

The continual interference on the part of the Spanish authorities in Cuba with American citizens and American commerce, culminating in the seizure of the *Black Warrior* in 1854, led pres. Pierce to appoint Messrs. Soulé, Buchanan, and Mason to meet and exchange views in reference to the purchase of the island of Cuba. The ministers drew up a paper known as the "OSTEND MANIFESTO," in which they reported their conclusion that "an immediate effort ought to be made by the U. S. to purchase Cuba from Spain at any price not exceeding the sum of $100,000,000." Spain refused to consider the proposition. The historic 10 years' struggle, although ending with the failure of the Cuban movement for independence, put a severe strain on the U. S., which suffered in its material interests and in national susceptibilities outraged by the wanton murder of the Americans in the *Virginius* expedition. When the new insurrection broke out in Feb. 1895, Spain poured corps after corps of her best soldiers into the island, but she made little headway. Marshal Campos was recalled for lack of energy, and gen. Weyler was sent out to inaugurate a vigorous policy. This took the form of fire and slaughter wherever his arms could penetrate, and the concentration of the non-combatant population into circumscribed zones, where they were left to die of starvation and disease. Congress, after several weeks' debate, adopted a joint resolution (6 Apr.) recognizing Cuba as a belligerent power. On the opening of the year 1898 the insurrection was still unsuppressed and the reconcentrados were still dying by hundreds. The government resolved to protect American interests by sending a war-vessel to Havana. Spain promptly notified the U. S., by way of reply, that its battle ship *Vizcaya* would pay a visit to New York. The battle-ship *Maine* was received with the usual courtesies, and was led to an anchorage by its hosts. On the night of

15 Feb. 1898, it was destroyed by an explosion in which 260 of its crew perished. It was this calamity that turned the direction of the current towards the war which was to be the final result An official examining board was in session in Havana and at Key West four weeks A unanimous decision was reached by the court 21 Mch

"That the loss of the *Maine* was not in any respect due to fault or negligence on the part of any of the officers or members of her crew, that the ship was destroyed by the explosion of a submarine mine, and that no evidence had been obtainable fixing the responsibility upon any person or persons"

The joint resolution of Congress, signed by the president on 20 Apr 1898, declared 1 That the people of Cuba are, and of right ought to be, free and independent 2 That the U. S demanded the withdrawal of Spain from Cuba. 3 That the president was empowered and directed to carry these resolutions into effect. 4 That the U S. disclaimed any disposition or intention to exercise sovereignty, jurisdiction, or control over Cuba, except for the pacification thereof, and asserted its determination to leave the government of the island in the hands of its inhabitants Porto Rico, the Philippine islands, and Guam were held by the U S, but Cuba was recognized as a free and independent republic

Hostile demonstrations at Havana by Spanish volunteers against Americans caused the governor general to place a guard around the U S consulate 15-20 Jan 1898
The battle ship *Maine* arrived at Havana on a friendly visit, 25 Jan "
A letter by min De Lome, in which he wrote disparagingly of pres McKinley, was published, on learning of the exposure the minister requested his government to accept his resignation . 8 Feb "
The U S Senate discussed intervention in Cuba 9 Feb "
Resolutions requesting the president to transmit information relative to the situation in Cuba were adopted by Congress, 14 Feb "
Señor Luis Polo y Bernabe was appointed Spanish minister to the U S to succeed señor De Lome 14 Feb "
The battle-ship *Maine* was blown up in the harbor of Havana, 260 American lives were destroyed 15 Feb "
Spain officially expressed regret for the *Maine* "incident," 16 Feb "
A naval court of inquiry into the cause of the destruction of the *Maine* was appointed by the U S 17 Feb "
The Spanish cruiser *Vizcaya* visited New York harbor, 18 Feb, she sailed for Havana 25 Feb "
The *Maine* court of inquiry began its session in Havana, 20 Feb "
The cruiser *Montgomery* proceeded to Havana 22 Feb "
Spain asked for the recall of con gen Lee, which was promptly refused by the U S government 5 Mch "
A bill appropriating $50,000,000 for the national defence was signed by the president 9 Mch. "
The war department began the mobilization of the army 11 Mch "
The battle ship *Oregon* sailed from San Franciseo to join the Atlantic squadron. 12 Mch "
Armistice was offered by Spain to the Cubans .. 12 Mch "
The Spanish fleet sailed from Cadiz 14 Mch "
Sen. Proctor's report on Spanish atrocities in Cuba was published 14 Mch "
The *Maine* court of inquiry completed its labors, 19 Mch, its report was delivered to the president, 25 Mch., and transmitted by him to Congress 28 Mch "
Com Schley took command of the flying squadron in Hampton Roads 25 Mch "
The president requested permission of Spain to relieve the reconcentrados, which was granted 30 Mch "
The Spanish fleet arrived at Cape de Verde islands 2 Apr "
The pope appealed to Spain in the interests of peace 4 Apr "
U S consuls in Cuba were recalled . 5 Apr "
The diplomatic representatives of the great powers of Europe waited on the president with a plea for peace .. 7 Apr "
Con gen Lee departed from Havana 9 Apr "
The president sent a message to Congress outlining the situation, declaring that intervention was necessary, advising against the recognition of the Cuban government, and requesting Congress to take action 11 Apr "
Congress adopted resolutions declaring Cuba independent and directing the president to use the forces of the U S to put an end to Spanish authority in Cuba 19 Apr "
The president signed the resolutions of Congress, an ultimatum to Spain was cabled to min Woodford . 20 Apr "
The Spanish Cortes met and received a warlike message from the queen regent . 20 Apr "
The Spanish government sent min Woodford his passports, thus beginning the war . . 21 Apr "
Great Britain notified by Spain that coal was contraband of war . 21 Apr "
Proclamation to the neutral powers announcing war was issued by the president . . . 22 Apr "
Adm Sampson's fleet sailed from Key West, the blockade of Cuban ports began 22 Apr "
The gun boat *Nashville* captured the Spanish ship *Buena Ventura*, the first prize of the war . . 22 Apr "
The president issued a call for 125,000 volunteers 23 Apr 1898
Six Spanish vessels captured 23, 24 Apr "
Great Britain issued a proclamation of neutrality, and was followed subsequently by the other powers, except Germany, 24 Apr "
Spain formally declares war 24 Apr "
Congress passed an act declaring that war had existed since 21 Apr 25 Apr "
Com Dewey's fleet sailed from Hong Kong for the Philippines, 25 Apr "
Spanish circular to the powers accusing the U S of aggression 25 Apr "
Lieut. A S Rowan lands on the S E coast of Cuba to arrange co operation with the insurgents about 26 Apr "
Congress passed an act for the increase of the regular army, 26 Apr "
Batteries at Matanzas were bombarded, *Guido*, Spanish steamer, captured 27 Apr "
The *Argonauta*, mail steamer, with 10 Spanish officers and soldiers, captured by the *Nashville* off Cuba 29 Apr "
Adm Cervera's fleet left the Cape de Verde islands for the West Indies. . 30 Apr "
Com Dewey destroyed the Spanish fleet at Manila, American loss, 6 men slightly wounded . 1 May, "
Riots in Spain 5-7 May, "
Com Dewey was made a rear admiral . 11 May, "
Attack on Cienfuegos and Cardenas, ensign Bagley and four men on the torpedo boat *Winslow* are killed 11 May, "
Adm Cervera's fleet appeared off Martinique 11 May, "
Adm Sampson bombarded San Juan de Porto Rico 12 May, "
American attempts to land at Cabañas, Cardenas, and Cienfuegos repulsed, forts destroyed by gun boats .12 May, "
The flying squadron left Hampton Roads for E Cuba, *via* Key West . 13 May, "
A new Spanish ministry, under señor Sagasta, came into office, 18 May, "
Adm Cervera's fleet arrived in the harbor of Santiago de Cuba 19 May, "
The cruiser *Charleston* sailed from San Francisco for Manila, 22 May, "
The battle ship *Oregon* reached Jupiter inlet, Florida 24 May, "
The president issued a second call for volunteers, the number being 75,000 25 May, "
The first Manila expedition from San Francisco started, 25 May, "
Adm Sampson's fleet arrived at Santiago from Porto Rico, 30 May, "
Forts of Santiago harbor are bombarded 31 May, "
The U S ship *Florida* lands 400 Cubans, with stores and ammunition, on the N coast of Santiago about 31 May, "
Lieut. Hobson sank the *Merrimac* in the entrance to Santiago harbor 3 June, "
Capt Gridley, of the *Olympia*, dies at Kobé, Japan . 4 June, "
Spanish cruiser *Reina Mercedes* sunk at Santiago 6 June, "
Marines landed at Guantanamo, and skirmished with the Spaniards the following day 11 June, "
War revenue bill was finally passed by Congress, 10 June, it was signed by the president 13 June, "
Gen Shafter's army of invasion, 16,000 strong, embarked at Key West for Santiago 12-14 June, "
There was fighting between marines and Spaniards at Guantanamo bay and a bombardment of the fort at Caimanera by war ships 14, 15 June, "
Adm Camara's fleet sailed from Cadiz for the Suez canal, 15 June, "
Santiago bombarded, forts dismantled, Americans repulsed on attempting to land at Punta Cabrera, W of Santiago, by col Aldea's column . . ... 16 June, "
The Ladrone islands were captured. 21 June, "
The auxiliary cruiser *St. Paul* repulsed a Spanish torpedo boat attack off San Juan, Porto Rico 22 June, "
Gen Shafter arrives with 47 U S ships and troops, S E of Santiago, 21 June, 6000 troops successfully landed at Daiquiri, under the direction of adm Sampson, gen Shafter, and gen Lawton, the country for 6 miles occupied by the Americans, with little or no resistance 20-23 June, "
Advance of American troops under gen Lawton, 24 June, a severe engagement fought near Santiago between about 1000 Americans, under gen Wheeler, col Wood, and gen Young, and 2000 Spaniards under gen Linares and gen Rubin, Spaniards driven back from Sevilla to the city, capt. Capron, serg H Fish, Mr Edw Marshall, correspondent, and about 34 others killed, Spanish loss, 265 . 24 June, "
Sharp engagement between 2000 Cubans, under Castillo, and the Spaniards at Guasima 24 June, "
Calixto Garcia, with 5000 Cubans, joins the Americans at Juragua 26 June, "
Adm Camara's fleet reached Port Said 26 June, "
Gen Merritt departed for Manila 28 June, "
Extension of the blockade by U S ships 28 June, "
The Spanish earthworks at El Caney and San Juan, Santiago, were carried by assault, with heavy loss, in which the Rough Riders and the 71st New York participated 1, 2 July, "
Gen Linares, severely wounded, gives up the command to gen Toral, San Juan captured by the Americans, the Spaniards retreat to Santiago 2 July, "
Adm. Cervera's squadron (ordered to sea by the Madrid government) leaves Santiago harbor and is destroyed by adm Sampson's squadron (1 ship only surrendered), Spanish loss, about 600, adm Cervera wounded and 692 Spaniards taken prisoners.. .... 3 July, "

Adm. Cervera's fleet, attempting to escape from Santiago, was destroyed by the American war-vessels............3 July, 1898

The surrender of Santiago was demanded............3 July, "

Alfonso XII., war-ship, attempting to escape from Havana, destroyed near Mariel..........................5 July, "

The archbishop of Santiago appeals to Madrid, advising the surrender of the city; the government determines on stubborn resistance.................................5 July, "

Hobson and his comrades were exchanged............6 July, "

Adm. Dewey's vessels took possession of Isla Grande, in Subig bay, near Manila..............................8 July, "

Bombardment of Santiago was resumed..............10 July, "

Armistice, till 9 July; gen. Toral's offer of honorable surrender declined; American reinforcements land to co-operate with Garcia, 10 July; bombardment resumed, and the line of investment extended, 9 A.M. till about noon; gen. Shafter sends a flag of truce, again demanding the unconditional surrender of the city; negotiations; gen. Miles arrives off Santiago; truce extended till 16 July..............11 July, "

Gen. Miles arrived at American headquarters in Cuba..11 July, "

Adm. Cervera and captured Spanish prisoners arrived at Portsmouth, N. H.......................................13 July, "

Yellow-fever (mild type) appears among the American troops; several deaths; Siboney ordered to be burned for sanitary reasons by gen. Miles; 18,000 refugees starving.....13 July, "

Surrender of Santiago and province successfully concluded, 16 July; Santiago evacuated by the Spanish troops; 20,000 surrendered; the U. S. flag hoisted, noon...........17 July, "

Naval engagement off Manzanillo; 3 Spanish merchantmen and 5 gun-boats destroyed; about 100 Spaniards killed, 18 July, "

Pres. McKinley issued instructions for the government, etc., of the province of Santiago.........................19 July, "

Guantanamo and Caimanera surrendered..........18, 19 July, "

Gen. Leonard Wood was appointed military governor of Santiago...20 July, "

Last naval engagement on the coast of Cuba; 4 U. S. war-ships entered the harbor of Nipe, and after a furious bombardment took possession of that port ....21 July, "

Surrender of Spanish troops at San Luis and Dos Palmas, 22 July, "

The Spanish cruiser *Jorge Juan* destroyed; reported..22 July, "

Gibara surrendered to the insurgents; Tunas and Zaza besieged by the Americans; reported..................24 July, "

Gen. Miles lands at Guanica, Porto Rico..............25 July, "

Castillo appointed military governor.................26 July, "

The Spanish government, through French ambassador Cambon, asked for terms of peace........................26 July, "

U. S. army, under gen. Miles, landed at Guanica, Porto Rico, 25 July; the town surrendered, and Ponce followed..28 July, "

Adm. Camara started to return through the Suez canal to Spain, 8 July; he reached Cadiz...................29 July, "

Gen. Merritt landed at Cavité, Manila harbor.........29 July, "

The president, through the French ambassador, stated the American terms ....30 July, "

The Americans repulsed the Spaniards, with loss on both sides, at Malate, near Manila..........................31 July, "

The Rough Riders left Santiago for Montauk Point....7 Aug. "

Gen. Ernst defeated a Spanish force at Coamo, Porto Rico, 9 Aug. "

Spain formally accepted the president's terms of peace..9 Aug. "

The peace protocol was signed and an armistice was proclaimed; terms: Spain to evacuate Cuba, and to cede to U. S. Porto Rico, her islands in the Antilles, and one of the Ladrones; U. S. to hold Manila temporarily........12 Aug. "

Manila surrendered to the American forces after a short land fight and bombardment by the fleet................13 Aug. "

Gen. Merritt sailed from Manila for Paris to attend the peace conference...30 Aug. "

The U. S. Cuban evacuation commissioners arrived at Havana..10 Sept. "

Adm. Cervera and other Spanish naval officers sailed for Spain..13 Sept. "

U. S. peace commissioners were appointed, 9 Sept.; they sailed for France ....17 Sept. "

Spanish peace commissioners were announced.......18 Sept. "

The evacuation of Porto Rico by the Spaniards began..20 Sept. "

A commission appointed by the president to investigate the conduct of the War Department began its sessions..24 Sept. "

The peace commissioners meet in Paris................1 Oct. "

The battle-ships *Oregon* and *Iowa* sailed from New York for Manila..12 Oct. "

Peace jubilee celebration at Chicago.................18 Oct. "

The American army and navy took formal possession of the island of Porto Rico at San Juan......................18 Oct. "

Time limit for the evacuation of Cuba by the Spaniards was extended to 1 Jan. 1899 ....24 Oct. "

After a long and earnest contention the Spanish peace commissioners accepted the American ultimatum not to assume the Spanish Cuban debt...............................27 Oct. "

The U. S. peace commissioners presented the demand of the U. S. for the Philippines ....31 Oct. "

The captured cruiser *Infanta Maria Teresa* was abandoned in a gale off San Salvador ....1 Nov. "

The Cuban assembly was organized at Santa Cruz del Sur; Domingo Mendez Capote was elected president......7 Nov. "

Spain abandons Cuba, the Philippines, and other islands for an indemnity of $20,000,000, 28 Nov.; treaty signed, 10 Dec.; ratified...6 Feb. 1899

American loss in the war: 336 men killed, 125 mortally wounded, 5277 died of disease.........1 May, 1898–18 Feb. "

Spanish loss, 80,000, the majority dying from disease; reported..25 Jan. 1899

Spanish era or **Era of the Cæsars,** is reckoned from 1 Jan. 38 B.C., the year following the conquest of Spain by Augustus. It was much used in Africa, Spain, and the south of France; but by a synod held in 1180 was abolished in all churches dependent on Barcelona. Pedro IV. of Aragon abolished it in his dominions in 1350; John of Castile in 1383. It was used in Portugal till 1415, if not till 1422. The months and days of this era are identical with the Julian calendar; and to turn the time into our era, subtract 38 from the year (if before the Christian era, 39).

Spanish Fury, the. ANTWERP.

Spanish grandees, the higher nobility, at one time almost equal to kings of Castile and Aragon, and often defying these, were restrained in 1474 on the union of the crowns by the marriage of Ferdinand and Isabella, who expelled many from the royal fortresses and domains. Charles V. reduced the grandees to 16 families (Medina-Sidonia, Albuquerque, etc.), dividing them into 3 classes.

Spanish language (*lengua Castellana*), derived from a dialect of Latin mingled with Arabic, which was the legal language till the 14th century. Spanish did not become general till the 16th century. LITERATURE.

Spanish main, the waters along the coast of South America, formerly so called because frequented by the Spanish vessels and somewhat under the jurisdiction of Spain.

Spanish Succession, War of the. When Charles II. of Spain died in 1700, leaving no heir, 4 European powers, France, Germany, Bavaria, and Savoy, with nearly equal rights, claimed succession. The last two retiring left the dispute to France and Germany; war ensued (1702–13), and England joined Germany. The French claimant, grandson of Louis XIV., was finally acknowledged as Philip V. of Spain. HOUSE OF BOURBON. This war, although distinguished by the achievements of the duke of Marlborough, earl of Peterborough, and prince Eugene, was without advantage to England.

Sparta, the capital of Laconia or Lacedæmon, the most considerable republic of the Peloponnesus, and the rival of Athens. Though without walls, it resisted its enemies by the valor of its citizens for 8 centuries. Lelex is supposed to have been first king. Lacedæmon, 4th king, and his wife Sparta, were the legendary founders of the city named for them. The Lacedæmonians were a nation of soldiers, and cultivated neither the arts or sciences, and paid but little attention to commerce or agriculture, all cultivation of the land being performed by slaves. The early history is mythical.

B.C.

Sparta founded (*Pausanias*)................................ 1490

Princes of Greece demand Helen in marriage; she makes choice of Menelaus of Mycenæ................................ 1216

Helen, daughter of Zeus and of Leda, the wife of Tyndarus, king of Sparta, stolen by Theseus, king of Athens, but recovered by her brothers Castor and Pollux.................. 1213

Paris, son of Priam, king of Troy, carries off Helen........... 1204

Trojan war (TROY).. 1194

After a war of 10 years, and a disastrous voyage of nearly 8, Menelaus and Helen return to Sparta..................... 1176

Kingdom seized by the HERACLIDÆ............................ 1104

Establishment of 2 kings, Eurysthenes and Procles, by their father Aristodemus.. 1100

Rule of Lycurgus, who establishes the senate, and enacts a code of laws (*Eusebius*). (Mythical).....................884–50

Charilaus declares war against Polymnestor, king of Arcadia.. 848

Alcamenes, known by his apophthegms, makes war on the Messenians.. 813

Nicander succeeds his father, Charilaus; war with the Argives, 800

Theopompus introduces the EPHORI.......................about 757

War against the Messenians; Amphia taken.................. 743

Partheniæ, sons of virgins, without the marriage rite......... 733

Battle of Ithome; Messenians beaten........................ 730

Ithome taken; the Messenians become vassals to Sparta, and the war of 19 years ends.................................. 724

Partheniæ, becoming a class, conspire with HELOTS to take Sparta.. 707

Conspiracy discovered, the Partheniæ sent to colonize Tarentum 706

Messenians revolt, and league with Elis, Argos, and Arcadia, against the Lacedæmonians. (This war lasted 14 years)..... 685

Carnian festivals instituted................................ 675

Messenians settle in Sicily................................ 669

War with the Argives, and celebrated battle between 300 select heroes of each nation.................................. 547

War with Athens.. 505

Spartans resist the king of Persia.......................... 491

States of Greece unite against the Persians 482
Leonidas with 300 Spartans, withstands the Persians at the defile of THERMOPYLÆ 480
Pausanias king, defeats the Persians at Platæa 479
He is put to death for treason, the Greeks choose an Athenian general 472
Earthquake at Sparta destroys 30,000 persons, rebellion of the Helots 466
Sparta joins Macedon against Athens 431
Platæa taken by the Spartans 429
Spartans, under Agis, enter Attica and lay waste the country, 426
Agis (king 427) defeats Argives and Mantineans 418
Lacedæmonian fleet under Mindarus, defeated at Cyzicum, and Mindarus slain 410
Spartans defeated by land and at sea, sue for peace, which is denied by the Athenians 409
Reign of Pausanias 408
Athenians defeated at Ægospotami by Lysander 405
Athens taken by him, end of Peloponnesian war 404
[Sparta at the height of its power]
Agesilaus (king 398) enters Lydia 396
Athenians Thebans, Argives and Corinthians league against the Spartans, Corinthian war begins 395
Lysander killed at Haliartus "
Agesilaus defeats the allies at Coronea 394
Lacedæmonian fleet under Peisander, defeated by Conon, Athenian commander, near Cnidos "
Peace of Antalcidas 387
Thebans drive the Spartans from Cadmea 378
Spartans lose dominion of the seas, their fleet destroyed by Timotheus 376
Spartans defeated at Leuctra 371
Epaminondas, heading 50,000 Thebans appears before Sparta 369
Battle of Mantinea, the Thebans victors 27 June, 362
Philip of Macedon overcomes Sparta 344
Pyrrhus defeated before Sparta 294
Agis IV endeavors to revive the laws of Lycurgus 244
Leonidas II vacates the throne, and flees 243
Recalled becomes sole sovereign, Agis killed 241
Reign of Cleomenes III the son of Leonidas 236
He re establishes most of the laws of Lycurgus 225
Antigonus defeats Cleomenes, and enters Sparta 222
Cleomenes retires to Egypt "
Spartans murder the Ephori 221
Machanidus king, abolishes the Ephori 210
He is defeated and slain by Philopœmen, prætor of the Achæan league 207
Cruel government of Nabis "
Romans besiege Sparta, Nabis sues for peace 197
Ætolians seize Sparta, Nabis assassinated 192
Laws of Lycurgus abolished 188
Sparta, under protection of Rome, again the leading state 147
A D
Taken by Alaric 396
Taken by Mahomet II 1460
Burned by Sigismund Malatesti 1463
Rebuilt at Misitra, Sparta is now part of Greece 1894

Spartacus's insurrection (or Servile war) Spartacus was a noble Thracian, who served in an auxiliary corps of the Roman army Having deserted and been apprehended, he was reduced to slavery and made a gladiator With some companions he made his escape, collected a body of slaves and gladiators, 73 B C, ravaged southern Italy, and defeated 4 consular armies sent against him Knowing the impossibility of successfully resisting the republic alone, he endeavored to conduct his forces into Gaul, there to invite Sertorius from Spain to join him, had this plan succeeded it would have endangered the republic, but his undisciplined followers compelled him to relinquish it and move towards Rome, when he was met by Crassus, his forces defeated, and himself slain, 71 B C

"Spasmodic school" of poetry, a name sarcastically given to Alex Smith, Sydney Dobell (d Aug 1874), Gerald Massey, and others (precursors of Morris, Algernon Swinburne, and Rossetti, sarcastically termed the "fleshly school"), ridiculed by prof Aytoun in his "Firmilian," pub 1854

speakers of the House of Commons. Peter de Montford, afterwards killed at the battle of Evesham, was the first speaker, 45 Hen III 1260, sir Thos Hungerford is said to have been the first named "speaker," 1372, but sir Peter de la Mare is supposed to have been the first regular speaker, 50 Edw III 1376

speakers of the House of Representatives of the UNITED STATES

"Speaker's Commentary." This edition of the Bible, with a revised text and a commentary by bishops and other theologians, edited by F C Cook, was planned, it is said, by John Evelyn Denison, speaker of the House of Commons, to refute the interpretations of dr Colenso, and was announced in Nov 1863 The publication began in 1871.

speaking-trumpet, a conical flaring mouth-tube employed in intensifying the sound of the voice, used in giving commands to persons at a distance, etc One is said to have been used by Alexander, 335 B C One was constructed from Kircher's description by Saland, 1652, philosophically explained and brought into notice by Morland, 1670.

spear, one of the most ancient weapons of war or hunting, consisting at first of a pointed wooden, then stone, afterwards bronze, and lastly iron or steel blade on a long shaft, similar to the PIKE

special or extra sessions of Congress. UNITED STATES

species. Much controversy among naturalists arose in consequence of the publication, in 1859, of Charles Darwin's "Origin of Species," containing proof that all the various species of animals were not created at one time, but have been gradually developed by what he terms "natural selection" and the struggle for life in which the strong overcome the weak "This preservation of favorable individual differences and variations, and the destruction of those which are injurious, I have called *natural selection* or the survival of the fittest"—*Darwin*

The idea of evolution was put forth by Lamarck in his "Philosophie Zoologique" 1809 Similar views appear in "Vestiges of Creation" 1844 Mr Darwin says that he infers "from analogy that probably all the organic beings which have ever lived on the earth have descended from some one primordial form, into which life was first breathed by the Creator" (DEVELOPMENT EVOLUTION) Prof G J Romanes s elaborate work, "Darwin and After Darwin," was pub 1892 LITERATURE

specific gravities. ELEMENTS, WEIGHTS

spectacles, an optical instrument used to assist or to correct defects of vision, unknown to the ancients, are generally supposed to have been invented by Alexander de Spina, a monk of Florence, in Italy, about 1285 According to dr Plott they were invented by Roger Bacon, about 1280 Manni attributes them to Salvino, who died 1317 On his tomb at Florence is the inscription, "Qui giace Salvino degli Armati, inventore degli occhiali Dio gli perdoni le peccata" ("Here lies Salvino degli Armati, inventor of spectacles may God pardon his sins")

"Spectator," a periodical The first number appeared in London on 1 Mch 1711, the last was No 635, 20 Dec 1714 The papers by Addison have one of the letters C. L I O at the end Most of the other papers are by sir Richard Steele, a few by Hughes, Budgell, Eusden, Miss Shephard and others The *Spectator* newspaper (philosophical, whig), begun 5 July, 1828

spec'troscope, an instrument for the forming and examining of spectra Its invention grew out of sir Isaac Newton's discovery of the solar spectrum, followed up by Wollaston's experiments, 1802, and by Fraunhofer, 1814-15. The instrument was greatly improved by profs Kirchhoff and Bunsen in 1859 as a means of chemical analysis. SPECTRUM

spec'trum, the image of the sun or any luminous body formed on a wall or screen, by a beam of light received through a small hole or slit, and refracted by a prism. The colors thus produced were regarded by Newton as 7 red, orange, yellow, green, blue, indigo, and violet. The phenomena were first explained by Newton, whose "Optics" was published in 1704. By many physicists, only 3 primary colors are recognized by Mayer (1775), red, yellow, and blue, by dr Thomas Young (1801), red, green, and violet, by prof. Clerk Maxwell (1860), red, green, and blue. As the color of a flame varies according to the substance burned in it, so the spectrum varies This fact was applied to chemical analysis by profs Bunsen and Kirchhoff (1860), who have discovered 2 new metals, and ascertained the presence of many substances in the atmosphere of the sun and stars, and even in the nebulæ, by comparing their spectra with those artificially produced by burning iron, sodium, and other substances For invisible rays, CALORESCENCE, FLUORESCENCE

Fraunhofer's lines In 1802 dr Wollaston observed several dark lines in the solar spectrum, in 1815 Joseph Fraunhofer constructed a map of 590 lines or dark bands. Brewster and others have increased the number to more than 2000.

Fox Talbot observed the orange line of strontium in the spectrum in 1826 sir David Brewster other lines, 1833-42-43 In 1862-63 William Huggins analyzed the light of the fixed stars and nebulæ, and in 1865 dr Bence Jones by spectrum analyses, detected minute quantities of metals in the living body, introduced a few minutes previously

Spectroscopic society in Italy pub a journal early in 1872

Lecoq de Boisbaudran's "Spectres Lumineux" 1874

Oxygen detected in the solar system by dr Draper of New York, 1877

Spectra of the stars photographed by dr Draper of New York, 1872 that of a comet's tail 1881

H Schellen's "Spectral Analyse" pub 1870, new edition 1883

H Roscoe's "Spectrum Analysis" pub 1867-85

Experiments of prof Dewar and others have shown that the spectra of various gases are affected by temperature and pressure 1888 89

"Spec'ulum Hu'manæ." BOOKS, PRINTING

sphere, an orb, a globe, a solid or volume bounded by a surface every point of which is equally distant from its central point Celestial and terrestrial spheres and sun-dials are said to have been invented by Anaximander 552 B.C., and the armillary sphere by Eratosthenes, about 225 B.C. The planetarium was constructed by Archimedes before 212 B.C. Pythagoras maintained that the motions of the 12 spheres must produce delightful sounds, inaudible to mortals, which he called the music of the spheres

Sphinx, The Great, near the Great Pyramid of Ghizeh, hewn of solid granite, represents the crouching body of a lion with the head of a man The body is 140 feet long from shoulders to rump, the fore-part, including the neck and head, 100 feet high, the head being 28 feet 6 inches, the fore-legs and paws 35 feet long Made about the time of the Great Pyramid EGYPT, IV Dynasty

sphyg'mograph (from the Gr σφυγμός, a pulsation), an instrument for recording the action of the pulse, invented by E J Marey, of Paris, and described by him in 1863

spin'et, a keyed musical instrument, resembling a clavichord, used in the 17th century, a modification of the VIRGINAL Bull, Gibbons, Purcell, and especially Domenico Scarlatti composed for this instrument

spinning, the drawing out and twisting into threads either by the hand or by machinery The first spinning was done by the spindle and distaff and was ascribed by the ancients to Minerva, the goddess of wisdom Arcas king of Arcadia, taught his subjects the art about 1500 B.C. Tradition reports that Lucretia with her maids was found spinning when her husband Collatinus visited her from the camp, that the wife of Tarquin was an excellent spinner, and that a garment made by her, worn by Servius Tullius, was preserved in the temple of Fortune Cotton was spun by the hand spinning-wheel, probably erroneously stated to have been invented at Nuremberg about 1530, till 1767, when Hargreaves, an ingenious mechanic near Blackburn, Engl. made a spinning-jenny, with 8 spindles, and also erected the first carding-machine, with cylinders Arkwright's machine for spinning by water was an extension of the principle of Hargreaves, but he also applied a large and small roller to expand the thread, for which he took out a patent in 1769 At first he worked his machinery by horses, but in 1771 he built a mill on the stream of the Derwent, at Cromford. In 1774-79, Crompton invented the MULE

Spino'zaism. PHILOSOPHY

Spires (*spirz*), capital of Rhenish Bavaria The German emperors held many diets at Spires after 1309, and it was the seat of the imperial chamber till 1688, when the city was burned by the French, and not rebuilt till after the peace of Ryswick, in 1697 The diet to condemn the reformers was held at Spires, called there by the emperor Charles V, 1529 It was taken by the French in 1792, and again in 1794 PROTESTANTS.

spirit-level, A straight bar, enclosing on its upper side a slightly curved glass tube containing alcohol (whence the name) In use by carpenters, masons, surveyors, etc. The invention is ascribed to J Melchisedec Thevenot, who first described it at Paris, 15 Nov 1666 Thevénot died 1692

spirits. DISTILLATION In all nations spirituous liquors have been considered as a proper subject of heavy taxation. ALCOHOL, BRANDY. The number of gallons of distilled spirits produced in the United States, 1890, was 111,101,738, 1891, 117,186,114 Internal-revenue receipts for the fiscal year ending 30 June, 1890, $81,682,970

spiritual'ism or **spirit'ism,** a word applied to the belief that certain phenomena or visible manifestations of power are produced by the spirits of the dead These phenomena have been witnessed and commented upon in all ages, notable instances within the last 250 years at Woodstock, 1649, at Tedworth, 1661, at the Epworth parsonage, in the family of Mr Wesley, the father of John Wesley, the founder of Methodism, the case of the COCK-LANE GHOST, in London, at Sunderland, at the residence of Mr Jobson, 1839 (all these in England) The Fox sisters in the United States, 1848 (noted below), and, as some suppose, in the Salem WITCHCRAFT cases of 1692 They have been attributed to diabolical agencies It is claimed that under favorable circumstances, by a force apparently residing in the subject itself, and with no external source, inanimate objects (articles of furniture, etc) are moved, rappings are heard, articles disappear from one closed apartment to appear in another, writing is produced purporting to be by spirits of the dead, and apparitions of the dead are recognized by voice and feature Multitudes of people, including many of education and intelligence, have embraced the vague beliefs taught by professional mediums, but the teachers have never agreed upon any coherent system of doctrine, nor have their practices been satisfactorily distinguished from delusion and imposture by scientific tests Emmanuel Swedenborg (1668-1772) asserted his intelligent communion with departed spirits and his direct knowledge of a spiritual world, reciting at length his detailed personal experience The more recent forms of spiritualism may be said to have begun in Hydesville, Wayne county, N Y, in 1848, when the daughters of John D Fox, Margaret (1834-93) and Kate (1836-92), first practised what is known as "spirit-rappings" From Hydesville, Fox soon after removed to Rochester The excitement aroused by the rappings soon spread far and wide Many "mediums" arose professing similar powers Andrew Jackson Davis pub "Principles of Nature," etc, 1845, said to have dictated to the rev William Fishbough in New York city, while the author was in a clairvoyant or trance state, many other works since on a variety of subjects, all ascribed to spirit dictation, but of no scientific value Judge John W Edmonds of New York (1799-1874) adopted the belief in 1851, and pub a work on "Spiritualism," 1853-55, as did dr. Robert Hare (1781-1858) of Philadelphia, who pub (1855) "Spiritual Manifestations Scientifically Demonstrated," among other noted persons who have avowed their belief that the phenomena are of spirit origin are dr Robert Chambers, Robert Owen (1771-1858), and his son, Robert Dale Owen, all of whom have written on the subject Of the many "mediums" (channels of communications), none ever attained to the celebrity, as a medium of this power, of Daniel D Home (b. 1833, d harmlessly insane, 1886, pub. "Incidents of My Life," 1863) A society termed "The London Society for Psychical Research," was founded in 1882, under the presidency of prof. H Sidgwick of Cambridge university, for the purpose of investigating that large group of debatable phenomena known as mesmeric, hypnotic, psychic, and spiritualistic Reports of a large number of varied and careful experiments in induced telepathic communication are published in their "Proceedings," branches of this society have been established elsewhere, notably in the U S In this connection also an international congress of experimental psychology has been formed 1st meeting, held in Paris, 1889, 2d, at University college, London, 1893, the next, the 3d, to be held at Munich in 1896 In a report of this congress 1893 it was stated that in a census of hallucinations undertaken by 410 members of the congress, 17,000 answers were obtained from Great Britain, France, America, Germany, etc, to the question, "Have you ever, while in good health and believing yourself to be awake, seen the figure of a person or animated object, or heard a voice which was not in your view referable to any external physical cause?" The answers in the negative numbered 15,311, and those in the affirmative 1689, out of these latter, after careful investigation, the committee classed 348 as actual apparitions of living persons, 155 of dead people, 273 as unrecognized A remarkable class of cases was that of collective apparitions, the same hallucination being experienced by 2 or more persons at the same time and place Some hold that all psychic phenomena, normal and abnormal, whether manifested as mesmerism, hypnotism, somnambulism, trance, spiritism, demonology or witchcraft genius or insanity, are in a way related, and are to be classed under some general law of nature yet to be discovered, which will withdraw them from the domain of the supernatural

Spitz'bergen, an archipelago in the Arctic ocean, discovered in 1553 by sir Hugh Willoughby, who called it Greenland, supposing it part of the western continent In 1595 Barentz and Cornelius, 2 Dutchmen, pretending to be original discoverers, visited and called it Spitzbergen, or sharp mountains, from its many sharp-pointed and rocky mountains Phipps.

spontaneous combustion of the human body, declared by chemists impossible, although many cases are reported The case of the countess of Gorlitz, 1847, disproved by confession of her murderer, Mch 1850

spontaneous generation. The origin of infusorial animalcules developed during putrefaction, etc, has been warmly debated by naturalists Spallanzani (about 1760), and especially M Pasteur and others of later times, assert that germs endowed with organic life exist in the atmosphere Needham (about 1747), and especially M Pouchet and his friends in our day, assert that these germs are spontaneously formed of organic molecules Pouchet's "Hétérogénie" appeared in 1859, Bastian's "Beginnings of Life," 1872 The researches of prof Tyndall, supporting Pasteur, and opposing Bastian, were published 1876-78 "Spontaneous generation" (also termed *generatio æquivoca* and *epigenesis*) has been further disproved by the microscopic investigations of the rev W H Dallinger, 1875-78 He found germs to stand much greater heat than perfect organisms.

sporting newspapers. Newspapers.

sports and **games.** The fullest development of ancient sports and games obtained among the Greeks, usually as a part of religious observances. (Olympian games, also Pythian, Isthmian, and Nemean) The Bacchanalia were introduced into Greece from Egypt Chariot races, gladiatorial combats, naval battles, etc., were held in the Circus Maximus at Rome (Circus) and at the Coliseum. In England, the first "Book of Sports," under the title, "The King's Majestie's Declaration to His Subjects Concerning Lawful Sports," to be used on Sundays after evening prayers, was published by king James I, 24 May, 1618, and led to long and bitter controversy among English divines (Sabbatarians) The book was ordered burned by the hangman, and the sports were suppressed by Parliament.

PRINCIPAL SPORTS AND GAMES OF AMERICA AND ENGLAND

(For history, etc , of each, see under their various titles)

Angling	Fox hunting (Hunting)
Archery	Golf
Backgammon	Hawking
Bagatelle	Hunting
Base ball.	Ice yachting (Sailing)
Bicycling	Lacrosse
Billiards	Lawn tennis.
Bowling	Pedestrianism
Boxing	Polo
Cards	Prize fighting (Boxing)
Checkers (Draughts)	Quoits
Chess	Horse racing
Cricket	Rowing
Croquet	Sailing
Curling	Skating
Dice	Stag hunting (Hunting)
Dominos.	Swimming
Draughts	Tennis
Falconry	Trap shooting
Fencing	Whist.
Foot ball.	Yachting (Sailing)

Spottsylvania, Va., Battle of. Grant's campaign in Virginia

Springfield, N. J., burned by the British troops. New Jersey, 1780.

spurs. Anciently knights were distinguished by wearing gilt spurs (*eques auratus*) from esquires with silver ones 2 sorts of spurs seem to have been in use at the time of the Conquest, one called a pryck, with a single point, the other a number of larger points. Spurs nearly of the present kind came into use about 1400.

Spurs, Battle of. Henry VIII of England, the emperor Maximilian, and the Swiss, in 1513, made an offensive alliance against France Henry VIII landed at Calais in the month of July, and soon formed an army of 30,000 men He was joined by the emperor with a good corps of horse and some foot, as a mercenary to the king of England, who allowed him a hundred ducats a day for his table! They invested Terouenne with an army of 50 000 men, and the duc de Longueville, marching to its relief, was signally defeated on 16 Aug, at Guinegate. This battle was called the battle of Spurs, because the French used their spurs more than their swords The English king laid siege to Tournay, which submitted in a few days —*Hénault* Courtrai

squatter sovereignty. Popular sovereignty

Squire's Letters. Literature, Forgeries of

SS. A symbol of unknown antiquity worn on the collars of the superior judges and lord mayors in England, formerly by persons attached to the royal household and others. It was assumed by certain classes, never bestowed, and had no connection with heraldry —*Stormonth* Some writers consider the symbol to be in honor of St Simplicius, a martyr, others, an adaptation of the widely spread and mysterious symbol of the entwined or contorted serpent, having the head and tail hanging downwards. On legal documents, SS. or ss. (*scilicet*) means, to wit, namely

Sta'bat Ma'ter, a Latin hymn, by Jacopone, 14th century, sung during Passion week in Catholic churches Rossini's music to this hymn (1842) is often performed

Stade dues. At a castle near the town of Stade, in Hanover, certain dues on goods were charged by the Hanoverian government The British government settled these dues in 1844 They were resisted by the Americans in 1855, and were abolished in June, 1861 Great Britain paid 160,000*l* as her share of the compensation (3,000,000*l*.)

stadt'holder. Holland.

stage-coaches, so called from the stages or inns at which the coaches stopped to refresh and change horses.—*Bailey* The custom of running stage-coaches in England was introduced from the Continent, but in what year the first stage run is not known, probably in the latter part of the 16th or early in the 17th century Introduced into Scotland in 1610 by Henry Anderson, running between Edinburgh and Leith In 1659 the Coventry coach is referred to, and in 1661 the Oxford stage-coach By the middle of the 18th century the stage-coach was in extensive use In 1757 the London and Manchester stage-coach made the trip, 187 miles, in 3 days regularly, afterwards reduced to 19 hours, and the London and Edinburgh stage coach ultimately made the distance between these cities, 400 miles, in 40 hours, including all stops, etc., the roads being excellent, the coaches and service admirable, and the number of horses equal to the number of miles, namely 400, and the relays frequent. The first mail-coach was set up at Bristol, by John Palmer, 2 Aug 1784. In the U. S. the first stage was run between New York city and Boston, 1732, probably not regularly and not long continued. In 1756 there was 1 stage-coach running between New York city and Philadelphia, distance 90 miles, time 3 days. In 1765 a second stage-coach was put on In 1796 the line was increased to 4 coaches, and in 1811 there were 4 coaches each way daily The 1st line, named the "Expedition," from Philadelphia to Paulus Hook—time, 12 hours, fare, $8 00 2d, "The Diligence" —time, 26 hours, fare, $5 50 3d, "Accommodation," left Philadelphia at 10 A.M, stopping overnight at Brunswick, N J, arriving at Paulus Hook 12 M next day, fare, $4 50 4th, "Mail Coach," left Philadelphia 1 P M., travelled all night, arrived at Paulus Hook at 6 A.M. At this time the coaches were poorly constructed for 8 to 10 passengers, each passenger allowed 14 pounds of luggage free—150 pounds the extent In later years the stage-coach was improved, but was never agreeable, as the roads were always bad, except in the finest weather.

Stag'irite. Aristotle, under Philosophy

Staked Plains or **Lla'no Estaca'do,** extensive table-lands in western Texas and eastern New Mexico, hose surface, gently undulating, is destitute of wood and ater, vegetation very scanty The name is derived from .e abundant growth of the *Yucca aloifolia*, or "Spanish iggers," the naked stems of which, growing to the height 10 feet, resemble stakes

Stalwart. POLITICAL PARTIES

Stamford-Bridge, York, Engl In 1066, Tostig, other of Harold II, rebelled against his brother and joined e invading army of Harold Hardrada, king of Norway hey defeated the northern earls, Edwin and Morcar, and ok York, but were defeated at Stamford-Bridge by Har-.l, 25 Sept, and were both slain The loss by this battle doubt led to Harold's defeat at HASTINGS, 11 Oct follow-g

Stamp act of 1765. STATE RECORDS, UNITED ATES

stamp-duties in England By 22 and 23 Charles II 670-71), duties were imposed on certain legal documents 1694 a duty was imposed upon paper, vellum, and parch ent The stamp-duty on newspapers began 1711, and every ar added to the list of articles paying stamp-duty

amp act, which led to the Revolution, passed 22 Mch 1765, repealed in 1766
amp duties in Ireland commenced 1774
amps on notes and bills of exchange in 1782
amp duties produced in England 3,126 535*l* 1800
[Many alterations made in 1853 and 1857 In June, 1855, he stamp duty on newspapers was abolished, the stamp on hem being henceforth for postal purposes]
July and Aug 1854, 19 115 000 newspaper stamps were is sued, in the same months only 6,870,000 in 1855
afts on bankers to be stamped 1858
ditional stamp duties were enacted in 1860 (on leases, bills of exchange, dock warrants, extracts from registers of births, etc), on leases, licenses to house agents, etc) 1861
amp duties reduced in 1864-65
fees payable in the superior courts of law after 31 Dec. 865, are to be collected by stamps, by an act passed in June, 865, also in Public Record office 1868
623 014 inland revenue penny stamps sold, besides other stamps. 1869
the Stamp acts, 10 Aug 1870, newspaper stamps were abol shed after 1 Oct 1870
w stamp duties imposed, came into effect. 1 Jan 1871
e penny receipt and postage stamps used for each other fter 1 June, 1881
.mp-duties imposed on foreign or colonial share certificates, bonds, etc , by custom act 1888

OUNT OF STAMP-DUTIES RECEIVED IN THE UNITED KINGDOM

0	£6,726,817	1876	£11,002,000
5	7,710 683	1881	11,933,114
0.	6,558,332	1882	12,348,175
5	6,805,605	1883	11,691,025
0	8,040,091	1885	11,886,185
5	9,542,645	1889	12 270,000
0	9,288,553	1891	13,460,000

standard for gold and silver in England fixed by law, 00 Standard gold is 22 parts out of 24 of pure gold, the er 2 parts, or carats, being silver or copper The standard silver is 11 oz 2 dwts. of fine silver alloyed with 18 dwts. copper, or 37 parts out of 40 pure silver, and 3 parts copper. 1300 these 12 oz of silver were coined into 20 shillings, in 12 they were coined into 30 shillings, and in 1527 into 45 llings In 1545, Henry VIII coined 6 oz of silver and 6 of alloy into 48 shillings; and the next year he coined 4 of silver and 8 oz of alloy into the same sum Elizabeth, 1560, restored the old standard in 60 shillings, and in 1601 62 shillings It is now 66 shillings The standard proportion of silver to gold at the royal mint is 15½ to 1. The ndard of plate and silver manufactures was affirmed, 6 Geo 1719 et seq COIN, GOLD, GOLDSMITHS, SILVER

Standard, Battle of the NORTHALLERTON

standard measures. In the reign of Edgar, a law s made in England to prevent frauds arising from the diversity of measures, and to establish a legal standard measure every part of his dominions The standard vessels made by ler of the king were deposited in the city of Winchester, and nce originated the term "Winchester measure" of the time Henry VII (1487) The bushel so made is still preserved the museum of that city. Henry I also, to prevent frauds the measurement of cloth, ordered a standard yard of the gth of his arm to be deposited at Winchester, with the standard measures of king Edgar The Guildhall contains the standard measures of succeeding sovereigns —*Camden.* The standard weights and measures were settled by Parliament in 1824 The pound troy was to be 5760 grains, and the pound avoirdupois 7000 grains The "Standard yard of 1760," in the custody of the clerk of the House of Commons, was declared to be the imperial standard yard and the unit of measures of extension This standard, supposed to have been burned at the fire of the parliament-house, 1834 (since discovered, July, 1891, in the *Journal* office), a new commission was appointed to reconstruct it, and researches for this purpose in conformity with the act, which directed the comparison of the standard with a pendulum vibrating seconds of time in the latitude of London, were begun by Francis Baily (d in 1844), continued by the rev R Sheepshanks till his death in 1855, and completed by G B Airy, astronomer royal. In 1855 was passed "An Act for Legalizing and Preserving Lost Standards of Weights and Measures" The parliamentary copies of the standard pound and yard are deposited at the Royal observatory, Greenwich The Standard Weights and Measures act was passed Aug 1866. The Standard Commission published reports, 1866 et seq

standard time. Chiefly for the convenience of railroads in the United States a standard of time was established by mutual agreement in 1883, on principles first suggested by Charles F Dowd, of Saratoga Springs, New York, by which trains are run and local time regulated The U S, beginning at its extreme eastern limit and extending to the Pacific coast, is divided into 4 time-sections eastern, central, mountain, and Pacific The eastern section, the time of which is that of the 75th meridian, lies between the Atlantic ocean and an irregular line drawn from Detroit Mich , to Charleston, S C The central, the time of which is that of the 90th meridian, includes all between the last-named line and an irregular line from Bismarck, N Dak , to the mouth of the Rio Grande. The mountain, the time of which is that of the 105th meridian, includes all between the last-named line and the western boundary of Montana, Idaho, Utah, and Arizona The Pacific, the time of which is that of the 120th meridian, includes all between the last-named line and the Pacific coast The difference in time between adjoining sections is 1 hour Thus, when it is 12 o'clock noon in New York city (eastern time), it is 11 o'clock A M (central time) at Chicago, and 10 o'clock A M at Denver (mountain time), and at San Francisco, 9 o'clock A M (Pacific time) The true local time of any place is slower or faster than the standard time as the place is east or west of the *time* meridian, thus, the true local time at Boston, Mass, is 16 minutes faster than eastern standard time, while at Buffalo, N Y, it is 16 minutes slower, the 75th *time* meridian being half-way between Boston and Buffalo Local time and standard time agree at Denver, Col , as Denver is on the 105th meridian, that of the mountain section

standards, a flag or ensign round which men rally or unite for a common purpose, also an emblem of nationality The practice of an army using standards dates from the earliest times The emblem of the cross on standards and shields is due to the asserted miraculous appearance of a cross to Constantine, previous to his battle with Maxentius, Eusebius says that he received this statement from the emperor himself, 312. The standard was named *labarum* For the celebrated French standard, AURIFLAMME The British imperial standard was first hoisted on the Tower of London, and on Bedford tower, Dublin, and displayed by the Foot Guards, on the union of the kingdoms, 1 Jan. 1801. BANNERS, FLAGS, SACRED STANDARD.

starch is a sediment falling when wheat is steeped in water, it is soft and friable, easily broken into powder, and is used to stiffen and clear linen, with blue, its powder is used on the hair The art of starching linen was brought into England by Mrs Dinghein, a Flemish woman, 1 Mary, 1553 —*Stow* Patents for obtaining starch from other substances have been taken out from potatoes by Samuel Newton and others, in 1707, from the horse-chestnut by William Murray, in 1796; from rice by Thomas Wickham, in 1823, from various matters by Orlando Jones, in 1839–40.

Star-chamber, Court of So called from its roof

being garnished with stars.—*Coke.* This court of justice w
called Star-chamber, not from the stars on its roof (whic
were obliterated even before the reign of queen Elizabeth
but from the Starra, or Jewish covenants, deposited there b
order of Richard I. No star was allowed to be valid exce
found in those repositories, and here they remained till t
banishment of the Jews by Edward I. The court was ins
tuted or revived, 3 Hen. VII. 1486, for trials by a committ
of the privy council, which was in violation of Magna Char
as it dealt with civil and criminal causes unfettered by t
rules of law. In Charles I.'s reign it punished several b
innovators, who gloried in their sufferings, and contributed
render government odious and contemptible. It was abolis
in 1640. There were in this court from 26 to 42 judges,
lord chancellor having the casting vote.

Star of India, a new order of knighthood for In
instituted by letters-patent 23 Feb., gazetted 25 *June,* 18
and enlarged in 1866. Motto, "*Heaven's light our guide.*"
comprised the sovereign, the grandmaster, 25 knights (Eu
peans and natives), and extra or honorary knights, such
the prince-consort, the prince of Wales, etc. Queen Victo
invested several knights on 1 Nov. 1861. The prince
Wales held a grand chapter at Calcutta, 1 Jan. 1876.

star-routes, routes on which contracts for carry
the United States mail are made upon bids which do
specify the mode of conveyance, but simply offer to carry
mails regularly, safely, and expeditiously. Such bids ar
garded by the post-office department as *inferior* to those w
specify *railroad, steamboat,* or *four-horse-coach* conveya
but as superior to those which specify only horseback carr
In 1881 second assistant postmaster-general Thomas J. Br
ex-senator Stephen W. Dorsey of Arkansas, and others,
accused of conspiracy to defraud the U. S. government in
management of these routes. They were brought to tr
June, 1882; 1st trial closed 11 Sept., jury not agreeing
trial began 4 Dec. 1882, closed 11 June, 188 . Verdict
guilty as indicted. UNITED STATES.

stars, the fixed. Each of those lu
the unassisted sight reveals to us by tho
heaven, which the telescope shows by
of space, shines with its own light, a
light and heat to a planetary system
were classed in constellations, it is su
Hicetas, of Syracuse, taught that the
motionless, and that the earth moves
B.C. (this is mentioned by Cicero, and
hint of this system to Copernicus).
mention several of the constellations.
Paris contains a Chinese chart of the
B.C., in which 1460 stars are correctly
tion of the stars was discovered by
of the stars were published by the S
of Useful Knowledge in 1839, and a
sued under the superintendence of th
emy, was completed in 1859. The sta
to apparent magnitude, those visible to
the 1st, 2d, 3d, 4th, 5th, and 6th magn

The following is a list of 20 of
which are commonly regarded as of
order of brightness:

	Name.	Constellation.		
1.	Sirius	Canis Major.	11.	Al
2.	Canopus	Argo.	12.	De
3.	Alpha (a)	Centaurus.	13.	Al
4.	Arcturus	Boötes.	14.	An
5.	Rigel	Orion.	15.	Al
6.	Capella	Auriga.	16.	Sp
7.	Vega	Lyra.	17.	Fo
8.	Procyon	Canis Minor.	18.	Bet
9.	Betelgeuse	Orion.	19.	Pol
10.	Achernar	Eridanus.	20.	Reg

Argelander gives the number of stars

1st	magnitude as	20	6th	mag
2d	"	65	7th	
3d	"	190	8th	
4th	"	425	9th	
5th	"	1100		

Ptolemy names 48 constellations: 21 n
15 southern. "Chambers's Astronomy," 1
Some as high as 109. CONSTELLATIONS.

ESTIMATED DISTANCE OF SOME OF THE FIXED STARS FROM THE EARTH.

[Arranged in the order of nearness, the parallax, etc.; the distance in multiples of the sun's distance, 91,400,000 miles, and estimating the movement of light at 186,000 miles per second.]

Star.	Parallax in seconds.	Sun's distance=1.	Light to reach the earth. Time.		Estimated by
a Centaurus	0.75	275,000	4.34	years	Gill, 1883-84
61 Cygnus	0.50	412,000	6.51	"	O. Struve, 1853
Sirius	0.38	543,000	8.57	"	Gill.
Vega	0.20	1,031,000	16.27	"	"
2 Ursa Major	0.13	1,586,000	25.04	"	C. A. F. Peters.
Arcturus	0.13	1,586,000	25.04	"	"
Polaris	0.07	2,947,000	46.50	"	"
Capella	0.04	5,157,000	81.37	"	"
Canopus	0.03	6,875,000	108.50	"	Elkin.

A number of new stars have appeared and disappeared at different times. A list of about 200, which vary greatly in brightness, has been published in George F. Chambers's "Hand-book on Astronomy," 1890. New stars noted in 1848, 1866, 1876, the last in 1885, 31 Aug., in the great nebula of Andromeda of the 6th magnitude.

"Star-Spangled Banner, The." This song was written by Francis Scott Key under the following circumstances: He had gone in the *Minden*, under a flag of truce, to solicit the rele nds who had been seized by adm. Cochrane on the city of Washington. Key fo out to attack more, and while Co the prisoners, d to let him the. The car- *nden* was cHenry, and Key s ept. 1814, of that e excitem and w *Minden* ery betwe that Ke ng. It w ack of return t ell.

gener a ancie e, firs to co the p evoluti 16 of 3 y. ve c d B Ma

Philadelphus and his court in the Serapeum of Alexander, 150 B.C. This philosopher's toy may be regarded as a forecast of the modern steam-engine.

Solomon de Caus, an eminent French mathematician and engineer, publishes a work describing a method of producing a jet of water by pressure of steam generated in a tight spherical vessel.......... 1615

Giovanni Branca, an Italian mathematician, publishes an account of a method of transmitting power by a wheel furnished with vanes and revolved by a jet of impinging steam.......... 1629

Marquis of Worcester describes in his "Century of Inventions" (original in the British museum), experiments in bursting plugged cannon by steam, and also a "water commanding engine," for forcing water into a tank by steam generated in tight vessels.......... 1663

Dr. Denys Papin of Blois introduces the safety-valve in his steam bone digester.......... 1684

Capt. Savery patents an engine to raise water from mines by alternate condensation and force of steam in air-tight cylinders furnished with valves..........25 July, 1698

Thomas Newcomen, a blacksmith of Dartmouth, Engl., patents an engine with a walking-beam, for pumping water from mines. It was operated by a boy who alternately admitted steam and a jet of cold water into a cylinder fitted with a piston.......... 1705

Boy named Humphrey Potter attaches a cord from the beam to the handles of the steam and cold-water stop-cocks in the Newcomen engine, and makes it self-acting..........about 1713

Henry Beighton of Newcastle-upon-Tyne constructs a self-acting engine on the Newcomen plan; the first with a steel-yard safety-valve.......... 1718

acob Leupold, a Saxon, constructs the first high-pressure steam-engine.......... 1720

ames Watt of England obtains a patent for a rotary steam-gine.......... 1769

-carriage for common roads built by Cugnot in France.. "

vents the separate condenser and air-pump (1765), and rtnership with Matthew Boulton sets up the first en- f this kind at Kinneil, Scotland.......... 1774

Hornblower of Penryn secures a patent for an en- th 2 cylinders.......... 1781

nts a double-acting engine.......... 1782

ilt with a fly-wheel above the piston, and no beam, eas Crowther of Newcastle-upon-Tyne.......... 1800

ans introduces the high-pressure engine in America.. "

a portable engine secured by rev. Edward Cart- f England.......... 1801

and Vivian of England patent a high-pressure en-.......... 1802

l steamboat by Symington.......... "

f Philadelphia, Pa., builds a high-pressure en-.......... 1803

mpound-engine improved by Woolf.......... 1804

omotive built by Trevethick.......... "

engine general in Cornwall mines.......... 1814

m-engine expounded by Carnot.......... 1824

t practical locomotive, by Stephenson.......... 1829

l of the Steam-engine," improves the scien- e subject.......... 1859

on marine-engine, by Kirk.......... 1874

ocomotive-engine introduced.......... 1881

mer, invented by James Nasmyth in by him 18 June, 1842. Its main feature er by which the elastic power of steam is and let fall the mass of iron constituting is attached direct to the end of a piston- the bottom of an inverted steam cylinder over the anvil.

applied his steam-hammer to driving piles, the execution of great public works. Owing ver, forged iron-work can now, by its means, and for a variety of purposes, with an ease viously possible. Parts of gigantic marine , and Armstrong guns, as well as the most mery, as in Enfield rifles, are executed by

en the largest known, completed at Wool- n weighs 40 tons, and when used with top e force of 91 tons, Apr. 1874. One at zot, France; weight between 75 and 80

May, 1890. His autobiography, edited n 1883.

n. The value of steam in navi- Denys Papin in a model steam- ssel, in 1707. This was soon de- nen. Jonathan Hulls of London, a patent obtained in 1736. Ber- a steamboat, using artificial fins, ng the duck's-foot propeller, in 1757. ated the Seine with a small steam- , comte de Jouffroy, constructed an boat on the Saône. NAVY.

STE

Jaes Rumsey of Sheppardstown, Va., invents a steamboat propelled by a steam-engine expelling water through a horizontal trunk opening in the stern (1782). He experiments publicly in the presence of gen. Washington, on the Potomac river..........Sept. 1784

Jn Fitch of Philadelphia, Pa., launches a steamboat worked by vertical paddles, 6 on each side, on the Delaware river.......... 1788

rick Miller of Dalswinton, Scotland, constructs a pleasure oat with paddle-wheels (1787), to which William Symington pplies a steam-engine.......... "

Jn Fitch sails a steamboat 18 ft. long on the Collect pond, New York city, where the "Tombs" now stands.......... 1796

Fi practical steamboat, the tug *Charlotte Dundas*, built by William Symington, and tried on the Forth and Clyde canal, cotland..........Mch. 1802

ert Fulton, in connection with Chancellor Livingston, U. S. mbassador in Paris, builds a steam paddle boat, 60 ft. long, hich is tried on the Seine..........9 Aug. 1803

Jn Stevens of Hoboken, N. J., builds a steamboat with win-screw propellers and an engine supplied by a boiler.......... 1804

ton's steamboat, the *Clermont*, 160 tons, runs from New York to Albany in 32 hours, thus securing the exclusive use the Hudson for steam navigation under grant of legislature made in 1798..........Aug. 1807

Phenix, a single screw propeller built by John Stevens, makes first sea voyage of a steam-vessel from New York to hiladelphia.......... 1808

Fi steamboat on the St. Lawrence river, the *Accommodation*, uns from Montreal to Quebec.......... 1809

Fi steamboat on the western rivers, a stern-wheeler, is uilt by Fulton at Pittsburg.......... 1811

Comet, first passenger steamboat built in Europe, by Henry ell, runs on the Clyde 7½ miles per hour..........18 Jan. 1812

am ferry between New York and Jersey City.......... "

Fi steam-vessel on the Thames, brought by Mr. Dodd from lasgow.......... 1815

Fi steamboat on the great lakes, the *Ontario*, built at Sackett's Harbor, N. Y.......... 1816

Walk-in-the-Water, a steamboat for lake Erie, launched at lack Rock (now part of Buffalo, N. Y.)..........28 May, 1818

Savannah, capt. Stevens Rogers, a steamboat of 350 tons, built New York city, crosses the Atlantic from Savannah to Liverpool in 26 days, during 18 of which she uses her paddles. cape Clear she is mistaken for a ship on fire, and pursued by the British cutter *Kite*. She sails from Savannah, (NEW YORK)..........24 May, 1819

Fi sea-going steam-vessel of iron, the *Aaron Manby*, is onstructed at the Horsley iron-works, Engl.......... 1821

Fi steam voyage to India made by the *Enterprise*, capt. Johnson, from London to Calcutta in 113 days, leaving Falmouth..........16 Aug. 1825

Fulton the First accidentally blown up at New York (NAVY, 1829)..........4 June, 1829

Steamboat *Royal William* crosses the ocean from Quebec.......... 1831

John Randolph, first iron vessel in American waters, built by ohn Laird of Birkenhead, and shipped in pieces at Liverpool, built in the Savannah river as a tugboat.......... 1834

Great Western Steamship company formed, and keel of the *Great Western* (1340 tons) laid at Bristol, Engl.......... 1836

Peninsular Steamship company founded.......... 1837

Capt. Ericsson's screw-steamer, *Francis B. Ogden*, makes 10 miles per hour on the Thames..........Apr. "

Fi voyage of the steamship *Great Western*, launched 19 July, 1837, from Bristol to New York..........8-23 Apr. 1838

Sirius, built at London, crosses the Atlantic in 18½ days, reaching New York under steam a few hours before the *Great Western*..........23 Apr. "

Francis Petit Smith's propeller first tried in England on a large scale in the *Archimedes* of 237 tons.......... 1839

Unicorn, first steam-vessel from Europe to enter Boston harbor, arrives..........2 June, 1840

Fi of the Cunard line, the *Britannia*, side-wheeler, crosses Boston in 14 days 8 hours, leaving Liverpool..........4 July, "

Pacific Steam Navigation company established.......... "

Screw steamer *Princeton* built for the U. S. navy.......... 1843

Screw steamer *Great Britain*, first large ship with iron hull, designed by I. K. Brunel (3443 tons, 322 ft. long, 51 ft. broad), launched 19 July, 1843, sails from Bristol..........23 Jan. 1845

Pacific Mail Steamship company organized.......... 1847

Collins line of American steamships formed and subsidized by the U. S. government.......... 1849

[It consisted of the *Arctic*, *Baltic*, *Atlantic*, and *Pacific*, and existed 8 years. The barber-shops on shipboard were a new feature.]

Inman line founded by William Inman, and the first vessel, iron screw steamer, *City of Glasgow*, put in commission.......... 1850

Emigrants first carried in steamships of the Inman line.......... "

Allan line organized.......... 1853

Fi trip around the world by a merchant steamer, the English screw steamship *Argo*.......... 1854

Hamburg-American and Anchor lines established.......... 1856

Great Western broken up for firewood at Vauxhall.......... 1857

North German Lloyd line established.......... "

GREAT EASTERN launched..........3 Nov. 1857-31 Jan. 1858

Iron-clad steamships introduced (NAVY).......... 1860

French line established.......... 1862

Great East, with 2 screw-propellers, launched at Millwall, 31 Oct. 1863

Guion line established.......... 1864

being garnished with stars.—*Cole.* This court of justice was called Star-chamber, not from the stars on its roof (which were obliterated even before the reign of queen Elizabeth), but from the Starra, or Jewish covenants, deposited there by order of Richard I. No star was allowed to be valid except found in those repositories, and here they remained till the banishment of the Jews by Edward I. The court was instituted or revived, 3 Hen. VII. 1486, for trials by a committee of the privy council, which was in violation of Magna Charta, as it dealt with civil and criminal causes unfettered by the rules of law. In Charles I.'s reign it punished several bold innovators, who gloried in their sufferings, and contributed to render government odious and contemptible. It was abolished in 1640. There were in this court from 26 to 42 judges, the lord chancellor having the casting vote.

Star of India, a new order of knighthood for India, instituted by letters-patent 23 Feb., gazetted 25 June, 1861, and enlarged in 1866. Motto, "Heaven's light our guide." It comprised the sovereign, the grandmaster, 25 knights (Europeans and natives), and extra or honorary knights, such as the prince-consort, the prince of Wales, etc. Queen Victoria invested several knights on 1 Nov. 1861. The prince of Wales held a grand chapter at Calcutta, 1 Jan. 1876.

star-routes, routes on which contracts for carrying the United States mail are made upon bids which do not specify the mode of conveyance, but simply offer to carry the mails regularly, safely, and expeditiously. Such bids are regarded by the post-office department as inferior to those which specify railroad, steamboat, or four-horse-coach conveyance; but as superior to those which specify only horseback carriers. In 1881 second assistant postmaster-general Thomas J. Brady, ex-senator Stephen W. Dorsey of Arkansas, and others, were accused of conspiracy to defraud the U. S. government in the management of these routes. They were brought to trial 1 June, 1882; 1st trial closed 11 Sept., jury not agreeing; 2d trial began 4 Dec. 1882, closed 11 June, 1883. Verdict, not guilty as indicted. UNITED STATES.

stars, the fixed. Each of those luminous points which the unassisted sight reveals to us by thousands in the vault of heaven, which the telescope shows by millions in the depths of space, shines with its own light, and may be a source of light and heat to a planetary system similar to ours. They were classed in constellations, it is supposed, about 1200 B.C. Hicetas, of Syracuse, taught that the sun and the stars are motionless, and that the earth moves round them, about 344 B.C. (this is mentioned by Cicero, and perhaps gave the first hint of this system to Copernicus). Job, Hesiod, and Homer mention several of the constellations. The Royal library at Paris contains a Chinese chart of the heavens, made about 600 B.C., in which 1460 stars are correctly inserted. The aberration of the stars was discovered by dr. Bradley, 1727. Maps of the stars were published by the Society for the Diffusion of Useful Knowledge in 1839, and a set of celestial maps, issued under the superintendence of the Royal Prussian academy, was completed in 1859. The stars are classed according to apparent magnitude, those visible to the naked eye forming the 1st, 2d, 3d, 4th, 5th, and 6th magnitude.

The following is a list of 20 of the most brilliant stars which are commonly regarded as of first magnitude in the order of brightness:

	Name.	Constellation.		Name.	Constellation.
1.	Sirius	Canis Major.	11.	Aldebaran	Taurus.
2.	Canopus	Argo.	12.	Beta (β)	Centaurus.
3.	Alpha (α)	Centaurus.	13.	Alpha (α)	Crux.
4.	Arcturus	Boötes.	14.	Antares	Scorpion.
5.	Rigel	Orion.	15.	Altaïr	Aquila.
6.	Capella	Auriga.	16.	Spica	Virgo.
7.	Vega	Lyra.	17.	Fomalhaut	Piscis Aust.
8.	Procyon	Canis Minor.	18.	Beta (β)	Crux.
9.	Betelgeuse	Orion.	19.	Pollux	Gemini.
10.	Achernar	Eridanus.	20.	Regulus	Leo.

Argelander gives the number of stars of the

1st magnitude as	20	6th magnitude as	3,200
2d "	65	7th "	13,000
3d "	190	8th "	40,000
4th "	425	9th "	192,000
5th "	1100		

Ptolemy names 48 constellations: 21 northern, 12 zodiacal, 15 southern. "Chambers's Astronomy," 1890, enumerates 85. Some as high as 109. CONSTELLATIONS.

ESTIMATED DISTANCE OF SOME OF THE FIXED STARS FROM THE EARTH.

[Arranged in the order of nearness, the parallax, etc.; the distance in multiples of the sun's distance, 91,400,000 miles, and estimating the movement of light at 186,000 miles per second.]

Star.	Parallax in seconds.	Sun's distance=1.	Light to reach the earth. Time.	Estimated by
α Centaurus	0.75	275,000	4.34 years.	Gill, 1883–84.
61 Cygnus	0.50	412,000	6.51 "	O. Struve, 1853.
Sirius	0.38	543,000	8.57 "	Gill.
Vega	0.20	1,031,000	16.27 "	"
2 Ursa Major	0.13	1,586,000	25.04 "	C. A. F. Peters.
Arcturus	0.13	1,586,000	25.04 "	"
Polaris	0.07	2,947,000	46.50 "	"
Capella	0.04	5,157,000	81.37 "	"
Canopus	0.03	6,875,000	108.50 "	Elkin.

A number of new stars have appeared and disappeared at different times. A list of about 200, which vary greatly in brightness, has been published in George F. Chambers's "Hand-book on Astronomy," 1890. New stars noted in 1848, 1866, 1876, the last in 1885, 31 Aug., in the great nebulæ of Andromeda of the 6th magnitude.

"Star-Spangled Banner, The." This song was written by Francis Scott Key under the following circumstances: He had gone in the cartel-ship *Minden*, under a flag of truce, to solicit the release of some friends who had been seized by adm. Cochrane during the attack on the city of Washington. Key found the British fleet about to attack Baltimore, and while Cochrane agreed to release the prisoners, he refused to let him or his friends return at once. The cartel-ship *Minden* was anchored in sight of fort McHenry, and from her deck Key saw, during the night of 13 Sept. 1814, the bombardment of that fortress. It was during the excitement of this attack, and while pacing the deck of the *Minden* with intense anxiety between midnight and dawn, that Key composed the song. It was first written on the back of a letter, and after his return to Baltimore copied out in full.

States-general of France. An ancient assembly of France, first met, it is said, in 1302 to consider the exactions of the pope. Previous to the Revolution, it had not met since 1614. The states consisted of 3 orders—the clergy, nobility, and commons. They were convened by Louis XVI., and assembled at Versailles, 5 May, 1789 (308 ecclesiastics, 285 nobles, and 621 deputies, or *tiers état*, third estate). A contest arose whether the 3 orders should make 3 distinct houses, or but one assembly. The commons insisted upon the latter, and, assuming the title of the National Assembly, declared that they were competent to proceed to business without the concurrence of the 2 other orders, if they refused to join them. The nobility and clergy found it expedient to concede the point, and they all met in one hall. NATIONAL ASSEMBLY.

States of the Church. ITALY, NAPLES, ROME.

stationers. Books and papers were formerly sold only at stalls, hence the dealers were called stationers. The company of stationers of London is of great antiquity, and existed long before printing was invented, yet it was not incorporated until 3 Philip and Mary, 1557. Their old dwelling was in Paternoster row.

statis'tics, the science of the state, political knowledge, is said to have been founded by sir William Petty, who died in 1687. The term is said to have been invented by prof. Achenwall of Göttingen in 1749. The first statistical society in England was formed at Manchester in 1833; the Statistical Society of London, which publishes a quarterly journal, was established 15 Mch. 1834, for the purpose of procuring, arranging, and publishing "facts calculated to illustrate the condition and prospect of society." Statistics of the United States are found in the census reports, first published in 1790 and every 10 years thereafter. These reports become more and more comprehensive at each census, giving statistics now of nearly every subject pertaining to state, political, or scientific facts. Mulhall's "Dictionary of Statistics," pub. 1891.

statues. SCULPTURE.

steam-engine. "The best-known mechanical arrangement for converting heat into work."—*A. Rigg*, 1878. The power of steam to impart motion was known to Hero of Alexandria, who, in his "Pneumatics," describes various methods of applying it. He exhibited an ÆOLIPILE to Ptolemy

…iladelphus and his court in the Serapeum of Alexander, …0 B C This philosopher's toy may be regarded as a fore…st of the modern steam engine

…lomon de Caus, an eminent French mathematician and engineer, publishes a work describing a method of producing a jet of water by pressure of steam generated in a tight spherical vessel 1615

…ovanni Branca an Italian mathematician, publishes an account of a method of transmitting power by a wheel furnished with vanes and revolved by a jet of impinging steam . 1629

…rquis of Worcester describes in his "Century of Inventions" (original in the British museum) experiments in bursting plugged cannon by steam and also a "water commanding engine" for forcing water into a tank by steam generated in tight vessels 1663

Denys Papin of Blois introduces the safety valve in his steam bone digester 1684

…pt Savery patents an engine to raise water from mines by alternate condensation and force of steam in air tight cylinders furnished with valves 25 July, 1698

…omas Newcomen, a blacksmith of Dartmouth Engl, patents an engine with a walking beam for pumping water from mines It was operated by a boy who alternately admitted steam and a jet of cold water into a cylinder fitted with a piston 1705

…y named Humphrey Potter attaches a cord from the beam to the handles of the steam and cold-water stop cocks in the Newcomen engine and makes it self acting about 1715

…nry Beighton of Newcastle upon Tyne constructs a self acting engine on the Newcomen plan, the first with a steel yard safety valve 1718

…ob Leupold a Saxon, constructs the first high pressure steam engine 1720

…nes Watt of England obtains a patent for a rotary steam engine . 1769

…eam-carriage for common roads built by Cugnot in France "

…att invents the separate condenser and air pump (1765), and in partnership with Matthew Boulton sets up the first engine of this kind at Kinneil Scotland 1774

…nathan Hornblower of Penryn secures a patent for an engine with 2 cylinders 1781

…att invents a double acting engine 1782

…gine built with a fly wheel above the piston, and no beam, by Phineas Crowther of Newcastle-upon Tyne 1800

…ver Evans introduces the high pressure engine in America "

…ent for a portable engine secured by rev Edward Cartwright of England. 1801

…rithick and Vivian of England patent a high pressure engine 1802

…st practical steamboat by Symington "

…ver Evans of Philadelphia, Pa builds a high pressure engine , 1803

…rnblower's compound engine improved by Woolf 1804

…st railway locomotive built by Trevethick "

…olf's pumping engine general in Cornwall mines 1814

…eory of the steam engine expounded by Carnot 1824

…he Rocket," first practical locomotive, by Stephenson 1829

…nkine's "Manual of the Steam engine," improves the scientific theory of the subject 1859

…st triple expansion marine engine by Kirk 1874

…bb's compound locomotive engine introduced 1881

…steam-hammer, invented by James Nasmyth in …38, and patented by him 18 June, 1842 Its main feature …the direct manner by which the elastic power of steam is …ployed to lift up and let fall the mass of iron constituting …hammer, which is attached direct to the end of a piston-…i passing through the bottom of an inverted steam cylinder …ced immediately over the anvil

…1842, Mr Nasmyth applied his steam hammer to driving piles, …which has facilitated the execution of great public works Owing …o its vast range of power, forged iron work can now, by its means, …e executed on a scale, and for a variety of purposes, with an ease …nd perfection not previously possible Parts of gigantic marine …team engines, anchors, and Armstrong guns, as well as the most …inute details of machinery, as in Enfield rifles, are executed by …he steam hammer

…team hammer, said then the largest known, completed at Wool…ich, the falling portion weighs 40 tons, and when used with top …team (51 tons) has the force of 91 tons, Ap 1874. One at …chneider's works, Creuzot, France, weight between 75 and 80 …ons, Dec. 1877

Nasmyth, aged 81, d 7 May, 1890 His autobiography, edited …y dr S Smiles, was pub in 1883

…steam navigation. The value of steam in navi…tion was demonstrated by Denys Papin in a model steam…at on the Fulda, near Cassel, in 1707. This was soon de…oyed by a mob of boatmen Jonathan Hulls of London, …gl, set forth the idea in a patent obtained in 1736 Ber…ulli experimented with a steamboat, using artificial fins, …l Genevois with one using the duck's-foot propeller, in 1757. …1775, M Perier navigated the Seine with a small steam…at, and in 1783, Claude, comte de Jouffroy, constructed an …gine which propelled a boat on the Saône NAVY

James Rumsey of Sheppardstown, Va, invents a steamboat propelled by a steam engine expelling water through a horizontal trunk opening in the stern (1782) He experiments publicly in the presence of gen Washington, on the Potomac river Sept 1784

John Fitch of Philadelphia, Pa, launches a steamboat worked by vertical paddles, 6 on each side, on the Delaware river 1788

Patrick Miller of Dalswinton, Scotland, constructs a pleasure boat with paddle wheels (1787), to which William Symington applies a steam engine "

John Fitch sails a steamboat 18 ft long on the Collect pond, New York city, where the "Tombs" now stands 1796

First practical steamboat, the tug *Charlotte Dundas*, built by William Symington, and tried on the Forth and Clyde canal, Scotland Mch 1802

Robert Fulton in connection with Chancellor Livingston U S ambassador in Paris builds a steam paddle boat, 60 ft long, which is tried on the Seine 9 Aug 1803

John Stevens of Hoboken N J, builds a steamboat with twin screw propellers and an engine supplied by a flue boiler 1804

Fulton's steamboat, the *Clermont* 160 tons runs from New York to Albany in 32 hours thus securing the exclusive use of the Hudson for steam navigation under grant of legislature made in 1798 Aug 1807

Phœnix, a single screw propeller built by John Stevens makes the first sea voyage of a steam-vessel from New York to Philadelphia 1808

First steamboat on the St Lawrence river, the *Accommodation*, runs from Montreal to Quebec 1809

First steamboat on the western rivers, a stern-wheeler, is built by Fulton at Pittsburg 1811

Comet, first passenger steamboat built in Europe, by Henry Bell runs on the Clyde 7½ miles per hour 18 Jan 1812

Steam ferry between New York and Jersey City "

First steam vessel on the Thames, brought by Mr Dodd from Glasgow 1815

First steamboat on the great lakes, the *Ontario*, built at Sackett's Harbor, N Y 1816

Walk in the Water, a steamboat for lake Erie, launched at Black Rock (now part of Buffalo, N Y) 28 May, 1818

Savannah capt Stevens Rogers a steamboat of 350 tons built in New York city, crosses the Atlantic from Savannah to Liverpool in 26 days, during 18 of which she uses her paddles Off cape Clear she is mistaken for a ship on fire, and pursued by the British cutter *Kite* She sails from Savannah, Ga. (NEW YORK) 24 May, 1819

First sea going steam-vessel of iron the *Aaron Manby*, is constructed at the Horsley iron works Engl 1821

First steam voyage to India made by the *Enterprise*, capt Johnson from London to Calcutta in 113 days, leaving Falmouth 16 Aug 1825

Fulton the First accidentally blown up at New York (NAVY, 1814) 4 June, 1829

Steamboat *Royal William* crosses the ocean from Quebec 1831

John Randolph, first iron vessel in American waters built by John Laird of Birkenhead, and shipped in pieces at Liverpool, built in the Savannah river as a tugboat 1834

Great Western Steamship company formed and keel of the *Great Western* (1340 tons) laid at Bristol, Engl 1836

Peninsular Steamship company founded 1837

Capt Ericsson's screw steamer, *Francis B Ogden*, makes 10 miles per hour on the Thames. Apr "

First voyage of the steamship *Great Western*, launched 19 July, 1837, from Bristol to New York 8-23 Apr 1838

Sirius built at London, crosses the Atlantic in 18½ days, reaching New York under steam a few hours before the *Great Western* 23 Apr "

Thomas Petit Smith's propeller first tried in England on a large scale in the *Archimedes* of 237 tons 1839

Unicorn, first steam vessel from Europe to enter Boston harbor, arrives 2 June, 1840

First of the Cunard line, the *Britannia*, side-wheeler, crosses to Boston in 14 days 8 hours, leaving Liverpool 4 July, "

Pacific Steam Navigation company established "

Screw steamer *Princeton* built for the U S navy 1843

Screw steamer *Great Britain*, first large ship with iron hull, designed by I K Brunel (3443 tons, 322 ft long, 51 ft. broad), launched 19 July, 1843, sails from Bristol 23 Jan 1845

Pacific Mail Steamship company organized 1847

Collins line of American steamships formed and subsidized by the U S government. 1849

[It consisted of the *Arctic*, *Baltic*, *Atlantic*, and *Pacific*, and existed 8 years. The barber shops on shipboard were a new feature]

Inman line founded by William Inman, and the first vessel, an iron screw steamer, *City of Glasgow*, put in commission 1850

Emigrants first carried in steamships of the Inman line "

Allan line organized . . . 1853

First trip around the world by a merchant steamer, the English screw steamship *Argo* 1854

Hamburg American and Anchor lines established 1856

Great Western broken up for firewood at Vauxhall. 1857

North German Lloyd line established "

GREAT EASTERN launched. . . 3 Nov 1857–31 Jan 1858

Iron clad steamships introduced (NAVY) 1860

French line established 1862

Far East, with 2 screw propellers, launched at Millwall, 31 Oct. 1863

Guion line established . . 1864

Trial trip of the *Nautilus*, with a hydraulic propeller (Ruthven's patent, 1849) worked by steam and no paddles or screw.....................................24 Mch. 1866
White Star line begins with the *Oceanic*, with saloons and state-rooms amidships instead of in the stern.................. 1870
Netherlands line established, 1872; Red Star line............ 1873
Steamship *Faraday*, 5000 tons, 360 ft. long, 52 ft. wide, and 36 ft. deep, launched at Newcastle (ELECTRICITY).......17 Feb. 1874
First export of live cattle by steamer, 373 head, shipped from U. S. to England in the steamship *European*..........July, “
Dead-meat trade between U. S. and England by refrigeration commences on White Star liners *Celtic* and *Britannic*...... “
Bessemer saloon-steamer launched at Hull, 24 Sept. 1874, makes first voyage to Gravesend....................5 Mch. 1875
Thingvalla line established.. 1879
Anthracite, a steamer 84 ft. long, planned by Loftus Perkins of England, with very high-pressure engines, crosses the Atlantic, 3316 miles in 22½ days, consuming only 25 tons of coal... 1880
Cunard steamer *Etruria* arrives at quarantine, port of New York, 1 hour before the McKinley bill goes into effect, and capt. Haines reaches the custom-house barely a minute before midnight, saving thousands of dollars in increased duties...midnight, 4 Oct. 1890
"Whaleback" *Charles W. Wetmore* steams from the head of lake Superior to Liverpool.. 1891
Campania, twin-screw Cunard liner, with a gross tonnage of 12,500 tons, 620 ft. long, 65 ft. 3 in. broad, and 43 ft. deep, launched on the Clyde...............................8 Sept. 1892

STEAM VESSELS OF THE WORLD (Lloyd's register, 1890-91).

Country.	Number.	Gross tonnage.	Value of vessels.	Value of trade carried.
Great Britain.....	6403	8,235,851	$550,000,000	$3,476,500,000
Germany.........	741	928,911	63,500,000	1,624,000,000
France...........	526	809,598	48,500,000	1,471,000,000
United States.....	416	517,394	42,000,000	1,462,500,000
Italy.............	212	300,625	22,000,000	415,000,000
Russia............	236	106,155	12,500,000	60,000,000

STATISTICAL TABLE OF SOME NOTED ATLANTIC STEAMERS.

Name of vessel.	Line.	Built.	Horse-power.	Tonnage.	Quickest passage.	Date.
Paddle-wheel.			Nominal.		days hrs. min.	
Sirius	......	1836	270	700	18 11 15	Apr. 1838
British Queen	......	1839	500	2,016	13 18 10	......
Liverpool	......	“	404	1,150	11 18 5	......
Great Western	......	1838	450	1,340	10 10 15	......
Screw.						
Pacific	......	1849	....	2,860	9 19 25	May, 1851
City of Richmond	Inman.	1873	700	4,780	7 18 50	......
City of Berlin	“	1874	1,000	5,526	7 14 12	......
			Indicated.			
Germanic	White Star.	1874	5,400	5,008	7 11 37	Apr. 1877
Britannic	“ “	“	“	5,004	7 10 53	Aug. 1877
Arizona	Guion.	1879	6,300	5,164	7 3 30	......
Servia	Cunard.	1881	10,300	7,392	6 23 50	......
Alaska	Guion.	“	10,000	6,932	6 18 37	1882
City of Rome	Anchor.	“	11,890	8,144	6 18 25	......
America	National.	1883	7,354	5,528	6 14 18	June, 1884
Oregon	Guion.	“	13,300	7,375	6 9 51	Aug. 1884
Umbria	Cunard.	1884	14,320	8,128	6 3 4	Nov. 1888
Etruria	“	“	“	8,120	6 1 44	Sept. 1889
City of New York	Inman.	1888	18,400	10,500	5 21 19	Oct. 1890
Majestic	White Star.	1889	17,000	9,861	5 18 8	Aug. 1891
Teutonic	“ “	“	“	9,686	5 16 30	Aug. 1891
City of Paris	Inman.	1888	20,100	10,500	5 14 24	Oct. 1892
Campania	Cunard.	1893	30,000	12,500	5 9 29	Aug. 1894
Lucania	“	“	“	“	5 7 48	Oct. 1894

LIST OF ATLANTIC STEAMSHIPS WHICH LEFT PORT AND WERE NEVER HEARD FROM.

Name of vessel.	Owners.	Nationality.	Persons on board.	Date of leaving port.
President	British and American S. N. company	British	136	11 Mch. 1841
Pacific	Collins line	American	240	23 Sept. 1856
Tempest	Anchor line	British	150	26 Feb. 1857
United Kingdom	“ “	“	80	17 Apr. 1868
City of Boston	Inman line	“	177	28 Jan. 1870
Scanderia	Anglo-Egyptian line	“	38	8 Oct. 1872
Ismailia	Anchor line	“	52	27 Sept. 1873
Colombo	Wilson line	“	44	Jan. 1877
Herman Ludwig		German	50	28 Sept. 1878
Homer		British	43	17 Dec. 1878
Zanzibar		“	48	11 Jan. 1879
Surbiton		“	33	18 Feb. 1879
Bernicia		“	45	19 Mch. 1879
City of Limerick		“	43	8 Jan. 1881
City of London		“	41	13 Nov. 1881
Straits of Dover		“	27	3 Jan. 1883
Coniston		“	27	24 Dec. 1884
Fernwood		“	25	20 Jan. 1885
Preston		“	29	20 Jan. 1885
Clandon		“	27	24 Jan. 1885
Humber		“	56	15 Feb. 1885
Erin	National line	“	72	31 Dec. 1889
Thanemore	Johnston line	“	43	26 Nov. 1890
Naronic	White Star line	“	....	Feb. 1893

steam-ploughs were patented by G. Callaway and R. A. Purkes, 1849; H. Cowing, 1850, and others. John Fowler's of 1854 is much approved.

stearine (from Gr. *στέαρ*, suet), that part of oils and fats which is solid at common temperature. The nature of fats was first made known by Chevreul, in 1823, who showed that they are compounds of peculiar acids, with a base termed *glycerine;* of these compounds the chief are stearine, margarine, and elaine. CANDLES.

steel, a compound of iron and carbon, exists in nature, and has been fabricated from the earliest times. It was certainly used by the Egyptians, Assyrians, and Greeks. It now largely replaces cast iron in shipbuilding, etc.

Réaumur discovered the direct process of making steel by immersing malleable iron in a bath of cast iron................ 1722
Manufactory for cast steel is said to have been set up by Benjamin Huntsman at Handsworth near Sheffield............. 1740
Manufacture of shear steel began in Sheffield...........about 1800
[German steel was made at Newcastle previously by Mr. Crawley. Mushat (1800), Lucas (1804), and Heath (1839) invented improvements in this manufacture. ENGRAVING.]
Reipe patented his "puddled steel"........................... 1850
[H. Bessemer made steel by passing cold air through liquid iron, 1856. By this method 20 tons of crude iron have been converted into cast steel in 23 minutes. For this invention he had received by royalties 1,057,748*l.* up to 1879; also many foreign honors; knighted, June, 1879.]
Subject investigated by M. Caron, 1861-65; attention excited by cutlery made from a metallic sand, from Taranaki or New Plymouth, in New Zealand.................................... 1860
Tungsten steel was made in Germany, 1859; and M. Frémy

made steel by bringing red-hot iron in contact with carbonate of ammonia ... 1861
Mr. Krupp exhibited an ingot of steel weighing 4500 lbs. in 1851, and one weighing 20 tons in ... 1862
A steel bridge, in connection with the exhibition, constructed at Paris by M. Joret ... 1866
Bessemer steel first manufactured in the U. S. in Wyandotte county, Mich., 1865. This first ingot was rolled into a rail at the North Chicago rolling-mill, 1865. The first rails made to order of Bessemer steel in the U. S. at the Cambria iron works, Johnstown, Pa ... 1867
John Heaton published his process ... 1867–8
Dr. Siemens's "regenerative gas furnaces" made excellent steel, cheap, in large masses ... 1875 et seq.
Cutlers' Company, London, opened; exhibition ... 1 May, 1879
Messrs. Bolchow, Vaughan & Co., of Middlesborough, by Thomas and Gilchrist's process, convert Cleveland iron ore into Bessemer steel, by lining the furnace with radial bricks of magnesian limestone, and adding cold basis material to remove phosphorus ... "
Process reported successful ... Oct. 1880
Number of steel works in the U. S. 73, and the number of tons made 1,145,711 ... "
J. S. Jeans published "Steel: its History, Manufacture, Properties, and Uses" ... Feb. "
The Garfield, a steel sailing-ship, 2220 tons, 292 ft. long, 24 ft. 9 in. deep, 41 ft. wide, launched at Belfast ... 7 Jan. 1882
Clapp-Griffith process introduced into the U. S. from Great Britain ... 1884
B. H. Thwaite of Liverpool, and A. Stewart of Bradford, announce an improved "rapid" process for making steel, Oct. 1887
Roberts-Bessemer process introduced into the U. S. from France ... 1888
Steel production of Great Britain, 3,669,960 tons; of the U. S. 3,385,732 tons; of Germany and Luxemburg, 2,046,147 tons; of the world, 10,746,126 tons in ... 1889

NUMBER OF STEEL WORKS AND THE NUMBER OF TONS MANUFACTURED IN THE PRINCIPAL STATES OF THE U. S. FOR 1890.

State.	No. of Works.	Tons.
Pennsylvania	73	2,768,258
Illinois	14	868,250
Ohio	18	446,808
West Virginia	2	183,225
New York	8	113,499
Massachusetts	6	30,252
New Jersey	8	17,999
Colorado	1	17,952
All other states	22	20,683
Total	158	4,466,926

For latest statistics on steel and iron, from 1898 to 1 Jan. 1904, see IRON.

steel pens. "Iron pens" are mentioned by Chamberlayne in 1685. Steel pens, made long before, began to come into use about 1820, when the first gross of three-slit pens were sold in England, wholesale, for *7l. 4s.* In 1830 the price was *8s.*, and in 1832, *6s.* A better pen is now sold for *6d.* a gross. Birmingham, in 1858, produced about 1,000,000,000 pens per annum. Women and children are principally employed in the manufacture. Perry, Mitchell, and Gillott are eminent makers. Joseph Gillott, originally a mechanic, made a large fortune by steel-pen making. He died 5 Jan. 1872, aged 72.

steelyard, an ancient weighing instrument, the same that is translated *balance* in the Pentateuch. The *statera Romana*, or Roman steelyard, similar to the one now in common use, is mentioned in 315 B.C.

Stef'ano, San, a small village on the sea of Marmora, southwest of Constantinople; here the grand-duke Nicholas established his headquarters, 24 Feb.; and here was signed a treaty of peace with Turkey, 3 Mch. 1878, modified by the treaty of Berlin, signed 13 July following. The Russians quitted San Stefano, 22 Sept. 1878.

The treaty made Montenegro, Servia, and Roumania independent; Bulgaria a tributary principality; required a heavy indemnity from Turkey for Russia, who was to gain a port on the Black sea and Kars; to exchange the Dobrudscha for Bessarabia; to obtain rights for Christians; to open the Bosporus and Dardanelles in peace and war, etc.

stenoch'romy. PRINTING IN COLORS.

stenog'raphy (from Gr. στένος, narrow), the art of short-hand, practised from antiquity, and improved by the poet Ennius, by Tyro, Cicero's freedman, and Seneca. The *Ars Scribendi Characteris*, written about 1412, is the oldest system extant. Dr. Timothy Bright's "Characterie, or the Art of Short, Swift, and Secret Writing," published in 1588, is the first English work on short-hand. Peter Bales, the famous penman, published on stenography in 1590; and John Willis published his "Stenographie" in 1602. There are many modern systems: John Byrom's (1767), T. Gurney's (1710), "Brachygraphy," based on Mason's (1750), "A Short-hand Dictionary" (1777), Taylor's (1786), Mavor's (1789), Pitman's (phonographic), 1837, A. M. Bell's "Stenophonography" (1852), Munson's "Complete Phonography" (1866), J. D. Everett's (1877), Pocknell's "Legible Short-hand" (1881), J. M. Sloan's (1882). PHONOGRAPHY. Sig. A. Michela's stenographic machine for graphic representation of phonetic sounds (about 200 words per minute), like a harmonium with a key-board, exhibited at the Turin exhibition of 1884; adopted by the Italian senate. International Short-hand congress, London, 1887 (482 systems noticed); Paris, 1889; Munich, 1890; Berlin, 1891.

Stephenson, Fort, Defence of. FORT STEPHENSON.

stereoch'romy, a mode of painting in which water-glass (an alkaline solution of flint, silex) connects the color with the substratum. Its invention is ascribed to Von Fuchs, who died at Munich on 5 Mch. 1856. Fine specimens by Kaulbach and Echter exist in the museum at Berlin and at Munich.

stereom'eter, an instrument to measure the liquid contents of vessels by gauging, invented about 1350.—*Anderson.* M. Say's stereometer, for determining the specific gravity of liquids, porous bodies, and powders as well as solids, was described in 1797.

ster'eoscope (from Gr. στερεός, solid, and σκοπεῖν, to see), an optical instrument for giving relief to pictures, by uniting one seen by each eye in a single image. The first stereoscope by reflection was constructed and exhibited by prof. Charles Wheatstone in 1838, who had announced its principle in 1833. Since 1854 stereoscopes have been greatly improved.

ster'eotype, a cast from a page of movable printing-types, so named by the Parisian printer, Didot, 1798. It is said that stereotyping was known in 1711. It was practised by William Ged of Edinburgh, about 1730. In the library of the Royal institution is an edition of Sallust, with this imprint: "Edinburgi, Gulielmus Ged, auri faber Edinensis, non typis mobilibus, ut vulgo fieri solet, sed tabellis seu laminis fusis, excudebat, 1744." (Printed at Edinburgh by William Ged, goldsmith of Edinburgh, not with movable types, as is commonly done, but with cast tablets or plates.) A Mr. James attempted to introduce Ged's process in London, but failed, about 1735.—*Nichols.* Stereotype printing was in use in Holland in the last century; and a quarto Bible and a Dutch folio Bible were printed there.—*Phillips.* It was revived in London by Wilson in 1804. It was introduced into the United States by David Bruce of New York in 1812. First work cast in the U. S. was the New Testament in bourgeois in 1814. Since 1850 the durability of stereotypes has been greatly increased by electroplating them with copper or silver. PRINTING.

sterling (money). Ducange says (1733), "Esterlingus, sterlingus, are English words relating to money, and hence familiar to other nations, and applied to the weight, quality, and kind of money." "Denarius Angliæ, quo vocatur sterlingus," stat. Edw. I. (The penny of England, which is called sterling.) Camden derives the word from *easterling* or *esterling*, observing that the money brought from Germany, in the reign of Richard I., was the most esteemed on account of its purity, being called in old deeds "*nummi easterling.*" Others derive the word from the Easterlings, the first moneyers in England.

steth'oscope (Gr. στῆθος, breast, and σκοπεῖν, to examine), an instrument for listening to the action of internal organs of the body. In 1816 Laënnec of Paris (1781–1826), by rolling a quire of paper into a cylinder, and applying the open end to the patient's chest and the other to his own ear, perceived the action of the heart in a much more distinct manner than by the immediate application of the ear. This led to his inventing the stethoscope or "breast-explorer," the principle of which, now termed "auscultation," was known by Hippocrates, 357 B.C., and by Robert Hooke, 1681.

steward of England, Lord High. The first grand

officer of the crown This office was established prior to the reign of Edward the Confessor, and was formerly annexed to the lordship of Hinckley, Leicestershire, belonging to the family of Montfort, earls of Leicester, who were, in right thereof, lord high stewards of England, but Simon de Montfort, the last earl of this family, having raised a rebellion against his sovereign, Henry III, was attainted, and his estate forfeited to the king, who abolished the office, 1265. It is now revived only *pro hâc vice*, at a coronation or the trial of a peer The first afterwards appointed was Thomas, second son of Henry IV The first for the trial of a peer was Edward earl of Devon, on the arraignment of the earl of Huntingdon, in 1400 The last was lord Denman, at the trial of the earl of Cardigan, 16 Feb 1841. The duke of Hamilton was lord high steward at the coronations of William IV, 1831, and Victoria, 1838

Stick'lestadt, a town of Norway Here Olaf II, aided by the Swedes, was defeated in his endeavors to recover his kingdom from Canute, king of Denmark, and slain 29 July, 1030 He was afterwards sainted, on account of his zeal for Christianity

Stirling, a burgh of S Scotland. The strong castle was taken by Edward I of England, 1304 Here James II stabbed the earl of Douglas, 13 Feb 1452, and James VI was crowned, 24 July, 1567 Stirling surrendered to Monk, 14 Aug 1651 The statue of king Robert Bruce unveiled, 24 Nov. 1877.

> "Ye towers! within whose circuit dread
> A Douglas by his sovereign bled"
> —*Scott*, "Lady of the Lake"

Stirling, Lord, William Alexander, general in the American army during the Revolution, and known by courtesy in American history as lord Stirling, was a son of James Alexander, heir presumptive to the Scottish title "earl of Stirling," which he forfeited by following in 1715 the Pretender, after whose fall he took refuge in America in 1716, and married His son, William Alexander, born in New York, 1726, was active in the French and Indian war of 1755, went to England, and instituted legal proceedings to obtain his earldom, though not successful, his right was generally conceded, and he was addressed as earl of Stirling Returning to America in 1761, he married a daughter of Philip Livingston, member of the Provincial council of New Jersey for several years That state made him colonel of its first regiment of militia, and in Mch 1776 Congress commissioned him brigadier-general He was conspicuous in the battle of Long Island in Aug, and in Feb 1777 was made major-general He exposed CONWAY to gen Washington He served throughout the war, at different times having in his command every brigade of the army except those of South Carolina and Georgia. He died at Albany, 15 Jan 1783.

stirrups were unknown to the ancients. Gracchus fitted the highways with stones to enable the horsemen to mount Warriors had projections on their spears for the same purpose Stirrups were used in the 5th century, but were not common even in the 12th

Stockbridge Indians, formerly occupying that part of Massachusetts about the Berkshire Hills A remnant of them now in Wisconsin INDIANS

Stock Exchange, the New York, grew out of an informal organization by the stock-brokers, May 17, 1792, and was formally instituted in 1817 Its sessions were held in various rented rooms till 1827, when it occupied part of the first "Merchants' Exchange," then completed This was burned, 16 Dec 1835 It then removed to Jauncey court (now 43 Wall street), in 1842 to the new Merchants' Exchange, now the Custom-house, in 1854 to the Old Corn Exchange Bank building, in 1856 to Lord's court in William street, and in 1865 to its own fine building in Broad, near Wall street. EXCHANGE.

Stock'holm, capital of Sweden (built on *holmen*, or islands), was fortified by Berger Jarl about 1254 Here the Swedish nobility were massacred by Christian II, in 1520 SWEDEN Pop 1890, 246,154

stockings of silk are said to have been first worn by Henry II of France, 1547 In 1560, queen Elizabeth was presented with a pair of knit black silk stockings by her silkwoman, Mrs. Montague, and she never wore cloth ones any more.—*Howell.* He adds, "Henry VIII wore ordinary cloth hose, except there came from Spain, by great chance, a pair of silk stockings, for Spain very early abounded with silk" Edward VI was presented with a pair of Spanish silk stockings by his merchant, sir Thomas Gresham, and the present was then much taken notice of—*Idem.* Others relate that William Rider, a London apprentice, seeing at the house of an Italian merchant a pair of knit worsted stockings from Mantua, made a pair like them, the first made in England, which he presented to the earl of Pembroke, 1564—*Stow* The art of weaving stockings in a *frame* was invented in England by the rev Mr Lee of Cambridge in 1589, 25 years after he had learned to knit them with wires or needles Cotton stockings were first made in 1730

stocks, properly the obligations of a government for its funded debt—government securities distinct from shares, but now commonly used to designate the property of a corporation, and the right to ownership in such property, represented by certificates distributed to the owners The public funding system originated in Venice, about 1173, and was introduced into Florence in 1340 The English funding system may be said to have had its rise in 1690.

"Bulls" are persons who buy stock and cause the market to rise, "Bears," those who sell and cause it to fall

Three per cent annuities created 1726
" " consols (i e, consolidated annuities) created 1731
" per cents reduced 1746
" per cent annuities, payable at South Sea house 1751
" and a half per cent annuities created. 1758
Long annuities 1761
Four per cent consols 1762
Foundation of the Stock Exchange in Capel court, London was laid . 18 May, 1801
Five per cent annuities 1797 and 1802
" " reduced to 4 1822
Old 4 per cents reduced to 3½ 1824
Act to prevent stock jobbing, Mch 1734, repealed 1860
Further reductions made in 1825, 1830, 1834, 1841, and 1844, the maximum being now 3 per cent.
Three per cents. convertible into 2¾, and 2½ per cent. by act of . 2 Sept. 1884

Stoics, disciples of Zeno PHILOSOPHY.

Stoke, East, near Newark, Nottinghamshire, Engl. Near here, on 16 June, 1487, the adherents of Lambert Simnel, who personated Edward, earl of Warwick, and claimed the crown, were defeated by Henry VII. John de la Pole, the earl of Lincoln, and most of the leaders, were slain Simnel was afterwards employed in the king's household

Stone, Charles P U S A, Case of The battle of BALL'S BLUFF, Va, was fought 21 Oct. 1861 The movement bringing on the battle was made under supervision of gen Stone, and resulted in the defeat of the federals An investigation followed, and on 5 Jan 1862, gen Stone was examined by the "Committee on the Conduct of the War," who, at the time, seemed to be satisfied with his explanations On suggestion of gen McClellan, he again appeared before the same committee on 31 Jan, and defended himself against a charge of disloyalty On 9 Feb 1862, he was arrested by brig gen Sykes on order of the secretary of war, addressed 28 Jan to gen McClellan Gen Stone asked of gen McClellan charges and specifications, 9 Feb, but received no answer He was kept in solitary confinement at fort Lafayette for 49 days, while no notice was taken of his repeated applications for a speedy trial, for a copy of charges, for change of locality, and for access to the records of his office, etc, and was then transferred to fort Hamilton, where he had opportunity for air and exercise. The cause of his arrest was still unexplained and his applications for service disregarded, but after 189 days of confinement he was released His wife was not permitted to visit him during his confinement. Meanwhile, his case attracted attention in Congress On 11 Apr 1862, Mr McDougall of California offered a resolution in the Senate, asking a trial for gen Stone. On 22 Apr, on motion of Mr Wilson, the resolution was amended and passed, "That the president of the United States be requested to communicate to the Senate any information touching the arrest and imprisonment of brig-gen Stone not deemed incompatible with the public interest" To this the president answered, in substance, 2 May, 1862, that the arrest was made by his authority and upon evidence which required such proceedings to be had against him, whether guilty or innocent, for the public safety. The president deemed it incompatible with the public interest and perhaps unjust to gen. Stone to make a more particular statement of the evidence. He had not been tried because the state of military operations at the time of his arrest and since would not warrant the withdrawal of officers to constitute a court-martial and witnesses from the army without serious injury to the service; that gen. Stone would be allowed a trial without unnecessary delay, and every facility would be afforded by the War department for his defence. Gen. Stone was not released, however, until 16 Aug. 1862, when by act of 17 July, 1862, it was illegal to hold him longer without trial. After his release he reported by telegram for orders; but, hearing nothing, he wrote on 25 Sept. to gen. L. Thomas, adjt.-gen. U. S. A., stating the case, and asking that charges be furnished him, or that he be placed on duty. Gen. Halleck answered, 30 Sept. 1862, that he was no longer under arrest, but that he could give him no orders, as he had not been assigned to him for duty; that he had no official information of the cause of his arrest, but understood it was made by the order of the president. No charges or specifications were on file against him as far as he (Halleck) could ascertain; that the matter was to be immediately investigated, and copies of charges when preferred would be furnished by the judge-advocate general. On 1 Dec. 1862, gen. Stone, hearing nothing further, wrote gen. McClellan that, as he could learn, the authority for his immediate arrest was from him, and respectfully requested that he be furnished with a copy of the charges. Gen. McClellan replied 5 Dec., stating that the order was given by the secretary of war; that the secretary said it was made at the solicitation of the Congressional Committee on the Conduct of the War, and based on testimony taken by them. That he (McClellan) had submitted to the secretary of war the written statement of a refugee from Leesburg. This information agreed to a certain extent with the evidence taken by the committee; he had further stated to the secretary that the charges were too indefinite for any case to be framed; that he had on several occasions called attention to the propriety of giving gen. Stone a prompt trial, but the reply had been, there was no time to attend to it, or that the Congressional court was still engaged in collecting evidence. Gen. Stone then asked gen. McClellan to furnish him with the name of the refugee, but to this request no answer was ever received. This is the substance of all the information gen. Stone was ever able to collect after persistent efforts. At last the government restored him to duty, making no acknowledgment of injustice done him. Gen. Stone continued to suffer under many annoyances until, towards the close of the war, he offered his resignation, which was promptly accepted. In view of the high character and military reputation (see gen. Grant's "Personal Memoirs") of gen. Stone, it is now universally believed that his treatment was unjust and that he was the victim of prejudice or mistake.

Stonehenge, on Salisbury Plain, Wiltshire, Engl., is said to have been erected on the counsel of Merlin, by Aurelius Ambrosius, in memory of 460 Britons who were murdered by Hengist the Saxon about 450.—*Geoffrey of Monmouth.* Erected as a sepulchral monument of Ambrosius, 500.—*Polydore Vergil.* An ancient temple of the Britons, in which the Druids officiated.—*Dr. Stukeley.* The Britons are said to have held annual meetings at Abury and Stonehenge, at which laws were made and justice administered. The cursus near Stonehenge was discovered by dr. Stukeley, 6 Aug. 1723. The origin and object of these remains are still very obscure. See W. M. Flinders Petrie's "Stonehenge: Plans, Description, and Theories," 1880.

Stone river. MURFREESBOROUGH, Battle of.

"Stonewall" Jackson (Thomas J. Jackson, b. 1824; d. 1863), a Confederate general, so called from the obstinate resistance made by the troops under his command at the battle of BULL RUN. CHANCELLORSVILLE.

Stonington, Defence of. This borough, on Long Island sound, in the eastern part of Connecticut, was assailed by the British, under com. Hardy, on 9 Aug. 1814. A cannonade and bombardment ensued for 2 or 3 days. Less than 20 men, with 3 cannon, successfully defended the place and prevented the British landing from boats. The Americans had 6 men wounded; the British, 21 killed and 59 wounded.

Stono Ferry, Battle of. The British army menacing Charleston, S. C., were attacked by gen. Lincoln at Stono Ferry, 10 miles below the city, on Stono river, or inlet, 20 June, 1779. The Americans were repulsed, with a loss of 146 killed and wounded. 3 days after the British evacuated the place, retiring to Savannah, Ga. Here, in a skirmish with a British foraging party from Charleston, Sept. 1782, capt. Wilmot, commanding the Americans, was killed. His was the last blood shed of the Revolution.

Stony creek, or **Burlington Heights,** at the west end of lake Ontario, in Upper Canada, was the scene of a night assault upon 1300 American troops under gen. Chandler, on 6 June, 1813, by a British force of about 800 men, under gen. Vincent. The Americans lost 17 men killed, 38 wounded, and 5 officers and 93 men made prisoners. Among the latter were gens. Chandler and Winder. The British loss was 178. After repulsing the attack the Americans retreated to fort George on the Niagara river.

Stony Point, Capture of. FORTS.

storms. A storm is "a decided or violent disturbance of the atmosphere, which undergoes translation from place to place." It may or may not be accompanied by rain, hail, or snow. The historical interest of storms depends largely upon their destructiveness to life and property. They are commonly designated as *typhoons, cyclones, tornadoes, hurricanes,* and *blizzards.* More or less destructive tornadoes are frequent in parts of the United States, and thousands of persons have been killed and injured by them. On one day (9 Feb. 1884) there occurred in the territory extending from Mississippi, Tennessee, Kentucky, and Illinois, eastward to the Atlantic, more than 60 tornadoes, which destroyed over 10,000 buildings, killed 800 persons, and wounded over 2500.

SOME DISASTROUS TORNADOES WHICH HAVE OCCURRED IN THE UNITED STATES.

Place.	Date.	Persons		Buildings destroyed.	Notes.
		Killed.	Injured.		
Northford, Conn.	19 June, 1794	...	...	...	Progress rapid.
Hancock, Ga.	4 Apr. 1804	...	...	...	Intense darkness.
Sunapee, N. H.	9 Sept. 1821	...	...	...	
Warner, N. H.	" "	...	...	...	Very destructive.
Kingston, Miss.	7 May, 1832	...	...	...	Great loss of property.
Adams county, Miss.	7 May, 1840	317	100	...	Loss, $1,260,000.
	16 June, 1842	500	...	...	
Louisville, Ky.	27 Aug. 1854	25	67	...	Very destructive.
Jefferson and Cook counties, Ill.	22 May, 1855	4	...	...	" "
Montevallo, Ala.	22 Nov. 1874	10	30	100	Town nearly destroyed.
Near Erie, Pa.	26 July, 1875	134	...	...	Loss, $500,000.
Saline county, Kan.	6 June, 1876	11	Many	...	Loss, $30,000.
Pensaukee, Wis.	7 July, 1877	8	...	...	Loss, $300,000.
Iowa county, Wis	23 May, 1878	30	...	...	
Ray county, Mo.	1 June, "	13	70	100	
New Haven county, Conn.	9 Aug. "	34	28	160	Loss, $2,000,000.
Walterborough, S. C.	16 Apr. 1879	16	...	50	
Kansas (several tornadoes)	30 May, "	...	...	...	Great loss of life.
Goodhue county, Minn.	3 July, "	9	30	...	
Barry, Stone, Webster, and Christian counties, Mo.	18 Apr. 1880	100	600	200	Loss, $1,000,000.
White county, Ark.	" "	10	20	...	
Taylorville, Ill.	24 Apr. "	6	20	25	
Noxubee county, Miss.	25 Apr. "	22	72	55	Loss, $100,000.

SOME DISASTROUS TORNADOES WHICH HAVE OCCURRED IN THE UNITED STATES.—*(Continued.)*

Place.	Date.	Persons Killed.	Persons Injured.	Buildings destroyed.	Notes.
Fannin county, Tex	28 May, 1880	40	83	49	
Pottawatomie county, Ia	10 June, "	20	...	35	
De Soto county, Miss	12 Apr. 1881	10	...	27	
Osage county, Kan	12 June, "	5	22	50	Loss, $150,000.
New Ulm, Minn	15 July, "	6	53	247	Loss, $300,000.
Henry and Saline counties, Mo	18 Apr. 1882	8	150	51	Loss, $150,000.
Grinnell, Ia	17 June, "	100	300	260	Loss, $1,000,000
Emmetsburg, Ia	24 June, "	100	...	...	
Kemper, Copiah, Simpson, Newton, and Lauderdale, Miss	22 Apr. 1883	51	200	100	Loss, $300,000.
Racine, Wis	18 May, "	16	100	52	Loss, $175,000.
Dodge and Olmstead counties, Minn	21 Aug. "	26	80	400	Loss, $700,000.
Izard, Sharp, and Clay counties, Ark	21 Nov. "	5	162	60	Loss, $300,000.
Illinois, Kentucky, Mississippi, Georgia, Tennessee, Virginia, North and South Carolina	9 Feb. 1884	800	2500	10,000	Unparalleled series of tornadoes, there being over 60 of them scattered over the territory after 10 A.M. on that day.
Richmond and Harnett counties, N. C.	19 Feb. "	18	125	55	
Miner, Lake, and Minnehaha counties, Dak	28 July, "	15	18	100	
Rock, Hennepin, Ramsey, and Washington counties, Minn. St. Croix, Polk, Chippewa, and Price counties, Wis	9 Sept. "	6	75	305	Loss, $4,000,000.
Camden county, N. J	3 Aug. 1885	6	100	500	Loss, $500,000.
Fayette county, O	8 Sept. "	6	100	300	" "
Dallas, Perry, and Bibbs counties, Ala	6 Nov. "	13	50	...	
Benton and Stearns counties, Minn	14 Apr. 1886	74	136	138	Loss, $385,000.
Green and Huron counties, O., 20 killed and 100 houses destroyed at Xenia	12 May, "	57	...	85	Loss, $1,300,000.
Prescott county, Kan	21 Apr. 1887	20	237	330	Loss, $1,000,000.
Mt. Vernon, Ill	15 Feb. 1888	39	125	...	Town nearly destroyed.
Still Pond, Md., and vicinity of Delaware	22 Aug. "	11	...	...	
Reading and Pittsburg, Pa	9 Jan. 1889	33	...	...	Suspension bridge for pedestrians and carriages wrecked at Niagara Falls.
In Missouri, Ohio, and Kentucky	10 Jan. 1890	18	...	...	
Louisville, Ky	27 Mch. "	76	200	900	Cut a path 1000 feet wide through the city. Loss, $2,150,000.
South Lawrence, Mass	26 July, "	9	40	...	Cut a path 200 feet wide through town. Most disastrous ever recorded in the New England states.
Mt. Carmel, Pa	26 June, 1891	7	...	...	
In Louisiana and Mississippi	6 July, "	10	50	...	
West Superior, Wis	16 July, "	...	...	...	Many killed.
Wellington, Kan	27 May, 1892	25	100	...	Many injured and much property destroyed.
In Minnesota	16 June, "	50	...	...	
Carey, O	4 July, "	...	...	50	
Red Bud, Ill	17 Nov. "	...	...	46	
Savannah, Ga., Charleston, S. C., and southern coast	28 Aug. 1893	1000	...	...	Great destruction of property.
Gulf coast of Louisiana	2 Oct. "	2000	...	...	" " " "
Kunkel, Williams county, O	17 May, 1894	7	30	50	Village quite destroyed.
Tacoma, Wash	4 June, "	...	...	30	Great damage to property.
Southern Minnesota and central Iowa	22 Sept. "	75	...	...	Many wounded; great destruction of property.

Cyclones or *hurricanes*, known as *typhoons* in the China sea, form a special class of storms, always accompanied by heavy rain. They follow parabolic paths, first to westward and then north and northeast in the southern hemisphere, but in the contrary direction in the northern. Some of the most disastrous of the past 30 years are as follows:

At Calcutta, India, followed by a storm wave over the delta of the Ganges; 45,000 lives lost and about 100 ships......5 Oct. 1864
Guadaloupe devastated..............................6 Sept. 1865
In the Bahamas, at Nassau, New Providence, 60 to 70 lives lost, 600 buildings destroyed, many ships wrecked.......1–2 Oct. 1866
In islands of Antigua and St. Kitts....................21 Aug. 1871
Near Madras, Hindostan................................1 May, 1872
"Nova Scotia cyclone" on Atlantic coast, U. S.; 1223 vessels destroyed; loss of life over 600; of property, $3,500,000, 14–17 Aug. 1873
At Macao, Hong-Kong, etc..............................22 Sept. 1874
Indianola, Tex., nearly destroyed; 126 lives lost; property destroyed, $1,000,000..............................15 Sept. 1875
At Backergunge, accompanied by a storm wave, covering the eastern edge of the delta of the Ganges with water from 10 to 50 ft. deep. Over 100,000 people perish..........31 Oct. 1876
At Buen Ayre and Curaçoa, many lives lost, damage over $2,000,000..............................23 Sept. 1877
In Havana, Wilmington, N. C., eastern Pennsylvania, and New England; very destructive.........................21–24 Oct. 1878
Along the Atlantic coast from Cape Lookout, N. C., to Eastport, Me. Over 100 large and 200 small vessels shipwrecked, and great damage done to inland property...........16–20 Aug. 1879
Nearly the whole of Jamaica devastated; over 12 lives lost and hundreds of buildings destroyed..................17–18 Aug. 1880
At Charleston, S. C., and along the coast, 400 lives lost and hundreds of buildings; value of property destroyed, $1,500,000, 23–28 Aug. 1881
In Haifong, etc., China; about 300,000 lives lost........8 Oct. "
In England, great destruction of life and property, including about 130 wrecks..............................14–19 Oct. "
All vessels wrecked, and nearly every house destroyed at Manzanilla; damage estimated, $500,000.................27 Oct. "
In Kansas, 12 killed..................................7 Apr. 1882
At McAllister, Ind. Ter.; 120 lives lost................10 May, 1882
At Galveston, Tex.....................................6 Sept. "
Hurricane crosses Cuba, killing 40 persons and thousands of cattle; passes along the Atlantic coast, wrecking 70 vessels off Labrador; 100 lives lost.........................8–14 Oct. "
At Manilla, Philippine islands; 60,000 families made homeless and 100 sailors drowned.................20 Oct. and 8 Nov. "
Oronogo, Mo., demolished..............................13 May, 1883
At Springfield, Mo....................................5 Nov. "
In Kentucky, 12 persons killed........................24 Mch. 1884
In Upper Austria and Hungary..........................7 Aug. "
In New York, Pennsylvania, and Ohio...................28 Sept. "
In Catania, Sicily, about 27 killed; damage, $1,000,000..7 Oct. "
At Charleston, S.C., 21 lives lost; damage to property, $2,000,000, 23–24 Aug. 1885
At Kansas City, Mo....................................11 May, 1886
In Madrid, Spain, 32 killed, 620 injured...............12 May, "
Newbury, Ind., destroyed...............................15 Aug. "
In gulf of Mexico and 200 miles inland; 38 lives lost; Indianola, Tex., completely destroyed; loss, $5,000,000...19–20 Aug. "
Great Britain; many lives lost........................14–15 Oct. "
Off coast of Australia, 550 pearl fishers said to have perished, 22 Apr. 1887
On coast of Madagascar; 11 vessels wrecked, 20 lives lost, 2 Mch. 1888
In Cuba; estimated loss of life, 1000..................13 Sept. "
At Muscat, Arabia; several hundred lives lost..........9 July, 1890
Near St. Paul, Minn.; over 100 lives lost..............13 July, "
At Slomni, Russia; 19 killed...........................22 July, "
Near Wilkesbarre, Pa., 200 houses wrecked, 15 lives lost, 19 Aug. "
On lake Ilman, Russia; many lumber vessels lost with their crews..31 May, 1891
At Martinique; all shipping in port wrecked, 340 lives lost; damage, $10,000,000...................................18 Aug. "
At Conneaut, O.; 30 buildings destroyed................27 Oct. "
Hurricane on and around the island of Mauritius, 1200 lives lost; 18 May, 1892
Cyclone sweeps the province of Ravigo, northern Italy; great loss of life and property...........................19 July, "
Hurricane occurs at Tonnatay, Madagascar, causing great loss of life; 10 vessels foundered in the harbor..........6 Mch. 1893

Severest wind-storm on record on lake Erie, many vessels and lives lost....................................17 May, 1893
Hurricane on the coast of Georgia and South Carolina, the Sea islands devastated and many lives lost.............28 Aug. "
Cyclone rages along the coast of Florida, Georgia, and South Carolina.......................................12 Oct. "
Great storm on the northwest coast of Europe, 237 lives lost and many vessels off the coast of England and 165 fishermen off Jutland.......................................20 Nov. "
Terrific gale on lake Michigan, 50 wrecks along the shore from Michigan City and Two Rivers, 25 lives lost, 20 schooners destroyed on the water front at Chicago, and 15 schooners and several steamers outside......................16 May, 1894

Hail-storms, like tornadoes, follow a path very narrow as compared with the distance traversed, often in parallel bands, between which rain, but no hail, falls. Some noteworthy hail-storms of which we have a record are as follows:

Near Chartres, France, hail fell on the marching army of Edward III.; horses and men suffered much from large hailstones 1339
Hail-storm passes from Touraine, France, to Belgium in 2 bands; one 5 miles wide and 500 long, the other 10 miles wide and 420 miles long. Property valued at $5,000,000 destroyed, 13 July, 1788
At Naina Tal, India, hailstones fell measuring from 9 to 13 inches in circumference, and weighing a pound.....11 May, 1855
Hail-storm follows a path 45 to 60 miles wide, from Bordeaux, France, to Belgium. In St. Quentin the fallen hail did not disappear for 4 days...............................9 May, 1865
Hailstones as large as oranges fell in the Yellowstone valley, 30 July, 1877
Great hail-storms in Pennsylvania, Massachusetts, Michigan, New Jersey, Ohio, and Dakota. At Yankton the hail was 9 to 12 inches deep...................................5 June, 1879
Hailstones 7 inches in circumference fell at Lanesborough, Mass..16 July, "
Hailstones 6 to 10 inches in circumference fell in Wisconsin, 26 July, "
Near Whiteball, Ill., hailstones fell of the size of goose eggs, and drifts from 8 to 12 inches deep were found the day after the storm ....2 June, 1881
In Iowa, hailstones as large as a man's fist fell, and drifts were formed 2 to 3 ft. deep...............................12 June, "
At Laredo, Tex., hailstones weighing one pound fell....8 June, 1882
At Dubuque, Ia., hailstones fell of great size, the largest weighing 28 oz..16 June, "
In Lac and Audubon counties, Ia., hailstones 13 inches in circumference were noted, and the hail drifted over the fence tops...7-8 Aug. 1883
Hail totally destroyed the crops in Walsh and Grand Fork counties, Dak.....................................26 June, 1886
In Dakota and Minnesota hail destroyed 250,000 acres of wheat. At Grafton, Minn., hailstones fell as large as hens' eggs, 24 July, "
At Fort Yates, Dak., hailstones fell 3½ inches in diameter, and having cylindrical protuberances on them...........10 Aug. "
At Moradabad, India, over 230 natives were killed by a hail-storm; drifts 1 to 2 feet in depth formed, and hailstones were of enormous size...................................30 Apr. 1888

Cloud-bursts or *Water-spouts*.—2 water-spouts fell on the Glatz mountains in Germany, and caused dreadful devastation to Hautenbach and many other villages; many persons perished, 13 July, 1827. A water-spout at Glanflesk, near Killarney, in Ireland, fell on a farm of John Macarthy, destroying farm-houses and other buildings; 17 persons perished, 4 Aug. 1831. The length of one seen near Calcutta, 27 Sept. 1855, was estimated to be 1000 feet. It lasted 10 minutes, and was absorbed upwards. One seen on 24 Sept. 1856, burst into heavy rain. The town of Miskolcz, Hungary, destroyed by a water-spout; great loss of life and property, 30 Aug. 1878. A water-spout destroyed the town of Paso de Cuarenta, Mexico, and 170 lives were lost, 8 May, 1885. Upwards of 100 persons were drowned by a cloud-burst on the Yang-tze river, China, 4 Feb. 1890.

CLOUD-BURSTS RECORDED IN THE UNITED STATES.

Place.	Date.	Notes.
Near Pittsburg, Pa.	25-26 July, 1874	134 drowned; loss, $500,000.
Fort Sully, Dak.	17 Aug. 1876	
Near Hayes City, Kan.	26 " "	
Chalk creek, Utah.	31 " "	
Colorado desert, Col.	12 Sept. 1877	400 ft. of railroad track destroyed.
Red Bluff, Cal.	16 Nov. "	
Beaver creek (90 miles south of Deadwood), Dak.	12 June, 1879	11 drowned.
Seven Star Springs, Mo.	11 June, 1881	5 "
Near Wickenburg, Ariz.	6 Aug. "	
Central City, Col.	8 " "	
An Indian settlement, Cal.	2 July, 1882	Destroyed.
Humboldt county, Nev.	10 June, 1884	
Near Jefferson, Mont.	22 " "	3 drowned.
Near Pike's Peak, Col.	26 July, 1885	2 "

HEAVIEST RAINFALLS RECORDED IN THE UNITED STATES.

Place.	Rainfall in inches.	Time.	Date.
Concord, Franklin county, Pa.	16	3 hours...	5 Aug. 1843
Newton, Delaware county, Pa.	5.50	40 min....	" "
Fort McPherson, Neb.	1.50	5 "	27 May, 1868
Galveston, Tex.	3.95	14 "	4 June, 1871
Biscayne, Fla.	4.10	30 "	28 Mch. 1874
Indianapolis, Ind	2.40	25 "	12 July, 1876
Sandusky, O.	2.25	15 "	11 July, 1879
Paterson, N. J.	1.50	8 "	13 July, 1880
Embarrass, Wis.	2.30	15 "	28 May, 1881
Huron, Dak.	1.30	10 "	26 July, 1885
Washington, D. C.	0.96	6 "	" "
Collinsville, Ill.	1.70	12 "	23 May, 1888
Tridelphia, W. Va.	6.09	55 "	19 July, "
Washington, D. C.	2.34	37 "	27 June, "

Snow-storms and *Blizzards*.—Snow is not unknown, though rare, in the southern portion of the United States. A heavy snow-fall was reported at New Orleans in 1852. At Punta Rassa, Fla., about 100 miles from Key West, snow fell for a few moments, 1 Dec. 1876. 5 inches, the most ever known, fell at Montgomery, Ala., 29-31 Dec. 1880. On 12-15 Jan. 1882, very heavy snow fell on the desert westward of Tucson, Ariz., which extended into Mexico and Lower California. At Leadville, Col., snow fell, 30 Aug. 1882; and slight falls of snow occurred in Great Britain as far south as the Isle of Wight on the night of 11 July, 1888. Nearly ¾ inch of snow fell *from a clear sky* at Bloomington, Ill., 15 Mch. 1885. The deposits of red snow in Greenland were discovered by capt. John Ross, British navy, in 1818, and snow the color of gold-dust fell in Peckeloh, Germany, 27 Feb. 1877.—A violent wind from the north, when the air is filled with drifting snow, is known as a *blizzard* in the U. S., the *purga* in the Yenisei valley, and the *bura* on the steppes of central Asia. The blizzard is mentioned by Henry Ellis, who wintered on Hudson Bay in 1746, and spoke of the northwest winds of York Factory being filled with fine particles of snow. The term *blizzard* was first used by the U. S. Signal Service in Dec. 1876. Noteworthy snow-storms and blizzards recorded since 1875 are as follows:

Severe snow-storm in Scotland, several lives lost.....1-3 Jan. 1878
Snow-storm in S. England...........................12 Mch. "
Blizzard in England and France; loss of life in England and Wales over 100; many of the streets of Paris were completely blocked with snow..............................18-19 Jan. 1881
Heavy snow-storms, with great loss of life by avalanches, etc., in Piedmont, near Mont Cenis, Italy..............16-28 Jan. 1885
Blizzard in Montana, Dakota, Minnesota, Kansas, and Texas; loss of life about 100...............................11 Jan. 1888
Blizzard in eastern U. S.; about 70 lives lost.......11-14 Mch. "
Blizzards in northwestern U. S., 29 Jan.-2 Feb., and 7-8 Feb. 1891
Blizzard in Great Britain; 70 deaths from cold, shipwreck, etc., 9-10 Mch. "

Miscellaneous.—The loss to shipping and life by gales and storms has been immense (WRECKS), and an enumeration of even the severest gales may not be here undertaken. A few historic storms are, however, to be added to the number mentioned above.

In London a storm destroyed 1500 houses..................... 944
Five hundred houses and many churches blown down in London ....5 Oct. 1091
Storm on east coast of England; 200 colliers and coasters lost, with most of their crews.................................. 1696
Great storm, one of the most terrible that ever raged in England. The loss in London was estimated at 2,000,000*l*. The number of persons drowned in the floods of the Severn and Thames, and lost on the coast of Holland, and in ships blown out to sea and never heard of afterwards, is thought to have been 8000. 12 men-of-war, with more than 1800 men on board, were lost within sight of their own shore. Trees were torn up by the roots, 17,000 of them in Kent alone. The Eddystone light-house was destroyed, and in it the ingenious contriver of it, Winstanley, and the persons who were with him. Multitudes of cattle were also lost; in one level 15,000 sheep were drowned............................26-27 Nov. 1703
Snow-storm in Sweden, in which, it is said, 7000 Swedes, marching to attack Drontheim, perished upon the mountains.. 1719
Thirty thousand persons perish and a great number of vessels are wrecked by a storm in India....................11 Oct. 1737
Hurricane in West Indies; 4000 houses destroyed and 1000 of the inhabitants..................................25 Oct. 1768
Seven thousand persons killed by a storm at Surat in India, 22 Apr. 1782
One hundred and thirty-one villages and farms laid waste in France... 1785
Hurricane at MADRAS.....................................May, 1811
Storm at Gibraltar; over 100 vessels destroyed.........18 Feb. 1828
Hurricane on west coast of England and Ireland......6-7 Jan. 1839

Minot's Ledge light house in Boston harbor destroyed by storm, 19 Apr 1851
Great storm in the Black sea causing much loss of life, shipping, and stores sent by England for the allied armies in the Crimea 13-16 Nov 1854
Part of Crystal palace, London, and the steeple of Chichester cathedral blown down 20-21 Feb 1861
One hundred and forty three vessels wrecked in storm on British coast 28 May, "
TAY BRIDGE blown into the river 28 Dec 1879
Gale in gulf of Mexico, 247 lives lost . 12 Oct 1886

Storthing, the Norwegian parliament, said to have been first held at Bergen by Haco V in 1223, now composed of 114 members, one fourth in the upper house (Lagthing) and three fourths in the lower house (Odelsthing)

stoves. The ancients used stoves which concealed the fire, as the German stoves yet do They lighted fires also in large tubes in rooms with open roofs. Apartments were warmed by portable braziers Stoves on this old principle, improved, continue in use in many houses and public establishments in England, and generally on the Continent. Dr. Franklin and count Rumford pointed out the waste of fuel in open fires, and dr Neil Arnott patented his "improvements in the production and agency of heat," 14 Nov 1821. CHIMNEYS Dr C William Siemens described his smokeless stove in *Nature* for 11 Nov 1880

Straight-out Democrats. POLITICAL PARTIES

Straits Settlements, including Malacca, Penang or Prince of Wales island, and Singapore, secured to Great Britain in 1824, were made a separate dependency in 1853 under the governor-general of India They were separated from India as an independent settlement by act passed 10 Aug. 1866, which took effect Apr 1867 The Cocos islands were placed under the Straits Settlements, 1 Feb 1886, and Christmas island, 8 Jan 1889 Singapore, the capital, is on the island of Singapore, which is about 27 miles long by 14 wide, with an area of 206 sq miles. The native states of Perak, Selangor, Sungei-Ujong, Negri Sembilan, Johor, and Pahang on the peninsula are also subject to some extent to the British rule The area of these states on the peninsula is over 32,000 sq. miles.

Stralsund, Pomerania, a strongly fortified Hanse town, built about 1230 It resisted a fierce siege by Wallenstein in 1628, was taken by Frederick William of Brandenburg in 1678, restored to the Swedes, 1679; recaptured by the Prussians and their allies, Dec. 1715 It surrendered to the French under Brune, 20 Aug 1807, was awarded to Prussia, 1815.

Strand, London. Houses were first built upon the Strand about 1353, when it was the court end of the town, or the communication between the 2 cities of London and Westminster, being then open to the Thames and to the fields

strangers in House of Commons. PARLIAMENT, May, 1875

Stras'burg, the Roman *Argentoratum*, the capital of Alsace, on the west bank of the Ill, near the left bank of the Rhine Here Julian defended the Alemanni, 357, who captured it, 455 It was annexed to Germany, 870 Louis XIV seized it 28 Sept 1681, and retained it by the treaty of Ryswick, 1697 The citadel and fortifications which he constructed have been augmented so that Strasburg is one of the strongest places in Europe It was confirmed to France by the peace of Ryswick in 1697, but captured by the Germans, 28 Sept. 1870, and retained at the peace, May, 1871 The cathedral, an epitome of Gothic art, was founded by Clovis, and reconstructed by Pepin and Charlemagne After destruction by lightning, 1007, it was principally rebuilt by Erwin de Steinbach and his son in the 14th century The lofty tower (468 feet high) was completed in 143[illegible] The celebrated astronomical clock, after a long stoppage, was repaired by M Schwilgué, and inaugurated 1 Jan 1843

Attempted insurrection by prince Louis Napoleon (afterwards emperor), aided by 2 officers and some privates . 30 Oct 1836
[They are arrested, and the prince shipped to America by the government]
Strasburg invested by Germans, principally from Baden, during the Franco Prussian war . 10 Aug 1870
Gen von Werder assuming command of the siege, bombardment began 14 Aug, a vigorous sally repulsed 16 Aug "
Gen Uhrich, the commander, after heroic resistance, a breach being made and an assault impending surrendered, 2 A M, at 8 A M 17,150 men and 400 officers laid down their arms, 27 Sept "

German loss was said to be 906 men, of whom 43 were officers, 28 Sept 1870
Germans entered Strasburg on the anniversary of its surprise by the French in 1681 30 Sept. "
Uhrich received the grand cross of the Legion of Honor Oct. "
Library was destroyed and the cathedral injured

Stratford-upon-Avon, a town of Warwickshire, Engl. SHAKESPEARE AND HIS PLAYS

Strathclyd, a kingdom formed by the Britons, who retired northward after the Saxon conquest, about 560 It extended from the Clyde to Cumberland The Britons in it submitted to Edward the Elder in 924

Strathmore estates. Miss Bowes of Durham, then the richest heiress in Europe, whose fortune was 1,040,000*l.*, with vast additions on her mother's death, and immense estates on the demise of her uncle married the earl of Strathmore, 25 Feb 1766 Having, after the earl's death, married Mr Stoney, she was forcibly carried off by him and other armed men, 10 Nov 1786 She was brought to the King's Bench by *habeas corpus* and released, and he committed to prison, 23 Nov. The lady recovered her estates, which she had assigned to her husband under terror, in May, 1788

Stratton Hill, Battle of, in Cornwall, Engl, 16 May, 1643, the royal army, under sir Ralph Hopton, defeated the forces of the parliament under earl of Stamford

strawberry. FLOWERS AND PLANTS.

Streight's raid. Col. A D Streight, 51st Indiana, with a force of 1700 men, mounted, was permitted by gen. Rosecrans to attempt the destruction of railroads and other property in northern Alabama and Georgia The raid commenced about 12 Apr and closed 3 May, 1863, by the capture of his entire command near Rome, Ga. This raid accomplished nothing, unless it was to illustrate the futility of attempting to accomplish much with little Col. Streight afterwards acquired some prominence by tunnelling out of Libby prison and escaping

Stre'litz, the imperial guard of Russia, established by Ivan IV about 1568 Becoming seditious, it was suppressed by Peter the Great; great numbers were killed, many by the czar's own hand, 1698–1704.

Strike, the abandonment of work by a body of workingmen, usually with a view of extorting terms from employers. Industrial arbitration originated in France in 1806, when Napoleon, at the request of the workingmen of Lyons, caused the creation by law of boards of arbitration and conciliation, which still exist under the title of "Conseils des Prud'hommes." The first voluntary tribunal of trade disputes in England was the Board of Arbitration and Conciliation in the glove and hosiery trade, which held its first meeting at Nottingham, Engl, 3 Dec. 1860 The first Board of Arbitration in the United States was organized by messrs Straiton & Storms, cigar manufacturers of New York city, in 1879 The Wallace act of Pennsylvania, in 1883, was the first legislation in this country providing for voluntary arbitration in industrial disputes between employers and employed The first recorded strike in the U S is that of the journeymen bakers of New York in 1741 The journeymen boot-makers of Philadelphia are mentioned as striking for increased wages in 1796, 1798, and 1799 The whole number of strikes and lockouts recorded in the U.S prior to 1881 is 1491, of which 316 were successful, 583 failed, and 154 were compromised Of 438 the results are unknown Since 1881 the yearly record has been as follows

Year	Strikes	Number involved	Year	Strikes	Number involved
1881	471	129,521	1886	1411	499,489
1882	454	154,671	1887	872	345 073
1883	478	149,763	1888	679	211 016
1884	443	147,054	1889	643	177,298
1885	645	242,705	1890	798	201,682

Strike of sailors in New York for increased wages, unsuccessful Nov 1803
Unsuccessful strike of the Shoemaking guild in Philadelphia, lasting 6–7 weeks 1805
Strike of 200 cordwainers in New York . Nov 1809
Printers strike in Albany, protesting against the employment of non union men . 1821
Strike of laborers on Chesapeake and Ohio canal . 1829
Strike and riot of laborers on Providence railroad Apr 1834
Mill strike at Paterson, N J, 26 weeks' idleness and loss of $24,000 in wages. 1835

rike of weavers at Moyamensing and Kensington, Philadelphia, Pa., on wages (amicably adjusted after 5 months), begins, Aug. 1842
Mechanics' bell," which hangs in a tower at the foot of Fourth st., East river, N. Y., was first erected in New York in 1831. It was recast and raised on a skeleton tower in Webb's shipyard (1844), to celebrate the first victorious strike in America for a 10-hour day, won by the journeymen ship-carpenters of Philadelphia....19 Mch. 1844
National congress of trade organizations held at Baltimore, Md.; 100 delegates represent about 50 trades unions..20 Aug. 1866

IMPORTANT STRIKES IN THE UNITED STATES SINCE 1845.

Class of trade.	Number involved.	Where begun.	Duration.	Successful.	Object of strike.	Loss in wages.	Date of beginning.
urneymen tailors....	1,200	Philadelphia, Pa........	4 mos.	Yes	For increase in wages.....	....	June, 1847
on workers.........	....	Pittsburg, Pa..........	2-3 "	No	Against reduced wages....	....	12 Jan 1850
eavers............	1,300	Fall River, Mass........	6 "	"	" " "	$140,000	20 Nov. "
oemakers	7,000	Lynn, Mass...........	5 wks.	"	For increase in wages.....	200,000	22 Feb. 1860
ip carpenters, etc...	10,000	Greenpoint, L. I.........	6 "	"	For 8-hour day	900,000	Apr. 1866
al miners..........	....	Scranton, Pa...........	4 mos.	Partly	Against reduced wages....	....	10 Jan. 1871
neral labor strike...	100,000	New York city	3 "	Yes	For 8-hour day	....	Mch. 1872
al miners	....	Tuscarawas valley, O......	6 "	Partly	Against 15 cents reduction per ton mined.........	....	Dec. 1873
al miners.	....	Mahoning valley, O.......	9 "	No	Against 15 cents reduction per ton mined.........	....	" "
tton mill operatives.	15,000	Fall River, Mass..........	9 wks.	"	Against reduced wages.....	746,700	1 Aug. 1875
neral railroad strike (PENNSYLVANIA)	Many thousands; extensive and wide-spread	Martinsburg, Md..........	3 mos.	"	" " "	Many millions in property	16 July, 1877
inners	14,000	Fall River, Mass..........	16 wks.	"	For increase in wages.....	100,000	26 June, 1879
on workers.........	317	Covington and Newport, Ky.	21 "	"	For new scale of prices	300,000	1 June, 1881
tton handlers.......	10,000	New Orleans, La..........	2 "	"	For increase in wages.....	50,000	2 Sept. "
eavers and spinners..	5,255	Lawrence, Mass...........	23 "	"	Against reduced wages....	800,000	14 Mch. 1882
al miners..........	2,174	Western Pennsylvania.....	20 "	"	" " "	500,000	1 Apr. "
tton mill hands.....	4,981	Cohoes, N. Y.............	19 "	"	" " "	541,250	17 Apr. "
lling-mill hands....	5,000	Cleveland, O.	95 days	"	For adoption of Association rules............	376,250	9 May, "
on workers (general).	30,000	Pittsburg, Pa............	4 mos.	"	For new scale of prices	3,300,000	1 June, "
icklayers.........	3,200	Chicago, Ill	68 days	Yes	Increase of wages.........	560,000	2 Apr. 1883
legraphers (general)	67,000	Pittsburg, Pa............	30 "	"	For 15% advance in wages..	....	19 July, "
ass blowers........	1,204	Western Pennsylvania.....	23 wks.	"	Against reduced wages....	526,000	1 Sept. "
inners.	4,755	Fall River, Mass..........	16 "	No	" " "	412,950	4 Feb. 1884
ners..	3,000	Brazil, Ind...............	14 "	"	" " "	300,000	26 Feb. "
inters	6,000	New York city...........	3 "	Yes	For increase in wages.....	324,000	17 Mch. "
ners	6,925	Western Pennsylvania.....	22 "	No	" " " "	727,480	16 June, "
ners...............	2,289	Hocking Valley, O.........	9 mos.	"	Against 20 cents reduction per ton mined....	473,500	23 June, "
rpet weavers.......	2,115	Philadelphia, Pa.........	22 wks.	Partly	Against reduced wages....	312,000	20 Nov. "
ners..	4,000	Western Pennsylvania.....	54 days	No	" " "	344,300	5 Mch. 1885
ners..	7,272	" "	29 "	Yes	For increase of wages.....	323,600	9 Mch. "
on workers	15,600	" "	16 "	"	Against reduced wages.....	442,733	1 June, "
lling-mill hands....	3,000	Cleveland, O.............	88 "	"	" " "	410,000	1 July, "
ners...............	4,500	Western Pennsylvania.....	4 mos.	No	For increase in wages.....	549,780	4 Sept. "
sters and bottomers..	5,755	Brockton, Mass...........	6 wks.	Partly	Against fixed rates........	430,000	14 Nov. "
ove makers........	7,374	Gloversville, N. Y.........	9 "	"	For increase in wages.....	648,900	1 Jan. 1886
ove moulders	1,750	Troy, N. Y...............	17 "	Yes	" " " "	400,000	27 Feb. "
issouri Pacific railroad system........	9,000	....	2 mos.	No	Ordered by Martin Jones...	1,400,000	6 Mch. "
ird Avenue Street-car line............	1,300	New York city............	60 days	Partly	Against hours of labor and discharge of men......	50,000	16 Apr. "
gar makers.........	20,000	" " "	1 day	No	For fewer hours...........	27,000	1 May, "
umber shovers.......	12,000	Chicago, Ill.............	2 wks.	"	For fewer hours, more pay..	270,000	10 May, "
reet-car lines.......	12,000	New York city...........	1 day	Yes	In sympathy with strikers..	25,000	5 June, "
eat packers.........	9,260	Chicago, Ill..............	11 days	No	Against 10-hour day........	175,000	9 Oct. "
eat packers.........	10,635	" "	10 "	"	Against increase of hours ..	169,680	6 Nov. "
al handlers.........	34,000	New York city...........	....	..	....	2,650,000	1887
eading railroad employees............	30,000	Pennsylvania	2 mos.	..	For advance in wages.....	3,620,000	24 Dec. "
icago, Burlington & Quincy railroad employees............	....	Illinois	....	..	Adjustment of wages	....	27 Feb. 1888
w York Central railroad (general)......	....	Albany, N. Y.............	1-4 wks.	..	Against dismissal of Knights of Labor	....	8 Aug. 1890
iners in coke district.	15,000	Connellsville, Pa..........	6 "	..	....	....	Mch. 1891
iners..............	3,000	Indiana..................	2 mos.	No	For wage scale............	875,000	1 May, "
rnegie steel works...	10,000	Homestead, Pa...........	5 "	"	" " "	2,000,000	25 June, 1892
vitchmen (Erie railroad)............	....	Buffalo, N. Y.............	10 days	"	....	....	14 Aug. "
iners, coal.........	28,000	Nanticoke, Pa............	3 mos.	Partly	For wage scale............	....	25 Feb. 1893
ainmen, Lehigh Valley railroad	2,000	....	18 days	"	General grievance.........	....	18 Nov. "
reat Northern and Montana Central railroad	....	....	16 "	"	Settled by arbitration......	....	15 Apr. 1894
ine workers; general throughout the U. S.	150,000 to 200,000	....	2 mos.	"	Against reduction of wages.	13,500,000	23 Apr. "
mployees of the Pullman Car Manufacturing company...	2,000	Chicago, Ill	4 "	No	" " " " .	....	11 May, "
merican Railway union orders railroad strike to support the boycott against the Pullman Car Co.....	....	Western railroads.........	2 "	"	Sympathetic..............	....	26 June, "

merican Railway Union, a powerful labor organization of railroad employees under the presidency of Eugene V. Debs, orders a sympathetic strike in favor of the Pullman Car company strikers on the western railroads, 26 June, 1894
apidly spreads....28 June, "
. S. government interferes on account of the mails..30 June, "
njunction against strikers from the U. S. courts.......2 July, "
ederal troops ordered to Chicago....3 July, "
Gov. Altgeld sends protesting telegrams to pres. Cleveland for sending the U. S. troops....4-5 July, 1894
Fierce rioting in Chicago during the strike; several million dollars' worth of railroad property destroyed......5-8 July, "
Debs, with Howard and other leaders, indicted and arrested for conspiracy, released on $10,000 bail....10 July, "
James R. Sovereign, president of the Knights of Labor, issues a call for the knights to strike—no general response, 10 July, "

Executive of the American Federation of Labor decides not to order a strike....................................13 July, 1894
[Strike greatly weakened by this decision.]
Debs arrested, charged with violating the Federal injunction, 17 July, "
Federal troops withdrawn from Chicago..............19 July, "
Pres. Cleveland appoints Carroll D. Wright, commissioner of labor, John D. Kernan, and Nicholas E. Worthington a committee to investigate the Pullman strike........25 July, "
Strike declared off by the strike committee of the American Railway Union....................................6 Aug. "
State troops ordered home by gov. Altgeld.............7 Aug. 1894
Committee of investigation begin their work in Chicago.15 Aug. "
Trial of Debs and other officers of the American Railway Union began in the U. S. courts, Chicago...........5 Sept. "
U. S. justice Harlan delivers his decision on strikes, Chicago, 1 Oct. "
Attorney-general Olney decides that the boycott of the Reading railroad against labor unions is unlawful............9 Nov. "
Committee of investigation report, exonerating the American Railway Union, and condemning the Pullman Company and the General Managers Association..................Nov. 12 "

IMPORTANT ENGLISH AND FOREIGN STRIKES.

Class of trade.	Number involved.	Where begun.	Duration.	Successful.	Object of strike.	Loss in wages.	Date of beginning.
Cotton spinners	30,000	Lancashire, Engl	4 mos.	No	For advance in wages	....	1810
Spinners	10,000	Manchester, Engl	6 "	"	Against new machinery	$1,250,000	1829
Spinners	30,000	Ashton and Staleysbridge	10 wks.	"	For advance in wages	1,250,000	1830
Builders	30,000	Manchester, Engl	6 mos.	"	Against contract building.	360,000	1833
Potters	3,300	Staffordshire, Engl	4 "	Yes	For advance in wages	250,000	Nov. 1834
Amalgamated Society of Operative Engineers	15,000	England	11 wks.	No	Against overtime	....	10 Jan. 1852
Spinners (lock-out)	17,000	Preston	9 mos.	"	For 10% increase in wages.	2,100,000	15 Oct. 1853
Colliers (lock-out)	3,200	West Yorkshire	2 "	Partly	Against reduced wages	500,000	1858
Building trade (lock-out).	25,000	London	7 "	No	For 9-hour day	....	6 Aug. 1859
Engineers	9,000	Newcastle	20 wks.	Yes	" " "	900,000	May, 1871
Cotton hands	35,000	Oldham	1 wk.	..		175,000	"
Colliers	18,000	South Wales	12 wks.	..		1,080,000	"
Agricultural union	....	Alderton, Suffolk, Engl	18 "	No		....	Mch. 1872
Building operatives	10,000	London	12 "	..	For 9-hour day	600,000	1 June, "
Colliers	70,000	South Wales	11 "	..	Against reduced wages	3,850,000	1 Jan. 1873
Miners (lock-out)	50,000	" "	5 mos.	No		....	2 Jan. 1875
Shipwrights	10,000	Clyde	"	Partly		....	May, 1877
Masons	1,700	London	33 wks.	..	More pay, less time	280,500	31 July, "
Cotton-mill hands	300,000	Lancashire	9 mos.	..	Against reduced wages	13,500,000	18 Apr. 1878
Nailers	25,000	Staffordshire	10 wks.	..		1,250,000	"
Cotton-mill hands	10,000	Oldham	4 mos.	No	Against reduced wages	200,000	25 Nov. "
Coal miners	70,000	Durham	....	Partly	" " "	....	5 Apr. 1879
Ship-builders	8,000	Tyne	3 mos.	..		120,000	"
Miners	30,000	S. Yorkshire and Midland	1 wk.	Yes	For advance in wages	....	1888
Coal miners	....	Westphalia, Germany	3 wks.	"	For increased pay and 8-hour day	....	3 May, 1889
Dock laborers	22 Aug. 25,000; 30 Aug. 80,000	London	4 "	Partly	For increased pay and other grievances	....	15 Aug. "
Factory hands	40,000	Barcelona, Spain	5 "	..	For reduction of time of labor	....	1890
Railroad	50,000	Cardiff, Wales	8 days	Partly	For reduction of time of labor	....	7 Aug. "
Shipping trade	80,000	Australia and New Zealand	....	..		....	29 Aug. "
Miners	36,000	Pas-de-Calais, France	....	..		....	15 Nov. 1891
Coal miners	60,000	England and Wales	1 mo.	Partly	Against 25% reduction in wages	....	28 July, 1893

One of the most notable strikes in recent times was that of the anthracite coal miners in Pennsylvania in 1902. The strike began 15 May, on demands for an increase of wages and an 8-hour working-day, and recognition of the unions. Lawlessness constantly increased until 30 July; by 5 Oct. the entire militia of the state had been called out. Pres. Roosevelt, on 1 Oct., invited the representatives of the labor unions and a number of the anthracite coal operators to confer with him. As a result of the conference the president appointed a commission on 13 Oct. to whom all questions at issue were referred. Work was resumed 23 Oct., and the commission met 24 Oct., judge George Gray presiding. During the year 1904 about 1800 strikes and lock-outs were reported, the most important of which were the strike of the miners in Colorado (unsuccessful), the textile workers in Fall River (compromised in 1905), the meat-packers in Chicago, and the employees of the subway railroad in New York City (successful). The subway employees, in a new strike during the early part of 1905, were utterly defeated. In May, 1905, the teamsters of Chicago began a sympathetic strike, which was met by the combined employers. The strikes of 1904 affected nearly 250,000 workmen, of which one-half were more or less successful.

WAGE LOSS OF EMPLOYEES, ASSISTANCE TO EMPLOYEES, AND LOSS OF EMPLOYERS, 1 JAN. 1881, TO 1 JAN. 1901.

Year.	Strikes.			Lock-outs.		
	Wage loss of employees.	Assistance by labor unions.	Loss of employers.	Wage loss.	Assistance by labor unions.	Loss of employers.
1881	$3,372,578	$287,999	$1,919,483	$18,519	$3,150	$6,960
1882	9,864,228	734,339	4,269,094	466,345	47,068	112,382
1883	6,274,480	461,233	4,696,027	1,069,212	102,253	297,097
1884	7,666,717	407,871	3,393,073	1,421,410	314,027	640,847
1885	10,663,248	465,827	4,388,893	901,173	89,488	455,477
1886	14,992,453	1,122,130	12,357,808	4,281,058	549,452	1,949,498
1887	16,560,534	1,121,554	6,698,495	4,233,700	155,846	2,819,736
1888	6,377,749	1,752,668	6,509,017	1,100,057	85,931	1,217,199
1889	10,409,686	592,017	2,936,752	1,379,722	115,389	307,125
1890	13,875,338	910,285	5,135,404	957,966	77,210	486,258
1891	14,801,505	1,132,557	6,176,688	883,709	50,195	616,868
1892	10,772,622	833,874	5,145,691	2,856,013	537,684	1,695,080
1893	9,938,048	563,183	3,406,195	6,659,401	364,268	1,034,420
1894	37,145,532	931,052	18,982,129	2,022,769	160,244	982,584
1895	13,044,830	559,165	5,072,282	791,703	67,701	584,155
1896	11,098,207	462,165	5,304,235	690,945	61,355	357,535
1897	17,468,904	721,164	4,868,687	583,606	47,326	298,044
1898	10,037,284	585,228	4,596,462	880,461	47,098	239,403
1899	15,157,965	1,096,030	7,443,407	1,485,174	126,957	379,365
1900	18,341,570	1,434,452	9,431,299	16,136,802	448,219	5,447,930
Total	$257,863,478	$16,174,793	$122,731,121	$48,819,745	$3,451,461	$19,927,983

LOCK-OUTS, BY YEARS, 1 JAN. 1881, TO 1 JAN. 1901.

Year.	Lock-outs.	Establishm'nts.	Average establishments.	Number employees.	Average duration (days).	Per cent. of success. Succeeded.	Suc'ded partly.	Failed.
1881	6	9	1.5	655	32	88.89	11.11	....
1882	22	42	1.9	4,131	105	64.29	....	35.71
1883	28	117	4.2	29,512	57	56.41	....	43.59
1884	42	354	8.4	18,121	41	27.97	.28	71.75
1885	50	183	3.7	15,424	27	38.25	3.28	58.47
1886	140	1,509	10.8	101,980	39	21.18	13.11	65.71
1887	67	1,281	19.1	59,630	49	34.19	1.25	64.56
1888	40	180	4.5	15,176	74	74.44	3.89	21.67
1889	36	132	3.7	10,731	57	40.91	25.76	33.33
1890	64	324	5.1	21,555	73	65.74	5.56	28.70
1891	69	546	7.9	31,014	37	63.92	14.29	21.79
1892	61	716	11.7	32,014	72	69.13	25.28	5.59
1893	70	305	4.4	21,842	34	41.90	18.31	39.79
1894	55	875	15.9	29,619	39	11.31	2.40	86.29
1895	40	370	9.3	14,785	32	13.24	.27	86.49
1896	40	51	1.3	7,668	65	80.39	1.96	17.65
1897	32	171	5.3	7,763	38	60.82	3.51	35.67
1898	42	164	3.9	14,217	48	63.41	.61	35.98
1899	41	323	7.9	14,817	37	18.01	.62	81.37
1900	60	2,281	38.0	62,653	265	94.30	.31	5.39
Total	1,005	9,933	9.9	504,307	....	50.79	6.28	42.93

STRIKES, BY YEARS, 1 JAN. 1881, TO 1 JAN. 1901.

Year.	Strikes.	Establishm'nts.	Average establishments.	Number employees.	Average duration (days).	Per cent. of establishments in which strikes— Succeeded.	Suc'ded partly.	Failed.
1881	471	2,928	6.2	129,521	13	61.37	7.00	31.63
1882	454	2,105	4.6	154,671	22	53.63	8.17	38.24
1883	478	2,759	5.8	149,763	21	58.17	16.09	25.74
1884	443	2,367	5.3	147,054	30	51.50	3.89	44.61
1885	645	2,284	3.5	242,705	30	52.80	9.50	37.70
1886	1,432	10,053	7.0	508,044	23	34.50	18.85	46.65
1887	1,436	6,589	4.6	379,676	20	45.64	7.19	47.17
1888	906	3,506	3.9	147,704	20	52.22	5.48	42.30
1889	1,075	3,786	3.5	249,559	26	46.49	18.91	34.60
1890	1,833	9,424	5.1	351,944	24	52.65	10.01	37.34
1891	1,717	8,116	4.7	298,939	35	37.88	8.29	53.83
1892	1,298	5,540	4.3	206,671	23	39.31	8.70	51.99
1893	1,305	4,555	3.5	265,914	21	50.86	10.32	38.82
1894	1,349	8,196	6.1	660,425	32	38.09	13.50	48.41
1895	1,215	6,973	5.7	392,403	20	55.24	9.94	34.82
1896	1,026	5,462	5.3	241,170	22	59.19	7.47	33.34
1897	1,078	8,492	7.9	408,391	27	57.31	28.12	14.57
1898	1,056	3,809	3.6	249,002	23	64.19	6.38	29.43
1899	1,797	11,317	6.3	417,072	15	73.24	14.25	12.51
1900	1,779	9,248	5.2	505,066	23	46.43	20.62	32.95
Total	22,793	117,509	5.2	6,105,694	....	50.77	13.04	36.19

stron'tium. The native carbonate of strontia was discovered at Strontian, in Argyleshire, in 1787. Sir Humphry Davy first obtained from it the metal strontium in 1808.

strych'nia, a poisonous vegetable alkaloid, discovered in 1818 by Pelletier and Caventou in the seeds of the *strychnos ignatia* and *nux-vomica*, and also in the upas poison. Half a grain blown into the throat of a rabbit occasions death in 4 minutes; it produces lockjaw. Much attention was given to strychnia in 1856, during the trial of William Palmer, who was executed for the murder of Cook, 14 June, 1856.

Stuart, properly **Stewart,** House of. ENGLAND, PRETENDERS, SCOTLAND.

stucco work, a plaster of pulverized marble and gypsum applied to walls and ceilings for decorative purposes. It was known to the ancients, and was much prized by them, particularly by the Romans, who excelled in it.—*Lenglet.* It was revived by D'Udine, about 1550; and in Italy, France, and England in the 18th century.

Stuhm, a town of W. Prussia. Here Gustavus Adolphus of Sweden defeated the Poles, 1628.

Stun'dists, a Puritan sect in south Russia, said to be descendants of Russian soldiers converted from the Greek church by German missionaries; some were cruelly persecuted by the bigoted peasantry of Vossnessensk in Kherson in 1879; 13 of the ringleaders were tried for the crime, 8 Nov. 1879.

Sturm und Drang ("storm and pressure") period or movement in German literature, a chaotic or volcanic period, without form or order, 1760–1800.

Stuttgart, capital of Würtemberg, first mentioned in 1229, was made his residence by count Eberhard, 1320; enlarged by Ulric, 1436; and made capital of the state, 1482. It has been greatly adorned during the last and present centuries. International rifle-meeting here, 1 Aug. 1875. Pop. 1890, 139,659.

style (Gr. στίζειν, to pierce, to stick, thence στύλος, a sharp-pointed iron), manner of writing, of doing, etc.; a mode of reckoning time. The style was altered by Augustus Cæsar's ordering leap-year to be once in 4 years, and the month Sextilis to be called Augustus, 8 B.C. AUGUST, NEW STYLE.

Styl'ites. MONACHISM.

Styr'ia, a province of Austria, part of the ancient Noricum and Pannonia, was held successively by the Romans, Ostrogoths, and Avars. It was conquered by Charlemagne, and divided among his followers, styled counts, among whom the count of Styria, about 876, was the most powerful. The count became margrave about 1060; and Ottocar VI., in 1180, was made duke. At his death, 1192, Styria was annexed to the duchy of Austria. In 1246 it was acquired by Bela IV. of Hungary; in 1253 by Ottocar II. of Bohemia, after whose defeat and death at Marchfeld, in 1278, it reverted to Rudolph of Hapsburg, and was annexed to his possessions.

submarine lamp, one invented by Siebe and Gorman, has been in use since 1850, especially at Cherbourg; Heinke and Davis's lamp was exhibited, 1871.

submarine telegraph. ELECTRICITY.

Succession, Wars of. AUSTRIAN SUCCESSION, SPANISH SUCCESSION.

Suevi (*swe'vi*), a warlike German tribe, which, with the Alani and the Visigoths, entered Spain about 408; were overcome and absorbed by the latter, about 584.

Suez canal. The caliph Omar about 640 opposed cutting the isthmus. A plan for a canal between the head of the Red sea and the bay of Pelusium was brought forward by M. Ferdinand de Lesseps in 1852. He undertook to cut a canal through 90 miles of sand (actual length, 87 miles; 66 miles canal and 21 miles lakes); to run out moles into the Mediterranean; to deepen the shallow waters; to create ports to receive the ships from India and Australia, and to adapt the canal to irrigation. The consent of the Egyptian, Turkish, Russian, French, and Austrian governments was gradually obtained, but not that of the British. A company was formed for the purpose, and the work commenced in 1858 by Daniel Lange (knighted 1870). The cost was estimated at 8,000,000*l.* Engineer, M. L. Monteit.

M. Delacour, a French engineer, after viewing works, "employing 25,000 men in the desert," expected that they would be completed in 4 or 5 years ....7 Nov. 1862
Waters of the Mediterranean admitted into a narrow channel communicating with lake Timsah....Dec. "
New town Timsah named Ismaila....4 Mch. 1863
Works visited by the sultan and by Mr. Hawkshaw.... "
Company compelled by the Egyptian government to give up compulsory labor; litigation ensued....Aug. "
M. de Lesseps reports that a vessel with 30 persons had been tugged from sea to sea....Feb. 1865
Delegates from British chambers of commerce visit the works, and report that success is only an affair of time and money....17 Apr. "
Flood-gates of smaller Suez canal opened, the fresh water of the Nile admitted; a coal-vessel passes from the Mediterranean to the Red sea ....15 Aug. "
Primo, 80 tons' burden, passes from the Mediterranean to the Red sea....17 Feb. 1867
A loan raised in France.... "
French and English vessels enter the canal....Nov. 1868
John Fowler, the engineer, reports the canal suitable for steamers and mail traffic, but not for vessels requiring tugs, 5 Feb. 1869
Mediterranean admitted to salt lakes ....18 Mch. "
Visited by the prince and princess of Wales....23 Mch. "
Canal opened in presence of the emperor of Austria, empress of the French, viceroy of Egypt, etc....17 Nov. "
M. de Lesseps entertained in London....4 July, 1870
Traffic in 1870-71 doubled....1872-73
Charges for vessels increased 50 per cent.; British appeal for a national conference....Apr. 1873
International conference on Suez dues meet at Constantinople; 21 sittings; report dated 18 Dec. Proposals of the sultan accepted by European powers....Dec. "
M. de Lesseps protests; lords of admiralty informed (by D. A. Lange) that canal will be closed unless old dues are paid, 22 Apr.; he yields....26 Apr. 1874
Col. Stokes, after survey, reports to earl of Derby the canal generally in a satisfactory state.... 20 Apr. "
British government authorize messrs. Rothschild to buy for 4,080,000*l.* the khedive's shares (176,602 shares of 20*l.*, out of 400,000) in the canal (at 5 per cent. till 1 July, 1894, after which dividends will be paid)....Nov. 1875
M. de Lesseps in a circular says he regards "as a fortunate circumstance the powerful union between English and French capitalists for the purely industrial and necessarily peaceful working of the universal maritime canal," 29 Nov. "
Subject discussed in the commons, 14 Feb.; money (4,080,000*l.*) voted, 21 Feb.; act passes....15 Aug. 1876
Neutrality of canal claimed by Great Britain....May, June, 1877
Its freedom secured by settlement of Egypt....1882-83
Receipts about 5,000,000 francs, 1870; 60,523,815 francs.... 1882
Second canal determined on by British ship-owners; syndicate appointed.... 10 May, 1883
Arrangements made by government for construction and advancement of capital, virtually under control of De Lesseps's company, announced 11 July; dissatisfaction and opposition in England, 12 July; proposed convention withdrawn, 23 July, "
Sir Stafford Northcote's resolution against De Lesseps's monopoly negatived (284-185)....31 July, "
De Lesseps visits London; agrees with steamship owners to enlarge present canal or create a new one, giving additional powers to the company, and to reduce dues, etc., 30 Nov. "
Agreement approved by the British government, 25 Feb.; the shareholders at Paris protest against it, but ratify it (2608-556)....29 May, "
Widening of the present canal decided on, after investigation by commission, Dec. 1884; plans adopted by the commission, 9 Feb. 1885
International commission sits at Paris; English and French schemes discussed....Apr.-May, "
Parts of these schemes incorporated in treaty....May, "
Arrangements with Egypt completed for widening the canal, 27 Dec. 1886
Convention at Paris for England and France, neutralizing the canal under a joint commission.... 24 Oct. 1887
Adhesion of the other powers announced, July; ratified by the sultan, 25 Oct.; by the powers....29 Oct. and 22 Dec. 1888

TRAFFIC THROUGH THE CANAL.

Year.	No. of ships.	Gross tonnage.	Gross receipts.
1870....	486	435,911	£255,488
1871....	765	761,467	464,091
1872....	1,082	1,439,169	758,659
1873....	1,173	2,085,073	971,882
1874....	1,264	2,423,672	1,029,492
1875....	1,494	2,940,709	1,204,387
1876....	1,457	3,072,107	1,229,157
1877....	1,663	3,418,950	1,337,617
1878....	1,593	3,291,535	1,272,435
1879....	1,477	3,236,942	1,214,443
Total, 10 years....	12,454	23,105,535	9,737,651
1880....	2,026	4,344,519	1,672,836
1881....	2,727	5,794,401	2,187,047
1882....	3,198	7,122,125	2,536,343
1883....	3,307	8,051,307	2,645,506
1884....	3,284	8,319,967	2,480,000
1885....	3,624	8,985,411	2,601,998
1886....	3,100	8,183,313	2,241,095
1887....	3,137	8,430,043	2,314,494
1888....	3,444	9,437,957	2,680,000
1889....	3,425	9,605,745	2,735,678
Total, 10 years....	31,272	78,274,788	24,094,997
1890....	3,389	9,749,129	2,679,340

The statutes of the Suez Canal company provide that all net earnings in excess of 5 per cent. interest on the shares shall be divided as follows:

1. 15 per cent. to the Egyptian government.
2. 10 " " to the founders' shares.
3. 2 " " for the employees of the company.
4. 71 " " as dividend on 394,677 shares.
5. 2 " " to the managing directors.

The net profits in 1890 were over 1,525,335*l.* Of the 3389 ships passed through the canal in 1890, 2522 belonged to Great Britain.

sugar (*Saccharum officinarum*) is supposed to have been known to the ancient Jews. Found in India by Nearchus, admiral of Alexander, 325 B.C.—*Strabo*. An Oriental nation in alliance with Pompey used the juice of the cane as a common beverage.—*Lucan*. It was prescribed as a medicine by Galen, 2d century. Brought into Europe from Asia, 625 A.D.; in large quantities, 1150. Attempted to be cultivated in Italy; not succeeding, the Portuguese and Spaniards carried it to America about 1510. It was long considered a neutral substance, without congeners, but has of late years become the head of a numerous family—viz.: cane-sugar (*sucrose*, from the sugar-cane; boiled with dilute acids it becomes *glucose*); fruit-sugar (from many recent fruits); grape-sugar (*glucose*, from dried fruits and altered starch); sugar of milk (*melitose*, from eucalyptus, by Berthelot in 1856); *sorbin* (from the berries of the mountain ash, by Pelouze); *inosite* (from muscular tissue, Scherer); *dulcose* (by Laurent); *mannite* (from manna, obtained from the *fraxinus ornus*, a kind of ash); *quercite* (from acorns); to these have been added *mycose*, by M. Mitscherlich, and *melezetose* and *trehalose*, by M. Berthelot.

Sugar-refining was made known to Europeans by a Venetian, 1503; and was first practised in England about 1659. The invaluable vacuum-pan was invented by Charles E. Howard, 1812. Dr. Scoffern's processes were patented in 1848-50.
Sugar-cane transported from Tripoli and Syria to Sicily and Madeira....about 1138
It is not known when sugar was introduced into England, but doubtless before Henry VIII. Mr. Whittaker, in the "History of Whalley," p. 109, quotes a mention.... 1497
A manuscript letter of sir Edward Wotton, dated Calais, notifies lord Cobham that he had taken up for him 25 sugar-loaves at 6 shillings a loaf, "whiche is eighte pence a pounde"....6 Mch. 1546
Sugar first taxed (by James II.).... 1685
The consumption of sugar per capita in the principal nations of Europe is, England, 78 pounds; Denmark, 41; Switzerland, 33; France, 28+; Holland, 28; Germany, 24; Norway and Sweden, 22+; Belgium, 21; Portugal, 14; others less. Average, 22.

SUGAR IN THE UNITED STATES.

Sugar-cane first grown in part of territory now constituting the U. S.... 1751
First American sugar-mill built near New Orleans.... 1758
Sugar first manufactured from sorghum.... 1882
A bounty was granted by Congress from 1 July, 1891, to 1 July, 1905, of 2 cents a pound on sugar not less than 90° by the polariscope from cane, beets, sorghum, and maple produced in the U. S., and testing less than 90° and not less than 80°, 1¾ cents....1 Oct. 1890
Bounty paid by U. S., $7,432,077.... 1891
[All bounties paid to sugar producers in the U. S. ceased from the date of the passage of the Tariff act, 27 Aug. 1894.]

Sugar production. Mulhall gives the following estimates of the production of cane and beet sugar in the world in English tons from 1840 to 1904, and Willett & Gray, New York, for the following years

Years	Cane	Beet	Total
	Tons	Tons	Tons
1840	1,100 000	50 000	1,150 000
1850	1,200 000	200,000	1 400 000
1860	1 830,000	400 000	2 230 000
1870	1,850 000	900 000	2 750 000
1880	1,860 000	1 810 000	3,670 000
1890	2 580 000	2 780 000	5,360,000
1898	2,850,000	4 650 000	7,500,000
1900	2,839 500	5,608,544	8,448 044
1901	3 657,416	6,066,939	9,724 355
1902	4,070,282	6,923,487	10,993 769
1903	4 118,059	5,717 332	9,835 391
1904	4 312,574	6 060,178	10,372,752

The production of sugar in 1903-4 by sugar growing countries, in tons of 2240 pounds, was

Countries	Cane Sugar
Louisiana	215,000
Porto Rico	130 000
Cuba.	1,033,708
British West Indies	134,758
Hayti and San Domingo	45,000
Peru and Brazil	367,000
Java	885,561
Hawaii	343,000
Queensland	91,828
Mauritius	215,000
Demerara	133,000
Argentina	140,719
Philippines	100,000
	Beet Sugar
United States	208,135
Germany	1,933 435
Austria	1 177,210
France	804,401
Russia	1,200,000
Belgium and Holland	326,997

The United States consumed in 1903 2,549,642 tons, a consumption per capita of over 71 pounds

suicide. Strabo, the historian, tells us that at Ceos, the country of Simonides, 500 B C., it was an established custom to allow suicide to those who had attained 60 years or were infirm In England until 1823 the body of the suicide was directed to be buried in a cross-road and a stake driven through it During 5 years, from 1882 to 1887, there were 8226 suicides in the United States The average annual suicide rate per 100,000 persons is estimated for various countries as follows Saxony, 31 1, Austria, 21 2, Switzerland, 20 2, France, 15 7, German Empire, 14 5, Prussia, 13 3, England and Wales, 6 9, United States, 3.5, Russia, 2 9, Ireland, 1 7, Spain, 1 4

An epidemic of suicide among the soldiers under Tarquin I, to avoid the menial task of excavating the sewers of Rome, is checked by an edict that the bodies of suicides be exposed to public view nailed on crosses B C. 606
Cato the Younger commits suicide at Utica, Africa 46
Jews, at the siege of Jerusalem by Titus, destroy themselves in large numbers in the fortress of Massada, to avoid falling into the hands of the Romans A D 70
Suicide condemned as a crime by the Council of Arles 452
First ecclesiastical rule as to suicide in England, made at the first Council of Braga, forbids a burial service for suicides 563
No commemoration of a suicide to be made in the Eucharist, and no psalms sung at the burial, by declaration of Council of Auxerre 578
Hara kiri (suicide by disembowelment) of persons of military class in Japan, condemned to death, instituted during the Ashikaga dynasty 1336-1568
By criminal law of Louis XIV of France, the body of a suicide is to be dragged at a cart's tail 1670
Epidemic of suicide at Versailles, 1793, at Rouen, 1806, and at Stuttgart 1811
In the British army an officer attempting suicide will be court martialed and cashiered, and a private imprisoned, by law of 1879
Law passed in New York, 26 July, 1881, making attempted suicide a felony, punishable by imprisonment not exceeding 2 years, or by a fine not exceeding $1000, or both, takes effect, 1 Dec. 1882
Lawrence Ballard sentenced to one year's imprisonment, for attempting suicide, first conviction under the law of 1882, 8 Feb. 1883

Sullivan, Fort. FORT MOULTRIE.

Sullivan's expedition against the Six Nations NEW YORK, 1779

sulphur has been known from the earliest times Basil Valentine mentions its production from green vitriol Sulphuric acid (vitriol) produced by him from burning sulphur, was introduced into England about 1720 Sulphur has been studied by eminent chemists during the present century, and many discoveries have been made—such as its allotropic condition, etc It is the inflammable constituent in gunpowder, and a deleterious ingredient in coal-gas The sulphur mines of Sicily have been wrought since the 16th century but the exportation was inconsiderable till about 1820, in 1838 the trade increased so much that Great Britain alone imported 38 654 tons In that year the Neapolitan government was induced to grant a monopoly of the trade to a French company, but a firm remonstrance from the British government led to a discontinuance of this impolitic restriction in 1841, which, however, gave a great and lasting impetus to the British sulphur manufacture In 1871, only 937,049 tons were imported into the United Kingdom

sultan, or ruler a Turkish title, from the Arabic, given to the grand-signior or emperor of Turkey It was first given to the Turkish princes, Angrolipez and Musgad, about 1055 —*Vatter* It was first given according to others, to the emperor Mahmoud, in the 4th century of the Hegira

Sulu islands or **archipelago,** under Spanish protection, by a protocol signed at Madrid, 7 Mch 1885, by representatives of Great Britain, Germany, and Spain, includes all islands between the western extremity of the island of Mindanao on the one side, and the islands of Borneo and Aragua on the other, excluding all Borneo and all lands within 3 maritime leagues of its coast The group contains about 60 islands, with an area of about 1000 sq miles

Suma'tra, an island in the Indian ocean, called Java Minor by Marco Polo, and visited by Nicolo di Conti prior to 1449 Mainly on account of the pepper trade, the Dutch formed a settlement at Padang about 1649, and the British at Bencoolen about 1685 The Dutch possessions with Java were acquired by the British in 1811, but were restored in 1816 In 1824 the Dutch acquired all the British settlements in Sumatra, in exchange for Malacca and some possessions in India Restrictions on their progress in Sumatra were removed by treaty Feb 1872 Severe fighting between the Dutch and the Achinese natives, with varying results, mostly in favor of the Dutch, Apr 1873 to 1879 Dutch successful in war Area, 149,555 sq miles. Pop about 3,500,000 ACHEEN

sumptuary laws restrain excess in dress, furniture, eating, etc The laws of Lycurgus were severe against luxury, probably about 881 B.C. Those of Zaleucus ordained that no sober woman should go attended by more than one maid in the street, or wear gold or embroidered apparel, 450 B.C.—*Diog Laert* The *Lex Orchia* among the Romans (181 B C) limited the guests at feasts, and the number and quality of the dishes at an entertainment, and it also enforced that during supper, which was the chief meal among the Romans, the doors of every house should be left open The English sumptuary laws, chiefly of the reigns of Edward III. and Henry VIII, were repealed in 1856. DRESS.

Sumter, Fort FORT SUMTER

sun, the, one of the so-called "fixed stars," is the centre of our solar system Its attraction controls the planet Neptune 2,745,998,000 miles away It would seem to be the parent of all the planets, but how or when they were formed science has as yet been unable to explain Pythagoras, about 529 B C., taught that the sun was one of the 12 spheres and that it was some 44,000 miles from the earth, Aristarchus of Samos, and afterwards Ptolemy, Copernicus, and Tycho Brabe supposed its distance about 4 800,000 miles Kepler increased it to some 15,000,000, while Cassini and La Caille approach the true distance by making it between 21,000 and 28,000 terrestrial radii The sun's distance from the earth, given until recently as 95,000,000 miles, has been shown to be somewhat less. The sun's horizontal parallax, as determined by different astronomers, is here given

		Parallax
Old value obtained by Encke from the transit of Venus	1761-69	8.571"
New value obtained by Hansen from the moon's parallactic equation.		8 916"

		Parallax
New value obtained by Le Verrier from the motion of Mars and Venus	1861	8 95″
New value obtained by Stone	1862	8 932″
" " " " from transit of Venus	1882	8 823″
" " " " Foucault from velocity of light,	1864	8 86″
" " " " Gill	1877	8 78″
" " " " Winnecke from observation of Mars		8 964″
New value obtained by Wolfe from transit of Venus	1882	8 808″

With a parallax of 8.8″ the distance would be about 92,890,000 miles from the earth, this is certainly within 150,000 miles of its true distance The sun's estimated diameter is 108 times that of the earth, or 852,900 miles Its surface exceeds that of the earth 11,900 times, and its volume 1,305,725 times, while its mass is 332,260 times that of the earth, and 750 times that of all the planets together Its density is about 25 that of the earth, or a little more than water One pound at the surface of the earth would weigh 27 9 lbs at the sun, and as a body falls through 16+ ft the first second of time here, it would there pass through 461+ ft. It revolves on its axis in 25 days 7 hrs 48 min, and its rotary velocity at its equator is 4477 miles per hour. Inclination of its axis to the plane of ecliptic, 82° 30′ Its light on the earth exceeds 620,000 full moons —*R A Proctor* As the distance from the earth to the sun varies, so do the light and heat of the sun at the earth vary If the mean intensity of the sun's light and heat at the earth be expressed by 1000, then 1034 will express its greatest light and heat, and 967 its least The sun is a perfect sphere as far as known, and is surrounded by an extensive and rare atmosphere (1) The photosphere, visible source of the solar light, (2) chromosphere, chiefly of incandescent hydrogen gas, (3) corona, a vast shell of unknown vapor, many thousand miles in thickness The study of the sun of late years has been greatly aided by the analysis of the solar spectrum

Adelmus, a Benedictine monk, discovers a spot on the sun (*Bede*) . 17 Mch 807

Averroes saw spots on the sun . . 1161

Hakluyt reported such 1590

Spots were observed by Fabricius, Harriot, and Galileo 1610

Dr Halley, by observing a sun spot, proved its motion round its own axis July and Aug 1676

Parallax of the sun, dr Halley . 1702

A spot 3 times the size of the earth passed the sun's centre, 21 Apr 1766

Dr Wilson observed the motion of a spot. 1769

He proves sun spots to be depressed 1774

Herschel measured 2 spots, whose length together exceeded 50,000 miles 19 Apr 1779

Schwabe discovered a cycle of changes (from maximum to minimum and minimum to maximum) in the number of spots in 11 years, confirmed by Wolf and others 1826–51

[According to dr R. Wolf of Zurich, for many years a standard authority on "sun spots," the monthly average of sun spots observed by him from 1879 is as follows 1879, 6, 1880, 31 6, 1881, 54 1, 1882, 59 3, 1883, 62 8, 1884, 63 3, 1885, 50 8, 1886, 25 7, 1887, 13 1, 1888, 6.7, 1889, 6 1, 1890, 7 11, 1891, 32 6]

Red flames, or protuberances, during an eclipse of the sun, observed by capt. Stannyan, 1706, by Halley, 1715, by F Baily (hence termed "Baily's beads") 1842

Warren De la Rue took 2 photographs at the time of total obscuration 18 July, 1860

James Nasmyth discovers the lenticular shaped objects on the sun (termed by him "willow leaves," by Stone "rice-grains") 28 Aug "

Mouchot constructed a solar boiler for distillation, etc Oct "

"Solar physics" especially studied by Warren De la Rue, Balfour Stewart, etc 1865–66

Red flames, or prominences, determined by M Janssen to be due to the accumulated hydrogen of the photosphere, at the solar eclipse (ECLIPSE) 18 Aug 1868

Mr Ericsson proposed condensation of the sun's rays and their employment as a motive power Oct "

[Observations in the eclipse of 22 Dec 1870 and 12 Dec 1871 suggested an unknown substance (represented in the spectrum by line 1474) in the sun]

Apparatus for cooking by the condensed solar rays in the Paris exhibition 1878

Solar eclipse well observed in the U S, the corona much brighter than in 1871 29, 30 July, "

M Mouchot at Algiers, by a mirror, collected solar rays, and boiled water, drove an engine, etc Mch 1880

Intensely red sunsets and after glow and very red sunrises seen in all parts of the globe Oct, Nov and Dec 1883

Attributed by some to the volcanic dust projected by the eruption of Krakatoa, Java . Aug "

Other causes such as cosmic dust suggested. Similar sunsets in the autumns of . 1884–85

Sun spots observed from the Royal observatory, Greenwich, with an estimated area of 3,360,000,000 sq miles on the sun's surface . Feb 1892

SUN

Sunday was the day on which, anciently, divine adoration was paid to the sun Among Christians, it is commonly called *Dies Dominica*, or Lord's day, on account of our Saviour's appearance on that day, after his resurrection. The first civil law that was issued for the observance of this day combined it with that of the seventh-day Sabbath and other festivals (Eusebius, "Life of Constantine"), and it was followed by several imperial edicts in favor of this day, which are extant in the body of Roman law, the earliest being that of Constantine the Great, dated 7 Mch 321 SABBATH, SABBATARIANS, SPORTS AND GAMES, WEEK. For Sunday letter, DOMINICAL LETTER

Council of Orleans prohibited farm labor on Sunday 538

Sabbath day was ordained to be kept holy in England from Saturday at 3 in the afternoon to Monday at break of day, 4th canon, Edgar 960

Act of parliament levying 1 shilling on every person absent from church on Sundays, 3 James I 1606

James I authorizes certain sports after divine service on Sundays (SPORTS) 1618

Act restraining amusements. 1 Charles I 1625

Act restraining the performance of servile works, and the sale of goods except milk at certain hours and meat in public-houses, and works of necessity and charity, on forfeiture of 5 shillings, 29 Charles II 1676

Massachusetts prohibits travel play, or work from the evening preceding Sunday, or any part of that day or evening following 1693

Sunday-schools. The modern revival of Sunday-schools is generally dated from the establishment at Gloucester, Engl., in July, 1780, of a school for the instruction of children in reading and the elementary truths of religion, held on Sunday, and conducted by paid teachers. This Sunday-school was instituted by Robert Raikes, editor and proprietor of the *Gloucester Journal*, and through the columns of his weekly paper his effort was made widely known There are now in the world over 200,000 Sunday-schools, with 2,500,000 teachers, and 18,000,000 scholars Of these there are in the United States about 110,000 schools, with 1,200,000 teachers, and 9,000,000 scholars Schools for Bible study were organized in Upper Egypt, Armenia, and elsewhere, early in the 4th century A canon attributed to the 6th general council of Constantinople, 680 A D, promotes the setting up of charity schools in all country churches St Carlo Borromeo left at his death, in 1584, Sunday-schools to the number of 743, which he had established in his cathedral at Milan, and in parish churches near and far A canon of the Church of England, in 1603, required the teaching of the catechism, etc., to children and ignorant persons by the parson, vicar, or curate every Sunday afternoon Rev Joseph Alleine established a Sunday-school at Bath, Engl, in 1665-68 They existed at Roxbury, Mass., 1674, Norwich, Conn, 1676, and Plymouth, Mass., 1680 One was conducted at Newtown, L I, by rev. Morgan Jones in 1683, and in England by bishop Frampton in 1693 Between 1740 and 1780 the following well-authenticated Sunday-schools were established

Place	Conductor	Established
Ephrata, Pa	Ludwig Höcker	1740
Bethlehem, Conn	Rev dr Joseph Bellamy	"
Philadelphia, Pa	Mrs. Greening	1747
Norham, Scotland	Rev Mr Morrison	1750
Brechin, Scotland	Rev David Blair	1763
Columbia, Conn	Rev Eleazer Wheelock	1764
Bedale, England	Miss Harrison	1765
High Wycombe, Engl	Miss Hannah Ball	1769
Doagh, Ireland	William Galt	1770
Bright Ireland	Rev dr Kennedy	1774
Little Lever, England	James Heys	1775
Mansfield, England.	Rev David Simpson	1778
Asbury, England	Rev Thomas Stock	about "
Dursley, England	William King	" "

Voluntary Sunday school teaching begun in Bolton, Engl 1785

Society for Promoting Sunday schools throughout the British Dominion, organized 7 Sept. "

Sunday school organized at the house of Thomas Crenshaw, Hanover county, Va., under direction of bishop Asbury 1786

First-day or Sunday school Society, for instructing poor children on Sunday, organized at Philadelphia 11 Jan 1791

London Sunday-school Union, to promote Sunday-schools having unpaid teachers, organized 13 July 1803

Sunday school in imitation of the Raikes schools in England started in New York city by Mr and Mrs Divie Bethune "

American Sunday-school Union organized . 1824

National convention of Sunday schools in New York city 1832

World's Sunday school convention in London, Engl . 1862

International lesson plan inaugurated 1873

Foreign Sunday-school Association, organized by Albert Woodruff of Brooklyn about 1863, incorporated 1878

Supralapsa'rians, a name given to the Gomarists or extreme Calvinists, the opposers of the Arminian party at the Synod of Dort, 1618 Their dogma is but a form of fatalism

supremacy over the church was claimed by pope Gelasius I as bishop of Rome, 494 On 15 Jan 1535, Henry VIII, by virtue of the act 26 Hen VIII c 1, formally assumed the style of "on earth supreme head of the church of England," which has been retained by all succeeding sovereigns The bishop of Rochester (Fisher) and the ex-lord chancellor (sir Thomas More) and many others were beheaded for denying the king's supremacy in 1535, and in 1578, John Nelson, a priest, and Thomas Sherwood, a young layman, were executed at Tyburn for the same offence The "act of Supremacy," repealed by 1 and 2 Phil and Mary, c. 8 (1554), was re-enacted 1 Eliz c 1 (1559)

Supreme court of Judicature of England was constituted by the Judicature act, 36 and 37 Vict c 66, passed 5 Aug 1873, to come into operation 1 Nov. 1874. In 1874 this was deferred to 1 Nov 1875

Existing courts were to be united into one Supreme court divided into the High court of Justice and the Court of Appeal The High court to consist of the lord chancellor the 2 lord chief justices, the vice chancellors, and the other judges (hereafter the court to consist of 21 judges)

Five divisions 1 Chancery, 2 Queen's Bench, 3 Common Pleas, 4 Exchequer, and 5 Probate, Divorce, and Admiralty, subject to alteration

Court of Appeal to consist of 5 *ex officio* judges (viz lord chancellor, 2 lord chief justices, lord chief baron, master of the rolls), and such others as may be appointed (§§ 20 21 22)

Appeals to the House of Lords or the judicial committee of the privy council to be discontinued.

Supreme court of Judicature (comprising the High court of Justice Chancery division, Queen's Bench, Common Pleas, and Exchequer subdivisions, Probate, Divorce, and Admiralty division) began 2 Nov 1875

By the Appellate Jurisdiction act (1876) the House of Lords remains the court of ultimate appeal, to consist of the lord-chancellor, 2 lords of appeal (to be created peers for life, with 6000*l* salary), and peers who are lawyers Act to come into operation 1 Nov 1876

At a meeting of the judges it was resolved to recommend the abolition of the Exchequer and Common Pleas and their consolidation into one, termed the "Queen's Bench division," under the lord chief-justice of England, 30 Nov, order in council 16 Dec. 1880

Carried into effect, old divisions at an end, Judicature act carried out for the first time 7 Mch. 1881

Supreme court of the United States COURTS OF THE UNITED STATES, JUSTICES

surgery (from surgeon = chirurgeon, Gr χείρ, the hand, and ἔργον, work, operation) The art and practice of curing or alleviating injuries and diseases of the body by manual operations It stands first among all the professions of science, its practice is not founded upon theory, but upon positive knowledge, its success upon the highest intelligence, great dexterity, and coolness under the most trying circumstances. Until the 13th century the bath-keepers and barbers were almost the only medical faculty and the sole surgeons in Germany In France the surgeons appear at an earlier period, as a graded and distinct class, and divided into guilds of inferior and superior surgeons An association of surgeons, influential in the development of modern surgery, was organized in France by Jean Pitard (1228-1315), which was called the "College de Saint Côme" The title of "surgeon" was first recognized by law in England in 1299 These "chirurgeons" or "surgeons" were educated in some institution of learning, and permitted to wear long robes and a peculiar style of hat, which distinguished them from the "barber-surgeons" of earlier date Field surgeons accompanied the English armies at the beginning of the 15th century. The practice of surgery was forbidden to barbers in France as early as 1425. The barber-surgeons in England were incorporated under the title of "Masters or Governors of the Mystery or Commonalty of Barbers of London," by charter dated 24 Feb. 1461. In 1540 an act was passed, providing "that no person using any shaving or barbery in London shall occupy any surgery, letting of blood or other matter, except only drawing of teeth," and surgeons were by this act prohibited from practising shaving. An act for making the surgeons and barbers of London 2 distinct and separate corporations was passed in 1745, and the same year a charter was given to the College of Surgeons A new charter was secured in 1800, again in 1843 (when it was styled "Royal College of Surgeons of England"), in 1852, and 1859 By the aid of anæsthetics, Lister's antiseptic dressings, and Esmarch's bandage, modern surgeons are able to operate in many cases without pain, without suppuration, and without bleeding Among surgeons, ancient and modern, who have attained eminence are the following

ANCIENT

Asclepiades of Prusa in Bithynia, 128-56 B C —Practised tracheotomy in angina

Archigenes of Apamea 48-117 A D —Described amputation with preliminary ligation of the main vessels and cauterization of small ones

Leonides of Alexandria fl about 200 A D

Antyllus, fl in 3d century —First to describe extraction of small cataracts

Philargius 300-75 —Removed stone by incision from above into the neck of the bladder

Paul of Ægina, about 625-90 —Obstetrician

ITALIAN.

Leonardo Bertapaglia, d 1460 —Operated for cancer, etc

Alexander Benedetti, d 1525 —First to mention artificial restoration of the nose

Bartolomeo Maggi, 1516-52 —Most important army surgeon of the day

Giacomo Berengario, d 1550

Cesare Magati, 1579-1647

Giuseppe Francesco Borri, 1625-95 —A skilful oculist.

Antonio Scarpa, 1752-1832

Bartolomeo Signorini, 1797-1844, Padua —Performed in 1832 the first total extirpation of the lower jaw

Luigi Porta, 1800-75 —Professor in Pavia.

Aloisio Vanzetti, b 1809 —Digital compression of arteries in treatment of aneurism

F Rizzoli, 1809-80

SPANISH

Francesco de Arce, 1493-1573

Bartolomæus Hidalgo de Aguerro, 1531-97

Andreas Alcazar, fl. about 1575

Antonio de Gimbernat, fl about 1790 —Anatomist and herniologist.

DUTCH.

Andreas Vesalius, 1514-64.

Cornelis van Solingen 1641-87

Joh Jac Rau, 1668-1719 —Lithotomist

Pieter Camper, 1722-89

Edward Sandifort, 1742-1814

Christian Bernard Tilanus, 1796-1883

Frans C Donders, 1818-89 —Ophthalmologist.

J Mezger, b 1839

GERMAN

Felix Wuertz, 1518-75

Florian Matthis, fl about 1602 —First to perform gastrotomy

Joh Leberecht Schmucker, 1712-86 —Surgeon general under Frederick II

Joh Ulrich Bilguer, 1720-96.—Performed first resection of wrist (1762)

Carl Caspar von Siebold, 1736-1807 —First in Germany to perform symphyseotomy in 1778

August Gottlieb Richter, 1742-1812.—"The greatest German surgeon of the 18th century"—*J H Baas*

Georg Jos. Beer, 1763-1821 —Oculist, first drew forth the iris and cut it off externally

Vincenz von Kern, 1769-1829

Conrad Johann Martin Langenbeck, 1776-1851 —Founder of German surgical or topographical anatomy, introduced iridokleisis.

Phil Franz von Walther, 1782-1849 —Founder of surgical clinics at Landshut and Bonn universities.

Cajetan von Textor, 1782-1860 — Inaugurator of conservative surgery (resection) in Germany

Carl Ferdinand von Graefe, 1787-1840 —Cultivated plastic surgery

Joseph, Baron von Wattmann, 1789-1847 —Operative surgery

Johann Friedrich Dieffenbach, 1794-1847 —Operative surgery

Georg Friedrich Louis Stromeyer, 1804-76 —Military surgeon, creator of operative orthopædia.

Franz Schuh, 1805-65 —Introduced the microscope in surgery

V von Bruns, 1812-83.

Friedrich Esmarch, b 1823 —Artificial anæmia.

R F Wilms, 1824-80

O Weber 1827-80 —Professor in Heidelberg

John Nepomuk von Nussbaum, b 1829

W König, b 1832

C Hueter, 1837-80

FRENCH

Guy de Chauliac, about 1300.—Successfully removed part of a man's brain

Jean Tagault, d. 1545.—Professor at Padua and Paris

Ambroise Paré, 1509-90.—Introduced ligation of arteries in amputation (1552) and staphyloplasty

Pierre Franco, fl about 1560 —Invented supra-pubic lithotomy

Jacques Baulot, 1651-1714 —Lithotomist

Jean Louis Petit 1674-1750 —Noted for his screw tourniquet and amputation à deux temps

François Gigot de la Peyronie 1678-1747 —Wounds of the intestines.

Henri François le Dran 1685-1770 —First disarticulation of the thigh.

Jacques Daviel, 1696-1762 —Introduces extraction of lens of the eye (1750)

Antoine Maitre Jean, fl about 1707 —Oculist.

Claude Nicolas le Cat, 1700-68.

François Chopart, 1743-95 —Foot amputation.

Pierre Joseph Desault, 1744-95.—Established the first surgical clinic in the Hôtel Dieu, Paris.
Alexis Boyer, 1757-1833
Jean Dominique Larrey, 1766-1842 —Invented *ambulances volantes*
Jacques Mathurin Delpech, 1777-1832.—Cultivator of orthopædic surgery and pioneer of autoplastic surgery in France.
Guillaume Dupuytren, 1777-1835 — "The Napoleon of surgery", first to make subcutaneous division of muscles and perform resection of the facial bones
Philibert Jos Roux 1780-1854
Jacques Lisfranc, 1790-1847 —First subcutaneous tenotomy of the tendo Achillis
Joseph François Malgaigne, 1806-65 —Noted as a writer on surgery
Auguste Nelaton, 1807-74 —Invented a probe
J. E. Petrequin 1808-76 —Galvano puncture in aneurisms.
Jules Nicolas Demarquay, 1814-75
Jules Rochard b 1819
Paul Broca, 1824-80 —Named the so called "Broca s convolution" in the brain
Jules Pean, b 1830 —Extirpation of spleen, resection of stomach
J L Reverdin, b 1842 —Skin grafting on ulcerated surfaces.

ENGLISH

John Ardern, about 1325-1400 —Treated fistula
Thomas Gale 1507-86 —Army surgeon
John Woodall, fl about 1613 —Surgeon general of the East India company
Richard Wiseman, fl 1603-25 —"The Pride of England"
John Greenfield, fl about 1677 —Lithotomist.
R Lowdham, fl about 1679 —Said to have been the first among the moderns to practise the flap method in amputation.
William Cheselden, 1688-1752 —Oculist and lithotomist
Alexander Monro, 1697-1767
Samuel Sharp, 1700-78
William Hunter, 1718-83.—Obstetrics
John Hunter, 1728-93 —First to describe phlebitis
Charles White, fl about 1768 —Performed first resection of the humerus
Sir William Blizard, 1743-1835 —First to tie the superior thyroid artery for relief of goitre
John Bell, 1763-1820
Sir Astley Paston Cooper, 1768-1841 —First to tie the abdominal aorta (1817), first paracentesis of the membrana tympani (1801)
Sir Charles Bell, 1774-1842
John Lezars, 1783-1860 —Extirpation of ovary and operation for chronic hydrocephalus.
Sir Benjamin Collins Brodie, 1783-1862
Sir William Lawrence, 1783-1867
George James Guthrie, 1785-1856.—Military surgeon.
Joseph Henry Green 1791-1863
Frederick Tyrrell, 1797-1843 —Ophthalmic surgeon
Sir Thomas Watson, 1792-1882
Sir Charles Locock, 1799-1875 — Physician—Accoucheur to queen Victoria, attended at each of her accouchements
William Coulson, 1802-77 —Specialist in lithotripsy and lithotomy
Sir William Fergusson, 1808-77 —"System of Practical Surgery," 1842
John Hutchinson, 1811-61
Thomas Blizard Curling, b 1811
John Erich Erichsen —Published "Science and Art of Surgery"
Sir James Paget, b 1814
Sir Henry Thompson, b. 1820 —Lithotomist, performed lithotomy upon the ex emperor Napoleon III, 1873.
Sir Joseph Lister, b 1827 —Inventor of antiseptic surgery
Sir William MacCormac, b. 1836.

AMERICAN.

Thomas Bond, 1712-84 —First professor of clinical medicine in U S.
John Jones, 1729-91 —Published the first native surgical work which appeared in the U S "Plain, Precise, Practical Remarks on the Treatment of Wounds and Fractures", medical attendant to Washington and Franklin, lithotomist.
Benjamin Church, 1734-76
William Shippin, jr, 1736-1808
Richard Bayley, 1745-1801 —Lithotomist and oculist.
John Warren, 1753-1815.—Founder of medical department of Harvard college
Nathan Smith, 1762-1829
Wright Post, 1766-1828
Philip Syng Physick, 1768-1837 —Called by Gross "the father of American surgery"
Ephraim McDowell, 1772-1830 —"Father of OVARIOTOMY"
John Collins Warren, 1778-1856.—Administered ether for surgical anæsthesia (1846)
Reuben Dimond Mussey, 1780-1866.—Removed entire scapula and clavicle (1837)
Amos Twitchell, 1781-1850 —Tied the primitive carotid artery
John Syng Dorsey, 1783-1818 —First American to tie the external iliac artery
William Gibson, 1784-1868.—First to tie the common iliac artery
Valentine Mott, 1785-1865 —First to tie the arteria innominata.
Benjamin W Dudley, 1785-1870 —Lithotomist.
Alexander Hodgdon Stevens 1789-1869 —Eminent clinical teacher
J Kearney Rodgers, 1793-1857 —Tied the left subclavian artery between the scaleni (1846)
George McClellan, 1796-1847 —Founder of Jefferson Medical college
Willard Parker, 1800-84 —"A bold and independent surgeon and popular teacher"
John Rea Barton, d 1871 —Lithotomist.
Dixi Crosby, 1801-73 —Removed the entire arm (1836).
Joseph Pencoast, 1805-82
Samuel D Gross, 1805-84
John Watson, 1807-62.—First in America to perform œsophagotomy (1844)
Gurdon Buck 1807-77 —Introduced extension by strips of adhesive plaster and weight and pulley (1851)
Thomas Dent Mutter 1811-59
J Marion Sims, 1813-83 —Gynæcologist
Frank Hastings Hamilton, 1813-86 —Practised skin grafting (1847)
Henry H Smith, 1815 90 —Fractures.
James Rushmore Wood, 1816-82 —Removed entire lower jaw (1856), previously performed by Horace A. Ackley, Cleveland, O See Italian surgeons above
John Murray Carnochan, 1817-87 —Ligation of femoral artery (1851), exsection of superior maxillary nerve beyond the ganglion of Meckel (1856)
David Hayes Agnew, 1818-92 —Attended president Garfield.
Henry J Bigelow —Performed first excision of hip joint in U S. (1852)
Lewis A Sayre, b 1820.—Orthopedic surgery
Cornelius Rea Agnew, 1830-88 —Ophthalmologist.
Henry Burton Sands 1830-88
Hunter McGuire, b 1835 – Tied the abdominal aorta (1868)
Samuel W Gross, 1837-89
J H Knapp, b Germany, 1832 —Founder of the Ophthalmic and Aural institute New York city, 1869
Nicholas Senn —Professor of surgery Rush Medical college, Chicago. Inventor of method of rectal insufflation of hydrogen gas in diagnosis of gastro intestinal injuries
John Ashurst, jr, professor of clinical surgery, University of Pennsylvania
William Detmold —College of Physicians and Surgeons, New York city Introducer of subcutaneous tenotomy into the U S
MEDICAL SCIENCE

Su'rinam, a colony of Dutch Guiana, South America, discovered by Columbus, 1498 The factories established by the English in 1640 were occupied by the Portuguese, 1643, by the Dutch, 1654, taken by the British, 1799, but restored to the Dutch at the peace of Amiens, 1802, again occupied by the English from 1804 to 1816, when it was returned at the peace of Paris, 1815 Area, 46,060 sq miles, pop. 1889, 55,968.

surname (Fr *surnom*, from *sur*, upon, and *nom*—Lat *nomen*—a name), the family name or name of the gens, to which is added or given the baptismal or Christian name, as William, John, etc, corresponding to the prænomen of the Latin NAMES were introduced into England by the Normans, and were adopted by the nobility about 1100 The old Normans used Fitz, which signifies son, as Fitzherbert. The Irish used O, for grandson, O'Neal, O'Donnell. The Scottish Highlanders used Mac, as Macdonald, son of Donald The northern nations added the word son to the father's name, as Williamson Many of the most common surnames, such as Johnson, Wilson, Dyson, Nicholson, etc, were taken by Brabantes and other Flemings, who were naturalized in the reign of Henry VI, 1435 M A. Lower's "Dictionary of English Surnames" was pub 1860

surplice, an outer robe worn by an officiating priest or clergyman in the Episcopal or Roman Catholic church, first worn by the Jewish priests, and said to have been first used in churches in the 4th century, and encouraged by pope Adrian, 786 "Every minister saying public prayers shall wear a comely surplice with sleeves," canon 58 The garb prescribed by stat. 2 Edw VI 1547, again 1 Eliz 1558, and 13 and 14 Chas II 1662 RITUALISM

Su'sa or **Shu'shan,** capital of Susiana, a province of Persia, was taken by Alexander the Great, 331 B.C.

suspension bridges. BRIDGES

Susquehan'na settlers. The charter of James I, in 1620, to the Plymouth company, covered the territory extending from the Atlantic to the Pacific and lying between 40° and 46° N lat. Connecticut purchased a part of this territory of the Plymouth company in 1631, with the boundary the same on the west and 41° lat. on the south. This sale was confirmed by Charles II in 1662 The grant of Charles II to Penn extended to 42° north Thus the Connecticut grant overlapped that of Pennsylvania 1 degree In 1753 the Susquehanna company was formed in Connecticut to explore and settle lands in this territory In 1754 they purchased of the Six Nations a tract including the Wyoming valley CONNECTICUT, 1754. Pennsylvania, while disputing this sale, made no effort to prevent a settlement In Aug 1762, 105 settlers came from Connecticut into the Wyoming valley, but, owing to the lateness of the season, soon returned Coming back early in May, 1763, they settled, but were obliged to return to Connecticut after a loss of 20 by an attack of the Indians in Oct of the same year The next attempt of Connecticut to form a settlement was in Jan 1769, when 40 settlers arrived in Wyoming Pennsylvania now determined to defend her territory, and arrested these settlers in Oct What might be termed a civil war (the Pennymite and Yankee war) followed for the next 6 years, with varied success and with the loss of a number of lives. The Connecticut settlers, however, reinforced from time to time, persisted, and organized an independent government by town meetings, as in Connecticut In 1774 they united 7 towns into one, Westmoreland, and attached it to Litchfield county, Conn This desultory strife continued with loss of life and much suffering until the struggle was suspended by the war of the Revolution These were the settlers that were killed and scattered in the fearful Wyoming massacre by the Tories and Indians in 1778. In 1779 and 1780 they again returned and occupied the valley In the meanwhile the titles of the Penns had passed to the state, and although the struggle was kept up after the Revolution, negotiations were more direct Pennsylvania finally confirmed the title of the Connecticut settlers on their payment of a nominal sum for their land, and compensated the Pennsylvania claimants with other lands and with money

suttee', the self-burning of widows This custom began in India from one of the wives of "Brahma, the Son of God," sacrificing herself at his death, that she might attend him in heaven 17 widows have burned themselves on the funeral pile of a rajah, and in Bengal alone 700 have thus perished in a year The English government, after long discouraging suttees, formally abolished them, Dec 1829, but they have since occasionally taken place The wife of the son of the rajah of Beygoon thus perished, June, 1864, and several wives of sir Jung Bahadoor, minister of Nepaul, 1 Mch 1877 Suttees still occur, one voluntary at Poona, Nov 1890

Swa'bia, a province in S Germany, was conquered by Clovis, and incorporated into the kingdom of the Franks, 496 After various changes of rulers, it was made a duchy by the emperor Conrad I, in 912, for Erchanger, according to some, in 916, for Burckhardt The duchy became hereditary in the house of Hohenstaufen in 1080 Duke Frederick III became emperor of Germany as Frederick I (usually styled Barbarossa, "red beard"), in 1152 Conradin, his descendant, was defeated at the battle of TAGLIACOZZO, in 1268, and beheaded shortly after The breaking-up of the duchy gave rise to many of the small German states, part of Swabia is included in Würtemberg and Switzerland Swabia was made a circle of the empire in 1387 and 1500 A league composed of Swabian cities and provinces, about 1254, was the germ of the great Swabian league, formed for the preservation of the peace of Germany, under the auspices of the emperor Frederick, in 1488

Swamp-angel, name given by the Federal soldiers to a 200-pound Parrott gun, mounted with great difficulty in a redoubt built in a morass between Morris and James islands, near Charleston, S C, 1863, by gen Gillmore, for the purpose of bombarding that city It threw 150-lb shells into the city, a distance of 5 miles The gun burst at the 36th discharge.

Swamp fight, The Great. MASSACHUSETTS, 1675.

Swanzey, Mass, Indian attack on MASSACHUSETTS, 1675

Swaz'iland, S Africa, a tract of about 8000 sq miles, nearly surrounded by the Transvaal territory. Pop. 1889, about 60,000 natives and 600 whites.

Swe'aborg, a strong fortress in Finland, the Gibraltar of the north, 3½ miles south of Helsingfors, it is situated on 7 rocky islands, the fortifications were commenced by the Swedes in 1748, and completed after Finland was united to Russia in 1809 On 6 Aug 1855, the English and French fleet anchored off Sweaborg, and bombarded it by mortar and gun-boats from the 9th to the 11th, causing the destruction of nearly all the principal buildings, including the dock-yard and arsenal Few casualties and no loss of life ensued in the allied squadron, but this success was not followed up

swearing on the Gospels, first used about 528, and introduced in judicial proceedings about 600 —*Rapin.*

sweating-sickness. PLAGUE.

Swe'den, a country of N Europe The ancient inhabitants were Finns, now the people of Finland, who retired thither on the appearance of the Scandinavians or Goths, who have ever since been masters of Sweden SCANDINAVIA. The internal state of this kingdom was little known previous to the 11th century By the union of Calmar, in 1397, Sweden became a province of Denmark, and was not wholly rescued from this subjection till 1521, when Gustavus Vasa recovered the kingdom from the Danish yoke He became king in 1523, and his descendants ruled till 1809 Norway ceded to Sweden by the treaty of Kiel, 14 Jan 1814. The government of Sweden is a limited monarchy The diet consists of 4 orders, the nobles, the clergy, the burghers, and the peasants, and meets every 3 years The king is, as in Great Britain, the head of the executive There are 2 universities, Upsal and Lund, and Sweden can boast among its great men Linnæus, Celsius, Scheele, Bergman, Berzelius, Thorwaldsen, Andersen, and Swedenborg Area, 170,979 sq miles Pop 1880, 4,518,901, 1890, 4,784,675, 1900, 5,221,291

		B C.
Odin said to have arrived in the north and to have died		70
His son Skiold reigns		40
Skioldungs reign till Olaf the infant is baptized, and introduces Christianity among his people	about	A D 1000
Waldemar I of Denmark subdues Rugen, and destroys the pagan temples.		1168
Stockholm founded		1260
Magnus Ladulæs establishes a regular government		1279
Crown, hitherto hereditary, is made elective, Steenchel Magnus surnamed Smek, or the foolish, king of Norway, is elected		1319
Waldemar lays Gothland waste.		1361
Albert of Mecklenburg reigns.		1363
Treaty or union of CALMAR, by which Sweden is united to Denmark and Norway, under Margaret		1397
University of Upsal founded		1476
Christian II of Denmark, "the Nero of the North," massacres the Swedish nobility		1520
Swedes delivered from the Danish yoke by the valor of Gustavus Vasa		1521
Gustavus Vasa raised to the throne		1523
He introduces Lutheranism and religious liberty		1527
Makes the crown hereditary		1544
Gustavus Adolphus heads the Protestant cause in Germany		1628
He takes Magdeburg and Munich, 1630, slain at Lutzen, 16 Nov		1632
Rugen ceded to Sweden by Denmark		1648
Abdication of Christina	16 June,	1654
Charles X overruns Poland		1655
Arts and sciences begin to flourish		1660
University of Lund founded		1666
Charles XII, "the Madman of the North," begins his reign, makes himself absolute, abolishes the senate, 1699, defeats the Russians at Narva	30 Nov	1700
Battle of POLTOWA, Charles defeated by czar of Russia,	8 July,	1709
He escapes to Bender where, after 3 years' protection, he is made a prisoner by the Turks.		1713
He is restored, and after numerous battles is killed at the siege of Frederickshald	11 Dec	1718
Queen Ulrica abolishes despotism		1719
Bremen and Verden ceded to Hanover	Nov	"
Royal Academy founded by Linnæus		1741
Conspiracy of counts of Brahe and Horne, who are beheaded		1756
Hats and Caps (French and Russian parties), 1738–57, put down by Gustavus III		1770
Despotism re established		1772
Order of the Sword instituted		"
Assassination of Gustavus III by count Ankerström at a ball, 16 Mch, he expires	29 Mch	1792
Regicide scourged with whips of iron thongs 3 successive days, his right hand cut off, then his head, and his body impaled	18 May,	"
Gustavus IV dethroned, government assumed by his uncle, duke of Sudermania (Charles XIII)	13 Mch	1809
Representative constitution established	7 June,	"
Sweden cedes Finland to Russia	17 Sept	"
Bernadotte, prince of Ponte Corvo (one of Bonaparte's marshals), chosen crown prince of Sweden	21 Aug	1810
Gustavus IV arrives in London	12 Nov	"
Swedish Pomerania seized by Napoleon	9 Jan	1812
Alliance with England	12 July,	"
Sweden joins the grand alliance against Napoleon	13 Mch	1813
Norway is ceded to Sweden by the treaty of Kiel, 14 Jan, carried into effect	Nov	1814
Bernadotte king, as Charles John XIV	5 Feb	1818
Canals and roads constructed		1822
Treaty of navigation between Great Britain and Sweden,	19 May,	1826
Death of Charles John, his son Oscar I. king	8 Mch	1844
Alliance with England and France	21 Nov	1855
Banishment decreed against Catholic converts from Lutheranism	Oct	1857
Demonstration in favor of Italy	17 Dec	1859
Increased religious toleration	May,	1860
Demonstration in favor of Poland	Apr	1863
Inauguration of free trade	1 Jan	1864
Sweden protests against the occupation of Schleswig by the allies.	22 Jan.	"

Foundation of a "National Scandinavian Society" at Stockholm to obtain by legal means a confederation of the 3 kingdoms for military and foreign affairs, reserving independent interior administration Dec 1864
New constitution passed by the chambers 4-8 Dec "
Severe famine in N Sweden Oct -Dec 1867
Princess Louisa married to Frederick, crown prince of Sweden, 28 July, 1869
Neutrality in Franco Prussian war proclaimed 4 Aug 1870
Queen d 13 Mch 1871
Death of king Charles XV 18 Sept. 1872
Diet opened by king Oscar II 20 Jan 1873
King and queen crowned 12 May, "
Crown prince made viceroy of Norway 19 Mch. 1884
Prince Oscar marries miss Munck at Bournemouth, Engl, 15 Mch 1888
Norway agitates for autonomy in foreign affairs, opposed by Sweden Feb 1892

KINGS OF SWEDEN (previously kings of Upsal)

1001 Olaf Schotkonung, or Olif Schœtkonung, the Infant, is styled king 1015
1026 Edmund Colbrenner
1051 Edmund Slemme
1056 Stenkill
1066 Halstan
1090 Ingo I, the Good
1112 Philip
1118 Ingo II
1129 Swerker, or Suercher I
1155 St Eric IX
1161 Charles VII, made prisoner by his successor
1167 Canute, son of Eric I
1199 Swerker or Suercher II, killed in battle.
1210 Eric X
1216 John I
1222 Eric XI the Stammerer
1250 Birger Jarl, regent
" Waldemar I
1275 Magnus I, Ladulæs
1290 Birger II
1319 Magnus II, Smæk, dethroned.
1350 Eric XII
1359 Magnus restored, deposed 1363.
1363. Albert of Mecklenburg, his tyranny causes a revolt of his subjects, who invite Margaret of Denmark to the throne
1389 Margaret, queen of Sweden and Norway, now also of Denmark, and Eric XIII
1397 [Union of Calmar, by which the 3 kingdoms are united under one sovereign]
1412 Eric XIII governs alone, deposed
1440 Christopher III
1448 Charles VIII Canuteson, king of Sweden only
1471 [Interregnum] Sten Sture, protector
1483 John II (I of Denmark)
1502 [Interregnum]
1503 Swante Sture, protector
1512 Sten Sture, protector
1520 Christiern, or Christian II of Denmark, styled the "Nero of the North", deposed for his cruelties.
1523 Gustavus I Vasa, by whose valor the Swedes are delivered from the Danish yoke
1560 Eric XIV, son, dethroned and slain by
1569 John III brother
1592 Sigismund III, king of Poland, son, disputes for the succession continued the whole of this reign
1604 Charles IX, brother of John III
1611 Gustavus II, Adolphus the Great, son, falls at the battle of Lutzen, 16 Nov 1632
1632 [Interregnum]
1633 Christina, daughter of Gustavus Resigns the crown to her cousin, 16 June, 1654, d at Rome in 1689
1654 Charles X, Gustavus, son of John Casimir, count palatine of the Rhine
1660 Charles XI, son, the arts and sciences flourish in this reign
1697 Charles XII, son, styled the "Alexander" and the "Mad man of the North", killed at Fredrickshald, 11 Dec. 1718
1718. Ulrica Eleanora, sister, and her consort Frederick I, landgrave of Hesse Cassel Ulrica relinquishes the crown, and in
1741 Frederick reigns alone
1751 Adolphus Frederick of Holstein Gottorp, descended from the family of Vasa.
1771 Gustavus III, Adolphus, son, assassinated by count Ankerström at a masked ball, 16 Mch, d 29 Mch 1792
1792 Gustavus IV, Adolphus, son, dethroned and the government assumed by his uncle, the duke of Sudermania.
1809 Charles XIII duke of Sudermania.
[Treaty of Kiel (1814), by which Norway falls under the sovereignty of Sweden]
1818 Charles (John) XIV, Bernadotte, the French prince of Ponte Corvo, d 8 Mch 1844
1844 Oscar I, son, b 4 July, 1799, d. 8 July, 1859
1859 Charles XV, son, b 3 May, 1826, d 18 Sept. 1872, a poet, brave and impulsive, much beloved.
1872 Oscar II, brother, b 21 Jan 1829, marries princess Sophia of Nassau, 6 June, 1857
Heir Gustavus, son, b 16 June, 1858, married to Victoria of Baden, 20 Sept 1881

Swe'denborg. PHILOSOPHY

Swedenbor'gians, or New Jerusalem Church, are those who adopt the theological teachings of Emanuel Swedenborg (b. at Stockholm, 29 Jan 1688, d in London, 29 Mch. 1772)

His disciples first meet as an organized body in London in 1788
They believe that the sole deity is centred in Jesus Christ, in whom is a trinity of essentials, that salvation is effected by faith and works combined, that, as man's soul is a spiritual body, he will never resume the material body, that the Last Judgment was effected in the spiritual world during Swedenborg's lifetime, and that the Lord's Second Coming has taken place through the revelation of a new system of truth from the inner sense of Scripture
Swedenborg Society instituted, 1810
Missionary and Tract Society of the New Church, 1821
This church, according to the U S census returns for 1890, numbers 154 organizations with 7095 members

swimming. Leander is said to have swum nightly across the Hellespont from Abydos to Sestos, about 1 mile, to meet Hero, and lord Byron and lieut Ekenhead did the same, 3 May, 1810

> "Across the Hellespont's wide weary space,
> Wherein he nightly struggled with the tide."
> —*Hood*, "Hero and Leander," stanza cxxiii.

Side stroke in swimming said to have been introduced by George Pewters. about 1850
Over hand stroke first used by Harry Gardner at Manchester, Engl 1862
Capt Matthew Webb swims from Blackwall to Gravesend, 20 miles, in 4 hrs. 53 min, 3 July, and from Dover to Calais, 35 miles in 21 hrs 45 min 24-25 Aug 1875
Agnes Beckwith, aged 14, swims from London bridge to Greenwich, 5 miles, in 1 h 8 min 1 Sept "
Emily Parker, aged 15, swims from London bridge to Blackwall, 7 miles, in 1 h 35 min 4 Sept "
Paul Boyton swims the strait of Gibraltar from Carnpa to Tangier in 5 hrs 5 min 20 Mch 1878
Capt. Matthew Webb swims from Gravesend to Woolwich and back to Rosherville, 40 miles, in 9 hrs. 57 min, Thames, Engl, 12 July, "
Miss Beckwith swims 20 miles in the Thames in 6 hrs. 25 min, 17 July, "
Capt Webb swims from Sandy Hook to Manhattan beach, Coney Island 13 Aug 1879
Miss Beckwith swims 30 continuous hours 7-8 May, 1880
Capt Webb drowned in attempting to swim through the whirlpool at Niagara falls 24 July 1883
J J Collier swims 1 mile in Hollingworth lake, Engl, in 28 min 19¾ sec. 23 Aug 1884
William J Kendall, wearing a cork jacket, swims through the Whirlpool rapids, Niagara falls 22 Aug 1886
Miss Edith Johnson swims from Bath to Antwerp, 16 miles, in 5 hrs 25 min, without resting. 29 Aug. "
Eugene Mercedier swims across the East river from the Navy-yard, Brooklyn, to Old Slip, New York with arms and legs bound and carrying a 2 lb dumb bell in each hand 22 June, 1890
Davis Dalton (Hahn) alleged to have swum on his back across the English channel from Boulogne to Folkestone, accompanied by a life boat. 17-18 Aug "
J Nuttall swims 1000 yards in 13 min 54⅕ sec —best on record—at Lambeth's baths, London 16 Oct. "
For Paul Boyton, LIFE BOAT

Swiss guards, bodies of hired Swiss troops formerly employed in many European countries as body-guards to the rulers In France formed in 1616 as the Royal Swiss guards, massacred while defending the Tuileries, 10 Aug 1792. Before the attack they numbered about 800 (not all, however, at the Tuileries at the time), under an able commander, Mandat, but he was murdered on the steps of the Hotel de Ville, where he had been called, just before the attack, to receive his orders, thus leaving them without a leader and without orders. How many were killed in the attack was never known. Many were killed afterwards in prison in the September massacres. Reorganized Sept 1815, defeated during the insurrection, 28 July, 1830, dismissed by Charles X., Aug. 1830.

Swithin's Day, St., 15 July. St Swithin lived in the 9th century, and, having been the preceptor to king Ethelwulf, was made bishop of Winchester in 852, and died 2 July, 862. The tradition states that it rained 40 days in consequence of the proposed removal of his remains from the churchyard to the cathedral

Switzerland, the ancient *Helvetia*, a federal republic of S. Europe, was conquered by the Romans, 15 B.C., and was successively subject to the Burgundians, Germans, and Franks. The canton of Schweitz was peopled by the Cimbrians, who, leaving their original habitation in Scandinavia, invaded Italy, and were defeated by the Roman general Marius, and fled into Helvetia about 100 B.C. This canton has given name to the whole confederacy. The Swiss confederation was founded, 1 Jan. 1308, by the 3 cantons of Uri, Schwyz or Schweitz, and

Unterwald. In 1353 it numbered 8 cantons, and in 1513, 13 cantons. This old confederation of 13 cantons was increased by the adherence of several subject territories, and existed till 1798, when it was replaced by the Helvetic republic, which lasted 4 years. In 1803 Napoleon I. organized a new confederation, composed of 19 cantons. This confederation was modified in 1815, when the number of cantons was increased to 22. The position of Switzerland in the history of the world is unique. It is the oldest republic on record, and has existed as such surrounded by forms of government entirely different. It has maintained its position not by extent of territory, population, or military power, but by the jealousy of the nations surrounding it. The present constitution came into force on 29 May, 1874. Area, 15,976 sq. miles; pop. 1860, 2,507,170; 1870, 2,669,147; 1880, 2,831,787; 1890, 2,933,612; 1900, 3,315,443. The present national council is elected every 3d year, at the rate of 1 member for every 2000 persons.

LIST OF CANTONS AND NUMBER OF REPRESENTATIVES TO THE "NATIONALRATH" FROM EACH.

Cantons.	Representatives.	Cantons.	Representatives.
Berne	27	Neufchâtel	5
Zurich	17	Geneva	5
Waadt (Pays de Vaud)	12	Solothurn	4
Aargau	10	Appenzell	4
St. Gall	11	Glarus	2
Lucerne	7	Schaffhausen	2
Ticino	6	Schweitz or Schwyz	3
Fribourg	6	Unterwalden	2
Basel	7	Uri	1
Grisons	5	Zug	1
Wallis (Valais)	5	Total	147
Thurgau	5		

B.C.

Helvetians invading Gaul severely defeated by Julius Cæsar .. 58

A.D.

Helvetians converted to Christianity by Irish missionaries.... 612
Helvetia ravaged by the Huns........ 909
Becomes subject to Germany........ 1032
Fribourg built by Berthold IV........ 1179
Berne built........ 1191
Men of Uri, Unterwalden, and Schwyz make a solemn league and covenant forever against the Austrians; this is regarded as the foundation of the Swiss confederation.........1 Aug. 1291
Tyranny of Gessler, heroism of William Tell, and revolt (demonstrated to be mythical), dated........ 1306
Confederation against Austria; declaration of Swiss independence confirmed by the leaders, Werner Stauffacher (of Schweitz), Walter Fürst (Uri), and Arnold von Melchthal (Unterwalden), determined to free their country.........4 Nov. 1307
A malignant fever carries off, in the canton of Basel, 1100 persons........ 1314
Form of government made perpetual........ 1315
Leopold of Austria defeated at Morgarten, 15 Nov........ "
Lucerne joins the confederacy........ 1335
Canton of Zurich joins and becomes head of the league........ 1350
Berne, Glarus, and Zug join........ 1351
Eight cantons form a perpetual league........ 1352
Leopold II. of Austria defeated and slain at Sempach (the Swiss led by Arnold von Winckelried, who loses his life in a desperate assault on the Austrian spearmen)........9 July, 1386
Austrians defeated at Näfels, 9 Apr. 1388; make peace........ 1389
Grisons league (CADDEE)........ 1400
Second league of the Grisons........ 1424
Third league of the Grisons........ 1436
Battle of St. Jacobs on the Birs, near Basel (1600 Swiss resist 30,000 French, and are all killed, the enemy losing 10,000), 26 Aug. 1444
Swiss defeat Charles the Bold at Granson, 5 Mch.; and at Morat........22 June, 1476
And aid the duke of Lorraine at Nancy, where Charles is slain........5 Jan. 1477
Swiss soldiers first enter into the pay of France, under Louis XI. 1480
Fribourg and Solothurn join confederation........ 1481
Maximilian I., emperor, acknowledges Swiss independence.... 1499
Schaffhausen and Basel join the union........ 1501
Appenzell joins the confederation (the 13th)........ 1513
Swiss invade Milan and defeat the French at Novara...6 June, "
Defeated by them at Marignano........13, 14 Sept. 1515
Swiss confederacy acknowledged by France and other powers........ 1516
Reformation begins at Basel; the bishop compelled to retire.. 1519
Reformation adopted by some cantons; battle of Cappel, Zwingli killed and reformers defeated........12 Oct. 1531
Grisons leagues join the Swiss confederacy as allies........ 1544
Appenzell joins the other cantons........ 1597
Charles Emanuel of Savoy enters Geneva by surprise, scaling the walls, but in the end is defeated........ 1602

[An annual festival commemorates this escape.]

Independence of Switzerland recognized by the treaty of WESTPHALIA........ 1648
Peace of Aargau, end of religious war........Aug. 1712

[From this period until the French revolution the cantons enjoyed tranquillity, disturbed only by the changes arising out of their various constitutions.]

Alliance with France........25 May, 1777
Strife in Geneva between the aristocratic and democratic parties; France interferes........ 1781
One thousand fugitive Genevese seek an asylum in Ireland (GENEVA)........ 1782
Swiss GUARDS ordered to quit France........ 1792
Helvetic confederation dissolved; its subjugation by France.. 1798
Helvetic republic formed........ "
Switzerland the seat of war........1799-1802
Number of cantons increased to 19, by the addition of Aargau, Graubünden (Grisons), St. Gall, Thurgau, Tessin, and Waadt (Vaud); the federal government restored, and a landamman appointed by France........ 1803
Uri, Schweitz, and Unterwalden separate from the republic.. "
Switzerland joins France with 6000 men........24 Aug. 1811
Allies enter Switzerland in the spring of........ 1814
Number of cantons increased to 22, by the addition of Geneva, Neufchâtel, Wallis (Valais), and the independence of Switzerland secured by the treaty of Vienna........ 1815
A colossal lion carved out of the solid rock at Lucerne after a model by Thorwaldsen, in honor of the Swiss guard who fell in defence of the Tuileries, Paris, 10 Aug. 1792; dedicated... 1821
Revision of the constitution of the cantons........ 1830
Law to make education independent of the clergy........ 1839
It leads to dissensions between Catholics and Protestants....1840-44
Dispute about the convents of Aargau, 1844; to put education into the hands of the Jesuits, etc.; opposition of the Protestant cantons........ 1846
Lucerne, Uri, Schweitz, Unterwalden, Fribourg, Zug, and Valais (Roman Catholic cantons) form a separate league (Sonderbund) to support education by the Jesuits, etc........ "
Insurrection at Geneva against Jesuit teaching; a temporary provisional government established........7 Oct. "
Diet declares the Sonderbund illegal, and dissolves it, 20 July; 7 cantons protest, 22 July; diet orders the expulsion of the Jesuits, 3 Sept.; communal assemblies held to resist it, 26 Sept., 3, 10 Oct.; appeal to arms........21 Oct. 1847
Diet prepares to repress the Sonderbund, 4 Nov.; Fribourg surrenders, 14 Nov.; civil war; Sonderbund defeated by gen. H. Dufour, near Lucerne, 23 Nov.; end of the Sonderbund; it submits to expulsion of Jesuits, and secularization of monastic property........29 Nov. "
New federal constitution........12 Sept. 1848
Dispute about NEUFCHÂTEL........ 1857
Declaration of neutrality in the Italian war........14 Mch. 1859
Mutiny and punishment of Swiss mercenary troops at Naples; confederation forbids foreign enlistment......July and Aug. "
Swiss government protests against annexation of Savoy to France........15 Mch. 1860
One hundred and fifty Swiss attempt to enter Savoy; stopped by Genevese government........30 Mch. "
M. Thorel, a Swiss, obtains a prize at the national shooting-match at Wimbledon........July, "
Government forbids the Swiss to enlist in foreign service without permission........30 July, "
French troops occupy Vallée des Dappes, 28 Oct.; Swiss announce the violation of their territory........5 Nov. 1861
Treaty of France settles question of the Vallée des Dappes by mutual cessions; no military works to be constructed on territory ceded; signed........8 Dec. 1862
Revision of the constitution; deliberations begin........23 Oct. 1865
Nearly all the revised articles of the federal constitution rejected by the vote of the Swiss burgesses........14 Jan. 1866
International peace and liberty congress at Geneva, 9-12 Sept. 1867; at Berne........22-26 Sept. 1868
Neutrality in the Franco-Prussian war proclaimed........July, "
New constitution adopted by Zurich........18 Apr. 1869
French army under Clinchant (84,000) crosses the frontiers and is disarmed........1 Feb. 1871
Extraordinary session of the federal assembly to revise the constitution........6 Nov. "
Plébiscite, a new constitution, reorganizing the army, and promoting uniform education, etc., rejected by a majority of 4967 out of 509,921........12 May, 1872
M. Favre engaged to construct a tunnel through St. Gothard in 8 years, for 2,000,000*l*........8 Aug. "
Revised federal constitution voted (321,870 for, 177,800 against), 19 Apr. 1874
Swiss national Catholic church constituted........about June, "
Nineteen Catholic priests deprived for refusal to take constitutional oath........5 Sept. "
International postal congress at Berne, 15 Sept.; protocol signed........9 Oct. "
Civil-marriage law and registration adopted by universal suffrage (212,854-204,700)........23 May, 1875
President of the national council for 3 years, J. Philippin, elected........6 June, 1877
Death of James Fazy, eminent statesman........6 Nov. 1878
National voting for St. Gothard railway and tunnel (161,000 majority)........19 Jan. 1879
Opening of St. Gothard's railway from Milan to Lucerne, 20-21 May, 1882
Invasion of the Salvation army........1883-84
Great powers protest against the asylum given to political criminals by the republic........June, 1889
Six hundredth anniversary of the founding of the Swiss confederation celebrated in the province of Schwytz...1-2 Aug. 1891

swords. The Roman swords were from 20 to 30 inches long. The broadsword and scimitar are of modern adoption. Damascus steel swords were most prized; the next the sword of Ferrara steel. Toledo sword-blades have been famed since the 15th century

> "The trenchant blade, Toledo trusty,
> For want of fighting was grown rusty"
> —*Butler*, 'Hudibras'

The Scotch Highlanders, from the artificer Andrea di Ferrara, called their swords *Andrew Ferraras* The large sword shown at Dumbarton castle as Wallace's is asserted to be one of Edward IV 's The broadsword was forbidden to be worn in Edinburgh in 1724 The 2 most famous swords of romance were the sword 'Excalibur," wrought for king Arthur "by the lonely maiden of the lake," and "Durandal," borne by Orlando or Roland, famed knight of the court of Charlemagne

Syb'aris, a Greek colony in S Italy, founded about 720 B.C , destroyed by the Crotonians about 510 B C The people were greatly addicted to luxury, hence the term Sybarite

Sydney, capital of New South Wales; founded by gov Philip on a cove on Port Jackson, 26 Jan 1788, as a British settlement for the colony of convicts originally intended for Botany Bay It was named after lord Sydney, secretary for the colonies. Pop 1891, including suburbs, 386,400

Legislative council first held	13 July, 1829
Lit with gas, the first place so lit in Australia	May, 1841
University founded	1852
Duke of Edinburgh at Port Jackson narrowly escapes assassination, O'Farrell a Fenian, who shot him in the back on 12 Mch , is convicted on 31 Mch , and executed	21 Apr 1868
J B Watson, termed the Australian "Quartz Reef king," dies at Sydney, said to have left 30,000 000*l* , the result of gold digging. railroad and other speculations	12 July, 1889

Syllabus of Errors in modern times, 80 paragraphs divided into 10 chapters, issued by pope Pius IX , with an encyclical letter, 8 Dec 1864 It condemned heresy, modern philosophy, and liberalism in politics, was forbidden to be read in French churches, and was generally opposed, but was adopted by the council at Rome, 1870

Symmes's theory. The theory or fancy that the earth is hollow and inhabited within was held with persistence by John Cleves Symmes (1779-1829), who claimed to believe that the earth was open at the poles for the admission of light and air, and contained within it other concentric hollow globes, all inhabited in like manner His belief in this theory was so strong, notwithstanding the general ridicule bestowed upon "Symmes's hole"—as it was popularly called—that he both wrote and lectured on the subject, and a petition was finally presented to Congress (1823), asking that an expedition be fitted out to investigate OHIO, UNITED STATES

sym'phonies, short pieces of instrumental music between songs in operas, early in the 17th century. These were gradually developed by the great masters, such as Lulli, into independent pieces, the symphonies of Corelli, Handel, Mozart, Haydn, and Beethoven are eminent examples

sympho'nion, an improved form of the musical-box, performing many more tunes, invented by Ellis Parr, 1887

syn'agogue (literally an assembly), a congregation of the Jews, and the place where such assembly is held for religious purposes When these meetings were first held is uncertain, some refer them to the times after the Babylonian captivity. In Jerusalem were 480 synagogues. A magnificent synagogue was consecrated at Berlin, 5 Sept 1866. JEWS

syn'dicate, originally a body of syndics, officers of a government or any ruling body; the term is now frequently used as synonymous with association, company, or body of trustees, 1888

syn'od (Gr. σύν, together, and ὁδός, way, i. e., meeting), an ecclesiastical convention, a council, the name now especially given to a convention of the Presbyterian church The first general synods were called by emperors, and afterwards by Christian princes, but the pope ultimately usurped this power, one of his legates usually presiding COUNCILS OF THE CHURCH The first national synod held in England was at Hertford, 673, the last was held by cardinal Pole in 1555 Made unlawful to hold synods but by royal authority, 25 Henry VIII 1533 DORT, THURLES

syn'onym, a word having the same or nearly the same meaning as another, as valor, courage. Books of Greek and Latin synonyms were early compiled G Crabbe's dictionary appeared 1816; dr P. M. Roget's excellent "Thesaurus of English Words and Phrases," 1852, and several editions since.

syph'ilis (from *Syphilus*, the name of a shepherd in the Latin poem of Fracastoro, "Syphilus sive Morbus Gallicus," which was pub 1530, from the Gr. σῦς, hog, swine, and φίλος, loving, the term was introduced into nosology by Sauvage), a venereal disease probably known to the ancients, and said to have been brought into Europe at the siege of Naples, 1495

Syracuse, a celebrated Greek city of SICILY, founded about 732 B.C by Archias, a Corinthian, and one of the Heraclidæ It became one of the most extensive cities of ancient Europe, second only to Athens in the splendor and magnificence of her public buildings, and one of the best-fortified cities of ancient times. Its government, first an oligarchy, fell under the rule of tyrants. Among its celebrities are some of the greatest names of Grecian history, viz Gelon, Hiero, Dionysius the Elder and Younger, Dion, Timoleon, Agathocles, and the great philosopher Archimedes. After a long period of wars with Athens, Carthage, and domestic turmoils, it fell into the hands of the Romans, being taken after a 3 years' siege by Marcellus, 312 B.C , at which Archimedes was killed. Since then Roman oppression, Gothic, Vandalic, and Saracenic fury, together with earthquakes, have effaced it from the catalogue of cities

Syria. The capital was originally Damascus, but after the battle of Ipsus, Seleucus founded Antioch Now a province of Asiatic Turkey Area of Syria, including Palestine, etc, 115,144 sq miles, pop 1885, 2 676,943

	B C
Alliance of David king of Israel, and Hiram, king of Syria	1049
Syria conquered by David	1040
Liberated by Rezin	980
Benhadad king of Syria, makes war on the Jews	898
Benhadad II reigns	about 830
Syria subjugated by Tiglath pileser, king of Assyria	740
Syria conquered by Cyrus.	537
And by Alexander	333
Seleucus *Nicator* enters Babylon	312
Æra of the SELEUCIDÆ	"
Great battle of Ipsus, death of Antigonus, defeated by Ptolemy, Seleucus, and Lysimachus	301
City of Antioch founded	299
Antiochus, son of Seleucus falling in love with his father's queen, Stratonice pines away, the secret being discovered, she is divorced by the father, and married by the son	297
Battle of Cyropedium, Lysimachus slain by Seleucus	281
Seleucus foully assassinated by Ceraunus, Antiochus I king	280
Antiochus I (*Soter*, or Saviour) defeats the Gauls	275
Antiochus II , surnamed by the Milesians *Theos* (God) king	261
Poisoned by Laodice	246
Seleucus II (king, 246) makes a treaty of alliance with Smyrna and Magnesia	243
Seleucus III (*Ceraunus*, or Thunder), king	226
Antiochus III the Great (king, 222) conquers Palestine but is totally defeated at Raphia	217
Again conquers Palestine, 198, but gives it to Ptolemy	193
Enters Greece, 192, defeated by the Romans at Thermopylæ, 191, and at Magnesia	190
Makes peace with the Romans, giving up to them Asia Minor	188
Seleucus Philopator, king	187
Antiochus IV , king who assumes the title of *Theos Epiphanes*, or the Illustrious God	175
He sends Apollonius into Judæa, Jerusalem is taken, the temple pillaged, 40,000 inhabitants destroyed, and 40,000 more sold as slaves	168
Antiochus V (Eupator) king, 164, murdered by Demetrius Sotor, who seizes the throne	162
Demetrius is defeated and slain by his successor Alexander Bala, 150, who is also defeated and slain by Demetrius Nicator	146
Antiochus VI (Sidetes), son of Demetrius Sotor, rules during the captivity of his brother Demetrius Nicator (after slaying the usurper Trypho)	137
Antiochus grants peace to the Jews, and placates the Romans, 133, invades Parthia, 129, and is defeated and slain	128
Demetrius Nicator restored	"
Cleopatra, the queen, murders her son Seleucus with her own hand	124
Her son Antiochus VII (Grypus), king, 125 whom she attempts to poison, but he compels his mother to swallow the deadly draught herself	123
Reign of Antiochus VIII (Cyzicenus) at Damascus, and of Grypus at Antioch.	111
Seleucus, king	95
Antiochus IX (Eusebes), king	94
Dethroned by Philip	85
Tigranes, king of Armenia, acquires Syria	83
Antiochus X. (Asiaticus) solicits the aid of the Romans.	75
Defeat of Tigranes by Lucullus, 69, he submits to Pompey, who enters Syria, and dethrones Antiochus Asiaticus	65
Syria made a Roman province	63

	A D
Syria invaded by the Parthians	162
By the Persians	256
Violent earthquakes	341
Invaded by the Saracens, 497, 502, 529, by the Persians	607
Conquered by the Saracens	638
Conquest of Syria by the Fatimite caliphs	970
Revolt of the emirs of Damascus	1067
Emirs of Aleppo revolt	1068
CRUSADES commence	1095
Desolated by the CRUSADES	1096–1272
Noureddin conquers Syria	1166
Saladin dethrones the Fatimite dynasty	1171
Tartars overrun all Syria	1259
Sultans of Egypt expel the Crusaders	1291
Syria overrun by Tamerlane	1400
Syria and Egypt conquered by the Turks	1516–17
Syria continued in possession of the Turks till the invasion by the French 1799, Bonaparte overruns the country, Gaza and Jaffa taken	Mch 1799
Siege of Acre begun by French 16 Mch, raised	20 May, "
Bonaparte returns to France from Egypt	23 Aug "
Egypt and Syria evacuated by the French	10 Sept 1801
Mehemet Ali attacks and captures Acre, and overruns the whole of Syria	1831
Ibrahim Pacha his son, defeats the grand signior at Konieh,	21 Dec 1832
Numerous battles with varying success, European powers intervene, peace is made	6 May, 1833
War renewed, May, Ibrahim defeats Turks at Nezib	24 June, 1839
Turkish fleet deserts to Mehemet Ali, reaching Alexandria	14 July, "
Five powers unite to support the Porte	July, "
Death of lady Hester Stanhope	23 June, 1840
Treaty of London (not signed by France)	15 July, 1840
Capture of SIDON	27 Sept "
Fall of BEYROUT	10 Oct "
Fall of ACRE	3 Nov "
Long negotiations, sultan grants hereditary rights to Mehemet, who gives up Syria	Jan 1841
Druses said to have destroyed 151 Christian villages, killing 1000 persons (DRUSES)	29 May to 1 July, 1860
Mahometans massacre about 3300 Christians at Damascus, many saved by Abd el Kader	9 July, et seq "
English and French governments intervene, convention at Paris, 12 000 men to be sent by France	3 Aug "
Vigor of Fuad Pacha, he punishes the Mahometans implicated in massacres at Damascus, 167 of all ranks including the governor, executed	20 Aug et seq "
Four thousand French soldiers, under gen Hautpoul, land at Beyrout	22 Aug "
Lord Dufferin, British commissioner in Syria, arrives at Damascus	6 Sept "
French and Turks advance against Lebanon, 14 emirs surrendered	Oct "
Pacification of the country effected	Nov "
French occupation ceases	5 June, 1861
Prince of Wales visits Syria	Apr 1862
Insurrection of Joseph Karam, Maronite, in Lebanon, suppressed	Mch 1866
Another suppressed, Karam flies to Algeria	31 Jan 1867
Midhat Pacha appointed governor-general to inaugurate reforms Nov 1878, experiences great difficulty, Oct, resigns, but continues	Oct 1879–June, 1880
Hamed Pacha, governor of Smyrna, and Midhat Pacha change places	Aug "
Midhat Pacha, charged with complicity in the murder of the sultan Abdul Aziz, surrenders (TURKEY, 1881)	about 17 May, 1881

T

T, a sharp mute consonant, and the 20th letter of the English alphabet, the τ (tau) of the Greek, thence from the Phœnician and Egyptian. "To a T"=exactly, with the greatest accuracy, a remark referring to the T-square, an instrument used by mechanics "We could manage the matter to a T."—*Sterne*, "Tristram Shandy," vol ii, chap v.

Tabella'riæ Le'ges, the laws which enabled the Roman commons to vote by ballot instead of *vivâ voce* Such laws diminished the power of the nobles Voting by ballot was allowed by the Gabinian law, A U C 614, in conferring honors, 2 years after at all trials except for treason, by the Cassian law, in passing laws, by the Papirian law, A U C. 622, and lastly, in trials for treason, by the Cœlian law, A U C 630

tab'ernacle, the holy place of the Israelites before the erection of Solomon's temple, supposed to have been constructed by divine direction, 1490 B.C. The tabernacle set up at Shiloh by Joshua 1444 B C. was replaced by the temple erected by Solomon, 1004 B.C

Tables, the Two, of the law in stone alleged to have been received by Moses from God on mount Sinai, 1491 B.C DECEMVIRI

Ta'bor, a city in Bohemia, was founded by Ziska in 1420, and became a chief seat of the HUSSITES.—A small mountain in Palestine, the headquarters of Barak prior to his victory over Sisera (Judges iv 14), and he supposed scene of the "Transfiguration"

Tadmor. PALMYRA

Tae-Pings. CHINA, 1851.

taf'fety, an early manufacture of silk, more prized formerly than now, woven very smooth and glossy It was worn by English queens, and was first made in England by John Tyce, of Shoreditch, London, 41 Eliz 1598.—*Stow*

Tagliacozzo (*tal ya cot'so*), a town in the Abruzzi mountains, S. Italy, where, on 23 Aug 1268, Charles of Anjou, usurping king of Naples, defeated and captured the rightful monarch, young Conradin (last of the Hohenstaufens, and grandson of emperor Frederick II), who had been invited into Italy by the Ghibelline or imperial party, their opponents, the Guelfs, or papal party, supporting Charles. Conradin was beheaded 29 Oct. following

Tagliamento (*tal-ya-men'to*), a river in Lombardy, N Italy, near which the Austrians, under the archduke Charles, were defeated by Bonaparte, 16 Mch. 1797.

Taherites, a dynasty of Persia, 813–72.

Tahiti (*ta-hee'tee*), the French abbreviated name for OTAHEITE

Taillebourg (*tai-ye-boorg'*), a village of W France. Near here Henry III of England was defeated and nearly captured by Louis IX of France, 20 July, 1242

Talave'ra de la Reyna, a city of central Spain, was taken from the Mahometans by Ordoño, king of Leon, 913. Here, 27, 28 July, 1809, the united British and Spanish armies under sir Arthur Wellesley met the French under marshals Victor and Sebastiani After a conflict on the 27th, both armies remained on the field till the French at break of day renewed the attack, and were repulsed by the allies with great slaughter At noon Victor charged the whole allied line, was repulsed at all points, and retreated with a heavy loss. As Soult, Ney, and Mortier were in the rear, the allies retired after the victory.

Tallade'ga, Battle at, near the Coosa river, in ALABAMA, between more than 2000 Americans, under gen Jackson, and 1000 Creek Indians, on 9 Nov 1813 The Indians left 290 dead on the field, and perhaps as many were wounded The Americans lost 15 killed and 86 wounded

Tallusahat'chee, Battle at, near the Coosa river, Alabama, between the Creek Indians and 900 mounted men, under gen Coffee, on 3 Nov 1813 The Indians lost 200 killed and 84 prisoners The Americans lost 5 killed and 41 wounded

Tal'mud (from *lamad*, to teach), the compendium of ancient Jewish oral or unwritten law, as distinguished from the Pentateuch, or written law, its origin is coeval with the return from the Babylonian captivity, 536 B.C Its compilation in Hebrew was begun by the Scribes, and by their successors the work was carried on till 220 B.C It is composed in prose and poetry, and contains 2 elements, legal and legendary The morality resembles that of the New Testament, and the philosophy is rather Platonic than Aristotelian

The Mishna, comprising the work of the rabbis, termed Thanaim, was compiled by Jehuda Hanassi in the middle of the 2d century A D., and forms the Jerusalem Talmud, written at Tiberias, in Palestine, about 230 The Babylonian Talmud contains also the Gemera or Ghemara, the work of the rabbis termed Amoraim, and criticisms and comments on the Mishna The part named *Halacha* is dogmatic, legal, and doctrinal, the *Agaba* is illustrative, narrative and legendary After being almost universally condemned, and the MSS. often burned, the defence of the Talmud was undertaken by the German reformer Reuchlin, in the 16th century, and between 1520 and 1523 the "Talmud Babylonicum," in 12 vols. fol., and the "Talmud Hierosolytanum," in 1 vol. fol., were printed at Venice. A discourse on the Talmud was given at the Royal Institution, 15 May, 1868, by Emanuel Deutsch. See his article in the *Quarterly Review*, Oct. 1867. A beginning of the first English translation of the Jerusalem Talmud (vol. i.) by dr. Moise Schwab appeared in 1886.

Tammany Society. This society was formed in 1789, chiefly through the efforts of William Mooney, an upholsterer in New York city, its first grand sachem, to oppose the Federalists. It has ever since been an important political body, largely controlling for many years the local government, and in state and national politics professing to adhere to the Democratic party. The name Tammany is said by tradition to have been taken from an aged, wise, and friendly Delaware chief, chosen for his virtues as the patron saint of the new republic. The first meeting was held 12 May, 1789. Act of incorporation passed 1805. The grand sachem and the 13 sachems represent the president of the U. S. and the 13 original governors. Although nominally a charitable and social organization, it is practically a combination to control the revenues and government of New York city, and has long been associated with every form of municipal jobbery and corruption. In Nov. 1894, for the first time in more than 20 years, it lost its control of the city by the triumphant election of a reform ticket.

Tan'agra, a ruined city of Bœotia, Greece. Here the Spartans defeated the Athenians 457 B.C., but were defeated by them in 456 and 426, when Agis II. headed the Spartans and Nicias the Athenians.

Tangier (*tan-jeer'*), a seaport town of Morocco, N.W. Africa, besieged by prince Ferdinand of Portugal, who was beaten and taken prisoner, 1437. It was conquered by Alfonso V. of Portugal, 1471, and given as a dower to princess Catherine, on her marriage with Charles II. of England, 1662; who in 1683 caused the works to be blown up and abandoned. It rapidly declined after coming into the possession of the Moors. Pop. 14,000.

tan'istry, in Ireland, the equal division of lands, after the decease of the owner, among his sons, legitimate or illegitimate. If one of the sons died, his son did not inherit, but a new division was made by the tanist or chief. Abolished 1604.—*Davies.*

Tanjore', a province of British India. About 1678, Vencajee, a Mahratta chief, brother of the great Sevajee, made himself rajah. In 1749 a British expedition endeavored to restore a deposed rajah without success; the reigning prince bought them off by cession of territories. Much intervention followed. In 1799 the East India company obtained possession of the country, engaging to support the rajah with nominal authority. The last is said to have died in 1855.

Tan'nenberg, E. Prussia. Here Ladislaus V. Jagellon of Poland defeated the Teutonic knights with great slaughter, the grandmaster being slain, 15 July, 1410. The order never recovered.

tanning leather with the bark of trees has been practised from the earliest ages in all countries, even in Africa; but the East until recently has produced the best leather. The manufacture of Morocco leather was introduced into Alsace, France, from the Mediterranean coast of Africa in 1749. The tanning of alligator skins was begun in New Orleans, La., about 1860. Great improvements have been recently made in tanning by chemical discoveries.

tan'talum, a rare metal, discovered in an American mineral by Hatchett, in 1801, and named by him columbium; and in a Swedish mineral by Ekeberg, who gave it its present name. Wollaston pointed out the identity of the 2 metals in 1809; and Berzelius prepared pure metallic tantalum in 1824. In 1846 Rose discovered that tantalum was really a mixture of 3 metals, which he named tantalum, niobium, and pelopium.—*Gmelin.*

Tâ'oism, one of the 3 religions of China. The name is derived from the Tâo, or "Way," a treatise written by Li Urh, a contemporary of Confucius, in the 6th century B.C. The "Way" is the quiet, passionless discharge of all duties, "Heaven" not being a ruler, but a pattern. Tâoism was modified by the introduction of Buddhism.

tap'estry, an art of weaving borrowed from the Saracens, and hence its original workers in France were called *Sarazinois.* The invention of tapestry hangings belongs (the date is not mentioned) to the Netherlands.—*Guicciardini.* Manufactured in France under Henry IV. by artists invited from Flanders, 1606. The art was brought into England by William Sheldon; and the first manufactory was established at Mortlake by sir Francis Crane, 17 James I. 1619.—*Salmon.* Under Louis XIV. the art of tapestry was much improved in France. GOBELIN TAPESTRY. Tapestry is mentioned by the ancient poets, and also in Scripture; so that the Saracens' manufacture is a revival of the art. Tapestry said to have been wrought by Matilda, queen of England. BAYEUX TAPESTRY.

Tapestry manufactory established at Windsor, Engl., by Mr. Henry, supported by the royal family and others; exhibition opened in the town-hall, 6 Dec. 1878.

Tappan, a village of New York, 24 miles north of New York city, and 1½ west of the Hudson river. Here, on 2 Oct. 1780, maj. John André was hanged as a British spy. NEW YORK.

tar, a very thick and viscous substance, black and strongly adhesive, obtained in a fluid form by distilling coal or wood. The wood tar is of varied use in the arts, entering into excellent varnishes, cements, etc., and being the best substance known to smear on ropes, canvas, etc., to make them waterproof. The chemist Becher first proposed to make tar from pit-coal—the earl of Dundonald's patent, 1781. Mineral tar was discovered at Colebrookdale, Shropshire, 1779; and in Scotland, Oct. 1792. Tar-water was first recommended for its medicinal virtues by dr. Berkeley, bishop of Cloyne, about 1744. From benzole, discovered in coal-tar, many brilliant dyes are now produced. ANILINE.

Ta'ra, a hill in Meath, Ireland, where the early kings of Ireland were inaugurated.

> "The harp that once through Tara's halls
> The soul of music shed."—*Moore.*

Near here, on 26 May, 1798, the royalist troops, 400 strong, defeated the insurgent Irish (4000 men), 500 killed. On 15 Aug. 1843, Daniel O'Connell held a monster meeting here (250,000 persons said to have been assembled).

Taren'tum, now **Taran'to,** a fortified city and seaport of S. Italy, was founded by the Greek Phalantus, 708 B.C. The people of Tarentum, assisted by Pyrrhus, king of Epirus, supported a war undertaken 281 B.C. by the Romans to avenge insults by the Tarentines to their ships; it was terminated after 10 years; 300,000 prisoners were taken, and Tarentum became subject to Rome. Except the citadel, Tarentum was captured by the Carthaginians, 212, but recovered by Fabius, 209 B.C. Tarentum has suffered in the revolutions of southern Italy till only ruins remain.

targums or **explanations** are ancient Chaldee paraphrases of the Old Testament. The most remarkable are those of Onkelos, Jonathan-ben-Uzziel, and Joseph the Blind. The Targum of Onkelos is referred by some to the 1st century A.D.

Tari'fa, a seaport town of S. Spain, the ancient *Joza* and *Julia Traducta,* where Muza landed when invading Spain, 712. It was taken from the Moors by Sancho IV. of Castile, 1291 or 1292; and was relieved, when besieged by them, after a great victory over the kings of Morocco and Granada, by Alfonso XI. of Castile and Alfonso IV. of Portugal, 28 or 30 Oct. 1340. The conflict is called the battle of Salado, having been fought on the banks of that river. Tarifa was taken by the French in 1823.

tariff. The tariff is a tax levied upon exports or (especially) imports. A duty was early collected by Moslem rulers at the Spanish port TARIFA, whence the modern name, on goods passing through the strait of Gibraltar. The word as used in the United States was adopted from the English tariffs, which before the reign of queen Elizabeth were prohibitory, and since used as a source of revenue. In the U. S. the tariff is for revenue and protection; there are no prohibitory duties except on chiccory, shoddy, doctored wines, and a few articles of like character. Before the adoption of the U. S. Constitution most of the American colonies had systems of taxation on imports. The first acts of the Dutch West India company with reference to the colony of New Netherlands provided for export and import duties, and specific rates were levied on furs and codfish by act of 7 June, 1629. In 1661 the council of Virginia laid an import tax on rum and sugar, and forbade unloading them except at appointed ports. The government of Massachusetts enacted a general import tax, Nov. 1668. Under the confederation, the Continental Congress made numerous unsuccessful attempts to induce the states to join in an import tax for the common treasury, only succeeding in securing, in 1786, an agreement from New York, granting to the U S certain imposts provided the other states did the same A measure for taxing imports, "for the support of the government, for the discharge of debts of the U S, and the encouragement and protection of manufactures," was introduced in the House of Representatives of the first Congress, by James Madison, 8 Apr 1789 From this dates tariff legislation in the U S

Congress passes first Tariff act, to continue in force until June, 1796, combining specific duties on some articles and *ad valorem* on others, equivalent to an 8½ per cent *ad valorem* rate, with drawback, except 1 per cent of duties, on all articles exported within 12 months, except distilled spirits other than brandy and geneva, signed by Washington 4 July, 1789

Act of Congress passed to regulate the collection of duties Each collection district to lie within a state Providing for collectors, deputy collectors, naval officers, surveyors, weighers measurers gaugers, and inspectors *Ad valorem* duties to be estimated by adding 20 per cent to the actual cost thereof if imported from the cape of Good Hope or any place beyond, and 10 per cent. if from any other country Duties to be paid in cash if under $50, if over might be secured by bond to run from 4 to 12 months, with 10 per cent discount for prompt payment 31 July, "

Act laying duties on importations extended to North Carolina, 8 Feb, and to Rhode Island 14 June, 1790

Act of 4 July 1789, repealed, and new law enacted raising duties to equal an 11 per cent *ad valorem* rate 10 Aug "

Tariff rate raised to equal 13½ per cent, by act of 2 May, 1792

Additional duties levied on imports, particularly tobacco, snuff and refined sugar, by acts of 5, 7 June, 1794

Tariff on brown sugar, molasses, and tea increased 3 Mch 1797

Duty on salt increased from 12 to 20 cents by act of 8 July, "

First elaborate act of Congress for taking possession of arriving merchandise and levying and collecting duties 2 Mch 1799

Additional duties imposed on wines, sugar, molasses, and such articles as have paid 10 per cent 13 May, 1800

Two and one half per cent *ad valorem* imposed on all importations in American vessels, and 10 per cent in foreign vessels in addition to existing rates for a fund to protect commerce and seamen against the Barbary powers, commonly called the "Mediterranean fund" 27 Mch 1804

All tariff duties increased 100 per cent, and 10 per cent additional on goods imported in foreign ships. 1 July, 1812

Double war duties continued until 30 June, 1816, and after that day an additional duty of 42 per cent. until a new tariff shall be formed 5 Feb 1816

Niles' Weekly Register advocates a protective tariff "

A J Dallas, secretary of the treasury, reports to Congress on the subject of a general tariff of increased duties 13 Feb "

Mr Lowndes of South Carolina reports a bill from the Committee of Ways and Means to regulate duties on imports and tonnage 12 Mch "

Tariff bill opposed by Mr Webster and most of the eastern states, and by John Randolph, and supported by messrs. Clay Calhoun and Lowndes. Among other provisions was one for the gradual reduction of the tax on cotton and woollen goods Act passes the House by a vote of 88 to 54, and the Senate by 25 to 7, and becomes a law 27 Apr "

Act passed deferring the time of reduction of tariff on woollens and cottons until 1826, and raising the duty on bar iron from $9 to $15 per ton 20 Apr 1818

Resolutions introduced in Congress for the abolition of drawbacks, and bills to shorten long credits on importations, to tax auction sales of imports, and to collect duties in cash debated, but fail to become laws 1819-22

Auction system, by which foreigners shipped goods to the U S, undervaluing them in the invoice, for which the auctioneer gave bonds and immediately sold for what they would bring, is remedied by deterrent legislation, which began in 1818 and concluded in act of 1 Mch 1823

Tariff bill with average rate of 37 per cent. duties, after a debate of 10 weeks, passes the House by vote of 107 to 102 The Senate adds amendments which the House rejects. The difference is settled by a committee of conference, and bill passes Senate by 25 to 22, approved 22 May, 1824

National convention called by the Pennsylvania Society for the Promotion of Manufactures and Mechanic Arts at Harrisburg, adopts resolutions in favor of more protection on iron, steel, glass, wool, woollens, and hemp 30 July, 1827

Tariff bill based on recommendation of Harrisburg convention, introduced in Congress 31 Jan 1828

New tariff with a 41-per cent. rate, favored by Daniel Webster, is debated from 4 Mch to 15 May, passed by House, 109-91, Senate, 26-21, and approved 19 May, "

[This became known as the "Tariff of Abominations." South Carolina protested against it as unconstitutional, oppressive, and unjust North Carolina also protested, and Alabama and Georgia denied the power of Congress to lay duties for protection]

Condy Raguet begins the publication of the *Free Trade Advocate*, afterwards known as the *Banner of the Constitution* 1829

Duties on coffee, cocoa, and tea reduced by act of 20 May, on molasses and salt by acts of 29 May, 1830

Secretary of the treasury Ingham, in his report, advocates "home" valuation in place of "foreign," the current value of goods in the U S to be the dutiable value 15 Dec. "

National Free trade convention meets at Philadelphia, 30 Sept. 1831

National Protection convention meets in New York 26 Oct "

George McDuffie, representative from South Carolina, from Committee on Ways and Means, reports a bill proposing *ad valorem* duties for revenue only 8 Feb 1832

John Quincy Adams reports a bill repealing the act of 1828, and reducing duties on coarse woollens, iron, etc 23 May, "

Tariff bill retaining the protective features of the tariff of 1828, but reducing or abolishing many taxes, is reported It reduced the tax on iron, increased that on woollens, made some raw wools free, and left cotton unchanged Duties of less than $200 to be paid in cash without discount, law to take effect 3 Mch 1833, approved 14 July, "

Representatives from South Carolina publish an address on the subject of the tariff, urging resistance 15 July, "

Convention meets in Columbia, S C, 19 Nov, and calls on the legislature to declare the tariff acts of 1824 and 1828 null and void in that state, and to prohibit the collection of duties there after 1 Feb 1833, law passed 24 Nov "

Secretary of the treasury, in his report recommends a reduction of duties to the requirements of revenue 5 Dec "

President proclaims intention to enforce the laws 11 Dec "

Mr Verplanck, from the Committee on Ways and Means reports a bill providing for the reduction of duties in the course of 2 years to about one half 8 Jan 1833

"Compromise Tariff bill" introduced by Mr Clay 12 Feb "

House strikes out Mr Verplanck's bill and substitutes Mr Clay's, which declares its object to be "to prevent the destruction of the political system, and to arrest civil war and restore peace and tranquillity to the nation" It provides for a gradual reduction in duties, and for "home valuation," all duties to be paid in cash Passed by vote of 118 to 84 in the House and 29 to 16 in the Senate and approved 2 Mch "

"Force bill" or "Bloody bill," to enforce the collection of duties, passed by Congress 2 Mch "

Nullification acts repealed by South Carolina 16 Mch "

Home league formed to agitate for high duties 1841

Several tariff bills, drafted and discussed fail to become laws during 1841 A general tariff act with average rate of duty about 33 per cent, and dropping the principle of "home valuation," is passed 11 Sept. "

Tariff law passed containing the much controverted and litigated "similitude section" (sec 20), imposing duties on non enumerated articles which may be similar in material, quality, texture, or use to any enumerated article 30 Aug 1842

Tariff bill passes the House by a vote of 114 to 95, and the Senate by the casting vote of the vice president Geo M Dallas Average rate of duty 25½ per cent 30 July, 1846

Warehouse system established by act of Congress 6 Aug "

Robert J Walker introduces the system of private bonded warehouses which is confirmed by act of Congress, 28 Mch 1854

Free trade policy declared in the platform of the Democratic party at Cincinnati 6 June, 1856

Tariff act passed lowering the average duty to about 20 per cent 3 Mch 1857

Republican convention at Chicago adopts a protective tariff platform 17 May, 1860

Tariff bill raising the tariff of 1857 about one third introduced in the House by Mr Morrill, passed and approved, 2 Mch 1861, goes into effect 1 Apr 1861

Amended tariff act raising duties passed 5 Aug "

Act passed increasing tariff on tea, coffee, and sugar 24 Dec "

Act passed raising tariff duties temporarily 14 July, 1862

Act passed "to prevent and punish frauds upon the revenue" etc which provides that all invoices of goods be made in triplicate, one to be given the person producing them, a second filed in the office of the consular officer nearest the place of shipment, and the third transmitted to the collector at the port of entry 3 Mch 1863

Joint resolution raising all duties 50 per cent. for 60 days, afterwards extended to 90 days 29 Apr 1864

General revision of tariff, increasing duties passed 30 June, "

Bill passed increasing tariff rates, 3 Mch 1865, and amended, 28 July, 1866

Transportation in bond of goods destined for Canada or Mexico through the U S, provided for by act of 28 July, "

Convention of woollen manufacturers at Syracuse ask increased duties They form an alliance with wool growers, and arrange a tariff which becomes a law by act of 2 Mch 1867

Duty on copper and copper ore increased by act of 24 Feb 1869

First law distinctly authorizing the appointment of special agents of the treasury in the custom service, passed, 12 May, 1870

Following a general debate on an act to reduce internal taxes, etc., a new tariff, retaining most of the protective features, becomes a law 14 July, "

Duties removed from tea and coffee after 1 July, 1872, by act of 1 May, 1872

General act passed reducing duties on imports and internal taxes 6 June, "

All provision moieties to informers repealed, and the proceeds of all fines, penalties, and forfeitures to be paid into the treasury, by act of 22 June, 1874

Tariff law amended by act of Congress 8 Feb. 1875

Salts and sulphate of quinine put on the free list 1 July, 1879

Act creating a Tariff commission of 9 civilians appointed by the president, to visit different sections of the country in the interest of tariff revision and report 15 May, 1882

Tariff commission, consisting of John L Hayes, pres, Henry W Oliver, jr, Austin M Garland, Jacob Ambler, Robert P Porter, John W H Underwood, Duncan F Kenner, Alexander R Boetler, and William H McMahon, organizes at the Ebbitt house Washington, D C 6 July, "

Report of Tariff commission submitted to Congress and referred to Ways and Means committee 4 Dec. "

Act passed repealing section 2501 of the Revised Statutes (levying an additional duty of 10 per cent. on goods from places west of the cape of Good Hope), 4 May, and amended, 23 Dec. 1882

Senate reports a tariff bill which is called up for consideration, 10 Jan.; House bill reported by Ways and Means committee, 16 Jan.; both bills discussed and amended for several weeks; a conference committee meets, 28 Feb.; after some resignations and reappointments of members, reports, 2 Mch., accepted in the Senate, 12.30 A.M., 3 Mch., by 32 to 31 votes, and in the House at 5.30 P.M., 3 Mch., by 152 to 116 votes, and signed by the president before adjournment, which was after midnight.......................................3 Mch. 1883

A bill "to reduce import duties and war-tariff taxes," introduced by Mr. Morrison, is reported in the House, 11 Mch., and defeated by vote of 159 to 155.......................15 Apr. 1884

A bill to reduce tariff taxes, introduced by Mr. Morrison, is lost by vote of the House, 157 to 140..................17 June, 1886

Mills bill, a measure "to reduce taxation and simplify the laws in relation to the collection of revenue," introduced in the House by Roger Q. Mills of Texas, chairman of the Ways and Means committee..............................2 Apr. 1888

Mills bill is taken up for discussion, 17 Apr., and debated until 19 July, and passes the House by vote of 149 to 14...21 July, "

[Referred in the Senate to the Finance committee, by whom a substitute was prepared, and failed to become a law.]

A bill "to equalize duties upon imports and to reduce the revenue of the government," introduced by Wm. McKinley, jr., of Ohio.......................................16 Apr. 1890

McKinley Customs Administration act approved......10 June, 1890

McKinley Tariff bill passes the House, 21 May; referred to Senate committee on Finance, 23 May; reported to the Senate with amendments, 18 June; passes Senate with amendments, 10 Sept.; reported by Conference committee to House, 26 Sept.; approved by the president, 1 Oct., and takes effect 6 Oct. "

Tariff (Wilson) bill made public.......................27 Nov. 1893

Submitted to the full committee of Ways and Means, 19 Dec. "

Debate on the bill begins in the House..................8 Jan. 1894

Internal revenue bill containing the income-tax reported to the House...24 Jan. "

Tariff bill with income-tax attached passes the House, 204 to 140...1 Feb. "

Revised tariff bill reported to the Senate from the Finance committee...20 Feb. "

Debate in the Senate on the tariff bill began by senator Voorhees..2 Apr. "

Senate passes tariff bill, 39 yeas (37 Democrats, 2 Populists), 34 nays (31 Republicans, 2 Populists, 1 Democrat, D. B. Hill), 3 July, "

Tariff bill received in the House with 633 Senate amendments, rates increased.......................................5 July, "

House disagreeing, a conference committee is appointed; the Senate compels the House to adopt its amendments..13 Aug. "

Bill sent to the president.............................17 Aug. "

Becomes a law without his signature..................27 Aug. "

YEARS OF TARIFF CHANGES, WITH AVERAGE RATE PER CENT. OF DUTIES FROM 1813.

Years of tariff changes.	Average rate per cent. of duty on dutiable imports, showing the general average for several years together from 1813.				Remarks.
1789 (first imposed.), 1790, 1792, 1794, 1797, 1804, 1812	....				Twine and pack-thread, $2 per cwt.; cordage, untarred, 90c. per cwt., tarred, 75c. Pickled fish, 75c. per bl. Hemp, 60c. per cwt. Boots, 50c. per pair. Unwrought steel, 50c. per cwt. Beer, ale, porter, and cider, in bottles, 20c. per doz. Green teas, 12c. per lb.; Hyson, 20c.; Black tea, 10c. Jamaica rum, and all wines except Madeira, 10c. per gal. Malt, 10c. per bu. Salt, 6c. per bu. Manufactured tobacco, 6c. per lb. Cheese, 4c. per lb. Cotton, 3c. per lb. Loaf sugar, 3c. per lb.; other sugar, except brown, 2½c.; brown sugar, 1c. Coffee 2½c. per lb. Coal, 2c. per bu. Glass, china, stone, and earthenware, gunpowder, paints, shoe and knee buckles, gold and silver lace and leaf, 10 per cent. *ad valorem*. Blank-books, paper, cabinet wares, leather ready-made, clothing, hats, gloves, millinery, combs, brushes, gold, silver, and plated ware, jewelry, buttons, saddles, slit and rolled iron and castings, anchors, tin and pewter ware, .07½ per cent. *ad valorem*. All other articles, including manufactured wool, cotton, and linen, .05 per cent. *ad valorem*.
1816, 1824	1813–24 inclusive,		34	per cent.	
1828, 1832	1825–32	"	40	"	Nullification acts in South Carolina owing to this tariff.
1833, 1841	1833–41	"	31.6	"	Compromise tariff bill of Henry Clay.
1846	1842–46	"	30.4	"	
1857	1847–57	"	24.2	"	Tariff bill of Robert J. Walker.
1861	1858–61	"	19.2	"	Comparatively free-trade.
1862, 1864	1862–64	"	35	"	Tariff bill of Justin S. Morrill of Vermont.
1866, 1869, 1870	1865–70	"	46.4	"	
1875, 1883	1871–90	"	43.2	"	
1890	1891–93	"	48.2	"	Tariff bill of William McKinley of Ohio.
1894	1894		37	"	Tariff bill of William L. Wilson of W. Virginia, reconstructed by Gorman of Maryland, and others in the Senate.

Tarpeian (*tar-pe'yan*) **rock,** Rome, owed its name to the tradition that Tarpeia, daughter of the keeper of the Roman citadel, was here crushed to death by the shields cast on her by the Sabines, whom she treacherously admitted, having bargained for the gift of what they wore on their left arms, meaning their bracelets, about 750 B.C. From its summit state criminals were afterwards thrown, notably Marcus Manlius Capitolinus, 381 B.C.

Tarrago'na, a seaport city of N.E. Spain, occupied as a naval station by the British before the capture of Gibraltar in 1704. It was stormed and sacked by French under Suchet, 29 Jan. 1811, and the inhabitants put to the sword.

tartan or **Highland plaid,** the dress of Scottish Highlanders, said to have been derived from the ancient Gauls, or Celtæ, the *Galli non Braccati*.

tartaric acid is said to have been the first discovery of the chemist Scheele, who procured it in a separate state by boiling tar with lime, and in decomposing the tartrate of lime by sulphuric acid, about 1770. In 1859, baron Liebig formed tartaric acid from other sources.

Tar'tary, a vast country of Asia and Europe. The Tatars, or Tartars, or Mongols, or Moguls, were known in antiquity as Scythians. During the decline of the Roman empire these tribes began to seek more fertile regions; and the first who reached the frontier of Italy were the Huns, the ancestors of the modern Mongols. The first acknowledged sovereign of this vast country was the famous Genghis Khan. His empire, by the conquest of China, Persia, and all central Asia (1206–27), became most formidable. It was during the reign of his son Ogdai that the Tartar invasion of eastern Europe occurred under Batu, capturing Pesth on Christmas, 1240, and, crossing the Danube on the ice, took Gran by assault, and defeated the Poles in a disastrous battle near Liegnitz, 12 Apr. 1241, then without delay moved southeastward into Moravia as far as the vicinity of Troppau, Silesia, when Batu was recalled by the death of the khan. The empire was split into parts in a few reigns. Timur, or Tamerlane, again conquered Persia, broke the power of the Turks in Asia Minor (1370–1400), and founded the Mogul dynasty in India, which began with Baber in 1525, and formed the most splendid court in Asia till the close of the 18th century. GOLDEN HORDE. The Kalmucks, a branch of the Tartars, expelled from China, settled on the banks of the Volga in 1672, but returned in 1771, and thousands perished on the journey. De Quincey gives a vivid description of this "exodus" in the "Flight of a Tartar Tribe."

Tasma'nia, an island south of Australia and separated from it by Bass's strait, formerly called Van Diemen's Land, after the governor of the Dutch East Indies. Name changed to Tasmania in 1853, in honor of Abel Jansen Tasman, who discovered it 24 Nov. 1642. Area, 26,215 sq. miles; pop. 1891, 146,667, mostly descendants of the English settlers, the aborigines being extinct; the last, a woman, dying in 1876.

Visited by Furneaux. 1773; capt. Cook........................ 1777
Proved to be an island by Flinders, who explores Bass's strait. 1799
Taken possession of for the English government by lieut. Bower, 1803
First settlement with convicts at Hobart Town.............. 1804
Transportation of convicts abolished........................ 1853

Taunton, a borough of Somerset, Engl., was taken by Perkin Warbeck, Sept. 1497; and here he was surrendered to Henry VII. 5 Oct. following. The duke of Monmouth was proclaimed king at Taunton, 20 June, 1685; and it was the scene of the "bloody assize" held by Jeffreys upon the rebels in August.

taverns may be traced to the 13th century. "In the raigne of king Edward the Third, only 3 taverns were allowed in London: one in Chepe, one in Walbrok, and the other in Lombard street."—*Spelman.* The Boar's Head, in Eastcheap, existed in the reign of Henry IV., and was the rendezvous of prince Henry and his dissolute companions. Shakespeare mentions it as the residence of Mrs. Quickly, and the scene of Falstaff's merriment.—*Shakespeare,* "Henry IV." The White Hart, Bishopsgate, established in 1480, was rebuilt in 1829.

At Fraunce's tavern, New York, gen. Washington bade farewell to the officers of the Continental army...............4 Dec. 1783

taxes were levied by Solon, the first Athenian legislator, 540 B.C. The first class of citizens paid an Attic talent of silver, about $270. Darius, the son of Hystaspes, levied a land-tax by assessment, which was deemed so odious that his subjects styled him, by way of derision, Darius the Trader, 480 B.C.—*D'Eon.* Taxes in specie were first introduced into England by William I., 1067, and he raised them arbitrarily. On 1 May, 1695, in England, a tax was imposed on bachelors and widowers, births, marriages, and burials, and continued until 1 Aug. 1706. The governmental revenue in the United Kingdom for 1890–91, derived from direct and indirect taxes, was as follows:

Source.	Imperial.	England.	Scotland.	Ireland.	United Kingdom.
Customs....	....	£15,221,672	£1,963,584	£2,294,744	£19,480,000
Excise.....	....	17,921,724	3,643,836	3,222,440	24,788,000
Stamps.....	£190,000	11,525,584	1,162,944	581,472	13,460,000
Land-tax...	....	995,392	34,608	....	1,030,000
Income-tax.	150,000	11,256,925	1,281,275	561,800	13,250,000
House duty.	....	1,476,899	93,101	....	1,570,000
Totals....	£340,000	£58,398,196	£8,179,348	£6,660,456	£73,578,000

In the United States taxes for the support of the federal government are mainly indirect taxes, such as customs and excise. The Constitution gives Congress "power to collect taxes, duties, imposts, and excises, to pay the debts and provide for the common defence and general welfare of the U. S.," subject to restrictions, no capitation or other direct tax to be laid unless in proportion to the census. The first direct tax ($2,000,000) was levied upon the 16 states, pro rata, in 1798, and there have been occasional repetitions since, noticeably in 1861, when a tax of $20,000,000 was levied, which has since been refunded. According to rulings of the Supreme court, Congress has no power to levy duties on exports, and the restriction upon direct taxation does not apply to an income tax. The systems and rates of state, county, and municipal taxation are numerous and constantly changing, but the taxes are direct, and are levied upon the assessed value of real estate and personal property. According to the single-tax theory, recently advocated by Henry George and others, taxation should be solely on land-value, exclusive of improvements. The history of federal taxation is outlined below. REVENUE, TARIFF, INCOME TAX in the U. S.

Duties laid upon spirits distilled within the U. S. from foreign and home material, 3 Mch. 1791, followed by an act further regulating these duties and imposing a tax on stills...8 May, 1792
Execution of the above laws leads to the WHISKEY INSURRECTION in Pennsylvania... 1794
Duties imposed on licenses for selling wines and foreign distilled spirituous liquors by retail; 8 cents per pound on all snuff manufactured for sale within the U. S.; 2 cents per pound on sugar refined within the U. S.; and specific duties as follows: On every coach, $10 yearly; chariot, $8; phaeton, $6; wagons used in agriculture or transportation of goods, exempt by act......................................5 June, "
Duties laid on property sold at auction..............9 June, "
Taxes on snuff repealed and duty laid on snuff-mills....3 Mch. 1795
Duties on carriages increased by act..................28 May, 1796
Duties laid on stamped vellum, parchment, and paper by act, 6 July, 1797
Direct tax of $2,000,000 laid, proportioned among the states, 14 July, 1798
Act to establish a general stamp-office at seat of government, 23 Apr. 1800
Duty on snuff-mills repealed............................24 Apr. "
Repeal of act taxing stills and domestic distilled spirits, refined sugar, licenses to retailers, sales at auction, carriages, stamped vellum, parchment, and paper after 30 June...........6 Apr. 1802
Act passed imposing duties of 1 per cent. on sales at auction of merchandise, and 25 per cent. on ships and vessels, on licenses to distillers of spirituous liquors; and on sugar refined within the U. S...............................24 July, 1813
Act passed imposing duties on licenses to retailers of wines, spirituous liquors, and foreign merchandise, and on notes of banks, etc., bonds and obligations discounted by banks, and on certain bills of exchange..........................2 Aug. "
Direct tax of $3,000,000 imposed on states by counties.. " "
Duties laid on carriages and harness, except those exclusively employed in husbandry............................15 Dec. 1814
Fifty per cent. added upon licenses to retailers of wines, etc., and 100 per cent. on sales by auction............... 23 Dec. "
Direct tax of $6,000,000 laid upon the U. S. annually.....9 Jan. 1815
Internal-revenue tax of $1 per ton imposed on pig-iron; 1 cent per pound on nails; also tax on candles, paper, hats, umbrellas, playing-cards, boots, tobacco, leather, etc., and an annual duty on household furniture, and gold and silver watches, by act of..18 Jan. "
Internal-revenue tax on gold and silver and plated ware, jewelry, and paste-work manufactured within the U. S.....27 Feb. "
Direct tax of $19,998.40 laid on the District of Columbia annually, by act.......................................27 Feb. "
Acts of 18 Jan. and 27 Feb, 1815 repealed..............22 Feb. 1816
Act of 9 Jan. 1815, and 27 Feb. repealed, and direct tax of $3,000,000 laid on the states, and direct tax of $9,999.20 laid on the District of Columbia..........................5 Mch. "
Duties on household furniture and watches kept for use removed by act of......................................9 Apr. "
Acts of 24 July, 1813, and 2 Aug., 15 and 23 Dec. 1814, repealed, 23 Dec. 1817
Act passed allowing states to tax public lands of the U. S. after they are sold by the U. S...........................26 Jan. 1847
Direct tax of $20,000,000 laid annually, and apportioned to the states by act of Congress (one tax to be levied previous to 1 Apr. 1865)..5 Aug. 1861
Act passed to provide internal revenue to support the government and to pay interest on the public debt, imposing taxes on spirits, ale, beer, and porter, licenses, manufactured articles and products, auction sales, yachts, billiard-tables, slaughtered cattle, sheep, and hogs, railroads, steamboats, ferry-boats, railroad bonds, banks, insurance companies, etc., salaries of officers in service of the U. S., advertisements, incomes, legacies, business papers of all kinds, like bank-checks, conveyances, mortgages, etc. (TOBACCO)..................1 July, 1862
Act to increase internal revenue passed................7 Mch. 1864
Act of 5 Aug. 1861, repealed...........................30 June, "
Act passed to reduce internal taxation.................13 July, 1866
U. S. Supreme court declares unconstitutional a capitation tax of $1 imposed by the state of Nevada on every person leaving the state by railroad train or other public conveyance...... 1868
Internal-revenue taxes reduced by acts of 14 July, 1870, and 6 June.. 1872
All special taxes imposed by law, accruing after 30 Apr. 1873, including taxes on stills, to be paid by stamps denoting the amount of tax, by act of............................24 Dec. "
Congress taxes real estate in the District of Columbia, 20 June, 1874
Internal-revenue tax on tobacco, snuff, and cigars, increased, and former tax of 70 cents per gallon on distilled spirits raised to 90 cents, by act of..........................3 Mch. 1875
Internal-revenue tax on tobacco reduced by act of......1 Mch. 1879
Henry George's "Progress and Poverty," advocating the "Single-tax" theory, published.................................. "
Act passed reducing internal-revenue taxes, and repealing tax on banks, checks, etc., matches, and medicinal preparations, 3 Mch. 1883
Special tax laid on manufacturers and dealers in oleomargarine, and a stamp tax of 2 cents per pound laid on the manufactured article..2 Aug. 1886
"Taxation in American States and Cities," by Richard T. Ely, pub.. 1888
Special internal-revenue tax on dealers in tobacco repealed, and tax on tobacco and snuff reduced by act...............1 Oct. 1890
Act passed to refund to the several states and territories the amount of direct tax paid under act of 5 Aug. 1861...2 Mch. 1891
Income-tax appended to the Wilson tariff bill and passed with it, becoming a law.................................27 Aug. 1894

[From 1 Jan. 1895 until 1 Jan. 1900 a tax of 2 per cent. levied on all incomes over and above $4000. U. S. Supreme Court holds it unconstitutional, 20 May, 1895. Also by the same act a tax of 2 cents on every pack of playing-cards; a tax of $1.10 on each proof gal. of distilled spirits, or wine gal. when below proof.]

Tay bridge, at Dundee, above 2 miles across the Tay; act passed 1870; work begun, June, 1871; Mr. De Bergue, first contractor, died; succeeded by messrs. Hopkins, Gilke & Co., of Middlesborough. Engineer, sir Thomas Bouch. It was much injured by a gale, 4 Feb. 1877; completed, 30 Aug.; tried,

25 Sept. 1877; opened, 31 May, 1878. Length, 10,612 feet; it consists of 85 spans, some above 90 feet above water-level; cost said to be 350,000*l.* Above 20 lives lost during its construction.

Bridge partly destroyed by a gale while a N. British mail-train was passing over it; a gap of about 3000 feet made; between 75 and 90 persons perished; about 7.15 P.M. Sunday...28 Dec. 1879
Forty-six bodies recovered....................up to 27 Apr. 1880
Plans for a new bridge approved....................Jan. 1882
Opened for public traffic.................... 20 June, 1887

Taylor, Zachary, administration of. UNITED STATES, 1849-50.

Tchad, or **Chad**, Lake, central Africa, 150 miles long by 130 wide. Area varies from 10,000 to 50,000 sq. miles. It contains many small islands, well inhabited; ordinarily no outlet except at high water.

Tcherna'ya, a river in the Crimea. On 16 Aug. 1855, the lines of the allied army at this place were attacked by 50,000 Russians under prince Gortschakoff, who were repulsed with the loss of 3329 slain, 1658 wounded, and 600 prisoners. The brunt of the attack was borne by 2 French regiments under gen. D'Herbillon. The loss of the allies was about 1200; 200 of these were from the Sardinian contingent, which behaved with great gallantry under gen. La Marmora. The Russian general Read and the Sardinian general Montevecchio were killed. The object of the attack was the relief of Sebastopol, then closely besieged by the English and French.

tea, an evergreen shrub of the order *Camellia*, at maturity from 3 to 4 feet in height, bearing white flowers and elliptical or lanceolate leaves, 2 species of which produce the teas of commerce. *Thea bohea* furnishing the various black teas, viz.: Pekoe, Caper, Oolong, Souchong, and Congou; and *Thea viridis* the green teas: Gunpowder, Hyson, Young Hyson, Imperial, etc. This shrub is a native of China and Japan, and while a decoction of its leaves has been a favorite beverage in those countries for centuries, it was wholly unknown to the more western nations until about the beginning of the 17th century; it is said to have been introduced by the Dutch about 1610. It is mentioned as having been used in England as a great rarity prior to 1657, and but little known for some time after. ["I sent for a cup of tea (a China drink), of which I had never drunk before."—"Pepys' Diary," 25 Sept. 1661.] At this time it was selling at 6*l.* and even 10*l.* the pound.

A duty of 8*d.* was charged upon every gallon of tea made for sale (12 Ch. II. c. 13).................... 1660
East India company first import it.................... 1669
[Brought into England in 1666, by lord Ossory and lord Arlington, from Holland; and, being admired by persons of rank, it was imported from thence, and generally sold for 60*s.* per pound, till the East India company took up the trade.—*Anderson.*]
Green tea began to be used.................... 1715
Price of black tea per pound, 13*s.* to 20*s.*; of green, 12*s.* to 30*s.*, 1728
Great Britain's tea trade monopolized by the East India company until.................... 1834
[Under the monopoly system the duty was about 200 per cent. ad valorem.]
About 120,000,000 lbs. of tea consumed in Great Britain....... 1890

Duty imposed on tea in America by Great Britain in 1767; this tax occasioned the destruction of 17 chests at New York, and 340 at BOSTON, Dec. 1773, and ultimately led to the Revolutionary war. Efforts have been made to introduce its cultivation in the highlands of the South Atlantic states; but while the climate and soil are considered adapted to its growth, the trouble and expense of preparing it for market in competition with China teas renders its cultivation as a remunerative industry impossible. Amount of tea consumed in the United States in 1870, about 47,000,000 lbs., or 1.2 lbs. per capita, and in 1893, 90,000,000 lbs., or about 1.45 lbs. per capita.

Duty removed from tea from....................1 July, 1872

"tearless victory" was won by Archidamus III., king of Sparta, over the Arcadians and Argives, without losing a man, 367 B.C.

Te Deum, a song of praise used by the Romish and English churches, beginning "*Te Deum laudamus*"—"We praise thee, O God"—supposed to be the composition of Augustin and Ambrose, about 390.

teeto'taler, a term applied to an abstainer from all fermented liquors, originated with Richard Turner, an artisan of Preston, Engl., who, contending for the principle at a temperance meeting, about Sept. 1833, asserted "that nothing but *te-te-total* will do." The word was immediately adopted. He died 27 Oct. 1846. These facts are taken from the *Staunch Teetotaler*, edited by Joseph Livesey, of Preston (an originator of the movement in Aug. 1832), Jan. 1867. ENCRATITES, GOOD TEMPLARS, TEMPERANCE, UNITED KINGDOM.

Teg'yra, a village of Bœotia. Here Pelopidas defeated the Spartans, 375 B.C.

tel'egraphs (from the Gr. τῆλε, afar, and γράφω, I write). Æschylus, in his Agamemnon (500 B.C.), describes the communication of intelligence by burning torches as signals. Polybius, the Greek historian (who died about 122 B.C.), calls the different instruments used by the ancients for communicating information, *pyrsiæ*, because the signals were always made by fire. In 1663, a plan was suggested by the marquess of Worcester, and a telegraph was suggested by dr. Hooke, 1684. M. Amontons is also said to have been the inventor of telegraphs about this period. James II., while duke of York, originated a set of navy signals, which were systematized by Kempenfeldt in 1780; and a dictionary was compiled by sir Home Popham. M. Chappe then invented the telegraph first used by the French in 1792, and 2 were erected over the admiralty office, London, 1796. The semaphore was erected there, 1816. The naval signals by telegraph enabled 400 previously concerted sentences to be transmitted from ship to ship, by varying the combinations of 2 revolving crosses. SIGNALS; for electric telegraph, ELECTRICITY; for wireless electricity, ELECTRICITY — LATEST DEVELOPMENTS. The electric telegraph in the United States is almost entirely in the hands of the Western Union Telegraph company.

GROWTH OF THE ELECTRIC TELEGRAPH IN THE U. S. SINCE 1867.

Year.	Miles of line.	Miles of wire.	Offices.	Messages.	Receipts.	Profits.
1867..	46,270	85,291	2,565	5,879,282	$6,568,925	$2,624,919
1871..	56,032	121,151	4,606	10,646,077	7,637,448	2,532,661
1881..	110,340	327,171	10,737	32,500,000	14,393,543	5,908,279
1891..	187,981	715,591	20,098	59,148,343	23,034,326	6,605,584
1904..	199,350	1,155,405	23,458	67,909,973	29,249,390	7,887,475

Tel-el-Ke'bir, a fortified seaport town of Egypt. Here, 13 Sept. 1882, sir Garnet Wolseley defeated Arabi Pacha. British force numbered 11,000 infantry and 2000 cavalry, 40 guns. The Egyptians were intrenched with about twice the force. British loss, 52 killed, 380 wounded; Egyptian, total loss, 1500.

telem'eter, an instrument for determining the distance between a gun and the object fired at. Lieut. von Ehrenberg and maj. Montaudon at Baden constructed a telemeter the size of a watch, by which the distance is determined and shown on a dial by the action of sound, 1878-85.—*Tel'elopom'eter*, another apparatus for ascertaining the distance from point to point, invented by dr. Luigi Cerebotani, was announced in Sept. 1885; 2 telescopes are employed.

telep'athy, "the supersensory transference of thoughts and feelings from one mind to another;" the principal subject of "Phantasm of the Living," edited by Edmund Gurney, Frederic Myers, and Frank Podmore, and issued by the Society for Psychical Research (SPIRITUALISM), about 30 Oct. 1886.

tel'ephone (from Gr. τῆλε, afar, and φωνή, voice, sound), a name now given to apparatus for transmitting articulate and musical sounds by means of wire, vibrating rods, threads, or magneto-electricity. ELECTRICITY, MICROPHONE, PHONOGRAPH.

Robert Hook conveyed sounds to a distance by distended wire, 1667
Wheatstone conveyed sounds of a musical-box from a cellar to upper rooms by a deal rod (termed "Enchanted Lyre").... 1821
C. G. Page produced galvanic musical tones by magnetizing and demagnetizing an iron bar.................... 1837
Philip Reis exhibits at Frankfort, Germany, an electrical instrument which transmits the pitch of a sound.........25 Apr. 1861
Alexander Graham Bell begins his investigation of electrical transmission and reproduction of articulate speech....July, 1874
Bell constructs an electrical telephone, with a diaphragm of gold-beater's skin, which transmits speech.............July, 1875
Thomas A. Edison, furnished by William Orton, president of the Western Union Telegraph company, with a description of Reis's telephone, begins experiments with a view to producing an articulating telephone....................July, "
Toy, called the "lovers' telegraph," being a string telephone, extensively sold in the U. S.... .... "

Elisha Gray files his caveat "to transmit the tones of the human voice through a telegraphic circuit," etc 14 Feb 1876
Prof Bell publicly explains his method before the American Academy of Arts and Sciences of Boston 10 May, "
Bell's telephone exhibited at the Centennial Exhibition, June, "
Iron diaphragm first used by Bell 30 June, "
Edison s carbon loud speaking telephone invented Jan 1877
Prof Bell exhibits at the Essex Institute, Salem, Mass, his telephone, by which speech into a similar telephone in Boston 16 miles distant, is distinctly audible in Salem 12 Feb "
First known telephone line connects the office of Charles Williams, electrician in Boston, and his house in Somerville, Apr "
First telephone exchange established in Boston, Mass "
One form of microphone invented by Edison 1 Apr "
Experiments begun in Brown university by prof Eli W Blake, prof John Pierce, and others result in the construction by dr William F Channing of the first portable telephone, Apr "
Handle telephone now generally in use made by dr Channing and Edson S Jones, at Providence R I May, "
Glass plate telephone invented by Henry W Vaughan, state assayer Providence, R I June, "
Bell telephone exhibited before the British association at Plymouth Engl, by W H Preece 23 Aug "
Singing and music of the Grand Opera, Paris, transmitted to the electrical exhibition Paris 1881
Pulsion telephone carrying speech by an ordinary wire without electricity, invented by Lemuel Mellett 1888
Telephone communication from London to Marseilles and Brussels completed 19 Apr 1891
Bell telephone patent expires 7 Mch 1893
American Bell Telephone company, practically controlling the telephone business in the U S, reports 240,412 miles of wire in use This company, with its subsidiary companies, represents $80,000,000 of capital, and the Long Distance Telephone company about $5,000,000 . 1891
The same company reports a total of 2,983 189 miles of wire, 798,901 circuits, 53,795 employés 1,525 167 stations, 3,779,517 instruments in use, average of daily calls 9 876,402, capital $154,179,300 (ELECTRICITY—LATEST DEVELOPMENTS), 1 Jan 1905

tel'ephotog'raphy, a process for transmitting to a distance images of objects by the agency of electricity and selenium, was invented by Shelford Bidwell early in 1881.

tel'erad'iphone, an arrangement of apparatus in which M Mercadier has adapted prof Graham Bell's photophone to telegraphy, announced Jan. 1882

tel'escopes. Their principle was described by Roger Bacon about 1250, and Leonard Digges (who d about 1573) is said to have arranged glasses magnifying very distant objects. The 4 principal kinds of reflecting telescopes are.

1 Gregorian, devised by James Gregory of Aberdeen 1663
2 Newtonian, invented by sir Isaac Newton 1669
3 Cassegrainian, invented by Cassegrain 1672
4 Herschelian, invented by sir William Herschel 1790

Telescopes constructed by John Lipperhey and Zacharias Jansen, spectacle makers of Middleburg, and James Metius of Alkmaer about 1608
Galileo (from a description of the above) constructed telescopes (May, 1609), gradually increasing in power, till he discovered Jupiter's satellites, etc Jan 1610
Telescope explained by Kepler 1611
Huyghens greatly improves the telescope, discovers the ring and satellites of Saturn, etc 1655–56
Telescopes improved by Gregory about 1663
Reflecting telescope invented by Newton 1668
Achromatic or refracting telescope, made by Chester More Hall, Harlow, Essex, Engl 1723
Obtains an image free from color 1729
Euler succeeds in 1747
John Dollond invents the "achromatic combination," for which he receives the Copley medal from the Royal Society 1758
Sir William Herschel (originally an organist at Bath) greatly improves telescopes, and discovers the planet URANUS, 21 Mch 1781, and a volcanic mountain in the moon, 1783, he completes his 40 ft.-focal length telescope and 48 in. mirror, 1789, and he discovers 2 other volcanic mountains, he lays before the Royal Society a catalogue of 5000 nebulæ and clusters of stars, 1802
Telescope made in London for the observatory of Madrid cost 11,000*l* "
Telescopes improved by Guinand and Fraunhofer 1805–14
Great telescope taken down, and one of 20-ft focal length erected by sir John Herschel, who afterwards used it at the cape of Good Hope . 1822
Earl of Rosse erected at Parsonstown, in Ireland, a telescope (at a cost exceeding 20,000*l*) 6 ft. in diameter and 54 ft. in length, it is moved with ease 1828–45
M Lassell constructs a telescope, 48 in mirror, by which he discovers the satellite of Neptune, 1846, and the 8 satellites of Saturn . 1848
One of gigantic size, 85 ft. in length (very imperfect), completed at Wandsworth by the rev John Craig . 1852
Magnificent equatorial telescopes set up at the national observatories at Greenwich and Paris 1860
M Foucault exhibits at Paris a reflecting telescope, the mirror 31½ in in diameter, the focal length 17½ ft . 1862
Mr Newall's telescope (with object-glass 25 in diameter, tube nearly 30 ft) set up at Gateshead by Cooke of York 1870
One at U S Observatory, Washington, object glass 26 in diameter, 33 ft. length
A Ainslie Common s reflecting telescope speculum 37½ in diameter, length 20 ft, said to be the most powerful in existence, Ealing, Middlesex, completed Sept 1879
Large refracting telescope, made by Howard Grubb at Dublin for Vienna, approved by the commissioners 16 Mch 1881
Largest reflecting telescope in the U S is at Harvard university, 28 in mirror
Largest refracting telescope in the world 40 in lenses, made by Alvin G Clark Cambridge, Mass, for the university of Chicago, to be completed during 1895
For other important refracting telescopes, OBSERVATORY

Tell, William, legendary Swiss hero, flourished about 1307 The popular stories respecting him were demonstrated to be mythical by prof Kopp of Lucerne, 1872

Tell-Amarna tablets, consisting of 320 tablets or portions of tablets covered with cuneiform writing, discovered by a peasant woman at Tell-Amarna, or the mound of Amarna, an important site 150 miles south of Cairo, Egypt, on the east bank of the Nile, 1887 The British museum obtained 48 tablets mostly in good condition, the Berlin museum 160, mostly fragments, the rest are at the museum of Cairo. *Their average size is* $8\frac{3}{4}$ *by* $4\frac{7}{8}$ *inches The largest contains* 98 lines, the smallest 10 lines Probably inscribed 1500 to 1450 B.C. A general record of letters written by the rulers of Egypt to rulers at Babylon, Palestine, Syria, etc, and replies—general gossip of governmental news.

tellu'rium, a rare metal, in its natural state associated with small quantities of iron and gold, was discovered by Muller of Reichenstein in 1782, and named by Klaproth

tel'odynam'ic transmitter, invented by M Hirn, is an arrangement of water-wheels, endless wires, and pulleys for conveying and using the power of waterfalls at a distance, and has been much used since 1850 The apparatus was shown at Paris in 1862

tel'pherage, an application of electrical motion, invented by profs Jenkin, Ayrton, and Perry for conveying heavy goods, shown at Millwall, Engl., 1884

Temeswar (*tem-esh-var'*), Hungary, capital of the Banat, often besieged by the Turks. On 10 Aug 1849, Haynau totally defeated the Hungarians besieging this town, and virtually ended the war

tem'nograph, an instrument designed to plot to any accurate scale a section of the ground over which it travels It works by frictional motion governed by 2 pendulous weights. Invented by A M Rymer-Jones in 1879.

temperance reform. Maurice, the landgrave of Hesse, founded an Order of Temperance, 25 Dec. 1600, a total abstinence society existed at Skibbereen, Ireland, in 1817, the Sober Society was formed at Allentown, N. J, in 1805, and this was followed by temperance societies organized, one at Moreau, Saratoga county, N Y, 30 Apr 1808, another at Greenfield, N. Y, in 1809, and another at Hector, N Y, 3 Apr. 1818 The Massachusetts Society for the Suppression of Intemperance was instituted at Boston, 5 Feb. 1813, but temperance reform as an organized movement began 13 Feb 1826, when the American Society for the Promotion of Temperance was organized at the Park Street church, Boston, Mass Drs Justin Edwards, Woods, Jenks, and Wayland, and messrs. John Tappan and S V. S Wilder were prominent in it

First Women's Temperance society organized in Ohio, close of 1828
New York State and Connecticut State Temperance societies organized 1829
Temperance society formed at New Ross, county Wexford, Ireland 14 Aug "
Young People's Temperance Society, with a pledge of total abstinence, organized at Hector, N Y 22 Aug "
First society in Scotland, the Mayhill Female Temperance Society, organized by Miss Graham and Miss Allen 1 Oct. "
Glasgow and West of Scotland Temperance Society organized, 12 Nov "
First temperance society in England organized at Bradford, the Bradford Society for Promoting Temperance 2 Feb 1830
London Temperance Society, organized about July, 1830, becomes the British and Foreign Temperance Society, 27 July, 1831
Paisley Youths' Total Abstinence Society organized 14 Jan 1832
Tradeston Total Abstinence Society organized at Glasgow, 15 Jan "
First temperance society in India organized at Fort William, Calcutta. 29 Aug "
Congressional Temperance Society organized at Washington, D. C . . . . 26 Feb 1833

First National Temperance convention meets at Philadelphia; 440 delegates from 22 states.....................24–27 May, 1833
Word "TEETOTALER" originates with Richard Turner, a workman at Preston, Engl., enters the English dictionary...about "
Independent Order of RECHABITES founded at Salford, Engl., 25 Aug. 1835
Father Mathew, Capuchin friar of Cork, Ireland, "the Apostle of Temperance," signs the pledge and begins his great work in Ireland.....................................10 Apr. 1838
First great medical declaration in favor of total abstinence signed by 79 members of the London medical faculty, 11 May, 1839
Order of Sons of Temperance organized in New York..29 Sept. 1842
John B. Gough signs the pledge at Worcester, Mass.....31 Oct. "
Father Mathew visits England in the cause of temperance, arriving at London...................................28 July, 1843
First National Temperance convention in Germany held at Hamburg...6–9 Aug. "
First World's Temperance convention in London......4–8 Aug. 1846
First "Band of Hope" organized at Leeds...............Oct. 1847
George Cruikshank in the cause of temperance issues a series of 8 engravings under the title, "The Bottle," 1847, and a second series of 8 entitled "Drunkards' Children".......... 1848
Father Mathew visits the U. S.; arriving in New York on the *Ashburton*, he is welcomed at the Irving house as the guest of the city...2 July, 1849
British and Foreign Temperance Society dissolved........... 1850
Maine Liquor law passed............................2 June, 1851
Order of GOOD TEMPLARS formed in New York state .... "
Father Mathew sails from Philadelphia on the *Pacific* for Ireland after an extended tour throughout the U. S......8 Nov. "
Rev. dr. Justin Edwards d..........................23 July, 1853
John B. Gough makes a 2 years' tour of England, delivering his first address in Exeter hall, London..............2 Aug. "
World's Temperance convention in Metropolitan hall, N.Y., 6–10 Sept. "
Father Mathew d. at Queenstown, Ireland..............8 Dec. 1856
Spirit rations in the navy of the U. S. abolished after...1 Sept. 1862
Statue of Father Mathew unveiled in Cork, Ireland.....10 Oct. 1864
National Temperance Society and publication house, with headquarters at New York, organized..................... 1865
National PROHIBITION PARTY organized at Chicago, Ill., 1–2 Sept. 1869
Inaugural meeting of the Church of England Temperance Society at Lambeth palace............................18 Feb. 1873
Blue-ribbon movement begun by Francis Murphy of Maine.... "
Woman's temperance crusade begins in Hillsborough, O., Dec. "
National Women's Christian Temperance Union organized, 18–20 Nov. 1874
British Women's Temperance Association organized at Newcastle-on-Tyne...21 Apr. 1876
Women's International Temperance congress in Philadelphia, Pa..12 June, "
International Temperance congress in Philadelphia, Pa., 13–14 June, "
Temperance Society of the Blue Cross organized in Geneva, Switzerland ....21 Sept. 1877
Department of Scientific Temperance in Public schools created in connection with the Woman's Christian Temperance Union, 1880
John B. Gough d. in Philadelphia, aged 69 ....17 Feb. 1886
Law for compulsory temperance education in public schools passed by Congress for District of Columbia and the territories (and by nearly every state legislature since).....17 May, "

temperature, heat or cold as related to sensation; the degree of heat or cold indicated by the thermometer. The temperature of any locality is the result of, 1st, the sun's rays; 2d, its latitude; 3d, the surface of the earth; 4th, oceanic currents; 5th, winds and their direction. The mean temperature of any locality for a year furnishes no adequate idea of its climate; the mean temperature may be 55° and not vary 5°, or it may be 55° and vary many degrees. But the average temperature of a place for any month may be regarded as a partial expression of its climate for that time; thus, the average temperature at El Paso, Texas, for January is the same as at Victoria, Vancouver's island. The temperature of space or "absolute zero" is placed at −493° Fahr., while the lowest recorded temperature of the atmosphere is −90° at Werchojansk, Siberia. The extreme range of temperature in the northern hemisphere is about 217.8°; maximum, 127.4° at Ouargle, Algeria, 17 July, 1879; minimum −90.4° at Werchojansk, Siberia, 15 Jan. 1885. Extreme range in one place, at Yakutsk, Siberia, 181.4°, and at Poplar Prairie, Montana, U. S., 172.7°. Lowest mean temperatures in the U. S. are at St. Vincent, Minn.; 10 years, annual 34°, for January 4.8° Fahr. Highest mean temperature, Rio Grande City, Tex., 7 years: annual, 73.1°; for June, 93.9° Fahr. At Point Barrow, Alaska, the temperature of the earth at a depth of 37 ft. was found to be 12°; estimating an increase of 1° in 50 ft., the earth would still be frozen at a depth of 1000 ft.; at Irkutsk, Siberia, the earth was found frozen at a depth of 382 ft. The annual temperature at the surface of the sea ranges from 75° Fahr., just north of the equator along the Gold Coast, Africa, to 28° in the great frozen sea north of Grinnell's Land. The mean equatorial temperature of land and water is about 81.5°, of the land alone about 83°; the hottest being in tropical Africa, 85.1°. Of sudden and great changes in temperature in the U. S., the following notable instances are given. Fall of 49.7° in 8 hours at fort Maginnis, Mont., 6 Jan. 1886; fall of 63.3° in 16 hours at Abilene, Tex., 27 Dec., 1886. Rise of 55.1° in 8 hours at Campo, San Diego county, Cal.; rise of 65° in 24 hours at Florence, Ariz., 22 June, 1881.

HIGHEST AND LOWEST TEMPERATURE, WITH TIME OF OBSERVATION AT SIGNAL STATIONS IN EACH STATE IN THE UNITED STATES.

Highest tem.	Place.	Time.	Lowest tem.	Place.	Time.
Fahr.			Fahr.		
106.9°	Montgomery, Ala	July, 1881	5°	Montgomery, Ala	Jan. 1886
119°	Fort McDowell, Ariz	June, 1887	—18°	Prescott, Ariz	Dec. 1879
104.5°	Fort Smith, Ark	July, 1884 Aug. 1886	—7°	Fort Smith, Ark	Jan. 1886
111.5°	Red Bluff, Cal	July, 1887	—25.5°	Fort Bidwell, Cal	" 1888
105.2°	Las Animas, Col	" 1885	—29°	Denver, Col	" 1875
100°	New Haven, Conn	Sept. 1881	—14°	New Haven, Conn	" 1873
98°	Delaware Breakwater, Del	Aug. 1885	1°	Delaware Breakwater, Del	Dec. 1880
104.3°	Washington, D. C	Sept. 1881	—14°	Washington, D. C	Jan. 1881
104°	Jacksonville, Fla	July, 1879	15°	Pensacola, Fla	" 1886
105°	Augusta, Ga	" 1878 Aug. "	—2°	Atlanta, Ga	" "
115°	Lapwai, Ida	" 1882	—38°	Eagle Rock, Id	" 1883
103°	Cairo, Ill	" 1881	—23°	Chicago, Ill	Dec. 1872
101°	Indianapolis, Ind	July, " Aug. "	—25°	Indianapolis, Ind	Jan. 1884
109°	Fort Gibson, I. T	July, 1879	—20°	Fort Reno, I. T	" 1886
104.4°	Des Moines, Ia	" 1886	—31.5°	Dubuque, Ia	" 1887
108°	Dodge City, Kan	" 1876	—29°	Leavenworth, Kan	" 1873
104.6°	Louisville, Ky	Aug. 1881	—19.5°	Louisville, Ky	" 1884
107°	Shreveport, La	July, 1875 Aug. 1881	—1.5°	Shreveport, La	" 1886
97°	Portland, Me	July, 1876	—21°	Eastport, Me	Dec. 1884
101.8°	Baltimore, Md	" 1887	—6°	Baltimore, Md	Jan. 1881
101.5°	Boston, Mass	Sept. 1881	—13°	Boston, Mass	" 1882
101°	Detroit, Mich	July, 1887	—33.4°	Mackinaw City, Mich	Feb. 1881
103.2°	St. Vincent, Minn	Aug. 1886	—53.5°	St. Vincent, Minn	Jan. 1888
101°	Vicksburg, Miss	June, 1881	3°	Vicksburg, Miss	" 1886
106.4°	St. Louis, Mo	July, "	—21.5°	St. Louis, Mo	" 1884
110.8°	Fort Benton, Mont	" 1886	—63°	Poplar Prairie, Mont	" 1885
107°	North Platte, Neb	" 1877	—34.6°	North Platte, Neb	" 1888
104°	Winnemucca, Nev	" "	—28°	Winnemucca, Nev	" "
93.3°	Manchester, N. H	" "	—11°	Manchester, N. H	Feb. 1886
101°	Sandy Hook, N. J	Sept. 1881	—10°	Barnegat, N. J	Jan. 1875
115°	Fort Bayard, N. M	July, 1882	—18°	Fort Stanton, N. M	Dec. 1887
100°	New York city, N. Y	Sept. 1881	—23°	Oswego, N. Y	Jan. 1885
107°	Kitty Hawk, N. C	July, 1887	—5°	Charlotte, N. C	Dec. 1880
105°	Bismarck, N. Dak	Aug. 1876	—44°	Bismark, N. Dak	Jan. 1887
103.5°	Cincinnati, O	July, 1881	—28°	Sandusky, O	Feb. 1884

HIGHEST AND LOWEST TEMPERATURE, ETC.—(*Continued.*)

Highest tem.	Place.	Time.	Lowest tem.	Place.	Time.
Fahr.			Fahr.		
110°	Umatilla, Ore	Aug. 1882	—39°	Fort Klamath, Ore	Jan. 1888
103°	Pittsburg, Pa	July, 1881	—16°	Erie, Pa	" 1887
92°	Narragansett Pier, R. I.	" 1885	—9°	Narragansett Pier, R. I.	Dec. 1884
104°	Charlotte, S. C.	" 1875	11°	Charlotte, S. C.	Jan. 1878
111°	Pierre, S. D.	June, 1876	—4.3°	Huron, S. Dak.	" 1885
104°	Nashville, Tenn.	Aug. 1874	—16°	Knoxville, Tenn	" 1884
113°	El Paso, Tex.	June, 1883	—14.2°	Fort Elliott, Tex	" 1888
104°	Fort Thornburg, Utah	July, 1884	—20°	Salt Lake City, Utah	" 1883
97°	Burlington, Vt	Aug. 1876	—25°	Burlington, Vt	" 1882
103°	Cape Henry, Va	" 1881	—5°	Lynchburg, Va	Dec. 1880
104°	Walla Walla, Wash.	July, 1886	—30.5°	Spokane Falls, Wash.	Jan. 1888
97°	Morgantown, W. Va.	" 1874	—10°	Morgantown, W. Va.	Feb. 1875
101°	La Crosse, Wis	" "	—42°	La Crosse, Wis	Jan. 1888
101°	Cheyenne, Wyo.	" 1881	—57°	Fort Wasakie, Wyo	Feb. 1883

DATE OF THE EARLIEST, LATEST, AND AVERAGE AUTUMNAL KILLING FROST IN DIFFERENT LOCATIONS IN THE UNITED STATES.

Place.	Latitude.	Killing frost.			Place.	Latitude.	Killing frost.		
		Earliest.	Latest.	Average.			Earliest.	Latest.	Average.
Washington, Ark	33° 44′ N.	30 Sept.	16 Nov.	28 Oct.	Oregon, Mo.	40° — N.	17 Sept.	3 Nov.	9 Oct.
Sacramento, Cal	38° 33′ "	17 Oct.	31 Dec.	19 Nov.	De Soto, Neb.	41° 28′ "	24 Sept.	31 Oct.	10 Oct.
Middletown, Conn.	41° 30′ "	10 Sept.	22 Oct.	2 Oct.	Cooperstown, N. Y.	42° 40′ "	3 Sept.	22 Oct.	27 Sept.
Forsyth, Ga.	32° 59′ "	17 Oct.	25 Nov.	8 Nov.	Portsmouth, Ohio	38° 45′ "	11 Sept.	14 Nov.	11 Oct.
Peoria, Ill.	40° 41′ "	1 Oct.	17 Nov.	27 Oct.	Brandon, Ore.	43° 50′ "	9 Sept.	18 Nov.	9 Oct.
Monticello, Ia	42° 45′ "	25 Aug.	13 Oct.	17 Sept.	Bethany, Pa.	41° 35′ "	30 Aug.	21 Oct.	23 Sept.
Lawrence, Kan.	39° — "	29 Sept.	18 Nov.	20 Oct.	New Ulm, Tex.	29° 40′ "	12 Nov.	15 Dec.	25 Nov.
Gardiner, Me	44° 12′ "	4 Sept	22 Oct.	1 Oct.	Lunenburg, Vt.	44° 27′ "	5 Aug.	16 Nov.	20 Sept.
Amherst, Mass.	42° 23′ "	10 Aug.	8 Oct.	20 Sept.	Wytheville, Va.	36° 56′ "	26 Aug.	14 Oct.	19 Sept.
Holly Springs, Miss.	34° 40′ "	10 Oct.	30 Nov.	30 Oct.	Manitowoc, Wis.	44° 5′ "	18 Sept.	13 Nov.	16 Oct.

LATITUDE AND MEAN TEMPERATURE OF THE PRINCIPAL CITIES OF EUROPE.

Cities.	Latitude.	Mean tem.	Remarks.
St. Petersburg, Russia	59° 55′	38.7°	Latitude nearly that of the mouth of Churchill river, Hudson's bay.
Stockholm, Sweden	59° 21′	42.3°	" " " "
Edinburgh, Scotland	55° 57′	47°	Latitude about that of fort York, central Hudson's bay.
Moscow, Russia	55° 40′	40°	" " " "
Berlin, Germany	52° 31′	48°	Latitude of the Saskatchewan district, Canada.
Amsterdam, Holland	52° 22′	49.8°	" " "
London, England	51° 31′	50.8°	Latitude of fort Moose, southern extremity of Hudson's bay.
Paris, France	48° 50′	51.3°	Latitude about 140 miles farther north than Quebec.
Vienna, Austria	48° 12′	51°	" " " "
Rome, Italy	41° 54′	60°	Latitude about that of Providence, R. I.
Constantinople, Turkey	41°	57.4°	" " New York city.
Madrid, Spain	40° 26′	58°	" " Philadelphia.
Alexandria, Egypt	31° 12′	69°	" " Baton Rouge.

Templars. The military order of "Soldiers of the Temple" was founded about 1118 by a Burgundian knight, Hugh de Paynes or Paganis (d. 1136), and 8 other knights at Jerusalem for the purpose of protecting pilgrims by guarding the public roads leading there. Baldwin II., then king of Jerusalem, granted them quarters and otherwise protected them. The order was confirmed by pope Honorius II., 1128. The Templars were numerous in several countries, and came to England before 1185. Their wealth having excited the cupidity of Philip IV. of France, the order was suppressed on charges of infidelity, gross immorality, and other crimes, by the council of Vienne, mostly through his efforts, and part of its revenues was bestowed upon other orders about 1312. The order suffered persecution throughout Europe, 1308–10, especially in France, where many were burned alive or hanged; 68 knights being burned at Paris, 1310. Pope Clement V. abolished the order, Apr. 1312. The grandmaster Molay was burned alive at Paris, 18 Mch. 1314. Their property in England was given to the Hospitallers, and the head of the order in England died in the Tower. As confessions were extorted under cruel torture, it is probable that most of the charges were false.

Temple, London, the dwelling of the Knights Templars, 1185, at the suppression of the order was purchased by the professors of the common law and converted into inns, 1311, afterwards called the Inner and Middle Temple. Essex house, also a part of the house of the Templars, was called the Outer Temple, because it was situated without Temple bar.

Temple hall was built.......... 1572
St. Mary's or the Temple church, situated in the Inner Temple, a Gothic stone building, erected by the Templars in 1240, is remarkable for its circular vestibule, and for tombs of crusaders. It was recased with stone by Mr. Smirke.......... 1828
New Middle Temple library opened by prince of Wales..31 Oct. 1861
Temple bar erected outside the gates; ordered to be rebuilt, 27 June, 1609; erected by sir C. Wren; completed Mch. 1672–73; cost 1397*l.* 10*s.*; room above contained books of Child & Co. for 200 years; reported dangerous, Mch.; began to sink, 30 July; shored up.......... 1868
[Its removal voted by the common council, 27 Sept. 1876; began 2 Jan. 1878; last stones removed 13 June, 1879 (set up in Epping forest).]
New Inner Temple hall opened by princess Louise.....14 May, 1870
Memorial to mark the site (including statues of the queen and prince of Wales); cost about 11,550*l.*; inaugurated by prince Leopold..........8 Nov. 1880

temple (Gr. τέμενος, Lat. *templum*), an enclosure or building set apart for religious rites; an edifice dedicated to the service of a deity or deities, and connected with a system of worship. The Egyptians were the first who erected temples to their gods.—*Herodotus.* The Greeks greatly excelled in this style of edifice. Most of the heathen temples were destroyed throughout the Roman empire by Constantine the Great and Theodosius, 331–392. 1st temple at Jerusalem built by Solomon, 1012–1004 B.C.; described by Josephus, bk. viii. chap. iii., Whiston's transl.; pillaged by Shishak, king of Egypt, 971; repaired by Joash, 856; destroyed by Nebuchadnezzar, king of Assyria, 586. 2d temple built by Zerubbabel, 536–30; much inferior to Solomon's; pillaged by Antiochus Epiphanes of Syria, 170; taken by Pompey, and its most holy place seen by him, 63. 3d temple built by Herod, the most magnificent of the 3, covering 19 acres, 18 B.C.; destroyed by Titus, 70 A.D. Fergusson's "Temples of the Jews," pub. London, 1878. ARCHITECTURE, DELPHI, DIANA, PARTHENON, PANTHEON.

Ten'edos, an island in the Ægean sea, off the coast of ancient Troas, whither the Greeks retired, as Virgil narrates, to surprise the Trojans (*Æn.* ii. 21, 254); now belonging to Turkey.

Teneriffe. CANARY ISLANDS.

Tennessee, one of the southern United States, lies between the Alleghany mountains on the east and the Mississippi river on the west. It is bounded on the north by Kentucky and Virginia, east by North Carolina, south by Georgia, Alabama, and Mississippi, and west by Arkansas and Missouri. It lies between 35° and 36° 35′ N. lat., and 81° 37′ and 90° 15′ W. lon. Area, 42,050 sq. miles. Pop. 1890, 1,767,518; 1900, 2,020,606. Capital, Nashville.

Louis Joliet and Père Jacques Marquette descend the Mississippi river to lat. 33°....... 1673
Robert Cavalier de La Salle builds fort Prud'homme on the 4th Chickasaw bluff of the Mississippi river....... 1682
M. Charleville, a French trader, builds a trading-house near the present site of Nashville on the west side of the Cumberland river....... 1714
French erect fort Assumption on the Mississippi at the 4th Chickasaw bluff....... "
Bienville makes a treaty of peace with the Chickasaw Indians at fort Assumption.......June, 1739
Party of Virginians, dr. Thomas Walker and others, discover the Cumberland mountains, Cumberland gap, and Cumberland river....... 1748
Fort Loudon founded near confluence of the Tellico and Little Tennessee rivers, about 30 miles from the present Knoxville....... 1756
Col. Bird builds Long Island fort on the Holston river, near its north fork, where the American army winters....... 1758
Cherokees capture fort Loudon. The garrison, after the surrender, start out for fort Prince George; after proceeding about 15 miles they are massacred by the Indians....7 Aug. 1760
Capt. James Smith and others explore the Cumberland and Tennessee rivers from above Nashville down to the Ohio.... 1766
By treaty at fort Stanwix (Utica, N. Y.) the Six Nations cede the country north and east of the Tennessee.......5 Nov. 1768
Capt. William Bean settles on Boone creek, near Watauga..... 1769
Company formed to hunt and explore middle Tennessee, with camp at Price's Meadows, Wayne county....... "
Written association formed for the government of the Watauga settlers, and 5 commissioners appointed as a governing court, 1772
Col. Richard Henderson, Nathaniel Hart, and Daniel Boone purchase from the Indians a tract of country between the Kentucky and Cumberland rivers, which they call Transylvania.......17 Mch. 1775
Watauga purchased from the Indians, and deed of conveyance to Charles Robertson executed.......19 Mch. "
Watauga settlers march against the advancing Cherokees, and disperse them in a battle near Long Island fort ....20 July, 1776
Cherokees under old Abraham attack the fort at Watauga, but are repulsed.......21 July, "
Forces under col. William Christian march against and destroy the Cherokee towns in E. Tennessee....... "
Washington county, including all of Tennessee, created by a law of North Carolina.......Nov. 1777
Richard Hogan, Spencer, Holliday, and others come from Kentucky and begin a plantation near Bledsoe's Lick....... 1778
Capt. James Robertson and others from Watauga cross the Cumberland mountains, pitch their tents near French Lick, and plant a field of corn where Nashville now stands....... 1779
Eleven Chickamauga Indian towns destroyed by troops under Isaac Shelby, who left Big creek, near the site of Rogersville, 10 Apr. "
Jonesborough laid off and established as the seat of justice for Washington county....... "
Colony under John Donelson, in open boats, leaving fort Patrick Henry on the Holston, descend the Tennessee and ascend the Cumberland to French Lick, where they found Nashborough.......24 Apr. 1780
Form of government for the Cumberland settlements drawn up and articles signed at Nashborough.......13 May, "
Battle of Boyd's creek, a confluent of the French Broad. Troops under col. John Sevier, returning from the battle of King's mountain, join in expedition against the Cherokees and disperse them on their way to massacre the Watauga settlers.......Oct. "
Indian atrocities and massacres of settlers in middle Tennessee, throughout this and the following year, begin by an attack on the house of maj. Lucas at Freeland's station, on the Cumberland, near Stone river.......15 Jan. 1781
Battle of the Bluffs, where Nashville now stands; an unsuccessful attack of the Cherokees on the fort.......2 Apr. "
Pre-emption right allowed to settlers on the Cumberland by legislature of North Carolina, 640 acres to each family or head of family.......Apr. 1782
Court of Oyer and Terminer held at Jonesborough for Washington and Sullivan counties.......15 Aug. "
Treaty at Nashborough, by which the Chickasaws cede to North Carolina a tract extending nearly 40 miles south from Cumberland river....... 1783
First Methodist preacher comes to the Holston circuit, which includes E. Tennessee....... 1783
Commissioners lay off on Duck river a grant of 2500 acres of land presented by North Carolina to gen. Nathaniel Greene.. "
Nashville established by the legislature to succeed Nashborough....... 1784
General Assembly of North Carolina cedes to the U. S. territory west of the Alleghany mountains on condition that Congress accepts it within 2 years.......2 June, "
Believing themselves no longer a part of North Carolina, settlers in Washington, Sullivan, and Greene counties meet in convention at Jonesborough, choose John Sevier president, and form a constitution for the state of FRANKLAND..14 Dec. "
Gov. Caswell of North Carolina pronounces the revolt of Frankland usurpation.......14 Apr. 1785
Constitution for Frankland, or the state of Franklin, accepted by a convention of the people, which meets at Greeneville, and chooses John Sevier as governor.......14 Nov. "
Capt. James White and James Connor settle on the site of Knoxville....... 1786
At a conference upon the legality of the state of Frankland it is agreed that the inhabitants are "at full liberty and discretion to pay their public taxes to either the state of North Carolina or the state of Frankland".......20 Mch. 1787
Legislature of Frankland meets for the last time at Greeneville, and government reverts to North Carolina.......Sept. "
First literary institution in Tennessee incorporated, the Martin academy, at Salem, afterwards (1795) Washington college, 1788
Deed, ratified in General Assembly of North Carolina Dec. 1789, conveying to the U. S. territory west of the Alleghany mountains, is presented in Congress by Samuel Johnston and Benjamin Hawkins, 25 Feb., and accepted by act approved.......2 Apr. 1790
William Blount appointed governor of the territory southwest of the Ohio river—the Southwestern territory.......7 Aug. "
First issue of the *Knoxville Gazette* published at Rogersville by George Roulstone.......5 Nov. 1791
Knoxville, chosen as the seat of government, is laid out..Feb. 1792
Attack of over 700 Indians on Buchanan's Station, 4 miles south of Nashville, repulsed by a garrison of 15.....30 Sept. "
General Assembly meets at Knoxville.......5 Aug. 1794
University of Tennessee at Knoxville, chartered 10 Sept. 1794 as Blount college, is opened....... 1795
State constitution, adopted without popular vote by a convention which sits at Knoxville.......11 Jan.–6 Feb. 1796
John Sevier inaugurated first governor of state.......30 Mch. "
Tennessee admitted into the union by act approved....1 June, "
William Blount of Tennessee expelled from the U. S. Senate on charge of instigating the Creeks and Cherokees to assist the British in conquering Spanish Louisiana.......July, 1797
Treaty with the Cherokees extinguishing claims to land in Tennessee granted to individuals by North Carolina....Sept. 1798
Great revival of religion, begun in Kentucky in 1800, spreads through Tennessee....... 1801
Nashville chosen as seat of government by legislature....... 1802
Gen. Wilkinson builds fort Pickering at Memphis....... 1803
Public reception given to Aaron Burr at Nashville.....28 May, 1805
Congress grants 1000 acres in one tract for academies in Tennessee, one in each county; 1000 acres more for 2 colleges, Blount in the east and Cumberland in the west....... 1806
Nashville bank, the first in Tennessee, chartered....... 1807
Cumberland Presbyterian church organized at the house of Mr. McAdow in Dickson county.......4 Feb. 1810
Pair of mummies exhumed in a cave in Warren county (described in the *Medical Repository*).......2 Sept. "
John Sevier dies near Fort Decatur, Ala.......24 Sept. 1815
Gens. Andrew Jackson and Isaac Shelby obtain by treaty from the Chickasaws a cession of their lands north of 35° lat. and east of the Mississippi river, known as the Jackson purchase, 19 Oct. 1818
First conveyance of town lots in Memphis made.......May, 1819
Madison county organized and Jackson settled....... 1820
Capital permanently fixed at Nashville....... 1826
University of Nashville, founded in 1785, incorporated as Cumberland college in 1806, reorganized in 1824, and name changed, 1827
Two mummies found in a cave in western Tennessee (*American Journal of Science*, vol. xxii.)....... 1828
Andrew Jackson elected president of the U. S.......11 Nov. "
John H. Eaton appointed secretary of war.......9 Mch. 1829
Act for a state system of internal improvements.......2 Jan. 1830
Joel Parrish, cashier of the state bank, proves a defaulter for $200,000, and the bank wound up soon after.......3 Jan. "
Memphis railroad chartered.......Dec. 1831
State penitentiary at Nashville opened....... 1832
Andrew Jackson re-elected president of the U. S.......13 Nov. "
Conviction of John A. Murrell of Madison county, the "great western land pirate" and leader of the "Mystic Clan," a band of outlaws, horse thieves, and negro runners, who was brought to justice by Virgil A. Stewart (TRIALS)....... 1834
Constitution framed by a convention which meets at Nashville, 19 May, and completes its labors 30 Aug. 1834; ratified by a popular vote of 42,666 to 17,691.......5–6 Mch. 1835
R. H. McEwen elected to the newly created office of superintendent of public schools....... 1836
During this and the previous year the state furnished 1651 volunteers for the Florida war....... 1837
Felix Grundy appointed attorney-general.......5 July, 1838
National Whig convention meets at Nashville.......17 Aug. 1840
State hospital for the insane opened near Nashville....... "
John Bell appointed secretary of war.......5 Mch. 1841
Cumberland university at Lebanon chartered and opened....... 1842

National Whig convention held at Nashville. 21 Aug 1844

Memphis Conference female institute at Jackson, chartered 1843 opened "

State school for the Blind at Nashville opened "

James K Polk elected president of the U S 12 Nov "

Cave Johnson appointed postmaster general 6 Mch. 1845

Act for self taxation of districts for common schools "

Tennessee School for Deaf and Dumb at Knoxville opened "

Andrew Jackson dies at the Hermitage aged 78 8 June, "

Jas K Polk dies at Nashville aged 54 15 June, 1849

Memphis incorporated as a city Dec "

Southern convention meets at Nashville 3 June, 1850

Convention meets at Nashville, 11 Nov 1850 and adjourns after recommending a congress of slave holding states by a vote of 6 states, Alabama Florida Georgia, Mississippi, South Carolina, and Virginia opposed to Tennessee, 19 Nov "

James Campbell appointed postmaster general 5 Mch 1853

Southern convention meets at Memphis 6 June, "

State Agricultural Bureau established 1854

State capitol, commenced in 1845 completed 1855

Aaron V Brown appointed postmaster general 6 Mch 1857

Memphis and Charleston railroad completed, joining the Atlantic ocean with the Mississippi river 27 Mch "

Southern commercial convention at Knoxville, by vote of 64 to 27, recommends abrogation of the 8th article of the Ashburton treaty which requires the U S to keep a naval force on the coast of Africa 10 Aug "

Constitutional Union convention at Baltimore, Md nominates John Bell of Tennessee for president 9 May, 1860

Call for a state convention at Nashville to consider secession, is defeated by a vote of the people 9 Feb 1861

Gov Isham G Harris replies to pres Lincoln's call for troops, "Tennessee will not furnish a single man for coercion but 50,000 if necessary for the defence of our rights, or those of our Southern brothers" 18 Apr "

Gov Harris orders the seizure of $75,000 worth of Tennessee bonds and $5000 in cash belonging to the U S government, in possession of the collector at Nashville 29 Apr "

Majority vote of the state favors a declaration of independence for Tennessee and the acceptance of the provisional government of the Confederate states 8 June, "

Eastern Tennessee Union convention at Greeneville declares its opposition to the Confederate government 21 June, "

Gov Harris proclaims Tennessee out of the Union 24 June, "

Confederate commissary and ordnance stores at Nashville destroyed by fire 22 Dec "

Com Foote defeats gen Lloyd Tilghman and captures fort Henry 6 Feb 1862

Bombardment of FORT DONELSON begins 13 Feb fort surrendered to gen Grant by gen Buckner with 13,829 prisoners, 16 Feb "

Seat of government removed to Memphis 20 Feb "

Confederates evacuate Nashville, and the federals under Nelson enter 23 Feb "

Andrew Johnson, commissioned brigadier general of volunteers and appointed military governor of Tennessee 5 Mch, arrives at Nashville 12 Mch "

Gov Johnson suspends the mayor and other officials in Nashville for refusing the oath of allegiance to the U S 5 Apr "

Two days' battle of PITTSBURG LANDING, or Shiloh 6–7 Apr "

Union meetings held at Nashville 12 May, and at Murfreesborough 24 May, "

Memphis surrendered to com Davis 6 June, "

Battle of MURFREESBOROUGH 31 Dec 1862-4 Jan 1863

Battle of Spring Hill, confederates under gen Earl Van Dorn victorious 5 Mch "

Van Dorn repulsed by federals under gen Gordon Granger at Franklin 10 Apr "

Federal raid under col. Abel D Streight starts from Nashville (STREIGHT'S RAID) 11 Apr "

Kingston and Knoxville, evacuated by confederates under gen Simon B Buckner, occupied by Federal troops under gen A E Burnside 1 Sept. "

Chattanooga abandoned by confederates under gen Braxton Bragg, 8 Sept., Cumberland gap surrendered to federals 9 Sept "

Confederates under gen James Longstreet defeat federals at Philadelphia, E Tenn 20 Oct "

Gen Grant arrives at Nashville 21 Oct, and at Chattanooga, 23 Oct. "

Gen W E Jones, confederate, defeats col Garrard at Rogersville 6 Nov "

Longstreet besieges Knoxville and is repulsed (FORT SANDERS), 17 Nov "

Grant defeats Bragg in battle of Chattanooga (CHATTANOOGA CAMPAIGN) 23–25 Nov "

Longstreet repulses federals under gen J M Shackelford at Bean's Station, E Tennessee 14 Dec. "

FORT PILLOW captured by confederates under gen N B Forrest, and garrison of colored troops annihilated 12 Apr 1864

Federals under gen A C Gillem surprise the Confederate gen John H Morgan at the house of a Mrs. Williams in Greeneville, E Tenn In attempting to escape he is killed 4 Sept. "

Federals under Schofield repulse confederates under Hood at FRANKLIN 30 Nov "

Federals retire from Franklin and occupy Nashville, 1 Dec, Hood advances and partially invests Nashville 3–14 Dec "

Thomas defeats Hood at NASHVILLE 15–16 Dec "

Constitutional amendment abolishing slavery framed by a convention which sits at Nashville 9 Jan to 26 Jan 1865, ratified by a vote of the people 21,104 to 40 22 Feb 1865

Legislature ratifies the XIII th Amendment to the Constitution of the U S 5 Apr 1865

Pres Lincoln dies, Andrew Johnson president 15 Apr "

Law disfranchising all citizens who have voluntarily borne arms for or aided the Confederate government 1866

Law making negroes and Indians competent witnesses "

Race riot in Memphis, 24 negroes killed 1–3 May, "

XIV th Amendment to Constitution of the U S ratified by the legislature 19 July, "

Tennessee readmitted into the Union by act approved, 24 July, "

All distinction of race or color in qualifications for electors abolished Feb 1867

Fisk university at Nashville, opened 1866 chartered "

Petition for removal of disabilities signed by nearly 4000 citizens, including leading men of the state, is presented to the legislature, but not granted 1868

Act to suppress the Ku klux klan entitled "An Act to Preserve the Public Peace," punishes membership by a fine of not less than $500 or imprisonment for 5 years "

University of the South at Sewanee, chartered in 1858 opened, "

Gov Brownlow calls out the state militia to suppress the Ku klux klan, and proclaims martial law in 9 counties 20 Feb. 1869

Southern Commercial convention held at Memphis, 1100 delegates from 22 states 18 May, "

Constitution framed by a convention which sat at Nashville 10 Jan to 22 Feb, ratified by a popular vote of 98 128 to 33,872 26 Mch 1870

Colored Methodist Episcopal church of America organized at Jackson by bishop Paine 16 Dec. "

Reunion and Reform association meets at Nashville 13 Oct. 1871

Le Moyne Normal institute at Memphis opened "

Office of Chief Commissioner of Immigration for the state created by act of legislature "

Agricultural Bureau organized under act of legislature, 14 Dec. "

Convention at Jackson to promote the formation of a new state, out of western Kentucky, Tennessee, and Mississippi, 29 July, 1873

Convention of colored people in Nashville, seeking their full rights as citizens of the U S, politically and socially, 28 Apr 1874

Sixteen negroes, 22 Aug, charged with shooting at 2 white men, are taken from Trenton jail and shot dead by disguised men, 26 Aug "

E Tennessee hospital for the insane located at Knoxville "

Andrew Johnson, ex president of the U S, dies near Jonesborough 31 July, 1875

Peabody Normal college at Nashville opened "

Vanderbilt university at Nashville, chartered 1873 opened "

Southwestern Baptist university at Jackson, chartered 1874, opened "

David McKendree Key appointed postmaster-general 12 Mch 1877

Yellow fever in Memphis (YELLOW FEVER) 1878–79

Bill passed, 28 Mch 1879, to settle the state debt at the rate of 50 cents on the dollar, with 4 per cent interest, is rejected by vote of the people, 30,920 to 19,669 7 Aug 1879

NEW RUGBY founded 1880

Centennial anniversary of the settlement of Nashville celebrated 17-24 May, and equestrian statue of gen Jackson unveiled on the capitol grounds 20 May, "

Horace Maynard appointed postmaster general 2 June, "

Normal academy at Morristown opened 1881

Act of 5 Apr 1881, to settle the state debt by issue of new compromise bonds bearing 3 per cent interest, and coupons receivable in payment for taxes and debts due the state, is declared unconstitutional Feb 1882

Quadrennial General conference of the Methodist church, South, meets at Nashville 3 May, "

Law of 1882 for settlement of state debt repealed, and a new law passed for funding at a discount of 24 per cent on 6 per cent bonds, and others in proportion 1883

West Tennessee hospital for the insane, located at Bolivar, Hardeman county 1886

Tennessee Industrial school for boys at Nashville opened for the reception of pupils 1887

Ward's seminary for young ladies at Nashville, opened 1865, chartered "

Prohibitory constitutional amendment lost by a vote of 117,504 in favor, to 145,197 against. Aug "

General Assembly at its session adopts the Australian ballot system, creates a State Board of Medical Examiners, and conveys to the Ladies' Hermitage association the homestead of Andrew Jackson and 25 acres of land 7 Jan -8 Apr 1889

National Teachers' Association meets at Nashville 15 June, "

Remains of John Sevier removed from Alabama, and interred at Knoxville "

National League of Republican clubs meets at Nashville 4 Mch 1890

Special session of the legislature held at Nashville by proclamation (11 Feb) of the governor 24 Feb -18 Mch "

First Monday in September (Labor day) made a legal holiday by the legislature at session ending 30 Mch 1891

Miners at Briceville attack the state militia, and secure the withdrawal of convict miners from the mines of the Tennessee Coal and Knoxville Iron companies 20 July, "

Miners refer the convict mining system to the legislature, 24 July, "

Sarah Childress Polk, widow of pres. Polk, b 1803, d. at Nashville 14 Aug "

Legislature meets in extra session to consider the convict labor system 31 Aug. "

Legislature resolves that it is powerless to abolish the convict lease system, but will not renew the lease 4–5 Sept "

Miners of Briceville set free 160 convicts, and 140 more at another prison....31 Oct. 1891
Over 200 convicts set free in E. Tennessee by miners...2 Nov. "
Ex-gov. Albert S. Marks dies suddenly at Nashville.....4 Nov. "
National Real Estate Association formally organized in Nashville....18 Feb. 1892
Mining troubles in Coal Creek valley settled; convicts to be replaced by white free miners....19 Feb. "
Steel cantilever bridge over the Mississippi at Memphis opened, 12 May, "
Confederate Soldiers' Home at the Hermitage formally opened, 12 May, "
Miners burn the convict stockade at Tracy City, 13 Aug., and make an attack on the stockade at Oliver Springs....16 Aug. "
Miners capture the stockade at Oliver Springs, and send the guards and convicts to Knoxville....17 Aug. "
Miners defeated and routed by militia under gen. Carnes, 19 Aug. "
Convention of National Farmers' Alliance opens in Memphis, 15 Nov. "

TERRITORIAL GOVERNOR.

William Blount, appointed governor of the territory southwest of the Ohio....7 Aug. 1790

STATE GOVERNORS.

John Sevier	assumes office	30 Mch.	1796
Archibald Roane	"	Sept.	1801
John Sevier	"	"	1803

STATE GOVERNORS.—(*Continued.*)

William Blount	assumes office	Sept.	1809
Joseph McMinn	"	"	1815
William Carroll	"	"	1821
Samuel Houston	"	"	1827
William Carroll	"	"	1829
Newton Cannon	"	Oct.	1835
James K. Polk	"	"	1839
James C. Jones	"	"	1841
Aaron V. Brown	"	"	1845
Neil S. Brown	"	"	1847
William Trousdale	"	"	1849
William B. Campbell	"	"	1851
Andrew Johnson	"	"	1853
Isham G. Harris	"	"	1857
Andrew Johnson	"	provisional, 12 Mch.	1861
W. G. Brownlow	"	Apr.	1865
DeWitt C. Senter	"	Oct	1869
John C. Brown	"	"	1871
James D. Porter, jr.	"	Jan.	1875
Albert S. Marks	"	"	1879
Alvin Hawkins	"	"	1881
William B. Bate	"	"	1883
Robert L. Taylor	"	"	1887
John P. Buchanan	"	"	1891
Peter Turney	"	"	1893
H. Clay Evans	"	"	1895

UNITED STATES SENATORS FROM THE STATE OF TENNESSEE.

Name.	No. of Congress.	Date.	Remarks.
William Blount	4th to 5th	1796 to 1797	Seated 5 Dec. Expelled for "high misdemeanor," 8 July, 1797.
William Cocke	4th " 9th	1796 " 1805	" "
Joseph Anderson	5th	1797 " 1798	Elected in place of Blount.
Andrew Jackson	"	" " "	Resigned 1798.
Daniel Smith	"	1798	Appointed in place of Jackson.
Joseph Anderson	6th to 14th	1799 to 1815	Elected in place of Jackson; elected president *pro tem.* 15 Jan., 28 Feb., and 2 Mch. 1805.
Daniel Smith	9th " 11th	1805 " 1809	Resigned 1809.
Jenkin Whiteside	11th " 12th	1809 " 1811	Elected in place of Smith. Resigned 1811.
George W. Campbell	12th " 13th	1811 " 1814	Elected in place of Whiteside. Resigned 1814.
Jesse Wharton	13th " 14th	1814 " 1815	Appointed in place of Campbell.
John Williams	14th " 18th	1815 " 1823	
George W. Campbell	14th " 15th	1815 " 1818	Resigned 1818.
John Henry Eaton	15th " 21st	1818 " 1829	Appointed in place of Campbell. Resigned 1829.
Andrew Jackson	18th " 19th	1823 " 1825	Resigned 1825.
Hugh Lawson White	19th " 26th	1825 " 1840	Elected in place of Jackson; elected president *pro tem.* 3 Dec. 1832 and 2 Dec. 1833. Resigned 1840.
Felix Grundy	21st " 25th	1829 " 1838	Elected in place of Eaton. Resigned 1838.
Ephraim H. Foster	25th " 26th	1838 " 1839	Appointed in place of Grundy.
Alexander Anderson	26th " 27th	1840 " 1841	Elected in place of White.
Felix Grundy	26th	1839 " 1840	Died in office.
Alfred O. P. Nicholson	26th to 28th	1841 " 1843	Appointed in place of Grundy.
Ephraim H. Foster	28th " 29th	1843 " 1845	
Spencer Jarnagin	28th " 30th	1843 " 1847	
Hopkins L. Turney	29th " 32d	1845 " 1851	
John Bell	30th " 36th	1847 " 1859	Nominated by the Union party for president of the U. S., 1860.
James C. Jones	32d " 35th	1851 " 1857	
Andrew Johnson	35th " 38th	1857 " 1862	Appointed military governor of Tennessee by pres. Lincoln, 1862. Elected vice-president U. S., 1864; succeeded to the presidency on death of Lincoln, 1865.
Alfred O. P. Nicholson	36th	1859 " 1861	Expelled, 3 July, 1861.
38th Congress, 1863 to 1865, vacant.			
Joseph S. Fowler	39th to 42d	1866 to 1871	
David T. Patterson	39th " 41st	1866 " 1869	
William G. Brownlow	41st " 44th	1869 " 1875	
Henry Cooper	42d " 45th	1871 " 1877	
Andrew Johnson	44th	1875	Served special session, 4–24 Mch. 1875; d. 31 July, 1875.
David McKendree Key	"	1875 to 1877	Appointed *pro tem.* in place of Johnson.
James E. Bailey	44th to 47th	1877 " 1881	Elected in place of Johnson.
Isham G. Harris	45th " ——	1877 " ——	Term expires 1901.
Howell E. Jackson	47th " 49th	1881 " 1886	Resigned 1886.
Washington C. Whitthorne	49th " 50th	1886 " 1888	Appointed in place of Jackson.
William B. Bate	50th " ——	1888 " ——	Term expires 1899.

tennis was played in France in a regular court, but with the bare hands, as illustrated in the "Book of Hours," 1496. It was played in England with a racket in 1505. In 1657 there were 114 tennis courts in Paris; in 1890 there were but 2.

First book giving an account of tennis published at Venice by Antonio Scaino da Salo.... 1555
Edmond Barre, greatest professional tennis player on record, dies at Paris....20 Jan. 1873
George Lambert, English champion, defeated at Hampton Court, in a 3 days' match, by Thomas Pettitt of Boston, Mass..... 1885

Tenure-of-Office act. UNITED STATES, Dec. 1866; Mch. 1867.

ter'bium, a rare metal, sometimes found with yttrium.

Terra del Fue'go ("land of fire"), an island south of South America, separated from the mainland by the strait of Magellan, who discovered it, 1520, and named it from the numerous fires seen on it at night.

Test act, directing all officers, civil and military, under government, to receive the sacrament according to the forms of the Church of England, and to take the oaths against transubstantiation, etc.; enacted by the British Parliament, 29 Mch. 1673. The Test and Corporation acts were repealed, 9 May, 1828. UNIVERSITY TESTS.

Testri, a village of N. France. Pepin d'Heristal, invited by malcontents, here defeated and captured Thierry III., king of Austrasia, and established himself as duke, 687.

Tettenhall, Staffordshire. It was probably at this place, then named Teotenheal, that the Danes were defeated by the Saxon king, Edward the Elder, 6 Aug. 910.

Tet'uan, a walled seaport town of Morocco, was entered by the Spaniards, 6 Feb. 1860, after a decisive victory on 4 Feb. The general, O'Donnell, was made a grandee of the first class.

Teutoberg forest (the *Teutobergiensis saltus.—Tacitus*), probably situate between Detmold and Paderborn, Germany, where Hermann, or Arminius, and the Germans defeated the Romans under Varus with very great slaughter, 9 A.D. Varus and many of his officers preferred suicide to captivity.

his defeat was regarded at Rome as a national calamity, ıd Augustus, in agony, cried, "Varus, give me back my leions!"

Teu'tones, a people of Germany, who with the Cimbri ıade incursions upon Gaul, and cut to pieces 2 Roman armies, 13 and 105 B.C. They were at last defeated by the consul Iarius at Aix, and a great number made prisoners, 102 B.C. CIMBRI, with whom authors commonly join the Teutones). he appellation came to be applied to the German nation in eneral.

Teuton'ic order, military knights established in ıe Holy Land about 1191, through the humanity of the Gerıans (Teutones) to the sick and wounded of the Christian ırmy in the Holy Land, under Guy of Lusignan, before Acre. he order was confirmed by a bull of pope Cœlestine III. On ıeir return to Germany, the knights were invited to subdue ıd Christianize the country now called Prussia and its neighorhood, and did so gradually. Their territories were invaded, ıd their army was defeated, with great slaughter, near Tanenberg, in E. Prussia, by Jagellon, duke of Lithuania, 15 uly, 1410, when the grandmaster and many of the knights ere slain. A large part of their possessions was incorporated ıto Poland in 1466, and into Brandenburg about 1521. In 525 the grandmaster was made a prince of the empire, and ıe order much weakened. Its remaining possessions were ized by Napoleon I. in 1809. PRUSSIA, etc.

Tewkes'bury, a borough of Gloucestershire, Engl., here Edward IV. crushed the Lancastrians, 4 May, 1471. ueen Margaret, the consort of Henry VI., was taken prisoner ıd her son killed.

> "Clarence is come—false, fleeting, perjur'd Clarence,
> That stabb'd me in the field by Tewksbury."
> —"Richard III.," act i. sc. iv.

he queen was conveyed to the Tower of London, where king Ienry expired soon after; being, as is generally supposed, ıurdered by the duke of Gloucester, afterwards Richard III. he queen was ransomed in 1475 by the French king, Louis I., for 50,000 crowns. ROSES.

bbey, founded by Robert Fitz-Hamon, cousin of William I., completed and consecrated 1123; grandly altered, 14th century; a monastery destroyed by Henry VIII.; the abbey spared; restored by G. G. Scott, 1877-79.

Texas, one of the southern states of the U. S., is bounded n the north by Oklahoma and the Indian territory, east by Arkansas and Louisiana, south by the gulf of Mexico and Mexico, and west by Mexico and New Mexico. It lies between 25° 51' and 36° 30' N. lat., and 93° 27' and 106° 40' W. lon. Area, 265,780 sq. miles, in 261 counties; pop. 1890, 2,235,523; 1900, 3,048,710. Capital, Austin.

Robert Cavalier de La Salle, sailing from France with 4 ships, 24 July, 1684, misses the Mississippi and lands near the entrance to Matagorda bay........18 Feb. 1685
a Salle builds fort St. Louis on the Lavaca..............July, "
a Salle murdered by 2 followers near the Neches river, 30 Mch. 1687
apt. De Leon, sent from Mexico against French settlers at fort St. Louis, on the Lavaca river, finds it deserted, 22 Apr. 1689
panish mission of San Francisco at fort St. Louis established.. 1690
on Domingo Teran de los Rios appointed governor of Coahuila and Texas.. 1691
an Antonio founded.. 1693
. St. Denis sent out by Lamothe Cadillac, governor of Louisiana, to open commercial relation with Mexico, reaches the mission of St. John the Baptist, on the Rio Grande, where he is arrested by the governor of Coahuila and imprisoned, Aug. 1714
panish mission established near the site of Nacogdoches..... 1715
panish mission established at La Bahia, now Goliad......... 1721
ienville, under orders from the company of the Indies, sends a colony by sea to Matagorda bay...................10 Aug. "
ettlement of San Antonio de Bexar increased by 13 families from the Canary islands sent by the Spanish government; they found "La Purissima Concepcion de Acuna"...5 Mch. 1731
on Manuel de Sandoval appointed governor of Texas........ 1734
Valls of the church of the Alamo erected at San Antonio de Bexar..May, 1744
Indians attack the mission of San Saba and massacre all...... 1758
France cedes Louisiana to Spain.........................3 Nov. 1762
Louisiana re-ceded to France by secret treaty...........1 Oct. 1800
Philip Nolan, an American, obtains a passport from the baron de Carondelet, governor of Louisiana, to buy horses in Texas, 17 July, 1797. In the belief that he was commissioned by gen. Wilkinson to reconnoitre and raise an insurrection, Mexicans under lieut. M. Muzquiz overtake him on the banks of the Blanco; Nolan is killed and his followers captured..21 Mch. 1801
Texas included in cession of Louisiana by France to the U. S., ratified at Washington..............................21 Oct. 1803
Spanish commander, gen. Herrera, enters into an agreement with gen. Wilkinson, establishing the territory between the Sabine and Arroyo Honda rivers as neutral ground, 22 Oct. 1806
Lieut.-col. Zebulon Pike arrives at San Antonio on his return from Chihuahua, whither he was taken by Spanish authorities to answer for building a fort on Spanish soil on the Rio del Norte, which he mistook for the Red river, July, 1807
Expedition under lieut. Augustus W. Magee, who conceived a plan of revolutionizing Texas, takes possession of Nacogdoches, July, 1812, which the Mexicans evacuate; reaches Goliad and takes possession, 1 Nov.; gov. Salcedo and gen. Herrera commence an investment of the town, 7 Nov.; engages in battles with the Americans, 20 Nov. 1812, 24 Jan., and 10 Feb. 1813; raise the siege.....................16 Feb. 1813
Magee dying of consumption, about 1 Feb. 1813, col. Kemper takes command, pursues the retreating Mexicans to San Antonio, which is surrendered to Kemper..............6 Mch. "
Salcedo, Herrera, and 10 officers are delivered to a company of Mexicans under Juan Delgado and massacred, 7 Mch. "
Battle of the Medina; Americans at San Antonio under don José Alvarez Toledo fall into ambush formed by Spaniards under gen. Arredondo..............................18 Aug. "
Galveston island occupied for Mexico by don José Manuel Herrera, minister of the Mexican patriots to the U. S.; a government is organized and don Luis Aury chosen governor of Texas and Galveston island.......................12 Sept. 1816
Jean Lafitte with a band of buccaneers occupies Galveston island during Aury's absence and calls his settlement Campeachy..Apr. 1817
Sabine river agreed upon as boundary between U. S. and Spanish possessions.....................................22 Feb. 1819
A company of volunteers under dr. James Long, raised at Natchez to invade Texas, occupy Nacogdoches, establish a provisional government, and issue a declaration proclaiming Texas to be a free and independent republic...........June, "
First printing-office in Texas established at Nacogdoches by Mr. Bigelow.. "
Lafitte is taken into the service of the Republican party of Mexico and appointed governor of Galveston............... "
Lafitte is compelled to evacuate Galveston island by lieut. Kearney of the U. S. brig *Enterprise*....................... 1821
Stephen F. Austin leaves Natchitoches, 10 June, and founds the colony for which his father, Moses Austin, recently deceased, received a grant from Mexico, on the Brazos river, July, "
He founds San Felipe de Austin as colonial town............. 1823
By decree of the Constituent Mexican congress, Coahuila and Texas are united in one state...........................7 May, 1824
Constitution of the united Mexican states proclaimed...4 Oct. "
Don José Antonio Saucedo appointed chief of the department of Texas, to reside at Bexar...........................1 Feb. 1825
Henry Clay, U. S. sec. of state, instructs the U. S. minister to endeavor to procure from Mexico the re-transfer of Texas, 26 Mch. "
Hayden Edwards, having procured a grant for a colony, locates at Nacogdoches..Oct. "
Edwards's grant annulled and the American settlers, known as "Fredonians," evacuate Nacogdoches and cross the Sabine, before Mexicans under Ahumada.....................31 Jan. 1827
Constitution for the state of Coahuila and Texas framed by a state congress at Satillo, proclaimed................11 Mch. "
Battle of Nacogdoches; Texans under col. Hayden Edwards defeat the Mexicans under col. Piedras.................2 Aug. "
Treaty of limits concluded between the U. S. and united Mexican states..12 Jan. 1828
First Sabbath-school in Texas established at San Felipe....... 1829
Name of La Bahia changed to Goliad by state congress..4 Feb. "
Vice-pres. Bustamente, succeeding Guerrero, deposed, by decree prohibits further immigration from the U. S.....6 Apr. 1830
Colonization laws repealed as to natives of the U. S....28 Apr. 1832
Fort of Velasco at the mouth of the Brazos taken by Texans under John Austin.................................26 June, "
Nacogdoches retaken by Texans........................2 Aug. "
First step towards independence, the framing of a state constitution, never recognized by the Mexican government and never put in operation, by a convention which met at San Felipe, 1 Apr., and adjourned........................13 Apr. 1833
Law passed forming Texas into 1 judicial circuit and 3 districts —Bexar, Brazos, and Nacogdoches.................17 Apr. 1834
Legislature of Coahuila and Texas, in session at Monclova, disperses on approach of army under gen. Martin P. de Cos, brother-in-law to gen. Santa Aña......................21 Apr. 1835
Committee of safety organized at Bastrop on the Colorado, 17 May, "
Lone-star flag made at Harrisburg and presented to the company of capt. Andrew Robinson.......................... "

Garrison of Anahuac captured by Texans under col William B Travis June, 1835

Commandant at Bexar having furnished the corporation of Gonzales with a brass 6 pounder against the Indians in 1831, the Mexicans call it a loan, the Texans a gift, the Texans win its possession in a fight 2 Oct "

Capture of Goliad from Mexicans under lieut col Sandoval, by patriot forces under capt George Collingsworth 9 Oct "

S F Austin appointed com in chief of the patriot forces, 10 Oct "

Permanent council of one from each of the committees of safety at San Felipe, chooses R R Royall president Oct "

Battle of Concepcion about 1½ miles from San Antonio, Texans under gen Austin and Mexicans under gen Cos, the latter retreating 28 Oct "

First permanent newspaper in Texas, the *Telegraph*, established at San Felipe Oct "

Assembly known as the General Consultation of Texas meets at San Felipe de Austin, establishes a provisional government with Henry Smith as governor, and sends Branch T Archer, S F Austin, and William H Wharton to the U S and solicit aid in the struggle for independence Nov "

Declaration of independence of Texas, and a provisional constitution framed by a convention which meets at San Felipe, 17 Oct, constitution signed 13 Nov "

One thousand four hundred Mexicans under gen Cos surrender to the Texans who attack San Antonio de Bexar 10 Dec. "

Colonists besiege the Mexican garrison of the Alamo at San Antonio, and, after a week s fighting, capture the fort, 16 Dec "

Declaration of independence made and signed by 91 Texans at Goliad 20 Dec "

Gen Santa Aña with 6000 troops leaves Monclova for Texas to drive out revolutionists and persons of foreign birth, 4 Feb 1836

Town of Bexar taken by Mexicans, and the Texans retire to the Alamo 21 Feb "

Declaration of independence adopted by a convention at Washington on the Brazos river 2 Mch "

Alamo invested 11 days by Santa Aña, the garrison, under col Travis, Bowie, and David Crockett, are overpowered and massacred, the bodies thrown into heaps and burned, 6 Mch "

Mexicans defeated in the first fight at the Mission del Refugio by Texans under capt King 9 Mch "

Second fight of the Mission del Refugio, col Ward attacks and drives back the Mexicans 10 Mch "

Constitution adopted for the republic of Texas by a convention which met at Washington, 1 Mch 17 Mch "

Col J W Fannin and 415 men, captured at Coleto by the Mexicans under gen Urrea, are taken to Goliad, and 330 shot by Santa Aña Sunday 27 Mch "

Col Ward retreats from Refugio 11 Mch, he surrenders his forces at Victoria, 24 Mch, and is massacred 28 Mch "

San Felipe de Austin burned by the Texans 31 Mch "

New Washington burned by the Mexicans 20 Apr "

Battle of San Jacinto, 750 Texans under gen Houston defeat 1600 Mexicans under Santa Aña, and capture him, 21 Apr "

Mexicans retreat beyond the frontier of Texas 24 Apr "

Congress meets at Washington, Mch, at Harrisburg, Mch, at Galveston, 16 Apr, and at Velasco May, "

Public and secret treaties with Santa Aña signed at Velasco, 14 May, "

Gen Sam Houston inaugurated as president of Texas at Columbia 22 Oct. "

Congress of U S acknowledges independence of Texas. Mch 1837

Congress meets at Houston May, "

Convention to fix the boundary line between the U S and Texas concluded at Washington, 25 Apr 1838, and ratifications exchanged 12 Oct and proclaimed 13 Oct 1838

Act of Congress approved for carrying into effect the convention of 13 Oct 1838 11 Jan 1839

By act of Texas Congress, 10 Dec 1836, the permanent flag of the republic bears 3 horizontal stripes of equal width, the upper one white, the middle one blue with a 5 pointed white star in the centre, and the lower one red 25 Jan "

Congress passes first educational act, appropriating certain lands for a general system of education 26 Jan "

France acknowledges the independence of Texas "

Congress meets at Austin, selected as the capital by a committee appointed Jan 1838, to locate a seat of government, Nov. "

England, Holland, and Belgium acknowledge the independence of Texas . 1840

Expedition under gen Hugh McLeod leaves Austin, 18 June, 1841, for Santa Fé When near San Miguel, his force is met by Mexican troops under Damacio Salazar, captured, and marched under guard to the city of Mexico 17 Oct. 1841

Twelve hundred Mexicans under gen Adrian Woll capture San Antonio, 11 Sept 1842, but are forced to retreat by Texan troops 18 Sept 1842

Congress meets at Washington Nov "

Battle at Mier on the Alcantra, Texans, under col Fisher, surrender to gen Ampudia 26 Dec "

Joint resolution for the annexation of Texas to the U S. passes the House of Representatives by 120 to 98, 25 Feb 1845, the Senate by 27 to 25, and is approved . . 1 Mch. 1845

Baylor female college at Belton chartered and opened . . . "

Charles A Wickliffe sent on a secret mission to Texas in the interest of annexation, by pres. Polk .... "

Joint resolution of Congress of U S is approved by Texan Congress 23 June, 1845

Ordinance of Texan Congress for annexation accepted by convention of people assembled at Austin 4 July, "

Convention at Austin frames a constitution which is ratified by the people, 4174 to 312 13 Oct "

Texas admitted into the Union by act approved 29 Dec. "

First state legislature convenes at Austin 16 Feb 1846

J P Henderson inaugurated first governor of the state, 19 Feb "

Fort Brown at Brownsville established 28 Mch "

Battles of Palo Alto, 8 May, and Resaca de la Palma, 9 May, "

Act of Congress sets apart one tenth of the general revenues of the state for educational purposes 13 May, "

Baylor university at Waco chartered 1845, and opened "

Treaty of Guadalupe Hidalgo concluded 2 Feb, ratification exchanged at Queretaro, 30 May, and proclaimed, 4 July, 1848

Austin city chosen as the seat of government for 20 years by vote of the people 1850

State penitentiary at Huntsville opened "

Texas formally accepts the boundary designated by the boundary bill for New Mexico, approved 9 Sept 1850, by which Texas is to receive $10,000,000 from the U S, 25 Nov 1852

Chappell Hill female college chartered and opened "

Aranama college at Goliad organized "

Waco female college at Waco chartered and opened 1856

St. Mary s university at Galveston, opened 1854, chartered. "

Texas Institution for the Blind at Austin opened "

Texas Deaf and Dumb asylum at Austin opened 1857

First overland mail from San Diego, Cal, arrives at San Antonio 6 Sept "

Enthusiastic union meeting held at Austin 23 Dec 1860

State Lunatic asylum at Austin opened 1861

Brig gen David E Twiggs surrenders to the state of Texas the U S. ordnance depot at San Antonio and contents, valued at $1,200,500 18 Feb "

State People's convention meets at Austin, 21 Jan, passes an ordinance of secession by vote of 166 to 7, 1 Feb, ratified by popular vote, 34,794 to 11,235 23 Feb "

Fort Brown, at Brownsville, evacuated and occupied by Texan troops 5 Mch "

Gov Sam Houston, opposing secession, and favoring separate state action, deposed, lieut gov Clark inaugurated, 20 Mch "

Constitution of the Confederate states ratified by legislature, 68 to 2 23 Mch. "

Col Earl Van Dorn captures 450 U S troops at Saluria, 25 Apr "

Gov Clark proclaims it treasonable to pay debts to citizens of states at war with the Confederate states 18 June, "

Galveston surrendered to com Renshaw 8 Oct 1862

Gen N J T Dana occupies Brazos, Santiago, and Brownsville with 6000 soldiers from New Orleans Nov "

Confederates under gen J B Magruder defeat Renshaw and capture Galveston 1 Jan 1863

Confederate privateer *Alabama* destroys the *Hatteras* in an engagement off Galveston 11 Jan "

Samuel Houston, b. Virginia, d at Huntersville, aged 70, 25 July, "

Battle of Aransas Pass, gen Ransom captures the Confederate works 18 Nov "

Battle of fort Esperanza, Matagorda bay, gen. C C Washburn defeats the confederates 30 Nov "

Last fight of the war, federals under col Barret defeated in western Texas by confederates under gen. Slaughter, 13 May, 1865

Gen Kirby Smith surrenders last Confederate army. 26 May, "

Gen A J Hamilton, appointed provisional governor by pres. Johnson, arrives at Galveston 21 July, "

Constitution, framed by a convention which met at Austin, 10 Feb and adjourned 2 Apr, is ratified by the people, 34,794 to 11,235 June, 1866

Gov J W Throckmorton enters upon his duties 13 Aug "

Gen P H Sheridan appointed commander of the 5th military district, comprising Louisiana and Texas. 19 Mch 1867

Gov Throckmorton removed, E M Pease appointed 30 July, "

Gen Sheridan relieved and gen Hancock substituted as commander of the 5th military district. . 17 Aug. "

Gen J Reynolds appointed to command of 5th military district. , 28 July, 1868

Constitution, framed by a convention called under the Reconstruction acts by gen Hancock, which sat at Austin, 1 June to Dec. 1868, is submitted to Congress, 30 Mch, and ratified by people, 72,395 to 4924 30 Nov–3 Dec. 1869

Legislature ratifies the XIV th and XV th amendments to the Constitution of the U S .... 18 Feb. 1870

Congress readmits Texas into the Union ,. 30 Mch. "

Trinity university at Tehuacana, opened 1869, chartered .. "

Public school system inaugurated . Sept. 1871

A special election for state officers, Richard Coke, Democrat, elected governor by 85,549 votes to 42,663 for gov Davis, Republican .. .. 2 Dec. 1873

Supreme court decides that the law authorizing the election of 2 Dec 1873, is unconstitutional . . ... 5 Jan 1874

New legislature organizes, not recognized by gov Davis, old legislature meets in the basement of the capitol . 13 Jan "

Old legislature adjourns , . 7 June, "

Southwestern university at Georgetown, opened 1873, chartered, 1875

'onstitution, framed by a convention which sat at Austin, 6 Sept. to 24 Nov. 1875, ratified by the people........17 Feb. 1876
tate Agricultural and Mechanical college of Texas at College Station, chartered 1871, opened........ "
.rmed band of Mexican outlaws enter Rio Grande City, break open the jail, release 2 notorious criminals, Esproneda and Garza, and escape with them to Mexico..............12 Aug. 1877
Iob of Mexicans and Texan citizens of Mexican birth attack state troops at San Elizario and 6 persons are killed, 13 Dec. "
'rairie View State Normal school at Hempstead opened, 6 Oct. 1879
am Houston State Normal school at Huntsville opened...... "
'illotson Collegiate and Normal Institute at Austin opened.... 1881
tate capitol destroyed by fire..................9 Nov. "
tate penitentiary at Rusk, established by law in 1875, in operation........ 1882
Iniversity of Texas at Austin, chartered 1881, opened........ 1883
'orner-stone of new capitol laid......................2 Mch. 1885
tate orphan asylum established at Corsicana by law.......... 1887
nstitution for the deaf and dumb and blind colored youth at Austin opened........ "
'ew state capitol dedicated......................16 May, 1888
tate reformatory near Gatesville opened...............1 Jan. 1889
.ct passed designating 22 Feb. as Arbor day.......... "
'onvention of delegates from 15 states and territories assembles at Topeka, Kan., to devise means for securing a deep harbor on the coast of Texas..............................1 Oct. "
nsane asylum at San Antonio established by law............ "
ohn T. Dickinson appointed secretary of the National World's Columbian commission........................27 June, 1890
'ongress appropriates $500,000 to improve Galveston harbor, and authorizes the secretary of war to contract for the completion of the work; estimated to cost $6,200,000......Sept. "
I. S. senator John H. Reagan resigns, to take effect 10 June, 24 Apr. 1891
Five constitutional amendments ratified at special election, 11 Aug. 1891
Experiments in rain-making by explosives conducted near Midland by R. G. Dyrenforth and his staff........18-26 Aug. "
Medical branch of the University of Texas opened at Galveston, 1 Oct. "
Horace Chilton appointed, qualifies as U. S. senator.....7 Dec. "
Southwest Texas lunatic asylum at Florine, 5 miles from San Antonio, opened..............................Dec. "
A small force of U. S. cavalry and infantry attack and break up the camp of Catarino Garza, Mexican revolutionist, at Retampal Springs..............................22 Dec. "
Roger Q. Mills chosen U. S. senator by the legislature, 22 Mch.; qualifies................................30 Mch. 1892
A band of revolutionists under Garza cross the border, burn a Mexican barrack, and return to Texas..............12 Dec. "
Town of Cisco destroyed by a tornado; 30 killed.......29 Apr. 1893

PRESIDENTS OF REPUBLIC.

Sam Houston..................	inaugurated	............22 Oct. 1836
M. B. Lamar..................	"	............10 Dec. 1838
Sam Houston..................	"	............13 Dec. 1841
Dr. Anson Jones..............	"	..............9 Dec. 1844

GOVERNORS OF THE STATE.

J. P. Henderson assumes office............19 Feb. 1846	J. W. Throckmorton, 13 Aug. 1866
George T. Wood.....21 Dec. 1847	E. M. Pease........30 July, 1867
P. Hansboro Bell......Dec. 1849	E. J. Davis.............Jan. 1870
E. M. Pease.......... " 1853	Richard Coke.......... " 1874
H. R. Runnels.......... " 1857	R. B. Hubbard........ " 1877
Sam Houston.......... " 1859	Oran M. Roberts...... " 1879
Edward Clark......20 Mch. 1861	John Ireland.......... " 1883
F. R. Lubbock.........Dec. "	Lawrence S. Ross..... " 1887
P. Murrah............ " 1863	J. S. Hogg........... " 1891
A. J. Hamilton....21 July, 1865	" .... " 1893
	David B. Culberson.... " 1895

UNITED STATES SENATORS FROM THE STATE OF TEXAS.

Name.	No. of Congress.	Date.	Remarks.
amuel Houston..................	29th to 36th	1846 to 1859	Seated, 30 Mch. 1846.
homas J. Rusk..................	29th " 35th	1846 " 1857	Seated, 26 Mch. 1846. President *pro tem.* 14 Mch. 1857. Died, 29 July, 1857.
. Pinckney Henderson..........	35th	1858	Elected in place of Rusk. Died, 1858.
Iatthias Ward..................	35th to 36th	1858 to 1859	Appointed *pro tem.* in place of Henderson.
ohn Hemphill..................	36th " 37th	1859 " 1861	Expelled, 10 July, 1861.
.ouis T. Wigfall..................	36th " 37th	1860 " 1861	Elected in place of Henderson. Expelled, 11 July, 1861.
	37th, 38th, 39th, and 40th		Congresses vacant.
. W. Flanagan..................	41st to 44th	1870 to 1875	Seated, 31 Mch. 1870
Iorgan C. Hamilton..............	41st " 45th	1870 " 1877	" " "
amuel Bell Maxey..............	44th " 50th	1875 " 1888	
:ichard Coke..................	45th " 54th	1877 " 1895	
ohn H. Reagan..................	50th " 52d	1888 " 1891	Resigned, 10 June, 1891.
Iorace Chilton..................	52d	1891 " 1892	Appointed *pro tem.* in place of Reagan.
toger Q. Mills..................	52d to ——	1892 " ——	Elected in place of Reagan. Term expires 1899.
Iorace Chilton..................	54th " ——	1895 " ——	

Tex'el, an island, town, and river at the mouth of the Zuyer Zee, Holland. Its vicinity has been the scene of memorable aval engagements. An engagement between the English under 3lake, Dean, and Monk, and the Dutch under Van Tromp and Je Ruyter, in which the latter were worsted and adm. Van 'romp was killed, 31 July, 1653. Again, at the mouth of the 'exel a sharp indecisive action took place between the allied Inglish and French fleets under prince Rupert and comte)'Estrées, and the Dutch fleet under De Ruyter, 11 Aug. 1673. 'he Dutch fleet was vanquished by adm. Duncan on 11 Oct. 797. CAMPERDOWN. The Dutch fleet of 12 ships of war nd 13 Indiamen surrendered to the British adm. Mitchell, rho, entering the Texel, possessed himself of them without firg a shot, 30 Aug. 1799.

thal'lium, a metal, occurring in the sulphuric-acid nanufacture, discovered by William Crookes by spectrum anlysis, Mch. 1861.

Thames, London, the Roman *Tamesis* or *Tamesa*, Saxn *Temese*, *Temesa*, rises in 4 springs, at Ullen farm, near 'oates, Gloucestershire. The head of the river in Wiltshire is .bout 170 miles from London bridge, and its whole course from ource to mouth about 220 miles. BRIDGES, LONDON, LONDON BRIDGE.

'onservation of the Thames given to the mayors of London... 1489
'hames made navigable to Oxford........................ 1624
'arliament gave the conservation of the Thames to the corporation of London; 12 conservators to be appointed—3 by the government.. 1857
'ontamination of the Thames by London sewage, in the summer of 1858, occasioned an act empowering the Metropolitan Board of Works to undertake new drainage................ 1858
'hames Navigation acts, appointing 5 more conservators, etc., and prohibiting pollution by sewage, etc., passed.......Aug. 1866
rs of the act extended up to Staines...................... 1867
-laws to protect the fish in the Upper Thames passed conservators..............................14 June, 1869
Highest tide known for many years; river overflowed from Gravesend to its tidal limit; great damage and distress in Blackfriars and Lambeth; Woolwich arsenal flooded and suffered; river said to have risen above 29 feet........15 Nov. 1875
Thames tunnel. TUNNELS.
Tower subway, an iron tube under the Thames, constructed by messrs. Barlow, begun 16 Feb. 1869, and privately opened, Apr. 1870, is said to have cost only 16,000*l.*
Thames embankment, recommended by sir Christopher Wren, 1666, and by William Paterson, founder of the bank of England, about 1694. The corporation embanked a mile in 1767. It was further recommended by Gwynne, 1767; by sir Frederick Eden, 1798; by sir Frederick Trench, 1824; by James Walker; by the duke of Newcastle, 1844; and by John Martin the painter, 1856. In 1860, the Metropolitan Board of Works recommended that the north bank of the Thames be embanked, whereby the bed of the river would be improved; a low-level sewer could be easily constructed beneath a broad roadway; docks to be constructed within the embankment wall; to be paid for by the city duties on coal, and by government. The principle was approved by Parliament, and a committee appointed, which first sat..........30 Apr. 1861
First stone of the northern (Victoria) embankment laid by Mr. Thwaites near Whitehall stairs, 20 July, 1864; the footway opened to the public, 30 July, 1868; the roadway opened by the prince of Wales.............................13 July, 1870
Proposal to build public offices upon the reclaimed land negatived by the House of Commons......................July, "
Other embankments since constructed on the south side.

Thames, Battle of, in Upper Canada, between 2500 Americans, under gen. Harrison, and 800 British regulars and 1200 Indians, under gen. Proctor, occurred on 5 Oct. 1813. The Indians were led by the celebrated Tecumseh or Tecumthé. The Americans were victorious, losing in killed and wounded only 29; the British lost in killed and wounded, including Indians (Tecumseh was slain), 57; and 560 men made prisoners, with 5000 small-arms and 6 pieces of cannon.

thane, a Saxon title of nobility, of which there were 2 orders, king's thanes or attendants at court and lords of manors, abolished in England at the Conquest, upon the introduction of the feudal system, and in Scotland by king Malcolm III, when the title of earl was adopted, 1057

Thanet, Kent, Engl, was the first permanent settlement of the Saxons, about 449 The Danes held a part of it, 853-865, and ravaged it 980, 988 et seq

Thanksgiving day, in the United States, originated in 1621 MASSACHUSETTS At first the practice of observing a day of thanksgiving in the autumn of every year was confined to New England, but it has now become national, the president appointing by proclamation the last Thursday in Nov as a day for national thanksgiving The first national English thanksgivings were offered at St Paul's cathedral for the defeat of the Spanish Armada, 8 Sept and 24 Nov 1588

Thapsus, a city of N Africa. Near here Julius Cæsar totally defeated the army of the party which supported the policy of Pompey, Feb 46 B C The suicide of Cato followed soon after

thatch-roof, a roof made of straw or rushes, unusual in the United States, common in Europe, mentioned by Herodotus If made of good material and well laid, a thatch-roof will last 100 years, some in Holland are 200 years old

theatre, a building appropriated to dramatic performances. That of Bacchus, at Athens, built by Philos, 420 B C, is said to have been the first erected Marcellus's theatre at Rome was begun by Cæsar, and dedicated by Augustus, 12 B C Theatres were erected in most cities of Italy Many of the inhabitants of Pompeii were assembled at a theatre on the night of 24 Aug 79, when an eruption of Vesuvius covered the city Scenes were introduced into theatres, painted by Balthazar Sienna, 1533 A D DRAMA, PLAYS, etc

theatres in England The first royal license for a theatre was in 1574, permitting master Burbage and 4 others, servants of the earl of Leicester, to act at the Globe, Bankside The first play-bill was issued on the opening of the Drury Lane theatre, 8 Apr 1663, of a comedy called "The Humourous Lieutenant, after naming the characters, it concludes thus "the play will begin at 3 o'clock exactly" The prices of admission in the reign of Elizabeth were, gallery, 2*d*, lord's rooms, 1s. The theatres were closed by Parliament from 1642 to 1660

Shakespeare's Globe theatre, London, near Bankside, built in horse shoe form, and partly covered with thatch erected 1594, burned during a performance of "Henry VIII," the spectators escaping unhurt 29 June, 1613
Lincoln's Inn theatre (the Duke's theatre) opened 25 Apr 1662
[Female parts, hitherto performed by boys, were from this time taken by women ACTRESSES]
Drury Lane theatre, London, opened 8 Apr 1663
Drury Lane theatre burned, Jan 1672, rebuilt by sir C Wren and reopened 26 Mch 1674
Italian Opera house, or Queen's theatre, opened 1705
Haymarket theatre built, 1702, and opened by French comedians 29 Dec 1720
Covent Garden theatre opened 7 Dec 1732
Beef steak Society founded 1735
Sadler's Wells theatre London, opened 1765
Covent Garden Theatrical Fund, established 1760, incorporated, 1774
Drury Lane Theatrical Fund, founded by David Garrick, 1766, incorporated 1775
Surrey theatre, London, originally the Circus opened 4 Nov 1783
Attempted assassination of king George III at Drury Lane theatre by one Hatfield (HATFIELD'S ATTEMPT) 11 May, 1800
Appearance of William Henry West Betty ("Infant Roscius") at Covent Garden theatre 1 Dec 1804
Olympic theatre, London, built by Mr Astley, opened, 18 Sept. 1806
Adelphi theatre, formerly the Sans Pareil, opened 27 Nov "
English Opera house, built by dr Arnold, 1794-95, opened as the Lyceum theatre 1809
Covent Garden theatre burned, 20 Sept. 1808 rebuilt, and on the reopening, 18 Sept. 1809, the higher scale of prices occasions "O P" (old price) riots until former prices are restored 16 Dec "
Horses first introduced at Covent Garden in "Bluebeard," 18 Feb 1811
Coburg, now Victoria, theatre, London, opened 1818
Strand theatre, London, first opened 1831
St James's theatre, London, first opened, under the management of Mr Braham 14 Dec. 1835
Princess's theatre, Oxford st., London, opened by J Maddox, 26 Dec 1842
General Theatrical Fund, established 1839, incorporated 1853
Several London theatres first opened on Sunday evenings for religious worship Jan 1860
"Colleen Bawn" presented at the Adelphi theatre, London, 10 Sept. "
Macfarren's "Robin Hood" brought out at Queen's theatre, 11 Oct 1860
First appearance of Mr Sothern at Haymarket theatre, London, as lord Dundreary in "Our American Cousins," 11 Nov "
Astley's amphitheatre, opened 1773, twice burned, and opened as Theatre Royal, Westminster, by Boucicault 26 Dec. 1862
Covent Garden leased by Dion Boucicault 29 Aug 1872
"Our Boys," by H J Byron (over 1350 representations) first played at the Vaudeville theatre, London 16 Jan 1875
Lyceum theatre, London, leased by Henry Irving Sept 1878
Opéra Comique, London opened, 29 Oct 1870, and "The Pirates of Penzance" first produced there 3 Apr 1880
Number of theatres in London, 55 Dec 1891

theatres in the United States The first recorded theatrical performance in North America was by amateurs, at Quebec, in 1694 The first in English was in the island of Jamaica in 1745 The first English play in New England was "The Orphans," given by amateurs at the Coffee-house in State st., Boston, in 1749, but a law of 1750 forbade such performances, fining spectators and actors 5*l* each etc. The first theatre in the Colonies opened at Williamsburg, Va, with "The Merchant of Venice," by an English company under Lewis Hallam, sr, 5 Sept 1752

First brick theatre in U S erected at Annapolis, Md, and opened with "The Beaux' Stratagem" 1753
First theatre in New York city opened in Nassau st, play, "The Conscious Lovers" 17 Sept. "
Warehouse fitted as a temporary theatre in an alley above Pine st, Philadelphia, Pa, first play, "The Fair Penitent," Apr 1754
First performance by professional actors in New England at a temporary theatre in Newport, R I, "The Provoked Husband," given, in spite of prohibition by a town meeting, 7 Sept. 1761
New theatre built in Chapel st., New York city, wrecked during a riot caused by the Stamp act Mch 1765
John Street theatre, New York city, opened with "The Stratagem" 7 Dec. 1767
First theatre in Albany, N Y, opened with "Venice Preserved" 3 July, 1769
First theatre built in Charleston, S C, by Mr Douglas Sept 1773
"The American Company," under Lewis Hallam, jr, leave for the West Indies, the Continental Congress advising that all public amusements be suspended 24 Oct. 1774
"Contrast," a comedy in 5 acts containing the first Yankee part for the stage, the first play written by an American (Royal Tyler, chief justice of Vermont) and acted by professionals, at John Street theatre, New York, by the old American company 16 Apr 1786
First theatre in Baltimore, Md, opened by Hallam and Henry, 16 Aug "
"The Father of an Only Child," the first accepted play of William Dunlap, the earliest American professional dramatist, produced 7 Sept. 1789
"New Exhibition Room" in Broad alley, near Hawley st., Boston, a theatre, opened 16 Aug. 1792
First theatrical riot in Boston, players giving "Douglas" and "The Poor Soldier," as "Moral Lectures" being arrested "
Massachusetts repeals the law against the theatre 1793
First regular theatre in Boston opens in Federal st, with "Gustavus Vasa" and "Modern Antiquities" (burned 1798), 4 Feb 1794
First theatre in Hartford, Conn, opened by Hodgkinson, with part of the old American company 1796
First theatre in Providence, R I, opened by part of same company "
"Starring" begun in the U S by T A Cooper 1800
"United States Theatre," first in Washington, D C, opened by Wignell "
First theatre in New Orleans built by a company of French comedians 1809
Theatre in Richmond, Va, destroyed by fire during the performance, 70 killed (VIRGINIA) 26 Dec 1811
First regular theatre in Cincinnati opened 1815
First Park theatre, New York city, opened, 1798, burned 1820, second Park theatre opened 1821
First American theatre in New Orleans, built by James H. Caldwell, opened with "The Dramatist" 1823
First theatre in St Louis, built by James H Caldwell, opened with "The Honeymoon" 30 June, 1827
First brick theatre in Pittsburg, Pa., opened with the "Busy Day" 2 Sept 1832
First theatre in Columbus, O, built. 1833
Eagle street theatre, Buffalo, N Y, opened 21 July, 1835
First theatre in Detroit opened by W Dinneford "
"Christy's Minstrels" organized by E P Christy at Buffalo, N Y 1842
Astor place opera-house opened 22 Nov 1847
[The scene of the Macready riot, evening of 10 May, 1849, when Macready attempted to play Macbeth NEW YORK CITY]
First theatre in Cleveland, O, built by J S Potter 1848
First theatre in San Francisco, opened by W Starke 1849
Assassination of pres. Lincoln, at Ford's theatre, Washington, D C, by J Wilkes Booth (BOOTH'S CONSPIRACY) 14 Apr 1865
Conway's Brooklyn theatre, Brooklyn, N Y, burned, 295 lives lost. 5 Dec. 1876

CHRONOLOGICAL LIST OF ENGLISH AND FOREIGN ACTORS, WITH DATE OF THEIR FIRST APPEARANCE AT PLACE NAMED.

Name.	Nation.	Born. Died.	First appearance.	Date.	First appearance in U. S.	Date.
James Quin	Engl.	1693-1766	Drury Lane theatre, London	4 Feb. 1715		
Charles Macklin	Irish	1699-1797	Lincoln's Inn Fields, "	4 Dec. 1730		
Katharine Clive	Engl.	1711-1785	Drury Lane theatre, "	about "		
David Garrick	"	1716-1779	Ipswich, 1741; Drury Lane theatre, London	May, 1742		
Margaret Woffington	Irish	1719-1760	Dublin and London	about 1737		
Spranger Barry	"	" -1777	Drury Lane theatre, London	Oct. 1746		
Samuel Foote	Engl.	1720- "	Haymarket theatre, "	6 Feb. 1744		
Thomas Sheridan	Irish	1721-1788	Smock Alley theatre, Dublin	1743		
Henry Mossop	"	1729-1773	" " " "	28 Nov. 1749		
George Anne Bellamy	Engl.	1727-1788	Covent Garden theatre, London	Nov. 1744		
Frances Barton Abington	"	1737-1815	Haymarket theatre, London	21 Aug. 1755		
Lewis Hallam, jr.	"	1740-1808		....	Williamsburg, Va.	5 Sept. 1752
John Henderson	Irish	1747-1785	Haymarket theatre, London	11 June, 1777		
Sarah Kemble Siddons	Engl.	1755-1831	Drury Lane theatre, "	29 Dec. 1775		
Geo. Frederick Cooke	"	1756-1812	Covent Garden theatre, "	31 Oct. 1800	Park theatre, New York	21 Nov. 1810
John Bernard	"	" -1828	" " " "	19 Oct. 1787	Greenwich St. theatre, New York	4 June, 1797
John Philip Kemble	"	1757-1823	Wolverhampton, Engl.	8 Jan. 1776		
Joseph Shepherd Munden	"	1758-1832	Covent Garden theatre, London	2 Dec. 1790		
Elizabeth Farren	"	1759-1829	Liverpool, 1773; London	9 June, 1777		
Dora Jordan	"	1762-1816	Drury Lane theatre, London	17 Oct. 1785		
François Joseph Talma	French	1763-1826	Théâtre-Français, Paris	21 Nov. 1787		
William Dowton	Engl.	1764-1851	Drury Lane theatre, London	11 Oct. 1796	Park theatre, New York	2 June, 1836
John Hodgkinson	"	1767-1805	Bristol, Engl.	....	Southwark theatre, Philadelphia	Sept. 1792
Robert William Elliston	"	1774-1831	Bath, "	14 Apr. 1791		
Charles Kemble	Welsh	1775-1854	Sheffield, "	1792	Park theatre, New York	17 Sept. 1832
Charles Mathews	Engl.	1776-1835	Haymarket theatre, London	15 May, 1803	Holliday St. theatre, Baltimore	2 Sept. 1822
John Liston	"	" -1846	" " "	14 June, 1805		
Thomas Apthorpe Cooper	"	" -1849	Edinburgh	1792	Chestnut St. theatre, Philadelphia	9 Dec. 1796
Charles Mayne Young	"	1777-1856	Liverpool	1798		
Edmund Kean	"	1787-1833	Drury Lane theatre, London	1813 or '14	Anthony St. theatre, New York	29 Nov. 1820
Eliza O'Neill	Irish	1791-1872	Drogheda, Ireland	1803		
Wm. Henry West Betty ("Infant Roscius")	Engl.	" -1874	Covent Garden theatre, London	1 Dec. 1804		
Robert Keeley	"	1793-1869	Richmond theatre, London	1813	Park theatre, New York	19 Sept. 1836
William Charles Macready	"	" -1873	Covent Garden theatre, London	16 Dec. 1816	" " "	2 Oct. 1826
James W. Wallack	"	1794-1864	Drury Lane theatre, London	1806	" " "	7 Sept. 1818
Mary Ann Dyke Duff	"	1795-1857	Dublin	1808	Boston, Mass.	31 Dec. 1810
Junius Brutus Booth	"	1796-1852	Covent Garden theatre, London	Oct. 1813	Richmond, Va.	13 July, 1821
Jane Marchant Fisher Vernon	"	" -1869	Drury Lane theatre, London	1817	Old Bowery theatre, New York	11 Sept. 1827
Eliza Lucy Bartolozzi Vestris	"	1797-1856	" " " "	19 Feb. 1820		1838
Benjamin Webster	"	1798-1882	Bath, Engl.	1814 or '15		
Susannah Paton Wood	Scotch	1802-1864	Haymarket theatre, London	1820	Park theatre, New York	9 Sept. 1833
John Baldwin Buckstone	Engl.	" -1879	Workington, Engl.	1821	" " "	July, 1840
Charles Mathews, jr.	"	1803-1878	Olympic theatre, London	7 Dec. 1835	" " "	1838
William E. Burton	"	1804-1860	Pavilion theatre, "	1831	Arch St. theatre, Philadelphia	3 Sept. 1834
Ellen Tree Kean	"	1805-1880	Drury Lane theatre, London	23 Sept. 1826	Park theatre, New York	12 Dec. 1836
John Brougham	Irish	1810- "	Tottenham St. theatre, "	July, 1830	" " "	Oct. 1842
Clara Fisher Maeder	Engl.	1811-	Drury Lane theatre, "	10 Dec. 1817	" " "	11 Sept. 1827
Frances Anne Kemble	"	" -1893	Covent Garden theatre, "	10 Oct. 1829	" " "	18 Sept. 1832
Charles John Kean	Irish	" -1868	Drury Lane theatre, "	1 Oct. 1827	" " "	1 Sept. 1830
G. V. Brooke	"	1819-1866	Theatre Royal, Dublin	May, 1833	Broadway theatre, New York	15 Dec. 1851
Elizabeth Rachael Felix	Swiss	1820-1858	Her Majesty's theatre, London	10 May, 1840	Metropolitan theatre, New York	3 Sept. 1855
Adelaide Ristori del Grillo	Italian	1821-	Italian Opera House, Paris	22 May, 1855	French theatre, New York	20 Sept. 1866
Barry Sullivan	Irish	1824-	Haymarket theatre, London	7 Feb. 1852	Broadway theatre, New York	22 Nov. 1858
Charles Albert Fechter	Engl.	" -1879	Princess theatre, London	27 Oct. 1860	Niblo's Garden, New York	10 Jan. 1879
Ernesto Rossi	Italian	1829-	Paris	1853		
Jean Margaret Davenport Landers	Engl.	1830-		Dec. 1844	Richmond theatre, New York	1838
Tommaso Salvini	Italian	"	Milan	1843		1874
Laura Keene	Engl.	"	Olympic theatre, London	Oct. 1851	Wallack's theatre, New York	20 Sept. 1852
Francesca Janauschek	Germ.	"				
E. A. Sothern (Douglas Stewart)	Engl.	" -1881	Haymarket theatre, London	11 Nov. 1861	National theatre, Boston	Sept. "
Henry Irving (John Henry Brodrib)	"	1838-	Sunderland theatre	29 Sept. 1856		1883
Sarah Bernhardt	French	1844-	Gaiety theatre, London	June, 1879		1881
Helen Modjeska	Polish	"	Bochnia	1861	California theatre, San Francisco	Aug. 1877
Ellen Alice Terry Kelly	Engl.	1848-	Princess theatre, London	28 Apr. 1856		Oct. 1883

CHRONOLOGICAL LIST OF NOTED AMERICAN ACTORS, WITH DATE OF THEIR FIRST APPEARANCE AT PLACE NAMED.

Name.	Born. Died.	First appearance.	Date.	First appearance in England.	Date.
John Howard Payne	1792-1852	Park St. theatre, New York	26 Feb. 1809	London	4 June, 1813
Henry Placide	1799-1870	Park theatre, New York	2 Sept. 1823	Haymarket theatre, London	1838
James H. Hackett	1800-1871	" " "	1 Mch. 1826	Covent Garden theatre, London	Apr. 1827
Solomon F. Smith	1801-1869	Vincennes, Ind.	1819		
Edwin Forrest	1806-1872	(Star) Chestnut St. theatre, Philadelphia	5 July, 1826	Drury Lane theatre, London	17 Oct. 1836
James E. Murdoch	1811-1893	Arch St. theatre, Philadelphia	13 Oct. 1829	Haymarket theatre, "	22 Sept. 1856
William Warren	1812-1888	Philadelphia	1832	Strand theatre, "	1845
Charlotte Cushman	1814-1876	Tremont theatre, Boston	8 Apr. 1835	Princess theatre, "	Feb. 1845
McKean Buchanan	1823-1872	St. Charles theatre, New Orleans	....	Standard theatre, "	5 Mch. 1859
F. S. Chanfrau	1824-1884	Mitchell's Olympic theatre, New York	1848		
John E. Owens	" -1886	National theatre, Philadelphia	about 1840		
Joseph Jefferson	1829-	(Star) Chanfrau's National theatre, New York	1 Sept. 1849	Adelphi theatre, London	4 Sept. 1865
William J. Florence (Bernard Conlin)	1831-1891	Richmond theatre, New York	6 Dec. "	Drury Lane theatre, London	Apr. 1856
Edwin T. Booth	1833-1893	Museum, Boston	10 Sept. "	London	30 Sept. 1861
John T. Raymond (John O'Brien)	1836-	Rochester, N. Y.	27 June, 1853	Haymarket theatre, London	1 July, 1867
John E. McCulloch	1837-1885	Arch St. theatre, Philadelphia	15 Aug. 1857		1881
Lawrence P. Barrett (Larry Brannigan)	1838-1891	Detroit	1853		1867

Among other prominent actors, most of them now on the stage, may be mentioned

	Where born	Birth
Neil Burgess	Boston, Mass	1846
Lotta Crabtree	New York city	1847
Kate J Bateman Crowe	Baltimore Md	1842
Fanny Davenport	London Engl	1850
Mrs. W H Kendal (Grimston)	Lincolnshire Engl	1849
Lily Langtry	St Helen s. Island of Jersey	1850
Richard Mansfield	Heligoland, Ger	1857
Robert B Mantell	Ayrshire	1854
Margaret Mather	Detroit Mich	1861
Frank Mayo	Massachusetts	1839
Maggie Mitchell	New York	1832
Clara Morris	Cleveland O	1846
Mary Anderson Navarro	Sacramento, Cal	1859
Mlle —— Rhéa	Brussels	1855
Ada Rehan	Limerick, Irel	1860
Sol Smith Russell	Brunswick, Mo	1848
Julia Marlowe	England	1866
James O Neil	Ireland	1848

Theban legion, according to tradition, composed of Christians who submitted to martyrdom rather than attack their brethren during the persecution of the emperor Maximin, or sacrifice to the gods, about 286 A D Their leader, Maurice, was canonized

Thebes or **Luxor,** a city of Egypt, called also Hecatompylos on account of its hundred gates, and Diospolis, as being sacred to Jupiter In the time of its splendor (1600-800 B.C.) it is said to have extended about 33 miles Thebes was ruined by Cambyses, king of Persia, 525 B.C, and by the foundation of Alexandria, 332 B C, it rebelled and was taken by Ptolemy Lathyrus, 86 B C, and few traces of it were seen in the age of Juvenal MEMNONIUM After centuries of neglect it has been much visited since the explorations of Belzoni, 1817

Thebes, N Greece, the capital of the country successively called Aonia, Messapia, Ogygia, Hyantis, and Bœotia, was called Cadmeia, from Cadmus, its founder, 1193 B C It became a republic about 1120 B C, and flourished under Epaminondas 378-362 B.C The "sacred band" formed by him, 377 B.C, was revived in 1877 Thebes's 7 gates are mentioned by Homer BŒOTIA, GREECE

theft was punished by heavy fines among the Jews, by death at Athens, by the laws of Draco DRACO'S LAWS The Anglo-Saxons nominally punished theft with death, if above 12d. value, but the criminal could redeem his life by a ransom In 9 Henry I, this power of redemption was taken away, 1108. The punishment of theft was very severe in England till mitigated by Peel's acts, 9 and 10 Geo IV 1829

Thellusson's will, a most singular document Peter Isaac Thellusson, a Genevese, and an affluent merchant of London, left 100,000*l* to his widow and children, and the remainder of his property, more than 600,000*l*, to trustees, to accumulate during the lives of his 3 sons, and of their sons, then the estates, to be purchased with the produce of the accumulated fund, were to be conveyed to the eldest lineal male descendant of his 3 sons, with the benefit of survivorship. Should no heir then exist, the whole was to be applied, by the sinking fund, to the discharge of the national debt It is said that Mr Thellusson held much property in trust, and that he desired a sufficient interval of time to elapse for the appearance of just claimants He died 21 July, 1797 His will incurred much public censure and was contested by the heirs-at-law, but finally established by a decision of the House of Lords, 25 June, 1805 The last surviving grandson died in Feb. 1856 A dispute then arose whether the eldest male descendant or the male descendant of the eldest son should inherit the property. The question was decided, on appeal, by the House of Lords (9 June, 1859), in favor of the latter, lord Rendlesham and Charles S Thellusson confirming the decision of the Master of the Rolls in 1858 In consequence of the legal expenses, the property is said not to exceed greatly its value in the testator's lifetime On 28 July, 1800, the Thellusson act was passed, making void any devise of property to accumulate for longer than 21 years after death Poe founded upon this case his imaginative sketch of "The Domain of Arnheim," in which the owner and beautifier of the domain, Seabright Ellison, has an estate of $450,000,000

theoc'racy, government by God The Israelites believed themselves so governed till Saul was made their king, about 1095 B C (1 Sam viii 7) Theocratic form of government established in Massachusetts, 1631

theod'olite (etym doubtful, from Gr θεώμαι=to see, ὁδός=way, and λιτός=plain, all conjectural), an instrument for measuring horizontal angles in surveying, consists of a telescope and a divided circle It was probably first constructed in the 17th century The first survey made by an instrument with a perfect circle is said to have been that of Zealand by Bugge, 1762-68 Jesse Ramsden, in 1787, completed a great theodolite employed in the trigonometrical survey of England and Wales by gen Roy

"Theolo'gia Germanica," or "Teutsche Theology" (printed 1528, Latin and French editions, 1558), a German mystical work, written about the 14th century In it, the "good man," disgusted with the corruptions in church and state, is led to seek for God in the temple of the heart Luther is said to have valued the work next to the Bible and St Augustin

theol'ogy (from Gr Θεος, God, and λογος, speech), the expressed views and ideas of the nature and attributes of God, of his relations to man, and of the manner in which they may be discovered These are known as either (1) *Inspired*, including the Holy Scriptures, their interpretation, etc, or (2) *Natural*, which lord Bacon calls the first part of philosophy Butler's "Analogy of Religion" (1736), and Paley's "Natural Theology" (1802), are eminent books on the latter subject Abelard (d 1142) wrote "Theologia Christiana" The "Summa Totius Theologiæ," by Thomas Aquinas (b about 1221), a standard Roman Catholic work, was printed with commentaries, etc, in 1596 PHILOSOPHY

theos'ophy, anciently called the "wisdom religion," is spoken of in Aryan literature and ancient religions and philosophies. The name was given to the school of Neo-Platonic philosophy opened at Alexandria by Ammonius Saccas, 232 A D, who is said to have urged the disregard of all class prejudices and minor differences of opinion in a union for the enlightenment of the world Followers of Paracelsus in the 16th century were called Theosophists Modern theosophy was founded in the United States by madame Helene Petrovna Blavatsky and col H. S. Olcott, with the motto, "There is no religion higher than the truth," 17 Nov 1875 Its object, (1) to form a nucleus of universal brotherhood, (2) to promote the study of Eastern literature, religion, and science, (3) to investigate the unexplained laws of nature and the physical powers of man, etc The number of lodges constituting the theosophical society has increased from 1, in 1875, to 11 in 1880, 121 in 1885, and 241 in 1890

Founders of the society go to India, leaving the work in the U S in the hands of William Q Judge	Dec. 1878
Madame Coulomb publishes "Some Accounts of my Intercourse with Madame Blavatsky," accusing her of fraud	1884
Madame Blavatsky publishes "The Secret Doctrine, the Synthesis of Science, Religion, and Philosophy," 1888, and "The Key to Theosophy"	1889
Madame Blavatsky dies in London, Engl	8 May, 1891

Ther'midor revolution. On the 9th Thermidor of the 2d year (27 July, 1794), the French convention deposed Robespierre, and next day he and 22 partisans were executed

thermo-electricity. ELECTRICITY, HEAT.

thermom'eter. The earliest account of an instrument for measuring heat is that of Hero's of Alexandria, 150 B.C. The invention of the modern thermometer is ascribed to Galileo before 1597, by Libri, to Drebbel of Alcmaer, 1609, by Boerhaave, to Paulo Sarpi, 1609, by Fulgentio, to Sanctorio, 1610, by Borelli. Edmund Halley suggested the use of quicksilver for the tube in 1680 The following are the principal thermometric scales in use

Fahrenheit's, freezing-point 32° above 0°, boiling-point 212° above 0° Devised by Gabriel D Fahrenheit (1686-1736) about 1726 In general use in the United States, Great Britain, and Holland

Reaumur's, freezing point 0°, boiling point 80° above Devised by Rene A F de Reaumur (1683-1757) about 1730

Centigrade, freezing point 0°, boiling point 100° above. Devised by Anders Celsius (1701-44) about 1742 Legalized in France in connection with the metric system, and widely used for scientific purposes in all countries.

De Lisle's, boiling point 0°, freezing point 150° below. In use somewhat in Russia.
Six's self-registering thermometer invented 1782, much improved since.

There are various forms of thermometers, as the air, balance, chemical, clinical, differential, electrical, marine, mercurial minimum, etc.

J. M. Casella issued a minimum thermometer in Sept. 1861. It registers degrees of cold by means of mercury.
Negretti and Zambra's registering minimum thermometers, adapted for deep-sea purposes, made known early in 1874.

ther'mophone, an apparatus in which sonorous vibrations are produced by the expansion of heated bodies, connected with an electro-magnet, was constructed by Theodor Wiesendanger, and described by him in Oct. 1878.

Thermop'ylæ, Doris, N. Greece. Leonidas, at the head of 300 Spartans and 700 Thespians, at the defile of Thermopylæ, withstood the whole force of the Persians under Xerxes during 3 days, 7, 8, 9 Aug. 480 B.C., until Ephialtes, a Trachinian, perfidiously led the enemy by a secret path up the mountains to the rear of the Greeks, who, between two assailants, perished gloriously on heaps of slaughtered foes. Only one Spartan, Aristodemus, returned home out of the 300, where he was treated with such scorn and contempt that he willingly sacrificed his life the next year at the battle of Platæa, after surpassing all his comrades in valor. The spirit that actuated these warriors at Thermopylæ is expressed in the distich in the Greek Anthology, by Simonides, their contemporary, thus translated:

"Go tell the Spartans, thou that passest by,
That here, obedient to their laws, we lie."

Here also Antiochus the Great, king of Syria, was defeated by the Romans under Acilius Glabrio 191 B.C.

Thermum, Thermus, or **Therma**, Greece, a strong city, the acropolis of Ætolia, N. Greece, was captured and ravaged by Philip V. of Macedon, 218 and 206 B.C., on account of its favoring the Romans.

Thesau'rus (Gr. θησαυρός=treasury, a lexicon), a common title, especially in the 17th and 18th centuries, of large collections on history and archæology, and of comprehensive lexicons of one or more languages, or branches of science. Some of the most celebrated are:

"Thesaurus Linguæ Latinæ," by Robert Stephens — 1531-35
"Thesaurus Linguæ Græcæ," by Henry Stephens — 1572
"Thesaurus Antiquitatum Græcorum," by J. Gronovius, 13 vols. fol. — 1697-1702
"Thesaurus Antiquitatum Romanorum," by J. G. Grævius, 12 vols. fol. — 1694
"Thesaurus Antiquitatum et Historicum Italiæ, Siciliæ," etc., by G. Grævius and P. Burmannus, 45 vols. fol. — 1725
"Thesaurus Antiquitatum Sacrarum," by B. Ugolinus, 34 vols. fol. — 1744-69

A Thesaurus of the Latin language, on a far larger scale than any similar work in existence, has been planned by an association of scholars in Europe and is expected to reach completeness in about 20 years. Preliminary studies for it have appeared for 8 years past in the "Archiv zur lateinischen Lexicographie," edited by E. Wölfflin.

Thes'piæ, a city of Bœotia, N. Greece. 700 of its citizens perished with Leonidas at Thermopylæ, Aug. 480 B.C. Through jealousy the Thebans destroyed its walls in 372 B.C.

Thessaloni'ca, now **Saloni'ca**, a city in Macedonia, N. Greece, originally Therme, but rebuilt by Cassander, and said to have been named after his wife, Thessalonica, daughter of Philip, after 315 B.C. Here Paul preached, 53, and to the church here he addressed 2 epistles in 54. In consequence of seditions, a great massacre was ordered here in 390 by the emperor Theodosius. Thessalonica partook of the changes of the Eastern empire. It was taken by the Saracens, with great slaughter, 30 July, 904, by the Normans of Sicily, 15 Aug. 1185, and after various changes was taken from the Venetians by the Turks under Amurath, 1430.

Thes'saly, N. Greece, the seat of many adventures described by poets. The first king known to tradition was Hellen, son of Deucalion, from whom his subjects, and afterwards all Greeks, were called Hellenes. From Thessaly came the Achæans, the Ætolians, the Dorians, the Hellenes, etc. The most remarkable legends of this country are the deluge of Deucalion, 1548 B.C. (DELUGE), and the expedition of the ARGONAUTS, 1263 B.C. Within its territory are mount Olympus and the "Vale of Tempe," here also was fought the battle of PHARSALIA. Thessaly long aimed at neutrality in Grecian affairs, but became involved through its rulers, the tyrants of Pheræ: Lycophron, about 404 B.C., his son Jason, 371, assassinated, 370, Alexander, the most eminent, defied Athens and Thebes, assassinated 359. Philip of Macedon, after a repulse (353 B.C.), defeated the tyrants, 352, and subjugated the country, 343. The Romans gave nominal freedom to Thessaly after their victory at Cynoscephalæ, 197. It now belongs to Greece by treaty signed 2 July, 1881.

Thieves' or **Robber synod**, at Ephesus 449, where the doctrines of Eutyches respecting Christ's incarnation were approved, so called because his opponents were silenced or excluded by force. EUTYCHIANS.

thimbles (from A.-S. *thuma*, a thumb). In 1693 a patent was granted to John Lofting (a native of Holland who established himself in London about 1688) for a machine for making thimbles, at Islington, near London, after which he made them of various metals with profit. Such a device is said to have been found at Herculaneum.

Thion'ville, the ancient *Theodonis villa*, a fortified city on the Moselle, N.E. France. It was an occasional residence of Charlemagne and his successors, and on the extinction of his race it was successively held by private lords, the counts of Luxemburg, the dukes of Burgundy, the house of Austria, and the kings of Spain. It was taken by the duke of Guise, 23 June, 1558, after an obstinate defence, and returned to Philip II. by the peace of Château Cambresis. It successfully resisted the marquis de Feuquières in 1637, but was taken after 4 months' siege by the duc D'Enghien, 10 Aug. 1643, and remained with France. It successfully resisted the Austrians in 1792, and the Prussians in 1814. It was invested by the Germans in Aug. 1870, and after bombardment, being in flames, surrendered, 24 Nov. following.

thirty tyrants, a term applied to the governors of Athens, in 404 B.C., who were expelled by Thrasybulus, 403, and also to the numerous aspirants to the imperial throne of Rome during the reigns of Gallienus and Aurelian, A.D. 259-274. TYRANTS.

Thirty Years' war, in Germany, between the Roman Catholics and Protestants. It began in Bohemia, 1619, by a resolve of the emperor of Germany, Ferdinand II., to make the Roman Catholic church supreme throughout the empire, and ended with the peace of Westphalia in 1648. Until the appearance of Gustavus Adolphus of Sweden, in 1630, as champion of the Protestant cause, the emperor's generals Tilly and Wallenstein were successful, but the defeat of Tilly by the Swedes at Breitenfeld, 1631, and again at Lech, 1632, and of Wallenstein at Lutzen, 1632, maintained the Protestant cause until the peace, which established the principle "that men should not be persecuted for their religious faith." For duration and for the suffering it caused this was one of the most memorable wars on record. At its commencement Germany probably numbered 20,000,000 people, at its close perhaps much less than 10,000,000. It was conducted with savage cruelty. Towns and villages were destroyed, and whole districts depopulated. Law and order disappeared, and starvation is said to have led to frequent cannibalism in certain districts. The most popular history of the war is by Schiller, pub. 1790-93, a fuller and far more trustworthy account by Von Ranke, 1869. BATTLES.

thirty-nine articles. ARTICLES OF RELIGION.

Thistle, Order of the, Scotland, founded by James V., 1540. It consisted originally of the sovereign and 12 knights, in memory of Christ and his 12 apostles. In 1542 James died, and the order was discontinued about the time of the Reformation. It was renewed by James VII. of Scotland (James II. of England), with 8 knights, 29 May, 1687, increased to 12 by queen Anne in 1703, to 16 by George IV. in 1827. Its motto "Nemo me impune lacessit."

Thistlewood's conspiracy. CATO-STREET CONSPIRACY.

Thomas, St. VIRGIN ISLES.

Thomas's, St., hospital, Southwark, Engl, was founded as an almshouse by Richard, prior of Bermondsey, in 1213, and surrendered to Henry VIII in 1538 In 1551 the mayor and citizens of London, having purchased of Edward VI the manor of Southwark, including this hospital, repaired and enlarged it, and admitted into it 260 poor, sick, and helpless persons, upon which the king, in 1553, incorporated it, together with Bethlehem, St Bartholomew's, etc It was rebuilt in 1693 In 1862 the site was sold to the Southeastern Railway company, and the patients were removed to Surrey music-hall The foundation-stone of the new hospital, erected at Stangate, near the Surrey side of Westminster bridge, was laid by queen Victoria, 13 May, 1868, and the new hospital was opened by her, 21 June, 1871

Thomists. SCOTISTS.

thorac'ic duct, discovered first in a horse by Eustachius about 1563, in man by Ol Rudbec, a Swedish anatomist Thomas Bartholine of Copenhagen and dr Joliffe of England also discovered it about 1654 LACTEALS

thor'ium, less correctly called **thori'num,** a very rare metal (a heavy gray powder), discovered by Berzelius in thoria, a Norway mineral, in 1828.

Thorn, a town on the Vistula, Poland, was founded by the Teutonic knights in 1231 Here they acknowledged themselves to be vassals of Poland in 1466 Thorn was taken by Charles XII of Sweden in 1703 Many Protestants were slain here (after a religious riot) at the instigation of the Jesuits, 7 Dec 1724 Thorn was acquired by the Prussians in 1793, taken by the French in 1806, restored to Prussia at the peace in 1815

Thoth, the Egyptian Hermes, god of speech and writing, and of wisdom, represented as a man with the head of an ibis, and with a crescent holding the full moon upon it

thought-reading, or **mind-reading.** In 1881 W. I Bishop professed to be able to read a person's thoughts by touching the skin On June 11, in the presence of G J Romanes, prof E Ray Lankester, F Galton, and others, he was successful with some persons, but failed with others (*Nature*, No 608)

Bishop challenged by Labouchere, M P, to operate under certain conditions at St James's hall, London, declined, 12 June, 1883
Other experiments by Bishop 3-4 June, 1884
Experiments by Stuart Cumberland reported successful, 19 July, "
Bishop sentenced to pay 10,000*l* damages to Mr Maskelyne for libel in *Truth* 23 July, "
Damages reduced to 500*l*. . 2 July, 1885
Bishop dies of catalepsy (?) in New York (SPIRITUALISM, TELEPATHY) 13 May, 1889

Thrace, now **Roume'lia,** a country of European Turkey, derived its name from Thrax, the son of Mars.—*Aspin.* The Thracians were a warlike people, and therefore Mars was said to have been born and to have had his residence among them —*Euripides* ODRYSÆ

B C.
Byzantium, the capital founded by Megarians about 675
Invasion of Darius I, 513, Thrace subdued by Megabyzus 508
Xerxes marches against Greece through Thrace, and retreats 480
Other Greek colonies established 450-400
Wars between Macedon and the ODRYSÆ . 429-343
Philip II acquires Amphipolis, 358, and gradually all the Greek colonies . 357-341
Death of Alexander, Thrace allotted to Lysimachus, 323, who builds Lysimachia. 309
Lysimachus defeated and slain by Seleucus at Corupedion 281
Thrace overrun by the Gauls 279
Lysimachia and the chief towns seized by the fleet of Ptolemy Euergetes . 247
Recovered by Philip V of Macedon . 205-200
Lost by him to the Romans 196
Seized by Antiochus III of Syria, who is defeated at Magnesia, 190, and surrenders Thrace . 188
Perseus defeated in attempt to regain Thrace 171-168
Thracian kings nominally under the Romans 148 et seq
Rebellion of Vologæsus quelled . 14

A. D
Rhœmetalces II, last king 38
Thrace made a Roman province . . about 47
Invaded by the Goths. . . 255
Settled by Sarmatians . . . 334-76
Ravaged by Alaric, 395, by Attila 447
Becomes a part of the Greek or Eastern Empire until conquered by the Turks, who made Adrianople their capital 1341-53
Constantinople captured by Mahomet II . . . 29 May, 1453

Thrasyme'ne or **Trasime'ne,** a lake about 90 miles north of Rome. Here the Carthaginians under Hannibal defeated the Romans under Flaminius, 217 B C, being the 3d battle and victory of Hannibal over the Romans. No less than 15,000 Romans were left dead on the field of battle, and 10,000 taken prisoners, or, according to Livy, 6000, or Polybius, 15,000 The loss of Hannibal was about 1500 men About 10,000 Romans escaped —*Livy, Polybius.*

threshing-machines. The flail was the only instrument formerly in use for threshing grain The Romans used a machine called the *tribulum*, a sledge loaded with stones or iron drawn over the grain sheaves by horses. Cattle and horses were used both in ancient and modern times to tread out the grain The first machines of modern times were invented by Hohlfield of Hermansdorf, Saxony, in 1711, and by Michael Menzies of Edinburgh in 1731 A rotary machine was invented by Leckie of Stirlingshire, Scotland, in 1758, but it was not until 1786 that the first practical machine for general use was invented by Andrew Meikle of Tyningham, Scotland American machines are built with spiked cylinders.

Meikle obtains a patent in Great Britain . . . 1788
In a trial of threshing machines on the farm of Mr Mechi, Tiptree Hall, Kelvedon, Engl, an American machine did nearly treble the work of any English machine Oct. 1853
In threshing contests at the Paris exposition, 6 men with flails threshed 36 liters of wheat in 1 hour, Pinet's French machine 150 liters, Duvoir's, French, 250, Clayton's, English, 410, Pitt s, American, 740 liters 1855
[Machines are now made in the U S. each capable of threshing 3000 bushels daily]

thugs, organized secret fanatical murderers in India, who considered their victims to be sacrifices to their gods. Their method was by strangulation The English attempted to suppress them about 1810, but did not succeed till about 1830, when a plan for the purpose was adopted by lord William Bentinck

thumb-screw, an instrument of torture by which the thumbs were compressed so as to cause intense pain, first used by the Spanish Inquisition In Great Britain, rev William Carstares, a Presbyterian minister, was the last who suffered by it, before the Scotch privy council, to make him divulge secrets which he firmly resisted After the revolution in 1688, the thumb-screw was presented to him by the council King William expressed a desire to see it, and tried it on, bidding a doctor turn the screw, but at the third turn he cried out, "Hold—*hold*' doctor, another turn would make *me* confess anything"

Thundering legion. During a contest with the invading Marcomanni the prayers of Christians in a Roman legion are said to have been followed by a thunder-storm, tending greatly to discomfit the enemy, and hence the legion received the name, 174.

Thu'rii or **Thu'rium,** a Greek city, S Italy, founded after the fall of Sybaris, about 452 B.C. It suffered from incursions of the Lucanians, by whom the Thurians were defeated, 390 B C It became eventually a dependent ally of Rome, was ravaged by Hannibal, 204, established as a colony by the Romans, 194, and captured by Spartacus in the Servile war, and subjected to heavy contributions, 72.

Thurin'gia, an early Gothic kingdom in central Germany, was overrun by Attila and the Huns. 451, the last king, Hermanfried, was defeated and slain by Thierry, king of the Franks, who annexed it, 530. It formed 2 duchies, 630-717 and 849-919, a margraviate, 960-1090, landgraviate and county, 1130-1247, and was, after various changes and many conflicts, absorbed into Saxony in the 15th century. In 1815 it was surrendered to Prussia. The grand-duchy of Saxe-Weimar, the duchies of Saxe Meiningen, Saxe-Coburg-Gotha, and Saxe-Altenburg, and the principalities of Schwarzburg-Rudolstadt, Schwarzburg-Sondershausen, Reuss-Greiz, and Reuss-Schleiz-Lobenstein are frequently grouped as the Thuringian states.

Thursday, the 5th day of the week, named from Thor, the most valiant son of Odin, a deified hero of the northern nations, particularly the Scandinavians and Celts. He was said to rule the winds, seasons, lightning and thunder, etc, Thursday is in Latin *dies Jovis*, or Jupiter's day.

Thyati'ra, Asia Minor, the place assigned for the bat-tie at which the rebel Procopius was defeated by the army of the emperor Valens, 366 SEVEN CHURCHES

Thymbra, a city of Asia Minor Here Cyrus the Great defeated the confederated army aiding Crœsus, and obtained supremacy in Asia, 548 B C

tia'ra, head-ornament of the ancient Persians. The name is given to the triple crown of the pope (anciently called *regnum*), indicative of his civil rank, as the keys are of his ecclesiastical jurisdiction The right to wear a crown is said to have been granted to the bishops of Rome by Constantine the Great, and by Clovis, founder of the French monarchy Their ancient tiara was a high round cap Pope Damasus II first caused himself to be crowned with a tiara, 1048 "Boniface VIII encompassed the tiara with a crown, Benedict XII added a second, and John XXIII a third"—*Rees*

Ti'ber, central Italy, the river on whose banks Rome was built In the flourishing times of the city the navigation of the river was important Livy says that the Tiber was frozen over 398 B.C A commission was appointed to dredge the bed of the river near Rome, Dec 1871 Garibaldi's scheme for improving the river, making a new port, etc, laid before the Italian parliament, 25 May, 1875, works begun, Mch 1877

Tibe'rias, a city in Palestine, built by Herod Antipas, and named after the emperor Tiberius 39 Near it Guy de Lusignan, king of Jerusalem, and the crusaders were defeated by Saladin, 3 4 July, 1187, and Jerusalem fell into his hands.

Ti'bet or **Thi'bet,** central Asia, is said to have been a kingdom 313 B.C., conquered by Genghis Khan, 1206, and gradually subdued by and annexed to China, 1255-1720 Area, 651,500 sq miles, pop. 6,000,000 Buddhism became the dominant religion about 905, and the lamas have absolute power in religious affairs Tibet was visited by Marco Polo, 1278, by Jesuits, about 1661-62, Bogle and Hamilton 1774, and Thomas Manning, 1810 An astronomical survey was carried on surreptitiously by 2 pundits of semi-Tibet origin, under the superintendence of capt Montgomerie, 1865-67

M Gabriel Bonvalot, prince Henry of Orleans and father Dedeken give an illustrated account of Tibet to the French Geographical Society at Paris 31 Jan 1891
Capt Bower, dr Thorold, and party cross Tibet, June, 1891, and arrive at Simla Apr 1892
Much geographical knowledge has been obtained and maps constructed

Ti'bur, now **Tiv'oli,** a Latin town more ancient than Rome, and frequently at war with it The Tiburtines were defeated 335 B.C, and the subjection of all Latium followed, for which Furius Camillus obtained a triumph and an equestrian statue in the forum

Tichborne case. TRIALS, 1871-74

Tici'no or **Tessin,** a Swiss canton south of the Alps, conquered by the Swiss early in the 16th century, made a separate canton in 1815 It suffered by internal disputes, 1839 and 1841

Tici'nus, a river in N Italy Here Hannibal, in his first battle with the Romans under P Cornelius Scipio, after crossing the Alps, defeated them, 218 B.C

ticket-of-leave. The English government in 1854 introduced a system whereby convicts might be liberated on a ticket-of-leave, though a portion of their term of imprisonment was unexpired. They were obliged to report, however, from time to time to the police until their sentence expired If fresh offence was committed, the ticket was recalled TRANSPORTATION

Ticondero'ga. FORT TICONDEROGA, NEW YORK.

tides. The periodical rise and fall of the waters of the ocean and its confluents, due to the attraction of the moon or sun When the water is rising it is termed *flood* tide, when falling, *ebb* tide At the time of the new moon and the full moon the flood tides rise higher, and the fall of the ebb tide is greater than at other times These tides are called spring-tides But when the moon is at her first or last quarter, or at the time of quadrature, the tides do not rise to their average height, and are called neap tides, from A-S. *nép*, signifying narrow, contracted, low. Homer is the earliest profane author who speaks of the tides Posidonius of Apamea referred the tides to the influence of the moon about 79 B C, and Cæsar speaks of them in his 4th book of the Gallic war The tides were first explained by Kepler, 1598, but the theory was first made complete by sir Isaac Newton about 1683 The conformation of the coast greatly affects the tides, for instance, near the entrance of the Bay of Fundy, Nova Scotia the tide rises 18 feet, while at its head it rises 70 feet, at St Johns, N B, 30 feet, at Campo Bello, Me, 25 feet, Eastport, Me, 15 feet, Boston, Mass, 10 feet, Providence, R I, 5 feet, Egg Harbor, N J, 5 feet, New York, 5 feet The tides along the southern United States do not exceed 7 feet, and reach 7 only at Savannah, Ga The tide in the Gulf of Mexico is small and also in the Pacific ocean At the mouth of the Columbia river Oregon, it rises to 7 feet In the west of England, in the Bristol channel and the mouth of the Severn at Chepstow, the spring-tide rises 60 feet The usual height along the coast of Wales is 36 feet The tides in the Mediterranean are hardly noticeable None of the larger fresh-water lakes have an appreciable tide

Tiers-État (*tyar-za-ta'*) STATES-GENERAL.

Tif'lis, Asiatic Russia, built about 469 by Vakhtang became the capital of Georgia. It was taken by Genghis Khan in the 12th century, by Mustapha Pacha, 1576, by the Persians, 1796, and by the Russians, 1801, who have made it the capital of their trans-Caucasian possessions

Tigranocer'ta, now **Sert** or **Iserd,** capital of Armenia, built by Tigranes the Great, and taken by Lucullus and the Romans after a great victory, 69 B C

Ti'gris, a river, the eastern boundary of Mesopotamia, celebrated for the cities founded on its banks Nineveh, Seleucia Ctesiphon, and Bagdad It was first explored by an English steamer in 1838

tile, a slab of clay, hardened by baking, and used for paving, roofing, and for constructing ovens, drains, etc Tiles are of ancient origin, being found in the ruins of Nineveh. They were in use in Greece, 620 B.C Pyrrhus, king of Epirus, was killed while fighting in the streets of Argos by a tile thrown from a roof by a woman, 272 B.C The art of glazing tile was brought to Spain by the Moors, 12th century, and from Spain was carried to Italy, and thence to Delft, Holland Tiles were used in England by the Romans during their occupation of that country. First made by the English probably about 1216 They were taxed in 1784, tax repealed in 1833

Tilsit, a town of Prussia on the river Niemen where, on a raft, the emperors of France and Russia met, 25 June, 1807. By a treaty between France and Russia, signed 7 July, Napoleon restored to the Prussian monarch one half of his territories, and Russia recognized the Confederation of the Rhine, and the elevation of Napoleon's 3 brothers, Joseph, Louis, and Jerome, to the thrones of Naples, Holland, and Westphalia

tilts. TOURNAMENTS

timber bending. Apparatus was invented for this purpose by T Blanchard of Boston, Mass, for which a medal was awarded at the Paris Exhibition of 1855 A company was formed for its introduction into England in 1856.

Timbuc'too, N. Africa a city built by Mansa Suleiman, a Mahometan, about 1214, and frequently subjugated by the sovereigns of Morocco. Since 1727 it has been partly independent. Major Laing visited this city in 1826 and was killed there René Caillie in 1828 won the prize of 10,000 francs offered by the Geographical Society of Paris to the first traveller who should give exact information regarding it It was again visited by Heinrich Barth during his explorations of the Soudan, 1849-55 Taken and occupied by the French, Jan 1894.

time. DAY, GLOBE, HOUR, MONTH, PLANETS, STANDARD TIME, WEEK, YEAR.

"Times," a newspaper of London On 13 Jan 1785, John Walter published the first number of the *Daily Universal Register*, price 2½d, printed on the logographic system (invented by Henry Johnson, a compositor), in which types containing syllables and words were employed instead of single letters

Paper is named the *Times* 1 Jan 1788
The *Times* is first printed by steam power (the invention of F Koenig) 1200 per hour, afterwards increased to 2000 and 4000 28 Nov 1814
[It is asserted that the *Times* was termed the *Thunderer* from an article by Edward Sterling, in which are the words, "We thundered forth articles on reform " etc]
Times express first conveyed to India overland by the agency of lieut Waghorn Oct 1845
"Walter press," printing about 15 000 an hour, perfected 1862-71
Weekly issue, price 2d began 5 Jan 1877
Rapid electric lamp adopted in the press room Nov 1878

tin, a white, lustrous, and malleable metal, very slow of oxidizing in the air, and therefore useful in a thin coating to prevent iron, etc, from rusting It has been known from earliest ages The ACCADIANS called it *anaku* 5000 years ago, it was used by the Egyptians when the first pyramids were built, it is mentioned in the Bible, 1452 B.C (Num xxxi 22) Homer often speaks of it (κασσιτερος) in describing arms and chariots, the Phœnicians traded in tin more than 1100 years B C, and Herodotus mentions the tin islands It is found in few and widely scattered places, chiefly in the provinces of Perak and Penang in Malacca, in Cornwall, Engl, in New South Wales, Saxony, Bohemia, and in smaller quantities in Mexico and Bolivia, and recently in California, South Dakota, Idaho, and West Virginia The world's annual production is about 40,000 tons Copper vessels were tinned by the Romans The art of tinning plate-iron was invented in Bohemia, whence it was carried into Saxony and other parts of Germany in 1620, and introduced into England in 1675

Existence of tin ore in New South Wales made known by rev W B Clarke, colonial geologist 1845
Rush of emigration to the tin mines of New South Wales 1871
Tin, previously known to exist as black sand in the gold ore from the Black Hills, S Dakota, is discovered there in commercial quantities by maj Andrew J Simmons of Rapid City, S Dak 1883
Tin discovered in West Virginia 17 Sept 1884
Sixty Welsh tin plate works shut down, throwing 25,000 hands out of employment 27 June, 1891

Tinchebray (*tinsh-bray'*), a town of N W France, where a battle was fought between Henry I of England, and his brother Robert, duke of Normandy England and Normandy were reunited under Henry, at the decease of William Rufus, who had already obtained Normandy by mortgage from his brother Robert, at his setting out for Palestine Robert, on his return, recovered Normandy by agreement with Henry, but after a quarrel Robert was defeated in the battle of Tinchebray, 28 Sept 1106, and Normandy was annexed to the crown of England —*Hénault.*

Tip'pecanoe', Battle of In the spring of 1811, Tecumseh or Tecumthé, a Shawnee chief, attempted to unite the Western and Southern Indians in war against the United States To meet this movement, gen Harrison, governor of the Indiana territory, marched towards Tippecanoe, the headquarters of the chief (near Lafayette, Ind), with about 650 men. There, on 7 Nov, he defeated over 600 Indians, under Tecumseh's brother, "The Prophet" Harrison lost 62 killed and 126 wounded, the Indians lost 150 killed.

Tip'permuir, near Perth, Scotland. Here the marquess of Montrose defeated the Covenanters under lord Elcho, 1 Sept. 1644

titan'ium, a rare metal, discovered by Gregor in menakite, a Cornish mineral, in 1791, and in 1794 by Klaproth, and since found in many iron ores Spectrum analysis has proved it to exist in the sun's atmosphere, and it occurs in some meteorites

tithes or **tenths,** a tenth part of anything, a tax of one tenth of the produce or its value, were commanded to be given to the tribe of Levi, 1490 B.C (Lev xxvii. 30) Abraham, returning from his victory over the kings (Gen xiv), gave tithes of the spoil to Melchisedek, king of Salem, priest of the most high God (1913 B C) For the first 800 years of the Christian church they were given purely as alms, and were voluntary —*Wickliffe* "I will not put the title of the clergy to tithes upon any divine right, though such a right certainly commenced, and I believe as certainly ceased, with the Jewish theocracy."—*Blackstone* They were established in France by Charlemagne about 800, and abolished 1789 Tenths were confirmed in the Lateran councils, 1215 —*Rainaldi* The payment of tithes appears to have been claimed by Augustin, the first archbishop of Canterbury, and to have been allowed by Ethelbert, king of Kent, under the term "God's fee," about 600

First written authority for them in England is a constitutional decree made in a synod enjoining tithes, 786.
Offa, king of Mercia, gave the church tithes of all his kingdom, to expiate his murder of Ethelbert king of the East Angles, 794
Tithes first granted to the English clergy in a general assembly held by Ethelwold, 844 —*Henry*
In England, in 1545, tithes were fixed at 2s 9d in the pound on rent, many later acts regulate them
Tithe Commutation act, passed 13 Aug 1836, was amended in 1837, 1840, 1846, 1860, and 1878
A *rector* takes all tithes, a *vicar* a small part or none
Several acts relating to tithes in Ireland, in 1832-47, alter and improve the system
Tithe redemption trust appointed, 1846
An act for the recovery of tithe rent charged in England and Wales passed, 26 Mch 1891 The liability for the payment of tithes is transferred from the tenant to the land-owner

tithing. The number or company of 10 men with their families in a society, all of them bound to the king of England for the peaceable and good behavior of each, of these companies there was one chief person, who, from his office, was called (toothingman) tithingman, but now he is nothing but a constable, formerly called the headborough.—*Cowel.*

titles royal. Henry IV had the title of "Grace" and "My liege," 1399 Henry VI, "Excellent grace," 1422. Edward IV, "Most high and mighty prince," 1461 Henry VII, "Highness," 1485, Henry VIII the same title, and sometimes "Grace," 1509 et seq Francis I of France addressed Henry as "Your majesty" at their interview in 1520 FIELD OF THE CLOTH OF GOLD Henry VIII was the first and last king who was styled "Dread sovereign" James I coupled to "majesty" the present "sacred," or "most excellent." "Majesty" was the style of the emperors of Germany, the first king to whom it was given was Louis XI of France, about 1463.

tobacco (*Nicotiana tabacum*) an American plant, of the nightshade family, whose leaves have strong narcotic effects, due to the alkaloid nicotine. It received its name from the Indian *tabaco*, the tube or pipe in which the natives smoked the plant, transferred by the Spaniards to the herb itself, others say the name is derived from Tabacco, a province of Yucatan, New Spain, or from the island of Tobago, one of the Caribbees, others from Tobasco, in the gulf of Florida. It is said to have been first observed at St. Domingo, in Cuba, 1492, and to have been used freely by the Spaniards in Yucatan in 1520 Tobacco was either first brought to Europe by Hermandez de Toledo or Francesco Fernandes, a physician sent by Philip II of Spain to investigate the products of Mexico in 1559, into England in 1565 by sir John Hawkins, or by sir Walter Raleigh and sir Francis Drake in 1586, to France by Jean Nicot (whence nicotine) The Pied Bull inn, at Islington, is said to have been the first house in England where tobacco was smoked The first settlers of Virginia cultivated tobacco, which soon became the chief agricultural staple, and within 10 years the standard currency, at a value of about 66 cents a pound. For 7 years, ending 1621, the annual exportation to England was 143,000 lbs James I tried to suppress its use, and wrote "A Counter-blast against Tobacco" In May, 1621, Parliament forbade its importation into England, except from Virginia and the Bermudas Tobacco is now raised not only in America but in Europe and India, although Kentucky raises more than any other state or country. The production in Java and Sumatra is rapidly increasing. The world's production is about 1,300,000,000 lbs., that of the United States about 540,000,000 lbs The great tobacco-producing states are

1	Kentucky	285,000,000 lbs
2	Virginia	65,000,000 "
3	Tennessee	46,000,000 "
4	Ohio	36,000,000 "
5	North Carolina	26,000,000 "
6	Pennsylvania	25,000,000 "

Other states raise from 1,000,000 to 16,000,000 lbs. each Crop of 1891 valued at about $44,000,000 Tax paid the U. S. from 1862 to 1891, $840,000,000

Toba'go, an island of the British West Indies, discovered by Columbus in 1498, settled by the Dutch, 1642 It as since changed hands several times, between England, 'rance, and Holland, but now belongs to England as part of he government of Trinidad Area, 114 sq miles, pop 20,727.

Tobolsk, capital of W Siberia, on the river Irtish. ettled by 500 Cossacks in 1587, pop about 22,000

Tohope'ka, Battle of ALABAMA, 1814

Tokay', a town of upper Hungary, which gives its ame to the sweet, heavy white wine of the district. This ine was first made here by dressers brought from Italy by Bela IV, king 1235-70 The best of the wine is sent to sovereigns, and 50 bottles were presented to queen Victoria at her ubilee, 1887

Toki'o, since 1869 the name of the former Jeddo or eddo, capital of Japan, on the island of Niphon Pop 1890, ,389,684

Tol'biac, now **Zulpich,** a town of Prussia, near he Rhine, where Clovis totally defeated the Allemanni, 496

Tole'do, the ancient *Toletum*, central Spain, made capal of the Visigothic kingdom by Athanagild, 554, taken by ne Saracens, 712 Toledo was taken after the war begun, 1081, y Alfonso I of Castile, 25 May, 1085 In 1088 the archbishop 'as made primate of Spain The university was founded in 199 Toledo sword-blades have been famed since the 15th entury. SWORDS.—The county seat of Lucas county, Ohio, ith its surrounding territory, claimed by Michigan until the oundary was settled in 1836 OHIO, 1802-36, MICHIGAN, 835-36

Toleration act, passed in 1689 to relieve Protestant issenters from the church of England Their liberties were, owever, greatly endangered in the latter days of queen Anne, ho died on the day that the Schism bill was to become a aw, 1 Aug 1714

he toleration granted was somewhat limited It exempted persons who took the new oath of allegiance and supremacy, and abjured popery, from penalties for absence from church and holding unlawful conventicles, and it allowed the Quakers to substitute an affirmation for an oath, but did not relax the Test act The party spirit of the times checked the king's liberal disposition

tolls were first paid by vessels passing the Stade, on the Elbe, 1109 They were first demanded by the Danes for passing the Sound, 1341 SOUND DUES, STADE DUES Toll-bars n England originated 1267, in the grant of a penny for every wagon that passed through a certain manor, and the first reglar toll was collected a few years after for mending the road n London between St Giles's and Temple Bar. Gathered for epairing the highways of Holborn-inn lane and Martin's lane now Aldersgate street), 1346 Toll gates or turnpikes were et up in 1663. In 1827, 27 turnpikes near London were reoved by Parliament, 81 turnpikes and toll-bars ceased on he north of London on 1 July, 1864, 61 on the south side eased on 31 Oct 1865, and many on the Essex and Middleex roads ceased on 31 Oct 1866, the remainder on the north f London ceased 1 July, 1872. The tolls on the commercial oads, London, E, were abolished 5 Aug 1871 The tolls on Waterloo and other metropolitan bridges abolished, 1878-79. WALES, 1843

Tolo'sa. On the plain named Las Navas de Tolosa, near the Sierra Morena, S Spain, Alfonso, king of Castile, aided by the kings of Aragon and Navarre, gained a great victory ver the Moors, 16 July, 1212, sometimes termed the battle of Muradal.

Toltecs, a people inhabiting Mexico and Central America prior to the Aztecs AMERICA

tomato (*Lycopersicum esculentum*), native of tropical S. America. In the United States it was a curiosity, and ommonly called love-apple until about 1830, a translation of the French name *pomme d'amour* But this is a corruption of the old Italian name, *poma dei Mori*, "Moor's apple," he tomato having come to Italy from Morocco It is now a staple vegetable, and a universal article of food

Tonga isles, Pacific, south of the equator, governed by a king Treaties of friendship with Great Britain, Germany, and the United States Area of the group, 374 sq. miles, pop 1889, 20,000

tonic sol-fa system. MUSIC.

tonom'eter, a delicate apparatus (consisting of 52 tuning-forks) for measuring and comparing the pitch of tones, by marking the number of vibrations It was invented by H Scheibler of Crefeld, and described in his "Tonmesser," 1834, but was little used till M Kœnig improved it, and exhibited it at the International Exhibition of 1862 in London.

Tonquin (*ton keen'*), S E ASIA, a province of Anam, subject to China, now under the protectorate of France Area, 34,740 sq miles, pop about 9,000 000

Liu Yang Fu declares war against French aggressors 8 May, 1883
Black Flags kill the French commander and 32 others at Hanoi, "
[The "Black Flags" originated with Li Hung Chang, an able leader of Canton rebels, who about 1864 with followers took refuge in Tonquin, where he was welcomed by the emperor of Anam, but grew strong enough to establish an independent government. They strenuously opposed the French]
Black Flags defeated 7 Aug "
Armistice granted, treaty signed recognizing the French government, ceding province of Bin Huam 25 Aug "
Adm Courbet begins actual occupation of Tonquin 3 Nov "
French take forts on the Red river, opposite Sontay 16 Dec "
Sontay captured, the Black Flags retire, French loss, 77 killed, 231 wounded 16-17 Dec "
Arrival of Chinese troops to defend Hainan against the French 20 Jan 1884
French capture Bacninh 12 Mch "
Treaty signed by capt Fournier and Li Hung Chang, French protectorate of Tonquin and Anam recognized The Chinese government repudiates the treaty 1 July, "
[Fighting throughout the remainder of the year]
Preliminaries of peace signed at Peking, Tonquin to be vacated by the Chinese, etc. 5 Apr 1885
Chief of the Black Flags rewarded for his services by the Chinese government Apr "
Establishment of the civil native guard for the suppression of piracy Sept 1888
Continued fighting with pirates 1889-92
French companies formed to work coal mines at Hongay and Kebao 1891
Expenditure of France for Anam and Tonquin was 10,450,000 francs in 1892, of which 450,000 francs were for the Tonquin submarine telegraph cable

tonsure, the clerical crown, shorn or shaven, it is said, in imitation of St Peter, or of Christ's crown of thorns It was regarded in the 4th century as proper only to penitents, and not made essential to priests till near the beginning of the 6th century

tontines, life-annuities with benefit of survivorship, so called from Lorenzo Tonti, a Neapolitan banker, who originated the plan in 1653, he died in the Bastile after 7 years imprisonment. A Mr Jennings of London was an original subscriber for a 100*l* share in a tontine company, and, being the last survivor of the shareholders, his share produced him 3000*l* per annum He died, aged 103 years, 19 June, 1798, worth 2,115,244*l*. By the termination of a tontine begun by M Lafarges in 1791, to diminish the national debt, the French government received 1,218,000 francs, Dec 1888. Henri de Tonti, companion of La Salle, was a son of Lorenzo, Henry died at fort St. Louis (now St Louis) in 1704 In recent years the name tontine has been given to a form of life-insurance, in which all profits from overpayments of premiums, lapses, etc., are accumulated until the end of a fixed period, and then divided among the survivors

to'paz, the second stone in the breastplate of the Jewish high-priest. AARON'S BREASTPLATE. Found in Cornwall, Engl., Scotland, Saxony, Siberia, Brazil, Mexico, and the United States. The finest are from Brazil, of a deep yellow, and sometimes resembling the diamond in lustre, and those from Siberia of a bluish color The yellow Brazilian stones when heated assume a rose color.

Toplitz, a town of Bohemia Here were signed, in 1813, 2 treaties—one between Austria, Russia, and Prussia, 9 Sept.; and one between Great Britain and Austria, 3 Oct.

top'ophone, an instrument invented by A M Mayer to determine the direction from which sound proceeds, as the sound of a bell, whistle, or fog-horn at sea in thick weather.

Torbanehill mineral. Mr Gillespie of Torbanehill granted a lease of all the coal in the estate to messrs.

Russell. In working it the lessees extracted a combustible mineral of value as a source of coal gas, and sold it as gas-coal. The lessor insisted that the mineral was not coal, but bituminous schist, and disputed the right of the lessees to work it. At the trial in 1853 there was a great array of scientific men and practical gas engineers, and the evidence was most conflicting. The judge set aside the scientific evidence, and the jury pronounced it coal. The authorities in Prussia have since pronounced it *not* to be coal.—*Percy.*

Tordesil'las, a town near Valladolid, Spain. Here was signed, 7 June, 1494, a treaty modifying the boundaries by which pope Alexander VI., in May, 1493, had divided the new world between Spain and Portugal.

Torgau (*tor'gow*), a town of Saxony, N. Germany, the site of a signal victory of Frederick II. (the Great) of Prussia over the Austrians; the Austrian general, count Daun, being wounded, 3 Nov. 1760. He had, in 1757, defeated the Prussian king at Kolin. Torgau was taken by the allies in 1814, and given to Prussia 1815.

Tories, a term given to a political party in England about 1678. WHIG. Dr. Johnson defines a Tory as one who adheres to the ancient constitution of the state and the apostolical hierarchy of the church of England. The Tories long maintained the doctrines of "divine hereditary indefeasible right, lineal succession, passive obedience, prerogative," etc.—*Bolingbroke.* CONSERVATIVES. During the American Revolution, Americans who adhered to the crown were called Tories.

tornadoes. STORMS.

Toronto, capital of the province of Ontario, Canada. Settled as York, 1794; name changed to Toronto, 1834. University, with its hall, library, and museum, burned, 14 Feb. 1890. Pop. 1886, 118,403; 1891, 181,220.

torpe'do-shells, a name given to explosives placed under water for the destruction of vessels, an invention ascribed to David Bushnell, an American, in 1777. His attempt to destroy the British ship *Cerberus* failed. The action of Fulton's torpedoes was successful in Britain, 1805; but their use was declined by the government. Torpedo-shells ignited by electricity were successfully employed in the United States during the civil war, 1861-65. On 4 Oct. 1865, messrs. M'Kay & Beardslee tried them at Chatham, Engl., before the duke of Somerset and others. An old vessel, the *Terpsichore*, was speedily sunk. The preliminary arrangements were complicated. Magneto-electricity was employed. Torpedoes made by prof. F. Abel of Woolwich were tried in May, 1866. A torpedo invented by Mr. Wightman and an Austrian tried and reported successful at Sheerness; an old hulk was sunk, 8 Oct. 1870. Torpedoes to be ignited from a distance by an electric battery are now made in the U. S. and at Woolwich, Engl. A Turkish monitor was blown up by a torpedo in the Danube (RUSSO-TURKISH WAR, 1877), 26 May, 1877.

New English torpedo-boat *Peacemaker* invented by J. H. L. Tuck.......... Aug. 1886
Powerful Brennan torpedo with the "Watkin position finder" successfully tried at Cliff End fort.......... 5 July, 1890
Controllable torpedo of Scott Sims & Edison tried at Portsmouth and reported successful.......... 3-15 Feb. 1892
NAVY, U. S.

Tor'res strait, dividing Australia from Papua or New Guinea, was discovered by Torres, a Spaniard, in June, 1606.

Tor'res Ve'dras, a city of Portugal. Near here Wellington, retreating from the French, took up a strong position, called the Lines of Torres Vedras, 10 Oct. 1810.

Torricellian experiment, by Evangelista Torricelli (1608-47). In 1643 he discovered that the weight of the air at the surface of the earth is equal to that of a column of mercury 30 in. in height; on this principle the barometer is constructed.

Torto'la. VIRGIN ISLES.

torture of slaves to obtain testimony was permitted by the Greeks, but not of citizens. By the Romans "torture to compel confession was only applied to slaves."—*Mommsen.* "The application of torture to witnesses and suspected persons pervaded nearly all the criminal jurisprudence of Europe until the last century."—*Grote,* "Hist. Greece," vol. vii. p. 39, note. It is the boast of the common-law of England that it never recognized torture as legal. "The rack itself, though not admitted in ordinary execution of justice, was frequently used upon any suspicion, by authority of a warrant from a secretary of the privy council."—*Hume.* Torture was applied to heretics, etc., by the Romish church as early as 1228, and continued until 1816, when it was suppressed by a papal bull, which provided that prosecutions should be public and the accuser should confront the accused. Torture was abolished in England, 1640; Scotland, 1690; Portugal, 1776; France, 1789; Sweden, 1786, and generally throughout Europe before 1800. Gen. Picton was convicted of allowing Louisa Calderon, in Trinidad, to be tortured under an old law of the island, at his trials, 21 Feb. 1806, and 11 June, 1808. The following are noted cases of torture under the sanction of a government:

Three of the soldiers who killed Cyrus the Younger at CUNAXA, Mithridates, a Persian, and 2 others. The slow method by which Mithridates was killed was termed the torture of the *boat.* He was 17 days dying.—*Plutarch,* "Artaxerxes."
Knights TEMPLARS, the church acquiescing.......... 1308-14
Balthazar Gerard, for the assassination of William, prince of Orange.......... 1584
François Ravaillac, for assassination of Henry IV. of France... 1610
Certain citizens of Milan, on suspicion of propagating the PLAGUE by ointments applied to the doors and walls of houses.......... 1630
Robert Francis Damiens, for the attempted assassination of Louis XV. of France.......... 1757
Count Ankerström, for the assassination of Gustavus III. of Sweden.......... 1792
Assassins of count Capo d'Istria, president of Greece (BURYING ALIVE).......... 1831
Instances of torture for heresy by the Romish church are very numerous. Ingenuity was strained to devise methods of torture for the Inquisition. Some methods are described in Poe's tale of "The Pit and the Pendulum."

to'tem, among savage tribes, especially the North American Indians, the token or symbol of a family or clan, usually an animal or some natural object selected for reverence and superstitious regard. It serves for a sort of surname of the family. Its importance lies in the notion that individuals trace their lineage from it. The turtle, the bear, and the wolf appear to be favored and honored totems among many tribes. The obligations growing out of a common totem are scrupulously regarded. Intermarriage among those having it was criminal. All such, of whatever clan or tribe, friendly or hostile, have the rights of hospitality, of succor in distress, and of friendship as blood-relations. The totem is never changed.

"*Uncas:* 'The Hurons' totem is a moose . . . the Delawares are the children of the tortoise. . . . My race is the grandfather of nations.' *Tamsemund:* 'Who art thou?' *Uncas:* 'A son of the great Unamis (turtle).' "—*Cooper,* "Last of the Mohicans."

Tot'nes, a town of Devon, England; thought to be the Roman *Ad Durium Amnem.* It was held by Judhael de Totneis, who built the castle about 1085. The parliamentary borough was disfranchised for gross corruption and bribery by the Reform act, 15 Aug. 1867.

Toul, the Roman *Tulli Leucorum,* a fortified town on the Moselle, N.E. France; one of the most ancient in the empire. The city and diocese acquired great privileges from Charles the Simple, 925, when it was united with the German empire. It was reunited with France, 1552. The fortifications, begun in 1238, were rebuilt and enlarged in 1700, according to the plans of Vauban. After a vigorous resistance to the Germans, commencing 14 Aug. 1870, Toul surrendered with its garrison of 3000 men, 23 Sept., when the town was burning in 23 places. The Germans thus acquired an uninterrupted railway communication to Paris.

Toulon', the ancient *Telo Martius,* S. France, an important military port. It was taken by the constable of Bourbon, 1524, and by the emperor Charles V. in 1536. In 1707 it was bombarded by the allies, both by land and sea. Most of the town was reduced to ruins, and several ships burned; but the allies were obliged to raise the siege. It surrendered 27 Aug. 1793, to the British admiral, lord Hood, who took possession both of the town and shipping, in the name of Louis XVII., under a stipulation to assist in restoring the French constitution of 1789. A conflict took place between the English and French forces, when the latter were repulsed, 15 Nov. 1793. Toulon was retaken by Bonaparte, 19 Dec., when such inhabitants as were thought to favor the British were cruelly handled. A naval battle off this port was fought 11 Feb. 1744, between the English under Mathews and Lestock, against the fleets of France and Spain. The victory was lost by a misunderstanding between the English admirals. Mathews was dismissed for misconduct. Pop. 1891, 77,747.

Toulouse (*too-looz'*), the ancient *Tolosa*, S. France, founded about 615 B.C.; was the capital of the Visigothic kings in 419 A.D.; and was taken by Clovis in 508. The dukes of Aquitaine reigned here, 631–761. A university was established here, 1229, and a parliament, 1302. The Inquisition was established here to extirpate heretics, 1229. The troubadours, or rhetoricians of Toulouse, had their origin about 850, and consisted of a fraternity of poets, whose art was extended throughout Europe, and gave rise to the Italian and French poetry. TROUBADOURS. The allied British and Spanish army entered this city on 12 Apr., immediately after the battle of Toulouse, fought between the British Peninsular army under lord Wellington, and the French led by marshal Soult, 10 Apr. 1814. The French were forced to retreat, after 12 hours' fighting. Neither of the commanders knew that Napoleon had abdicated the throne of France. Pop. 1891, 149,791.

Toulouse, a county of S.E. France, was created out of the kingdom of Aquitaine by Charlemagne, in 778. It enjoyed great prosperity till the dreadful war of the ALBIGENSES, when the count Raymond VI. was expelled, and Simon de Montfort became count. At his death, in 1218, Raymond VII. obtained his inheritance. His daughter Jane and her husband Alphonse (brother of Louis IX. of France) dying without issue, the county of Toulouse was united to the French monarchy in 1271. A large part of Toulouse destroyed by an inundation of the Garonne (St. Cyprian like a sepulchre), 21–26 June, 1875.

Touraine (*too-rān'*), the garden of France, was conquered by the Visigoths about 480. It was ceded to Geoffroy, count of Anjou, 1044, and thus became the property of the Plantagenet kings of England. It was seized by Philip Augustus in 1203, and was made a duchy by John, 1360. It was finally united to the crown on the death of the duke of Anjou, 1584.

tour'naments or **jousts** were martial sports of the ancient cavaliers. Tournament is derived from the French word *tourner*, "to turn round." Tournaments were frequent about 890; and were regulated by the emperor Henry I., about 919. Tournaments were introduced into England early in the 12th century; prohibited by Henry II., but revived by Richard I., his son. Solemn tournaments were held by Edward III., 25 Sept. 1329, in London; and 19 Jan. 1344, at Windsor; and by Richard II. near the end of the 14th century; and also by Henry VIII., in May, 1513. The Lateran council protested against their continuance in 1136. Henry II. of France, in a tilt with the comte de Montgomerie, had his eye struck out; an accident which caused the king's death in a few days, 29 June, 1559. Tournaments were then abolished in France. A magnificent feast and tournament, under the auspices of Archibald, earl of Eglintoun, took place at Eglintoun castle, 29 Aug. 1839, and the following week; many of the visitors (among whom was Louis Napoleon Bonaparte) appeared as ancient knights, lady Seymour being the "Queen of Beauty." Among the festivities at the marriage of prince Humbert, at Turin, was a tournament, 24 Apr. 1868. Tournaments held at the Agricultural hall, London, N. (for benefit of soldiers' widows, etc.), 21 June et seq. 1880, and 25 June et seq. 1881.

Tournay', a city of S. Belgium, was very flourishing till ravaged by barbarians in the 5th century. It has sustained many sieges. Taken by the allies in 1709, and ceded to the house of Austria by the treaty of Utrecht; but the Dutch were allowed to garrison it, as one of the barrier towns. It was taken by the French under gen. La Bourdonnaye, 8 Nov. 1792. Several battles were fought near Tournay in May, 1793, and May, 1794.

tourniquet (*toor-nee-kay'*; from *tourner*, to turn), an instrument for stopping the flow of blood in a limb, by tightening the bandage in amputations, is said to have been invented by Morelli at the siege of Besançon, 1674. J. L. Petit, in France, invented the screw tourniquet in 1718. Greatly improved by Savigney of London, 1800, and by others since.

Tours (*toor*), an ancient city, central France, near which Charles Martel gained a great victory over the Saracens, and saved Europe, 10 Oct. 732, and from which he acquired the name of Martel, signifying hammer. This conflict is also called the battle of Poitiers. When Paris was invested by the Germans, M. Crémieux and several of the members of the French government of defence went to Tours, together with the representatives of foreign powers, 18 Sept. 1870. On 9 Oct. these were joined by Gambetta, minister of the interior, afterwards of war (who escaped from Paris by a balloon, 7 Oct.). In consequence of the defeat of the army of the Loire near Orleans, the government removed to Bordeaux, 11 Dec.

Tower of London. The tradition that Julius Cæsar founded a citadel here (about 54 B.C.) is very doubtful.

> "Ye towers of Julius, London's lasting shame,
> With many a foul and midnight murder fed."—*Gray.*

A royal palace, on the present site of the White tower, which appears to have been first marked out by William the Conqueror, 1076, was commenced in 1078, and completed by William Rufus, who, in 1098, surrounded it with walls and a ditch. Several succeeding princes made additions, and king Edward III. built the church. In 1638 the old White tower was rebuilt; and under king Charles II. it was thoroughly repaired, 1680–85, and many additions built. Here are the armory, jewel-office, and various other divisions and buildings of peculiar interest: notably, the Bloody tower, Wakefield tower, Bell tower, and Beauchamp tower.

CHRONOLOGICAL LIST OF IMPORTANT IMPRISONMENTS IN THE TOWER.

Name.	Disposal.	Date.	Whose reign.	Remarks.
David, king of Scotland	Released	1357	Edward III.	After 11 years in the Tower.
John, king of France	....	"	"	PRISONERS.
James, son of Robert III. of Scotland	Released	1423	Henry V.	Afterwards James I. of Scotland; 18 years a captive.
Henry VI.	Murdered	1471	Edward IV.	Supposed to have been killed by the duke of Gloucester, afterwards Richard III.
George, duke of Clarence, brother of the king	"	1478	"	Drowned in a butt of Malmsey.
Lord Hastings	Beheaded	1483	Richard III.	Arrested in the Tower, and beheaded at once.
Edward V. and duke of York	Murdered	"	"	Children; buried in the Tower.
Perkin Warbeck	Beheaded	1499	Henry VII.	For personating the duke of York.
Edward Plantagenet, earl of Warwick	"	"	"	His life had been spent in the Tower.
Dudley and Empson	"	1509	"	Ministers of the king.
Earl of Suffolk	"	1513	Henry VIII.	The king carried out the wishes of Henry VII.
Fisher, bishop of Rochester	"	1535	"	For refusing to acknowledge the king's supremacy.
Sir Thomas More	"	"	"	" " " " " " "
Anne Boleyn	"	1536	"	Wife of Henry VIII.
Thomas Cromwell	"	1540	"	Minister of Henry VIII.
Lady Catharine Howard	"	1542	"	Wife of Henry VIII.
Earl of Surrey	"	1547	"	Son of the duke of Norfolk.
Duke of Norfolk	Released	"	"	Escaped execution, the king dying the night the warrant was issued, 1547. The lieutenant of the Tower held the warrant, and he was liberated by queen Mary, 6 years afterwards.
Sir Thomas Seymour	Beheaded	1549	Edward VI.	Treason. His brother, Edward Seymour, duke of Somerset, being lord protector of England during the minority of Edward VI., signed the warrant for his execution.

CHRONOLOGICAL LIST OF IMPORTANT IMPRISONMENTS IN THE TOWER.—(*Continued.*)

Name.	Disposal.	Date.	Whose reign.	Remarks.
Edward Seymour, duke of Somerset	Beheaded	1552	Edward VI.	(Brother of sir Thomas) convicted of treason.
Earl of Courtney	Released	1553	Mary	
Duke of Northumberland	Beheaded	"	"	For placing lady Jane Grey on the throne.
Lord Guilford Dudley	"	1554	"	Husband of lady Jane Grey.
Lady Jane Grey	"	"	"	Daughter of the earl of Suffolk.
Earl of Suffolk	"	"	"	For making lady Jane Grey queen.
Sir Thomas Wyatt	"	"	"	Attempted insurrection.
Princess Elizabeth	Released	"	"	For a short time after the Wyatt insurrection.
Earl of Hertford and his wife	"	1561	Elizabeth	Imprisoned for marrying without the consent of Elizabeth; the earl was released after the death of his wife, 1570.
Lady Catherine Grey	"	"	"	
Duke of Norfolk	Beheaded	1571 / 1572	"	Treason with Spain.
Duke of Northumberland	"	1572	"	For treason.
Robert Devereux, earl of Essex	"	1601	"	Treason. Attempted insurrection.
Sir Thomas Overbury	Murdered	1613	James I.	Poisoned by the earl and countess of Somerset.
Sir Walter Raleigh	Beheaded	1618	"	After many years' imprisonment.
Sir Francis Bacon	Released	1621	"	For bribery.
Thomas Wentworth, earl of Stafford	Beheaded	1641	Charles I.	Impeached by Parliament.
Archbishop Laud	"	1645	"	" " "
Sir Henry Vane	"	1662	Charles II.	Treason.
Lord Russell	"	1683	"	Implicated in the Rye House plot.
Algernon Sidney	"	1683	"	" " " " " "
Arthur, earl of Essex	Murdered or committed suicide.	1683	"	" " " " " "
Duke of Monmouth	Beheaded	1685	James II.	Natural son of Charles II. and Lucy Waters; b. Rotterdam, 1649. For treason. SEDGMOOR.
George Jeffreys, chief justice	Died	1689	William III.	Arrested and placed in the Tower to save him from the mob, Dec. 1688.

tower, a structure lofty in proportion to its base, generally round or square. That of BABEL, the first on record, built in the plains of Shinar (Gen. xi.), 2257 B.C. The Tower of the Winds at Athens, built 550 B.C.; the Tower of PHAROS, 280 B.C. The *round towers* in Ireland were the only structures of stone found on the arrival of the English, 1169, except some buildings in the maritime towns founded by Danes. They are tall hollow pillars, nearly cylindrical, but narrowing towards the top; pierced with lateral holes to admit the light, and covered with conical roofs. 56 still remain, from 50 to 130 feet high. An old tower at Newport, R. I., has long been a subject of controversy as to by whom and when erected. Lossing introduces this subject in his "Field Book of the Revolution," vol. i. p. 633–34, with illustration. *Scribner's Monthly*, vol. xvii., 1879, and the *American Historical Magazine*, vol. iii., 1879, have articles relating to this tower.

> "Some there are who say,
> Thou wert an ancient windmill."
> —*Mrs. L. H. Sigourney*, "The Newport Tower."

MARTELLO, PISA.

Townley marbles, sculptures which Charles Townley collected at Rome between 1765–72. He died in 1805, when his collection (350 pieces) was purchased for the British museum.

Towton, a township of Yorkshire, Engl., where a sanguinary battle was fought, 29 Mch. 1461, between the houses of York (Edward IV.) and Lancaster (Henry VI.); fatal to the latter, who lost more than 37,000 men. Edward gave no quarter, and a merciless slaughter ensued. Henry and his queen, Margaret, fled to Scotland; and Edward IV. was settled on the throne.

Toxoph'ilites (from τόξον, a bow, and φίλος, a lover), a society established by sir Aston Lever in 1781. In 1834 they took grounds in the inner circle of Regent's park, and built the archery lodge. They possess a curious piece of plate, given by Catherine, queen of Charles II., to be shot for by the Finsbury archers, whom the Toxophilites represent.

tract societies. The Society for Promoting Christian Knowledge was founded in 1698; the Religious Tract Society, London, in 1799; and other similar societies since. The first undenominational tract society in the United States was formed in Boston, 1803, and one at Andover, Mass., 1814, which removed to Boston, 1823, under the name of the "American Tract Society." In 1825 another was formed in New York, and soon after a union of all was effected.

tractarianism, a set of opinions on church matters propounded in the "Tracts for the Times," of which 90 numbers were published, 1833–41. The principal writers were the revs. dr. E. Pusey, J. H. Newman, J. Keble, J. Froude, and I. Williams—all of the University of Oxford. PUSEYISM. The tracts (specially No. 90) were condemned by the authorities at Oxford, 15 Mch. 1841.

traction-engines, locomotive engines for drawing heavy loads, were used on common roads in London in 1860, but afterwards restricted. In Aug. 1862 one of Bray's traction-engines conveyed through the city a mass of iron which would require 29 horses. RAILWAYS.

Trade and Plantations, Board of. Cromwell seems to have given the first notions of a board of trade; in 1655 he appointed his son Richard, with many lords of his council, judges, and gentlemen, and about 20 merchants of London, York, Newcastle, Yarmouth, Dover, etc., to meet and consider by what means the trade and navigation of the republic might be best promoted.—*Thomas's* "Notes of the Rolls." Charles II., on his restoration, established a council of trade for keeping a control over the whole commerce of the nation, 1660; he afterwards instituted a board of trade and plantations, which was remodelled by William III. This board was abolished in 1782; and a new council for the affairs of trade on its present plan was appointed, 2 Sept. 1786.

trade dollar. COIN AND COINAGE, U. S.

trades' unions, England. By 6 Geo. IV. c. 129 (1825), the combination laws were repealed, and other provisions made. As trades' unions formed for maintaining wages, etc., are not recognized by law, a commission (including lord Elcho, Thomas Hughes, and others, with sir Wm. Erle as chairman) was appointed to inquire into their constitution, 14 Feb. 1867, and an act to facilitate its proceedings was passed 5 Apr. following. It reported during the year, disclosing the existence of murderous practices, with much intimidation. MANCHESTER, SHEFFIELD. An act to protect union funds from embezzlement was passed in 1869. A trade-union act passed 29 June, 1871; amended by act passed 30 June, 1876. To counteract the influence of trades' unions, the National Federation of Employers was formed, Dec. 1873. LABOR, American Federation of; WORKINGMEN.

Trafalgar', Cape, S. Spain, off which a great naval victory was gained by the British, under Nelson, over the combined fleets of France and Spain, commanded by adm. Villeneuve and 2 Spanish admirals, 21 Oct. 1805. The enemy's force was 18 French and 15 Spanish vessels, all of the line; that of the British, 27 ships. After a protracted fight, Villeneuve and the other admirals were taken, and 19 of their ships captured, sunk, or destroyed. Nelson was killed, and adm. Collingwood succeeded to the command. Nelson's ship was the *Victory;* and his last signal was, "England expects every man to do his duty." NELSON'S VICTORIES.

Trafalgar square, London, begun 1829; completed 1845. Grand hotel opened by lord mayor, 29 May, 1880.

tragedy. DRAMA, SHAKESPEARE.

Trajan's column (in Rome), erected 114, by the Roman senate and people, to commemorate his victories over the Dacians, and executed by Apollodorus It was built in the square called the *Forum Trajanum*, it is of the Tuscan order, and from its base, exclusive of the statue and pedestal, is 127½ feet high

tram-roads, a road with a track for wheels, now generally made of iron, but formerly of wooden rails or stone As Benjamin Outram father of sir James, the Indian general, in 1800 made improvements in this system of railways for common vehicles in the north of England, the name is sometimes ascribed to him, but it is said to have existed in Derbyshire as early as 1602 The iron tram-road from Croydon to Wandsworth was completed on 21 July, 1801 STREET RAILWAYS

transcenden'talism, the philosophy which finds all reality, not in the observation of external and objective fact, but in the mind and its processes The word was first applied to the teachings of Kant, but more specially and accurately afterwards to those of Schelling and his followers, and in America to the school of Emerson PHILOSOPHY

transfigura'tion, the change of Christ's appearance on mount Tabor, in the presence of Peter, James, and John, 32 A D (Matt. xvii). The feast of the Transfiguration, kept on 6 Aug, was instituted by pope Calixtus II in 1455.

transfusion of blood. BLOOD

transit. MERCURY, SUN, VENUS

translation to heaven The supposed translation of Enoch to heaven at the age of 365 years, 3017 B.C The prophet Elijah was, as some assert, translated to heaven in a chariot of fire, 896 B C The possibility of translation to the abode of eternal life has been maintained by some enthusiasts The Irish House of Commons expelled Mr Asgill for writing a book asserting the possibility of translation to the other world without death, 1703

Transpa'dane republic, comprising Lombardy and part of the Venetian territories, was established by Bonaparte after his victory at Lodi, 10 May, 1796 With the Cispadane republic it merged into the Cisalpine republic, Oct 1797

transporta'tion. British judges were given the power of sentencing offenders to transportation "into any of his majesty's dominions in North America," by 18 Charles II c. 3 (1666), and by 4 Geo I c 11 (1718) Transportation ceased in 1775, but was revived in 1786 The reception of convicts was successfully resisted by the Cape of Good Hope (in 1849) and the Australian colonies (1864) Transportation, even to W Australia, where labor is wanted, ceased after a few years, through the fierce opposition of the eastern colonies. In consequence of the difficulty then experienced in transporting felons, 16 and 17 Vict c 99 was passed, substituting penal servitude, empowering the crown to grant pardon to offenders under certain conditions, and licenses to others to be at large, such licenses to be revoked if necessary, and many have been Such a license is termed "TICKET-OF-LEAVE" The system was assailed in Oct and Nov. 1862, on account of crimes traced to ticket-of leavers. CRIME

John Eyre, esq, a man of fortune, was sentenced to transportation for stealing a few quires of paper (*Phillips*) 1 Nov 1771

Rev dr Halloran, tutor to earl of Chesterfield, transported for forging a frank (10*d* postage) 9 Sept 1818

First transportation of felons to Botany Bay was in May, 1787, where gov Phillip arrived with about 800 on 20 Jan 1788, convicts were afterwards sent to Tasmania, Norfolk Island, etc.

Returning from transportation was punishable with death until 5 Will IV c 67, Aug 1834 afterwards by transportation for life

A shipment of convicts to W Australia (which had already received 10,000) in 1867

transubstan'tiation, the doctrine of the "real presence" That the bread and wine in the Eucharist are changed into the very flesh and blood of Christ by the consecration, was asserted in the days of Gregory III. (731) and by Amalarius and Radbertus (about 830), but denied by Rabanus Maurus, Johannes Scotus Erigena, Berengarius, Wickliffe, and others In the Lateran council, held at Rome by Innocent III., the word "transubstantiation" was used to express this doctrine, decreed to be incontrovertible, all who denied it were condemned as heretics. This was confirmed by the council of Trent, 18 Jan 1562 John Huss, Jerome of Prague, and other martyrs of the Reformation, suffered for denying this dogma, which is renounced by the church of England (28th article), and by all Protestant dissenters. The declaration against transubstantiation, invocation of the saints, and the sacrifice of the mass, on taking any civil office, was abolished in Great Britain by an act passed 25 July, 1867 SACRAMENT.

Luther maintained the doctrine of *consubstantiation*—viz that after consecration, the body and blood of Christ are substantially present in the bread and wine. He was opposed by Bucer, Carlstadt, Zwingle and others (termed sacramentarians), who asserted that the Lord's supper is only a commemorative rite

Transvaal or **South African Republic,** founded by the Dutch farmers (Boers) about 1848 After several years' severe conflict with the natives, its independence was declared, 17 Jan 1858 The executive is vested in a president, elected for 5 years Area, 113,642 sq miles Pop 1890, whites, 119,128, natives estimated at 560,000 Capital, Pretoria

War with the Kaffirs begun, Cetywayo, king, Secocoeni (Sickakuni), an eminent chief July, 1876

Boers assisted by the Amazwasies, a warlike tribe, who check Kaffirs Sept "

Sir T Shepstone well received, a desire expressed for federation, Feb, opposition to it Mch 1877

Anarchy in the Transvaal, annexation (for protection) to the British dominions proclaimed by sir T Shepstone, 12 Apr, he is sworn in as administrator 30 May, "

Great opposition to British rule, appeased after much discussion 12 Apr 1879

Sir G Wolseley appointed governor of Natal, etc May, "

Transvaal declared a crown colony Dec "

Boers meet and claim independence, Bok, Kruger, and Pretorius arrested for signing a document issued by the Boer committee Dec 1879, and Jan 1880

Boers seize Heidelburg, 16 Dec, establish the South African Republic, Paul Kruger, president 17 Dec "

A party of Boers stop at Bronker's Spruit about 250 British troops of the 94th regiment who resist, some killed or wounded, others disarmed and dismissed 20 Dec "

Potchefstrom seized by Boers, who retire when the place is shelled, col Bellairs besieged in it 27 Dec et seq "

South African Republic proclaimed by a triumvirate—Kruger, Joubert, and Pretorius 30 Dec "

Troops sent from Britain, etc Dec 1880, and Jan 1881

Sir George P Colley (appointed governor of Natal, 1880) takes command in the war Jan "

Gen Colley's attack on Laing's Nek, a pass, repulsed with heavy loss 28 Jan "

Severe conflict on the Ingogo river, the British 12 hours under fire, repulsed with heavy loss 8 Feb "

Sir Evelyn Wood brings reinforcements to gen Colley 17 Feb "

Orange Free State proclaims neutrality and mediation, about 22 Feb "

Gen Colley marches in the night to Majuba Hill, defeated and killed after a desperate conflict 27 Feb "

Gen sir F Roberts sent to Africa . 28 Feb "

Armistice proposed by the Boers, accepted for 6–14 Mch, armistice extended, 14 Mch, Boers agree to British terms, 21, 22 Mch, peace proclaimed, the Boers disperse, gen Roberts recalled . 24 Mch "

Potchefstrom surrenders with honors of war, 21 Mch, given up as occupied by mistake Apr "

Vote of censure on the government in commons negatived (314–205) 25, 26 July, "

Commissioners to carry out treaty of peace appointed, 5 Apr, agree to convention ceding virtually all the territory to "The Transvaal State" on 8 Aug, subject to suzerainty of queen Victoria and a British resident, with debt of about 420,867*l*., etc., independence of the Swazies guaranteed, signed by royal commissioners and Martin W Pretorius and Peter J Joubert (Stephen J P Kruger not present), 3 Aug, effected 8 Aug "

Meeting of the Volksraad, 21 Sept, treaty confirmed 25 Oct. "

War with the natives .. 1882–83

Paul Kruger president 1883–88

Amended boundary lines accepted, 2 Feb, convention signed, the republic to be styled the "South African Republic," under British suzerainty 27 Feb 1883

Convention adopted by the Transvaal assembly 8 Aug "

Johannesburg founded by gold miners . 1887

SOUTH AFRICAN WAR.

Transylva'nia, an Austrian province, was part of the ancient DACIA, so named by the Romans, meaning the country beyond the forest In 1526, John Zapoly rendered himself independent of the emperor Ferdinand I by the aid of the Turks. His successors ruled with much difficulty till Jan 1699, when the emperor Leopold I, by the treaty of Carlowitz, finally incorporated Transylvania into the Austrian dominions The Transylvanian deputies did not take their seat in the Austrian parliament till 20 Oct. 1863 A decree for the convocation of the Transylvanian diet was issued 12 Sept 1865 The inhabitants are about 1,100,000 ignorant

Roumanians, 1,500,000 Saxon colonists, and 550,000 Magyars, the last being the ruling class. The union of Transylvania with Hungary in 1848, which has caused much discontent, was ratified by the Transylvanian diet, 25 Dec. 1866.

Trappists, monks of the order of Cistercians. The first abbey of La Trappe in Normandy was founded, in 1140, by Rotrou, comte de Perche. The present order of Trappists owes its origin to the learned Jean le Bouthillier de la Rancé (editor of *Anacreon* when aged 14), who renounced the world and sold all his property, giving the proceeds to the abbey of La Trappe, to which he retired in 1662, to live there in great austerity. After several efforts he succeeded in reforming the monks, and in establishing new rules of silence, prayer, reading, and manual labor, and forbidding study, wine, fish, etc. Rancé was born in 1620, and died in 1700. The Trappists' new building was consecrated in Aug. 1833.

trap-shooting. Shooting at a stuffed parrot on a pole, known as popinjay shooting, was practised by the ancient Greeks; sometimes a living bird was attached to the pole by a cord. Pigeon-shooting, patronized by lord Huntingfield and other noblemen, became fashionable sport in England about 1856. Trap-ball shooting was developed in the United States by Ira Payne and capt. A. H. Bogardus to supplant pigeon-shooting, prohibited by law in many states as cruel.

990 glass balls broken out of 1000 shot at, by A. H. Bogardus (14 yds.), at Bradford, Pa....20 Nov. 1879
5500 glass balls broken out of 5854, at 15 yds., by A. H. Bogardus in New York city....20 Dec. "
99 pigeons killed out of 100 single, 30 yds. rise; A. H. Bogardus, at Coney Island....2 July, 1880
100 single pigeons killed in succession, 30 yds. rise, by Al. Bandle, at Cincinnati, O....25 Dec. 1888
60,000 wooden balls hit, out of 60,670 shot at, by W. F. Carver, at Minneapolis, Minn....24-30 Dec. "
100 single pigeons shot in succession at 28 yds. rise, by A. L. Fulford, at Marion, N. J....17 Nov. 1891

tread-mill, an invention of the Chinese to raise water for irrigating fields. The complicated tread-mill in the prisons of Great Britain is the invention of Mr. (afterwards sir William) Cubitt, of Ipswich. It was erected at Brixton jail, 1817, and soon afterwards in other large prisons.

treason. HIGH-TREASON.

treason, petty, in English law (a term abolished in 1828, defined by the statute of 25 Edw. III. 1352), was a wife's murder of her husband, a servant's murder of his master, and an ecclesiastical person's murder of his prelate or other superior.

treason-felony, Engl. By the Crown and Government Security act, 11 Vict. c. 12 (1848), certain treasons heretofore punishable with death were mitigated to felonies, and subjected to transportation or imprisonment. The Fenians in Ireland were tried under this act.

treasurer of England, Lord high, the third great officer of the crown, a lord by virtue of his office, having the custody of the king's treasure, governing the upper court of exchequer, and formerly sitting judicially among the barons. The first lord high treasurer in England was Odo, earl of Kent, in the reign of William I. This great trust is now confided to a commission of 5 persons, called "lords commissioners for executing the office of lord high treasurer," and of these the chancellor of the exchequer is usually one, the first lord being usually the premier. A third lord of the treasury (Mr. Stansfeld) was appointed, Dec. 1868, succeeded by W. H. Gladstone, Dec. 1869.

First of this rank in Ireland was John de St. John, Henry III. 1217; the last, William, duke of Devonshire, 1766; vice-treasurers were appointed till 1789; then commissioners till 1816, when the revenues of Great Britain and Ireland were united.
First lord high treasurer of Scotland was sir Walter Ogilvie, appointed by James I. in 1420; the last, in 1641, John, earl of Traquair; afterwards commissioners were appointed.

treasury, United States, Secretaries of. UNITED STATES, ADMINISTRATIONS OF.

treaties, compacts or agreements, especially between 2 nations or governments. The first formal written treaty made by England with another nation was at Kingston, between Henry III. and the dauphin of France (then in England), 11 Sept. 1217. The first commercial treaty was with Guy, earl of Flanders, 1274; the second with Portugal and Spain, 1308.—*Anderson.*

MOST IMPORTANT OF FOREIGN TREATIES.

Where concluded.	Treaty.	Date.
Adrianople	Peace: Russia and Turkey	14 Sept. 1829
Aix-la-Chapelle	Peace: France and Spain	2 May, 1668
"	Peace: Terminating the war of the AUSTRIAN SUCCESSION	7 Oct. 1748
Amiens	Peace: Great Britain, Holland, France, and Spain	27 Mch. 1802
Augsburg	Peace of Religion: Catholic and Protestant	15 Sept. 1555
Belgrade	Peace: Turkey and Austria	18 Sept. 1739
Berlin	Settling the Eastern question: Germany, Russia, Turkey, Great Britain, Austria, France, and Italy	13 July, 1878
Bretigny	Peace: England and France	8 May, 1360
Bucharest	Peace: Russia and Turkey	28 May, 1812
Cambray	"Paix des Dames": Francis I. of France and Charles V. of Germany	5 Aug. 1529
Campo Formio	Cession by Austria to France	17 Oct. 1797
Carlowitz	Peace: Turkey with Germany, Russia, Poland, and Venice	26 Jan. 1699
Dresden	Peace: Hungary, Prussia, and Saxony	25 Dec. 1745
Frankfort-on-Main	Peace: France and Germany	10 May, 1871
Hubertsburg	Peace: Saxony, Prussia, and Bavaria	15 Feb. 1763
Kutschouc Kainardji	Independence of Crimea, etc.: Russia and Turkey	July, 1774
London	On behalf of Greece: Great Britain, Russia, and France	6 July, 1827
"	Settlement of Belgian question (5 great powers)	15 Nov. 1831
"	Settling the relations between Turkey and Egypt	15 July, 1840
Luneville	Peace: French Republic and Germany	9 Feb. 1801
Nimeguen	Peace: France and United Provinces	10 Aug. 1678
Nystadt	Cession by Sweden to Russia	30 Aug. 1721
Oliva	Peace: Sweden, Poland, Brandenburg, and Prussia	3 May, 1660
Paris	Cession of Canada to Great Britain by France and Florida by Spain	10 Feb. 1763
"	Peace: Cession by France to Sweden	6 Jan. 1810
"	Peace: France and allied powers	11 Apr. 1814
"	Confiding care of Napoleon (prisoner of war) to England: Signed by Great Britain, Austria, Russia, and Prussia	2 Aug. 1815
"	Peace: Russia, Turkey, England, France, and Sardinia	30 Mch. 1856
Passarowitz	Commercial and land cessions between Germany, Venice, and the Turks	21 July, 1718
Passau	Between Charles V. and the Protestant princes of Germany, granting religious freedom	12 Aug. 1552
Prague	Peace: Ferdinand II. and Saxony	30 May, 1635
"	Peace: Austria and Prussia	23 Aug. 1866
Presburg	Peace: France and Austria	26 Dec. 1805
Pyrenees	Peace: France and Spain	7 Nov. 1659
Ryswick	Peace: England, France, Spain, Holland, and Germany	Sept.-Oct. 1667
San Stefano	Peace: Russia and Turkey	3 Mch. 1878
Tien-Tsin	Peace: France and China	26 June, 1858
"	" " " "	9 June, 1885
Tilsit	Peace: France and Russia	7 July, 1807
Troyes	Stipulating marriage of Henry V. with Catharine, etc.: England, France, and Burgundy	21 May, 1420
Utrecht	Terminating the war of the SPANISH SUCCESSION	11 Apr. 1713
Vienna	Peace: Charles VI. of Germany and Louis XV. of France	18 Nov. 1738
"	Peace: France and Austria	14 Oct. 1809
"	Confirming treaty of Chaumont, 1 Mch. 1814: Great Britain, Austria, Russia, and Prussia	23 Mch. 1815
"	Peace: Austria and Prussia with Denmark	30 Oct. 1864
"	Peace: Austria and Italy	3 Oct. 1866
Westphalia	Ending the Thirty Years' war.	24 Oct. 1648
Zurich	Peace: Austria, France, and Sardinia	10 Nov. 1859

TRE

Other important treaties are mentioned under the following articles:

Abo.
Akerman.
Allahabad.
Antalcidas.
Antwerp.
Armed neutrality.
Arras.
Barrier.
Basel.
Berlin.
Chaumont.
Conflans.
Constantinople.
Fontainebleau.
Fuessen.
Gastein.
Grand alliance.
Hague, The
Holy alliance.
Japan (1858).
Kiel.
Leagues.
Methuen.
Milan.
Munster.
Paris.
Partition treaties.
Peterswald.
Pilnitz.
Quadruple treaty.
Rastadt.
Ratisbon.
Reichenbach.
St. Ildefonzo.
St. Petersburg.
Smalcald.
Stockholm.
Suncion.
Tolentino.
Töplitz.
Transvaal.
Triple alliance.
Ulm.
Valençay.
Versailles.
Vossem.
Warsaw.

PRINCIPAL TREATIES AND CONVENTIONS OF THE UNITED STATES WITH OTHER POWERS (EXCLUSIVE OF POSTAL CONVENTIONS).

NOTE.—Treaties indicated by T. Conventions by C.

Foreign power and object of treaty.	Where concluded.	Date.
Algiers:		
T. Peace and amity	Algiers	5 Sept. 1795
T. " " "	"	6 July, 1815
T. " " "	"	24 Dec. 1816
Argentine Confederation:		
T. Free navigation of Parana and Uruguay	San José	10 July, 1853
T. Friendship, commerce, navigation	"	27 July, "
Austria:		
T. Commerce, navigation	Washington	26 Aug. 1829
T. Commerce and navigation	"	8 May, 1848
C. Extradition	"	3 July, 1856
Austro-Hungary:		
C. Rights of consuls	Washington	11 July, 1870
C. Naturalization	Vienna	20 Sept. "
C. Trade-marks	"	25 Nov. 1871
Baden:		
C. Extradition	Berlin	30 Jan. 1857
T. Naturalization	Carlsruhe	19 July, 1868
Bavaria:		
C. Abolishing droit d'aubaine and taxes on emigration	Berlin	21 Jan. 1845
C. Extradition	London	12 Sept. 1853
T. Citizenship of emigrants	Munich	26 May, 1868
Belgium:		
T. Commerce and navigation	Brussels	10 Nov. 1845
C. Peace, amity, commerce, etc.	Washington	17 July, 1858
C. Completing treaty of 1858	Brussels	20 May, 1863
T. To extinguish Scheldt dues	"	20 July, "
C. Naturalization	"	16 Nov. 1868
C. Trade-marks	"	20 Dec. "
C. Extradition	Washington	19 Mch. 1874
T. Commerce and navigation	"	8 Mch. 1875
C. Consular rights	"	9 Mch. 1880
C. Trade-marks	"	7 Apr. 1884
Bolivia:		
T. Peace, friendship, commerce, navigation	La Paz	13 May, 1858
Borneo:		
C. Peace, friendship, good understanding	Bruni	23 June, 1850
Brazil:		
T. Peace and amity	Rio de Janeiro.	12 Dec. 1828
C. Satisfying U. S. claims	"	27 Jan. 1849
C. Trade-marks	"	24 Sept. 1878
Brunswick and Luxemburg:		
C. Rights of citizens	Washington	21 Aug. 1854
Central America:		
C. Peace, amity, navigation, etc.	Washington	5 Dec. 1825
Chili:		
C. Peace, commerce, and navigation	Santiago	16 May, 1832
C. Arbitration of Macedonian claims	"	10 Nov. 1858
China:		
T. Peace, amity, and commerce	Wang-Hiya	3 July, 1844
T. " " " "	Tien-Tsin	18 June, 1858
C. Adjustment of claim	Shang-Haï	8 Nov. "
C. Additions to treaty of 18 June, 1858	Washington	28 July, 1868
T. Immigration	Peking	17 Nov. 1880
T. Commercial and judicial	"	" "
Colombia:		
C. Peace, amity, commerce, navigation	Bogota	3 Oct. 1824
C. Extradition	"	7 May, 1888
Corea:		
T. Peace, amity, commerce, navigation	Yin-Chuen	22 May, 1882
Costa Rica:		
T. Friendship, commerce, navigation	Washington	10 July, 1851
C. Adjustment of claims	San José	2 July, 1860
Denmark:		
C. Friendship, commerce, navigation	Washington	26 Apr. 1826
C. To indemnify the U. S	Copenhagen	28 Mch. 1830

PRINCIPAL TREATIES AND CONVENTIONS, ETC.—(*Continued.*)

Foreign power and object of treaty.	Where concluded.	Date.
Denmark (continued):		
C. Discontinuance of Sound dues	Washington	11 Apr. 1857
C. Naturalization	Copenhagen	20 July, 1872
Dominican Republic:		
C. Amity, commerce, navigation, extradition	Santo Domingo.	8 Feb. 1867
Ecuador:		
T. Friendship, commerce, navigation	Quito	13 June, 1839
C. Mutual adjustment of claims	Guyaquil	25 Nov. 1862
C. Naturalization	Washington	6 May, 1872
T. Extradition	Quito	28 June, "
Egypt:		
C. Concerning commerce and customs	Cairo	16 Nov. 1884
France:		
T. Alliance	Paris	6 Feb. 1778
T. Amity and commerce	"	" "
C. Payment of loan	Versailles	16 July, 1782
C. Power of consuls	"	14 Nov. 1788
C. Navigation and commerce	Washington	24 June, 1822
C. Claims for indemnity	Paris	4 July, 1831
C. Extradition	Washington	9 Nov. 1843
C. Consular	"	23 Feb. 1853
C. Trade-marks	"	16 Apr. 1869
C. Claims	"	15 Jan. 1880
French Republic:		
C. Terminating difficulties	Paris	30 Sept. 1800
T. Regarding treaty of 27 Oct. 1795	"	30 Apr. 1803
Guatemala:		
C. Peace, amity, commerce, navigation	Guatemala	3 Mch. 1849
German Empire:		
C. Consuls and trade-marks	Berlin	11 Dec. 1871
Great Britain:		
C. Armistice	Versailles	20 Jan. 1783
T. Peace	Paris	3 Sept. "
T. Amity, commerce, navigation	London	19 Nov. 1794
C. Regarding treaty of 1794	"	8 Jan. 1802
T. Peace and amity	Ghent	24 Dec. 1814
C. Regulating commerce	London	3 July, 1815
C. Naval force on great lakes, U.S.	Washington	Apr. 1817
C. Fisheries, northern boundary, etc	London	20 Oct. 1818
T. Indemnification	St. Petersburg	12 July, 1822
C. Award	London	13 Nov. 1826
C. Boundary	"	29 Sept. 1827
T. Boundary, slave-trade, extradition	Washington	9 Aug. 1842
T. Oregon boundary, etc	"	15 June, 1846
C. Nicaragua ship canal	"	17 Apr. 1850
C. Settlement of claims	London	8 Feb. 1853
T. Fisheries, etc	Washington	5 June, 1854
T. Suppression of slave-trade	"	7 Apr. 1862
T. Hudson's bay and Puget's sound claims	"	1 July, 1863
C. Naturalization	London	13 May, 1870
C. Slave-trade	Washington	3 June, "
T. Fisheries, Alabama claims, etc.	"	8 May, 1871
C. Trade-marks	London	24 Oct. 1878
C. Supplementing extradition treaty of 9 Aug. 1842	Washington	12 July, 1889
Greece:		
T. Commerce and navigation	London	10–22 Dec. 1837
Hamburg, Bremen, and Lubeck:		
C. Friendship, commerce, and navigation	Washington	20 Dec. 1827
C. Extending jurisdiction of consuls	"	30 Apr. 1852
Hanover:		
T. Commerce and navigation	Berlin	20 May, 1840
T. " " "	Hanover	10 June, 1846
C. Extradition	London	18 Jan. 1855
T. Stade or Brunshausen dues abolished	Berlin	6 Nov. 1861
Hawaiian islands:		
T. Friendship, commerce, navigation	Washington	20 Dec. 1849
C. Commercial reciprocity	"	30 Jan. 1875
Hayti:		
T. Amity, commerce, navigation, etc	Porte-au-Prince	3 Nov. 1864
Hesse-Cassel:		
C. Droit d'aubaine and tax on emigration abolished	Berlin	26 Mch. 1844
Hesse-Darmstadt:		
T. Naturalization	Darmstadt	1 Aug. 1868
Italy:		
C. Consular	Washington	8 Feb. "
C. Extradition	"	23 Mch. "
T. Commerce and navigation	Florence	26 Feb. 1871
C. Consular privileges	Washington	8 May, 1878
C. Consular rights	"	24 Feb. 1881
Japan:		
T. Peace, amity, commerce, etc.	Kanagawa	31 Mch. 1854
T. Commercial; ports opened	Simoda	17 June, 1857
T. Peace, amity, and commerce	Yedo	29 July, 1858

PRINCIPAL TREATIES AND CONVENTIONS, ETC.—(*Continued.*)

Foreign power and object of treaty.	Where concluded.	Date.
Japan (continued):		
C. Reducing import duties	Yedo	28 Jan. 1864
C. Indemnities. (U. S., Great Britain, France, and Holland sign)	Yokohama	22 Oct. "
C. Regarding expense of shipwrecks	Tokio	17 May, 1880
T. Extradition	"	29 Apr. 1886
Loo-Choo:		
C. Permitting unobstructed trade.	Napa	11 July, 1854
Liberia:		
T. Commerce and navigation	London	21 Oct. 1862
Luxemburg:		
T. Extradition	Berlin	29 Oct. 1883
Madagascar:		
T. Commerce	Antananarivo	14 Feb. 1867
Mexico:		
T. Extradition	Mexico	11 Dec. 1861
C. Adjustment of claims	Washington	4 July, 1868
C. Citizenship of emigrants	"	10 July, "
C. Mutual right to pursue Indians across the boundary	"	29 July, 1882
C. Commercial	"	20 Jan. 1883
C. International boundary	"	12 Nov. 1884
Mexican Republic:		
C. Adjustment of claims	Washington	11 Apr. 1839
T. Peace, friendship, limits	Guadalupe Hildago	2 Feb. 1848
T. Boundary, etc	Mexico	30 Dec. 1853
Morocco:		
T. Peace and friendship		Jan. 1787
T. Peace		16 Sept. 1836
C. To maintain light-house at cape Spartel. (Signed by U. S., Austria, Belgium, Spain, France, Great Britain, Italy, Netherlands, Portugal, Sweden)	Tangier	31 May, 1865
C. Protection (signed by 13 powers)	Madrid	3 July, 1880
Muscat:		
T. Amity and commerce	Muscat	21 Sept. 1833
Nassau:		
C. Abolishing droit d'aubaine	Berlin	27 May, 1846
Netherlands:		
T. Amity and commerce	The Hague	8 Oct. 1782
T. Commerce and navigation	Washington	19 Jan. 1839
C. Commercial	"	26 Aug. 1852
C. Consular	The Hague	22 Jan. 1855
C. "	Washington	23 May, 1878
C. Extradition	"	22 May, 1880
C. "	"	2 June, 1887
New Granada:		
T. Peace, amity, navigation, commerce	Bogota	12 Dec. 1846
C. Consular powers	Washington	4 May, 1850
C. Claims	"	10 Sept. 1857
Nicaragua:		
T. Friendship, commerce, navigation	Managua	21 June, 1867
C. Extradition	"	25 June, 1870
Orange Free State:		
C. Friendship, commerce, extradition	Bloemfontein	22 Dec. 1871
Ottoman Empire:		
T. Commerce and navigation	Constantinople	25 Feb. 1862
C. Extradition	"	11 Aug. 1874
Ottoman Porte:		
T. Friendship		7 May, 1830
Paraguay:		
C. Friendship, commerce, navigation	Asuncion	4 Feb. 1859
Persia:		
T. Friendship and commerce	Constantinople	13 Dec. 1856
Peru:		
C. Peru to pay claims of $300,000.	Lima	17 Mch. 1841
T. Friendship, commerce, navigation	"	26 July, 1851
C. Rights of neutrals at sea	"	22 July, 1856
C. Claims	"	20 Dec. 1862
C. "	"	12 Jan. 1863
C. Adjustment of claims	"	4 Dec. 1868
T. Friendship, commerce, navigation	"	6 Sept. 1870
T. Extradition	"	12 Sept. "
T. Friendship, commerce, navigation	"	31 Aug. 1887
Peru-Bolivia Confederation:		
C. Peace, friendship, commerce, navigation	Lima	30 Nov. 1836
Portugal:		
T. Commerce and navigation	Lisbon	26 Aug. 1840
C. Portugal to pay $91,727 claims, etc.	Washington	26 Feb. 1851
Prussia:		
T. Amity and commerce		July–Sept. 1785

PRINCIPAL TREATIES AND CONVENTIONS, ETC.—(*Continued.*)

Foreign power and object of treaty.	Where concluded.	Date.
Prussia (continued):		
T. Amity and commerce	Berlin	11 July, 1799
T. Commerce and navigation	Washington	1 May, 1828
T. Regulating citizenship of emigrants	Berlin	22 Feb. 1868
Prussia and German Confederation:		
C. Extradition	Washington	16 June, 1852
Roumania:		
C. Consular	Bucharest	5–17 June, 1881
Russia:		
C. Navigation, fishery, boundary.	St. Petersburg	5–17 Apr. 1824
T. Navigation and commerce	"	6–18 Dec. 1832
C. Rights of neutrals	Washington	22 July, 1854
T. Cession of Russian possessions.	"	30 Mch. 1867
Addition to treaty of 1832	"	27 Jan. 1868
T. Extradition	"	21 Apr. 1893
San Salvador:		
T. Amity, navigation, commerce.	Leon	2 Jan. 1850
C. Extradition	San Salvador	23 May, 1870
T. Amity, commerce, consular privileges	"	6 Dec. "
Samoan islands:		
T. Friendship and commerce	Washington	17 Jan. 1878
Sardinia:		
T. Commerce and navigation	Genoa	26 Nov. 1838
Saxony:		
C. Abolition of droit d'aubaine	Berlin	14 May, 1845
Siam:		
T. Amity and commerce	Bankok	20 Mch. 1833
T. Friendship, commerce, etc	"	29 May, 1856
Regulating liquor traffic in Siam.	Washington	14 May, 1884
Spain:		
T. Friendship, limits, navigation.	San Lorenzo el Real	27 Oct. 1795
C. Indemnification	Madrid	11 Aug. 1802
T. Amity, settlement, limits	Washington	22 Feb. 1819
C. Settlement of claims	Madrid	17 Feb. 1834
C. Extradition	"	5 Jan. 1877
Sweden:		
T. Amity and commerce	Paris	3 Apr. 1783
T. Friendship and commerce	Stockholm	4 Sept. 1816
Sweden and Norway:		
T. Navigation, commerce, consular powers	Stockholm	4 July, 1827
C. Extradition	Washington	21 Mch. 1860
C. Naturalization	Stockholm	26 May, 1869
Swiss Confederation:		
C. Abolishing droit d'aubaine and taxes on emigration	Washington	18 May, 1847
C. Friendship, commerce, etc	Berne	25 Nov. 1850
Texas:		
C. Indemnity	Houston	11 Apr. 1838
C. Boundary	Washington	25 Apr. "
Tonga:		
T. Amity, commerce, navigation.	U. S. steamer *Mohican*	2 Oct. 1886
Tripoli:		
T. Peace and friendship	Tripoli	4 Nov. 1796
T. Peace and amity	"	4 June, 1805
Tunis:		
T. Peace and friendship	Tunis	26 Mch. 1799
Two Sicilies:		
C. Regarding depredation of Murat	Naples	14 Oct. 1832
T. Commerce and navigation	"	1 Dec. 1845
C. Rights of neutrals at sea	"	13 Jan. 1855
C. Peace, friendship, commerce, etc	"	1 Oct. "
United Mexican States:		
T. Limits	Mexico	12 Jan. 1828
T. Amity, commerce, navigation.	"	5 Apr. 1831
Venezuela:		
T. Peace, friendship, navigation, commerce	Caracas	20 Jan. 1836
C. Satisfying Aves island claims.	Valencia	14 Jan. 1859
T. Amity, commerce, navigation, extradition	Caracas	27 Aug. 1860
C. Referring claims	"	25 Apr. 1866
Würtemberg:		
C. Abolishing droit d'aubaine and taxes on emigration	Berlin	10 Apr. 1844
T. Naturalization	Stuttgart	27 July, 1868
Zanzibar:		
C. Enlarging treaty with Muscat, 1833	Zanzibar	3 July, 1886

GENERAL CONVENTIONS.

C. With Belgium, Brazil, Dominican Republic, France, Great Britain, Guatemala, Italy, the Netherlands, Norway, Portugal, Salvador, Servia, Spain, Sweden, Swiss Confederation, and Tunis; convention for the protection of industrial property, signed at Paris ....20 Mch. 1883

C. With Belgium, Brazil, Italy, Portugal, Servia, Spain, and Switzerland, for exchange of official documents and literary publications; signed at Brussels...............15 Mch. 1886

C. With Germany, Great Britain and Ireland, general act

for neutrality of Samoan islands, signed at Berlin. 14 June, 1889

C With foreign powers for an international union to publish customs tariffs, signed at Brussels 5 July, 1890

Trebia, now **Trebbia,** a river in N Italy, near the mouth of which Hannibal defeated the Roman consul Sempronius 218 B C, his second battle and victory after crossing the Alps, here also Suwarrow defeated the French marshal Macdonald and compelled him to retreat, 17-19 June, 1799

Treb'izond, formerly **Trape'zus,** a port of Asia Minor in the Black sea, was colonized by the Greeks and became subject to the kings of Pontus It was the first Greek colony reached by the "Ten Thousand Greeks" on their retreat after the battle of Cunaxa It enjoyed self-government under the Roman empire, and when the Latins took Constantinople, in 1204, it became the seat of an empire which endured till 1461 when it was conquered by the Turks under Mahomet II

trees. ARBOR DAY, FLOWERS AND PLANTS. For Charter Oak, CONNECTICUT, 1687 and 1856, and Penn's Treaty Elms' PENNSYLVANIA, 1682

Trent, the ancient *Tridentum* a city of the Tyrol, Austria The council held here is reckoned in the Roman Catholic church as the 18th general council Its decisions have been implicitly received as the standard of faith, morals, and discipline in that church It first sat 13 Dec 1545, and continued (with interruptions) under popes Paul III, Julius III, and Pius IV to 4 Dec 1563, its last sitting, the 25th A jubilee in relation to this council was celebrated in June, 1863

At this council was decreed with anathemas the canon of Scripture (including the Apocrypha) and the church its sole interpreter, the traditions to be equal with Scripture, the seven sacraments (baptism confirmation the Lord's supper, penance, extreme unction, orders and matrimony) transubstantiation, purgatory, indulgences, celibacy of the clergy, auricular confession etc

Trent affair. On 7 Nov 1861, James M Mason of Virginia, Confederate envoy to Great Britain, and John Slidell of Louisiana, accredited to France, embarked at Havana in the British mail steamer *Trent* for England The U S steamship *San Jacinto*, capt Wilkes, was watching for the *Trent* in the Bahama channel, 240 miles from Havana, capt Wilkes having decided, on his own responsibility, to seize the 2 Confederate envoys The *San Jacinto* met the *Trent* on the forenoon of 8 Nov, signalled her to stop in vain, and then fired a shot across her bow Her captain unwillingly allowed Mason and Slidell, with their secretaries, to be taken on board the *San Jacinto* Capt Wilkes reached Boston on 19 Nov, and the 2 ministers were confined in fort Warren. This seizure was received with favor in the U S, but Great Britain demanded from the government at Washington a formal apology and the immediate release of the prisoners, Lord John Russell instructing the minister, lord Lyons, at Washington, 30 Nov 1861, that unless a satisfactory answer were given within 7 days he might, at his discretion, withdraw the legation and return to England This despatch was received on 18 Dec, on the 19th lord Lyons called on Mr Seward, and in a personal interview an amicable adjustment was made possible by the moderation of both diplomats. On 26 Dec Mr Seward transmitted to lord Lyons the reply of the U S, in which the illegality of the seizure was recognized, while the satisfaction of the U S government was expressed in the fact that a principle for which it had long contended was thus accepted by the British government. Mason and Slidell were at once released, and sailed for England 1 Jan. 1862

Trenton, Battle of At the close of Nov. 1776, the British occupied New Jersey, and only the Delaware river shut off Cornwallis from Philadelphia. Washington had crossed the Delaware 2 Dec, securing every boat, so that the British were unable to follow. The British army, in fancied security, held an extended line. A detachment of Hessians, 1500 strong, under col Rahl, with a force of 500 cavalry, were at Trenton, while count Donop, with another force of 2000 men, was at Bordentown. Washington determined to surprise col Rahl On the evening of 25 Dec. 1776, with 2400 men and 20 pieces of artillery, he recrossed the Delaware a few miles above Trenton. Owing to the darkness and the floating ice in the river it was 4 o'clock on the morning of the 26th before the entire force had crossed, and although the Americans did not reach Trenton until after daylight, the enemy were surprised A severe engagement ensued. The British cavalry and some infantry escaped, but about 1000 men with 6 pieces of artillery were captured Among the fatally wounded was col Rahl, the commander Washington recrossed the river to his camp before midnight of the 26th PRINCETON

Trèves (*trāv*) or **Trier,** the Roman *Treviri*, in Rhenish Prussia, was a prosperous city of the Gauls, 12 B C The emperor Gallienus held his court here, 255 A D The church of St Simeon dates from the 4th century Treves was made an electorate in the 14th century, and became subject to the archbishop in 1585 Councils held here 385-1423 The archbishopric is said to have been founded before the 7th century, and to be the oldest in Germany After various changes, Trèves was acquired by Prussia, June, 1815 In 1844, much excitement was occasioned by miracles said to have been wrought by a "holy coat"

"Tria Juncta in Uno" ("three joined in one"), motto of the knights of the military order of the Bath, Engl., signifying "faith, hope, and charity" BATH.

trial (Gr τείρω, Lat *tero*, to wear out, to distress, to afflict) Examination by tests or experiments —The formal examination before a judge and generally before a jury, by means of witnesses in a court of law, as to whether certain alleged facts or charges are true or not, as below Regulations for conducting trials were made by Lothaire and Edric kings of Kent, about 673 to 680 Alfred the Great is said to have begun trials by jury, but there is good evidence of such before his time —*Trial at bar* signifies by the whole court or a plurality of judges This plan was adopted at Bristol after the riots of 1832, also at O Connell's trial, 1844, and arranged for the trial of the claimant of the Tichborne estates for perjury, in Apr. 1873

FAMOUS ENGLISH TRIALS

GUNPOWDER-PLOT conspirators, Digby, R Winter Grant, and Bates, 30 Jan, T Winter, Rookwood, Keys, and Fawkes, 31 Jan, Henry Garnett, Jesuit, at London	3 May,	1606
Earl and countess of Somerset and others for the murder of sir Thomas Overbury		1613
John Felton, for murder of duke of Buckingham, hanged at Tyburn	28 Nov	1628
King Charles I, 20 Jan, beheaded	30 Jan	1649
OATES'S PLOT: Edward Coleman convicted, 27 Nov, William Ireland and other priests	17 Dec.	1678
OATES'S PLOT: Robert Green and others, 10 Feb, Thomas Whitebread and other Jesuits, 13 June, Richard Langhorne, counsellor	14 June,	1679
OATES'S PLOT: Sir George Wakeman, queen's physician acquitted	13 July,	"
OATES'S PLOT: Viscount Stafford convicted	30 Nov -7 Dec.	1681
RYE HOUSE PLOT convicted, William (lord) Russell, 13 July, Algernon Sidney	21 Nov	1683
Charnock, King, and Keys, 18 Mch, sir John Friend and sir William Perkins ("assassination plot")	3 Apr	1696
Capt William Kidd and 3 others, piracy	23 May,	1701
James, earl of Derwentwater, and William, earl of Kenmure, rebellion, Tower hill	24 Feb	1716
John Price the hangman, murder, Bunhill row	21 May,	1718
Jack Sheppard, highwayman, Tyburn	16 Nov	1724
Richard Turpin, highwayman, York	7 or 10 Apr	1739
Jenny Diver, for felony, executed	18 Mch	1740
William Duell, executed for murder at Tyburn, came to life when about to be dissected at Surgeons' hall	24 Nov	"
Lords Kilmarnock and Balmerino, for high treason	28 July,	1746
Mary Hamilton, for marrying with her own sex, 14 wives, 7 Oct		"
Lord Lovatt, 80 years of age, for high treason, beheaded, 9 Mch		1747
Freney, the celebrated Irish robber, who surrendered himself,	9 July,	1749
Amy Hutchinson, burned at Ely, for the murder of her husband	5 Nov	1750
Miss Blandy, for the murder of her father, hanged	3 Mch	1752
Ann Williams, for murder of her husband, burned alive.	11 Apr	1753
Richard William Vaughan, first forger of Bank of England notes	11 May,	1758
Eugene Aram, murder, York	6 Aug	1759
Earl Ferrers, murder of his steward, Tyburn	5 May,	1760
John Perrott, fraudulent bankrupt, Smithfield	11 Nov	1761
Ann Bedingfield, for murder of husband, burned alive	6 Apr	1763
Elizabeth Brownrigg, murder of her apprentice, Tyburn,	14 Sept.	1767
Great cause between the families of Hamilton and Douglas,	27 Feb	1769
Great Valencia cause in Irish house of peers.	18 Mch	1772
Cause of Somerset, the slave (SLAVERY)	22 June,	"
Elizabeth Herring, for the murder of her husband, hanged and burned at Tyburn	13 Sept.	1773
Daniel and Robert Perreau, wine-merchants, forgery, Tyburn,	17 Jan	1776

Rev dr Dodd, found guilty of forging a bond in the name of lord Chesterfield, for 4200*l*. High influence was exerted to save him, but before the council, the minister of the day said to George III, "If your majesty pardon dr Dodd, you will have murdered the Perreaus" . 27 June, 1777

Lord George Gordon, acquitted of high-treason 5 Feb 1781

Warren Hastings, a trial which lasted 7 years and 3 months (HASTINGS'S TRIAL), commenced 13 Feb 1788

Christian Murphy (or Bowman), a woman, strangled and burned for coining 18 Mch 1789

Thomas Paine, political writer and deist, for libels in the "Rights of Man," convicted . 18 Dec 1792

Messrs Hardy, Horne Tooke, Thelwall, and Joyce, for high treason, acquitted 29 Oct. 1794

Parker, mutineer at the Nore, called adm Parker (MUTINY), 27 June, 1797

Sir Harry Brown Hayes, for carrying off Miss Pike of Cork, 13 Apr 1800

Hatfield, for shooting at George III (HATFIELD'S ATTEMPT), 26 June, "

Mutineers at BANTRY BAY, hanged . . 8 Jan 1802

Gov Wall, for cruelty and murder 20 years before (tried under 33 Hen VIII c 23) 20 Jan "

Col Despard and associates, for high treason, hanged on the top of Horsemonger lane jail (DESPARD'S CONSPIRACY), 7 Feb 1803

Robert Aslett cashier at bank of England, for embezzlement and frauds, loss to the bank, 320,000*l.*, acquitted, the bills being invalid 18 July, "

John Hatfield (a rank impostor, who married by deceit the celebrated "Beauty of Buttermere"), forgery, Carlisle 3 Sept. "

Robert Emmett, at Dublin, for high treason, executed next day 19 Sept "

William Cooper, the Hackney monster, for offences against females 17 Apr 1805

Warrington gang, for unnatural offences, executed 23 Aug "

Gen Picton, for torture of Louisa Calderon, to extort confession, at Trinidad (under 42 Geo III c 85) in King's Bench, guilty (new trial, same verdict, 11 June, 1808) 24 Feb 1806

Hon capt Lake, for landing Robert Jeffery, a British seaman, at SOMBRERO, dismissed the service . 10 Feb 1810

Lord Louth, in Dublin, sentenced to imprisonment and fine, for oppressive conduct as a magistrate 19 June, 1811

Berkeley cause house of peers, concluded 28 June, "

Bellingham, for murder of Mr Perceval, prime minister, 15 May, 1812

Hugh Fitzpatrick, for publishing Scully's "History of the Penal Laws" . 6 Feb 1813

Eliza Fenning, poisoning, Old Bailey 26 July, 1815

[Believed to be innocent, she denied her guilt on the scaffold, and thousands accompanied her funeral In the *Annual Register* for 1857, p 143, it is stated, on the authority of Mr Gurney, that she confessed the crime to James Upton, a Baptist minister, before her execution]

Vaughan, a police officer, Mackay, and Browne, for conspiracy to instigate felonies to obtain the reward, convicted, 21 Aug 1816

Hone, bookseller, for parodies, 3 trials before lord Ellenborough, extemporaneous and successful defence 18-20 Dec 1817

Appeal of murder case, Ashford, brother of Mary Ashford, against Abraham Thornton, accused of her murder (APPEALS) and acquitted 16 Apr 1818

Rev dr O Halloran, for forging a frank (TRANSPORTATION), 9 Sept. "

Robert Johnston, at Edinburgh, his dreadful execution, 30 Dec "

Carlile, for publishing Paine's "Age of Reason," etc 15 Oct 1819

Thistlewood, Ings Brunt, Davidson, and Tidd for conspiracy to murder the king's ministers, commenced (CATO STREET CONSPIRACY) . 17 Apr 1820

Queen Caroline, house of lords for adultery, commenced 16 Aug, ended (QUEEN CAROLINE'S TRIAL) 10 Nov "

David Haggart, an extraordinary robber, and a man of eventful life, at Edinburgh, for the murder of a turnkey 9 June, 1821

Josiah Cadman, forgery, hanged . 21 Nov "

"Earl of Portsmouth's case" commenced . 18 Mch 1823

Henry Fauntleroy, banker of London, for forgery, hanged, 30 Oct 1824

Edward Lowe, coining (the last coiner drawn on a sledge to the scaffold), Old Bailey 22 Nov 1827

Capt Charles Montgomery, ordered for execution for forgery, took an ounce and a half of prussic acid to escape the gallows, and was found dead in his cell 4 July, 1828

Burke, at Edinburgh for the Burking murders, Hare, his accomplice, became informer (BURKING) 24 Dec "

Thomas Maynard, the last executed for forgery 31 Dec. 1829

Clune, etc, at Ennis, for cutting out the tongues of the Doyles, 4 Mch 1830

Mr Comyn, for burning his house in county Clare, hanged, 6 Mch "

Rev Robert Taylor (called "the Devil's chaplain") for reviling the Redeemer, convicted . . 6 July, 1831

John Any Bird Bell 14 years of age, for the murder of Richard Taylor aged 13, hanged at Maidstone 1 Aug "

Bishop and Williams, for murder of the Italian boy (BURKING), 3 Dec "

Elizabeth Cooke, for murder of Mrs. Walsh by "burking," 6 Jan. 1832

Rev Edward Irving, by the Scots church for heresy, expelled (IRVINGITES) . . 13 Mch. 1833

Hon G C Norton *v* lord Melbourne, in Common Pleas, for *crim con.* with hon Mrs Norton, acquitted . 22 June, 1836

Edward OXFORD attempts the life of queen Victoria, adjudged insane and confined in Bethlehem 9, 10 July, 1840

Allen Bogle *v* Lawson, publisher of the *Times*, for libel in stating the plaintiff to be connected with bank forgers throughout Europe in schemes to defraud messrs. Glyn & Company, bankers of London, by fictitious letters of credit, damages, one farthing This exposure, so honorable to the *Times*, leads to the *Times testimonial* 16 Aug 1841

Beaumont Smith, for large forgery of exchequer bills, pleads guilty, sentenced to transportation for life 4 Dec "

John FRANCIS, attempt to assassinate queen Victoria 17 June, 1842

Samuel Sidney Smith, forgery, transported for life 29 Nov "

Rev W Bailey LL D, forgery, transported for life 1 Feb 1843

Mary Furley for murder of her child in despair 16 Apr 1844

William Henry Barber, Joshua Fletcher, Georgiana Dorey, William Saunders, and Susannah, his wife, all convicted of forging a will, 15 Apr, sentenced 22 Apr "

[In 1848 Mr Barber returned to England with a free pardon, his innocence acknowledged by his prosecutors, he was readmitted to practice as an attorney, and on 3 Aug 1859, by recommendation of a select committee of the House of Commons, the sum of 5000*l.* was voted him "as a national acknowledgment of the wrong he had suffered from an erroneous prosecution "]

Spanish pirates, for murder of 10 Englishmen at sea 26 July, 1845

Rev dr Wetherall, *for crim con.* with Mrs Cooke, his daughter . . 16 Aug "

Mitchell, the Irish confederate, transported for 14 years (IRELAND) 26 May, 1848

William Smith O'Brien, Meagher, and confederates, sentence, death, afterwards commuted to transportation (pardoned in 1856) 9 Oct "

Gorham *v* the bishop of Exeter, ecclesiastical case, judgment in the court of arches against plaintiff 2 Aug 1849

[The bishop refused to institute Mr Gorham into the living of Brampton Speke, in Devonshire, alleging want of orthodoxy in denying baptismal regeneration, the court held the charge of false doctrine proved Mr Gorham appealed to the judicial committee of the privy council, which pronounced its opinion (8 Mch 1850) that "the doctrine held by Mr Gorham was not contrary or repugnant to the declared doctrine of the church of England and that Mr Gorham ought not, by reason of the doctrine held by him, to have been refused admission to the vicarage of Brampton Speke" On appeal to 3 courts of law, each court refused to interfere, and Mr Gorham was instituted into his vicarage, 7 Aug 1850]

Sloanes, man and wife, for starving their servant, Jane Wilbred . 5 Feb 1851

Sarah Chesham, for poisoning her husband, she had poisoned several of her children and others, hanged 6 Mch "

Doyle *v* Wright, for personal custody of miss Augusta Talbot, a Roman Catholic ward of chancery, before the lord chancellor, protracted case 22 Mch "

Pierce Somerset Butler *v.* viscount Mountgarret, gaining a peerage, defendant being proved illegitimate . Aug 1854

Courts martial on sir E Belcher, capt McClure, etc., for abandoning their ships in the Arctic regions, acquitted Oct "

William Palmer, for murder of J P Cook by poison 14-27 May, 1856

[He was executed at Stafford on 14 June, in the presence of 50,000 persons If he had been acquitted, he would have been tried for the murder of his wife and brother]

Leopold Redpath, for forgeries (to 150,000*l*) upon Great Northern Railway company, transported for life . 16 Jan 1857

Jem Saward, a barrister (called the Penman), William Anderson, and others, convicted of extensive forgery of bankers' checks 5 Mch "

Patience Swynfen *v* F H Swynfen, a will affirmed 27 July, 1858

[Plaintiff was Patience Swynfen, widow of Henry John Swynfen, son of the testator, Samuel Swynfen Her husband died 15 June, 1854, and his father on 16 July following, having made a will 19 days before his death, devising the Swynfen estate (worth about 60,000*l*) to his son's wife, but leaving a large personal estate undisposed of The defendant F H Swynfen, son of the testator's eldest half brother, claimed the estate as heir at law on the ground of the testator's insanity The issue was brought to trial in Mch. 1856, but proceedings were stayed by agreement of Mrs. Swynfen's counsel sir F Thesiger, with the opposite counsel, sir Alexander Cockburn, without her consent, and in defiance of her instructions After various proceedings, the court of chancery ordered a new trial She gained her cause, mainly through the energy of her counsel, Charles R Kennedy, to whom she had promised to pay 20,000*l*, but she married a Mr Broun, and repudiated Mr Kennedy's claim The latter obtained a verdict in his favor on 29 Mch 1862 which was, on appeal, finally reversed in Feb 1864 Mrs. Swynfen was nonsuited in an action brought against her counsel (afterwards lord Chelmsford and lord chancellor), in July, 1859, and June, 1860.]

THELLUSSON will case decided 9 June, 1859

Thomas Smethurst, surgeon, for poisoning Isabella Bankes, whom he had married during his wife's life, convicted, 15-19 Aug "

[He was reprieved on the ground of insufficient evidence, but was convicted of bigamy 16 Nov 1859 On 11 Nov 1862, he proved Miss Bankes's will, and obtained her property]

Eugenia Plummer, 11 years, convicted of perjury against rev Mr Hatch . . . . . 14 May 1860

Thomas Hopley, schoolmaster, convicted of manslaughter of Reginald Cancellor, by flogging 23 July, "

Miss Shedden *v* Patrick (the plaintiff ably pleads her own cause, but fails to prove the legitimacy of her father), 9 Nov et seq "

Thelwall *v* hon maj Yelverton The plaintiff sues for expenses incurred by defendant's wife, the major denies the validity of the marriage, having since married the widow of prof Edward Forbes, the eminent naturalist. The court in Dublin supports the first marriage 21 Feb to 4 Mch 1861

[Miss Longworth endeavored to establish her marriage On appeal, the Scotch court annulled the marriage, July, 1862, and this judgment was affirmed by the House of Lords, 28 July 1864 and again finally, 30 July, 1867 An attempt to set aside the judgment of the House of Lords rejected by the court of session, 29 Oct 1868]

Brook *v* Brook. MARRIAGE The House of Lords on appeal decides against the validity of such a marriage even in a foreign country 18 Mch 1861

Beamish *v* Beamish, the lords on appeal decide that a clergyman cannot celebrate marriage for himself 22 Apr "

Emperor of Austria *v* Day, verdict for plaintiff The defendant printed 100 000 000 florin notes on the bank of Hungary, for Louis Kossuth The notes are ordered to be destroyed within 1 month, 6 May, judgment affirmed, 12 June, "

Cardross case John MacMillan, a free church minister is expelled for drunkenness and misconduct, May, 1858 The Glasgow synod and the general assembly of the free church affirm the sentence On appeal the court of session sets aside the decree (which involved temporalities), asserting that the assembly had only spiritual authority July, "

Martin Doyle, barbarous attempted murder (last execution for this crime) 27 Aug "

Inquiry into sanity of William Frederick Wyndham (on behalf of his relatives) to annul an injudicious marriage, trial lasts 34 days, 140 witnesses examined, verdict, sane mind 16 Dec 1861, and 30 Jan 1862

[Each party to pay its own costs, Mch 1862]

Capt Robertson, by court martial, convicted of submitting to ungentlemanly conduct from his brother officers, 30 days' inquiry ended 24 Mch "

[The court severely criticised, and sentence annulled.]

Queen on appeal of earl of Cardigan *v* col Calthorpe, for libel, charging the earl with deserting his men at Balaklava, 25 Oct 1855, verdict for defendant (who, however, admits his error) 9, 10 June, 1863

Attorney general *v* Sillim and others, for building the *Alexandra* for the confederates, against the Enlistment act, verdict for defendants 25 June, "

[Decision affirmed on appeal to lords, 6 Apr 1864]

Franz Müller, for the murder of Mr Briggs in a railway carriage, 9 July, convicted 27–29 Oct 1864

Queen *v* William Rumble for infringement of Foreign Enlistment act, in equipping the *Rappahannock* for the Confederate government, acquitted 4 Feb 1865

Bishop Colenso's appeal to privy council, decision of bishop of Capetown, deposing him, is annulled 21 Mch "

Trials of Fenians for treason felony, Thomas Clarke Luby, sentenced to 20 years' penal servitude, 28 Nov -1 Dec., O Leary and others convicted, O'Donovan Rossa (previously convicted) sentenced to imprisonment for life, 13 Dec; others convicted at Cork (TRIALS, U S, 30 June, 1885) Dec "

Ryves & Ryves *v* the attorney general, an endeavor to prove the marriage of king George III with Hannah Wilmot, and that of his brother Henry, duke of Cumberland, with Olive Wilmot, the jury decides against the claim, and that Olive Serres the alleged mother of Mrs Ryves, was not the legitimate daughter of the duke of Cumberland, and that the 82 documents brought in evidence were forged (Mrs Ryves d 7 Dec. 1871) 13 June, 1866

Banda and Kirwee prize case (Indian mutiny), court of admiralty awards 700 000*l*, to be divided among the soldiers of gens Whitelocke, Rose, Roberts, and others 30 June "

Bishop Colenso *v* Gladstone and others, trustees of colonial bishopric fund (for withholding his stipend), verdict for plaintiff, with costs. 6 Nov "

George Druitt, M Lawrence, and John Anderson, leaders of the operative tailors' association, convicted of a misdemeanor (organizing the system of "picketing," or watching men on strike, and intimidating non-unionists, which began 24 Apr 1867) .. 21 Aug 1867

Thirteen tailors convicted of "picketing" . 22 Aug "

Rigby Wason *v* Walter (for publication of an alleged libel in the *Times*—viz, a correct report of a debate in the House of Lords, etc), verdict for defendant, settling that such a report is privileged . 18–20 Dec "

[Reaffirmed, 25 Nov 1868 Mr Wason d July, 1875]

Martin *v* Mackonochie (for ritualistic practices), before dean of arches 4 Dec 1867, closed . . 18 Jan 1868

Flamank *v* Simpson, similar case, begun 5 Feb, verdict against elevation of sacrament, use of incense, and mixture of water with wine in the communion . 28 Mch "

Trial of FENIANS for Clerkenwell outrage, begun 20 Apr, all acquitted except Michael Barrett . 20–27 Apr "

Barrett's the last public execution in England 26 May, "

Lyon *v* Home (the spiritual medium) The plaintiff, a widow, seeks to recover 60,000*l* stock, given to Home at the alleged command of her husband's spirit, between Oct 1866 and Feb. 1867, instituted 15 June, 1867, trial, 21 Apr to 1 May, 1868, judgment for plaintiff, by the vice chancellor, sir G M. Giffard, 22 May, "

[The judge said of spiritualism, "the system, as presented by the evidence, is mischievous nonsense, well calculated on the one hand to delude the vain, the weak, the foolish, and the superstitious, and on the other to assist the projects of the needy and the adventurer "]

Mornington *v* Wellesley, and Wellesley *v* Mornington, 29 years in chancery, decided (costs above 30,000*l*.), 22 000*l*. awarded the countess of Mornington . . 7 May, "

Thomas Wells, for murder of Mr Walsh, station-master at Dover (*first private execution*) .. ..13 Aug "

Chronford *v* Lingo female suffrage declared illegal 7-9 Nov 1868

Baxter *v* Langley Sunday evening lectures declared not illegal . 19 Nov "

Cooper *v* Gordon, verdict for plaintiff, vice chancellor decides that the majority of a congregation of dissenters may dismiss their minister for any cause 28 May, 1869

Smith *v*. Earl Brownlow after long litigation, decision against the enclosure of the common at Berkhampstead by lord of the manor 14 Jan. 1870

Sir Charles Mordaunt *v* lady Mordaunt and others, for divorce preliminary trial of her sanity (declared insane, 30 Apr 1869), 16–25 Feb 1870, appeal, 27 Apr 1870, judgment affirmed, 2 June, "

Bishop Goss (Roman Catholic) *v* Hill and Whittaker will case, Mr Moreton's will, bequeathing the chief of his property to the bishop, set aside 16 June, "

Phillips *v* Eyre, for imprisonment during Jamaica rebellion, verdict for defendant. 23 June, "

Michael Davitt and John Wilson, treason felony (FENIANS), 18 July, "

Tichborne Case

Tichborne *v* Lushington the plaintiff declared himself to be sir Roger Charles Tichborne, supposed to have been lost at sea, and claimed the baronetcy and estates, worth about 24 000*l* a year

Roger Charles Tichborne, son of sir James, born 1829

Educated in France till about 1843

Enters the army 1849

Proposes marriage to his cousin Kate Doughty, declined Jan 1852

Sails from Havre for Valparaiso (Mch), and arrives there, 19 June, 1853

Sails from Rio Janeiro in the *Bella*, which founders at sea, 20 Apr 1854

[In a chancery suit his death was legally proved]

His mother advertises for her son 19 May, 1865

Claimant (found by Gibbes and Cubitt in Australia) asserts that he, saved with 8 others from the wreck, went to Australia, and lived there, roughly, 13 years under the name of Castro, marries as Castro, Jan, as Tichborne 3 July, 1866

He is accepted by the dowager lady Tichborne as her son at Paris Jan 1867

[No others of the family accepted him, but sir Clifford Constable and some brother officers did]

His claim is resisted on behalf of sir Henry (a minor), son of sir Alfred Tichborne, and after chancery proceedings (begun Mch. 1867) a trial begins in the court of Common Pleas before chief justice Bovill 11 May, 1871

Claimant is examined 22 days, the trial adjourns on 40th day, 7 July, resumed 7 Nov, case for claimant closes 21 Dec. "

Trial resumed 15 Jan, the attorney general sir J D Coleridge, speaks 26 days on 4 Mch the jury express themselves satisfied that the claimant is not sir Roger, on the 103d day he is declared nonsuited 6 Mch 1872

[Case said to have cost the estate nearly 92,000*l*]

He is lodged in Newgate to be tried for perjury, 7 Mch, indicted as Thomas Castro, otherwise Arthur Orton for perjury and forgery . 9 Apr "

Court of Queen's Bench decides that he may be admitted to bail, 23 Apr, released 26 Apr "

Trial of the claimant for perjury and forgery begun before chief justice Cockburn, and justices Mellor and Lush at bar, 23 Apr, case for the prosecution closes, 10 July, resumed (for defence) 21 July, "

Lady Doughty, mother of sir Henry Tichborne dies 13 Dec "

[Up to 27 June (47th day of the trial) out of 150 witnesses above 100 had sworn that the claimant was not Tichborne, and about 40 that he was Arthur Orton]

Guildford Onslow and G H Whalley, M P's fined for contempt of court in speeches of 20 Jan, Mr Skipworth, barrister, for same offence, imprisoned 3 months and fined, claimant to give securities for 1000*l* for a similar offence 29 Jan 1873

Claimant forbidden to attend public meetings. 19 Sept "

Cheltenham Chronicle fined 150*l*. for commenting on trial, 23 Sept. "

Case for defence closes on 124th day, 27 Oct., adjourns from 31 Oct to 17 Nov, then to 27 Nov, rebutting evidence heard, 27, 28 Nov "

Dr Kenealy's summing up, 2 Dec. 1873–14 Jan 1874, Mr Hawkins's reply .. 15–28 Jan 1874

[Mr Whalley, M P, fined for contempt of court, 250*l*, 23 Jan]

Chief justice's summing up 29 Jan –28 Feb "

Verdict that the claimant did falsely swear that he was Roger Charles Tichborne, that he seduced Catherine N E Doughty in 1851, and that he was not Arthur Orton, sentence, 14 years' imprisonment with hard labor 28 Feb "

[Longest trial known in England]

Charles Orton declares the claimant to be his brother Arthur, at the *Globe* office 10 Mch. "

Jean Luie (Lindgren) and "capt." Brown for perjury in the Tichborne trial, get 7 years and 5 years penal servitude, 9, 10 Apr "

New trial refused Orton by the judges. 29 Apr "

On appeal, sentence affirmed by the lords 10, 11 Mch 1881

Released on TICKET OF LEAVE 20 Oct 1884

Rev John Selby Watson, eminent scholar, kills his wife in passion, 8 Oct, convicted and imprisoned for life 10–12 Jan 1872

Baker *v* Loader, widow, to whom 107,000*l* had been bequeathed, in 10 years is reduced to poverty by imposition, she sues the widow of her friend Loader and solicitors, vice chancellor Malins orders deeds to Loader to be cancelled, the solicitor to pay his own costs ..20 Nov "

Andrews v Salt, decision by lord chancellor that a child shall be educated as a Protestant by grandmother not by Roman Catholic uncle, confirmed on appeal 6 May, 1873

Mordaunt v Moncrieff (see 1870), divorce court 3 judges hold insanity no bar to suit for divorce, 2 judges that it is. 15 May, "

Rev O'Keeffe v cardinal Cullen (for libel and virtually suspending him from his office), consideration of demurrer, judges (at Dublin) disagree 3 hold that the papal ordinance on which the cardinal relied was prohibited by the statutes of Elizabeth, demurrer set aside, 7 May, the trial begun 12 May, verdict for plaintiff, 1 farthing damages 27 May, "

[Mr O Keeffe submitted to the cardinal May 1876]

Todd v Lyne (father Ignatius), son of the plaintiff rescued from convent (where he had taken vows) by chancery. 25 July, "

Bank forgery Austin Biron Bidwell, George Macdonnell, George Bidwell and Edwin Noyes Americans, forge bills for discount at bank of England, West Branch and obtain 102,217*l*., detected through not dating one bill, convicted, penal servitude for life (vain effort to escape by bribing warders) 18-26 Aug "

Epping forest case decision against the enclosures of the lords of the manor as illegal (COMMONS) 10 Nov "

Rubery v baron Albert Grant and M B Sampson (long city editor of the *Times*) for libel, the *Times*, 18, 20 Nov and 20 Dec. 1872, charged Rubery with fraud in a diamond mine in Colorado, 10 days' trial, Grant cleared, Sampson fined 500*l* 18 Jan 1875

[These articles protected the public from a bad scheme]

Alleged false prospectus case (Canadian Oil works corporation), Charlton v sir John Hay, Mr Eastwick and others grossly deceived, 17 days' trial, jury divided, discharged, no verdict 24 Feb "

[Oil wells in Ontario, Canada property of Prince's company got up to buy them by Longbottom scheme not accepted in the City, taken up at West End, sir John Hay M'Cullagh Torrens, Mr Eastwick and others induced to become directors, wells bought, company collapsed]

Mordaunt v Mordaunt and viscount Cole (see above, May, 1874), divorce granted 11 Mch "

Terry v Brighton Aquarium company, for opening on Sundays, verdict, penalty 200*l* (SUNDAY) 27 Apr "

Keith Johnston v proprietors of *Athenæum*, for libel in criticism of an atlas, Edinburgh, damages 1275*l*, 24 Mch, new trial, damages 100*l* 16 June, "

Jenkins v rev Flavel Cook (for exclusion from communion for heresy [denying personality of Satan and eternal punishment], verdict for defendant in court of arches) 16 July, "

Col Valentine Baker sentenced to fine of 500*l*. and 12 months' imprisonment for indecent assault on Miss Dickenson in a railway carriage (afterwards enters the service of the khedive of Egypt, where he is made a pacha and dies 17 Nov 1887, aged 62 years) (EGYPT) 2 Aug "

W K Vance and Ellen Snee, conspiracy to murder (ostensibly herself), singular case, sentenced to imprisonment, 1 June, 1876

Lewis v Higgins, for alleged slander in speech as counsel, verdict for defendant, affirming privilege of counsel 4 Dec "

Queen v Charles Bradlaugh and Annie Besant, for publication of "Fruits of Philosophy," by Dr Knowlton, which they defend, on grounds of humanity, in long speeches, verdict, the book calculated to deprave, but not intended, 18-21 June, sentence (defendants not submitting to the court), 6 months' imprisonment, 200*l* fine for both, 28 June, appeal, alleging informality, disallowed by Queen's Bench 16 Nov 1877

Forged leases Frederick Dimsdale solicitor, Charles Burrell Moore, clerk, and others, forge leases, and borrow money on them (above 300,000*l*), many lenders do not appear, plead guilty, sentence, Dimsdale, penal servitude for life, Moore, 7 years, others less 16, 17 Jan 1878

Madame Rachel (Levison or Leverson), convicted of misdemeanor, obtains money and jewels from Mrs Pearce, for "beautifying," 5 years' penal servitude 10, 11 Apr "

In re Agar Ellis, the husband's promise before marriage that his children should be brought up Romanists, permitted to be withdrawn by chancery 6 Aug "

Paul and others v Summerhayes, appeal, sentence against plaintiffs affirmed (fox hunters may not trespass), Queen's Bench 16 Nov "

Whistler v Ruskin, for libellous criticism in "Fors Clavigera," 1 farthing damages 25, 26 Nov "

Rev Christopher Newman Hall v Mrs Hall and Mr Richardson, long trial, divorce granted 8 Aug 1879

Adolphus Rosenberg, for libelling Mrs Langtry and Mrs West, in *Town Talk*, 18 months' imprisonment 25-27 Oct. "

Phillips, surgeon, v S W Railway company for injury, awarded 7000*l*. by justice Field, new trial, awarded 16,000*l*. by lord chief justice Coleridge, Common Pleas, 3d trial refused, 6 Dec "

Debenham & Freebody v Mellon, appeal, lords decide that a husband who supplies his wife with proper means is not responsible for her debts. 27 Nov 1880

Dysart peerage legitimacy case Wm John Manners claims by an English marriage of lord Huntingtower, Albert Edwin Tollemache by a Scotch marriage (not proved), House of Lords . 7 Mch 1881

Spiritualist case Susan Wills Fletcher (wife of a spiritualist doctor in America) for obtaining, by false pretences, about 10,000*l*. (in jewelry, etc.) of Mrs Hart Davies, 12 months' imprisonment with hard labor . . 12 Apr "

Johann Most, for libel against Alexander II of Russia, and incitement to murder in the *Freiheit* for 19 Mch, 25 May, sentence affirmed on appeal, 18 June, 16 months' imprisonment with hard labor 29 June, 1881

Phœnix park murders (IRELAND) Apr -May, 1883

Dynamite plot Thomas Gallagher Henry Wilson, John Curtin and Alfred Whitehead for treason felony, sentenced to penal servitude for life 11-14 June, "

Patrick O'Donnell, for murder of James Carey, the informer (IRELAND) 30 Nov -1 Dec "

Earl v countess of Euston, for divorce because she had a husband living when married, but that husband had a wife living when he married her, and divorce is refused 4 Apr 1884

Adams v hon B Coleridge, for libel in a letter to miss M Coleridge, verdict for plaintiff, 3000*l*, set aside by judge Manisty, the letter being privileged 21, 22 Nov "

Edmund Yates sentenced to 4 months' imprisonment for libel of earl Lonsdale (in the *World*), July, 1883-Apr 1884, appeal disallowed 16 Jan 1885

Irving Bishop fined 10,000*l* for libel (THOUGHT READING), 15 Jan "

John Lee, footman, for murder of miss Emma A W Keyse, his mistress (at Babbicombe near Torquay, 15 Nov), 2-4 Feb, to be hanged at Exeter, but the drop fails 3 times, and Lee is reprieved 23 Feb "

Earl of Durham's petition to annul his marriage for insanity of the wife at the time, dismissed by sir James Hannen after 8 days' trial 10 Mch "

W T Stead editor of *Pall Mall Gazette* (3 months' imprisonment), Sampson Jacques, assistant (1 month), Bramwell Booth, of Salvation Army (acquitted), Rebecca Jarrett (6 months), and Louisa Mourey (6 months with hard labor), for complicity in abduction, etc, of Eliza Armstrong under 16 23 Oct -10 Nov "

Crawford v Crawford, divorce decreed, 12 Feb, confirmed, charges against sir Charles Dilke denied by him, but accepted by jury 23 July, 1886

Mary Lena Sebright (formerly Scott) v Arthur Sebright, a marriage contract by plaintiff under terror annulled, 16 Nov "

Adams v lord Coleridge and his son, the hon B Coleridge, for libel in letters sent to an arbitrator (lord Monkswell), wrongly delivered, verdict for defendants 17-25 Nov "

Lord and lady Colin Campbell divorce, double suit (after judicial separation), dismissed 27 Nov -20 Dec. "

Prof Caird v Syme (a bookseller), after conflicting decisions in lower courts the lords on appeal, hold unauthorized publication of university lectures unlawful 13 June, 1887

Cunninghame Graham, M P and John Burns for assaulting police etc, on 13 Nov 1887 (RIOTS), convicted of unlawful assembly, 6 weeks' simple imprisonment 16-18 Jan 1888

Slater v Slater, a chancery forgery, court defrauded of 4000*l*, property of miss Rose Maud Maxwell, by William Bowden, a solicitor's clerk, the money ordered repaid to her by the court, Bowden in Nebraska, John Francis Lidiard, a solicitor, his friend, to repay the court 4 Feb "

Marquis of Abergavenny v bishop of Llandaff, bishop's refusal to induct the rev Robert W Gosse, ignorant of the Welsh language, sustained 22 Feb "

O'Donnell v Walter and another (for libel in the *Times*), verdict for defendants (PARNELL) 2-5 July, "

Regent's park murderers July, "

Anthony Isidor Glika sentenced to 10 years' penal servitude for defrauding his employers, messrs Vagliano Bros, and the Bank of England, of 71,500*l*, 27 June-7 July, the Queen's Bench division throws the loss on the bank 2 Nov "

[Sentence confirmed by court of appeal, 21 May, 1889, reversed by lords, 5 Mch 1891]

Charles Richardson and Edgell confess burglary at Edlingham vicarage, near Alnwick, on 7 Feb 1879, sentence, 5 years' penal servitude 24 Nov "

[Michael Brannagham and Peter Murphy, wrongfully convicted of this crime, with attempt to murder, and sentenced to penal servitude for life, Apr 1879, received 800*l*. each as compensation, Dec 1888, police acquitted of perjury, confession of Richardson and Edgell doubted, Feb 1889]

Florence Elizabeth Maybrick, for poisoning her husband, James Maybrick, at Aigburth, by arsenic, tried at Liverpool by justice Stephen, 21 July-7 Aug, sentence of death commuted to penal servitude for life 22 Aug 1889

Herbert J Gladstone v col George B Malleson, for libel in *Allahabad Morning Post*, damages awarded 1000*l* 16 Jan 1890

Crewe murder Richard and George Davies, aged 19 and 16, kill their father, Richard Davies, a clothier, 25 Jan, while riding home in a pony chaise, trial 20-21 Mch, Richard executed, George reprieved (penal servitude for life). 8 Apr "

Miss Gladys Knowles v. Leslie Duncan, proprietor and editor of the *Matrimonial News*, for breach of promise of marriage, damages awarded, 10,000*l* . 11, 12 Aug "

Capt. O'Shea v. Mrs C. O'Shea and C S Parnell, M.P., divorce granted . 15-17 Nov "

Baccarat case sir William Gordon Cumming v Mr and Mrs. Lycett Green and others, for slander, charging him with cheating at baccarat, in the house of Arthur Wilson, Tranby Croft, near Doncaster, Sept 1890, for plaintiff, sir Edward Clarke, for defendants, sir Charles Russell and others, Queen's Bench division, lord Coleridge, prince of Wales a witness, verdict for defendants. . . 1-9 June, 1891

Berkeley peerage case decided . . 31 July, "

Miss Ethel Florence Elliot (afterwards Mrs. Osborne) v major and Mrs. Hargreaves, for slanderous charge of stealing jewels while their guest at Torquay, 9-18 Feb, verdict by consent for defendants. 15-22 Dec. "

[It was proved that miss Elliot sold the jewels to messrs

Spinks, in Gracechurch street, for 550*l*, 19 Feb, cashed the check for gold at the bank of Glyn, Mills & Co, 23 Feb, through messrs Benjamin of Conduit street, W, changed gold for bank notes, at the National and Provincial bank, in St James's square, early in Mch, endorsed one of these notes for 50*l* and paid it to messrs Maple, and it passed into the Bank of England On information to justice Denman the trial was suspended 19 Dec It was admitted by all that capt Osborne plaintiff's husband acted honorably throughout Mrs Osborne, for larceny and perjury, was sentenced to 9 months' imprisonment with some hard labor, 9 Mch, released in the summer, 1892 The jewels were sold by auction for major Hargreaves for 1076*l*, 29 Mch 1892]

Alexander Jacob jeweller of Simla, charged at Calcutta by the Nizam of Hyderabad of criminally misappropriating 23 lacs of rupees (above 100,000*l*) deposited as earnest money for purchase of the "imperial diamond," after a long trial, acquitted 22 Dec 1891

Concha, pauper, *v* Concha and wife, intricate property suits, begun in 1858, the lords vary the decision of the court of Appeal 28 Mch 1892

Mrs Montague sentenced at Dublin to 1 year's imprisonment for manslaughter in killing her daughter, aged 3 4 Apr "

Melbourne murder Frederick Bailey Deeming (alias Albert Oliver Williams) marries Emily Mather at Liverpool 17 Oct, brings her to Australia 15 Dec, kills her at Windsor near Melbourne about 25 Dec 1891, convicted 28 Apr -2 May, executed 23 May, "

[In Feb 1881, he married Marie James went with her to Sydney was there convicted of fraud in 1882, he took Dinham Villa, Rainhill, near Widnes, Lancashire, Engl, 23 July, 1891 and there murdered his wife and 4 children about 26, 27 July 1891, so the coroner's jury found, 28 Mch 1892 WHITECHAPEL]

Mrs Carhill *v* the Carbolic Smoke Ball company, recovers 100*l* promised by the company to any person who used the smoke ball in vain to prevent influenza (by advertisement 13 Nov 1891) 4 July, "

Mr Bottems contractor, *v* Corporation of York, court of Appeals requires plaintiff to fulfil a ruinous contract 16 July, "

TRIALS IN THE UNITED STATES

Anne Hutchinson, sedition and heresy (the Antinomian controversy) imprisoned and banished (MASSACHUSETTS) 1637

Trials of QUAKERS in Massachusetts 1656–61

Jacob Leisler, New York, convicted and executed for treason (NEW YORK) 16 May, 1691

Trials for WITCHCRAFT, Massachusetts 1692

Thomas Maule, for slanderous publications and blasphemy, Massachusetts 1696

Nicholas Bayard, treason 1702

John Peter Zenger, for printing and publishing libels on the colonial government, Nov 1734, acquitted (NEW YORK) 1735

Michael Corbett, Massachusetts, murder on the high seas, discharged 1767

William Wemms, James Hartegan, William McCauley, and other British soldiers, in Boston, Mass, for the murder of Crispus Attucks, Samuel Gray, Samuel Maverick, James Caldwell, and Patrick Carr (BOSTON MASSACRE) 5 Mch 1770

Col David Henley, Massachusetts, for improper conduct as an officer of the army, discharged 1778

Maj-gen Charles Lee, court martial after the battle of Monmouth, found guilty of, 1st, disobedience of orders in not attacking the enemy, 2d, unnecessary and disorderly retreat, 3d, disrespect to the commander in chief, suspended from command for 1 year, tried 4 July, "

Bathsheba Spooner and others, for murder of Joshua Spooner, Massachusetts, convicted "

John Hett Smith, for assisting Benedict Arnold, New York, not guilty 1780

Maj John André, adjutant general, British army seized as a spy at Tappan, N Y, 23 Sept 1780, tried by military court and hung (NEW YORK) 2 Oct "

Sweeting (Whiting) at Albany, for murder of Darius Quimby, executed 16 Aug 1791

Gideon Henfrield, convicted of illegal privateering, Pennsylvania 1793

John E Guinett, convicted of illegal privateering, Pennsylvania, 1795

Stewart, Wright, Porter, Vigol, and Mitchell, western insurgents, found guilty "

William Blount, U S Senate, impeached for misdemeanor 1797

William Corbett, for libelling the king of Spain and his ambassador, writing as Peter Porcupine in *Porcupine's Gazette*, 17 July, before Supreme court of Pennsylvania, acquitted "

Francis Villato, for illegal privateering, discharged "

John Haner and others, for murder of Francis Shitz, Pennsylvania, executed 1798

Robert Worrell, bribery, imprisoned "

Thomas Cooper of Northumberland, Pa., convicted under the Sedition act of libel on the administration of pres Adams in Reading *Advertiser* of 26 Oct. 1799, imprisonment for 6 months and $400 fine 1799

Duane, Reynolds, Moore, and Cumming acquitted of seditious riot, Pennsylvania "

Anthony Haswell, publisher of *Vermont Gazette*, for libel, fine of $200 and 60 days in jail "

Matthew Lyon convicted in Vermont, Oct 1798, of writing for publication a letter calculated "to stir up sedition and to bring the president and the government into contempt," confined 4 months in Vergennes jail, fine of $1000 paid by friends and Lyon released 9 Feb. "

Isaac Williams, illegal privateering, Connecticut 1799

J T Callender, for libel of pres Adams in a pamphlet, "The Prospect Before Us," tried at Richmond, Va, fined $200, and sentenced to 9 months' imprisonment (UNITED STATES), 6 June, 1800

Thomas Daniel, for opening letters of a foreign minister "

Levi Weeks, for the murder of Gulielma E Sands, (Manhattan well murder) 31 Mch - 2 Apr 1801

["Norman Leslie," a novel by T S Fay, founded on this case]

Jason Fairbanks, for murder of miss Elizabeth Fales "

Judge John Pickering impeached before the U S Senate, 3 Mch 1803, for malfeasance in the New Hampshire District court in Oct and Nov 1802, in restoring ship *Eliza*, seized for smuggling, to its owners, judge Pickering though doubtless insane, is convicted and removed from office 4 Mch 1804

Joshua Nettles and Elizabeth Cannon, for the murder of John Cannon night of 24 Oct "

Judge Samuel Chase impeached before the U S Senate, acquitted (UNITED STATES, 1804) 1805

William S Smith and Samuel G Ogden tried for misdemeanors in New York in Circuit court of the U S July, 1806

Thomas O Selfridge tried for murder of Charles Austin on the Public exchange in Boston 4 Aug "

Aaron Burr, for treason, Virginia, acquitted (BURR'S CONSPIRACY), 27 Mch -7 Sept 1807

Mary Cole, for murder of Agnes S Teaurs 1812

Col Thomas H Cushing, by court martial at Baton Rouge, on charges of brig gen Wade Hampton "

King of Spain *v* D Parish, for $180 000 duties on trade between the Spanish colonies and the U S by license of Spanish crown, plaintiff nonsuited at Philadelphia. 8-21 Apr "

Patrick Byrne, for mutiny, by general court-martial at fort Columbus, sentenced to death 22 May, 1813

Gen W Hull commanding the northwestern army of the U S, for cowardice in surrender of Detroit 16 Aug, etc, by court martial, held at Albany, sentenced to be shot, sentence approved by the president, but execution remitted (UNITED STATES) 3 Jan 1814

Levi and Laban Kenniston, for highway robbery of maj Elijah P Goodridge, Massachusetts 19 Dec 1816, acquitted 1817

[Daniel Webster for the defence]

Dartmouth college case, defining the power of states over corporations . 1817-18

[Daniel Webster for the college.]

ARBUTHNOT and AMBRISTER, by court martial, 26 Apr 1818, for inciting Creek Indians to war against the U S, executed by order of gen Jackson 30 Apr 1818

Stephen and Jesse Boorn, at Manchester, Vt, Nov 1819, for the murder of Louis Colvin, who disappeared in 1813, sentenced to be hung 28 Jan 1820

[Six years after Colvin disappeared, an uncle of the Boorns dreamed that Colvin came to his bedside, declared the Boorns his murderers, and told where his body was buried, this was 27 Apr 1819 The Boorns were arrested, confessed the crime circumstantially, were tried and convicted but not executed, because Colvin was found alive in New Jersey Wilkie Collins's novel, "The Dead Alive," founded upon this case]

Robert M Goodwin, for manslaughter in killing James Stoughton, esq, in Broadway, New York "

Michael Powers, for the murder of Timothy Kennedy "

Daniel D Farmer, for murder of Anna Ayer, at Goffstown, 4 Apr 1821

James Prescott, judge of probate for county of Middlesex, impeached before the senate of Massachusetts "

Israel Nelson, and Isaac Thayer, brothers, "the three Thayers," arrested in Boston, Erie county, N Y for murder of John Love, a lake carrier and petty money lender who held their notes for $250, and whose body was found buried near the Thayers's dwelling Tried at court house in Buffalo, 21 to 24 Apr, and hung 17 June, 1825

Capt David Porter, by court martial at Washington, for exceeding his powers, in landing 200 men on Porto Rico and demanding an apology for arrest of the commanding officer of the *Beadle*, sent by him, Oct 1824 to investigate alleged storage of goods on the island by pirates, suspended for 6 months 7 July, "

People *v* Henry Eckford, Joseph G Swift, Matthew L. Davis, etc, at court of Oyer and Terminer, New York 26 Sept. 1826

Jesse Strang, for murder of John Whipple, Albany, N Y 1827

Alexander Drew, drunkenness 1828

George Swearingen, for murder of his wife, hanged 1829

John F Knapp, murder of Joseph White, Salem, Mass. 6 Apr 1830

[Trial Aug 1830, Daniel Webster for the state]

James H Peck, judge of U S District court for the district of Missouri, impeached for alleged abuse of judicial authority, trial begins 4 May, 1830, acquitted 31 Jan 1831

Dr Butler and Mr Worcester, Presbyterian missionaries arrested under Georgia law forbidding white men to reside in Cherokee possessions without a license (GEORGIA)

Lucretia Chapman or Lucretia Espos y Mina 1832

Rev Ephraim K Avery, for the murder of Sarah M Cornell, Newport, R I, acquitted Mch 1833

John A Murrell, the great western land pirate, chief of noted bandits in Tennessee and Arkansas, whose central committee, called "Grand Council of the Mystic Clan," is broken up by arrest of its leader 1834

[Murrell lived near Denmark, Madison county, Tenn He was a man without fear, physical or moral His favorite operations were horse-stealing and "negro running" He promised negroes their freedom if they allowed him to conduct them north, selling them on the way by day and stealing them back by night, always murdering them in the end. He was captured by Virgil A Stewart in 1834 convicted, and sentenced to the penitentiary where he died]

Spanish pirates (12 in number), for an act of piracy on board the brig *Mexican*, trial at Boston, 7 found guilty, 5 acquitted 11-25 Nov 1834

Heresy trial, rev Lyman Beecher, Presbyterian, before the presbytery and synod of Cincinnati, on charges preferred by dr Wilson, of holding and teaching Pelagian and Arminian doctrines, acquitted 9 June et seq 1835

John Earls for murder of his wife, Williamsport 1836

Abraham Prescott for murder of Mrs Sally Cochran of Pembroke N H, 23 June, 1833 Executed at Hopkinton 6 Jan "

Rev Albert Barnes, Presbyterian for heresies in "Notes on the Epistle to the Romans," tried and acquitted by presbytery of Philadelphia, 30 June-8 July 1835, condemned by the synod and suspended for 6 months, but acquitted by the general assembly "

Richard P Robinson tried for murder of Helen Jewett (Dorcas Doyen) in New York, 11 Apr 1836 acquitted 7 June, "

[The jury were accused of corruption, and one perjured witness committed suicide soon after]

Case of slave schooner AMISTAD 1839-40

Samuel R Wood for perjury 1840

Charles Cook Oct 1840 for the murder of Mrs Merry, his employer's wife at Glenville, near Schenectady, N Y, 22 Sept 1840 Though probably insane he is hung 18 Dec "

Major McElroy, for murder of Rainsford Otis whose body is found in the ruins of a burned barn in Concord Erie county, N Y, 23 Apr 1840 Convicted Nov 1840, on circumstantial evidence, and hung at Buffalo, N Y 19 Jan 1841

Alexander McLeod, a Canadian charged as an accomplice in burning the steamer *Caroline* in the Niagara river, and in the murder of Amos Durfee, is taken from Lockport to New York on *habeas corpus*, May, 1841 Great Britain asks his release in extra session of Congress, Mr Webster advocates his discharge. A special session of the Circuit court, ordered by the legislature of New York at Utica, tries and acquits him 4-12 Oct "

A W Holmes, of the crew of the *William Brown* (WRECKS) for murder on the high seas (44 of the passengers and crew escaping in the long boat the sailors threw some passengers overboard to lighten the boat, 19 Apr 1841), convicted, but recommended to mercy May, 1842

Monroe Edwards, for forgery, New York city, sentenced to 10 years' imprisonment 6-12 June, "

[William M Evarts, in defence, laid the foundation of his fame as an advocate Edwards paid for his services a forged check]

Thomas W Dorr Rhode Island, treason (DORR'S REBELLION). "

Alexander S Mackenzie (SOMERS'S MUTINY) "

John C Colt, book-keeper, for murder of Samuel Adams, a printer, in New York He packs the body in a box and ships it to New Orleans, the vessel is delayed the box discovered, Colt convicted and sentenced to death He commits suicide in the Tombs by stabbing himself with a knife on the day appointed for his execution 18 Nov "

Benjamin D White, Batavia 1843

Bishop Benjamin T Onderdonk of New York, for immoral conduct, by ecclesiastical court suspended 10 Dec 1844-3 Jan 1845

H Daniel, for murder of Clifton R Thomson, Cincinnati "

Ex senator J C Davis of Illinois T C Sharp editor of *Warsaw Signal*, Mark Aldrich, Wm N Grover, and col Levi Williams, for murder of Hiram and Joe Smith (Mormons), trial begins at Carthage, Ill, acquitted 21 May, "

Henry G Green for poisoning his wife (called "the murdered bride"), Berlin, N Y "

Albert J Tirrell (the somnambulist murderer), for killing Maria A Bickford 1846

[Acquitted on the plea that the murder was committed while he was sleep-walking]

Margaret Howard, for the murder of Mrs M E Smith, her husband's paramour, Cincinnati 1849

Reuben Dunbar, for murder of S V and D L Lester, his young nephews, Albany county, N Y, tried and executed at Albany 1850

Dr John W Webster, for the murder of dr George W Parkman in the medical college, Boston, 23 Nov 1849 Webster partly burns his victim The remains identified by a set of false teeth Webster convicted and hung, trial 19-30 Mch "

Stephen Arnold, for the murder of Betsy Van Amburgh, a child 6 years of age, in Cooperstown 4 June, "

Conspiracy for injuring the property of the Michigan Central railroad, 40 indicted, 12 convicted and sent to prison from 5 to 10 years, among the counsel for the defence is Wm H Seward, trial concluded at Detroit Sept. 1851

Catherine N Forrest *v* Edwin Forrest, divorce and alimony granted to Mrs Forrest 16 Dec. 1851-26 Jan 1852

Arthur Spring, for murder of Mrs Shaw and Mrs Lynch in Federal st Philadelphia, 10 Mch (one of the bodies stabbed in 43 places) sentenced to be hung 16 Apr 1853

John Hendrickson, convicted of poisoning his wife Maria at Bethlehem, Albany county, N Y, 6 Mch, trial June-July, "

Matt. F Ward, acquitted of the murder of Wm H G Butler, principal of the Louisville (Ky) high school, 2 Nov 1853, in the school room in presence of pupils, trial at Elizabethtown, 18-27 Apr 1854

Anthony Burns, fugitive slave case, Boston (MASSACHUSETTS), 27-31 May, "

Robert Scott for murder of Ann King, San Francisco 1854

Dr Stephen T Beale, ether case 1855

U S *v* Henry Hertz *et al*, for hiring and retaining persons to go out of the U S to enlist in the British Foreign Legion for the Crimea, tried in the District court of the U S for East District of Pennsylvania "

David F Mayberry for murder of Andrew Alger, before the Rock county (Wis.) Circuit court, killed by a mob "

Lewis Baker, James Turner, Cornelius Linn, Charles Van Pelt, John Huyler, John Morrissey, James Irving and Patrick McLaughlin *alias* Pawdeen for the murder of William Poole in Stanwix hall, opposite the Metropolitan hotel, on Broadway, N Y, 24 Feb 1855, jury disagree (BOXING) "

Ellen Irving, murderer of 16 persons, Baltimore 1856

Slave case in Cincinnati, O (see *Harper's Magazine*, vol xii p 691) Apr "

James P Casey for shooting James King of William editor of the San Francisco *Bulletin*, and Charles Cora murderer of U S marshal Richardson, tried and hung by the Vigilance committee in San Francisco 20 May, "

DRED SCOTT case "

Charles B Huntingdon, for forgery, guilty "

R J M Ward ("the most extraordinary murderer named in the calendar of crime"), Cleveland, O 1857

Emma A Cunningham for the murder of dr Burdell in New York city 30 Jan 1856, acquitted May, "

Edward W Hawkins for murder of James M Land and Jesse Arvine (he committed 4 murders, many thefts and forgeries, and married 6 young women before he was 21), executed in Estill county, Ky 29 May, "

Daniel E Sickles for killing Philip Barton Key, Washington, D C, acquitted (UNITED STATES) 4-26 Apr 1859

John Brown, for insurrection in Virginia tried 29 Oct and executed at Charlestown, Va (BROWN'S INSURRECTION), 2 Dec. "

Jacob S Harden, for the murder of his wife at Belvidere N J, hung 6 July, 1860

Albert W Hicks, pirate, tried at Bedloe's island, 18-23 May, convicted of triple murder on the oyster-sloop *Edwin A Johnson* in New York harbor, hung 13 July, "

Burch divorce case, adultery, Mrs. Burch exonerated, Chicago, Dec "

Hersey, "the Yankee Bluebeard" (supposed to have killed 2 wives) for murder of Betsy F Tyrrell, Boston, trial, 28-31 May, hung 8 Aug. 1861

Officers and crew of the privateer *Savannah*, on the charge of piracy, jury disagree 23-31 Oct. "

Nathaniel Gordon, for engaging in the slave trade, 6-8 Nov 1861, hanged at New York 21 Feb 1862

Parish Will case, to set aside certain codicils added to the will of Henry Parish of New York after an attack of paralysis in Wall st, 19 July, 1849 and giving his estate mainly to his wife, he dies 2 Mch 1856, the codicils set aside by the surrogate, decision affirmed by court of Appeals June, "

Fitz John Porter tried by military court (PORTER, Case of), Nov 1862-Jan 1863

C L Vallandigham, for treasonable utterances, by court martial in Cincinnati sentence of imprisonment during the war commuted to banishment to the South (UNITED STATES). 5-16 May, "

Pauline Cushman Union spy, sentenced to be hung by a court martial held at gen Bragg's headquarters, is left behind at the evacuation of Shelbyville, Tenn, and rescued by Union troops June, "

For conspiracy against the U S, in organizing the Order of American Knights or Sons of Liberty about 16 May, tried by a military commission at Indianapolis, Ind, beginning 27 Sept, William A Bowles, L P Milligan, and Stephen Horsey sentenced to be hung (MILLIGAN, CASE OF) 17 Oct. 1864

J Y Beall, tried at fort Lafayette by a military commission, for seizing the steamer *Philo Parsons* on lake Erie, 19 Sept., and other acts of war, without visible badge of military service, sentenced to death and hung, trial occurs Dec. "

Miss Mary Harris for the murder of A J Burroughs in Washington, D C, acquitted, trial July 1865

Capt Henry Wirtz commander of Andersonville prison during the war, for cruelty, trial begins 21 Aug, Wirtz hung, 10 Nov "

Conspirators for assassination of pres. Lincoln (BOOTH'S CONSPIRACY) "

Dr John W Hughes hanged for murder of miss Tamzen Parsons, Cleveland 1866

Antoine Probst, for the murder of the Deering family (father, mother, 4 children, and 2 other children in the family) on 7 Apr, executed at Philadelphia 8 June, "

John H Surratt (BOOTH'S CONSPIRACY) 1867

In the case of William H McCardle of Mississippi, testing the constitutionality of the Reconstruction act of 1867, Matt. H Carpenter of Wisconsin, Lyman Trumbull of Illinois, and Henry Stanberry attorney general, appear for the government, and judge Sharkey Robert J Walker of Mississippi, Charles O'Conor of New York Jeremiah S Black of Pennsylvania, and David Dudley Field for McCardle, Reconstruction act repealed during the trial *habeas corpus* issued 12 Nov "

Andrew Johnson, impeachment (UNITED STATES) 1868

George S Twitchell, jr, for murder of his mother in law Mrs. Mary E Hill, Sunday, 22 Nov 1868, sentenced to death, 30 Jan, commits suicide in Philadelphia 8 Apr 1869

Col Yerger, for murder of col Crane, U S army, at Jackson, Miss 8 June, "

Wm H. Holden, governor of North Carolina, impeached and removed 22 Mch 1870

Daniel MacFarland, for the murder of Albert D. Richardson, 25 Nov. 1869, in New York city; acquitted....4 Apr.–10 May, 1870

David P. Butler, governor of Nebraska, impeached for appropriating school funds, and suspended..................2 June, "

Benjamin Nathan, a prominent Hebrew of New York, is found murdered in his home, his head beaten in by a heavy iron bar; one of his sons suspected, but never brought to trial, night of 29–30 July, "

"The Bible in the Public Schools," Case of; J. D. Miner *et al.* v. the Board of Education of Cincinnati *et al.*; tried in the Superior court of Cincinnati; arguments for the use of the Bible in the public school by Wm. M. Ramsey, George R. Sage, and Rufus King; against, J. B. Stallo, George Hoadly, and Stanley Matthews.................................... "

James W. Smith, first colored boy admitted to the U. S. Military academy; by court-martial for striking a cadet, 7–12 Jan. 1871

Laura D. Fair, for murder of A. P. Crittenden in San Francisco, Cal., 3 Nov. 1870; acquitted...............27 Mch.–26 Apr. "

Edward H. Ruloff, philologist ("the modern Eugene Aram"), for murder; hung at Binghamton, N. Y................18 May, "

Aratus F. Pierce, for murder of William Bullock at Lockport, N. Y.; acquitted.. "

George Vanderpool, for the murder of Herbert Field at Manistee, Mich., 5 Sept. 1869; 1st trial, prisoner found guilty and sentenced to life imprisonment at Jackson; 2d trial, jury disagree; acquitted on the 3d trial.........................Aug. "

Fanny Hyde, for murder of George W. Watson, N. Y........ 1872

Mrs. Wharton, for murder of gen. W. S. Ketchum, U. S. A., at Washington, 28 June, 1871; acquitted....4 Dec. 1871–24 Jan. "

George C. Barnard (judge of Supreme court, New York) impeached, 13 May, for corruption, and deposed.......18 Aug. "

Jacob Rosenzweig (abortionist), for killing Alice A. Bowlesby in New York; the body is found in a trunk shipped to Chicago; verdict, manslaughter in 2d degree; sentence, state-prison for 7 years......................26 Oct. et seq. "

John Scanlan, for murder of T. Donohue in New York..2 Nov. "

Lydia Sherman, convicted of poisoning 3 husbands and 8 children, Philadelphia.................................... 1873

William Foster (car-hook murderer), for killing Avery D. Putnam, 26 Apr. 1871, in New York city; tried, 22 Mch.–26 May, 1871; convicted and hung.........................21 Mch. "

Frank H. Walworth (the "boy parricide"), for killing his father in New York city; sentenced to imprisonment for life; afterwards pardoned.......................24 June–5 July, "

Capt. Jack and 3 other Modoc Indians tried 3 July for the massacre of gen. E. R. S. Canby, U. S. A., and rev. dr. Thomas (commissioner), 11 Apr.; convicted and hung at Fort Klamath, Or..3 Oct. "

E. S. Stokes, for the murder of James Fisk, jr., in New York, 6 Jan. 1872; first jury disagree, 19 June, 1872; second trial (guilty and sentenced to be hanged 28 Feb. 1873), 18 Dec. 1872–6 Jan. 1873; third trial (guilty of manslaughter in 3d degree; sentence, 4 years in prison at Sing Sing)..13–29 Oct. "

W. M. Tweed, for frauds upon the city and county of New York; sentenced to 12 years' imprisonment.........19 Nov. "

A. Oakey Hall, ex-mayor of New York, for complicity with the Tweed "ring" frauds; jury disagree, 1–21 Mch. 1872; second trial, jury disagree 1 Nov.; acquitted........24 Dec. "

Emil Lowenstein, for murder of John D. Weston at West Albany, 5 Aug. 1873; hung at Albany, N. Y.........10 Apr. 1874

David Swing, for heresy before the Chicago Presbytery, 15 Apr. et seq., in 28 specifications by prof. Francis L. Patton; acquitted after a long trial..................................... "

[Prof. Swing withdrew from the Presbyterian church and formed an independent congregation.]

William E. Udderzook (the insurance murderer), for the murder of W. S. Goss, 2 Feb. 1872, at West Chester, Pa.; tried 27 May–9 Nov. 1873, and found guilty; hung........12 Nov. "

[Goss, whose life was insured for $25,000, ran away, and Udderzook, his brother-in-law, by perjury, collected the money for Goss's wife; Goss reappearing, Udderzook killed him to avoid exposure.]

Belfry murder in Boston; little Mabel H. Young butchered by the sexton of the Warren Ave. Baptist church.............. 1875

James M. Lowell, for wife murder.............................. "

Theodore Tilton v. Henry Ward Beecher, for adultery, Brooklyn, N. Y.; jury disagree; case ended...............2 July, "

Jesse Pomeroy, the Boston boy murderer, for killing of Horace W. Millen, 22 Apr. 1874, supposed to be Pomeroy's fourth victim... "

Gen. O. E. Babcock, private secretary of pres. Grant, tried at St. Louis for complicity in whiskey frauds; acquitted, 7 Feb. 1876

[Babcock was drowned off the Florida coast, 3 June, 1884.]

Pasach N. Rubenstein, for murder of Sarah Alexander, 12 Dec. 1875, in Brooklyn, N. Y.; tried 31 Jan.–12 Feb.; sentenced to be hanged, but dies in jail..........................9 May, "

W. W. Belknap, U. S. secretary of war, impeached (United States); acquitted...............................1 Aug. "

John D Lee, for the Mountain Meadow massacre, 15 Sept. 1857; convicted and executed.......................23 Mch. 1877

Jesse Billings, jr., for murder of his wife at Saratoga, N. Y., 4 June; acquitted.......................................Oct. 1878

Rev. H. H. Hayden, for murder of Mary Stannard, New Haven, Conn... 1879

Benjamin F. Hunter, for murder of J. F. Armstrong in Camden, N. J., 23 Jan. 1878; hung in Camden.................10 Jan. "

John P. Phair tried for murder of Ann E. Frieze of Rutland, Vt., 9 June, 1874; sentenced to be hung, 6 Apr. 1877; reprieved until 4 Apr.; hung at Windsor, Vt., protesting his innocence..10 Apr. "

TRI

Col. Thomas Buford, for killing judge Elliott at Frankfort, Ky.; acquitted on ground of insanity; trial.................July, 1879

Chastine Cox, negro, for murder of Mrs. Jane Deforest Hull, in New York city, 10 June, 1879; hung.............16 July, 1880

Whittaker, colored cadet at West Point, by military court for injuring himself on pretence of being hurt by others, 6 Apr.; expelled.. "

Pietro Balbo, for the murder of his wife, New York; executed, 6 Aug. "

Monroe Robertson, murderer of 9 men, the last, his wife's brother, Wiley Coulter, a boy of 19, in Oct. 1879; hung at Greenville, O......................................20 Aug. "

George Smith and Mrs. Catherine Miller, for murder of Andrew Miller (the latter's husband), at the instigation of Mrs. Miller, 18 Mch. 1880, near Jersey Shore, Pa.; hung at Williamsport, Pa......................................3 Feb. 1881

Joseph Stevens, colored, for murder of Andrew Mobley, colored, 20 May, 1878, by stabbing in the breast at a prayer-meeting because he felt a severe pain in his arm when shaking hands with him. A sorceress, "old Nell Gyles," of Augusta, had told him he would feel a sharp pain in the arm when he shook hands with the person causing his aches and pains; hung at Edgefield, S. C............20 May, "

James Malley, for the murder of Jennie E. Cramer, New Haven, Conn., *Aug.* 5, 1881; acquitted...................June, 1882

Lieut. Flipper, colored, by military court, for embezzlement and false statements, Nov. 1881; dismissed from the service.... "

Charles F. Kring, for murder of Mrs. Dora C. J. Broemser, St. Louis... "

Charles J. Guiteau, for the assassination of pres. Garfield (United States, 1881); convicted, 26 Feb.; hanged, 30 June, "

Star Route trials... "

John Cockrill, managing editor of the St. Louis *Post-Despatch*, for fatally shooting col. Slayback (acquitted).........13 Oct. "

N. L. Dukes, for murder of col. Nutt, Uniontown, Pa. (acquitted)...21 Mch. 1883

Edward N. Rowell of Batavia, for fatally shooting Johnson L. Lynch of Utica, his wife's paramour (acquitted).....30 Oct. "

Debris suit (California), decided against hydraulic miners, judge Sawyer of the U. S. court, San Francisco, Cal., granting a perpetual injunction..............................7 Jan. 1884

William Berner, convicted at Cincinnati of manslaughter in killing William H. Kirk..........................28 Mch. "

[Berner was a confessed murderer; the verdict of manslaughter, when 20 untried murderers were in the city jail, led to a 6 days' riot, during which the court-house and other buildings were set on fire, 45 persons were killed, and 138 injured.]

Brig.-gen. D. G. Swaim, judge-advocate general of the army, tried by court-martial for attempt to defraud a banking firm in Washington, and failing to report an army officer who had duplicated his pay account; sentenced to suspension from duty for 12 years on half-pay; trial opens.....15 Nov. "

James D. Fish, president of the Marine bank of New York, secretly connected with the firm of Grant & Ward, convicted of misappropriation of funds, 11 Apr., and sentenced to 10 years at hard labor in Sing Sing, N. Y..............27 June, 1885

Mrs. Lucilla Dudley, tried at New York for shooting O'Donovan Rossa in Chambers st., 2 Feb.; the shot not fatal, and Mrs. Dudley acquitted as insane.....................30 June, "

Ferdinand Ward, of the suspended firm of Grant & Ward, New York city, indicted for financial frauds, 4 June; convicted and sentenced to 10 years at hard labor in Sing Sing, 31 Oct. "

[Released, 30 Apr. 1892.]

Henry W. Jaehne, vice-president of the New York common council, for receiving a bribe to support Jacob Sharp's Broadway surface road on 30 Aug. 1884; sentence, 9 years and 10 months in Sing Sing (New York)......................20 May, 1886

Alfred Packer, one of 6 miners, who killed and ate his companions when starving in their camp on the site of Lake City, Col., in 1874; convicted at New York of manslaughter, and sentenced to 40 years' imprisonment...................Aug. "

Mrs. Roxalana Druse and daughter, for murder of Mr. Druse in 1884; Mrs. Druse convicted and hung at Herkimer, N. Y.; daughter imprisoned for life...............................Feb. 1887

Tillie Smith, a serving-maid in an educational institute, is found murdered at Hackettstown, N. J., 9 Apr. 1886; innocent persons suspected, but the crime proved on one Titus, the janitor, who is convicted 15 Oct. 1886, and sentenced to death; commuted to imprisonment for life.......21 Mch. "

Trial of Jacob Sharp; found guilty of bribery and sentenced to 4 years' imprisonment and a fine of $5000........14 July, "

[Sentence reversed by court of Appeals.]

Anarchists at Chicago (United States): 22 indicted, 27 May, 1886; 7 convicted of murder, 20 Aug.; 4 (Spies, Parsons, Fischer, and Engle) hung; and 1 (Lingg) commits suicide, 11 Nov. "

[Gov. Altgeld pardoned all the anarchists (Schwab, Neebe, and Fielden) in prison, 26 June, 1893.]

Maxwell, an Englishman, *alias* Brook, *alias* Lennox, under conviction for more than 2 years for murder of Mr. Preller, executed at St. Louis..............................10 Aug. 1888

David Walker, William Walker, and John Matthew, noted "bald knobbers" (Missouri, 1887–89), sentenced 18 May, 1888; executed at Ozark..............................10 May, 1889

City of New Orleans against administratrix of the estate of Myra Clark Gaines, deceased, 9 Jan. 1885, in Supreme court of U. S.; judgment against the city for over $500,000, 13 May, "

[About 1836 Myra Clark Gaines filed a bill in equity to recover real estate in the possession of the city of New Orleans. Her father, Daniel Clark, who died in New Orleans a reputed bachelor, 16 Aug. 1813, by will dated 20 May, 1811, gave the property to his mother, and by memorandum for a will (which was never found) made in 1813, gave it to his daughter Myra. The latter will was received by the Supreme court of Louisiana 18 Feb. 1856, and the legitimacy of Myra questioned. Judge Billings of the U. S. Circuit court at New Orleans rendered a decision which recognized the probate of the will of 1813, in Apr. 1877; an appeal was taken, and in 1883 judgment was again given in favor of Mrs. Gaines for $1,925,667 and interest. The final appeal, June, 1883, resulted as above. In 1861 the value of the property was estimated at $35,000,000.]

Dr. Patrick Henry Cronin, Irish dynamite nationalist (expelled from the Clan-na-Gael, and denounced as a spy by Alex. Sullivan and the leaders, termed the "Triangle," and condemned to death by them for accusing them of embezzling funds allotted for dynamiting in England in Feb., 4 May), found murdered at Lake View, Chicago.............22 May, 1889

Coroner's jury declare the murder to be the result of a conspiracy of which Alexander Sullivan, P. O'Sullivan, Daniel Coughlin, and Frank Woodruff (connected with the Clan-na-Gael) were the principals. Alex. Sullivan and others arrested, 12 June; Sullivan released on high bail......15 June, "

Martin Burke arrested at Winnipeg, Canada, indicted about 20 June. The grand jury at Chicago, after 16 days' investigation, indict Martin Burke, John F. Beggs, Daniel Coughlin, Patrick O'Sullivan, Frank Woodruff, Patrick Cooney, and John Kunz, with others unknown, of conspiracy and of the murder of Patrick Henry Cronin.....................29 June, "

Coughlin, Burke, O'Sullivan, Kunz, and Beggs for murder of Cronin in Chicago, 6 May; trial begins 30 Aug.; the first 3 are sentenced to imprisonment for life, Kunz for 3 years, and Beggs discharged.............................16 Dec. "

[Second trial of Daniel Coughlin began 3 Nov. 1893; acquitted by jury, 8 Mch. 1894.]

Commander B. H. McCalla of U. S. S. *Enterprise*, by court-martial for malfeasance and cruelty, 22 Apr., on finding of a court of inquiry held in Brooklyn navy-yard, 11 Mch.; suspended from rank and duty for 3 years; sentence approved by sec. Tracy...15 May, 1890

William Kemmler, for murder of his paramour at Buffalo, N. Y.; the first execution by electricity, at Auburn prison, N. Y...6 Aug. "

Dr. T. Thacher Graves, for murder of Mrs. Josephine Barnaby of Providence, R. I., by poison, at Denver, Col............... 1891

[While awaiting his second trial he committed suicide in the county jail at Denver, 3 Sept. 1893.]

Rev. Charles A Briggs, charged by the presbytery of New York, 5 Oct. 1891, with teaching doctrines "which conflict irreconcilably with, and are contrary to, the cardinal doctrines taught in the Holy Scriptures," in an address at the Union Theological seminary in New York, 20 Jan. 1891; case dismissed, 4 Nov.; prosecuting committee appeal to the General Assembly, 13 Nov.; judgment reversed and case remanded to the presbytery of New York for new trial, 30 May, 1892; prof. Briggs acquitted after a trial of 19 days..30 Dec. 1892

Dr. Robert W. Buchanan, tried in New York city for wife poisoning; verdict, "guilty of murder in 1st degree"....26 Apr. 1893

Carlyle W. Harris, for murder of Helen Potts, 1 Feb. 1891, to whom he was secretly married, 8 Feb. 1890; she dies of an overdose of morphine, and Harris is convicted on circumstantial evidence, 2 Feb. 1892; executed by electricity at Sing Sing...8 May, "

George H. Abbott, *alias* Frank C. Almy, for murder of Christie Warden, near Hanover, N. H., June, 1891; hung at Concord, N. H...16 May, "

Lizzie Borden, arrested in Fall River, 11 Aug. 1892, for murder of her father and step-mother on 4 Aug. 1892; arraigned at New Bedford, pleads not guilty, 8 May, 1893; acquitted..20 June, "

[Defended by ex-gov. Robinson of Massachusetts.]

John Y. McKane, Gravesend, L. I., for election frauds; convicted and sentenced to Sing Sing for 6 years........19 Feb. 1894

Miss Madeline V. Pollard, for breach of promise, against representative W. C. P. Breckenridge of Kentucky; damages, $50,000; trial begun 8 Mch. 1894, at Washington, D. C.; verdict of $15,000 for miss Pollard, Saturday............14 Apr. "

Patrick Eugene Prendergast, for the murder of Carter Harrison, mayor of Chicago, 28 Oct. 1893; plea of defence, insanity; jury find him sane and he is hung...................13 July, "

George A. Bartholomy for the murder of William E. Delaney, ex-city clerk, Buffalo, N. Y., 14 June, 1894; sentenced to Auburn state-prison for life..........................10 Oct. "

tribunes of the people (*tribuni plebis*), magistrates of Rome, first chosen from among the commons to represent them, 494 B.C., when the people, after a quarrel with the patricians, had retired to Mons Sacer. The first 2 tribunes were C. Licinius and L. Albinus, but the number was soon raised to 5, and 37 years later to 10. The office was annual, and as the first had been created on the 4th of the ides of Dec., that day was chosen for the election. In A.D. 1347 Nicolo di Rienzi assumed absolute power in Rome as tribune of the people, and reformed many abuses; but his extravagances destroyed his popularity and he abdicated, returned to Rome, and was assassinated, 8 Sept. 1354.

trichiniasis (*trick-i-ni'a-sis*), a disease, often fatal, occasioned by eating raw or underdone pork containing a minute worm named *Trichina spiralis*. Prof. Owen discovered these worms in cysts, in human muscle, in 1832. The trichinæ are thoroughly destroyed by proper cooking. The disease excited much attention in 1865, and was the subject of a lecture by dr. Thudichum at the Society of Arts on 18 Apr. 1866.

tricolor flag (red, white, and blue), adopted by France 1789.

tricoteuses (*tree-co-tuz'*), knitters, a name given to fanatical women in Paris, in 1792, who zealously attended political meetings and executions, knitting at intervals. A notable example, madame Defarge in Dickens's "Tale of Two Cities."

Trieste (*tree-est'*), an Austrian port on the Adriatic, declared a free port by the emperor Charles VI., 1719, confirmed by Maria Theresa in 1750. It was held by the French in 1797 and 1805. Since the establishment of the overland mail to India it has risen to great commercial importance. After various changes of rulers it was restored to Austria in 1814. Pop. 1890, 158,344.

trimmer, a term applied to Charles Montague, earl of Halifax, and others who held similar political opinions, midway between the extreme Whigs and Tories, in the latter part of the 17th century. He accepted the title as an honor, asserting that it belonged to the British constitution and church. Macaulay regarded Halifax as a trimmer on principle, and not a renegade. He died in 1715.

Tri-mountain. BOSTON, 1630; MASSACHUSETTS.

Trinac'ria (3-cornered), a name of Sicily. The title "King of Trinacria" was temporarily assumed by Frederick II. (1302) and Frederick III. (1373).

Trin'idad, an island of the British West Indies, discovered by Columbus in 1498, was taken from the Spaniards by sir Walter Raleigh in 1595; by the French from the English in 1676. Taken by the British, with 4 ships of the line and a military force under sir Ralph Abercromby, to whom the island capitulated, 18 Feb. 1797; they captured 2 and burned 3 Spanish ships of war in the harbor. This possession was confirmed to England by the peace of Amiens in 1802. The insurrection of the negroes occurred 4 Jan. 1832. A large lake of pitch or bitumen on the island is extensively worked. ASPHALT. Area, 1754 sq. miles; pop. 1890, 208,030.

Trinity and **Trinita'rians.** Theophilus, bishop of Antioch, who flourished in the 2d century, was the first who gave the term Trinity to the supposed 3 persons in the Godhead. His "Defence of Christianity" was edited by Gesner, at Zurich, in 1546.—*Watkins.* An order of the Trinity, termed Mathurins, was founded about 1198 by John de Matha and Felix de Valois. A Trinity fraternity of 15 persons was instituted at Rome by St. Philip Neri in 1548. In England the act to exempt from penalties persons denying the doctrine of the Trinity (such as Unitarians and Swedenborgians) passed in 1813.

Trinity church, New York city, Protestant-Episcopal, the wealthiest church corporation in the United States. First building 1696, enlarged 1737, burned 1776, rebuilt 1788, taken down 1839; present edifice consecrated, 21 May, 1846; height of spire, 284 ft.

Trinity colleges. CAMBRIDGE, OXFORD. Trinity college, Dublin, called the university; grant of the Augustine monastery of All-Saints within the suburbs for erecting this college conferred by queen Elizabeth, 1591. First stone laid by Thomas Smith, mayor of Dublin, 1 Jan. 1593. New charter, 1637. Made a barrack for soldiers, 1689.—*Burns.* The principal or west front erected, 1759. Library erected, 1732. This college grants degrees upon examination without residence. The Roman Catholics desire exemption from mixed education and special privileges. Great changes were proposed by an Irish University bill brought into Parliament Feb. 1873, but withdrawn. Religious tests were abolished in the same year.

Proposal to establish a Roman Catholic college within the university negatived by senate (74–7)..................18 May, 1874

Trinity Sunday, the next after Whitsunday. The festival of the Holy Trinity was instituted by pope Gregory IV. in 828, on ascending the papal chair, and is observed by the Latin and Protestant churches originally as an octave of

Pentecost or Whitsunday. The observance was first enjoined in the council of Arles, 1260. It was fixed on the present day by pope John XXI in 1334

Trinoban'tes, a British tribe which occupied Middlesex and Essex, and joined in opposing the invasion of Julius Cæsar, 54 B.C., but soon submitted. They joined Boadicea, queen of the ICENI, and were defeated by Suetonius Paulinus near London, 61

Tripar'tite treaty, name given to treaty of Paris, 1856

Triple alliance was ratified between the States-general and England against France for the protection of the Spanish Netherlands, Sweden afterwards joining the league, it was known as the Triple alliance, 23 Jan 1668. Another Triple alliance was that between England, Holland, and France against Spain, Jan 1717. Another between Great Britain, Russia, and Austria, 28 Sept 1795. Germany, Austria, and Italy against France and Russia, 13 Mch 1887

Trip'oli ("3 cities") (1) In Syria, comprised three quarters built by the Tyrians, Sidonians, and Arabians, was taken by the crusaders 1109, and made a county for Raymond of Toulouse. It was conquered by Egyptians in 1832, restored to the Porte, 1835, surrendered to the British, 1841. (2) A Turkish province, N Africa, comprised the cities Sabrata, Œa (the present Tripoli, the capital), and Leptis (the ancient Tripolitana), after having been held by Greeks, Romans, Vandals, and Saracens, it was conquered and annexed by the Turks, 1551. Hamet Bey, pacha in 1741, made himself independent, and the government remained in his family till 1835, when Tripoli was restored to nominal subjugation to the sultan. NAVAL BATTLES, UNITED STATES, 1800, etc.

tri'remes, galleys with 3 banks of oars, said to have been invented by Corinthians, 784 or 700 B.C.

triumphs were granted by the Roman senate to generals of armies after important victories. They were welcomed into the city with magnificence and public acclamations. The greater of these festivals of welcome was called the triumph, and the less, the OVATION

trium'virates, Roman. In 60 B.C., Julius Cæsar, Pompey, and Crassus formed a coalition to rule the state. This lasted 10 years, and civil war ensued. The second triumvirate, 43 B.C., formed by Octavius Cæsar, Mark Antony, and Lepidus, destroyed the liberty of the Romans. Lepidus was expelled in 36. Antony was subdued in 31, and Octavius made himself absolute. ROME. In Feb 1849, a triumvirate was appointed at Rome, consisting of Joseph Mazzini, Armellini, and Saffi, which resigned on 1 July, 1849, when the city was taken by the French

trog'lodytes (Gr τρωγλοδύτης, one who creeps into holes, a cave dweller, from τρωγλη, a cave, and δύω, to enter, to creep in). A name given by the ancient Greeks to various races of savages who lived in caverns or abodes excavated in the earth, generally applied to the inhabitants of southern Egypt, Ethiopia and the mountain districts of Arabia, but all cave dwellers may be so denominated, all prehistoric people were probably troglodytic. Figuratively applied to one who secludes himself from the affairs of the world

trou'badours and **trouvères'** (from *troubar*, *trouver*, to find or invent), the poets of the middle ages (11th to 15th centuries). The former flourished in the south of France and north of Spain, and used the langue d'oc (that is, *oc* for *oui*, yes), the latter flourished in the north of France, and used the langue d'oil (that is, *oïl* for *oui*). The troubadours produced romances, but excelled chiefly in lyric poetry, the trouvères excelled in romances, several of which are extant as the "Brut d'Angleterre" and the "Rou," by Wace, the "Romance of the Rose," by Guillaume de Lorris and Jean de Meung. The troubadours were usually accompanied by *jongleurs*, who sang their masters' verses, with the accompaniment of the guitar. Histories of these French poets and specimens of their works have been published in France. These poets, although frequently very licentious, tended to promote civilization during those warlike times

Troy or **Ilium,** capital of Troas, Asia Minor; HOMER'S "ILIAD" and "ODYSSEY." Its history mythical.

B C

Arrival of Scamander in Phrygia (*Blair*) 1546

Teucer succeeds his father 1502

Dardanus succeeds, builds Dardania. 1480

Reign of Erichthonius 1449

Reign of Tros, from whom the people are called Trojans, and the city Troas 1374

Ilus his son, reigns, the city called Ilium 1314

Reign of Laomedon 1260

Arrival of Heracles in Phrygia. Hesione delivered from the sea monster (*Blair*, *Usher*) 1225

War of Heracles and Laomedon 1224

Reign of Priam or Podarces "

Rape of Helen, by Alexander Paris, son of Priam, 20 years before the sacking of Troy (*Homer's Iliad*, book xxiv) 1204

Commencement of the invasion of the Greeks to recover Helen, 1193

Troy taken and burned in the night, 11 June, i e, 23d of the month Thargelion.—*Parian Marbles*. 408 years before the 1st Olympiad.—*Apollodorus*, *Hales*, and *Clinton*, 1183, others 1184

[W E Gladstone dates the war 1316-07]

Æneas arrives in Italy (*Lenglet*) 1183

[Some time after the destruction of Troy a new city was built with the same name about 30 stadia distant. It was favored by Alexander the Great in his Asiatic expedition, but never rose to much importance, and in the age of Strabo was nearly in ruins.—*Priestley*.]

A D

Dr H Schliemann at Hissarlik in the Troad excavates a very ancient buried city, which he names "Novum Ilium" 1872-73

He pub "Troy and its Remains" (transl by dr P Smith) 1875

His Trojan antiquities arranged at South Kensington museum, Dec 1877

Dr Schliemann resumes excavations at Hissarlik, discovers Trojan houses and many antiquities, a dagger, earrings, bracelets, idols shells etc 30 Sept.-1 Dec 1878

Again with prof Virchow and M Burnouf, 1 Mch, makes fresh discoveries described in a letter, 5 June, 1879, pubs his book, "Ilios" 1880

troy weight. The Romans introduced their ounce, the avoirdupois ounce, into Britain. The present ounce was brought from Grand Cairo into Europe, about the time of the crusades, 1095, and was first adopted at Troyes, a city of France, whence the name. It is used to weigh gold, silver, and precious stones. The troy weight, Scots, was established by James VI. (James I of England) in 1618. STANDARDS

Troyes (*troi*), central France, where a treaty was concluded between England, France, and Burgundy, whereby it was stipulated that Henry V should marry Catherine, daughter of Charles VI, be appointed regent of France, and, after the death of Charles, should inherit the crown, 21 May 1420.

truce of God (*frera*, or *treuga Dei*), a term given to a cessation of the private feuds and conflicts so general during the middle ages all over Europe, said to have been advocated by the bishop of Aquitaine in 1032. The clergy gave their influence for it. A synod at Roussillon, 1027, decreed that none should attack his enemy between Saturday evening (at nones) and Monday morning (at the hour of prime). Similar regulations were adopted in England, 1042 (sometimes Friday and Wednesday being chosen for the time). The truce of God was confirmed by many councils of the church, especially the Lateran council in 1179.

truck-farming is raising vegetables for the markets, usually on a larger scale than what is called market-gardening, and is dependent on transportation companies and commission merchants to place its products on sale. Before 1860 this industry was but little known, and confined to the immediate vicinity of the cities, now many of its products are transported from 500 to 2000 miles for consumption. Late in the autumn and early in the spring the Gulf states and the lower Mississippi valley supply the enormous demand for green vegetables to the northern cities until the season, advancing at the rate of 13 miles a day, gradually brings the growth northward, so that now at no season of the year are the great northern cities without fresh summer fruits and vegetables. The first report of the Census Bureau on truck farms, made in 1890, shows that in 1889 the value of products sold, after deducting freight and commissions, was $76,518,155, after deducting for labor, seed, etc., the net income was $51,909,265, from the following acreage in different districts.

District.	Acres.
1 New England	6,838
2 New York, New Jersey, Pennsylvania	108,135
3. Delaware, Maryland, Virginia (east of Chesapeake bay)	25,714
4. Southeastern counties of Virginia and northeastern counties of North Carolina	45,375
5. Western Maryland and western Virginia	37,181
6 North Carolina, South Carolina, Georgia, Florida	111,441
7 Alabama, Mississippi, Louisiana, Tennessee, Kentucky	36,180

District	Acres
8 Texas, Arkansas Missouri, Kansas	36,889
9 Ohio, Indiana, Michigan, Wisconsin Iowa, Nebraska	107,414
10 Minnesota North Dakota, South Dakota	1,083
11. Idaho Wyoming Utah, Nevada Colorado, New Mexico Arizona	3,833
12 California, Oregon, Washington	14,357
Total	534,440

The principal vegetables grown are here mentioned in order of the values sold

1 Watermelons	6 Sweet potatoes
2 Cabbage	7 Tomatoes
3 Pease	8 Spinach
4 Asparagus	9 Irish potatoes
5 Melons other than water melons	10 Celery
	11 String beans

Other vegetables connected with this industry are beets, cucumbers, cauliflower, carrots, egg-plant, kale, lettuce, Lima beans, onions, parsnips, radishes, rhubarb, squashes, sweet corn, and turnips

trumpet, a wind instrument of great antiquity, properly of metal, with a flaring opening for the sound to issue Some of the Greek historians ascribe the invention of the trumpet to the Tyrrhenians, and others to the Egyptians It was in use in the time of Homer Shells of fish, sounded like trumpets, were in use as signals among most primitive peoples. —*Potter* The Jewish feast of trumpets was appointed 1490 B.C (Lev xxiii 24) Offa, king of Mercia, is said to have had trumpets sounded before him when travelling, about 790 A D SPEAKING-TRUMPET

trusts and **combines.** Terms applied in the United States originally to organizations and agreements, by which a body of trustees held the stock of a number of corporations, or a controlling interest in each, and administered them in common A trust may be defined as "embracing every act, agreement, or combination of persons or capital, believed to be done, made, or formed with the intent, power, or tendency to monopolize business, to restrain or interfere with competitive trade, or to fix, influence, or increase the prices of commodities." To this definition may be added "largeness," and in most instances "with a monopoly" such monopoly being either public franchises, patents, trade marks, secret processes of manufacture, tariff benefits, control of material or of necessary real estate, good-will, personal efficiency in management, etc The latest published statistics regarding trusts will be found in Moody's "The Truth About the Trusts" (1904), from which book the following tables are taken. With a few exceptions, trusts having a capitalization of less than $2,000,000 are omitted

	No of Plants.	Capitalization
Totals of the 7 greater industrial trusts	1528	$2,662,752,100
Totals of the 298 lesser industrial trusts	3426	4,055,039,433
Totals of the 13 industrial trusts in progress of reorganization	334	528,551,000
	5288	$7,246,342,533
Totals of the 111 franchise trusts	1336	3,735,456,071
Totals of the 6 great steam railroad groups,	790	9,017,086,907
Totals of 10 "allied independent" steam railroad systems	250	380,277,000
	2376	$13,132,819,978
Grand totals of 445 trusts—industrial, franchise, transportation, etc . . .	7664	$20,379,162,511

Tuam, a town of W Ireland St Jarlath the son of Loga, who lived about 501, is looked upon as the first founder of the cathedral of Tuam. The church was anciently called *Tuaim-da-Gualand.* ARCHBISHOPS, BISHOPS in Ireland.

tuberculo'sis, a disease consisting of the degeneration of tissue and growth of tubercles, masses of diseased matter, in the lungs (phthisis or consumption) or other parts of the body.

Dr Robert Koch of Berlin discovers in a minute organism, named *bacillus tuberculosis*, the cause of the disease	1882
Koch announces a lymph by the injection of which, as in vaccination, he hopes to cure the disease . autumn of	1890
Full account of dr Koch's method pub . Nov	"
Exaggerated reports of success discussed.	1890–91
Dr Koch explains his lymph, *tuberculine*, as a glycerine extract from the pure cultivation of the tubercle bacilli, 15 Jan	1891
Prof Badenheuer of Cologne asserts that out of 100 surgical cases no perfect cure has been effected by the lymph. Jan	"
Prof Virchow, Berlin, reports in 21 cases of injection of lymph unfavorable results . . . . Jan.	"
Drs. Bertin, Picq, and Bernheim propose the cure of tuberculosis by the transfusion of goat's blood Jan , Feb	1891
Dr Koch acknowledges the failure of his remedy, and proposes an improvement by the addition of alcohol 22 Oct.	"

The use of *tuberculine,* though not curative, has proved to be of the highest importance in the diagnosis of the disease. In cases in which tuberculosis has found a lodgement, an injection of this substance into the circulation is at once followed by a marked rise of the temperature, even though no other symptom of the disease is exhibited. It is by this means that suspected cattle are examined, and diseased ones distinguished

Tu'bingen school of Theology (Old), connected with the Tubingen university Its first representative, Gottlob Christian Storr (1746–1805), aimed to fix faith firmly on the authority of revelation as in the Scriptures, miracles, etc, in opposition to the philosophy of Kant, Fichte, Schelling, etc *Modern school,* founded by Ferdinand Christian Baur (1792–1860), introduced a rigid criticism of the books of the New Testament and strove to free Christianity from supernaturalism, i e, miracles, etc.

tubular bridges. BRIDGES

Tuesday (Lat *Dies Martis,* the day of Mars), the 3d day of the week, so called from *Tuisto, Tiw,* or *Tuesco,* a Saxon deity, worshipped on this day. Tuisto is mentioned by Tacitus. WEEK-DAYS.

Tuileries (*tweel-ree'*), Paris, the imperial palace of France, commenced by Catherine de Medicis, after the plans of Philibert de l'Orme, 1564, continued by Henry IV, and finished by Louis XIV This palace was stormed by the mob, 10 Aug 1792, and ransacked in the revolutions of July, 1830, and Feb 1848 Louis Napoleon made it his residence in 1851, and greatly renovated it The restoration of the Tuileries (much injured by fire by the Communists, May, 1871) was determined on, Oct 1872, but not proceeded with. The ruins were sold for $161,000 to M. Picard, 4 Dec 1882

tulips, indigenous in the east of Europe, were taken to England from Vienna about 1578 It is recorded in the register of Alkmaer, in Holland, that in 1639 120 tulips, with the offsets, sold for 90,000 florins, and that one, called the Viceroy, sold for 4203 guilders! The government stopped this ruinous traffic.—The tulip-tree, *Liriodendron tulipifera,* was carried to England from America, about 1663 FLOWERS AND PLANTS.

Tullaho'ma campaign. The Confederate commander Bragg, after the battle of MURFREESBOROUGH, retreated to Shelbyville, about 25 miles south from Murfreesborough, and part of his army to Tullahoma, somewhat farther away. Here he intrenched to resist the Federal advance It was not until 24 June, 1863, that gen Rosecrans advanced from Murfreesborough, and in a short campaign of 15 days (24 June–7 July), without severe fighting, compelled Bragg to evacuate middle Tennessee and retreat across the Tennessee river CHICKAMAUGA.

tumulus, pl **tumuli** (Lat), a mound, a heap They are found in all parts of the world, and date from prehistoric times. Mentioned in the Bible, Josh. vii. 26, viii. 29, 2 Sam xviii 17 Erected over the dead by the ancient Greeks, thus Homer, speaking of the burial of Patroclus

> "Then drew a circle for the sepulchre
> And, laying its foundations to enclose
> The pyre, they heaped the earth, and having reared
> A mound, withdrew" —"Iliad," bk xxiii, lines 314–17

Artificial mounds vary in size from a few feet to over 200 feet in height, the highest in England, at Silbury hill, is 170 feet. The utensils found in them indicate that they belong to the neolithic (stone), bronze, or iron age, and are probably uncivilized attempts at pyramid building MOUND BUILDERS.

tungsten (also called *wolfram* and *scheelium*), a hard, whitish, brittle metal. From tungstate of lead, Scheele, in 1781, obtained tungstic acid, whence the brothers De Luyart, in 1786, obtained the metal In 1859 it was employed in making a new kind of steel

Tu'nis, a seaport town and state of N Africa, stands nearly on the site of Carthage. Tunis was besieged by Louis IX. of France, who died near it, 25 Aug. 1270. It remained under African kings till taken by Barbarossa, for Solyman the

TUN

Magnificent, 1531. Barbarossa was expelled by the emperor Charles V, when 10,000 Christian slaves were set at liberty, June, 1535 The country was recovered by the Turks under Selim II, 1575 The bey of Tunis was first appointed in 1574 Tunis was reduced by adm Blake on the bey refusing to deliver up the British captives, 1655 The Hussein dynasty was founded 1705 In July, 1856, the bey agreed to make constitutional reforms He died 22 Sept 1859, and his brother and successor, Mohamed-es Saduk, took the oath of fidelity to the constitution Died 1882, succeeded by his brother, Sidi-Ali, 28 Oct 1882 Area, 45,000 sq miles, pop 1890, 1,500,000 It is now under French protection

Tunis incorporated with the Turkish empire 25 Oct 1871

Dispute with France, predatory incursions of the Kroumirs, nomadic shepherd tribes on Algerian territory, Mch, military expedition sent from France, lands in Tabarka, 25 Apr, bombards fortress and occupies Bizerta 30 Apr 1881

Bey appeals to Turkey 11 Apr, and the great powers, 27 Apr "

French approach Tunis alleging the object to be to restrain warlike tribes and protect their frontier 11 May, "

Treaty with France signed, France to occupy the positions which she deems necessary for the maintenance of order and the security of the frontier and the coast, and to send a resident minister to the capital French government guarantees to the bey the security of his person his states, and his dynasty, and the maintenance of existing treaties with the European powers, while the bey undertakes not to conclude any international convention without a previous understanding with the French government, and to prevent the introduction of arms into Algeria through Tunis Financial system of the regency to be regulated by France in concert with the bey 12 May, "

M Roustan, the consul appointed French resident minister (said to be virtual ruler, replacing bey), French army returning home June, "

Mustapha ben Ismail, the bey's chief minister, received by pres Grévy at Paris . . . . 21 June, "

French courts of law established 1 Jan 1884

Canal from Tunis to its port Goletta, a distance of 7 miles, is being built, to be finished 1894

Tunkers, a sect of American Baptists, called also Dunkers or Tumblers (from their mode of baptism by putting converts, while kneeling, head-foremost into the water), are an offshoot of a German Baptist community at Schwartzenau, on the river Eder, a number of whom emigrated to America under Conrad Beissel (or Peysel) and others, about 1719 Peysel afterwards founded a separate settlement at Ephrata, about 50 miles from Philadelphia, where celibacy and monasticism were encouraged but not made obligatory

tunnage and **poundage** were ancient duties levied on every tun of wine and pound of other goods, imported or exported, and were the origin of "customs" They commenced in England about 1346, and were granted to the kings for life, beginning with Edward IV Charles I gave offence by levying them on his own authority, 1628 They were granted to Charles II for his lifetime, 24 June, 1660 By the act 27 Geo III c 13, these and other duties were repealed, 1787, and the present system of excise and customs introduced.

tunnel, an underground passage or roadway through a mountain or hill or under the bed of a stream, etc. Herodotus speaks of a tunnel 7 furlongs long and 8 feet high through a hill on the island of Samos The Romans constructed a tunnel 6000 feet long by 7 high and 5 wide to tap lake Albanus, 359 B.C Lake Fucino in Italy was drained by a tunnel 3 miles long, 20–30 feet high, and about 30 feet wide, devised by Julius Cæsar and executed by Claudius, 52 A D One of the earliest known tunnels, said to have been constructed to drain the plateau on which stands the city of Mexico, pierced the Nochistengo ridge for 6 miles It was destroyed during a flood and replaced by an open cut, with a maximum depth of 200 feet, in 1608 The first canal tunnel constructed in England was the Harecastle, 1 mile 5 furlongs in length, for the Trent and Mersey canal, in 1766–77 Among other noted tunnels built for canal purposes are Thames and Medway, 3720 yards, Tipton Green, 2926 yards, Bilsworth (Grand Junction), 3080 yards, Sapperton (Thames and Severn), 4180 yards, Soussey (Bourgogne), 3852 yards, Nauvages (Canal du Marne au Rhin), 5320 yards, Lapal (Dudley canal), 3776 yards, Ripley (Cromford canal), 2966 yards, Marsden (Huddersfield), 5500 yards, Noirieu (St. Quentin), 13,128 yards, Pouilly (Bourgogne), 3660 yards. Railroad tunnels are innumerable, besides those detailed below, there may be noted the Woodhead tunnel, between Manchester and Sheffield, Engl., 3 miles in length, Standedge, on London and Northwestern railroad, over 3 miles, at Nerthe, France, about 3 miles, at Blaisy, France, about $2\frac{1}{2}$ miles in length, and many in the United States

First tunnel in the U S near Auburn, Pa, for the Schuylkill Navigation company's canal, 450 feet long, 20 wide and 18 high, begun 1818, completed 1821

Alleghany Portage railroad tunnel in Pennsylvania, one of the first in the U S, 900 feet in length begun 1831 completed 1833

Black Rock tunnel, on the Reading railroad, Pennsylvania, 1932 feet long, constructed . . 1836

Thames tunnel, between Rotherhithe and Wapping, length, 1200 feet width, 35 feet, height, 20 feet, cost about $5500 per lineal yard, planned by I K Brunel in 1823, excavation begun, Dec 1825, irruptions of river 18 May, 1827 and 12 Jan 1828, when 6 workmen were drowned, thickness of earth between the crown of the tunnel and the bed of the river, about 15 feet, opened for foot passengers 25 Mch 1843

[It was purchased by the East London railway and closed to others, 21 July, 1866]

Machine rock drill invented by J J Couch an American 1849, and machine drills first used practically in tunnelling Mont Cenis 1861

Nitro glycerine first applied to blasting 1863

Machine rock drill first practically used in tunnelling in the U S in the Hoosac tunnel Nov 1866

Tunnel extending 2 miles under lake Michigan at Chicago, to supply the city with water, the first of its kind, begun 17 Mch 1864, and completed 17 Dec. "

[A second tunnel was built 1872-74]

Dynamite invented by Nobel 1867

Great tunnel of the Central Pacific railroad at the summit of the Sierra Nevada opened Jan 1868

First river tunnel in the U S constructed under the Chicago river, length 810 feet, completed Dec "

Mont Cenis tunnel, nearly 8 miles long extends from Modane to Bardonnèche under the Col de Fréjus, site was indicated in 1840, cost about $1100 per lineal yard, engineers messrs Grattoni, Grandis, and Sommeiller, work begun by king Victor Emmanuel, 31 Aug 1857, blasting by hand until 1860 at the south heading, and 1862 at the north when rock drills were introduced, 2 headings meet, with a difference of 1 foot in level, 25 Dec 1870, tunnel opened 17 Sept. 1871

Hoosac tunnel, through the Hoosac mountains, near North Adams, Mass, is $4\frac{3}{4}$ miles long averages 25×25 feet, and cost about $14 000,000 Massachusetts legislature reports in favor of a canal tunnel, 1825, railroad tunnel located, 1850, act of legislature authorizing its construction and lending state aid passed, 1854, tunnel driven 2400 feet at the east heading and 610 feet at the west, 1855–61, abandoned by contractors, July 1861, work resumed by state, Oct 1863, head house, etc, destroyed by fire, the result of an explosion, and 13 lives lost, Oct. 1867, headings of tunnel meet, 27 Nov 1873

Tunnel under the Detroit river, begun in 1872, to connect the Michigan Central railroad with the Great Western of Canada, abandoned on account of irruption of sand and water from the river . .. "

Hallet's Point reef "Hell Gate" East river N Y, honey combed with tunnels and blown up, work begun, Aug 1869, total length of tunnels, 7425 feet, explosion conducted by gen John Newton, U S A . 24 Sept. 1876

Rothschönberg tunnel, to drain the Freiberg mines, Saxony, $31\frac{1}{8}$ miles in length and about 10 feet high, begun in 1844, completed 1877

Sutro tunnel, 4 miles long, to drain the Comstock Lode, Nevada, at a depth of 1600 feet, company chartered 4 Feb 1865, completion celebrated in Carson Valley 30 June, 1879

Ancient aqueduct tunnel, about 11 miles long built in the time of Augustus, to supply Bologna with water from the Setta, is restored by count Gozzadini and reopened 5 June, 1881

St Gothard tunnel, piercing the Alps, actual length, $9\frac{1}{4}$ miles, cost about $700 per lineal yard, work begun at each end, Sept 1872, machinery used after Apr and July, 1873 headings joined, 29 Feb 1880, with a horizontal difference at joining of only 2 inches, and a lateral of 13 inches, first passenger train through . . 1 Nov "

Rack a rock blasting powder invented by S R Divine . 1882

Hudson river tunnel, New York to Jersey City, begun 1874, 20 workmen drowned by irruption of water, July 1880, work stopped for lack of funds on New Jersey side Nov 1882, and on the New York side, July, 1883 and tunnel abandoned after an expenditure of over $1,000,000 July, 1883

Arlberg tunnel, under the Alps, at the Arl mountain, from Langen to St Anton, $6\frac{1}{3}$ miles, cost about $500 per lineal yard, work begun, July, 1880, headings joined, Nov 1883, railway opened. .. . . Sept 1884

Tunnel under the Mersey, between Liverpool and Birkenhead, Engl., was authorized by Parliament, 1866, dimensions width, 26 feet, height, 19 feet; length, $1\frac{1}{8}$ miles, experimental work begun, Dec 1879, regular work begun, 1881, tunnel opened. . . . 13 Jan 1886

Big Bend tunnel, Cal, to drain a section of the Feather river for gold mining was begun Nov 1882, length, 12,000 feet; cross section, 12×16 feet, work completed . . . Apr "

Company chartered by New York to construct a tail race tunnel about $1\frac{1}{8}$ miles in length, in the bank of Niagara river, from a point above to a point below the falls, to supply water power for mills, electric plants, etc . . . . .. "

Severn tunnel, built for the Great Western railway, from Monmouthshire to Gloucestershire, total length, 4 miles 626 yards; work begun, 1873, submerged by irruption from river for 1 year from Oct. 1879, lining with brick work begun, 1881;

flooded again, Oct. 1883; connections made, Oct. 1884; opened for traffic.......................................1 Sept. 1886
Tunnel through the Cascade range in Washington, 9850 feet long; cross section, 16×20½ feet; work begun, Apr. 1886; completed.......................................June, 1888
New Croton aqueduct, which is 33¼ miles long, built to supply water to New York city, contains 30¾ miles of tunnels; this portion of the work completed (CROTON AQUEDUCT).......... "
Sarnia tunnel, under the St. Clair river, from Sarnia to Port Huron; a cast-iron tube, over 6000 feet in length, 21 feet in diameter and lined with masonry; opened for railroad traffic, 1890
Tunnel under the Channel between Dover and Calais, proposed 1869; experimental boring begun in France, 1876; in England, 1882; Channel tunnel disapproved by sir G. Wolseley and other officers, British and foreign, Mch. 1882; work stopped by the government, 6 July, 1882; sir E. Watkin's bill for experimental works opposed by the government and rejected in the Commons, June, 1888, and again.......June, "

Tura'nian, a subdivision of the Mongolian race. ETHNOLOGY, LANGUAGE.

turbine wheel (Lat. *turbo*, a reel, a whirl, etc.), a form of a water-wheel invented by Benoit Fourneyson, 1823; first built, 1827. The varieties are now numerous.

Tu'rin, the ancient *Augusta Taurinorum* in Liguria. Under the name of Taurasia it was taken by Hannibal, 218 B.C. Capital of Piedmont, of the Sardinian states, and of the kingdom of Italy till 1864, when it was superseded by Florence. Its importance dates from the permanent union of Savoy and Piedmont in 1416. The French besieged this city; but prince Eugene defeated their army and compelled them to raise the siege, 7 Sept. 1706. In 1798 the French republican army took possession of Turin, seized all the strong places and arsenals of Piedmont, and obliged the king and his family to remove to the island of Sardinia. In 1799 the French were driven out by the Austrians and Russians; but the city and all Piedmont surrendered to the French, June, 1800. In May, 1814, it was restored to the king of Sardinia. ITALY, 1864. University founded 1405. Louis Kossuth, the Hungarian patriot, died here, 20 Mch. 1894, aged 92 years. Pop. 1890, 320,808.

Turin Papyrus, The, or "Book of Kings," a fragmentary list of Egyptian kings, brought from Thebes by an Italian named Drovetti. A fac-simile is preserved in the Royal Society of Literature, London.

Turkestan', called by the Persians Turan, Independent Tartary, the original country of the Turks, in central Asia, was reached by Alexander, 331 B.C. The Russians are gradually encroaching on this country; on 14 Feb. 1865, a new province, Turkestan, was created by decree, and gen. Kauffmann made governor, 26 July, 1867. It includes Samarcand, Ferghanah, Semiryetchensk, and Syr-Daria. Area, 409,414 sq. miles; pop. 3,400,000.

Turkey or the **Ottoman Empire.** The Turks were originally a tribe of Tartars; but, by incorporation with the peoples they have conquered, have become a mixed race. About 760 they obtained possession of a part of Armenia, called from them Turcomania. They first appeared in Europe in 1080, crossing the Bosporus to assist the emperor Botoniates against his rival. Under Othman or Osman, the founder of the present dynasty, they made themselves masters of several places in Asia, captured Nicea, and made Broussa their capital (1326). By the end of the 14th century they controlled Thessaly, Macedonia, and Bulgaria in Europe and nearly all western Asia. After the fall of Constantinople in 1453, Mahomet II., its conqueror, proceeded to subdue Trebizond, Wallachia, Bosnia, Illyria, and the Morea. Egypt, Syria, Circassia, and Moldavia passed under Turkish rule, 1481–1512. In 1522 they subdued Rhodes, and in 1525 invaded Hungary and invested Vienna, from which they were repulsed, 1529. At this time they were at the height of their power, ruling an area in Europe of 230,000 sq. miles. Their power has since rapidly declined. It has not been the custom of the sultans of Turkey for some centuries to contract regular marriages. The inmates of his harem are not Turkish subjects, but come by purchase or free will from other districts, chiefly from Circassia. From these inmates the sultan selects a certain number, generally 7, to be "kadyn" or ladies of the palace; the rest, called "odalik," remain as servants to them. But one, and only one, lady of the palace, bearing the title of Harnadar-Kadyn, and she always old, keeps any intercourse with the outer world, and this only through the chief of the guard of eunuchs, called Kyzlar-Agassi, bearing the same rank as the grand-vizier. The will of the sultan is absolute in so far as it is not in opposition to the teachings of the Koran. Forms of constitution, after the model of the western European states, have been drawn up, the first proclaimed 18 Feb. 1856, and a second as a decree of sultan Abdul-Hamid II., Nov. 1876, but it appears impossible to carry them out in the present condition of the Ottoman empire.

AREA AND POPULATION OF THE IMMEDIATE POSSESSIONS OF THE OTTOMAN EMPIRE.

Country.	Sq. miles.	Population.
Europe	61,200	4,780,000
Asia	687,640	21,608,000
Africa	398,738	1,300,000
Total	1,147,578	27,688,000

[This does not include Bulgaria, which is virtually free from Turkey, nor Bosnia and Herzegovina, now governed by Austro-Hungary, nor Egypt.]

Alp Arslan and the Turks conquer Armenia and Georgia....1065–68
Asia Minor conquered, 1074–84; Jerusalem taken............ 1076
Solyman Shah drowned in the Euphrates on the march; his son Ertoghul, granted territories near Angora, d........... 1288
Othman, his son, emir of the sultan of Iconium, founded the Ottoman empire at Prusa, Bithynia....................... 1299
Organization of Janissaries by Orcan....................about 1330
Nicæa conquered, 1330; and the Morea.......................... 1346
Turks penetrate into Thrace and take Adrianople............. 1361
Amurath I. remodels the Janissaries............................ 1362
Bajazet I. overruns provinces of Eastern empire........1389 et seq.
He defeats Sigismund of Hungary at Nicopolis........28 Sept. 1396
He besieges Constantinople; but interrupted by Tamerlane (or Timour), defeated and made prisoner, at Ancyra....28 July, 1402
Macedonia annexed.. 1430
Ladislas of Hungary defeated and slain at Varna by Amurath, 10 Nov. 1444
Amurath defeats John Hunniades at Kossova.............Oct. 1448
Turks, invading Hungary, repelled by Hunniades............ 1450
Constantinople taken by the Turks under Mahomet II., which ends the Eastern or Greek empire..................29 May, 1453
Belgrade relieved by Hunniades's victory over the Turks, July, 1456
GREECE subjected to the Turks..............................1458–60
Turks take Otranto, spreading terror in Europe............. 1480
Selim I. raised to the throne by the Janissaries; murders his father, brothers, etc.. 1512
He takes the islands of the Archipelago......................... 1514
He overruns Syria.. 1515
Gains Egypt by defeat of Mamelukes....................Aug. 1516
Solyman takes Belgrade, Aug. 1521; and Rhodes..........Dec. 1522
Defeats Hungarians at Mohatz.........................29 Aug. 1526
Repulsed before Vienna....................................Oct. 1529
Peace with Austria.. 1533
Cyprus taken from the Venetians........................Aug. 1571
Great battle of LEPANTO......................................7 Oct. "
Treaty of commerce with England................................ 1579
Turks driven out of Persia by shah Abbas....................... 1585
War with the Cossacks, who take Azof........................... 1637
Turks defeat Persians and take Bagdad........................ 1638
Candia (Crete) taken from Venice, after a 25-years siege...... 1669
Vienna besieged by Mahomet IV., but relieved by John of Poland...12 Sept. 1683
Peace of Carlovitz..26 Jan. 1699
Mustapha II. deposed by Janissaries............................ 1703
Morea retaken by the Turks...................................... 1715
Turks defeated at Peterwardein................................. 1716
They lose Belgrade, and their power declines................ 1717
Peace of Erivan (with Persia)................................... 1732
Belgrade taken from Austria, Russia relinquishes Azof........ 1739
Turks defeated at Kars.. 1745
Insurrection of Wahabees.. 1749
Great sea-fight in the channel of Scio; Russian fleet defeats the Turkish.. 1770
Crimea ceded to Russia......................................Jan. 1784
War with Russia and Austria; Turks lose more than 200,000 men...1787–91
Cession of Oczacow.. 1791
War with the French, who invade Egypt....................... 1798
Insurrection of Mamelukes at Cairo............................ 1803
War against Russia and England.........................7 Jan. 1807
Passage and repassage of the DARDANELLES by the British fleet, with great loss...19 Feb. "
Murder of Hali Aga...25 May, "
Janissaries massacre the newly disciplined troops........... 1808
Russians defeated at Silistria.................................... 1809
Treaty of Bucharest..28 May, 1812
Caravan of 2000 souls on return from Mecca destroyed by hot wind in Arabian desert; 20 saved..........................9 Aug. "
Subjugation of the Wahabees....................................1818–19
Ali Pacha of Janina, in Greece, declares himself independent.. 1820
Insurrection in Moldavia and Wallachia....................6 Mch. 1821
Persecution of Christians, 6 Mch.; the Greek patriarch murdered at Constantinople (GREECE)......................23 Apr. "
Horrible massacre at Scio (CHIOS)............................" 1822
Sea-fight near Mitylene; Turks defeated..................6 Oct. 1824

New Mahometan army organized 29 May, 1826

Insurrection of the Janissaries at Constantinople, they are suppressed and massacred 14-16 June, "

Battle of NAVARINO, Turkish fleet destroyed by those of England France and Russia 20 Oct. 1827

Banishment of 132 French 120 English, and 85 Russian settlers from the empire 5 Jan 1828

War with Russia 26 Apr "

Czar Nicholas takes the field 20 May, "

Capitulation of Brahilow 19 June, "

Surrender of Anapa 23 June "

Eminences of Shumla taken by Russians 20 July, "

Czar arrives before Varna 5 Aug "

Battle of Akhalzic 24 Aug "

Fortress of Bajazet taken 9 Sept "

Sultan proceeds to the camp with the sacred standard 26 Sept "

Dardanelles blockaded 1 Oct "

Surrender of Varna 11 Oct "

Russians retreat from Shumla 16 Oct "

Surrender of castle of the Morea to French 30 Oct "

Siege of Silistria raised by Russians 10 Nov "

Victory of Russians at Kulefscha, near Shumla 11 June, 1829

Battle near Erzeroum 2 July, "

Adrianople entered by Russians 20 Aug, armistice 29 Aug "

Treaty of peace at Adrianople 14 Sept "

Porte acknowledges independence of Greece 25 Apr 1830

Treaty with America 7 May, "

Military "order of glory" (Nischan) founded 19 Aug 1831

St Jean d'Acre taken by Ibrahim Pacha son of Mehemet Ali of Egypt 2 July, 1832

He defeats the army of the sultan at Konieh 21 Dec "

Ibrahim Pacha marches within 80 leagues of Constantinople, and the sultan asks the aid of Russia Jan 1833

Russians enter Constantinople 3 Apr "

Treaty with Russia, offensive and defensive 8 July, "

Office of grand vizier abolished 10 Mch 1838

Treaty of commerce with England concluded by lord Ponsonby, ratified 16 Aug "

War with Egypt SYRIA 1839-41

Christians admitted to office in Turkey June, 1849

Turkey, countenanced by England, refuses to surrender Hungarian and Polish refugees on joint demand of Russia and Austria 16 Sept "

Russia suspends intercourse with the Porte 12 Nov "

British fleet, under sir W Parker, anchors in Besika bay, 13 Nov "

Diplomatic relations between Russia and the Porte resumed, 31 Dec, refugees sent to Konieh Jan 1850

Turkish Croatia in a state of rebellion " 1851

Treaty with France on HOLY PLACES 13 Feb 1852

Imperial order of Medjidie founded Aug "

Prince Menschikoff at Constantinople as Russian negotiator, 28 Feb, his demands rejected 19 Apr 1853

Reschid Pacha becomes foreign minister, the ultimatum rejected, Menschikoff quits Constantinople 21 May, "

Hatti scheriff issued, confirming rights of Greek Christians, 6 June, "

Russian manifesto against Turkey 26 June, "

Russian army crosses the Pruth 2 July, "

Grand national council, war to be declared if the principalities are not evacuated . 26 Sept. "

War declared against Russia (RUSSO TURKISH WAR, Crimean) 5 Oct. "

Commencement of national debt (LOANS, 1854) 1854

Insurrection in Epirus and Albania favored by government at Athens, Hellenic empire proclaimed 27 Jan "

Volunteers from Athens join it 14 Mch "

Rupture between Greece and Turkey 28 Mch "

[Several conflicts ensue with varied success]

Osman Pacha storms Peta, the centre of insurrection 25 Apr "

English and French governments, after remonstrances, send troops to Piræus, the king of Greece submits, promising strict neutrality, Greek volunteers recalled 25 and 26 May, "

Convention between Turkey and Austria 14 June, "

Abdi Pacha and Fuad Effendi take the intrenched camp at Kolampaka, insurrection ends 18 June, "

Reschid Pacha retires, 3 June, resumes office 1 July, "

Russians leave the principalities, Austrians enter Sept. "

Turkish LOANS Aug 1855

Firman authorizing free exercise of religion 18 Feb 1856

Peace with Russia by treaty of Paris. 30 Mch "

Great Britain, France, and Austria guarantee integrity of Turkish empire 15 Apr "

Austrians quit the principalities Mch 1857

Misunderstanding among the allied powers respecting Moldavian elections which are annulled July, "

Massacre of Christians at Jedda. 15 June, 1858

Conflicts in Montenegro between natives and Turks July, "

Turkish financial reforms begun Aug "

First Turkish railway opened, Aidan to Smyrna 19 Sept "

Electric telegraph completed, Aden to Suez May, 1859

Conspiracy against sultan, 17 Sept, his brother implicated, several condemned to die, reprieved Sept and Oct. "

Alleged ill treatment of Christians in Turkey, proposed intervention of great powers, 5 May, Turkish government promises redress, 30 May, all powers satisfied except Russia, June, 1860

War between DRUSES and Maronites in Lebanon, massacres, June, "

Massacre of Christians at DAMASCUS (SYRIA) 9-11 July, "

Convention of the great powers at Paris, French armed intervention agreed to 2 Aug "

Sultan Abdul Medjid d, Aziz his brother succeeds 25 June. 1861

Imperial order of knighthood (Osmaneh), to include civil as well as military persons, founded Sept "

Treaties of commerce with Sweden, Spain, etc Mch 1862

Insurgents in Herzegovina submit, peace made with Montenegro 23 Sept "

Dispute with Servia settled 7 Oct "

Cholera at Constantinople, nearly 50 000 deaths, Aug, subsides Sept 1865

Revolt of the Maronites under Joseph Karam 30 Dec. "

Revolution in Bucharest (ROUMANIA) "

Insurrection in Candia Aug 1866

Maronite revolt under Joseph Karam suppressed, his flight, Jan, Turks leave 28 Mch 1867

Recommendation of the European powers to the sultan to give up Candia finally declined 31 Mch "

Sultan, with his son and nephew, visits Paris 1-12 July, London 12 July, entertained by the queen at Windsor, 13 July, by the lord mayor, 18 July, returns to Constantinople 7 Aug "

Sultan declines a proposition of Russia to suspend hostilities in Crete, and an international commission 4 Sept "

Meeting of the new council of state (including Jews and Christians), with legislative, but not executive functions 18 May, 1868

Porte requests the European powers to abolish consular jurisdictions, termed "capitulations" June, 1869

Khedive or viceroy of Egypt censured for encroaching on the sovereignty of the sultan Aug "

System of compulsory education promulgated Oct. "

Khedive submits to the sultan Dec "

Modification of the "capitulations" Apr 1870

Russia repudiates the treaty of Paris, 1856 31 Oct "

Note delivered to the Porte (RUSSIA) 15 Nov "

Sultan agrees to a conference on the Black Sea question alone, about 3 Dec "

Black Sea question settled by the conference at London (RUSSIA) 13 Mch 1871

Tunis incorporated with the empire by decree 23 Oct. "

Political reforms inaugurated by the new ministry Nov "

Roumelian railway connecting Constantinople, Adrianople, etc., opened 17 June, 1873

Sultan's jewels, etc, valued at 8,000,000*l*, exhibited at Vienna, Aug "

Inability to raise a loan, the sultan gives up a large sum, great financial reforms proposed Oct "

Turkish aggressions on South Arabia checked by Great Britain, Nov "

Great improvements in the army, formation of reserves "

Sultan ill, he recognizes his nephew Murad as successor, about 5 Oct. 1874

Austria, Germany and Russia assert to Turkey their right to treat separately with Roumania 20 Oct "

Mésoudiye or *Mesoudiyé*, Turkish iron clad, launched at Blackwall, Engl 28 Oct. "

Turkish debt 3,000 000*l* in 1854, 180,000,000*l* "

Budget estimated receipts, 21,711,764*l*, expenditure, 26 299,-178*l* June, 1875

Insurrection in Herzegovina, excitement in Bosnia, Servia, and Montenegro July-Aug "

Decree (deficit of 5,000,000*l*. in the budget) for 5 years' half interest on the debt, to be paid in cash, half in 5 per cent bonds 6 Oct "

Circular note remitting taxes and promising economical and commercial reform, 7 Oct, another, stating purpose of the government to stop onerous loans, develop the resources of the empire, etc 20 Oct. "

Remonstrance of British and Russian ambassadors with the government respecting expenditure and treatment of Christian subjects Sept.-Nov "

Firman issued, ordering reforms, equality of rights to Christians etc Dec "

Note of Andrassy, Austrian minister, respecting reforms, 30 Dec, adopted by Germany and Russia, Jan, by Great Britain, 18 Jan, transmitted to the Porte about 7 Feb, agreed to 10 Feb 1876

Insurrection in Bulgaria, promoted by foreign agitators, 1, 2 May, quickly suppressed by troops sent, 7 May, about 65 villages burned by the Bashi bazouks and other Turkish troops, several towns destroyed, about 15 000 persons killed, cruelties to women and children, a few Turks killed by Bulgarians in self defence (report by Mr Schuyler) May, "

Riots at Constantinople, the softas fanatical students, and others, demand reforms, and "Turkey for the Turks," ministerial changes, Mahmoud Pacha, the grand vizier, replaced by Mehemet Ruchdi, Europeans alarmed 10 May et seq "

British fleet arrives in Besika bay 26 May, "

At Berlin, ministers of Austria, Germany, and Russia meet, adopt a note to Turkey requiring an armistice of 2 months, and other measures, 11, 12 May, note accepted by France and Italy, not by Great Britain, 19 May, not presented because of the revolution 30 May, "

Grand vizier Mehemet Ruchdi, Hussein Avni, and Midhat Pacha request of the sultan some of his treasure to save the nation, he refuses, and is deposed, 29 May, his nephew proclaimed as Murad V, accepted by people, and recognized by Western powers. 30 May et seq "

Manifesto recognizing the danger of the empire through misgovernment, and promising amendment. . 2 June, "

Abdul Aziz recognizes Murad, his reported suicide by cutting arteries in the arm when insane (*see below*, June, 1881), 4 June, "

War declared by Servia, 1 July, by Montenegro. . 2 July, "

Tchernayeff and Servians enter Turkey, battle at Saitschar, or Zaicar, Turks have the advantage 3 July, 1876

Severe fight with Servians at Yavor, near Novi Bazar 6 July, with Montenegrins at Nevesinje 27 July, "

League in aid of Turkish Christians formed in London " "

Mukhtar Pacha defeated by prince Nikita, at Urba or Urbitza, in Herzegovina 28 July, "

Several days' conflict, Turks enter Servia, and capture Gurgosavatz Servians retreat 7 Aug. "

Turkish barbarities in Bulgaria reported by *Daily News* correspondent, substantiated by Mr Schuyler, American commissioner from Constantinople, dated 10 Aug "

Asserted victory of prince Nikita at Medun, near Kutchi, about 14 Aug "

Advance of the Turks under Abdul Kerim Pacha upon Alexinatz, severe fighting, 9 Aug 19-30 Aug "

Servia invites the mediation of the guaranteeing powers, about 24 Aug "

Murad V deposed on account of bad health, his brother Abdul-Hamid II proclaimed 31 Aug "

Armistice till 25 Sept agreed to about 17 Sept "

Prince Milan proclaimed king by the army at Deligrad, disapproved 16 Sept "

Report of Mr Baring, the British commissioner in Bulgaria, published 19 Sept "

[It established the facts "that a ferocious Mussulman soldiery, in revenge for a feeble and abortive insurrection were let loose on the inhabitants of a large province, that the population were barbarously massacred men women, and children included, and that during the storm of savage fury crimes of all descriptions and outrages unmentionable, were perpetrated on the inhabitants "—*Times*]

Firm despatch lord Derby to sir H Elliot, referring to Mr Baring's report, proposing longer armistice etc 21 Sept "

Porte receives propositions of 6 great powers 26 Sept "

Lord Derby informs deputation from city of London that the government seeks local self government for Turkish provinces in Europe, equal treatment of Mahometans and Christians, better administration for both, security for life and property, and effectual guarantees against outrages 27 Sept "

Servia rejects renewal of armistice, Tchernayeff and army dominant, fighting renewed 26, 27 Sept "

Servian attacks on Turks near Alexinatz repulsed 28, 29 Sept. "

In reply to Great Powers the Porte declines armistice, opposes administrative autonomy to provinces as impracticable, proposes a senate, and guarantees reforms 2 Oct "

Montenegrin victory at Danilograd 13 Oct "

Turkey proposes armistice for 6 months, 10 Oct , declined by Russia who proposes 4 to 6 weeks, longer being injurious to commerce etc 14 Oct "

Continued fighting, unfavorable to Servians 15-19 Oct "

Medun surrenders to Montenegrins 20 Oct "

Krevet taken by Turks 21 Oct. "

Result of fighting very favorable to Turks 19-21 Oct "

Turkish successes in the valley of the Morava " "

Servians and Russians defeated, armies under Tchernayeff and Horvatitch divided, 19-21 Oct , Djunis taken by Turks, Deligrad untenable, severe Russian loss 29 Oct "

Alexinatz captured by Turks, Russian ultimatum demands 6 weeks' armistice within 48 hours dated 31 Oct "

Armistice for 2 months signed 1 Nov "

Deligrad captured by Turks, now virtually masters of Servia, 1 Nov "

Deligrad evacuated by Turks 4 Nov "

Czar's speech at Moscow, he will act independently if guarantees are not obtained . 10 Nov "

Preliminary meetings of conference of representatives of 6 great powers begin (Great Britain, Russia, Austria, Germany, France, and Italy) 12 Dec "

Armistice extended to Feb 1877 Dec. "

New political constitution proclaimed (chief provisions indivisibility of the empire, the sultan supreme, individual liberty, freedom of all creeds, of the press, and of education, equal legal taxation, a senate and 2 chambers, general elections by ballot every fourth year, irremovable judges, etc), 23 Dec. "

Opening of the conference " "

Armistice extended to 1 Mch 28 Dec. "

Great national council of Turkey rejects the propositions of the conference, 18 Jan , it closes, 20 Jan , chief ambassadors leave soon after 22 Jan 1877

Negotiations for peace opened with Servia and Montenegro, about 26 Jan "

Gortschakoff's circular to great powers, inquiring their purposes, signed 19 Jan , published about 7 Feb "

Protocols of the conference published in *Times*, etc , early in Feb "

In Turkey "there is no aristocracy, no governing class, no organized democracy, no representative government" (*Marquess of Salisbury*) 20 Feb "

Peace with Servia signed 1 Mch "

First Turkish parliament opened, 30 senators, 90 deputies, speech from the sultan 19 Mch "

Protocol signed for 6 powers, principles—to wait for Turkish reforms and watch, conditional disarmament in Russia and Turkey (voidable under certain conditions) 31 Mch "

Protocol rejected by Turkey, 12 Apr , justificatory circular sent to the powers . Apr "

War declared by Russia (RUSSO TURKISH WAR, 1877) 24 Apr "

JIHAD or holy war against Russia propounded by the Sheikh-ul Islam about 28 May, "

Proclamation for increase of army by 150,000—Christians and others to serve 26 Nov 1877

Surrender of Plevna 10 Dec , circular note to the great powers requesting mediation 12 Dec "

Parliament opened, the sultan's speech censures the war and praises his generals and soldiers 13 Dec "

British fleet enter the Dardanelles without permission of the sultan 13 Feb 1878

Parliament dissolved by the sultan 14 Feb "

Insurrection in Crete Thessaly, Epirus, etc Feb , Mch "

Treaty of peace with Russia signed at San Stefano (STEFANO, SAN) 3 Mch , ratified at St. Petersburg 17 Mch "

Osman Pacha honorably received by sultan 24 Mch "

Grand duke Nicholas and the sultan exchange visits at Constantinople 26 Mch "

Secret British convention with Turkey (defensive alliance), if, by treaty of Berlin, Russia acquires Kars Ardahan, or Batoum Great Britain to join the sultan in arms in defending his dominions, he engaging to reform his government, Cyprus to be held by Great Britain till Russia returns its acquisitions 4 June, "

Cyprus ceded to Great Britain . 3 July, "

Berlin conference meets, 13 June, treaty signed (BERLIN), 13 July "

Ratification of the treaty of Berlin announced 4 Aug "

Definitive treaty of peace with Russia signed 8 Feb 1879

British fleet leaves the sea of Marmora Mch "

Definitive treaty with Austria, published 26 May, "

Russians evacuate Turkey July, Aug "

Pressure for reforms by British, adm Hornby and the fleet enter Turkish waters, quit early in Nov "

Baker Pacha appointed inspector general of gendarmerie in Asia Minor announced 18 Nov "

Official relations with Great Britain temporarily suspended on account of the imprisonment of dr Köller a German missionary and Ahmed Tewfik who assisted him in translations, 31 Dec "

Successful intervention of sir A H Layard 1-10 Jan 1880

Col and Mrs Synge (distributers of relief to Mussulmans) captured by Greek brigands, near Salonica, about 19 Feb , released for 10,000*l* about 24 Mch "

Collective note of Berlin conference presented 15 July, "

Madame Skobeleff mother of the Russian general, robbed and murdered near Philippopolis by Ouzalis a Russian 18 July, "

Collective note from powers urging cession of Dulcigno etc , to Montenegro, and proposing to aid the prince in taking possession 3 Aug "

Final note from powers respecting cession of Dulcigno to Montenegro, delivered 15 Sept "

Adm Beauchamp Seymour, commander of combined fleet at Ragusa, sent for a demonstration near Dulcigno 20 Sept "

Sultan refuses to surrender Dulcigno, French decline to partake in attack about 27 Sept "

Note from the sultan limiting his concessions and resisting coercion, presented 3 Oct "

Immediate cession of Dulcigno ordered by the sultan, about 23 Oct , effected 26 Nov "

Combined fleet disperses 4 Dec "

Note from the sultan to powers respecting the Greek arming, 14 Dec "

Circular from powers recommending arbitration, 24 Dec. 1880, declined by Turkey and Greece early in Jan 1881

Circular from Turkey proposing conference at Constantinople, etc about 15 Jan "

Notes from the powers presented 21 Feb "

Conference at Constantinople, agreement between Turkey and powers, proposals referred to Athens 30 Mch "

Sultan protests against French invasion of Tunis May, "

Turkey protests against the Tunis treaty of 12 May " "

Convention between Turkey and Greece arranged at Constantinople, settling frontiers, Thessaly ceded by Turkey 24 May, "

Trial of Midhat Pacha and others for murder of Abdul Aziz, June 4, 1876, convicted, Mustapha Fahri Bey and Hadji Mehmed actual assassins, others, Mahmoud and Nouzi Pachas the sultan's brothers in law, Midhat Pacha, and others, accomplices . 27, 28 June, "

Sentence, death to all, except 2 subordinates to imprisonment, 29 June, "

Turco-Greek convention ceding Thessaly to Greece, signed at Constantinople 2 July, "

Trial of Midhat and others said to be a mockery, pardon expected July, "

Midhat Pacha and his companions sentenced to death, punishment commuted to exile, on intercession of British government, announced 31 July, "

Henry Suter, engaged in mining, seized by brigands at Cassandria, Salonica, about 8 Apr 1881, liberated on paying 15,000*l* ransom, 23 May, brigands captured in Greece, 15 Aug "

German vessel *Vulcan* laden with dynamite (said to belong to Russia), cargo discharged near Constantinople about 8 Oct. "

Decree signed for a satisfactory settlement of the national debt, 28 Dec "

Sultan protests against bombardment of forts at Alexandria, about 11 July, 1882.

Turkish note to the powers against British Egyptian circular, about 23 Jan 1883

Death of Midhat Pacha, great statesman and reformer, in exile, aged 62 . . . . . . May, 1884

Circular to the 6 great powers announcing the stoppage of the post offices in Constantinople, 20 July, resisted, Turkish arrangements fail, and are withdrawn . Aug "

reek patriarch elected ....13 Oct. 1884
urkey protests against Italian occupation of Massowah on the Red sea..............................about 23 Feb. 1885
evolution in Roumelia ....18 Sept. "
urkey asks assistance of powers to settle the Roumelian affair..............................19 Oct. "
ultan ratifies treaty between Bulgaria and Servia....13 Mch. 1886
obart Pacha, Turkish admiral, dies, aged 64..........19 June, "
irect railway communication between London and Constantinople, *via* Dover and Calais, in 94 hours; first train from Vienna ....12–14 Apr. 1888
erman emperor and empress warmly received by the sultan at Constantinople, 2 Nov.; a review..............3–6 Nov. 1889
ive new war vessels launched at Constantinople......30 Jan. 1890
ussian government demands the arrears of the Russo-Turkish war indemnity..............................about 15 May, "
urkey defers payment of indemnity till Nov.; Russia demands immediate payment; note sent..............18 June, "
ritish cotton and yarn spinning factory opened at Constantinople ....22 June, "
urkish frigate *Ertogoul* founders off the south coast of Japan during a gale; of 653 persons 584 perish, among them vice-adm. Osman Pacha..............................18 Sept. "
rthodox churches reopened throughout European Turkey in time to permit the churches to celebrate Christmas, o.s., 5 Jan. 1891
ailroad train from Constantinople to Adrianople attacked by brigands and 5 passengers carried off; ransomed for 200,000 francs (8000*l.*) ....5 June, "
apture by brigands of a French engineer, Eugène de Raymond; ransomed by the sultan for 5000*l.*..............Aug. "
Kiamil Pacha, dismissed as grand-vizier, succeeded by Djevad Pacha (a change favoring Russia) ....Sept. "
ussia proposes that all Russian vessels flying the commercial flag between Russian ports have the right of free passage through the strait; objected to as contrary to international treaties; England supports the objection and demands the same privilege for herself if granted; proposition dropped.... 1892
isturbance in Armenia 1893
isturbance continued; reported massacre of several thousand Armenians by the Turks..............................Nov. 1894

TURKISH SULTANS.

299. Othman, Osman, or Ottoman, founded the empire, retained the title "emir," but ruled despotically.
326. Orchan, son, took the title "sultan."
360. Amurath (or Murad) I.; stabbed by a soldier, of which wound he died.
389. Bajazet I., Ilderim, son; defeated by Tamerlane, and died imprisoned.
403. Solyman, son; dethroned by his brother.
410. Musa-Chelebi; strangled.
413. Mahomet I., son of Bajazet.
421. Amurath II., son.
451. Mahomet II., son; took Constantinople, 1453.
481. Bajazet II., son.
512. Selim I., son.
520. Solyman I. or II., the Magnificent, son.
566. Selim II., son.
574. Amurath III., son; killed his 5 brothers; their mother, in grief, stabbed herself.
595. Mahomet III., son; strangled all his brothers, and drowned his father's wives.
603. Ahmed (or Achmet) I., son.
617. Mustapha I., brother; deposed by the Janissaries, and imprisoned.
618. Osman II., nephew; strangled by Janissaries.
622. Mustapha I. again; again deposed, sent to the Seven Towers, and strangled.
623. Amurath IV., brother of Osman II.
640. Ibrahim, brother; strangled by the Janissaries.
648. Mahomet IV., son; deposed by
687. Solyman II. or III., brother.
691. Ahmed (or Achmet) II., son of Ibrahim, nephew.
695. Mustapha II., eldest son of Mahomet IV.; deposed.
703. Ahmed (or Achmet) III., brother; deposed, and died in prison in 1736.
730. Mahmud I. (or Mahomet V.), son of Mustapha II.
754. Osman III., brother.
757. Mustapha III., brother.
774. Abdul-Ahmed, or Hamid I. (or Achmet IV.), brother.
789. Selim III., son of Mustapha III.; deposed by the Janissaries.
807. Mustapha IV., son of Abdul-Ahmed; deposed, and, with the late sultan Selim, murdered.
808. Mahmud II., or Mahomet VI., brother.
839. Abdul-Medjid (son), 2 July (b. 23 Apr. 1823); d. 25 June, 1861.
861. Abdul-Aziz, brother, b. 9 Feb. 1830; deposed 29 May; murdered 4 June, 1876 (see 1881).
876. Amurath V. (Murad), son of Abdul-Medjid, b. 21 Sept. 1840; proclaimed 30 May; deposed for bad health, 31 Aug.
" Abdul-Hamid II., brother, 31 Aug.; b. 22 Sept. 1842.
["He is not a tyrant, he is not dissolute, he is not a bigot or corrupt."—*Lord Beaconsfield*, 27 July, 1878.]
Son: Mehemed Selim, b. 11 Jan. 1870.

turkey, an American gallinaceous bird of the genus *Meleagris*, called turkey because at first it was supposed to be a native of Turkey, Tartary, or Asia, and even of Africa; frequently confounded with the guinea-hen. There are 2 species, the *M. americana* and the *M. mexicana*. The first is found in the northern and middle U.S. and Canada; the second in Texas, Mexico, and Central America. The *M. americana* is larger than the southern species, weighing from 12 to 20 lbs. when dressed. It was carried to Europe as early as 1523.

Türk'heim, a town of Alsace, Germany. Here the elector of Brandenburg and the imperialists were defeated by the French under Turenne, 5 Jan. 1675.

Turk's islands, a group of small islands, geographically a portion of the Bahamas, but under the government of Jamaica.

Turner's Falls, fight with the Indians at. MASSACHUSETTS, 1676.

Turner's legacies. Joseph M. W. Turner, the landscape-painter, was born in Apr. 1775, and died 19 Dec. 1851. He bequeathed to the British nation all the pictures and drawings collected by him and deposited at his residence, 47 Queen Anne street, on condition that a suitable gallery should be erected for them within 10 years; and directed his funded property to be expended in founding an asylum at Twickenham for aged and infirm artists. The will was disputed by his relatives, but a compromise was made. The oil-paintings (100 in number) and the drawings (1400) were obtained by the nation, and the engravings and some other property were transferred to the next of kin. The drawings were cleaned and mounted under the careful superintendence of Mr. Ruskin, and the pictures were sent to Marlborough House for exhibition. In 1861 many of the pictures were removed from the South Kensington Museum to the National Gallery, others in 1869. The sketches, plates, etc., of Turner's "Liber Studiorum" were sold for about 20,000*l.*, 28 Mch. 1873.

turning. LATHE. In British dock-yards, blocks and other materials for ships of war are now produced by an almost instantaneous process, from rough pieces of oak, by the machinery of Mr. (afterwards sir Mark Isambard) Brunel (d. 1849).

turnpikes. TOLLS.

turpentine (Gr. τερέβινθος, terebinth), an oily, resinous substance secreted by the wood or bark of a number of trees, all *coniferæ* except the terebinth (*Pistacia terebinthus*), which yields the Chian or Scio turpentine. The *Pinus palustris*, yellow pine or long-leaved pine of the southern U. S., Virginia to Florida, furnishes most of the turpentine of commerce. North Carolina, popularly known as the "turpentine state," exports several millions of gallons annually. Spirits of turpentine first applied with success in England to the rot in sheep (mixture, $\frac{1}{2}$ spirits to $\frac{2}{3}$ water) in 1772.

tur'quoise, a bluish-green mineral which, when highly colored, is esteemed as a gem. So called because it first came from Turkey. The turquoise mines near Santa Fé, New Mexico, were worked by the Spaniards, and furnished the regalia of Spain with the finest turquoises in Europe.

Tuscan order of architecture, a debased Doric, used in Tuscany for buildings in which strength is chiefly required.—*Wotton.*

Tus'cany, formerly a grand-duchy in central Italy, the northern part of the ancient ETRURIA. It formed part of the Lombard kingdom, after the conquest of which by Charlemagne, 774, it was made a marquisate for Boniface about 828. His descendant, the great countess Matilda, bequeathed the southern part of her domains to the pope (1115). In the northern part (then called Tuscia), the cities of Florence, Pisa, Sienna, Lucca, etc., gradually became flourishing republics. FLORENCE became the chief under the government of the Medici family. The duchy in that family began in 1531, and the grand-duchy in 1569. After the extinction of the Medicis in 1737, Tuscany was given by the treaty of Vienna (1738) to Francis, duke of Lorraine (married to Maria Theresa of Austria in 1736), who had ceded his hereditary estates to France. Area, 9287 sq. miles. Pop. in 1860, 1,826,830; 1890, estimated, 2,274,191.

French enter Florence ....28 Mch. 1799
Grand-duke is dispossessed, and his dominions given to Louis, duke of Parma (of the royal house of Spain), with the title of king of Etruria.............................. 1801
Tuscany incorporated with the French empire................ 1807
Grand-duchy given to Eliza, sister of Napoleon.............. 1808

Ferdinand III. restored 1814
Lucca united to Tuscany 1847
Leopold II. grants a free constitution .... 15 Feb. 1848
Insurrection at Florence; republic proclaimed; the grand-duke flies .... 11 Feb. 1849
He is restored by the Austrians .... July, 1850
Rigorous imprisonment of the Madiai, husband and wife, converts to Protestantism, for reading the Bible .... May, 1852
Earls of Shaftesbury and Roden and others in vain intercede for them at Florence .... Oct. "
They are released on intervention of Great Britain .... Mch. 1853
[An annuity was given them by subscription.]
Tuscan army demand alliance with the Sardinians; the grand-duke refuses, and departs to Bologna; king of Sardinia proclaimed dictator, and provisional government formed, 27 Apr. 1859
King assumes command of the army, but declines the dictatorship .... 30 Apr. "
Sardinian commissary Buoncompagni invested with the powers of government .... 11 May, "
Prince Napoleon arrives at Leghorn, addresses the Tuscans, and erects his standard .... 23 May, "
Grand-duke Leopold II. abdicates in favor of his son Ferdinand, 21 July, "
Tuscan constituent assembly meets .... 11 Aug. "
It declares against the house of Lorraine, and votes for annexation to Sardinia .... Sept. "
Prince Eugene of Savoy-Carignan elected governor-general of central Italy; he declines, but recommends Buoncompagni, Nov., who is accepted by the Tuscans .... 8 Dec. "
Annexation to Sardinia voted by universal suffrage, 11, 12 Mch.; decreed .... 22 Mch. 1860
Prince Eugene appointed governor .... 25 Mch. "
Florence made the capital of Italy, by decree published 11 Dec. 1864
FLORENCE, ITALY.

SOVEREIGNS OF TUSCANY.

DUKES.

1531. Alexander I.
1537. Cosmo I.

GRAND-DUKES.

1569. Cosmo I., *Medici.*
1574. Francis I.
1587. Ferdinand I.
1608. Cosmo II.
1621. Ferdinand II.
1670. Cosmo III. (visited England, and wrote an account of his travels).
1723. John Gaston (last of the Medici).
1737. Francis II. (duke of Lorraine); became emperor of Germany in 1745.
1765. Leopold I. (emperor in 1790).
1790. Ferdinand III. (second son of Leopold I.); expelled by the French in 1800.

KINGS OF ETRURIA.

1801. Louis I., duke of Parma.
1803. Louis II.

GRAND-DUCHESS.

1808-14. Eliza Bonaparte (married to Bacciocchi, made prince of Lucca).

GRAND-DUKES.

1814. Ferdinand III. restored.
1824. Leopold II., 18 June (b. 3 Oct. 1797; abdicated, 21 July, 1859); d. 29 Jan. 1870.
1859. Ferdinand IV., 21 July (b. 10 June, 1835); protested against the annexation of his grand-duchy, 26 Mch. 1860.
Son: Leopold Ferdinand, b. 2 Dec. 1868.

Tuscaro'ras, one of the "Six Nations." INDIANS; NEW YORK, 1712.

Tus'culum, now **Frasca'ti,** a city of Latium, S. Italy. The Tusculans supported Tarquinius Superbus against the Romans, by whom they were defeated, 497 B.C. The Tusculans, for their friendship with Rome, suffered much from other Latins, who took the city, 374, but were chastised for it. Here Cicero during his retirement wrote "Tusculanæ Disputationes," about 46 B.C.

Twelfth-day, the feast of the Epiphany, or manifestation of Christ to the Gentiles, 6 Jan. EPIPHANY.

Twelve tables. DECEMVIRI.

Ty'burn, at the west end of Oxford street, W. London; a noted place of execution for criminals convicted in Middlesex county, including London, down to 1 Nov. 1783, when the place of execution was transferred to NEWGATE, where the 1st execution took place 9 Dec. the same year. The name is derived from a brook called Tyburn, which once flowed from Hampstead into the Thames.—*Chambers.*

Tyler, John, administration of. UNITED STATES, 1841.

Tyler's insurrection, against a poll-tax imposed in England on all persons above 15, 5 Nov. 1380. One of the collectors, acting with indecent rudeness to Wat Tyler's daughter, was struck dead by the father, June, 1381. His neighbors took arms, and almost the whole population of the southern and eastern counties soon rose, extorting freedom from their lords, and plundering. On 12 June, 1381, they gathered upon Blackheath to the number of 100,000 men, and on 14 June murdered Simon of Sudbury, archbishop of Canterbury, and sir Robert Hales, the royal treasurer. The king, Richard II., invited Tyler to a parley, which took place on the 15th at Smithfield, where the latter addressed the king in a menacing manner, now and again lifting up his sword. On this the mayor, Walworth, stunned Tyler with a blow of his mace, and one of the king's knights despatched him. Richard temporized with the multitude, promising a charter, and thus led them out of the city, when sir R. Knollys and a band of knights attacked and dispersed them with great slaughter. The insurrection in Norfolk and Suffolk was subdued by the bishop of Norwich, and 1500 of the rebels were executed.

type-composing machine. Linotype, under PRINTING, 1888.

type-writers. M. Foucault sent to the Paris exhibition of 1855 a writing-machine for the blind; and several were invented by Wheatstone. After successive improvements, messrs. Remington, in the United States, in 1873, contracted to construct 25,000. The speed is said to have been raised to 75 words a minute. Many improved patents since.

Action of the type-writer somewhat resembles that of a pianoforte. Pressure upon a key marked with a letter raises a hammer with a type-cut letter, which presses upon paper; provision is made for inking the type, shifting the paper, etc.

tyrant (Gr. τύραννος). In early Greek history, the term was applied to any man who obtained despotic power in a state. The term was applied by the Greeks to the mild Pisistratus, but not to the autocrats of Persia. It became a term of reproach, because of the unjust manner in which the despots of cities often obtained and exercised their powers. Solon objected to the term, and chose the name ἀρχόν ("ruler"), 594 B.C. The earliest tyrants were those at Sicyon, beginning with Cleisthenes, in the 7th century B.C. Tyranny declined in Greece about 490 B.C., and revived after the close of the Peloponnesian war, 404 B.C. THIRTY TYRANTS.

Tyre in Phœnicia, a great city, said to have been first built by Agenor. Another city was built 1257 (about 2267 *Hales*) B.C. It was besieged by the Assyrians, who retired from before it, after a siege of upwards of 5 years, 713 B.C. Taken by Nebuchadnezzar, 572 B.C., after a siege of 13 years and the city demolished, when the Tyrians removed to an opposite island, and built a new and magnificent city. It was taken by Alexander with much difficulty, after a siege of 7 months, July, 332 B.C. He joined the island to the continent by a mole.—*Strabo.* Tyre was captured by the crusaders 7 July, 1124, and formed a royal domain of the kingdom of Jerusalem, as well as an archiepiscopal see. The first archbishop was an Englishman, William of Tyre, the well-known historian. In 1289 it was retaken by the Saracens; by the French, 3 Apr. 1799; and by the allied fleet, during the war against Mehemet Ali, 1841.

Tyre, Era of, began on 19 Oct. 125 B.C., with the month of Hyperberetæus. The months were the same as in the Grecian era, and the year is similar to the Julian year. To reduce this era to ours, subtract 124. But for a year less than 125, deduct the number from 125, and the remainder will be the year before Christ.

Tyr'ol, the eastern part of ancient Rhætia, now a province of the Austrian empire, was ceded to the house of Hapsburg in 1359 by Margaret, the heiress of the last count. It became an appanage of the younger (or Tyrol) branch of the imperial house, which came to the throne in the person of Maximilian II., in 1618. The French conquered the Tyrol in 1805, and united it to Bavaria; but in 1809 an insurrection broke out, headed by Andreas Hofer, an innkeeper, who drove the Bavarians out of the Tyrol, thoroughly defeated some French detachments, but laid down his arms at the treaty of Vienna. He was subsequently accused of corresponding with the Austrians, captured and sent to Mantua, and there shot by order of the French government, 20 Feb. 1810. The Austrian emperor ennobled his family in 1819, and erected his statue in Innspruck in 1834. The Tyrolese riflemen were very effective in the Italian war in 1859.

Tyrrhe'ni included the ancient Etruscans, and othe

tribes, said to have come from Lydia, Asia Minor, under Tyrrhenus, a son of Atys, king of Lydia, long before the destruction of Troy.—*Herodotus.* "Neither do I think the Tyrrhenes a colony of Lydians, for there is no resemblance here in language. These 2 peoples differ in laws, in manners, and institutions. That opinion then seems the most probable which supposes them an indigenous race in Italy."—*Clinton,* "Chronology of Greece."

U

U, the 21st letter of the English alphabet, and its 5th vowel. The *υ* (upsilon) added by the Greeks to the alphabet borrowed from the Phœnicians.

Ubiquita'rians or **Ubiqua'rians,** a small German sect, originated by John Brentius about 1560, who asserted that the body of Christ is present everywhere (*ubique*).

Uchees. Indians.

Ugan'da, a kingdom of equatorial Africa, near the head of the Nile, bordering on lake Victoria Nyanza. Capital, Mengo.

Missionaries sent out by the Church Missionary Society..July, 1877
French Roman Catholic missionaries arrive.................. 1879
Uganda placed under British influence by Anglo-German treaty, 1 July, 1890
Trouble between Protestant and Roman Catholic missionaries; disorder and bloodshed.................. 1891
Order restored at Mengo; the British East African company predominant.................. 1892

Uhlans, the national Polish lancers, adopted after the partition of Poland in the Austrian and German armies; efficient in the Franco-Prussian war of 1870.

U'kraine (Polish for frontier), a vast fertile plain in Russia, ceded to the Cossacks by Poland in 1672, and obtained by Russia in 1682. The country was divided, Poland having the west side of the Dnieper, and Russia the east. The whole was assigned to Russia by the treaty of partition in 1795.

"Among the rest Mazeppa . . .
The Ukraine's hetman, calm and bold."
—*Byron,* "Mazeppa."

Ulm, a town of Würtemberg, S. Germany, where a peace was signed, 3 July, 1620, by which Frederick V. lost Bohemia (having been driven from it previously). Ulm was taken by the French in 1796. After a battle between the French and Austrians, in which the latter, under gen. Mack, were defeated with dreadful loss by marshal Ney, Ulm surrendered with 28,000 men, the flower of the Austrian army, 17–20 Oct. 1805.

The cathedral was built 1377–1494. Last stone of the spire, 530 ft. high, said to be the loftiest in the world, laid with great rejoicing..................31 May, 1890

Ul'philas's Bible. Bible.

Ulster, the N. division of Ireland. After the death of Strongbow, 1176, John de Courcy was made earl of Ulster; Hugh de Lacy was earl in 1243, and Walter de Burgh in 1264, whose descendant, Elizabeth, married Lionel, son of Edward III., 1352. He thus became earl of Ulster. In 1611, the British colonization of the forfeited lands (termed the Ulster settlements or plantations) began, much land being granted to the corporation of London. The consequent rebellion of the Irish chieftains, Roger More, Phelim O'Neale, McGuire, earl of Inniskillen, and others, broke out on 23 Oct. 1641 (Ireland). Ulster king-at-arms appointed for Ireland, 1553. By the ancient "Ulster tenant-right," the outgoing tenant of a farm received from his successor a sum of money for the privilege of occupancy. A modified form of this right was adopted in the Irish Land act, passed 8 July, 1870. Ulster convention, proposed 8 Apr., met at Belfast, 17 June, 1892. 12,000 delegates present; duke of Abercorn presided. 5 resolutions for firmly maintaining the union of Great Britain and Ireland, in opposition to the scheme for home rule, were passed unanimously.

Ultramon'tanists (from *ultramontanus,* beyond the mountains), a term originally applied in France to those who upheld the authority of the pope against the freedom of the Gallican church, which had been secured by various bulls, and especially by the concordat of 15 July, 1801. Ultramontanists now are those who maintain the *official* infallibility of the pope of Rome. Gallicanism.

umbrella, described in early dictionaries as "a portable penthouse to carry in a person's hand to screen him from violent rain or heat." Umbrellas appear in the carvings at Persepolis. Niebuhr saw a great Arabian prince returning from a mosque, he and each of his family having a large umbrella carried by their side. Old chinaware shows the Chinese shaded by umbrellas. First used in the United States in Baltimore, brought from India, 1772. It is said that the first person who commonly carried an umbrella in London was the benevolent Jonas Hanway, who died in 1786.

John Macdonald, a footman, who wrote his own life, informs us that he had "a fine silk umbrella, which he brought from Spain; but he could not with any comfort to himself use it, the people calling out, 'Frenchman! why don't you get a coach?'" The hackney-coachmen and chairmen were clamorous against their rival. The footman says he "persisted for three months, till they took no further notice of this *novelty. Foreigners* began to use theirs; and then the English." 1778.

"Uncle Sam." The United States government is sometimes personified under this name, the origin of which is uncertain, though sometimes attributed to an incident in the commissary department in the state of New York during the war of 1812, where casks, etc., of provisions were marked U. S., supposed to stand for "Uncle Sam," as Samuel Wilson, who had charge of the stores, was called.

"Uncle Tom's Cabin," by Mrs. Stowe, first published in portions in *National Era* at Washington, 1851–52, and complete in Boston, 1852. The rev. Josiah Henson, the original "Uncle Tom," died at Dresden, Ont., 5 May, 1883, aged 93.

unction, Extreme. Anointing.

Underground railroad, a popular designation (1850–60) of the secret means by which slaves fleeing from their masters to the northern or free states were forwarded into Canada and thus made secure from the slave-hunters.

un'dulatory theory of light supposes a progressive wave-like motion from the source of light to the eye. It is said to have been suggested by Francisco Grimaldi about 1665, and was propounded by Robert Hooke and Huyghens about 1672; opposed by Newton; but confirmed by Thomas Young's experiments in 1801, and since fully demonstrated. Emission theory, Light.

uniform, the particular distinguishing dress of soldiers. The army of Timour or Tamerlane, who defeated the sultan Bajazet at Angora, 28 July, 1402, wore uniforms. At the relief of Neuss, 1471, the bishop of Münster's troops (7400 men) had green uniforms. Military uniforms were first used in France "in a regular manner" by Louis XIV., about 1668, and were soon after adopted in England. In the English navy uniforms were not definitely fixed until the beginning of the reign of George III. Scarlet is the prevailing color of the British army; blue of the French; white of the Austrian; green of the Muscovite and Spanish, and brown of the Portuguese. Uniforms in the American Revolution were of every variety, brown and white, blue and red, black and red, green and red, blue and white, etc. In 1777 gen. Knox's artillery wore black coats turned up with red, white wool jackets, and hats trimmed with yellow. The uniform of col. Heartley's foot-guards is described as blue regimental coat, white cape, white jacket, buckskin breeches, stockings and shoes. In 1778 col. Lee's regiment wore blue faced with white, white waistcoats and black breeches. In 1779 capt. Scott's company (gen. Putnam's division) wore blue regimental coat turned up with red, buttons marked U. S., flannel jacket and drawers, coarse white linen stockings, and shoes. Revolutionary "blue and buff" is spoken of as the American uniform worn at the Inauguration ball, 30 Apr. 1789. In "Duane's Military Dictionary," pub 1810, blue is said to be the established uniform in the U S, and "Hoyt's Military Dictionary" of the same date says, "the uniform of the infantry of the American army is blue with red facings"

New uniform for the army of the U S ordered to be worn on and after ... 1 Jan 1852
Uniform for the navy established ... 4 July, "

[Uniform of the U S army during the civil war, enlisted men dark blue blouse light blue trousers and overcoats, officers dark blue of the confederates, gray Prevailing color of present uniform in both army and navy of the U S, dark blue]

Uniformity acts. That of 2 and 3 Edward VI, 15 Jan 1549 ordained that the order of divine worship drawn up by Cranmer and others, "with the aid of the Holy Ghost," should be the only one after 20 May, under penalties of fine and imprisonment This act was confirmed in 1552, repealed by Mary, 1554, and re-enacted by Elizabeth in 1559 The act of Uniformity, 14 Caro II c 1, was passed in 1662 It enjoined uniformity in matters of religion, and obliged all clergy to subscribe the 39 articles, and use the same form of worship and book of common prayer Its enforcement on 24 Aug 1662, termed Black Bartholomew's day, caused, it is said, upwards of 2000 ministers to quit the church of England This day was commemorated by dissenters in 1862 The Act of Uniformity Amendment act, whereby shortened services were authorized and other changes made, was passed 18 July, 1872 The Uniformity of Process act, which made many law changes, was passed 23 May, 1832

Union, American UNITED STATES

Union college. Founded at Schenectady, N Y, Feb 1795, the second in the state Columbia college, New York city, being the first. Called Union, as indicating its freedom from sectarian influence. 1st president, rev John Blair Smith of Philadelphia, 2d rev Jonathan Edwards, 3d, rev Jonathan Maxcy, 4th, rev Eliphalet Nott, 1804-66, 5th, dr Laurens P Hickok, 1866-68, 6th, rev Charles A A Aiken, D D, 1869-71, 7th rev Eliphalet Nott Potter, D D, 1872-87, 8th, Harrison E Webster, LL D 1888 1st commencement, 1797, 3 graduates It is claimed for Union college that it was the first to provide a scientific course of study, substituting, in 1835, modern languages and an increased amount of mathematics and physical science for part of the Greek and Latin classical course. By a law of 1873, Union college, the Medical college, the Law school, Dudley Observatory, and the college of Pharmacy at Albany, were authorized to unite for their mutual benefit in one university corporation as Union university

union-jack. The original flag of England was the banner of St George, i e, white with a red cross, which, 12 Apr 1606 (3 years after James I ascended the throne), was incorporated with the banner of Scotland, i e, blue with a white diagonal cross This combination obtained the name of "union-jack," in allusion to the union with Scotland, and the word jack is considered a corruption of the word Jacobus, Jacques, or James This arrangement continued until the union with Ireland, 1 Jan 1801, when the banner of St. Patrick, i e, white with a diagonal red cross, was amalgamated with it, and forms the present British Union flag The union-jack of the United States or American jack is a blue field with white stars, denoting the union of the states. It is without the fly, which is the part composed of alternate stripes of white and red

Union of England and Scotland by the accession of James VI of Scotland as James I of England, 24 Mch 1603 The legislative union of the 2 kingdoms (as Great Britain) was attempted, but failed in 1604 and 1670, in the reign of Anne commissioners were appointed, the articles discussed, and, notwithstanding a great opposition made by the Tories, every article in the union was approved by a great majority, first in the House of Commons, and afterwards by the peers, 22 July, 1706, ratified by the Scottish Parliament, 16 Jan 1707, and became law 1 May, same year

Union of Great Britain and Ireland effected 2 July, 1800

Proposed in the Irish Parliament . . . . 22 Jan 1799
Act passes in the British Parliament. . 2 July, 1800
Imperial united standard first displayed at the Tower of London and upon Bedford Tower, Dublin Castle, on the act of legislative union becoming operative . 1 Jan 1801

Union Pacific railroad. PACIFIC RAILROAD

Unita'rians, termed Socinians from Lælius Socinus, who founded a sect in Italy about 1546 They profess to believe in and worship one only self-existent God, in opposition to those who worship the Trinity in unity They consider Christ to have been a mere man, and do not admit the need of atonement or of the complete inspiration of the Scriptures Michael Servetus printed a tract in disparagement of the doctrine of the Trinity In 1553, proceeding to Naples through Geneva, Calvin induced the magistrates to arrest him on a charge of blasphemy and heresy Servetus, refusing to retract his opinions, was condemned to the flames, which sentence was carried into execution, 27 May, 1553 Servetus is numbered among anatomists who came near the explanation of the circulation of the blood, before Harvey made the theory complete Matthew Hamont was burned at Norwich for denying Christ to be the son of God, 1 June, 1579 One of the first churches nominated Unitarian in England was established in Essex street, London, in 1774, by rev Theophilus Lindsey Dr Joseph Priestley for preaching the doctrine, was driven out of Birmingham, 1794 Unitarians were not included in the Toleration act till 1813 Their tenets resembled those of the Arians and Socinians The Unitarian Marriage bill was passed in Great Britain June, 1827. In Dec 1833, by a decision of the vice-chancellors, the Unitarians (as such) lost the possession of lady Hewley's charity, the decision was affirmed on appeal in 1842 British and Foreign Unitarian Association founded to promote Unitarianism, 1825 There were between 300 and 400 Unitarian churches in the United Kingdom in 1891 In America dr James Freeman of King's chapel, Boston, in 1783, removed from the "Prayer Book of Common Prayers" all reference to the Trinity or Deity and worship of Christ, his church became distinctly Unitarian in 1787 In 1801 the Plymouth church declared itself Unitarian Dr William Ellery Channing (1780-1842) was the acknowledged head of this church until his death The American Unitarian association was formed 24 May, 1825, headquarters at Boston, Mass The Western conference organized 1852, and a National Unitarian conference at New York city, 5 Apr 1865 There are about 400 churches in the United States, 2 theological schools, one at Cambridge, Mass, and one at Meadville, Pa

United Brethren. MORAVIANS.

United Kingdom. England and Wales were united in 1283, Scotland to both in 1707, and the British realm was named the United Kingdom on the union of Ireland, 1 Jan 1801 UNION OF ENGLAND AND SCOTLAND

United Presbyterians. In 1732 Ebenezer Erskine and others seceded from the church of Scotland Differing in interpretation of the oath administered to the burgesses, to profess "the true religion, presently professed within this realm and authorized by the laws thereof," they divided into Burghers and Anti-Burghers in 1747 In 1820 they reunited as the United Associate Synod of the Secession church, which joined the Relief church, 13 May, 1847, to form the United Presbyterian church in Scotland The United Presbyterian church of North America was formed in May, 1858, by the union of the Associated Presbyterian church and Associate Reformed Presbyterian church, and their first General Assembly met at Xenia, O, in May, 1859 The United Presbyterian Theological seminary at Xenia, O, was founded at Canonsburg, Pa, in 1794, removed to Xenia in 1860, and chartered in 1877 The Seminary of the United Presbyterian church was established at Alleghany City, Pa, in 1825, and chartered in 1868 The present (1891) strength of the United Presbyterian church in the United States is as follows Presbyteries, 59, ministers 782, churches, 815, members, 106,385.

United States of America. On 9 Sept 1776, the Continental Congress resolved "that in all continental commissions where heretofore the words 'United Colonies' have been used, the style be altered for the future to United States" This domain now numbers 45 states, 5 territories, and 1 district The area of the states is 2,718,780 sq miles, of the territories, 883,490, and of the district, 70, in all 3,602,340 sq miles In latitude it extends from Key West, its most southerly point, 24° 33′ N, to the 49th parallel of north latitude From this latitude, on the Pacific coast, the territory belongs to Canada to 54° 40′, where Alaska begins, extending to the Arctic ocean and embracing an area of over 577,000 sq. miles. In longitude it extends from the most easterly point of Maine, 66° 48′ W., to 125° 20′ W., and if Atoo, the most westerly of the Aleutian islands, be taken for its western limits, it extends to the 174th meridian. The population of this territory in 1890, not including Alaska or the Indian territory, was 62,622,250. In 1900, including Alaska and Indian territory, 76,303,387. Each state has an independent legislature for its local affairs, but all are legislated for, in national matters, by 2 houses of congress: the Senate, whose members are elected for 6 years by the state legislatures, and the House of Representatives, elected for 2 years by the people of the different states. Representation in the Senate is by states, without regard to population; in the House of Representatives the representation is in proportion to population. The president of the United States is elected every 4th year by electors chosen by the people, each state having as many electoral votes as it has senators and representatives in Congress. For its general history, administration, etc., see *infra;* for the colonies and states see under their proper heads; also ARMY, CABINET, COIN, CUSTOMS, EXPENDITURES, NATIONAL DEBT, NAVY, POPULATION, PRESIDENT, REPRESENTATIVES, REVENUE, SENATE, TARIFF, etc.

Under the Continental Congress.

[For previous history see each state separately.]

Pursuant to arrangements made by committees appointed in the several colonies to confer with each other regarding the mutual interests and safety of the colonies, and termed "Committees of Correspondence," delegates were chosen for the First Continental Congress, to meet at Philadelphia about 1 Sept. 1774.

First Continental Congress meets at Carpenter's hall, Philadelphia (44 delegates present, representing all the states except Georgia and North Carolina; see below) ....Monday, 5 Sept. 1774

[Peyton Randolph of Virginia, president; Charles Thomson, secretary. Mr. Thomson remained secretary of the Continental Congress from its beginning to its close, 1774–89.]

DELEGATES TO THE FIRST CONTINENTAL CONGRESS.

Delegates.	State represented.	Credentials signed.
1. Maj. John Sullivan....	New Hampshire.........	21 July, 1774
2. Col. Nathaniel Folsom		
3. Hon. Thomas Cushing	Massachusetts Bay......	17 June, 1774
4. John Adams.........		
5. Samuel Adams.......		
6. Robert Treat Paine....		
7. Hon. Stephen Hopkins	Rhode Island and Providence Plantations...	10 Aug. 1774
8. Hon. Samuel Ward....		
9. Hon. Eliphalet Dyer..	Connecticut............	13 July, 1774
10. Hon. Roger Sherman..		
11. Silas Deane..........		
12. James Duane	City and county of New York, and other counties in province of New York........	28 July, 1774
13. Philip Livingston		
14. John Jay............		
15. Isaac Low...........		
16. John Alsop..........		
17. John Herring........		
18. Simon Boerum.......		
19. Henry Wisner........		
20. Col. William Floyd....	County of Suffolk in province of New York	28 July, 1774
21. James Kinsey........	New Jersey.............	23 July, 1774
22. John De Hart........		
23. Richard Smith.......		
24. William Livingston...		
25. Stephen Crane.......		
26. Hon. Joseph Galloway	Pennsylvania...........	22 July, 1774
27. Samuel Rhodes		
28. Thomas Mifflin......		
29. John Morton.........		
30. Charles Humphreys..		
31. Edward Biddle.......		
32. George Ross.........		
33. John Dickinson......		
34. Hon. Cæsar Rodney...	Newcastle, Kent, and Sussex on the Delaware...............	1 Aug. 1774
35. Thomas McKean.....		
36. George Read.........		
37. Robert Goldsborough .	Maryland...............	22 June, 1774
38. William Paca		
39. Samuel Chase........		
40. Thomas Johnson.....		
41. Matthew Tilghman....		

UNI

DELEGATES TO FIRST CONTINENTAL CONGRESS.—(*Continued.*)

Delegates.	State represented.	Credentials signed.
42. Hon. Peyton Randolph	Virginia...............	5 Aug. 1774
43. Patrick Henry		
44. Benjamin Harrison...		
45. George Washington...		
46. Richard Bland		
47. Edmund Pendleton...		
48. Richard Henry Lee...		
49. Henry Middleton.....	South Carolina..........	6 July, 1774
50. Christopher Gadsden .		
51. Edward Rutledge.....		
52. John Rutledge.......		
53. Thomas Lynch.......		
54. Richard Caswell......	North Carolina..........	25 Aug. 1774
55. Joseph Hewes.......		
56. William Hooper......		
Delegates mentioned above not present at 1st day of meeting.		Date of joining.
Richard Henry Lee......	..Virginia...............	6 Sept. 1774
Thomas Johnson........	..Maryland..............	" "
Matthew Tilghman......	.. "	12 Sept. "
Henry Wisner..........	New York..............	14 Sept. "
John Alsop............		
George Ross...........	..Pennsylvania...........	" "
Joseph Hewes..........	North Carolina.........	" "
William Hooper........		
Richard Caswell.......	.. "	17 Sept. "
John Dickinson	..Pennsylvania..........	" "
John Herring	..New York.............	26 Sept. "
Simon Boerum.........	.. "	1 Oct. "

Congress resolves "that in determining questions, each colony or province shall have one vote" ...6 Sept. 1774

Rev. Jacob Duché (Episcopal) opens Congress with prayer...............................7 Sept. "

[Mr. Duché afterwards went over to the British and retired to England, 1778; but returned to the U. S. 1790, and died in Philadelphia, 1794.]

Resolution of Suffolk, Mass., convention (6 Sept.), "that no obedience is due to any part of the recent acts of Parliament," approved by Congress, 10 Sept. "

Congress rejects a plan for union with Great Britain, proposed by Joseph Galloway of Pennsylvania, as intended to perpetuate dependence....... 28 Sept. "

Battle of Point Pleasant, west Virginia (VIRGINIA), 10 Oct. "

Congress adopts a "Declaration of Colonial Rights," claiming self-government...............14 Oct. "

American Association, denouncing foreign slave-trade, and pledging the signers to non-consumption and to non-intercourse with Great Britain, Ireland, and the British West Indies, signed by 52 members of Congress...........................20 Oct. "

"Address to the People of Great Britain," prepared by John Jay, approved by Congress.........21 Oct. "

Congress adopts a "Memorial to the Several Anglo-American Colonies" ....21 Oct. "

A letter to the unrepresented colonies of St. John, N.S., Georgia, and east and west Florida, despatched by Congress............................ 22 Oct. "

Randolph resigning on account of indisposition, Henry Middleton of South Carolina succeeds him as president of Congress.......................22 Oct. "

"Petition to the King" drawn by John Dickinson, ordered sent to colonial agents in London by Congress............................ 25 Oct. "

Congress adopts "An Address to the People of Quebec," drawn by Dickinson....................26 Oct. "

First Continental Congress dissolved; 52 days' session (actual session 31 days)..................... 26 Oct. "

[Proceedings of First Continental Congress endorsed by the colonies: Connecticut, Nov. 1774; Massachusetts, 5 Dec. 1774; Maryland, 8 Dec. 1774; Rhode Island, 8 Dec. 1774; Pennsylvania, 10 Dec. 1774; South Carolina, 11 Jan. 1775; New Hampshire, 25 Jan. 1775; Delaware, 15 Mch. 1775; Virginia, 20 Mch. 1775; North Carolina, 7 Apr. 1775 New Jersey, 26 May, 1775.]

Rhode Island colonists seize 44 pieces of ordnance at Newport.............................6 Dec. "

Maryland convention enrolls the militia and votes 10,000*l.* to purchase arms.............8–12 Dec. "

New Hampshire freemen seize 100 barrels of powder and some ordnance at Portsmouth........11 Dec. 1774
Benjamin Franklin returns from England (PENNSYLVANIA).................................Apr. 1775
Delegates from Georgia to Congress by letter express loyalty, and explain inability to attend.....8 Apr. "
First anti-slavery society in the U. S. formed by Quakers of Philadelphia................14 Apr. "
Battle of LEXINGTON, Mass., at dawn of......19 Apr. "
Letters from England to public officials in America, expressing determination of England to coerce the colonies, intercepted at Charleston, S. C.....19 Apr. "
Col. Samuel H. Parsons and Benedict Arnold plan, at Hartford, Conn., the capture of fort Ticonderoga, N. Y..............................27 Apr. "
Arnold leads his company from New Haven to Boston, arriving............................29 Apr. "

Second Continental Congress meets at Independence hall, Philadelphia ....10 May, "
[Peyton Randolph, president; Charles Thomson, secretary.]

COLONIES REPRESENTED IN SECOND CONTINENTAL CONGRESS.

Colonies represented.	Delegates.	When chosen.
Connecticut	5	3 Nov. 1774
Massachusetts..................	5	5 Dec. "
Maryland.......................	7	8 Dec. "
Pennsylvania...................	6	15 Dec. "
New Jersey.....................	5	24 Jan. 1775
New Hampshire..................	2	25 Jan. "
South Carolina.................	5	3 Feb. "
Delaware.......................	3	16 Mch. "
Virginia.......................	7	20 Mch. "
North Carolina	3	5 Apr. "
New York.......................	12	22 Apr. "
Pennsylvania (additional)	3	6 May, "
Rhode Island...................	2	7 May, "

FORT TICONDEROGA captured by Ethan Allen, 10 May, "
CROWN POINT, N. Y., captured by Americans, 12 May, "
Lyman Hall seated in Congress as delegate from Georgia............................13 May, "
Americans under Benedict Arnold capture St. John, Canada............................16 May, "
Articles of Union and Confederation (CONFEDERATION, ARTICLES OF) agreed upon in Congress...20 May, "
Mecklenburg declaration of independence signed and forwarded to Congress (NORTH CAROLINA), 20 May, "
John Hancock of Massachusetts chosen president of Congress...........................24 May, "
[Randolph having resigned on account of ill-health.]
British generals Howe, Clinton, and Burgoyne arrive at Boston from England with troops......25 May, "
Congress adopts an "Address to the Inhabitants of Canada"...........................29 May, "
Congress votes to raise 20,000 men.........14 June, "
George Washington, nominated by Thomas Johnson of Maryland, is unanimously elected by Congress commander-in-chief of the American forces, 15 June, "
Battle of Bunker Hill (MASSACHUSETTS, 16-17 June, 1775) and burning of Charlestown.......17 June, "
Resolved by Congress, "That a sum not exceeding two million of Spanish milled dollars be emitted by Congress in bills of credit for the defence of America"...............................22 June, "
Washington takes command of the army at Cambridge (he left Philadelphia 21 June)............3 July, "
Declaration by Congress, the causes and necessity for taking up arms........................6 July, "
Congress adopts a second petition to the king..8 July, "
First provincial vessel commissioned for naval warfare in the Revolution, sent out by GEORGIA..10 July, "
Congress organizes a systematic superintendence of Indian affairs, creating 3 departments, northern, middle, and southern..................12 July, "
Importation of gunpowder, saltpeter, sulphur, and fire-arms permitted by act of Congress........15 July, "
Georgia joins the United Colonies..........20 July, "

UNI

Franklin's plan of confederation and perpetual union, "The United Colonies of North America," considered by Congress..................21 July, 1775
Benjamin Franklin, first postmaster-general, establishes posts from Falmouth, Me., to Savannah, Ga., 26 July, "
Congress resolves to establish an army hospital, 27 July, "
Congress adopts an "Address to the People of Ireland," 28 July, "
Resolved by Congress, "That Michael Hillegas and George Clymer, Esqs., be joint treasurers of the United Colonies"......................29 July, "
British vessel, the *Betsy*, surprised by a Carolina privateer off St. Augustine bar, and 111 barrels of powder captured (GEORGIA)..........................Aug. "
King issues a proclamation for suppressing rebellion and sedition in the colonies ....23 Aug. "
American troops under gen. Richard Montgomery sent into Canada to cut off British supplies.........Sept. "
Col. Benedict Arnold, with a force of about 1100 men, marches against Quebec *via* Kennebec river ..Sept. "
English ship seized off Tybee island, Ga., by the Liberty people, with 250 barrels of powder....17 Sept. "
British capture col. Ethan Allen and 38 men near Montreal ....25 Sept. "
Bristol, R. I., bombarded (RHODE ISLAND).....7 Oct. "
Gen. William Howe supersedes gen. Gage as commander of the British army in America, who embarks for England.....................10 Oct. "
Falmouth, Me., burned by British (MAINE) ...18 Oct. "
Peyton Randolph d. at Philadelphia.........22 Oct. "
St. John, Canada, surrenders to Americans under Montgomery...............................2 Nov. "
Congress orders a battalion to protect Georgia, 4 Nov. "
British fleet repulsed at Hampton, Va., 25 Oct. 1775, and lord Dunmore declares open war.......7 Nov. "
Night attack of the British vessels *Tamar* and *Cherokee* on the schooner *Defence*, in Hog Island channel, S. C. (SOUTH CAROLINA)..................12 Nov. "
Americans under Montgomery capture Montreal, 13 Nov. "
Benjamin Harrison, Benjamin Franklin, Thomas Johnson, John Dickinson, and John Jay, appointed by Congress a committee for secret correspondence with friends of America in Great Britain, Ireland, and other foreign nations...............29 Nov. "
Battle of Great Bridge (VIRGINIA) ....9 Dec. "
Congress appoints Silas Deane, John Langdon, and Christopher Gadsden, a committee to fit out 2 vessels of war, 25 Nov., orders 13 vessels of war built and appoints Esek Hopkins commander (NAVY, U.S.), 13 Dec. "
British vessels driven from Charleston harbor, S. C., by artillery company under col. Moultrie, stationed on Haddrell's Point...........................Dec. "
American forces united under Montgomery and Arnold repulsed at Quebec; gen. Montgomery killed, 31 Dec. "

Washington unfurls the first union flag of 13 stripes at Cambridge, Mass. (FLAG)................1 Jan. 1776
Norfolk, Va., partly burned by gov. Dunmore .. " "
Thomas Paine publishes "Common Sense" (PENNSYLVANIA)..........................8 Jan. "
Battle of Moore's Creek, N. C.; McDonald's loyalists routed by militia; 70 killed and wounded..27 Feb. "
Silas Deane appointed political agent to the French court..................................2 Mch. "
Howe evacuates Boston (MASSACHUSETTS)...17 Mch. "
Congress authorizes privateering...........23 Mch. "
Congress orders the ports open to all nations...6 Apr. "
North Carolina declares for independence ....22 Apr. "
American forces under gen. John Thomas retire from the siege of Quebec...................6 May, "
Rhode Island, 4 May; Massachusetts, 10 May; and Virginia, 14 May, declare for independence .... "
Congress advises each colony to form a government independent of Great Britain............15 May, "
Gen. Thomas d. of small-pox at Chambly.....2 June, "
Resolution introduced in Congress by Richard Henry Lee, that "the United Colonies are and ought to be

free and independent states, that they are absolved from all allegiance to the British crown, and that their political connection with Great Britain is and ought to be totally dissolved " 7 June, 1776

Committee appointed by Congress to prepare a form of confederation (CONFEDERATION, ARTICLES OF), 11 June, "

Committee appointed by Congress to draw up a Declaration of Independence 11 June, "

Board of War and Ordnance appointed by Congress, consisting of 5 members, viz John Adams, Roger Sherman, Benjamin Harrison, James Wilson, and Edward Rutledge, Richard Peters elected secretary, 12 June, "

[This board several times changed, continued until Oct 1781, when Benjamin Lincoln was appointed secretary of war, an office created by Congress in Feb]

American forces under gen Sullivan retire from Canada to Crown Point, N Y 18 June, "

Unsuccessful attack on FORT MOULTRIE by British fleet under sir Peter Parker 28 June, "

DECLARATION OF INDEPENDENCE adopted by Congress, 4 July, "

Declaration of Independence read to the army in New York by order of gen Washington 9 July, "

[The same night the statue of George III in Bowling Green was thrown down, and the lead in it afterwards cast into 42 000 bullets for the patriot army]

Engrossed Declaration signed by 54 delegates 2 Aug "

British gen lord Howe lands 10 000 men and 40 guns near Gravesend, L I 22 Aug "

Battle of LONG ISLAND (NEW YORK) 27 Aug "

Washington withdraws his forces from Long Island to the city of New York 29-30 Aug "

First society of SHAKERS in the United Colonies reach New York, 1774, and settle at Watervliet, N Y, Sept. "

Congress resolves "that all Continental commissions in which heretofore the words 'United Colonies' have been used, bear hereafter the words 'UNITED STATES'" 9 Sept. "

Americans evacuate New York city 14 Sept. "

British repulsed at HARLEM HEIGHTS 16 Sept. "

Benjamin Franklin, Silas Deane, and Arthur Lee appointed ambassadors to the court of France, 22 Sept. "

Nathan HALE executed as a spy at New York, 22 Sept "

Battle on lake Champlain, British victory (NEW YORK) 11-13 Oct "

Thaddeus Kosciuszko, a Pole, arrives, recommended to Washington by dr Franklin, appointed col of engineers by Congress 18 Oct "

Battle of WHITE PLAINS, N Y, British victory, 28 Oct "

Franklin sails for France in the *Reprisal*, of 16 guns, one of the new Continental frigates, the first national vessel to appear in the eastern hemisphere Oct "

Congress authorizes the raising of $5,000,000 by lottery for expenses of the next campaign 1 Nov. "

FORT WASHINGTON on the Hudson captured by the British 16 Nov "

Americans evacuate FORT LEE, 18 Nov, and retreat across New Jersey to Pennsylvania Nov "

Eight thousand British troops land and take possession of Rhode Island . . 28 Nov. "

Washington with his forces crosses the Delaware into Pennsylvania . . 8 Dec. "

Sir Peter Parker takes possession of Rhode Island, and blockades the American fleet at Providence 8 Dec "

Second Continental Congress (Philadelphia) adjourns, 582 days' session 12 Dec "

Maj -gen Charles Lee captured by British at Baskingridge, N J 12 Dec "

Third Continental Congress meets at Baltimore, Md., 20 Dec. "

[John Hancock president.]

Battle of TRENTON, N. J . 26 Dec "

Congress resolves to send commissioners to the courts of Vienna, Spain, Prussia, and Tuscany .30 Dec. "

Battle of PRINCETON . . .3 Jan 1777

Washington's army encamps for the winter at Morristown . . . . . . Jan. "

UNI

Voted in Congress "that an authentic copy, with names of the signers of the Declaration of Independence, be sent to each of the United States" 20 Jan 1777

Americans under gen Maxwell capture Elizabethtown, N J 23 Jan "

Letters of marque and reprisal granted by England against American ships 6 Feb "

Five vessels belonging to a British supply fleet are sunk near Amboy, N J 26 Feb "

Third Continental Congress (Baltimore) adjourns 75 days' session 4 Mch "

Fourth Continental Congress meets at Philadelphia 4 Mch "

[John Hancock president]

Vermont declares itself an independent state, Jan 1777, and presents a petition to Congress for admission into the confederacy, which was denied 8 Apr

Danbury, Conn, destroyed by troops under ex-gov Tryon 26 Apr "

Col Meigs with whale boats from Guilford, attacks the British forces at Sag Harbor destroying vessels and stores and taking 90 prisoners 23 May, "

Stars and Stripes adopted by Congress (FLAG), 14 June, "

British under gen Howe evacuate New Jersey, crossing to Staten Island 30 June, "

British under Burgoyne appear before Ticonderoga, 1 July, "

American garrison withdraw (NEW YORK) 6 July, "

Battle of HUBBARDTON, Vt. (VERMONT) 7 July, "

British gen Richard Prescott surprised and captured near Newport by lieut -col Barton (RHODE ISLAND), 10 July, "

Miss Jane McCrea captured by Indians in British employ at fort Edward, N Y, and shot and scalped (NEW YORK) 27 July, "

On the approach of Burgoyne gen Schuyler evacuates fort Edward, and retreats down the Hudson valley, 29 July, "

Gen Lafayette, who volunteers his services to Congress, is commissioned major-general 31 July, "

Lafayette introduced to Washington in Philadelphia, and attached to his personal staff 3 Aug "

Battle of ORISKANY, N Y 6 Aug "

Battle of BENNINGTON, Vt. 16 Aug "

Gen Philip Schuyler succeeded by gen Horatio Gates in command of the northern army 19 Aug. "

Gen Arnold sent to relieve FORT SCHUYLER, invested by British under St Leger, who retreats and returns to Montreal 22 Aug "

Battle of BRANDYWINE, Washington defeated, 11 Sept. "

Count Pulaski commissioned brigadier-general by Congress 15 Sept "

Fourth Continental Congress adjourns, 199 days' session, 18 Sept. "

Battle of Stillwater, N Y, indecisive (BEMIS'S HEIGHTS) 19 Sept "

Three hundred of Wayne's troops slaughtered at PAOLI 20-21 Sept. "

British army occupies Philadelphia 27 Sept "

Fifth Continental Congress meets at Lancaster, Pa, and adjourns, one day's session 27 Sept "

[Hancock president]

Sixth Continental Congress meets at York, Pa, 30 Sept "

[Hancock president]

Battle of GERMANTOWN, Americans repulsed 4 Oct. "

Forts CLINTON and MONTGOMERY captured by the British 6 Oct "

Battle of Saratoga, N Y (BEMIS'S HEIGHTS) 7 Oct "

Gen Burgoyne's army surrenders (CONVENTION TROOPS) 17 Oct. "

Successful defence of FORT MIFFLIN and FORT MERCER . 22-23 Oct. "

Congress creates a new Board of War, gen Gates presiding Oct "

[The "CONWAY CABAL," a conspiracy to remove Washington, followed]

Henry Laurens of South Carolina chosen president of Congress to succeed Hancock, resigned on account of ill health 1 Nov 1777
Articles of Confederation adopted (CONFEDERATION, ARTICLES OF) 15 Nov "
Forts MIFFLIN and MERCER besieged by the British and captured 16-20 Nov "
Congress recommends to the several states to raise by taxes $5,000,000 for the succeeding year . Nov "
Howe leaves Philadelphia with 14,000 men to drive Washington from his position at Whitemarsh, but does not attack . 4 Dec "
Howe hurriedly returns to Philadelphia 8 Dec "
American army goes into winter quarters at VALLEY FORGE, on the Schuylkill 18 Dec. "
Gen Chas. Lee released in exchange for gen Prescott, Dec "
Battle of the KEGS . 5 Jan 1778
Gen John Cadwallader seriously wounds gen Conway in a duel (CONWAY CABAL) . 5 Feb "
Louis XVI acknowledges the independence of the colonies, and signs a treaty of alliance and commerce, 6 Feb "
Congress prescribes an oath for officers of the army, Feb "
Baron Steuben joins the camp at Valley Forge (ARMY, List of general officers, NEW YORK, 1791) Feb "
Bill introduced by lord North in Parliament concerning peace negotiations with America reaches Congress 15 Apr, and is rejected 22 Apr "
French treaty reaches Congress by messenger 2 May, "
Deane's treaty with France ratified 4 May, "
Mischianza, a festival, is given at Philadelphia by the British officers in honor of sir William Howe (who had been succeeded by sir Henry Clinton), 6 days before his return to England 18 May, "
[Maj John André was the chief inventor of the pageant, which consisted of a regatta on the Delaware river, a tournament grand ball, and supper, and concluded with a great display of fireworks.]
Affair at BARREN HILL . 20 May, "
British raid in Warren and Bristol, R I 25 May, "
Col Ethan Allen, released from imprisonment, returns to Bennington, Vt 31 May, "
Count Pulaski raises a legion in MARYLAND "
Earl of Carlisle, George Johnstone, and William Eden appointed peace commissioners to America, with prof Adam Ferguson as secretary, on reaching Philadelphia they address a letter to Congress (see below, 11 Aug) 10 June, "
British evacuate Philadelphia and retire across the Delaware into New Jersey 18 June, "
Americans break camp at VALLEY FORGE and follow, 18 June, "
Sixth Continental Congress adjourns, 272 days' session, 27 June, "
Battle of MONMOUTH COURT-HOUSE, N J, British retreat 28 June, "
"Molly Pitcher" commissioned sergeant by Washington for bravery at Monmouth .29 June, "

Seventh Continental Congress meets at Philadelphia, [Henry Laurens, S C., president] 2 July, "
Massacre of inhabitants in WYOMING VALLEY, Pa, by Indians and Tories 4 July, "
Expedition from Virginia under maj George Roger Clarke captures the British fort at Kaskaskia (ILLINOIS) . . 4 July, "
Articles of Confederation signed by delegates from 8 states—New Hampshire, Massachusetts, Rhode Island, Connecticut, Pennsylvania, New York, Virginia, and South Carolina . 9 July, "
Delegates from North Carolina sign them 21 July, "
Delegates from Georgia sign them 24 July, "
Francis Hopkinson elected treasurer of loans by Congress . 27 July, "
French fleet, under count D'Estaing, enters Narragansett bay 29 July, "

M. Gerard, minister from France to America, received in Congress . . .6 Aug 1778
Congress rejects the bills of Parliament, and refuses to negotiate with Great Britain until her fleets and armies are withdrawn, and she acknowledges the independence of the colonies . 11 Aug "
Gen Charles Lee by court-martial for disobedience, misbehavior, and disrespect to Washington, suspended from command for one year. 12 Aug "
Battle of Rhode Island . 29 Aug "
Americans evacuate Rhode Island 30 Aug., and British occupy Newport . 31 Aug "
British under gen Grey burn Bedford village, in Dartmouth, Mass, and 70 American vessels lying at the wharfs 5 Sept. "
Benjamin Franklin appointed minister to the court of France 14 Sept. "
Territory northwest of the Ohio, occupied for Virginia by maj Clarke, is constituted a county of Virginia by the assembly, and named Illinois Oct. "
Congress advises the several states to take measures for the suppressing of "theatrical entertainments, horse-racing, gaming, and such other diversions as are productive of idleness, dissipation and general depravity of principles and manners" 12 Oct "
Massacre by Indians and Tories at CHERRY VALLEY, N Y 10 Nov. "
Delegates from New Jersey sign the Articles of Confederation 26 Nov. "
John Jay of New York chosen president of Congress, 10 Dec. "
British troops under Howe capture Savannah, the Americans retreat across the Savannah river (GEORGIA) 29 Dec "
Thomas Hutchins of New Jersey appointed "geographer-general of the United States" by act of Congress, which office he holds until his death at Pittsburg, 28 Apr 1789 "
Northern American army hutted in cantonments from Danbury, Conn, to Elizabethtown, N J, for the winter 1778-79
First society of Universalists in the U. S. organized at Gloucester, Mass. 1 Jan. 1779
Maj-gen Benjamin Lincoln, commanding the southern forces, establishes his first post at Purysburg, on the Savannah river . "
Congress calls upon the states for their quotas of $15,000,000 for the year, and $6,000 000 annually for 18 years to follow as a sinking-fund 2 Jan. "
Vincennes, Ind, captured by the British Jan. "
British under gen. McLane take possession of Castine (MAINE) 12 Jan. "
British under maj Gardiner driven from Port Royal island by gen Moultrie (SOUTH CAROLINA), 3 Feb. "
Franklin commissioned sole minister plenipotentiary to France and Adams recalled . . Feb. "
Battle of Kettle Creek, Ga, American victory, 14 Feb. "
Americans under maj Clarke capture Vincennes, 20 Feb "
Battle of Brier Creek, Ga, British victory 3 Mch. "
Salt works at Horseneck, Conn, destroyed by gen Tryon . 26 Mch "
American ministers recalled, except at Versailles and Madrid . . Apr "
Articles of Confederation signed by Thomas McKean of Delaware, 12 Feb., and by John Dickinson of Delaware . . 5 May, "
Americans repulsed at Stono Ferry, S C. 20 June, "
Spain declares war against Great Britain June, "
British under Tryon plunder New Haven, 5 July, and burn Fairfield, 8 July, and Norwalk . . .12 July, "
Americans under Wayne take by storm FORT STONY POINT, N. Y . 16 July, "
Expedition against the British at fort Castine, Me, repulsed . . 25 July, "
American fleet arrive at Penobscot, 25 July, and are dispersed by British fleet (MAINE) 13 Aug "
Congress agrees to a basis of terms for a peace with Great Britain . . . 14 Aug. "

Gen Sullivan's campaign against the Six Nations, the Indian villages of the Genesee valley destroyed (New York) July-Sept 1779

British fleet at Tybee captured by count D'Estaing (Georgia) 3 Sept "

Congress votes thanks and a gold medal to maj Lee, for surprising and capturing (19 Aug) the British garrison at Paulus's Hook Sept "

Congress guarantees the Floridas to Spain if she takes them from Great Britain, provided the U S should enjoy the free navigation of the Mississippi river, 17 Sept "

Naval engagement off Flamborough Head, Engl, the *Bonhomme Richard* (American), Paul Jones commander, captures the British gun-ship *Serapis* (Naval Battles of the U S) 23 Sept. "

John Jay appointed minister to Spain, and John Adams to negotiate a peace with Great Britain 27 Sept "

Samuel Huntington of Connecticut chosen president of Congress 28 Sept "

Siege of Savannah, Ga, by Americans and French, fails, Pulaski killed (Georgia) 23 Sept-9 Oct. "

A company of British regulars and 4 armed vessels in the Ogeechee river, Ga, surrenders to Col White, 1 Oct "

British evacuate Rhode Island 11-25 Oct "

M Gerard succeeded by the Chevalier de la Luzerne as minister from France to the U S 17 Nov. "

American army winters at Morristown Dec "

Gen Clinton sails from New York against Charleston, 26 Dec "

Washington reprimands gen Arnold, by order of Congress, for misconduct charged by the council of Philadelphia Jan 1780

[Arnold had been already for months in secret correspondence with maj Andre of gen Clinton's staff]

Gen Charles Lee dismissed from the army 10 Jan "

Legislature of New York empowers its delegates to cede to Congress a portion of its western territory for the common benefit 19 Feb "

Bank of Pennsylvania, the first in the U S, chartered and located at Philadelphia 1 Mch "

Congress sends gen Gates to succeed Baron de Kalb, who, by the surrender of gen Lincoln, had been commander-in-chief in the south Mch "

Gen Clinton lays siege to Charleston 10 Apr "

Battle at Monk's Corner, S C 14 Apr "

Lafayette rejoins the army, after a visit to France, bringing a commission from the French government to Washington as lieutenant-general and vice-admiral of France, so that he may be commander-in-chief of the united forces of France and the U S, 11 May, "

Fort Moultrie, S. C., surrendered to capt Hudson of the British navy .. 6 May, "

Charleston, S C, capitulates (South Carolina), 12 May, "

"Dark day" in New England (Massachusetts), 19 May, "

Massacre of Americans under col Buford at Waxhaw, on the North Carolina border, by British under Tarlton 29 May, "

Gen Clinton proclaims South Carolina subject to England 3 June, "

Battle of Ramsour's Mills, N C 20 June, "

Battle at Springfield, N J, gen Clinton burns the town 23 June, "

French army of 6000 men, under Rochambeau, reaches Newport harbor, R I 10 July, "

Battle of Rocky Mount, S C 30 July, "

Command in the highlands of the Hudson with West Point given to gen Benedict Arnold 3 Aug "

Battle of Hanging Rock, S. C 6 Aug "

Battle of Camden, S. C.; Gates defeated . 16 Aug "

Battles of Musgrove Mills and Fishing Creek, S C., 18 Aug "

Congress advises states to surrender their territorial claims to western land for the general benefit, 6 Sept "

UNI

Maj John Andre, British adjutant-general, meets Benedict Arnold near Stony Point, N Y (New York), 21 Sept 1780

Maj André captured near Tarrytown 23 Sept "

Arnold escapes to the British vessel *Vulture* 24 Sept "

Battle of Charlotte, N C 26 Sept "

Andre convicted as a spy by military board, gen Nathaniel Greene, president, 29 Sept, and hung at Tappan, N Y 2 Oct "

Congress votes John Paulding, David Williams, and Isaac Van Wart, captors of Andre, its thanks a silver medal, and a pension of $200 each yearly, for life Oct "

Henry Laurens, minister from U S, seized on his way to Holland by a British frigate, 3 Sept, and imprisoned in the Tower of London 6 Oct "

Battle of King's Mountain, S C 7 Oct "

Congress resolves that western lands to be ceded shall be formed into republican states, and become equal members of the Union 10 Oct "

Gen Nathaniel Greene appointed to command of the armies in the south superseding gen Gates 14 Oct "

Congress sends the ministers to France and Spain a statement of the claims of the U S to lands as far as the Mississippi river 17 Oct "

Col John Laurens appointed a special minister to France to secure a loan Dec "

Pennsylvania troops break camp at Morristown, 1 Jan, demanding back pay Congress appoints a commission, which accedes to their demand (Mutiny), 1 Jan 1781

Benedict Arnold plunders Richmond, Va 5-6 Jan "

Robert R Livingston appointed secretary of foreign affairs by Congress. Jan "

Battle of Cowpens, S C, American victory 17 Jan "

Mutiny of New Jersey troops quelled by gen Robert Howe 23-27 Jan "

Young's house, near White Plains, surprised by British, 2 Feb "

Robert Morris appointed superintendent of finances by Congress 20 Feb "

Skilful retreat of Americans under gen Greene from Cowpens to the river Dan, pursued by Cornwallis, 28 Jan.-13 Feb "

[The distance traversed was over 200 miles over roads almost impassable]

Delegates from Maryland sign the Articles of Confederation 1 Mch "

Final ratification of Articles of Confederation announced by order of Congress 1 Mch "

Battle of Guilford Court-house N. C. 15 Mch "

British under gens Phillips and Benedict Arnold occupy Petersburg (Virginia) 24 Apr "

Battle of Hobkirk's Hill, S C 25 Apr "

Union of Vermont with the British proposed to col Ira Allen at Isles aux Noix, Canada May, "

Cornwallis joins Arnold at Petersburg, Va 20 May, "

Augusta, Ga, taken by col Clark, 14 Sept 1780, retaken by British, 17 Sept 1780, capitulates to Americans 5 June, "

Gen Wadsworth captured, and imprisoned at Castine (Maine) 18 June, "

British abandon Fort Ninety-six 21 June, "

Jonas Fay, Ira Allen, and Bazaleel Woodward appointed to represent the cause of Vermont in the Continental Congress 22 June, "

Gen Lafayette attacks Cornwallis, near Green Springs, Va, and is repulsed 6 July, "

Thomas McKean of Delaware elected president of the Continental Congress 10 July, "

Cornwallis retires with his army to Yorktown 4 Aug "

R. R. Livingston appointed secretary of foreign affairs by Congress Aug "

Congress requires Vermont to relinquish territory east of the Connecticut and west of the present New York line before admission as a state 20 Aug "

Combined armies of Americans and French start for Yorktown, Va, from the Hudson river 25 Aug. "

Count de Grasse, with the French fleet, arrives in the Chesapeake..........................30 Aug. 1781
Lafayette joins French troops under count de St. Simon at Green Springs, 3 Sept., and they occupy Williamsburg, about 15 miles from Yorktown..5 Sept. "
Benedict Arnold plunders and burns New London, Conn., and captures FORT GRISWOLD.......6 Sept. "
British fleet under adm. Graves appears in the Chesapeake..............................7 Sept. "
Indecisive battle of EUTAW SPRINGS, S. C.... 8 Sept. "
Washington and count Rochambeau reach Williamsburg...............................14 Sept. "
Siege of Yorktown (VIRGINIA)............5-19 Oct. "
Cornwallis surrenders at Yorktown..........19 Oct. "
Sir Henry Clinton, with fleet of 35 vessels and 7000 troops, arrives at the Chesapeake, 24 Oct., and returns to New York.....................29 Oct. "
Benjamin Lincoln appointed secretary of war by Congress...............................30 Oct. "
John Hanson of Maryland chosen president of Continental Congress.......................5 Nov. "
Day of public thanksgiving and prayer observed throughout the U. S...................13 Dec. "
Lafayette sails for France from Boston in the *Alliance*. [Again in the U. S. in 1784 and in 1824.] 22 Dec. "
Henry Laurens released from imprisonment in the Tower of London......................31 Dec. "
Bank of North America established at Philadelphia (BANKS in the U. S.)..................31 Dec. "
Holland recognizes the independence of U. S. . 19 Apr. 1782
Sir Guy Carleton, appointed to succeed Clinton, lands in New York..........................5 May, "
Congress adopts a GREAT SEAL for the U. S. . 20 June, "
Savannah, Ga., evacuated by the British.....11 July, "
Treaty of amity and commerce concluded by Mr. Adams, on part of the U. S., with Holland...8 Oct. "
First manufacture of fustians and jeans in the U. S. begins at Philadelphia......................... "
Elias Boudinot of New Jersey chosen president of the Continental Congress...................4 Nov. "
Preliminary articles of peace signed at Paris by Richard Oswald for Great Britain, and by John Adams, Benjamin Franklin, John Jay, and Henry Laurens for the U. S. ....30 Nov. "
British evacuate Charleston, S. C...........14 Dec. "
French army embarks from Boston for St. Domingo, having been in the U. S. 2 years 5 months and 14 days..................................24 Dec. "
Sweden recognizes independence of U. S......5 Feb. 1783
Denmark recognizes independence of U. S....25 Feb. "
Congress being unable to pay either officers or men of the army, an anonymous address is circulated, 11 Mch. 1783, advising the army at Newburg, N. Y., to enforce its claims. The situation is critical, but Washington, by an admirable address, obtains from the officers a declaration of confidence in Congress and the country......................15 Mch. "
[The author of the "Anonymous Address" was maj. John Armstrong, afterwards secretary of war.]
Congress grants 5 years' full pay to officers in lieu of half-pay for life, promised 21 Oct. 1780....22 Mch. "
Spain recognizes independence of U. S......24 Mch. "
Congress ratifies the preliminary treaty with Great Britain..............................15 Apr. "
Congress proclaims a cessation of hostilities, 11 Apr. 1783, which is read to the army..........19 Apr. "
Constitution for the Society of the CINCINNATI, formed at the army quarters on the Hudson river..13 May, "
First vessel to carry the flag of the U. S. to a Russian port enters Riga........................1 June, "
Washington writes on the situation to each of the state governors.........................8 June, "
Seventh Continental Congress adjourns; session, 1816 days, 21 June, "
[The longest session ever held in the U. S.]

Eighth Continental Congress meets at Princeton, 30 June, "
[Elias Boudinot president.]

Independence of the U. S. recognized by Russia..July, 1783
Definitive treaty signed by David Hartley on the part of Great Britain, and by Benjamin Franklin, John Adams, and John Jay on the part of the U. S., 3 Sept. "
Washington issues his "Farewell Address to the Army" from Rocky Hill, near Princeton, N. J......2 Nov. "
Thomas Mifflin of Pennsylvania chosen president of the Continental Congress................3 Nov. "
By general order of Congress, proclaimed 18 Oct., the army is disbanded, a small force remaining at West Point..................................3 Nov. "
Eighth Continental Congress adjourns; 127 days' session, 4 Nov. "
British evacuate New York city............25 Nov. "

Ninth Continental Congress meets at Annapolis, Md., 26 Nov. "
[Thomas Mifflin president.]

Gen. Washington bids farewell to his officers at Fraunce's tavern, cor. Pearl and Broad sts., New York city..............................4 Dec. "
British evacuate Long Island and Staten Island (withdrawing their last armed man sent for the purpose of reducing the colonies to subjection)......4 Dec. "
Washington resigns his commission as commander-in-chief at the state-house, Annapolis, Md., and retires to Mount Vernon......................23 Dec. "
Congress ratifies the definitive treaty of peace..14 Jan. 1784
Congress accepts cession of northwest territory by Virginia; deed signed by Virginia delegates.1 Mch. "
American Daily Advertiser, first daily newspaper in America, issued at Philadelphia by Benjamin Franklin Bache.................................. "
Fiscal affairs of the U. S. placed in the hands of 3 commissioners appointed to succeed Robert Morris.. "
John Jay appointed secretary of foreign affairs in place of Livingston, resigned......................Mch. "
Ninth Continental Congress adjourns; 189 days' session, 3 June, "
General Assembly of North Carolina cedes her western lands to the U. S. on condition of acceptance within 2 years, Apr. 1784, but repeals the act......22 Oct. "
Washington makes a tour of the western country to ascertain by what means it could be most effectually bound to the Union.............................. "

Tenth Continental Congress meets at Trenton, N. J., 1 Nov. "

Richard Henry Lee of Virginia chosen president of Continental Congress..................30 Nov. "
Tenth Continental Congress adjourns; 54 days' session, 24 Dec. "
Methodist Episcopal church organized at a Christmas conference in Baltimore, Md...24 Dec. 1784-2 Jan. 1785

Eleventh Continental Congress meets at New York, 11 Jan. "
[Richard H. Lee president.]

Gen. Henry Knox appointed sec. of war with added duties of sec. of navy.................. 8 Mch. "
[He was continued sec. of war under Washington's administration until 1795.]
Franklin, minister to France, obtains leave to return; Jefferson is appointed..................10 Mch. "
Dispute between the U. S. and Spain on navigation of the Mississippi river and the boundaries of the Floridas... "
City directory of Philadelphia, first in America, pub.. "
Massachusetts cedes to the U. S. her claims to lands west of the Niagara river, in accordance with an act of legislature of 13 Nov. 1784.............19 Apr. "
John Adams appointed minister plenipotentiary to Great Britain, 24 Feb., and received at the court of George III..............................1 June, "
Don Diego Gardoqui, minister from Spain to the U. S., recognized by Congress..................2 July, "
First Episcopal ordination held in the U. S., that of rev. Ashbel Baldwin at Middletown, Conn...3 Aug. "
Treaty of amity and commerce concluded between the king of Prussia and the U. S., and signed by Thomas

Jefferson at Paris, 28 July, Benjamin Franklin at Passy, 9 July, and J Adams at London 5 Aug. 1785
Franklin returns to Philadelphia from France, after an absence of 9 years, landing 13 Sept "
State of FRANKLAND formed from western lands of North Carolina Nov "
Eleventh Continental Congress adjourns, 298 days' session, 4 Nov "
Twelfth Continental Congress meets at New York, 7 Nov "
John Hancock of Massachusetts chosen president of the Continental Congress 23 Nov "
[Did not serve owing to continued illness]
James Rumsey succeeds in propelling a boat by steam and machinery on the Potomac . Mch 1786
First spinning-jenny in the U S put in operation by Daniel Jackson of Providence, R I "
Nathaniel Gorham chosen president of the Continental Congress 6 June, "
Gen Nathaniel Greene dies at Mulberry Grove, 14 miles from Savannah, Ga 19 June, "
Ordinance establishing the coinage passed Aug "
Delegates from Virginia, Pennsylvania, Delaware, New Jersey, and New York, at Annapolis, Md, consider the condition of the nation, and request all the states to send delegates to a convention at Philadelphia in May following 11 Sept "
Connecticut makes a qualified cession to the U S of all territory south of 41° N lat, and west of a line 120 miles west of Pennsylvania . 14 Sept. "
SHAYS'S REBELLION in Massachusetts "
Ordinance establishing a U S mint passed by Congress 16 Oct. "
Twelfth Continental Congress adjourns, 362 days' session, 3 Nov "
Thirteenth Continental Congress meets at New York, 6 Nov "
Arthur St Clair of Pennsylvania chosen president of Congress 2 Feb. 1787
Congress advises the states to send delegates to a convention in Philadelphia to revise the Articles of Confederation, to meet 14 May (CONSTITUTION OF THE UNITED STATES) 21 Feb "
Congress by ordinance provides government for the territory northwest of the Ohio (now Ohio, Indiana, Illinois, Michigan, and Wisconsin) 13 July, "
Treaty between the U S and the emperor of Morocco, negotiated Jan 1787 by John Adams and Thomas Jefferson, is ratified by Congress 18 July, "
South Carolina cedes to the U S. her claims to a strip 12 miles wide, west of a line from the head of the Tugaloo river to the North Carolina border, 9 Aug "
Delegates to the convention sign the CONSTITUTION, 17 Sept. "
Manufacture of cotton first attempted in the U S at Beverly, Mass "
Manufacture of salt from the Onondaga springs at Syracuse, N Y, began "
Ship *Columbia*, capt. John Kendrick, and the sloop *Washington*, capt Robert Gray, sail from Boston for the northwest coast, where they exchange ships, and Gray proceeds to Canton on his way around the world .. .. 30 Sept "
Thirteenth Continental Congress adjourns, 359 days' session .. .. . 30 Oct. "
Fourteenth Continental Congress meets at New York, 5 Nov. "
Spanish intrigues in KENTUCKY 1788
Cyrus Griffin of Virginia chosen president of Continental Congress . ... 22 Jan. "
Method for putting the new government into operation reported by the committee adopted by Congress (CONSTITUTION) .. 13 Sept "
Fourteenth and last Continental Congress adjourns; 353 days' session . .. .. 21 Oct. "
Electors in the several states vote for president and vice-president . .. Feb. 1789

History knows of few bodies more remarkable than the Continental Congress It is often compared with the Long Parliament of Charles I and the French National Assembly Coming together at first as a gathering for consultation, the delegates had boldly seized the reins of power, assumed the leadership of the insurgent states, issued bills of credit, raised armies, declared independence, negotiated foreign treaties, carried the nation through seven years of war, finally, had extorted from a powerful ruling government an acknowledgment of the authority so daringly assumed and so indomitably maintained But its career was not destined to end gloriously Its decline began during the war Exhausted by its early efforts, smitten with poverty, insolvent almost from the beginning, pensioner on the bounty of France, without sympathy at home or abroad, unable to fulfil the treaties it had made, issuing fruitless requisitions which it had no power to enforce, vainly begging for more authority to prolong its existence—even while all eyes were turned towards the rising splendors of the new government, with hardly a respectful word uttered in its behalf or a recollection of the incomparable good wrought in its early days, the Continental Congress passed into history

Under the Constitution

The Constitution of the United States takes effect in the 11 states which have ratified it, forming a nation of Delaware Pennsylvania, New Jersey, Georgia, Connecticut, Massachusetts, Maryland, South Carolina, New Hampshire, Virginia, and New York, 4 Mch 1789

First Administration—Federal. 4 Mch 1789 to 3 Mch 1793

Seat of Government, New York city, 1789, and Philadelphia from 6 Dec 1790

George Washington, Va, president
John Adams, Mass, vice-president

CABINET

Thomas Jefferson, Va., sec of state, from 21 Mch 1790
Alexander Hamilton, N. Y, sec of treas from 11 Sept 1789.
Henry Knox, Mass, sec of war, from 12 Sept 1789.
Edmund Randolph, Va, attorney-gen, from 26 Sept 1789

Samuel Osgood, Mass., postmaster-gen from 26 Sept. 1789
Timothy Pickering, Mass, postmaster-gen from 12 Aug 1791.
[The postmaster-gen not a member of the cabinet until 1829 CABINET COUNCIL]

First Congress, *First Session*, meets, New York 6 Apr. 1789
Speaker of the House, F A Muhlenberg, Pa.
Electoral vote counted George Washington of Va receives the entire electoral vote, 69, and is chosen president, and John Adams of Mass receives 34 votes and becomes vice-president 6 Apr "
President takes the oath of office, New York. 30 Apr "
First tariff bill passes (TARIFF) 4 July, "
Department of Foreign Affairs organized . 27 July, "
This name is changed to State department 15 Sept "
Act organizing the War (and Navy) department, 7 Aug "
Treasury department organized 2 Sept "
Post-office department temporarily established 22 Sept "
Office of attorney-general organized 24 Sept. "
Supreme court of the U S established, with John Jay of N Y as chief-justice Sept "
Twelve Amendments to the Constitution submitted to the states for ratification 25 Sept. "
[Ten of these ratified, taking effect 15 Dec. 1791.]
Thomas Jefferson of Va, the minister to France, appointed secretary of state 26 Sept. "
First Session adjourns 29 Sept. "
President visits northern and eastern states 15 Oct "
North Carolina ratifies the Constitution. 21 Nov "
John Fenno's *Gazette of the United States* began (supports the principles of the *Federalist*) .... "
Second Session meets, New York . 4 Jan 1790
First annual message from the president " "
Secretary Hamilton reports on the public debt 14 Jan "
[He proposed that the government (1) fund

and pay the foreign debt of the Confederation ($12,000,000); (2) fund and pay the domestic debt ($40,000,000); (3) assume and pay the unpaid war debt ($21,500,000) of the states. The last proposition was strongly opposed, but was finally carried: Senate, 14 to 12; House, 34 to 28.]

An act ordering a census passed............1 Mch. 1790

Franklin dies at Philadelphia, aged 84......17 Apr. "

Rhode Island ratifies the Constitution...... 29 May, "

[The last of the 13 colonies.]

An act passed by 32 to 29—House—authorizing the acquisition of the DISTRICT OF COLUMBIA for the seat of government..................10 July, "

First mechanical patent issued to Samuel Hopkins for making potash and pearlash............31 July, "

First national census begun; population enumerated as of..............................1 Aug. "

Treaty with the Creek Indians..............7 Aug. "

Tariff bill amended by increasing duties......10 Aug. "

Capt. Robert Gray, in the *Columbia*, returns to Boston from his voyage around the world (see 1787), 10 Aug. "

[The first American ship to sail around the world.]

Second Session adjourns....................12 Aug. "

Gen. Harmar's and col. Hardin's expedition against the Indians defeated in northwestern OHIO..17-20 Oct. "

Third Session, Philadelphia, opens............6 Dec. "

Act incorporating Bank of the United States...8 Feb. 1791

[Bank to be at Philadelphia; might establish branches; chartered for 20 years; capital, $10,000,000.]

Vermont, the 14th state, admitted..........18 Jan. "

An act taxing imported spirits, with new duty on domestic spirits................................ "

First Congress adjourns....................3 Mch. "

[An able Congress. In 2 years it provided a competent revenue, funded the public debt, and gave the young nation a respectable standing in the world.]

Great Britain appoints her first minister, George Hammond, to the U. S.......................7 Aug. "

***Second Congress**, First Session*, opens at Philadelphia..................................24 Oct. "

Speaker of the House, Jonathan Trumbull of Conn.

Gen. Arthur St. Clair's expedition against the Indians of OHIO surprised and routed..............4 Nov. "

Philip Freneau's *National Gazette* started at Philadelphia in the interest of the Republican party...... "

Congress grants a bounty for fishing-vessels...16 Feb. 1792

Post-office department reorganized..........20 Feb. "

U. S. Mint established (COIN)...............2 Apr. "

Apportionment act, gives one representative to 33,000 inhabitants; 105 in all..................14 Apr. "

Tariff amended..........................2 May, "

Laws organizing the militia................8 May, "

First Session adjourns.................... " "

Capt. Robert Gray, in the *Columbia*, discovers the mouth (lat. 46°10′ N.) of the river Columbia, 11 May, "

[This discovery strengthened the U. S. claim to the Oregon territory.]

Kentucky admitted (the 15th state)........ 1 June, "

Second Session opens at Philadelphia..........5 Nov. "

Second presidential election................6 Nov. "

President's salary fixed at $25,000..........8 Feb. 1793

Electoral count..........................13 Feb. "

[George Washington of Va. received 132 electoral votes (all); John Adams of Mass. 77 votes; and George Clinton, opposition, 50.]

Second Congress adjourns....................2 Mch. "

Second Administration—Federal. 4 Mch. 1793 to 3 Mch. 1797.

Seat of Government, Philadelphia, Pa.

George Washington, Va., president.
John Adams, Mass., vice-president.

CABINET.

Thomas Jefferson, Va., sec. of state, continued from 1790 to 1793. Resigns.

Edmund Randolph, Va., sec. of state, from 2 Jan. 1794. Resigns.

Timothy Pickering, Mass., sec. of state, from 10 Dec. 1795.

Alexander Hamilton, N. Y., sec. of treas., continued from 11 Sept. 1789. Resigns.

Oliver Wolcott, Conn., sec. of treas., from 2 Feb. 1795.

Henry Knox, Mass., sec. of war, continued from 12 Sept. 1789. Resigns.

Timothy Pickering, Mass., sec. of war, from 2 Jan. 1795.

James McHenry, Md., sec. of war, from 27 Jan. 1796.

Edmund Randolph, Va., attorney-gen., continued from 26 Sept. 1789. Resigns.

William Bradford, Pa., attorney-gen., from 8 Jan. 1794. Dies in office.

Charles Lee, Va., attorney-gen., 10 Dec. 1795.

Timothy Pickering, Mass., postmaster-gen., continued from 1791.

Joseph Habersham, Ga., postmaster-gen. from 25 Feb. 1795.

"Citizen" Genet of France, as minister to the U. S., arrives at Charleston, S. C.; warmly received, 9 Apr. 1793

Eli Whitney invents the cotton-gin; marked effect on slavery.................................. "

President issues his celebrated proclamation of neutrality (severely criticised by the opposition), 22 Apr. "

French government directs the seizure of vessels carrying supplies to an enemy's port.........9 May, "

Great Britain orders her ships of war to stop all vessels laden with French supplies and turn them into British ports..........................8 June, "

Minister Genet's recall asked for by the government, Aug. "

Corner-stone of the U. S. Capitol laid by Washington, 18 Sept. "

Followers of Jefferson begin to assume the name of Republicans, in opposition to the Federalists, under leadership of Alexander Hamilton.............. "

***Third Congress**, First Session*, opens at Philadelphia, Pa...............................2 Dec. "

Speaker of the House, F. A. Muhlenberg, Pa.

Thomas Jefferson retires from State department..Dec. "

[A place he could no longer consistently hold, owing to his opposition to the administration, an opposition which, aided by dissensions among the Federalists themselves, finally resulted in that party's overthrow.]

An Amendment (XI.) to the Constitution approved by Congress, securing states against suits in the U. S. courts..............................5 Mch. 1794

[Declared in force, 8 Jan. 1798.]

Act authorizing the construction of 6 ships of war, the foundation of the U. S. navy..............11 Mch. "

[Three 44 guns; three 38 guns. Of these, 3 were finally finished: *Constitution*, 44 guns, at Boston, launched 20 Sept. 1797; *United States*, 44 guns, at Philadelphia, launched 10 July, 1797; and *Constellation*, 38 guns, at Baltimore, 7 Sept. 1797.]

An act is passed forbidding any American vessel to supply slaves to another nation, under penalty of forfeiture of the vessel and fine of $2000, 22 Mch. "

In retaliation against England, an embargo is laid on all shipping, continued for 60 days.......26 Mch. "

Senate ceases to sit with closed doors........27 Mch. "

President nominates John Jay as envoy extraordinary to England, with a view to a treaty, 16 Apr. "

Gouverneur Morris recalled as minister to France, and James Monroe appointed...........27 May, "

An act relating to neutrality passed.........5 June, "

[This was necessary because popular sympathy with the French and the French minister Genet threatened to embroil the country with England.]

Post-office department permanently established..... "

Tariff act of 1792 further amended by increasing the *ad valorem* rates of duty 7 June, 1794
First Session adjourns 9 June, "
Whiskey insurrection in western PENNSYLVANIA, July-Nov "
Gen Anthony Wayne defeats the Indians near Maumee Rapids, in OHIO 20 Aug "
French minister Fauchet's despatch, supposed to compromise Edmund Randolph, sec of state, intercepted by the British and shown to the U S government, Randolph resigns "
Second Session opens at Philadelphia, Pa 3 Nov "
Draft of treaty with England agreed to by John Jay, special envoy 19 Nov "
Stringent naturalization law passed, requiring renunciation of titles of nobility 29 Jan 1795
Act passed for gradual redemption of public debt "
Hamilton secretary of the treasury, resigns Jan "
Third Congress adjourns 3 Mch "
President calls the Senate together to consider the Jay treaty with England 8 June, "
[Senate favored it by a two-thirds majority, violent popular remonstrances against it]
Washington signs the treaty 14 Aug "
Gen Wayne's treaty with the Ohio Indians at Greenville, they cede 25,000 sq miles 3 Aug "
Treaty with Algiers to ransom prisoners taken by corsairs, and to pay annual tribute of $23,000 to the dey 5 Sept "
Treaty with Spain, opening the Mississippi and establishing boundaries 20 Oct "

Fourth Congress, First Session, opens at Philadelphia, Pa . 7 Dec "
Speaker of the House, Jonathan Dayton of N. J, Federalist
Proclamation of the Jay treaty 1 Mch 1796
House demands the papers relating to the Jay treaty, 24 Mch "
[President declined, the House being no part of the treaty-making power]
Jefferson writes the famous "Mazzei letter," about 21 Apr. "
[The publication of this letter, about a year later, severs all friendly relations between Washington and Jefferson]
Fisher Ames's speech before the House on the Jay treaty with England 28 Apr. "
["The most eloquent speech ever heard in Congress by his generation"—*Schouler's* "Hist U S," vol i p 313]
House agrees to sustain Jay's treaty . . 30 Apr "
Tennessee admitted (the 16th state). . . 1 June, "
First Session adjourns . . . . . " "
New treaty with the Creek Indians 29 June, "
Washington's "Farewell Address" issued, refusing to accept office again 19 Sept. "
Charles C. Pinckney succeeds James Monroe as minister to France . . Sept "
Third presidential election . 8 Nov "
[Federals, John Adams, Mass , and Thomas Pinckney, S C., Republicans, Thomas Jefferson, Va., and Aaron Burr, N Y.]
Second Session opens at Philadelphia, Pa . 6 Dec "
Congress assembles in the House for the purpose of counting the electoral vote . . 8 Feb. 1797
[Of the 138 votes cast, John Adams of Mass. received 71, Thomas Jefferson of Va. 68, Thomas Pinckney of S C 59, and Aaron Burr, 30]
[At this time was illustrated one of the great faults in the Constitution relative to the election of president and vice-president prior to the XIIth Amendment—Adams, a strong Federalist, president, and Jefferson, in direct opposition to that party, vice-president.]
Charles C. Pinckney, U S. minister, not received by the French government, leaves France . Feb. "
Fourth Congress adjourns. . . . . 3 Mch. "

Third Administration—Federal. 4 Mch 1797 to 3 Mch 1801

Seat of Government, Philadelphia, until 1800 then transferred to Washington, D C

John Adams, Mass., president
Thomas Jefferson, Va, vice-president

CABINET

Timothy Pickering, Mass., sec of state, continued from 10 Dec 1795 Resigns
John Marshall, Va., sec of state, from 13 May, 1800
Oliver Wolcott, Conn , sec of treas , continued from 2 Feb 1795.
Samuel Dexter, Mass , sec of treas , from 1 Jan 1801
James McHenry, Md , sec of war, continued from 27 Jan 1796. Resigns
Samuel Dexter, Mass , sec of war, from 13 May, 1800
Roger Griswold, Conn , acting sec of war from 3 Feb 1801
George Cabot, Mass., sec of navy, 3 May, 1798 Declined
Benjamin Stoddert, Md , sec of navy, from 3 May, 1798
Charles Lee, Va , attorney-gen , continued from 10 Dec 1795

Joseph Habersham, Ga , postmaster gen , continued from 25 Feb 1795

Special session of Congress called to consider the threatening relations with France 25 Mch 1797

Fifth Congress, First Session (extra), assembles at Philadelphia, Pa. 15 May, "
Speaker of the House, Jonathan Dayton of N J , Federalist
Congress subjects to a fine of $10,000 and 10 years' imprisonment any citizen concerned in privateering against a friendly nation 14 June, "
Congress authorizes the president to raise 80,000 militia for 3 months — the quota from Tennessee, the smallest, 806, and Massachusetts, the largest, 11,836, 24 June, "
President empowered to employ the frigates *Constitution, Constellation*, and *United States* (*see* 1794), 1 July, "
Duties on stamped vellum parchment and paper, receipts, bonds, bills, insurance policies, certificates, etc , by act of 6 July, "
A duty on salt levied 8 July, "
Senate expels William Blount of Tennessee 9 July, "
[Committee of Ways and Means organized in the House for the first time at this session]
First Session adjourns 10 July, "
President appoints John Marshall of Va and Elbridge Gerry of Mass. with C C Pinckney, as commissioners to treat with France, they meet at Paris, 4 Oct "
[Commissioners asked to bribe members of French Directory, but indignantly refuse Talleyrand, the French minister of foreign affairs, implicated Mr Marshall and Mr Pinckney ordered out of France C C Pinckney declared that the U S had "millions for defence, but not one cent for tribute "]
Second Session assembles at Philadelphia, Pa 13 Nov "
First personal encounter in Congress between Matthew Lyon of Vt. and Roger Griswold of Conn , the House fails to censure or punish 12-15 Feb 1798
Mississippi territory organized 3 Apr "
Navy department organized 30 Apr. "
Secretary of the navy appointed 3 May, "
Harper's Ferry selected as site for a government armory and manufactory 4 May, "
Congress authorizes a PROVISIONAL ARMY, and empowers the president, in case of an actual declaration of war or invasion, to enlist, for 3 years, 10,000 men, and to appoint one lieutenant-general, to be chief commander of the army, and one inspector-general, with other necessary officers , all to remain in the service only so long as the president deems necessary for the public safety 28 May, "
Congress authorizes the president to instruct commanders of ships of war to seize French armed vessels attacking American merchantmen or hovering about the coast for that purpose . 28 May "
Song "HAIL, COLUMBIA!" first sung. May, "

Imprisonment for debt abolished 6 June, 1798
Commercial intercourse with France suspended 12 June, "
Washington accepts appointment as commander-in-chief, with rank of lieutenant-general (ARMY), 17 June, "
Uniform rule of naturalization adopted. 18 June, "
President announces the failure of the commission sent to France to make peace 21 June, "
Alien act passed (ALIEN AND SEDITION LAWS) 25 June, "
All French treaties declared void 6 July, "
[The tenor of judicial opinion has been that France and the U S. were not at war, although naval engagements took place — "Narrative and Critical History of America," vol vii. p 473]
Marine corps first organized by act of 11 July, "
Sedition laws passed (ALIEN AND SEDITION LAWS), 14 July, "
Second Session adjourns 16 July, "
[Jefferson looked anxiously for this adjournment, as affording the opposition (of which he was the head) the only chance to rally —*Hildreth's* "U S," vol v p 236]
By treaty the Cherokees allow a free passage through their lands in Tennessee to all travellers on the road to Kentucky passing through Cumberland Gap, 2 Oct "
Trial of Matthew Lyon of Vt. before judge Patterson, under the sedition law (TRIALS) 7 Oct "
Third Session assembles at Philadelphia, Pa 3 Dec. "
"Wieland," the first novel of Charles Brockden Brown, appears "
U. S frigate *Constellation*, com Thomas Truxtun, captures the French ship of war *L'Insurgente*, off the island of St Kitts 9 Feb 1799
General post-office established by act of 2 Mch "
Act to regulate the collection of duties and tonnage, and to establish ports of entry 2 Mch "
Estimates for the year amount to over $13,000,000 "
Fifth Congress adjourns . 3 Mch "
Upon assurance from France that a representative from the U S. will be received with the "respect due a powerful nation," president nominates William Van Murray as minister to France, and associates with him chief-justice Ellsworth of Connecticut and gov. Davie of North Carolina, all are received by Napoleon, first consul . 30 Mch. "

Sixth Congress, *First Session*, assembles at Philadelphia, Pa . 2 Dec. "
Speaker of the House, Theodore Sedgwick, Mass
John Randolph of Roanoke, Va., enters Congress, 2 Dec. "
George Washington d. 14 Dec "
Eulogy before Congress by Henry Lee of Va calling him "First in war, first in peace, and first in the hearts of his countrymen" 26 Dec "
U. S. frigate *Constellation*, com Thomas Truxtun, defeats the French frigate *La Vengeance* 1 Feb 1800
[Congress honored Truxton with a gold medal]
General Bankruptcy act 4 Apr "
Territory of Indiana organized . 7 May, "
Stricter law against the slave-trade 10 May, "
Congress establishes 4 land offices for the sale of public lands in the Northwest territory (OHIO) 10 May, "
First Session (last meeting in Philadelphia) adjourns, 14 May, "
President Adams removes Timothy Pickering, sec. of state, and James McHenry, sec. of war May, "
U S government removes from Philadelphia to the new capital, Washington . July, "
[One packet-sloop carried from Philadelphia all the furniture of the several departments, together with the archives of the Federal government, which filled "7 large boxes and 4 or 5 smaller ones."]
Frigate *George Washington*, capt. William Bainbridge, carries to Algiers the dey's tribute-money, and is required to carry the dey's ambassador to Constantinople . . . Sept. "
[First U. S. man-of-war in the Bosporus.]

Envoys to France negotiate a convention for 8 years, preventing open war 30 Sept 1800
[Ratified by France, 31 July, 1801, and by the U S., 19 Dec 1801 Under this treaty the claims for indemnity, known as the "French Spoliation Claims," have been the subject of frequent reports and discussions in Congress, with no result until referred to the court of Claims by the act of 20 Jan 1885]
Spanish government cedes Louisiana to France by the secret treaty of St. Ildefonso 1 Oct. "
Fourth presidential election 11 Nov "
[Democratic-Republican candidates, Thomas Jefferson and Aaron Burr, Federalists, John Adams and Charles C Pinckney]
Second Session (first meeting in Washington, D C.), 17 Nov "
Capitol building burned at Washington. 19 Jan 1801
John Marshall appointed chief-justice 20 Jan "
Electoral votes counted 11 Feb. "
[Thomas Jefferson received 73, Aaron Burr, 73, John Adams, 65, Charles C Pinckney, 64, John Jay, 1 The tie between Jefferson and Burr remained for the House of Representatives to decide. Balloting began Wednesday, Feb 11, and continued for 7 days, until a choice was effected Seats were provided for the president and Senate, but the gallery was cleared and the doors were closed On the first ballot, New York, New Jersey, Pennsylvania, Virginia, North Carolina, Georgia, Kentucky, and Tennessee voted for Jefferson, while New Hampshire, Massachusetts, Rhode Island, Connecticut, Delaware, and South Carolina voted for Burr Vermont and Maryland were divided 104 members were present In the afternoon of 17 Feb, on the 36th ballot, Delaware and South Carolina cast blanks, while Vermont and Maryland voted for Jefferson and elected him]
Congress assumes jurisdiction over the District of Columbia 27 Feb "
Navy reduced to 13 vessels, the rest to be disarmed and sold 3 Mch "
[Among those reserved were the frigates *United States, Constitution, President, Chesapeake, Philadelphia, Constellation, Congress*]
Sixth Congress adjourns . . . . 3 Mch "

Fourth Administration—Democratic-Republican.
4 Mch. 1801 to 3 Mch 1805.
Seat of Government at Washington, D C.

Thomas Jefferson, Va , president.
Aaron Burr, N Y , vice-president.

CABINET

James Madison, Va., sec. of state, from 5 Mch 1801.
Samuel Dexter, Mass., sec. of treas , continued.
Albert Gallatin, Pa., sec. of treas., from 15 May, 1801
Henry Dearborn, Mass , sec. of war, from 5 Mch. 1801.
Benjamin Stoddert, Md., sec. of navy, continued.
Robert Smith, Md , sec. of navy, from 26 Jan. 1802.
Jacob Crowninshield, Mass., sec. of navy, from 2 Mch 1805.
Levi Lincoln, Mass., attorney-gen , from 5 Mch 1801.
Robert Smith, Md , attorney-gen , from 2 Mch. 1805

Joseph Habersham, Ga., postmaster-gen , continued
Gideon Granger, Conn , postmaster-gen. from 28 Nov 1801.
Three frigates and one sloop-of-war sent to the Barbary coast to protect our commerce, commanded by com Richard Dale . . . 20 May, 1801
Tripoli declares war against the U.S . 10 June, "

Seventh Congress, *First Session*, convenes. . 7 Dec "
Speaker of the House, Nathaniel Macon, N C.
President Jefferson sends a written message to Congress and announces that no answer is expected No president has since addressed Congress orally.
Congress appoints John Beckley of Va librarian, with a room of the Capitol for the library.... 26 Jan. 1802

Congress recognizes the war with Tripoli ...6 Feb 1802
Repeal of the new Circuit act 8 Mch "
Congress reduces the army to the peace establishment of 1796—1 regiment of artillery and 2 of infantry—and organizes a military academy at West Point 16 Mch. "
Excise tax repealed 16 Mch. "
Naturalization laws of 1798 repealed, those of 1795 restored 14 Apr "
[That of 1795 required 5 years' residence, and application 3 years prior to naturalization, that of 1798 required 14 years' residence, and application 5 years prior to naturalization]
Judicial system of the U S amended 29 Apr. "
Library of Congress catalogued, containing 964 volumes and 9 maps Apr "
First Session adjourns 3 May, "
Washington incorporated as a city " "
Ohio adopts a state constitution 29 Nov "
[Political intrigues in the state of New York and at Washington against Aaron Burr, destroying his political prospects, culminated during 1802 "Never in the history of the United States did so powerful a combination of rival politicians unite to break down a single man as that which arrayed itself against Burr, for, as the hostile circle gathered about him, he could plainly see Jefferson, Madison, and the whole Virginia legion, with DeWitt Clinton and others of New York, and among them Alexander Hamilton, joining hands with his own bitterest enemies to complete the ring and bring about his political ruin"—*Henry Adams's* "Hist. U S," vol i p. 332]
Second Session convenes . 6 Dec "
Ohio admitted as a state (the 17th) 19 Feb. 1803
Seventh Congress adjourns . . 3 Mch "
Treaty with France the U S. purchases Louisiana for $15,000,000 . 30 Apr "

Eighth Congress, First Session, convenes 17 Oct. "
Speaker of the House, Nathaniel Macon, N C.
Senate ratifies the treaty with France, by vote of 24 to 7 ..... 20 Oct "
President authorized by Congress to take possession of Louisiana . 30 Oct "
Frigate *Philadelphia*, 44 guns, capt Bainbridge, pursuing Tripolitan ship of war, strikes a rock in the harbor of Tripoli and is captured 31 Oct "
Independence of Hayti proclaimed. 29 Nov "
XIIth Amendment to the Constitution, relative to electing the president and vice-president, passed by the Senate, 22 to 10 . 2 Dec "
[By this amendment the electors are required to ballot separately for president and vice-president The election of 1804 the first under the amendment]
Same passed by the House—83 to 42 . 12 Dec "
New Orleans delivered to the U. S. . 20 Dec. "
Lieut Stephen Decatur, with the ketch *Intrepid*, destroys the *Philadelphia* in the harbor of Tripoli under the guns of the castle, without losing a man, night of 16 Feb 1804
Impeachment of Samuel Chase, associate justice of the Supreme court, trial began Feb "
[Acquitted Mch. 1805]
Louisiana purchase divided into the territory of Orleans and the District of Louisiana . . . . 26 Mch. "
First Session adjourns . . 27 Mch. "
Capt Meriwether Lewis, of the First Infantry, and lieut William Clark, appointed to explore the Missouri river and seek water communication with the Pacific coast, enter the Missouri river, 14 May, "
Burr, vice-president, mortally wounds Alexander Hamilton in a duel at Weehawken, N. J, Hamilton having fired in the air (BURR'S CONSPIRACY, DUELS), 11 July, "
XIIth Amendment being accepted by two thirds of the states—Massachusetts, Connecticut, and Delaware only dissenting—is declared ratified, 25 Sept 1804
Second Session convenes 4 Nov "
[7 Federal senators and 25 representatives]
Fifth presidential election 13 Nov
Territory of Michigan formed from Indiana 11 Jan 1805
[Division to take place 30 June, 1805]
Electoral vote counted 13 Feb "
[For president, Thomas Jefferson, Va, 162 votes, for vice-president, George Clinton, N Y, 162 votes, both Democratic-Republicans Charles C Pinckney, S C, for president, and Rufus King, N Y, for vice-president, Federal, each receiving 14 votes]
Twenty-five gunboats ordered for the protection of ports and harbors 2 Mch "
[This measure was urged by President Jefferson, but proved to be useless]
Genesee and Buffalo Creek, N Y, made ports of entry 3 Mch. "
Eighth Congress adjourns " "
[With this Congress closes the political life of Aaron Burr]

Fifth Administration—Democratic-Republican.

4 Mch 1805 to 3 Mch 1809

Thomas Jefferson, Va, president
George Clinton, N Y, vice-president

CABINET.

James Madison, Va, sec. of state, continued
Albert Gallatin, Pa, sec of treas., continued.
Jacob Crowninshield, Mass., sec of navy, from 3 Mch. 1805.
Henry Dearborn, Mass, sec of war, continued
Robert Smith, Md, attorney-gen, from 3 Mch 1805
John Breckinridge, Ky, attorney-gen, from 25 Dec 1805.
Cæsar A Rodney, Del, attorney-gen, from 20 Jan 1807

Gideon Granger, Conn, postmaster-gen, continued

Treaty of peace with Tripoli 3 June, 1805
Abiel Holmes's "American Annals" first pub. "

Ninth Congress, First Session, convenes 2 Dec. "
Speaker of the House, Nathaniel Macon, N C.
Commission authorized to lay out a national road from Cumberland, Md, to the Ohio river 29 Mch 1806
First Session adjourns 21 Apr "
Leander, a British naval vessel, fires into an American coaster, the *Richard*, off Sandy Hook, and kills the helmsman 25 Apr. "
Great Britain issues an "order in council" declaring the whole coast of Europe, from the Elbe to Brest, in France, under blockade 16 May, "
Napoleon issues the BERLIN DECREE 21 Nov "
Second Session convenes 1 Dec "
Treaty with Great Britain signed by commissioners, but the president did not even send it to the Senate, 3 Dec "
Aaron Burr's supposed conspiracy culminates "
Burr arrested by lieut. Gaines, near fort Stoddart, Ala 19 Feb 1807
Act to prohibit import of slaves from 1 Jan 1808 passes the House 7 Feb 1807, by 113 to 5, approved, 2 Mch "
Duty on salt repealed 3 Mch "
Ninth Congress adjourns " "
Burr brought to Richmond, Va, early in . Mch "
His trial for treason begins there (BURR'S CONSPIRACY, TRIALS) .. 22 May, "
British frigate *Leopard*, 50 guns, capt. Humphreys, fires into the U S frigate *Chesapeake*, com Barron, off Chesapeake bay, killing 3 and wounding 8, and takes 4 seamen, claiming them as British subjects, 22 June, "
[Barron was suspended by a court-martial for 5 years without pay and emoluments, for making no resistance and surrendering his ship]
American ports closed to the British, and British ships ordered from American waters . July, "

First steamboat, the *Clermont* (Fulton's), starts from New York for Albany 14 Sept 1807
[From this time regular trips were made on the Hudson at about 5 miles an hour]
Aaron Burr acquitted 15 Sept "

Tenth Congress, First Session, convenes 26 Oct. "
Speaker of the House, Joseph B. Varnum, Mass
A British "order in council" forbids neutral nations to trade with France or her allies except under tribute to Great Britain 11 Nov "
Napoleon's Milan decree forbids trade with England or her colonies and confiscates any vessel paying tribute or submitting to English search 17 Dec. "
Congress authorizes the building of 188 gunboats, at a cost of not over $852,000 18 Dec. "
[This made, with those previously built, 257]
Embargo act prohibits foreign commerce 22 Dec. "
[On the mere recommendation of the executive, with little debate, with closed doors, with scarcely any warning to the public, or opportunity of advice by those most able to give it, this act was forced through by night sessions, and by the overbearing determination of a majority at once pliant and obstinate—an act striking a deadly blow at the national industry and at the means of livelihood of great numbers, the real nature and inevitable operation of which seems to have been equally misapprehended by the president and the cabinet recommending it, and by the majority enacting it — *Hildreth's* "Hist U S," vol vi p 37]
Second and more stringent Embargo act (commonly called, reading the title backward, the "O grab me act") 9 Jan. 1808
Embargo modified, the president authorized to permit vessels to transport American property home from foreign ports 12 Mch. "
Army raised to 5 regiments of infantry, 1 of riflemen, 1 of light artillery, and 1 of light dragoons, to be enlisted for 5 years ..12 Apr "
"Salmagundi," first work of Washington Irving, pub "
First Session adjourns 25 Apr "
Burr leaves New York for Europe 9 June, "
Sixth presidential election 8 Nov. "
Second Session convenes 7 Nov "
Territory of Illinois established 3 Feb. 1809
[Now the states of Illinois and Wisconsin]
Electoral vote counted in the House 8 Feb. "
[Candidates Democratic-Republicans, James Madison of Va for president, 122, George Clinton of N Y for vice-president, 113 Federalists, Charles C Pinckney of S C for president, 47, Rufus King of N Y for vice-president, 47, scattering, 21]
Embargo act repealed 1 Mch. "
Non-intercourse act forbids commercial intercourse with Great Britain, France, and their dependencies after May 20 1 Mch. "
Tenth Congress adjourns 3 Mch. "

Sixth Administration—Democratic-Republican.

4 Mch 1809 to 3 Mch. 1813.

James Madison, Va., president.
George Clinton, N. Y, vice-president.

CABINET.

Robert Smith, Md, sec. of state, from 6 Mch 1809
James Monroe, Va., sec. of state, from 2 Apr 1811
Albert Gallatin, Pa., sec. of treas, continued
William Eustis, Mass., sec. of war, from 7 Mch 1809
John Armstrong, N Y, sec of war, from 13 Jan 1813.
Paul Hamilton, S C., sec. of navy, from 7 Mch 1809
William Jones, Pa., sec. of navy, from 12 Jan. 1813
Cæsar A Rodney, Del., attorney-gen, continued.
William Pinkney, Md, attorney-gen, from 11 Dec. 1811.

Gideon Granger, Conn, postmaster-gen., continued.

President proclaims that both England and France have revoked their edicts as to neutrals, and terminates the Non-intercourse act 19 Apr 1809

Eleventh Congress, First Session (extra), convenes, 22 May, "
Speaker of the House, Joseph B. Varnum, Mass
Francisco Miranda, a native of South America, aiming to overthrow the Spanish power in Caracas, S. A., engages a vessel, the *Leander,* and with about 250 men sails from New York, Feb 1806 Although reinforced by some other vessels, and gaining some advantages, the expedition results in failure. The Americans of the expedition captured by the Spaniards, while confined at Carthagena, petition their government for relief, 9 June A resolution requesting the president to take measures for their liberation, if satisfied that they are entitled to it, is offered in the House, it is lost (61 to 61) by the speaker's casting vote 14 June, "
John Quincy Adams, minister to Russia, continued until 1813 "
First Session (extra) adjourns 28 June, "
Great Britain not revoking her "Orders in Council" of 1807, the president proclaims the Non-intercourse act still in force towards that country 9 Aug "
David M Erskine, British minister to U S., recalled, and Francis J Jackson appointed arrives Sept. "
[British minister F J Jackson left Washington, and from New York asked for his passport His relations with this government being unsatisfactory, his recall was asked for]
Second Session convenes 27 Nov. "
Committee appointed by the House to inquire into the charge that brig gen James Wilkinson had received a bribe from the Spanish government, or was an accomplice, or in any way concerned, with the agent of any foreign power, or with Aaron Burr (see this record, 1811) 3 Apr 1810
General post office established at Washington under the postmaster-general (POSTAL SERVICE) 30 Apr "
British and French armed vessels excluded from American waters by act approved 1 May, "
Second Session adjourns " "
Napoleon's Rambouillet decree, dated Mch 23, issued, May, "
[Ordered the sale of 132 American vessels captured, worth, with their cargoes, $8,000,000 (see *McMaster's* "Hist of the People of the U. S.," vol iii, p 367, note)]
France proclaims the revocation of the Berlin and Milan decrees, to take effect after 1 Nov. "
[The revocation was not carried into effect, but American vessels still continued to be seized by French cruisers and confiscated]
Third Session convenes 3 Dec. "
Recharter of the U. S bank passed by the House, 65 to 64, fails in the Senate, 17 to 17, by the casting vote of president of the Senate, George Clinton, 20 Feb 1811
Trading-posts first established among the Indians by Congress, act approved . . . . 2 Mch "
Eleventh Congress adjourns 3 Mch "
William Pinkney, U S. minister to England, returns to the U. S May, "
President, U S. frigate, 44 guns, com. John Rodgers commanding, meets the British sloop-of-war *Little Belt* in lat. 37°, about 40 miles off cape Charles 16 May, "
[In this engagement (both parties denied beginning it) the *Little Belt,* a much weaker vessel than the *President,* was badly riddled, action continued about 15 minutes The conduct of both commanders was approved by their governments.]

Twelfth Congress, First Session, convenes . . . 4 Nov. "
Speaker of the House, Henry Clay of Ky (first appearance in the House, previously in the Senate. KENTUCKY, senators)
[John C. Calhoun of S C appeared in Congress

for the first time this session, being elected as a War Democrat]

Gen Wm H Harrison defeats the Indians under the Prophet at TIPPECANOE, within the present state of Indiana 7 Nov 1811

Brig gen James Wilkinson is tried by a general court-martial, convened at Fredericktown, Md, 2 Sept., and acquitted (see this record, 1810) 25 Dec "

Theatre at Richmond burned, the governor and many eminent citizens perish (VIRGINIA) Dec "

Case of John Henry and the Federalists of New England, papers laid before the Senate by the president 9 Mch. 1812

President requested to lay before the Senate any information, which may be communicated without prejudice to the public interest, bearing on the case of John Henry 10 Mch. "

[John Henry, a political adventurer born in Ireland, came over about 1793 He claimed to have important facts on the disaffection of New England states before the war, and implicating the British government in an attempt to alienate these states from the U S The president paid him $50,000, Feb. 10, 1812, for worthless papers, said to prove these assertions. Henry sailed for France, 9 Mch 1811. See *Henry Adams's* "Hist U S.," vol vi ch ix]

Embargo on all vessels in the U S for 90 days .4 Apr "

Louisiana admitted as the 18th state, to date from 30 Apr, approved 8 Apr "

[One of the conditions of admission was that the Mississippi river shall be forever free to citizens of the U S]

That part of west Florida west of Pearl river is annexed to Louisiana . . 14 Apr. "

George Clinton, vice-president, dies at Washington, aged 73 20 Apr. "

[Wm H Crawford of Ga. president *pro tem* of the Senate]

Joel Barlow, minister to France. . . . . . "

Pres Madison renominated . 18 May, "

[Madison is renominated by the Democratic-Republican party under promise of a declaration of war with England]

President sends a war-message to Congress. 1 June, "

Report of the minority against the war presented to the House 3 June, "

Motion to make the debate public lost . " "

Territory of Missouri established 4 June, "

Aaron Burr returns to New York from Europe, 8 June, "

Cartel-ship from Great Britain, with the survivors (2) of the 4 seamen taken by force from the *Chesapeake* by the *Leopard* in 1807, arrives at Boston, and delivers the men to the U S 12 June, "

"Orders in Council" abandoned by England 17 June, "

War declared against Great Britain (vote in the Senate, 19 to 13, in the House, 79 to 49) 18 June, "

["Amount of direct pecuniary spoliation inflicted by France and other nations under her influence upon the commerce of the U S. exceeded that from Great Britain"—*Hildreth's* "Hist. U S.," vol vi p 312]

["Never surely was an unfortunate country precipitated into an unequal and perilous contest under circumstances more untoward"—*Hildreth's* "Hist. U S.," vol. vi p 316]

["That the war was as just and necessary as any war ever waged seemed so evident to Americans of another generation that only with an effort could modern readers grasp the reasons for the bitter opposition of large and respectable communities which left the government bankrupt and nearly severed the Union, but if students of national history can bear with patience the labor of retaining in mind the threads of negotiation which pres. Madison so thoroughly tangled before breaking, they can partially enter into the feelings of citizens who held themselves aloof from Madison's war"—*Henry Adams's* "Hist. U S.," vol. vi., pp 224, 225. "Madison had challenged a danger more serious than he ever imagined, for he stood alone in the world in the face of victorious England"—*Ibid.*, p 266 But, while England was victorious, her efforts had weakened her almost to prostration]

Army raised to 25 regiments of infantry, 4 regiments of artillery, 2 regiments of dragoons, and 1 of riflemen, total, 36,700 on paper 26 June, 1812

Duties on imports doubled 1 July, "

First Session adjourns 6 July, "

[This Congress had passed 138 acts in a session of 245 days In the House Josiah Quincy of Mass and John Randolph of Roanoke were the leaders in the opposition to the war, Henry Clay of Ky and John C Calhoun of S C in favor of it]

Office of the *Federal Republican* at Baltimore Md, attacked by a mob, for denouncing the declaration of war with England 12 June and 27 July "

On promise of protection by the military, the defenders of the office surrender and are taken to jail The mob reassemble and break open the jail, kill gen Lingan, an officer of the Revolution, and mangle 11 others, leaving 8 for dead 28 July, "

[Arrests were made, but no one was punished]

Action at Brownstown (MICHIGAN) 5 Aug "

Action at MAGUAGA, 14 miles below Detroit 9 Aug "

Surrender of fort Dearborn and massacre (CHICAGO), 15 Aug "

Surrender of Detroit by gen William Hull (MICHIGAN), 16 Aug "

Great meeting in opposition to the war in New York city, John Jay, Rufus King, Gouverneur Morris, and other prominent citizens in attendance 19 Aug "

Frigate *Constitution* captures British frigate *Guerriere* (NAVAL BATTLES of the U. S.) 19 Aug "

[Consult *Henry Adams's* "Hist U S," vol vi p. 373 et seq]

Defence of fort Harrison, Ind., capt. Zachary Taylor commanding 4 Sept "

Battle of QUEENSTOWN 13 Oct. "

Sloop of war *Wasp* captures British sloop *Frolic*, 18 Oct "

Action at St Regis, N Y . 23 Oct "

Frigate *United States* captures British frigate *Macedonian* (NAVAL BATTLES of the U S) . 25 Oct "

Second Session convenes 2 Nov "

Presidential election 10 Nov "

Affair at Black Rock, N Y, attempted invasion of Canada by the Americans under gen. Alexander Smyth 28 Nov. "

Frigate *Constitution* captures British frigate *Java* off the coast of Brazil (NAVAL BATTLES of the U S) 29 Dec. "

Schooner *Patriot* sails from Charleston, S C for New York .. .. 30 Dec "

[This vessel, having on board Theodosia, the wife of gov. Alston and only child of Aaron Burr, is never heard of afterwards]

Congress appropriates $2,500,000 to build 4 74-gun ships and 6 44-gun ships .. .. 2 Jan. 1813

Action at Frenchtown, now Monroe, Mich (MICHIGAN), 18 Jan "

Defeat and capture of gen. Winchester at the river Raisin (MICHIGAN) . . 22 Jan "

British fleet, vice-adm Cockburn, attempts to blockade the Atlantic coast .. . Jan et seq "

Electoral vote counted in the Senate chamber 10 Feb "

[James Madison, Democratic-Republican, favoring war with England, received 128 votes for president, Elbridge Gerry of Mass, 131 for vice-president, De Witt Clinton of N Y, supported by the Democratic-Republicans united with the Federalists in opposition to war with England, 89 for president; Jared Ingersoll of Pa., 86 for vice-president POLITICAL PARTIES]

Total strength of the army, limited by Congress, 58,000, according to the returns of adjt.-gen., including staff and regimental officers, 18,945 16 Feb. "

Sloop-of-war *Hornet* captures and sinks British sloop *Peacock* near the mouth of the Demerara river, South America (NAVAL BATTLES of the U S), 24 Feb 1813

A proclamation and circular letter from the governor of Bermuda is laid before Congress by the president, which recites a "British Order in Council," providing for colonial trade, with instructions to colonial governors to show special privileges to the eastern (New England) states 24 Feb "

Congress passes an act to encourage vaccination, 27 Feb "

[An agent was to be appointed to keep and dispense genuine vaccine matter for public use, etc]

President vested with the power of retaliation on British subjects, soldiers, or Indians 3 Mch "

Twelfth Congress adjourns " "

Seventh Administration — Democratic - Republican.

4 Mch 1813 to 3 Mch 1817

James Madison, Va, president
Elbridge Gerry, Mass, vice-president

CABINET

James Monroe, Va, sec. of state, continued from 2 Apr 1811
Albert Gallatin, Pa, sec of treasury, continued from 14 May, 1801
George W Campbell, Tenn, sec of treasury, from 9 Feb 1814
Alexander J Dallas, Pa, sec. of treasury, from 6 Oct 1814.
John Armstrong N Y, sec of war, continued from 13 Jan 1813.
James Monroe, acting sec. of war, from 26 Sept 1814
William H Crawford, Ga, sec of war, from 3 Mch 1815
William Jones, Pa., sec of navy, continued from 12 Jan 1813.
Benjamin W Crowninshield, Mass, sec of navy, from 19 Dec 1814
William Pinkney, Md, attorney-gen, continued from 11 Dec 1811
Richard Rush, Pa., attorney-gen, from 10 Feb 1811

["The attorney-generalship now became a cabinet office"—*Hildreth's* "Hist. U S," vol vi p 458 "Up to this time the attorney-gen had not been regarded as standing on the same footing with the other members of the cabinet His salary was much less, and he had neither office room or clerks, and was not required to reside permanently at Washington"—*Henry Adams's* "Hist. U S" vol. vii. p 398.]

Gideon Granger, Conn, postmaster-gen., continued from 28 Nov. 1801
Return J Meigs, O, postmaster-gen, from 17 Mch 1814.

Russia offers mediation between the U. S. and Great Britain Mch 1813

U S divided into 9 military districts 19 Mch. "

William H Crawford, Ga., appointed to succeed Joel Barlow (d 26 Dec 1812) as minister to France, Apr. "

Gen Wilkinson takes possession of the Spanish fort at Mobile 15 Apr "

York (now Toronto), Upper Canada, captured 27 Apr. "

Defence of FORT MEIGS (O) by gen. Harrison, 28 Apr-9 May, "

Gen Green Clay is checked in attempting to reinforce fort Meigs . 5 May, "

Albert Gallatin, Pa, and James A. Bayard, Md, appointed as peace commissioners with John Quincy Adams at the Russian court to negotiate a peace, they sail. .. . 9 May, "

Thirteenth Congress, First Session (extra), convenes,

Speaker of the House, Henry Clay, Ky. 24 May, "

[Daniel Webster entered Congress at this session.]

Fort George, on the west side of Niagara river, near its mouth, is captured by the American troops under gen Dearborn (FORT GEORGE) .. . . 27 May, "

Frigate *Chesapeake* surrenders to the British ship *Shannon* (NAVAL BATTLES of the U. S.) .1 June, "

Action at STONY CREEK, Upper Canada . ..6 June, "

Affair at BEAVER DAMS, Upper Canada 24 June, "

Legislature of Massachusetts remonstrates against the continuance of the war .. .. ..15 July, "

UNI

Maj George Croghan's gallant defence of FORT STEPHENSON 2 Aug 1813

Congress authorizes the loan of $7,500,000 " "

Congress lays a direct tax of $3 000,000, number of states, 18, New York assessed the most, being $430,141 62, Louisiana the least, $28,295 11 2 Aug. "

First Session (extra) adjourns " "

British sloop-of-war *Pelican* captures the brig *Argus* in the British channel (NAVAL BATTLES of the U. S), 14 Aug "

Massacre at FORT MIMMS, Ala, by the Creek Indians, 30 Aug "

Brig *Enterprise* captures British brig *Boxer* off the coast of Maine (NAVAL BATTLES of the U S) 5 Sept "

Perry's victory on lake Erie (NAVAL BATTLES of the U S) 10 Sept "

Detroit, Mich, reoccupied by the U S forces, 28 Sept. "

Battle of the THAMES, Upper Canada, Harrison defeats Proctor, death of Tecumseh 5 Oct "

Action at CHRYSLER'S FIELD, on the northern shore of the St Lawrence, about 90 miles above Montreal, 11 Nov. "

Jackson's campaign against the Creek Indians (CREEK WAR) . Nov "

Second Session convenes 6 Dec. "

Gen George McClure, commanding a brigade on the Niagara frontier, burns the village of Newark, Canada, and evacuates fort George, opposite fort Niagara (he is severely censured) 10 Dec. "

Embargo established by Congress until 1 Jan 1815, 17 Dec. "

Fort Niagara captured by the British (FORT NIAGARA, NEW YORK) 19 Dec. "

BUFFALO and Black Rock burned by the British and Indians 30 Dec "

Pres Madison orders a general court-martial at Albany, N Y, upon brig -gen Wm Hull for the surrender of Detroit He is tried on charges of (1st) treason, (2d) cowardice, and (3d) neglect of duty and unofficer-like conduct 3 Jan. 1814

An English vessel, the *Bramble*, under a flag of truce, arrives at Annapolis, Md, with offers of peace, 6 Jan "

Congress authorizes increasing the army to 63,000 regular troops, and 5 years' service Jan "

Daniel Webster's first speech in the House on the enlistment bill . 14 Jan "

Henry Clay resigns as speaker of the House 19 Jan "

[He was appointed one of the peace commissioners, to meet at Ghent.]

Langdon Cheves of S C elected speaker 19 Jan "

Resolution tabled in Congress for a committee to investigate the BLUE LIGHTS 24 Jan "

President transmits to the House a report from the sec of war explaining the failure of the army on the northern frontier 2 Feb "

[It was founded on letters and reports from the sec of war (John Armstrong), gen Henry Dearborn, gen Jas Wilkinson, gen Wade Hampton, gen Lewis Cass, gen William H Harrison, and gen George B. McClure (see "Annals of the XIII th Congress," p. 2353)]

Massachusetts forbids the confinement in her jails of persons not committed by her judicial authorities, 7 Feb "

[The object was to free herself from confining British captives]

Loan of $25,000,000 and an issue of treasury notes for $10,000,000 authorized by Congress 24 Mch. "

Brig-gen. Wm Hull is found guilty on the 2d and 3d charges, and sentenced to be shot (see 3 Jan. 1814), 26 Mch "

[This sentence was approved by the president, but the execution remitted]

Gen. Jackson defeats and crushes the Creek Indians at Great Horse Shoe Bend, on the Tallapoosa 27 Mch "

Frigate *Essex*, capt David Porter, surrenders to the British ships *Phœbe* and *Cherub* in the harbor of Valparaiso, Chili (NAVAL BATTLES of the U S.), 28 Mch. "

Gen Wilkinson, with about 2000 troops, attacks a party of British, fortified in a stone mill, at La Colle, Lower Canada, near the north end of lake Champlain, and is repulsed 30 Mch 1814

[Gen Wilkinson was relieved from command, a court of inquiry was granted, which exculpated him, but he was never restored to command]

Repeal of the embargo 14 Apr "

Congress authorizes the purchase of the British vessels captured on lake Erie 10 Sept 1813, for $255,000 to be distributed as prize money among the captors, com Oliver H Perry to be paid $5000 in addition 18 Apr "

Congress authorizes the collection and preservation of flags, standards, and colors captured by the land or naval forces of the U S 18 Apr "

Second Session adjourns " "

British blockade extended to the whole coast of the U S 23 Apr "

Sloop-of-war *Peacock* captures the British brig *Epervier* off the coast of Florida with $118,000 in specie (NAVAL BATTLES of the U S) 29 Apr "

British attack and destroy the fort at Oswego, NEW YORK 6 May, "

Action at Big Sandy Creek, NEW YORK 29 May, "

Sloop-of-war *Wasp* captures the British sloop *Reindeer* in the British channel (NAVAL BATTLES of the U S), 28 June, "

FORT ERIE, with about 170 British soldiers, surrenders to gen Winfield Scott and gen Ripley 3 July, "

Battle of CHIPPEWA, Upper Canada 5 July, "

Battle of Lundy's Lane, or Bridgewater, Upper Canada (NEW YORK, 1814) 25 July, "

Congress appropriates $320,000 for one or more floating-batteries, designed by Robert Fulton, one finished July, "

[This was the first steam vessel of war built. BATTERIES]

Expedition from Detroit against FORT MACKINAW fails 4 Aug. "

British troops land at Pensacola, FLORIDA " "

British troops, 5000 strong, under gen Drummond, invest FORT ERIE 4 Aug "

American commissioners to negotiate a peace with Great Britain John Quincy Adams and Jonathan Russell, Mass , Albert Gallatin, Pa , James A Bayard, Del , and Henry Clay, Ky These commissioners meet adm lord Gambier, Henry Goulbourn, and William Adams, British commissioners, at Ghent, Belgium 8 Aug "

Creek Indians, by treaty, surrender a great part of their territory to the U S 9 Aug "

STONINGTON, Conn , bombarded by the British fleet under com Hardy 9-12 Aug "

British fleet, with 6000 veterans from Wellington's army under gen Ross, appears in Chesapeake bay, 14 Aug. "

Midnight assault by the British on fort Erie repulsed (FORT ERIE) 15 Aug. "

Battle of BLADENSBURG, the Capitol at Washington burned .... . 24 Aug. "

Banks in the District of Columbia suspend 27 Aug. "

Nantucket island stipulates with the British fleet to remain neutral 31 Aug "

Sloop-of-war *Wasp* sinks the British sloop *Avon* (NAVAL BATTLES of the U S.) . . 1 Sept "

British gen Prevost crosses the Canadian frontier towards Plattsburg, N Y , with 12,000 veteran troops, 1 Sept. "

John Armstrong, secretary of war, resigns 3 Sept. "

[He was blamed for the capture of Washington]

Fleet on lake Champlain under com Thomas McDonough defeats the British under com Downie (NAVAL BATTLES of the U S.) . 11 Sept. "

[Army under Prevost retired without a general engagement, though with a loss in its advance and retreat of over 1500 men]

British approaching Baltimore, Md , under gen. Ross, he is killed at North Point 12 Sept "

They find the city too well fortified, and retire, 13 Sept 1814

British fleet bombard FORT MCHENRY " "

[During this attack Francis Scott Key wrote "THE STAR-SPANGLED BANNER "]

British attack on FORT BOWYER, Mobile bay, repulsed, 15 Sept "

Garrison at FORT ERIE by a sortie break up the siege, 17 Sept "

Third Session convenes .... 19 Sept "

Gen Drummond raises the siege of fort Erie 21 Sept "

Wasp captures the British brig *Atlanta* (NAVAL BATTLES of the U S) 21 Sept "

Gallant fight of the privateer, the *Gen Armstrong*, with the British 74-gun ship-of-the-line, the *Plantagenet*, in the harbor of Fayal, one of the Azores (NAVAL BATTLES of the U S) 26 Sept "

Gen Geo Izard, on the Niagara frontier, moves on Chippewa with a force of 6000 men 13 Oct "

A resort of pirates and smugglers at BARATARIA BAY broken up, without resistance, by com Patterson, 16 Oct "

Gen Izard, after a skirmish with the British near Chippewa, 19 Oct , retires to the Niagara river, opposite Black Rock 21 Oct "

"THE STAR-SPANGLED BANNER" first sung at the Holliday Street theatre, Baltimore Oct "

Fort Erie abandoned and blown up by the U S troops, 5 Nov. "

Gen Jackson occupies Pensacola 6 Nov "

Elbridge Gerry of Mass , 5th vice-president of the U S., dies at Washington, D C., aged 70 years 23 Nov "

John Gaillard of S. C. elected president of the Senate, 25 Nov "

HARTFORD CONVENTION meets at Hartford, Conn , 15 Dec "

Martial law proclaimed in New Orleans by gen Jackson 15 Dec "

British approach New Orleans 22 Dec "

Gen Jackson attacks the command of gen Keane on Villere's plantation, about 9 miles below the city, and checks its advance on the night of 23 Dec. "

He intrenches about 7 miles below the city 24 Dec. "

[His line, extending at right angles to the river, reached to a cypress swamp about 1½ miles distant, and was protected by rudely constructed breastworks of cotton bales and earth, with a shallow ditch in front. At the extreme left of this line was stationed the brigade of gen Coffee, 800 strong, then came Carroll's brigade, about 1400 men, while the right towards the river was held by 1300 men under col Ross, including all the regulars, gen Adair was placed in the rear with about 500 men as a reserve Along the line was placed at intervals 18 guns, carrying from 6 to 23 pound balls, and several guns across the river under Patterson Anticipating an advance on the west bank of the river as well, Jackson had placed gen. David B. Morgan with about 1200 men, and 2 or 3 guns, a little in advance of his own position.]

Treaty of peace signed by the commissioners at Ghent, 24 Dec "

British attack gen Jackson with artillery, but are forced to retire 28 Dec. "

Another attempt made 1 Jan 1815

Final assault fails . 8 Jan "

[The British commander, sir Edward Pakenham, in his final assault designing to attack on both sides of the river at once, ordered col William (afterwards sir) Thornton to cross on the night of 7 Jan with 1200 men, and attack gen. Morgan at early dawn. The main assault under Pakenham was made as early as 6 A M , the 8th, in 2 columns, the right under maj.-gen sir Samuel Gibbs, the left under maj -gen. John Keane, and the reserve under maj -gen John Lambert, total force probably numbered about 7000 men. Gen Gibbs's column in close ranks, 60 men front, came under fire first, which was so severe and deadly that a few platoons only reached the edge of the ditch and broke.

In this advance Gibbs was mortally wounded, and Pakenham, in his attempt to rally the men, was almost instantly killed. The left advance under Keane fared no better, Keane being severely wounded and carried off the field, and his column routed. By 8 A.M. the assault was at an end. Col. Thornton's attack on the west side of the river was successful, for he routed gen. Morgan's militia, which were poorly armed, and drove them beyond Jackson's position towards the city, and compelled Patterson to spike his guns and retire, but owing to the failure of the main assault, together with the loss of the chief officers, gen. Lambert, now chief in command, recalled Thornton from his successes, and on 9 Jan. began preparation for retreating. Of the 7000 British troops probably engaged in the assault, 2036 were killed and wounded, the killed being estimated at over 700; Americans lost 8 killed and 13 wounded in the main assault; total loss on both sides of the river, 71.]

Congress levies a direct tax of $6,000,000 (number of states 18)....9 Jan. 1815
[The largest assessment, that of New York state, was $864,283.24; the smallest, of Delaware, $64,-092.50.]
Christopher Gore of Mass. opposes this bill in the Senate....5 Jan. "
Frigate *President*, 44 guns, com. Decatur commanding, is captured by the British frigates *Endymion*, 40 guns, the *Pomone*, *Tenedos*, and *Majestic* (NAVAL BATTLES of the U. S.)....15 Jan. "
Congress imposes duties on household furniture and on gold and silver watches....18 Jan. "
[Tax on a gold watch, $2; on a silver watch, $1; on $1500 worth of household furniture, $6; $3000, $17; $4000, $28; $6000, $45; $10,000, $100. Beds, bedding, kitchen furniture, and family pictures, exempt.]
U. S. purchases Jefferson's library, about 7000 volumes, for the use of Congress for $23,000 (vote of the House 81 to 71)....26 Jan. "
Bill to incorporate the Bank of the U. S. is vetoed by pres. Madison....30 Jan. "
Treaty of peace reaches New York in the British sloop-of-war *Favorite*....11 Feb. "
It is ratified....17 Feb. "
Frigate *Constitution* captures the *Cyane* and the *Levant*, British sloops-of-war (NAVAL BATTLES of the U. S.), Feb. "
Fort BOWYER, invested by the British fleet, surrenders....12 Feb. "
ARMY reduced to a peace footing of 10,000 men, 2 major-generals, and 4 brigadier-generals....3 Mch. "
[The major-generals were Jacob Brown and Andrew Jackson; the brigadier-generals were Winfield Scott, Edmund Gaines, Alexander Macomb, and Eleazar W. Ripley.]
Non-intercourse and Non-importation acts repealed, 3 Mch. "
U. S. declares war against Algiers.... " "
Thirteenth Congress adjourns.... " "
Sloop-of-war *Hornet*, capt. James Biddle, captures the British brig-of-war *Penguin*, off cape of Good Hope (NAVAL BATTLES of the U. S.)....23 Mch. "
Gen. JACKSON, at New Orleans, is fined $1000 for contempt of court....31 Mch. "
American prisoners-of-war at DARTMOOR, Engl., are fired upon by prison guards; 5 killed and 33 wounded, 2 mortally....6 Apr. "
Com. Decatur sails from New York for Algiers with the frigates *Guerrière*, *Macedonian*, and *Constellation*, 1 sloop-of-war, 4 brigs, and 2 schooners....19 May, "
Guerrière captures an Algerian frigate of 44 guns off Gibraltar....17 June, "
Dey, in a treaty of peace, renounces all claims to tribute, or presents, or to hold prisoners-of-war as slaves, 30 June, "
At a grand Indian council at Detroit, Mich., a treaty is made with 8 of the principal tribes east of the Mississippi....1 Sept. 1815
Total debt of the U. S., $119,600,000....30 Sept. "
[Estimated cost of the war, $85,500,000.]

Fourteenth Congress, First Session, convenes....4 Dec. "
President of the Senate *pro tem.*, John Gaillard of S. C.
Speaker of the House, Henry Clay of Ky.
North American Review starts in Boston, Mass., William Tudor, editor.... "
Congress fixes the pay of its members at $1500..19 Mch. 1816
[President of the Senate *pro tem.* and the speaker of the House $3000 each.]
Repeal of the act of 18 Jan. 1815, taxing household furniture, watches, etc....9 Apr. "
U. S. bank, capital $35,000,000, chartered by Congress for 20 years....10 Apr. "
Indiana authorized by Congress to form a constitution and state government....19 Apr. "
An act for the relief of the relatives and representatives of the crew of the sloop-of-war *Wasp*, believed to be lost, passed (NAVAL BATTLES of the U. S., 1814), 24 Apr. "
[12 months' wages and $50,000 prize-money awarded.]
Act passed regulating duties on imports....27 Apr. "
Congress appropriates $1,000,000 a year for 8 years to increase the navy....29 Apr. "
First Session adjourns....30 Apr. "
Presidential election held....12 Nov. "
[Democratic-Republican candidate for president, James Monroe of Va.; for vice-president, Daniel D. Tompkins of N. Y. Federal candidate for president, Rufus King of N. Y.; no nominee for vice-president.]
Second Session convenes....2 Dec. "
Indiana admitted into the Union (the 19th state), 11 Dec. "
American Colonization Society formed in Washington, D. C....Dec. "
U. S. bank begins operations....Jan. 1817
Congress authorizes the president to employ John Trumbull of Conn. to paint 4 scenes of the Revolution for the Capitol....6 Feb. "
[These paintings are "The Declaration of Independence," "Surrender of Burgoyne at Saratoga," "Surrender of Cornwallis," and the "Resignation of Washington at Annapolis."]
Electoral vote counted....12 Feb. "
[James Monroe of Va. (Dem.-Rep.) for president received 183; Daniel D. Tompkins of N. Y., for vice-president, 183; Rufus King of N. Y. (Federal) for president, 34; scattering, 34.]
Act dividing the Mississippi territory; the western part to form a state government, and to admit such state into the Union, and erecting the eastern portion into the territory of Alabama....1 Mch. "
Fourteenth Congress adjourns....3 Mch. "

Eighth Administration—Democratic-Republican.

4 Mch. 1817 to 3 Mch. 1821.

James Monroe, Va., president.
Daniel D. Tompkins, N. Y., vice-president.

CABINET.

John Quincy Adams, Mass., sec. of state, from 5 Mch. 1817.
William H. Crawford, Ga., sec. of treas., " " "
Isaac Shelby, Ky., sec. of war, from 5 Mch. 1817; declined appointment.
George Graham, Va., sec. of war, from 7 Apr. 1817.
John C. Calhoun, S. C., sec. of war, from 8 Oct. 1817.
Benjamin W. Crowninshield, Mass., sec. of navy, continued from 19 Dec. 1814.
Smith Thompson, N. Y, sec. of navy, from 9 Nov. 1818.
Richard Rush, Pa., attorney-gen., continued from 10 Feb. 1814.
William Wirt, Va., attorney-gen., from 13 Nov. 1817.

Return J. Meigs, O., postmaster-gen., continued from 17 Mch. 1814.

Indians attack a boat on the Appalachicola river, Fla., containing 40 men, with women and children, killing all but 6 men and 1 woman 30 Nov. 1817

fteenth Congress, First Session, convenes. 1 Dec. "

Speaker of the House, Henry Clay, Ky

Mississippi, the 20th state, admitted into the Union, 10 Dec. "

Gen Jackson takes the field against the Florida Indians 19 Feb. 1818

Pensions granted $20 a month to officers and $8 a month to privates who had served 9 months or more in the Continental army or navy, on proof of need 18 Mch "

Act establishing the flag of the U S 13 horizontal stripes, representing the original states, alternately red and white, with a white star in a blue field, for each state (FLAG) approved 4 Apr "

Gen Jackson captures the Spanish fort of St Marks, Fla 7 Apr "

An act to enable the people of Illinois to form a state government, and for the admission of such state, approved 18 Apr "

irst Session adjourns 20 Apr "

At the capture of the Spanish fort of St Marks, Jackson secures Alexander Arbuthnot and Robert C. Ambrister, and hangs them under sentence of a military court (ARBUTHNOT and AMBRISTER, Case of) 30 Apr "

Gen Jackson takes possession of Pensacola 24 May, "

Captures the fortress at Barrancas 27 May, "

Centre foundation of the Capitol at Washington laid, 24 Aug "

Indians of Ohio cede their remaining lands (about 4,000,000 acres), mostly in the Maumee valley, 27 Sept. "

Chickasaw Indians cede all land between the Mississippi river and the northern course of the Tennessee river . "

Treaty with England made 20 Oct "

[Commissioners of the U S, Richard Rush and Albert Gallatin The boundaries between the U S and British America from the lake of the Woods to the Rocky mountains settled, the territory west of the Rocky mountains to remain in the joint occupancy of both parties for 10 years, the commercial convention of 1815 to continue 10 years longer]

Second Session convenes . 16 Nov "

Illinois admitted (the 21st state) . 3 Dec "

Memorial from the territory of Missouri, asking permission to frame a state government, and for admission into the Union . 18 Dec "

Committee of 5 appointed by the Senate to inquire into the course of gen Jackson, in taking possession of fort St Marks and Pensacola, and in executing Arbuthnot and Ambrister 18 Dec. "

[The committee disapproved his acts, but the Senate postponed action indefinitely The House referred the matter to the Committee on Military Affairs, which also disapproved of Jackson's action, but the House, after debate from 12 Jan to 8 Feb., failed to support the report]

Bill introduced for the admission of Missouri 13 Feb 1819

Bill introduced to organize the territory of Arkansas, 16 Feb "

[When this bill was taken up, John W Taylor of N Y moved a proviso "that neither slavery nor involuntary servitude should hereafter be introduced into any part of the territories of the U S north of 36° 30′ N lat." Taylor finally withdrew his motion Thus the proposition of the "Missouri compromise," which was finally agreed to, was originated by a northern member, and not by Henry Clay of Ky, as is generally supposed —See *Lossing's* "Cyclopædia of U S Hist," *Missouri Compromise*, *Hildreth's* "Hist of the U. S," vol vi p 662, *Blaine's* "Twenty Years of Congress," vol. i p 19]

Bill for admission of Missouri taken up by the House, 16 Feb "

James Tallmadge, jr., of N. Y, moves an amendment, declaring free all children born in Missouri after admission into the Union, and providing for the gradual emancipation of the slaves This is modified to declare all slave children born in the state after its admission free at the age of 25 The bill so amended, passes the House, 87 to 76 17 Feb 1819

Treaty with Spain concluded 22 Feb "

Approved by the president 25 Feb "

[By this treaty Spain ceded to the U S all territory east of the Mississippi called E and W Florida, with adjacent islands, for $5,000 000 West of the Mississippi the new boundary-line began at the mouth of the Sabine river on the gulf of Mexico, thence north along the line of that river to 32° lat, thence north to the Red river, thence west along the line of this river to 100° W lon, thence north to the Arkansas river, thence westerly along the line of this river to 106° W lon, thence north to 42° N lat, thence west along the line of this parallel to the Pacific Not ratified by Spain until 20 Oct 1820]

Senate rejects the proviso of the House on the admission of Missouri, 31 to 7 27 Feb "

Senate returns the bill with amendments House adheres, 78 to 76, and the bill fails 2 Mch "

Alabama authorized to form a state government and to be admitted into the Union 2 Mch "

Arkansas organized as a territory " "

Congress authorizes the president to occupy E. and W. Florida 3 Mch "

Fifteenth Congress adjourns " "

Side-wheel steamer *Savannah* leaves Savannah, Ga, for Liverpool, Engl . 24 May, "

She arrives at Liverpool 20 June, "

[From Liverpool she sailed to St. Petersburg, Russia Having exhausted her coal on the Atlantic, she finished her voyage under canvas (NEW YORK)]

Maine separated from Massachusetts by the Massachusetts legislature 19 June, "

First published specimen of American lithographic printing (stone procured from Munich) appears in the *Analectic Magazine* July, "

Com Oliver Hazard Perry dies at Trinidad, West Indies, of yellow-fever . 23 Aug "

Sixteenth Congress, First Session, convenes 6 Dec "

Henry Clay, speaker of the House

Memorial from the people of Maine, praying for admission into the Union, presented 7 Dec "

Memorial from Missouri, asking for admission, again presented in the House 7 Dec "

Alabama admitted (the 22d state) 14 Dec "

Bill for the admission of Maine passes the House, 3 Jan 1820

Senate adds to the bill admitting Maine a clause for the admission of Missouri and an amendment proposed by senator Thomas, Ill, prohibiting the introduction of slaves into Louisiana north of the Arkansas boundary, 36° 30′, except in Missouri Thomas proviso passes the Senate, 30 to 10, and the bill as amended passes the Senate, 24 to 20 . 18 Feb "

House rejects the amendments, Senate asks for a committee of conference, House passes Missouri bill with a clause prohibiting the further introduction of slaves, 93 to 84 29 Feb "

Senate returns the Missouri bill to the House with slavery clause struck out and senator Thomas's territorial proviso inserted 2 Mch "

Committee of conference advises the Senate to recede from its amendment to the Maine bill, and the House to pass the Senate Missouri bill, House strikes out from the Missouri bill the prohibition of slavery, 90 to 84, and inserts the "Thomas proviso," 134 to 42 . 2 Mch "

Maine admitted (the 23d state) by act of Congress approved 3 Mch "

[To take effect 15 Mch]

Congress authorizes the people of Missouri to form a state government . 6 Mch "

Duel between com Stephen Decatur and com James Barron at Bladensburg, Md 22 Mch 1820
[Decatur was mortally and Barron severely wounded]
Congress abolishes the sale of public lands on credit, 24 Apr "
Congress organizes the first committee on agriculture, 3 May, "
Congress authorizes a loan of $3,000,000 15 May, "
First Session adjourns " "
First steamship line between New York and New Orleans established June, "
Daniel Boone dies at Charrette, Mo, aged 85, 26 Sept. "
Spain ratifies her treaty with the U S whereby she cedes Florida 20 Oct. "
Second Session convenes 13 Nov. "
Henry Clay resigns the speakership, John W Taylor of N Y elected on the 22d ballot by a majority of 1, 14 Nov. "
Presidential election held " "
[James Monroe of Va., Democratic-Republican, for president, Daniel D Tompkins of N Y for vice-president No opposition]
Missouri, in her constitution, requires her legislature to prohibit free colored persons from settling in the state The Senate adds a proviso that nothing contained in the constitution shall be construed as conflicting with that clause in the Constitution of the U S which declares "the citizens of each state shall be entitled to all the privileges and immunities of citizens in the several states." The bill admitting Missouri, with her constitution as amended, passes the Senate, 26 to 18 11 Dec. "
Electoral votes counted 14 Feb 1821
[James Monroe of Va. for president, 231, John Q Adams, 1 Daniel D Tompkins of N Y for vice-president, 218, scattering, 14]
House not agreeing with the Senate, 22 Feb, on the Missouri bill, Henry Clay of Ky moves a committee to act with a committee of the Senate "to consider whether it is expedient to admit Missouri into the Union, and for the due execution of the laws of the U S, and if not, whether any other or what provision should be made" The joint committee consists of 7 senators and 23 representatives. Clay reports a joint resolution from the committee 26 Feb. 1821
This resolution—"that Missouri shall be admitted on the fundamental condition that the 4th clause (respecting free negroes) shall never be construed to authorize the passing of any law, and no law shall be passed, by which any citizen of any of the states shall be excluded from the enjoyment of any of the privileges to which he is entitled by the Constitution of the U S, provided the legislature, by a solemn public act, shall declare and transmit to the president its assent to the amendment recommended by the select committee"—passes the House, 87 to 81, 26 Feb. "
Senate concurs, 26 to 15 27 Feb "
Resolution passed by Congress admitting Missouri into the Union (the 24th state) approved 2 Mch "
[It was 3 years after the question of admitting Missouri came before Congress that the final compromise and resolution of admission passed]
Congress authorizes a loan of $5,000,000 3 Mch. "
Sixteenth Congress adjourns " "
[It was during this and the preceding Congress, and in the discussions on the admission of Missouri, that the Southern slave interest outlined its future course as a political power.]

Ninth Administration—Democratic-Republican.

5 Mch 1821 to 3 Mch 1825

James Monroe, Va., president.
Daniel D. Tompkins, N Y, vice-president.

CABINET

John Quincy Adams, Mass., sec. of state, continued from 1817.
William H Crawford, Ga., sec. of treas., continued from 1817.
John C Calhoun, S C., sec. of war, continued from 1817
Smith Thompson, N Y, sec. of navy, continued from 1818
John Rogers, Mass, pres of navy committee, 1 Sept 1823.
Samuel J Southard, N J, sec of navy, 16 Sept 1823
William Wirt, Va., attorney-gen, continued from 1817.

Return J Meigs, O., postmaster-gen, continued from 1814.
John McLean, O, postmaster-gen, 26 June, 1823

President appoints gen Andrew Jackson governor of Florida Apr 1821
Gen Jackson takes possession of Florida 1 July, "
Pres Monroe proclaims the admission of Missouri as the 24th state 10 Aug "
Seventeenth Congress, *First Session*, convenes 3 Dec. "
Philip P Barbour, Va, elected speaker of the House
Thomas H Benton enters the Senate from Missouri, 6 Dec "
William Pinkney of Md dies, aged 58 25 Feb 1822
Apportionment bill passed (REPRESENTATIVES, House of) . 1 Mch "
President, by message, recommends the recognition of the independence of the South American states and Mexico 8 Mch "
Bankrupt bill defeated in the House by a vote of 72 to 99 12 Mch "
Resolution recognizing the independence of the American provinces of Spain passed by the House, 167 to 1 28 Mch "
[Mr Garnett of Va voted against the measure]
Territorial government established in Florida, 30 Mch. "
President vetoes an appropriation of $9000 for preserving and repairing the CUMBERLAND ROAD 4 May, "
President submits to Congress his objection to national appropriations for internal improvements 4 May, "
["This important state paper, together with the veto, interposes a breakwater to the popular policy of the day"—*Schouler's* "Hist. of the U S," vol III. p 254]
First Session adjourns 8 May, "
Second Session convenes . 2 Dec. "
A petition to Congress asks that capt John Cleves Symmes's theory be verified by a voyage to the north, and that capt. Symmes be intrusted with the conduct of the expedition (SYMMES'S THEORY), 27 Jan. 1823
Stephen F. Austin obtains from Mexico a grant of land in Texas for colonization . . Feb "
[The settlement named Austin, now the capital of the state TEXAS.]
Seventeenth Congress adjourns . . 3 Mch. "
Eighteenth Congress, *First Session*, convenes . 1 Dec. "
Henry Clay of Ky. elected speaker
Pres Monroe, in his message, proclaims the "Monroe Doctrine" in the following words "We owe it to candor, and to the amicable relations existing between the United States and those great European powers, to declare that we should consider any attempt on their part to extend their system to any portion of this hemisphere as dangerous to our peace and safety. With the existing colonies and dependencies of any European power we have not interfered, and shall not interfere, but with the governments who have declared their independence and maintained it and whose independence we have on great considerations and on just principles acknowledged, we could not view any interposition for the purpose of oppressing them, or controlling in any other manner their destiny, by any European power, in any other light than as a manifestation of an unfriendly disposition towards the United States." This is known as the "Monroe doctrine" 2 Dec. "
A resolution authorizing an embassy to Greece offered in the House by Daniel Webster of Mass 8 Dec. "
[This resolution was defeated 26 Jan 1824, although ably supported by Clay, Webster, and others. John Randolph opposed it in speeches full of sense

and sarcasm. "Of the three distinct types of our congressmen's oratory, no better specimens to this day can be found than in the several speeches which Clay, Webster, and Randolph delivered in the winter of 1823-24 on the spur of Webster's resolution." —*Schouler's* "Hist. of the U. S.," vol. iii. p. 304.]

Tariff (protective) bill brought before the House, 9 Jan. 1824

[Clay and Buchanan supported the bill, while Webster opposed it.]

Congress by resolution offers the marquis de Lafayette a ship to bring him to the U. S., approved 4 Feb. "

Act to survey routes for canals and roads.......Feb. "

Ninian Edwards presents an address to the House bringing charges against secretary Crawford. This is known as the A. B. PLOT............19 Apr. "

[A committee of 7 appointed to investigate.]

Tariff bill passes the House, 125 to 66......19 May, "

Approved............................22 May, "

[37 per cent. was the average rate of duty.]

Report of committee exonerating secretary Crawford from the charges of Mr. Edwards........25 May, "

rst Session adjourns.....................27 May, "

Lafayette, with his son, arrives at New York. 15 Aug. "

[He declined the offer of a government vessel.]

Tenth presidential election................9 Nov. "

[There were 4 Dem.-Rep. candidates: John Q. Adams of Mass., sec. of state; William H. Crawford of Ga., sec. of treasury; Henry Clay of Ky., speaker of the House; and Andrew Jackson of Tenn. John C. Calhoun of S. C. was the candidate for vice-president.]

cond Session convenes....................6 Dec. "

Lafayette welcomed to the House of Representatives, in an address by the speaker, Mr. Clay.....10 Dec. "

Congress (the House by 166 to 26, the Senate unanimously) votes to Lafayette $200,000 and a township of land in any part of the U. S. he might select, now unoccupied...................22 Dec. "

Treaty with Russia ratified...............11 Jan. 1825

[Establishing the boundary-line between the U. S. and Russia at 54° 40′ N. lat.]

Electoral votes counted....................9 Feb. 1825

[Of these votes for president Andrew Jackson received 99, John Quincy Adams 84, William H. Crawford 41, Henry Clay 37. John C. Calhoun, for vice-president, received 182; scattering, 78. As no candidate for president had a majority, the House proceeded to vote for the three highest—Jackson, Adams, and Crawford. This vote was taken by states, each state having 1 vote. Of these John Q. Adams received 13, Andrew Jackson 7, and William H. Crawford 4; and Adams was elected, Clay throwing his influence for him. This produced great excitement, as the country expected Jackson to be chosen.]

Treaty with the Creek Indians termed the "Indian Spring treaty"......................12 Feb. "

[This treaty was signed by their chief McIntosh, and provided for the cession of all the Creek territory in Georgia and several million acres in Alabama for $400,000. The Indians repudiated this cession and killed McIntosh, about 30 Apr.—"Niles's Register," 21 May, 1825.]

An act appropriating $150,000 to extend the CUMBERLAND ROAD from Canton, on the Ohio, opposite Wheeling, to Zanesville, O......approved 3 Mch. "

An act of Congress for strengthening the laws of the U. S.........................approved 3 Mch. "

ighteenth Congress adjourns................ " "

enth Administration.—Democratic-Republican (coalition) 4 Mch. 1825 to 3 Mch. 1829.

John Quincy Adams, Mass., president.
John C. Calhoun, S. C., vice-president.

CABINET.

enry Clay, Ky., sec. of state, from 7 Mch. 1825.
ichard Rush, Pa., sec. of treas., from 7 Mch. 1825.
James Barbour, Va., sec. of war, from 7 Mch. 1825.
Peter B. Porter, N. Y., sec. of war, from 26 May, 1828.
Samuel L. Southard, N. J., sec. of navy, continued from 16 Sept. 1823.
William Wirt, Va., attorney-gen., continued from 13 Nov. 1817.

John McLean, O., postmaster-gen., continued from 26 June 1823.

[Senate confirmed the cabinet officers unanimously, except the secretary of state. The vote upon his nomination was 27 to 14. The opposition charged Clay with defeating Andrew Jackson by a coalition with Mr. Adams.]

Corner-stone of Bunker Hill monument laid..17 June, 1825

[Lafayette was present, and Daniel Webster delivered the oration.]

Lafayette leaves Washington for France in the new frigate *Brandywine*, furnished him by the government..............................7 Sept. "

[He had visited every state (24) of the Union.]

Mordecai M. Noah selects Grand Island, in the Niagara river, as a site for a city of refuge for the Jews, to be called Ararat......................17 Sept. "

[The only remaining relic of this scheme, now in possession of the Buffalo Historical Society, is a stone tablet bearing a Hebrew inscription, and the name of the founder, etc.]

Illuminating gas comes into general use in New York. "

Com. David Porter, while cruising, lands a force at Porto Rico and exacts an apology for an insult to the American flag. He is recalled and suspended for 6 months.............................. "

Erie canal finished (NEW YORK)...........26 Oct. "

Nineteenth Congress*, First Session*, convenes...5 Dec. "

Speaker of the House, John W. Taylor, N. Y.

[Edward Everett entered Congress this session from Mass., and James K. Polk from Tenn.]

Dispute between the state of Georgia and the U. S. upon the removal of the Creek Indians........1825-29

John Gaillard, U. S. senator from S. C. from 1804-26, and from 14 Apr. 1814 to 9 Mch. 1825, president *pro tem.* of the Senate, dies at Washington.....26 Feb. 1826

South American states call a general congress, to meet at Panama in June, 1826, and to consider the rights of those states, and invite delegates from the U. S. Congress appropriates $40,000, and appoints Richard C. Anderson, minister to Colombia, and John Sargeant of Philadelphia, delegates, 14 Mch. 1826

During the debate on the "Panama congress" in the Senate, John Randolph refers to the coalition of Adams and Clay as that of "the Puritan and the blackleg." A duel followed between Clay and Randolph (DUELS)..........................8 Apr. "

First Session adjourns.....................22 May, "

John Adams, b. Braintree, Mass., 19 Oct. 1735, and Thomas Jefferson, b. Monticello, Va., 2 Apr. 1743, die on the 50th anniversary of American independence..............................4 July, "

Abduction of William Morgan from Canandaigua, N. Y..............................12 Sept. "

[Gave rise to a political party — the Anti-Masonic—that became national in importance, though short-lived. MORGAN, William; NEW YORK; POLITICAL PARTIES.]

Convention with Great Britain concerning indemnities for the war of 1812-14..................13 Nov. "

Second Session convenes....................4 Dec. "

Congress makes an appropriation for the payment of Revolutionary and other pensions.........29 Jan. 1827

Nineteenth Congress adjourns.................3 Mch. "

Gen. Gaines ordered into the Creek Indian country... "

Protectionists hold a convention at Harrisburg, Pa., and demand a higher tariff..........30 July, "

U. S. and Great Britain by treaty agree to extend or renew the commercial agreements of 1818, and the Oregon boundary to continue indefinitely, 6 Aug. "

First railroad in the U S., running from Quincy, Mass, to the Neponset river, 3 miles, commenced 1826, completed (operated by horse-power) 1827
Boundary differences between the U S and the British possessions to be referred to an arbiter 29 Sept "

Twentieth Congress, First Session, convenes 3 Dec "
Speaker of the House, Andrew Stevenson of Va
By another treaty Creek Indians cede their remaining lands in Georgia for $47,491 Ratified Jan 1828
Maj-gen Jacob Brown dies at Washington 24 Feb "
Debate on the tariff bill begun in the House 4 Mch "
Debate in the Senate 5-14 May, "
Tariff bill passed by the House 15 May, "
Approved known as the "Tariff of Abominations" (TARIFF) 19 May, "
[Principal speakers in the Senate on this bill were Thomas H Benton, Mo , M Dickerson, N J , Robert Y. Hayne, S C , Daniel Webster, Mass , Levi Woodbury, N H , and Samuel Smith, Md]
Congress by resolution grants Charles Carroll of Carrollton only surviving signer of the Declaration of Independence, the franking privilege, 23 May, "
First Session adjourns 26 May, "
Second railroad in the U S from Mauch Chunk, Pa , to the Lehigh river, 9 miles, commenced 1827, and finished "
Eleventh presidential election 11 Nov "
[Candidates Democrats, for president, Andrew Jackson Tenn , vice-president, John C. Calhoun, S C National-Republicans, for president, John Q Adams, Mass., vice-president, Richard Rush, Pa]
Second Session convenes 1 Dec "
Electoral votes counted in the House 11 Feb 1829
[Democrats, Andrew Jackson, Tenn , for president, 178, John C. Calhoun, S C , vice-president, 171 National-Republicans, John Quincy Adams, Mass , for president, 83, Richard Rush, Pa , vice-president, 83 Nullifiers, William Smith, S C, for vice-president, 7]
Twentieth Congress adjourns. 3 Mch. "

Eleventh Administration—Democratic. 4 Mch 1829 to 3 Mch 1833.

Andrew Jackson, Tenn , president.
John C Calhoun, S C , vice-president

CABINET

Martin Van Buren, N Y , sec. of state, from 6 Mch. 1829. Resigned
Edward Livingston, La., sec of state, from 24 May, 1831.
Samuel D Ingham, Pa , sec of treas , from 6 Mch 1829
Louis McLane, Del , sec. of treas , from 8 Aug 1831
John H Eaton, Tenn , sec of war, from 9 Mch 1829
Lewis Cass, Mich , sec of war, from 1 Aug 1831.
John Branch, N C , sec of navy, from 9 Mch 1829
Levi Woodbury, N H , sec of navy, from 23 May, 1831
John McPherson Berrien, Ga., attorney-gen , from 9 Mch. 1829
Roger B Taney, Md , attorney-gen , from 27 Dec 1831.
William T. Barry, Ky , postmaster gen , from 9 Mch 1829
[Postmaster-gen had not hitherto been recognized as a member of the cabinet]

John Jay, statesman, dies at Bedford, N. Y 19 May, 1829
James L. M Smithson, founder of the SMITHSONIAN INSTITUTION, dies in Genoa, Italy 27 June, "
"Stourbridge Lion," the first locomotive run in the U S , is purchased in England and arrives in New York in June, 1829 , shipped to Carbondale, and tried on the track at Honesdale 8 Aug "
William Lloyd Garrison publishes the *Genius* at Baltimore, Md , advocating immediate emancipation. "
[Benjamin Lundy associate editor]

Twenty-first Congress, First Session, convenes. 7 Dec "
Speaker of the House, Andrew Stevenson of Va
Robert Y Hayne's (S C) great speech in defence of state rights in the Senate on "the Foote resolution," limiting the sale of public lands. 25 Jan. 1830
Daniel Webster's reply defends the Constitution, 26-27 Jan. 1830
[Perhaps the most eloquent speeches ever made in Congress]
Jared Sparks begins his "American Biography" "
Bill before the House for a national road from Buffalo, N Y , to New Orleans, La , *via* Washington, 23 Mch "
Treaty with Denmark, indemnity claims 28 Mch "
Pres Jackson at a public dinner in Washington on Jefferson's birthday gives this toast, "Our Federal Union, it must be preserved" Vice-pres Calhoun responded "Liberty dearer than Union" 13 Apr "
Bill for a national road from Buffalo, N Y , to New Orleans, La., rejected in House by 88 to 105..14 Apr. "
Treaty with the Ottoman empire. . 7 May, "
Final rupture between Jackson and Calhoun May, "
[Van Buren set to work to destroy the friendship and confidence that existed between Calhoun and the president —*Blaine's* "Twenty Years of Congress," vol i p 28]
Duties on coffee, tea, and cocoa reduced 20 May, "
President vetoes the Maysville and Lexington, Ky, road bill (VETO) . . 27 May, "
Massachusetts obtains from the U S. $430,748 26 for services of her militia 1812-14 . 31 May, "
First Session adjourns " "
John Randolph sails as minister to Russia June, "
[He remained in Russia for 10 days, went to England for nearly a year, returned in Oct 1831, and drew $21,407 as pay —*Schouler's* "Hist of the U S," vol iii p 461]
Anti-Masonic party hold the first national convention in the U S at Philadelphia, Pa., Francis Granger of New York presiding Sept. "
Second Session convenes 6 Dec. "
Senate rejects the award of the king of the Netherlands as arbitrator of the boundary between Maine and Great Britain (MAINE) 10 Jan 1831
First locomotive built in the U S , "The Best Friend," at the West Point foundery shops in New York city , first trip on the South Carolina railroad 15 Jan "
Twenty-first Congress adjourns . . 3 Mch "
John H Eaton, sec. of war, resigns 7 Apr "
Martin Van Buren, sec of state, resigns . " "
Ex-pres. James Monroe dies in New York, aged 73, 4 July, "
Negro insurrection led by Nat Turner in Southampton county......... . . . Aug. "
Pres. Jackson re-forms his cabinet . "
Anti-Masonic party hold a national convention at Baltimore, Md and nominate William Wirt of Va. for president and Amos Ellmaker of Pa. for vice-president, number of delegates 112 . 26 Sept. "
Free-trade convention held at Philadelphia 5 Oct. "
High-tariff convention held at New York 26 Oct. "
Copyright law radically amended, making the term 28 years instead of 14, with renewal of 14 years more, and wife and children of author, in case of his death, entitled to a renewal . . . . "
William Lloyd Garrison begins the publication of the *Liberator* at Boston. . . .. . "

Twenty-second Congress, First Session, convenes, 5 Dec. "
Speaker of the House, Andrew Stevenson of Va
[Thomas Corwin's first appearance in Congress as a member from Ohio.]
National-Republican party hold a national convention at Baltimore, Md , and nominate Henry Clay of Ky. for president and John Sergeant of Pa for vice-president , number of delegates 155 12 Dec. "
[This party advocated higher tariff and internal improvements.]
Memorial for the renewal of the charter of the National bank presented to Congress .. . 9 Jan. 1832
William L Marcy of N Y , while urging the Senate to confirm Martin Van Buren as minister to England, says, "They see nothing wrong in the rule that to the victors belong the spoils of the enemy," 25 Jan "

Henry Clay advocates the 'American system" of protection in the Senate, supported by the senators from Delaware, Maine, Massachusetts, New Jersey, Ohio, Pennsylvania, and Rhode Island Jan - Feb 1832

Democratic (first so called) National convention meets in Baltimore 21 May, "

[Nominated Jackson for president, and Martin Van Buren of N Y for vice-president, he having been rejected as minister to England in the Senate by the vote of vice-pres Calhoun In this convention it was resolved "that two thirds of the whole number of votes in the convention shall be necessary to constitute a choice' This was the origin of the famous two-thirds rule]

Ratio of representation agreed upon by Congress according to the 5th census, 47,700 22 May, "

[Number of REPRESENTATIVES, 240]

BLACK HAWK WAR May - Aug "

Gen Thomas Sumter, distinguished Revolutionary soldier, dies near Camden, S C aged 98 1 June, "

Bill re-chartering the National bank passes the Senate, 28 to 20 11 June, "

And the House, 107 to 85 3 July, "

Commissioner of Indian affairs first appointed 9 July, "

President vetoes the Bank bill 10 July, "

Senate fails to pass the Bank charter over the president's veto 13 July, "

Source of the Mississippi discovered by an exploring party under Henry R Schoolcraft 13 July, "

Partial repeal of the tariff measures of 1828 14 July, "

[This repeal reduced many of the revenue taxes, but the protective taxes were not materially altered Woollen yarn was now first taxed]

rst Session adjourns 16 July, "

Cholera first appears in the U S "

[First case in Quebec, 8 June, in New York, 27 June]

Treaty with the Two Sicilies, indemnity 14 Oct "

Presidential election 13 Nov "

[Candidates Democrats, for president, Andrew Jackson of Tenn for vice-president, Martin Van Buren of N Y National-Republicans, for president, Henry Clay of Ky for vice-president, John Sergeant of Pa Anti-Masons, for president, William Wirt of Va for vice-president, Amos Ellmaker of Pa Nullifiers (S C.), for president, John Floyd of S C, for vice-president, Henry Lee of Va]

Charles Carroll of Carrollton, Md, last surviving signer of the Declaration of Independence, dies at Baltimore, aged 95 14 Nov "

Convention is held at Columbus, S C, which by ordinance declares the Tariff acts of 1828 and 1832 null and void 19 Nov "

[The term "nullification" was borrowed from the Virginia and Kentucky RESOLUTIONS of 1798]

econd Session convenes 3 Dec. "

Pres. Jackson issues a proclamation to the people of South Carolina 10 Dec "

[An able and eloquent paper, written by Livingston, sec of state, after an original draft by Jackson]

John C Calhoun, vice-president, resigns 28 Dec. "

[Hugh L White of Tenn. president *pro tem.* of the Senate]

Pres Jackson, by message, informs Congress of the proceedings of South Carolina, and asks power to enforce the collection of the revenue 16 Jan 1833

John C Calhoun, now a senator from S C, introduces resolutions that the theory that the people of the U S are now or ever have been united in one nation is erroneous, false in history and reason 22 Jan "

Henry Clay introduces the "compromise tariff" in the Senate as a solution of all pending troubles between the manufacturing states and the South. 12 Feb. "

Electoral votes counted 13 Feb. "

[Andrew Jackson, Tenn, for president, 219, Martin Van Buren, N Y, for vice-president, 189, Henry Clay, Ky, for president, 49 (Mass, R I, Conn, Del., Ky, Md) John Sergeant, Pa., for vice-president, 49 (Mass., R. I., Conn, Del, Ky, Md) William Wirt, Va., for president, 7 (Vt), Amos Ellmaker, Pa., for vice-president 7 (Vt), John Floyd, S C, for president, 11 (S C), Henry Lee, for vice-president, 11 (S C), William Wilkins, Pa, for vice-president, 30 (Pa)]

"Compromise tariff" passes the House, 119 to 85, 26 Feb 1833

And the Senate, 29 to 16 1 Mch. "

Becomes a law 3 Mch "

[This law scaled down all duties so that 20 per cent should be the standard duty in 1842]

Twenty-second Congress adjourns 3 Mch "

Twelfth Administration — Democratic. 4 Mch 1833 to 3 Mch 1837

Andrew Jackson, Tenn, president

Martin Van Buren, N Y, vice-president

CABINET

Louis McLane, Del, sec of state, from 29 Mch 1833

John Forsyth, Ga. sec of state, from 27 June, 1834

Louis McLane, Del, sec of treas, continued from 8 Aug 1831

William J Duane, Pa, sec of treas, from 29 May, 1833

Roger B Taney, Md, sec of treas, from 23 Sept 1833 Not confirmed by the Senate

Levi Woodbury, N H sec of treas, from 27 June, 1834

Lewis Cass, Mich, sec of war, continued from 1 Aug 1831

Levi Woodbury, N H, sec of navy, continued from 23 May, 1831

Mahlon Dickerson, N J, sec of navy, from 30 June, 1834.

William T Barry, Ky, postmaster-gen, continued from 9 Mch. 1829

Amos Kendall, Ky, postmaster-gen, from 1 May, 1835

Roger B Taney, Md., attorney-gen, continued from 27 Dec 1831.

Benjamin F Butler, N. Y, attorney-gen, from 24 June, 1834

South Carolina repeals the ordinance of nullification in a convention held 16 Mch 1833

John Randolph of Va dies in Philadelphia, aged 60, 24 May, "

Pres Jackson lays near Fredericksburg, Va, the corner-stone of a monument to Washington's mother, Mary Washington May, "

Pres Jackson makes a tour of the eastern states as far as Concord, N H, returning to Washington, 3 July, "

[Harvard university conferred upon him the degree of LL D]

Gen John Coffee d near Florence, Ala, aged 61, 7 July, "

Com William Bainbridge dies in Philadelphia, aged 59 28 July, "

Sun, newspaper, first pub in New York, price 1 cent, Benjamin H Day publisher 3 Sept. "

President removes W. J Duane, sec of treas, for refusing to withdraw the deposits from the National bank, and appoints Roger B Taney of Md in his place 23 Sept "

Pres Jackson directs the secretary of the treasury to withdraw the deposits, about $10,000,000, from the National bank 26 Sept. "

Indian chief Black Hawk is taken through the principal eastern cities autumn of "

Bank deposits removed from the National bank 1 Oct "

[This action of pres Jackson caused great dissatisfaction.]

Anti-slavery society organized in New York city, 2 Oct "

First severe railway accident in the U S on the Amboy and Bordentown railroad, several killed 8 Oct "

Great display of shooting stars morning of 13 Nov. "

[Generally visible in North America, though most brilliant in the eastern U S., commencing at midnight and continuing until sunrise]

***Twenty-third Congress**, First Session*, convenes 2 Dec. "

Speaker of the House, Andrew Stevenson of Va

American Anti-slavery society organized at Philadelphia, Beriah Green president, and John G Whittier one of the secretaries 6 Dec. "

Mr. Clay offers a resolution, 10 Dec., inquiring of the president whether a paper read to heads of departments under date of 18 Sept. 1833, relative to the deposits of the public money, was genuine, and requesting that said paper be laid before the Senate. This resolution passes the Senate, 23 to 18..11 Dec. 1833
Senate appoints a committee to investigate the National bank....................................4 Feb. 1834
Treaty with Spain, indemnity..............17 Feb. "
William Wirt, orator, lawyer, and author, dies at Washington, D. C., aged 62..................18 Feb. "
Senate resolves that in removing the deposits the president had assumed authority not conferred by the Constitution and the laws...............28 Mch. "
House resolves that the National bank shall not be rechartered nor the deposits restored..........4 Apr. "
President protests against the resolution of 28 Mch., but the Senate refuses to enter the protest in its minutes, 15 Apr. "
Gen. Lafayette dies in France (FRENCH REVOLUTION), 20 May, "
Senate, by resolution, censures the president for removing the deposits.....................June, "
Coinage of the U. S. changed (COIN).......28 June, "
Indian territory established by Congress.....30 June, "
First Session adjourns..................... " "
"Whig" party [first so called, NEW YORK, 1832] fully organized. POLITICAL PARTIES............... "
[Name pleased the Federals of New England and the State-rights men of the South.]
Treaty is made with the Seminole Indians at Payne's Landing, 9 May, 1833, and an additional treaty at fort Gibson, 28 Mch. 1834, for their removal to the INDIAN TERRITORY; Indians reject the treaty of their chiefs. Gen. Thompson sent by the U. S. to insist on its execution..................28 Oct. "
[Seminole war began, 1835-42. FLORIDA, 1832-42.]
Second Session convenes.....................1 Dec. "
John Bell of Tenn. speaker in place of Andrew Stevenson, resigned; John Hubbard of N. H. speaker *pro tem.* during this session.
Over 500 local banks in the U. S.................. "
["The government revenues were deposited in banks selected by the treasury. Neither these nor their unselected rivals were under any sort of supervision by the state which chartered them or by the federal government, and no bank-note had any certainty of value."—"Narrative and Critical Hist. of America," vol. vii. p. 289.]
President in his message announces the extinguishment of the national debt.......................Dec. "
John Quincy Adams, member from Mass., delivers an oration on Lafayette before Congress.......31 Dec. "
Attempted assassination of pres. Jackson at the Capitol by Richard Lawrence...................30 Jan. 1835
[Lawrence tried in Apr., but proved insane.]
Congress awards a gold medal to col. George Croghan for his gallant defence of FORT STEPHENSON 22 years before..........................13 Feb. "
Senate appoints a committee of 5 to inquire into the alleged complicity of sen. Poindexter of Miss. in the attempt to assassinate the president........22 Feb. "
[Investigation showed sen. Poindexter innocent.]
Congress establishes branch mints at New Orleans, La., Charlotte, N. C., and Dahlonega, Ga........3 Mch. "
Twenty-third Congress adjourns................ " "
New York *Herald* appears, James Gordon Bennett publisher....................................6 May, "
National Democratic convention at Baltimore, Md., May, "
[Martin Van Buren of N. Y. nominated for president; Richard M. Johnson of Ky. for vice-president.]
Antislavery documents taken from the mail and burned at Charleston, S. C......................Aug. "
Name "Loco-focos" first applied to the Democratic party (LOCO-FOCO)........................... "
Gen. William H. Harrison of O. nominated for president, with Francis Granger of N. Y. for vice-president, by a state Whig convention at Harrisburg, Pa....... 1835
[Gen. Harrison also received the nomination at the Whig state conventions of New York, Ohio, Maryland, and other states. No national Whig convention was held. Hugh L. White of Tenn. was supported by the states of Tennessee and Georgia, Daniel Webster receiving the vote of Massachusetts, and W. P. Mangum of N. C. the vote of South Carolina.]
Samuel Colt patents a "revolving pistol".......... "

Twenty-fourth Congress, First Session, convenes, 2 Dec. "
Speaker of the House, James K. Polk of Tenn.
The president, in his message, suggests laws to prohibit the circulation of anti-slavery documents through the mails.
Great fire in New York city............16-17 Dec. "
Gen. Thompson, lieut. C. Smith, and others massacred by the Seminole Indians at fort King, 60 miles southwest of St. Augustine, Fla..............28 Dec. "
[Osceola, whom gen. Thompson had shortly before put in irons for a day, led this war-party.]
Maj. F. L. Dade, with 100 men, moving from fort Brooke to the relief of gen. Clinch, is waylaid and the entire party killed except 4, who afterwards die of injuries there received...............28 Dec. "
Treaty with the Cherokee Indians in Georgia; they cede all their territory east of the Mississippi for $5,000,000..........................29 Dec. "
Memorial presented to Congress praying for the abolition of slavery within District of Columbia..11 Jan. 1836
Texas declares her independence...........2 Mch. "
Mexicans under Santa Aña capture the ALAMO, San Antonio, Tex., and massacre the garrison. David Crockett killed here.....................6 Mch. "
Battle of San Jacinto, defeat of Santa Aña...21 Apr. "
Mexico acknowledges independence of Texas.14 May, "
House resolves, by a vote of 117 to 68, that everything presented to that body in any way relating to slavery or its abolition shall be laid on the table without further action or notice.................26 May, "
[This was the first of the "gag rules" of Congress.]
Arkansas admitted as the 25th state........15 June, "
Act authorizing the different states to become depositories, in proportion to their respective representation, of the surplus funds in the U. S. treasury over $5,000,000. This money subject to recall by the U. S. treasurer at any time, but not in sums of over $10,000 per month. Money to be paid to the states quarterly, viz., 1 Jan., 1 Apr., 1 July, 1 Oct., 1837. Although but 3 instalments were paid, it aggregated $28,000,000. This money has never been recalled, and is carried on the treasurer's report as unavailable funds. Approved............23 June, "
James Madison dies at Montpelier, Va., aged 85, 28 June, "
Territory of Wisconsin organized................. "
First Session adjourns.......................4 July, "
First observatory in the U. S. built at Williams college, Mass.. "
Treasury issues a "specie circular," requiring collectors of the public revenue to receive only gold and silver............................... 11 July, "
[This proceeding hastened the panic of 1837.]
Aaron Burr dies at Staten Island, aged 80....14 Sept. "
Samuel Houston elected first president of the republic of TEXAS........................... 22 Oct. "
Presidential election.......................8 Nov. "
[Candidates: Democrats, for president, Martin Van Buren, N. Y.; for vice-president, Richard M. Johnson, Ky. Whigs, for president, William Henry Harrison, O., Hugh L. White, Tenn., Daniel Webster, Mass., W. P. Mangum, N. C.; for vice-president, Francis Granger, N. Y., John Tyler, Va., Wm. Smith, Ala.]
Second Session convenes.....................5 Dec. "
Resolution of Senate, June, 1834, censuring pres. Jack-

son for removing the public money from the National bank, expunged from the records....16 Jan. 1837
Coinage of the U. S. again changed ....18 Jan. "
Michigan admitted into the Union, the 26th state in order.....................................26 Jan. "
Electoral vote counted....................8 Feb. "
[Martin Van Buren, N. Y., for president, 170; Richard M. Johnson, Ky., for vice-president, 147; William Henry Harrison, O., for president, 73; Hugh L. White, Tenn., for president, 26; Daniel Webster, Mass., for president, 14; W. P. Mangum, N. C., for president, 11; Francis Granger, N. Y., for vice-president, 77; John Tyler, Va., for vice-president, 47; Wm. Smith, Ala., for vice-president, 23. No candidate having a majority for vice-president, the Senate elected Richard M. Johnson by a vote of 33 to 16 for Francis Granger.]
Twenty-fourth Congress adjourns..............3 Mch. "

Thirteenth Administration—Democratic. 4 Mch. 1837 to 3 Mch. 1841.

Martin Van Buren, N. Y., president.
Richard M. Johnson, Ky., vice-president.

CABINET.

John Forsyth, Ga., sec. of state, continued from 27 June, 1834.
Levi Woodbury, N. H., sec. of treas., continued from 27 June, 1834.
Joel R. Poinsett, S. C., sec. of war, from 7 Mch. 1837.
Mahlon Dickerson, N. J., sec. of navy, continued from 30 June, 1834.
James K. Paulding, N. Y., sec. of navy, from 20 June, 1838.
Amos Kendall, Ky., postmaster-gen., continued from 1 May, 1835.
John M. Niles, Conn., postmaster-gen., from 18 May, 1840.
Benj. F. Butler, N. Y., attorney-gen., continued from 24 June, 1834.
Felix Grundy, Tenn., attorney-gen., from 7 July, 1838.
Henry D. Gilpin, Pa., attorney-gen., from 10 Jan. 1840.

Great commercial panic begins by the failure of Herman Briggs & Co., New Orleans, La.........Mch. 1837
[This panic reached its height in May.]
All the banks in New York city suspend specie payment..............................10 May, "
[Banks in Boston, Philadelphia, and Baltimore followed.]
An extra session of Congress called to meet first Monday in Sept..........................15 May, "
Victoria, daughter of the duke of Kent, succeeds to the throne of England on the death of William IV., 28 June, "
***Twenty-fifth Congress**, First Session* (extra), assembles, 4 Sept. "
Speaker of the House, James K. Polk, Tenn.
President's message advocates the sub-treasury. First Sub-treasury bill reported in the Senate...14 Sept. "
Passes the Senate by a small majority........4 Oct. "
Defeated in the House (see 6 Aug. 1846).....14 Oct. "
"Patriot war" in Canada commences.............. "
First Session (extra) adjourns................16 Oct. "
Osceola, the Seminole chief, with a party of 70 warriors, visits the camp of gen. Jessup under stipulations of safety, and is detained as prisoner..21 Oct. "
[He was confined in fort Moultrie, Charleston, S. C., where he died, 31 Jan. 1838.]
Many citizens of the U. S. along the borders of Canada join the insurgents in the Patriot war during the autumn...................................... "
Elijah P. Lovejoy shot while defending his printing-press and paper at Alton, Ill., from the attack of a pro-slavery mob (ALTON RIOT, ILLINOIS)...7 Nov. "
Second Session assembles.....................4 Dec. "
Wendell Phillips's first "abolition" speech in Faneuil hall, Boston, to protest against the murder of Elijah P. Lovejoy.............................8 Dec. "
Col. Zachary Taylor defeats the Seminole Indians at Okeechobee swamp, Fla................25 Dec. "
American steamer *Caroline* is attacked and burned by Canadian troops at Schlosser's Landing, above Niagara falls, on the American side (NEW YORK), 29 Dec. 1837
President issues a proclamation of neutrality as regards the disturbance in Canada...........5 Jan. 1838
Duel between William J. Graves of Ky. and Jonathan Cilley of N. H., members of the House....24 Feb. "
[Fought with rifles; Cilley killed at the 3d shot.]
First regular passage by steamer across the Atlantic completed by the *Great Western* and *Sirius*. *Sirius* 17 days from London, and *Great Western* 15 days from Bristol. Both arrive at New York city, 23 Apr. "
Banks in New England and New York resume specie payments.............................10 May, "
Iowa receives a territorial government......12 June, "
Second Session adjourns.....................9 July, "
U. S. Exploring expedition to the Antarctic and Pacific oceans, under command of lieut. Charles Wilkes, sails from Hampton Roads..............18 Aug. "
[The expedition consisted of the sloops-of-war *Vincennes* and *Peacock*, brigs-of-war *Porpoise* and *Relief*, and the schooners *Flying Fish* and *Sea Gull*.]
Third Session assembles......................3 Dec. "
Charles G. Atherton of N. H. introduces a resolution in the House, known as the "ATHERTON GAG," to prevent the discussion of slavery. It passes by a vote of 127 to 78 (see 1836)................11 Dec. "
Loss of steamboats on the western rivers: Mississippi, 55; Ohio, 13; Missouri, 2; Illinois, 2; Arkansas, 1; Red, 1; and 4 others during the year ("Niles's Register," vol. lvii. p. 32)........................ "
Unsettled boundary between Maine and the British provinces results in the "AROOSTOOK war". .Feb.–Mch. 1839
Rev. Zerah Colburn d. at Norwich, Vt., aged 35, 2 Mch. "
[A mathematical prodigy.]
Twenty-fifth Congress adjourns...............3 Mch. "
L'Amistad ("Friendship") is captured off Montauk point by the U. S. brig *Washington*, lieut. Geding commanding (AMISTAD, case of; CONNECTICUT), 29 Aug. "
Daguerrotypes first taken in the U. S. by prof. J. W. Draper .... "
Jesse Buell, agriculturist, dies at Danbury, Conn., aged 61 ....6 Oct. "
Liberty party, in convention at Warsaw, N. Y., nominates James G. Birney for president and Thomas Earle of Pa. for vice-president...........13 Nov. "
[This was the first appearance of a national anti-slavery party, and although Mr. Birney declined the nomination, it polled over 7000 votes.]
Ulysses, a Portuguese brig, built at Baltimore, is captured by the British war-schooner *Skipjack* off the Isle of Pines with a cargo of 556 Africans..30 Nov. "
[These negroes were confined in a space of 2 ft. 4½ in. each and had been 50 days at sea.]

***Twenty-sixth Congress**, First Session*, assembles, 2–16 Dec. "
Robert M. T. Hunter of Va., Whig, elected speaker of the House on the 11th ballot, receiving 119 votes out of 232.
Whig National convention at Harrisburg, Pa...4 Dec. "
[First ballot, Clay, 103; Harrison, 94; and Scott, 57. Fifth ballot, Clay, 90; Harrison, 148; and Scott, 16. The nomination of Harrison was made unanimous, and John Tyler nominated for vice-president.]
Steamer *Lexington* burned on Long Island sound, between New York and Stonington.........13 Jan. 1840
[140 lives lost.]
Lieut. Charles Wilkes discovers the antarctic continent, 66° 20′ S. lat., 154° 18′ E. lon......19 Jan. "
[He coasted westward along this land 70 degrees.]
Washingtonian Temperance Society founded in Baltimore.. "
Democratic National convention at Baltimore, Md. Martin Van Buren nominated for president, leaving the states to nominate for vice-president...5 May, "
Sub-treasury or Independent Treasury bill passed and approved...........................4 July, "

Britannia, the first regular steam-packet of the Cunard line, arrives at Boston, 14 days and 8 hours from Liverpool......................19 July, 1840

First Session adjourns......................21 July, "

"Log-cabin" and "Hard-cider" campaign, in the interest of William Henry Harrison, begins....July, "

[Modern methods of conducting a presidential campaign were now introduced.]

Steamship *Arcadia* arrives at Boston from Liverpool in 12 days and 12 hours, the shortest passage up to that time......................17 Oct. "

Alexander MacLeod arrested in the state of New York for complicity in the destruction of the steamer *Caroline*, 29 Dec. 1837......................Nov. "

[He was tried and acquitted 12 Oct. 1841.]

Log-cabin, a Whig campaign paper, edited by Horace Greeley, reaches a circulation of 80,000 during the autumn...................... "

Fourteenth presidential election............10 Nov. "

[Candidates: Whigs, for president, William Henry Harrison, O.; for vice-president, John Tyler, Va. Democrats, for president, Martin Van Buren, N. Y.; for vice-president, Richard M. Johnson, Ky. Liberty party, for president, James G. Birney, N. Y.; for vice-president, Thomas Earle, Pa.]

Treaty of commerce between Texas and Great Britain made......................14 Nov. "

Second Session assembles......................7 Dec. "

Electoral votes counted......................19 Feb. 1841

[For president, Harrison, 234, Van Buren, 60; for vice-president, Tyler, 234, Johnson, 48.]

Twenty-sixth Congress adjourns................3 Mch. "

Fourteenth Administration—Whig. 4 Mch. 1841 to 3 Mch. 1845.

William Henry Harrison, O., president.
John Tyler, Va., vice-president.

CABINET (until 11 Sept. 1841).

Daniel Webster, Mass., sec. of state, from 5 Mch. 1841.
Thomas Ewing, O., sec. of treas., from 5 Mch. 1841.
John Bell, Tenn., sec. of war, from 5 Mch. 1841.
George E. Badger, N. C., sec. of navy, from 5 Mch. 1841.
Francis Granger, N. Y., postmaster-gen., from 6 Mch. 1841.
John J. Crittenden, Ky., attorney-gen., from 5 Mch. 1841.

Steamer *President* sails from New York city with 109 passengers and is never heard of again....11 Mch. 1841

[This vessel, when launched, 1840, was considered the largest ship afloat, being 268 ft. in length, 64 ft. in width, including paddle-boxes, engine 500 horse-power, 2360 tons' register.]

President calls an extra session of Congress for 31 May, 17 Mch. "

Pres. Harrison d. aged 68 years............4 Apr. "

Vice-pres. Tyler takes the oath of office as president, 6 Apr. "

CABINET.

Daniel Webster, Mass., sec. of state, continued from 5 Mch. 1841.
Hugh S. Legaré, S. C., sec. of state, from 9 May, 1843.
Abel P. Upshur, Va., sec. of state, from 24 July, 1843.
John Nelson, Md., sec. of state, acting, from 29 Feb. 1844.
John C. Calhoun, S. C., sec. of state, from 6 Mch. 1844.
Thomas Ewing, O., sec. of treas., continued from 5 Mch. 1841.
Walter Forward, Pa., sec. of treas., from 13 Sept. 1841.
Caleb Cushing, Mass., sec. of treas., rejected by the Senate.
John C. Spencer, N. Y., sec. of treas., from 3 Mch. 1843.
George M. Bibb, Ky., sec. of treas., from 15 June, 1844.
John Bell, Tenn., sec. of war, continued from 5 Mch. 1841.
John McLean, O., sec. of war, declined from 13 Sept. 1841.
John C. Spencer, N. Y., sec. of war, from 12 Oct. 1841.
James M. Porter, Pa., sec. of war, rejected by the Senate, 8 Mch. 1843.
William Williams, Pa., sec. of war, from 15 Feb. 1844.
George E. Badger, N. C., sec. of navy, continued from 5 Mch. 1841.
Abel P. Upshur, Va., sec. of navy, from 13 Sept. 1841.
David Henshaw, Mass., sec. of navy, rejected by the Senate, 24 July, 1843.
Thomas W. Gilmer, Va., sec. of navy, from 15 Feb. 1844.
John Y. Mason, Va., sec. of navy, from 14 Mch. 1844.
Francis Granger, N. Y., postmaster-gen., continued from 6 Mch. 1841.
Charles A. Wickliffe, Ky., postmaster-gen., from 13 Sept. 1841.
John J. Crittenden, Ky., attorney-gen., continued from 5 Mch. 1841.
Hugh S. Legaré, S. C., attorney-gen., from 13 Sept. 1841.
John Nelson, Md., attorney-gen., from 1 July, 1843.

Corner-stone of the Mormon temple at Nauvoo, Ill., laid......................6 Apr. 1841

Horace Greeley issues the first number of the New York *Daily Tribune*......................10 Apr. "

[A small sheet selling for 1 cent. The *Weekly Tribune* was issued the following autumn.]

Twenty-seventh Congress, *First Session* (extra), assembles......................31 May, "

Samuel L. Southard, N. J., president *pro tem.* of the Senate and acting vice-president of the U. S. until his death, 22 May, 1842.

W. P. Mangum, N. C., president *pro tem.* of the Senate and acting vice-president of the U. S. from 31 May, 1842, to the end of pres. Tyler's term.

Speaker, John White, Ky.

Act to appropriate the proceeds of the public lands and pre-emptive rights granted, passed........6 July, "

U. S. sloop-of-war *Peacock*, of the Wilkes U. S. Exploring expedition, is lost at the mouth of the Columbia river, Or......................18 July, "

Sub-treasury or Independent Treasury act repealed, 9 Aug. "

Pres. Tyler vetoes the bill to incorporate the Fiscal Bank of the U. S......................16 Aug. "

Bankruptcy bill passed......................19 Aug. "

Pres. Tyler vetoes the Fiscal Corporation bill..9 Sept. "

Party of British volunteers from Canada carry off col. Grogan......................9 Sept. "

[This seizure was unauthorized by the British government, and Grogan was promptly released. The seizure, however, caused great excitement.]

Cabinet resigns, except the sec. of state......11 Sept. "

[Because of the veto of the Fiscal Corporation bill.]

First Session (extra) adjourns................13 Sept. "

President's proclamation forbids American citizens to invade British possessions..............25 Sept. "

Failure of the U. S. bank under the Pennsylvania charter......................11 Oct. "

Brig *Creole*, Ensor, master, sails from Richmond, Va., for New Orleans with merchandise and 135 slaves; some of the slaves attack the captain and crew, and capture the vessel......................7 Nov. "

[They proceeded to the island of New Providence, belonging to Great Britain; the magistrates refused to give the negroes up, and they were finally liberated. Serious dispute with England followed.]

Second Session assembles...................... 6 Dec. "

Joshua R. Giddings, member from Ohio, presents resolutions concerning the brig *Creole* and adverse to slavery......................21 Mch. 1842

[Being censured by the House by a vote of 125 to 69, he immediately resigned, returned to Ohio, and was re-elected by a large majority.]

Henry Clay resigns from the Senate...... 31 Mch. "

Influenza, called "la grippe," widely prevalent..... "

Col. John C. Frémont's first exploring expedition to the Rocky Mountains commences..........2 May, "

U. S. Exploring expedition under lieut. Charles Wilkes —which penetrates to 66° S. lat., and discovers the antarctic continent (now known as Wilkes's Land), along which it coasts 70°—after a voyage of 4 years and over 90,000 miles, returns to New York (see this record, 1838)......................10 June, "

Dorr's rebellion in Rhode Island, caused by the disagreement between the Charter and Suffrage parties (DORR'S REBELLION)..............May–June, "

Statue of Washington, by Horatio Greenough, placed in the Capitol 1842

[It was executed in Italy, and in position cost $45,000.]

Charles Dickens visits the U S "

Earliest actual finding of gold in California in Los Angeles district (CALIFORNIA) "

"Ashburton treaty" with England for settling the boundaries between Maine and the British provinces also for suppressing the slave-trade and extradition, negotiated at Washington between lord Ashburton, special minister of Great Britain, and Daniel Webster, sec of state, and signed 9 Aug "

End of the Indian war in Florida proclaimed 14 Aug "

Ashburton treaty ratified by the Senate, 39 to 9 20 Aug "

Beginning of the fiscal year changed from 1 Jan to 1 July by law of 28 Aug "

[To take effect from 1 July 1843]

After vetoing 2 tariff bills, pres Tyler signs the 3d, 30 Aug "

[The prevailing rate of this tariff was 20 per cent]

ond Session adjourns 31 Aug "

[It passed 95 acts, 13 joint resolutions, and 189 private bills, sitting 269 days — the longest session since the beginning of Congress]

New ratio of representation, based on the census of 1840, gives 1 representative for every 70 680 population "

William Ellery Channing, Unitarian minister, dies at Bennington, Vt, aged 62 2 Oct. "

Alexander Slidell Mackenzie, commanding the U S. brig *Somers*, while on a short cruise, hangs at the yard-arm Philip Spencer, a midshipman and son of John C Spencer, then sec of war, Samuel Cromwell, a boatswain's mate, and Elijah H Small, for an alleged conspiracy (SOMERS, U S BRIG-OF-WAR, Mutiny on) 1 Dec. "

ird Session assembles . 5 Dec "

Samuel Woodworth (author of the "Old Oaken Bucket") dies at New York city, aged 57 9 Dec "

Resolution offered by John M Botts of Va, for the impeachment of pres Tyler for gross usurpation of power, wicked and corrupt abuse of the power of appointments, high crimes and misdemeanors, etc 10 Jan 1843

[Rejected by a vote of 83 to 127]

Francis S Key, author of "STAR-SPANGLED BANNER," dies at Baltimore, Md, aged 64 11 Jan "

Com Isaac Hull dies at Philadelphia, Pa, aged 68 (NAVAL BATTLES of the U S) 13 Feb "

Dr Marcus Whitman, learning of the intention of the British government to permanently occupy the Oregon territory, and desirous of a personal interview with the U S government, to give warning and also to announce the practicability of overland emigration to that region, leaves Walla Walla Oct 1842, and reaches Washington, D C 3 Mch "

[This information aided the U S government in retaining this territory Dr Whitman was appointed a missionary commissioner to the Oregon Indians, and with his wife and the rev Henry Spaulding and his wife, made the first journey over the Rocky mountains in a wagon, 1835-36 Dr Whitman, his wife, and several others were massacred by the Cayuse Indians, 1847 OREGON, 1850]

Bankruptcy act of 1841 repealed 3 Mch "

Congress appropriates $30,000 to build Morse's electric telegraph from Washington to Baltimore 3 Mch "

venty seventh Congress adjourns " "

John Armstrong, sec of war 1812, dies at Red Hook, N Y, aged 85 . 1 Apr "

Col John C. Frémont starts on his second exploring expedition with 39 men . May, "

[Reached Salt lake, 6 Sept., and the Pacific coast, at the mouth of the Columbia river, Nov. 10, returned July, 1844]

Bunker Hill monument completed and dedicated, 17 June, "

[Pres Tyler was present, and Daniel Webster delivered the address.]

National Liberty party, in convention at Buffalo, N Y, nominates James G Birney for president, and Thomas Morris of O for vice-president 30 Aug 1843

Twenty-eighth Congress. *First Session*, convenes 4 Dec "

John W Jones of Va elected speaker

Explosion of a large gun, "the Peace-maker," on the U.S. war-steamer *Princeton*, on the Potomac, carrying, with many excursionists, the president and several of his cabinet, kills Mr Upshur, sec of state, Mr Gilmer sec of navy, David Gardiner, and others, besides wounding 12 of the crew 28 Feb 1844

Treaty of annexation with Texas signed 12 Apr "

[Rejected by the Senate, 35 to 16]

National Whig convention at Baltimore 1 May, "

[Henry Clay of Ky nominated for president, and Theodore Frelinghuysen of N J for vice-president]

Riots in PHILADELPHIA between native Americans and the Irish 6-8 May, "

National Democratic convention at Baltimore, Md, 27 May, "

[Martin Van Buren of N Y received on the 1st ballot 146 out of 266 votes, but failed to get the required two-thirds vote, his name was withdrawn on the 8th ballot, and James K Polk of Tenn was nominated on the 9th, Silas Wright of N Y was nominated for vice-president, but declined, and George M Dallas of Pa was nominated]

First telegraphic communication in the U S during this convention, on the experimental line erected by the government between BALTIMORE and Washington (ELECTRICITY) 27 May, "

First Session adjourns . 17 June, "

"Joe" Smith, the Mormon prophet, with his brother Hiram, murdered by a mob at the jail in Carthage, Ill 27 June, "

Treaty with China, of peace, amity, and commerce, 3 July, "

Henry Clay's ALABAMA LETTER, published in the *North Alabamian*, alienates the northern Whigs 16 Aug "

Fifteenth presidential election 12 Nov "

[Candidates Democrats, for president, James Knox Polk of Tenn, for vice-president, George Mifflin Dallas of Pa Whigs, for president, Henry Clay of Ky, for vice-president, Theodore Frelinghuysen of N.J Liberty party, for president, James G. Birney of N Y., for vice-president, Thomas Morris of O]

Second Session assembles 2 Dec. "

On motion of John Quincy Adams the "gag rule," prohibiting the presentation of Abolition petitions, is rescinded, 108 to 88. 3 Dec. "

Samuel Hoar, sent by Massachusetts to South Carolina in aid of the Massachusetts colored citizens imprisoned at Charleston, S. C., is expelled from Charleston by citizens (MASSACHUSETTS) . . 5 Dec "

Congress appoints the Tuesday following the first Monday in Nov for the national election day 23 Jan 1845

Electoral votes counted 12 Feb "

[For president, Polk, 170, Clay, 105, for vice-president, Dallas, 170, Frelinghuysen, 105 Liberty party, popular vote, 62,300]

Pres. Tyler vetoes a bill forbidding the building of any steam-vessel for the revenue service unless by special appropriation . . . 20 Feb "

[This bill passed both branches of Congress over the veto, the first veto overruled by Congress.]

Texas annexed by a joint resolution. 28 Feb. "

Which the president approves .. 1 Mch "

Florida admitted as the 27th state. 3 Mch "

Congress reduces postage on letters to 5 cents within 300 miles and 10 cents for greater distances 3 Mch. "

Twenty-eighth Congress adjourns " "

Fifteenth Administration — Democratic. 4 Mch. 1845 to 3 Mch. 1849

James Knox Polk, Tenn., president

George Mifflin Dallas, Pa., vice-president.

CABINET

James Buchanan, Pa, sec of state, from 5 Mch 1845.
Robert J Walker, Miss, sec of treas, from 5 Mch. 1845
William L. Marcy, N Y, sec. of war, from 5 Mch. 1845.
George Bancroft, Mass, sec of navy from 10 Mch 1845.
John Y Mason, Va, sec of navy, from 9 Sept 1846
Cave Johnson, Tenn, postmaster-gen, from 5 Mch 1845.
John Y Mason, Va. attorney gen, from 5 Mch 1845
Nathan Clifford, Me, attorney-gen., from 17 Oct 1846
Isaac Toucey, Conn, attorney-gen, from 21 June, 1848

Mexican minister demands his passport 6 Mch 1845
Steamboat *Swallow*, from New York for Albany, wrecked on a rock near Athens, the stern sinking, many passengers are drowned 7 Apr "
Andrew Jackson, 7th president, dies at the Hermitage, near Nashville, Tenn, aged 78 8 June, "
By an act of amnesty the Rhode Island legislature releases Thomas W Dorr, who was under a life sentence for treason 27 June, "
Naval school established at Annapolis Md, while George Bancroft is sec of navy "
Annexation ratified by Texas in convention 4 July, "
Texas in convention adopts a constitution 27 Aug "
Gov Silas Wright of N Y proclaims Delaware county in a state of insurrection from anti-rent difficulties, 27 Aug "
Joseph Story, associate-judge of the U S Supreme court, dies at Cambridge, Mass, aged 66 10 Sept "
Texas state constitution ratified by the people 13 Oct "

Twenty-ninth Congress, *First Session*, assembles 1 Dec "
John W Davis of Ind elected speaker
Texas admitted as the 28th state 29 Dec "
American army of occupation, gen Zachary Taylor, 3500 strong, reaches the Rio Grande, and takes post opposite Matamoras 28 Mch 1846
Hostilities begun between Mexico and the U S, a small force of U S. troops captured by the Mexicans (MEXICAN WAR) . 25 Apr. "
Battle of PALO ALTO 8 May, "
Battle of RESACA DE LA PALMA 9 May, "
Pres. Polk, by special message to Congress, announces that war exists by the act of Mexico 11 May, "
Congress authorizes the president to raise 50,000 men and $10,000,000 for the war . 13 May, "
Treaty with Great Britain signed, establishing the boundaries west of the Rocky mountains on the 49th parallel of N lat, and thus settling the "Oregon difficulty" . 15 June, "
[The U S claimed the whole territory to 54° 40′ N lat by the right of discovery and entrance of the Columbia river by capt Grey in 1792, which river and its tributaries water all that region]
Com John D. Sloat, of the Pacific squadron, occupies Monterey, Cal, and proclaims the country annexed to the U. S 6 July, "
Congress re cedes to Virginia the southern part of the DISTRICT OF COLUMBIA 9 July, "
Collection district of Chicago established, Chicago made a port of entry 16 July, "
Tariff of 1842 repealed, and a revenue tariff passed (in the Senate by the casting vote of vice-pres George M Dallas) approved 30 July, "
"Warehouse system" established by Congress 6 Aug "
Independent Treasury system re-enacted " "
Wisconsin authorized to form a constitution and state government. . . . 6 Aug "
Bill with the "WILMOT PROVISO" attached passes the House by 85 to 79 (no vote in the Senate) 8 Aug "
Act establishing the SMITHSONIAN INSTITUTION approved 10 Aug "
First Session adjourns . . " "
Brig-gen Kearny takes peaceable possession of Santa Fé . .. 18 Aug "
Gen Zachary Taylor captures Monterey, Mexico, after a three days' battle or siege . . .. 24 Sept "
Second Session assembles . ...7 Dec "
Iowa admitted as the 29th state . ... . 28 Dec "

Battle of San Gabriel, CALIFORNIA, fought 8 Jan 1847
Congress authorizes 10 additional regiments for the regular army 11 Feb "
Battle of BUENA VISTA 22-23 Feb. "
Battle of Sacramento . . .28 Feb "
Congress resolves to light with gas the Capitol and Capitol grounds 3 Mch "
Twenty-ninth Congress adjourns " "
Gen Scott lands at Vera Cruz, Mexico, with 13,000 men 9 Mch "
Vera Cruz surrenders after a bombardment of 9 days, 29 Mch. "
Army moves from Vera Cruz towards the city of Mexico under gen Twiggs 8 Apr. "
Battle of CERRO GORDO fought 18 Apr. "
Army enters Puebla 15 May, "
Pres Polk visits the eastern states as far as Augusta, Me, and returns to Washington 7 July, "
Battles of CONTRERAS and Churubusco 20 Aug "
Armistice granted the Mexicans by gen Scott, from 21 Aug to 7 Sept. "
Salt Lake City founded by the Mormons "
Battle of EL MOLINO DEL REY ("The King's Mill"), 8 Sept. "
Fortress of CHAPULTEPEC carried by storm, and the city of Mexico occupied by the U S troops 13 Sept "
Gen Zachary Taylor returns to the U S Nov. "
Springfield Republican appears at Springfield, Mass., Samuel Bowles publisher "

Thirtieth Congress, *First Session*, assembles 6 Dec. "
Speaker of the House, Robert C Winthrop, Mass
By resolution Congress authorizes the erection on public grounds in Washington of a monument to George Washington 31 Jan 1848
Treaty of peace, friendship, limits, claims, etc., between the U S and Mexico signed at Guadalupe Hidalgo, 2 Feb. "
[Ratified 19 May, and proclaimed by pres Polk, 4 July. The U S. stipulated to pay $15,000,000 for New Mexico and California, and assume debts due citizens of the U. S. from Mexico of $3,500,000]
John Quincy Adams, 6th president, dies at Washington, aged 81 23 Feb. "
[He was in his seat in the House when stricken with apoplexy, 21 Feb]
John Jacob Astor dies in New York, aged 85, 29 Mch. "
Congress authorizes a loan of $16,000,000 31 Mch. "
By resolution Congress tenders the congratulations of the people of the U. S to the French people on becoming a republic. 13 Apr. "
Democratic National convention at Baltimore nominates upon the 4th ballot, under the two-third rule Lewis Cass of Mich. for president, and William O. Butler of Ky. for vice-president . 22-26 May, "
Wisconsin admitted as the 30th state by act approved, 29 May, "
Congress appropriates $25,000 to buy the unpublished papers of James Madison . 31 May, "
Whig National convention at Independence hall, Philadelphia, on the 4th ballot nominates maj-gen. Zachary Taylor of La. for president, Millard Fillmore of N. Y. for vice-president. 7-8 June, "
Corner-stone of the Washington monument laid at Washington, D. C. . 4 July, "
[Robert C. Winthrop of Mass, speaker of the House, delivered the address. WASHINGTON MONUMENT]
Free-soil National convention at Buffalo, N Y, nominates Martin Van Buren of N. Y. for president, and Charles Francis Adams of Mass. for vice-president, 9-10 Aug. "
So much of the Cumberland road as lies in Indiana is surrendered to that state by act approved, 11 Aug "
Territorial government established in Oregon by act approved .... 14 Aug. "
First Session adjourns. . . ... . " "

Sixteenth presidential election . . . . 7 Nov. 1848
[Candidates: Democrats, Lewis Cass, Mich., for president; William O. Butler, Ky., for vice-president. Whigs, Zachary Taylor, La., for president; Millard Fillmore, N. Y., for vice-president. Free-soilers, Martin Van Buren, N. Y., for president; Charles Francis Adams, Mass., for vice-president.]
Second Session assembles . . . . 4 Dec. "
First gold from California (1804.59 ounces troy, average value per ounce, $18.05½) deposited at the U. S. mint by David Carter . . . . 8 Dec. "
Postal treaty with Great Britain . . . . 15 Dec. "
Electoral votes counted . . . . 14 Feb. 1849
[For president, Taylor, 163; Cass, 127. For vice-president, Fillmore, 163; Butler, 127. Free-soilers, popular vote, 291,263.]
Act granting swamp-lands to the state of Louisiana, approved (see Mch. 1857) . . . . 2 Mch. "
Territorial government of Minnesota established by act approved . . . . 3 Mch. "
Coinage of the gold dollar and double-eagle authorized, 3 Mch. "
Department of Interior created by act approved . " "
Work of census office, previously under secretary of state, transferred to the Interior by act of . . 3 Mch. "
Thirtieth Congress adjourns . . . . " "

Sixteenth Administration—Whig. 5 Mch. 1849, to 3 Mch. 1853.

Zachary Taylor, La., president.
Millard Fillmore, N. Y., vice-president.

CABINET.

John M. Clayton, Del., sec. of state, from 7 Mch. 1849.
William M. Meredith, Pa., sec. of treas., from 7 Mch. 1849.
George W. Crawford, Ga., sec. of war, from 7 Mch. 1849.
William B. Preston, Va., sec. of navy, from 7 Mch. 1849.
Thomas Ewing, O., sec. of interior, from 7 Mch. 1849.
Jacob Collamer, Vt., postmaster-gen., from 7 Mch. 1849.
Reverdy Johnson, Md., attorney-gen., from 7 Mch. 1849.

Gen. William J. Worth, U. S. A., dies at San Antonio, Tex., aged 55 . . . . 7 May, 1849
Gen. Edmund P. Gaines dies at New Orleans, aged 72, 6 June, "
James K. Polk, 11th president, dies at Nashville, Tenn., aged 54 . . . . 15 June. "
Pres. Taylor issues a proclamation against filibustering expeditions to Cuba under Lopez (FILIBUSTERS), 11 Aug. "
Albert Gallatin, distinguished statesman, dies at Astoria, L. I. . . . . 12 Aug. "
Thirty-first Congress, First Session, assembles . . 3 Dec. "
Senate strongly Democratic, and in the House the Free-soilers hold the balance of power between the Democrats and Whigs. After 63 ballots for speaker, 22 Dec., Howell Cobb of Ga. chosen by a plurality of 102 to 99 for Robert C. Winthrop of Mass. Organization of the House not completed until 11 Jan. 1850
[This Senate was illustrious for talent, including Webster, Clay, Calhoun, Benton, King of Ala., Davis and Foote of Miss., Hamlin of Me., Cass of Mich., Seward and Dickinson of N. Y., Chase and Corwin of O., Douglas of Ill., Frémont of Cal., Soulé of La., Hale of N. H., Mangum of N. C., Hunter and Mason of Va., and Bell of Tenn., besides others of note.]
Henry Clay introduces 6 resolutions as a basis for compromise of the slavery controversy . . . . 29 Jan. "
[These resolutions related to (1) admission of California as a free state; (2) territorial governments for Utah and New Mexico without conditions as to slavery; (3) boundaries of Texas; (4) payment of Texas debt; (5) suppression of the slave-trade in the District of Columbia; (6) fugitive-slave laws.]
Clay advocates his resolutions in the Senate . . 5–6 Feb. "
Resolution of Congress for purchasing the manuscript of Washington's "Farewell Address" . . . . . . 12 Feb. "

Abolitionists attacked by Daniel Webster in debating the Compromise bill . . . . 7 Mch. 1850
[This speech much weakened Webster's influence at the north.]
John C. Calhoun, statesman and member of the Senate, dies at Washington, aged 68 . . . . 31 Mch. "
Bulwer-Clayton treaty with Great Britain, for a joint occupancy of the proposed ship-canal through Central America, signed . . . . 19 Apr. "
After a debate of over 2 months, Clay's Compromise resolutions are referred to a committee of 13, with Clay as chairman . . . . 19 Apr. "
[Committee consisted of 6 Democrats and 7 Whigs.]
Collins line of steamers between Great Britain and the U. S. goes into operation . . . . 27 Apr. "
Committee on the Compromise resolutions submits an elaborate series of bills embodying the substance of the resolutions of Jan. 29 . . . . 8 May, "
[These several bills are known as the Compromise or "Omnibus" bill, the last passed 20 Sept.]
Narcisso Lopez, a South American adventurer, makes a filibustering expedition to Cuba from New Orleans in the steamer *Creole*, and lands at Cardenas 19 May, with about 600 men; is repulsed and retires to the steamer with a loss of 30 killed and wounded; is pursued by the Spanish war-steamer *Pizarro* to Key West, where he escapes (FILIBUSTERS), 21 May, "
Advance, 140 tons, and *Rescue*, 90 tons, equipped by Henry Grinnell of New York to search for sir John Franklin, sail from New York city, under lieut. E. J. De Haven, with dr. Elisha Kent Kane as surgeon . . . . 23 May, "
Pres. Taylor dies at Washington, aged 66 . . . . . 9 July, "
Vice-pres. Fillmore takes the oath of office as president . . . . 10 July, "
Wm. R. King of Ala. president *pro tem.* of the Senate, 11 July, "

PRES. FILLMORE'S CABINET.

Daniel Webster, Mass., sec. of state, from 20 July, 1850.
Edward Everett, Mass., sec. of state, from 9 Dec. 1852.
Thomas Corwin, O., sec. of treas., from 20 July, 1850.
Charles M. Conrad, Va., sec. of war, from 20 July, 1850.
Wm. A. Graham, N. C., sec. of navy, from 20 July, 1850.
John P. Kennedy, Md., sec. of navy, from 22 July, 1852.
James A. Pearce, Md., sec. of interior, from 20 July, 1850.
Alex. H. H. Stuart, Va., sec. of interior, from 12 Sept. 1850.
N. K. Hall, N. Y., postmaster-gen., from 20 July, 1850.
Samuel D. Hubbard, Conn., postmaster-gen., from 31 Aug. 1852.
John J. Crittenden, Ky., attorney-gen., from 20 July, 1850.

Treaty between the U. S. and the Hawaiian or Sandwich islands, signed 20 Dec. 1849; ratified, 24 Aug. 1850
Territory of Utah created, and territorial government established (UTAH) . . . . 9 Sept. "
Territorial government established in New Mexico, 9 Sept. "
[The act provided that the territory or any portion of it should be received into the Union with or without slavery, as its constitution might prescribe at the time of its admission.]
California admitted as the 31st state, her constitution excluding slavery . . . . 9 Sept. "
Northern and western boundaries of Texas established. Texas cedes all claim to territory beyond this boundary, and relinquishes all claim for debt, compensation, or indemnity for the surrender of all U. S. property; $10,000,000 to be paid by the U. S. government in stocks bearing 5% interest, and redeemable at the end of 14 years . . . . 9 Sept. "
Jenny Lind gives her first concert at Castle Garden, New York . . . . 12 Sept. "
Amendments of great stringency to the Fugitive Slave laws of Feb. 12, 1793, pass the House by 109 to 75, 12 Sept. 1850; approved . . . . 18 Sept. "
Slave-trade suppressed from 1 Jan. 1851, in the District of Columbia, by act approved . . . . 20 Sept. "
Flogging abolished in the navy and on vessels of commerce by act approved . . . . 28 Sept. "

Act granting swamp-lands to Arkansas and other states, approved (see 3 Mch. 1857)............28 Sept. 1850

First Session (302 days) adjourns............30 Sept. "

[This session the longest up to this time.]

City council of Chicago passes a resolution nullifying the Fugitive Slave law, and releasing the police from obedience to it........................22 Oct. "

[They subsequently reconsidered it.]

Second Session assembles....................2 Dec. "

British consul at Charleston, S. C., in a communication to the governor, calls attention to the state law under which a class (negroes) of her majesty's subjects, entering the ports of South Carolina on the guarantee of a national treaty, in trading vessels or in distress, are taken from the protection of the British flag and imprisoned, and hopes that the state will abrogate such portion of the law as applies to British subjects (see this record, 5 Dec. 1844, and MASSACHUSETTS, 1844)............................14 Dec. "

John James Audubon, distinguished ornithologist, dies near New York city, aged 71............27 Jan. 1851

Pres. Fillmore issues a proclamation relative to the rescue of Shadrach, a negro, at Boston, Mass., who had been arrested as a fugitive slave, 15 Feb. 1851, calling on all officers and citizens to aid in recapturing him, and commanding the arrest of all persons aiding in his escape (MASSACHUSETTS)....18 Feb. "

Letter postage reduced to 3 cents for 3000 miles or less, if prepaid, and 5 cents if not; over 3000 miles double rate. Coinage of 3-cent piece authorized...3 Mch. "

Congress authorizes the president to employ a public vessel, then cruising in the Mediterranean, to convey to the U. S. Louis Kossuth and his associates in captivity, if they wish to emigrate to the U. S., and if the sultan of Turkey will consent..........3 Mch. "

Thirty-first Congress adjourns................ " "

[At this time it was decided that Congress expires at noon on the 4th day of March.]

Com. James Barron dies at Norfolk, Va., aged 83, 21 Apr. "

Pres. Fillmore issues a proclamation against the promoters of a second expedition against Cuba, and the ship *Cleopatra*, with military supplies for that island, is seized..........................25 Apr. "

First train on the Erie railway, New York to Dunkirk, 28, 29 Apr. "

Extension of the U. S. Capitol; corner-stone laid by the president; oration by Daniel Webster......4 July, "

[Extensions finished Nov. 1867.]

Gen. Lopez's second expedition against Cuba (FILIBUSTERS)...........................3 Aug. "

Louis Kossuth and suite received on the U. S. war steamer *Mississippi* at the Dardanelles....10 Sept. "

James Fenimore Cooper, author, dies at Cooperstown, N. Y., aged 62........................14 Sept. "

Hudson River railroad opened from New York to Albany.............................8 Oct. "

Kossuth leaves the *Mississippi* at Gibraltar and embarks on the *Madrid*, an English passenger steamer, for Southampton, Engl....................15 Oct. "

Pres. Fillmore issues a proclamation forbidding military expeditions into Mexico............22 Oct. "

Grinnell expedition, sent out in search of sir John Franklin, May, 1850, returns to New York.....Oct. "

Thirty-second Congress, *First Session*, assembles, 1 Dec. "

Speaker of the House, Linn Boyd of Ky.

Kossuth arrives at New York from England....5 Dec. "

[He was received with enthusiasm.]

Resolution of welcome to Louis Kossuth by Congress approved..........................15 Dec. "

Henry Clay resigns his seat in the Senate (to take effect Sept. 1852).....................17 Dec. "

A fire in the library of Congress destroys 35,000 of its 55,000 volumes.......................24 Dec. "

Kossuth arrives at Washington, D. C., on the invitation of Congress.....................30 Dec. "

A memorial presented to the Senate from citizens of the U. S. (about 160 in number), captured by the Spanish government in Cuba while engaged in the expedition of Lopez, sent to Spain as prisoners, and there liberated by queen Isabella II., asking Congress for transportation to the U. S..............7 Jan. 1852

Congress appropriates $6000 to return them to the U. S., 10 Feb. "

Congress appropriates $72,500 for the repair of the Congressional library.....................19 Mch. "

Democratic National convention held at Baltimore, the two-third rule governing................1 June, "

[Four principal candidates for the presidency at this convention were gen. Lewis Cass, Mich., James Buchanan, Pa., ex-gov. William L. Marcy, N. Y., and Stephen A. Douglas, Ill. On the 35th ballot the name of Franklin Pierce of N. H. was first presented and received 15 votes, and on the 49th ballot he was nominated, receiving 282 votes. William R. King of Ala. nominated for vice-president.]

Whig National presidential convention meets at Baltimore.............................16 June, "

[Candidates for the presidency were Millard Fillmore, N. Y., gen. Winfield Scott, Va., and Daniel Webster, Mass. On the first ballot Fillmore had 133 votes, Scott 131, and Webster 29; these proportions were maintained very steadily until the 53d ballot, when gen. Scott received 159 votes to 112 for Fillmore and 21 for Webster. William A. Graham, N. C., was on the 2d ballot nominated for vice-president.]

Henry Clay dies at Washington, D. C., aged 75.29 June, "

Branch of the U. S. mint established at San Francisco, Cal.............................3 July, "

Free-soil convention at Pittsburg, Pa........11 Aug. "

[Named John P. Hale, N. H., for president, and George W. Julian, Ind., for vice-president.]

First Session adjourns (after a session of 275 days), 31 Aug. "

Daniel Webster dies at Marshfield, Mass., aged 70.24 Oct. "

Seventeenth presidential election takes place...2 Nov. "

[Candidates: Democrats, Franklin Pierce, N. H., for president; William R. King, Ala., for vice-president. Whigs, gen. Winfield Scott, Va., for president; William A. Graham, N. C., for vice-president. Free-soilers, John P. Hale, N. H., for president; George W. Julian, Ind., for vice-president.]

Second Session assembles.....................6 Dec. "

William R. King, Ala., president *pro tem.* of the Senate, resigns, and David R. Atchison, Mo., chosen..20 Dec. "

Caloric ship *Ericsson* makes a trial trip from New York to the Potomac.....................11 Jan. 185

Congress transfers all that portion of the Cumberland road which lies between Springfield, O., and the western boundary of that state to Ohio, by act approved.............................20 Jan. "

Electoral vote counted.....................9 Feb. "

[For president, Pierce, 254; Scott, 42; for vice-president, King, 254; Graham, 42. Free-soilers, pop. vote, 156,149.]

Coinage of $3 gold-pieces authorized, and the weight of the half-dollar fixed at 192 gr., and the quarter-dollar, the dime, and half-dime at proportionate amounts, by act approved (COIN)........21 Feb. "

Territory of Washington formed by act approved, 2 Mch. "

Further purchase of ailanthus-trees for the public grounds forbidden by Congress (FLOWERS AND PLANTS)...........................3 Mch. "

Congress authorizes a survey for a railway from the Mississippi to the Pacific................3 Mch. "

Thirty-second Congress adjourns.............. " "

Seventeenth Administration — Democratic. 4 Mc[h.] 1853 to 3 Mch. 1857.

Franklin Pierce, N. H., president.
William R. King, Ala., vice-president.

Oath of office is administered to the vice-president elect by U. S. consul Sharkey, at Cumbre, near Matanzas, on the island of Cuba.......... 24 Mch. 18[53]

[A special act of Congress authorized Mr. Sharkey to do this.]

CABINET

illiam L. Marcy, N Y, sec of state, from 5 Mch 1853
mes Guthrie, Ky sec of treas, from 5 Mch 1853
fferson Davis Miss sec of war, from 5 Mch 1853
mes C Dobbin, N C, sec of navy, from 5 Mch 1853
bert McClelland, Mich, sec of interior, from 5 Mch 1853
mes Campbell, Pa, postmaster-gen, from 5 Mch 1853
leb Cushing, Mass, attorney-gen, from 5 Mch 1853

Wm R King, 13th vice-president of the U S, dies at Cahawba, Ala aged 67 — 18 Apr 1853

Kane sails from New York in the brig *Advance*, under the auspices of the U S navy, in search of sir John Franklin — 30 May, "

[Reached 78° 43' N in 1855 See this record, 1855]

KOSZTA AFFAIR, at Smyrna, Turkey — 21 June, "

Com M C Perry, a brother of Oliver Hazard Perry, with a fleet of 7 vessels, proceeds to Japan with a letter from pres Fillmore to the tycoon, soliciting a treaty Com Perry arrives at the bay of Yedo (JAPAN, and this record, 1854) — 14 July, "

World's Fair, Crystal palace, opening at New York city, pres Pierce present — 14 July, "

William Walker's filibustering expedition to Sonora, Mexico (FILIBUSTERS) — July, "

irty-third Congress. First Session, assembles — 5 Dec "

David R Atchison president *pro tem* of the Senate, and acting vice-president of the U S in place of Wm R King deceased, Linn Boyd of Ky speaker of the House

James Gadsden of S C, minister to Mexico, by treaty purchases her territory south of the Gila river, now known as the "Gadsden purchase," and included in Arizona, containing 45,535 sq miles, for $10,000,000 Treaty and purchase approved — 30 Dec "

Stephen A Douglas of Ill introduces a bill in the Senate, organizing the territory of Nebraska — 4 Jan 1854

A Dixon of Ky gives notice of an amendment exempting the territory from the Missouri compromise prohibiting slavery — 16 Jan "

Proclamation of pres Pierce against the invasion of Mexico (called out by Walker's expedition into Sonora and Lower California FILIBUSTERS), 18 Jan "

Sen Douglas of Ill reports a bill creating 2 territories, Kansas and Nebraska, of the same territory as the former Nebraska bill, with a section virtually repealing the Compromise of 1820 — 23 Jan "

U S steamer BLACK WARRIOR seized by the Cuban authorities at Havana — 28 Feb "

Kansas-Nebraska bill passes the Senate, 37 to 14 — 3 Mch "

First treaty between the U S and Japan, of peace, amity, and commerce, concluded and signed at Kanawaga, Japan — 31 Mch "

[Two ports of entry opened to the U S., Hakodadi and Simoda]

Massachusetts Emigrant Aid Society organized by Eli Thayer, and incorporated (to aid emigration to Kansas) — 20 Apr "

Kansas-Nebraska bill taken up in the House — 8 May, "

Bill passes the House as an original measure, by 112 to 99 — 24 May, "

It passes the Senate, 35 to 13, and approved — 30 May, "

[The Missouri Compromise measures of 1820 repealed by sec 14 of this act]

Pres Pierce issues a proclamation against the invasion of Cuba — 31 May, "

Anthony Burns, arrested as a slave at Boston, Mass., is taken by the revenue cutter *Morris*, by order of pres Pierce, conveyed to Norfolk, Va, and delivered to his alleged master, a Mr Suttle (MASSACHUSETTS), — 2 June, "

Treaty with Great Britain, reciprocity, the fishery difficulty settled — 5 June, "

George N Hollins, commander of the ship *Cyane*, bombards and destroys the small town of Greytown on the Mosquito coast, Central America — 13 June, "

[This was an attempt to obtain redress for a personal insult to one of the officers of the government, and to enforce a claim of $24,000 indemnity]

Merrimac, a new steam war-frigate, launched at the Charleston navy-yard — 14 June, 1854

[This was one of the vessels seized by the confederates at the Norfolk navy-yard, Apr 1861]

Medal presented to capt Ingraham, U S N, by a resolution of Congress, as a testimonial of the high sense entertained of his gallant and judicious conduct on 2 July, 1853, in rescuing Martin Koszta from illegal seizure and imprisonment on board the Austrian brig *Huzzar*, approved (KOSZTA AFFAIR) — 4 Aug "

[Ingraham resigned in 1861 and joined the Confederate navy, d in Charleston, S C, 16 Oct 1891, aged 89]

First Session adjourns — 7 Aug "

OSTEND MANIFESTO issued — 18 Oct "

Andrew H Reeder of Pa appointed governor of Kansas by pres Pierce (KANSAS) "

Second Session assembles — 4 Dec "

Jesse D Bright of Ind elected president *pro tem* of the Senate — 5 Dec "

Congress assents to the cession by Massachusetts to New York of "Boston Corner," the southwesterly corner of Berkshire county, approved — 3 Jan 1855

Annexation of the Sandwich islands discussed in Congress (strongly opposed by England) — Jan "

Panama railroad completed, first train from ocean to ocean — 28 Jan "

Rights of citizenship secured to children of citizens born in foreign territory by an act approved — 10 Feb "

Grade of lieutenant-general by brevet revived by a resolution approved — 15 Feb. "

[This rank was immediately conferred upon maj-gen Winfield Scott]

Right of way granted to Hiram O Alden and James Eddy for a line of telegraph from the Mississippi river to the Pacific by an act approved — 17 Feb "

Thirty-third Congress adjourns — 3 Mch "

Gov Reeder of Kan removed by pres Pierce, Wilson Shannon of O appointed in his place — 28 July, "

William Walker lands in Nicaragua with 160 men, — 3 Sept "

Col Henry L. Kinney made civil and military governor of Greytown, Nicaragua, by citizens, — 12 Sept "

Expedition in search of dr Kane, under lieut Hartstene, U S N, finds at the isle of Disco, Greenland, Kane and his companions, who had left the ship in the ice, 17 May, and reached Disco 8 Aug, — 13 Sept "

This expedition returns to New York city — 11 Oct "

Thirty-fourth Congress, First Session, assembles — 3 Dec "

After a contest of 9 weeks, on the 133d ballot, Nathaniel P Banks of Mass is elected (2 Feb 1856) speaker by a plurality of 3 votes over William Aiken of S C.

["It was a distinctive victory of the free states over the consolidated power of the slave states It marked an epoch"—*Blaine's* "Twenty Years of Congress," vol i. p 122 This session was the stormiest ever held]

Proclamation of pres. Pierce against the invasion of Nicaragua — 8 Dec "

Pres Pierce, in special message, recognizes the pro-slavery legislature of the territory of Kansas, and calls the attempt to establish a free-state government an act of rebellion (KANSAS) — 21 Jan 1856

Pres. Pierce by proclamation warns all persons against unlawful combinations against the constituted authorities of Kansas — 11 Feb "

American National convention at Philadelphia, Pa, on the 1st formal ballot nominates Millard Fillmore of N Y for president, and Andrew J Donelson of Tenn for vice-president — 22 Feb "

Capture and sack of Lawrence, Kan, by the pro-slavery party (KANSAS) — 21 May, "

Charles Sumner of Mass beaten down in the Senate

chamber by Preston S. Brooks, of S. C., because of his speech, "The Crime against Kansas" . . 22 May, 1856

[Brooks accompanied by L. M. Keitt of S. C.]

House committee recommends the expulsion of Brooks and censure of Keitt, but the resolution fails, 121 to 95 (two-thirds required); Brooks and Keitt resign, 2 June, "

Democratic National convention meets at Cincinnati, O. . . . . .3 June, "

[James Buchanan of Pa. nominated for president on the 17th ballot, and John C. Breckinridge of Ky. for vice-president. Franklin Pierce and Stephen A. Douglas were also candidates for the presidency, but were withdrawn on the 15th and 16th ballots.]

First Republican National convention held at Philadelphia. . . . . .17 June, "

[On the 1st formal ballot John Charles Frémont of Cal. was nominated for president, 329 votes to 37 for McLean of O., and 1 for W. H. Seward; Wm. L. Dayton of N. J. was nominated for vice-president.]

John W. Geary of Pa. appointed governor of Kansas in place of Shannon. . . . . .1 July, "

Committee appointed by the House, 19 Mch. 1856, consisting of John Sherman of O., Wm. A. Howard of Mich., and M. Oliver of Mo., to *inquire into the* Kansas troubles, reports: (1) that the election held by the free-state party was not illegal; (2) that the elections under the alleged territorial laws were carried by invaders from Missouri; (3) that the alleged territorial legislature was illegal; (4) that its acts were intended for unlawful ends; (5) that neither of the delegates to Congress was entitled to a seat; (6) that no election could be held without a new census, a stringent election law, impartial judges of election, and U. S. troops at every polling place; (7) that the constitution framed by the convention embodies the will of the majority of the people, 1 July, "

[Mr. Oliver of Mo. made a minority report.]

Grand-jury at Washington indicts Preston S. Brooks for assault and battery upon Charles Sumner, 22 June; on trial Brooks admits the facts, and is fined $300. . . . . .8 July, "

Preston S. Brooks challenges to a duel Anson Burlingame, member from Mass. Mr. Burlingame in reply agrees to meet him at the Clifton house, Niagara Falls, on 26 July at noon, when differences between them can be adjusted. Burlingame leaves Washington for the rendezvous; Brooks declines to pursue the matter further. . . . . .21 July, "

Preston S. Brooks and L. M. Keitt are returned to Congress from South Carolina. . . . . .28 July, "

First Session adjourns. . . . . .18 Aug. "

Army appropriation bill failing to pass, owing to a proviso that the army be not used to aid the pro-slavery legislature of Kansas, an extra session of Congress is called for 21 Aug. . . . . .19 Aug. "

Second Session (extra) convenes. . . . . .21 Aug. "

Governor of Kansas proclaims the territory in insurrection. . . . . .25 Aug. "

Army appropriation bill passes without the proviso, 30 Aug. "

Second Session (10 days) adjourns. . . . . " "

[The shortest session of any Congress.]

Whig National convention meets at Baltimore, 17 Sept. "

[It adopted the nominees of the American party for president, Fillmore and Donelson. Last appearance of the Whig party in politics.]

Eighteenth presidential election held. . . . . . . .4 Nov. "

Third Session convenes. . . . . .1 Dec. "

Dispersion of the Free-state legislature at Topeka, Kan., by federal troops. . . . . 6 Jan. 1857

Electoral votes counted. . . . . 11 Feb. "

[Democrats, James Buchanan, Pa., for president, 174; John C. Breckinridge, Ky., for vice-president, 174. Republicans, John C. Frémont, Cal., for president, 114; Wm. L. Dayton, N. J., for vice-president, 114. Americans, Millard Fillmore, N. Y., for president, 8; Andrew J. Donelson, Tenn., for vice-president, 8.]

Death of Elisha Kent Kane (arctic explorer), at Havana, Cuba, aged 35. . . . . .16 Feb. 1857

Act to confirm to the several states the swamp and overflowed lands selected under act of 2 Mch. 1849, which granted to the state of Louisiana all such lands found unfit for cultivation, and under act of 28 Sept. 1850, which made similar grants to Arkansas and other states; approved. . . . . .3 Mch. "

[Excepted California, Michigan, Minnesota, and Wisconsin, these lands have been selected by agents of the state, who furnish to the U. S. proofs of their unfitness for cultivation, etc. It was estimated in 1849-50 from government surveys that the total area of swamp-lands would not exceed 21,000,000 acres. But these acts and grants have led to complaints of fraud and deceit. Millions of acres have been listed as swamp-land which are now held for further investigation. The area claimed by the states under the various acts amounts to over 80,000,000 acres to 30 June, 1891, of which 58,000,000 acres have been patented to the states. Of the principal states claiming such lands under the several acts, Alabama, Arkansas, California, Florida, Illinois, Indiana, Iowa, Louisiana, Michigan, Minnesota, Mississippi, Misouri, Ohio, Oregon, and Wisconsin, Florida has received the most, 22,500,000 acres, and Ohio the least, 117,000 acres.—Report of the sec. of the interior, 1891.]

Act passed materially reducing duties. . . . . 3 Mch. "

Thirty-fourth Congress adjourns . . . . " "

Eighteenth Administration—Democratic, 4 Mch. 1857 to 3 Mch. 1861.

James Buchanan, Pa., president.

John C. Breckinridge, Ky., vice-president.

CABINET.

Lewis Cass, Mich., sec. of state, from 6 Mch. 1857.
Jeremiah S. Black, Pa., sec. of state, from 17 Dec. 1860.
Howell Cobb, Ga., sec. of treas., from 6 Mch. 1857.
Philip F. Thomas, Md., sec. of treas., from 12 Dec. 1860.
John A. Dix, N. Y., sec. of treas., from 11 Jan. 1861.
John B. Floyd, Va., sec. of war, from 6 Mch. 1857.
Joseph Holt, Ky., sec. of war, from 18 Jan. 1861.
Isaac Toucey, Conn., sec. of navy, from 6 Mch. 1857.
Jacob Thompson, Miss., sec. of interior, from 6 Mch. 1857.
[Resigned 8 Jan. 1861; no one appointed in his place.]
Aaron V. Brown, Tenn., postmaster-gen., from 6 Mch. 1857.
Joseph Holt, Ky., postmaster-gen., from 14 Mch. 1859.
Horatio King, Me., postmaster-gen., from 12 Feb. 1861.
Jeremiah S. Black, Pa., attorney-gen., from 6 Mch. 1857.
Edwin M. Stanton, O., attorney-gen., from 20 Dec. 1860.

Chief-justice Taney, of the Supreme court, delivers his decision in the Dred Scott case. . . . . .6 Mch. 1857

Robert J. Walker of Miss. appointed governor of Kansas in place of Geary of Pa., resigned. . . . .Apr. "

Second treaty with Japan; the third port, Nagasaki, opened to the U. S. . . . . .17 June, "

Shore end of the Atlantic submarine telegraph cable is fixed by the U. S. steam-frigate *Niagara* at Valencia bay, Ireland. . . . . .5 Aug. "

Cable breaks after paying out 335 miles. . . . .11 Aug. "

[It was abandoned until the next year.]

Brigham Young, governor of Utah, by proclamation forbids any armed force coming into Salt Lake City, and orders the troops in readiness to repel such invasion and declares martial law. . . . . .15 Sept. "

Mountain Meadow massacre (Utah, 1857-77), 18 Sept. "

Mormons attack the government trains and destroy 78 wagons. . . . . 5 Oct. "

Great financial distress; banks in New York city and Boston suspend. . . . . .13-14 Oct. "

Pres. Buchanan removes Brigham Young, and appoints Alfred Cumming of the U. S. army as governor of Utah. . . . . "

William Walker makes his third filibustering expedition to Nicaragua from New Orleans. . . . . .11 Nov. "

Lands on the Nicaraguan coast with 400 men, 25 Nov. 1857
Com Paulding of the U S navy arrests Walker at Greytown, Nicaragua, and he is taken to New York as prisoner 3 Dec "

irty-fifth Congress, First Session, assembles 7 Dec. "
James L Orr of S C elected speaker of the House
[House, 131 Democrats, 92 Republicans, and 14 Americans Senate, 39 Democrats, 20 Republicans, 5 Americans]
Stephen A Douglas of Ill in the Senate opposes forcing the Lecompton constitution on Kansas 9 Dec. "
[He thus parted from the southern Democracy]
Robert J Walker, governor of Kansas, resigns, 15 Dec. "
The House of Representatives met for the first time in the new hall of representatives in the south wing of the extension 16 Dec. "
[By an act approved 2 July, 1864, the old hall of representatives was set apart as a national statuary hall, and each state invited to furnish in marble or bronze statues of 2 of its most distinguished citizens]
James H Hammond of S. C. makes a "memorable speech ' in the Senate in reply to W. H. Seward, 4 Mch. 1858
[This speech expressed the confidence of the South in her ability to organize a government and defend it, and in its bold stand for the perpetuation of slavery In this speech originated the term "mud-sills of society ']
Pres. Buchanan issues a proclamation respecting the Mormon rebellion in Utah 6 Apr "
Thomas H Benton dies at Washington, aged 76, 10 Apr "
An act to admit Kansas under the Lecompton constitution 4 May, "
Minnesota admitted as the 32d state 11 May, "
Congress authorizes a loan of $20,000,000 14 June, "
rst Session adjourns " "
Second treaty with China of peace, amity, and commerce 18 June, "
Debates in the senatorial contest in Illinois between Abraham Lincoln and Stephen A Douglas during June and July, "
Remains of James Monroe, 5th president of the U S, buried at New York, 1831, taken up and conveyed to Virginia 2 July, "
Street deposit boxes (iron) for letters for the mails first used in Boston, Mass .. 2 Aug. "
Lecompton constitution for Kansas rejected by the people of Kansas, 11,088 to 1788 2 Aug. "
Atlantic submarine telegraph completed 5 Aug "
First message from queen Victoria to pres Buchanan, 16 Aug "
[After 23 days, 400 messages having been transmitted, the cable lost its conducting power]
Seizure of the *Echo*, a slaver, with 318 slaves, by the U S brig *Dolphin*, lieut John H. Maffit commanding (SOUTH CAROLINA) 21 Aug "
Fifteen hundred U S troops leave fort Laramie for the suppression of Mormon troubles in Utah Sept "
Crystal palace burned in New York 5 Oct "
First mail overland from San Francisco reaches St. Louis, 24 days 18 hours in transit 9 Oct "
Donati's comet, first appearing in June, attains its greatest brilliancy (COMETS) 9 Oct. "
Pres Buchanan issues a proclamation respecting an apprehended invasion of Nicaragua 30 Oct. "
Paul Morphy of New Orleans becomes the champion CHESS-player of the world "
Grand-jury of Columbia, S C., refuses to indict the crew of the slaver *Echo* 30 Nov. "
cond Session assembles 6 Dec "
Senate leaves the old to occupy the new Senate chamber in the north wing of the extension 4 Jan 1859
[Before leaving a memorial address was delivered by vice-president Breckinridge reviewing the history of the old chamber. Since Dec 1860, it has been occupied by the Supreme court of the U S]

A bill presented in the Senate giving the president $30,000,000 to purchase Cuba 24 Jan 1859
William H Prescott, author, dies at Boston, Mass, aged 63 28 Jan "
Oregon admitted as the 33d state 14 Feb "
Daniel E Sickles, congressman from New York, kills Philip Barton Key at Washington for adultery with his wife 27 Feb "
Thirty-fifth Congress adjourns 3 Mch "
Trial of Daniel E Sickles begun at Washington, D C., 4 Apr "
[It lasted 18 days and resulted in his acquittal]
A rich gold mine opened in COLORADO. on the north fork of Clear creek, by John H Gregory 10 May, "
Unexampled frost throughout the northern U S., night of 4 June, "
M Blondin for the first time crosses the Niagara river just below the falls on a tight-rope 30 June, "
San Juan islands occupied by gen Harney, U S army (though claimed by Great Britain as belonging to Vancouver island) 9 July, "
Little John, a negro, arrested at Oberlin, O, as a slave, and rescued at Wellington (OHIO) 13 Sept "
Senator David C Broderick of Cal, mortally wounded in a duel with judge Terry near lake Merced, Cal, 13 Sept, d 16 Sept "
U. S steamship *Niagara* sails from Charleston, S C, for Liberia, Africa, with the negroes taken from the slaver *Echo*, 271 are returned out of 318 20 Sept "
Jefferson Davis addresses the Democratic State convention of Mississippi in behalf of slavery and the extension of slave territory Oct. "
BROWN'S INSURRECTION at Harper's Ferry, W Va, 16-18 Oct. "
Gen Winfield Scott is ordered to the Pacific coast in view of the British claims to San Juan, he arrives at Portland, Or 29 Oct "
Washington Irving dies at Tarrytown, N Y, aged 76, 28 Nov "
John Brown (BROWN'S INSURRECTION) hanged at Charlestown, W Va . 2 Dec. "

Thirty-sixth Congress, First Session, assembles 5 Dec "
[Senate Democratic, House with no clear majority for any party John Sherman of O was the Republican candidate for speaker and Thomas S Bocock of Va. the Democratic After 8 weeks' balloting Mr Sherman withdrew, and William Pennington of N J was elected on the 44th ballot, 1 Feb 1860]
Green, Copeland, Cook, and Coppoc, Harper's Ferry insurgents, hanged (BROWN'S INSURRECTION), 16 Dec. "
Mr Clark of Mo introduces a resolution in the House that no one who had approved Helper's "The IMPENDING CRISIS" was fit to be speaker Dec "
House adopts resolutions offered by John Covode of Pa, for a committee to investigate the conduct of the president 5 Mch. 1860
A C Stephens and Albert Hazlett hanged at Charlestown, W Va 16 Mch. "
[These were the last of the prisoners captured at Harper's Ferry in the John Brown insurrection.]
National Democratic convention meets in Charleston, S. C 23 Apr "
After much discord the southern members secede, and the convention, after 57 ballotings without nominating, adjourns to meet at Baltimore 18 June, 3 May, "
"Constitutional Union" party holds a national convention in Baltimore 9 May, "
[John Bell of Tenn and Samuel Houston of Texas were the candidates for nomination, on the 2d ballot Bell received 138 votes and Houston 69 Edward Everett of Mass unanimously nominated for vice-president.]
Morrill Tariff bill passes the House 10 May, "
[It was protective, the duties being high and specific, it passed the Senate after the southern members withdrew, approved 2 Mch 1861.]

Japanese embassy, numbering 72, of all grades, arrive at Hampton Roads and reaches Washington, 14 May, 1860

National Republican convention meets at Chicago, 16 May, "

[All the free states were strongly represented, besides delegates from Delaware, Maryland, Virginia, Kentucky, Missouri, District of Columbia, and territories of Kansas and Nebraska. George Ashmun of Mass. was chosen president; convention decided that a majority nominate; platform protested against the indefinite extension of slavery in the territories, but proposed no interference with it in the states. Balloting began 18 May, with 465 delegates; necessary to a choice, 233. Candidates were Abraham Lincoln of Ill., William H. Seward of N. Y., Simon Cameron of Pa. (withdrew after the 1st ballot), Salmon P. Chase of O., and Edward Bates of Mo. Mr. Seward received on the 1st ballot 173½ votes; 2d, 184½; 3d, 180; Mr. Lincoln, 1st ballot, 102 votes; 2d, 181; 3d, 231½; changes then made gave Mr. Lincoln 354 votes. Hannibal Hamlin of Me. was nominated for vice-president on the 2d ballot.]

Southern seceders from the Charleston Democratic convention meet at Richmond, Va., and adjourn to await the decision of the Baltimore convention, 11 June, "

Seceders, with the rejected delegates, meet at Baltimore....18 June, "

[Twenty-one states were represented by 105 delegates. John C. Breckinridge of Ky. was nominated for president and Joseph Lane of Or. for vice-president, 23 June.]

National Democratic convention assembles at Baltimore pursuant to adjournment....18 June, "

After some days of debate over credentials of delegates, many delegates withdraw, and the chairman, Caleb Cushing of Mass., resigns. David Tod of O. is chosen chairman and balloting begins ....22 June, "

[On the 2d ballot Stephen A. Douglas of Ill. received 181½ votes. Benjamin Fitzpatrick of Ala. was nominated for vice-president, but declined, and the National committee nominated Herschel V. Johnson of Ga.]

A loan of $21,000,000 authorized by Congress.22 June, "

Homestead bill vetoed by the president...... " "

[Senate fails to pass it over the veto by 3 votes.]

First Session adjourns....25 June, "

Steamship Great Eastern sails from England, 17 June, reaching New York in 11 days, 2 hours, 28 June, "

Kansas elects a convention to draft a second constitution; it meets....5 July, "

[Under this, the Wyandotte constitution, prohibiting slavery, Kansas was afterwards admitted.]

Lady Elgin, a steamer on lake Michigan, sunk by collision with the schooner *Augusta*, morning of 8 Sept. "

[Out of 385 persons on board, 287 were lost. Wrecks.]

William Walker, Nicaraguan filibuster, captured and shot at Truxillo, Nicaragua (Filibusters). 12 Sept. "

Prince of Wales arrives at Detroit, Mich., from Canada, 21 Sept. "

After visiting Chicago, St. Louis, Cincinnati, Washington, Baltimore, Philadelphia, New York, and Boston, he embarks for England from Portland, Me., 20 Oct. "

Nineteenth presidential election held....6 Nov. "

[Candidates and popular votes: Republicans, Abraham Lincoln of Ill., for president, and Hannibal Hamlin of Me., for vice-president, 1,866,352 votes. Democrats: Stephen A. Douglas of Ill., for president, and Herschel V. Johnson of Ga., for vice-president, 1,375,157. Seceding Democrats: John C. Breckinridge of Ky., for president, and Joseph Lane of Or., for vice-president, 847,514. Constitutional Union: John Bell of Tenn., for president, and Edward Everett of Mass., for vice-president, 587,830.]

Second Session assembles....3 Dec. "

President's message contends that the south has no legal right to secede, and the government no power to prevent secession....4 Dec. 1860

A special committee of 33, one from each state, appointed by the House upon the condition of the country....4 Dec. "

[This committee submitted 5 propositions, 14 Jan. 1861; but one, that proposing a constitutional amendment, ever reached the Senate.]

Howell Cobb of Ga., sec. of treasury, resigns ..10 Dec. "

Lewis Cass of Mich., sec. of state, resigns because the president refused to reinforce maj. Anderson at fort Moultrie, S. C....14 Dec. "

A loan of $10,000,000 authorized by Congress, 17 Dec. "

Senate appoints a committee of 13 upon the condition of the country, and to report a plan on adjusting the difficulty....18 Dec. "

[On 31 Dec. the chairman reported that the committee were unable to agree.]

John J. Crittenden of Ky. speaks for union in the Senate, and offers resolutions for amending the Constitution, 18 Dec. "

[These resolutions, known as the Crittenden Compromise measure of 1860-61, proposed to restore the compromise of 1820 and strengthen the Fugitive-Slave law of 1850. They were rejected after a continued debate by 19 to 20, 2 Mch. 1861.]

State of South Carolina unanimously passes the ordinance of secession (South Carolina)....20 Dec. "

Robert W. Barnwell, James H. Adams, and James L. Orr, appointed commissioners by South Carolina, to treat for the possession of U. S. property within the limits of South Carolina....21 Dec. "

[On their arrival at Washington they addressed a diplomatic letter to the president, 28 Dec. The president replied, 30 Dec., but persistently refused to receive them officially.]

Maj. Robert Anderson, in command at fort Moultrie, Charleston harbor, S. C., abandons that fort and, with its garrison, consisting of 7 officers, 61 non-commissioned officers and privates, and 13 musicians, occupies Fort Sumter ....night of 26 Dec. "

Ralph Farnham, last survivor of the battle of Bunker Hill, dies at Acton, ~~N. H.~~, aged 104½....27 Dec. "

Castle Pinckney and fort Moultrie seized by South Carolina state troops....27 Dec. "

U. S. arsenal, with 75,000 stands of arms, seized by South Carolina state troops at Charleston...30 Dec. "

Edward D. Baker of Or. answers the plea of Judah P. Benjamin of La. in the Senate for the right of secession....2 Jan. 1861

Fort Pulaski, at the mouth of the Savannah river, Ga., seized by Georgia state troops....3 Jan. "

U. S. arsenal seized at Mt. Vernon, Ala., by the Alabama state troops....4 Jan. "

Forts Morgan and Gaines, at the entrance of Mobile bay, seized by the Alabama state troops....5 Jan. "

Fernando Wood, mayor of N. Y., recommends secession to the common council....6 Jan. "

U. S. arsenal at Appalachicola, Fla., seized by Florida state troops....6 Jan. "

Fort Marion and fort St. Augustine, Fla., seized by Florida state troops....7 Jan. "

Robert Toombs, senator from Ga., delivers his last speech in the Senate....7 Jan. "

Star of the West, sent by the U. S. government to reinforce fort Sumter with 200 men under lieut. Chas. R. Wood of the 9th infantry, is fired on from Morris island and forced to retire....9 Jan. "

Ordinance of secession of Mississippi adopted in convention, 84 to 15....9 Jan. "

Fort Johnston seized by citizens of Smithville, N. C., 9 Jan. "

Fort Caswell seized by citizens of Smithville and Wilmington, N. C....10 Jan. "

Ordinance of secession of Florida adopted in convention, 62 to 7....10 Jan. "

U. S. arsenal and barracks at Baton Rouge, La., seized by Louisiana state troops....10 Jan. "

Fort Jackson and fort Philips below New Orleans, seized by Louisiana state troops 11 Jan 1861
Ordinance of secession of Alabama adopted in convention, 61 to 39 11 Jan "
Florida demands the surrender of fort Pickens, at the entrance of Pensacola bay Fla, with the garrison of 81 men, under lieut Slemmer refused 12 Jan "
Fort Taylor, Key West, garrisoned by U S. troops, 14 Jan "
Ordinance of secession of Georgia adopted in convention, 208 to 89 19 Jan. "
U S senators Clement C Clay of Ala, Thomas L. Clingman of N C., Jefferson Davis of Miss Stephen R. Mallory and David L Yulee of Fla withdraw from the Senate with speeches of defiance 21 Jan "
U S arsenal at Augusta Ga, seized by Georgia troops, 24 Jan "
Ordinance of secession of Louisiana adopted in convention, 113 to 17 . 26 Jan "
Alfred Iverson of Ga. withdraws from the Senate in a speech of defiance 28 Jan "
Kansas admitted as the 34th state 29 Jan "
Ordinance of secession of Texas adopted in convention, 166 to 7 . 1 Feb. "
Peace conference held at Washington, D C, at the request of the legislature of Virginia 4 Feb. "
[21 states represented, ex-pres Tyler chosen president It adjourned 27 Feb, after proposing amendments to the Constitution, which were offered in the Senate 2 Mch, and rejected by a vote of 3 to 34]
U S senators Judah P Benjamin and John Slidell of La withdraw from the Senate with speeches, 4 Feb "
Confederate congress meets at Montgomery, Ala " "
[6 states represented, 8 delegates from South Carolina, 10 from Georgia, 9 from Alabama, 7 from Mississippi, 5 from Louisiana, and 3 from Florida. (CONFEDERATE STATES)]
Choctaw nation adheres to the Confederate States, 7 Feb "
Congress authorizes a loan of $25,000,000 8 Feb. "
U S arsenal seized at Little Rock, Ark, by the state troops . 8 Feb. "
Jefferson Davis of Miss. chosen president, and Alex H. Stephens of Ga vice-president, by the Confederate congress (CONFEDERATE STATES) .. 9 Feb. "
Electoral vote counted 13 Feb. "
[Lincoln for president and Hamlin for vice-president, 180 Breckinridge for president and Lane for vice-president, 72 Bell for president and Everett for vice-president, 39 Douglas for president and Johnson for vice-president, 12.]
U S arsenal and barracks seized at San Antonio by the Texas state troops . 16 Feb. "
U.S military posts in Texas surrendered to the state by gen Twiggs, U S A . .. 18 Feb. "
[The amount of U S stores surrendered estimated at £1,300,000, of which $55,000 was specie, 35,000 stands of arms and 70 pieces of artillery, besides commissary and quartermaster's stores.]
Jefferson Davis inaugurated president of the Confederacy (CONFEDERATE STATES) . 18 Feb. "
Territorial government established in Colorado, 28 Feb. "
Gen D E Twiggs dismissed from the army 1 Mch. "
Territorial governments established in Dakota and Nevada . 2 Mch. "
[No restrictions as to slavery in the acts establishing these governments]
Gen Winfield Scott, in a letter to Mr. Seward, submits 4 plans of dealing with the seceding states (1) by conciliation, as proposed by Mr Crittenden or the Peace convention, (2) collect duties on foreign goods outside the ports of the seceding states and blockade them, (3) conquer the seceding states (which will take 300,000 men) and hold them as conquered provinces, or (4) say to the seceding states, "Wayward sisters, go in peace" . 3 Mch. "
hirty-sixth Congress adjourns . . . . . . 4 Mch. "

Nineteenth Administration—Republican. 4 Mch. 1861 to 3 Mch 1865

Abraham Lincoln, Ill, president
Hannibal Hamlin, Me, vice-president

CABINET

William H Seward, N. Y, sec of state, from 5 Mch 1861.
Salmon P. Chase, O, sec of treas., from 7 Mch 1861
Simon Cameron, Pa, sec of war, from 5 Mch 1861.
Edwin M Stanton, O, sec of war, from 15 Jan 1862.
Gideon Welles, Conn, sec of navy, from 5 Mch 1861.
Caleb B Smith, Ind, sec of interior, from 5 Mch 1861.
John P Usher, Ind, sec of interior, from 8 Jan 1863
Montgomery Blair, Md, postmaster-gen, from 5 Mch 1861.
William Dennison, O, postmaster-gen, from 24 Sept 1864
Edward Bates, Mo, attorney-gen, from 5 Mch 1861
T J Coffey, *ad int.*, attorney-gen, from 22 June, 1863.
James Speed, Ky., attorney-gen, from 2 Dec 1864

State of Louisiana seizes the bullion in the New Orleans mint, $536,000, for the Confederate government (COIN, Confederate) 7 Mch 1861
John Forsyth of Ala and Martin J Crawford of Ga. present credentials as commissioners of the Confederate States to the secretary of state 12 Mch "
He declines official intercourse with them 15 Mch "
Gen P T G Beauregard summons fort Sumter to surrender 11 Apr "
Fire opened on fort Sumter on the morning of 12 Apr. "
[First gun fired by Edmund Ruffin, a Virginian, 75 years of age He survived the war, in which he lost all his property, but committed suicide soon after SOUTH CAROLINA]
FORT SUMTER surrenders on Sunday, 14 Apr "
President by proclamation calls for 75,000 troops, and convenes Congress for 4 July 15 Apr "
Governor of North Carolina refuses to furnish quota of militia (2 regiments) to the U S 15 Apr "
Forts Caswell and Johnston of North Carolina taken possession of by state troops 16 Apr. "
Ordinance of secession of Virginia adopted in convention by 88 to 55 17 Apr. "
Governor of Missouri refuses to furnish quota of militia (4 regiments) to the U. S 17 Apr "
U S armory at Harper's Ferry, W Va, abandoned and burned by its garrison (VIRGINIA) 18 Apr "
U. S arsenal seized at Liberty, Mo, by state troops, 18 Apr. "
Conflict between the Sixth Massachusetts and mob in Baltimore, Md (MARYLAND) 19 Apr. "
President proclaims the blockade of all ports of the seceding states . 19 Apr. "
Gen Benj F. Butler's command arrives at Annapolis, Md 20 Apr "
U S officers seized at San Antonio, Tex, as prisoners of war 23 Apr. "
Governor of Arkansas refuses to furnish quota of militia (1 regiment) to the U. S 23 Apr "
John A Campbell of Ala., associate-justice of the Supreme court of the U. S., resigns about 1 May, "
[Campbell alone of the 3 Southern justices joined the Confederacy He became assist-sec. of war of the Confederate States, d 1889]
Pres Lincoln calls for 42,034 volunteers for 3 years, and adds 22,714 men to the regular army and 18,000 to the navy . 3 May, "
U S. ordnance stores seized at Kansas City 4 May, "
Ordinance of secession of Arkansas adopted in convention by 69 to 1 6 May, "
President proclaims martial law and suspends the *habeas corpus* in Key West, the Tortugas and Santa Rosa 10 May, "
Baltimore, Md, occupied by U S. troops 13 May, "
Gen Geo B McClellan, U S army, assumes command of the department of the Ohio, embracing a portion of W Virginia 13 May, "
Engagement at Sewell's Point, Va 18-19 May, "
Ordinance of secession of NORTH CAROLINA adopted in convention, vote unanimous 21 May, "

U S troops advance into Virginia and occupy Arlington Heights and Alexandria 24 May, 1861
Col E E Ellsworth, of the New York Fire Zouaves, shot at Alexandria, Va (VIRGINIA) 24 May, "
Gen Irwin McDowell, U S army, assumes command of the department of N E Virginia 28 May, "
Grafton, W Virginia, occupied by U S troops, 30 May, "
Ordinance of secession of the state of Tennessee adopted by the legislature (TENNESSEE) 8 June, "
Virginia state troops transferred to the Confederate government 8 June, "
Engagement at BIG BETHEL, Va (VIRGINIA), 10 June, "
Governor of Missouri calls for 50,000 state militia to repel invasion 12 June, "
Harper's Ferry abandoned by the confederates, 15 June, "
Gen Banks arrests George P Kane, chief of police, at Baltimore 27 June, "
And police commissioners (HABEAS CORPUS) 1 July, "
Western department constituted (MISSOURI) 3 July, "

Thirty-seventh Congress, First Session (extra), assembles 4 July, "
Galusha A Grow of Pa elected speaker of the House
[States not represented in the 37th Congress Alabama, Arkansas, Florida, Georgia, Mississippi, North Carolina, South Carolina, Texas, from Louisiana 2 representatives were present from Feb 1863, Tennessee was represented in the Senate by Andrew Johnson, and in the House by 3 members, 2 of them from Feb 1863]
President's first message to Congress 4 July, "
Engagement at Carthage, Mo (MISSOURI), between the federals under col Franz Sigel and confederates under gen Jackson, Sigel retreats 5 July, "
Senate, by a vote of 32 to 10, expels Mason and Hunter of Va, Clingman and Bragg of N C, Chestnut of S C, Nicholson of Tenn, Sebastian and Mitchell of Ark, Hemphill and Wigfall of Tex 11 July, "
[These senators had vacated their seats at the previous session]
Congress authorizes a loan of $250,000,000 17 July, "
Battle of BULL RUN 21 July, "
Gen George B. McClellan ordered to Washington, 22 July, "
Congress authorizes the enlistment of 500,000 men, 22 July, "
Gen William S Rosecrans assumes command of the department of the Ohio 23 July, "
Gen John C. Fremont assumes command of the western department 25 July, "
Gen George B McClellan assumes command of the division of the Potomac 27 July, "
State troops of Tennessee transferred to the Confederate government 31 July, "
First (extra) *Session* (34 days) adjourns 6 Aug "
[The second shortest session of any Congress]
An act confiscating the property, including slaves, of enemies of the U S 6 Aug "
Gen U S Grant assumes command of the district of Ironton, Mo. 8 Aug "
Battle of Springfield or Wilson's Creek, Mo., and death of gen Lyon (MISSOURI, WILSON'S CREEK), 10 Aug "
Kentucky and Tennessee constituted the department of the Cumberland, under command of gen Robert Anderson 15 Aug "
President by proclamation forbids commercial intercourse with seceding states 16 Aug "
Departments of northeastern Virginia, of Washington, and of the Shenandoah merged into the department or army of the Potomac 17 Aug "
Gen Butler captures forts Hatteras and Clark, at the entrance of Hatteras inlet, with 715 prisoners and 25 guns 29 Aug "
Gen Fremont proclaims martial law in Missouri, with freedom to the slaves of active rebels 31 Aug "
[This act was disapproved by the president]
Gen Grant assumes command of southeastern Missouri, 1 Sept. "
Advance of the confederates into Kentucky, and capture of Columbus 3-12 Sept 1861
Paducah, Ky, occupied by gen Grant 6 Sept "
Gen George H Thomas assigned to command at camp "Dick Robinson," E Kentucky 10 Sept "
Siege and surrender of LEXINGTON, Mo 11-20 Sept "
Bowling Green, Ky, occupied by the confederates, 18 Sept "
Gen O M Mitchel assumes command of the department of the Ohio 21 Sept "
Gen William T Sherman supersedes gen Anderson in the department of the Cumberland 8 Oct "
Gen O M Mitchel organizes an expedition for the occupation of E Tennessee 10 Oct. "
James M Mason of Va, John Slidell of La, Confederate envoys to Great Britain and France, run the blockade of Charleston harbor, S C., in the steamship *Theodora* (TRENT AFFAIR), on the night of, 12 Oct "
Battle of BALL'S BLUFF, Va 21 Oct. "
Gen Scott retired, aged 75 1 Nov. "
Gen David Hunter, U S army, relieves gen Fremont at St Louis, Mo 2 Nov "
Battle of BELMONT, Mo 7 Nov. "
British royal mail-contract packet *Trent* leaves Havana, Cuba, for England, 7 Nov, with Mason and Slidell on board, she is stopped by the U S war steamer *San Jacinto*, capt Wilkes and the envoys taken from her (TRENT AFFAIR) 8 Nov "
Department of Missouri constituted 9 Nov "
Department of the Ohio reorganized to include Kentucky and Tennessee, 9 Nov, gen Don Carlos Buell assumes command 15 Nov "
Gen Halleck assumes command of the department of Missouri 19 Nov "
Second Session assembles 2 Dec "
Pres Lincoln's first annual message to Congress, 3 Dec. "
John C Breckinridge, Ky, expelled from the Senate, 4 Dec "
[He had remained in the Senate until the end of the previous session]
Senate resolves that a joint committee of 3 members from the Senate and 4 from the House be appointed to inquire into the conduct of the war, with power to send for persons and papers, and to sit during the session (33 yeas to 3 nays) 9 Dec. "
House concurs 10 Dec "
This committee consists of senators Benj F Wade of O, Zachariah Chandler of Mich, and Andrew Johnson of Tenn, 17 Dec, and congressmen Daniel W Gooch of Mass, John Covode of Pa, George W Julian of Ind, and Moses F. Odell of N Y, 19 Dec "
Committee convenes, Mr Wade chairman 20 Dec "
Affair at Dranesville, Va " "
Government suspends specie payment 1 Jan 1862
Department of North Carolina established, gen A E Burnside commander. 7 Jan "
Burnside's expedition arrives at Hatteras inlet, N. C, 13 Jan "
Engagement at Logan's Cross Roads or MILL SPRING, Ky 19 Jan "
Jesse D Bright of Ind expelled from the Senate on a charge of disloyalty, by 32 to 14 20 Jan "
Capture of FORT HENRY, Tenn, by forces under gen Grant and com Foote 6 Feb "
Battle of Roanoke Island, by troops under command of gen Burnside 8 Feb "
Gen Grant assigned to command of district of W Tennessee 14 Feb "
Surrender of fort Donelson, Tenn, to Federal forces under gen Grant (FORT DONELSON) 16 Feb. "
Nashville, Tenn, occupied by Federal forces, 25 Feb "
Congress authorizes $150,000,000 U S notes, the Legal-tender bill 25 Feb "
Battle of Pea Ridge, Ark (ARKANSAS, 1862), 6-8 Mch. "
Naval engagement at Hampton Roads, Va., and destruction of the U. S. frigate *Congress* and sloop-of-war *Cumberland* by the Confederate iron-clad *Virginia*, formerly the U S. frigate *Merrimac* 8 Mch. "

Fight between the *Merrimac* and *Monitor* (HAMPTON ROADS), the *Merrimac* retires 9 Mch 1862
Advance of the army of the Potomac to Manassas Junction, Va 7-11 Mch "
Gen McClellan relieved from command in chief, retaining the army of the Potomac 11 Mch "
Departments of Kansas, of Missouri, and part of Ohio merged into the department of the Mississippi under maj-gen Halleck 11 Mch "
All persons in the service forbidden to return escaped slaves to Confederate owners, by a new article of war 13 Mch "
New-Berne, N C occupied by the U S forces, 14 Mch. "
Embarkation of the army of the Potomac for the Peninsula commenced at Alexandria (PENINSULAR CAMPAIGN) 17 Mch "
Battle of Kernstown or Winchester, Va, brig-gen James Shields defeats "Stonewall" Jackson 23 Mch "
Siege of Yorktown, Va, commenced by gen McClellan, 5 Apr "
Battle of PITTSBURG LANDING, Tenn . 6-7 Apr "
Island No 10, in the Mississippi, evacuated by the confederates 7 Apr "
Huntsville, Ala., occupied by the U S forces under gen O M Mitchel 11 Apr "
Bill abolishing slavery in the District of Columbia passes the Senate Apr 3, 29 to 14, and the House Apr 11, 92 to 39, approved 16 Apr "
[The average compensation paid by the government for each slave was $300]
Adm Farragut with his fleet passes FORTS JACKSON and ST PHILIP, the two forts guarding the Mississippi below New Orleans (LOUISIANA) 24 Apr "
Adm Farragut occupies New Orleans (LOUISIANA), 25 Apr "
Gen B F. Butler occupies New Orleans with his troops, 1 May, "
Gen Magruder evacuates Yorktown, Va 4 May, "
Battle of Williamsburg, Va (PENINSULAR CAMPAIGN), 5 May, "
Gen David Hunter proclaims emancipation of slaves, and authorizes arming all able-bodied negroes in Florida, Georgia, and South Carolina 9 May, "
[These orders were not approved by the president]
Norfolk, Va, occupied by U S forces under gen. Wool 10 May, "
Merrimac blown up by the confederates . 11 May, "
Department of Agriculture established 15 May, "
Gen. Butler issues General order No. 28 at New Orleans regarding the conduct of the women of that city 15 May, "
[This order produced great excitement in the south, and with other acts of the general, called forth a proclamation from the president of the Confederacy. See 23 Dec 1862]
Gen McDowell moves towards Richmond to co-operate with gen McClellan (PENINSULAR CAMPAIGN), 17 May, "
President approves the Homestead act 20 May, "
Education of colored children provided for in the District of Columbia by act of 21 May, "
Battle of Hanover Court-house, Va (PENINSULAR CAMPAIGN) . 24 May, "
Corinth, Miss, evacuated by the confederates, and occupied by the U S forces under maj-gen. Halleck (MISSISSIPPI, TENNESSEE) 30 May, "
Battle of "Seven Pines or Fair Oaks," near Richmond, Va (PENINSULAR CAMPAIGN) 31 May-1 June, "
Maj gen Robert E Lee assigned to command the Confederate forces about Richmond 3 June, "
President authorized to appoint diplomatic representatives to the republics of Hayti and Liberia 5 June, "
Treaty with Great Britain for the suppression of the African slave-trade 7 June, "
Gen Butler hangs Wm Mumford at New Orleans, 7 June, "
Battle of Cross Keys, Va (PENINSULAR CAMPAIGN, VIRGINIA) . .. 8 June, "
Battle of Port Republic, Va (PENINSULAR CAMPAIGN, VIRGINIA) 9 June, 1862
Confederate cavalry, 1500 men, under gen J E B Stuart, pass around army of the Potomac, 12-13 June, "
Slavery forever prohibited in the territories 19 June, "
Army of Virginia formed and placed under command of maj-gen John Pope (POPE'S VIRGINIA CAMPAIGN) 26 June "
Seven days' fighting and retreat of the army of the Potomac from before Richmond to Harrison's Landing on the James river 26 June-2 July, "
[Battles fought Mechanicsville, 26 June, Gaines's Mill, 27 June, Savage Station, 29 June, Glendale, 30 June, Frazier's Farm or White Oak Swamp, 30 June, Malvern Hill, 1 July PENINSULAR CAMPAIGN]
Vicksburg canal begun, designed by gen Thomas Williams to change the course of the Mississippi and isolate Vicksburg (VICKSBURG CAMPAIGN) 27 June, "
[Gen Grant recommenced work on this canal, 22 Jan 1863, but it proved a failure]
Act for a railroad and telegraph line from the Missouri river to the Pacific ocean, approved 1 July, "
Office of Commissioner of Internal Revenue created (INCOME-TAX in the U S) 1 July, "
Pres Lincoln calls for 300 000 volunteers for 3 years, 2 July, "
Gen McClellan's letter to pres Lincoln from Harrison's Landing, Va, giving advice on the policy of the government 7 July, "
Maj-gen Halleck commander-in-chief 11 July, "
By resolution Congress provides 2000 "medals of honor" for distribution to non-commissioned officers and privates who shall distinguish themselves (MEDALS), 12 July, "
Maj-gen John Pope takes command of the army of Virginia (POPE'S VIRGINIA CAMPAIGN) 14 July, "
Congress authorizes the enrolment of the militia between 18 and 45, the appointment of a judge advocate-general, the president to organize army corps at his discretion, persons of African descent to be admitted to the army, act approved 17 July, "
Congress authorizes the seizure and confiscation of rebel property 17 July, "
Second Session adjourns " "
Ex-pres Martin Van Buren dies at Lindenwold, N Y, aged 80 24 July, "
Pres Lincoln calls for 300,000 9-months militia 4 Aug "
[A special draft ordered in states whose quotas are not filled by 15 Aug]
Battle of Cedar Mountain, Va. (POPE'S VIRGINIA CAMPAIGN) 9 Aug "
Property in Louisiana belonging to John Slidell, Confederate commissioner to France, confiscated by order of gen Butler 11 Aug "
Army of the Potomac evacuates Harrison's Landing (PENINSULAR CAMPAIGN) 16 Aug "
Sioux Indians attack the frontier settlements of MINNESOTA 19 Aug "
Confederates, under gen Braxton Bragg, invade Kentucky, crossing the Tennessee river at Harrison, above Chattanooga (BRAGG'S KENTUCKY CAMPAIGN) . 21-24 Aug. "
Secretary of war directs the military governor of the coast islands of South Carolina to enlist 5000 volunteers of African descent . 25 Aug. "
[The first permission by the government to employ negroes as soldiers]
Battle of Groveton, Va, between the advance of gen Lee's army and gen Pope 29 Aug "
Battle of Manassas or "second Bull Run," a continuation of Groveton (POPE'S VIRGINIA CAMPAIGN), 30 Aug "
Kirby Smith, with Bragg's right, advances on Richmond, Ky, and defeats the Union forces 30 Aug. "
Battle of Chantilly, Va (POPE'S VIRGINIA CAMPAIGN), 1 Sept "
Gen Pope asks to be relieved from his command of the

army of Virginia, and transferred to the department of the Northwest 3 Sept 1862
Joseph Holt of Ky appointed JUDGE-ADVOCATE-GENERAL of the U S 3 Sept. "
Confederate forces cross the Potomac and occupy Frederick City, Md 4-5 Sept. "
Department of the Northwest created of Iowa, Minnesota Wisconsin, and the territories of Dakota and Nebraska, gen Pope commanding 6 Sept. "
Gen Lee issues a proclamation on entering Maryland, 8 Sept. "
Harper's Ferry surrenders to "Stonewall" Jackson, (MARYLAND CAMPAIGN) . 15 Sept "
Battles of SOUTH MOUNTAIN, Md " "
Capture of Munfordville, Ky, by the Confederate forces under Bragg (BRAGG'S KENTUCKY CAMPAIGN) 14-16 Sept. "
Advance of gen Kirby Smith appears before Covington, Ky, but immediately retires 15 Sept. "
Battle of Antietam (MARYLAND CAMPAIGN), 16-17 Sept "
Confederate army retreat across the Potomac on the night of 18-19 Sept. "
Battle of Iuka, Miss, gen Rosecrans forces Confederate gen Price to retreat 19-20 Sept. "
Preliminary proclamation of pres Lincoln announcing that in territory still in rebellion on 1 Jan 1863, the slaves will be declared forever free 22 Sept "
Convention of governors from 14 loyal states, with proxies from 3 others, meet at Altoona, Pa, and approve the emancipation proclamation 24 Sept. "
Gen Buell with the U S. forces arrives at Louisville, Ky, in advance of the Confederate forces 25 Sept "
Office of provost-marshal general created by the secretary of war 26 Sept "
Brig gen Jeff C Davis, U S A, shoots and mortally wounds gen William Nelson at the Galt House, Louisville, Ky 29 Sept "
[No notice was ever taken of this affair by the government]
Battle of Corinth, Miss (CORINTH) 3-4 Oct. "
Battle of Perryville, Ky (BRAGG'S KENTUCKY CAMPAIGN) 8 Oct. "
Eighteen hundred Confederate cavalry, with 4 pieces of artillery, under gen J E B Stuart, cross the Potomac for a raid into Pennsylvania . 10 Oct. "
They reach and occupy Chambersburg, Pa., on 11 Oct., and return to Virginia through Maryland, crossing the Potomac at White's Ford, without the loss of a man killed, and having secured 1000 horses, 12 Oct "
Ten Confederate prisoners at Palmyra, Mo., shot by order of gen McNiel (ALLSMAN, Andrew, Case of), 18 Oct. "
Gen McClellan assumes the offensive, and crosses the Potomac from Maryland . 26 Oct. "
Rear of the Confederate army under gen Bragg passes through Cumberland Gap on its retreat from Kentucky . .. 26 Oct. "
Death of gen O M Mitchel, U. S. A., at Beaufort, S C., aged 52 30 Oct "
Maj-gen Buell, commanding army of the Ohio, superseded by maj-gen Rosecrans . 30 Oct. "
Large Democratic gains in elections in northern states, 4 Nov. "
[Horatio Seymour, Democrat, elected governor of New York]
Gen McClellan relieved of command of army of the Potomac, and ordered to Trenton, N. J, gen Burnside appointed (FREDERICKSBURG, Battle of), 5 Nov. "
Gen. Porter ordered to Washington to answer charges of gen Pope (PORTER, FITZ-JOHN, Case of), 8 Nov. "
Gen B F Butler relieved from command of New Orleans . 9 Nov "
Lord Lyons, British minister to the U S., reports to his government upon the prospects of the confederates; the intentions of the conservative (Democratic) party, and the probability of success of mediation by foreign governments in the war. . 17 Nov. "
Third Session convenes 1 Dec 1862
[The president's message recommended a plan of emancipation in the loyal states (1) Any state abolishing slavery prior to 1 Jan 1900 should receive compensation, (2) slaves made free by the war to be forever free, loyal owners to be compensated.]
Battle of Prairie Grove, ARKANSAS . 7 Dec. "
Gen Burnside moves the army of the Potomac to the Rappahannock, opposite Fredericksburg 10 Dec. "
Army crosses the river . 11-12 Dec. "
Battle of FREDERICKSBURG .. 13 Dec "
Gen. N P. Banks assumes command of the Department of the Gulf, headquarters at New Orleans 16 Dec "
Gen. Grant expels Jews from his department 17 Dec. "
Pres Davis proclaims gen Benj. F Butler a felon, outlaw, and common enemy of mankind, directing that if captured he be hung immediately without trial, and all his commissioned officers or others serving with armed slaves, if captured, be reserved for execution 23 Dec "
Thirty-eight Indians hung at Mankato, Minn, for participation in the massacres (see 19 Aug) 26 Dec. "
Gen W. T. Sherman, aided by adm Porter, assaults Vicksburg on the north .27-28 Dec. "
[Known as the battle of "Chickasaw Bayou."]
Monitor founders off cape Hatteras in a storm, with a loss of 16 of her crew, night of 30 Dec "
Act admitting West Virginia, to date from 20 June, 1863 (the 35th state), approved . 31 Dec "
Battle of MURFREESBOROUGH or Stone River, 31 Dec. 1862-2 Jan 1863
Pres Lincoln proclaims all slaves free in the seceding states (SLAVERY in the U S) ... . 1 Jan "
Absent from duty in the army 8987 officers and 280,073 enlisted men .. 1 Jan "
Galveston, Tex, captured by the confederates " "
Gold at New York 133¼@133⅞ 2 Jan "
M Drouyn de l'Huys, French minister of foreign affairs, addresses M Mercier, French minister at Washington, concerning mediation between the U. S government and Confederate .. . 9 Jan. "
Arkansas post captured by the U S forces under W T. Sherman and McClernand, with a fleet of gunboats under adm Porter . 11 Jan "
Gen. Burnside resumes active operations, but is foiled by storms (FREDERICKSBURG, Battle of). 20-24 Jan "
Gen Fitz-John Porter cashiered and dismissed from the service of the U S. under the 9th and 52d articles of war (PORTER, Fitz-John, Case of) . 21 Jan. "
Organization of the 1st South Carolina colored loyal volunteers, col. T W. Higginson commander 25 Jan. "
Maj.-gen Burnside relieved by maj-gen. Hooker, 25 Jan. "
A. D. Boileau, proprietor of the Philadelphia *Evening Journal*, arrested and taken to Washington 27 Jan. "
Sec Seward replies to the French government upon mediation (see 9 Jan) .. .. 6 Feb. "
Commissary-general of subsistence first appointed, with the rank of brigadier-general . . . 9 Feb "
Territorial government established in ARIZONA, 24 Feb. "
Congress provides a national currency secured by U S. bonds . . approved 25 Feb. "
[Vote in the Senate, 23 to 21, House, 78 to 64]
Destruction of the Confederate war-steamer *Nashville* by the *Montauk*, in the Ogeechee river, Ga., 28 Feb. "
Congress authorizes, besides the 4 major-generals and 9 brigadier-generals for the regular army, 40 major-generals and 200 brigadier-generals for the volunteer service, there may be appointed 30 major-generals and 75 brigadier-generals for the volunteers, 2 Mch. "
Congress resolves that it is the unalterable purpose of the U S to prosecute the war vigorously until the rebellion is suppressed . . That any attempt at mediation will prolong instead of shortening the war . . . That the rebellion is now sustained by the hope of such intervention . 3 Mch. "
Congress empowers the president to suspend the writ of *habeas corpus* . . . . 3 Mch "

Congress authorizes loans of $300,000,000 for 1863, and $600,000,000 for 1864. . . . . 3 Mch. 1863

irty-seventh Congress adjourns. . . . . .4 Mch. "

[This Congress faced extraordinary difficulties, and solved unprecedented problems of statesmanship with wisdom and patriotism.]

Proclamation of the president relative to desertions in the army. . . . . 10 Mch. "

Maj.-gen. Burnside supersedes maj.-gen. H. G. Wright in the department of the Ohio. . . . . .25 Mch. "

Adm. Farragut passes the Confederate batteries at Grand Gulf, Miss., with 3 gun-boats. . . . . . . 1 Apr. "

Raid of mounted infantry from Tuscumbia, Ala., towards Rome, Ga. The entire force, 1700 men, with col. A. D. Streight, captured by the confederates (STREIGHT'S RAID). . . . . .7 Apr.–3 May, "

Maj.-gen. Burnside orders that death shall be the penalty for aiding the confederates, sympathizers with rebellion be sent into the Confederate lines, 13 Apr. "

Adm. Porter, with 8 gun-boats and 3 steam transports, passes (down) the Confederate batteries at Vicksburg. . . . . 16 Apr. "

Maj.-gen. Hooker crosses the Rappahannock at Kelly's Ford. . . . . .28–29 Apr. "

Gen. Grant crosses the Mississippi at Bruinsburg, below Vicksburg (VICKSBURG CAMPAIGN). . . . . . .30 Apr. "

Battle of CHANCELLORSVILLE, Va. . . . . 2-4 May, "

["Stonewall" Jackson (Confederate general), mortally wounded on the 2d, died on the 10th.]

Grand Gulf, below Vicksburg, abandoned by the confederates. . . . . .3 May, "

Clement L. Vallandigham arrested at Dayton, O., for treasonable utterances, by orders from gen. Burnside, 4 May, "

Gen. Hooker recrosses the Rappahannock. . . . .5 May, "

Gen. Grant occupies Jackson, Miss. . . . . .14 May, "

C. L. Vallandigham, convicted by court-martial at Cincinnati, of disloyal utterances, and sentenced to close confinement during the war in some fortress of the U. S. Gen. Burnside approves, and designates fort Warren, Boston. . . . . .16 May, "

Battle of Champion Hills, Miss. (VICKSBURG CAMPAIGN). . . . . .16 May, "

Battle of Big Black River, Miss. . . . . .17 May, "

Confederates retire within the defences of Vicksburg, and the siege begins. . . . . 18 May, "

U. S. forces assault the works at Vicksburg without success. . . . . .21–22 May, "

President rescinds gen. Burnside's order concerning C. L. Vallandigham, and sends him into the confederacy. . . . . .22 May, "

Maj.-gen. Banks, investing the Confederate works at Port Hudson, assaults them without success, 27 May, "

Fifty-fourth Massachusetts (colored), the first negro regiment sent from the north, departs for Hilton Head, S. C. . . . . .28 May, "

Gen. Lee begins his movement for the invasion of the north (GETTYSBURG, Pa., Battle of). . . . . . .3 June, "

Cavalry battle at Beverly's Ford, Va., between gens. Pleasanton, Buford, and Gregg, and the Confederate gen. J. E. B. Stuart. . . . . .9 June, "

C. L. Vallandigham nominated for governor by the Ohio Democratic convention. . . . . .11 June, "

Gen. Hooker begins the movement of his army northward from the Rappahannock. . . . . .13–15 June, "

Battle of Winchester, Va.; gen. Ewell defeats the U. S. troops under gen. Milroy. . . . . .14–15 June, "

Pres. Lincoln calls for 100,000 men for 6 months to resist the invasion of Pennsylvania. . . . .15 June, "

[Maryland to furnish 10,000, Pennsylvania 50,000, W. Virginia 10,000, and Ohio 30,000. These men were not used.]

Chambersburg, Pa., raided by Confederate cavalry, 15 June, "

Confederate army crosses the Potomac. . .24–25 June, "

Gen. Rosecrans finishes the TULLAHOMA CAMPAIGN, Tenn., forcing the confederates across the Tennessee at Bridgeport, Ala. . . . . 24 June–7 July, "

UNI

Gen. Rosecrans advances from Murfreesborough against gen. Bragg at Tullahoma, Tenn. . . . . .24 June, 1863

Army of the Potomac crosses the Potomac. . .26 June, "

Confederates advance to within 13 miles of Harrisburg, Pa. . . . . .27 June, "

Maj.-gen. Hooker relieved of command of the army of the Potomac, and maj.-gen. George G. Meade succeeds. . . . . .27 June, "

U. S. and Confederate forces concentrating at Gettysburg, Pa., battle of Gettysburg begins 1 July, and continues with the defeat of confederates (GETTYSBURG, Pa., Battle of. . . . . .2–3 July, "

Franklin Pierce, ex-president of the U. S., addresses a Democratic mass-meeting at Concord, N. H., 4 July, "

[Extract: "In this republic . . . it is made criminal . . . for that noble martyr of free speech, Mr. Vallandigham, to discuss public affairs in Ohio—ay, even here the temporary agents of the sovereign people, the transitory administration of the government, tell us that in time of war the mere arbitrary will of the president takes the place of the Constitution; and the president himself announces to us that it is treasonable to speak or to write otherwise than he may prescribe—nay, that it is treasonable even to be silent."]

Vicksburg surrenders to gen. Grant (VICKSBURG CAMPAIGN). . . . . .4 July, "

Four thousand Confederate raiders, with 10 guns, under John H. Morgan, cross the Ohio river at Brandenburg, Ky., into Indiana (MORGAN'S RAID). . .7 July, "

Port Hudson surrenders to gen. Banks (PORT HUDSON), 8 July, "

Confederate army recrosses the Potomac at Williamsport during the night of. . . . . .13 July, "

Draft riot in New York city. . . . . .13–16 July, "

Repulse of the U. S. troops in their assault on FORT WAGNER, Morris Island, S. C. . . . . .18 July, "

Samuel Houston dies at Huntersville, Tex., aged 70, 25 July, "

John J. Crittenden dies at Frankfort, Ky., aged 77, 26 July, "

Pres. Lincoln proclaims protection of colored soldiers against retaliation by the confederates. . . . .30 July, "

Gov. Seymour of N. Y. requests pres. Lincoln to suspend the draft for troops in that state. . . . . .3 Aug. "

John B. Floyd, ex-sec. of war and confederate brigadier-general, dies at Abingdon, Va. . . . . . . .26 Aug. "

Army of the Cumberland crosses the Tennessee in pursuit of gen. Bragg. . . . . .29 Aug.–3 Sept. "

Advance of gen. Burnside's command occupies Knoxville, E. Tenn. . . . . .4 Sept. "

Confederates evacuate fort Wagner on the night of, 7 Sept. "

Gen. Wood's division of the 21st corps, army of the Cumberland, occupies Chattanooga, Tenn. . .9 Sept. "

Pres. Lincoln suspends the writ of *habeas corpus* by proclamation. . . . . .15 Sept. "

Battle of CHICKAMAUGA. . . . . .19–20 Sept. "

11th and 12th corps, army of the Potomac, maj.-gen. Hooker, ordered to Middle Tennessee to reinforce the army of the Cumberland. . . . . .23 Sept. "

20th and 21st corps consolidated into the 4th corps, maj.-gen. Gordon Granger commander; maj.-gens. Alex. McDowell McCook of the 20th corps and T. L. Crittenden of the 21st corps relieved, and ordered to Indianapolis, Ind., to await a court of inquiry upon their conduct at Chickamauga. .28 Sept. "

Engagement at Bristow Station, Va., between the rear of the Potomac army and A. P. Hill. . . . . . .14 Oct. "

Maj.-gen. U. S. Grant appointed to the division of the Mississippi, including the departments of the Tennessee, Cumberland, and Ohio; maj.-gen. Wm. S. Rosecrans relieved of command of the army of the Cumberland, and maj.-gen. George H. Thomas succeeds, by general order No. 337, War department, 16 Oct. "

Pres. Lincoln calls for 300,000 men for 3 years. .17 Oct. "

Regulations issued for the re-enlistment of soldiers in the field in "veteran volunteer regiments," 23 Oct. 1863

Gen Hooker crosses the Tennessee at Bridgeport, Ala, 23 Oct., and advances to the Wauhatchie valley, at the foot of Lookout mountain, on the west 27 Oct "

Pontoon bridge thrown across the Tennessee at Brown's Ferry, below Chattanooga 27 Oct "

Battle of Wauhatchie (CHATTANOOGA CAMPAIGN), 27 Oct "

Gen Longstreet, detached from the Confederate army before Chattanooga, advances towards Knoxville, E Tennessee (CHATTANOOGA CAMPAIGN) 4 Nov "

Engagement at Rappahannock Station and Kelly's Ford, Va The Potomac army succeeds in crossing the Rappahannock, Lee retiring to the line of the Rapidan 7 Nov. "

Confederate forces under gen Longstreet before Knoxville 19 Nov "

Battle of Lookout Mountain (CHATTANOOGA CAMPAIGN) 24 Nov "

Battle of Chattanooga or Missionary Ridge (CHATTANOOGA CAMPAIGN) 25 Nov "

At Mine Run, Orange county, Va, the advance of the army of the Potomac under gen Meade meets the confederates under gen Lee. Attacks desultory, Meade retires 27-30 Nov. "

Gen Longstreet assaults the defences of Knoxville, especially FORT SANDERS, repulsed with heavy loss 29 Nov "

Gen Longstreet raises the siege of Knoxville, retreats towards Virginia, remaining in northeastern Tennessee during the winter, in the spring he joins gen. Lee at Richmond 1-4 Dec "

Gen Sherman's command and the 4th corps, army of the Cumberland, reinforce Knoxville from Chattanooga 3-6 Dec. "

Thirty-eighth Congress, First Session, convenes 7 Dec "

Schuyler Colfax of Ind elected speaker Pres. Lincoln proclaims amnesty to all confederates on returning to their allegiance 8 Dec "

Total debt of confederacy, $1,220,866,042 50 1 Jan 1864

Isaac Murphy inaugurated provisional governor of Arkansas 22 Jan "

President calls for 500,000 men for 3 years 1 Feb "

Sherman's Meridian expedition leaves Vicksburg, Miss 3 Feb "

More than 100 Union prisoners, including cols. Thomas E Rose and col. Streight, escape from Libby prison, Richmond, Va, by tunnelling under the walls (STREIGHT'S RAID) 9 Feb "

First Federal prisoners received at ANDERSONVILLE prison, Ga. . . . 15 Feb. "

Second Confederate congress meets at Richmond, 19 Feb "

Battle of OLUSTEE, Fla 20 Feb "

Battle of Tunnel Hill, Ga 22-25 Feb. "

Congress votes to every Union master whose slave enlists in the Federal army a compensation not exceeding $300, the volunteer to be free 24 Feb "

Congress revives grade of lieutenant-general in the army 29 Feb. "

Secretary of the treasury authorized to borrow $200,000,000 upon "5 40 bonds" 3 Mch "

Kilpatrick attempts in vain to release Union prisoners at Libby prison, 28 Feb Col. Dahlgren loses his life in a raid . 4 Mch. "

Ulysses S Grant commissioned lieutenant-general, 9 Mch, takes chief command . 10 Mch. "

Draft for 200,000 men for the navy and the reserve ordered for 15 Apr. by the president 14 Mch "

Gov Michael Hahn appointed military governor of Louisiana .. .. . 15 Mch. "

Enabling act for admission of Nevada and Colorado, 21 Mch "

New York Sanitary Commission fair (receipts $1,200,000) opened . 4 Apr. "

Battles of Sabine Cross Roads, Pleasant Grove, and Pleasant Hill, La (RED RIVER CAMPAIGN), 8-9 Apr 1864

Fort Pillow, Tenn, captured by confederates under Forrest, and colored garrison slaughtered 12 Apr. "

Enabling act to admit Nebraska approved 19 Apr. "

Motto "In God we Trust" first stamped upon the bronze two-cent coins authorized by act of 22 Apr. "

Hon Daniel Clark of N H elected president of the Senate *pro tem* . 26 Apr "

Army of the Potomac, 130,000 strong, crosses the Rapidan (GRANT'S CAMPAIGN IN VIRGINIA) 4 May, "

Sherman advances southward from Chattanooga (ATLANTA CAMPAIGN) 4 May, "

Sassacus defeats the Confederate ram *Albemarle*, in Albemarle sound 5 May, "

Battle of the Wilderness, Va 5-6 May, "

Battle of Spottsylvania Court-house, Va 10 May, "

Battle at New Market, Va, Sigel repulsed by confederates 15 May, "

Confederates under Johnston evacuate Resaca, Ga (ATLANTA CAMPAIGN) .. 15 May, "

Act for a postal money-order system 17 May, "

Offices of the New York *Journal of Commerce* and *World*, which had published a forged proclamation of the president, calling for 400,000 troops, seized and held several days by order of the secretary of war . 19 May, "

[On 1 July gen John A Dix and others were arrested, in accordance with a letter from gov Seymour to district-attorney A Oakey Hall, for seizing these offices]

Nathaniel Hawthorne dies at Plymouth, N H, aged 60 19 May, "

Battles near Dallas, Ga 25-28 May, "

Act creating Montana territory out of part of Idaho, approved 26 May, "

Convention of radicals at Cleveland, O, protests against the government's policy, and nominates gen John C Fremont for president and gen John Cochrane for vice-president, by acclamation 31 May, "

Morgan raids Kentucky (MORGAN'S RAID) June, "

Battle of Cold Harbor, Va 1-3 June, "

Currency bureau of the treasury established, with a comptroller of the currency, appointed by president by act 3 June, "

Philadelphia Sanitary fair (receipts $1,080,000) opens, 7 June, "

Union National convention meets at Baltimore, Md, on call of the National executive committee, 22 Feb, appoints hon William Dennison of O president, admits delegates from Virginia and Florida to seats without votes, and rejects delegates from South Carolina . 7 June, "

National Republican convention meets at Chicago, 7 June, "

[On the 1st ballot for president, Lincoln received all the votes, except those of Missouri for Grant, which were changed to Lincoln before the result was announced. 1st ballot for vice-president, Andrew Johnson 200, D S Dickinson 108, H Hamlin 150, scattering 61; after many changes the vote was announced. Johnson 494, Dickinson 17, Hamlin 9]

Vallandigham returns to Dayton, O, from Canada, 15 June, "

General assault of federals on Petersburg, Va, 16-18 June, "

Confederate cruiser ALABAMA fights the U. S ship KEARSARGE off Cherbourg, France, and surrenders in a sinking condition . . . . 19 June, "

Battle of Weldon Railroad, Va . 21-22 June, "

Lincoln accepts the renomination by letter, dated Washington . . . . . 27 June, "

Battle of Kenesaw Mountain, Ga (ATLANTA CAMPAIGN). . . . . 27 June, "

Repeal of Fugitive Slave law of 1850 approved, 28 June, "

Act authorizing the issue of bonds not to exceed $400,000,000, or treasury notes not to exceed $200,000,000 and bonds for same amount 30 June, 1864
Congress grants Yosemite valley and Mariposa Big Tree grove to California for a public park 30 June, "
Secretary Chase resigns 30 June, William P Fessenden appointed 1 July, "
Confederates evacuate Marietta, Ga " "
Act prohibiting the coast-wise slave-trade forever approved 2 July, "
irst Session adjourns " "
President suspends the *habeas corpus* in Kentucky, and proclaims martial law 5 July, "
President, under resolution of Congress, appoints the 1st Thursday of August as a day of humiliation and prayer 7 July, "
President by proclamation explains veto, 2 July, of a Reconstruction bill passed less than an hour before the adjournment of Congress 8 July, "
Battle of Monocacy, Md 9 July, "
Repulse of gen Early (confederate) at fort Stevens, 6 miles from Washington 12 July, "
Gold reaches 285 per cent, the maximum 16 July, "
Hood supersedes Johnston in defence of Atlanta, 17 July, "
President calls for 500,000 volunteers for 1, 2, or 3 years, 18 July, "
On 5 July Horace Greeley received a letter from George N Sanders, Clifton, Canada, averring that Clement C Clay of Ala, Jas P Holcombe of Va, and the writer, confederates in Canada, would proceed to Washington in the interest of peace if full protection were accorded them Greeley referred this letter to the president, suggesting with it a plan of adjustment The president requested him to proceed to Niagara falls and communicate with the parties in person 18 July, "
[A fruitless conference was the result]
Battle of Peach Tree Creek, Ga (ATLANTA CAMPAIGN) 20 July, "
Battle of Decatur or Atlanta, Ga 22 July, "
Battle of Ezra's Church, Ga 28 July, "
Chambersburg, Pa, raided and mostly burned (GRANT'S VIRGINIA CAMPAIGN) 30 July, "
Unsuccessful mine explosion under a Confederate fort, near Petersburg, Va, conducted by gen Burnside (MINE EXPLOSION) 30 July, "
Confederate steamer *Tallahassee*, built in England, destroys many U S merchantmen July-Aug "
Successful attack on the harbor of Mobile, forts Gaines, Morgan, and Powell captured by fleet under Farragut and land forces under Granger 5-22 Aug "
Maj-gen Philip H Sheridan appointed to the army of the Shenandoah (GRANT'S VIRGINIA CAMPAIGN), 7 Aug "
English-built cruiser *Georgia* captured at sea by the *Niagara* 15 Aug "
Gen Grant seizes the Weldon railroad 18 Aug "
Democratic National convention meets at Chicago, 29 Aug, Horatio Seymour chosen president of the convention and platform adopted, 30 Aug On 1st ballot for president, gen George B McClellan of N J has 174 votes (as revised and declared, 202½), nomination made unanimous George H Pendleton of O nominated on the 2d ballot for vice-president 31 Aug "
Battles at Jonesborough, Ga (ATLANTA CAMPAIGN), 31 Aug-1 Sept. "
Hood evacuates Atlanta, Ga. " "
Gen John H Morgan killed at Greeneville, Tenn, 4 Sept. "
Gen McClellan's letter accepting nomination, dated Orange, N J. 8 Sept "
Frémont withdraws in favor of Lincoln and Johnson, by letter 17 Sept "
Battle of WINCHESTER, Va 19 Sept. "
Battle of FISHER'S HILL, Va 22 Sept "
Gen. Price invades MISSOURI 24 Sept-28 Oct. "
English-built cruiser *Florida* captured in the Brazilian harbor of Bahia by the U S war-ship *Wachusett*, and taken to Hampton Roads, where she is sunk by a collision a few days after (BRAZIL) 7 Oct 1864
Chief-justice Roger B Taney dies in Washington, 12 Oct. "
Battle of CEDAR CREEK, Va 19 Oct. "
Raid on St Albans, Vt., by confederates from Canada (VERMONT) 19 Oct. "
Confederates under Price enter Linn county, Kan, 23 Oct "
Confederate ram *Albemarle* blown up by lieut Cushing, U S navy, at Plymouth, N C. 27 Oct "
Battle of Hatcher's Run, Va " "
Nevada, the 36th state in order, admitted into the Union by proclamation of the president 31 Oct "
Mr Seward telegraphs the mayor of New York of a conspiracy to burn the principal cities of the North, 2 Nov "
Second session of second Confederate congress convenes at Richmond 7 Nov "
McClellan resigns his command in the army 8 Nov "
At the general election, Lincoln and Johnson, Republican, carry 22 states, McClellan and Pendleton, 3 (New Jersey, Delaware, and Kentucky), 11 not voting 8 Nov. "
Atlanta burned, and Sherman begins his march to the sea 14 Nov "
Blockade of Norfolk, Va, Fernandina, and Pensacola, raised by proclamation of president 19 Nov. "
Benjamin Silliman, LL D, born 1779, dies at New Haven, Conn 24 Nov "
Confederate incendiaries fire many hotels in New York, 25 Nov. "
Battle of FRANKLIN 30 Nov. "
Second Session convenes 5 Dec "
Fourth annual message of pres Lincoln 6 Dec "
Henry Rowe Schoolcraft, LL D, born 1793, died at Washington, D C 10 Dec "
Fort McAllister, Savannah, Ga, captured by Hazen's division of Sherman's army 13 Dec "
Thomas defeats Hood at NASHVILLE, Tenn, 15-16 Dec. "
Pres. Lincoln calls for 300,000 volunteers to make up deficiency in call 18 July, 1864 If not obtained before 15 Feb, 1865, a draft to be made 19 Dec "
Savannah, evacuated by confederates 20 Dec, occupied by Sherman 21 Dec "
Grade of vice-admiral established for the U S NAVY by act of Congress 21 Dec "
Fort Fisher, N C, bombarded by gen Porter, 24 Dec, and unsuccessfully attacked by gens Butler and Porter 25 Dec "
Vice pres. Hamlin resumes the chair in the Senate, 5 Jan 1865
Gen Grierson's raid, after destroying 100 miles of railroad, taking 600 prisoners and 1000 contrabands, he arrives at Vicksburg 5 Jan "
FORT FISHER captured 15 Jan "
Edward Everett dies at Boston, aged 71 " "
Monitor *Patapsco* sunk off Charleston by a torpedo, 15 Jan "
Joint resolution, proposing a XIIIth Amendment to the Constitution, abolishing slavery, passes the House, 119 to 56 31 Jan. "
Sherman leaves Savannah and starts northward, 1 Feb. "
President and sec Seward meet Alexander H. Stephens, vice-president of the confederacy, and commissioners R M T Hunter and judge Campbell, to treat for peace, in Hampton Roads 2-3 Feb "
Bennett G Burley, the Confederate raider on lake Erie, surrendered to the U. S by the Canadian government 3 Feb "
Battle of Hatcher's Run, Va 5 Feb "
Electoral votes counted, necessary to a choice, 117
For president and vice-president, Lincoln and Johnson receive 212, McClellan and Pendleton 21. 8 Feb "
Gen. J M Schofield appointed to command depart-

ment of North Carolina, with headquarters at Raleigh 9 Feb 1865
President calls an extra session of the Senate, 4 Mch 1865 17 Feb "
Columbia, S C, surrenders to gen Sherman " "
Lee takes command of the Confederate armies, 18 Feb "
Charleston, S C, evacuated and burned by gen Hardee, 17 Feb, is occupied by Federal troops 18 Feb "
Fort Anderson captured by federals under gen Cox, 18 Feb "
Wilmington, N C, captured by gen Schofield, 22 Feb. "
Secretary of the treasury authorized to borrow $600,000,000 on bonds at not exceeding 6 per cent in coin, 3 Mch. "
Act passed to establish a bureau for the relief of freedmen and refugees 3 Mch. "
A tax of 10 per cent imposed on notes of state banks paid out after 1 July, 1866 3 Mch "
Confederate debt disowned by U S Senate, 17 Feb, by House of Representatives 3 Mch. "
Andrew Johnson inaugurated vice-president, oath administered by H. Hamlin in the Senate chamber, 3 Mch "
Thirty-eighth Congress adjourns " "
Senate assembles in special session 4 Mch "
Lincoln inaugurated president " "
[Second term, oath administered by chief-justice Chase at the Capitol In his inaugural address occur the words "With malice towards none, with charity for all, with firmness in the right, as God gives us to see the right, let us strive on to finish the work we are in, to bind up the nation's wounds, to care for him who shall have borne the battle, and for his widow and his orphan, to do all which may achieve and cherish a just and a lasting peace among ourselves and with all nations."]

Twentieth Administration—Republican. 4 Mch 1865 to 3 Mch 1869

Abraham Lincoln, Ill., president
Andrew Johnson, Tenn, vice-president.

CABINET (until 15 Apr 1865)

William H Seward, N. Y., sec. of state, continued
Hugh McCulloch, Ind, sec of the treasury, appointed 7 Mch. 1865
Edwin M Stanton, O, sec of war, continued
Gideon Welles, Conn, sec of the navy, continued
John P Usher, Ind., sec of the interior, continued.
William Dennison, O, postmaster-gen, continued
James Speed, Ky, attorney-gen, continued

L. S. Foster of Conn elected president *pro tem* of the Senate (serves through the session) 7 Mch 1865
Special session of Senate adjourns .. 11 Mch "
Battle of Averysborough, N C. ... 15 Mch. "
Confederate Congress adjourns *sine die* 18 Mch "
Battle of Bentonville, N C. . . 19 Mch "
Armies of Sherman, Terry, and Schofield join at Goldsborough, N C . . 23 Mch. "
Battle of Five Forks, Va . 31 Mch-1 Apr "
Richmond evacuated by confederates and partly burned ... . . 2 Apr. "
Selma, Ala, captured with large stores " "
Ewell's division, some 8000 men, cut off, surrounded, and captured at Sailor's creek, Va . 6 Apr "
Correspondence between U S minister Adams in London and earl Russell, respecting the *Alabama*, begins . . . . 7 Apr "
Lee surrenders to Grant at Appomattox Court-house, Va . . . . 9 Apr "
Montgomery, Ala, surrenders to Wilson .. 11 Apr "
Mobile evacuated by confederates .12 Apr "
Secretary of war issues orders to stop drafting and further purchase of war materials . . . 13 Apr. "
Gen Sherman occupies Raleigh, N C . . . . " "
"Stars and Stripes" raised over FORT SUMTER, Charleston ... . 14 Apr. "

UNI

Pres Lincoln shot by J Wilkes Booth in Ford's theatre, Washington (BOOTH'S CONSPIRACY), 14 Apr 1865
Sec Seward and his son wounded in his own house by an assassin . 14 Apr. "
Pres Lincoln dies at about 7 30 A M. .15 Apr "
Chief-justice Chase administers the oath of office as president to Andrew Johnson 15 Apr "

PRES JOHNSON'S CABINET

William H Seward, N Y, sec of state, continued.
Hugh McCulloch, Ind, sec of treas, continued
Edwin M Stanton, O, sec of war, continued
U S Grant, Ill., sec of war (*ad interim*), from 12 Aug 1867.
Lorenzo Thomas, sec. of war (*ad interim*), from 21 Feb 1868
John M Schofield, N Y, sec of war, from 30 May, 1868
Gideon Welles, Conn, sec of navy, continued.
John P Usher, Ind, sec of interior, continued.
James Harlan, Ia, sec of interior, from 15 May, 1865.
Orville H Browning, Ill, sec. of interior, appointed 27 July, served from 1 Sept 1866
James Speed, Ky, attorney-gen, continued
Henry Stanbery, Ky, attorney-gen, from 23 July, 1866
William M. Evarts, N Y, attorney-gen, from 15 July, 1868.
William Dennison, O, postmaster-gen, continued
Alexander W Randall, Wis, postmaster-gen, from 25 July, 1866.

Funeral services of pres Lincoln at the Executive mansion at noon, and appropriate memorial services held throughout the country . . 19 Apr 1865
[Remains of the president, after lying in state at the Capitol through the 20th, conveyed to Springfield, Ill, *via* Baltimore, Harrisburg, Philadelphia, New York, Albany, Buffalo, Cleveland, Columbus, Indianapolis, and Chicago, buried at Springfield (LINCOLN'S MONUMENT), 4 May]
Macon, Ga, occupied by Union forces 20 Apr. "
J Wilkes Booth, discovered in a barn near Bowling Green, Va, shot by serg Boston Corbett, and his accomplice Harold captured 26 Apr "
Memorandum for a peace, signed by gens Sherman and Johnston at Durham Station, N C, 18 Apr, is rejected at Washington 21 Apr Grant arrives at Raleigh 24 Apr, and gen Johnston surrenders to Sherman at Bennett's house, near Durham Station, 26 Apr "
Executive order for trial by military commission of alleged assassins of pres Lincoln issued 1 May, "
Reward of $100,000 offered for the capture of Jefferson Davis by proclamation of president ...2 May, "
Confederate gen. Richard Taylor surrenders at Citronelle, near Mobile, Ala . 4 May, "
Executive order re-establishing authority of the U S in Virginia, recognizes Francis H Pierpont as governor ... 9 May, "
Jefferson Davis captured, with his wife, mother, postmaster-gen Reagan, col Harrison, Johnson, and others, by 4th Michigan cavalry under col. Pritchard, at Irwinsville, Ga . . . 10 May, "
[Davis taken to fortress Monroe]
Last fight of the war near Palo Pinto, Tex., a Federal force under col Barret defeated by confederates under gen Slaughter . . . 13 May, "
Confederate ram *Stonewall* surrenders to Spanish authorities in Cuba .. .... 20 May, "
Pres Johnson proclaims southern ports open 22 May, "
Grand review of the armies of the Potomac, Tennessee, and Georgia at Washington, D C . ..22-23 May, "
Gen E Kirby Smith surrenders his trans-Mississippi army .. . . 26 May, "
President proclaims general amnesty to rebels, with exceptions, on taking oath of allegiance 29 May, "
William W Holden proclaimed provisional governor of North Carolina by pres Johnson . 29 May, "
Day of humiliation and mourning on account of the assassination of Lincoln . . 1 June, "
British government rescinds its recognition of the confederates as belligerents ... . 2 June, "

Galveston, Tex , the last seaport held by the South, surrenders 5 June, 1865
French government rescinds its recognition of the confederates as belligerents 6 June, "
Judge William L Sharkey appointed provisional governor of Mississippi by pres. Johnson 13 June, "
Proclamation of president removing restrictions on trade east of the Mississippi after 1 July, and declaring insurrection in Tennessee suppressed 13 June, "
Gen A J Hamilton appointed provisional governor of Texas by president 17 June, "
James Johnson appointed provisional governor of Georgia 17 June, "
Lewis E Parsons proclaimed provisional governor of Alabama 21 June, "
Proclamation of the president rescinding the blockade, 23 June, "
Restriction of trade west of the Mississippi removed by proclamation of president 24 June, "
Benjamin F Perry proclaimed provisional governor of South Carolina 30 June, "
Execution of Lewis Payne, G A Atzerodt, David E Harold, and Mary E Surratt, implicated in the assassination of Lincoln 7 July, "
William Marvin proclaimed provisional governor of Florida 13 July, "
Confederate privateer *Shenandoah* (capt Waddell) destroys about 30 Federal vessels during Aug "
Mississippi nullifies the ordinance of secession, 22 Aug "
All restrictions on southern ports removed after 1 Sept by proclamation of president 29 Aug "
South Carolina repeals ordinance of secession, 15 Sept. "
Alabama annuls the ordinance of secession 25 Sept "
North Carolina annuls the ordinance of secession, 7 Oct "
Alexander H Stephens of Ga, John H Reagan of Texas, John A. Campbell of Ala, George A Trenholm of S. C, and Charles Clark of Miss, paroled by executive order 11 Oct. "
President proclaims end of martial law in Kentucky, 12 Oct "
Great Fenian meeting at Philadelphia, the Irish republic proclaimed 16-24 Oct "
Florida repeals ordinance of secession 28 Oct "
Georgia repeals ordinance of secession 30 Oct "
National thanksgiving for peace 2 Nov "
Shenandoah, capt Waddell, reaches Liverpool, Engl, 6 Nov, he had first heard of the peace 2 Aug, vessel given up to British government and crew paroled 8 Nov, and the vessel given to the American consul 9 Nov "
Capt Wirz, after military trial, begun 21 Aug, is convicted of cruelty to Federal prisoners in Andersonville, and hung 10 Nov "
Ex-pres Buchanan publishes a vindication of his administration Nov. "
Habeas corpus restored in the northern states by president's proclamation 1 Dec "

[Th]irty-ninth Congress, First Session, convenes 4 Dec. "
Lafayette S Foster, president *pro tem.* of the Senate
Schuyler Colfax elected speaker of the House by a vote of 139 to 36 for James Brooks of New York
President's annual message presented 4 Dec "
House appoints as committee on reconstruction messrs Stevens, Washburn, Morrill, Grider, Bingham, Conkling, Boutwell, Blow, and Rogers 14 Dec. "
Sec Seward declares the XIII th Amendment to the Constitution, abolishing slavery, ratified by Illinois, Rhode Island, Michigan, Maryland, New York, West Virginia, Maine, Kansas, Massachusetts, Pennsylvania, Virginia, Ohio, Missouri, Nevada, Indiana, Louisiana, Minnesota, Wisconsin, Vermont, Tennessee, Arkansas, Connecticut, New Hampshire, South Carolina, Alabama, North Carolina, and Georgia, 27 states 18 Dec. "
President sends a message to Congress on the insurgent states, with report of gen. Grant 18 Dec. "

Senate appoints as committee on reconstruction messrs Fessenden, Grimes, Harris, Howard, Johnson, and Williams 21 Dec 1865
Gov Holden of N C relieved by pres Johnson, and governor-elect Jonathan Worth appointed 23 Dec "
Death of Joseph Crele, said to be 141 years of age, born at site of Detroit in 1725, dies at Caledonia, Wis 27 Jan 1866
Freedmen's Bureau bill passed by Senate, 25 Jan, by House, 6 Feb 1866, vetoed 19 Feb "
[The Senate fails to pass this bill over the president's veto, vote being 30 for to 18 against]
President denounces Congress and the Reconstruction committee, in a speech at the executive mansion, 22 Feb "
Civil Rights bill passed 16 Mch, vetoed 27 Mch "
President proclaims the insurrection at an end in Georgia, South Carolina, Virginia, North Carolina, Tennessee, Alabama, Louisiana, Arkansas, Mississippi, and Florida 2 Apr "
First post of the Grand Army of the Republic organized at Springfield, Ill (GRAND ARMY) 6 Apr "
Civil Rights bill passed over the president's veto, 9 Apr "
Fair held in Baltimore for the relief of the destitute in the southern states nets $164,569 97 Apr "
Race riot in Memphis, Tenn 1-2 May, "
Boundary of Nevada extended 1 degree east, by act of Congress 5 May, "
Jefferson Davis indicted for complicity in the assassination of pres Lincoln, in the U S Circuit court of Virginia 8 May, "
Fourth Wisconsin cavalry mustered out, after serving 5 years and 1 day, the longest term of volunteers on record 28 May, "
Death of gen Winfield Scott at West Point, aged 80, 29 May, "
Customs officers seize 1200 stands of Fenian arms at Rouse's Point, N. Y., 19 May, and 1000 at St Alban's, Vt 30 May, "
Fenian raid into Canada, about 1200 men cross the Niagara river at Buffalo, N Y, landing near old fort Erie, 31 May, 1866 After a skirmish near Ridgeway they withdraw to the U S, where many are arrested for violating the neutrality laws, and over 1000 paroled 2 June, "
President's proclamation against the invasion of Canada by Fenians 6 June, "
Over 1000 Fenians attack St Armand, Quebec, and are routed 9 June, "
XIV th Amendment to Constitution passes the Senate 8 June, the House 13 June, reaching the State department 16 June, "
Majority of Reconstruction committee report the late Confederate States not entitled to representation in Congress 18 June, "
Message from the president to Congress adverse to presenting the XIV.th Amendment to the states, 22 June, "
Great fire in Portland, Me 4 July, "
James H Lane, senator from Kansas, commits suicide, 11 July, "
[For cause, see Blaine's "Twenty Years of Congress," vol ii p 185-6]
Tennessee readmitted by joint resolution of Congress, approved 24 July, "
Congress creates the grades of admiral and vice-admiral in the navy, and revives that of general in the army (ARMY, NAVY) 25 July, "
Atlantic telegraph completed 27 July, "
Act increasing and fixing the military peace establishment 28 July, "
First Session adjourns " "
Race riot in New Orleans, many negroes killed 30 July, "
National Union convention of Conservatives in Philadelphia, senator James R Doolittle, president, 14 Aug "

This convention adopts a declaration of principles vindicating the president.................17 Aug. 1866

[The previous political character of its members made this convention somewhat noted; it contained prominent citizens whose course throughout the rebellion had been patriotic, such as Thurlow Weed, Marshall O. Roberts, Henry J. Raymond, John A. Dix, and Robert S. Hale of N. Y., Cowan of Pa., Doolittle of Wis., and others of previous good standing in the Republican party, together with Vallandigham of O., Fernando Wood and Jas. Brooks of N. Y., Burke and Sinclair of N. H., Phelps of Vt., Campbell of Pa., Carmichael of Md., and others, who had been known as "copperhead" or "secessionist," and other more conservative Democrats, such as Tilden, Dean Richmond, and Sanford E. Church of N. Y., Stockton and Parker of N. J., Porter, Bigler, and Packer of Pa., English of Conn., Johnson of Md., and many others.]

President proclaims the decree of Maximilian, 9 July, 1866, closing Matamoras and other Mexican ports, null and void as against the U. S........ 17 Aug. "

Insurrection in Texas at an end by proclamation of the president.......................... 20 Aug. "

Pres. Johnson visits Philadelphia, New York, Chicago, etc., speaking in favor of his policy and against Congress.....................24 Aug.–18 Sept. "

[In this journey, then popularly known as "swinging around the circle," the president was accompanied by sec. Seward, sec. Welles, postmaster-gen. Randall, gen. Grant, adm. Farragut, and other army officers and civilians.]

Convention of Southern Loyalists, held at Philadelphia..............................3-7 Sept. "

[This convention united with the convention of the congressional party opposing the president's policy.]

Corner-stone of monument to Stephen A. Douglas laid in Chicago........................... 6 Sept. "

National mass convention of soldiers and sailors held in the interest of the president at Cleveland, in resolutions reported by col. L. D. Campbell, approve unanimously the action of the Philadelphia convention of 17 Aug.......................18 Sept. "

Pittsburg convention of soldiers and sailors held in opposition to the president's policy.....25-26 Sept. "

Peabody Institute, Baltimore, Md., inaugurated; George Peabody present.........................24 Oct. "

Soldiers first admitted to the National Home for Disabled Volunteers, located at Togus, near Augusta, Me..................................10 Nov. "

A gold medal for Mrs. Abraham Lincoln, the gift of 40,000 French citizens, is delivered to minister Bigelow at Paris...........................1 Dec. "

Second Session convenes; president's message received, 3 Dec. "

Geo. H. Williams of Or. introduces bill "to regulate the tenure of civil offices"...............3 Dec. "

Massacre by Indians of U. S. troops at fort Philip Kearney, near Big Horn, Wyoming; 3 officers and 90 men killed and scalped.................21 Dec. "

In the House of Representatives, James M. Ashley of O. charges pres. Johnson with usurpation, corrupt use of the appointing, pardoning, and veto powers, and corrupt disposition of public property, and interference in elections. The case is referred to the judiciary committee by 108 to 39..........7 Jan. 1867

Bill extending suffrage to negroes in the District of Columbia, passed by Congress 14 Dec. 1866, vetoed 5 Jan.; passed over the veto............ 8 Jan. "

N. P. Willis, born 1807, dies at Idlewild on the Hudson................................20 Jan. "

Evangelical Alliance of the U. S. organized in New York, with William E. Dodge as president. .30 Jan. "

Congress admits Nebraska as a state over the president's veto..........................9 Feb. "

Alexander Dallas Bache, LL.D., A.A.S., born 1806, dies at Newport, R. I......................17 Feb. "

UNI

Nebraska, the 37th in order, proclaimed a state by the president............................ 1 Mch. 1867

Tenure of Civil Office bill passed over the president's veto; Senate, 35 to 11; House, 133 to 37...2 Mch. "

Military Reconstruction act introduced in the House by Thaddeus Stevens, Feb. 6, providing for the division of the insurrectionary states into 5 military districts, as follows: 1st, Virginia; 2d, North and South Carolina; 3d, Georgia, Florida, and Alabama; 4th, Mississippi and Arkansas; 5th, Louisiana and Texas. Passed over the president's veto; House, 138 to 51; Senate, 38 to 10..............2 Mch. "

National Bankruptcy bill passed............ " "

Department of Education established by act of Congress...............................2 Mch. "

Peonage in the territory of New Mexico abolished and forever prohibited by act of Congress......2 Mch. "

Committee on the Judiciary reports, concerning impeachment, its inability to conclude its labors (report presented at 3 A.M. Sunday, 3 Mch.), and recommends a continuance of investigation....2 Mch. "

B. F. Wade of O. elected president *pro tem.* of the Senate, Mr. Foster retiring...............4 Mch. "

Thirty-ninth Congress adjourns.............. " "

Fortieth Congress, First Session, convenes..... " "

Schuyler Colfax re-elected speaker by a vote of 127 to 30 for Samuel S. Marshall of Ill.

[The 1st session of the 40th Congress was continued by repeated adjournments, sitting 1st, 4–29 Mch.; 2d, 3-20 July; 3d, 21 Nov.–2 Dec., when it adjourned *sine die.* Congress distrusting the president, it was deemed advisable "that the president should not be allowed to have control of events for 8 months without the supervision of the legislative branch of the government." Benj. F. Butler enters Congress for the first time at this session as Republican representative from Massachusetts.]

Charles F. Browne (Artemus Ward), born 1834, dies at Southampton, Engl...................6 Mch. "

General orders No. 10, issued from army headquarters by direction of the president, assigning gen. J. M. Schofield to command 1st military district; gen. D. E. Sickles to command 2d military district; gen. G. H. Thomas to command 3d military district; gen. E. O. C. Ord to command 4th military district; gen. P. H. Sheridan to command 5th military district.............................11–12 Mch. "

Gen. John Pope assigned to 3d military district, gen. Thomas to command department of the Cumberland, 15 Mch. "

Henry Barnard, LL.D., appointed commissioner of education................................16 Mch. "

Peabody Southern Educational Fund (a gift of $2,100,000 from George Peabody) transferred to a board of trustees, rev. dr. Barnas Sears superintendent................................ 22 Mch. "

Supplementary Reconstruction act concurred in 19 Mch., vetoed by president 23 Mch.; is passed over his veto by the House, 114 to 25, and by the Senate, 40 to 7.............................23 Mch. "

Congress adjourns to 3 July, after a session of 26 days, 29 Mch. "

Special session of the Senate in accordance with president's proclamation, 30 Mch., meets........1 Apr. "

Special session of the Senate adjourns *sine die,* 19 Apr. "

Expedition against the Indians in western Kansas, led by gens. Hancock and Custer.........30 Apr. "

Jefferson Davis taken to Richmond on *habeas corpus* and admitted to bail in $100,000; sureties, Horace Greeley and Augustus Schell of New York; Aristides Welsh and David K. Jackman of Philadelphia; W. H. McFarland, Richard B. Haxall, Isaac Davenport, Abraham Warwick, G. A. Myers, W. W. Crump, James Lyons, J. A. Meredith, W. H. Lyons, John M. Botts, Thomas W. Boswell, and James Thomas, jr., of Virginia.................... 13 May, "

Congress reassembles......................3 July, "

Supplementary Reconstruction bill, reported 8 July, vetoed and passed over the veto 19 July, 1867

Congress adjourns to 21 Nov, after a session of 18 days 20 July, "

Catharine Maria Sedgwick, authoress, born 1789, dies near Roxbury, Mass 31 July, "

John H Surratt, implicated in assassination of pres Lincoln is arrested in Alexandria, Egypt, and placed on the American vessel *Swatara*, 21 Dec 1866, his trial begins 10 June, 1867, in the Criminal court for District of Columbia, the jury, disagreeing, are dismissed 10 Aug "

E M Stanton, sec of war, refusing to resign at the request of the president, 5 Aug, is suspended, and gen. Grant appointed secretary *pro tem*, Stanton submitting under protest 12 Aug. "

Sheridan relieved of command in 5th military district, and gen Hancock appointed 17 Aug "

Gen Sickles succeeded by gen E R S. Canby as commander of 2d military district 26 Aug. "

Woman's Suffrage campaign in Kansas conducted by Lucy Stone, Susan B Anthony, Elizabeth Cady Stanton, and George Francis Train with the Hutchinson family of singers Sept.-Oct "

General amnesty proclaimed by the president 7 Sept "

National cemetery at Antietam dedicated 17 Sept "

Gold discovered in Wyoming, and South Pass City established Oct "

Elias Howe, inventor, born 1819, dies at Brooklyn, L I, 3 Oct "

Formal transfer of Alaska by Russia to gen Rousseau of the U S service at New Archangel, Sitka, 9 Oct "

Congress reassembles 21 Nov "

Congress adjourns *sine die* after a 12 days' session, 2 Dec "

Second Session meets " "

President s message received by Congress 3 Dec "

Resolution to impeach the president negatived in the House of Representatives 7 Dec "

Maj-gen George C Meade appointed to command of 3d military district, succeeding Pope, removed, 28 Dec "

Senate refuses to approve of the suspension of secretary Stanton 13 Jan 1868

Act exempting cotton from internal tax 3 Feb "

Pres Johnson removes Stanton, and appoints gen Lorenzo Thomas secretary of war *ad interim*, act declared illegal by the Senate 21 Feb. "

Mr Stanton refuses to vacate, and has Thomas arrested and held to bail (discharged 24 Feb.) 22 Feb "

House of Representatives votes to impeach the president, 124 to 42 24 Feb "

Impeachment reported at the bar of the Senate by Thaddeus Stevens and John A Bingham 25 Feb "

Articles of impeachment adopted by the House, and Thaddeus Stevens, B F Butler, John A. Bingham, George S Boutwell, James F Wilson, Thomas Williams, and John A Logan elected managers, 2 Mch "

Senate organizes as a court of impeachment 5 Mch "

Gen Hancock succeeded by gen Buchanan as commander of 5th military district 18 Mch "

Answer of pres. Johnson to articles of impeachment read in court by his counsel 23 Mch. "

Prosecution begun by B. F Butler 30 Mch. "

Chinese embassy, headed by Anson Burlingame, arrives at San Francisco 31 Mch. "

Benjamin R Curtis opens the defence in court of impeachment 9 Apr. "

Memorial monument and statue of pres. Lincoln unveiled at Washington 15 Apr "

Public dinner to Charles Dickens given in New York city . 18 Apr "

Dickens arrived at Boston, Mass, 19 Nov 1867 (his 2d visit to the U. S., his first being in 1842) He gives readings from his own works in most of the larger cities of the U S., and sails from New York city on his return voyage 22 Apr. "

Grand Army of Republic institutes Memorial or Decoration day by order designating 30 May for observance 5 May, "

Senate votes upon 11th article of impeachment, 35 (not two thirds) for conviction, 19 for acquittal 16 May, 1868

Republican National convention assembles at Chicago, and Joseph R Hawley of Conn chosen permanent president, 20 May, Ulysses S Grant nominated for president on first ballot, on the fifth ballot for vice president, Schuyler Colfax of Ind receives 541 votes, Benjamin F Wade of O, 38, Reuben E Fenton of N Y, 69 21 May, "

Court of impeachment acquits the president on articles ii and iii by same vote as on article xi, and adjourns *sine die* by vote of 34 to 16 26 May, "

Mr Stanton resigns as secretary of war, 26 May, and is succeeded by gen Schofield 30 May, "

Ex-pres James Buchanan, born 1791, dies at Wheatland, Pa 1 June, "

Gen George Stoneman assigned to 1st military district, to replace Schofield 1 June, "

Gen Irvin McDowell appointed to command 4th military district, 28 Dec 1867, assumes his duties, 4 June, "

Arkansas admitted to representation by Congress over president's veto 22 June, "

Eight hours to constitute a day's work for all laborers, workmen, and mechanics in government employ, by act of 25 June, "

North Carolina, South Carolina, Louisiana, Georgia, Alabama, and Florida admitted to representation in Congress over president's veto 25 June, "

McDowell relieved and gen Alvan C Gillem appointed to command of 4th military district 30 June, "

So called "Burlingame treaty" with China signed at Washington 4 July, "

Amnesty proclamation by the president pardoning all late rebels not under presentment or indictment in U S courts 4 July, "

National Democratic convention meets in Tammany Hall, New York, 4 July, and Horatio Seymour chosen permanent president, 6 July, Horatio Seymour nominated for president on 22d ballot, gen Frank P Blair for vice-president unanimously on first ballot, 9 July, "

Act removing legal and political disabilities imposed by U S on several hundred persons in the southern states as mentioned in act 20 July, "

Sec Seward announces the XIVth Amendment to the Constitution adopted by the votes of 29 states (Connecticut, New Hampshire, Tennessee, New Jersey, Oregon, Vermont, New York, Ohio, Illinois, West Virginia, Kansas, Maine, Nevada, Missouri, Indiana, Minnesota, Rhode Island, Wisconsin, Pennsylvania, Michigan, Massachusetts, Nebraska, Iowa, Arkansas, Florida, North Carolina, Louisiana, South Carolina, and Alabama) 20 July, "

Bill for payment of national debt and reduction of rate of interest passed by Congress 25 July, "

Territory of Wyoming created of parts of Dakota, Utah, and Idaho 25 July, "

FREEDMEN'S BUREAU discontinued after 1 Jan 1869, by act of 25 July, "

U S laws relating to customs, commerce, and navigation extended over Alaska, by act of 27 July, "

Act for protection of naturalized citizens abroad, " "

Second Session adjourns to 21 Sept, after sitting 239 days 27 July, "

XIVth Amendment ratified by Georgia, 21 July, 1868, proclaimed by president 27 July, "

Gen J Reynolds appointed to command 5th military district (Texas) 28 July, "

Thaddeus Stevens, born 1793, dies at Washington, 11 Aug "

Ordinance of secession declared null and void in Louisiana by constitution, ratified by the people, 17-18 Aug "

Col George A Forsyth engages in an 8-days fight with Indians on the north fork of the Republican river, Kan . . Sept. "

Second Session reassembles for one day and adjourns to 16 Oct . 21 Sept. "

Congress meets and adjourns to 10 Nov. 16 Oct. "

Grant and Colfax, Republicans, elected president and vice-president by votes of 26 states and a popular vote of 3,015,071; Seymour and Blair, Democrats, receive votes of 8 states and a popular vote of 2,709,-613 ....3 Nov. 1868

Second Session meets and adjourns....10 Nov. "

Third Session meets ....7 Dec. "

President proclaims unconditional pardon and amnesty to all concerned in the late insurrection....25 Dec. "

Colored National convention, Frederick Douglass president, meets at Washington....13 Jan. 1869

Objection to counting electoral votes of Georgia made in the House of Representatives by Mr. Butler of Mass....10 Feb. "

Electoral votes counted by Congress: for Grant and Colfax, Republicans, 214; for Seymour and Blair, Democrats, with Georgia, 80, without Georgia, 71, 10 Feb. "

A *nolle prosequi* entered in case of Jefferson Davis, 11 Feb. "

Loans of money on U. S. notes by national banks forbidden by act of....19 Feb. "

XV.th Amendment to the Constitution, forbidding states to restrict the elective franchise because of race, color, or previous condition of servitude, proposed by resolution of Congress, received at department of state, 27 Feb. "

St. Paul and St. George islands, Alaska, declared a special reservation for protection of fur seal, and landing thereon forbidden, by act....3 Mch. "

Speaker Colfax resigns, T. M. Pomeroy unanimously elected speaker....3 Mch. "

Oath of office administered to vice-president Colfax, 4 Mch. "

Fortieth Congress adjourns.... " "

Gen. Grant inaugurated president.... " "

Twenty-first Administration — Republican. 4 Mch. 1869 to 3 Mch. 1873.

Ulysses S. Grant, Ill., president.
Schuyler Colfax, Ind., vice-president.

CABINET.

Elihu B. Washburn, Ill., sec. of state, 5 Mch. 1869.
Hamilton Fish, N. Y., sec. of state, 11 Mch. 1869.
George S. Boutwell, Mass., sec. of treasury, 11 Mch. 1869.
John A. Rawlins, Ill., sec. of war, 11 Mch. 1869.
William T. Sherman, O., sec. of war, 9 Sept. 1869.
William W. Belknap, Ia., sec. of war, 25 Oct. 1869.
Adolph E. Borie, Pa., sec. of navy, 5 Mch. 1869.
George M. Robeson, N. J., sec. of navy, 25 June, 1869.
Jacob D. Cox, O., sec. of interior, 5 Mch. 1869.
Columbus Delano, O., sec. of interior, 1 Nov. 1870.
John A. J. Creswell, Md., postmaster-gen., 5 Mch. 1869.
E. Rockwood Hoar, Mass., attorney-gen., 5 Mch. 1869.
Amos T. Akerman, Ga., attorney-gen., 23 June, 1870.
George H. Williams, Or., attorney-gen., 14 Dec. 1871.

Forty-first Congress, *First Session*, meets....4 Mch. 1869

James G. Blaine elected speaker by 135 to 57 for Michael C. Kerr of Ind.

Gen. Gillem removed from 4th military district (Mississippi), and gen. Adelbert Ames appointed..Mch. "

A. T. Stewart, nominated and confirmed as secretary of the treasury, 5 Mch., resigns because of act of 2 Sept., 1789, which forbids any one interested in importing to hold the office....9 Mch. "

Earliest practicable redemption of U. S. notes in coin promised by act....18 Mch. "

H. B. Anthony of R. I. elected president *pro tem.* of the Senate....23 Mch. "

President's message to the Senate on claims upon Great Britain....7 Apr. "

President calls a special session of the Senate for 12 Apr....8 Apr. "

First Session adjourns....10 Apr. "

Special session of the Senate meets....12 Apr. "

Gen. E. R. S. Canby assumes command of the military district of Virginia....20 Apr. "

UNI

Special session of Senate adjourns....23 Apr. 1869

Union Pacific railroad opened for traffic (PACIFIC RAILROADS)....10 May, "

Filibustering expedition under gen. Thomas Jordan, fitted out in New York, lands on north coast of Cuba, 12 May, "

Southern Commercial convention meets at Memphis, Tenn.; 1100 delegates from 22 states....18 May, "

National Commercial convention meets at New Orleans, 25 May, "

Great peace jubilee at Boston, Mass. (MUSIC), 15 June, "

Adolph E. Borie, sec. of navy, resigns....22 June, "

Expedition for Cuba under col. Ryan, sailing from New York, 26 June, is captured by a U. S. revenue cutter, 27 June, "

Soldiers' National monument at Gettysburg dedicated, 1 July, "

Irish National Republican convention meets in Chicago; 221 delegates....4–5 July, "

U. S. end of the Franco-American cable landed at Duxbury, Mass., 23 July, and event celebrated..27 July, "

National Labor convention meets in Philadelphia, 16 Aug. "

National Temperance convention (500 delegates) meets in Chicago....1–2 Sept. "

John A. Rawlins, sec. of war, and gen. Grant's adjutant-general throughout the war, born 1831, dies at Washington, D. C....6 Sept. "

One hundred and eight men suffocated in a burning coal-mine at Avondale, Pa....6 Sept. "

Commercial convention meets at Keokuk, Ia..7 Sept. "

William Pitt Fessenden, born 1806, dies at Portland, Me....8 Sept. "

Financial panic in New York city culminates in "Black Friday"; gold quoted at 162½....24 Sept. "

George Peabody lands at New York, 10 June; he endows several institutions, adds $1,400,000 to his Southern Education fund, and leaves for London, 30 Sept. "

Northwestern branch of the National Home for Disabled Volunteer Soldiers, near Milwaukee, Wis., dedicated....Oct. "

Franklin Pierce, ex-president, born 1804, dies at Concord, N. H....8 Oct. "

Commercial convention held at Louisville, Ky., 520 delegates from 22 states, ex-pres. Millard Fillmore presiding....13 Oct. "

Père Hyacinthe arrives at New York, 18 Oct., and is introduced in public by Henry Ward Beecher, 24 Oct. "

Steamboat *Stonewall* burned on the Mississippi below Cairo; about 200 persons perish....27 Oct. "

U. S. branch mint at Carson City, Nev., founded 1866, begins operations....1 Nov. "

Adm. Charles Stewart, born 1778, dies at Bordentown, N. J....6 Nov. "

Maj.-gen. John Ellis Wool, born 1784, dies at Troy, N. Y....10 Nov. "

Reunion of Old and New School Presbyterian churches at Pittsburg, Pa....12 Nov. "

National Woman Suffrage convention meets at Cleveland, O. (183 delegates from 16 states, Rev. Henry Ward Beecher president), and organizes American Woman's Suffrage Association....24 Nov. "

Second Session opens....6 Dec. "

National Colored Labor convention meets at Washington....10 Dec. "

Wyoming gives women the right to vote and hold office....10 Dec. "

George H. Peabody, born South Danvers, Mass., 1795, dies in London, 4 Nov.; funeral services held in Westminster Abbey, 12 Nov., and body placed on the British steamship *Monarch* for transportation to the U. S....11 Dec. "

Act removing legal and political disabilities from large classes of persons in the southern states...14 Dec. "

Edwin M. Stanton, born 1814, dies at Washington, D. C....24 Dec. "

Telegraph operators' strike throughout the country, 4 Jan 1870
Statue of Nathaniel Greene, placed in the old hall of House of Representatives by Rhode Island, accepted by resolution of Congress 20 Jan "
British Peninsular and Oriental steamship *Bombay* collides with and sinks the U S corvette *Oneida*, about 20 miles from Yokohama, Japan, 112 lives lost 23 Jan "
Prince Arthur of Great Britain reaches New York, 21 Jan, and is presented to pres Grant 24 Jan "
Virginia readmitted by act approved 26 Jan and government transferred to civil authorities by gen Canby 27 Jan "
George Peabody buried at Peabody (South Danvers), Mass 8 Feb "
Congress authorizes the secretary of war to establish a weather bureau for the U S 9 Feb "
Northern Pacific railroad begun at the Dalles of the St Louis, Minn 15 Feb "
Anson Burlingame, born 1822, dies at St Petersburg Russia 23 Feb "
Mississippi readmitted by act approved " "
Hiram R Revels of Miss, first colored member of the Senate, sworn 25 Feb. "
Act removing legal and political disabilities from many persons in the southern states 7 Mch "
Grand jury of men and women impanelled at Laramie, Wyo 7 Mch "
Texas *readmitted by act approved* 30 Mch "
Sec Fish proclaims the ratification of XV th Amendment by 29 states North Carolina, West Virginia, Massachusetts, Wisconsin, Maine, Louisiana, Michigan, South Carolina, Pennsylvania, Arkansas, Connecticut, Florida, Illinois, Indiana, New York, New Hampshire, Nevada, Vermont, Virginia, Alabama, Missouri, Mississippi, Ohio, Iowa, Kansas, Minnesota, Rhode Island Nebraska, Texas 30 Mch "
Mass-meeting of Mormons at Salt Lake City protest against interference by Congress with polygamy, 5 Apr. "
American Anti-Slavery Society, after an existence of 37 years, is dissolved 9 Apr. "
Point of junction of Union and Central Pacific railroads fixed northwest of the station at Ogden, Utah, by act of 6 May, "
Proclamation of president against Fenian invasion of Canada 24 May, "
Fenian army of 500 invade Canada from Fairfield, Vt, and are driven back 25-27 May, "
Act to enforce the right to vote under the XV th Amendment 31 May, "
Attorney-gen Hoar resigns 15 June, "
U S department of justice organized by act of 22 June, "
Treaty to annex Dominican Republic and lease bay and peninsula of Samana concluded, 29 Nov 1869, rejected by the Senate 30 June, "
Congress grants the widow of pres Lincoln a pension of $3000 per annum 14 July, "
Stone presented to pres Lincoln by patriots of Rome is given to the Lincoln Monument Association at Springfield, Ill, by Congress 14 July, "
Act to authorize refunding the national debt at 5, 4½, and 4 per cent 14 July, "
Georgia readmitted by act approved 15 July, "
Act reducing the U S army to a peace footing, " "
Second Session adjourns " "
First through-car from the Pacific reaches New York, 24 July, "
Adm David C Farragut, born 1801, dies at Portsmouth, N H 14 Aug "
National Labor congress meets in Cincinnati 15 Aug "
President proclaims neutrality in the Franco-Prussian war 22 Aug "
Irish National congress assembles at Cincinnati, 23 Aug "
National Commercial convention meets at Cincinnati, O, 4 Oct. "

Gen Robert E Lee, born 1807, dies at Lexington, Va, 12 Oct 1870
President's proclamation forbidding military expeditions against nations at peace with the U S, 12 Oct "
Oliver P Morton, appointed minister to Great Britain, declines for political reasons 25 Oct. "
Jacob D Cox, secretary of interior, resigns 30 Oct "
John Lothrop Motley, minister to England, asked to resign by the president, July, 1870, disregarding the request, is recalled Nov "
Third Session opens 5 Dec. "
President's annual message presented " "
J H Rainey of S C, first colored member of House of Representatives, is sworn in 12 Dec "
Colored Methodist Episcopal church in America organized by bishop Paine at Jackson, Tenn 16 Dec "
Gen Robert Schenck appointed minister to Great Britain 22 Dec "
Resolution authorizing a San Domingo commission approved (B F Wade of O, A D White, president of Cornell university, and S G Howe of Mass, named) 12 Jan 1871
Supreme court decides the Legal Tender act of 1862 constitutional 16 Jan "
Statue of Lincoln in the rotunda of the Capitol unveiled 25 Jan "
George Ticknor, historian, born 1791, dies at Boston, 26 Jan. "
Act for a commission of fish and fisheries (Spencer F. Baird appointed) 9 Feb "
District of Columbia made a territorial government, by act of 21 Feb "
Act for celebration of centennial of Independence by an international exhibition at Philadelphia in 1876, 3 Mch "
Forty-first Congress adjourns 4 Mch. "

Forty-second Congress, *First Session*, meets " "
Speaker of the House James G Blaine of Me.
Charles Sumner, chairman of Senate Committee on Foreign Relations, replaced by sen Cameron of Pa, 10 Mch "
President's proclamation against unlawful combinations of armed men in South Carolina (Ku-klux), 24 Mch. "
Sen Sumner's speech on the resolutions regarding the employment of the navy on the coast of San Domingo during negotiations for the acquisition of part of that island 27 Mch "
[The acquisition of San Domingo by annexation was favored by the president, but was not by either the House or the Senate. The speeches of sen. Sumner were so bitter towards the measure and the administration that all personal intercourse ceased between him and the president]
First Civil-service commission, George William Curtis, Alexander G Cattell, Joseph Medill, D A Walker, E B Ellicott, Joseph H Blackfan, and David C Cox, appointed by president Mch "
William H Gibson (colored), U S mail agent on the Lexington and Louisville railroad, assaulted at North Benson, Ky, 26 Jan, U S troops sent into Kentucky, and mail withdrawn on that route for one month Mch "
San Domingo commission's report sent to Congress with a special message by the president 5 Apr "
Act to enforce the XIV th Amendment (Ku-klux act), 20 Apr "
Branch mint at Dahlonega, Ga, conveyed to trustees of the North Georgia Agricultural college for educational purposes, by act of 20 Apr. "
First Session adjourns " "
Under call, dated 20 Apr, Senate meets in special session 10 May, "
Henry B Anthony elected president *pro tem.* of the Senate 23 May, "
International Young Men's Christian Association meets at Washington, D C. 24 May, "
Extra session of Senate adjourns *sine die* 27 May, "

Hall's Arctic expedition sails from New York (NORTH-EAST AND NORTHWEST PASSAGES) 29 June, 1871
Riot in New York city between Irish Orangemen and Catholics 12 July, "
First narrow-gauge (3 feet) locomotive built in the U S shipped from Philadelphia for the Denver and Rio Grande railroad 13 July, "
Tweed Ring frauds first exposed in the New York *Times*, 22 July, "
Boiler on Staten Island ferry-boat *Westfield* at New York explodes, 100 killed, 100 wounded 30 July, "
Political disturbance in Louisiana begins (LOUISIANA, 1871-75) 8 Aug "
National Labor congress held in St Louis 10 Aug "
Mass-meeting in New York held to consider the Tweed Ring frauds, committee of 70 appointed 4 Sept. "
Pres Lincoln's body removed to the permanent vault at Springfield, Ill 19 Sept. "
National Commercial convention meets at Baltimore, Md 26 Sept. "
Brigham Young arrested in Salt Lake City for polygamy 2 Oct. "
Chicago fire breaks out Sunday evening 8 Oct "
Forest fires in vicinity of Green Bay (WISCONSIN), 8-9 Oct "
Proclamation by the president against Ku-klux in South Carolina 12 Oct "
William M Tweed arrested and released on $2,000,000 bail 27 Oct "
Capt Charles Francis Hall, Arctic explorer, dies on the *Polaris* 8 Nov "
Grand-duke Alexis of Russia arrives at New York with a fleet of war vessels, 19 Nov, public reception, 21 Nov "
Russian envoy to the U S, Catacazy, recalled, owing to personal differences with sec Fish 25 Nov. "
Second Session convenes. 4 Dec "
Fish-Catacazy correspondence published 6 Dec. "
Attorney-gen A T Akerman resigns his office, 13 Dec "
Tweed committed to the Tombs, but released on writ of *habeas corpus* 16 Dec "
President's message with report of Civil-service Reform commission 19 Dec "
Brigham Young arrested in Salt Lake City as implicated in murder of Richard Yates 2 Jan. 1872
Col James Fisk, jr, shot in the Grand Central Hotel, New York, by Edward S Stokes, 6 Jan, dies (TRIALS) 8 Jan. "
Congress accepts from Rhode Island a statue of Roger Williams 11 Jan "
Sen Sumner's speech on civil rights 15 Jan "
Liberal Republican movement begins with a convention held at Jefferson City, Mo 24 Jan "
Martin J Spalding, Roman Catholic archbishop of Baltimore and primate of the church in America, born 1810, dies 7 Feb "
Sen Sumner offers resolutions to investigate sales of ordnance stores by the government during the Franco-German war 12 Feb. "
Labor Reform convention meets at Columbus, O, 21 Feb, and nominates judge David Davis of Ill for president, and judge Joel Parker of N J for vice-president 22 Feb. "
National Prohibition convention at Columbus, O, nominates James Black of Pa for president, and John Russell of Mich. for vice-president 22 Feb "
Yellowstone National park established by act approved . 1 Mch. "
Imperial Japanese embassy, of 114 persons, is presented to the president at the Executive mansion 4 Mch. "
U S Centennial commissioners and alternates meet in Philadelphia and organize, electing Joseph R Hawley president 4 Mch "
Statues of Jonathan Trumbull and Roger Sherman presented to the Senate by Connecticut for the old Hall of Representatives 8 Mch. "
Pres. Grant appoints gen A A Humphreys, U S A., prof Benjamin Pierce, U S coast survey, and capt. Daniel Ammen, U S N, a commission to examine plans and proposals for an interoceanic canal across the Isthmus of Darien Mch 1872
Prof S F B. Morse, born 1791, dies in New York, 2 Apr "
National convention of colored men at New Orleans, Frederick Douglass, chairman 10-14 Apr "
Assassination of judge J C Stephenson, Thomas E Detro, and James C Cline at Gun City, Mo. (MISSOURI) 24 Apr "
Sen elect Matthew W Ransom from N C admitted to a seat, and the Senate for the first time since 1861 is full 24 Apr "
Brigham Young taken to camp Douglas, 21 Mch, and released 30 Apr "
Duty on tea and coffee repealed by act of 1 May, "
National Liberal Republican convention meets in Cincinnati O, Carl Schurz permanent president. Horace Greeley of N Y nominated for president on the 6th ballot, 3 May, gov B. Gratz Brown of Mo for vice-president 1-3 May, "

[The result of the balloting in the nomination of Greeley created surprise and disappointment. 'That a convention which owed its formal call to a body of active and aggressive free-traders, should commit its standard to the foremost champion of protection in the country That a convention, composed largely of Democrats, should select him who had waged incessant and unsparing war against them from the hour he first entered political life, who had assailed them with all the terms of abuse found in his well-filled armory of denunciation, was not only singular but incongruous"—*Blaine's* "Twenty Years of Congress," vol ii p 524]

Greeley's letter of acceptance dated 20 May, "
Political disabilities under article 3 of the XIVth Amendment removed, except from senators and representatives in 36th and 37th Congresses, and officers of the judicial, military, and naval service of the U. S, heads of departments, and foreign ministers of the U S, by act of 22 May, "
Workingmen's National convention at New York nominates Grant and Wilson for president and vice-president 23 May, "
Sumner assails the president in the Senate 31 May, "

["Sumner seeks to prevent the renomination of gen Grant by concentrating, in one massive broadside, all that should be suggested against him"—*Blaine's* "Twenty Years of Congress," vol ii p 533]

B Gratz Brown accepts the nomination for vice-president 31 May, "
Dispute with Spain respecting the imprisonment of dr Howard, an American citizen, in Cuba since 13 Dec 1870, settled, and dr Howard released June, "
General labor strike in New York settled (STRIKE), June, "
Centennial Board of Finance incorporated by act of, 1 June, "
James Gordon Bennett, founder of the New York *Herald*, born 1795 dies at New York. 1 June, "
National Republican convention at Philadelphia, 5 June, Thomas Settle of N C. permanent president Grant renominated by acclamation, and on 1st ballot Henry Wilson of Mass nominated for vice-president by 364½ votes to 321½ votes for Schuyler Colfax, 6 June, "
Henry B Anthony chosen president *pro tem.* of the Senate . 8 June, "
Second Session adjourns 10 June, "
Grant accepts the Republican nomination . " "
Sen Wilson's letter of acceptance dated . . 14 June, "
World's Peace Jubilee at Boston (MUSIC), 17 June-4 July, "
Liberal Republican Revenue Reformers' convention at New York nominates William S Groesbeck of O for president, and Frederick Law Olmstead of N Y for vice-president . 21 June, "
Judge David Davis declines the Labor Reform nomination for president . . 24 June, "

Joel Parker, nominated for vice-president by Labor Reform convention, declines 28 June, 1872

National Democratic convention meets at Baltimore, Md, 9 July, James R Doolittle of Wis chairman Horace Greeley of N Y nominated for president on 1st ballot by 686 votes out of 732, and B Gratz Brown of Mo for vice-president by 713 votes out of 732 9-10 July, "

Mr Greeley accepts the nomination 12 July, "

Jesse Olney, geographer, born 1798, dies at Stratford, Conn 30 July, "

B Gratz Brown accepts the Baltimore nomination, 8 Aug "

National Labor Reform convention at Philadelphia nominates Charles O Conor for president, and Eli Saulsbury for vice-president 22 Aug "

O Conor declines the nomination 27 Aug "

National convention of "Straight out" Democrats in Louisville, Ky, repudiates the Baltimore nominees, and nominates Charles O Conor of N Y for president, and John Quincy Adams of Mass for vice-president (both decline) 3-5 Sept. "

National Industrial Exposition opens at Louisville, Ky, 3 Sept. "

Tribunal at Geneva, under article vii of the treaty of Washington, 8 May, 1871, awards to the U S $15,500 000 as indemnity from Great Britain 14 Sept. "

Colored Liberal Republican National convention at Louisville, Ky delegates from 23 states, Greeley and Brown nominated 25 Sept "

William Henry Seward, born 1801, dies at Auburn, N Y 10 Oct. "

"Epizootic," affecting horses throughout the country, reaches the city of New York 23 Oct. "

Emperor of Germany, arbitrator in the San Juan difficulty, awards the islands to the U S (JUAN, SAN), 23 Oct. "

General election Grant and Wilson carry 31 states, popular vote, 3,597,070, Greeley and Brown, 6 states, popular vote, 2,834,079, Black and Russell, 5608 5 Nov. "

Great fire in Boston, loss $80,000,000 . . 9-10 Nov. "

Susan B Anthony and 14 other females prosecuted for illegal voting in Rochester, N Y . 18 Nov. "

Modoc war in California 29 Nov. "

Horace Greeley, born 1811, dies at Pleasantville, N Y, 29 Nov. "

Nicaragua expedition, in charge of commander E P. Lull, sails from the U. S (returns July, 1873) Dec. "

Third Session begins 2 Dec. "

President's annual message received " "

Resolutions of Mr Blaine adopted in the House, to investigate the accusation in the public press that members of the House had been bribed in behalf of the Union Pacific railroad by stock in the CREDIT MOBILIER of America, and Luke P Poland of Vt, Nathaniel P Banks of Mass, James B. Beck of Ky, William E Niblack of Ind, and George W McCrary of Ia., appointed the committee 2 Dec "

Edwin Forrest, the tragedian, born 1806, dies at Philadelphia . . 12 Dec. "

CRÉDIT MOBILIER investigation to be henceforth conducted in open session by resolution of the House, 6 Jan 1873

Resolution adopted by the House to investigate the relations of the Credit Mobilier and the Union Pacific railroad company to the government 6 Jan "

Committee appointed to investigate: J M Wilson, Ind, Samuel Shellabarger, O, Henry W Slocum, N Y., Thos. Swann, Md, and Geo F Hoar, Mass. 7 Jan. "
[This committee reported 20 Feb]

William M Tweed placed on trial 8 Jan. "

Act to abolish the grades of admiral and vice admiral in the U S navy; no future appointments to be made . . . 24 Jan "

Jury disagree in the Tweed trial 31 Jan "

Postal franking privilege abolished by act of Congress, 31 Jan "

"Trade dollar" ordered and silver demonetized by act passing the Senate 6 Feb and the House 7 Feb 1873

Electoral votes counted 12 Feb "
[Whole number of electors, 366, majority, 184. The electoral votes of Louisiana and Arkansas were not counted, and the 3 votes of Georgia, cast for Horace Greeley for president, were excluded Number of votes counted for president, 349, for vice-president, 352, distributed as follows For president, Ulysses S Grant, Ill, 286, B Gratz Brown, Mo, 18, Thomas A. Hendricks, Ind, 42, Charles J Jenkins, Ga, 2, David Davis, Ill, 1 For vice-president, Henry Wilson, Mass., 286, B Gratz Brown, Mo 47, Nathaniel P Banks, Mass., 1, George W Julian, Ind, 5, Alfred H Colquitt, Ga, 5, John M Palmer, Ill, 3, Thomas E Bramlette, Ky, 3, William S Groesbeck, O, 1, Willis B Machen, Ky, 1]

March 4, 1873, designated for extraordinary session of Senate by proclamation of president 21 Feb "

Alexander H Stephens elected to 43d Congress from Georgia 26 Feb "

Resolutions of the House censuring Oakes Ames of Mass, and James Brooks of N Y, for connection with CRÉDIT MOBILIER 27 Feb "

Act by which hereafter no Indian nation or tribe within the territory of the U S shall be acknowledged or recognized as an independent nation, tribe, or power with whom the U S may contract by treaty, 3 Mch "

Amendment to appropriation bill offered by B F Butler, fixing salary of the president of the U S at $50,000 per year, vice-president $10,000, and senators, representatives, and delegates, including those of the 42d Congress, $7500, besides travelling expenses (the "Salary Grab" bill) passed 3 Mch "

Act to establish 10 life-saving stations on the coast of Maine, New Hampshire, Massachusetts, Virginia, and North Carolina 3 Mch "

Oath of office administered to vice pres Wilson, 4 Mch "

Forty-second Congress adjourns " "

Senate convenes in special session " "

Pres. Grant reinaugurated . . " "

Twenty-second Administration—Republican. 4 Mch. 1873 to 3 Mch 1877.

Ulysses S Grant, Ill., president.
Henry Wilson, Mass, vice-president.

CABINET

Hamilton Fish, N Y, sec. of treas., continued
William A Richardson, Mass., sec. of treas, from 17 Mch 1873.
Benjamin H Bristow, Ky, sec of treas, from 4 June, 1874
Lot M Morrill, Me., sec of treas, from 7 July, 1876
Columbus Delano, O, sec of interior, continued.
Zachariah Chandler, Mich, sec of interior, from 19 Oct. 1875.
W. W. Belknap, Ia, sec of war, continued
Alphonso Taft, O, sec of war, from 8 Mch 1876
James D Cameron, Pa, sec of war, from 22 May, 1876
George M. Robeson, N J, sec of navy, continued
John A J. Creswell, Md, postmaster-gen, continued
James W Marshall, Va, postmaster-gen, from 7 July, 1874.
Marshall Jewell, Conn, postmaster-gen, from 24 Aug 1874
James N Tyner, Ind, postmaster-gen, from 12 July, 1876.
George H Williams, Or, attorney-gen, continued
Edwards Pierrepont, N. Y, attorney-gen, from 26 Apr 1875.
Alphonso Taft, O., attorney-gen, from 22 May, 1876.

Special session of Senate adjourns 26 Mch 1873

White Star steamship *Atlantic* wrecked on Marr's Rock, off Nova Scotia, 547 lives lost 1 Apr "

Massacre by Indians under capt Jack of gen. Canby, in the lava beds near fort Klamath, Cal 11 Apr. "

James Brooks of N Y, born 1810, dies at Washington . 30 Apr. "

Rescue of 19 persons (late of the *Polaris*) from floating ice in Baffin's bay, by the sealing-vessel *Tigress*, capt. Bartlett of Conception bay, Newfoundland, 30 Apr. "

One-cent postal-cards issued by the U. S. government, 1 May, 1873
National Cheap Transportation Association organized in New York........................6 May, "
Chief-justice Salmon P. Chase, born 1808, dies in New York city..........................7 May, "
Oakes Ames, member of Congress from Mass., "father of the Crédit Mobilier," born 1804, dies.....8 May, "
President's proclamation dispersing disorderly bands in Louisiana..........................22 May, "
U. S. Agricultural congress, organized in St. Louis, 1872, meets at Indianapolis, Ind.........28 May, "
Nearly all the Modocs surrender, 22 May; capt. Jack and the remainder surrender.............1 June, "
Susan B. Anthony fined $100 for illegal voting at Rochester..........................18 June, "
Ravenscraig of Kirkcaldy, Scotland, in 75° 38′ N. lat., and 65° 35′ W. lon., rescues the remainder of the crew of the *Polaris*..................23 June, "
Hiram Powers, sculptor, born 1805, dies at Florence, Italy..............................27 June, "
Centennial exposition at Philadelphia, to open 19 Apr. 1876, and close 19 Oct. following, by proclamation of president............................3 July, "
Site of Exposition buildings in Fairmount park, Philadelphia, transferred to the Centennial commission, 4 July, "
England pays the Alabama award ($15,500,000), 5 Sept. "
Panic begins in the Stock exchange, New York city, 19 Sept. "
New York Stock exchange closed Sept. 20; reopens, 30 Sept. "
Execution of capt. Jack and other Modocs.....3 Oct. "
Evangelical Alliance of the World holds a session in New York..........................3–11 Oct. "
Virginius, an American schooner, suspected of conveying men and arms from New York to the insurgents in Cuba, is captured by the Spanish gun-boat *Tornado*, and conveyed to Cuba.............31 Oct. "
Above 90 insurgents and sailors tried; many insurgents and 6 British and 30 Americans shot.4–7 Nov. "
William M. Tweed convicted (NEW YORK)...19 Nov. "
Hoosac tunnel completed (TUNNEL).........27 Nov. "

Forty-third Congress, *First Session*, opens.....1 Dec. "
Vote for speaker of the House: James G. Blaine, 189; Fernando Wood, 76; S. S. Cox, 2; Hiester Clymer, 1; Alexander H. Stephens, 1.................1 Dec. "
Matthew H. Carpenter of Wis. chosen president *pro tem.* of Senate........................11 Dec. "
Prof. Louis J. R. Agassiz, scientist, born 1807, dies at Cambridge, Mass.......................14 Dec. "
Virginius surrendered to the U. S. by Spain; she founders at sea off cape Fear while on her way to New York..........................19 Dec. "
Ex-mayor Hall of New York acquitted......24 Dec. "
Survivors of the *Virginius* massacre, 102, surrendered to the U. S. authorities at Santiago de Cuba, 18 Dec., reach New York on the *Juniata*..........28 Dec. "
Leavenworth, Kan., selected as the site for the National Military prison.......................29 Dec. "
Women's Temperance crusade begins at Hillsborough, O.......................................Dec. "
Chang and Eng, the Siamese twins, born in Siam, 15 Apr. 1811, came to the U. S. 1828, die at their home near Salisbury, N. C., Eng surviving Chang about 2 hours..............................17 Jan. 1874
Act of 3 Mch. 1873 ("Salary Grab" bill), repealed, except as to salaries of the president and justices of the Supreme court.......................20 Jan. "
Morrison R. Waite appointed and confirmed chief-justice of the Supreme court...............21 Jan. "
Act authorizing coinage at the mint of coins for foreign nations..........................29 Jan. "
Act providing for busts of chief-justices Taney and Chase, to be placed in the Supreme Court room of the U. S...........................29 Jan. "

UNI

Ex-pres. Millard Fillmore, born 1800, dies at Buffalo, N. Y...............................8 Mch. 1874
Charles Sumner, born 1811, dies at Washington, D. C., 11 Mch. "
Bill to inflate the currency, fixing the maximum limit at $400,000,000, passed by Senate, 6 Apr., by 29 to 24, and House, 14 Apr., by 140 to 102, vetoed.22 Apr. "
Condition and status of the fur trade in Alaska to be investigated by special government agent, by act, 22 Apr. "
Proclamation of president commanding turbulent and disorderly gatherings in Arkansas to disperse, 15 May, "
Reservoir dam on Mill river, Mass., bursts: loss of property $1,500,000; of life nearly 200 persons, 16 May, "
W. A. Richardson, sec. of the treasury, resigns.1 June, "
President to invite foreign governments to take part in the Centennial Exhibition, by act........5 June, "
Territorial government for the District of Columbia abolished, and a board of 3 governing regents provided for, by act of....................20 June, "
Congress appropriates $300 or less to purchase and restore to the family of Lafayette the watch presented him by gen. Washington, lost during his visit to the U. S. in 1825, and since found........22 June, "
"Hazing" at the Annapolis Naval academy to be investigated by court-martial, and punished by dismissal, by act........................23 June, "
Court of Commissioners of Alabama claims constituted by act of Congress...................23 June, "
Law to punish by imprisonment and fine the bringing into the U. S., and selling or holding in involuntary servitude inveigled or kidnapped foreigners, 23 June, "
First Session adjourns.................... " "
Postmaster-gen. A. J. Creswell resigns......24 June, "
Great distress in Minnesota, Kansas, and Nebraska by the grasshopper plague..............July–Oct. "
Mysterious abduction of Charley Ross, aged 4 years, from his father's home in Germantown, Pa. (never found)........................1 July, "
Illinois and St. Louis railroad bridge over the Mississippi at St. Louis opened...............4 July, "
Rev. Henry Ward Beecher demands an investigation of Theodore Tilton's charges against him...7 July, "
Sixteen negroes forcibly taken out of the Trenton, Tenn., jail by disguised men and shot...........26 Aug. "
Rev. H. W. Beecher acquitted by a committee of his church...............................28 Aug. "
Headquarters of the U. S. army removed to St. Louis, 1 Oct. "
Lincoln monument at Springfield, Ill., dedicated, 15 Oct. "
National Woman's Christian Temperance Union organized at Cleveland, O...................19 Nov. "
Second Session opens.......................7 Dec. "
President's message received.............. " "
Race riot at Vicksburg, Miss.; 75 negroes killed, " "
Death of hon. Ezra Cornell, born 1807, occurs at Ithaca, N. Y..................................9 Dec. "
Official reception given king Kalakaua of the Hawaiian islands by Congress...................18 Dec. "
President by proclamation orders turbulent and disorderly gatherings in Mississippi to disperse..21 Dec. "
Gerrit Smith, philanthropist, born 1797, dies at New York city...........................28 Dec. "
Sen. Sherman's bill for resumption of specie payment, 1 Jan. 1879, approved, with special message.14 Jan. 1875
President calls the Senate for 5 Mch.........17 Feb. "
Indemnity from the Spanish government for families of men shot in the *Virginius* massacre fixed at $80,000.................................27 Feb. "
Civil Rights bill, to enforce equal enjoyment of inns, public conveyances, theatres, etc., approved..1 Mch. "
Contract with James B. Eads for jetty-work at the mouth of the Mississippi river, by act of....3 Mch. "
Enabling act for Colorado passed........... " "
Supplementary Immigration act passed........ " "
Act authorizing twenty-cent pieces of silver... " "
Part of island of Mackinac made a national park, by act of...................................3 Mch. "

rty-third Congress adjourns................4 Mch. 1875
Special session of Senate convenes, T. W. Ferry president *pro tem.*.........................5 Mch. "
Gold discovered in Deadwood and Whitewood gulches, S. Dakota..........................14 Mch. "
Special session of Senate adjourns..........24 Mch. "
Wheeler adjustment of Louisiana state government (LOUISIANA, 1871-75)..................14 Apr. "
Centenary of the battle of Lexington........19 Apr. "
Archbishop John McCloskey invested with the biretta of a cardinal of the Roman Catholic church, in St. Patrick's cathedral, N. Y...............27 Apr. "
Whiskey frauds in western states, causing a loss to the U. S. of $1,650,000 in revenue in 10 months, exposed..............................1 May, "
Secret investigation of the Whiskey ring by sec. Bristow, aided by Myron Colony, leads to seizure of 16 distilleries and many rectifying-houses in St. Louis, Milwaukee, and Chicago..........10 May, "
George H. Williams, attorney-general, resigns, 22 Apr., to take effect.......................15 May, "
John C. Breckinridge, born 1821, dies at Lexington, Ky..................................17 May, "
Pres. Grant's letter on the "Third term" appears, 29 May, "
Centenary of the battle of Bunker Hill..... 17 June, "
Jury in the case of Tilton *vs.* Beecher disagree and are discharged..........................2 July, "
Andrew Johnson, born 1808, dies near Jonesborough Tenn..................................31 July, "
Hon. Horace Binney, born 1780, graduate of Harvard, 1797, and oldest member of Philadelphia bar, dies at Philadelphia.......................12 Aug. "
Com. Perry's flag-ship, the *Lawrence*, sunk for preservation in Misery bay, lake Erie, in July, 1815, is raised for transportation to the Centennial exposition...............................14 Sept. "
Democratic conventions of New York declare for specie resumption.......................16 Sept. "
Columbus Delano, secretary of the interior, resigns 5 July; resignation accepted...........22 Sept. "
Pres. Grant speaks against sectarian schools in Des Moines, Ia..........................29 Sept. "
Steamship *Pacific* founders between San Francisco and Portland; 200 lives lost..................4 Nov. "
Henry Wilson, vice-president, born 1812, dies at Washington, D. C..........................22 Nov. "
Thomas W. Ferry of Mich., president *pro tem.* of the Senate, becomes acting vice-president.....22 Nov. "
William B. Astor, born 1792, dies in New York, 24 Nov. "

rty-fourth Congress, First Session, meets ....6 Dec. "
Democratic majority in the House of Representatives for the first time in 15 years; Michael C. Kerr chosen speaker by 173 to 106 for James G. Blaine, 6 Dec. "
Seventh annual message of pres. Grant advocates unsectarian and compulsory education........7 Dec. "
Extensive forgeries of E. D. Winslow of Boston discovered, and he flees the country.........25 Jan. 1876
Reverdy Johnson, born 1796, dies at Annapolis, Md., 10 Feb. "
Congress appropriates $1,500,000 to complete Centennial buildings, etc., at Philadelphia ....16 Feb. "
Charlotte Cushman, born 1816, dies at Boston, Mass., 18 Feb. "
W. W. Belknap, secretary of war, resigns; the House, by resolution, impeaches him............2 Mch. "
Articles of impeachment presented in Senate..4 Apr. "
Charles A. Dana, appointed minister to Great Britain, rejected by the Senate.................. 5 Apr. "
Alexander T. Stewart, born in Belfast, Ireland, 1803, dies at New York.....................10 Apr. "
Statue of Abraham Lincoln, from contributions of freedmen, unveiled in Lincoln park, Washington (SCULPTURE, Ward, John Q. A.).........14 Apr. "
Pres. Grant vetoes Senate bill to reduce his salary after 4 Mch. 1877, from $50,000 to $25,000......19 Apr. "
Message from pres. Grant justifying his absence from the seat of government by precedents......4 May, 1876
Dom Pedro II., emperor of Brazil, with the empress Theresa, arrives in New York 15 Apr., and is presented to pres. Grant....................7 May, "
Centennial exposition at Fairmount park, Philadelphia, opened by pres. Grant and dom Pedro, 10 May, "
Prohibition convention at Cleveland, O., nominates gen. Green Clay Smith of Ky. for president, and G. T. Stewart of O. for vice-president........17 May, "
National Greenback convention at Indianapolis, Ind., nominates Peter Cooper of N. Y. for president; U. S. sen. Newton Booth, nominated for vice-president, declines, and Samuel F. Cary of O. substituted, 18 May, "
Alphonso Taft, secretary of war, resigns, being appointed attorney-general.................22 May, "
Peter Cooper's letter of acceptance..........31 May, "
Edwards Pierrepont, attorney-general, resigns, 1 June, "
Site for observatory of Mount Hamilton, Santa Clara county, Cal., granted to the trustees of Lick observatory by Congress....................7 June, "
Ezra D. Winslow, the American forger, surrendered by Great Britain (EXTRADITION)...........15 June, "
Republican National convention meets at Cincinnati, O., 14 June. Edward McPherson of Pa. permanent president. On the 16th, 9 nominations for president are made; votes necessary to a choice, 378; on the 1st ballot, Rutherford B. Hayes has 61; Jas. G. Blaine, 285; B. H. Bristow, 113; on the 7th ballot, Hayes, 384; Blaine, 351; Bristow, 21; for vice-president, William A. Wheeler of N. Y. unanimously elected on first ballot..................16 June, "
B. H. Bristow, sec. of the treasury, resigns...20 June, "
Massacre of gen. George A. Custer and 276 men, by Indians under Sitting Bull, near the Little Big Horn river, Montana.......................25 June, "
President suggests public religious services on 4 July, 1876, by proclamation.................26 June, "
Democratic National convention at St. Louis, gen. John A. McClernand permanent president, 27 June; six nominations for president made; 1st ballot gives Samuel J. Tilden of N. Y. 417, Thomas A. Hendricks of Ind. 140; on the 2d ballot Tilden receives 535 votes, and his nomination made unanimous, 28 June; Thomas A. Hendricks nominated for vice-president by acclamation................29 June, "
Centenary of American independence........4 July, "
R. B. Hayes accepts Republican nomination...8 July, "
Shooting of 5 negro militiamen by whites at Hamburg (SOUTH CAROLINA)................9 July, "
Postmaster-general Jewell resigns..........11 July, "
W. A. Wheeler's letter of acceptance........15 July, "
Congress authorizes the minting of not less than $10,000,000 in silver coin to exchange for legal-tender notes, and declares the trade dollar no longer a legal tender.........................22 July, "
Hendricks's letter of acceptance dated.......24 July, "
Tilden's letter of acceptance dated..........31 July, "
W. W. Belknap acquitted by the Senate; vote on first article, 35 guilty, 25 not guilty.............1 Aug. "
Colorado, the 38th state in order, admitted by act of 3 Mch. 1875, and by proclamation of president, 1 Aug. "
Congress appropriates $200,000 to complete the Washington monument.......................2 Aug. "
First Session adjourns......................15 Aug. "
Hon. M. C. Kerr, speaker of House of Representatives, born 1827, dies at Rockbridge Alum springs, Va., 19 Aug. "
Bronze statue of Lafayette, the gift of the French republic to New York city, is unveiled.......6 Sept. "
Hallet's Point reef, "Hell gate," blown up...24 Sept. "
Gen. Braxton Bragg, born about 1815, dies at Galveston, Tex............................27 Sept. "
By proclamation pres. Grant commands disorderly and turbulent gatherings in South Carolina to disperse, 17 Oct. "

Popular vote at presidential election Hayes, Republican 4,033,295 Tilden, Democratic 4,284,265. Cooper, Greenback, 81,737, Smith, Prohibition, 9522, 7 Nov 1876
International exhibition at Philadelphia closes, 10 Nov "
Second Session meets, Thomas W Ferry presiding in the Senate 4 Dec. "
In the House, Samuel J Randall is elected speaker by 162 to 82 for James A Garfield 4 Dec "
Pres Grant's 8th annual message 5 Dec "
Brooklyn theatre burned during a performance of "The Two Orphans," and 295 lives lost 5 Dec "
First incineration in the U S. of body of baron De Palm, at the crematory in Washington, Pa 6 Dec "
Returning-boards give Hayes 185 electoral votes, Tilden 184, election disputed (the country in great excitement till the following March) 6 Dec "
Com Cornelius Vanderbilt, born 1794, dies at New York, 4 Jan. 1877
Two governors, Nicholls (Dem) and Packard (Rep), inaugurated in LOUISIANA 8 Jan "
Joint congressional committee agrees upon a plan for counting the electoral votes 17 Jan "
Act passed by Senate, 25 Jan, by 47 to 17, and by House, 26 Jan, by 191 to 86, provides for an electoral commission of 5 members of each House, elected *viva-voce* on the Tuesday before the first Thursday in Feb 1877, with 4 associate justices of the Supreme court from the 1st, 3d, 8th, and 9th circuits, together with a 5th associate justice selected by the other 4, the commission not to be dissolved when organized, and no withdrawal of members permitted except by death or physical disability, approved 29 Jan "
Senate elects as members George F Edmunds, Oliver P Morton, Frederick T Frelinghuysen, Allen G Thurman, Thomas F Bayard, the House elects Henry B Payne, Eppa Hunton, Josiah G Abbot, James A Garfield, George F Hoar, the justices of the Supreme court designated are Nathan Clifford, Samuel F Miller, Stephen J Field, and William Strong, and select Joseph R Bradley as the 5th, in all 8 Republicans, 7 Democrats 30 Jan "
Three certificates from Florida referred to the Electoral commission, and the vote awarded to the Republicans by 8 to 7 9 Feb "
Prof A Graham Bell exhibits his TELEPHONE at Salem, Mass . 12 Feb "
Commission awards the electoral vote of Louisiana to the Republicans by vote 8 to 7 16 Feb "
Contested vote of Oregon counted for the Republicans by the commission, 8 to 7 23 Feb "
Political disabilities of Joseph E Johnston of Va, under the XIV th Amendment, removed by act of, 23 Feb "
Sen Francis Kernan of N Y substituted on Electoral commission for sen. Thurman, physically unable to serve 26 Feb "
Contested vote of South Carolina awarded to Republicans by Electoral commission, 8 to 7 27 Feb "
Election of R B Hayes as president and William A Wheeler as vice-president confirmed, and joint meeting of 2 Houses of Congress dissolves at 4 10 A M, 2 Mch "
Act to remove political disabilities of John S Marmaduke approved 2 Mch "
President calls special session of the Senate for 5 Mch 1877 . 2 Mch "
House of Representatives resolves that Samuel J Tilden and Thomas A. Hendricks received 196 electoral votes for president and vice-president, and were elected, 136 yeas, 88 nays, 66 not voting 3 Mch "
R B Hayes privately takes oath of office as president, 7.05 P M., Saturday, 3 Mch. "
Forty-fourth Congress adjourns . 4 Mch. "
R. B Hayes inaugurated and publicly takes the oath of office 5 Mch. "
Special session of Senate convenes, vice-president Wheeler sworn in . . 5 Mch "

Twenty-third Administration — Republican. 4 Mch. 1877 to 3 Mch 1881

Rutherford B. Hayes, O, president
William A Wheeler, N Y, vice-president.

CABINET

William M Evarts N Y, sec of state, from 12 Mch 1877.
John Sherman, O, sec of treas, from 12 Mch 1877.
George W McCrary, Ia, sec of war, from 12 Mch 1877.
Alexander Ramsey, Minn, sec of war, from 10 Dec 1879.
Richard W Thompson, Ind, sec of navy, from 12 Mch 1877.
Nathan Goff, jr, W Va, sec of navy, from 6 Jan 1881.
Carl Schurz, Mo, sec of interior, from 12 Mch 1877.
David McK Key, Tenn, postmaster-gen, from 12 Mch 1877.
Horace Maynard, Tenn, postmaster-gen, from 2 June, 1880
Charles Devens, Mass., attorney gen, from 12 Mch 1877

Special session of Senate adjourns 17 Mch 1877
John D Lee, convicted of complicity in the Mountain Meadow massacre, executed (MASSACRES, U S, UTAH) 23 Mch "
Packard legislature in LOUISIANA breaks up 21 Apr "
Forty-fourth Congress adjourning without making the usual appropriations for the army for the year ending 30 June, 1878, the president calls on the 45th Congress to meet 15 Oct 5 May, "
Ex-pres Grant leaves Philadelphia for an extended European tour 17 May, "
John L Motley, historian, born 1814, dies at Dorsetshire, Engl 29 May, "
Ten MOLLY MAGUIRES hung, 6 at Pottsville and 4 at Mauch Chunk, Pa 21 June, "
Civil-service order issued by pres Hayes "No officer should be required or permitted to take part in the management of political organizations or election campaigns" 22 June, "
Strike on the Baltimore and Ohio railroad begins at Martinsburg, W Va (MARYLAND, PENNSYLVANIA, WEST VIRGINIA, and other states) 16 July, "
Proclamations of president against domestic violence in West Virginia (dated 18 July), in Maryland (21 July), and Pennsylvania . 23 July, "
Two satellites of Mars discovered by prof Asaph Hall of the U S nights of 11 and 17 Aug "
Armed band of Mexican outlaws forcibly release 2 notorious criminals, Esproneda and Garza, from jail in Rio Grande City, Tex, escaping to Mexico, 12 Aug "
Brigham Young, b 1801, dies at Salt Lake City, 29 Aug "
Monument to John Brown dedicated at Ossawatomie, Kan 30 Aug. "
War with the Nez Perces Indians breaks out in Idaho, 15 June, closed by surrender of Indians to col Miles, 30 Sept. "
***Forty-fifth Congress**, First Session* (extra), opens, 15 Oct. "
Samuel J Randall elected speaker of House by 149 to 132 for James A Garfield.
Pres Hayes's message 16 Oct. "
Bill for free coinage of the standard silver dollar as a legal tender introduced in the House by Mr Bland of Mo . . 5 Nov. "
Fisheries commission, under treaty of Washington, awards $5,500,000 in gold to be paid by the U S to Great Britain for fisheries privilege .. 23 Nov. "
U S sloop-of-war *Huron* wrecked in a gale off the coast of North Carolina near Oregon Inlet, over 100 lives lost .. .. . 24 Nov. "
First Session adjourns . . . . 3 Dec. "
Second Session meets " "
President's message recommends resumption of specie payment, 1 Jan 1879 . . 3 Dec. "
President and Mrs Hayes celebrate their silver wedding at the White House . . 31 Dec "
About 100 lives, chiefly railroad engineers and artisans bound for Brazil, lost by wreck of the steamship *Metropolis* near Kitty Hawk, N C ... 31 Jan 1878
Greenback National convention in Toledo, O, organizes a National Greenback party, with judge Francis W. Hughes as president. ... .. 22 Feb. "

BLAND SILVER BILL, as amended, passed over the president's veto 28 Feb 1878
Benjamin F Wade, born 1800, dies at Jefferson, O, 2 Mch "
American register to be issued to, and naval officers detailed for the *Jeannette* (fitted for a Polar expedition by James Gordon Bennett), by act of 18 Mch "
William M Tweed, born 1823, dies in Ludlow Street jail, New York 12 Apr "
Thomas W Ferry chosen president *pro tem* of the Senate 17 Apr. "
First train on the Gilbert Elevated railroad, New York, is run on Sixth avenue 29 Apr "
Coinage of 20 cent silver pieces stopped by act of 2 May, "
Prof Joseph Henry of the Smithsonian Institution, born 1797, dies 13 May, "
Select committee appointed in the House on motion of Mr Potter to investigate alleged frauds in the presidential election in Louisiana and Florida 17 May, "
Further retirement of legal-tender notes forbidden, the balance, $350,000,000, to be kept in circulation, by act of 31 May, "
Bill to repeal the Bankrupt law passed 7 June, "
Act providing for government of the District of Columbia by 3 commissioners 11 June, "
William Cullen Bryant, born 1794, dies in New York, 12 June, "
It is made unlawful to employ the army as a *posse comitatus* to execute laws except as expressly authorized by the Constitution 18 June, "
Act for additional life-saving stations and for organizing the LIFE-SAVING SERVICE 18 June, "
Act to relieve political disabilities of gen E Kirby Smith 19 June, "
Second Session adjourns 20 June, "
YELLOW-FEVER prevails in the southern states, beginning at New Orleans about 10 to 15 July, "
Gen B F Butler joins the Greenback party 10 Aug "
Repeal of Bankrupt laws of 1867 and 1874 takes effect, 1 Sept. "
First resident embassy of China to the U S, Chen Lan Pin, Yung Wing, and 36 others, arrive at Washington 20 Sept, and present their credentials 28 Sept "
Proclamation of president warning all persons to desist from violence in New Mexico 7 Oct. "
Remains of the late A. T. Stewart mysteriously stolen from the vault in St. Mark's churchyard, N Y, 7 Nov. "
Third Session meets, and pres. Hayes's second annual message received 2 Dec. "
Gold reaches par in Wall st, N Y, for the first time since 13 Jan 1862 17 Dec. "
Bayard Taylor, born 1825, dies at Berlin, Germany, 19 Dec. "
Government resumes specie payment 1 Jan 1879
Caleb Cushing, born 1800, dies at Newburyport, Mass, 2 Jan "
Potter committee of House of Representatives begins the "Cipher Despatches" inquiry at Washington, 21 Jan. "
Act to incorporate the Society of the Jesuit Fathers of New Mexico, passed by the legislative assembly of New Mexico over the governor's veto, 18 Jan, is declared void by act approved 3 Feb "
During the debate on the Chinese Immigration bill in the Senate, for the first time a colored senator, B. K. Bruce of Miss., occupies the chair 14 Feb. "
Women permitted to practise before the Supreme court by act of . 15 Feb. "
Sec of navy authorized to accept for a voyage of exploration by Behring's strait the ship *Jeannette*, tendered by James Gordon Bennett, by act of 27 Feb. "
Bill to restrict Chinese immigration passes the Senate 15 Feb the House 22 Feb, is vetoed 1 Mch. "
Congress appropriates $250,000 as a perpetual fund for the American Printing-house for the Blind at Louisville, Ky (incorporated 1858) 3 Mch. "
Act for taking the 10th and subsequent censuses, " "
National Board of Health of 7 members (one from a state), to be appointed by the president by act of, 3 Mch 1879
Forty-fifth Congress adjourns " "
Congress not having made the necessary appropriations, pres Hayes calls an extra session for 18 Mch, 4 Mch "

Forty-sixth Congress, *First Session* (extra), meets 18 Mch "
Samuel J Randall is chosen speaker of the House by 143 to 125 for James A Garfield 18 Mch. "
["For the first time since the Congress that was chosen with Mr Buchanan in 1856, the Democratic party was in control of both branches"—*Blaine's* "Twenty Years of Congress," vol ii p 642]
Negro exodus from southern states to Kansas, Mch-Apr "
Allen G Thurman of O elected president *pro tem* of the Senate 15 Apr "
Proclamation of president ordering the removal of squatters from Missouri and Texas settling in Oklahoma 26 Apr "
Army Appropriation bill vetoed 29 Apr "
William Lloyd Garrison, abolitionist, born 1804, dies in New York 24 May, "
Veto of the Legislative, Executive, and Judicial Appropriation bill 29 May, "
Joint resolution to erect a monument at the birthplace of George Washington 14 June, "
Second Army Appropriation bill approved by the president 23 June, "
Commission of 7 members for the improvement of Mississippi river to be appointed by the president, by act of 28 June, "
First Session adjourns 1 July, "
Yacht *Jeannette* sails from San Francisco for the Arctic regions (NORTHEAST AND NORTHWEST PASSAGES), 8 July, "
Confederate gen John B Hood, born 1831, dies at New Orleans 30 Aug "
Excitement over elections in MAINE begins 8 Sept. "
Indian massacre at the White River agency, Col, of N C Meeker and 12 others 29 Sept "
Henry C Carey, political economist, born 1793 dies at Philadelphia 13 Oct. "
French ocean cable landed at North Eastham, Mass., 15 Nov. "
Second Session meets, pres Hayes's third annual message received 1 Dec. "
Sec of war McCrary resigns 10 Dec. "
Parnell and Dillon arrive at New York 2 Jan, and Parnell addresses a large meeting 4 Jan 1880
Second proclamation of president to prevent settlement of Oklahoma 12 Feb. "
Ferdinand de Lesseps banqueted in New York, 1 Mch. "
Denis Kearney, sand-lots agitator of San Francisco, sentenced to 6 months' imprisonment and $1000 fine (CALIFORNIA) 15 Mch "
U S steamer *Constellation*, commissioned under act of 25 Feb 1880, to carry contributions for relief of suffering poor in Ireland, sails from New York, 30 Mch "
Allen G Thurman, elected president of the Senate *pro tem*, serving till 15 Apr 7 Apr "
Congress accepts from Thomas Jefferson Coolidge and others, of Mass., the desk used by Thomas Jefferson in writing the Declaration of Independence, to be deposited in the Department of State 28 Apr "
Pres Hayes authorized to accept the steamship *Gulnare* from H W. Howgate, and fit her up to establish a temporary station for Arctic scientific observation at some point north of 81°, or on or near the shore of Lady Franklin bay 1 May, "
Appropriation bill vetoed because of a clause modifying the election laws . . 4 May, "
Republican Anti-Third-Term convention held at St Louis, gen John B Henderson presiding 6 May, "
Allen G. Thurman chosen president *pro tem* of the Senate . . 6 May, "
Postmaster-gen. Key resigns. . . . . . May, "

Republican National convention meets at Chicago, 2 June, George F Hoar permanent president, 3 June, 14 nominations made for president On the 2d ballot James A Garfield's name appeared, with 1 vote. Until the 34th ballot the votes remained substantially unchanged, the 5 most important ballots are given

	1st.	2d	34th	35th	36th
James A Garfield		1	17	250	399
U S Grant	304	305	312	313	306
James G Blaine	284	282	275	57	42
John Sherman	93	94	107	99	3

Garfield nominated for president, and gen Chester A. Arthur of N Y on the 1st ballot, for vice-president, 7 June, 1880

Congress appropriates $100,000 or less to carry into effect its resolution of nearly 100 years previously (29 Oct 1781), to erect a marble column at Yorktown Va, "inscribed with a succinct narrative of the surrender of earl Cornwallis to his excellency gen Washington" 7 June, "

Act to pay the Oneida Historical Society $4100, according to resolution of the Continental Congress, 4 Oct 1777, to erect a monument to brig-gen Herkimer, killed at the battle of Oriskany 8 June, "

Greenback National convention meets at Chicago, 9 June, Richard Trevellick of Mich president. After an informal ballot, James B Weaver of Ia. receives the entire vote (718) for president, and B J Chambers of Tex 403 for vice-president to 311 for gen A M West of Miss 11 June, "

Second Session adjourns 16 June, "

Neal Dow of Me nominated for president, and A M. Thompson of O for vice-president, by Prohibition National convention at Cleveland, O. . 17 June, "

Samuel J Tilden declines to be a candidate for president, by letter of 18 June, "

Democratic National convention meets in Cincinnati, 22 June, John W Stevenson of Ky chosen permanent president on the 1st ballot Winfield S Hancock has 171 and Thomas F Bayard 153½ out of 728½ cast, 23 June, 2d ballot Hancock 320, Samuel J Randall 128½, Bayard 113, and nomination of Hancock made unanimous For vice-president, William H English of Indiana nominated by acclamation, 24 June, "

Gen Weaver accepts Greenback nomination 3 July, "

Gen Garfield accepts Republican nomination 12 July, "

Steamer *Dessong*, with Egyptian obelisk "Cleopatra's Needle," arrives in NEW YORK . 20 July, "

Neal Dow accepts Prohibition nomination .. " "

Gen Hancock accepts Democratic nomination, 29 July, "

Dr. Henry S Tanner of Minneapolis, Minn, completes at New York a fast of 40 days, living upon water alone . .. . .7 Aug "

International sheep-and-wool show held at Philadelphia, Pa Sept. "

Return of the Schwatka Arctic Exploration expedition to New York 23 Sept. "

Arctic steamer *Gulnare* returns to Washington, 10 Oct. "

Publication of forged letters on the Chinese question (MOREY LETTERS) attributed to gen Garfield, addressed to a mythical person, H L Morey of Lynn, 20 Oct "

Popular vote at presidential election James A Garfield, Republican, 4,450,921, Winfield S Hancock, Democrat, 4,447,888, James B Weaver, Greenback, 307,740, Neal Dow, Prohibition, 10,305 2 Nov. "

Lucretia Mott, born 1793, dies in Montgomery county, Pa . .. . . 11 Nov. "

Electoral votes of states, except Georgia, cast 6 Dec. "

Third Session meets . " "

Samuel J Randall speaker of House

President Hayes's 4th annual message presented " "

Electoral vote of Georgia, 11 for Hancock and English, cast . . .. 8 Dec. "

R. W. Thompson, secretary of navy, resigns 15 Dec. "

Nearly 1 mile of Broadway, N Y, is lighted by electricity, Brush system ....20 Dec. "

UNI

International Sanitary Conference, called by resolution of Congress, 14 May, 1880, meets at Washington, D C. 5 Jan 1881

"Cleopatra's Needle" set up in Central park, N Y, 22 Jan. "

Electoral votes counted in Congress, the reading of the formal parts of the certificates being omitted for Garfield and Arthur, Republicans, 214, for Hancock and English, Democrats, with Georgia, 155, without, 144 Garfield and Arthur declared elected, 9 Feb. "

Pres Hayes calls the Senate in extra session for 4 Mch 1881 28 Feb "

President vetoes the "Funding act of 1881" 3 Mch. "

Forty-sixth Congress adjourns " "

Special session of Senate convenes, Chester A Arthur presiding 4 Mch "

James A Garfield inaugurated president " "

Twenty-fourth Administration—Republican. 4 Mch. 1881 to 3 Mch 1885

James A. Garfield, O, president.
Chester A Arthur, N Y, vice-president.

CABINET

James G Blaine, Me, sec of state, from 5 Mch 1881
William Windom Minn, sec of treas, from 5 Mch 1881
Samuel J Kirkwood, Ia., sec. of interior, from 5 Mch 1881.
Robert T Lincoln, Ill, sec of war, from 5 Mch 1881
William H Hunt, La, sec of navy, from 5 Mch 1881.
Thomas L James, N. Y, postmaster-gen, from 5 Mch 1881.
Wayne McVeagh, Pa, attorney-gen, from 5 Mch 1881.

Postmaster-gen James presents to president the protest of himself, vice-pres Arthur, and U S sens. Conkling and Platt of N Y against the removal of gen Merritt from the collectorship at New York, and appointment of Mr Robertson, without consulting said senators 28 Mch 1881

Investigation of alleged "Star Route" frauds leads to resignation of second assistant postmaster-general Thomas A Brady 20 Apr. "

Vinnie Ream-Hoxie's bronze statue of adm. Farragut unveiled at Washington, D C . 25 Apr "

Sens Conkling and Platt of N Y resign 16 May, "

Special session of Senate adjourns *sine die* 20 May, "

Arctic steamer *Jeannette*, crushed in the ice in lat. 77° N., lon 157° W, is abandoned and sinks (NORTHEAST AND NORTHWEST PASSAGES) . 12 June, "

Steam-whaler *Rodgers* despatched from San Francisco by the Navy department in search of the *Jeannette*, 15 June, "

Sec. Blaine writes to American ministers at principal European courts that any movement to jointly guarantee the neutrality of the interoceanic canal at Panama would be regarded by the U S as an uncalled-for interference 24 June, "

American Association of the Red Cross, organized 9 June, with miss Clara Barton as president, incorporated (RED CROSS) 1 July, "

Pres Garfield shot by Charles Jules Guiteau in the Baltimore and Potomac railroad station at Washington, D C., . . 2 July, "

Lieut Adolphus W. Greely, with a party of 25 in all, sails from St John's, Newfoundland, in the *Proteus* to establish 1 of 13 circumpolar stations for scientific purposes in accordance with European plans (ABSTINENCE, NORTHEAST AND NORTHWEST PASSAGES) . . . .. . 7 July, "

Warner Miller of N Y elected to Senate to succeed Platt . . . 16 July, "

Elbridge G. Lapham of N Y elected to Senate to succeed Conkling 22 July, "

Nathan Clifford, U.S Supreme court judge, born 1803, dies at Cornish, Me . ... 25 July "

Wrangell island or land, off the Siberian coast, taken possession of in name of the U S. by capt Hooper and Mr Reynolds of the revenue cutter *Corwin*, 12 Aug. "

Forest fires in Huron and Sanilac counties, Mich.,

spread over 1800 sq. miles, making 2900 families homeless, and destroying 138 lives. .... Sept. 1881

'res. Garfield removed from Washington to the Francklyn cottage, Elberon, N. J .... 6 Sept. "

ien. Ambrose E. Burnside, born 1824, dies at Bristol, R. I .... 13 Sept. "

'res. Garfield dies 10.35 P.M. .... 19 Sept. "

'ice-pres. Arthur sworn as president at his residence in New York city between 2 and 3 o'clock A.M. by judge John R. Brady .... 20 Sept. "

'res. Arthur formally takes the oath of office in Washington .... 22 Sept. "

PRES. ARTHUR'S CABINET.

ies G. Blaine, Me., sec. of state, continued.
'. Frelinghuysen, N. J., sec. of state, from 12 Dec. 1881.
'liam Windom, Minn., sec. of treas., continued.
rles J. Folger, N. Y., sec. of treas., from 27 Oct. 1881.
lter Q. Gresham, Ind., sec. of treas., from 24 Sept. 1884.
h McCulloch, Ind., sec. of treas., from 28 Oct. 1884.
uel J. Kirkwood, Ia., sec. of interior, continued.
ry M. Teller, Col., sec. of interior, from 6 Apr. 1882.
ert T. Lincoln, Ill., sec. of war, continued.
'liam H. Hunt, La., sec. of navy, continued.
'liam E. Chandler, N. H., sec. of navy, from 1 Apr. 1882.
mas L. James, N. Y., postmaster-gen., continued.
othy O. Howe, Wis., postmaster-gen. from 20 Dec. 1881.
lter Q. Gresham, Ind., postmaster-gen., from 3 Apr. 1883.
nk Hatton, Ia., postmaster-gen., from 14 Oct. 1884.
yne McVeagh, Pa., attorney-gen., continued.
jamin H. Brewster, Pa., attorney-gen., from 19 Dec. 1881.

'resident calls the Senate in extra session for 10 Oct., 23 Sept. 1881

uneral train, bearing the remains of pres. Garfield, leaves Washington for Cleveland, O .... 23 Sept. "

)bsequies of pres. Garfield at Cleveland; day of mourning observed throughout the country under proclamation of president, dated 22 Sept .... 26 Sept. "

nternational Cotton exposition opens at Atlanta, Ga., 5 Oct. "

pecial session of Senate convenes .... 10 Oct. "

'homas F. Bayard elected president *pro tem.* of Senate, 10 Oct. "

. G. Holland, poet and author, born 1819, dies at New York city .... 12 Oct. "

'avid Davis elected president *pro tem.* of Senate, 13 Oct. "

'ne hundredth anniversary of the surrender of lord Cornwallis celebrated at Yorktown, Va ..... 19 Oct. "

pecial session of Senate adjourns .... 25 Oct. "

ec. of treas. Windom resigns .... 14 Nov. "

esignation of attorney-gen. McVeagh accepted, " "

'rial of Charles J. Guiteau for murder begins at Washington .... 14 Nov. "

ty-seventh Congress, First Session, opens ... 5 Dec. "

'avid Davis presiding in Senate; Joseph Warren Keifer of O. elected speaker by 148 votes to 129 for Samuel J. Randall of Pa .... 5 Dec. "

'res. Arthur's annual message .... 6 Dec. "

ec. of state Blaine resigns .... 15 Dec. "

'r. Isaac I. Hayes, Arctic explorer, born 1832, dies in New York city .... 17 Dec. "

'ranking privilege granted to Lucretia, widow of James A. Garfield, by act of .... 20 Dec. "

'xodus of colored people from Edgefield county, S. C., 24–31 Dec. "

'ostmaster-gen. James surrenders his department to his successor .... 6 Jan. 1882

'ongress tenders the thanks of the U. S. to the khedive of Egypt for the obelisk known as "Cleopatra's Needle" .... 12 Jan. "

'uiteau convicted of murder .... 25 Jan. "

.ct granting an additional pension to Mary, widow of Abraham Lincoln .... 2 Feb. "

'uiteau sentenced to be hanged 30 June ...... 4 Feb. "

'ational memorial services in the hall of House of Representatives; James G. Blaine delivers a eulogy upon the late pres. Garfield .... 27 Feb. "

Act passed for the apportionment, after 3 Mch. 1883, of representation by the census of 1880, increasing the number of representatives to 325 .... 28 Feb. 1882

Floods in the Mississippi valley .... Feb.–Mch. "

In the Criminal court of the District of Columbia John W. Dorsey, John M. Peck, John R. Miner, Stephen W. Dorsey, M. C. Rerdell, Thomas J. Brady, William H. Turner, and J. L. Sanderson are indicted for frauds and conspiracy to defraud the government in bids for mail service on STAR ROUTES ...... 4 Mch. "

Edmunds's law, excluding bigamists and polygamists in the territories from voting or holding office, passed, 22 Mch. "

Engineer Melville finds the bodies of DeLong and 11 of his men, near the mouth of the river Lena, Siberia, 23 Mch. "

Henry W. Longfellow, born 1807, dies at Cambridge, Mass .... 24 Mch. "

Northern boundary of Nebraska extended to 43d parallel by act of .... 28 Mch. "

Annual pension of $5000 each granted to widows of James A. Garfield, James K. Polk, and John Tyler, by act of .... 31 Mch. "

Jesse James, notorious desperado, killed at St. Joseph, Mo., by the Ford brothers .... 3 Apr. "

Pres. Arthur vetoes bill restricting Chinese immigration for 20 years .... 4 Apr. "

Sec. of the interior Kirkwood resigns .... Apr. "

Sec. of the navy Hunt resigns .... " "

Elephant "Jumbo" arrives in New York from England .... 9 Apr. "

Congress appropriates $10,000 for a monument at the grave of Thomas Jefferson at Monticello, Va., 18 Apr. "

Ralph Waldo Emerson, b. 1803, dies at Concord, Mass., 27 Apr. "

Proclamation of president against violence in Arizona, referring to the "cowboys" .... 3 May, "

Pres. Arthur remits the unexecuted part of the sentence disqualifying gen. Fitz-John Porter .. 4 May, "

Immigration of Chinese laborers to the U. S. suspended for 10 years, and admission of Chinese to citizenship prohibited by act of .... 6 May, "

Lt. James B. Lockwood and sergeant Brainard of the Greely expedition reach 83° 23′ 8″ N. lat. (NORTH-EAST AND NORTHWEST PASSAGES) .... 13 May, "

Bill to appoint a Tariff commission approved, 15 May, "

New indictment in the Star-route trial presented, with Sanderson's name omitted .... 20 May, "

Lieut. Danenhower, dr. Newcomb, Cole, and Long Sing, part of the survivors of the *Jeannette*, arrive in New York .... 28 May, "

Deadlock in the House of Representatives begins 25 May, over contested election of E. M. Mackey of S. C. *vs.* Samuel Dibble; the former finally seated, 31 May, "

New STAR-ROUTE trial begins .... 1 June, "

Iron-workers' strike begins .... " "

Guiteau executed at Washington, D. C ...... 30 June, "

Tariff commission meets at Washington; John L. Hayes, president .... 6 July, "

Mrs. Lincoln, widow of pres. Lincoln, dies at Springfield, Ill .... 16 July, "

Veto of River and Harbor Appropriation bill .. 1 Aug. "

[Extract from the president's veto message: "The appropriations for river and harbor improvements have, under the influences to which I have alluded, increased out of proportion to the progress of the country, great as it has been. In 1870 the aggregate appropriations for this purpose were $3,975,900; 1875, $6,648,517; 1880, $8,976,500; 1881, $11,451,000; while the present act appropriates $18,743,875." RIVER AND HARBOR BILLS.]

River and Harbor Appropriation bill passed over the veto .... 2 Aug. "

President authorized to call an international conference at Washington, to fix on a common prime meridian for the world .... 3 Aug. "

First Session adjourns .... 8 Aug. "

National Mining and Industrial exposition held at Denver, Col Aug. 1882
Verdict in Star-route case Peck and Turner not guilty, Miner and Rerdell guilty, jury disagree on the others 11 Sept. "
Engineer G W Melville of the *Jeannette* and seamen William Noros and William Ninderman arrive at New York . 13 Sept "
Iron-workers' strike ended . . 20 Sept. "
Bi-centennial of the landing of William Penn celebrated in Philadelphia 22-27 Oct. "
Thurlow Weed, politician and journalist, born 1798, dies, 22 Nov "
Second Session convenes 4 Dec. "
David Davis presiding in Senate
Tariff commission submits an exhaustive report, " "
New trial of Star-route cases begins " "
Newhall House, Milwaukee, Wis, burned, nearly 100 lives lost 10 Jan 1883
Lot M Morrill, born 1813, dies at Augusta, Me " "
Act to regulate and improve the civil service of the U S., under which Dorman B Eaton of N. Y, John M Gregory of Ill., and Leroy D Thoman of O were appointed a Civil-service commission 16 Jan "
William E Dodge, born 1805, dies at New York, 9 Feb "
In Star-route case Rerdell pleads guilty, and offers to testify touching the conspiracy 15 Feb. "
Ohio river flood, at Cincinnati the water reaches the height of 66 ft 4 in 15 Feb "
George F Edmunds elected president *pro tem* of the Senate 3 Mch "
Tariff bill approved " "
Forty-seventh Congress adjourns 4 Mch "
Alexander H Stephens, born 1812, dies at Atlanta, Ga., 4 Mch. "
Envoys from the queen of Madagascar presented to pres Arthur in Washington 7 Mch. "
Postmaster-gen. T. O Howe, born 1816, dies at Kenosha, Wis . . 25 Mch "
Four survivors of the *Jeannette* arrive at New York, 27 Mch "
Peter Cooper, born 1791, dies at New York city 4 Apr "
Brig-gen Joseph K Barnes, surgeon-general of the U S. army 1864-82, dies at Washington, D C, 5 Apr "
Ex-sen William P. Kellogg of La indicted for complicity in Star-route frauds by grand-jury at Washington 18 Apr "
Irish-American National convention at Horticultural hall, Philadelphia, nearly 1600 delegates, Alexander Sullivan of Chicago permanent president. Object, to sustain the league in Ireland and to promote a clearer understanding by the American people of the Irish question 26 Apr "
New Civil-service rules published by the president, 8 May, "
New York and Brooklyn bridge opened 24 May, "
National exposition of railway appliances opened in Chicago . . 24 May, "
Panic on the New York and Brooklyn bridge, 12 killed, 29 injured . 30 May, "
Remains of John Howard Payne, author of "Home, Sweet Home," who died at Tunis, 1 Apr 1852, are brought, by aid of W W Corcoran of Washington, and interred in Oak Hill cemetery, Washington, 9 June, "
Verdict of not guilty in the Star-route case 14 June, "
Celebration of the 333d anniversary of Santa Fe, New Mexico . 2 July, "
Charles H Stratton (Tom Thumb), born 1838, dies at Middleborough, Mass . ... 15 July, "
General strike of telegraph operators, 1200 quit work, 12 o'clock noon ... 19 July, "
Brig-gen E O C Ord, born 1818, dies at Havana, Cuba . 22 July, "
Capt Matthew Webb drowned in swimming the whirlpool below Niagara (body found at Lewiston 4 days later) . ..24 July, "

UNI

Southern exposition opened at Louisville, Ky, by pres Arthur . . 1 Aug 1883
American Forestry congress meets at St Paul, Minn, 8 Aug "
Boston Foreign exhibition opens 3 Sept "
Last spike of the Northern Pacific Railroad driven opposite mouth of Gold creek, Mont, by Henry Villard (PACIFIC RAILROADS) 9 Sept "
U S steamer *Yantic* and Arctic steamer *Proteus* leave St John's, Newfoundland, for relief of Greely expedition, 29 June, the *Proteus* is crushed in the ice at entrance to Smith's sound, 23 July, the *Yantic*, returning, arrives at St John's 13 Sept "
Pres Arthur receives the Corean ambassadors at the Fifth Avenue hotel, New York city 18 Sept "
Direct telegraphic communication between U S and Brazil *via* Central America opened, message by pres Arthur to the emperor 21 Sept "
National convention of colored men—300 delegates from 27 states—meets at Louisville, Ky 24 Sept "
Centennial of the disbanding of the Army of the Revolution celebrated at Newburg, N Y 18 Oct "
Lieut-gen Philip H Sheridan succeeds gen W T Sherman, retired, in command of U S army, 1 Nov "
Dr J Marion Sims, surgeon, born 1813, dies 13 Nov "
Standard railroad time in the U S goes into effect (STANDARD TIME) 18 Nov "

Forty-eighth Congress, *First Session*, convenes, 3 Dec. "
George F Edmunds presiding in Senate, John G Carlisle chosen speaker of the House by 190 votes, to 113 for J Warren Keifer
Pres Arthur's third annual message . .. 4 Dec "
New cantilever bridge opened over the gorge at Niagara falls 20 Dec "
President, by proclamation, recommends observance by appropriate exercises of the 100th anniversary of the return by George Washington to the Continental Congress at Annapolis (23 Dec. 1783) of his commission as commander-in-chief 21 Dec. "
Dr. Edward Lasker, distinguished German liberal, dies suddenly in New York city 4 Jan 1884
George F Edmunds continued as president *pro tem* of the Senate, sen H. B Anthony, elected, having declined 14 Jan. "
Steamship *City of Columbus* wrecked on Devil's Bridge, off Gay Head, Mass, 97 lives lost 18 Jan. "
Wendell Phillips, born 1811, dies at Boston, Mass, 2 Feb. "
Morrison Tariff bill introduced in the House 4 Feb. "
Arnold Henry Guyot, geographer, born 1807, dies at Princeton, N J 8 Feb. "
Joint resolution for an expedition to the coast of Greenland to relieve the Greely Arctic expedition, 13 Feb. "
Floods in the Ohio valley, the river rises 71 feet at Cincinnati 14 Feb. "
Congress appropriates $300,000, 12 Feb., and $200,000 additional, 15 Feb, for relief of flood sufferers in the Ohio valley . 12 and 15 Feb "
Funeral services in New York, at the Church of the Holy Trinity, for victims of the *Jeannette* Arctic expedition (brought to New York) . 22 Feb "
Pres Arthur, by special message to Congress, asks appropriation to reconstruct the navy. 26 Mch. "
Three days of mob rule in Cincinnati, arising from a verdict of manslaughter against William Berner for complicity in the murder of his employer, W. H. Kirk 28-30 Mch. "
Government offers $25,000 for the discovery and rescue, or ascertaining the fate, of the Greely Arctic expedition, by act of 17 Apr "
Steamer *Thetis* leaves Brooklyn navy-yard for relief of Greely . ..1 May, "
Morrison Tariff bill rejected in House of Representatives . .. . 6 May, "
Failure of the Marine bank and firm of Grant & Ward in New York city , 6 and 7 May, "
Statue of chief-justice John Marshall unveiled at Washington, D C . . . 10 May, "

Alert, the last Greely relief steamer, sails from Brooklyn navy-yard ....10 May, 1884
Charles O'Conor, born 1804, dies at Nantucket, 12 May, "
Bill repealing the test oath of 1862 approved . " "
Financial crisis in New York city ....14 May, "
National Anti-monopoly convention in Chicago nominates gen. B. F. Butler for president; the candidate for vice-president left to the committee....14 May, "
Act passed providing for the civil government of Alaska ....17 May, "
National Greenback-Labor convention meets in Indianapolis, Ind., 28 May; James B. Weaver permanent president; B. F. Butler nominated for president, and gen. A. M. West of Miss. for vice-president..29 May, "
Republican National convention meets at Chicago, 3 June; John B. Henderson of Mo. permanent president, 4 June; nominations made for presidential candidates, 5 June; 4 ballots cast, 6 June; of the 8 candidates, James G. Blaine receives on the 1st ballot 334½ votes, and on the 4th, 541; Chester A. Arthur on the 1st, 278, on the 4th, 207; the votes necessary to a choice being 411, the nomination of Blaine is made unanimous. John A. Logan nominated for vice-president.........................6 June, "
Gen. B. F. Butler endorses the Greenback-Labor platform...............................12 June, "
American Prohibition National convention at meeting in Chicago nominates Samuel C. Pomeroy of Kan. for president, and John A. Conant of Conn. for vice-president (candidates withdraw in favor of St. John and Daniel in Aug. following)...........20 June, "
Lieut. A. W. Greely and 6 others found alive by search party in *Thetis* and *Bear*, under W. S. Schley, in Smith sound, 5 miles off cape Sabine (ABSTINENCE, NORTHEAST AND NORTHWEST PASSAGES), 22 June, "
Act passed to establish a bureau of labor in the department of the interior...................27 June, "
Proclamation by president warning persons not to settle on Oklahoma lands....................1 July, "
Gen. West accepts nomination of Greenback-Labor party.................................3 July, "
Bill for relief of Fitz-John Porter vetoed, and passed over the veto by House, 2 July, is killed in the Senate.................................3 July, "
Bureau of navigation in the department of the treasury, created by act of Congress, approved.......5 July, "
1st Session adjourns ....7 July, "
Paul Morphy, famous CHESS-player, dies at New Orleans, La., aged 47.....................10 July, "
Democratic National convention meets in Chicago, 8 July; William F. Vilas chosen permanent president of convention, 9 July; balloting for 9 candidates; necessary to a choice, 547 votes: on 1st ballot Grover Cleveland of N. Y. receives 392 votes, T. F. Bayard, 170, and Thomas A. Hendricks, 1, 10 July; 2d ballot: Grover Cleveland 475, amended 683; T. F. Bayard 150½, amended 81½; Thomas A. Hendricks 124½, amended 45½. Thomas A. Hendricks of Ind. nominated for vice-president by Democratic convention, unanimously................11 July, "
Blaine's letter of acceptance...............18 July, "
Gen. Logan's letter of acceptance published...22 July, "
National Prohibition convention meets in Pittsburg, Pa., 23 July; ex-gov. John P. St. John of Kan. nominated for president, and William Daniel of Md. for vice-president.....................24 July, "
National Labor party at Chicago adopts the Democratic nominees for president and vice-president..30 July, "
Lieut. Greely and his men reach Portsmouth, N. H., 2 Aug., and are publicly welcomed..........4 Aug. "
Corner-stone of pedestal of the statue of "Liberty Enlightening the World" laid on Bedloe's island, New York harbor ....5 Aug. "
Thetis, *Bear*, and *Alert*, with bodies of the dead of the Greely expedition, arrive at New York .....8 Aug. "
Gen. A. M. West of Miss. nominated for vice-president of U. S. by National committee of the Anti-monopoly party...............................16 Aug. "

Butler's letter of acceptance published......,19 Aug. 1884
Cleveland's letter of acceptance published.... " "
Hendricks's letter of acceptance published....20 Aug. "
St. John and Daniel announce their acceptance of the prohibition nomination at a temperance camp-meeting at Cuba, N. Y.......................25 Aug. "
International Electrical exhibition opens at Philadelphia.................................2 Sept. "
Charles J. Folger, ex-secretary of the treasury, born 1818, dies at Geneva, N. Y...............4 Sept. "
Mrs. Belva Lockwood of Washington accepts the nomination of the California Woman's Rights convention for president............................Sept. "
Messrs. Fisher and Mulligan publish letters of J. G. Blaine, upon which he is charged with corruption in legislation favoring the Little Rock and Fort Smith railroad in 1876.......................16 Sept. "
International Prime Meridian conference opens in Washington, D. C., 1 Oct., 25 nations represented; the meridian of Greenwich is recommended by 21 nations, San Domingo opposing it, and France and Brazil not voting......................13 Oct. "
Secretary of the treasury Gresham resigns....28 Oct. "
Famous alliterative sentence of dr. Burchard, who, at the reception by Mr. Blaine of a delegation of clergymen in New York city, refers to the Democracy as the party whose antecedents have been "rum, Romanism, and rebellion"...............29 Oct. "
Popular vote for president: Cleveland and Hendricks, Democrats, 4,911,017; Blaine and Logan, Republicans, 4,848,334; Butler and West, Greenback and Anti-Monopoly, 133,825; St. John and Daniel, Prohibition, 151,809......................4 Nov. "
Capt. David L. Payne, famous leader of OKLAHOMA boomers, dies at Wellington, Kan........29 Nov. "
Second Session meets; sen. Edmunds presiding in Senate; president's annual message presented.......1 Dec. "
Capstone of the Washington monument, Washington, D. C. (foundation first laid, 4 July, 1848), is embedded....................................6 Dec. "
World's Industrial Cotton Centennial exposition opens at New Orleans; machinery set in motion by pres. Arthur by telegraph from Washington, and opening address sent by telegraph ....16 Dec. "
Pres.-elect Cleveland resigns as governor of New York; David B. Hill, lieut.-gov., succeeds....6 Jan. 1885
Schuyler Colfax, born 1823, dies at Mankato, Minn., 13 Jan. "
Electoral votes of Iowa and Oregon not reaching the sec. of state before the first Wednesday in January, Congress appropriates $1000 to send special messengers for them.........................17 Jan. "
Act to ascertain claims of American citizens for spoliations by the French prior to 31 July, 1801..20 Jan. "
"Liberty bell," sent from Philadelphia, arrives at the New Orleans exhibition.................25 Jan. "
President announces the expiration on 1 July of the treaty with Great Britain concluded 8 May, 1871 (TREATIES).........................31 Jan. "
Electoral votes counted in Congress: For Cleveland and Hendricks, 219; for Blaine and Logan, 182. In announcing the votes for Cleveland and Hendricks, sen. Edmunds, president of the Senate *pro tem.*, uses the expression, "and so *appear* to have been elected;" and adds that the president of the Senate makes this declaration only as a public statement of the contents of papers opened and read, and not as possessing any authority in law to declare any legal conclusions whatever.....................11 Feb. "
Act to authorize a retired list at three-quarter pay for private and non-commissioned officers in U. S. army or marine corps who have served 30 years..14 Feb. "
Dedication of Washington monument at Washington, D. C.; orations by Robert C. Winthrop of Mass. and John W. Daniels of Va.....................21 Feb. "
Court convened 15 Nov. 1884, for the trial of brig.-gen. David G. Swaim; judge-advocate-gen. concludes its work, and sentences him to suspension from the du-

ties of his office on half-pay for 12 years (see 1 Dec 1894) 24 Feb 1885

President-elect, in a letter to congressmen, advises suspension of the purchase and coinage of silver 24 Feb "

Act to prohibit the importation and migration of aliens under contract or agreement to perform labor, except domestic service, or skilled labor in new industries not otherwise obtainable 26 Feb "

Special session of Senate called for 4 Mch 27 Feb "

Act to appoint 1 person from those who have been generals or generals-in-chief of the army of the U S on the retired list with rank and full pay (gen U S Grant so appointed by pres Arthur), approved, 3 Mch "

Act approved appropriating $1 895,000 for 4 new vessels for U S navy 2 cruisers and 2 gun-boats 3 Mch "

Oath of office as vice-president administered to Mr Hendricks by sen Edmunds 3 Mch. "

Forty-eighth Congress adjourns " "

Special session of Senate, vice-president presiding, 4 Mch "

Cleveland inaugurated president, oath administered by chief-justice Waite . 4 Mch "

Twenty-fifth Administration—Democratic. 4 Mch 1885 to 3 Mch 1889

Grover Cleveland, N Y, president
Thomas A. Hendricks, Ind, vice-president

CABINET

[Named in order of succession established by act of Congress, 19 Jan 1886 (see below), the Department of Agriculture was not created until 9 Feb 1889]

Thomas F Bayard, Del, sec of state, from 6 Mch 1885
Daniel Manning, N Y, sec of treas, from 6 Mch 1885
Charles S Fairchild, N Y, sec of treas, from 1 Apr 1887
William C Endicott, Mass, sec of war, from 6 Mch 1885
Augustus H Garland, Ark, attorney-gen from 6 Mch 1885.
William F Vilas, Wis. postmaster-gen, from 6 Mch 1887
Don M Dickinson, Mich postmaster-gen, from 16 Jan 1888.
William C Whitney, N Y, sec of navy, from 6 Mch 1885.
Lucius Q C Lamar, La, sec of interior, from 6 Mch 1885
William F Vilas, Wis, sec of interior, from 16 Jan 1888
Norman J Coleman, Mo, sec of agriculture, from 12 Feb 1889

Proclamation of president warning persons against attempting to settle on Oklahoma lands 13 Mch 1885

U S government determines to guarantee free and uninterrupted transit across the isthmus of Panama, now threatened by insurgents 2 Apr. "

Special session of Senate adjourns " "

Richard Grant White, Shakespearian critic and philologist, born 1822, dies in New York city 8 Apr "

Five hundred U S troops enter Panama, arrest Aizpuru, leader of insurgents, and protect American property, 24 Apr "

Revised version of the Old Testament published in London and New York (BIBLE) 15 May, "

Apache Indian outbreak under Geronimo in New Mexico and Arizona 17 May, "

F. T Frelinghuysen, ex-sec. of state, born 1817, dies in Newark, N J 20 May, "

Cotton Centennial exposition at New Orleans closes, 31 May, "

Benjamin Silliman, chemist, born 1816, dies at New Haven, Conn 14 June, "

James D Fish, president of the suspended Marine bank of New York city, sentenced to 10 years' imprisonment at Sing Sing 27 June, "

Niagara Falls reservation formally opened to the public 15 July, "

Samuel Irenæus Prime, American journalist, born 1812, dies at Manchester, Vt 18 July, "

Investigation of contract for ship-building with John Roach instituted by sec of navy Whitney, in Mch., payments to Mr Roach suspended 19 July, "

Gen U S. Grant dies at Mount McGregor, near Saratoga, N Y, 8 08 A M . 23 July, "

Proclamation of president suspending all public business on the day of funeral of gen Grant . 23 July, "

Gen. Grant buried at Riverside park, New York city, 8 Aug 1885

James W Marshall, the discoverer of gold in California, dies there in poverty 8 Aug "

Helen Hunt Jackson, author, born 1831, dies at San Francisco, Cal 12 Aug "

Massacre of Chinese at Rock Springs, Wyo , 50 killed by the opposing miners 2 Sept. "

Maj Aaron Stafford, last surviving officer of the war of 1812, dies at Waterville, N Y, aged 95 6 Sept "

American sloop *Puritan* wins the *America's* cup in a race with the British cutter *Genesta* at New York, 14-16 Sept. "

William Page, American artist, born 1811, dies at Tottenville, N Y 1 Oct "

John McCloskey, first American cardinal, born 1810, dies at New York 10 Oct "

Breaking up at 1 blast of Flood rock, Hell Gate, N. Y, covering 9 acres, 282,730 pounds of explosive used, conducted by gen John Newton, U. S A (total cost, $106,509 93) 10 Oct. "

H W Shaw ("Josh Billings"), born 1818, dies at Monterey, Cal 14 Oct "

Gen George B McClellan, born 1826, dies at Orange, N. J 29 Oct "

Ferdinand Ward, of firm of Grant & Ward, New York city, indicted 4 June, sentenced to 10 years in Sing Sing 31 Oct "

All insurgents and unlawful assemblages in Washington territory commanded to disperse by proclamation of president 7 Nov "

John McCulloch, actor, born 1837, dies at Philadelphia, Pa 8 Nov "

North, Central, and South American exposition opened at New Orleans. . 10 Nov. "

Elizur Wright, abolitionist, born 1804, dies at Medford, Mass . 22 Nov "

Vice-pres Thomas A Hendricks, born 1819, dies at Indianapolis, Ind 25 Nov "

[His death left the country without any one in the line of succession of the president, there being no president *pro tem* of the Senate or speaker of the House]

Farmers' congress, at its 5th annual meeting, held at Indianapolis, Ind, organizes with Robert Beverly of Va. as president 3 Dec. "

***Forty-ninth Congress, First Session,* meets** 7 Dec. "

John Sherman of O elected president *pro tem* of the Senate, and John G Carlisle of Ky speaker of the House 7 Dec "

Pres Cleveland's first annual message 8 Dec. "

W H Vanderbilt, born 1821, dies in New York city, 8 Dec "

Robert Toombs, Confederate sec. of state, born 1810, dies at Washington, Ga. 15 Dec. "

Pension of $5000 per annum granted to Julia D Grant, widow of gen Grant 26 Dec. "

Capt. Emmet Crawford, U S A., shot by Mexicans probably by mistake while in pursuit of Apaches, 50 miles southwest of Nacori, Mex, 11 Jan, dies, 18 Jan 1886

Act providing that, in case of removal, death, resignation, or inability, both of the president and vice-president, the cabinet officers succeed in the following order Sec. of state, sec of treas., sec of war, attorney-gen, postmaster-gen, sec of navy, and sec. of interior . 19 Jan. "

Four hundred Chinamen driven out of Seattle, Washington territory, without violence, and sent to San Francisco, 7 Feb, riots result, and U. S. troops ordered out .. 7-9 Feb. "

Proclamation of president orders unlawful assemblages in Washington territory to disperse .. 9 Feb. "

Maj-gen W. S. Hancock, born 1824, dies at Governor's island, N. Y... 9 Feb. "

Horatio Seymour, born 1810, dies at Utica, N. Y, 12 Feb. "

Mr. Morrison introduces his tariff bill in the House, 15 Feb "

John B. Gough, temperance lecturer, born 1817, dies at Frankford, Pa. . . . . 18 Feb. 1886
Lay Sang, Chinese merchant, member of a business firm in San Francisco, returning from Hong-Kong, is refused permission to land at San Francisco, although presenting a certificate from the U. S. consul at Hong-Kong. . . . . 21 Feb. "
House of Representatives appoints a committee to investigate the "Pan-Electric scandal," attorney-gen. Garland being accused of connivance, in a government suit against the Bell Telephone company, with a company in which stock was given him. . 26 Feb. "
Message of pres. Cleveland to the Senate on suspension from office and the constitutional competence of Congress to have access to official papers and documents. The phrase "innocuous desuetude" is here applied to unenforced laws. . . . . 1 Mch. "
President informs Congress that the nation is probably not liable for the Rock Springs Chinese outrages, but suggests indemnity. . . . . 2 Mch. "
Blair Educational bill considered and passed in the Senate. . . . . 5 Mch. "
Knights of Labor strike on the Gould southwestern railway system. . . . . 6 Mch. "
Blair Educational bill referred to House committee on education. . . . . 9 Mch. "
Masked strikers disable 12 locomotives at Kansas City, Mo. . . . . 23 Mch. "
U. S. troops ordered to St. Louis and other points, to prevent interruption of mail transportation, 26 Mch. "
Pension of $2000 per annum granted to the widow of gen. W. S. Hancock. 29 Mch. "
Bill for the free coinage of silver (without limit) defeated in the House by 163 to 126. . . . . 8 Apr. "
Six strikers killed in a collision with sheriff's officers at East St. Louis, Ill. 9 Apr. "
Gov. Alger of Mich., by proclamation, designates "Arbor day" to be celebrated by general tree-planting, 11 Apr. "
Mr. Morrison reports from the committee on ways and means his tariff bill. . . . . 12 Apr. "
President's message suggesting a Commission of Labor, to consider and settle, when possible, controversies between labor and capital. . . . . 22 Apr. "
Great railroad strike formally declared at an end by Knights of Labor. . . . . 4 May, "
Anarchist riot, "Haymarket massacre," in Chicago, Ill. . . . . 4 May, "
Act of Congress to provide for study of alcoholic drinks and narcotics, and their effect on the human system, in public schools of territories, District of Columbia, and in military and naval academies and Indian and colored schools of the U. S. . . . . 20 May, "
Henry W. Jaehne, vice-president of the New York city common council, sentenced to 9 years and 10 months in Sing Sing, for receiving a bribe from Jacob Sharp's Broadway surface road, 30 Aug. 1884 (New York), 20 May, "
Dr. Dio Lewis, born 1823, dies at Yonkers, N. Y., 21 May, "
Twenty-two anarchists indicted at Chicago for murder, 27 May, "
Pres. Cleveland married to Frances Folsom at the White House, Washington, D. C. . . . . 2 June, "
Johann Most, anarchist, sentenced in New York city to 1 year's imprisonment and $500 fine for inciting to murder, etc., and his companions Schenck and Braunschweig to 9 months' imprisonment. . . 2 June, "
General "tie-up" of New York city street-car lines by Knights of Labor. . . . . 5 June, "
Morrison Tariff bill defeated in House of Representatives by 157 to 140. . . . . 17 June, "
Judge David Davis, born 1815, dies at Bloomington, Ill. . . . . 26 June, "
Franking privilege granted to the widow of gen. U. S. Grant by act of Congress. . . . . 28 June, "
Act to legalize incorporation of national trade unions, headquarters in District of Columbia. . . . . 29 June, "
James Gibbons created archbishop of Baltimore, 7 June, and invested with the biretta. . . . . 30 June, 1886
Act restoring gen. Fitz-John Porter to the army, approved. . . . . 1 July, "
Paul Hamilton Hayne, the southern poet, born 1831, dies near Augusta, Ga. . . . . 7 July, "
C. D. Graham, cooper, passes through the Whirlpool rapids at Niagara falls in a barrel of his own construction. . . . . 11 July, "
Order of pres. Cleveland warning office-holders and subordinates against the use of official positions to influence political movements. . . . . 14 July, "
Bi-centennial of the founding of the city of Albany, N. Y., celebrated. . . . . 18–22 July, "
A. K. Cutting, an American and editor of a paper in Texas, imprisoned by Mexican authorities at Paso del Norte for libel, in calling a Spanish-Mexican, Emilio Medina, a "fraud and a dead-beat". . 23 July, "
Act taxing and regulating the manufacture of oleomargarine. . . . . 2 Aug. "
Sec. Bayard demands the immediate release of Cutting, which is refused, and the secretary and president having exhausted their powers, the case is referred to Congress. . . . . 2 Aug. "
Fitz-John Porter appointed to a colonelcy in the army (Porter, Case of). . . . . 2 Aug. "
Act to increase the navy, providing for 4 double-turreted monitors, and 2 armed vessels, a cruiser and a torpedo-boat, to be built of American steel and domestic armor-plate. . . . . 3 Aug. "
Congress authorizes 1, 2, and 5 dollar silver certificates. . . . . 4 Aug. "
Samuel J. Tilden, born 1814, dies at Greystone, N. Y., 4 Aug. "
By joint resolution, Congress accepts from Mrs. Grant and W. H. Vanderbilt the presents of various foreign governments to the late gen. U. S. Grant, 5 Aug. "
First Session adjourns. . . . . " "

[During this session of Congress, pres. Cleveland vetoed 145 bills out of 1649 passed; of 977 private pension bills he vetoed 123.]

Cutting found guilty by Mexican court, 6 Aug., and sentenced to 1 year's imprisonment and $600 fine, 7 Aug. "
Two men in a cask pass in safety through the Whirlpool rapids below Niagara falls. . . . . 8 Aug. "
Seven Chicago anarchists convicted of murder: August Spies, Michael Schwab, Samuel Fielden, Albert A. Parsons, Adolph Fischer, George Engel, and Louis Lingg, sentenced to death; Oscar W. Neebe to 15 years' imprisonment. . . . . 20 Aug. "
William J. Kendall of Boston swims through the Niagara rapids and whirlpool with cork life-preserver, 22 Aug. "
Cutting set at liberty by Mexican authorities, 23 Aug. "
Lightning ignites 70,000 pounds of dynamite and 70 tons of powder at Laflin & Rand's powder-magazine near Chicago, Ill.; 5 killed, 25 injured, 29 Aug. "
Charleston Earthquake. 31 Aug. "
Apache Indian chief Geronimo, with his band, surrenders to gen. Miles at Skeleton cañon, Arizona, 4 Sept. "
American yacht *Mayflower* defeats the British yacht *Galatea* off New York, in international race for *America's* cup. . . . . 7 and 11 Sept. "
First national convention of anti-saloon Republicans meets at Chicago; 800 delegates. . . . . 16 Sept. "
Asher Brown Durand, line engraver and painter, born 1796, dies at South Orange, N. J. . . . . 17 Sept. "
Disastrous gale on gulf of Mexico and floods in Texas; 250 lives lost, 2000 persons left desolate. . . . 12 Oct. "
"Boodle" aldermen in New York city arraigned for bribery. . . . . 19 Oct. "
Bartholdi's statue of Liberty Enlightening the World unveiled. . . . . 28 Oct. "
Reception to French delegates to the Bartholdi statue dedication given at the White House, Washington, 4 Nov. "
Ex-pres. Chester A. Arthur, born 1830, dies at New York. . . . . 18 Nov. "

Charles Francis Adams, sr, born 1807, dies at Boston, Mass 21 Nov. 1886
Henry M Stanley, the African explorer, received in New York 27 Nov. "
ARBOR DAY celebrated in San Francisco by school children, 40,000 young trees supplied by Adolph Sutro for the occasion 27 Nov. "
Second Session begins 6 Dec. "
John Sherman of O president *pro tem* of the Senate.
President's message presented 6 Dec. "
Isaac Lea, LL.D, naturalist, born 1792, dies at Philadelphia, Pa 8 Dec "
Gen John A Logan, born 1826, dies at Washington, D C 26 Dec. "
John Roach, ship-builder, born 1813, dies at New York city 10 Jan. 1887
Remnant of Table Rock at Niagara falls, 100 ft long, 76 wide, and 170 deep, falls 12 Jan "
Edward L Youmans, scientist, born 1821, dies at New York 18 Jan. "
Mexican-war Pension bill approved 29 Jan. "
Act fixing 2d Monday in January for meeting of electors of each state at such place as legislatures may direct, and 2d Wednesday in February for counting electoral votes in Congress 3 Feb "
Interstate Commerce bill, appointing 5 commissioners to regulate commerce between the states, approved, [Salary of each $7000 per annum] 4 Feb "
Pension bill for relief of dependent parents and honorably discharged soldiers and sailors who served 3 months in the civil war, now disabled and dependent upon their own labor, vetoed 11 Feb "
Daniel Manning resigns as secretary of the treasury, 14 Feb "
Union Labor party organized at Cincinnati, O, 22 Feb "
Bill to prohibit importation of opium from China approved 23 Feb "
Act prohibiting the hiring or contracting out of the labor of prisoners under the laws of the U S, 23 Feb. "
Veto of the Dependent Pension bill sustained in the House 24 Feb "
Congress appropriates $147,748 to indemnify Chinese subjects for the Rock Springs massacre 24 Feb. "
John J Ingalls elected president *pro tem* of the Senate, in place of John Sherman resigned 26 Feb "
Act to organize the Hospital corps of the army of the U S 1 Mch "
Act to establish agricultural experiment stations in colleges established by act of 2 July, 1862, in the several states 2 Mch "
President authorized to adopt retaliatory measures in the fishery dispute with Canada 2 Mch "
Act authorizing the president to deliver the so-called "Twiggs swords," captured or seized by gen B F Butler in 1862, to such person as the court of claims may decide to be the owners 3 Mch "
Tenure of Office act repealed " "
Act for return and recoinage at par of trade dollars, 3 Mch "
Forty-ninth Congress adjourns " "
Henry Ward Beecher, stricken with apoplexy 2 Mch, dies in Brooklyn 8 Mch. "
James B Eads, engineer, born 1820, dies at Nassau, N P (MISSISSIPPI RIVER) 8 Mch "
Interstate Commerce commission appointed by the president 22 Mch "
Transatlantic yacht race from Sandy Hook to Queenstown, between the *Coronet* and *Dauntless*, won by the former in 14 days 19 hrs 3 m 14 sec., sailing 2934 miles 27 Mch "
John G Saxe, poet, born 1816, dies at Albany, N. Y, 31 Mch. "
Body of Abraham Lincoln, carefully guarded since an effort to steal it from the sarcophagus of the Lincoln monument, Springfield, Ill, made in 1876, is buried in a grave dug in the crypt and covered with 6 feet of cement, the sarcophagus being replaced 14 Apr. "
Monument to James A Garfield unveiled in Washington, D C 12 May, 1887
Fire in horse-car barns, New York city, 1200 horses suffocated 27 May, "
William A Wheeler, ex-vice-president, born 1819, dies at Malone, N Y 4 June, "
A recommendation made by adjt-gen Drum on 30 Apr, to return flags, both Union and Confederate, captured in the civil war and stored in the War Department, approved by the president and endorsed by the secretary of war, is revoked by pres Cleveland as not authorized by law nor justifiable as an executive act 16 June, "
Reunion of Union and Confederate soldiers, survivors of the Philadelphia brigade and Pickett's division, is held at Gettysburg, Pa 2-4 July, "
Jacob Sharp, found guilty of bribing New York aldermen, is sentenced to 4 years' imprisonment and a fine of $5000 14 July, "
Miss Dorothea L Dix, philanthropist, born 1805, dies at Trenton, N J 19 July, "
Failure of H S Ives & Co, of New York, stock-brokers, liabilities, $20,000,000 11 Aug. "
Spencer F Baird, naturalist, born 1823, dies at Wood's Holl, Mass 19 Aug. "
Ninth international medical congress meets at Washington, D C 5 Sept "
Labor day observed as a legal holiday for the first time in New York 5 Sept. "
Three days' centennial celebration of the formation of the Constitution begins at Philadelphia 15 Sept "
American party organized in Philadelphia. 17 Sept "
American sloop *Volunteer* wins the international yacht race over the British cutter *Thistle* 27 and 30 Sept. "
Pres and Mrs Cleveland leave Washington for a tour of the West and South 30 Sept "
Elihu B. Washburne, born 1816, dies at Chicago, Ill, 22 Oct. "
Sentence of anarchists Fielden and Schwab commuted to imprisonment for life, Lingg kills himself by exploding a bomb in his mouth 10 Nov "
Chicago anarchists Spies, Fischer, Engel, and Parsons hanged 11 Nov. "
Johann Most, anarchist, of New York, arrested for incendiary language 17 Nov. "
Fiftieth Congress, First Session, opens 5 Dec 1887, John J Ingalls of Kan president *pro tem* of the Senate, John G Carlisle of Ky. elected Speaker of the House by 163 to 147 for Thomas B Reed 5 Dec. "
Pres Cleveland's third annual message 6 Dec. "
Anarchist Most sentenced to 1 year's imprisonment, 8 Dec "
Cigar-shaped raft 560 ft. long, 65 wide, 38 high, with draught of 19 ft. and containing 27,000 logs, which cost $30,000, and launched in the bay of Fundy, bound for New York, goes to pieces off Nantucket shoals during a storm about 20 Dec. "
Ferdinand Vandeveer Hayden, geologist, born 1829, dies at Philadelphia 22 Dec "
Ex-sec. of the treas. Manning, born 1831, dies at Albany, N. Y 24 Dec "
Sec. Lamar resigns 7 Jan 1888
Asa Gray, botanist, born 1810, dies at Cambridge, Mass., 30 Jan. "
David R. Locke, "Petroleum V. Nasby, Confederate X Roads," born 1833, dies at Toledo, O 15 Feb. "
W. W Corcoran, philanthropist, born 1798, dies at Washington, D. C 24 Feb. "
A. Bronson Alcott, born 1799, dies at Boston, Mass., 4 Mch, and Louise M Alcott, his daughter, novelist, born 1832, dies at Boston... 6 Mch. "
"Blizzard" on the Atlantic coast, 30 lives lost; $10,000,000 worth of property destroyed, about 4 feet of snow falls in New York city and drifts in the streets 10 to 20 feet deep (STORMS) 12-13 Mch "
Chief-justice Morrison R Waite, born 1816, dies at Washington, D. C. . . . . . . 23 Mch "

agress votes $1000 to reward the Esquimaux of the Asiatic coast of the Arctic ocean for acts of humanity to shipwrecked seamen . 2 Apr 1888

ghton Beach hotel, Kings county, N Y, a wooden structure 465 ft long, 150 deep, and 3 stories high, estimated weight 5000 tons is moved back from the ocean 600 feet by 112 platform cars on 24 parallel racks drawn by 4 locomotives attached by tackle, 3 Apr et seq. "

scoe Conkling, statesman, born 1829, dies at New York . . 18 Apr. "

nvention of delegates from nearly all the Southern states east of the Mississippi meets at Hot Springs, N C, to promote immigration 25 Apr. "

lva A Lockwood, nominated for president by Equal Rights convention at Des Moines, Ia . 15 May, "

son J Streeter of Ill nominated for president, and C. E Cunningham of Ark for vice-president, by Union Labor party, at Cincinnati, O 16 May, "

bert H Cowdrey of Ill nominated for president, and W H T Wakefield of Kan for vice-president by United Labor convention at Cincinnati, O, 17 May, "

nton B Fisk of N J nominated for president, and John A Brooks of Mo for vice-president by Prohibition National convention at Indianapolis, 31 May, "

ade of lieut-gen in the army merged into grade of general, and president authorized to appoint a general of the army by act .. 1 June, "

H Sheridan commissioned general of the army, 1 June, "

k Observatory, 13 miles east from San Jose, Cal, transferred by the trustees to the University of California 1 June, "

t providing for execution of murderers by electricity in New York state signed by gov. Hill .4 June, "

mocratic National convention meets in St Louis, Patrick A Collins of Mass permanent president, 5 June, Grover Cleveland nominated for president by acclamation, 6 June, Allen G Thurman of O nominated for vice president by 690 to 105 for Isaac P. Gray of Ind and 25 for John C Black of Ill, 7 June, "

partment of Labor, in charge of a commissioner of labor to be appointed by the president, established by act of . . .13 June, "

publican National convention opens in Chicago, 19 June M M Estee of Cal made permanent president, 20 June, 19 candidates are balloted for—necessary to a choice 416 2 ballots are cast 22 June, 3 on 23 June, and 3 on 25 June The result of the 1st and 8th ballots for the 4 principal candidates as follows.

	1st	8th
Benjamin Harrison of Ind	80	544
John Sherman of O . . .	229	118
Russell A Alger of Mich. .	84	100
Walter Q Gresham of Ill . .	111	59

Levi P Morton of N Y nominated for vice-president . . .... 25 June, "

nument to Francis Scott Key unveiled in Golden Gate park, San Francisco, Cal ... . . .4 July, "

ntennial exposition of the Ohio valley and central states, continuing until 28 Oct., is opened at Cincinnati, O . . . . 4 July, "

bate on Mills Tariff bill in the House closed, 19 July, and bill passed by 162 to 149 .. 21 July, "

cond timber-raft launched at Toggins, bay of Fundy, 25 July, containing 22,000 logs averaging 40 ft. in length, is towed in safety to New York, arriving about 5 Aug "

n P. H Sheridan, born 1831, dies at Nonquitt, Mass. .. .. 5 Aug "

ndidates of Prohibition party publish letters of acceptance ... .6 Aug. "

n J M. Schofield succeeds to command of army of the U. S ... . 14 Aug. "

mes Langdon Curtis of N. Y. nominated for president, and James R Geer (replaced by P D. Wigginton, 2 Oct) for vice-president by the American party in convention at Washington . . . . . .15 Aug "

President's message outlining a plan of retaliation in the matter of the Fishery treaty . 23 Aug 1888

Grover Cleveland's letter of acceptance .. 8 Sept "

Canadian Retaliation bill passes House of Representatives by 176 to 4, 8 Sept, referred to the Senate committee on foreign relations 10 Sept "

Benjamin Harrison's letter of acceptance . 11 Sept "

Richard A Proctor, astronomer, born, Engl., 1837, dies at New York city . 12 Sept "

Immigration of Chinese into the U S, except officials, teachers, students, merchants, or travellers for pleasure, prohibited by act approved 13 Sept "

Hodju Hussein Ghooly Khan, first minister from Persia to the U S., arrives at New York . 30 Sept "

Levi P Morton's letter of acceptance . 2 Oct. "

Melville W Fuller, appointed chief-justice of the U S 30 Apr, is confirmed, 20 July, and sworn in, 8 Oct. "

Allen G Thurman's letter of acceptance . 12 Oct "

First Session (321 days) adjourns .. 20 Oct "

[This was the longest session on record 15,585 bills and joint resolutions were introduced, of which 1237 bills and 57 joint resolutions became laws]

Indiscreet letter on American politics from the British minister, lord Sackville West, dated Beverly, Mass, 13 Sept 1888 to Charles F Murchison of Pomona, Cal, a naturalized Englishman who had asked advice how to vote, published . 25 Oct. "

Recall of minister Sackville suggested, and the president refuses to recognize him officially 30 Oct. "

General election, popular vote Cleveland, Democrat, 5,540 329, Harrison, Republican, 5,439,853, Fisk, Prohibition, 249,506, Streeter, Union Labor, 146,-935, Cowdry, United Labor, 2818, Curtis, American, 1591 Cleveland's plurality, 100,476 6 Nov. "

Second Session meets . . . 3 Dec. "

President's annual message presented " "

Oyster war in Chester river, etc (MARYLAND), 11 Dec. "

Act incorporating the American Historical Association .. 4 Jan 1889

Upper Suspension bridge at Niagara falls torn from its cables and blown into the river during a gale, 10 Jan. "

Substitute for the Mills Tariff bill passes the Senate, 22 Jan, is debated in the House and referred to committee on ways and means . 26 Jan "

John M Clayton, Republican candidate for Congress from second district, Arkansas, assassinated at Plummersville, Ark . 29 Jan. "

New executive department, "the Department of Agriculture," created by act of 9 Feb "

John Call Dalton, physiologist, born 1825, dies at New York city . . 12 Feb. "

Norman J Coleman of Mo appointed first secretary of agriculture 12 Feb. "

Electoral votes counted in Congress Benjamin Harrison of Ind and Levi P. Morton of N Y, Republicans, receive 233 votes, Grover Cleveland of N Y. and Allen G. Thurman of O, Democrats, receive 168 votes . . .. . 13 Feb. "

Act to create the Maritime Canal company of Nicaragua . . .. 20 Feb "

Act dividing Dakota into 2 states, and enabling the people of North and South Dakota, Montana, and Washington to form constitutions and state governments .. . . 22 Feb. "

Congress appropriates $250,000 to aid American workmen thrown out of employment by stoppage of work on the Panama canal .. .. 25 Feb "

President calls the Senate in extraordinary session, 4 Mch . . . . .26 Feb. "

Bill passed retiring gen William S. Rosecrans, 27 Feb "

Act to provide for taking the 11th and subsequent censuses . . . . 1 Mch. "

Congress appropriates $100,000 for a permanent coaling station at Pago Pago, Tutuila, Samoa. .2 Mch "

Bill to refund to the states and territories the direct tax levied by act of 5 Aug 1861, vetoed by pres. Cleveland, 2 Mch., is passed by the Senate, but lost in the House . ... 2 Mch "

Act *to* punish the use of the mails in "the sawdust swindle" or "counterfeit-money fraud," or by dealing in "green articles," "green coin," "bills," "paper goods," "green cigars," etc., by fine and imprisonment ....2 Mch. 1889
Levi P. Morton, vice-president elect, takes the oath of office in the Senate..................4 Mch. "
Fiftieth Congress adjourns.................. " "
Special session of the Senate convenes, vice-pres. Morton presiding ....4 Mch. "
Pres. Harrison inaugurated .... " "

Twenty-sixth Administration—Republican. 4 Mch. 1889 to 3 Mch. 1893.

Benjamin Harrison, Ind., president.
Levi P. Morton, N. Y., vice-president.

CABINET.

James G. Blaine, Me., sec. of state, from 5 Mch. 1889.
John W. Foster, Ind., sec. of state, from 29 June, 1892.
William Windom, Minn., sec. of treasury, from 5 Mch. 1889.
Charles Foster, O , sec. of treasury, from 24 Feb. 1891.
Redfield Proctor, Vt., sec. of war, from 5 Mch. 1889.
Stephen B. Elkins, W. Va., sec. of war, from 24 Dec. 1891.
William H. H. Miller, Ind., attorney-gen., from 5 Mch. 1889.
John Wanamaker, Pa., postmaster-gen., from 5 Mch. 1889.
Benjamin F. Tracy, N. Y., sec. of navy, from 5 Mch. 1889.
John W. Noble, Mo., sec. of interior, from 5 Mch. 1889.
Jeremiah M. Rusk, Wis., sec. of agriculture, 5 Mch. 1889.

Sen. Ingalls re-elected president *pro tem.* of Senate, presiding until 18 Mch ....7 Mch. 1889
John Ericsson, scientist and inventor, born 1803, dies in New York city......................8 Mch. "
U. S. steamers *Trenton* and *Vandalia* wrecked and the *Nipsic* stranded in a storm near Apia, SAMOAN ISLANDS ....16 Mch. "
Proclamation of the president warning persons against entering Behring sea for unlawful hunting of fur-bearing animals ....21 Mch. "
Stanley Matthews, associate justice of Supreme court of U. S., born 1824, dies in Washington, D. C., 22 Mch. "
Extra session of Senate closes...............2 Apr. "
Proclamation of president designates 30 Apr. 1889, the centennial of the inauguration of Washington as president, as a day of special thanksgiving...4 Apr. "
Oklahoma, by proclamation of president, 23 Mch. 1889, is opened for settlement at noon, and city of Guthrie established..........................22 Apr. "
Simpson dry-dock at Newport News, Va., the largest in the U. S., formally opened..............24 Apr. "
Centennial of inauguration of pres. Washington celebrated in New York city and elsewhere, 29 Apr.–1 May, "
Body of dr. Cronin of Chicago, who had disappeared 3 weeks previously, found in a sewer; murdered. (TRIALS) ....22 May, "
JOHNSTOWN FLOOD ....31 May, "
John Brown's fort, near Harper's Ferry, swept away by flood on the Potomac....................June, "
City of Seattle, W. T., nearly destroyed by fire; 30 acres burned over; loss, $5,000,000........6 June, "
Simon Cameron, statesman, born 1799, dies in Donegal, Lancaster county, Pa..................26 June, "
Maria Mitchell, astronomer, born 1818, dies at Lynn, Mass...................................28 June, "
Theodore Dwight Woolsey, ex-president of Yale college, born 1801, dies at New Haven, Conn...1 July, "
Mayor of New York calls a meeting with a view to holding a World's Fair in 1892...........18 July. "
Sioux reservation in Dakota (11,000,000 acres) ceded to the U. S ....6 Aug. "
Mayor Grant of New York city appoints committees for the World's Fair in 1892..............11 Aug. "
David S. Terry, assaulting judge Stephen Field at Lathrop, Cal., is shot dead by U. S. marshal Nagle, 14 Aug. "
Cronin murder trial begins in Chicago (TRIALS), 30 Aug. "

Deep Harbor convention, with delegates from 15 states and territories, meets at Topeka, Kan., to consider the security of a harbor on the Texas coast ..1 Oct. 1889
Pan-American congress organizes in Washington, D.C., 2 Oct. "
International Marine conference meets in Washington, D. C...............................16 Oct. "
Work formally begun on the Nicaragua canal .22 Oct. "
North and South Dakota admitted into the Union as states (39th and 40th in order), by proclamation of the president..........................2 Nov. "
Maritime exhibition opens in Boston, Mass....4 Nov. "
Montana (41st state in order) admitted into the Union by proclamation of president.............8 Nov. "
Washington (42d state in order) admitted into the Union by proclamation of president.......11 Nov. "
Pan-American delegates, after visiting all sections of the country, a journey of 6000 miles, return to Washington..............................13 Nov. "
Great fire in Lynn, Mass.; 80 acres burned over; 296 buildings destroyed; loss over $4,000,000..26 Nov. "

Fifty-first Congress, First Session, meets......2 Dec. "
Thomas B. Reed of Me. elected speaker of the House.
Pres. Harrison's first annual message ....3 Dec. "
Jefferson Davis, ex-president of the Confederacy, born 1808, dies at New Orleans................6 Dec. "
Committees representing the Farmers' Alliance and Industrial Union and the Knights of Labor meet at St. Louis and adopt a platform of principles demanding the free and unlimited coinage of silver, the abolition of national banks and issue of legal-tender treasury notes, prohibiting alien ownership of land and dealing in futures of agricultural and mechanical products..................................6 Dec. "
Auditorium building and opera-house, Chicago, dedicated.................................9 Dec. "
Coughlin, O'Sullivan, and Burke sentenced to life imprisonment, and Kunze to 3 years, for complicity in murder of dr. Cronin of Chicago, and Beggs acquitted, 16 Dec. "
"La grippe" invades the U. S.............21 Dec. "
Horatio Allen, first locomotive engineer in the U. S., dies at Montrose, N. J., aged 88...........1 Jan. 189
State dinner given by the president to the vice-president and cabinet ....7 Jan. "
William D. Kelley, born 1814, the oldest member of the House of Representatives in term of service (since 1860) as well as in years, dies........9 Jan. "
Adam Forepaugh, veteran circus manager, born 1831, dies at Philadelphia....................22 Jan. "
Woman's Christian Temperance league organized at Cleveland, O..........................23 Jan. "
"Nellie Bly" (miss Pink E. Corkran), of the New York *World*, completes a trip around the world eastward in 72 days, 6 hrs. 11 min.................25 Jan. "
House of Representatives disputes on the power of the speaker to count a quorum when members present refuse to vote...........................29 Jan. "
Wife and daughter of sec. of the navy Tracy lose their lives in the burning of their residence at Washington, D. C...............................3 Feb. "
Gentiles at Salt Lake City, Utah, for the first time obtain control in a local election............10 Feb. "
Proclamation of the president opening part of the Great Sioux reservation for settlement..........10 Feb. "
Proclamation by the president against the use of the Cherokee strip for grazing by whites under private contract with the Cherokees.............17 Feb. "
John Jacob Astor, born 1822, dies at New York, leaving a vast fortune..........................22 Feb. "
Vote in the House of Representatives on a site for the World's Columbian exposition results: Chicago, 157; New York, 107; St. Louis, 26; Washington, D. C., 18; necessary to a choice, 155..................24 Feb. "
U. S. steamer *Enterprise* arrives at New York with the body of the late George H. Pendleton, who died at Brussels, 24 Nov. 1889.....................27 Feb. "

rth American Commercial company secures the Alaskan fur seal rights (ALASKA) 28 Feb 1890
tional league of Republican clubs meets at Nashville, Tenn 4 Mch "
t authorizing an assistant sec of war at a salary of $4500 5 Mch "
ring to British seal-poaching in American waters, and refusal of Great Britain to recognize a close season, the president by proclamation warns persons against entering Behring sea for the purpose of unlawfully killing fur-bearing animals 15 Mch "
rge number of "boomers" invade the Cherokee strip 23 Mch "
n Robert C Schenck born 1809, dies at Washington, D C 23 Mch "
uisville tornado (STORMS) 27 Mch "
istralian ballot system successfully introduced at a state election in Rhode Island 2 Apr "
nic in the Chicago Board of Trade 12 Apr "
muel J Randall, born 1828, dies at Washington, D C, 13 Apr "
Kinley Tariff bill introduced from the committee on ways and means 16 Apr "
n-American conference, in which was represented Hayti, Nicaragua, Peru, Guatemala, Colombia Argentine Republic, Costa Rica Paraguay, Brazil, Honduras, Mexico, Bolivia, United States, Venezuela, Chili, San Salvador, and Ecuador, adjourns, 19 Apr "
hn C Fremont *placed on the army retired list*, with the rank of major-general by act of 19 Apr, approved 21 Apr "
n-Electric suit decided by the Supreme court in favor of ex attorney-gen Garland 21 Apr "
mmander B H McCalla of U S S *Enterprise* court-martialled on charges of malfeasance, based on findings of a court of inquiry which met 11 Mch at Brooklyn navy-yard 22 Apr "
ngress appropriates $150,000 for relief of sufferers from floods on the Mississippi 25 Apr "
t passed to provide for celebrating the 400th anniversary of the discovery of America by Christopher Columbus by an international exhibition of arts, industries, manufactures, and products of the soil, mines, and sea, at Chicago, Ill 25 Apr "
preme court decides that imported liquors may be carried into any state, and sold in the original packages, without reference to local prohibitory or restrictive laws 28 Apr "
t to provide for a temporary government in the territory of Oklahoma 2 May, "
mmander B H McCalla sentenced to be suspended from rank and duty for 3 years, sentence approved by sec. Tracy 15 May, "
cKinley Tariff bill debated in the House of Representatives 7-10 May, and passed by the House, 164 to 142 21 May, "
ork of taking the U S census begins 2 June, "
cKinley Tariff bill reported in the Senate 18 June, "
tional Commission of the World's Columbian exposition appointed by the president, elects ex-sen Thomas W Palmer of Detroit permanent chairman, and John T Dickinson of Tex permanent secretary, 27 June, "
ll passes granting pensions to soldiers and sailors who served 90 days in the civil war, now or hereafter disabled, and to widows and minor children and dependent parents 27 June, "
ll to protect trade and commerce against unlawful restraints of trusts, monopolies, etc, approved, 2 July, "
ct admitting Idaho as a state (the 43d) 3 July, "
en. Clinton B Fisk, born 1828, dies at New York city, 9 July, "
t admitting Wyoming as a state (the 44th), 10 July, "
ct authorizing a bridge over the Hudson river between New York and New Jersey, and incorporating the North River Bridge company 11 July, "

Maj-gen John C Frémont, born 1813, dies at New York 13 July, 1890
Act authorizing the purchase of not more than 4,500,000 ounces of silver per month at not more than $1 for $371\frac{25}{100}$ grains, and to issue treasury notes therefor, and coinage of 2,000,000 ounces per month until 1 July, 1891, and thereafter as necessary 14 July, "
C H F Peters, American astronomer, discoverer of 50 asteroids, born 1813, dies 18 July, "
Message of pres Harrison recommends legislation closing the mails and express lines of the U S against lottery companies 29 July, "
Post-office department excludes from the mails Tolstoi's "Kreutzer Sonata" as an immoral work 1 Aug "
William Kemmler, murderer, executed by electricity at Auburn prison N Y (TRIALS) 6 Aug "
Strike of 3000 trainmen on the New York Central railroad 8 Aug "
Wilson bill as amended authorizing the states to prohibit sale of imported liquors in "original packages," approved 8 Aug "
John Boyle O Reilly, Irish patriot and poet, born 1844, dies at Hull, Mass 10 Aug "
First annual convention of letter-carriers of the U S held at Boston, Mass, 100 delegates 13 Aug "
Act establishing a National military park at the battle-field of Chickamauga 19 Aug "
Body of capt John Ericsson sent to Sweden on the U S S *Baltimore* 23 Aug "
Act for inspection by the Department of Agriculture of salted pork and bacon for export and of foods and drink and cattle imported, and empowering the president to retaliate upon foreign nations discriminating against the U S 30 Aug "
Act for an annual appropriation of moneys received from the sale of public lands to Colleges of Agriculture and Mechanics' Arts established by act of Congress 2 July, 1862, each state and territory to receive $15,000 the first year, increased by $1000 annually, until $25,000 is reached, which shall be a permanent annual donation 30 Aug
Single Tax convention meets in New York city 2 Sept. and adopts a platform 3 Sept "
Criminal jurisdiction of U S Circuit and District courts extended to the Great Lakes and connecting waters by act of 4 Sept "
Direct Trade convention, with delegates from 6 cotton-producing states, organizes at Atlanta, Ga 10 Sept "
Strike of trainmen on the N Y Central railroad declared off 17 Sept "
Dion Boucicault, dramatist, born 1822, dies at New York city 18 Sept "
Act amending sec 3894 of Revised Statutes, relating to advertising of lottery tickets, approved 19 Sept "
River and Harbor bill, appropriating $24,981,295, approved 19 Sept "
George R Davis of Ill selected as director-gen of the World's Fair 19 Sept "
Bronze statue of Horace Greeley, by John Quincy Adams Ward, unveiled in front of the Tribune building, New York city 20 Sept "
Act reserving as a public park the big-tree groves in townships 17 and 18 south, in California 25 Sept. "
Coinage of 3-dollar and 1-dollar gold pieces, and 3-cent nickel pieces discontinued by act of (COIN), 26 Sept. "
Celebration at Providence, R I., of the centennial of the introduction of cotton spinning into America, 29 Sept "
Pension of Sarah Dabney, widow of John Q Dabney, Revolutionary soldier, increased from $12 to $30 per month by act 20 June, also of Asenath Turner, widow of Samuel Dunham, and Mary Snead, widow of Bowdoin Snead, Revolutionary pensioners, 30 Sept. "
McKinley Tariff bill approved . 1 Oct "
Act of Congress setting apart certain tracts of land in California as forest reservations. . 1 Oct. "
Act transferring the Weather bureau to the department of agriculture .. .. 1 Oct. "

passed by House of Representatives 2 July, 1890, closes in the Senate.......................19 Jan.

Aldrich cloture rule, to limit debate, submitted 29 Dec. 1890, is considered in Senate.......................20 Jan.

King Kalakaua, born 1836, dies at San Francisco, 20 Jan.

Representatives of the Farmers' Alliance and Industrial Union in Washington, D. C., agree upon a confederation of the labor organizations.......................22 Jan.

Aldrich cloture resolution displaced in Senate by bill for apportionment of representation, by 35 to 34, 26 Jan.

Over 100 miners killed by an explosion of fire-damp in the coke mines near Mt. Pleasant, Pa.......................27 Jan.

Sec. of treas. Windom, born 1827, dies suddenly of heart-disease at a banquet at Delmonico's, New York city, 29 Jan.

Act apportioning representatives in Congress, 356 after 3 Mch. 1893, approved.......................7 Feb.

Strike involving 13,000 miners begins in Connellsville coke region, Pa.......................9 Feb.

Admiral David Dixon Porter, born 1814, dies at Washington, D. C.......................13 Feb.

[With him expired the grade of admiral in the navy.]

Gen. William T. Sherman, born 1820, dies at New York, 14 Feb.

Gen. Nathaniel P. Banks placed upon the pension roll at the rate of $100 per month.......................18 Feb.

Sen. Ingalls chosen president of the Senate pro tem., 25 Feb. 1888, and continued by successive elections until 3 Apr. 1890. On 13 Mch. 1890, he is unanimously designated to preside during the future absence of the vice-president and at the pleasure of the Senate, a function never before exercised by any member of the Senate; he resigns this office.......................17 Feb.

Prof. Alexander Winchell, geologist, born 1824, dies at Ann Arbor, Mich.......................19 Feb.

First triennial of National Council of Women of the U. S. meets at Washington, D. C.......................22 Feb.

Act to refund to the states $15,227,632.28 collected under the direct-tax act of 1861 [illegible] $20,000,000, 2 Mch.

Act authorizing 2 U. S. [illegible] another south of 39° and east of the [illegible] the 3d west of the Rocky mountains.......................3 Mch.

Convention of International Young Women's Christi[illegible] **Association at Scranton**, Pa. . . . . .24-2[illegible] A[illegible] 1891

China formally objects to Henry W. Blair as m[illegible]**ister from the U. S.**, because of his speech in C[illegible]**gress against the Chinese** . . . . .28 A[illegible] "

Verdict of "not guilty" in Milington murder case[illegible] **Denver, Col** . . . . .2[illegible] A[illegible] "

Charles Pratt, philanthropist, born 1830, dies in N[illegible] **York city** . . . . .4 M[illegible] "

U. S. marshal, at the request of Chilian minister, se[illegible] **the Chilian insurgent** transport *Itata* at San Di[illegible] **Cal** . . . . .6 M[illegible] "

Itata **sails from San Diego**, carrying off the U. S. d[illegible]**uty marshal** . . . . .7 M[illegible] "

[**The marshal** was landed some 8 miles south [illegible] **San Diego, and the** *Itata* took from the Americ[illegible] **schooner** *Robert and Minnie* a cargo of arms shipp[illegible] **from Ilion, N. Y.**]

U. S. cruiser *Charleston* sails in pursuit of the *Itata* . . . . .9 M[illegible] "

Pres. Harrison returns to Washington . . . . . . .15 M[illegible] "

Rear-adm. McCann given command of the Americ[illegible] **vessels in the South Pacific** . . . . .17 M[illegible] "

Trans-Mississippi Commercial congress (1200 delega[illegible]) **opens at Denver, Col** . . . . .19 M[illegible] "

People's party organized at the National Union c[illegible]**ference (1418 delegates from 32 states) at Cinc[illegible]nati, O** . . . . .19 M[illegible] "

President opens to settlement about 1,[illegible] acres [illegible] **the Fort Berthold Indian reservation**, N. Dak., 20 M[illegible] "

Charleston **reaches Callao without having** seen [illegible] *Itata* . . . . .27 M[illegible] "

First Sunday opening of the New York Metropoli[illegible] museum; 10,000 visitors . . . . .31 M[illegible] "

Benson John Lossing, historian, born 1813, dies [illegible] **Chestnut Ridge, Dutchess county, N. Y.** . . . .3 Ju[illegible] "

Itata **surrenders to adms. McCann and Brown** in [illegible] **harbor of Iquique with a cargo of 5000 rifles**, 4 Ju[illegible] "

Lieut. R. E. [illegible] wife (the first lady to jo[illegible] Polar expedition [illegible] Arctic regions, 6 Ju[illegible] "

Great Britain agrees [illegible] a close sea[illegible] and limited privile[illegible] fisheries, un[illegible] [illegible] 15 Ju[illegible] "

[illegible]

Cherokee strip closed to the whites by order of the president . . . . .13 Aug. 1891

Sarah Childress Polk, widow of ex-pres. James K. Polk, born 1803, dies at Nashville, Tenn. . . . . . .14 Aug. "

Battle monument, 308 feet high, at Bennington, Vt., dedicated; address by pres. Harrison . . . . . .19 Aug. "

Over 60 persons killed by a falling building in Park place, New York city .22 Aug. "

R. G. Dyrenforth and staff experiment in artificial rain production by dynamite bombs exploded in the air, etc., near Midland, Tex . . . . .18-26 Aug. "

First reunion of survivors of the Black Hawk war of 1832 held at Lena, Ill.; 47 veterans over 70 years old present . . . . .28 Aug. "

Germany removes restrictions on imports of American pork . . . . .3 Sept. "

New Chilian government, with Jorge Montt as president, officially recognized by the department of state at Washington, D. C. . . . . .7 Sept. "

Denmark revokes prohibition of import of American pork . . . . .8 Sept. "

Forest reservation in Wyoming, adjoining Yellowstone National park, set apart by proclamation of pres. Harrison, 30 Mch., and supplementary proclamation, 10 Sept. "

William Ferrel, meteorologist, born 1817, dies at Maywood, Kan. . . . . .18 Sept. "

President proclaims the ceded Indian lands in Oklahoma territory open to settlement on 22 Sept., 18 Sept. "

Opening of the St. Clair river tunnel celebrated at Port Huron and Sarnia . . . . .19 Sept. "

Russian man-of-war *Aleut* seizes an American sealer, the *Lewis*, at Behring's island and carries the crew to Vladivostock for trial . . . . .2 Oct. "

Human Freedom league organized in Independence hall, Philadelphia . . . . .12 Oct. "

Boatswain, mate, and 6 sailors of the U. S. cruiser *Baltimore* injured by a mob in the streets of Valparaiso, Chili, resulting in death of 2 sailors (see this record, 21 Jan.–17 July, 1892) . . . . .16 Oct. "

Nathaniel Duncan Ingraham, formerly of the U. S. navy (KOSZTA AFFAIR), afterwards in the Confederate service, dies at Charleston, S. C. . . . . . .16 Oct. "

James Parton, author, born 1822, dies at Newburyport, Mass. . . . . .17 Oct. "

Italy withdraws her prohibition of American pork, 21 Oct. "

Officers of the Louisiana State lottery indicted under U. S. law by the grand jury in Sioux Falls, N. Dak., 23 Oct. "

First Empire State express train runs from New York to Buffalo *via* N. Y. C. & H. R. R. R. in 8 hours 42 min. . . . . .26 Oct. "

Southern States exposition opens at Augusta, Ga., 2 Nov. "

[illegible] case submitted by counsel in the U. S. court at [illegible] Angeles, Cal. . . . . .5 Nov. "

[illegible] Pedro Montt, minister from Chili, officially pre[illegible] to pres. Harrison . . . . .14 Nov. "

[illegible] enters the office of Russell Sage in New York [illegible] a hand-bag, demands $1,250,000, and on [illegible] the bag filled with explosives, killing [illegible] a bystander, injuring others, and wreck[illegible] building . . . . .4 Dec. "

[illegible] Redfield Proctor resigns . . . . .5 Dec. "

[illegible] restrictions on American pork . .6 Dec. "

[illegible] murderer, executed at Sing Sing by [illegible] . . . . .7 Dec. "

[illegible] *First Session*, meets . . . . " "

[illegible] (democrat) of Ga. elected speaker of [illegible] . . . . .8 Dec. "

[illegible] Harrison .9 Dec. "

[illegible] general act passed by the Anti[illegible] Brussels, 2 July, 1890, 11 Jan. 1892

[illegible] set apart by proclama[illegible] . . . . .11 Jan. "

First Session (304 days) adjourns 1 Oct. 1890
[This was the second longest session ever held, 16,972 bills introduced nearly 1400 became laws.]
Louis Philippe Albert d'Orléans, comte de Paris, volunteer aide on gen McClellan's staff during the civil war, arrives in New York 3 Oct. "
Polygamy abolished as an institution of the church of Latter-day Saints at a general conference in Salt Lake City, Utah 6 Oct. "
Daughters of the American revolution organized at Washington 11 Oct "
Associate-justice Samuel Miller of the Supreme court, struck with paralysis 10 Oct, dies at Washington, 13 Oct "
William W Belknap ex-sec of war, born 1829, dies at Washington D C 13 Oct "
Chief of police David C Hennessy of New Orleans waylaid before his own home by Italian 'Maffia," to whose band he had traced a number of crimes, and killed, receiving 6 wounds 15 Oct. "
Religious excitement among the Indians of the Northwest ('Messiah craze") first appears 3 June, when 3 Indian chiefs, representing the Comanches, Cheyennes, and Arapahoes, meet near the Crow agency in Montana to behold the Great Spirit on the rocks, it develops into the "ghost dances" among the Sioux tribes the latter part of . Oct "
Henry M Stanley begins a lecture tour at New York city 12 Nov "
Benjamin Penhallow Shillaber, 'Mrs Partington," born 1814, dies at Chelsea, Mass 25 Nov "
Second Session convenes 1 Dec. "
President's message read " "
David Kalakaua, king of the Sandwich islands lands at San Francisco, Cal 4 Dec "
Tatonka Otanka 'Sitting Bull,' born in Dakota, 1837, who posed as leading apostle in the ghost dances, is arrested and is killed during an attempt of Indians to rescue him, near Grand river, about 40 miles from Standing Rock agency, N Dak. .15 Dec. "
Maj-gen Alfred H Terry, born 1827, dies at New Haven, Conn 16 Dec. "
Sec Blaine proposes to the British minister at Washington arbitration in the Behring Sea difficulty (our government contending that the phrase 'Pacific ocean" in the Russo-American and Anglo-Russian treaties of 1824 and 1825, does not include 'Behring sea') . . 17 Dec. "
Giovanni Succi concludes a fast of 45 days at New York (ABSTINENCE) 20 Dec. "
By proclamation the president appoints 1 May, 1893, as the opening and the last Thursday of Oct. 1893 as the closing day of the World's Columbian exposition at Chicago . 24 Dec. "
Battle with "Big Foot's" band of Indians on Wounded Knee creek, S. Dak, among the Indians killed were 44 squaws and 18 pappooses, loss to U S. troops, 32 killed, 39 wounded .29 Dec. "
Gen Francis E Spinner, U S. ex-treasurer, born 1802, dies at Jacksonville, Fla . 31 Dec. "
International Monetary conference meets at Washington . . . . . . 7 Jan. 1891
Motion for leave to file a petition for a writ of prohibition against the condemnation of the Canadian sealer *W P Sayward*, condemned by the U S District court in Alaska in 1887 for violating U. S. laws, by taking seals in Behring sea, and appealed to the Supreme court, is entered on behalf of the attorney-general of Canada.. .. .. 12 Jan. "
Senate passes a Free Coinage bill, adopted 17 June, 1890, as a substitute for the Financial bill, and takes up the Federal Election bill by 34 to 33. ..14 Jan. "
George Bancroft, historian, born 1800, dies at Washington ... .17 Jan. "
Indian chiefs at Pine Ridge agency, 14 Jan., agree to surrender to gen. Miles, who declares the Indian outbreak ended . ... 19 Jan. "
Discussion of the Federal Election bill (H. R. 11,045), passed by House of Representatives 2 July, 1890, closes in the Senate 19 Jan 1891
Aldrich clôture rule, to limit debate, submitted 29 Dec. 1890, is considered in Senate 20 Jan. "
King Kalakaua, born 1836, dies at San Francisco, 20 Jan. "
Representatives of the Farmers' Alliance and Industrial Union in Washington, D C, agree upon a confederation of the labor organizations 22 Jan "
Aldrich clôture resolution displaced in Senate by bill for apportionment of representation, by 35 to 34, 26 Jan "
Over 100 miners killed by an explosion of fire-damp in the coke-mines near Mt. Pleasant, Pa 27 Jan. "
Sec. of treas Windom, born 1827, dies suddenly of heart-disease at a banquet at Delmonico's, New York city, 29 Jan "
Act apportioning representatives in Congress, 356 after 3 Mch 1893, approved . 7 Feb. "
Strike involving 10,000 miners begins in Connellsville coke regions, Pa 9 Feb. "
Adm David Dixon Porter, born 1814, dies at Washington, D. C. 13 Feb. "
[With him expired the grade of admiral in the navy.]
Gen William T Sherman, born 1820, dies at New York, 14 Feb "
Gen Nathaniel P Banks placed upon the pension roll at the rate of $100 per month. . . 18 Feb. "
Sen. Ingalls chosen president of the Senate *pro tem*, 25 Feb 1886, and continued by successive elections until 3 Apr 1890 On 12 Mch 1890, he is unanimously designated to preside during the future absences of the vice-president and at the pleasure of the Senate, a function never before exercised by any member of the Senate he resigns this office 19 Feb "
Prof Alexander Winchell, geologist, born 1824, dies at Ann Arbor Mich . 19 Feb. "
First triennial of National Council of Women of the U S meets at Washington, D C 23 Feb "
Act to refund to the states $15,227,632.03 collected under the direct-tax act of 1861, levying $20,000,000, 2 Mch. "
Act authorizing 3 U S. prisons: 1 north another south of 39° and east of the Rocky mountains, the 3d west of the Rocky mountains . .3 Mch. "
Congress appropriates $15,000 for experiments in forestry and artificial rain-making . .. .. 3 Mch "
Act creating 9 Courts of Appeal and 9 additional U. S. Circuit Court judges approved . . 3 Mch. "
Act granting registry to certain foreign-built vessels with subsidies, the mails to be carried when required without additional compensation, and new vessels to be built suitable for conversion into auxiliary cruisers or transports. .. . .3 Mch. "
International Copyright act approved. " "
Fifty-first Congress adjourns.. .. ..4 Mch. "
[The 51st Congress was nicknamed the "Billion Dollar Congress" from the grand total of its appropriations.]
Eleven Italians confined in the parish prison, New Orleans, on charge of the murder of chief Hennessy, 6 of whom had just been acquitted by jury trial, are massacred ... . 14 Mch. "
Baron Fava, Italian minister at Washington, protests against the New Orleans lynching. .....15 Mch. "
Gen. Joseph E. Johnston, born 1807, dies at Washington, D C .. ..21 Mch. "
Italian minister Fava recalled ... . 31 Mch. "
Gen. Albert Pike, born 1809, dies at Washington, D C., 2 Apr. "
Sen George F. Edmunds resigns, to take effect 1 Nov., 6 Apr. "
Phineas T Barnum, born 1810, dies at Bridgeport, Conn. .. ..7 Apr. "
Patent centennial opened in Washington by pres. Harrison. ....8 Apr. "
Pres. Harrison and party leave Washington for an extended trip in the South and West........14 Apr. "
Resignation of sen. John H. Reagan of Tex., to take effect 10 June..........................24 Apr. "

Convention of International Young Women's Christian Association at Scranton, Pa 24-26 Apr 1891
China formally objects to Henry W Blair as minister from the U S, because of his speech in Congress against the Chinese 28 Apr "
Verdict of "not guilty" in Millington murder case at Denver, Col . 29 Apr "
Charles Pratt, philanthropist, born 1830, dies in New York city 4 May, "
U S marshal, at the request of Chilian minister, seizes the Chilian insurgent transport *Itata* at San Diego, Cal 6 May, "
Itata sails from San Diego, carrying off the U S deputy marshal 7 May, "
[The marshal was landed some 8 miles south of San Diego, and the *Itata* took from the American schooner *Robert and Minnie* a cargo of arms shipped from Ilion, N Y]
U S. cruiser *Charleston* sails in pursuit of the *Itata*, 9 May, "
Pres. Harrison returns to Washington 15 May, "
Rear-adm McCann given command of the American vessels in the South Pacific 17 May, "
Trans-Mississippi Commercial congress (1200 delegates) opens at Denver, Col 19 May, "
People's party organized at the National Union conference (1418 delegates from 32 states) at Cincinnati, O . 19 May, "
President opens to settlement about 1,600,000 acres of the Fort Berthold Indian reservation, S Dak, 20 May, "
Charleston reaches Callao without having seen the *Itata* 27 May, "
First Sunday opening of the New York Metropolitan museum, 10,000 visitors 31 May, "
Benson John Lossing, historian, born 1813, dies at Chestnut Ridge, Dutchess county, N. Y 3 June, "
Itata surrenders to adms McCann and Brown in the harbor of Iquique with a cargo of 5000 rifles, 4 June, "
Lieut R E Peary and wife (the first lady to join a Polar expedition) sail for the Arctic regions, 6 June, "
Great Britain agrees to a *modus vivendi*, a close season and limited privilege in the seal fisheries, until 1 May, 1892 Proclaimed by president 15 June, "
Monument, inscribed, "On this spot Christopher Columbus first set foot upon the soil of the New World," erected on Watling island by the Chicago *Herald* . 15 June, "
Nine new U. S Circuit courts of Appeal formally organized .. 16 June, "
Rain-making experiments begun in Texas under the department of agriculture 23 June, "
Discovery recorded of a new lake forming in Salton Sink, Ariz, owing to floods on the Colorado, 29 June, "
Weather bureau transferred from war department to department of agriculture, prof Mark W Harrington appointed chief. 30 June, "
Ex-vice-pres. Hannibal Hamlin, born 1809, dies at Bangor, Me 4 July, "
Charleston and *Itata* arrive at San Diego, Cal, " "
Four murderers, Slocum, Smiler, Wood, and Jugiro, executed by electricity at Sing Sing, N Y 7 July, "
Secretary of the treasury accepts $500 from the *Itata* for violation of the navigation laws 8 July, "
Cargo of arms and ammunition on the *Itata* libelled by the U S. marshal at San Diego, Cal. 14 July, "
Statue of gen Stonewall Jackson unveiled at Lexington, Va., 15,000 Confederate veterans present, oration by gen Early . . . . . . 21 July, "
Smokeless powder used for the first time in this country in experiments at Sandy Hook, N J 25 July, "
Thomas W Bocock, born 1815, for 14 years in congress from Virginia and for 4 years speaker of Confederate congress, dies in Appomattox co, Va . 5 Aug "
Two vessels seized in Behring sea for unlawful sealing. . . . . 7 Aug "
James Russell Lowell, born 1819, dies at Cambridge, Mass. . . . . 12 Aug "

UNI

Cherokee strip closed to the whites by order of the president 13 Aug 1891
Sarah Childress Polk, widow of ex-pres James K Polk, born 1803, dies at Nashville, Tenn 14 Aug "
Battle monument, 308 feet high at Bennington, Vt, dedicated, address by pres Harrison 19 Aug "
Over 60 persons killed by a falling building in Park place, New York city 22 Aug "
R G Dyrenforth and staff experiment in artificial rain production by dynamite bombs exploded in the air, etc, near Midland, Tex . 18-26 Aug "
First reunion of survivors of the Black Hawk war of 1832 held at Lena, Ill, 17 veterans over 70 years old present 28 Aug "
Germany removes restrictions on imports of American pork 3 Sept. "
New Chilian government, with Jorge Montt as president, officially recognized by the department of state at Washington, D C 7 Sept "
Denmark revokes prohibition of import of American pork 8 Sept. "
Forest reservation in Wyoming, adjoining Yellowstone National park, set apart by proclamation of pres Harrison, 30 Mch, and supplementary proclamation, 10 Sept "
William Ferrel, meteorologist, born 1817, dies at Maywood, Kan 18 Sept "
President proclaims the ceded Indian lands in Oklahoma territory open to settlement on 22 Sept, 18 Sept. "
Opening of the St Clair river tunnel celebrated at Port Huron and Sarnia 19 Sept. "
Russian man-of-war *Alente* seizes an American sealer, the *Lewis*, at Behring's island and carries the crew to Vladivostocks for trial 2 Oct "
Human Freedom league organized in Independence hall, Philadelphia 12 Oct "
Boatswain, mate, and 6 sailors of the U S cruiser *Baltimore* injured by a mob in the streets of Valparaiso, Chili, resulting in death of 2 sailors (see this record, 21 Jan.-17 July, 1892) 16 Oct "
Nathaniel Duncan Ingraham, formerly of the U S navy (KOSZTA AFFAIR), afterwards in the Confederate service, dies at Charleston, S. C. 16 Oct "
James Parton, author, born 1822, dies at Newburyport, Mass 17 Oct "
Italy withdraws her prohibition of American pork, 21 Oct "
Officers of the Louisiana State lottery indicted under U S law by the grand jury in Sioux Falls, N Dak, 23 Oct "
First Empire State express train runs from New York to Buffalo *via* N Y. C. & H R. R R in 8 hours 42 min 26 Oct "
Southern States exposition opens at Augusta, Ga, 2 Nov "
Itata case submitted by counsel in the U S. court at Los Angeles, Cal 5 Nov "
Señor Pedro Montt, minister from Chili, officially presented to pres. Harrison 14 Nov "
A lunatic enters the office of Russell Sage in New York city with a hand-bag, demands $1,250,000, and on refusal drops the bag filled with explosives, killing himself and a bystander, injuring others, and wrecking the building 4 Dec "
Sec of war Redfield Proctor resigns 5 Dec. "
France removes restrictions on American pork 6 Dec. "
Martin D Loppy, murderer, executed at Sing Sing by electricity . .. 7 Dec. "

Fifty-second Congress, First Session, meets " "
Charles F Crisp (Democrat) of Ga. elected speaker of the House . . . 8 Dec. "
Annual message of pres. Harrison . 9 Dec. "
U S Senate ratifies the general act passed by the Anti-slavery conference in Brussels, 2 July, 1890, 11 Jan 1892
Forest preserve in New Mexico set apart by proclamation of president . . 11 Jan. "

Randolph Rogers, sculptor, born 1825, dies at Rome, N Y 14 Jan 1892
Cong Bland introduces a Free Coinage bill in the House 21 Jan. "
Ultimatum of the U S served on the Chilian government by sec Blaine, through minister Montt, demanding an apology for the assault upon the sailors of the *Baltimore* in the streets of Valparaiso, an indemnity, and the withdrawal of the insulting circular of minister Matta . 21 Jan "
Satisfactory answer to the ultimatum from Chili submitted to Congress with a message from the president 27 Jan. "
James G Blaine writes to chairman Clarkson of the Republican National committee, refusing to be a candidate for president 6 Feb. "
Senate Financial committee reports against 3 Free Silver Coinage bills 9 Feb "
France, Italy, and Sweden chosen as Behring Sea arbitrators 10 Feb "
Bland Free Coinage Silver bill reported favorably by the House 10 Feb. "
Resolution for investigation of the so-called "sweating system" of tenement labor upon manufacture of clothing, etc 13 Feb. "
National Real Estate association formally organized in Nashville, Tenn 18 Feb "
First Continental congress of the National Society of the Daughters of the American Revolution, Mrs Harrison president-general, opens in Washington, 22 Feb. "
National Industrial conference meets in St Louis, Mo, with delegates from Farmers' Alliance, 246, Farmers' Mutual Benefit Association, 53, Knights of Labor, 82, National Farmers' Alliance, 97, National Citizens' Alliance, 25, Colored Farmers' Mutual Benefit Association, 97, National Citizens' Independent Alliance, 27, Patrons of Industry, 25, National Woman's Christian Temperance Union, 4 Delegates decide to act with the People's party in the presidential canvass 22 Feb "
Treaty signed at state department, Washington, by sir Julian Pauncefote and sec Blaine referring the Behring Sea dispute to an international arbitration commission of 7 members 29 Feb "
Ex-sec Bayard opposes the free coinage of silver in an open letter 14 Mch "
Forest reserve, Pike's peak, Col., set apart by proclamation of pres Harrison 11 Feb and 18 Mch "
Standard oil trust dissolved 21 Mch "
David Hayes Agnew, surgeon, born 1818, dies at Philadelphia, Pa. 22 Mch "
Debate on the Silver bill closes in House of Representatives and fails of a vote 24 Mch "
Walt Whitman, poet, born 1819, dies at Camden, N J., 26 Mch "
Treaty with foreign powers for repressing the slave-trade in Africa and the importation of fire-arms, ammunition, and spirituous liquors, signed at Washington 2 Apr "
Steamer *Missouri*, which sailed from New York, 15 Mch, carrying food supplies to starving Russians, arrives at Libau 3 Apr "
President proclaims open to settlement the greater part of Lake Traverse Indian reservation in North Dakota, 15 Apr 11 Apr. "
President proclaims open to settlement Cheyenne and Arapahoe Indian lands in Oklahoma, 19 Apr, about 3,000,000 acres 12 Apr "
Under instruction from pres Harrison, sec Blaine tenders the Italian government, as a voluntary offering for distribution among the relatives of Italians lynched in New Orleans, 14 Mch 1891, $25,000, which is accepted and paid 14 Apr. "
Baron Fava ordered to resume his position as minister to the U. S by the Italian government. 16 Apr. "
Sec Blaine and sir Julian Pauncefote conclude a new *modus vivendi* for the Behring sea 18 Apr. "
Bill introduced in the House by Mr. Geary of California, 6 Jan, to prohibit absolutely the coming of Chinese into the U S, whether subjects of the Chinese empire or otherwise, referred to the committee on foreign affairs On 19 Feb he reports a substitute from the committee, which, taken up and debated, 4 Apr, passes the House, 179-43, 107 not voting Senate and House not able to agree, a conference is held and a bill presented, which passes the House, 3 May, and the Senate, 4 May, and approved 5 May, 1892
Behring Sea Arbitration treaty ratified 9 May, "
Act to encourage American shipping approved, 10 May, "
Steamer *Conemaugh* sent from New York and Philadelphia with provisions for the starving Russians, arrives at Riga 12 May, "
Spain removes restriction on American pork 22 May, "
Sen Stewart's bill for free coinage of silver taken up by the Senate 26 May, "
Provision for closing the World's Fair government exhibit on Sundays adopted by the House of Representatives 26 May, "
James G Blaine, secretary of state, resigns 4 June, "
Dam at Spartansburg, Pa, bursts, causing a flood and the breaking of tanks of gasoline, which ignites on Oil creek between Titusville and Oil City, flood and fire result in the loss of over 100 lives 5 June, "
Republican National convention assembles at Minneapolis, Minn, 7 June, gov. McKinley of O permanent chairman, 8 June, on 1st ballot Benjamin Harrison receives 535⅙ votes, Blaine, 182⅙, McKinley, 182, Reed, 4, Robert T Lincoln, 1 On motion of Charles McKinley the nomination of Harrison is made unanimous At the evening session Whitelaw Reid of N Y is nominated for vice-president by acclamation . 10 June, "
Pres. Harrison, by message to Congress, recommends retaliation against Canada for discrimination against American vessels . 20 June, "
Democratic National convention meets in Chicago, Ill., 21 June, W L. Wilson of W. Va. chosen permanent chairman, 22 June, First ballot for president cast 23 June Cleveland 617⅓, Hill, 115, Boies, 103, Gorman, 36½, Carlisle, 14, Cleveland declared nominated, and for vice-president Adlai E. Stevenson of Ill. chosen unanimously on first ballot 23 June, "
National Prohibition convention meets at Cincinnati, O . . 29 June, "
Congress authorizes the president to proclaim a general holiday commemorating the 400th anniversary of the discovery of America 29 June "
John W Foster of Ind confirmed by the Senate as sec. of state 29 June, "
Gen. John Bidwell of Cal nominated for president, and J B. Cranfell of Tex for vice-president by the Prohibition convention . 30 June, "
Lock-out of strikers at the Carnegie Steel company's mills at Homestead, Pa, begins .. 1 July, "
Catholic Sioux congress opens at the Cheyenne agency, S Dak., 6000 Sioux Indians present 3 July, "
First National convention of the People's party meets at Omaha, Neb, 2 July, H. L. Loucks of S Dak. permanent chairman Gen James B Weaver of Ia. nominated for president, 4 July, gen James G Field of Va. for vice-president . 5 July, "
Congress appropriates $50,000 for site and pedestal for a statue of gen. W. T. Sherman 5 July, "
Pinkerton detectives, attempting to land from a barge at the Carnegie mills, Homestead, Pa, are attacked by strikers, several detectives and strikers killed or wounded 6 July, "
Entire National Guard of Pennsylvania is ordered to Homestead by gov Pattison . . . 10 July, "
Lock out involving 3000 striking miners begins in the Cœur d'Alene mining district, in Shoshone county, Id., 1 Apr, an attack is made by union men on new hands employed in the Gem mine, in which several are killed . ... . 11 July, "
Cyrus W. Field, born 1819, dies at Ardsley, N. Y., 12 July, "

River and Harbor bill, appropriating $21,153,618 and authorizing in contracts $31,555,401, approved, 13 July, 1892

Bland-Stewart Free Silver bill, passed by the Senate, 29 to 25, 1 July, is refused consideration in the House by 154 to 136 13 July, "

Proclamation of president commanding all persons in insurrection in Idaho to disperse 16 July, "

Indemnity of $75,000 in the matter of the Chilian affair of 16 Oct 1891, accepted from Chili by U S minister Eagan (the money to be distributed among the relatives of the 2 sailors killed and those who were injured) 17 July, "

Proviso for closing the World's Fair on Sunday confirmed by Senate 14 July, and concurred in by House 19 July, "

President authorized to contract for 1 armored cruiser of about 8000 tons and 1 coast-line battle-ship of 9000 tons, by act approved 19 July, "

Two thousand U S troops, sent by pres Harrison to the Cœur d'Alene mining district, Id., occupy Wardner, 14 July, order restored among the strikers, and soldiers ordered home 23 July, "

H C Frick, chairman of the Carnegie Steel company, shot and twice wounded by a Russian-Hebrew anarchist named Berkman 23 July, "

Private Iams of Company K, 10th regiment calling for three cheers for the assassin, is hung up by his thumbs for 30 minutes by order of col Streeter 23 July, "

Act authorizing the president in retaliation to demand tolls for, or prohibit the passage of, St. Mary's Falls canal by foreign vessels, in his discretion 26 July, "

Act granting pensions of $8 per month to survivors of the Indian wars of 1832-42 (Black Hawk war, Creek war, Cherokee disturbance, and Seminole war), approved 27 July, "

Act changing date of the dedication of the World's Fair buildings from 12 Oct to 21 Oct 4 Aug "

Act granting pensions of $12 per month to all nurses during the civil war, now dependent 5 Aug "

Bill for coinage of 5,000,000 half-dollar silver pieces as souvenirs for the benefit of the Columbian exposition, on condition that the exposition shall not be opened on Sunday 5 Aug "

Train in charge of the U S government, carrying $20,000,000 in gold, leaves San Francisco for New York 5 Aug "

Resolution of Congress inviting the king and queen of Spain and the descendants of Columbus to the World's Columbian exposition . 5 Aug "

First Session adjourns. " "

Miss Lizzie Borden arrested in Fall River, Mass, charged with the murder (4 Aug) of her father and step-mother (TRIALS) 11 Aug "

Violence by miners in Tennessee opposed to convict labor, quelled by National Guard . 13-16 Aug. "

Switchmen's strike on Erie railroad begins at Buffalo, N Y, where the strikers burn freight trains, destroying about a million dollars' worth of railroad property 14 Aug "

Gen Doyle orders out the 65th and 74th regiments of National Guard at Buffalo 15 Aug "

In response to appeal from sheriff and mayor of Buffalo, gov Flower of N Y orders out about 8000 of the National Guard from New York, Brooklyn, and elsewhere to protect property at Buffalo, N.Y 17 Aug. "

Pres. Harrison, in retaliation against Canadian measures, proclaims that a toll of 20 cents per ton be collected from 1 Sept until further notice, on all freight passing through St. Mary's Falls canal to any port of the dominion of Canada 20 Aug. "

Switchmen's strike at Buffalo declared off by grandmaster Sweeney 24 Aug. "

John Bidwell's letter of acceptance 25 Aug "

Eight delegates of Socialistic Labor party in New York city nominate Simon Wing of Mass for president, and Charles H Matchett of N. Y. for vice-president of U. S . . . . . .28 Aug. "

Hamburg-American steamship *Moravia* brings to New York the first cases of cholera (out of 385 steerage passengers, 22 die during the voyage) 30 Aug 1892

George William Curtis, born 1824, dies at West Brighton Staten Island 31 Aug "

Pres Harrison orders 20 days' quarantine of all immigrant vessels from cholera-infected ports 1 Sept "

Pres Harrison's letter of acceptance published 5 Sept "

John Greenleaf Whittier, poet, born 1807, dies at Hampton Falls, N H 7 Sept. "

Ex-sen Francis Kernan born 1816, dies at Utica, N Y, 7 Sept "

John L Sullivan, pugilist, defeated by James J Corbett at the Olympic club, New Orleans, in 21 rounds (BOXING) 7 Sept "

Lieut Peary and party arrive at St John's, N F, on the steamer *Kite*, sent to the Arctic regions in search of them 11 Sept "

Cabin passengers of the *Normannia* prevented from landing at Fire island, by injunction restraining the health authorities from using the island for quarantine purposes, 12 Sept, injunction dissolved, and 2 regiments of National Guard and Naval reserves ordered out by gov Flower, passengers are finally suffered to land 13 Sept "

Gens Weaver and Field accept the nomination of the People's party 17 Sept "

Gen John Pope, born 1823, dies at Sandusky, O, 23 Sept. "

Patrick S. Gilmore, leader of Gilmore's band, born 1829, dies at St Louis 24 Sept "

Grover Cleveland's letter of acceptance 26 Sept. "

Encounter at Coffeyville, Kan, the famous Dalton gang, attempting to rob the banks, are annihilated by a marshal's posse, in which affray 4 citizens are killed by the desperadoes 5 Oct "

Columbus day celebration in New York city and elsewhere 12 Oct. "

Opening exercises of the World's Columbian exposition at Chicago 21 Oct "

Presidential election held 8 Nov "

[Popular vote Cleveland and Stevenson, Democratic, 5,556,533, Harrison and Reid, Republican, 5,440,216, Weaver and Field People's party, 1,122,015, Bidwell and Cranfill, Prohibition, 279,191, Wing and Matchett, Social Labor party, 21,191]

Strike at the Carnegie mills, Homestead, Pa, declared off 20 Nov "

Continental congress of the Salvation Army opens in New York 21 Nov "

Jay Gould, born 1836, dies in New York city, leaving a fortune estimated at $72,000,000 2 Dec "

U S, England, and Germany agree to common action in restoring order in Samoa . 5 Dec "

Second Session opens. " "

Joint resolution, introduced in House by Mr Durborow of Ill to open the Exposition on Sunday, referred to committee on Columbian exposition 5 Dec. "

President's message read in House and Senate 6 Dec. "

Proclamations of the president setting apart the South Platte Forest reserve in Colorado, 9 Dec, San Gabriel Timber reservation, California, 20 Dec., Battlement Forest reserve, Colorado, 24 Dec., and Afognak Forest and Fish Culture reserve in Alaska. 24 Dec "

President issues a proclamation of amnesty to Mormons liable to prosecution for polygamy on condition of future obedience to law 4 Jan 1893

Pensioners of Mexican war now drawing $8 to receive $12 per month, by act of 5 Jan. "

Great Northern railroad completed to Pacific 6 Jan. "

Presidential electors meet at state capitals and vote, 9 Jan. "

Gen Benjamin F. Butler, born at Deerfield, N H, 5 Nov 1818, dies suddenly at Washington 11 Jan. "

Ex-pres Rutherford B. Hayes, born at Delaware, O, 1822, dies at his home at Fremont, O 17 Jan. "

L. Q C Lamar, ex-Confederate general, ex-senator, secretary of the interior in Cleveland's first cabi-

net, and associate-justice of the Supreme court, dies near Macon, Ga........................23 Jan. 1893
Phillips Brooks, Protestant-Episcopal bishop of Massachusetts, born at Boston, 13 Dec. 1835, dies there, 23 Jan. "
James G. Blaine, born 1830, dies at his home in Washington...............................27 Jan. "
H. E. Jackson of Tenn., judge of the 6th Federal district, nominated to succeed justice Lamar........2 Feb. "
Bill to repeal the silver purchase clause of the Sherman act called up by sen. Hill.................6 Feb. "
Electoral votes counted....................8 Feb. "
[For Cleveland and Stevenson, 277; for Harrison and Reid, 145; for Weaver and Field, 22.]
Hawaiian commission reaches Washington, 3 Feb.; treaty of annexation signed, 14 Feb., and laid before the Senate............................15 Feb. "
Act for a national quarantine against cholera approved, 15 Feb. "
Gen. P. T. G. Beauregard, born near New Orleans, 28 May, 1818, dies at New Orleans, La........20 Feb. "
President suspends part of the proclamation of 18 Aug. 1892, imposing tolls on freight for Canada through the St. Mary's Falls canal...............21 Feb. "
Inman line steamers *City of New York* and *City of Paris* transferred from British to American registry; the stars and stripes raised on the *City of New York* by pres. Harrison.........................22 Feb. "
Sec. of state Foster resigns to sit on the Behring Sea tribunal at Paris......................23 Feb. "
Proclamations of president setting apart the Sierra Forest reserve, Cal., 14 Feb.; Pacific Coast reserve, Washington, 20 Feb.; Grand Cañon Forest reserve, Arizona, 20 Feb.; Trabuco Cañon Forest reserve and another timber reserve in California, 25 Feb. "
Diplomatic Appropriation act, authorizing the president at his discretion to confer on the envoys to any government the same rank as its representative in the U. S., approved.....................1 Mch. "
Act requiring inter-state railroads after 1 Jan. 1898 to use only cars with automatic couplers and engines with air-brakes approved...................2 Mch. "
Fifty-second Congress appropriates $1,026,822,049.72, more by $38,400,000 than the 51st, the so-called "Billion Dollar" Congress..............3 Mch. "
Fifty-second Congress adjourns................4 Mch. "

Twenty-seventh Administration—Democratic. 4 Mch. 1893 to 3 Mch. 1897.

Grover Cleveland, N. Y., president.
Adlai E. Stevenson, Ill., vice-president.

CABINET.

Walter Q. Gresham, Ill., sec. of state, from 6 Mch. 1893.
John G. Carlisle, Ky., sec. of treas., " " "
Daniel S. Lamont, N. Y., sec. of war, " " "
Richard Olney, Mass., attorney-gen., " " "
Wilson S. Bissell, N. Y., postmaster-gen., " " "
William L. Wilson, W. Va., " " 1 Mch. 1895.
Hilary A. Herbert, Ala., sec. of navy, from 6 Mch. 1893.
Hoke Smith, Ga., sec. of interior, " " "
J. Sterling Morton, Neb., sec. of agriculture, from 6 Mch. 1893.
Richard Olney, Mass., sec. of state from 7 June, 1895.
Judson Harmon, Ohio, attorney-gen. " " "
David R. Francis, Mo., sec. of interior, from 22 Aug. 1896.

Senate assembles in extra session...........4 Mch. 1893
President withdraws the Hawaiian treaty....9 Mch. "
Hawaiian princess Kaiulani and suite reach Washington, 8 Mch., and are received at the White House, 13 Mch. "
Extradition treaty with Sweden ratified....18 Mch. "
Ex-representative Blount sails from San Francisco for Honolulu on the revenue cutter *Rush* on his special mission to Hawaii....................20 Mch. "
Great Britain and France have raised their representatives to the U. S. to the rank of ambassadors, 24 Mch. "
A threatening outbreak on the Choctaw reservation, Ind. Ter., between rival Indian factions, results in a battle; several are wounded.............28 Mch. 1893
Edmund Kirby Smith, Confederate general, born at St. Augustine, Fla., 16 May, 1824, dies in Sewanee, Tenn..............................28 Mch. "
Gen. Hiram Berdan, inventor of a long-range rifle, dies at Washington, D. C..................31 Mch. "
Thomas F. Bayard of Del. nominated ambassador to the court of St. James (the first ambassador of the U. S.), 30 Mch.; he takes the oath of office........3 Apr. "
Arguments of English and American representatives begun before the Court of Arbitration in the Behring Sea dispute..........................4 Apr. "
Minister Hicks telegraphing that the consular agency at Mollendo, Peru, was attacked, 25 Mch., and the agent shot, sec. Gresham directs a protest and a demand for reparation.....................6 Apr. "
Chief of the diplomatic service to France, James B. Eustis of La., raised to the rank of ambassador, 8 Apr. "
Caravel *Santa Maria*, a reproduction of the flag-ship of Columbus, given to the U. S. by Spain, 26 Mch., reaches Havana........................9 Apr. "
Sir Julian Pauncefote received by the president as ambassador from Great Britain.............11 Apr. "
American Railway union organized at Chicago, 12 Apr. "
M. Patenotre received by the president as ambassador from France..........................12 Apr. "
Duke of Veragua and party arrive at New York and are publicly received...................15 Apr. "
Senate special session adjourns............. " "
Spanish caravels reach Hampton Roads, 21 Apr.; New York harbor..........................24 Apr. "
Original Paul Jones flag raised and saluted at the Highlands of Navesink, N. J...................25 Apr. "
Gen. John M. Corse, the hero of ALLATOONA, Ga., dies at the "Hemlocks," Mass................27 Apr. "
International Columbian naval review in New York harbor and Hudson river; pres. Cleveland reviews the fleet on the *Dolphin*, passing between lines of ships 3 miles in length; 10 nations represented by 36 war-ships and over 10,000 officers and men, 27 Apr. "
Liberty bell received at Chicago with honors (BELLS), 29 Apr. "
World's Columbian exposition formally opened at Chicago by pres. Cleveland..............1 May, "
Secretary of the treasury issues an order, supplemented by a circular from the attorney-general, suspending arrests under the Chinese Exclusion act until further orders..............................4 May, "
James H. Blount of Ga. appointed minister to Hawaii to succeed John L. Stevens, resigned.......9 May, "
Joseph Francis, inventor of the life-saving car, for which a special gold medal was awarded, 27 Aug. 1888, and presented by Congress, 12 Apr. 1890, dies at Cooperstown, N. Y., aged 92...................10 May, "
Locomotive engine No. 999 of the New York Central & Hudson River railroad runs a mile in 32 sec. between Rochester and Buffalo, N. Y.............11 May, "
Geary Chinese Exclusion act upheld as constitutional by the Supreme court in special session; arguments begun, 10 May; decision reached.........15 May, "
Secretary of state defers deportation of Chinese under the Geary act until Congress shall appropriate sufficient funds.........................17 May, "
Infanta Eulalie arrives in New York with her husband, prince Antoine, to represent the queen regent of Spain at the World's Fair..............18 May, "
Cherokee strip between Kansas and Oklahoma, containing 6,072,754 acres, purchased by the government for $8,596,736, to be added to Oklahoma...18 May, "
Jefferson Davis's remains removed from New Orleans, 28 May, and reinterred in Hollywood cemetery, Richmond, Va..........................31 May, "
Official notice that the Italian and German legations at Washington are made embassies...2 and 3 June, "

President promulgates the extradition treaty with Russia, ratified at St. Petersburg, 21 Apr., to go into effect 24 June.........................5 June, 1893
Edwin T. Booth, actor, born near Baltimore, Md., 13 Nov. 1833, dies in New York city.........7 June, "
Gold reserve in the U.S. treasury falls below $89,600,000..................................8 June, "
Floor of Ford's theatre, Washington, D. C., used by the pension record division of the war office, falls while nearly 400 government clerks are at work in the building; 21 killed, 68 injured...........9 June, "
Battle-ship *Massachusetts* launched at messrs. Cramp & Sons' ship-yards in Philadelphia.......10 June, "
Viking ship, representing Lief Ericson's "Cockstab Find," which left Bergen, Norway, 30 Apr., for the World's Fair at Chicago, reaches New York, 17 June, "
U. S. sen. Leland Stanford, ex-governor of California, born 1824, dies at Palo Alto, Cal..........20 June, "
Gov. Altgeld of Ill. pardons Fielden, Schwab, and Neebe, anarchists engaged in the Haymarket riot, 26 June, "
Pres. Cleveland calls an extra session of Congress to meet 7 Aug..........................30 June, "
Frequent failures among national, state, and private banks...........................July–Sept. "
Lieut. Peary leaves New York on his 2d Greenland expedition..............................2 July, "
First summer meeting for university extension students called in Philadelphia by the Society for the Extension of University Teaching.........5 July, "
Justice Blatchford, of the Supreme court, born 9 Mch. 1820, dies at Newport, R. I..............7 July, "
Colorado Silver convention opens in Denver, and issues an appeal to the people of the U. S.......11 July, "
Institute of Christian Sociology organized at Chautauqua, prof. R. T. Ely, Ph.D., LL.D., of the University of Wisconsin, first president....19–20 July, "
Ex-gov. G. C. Perkins appointed by gov. Markham of California to fill the unexpired term of the late sen. Stanford...........................22 July, "
First convention of the National Bimetallic league in Chicago..............................1 Aug. "

Fifty-third Congress. *First Session* (extra) assembles, 7 Aug. "

Senate composed of 44 Democrats, 37 Republicans, 4 Populists, with 3 vacancies. House composed of 216 Democrats, 125 Republicans, 11 Populists, with 4 vacancies. C. F. Crisp of Ga. elected speaker, 7 Aug. "
President's message, recommending the repeal of the purchase clause of the Sherman Silver act...8 Aug. "
"Currency famine" early in August; premiums for small bills reach $25 per $1000...........10 Aug. "
Wilson bill to repeal the Silver Purchase law introduced in the House.................. 11 Aug. "
U. S. cruiser *Minneapolis* launched at Cramp & Sons' ship-yards, Philadelphia................12 Aug. "
Decision of Behring Sea Court of Arbitration, denying the right of the U. S. to a close sea, but adopting regulations forbidding the killing of seals within 50 miles of Pribylov islands, or outside that limit from 1 May to 31 July.................15 Aug. "
Legislatures of Montana, Washington, and Wyoming adjourning without electing senators for 6 years, beginning 4 Mch. 1893, the Senate decides that when a state legislature has the opportunity to elect and fails, an appointment by the governor is void. This left 3 vacancies in the Senate............23 Aug. "
Severe hurricane in South Atlantic states; more than 600 lives lost at Beaufort, Port Royal, and adjacent places..................................28 Aug. "
Wilson bill, repealing the purchasing clause of the "Sherman act," passes the House; yeas, 239; nays, 109; not voting, 5...................... 28 Aug. "
Wilson bill reported in the Senate from the finance committee, with amendments, pledging the government to maintain bimetalism, by sen. Voorhees of Ind...............................29 Aug. 1893
Official data show 560 state and private bank suspensions and 72 resumptions and 155 national bank suspensions and 70 resumptions from 1 Jan. to 1 Sept. "
Albert S. Willis of Ky. appointed minister to Hawaii, to succeed Mr. Blount.................3 Sept. "
Second World's Sunday-school convention meets at St. Louis..............................4 Sept. "
Pan-American Medical congress opened at Washington, D. C., by pres. Cleveland; over 1000 physicians in attendance..............................5 Sept. "
Hamilton Fish, LL.D., statesman, born 3 Aug. 1808, dies at Garrisons, N. Y..................7 Sept. "
Envoy to Germany made an ambassador.....8 Sept. "
World's Parliament of Religions begins its sessions in Chicago, Ill...................11 Sept. "
Twenty masked robbers hold up a train on the Lake Shore railroad, near Kendallville, Ind., shoot the engineer, and, by dynamite, secure nearly $20,000 from the express car...................12 Sept. "
Five thousand ounces of gold, worth $134,000, missed from the U. S. mint at Philadelphia, in a vault not opened since 1887. The money was stolen by weigh clerk H. S. Cochran, who restores $107,000, 14 Sept. "
Cherokee outlet, Oklahoma, opened to settlement under proclamation of the president, 19 Aug. 1893; 100,000 persons make a rush for the 6,000,000 acres of land..........................16 Sept. "
Centennial of the laying of the corner-stone of the Capitol celebrated at Washington; William Wirt Henry of Va. chief orator...............18 Sept. "
Destructive storm on the gulf of Mexico; over 2000 lives lost along the coast, with a large loss of property.................................2 Oct. "
Pan-American Bimetallic convention meets at St. Louis...................................3 Oct. "
Tucker bill to repeal the Federal Election laws passes the House by 201 to 102; not voting, 50, 10 Oct. "
Senate sits continuously to force a vote on the Repeal bill, from 11 A.M. Wednesday, 11 Oct., to 1.45 A.M. Friday, when it adjourns for want of a quorum. Sen. Allen of Neb. holds the floor for 14 hours, in the longest continuous speech ever made in the Senate, 13 Oct. "
American yacht *Vigilant* wins the 3d of 5 races for the *America's* cup, off Sandy Hook, N. J., defeating the English *Valkyrie*......................13 Oct. "
Sec. Gresham issues confidential instructions to minister Willis, outlining the plan of the president for reinstating the queen at Hawaii by moral force, under certain conditions.................. 18 Oct. "
Lucy Stone (Blackwell), founder of the American Woman Suffrage association, born 13 Oct. 1818, dies at Dorchester, Mass.....................18 Oct. "
Philip Schaff, scholar and clergyman, born in Switzerland, 1819, dies in New York city.........20 Oct. "
Rear-adm. Stanton removed from command of the South Atlantic squadron, on charge of saluting the flag-ship of adm. Mello, leader of the Brazilian revolutionists (Rio Janeiro)...............25 Oct. "
Battle-ship *Oregon* launched at San Francisco, 26 Oct. "
World's Columbian Exposition closed....30 Oct. "
Senate passes the Wilson bill to repeal the Silver Purchase law, with the Voorhees amendment, by 43 to 32 (23 Republicans, 20 Democrats for; 19 Democrats, 9 Republicans, 4 Populists against; 10 not voting), 30 Oct. "
Wilson bill as amended passes the House by 193 to 94; not voting, 66; and is approved...........1 Nov. "
McCreary Chinese Exclusion bill, as amended by Mr. Geary, passes the House by 178 to 9, 16 Oct., and Senate 2 Nov. The bill extends the time of registration 6 months from date; approved....3 Nov. "

First Session (extra) adjourns 3 Nov 1893
Francis Parkman, American historian, born 1823, dies at Jamaica Plains, near Boston 8 Nov. "
Extradition treaty with Norway ratified 8 Nov, and proclaimed . 9 Nov. "
Supreme court decides that the great lakes of this country and their connecting waters are included in the term "high seas" 20 Nov "
Jeremiah M Rusk, ex-secretary of agriculture, dies at his home in Viroqua Wis, aged 53 21 Nov "
J R Sovereign of Ia appointed to succeed grand-master workman Powderly (for 15 years at the head of the Knights of Labor), at the annual convention at Philadelphia Pa 14-28 Nov "
Pauline Cushman (Fryer), actress, scout, and spy in the Federal army during the civil war, dies in San Francisco, Cal, aged 60 . 2 Dec "
Supreme court declares the alien contract labor law constitutional . 4 Dec. "
Second Session assembles President's message received and read 4 Dec. "
Bill to admit Utah to the Union passes the House, 13 Dec. "
Bill to admit Arizona to the Union passes the House, 15 Dec, referred to the committee on territories in the Senate . 18 Dec "
President's message to Congress defining his position in the Hawaiian controversy 18 Dec "
Wilson Tariff bill reported in the House from the ways and means committee 19 Dec "
Rear-adm Stanton restored to rank, and assigned to command of the North Atlantic squadron, 21 Dec. "
Senate committee begins the investigation of pres. Cleveland's Hawaiian policy 27 Dec "
Debate on the Wilson Tariff bill begins in the House, 8 Jan 1894
William B Hornblower of N Y nominated associate-justice of the Supreme court in place of Blatchford, deceased, 19 Sept 1893, rejected by the Senate, through the influence of sen Hill of N Y, by 30 to 24 15 Jan "
John H Gear of Ia elected U S senator 16 Jan "
Sec Carlisle announces an issue of $50,000,000 10-year 5 per cent. bonds, payable in coin 17 Jan. "
U. S sen Edward C Walthall from Mississippi resigns, 18 Jan "
Income tax clause attached to the Tariff bill in the House by 175 to 56, 31 Jan, and the bill amended passed by 204 to 140, not voting 8 . 1 Feb "
Old corvette KEARSARGE, which fought and sank the ALABAMA off Cherbourg, France, during the civil war, is wrecked on Roncardo reef about 200 miles N E from Bluefields, Nicaragua, no lives lost, 2 Feb "
Bland Silver bill, providing for the coinage of seigniorage to the amount of $55,000,000, introduced in the House .7 Feb. "
McCreary resolutions on Hawaii, upholding the administration policy, pass the House by 177 to 76, not voting, 98 . . 7 Feb "
Federal Election Laws Repeal bill passes the Senate by 39 to 28 7 Feb, approved . . 8 Feb "

[This bill repealed all statutes relating to supervisors and special deputy-marshals. The election laws, often called "the Force Bills," were originally passed 31 May, 1870, and further strengthened by act of 20 Apr 1871, to protect the colored voter at the polls]

Wheeler H Peckham of N Y nominated associate-justice of the Supreme court, 22 Jan, nomination rejected by the Senate, through the influence of sen Hill of N Y, by 41 to 32 . 16 Feb. "
Sen E D White of La nominated as associate-justice and confirmed . . . . . 19 Feb "
Bland Silver bill passes the House by 168 to 129; not voting, 56 . . . . 1 Mch. "
N. C Blanchard, representative in Congress, appointed by the governor of Louisiana, qualifies as successor to sen White 12 Mch 1894
Bland bill passes the Senate by 44 to 31, not voting, 10 15 Mch "
Tariff bill, with amendments, reported in the Senate from the committee on finance by sen Voorhees, 20 Mch "
J. S Coxey's Army of the Commonweal starts from Massillon, O, for Washington with about 100 men, 25 Mch "
Alfred Holt Colquitt, U S senator from Ga, dies at Washington, D C, in his 70th year .26 Mch. "
Pres. Cleveland vetoes the Bland bill for coinage of seigniorage 29 Mch. "
Sen. Voorhees opens the tariff debate in the Senate, 2 Apr "
Kelly's Industrial army, 350 strong, leaves San Francisco for Oakland on its way to Washington, 3 Apr "
Bill to carry out the terms of the Behring Sea tribunal passes the Senate, 3 Apr, and is approved, 6 Apr "
President proclaims the award of the Behring Sea tribunal . 9 Apr "
Patrick Walsh, editor of the Augusta *Chronicle*, appointed by the governor of Ga to succeed U S. sen. Colquitt, 2 Apr, qualifies 9 Apr. "
Kelly's army, augmented to 1200 men, seizes a Union Pacific railroad train of 20 coal-cars and proceeds eastward 12 Apr "
Sen Zebulon B Vance of N C dies in Washington, D C, aged 64 14 Apr "
Gen Henry W Slocum dies at his home in Brooklyn, aged 66 . . 14 Apr "
Henry S. Ives, nicknamed the "Napoleon of finance," dies of consumption near Asheville, N C 17 Apr. "
Ex-gov Thomas J Jarvis, appointed 19 Apr to succeed the late sen Vance of N C., qualifies 26 Apr. "
Gen Coxey's army of Commonwealers arrives at Brightwood park, near Washington, D C 29 Apr. "
Francis B Stockbridge, U S. senator from Michigan, dies at Chicago, aged 68 . 30 Apr "
Leaders of Coxey's army arrested for trespassing on the grounds of the Capitol, and imprisoned, 1 May, "
Canadian revenue cutter *Petrel* seizes 2 American steamboats on lake Erie and arrests 48 residents of Ohio on charge of illegal fishing in Canadian waters, 9 May, "
John Patton, jr, appointed U S senator, to succeed F B Stockbridge, by gov Rich of Mich, 5 May, qualifies . . . 10 May, "
Days of grace on notes, drafts, etc, in New York abolished after 1 Jan 1895, by act of . 10 May, "
Richard Croker resigns as a member of the executive, and as chairman of the finance committee of Tammany Hall, John McQuade succeeds him, 10 May, "
W H. Edwards, consul-general at Berlin, dies, 16 May, "
General assembly of the Presbyterian church convicts prof Henry P Smith of heresy by a vote of 396 to 101 . . . . . . 26 May, "
Kelly's Industrial army, 1100 strong, reaches St. Louis, 28 May, divides, and proceeds down the Mississippi and up the Ohio towards Washington, 31 May, "
Frye's California army arrives in detachments at Washington . early part of June, "
Rhode Island legislature elects ex-gov George P. Wetmore as successor to U S. sen. Dixon 12 June, "
American Railway union boycott of the Pullman Palace Car company grows into a general western railroad strike (STRIKE) . . . . 27 June, "
Bill making the 1st Monday in Sept. a legal holiday, "Labor day," in the U S, approved 28 June, "
Rear-adm William Grenville Temple, U S. N, dies at Washington, aged 70 . . . . . 28 June, "

Kelly's army reaches the vicinity of Washington, about 1 July, 1894
U S judges Groscup and Woods of the northern district of Illinois enjoin pres Debs of the American Railway union and others from interference with trains carrying U S. mails 2 July, "
Secretary of war announces that the U S troops at fort Sheridan—8 companies of infantry, 2 troops of cavalry, and a battery of light artillery—have been ordered to Chicago to enforce the laws of the U S, 3 July, "
Gorman Compromise Tariff bill passes the Senate yeas, 39 (37 Democrats, 2 Populists), nays, 34 (31 Republicans, 2 Populists, 1 Democrat [Mr Hill of N Y]), with 634 amendments to the original Wilson bill of the House 3 July, "
Gov Altgeld of Illinois protests against ordering Federal troops into the state 5 July, "
National convention in interest of good roads opens at Asbury Park, N J 5 July, "
Proclamation of president warning unlawful assemblages in the state of Illinois to disperse, 8 July, and a second proclamation referring to states in the northwest 9 July, "
Pres Debs vice-pres Howard, and other leaders in the American Railway union strike, indicted by the Federal grand jury for conspiracy to obstruct the mails and hinder the execution of laws 10 July, "
Joint committee of the Senate and House on naval affairs agrees on a scheme of promotion in the navy, 13 July, "
Pres Cleveland signs the Enabling act to admit Utah into the Union 17 July, "
Representative Wilson from West Virginia reads in the House a personal letter from the president condemning the Senate tariff bill 19 July, "
Gen Coxey, after a short term in the district jail, disbands his army, stating that his plan had failed and that they would have to look out for themselves, 26 July, "
Ex-judge advocate-gen Joseph Holt, U S army retired, born Jan 1807 dies in Washington, D C, 1 Aug "
American Railway union strike virtually ended 14 July, when the strikers returned to work in large numbers, is formally declared off 3 Aug. "
U S treasury gold reserve reaches the lowest point since the resumption of specie payments, namely, $52,189,500 7 Aug "
Pres Cleveland recognizes the new republic of Hawaii, 8 Aug "
A detachment of militia drives the remnant of the Kelly and Frye industrial armies across the Potomac 11 Aug "
[They were finally furnished transportation to their western homes by the government]
U S. Senate ratifies the new Chinese treaty regulating immigration, signed Mch, by 47 to 20 13 Aug. "
[Formally proclaimed by the president, 8 Dec.]
House passes the Senate Tariff bill by 182 yeas (175 Democrats, 7 Populists) to 106 nays (93 Republicans, 13 Democrats), and passes bills for free coal, iron, barbed wire, and sugar . 13 Aug. "
Tariff bill becomes a law without the president's signature (TARIFF) . midnight 27 Aug. "
Second Session (268 days) adjourns . 28 Aug "
Ten towns in Minnesota, 6 in Wisconsin, and 3 in Michigan totally destroyed by forest fires .Aug "
Gen N P Banks, born 30 Jan 1816, dies at Waltham, Mass . 1 Sept. "
Samuel J Kirkwood, U S ex-senator, ex-secretary of the interior, and war governor of Iowa, dies at Des Moines, aged 81 . . 1 Sept. "
Maj.-gen George Stoneman, ex-governor of California, born 8 Aug 1822, dies at Buffalo, N Y 5 Sept. "
Successful strike of United Garment Workers and United Brotherhood of Tailors in New York, Brooklyn, and vicinity .. 4 to 13 Sept. "
Pres. Cleveland proclaims amnesty to persons convicted of polygamy under the Edmunds act . 27 Sept 1894
Proclamation of president setting apart the Ashland Forest reserve in Oregon 28 Sept "
Brig-gen John P Hawkins commissary-gen of subsistence, U S army, retired 29 Sept "
Oliver Wendell Holmes, born in Cambridge, Mass, 29 Aug 1809 dies at his residence in Boston 7 Oct. "
Andrew G Curtin, war governor of Pennsylvania, dies at Bellefonte, Pa, aged 77 7 Oct. "
Col Michael Morgan made commissary gen, U S army, and brig-gen 8 Oct "
Corner-stone of the Commercial Travellers' Home of the U S laid at Binghamton, N Y 9 Oct "
Train on the Fredericksburg and Potomac railroad held up 41 miles south of Washington, D C, and robbed of $150,000 12 Oct "
Memorial tablet to memory of Robert C Morris, the financier of the Revolution, unveiled at Batavia, N Y, oration by sec of treas Carlisle 13 Oct "
Sec Carlisle offers for sale $50,000 000 of U S 5-per-cent 10-year bonds 13 Nov "
[Awarded to the Stewart syndicate of New York city, 26 Nov]
Dr James McCosh, ex-president of Princeton college, dies in Princeton, N J, aged 83 16 Nov "
Rev dr W G T Shedd, theologian and scholar, dies in New York city, aged 74 17 Nov "
New treaty with Japan signed at Washington, 23 Nov "
President remits the unexpired portion of brig-gen Swaim's sentence (see Feb 1885) 1 Dec "
John Burns, the English labor leader and member of Parliament, arrives at New York 1 Dec "
[Returned to England 3 Jan 1895]
Third Session convenes 3 Dec "
Emigrant convention with China ratified 7 Dec "
During the year 1893 charges were made accusing superintendent Z R Brockway of the Elmira reformatory, N Y, of mismanagement, together with cruel and inhuman treatment of the prisoners To investigate these charges, gov Flower appointed a committee of 3 which met at Elmira, 11 May, 1894. After a thorough and extended investigation, 2 of the committee report favorably to Brockway and the 3d unfavorably. Gov Flower dismisses the charges, 10 Dec "
Ex-gov B R Tillman elected U S senator by South Carolina legislature to succeed M C Butler, 11 Dec "
Pres Cleveland issues an order placing in the classified civil service the internal-revenue force 12 Dec "
Eugene V Debs sentenced to 6 months' imprisonment, and his associates to 3 months' imprisonment for contempt of court (sentence to begin 8 Jan 1895), 14 Dec "
Mosquito reservation formally incorporated with Nicaragua 17 Dec "
Brig-gen Swaim, judge advocate-gen, retired, 21 Dec "
Philological congress in the U S opens at the University of Pennsylvania, Philadelphia 27 Dec "
Act to establish a National Military park at the battlefield of Pittsburg Landing or Shiloh approved, 28 Dec "
James G Fair, U S ex-senator from California, dies at San Francisco, aged 63 29 Dec "
[Estate estimated at $40,000,000]
Lexow committee, investigating the methods of the police department of New York city, holds its last session 29 Dec "
[This committee was appointed under a resolution offered by Clarence Lexow in the Senate of New York, 24 Jan 1894, and passed unanimously, charges against the police of the city of New York having been made publicly by the rev dr Charles H Parkhurst of that city The committee was appointed 31 Jan, with sen. Lexow chairman Investigation commenced on 9 Mch, at the court-room of the County court house in New York, with William A Sutherland as counsel for the committee until 13 Apr, when John W Goff appeared as counsel. At

the end of June the committee adjourned until 10 Sept., and continued with one or two short intermissions until 29 Dec The evidence confirmed the charges The committee submitted its report to the legislature at Albany, 18 Jan 1895 The examination and testimony of the 700 witnesses making 10,576 printed pages]

President nominates col. G N Lieber to be judge advocate gen in place of brig-gen David G Swaim, retired 3 Jan 1895

Royalist uprising at Waikiki Beach, about 5 miles from Honolulu, for the purpose of overthrowing the government (easily suppressed) 6 Jan "

Brooklyn street car strike, attended with great loss of property and several lives, without beneficial result to the strikers 10 Jan "

Senate passes the Urgency Deficiency bill, including appropriations for collecting the income tax, 15 Jan "

Nicaragua canal bill passes the Senate 25 Jan "

Springer (administration) Finance bill, authorizing the issue of $500,000,000 of gold bonds, etc, defeated in the House (162 to 135) 5 Feb. "

Joint resolution passed to revive the grade of lieut-gen in the army for the benefit of maj-gen John M Schofield, signed by the president, and confirmed 6 Feb "

President sends a message to Congress advising it of a loan of $62,400,000 @ 4 per cent for 30 years, under provision of the act of 14 Jan 1875 8 Feb "

Frederick Douglass, colored, celebrated in the history of the country, dies at Anacostia, D. C, aged about 78 years 20 Feb "

Postmaster-gen Wilson S Bissell resigns 27 Feb "

Wm. L. Wilson of West Virginia, appointed postmaster-gen, and confirmed 1 Mch "

Fifty third Congress adjourns 4 Mch "

[Appropriations allowed for the year $498,952,524, of which $141,381,570 was for persions.]

An act to reduce taxation, to provide revenue, etc (the tariff bill) "

[It became a law without the president's approval]

Steamship *Alliança* fired upon by Spanish cruiser *Conde de Venduito* 5 Mch "

Riot and massacre on the levee, New Orleans, 12 Mch "

Spain gives satisfaction in the *Alliança* affair, 26 Apr. "

Income tax declared null and void by the Supreme Court 20 May, "

Richard Olney appointed secretary of state and Judson Harmon attorney general 7 June, "

The president issues a proclamation against the Cuban filibusters 12 June, "

Maj-gen Miles assumes command of the army, 5 Oct "

Members of the Venezuela boundary commission named by the president 1 Jan 1896

The secretary of the treasury calls for bids for $100,000,000 in bonds as a popular loan 6 Jan "

The American ship *St. Paul* goes ashore off Long Branch, N J 24 Jan "

[She was released 4 Feb]

The U. S consulate at Barcelona, Spain, mobbed, 2 Mch. "

American college athletes win many victories in the Olympian games in Greece 6 Apr. "

International arbitration congress meets at Washington 22 Apr "

John Hays Hammond and other Americans convicted of high treason in the Transvaal republic, sentenced to death 28 Apr. "

[They were subsequently banished]

Republican national convention meets at St. Louis, Mo June, "

Democratic national convention meets at Chicago, Ill, platform adopted 9 July, "

UNI

The Venezuelan arbitration correspondence made public 17 July, 1896

The People's party national convention meets at St Louis, Mo 24 July, "

The president issues a proclamation against Cuban filibusters 30 July, "

The rev. Sebastian Martinelli appointed papal delegate in the U S. 30 July, "

Hoke Smith, secretary of the interior, resigns, David R Francis appointed his successor 22 Aug "

Li-Hung Chang arrives in New York 28 Aug "

[Received by the president, 29 Aug]

National Democratic party meets at Indianapolis, Ind, declares for the gold standard 3 Sept "

Arbitration treaty between the U S. and Great Britain signed at Washington, D C 11 Jan 1897

National monetary association meets at Indianapolis, Ind 12 Jan "

Intoxicating drinks to Indians prohibited 30 Jan "

Postal laws providing indemnity for loss of registered mail matter 27 Feb. "

Twenty-eighth Administration—Republican. 4 Mch 1897 to 4 Mch 1901

William McKinley, Ohio, president.
Garret A. Hobart, N J, vice-president.

CABINET

John Sherman, Ohio, sec of state, from 4 Mch 1897
William R Day, Ohio, " " " 26 Apr 1898.
John Hay, Ohio, " " " 30 Sept 1898.
Lyman J. Gage, Ill, sec of treas, " 4 Mch 1897.
Russell A Alger, Mich, sec of war, " " "
Elihu Root, N Y, " " " 22 July, 1899
Joseph McKenna, Cal, attorney-gen, from 4 Mch 1897.
John W Griggs, N J, " " " 25 Jan 1898
James A Gary, Md., postmaster-gen, " 4 Mch 1897.
Charles E Smith, Pa, " " " 21 Apr. 1898.
John D Long, Mass, sec of navy, " 4 Mch 1897.
Cornelius N Bliss, N Y, sec. of interior, " " "
Ethan A. Hitchcock, Mo., " " " 21 Dec 1898
James Wilson, Iowa, sec of agriculture, " 4 Mch 1897.

Congress at Venezuela ratifies arbitration treaty, 30 Mch. 1897

Universal Postal Union congress opens at Washington, D C 2 May, "

Arbitration treaty with Great Britain rejected by the Senate 5 May, "

Berliner telephone case decided by U S Supreme Court in favor of Bell Company 10 May, "

Belligerency of Cuba recognized 20 May, "

Fifty thousand dollars appropriated for the relief of U. S. destitute citizens in Cuba 24 May, "

Severe earthquake in Central States 31 May, "

Venezuela boundary treaty ratified at Washington, 14 June, "

An act to provide revenue for the government, and to encourage the industries of the U. S (the tariff bill) 24 July, "

Authority given to the president to suspend discriminating duties imposed on foreign vessels and commerce 24 July, "

Hawaii ratifies annexation treaty 14 Sept. "

Bering sea treaty signed at Washington 8 Nov. "

Postal Union treaty signed at Washington 16 Nov. "

Yellow-fever returns from the Mississippi coast show 4286 cases, of which 446 were fatal 21 Nov. "

The killing of seals in the waters of the North Pacific prohibited 29 Dec. "

The monetary convention meets at Indianapolis, 25 Jan 1898

Free silver beaten in the House of Representatives by a vote of 182 to 132 31 Jan "

The letter written by the Spanish minister at Washington (De Lome) reflecting on the president, published 8 Feb. "

The battle-ship *Maine* blown up in the harbor of Havana 15 Feb "

Joint resolution providing for a survey upon the practicability of securing a channel of 35 ft. depth through the southwest pass of the Mississippi River, approved . . . . 17 Feb. 1898
Joint resolution providing for the recovery of the remains of the officers and men on the U. S. battle-ship *Maine*, approved . . . . 23 Feb. "
A law prohibiting the passage of local or special laws in the territories, and limiting territorial indebtedness, amended . . . . 4 Mch. "
Relief for the sufferers by the destruction of the U. S. ship *Maine* authorized . . . . 26 Mch. "
Joint resolution for the recognition of the independence of the people of Cuba, demanding that the government of Spain relinquish its authority and government in the island of Cuba, and to withdraw its land and naval forces from Cuba and Cuban waters, and directing the president of the U. S. to use the land and naval forces of the U. S. to carry the resolution into effect . . . . 20 Apr. "
[For chronological record, see SPANISH-AMERICAN WAR.]
Charles Emory Smith appointed postmaster-general, 21 Apr. "
Volunteer brigade of engineers, and an additional force of 10,000 men, authorized . . . . 11 May, "
Volunteer signal corps authorized . . . . 18 May, "
Battle-ship *Alabama* launched at Chester, Penn., 18 May, "
An act to provide assistance to the inhabitants of Cuba, by arms, munition, and military stores . . . . 18 May, "
U. S. auxiliary naval force authorized . . . . 26 May, "
Commercial treaty with France signed . . . . 30 May, "
The Trans-Mississippi International Exposition in Omaha, Neb . . . . 1 June, "
Congress authorizes the secretary of the navy to present a sword of honor to com. George Dewey, and bronze medals to the officers and men of the ships of the Asiatic squadron . . . . 3 June, "
House document No. 396, relating to the beet-sugar industry in the U. S., authorized by joint resolution to be printed . . . . 4 June, "
Disabilities imposed by section 3 of the 14th amendment to the constitution removed . . . . 6 June, "
Appropriation to pay the Bering sea awards, 15 June, "
Commission appointed to collate information and to consider and recommend legislation to meet the problems presented by labor, agriculture, and capital, authorized . . . . 18 June, "
The bankruptcy law approved . . . . 1 July, "
Joint resolution annexing the Hawaiian islands to the U. S. approved . . . . 7 July, "
Anglo-American League organized in London . . 13 July, "
U. S. and Canadian joint high commission meet in Quebec . . . . 23 Aug. "
John Hay appointed secretary of state . . . . 30 Sept. "
Battle-ship *Illinois* launched at Newport News, 4 Oct. "
U. S. Supreme Court decides Joint Traffic Association case against the railroads . . . . 24 Oct. "
The captured Spanish cruiser *Infanta Maria Theresa* abandoned in a gale . . . . 1 Nov. "
General elections result in a small Republican majority in the next House of Representatives . . . 8 Nov. "
Gen. Wood succeeds gen. Brooke in Cuba 1899
The American flag raised at Guam; com. Taussig, of the *Bennington*, first governor . . . . 1 Feb. "
Fire in Brooklyn navy-yard; loss, $1,000,000 . . 15 Feb. "
An act making an appropriation to carry out the obligations of the treaty of 10 Dec. 1898, between the U. S. and Spain . . . . 2 Mch. "
The Mount Rainier National Park authorized, 2 Mch. "
The office of admiral of the navy created . . . . 2 Mch. "
An act providing for the erection of a new custom-house in the city of New York, approved . . . 3 Mch. "
[The secretary of the treasury authorized to acquire the Bowling Green site at a cost not to exceed $3,000,000, and the custom-house property on Wall street to be sold for not less than $3,000,000.]
The navy and marine corps reorganized (the navy personnel act) . . . . 3 Mch. 1899
Pan-American Exposition of 1901 authorized . . 3 Mch. "
Attack on British and American sailors at Samoa, by Mataafa's followers . . . . 1 Apr. "
Stephen J. Field, associate justice U. S. Supreme Court, dies at Washington, D. C. . . . . 9 Apr. "
First formal meeting of the Venezuela arbitration commission . . . . 15 June, "
The president calls for 10 regiments to quell Philippine insurrection . . . . 7 July, "
[For an account of the insurrection, and chronology of the main events, see AGUINALDO; PHILIPPINES, etc.]
Elihu Root succeeds Russell A. Alger as secretary of war . . . . 22 July, "
Reciprocity treaty with France signed . . . . 24 July, "
Hurricane at Porto Rico; many hundreds of lives lost . . . . 8 Aug. "
Great naval parade in honor of adm. Dewey in New York . . . . 29 Sept. "
Venezuela commission announced its award . . . 2 Oct. "
Temporary boundary-line of Alaska agreed upon with England . . . . 12 Oct. "
U. S. cruiser *Charleston* wrecked off the Philippines, 7 Nov. "
England relinquishes her territorial claims in Samoa, 8 Nov. "
Vice-pres. Hobart died at Paterson, N. J. . . . 21 Nov. "
Samoan partition treaty signed at Washington . . 2 Dec. "
Fifty-sixth Congress meets . . . . 4 Dec. "
Sec. Hay announced the success of the "open-door" policy in China . . . . 2 Jan. 1900
The British government notified that the seizures of American flour at Delagoa Bay are illegal, 2 Jan. "
[The British government reply that food-stuffs are not contraband of war unless intended for the enemy.]
Samoan treaty ratified . . . . 16 Jan. "
The Hay-Pauncefote treaty signed at Washington, 5 Feb. "
William H. Taft appointed chairman of commission to establish civil government in the Philippines, 6 Feb. "
Congress orders the frigate *Constitution* preserved, 14 Feb. "
The gold standard currency bill signed . . . . 14 Mch. "
Gen. MacArthur succeeded gen. Otis in the Philippines . . . . 7 Apr. "
Charles N. Allen appointed governor of Porto Rico, 12 Apr. "
The Senate refuses seat to Matthew Quay, appointed U. S. Senator by the governor of Pennsylvania, 24 Apr. "
Act creating the senior major-general of the army lieutenant-general . . . . 6 June, "
Civil government act for the "District" of Alaska enacted . . . . 6 June, "
Gen. MacArthur proclaims amnesty to the Filipino insurgents . . . . 15 June, "
Siege of the legations at Peking begins . . . . 20 June, "
[For events of this war between China and the U. S. and European powers see CHINO-EUROPEAN (BOXER) WAR.]
Republican convention at Philadelphia nominates McKinley and Roosevelt . . . . 21 June, "
U. S. battle-ship *Oregon* grounded at Chefoo, China, 29 June, "
[Subsequently taken off without any serious damage.]
Democratic national convention at St. Louis nominates Bryan and Stevenson . . . . 5 July, "
Six thousand two hundred troops ordered to China, 8 July, "

Ex-sec. of state Jacob D. Cox dies at Oberlin, O., 4 Aug. 1900

Relief for the destitute miners at Cape Nome authorized ....31 Aug. "

Ex-sec. of state John Sherman dies at Washington, 22 Oct. "

U. S. cruiser *Yosemite* wrecked at Guam ....13 Nov. "

The centenary of John Marshall's inauguration as chief-justice of the U. S. Supreme Court celebrated ....4 Feb. 1901

War department closes canteens ....4 Feb. "

Russia adds 30 per cent. to customs duties on certain American goods in retaliation for U. S. duty on sugar..............................16 Feb. "

Incorporation of the United States Steel Corporation in New Jersey ....21 Feb.

Decision against the Bell Telephone Company in the Berliner patent case decided ....27 Feb. "

Twenty-ninth Administration—Republican. 4 Mch. 1901, to 4 Mch. 1905.

William McKinley, Ohio, president.

Theodore Roosevelt, N. Y., vice-president.

CABINET.

John Hay, Ohio, sec. of state, continued.
Lyman J. Gage, Ill., sec. of treas, "
Leslie M. Shaw, Iowa," " from 8 Jan. 1902.
Elihu Root, N. Y., sec. of war, continued.
William H. Taft, Ohio, sec. of war, from 25 Aug. 1903.
Philander C. Knox, Pa., attorney-gen., " 5 Apr. 1901.
William H. Moody, Mass., " " " 24 June, 1904.
Charles E. Smith, Pa., postmaster-gen., continued.
Henry C. Payne, Wis., " " from 8 Jan. 1902.
Robert J. Wynne, Pa., " " " 10 Oct. 1904.
John D. Long, Mass., sec. of navy, continued.
William H. Moody, Mass., sec. of navy, from 10 Mch. 1902.
Paul Morton, Ill., " " " 24 June, 1904.
Ethan A. Hitchcock, Mo., sec. of interior, continued.
James Wilson, Iowa, sec. of agriculture, "
George B. Cortelyou, N. Y., sec. of com. and labor, from 16 Feb. 1903.
Victor H. Metcalf, Cal., sec. of com. and labor, from 24 June, 1904.

Extra session of the Senate called ....4 Mch. 1901

The river and harbor appropriation bill, amounting to $28,565,696, fails to become a law........4 Mch. "

Andrew Carnegie gives $4,000,000 as a fund for disabled and superannuated workmen of the Carnegie Company...........................13 Mch. "

Benjamin Harrison, ex-president, dies......13 Mch. "

The U. S. government purchased from Spain the islands of Cagayan and Cibutu............23 Mch. "

Aguinaldo, Filipino insurgent chief, is captured by gen. Funston in Isabella, Luzon........23 Mch. "

Philander C. Knox appointed attorney-general, 5 Apr. "

Leyland Steamship Company in England purchased by J. P. Morgan & Co.................29 Apr. "

Pan-American Exposition is opened at Buffalo..1 May, "

Porto Rico tariff law declared constitutional, 27 May, "

The Cuban convention adopts the Platt amendment, 12 June, "

W. H. Taft appointed first civil governor of Philippines..............................21 June, "

Gen. Chaffee appointed military governor of Philippines..............................22 June, "

Turkey settles the U. S. indemnity claims...2 July, "

Sec. of navy orders court of inquiry on conduct of rear-adm. Schley at Santiago...........24 July, "

Porto Rico adopts resolutions providing for free trade with U. S..........................25 July, "

William H. Hunt appointed governor of Porto Rico, 30 Aug. "

Pres. McKinley makes an address at the Buffalo Exposition, Sept. 5; is shot while holding a reception, Sept. 6; dies........................14 Sept. "

Pres. Roosevelt takes the oath of office as president, 14 Sept. 1901

Pres. Roosevelt proclaims a day of mourning, 19 Sept. "

Pres. McKinley's body is taken to Washington, where it lies in state in the Capitol, and then to Canton, O., where last ceremonies are held.......19 Sept. "

Czolgosz placed on trial in Buffalo.........23 Sept. "

[He is found guilty 24 Sept. and is electrocuted at Auburn, 29 Oct.]

The body of pres. Lincoln is entombed at Springfield, 26 Sept. "

The Cuban constitutional convention dissolved by gen. Wood ....3 Oct. "

Yale university celebrates its bi-centennial.22–24 Oct. "

Fifty-seventh Congress meets...............2 Dec. "

Pres. Roosevelt's first message to Congress....3 Dec. "

Court of inquiry decides against rear-adm. Schley; adm. Dewey dissents...................13 Dec. "

Hay-Pauncefote treaty ratified.............16 Dec. "

Panama canal offered to the U. S. for $40,000,000, 4 Jan. 1902

Henry C. Payne succeeds as postmaster-general, 15 Jan. "

Panama canal commission recommend purchase of Panama canal for $40,000,000 ....20 Jan. "

Denmark agrees to transfer the Danish West Indies to the U. S. for $4,000,000..............23 Jan. "

[Treaty not ratified by Denmark.]

Andrew Carnegie gives $10,000,000 to the U. S. for advanced study and original research......29 Jan. "

Schley court of inquiry met 12 Sept. 1901; decision published 13 Dec. 1901; Schley's appeal rejected, 30 Jan. "

Leslie M. Shaw succeeds as secretary of the treasury, 1 Feb. "

Miss Ellen M. Stone released by Macedonian brigands, 23 Feb. "

The Philippine tariff bill signed............8 Mch. "

Prince Henry, representing the German emperor, arrives in New York, Feb. 22; makes a tour of the U. S., and returns to Germany..........11 Mch. "

West Point ordered rebuilt at a cost of $6,000,000, 15 Apr. "

William H. Moody succeeds J. D. Long as secretary of the navy...........................1 May, "

Strike of anthracite coal-miners...........12 May, "

[Pres. Roosevelt appoints a commission, 24 Oct.; strike called off, 21 Nov.; commission reported, 18 Mch. 1903; see STRIKES.]

The U. S. retires from Cuba...............20 May, "

The U. S. army reduced to 66,497 men......31 May, "

Centennial of West Point Academy celebrated, 9 June, "

The president proclaims peace and amnesty in the Philippines..........................3 July, "

Sec. Hay urges relief for Rumanian Jews....17 Sept. "

Hague tribunal decides Pious Fund case in favor of the U. S.............................14 Oct. "

King Oscar decides adversely to the U. S. on the Samoan controversy........................21 Oct. "

Reciprocity treaty between U. S. and Newfoundland signed..................................8 Nov. "

Russia condemned by arbitration to pay damages for seizure of American sealers...............29 Nov. "

Venezuela appeals to the U. S. for arbitration of European claims...........................15 Dec. "

Pres. Roosevelt greets king Edward by wireless telegraphy.................................18 Jan. 1903

Panama canal treaty between the U. S. and Colombia signed..................................22 Jan. "

[Treaty not ratified by Colombia. For further history see PANAMA CANAL.]

Department of Commerce and Labor created..14 Feb. "

Pres. Roosevelt signs bill for a general staff in the army.................................14 Feb. "

Cuban reciprocity treaty, with amendments, ratified by U. S................................17 Mch. "

Award of Anthracite coal-strike commission goes into effect 1 Apr 1903
Andrew Carnegie gives $1,500,000 for Temple of Peace at The Hague 20 Apr "
U S Supreme Court sustains Alabama constitution in disfranchising negroes 27 Apr "
Grounds of Louisiana Purchase Exposition, St Louis, are dedicated 30 Apr "
European squadron, U S navy, is received by German emperor at Kiel 23-26 June, "
Cuba cedes two naval stations, and Isle of Pines adjudged to Cuba 2 July, "
Pacific cable completed, pres. Roosevelt sends the first message to the Philippines, the second around the world, time, 12 min 4 July, "
Battle-ship *Kearsarge* crosses the Atlantic in 9 days, 4½ hours .. July, "
Russia refuses to receive the Kishineff petition from the U S 16 July, "
Bristow reports on the Tulloch charges 17 July, "
Lieut gen Miles retires 7 Aug "
Lou Dillon trots a mile in 2 m, breaking world's record 24 Aug. "
The *America* cup races won by *Reliance*, 22, 25 Aug, 3 Sept "
G W Beavers, A W. Machen, and others indicted for postal frauds 8 Sept "
Commercial treaty between the U S and China signed 8 Oct "
[Ratified 13 Jan 1904]
Alaskan boundary commission decides in favor of the U S 17 Oct. "
[See ALASKAN BOUNDARY]
National employers' association organized 30 Oct "
Republic of Panama recognized as an independent power 6 Nov "
Fifty-eighth Congress meets in extraordinary session to consider the Cuban reciprocity treaty 9 Nov "
Hay Varilla isthmian treaty signed 18 Nov "
[Treaty ratified 23 Feb 1904]
Fifty eighth Congress meets in regular session 7 Dec "
Nearly 600 lives are lost by burning of Iroquois theatre, Chicago 30 Dec. "
U S Supreme Court decides that Porto-Ricans are not aliens 4 Jan 1904
William H Taft succeeds Elihu Root as secretary of war 1 Feb "
The U S proposes the neutralization of China, except Manchuria 8 Feb "
[Accepted by Japan and Russia]
Bates treaty with sultan of Sulu abrogated 7 Mch "
U S Supreme Court decides Northern Securities Company illegal 14 Mch "
Pres Roosevelt rules that civil war pensioners 62 years of age are "disabled" 16 Mch "
U S Senate ratifies Cuban treaty embodying the Platt amendment . 22 Mch "
Chicago votes for municipal ownership of street-railways . 5 Apr. "
Andrew Carnegie founds a hero-fund with $5,000,000, 15 Apr. "
Contract for transfer to U S. of Panama canal property is signed at Paris 22 Apr. "
Louisiana Purchase Exposition is opened at St Louis, 30 Apr. "
U S squadron ordered to Tangier in consequence of the kidnapping of Ion Perdicaris 20 May, "
[Perdicaris was released 24 June, 1904]
Steamer *General Slocum* burned in New York harbor, over 1000 lives lost 15 June, "
Republican convention at Chicago nominates Roosevelt and Fairbanks . .. . 21 June, "
Prohibition convention at Indianapolis nominates Swallow and Carroll 30 June, "
People's convention at Springfield, Ill., nominates Watson and Tibbles . .. 5 July, "
Democratic convention at St. Louis nominates Parker and Davis . . .. 9, 10 July, "
Great textile mills strike begins at Fall River, Mass, 21,000 operatives out 25 July, 1904
U S protests against seizure of asphalt properties by Venezuela 1 Aug "
Military manœuvres on Bull Run, Va, battle field began 7 Sept "
Thirteenth International Peace Conference opened at Boston 3 Oct "
The New York city subway opened 27 Oct "
Arbitration treaty between France and the U S signed 1 Nov "
Republican national candidates elected 8 Nov "
Arbitration treaty between Germany and the U S signed 15 Nov "
Statue of Frederick the Great, presented to the U S by German emperor, is unveiled at Washington, 19 Nov "
All differences between the U S and Panama adjusted by sec Taft and pres Amador 2 Dec "
Fifty-eighth Congress meets in regular session 5 Dec "
Hay's note suggesting a second Hague conference made public 23 Dec "
Attorney-general decides that U S laws do not apply to the Panama canal zone 27 Dec "
Sec Hay receives assurance from the powers that they will respect China's territorial integrity at the close of the war 19 Jan 1905
Sec Hay publishes a statement as to the U S agreement with Santo Domingo 22 Jan "
Att-gen Miller decides that 99 per cent of the duty on imported wheat may be allowed as a drawback on exports of flour 1 Feb "
A T & S F R R declared guilty of violation of law in making rebates 3 Feb "
In the revised protocol between the U S and Santo Domingo, the former agrees to respect the territorial integrity of the latter 8 Feb "
Parcels post treaty between the U S and Great Britain signed . 17 Feb "
Engineering committee of the Panama canal commission recommend a sea-level canal at a cost of $230,500,000 26 Feb "
Judge Swayne acquitted by the U S Senate, 27 Feb "

Thirtieth Administration—Republican. 4 Mch 1905, to 4 Mch 1909

Theodore Roosevelt, N Y, president
Charles Warren Fairbanks, Ind., vice-president

CABINET

John Hay, Ohio, sec of state, continued.
Leslie M Shaw, Iowa, sec. of treas "
William H Taft, Ohio, sec of war, "
William H Moody, Mass, attorney gen continued
George B Cortelyou, N Y, postmaster-gen from 6 Mch. 1905.
Paul Morton, Ill, sec of navy, continued
Charles J Bonaparte, Md., sec of navy, from 1 July, 1905
Ethan A Hitchcock, Mo, sec of interior, continued
James Wilson, Iowa, sec. of agriculture, "
Victor H Metcalf, Cal, sec of commerce and labor, continued

U S Senate meets in special session 4 Mch 1905
U S. Supreme Court decides Northern Securities case in favor of James J Hill 6 Mch "
George B Cortelyou takes office as postmaster-general 7 Mch "
Sec Taft announces indefinite retention of Philippines as the policy of the administration, 16 Mch "
U S Senate adjourns without deciding the Santo Domingo problem 18 Mch "
Arrangement made by U S min Dawson with Santo Domingo for collection of revenues by a U S commissioner 24 Mch "
Pres Castro refuses U S demand for arbitration of asphalt controversy 24 Mch "
Pres Castro declares French and Bermudez cable companies in league with revolutionists 30 Mch "

Pres. Roosevelt appoints new Panama canal commission . . . 3 Apr. 1905
Extradition treaty between the U. S. and Norway and Sweden . . . 4 Apr. "
Body of John Paul Jones found at Paris . . . 14 Apr. "
[To be interred at naval academy, Annapolis.]
Right of trial by common law jury affirmed . . 10 Apr. "
Panama canal commissioners' decision to buy in cheapest market at home or abroad causes great dissatisfaction among protectionist manufacturers, May, "
Interstate commerce commission files complaints against common carriers . . . 2 May, "
Interstate commerce commission to investigate rebates to private car lines . . . 4 May, "
U. S. attorney-general decides Congress has power to fix railroad rates and can delegate its power . . 5 May, "
Pres. Roosevelt orders investigation of tobacco trust, 5 May, "
Immigration records broken by arrival of 12,039 immigrants, mostly Italians, on 10 liners, on one day, in New York City . . . 7 May, "
U. S. Supreme Court decides that dealing in futures is not gambling . . . 8 May, "
Federal government asks U. S. Supreme Court for rehearing on Philippine tariff cases . . . 16 May, "
Eleven yachts start from N. Y. on ocean race (won by American yacht *Atlantic*) . . . 17 May, "
Senate interstate commerce commission closes hearings on the railroad rates . . . 23 May, "
U. S. Supreme Court upholds New York special franchise law . . . 29 May, "
Lewis and Clark Exposition at Portland, Ore., opened, 31 May, "
Three Russian cruisers at Manila ordered interned, 5 June, "
Federal grand jury instructed to continue beef-trust investigation . . . 7 June, "
U. S. attorney-general decides the 8-hour law applies to laborers on Panama canal, but not to railroad or office forces . . . 8 June, "
Identical note to Japan and Russia, urging them to make peace, sent by pres. Roosevelt . . . 9 June, "
[Accepted by both powers.]
Amer.-Asiatic association protests to the president against Chinese exclusion laws . . . 12 June, "
Investigation of Bowen-Loomis case ends in dismissal of Mr. Bowen and reproof to Mr. Loomis . . 20 June, "
Pres. Roosevelt directs moderation in enforcement of Chinese exclusion laws . . . 24 June, "
Charles J. Bonaparte succeeds Paul Morton as secretary of the navy . . . 1 July, "

United Workmen, Ancient Order of, founded 1868. Object, fraternal and beneficiary; number of grand lodges, 1894, 32; number of sub-lodges, 4831; number of members, 341,371. Benefits disbursed since organization for beneficiary fund, $51,050,124; benefits disbursed last fiscal year, $6,479,175. The chief officer is termed supreme master-workman. This order stands fourth in the list of fraternal organizations, in the number of members being exceeded by the Freemasons, Oddfellows, and Knights of Pythias.

unity. CHRISTIAN UNITY.

universal suffrage (*plebiscitum*), one of the 6 points of the charter (CHARTISTS), was adopted in the constitution of France in 1791, and used in the election of president in 1851 and of emperor in 1852, and by the Italian states in voting for annexation to Sardinia in 1860, 1861, 1866, and 1870.

Universalists, a sect who believe in the final salvation of all. This doctrine, declared in the Talmud, and ascribed to Origen about 230, was advocated by other early fathers, but opposed by St. Augustine, about 420; and condemned by the 5th general council at Constantinople, May, June, 553. It was received by the Unitarians in the 17th century, and avowed by many clergymen of the church of England. James Relly, who published his "Union" in 1760, founded the sect of Universalists in Britain; and John Murray, in America, about 1770. The sect barely exists in Great Britain, but flourishes in the United States. Before 1818, many Universalists in the United States were believers in future retribution, and the terms Restorationists and Universalists were used synonymously. In 1818 Hosea Ballou taught that retribution is confined to this life, and those who could not accept this doctrine formed a distinct sect and took the name of Universal Restorationists at Mendon, Mass., 17 Aug. 1831. The present strength of the Universalists in the U. S. (1891) is: parishes, 947; church-members, 41,177.

university, a school for universal knowledge, an association of men for the purpose of study empowered to confer degrees which are recognized throughout Christendom, often endowed by the State. The most ancient universities in Europe are those of Cambridge, Paris, Oxford, Cordova, and Bologna. In old Aberdeen was a monastery, in which youths were instructed in theology, the canon law, and the school philosophy, at least 200 years before the university and King's college were founded. DEGREES. For leading universities in the U. S., COLLEGES and states separately.

DATES OF THE FOUNDING OF THE PRINCIPAL UNIVERSITIES IN EUROPE.

(Arranged according to dates, some of them now extinct.)

Name.	Country.	Founded.	Name.	Country.	Founded.
Cambridge	England	(?) 635	Siguenza	Spain	1517
Paris	France	792	Compostella	"	"
Oxford	England	879	Marburg	Prussia	1527
Cordova	Spain	968	Debreczin	Hungary	1531
Bologna	Italy	1116	Evora	Portugal	1533
Valencia	Spain	1209	Grenada	Spain	1537
Arezzo	Italy	1215	Strasburg	Germany	1538
Naples	"	1224	Königsberg	"	1544
Padua	"	1228	Jena	Thuringia	1547
Toulouse	France	1229	Greifswald	Germany	"
Salerno	Italy	1233	Rheims	France	1548
Salamanca	Spain	1239	Pisa	Italy	1552
Genoa	Italy	1243	Urbino	"	1564
Rome	"	1245	Milan	"	1565
Sorbonne	France	1253	Dillingen	Swabia	"
Coimbra	Portugal	1279	Douay	France	1568
Montpellier	France	1289	Ingolstadt	Bavaria	1573
Lyons	"	1300	Helmstadt	Brunswick	1575
Lerida	Spain	"	Leyden	Holland	"
Avignon	France	1303	Edinburgh	Scotland	1582
Orleans	"	1305	Franeker	Belgium	1585
Perugia	Italy	1307	Graz	Austria	1586
Cahors	France	1332	Dublin	Ireland	1591
Grenoble	"	1339	Paderborn	Germany	1592
Valladolid	Spain	1346	Venice	Italy	"
Prague	Bohemia	1348	Pavia	"	1599
Huesca	Spain	1354	Harderwijk	Holland	1600
Cracow	Poland	1364	Giessen	Hesse-Darmstadt	1607
Angers	France	"			
Vienna	Austria	1365	Groningen	Holland	1614
Fünfkirchen	Hungary	1367	Salzburg	Austria	1623
Geneva	Switzerland	1368	Mantua	Italy	1625
Sienna	Italy	1380	Dorpat	Livonia	1632
Cologne	Germany	1385	Utrecht	Holland	1634
Heidelberg	"	1386	Buda-Pest	Hungary	1635
Erfurt	Thuringia	1390	Bamberg	Bavaria	1648
Ferrara	Italy	1391	Kiel	Germany	1665
Würzburg	Germany	1403	Bruges	Belgium	"
Turin	Italy	1405	Lund	Sweden	1668
Leipsic	Saxony	1409	Besançon	France	1676
St. Andrews	Scotland	1411	Innsbruck	Tyrol	1692
Rostock	Mecklenberg	1419	Dresden	Saxony	1694
Dole	Burgundy	1422	Hallo	"	"
Louvaine	Belgium	1426	Breslau	Prussia	1702
Poitiers	France	1431	Dijon	France	1722
Florence	Italy	1439	Pan	Italy	"
Mechlin	Belgium	1440	Camerino	"	1727
Palermo	Italy	1447	Göttingen	Hanover	1735
Glasgow	Scotland	1450	Erlangen	Bavaria	1743
Valence	France	1454	Nancy	France	1769
Freibourg	Germany	1460	Stuttgart	Germany	1775
Nantes	France	"	Lemberg	Austria	1784
Basle	Switzerland	"	Wilna or Vilna	Russia	1803
Bourges	France	1463	Kieff	"	"
Mentz or Mainz	Germany	1467	Moscow	"	"
			Caen	France	"
Bordeaux	France	1472	Kasan	Russia	1804
Treves	Germany	1473	Kharkoff	"	"
Saragossa	Spain	1474	Berlin	Germany	1810
Upsal	Sweden	1476	Christiania	Norway	1811
Copenhagen	Denmark	"	Ghent	Belgium	1816
Tübingen	Germany	1477	Liege	"	"
Parma	Italy	1482	Bonn	Germany	1818
Münster	Prussia	1491	St. Petersburg	Russia	1819
Aberdeen	Scotland	1494	London	England	1826
Toledo	Spain	1499	Helsingfors	Finland	"
Alcala	"	"	Munich	Bavaria	"
Wittenberg	Germany	1502	Durham	England	1831
Seville	Spain	1504	Zurich	Switzerland	1832
Frankfort-on-the-Oder	Prussia	1506	Brussels	Belgium	1834
			Berne	Switzerland	"

DATES OF THE FOUNDING OF THE PRINCIPAL UNIVERSITIES IN EUROPE.—(*Continued.*)

Name.	Country.	Founded.	Name.	Country.	Founded.
Madrid	Spain	1836	Czernowitz	Austria	1875
Athens	Greece	"	Amsterdam	Holland	1877
London	England	1837	Irish	Ireland	1879
Barcelona	Spain	1841	Victoria	Manchester, Engl.	1880
Odessa	Russia	1865			
Agram	Austria	1869			

OF THE BRITISH COLONIES.

Name.	Country.	Founded.	Name.	Country.	Founded.
McGill	Montreal, Can.	1821	Calcutta	India	1857
			Bombay	"	"
Toronto	Toronto, Can.	1827	Madras	"	"
			New Zealand	New Zealand	1870
Queens	Kingston, Can.	1841	Adelaide	South Australia	1872
Sidney	New South Wales	1852	Cape Colony	Cape of Good Hope	1873
Melbourne	Victoria	1855	Punjab	India	1883

university boat-races. BOAT-RACES.

university extension, a plan originating at the University of Cambridge, England, in 1872, for extending the advantages of university instruction by lectures and classes at important centres. The popular favor and success of the scheme in England encouraged Provost William Pepper, of the University of Pennsylvania, to introduce it in the United States in 1890. From this beginning the movement has spread through the country. The plan of instruction includes a course of from 6 to 12 lectures on different branches of education, some attention being given to class work, as reference reading, examinations, etc. It must be admitted that the plan of instruction is too limited as well as too general in its topics to be of much disciplinary service; but it is popular and doubtless useful in awakening interest in many subjects of study.

unknown tongues. IRVINGITES.

Upsa'la, a city of Sweden. The Swedish rulers were kings of Upsala till 1001. The university was founded in 1476, by Sten Sture, the "protector," and opened 21 Sept. 1477. Celebration of foundation of university, Sept. 1877.

ura'nium, a brittle gray metal discovered by Klaproth in 1789, in the mineral pitchblende; lately employed in manufacturing glass for philosophical purposes.

U'ranus, a planet with 4 satellites, was discovered by William Herschel, 13 Mch. 1781; first called Georgium Sidus, after George III.; next Herschel; and finally Uranus. Its mean distance from the sun is 1,753,869,000 miles, and its diameter is 32,250 miles, density about that of ice. It receives from the sun about $\frac{1}{370}$ of the heat received by the earth. The completion of its first revolution (in 84 years 7 days) since discovery was celebrated on 20 Mch. 1865. Its perturbations led to the discovery of Neptune in 1846. Uranus is accompanied by at least 4 satellites; Herschel discovered 2, 11 Jan. 1787, Lassell 1, 14 Sept. 1847, and O. Struve 1, 8 Oct. 1847. Herschel thought he had discovered 6, which, with the 2 discovered later, would make 8, but 4 of them are unverified.

Urbi'no, the ancient *Urbinum Hortense*, central Italy, capital of a duchy created for Malatesta, 1474. It was treacherously seized by Cæsar Borgia, 1502; captured by Julius II., 1503, and given to Borgia, 1504; given to Lorenzo de' Medici by Leo X., 1516; after many vicissitudes recovered by the duke Francesco, 1522; on the duke's resignation annexed to the Papal States, 1631; annexed to Italy, 1860.

Urim and Thummim, "Light and Perfection" (Exod. xxviii. 30), words connected with the breastplate worn by the high-priest when he entered the holy place to obtain an answer from God (1490 B.C.).

Ursa Major, "Great Bear" constellation, one of the most familiar in the heavens. It contains the "Pointers," and is popularly known as the "Butcher's Cleaver" and "Charles's Wain."

"And we danced about the May-pole and in the hazel copse,
Till Charles's Wain came out above the tall white chimney-tops."
—*Tennyson's* "May Queen."

Ur'suline nuns (so called from St. Ursula), founded originally by St. Angela of Brescia, about 1537. Several communities existed in England, and some still exist in Ireland. First convent in America built at Quebec, founded by madame de la Peltrie, 1641.

U'ruguay, Banda Orientale (the "Eastern side"), a republic in South America, formerly part of the viceroyalty of Buenos Ayres; declared its independence, 25 Aug. 1825; recognized, 4 Oct. 1828; constitution proclaimed, 18 July, 1830. Area, 72,110 sq. miles; pop. 1890, 684,000. In form the government is similar to that of the United States.

Ushant (*ush'-ung*), an island near Brest, N.W. France, near which 2 naval battles were fought between the British and French fleets. The first, 27 July, 1778, indecisive. The English under adm. Keppel, the French under count d'Orvilliers. The second fought 1 June, 1794. The English under lord Howe, with 25 ships, defeated the French, 26 ships, under Villaret-Joyeuse. As the battle saved to the French a large fleet of merchantmen, they claimed the honors of the day.

u'sury is payment for the use of money, interest; but is commonly applied to an excess of interest above the legal rate. The Jews might take interest from strangers, but not from their brethren, 1491 B.C. (Exod. xxii. 25; Deut. xxiii. 19). This law was enforced by Nehemiah, 445 B.C. (Neh. v.). Usury was prohibited by the English Parliament, 1341. Until the 15th century no Christians were allowed to receive interest of money, and Jews were the only usurers, and therefore often banished and persecuted; JEWS. By 37 Hen. VIII. the rate of interest was fixed at 10 per cent., 1545. This statute was repealed by Edward VI., but re-enacted 13 Eliz. 1570. INTEREST.

Utah, a state of the United States, the 45th in admission, is bounded on the north by Idaho and Wyoming, east by Wyoming and Colorado, south by Arizona, and west by Nevada. Area, 84,970 sq. miles, lying between 109° and 114° W. lon., and north of 37° N. lat. Pop. 1890, 207,905; 1900, 276,749. Capital, Salt Lake City.

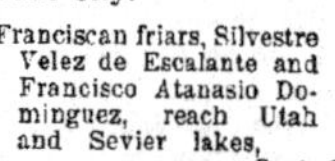

Franciscan friars, Silvestre Velez de Escalante and Francisco Atanasio Dominguez, reach Utah and Sevier lakes, Sept. 1776
Great Salt lake discovered by James Bridger, a trapper on Bear river 1825
One hundred and twenty men under William H. Ashley come to Utah lake from St. Louis through South pass, and build fort Ashley "
Jedediah S. Smith and 15 trappers march from Great Salt lake to Utah lake, and thence crossing the Sevier river westward to San Gabriel mission, Cal., 1826, return to Utah 1827
J. Bartleson and 27 emigrants for California proceed from Soda springs to Corrine and thence into Nevada Aug. 1841
Marcus Whitman and A. L. Lovejoy, on their way from Oregon to the U. S., pass through Utah from fort Hall by way of Uintah, Taos, and Santa Fé 1842
Col. John C. Frémont, with Kit Carson and 3 others, explores Great Salt lake in a rubber boat 8 Sept. 1843
Brigham Young and 142 Mormons, in search of a location for their new Zion, journey from the Mormon camp, near Council Bluffs, up the Platte valley and through South pass to the site of Salt Lake City 21 July, 1847
Mormons to the number of 1553, with 580 wagons, leave Council Bluffs, 4 July, and reach Salt lake Sept. "
Utah included in the cession by Mexico to the U. S. by the treaty of Guadalupe Hidalgo 2 Feb. 1848
James Brown purchases the tract where Ogden now stands from Miles M. Goodyear, who held it by Spanish grant as early as 1841 6 June, "
Provisional government for the state of Deseret, with capital at Salt Lake City, formed by a convention which met at Salt Lake City 4 Mch., and chose Brigham Young governor, 12 Mch. First general assembly convenes 2 July, 1849
City of Provo founded "
Perpetual Emigration Fund company, to aid poor emigrants from Europe, is organized at Salt lake 6 Oct. "
First number of the *Deseret News* published at Salt Lake City, Willard Richards editor 15 June, 1850
City of Ogden laid out by Brigham Young and others Aug. "
Territory of Utah created by act of Congress 9 Sept. "
Salt Lake City incorporated Jan. 1851
Coal discovered on Coal creek at Cedar City May, "
Capt. J. W. Gunnison, engaged in a government survey in Utah, massacred by the Pah Utes while exploring lake Sevier, with 5 out of 10 companions 26 Oct. 1853
A mob of armed Mormons compels associate-judge W. W. Drummond of the U. S. District court, who had become unpopular, to adjourn his court *sine die* Feb. 1856
First "hand-cart" emigrants reach Great Salt lake on foot

from Iowa with 20 hand carts and 1 wagon to each 100 emigrants.....26 Sept. 1856

Judge Drummond resigns.....30 Mch. 1857

Army of Utah, sent by pres. Buchanan as a *posse comitatus* to sustain the governor, begins to assemble at fort Leavenworth, June, "

Nauvoo legion, organized in 1840, is reorganized in Utah..July, "

Alfred Cumming appointed governor of Utah.....11 July, "

Mountain Meadows massacre, about 30 miles southwest from Cedar City; Arkansas emigrants, 30 families, are fired upon by Indians, 7 Sept.; forming a corral, after a siege of 4 days they surrender to a company of the Mormon Nauvoo legion, headed by John D. Lee, who promises protection, but all except 17 children under 7 years of age are massacred by Indians and Mormons.....11 Sept. "

Brigham Young by proclamation forbids armed forces to enter Salt Lake City, directs the troops in the territory to repel such invasion, and declares martial law.....15 Sept. "

Mormons under maj. Lot Smith destroy on the Green river and Big Sandy 3 or more supply trains destined for the army of Utah.....5-6 Oct. "

Army of Utah, under col. Albert Sidney Johnston, is ordered to fort Badger, and into winter-quarters at camp Scott, 2 or 3 miles from fort Badger and 115 from Salt Lake City....Nov. "

Gov. Cummings at camp Scott proclaims the territory in rebellion.....27 Nov. "

Col. Thomas L. Kane arrives at Salt Lake City as a peacemaker, with credentials from pres. Buchanan.....25 Feb. 1858

Gov. Cummings visits Salt Lake City with col. Kane, leaving camp Scott.....5 Apr. "

A constitution for the state of Deseret, formed by a people's convention at Salt Lake City in Mch. 1856, is tabled in the U. S. Senate.....20 Apr. "

Proclamation by pres. Buchanan offering amnesty to Mormons who submit to federal authority, issued 6 Apr., is accepted by the Mormon leaders.....2 June, "

Van of the army of Utah finds Salt Lake City deserted; 30,000 Mormons had moved southward.....26 June, "

Gov. Cumming resigns and leaves Salt Lake City.....May, 1861

Another convention meets 20 Jan., finishes a constitution for the state of Deseret, 23 Jan., ratified by the people...3 Mch. 1862

Act of Congress passed to punish and prevent polygamy in the territories.....1 July, "

Mormon apostates, known as Morrisites, indicted for armed resistance to law, when summoned to surrender by the sheriff, resist for 3 days, 13-16 June, 1862, until their leader, Joseph Morris, and others are killed; tried before judge Kinney, 7 are convicted of murder in the second degree.....Mch. 1863

Gov. James Duane Doty d.....13 June, 1865

University of Deseret at Salt Lake City, chartered 1850, organized.....8 Mch. 1869

Mass-meeting of Mormons at Salt Lake City to protest against interference by Congress with polygamy.....5 Apr. 1870

Gov. J. Wilson Shaffer by proclamation forbids the review of the Nauvoo legion of 13,000 men.....15 Sept. "

Vernon H. Vaughan succeeds gov. Shaffer, who d.....Oct. "

Zion's Co-operative Mercantile institution incorporated .1 Dec. "

Companies of the Nauvoo legion, assembling, are dispersed by federal authority.....4 July, 1871

Brigham Young, ordered to be tried for bigamy, escapes; Hawkins, an elder, sentenced to 3 years' imprisonment for adultery..... "

Brigham Young surrenders for trial; proceedings annulled by the Supreme court..... 1872

Brigham Young resigns temporal power.....10 Apr. 1873

Brigham Young again indicted for polygamy.....Oct. 1874

Adjudged to support one of his wives while she sues for divorce, Mch.; imprisoned in his own house for non-compliance, Nov.; discharged.....Dec. 1875

John D. Lee, convicted of murder in the first degree for the Mountain Meadows massacre, 11 Sept. 1857, is shot on the site of it.....23 Mch. 1877

Brigham Young d.....29 Aug. "

Brigham Young college at Logan opened.....Sept. 1878

School districts formed and a tax levied for school buildings... 1880

Edmunds law against polygamy, amending law of 1862, 22 Mch. 1882

Utah Deaf Mute institute at Salt Lake City opened..... 1884

Asylum for the insane near Provo opened..... 1885

Congress authorizes an Industrial home at Salt Lake City for women renouncing polygamy, and their children..... 1886

Edmunds-Tucker Anti-polygamy law approved.....3 Mch. 1887

Reform school at Ogden opened.....31 Oct. 1889

Site for Agricultural college selected at Logan; construction begun, June, 1889; college opened.....4 Sept. 1890

New school-law making public-schools free..... "

Methodist university at Ogden founded..... "

Gentiles for the first time control a municipal election in Salt Lake City.....10 Feb. "

New free-school law, a territorial bureau of statistics established, and 8 per cent. made the legal rate of interest by legislature at session.....13 Jan.-13 Mch. "

Mormon church renounces polygamy at a general conference in Salt Lake City.....6 Oct. "

Territorial Reform school destroyed by fire.....24 June, 1891

First election under national party lines; Mormon Republican and Democratic votes about equal.....4 Aug. "

Irrigation convention; delegates from nearly every state and territory west of the Mississippi at Salt Lake City..15 Sept. "

Cap-stone of temple in Salt Lake City laid by pres. Woodruff of the church of the Latter-Day Saints.....6 Apr. 1892

Congress abolishes the Utah commission of 5, under act of 22 Mch. 1882, and transfers their duties to the governor, chief-justice, and secretary of Utah.....14 July, "

President issues a proclamation of amnesty to Mormons liable to prosecution for polygamy..... 4 Jan. 1893

New temple at Salt Lake City, begun 40 years before, dedicated, 6 Apr. "

Bill passes the House of Representatives admitting Utah, 13 Dec. "

Bill passes the Senate admitting Utah.....10 July, 1894

[The admission being under certain conditions, one of which is "*that polygamous or plural marriages are forever prohibited.*"]

Act permitting Utah to hold a constitutional convention and become a state, signed.....17 July, "

GOVERNORS.

Brigham Young	assumes office	1851
Alfred Cumming	"	1857
John W. Dawson	"	1861
Stephen S. Harding	"	1862
James Duane Doty	"	1863
Charles Durkee	"	1865
J. Wilson Shaffer	"	1870
Vernon H. Vaughn	"	"
George L. Woods	"	1871
S. B. Axtell	"	1874
George W. Emery	"	1875
Eli H. Murray	"	1879
Caleb W. West	"	1886
Arthur L. Thomas	"	1889
Caleb W. West	"	1893

Utes. INDIANS.

U'tica (N. Africa), an ancient Tyrian colony, an ally of Carthage, named in the treaty with the Romans, 348 B.C. Here Cato the Younger, after the defeat of the partisans of Pompey at Thapsus, committed suicide, 46 B.C. Utica flourished after the fall of Carthage, and was made a Roman city by Augustus on account of its favoring Julius Cæsar. It suffered by the invasion of the Vandals, 439, and of the Saracens, about 700.

Utilita'rianism, termed the "greatest happiness principle," the philosophy which proposes as the test of moral good *the greatest happiness of the greatest number*; a doctrine ascribed to Priestley by Bentham. The doctrine is found in the writings of Locke, Hartley, Hume, and Paley; but was formed into an ethical system by Jeremy Bentham in his "Introduction to the Principles of Morals and Legislation," 1780-89, and by John Stuart Mill, who died 8 May, 1873. Mill founded a small "utilitarian society" in 1822. He took the name from an expression in Galt's "Annals of the Parish."

Uto'pia (Gr. οὐ, not, and τόπος, place; properly "nowhere"), a name given by sir Thomas More to an imaginary island representing the "best state of a public weale," described *in a book in Latin published* 1548. *The work is* considered a satire on the state of Europe at the time. An English translation was published in 1551.

U'trecht (the Roman *Trajectum ad Rhenum*) became an independent bishopric about 695. The last prelate, Henry of Bavaria, weary of his turbulent subjects, sold his temporal government to the emperor Charles V. in 1528. The union of the 7 united provinces—viz., Holland, Zealand, Utrecht, Friesland, Groningen, Overyssel, and Guelderland—was formed here for their mutual defence against Spain, 23 Jan. 1579; 300th anniversary celebrated 23 Jan. 1879. The treaty of Utrecht, which terminated the wars of queen Anne, was signed by the ministers of Great Britain and France and the other allies, except the empire, 11 Apr. 1713. It secured Protestant succession in England, separation of the French and Spanish crowns, destruction of the works of Dunkirk, enlargement of the British colonies and plantations in America, and full satisfaction for the claims of the allies. Utrecht surrendered to the Prussians, 9 May, 1787; was acquired by the French, 18 Jan. 1795; and restored at the peace, 1814.

Ux'mal, a place with extensive ruins in Yucatan. Their origin is unknown. They are evidently due to a more advanced civilization than that found there by the Spaniards. They cover several square miles. AMERICA, COPAN, and PALENQUE.

V

V, a character derived from the Greek Υ, upsilon The 22d letter in the English alphabet is the older form of the letter u, and only recently distinguished from it, but while u is a vowel, v is always a consonant The letter v designates the number 5

vaccina'tion (from *Variola vaccina*, the cow pox), discovered by dr Edward Jenner He was born in Berkeley, Gloucestershire, Engl., 17 May, 1749, and educated in medicine, partly by John Hunter Having heard that milkmaids who had had cow-pox never took small pox, he, about 1780, conceived the idea of vaccination He made the first experiment on a healthy child at Berkeley, 14 May, 1796, with pus from a milkmaid who had caught cow-pox from cows He announced his success, 1798, and vaccination, begun 21 Jan 1799, soon became general, after much opposition Dr Jenner received 10,000*l* from the British Parliament, 2 June 1802, and 20,000*l* in 1807 The first national institution for vaccination, the Royal Jennerian Institution, was founded in London, 19 Jan 1803 The emperor Napoleon valued dr Jenner highly, and liberated dr Wickham, a prisoner of war, at his request, and subsequently whole families of English, refusing nothing that he asked Vaccination, although much opposed, extended throughout Europe before 1816 Dr Jenner died suddenly, 26 Jan 1823

Royal Jennerian and London vaccine institution founded 1803
Vaccination act, 3 and 4 Vict passed 23 July, 1840
John Badcock, of Brighton, begins to inoculate cows with small pox to produce new lymph for vaccination about "
Blue book of "Papers on the History and Practice of Vaccination" edited by John Simon, is published by the board of health 1857
Statue subscribed for by all nations, is erected to Jenner's memory in Trafalgar square 30 Apr 1858
It is removed to Kensington 1862
Vaccination is made compulsory in England in 1853, and in Ireland and Scotland 1863
Statue to Jenner erected by the French at Boulogne, inaugurated 11 Sept. 1865
Vaccination direct from the cow or calf advocated and practised in Brussels, etc 1879-81
Successful vaccination of 68,000 sheep by M Pasteur of Paris up to 1 Oct 1881
Grocers' company of London offers 1000*l* for a method of propagating vaccine contagion apart from the animal body, 30 May, 1883
Estimate published 750,000 infants vaccinated, 50 die of disease in consequence Oct 1887
Royal commission of inquiry appointed, England. 29 May, 1889
HYDROPHOBIA

vacuum, partial, reducing the pressure of the atmosphere, vastly increases its absorption of moisture This principle has been utilized by M Emil Passburg of Breslau in an apparatus for drying grain, used since 1888

Vadimo'nis la'cus, the Vadimonian lake, Umbria, central Italy, near which the Etruscans were totally defeated in 2 severe engagements by the Roman consuls—1, by Fabius Maximus, 309 B C, 2, by Cornelius Dolabella, 283

vagrant (Lat. *vagor*, to wander), a person aimlessly wandering from place to place, a vagabond, a tramp By English law a vagrant was whipped and sworn to return to the place where he was born, or had last dwelt for 3 years, 1530 A vagrant a second time convicted was to lose the upper part of the gristle of his right ear, 1535, a third time convicted, death. A vagabond to be branded with a V, and be a slave for 2 years, 1547 If he absconded and was caught, he was to be branded with S, and be a slave for life Vagrants were punished by whipping, jailing, boring the ears, and death for a second offence, 1572 Milder statutes were enacted during the reigns of George II and George III The present Vagrant act was passed in England in 1824

Valençay (*val-an-say'*), a château near Châteauroux, central France, where Napoleon I imprisoned Ferdinand of Spain from 1808 to 1813 The kingdom was restored to Ferdinand by treaty signed 8 Dec 1813

Valen'cia, a city of E Spain, the *Valentia Edetanorum* of the Romans, became the capital of a Moorish kingdom, 1000, annexed to Aragon, 1238 Its university founded, it is said, in the 13th century, was revived in the 15th Valencia was taken by the earl of Peterborough in 1705 but submitted to the Bourbons after the unfortunate battle of Almanza, in 1707 It resisted the attempts of marshal Moncey, but was taken from the Spaniards with a garrison of more than 16 000 men, and immense stores, by the French under Suchet, 9 Jan 1812

Valenciennes (*val-en-see-en'*), N France This city (the Roman *Valentiana*), after many changes, was taken by Louis XIV in 1677, and annexed 1678 It was besieged from 23 May to 28 July, 1793, when the French garrison surrendered to the allies under the duke of York It was retaken together with Condé by the French, 27-30 Aug 1794, on capitulation, the garrison and 1100 emigrants were made prisoners, with immense stores

Valen'tia, a Roman province, including the country between the walls of Severus and Adrian, was reconquered from the Picts and Scots by Theodosius and named after Valentinian I, the reigning emperor, 368

Valentine's day (14 Feb) Valentine is said to have been a bishop, martyred under Claudius II at Rome, others say under Aurelian, in 271 The origin of the ancient custom of "choosing a valentine" has been much controverted

"To morrow is Saint Valentine's day
All in the morning betime,
And I a maid at your window,
To be your Valentine"
—*Shakespeare*, "Hamlet," act iv sc v

Valentin'ians, followers of Valentine, a priest who, on being disappointed of a bishopric, forsook the Christian faith, declaring there were 30 gods and goddesses, 15 of each sex, which he called Æones, or Ages He taught in the 2d century, and published a gospel and psalms, his followers added other errors

Valhalla (Icel *valhöll*, gen *valhallar*, lit the hall of the slain, from *valr*, the slain, and *höll*, hall) In Scandinavian mythology the place of immortality for the souls of heroes slain in battle, selected by female deities called in Icelandic *Valkyrur*, choosers of the slain Here they feast daily with Odin, eating boar's flesh and drinking mead from the skulls of their slain enemies A name given to the Pantheon or Temple of Fame, built by Louis I of Bavaria at Donaustauf, near Ratisbon Begun 18 Oct 1830, and dedicated 18 Oct 1842 It is consecrated to the great men of Germany, and contains statues and memorials of them

Valkyriur. VALHALLA.

Valladolid', a city of Spain, the Roman *Pintia* and the Moorish *Belad Walid*, was recovered for the Christians by Ordoño II, the first king of Leon, 914-23 It became the capital of Castile in the 15th century It was taken by the French, Jan 1808, and captured by the English, 4 June, 1813. Here died Christopher Columbus, 20 May, 1506.

Vallambro'sa, a town of central Italy. A Benedictine abbey was founded here by John Gualbert, about 1038 The monks were termed Vallambrosians.

Vallandigham, Arrest of UNITED STATES, 1863

Valley Forge, encampment of the army of 11,000 Americans during the winter of 1777-78, from 19 Dec to 18 June, about 20 miles northwest from Philadelphia, on the Schuylkill Famous for the suffering and privations of the American troops (in log huts 14 by 16 ft) during the severe winter

Valmy, a village of N E France Here the French under Kellermann defeated the Prussians under the duke of Brunswick, 20 Sept 1792 The victory was of immense advantage to the republican cause, and Kellermann was made duke of Valmy in 1808

Valois (*val-wah'*) a county in N France given by Philip III. to his younger son Charles, whose son Philip became king as Philip IV in 1328 FRANCE

Valparai'so, principal port of Chili, South America

Here com. Porter, after a desperate fight, surrendered his vessel, the *Essex*, to the British ships *Cherube* and *Phœbe*, 28 Mch. 1814. NAVAL BATTLES. Pop. 1891, 105,000.

Valtel'line, N. Italy, a district near the Rhætian Alps, seized by the Grison league, 1512, and ceded to it, 1530. At the instigation of Spain, the Catholics rose and massacred the Protestants, 19-21 July, 1620. After much contention between the French and Austrians, the neutrality of the Valtelline was assured in 1639. It was annexed to the Cisalpine Republic in 1797; to Italy, 1807; to Austria, 1814; to Italy, 1860.

val'vasor or **vav'asor.** The first dignity in England beneath a peer was anciently that of *vidames, vice-domini*, or *valvasors*. Valvasors are mentioned by ancient lawyers as *viri magnæ dignitatis*, and sir Edward Coke speaks highly of them. Now, the first personal dignity after the nobility is a knight of the Garter.—*Blackstone*.

Valverde, Battle of. NEW MEXICO, 1862.

Van Buren, Martin, Administration of. UNITED STATES, 1837.

vana'dium (from *Vanadis*, the Scandinavian Venus), metal discovered by Sefström, in 1830, in iron ore. A similar metal, discovered in lead ore by Del Rio in 1801, and named *erythronium*, was proved by Wöhler to be vanadium. Vanadium was discovered in the copper-bearing beds in Cheshire, in 1865, by H. E. Roscoe, by whom its peculiarities were further studied, and published in 1867-68. It is likely to be useful in photography and dyeing.

Vancou'ver's island, North Pacific ocean, near the mainland of the state of Washington, U. S., and British Columbia, from which it is separated by the gulf of Georgia. It is about 300 miles long, and was named after capt. Geo. Vancouver, an English navigator, who was sent on a voyage of discovery to seek any navigable communication between the North Pacific and North Atlantic oceans. He sailed 7 Jan. 1791, and returned 24 Sept. 1795. He compiled an account of his survey of the northwest coast of America, and died in 1798. Settlements, made here by the English in 1781, were seized by the Spaniards in 1789, but restored. By treaty with the U. S., in 1846, the island was secured to Great Britain. It has become of importance since the discovery of gold in the neighboring mainland, in 1858, and the colonization of British Columbia. The island was united with British Columbia in Aug. 1866; and on 24 May, 1868, Victoria, founded in 1857, was declared the capital.

Van'dals, a Germanic race, attacked the Roman empire in the 3d century, and began to ravage Germany and Gaul, 406-14; their kingdom in Spain was founded in 411; under Genseric they invaded and conquered the Roman territories in Africa, 429, and took Carthage, Oct. 439. They were subdued by Belisarius in 534. They were driven out by the Saracen Moors. The dukes of Mecklenburg style themselves princes of the Vandals.

VANDAL KINGS IN AFRICA.

429. Genseric (MECKLENBURG).	496. Thrasimund.
477. Hunneric, his son.	523. Hilderic.
484. Gundamund.	531. Gelimer.

Van Diemen's Land. TASMANIA.

Varan'gians, northern pirates who invaded Flanders about 813; France about 840; Italy, 852. Their leader, Ruric, invited by the Novgorodians to help them, founded the Russian monarchy, 862.

Varennes (*va-ren'*), a town in N.E. France, is celebrated for the arrest of Louis XVI., his queen, sister, and 2 children. They fled from the Tuileries on 21 June, 1791; were overtaken here next day, and conducted back to Paris, mainly through Drouet, the postmaster, who at an intermediate town recognized the king.

variable stars. Those which change in brilliancy; mostly in regular periods, varying from 70 years or more to a few hours. The first observed was a small star of Cetus, or the Whale, by Daniel Fabricius, 13 Aug. 1596. In October of same year the star had vanished. Since then many similar variations have been observed by Goodricke, Herschel, and other astronomers, until the number of variable stars included in standard catalogues is 234, with 126 "suspected," and new ones are discovered every year. In many cases the change is explained by the revolution of a dark or less bright companion, intercepting part of its light; but some astronomers incline to think all the fixed stars affected in brilliancy by internal commotions, and that these variations may be important enough in some of them to account for changes of magnitude.

Varna, a fortified seaport in Bulgaria, formerly European Turkey. A great battle was fought near this place, 10 Nov. 1444, the Turks under Amurath II. defeating the Hungarians under king Ladislaus and John Hunniades, with great slaughter, killing the king and capturing Hunniades, who had urged the Christians to keep the truce recently made at Szegedin for 10 years. The emperor Nicholas of Russia arrived before Varna, the headquarters of his army, besieging the place, 5 Aug. 1828. The Turkish garrison made a vigorous sortie, 7 Aug.; and another on the 21st, but were repulsed. Varna surrendered 11 Oct. 1828. It was restored at the peace in 1829; its fortifications were dismantled, but have been restored. The allied armies disembarked at Varna, 29 May, 1854, and sailed for the Crimea, 3 Sept. They suffered severely from cholera. Under the treaty of Berlin, Varna was evacuated by the Turks, and occupied by Russians, autumn, 1878.

vassalage. FEUDAL LAWS, SLAVERY.

Vassar college, the first institution in the world designed to give women a full collegiate education, was founded at Poughkeepsie, N. Y., in 1861, by Matthew Vassar. His first bequest was $408,000, with additions of as much more. It was opened, Sept. 1865, with a full faculty and 350 students. It has been successful, and is considered a model institution.

Vassy (*vas-see'*), a town of N.E. France. The massacre of the Protestants at this place by the duke of Guise, on 1 Mch. 1562, led to desolating civil wars.

Vat'ican, Rome, the ancient Mons Vaticanus, a hill of Rome. The foundation of the palace is ascribed to Constantine, Liberius, and Symmachus. It became the residence of the pope at his return from Avignon, 1377. It is said to contain 7000 rooms, rich in works of art, ancient and modern. The library, founded by pope Nicholas V., 1448, is rich in printed books and MSS.—Pistolesi's description of the Vatican, with numerous plates, pub. 1829-38.—The phrase "Thunders of the Vatican" was first used by Voltaire, 1748. The ancient Vatican codex of the Old and New Testament in Greek was published at Rome in 1857. "Vatican Decrees," COUNCILS OF THE CHURCH.

Vaud (*vō*), a Swiss canton, long held by the Franks, the kings of Burgundy, emperors of Germany, dukes of Zähringen, and dukes of Savoy, was conquered by the Bernese, Jan. 1536, and annexed, 1554. Vaud, made independent in 1798, joined the confederation in 1815. A new constitution was obtained in 1830, after agitation.

Vaudois. WALDENSES.

Vedas, the sacred books of the Hindus, in Sanscrit, were probably written about 1000 B.C. Veda means knowledge. These writings comprise hymns, prayers, and liturgical formulæ, supposed to have been revealed to certain Brahmins. They are divided into 4 parts or books, called (in the order in which they were written) the Rig-Veda, Sama-Veda, Yajur-Veda, and the Atharva-Veda. Often spoken of as separate Vedas. Prof. Max Müller published them under the patronage of the East India company in 1849-74. 4 volumes of a translation by H. H. Wilson, pub. 1850-67; vols. v. and vi., completing the work, pub. 1889. A new edition of Max Müller's text in progress, 2 vols. pub. 1890.

Vehmic tribunals (Ger. *Vehmgerichte, Fehmgerichte*, or *Femgerichte*), secret tribunals in Westphalia to maintain religion and the public peace, founded in the time of Charlemagne, rose to importance in 1182, when Westphalia became subject to the archbishop of Cologne. Persons of exalted rank were at times seized, tried, and executed by them. The emperors endeavored to suppress them, but did not succeed till the 16th century. Their last court, it is said, was held in 1568 Sir W Scott has described them in "Anne of Geierstein" A remnant of this tribunal was abolished by Jerome Bonaparte, king of Westphalia, in 1811

Veii (*ve'i*), an independent Latin city near Rome Between the Romans and Veientes frequent wars occurred, till Veii was destroyed, after 10 years' siege, 396 B.C A Roman family, the FABII, who had seceded from Rome for political reasons, were surprised and destroyed at the river Cremera by the Veientes, 477 B C

veloc'ipedes. BICYCLE

velvet (from O It *veluto*), a cloth made from silk or cotton with a close pile The manufacture, long confined to Genoa, Lucca, and other places in Italy, was carried to France, and thence to England, about 1685 Velvet is mentioned by Joinville in 1272, and Richard II, in his will, directed his body to be clothed "in velveto," 1399 Jerome Lanyer in London patented "velvet paper" in 1634

Vendée. LA VENDÉE

Vendémiaire 12, 13, 14 (3, 4, 5 Oct), 1795, Barras and Napoleon Bonaparte suppressed a royalist revolt against the convention

Vendôme column (132 feet 2 inches high), erected in the Place Vendôme, Paris, by Napoleon I in 1806 to commemorate his successful campaign in Germany in 1805 On its side were bass-reliefs by Launay It was pulled down by the communists "in the name of international fraternity," 16 May, 1871, restored by the National Assembly, 31 Aug 1874, statue of Napoleon I. on the top replaced, 28 Dec. 1875

Ven'eti, maritime Gauls, of uncertain origin, inhabiting Armorica, N W France They rose against the Romans, 57 B C, and were quelled by Julius Cæsar, who defeated their fleet, 56, and exterminated an active commercial race

Vene'tia. VENICE

Venezue'la. When the Spaniards landed in 1499, they gave it the name of Venezuela, or Little Venice In July, 1814, Venezuela declared itself independent It formed part of the republic of Colombia till Nov 1829 The fundamental law in force from 1830, and re-proclaimed with alterations on 28 Mch 1864, and Apr 1881, is modelled on the Constitution of the United States Area, 594,165 sq miles, pop. 1890, 2,285,054

Independence recognized by Spain 1845
Renunciation of papal authority Sept 1876
In a message to Congress, pres. Cleveland intervenes between Venezuela and Great Britain 17 Dec. 1895
Arbitration treaty commission meets in Paris 15 June, 1899
The commission draws the boundary line between Venezuela and British Guiana 3 Oct "
Germany, Great Britain, and Italy attempt to collect claims by war-ships, Puerto Cabello is bombarded Dec 1902
The claims are referred to the Hague Arbitration Court, which decides against Venezuela 22 Feb. 1904
Venezuela agrees to prefer claims of Germany and Great Britain to the amount of $26,000,000 21 Mch 1905

Venice, a city of N Italy in the province of Venetia The Veneti, said to be descendants of Antenor, a Trojan prince, who settled here with a colony of Paphlagonians after the fall of Troy, made an alliance with the Romans, 215 B.C, who founded Aquileia, 181, and gradually acquired the whole country Under the empire, Venetia included Padua, Verona, and other important places. Population of Venice in 1857, 118,173, in 1890, 158,019, and of the province, 2,985,036. Area of the province, 9059 sq miles. New line of steamers for the East started from Venice by the Peninsular and Oriental company, July, 1872

Venice founded by families from Aquileia and Padua fleeing from Attila . about 452
First doge (or duke) chosen, Anafesto Paulutio 697
Bishopric founded 733
Doge Orso slain, an annual magistrate (*maestro di militi*, master of the militia) appointed . 737
Diodato, son of Orso made doge 742
Two doges reign Maurizio Galbaio and his son Giovanni 777
Rialto made the seat of government . 811
Venice independent of the Eastern empire, and acquires the maritime cities of Dalmatia and Istria 997
Its navy and commerce increase 1000-1100
Venetians aid capture of Tyre and acquire the third part, 1124, and ravage the Greek archipelago . 1125
Bank of Venice established 1157
Ceremony of wedding the ADRIATIC instituted about 1177
Zara captured by the Venetians 24 Nov 1202
Venetians aid crusaders with men, horses, and ships "
Crete purchased 1204
Venice helps in the Latin conquest of Constantinople, and obtains power in the East 1204-5
Four bronze horses by Lysippus, from Constantinople placed at St. Mark's by doge Pietro Ziani d 1229
Venetians defeat Genoese near Negropont 1263
War with Genoa 1293
Venetian fleet defeated by Genoese in the Adriatic, 8 Sept 1298, peace 1299
Louis of Hungary defeated at Zara 1 July 1346
Severe contest with Genoa 1350-81
Doge Marino Faliero, to avenge an insult, conspires against the republic, beheaded 17 Apr 1355
Venetians lose Istria and Dalmatia 1358
War with Genoese, who defeat Venetians at Pola, and attack Venice vigorous defence 1377
Genoese fleet captured at Chiozza 1380
Peace concluded 1381
Venice flourishes under Antonio Vernieri 1382-1400
War with Padua, conquest of Padua and Verona 1404
With Milan, conquest of Brescia, 1425, of Bergamo 1428
Plague in Venice 1447
War against Milan, 1430 conquest of Ravenna 1454
War with Turks, many Eastern possessions lost 1461-77
Venetians take Athens, 1466 and Cyprus 1475
Venice excommunicated, 1483 joins league against Naples 1493, helps to overcome Charles VIII of France 1495
Injured by the discovery of America (1492) and the passage to the Indies 1497
Venetians nearly ruined by the League of Cambray 1508
They assist in defeating the Turks at Lepanto 7 Oct 1571
Turks retake Cyprus "
Destructive fire at Venice 1577
"Bridge of Sighs," a single span (enclosed) connecting the ducal palace with the prisons, built, some say, by the builder of the Rialto and others by the architect San Sovino about 1580

[Those who passed over it after trial were prisoners on their way to execution, hence the name.

"I stood in Venice on the Bridge of Sighs,
A palace and a prison on each hand"
—*Byron*, "Childe Harold," canto iv stanza 1]

Rialto bridge and Piazza di San Marco erected about 1592
Paul V 's interdict on Venice (1606) disregarded 1607
Naval victories over Turks at Scio, 1651, and in the Dardanelles 1655
Turks take Candia after 24 years' siege 1669
Venice recovers part of the Morea, 1683-99, loses it 1716-39
Bonaparte seizes Venice, and by treaty at Campo Formio gives part to Austria, and the rest to the Cisalpine republic 1797
Venice annexed to Italy by treaty of Presburg 26 Dec. 1805
Transferred to empire of Austria 1814
Venice declared a free port 24 Jan 1830
Insurrection, 22 Mch 1848, the city defended by Daniel Manin, surrenders to Austrians after a long siege 22 Aug 1849
Venetia surrendered to Napoleon III, for Italy (by treaty of Vienna), 3 Oct, transferred to Italy 17 Oct 1866
Plebiscitum 651,758 votes for annexation to Italy, 69 against, 22 Oct. "
Masterpiece of Titian ("Death of Peter Martyr") destroyed by the burning of a chapel 15 Aug 1867
Remains of Daniel Manin (brought from Paris) buried in St Mark's 23 Mch 1868
His statue unveiled . 22 Mch 1875
Restoration of palace of the doges completed and opened Nov 1889

[Venice has had 122 doges Anafesto, A D 697, to Luigi Manin, 1797]

ventilators were invented by the rev dr Hales, and described to the Royal Society of London, May, 1741, and a ventilator for ships was announced by Mr. Triewald in Nov same year The marquess of Chabannes's plan for warming and ventilating theatres and houses for audiences was applied in London about 1819 The systems of dr Reid (about 1834) and others followed, with much controversy Dr Arnott's work on this subject was published in 1838

ventril'oquism ("speaking from the belly") is evidently described in Isa xxix 4 (about 712 B C) Among eminent ventriloquists were baron Mengen and M. Saint Gille, about 1772 (whose experiments were examined by a commission of the French academy), Thomas King (about 1716), Charles Mathews (1824), and M. Alexandre (1822)

Venus, the second planet from the sun, its mean distance being 66,134,000 miles, and its orbit almost a circle Its period is 224 days 17 hours, its orbital velocity 78,000 miles an hour Its diameter is about 7510 miles, and its daily revolution was determined by Cassini in 1667 at 23 hours 21 minutes 23 seconds, but there is some uncertainty from recent observations. The rare transits of Venus across the sun's disc are watched by astronomers with great interest, as one of the best means of determining the sun's distance from us Transits occur in pairs, 8 years apart, at intervals of more than a century. Transits occurred 5 June, 1761, 3 June, 1769, 8 Dec. 1874, 6 Dec. 1882; next transits 8 June, 2004, 6 June, 2012, the pairs occurring alternately in Dec. and in June. The transit of Venus over the sun was predicted by Kepler, but not observed. The first ever observed was by the rev. Jeremiah Horrox, or Horrocks, and his friend William Crabtree, on 24 Nov. 1639, as predicted by Horrox in 1633. The astronomer-royal Maskelyne observed one at St. Helena, 6 June, 1761. Capt. Cook made his first voyage in the *Endeavor* to Otaheite to observe a transit of Venus, 3 June, 1769.

Halley explains the method of determining the distance of the sun by the transit 1716
Another method by Delisle ....about 1743
Both plans used ....Dec. 1874
Expeditions for accurate observation on 8 Dec. astronomical day (ordinary day, 9 Dec.), are sent to different parts of the globe by all the great powers .... "
Transit observed at Bath, Penzance, Cork, Cape Town, Washington, D. C., Melbourne, and many other places (Sun), 6 Dec. 1882

Venus, the Roman goddess of love and beauty, identified with the Greek *Aphrodite*. To represent her in marble has always been a favorite work of famous sculptors, the most celebrated statues being the Venus di Medici found near Tivoli early in the 17th century, and at first placed in the Medici palace in Rome (whence the name), removed to Florence, 1680, and the Venus of Melos, or Milo, discovered on the island of Melos by a farmer in 1820, placed in the Louvre, 1834, supposed to be the work of the 4th century B.C. Of less note are the Venus of Arles, the Venus of Capua, the Venus of the Capitol, and later the Venus Borghese by Canova, whose model was Pauline Bonaparte. SCULPTURE.

Vera Cruz, a seaport town of Mexico, built about 1600, was taken by U. S. troops in 1847, and by the allies on 17 Dec. 1861, during the intervention; retaken by the liberals under Juarez, 27 June, 1867.

Vercel'li (the ancient *Vercellæ*), a town of Piedmont, near which Marius defeated the Cimbri, 101 B.C., was the seat of a republic in the 13th and 14th centuries. It was taken by the Spaniards, 1630; French, 1704; and allies, 1706; and afterwards shared the fortunes of Piedmont.

Ver'den, a town of Hanover. Here Charlemagne massacred about 4500 Saxons, who had rebelled and relapsed into idolatry, 782.

Verdun' (the ancient *Verodunum*), a first-class fortress on the Meuse, N.E. France, made a magazine for his legions by Julius Cæsar. It was acquired by the Franks in the 6th century, and formed part of the dominions of Lothaire by the treaty of Verdun, 843, when the empire was divided between the sons of Louis I. It was taken and annexed to the empire by Otho I. about 939. It surrendered to France in 1552, and was formally ceded in 1648. It was taken and held by the Prussians 43 days, Sept.–Oct. 1792. Gen. Beaurepaire, the commandant, committed suicide before the surrender, and 14 ladies were executed on 28 May, 1794, for appealing to the king of Prussia for the town. Verdun surrendered to the Germans, 8 Nov. 1870, after a brave defence. It was the last place held by the Germans, and was given up 15, 16 Sept. 1873, and the troops retired.

Vermont, a New England state, is bounded on the north by the province of Quebec, east by New Hampshire, south by Massachusetts, and west by New York and lake Champlain. It lies between 42° 44′ to 45° 43′ N. lat., and 71° 38′ to 73° 25′ W. lon. Area, 9565 sq. miles. Pop. 1890, 332,422; 1900, 343,641. Capital, Montpelier.

Samuel de Champlain explores the lake bearing his name 1609
About 44,000 acres in southern Vermont, granted to the colony of Connecticut, in 1715, as an equivalent for lands granted by Massachusetts in Connecticut territory, transferred to William Dummer, Anthony Stoddard, William Brattle, and John White 1716
Fort Dummer built by the colony of Massachusetts on the Connecticut river at Brattleborough 1724
French settle at Chimney Point, Addison township, Vt. 1730
Township Number One, now Westminster, laid out between the great falls and the land grant of 1716, by the general court of Massachusetts ....19 Nov. 1736
Grant of Walloomsack, 1200 acres, mostly in New York, but extending into the township of Bennington 1739
Gov. Wentworth of New Hampshire makes a grant of Bennington 1749
Bennington settled 1761
Northern boundary of Vermont fixed at 45° N. lat. 1763
Proclamation by lieut.-gov. Colden of New York claiming the territory west of the Connecticut, now Vermont, under grants from Charles II. to the duke of York, and ordering the sheriff to return the names of those who had settled on it under titles from New Hampshire ....28 Dec. "
[This claim was not settled until 1790.]
Gov. Wentworth, after granting about 130 townships west of the Connecticut, proclaims the claims of New York obsolete, and jurisdiction belongs to New Hampshire ....13 Mch. 1764
New York appeals to the king, who decides the Connecticut river to be the eastern boundary of New York ......20 July, "
Lieut.-gov. Colden proclaims *Vermont* annexed to New York, 10 Apr. 1765
First New York patent for lands in Vermont, under Colden's proclamation, for 26,000 acres, called Princetown, in the valley of the Battenkill, between Arlington and Dorset, 21 May, "
Samuel Robinson, appointed by 1000 settlers under the New Hampshire grants to present their petition to the king, sails from New York for England ....25 Dec. 1766
King George III. forbids New York, until authorized, to grant land in Vermont ....24 July, 1767
Lieut.-gov. Colden disregards the order, and between Sept. 1769 and Oct. 1770, grants 600,000 acres 1769–70
New-Yorkers, claiming the farm of James Breakenridge in the township of Bennington (part of the Walloomsack grant of 1739), send commissioners and surveyors who are dispersed by friends of Breakenridge ....19 Oct. 1769
Ejectment suits for lands claimed by New York at Albany are decided against settlers under New Hampshire grants. .June, 1770
Sheriff Ten Eyck, with a posse of about 300 citizens of Albany, attempts to take Breakenridge's farm for New York claimants, but is driven off by armed settlers ....19 July, 1771
Organization of the "Green Mountain Boys" under command of col. Ethan Allen, for opposing "the Yorkers" .... "
Jehiel Hawley and James Breakenridge appointed by deputies of Bennington at Manchester, 21 Oct., to petition the king to confirm their grants from New Hampshire ....21 Oct. 1772
Green Mountain Boys visit Durham (Clarendon) twice, armed and with threats, to compel the inhabitants to acknowledge the New Hampshire title ....Oct.–Nov. 1773
Gov. Tryon of New York, by proclamation, commands Ethan Allen, Seth Warner, Remember Baker, Robert Cochran, Peleg Sunderland, Silvanus Brown, James Breakenridge, and John Smith to surrender within 30 days, offering 150*l*. for capture of Allen, and 50*l*. each for capture of the others ......9 Mch. 1774
Convention at Manchester resolves that whoever takes a commission of the peace from New York will be deemed an enemy to his country and the common cause .....12–13 Apr. "
Benjamin Hough, an inhabitant of New Hampshire grants, favoring New York, procures a commission as justice of the peace. He is found guilty of violating the resolution of Apr. 1774, publicly whipped, and sent to New York ......30 Jan. 1775
People, to resist the holding of court under royal authority at Westminster appointed for 14 Mch. 1775, assemble at the court-house, 13 Mch. A guard left during the night is fired upon by sheriff Patterson and his posse a little before midnight, wounding 10, 2 mortally, and 7 are taken prisoners. In the morning court is opened, but the judge and officers are imprisoned at Northampton by the mob ....14 Mch. "
Ethan Allen, with 83 men, captures FORT TICONDEROGA, 10 May, "
Ethan Allen and 38 men, captured in an attack on Montreal, sent in irons to England ....25 Sept. "
Convention of the New Hampshire grants at Dorset; 56 delegates from 33 towns, to form a separate state ....25 Sept. 1776
Convention at Westminster declares Vermont "a separate, free, and independent jurisdiction or state, as 'New Connecticut,'" 17 Jan. 1777
Convention at Windsor names the state Vermont, adopts a constitution, and appoints a provisional council of safety for the state ....2–8 July, "
British troops under gens. Fraser and Riedesel attack and disperse the rear guard of St. Clair's army under cols. Francis and Warner at HUBBARDTON ....7 July, "
Council of Vermont appoints "commissioners of sequestration" to seize property of "all persons in the state who had repaired to the enemy" ....28 July, "
Battle of BENNINGTON; gen. Burgoyne sends about 1000 German troops under cols. Baume and Breyman to seize provisions at Bennington; they are routed by Americans under gen. Stark, 16 Aug. "
Legislature at Windsor divides the state into 2 counties; one east of the Green mountains, called Cumberland, and another west, called Bennington ....12 Mch. 1778
Stockade fort and blockhouse erected at Rutland ....Apr. "
Col. Ethan Allen, prisoner of the British since 1775, exchanged, is welcomed to Bennington by a salute of 14 guns, "one for young Vermont" ....31 May, "

 VER

Convention of towns on both sides of the Connecticut river, including 8 from Vermont at Cornish N H, proposes to form a state with capital on the Connecticut 9 Dec 1778

Assembly of Vermont declares the union of 1778 with the 16 towns east of the Connecticut null and void 12 Feb 1779

Legislature of New York refers to Congress to determine equitably the controversy between New York and Vermont 21 Oct "

Pamphlet, "Vermont's Appeal to the Candid and Impartial World," for independence, pub at Hartford by Hudson & Goodwin Dec "

Town of Royalton attacked by 300 Indians from Canada, many buildings burned 16 Oct 1780

Massachusetts assents to the independence of Vermont Mch 1781

Towns east of the Connecticut annexed to Vermont at their request Apr "

First newspaper in Vermont, the *Vermont Gazette or Green Mountain Post boy* printed at Westminster by Judah Paddock Spooner and Timothy Green "

Col Ira Allen commissioner to exchange prisoners with the British reaches Isle aux Noix a few miles north of the Canadian line about 8 May and spends 17 days in conference, a union of Vermont with the British is proposed under instructions from gen Haldimand, by encouraging which Allen effects an exchange of prisoners and cessation of hostilities on the border May, "

Jonas Fay, Ira Allen, and Bazaleel Woodward sent by the legislature to represent the cause of Vermont to the Continental Congress 22 June, "

Congress resolves that an indispensable preliminary to the admission of Vermont as a state should be the relinquishing of territory east of the Connecticut and west of the present New York state line 20 Aug 1781, the legislature dissolves its eastern and western unions 22 Feb. 1782

Residents of Brattleborough Guilford, and Halifax in a petition prepared by Charles Phelps to gov Clinton of New York, complain of the Vermont government, and ask New York to assume jurisdiction over Windham county 30 Apr "

Gov Chittenden commissions gen Ethan Allen, 2 Sept, to raise 250 volunteers, and march into Windham county as a *posse comitatus* to enforce Vermont laws. This force, doubled by volunteers from Windham county arrests some 20 leaders of the rebellion, Charles Phelps escaping, 10 Sept, these leaders are tried at Westminster and banished from the state, 11 Sept. "

First school law, towns are empowered to form school districts and to elect trustees 22 Oct "

Legislature establishes post offices and a postmaster general, "the rates of postage to be the same as in the U S" 1784

Grant to Reuben Harmon, jr, of Rupert, of the exclusive privilege of coining copper for a limited period . 1785

As provided by state constitution, the first council of censors meets and suggests changes in the constitution, and calls a convention . "

Constitution framed by a convention, 4 July, 1786, is adopted by the legislature and declared Mch 1787

Ethan Allen, b at Litchfield Conn, 10 Jan 1737, d at Burlington 12 Feb 1789

New York consents to the admission of Vermont into the Union, renouncing her claims for $30,000, and the legislature of Vermont ratifies the agreement . 28 Oct 1790

Vermont adopts the Constitution of the U S without amendments .. 10 Jan 1791

Vermont admitted by act of Congress of 18 Feb, to take effect, 4 Mch "

Constitutional convention meets at Windsor, 4 July, completes its labors 9 July, 1793

Constitution of 1793 adopted by the legislature 2 Nov 1796

Gov Thomas Chittenden resigns on account of failing health (1797) and d at Williston 25 Aug 1797

University of Vermont and State Agricultural school at Burlington chartered 1791, opened 1800

Middlebury college at Middlebury, chartered 1800, opened 1801

Legislature meets at Montpelier as the capital . 1808

State prison at Windsor established by law "

Steamboat *The Vermont* launched at Burlington by John and James Winans 1809

Flag ship *Saratoga*, of 26 guns, and several small vessels built upon Otter creek during the winter of 1813-14, under Thomas McDonough, engage in the battle of Plattsburg and lake Champlain, Americans victorious 11 Sept 1814

Pres James Monroe makes a tour through Vermont 1817

Death of dr Jonas Fay at Burlington, aged 81 . 6 Mch 1818

Norwich university founded at Norwich 1819

Resolutions of the Vermont legislature presented in the U S Senate, declaring slavery a moral and political evil, and that Congress has the right to prohibit its extension 9 Dec. 1820

Thaddeus Fairbanks starts a foundery at St Johnsbury 1823

Gen Lafayette lays the corner stone of the new university building at Burlington, to replace that destroyed by fire in 1824 . 29 June, 1825

Act for the establishment of common schools 1827

Chester A Arthur born at Fairfield 5 Oct. 1830

Anti Masonic governor, William A Palmer, elected . 1831

House of Representatives divided into a Senate and General Assembly . . . 1836

Vermont asylum for the insane at Brattleborough, incorporated Nov 1834, is opened . . Dec. "

Legislature [illegible] anti slavery resolutions . . 1837

[illegible] pelier completed . . "

[illegible] patriots, organized on the Canada side of the Vermont line to invade the province, threatened by 1600 or 1700 Canadian troops, decide to return to Vermont, but are compelled to surrender by gen Wool Dec 1838

Marble first quarried at Rutland 1844

License law passed "

School fund abolished to pay the state debt 1845

First slate quarry in the state opened at Fairhaven, Rutland county "

Act providing state superintendent of common schools, with town superintendents and district committees 5 Nov "

Local Option law passed 1846

Two brass field pieces captured at Bennington, given Vermont by Congress 10 July, 1848

Jacob Collamer appointed postmaster general 8 Mch 1849

Railroad jubilee at Burlington, celebrating the union of the lakes and the Atlantic by railroad through Vermont 25 June 1850

Vermont State Teachers' Association organized "

Maine Prohibition law passed 20 Dec 1852

State Board of Education established 1856

Capitol at Montpelier burned 6 Jan 1857

Personal Liberty bill, "to secure freedom to all persons within the state," passed 25 Nov 1858

Under the call of pres Lincoln and gov Fairbanks 15 Apr the first Vermont regiment reaches New York city 10 May, 1861

Personal Liberty bill of 1858 repealed as inconsistent with the Constitution of the U S "

Southern refugees in Canada under lieut Bennett H Young, rob the banks of St Albans, escaping into Canada with over $200,000 19 Oct. 1864

Vermont Reform school at Waterbury opened June, 1866

Home for destitute children established at Burlington "

Norwich university removed to Northfield "

Vermont ratifies the XIV th Amendment 9 Nov "

State Normal school at Castleton opened 1867

State Normal School at Johnson opened "

Vermont State Normal school at Randolph opened "

Vermont ratifies the XV th Amendment. 21 Oct. 1869

Gov P J Washburn d, lieut gov W Hendee succeeds, 7 Feb 1870

Five hundred Fenians, marshalled and armed at Fairfield, invade Canada and are driven back by Canadian militia, May, "

State constitution amended council of censors abolished, legislative sessions and state elections made biennial 1871

Board of Education abolished and the office of State Superintendent of Education, filled by the legislature created 1874

State Reform school at Waterbury destroyed by fire 12 Feb "

Vergennes selected as location for the new State Reform school, Jan 1875

Estate, valued at $250,000 left to the state as a common school fund by Arunah Huntington, who d at Brantford, Canada, 10 Jan 1877

Celebration at Bennington of 100th anniversary of the battle of Bennington 15-16 Aug "

Revision of state laws of Vermont under act of 1878 completed, 1880

Manufacture and sale of intoxicating liquors prohibited 1882

State Soldiers' Home located at Bennington 5 Feb 1887

$100 000 appropriated for a state insane asylum at Waterbury, 1888

State Board of Trade organized "

Redfield Proctor appointed secretary of war 5 Mch 1889

Australian Ballot law passed at session 1 Oct -25 Nov 1890

Geo F Edmunds resigns from the U S Senate, to take effect 1 Nov 6 Apr 1891

Ex gov Paul Dillingham d at Waterbury 26 July, "

Celebration of centennial of admission of Vermont into the Union and dedication of the battle monument (308 ft high) at Bennington 19 Aug "

Legislature called in special session concerning direct tax money refunded by Congress 25 Aug "

Ex gov John Gregory Smith d at St Albans 6 Nov "

Redfield Proctor appointed U S senator, 25 Aug, qualifies, 7 Dec "

Redfield Proctor elected U S senator 19 Oct 1892

GOVERNORS

	Assumes office		Assumes office
Thomas Chittenden	1777	Stephen Royce	1854
Moses Robinson	1789	Ryland Fletcher	1856
Thomas Chittenden	1790	Hiland Hall	1858
Paul Brigham	1797	Erastus Fairbanks	1860
Isaac Tichenor	"	Frederick Holbrook	1861
Israel Smith	1807	J Gregory Smith	1863
Isaac Tichenor	1808	Paul Dillingham	1865
Jonas Galusha	1809	John B Page	1867
Martin Chittenden	1813	Peter T Washburn	1869
Jonas Galusha	1815	G W Hendee	1870
Richard Skinner	1820	John W Stewart	"
C P Van Ness	1823	Julius Converse	1872
Ezra Butler	1826	Asahel Peck	187-
Samuel C Crafts .	1828	Horace Fairbanks	1876
William A Palmer	1831	Redfield Proctor	1878
S H Jenison	1835	Roswell Farnham	1880
Charles Paine .	1841	John L Barstow	1882
John Mattocks	1843	Samuel E Pingree	1884
William Slade	1844	Ebenezer J Ormsbee	1886
Horace Eaton	1846	William P Dillingham	1888
Carlos Coolidge	1848	Carroll S Page	1890
Charles K Williams .	1850	Levi K Fuller	1892
Erastus Fairbanks	1852	Urban A Woodruff	1894
John S Robinson	1853		

UNITED STATES SENATORS FROM THE STATE OF VERMONT.

Name.	No. of Congress.	Date.	Remarks.
Stephen R. Bradley	2d to 4th	1791 to 1795	
Moses Robinson	2d " 4th	1791 " 1796	Resigned 1796.
Isaac Tichenor	4th " 5th	1796 " 1797	Elected in place of Robinson. Resigned 1797.
Elijah Paine	4th " 7th	1795 " 1801	Resigned 1801.
Nathaniel Chipman	5th " 8th	1797 " 1803	
Stephen R. Bradley	7th " 13th	1801 " 1813	Elected in place of Paine; elected president *pro tem.* 14 Dec. 1802–25 Feb. and 2 Mch. 1803–28 Dec. 1808.
Israel Smith	8th " 10th	1803 " 1807	Resigned 1807.
Jonathan Robinson	10th " 14th	1807 " 1815	Elected in place of Smith.
Dudley Chace	13th " 15th	1813 " 1817	Resigned 1815.
Isaac Tichenor	14th " 17th	1815 " 1821	
James Fisk	15th	1817 " 1818	Elected in place of Chace. Resigned 1818.
William A. Palmer	15th to 19th	1818 " 1825	Elected in place of Fisk.
Horatio Seymour	17th " 23d	1821 " 1833	
Dudley Chace	19th " 22d	1825 " 1831	
Samuel Prentiss	22d " 27th	1831 " 1842	Resigned 1842.
Benjamin Swift	23d " 26th	1833 " 1839	
Samuel S. Phelps	26th " 32d	1839 " 1851	
Samuel C. Crafts	27th	1842 " 1843	Appointed *pro tem.* in place of Prentiss.
William Upham	28th to 33d	1843 " 1853	Died 1853.
Samuel S. Phelps	33d	1853 " 1854	Appointed in place of Upham.
Solomon Foot	32d to 39th	1851 " 1866	President *pro tem.* 16 Feb. and 18 July, 1861; 23 Feb. 1864. Died 1866.
Lawrence Brainerd	33d	1854 " 1855	Elected in place of Upham.
Jacob Collamer	34th to 39th	1855 " 1865	Died 1865.
George F. Edmunds	39th " 52d	1866 " 1891	Elected in place of Foot. Resigned 1891.
Luke P. Poland	39th	1865	Appointed in place of Collamer.
Justin S. Morrill	40th to ——	1867 to ——	Term expires 1897.
Redfield Proctor	52d " ——	1891 " ——	Elected in place of Edmunds. Term expires 1899.

Vero'na, a fortified city of N. Italy, was founded by the Gauls or Etruscans. CAMPUS RAUDIUS. It was the birthplace of the poet Catullus and the celebrated architect Vitruvius, and probably of the biographer Cornelius Nepos and the elder Pliny. The amphitheatre was built by Titus, A.D. 82. Verona has been the site of many conflicts. It was taken by Constantine, 312; and on 27 Sept. 489, Theodoric defeated Odoacer, king of Italy. Verona was taken by Charlemagne, 774. About 1260 Mastino della Scala was elected podestà, and his descendants (the Scaligeri) ruled till subdued by the Visconti, dukes of Milan, 1387. Verona was conquered by the Venetians, 1405, and held by them, with some intermissions, till its capture by the French general Massena, 3 June, 1796. Near to it Charles Albert of Sardinia defeated the Austrians, 6 May, 1848. Verona was 1 of 4 strong Austrian fortresses termed the Quadrangle, or QUADRILATERAL. It was surrendered to the Italian government, 16 Oct. 1866. Above 50,000 coins of Gallienus and other emperors, chiefly bronze, discovered near Verona, Jan. 1877.

Versailles (*ver-say'-ye*), near Paris, was a small village, in a forest 30 miles in circuit, where Louis XIII. built a hunting-seat about 1632. Louis XIV., between 1661 and 1687, enlarged it into a magnificent palace, which became the usual residence of the kings of France. By the treaty between Great Britain and the revolted colonies of North America, signed at Paris, the United States was admitted to be sovereign and independent, 3 Sept. 1783. On the same day a treaty was signed at Versailles between Great Britain, France, and Spain, by which Pondicherry and Carical, with other possessions in Bengal, were restored to France, and Trincomalee restored to the Dutch. Here was held the military festival of the royal guards, 1 Oct. 1789, which was followed (on the 5th and 6th) by the attack of the mob, who massacred the guards and brought the king back to Paris. Versailles became the residence of Louis Philippe in 1830. The historical gallery was opened in 1837. Versailles, with the troops there, surrendered to the Germans, 19 Sept. 1870, and the crown-prince of Prussia entered the next day; and on 26 Sept. he awarded the iron cross to above 30 soldiers at the foot of the statue of Louis XIV. The palace was converted into a hospital. The royal headquarters were removed here from Ferrières, 5 Oct. After the peace Versailles became the seat of the French government (FRANCE), Mch. 1871.

verse (Lat. *versus*, a line, a row—in particular, a line of poetry, a succession of feet written or printed in one line; metrical composition in general, rhymed or unrhymed). Surrey's translation of part of Virgil's "Æneid" into blank verse is the first English composition of the kind, omitting tragedy, extant in the English language (pub. in 1547). The verse previously used in grave compositions was the stanza of 6 lines, the *ottava rima* (adopted, with the addition of one line, in the "Faërie Queene," by Spenser, who probably borrowed it from Ariosto and Tasso). Boccaccio introduced it into Italy in his "Teseide," having copied it from the old French *chansons*. Trissino is said to have been the first introducer of blank verse among the moderns, about 1508.—*Vossius*. ELEGY, HEXAMETER, IAMBIC, LITERATURE, POETRY, etc.

Veseronce', a village of S.E. France, near Vienne. Here Gondemar, king of the Burgundians, defeated and killed Clodomir, king of Orleans, and revenged the murder of his brother Sigismond and his family, 524. This conflict is called also the battle of Voiron.

Vespucius, Americus. AMERICA.

Vesta, a goddess among the Romans, identified with the Greek Hestia, presiding over public and private hearths.—One of the asteroids discovered by dr. Olbers of Bremen, 29 Mch. 1807.

vestals, virgin priestesses, took care of the perpetual fire consecrated to Vesta. The mother of Romulus was a vestal. Numa is said to have appointed 4, 710 B.C., and Tarquin added 2, and the number remained 6 ever after. If any of them violated her vow of chastity, she was buried alive in the Campus Sceleratus. Minutia was so buried for breaking her virgin vow, 337 B.C.; Sextilia, 273 B.C.; and Cornelia Maximiliana, 92 A.D. CHASTITY. The order was abolished by Theodosius, 389.

"Vestiges of the Natural History of Creation," a work which upholds the doctrine of progressive development in organic creation, first appeared in 1844, and occasioned much controversy. The author, long unknown, proved to be Robert Chambers.

Vesuvius, an active and destructive volcano, near Naples in Italy.

		A.D.
Cities of Pompeii and Herculaneum are overwhelmed, and more than 200,000 persons perish, among them Pliny the elder	24 Aug.	79
Torre del Greco with 4000 persons destroyed	17 Dec.	1631
Violent eruption	24 Nov.	1759
Another, being the 34th from the time of the destruction of Pompeii and Herculaneum	8 Aug.	1767
Destructive eruption, the lava flowing over 5000 acres of rich vineyards and cultivated land, and Torre del Greco again burned; the top of the mountain falls, forming a crater 2 miles in circumference	June,	1794
Severe eruption	Oct.	1822
Another "	May,	1855
Destructive eruption	May–June,	1858
Torre del Greco again destroyed	Dec.	1861
Severe eruption	Feb.	1865
Almost constant eruption, commencing 12 Nov. 1867, and continuing throughout		1867–68
Phenomena observed by profs. Tyndall, Miller, sir John Lubbock, and other scientific men	Apr.	1868
Severe eruption, 60 lives lost	23 Apr.–3 May,	1872
Active		1876
Another eruption; lava thrown to the height of 300 ft.	20 Sept.	1878

nother.......................................11 June, 1879
itermittent..................................2 May, 1885
ew crater formed.............................8 June, 1891
razilian tourist falls into the crater.......July, "
ctive..13 Sept. 1892

veto (a Lat. verb, *I forbid*), the power of the executive i a government to negative legislation. The president of the 'nited States may treat a bill passed by Congress in any of 5 ways: (1) Sign it; (2) sign it with a protest; (3) if presented more than 10 days before the close of the session, and he takes no action, at the expiration of 10 days it becomes a law without his signature; (4) if presented within 10 days of the close of the session, and he fails to return it, it does not become a law; this is termed a "pocket veto"; (5) *veto it, giving his* reasons to Congress.

BILLS VETOED BY THE PRESIDENTS OF THE UNITED STATES.

President.	No.	Date.	Subject of bill.	Remarks.
Washington, 2	1	5 Apr. 1792	Apportionment of Representation.	
	2	28 Feb. 1797	Reduction of the Army.	
	3	21 Feb. 1811	Incorporating Church at Alexandria.	
	4	28 Feb. "	Relief.	
Madison, 6	5	3 Apr. 1812	Trials in District Courts.	
	6	6 Nov. "	Naturalization	Pocketed.
	7	30 Jan. 1815	*Incorporation of National Bank.*	
	8	3 Mch. 1817	Internal Improvements.	
Monroe, 1	9	4 May, 1822	Internal Improvements, Cumberland Road.	
	10	27 May, 1830	Internal Improvements, Maysville Road, Ky.	
	11	31 May, "	Internal Improvements, Turnpike Stock.	
	12	6 Dec. "	Internal Improvements, Light-houses and Beacons	Pocketed.
	13	" "	Internal Improvements, Canal Stock	Pocketed.
	14	10 July, 1832	Extension of Charter of U. S. Bank.	
Jackson, 12	15	6 Dec. "	*Interest of State Claims*	Pocketed.
	16	" "	River and Harbor	Pocketed.
	17	4 Dec. 1833	Proceeds of Land Sales	Pocketed.
	18	1 Dec. 1834	Internal Improvements, Wabash river	Pocketed.
	19	3 Mch. 1835	Compromise Claims against the Two Sicilies.	
	20	9 June, 1836	Regulations for Congressional Sessions.	
	21	3 Mch. 1837	Funds receivable from U. S. Revenue	Pocketed.
	22	16 Aug. 1841	Incorporating Fiscal Bank.	
	23	9 Sept. "	Incorporating Fiscal Corporation.	
	24	29 June, 1842	First Whig Tariff.	
	25	9 Aug. "	Second Whig Tariff.	
Tyler, 9	26	14 Dec. "	Proceeds of Public Land Sales	Pocketed.
	27	" "	Testimony in Contested Elections	Pocketed.
	28	18 Dec. "	Payment of Cherokee Certificates	Pocketed.
	29	11 June, 1844	River and Harbor.	
	30	20 Feb. 1845	Revenue Cutters and Steamers for Defence	Passed over the veto, *the first.*
	31	3 Aug. 1846	River and Harbor.	
Polk, 3	32	8 Aug. "	French Spoliation Claims.	
	33	15 Dec. 1847	Internal Improvements	Pocketed.
	34	3 May, 1854	Land Grant for Indigent Insane.	
	35	4 Aug. "	Internal Improvements.	
	36	17 Feb. 1855	*French Spoliation Claims.*	
	37	3 Mch. "	Subsidy for Ocean Mails.	
Pierce, 9	38	19 May, 1856	Internal Improvements, Mississippi	Passed over veto.
	39	" "	Internal Improvements, St. Clair Flats, Mich	Passed over veto.
	40	22 May, "	Internal Improvements, St. Mary's river, Mich	Passed over veto.
	41	11 Aug. "	Internal Improvements, Des Moines river, Mich	Passed over veto.
	42	14 Aug. "	Internal Improvements, Patapsco river, Md	Passed over veto.
	43	7 Jan. 1859	Overland Mails	Pocketed.
	44	24 Feb. "	*Land Grants for Agricultural Colleges.*	
	45	1 Feb. 1860	Internal Improvements, St. Clair Flats, Mich	Pocketed.
Buchanan, 7	46	6 Feb. "	Internal Improvements, Mississippi river	Pocketed.
	47	17 Apr. "	Relief of A. Edwards & Co.	
	48	22 June, "	Homestead.	
	49	25 Jan. 1861	Relief of Hockaday & Legget.	
	50	23 June, 1862	Bank Notes in District of Columbia.	
Lincoln, 3	51	2 July, "	Medical Offices in the Army.	
	52	5 Jan. 1865	*Correcting Clerical Errors*	Pocketed.
	53	19 Feb. 1866	Freedmen's Bureau.	
	54	27 Mch. "	Civil Rights	Passed over veto.
	55	15 May, "	Admission of Colorado.	
	56	15 June, "	Public Lands (Montana Iron company).	
	57	15 July, "	Continuation of Freedmen's Bureau	Passed over veto.
	58	28 July, "	Survey District of Montana.	
	59	5 Jan. 1867	Suffrage in District of Columbia	Passed over veto.
	60	29 Jan. "	Admission of Colorado.	
	61	" "	Admission of Nebraska	Passed over veto.
	62	2 Mch. "	Tenure of Office	Passed over veto.
Johnson, 21	63	" "	Reconstruction	Passed over veto.
	64	23 Mch. "	Supplemental Reconstruction	Passed over veto.
	65	19 July, "	Supplemental Reconstruction	Passed over veto.
	66	" "	Joint Resolution Reconstruction	Passed over veto.
	67	25 Mch. 1868	Amending Judiciary	Passed over veto.
	68	20 June, "	Admission of *Arkansas (reconstructed)*	Passed over veto.
	69	25 June, "	Admission of Southern States	Passed over veto.
	70	20 July, "	Exclusion of Electoral Votes of Unreconstructed States	Passed over veto.
	71	25 July, "	Discontinuance of Freedmen's Bureau	Passed over veto.
	72	13 Feb. 1869	Trustees of Colored Schools in District of Columbia.	
	73	22 Feb. "	Tariff on Copper	Passed over veto.
	74	11 Jan. 1870	Relief, Private	Passed one House over veto.
	75	14 July, "	Southern Union Troops.	
	76	4 Jan. 1871	Relief.	
	77	7 Feb. "	Relief.	
	78	1 Apr. 1872	Relief.	Passed one House over veto.
	79	" "	Relief.	
	80	10 Apr. "	Relief.	
Grant, 43	81	15 Apr. "	Pension, Private.	
	82	22 Apr. "	Pension.	
	83	14 May, "	Pension, Mary Ann Montgomery	Passed over veto.
	84	1 June, "	Pension.	
	85	7 June, "	Relief.	
	86	6 Jan. 1873	Relief.	
	87	22 Jan. "	New Trial in Court of Claims.	
	88	29 Jan. "	Relief of East Tennessee University.	

BILLS VETOED BY THE PRESIDENTS OF THE UNITED STATES.—(*Continued.*)

President.	No.	Date.	Subject of bill.	Remarks.
	89	8 Feb. 1873	Relief.	
	90	" "	Relief.	
	91	10 Apr. 1874	Relief.	
	92	22 Apr. "	Inflation of Currency.	
	93	12 May, "	Relief.	
	94	30 Jan. 1875	Relief.	
	95	12 Feb. "	Pension.	
	96	3 Feb. 1876	Custody of Indian Trust Funds.	
	97	27 Mch. "	Relief.	
	98	31 Mch. "	Relief of G. B. Tyler and E. H. Luckett	Passed over veto.
	99	18 Apr. "	Reduction of President's Salary.	
	100	26 May, "	Recording in the District of Columbia.	
	101	9 June, "	Relief.	
	102	30 June, "	Internal Improvements.	
Grant, 43	103	11 July, "	Relief of Nelson Tiffany	Passed over veto.
	104	13 July, "	Pension.	
	105	20 July, "	Post-office Statutes.	
	106	4 Aug. "	Relief.	
	107	15 Aug. "	Paving Pennsylvania ave.	
	108	" "	Sale of Indian Lands	Passed over veto.
	109	" "	Relief.	
	110	15 Jan. 1877	Homestead Entries.	
	111	23 Jan. "	District of Columbia's Police	Passed in the House over veto.
	112	26 Jan. "	Diplomatic Congratulations.	
	113	" "	Relief.	
	114	14 Feb. "	Relief.	
	115	" "	Advertising of Executive Department.	
	116	28 Feb. "	Relief.	
	117	" 1878	Standard Silver Dollar	Passed over veto.
	118	6 Mch. "	Special Term of Courts in Mississippi.	
	119	1 Mch. 1879	Restriction of Chinese Immigration.	
	120	29 Apr. "	Army Appropriation.	
	121	12 May, "	Interference at Elections.	
Hayes, 12	122	29 May, "	Civil Appropriations.	
	123	23 June, "	Payment of Marshals.	
	124	27 June, "	Relief.	
	125	....	Payment of Marshals.	
	126	4 May, 1880	Payment of Marshals.	
	127	15 June, "	Payment of Marshals.	
	128	3 Mch. 1881	Refunding the National Debt.	
	129	4 Apr. 1882	Chinese Immigration.	
	130	1 July, "	Carriage of Passengers at Sea.	
Arthur, 4	131	1 Aug. "	RIVER AND HARBOR BILL	Passed over the veto.
	132	2 July, 1884	Relief of Fitz-John Porter	Passed over the veto in the House, 168-78; vote in the Senate, 27-27.
	133	10 Mch. 1886	Relief.	
	134	11 Mch. "	Settlers' Titles to Des Moines Public Lands	Passed over the veto in the Senate.
	135	26 Apr. "	Bodies for Dissection.	
	136	30 Apr. "	Omaha a Port of Entry.	
	137, 138	8 May, "	Pensions.	
	139	17 May, "	Springfield a Port of Entry.	
	140 to 156	May, " to 19 June, "	Pensions, Private.	
	157	" "	Public Building at Sioux City, Ia.	Passed over the veto in the Senate.
	158	" "	Public Building at Zanesville, O.	
	159 to 226	June, " to 6 July, "	Pensions and Reliefs, Private.	
	227	" "	Public Building at Duluth, Minn.	
	228 to 231	" "	Pensions and Reliefs, Private.	
	232	7 July, "	Right of Way to Railroad in North Montana.	
	233	9 July, "	Pension, Private.	
	234	" "	Public Building in Dayton, O.	Passed over veto.
	235	10 July, "	Public Building in Asheville, N. C.	
	236	30 July, "	Bridge across Lake Champlain.	
	237	" "	Public Building at Springfield, Mass.	
Cleveland, 301	238 to 261	31 July, " to 11 Feb. 1887	Pensions and Reliefs, Private.	
	262	16 Feb. "	Texas Seed Bill.	
	263 to 272	19 Feb. " to 24 Feb. "	Pensions.	
	273	25 Feb. "	Public Building at Lynn, Mass.	
	274, 275	26 Feb. "	Pensions, Private.	
	276, 277	" "	Public Building at Portsmouth, O., and Lafayette, Ind.	
	278 to 292	4 Apr. 1888 to 3 May, "	Pensions and Reliefs.	
	293	7 May, "	Sale of Indian Land.	
	294	9 May, "	Public Building at Allentown, Pa.	
	295 to 297	" " to 18 May, "	Pensions.	
	298	" "	Use of Castle Island, Boston Harbor.	
	299 to 307	" " to 26 May, "	Pensions.	
	308	28 May, "	Public Building at Youngstown, O.	
	309 to 311	" "	Pensions.	

BILLS VETOED BY THE PRESIDENTS OF THE UNITED STATES.—(*Continued.*)

President.	No.	Date.	Subject of bill.	Remarks.
Cleveland, 301	312	29 May, 1888	Public Building at Columbus, Ga.	
	313	5 June, "	Public Building at Bar Harbor, Me.	
	314	" "	Government Land Purchase, Council Bluffs, Ia.	
	315 to 344	" " to 26 July, "	Pensions and Reliefs, Private.	
	345	" "	Right of Way for Railroad through Indian Lands.	
	346	3 Aug. "	Relief	
	347	7 Aug. "	Land Grant to Tacoma, Wash.	
	348 to 361	9 Aug. " to 10 Aug. "	Pensions, Private.	
	362	14 Aug. "	Additional Copies of U. S. Map for 1886.	
	363 to 373	" " to 27 Aug. "	Pensions and Reliefs.	
	374	" "	Public Building, Sioux City, Ia.	
	375 to 385	" " to 13 Sept. "	Pensions and Reliefs, Private.	
	386	24 Sept. "	Land Grant to Kansas.	
	387	" "	Sale of Military Reservation in Kansas.	
	388 to 424	10 Oct. " to 14 Feb. 1889	Pensions and Reliefs, Private.	
	425	21 Feb. "	Quieting Settlers' Titles on the Des Moines river.	
	426 to 432	23 Feb. " to 26 Feb. "	Pensions and Reliefs, Private.	
	433	2 Mch. "	Refunding the Direct Tax..........................	Passed over the veto in the Senate.
Harrison, 19	434	26 Apr. 1890	City of Ogden Increased Indebtedness.	
	435	29 Apr. "	Public Building, Dallas, Tex.	
	436	4 June, "	Public Building, Hudson, N. Y.	
	437	12 June, "	Public Building, Tuscaloosa, Ala.	
	438	17 June, "	To change boundary of Uncompahgre Reservation.	
	439	20 June, "	Bonds issued by Maricopa county, Arizona, for certain Railroad.	
	440	9 July, "	Indian Payment.	
	441	30 Sept. "	Relief of Capt. Charles B. Stivers.	
	442	1 Oct. "	Relief of the Portland Company.	
	443	" "	Relief of Charles B. Chouteau.	
	444	" "	Pool Selling in the District of Columbia.	
	445	24 Dec. "	Public Building, Bar Harbor, Me.	
	446	26 Jan. 1891	Bonds, Oklahoma City, Oklahoma Territory.	
	447	26 Feb. "	Act to Establish the Record and Pension of the War Department, etc.	
	448	2 Mch. "	Relief of George W. Lawrence	
	449	19 July, 1892	An Act to Establish Circuit Court of Appeal, etc.	
	450	29 July, "	Relief of William McGarrahan.......................	Senate fails to pass it over the veto, 17 Jan. 1893
	451	3 Aug. "	An Act to provide for bringing Suit against the United States.	
	452	27 Feb. 1893	An Act to prescribe the number of District Attorneys and Marshal's in the Judicial Districts of the state of Alabama..................................	Passed over the veto, 2 Mch. 1893.

vice or **vise,** an instrument which Archytas of Tarentum, disciple of Pythagoras, is said to have invented, with the pulley and other implements, 420 B.C.

Vicenza (*vee-chen'-tsu*), the ancient *Vicentia*, N. Italy, was the seat of a republic in the 12th century. It suffered by ravages of Alaric, 401, and Attila, 452. Having joined the Lombard league, it was sacked by Frederic II., 1236. After many changes it was subjected to Venice, and with it fell under the French domination, 1796; and was given to Austria in 1814. Having revolted, it was retaken by Radetzky, 11 June, 1848. It was annexed to the kingdom of Italy, Oct. 1866.

vice-president of the United States. He presides in the Senate, and on the death, resignation, or disability of the president, succeeds him. 4 vice-presidents have in this way become presidents: John Tyler, succeeding William Henry Harrison, who died 4 Apr. 1841; Millard Fillmore, succeeding Zachary Taylor, who died 9 July, 1850; Andrew Johnson, succeeding Abraham Lincoln, who died 15 Apr. 1865; Chester A. Arthur, succeeding James A. Garfield, who died 19 Sept. 1881. For their administrations, UNITED STATES for the years as above.

Vicksburg, Miss., Campaigns for the possession of. Vicksburg, about 400 miles above New Orleans, and about the same distance from Cairo, stands on a high bluff on the east side of the Mississippi river, which just above the town runs for several miles in a northeasterly direction, then, suddenly changing its course, it passes Vicksburg, flowing southwesterly, forming a peninsula several miles in length and from three-quarters to a mile in width directly opposite the town. It was connected with Jackson, the capital of the state, about 45 miles to the east, by the Vicksburg and Jackson railroad, and west of the river it drew the land-commerce of northern Louisiana and Texas by the Vicksburg and Shreveport railroad, the only railroad communication the confederacy had with her territory west of the Mississippi, thus making Vicksburg the most important point to the confederacy on the river. The place is easily defensible, the high bluffs extending along the river banks from Warrenton, about 8 miles below, to Haines's Bluff, 15 miles above, where they terminate at the Yazoo river. The country to the north on the same side of the river is filled with swamps, lagoons, sloughs, and bayous, through which flows the sluggish Yazoo, which empties into the Mississippi 9 miles above Vicksburg. The country west of Vicksburg across the Mississippi is also covered with swamps and bayous; to the east the ground is higher, but much broken, the Big Black river flowing through it.

First advance against Vicksburg made from New Orleans, after its occupancy by gen. Butler, when Samuel P. Lee, commanding the advance naval division of Farragut's squadron, demanded its surrender and was refused. M. L. Smith commands the military defences with 10,000 men.......18 May, 1862

Gen. Thomas Williams, with 4 regiments and 8 guns, from Baton Rouge, occupies the peninsula opposite......24 June, "

Gen. Williams begins to cut a canal across the peninsula opposite Vicksburg, to change the course of the river....27 June, "

Farragut runs the Vicksburg blockade to join Davis, and bombards Vicksburg..................................28 June, "

Van Dorn takes command at Vicksburg...............28 July, "

Expedition up the Yazoo to destroy the ram *Arkansas* meets her coming down and retires; the ram enters the Mississippi and takes refuge under the guns of Vicksburg.......15 July, "

Ellet and W. D. Porter, with the *Queen of the West* and *Essex*, attack the ram, are repulsed, and with difficulty escape, 22 July, "

Williams's canal proves a failure.......................... " "

Williams's force leaves for Baton Rouge..............24 July, "

Breckenridge attacks gen. Williams's force at Baton Rouge, but is repulsed; gen. Williams killed.....................5 Aug. "

Destruction of the ram *Arkansas* by com. Porter in the *Essex*, 6 Aug. 1862

Vicksburg's defences strengthened and a line of works built along the bluff from Haines's Bluff to Warrenton..Aug.-Oct. "

Department of Mississippi and East Louisiana constituted (Confederate) under maj.-gen. John C. Pemberton, who supersedes Van Dorn and assumes command at Vicksburg, 14 Oct. "

Grant's Campaign against Vicksburg......................1862-63

[Grant's advance was at Bolivar, S.W. Tennessee, while Sherman was at Memphis. The confederates occupied Grand Junction on the Memphis and Charleston railroad, and the entire line of the Mississippi Central south from that point. Grant moved by the Mississippi Central against Vicksburg, 2 Nov. 1862. Occupied Grand Junction 8 Nov. and Holly Springs, 13 Nov., the confederates in the meanwhile retiring south of the Tallahatchie.]

Grant at Oxford, Miss., and his advance at Coffeeville....5 Dec. 1862

From this point he suggests to Halleck the importance of moving against Vicksburg from Memphis and Helena by the Mississippi river; gen. Sherman ordered by Grant to proceed against Vicksburg with 30,000 men by the river.......8 Dec. "

Col. R. C. Murphy, 8th Wisconsin, with 1500 men, guarding Grant's supply depot at Holly Springs, surrenders to gen. Van Dorn without defence; entire stores destroyed..20 Dec. "

[Murphy was dismissed from the service.]

Grant compelled by this disaster to retire.................Dec. "

Sherman embarks from Memphis with 20,000 men, 20 Dec.; is reinforced by 12,000 men at Helena; convoyed up the Yazoo by Porter's fleet, 26 Dec.; lands near Chickasaw bayou, about 12 miles from the mouth of the Yazoo, 27 Dec.; advances against the defences on the bluffs, about 5 miles to the north of Vicksburg; assaults, and is repulsed with a loss of 208 killed, 1005 wounded, 563 missing; total, 1776....27-28 Dec. "

Maj.-gen. John A. McClernand supersedes Sherman in command before Vicksburg..............................2 Jan. 1863

Expedition re-embarks and returns to Milliken's Bend, about 20 miles above Vicksburg on the Mississippi..........2-3 Jan. "

This expedition, McClernand in command, moves against Arkansas post (ARKANSAS, 1863).........................4 Jan. "

Which it captures...18 Jan. "

Occupation of Young's Point, 9 miles above Vicksburg, on the opposite bank...21 Jan. "

Work commenced reopening Williams's canal across the peninsula for getting below Vicksburg.....................22 Jan. "

Grant reaches Young's Point and assumes command...29 Jan. "

Queen of the West, capt. C. R. Ellet, runs by the Vicksburg batteries...10 Feb. "

Queen of the West captured by confederates............13 Feb. "

Iron-clad *Indianola* passes the Vicksburg batteries, night of 13 Feb. "

Confederates capture the *Indianola*....................24 Feb. "

Porter sends his "dummy" past Vicksburg; in the panic which follows the confederates destroy the *Queen of the West* and the *Indianola*, which they were repairing.......24 Feb. "

Mississippi breaks the levee and stops work on the canal; the project abandoned.................................8 Mch. "

Attempt to open a route below Vicksburg by lake Providence, about 40 miles above Young's Point; abandoned....16 Mch. "

Third attempt to gain the rear of Vicksburg by the Yazoo pass; this pass leaves the Mississippi a few miles below Helena, Ark.; by means of this pass and the bayous, etc., it was thought possible to gain the Yazoo river and thus the highlands in the rear of Vicksburg; abandoned..........23 Mch. "

Fourth attempt to gain the rear of Vicksburg, by the Steele bayou route; Steele bayou starts about 30 miles above Young's Point, and connecting with other bayous, creeks, etc., empties into the Yazoo about 25 miles above Vicksburg; abandoned...20 Mch. "

After these failures 3 plans are suggested: (1) assault the Confederate batteries; (2) return to Memphis and renew the campaign by the Mississippi Central railroad; (3) cross the Mississippi below Vicksburg and gain its rear, trusting to the country for supplies. Grant decides on the last, and McClernand, with the 13th corps, starts from Milliken's Bend for New Carthage, about 20 miles below Vicksburg, 29 Mch., arriving with 1 division and its artillery................6 Apr. "

[Stopped at New Carthage by a break in the levee; Grant decided to cross at Hard Times, a little below Grand Gulf, about 70 miles south from Milliken's Bend.]

At Grand Gulf the confederates well fortified; to silence these batteries adm. Porter, with the river fleet, runs the batteries at Vicksburg...............................night of 16 Apr. "

To support Porter in attacking Grand Gulf, Grant orders gen. Sherman, who had been left above Vicksburg, to make a feint on the Confederate batteries at Haines's Bluff, while Porter attacks Grand Gulf with 8 gun-boats..........29 Apr. "

Porter unable to silence the guns at Grand Gulf, but at Bruinsburg, a few miles below, McClernand crosses, followed by McPherson...30 Apr. "

Confederates under Bowen defeated at Port Gibson.....2 May, "

Grierson's raid to help Grant below Vicksburg, from La Grange, Tenn., 17 Apr., to Baton Rouge, La., 600 miles in 16 days, fighting and destroying railroads.....................2 May, "

[Grant says, "This raid was of great importance" as it "attracted the attention of the enemy from the main movement against Vicksburg."—"Personal Memoirs."]

Confederates evacuate Grand Gulf......................3 May, "

Sherman joins Grant...................................6-8 May, "

[Corps under Grant during the campaign in the rear of Vicksburg and during the siege were the 13th, maj.-gen. John A. McClernand commanding; 15th corps, W. T. Sherman, and the 17th, James B. McPherson, in all about 50,000 men, including infantry, cavalry, and artillery.]

McPherson defeats Gregg and Walker at Raymond, near Jackson, 12 May, 1863

Capture of Jackson by Sherman and McPherson.......14 May, "

Grant, ascertaining that Pemberton is advancing from Vicksburg, recalls Sherman and McPherson from Jackson to anticipate this attack; meets Pemberton at CHAMPION HILLS, 25 miles west of Jackson, and defeats him (BATTLES), 16 May, "

Pemberton makes a stand on the banks of the Big Black river and is defeated.....................................17 May, "

Pemberton retires within the fortifications of Vicksburg, 17 May, "

Grant invests Vicksburg; Sherman establishes himself on the Yazoo; Porter opens communications for Grant's army by the Yazoo..18 May, "

First assault on Vicksburg repulsed..................19 May, "

Second assault on Vicksburg repulsed.................22 May, "

McClernand relieved of command of the 13th corps....18 June, "

[For issuing a congratulatory order to his command, 30 May. See Official Records, "War of the Rebellion," series I. vol. xxiv. part 1. Reports, pp. 137-86.]

Surrender of Vicksburg with 27,000 men, 128 pieces of artillery, and 80 siege-guns.......................................4 July, "

UNION LOSSES FROM 1 MAY UNTIL THE SURRENDER OF VICKSBURG.

	Killed.	Wounded.	Missing.	Total.
Port Gibson	131	719	25	875
Raymond	66	339	37	442
Jackson	42	251	7	300
Champion Hills	410	1844	187	2441
Big Black	39	237	3	279
Skirmishes before Vicksburg, 18, 20, 21 May	45	194	2	241
1st assault, 19 May	157	777	8	942
2d " 22 May	501	2551	147	3199
Siege, 23 May-4 July	120	484	37	641
Total	1511	7396	453	9360

Confederate losses about 10,000 prior to the surrender.

Confederate gen. Johnston, on hearing of the surrender of Vicksburg, falls back and occupies Jackson; Grant orders Sherman to proceed against him, and by 11 July he is close to the defences of the city; on the 17th Johnston evacuates and retires eastward. CHATTANOOGA CAMPAIGN.

Victoria, formerly **Port Phillip,** a British colony in S. Australia, between New South Wales and South Australia. In 1798, Bass, in his whale-boat expedition, visited Western Port, one of its harbors; and in 1802 Flinders sailed into Port Phillip bay. The legislative authority is vested in a parliament of 2 chambers, and the executive in a governor appointed by the crown. Area, 87,884 sq. miles; pop. 1836, 224; 1846, 32,879; 1857, 403,519; 1871, 729,654; 1891, 1,140,411.

Col. Collins lands with convicts to found a settlement at Port Phillip, but afterwards removed to Van Diemen's Land..... 1804

Messrs. Hume and Hovell, stock-owners from New South Wales, explore part of the country, but do not discover its great advantages.. 1824

Edward Henty (of a Sussex family) comes from Tasmania with cattle, sheep, shepherds, etc., and settles in Portland bay; his brothers, Stephen, George, and John, follow soon........ 1832

John Batman enters between the heads of Port Phillip, and purchases a large tract of land from the aborigines for a few gewgaws and blankets; he soon after, with 15 associates from Hobarton, takes up 600,000 acres in the present Geelong country..May, 1835

Launceston associates, and John Pascoe Falkner, ascend the Yarra-Yarra (or ever-flowing) river, and encamp on the site of Melbourne.. "

Colonists (450 in number) possess 140,000 sheep, 2500 cattle, and 150 houses; sir R. Bourke, governor of New South Wales, visits the colony, determines the sites of towns, and causes the land to be surveyed and resold, setting aside contending claims; he appoints capt. Lonsdale chief-magistrate........ 1837

Colony named Victoria.................................... 1839

Province declared independent of New South Wales; a reward of 200*l.* offered for the discovery of gold in Victoria, which is soon found near Melbourne, and profitably worked....Aug. 1851

[From 30 Sept. to 31 Dec. 1851, 30,311 ounces of gold were obtained from Ballarat; and from 29 Oct. to 31 Dec. 94,524 ounces from mount Alexander—total, 124,835 ounces.]

Representative constitution granted........................ 1855

Parliament opened.................................26 Nov. 1857

Great opposition to reception of convicts in any part of Australia; a ship containing them sent back.............Oct. 1864

First woollen and paper manufactories established.......May, 1868

Payment (300*l.* a year) to members of Parliament begins...... 1872

International exhibition at Melbourne opened..........1 Oct. 1880

Chinese immigrants virtually excluded...................... 1886

Government submits to the protectionists; the import duties increased and new ones imposed...................13 Sept. 1889

Irrigation conference at Melbourne; 250,000*l.* advanced by the state...25 Mch. 1890

Victoria cross, an order of merit instituted by the

English government to reward gallantry in all ranks of the army and navy, 5 Feb 1856 It is a Maltese cross made of Russian cannon from Sebastopol Queen Victoria conferred the honor on 62 persons (of both services) on Friday, 26 June, 1857, and on many of the Indian army, 2 Aug 1858

Victoria Nyanza. AFRICA, 1863, '75, etc

Victoria Railway bridge. BRIDGES

Victoria regia, the magnificent water-lily taken to England from Guiana by sir Robert Schomburgk, in 1838, and named after the queen Fine specimens are at the Botanic gardens at Kew, Regent's park, etc It was grown in the open air in 1855 by messrs Weeks of Chelsea

vict'uallers, an ancient trade in England The Vinters' company of London was founded 1437, their hall rebuilt in 1823

None shall sell less than one full quart of the best beer or ale for 1*d* and two quarts of the smaller sort for 1*d* 1603
Power of licensing public houses granted to sir Giles Mompesson and sir Francis Mitchel 1621
Number in England then about 13 000 "
In Great Britain about 70,000 public houses 1790
Licensed victuallers in the United Kingdom 99 165 1872
New licensing act, regulating hours of opening and shutting, etc, passed and came into execution 10 Aug "
[It caused much irritation, and was said to have conduced to the fall of the Gladstone ministry, 1874]

Vienna (the Roman *Vindobona*), capital of the margraviate of Austria, 981, virtual capital of the German empire, 1273, since 1806 capital of the Austrian provinces only Pop. in 1857, 476 222, 1872, 901,000, 1880, 1,103,857, 1890, 1,364,548, 1900, 1,674,957

Vienna made an imperial city 1136
Walled and enlarged with the ransom paid for Richard I of England 40 000*l* 1194
Besieged by the Turks under Solyman the Magnificent, with 300 000 men, forced to raise the siege with the loss of 70 000 of his best troops 1529
Besieged by the Turks July, 1683
Siege raised by John Sobieski, king of Poland, who defeats the Turkish army of 100 000 12 Sept. "
Vienna taken by the French under prince Murat, 14 Nov 1805, evacuated 12 Jan 1806
Captured by Napoleon I 13 May, 1809
Restored on the conclusion of peace 14 Oct. "
Congress of sovereigns at Vienna Nov 1814
Imperial Academy of Sciences founded 1846
Vienna bombarded by Windischgrätz and Jellachich, 28 Oct., it capitulates 30 Oct. 1848
Conferences on Russo Turkish war held at Vienna 1853-55
Fortifications demolished, the city enlarged and beautified 1857-58
Imperial parliament (Reichsrath) meets here 31 May, 1860
Prussians encamp near Vienna, state of siege proclaimed, July, 1866
Ring theatre burned, 447 persons perish out of 2000 8 Dec. 1881
Joseph Pircher a gilder, climbs the spire of St Stephen's cathedral, 432 feet high, and places a banner on the cross, 18 Aug 1886
City enlarged by incorporating the suburbs Dec 1891

TREATIES OF VIENNA

1 Between the emperor of Germany and the king of Spain, confirming to each other such parts of the Spanish dominions as they respectively possessed, and by a private treaty the emperor engaged to use his powers to procure the restoration of Gibraltar to Spain, and to place the Pretender on the throne of Great Britain Spain guaranteed the Pragmatic Sanction 30 Apr 1725
2 Alliance between the emperor of Germany, Charles VI, George II, king of Great Britain, and the states of Holland, by which the Pragmatic Sanction was guaranteed, and the disputes as to the Spanish succession terminated (Spain acceded to the treaty on 22 July) Signed 16 Mch 1731
3 Peace between the emperor Charles VI of Germany and the king of France, Louis XV, the latter power guaranteed the Pragmatic Sanction, and Lorraine was ceded to France Signed 18 Nov 1738 PRAGMATIC SANCTION
4 Between Napoleon I of France and Francis (II of Germany) I of Austria Austria ceded to France the Tyrol, Dalmatia, and other territories, which were shortly after declared united to France as the Illyrian Provinces, and engaged to adhere to the prohibitory system adopted towards England by France and Russia 14 Oct 1809
5. Between Great Britain, Austria, Russia, and Prussia, confirming the principles of the treaty of Chaumont, 1 Mch 1814 Signed 23 Mch 1815.
6 Between the king of the Netherlands on the one part and Great Britain, Russia, Austria, and Prussia on the other, enlarging the Dutch territories, and vesting the sovereignty in the house of Orange. 31 May, 1815
7 Denmark ceded Swedish Pomerania and Rugen to Prussia, in exchange for Lauenburg, 4 June, 1815
8 Commercial treaty for 12 years between Austria and Prussia. Signed at Vienna, 19 Feb 1853.
9. For the maintenance of Turkey by Great Britain, France, Austria, and Russia Signed 9 Apr 1854
10 Between Austria, Prussia, and Denmark, Denmark ceding the duchies 30 Oct 1864
11 Peace between Austria and Italy, Venetia given up to Italy 3 Oct 1866

Vienne (*vi-en'*), the ancient *Vienna Allobrogum*, a town of S E France. Here the emperor Valentinian II was put to death by Arbogastes, 15 May, 392, and a short reaction in favor of paganism followed Vienne was capital of the kingdom of Burgundy in 432 and 879, and sometimes gave its name to the kingdom A general council was held here in 1311 Vienne was annexed to the French monarchy, 1418

Vigilance committee. CALIFORNIA, 1851-56

Vigo (*vee'go*), a seaport town of N W Spain, was attacked and burned by the English under Drake and Norris in 1589 Sir George Rooke, with the combined English and Dutch fleets, attacked the French fleet and the Spanish galleons in the port of Vigo, when several men-of-war and galleons were taken, and many destroyed, and abundance of plate and other valuable effects fell into the hands of the conquerors, 12 Oct 1702 Vigo was taken by lord Cobham in 1719, but relinquished after raising contributions. It was again taken by the British 27 Mch 1809

vikings, Scandinavian chiefs, Swedes, Danes, and Norsemen, who in the 4th century migrated—eastward, to the countries beyond the Baltic, westward and southward, chiefly to the British Isles Paul B du Chaillu, in his "Viking Age," describes the vikings as the ancestors of the English

Villeré's plantation, La., about 9 miles south from New Orleans, where an indecisive engagement was fought on the night of 23 Dec 1814, between American forces under Jackson and British under gen Keene The Americans numbered about 1800 and the British 2500 The British lost 400 and the Americans over 200, both retired. UNITED STATES, 1814.

Ville'ta, a town of Paraguay, South America Here Lopez and the Paraguayans were defeated by the Brazilians and their allies, 11 Dec. 1868 Lopez and 200 men fled, 3000 prisoners were made, and the war was ended

Vimeira (*ve-ma'ē-ra*), a town of Portugal, where the British and Spanish forces, under sir Arthur Wellesley, defeated the French, under marshal Junot, duke of Abrantes, 21 Aug 1808 The attack, made and repulsed with great bravery, was then repeated by Kellermann with the French reserve in vain. The French, charged with the bayonet, withdrew on all points in confusion, leaving many prisoners.

Vincennes (*vin-sen'*), a strong castle near Paris, a residence of the French kings from the 12th to the 14th century. Henry V of England died at the Bois de Vincennes, 31 Aug 1422 At the fosse of the castle, Louis duc d'Enghien was shot by order of Napoleon, after a hasty trial, early on the morning of 22 Mch 1804 INDIANA

Vincent de Paul, St., Charitable Society of, founded in 1833, in France, by 12 young men It extends its beneficial operations into Britain The jealousy of the French government suppressed its central committee of Paris in Oct 1861. St. Vincent de Paul was born 1576, established the congregation of Lazarists, or Vincentines, 1625, Sisters of Charity, 1634, a foundling hospital, 1648 He died 1660

Vincent, St., West Indies, long a neutral island, but at the peace of 1763 the French agreed that the right to it should be vested in the English The latter soon after engaged in war against the Caribs, on the windward side of the island, and forced them to a peace, ceding a large tract to the British crown In 1779 the Caribs greatly aided the French in the reduction of the island, but they restored it in 1783 In 1795 the French landed troops, and again instigated the Caribs to an insurrection, which was not subdued for several months A great eruption of the Souffrière mountain, after the lapse of nearly a century, occurred in 1812. Area, 132 sq. miles. Pop. 1861, 31,755, 1891, 41,054

Viney, N. France. Here Charles Martel defeated the Neustrians, 21 May, 717, and acquired their country

vine (Lat. *vinea*, a climbing plant with a woody stem of the genus *vitis*, the fruit is the grape) The vine was planted by Noah, 2347 B.C. (Gen. ix. 20) A colony of vine-dressers from Phocea, in Ionia, settled at Marseilles, and instructed the South Gauls in tillage, vine-dressing, and commerce, about 600 B.C. Some think the vine a native of Languedoc, Provence, and Sicily; and growing spontaneously on the Mediterranean shores of Italy, France, and Spain. The vine was carried into Champagne, and part of Germany, by the emperor Probus, about 279 A.D. The vine and sugar-cane were planted in Madeira in 1420. In the gardens of Hampton-court palace is an old vine, said to surpass any in Europe. The Tokay vines were planted in 1350. FLOWERS AND PLANTS.

Vine disease. In the spring of 1845 E. Tucker, of Margate, observed a fungus (since named *oïdium Tuckeri*) on grapes in the hot-houses of Mr. Slater, of Margate. *It is a whitish mildew*, and totally destroys the fruit.
The spores of this *oïdium* were found in the vineries at Versailles in 1847. The disease soon reached the trellised vines, and in 1850 many lost all their produce.
In 1852 it spread over France, Italy, Spain, Syria, and in Zante and Cephalonia attacked the currants, reducing the crop to one twelfth of the usual amount.
Through its ravages the wine manufacture in Madeira ceased for several years.
Attempts to arrest the progress of this disease have had little success. Sulphur-dust is the most efficacious remedy.
The disease had much abated in France, Portugal, and Madeira in 1863. In 1862 Californian vines were introduced into the two latter.
New malady (microscopic insect, *phylloxera vastatrix*) in S. France, observed.... 1865
Remedy, sulphuret of carbon, recommended by M. Dumas, Aug. 1873
Not successful; great destruction; 12,000*l.* offered for a remedy, July, 1876
Phylloxera prevalent in Malaga and France; reported July-Aug. 1878; Portugal, Italy, Spain, Sept.-Nov. 1879; appears in Victoria, Australia.... Nov. 1880
Phylloxera congress at Bordeaux.... 10-15 Oct. 1881
Phylloxera driven out of W. France through the researches of M. Pasteur.... 1883-91
GRAPES, WINE.

vinegar, dilute acetic acid obtained by the acetous fermentation of spirits. The ancients had several kinds, which they used for drink. The Roman soldiers were accustomed to take it in their marches. The Bible represents Boaz, a rich citizen of Bethlehem, as providing vinegar for his reapers (1312 B.C.), a custom still prevalent in Spain and Italy.

Vinegar Hill, near Enniscorthy, in Wexford, S.E. Ireland. Here the Irish rebels, headed by father John, a priest, encamped and committed outrages on the surrounding country. They were gradually surrounded by the British troops, commanded by Lake, 21 June, 1798; and after a fierce struggle, with much slaughter, dispersed.

viol and **violin.** The lyre of the Greeks became our harp, and the viol of the middle ages became the violin. The violin is mentioned as early as 1200, in the legendary life of St. Christopher. It was introduced into England, some say, by Charles II. Straduarius (or Stradivarius) of Cremona was a renowned violin-maker (1700 to 1722). The eminent violinist Paganini died at Nice, 27 May, 1840.

Virgin Islands, West Indies, an eastern group discovered by Columbus (1494): Virgin Gorda, Tortola, Anegada, etc., and the Danish isles, St. Thomas, Santa Cruz, and St. John.
Tortola settled by Dutch buccaneers about 1648; expelled by the English (who have held it since).... 1666
Earthquake at St. Thomas and other isles; much damage; few lives lost.... Nov. 1867
St. Thomas settled by Danes 1672, and St. John a few years after; held by the British 1801-2, 1807-15; proposed sale to the U. S. for 1,500,500*l.* to be made a "territory." Danish proclamation, 25 Oct. 1867; purchase declined by U. S. Senate, 23 Mch.-May, 1870
[By a hurricane off St. Thomas, the British mail steamers *Rhone* and *Wye* were wrecked; the *Conway* and *Derwent*, and above 50 other vessels, driven ashore; about 1000 persons said to have perished.]
Santa Cruz. A negro insurrection; M. Fontaine, a planter, killed; Frederickstad and 36 out of 50 sugar plantations burned, and about 3000 whites rendered homeless; suppressed by col. Garde, the governor; about 200 negroes killed, 1-5 Oct. 1878

Virgin Mary. The Assumption of the Virgin is a festival in the Greek and Latin churches, in honor of the supposed ascent of Mary into heaven, 15 Aug. 45 A.D. The Presentation of the Virgin is a feast celebrated 21 Nov., said to have been instituted among the Greeks in the 11th century; its institution in the West is ascribed to pope Gregory XI., 1372. ANNUNCIATION; CONCEPTION, IMMACULATE.

vir'ginals, an early keyed instrument of the kind termed clavichords; used in the 16th and 17th centuries; played on by queen Elizabeth and Mary queen of Scots. According to Johnson, named from young women being the usual performers. Tallis, Morley, Purcell, Gibbons, and Bull composed for this instrument.

Virginia. DECEMVIRI.

Virginia, one of the 13 original states of the U. S., lies between 36° 30′ and 39° 40′ N. lat. and 75° 25′ and 83° 34′ W. lon. It is bounded north and west by Kentucky and West Virginia, north and east by Maryland, Chesapeake bay, and the Atlantic ocean, and on the south by North Carolina and Tennessee. It is 425 miles in length east and west and 205 miles in breadth north and south. Area, 40,125 sq. miles. Pop. 1890, 1,655,980; 1900, 1,854,184. Capital, Richmond.

Lucas Vasquez de Ayllon's supposed entry of the James river (AMERICA, Principal persons connected with discovery, etc.).... 1527
Capt. Philip Amidas and Arthur Barlow leave the Thames in 2 small vessels fitted out by sir Walter Raleigh.... 27 Apr. 1584
They enter Ocracock inlet and land on the island of Wocoken in Albemarle sound.... 13 July, "
After exploring Albemarle and Pamlico sounds and the island of Roanoke, they take 2 natives, Manteo and Wauchese, to England.... Sept. "
[This country, lying between 34° and 45° of N. lat., called Virginia, in honor of queen Elizabeth.]
Sir Walter Raleigh despatches 7 vessels from Plymouth under sir Richard Grenville to plant settlements in the territory, 9 Apr. 1585
Grenville lands on the island of Wocoken.... 26 July, "
Leaving 108 men under Ralph Lane as colonists, Grenville returns to England.... 25 Aug. "
Sir Francis Drake with 23 ships anchors outside of Roanoke inlet.... 10 June, 1586
Drake sails for England with all the colonists, who had become very despondent, thus ending the first settlement of the English in America.... 19 June, "
Another ship of 100 tons, sent by sir Walter Raleigh at his own expense with supplies, arrives at Roanoke a few days later; finding the colonists gone she returns to England.... June, "
Sir Richard Grenville with 3 ships visits Roanoke about 15 days after the departure of Drake, and leaves 15 men plentifully supplied for 2 years to keep the land.... "
New colony of 150, sent by sir Walter Raleigh in charge of John White, leaves Plymouth.... 26 Apr. 1587
They reach Roanoke to find that the men left by Grenville have been murdered by Indians.... 22 July, "
Eleanor Dare, wife of one of the assistants, gives birth to the first English child on American soil (named Virginia Dare), 18 Aug. "
John White returns to England at request of colonists for supplies, leaving behind 89 men, 17 women, and 2 children, 27 Aug. "
John White returns to Roanoke.... 9 Aug. 1590
[He found the settlement deserted. Its fate is conjectural. White's delay in returning was due to the engrossing efforts of England to repel the Spanish armada.]
James I. of England grants the London company, including sir Thomas Gates, sir George Somers, Richard Hakluyt (the historian), and Edward M. Wingfield the exclusive right to occupy the land from 34° to 38° N. lat.... 10 Apr. 1606
Three vessels—*Susan Constant*, of 100 tons, capt. Christopher Newport; *Good-speed*, of 40 tons, capt. Bartholomew Gosnold; and *Discovery*, 20 tons, capt. John Ratcliffe—with 105 emigrants sail from the Downs, Engl., destined for Virginia, 19 Dec. "
They enter Chesapeake bay, naming the capes at its entrance Charles and Henry, after the sons of king James.... 26 Apr. 1607
They enter the James river and land at a place they name Jamestown.... 13 May, "
Edward M. Wingfield chosen president.... "
Christopher Newport sails to England for provision and more settlers.... 15 June, "
Bartholomew Gosnold, the projector of the settlement, dies and is buried at Jamestown.... 22 Aug. "
Before autumn 50 more die; Wingfield is deposed and John Ratcliffe chosen president, whose incompetence gives the control to capt. John Smith during the autumn of.... "
Capt. John Smith, in exploring the Chickahominy, is attacked by Indians and captured; his companions killed.... Dec. "
Condemned to death by Powhatan, he is saved by his daughter Pocahontas.... Dec. "
[The truth of this story is disputed. See Charles Deane's introduction to Smith's "True Relation."]
Capt. Newport returns with supplies and 120 immigrants, 8 Jan. 1608
Newport returns to England with a ship-load of worthless earth, supposed to contain gold.... 10 Apr. "
Capt. John Smith explores the region of the Chesapeake bay, nearly 3000 sq. miles, as far north as Wyoming valley, 24 July, "
[His map is so exact that it was adduced as authority as late as 1873.—"Narrative and Critical History of America," vol. iii. p. 132.]

Smith returns to Jamestown 7 Sept 1608

He is made president of the council 10 Sept "

Newport arrives with supplies and about 70 immigrants, among them 2 women, the first in this colony Sept "

Smith compels the colonists to labor 6 hours each day 1608-9

New charter granted the London company under the title of "Adventurers and Planters of the City of London" with ampler privileges 23 May, 1609

["The new charter transferred to the company the powers which had before been reserved to the king The lives liberty and fortune of the colonists were placed at the arbitrary will of a governor who was to be appointed by a commercial corporation —*Bancroft's* "Hist U S, vol i p 137, 9th ed]

Nine vessels, with more than 500 emigrants many swine and a few horses sail from England for Virginia 12 June, "

[Two of the vessels were driven on the Bermudas and wrecked, the rest reached Virginia]

Capt John Smith, disabled by an explosion of gunpowder embarks for England about 29 Sept. "

[He never returned to Virginia]

Colony reduced from 490 to 60 in 6 months 1609-10

[This is known in Virginia history as "the starving time"]

Sir Thomas Gates and the passengers wrecked on the Bermudas construct 2 vessels and reach Jamestown 24 May 1610

In their destitution the whole colony leave Jamestown for Newfoundland in their few small vessels, near the mouth of the river they meet a boat of lord Delaware's whose ships had just arrived with more colonists and supplies and together they return to Jamestown 8 June, "

Lord Delaware the first executive of Virginia called governor, owing to ill health he embarks for England 28 Mch 1611

Sir Thomas Dale reaches Jamestown from England with 3 vessels and ample supplies and assumes the government, 12 May "

Sir Thomas Gates with his wife and daughters bringing in 6 ships 300 settlers, 100 cows and other cattle and an abundant supply of provisions, arrives at Jamestown early in Aug "

Third charter granted transfers the control from the council or the king to the London company 12 Mch 1612

Capt Samuel Argall in a foraging expedition entices Pocahontas, daughter of Powhatan, on his vessel and brings her to Jamestown "

Marriage of Pocahontas to John Rolfe by the rev Alexander Whitaker at Jamestown (she had previously been baptized and named Rebecca) 5 Apr 1613

First establishment of fixed property in the soil, the company granting 50 acres to every freeman in fee simple (Laws) 1615

Sir Thomas Dale embarks with John Rolfe and his wife Pocahontas, reaching Plymouth 12 June, 1616

[Pocahontas soon after presented at the court of James]

Pocahontas dies at Gravesend Kent, when about to embark for Virginia, aged 22, leaving one child 21 Mch 1617

["From her child, a son, can be traced descendants both in England and America "—"Narrative and Critical History of America" vol iii p 141]

Capt. Samuel Argall returns to Virginia as deputy-governor with 100 settlers, and John Rolfe as secretary 15 May, "

First seal (colonial) of Virginia "

Lord Delaware embarks in the *Neptune* with 200 settlers and supplies, he dies on the passage 18 Apr 1618

Powhatan d "

Deputy gov Argall convicted of malfeasance and oppressive exaction escapes 9 Apr 1619

Sir George Yeardley succeeds Lord Delaware as governor, and arrives at Jamestown 19 Apr "

First representative legislative assembly ever held in America meets at Jamestown 30 July, "

[It was composed of 22 burgesses, all interests of the colony were debated No legislation was of force till ratified by the company in England]

Dutch man of war sells colonists at Jamestown 20 negroes, Aug "

["This is the epoch of the introduction of negro slavery in the English colonies "—*Bancroft's* "Hist. of the U S," vol i p 177]

Earl of Southampton, the early patron of Shakespeare, elected treasurer of the London company 28 June, 1620

Population estimated at 4000, and 40,000 pounds of tobacco shipped to England "

England claims a monopoly of trade of her plantations Oct 1621

London company begins to ship respectable young women to supply the colonists with wives "

[They were sold for 120 lbs of tobacco each, or the cost of bringing them over Offers were made and matches agreed upon, the men paying for their partners, whom they immediately married These unions were often happy]

Sir Francis Wyatt chosen governor, and with 9 ships with emigrants and supplies, reaches Virginia Oct "

Cotton seed planted as an experiment for the first time "

Indians rise and massacre the whites at nearly all the plantations, extending 140 miles on both sides of the river, only Jamestown and the nearest settlements saved, a converted Indian revealing the plot 22 Mch 1622

[About 347 persons were killed in a few hours, 80 plantations were reduced to 8 A war ensued, with little loss to the colonists, no settled peace for 14 years.]

Dissensions arising in the Virginia company, and king James wishing to annul the charter, appoints commissioners to investigate it who advise a dissolution May, 1623

Charter annulled by the King's Bench 16 June, 1624

[The company had spent $750,000, had sent 9000 emigrants to Virginia, and granted the colony free government.]

Death of James I and accession of Charles I. 27 Mch. 1625

Sir Francis Wyatt succeeded by sir George Yeardley as governor May, 1626

Gov Yeardley d 14 Nov 1627

Council elects Francis West, a younger brother of lord Delaware, governor 15 Nov "

Gov West goes to England, dr John Potts succeeds 5 Mch 1628

Population, 5000 1629

George Calvert, Lord Baltimore, arrives in Virginia in the autumn of "

[He visited the territory about Chesapeake bay and returning to England, obtained a patent for the territory now Maryland]

Ministers of the gospel are ordered to conform in all things to the canons of the church of England 1629-30

Gov Potts superseded as governor by sir John Harvey Mch 1630

Trouble with Maryland as to land titles 1632-44

Virginia divided into 8 counties or shires, viz, Elizabeth City, Warwick, James City, Charles City, Henrico, Isle of Wight, York, and Accomac 1634

William Clayborne, a Virginia contestant sent to England by gov Harvey to answer for attempting to establish his claim against Maryland 1635

Gov Harvey deposed by the Virginia assembly and commissioners appointed to impeach him in England He accompanies the commission "

John West acting governor during the absence of gov Harvey, 1635-36

Harvey, reinstated by Charles returns 1837

Sir Francis Wyatt succeeds Harvey as governor Nov 1639

Sir William Berkeley appointed governor, and arrives in Virginia Feb 1642

Massachusetts sends 3 clergymen to Virginia at the request of Puritans there "

Virginia assembly enacts that all ministers in the colony shall conform to the order and constitution of the church of England or depart 1643

Indians incited by Opechancanough sachem of the Powhatans, attack the outlying settlements and massacre 300 colonists, 18 Apr 1644

Indians are quickly overcome and the aged Opechancanough is captured and dies in prison "

Gov Berkeley sails for England for a year's visit, and leaves Richard Kemp as deputy June, "

Virginia in sympathy with the Cavaliers of England Population consists of 20,000 whites and 300 negroes, average yearly export of tobacco, 1,500,000 lbs 1648

Dissenters having increased to 118, encounter all the rigor of colonial authority, and are suppressed by imprisonment and banishment "

Virginians continue their allegiance to Charles II after the execution of Charles I 30 Jan 1649

Three hundred and thirty adherents of Charles I come to Virginia near the close of "

Gov Berkeley sends col Henry Norwood to Breda to invite Charles II to Virginia 1650

King Charles II sends a new commission to Berkeley as governor, dated 3 June, "

Capt Robert Dennis, one of the commissioners of the commonwealth to reduce Virginia, arrives at Jamestown Mch 1652

Colony surrenders 12 Mch "

Provisional government organized, Richard Bennett governor, 30 Apr "

Richard Bennett succeeded by Edward Digges as governor 1655

Col Edward Hill attacks the Indians at the falls of James river and is repulsed with loss 1656

[Bloody Run, near Richmond, received its name from this encounter]

Samuel Matthews succeeds Edward Digges as governor 1657

Gov Matthews d Jan 1659

Sir William Berkeley elected governor 23 Mch 1660

Charles II monarchy re established in England 29 May, "

New commission as governor transmitted to Berkeley by Charles II 31 July, "

Gov Berkeley goes to England to defend the colony against the Navigation act 30 Apr 1661

Col Francis Morrison acting governor 1661-62

Quakers and other separatists persecuted by fines and banishment 1662

Virginia assigned for 31 years to lords Arlington and Culpepper by Charles II, at the yearly rental of 40 shillings 1673

[This grant covered not merely the wild lands, but private plantations long settled and improved]

Colonists become dissatisfied with their oppressive and unequal taxes "To produce an insurrection nothing was wanting but an excuse for appearing in arms" 1674-75

Susquehanna Indians driven from the head of the Chesapeake, commence depredations on the colonists of Virginia and Maryland 1675

These Indians are attacked in their fort, near the present site of Washington, by 1000 men from Virginia and Maryland, under col John Washington, great grandfather of George Washington "

Six Indian chiefs sent out the fort for a parley, are killed "

Indians escape from the fort and spread dismay and havoc upon the plantations along the James and Rappahannock "

Assembly meets and declares war against them 500 men gathered under sir Henry Chicheley Mch 1676

When about to march gov Berkeley orders the force disbanded, "

Alarmed colonists choose Nathaniel Bacon (b. in Suffolk, Engl) as their leader, he, failing to procure a commission from the governor, marches against the Indians without one and defeats them May, "

Gov. Berkeley proclaims Bacon a rebel..............29 May, 1676
Bacon elected a member of the new assembly.............. "
He is captured on his way to Jamestown, tried before the governor and council, and released on parole.............June, "
Bacon before the assembly asks the governor for pardon, which is granted..5 June, "
Bacon leaves Jamestown.................................June, "
He returns with 600 men and again demands a commission against the Indians. He is made commander-in-chief and authorized by the assembly to raise 1000 men, and this is ratified by the governor........................June, "
Bacon, while engaged in a successful campaign against the Indians, is again proclaimed a rebel and a traitor by gov. Berkeley.....................................29 July, "
Governor, unable to resist Bacon, is compelled to retreat to Accomac..Aug. "
Gathering some vessels and about 1000 men, the governor returns to Jamestown.............................7 Sept. "
Bacon marches to Jamestown and drives out the governor and his followers.....................................18 Sept. "
He burns Jamestown...................................19 Sept. "

[It consisted of a state-house, church, and about 18 houses, mostly of brick.]

Gov. Berkeley retires again to Accomac, while Bacon suddenly sickens of a malignant fever, a result of exposure and anxiety, and d.......................................26 Oct. "

["Nobody of later times knew where Nathaniel Bacon was buried." The death of Bacon ended the rebellion, as there was no competent leader left. 23 were executed for this rebellion, more than those killed on both sides during the war.]

News of this rebellion in England prevents the issue of the promised liberal charter, just ready to pass the seals....Oct. "
Three commissioners despatched to Virginia and 1 regiment of soldiers arrive...................................29 Feb. 1677
Gov. Berkeley, being recalled by the king, sails for England greatly disliked.................................27 Apr. "
Gov. Berkeley succeeded by sir Herbert Jeffreys, who d..Dec. 1678
William Byrd builds a mill and trading-house upon the present site of Richmond, the place known as "Byrd's warehouse," 1679
Sir Henry Chicheley governor until...............10 May, 1680

[Succeeded by lord Culpepper.]

John Buckner brings a printing-press to Virginia and prints the session laws, but is called to account by gov. Culpepper and the council, and obliged to give bonds to print nothing more till the king's pleasure be known; all printing forbidden in the colony.. 1682
Lord Culpepper succeeded by lord Howard of Effingham..... 1684
Gov. Effingham visits gov. Dongan of New York, and at Albany concludes a treaty with the Iroquois chiefs...........July, "
Accession of James II. to the throne..................6 Feb. 1685
Many persons engaged in the rebellion of the duke of Monmouth transported to Virginia.............................. "
Gov. Effingham embarks for England, and the assembly sends col. Ludwell to lay the grievances of the colony before the English government... 1688
William and Mary proclaimed in Virginia...............Apr. 1689
Huguenots of France first come to Virginia................. 1690
Francis Nicholson, formerly governor of New York, appointed governor of Virginia............................3 June, "
First assembly under William and Mary at Jamestown....Apr. 1691
Rev. James Blair obtains from William and Mary a charter for William and Mary college at Williamsburg...........Feb. 1692

[The plan of the building was drawn by sir Christopher Wren. It was amply endowed. Rev. Mr. Blair was its first president.]

Sir Edmund Andros, formerly governor of New York and New England, succeeds Nicholson as governor of Virginia...Feb. "
Francis Nicholson again governor of Virginia...........Nov. 1698
Williamsburg settled...................................... 1699
First commencement at William and Mary college............ 1700
Williamsburg made the capital.............................. "
Edward Nott appointed lieut.-governor..............13 Aug. 1704
Gov. Nicholson recalled.................................... 1705
George Hamilton, earl of Orkney, appointed governor of Virginia.. "

[From this time the office became a pensionary sinecure, the governor residing in England, and out of a salary of 2000*l*. paid his deputy, the actual governor, 800*l*.]

Edward Nott d. in office.............................Aug. 1706
Robert Hunter appointed lieut.-governor, but is captured on the voyage by the French................................ 1708
Affairs of the colony managed by the council, Edward Jennings president...1705–10
Col. Alexander Spotswood arrives in Virginia as lieut.-governor...June, 1710

[He was received with satisfaction by the people, and granted the right of *habeas corpus*, hitherto withheld.]

Gov. Spotswood explores the country west as far as the Shenandoah valley, crossing the Blue Ridge; the expedition occupies 6 weeks....................................Aug.–Sept. 1716
Gov. Spotswood sends lieut. Maynard of the British navy with 2 small vessels into Pamlico bay in pursuit of the pirate John Teach or "Blackbeard"..........................21 Nov. 1718

[Maynard sailed back with the head of the pirate chief as a trophy. 13 captured pirates hung at Williamsburg. Benjamin Franklin, then a printer's apprentice at Boston, Mass., wrote a ballad on Blackbeard's fate, which was sold in the streets of that city.]

Gov. Spotswood effects a treaty with the Iroquois............ 1722
Gov. Spotswood succeeded by Hugh Drysdale................. "
Gov. Drysdale succeeded by William Gooch.................. 1727

VIR

Boundary established between Virginia and North Carolina... 1728
Alexander Spotswood appointed deputy postmaster-general of the colony, and through him Benj. Franklin is appointed postmaster of Pennsylvania.................................. 1730
First settler in the Shenandoah valley Joist Hite, who takes up 40,000 acres and enters upon possession with a party from Pennsylvania... 1732
Richard Henry Lee b. at Stratford on the Potomac.....20 Jan. "
Geo. Washington b. Westmoreland county............22 Feb. "
Patrick Henry b. at Studley, Hanover county.........29 May, 1736
First newspaper in Virginia, the *Virginia Gazette*, published by William Parks, weekly, at 15*s*. per annum, appears at Williamsburg..Aug. "
Richmond settled by William Byrd........................... 1739
Virginia raises a regiment to assist in the reduction of Carthagena, W. Indies. Lawrence Washington, half-brother of George Washington, is a captain in it, embarking.......... 1740
Mount Vernon named by Lawrence Washington after adm. Vernon, who commanded the fleet against Carthagena...... "
George Whitefield comes to Virginia........................ "
Richmond incorporated...................................... 1742
Augustine Washington, father of George Washington, d...Apr. 1743
Thomas Jefferson b. in Albemarle county.............2 Apr. "
Dr. Thomas Walker, of the council of Virginia, crosses and names the Cumberland mountains.......................... 1747
Harper's Ferry named after Robert Harper, an English millwright, who obtains a grant of it from lord Fairfax......... 1748

[The first survey of it was made by Washington.]

Thomas Lee, of the council, proposes to form the Ohio company, consisting of himself and 12 others, among them Lawrence and Augustine Washington......................... "
They obtain a grant of 600,000 acres west of the mountains and south of the Ohio river between the Monongahela and the Kanawha..Mch. 1749
William Gooch, governor of Virginia for 22 years, retires to England..Aug. "
Christopher Gist is sent to explore the Ohio country as far as the falls of the Ohio by the Ohio company................1750–51
John Robinson, president of the council, acting governor, dying, is succeeded first by Thomas Lee, then by Lewis Burwell..1750–51
Robert Dinwiddie appointed lieut.-governor, and arrives in Virginia early in.. 1752
By treaty the western Indians at Logstown, a trading-post about 17 miles northwest from Pittsburg, agree not to molest any settlement on the south side of the Ohio.......13 June, "
Gov. Dinwiddie sends Washington (then 21 years old) as a commissioner to investigate the proceedings of the French on the Ohio; Washington leaves Williamsburg with a few attendants..30 Oct. 1753
Christopher Gist meets Washington at Cumberland and accompanies him...14 Nov. "
They arrive at Logstown...............................24 Nov. "
They reach fort Le Bœuf on French creek, Pa., about 15 miles south of lake Erie.....................................11 Dec. "
Deliver gov. Dinwiddie's letter to St. Pierre, commandant at Le Bœuf, receive a written reply, and return........16 Dec. "
Reach Williamsburg in 11 weeks, after a journey of 1500 miles through an almost trackless wilderness..............16 Jan. 1754

[The answer of the French was evasive and unsatisfactory.]

Assembly vote 10,000*l*. for an expedition to protect the Ohio company in settling the territory on the Ohio and building fortifications..Feb. "
Washington, with 2 companies, sent by gov. Dinwiddie to the Great Meadows...Apr. "
Washington attacks a small party of French near the Great Meadows...28 May, "

[The leader, M. De Jumonville, was killed; first bloodshed in this war.]

Washington surrenders fort Necessity, a rude stockade at the Great Meadows, to the French after a spirited defence, and with military honors leads out its garrison..........3 July, "

["In the whole valley of the Mississippi, to its head-springs in the Alleghanies, no standard floated but that of France."—*Bancroft's* "Hist. U. S."]

Fort Cumberland, about 55 miles northwest of Winchester, built.. "
Gen. Edward Braddock arrives in Virginia as commander-in-chief of all the forces in America......................Feb. "
Gen. Braddock starts from fort Cumberland for fort Duquesne with 2150 men (PENNSYLVANIA)..................7–8–10 June, "
Consternation on the western frontier of Virginia in consequence of Braddock's defeat.................................. "
Virginia assembly votes 40,000*l*. for the public service; calls out 1500 men for active duty, and appoints Washington commander-in-chief..Aug. "
Assembly allows Washington 300*l*. as a compensation for his losses at the battle of Monongahela (PENNSYLVANIA, 1755), Aug. "
Washington visits gov. Shirley at Boston to deliver to him a memorial from the officers of the Virginia regiment asking king's commissions, and also to acquaint himself with the governor's military plans.........................Feb.–Mch. 1756

[During this journey made on horseback, while a guest of his friend Beverly Robinson, Washington became acquainted with miss Mary Phillipse, afterwards wife of col. Roger Morris, an officer in the British army.]

Winchester incorporated 1752; the only settlement not deserted west of the Blue Ridge..................................... "
Gov. Robert Dinwiddie retires.........................Jan. 1758

[John Blair, president of the council, acting governor.]

Francis Fauquier, appointed governor, arrives.........7 June, "

Gen John Forbes's expedition against fort Duquesne (PENNSYLVANIA) July, 1758

Washington commands a regiment, and from it garrisons fort Pitt (formerly Duquesne), then considered within the jurisdiction of Virginia. He marches back to Winchester and takes his seat in the assembly, resigning his commission after more than 5 years' continuous service Dec "

He marries Martha, widow of John Parke Custis, and daughter of John Dandridge 6 Jan 1759

Patrick Henry's speech in the "Parsons' case" 1 Dec 1763

Stamp act approved by the king 22 Mch 1765

Patrick Henry introduces in the Virginia assembly 5 resolutions against the Stamp act 30 May, "

[During the debate, referring to the fate of Tarquin, Cæsar, and Charles I, he boldly exclaimed that George III might profit by their example The resolutions passed by a close vote, the 5th by a majority of 1]

Virginia prevented by gov Fauquier from sending delegates to the congress in New York to oppose the Stamp act Oct "

George Mercer appointed distributer of stamps but not permitted to serve Oct "

Repeal of the Stamp act Mch 1766

Gov Fauquier d 1768

Norborne Berkeley, baron de Boutetourt, arrives in Virginia as governor Nov "

Gov Boutetourt d Oct 1770

[William Nelson, president of the council, acting governor]

John Murray, earl of Dunmore governor, arrives at Williamsburg 1772

Virginia House of Assembly appoints a "Committee of Correspondence" and recommends similar appointments to the other colonies to promote union Mch 1773

Gov Dunmore dissolves the house of burgesses for setting apart 1 June as a day of fasting and prayer, in sympathy with the people of Boston 25 May, 1774

First Continental Congress meets at Philadelphia, Peyton Randolph of Virginia president 5 Sept "

Indian war "

[Gov Dunmore's conduct of the expedition from fort Pitt to meet gen Lewis at the mouth of the Great Kanawha suggests premeditated treachery (See "Narrative and Critical History of America," vol vi p 716) This war was caused by the cold blooded murder of the family and relatives of Logan, chief of the Mingoes, and other atrocities by the frontier men]

Battle of Point Pleasant at the junction of the Great Kanawha and Ohio, opposite the present town of Gallipolis, O 10 Oct. "

[About 1200 Virginians under gen Andrew Lewis were attacked by 1500 Indians led by Cornstalk and Logan The Indians, after fighting all day, retreated. The Virginians lost 75 killed and 140 wounded]

Speech of Patrick Henry before the convention in the old church at Richmond, urging resistance to England 20 Mch 1775

Gov Dunmore removes the gunpowder at Williamsburg to a British man of war in the James river 20 Apr "

Gov Dunmore leaves Williamsburg taking refuge on board the *Fowey*, a British ship, at Yorktown 8 June, "

George Washington appointed commander in chief of the American forces by Congress 15 June, "

Virginia convention appoints a Committee of Safety, with Edmund Pendleton president July, "

This convention appoints Patrick Henry commander in chief of the Virginian forces "

Battle of Great Bridge, near the Dismal Swamp, 12 miles from Norfolk 9 Dec "

[Col William Woodford's successful defence against troops of lord Dunmore, who lost 55 killed and wounded John Marshall, afterwards chief justice of the U S, was a lieutenant under Woodford This was the first bloodshed of the Revolution in Virginia]

Lord Dunmore burns Norfolk 1 Jan 1776

Patrick Henry, feeling slighted, resigns as commander-in chief, Feb "

Patrick Henry elected a delegate to the convention Apr "

Convention instructs her delegates to Congress to advocate independence 15 May, "

Declaration of rights by George Mason adopted by the convention 12 June, "

Patrick Henry elected governor of Virginia June, "

State constitution adopted, and colonial government ceases in Virginia 29 June, "

Kentucky made a county of Virginia "

Henry Clay born in "The Slashes," Hanover county 12 Apr 1777

Maj George Roger Clarke sent by gov Henry with an expedition against the British fort at Kaskaskia (now in Illinois) and captures it 4 July, 1778

He also occupies Vincennes (ILLINOIS) Aug "

All territory northwest of the Ohio river occupied by Clarke is made by the Virginia assembly into the county of Illinois Oct. "

Col John Todd appointed its county lieutenant 12 Dec "

Richmond becomes the capital of the state 1779

Virginia tenders to Congress the entire region beyond the Ohio, 1780

[This vast domain extended to the Mississippi Virginia retained the jurisdiction of the remaining territory east of the Mississippi river and north of 35° 30']

Virginia charters the town of Louisville, Ky "

Virginia issues $30,000,000, and makes it legal tender at $40 for $1 "

Benedict Arnold, with 1600 men, enters the James river by order of sir Henry Clinton 2 Jan. 1781

He plunders Richmond and destroys stores 5-6 Jan "

He fixes headquarters at Portsmouth 20 Mch 1781

Gen Phillips, with 2000 men, reinforces him 27 Mch "

Phillips and Arnold leave Portsmouth 18 Apr and occupy Petersburg driving out baron Steuben and gen Nelson 24 Apr "

Gen Lafayette approaches Petersburg 11 May, "

Gen Phillips dies at Petersburg 13 May, "

Lord Cornwallis reaches Petersburg 19 May, "

Cornwallis sends Arnold to New York May, "

Cornwallis starts in pursuit of Lafayette " "

Lafayette and Wayne unite their forces 7 June, "

Cornwallis retires to Williamsburg 25 June, "

[Estimated destruction of property by the British during this campaign in Virginia, $15,000,000]

Lafayette attacks Cornwallis near Green Springs and is repulsed 6 July, "

Cornwallis crosses the James and reaches Portsmouth 9 July, "

Cornwallis retires with his army to Yorktown 4 Aug "

Gen Lafayette at the forks of the Pamunky and Mattapony 13 Aug "

American and French army starts for Yorktown, Va, from the Hudson river 25 Aug "

Count de Grasse arrives in the Chesapeake with 26 French ships of the line, besides frigates and transports 30 Aug "

Combined army passes Philadelphia on the way to Yorktown 2 Sept "

Count de St Simon lands 3200 French at Jamestown island and Lafayette joins him at Green Spring 3 Sept. "

They occupy Williamsburg, about 15 miles from Yorktown, 5 Sept. "

British fleet under adm Graves appears off the Chesapeake and skirmishes with the French fleet 7 Sept "

Washington reaches Williamsburg 14 Sept "

He visits count de Grasse to plan the siege 18 Sept "

French and American army (about 16,000) advances within 2 miles of the British outposts. 28 Sept "

First parallel of the American opened on Yorktown 5-6 Oct "

Storming parties (American under col Alexander Hamilton and French under baron de Viomenil) carry 2 British redoubts, 14 Oct "

Lieut col Abercrombie vainly assaults the French batteries on the morning of 16 Oct "

Cornwallis attempts to escape across the river to Gloucester Point on the night of 16 Oct. "

[He was prevented by a storm]

Negotiations for capitulation begin 17 Oct. "

Cornwallis surrenders 7247 men, 75 brass guns, 69 iron guns, 19 Oct "

[Several vessels, with 900 officers and men, surrendered to the French fleet Casualties during the siege Americans, 23 killed, 65 wounded French 52 killed, 134 wounded, British 156 killed, 326 wounded, 70 missing This victory largely due to chance, virtually ended the war — "Narrative and Critical Hist of America," vol vi p 504]

Adm Digby appears off the capes of the Chesapeake with 25 ships of the line, 2 50 gun ships, and 8 frigates, carrying sir Henry Clinton and 7000 troops 24 Oct "

Learning of the surrender, he returns to New York 29 Oct "

Thomas Fairfax, 6th lord and baron of Cameron dies at his lodge, Greenway court, Frederick county, aged 90 years, 12 Dec "

[He was a stanch loyalist, but took no part in the war Learning that his friend Washington had compelled Cornwallis to surrender, he was overcome with emotion, exclaiming, "It is time for me to die"]

Northwest territory, ceded by Virginia to the U S, accepted by Congress 1784

Religious Freedom act passed 1785

It is made treason to erect a new state in the territory of Virginia without permission from the assembly Oct "

Legislature authorizes the 5 counties of Kentucky to elect 5 delegates each to consider an independent government Nov "

James Rumsey moves a boat by steam on the Potomac Mch 1786

Lynchburg on the James river laid out "

Kentucky favors separation at a convention held at Danville 7 Sept 1787

Convention at Richmond on the Federal Constitution 2 June, 1788

Patrick Henry, James Monroe, George Mason, etc, oppose it, James Madison, Edmund Pendleton, John Marshall, etc, advocate it It is ratified 89 to 79 25 June, "

Virginia cedes 40 sq miles south of the Potomac to the U S for a Federal district 1790

[This land was restored to Virginia by Congress in July, 1846 DISTRICT OF COLUMBIA]

Government armory and manufactory located at Harper's Ferry 4 Mch 1798

Patrick Henry d. 6 June, 1799

George Washington d 14 Dec "

Insurrection of the negroes under one Gabriel, slave of a planter near Richmond 1800

[Most of the negroes were captured and executed]

John Marshall of Virginia appointed chief justice of the Supreme court 31 Jan 1801

Richmond *Enquirer* appears at Richmond 9 Mch 1804

Trial of Aaron Burr for high treason at Richmond 1 Sept 1807

Verdict, not proven, returned (BURR'S CONSPIRACY) 9 Sept. "

Theatre at Richmond burned 26 Dec 1811

[During a play called "The Bleeding Nun" about 70 perished, among them the governor, George W Smith]

Chesapeake and Ohio Canal company chartered 27 Jan 1824

University of Virginia opened 25 Mch 1825

[It was chartered 1819]

The *Whig* newspaper appears in Richmond 1826

Assembly condemns the tariff as unconstitutional 21 Feb 1829

Geological survey of Virginia ordered (completed in 6 years) 1836

Sixty gold mines or "diggings" worked in Virginia (26 in Spottsylvania and 15 in Orange county) 1839

John Brown with several men, rents a small farm near Harper's Ferry June 1859

Brown, with 16 whites and 6 blacks, captures the U S armory building at Harper's Ferry on the night of 16 Oct "

Attacked by U S troops under col Robert E Lee, he is captured with the survivors 18 Oct "

He is hung at Charleston, Va (BROWN'S, John, INSURRECTION), 2 Dec "

Gov Letcher calls an extra session of the legislature which orders a convention 13 Jan 1861

Convention rejects an ordinance of secession, 89 to 45 4 Apr "

It chooses 3 commissioners to ask of the president his policy towards the Confederate States 4 Apr "

First shot at fort Sumter from Stevens's battery, fired by Edmund Ruffin of Virginia at his earnest request (UNITED STATES) 12 Apr "

Virginian commissioners present their credentials to the president 13 Apr "

President answers the commissioners, refusing to acknowledge the Confederate States 15 Apr "

Gov Letcher refuses to furnish troops at the call of the president 16 Apr "

Virginia State convention passes a secession ordinance, 88 to 55, subject to a vote of the people 17 Apr "

Gov Letcher by proclamation recognizes the Confederacy and orders the state troops in readiness 17 Apr "

Norfolk harbor obstructed by sinking vessels, by order of gov Letcher 17 Apr "

Gen W B Taliaferro assigned to the command of the Virginia troops at Norfolk 18 Apr "

Harper's Ferry, threatened by Virginia militia, is evacuated by lieut Jones and 45 regulars, after destroying public property 18 Apr "

Norfolk navy yard evacuated and property destroyed 20 Apr "

[Among the ships scuttled and sunk was the *Merrimac*, afterwards raised and iron clad See 9 Mch 1862]

Robert E Lee nominated by the governor and confirmed by the convention as commander of the state forces 21 Apr "

Virginia convention sends commissioners to Alexander H Stephens vice president of the Confederacy, to treat for the annexation of Virginia 24 Apr "

Governor's proclamation that Virginia is a member of the Confederacy (subject to popular vote in May) 25 Apr "

Richmond becomes the capital of the Confederacy and general rendezvous of southern troops May, "

Virginia incorporated with the Confederacy, and gen Robert E Lee in command of the Virginia Confederate forces, 6 May, "

Gen Benj F Butler takes command at fortress Monroe, 22 May, "

People confirm the secession ordinance 23 May, "

First advance of the federals into Virginia. 24 May, "

[3 regiments crossed at Georgetown, 4 at Washington, and 1 (Ellsworth Zouaves) at Alexandria.]

Col E E Ellsworth enters Alexandria in command of the New York Fire Zouaves, and is shot by Jackson a hotel keeper at Alexandria, while taking down a Confederate flag. 24 May, "

[Jackson was instantly shot by Francis E Brownell, one of the Zouaves]

Slaves around fortress Monroe entering the Federal lines are declared "contraband" by gen B F Butler 27 May, "

Occupation of Newport News by the federals. 27-29 May, "

Federal troops cross the Ohio at Wheeling and at Parkersburg, 27 May, "

Occupy Grafton, W Va 30 May, "

Affair at Philippi, confederates retreat to Beverly 3 June, "

Gen P G T Beauregard proclaims to the people of Loudoun, Fairfax, and Prince William counties that the federals are warring for "Beauty and Booty" 5 June, "

Virginia troops transferred to the Confederate government by the governor 8 June, "

Affair at Big Bethel, near fortress Monroe 10 June, "

[Maj Theodore Winthrop, aid to gen Butler, killed The federals repulsed with slight loss]

Gen Patterson crosses the Potomac at Williamsport 2 July, "

[His advance defeated gen Jackson's brigade at Falling Water]

Affair at Rich Mountain, W Va: the confederates under col George H Pegram defeated by the federals under gen Rosecrans 11 July, "

Battle at Carricksford, W Va., confederates defeated with the loss of their general, Robert S Garnett 14 July, "

Battle of BULL RUN 21 July, "

Gen Patterson relieves gen Nathaniel P Banks in command of the department of the Shenandoah 25 July, "

Maj gen George B McClellan appointed to the army of the Potomac 27 July, "

Holding or accepting office under the Federal government declared treason by the state 1 Aug "

Battle of BALL'S BLUFF 21 Oct "

West Virginia votes for a separation from Virginia, vote substantially unanimous 24 Oct "

Confederate armies in Virginia reorganized under gen Joseph F Johnston 9 Nov "

Union troops occupy Big Bethel 3 Jan 1862

At Hampton Roads the Confederate ram *Merrimac* capt Franklin Buchanan sinks the Federal ship *Cumberland*, captures the *Congress*, and forces the *Minnesota* aground 8 Mch 1862

Battle between the *Merrimac* and *Monitor*, lieut Worden commander, *Merrimac* retires 9 Mch "

Manassas Junction evacuated by the confederates 10 Mch. "

Battle of Winchester or Kernstown, gen James Shields commanding Federal forces gen "Stonewall" Jackson confederates, confederates retire 23 Mch "

Peninsular campaign in Virginia begun " "

Norfolk reoccupied by Union troops 11 May, "

Confederates under "Stonewall" Jackson drive gen Banks from Winchester 25 May, "

Gen Robert E Lee assumes command of the Confederate forces in Virginia 3 June, "

Battle of Cross Keys gen Frémont attacks a part of Jackson's command under gen Ewell, but retires (CROSS KEYS PENINSULAR CAMPAIGN) 8 June, "

Battle of Port Republic the federals with 2 brigades (3000) defeated by "Stonewall" Jackson (8000) (PENINSULAR CAMPAIGN) 9 June, "

Maj gen John Pope appointed to the army of Virginia (POPE'S VIRGINIA CAMPAIGN) 26 June, "

Lee advances into Maryland, "Stonewall" Jackson crosses the Potomac at White's ford, near Leesburg 5 Sept. "

"Stonewall" Jackson captures Harper's Ferry (MARYLAND CAMPAIGN) 15 Sept "

Battle of FREDERICKSBURG 13 Dec "

Battle of CHANCELLORSVILLE 2, 3, 4 May, 1863

Federals under Milroy driven out of WINCHESTER by the Confederate gen Ewell (GETTYSBURG) 15 June, "

GRANT'S CAMPAIGN IN VIRGINIA begins 4 May, 1864

Gen B F Butler forbids civil government in Norfolk by F H Pierpont as loyal governor of Virginia 30 June, "

[On appeal the president sustained gen Butler]

Maj gen Philip H Sheridan appointed to the army of the Shenandoah 7 Aug "

Battle of WINCHESTER 19 Sept. "

Battle of FISHER'S HILL 22 Sept. "

Battle of CEDAR CREEK 19 Oct "

Confederates abandon and partly burn Richmond 2 Apr 1865

Surrender of Lee at Appomattox (GRANT'S VIRGINIA CAMPAIGN), 9 Apr "

Francis H Pierpont recognized as governor of Virginia by a proclamation of pres Johnson 9 May, "

Gov Pierpont assumes office 26 May, "

XIV th Amendment rejected by Virginia 1866

By act of Congress the Federal government assumes the government of Virginia 2 Mch 1867

Gen Schofield assigned to the 1st Military District 13 Mch "

Gen Schofield prescribes regulations for registering voters for a state convention 13 May, "

Election for a convention to frame a constitution 22 Oct. "

[Vote for, 107,342, against, 61,887]

Convention meets 3 Dec., adjourns 20 Dec. 1867, to 2 Jan 1868

Convention reassembles " "

Convention adopts a constitution by 51 to 36 17 Apr "

[It was to be submitted to the people 2 June, state officers and representatives of Congress to be elected at the same time The assembly to meet 24 June No election was held, the state remaining under military authority]

Gen Schofield relieved, and gen George Stoneman assigned to the command 1 June, "

Gen George Stoneman relieved, and gen E R S Canby assumes command 20 Apr 1869

Virginia adopts her new constitution at an election by a majority of 39,957 6 July, "

[It recognizes equal civil rights irrespective of race color, or former condition Gilbert C Walker elected governor]

Legislature assembles at Richmond 5 Oct "

[The first deliberative assembly of the state for 3 years, and the first regular legislature for 10]

XIV th and XV th Amendments to the Federal Constitution ratified 8 Oct "

Act admitting Virginia into the Union without further conditions approved 26 Jan 1870

Gen Canby turns the state over to the civil authorities, 27 Jan "

Gov Walker proclaims the final reconstruction of the state, 8 Feb. "

Capitol at Richmond falls, the galleries giving away, about 60 persons killed and 120 injured 27 Apr "

Freshets in the James and Shenandoah valleys, $5,000 000 worth of property destroyed Sept. "

Burning of the Spotswood hotel at Richmond 25 Dec "

State Board of Health organized in Virginia 1872

Gen Grant has a majority for president of 1975 over Horace Greeley "

State Board of Immigration established 1873

Completion of the Chesapeake and Ohio railroad between Richmond and Huntington on the Ohio, length 421 miles. "

Richmond and Atlantic "Air Line" railroad opened "

James river free bridge at Richmond completed "

Constitutional amendment abolishing the township system ratified 1874

Educational convention (colored) meets at Richmond 24 Aug. 1875

Statue of gen Thomas ("Stonewall") Jackson unveiled on Capitol square at Richmond 26 Oct. "

Violent earthquake shock at Richmond 22 Dec. "

W W Corcoran of Washington gives the University of Virginia $55,000 1876

Twenty-four U. S. soldiers posted at Petersburg to protect the polls.......4–13 Nov. 1876

Readjusters, formerly Democrats, organize as a party...25 Feb. 1879

Readjusters hold a state convention at Richmond.......7 July, 1880

One hundredth anniversary of the surrender of Cornwallis celebrated at Yorktown.......19 Oct. 1881

[Robert C. Winthrop of Massachusetts delivered the oration. Representatives of the families of Lafayette, count Rochambeau, and baron Steuben were present. The corner-stone of the monument (122 ft. high), to commemorate this victory, was laid 18 Oct. 1881; military review 20, and naval 21 Oct.]

Act passed making receivable for taxes only gold, silver, U. S. Treasury notes, national bank-notes, and currency (excluding coupons on state bonds).......26 Jan. 1882

"Riddleberger act" passed, offering terms of settlement with state bond-holders.......14 Feb. "

All acts for punishment by stripes repealed, and other punishment substituted....... "

Legislature meets in extra session.......7 Mch.–22 Apr. "

Amendment to state constitution abrogating capitation tax as a condition of voting ratified by vote, 107,303 to 66,131, at election.......Nov. "

Virginia Normal and Collegiate institute established at Petersburg....... 1883

Extra session of the legislature.......Aug.–Dec. 1884

Southwestern Lunatic asylum provided for by law....... "

State Woman Normal school established at Farmville....... "

U. S. Supreme court decides that coupons are a good tender in payment of taxes in Virginia.......20 Apr. 1885

Act to establish an Agricultural Experiment station at the Virginia Agricultural and Mechanical college at Blacksburg; one appointing a commission to fix the boundary line with North Carolina, and a Local Option act passed by legislature, which adjourns.......5 Mch. 1886

Legislature convenes in extra session 16 Mch. 1887; among other acts passes one to punish persons fraudulently using coupons, and adjourns.......24 May, 1887

Board of Agriculture established by legislature, which adjourns.......5 Mch. 1888

College of William and Mary becomes State Male Normal college by act approved.......5 Mch. "

Nineteenth Jan. (gen. Robert E. Lee's birthday) made a legal holiday by legislature at session ending.......1 Mch. 1890

Mercie's equestrian statue of gen. Robert E. Lee unveiled at Richmond.......29 May, "

Monument to the Confederate dead unveiled at Fredericksburg.......10 June, 1891

Statue of gen. Stonewall Jackson unveiled at Lexington; 15,000 Confederate veterans present; oration by gen. Early, 21 July, "

Thomas W. Bocock, born 1815, for 14 years a congressman and for 4 years speaker of the Confederate Congress, dies in Appomattox county.......5 Aug. "

Appomattox Court-house building destroyed by fire.....3 Feb. 1892

Legislature ratifies a final settlement of the State debt with the bond-holders. $19,000,000 in bonds, to run 100 years at 2 per cent. for 10 years and 3 per cent. for 90 years, to be issued for the $28,000,000 outstanding.......Feb. "

Senator John S. Barbour dies suddenly in Washington, 14 May, "

Eppa Hunton of Warrenton, under executive appointment 28 May, qualifies as U. S. senator.......1 June, "

Corner-stone of new Chamber of Commerce laid at Richmond, 25 Aug. "

Convention of Southern governors meet at Richmond in the interest of the South.......12 Apr. 1893

Remains of Jefferson Davis, brought from New Orleans, buried in Hollywood cemetery, Richmond.......31 May, "

Jubal A. Early, confederate general, dies at Lynchburg, 2 Mch. 1894

Monument at Fredericksburg, erected to the memory of the mother of Washington, unveiled.......10 May, "

GOVERNORS UNDER THE COLONIAL GOVERNMENT.

PRESIDENTS OF THE COUNCIL.

Name.	Date.	Remarks.
Edward Maria Wingfield....	1607	Deposed from the office by the colonists.
John Ratcliffe..........	1607 to 1608	Relieved.
Capt. John Smith..........	1608 " 1610	Returns to England.
George Percy..........	1610 " 1611	

GOVERNORS.

Name.	Date.	Remarks.
Lord Delaware..........	1611	Returns to England.
Sir Thomas Dale..........	1611	Dep. gov. Superseded by sir Thomas Gates.
Sir Thomas Gates..........	1611 to 1614	Dep. gov. Returns to England.
Sir Thomas Dale..........	1614 " 1616	Dep. gov. Returns to England.
George Yeardley..........	1616 " 1617	Dep. gov.
Samuel Argall..........	1617 " 1619	" Deposed.
Sir George Yeardley..........	1619 " 1621	
Sir Francis Wyatt..........	1621 " 1626	Returns to England.
Sir George Yeardley..........	1626 " 1627	Dies in office.
Francis West..........	1627 " 1629	Acting.
John Potts..........	1629	" Relieved by John Harvey.

VIR

GOVERNORS.—(*Continued.*)

Name.	Date.	Remarks.
John Harvey..........	1629 to 1635	Goes to England to answer charges.
John West..........	1635 " 1636	Acting.
John Harvey..........	1636 " 1639	
Sir Francis Wyatt..........	1639 " 1641	
Sir William Berkeley..........	1641 " 1652	Appointed by the Commonwealth of England.
Richard Bennett..........	1652 " 1655	
Edward Digges..........	1655 " 1656	Appointed by the Commonwealth of England.
Samuel Matthews..........	1656 " 1660	Dies in office.
Sir William Berkeley..........	1660 " 1661	Returns to England.
Col. Francis Moryson..........	1661 " 1663	Acting.
Sir William Berkeley..........	1663 " 1677	Retires to England to remain.
Sir Herbert Jeffreys..........	1677 " 1678	Lt.-gov. Dies in office.
Sir Henry Chicheley..........	1678 " 1680	Dep. gov.
Lord Culpepper..........	1680 " 1684	Recalled and deprived of his office.
Lord Howard of Effingham.	1684 " 1688	Retires to England.
Nathaniel Bacon..........	1688 " 1690	Acting.
Francis Nicholson..........	1690 " 1692	
Sir Edmund Andros..........	1692 " 1698	Removed.
Francis Nicholson..........	1698 " 1705	"
Edward Nott..........	1705 " 1706	Dep. gov. Dies in office.
Edmund Jennings..........	1706 " 1710	"
Alexander Spotswood..........	1710 " 1722	Lt.-gov. Removed.
Hugh Drysdale..........	1722 " 1726	" Dies in office.
William Gouch..........	1726 " 1749	"
Thomas Lee and..........	1749 " 1752	Acting.
Lewis Burwell..........	1749 " 1752	
Robert Dinwiddie..........	1752 " 1758	Lt.-gov.
Francis Fauquier..........	1758 " 1768	"
Lord Boutetourt..........	1768 " 1770	" Dies.
William Nelson..........	1770 " 1772	
Lord Dunmore..........	1772 " 1775	Last of the royal governors.

Provisional convention.........from 17 July, 1775, to 12 June, 1776

GOVERNORS UNDER THE CONTINENTAL CONGRESS AND THE CONSTITUTION.

Name.	Date.	Remarks.
Patrick Henry..........	1776 to 1779	
Thomas Jefferson..........	1779 " 1781	
Thomas Nelson..........	1781	
Benjamin Harrison..........	1781 to 1784	
Patrick Henry..........	1784 " 1786	
Edmund Randolph..........	1786 " 1788	Resigns.
Beverly Randolph..........	1788 " 1791	
Henry Lee..........	1791 " 1794	
Robert Brooke..........	1794 " 1796	
James Wood..........	1796 " 1799	
James Monroe..........	1799 " 1802	
John Page..........	1802 " 1805	
William H. Cabell..........	1805 " 1808	
John Tyler..........	1808 " 1811	
James Monroe..........	1811	
George W. Smith..........	1811 to 1812	
James Barbour..........	1812 " 1814	
Wilson C. Nicholas..........	1814 " 1816	
James P. Preston..........	1816 " 1819	
Thomas M. Randolph..........	1819 " 1822	
James Pleasants..........	1822 " 1825	
John Tyler..........	1825 " 1826	
William B. Giles..........	1826 " 1829	Democrat.
John Floyd..........	1829 " 1833	"
Littleton W. Tazewell..........	1833 " 1836	Resigns.
Wyndham Robertson..........	1836 " 1837	Democrat.
David Campbell..........	1837 " 1840	
Thomas W. Gilmer..........	1840 " 1841	
John Rutherford..........	1841 " 1842	
John M. Gregory..........	1842 " 1843	
James McDowell..........	1843 " 1846	
William Smith..........	1846 " 1849	
John B. Floyd..........	1849 " 1851	
John Johnson..........	1851 " 1852	
Joseph Johnson..........	1852 " 1856	
Henry A. Wise..........	1856 " 1860	
John Letcher..........	1860 " 1864	Also governor under the Confederacy.
William Smith..........	1864 " 1865	Confederate governor.
Francis A. Pierpont..........	1863 " 1867	
Henry A. Wells..........	1867 " 1869	Provisional governor. Resigns Sept. 1869.
Gilbert C. Walker..........	1869 " 1874	Provisional governor from Sept. 1869, to Jan. 1870.
James L. Kemper..........	1874 " 1878	Democrat. Maj.-gen. Confederate army.
F. W. M. Holliday..........	1878 " 1882	Democrat.
W. E. Cameron..........	1882 " 1886	Readjuster Democrat.
Fitz-Hugh Lee..........	1886 " 1890	
Philip W. McKinney..........	1890 " 1894	
Charles T. O'Ferrall..........	1894 " 1898	Democrat.

UNITED STATES SENATORS FROM THE STATE OF VIRGINIA.

Name.	No. of Congress.	Date.	Remarks.
Richard Henry Lee	1st to 2d	1789 to 1792	President *pro tem.* 18 Apr. 1792. Resigned 1792.
William Grayson	1st	1789 " 1790	Died 1790.
John Walker	1st	1790	Appointed *pro tem.* in place of Grayson.
James Monroe	1st to 4th	1790 to 1795	Elected in place of Grayson.
John Taylor	2d " 3d	1792 " 1794	Elected in place of Lee. Resigned 1794.
Henry Tazewell	3d " 5th	1794 " 1799	Elected in place of Taylor; president *pro tem.* 7 Dec. 1795; died 1799.
Stevens Thomson Mason	4th " 8th	1795 " 1803	Died 1803.
Wilson Cary Nicholas	6th " 8th	1800 " 1804	Resigned 1804.
Andrew Moore	8th " 11th	1804 " 1809	
William B. Giles	8th " 14th	1804 " 1815	Resigned 1815.
John Taylor	8th	1803	Appointed *pro tem.* in place of Mason.
Abraham B. Venable	8th	1803 to 1804	Resigned 1804.
Richard Brent	11th to 13th	1809 " 1814	Died in office 1814.
James Barbour	13th " 19th	1815 " 1825	President *pro tem.* 15 Feb. 1819. Resigned 1825.
Armistead T. Mason	14th	1816 " 1817	Elected in place of Giles.
John W. Eppes	15th	1817 " 1819	Resigned 1819.
James Pleasants	16th to 17th	1819 " 1822	Elected in place of Eppes. Resigned 1822.
John Taylor	17th " 18th	1822 " 1824	Elected in place of Pleasants. Died 1824.
Littleton W. Tazewell	18th " 22d	1824 " 1832	Elected in place of Taylor. President *pro tem.* 9 July, 1832. Resigned 1832.
John Randolph	19th " 20th	1825 " 1827	Elected in place of Barbour.
John Tyler	20th " 24th	1827 " 1836	Defeated Randolph for the Senate. President *pro tem.* 3 Mch. 1835. Resigned 1836.
William C. Rives	22d " 23d	1833 " 1834	Resigned 1834.
Benjamin W. Leigh	23d " 24th	1834 " 1836	Elected in place of Rives. Resigned 1836.
Richard E. Parker	24th " 25th	1836 " 1837	Elected in place of Leigh. " 1837.
William C. Rives	24th " 29th	1836 " 1845	Elected in place of Tyler.
William H. Roane	25th " 27th	1837 " 1841	Elected in place of Parker.
William S. Archer	27th " 30th	1841 " 1847	
Isaac S. Pennybacker	29th " 30th	1845 " 1847	
James M. Mason	29th " 37th	1847 " 1861	Elected in place of Pennybacker; president *pro tem.* 6 Jan. and 4 Mch. 1857; expelled July, 1861.
Robert M. T. Hunter	30th " 37th	1847 " 1861	Expelled July, 1861.
John S. Carlile	37th	1861	Elected in place of Hunter.
Waiteman T. Willey	37th	1861 to 1863	Elected in place of Mason.
John J. Bowden	38th	1863 " 1864	Died.
39th and 40th Congresses vacant.			
John W. Johnston	41st	1870 to 1883	
John F. Lewis	41st to 44th	1870 " 1875	
Robert E. Withers	44th " 47th	1875 " 1881	
William Mahone	47th " 50th	1881 " 1887	
H. H. Riddleberger	48th " 51st	1883 " 1889	
John W. Daniel	50th " ——	1887 " ——	Term expires 1899.
John S. Barbour	51st " 52d	1889 " 1892	Died 1892.
Eppa Hunton	52d " 54th	1892 " 1895	
Thomas S. Martin	54th " ——	1895 " ——	Term expires 1901.

Virginius. UNITED STATES, Oct.-Dec. 1873.

Visconti (*vis-con'tī*), a noble Italian family, which ruled in Milan from about 1277 to 1447; the heiress of the family married Francesco Sforza, who became duke 1450.

viscount (*vī'count*) (*Vice Comes*), anciently the deputy of an earl. The first viscount in England created by patent was John, lord Beaumont, whom Henry VI. created viscount Beaumont, giving him precedence above all barons, 10 Feb. 1440.—*Ashmole.* This title is of older date in Ireland and France. John Barry, lord Barry, was made viscount Buttevant, in Ireland, 9 Rich. II. 1385.—*Beatson.*

Vish'nu, the second person of the Hindu triad sustaining the rôle of Preserver. In the earlier Vedas he appears as a manifestation of the sun. When necessary in certain crises he assumes the human form and preserves by his power the human race.

visible speech, as Alex. Melville Bell calls his "Universal Self-Interpreting Physiological Alphabet," comprises 30 symbols representing the forms of the mouth when uttering sounds. About 50 symbols, he asserts, would be required to represent the sounds of all known languages. He expounded his system to the Society of Arts, London, 14 Mch. 1866, and published a book in 1867.

Visigoths, or western Goths, separated from the Ostrogoths about 330. GOTHS. The emperor Valens, about 369, allowed them to cross the Danube and settle in Roman territories on condition of serving when wanted in the Roman armies; and Theodosius the Great permitted them to form distinct corps with their own officers. In 400, under Alaric, they invaded Italy, and though at first defeated by Stilicho, they took Rome, 410. They founded the kingdom of Toulouse, 414; conquered the ALANI, and extended their rule into Spain, 414, which they occupied until conquered by the Saracens under Muza, 711, when their last king, Roderic, was defeated and slain. SPAIN. Their rule in France ended with their defeat by Clovis at Vouglé, 507.

vital force, defined by Humboldt as "an unknown cause preventing the elements from obeying primitive affinities." This theory is rejected by many physiologists, and animal motion is attributed to muscular and nervous irritability, illustrated by the researches of Galvani, Humboldt, sir Charles Bell, Marshall Hall, and others. The subject is fully discussed by Huxley and other physiologists.

Vitto'ria, a town of N. Spain, the site of a victory of Wellington over the French armies of Joseph Bonaparte, king of Spain, and marshal Jourdan, 21 June, 1813. The hostile armies were nearly equal, from 70,000 to 75,000 each. After a long struggle, the French were driven, towards evening, through the town of Vittoria, and were thrown into irretrievable confusion. The British loss was 22 officers and 479 men killed; 167 officers and 2640 men wounded. Marshal Jourdan lost 151 pieces of cannon, 451 wagons of ammunition, his baggage, provisions, cattle, and treasure, with his baton as a marshal of France. Continuing the pursuit on the 25th, Wellington took Jourdan's only remaining gun.

vivisec'tion (Lat. *vivus*, alive, and *secare*, to cut), the dissection of living subjects. Physiological experiments upon living animals having much increased, societies for the prevention of cruelty to animals in Dresden and Paris in 1859 asked of several eminent scientific men the value of knowledge thus acquired. Their judgment was not unanimous. The London society took up the question in 1860, and printed a pamphlet by G. Macilwain against vivisection. In Aug. 1862, an international conference to discuss the question was held at the Crystal palace, Sydenham. After another discussion in 1866, a prize was awarded by the London society. Sir Charles Bell's opinion of vivisection was that it either obscured the subject it was meant to illustrate, or misled men into serious practical errors. But of late years discoveries of vast importance in the treatment of disease have been made by experiments on living organisms, and scientific opinion is practically unanimous that this method is valuable and indispensable to the progressive art of healing, though so liable to abuse that it ought to be practised with caution and limited by necessity.

Discussion revived by prosecution of dr. Schiff in Florence, who justified vivisection under anæsthetics.............1873-76

Rival societies: 1. Society for the Abolition of Vivisection,

1875; 2. International Association for Total Suppression of Vivisection.. 1876

[Commission (viscount Cardwell, prof. Huxley, and others) to inquire into the practice, appointed 23 June, 1875; report signed, 8 Jan.; pub. Mch. 1876; bill to regulate vivisection (Cruelty to Animals act) introduced in Parliament; opposed by the medical profession, June, July; passed, 15 Aug. 1876. Vivisectors to have a license or certificate.]

Resolutions in favor of vivisection, by the International Medical congress, London..............................9 Aug. 1881

Prof. Ferrier (who experimented on brains of monkeys under anæsthetics) and others prosecuted; no conviction.....Nov. "

Dr. Koch of Berlin demonstrates the cause of tubercular disease to be minute organisms termed bacilli................ 1882

Bill before the British Parliament to prohibit vivisection talked out...4 Apr. 1883

Four hundred and forty-one experiments in Great Britain in.. 1884

Instructed by dr. Ferrier's vivisection experiments, dr. Hughes Bennett localizes in a man's brain a tumor, which is removed by dr. Godlee..............................25 Nov. "

One thousand and sixty-nine experiments in Great Britain in 1888

Dr. Nicolaier, a German, experiments with live animals, inoculating them for tetanus (lock-jaw), 1884; further discoveries in dr. Koch's laboratory at Berlin, and at Bologna by prof. Tizzoni and Cattani.. 1889

[These and all other investigations in this direction place it beyond doubt that all forms of tetanus are due to the drum-stick-shaped bacillus of Nicolaier.]

Pasteur's experiments with animals inoculated for hydrophobia result in a cure for it..................................1885-90

MEDICAL SCIENCE.

vizier', grand, an officer of the Porte, said to have been first appointed by Amurath I., about 1386. The office was abolished in 1838, but has since been frequently revived and suppressed.

volapük (*vo-la-pük'*), from 2 words in the new language: *vol*, world, universe, and *puk*, speech, discourse, etc. An attempt to form a universal language by Johann M. Schleyer, a German teacher at Constance, Germany, about 1879, by a selection of words or roots from most of the modern European languages, and from Latin. Its peculiarities are: (1) Alphabet consists of 27 letters, 8 vowels and 19 consonants. (2) Each letter has but one sound. (3) Consonants are sounded as in English, except *c* and *j*; *g* is always hard, and *h* is an aspirate. (4) Accent invariably on the last syllable. (5) One conjugation and no irregular verbs. (6) All word forms and inflections are regular. (7) Adjectives, verbs, and adverbs regularly formed from substantives. (8) *w* becomes *v*, and *l* is substituted for *r*. (9) Words are as far as possible reduced to one syllable. (10) Nouns have one declension and 4 cases. (11) Adjectives are formed by adding *ik* to the substantive, and adverbs by adding *o* to the adjective, as *fam*, glory; *famik*, glorious; and *famiko*, gloriously. It was adopted for international correspondence by many business houses, and schools of volapük were opened in many cities; but it is now nearly forgotten.

volca'no (Ital., from Lat. *Volcanus*, Vulcan, god of fire), originally the name of Etna, in which Roman mythology placed the forge where Vulcan wrought the thunderbolts of Jupiter; later a general name for a mountain with a crater or opening into a mass of molten rock within the earth. Such mountains are widely distributed over the globe, but are mostly near the sea. They are very variable in activity, and usually intermittent; sometimes quiet for many years or even centuries, and again extremely violent, throwing high in the air vast columns of smoke and fire with cinders, and pouring through crevices streams of lava or melted rocks, which at times cover large tracts of land. Many volcanoes, once active, have been quiescent from the dawn of history. The following is a list of active and extinct volcanoes located by groups. Under the 2 systems of central and linear, the former consisting of several vents grouped together, but one of which is usually in eruption at any one time. The latter system consists of vents extending in one direction along a range of mountains, as the Andes in South America, and extending into North America as the Rocky Mountains. Some, long regarded as extinct, have suddenly become active.

CENTRAL SYSTEM—GROUPS.

Name of group.	No.	Remarks.
MEDITERRANEAN SEA.		
I. ETNA, Sicily........	1	Active.
II. VESUVIUS, Italy	1	"
III. Lipari islands......	2	Stromboli the principal, always active, called the Light-house of the Mediterranean.
ATLANTIC OCEAN.		
IV. Jan Mayen island...	2	Active. Most northern volcanoes on the globe. Lat. 70° 49′ N.
V. Iceland	8	HECLA the principal. All active.
VI. Azores............	2	1 active.
VII. Canary islands.....	5	" (Teneriffe quiet.)
VIII. Cape Verde islands.	1	Active.
IX. Ascension "	1	
X. Tristan d'Acunha islands.........	1	
XI. Trinidad island.....	1	
XII. Traverse isles......	2	1 active.
INDIAN OCEAN.		
XIII. Mauritius and Bourbon isles........	3	1 active.
PACIFIC OCEAN.		
XIV. Hawaii archipelago.	4	3 active. Mauna Loa the principal.
XV. Galapagos islands...	1	Active.
XVI. Marquesas " ...	1	
XVII. Society " ...	1	
XVIII. Easter " ...	1	
WESTERN ASIA.		
XIX. El Burs, Ararat, etc.	3	1 active.
EASTERN AFRICA.		
XX. Zanguebar	2	

LINEAR SYSTEM—GROUPS.

Name of group.	No.	Remarks.
MEDITERRANEAN SEA.		
I. Santorini, Gr. islands	1	Active.
ASIA.		
II. Thian-Shan	2	Active.
III. Red sea............	2	1 active.
IV. Kamtchatka	21	All active.
PACIFIC OCEAN, SOUTH.		
V. Friendly isles	4	2 active.
VI. Australasian isles...	13	All active.
PACIFIC OCEAN, NORTH.		
VII. Moluccas, Philippine, Formosa...	37	At least 25 active.
VIII. Ladrone isles......	7	3 active.
IX. Bonin Sima isles....	2	Active.
X. Japan.............	23	From 15 to 19 active.
XI. Kurile isles	18	11 active.
XII. Aleutian isles.......	35	23 "
INDIAN OCEAN, SUNDA.		
XIII. Sunda isles.........	80	47 are on the island of Java, 16 of them active, and 7 on the island of Sumatra. On the island of Krakatoa the greatest eruption of modern times occurred, 26-28 Aug. 1883. JAVA.
AMERICA.		
XIV. North Pacific coast..	10	4 active.
XV. Mexico............	[illegible]	5 "
XVI. Central	36	25 "
XVII. West Indies........	10	7 "
XVIII. South, Quito........	17	10 "
XIX. " Peru and Bolivia	12	9 " Highest in the world.
XX. " Chili	22	17 "
XXI. Terra del Fuego	3	
XXII. Antarctic continent.	3	Active. Erebus, on Victoria Land, 77° 32′ S. lat., is the most southern volcano known.
	408	

Volsci (*wols'kee* or *vol'sē*), an ancient Latin people, frequently at war with the Romans. From their capital, Corioli, Caius Martius (who defeated them about 490 B.C.) derived his name Coriolanus. The legend of his banishment by his ungrateful countrymen, of his revenge by bringing the Volsci to the gates of Rome, yet afterwards sparing the city at the entreaties of his mother Volumnia (487 B.C.), is immortalized in Shakespeare's tragedy of "Coriolanus." The Volsci and their allies were subdued at Sutrium by the consul Valerius Corvus (346 B.C.), and incorporated with the Roman people about 338 B.C.

voltaic pile or **battery** was constructed by Galvani. GALVANISM under ELECTRICITY. The principle was discovered by Alessandro Volta, of Como (b. 1745), for 30 years professor of natural philosophy at Pavia, and announced by him to the Royal Society of London in 1793. The battery was first set up in 1800. Volta was made an Italian count and senator by Napoleon Bonaparte, and was greatly honored. While young he invented the electrophorus, electric pistol, hydrogen lamp. He died in 1826, aged 81. The form of voltaic battery has been greatly improved by recent electricians. The nitric-acid battery of sir W. R. Grove was constructed in 1839; Alfred Smee's battery in 1840; the carbon battery of prof. Robert Bunsen in 1842. Grove's is best known in England; Bunsen's on the European continent. COPPER.

voluntary contributions, public and private, to the United States government during the civil war, 1861–1865, were not less than $500,000,000.—*Greeley's* "American Conflict," vol. ii. appended notes ii. This came in all amounts, from one cent up to Cornelius Vanderbilt's gift of a fully equipped war-steamer valued at $800,000. JOHNSTOWN FLOOD, SANITARY COMMISSION, etc.

volunteers. ARMY, UNITED STATES.

vote. POPULAR VOTE; for electoral, UNITED STATES.

Vouglé or **Vouillé** (*vool-ya'*), a town of S.W. France, near Poitiers, where Alaric II., king of the Visigoths, was defeated and slain by Clovis, king of France, 507, who subdued the whole country from the Loire to the Pyrenees. Peace followed between the Franks and Visigoths, who had been settled above 100 years in that part of Gaul called Septimania. Clovis soon after made Paris his capital.

voyages. AMERICA, CIRCUMNAVIGATORS, EXPEDITIONS, NORTHEAST AND NORTHWEST PASSAGES, etc.

Vul'can (Lat. *Volcanus*), the Roman god of fire and the worker of metals, the same with Hephæstus of the Greeks; according to Homer, the son of Zeus and Hērē. Vulcan is the "Tubal-Cain" of heathen mythology.—This name has also been given to a conjectural planet between the orbit of Mercury and the sun; first reported by M. Lescorbault, a physician of Orgeres, France, 26 Mch. 1859. The French astronomer Le Verrier accepted it, but nothing has been seen of it by other astronomers.

Vul'gate (from *vulgatus*, published), a term applied to the Latin version of the Scriptures which is authorized by the council of Trent (1546), and which is attributed to St. Jerome, about 384. The older version, called the Italic, is said to have been made in the beginning of the 2d century. A critical edition was printed by order of pope Sixtus V. in 1590, which, being considered inaccurate, was superseded by the edition of pope Clement V. in 1592. The earliest printed Vulgate is without date, by Gutenberg and Faust, probably about 1455; the first dated (Faust and Schöffer) is 1462. BIBLE.

W

W, the 23d letter and 18th consonant of the English alphabet. It began to be used in the 11th century, and owes its origin to the upsilon of the Greeks. It was made by doubling the u or v sign.

"Wacht des Deutschen Vaterlands" ("Watch of the German Fatherland"). German national hymn, by Reichardt, first performed 2 Aug. 1825. Very popular during the war 1870–71.

Wadai, Sultanate of, [illegible] present the most powerful state in Central Soudan, and occupies, with its tributary states, the whole region between Dar-Fur and lake Chad, and from the southern verge of the Sahara southward to the divide, between lake Chad and the Congo basin. Area, 172,000 sq. miles; pop. 2,600,000.

wager of battle. APPEAL.

wages, earnings of persons in the employment of others. —*Atkinson.* The purchasing power of money, cost of living, etc., cannot be excluded in considering the subject of wages. On comparing wages now customary, with those formerly paid, it will be seen that they have materially increased, especially in the United States, while the average price of provisions has remained about the same; some articles as beef, potatoes, apples, butter, eggs, milk, and coffee, being dearer, while the cereals, sugar, and tea, are cheaper. The following tables show the facts in detail.

COMPARISON OF AVERAGE WAGES PAID PER DAY IN THE UNITED STATES FOR THE YEARS 1800, 1840, 1890, IN THE OCCUPATIONS MENTIONED.

	Blacksmiths.	Carpenters.	Laborers: Farm, etc.	Masons, bricklayers, plasterers.	House painters.	Plumbers.	Printers.	Weavers.	Tailors.	Shoemakers.
1800	$0.75	$1.00	$0.60	$1.00	$1.00	....	$1.00	$0.50	$0.75	$0.75
1840	1.40	1.40	0.90	1.50	1.50	[illegible]	[illegible]	0.90	1.25	1.00
1890	2.50	2.60	1.50	3.00	2.50	[illegible]	2.25	1.50	2.00	2.00

COMPARISON OF THE PRICE OF PROVISIONS IN THE UNITED STATES FOR THE YEARS 1800, 1840, 1890, 1895.

	Beef.	Ham.	Pork.	Lard.	Corn-meal.	Rice.	Flour, wheat.	Potatoes.	Apples.	Beans.	Butter.	Cheese.	Eggs.	Milk.	Sugar.	Coffee.	Tea.
	per lb.	per lb.	per lb.	per lb.	per lb.	per lb.	per bl.	per bu.	per bu.	per qt.	per lb.	per lb.	per doz.	per qt.	per lb.	per lb.	per lb.
1800	$0.08	$0.12	$0.11	$0.13	$0.04	$0.06	$9.00	$0.50	$0.35	$0.05	$0.16	$0.14	$0.12	$0.04	$0.16	$0.27	$0.95
1840	0.09	0.11	0.09	0.10	0.02	0.05	7.00	0.60	0.80	0.07	0.18	0.10	0.16	0.05	0.11	0.20	0.75
1890	0.14	0.13	0.11	0.10	0.02	0.08	6.00	0.75	1.00	0.10	0.26	0.15	0.22	0.06	0.06	0.30	0.50
1895	0.14	0.13	0.11	0.10	0.02	0.08	4.50	0.75	1.00	0.08	0.26	0.15	0.22	0.06	0.045	0.30	0.50

Thus wages have increased more than 100 per cent. during the last 90 years. The progression of division of labor in large establishments prevents an exact comparison in many cases; but the instances recorded represent a fair average concerning the wages of the skilled artisan and common laborer. "A man who performed what is now called unskilled labor—sawing wood, digging ditches, mixing mortar, cutting hay, etc.—received 2*s.* or 25 cents per day in 1784, yet the pay was twice as great as in 1774."—*McMaster's* "Hist. U. S.," vol. i. p. 96. "Hours of labor from sunrise to sunset, at 40 cents per day, in 1800; or by the month, $6 in the summer, and $5 in the winter, with board—$65 a year average, with board and perhaps lodging." —*Ibid.*, vol. ii. p. 617. "A few classes of artisans greatly in demand, as ship-carpenters, were paid $2 per day, 1810–20, but they were the exception."—*Ibid.*, vol. iii. p. 510.

Wa'gram, a village near Vienna, where Napoleon I. defeated the archduke Charles, 5, 6 July, 1809, with great slaughter on both sides; 20,000 Austrians were taken by the French, and the defeated army retired to Moravia. An armistice was signed on the 12th; and on 24 Oct., by a treaty of peace, Austria ceded all her sea-coast to France; the kingdoms of Saxony and Bavaria were enlarged at her expense; part of Galicia was ceded to Russia, and Joseph Bonaparte was recognized as king of Spain.

Waha'bees or **Waha'bites,** a warlike Mahometan reforming sect, claiming to be the only true followers of the prophet, established themselves in Arabia about 1750, under Abd-el-Wahab, who died 1787. His grandson, Saoud, in 1801, defeated an expedition headed by the caliph of Bagdad. In 1803 this sect seized Mecca and Medina, and continued their conquests, although their chief was assassinated in the midst of his victories. His son, Abdallah, long resisted Mahommed Ali, pacha of Egypt, but in 1818 was defeated and taken prisoner by Ibrahim Pacha, who sent him to Constantinople, where he was put to death. The sect, now flourishing, is described by W. Gifford Palgrave, in his "Journey and Residence in Arabia in 1862–63," published in 1865. It is influential in India, and is suspected of a tendency to insurrection.

waits, a name given in England to night minstrels who perform shortly before Christmas. The name was given to the musicians attached to the court of the king. A company of waits was established at Exeter in 1400 to "pipe the watch." The waits in London and Westminster were long officially recognized by the corporation.

Wakefield, W. Yorkshire, Engl. Near it a battle was fought between the adherents of Margaret, the queen of Henry VI., and the duke of York, in which the latter was slain, and 3000 Yorkists fell upon the field, 31 Dec. 1460. The earl of Warwick supported the cause of the duke's son, afterwards Edward IV., and the civil war was continued.

Wakefield estate, Va., on which Washington was born, about half a mile from the junction of Pope's creek with the Potomac, in Westmoreland county.

Wake island. The United States flag was hoisted over Wake island in Jan. 1899, by com. Taussig, of the *Bennington*, while proceeding to Guam. It is a small island in the direct route from Hawaii to Hong-Kong, about 2000 miles from the first and 3000 miles from the second. The United States possesses a number of scattered small islands in the Pacific Ocean, some hardly more than rocks or coral reefs. They are of little present value and mostly uninhabited. The largest are Christmas, Gallego, Starbuck, Penrhyn, Phœnix, Palmyra, Howland, Baker, Johnston, Gardner, Midway, Morell, and Marcus islands. The Midway islands are occupied by a colony of telegraphers in charge of the relay in the cable line connecting the Philippines with the United States and a camp of United States marines, in all about forty persons.

wakes. (1) The ancient parish festivals on the saint's day to commemorate the dedication of the church; regulated in 1536, but gradually became obsolete. (2) Watching with a dead body prior to burial, by friends and neighbors of the deceased. Custom formerly prevalent in Scotland and still in Ireland.

Walcheren, an island at the mouth of the Scheldt, Holland. The unfortunate expedition of the British to this isle in 1809 consisted of 35 ships of the line, 200 smaller vessels, 40,000 land forces, under the earl of Chatham, the fleet under sir Richard Strachan. Flushing was invested in Aug.; a bombardment followed, and the place was taken 15 Aug.; but neither the naval commander nor his own officers could drive the earl to vigorous action until the chance of success was gone, and he had to return with such troops as disease had spared. The place was evacuated 23 Dec. 1809.

Wal'denses (also called Valdenses, Vallenses, and Vaudois), a sect inhabiting the Cottian Alps, derive their name, according to some authors, from Peter de Waldo, of Lyons (1170). They were known, however, as early as 1100, their confession of faith published 1120. Their doctrine condemned by the council of Lateran, 1179. They had a translation of the Bible, and allied themselves to the ALBIGENSES, whose persecution led to the establishment of the Holy Office or Inquisition. The Waldenses settled in the valleys of Piedmont about 1375, but were frequently dreadfully persecuted, notably 1545–46, 1560, 1655–56, when Oliver Cromwell, by threats, obtained some degree of toleration for them; again in 1663–64 and 1686. They were permitted to have a church at Turin, Dec. 1853. In Mch. 1868, it was stated that there were in Italy 28 ordained Waldensian ministers and 80 other teachers. Early in 1893 a delegation was sent to the United States to investigate the advantages of forming a settlement in some favorable locality. It resulted in their purchasing several thousand acres of land in Burke county, N. C., and establishing a colony the same year, calling the place Waldese.

Wales, Cambria, Cymru, the land of the Cymry, called by the Romans *Britannia Secunda*. Welsh and Wales are corruptions of Teutonic epithets of foreigners, especially Gauls. After the Roman emperor Honorius gave up Britain, Vortigern was elected king of South Britain. He invited the Saxons over to defend his country against the Picts and Scots; but the Saxons perfidiously sent for reinforcements, consisting of Saxons, Danes, and Angles, and made themselves masters of South Britain. Many of the Britons retired to W. defended against the Saxons their inaccessible mou. about 447. Thus Wales remained unconquered till Henr. subdued South Wales in 1157; and in 1282 Edward I. redu the whole country, its independence ending by the death o Llewelyn, the last prince. In 1284 the queen gave birth to a son at Caernarvon, whom Edward styled prince of Wales—a title since given to the heir-apparent to the crown of Great Britain. Wales was incorporated with England by act of Parliament, 1536. Area, 7363 sq. miles, in 12 counties; pop. 1891, 1,518,914. BARDS, BRITAIN.

	A. D.
Ostorius Scapula, propraetor of Britain, defeats the Cymry....	50
Supreme authority in *Britannica Secunda* intrusted to Suetonius Paulinus, who causes desolating wars..................	58–61
Conquests by Julius Frontinus..................	70
Silures totally defeated..................	"
Roman Julius Agricola commands in Britain..................	78
Bran ab Llyr, the Blessed, dies about..................	80
Druidical class gradually dissolved by the influence of Christianity in..................	300–400
Britons defeat the Saxons..................	447–448
Vortigern king..................	"
Renowned Arthur elected king..................about	500
Defeats Saxons..................about	527
Cadwallawn, king of Gwynedd, defeated and slain by the Saxons at Denisburn..................about	634
Dyvnwal Moelmud, from Armorica, said to have reigned west of the Tamar and Severn over the Cymry..................about	640
Reign of Roderic the Great..................	844
He unites the petty states into one principality; d..................	877
Division of Wales—into north, south, and central (or Powysland)..................	"
Welsh princes submit to Alfred..................	885
Danes land in Anglesey..................	900
Laws enacted by Howel Dha, prince of all Wales..................about	920
Athelstan subdues the Welsh..................	933
Civil wars at his death..................about	948
Sons of Howel Dha defeated by sons of Idwal Voel..................	954
Edgar invades Wales..................about	973
Devastations committed by Edwin, the son of Eincon..................	980
Danes invade Wales; lay Anglesey waste, etc..................	980–1000
Country reduced by Aedan, prince of North Wales..................	"
Aedan, the usurper, slain in battle by Llewelyn..................	1015
Part of Wales laid waste by the forces of Harold..................	1063
William I. claims feudal authority over Wales..................	1070
Rhys ab Owain kills king Bleddyn, 1073; defeated and slain...	1077
Ravaging invasion of Hugh, earl of Chester..................	1079–80
Invasion of the Irish and Scots..................	1080
William I. invades Wales..................	1081
Battle of Llechryd..................	1087
[The sons of Bleddyn ab Cynvyn were slain by Rhys ab Tewdwr, the reigning prince.]	
Rhys ab Tewdwr slain; S. Wales conquered by the English....	1090
Invasion of the English under William II..................	1095–97
Settlement in Wales of a colony of Flemings..................	1106
Nest, wife of Gerald de Windsor, seized by Owain, son of Cadwgan ab Bleddyn..................	1108
Cardigan conquered by Strongbow..................	1109
Cadwgan assassinated..................	1112
Gruffydd ab Rhys lays claim to the sovereignty..................	1113
Another body of Flemings settle in Pembrokeshire..................	"
[Their posterity differ from the true British in language, manners, and customs.]	
Civil war in South Wales and Powysland; the English occupy the country; Henry I. erects castles in Wales..................	1114 et seq.
Owain killed in battle with Gerald de Windsor..................	1116
Revolt of Owen Gwynedd on the death of Henry I.; part of South Wales laid waste..................	1135
English defeated in several battles..................	1136
Strongbow, earl of Pembroke, invested with the powers of a count palatine in Pembroke..................	1138
Henry II. invades Wales; resisted by Owen Gwynedd; subdues South Wales..................	1157
Princes of Wales combine to recover independence..................	1164
Prince Madoc said to have emigrated to America..................about	1169
Anglesey devastated..................	1173
Crusades preached by Baldwin, archbishop of Canterbury.....	1188
Earl of Chester's inroad into North Wales..................	1210
King John invades Wales, laying waste a great part; exacts tribute and allegiance..................	1211
Pope incites the Welsh to resist John..................	1212
Revolt of the Flemings..................	1220
Llewelyn, prince of North Wales, commits great ravages; repulses Henry III..................	1228
Earl of Pembroke and other nobles join Llewelyn against Henry III., 1233; a truce..................	1234
Prince David ravages the marches, etc..................	1244
Invasion of Henry III..................	1245
Anglesey cruelly devastated by the English..................Sept.	"
Llewelyn ap Griffith, the last prince..................	1246
Welsh princes combine against the English..................	1256
Invasion by the English, who retreat with loss..................	1257
Welsh offers of peace refused..................	1257–62
Llewelyn's incursions into English territory..................	1263
Reported conference between him and Simon de Montfort against the Plantagenets..................	1265
Llewelyn does homage to Henry III. for a treaty..................Sept.	1267

. summons Llewelyn to Westminster, on his refusal, ...es him, 1276, and invades Wales June, 1277
...lyn submits and obtains good terms 10 Nov "
...marries Eleanor de Montfort 13 Oct. "
...ns of Gruffydd treacherously drowned in the Dee by earl Warrenne and Roger Mortimer, insurrection 1281
Hawarden castle taken by surprise by Llewelyn and his brother David, 21 Mch , they destroy Flint and Rhuddlan castles Fruitless negotiations Nov 1282
Battle between Llewelyn and the English near Aber Edw, Llewelyn slain, after the battle by Adam Frankton 11 Dec "
Prince David surrenders, and is executed 1283
Wales finally subdued by Edward I "
First English prince of Wales, son of Edward, born at Caernarvon castle 25 Apr 1284
Statute of Wales enacted 19 Mch "
Insurrections suppressed and leaders executed 1287-1320
Owain Glyndwr or Owen Glendower (descendant of the last prince, Llewelyn), rebels 1400
Radnor and other places taken by Owain Glyndwr 1401
Allies with Scots and the Percies, besieges Caernarvon 1402
And seizes Harlech castle 1404
Makes a treaty with France 10 May, "
Harlech castle retaken by the English forces 1407
Loses his allies by their defeat at Branham moor 19 Feb 1408
Ravages the English territories 1409
Refuses to ask for terms or submit, d 21 Sept 1415
His son submits 24 Feb 1416
Margaret of Anjou, queen of Henry VI , takes refuge in Harlech castle 1459
Town of Denbigh burned 1460
Earl of Richmond afterwards Henry VII , lands in Pembroke, and is aided by the Welsh Aug 1485
Palatine jurisdictions in Wales abolished by Henry VIII 1535
Monmouth made an English county, counties of Brecknock, Denbigh, and Radnor formed "
Act for "laws and justice to be administered in Wales in same form as in England," 27 Hen VIII "
Wales incorporated into England by Parliament 1536
Divided into 12 counties 1543
Dr Ferrar, bishop of St David's burned for heresy 30 Mch 1555
Lewis Owain, a baron of the exchequer, attacked and murdered on his assize tour "
Bible and prayer book ordered translated into Welsh, and divine service to be in that language 1562
Welsh Bible printed 1588
First congregation of dissenters assembled in Wales, Vavasour Powel apprehended while preaching 1620
Beaumaris castle garrisoned for king Charles I 1642
Powys castle taken by sir Thomas Myddelton Oct 1644
Dr Laud, formerly bishop of St David's beheaded on Tower hill 10 Jan 1645
Surrender of Hawarden castle to parliament general Mytton "
Charles I takes refuge in Denbigh . "
Rhuddlan castle surrenders "
Harlech castle surrenders to Cromwell's army under Mytton 1647
Battle of St Fagan's, the Welsh defeated by col Horton, Cromwell's lieutenant 8 May, 1648
Beaumaris castle surrenders to Cromwell "
Pembroke castle taken 1649
Lords marchers' court suppressed 1688
"Charitable Society of Ancient Britons" and Welsh charity schools, established (now at Ashford) 1715
Cymmrodorion Society (charitable) established 1751-81
French land in Pembrokeshire, and are made prisoners Feb 1797
Rebecca or "Becca" riots against toll gates, Feb., an old woman, a toll keeper, murdered, 10 Sept., many persons tried and punished Oct. 1843
Cambrian Archæological Association founded 1846
Subscriptions begun for a university in Wales Dec 1863
National unsectarian university college at Aberystwyth opened, 9 Oct. 1872
Cymmrodorion Society, to promote literature and art, re-established 1877
"Rebecca" riots, people of Rhayader on the Wye capture fish illegally and resist water bailiffs. Dec 1878–Jan 1879
National council of Wales meets at Aberystwyth, advocates disestablishment and disendowment of the church, home rule, etc 7 Oct. 1887
Mr Dillwyn's motion for disestablishment of church in Wales rejected by the commons (284-231) 14 May, 1889
Tithes collected by the help of the military Aug 1890
Proposed disestablishment of the church in Wales negatived by the commons (235-203), 20 Feb 1891, and again (267-220), 23 Feb 1892

SOVEREIGNS OF WALES

630 Cadwallawn, king of Gwynedd
634 Cadwaladyr, his son
661 Idwal, son
728 Rhodri, or Roderic, heroic defender
755. Cynan and Howel, sons, incessant war
818. Mervyn, son in law and Essylt (wife).
844 Roderic the Great, son

PRINCES OF GWYNEDD, OR NORTH WALES, AND FREQUENTLY OF ALL WALES

877 Anarawd, son of Roderic
915. Idwal Voel
943 Howel Dha the Good, prince of all Wales.
948 Iefan and Iago, sons of Idwal

972 Howel ap Iefan, the Bad
984 Cadwallon, brother
985 Meredith ap Owen ap Howel Dha.
992 Idwal ap Meyric ap Edwal Voel, able, brave.
998 Aedan, a usurper
1015 Llewelyn ap Sitsyllt, good sovereign
1023 Iago ap Idwal ap Meyric
1039 Griffith ap Llewelyn ap Sitsyllt, killed
1067 Bleddyn
1073 Trahaern ap Caradoc
1079 Griffith ap Cynan, able, warlike, generous
1137 Owain Gwynedd, energetic, successful warrior
1169 Howell, son
" David ap Owain Gwynedd, brother, married sister of Henry II
1194 Llewelyn the Great.
1240 David ap Llewelyn
1246. Llewelyn ap Griffith, last prince of the blood, slain after battle, 11 Dec 1282

ENGLISH PRINCES OF WALES

1284. Edward Plantagenet (afterwards king Edward II), son of Edward I , born in Caernarvon castle on 25 Apr 1284 It is asserted that immediately after his birth the king held him in his arms before the Welsh chieftains as their future sovereign, saying, in the Welsh language "Eich Dyn," literally, "This is your man"—that is, "This is your countryman and king" ICH DIEN
1301 Edward of Caernarvon, made prince of Wales and earl of Chester
1343 Edward the Black Prince
1376 Richard his son (afterwards Richard II)
1399 Henry (afterwards Henry V) son of Henry IV
1454 Edward son of Henry VI , slain at Tewkesbury, 4 May, 1471
1471 Edward (afterwards Edward V), son of Edward IV
1483. Edward, son of Richard III , d 1484
1489 Arthur, son of Henry VII , d. 1502
1503 Henry, his brother (afterwards Henry VIII)
Edward, his son (afterwards Edward VI), was duke of Cornwall, and not prince of Wales.
1610 Henry Frederic, son of James I , d 6 Nov 1612.
1616. Charles, his brother (afterwards Charles I)
Charles, his son (afterwards Charles II), never created prince of Wales
1714. George Augustus (afterwards George II)
1729 Frederic Lewis, his son, d 20 Mch 1751
1751 George, his son (afterwards George III)
1762 George, his son (afterwards George IV), b 12 Aug
1841 Albert Edward, son of queen Victoria, b 9 Nov

Walhal'la. VALHALLA

Walker's expeditions. FILIBUSTERS.

Wallabout bay. NEW YORK, 1623

Walla'chia, one of the former DANUBIAN PRINCIPALITIES of Europe On 23 Dec 1861, the union of Wallachia and Moldavia, under the name of Roumania, was proclaimed at Jassy and Bucharest

Waller's plot. Edmund Waller, the poet, and others, conspired to disarm the London militia and let in the royalists, May, 1643 The plan was detected and punished, June–July, 1643 Waller betrayed his confederates, and was suffered to emigrate

Wallis's voyage. Capt Wallis sailed from England on his voyage round the world, 26 July, 1766, and returned to England, 19 May, 1768

Walloons', descendants of the ancient inhabitants of the Low Countries. Some of them fled to England from the persecution of the duke of Alva, the governor of the Low Countries for Philip II of Spain, 1566 A church was given to them by queen Elizabeth at Sandwich, and they still have one at Canterbury Their language is considered to be based on that of the ancient Gauls. NEW YORK, 1623

walls. HADRIAN'S, ROMAN and CHINESE.

Walpur'ga, Saint, traditional character of the 8th century, England and Germany. The name has been associated with noted popular German superstitions, as Walpurgis-Night, 30 Apr , 1 May, Witch's Sabbath meeting, with the devil as master of ceremonies. Famous from Goethe's "Faust"

" *Faust.* We climb the Brocken's top in the Walpurgis Night "
—*Goethe's* "Faust" (Taylor's translation)

waltz, the popular German national dance, was introduced into England by baron Neuman and others in 1813 —*Raikes.*

Wandering Jew. JEW, THE WANDERING

Wan'diwash, a town of S India Here the French, under Lally, were defeated by col Eyre Coote, 22 Jan 1760.

war, called by Erasmus "the malady of princes." Osymandyas of Egypt, the first warlike king, passed into Asia, and conquered Bactria, 2100 B.C —*Usher*

LIST OF MOST CELEBRATED WARS.

Name.	Continuance.	Results.	Principal battles.	Chief leaders.
	B.C.			
Trojan	1193–1184	Greeks capture Troy	Siege	Hector, Agamemnon.
Messenian	743–669	Sparta conquers Messenia.		
Persian-Grecian	504–469	Greece successfully resists Persia.	Marathon, Thermopylæ, Salamis, Platæa, Mycale	Miltiades, Leonidas, Themistocles, Pausanias, Leotychides—Greek.
Sacred 1st	595–586	Intestine Greek; without result.		
Sacred 2d	448–447			
Sacred 3d	357–346			
Peloponnesian	431–404	Lacedæmonians take Athens	Naval	Pericles, Alcibiades, Lysander.
Greco-Persian	334–331	Greece conquers Persia	Granicus, Issus, Arbela	Alexander the Great, Darius.
Samnite	343–290	Romans subjugate the Samnites	Caudine Forks, Sentinum	Fabius Maximus, Caius Pontius.
Punic, 1st, 2d, 3d	264–146	Romans destroy Carthage	Ticinus, Trebia, Thrasymenus, Cannæ, Metaurus, Zama	Fabius, Scipio, Hannibal.
Roman-Grecian	200–146	Rome subdues Greece	Cynoscephalæ, Pydna	Flaminius, Æmilius Paulus, Mummius, Perseus.
Jugurthine	112–106	Romans conquer Numidia		Metellus, Marius
Social	90–88	The Socii obtain right of Roman citizenship.		
Mithridatic	88–63	Mithridates defeated	Chæronea, Cabeira	Lucullus, Pompey, Sulla.
Gladiatorial	73–71	Gladiators defeated	Petelia	Spartacus, Crassus.
Gallic	58–51	Gaul conquered		Cæsar.
Civil, Roman	50–31	Establishment of the Roman empire	Pharsalia, Thapsus, Munda, Philippi, Actium	Pompey, Cæsar, Brutus, Cassius, Anthony, Augustus.
	A.D.			
Jewish	70	Jerusalem taken; temple destroyed	Siege	Titus.
Dacian	86–109	Country beyond the Danube conquered		Trajan.
Barbarian	410–553	Barbarians capture Rome and ravage Italy		Alaric, Genseric, Totila.
Saracen or Moslem	710–1492	Occupy Spain, but driven from France	Xeres, Tours, Tarifa, Grenada	Musa, Tarik, Charles Martel, Cid Rodrigo.
Crusades	1095–1291	Christians take Jerusalem and occupy ports of Sepia, but are finally driven out by the Moslems		CRUSADES.
Hundred Years, in France	1337–1453	English lose all their possessions in France but Calais, although France suffers sorely	Crécy, Calais taken, Poictiers, Agincourt	Edward III. of England; Edward, Black prince, of England; Henry V. of England.
Austro-Swiss	1385–1389	Swiss secure their independence	Sempach, Näfels	Arnold von Winckelried, Leopold II.
Hussite	1419–1436	Religious toleration	Prague	John Ziska, Sigismund.
Roses, England	1455–1485	House of York supplants House of Lancaster	St. Albans, Bloreheath, Wakefield, Towton, Barnet, Tewkesbury, Bosworth	Richard, duke of York; Edward, duke of York; earl of Warwick; queen Margaret; Henry VI.; Richard III.
Civil, in France	1562–1593	Edict of Nantes	Dreux, St. Denis, Jarnac, Moncontour, Ivry	Duke of Anjou, Henry III.; Henry IV., Condé.
Spanish, Netherlands	1567–1609	Netherlands made independent of Spain	Zutphen, Nieuport, sieges and naval	William I., prince of Orange; Maurice; duke of Alva; Alexander Farnese, duke of Parma.
Thirty Years	1618–1648	Freedom of religious faith. Peace of Westphalia	Dessau, Leipsic, 1–2, Lech, Lutzen, Nordlingen, 1–2	Gustavus Adolphus, Wallenstein, Tilly, Turenne.
Civil, in England	1642–1660	Establishment of the Commonwealth	Edgehill, Marston Moor, Naseby, Dunbar, Worcester.	Prince Rupert, Fairfax, Charles I., Cromwell.
Spanish Succession	1701–1714	Treaty of Utrecht	Blenheim, Ramillies, Turin, Oudenarde, Malplaquet	Duke of Marlborough, prince Eugene, marshal Tallard, marshal Villars.
Swedish-Russian	1700–1709	Defeat of Charles XII	Narva, Pultowa	Charles XII. of Sweden, Peter the Great of Russia.
Austrian Succession	1740–1748	Peace of Aix-la-Chapelle	Dettingen, Fontenoy, Placentia, Laffeldt	Marshal Saxe, George II. of England, duke of Cumberland.
Seven Years	1756–1763	Peace of Paris. Prussia holds part of Silesia	Prague, Kollin, Rosbach, Lissa, Torgau	Daun, Frederick the Great.
Revolution, American	1775–1783	Peace of Paris. Independence of the English colonies	Bunker Hill, Saratoga, Monmouth, Yorktown	Washington, Burgoyne, Clinton, Howe.
French Revolution	1792–1799	Successful resistance to the reinstatement of the Bourbons on the French throne	Valmy, Jemmapes, Wattignies, Loano, Lodi, Arcola, Pyramids	Kellermann, Dumouriez, Jourdan, Moreau, Hoche, Napoleon.
Napoleonic	1800–1815	Revives Europe and places France in the first position	Marengo, Trafalgar, Austerlitz, Jena, Eylau, Friedland, Wagram, Borodino, Leipsic, Ligny, Waterloo	Napoleon, Wellington, Nelson, Blucher, Alexander I., Francis I., and Frederic William III., etc.
United States-England	1812–1815	United States entirely independent of Great Britain	Mostly naval, with the exception of New Orleans.	
Greek of Independence	1821–1828	Independence of Greece secured	Navarino, naval.	
Mexican	1846–1847	Boundaries established	Buena Vista, Cerro Gordo, Capture of the City of Mexico	Taylor, Scott, Santa Aña.
Crimean	1854–1856	Peace of Paris	Alma, Balaklava, Inkermann, Malakhoff	Lord Raglan, marshal St. Arnaud, prince Menschikoff, gen. Canrobert.
Italian	**1859**	**Peace of Villafranca**	Magenta, Solferino	**Napoleon III., Victor Emmanuel, Francis Joseph I.**
Civil, United States	**1861–1865**	**Abolition of slavery**	Bull Run, Shiloh, Seven Days, Bull Run, 2d, Antietam, Murfreesborough, Chancellorsville, Vicksburg, Gettysburg, Chickamauga, Chattanooga, Virginia campaign, Atlanta campaign, etc.	**McClellan, Grant, Sherman, Sheridan, Thomas, Lee, Johnston.**
Seven Weeks	**1866**	**Prussia defeats Austria and becomes supreme in Germany.**	Königgrätz or Sadowa	**Marshal Benedek, William I.**
Franco-Prussian	**1870**	**Germans defeat French, take Paris, and add Alsace and Lorraine to Germany**	Wörth, Gravelotte, Sedan, Metz, Paris, etc.	**William I., Von Moltke, crown-prince Frederick, prince Frederick Charles, Napoleon III., MacMahon, Bazaine, Trochu.**
Russo-Turkish	**1877**	**Peace of San Stefano. Treaty of Berlin**	Plevna, Shipka Pass, Kars, etc.	**Grand duke Nicholas, Gourko, Skobeleff, Todleben, Osman Pacha, Mukhtar Pacha.**
Chinese-Japanese	**1894–1895**	**Treaty of Shimonoseki**	Japanese occupy Korea, Port Arthur, Wei-Hai-Wei, Nin-Chang.	**Count Oyama, prince Arisugawa, prince Komatsu.**

For a fuller account consult the nations mentioned. **ARMY, BATTLES.**

arbeck's insurrection. Perkin Warbeck, son of a Florentine Jew, to whom Edward IV. had stood godfather, was persuaded by Margaret, duchess of Burgundy, sister to Richard III., to personate her nephew Richard, Edward V.'s brother, which he did first in Ireland, where he landed, 1492. The imposture was discovered by Henry VII., 1493. Some writers have defended Warbeck's claims.

Warbeck attempts to land in Kent with 600 men; 169 are taken prisoners and executed.......................July, 1495
Recommended by the king of France to James IV. of Scotland, who gives him his kinswoman, lord Huntley's daughter, in marriage, when he assumes the title of Richard IV. James IV. invades England in his favor.......................... 1496
Leaves Scotland and goes to Bodmin in Cornwall, where 3000 join him..Sept. 1497
On the approach of Henry takes sanctuary at Beaulieu; surrenders; taken to London...........................Oct. "
Said to have been set in the stocks at Westminster and Cheapside, and sent to the Tower........................June, 1499
Accused of plotting with the earl of Warwick to escape by murdering the lieutenant, Aug.; the plot fails, and he is hanged at Tyburn, 23 Nov.; earl beheaded.........28 Nov. "

Wardian cases. In 1829 N. B. Ward, from observing a small fern and grass growing in a closed glass bottle, in which he had placed a chrysalis covered with moist earth, was led to construct his well-known closely glazed cases, which afford to plants light, heat, and moisture, and exclude deleterious gases, smoke, etc. They are particularly adapted for ferns. In 1833 they were first employed for the transmission of plants to Sydney, etc., with success, and prof. Faraday lectured on the subject, 1838.

War'saw, the metropolis of Poland up to 1772, now the capital of Russian Poland. The diet was transferred to this city from Cracow in 1566, and it became the seat of government in 1689. Pop. 1859, 162,777; 1900, 638,209.

Poles defeated in 3 days' battle by the Swedes......28-30 July, 1656
Alliance at Warsaw of Austria and Poland against Turkey, in pursuance of which John Sobieski assists in raising the siege of Vienna (Sept. following); signed............31 Mch. 1683
Warsaw surrenders to Charles XII........................... 1703
Treaty of Warsaw between Russia and Poland.........24 Feb. 1768
Russian garrison expelled with loss of 2000 killed and 500 wounded, and 36 pieces of cannon..................17 Apr. 1794
Poles defeated by the Russians at Maciejovice..........4 Oct. "
King of Prussia besieges Warsaw, July; compelled to raise the siege, Sept.; it is taken by the Russians..............Nov. "
Suwarrow, Russian general, after the destruction of Warsaw, cruelly butchers 30,000 Poles..........................4 Nov. "
Warsaw made a duchy and given to the house of Saxony, Aug. 1807
Duchy overrun by the Russians; Warsaw made the residence of a Russian viceroy....................................... 1813
Last Polish revolution at Warsaw begins..............29 Nov. 1830
Battle of Grochow, near Warsaw, the Russians driven back with the loss of 7000 men ....25 Feb. 1831
Battle of Warsaw; after 2 days' hard fighting the city capitulates, and is occupied by the Russians; Polish army retires towards Plock and Modlin.............................6-8 Sept. "
Czar meets the emperor of Austria and the regent of Prussia; no result......................................20-25 Oct. 1860
POLAND, 1861-65.

Wartburg, a castle in Saxony, N. Germany, where Luther was conveyed for safety by the elector Frederick after the diet of Worms, Apr. 1521, and translated the Bible into German.

Washington, a western frontier state of the United States, between lat. 45° 40′ and 49° N., and lon. 117° and 124° W., is bounded on the north by the strait of Juan de Fuca and British America, east by Idaho, south by Oregon, and west by the Pacific ocean. Area, 69,180 sq. miles. Pop. 1890, 349,390; 1900, 518,103. Capital, Olympia.

Juan Perez, in the ship *Santiago*, coasts the shore of Washington and discovers mount Olympus, 10-11 Aug. 1773
Bruno Heceta, at the head of a Spanish expedition, discovers the mouth of the Columbia river.. 1775
Strait of Juan de Fuca explored and named by capt. Meares after a Greek mariner of that name....................... 1788
Capt. Meares sails from Nootka southward, names mount Olympus, and discovers and names Shoal-water bay..5 July, "
Capt. Robert Gray discovers Gray harbor, which he names Bulfinch harbor, and Columbia river, which he enters...11 May, 1792
Lieut. Broughton, of the British navy, ascends Columbia river about 100 miles....................................Oct.-Nov. "
Lewis and Clarke U. S. government exploring expedition descends the Columbia river, reaching its mouth.......5 Nov. 1805
Capt. Meriwether Lewis explores the coast from Columbia river to Shoalwater bay....................................18 Nov. "
Fort Okanagan, built by David Stuart on the Okanagan, a branch of the Columbia..................................Aug. 1811
Pierre Dorion and 2 others massacred by Indians on the Snake river...Jan. 1814
Fort Walla Walla, on the Columbia river, built by the Hudson Bay company... 1818
Exploring party under James McMillan leaves Astoria, 18 Nov. 1824; ascends the Chehalis river to Black river, thence to Tumwater lake; thence by an Indian portage it descends the Eld inlet to Puget sound.........................Dec. 1824
Convention with Russia at St. Petersburg, 5-7 Apr. 1824, regulating fishing and trading on the Pacific coast, and fixing 54° 40′ as the northern boundary of the U. S.; ratified...12 Jan. 1825
Fort Colville built by Hudson Bay company at Kettle falls, on the Columbia .... "
Nathaniel J. Wyeth, with 21 men, starts from Boston overland for Oregon, and with a remnant of his party descends the Columbia, arriving at fort Vancouver................29 Oct. 1832
Fort Nisqually built by Archibald McDonald 4 or 5 miles from the mouth of the Nisqually river.......................... 1833
Mission station established at Waiilatpu, near Walla Walla, by the revs. Whitman, Spalding, and Gray...................... 1835
Lieut. R. E. Johnson, of the U. S. exploring expedition, with 3 men from Nisqually, visits forts Okanagan, Colville, Lapwai, and Walla Walla, and returns by Yakima river....May-July, 1841
Michael T. Simmons, with 5 families, settles at Tumwater, at the head of Budd inlet, naming it New Market..........Oct. 1845
Congress notifies Great Britain that the conventions of 1818 and 1827, for joint occupation of Oregon territory (including Washington) will terminate after 12 months..........9 Feb. 1846
Smithfield, afterwards (1850) Olympia, founded by Levi L. Smith.. "
Indian massacre at the Presbyterian mission at Waiilatpu; dr. M. Whitman and family killed......................29 Nov. 1847
Fort Steilacoom, on Puget sound, established............July, 1849
Convention of 26 delegates at Cowlitz landing memorializes Congress for a separate government for "Columbia" (Oregon north of the Columbia)..............................29 Aug. 1851
Seattle founded; named from a noted Indian chief........... 1852
Coal discovered near Bellingham bay by William Pattle...... "
First number of the *Columbian*, a weekly newspaper, issued at Olympia..11 Sept. "
Congress establishes a territorial government for Washington (Oregon north of the Columbia), and confirms titles of lands held by missionary stations before the establishment of Oregon, not exceeding 640 acres each, to their religious societies, 2 Mch. 1853
T. J. Dryer and party ascend mount St. Helen, which they discover to be an expiring volcano............................ "
Wagon road opened over the Cascade mountains, and 35 wagons, with 100 or 200 emigrants, reach Puget sound.......... "
I. I. Stevens, appointed governor of the territory, arrives at Olympia, 26 Nov., and organizes the government....28 Nov. "
First Federal court held in Washington at Cowlitz landing by judge Monroe......................................2 Jan. 1854
Treaty at Point Elliott, near the mouth of Snohomish river, with 2500 Indians, agreeing upon a reservation on the Lumini river, 22 Jan., and later with the tribes farther north, selecting a reservation about the head of Hood canal.........Jan. "
Capital fixed at Olympia by act of legislature................. "
Gold discovered near fort Colville................................ 1855
Treaty with the Nez Percés, Cayuses, Walla Wallas, and Yakimas at Waiilatpu, by commissioners from gov. Stevens..11 June, "
Indian war begins; Indians attack 84 soldiers under maj. G. O. Haller, sent from fort Dallas, 3 Oct., for the Yakima country, 6 Oct. "
Three families massacred by Indians in White River valley, 28 Oct. "
Indians under Leschi, Owhi, Tecumseh, and Curley, attacking Seattle, dispersed by shells from the sloop-of-war *Decatur*, 26 Jan. 1856
Indians defeated in an attack on troops at White river, 8 Mch. "
Yakimas and Klikitats sweep down upon the Cascades, massacre the family of B. W. Brown, 26 Mch., and besiege the garrison until relieved by troops under col. Wright, 28 Mch. "
Leschi, arrested Nov. 1856, is 3 times tried for murder and condemned, and is finally hanged....................19 Feb. 1858
Col. George Wright subdues the Cœur d'Alènes and Spokanes, and executes treaties of peace at the mission on a branch of the Cœur d'Alènes.............................17-23 Sept. "
Light-house on cape Shoalwater, first illuminated.......1 Oct. "
First vessel direct from China to enter Puget sound, the *Lizzie Jarvis*, arrives and secures a cargo of spars...........Oct. "
That part of Oregon territory not included in the state is added to Washington territory by Congress.............14 Feb. 1859
Fort Colville established a few miles east of the old Hudson Bay company's fort.................................20 June, "
First cargo of yellow-fir spars shipped to Atlantic ports of the U. S. from Port Gamble, in the *Lawson*, of Bath, Me......... 1860
University of Washington at Seattle, chartered 1861, opened.. 1862
Act of Congress approved, organizing as the territory of Idaho that part of Washington east of Oregon and of the 117th meridian of west longitude.................................3 Mch. 1863

Capitol at Olympia completed 1863
William and George Hume and A. S. Hapgood erect the first factory at Eagle Cliff, on the Columbia river, for canning salmon 1866
Penitentiary located on McNeil's island, near Steilacoom, by commissioners appointed 1869
Government buildings at fort Steilacoom converted into a territorial insane asylum, and occupied .... Aug. 1871
Tacoma on Commencement bay, Puget sound, selected as the Western terminus of the Northern Pacific Railroad 1872
[Then the site of a sawmill and a few cabins.]
First settler at Spokane Falls 1878
Constitutional convention meets at Walla Walla 11 June, 1878, sits 24 days. Constitution ratified by the people .... Nov. "
Whitman college at Walla Walla, opened 1882, chartered 1883
Attempts of Knights of Labor to expel the Chinese from Washington lead to riots. Gov. Squire, by proclamation, calls on citizens to preserve peace, 5 Nov. 1885; and a riot occurring in Seattle, 7 Feb. 1886, he declares martial law .... 8 Feb. 1886
Northwest Normal school at Lynden opened .... "
Washington School for Defective Youth at Vancouver opened, "
Penitentiary at Walla Walla completed 1887
New insane asylum at Steilacoom completed 1888
Washington admitted to the Union .... 22 Feb. 1889
Constitution framed by a convention which meets at Olympia, 3 July; ratified by the people 40,152 to 11,879. Articles for woman suffrage and prohibition are rejected .... 1 Oct. "
President proclaims Washington a state from .... 11 Nov. "
New insane asylum at Medicine lake erected 1889-90
Legislature passes the Australian Ballot bill .... 19 Mch. 1890
New legislative apportionment law, on the census of 1890, enacted by the legislature at special session ..... 3-11 Sept. "
Forty-five men buried under 20,000 cubic feet of rock by the premature explosion of a blast at Spokane Falls ...... 7 Sept. "
Work begun at excavating for commerce a solid deposit of borax in Douglas county, 8½ feet thick, 1½ miles long, and ½ mile wide, discovered in 1875 1891
New U. S. naval station established at Port Orchard ..... Sept. "
Centennial of the discovery of Puget sound celebrated at Port Townsend .... 7 May, 1892

TERRITORIAL GOVERNORS.

I. I. Stevens .... assumes office .... 28 Nov. 1853
Fayette McMullen .... " .... Sept. 1857
C. H. Mason, acting .... " .... July, 1858
Richard D. Gholson .... " .... " 1859
Henry M. McGill, acting ... " .... May, 1860
W. H. Wallace .... " 1861
L. J. S. Turney, acting ..... " .... "
William Pickering .... " .... June, 1862
Marshall F. Moore .... " 1867
Alvan Flanders .... " 1869
Edward S. Salomon .... " 1870
Elisha Pyre Ferry .... " 1872
William A. Newell .... " 1880
Watson C. Squire .... " 1884
Eugene Semple .... " 1887
Miles C. Moore .... " 1888

STATE GOVERNORS.

Elisha P. Ferry .... assumes office .... 18 Nov. 1889
John H. McGraw .... " .... Jan. 1893

UNITED STATES SENATORS FROM THE STATE OF WASHINGTON.

Name.	No. of Congress.	Date.	Remarks.
John B. Allen	51st to 53d	1890 to 1893	
Watson C. Squire ..	51st " ——	1890 " ——	Term expires 1897.
Vacant *	53d " ——	—— ——	
John L. Wilson	54th " ——	1895 ——	Term expires 1899.

* The state legislature having failed to elect a U. S. senator 1893, the governor appointed John B. Allen, whom the U. S. Senate refused to seat.

Washington, City of. DISTRICT OF COLUMBIA.

"Washington crossing the Delaware," a celebrated painting by Thomas Sully (b. England, 1783; d. Philadelphia, 1872) painted about 1820. Now in possession of Boston museum.

Washington, Fort. FORT WASHINGTON.

Washington, George, Administration of. UNITED STATES, 1789-97.

Washington monument, at Washington, D. C. The corner-stone was laid, 4 July, 1848, with Masonic rites, Robert C. Winthrop delivering the oration. The work proceeded until 1854, when it ceased for want of funds. In 1880 it was resumed by the government, and completed 1884, the entire cost being $1,200,000. It is a white obelisk, 555 ft. high, being the loftiest structure in the world, except the Eiffel tower in Paris. The base is 55 ft. square, with walls 15 ft. thick. The exterior is of crystal Maryland marble; while the interior, lighted by electricity, is occupied by a stairway of 800 steps, extending from the bottom to the top, and an elevator which rises in 7 minutes.

Washington's birthday. First recorded celebration occurred in Richmond, Va., Feb. 11 (o. s.) 1782. It was celebrated there and in other places on 11 Feb. each year until 1793, when 22 Feb. was adopted, according to the new style.

Washington's, George, record.

Birth, WAKEFIELD estate, VIRGINIA 1732
In the French war (VIRGINIA) .... 1753 et seq.
Marriage, etc., p. 658.
ARMY, pp. 49 and 54.
Nominated commander-in-chief (UNITED STATES) 1775
At Cambridge, Mass. (UNITED STATES) .... "
Unfurls flag (UNITED STATES) 1776
MONMOUTH, battle of; also, UNITED STATES,
CONWAY CABAL. 28-29 June and 12 Aug. 1778
At Newburg (UNITED STATES) 1783
Addresses state governors (UNITED STATES) .... "
Issues farewell address (UNITED STATES) .... "
Takes leave of officers (UNITED STATES) .... "
At constitutional convention, p. 200.
Arrives at New York, takes oath of office, etc. (NEW YORK) 1789
Eulogy on (UNITED STATES) .... Dec. 1799

Wasp and Frolic. NAVAL BATTLES.

Wasp, Cruise of the. NAVAL BATTLES; UNITED STATES, 1816.

Wat Tyler's insurrection. TYLER'S INSURRECTION.

watch of London, at night, appointed 1253, proclaimed the hour with a bell before the introduction of public clocks.—*Hardie.* The old watch was discontinued, and a new police (on duty night and day) commenced, 29 Sept. 1829. POLICE.

watches are said to have been invented at Nuremberg, 1447; although tradition asserts that Robert, king of Scotland, had a watch about 1310.

Watches first used in astronomical observations by Purbach .. 1500
Authors assert that the emperor Charles V. was the first who had a real watch, though some call it a small table-clock ... 1530
Watches first brought to England from Germany 1577
A watch which belonged to queen Elizabeth is preserved in the library of the Royal Institution, London.
Spring pocket-watches (watches properly so called) are ascribed to dr. Hooke by the English, and to M. Huyghens by the Dutch. Dr. Derham, in his "Artificial Clockmaker," says that dr. Hooke was the inventor; and he appears to have produced the pendulum watch about 1658; an inscription on one of the double-balance watches presented to Charles II. reads, "Rob. Hooke, inven. 1658; T. Tompion, fecit, 1675."
Repeating watches invented by Barlowe 1676
Harrison's first timepiece produced (HARRISON'S TIMEPIECE) ... 1735

Watches for the United States were formerly supplied from England, France, and Switzerland. In 1850 Aaron Dennison of Boston and Edward Howard, experts in watch and clock work, began making watches by machinery. They soon removed their works to Waltham, Mass., where they have become the largest in the world, with about 2800 operatives, turning out daily 2000 watches. A second centre of watch manufacture is at Elgin, Ill. CLOCK.

water. Thales of Miletus, founder of the Ionic sect, considered water to be the original principle of everything, about 594 B.C.—*Stanley.* In the Roman church water was first mixed with the sacramental wine, 122.—*Lenglet.* In cooling water contracts till it is reduced to 40° Fahr.; it then begins to expand till it becomes ice at 32°. A cubic foot of water weighs 62.5 lbs. avoirdupois; a cubic foot of ice weighs 57.25 lbs.

Cavendish and Watt demonstrate that water is composed of 8 parts of oxygen and 1 part of hydrogen 1781-84
Water decomposed into oxygen and hydrogen gases by Lavoisier, 1783; by the voltaic battery by Nicholson and Carlisle, 1800; by the heat of the oxy-hydrogen flame by W. R. Grove, 1846
AQUEDUCTS, CROTON AQUEDUCT, etc.

water-bed. BED.

water-clock. CLOCK.

water-color painting has been gradually raised from the hard, dry style of the last century to its present brilliancy, by the efforts of Nicholson, Copley Fielding, Sandby, Varley, the great Turner, Pyne, Cattermole, Prout, etc. The Water-color Society's exhibition (England), which began in 1805, was made royal in 1881; the diplomas were to be signed by the queen after Nov. 1882. The Institute of Painters in Water-colors established about 1831 (made royal in 1883). The first organized movement in associating water-color painters in the United States was made in 1850, it was unsuccessful and ceased in 1854 In 1866 the Artists' Fund Society, in its annual exhibition held in the National Academy of Design, New York, made a feature of this branch of art, and exhibited a collection of works by native and foreign painters The result was the organization, in Dec 1866, of the American Society of Painters in Water Colors.

water-glass, a liquid mixture of sand (silex) and one of the alkalies (potash or soda) Glauber (*De Lithuse*) mentions a similar mixture in 1644 Dr Von Fuchs, the modern inventor, gave an account of his process in 1825, and Frederick Ransome, of Ipswich, ignorant of Von Fuchs's discovery, patented a mode of preparing water glass in 1845, which he has since greatly improved In 1857, M Kuhlmann, of Lille, published a pamphlet setting forth the advantageous employment of water-glass in hardening porous stone and in stereochromy. It has been applied to the exterior of many buildings in France and England The memoirs of Von Fuchs and Kuhlmann were translated and printed in England in 1859, by direction of the prince-consort

Wat'erloo, a village of Belgium, the site of the great battle, on Sunday, 18 June, 1815, between 71,947 French, with 246 guns, under Napoleon, and the allies under the duke of Wellington, with 67,661 men and 156 guns The French continued their attacks from about 10 in the morning until 5 in the afternoon, when 1( )0 Prussians reached the field, and by 7, the force under Blucher amounted to above 50,000 men, with 104 guns. Wellington then moved forward his whole army A rout ensued, with great carnage Of the British (23,991), 93 officers and 1916 men were killed and missing, and 363 officers and 4560 men wounded—total, 6932, and the total loss of the allied army amounted to 4206 killed, 14,539 wounded, and 4231 missing, making 22,976 *hors de combat*. Napoleon, quitting the wreck of his army, returned to Paris, and, finding it impossible to raise another, abdicated.—*P Nicolas* Napoleon attributed his defeat to the failure of marshal Grouchy to keep Blucher from reinforcing Wellington It is now conceded that this is correct, that Napoleon would have defeated Wellington by 4 P M. had it not been (1) for the anticipated reinforcements and (2) for the actual. It was without doubt known at an early hour to Wellington that Blucher would be on the field as early as 2 P M, if not before, and it was about this time that detachments of the Prussian army appeared on the French left. With this expected and certain aid the British held on, bearing blow after blow with dogged resolution, knowing that help was approaching Had Grouchy placed his forces (35,000) between the British and Prussian armies, the battle of Waterloo would have been a French victory

Waterloo monument, over the remains of the officers and men who fell in the campaign of 1815 erected by queen Victoria in a cemetery at Brussels, unveiled by the duke of Cambridge 26 Aug 1890
Gen Geo. Whichcote, b. 21 Dec. 1794, who fought in the Spanish campaigns and at Waterloo, d 26 Aug 1891
William Hewitt, lieutenant colonel, last surviving British officer at this battle, d. aged 96 26 Oct. "

Waterloo bridge (London) A bridge here over the Thames was repeatedly suggested during the last century, but no actual preparations for it were made till 1806, when G Dodd procured an act of Parliament, and gave the present site, plan, and dimensions of the bridge, but, under some disagreement with the committee, he was superseded by John Rennie, who completed this noble structure It was commenced 11 Oct 1811, and opened 18 June, 1817, on the anniversary of the battle of Waterloo, the prince-regent, the duke of Wellington, etc., being present Its length within abutments is 1242 feet, its width within balustrades is 42 feet, and the span of each of the 9 arches is 120 feet Bought for 475,000*l* by the Metropolitan Board of Works, opened toll-free, 5 Oct 1878, lit by electric light from 10 Oct 1879

water-mills, for grinding corn, are said to have been invented by Belisarius, the general of Justinian, while besieged in Rome by the Goths, 555. The ancients parched their corn, and pounded it in mortars. Afterwards mills were invented, which were turned by men and beasts with great labor, yet Pliny mentions wheels turned by water. TELODYNAMIC TRANSMITTER.

water-spouts. STORMS

Watling street. ROMAN ROADS

Wattignies (*wat-teen'yie*), a village of N France. Here Jourdan and the French republicans defeated the Austrians under the prince of Coburg, and raised the siege of Maubeuge, 14-16 Oct. 1793

Wauhatch'ie, Battle of CHATTANOOGA CAMPAIGN

wave principle (in accordance with which the curves of the hull of a ship should be adapted to the curves of a wave of the sea) formed the subject of experiments begun by John Scott Russell in 1832, for increasing the speed of ships Col Beaufoy is said to have spent 30,000*l* in researches upon this matter It was taken up by the British Association, who have published reports. The principle has been adopted by naval architects. LIGHT, UNDULATORY THEORY

Wa'verley novels. The publication of the series began with "Waverley, or, 'Tis Sixty Years Since," in 1814, and closed with "Tales of my Landlord," 4th series, in 1831. The authorship was acknowledged by sir Walter Scott, at a dinner, 23 Feb 1827 The original MSS of several of Scott's poems and novels were sold by auction by Christie & Manson for 1255 guineas, 6 July, 1867. LITERATURE.

Wavre (*vav'r*), a village in Belgium, 15 miles southeast from Brussels Here Grouchy attacked the Prussians under Thielman, 18 June, 1815, instead of hastening to the support of Napoleon at WATERLOO

Wawz or **Wawre,** a town of Poland. The Poles under Skrzynecki attacked the Russians at Wawz, and after 2 days' hard fighting all the Russian positions were carried by storm, and they retreated, with the loss of 12,000 men and 2000 prisoners, 31 Mch 1831. The loss of the Poles was small, but their triumph was soon followed by defeat and ruin.

wax (A S *weax*, Ger *Wachs*), a substance secreted by bees and used in constructing their cells, also a substance formed in leaves and fruit and certain plants It came into use for candles in the 12th century, and wax candles were esteemed a luxury in 1300, and were rare In China, candles of vegetable wax have been in use for centuries. CANDLES The wax tree, *Ligustrum lucidum*, was taken to England from China before 1794 —Sealing-wax was not brought into use in England until about 1556. Its use has been almost superseded by adhesive envelopes, since 1844.

waxwork. Exhibitions of models in wax were popular in the 17th and 18th centuries. The collection of wax figures exhibited by Mrs Salmon at Aldgate, early in the last century, was removed to Fleet street, London, and shown there till 1812, when it was sold, it is said, for 50*l*. Mme. Tussaud, a skilful modeller, exhibited her collection of models and casts of eminent persons, with costumes and other relics, in the boulevard du Temple, Paris, 1785 In 1802 she exhibited it at the Lyceum, Strand, London, and afterwards at other places The interest of the exhibition has been energetically sustained for many years at Baker street, London, W., and latterly at Marylebone road, by Mme. Tussaud and her family, she died 15 Apr 1850, aged 90 Early in 1889 the collection was purchased by a company, John Tussaud being engaged as manager Louis Tussaud opened a new exhibition of waxworks at 207 Regent street, 24 Dec 1890, it was destroyed by fire, 20 June, 1891, estimated loss 10,000*l*.

Wayne's Indian campaign. OHIO, 1793.

we. Sovereigns generally use *we* for *I*, a style which began with king John, 1199 —*Coke*. The German emperors and French kings used the plural about 1200.

Weald of Kent and Sussex, the site of very large, ancient forests, St Leonard's still remaining, near which, in the Wealden formation, dr G. A Mantell discovered the remains of huge extinct animals, 1825 et seq R. Furley published an exhaustive "History of the Weald of Kent," 1871-74.

"Wealth of Nations," an inquiry into the cause of, by Adam Smith, pub 1776 Of this work Buckle says, "probably the most important book which has ever been written, whether we consider the amount of original thought it contains or its practical influence."

Weather bureau. The United States Weather bureau, from its organization in 1870 until 30 June, 1891, when it was transferred to the Department of Agriculture, was a division of the U S Signal service under the War department It was organized by chief signal officer brig-gen Albert J Myer, under act of Congress 9 Feb 1870, the first legislation of the U S for a national weather service Meteorological reports had been collected and maps sent out daily by prof Henry at the Smithsonian Institution in 1854, and European governments had issued storm warnings in Holland, France, and England, but prof Cleveland Abbe, meteorologist, of Cincinnati, originated the present system of weather forecasts Prof Abbe began the publication of the *Weather Bulletin of the Cincinnati Observatory*, for the benefit of the Cincinnati Chamber of Commerce, 1 Sept 1869 His success led prof Lapham of Milwaukee to cause memorials for a national system, to be indorsed by all chambers of commerce and boards of trade, and presented to Congress with a bill by gen H E Paine, resulting in the act of 1870 The great value of the service lies in *simultaneous* weather observations throughout the U S, transmitted twice daily by telegraph to Washington, from which are made synoptic weather maps and press reports telegraphed to all points Cautionary storm-signals are displayed for the shipping at all seaport and lake stations, and special flood reports at river stations For the benefit of agriculture, special *Farmers' Bulletins* are issued from the Washington office at 1 A M, and distributed by the "Railway Weather Bulletin service," so that, in the remotest sections, the farmer may know at an early hour the "probabilities" for the day The title "Old Probabilities," familiarly applied to the head of the Weather bureau, was first given in 1869 to prof Abbe, and he was chosen in 1870 by gen Myer to prepare "probabilities" or storm-warnings.

First weather bulletins of simultaneous observations issued and telegraphed to more than 20 cities 4 Nov 1870
First storm warning bulletins along the lakes issued about, 10-15 Nov "
Systematic tri daily weather predictions begun 12 Feb 1871
Display of cautionary signals on the sea coasts and lakes begun 24 Oct "
Signal service charged to extend its researches in the interest of agriculture, by act approved 10 June, 1872
Signal service stations established at light house and life saving stations on the lakes and sea coast, by act of 3 Mch 1873
Monthly Weather Review first published "
System of international co operative simultaneous weather observation, proposed by gen Myer at the congress of meteorologists convened at Vienna, is begun Sept "
All Smithsonian weather observers transferred to the signal service at the instance of prof Joseph Henry 2 Feb 1874
Meteorological reports of army post surgeons ordered by the surgeon general to be sent to the chief signal office 19 June, "
Daily publication of *Bulletin of International Simultaneous Meteorological Observations of the Northern Hemisphere* begun at Washington 1 Jan 1875
Publication of graphic synoptic *International Weather Maps of Simultaneous Observations* begun by gen Myer 1 July, 1878
Gen Albert J Myer, b. 1828 d at Buffalo, N Y 24 Aug 1880
Brig gen W B Hazen appointed chief signal officer 6 Dec "
Gen Hazen, b 1830, d at Washington 16 Jan 1887
Gen A W Greely appointed chief signal officer 3 Mch "
Weather bureau transferred to the Department of Agriculture, and prof Mark W Harrington appointed chief 30 June, 1891

weaving (weave, Dut *weven*, Ger *weben*, Sanscr *vap*), the art of forming cloth in a loom, appears to have been practised in China more than a thousand years before it was known in Europe or Asia The Egyptians ascribed the art to Isis, the Greeks to Pallas Athene, and the Peruvians to the wife of Manco Capac Our Saviour's vest, or coat, is reported to have had no seam, being woven from the top throughout in one whole piece. The print of a frame for weaving such a vest may be seen in Calmet's "Dictionary," under the word *Vestments* 2 weavers from Brabant settled at York, Engl., where they manufactured woollens, which, says king Edward, "may prove of great benefit to us and our subjects" (1331) Flemish dyers, cloth-drapers, linen-makers, silk-throwsters, etc, settled at Canterbury, Norwich, Colchester, Southampton, and other places, on account of the duke of Alva's persecution, 1567 LOOM.

wedding-rings were used by the ancients, and put upon the left third finger, from a supposed connection of a vein there with the heart. According to Pliny, they were made of iron; in the time of Tertullian of gold Wedding-rings in England are of standard gold by statute, 1855 ADRIATIC.

weddings. Silver weddings are celebrated after a union of 25 years, golden weddings after 50 years, and diamond weddings after 60 years.

Wedgwood ware, pottery and porcelain produced by Josiah Wedgwood of Staffordshire, Engl, in 1762 His potteries, termed Etruria, were founded in 1771 Previous to 1763 much earthenware was imported from France and Holland POTTERY

Wednesday, the 4th day of the week, so called from the Saxon idol Woden, or Odin, worshipped on this day Woden was the reputed author of magic and the inventor of all the arts, and was thought to answer to the Mercury of the Greeks and Romans

week, a period of 7 days, supposed to have been first used among the Jews, who observed as holy the sabbath or 7th day They had 3 sorts of weeks—the common one of 7 days, the 2d of 7 years, the 3d of 7 times 7 years, at the end of which was the jubilee All the present English names of days are derived from the Saxon names of gods, and it is for this reason that Quakers regard it as idolatry to use these names, and substitute numbers (1st day, etc) for them

Latin.		*French*
Dies Solis	Day of the Sun,	Dimanche
Dies Lunæ,	Day of the Moon,	Lundi
Dies Martis,	Day of Mars,	Mardi
Dies Mercurii,	Day of Mercury,	Mercredi
Dies Jovis,	Day of Jupiter,	Jeudi
Dies Veneris,	Day of Venus,	Vendredi
Dies Saturni,	Day of Saturn,	Samedi

English	*Saxon*	*German*
Sunday,	Sun's day,	Sonntag
Monday,	Moon s day,	Montag
Tuesday	Tiw s day	Dienstag
Wednesday,	Woden's day,	Mittwoche (mid week, originally Woden's Tag)
Thursday,	Thor's day,	Donnerstag
Friday,	Friga's day,	Freitag
Saturday,	Saterne's day,	Samstag or Sonnabend

weeping willow (Lat *Salix Babylonica*) Said to have been introduced into England from the East in 1722, and into the United States in 1775, by one of the British officers who came to Boston with the army, bringing a twig This twig came into possession of John Parke Custis, who planted it on his estate at Abingdon, Va., where it became the progenitor of this species in the U S.

weights and **measures.** These and the stamping of gold and silver money are attributed to Pheidon, tyrant of Argos, 895 B C ARUNDELIAN MARBLES Weights were originally taken from grains of wheat, the lowest being still called a grain —*Chalmers* CUBIT, METRIC SYSTEM, and STANDARD MEASURES

Much information is given by H W Chisholm in his work "On the Science of Weighing and Measuring" 1877
Jews ascribed weights and measures to Cain, Egyptians to Theuth, or Thoth, Greeks to Hermes (the Roman Mercury)
Basis of ancient measures was the natural dimensions of the human body, the digit, or breadth of the middle part of the first joint of the forefinger, being the lowest unit of the scale
Egyptian cubit (6 palms), under the Pharaohs was about 18 24 English inches, cubit of Ptolemy about 21 87 inches, he determined the length of a stadium and of a degree
Sacred cubit of the Jews (Newton) 24 7 inches
Assyrian weights are described by Mr Layard in his "Nineveh"
Grecian πούς = 1 01 ft, and a στάδιον or great measure = 607 ft
Roman *pes* = 11 65 in, while the *milliare* = 11/12 of a mile
Grecian δράχμη = 2 46 drs avoirdupois, while the Roman *libra* = 11 oz 8 6 drs avoirdupois
Standard measure was originally kept at Winchester, Engl, by the law of king Edgar 972
Standard weights and measures were provided for the kingdom of England by the sheriffs of London, 9 Rich I 1197
Public weighing machine was set up in London and all commodities ordered to be weighed by the city officer, called the weigh master, who was to do justice between buyer and seller stat 3 Edw II (*Stow*) 1309
Edward III ordered that there should be "one weight, measure, and yard" throughout the kingdom 1353
First statute, directing the use of *avoirdupois* weight, of 24 Hen VIII 1532
Weights and measures ordered to be examined by the justices at quarter sessions, 35 Geo III 1795
Again regulated 1800
Statute for establishing uniformity of weights and measures, 1824, took effect throughout the United Kingdom 1 Jan 1826
Specific gravities ELEMENTS

Weinsberg, City of GUELPHS.

Weldon Road, Battle of. GRANT'S CAMPAIGN IN VIRGINIA.

Welland canal. CANALS

wells were dug by Abraham, 1892 B C, and Isaac, 1804

(Gen. xxi. 30, and xxvi. 19). Danaus is said to have introduced well-digging into Greece from Egypt. Norton's "tube-well," patented Oct. 1867, is said to be the invention of Hiram J. Messenger, Stephen Brewer, and Byron Mudge, Americans, of the state of New York. The apparatus consists of an iron tube perforated with holes at the lower end, and shod with a steel point, which readily enters the hardest soil when forcibly driven. It was used with great advantage during the civil war, 1861-64; by the British in their campaign in Abyssinia, 1867-1868; and by the Russians in Khiva, 1873. ARTESIAN WELLS.

Wends, a branch of the Slavonic family which spread over Germany in the 6th century, and settled especially in the northeastern parts.

Wesleyan Methodists. The term "Wesleyan" is applied to all Methodists in England, but in the United States only to an organization that withdrew from the Methodist Episcopal church in 1843, dissatisfied with the attitude of the Methodist Episcopal church towards slavery. It has no distinctive doctrines, and has not increased in strength or importance. According to the census of 1890 it has in the U. S. 341 churches, with 16,492 members. METHODISM.

West African settlements under the English government and protection. *Gold Coast* extends along the gulf of Guinea 350 miles. Area, 15,000 sq. miles (under English protection, 46,600 sq. miles); pop. 1,905,000. *Lagos*, an island on the slave coast, with a protectorate extending some distance inland. Area, 1071 sq. miles; pop. 100,000. *Gambia*, at the mouth of the river Gambia. Area, 2700 sq. miles; pop. 50,000. *Sierre Leone*, area, 15,000 sq. miles; pop. 180,000. Each with a governor appointed by the British crown.

West Indies, islands discovered by Columbus (AMERICA), form a long archipelago reaching from Florida and Yucatan to the shores of Venezuela, South America, separating the open Atlantic from the gulf of Mexico and the Caribbean sea. So called because they were supposed to be a part of India. 3 great divisions are recognized in this archipelago:

I. Greater Antilles: CUBA, HAYTI, PORTO RICO, and JAMAICA.

II. BAHAMAS: Extending from about 20° to 27° N. lat., forming a British colonial possession, few inhabited; Nassau, on Providence island, the capital. They form a barrier which throws the Gulf stream upon the Atlantic coast of the U. S., thus greatly modifying the climate of the eastern U.S. and northern Europe.

		Names.	Possessors.
III. Lesser Antilles.	Leeward isles.	Virgin islands....	British, Danish, Spanish.
		Anguilla..........	British.
		St. Christopher (St. Kitt's)..........	"
		St. Martin..........	French, Dutch.
		St. Bartholomew....	French.
		Saba..............	Dutch.
		St. Eustatius........	"
		Nevis..............	British.
		Barbuda............	"
		Antigua............	"
		Montserret..........	"
		Guadeloupe..........	French.
		Marie-Galante......	"
		Dominica..........	British.
	Windward isles.	Martinique..........	French.
		St. Lucia..........	British.
		St. Vincent..........	"
		Grenada..........	"
		Barbadoes..........	"
		Tobago..........	"
		Trinidad..........	"
		Oruba..........	Dutch.
		Curaçoa..........	"
		Buen Ayre..........	"
		Aves (Bird) islands	Venezuela.
		Los Roques.......	
		Orchilla..........	
		Blanquella..........	

For special information see each separately.

West Point, Orange county, N. Y., a town on the west bank of the Hudson river, 52 miles from New York city; pop. about 1400. Site of forts Clinton and Putnam, built during the Revolution; also scene of Arnold's treason. UNITED STATES, 1780.

West Point military academy, the only school to educate officers for the army of the United States, occupies 2200 acres at West Point. The 27 sec. of the act of Congress, 16 Mch. 1802, by which the military peace establishment was determined, provided for a corps of engineers to be stationed at West Point, N. Y., and to constitute a military academy, the senior engineer officer, Jonathan Williams, maj. of engineers, to be superintendent. By act of 25 Feb. 1803, the president was empowered to appoint a teacher of French and one of drawing. Further provisions made by Congress for it 29 Apr. 1812, defining the principles upon which the school has since been conducted. This act established the following departments: Engineering, philosophy, mathematics, French, Spanish, drawing, geography, history, ethics, chemistry, mineralogy, geology, infantry tactics, practical engineering, artillery and cavalry practice, ordnance and gunnery, equitation, fencing, and bayonet exercise. Requirements for admission, time of study and service, rate of pay and emoluments prescribed. On 28 July, 1817, brevet-maj. Sylvanus Thayer, of the corps of engineers, known as "the Father of the academy," assumed control as superintendent. "From this period the commencement of whatever success as an educational institution and whatever reputation the academy may possess throughout the country and abroad for its strict, impartial, salutary, elevating, and disciplinary government must be dated." —*Capt. Edward C. Boynton*, "History of West Point," p. 217.

First graduates, Joseph G. Swift and Simon M. Levy...12 Oct. 1802

3	graduates..........	1803	15	graduates.......	1808
2	"	1804	7	"	1809
3	"	1805	—	"	1810
15	"	1806	19	"	1811
5	"	1807			

[Total, 1802-94 inclusive, 3616.]

Permanent superintendent appointed.......................... 1815

Board of visitors appointed.......................... 1816

[Board of visitors are appointed annually. 7 by the president, 2 by the president of the Senate, and 3 by the speaker of the House. They visit the academy in June and are present at the graduation of the class.]

Uniforms prescribed.......................... "

Class rank inaugurated.......................... 1818

Martial law introduced; first court-martial.................. "

[Cadets held to be subject to the rules and articles of war. Opinion confirmed by pres. Monroe and Calhoun, sec. of war.]

Severer regulations introduced.......................... "

[By sec. 28, act of Congress, 5 July, 1838, cadets to serve the government 8 years unless sooner discharged.]

[Congress organized a commission of 2 senators, 2 representatives, and 2 army officers to examine the academy, to ascertain what changes, if any, were necessary, etc. It consisted of Jefferson Davis and Solomon Foot, of the Senate; John Cochrane and Henry W. Davis, of the House; maj. Robert Anderson and capt. A. A. Humphreys, U. S. army. They met at West Point, 17 July, 1860, and on 13 Dec., in a report of 350 pages, recommended the reorganization of the academy.]

Total number of cadets present at the academy on 1 Nov. 1860.......................... 278

From the southern states.......................... 86

Of these from the south, the number discharged, dismissed, and resigned, from causes connected with the civil war, was.......................... 65

Leaving at the academy from the south to prosecute their studies.......................... 21

Of the 1249 living graduates at the beginning of the civil war,
919 remained loyal,
283 joined the confederates,
47 neutral or unknown;
1249 total.

By act of Congress, 3 Aug. 1861, the oath of allegiance was amended so as to abjure all allegiance, sovereignty, or fealty conceived to be due any state, county, or country whatsoever, and pledge an unqualified support to the Constitution and the national government. By provision of law, each congressional district and territorial district, as well as the District of Columbia, is entitled to 1 cadet. Appointments from the first two are made on the nomination to the sec. of war by the representative in Congress from his own district. However large the number of applicants from any district, the appointee is selected at the instance of the representative. The pres. of the U. S. is authorized to appoint 10 cadets at large independent of residence. Candidate must be over 16 and under 21 years of age, and at least 5 ft. high; must be able to read and write well, and grounded in the first 4 rules of arithmetic, etc.; subject to examination by the medical board at West Point.

SUPERINTENDENTS OF WEST POINT.

1. Jonathan Williams...1802-12
2. Joseph G. Swift......1812-17
3. Sylvanus Thayer....1817-33
4. Rene E. De Russy....1833-38
5. Richard Delafield....1838-45
6. Henry Brewerton....1845-52
7. Robert E. Lee........1852-55
8. John G. Barnard.....1855-56
9. Richard Delafield....1856-61
10. P. G. T. Beauregard..1861 [Served 5 days. Appointed by John Floyd, sec. of war; relieved by Joseph Holt.]
11. Alexander H. Bowman............1861-64
12. Zealous B. Tower....1864
13. George W. Cullum....1864-66
14. Thomas G. Pitcher....1866-71
15. Thos. H. Ruger......1871-76
16. Gen. John M. Schofield............1876-81
17. Gen. Oliver O. Howard...............1881-82
18. Wesley Merritt......1882-87
19. John G. Parke.......1887-89
20. Jas. M. Wilson......1889-94
21. O. H. Ernst..........1894

GRADUATES RANKING No. 1 FROM 1818 TO 1861 (NO CLASS RANK PRIOR TO 1818), WITH THE CLASS AND GRADUATING RANK OF OTHERS WHO BECAME DISTINGUISHED IN THE CIVIL WAR.

Class rank, No. 1. Name.	Year of graduation.	No. in Class.	Remarks.	Class rank of distinguished officers graduating at the time.
Richard Delafield	1818	23	Retired	
William A. Eleason	1819	29	Died, 1839.	
Stephen Tuttle	1820	30	Died, 1835.	
Edward A Courtenay	1821	24	Resigned, 1834.	
George Dutton	1822	40	Died, 1857	David Hunter 25 Joseph K. T. Mansfield 2
Alfred Mordecai	1823	35	Resigned, 1861.	
Dennis A. Mahan	1824	31		
Alexander D. Bache	1825	37	Died, 1867	Robert Anderson 15 Charles F. Smith 19
William H. C Bartlett	1826	41	Resigned, 1829	Albert Sidney Johnston 8 S. P. Heintzelman 17
Ebenezer S. Sibley	1827	38	Resigned, 1864	Leonidas Polk 8
Albert E. Church	1828	33		Jefferson Davis 23
Charles Mason	1829	46	Resigned, 1831	O. McKnight Mitchel 15 Joseph E. Johnston 13 Robert E. Lee 2
Alexander J. Swift	1830	42	Died, 1847	J. B. Magruder 15
Roswell Park	1831	33	Resigned, 1836	Samuel R. Curtis 27 A. A. Humphreys 13
George W. Ward	1832	45	Resigned, 1836.	
Frederic A. Smith	1833	43	Died, 1852	George W. Cullum 3
Wm. D. Fraser (named Wm. Smith at graduation)	1834	36	Died, 1856.	
George W. Morell	1835	56	Resigned, 1837; re-entered the army, 1861	George G. Meade 19 Gordon Granger 35
George L. Welcker	1836	49	Died, 1848	Thomas W. Sherman 18
Henry W. Benham	1837	50		Joseph Hooker 29 John Sedgwick 24 Braxton Bragg 5 Jubal A. Early 18 J. C. Pemberton 27 William H. French 22
William H. Wright	1838	45	Died, 1845	Irvin McDowell 23 Andrew J. Smith 36 P. G. T. Beauregard 2 William J. Hardee 26
Isaac J. Stevens	1839	31	Resigned, 1853; re-entered the army, 1861; killed at Chantilly, 1862	Edward R. S. Canby 30 Henry W. Halleck 3 Edward O. C. Ord 17 Henry J. Hunt 19
Paul O. Hebert	1840	42	Resigned, 1845; reappointed, 1847; resigned, 1848; joined the rebellion	William Tecumseh Sherman 7 George H. Thomas 12 Richard S. Ewell 13
Zealous B. Tower	1841	52		John F. Reynolds 26 Don Carlos Buell 32 Nathaniel Lyon 11 Horatio G. Wright 2 John M. Brannan 23
Henry L. Eustis	1842	56	Resigned, 1864	John Newton 2 William S. Rosecrans 5 John Pope 17 George Sykes 39 D. H. Hill 28 James Longstreet 54 Earl Van Dorn 52
William B. Franklin	1843	39	Resigned, 1866	Christopher G. Auger 16 Ulysses S. Grant 21 Frederick Steele 30
William G. Peck	1844	25	Resigned, 1865	Winfield S. Hancock 18 Alfred Pleasanton 7 S. B. Buckner 11
William H. C. Whiting	1845	41	Resigned, 1861; joined the rebellion	Fitz-John Porter 8 Charles P. Stone 7 Thomas J. Wood 5 William F. Smith [illegible] Edmund Kirby Smith 25
C. Seaforth Stewart	1846	59		George B. McClellan 2 George Stoneman 33 Darius Couch 13 John G. Foster 4 Thomas J. Jackson, "Stonewall" 17 George Pickett 59
John C. Symmes	1847	38	Retired, 1861	Ambrose E. Burnside 18 Orlando B. Wilcox 8 Charles Griffin 23 John Gibbon 20 Romeyn B. Ayres 22 Ambrose P. Hill 15
William P. Trowbridge	1848	38	Resigned, 1856.	
Quincy A. Gilmore	1849	43		John G. Parke 2 Absalom Baird 9
Frederick E. Prime	1850	44		G. K. Warren 2
George L. Andrews	1851	42		
Thomas Lincoln Casey	1852	43		David Stanley 9 Henry W. Slocum 7 Alexander McDowell McCook 30 George W. Crook 32
James B. McPherson	1853	52	Killed before Atlanta, Ga., 1864, aged 35.	John M. Schofield 7 Philip H. Sheridan 34 J. B. Hood 44
G. W. Custis Lee	1854	46	Resigned, 1861; joined the rebellion	O. O. Howard 4 J. E. B. Stuart 13
Cyrus B. Comstock	1855	34		William B. Hazen 28 Godfrey Weitzel 2 William B. Averell 26 David McM. Gregg 8 Alfred T. O. Torbert 21

GRADUATES RANKING No. 1, ETC., WHO BECAME DISTINGUISHED IN THE CIVIL WAR.—(*Continued.*)

Class rank, No. 1. Name.	Year of graduation.	No. in Class.	Remarks.	Class rank of distinguished officers graduating at the time.
George W. Snyder	1856	49	Died, 1861.	
John C. Palfrey	1857	38		
William C. Paine	1858	27	Resigned, 1863.	
William E. Merrill	1859	22		
Walter McFarland	1860	41		Wesley Merritt....22 James H. Wilson....6
Henry A. Dupont	1861	34		Judson Kilpatrick....17 Emory Upton....8 George A. Custer....34

West Saxons. BRITAIN.

West Virginia, a state of the United States formed from Virginia west of the Alleghany mountains, is of irregular shape, a narrow strip known as the Panhandle extending north between Pennsylvania and Ohio some 70 miles, and Maryland cutting a triangle out of the northeastern portion. It lies between lat. 37° 5′ and 40° 37′ N., and lon. 77° 4′ and 82° 40′ W. Its general boundary is Pennsylvania and Maryland on the north, Virginia on the east and south, and Kentucky and Ohio on the west. Area, 24,780 sq. miles, in 54 counties. Pop. 1890, 762,794; 1900, 958,800. Capital, Charleston. VIRGINIA.

Harper's Ferry established as a ferry.... 1748
Baptist church formed at Opequon, Berkeley county, under charge of rev. John Gerard from New England.... 1754
Battle of the Trough, near Moorefield. A small band of settlers pursuing Indians under Kill Buck are hemmed in between mountain and river, and obliged to retreat with loss of half their number....spring of 1756
Massacre of the garrison of fort Seybert, 12 miles from site of Franklin, by Indians....May, 1758
Romney laid out and named by lord Fairfax....Nov. 1762
Capt. William Arbuckle, the first white man to traverse the Kanawha valley, reaches the site of Point Pleasant.... 1764
English exploring expedition under col. Crogan descends the Ohio, encamping at West Columbia and Little Guyandotte river....May, 1765
George Washington, on a surveying expedition to the Ohio, passes through Romney....9 Oct. 1770
Indians attack the crew of a trading canoe from Pittsburg on the Ohio, near Wheeling, killing 1 man, thus breaking a 10 years' truce, 16 Apr. The settlers declare war and engage in a battle near the mouth of Captina creek....27 Apr. 1774
Fort Union built on site of Lewisburg.... "
Fort Fincastle, afterwards fort Henry, at Wheeling, built.... "
Battle of Point Pleasant, at the mouth of the Great Kanawha (VIRGINIA)....10 Oct. "
Fort Randolph, at Point Pleasant, begun.... " "
John Harvie and John Nevill, chosen to represent western Virginia in the Virginia convention, are admitted to seats, 21 Mch. 1775
Convention of Virginia frontiersmen west of the Alleghany mountains at Pittsburg elects John Harvie and George Rodes delegates to Continental Congress....16 May, "
Tory insurrection under John Claypole, a resident of Hardy county, suppressed by troops under gen. Morgan....June, "
Capt. Foreman and 21 men massacred by Indians about 4 miles from Moundsville....25 Sept. 1777
FORT HENRY unsuccessfully besieged by Indians under Simon Girty....27–28 Sept. "
Cornstalk, Shawnee chief, murdered at Point Pleasant, 10 Nov. "
Fort Randolph besieged by Indians....May, 1778
Attack by the Indians on Donnally's fort, 10 miles northwest of Lewisburg....May, "
By grant to William Penn in 1681, the western boundary of Pennsylvania is the meridian 5 degrees west of the Delaware. Virginia in ceding to the U. S. lands beyond the Ohio, in 1784, reserved a strip about 70 miles long upon the Ohio west of Pennsylvania, now known as the Panhandle..1 Mch. 1784
General assembly directs the establishment of Morgantown, Oct. 1785
Wheeling laid out in town lots by col. Ebenezer Zane.... 1793
Charleston created by act of legislature....19 Dec. 1794
Aaron Burr visits Herman Blennerhassett at his island in the Ohio, 2 miles below Parkersburg (BLENNERHASSETT'S ISLAND; UNITED STATES).... 1805
First steamboat on the Great Kanawha, the *Robert Thompson*, ascends the river from Point Pleasant to Red House shoals.. 1819
Bethany college at Bethany, chartered 1840, opened.... 1841
Wheeling female college at Wheeling, chartered 1848, opened.. 1850
John Brown, seeking "to free the slaves," captures Harper's Ferry (BROWN'S, JOHN, INSURRECTION; VIRGINIA)..16–17 Oct. 1859
Petroleum discovered at Burning Springs, on the north bank of the Kanawha.... 1860
First public Union meeting in West Virginia, declaring against secession, held at Preston....12 Nov. "
Forty-six delegates from what is now West Virginia vote on the ordinance of secession; 9 for, 29 against; 7 are absent, 1 excused....17 Apr. 1861
Garrison at Harper's Ferry burn the arsenal and flee into Maryland....21 Apr. "
West Virginia declares for the Union.... " "
First Wheeling convention on the future of western Virginia meets in Washington hall, Wheeling....13 May, "
First Virginia federal infantry mustered in on Wheeling island by maj. Oaks....15 May, "
Second Wheeling convention meets at Washington hall, Wheeling, 11 June, 1861; adopts a declaration of rights, 13 June; an ordinance to reorganize the state government, 19 June; and elects Francis H. Pierpont governor....20 June, "
Gen. Rosecrans defeats confederates under gen. R. S. Garnett, in the battle of Rich mountain....11 July, "
Battle of Carnifex Ferry; confederates under gen. H. A. Wise attacked by federals under Rosecrans....10 Sept. "
Gen. Reynolds repulses confederates under Lee in battle at Cheat mountain....12–14 Sept. "
Convention at Wheeling passes an ordinance to form a new state in western Virginia called Kanawha, 20 Aug. 1861; ordinance ratified by popular vote of 18,408 to 781....24 Oct. "
Federals burn Guyandotte....11 Nov. "
Constitution for a new state, named West Virginia, framed by convention which meets at Wheeling, 26 Nov. 1861, and completes its labors, 18 Feb.; constitution ratified by popular vote of 18,862 to 514....Apr. 1862
General assembly of reorganized Virginia at Wheeling assents to the erection of the new state of West Virginia....12 May, "
Harper's Ferry surrendered by gen. Dixon H. Miles to confederates under Stonewall Jackson (MARYLAND CAMPAIGN), 15 Sept. "
Gen. J. A. J. Lightburn retreats through the Kanawha valley, pursued by confederates under gen. Loring.... "
Congress admits West Virginia into the Union from 20 June, 1863....31 Dec. "
Confederates under gen. Jones burn 100,000 barrels of petroleum at Burning Springs....9 May, 1863
Inauguration of new state government takes place at Wheeling....20 June, "
Supreme court of appeals organized at Wheeling....9 July, "
Gen. W. W. Averill defeats maj. John Echols in battle of Droop mountain....6 Nov. "
Hospital for the insane at Weston opened.... 1864
Transfer of the counties of Berkeley (5 Aug. 1863) and Jefferson (2 Nov. 1863) from the state of Virginia to West Virginia is recognized by joint resolution of Congress....10 Mch. 1866
Amendments to state constitution ratified excluding from citizenship all who had, subsequent to June, 1861, given voluntary aid to the southern Confederacy....24 May, "
State penitentiary located at Moundsville by act of 7 Feb. 1866, begun....July, "
Legislature ratifies the XIV.th Amendment to federal Constitution....16 Jan. 1867
Fairmount State Normal school at Fairmount opened.... "
Storer college at Harper's Ferry opened.... "
West Virginia university at Morgantown opened....17 June, "
Marshall college, State Normal school at Huntington, opened.. 1868
Legislature ratifies the XV.th Amendment to federal Constitution....3 Mch. 1869
Charleston chosen as seat of government by legislature, 20 Feb. 1869, from....30 Apr. 1870
State Normal school at West Liberty opened.... "
West Virginia School for the Deaf and the Blind at Romney opened.... "
Amendment to sec. i. art. iii. of the state constitution, rehabilitating citizens disfranchised, ratified by the people...27 Apr. 1871
Constitution framed by a convention which meets at Charleston, 16 Jan. 1872, and completes its labors, 9 Apr. 1872; ratified by the people....22 Aug. 1872
Shepherd college, State Normal college at Shepherdtown, opened.... "
State Normal school at Glenville opened.... 1873
Legislature meets at Wheeling as temporary seat of government by act of 20 Feb. 1875....10 Nov. 1875
Broaddus college at Clarksburg, opened 1871, chartered.... 1877
Strike on the Baltimore and Ohio railroad begun at Martinsburg....16 July, "
At election held by act of 21 Feb. 1877, to locate the state capital after 1 May, 1885, Charleston has 41,288 votes, Clarksburg, 30,812, Martinsburg, 8049....7 Aug. "
Nathan Goff, jr., appointed secretary of the navy....6 Jan. 1881

Act striking the word "white" out of the "Woods Jury law" of 1872–73 1881
Act passed establishing a state Board of Health .... 11 June, "
West Virginia Normal and Classical Academy at Buckhannon opened 1882
West Virginia Immigration and Development Association organized at Wheeling .... 29 Feb. 1888
Returns of election for governor in Nov. 1888 were: Nathan Goff, Rep., 78,714; A. B. Fleming, Dem., 78,604. Fleming contests for fraudulent returns, and is declared elected by a party vote of the legislature, 43 to 40 .... 4 Feb. 1890
State Reform school opened .... July, "
Hatfield-McCoy feud ended by a marriage .... 21 Mch. 1891
First state Board of Agriculture meets at the capitol in Charleston .... 4 May, 1891
Stephen B. Elkins qualifies as U. S. secretary of war .... 24 Dec. "

GOVERNORS OF WEST VIRGINIA.

Arthur I. Boreman .... inaugurated 1863
William E. Stevenson .... " 1869
John J. Jacob .... " 1871
Henry M. Mathews .... " 1877
Jacob B. Jackson .... " 1881
E. Willis Wilson .... " 1885
A. B. Fleming .... " 1890
William A. McCorkle .... " 1893

UNITED STATES SENATORS FROM THE STATE OF WEST VIRGINIA.

Name.	No. of Congress.	Date.	Remarks.
Waitman T. Willey	38th to 42d	1863 to 1871	Seated 7 Dec.
Peter G. Van Winkle	38th " 41st	1863 " 1869	" "
Arthur I. Boreman	41st " 44th	1869 " 1875	
Henry G. Davis	42d " 48th	1871 " 1883	
Allen T. Caperton	44th	1875 " 1876	Died in office.
Samuel Price	44th	1876	Appointed *pro tem.* in place of Caperton.
Frank Hereford	44th to 47th	1877 to 1881	Elected in place of Caperton.
Johnson N. Camden	47th " 50th	1881 " 1887	
John E. Kenna	48th " 52d	1883 " 1893	Died in office, 11 Jan. 1893.
Charles E. Faulkner	50th " ——	1887 " ——	Term expires 1899.
Johnson N. Camden	53d " 54th	1893 " 1895	Elected in place of Kenna.
Stephen B. Elkins	54th " ——	1895 " ——	Term expires 1901.

Western Australia, formerly **Swan River settlement,** projected by col. Peel in 1828. Regulations issued from the colonial office, and capt. Stirling, appointed lieutenant-governor, 17 Jan. 1829, arrived at the appointed site in Aug. The 3 towns of Perth, Freemantle, and Guildford were founded the same year. In Mch. 1830, 50 ships, with 2000 emigrants, with property amounting to 1,000,000*l.*, had arrived before many dwellings had been erected or land surveyed. The more energetic settlers left for home or the neighboring colonies, and the colony languished for 20 years for want of suitable inhabitants—the first settlers, from their previous habits and rank, proving unfit for the rough work of colonization. In 1848 the colonists requested that convicts might be sent out, and in 1849 a band arrived, who were kindly received and well treated. The best results ensued. By 1853 2000 had arrived, and the inhabitants of Perth had requested that 1000 should be sent annually. The reception of convicts was stopped because of energetic opposition by other Australian colonies (1865).—The settlement of King George's sound was founded in 1826 by the government of New South Wales. It was used as a military station for 4 years. In 1830 the home government ordered the settlement to be transferred to Swan River. Since steam communication began, the little town of Albany here, from a coaling-station, has become a thriving seaport. It has an excellent harbor, used by whalers. A journal called the *Freemantle Gazette* was published here in Mch. 1831. In 1890 it became self-governing; power vested in a governor, legislative council, and assembly. Area, 1,060,000 sq. miles; pop. 1891, 49,782. Capital, Perth; pop. 1891, 9617.

Western church, called also the **Latin** or **Roman,** broke off communion with the Greek or Eastern church 653. GREEK CHURCH. Its history is mainly that of the POPES and of the European kingdoms. This church was disturbed by the Arian heresy about 345 and 500; by Pelagianism, about 409; by image-worship about 600; by the celibacy of the clergy and the rise of monastic orders, about 649; by the contests between emperors and popes on ecclesiastical investitures between 1073 and 1173; by the Reformation of the 15th and 16th centuries; by the contests of Jesuits and Jansenists in the 17th and 18th centuries; and by modern philosophy, rationalism, and ultramontanism in the 19th.

Western empire. The Roman empire was divided into Eastern and Western by Diocletian in 296; but was reunited under Constans in 340. It was again divided into Eastern and Western by Valentinian and Valens, the former having the Western portion, or Rome, 364. EASTERN EMPIRE, ITALY, ROME.

EMPERORS.

364. Valentinian, son of Gratian, takes the Western, and his brother Valens the Eastern empire.
367. Gratian, a youth, son of Valentinian, made a colleague by his father.
375. Valentinian II., another son, very young, is, on the death of his father, associated with Gratian, who is assassinated by his general, Andragathius, in 383. Valentinian murdered by an officer, Arbogastes, in 392.
392. Eugenius, a usurper, assumes the imperial dignity; he and Arbogastes are defeated by
394. Theodosius the Great, who becomes sole emperor. [Andragathius threw himself into the sea, and Arbogastes died by his own hand.]
395. Honorius, son of Theodosius, reigns, on his father's death, in the West, and his brother Arcadius in the East. Honorius dies, 423.
423. John, the Notary, usurper, defeated and slain near Ravenna.
425. Valentinian III., son of the empress Placidia, daughter of Theodosius the Great; murdered at the instance of
455. Maximus: he marries Eudoxia, widow of Valentinian, who, to avenge her first husband, invites the African Vandals into Italy, and Rome is sacked. Maximus stoned.
" Marcus Mæcilius Avitus; forced to resign, and dies in his flight towards the Alps.
457. Julius Valerius Majorianus; murdered at the instance of his minister, Ricimer, who raises
461. Libius Severus to the throne, but holds the supreme power; Severus poisoned by Ricimer.
465. [Interregnum. Ricimer retains the authority, without the title of emperor.]
467. Anthemius, chosen by the senate and army; murdered by Ricimer, who dies soon after.
472. Flavius-Anicius Olybrius; slain by the Goths soon after.
473. Glycerius; forced to abdicate by
474. Julius Nepos: deposed by his general, Orestes, and retires to Salonæ.
475. Romulus (called Augustulus, or Little Augustus), son of Orestes. Orestes is slain, and the emperor deposed by
476. Odoacer, king of the Heruli; takes Rome, assumes the style king of Italy; end of the Western empire.

GERMANY, ITALY, ROME.

Western Reserve, Ohio. CONNECTICUT, 1786, 1792, '95, 1800.

Westminster abbey, originally the church erected by Edward the Confessor as part of an abbey within his palace-grounds, is on the site of still earlier churches; and from the time of Harold has been the coronation church of the monarchs of England. Christopher Wren, in his survey of the present edifice, found nothing to show that it was erected on the ruins of a pagan temple. The earliest edifice, of the 7th century, is ascribed to St. Sebert, king of Essex.

Church, becoming ruinous, splendidly rebuilt by Edward the Confessor (1055–65) and filled with monks from Exeter (Pope Nicholas II. assigned it for the inauguration of the kings); dedicated .... 28 Dec. 1065
Rebuilt in a magnificent style by Henry III 1220–69
In the reigns of Edward II., Edward III., and Richard II., the great cloisters, abbot's house, and principal monastic buildings erected 1300–1400
Western parts of the nave and aisles rebuilt between .. 1340 and 1483
West front and the great window built by Richard III. and Henry VII.; the latter commenced the chapel which bears his name; the first stone laid .... 24 Jan. 1502–3
Abbey dissolved and made a bishopric 1540
Made a collegiate church by Elizabeth 1560
Made a barrack for soldiers (*Mercurius Rusticus*) .... July, 1643
Great west window and the western towers rebuilt in the reigns of George I. and II. 1714–60
Choir injured by fire .... 9 July, 1803
Mr. Wyatt commences restoring the dilapidated parts, at an expense of 42,000*l.* 1809
Eight hundredth anniversary of the foundation celebrated, 28 Dec. 1865

Westminster Confession of Faith and **Catechisms** were drawn up by the "Assembly of Divines" (partly consisting of laymen), who sat by authority of Parliament in Henry VII.'s chapel, Westminster, from 1643 to 1647. These have ever since been the doctrinal standards of Scotch Presbyterians.

Westminster Hall, London, first built by William Rufus in 1097, for a banqueting-hall; and here, in 1099, on his return from Normandy, "he kept his feast of Whitsuntide very royally." The hall became ruinous before the reign of Richard II., who repaired it in 1397, raised the walls, altered the windows, and added a new roof, a stately porch, and other buildings. In 1236, Henry III., on New Year's Day, caused 6000 poor persons to be entertained in this hall, and in the other rooms of his palace, as a celebration of queen Eleanor's coronation; and here Richard II. held his Christmas festival in 1397, when the number of the guests each day the feast lasted was 10,000.—*Stow.* The courts of law were established here by king John.—*Idem.* Removed to the new buildings in the Strand, Jan. 1883. Westminster Hall was long believed to be the largest room in Europe unsupported by pillars (except a hall of justice at Padua); it is 270 feet in length, 74 feet broad. The roof and windows greatly injured by an explosion of dynamite, 24 Jan. 1885.

Westpha'lia, Germany. This duchy belonged in former times to the dukes of Saxony, and afterwards became subject to the archbishop of Cologne. On the secularization, in 1802, it was made over to Hesse-Darmstadt; and in 1814 was ceded for an equivalent to Prussia. The *kingdom* of Westphalia, one of the temporary kingdoms of Bonaparte, composed of conquests from Prussia, Hesse-Cassel, Hanover, and the smaller states to the west of the Elbe, was created by decree 18 Aug. 1806, and Jerome Bonaparte appointed king 1 Dec. 1807. Hanover was annexed to it, 1 Mch. 1810. The kingdom was abolished in 1813, and the countries were restored to their former rulers.

Westpha'lia or **Münster,** Peace of, the treaties signed at Osnaburg, 6 Aug., and at Münster, 24 Oct. 1648, between France, the emperor of Germany, and Sweden; Spain continuing the war against France. By this peace (ending the Thirty Years' war) the principle of a balance of power in Europe was first recognized; Alsace given to France, and part of Pomerania and some other districts to Sweden; the Lower Palatinate restored to the elector palatine; the religious and political rights of the German states established; and the independence of the Swiss Confederation recognized by Germany.

wheat, a grain of the order *Gramineae* of the species *Triticum* (from the Lat. *tritum*, "rubbed" or "ground," alluding to the manner of preparing it for food), and closely related to barley and rye. It is the most valuable of cereals for food, and has been in use from the remotest ages. It may have been derived from the species *Ægilopsoota* of the Mediterranean region. It was introduced into England about the 6th century, and into America by the Spaniards in 1530, and by the English into their colonies at their first settlements. The 2 principal varieties are spring wheat, sown in the spring and ripening the same summer, and winter wheat, sown in the early autumn and ripening the next summer. It can be cultivated as far north as 45° and in southern latitudes to the height of 2000 ft. above the level of the sea.

PRODUCTION OF WHEAT IN THE PRINCIPAL WHEAT-GROWING COUNTRIES IN THE WORLD FOR THE YEAR 1891.

	Bushels.
United States	612,000,000
India	250,000,000
France	230,000,000
Russia	190,000,000
Austro-Hungary	160,000,000
Italy	105,000,000
Germany	90,000,000
Spain	76,000,000
Great Britain	72,000,000
Roumania	65,000,000
Canada	62,000,000
Australia	45,000,000
Argentine Republic	40,000,000
Egypt and Algeria	40,000,000
Total	2,037,000,000
Other countries	150,000,000
Grand total	2,187,000,000

The wheat crop in the United States for 1892 was 515,949,000 bu., acreage, 38,554,430; 1893, 396,131,725 bu., the smallest crop since 1885, acreage, 34,629,418. AGRICULTURE.

wheel, Breaking on the. A barbarous mode of death, of great antiquity, ordered by Francis I. for robbers, about 1535.

Whigs. In the reign of Charles II. of England the name *Whig* was a term of reproach given by the court party to their antagonists for holding the principles of the "Whigs," or fanatical Covenanters in Scotland; and in return the name *Tory* was given to the court party, comparing them to the tories, or popish robbers in Ireland.—*Baker.* The distinction arose out of the discovery of the MEAL-TUB PLOT in 1678. Upon bringing up the meal plot before Parliament, 2 parties were formed: those who doubted the plot styled those who believed in it *Whigs;* these styled their adversaries *Tories.* In time these names, given as marks of opprobrium, became honored distinctions.—*Hume.* The Whigs brought about the revolution of 1688-89, and established the Protestant succession. They were chiefly instrumental in obtaining the abolition of the slave-trade and slavery, the repeal of the Test and Corporation act, Catholic emancipation, parliamentary and municipal reform, the repeal of the corn laws, and similar measures. The Whig club was established by Charles James Fox. The principal Whig ministries of England were: Godolphin's, Halifax's, Walpole's, Rockingham's, Grenville's, Grey's, Melbourne's, Russell's, Palmerston's, and Gladstone's. For Whigs in the United States, see POLITICAL PARTIES.

whip, the popular title of the patronage secretary of the treasury of Great Britain, whose duty it is to collect members to make a house on important occasions, etc. Sir Wm. Hayter, the Liberal "whip," 1850-58, received a testimonial for his energetic services early in 1861. The right hon. Wm. P. Adam, an able whip, died governor of Madras, 24 May, 1881.

The management of the House of Commons by bribery is said to have begun with Clifford of the "Cabal" ministry, and continued by Whigs and Tories. Mr. Roberts (under Henry Pelham) is said to have paid members sums of 1000*l.*, 500*l.*, etc., to each at the close of a session for their support.—*Wraxall.*

Whiskey insurrection, a popular outbreak in western Pennsylvania, in the summer of 1794, on account of the imposition of duties on domestic distilled spirits. The insurgents put 16,000 men in the field, maltreated the excise officers, committed many outrages, and defied the national government. The governor of Pennsylvania refusing to act, Washington, as president of the United States, called out 13,-000, afterwards increasing the number to 15,000, militiamen of Virginia, Maryland, Pennsylvania, and New Jersey; and, putting gen. Henry Lee of Virginia in command, ordered a movement against the insurgents on 1 Sept. 1794. The prompt response to the call for militia intimidated the insurgents into complete submission. Among the leaders in this insurrection was Albert Gallatin, afterwards sec. of the treasury. It cost the national government $1,500,000, but was useful by showing its power to cope with so formidable an outbreak.

whist, a game at cards, became popular at the end of the 17th century.

"Whist," a poem	1791
Laws by "Cavendish," compiled	about 1861
Edmund Hoyle, who published his "Short Treatise" about 1742, died in 1769, aged 97; lord Peterborough introduced short whist early in the present century; the laws revised	1864
James Clay, M.P., an eminent player, d.	26 Sept. 1871

White Friars. CARMELITES.

"White Horse." ASHDOWN.

White House, Washington, the residence of the president, gives name to the executive of the United States, as St. James's palace does to that of Great Britain. The corner-stone was laid 1792; building first occupied, by pres. Adams, 1800; burned by the British, 1814; restoration completed, 1818.

White House, on the Pamunkey, Va., belonging to Mrs. Robert E. Lee, was made the headquarters of gen. McClellan, and its vicinity the depot of supplies while engaged in his advance on Richmond in 1862.

White Mountains, in New Hampshire, covering 1300 sq. miles in several short ranges. In the Presidential range tower the peaks of mounts Washington, 6292 ft., Adams, 5794, Jefferson, 5714, Madison, 5365, Monroe, 5384, Jackson, and others. They were called *Waumbek Methna* by the Indians, a name adopted by Whittier in his ballad of "Mary Garvin."

"From the heart of Waumbek Methna,
From the lake that never fails
Falls the Saco in the green lap
Of Conway's intervales."

Mount Washington has a carriage-road ascending its rocky slope to the summit. The first cog-rail mountain railway in the world was built to the summit in 1868-69, rising 3730 ft. in less than 3 miles, the steepest grade being 13½ ins. in a yard. APPALACHIAN MOUNTAINS.

White Plains, a post-village of New York. Here Washington opposed the advance of the British forces under sir William Howe, 28 Oct. 1776. It terminated in the defeat of the Americans, whose losses were about 300 in killed, wounded, and prisoners. NEW YORK, UNITED STATES.

White tower, the keep or citadel in the Tower of London, a large, square, irregular building, erected in 1070 by abbot Gundulph, afterwards bishop of Rochester. It measures 116 feet by 96, and is 92 feet in height; the walls are 11 feet thick, with a winding staircase along 2 sides, like that in Dover Castle. It contains an extensive armory. Within this tower is the ancient chapel of St. John, originally used by the English monarchs. The turret at the northeast angle, the highest of the 4, was used for astronomical purposes by Flamsteed before the erection of the royal observatory at Greenwich.

Whitechapel, a parish in E. London. In this parish much excitement was caused by the murder and brutal mutilation of unfortunate women at different times and apparently by the same person. Smith, 3 Apr., Martha Turner, 7 Aug., Nichols, 31 Aug., Chapman, 8 Sept., Watts and Conway, 30 Sept., Mary Jane Kelly, 9 Nov., and Rose Millet, 28 Dec. 1888. Alice McKenzie, 17 July, and another woman, 10 Sept. 1889. Frances Coles, 13 Feb. 1891. The evidence showed a murderer possessed of surgical knowledge. Active measures were taken to discover the perpetrator of these murders in vain, but there is reason to believe that it was Frederick Bailey Deeming *alias* Albert Oliver Williams, executed at Melbourne, Australia, 1892. TRIALS, 1892.

Whitefieldites. George Whitefield, the founder of the "Calvinistic Methodists," born in England, 1714, was the son of an innkeeper at Gloucester, where he received his first education. He was admitted a servitor at Oxford in 1732, became a companion of the Wesleys there, and aided them in founding Methodism. He left them in 1741, on account of their rejection of the doctrine of election. He was the most eloquent preacher of his day. His first sermon was preached in 1736, and he commenced field-preaching in 1739. He is said to have delivered 18,000 sermons in 34 years. He visited America in 1738, 1739, 1744, and several times after, and died at Newburyport, Mass., 30 Sept. 1770. His followers are termed "the countess of Huntingdon's connection," from his having become her chaplain in 1748, and from her energetic support of the sect by establishing a college at Trevecca, 1767. There were 109 chapels of this connection in 1851, but many of his followers have joined the Independents. GEORGIA, 1739-40, MASSACHUSETTS; PENNSYLVANIA.

Whitsuntide, a festival appointed to commemorate the descent of the Holy Ghost upon the apostles, the newly baptized persons, or catechumens, are said to have worn white garments on Whit-Sunday. This feast is movable, being always exactly 7 weeks after Easter. Rogation week is the week before Whit-Sunday.

Whittington's charities. Sir Richard Whittington, a citizen and mercer of London, served the office of lord mayor 3 times, the last in 1419. Many false stories are connected with his name, and his munificent charities are little known. He founded his college, dedicated to the Holy Ghost and the Virgin Mary, in 1424, and his almshouses in 1429, the latter, originally built in London, now stand on Highgate hill (built 1808), near the supposed site of the famous stone which commemorated the legend of his return to London, after leaving it in despair. Stopping to rest on this stone, immediately after his departure from London, his ear caught the sound of the London bells which, to his disturbed fancy, repeated over and over again, "Turn again, Whittington, thrice lord mayor of London." Heeding the words he returned, his success in later years fulfilling the prophecy.

Wick'liffites, the followers of John Wickliffe (b. 1324), a professor of divinity in the university of Oxford and rector of Lutterworth in Leicestershire. He was a forerunner of the reformation of the English church, being among the first who opposed the authority of the pope, transubstantiation, the celibacy of the clergy, etc. Wickliffe, protected by John of Gaunt, Edward's son and Richard's uncle, was virulently persecuted by the church, and only saved from martyrdom by a paralytic attack, which caused his death, 31 Dec. 1384, in his 60th year. The council of Constance, in 1414, decreed his bones to be disinterred and burned, which was done by the bishop of Lincoln, and his dust was cast into the river Swift, 1415. Wickliffe's English version of the Bible was commenced in 1380, a noble edition of it was printed at Oxford in 1850. LOLLARDS.

widows. The Jewish law required a man's brother to marry his widow (1490 B.C.). For the burning of widows in India, SUTTEES. According to Swedenborg, widows signify in the Scriptures those without truth but desiring it.

Wight, Isle of, the Roman *Vecta*, or *Vectis*, an island in the British channel, was conquered by Vespasian in the reign of Claudius. It was conquered by the Saxons under Cerdic about 530, by the Danes, 787, and in 1001, when they held it for several years. It was invaded by the French July, 1377, and his several times suffered from invasion by them. In 1442, Henry VI. alienated the isle to Henry de Beauchamp first premier earl of England and then duke of Warwick, and afterwards crowned him king of the Isle of Wight with his own hands, but for want of heirs male his regal title died with him, and the isle reverted to the crown. Charles I., after his flight from Hampton court, was a prisoner in Carisbrooke castle, in 1647. In the time of Charles II. timber was very plentiful. In this isle is queen Victoria's marine residence, Osborne house, also the former residence of Tennyson.

Wilderness battles. GRANT'S CAMPAIGN IN VIRGINIA, UNITED STATES, May, 1864.

Wilkes's Exploring expedition. UNITED STATES, 1838 and 1842.

Williams, Eleazar, was a reputed son of Thomas Williams, son of Eunice, daughter of rev. John Williams (MASSACHUSETTS, 1704). In 1853-54 rev. Mr. Hanson published a series of papers in *Putnam's Monthly*, under the title "Have We a Bourbon Among Us?" and afterwards in a volume, entitled "The Lost Prince," asserting the identity of Mr. Williams with the son of Louis XVI., whose death from neglect in prison, 8 June, 1795, has often been doubted, many rumors being current regarding his fate. One story was that he had been secretly conveyed to the United States and placed among the Indians, etc. So strong was the case presented by Mr. Hanson, that in 1854 the prince de Joinville visited Mr. Williams at Green Bay, Wis., but without definite results. Mr. Williams died at Hogansburg, N. Y., 28 Aug. 1858, aged 72. He was from 1826 an ordained Episcopal missionary, and labored in northern New York and Wisconsin among the Indians, translating the "Book of Common Prayers" into the Mohawk language, and also prepared an Iroquois spelling-book.

Williamsburg, Va., Battle of. PENINSULAR CAMPAIGN.

willow-leaves. SUN.

wills and **testaments,** as indicating in writing what a person desires to be done with his real and personal estate after death, are of high antiquity (Gen. xlviii.). Solon introduced them at Athens, 578 B.C. There are regulations respecting wills in the Koran. Trebatius Testa, the civilian, introduced codicils to wills at Rome, 31 B.C. The power of bequeathing lands by will was confirmed to English subjects, 1 Hen. I. 1100, but with restrictions and limitations respecting the feudal system, which were taken off by the statute of 32 Hen. VIII. 1541.—*Blackstone's Commentaries.* The first will of a sovereign on record is said to be that of Richard II 1399, but in fact Edward the Confessor made a will, 1066

The will of *Peter the Great*, described in the *Memoires de la Chevaliere d'Eon* as a "plan for compassing European supremacy," left for his successors and deposited in the archives of the palace of Peterhoff near St Petersburg It advocated 'approach as near as possible to Constantinople and towards the Indies, wars with Turkey and Persia, possession of the shores of the Black sea and the Baltic.' etc The existence of the will (denied by the czars) was first announced by M Lesur, in his "Progres de la Puissance Russe," published at Paris in 1812 In 1863, dr Berkholz of Riga asserted that the will was a forgery, probably dictated by Napoleon I W J Thoms, the antiquary and others, contend for the genuineness of the will, June, 1878

Extracts from the Last Will of Napoleon I, Emperor of France.

[He died 5 May 1821, 11 days after he had signed these documents The original in French, occupies about 26 pages in Peignot s 'Testaments Remarquables ' 1829]

"This day, 24 April, 1821, at Longwood, in the island of St Helena. This is my testament, or act of my last will

"I leave the comte Montholon 2 000,000 francs as a proof of my satisfaction for the attentions he has paid to me for these 6 years, and to indemnify him for the losses which my residence in St Helena has occasioned him I leave to the comte Bertrand 500,000 francs I leave to Marchand my first valet de chambre, 400 000 francs, the services he has performed for me are those of a friend I desire that he may marry a widow sister, or daughter of an officer or soldier of my old guard To St Denis 100 000 francs To Novarre 100,000 francs To Pieron 100,000 francs To Archambaud, 50,000 francs To Curier 50,000 francs To Chandelle, *idem*

"To the Abbé Viguali 100,000 francs I desire that he may build his house near Ponte Novo de Rossino To the comte Las Casas, 100,000 francs. To comte Lavalette, 100 000 francs To the surgeon in chief Larrey, 100,000 francs He is the most virtuous man I have known To gen Brayer 100 000 francs

"To gen Lefevre Desnouettes 100,000 francs To gen Drouet, 100 000 francs To gen Cambronne 100 000 francs To the children of gen Muton Duvernais 100,000 francs To the children of the brave Labedoyère, 100 000 francs To the children of gen Girard, killed at Ligny, 100,000 francs To the children of gen Chartrand, 100,000 francs To the children of the virtuous gen Travost, 100,000 francs To gen Lallemand, the elder, 100 000 francs To gen Clausel 100 000 francs To Costa Bastilica also 100,000 francs To the baron de Menevalle 100,000 francs To Arnault, author of 'Marius,' 100,000 francs

"To col Marbot, 100,000 francs, I request him to continue to write for the defence and glory of the French armies and to confound the calumniators and the apostates To the baron Bignon, 100 000 francs, I request him to write the history of French diplomacy from 1792 to 1815 To Poggi de Talaro, 100,000 francs To the surgeon Emmery, 100,000

"These sums shall be taken from the 6 000 000 which I deposited on leaving Paris in 1815, and from the interest at the rate of 5 per cent since July, 1815, the account of which shall be adjusted with the bankers by the comtes Montholon and Bertrand and by Marchand

"These legacies, in case of death, shall be paid to the widows and children, and in their default shall revert to the capital I institute the comtes Montholon, Bertrand, and Marchand my testamentary executors This present testament, written entirely by my own hand, is signed and sealed with my arms "NAPOLEON

"24 April, 1821, Longwood "

The following are part of the 8 *codicils* to the preceding will of the emperor

"On the liquidation of my civil list of Italy—such as money, jewels, plate, linen, coffers, caskets of which the viceroy is the depositary, and which belong to me—I dispose of 2,000,000, which I leave to my most faithful servants I hope that, without their showing any cause my son Eugene Napoleon will discharge them faithfully He cannot forget the 40,000,000 which I have given him in Italy, or by the right (*parage*) of his mother's inheritance

"From the funds remitted in gold to the empress Maria Louisa, my very dear and well beloved spouse at Orleans, in 1814, there remain due to me 2,000 000, which I dispose of by the present codicil in order to recompense my most faithful servants, whom I beside recommend to the protection of my dear Maria Louisa I leave 200,000 francs to comte Montholon, 100,000 francs of which he shall pay into the chest of the treasurer (Las Casas) for the same purpose as the above, to be employed according to my dispositions in legacies of conscience

"10 000 francs to the sub officer Cantillon [d July, 1869], who has undergone a prosecution, being accused of a desire to assassinate lord Wellington of which he has been declared innocent. Cantillon had as much right to assassinate that oligarch, as the latter had to send me to perish on the rock of St Helena," etc

Letter to M Lafitte

"Monsieur Lafitte,—I remitted to you in 1815, at the moment of my departure from Paris, a sum of nearly 6,000,000, for which you gave me a double receipt I have cancelled one of these receipts, and I have charged comte Montholon to present to you the other receipt, in order that you may, after my death, deliver to him the said sum with interest at the rate of 5 per cent, from the 1st of July, 1815 deducting the payments with which you have been charged in virtue of my order I have also remitted to you a box containing my medallion I beg you will deliver it to comte Montholon

"This letter having no other object, I pray God, monsieur Lafitte, that he may have you in his holy and worthy keeping "NAPOLEON

"Longwood, in the island of St Helena, 25 April, 1821."

The following will of *Napoleon III* was published in the *Times*, 30 Apr 1873 "April 24, 1865

"This is my will I commend my son and my wife to the high constituted authorities of the state (*aux grands corps de l'etat*), to the people and the army The empress Eugenie possesses all the qualities requisite for conducting the regency well and my son displays a disposition and judgment which will render him worthy of his high destinies Let him never forget the motto of the head of our family, 'Everything for the French people' Let him fix in his mind the writings of the prisoner of St Helena, let him study the emperor s deeds and correspondence, finally let him remember, when circumstances so permit, that the cause of the peoples is the cause of France. Power is a heavy burden because one cannot always do all the good one could wish, and because your contemporaries seldom render you justice, so that, in order to fulfil one's mission, one must have faith in and consciousness of one s duty It is necessary to consider that from heaven on high those whom you have loved regard and protect you, it is the soul of my illustrious uncle that has always inspired and sustained me The like will apply to my son, for he will always be worthy of his name I leave to the empress Eugenie all my private property It is my desire that on the majority of my son she shall inhabit the Elysée and Biarritz I trust that my memory will be dear to her, and that after my death she will forget the griefs I may have caused her With regard to my son, let him keep as a talisman the seal I used to wear attached to my watch, and which comes from my mother, let him carefully preserve everything that comes to me from the emperor, my uncle and let him be convinced that my heart and my soul remain with him I make no mention of my faithful servants I am convinced that the empress and my son will never abandon them I shall die in the Catholic, Apostolic, and Roman religion, which my son will always honour by his piety Done, written, and signed with my hand at the palace of the Tuileries, the 24th of April, 1865 "NAPOLEON"

The will of *Prince Louis Napoleon* was written with his own hand, and signed 26 Feb 1879 the night before he sailed for South Africa (where he was killed while on a reconnoitring party, 1 June, 1879) He states that he dies in the Catholic religion, expresses his love for his country his mother the empress, and his friends, and his gratitude to the queen and royal family of England, and to the English people for their cordial hospitality He constitutes his mother sole legatee, bequeaths legacies and memorials to prince J N Murat, M F Pietri, baron Corvisart M Rouher and others, and assigns to Victor, the eldest son of prince Napoleon Jerome, the task of continuing the work of Napoleon I and Napoleon III. Executors, MM Rouher and Pietri

Wil'mington, a town of North Carolina, was held by the confederates, resisted severe attacks of the federals in Dec 1864 FORT FISHER was taken by assault on 15 Jan, and Wilmington was evacuated by the confederates, 22 Feb. 1865

Wilmot proviso. While a bill was pending in Congress to authorize the president to purchase territory in negotiating peace with Mexico, David Wilmot of Pennsylvania offered an amendment, 8 Aug 1846, providing "that, as an express and fundamental condition to the acquisition of any territory from the republic of Mexico, neither slavery nor involuntary servitude should ever exist in any part of said territory" This "proviso" was adopted by the House of Representatives, but rejected by the Senate It became the doctrinal foundation of the Free-soil party in 1848, and of the Republican party in 1856

Wilson's Creek, Battle of, a few miles from Springfield, Mo Here, early on the morning of 10 Aug 1861, the Union forces, about 6000 men, under gen Nathaniel Lyon, attacked the confederates, 20,000 strong, under McCulloch and Price, but were obliged to retire, after severe fighting and the death of gen Lyon, with a loss of 1235 in all, Confederate loss about the same

Winchester, Hampshire, Engl, an ancient city perhaps founded by Celtic Britons, with the fabulous date 392 B.C It was made the capital of the West Saxon kingdom under Cerdic, about 520, and of England by Egbert, 827, it became the residence of Alfred, 879-901. In the reign of William I. London began to rival it, and the destruction of religious houses by Henry VIII almost ruined it. Several kings resided at Winchester, and many parliaments were held there. Memorials of its ancient superiority exist in the national denomination of measures of quantity, as Winchester ell, Winchester bushel, etc., the use of which has been replaced by imperial measures. The cathedral church was first founded and endowed by Cynegils, or Kenegilsus, the first Christian king of the West Saxons. Becoming ruinous, the present fabric was begun by bishop Walkelyn, the 34th bishop, 1073. The church was first dedicated to St Amphibalus, then to St. Peter, and afterwards to St. Swithin, once bishop here Dedicated to the Holy Trinity by Henry VIII St Birinus was the first bishop of the West Saxons, his seat Dorchester, 636; Wina, in 660, was the first bishop of Winchester.

Winchester, Va. This town is situated in the Shenandoah valley. During the civil war there were several conflicts here of greater or less importance. Here, on 23 Mch. 1862, gen. Shields repulsed "Stonewall" Jackson. Jackson attacked gen. Banks at this place, 25 May, and forced him to retreat. Gen. Milroy held the town with 7000 men at the time of Lee's invasion, June, 1863. On the approach of the confederates he retreated, 15 June, and a column of the enemy gaining his rear, while another attacked in front, he was defeated, his force dispersed, and 2300 captured. In the autumn of 1864, gen. Sheridan, commanding the army of the Upper Potomac, held a strong position near the railroad from Harper's Ferry towards Winchester. The confederate general Early commanded a large force in the valley of the Shenandoah, and on 18 Sept. was posted on the Opequan creek, near Winchester. Sheridan gained the rear of the confederates, and on 19 Sept. defeated them, capturing 4500 prisoners. On the Confederate side gens. Rhodes and Godwin were killed; on the Federal, gen. D. A. Russell was killed, and gens. Upton, McIntosh, and Chapman were wounded. The Federal loss was over 3000. The Confederate loss in killed and wounded was 3500. GRANT'S CAMPAIGN IN VIRGINIA, PENINSULAR CAMPAIGN, etc.

Winchester school, founded by bishop William of Wykeham, 1382-87; the 500th anniversary of the laying of the first stone of New college, 26 Mch. 1387, celebrated 26 Mch. 1887.

wind. METEOROLOGY, STORMS.

windmills are of great antiquity, said to be of Roman or Saracen invention, and originally introduced into Europe by the knights of St. John, who had seen them in the crusades.—*Baker.* Windmills were first known in Spain, France, and Germany, in 1299.—*Anderson.* Wind saw-mills were invented by a Dutchman in 1633, when one was erected near the Strand, in London.

windows. There were glass windows in Pompeii, 79 A.D., as is evident from its ruins. It is certain that windows of some kind were glazed so early as the 3d century, if not before, though the fashion was not introduced until it was done by Benedict Biscop, about 650. In England windows of glass were used in private houses, but the glass was imported, 1177.—*Anderson.*

Windsor castle, Berkshire, Engl., a residence of the British sovereigns, begun by William the Conqueror, and enlarged by Henry I. about 1110. Edward III., who was born here, 13 Nov. 1312, caused the old building, except 3 towers at the west end, to be taken down, re-erected the whole castle under the direction of William of Wykeham, 1356, and built St. George's chapel. He assessed every county in England to send him workmen. James I. of Scotland was imprisoned here, 1406-23. Several additions were made by Henry VIII. Elizabeth made the grand north terrace; and Charles II. repaired and beautified it, 1676-80.

Windsor Forest, south and west of the town of Windsor, was formerly 120 miles in circumference; in 1607 it was 77½ miles round, but it has since been reduced in its bounds to about 56 miles. It was surveyed in 1789, and found to contain 59,600 acres.

On the south side is Windsor Great park, of about 3800 acres.

Little Park, on the north and east sides of the castle, contains about 500 acres. The fine gardens have been improved by the addition of the house and gardens of the duke of St. Albans, purchased by the crown.

Windward isles. WEST INDIES.

wine, properly the fermented juice of the grape; but that of other fruits is sometimes called by this name. "Noah planted a vineyard, and drank of the wine," 2347 B.C. (Gen. ix. 20). VINE. Ching-Noung, emperor of China, is said to have made rice wine, 1998 B.C. The art of making wine is said to have been brought from India by Bacchus. Christ changed water into wine at the marriage of Cana in Galilee, 30 A.D. (John ii. 3-10).

Wine sold in England by apothecaries as a cordial in 1300 and after, although there is mention of "wine for the king" so early as John.

Wine produced in the U. S. 1889-90 was 24,306,905 gals., of which 14,626,000 gals. were produced in California; New York follows next with 2,528,250 gals. Florida has recently given promise of becoming an important wine-producing state, although she does not appear in the report cited.

Winnebagoes, a tribe of the Dakotas. INDIANS.

wire. The invention of drawing wire is ascribed to Rodolph of Nuremberg, about 1410. Mills for this purpose were first set up at Nuremberg in 1563. The first wire-mill in England was erected in Mortlake in 1663.—*Mortimer.*

Wisconsin, one of the western states of the United States, lying between lat. 42° 27′ and 47° N. and lon. 86° 53′ and 92° 53′ W., is bounded on the north by lake Superior and Michigan, on the east by Michigan and lake Michigan, on the south by Illinois, and west by Iowa and Minnesota, the Mississippi and St. Croix rivers marking almost the entire boundary-line on the west. Area, 56,040 sq. miles. Pop. 1890, 1,686,880; 1900, 2,069,042. Capital, Madison.

Jean Nicolet, interpreter at Three Rivers, explores the Fox river.............. 1634
Sieur Radisson and sieur des Groseilliers, French traders, winter in the Green Bay country.............. 1658
Radisson and Groseilliers ascend the Fox river.............. 1659
Radisson and Groseilliers build a stockade on Chequamegon bay where Ashland now is.............. 1661
Jesuit missionary to the Hurons, René Ménard, loses his life near the Black river..............June, 1662
Father Claude Allouez establishes a mission at La Pointe, on Chequamegon bay.............. 1665
Mission established at the Rapids de Père on the Fox river, near Green bay, by father Allouez.............. 1670
Father Marquette and M. Joliet from Michilimackinac enter Green bay and pass Fox river portage to the Wisconsin river, 10 June, and down the Wisconsin, discovering the Mississippi..............17 June, 1673
Marquette coasts lake Michigan from Green bay, reaching the site of Chicago..............4 Dec. 1674
La Salle, leaving his ship the *Griffin* at Green bay, sails up the coast of lake Michigan.............. 1679
Daniel Grayson Duluth ascends the Bois Brulé from lake superior, and descends the St. Croix to the Mississippi river..... 1680
Father Louis Hennepin, with Duluth, journeys from lake St. Francis to Green bay by way of the Wisconsin and Fox rivers, "
Pierre le Sueur reaches the Mississippi river *via* the Fox and Wisconsin.............. 1683
Nicholas Perrot, appointed commandant of the West, winters near Trempeleau, which he reaches *via* the Fox and Wisconsin rivers from Green bay.............. 1685
Father St. Cosme visits site of Milwaukee on his way by boat from Green bay to the Mississippi river..............7 Oct. 1699
Le Seuer discovers lead mines in southwestern Wisconsin.... 1700
Marin, the French leader, sent by the Quebec government, attacks the Fox Indians at Winnebago Rapids (Neenah), winter of 1706-7
De Louvigny, sent to destroy the Fox tribes, leaves Quebec 14 Mch.; fights the battle of Buttes des Morts on the Fox river, and reaches Quebec again..............12 Oct. 1716
Francis Renault engages in mining on the Mississippi above the mouth of the Wisconsin.............. 1719
De Lignery makes a treaty with the Sacs, Foxes, and Winnebagoes by which the French may cross Wisconsin to trade with the Sioux on lake Pepin..............7 June, 1726
Cardinell, a French soldier, and his wife, settle at Prairie du Chien.............. "
Fort Beauharnois, on lake Pepin, established by the French, with sieur de la Perrière as commandant.............. 1727
Fort St. Francis, at Green bay, on site of fort Howard about 1718-21, is destroyed, to keep it from the Indians.......... 1728
Expedition fitted against the Fox Indians by the marquis de Beauharnois ascends the Fox river, burning deserted Indian villages..............Aug. "
Expedition against the Fox Indians under De Villiers........ 1730
Fort La Baye built by the French on the site of fort Howard.. "
Expedition against the Sacs and Foxes by the French under De Noyelle.............. 1735
Legardeur Saint Pierre, commandant at lake Pepin, evacuates his post, fearing massacre by the Indians.............. 1737
Massacre of 11 Frenchmen at Green bay, by the Menomonee Indians.............. 1758
Wisconsin becomes English territory..............8 Sept. 1760
Capt. Belfour and lieut. Gorrell with English troops occupy Green Bay, which Belfour names fort Edward Augustus, 12 Oct. 1761
English abandon fort Edward Augustus on account of the Pontiac war, cross lake Michigan to L'Arbre Croche and thence to Montreal..............21 June, 1763
Trade with the Chippewas at Chequamegon bay reopened by Henry, an English trader.............. 1765
Augustin de Langlade and his son Charles Michel settle permanently at Green Bay.............. 1766
Jonathan Carver, exploring the northwest as a trader and traveller, by way of Green bay and the Fox and Wisconsin rivers, reaches Prairie du Chien..............15 Oct. "
John Long, an English trader, visits Green Bay and Prairie du Chien..............June, 1780

WIS

Bazil Girard, Augustin Angé, and Pierre Antaya settle Prairie du Chien . . . 1781

Laurent Barth engages in the carrying trade at the portage from the Fox to the Wisconsin rivers 1793

Trading posts established at Kewaunee, Sheboygan, Manitowoc, and Milwaukee, by Jacques Vieau . 1795

Western posts surrendered by England to the U S 1 June, 1796

Wisconsin included in the territory of Indiana, created by act approved 7 May, 1800

Judge Charles Reaume appointed justice of the peace at Green Bay by gov William Henry Harrison of Indiana 1803

By treaty of St Louis the united Sacs and Foxes cede to the U S land, a portion of which lies in southern Wisconsin 3 Nov 1804

Wisconsin included in the territory of Illinois, created by act approved . 3 Feb 1809

Thomas Nuttall and John Bradbury, naturalists, explore Wisconsin . "

Gov Clarke takes possession of Prairie du Chien and builds fort Shelby 1813

Fort Shelby surrendered to the British under col McKay 19 July, 1814

U S troops occupy Prairie du Chien and commence fort Crawford on the site of fort McKay, formerly fort Shelby June, 1816

Fort Howard, on Green bay, built and garrisoned by American troops under col John Miller . . "

First grist mill in western Wisconsin built at Prairie du Chien by John Shaw . . . 1818

Solomon Juneau arrives at Milwaukee 14 Sept "

Wisconsin attached to Michigan territory upon admission of Illinois into the Union . 3 Dec. "

Col William S Hamilton having a contract to supply the garrison at fort Howard with provisions, drives several hundred cattle from lower Illinois north along the west shore of lake Michigan to Green Bay . . 1823

Episcopal mission established near Green Bay "

First term of U S District court held at Green Bay, James D Doty, judge . 4 Oct 1824

Winnebago Indians massacre 3 whites at Prairie du Chien, 28 June, 1827

Treaty concluded with the Menomonee and other Indian tribes at Butte des Morts 11 Aug "

Fort Winnebago built at the portage between the Fox and Wisconsin rivers . 1828

Methodist mission established at Green Bay 1829

Battle of Wisconsin Heights, Black Hawk attacked by Illinois troops under gen James D Henry, and Wisconsin rangers under maj Henry Dodge 21 July, 1832

Black Hawk's band destroyed by U S troops and crew of government steamboat *Warrior*, at mouth of Bad Axe river, 2 Aug "

Black Hawk delivered to gen Street, agent of the Winnebagoes, by his captors, Chaetar and One-eyed Decorra 27 Aug "

Treaty with the Winnebagoes at Rock Island, ceding to U S their lands east of the Mississippi and west of Green bay, 15 Sept. "

First newspaper the *Green Bay Intelligencer*, published at Green Bay . 11 Dec 1833

Land offices established at Mineral Point and Green Bay . 1834

Military road from fort Howard to fort Crawford begun 1 June, 1835

First steamboat makes port at Milwaukee 17 June, "

Territory of Wisconsin created by act of 20 Apr, and government organized at Mineral Point .. 4 July, 1836

Milwaukee Advertiser published at Milwaukee . 14 July, "

Real estate speculation at Kewaunee, owing to discovery of gold, at its height . . "

First session of the assembly held at Belmont, Iowa county, 25 Oct "

First permanent settlement of Madison . . Apr 1837

Corner stone of capitol at Madison laid 4 July, "

Gov Dodge of Wisconsin territory, by treaty with the Ojibways at fort Snelling, obtains cession to the U S of the pine forests of the valley of the St Croix and its tributaries 29 July, "

Assembly meets at Burlington, Des Moines county 6 Nov "

Portage canal, connecting Wisconsin and Fox rivers, begun by the U S. . . 1838

Legislature assembles at Madison .. 26 Nov "

Mitchell's bank at Milwaukee established . . 1839

"The Wisconsin Phalanx," a community on Fourier's system, established at Ceresco, now Ripon May, 1844

Mormon colony, an offshoot from Nauvoo, led by James Jesse Strang, is founded on White river at Voree . . 1845

Enabling act for the state of Wisconsin passed by Congress, 6 Aug 1846

State constitution prohibiting banks and banking, framed by a convention at Madison, 5 Oct. to 16 Dec 1846, is rejected by the people . Apr 1847

Troops from Michigan and Wisconsin leave Detroit by boat for Vera Cruz enlisted in the Mexican war . . 24 Apr "

Beloit college at Beloit chartered 1846, opened "

First railroad charter in Wisconsin granted to the Milwaukee and Waukesha Railroad company . . "

Convention assembles at Madison, 15 Dec 1847, frames a constitution, and adjourns, 1 Feb 1848 Constitution ratified by a popular vote of 16,442 to 6149 . . 13 Mch 1848

Wisconsin admitted into the Union by act approved . 29 May, "

First state legislature convenes 5 June, and officers take the oath . . 7 June, "

First telegram received at Milwaukee from Chicago . 17 Jan 1849

State Historical Society organized at Madison .. 30 Jan. "

Lawrence university at Appleton chartered and opened "

University of Wisconsin at Madison, chartered 1848, opened "

Amendment to the constitution conferring suffrage on colored men receives a majority of votes cast, but not a majority of all who voted for state officers, and the canvassers declare it rejected 6 Nov 1849

Wisconsin School for the Blind at Janesville opened 1 Aug 1850

First railroad train between Milwaukee and Waukesha Feb 1851

Question of banks or no banks submitted to the people of Wisconsin by act of 5 Mch 1851, 31,219 votes in favor to 9126 opposed .. "

State prison at Waupun opened 1852

Wisconsin School for the Deaf at Delavan opened "

St Clara academy at Sinsinawa Mound, opened 1845, chartered, "

Capital punishment in Wisconsin abolished July, 1853

Milwaukee college at Milwaukee chartered and opened . . "

Meeting at Ripon, called by A E Bovay, Jedidah Bowen, and others to organize the Republican party, and Mr Bovay suggests the name "Republican" . . 28 Feb 1854

Title "Republican" adopted for the party at a mass convention in Capitol park at Madison 13 July, "

A negro Joshua Glover, claimed as a slave by a Missourian named Garland, being forcibly released from prison in Milwaukee, federal and state authorities dispute on the legality of the Fugitive Slave law "

Act passed to extinguish the title of the Chippewa Indians to lands owned and claimed by them in Wisconsin and the territory of Minnesota 19 Dec "

Sherman M Booth of Milwaukee, convicted in the Federal District court of Wisconsin of violating the Fugitive Slave law by aiding in the liberation of Glover, and fined and imprisoned, is discharged by the Supreme court, which pronounces the law unconstitutional 3 Feb 1855

Downer college at Fox lake chartered and opened "

William A Barstow, Dem, ex governor and Coles Bashford, Rep, each claiming to be elected governor by the people, take the oath of office, the one at the capitol, the other in the Supreme court room 7 Jan 1856

Assembly recognizes Barstow as governor and the Senate as governor *de facto* 10 Jan "

Supreme court of Wisconsin summons Barstow to show by what authority he claims to hold the office 17 Jan "

Supreme court decides that Barstow has been counted in upon fraudulent returns, lieut. gov McArthur fills the office for 4 days, when Coles Bashford assumes office 21 Mch "

Seminary of St Francis of Sales, at St. Francis, chartered and opened "

First railway reaches the Mississippi river at Prairie du Chien, 15 Apr 1857

Wisconsin Industrial School for Boys, at Waukesha, opened 23 July, 1860

Hospital for the insane at Madison opened "

First Wisconsin regiment, mustered into service 17 May, 1861, receives marching orders 7 June, 1861

About 700 Confederate prisoners are received at camp Randall, Madison Apr 1862

Gov Harvey dies on his way to the battlefield of Shiloh to look after the welfare of Wisconsin soldiers Apr "

Personal Liberty law repealed July, "

Negro suffrage amendment to the constitution rejected by vote of 55,591 to 46,588 Nov 1865

Home for soldiers' orphans opened 1 Jan 1866, established by private subscription, becomes a state institution 31 Mch 1866

Fourth regiment Wisconsin cavalry mustered out after a service of 5 years and 1 day, the longest term on record of a volunteer organization 28 May, "

Alexander W Randall appointed postmaster-general 25 July, "

Supreme court sustains the amendment to the constitution giving suffrage to colored men, as ratified by the people in 1849, "

State Normal school at Platteville opened "

Northwestern university at Watertown, opened 1865, chartered, 1867

State Normal school at Whitewater opened . 1868

Legislature ratifies the XV th Amendment to Constitution of the U S. . 9 Mch 1869

Northwestern branch of the National Home for Disabled Volunteer Soldiers, near Milwaukee, dedicated Oct "

Catholic Normal School of the Holy Family, at St. Francis, opened, 1871

A "whirlwind of fire" 10 miles in width sweeps over the counties bordering on Green bay Loss of life, 1000 persons, burned, drowned, or smothered, of property, over $3,000 000, 8-9 Oct. "

State Board of Charities and Reform appointed by gov Fairchild, 4 men and 1 woman . "

College for women opened at Madison in connection with the state university . 20 Dec "

Act punishing intoxication by fine and imprisonment 1872

Northern Hospital for the Insane at Oshkosh opened Apr 1873

First state meeting of the "American Constitutional Union," 666 delegates, at Milwaukee . 7 Aug "

"Potter Railroad law," relating to railroads, express, and telegraph companies, fixing rates of transportation, and providing for railroad commissioners . . . 11 Mch 1874

St. Paul and Northern railroads announce to the governor that they cannot obey the Potter law 27 Apr "

Supreme court sustains the Potter law Sept "

First cotton cloth manufactured in Wisconsin, at Janesville 1875

Real estate of soldiers' orphans' home transferred to the regents of the state university for a medical college "

Wisconsin Industrial School for Girls at Milwaukee opened . "

State Normal school at River Falls opened "

Supreme court rejects the application of miss Lavinia Goodell for admission to the bar, as a calling inconsistent with the duties of the sex . . : . Jan. 1876

Potter Railroad law of 1874 made much less stringent 18 Feb "

St John's Catholic Deaf Mute institution at St Francis opened, "

Legislature enables women to practise law 1877

State park established in Lincoln county by act of legislature.. 1878
National German-American teachers' seminary at Milwaukee opened .... "
Legislature passes a compulsory Education law.............. 1879
Death of "Old Abe," the Wisconsin war eagle, belonging to company C, Eighth Wisconsin infantry, the survivor of 36 battles and numerous wounds.........................Mch. 1881
Timothy O. Howe appointed postmaster-general.......20 Dec. "
Milwaukee Day School for the Deaf at Milwaukee opened..... 1883
Science hall of the state university destroyed by fire; loss $200,000...1 Dec. 1884
William F. Vilas appointed postmaster-general.........6 Mch. 1885
Women empowered to vote at school elections.................. "
Legislature appropriates $5000 yearly to hold farmers' institutes, "
State Normal school at Milwaukee opened........................ "
Anarchist riots in Milwaukee..............................5 May, 1886
State public school at Sparta opened.................13 Nov. "
Oral department of public schools at La Crosse opened........ 1887
State Normal school at Oshkosh opened.............................. "
William F. Vilas appointed secretary of the interior....16 Jan. 1888
Jeremiah M. Rusk appointed secretary of agriculture...5 Mch. 1889
Annual meeting of the Grand Army of the Republic held at Milwaukee...27 Aug. "
Acts passed to secure a secret ballot at elections..................... "
Local Option law passed, providing for a vote on the question of license on petition of 10 per cent. of the voters in any town or village... "
Ex-sec. Vilas chosen U. S. senator...........................27 Jan. 1891
Bennet School law of 1889, requiring schools recognized by the state to teach reading, writing, arithmetic, and U. S. history in English, is repealed... "
Ex-gov. Harrison Ludington dies at Milwaukee, aged 78, 17 June, "
Dr. Isaac Leo Nicholson enthroned as bishop of Milwaukee, the first ceremony of the kind in the U. S...........10 Nov. "
Charles Kendall Adams, ex-president of Cornell university, accepts the presidency of the University of Wisconsin..30 July, 1892
Legislature in special session to reapportion the state..17 Oct. "
Destructive fire in Milwaukee; over 300 buildings destroyed and 10 lives lost; loss in property over $5,000,000....28 Oct. "
Dr. P. R. Hoy, naturalist, dies at Racine, aged 76........8 Dec. "

TERRITORIAL GOVERNORS.

Henry Dodge.......................assumes office..........1836
James D. Doty.......................... " 1842
Nathaniel P. Tallmadge............ " 1844
Henry Dodge............................ " 1845

STATE GOVERNORS (term 2 years).

Nelson Dewey......................assumes office..........1848
Leonard J. Farwell.................. " 1852
William A. Barstow.................. " 1854
Coles Bashford .... " 1856
Alexander W. Randall............... " 1858
Louis P. Harvey........................ " 1862
Edward Salomon........................ " .... "
James T. Lewis.......................... " 1864
Lucius Fairchild........................ " 1866
C. C. Washburn......................... " 1872
William R. Taylor...................... " 1874
Harrison Ludington.................... " 1876
William E. Smith....................... " 1878
Jeremiah M. Rusk...................... " 1882
William D. Hoard...................... " 1889
Geo. W. Peck............................ " 1891
William H. Upham..................... " 1895

UNITED STATES SENATORS FROM THE STATE OF WISCONSIN.

Name.	No. of Congress.	Date.	Remarks.
Henry Dodge.....	30th to 35th	1848 to 1857	Seated 23 June.
Isaac P. Walker ..	30th " 34th	1848 " 1855	Seated 26 June.
Charles Durkee...	31th " 37th	1855 " 1861	
James R. Doolittle	35th " 41st	1857 " 1869	
Timothy O. Howe.	37th " 46th	1861 " 1879	
Matt. H. Carpenter	41st " 44th	1869 " 1875	Pres. *pro tem.* 12 Mch. 1873.
Angus Cameron...	44th " 46th	1875 " 1881	
Matt. H. Carpenter	46th	1879 " 1881	Died in office, 24 Jan. 1881.
Philetus Sawyer..	46th to 53d	1881 " 1893	
Angus Cameron...	46th " 49th	1881 " 1885	Elected in place of Carpenter.
John E. Spooner..	49th " 52d	1885 " 1891	
William F. Vilas..	52d " ——	1891 " ——	Term expires 1897.
John L. Mitchell..	53d " ——	1893 " ——	Term expires 1899.

witchcraft, the practices and powers of a witch, a woman supposed to have supernatural power and knowledge given her by evil spirits. The Jewish law (Exod. xxii. 18), 1491 B.C., decreed, "Thou shalt not suffer a witch to live." Saul, after banishing or condemning witchcraft, consulted the witch of Endor, 1056 B.C. (1 Sam. xxviii.). Bishop Hutchinson's historical "Essay on Witchcraft" was published 1718. Pope Innocent VIII. issued a bull against witchcraft, 1484. Thousands of innocent persons were burned, and others killed by the tests applied.

Many Templars burned at Paris for witchcraft, etc............ 1309
Joan of Arc burned at Rouen as a witch.............30 May, 1431
About 500 witches burned in Geneva in 3 months.............. 1515
Great number in France, when 1 sorcerer confessed to having 1200 associates..about 1520
Many witches burned in the diocese of Como in a year..about 1524
Nine hundred burned in Lorraine...................................1580-95
One hundred and fifty-seven burned at Würzburg, old and young, learned and ignorant...........................between 1627-29
Grandier, the parish priest at Loudon, burned on a charge of having bewitched a whole convent of nuns..................... 1634
In Bretagne 20 poor women put to death as witches.......... 1654
Maria Renata burned at Würzburg.................................. 1749
At Kalisk, in Poland, 9 old women, charged with having bewitched and rendered unfruitful the lands belonging to that palatinate, were burned.............................17 Jan. 1775
Five women condemned to death by the Brahmans, at Patna, for sorcery, and executed ....15 Dec. 1802

WITCHCRAFT IN GREAT BRITAIN.

Statutes made all witchcraft and sorcery felony without benefit of clergy, 33 Hen. VIII. 1541, 5 Eliz. 1562, and 1 James I. 1603.
The 73d canon of the church prohibits the clergy from casting out devils, 1603.
Barrington estimates the judicial murders for witchcraft in England in 200 years at 30,000.
Matthew Hopkins, "witch-finder," causes judicial murder of about 100 persons in Essex, Norfolk, and Suffolk, 1645-47.
Sir Matthew Hale burned 2 persons for witchcraft in 1664.
Seventeen or 18 persons burned at St. Osyths, in Essex, about 1676.
Two pretended witches were executed at Northampton in 1705, and 5 others 7 years afterwards.
In 1716 Mrs. Hicks, and her daughter, aged 9, were hanged at Huntingdon.
Northamptonshire and Huntingdon preserved the superstition about witchcraft later than other counties.
In Scotland thousands of persons were burned in about 100 years; among them persons of high rank, while all orders in the state concurred. James I. even caused a whole assize to be prosecuted for an acquittal. The king published his "Dæmonologie" in Edinburgh, 1597. The last sufferer was at Dornoch in 1722.
Laws against witchcraft had lain dormant for many years, when, an ignorant person attempting to revive them (by a bill against a poor old woman in Surrey for witchcraft), they were repealed, 10 Geo. II. 1736. Belief in witchcraft still abounds in the country districts of England. On 4 Sept. 1863, a poor old paralyzed Frenchman died from being ducked as a wizard at Castle Hedingham, Essex, and similar cases have since occurred.
Ann Turner, old; killed as a witch by a half-insane man at Long Compton, Warwickshire, 17 Sept. 1875.

witchcraft, Salem. A grewsome chapter in the history of popular delusions is the record of that which is known in American history as Salem witchcraft. The people of Massachusetts generally believed in witchcraft. It had taken strong hold upon their feelings, and in Mch. 1692, excitement suddenly broke out at Danvers (part of Salem), Mass., and spread like an epidemic. It commenced in the family of the rev. Samuel Parris. The principal accusers and witnesses in the witchcraft prosecution were 8 females, nearly all young girls, viz.: Abigail Williams, aged 11 years; Mary Walcut, 17; Ann Putnam, 12; Mary Lewis, a servant, 17; Mary Warren, 20; Elizabeth Booth, 18; Sarah Churchill, 20; and Susannah Sheldon. But 2 of these could write their names.—*Drake's* "Annals of Witchcraft in New England."

First person tried is Bridget Bishop, on charges by the rev. Samuel Parris, and she is hanged as a witch........10 June, 1692
Susannah Martin hanged as a witch........................19 July, "
Sarah Good hanged as a witch.......................... " "
[She is said to have exclaimed, at the time of her execution, to the rev. Nicholas Noyes, who was very active in these prosecutions, "If you take my life, God will give you blood to drink." Hawthorne has put this expression in the mouth of "Old Matthew Maule," in "The House of the Seven Gables."]
Sarah Wildes hanged as a witch.........................19 July, "
Elizabeth How hanged as a witch.......................... " "
Rebecca Nourse hanged as a witch......................... " "
[Mrs. Nourse was acquitted, but the court, being determined on her death, sent the jury out again and forced a verdict of guilty. She was a lady of worth, but old and in ill-health.]
George Burroughs executed................................19 Aug. "
[He was a graduate of Harvard college, 1670. Had been a minister at Salem.]
John Proctor executed..19 Aug. "
John Willard executed.. " "
[He was a resident of Salem, and had been a deputy in making arrests; becoming satisfied that the persons accused were innocent, he was "cried out upon," and in atte[illegible]ng to escape he was captured and executed.]
Martha Carrier executed....................................1[illegible] Aug. "
[Her children forced by torture to testify against her.]
George Jacobs, sen., executed...............................19 Aug. "
[His granddaughter testified against him at his trial, but acknowledged her perfidy in a piteous letter when too late.—*Bancroft's* "Hist. of U. S."]
Giles Corey, upwards of 80 years of age, refusing to plead, is pressed to death; the only instance of this horrible punishment in New England..17 Sept. "

"Then by the statute you will be condemned
To the *peine forte et dure!* To have your body
Pressed by great weights until you are dead."
—*Longfellow,* "Giles Corey" ("New England Tragedies"), act iv.

Martha Corey, wife of Giles Corey, Mary Easty, Alice Parker, Mary Parker, Ann Pudeator (70 years old), Willmot Reed,

Margaret Scott, and Samuel Wardwell (the first confessed, the only one to do so but declared his innocence at his execution) are hanged 22 Sept. 1692

[At the execution of these victims Nicholas Noyes, the minister at Salem, is said to have exclaimed, pointing to the bodies swinging, "There hang 8 fire brands of hell"]

Cotton Mather's narrative of "The Wonders of the Invisible World," a plea for the truth of witchcraft Oct "

[This book was approved by the president of Harvard college, gov Phipps, and William Stoughton, then lieutenant governor of Massachusetts, and afterwards chief justice of the Superior court.—*Bancroft's* "Hist of the U S"]

Mrs Hale wife of the minister of the First church at Beverly, accused of being a witch Oct "

[The whole community became convinced that the accusers, in crying out upon Mrs Hale, had perjured themselves, and from that moment their power was destroyed the awful delusion was dispelled, and a close put to one of the most tremendous tragedies in the history of real life—the wildest storm that ever raged in the moral world"—*Upham's* "Witchcraft in Salem" vol ii p 346]

An attempt is made to convict Sarah Daston a woman of 80, who for 20 years had been reputed a witch, but the common mind is disenthralled, the jury acquits her Feb 1693

Prosecutions for witchcraft cease Apr "

Sir William Phipps by proclamation discharges all imprisoned for witchcraft May "

[The number released is said to have been about 150 The total number executed for witchcraft in Salem at this time was 21, others had been executed before, notably Anne Hibbins, 1656, but none after "All things considered, the outbreak of witchcraft in 1692 is one of the most surprising events of history—the smallness of the number of those engaged in it at its beginning their youth and position in society, and their ability to deceive everybody so long In any view that has yet been taken of it its narrator has found himself baffled to a degree beyond that of any other event in the whole range of history to account satisfactorily for the conduct of the young females through whose instrumentality it was carried on It required more devilish ability to deceive, adroitness to blind the understanding, and keep a consciousness of that ability among themselves, than ever fell to the lot of a like number of impostors in any age of which the writer has ever read The most active participants in pushing the prosecutions were the rev Samuel Parris rev Nicholas Noyes and the rev Cotton Mather, and among the judges William Stoughton, Samuel Sewell, and John Hathorne The accusers were never punished, and of those who caused the prosecutions, says Hutchinson, some proved profligate, abandoned to all vice, others passed their days in obscurity and contempt"—*Drake's* "Annals of Witchcraft in New England" "It is safe to say that if gov Bradstreet had not been superseded by the arrival of sir William Phipps as governor under the new charter, the witch prosecution of 1692 would never have taken place"—*Upham's* "Salem Witchcraft" vol i p 431 "A little attention must force conviction that the whole was a scene of fraud and imposition, begun by young girls, who at first perhaps thought of nothing more than being pitied and indulged, and continued by adult persons, who were afraid of being accused themselves. The one and the other, rather than confess their fraud suffered the lives of so many innocents to be taken away through the credulity of judges and juries."—*Hutchinson's* "History of Massachusetts Bay"]

wi'tena-mot', wi'tena-gemot', or **wi'tan,** the assembling of the wise men, the great council of the Anglo-Saxons. A witena-mot was called in Winchester by Egbert, 800, and in London, 833, to consult on the proper means to repel the Danes, and, among others, one in 1066, choosing Harold as king PARLIAMENT.

Witepsk', a town of Russia, near which a battle was fought between the French under marshal Victor, duke of Belluno, and the Russians, commanded by gen Wittgenstein The French were defeated after a desperate engagement, with the loss of about 3000 men on both sides, 14 Nov. 1812

witness (from A. S *witnes* = one that knows, from *witan*, to know, to attest, to give testimony) Two or more witnesses were required by the law of Moses, 1451 B.C (Deut. xvii 6), and by the early Christian church in cases of discipline (2 Cor xiii 1), 60 A.D. The evidence of 2 witnesses required to attaint for high-treason, 25 Edw. III 1352. Lord Ellenborough ruled that no witness is obliged to give answers which may tend to degrade himself, 10 Dec 1802.

wives. MARRIAGE

Wizard of the North, a name given to sir Walter Scott, on account of his romances, also to Mr Anderson, the conjurer, who died 3 Feb. 1874.

Robert Houdin's "Confidences d'un Prestidigitateur," pub. 1859

Herr Herrmann, an eminent conjurer or prestidigitateur, b Hanover, d at Carlsbad, aged 71 8 Jan. 1887

Woman's Christian Temperance Union was an outgrowth of the woman's crusade against the saloons, which began in Hillsborough, O, 23 Dec. 1873 The National Association was organized at Cleveland, O, 17-18 Nov. 1874 It now has a membership of nearly 200 000 The Children's Society under its auspices, with a membership of 200,000 to 300 000, is known as the Loyal Temperance Legion The Woman's Christian Temperance Union has a publishing house in Chicago and national headquarters at Evanston, Ill In 1883 was formed an international union with the title, "The World's Woman's Christian Temperance Union," of which Mrs Margaret Bright Lucas, sister of John Bright, was chosen president.

women, Advancement of But few names of women appear in history In most lands and times they have been without share in public life or in government, and have been deprived by law of equality in the acquisition and ownership of property The history of woman is mostly "domestic" history, that of the patient "Griselda"—largely a story of suffering and wrong at the hands of masculine rulers, fathers, and husbands, and without legal redress The sex has been from the first unrepresented in governing bodies. But the progress of civilization has been marked by the steady increase of the intelligence and influence of women in all departments of activity which they have entered, and multitudes of social thinkers now advocate the abolition of all distinctions in civil and political rights founded on sex.

ADVANCEMENT OF WOMEN IN ENGLAND

Mary Wollstonecraft's "Vindication of the Rights of Women," pub 1791

Great advance in the legal rights, position, and employment of women 1837-92

Women's hospitals founded, Soho 1842

Woman's Medical Society and Obstetrical college founded, about 1864

Woman's suffrage for members of Parliament proposed by J S. Mill, negatived by 196 against 73 20 May, 1867

Lily Maxwell, a shopkeeper at Manchester, votes for Jacob Bright 26 Nov "

First annual meeting of the Manchester National Society for Women's Suffrage 30 Oct 1868

Female suffrage held illegal by the court of common pleas, 7-9 Nov "

John S Mill's "Subjection of Women," pub 1869

Women's Club and Institute, Newman street, London, W, opened Jan "

Women's Disabilities Removal bill rejected by the Commons (220 to 94) 12 May, 1870

[It was presented every year, and the vote stood 217 to 103, 7 Mch 1879]

Woman's hospital founded at Marylebone 1871

Miss Garrett and miss Davies elected members of the metropolitan school board 29 Nov 1871

Medical school for women opened Oct. 1874

Miss Merington elected guardian of the poor for Kensington (the first case in London) Apr 1876

Women permitted to be registered under "Medical act" by 39 and 40 Vict c. 41 11 Aug "

University of London, senate votes for granting degrees to women, 28 Feb, convocation votes against it, 8 May, and July, 1877, votes for a supplemental charter granting it (242-132), 15 Jan, charter granted 28 Mch 1878

Great meeting for woman's suffrage, St James's hall 6 May, 1880

Women to be admitted to examinations for honors at Oxford, by statute 29 Apr 1884

Woman's householders' suffrage (widows and spinsters) proposed by Mr Woodall in the commons, 10 June, negatived (271-135), 12-13 June, miss H Müller refuses to pay queen's taxes, and her goods are distrained 2 July, "

Woman's suffrage granted in Madras presidency, India, 28 Sept. 1885

Woman's Suffrage Society, first annual meeting July, 1886

Women's hospital with female practitioners founded by the princess of Wales in Euston road 7 May, 1889

Mrs Scharlieb made M D 16 May, "

International "Council of Women," advocating women's rights, meets at Paris 25 June, "

Miss A F Ramsay and miss B M Hervey obtain high university honors 18 June, 1887, and miss G P Fawcett 7 June, 1890

Two ladies elected for the London common council This declared illegal, a bill to legalize it rejected by the lords, 20 May, 1889, and 9 June, 1890, by the commons 26 May, 1891

Women in New Zealand authorized to serve in parliament and vote at elections, bill passed 4 Sept., rejected by the legislative council 10 Sept "

Woman's Suffrage bill, lords read first time 3 July, negatived, 10 July, 1884, again, 28 July, 1885, again negatived by the lords, 16 Mch. 1886, again, 13 Sept. 1887, 13 Apr 1888, 18 Mch 1889, again 1891-92

Sir Albert Rollit's bill for the extension of the parliamentary franchise to women rejected by the commons (175-152), 27 Apr 1892

ADVANCEMENT OF WOMEN IN THE UNITED STATES.

Oberlin college, O, made no distinction as to sex from its foundation 1833

[Many colleges in the U S now admit female students under the same conditions as males.]

Elizabeth Blackwell graduates from the medical department, Geneva college (the first M D. in the U S.) 1849

Her sister Emily graduates from the Cleveland Medical college, 1852

First woman's hospital in the world founded at New York city by dr. Marion Sims ... 1857
[In Philadelphia, 1862; in Boston, incorporated, 1863; in Chicago, 1865; in San Francisco, 1875; in Minneapolis, 1882.]
Arabella A. Mansfield of Mt. Pleasant, Ia., admitted to the practice of law ... June, 1869
Mrs. Myra Bradwell of Chicago applies for a license as an attorney-at-law ... "
[The Superior court of Illinois refused, and the Supreme court of the U. S. affirmed the decision. Women now admitted to the practice of law in Illinois by statute.]
American Woman's Suffrage Association formed by Lucy Stone Blackwell ... "
First convention held at *Case hall*, *Cleveland*, O. ... 24 Nov. "
[Unites with the National Woman's Suffrage Association, forming the National American Woman's Suffrage Association, 1890.]
Marilla M. Ricker of Dover, N. H., attempts to vote; her vote refused for non-registration, although her name had been offered for registry ... Mch. 1870
Mrs. Ada H. Kepley of Effingham, Ill., the first graduate from a law-school, Union College of Law, Chicago ... 30 June, "
Women admitted into the department of medicine and surgery in the University of Michigan at Ann Arbor ... 1871
Illinois enacts that no person shall be precluded or debarred from any occupation, profession, or employment (except military) on account of sex ... Mch. 1872
[Women are now admitted to many medical colleges throughout the U. S.]
Susan B. Anthony votes at the presidential election at Rochester, N. Y. ... 5 Nov. "
She is convicted of illegal voting and fined $100 ... 18 June, 1873
Dr. Sarah H. Stevenson of Chicago admitted as a delegate (the first woman) to the American Medical Association at Philadelphia ... 1876
Mrs Belva Lockwood admitted to practice before the Supreme court of the U. S. 1879; disability removed by an act of Congress approved ... 15 Feb. 1879
[Others since admitted: Laura De Force Gordon of Stockton, Cal.: Ada M. Bittenbender of Lincoln, Neb.; Carrie Barnham Kilgore of Philadelphia; Clara M. Foltz of San Diego, Cal.; Lelia Robinson-Sawtelle of Boston; Emma M. Gillet of Washington, D. C.]
Mrs. Belva Lockwood accepts the nomination for president of the U. S. from the California Woman's Suffrage convention, Sept. 1884
A select committee of the U. S. Senate, Feb. 7, 1889, and the House judiciary committee, May 29, 1890, reported in favor of amending the Constitution to permit woman suffrage. Congress did not act upon these reports.
School suffrage for women exists in some form in most of the states where asked for; the number is now 32.
Women vote on equal terms with men in Wyoming, since 1870, under the state constitution, ratified by the people before admission by Congress, 10 July, 1890.
Women voted in Utah until excluded by the Edmunds law.
In adopting a state constitution in Washington, women were debarred from voting, although previously allowed.
In Kansas women have suffrage in municipal elections, and the number of voters is constantly increasing; in 1891 60,000 women voted in that state.
People vote in favor of woman's suffrage in Colorado in the state election of ... 1893
Montana women who are tax-payers have the same privileges at the polls as the men.
New York state convention to revise the constitution decided against a woman's suffrage amendment by a vote of 97 to 58. 1894
Supreme court of New Jersey decides against the right of women to vote at school elections ... 1894
Twenty-seventh annual convention of the American Woman's Suffrage Association begins at Atlanta, Ga ... 31 Jan. 1895
[Susan B. Anthony, president.]
Second triennial session of the National "Council of Women" of the *U. S. begins* at Washington, D. C., 18 Feb.; ends. 2 Mch. 1895
Area of countries in the whole world in which women have acquired at least partial suffrage within 25 years is about 20,000,000 sq. miles, with a population of over 385,000,000.

wonders (seven) of the world. These have been reputed to be: 1. The pyramids of Egypt. 2. The mausoleum or tomb built for Mausolus, king of Caria, by Artemisia, his queen. 3. The temple of Diana, at Ephesus. 4. The walls and hanging gardens of the city of Babylon. 5. The vast brazen image of the sun at Rhodes, called the Colossus. 6. The ivory and gold statue of Jupiter Olympus. 7. The pharos or watch-tower, built by Ptolemy Philadelphus, king of Egypt. Some place the great wall of China in the list. See separate articles.

wood. The following table shows the specific gravity of timber in general use, water being 100:

Name.	Specific gravity.	Name.	Specific gravity.
Lignum-vitæ	133	Oak, English	93
Ebony	133	Logwood	91
Box, French	132	Beech	85
Oak, Live	126	Hazel	85
Cocoa palm	106	Ash	84
Mahogany	106	Gum	84
" Spanish	85	Hickory	80
Plum	79	Hackmatack	59
Apple	79	Elm	59
Dogwood	75	Pine, Red	59
Maple, Hard	75	Birch	56
Locust	72	Cedar	56
Rosewood	72	Larch	54
Teak	72	Poplar, white-wood	52
Cherry	71	Black-walnut	50
Persimmon	71	Fir, Norway spruce	50
Pear	66	Sassafras	48
Pine, Pitch	66	Poplar, common	38
Cypress	64	Tamarack	38
Sycamore	62	Butternut	37
Chestnut	61	Hemlock	36
Basswood, Linden	60	Cork	24

The solid portion (*lignin*) of all woods whatever, under all circumstances of growth, is nearly the same; the specific gravity being as 1.46 to 1.53. The comparative value of the different woods in common use for fuel is as follows:

Shell-bark hickory	1.	Hard maple	.6
Red-heart "	.81	New Jersey pine	.54
White oak	.81	Spruce	.52
Beech	.7	Hemlock	.44
Red oak	.69		

The age and growth of a tree are indicated by the number and width of the rings of annual increase shown by a cross-section. Timber requires from 2 to 8 years to be seasoned thoroughly, according to its dimensions. In a perfectly dry atmosphere the durability of woods is almost unlimited. Rafters of roofs are known to have existed 1000 years, and piles submerged in fresh water have been found perfectly sound 800 years after driving.

wood pavement. PAVEMENTS.

wood-cuts. ENGRAVING.

woods. FORESTS.

Wood's half-pence, for circulation in Ireland and America, were coined by virtue of a patent, passed 1722-23. Against them, dr. Jonathan Swift, by his "Drapier's Letters," raised such opposition that Wood was virtually banished the kingdom. The half-pence were assayed in England by sir Isaac Newton, and proved to be genuine, in 1724. COIN; UNITED STATES, 1722.

Woodstock, a town of Oxfordshire, Engl. In Woodstock, now Blenheim park, originally stood a royal palace, in which king Ethelred held a parliament and Alfred the Great translated "Boethius de Consolatione Philosophiæ," 888. Henry I. beautified the palace; and here resided Rosamond, mistress of Henry II., 1154. In it were born Edmund, second son of Edward I., 1301, and Edward, eldest son of Edward III., 1330; and here the princess Elizabeth was confined by her sister Mary, 1554. A splendid mansion, built at the expense of the nation for the duke of Marlborough, was erected here to commemorate his victory at Blenheim in 1704. At that time every trace of the ancient edifice was removed, and 2 elms were planted on its site. BLENHEIM. Scott's romance, "Woodstock," was pub. June, 1826; Marshall's "Hist. of Woodstock," 1873.

wool. From the earliest times to the reign of queen Elizabeth the wool of Great Britain was not only superior to that of Spain, but accounted the finest in the world; and even in the times of the Romans a manufacture of woollen cloths was established at Winchester for the use of the emperors.—*Anderson.* In later times wool was manufactured in England, and is mentioned 1185, but not in any quantity until 1331, when the weaving of it was introduced by John Kempe and other artisans from Flanders. This was the real origin of English manufacture, 6 Edw. III. 1331.—*Rymer's* "Fœdera." For the introduction of sheep into the United States, SHEEP.

WOOL PRODUCTION IN THE UNITED STATES FOR THE YEARS GIVEN.

Year.	Production.	Imports.	Total production and imports.	Retained for home consumption.	Per cent. of imports.
	lbs.	lbs.	lbs.	lbs.	
1870...	162,000,000	49,230,199	211,230,199	209,367,254	23.3
1875...	181,000,000	54,901,700	235,991,700	232,156,099	23.3
1877...	200,000,000	42,171,192	242,171,192	239,002,636	17.4
1880...	232,500,000	128,131,747	360,631,747	356,791,676	35.5
1883...	290,000,000	70,575,478	360,575,478	356,500,961	19.7
1885...	308,000,000	70,596,170	378,596,170	375,392,825	18.8
1886...	302,000,000	129,084,958	431,084,958	422,412,452	30.6
1888...	269,000,000	113,558,753	382,558,753	378,176,858	30.0
1890...	265,000,000	105,431,281	370,431,281	366,911,772	27.7
1892...	340,000,000	167,784,000	507,784,000	503,474,500	33

Total production of wool in the world in 1891 was 2,456,773,-600 lbs., Australia standing 1st, Argentine Republic 2d, and the U. S. 3d.

woollen cloth. Woollen cloths were made an article of commerce in the time of Julius Cæsar, and are familiarly alluded to by him. WEAVING.

	B.C.
Jews forbidden to wear garments of woollen and linen together	1451
	A.D.
Seventy families of cloth-workers (from the Netherlands) settled in England by Edward III. (*Rymer*)	1331
Worsted manufacture in Norfolk	1340
Blankets first made in England (*Camden*)...about	"
Woollens made at Kendal	1390
No cloth but of Wales or Ireland to be imported into England	1463
Medleys, or mixed broadcloth, first made	1614
Manufacture of fine cloth begun at Sedan, in France, under the patronage of cardinal Mazarin	1646
Broadcloth first dressed and dyed in England, by Brewer, from the Low Countries	1667
British and Irish woollens prohibited in France	1677
All persons to be buried in woollens, and the persons directing burial otherwise to forfeit 5*l.*, 29 Charles II	1678

In the United States, prior to the Revolution, the manufacture of woollen cloth was confined to the private loom, and was of a "home" or "domestic" character; but after the war factories were erected, and the manufacture of woollen goods rapidly developed down to the period of the embargo. American woollens, selling for $1.06 per yard, equalled in quality British goods of double the width, costing $3.50 per yard. After the war of 1812-15 the woollen industry revived and rapidly extended until 1827, but the increase has since been less rapid and less remunerative.

woolsack, the seat of the lord high chancellor of England in the House of Lords, a large square bag of wool, without back or arms, covered with red cloth. Wool was the staple commodity of England in the reign of Edward III., when the woolsack first came into use.

Woolwich, Kent, the most ancient military and naval arsenal in England. Its royal dockyard, where men-of-war were built in the reign of Henry VIII., was closed 1 Oct. 1869. Here *Harry Grâce de Dieu* was built, 1512; and here she was burned in 1552. The royal arsenal was formed about 1720, on the site of a rabbit-warren; it contains vast magazines of great guns, mortars, bombs, powder, and other warlike stores; a foundry, with many furnaces, for casting ordnance; and a great laboratory, where fireworks, cartridges, grenades, etc., are made for the government. The Royal Military academy was erected in the royal arsenal, but was not completely formed until 19 Geo. II. 1745.

Worcester (*woos'ter*), Battle of, 3 Sept. 1651, when the Scots army which came to England to reinstate Charles II. was defeated by Cromwell, who called it his *crowning mercy.* Charles with difficulty escaped to France. More than 2000 royalists were slain, and most of the 8000 prisoners were sold as slaves to American colonists. BOSCOBEL.

Wordsworth Society, formed "as a bond of union among those who are in sympathy with the general teaching and spirit of Wordsworth," and "to promote and extend the study of the poet's works," etc., was founded at Grasmere, Westmoreland, 30 Sept. 1880. President, dr. Charles Wordsworth, bishop of St. Andrews.

workingmen. KNIGHTS OF LABOR, LABOR, SOCIALISM, WAGES, etc.

world. CREATION, GLOBE.

World's Columbian Exposition, held at Chicago, Ill., 1 May to 30 Oct. 1893, surpassed, except in attendance, which fell short of the Paris Exposition of 1889 by a daily average of about 22,000, all previous world's fairs. Jackson park and the Midway Plaisance, the site of the exposition, cover 633 acres of land on the shore of lake Michigan, and of this about 190 acres were under roof. The 28 main exposition buildings occupied 142½ acres, the balance being covered by state and foreign buildings and concessions. A plat of the grounds was submitted by the Board of Consulting Architects, 1 Dec. 1890. Ground was broken in Feb. following; and about 1,500,000 cubic yards of earth were handled in carrying out the design, which called for a system of lagoons joined by canals, the principal buildings each having a water as well as a land frontage. The entrance from the lake was through a peristyle 600 ft. long, 60 ft. wide, and 60 ft. high, the grand archway at its centre forming a portal from lake Michigan to the basin in the Grand Central Court. A few statistics of one of the main buildings, that assigned to the departments of manufactures and liberal arts, will serve to illustrate the magnificent scale upon which the exposition was laid out. This building, the largest in the world, measured 1687 by 787 ft., and covered 30½ acres. The central hall, 1280 by 380 ft., was open to the roof (237.6 ft.) without a supporting pillar. The walls of the 4 central pavilions were 122 ft. high, the 4 corner pavilions 97 ft., and the main walls 66 ft. There were 11 acres of skylight, and 40 car-loads of glass in the roof, and it required 7,000,000 ft. of lumber and 5 car-loads of nails to lay the floor. Including the galleries, there were 44 acres of exhibition space in the building, and from necessity the Anthropological building, covering 2.2 acres, was afterwards erected to supply the space demanded by exhibitors in these two departments. Painting of this building, by means of spraying machines, was begun 8 Dec. 1892, and completed in about 6 weeks, 50 tons of paint being used. The exterior was covered with staff, a composition of plaster, cement, and hemp or similar fibre moulded for ornamentation and treated to represent marble. Most of the World's Fair buildings were covered with this material, 30,000 tons being used for the purpose; hence the fair became familiarly known as the "White City." Tables giving items of interest about the main buildings and those erected by the several states and territories will be found below. Among other special buildings and exhibits may be mentioned: Music Hall Peristyle and Casino, Choral Hall, Children's building, the Saw Mill, Cold Storage building, Convent of La Rabida, Battle-ship *Illinois*, the Krupp Gun Exhibit, and the Ferris Wheel. The last named was located near the western approach to the Midway Plaisance noted above; a strip of land 600 ft. wide and ⅞ of a mile long, connecting Jackson and Washington parks, given up to private concessions and amusement attractions. 52 foreign powers officially participated in the Exposition, their appropriations amounting to over $6,000,000; and 14 more had individual exhibitions in the several great departments or on the Midway Plaisance. Foreign powers which appropriated $100,000 or more were as follows:

Argentine Republic	$100,000	Ceylon	$125,000
Austria	110,000	New South Wales	150,000
Brazil	600,000	Guatemala	200,000
Costa Rica	150,000	Japan	630,000
Ecuador	125,000	Netherlands	100,000
France	733,000	Paraguay	100,000
Germany	800,000	Spain	200,000
Great Britain	291,000	Sweden	108,000
Canada	450,000		

COMPARATIVE STATISTICS OF WORLD'S FAIRS.

Where held.	Year.	Acres of buildings.	Days open.	Number of exhibitors.	Number of admissions.	Total receipts.
London	1851	21	144	17,900	6,170,000	$2,530,000
Paris	1855	24½	185	23,950	5,162,330	1,280,000
London	1862	23⅓	171	28,653	6,211,103	2,942,410
Paris	1867	37	217	50,236	10,200,000	2,103,675
Vienna	1873	40	186	42,000	7,254,687	1,030,000
Philadelphia	1876	56	159	60,000	9,789,392	3,813,749
Paris	1878	60	194	52,000	16,032,725	2,531,650
"	1889	75½	183	60,000	32,354,111	8,380,000
Chicago	1893	142½	178	65,422	27,529,400	14,117,332

ATTENDANCE AT WORLD'S COLUMBIAN EXPOSITION, 1893.

Month.	Days open.	Paid admissions.			Free admissions.	Total admissions.
		Adults.	Children.	Total.		
May	28	1,027,212	22,825	1,050,037	481,947	1,531,984
June	30	2,541,958	133,155	2,675,113	902,721	3,577,834
July	30	2,619,605	140,658	2,760,263	1,217,239	3,977,502
August	31	3,328,522	186,971	3,515,493	1,172,215	4,687,708
September	30	4,477,467	182,404	4,659,871	1,149,071	5,808,942
October	30	6,228,510	587,925	6,816,435	1,128,995	7,945,430
Totals	179	20,223,274	1,253,938	21,477,212	6,052,188	27,529,400

Dr. Charles M. Zaremba of Chicago claims to have conceived and suggested the idea of celebrating the 4th centenary of the discovery of America by Columbus by a world's fair, 9 Sept. 1876

Alexander D. Anderson, sec. of the Board of Trade at Washington, D. C., claims to have presented the project of a world's fair, to be held in the city of Washington, at a public meeting held there....25 Feb. 1886

Hon. Perry Belmont of New York submits to the House of Representatives, in behalf of a committee, a unanimous report (No. 2601, 50th Congress, first session) in favor of the project, designating Washington as the place, 16 June, 1888

Mayor of New York city issues invitations to 500 prominent citizens, requesting them to meet and discuss plans to secure the fair....17 July, 1889

Committee of 100, appointed by mayor De Witt C. Cregier of Chicago to secure the fair for that city, meets in the council chamber and appoints an executive committee, 1 Aug. “

Business men of St. Louis assemble at the invitation of the mayor of that city, and decide to attempt to secure the fair, 11 Aug. “

License granted to a corporation styled "The World's Exposition of 1892," with a capital of $5,000,000, at Springfield, Ill., for the holding of an international exposition at Chicago, 14 Aug. “

St. Paul, Minn., through its Board of Trade, enters the lists, 1 Oct. “

World's Fair bill introduced in the Senate by U. S. senator Cullom of Illinois....19 Dec. “

Hearing before Senate committee on selection of site; New York represented by Chauncey M. Depew, Chicago by mayor Cregier....11 Jan. 1890

House of Representatives votes on the question of filling in the blank in the World's Fair bill with the name of a city in which *the exposition* should be held. First ballot, Chicago, 115; New York, 70; St. Louis, 61; Washington, 58; Cumberland Gap, 1. Eighth ballot, Chicago, 157; New York, 107; St. Louis, 25; Washington, 18. Necessary to a choice, 154, and site secured for Chicago, 21 Feb. “

First meeting of the board of directors of the World's Columbian Exposition held at the Sherman house....12 Apr. “

World's Fair bill, fixing date of opening of the fair 1 May, 1893, signed by the president....28 Apr. “

Board of directors elect permanent officers: Lyman J. Gage, president; Thos. B. Bryan, 1st vice-president; and Potter Palmer, 2d vice-president....30 Apr. “

Pres. Harrison appoints members of the national commission on nominations made by the governors of the several states and territories....26 May, “

First session of the national commission held at the Grand Pacific hotel, Chicago....26 June, “

Hon. Thomas W. Palmer of Michigan elected president of the national commission....27 June, “

National commission formally accepts Jackson park and Midway Plaisance as the site for the exposition....2 July, “

Bill amending the constitution of Illinois, to authorize Chicago to issue $5,000,000 of bonds in aid of the exposition; signed by gov. Fifer....5 Aug. “

Col. George R. Davis of Chicago elected director-gen. of the exposition....19 Sept. “

D. H. Burnham of Chicago appointed chief of construction, Oct. “

Board of lady managers organized; Mrs. Potter Palmer of Chicago elected president....20 Nov. “

Proclamation issued by pres. Harrison declaring that the exposition will open 1 May, 1893, and in the name of the government and people of the U. S. inviting "all nations of the earth to participate in the commemoration of an event that is pre-eminent in human history, and of lasting interest to mankind"....24 Dec. “

Wm. T. Baker elected to succeed Lyman T. Gage as president of Board of Directors....14 Apr. 1891

Proviso for closing the fair on Sunday passed by the Senate in committee of the whole, 14 July, and concurred in by the House....19 July, 1892

Date of dedication of World's Fair buildings changed from 12 Oct. to 21 Oct....4 Aug. “

Congress by resolution extends an invitation to the king and queen of Spain and the descendants of Columbus to participate in the World's Columbian Exposition, 5 Aug. “

Congress passes a bill authorizing a gift of $2,500,000 to the exposition in souvenir silver half-dollars....5 Aug. “

Pres. W. T. Baker resigns, and H. N. Higinbotham is elected in his stead....18 Aug. “

Title of "director of works" conferred on chief of construction, D. H. Burnham....Oct. “

Buildings dedicated....21 Oct. “

[The programme comprised: 1, "Columbian march," composed by John K. Paine of Cambridge; 2, Prayer by bishop Fowler; 3, Address, director-gen. Davis; 4, Dedicatory ode, by miss Harriet Stone Monroe, read by Mrs. LeMoyne; 5, Addresses by pres. Higinbotham, D. H. Burnham, pres. Palmer, Mrs. Potter Palmer, and vice-pres. Levi P. Morton, who represented pres. Harrison; 6, Dedicatory oration, Henry Watterson; 7, Anthem, "Star-Spangled Banner;" 8, Oration, Chauncey M. Depew; 9, Prayer, cardinal Gibbons; 10, Benediction, rev. H. C. McCosh; 11, National salute.]

Joint resolution for opening the fair on Sunday introduced in the House of Representatives by congressman Burborow of Illinois and referred to committee....5 Dec. “

Pres. Cleveland, the duke of Veragua, and the Liberty bell received at Chicago with honors....29 Apr. 1893

Opening exercises held in front of Administration building, 1 May, 1893

[Programme: 1, "Columbian march;" 2, Prayer, rev. William H. Milburn, chaplain U. S. Senate; 3, Poem, "The Prophecy," Wm. A. Croffut, read by miss Jessie Couthoui; 4, Overture from "Rienzi;" 5, History of growth and development of the exposition, director-gen. Geo. R. Davis; 6, Address, pres. Cleveland (at the close of his address pres. Cleveland touched an electric button, and the machinery of the great fair was set in motion at 12.04 P.M.); 7, Hallelujah chorus, "America." (Total attendance 1 May, 137,557.)]

Sunday, fair closed....7 May, “

First illumination of buildings by electricity and search-lights, 8 May, “

Local directory votes to open the grounds, but *not the exhibition* buildings, on Sunday....12 May, “

Sunday, fair closed....14 May, “

Congress of Woman's Progress opens....15 May, “

Public Press congress opens....18 May, “

Sunday, fair closed....21 May, “

First *open air concert* by Sousa's military band....22 May, “

World's Fair National commissioners vote to adopt the judiciary committee's minority report in favor of Sunday opening, 23 May, “

Haydn's "Creation" given by Columbian chorus in Festival hall....25 May, “

Sunday, gates open all day; paid admissions, 77,212; 15 state buildings closed, also the U. S. government, British government, and other foreign exhibitions....28 May, “

Congress of Medicine and Surgery opens....29 May, “

Decoration day: attendance, 139,979; Montana silver statue, Ada Rehan, in Mines building, unveiled....30 May, “

Argument on the proceeding of the government to close the gates of the fair on Sunday begun in the Federal court in Chicago....31 May, “

Congress of Temperance opens....5 June, “

Infanta Eulalia visits the exposition; total attendance, 168,996, 8 June, “

Congress of Moral and Social Reform opens....12 June, “

German-American day: attendance, 200,718....15 June, “

Federal Court of Appeals, chief-justice Fuller, decides that the World's Fair corporation has the right to open the gates on Sunday....17 June, “

Congress of Commerce and Finance opens....19 June, “

Formal opening of the Ferris wheel....21 June, “

Religious services held *in Festival hall, Sunday*....25 June, “

Children's chorus, 1200 voices, at Festival hall....26 June, “

Congress of Music opens....3 July, “

Grand Fourth-of-July celebration from sunrise to sunset; total attendance, 339,542....4 July, “

[Addresses by vice-pres. Stevenson, Hampton L. Carson of Philadelphia, and mayor Harrison; Paul Jones flag unfurled; monument of souvenir coins in Manufactures building unveiled.]

Spanish caravels arrive in Chicago....7 July, “

Cold Storage building burned; 17 firemen lose their lives in the fire....10 July, “

Congress of Literature opens.... “ “

Viking ship arrives at the pier near battle-ship *Illinois*, 12 July, “

Congress of Education opens....17 July, “

Sunday, fair closed by order of directors....23 July, “

Congresses of Engineering, Art, Architecture, etc., open, 31 July, “

Directors fined by judge Stein for contempt of court in closing the fair on Sunday, 23 July....2 Aug. “

Congress of Government, Law Reform, Political Science, etc., opens....7 Aug. “

British Empire day: total attendance, 213,436....19 Aug. “

Congress of Science and Philosophy opens....21 Aug. “

Colored people's day: *attendance*, 180,225....25 Aug. “

[Oration by hon. Frederick Douglass.]

Congress of Labor opens....28 Aug. “

New Columbian liberty bell dedicated....9 Sept. “

Parliament of Religions opens in Chicago....11 Sept. “

Spanish caravels, transferred to the U. S. government by capt. Concas on behalf of the Spanish government....12 Sept. “

Knights of Honor day: attendance, 256,930....23 Sept. “

Odd Fellows' day: attendance, 238,360....26 Sept. “

Chicago day: attendance, 761,942....9 Oct. “

Firemen's day: attendance, 349,491....10 Oct. “

Special days and amusements for children....18, 19, 20 Oct. “

[While the average daily attendance of children was about 5 per cent. of the paid admissions, it rose to over 20 per cent. on these days, the paid admissions being 65,199 children and 240,762 adults on 19 Oct.]

Manhattan day: attendance, 339,811....21 Oct. “

Marshall Field subscribes $1,000,000 conditionally for a Memorial museum on the World's Fair grounds....27 Oct. “

Fair officially closed....30 Oct. “

Roof of Manufactures and Liberal Arts building gives way under a weight of snow and ice....9 Dec. “

One of several fires *among the buildings destroys the* Casino, Peristyle, and Music hall, and damages the Manufactures and Liberal Arts building....8 Jan. 1894

Field Columbian *museum dedicated*....2 June, “

Fire destroys the Terminal station, Administration building, Manufactures, Electricity and Mining, Agriculture and Machinery buildings; the supposed work of incendiaries, 5 July, “

STATISTICS OF STATE BUILDINGS OF THE WORLD'S COLUMBIAN EXPOSITION.

[In states and territories not mentioned about $353,000 was raised for fair purposes, chiefly by private subscription, for the most part used for state exhibits in sections of the main exhibition buildings.]

State.	Chief commissioner.	Fund raised for fair purposes.	Description of state building.	Cost of state building.	When dedicated.	Architect.	Special state day.	Attendance on special state day.
Arkansas	James Mitchell	$ 55,000	French rococo	$18,000	15 June, 1893	Mrs. Jean Douglas.	....	....
California	Irving M. Scott	550,000	Old California mission.	75,000	19 June, "	A. Page Brown	9 Sept.	277,118
Colorado	Gov. Davis H. Waite	167,000	Spanish renaissance	35,000	....	H. T. E. Wendell	12 Sept.	206,931
Connecticut	Gov. L. B. Morris	75,000	Colonial	15,000	....	J. W. Northrup	11 Oct.	349,877
Delaware	Thos. B. Smith	20,000	Southern colonial (native woods)	8,000	....	....	23 Aug.	192,003
Florida	Arthur C. Jackson	50,000	Miniature of old fort Marion at St. Augustine	20,000	22 Oct. 1892	....	13 Sept.	202,527
Idaho	James M. Wells	100,000	3-story log-cabin (Swiss style)	30,000	....	....	....	....
Illinois	Lafayette Funk	800,000	Italian renaissance	250,000	18 May, 1893	W. W. Boynton & Co.	24 Aug.	288,921
Indiana	Clem Studebaker	135,000	French Gothic	75,000	15 June, "	....	27 Sept.	238,289
Iowa	James O. Crosby	130,000	French château	35,000	22 Oct. 1892	....	20 Sept.	220,260
Kansas	M. W. Cobun	165,000	2-story frame and staff, with elliptical glass dome	25,000	" "	Seymour Davis	11 Sept.	202,932
Kentucky	W. H. Dulaney	175,000	Southern colonial	18,000	1 June, 1893	Maury & Dodd	1 June	61,727
Louisiana	A. A. Woods	36,000	Colonial (imitation of Creole home)	18,000	10 Aug. "	....	....	....
Maine	Hall C. Burleigh	57,000	Lower story, granite (octagonal). Upper story, wood (square)	22,000	24 May, "	C. S. Frost.	....	....
Maryland	Gov. Frank Brown.	60,000	Free classic	12,000	....	....	12 Sept.	206,931
Massachusetts	Gen. Francis A. Walker	175,000	Modelled after the John Hancock house, Beacon st., Boston	65,000	22 Oct. 1892	Peabody & Stearns	17 June	184,775
Michigan	Isaac M. Weston	275,000	Renaissance (native material)	50,000	....	....	13 Sept.	202,527
Minnesota	D. A. Monfort	150,000	Italian renaissance	30,000	17 May, 1893	W. C. Whitney	13 Oct.	255,743
Missouri	N. A. Gentry	150,000	Spanish "	50,000	19 July, "	....	30 Aug.	197,493
Montana	Stephen DeWolfe	100,000	Romanesque	20,000	....	Galbraith & Fuller	20 Sept.	220,260
Nebraska	Chas. A. Coe	85,000	Corinthian order	20,000	8 June, "	Henry Voss	8 June	168,996
New Hampshire	Chas. H. Amsden	25,000	Swiss cottage	10,000	26 June, "	G. B. Howe.	....	....
New Jersey	Stephen J. Meeker.	130,000	Modelled after Washington's headquarters at Morristown, N. J.	40,000	1 May, "	Chas. Alling Gifford.	....	....
New York	Chauncey M. Depew	600,000	Pompeiian	150,000	22 Oct. 1892	McKim, Meade & White	4 Sept.	198,858
North Dakota	Martin Hector	70,06?	2-story, with gable ends of brick and sides timber and plaster	18,000	20 May, 1893	J. L. Silsbee	10 Oct.	349,491
Ohio	W. W. Peabody	200,000	Colonial	35,000	22 Oct. 1892	Jas. W. H. McLaughlin	14 Sept.	238,718
Pennsylvania	Gov. Robert E. Pattison	360,000	Colonial (front a reproduction of Independence hall)	80,000	....	Theo. P. Lonsdale	7 Sept.	245,467
Rhode Island	E. Benjamin Andrews	57,500	Greek (amphiprostyle)	8,000	" "	Stone, Carpenter & Wilson	5 Oct.	222,452
South Dakota	L. G. Ochsenreiter	85,000	Romanesque	20,000	12 July, 1893	....	....	....
Texas	H. B. Andrews	40,000	Spanish	30,000	20 July, "	J. R. Gordon	16 Sept.	246,717
Vermont	B. B. Smalley	39,750	Pompeiian	8,000	10 May, "	....	15 Sept.	198,414
Virginia	A. S. Buford	75,000	Washington's home, Mt. Vernon (reproduced)	25,000	....	....	9 Aug.	145,533
Washington	N. G. Blalock	100,000	Foundation of immense logs; entrance a great stone arch	50,000	17 May, "	....	....	....
West Virginia	W. N. Chancellor	40,000	Colonial (W. Va. residence)	20,000	20 June, "	J. L. Silsbee	23 Aug.	192,003
Wisconsin	A. Ledyard Smith	212,000	Representation of a Wisconsin home	30,000	23 May, "	Wm. Waters	6 Sept.	217,083
Wyoming	John S. Harper	30,000	French château	20,000	....	Van Brunt & Howe.	....	....
Utah	R. C. Chambers	50,600	Façade (modern renaissance)	15,000	8 Sept. "	Dallas & Hedges	9 Sept.	277,118
Arizona	S. P. Behan	30,000	Composite (lower story supported by Doric columns; 3 departments, 1 for each territory)	7,500	....	Seymour Davis	16 Sept.	246,717
New Mexico	W. T. Thornton	35,000						
Oklahoma	Gov. A. J. Seay	17,500						

STATISTICAL TABLE OF MAIN EXHIBITION BUILDINGS.

[Total cost of buildings, $7,290,000.]

Name of building.	Dimensions.	Acres covered.	Cost.	Style of architecture.	Name of architect.	Contract let.
Administration	262×262	1.6	$450,000	French renaissance	Richard M. Hunt, New York	25 May, 1891
Agriculture	500×800	9.2	618,000	Classic "	McKim, Meade & White, New York	18 July, "
Annex	300×550	3.8				
Assembly hall, etc.	125×450	1.3	100,000			
Live-stock pavilion	280×440	2.8	335,000	....	Holabird & Roche, Chicago, Ill.	
Sheds, etc.	....	40.9				
Dairy	100×200	.5	30,000	....	C. B. Atwood	24 Oct. "
Electricity	345×690	5.5	400,000	Corinthian	Van Brunt & Howe, Kansas City	20 May, "
Fine Arts	320×500	3.7	670,000	Classic	Charles B. Atwood	19 Sept. "
Two annexes	120×200	1.1				
Fisheries	165×365	1.4	224,000	Spanish Romanesque	Henry Ives Cobb, Chicago	12 Aug. "
Two annexes	135 diam.	.8				
Forestry	208×528	2.5	100,000	Rustic	C. B. Atwood	18 Sept. "

STATISTICAL TABLE OF MAIN EXHIBITION BUILDINGS.—(*Continued.*)

Name of building.	Dimensions.	Acres covered.	Cost.	Style of architecture.	Name of architect.	Contract let.
U. S. government	345×415	3.3	$400,000	Classic	Windrim & Edbrooke	
Horticulture	250×988	5.7	300,000	Venetian renaissance	W. L. B. Jenney, Chicago	9 June, 1891
Eight greenhouses	24×100	.5	5,000			
Machinery hall	492×846	9.6 }	1,200,000	Renaissance of Seville	Peabody & Stearns, Boston	24 Sept. "
Annex	490×550	6.2 }				
Power house	100×461 }					
Pumping works	77×84 }	2.1	85,000			
Machine shop	146×250 }					
Manufactures and Liberal Arts	787×1687	30.5	1,500,000	Corinthian	George B. Post, New York	25 May, "
Anthropological	255×415	2.2	100,000			
Mines and Mining	350×700	5.6	265,000	Italian renaissance	S. S. Beman, Chicago	14 May, "
Transportation	256×960	5.6 }	370,000	Romanesque (approximately)	Adler & Sullivan, Chicago	24 June, "
Annex	425×900	8.8 }				
Woman's	199×388	1.8	138,000	Italian renaissance	Miss Sophia B. Hayden, Boston	3 June, "

Worms, a city on the Rhine, in Hesse-Darmstadt. The Roman city, Borbetomagus, was plundered by the Alemanni, 354, and by Attila, 451; rebuilt by Clovis I. about 475. Here Charlemagne resided in 806. Here was held the imperial diet before which Martin Luther was summoned, 4 Apr. 1521, and by which he was proscribed. Luther was met by 2000 persons on foot and on horseback, at the distance of a league from Worms. When Spalatin sent to warn him of his danger, he answered, "If there were as many devils in Worms as there are tiles upon the roofs of its houses, I would go on." He appeared before the emperor, the archduke Ferdinand, 6 electors, 24 dukes, 7 margraves, 30 bishops and prelates, and many princes, counts, lords, and ambassadors, 17 Apr., acknowledged his writings and opinions, and left Worms, in fact, a conqueror. Yet, to save his life, he had to remain in seclusion under the protection of the elector of Saxony for about a year. The edict putting him under the ban of the empire was issued 26 May, 1521. Worms was burned, by order of Louis XIV., 1689, the cathedral excepted; and was taken by the French, under Custine, 4 Oct. 1792. A memorial statue of Luther at Worms was uncovered, 25 June, 1868, in the presence of the king of Prussia and other sovereigns.

worship. The first worship mentioned is that of Abel, 3872 B.C. (Gen. iv.). "Men began to call on the name of the Lord," 3769 B.C. (Gen. iv.). The Jewish order of worship was set up by Moses, 1490 B.C. Solomon consecrated the temple, 1004 B.C. To the corruptions of the simple worship of the patriarchs all the Egyptian and Greek idolatries owed their origin. Athotes, son of Menes, king of Upper Egypt, 2112 B.C., is supposed to be the *Copt* of the Egyptians, and the *Toth*, or *Hermes*, of the Greeks, the *Mercury* of the Latins, and the *Teutates* of the Celts or Gauls.—*Usher.*

worship in England. The Druids were the priests here, at the invasion of the Romans (55 B.C.), who eventually introduced Christianity, which was almost extirpated by the victorious Saxons (455), who were pagans. The Roman Catholic form of Christianity was introduced by Augustine, 596, and continued till the Reformation. SECTS.

worsted, spun wool, obtained its name from having been first spun at a town called Worsted, in Norfolk, in which the inventor lived, and where manufactures of worsted are still extensively carried on, 14 Edw. III. 1340.—*Anderson.* "A worsted-stocking knave" is a term of reproach or contempt used by Shakespeare.

Wörth sur Sauer (*vört sür sō-air'*), a town in the department of the Lower Rhine, N.E. France. After storming Wissembourg, on 4 Aug. 1870, the crown-prince of Prussia, with the 3d army (about 150,000), marched rapidly forward and surprised part of the French army under marshal MacMahon, including the corps of Canrobert and part of that of Failly (about 47,000), and defeated it in a long, desperate, and sanguinary engagement near this place, 6 Aug. The battle lasted from 9 A.M. till 4 P.M. The chief struggles occurred in the country round Reichshoffen and in the village of Froeschweiler; the French are said to have charged the German line 11 times, each time breaking it, but always finding a fresh mass behind. The ridge on which Wörth stands was not captured until the French were taken in flank by the Bavarians and Wurtembergers. Nearly all MacMahon's staff were killed, and the marshal himself, unhorsed, fell fainting into a ditch, from which he was rescued by a soldier. He then, on foot, directed the retreat towards Saverne, to cover the passes of the Vosges. The victory is attributed to the great numerical superiority of the Germans as well as to their excellent strategy. The French loss has been estimated at 5000 killed and wounded, and 55,000 prisoners, 2 eagles, 6 mitrailleuses, 35 cannon, and much baggage. The Germans are stated to have had above 8000 men put *hors de combat.* It was admitted that MacMahon acted as an able and brave commander.

worthies, nine, a term long ago applied to the following eminent men:

Jews.	Died B.C.	Heathens.	Died B.C.
Joshua	1426	Hector of Troy	1184
David	1015	Alexander the Great	393
Judas Maccabæus	161	Julius Cæsar	44

Christians.	Died A.D.
King Arthur of Britain	542
Charlemagne of France	814
Godfrey of Bouillon	1100

In some lists, Gideon and Samson are given instead of Hector and Arthur. In Shakespeare's "Love's Labor's Lost," act v. sc. ii., Hercules and Pompey appear as worthies.

wrecks. Statistics of wrecks and shipping disasters on or near the coasts and on the rivers of the United States and to American vessels in foreign waters, collected under act of Congress, 20 June, 1874, are published in the "Annual Reports of the U. S. Life-saving Service." During 10 years, from 1 June, 1879, to 1 June, 1889, they show a yearly average of 1919 wrecks, involving the loss of 535 lives. During the same period of 10 years, of British vessels (exclusive of the royal navy), there were 6641 totally wrecked, while the loss to life by wrecks and casualties of all kinds on British vessels, navy excluded, was 19,130. During the same 10 years 1777 German vessels were wrecked, with a loss of 3460 lives; and on the German coast 2640 wrecks occurred, involving the loss of 391 lives. On the French coast, during 5 years (1877–81), 1346 wrecks occurred, with loss of 949 lives; and on the Italian coast, for the years 1886 to 1890 inclusive, the records show 483 wrecks, with loss of 116 lives.

WRECKS AND CASUALTIES IN AMERICAN WATERS, AND DISASTERS TO AMERICAN VESSELS IN FOREIGN WATERS.

Year.	Atlantic and gulf coast.		Pacific coast.		Great lakes.		Rivers.		At sea or in foreign waters.		Totals.	
	Wrecks.	Lives lost.	Wrecks.	Lives lost.	Wrecks.	Lives lost.	Wrecks.	Lives lost.	Wrecks.	Lives lost.	Wrecks.	Lives lost.
1879–80	1,008	107	112	7	552	35	211	38	435	230	2,318	417
1880–81	798	95	74	5	545	128	238	52	374	325	2,029	605
1881–82	937	59	93	2	506	73	236	118	323	242	2,095	494
1882–83	801	63	88	42	468	60	241	168	361	186	1,959	519
1883–84	970	201	65	7	433	83	250	42	452	465	2,170	798
1884–85	834	40	68	11	358	18	255	44	385	175	1,900	288
1885–86	1,158	133	75	20	330	78	268	38	464	262	2,296	531
1886–87	640	69	56	41	323	103	177	89	298	227	1,494	529
1887–88	651	64	58	72	301	83	165	16	286	303	1,461	538
1888–89	662	106	74	44	258	26	164	77	310	385	1,468	638
Totals	8,459	937	763	251	4,074	687	2,205	682	3,688	2,800	19,189	5,357

NOTABLE WRECKS AND SHIPPING DISASTERS IN NORTH AND SOUTH AMERICAN WATERS.

Atlantic Ocean, Gulf of Mexico, etc.

British powder ship *Morning Star* struck by lightning and blown up in New York harbor.......................9 Aug. 1778

Thunderer, 74 guns; *Stirling Castle*, 64; *Defiance*, 64; *Phœnix*, 44; *La Blanche*, 32; *Laurel*, 28; *Shark*, 28; *Andromeda*, 28; *Deal Castle*, 24; *Penelope*, 24; *Scarborough*, 20; *Barbadoes*,

14, *Chameleon* 14, *Endeavour*, 14, and *Victor*, 10—all lost in the same storm in the West Indies Oct. 1780

La Tribune, 36 guns wrecked off Halifax, 300 lives lost, 16 Nov 1797

Transport *Æneas* wrecked off Newfoundland, 340 lives lost, 23 Oct 1805

Transport *Harpooner* wrecked near Newfoundland, 200 lives lost 10 Nov 1816

Magazine of steam frigate *Fulton* explodes at Brooklyn navy yard, vessel entirely destroyed, 26 lives lost. 4 June, 1829

Brig *Billow* lost in storm on Ragged island, N S, all on board, 137 in number, perish 9 Apr 1831

Lady Sherbrooke, from Londonderry to Quebec, lost near cape Ray, 273 persons perish, 32 only saved 19 Aug "

Ship *Lady of the Lake* on passage to Quebec, wrecked on an iceberg, 215 lives lost 11 May, 1833

Steamboat *Royal Tar*, of St John's, N B, destroyed by fire in Penobscot bay, 32 lives lost 25 Oct 1836

Ship *Bristol* on passage from Liverpool to New York, wrecked near Rockaway, L I, 70 lives lost 20 Nov "

Ship *Mexico*, from Liverpool wrecked on Hampstead beach, L I, 108 lives lost 3 Jan 1837

Steamboat *Home*, on passage from New York to Charleston, S C, wrecked in a gale near Ocracoke, about 100 lives lost, 9 Oct "

Steamboat *Pulaski*, from Savannah to Baltimore, bursts a boiler off coast of North Carolina, of nearly 200 passengers and crew only 60 are saved 14 June, 1838

Steamboat *Lexington*, New York to Stonington, burned off Eden's Neck, L I, 140 lives lost. 13 Jan 1840

Brig *Florence* Rotterdam to New York, wrecked off southeast coast of Newfoundland, 50 lives lost 9 Aug "

Steamer *President*, New York to Liverpool, sailed 11 Mch with 136 persons on board, not heard from after storm of, 13 Mch 1841

Steamboat *Medora* of Baltimore explodes her boiler just after leaving the wharf, 28 killed and 40 injured 14 Apr 1842

Phœnix wrecked in a storm off the coast of Newfoundland, many lives lost 26 Nov 1843

Steamer *Tweed* lost off Yucatan, 60 lives lost 12 Feb 1846

Brig *Sutley*, from Picton, N S to Fall River, Mass, wrecked in Vineyard sound, 30 drowned 27 June, "

Steamer *New York*, from Galveston to New Orleans, founders at sea, about 20 lives lost 7 Sept "

All but 12 out of 104 vessels in port at Havana sink or are wrecked, and 50 coastwise vessels destroyed by a hurricane, 10-11 Oct "

U S brig *Somers* struck by a squall off Vera Cruz and sunk, 41 lives lost (SOMERS, MUTINY ON, MEDALS) 8 Dec "

American emigrant ship *William and Mary* wrecked on a sunken reef near the Bahamas, about 170 persons perish, 3 May, 1853

Aurora of Hull sails from New York 26 Apr and founders, about 25 lives lost 20 May, "

Ship *Staffordshire*, from Liverpool to Boston, strikes on Blande rock south of Seal island, 178 lives lost 30 Dec. "

Steamer *San Francisco* bound for California with 700 U S. troops, founders at sea, and 240 of the soldiers are swept from the deck and perish 23–31 Dec. "

Steamer *Georgia*, from Montgomery, Ala, destroyed by fire at New Orleans, 60 lives lost 28 Jan 1854

Ship *Powhatan*, from Havre to New York, with 311 emigrants, goes ashore in a gale on Long Beach, 7 miles north of Egg Harbor light, and is wrecked, no passenger saved 16 Apr "

Steamer *Arctic* from Liverpool, struck by the *Vesta*, 40 miles off cape Race, Newfoundland, in a fog, and sinks, over 350 lives lost . .27 Sept. "

Steamship *Pacific*, Collins line, 240 persons on board, never heard from after leaving port 23 Sept. 1856

French steamer *Le Lyonnais* sunk off Nantucket by collision with the bark *Adriatic*, 260 lives lost 2 Nov "

Steamship *Tempest*, Anchor line, 150 persons on board, never heard from after leaving port. .26 Feb. 1857

Steamship *Louisiana*, from New Orleans to Galveston, burned near Galveston, 55 lives lost. . . 31 May, "

Steamer *J W Harris* sunk in collision with steamer *Metropolis* in Long Island sound, 14 lives lost 8 Aug "

Steamer *Central America*, from Havana to New York, springs a leak in a heavy storm, 8 Sept., 100 persons are taken off by a passing vessel, 12 Sept., and soon after she sinks, carrying down over 400 persons. 12 Sept. "

Steamship *Indian*, from Liverpool to Portland, strikes on Seal ledge, about 65 miles east of Halifax, and breaks in two amidships, 24 lives lost. . . . 21 Nov 1859

New mail steamer *Hungarian* wrecked near cape Sable, N S, all on board (205) lost . . night of 19–20 Feb. 1860

Steamer *Canadian* strikes on ice field in strait of Belle Isle, Newfoundland, and founders in half an hour, 35 lives lost, 4 June, 1861

British mail steamer *Anglo Saxon* wrecked in a dense fog on reef off cape Race Newfoundland, about 237 out of 446 lives lost . 27 Apr 1863

Steamer *Constitution* wrecked on cape Lookout shoals, 40 lives lost . . . . 25 Dec 1865

Steamer *Evening Star*, from New York to New Orleans, founders at sea, about 250 lives lost . .. 3 Oct. 1866

Royal mail steamers *Rhone* and *Wye* entirely wrecked, and more than 50 other vessels driven ashore at St Thomas, West Indies, by a hurricane, about 1000 lives lost 29 Oct 1867

Steamship *City of Boston*, Inman line, 177 persons on board, never heard from after leaving port 28 Jan. 1870

Steamer *Varuna*, New York for Galveston, founders off Florida coast with 36 passengers and all the crew except 5, 20 Oct. 1870

Steamer *Kensington* collides with bark *Templar* off cape Hatteras, both wrecked and many lives lost 27 Jan 1871

Staten Island ferry boat *Westfield* explodes at New York, 100 lives lost, 200 persons injured 30 July "

Steamer *America*, from Buenos Ayres to Montevideo, burned, 60 lives lost . 23 Dec "

Steamer *Metis* sunk in collision on Long Island sound, 50 lives lost . . 30 Aug 1872

Steamer *Missouri*, from New York to Havana, burned at sea, 32 lives lost. 22 Oct "

White Star steamer *Atlantic* strikes on Marr's rock, off Nova Scotia, 547 lives lost out of 976 . 1 Apr 1873

French steamer *Ville du Havre* from New York to Havre, sunk in 16 minutes in mid ocean by collision with ship *Loch Earn*, 230 lives lost out of 313 23 Nov "

American steamer *City of Waco* burned off Galveston bar 53 lives lost 9 Nov 1875

Loss of 12 American whaling ships in Arctic ice, reported by whaling bark *Florence*, about 100 lives lost 12 Oct 1876

British ship *Circassian* stranded on Bridgehampton beach, L I, 28 lives lost . 29 Dec "

American steamer *George Cromwell* stranded off cape St. Mary's, Newfoundland, 30 lives lost 5 Jan 1877

American steamer *George Washington* stranded off Mistaken Point, Newfoundland, 25 lives lost . .20 Jan "

American steamer *Leo* burned 83 miles south of Tybee light, Ga, 23 lives lost 13 Apr "

U S sloop of war *Huron* wrecked on coast of North Carolina, about 100 lives lost . . 24 Nov "

Steamer *Metropolis* wrecked on North Carolina coast, about 100 lives lost 31 Jan 1878

American steamer *Emily B Souder* founders off cape Hatteras, N C, 38 lives lost 10 Dec. "

Thirteen American fishing schooners founder off George's bank, Newfoundland, 144 lives lost 12–16 Feb 1879

American steamer *Champion* wrecked in collision with ship *Lady Octavia*, 15 miles from Delaware light ship, 31 lives lost 7 Nov "

American steamer *Narragansett* wrecked in collision near Cornfield Point shoal, Long Island sound, 27 lives lost, 11 June, 1880

American steamer *Seawanhaka* burned off Ward's island, N Y, 24 lives lost . . .28 June, "

American steamer *San Salvador* lost at sea from Honduras to Cuba, 29 lives lost Aug "

Steamer *City of Vera Cruz* founders off Florida coast, 68 lives lost . 29 Aug "

Steamer *Bahama* founders between Porto Rico and New York, 20 lives lost 4 Feb. 1882

Thirty five wrecks during a storm off Newfoundland, about 19 Dec "

Six American schooners founder off St. George's bank, 76 lives lost Nov 1883

American steamship *City of Columbus* wrecked on Devil's bridge, off Gay Head light, Mass, 99 lives lost . . . 18 Jan 1884

Belgian White Cross line steamship *Daniel Steinman* struck on rock off Sambro head, N S, 131 lives lost 3 Apr "

Three American schooners lost at sea between Gloucester and St. George's bank, 42 lives lost . . 26 Dec 1885

Cunard steamer *Oregon*, from Liverpool to New York, run into by an unknown schooner, 18 miles east of Long Island, all the passengers (631) and crew (205) taken off in safety, the ship sinking 8 hours afterwards .. . . . 14 Mch 1886

Three Atlantic steamers stranded in one day_ the *Persian Monarch* on the Portland breakwater, the Cunard steamer *Pavonia* on High Pine ledge, Massachusetts bay, and the Beaver line steamer *Lake Huron* on Madame island, 7 miles below Quebec, each owing to heavy fog 29 Oct. "

German ship *Elizabeth* stranded near Dam Neck mills, Va, 22 lives lost .. . . 8 Jan 1887

Kapunda, from London for western Australia, collides with the bark *Ada Melmore* off coast of Brazil and founders, more than 300 lives lost . 20 Jan "

American sloop yacht *Mystery*, on a pleasure trip, capsizes off Barren island, Jamaica bay, N Y, 25 lives lost. . 10 July, "

Steamer *Vizcaya*, from New York to Havana, run into by schooner *Cornelius Hargraves* near Barnegat light, N J, both vessels sink within 7 minutes, about 70 lives lost, 29 Oct. 1890

Brazilian turret ship wrecked near the mouth of the La Platta, 120 lives lost. .. 22 May, 1892

Haytian war-ship *Petron* wrecked off cape Tiburon, 79 lives lost. .. . . 6 Sept. 1893

Dynamite cruiser *Vesuvius* ordered to destroy all derelicts along the Atlantic coast 5 Oct. "

Ward line steamer *City of Alexandria*, from Havane to New York, burned at sea, 30 lives lost .. . . . 2 Nov "

Steamer *Jason* wrecked off cape Cod, Mass, 20 lives lost. 6 Dec "

U S corvette KEARSARGE wrecked on Roncardo reef, about 200 miles northeast from Bluefield, Nicaragua . 2 Feb 18[illegible]

[illegible] c Ocean.

Independence wrec[illegible]etta island, off coast of Lower California, the v[illegible]re, 140 persons drowned or burned to death [illegible]ng with great suffering on a barren shore .. .. 16 Feb 18[illegible]

Explosion of stea[illegible]at Canemah, Or, 21 killed and many wounded. . . . . . . 8 Apr 18[illegible]

Steamboat *Secretary*, crossing San Pablo bay from San Francisco to Petaluma, bursts her boiler; more than 50 lives lost, 15 Apr. 1854

Chilian war-steamer *Cazador*, leaving Talcahuano with 358 persons on board, strikes a rock and sinks; 314 lives lost, 30 Jan. 1856

Steamer *Northerner* wrecked on a rock near cape Mendocino, between San Francisco and Oregon; 38 lives lost......6 Jan. 1860

American steamer *Pacific* collides, 30 miles southwest of cape Flattery; 236 lives lost..........4 Nov. 1875

American schooner *Sunshine* stranded near cape Foulweather, Or.; 20 lives lost..........18 Nov. "

English Pacific Steam Navigation company's steamship *Eten* wrecked about 70 miles north of Valparaiso; about 100 out of 160 lost; many rescued by English ship *Amethyst*, 15 July, 1877

Steamer *Atacama* wrecked 22 miles south of Caldera, near Copiapo, Chili; about 104 lives lost..........end of Nov. "

American bark *Malleville* stranded on Vancouver's island; 19 lives lost..........10 Oct. 1882

Grappler burned near Bute inlet, Vancouver island; about 70 lives lost..........about 3 May, 1883

American schooner *Flying Scud*, bound for Kadiak, Alaska, never heard from; 24 persons on board..........Nov. 1886

American schooner *Harvey Mills* founders, 60 miles southwest of cape Flattery, Wash.; 23 lives lost..........14 Dec. "

American bark *Atlantic* stranded at entrance to Golden Gate, Cal.; 27 lives lost..........17 Dec. "

American ship *St. Stephen*, from Port Townsend to San Francisco, founders at sea; 27 lives lost..........Apr. 1887

British bark *Abercorn* stranded on Damon's Point, north of Gray's harbor, Wash.; 22 lives lost..........30 Jan. 1888

American ferry-boat *Julia* explodes her boiler at South Vallejo, Cal.; 30 lives lost..........27 Feb. "

American bark *Ohio* stranded near Point Hope, Alaska; 25 lives lost..........3 Oct. "

American steamer *Alaskan* founders at sea between Astoria, Or., and San Francisco; 26 lives lost..........13 May, 1889

Ship *Elizabeth* wrecked at entrance to San Francisco harbor; 18 lives lost..........22 Feb. 1891

Blanco Encalada, flagship of the revolutionary party in Chili, is blown up by a torpedo in Caldera bay; upwards of 200 lives lost..........22 Apr. "

Great Lakes.

Steamboat *Washington* takes fire on lake Erie, near Silver creek; 40 to 50 lives lost..........16 June, 1838

Steamboat *Erie* burned on lake Erie about 33 miles from Buffalo; about 170 lives lost..........9 Aug. 1841

Steamer *Phœnix* burned on lake Michigan, 15 miles off Sheboygan; about 240 lives lost, mostly emigrants from Holland, 21 Nov. 1847

Steamer *Anthony Wayne*, from Sandusky to Buffalo on lake Erie, explodes her boiler and sinks; 38 killed or missing, 27 Apr. 1850

Steamer *Griffith*, from Erie to Cleveland, burned; only 30 or 40 out of 330 lives saved..........17 June, "

Steamer *Atlantic* collides with propeller *Ogdensburg* on lake Erie and sinks in half an hour; 250 lives lost..........20 Aug. 1852

Steamer *E. K. Collins*, from Sault Ste. Marie to Cleveland, takes fire on the lake and is burned; 23 lives lost..........8 Oct. 1854

Steamer *Northern Indiana* burned on lake Erie; over 30 lives lost..........17 July, 1856

Steamer *Niagara* burned on lake Michigan; 60 to 70 lives lost, 24 Sept. "

American steamer *Lady Elgin* sunk in collision with schooner *Augustus* on lake Michigan; of 385 persons on board, 287 lost, including Herbert Ingram, M. P., founder of the *Illustrated London News*, and his son..........8 Sept. 1860

Steamer *Sea Bird* burned on lake Michigan; 100 lives lost, 9 Apr. 1868

Steamer *Hippocampus* wrecked in lake Michigan; many lives lost..........8 Sept. "

American steamer *Equinox* founders on lake Michigan, 8 miles off Point Au Sable; 26 lives lost..........9 Sept. 1875

American steamer *St. Clair* burned on lake Superior, near Fourteen Mile Point..........9 July, 1876

American steamer *Alpena* founders on lake Michigan; 60 lives lost..........16 Oct. 1880

Northwest transit service steamer *Asia* founders between Ontario and Sault Ste. Marie; about 98 lives lost..........14 Sept. 1882

American steamer *Manistee* founders off Eagle Harbor, lake Michigan; 30 lives lost..........14 Nov. 1883

British steamer *Algoma* stranded on south shore Isle Royal, lake Superior; 48 lives lost..........7 Nov. 1885

American steamer *Champlain* burned off Fisherman's island, lake Michigan; 22 lives lost..........17 June, 1887

American steamer *Vernon* founders on lake Michigan; 41 lives lost..........29 Oct. "

Steel steamer *Western Reserve* breaks in two on lake Superior; 26 persons drowned..........1 Sept. 1892

Propeller *Wocoken* ashore off Long Point, lake Erie; 14 lives lost..........14 Oct. 1893

Propeller *Dean Richmond* founders off Dunkirk, lake Erie; 23 lives lost..........14 Oct. "

Propellers *Philadelphia* and *Albany* collide off Pt. Aux Barques, lake Huron; 24 lives lost..........7 Nov. "

Mississippi River.

Steamboat *Brandywine* burned near Memphis; about 110 lives lost..........9 Apr. 1832

Steamer *Rob Roy* explodes near Columbia, about 20 lives lost, 9 June, 1836

Steamer *Ben Sherrod*, racing with steamer *Prairie*, takes fire 30 miles below Natchez; 175 lives lost..........9 May, 1837

Steamer *Dubuque* explodes near Bloomington, Wis.; 26 lives lost..........15 Aug. "

Steamer *Monmouth* collides with ship *Trenton*, in tow of steamer *Warren*, near Prophet island, and sinks; of 490 emigrant Creek Indians, 234 perish..........29 Oct. "

Steamer *Gen. Brown* explodes at Helena; 60 killed and injured, 25 Nov. 1838

Steamer *Edna* collapses flues near mouth of Missouri; 33 lives lost..........28 June, 1842

Steamer *Eliza* strikes on snag 2 miles below mouth of the Ohio and sinks; 30 to 40 lives lost..........13 Oct. "

Steamer *Clipper* bursts her boiler at bayou Sara, La.; 20 killed, 19 Sept. 1843

Steamer *Shepherdess* strikes a snag below St. Louis; 20 to 30 drowned..........4 Jan. 1844

Steamers *De Soto* and *Buckeye* collide; the latter sinks and more than 60 persons are drowned..........28 Feb. "

Steamer *Belle of Clarksville* run down by the *Louisiana* and sunk; more than 30 drowned..........14 Dec. "

Steamer *Edward Bates* collapses 2 boiler flues; 28 killed, 12 Aug. 1848

Twenty-three steamboats with their cargoes burned at St. Louis..........17 May, 1849

Steamer *Louisiana* explodes at New Orleans; 60 killed, 80 injured, and 12 missing..........16 Nov. "

Steamer *Anglo-Norman* explodes at New Orleans; 75 to 100 killed, wounded, or missing..........13 Dec. 1850

Eight steamboats destroyed by fire at New Orleans; 37 lives lost..........4 Feb. 1854

Steamer *Caroline* burned at the mouth of the White river; 45 lives lost..........5 Mch. "

Steamer *Pennsylvania* bursts her boiler 80 miles below Memphis; about 100 lives lost..........13 June, 1858

Steamer *Princess* explodes boiler and burns near Baton Rouge, 25 killed, 35 injured..........27 Feb. 1859

Steamer *Ben W. Lewis* bursts boiler at Cairo; 50 lives lost, 24 June, 1860

Steamer *Miami* explodes boilers, burns, and sinks; 150 lives lost..........30 Jan. 1866

Steamer *Stonewall* burned below Cairo; 200 lives lost...27 Oct. 1869

Steamer *T. L. McGill* burned; 58 lives lost..........14 Jan. 1871

Steamer *H. R. Arthur* explodes; 37 lives lost..........28 Jan. "

Steamer *Oceanus* explodes; 40 lives lost..........11 Apr. 1872

Steamer *George Wolfe* explodes; 30 lives lost..........23 Aug. 1873

Steamer *Golden City* burned near Memphis; 20 lives lost, 30 Mch. 1882

Steamer *Robert E.* [illegible] burned 30 miles below Vicksburg; 21 lives lost..........30 Sept. "

Steamer *Yazoo* strikes a log 35-mile point above New Orleans, and sinks; 19 lives lost..........4 Mch. 1883

Flues of steamer *La Mascotte* collapse and vessel burned near Crawford's Landing, Mo.; 34 lives lost..........5 Oct. 1886

Steamer *Kate Adams* burned near Commerce Landing; 33 lives lost..........24 Dec. 1888

Steamer *John H. Hanna* burned opposite Plaquemine, La.; 22 lives lost..........24 Dec. "

Steamer *Corona* explodes; 38 lives lost..........3 Oct. 1889

Ohio and other American Rivers.

Steamer *Benjamin Franklin* explodes near Montgomery, Ala.; 25 to 30 killed and injured..........13 Mch. 1836

Boiler of steamer *Moselle* explodes soon after leaving her dock at Cincinnati; over 100 lives lost..........25 Apr. 1838

Steamer *Shamrock* bursts her boiler on the St. Lawrence river and sinks; 68 lives lost..........9 July, 1842

Steamer *Lucy Walker* explodes 3 boilers simultaneously at New Albany, Ind.; 50 to 60 killed and about 20 wounded, 23 Oct. 1844

Steamer *Swallow* is broken on a rock in the Hudson river, near Athens..........7 Apr. 1845

Steamer *Tuscaloosa*, 10 miles above Mobile, bursts 2 boilers; about 20 killed and many injured..........28 Jan. 1847

Brig *Carrick* wrecked in a gale in the St. Lawrence; 170 emigrants perish..........19 May, "

Steamer *Talisman* collides with the *Tempest* on the Ohio between Pittsburg and St. Louis; more than 100 lives lost, 19 Nov. "

Boilers of steamer *Blue Ridge* on the Ohio river explode; 30 lives lost..........8 Jan. 1848

Steamer *Orville St. Johns* burned near Montgomery, Ala.; 30 lives lost..........7 Mch. 1850

Steamboat *Henry Clay* burned on the Hudson river; over 70 lives lost..........27 July, 1852

Boiler of steamer *Reindeer* on the Hudson explodes; 38 lives lost, 20 injured..........4 Sept. "

Steamer *Reindeer* bursts a flue at Cannelton, Ind., Ohio river; 50 killed or injured..........14 Mch. 1854

Steamer *Montreal*, from Quebec to Montreal, burned; nearly 250 lives lost, mostly emigrants..........26 June, 1857

Steamer *Missouri* explodes her boilers on the Ohio; 100 lives lost..........30 Jan. 1866

Steamer *Magnolia* explodes boilers on the Ohio river; 80 lives lost..........18 Mch. 1868

Steamers *United States* and *America* collide in the Ohio river near Warsaw and burn; great loss of life..........4 Dec. "

Steamer *Wawasset* burned in the Potomac river; 75 lives lost, 8 Aug. 1873

Steamer *Pat Rogers* burned on the Ohio; 50 lives lost, 26 July, 1874
Steam-yacht *Mamie* cut in two by steamer *Garland* on the Detroit river; 16 lives lost........................22 July, 1880
Steamer *Victoria* capsized on Thames river, Canada; 200 drowned..24 May, 1881
Steamer *West Point* burned in York river, Va.; 19 lives lost, 26 Dec. "
Steamer *Sciota* wrecked in collision on the Ohio river; 57 lives lost..4 July, 1882
Steamer *W. H. Gardner* burned on the Tombigbee river, 3 miles below Gainesville, Ala.; 21 lives lost..........1 Mch. 1887

NOTABLE WRECKS AND SHIPPING DISASTERS IN FOREIGN WATERS.

Atlantic Ocean, Mediterranean Sea, etc.

Mary Rose, 60 guns, from Portsmouth to Spithead, upset in a squall; all on board perish........................20 July, 1545
Stirling Castle, 70 guns; *Mary*, 70 guns; *Northumberland*, 70 guns, lost on the Goodwin sands; *Vanguard*, 70 guns, sunk at Chatham; *York*, 70 guns, lost near Harwich, all lost but 4 men; *Resolution*, 60 guns, coast of Sussex; *Newcastle*, 60 guns, at Spithead, 193 drowned; *Reserve*, 60 guns, at Yarmouth, 173 perish........................night of 26 Nov. 1703
Association, 70 guns, sinks with 800 men, and other vessels wrecked off SCILLY ISLES..........................22 Oct. 1707
Prince George, 80 guns, burned in lat. 48° N. on way to Gibraltar; about 400 perish............................13 Apr. 1758
Lichfield, 50 guns, lost on the coast of Barbary; 130 of the crew perish..29 Nov. "
Sloop-of-war *Swan* wrecked off Waterford; 130 drowned, 4 Aug. 1782
Man-of-war *Royal George*, 108 guns, while keeled over to repair a pipe at Spithead, is foundered by a gust of wind and sinks; about 600 persons perish..........................29 Aug. "
[Portions of vessel and cargo were raised under superintendence of sir Charles Pasley about 58 years later.]
East Indiaman *Count Belgioioso* wrecked off Dublin bay; 147 lives lost..13 Mch. 1783
Charlemont packet, from Holyhead to Dublin, wrecked; 104 drowned..22 Dec. 1790
Amphion, 38 guns, blown up while at anchor in Plymouth sound, and all the crew on board, 250 persons, perish.......22 Sept. 1796
Nassau, 64 guns, wrecked on Haak bank, Texel; 100 perish, 25 Oct. 1799
Sceptre, 64 guns, wrecked in Table bay, cape of Good Hope; 291 of the crew perish..............................5 Nov. "
Ship-of-war *Queen Charlotte*, 110 guns, burned off Leghorn; 673 lives lost by fire or drowning...................17 Mch. 1800
Invincible, 74 guns, wrecked near Yarmouth: capt. John Rennie and the crew, except 126, perish................16 Mch. 1801
East Indiaman *Abergavenny* wrecked on the Bill of Portland; more than 300 persons perish........................6 Feb. 1805
Transport *Aurora* lost on Goodwin sands; 300 perish..21 Dec. "
Packet *King George* lost on the Hoyle bank; 125 persons drowned..21 Sept. 1806
Athénien, 64 guns, wrecked near Tunis; 347 perish.....27 Oct. "
Ajax, 74 guns, burned off the island of Tenedos; 250 lives lost, 14 Feb. 1807
Park-gate packet *Prince of Wales* and transport *Rochdale* wrecked on Dunleary point near Dublin; nearly 300 lives lost..19 Nov. "
Minotaur, 74 guns, wrecked on the Haak bank, Texel; 360 lives lost..22 Dec. 1810
Frigate *Saldanha* wrecked on the Irish coast; 300 persons perish..4 Dec. 1811
St. George of 98 and *Defence* of 74 guns and the *Hero* stranded on the coast of Jutland; adm. Reynolds and all the crews (about 2000 men) perish, except 18 seamen..........24 Dec. "
Transport *Seahorse* wrecked near Tramore bay; 365 persons, chiefly soldiers, and most of the crew, drowned.......30 Jan. 1816
Transports *Lord Melville* and *Boadicea*, with upwards of 200 soldiers with their wives and children, lost near Kinsale, Ireland; almost all perish..........................31 Jan. "
Medusa, French frigate, bound for Senegambia, wrecked off cape Finisterre..22 June, "
[400 on board. A raft is built to hold about 200, and the rest embark in boats, 17 July; 15 are rescued from the raft alive. "A scene from the wreck of the *Medusa*," a greatly noted painting by Géricault.]
Kent, East Indiaman, burned in the bay of Biscay.....29 Feb. 1825
Steam-packet *Rothsay Castle* wrecked near Liverpool; more than 100 lives lost................................19 Aug. 1831
Ship *Amphitrite*, with women convicts to New South Wales, lost on Boulogne sands; out of 131 persons only 3 are saved, 30 Aug. 1833
English ship *Jane and Margaret*, from Liverpool to New York, wrecked near the Isle of Man; over 200 lives lost.......Feb. 1837
Steamer *Forfarshire*, from Hull to Dundee, wrecked in a gale; 38 persons drowned; 15 persons saved by the keeper of the Outer-Fern light-house, James Darling, and his heroic daughter Grace, who venture out to their rescue in a coble, notwithstanding a tremendous sea..................6 Sept. 1838
Steamer *Thames*, from Dublin to Liverpool, wrecked off St. Ives; the captain and 55 persons perish..............4 Jan. 1841
Governor Fenner, from Liverpool to America, run down off Holyhead by the steamer *Nottingham*, out of Dublin; 122 lives lost..19 Feb. "
William Browne of Philadelphia wrecked by striking ice on her passage from England to America; about 70 lives lost; 16 passengers, who had been received into the long-boat, are thrown overboard by the crew to lighten her........19 Apr. 1841
Transports *Abercrombie*, *Robinson*, and *Waterloo* wrecked in Table bay, cape of Good Hope; of 330 persons on board the latter vessel, 189, principally convicts, perish........28 Aug. 1842
East Indiaman *Reliance*, from China to London, wrecked off Merlemont, near Boulogne; of 116 persons on board only 7 are saved..13 Nov. "
Emigrant ship *Exmouth*, from Londonderry to Quebec, wrecked; of 240 persons on board nearly all are drowned.......28 Apr. 1847
British steam-frigate *Avenger* wrecked off north coast of Africa; officers and crew of nearly 200 lost..................20 Dec. "
American emigrant ship *Ocean Monarch* burned to the water's edge off Great Orme's Head, Carnarvonshire, N. Wales; of the nearly 400 persons on board 178 perish, and 156 of the remainder are saved by crews and passengers of the Brazilian steam-frigate *Alfonso* and the yacht *Queen of the Ocean*; the ship had sailed from Liverpool........................24 Aug. 1848
Emigrant ship *Caleb Grimshaw* takes fire, 12 Nov.; 60 passengers leave on a raft the following day and are lost; the remaining 400 are rescued by capt. Cook of the British bark *Sarah*..16 Nov. 1849
Steamer *Royal Adelaide* wrecked on the Tongue sands off Margate; upwards of 400 lives lost..................30 Mch. 1850
Steamship *Orion* strikes on a sunken rock on shore northward of Portpatrick and instantly fills; of 200 passengers more than 50 are drowned..18 June, "
Emigrant ship *Edmund*, with nearly 200 passengers from Limerick to New York, wrecked off the western coast of Ireland; about 100 lives lost................................12 Nov. "
West India mail steamer *Amazon* destroyed by fire at sea about 110 miles W.S.W. of Scilly..........................4 Jan. 1852
[Out of 161 persons on board, 102 perished by fire or drowning, 21 saved by life-boats, 25 picked up by passing Dutch vessel, and 13 picked up in the bay of Biscay.]
Troop-ship *Birkenhead*, from Queenstown to cape of Good Hope, strikes on a pinnacle rock off Simon's bay, South Africa; out of 638, 454 of the crew and soldiers perish, 26 Feb. "
Steamship *St. George*, from Liverpool to New York, with 121 emigrants and a crew of 29 seamen, destroyed by fire at sea (the crew and 70 of the passengers saved by the American ship *Orlando* and conveyed to Havre)......................24 Dec. "
Steamship *Queen Victoria*, from Liverpool, wrecked off the Bailey light-house, near Dublin, in a snow-storm; 67 lost out of 120..15 Feb. 1853
Emigrant vessel *Annie Jane*, of Liverpool, driven on shore on the Barra islands, on the west coast of Scotland; about 348 lives lost..29 Sept. "
Emigrant ship *Tayleur* driven on the rocks off Lambay island, north of Howth; about 380 lives lost..............20 Jan. 1854
British steamer *City of Glasgow* sails from Liverpool for Philadelphia with 480 passengers and is never heard from, Mch. "
Eleven transports wrecked, 6 disabled, and the new steamship *Prince* sunk, with total loss of nearly 500 lives and a cargo of supplies for the army in the Crimea valued at 500,000*l*., in the storm on the Black sea......................13-16 Nov. "
Emigrant vessel *John* wrecked on the Muncles rocks off Falmouth; 200 lives lost..............................1 May, 1855
Collins line steamer *Pacific* leaves Liverpool for New York with 240 persons on board and is never heard from..23 Sept. 1856
Steam emigrant-ship *Austria*, from Hamburg to New York, burns in the middle of the Atlantic ocean; of 538 persons on board only 67 are saved..........................13 Sept. 1858
American ship *Pomona*, Liverpool to New York, wrecked on Blackwater bank, the master mistaking the Blackwater for the Tuskar light; only 24 out of 419 persons saved, night of 27-28 Apr. 1859
Screw steamer *Royal Charter* totally wrecked off Moelfra on the Anglesea coast; 446 lives lost, with 800,000*l*. of gold ($4,000,000), much of which has been recovered, night of 25-26 Oct. "
Steamer *Ondine* lost through collision with the *Heroine* of Bideford, abreast of Beachy Head; 60 lives lost......19 Feb. 1860
American emigrant vessel *Luna* wrecked on rocks off Barfleur; about 100 lives lost..............................19 Feb. "
Steamer *London*, on her way to Melbourne, founders in the bay of Biscay; about 220 lives lost..................11 Jan. 1866
British steamship *City of Boston* sails from New York for Liverpool, 28 Jan. 1870; never since seen; a board, stating that she was sinking, found in Cornwall....................11 Feb. 1870
British iron-clad *Captain* founders in a squall off Finisterre; 18 of the crew saved; 472 lives lost....................7 Sept. "
Iron screw steamer *Cambria* lost in a storm off Inishtrahul island, northwest of Ireland; about 170 lives lost.....19 Oct. "
Steamer *Delaware* wrecked off Scilly rocks; only 2 out of 47 saved..20 Dec. 1871
Northfleet, laden with railway iron for Van Diemen's Land, run into by a foreign steamer (probably a Spanish vessel, the *Murillo*) off Dungeness; about 300 lives lost............22 Jan. 1873
Hamburg mail-steamer *Schiller* wrecked in a fog on rocks off the Scilly isles; 200 lives lost........................7 May, 1875
Atlantic steamer *Deutschland*, from Bremen to New York, during a gale, wrecked on sand-bank, the Kentish Knock, at mouth [illegible] Thames; 157 lives lost (many emigrants), 6 Dec. "
American ship *Harvest Queen* wrecked by collision about 45 miles from Queenstown; 27 lives lost..................31 Dec. "
American ship *George Green* stranded near Dartmouth, Engl.; 24 lives lost..22 Jan. 1877

Frigate *Eurydice*, British training ship returning from the Bermudas, founders off Dunnose headland near Ventnor, Isle of Wight, through a squall about 300 lives lost, 24 Mch 1878

Iron saloon steamer *Princess Alice*, with about 900 persons principally women and children from Sheerness, immediately sunk by collision with the large screw steamer *Bywell Castle*, in the Thames, about a mile below Woolwich arsenal, less than 200 persons saved 640 bodies recovered 3 Sept "

French steamer *Byzantin* sunk in collision with the English steamer *Rinaldo* in the Dardanelles during a gale, over 200 lives lost 18 Dec "

Dominion steamer *Borussia* springs aleak in the Atlantic after leaving Corunna, Spain, and sinks, 10 out of 184 saved, 2 Dec 1879

British training ship *Atalanta* leaves the Bermudas on a trial voyage with 15 officers and 265 men and boys, and is never heard from 31 Jan 1880

French steamer *Oncle Joseph* sinks by collision with Italian steamer *Ortigia* off Spezzia, about 50 out of 300 saved 24 Nov "

Screw mail steamer *Teuton* strikes on a rock near cape Agulhas, cape of Good Hope and founders, nearly 200 lives lost, 30 Aug 1881

Coasting steamer *Daphne* keels over during launch in the Clyde, about 124 drowned 3 July, 1883

Bark *Ponema* collides with the steamship *State of Florida* about 1200 miles from coast of Ireland, both vessels sink, only 35 out of 180 persons saved 18 Apr 1884

Collision between Spanish steamer *Gijon* and British steamer *Laxham* off cape Finisterre, both sink, over 150 lives lost 22 July "

British gun boat *Wasp* wrecked on north side of Tory island off Donegal, 52 lives lost 22 Sept "

Red Star steamer *W A Scholten* collides with the steamer *Mary Rosa* in the English channel near Dover, during a fog, the *Scholten* sinks, loss of life, 134 19 Nov 1887

American ship *Alfred D Snow* stranded off coast of Ireland, 30 lives lost 4 Jan 1888

Collision between the steamship *Geiser* and *Thingvalla* of the Danish line, 105 lives lost by sinking of the *Geiser* 14 Aug "

Collision between Italian steamship *Sud America* and French steamer *La France* near Port Luz (Grand Canary), 89 lives lost 13 Sept. "

Steamer *Persia* goes ashore on the island of Corsica, about 130 lives lost. 2 Jan 1890

British torpedo cruiser *Serpent* wrecked in a storm off north west coast of Spain about 20 miles from Corunna, only 3 out of 170 officers and men saved 10 Nov "

Anchor line steamer *Utopia*, with 850 passengers and crew, collides with British steamer *Anson* off Ragged Staff, Gibraltar, *Utopia* sinks and 574 persons are drowned 17 Mch 1891

Italian mail steamer *Taormina* run down off cape Sunium (Colonna) by Greek steamer *Thessalia*, about 50 lives lost, 10 Sept "

British ship *Thracian* founders off the Isle of man, 23 lives lost, 15 Aug 1892

Anchor line steamer *Roumania* wrecked off the Portuguese coast, 113 lives lost out of 122 28 Oct. "

Anchor line steamer *Trinacria* wrecked on the Bermellas rocks on the west coast of Spain, 30 of a crew of 37 and all the passengers lost. 8 Feb 1893

British battle ship *Victoria* sunk by a collision with her sister ship *Camperdown*, during a manœuvre off Tripoli, Syria, vice adm sir George Tryon, 22 officers, and 336 of the crew drowned 22 June, "

German Lloyd steamer *Elbe* sunk by a collision with British steamer *Crathie* in the North sea, out of 355 passengers and crew only 20 saved, one a woman 30 Jan 1895

Spanish cruiser *Reina Regenta* foundered in the Atlantic at the entrance of the Mediterranean, over 400 persons drowned, 11 Mch "

Pacific Ocean, etc

Clipper *Dunbar* wrecked on the rocks near Sydney, Australia, out of 121 persons on board only 1 saved, who was on the rocks for 30 hours 20 Aug 1857

St. Paul, from Hong Kong to Sydney, Australia, with 327 Chinese emigrants, wrecked on the island of Rossel, 30 Sept. 1858, the captain and 8 of the crew, who left the island for assistance, are picked up by the schooner *Prince of Denmark* French steamer *Styx*, sent to the island, finds that the emigrants and crew have been massacred and devoured by the natives, except one Chinaman rescued 25 Jan 1859

British steamer *Orpheus*, a new vessel, wrecked on Manakau bar, west coast of New Zealand, 70 persons saved, about 190 perish 7 Feb 1863

British steamer *Racehorse* wrecked off Chefoo cape, Chinese coast, 99 lives lost 4 Nov 1864

General Grant wrecked off Auckland isles on voyage from Melbourne to London, only 13 out of about 100 saved May. 1866

American vessel *Oneida* run down by Peninsular and Oriental steamer *Bombay*, off Yokohama, about 115 lives lost, 24 Jan 1870

Emigrant vessel *Cospatrick*, on her way to Auckland, New Zealand, takes fire at midnight, 17 Nov, only 5 or 6 out of 476 escape, who are picked up 27 Nov, and arrive at St Helena, 6 Dec. 1874

Australian Steam Navigation company's steamer *Ly-ee-moon* wrecked off Green cape on voyage from Melbourne to Sydney, 70 lives lost 30 May, 1886

American ship *Abbie Carver*, from Hong-Kong to Callao, Peru, lost at sea, 20 persons perish .. 13 Aug "

British steamer *Wah Yeung*, trading between Canton and Hong-Kong, burns, 400 lives lost . . .. 15 Nov 1887

U S steamers *Trenton* and *Vandalia* wrecked, and the *Nipsic* stranded, in a storm at Apia, Samoan islands, 51 lives lost In the same storm the German steamers *Adler* and *Eber* are wrecked with a loss of 96 lives 16 Mch 1889

British steamer *Duburg* wrecked in the Chinese sea, 400 lives lost 17 Feb 1890

Quetta, of the Queensland line, strikes on a rock off cape York, Torres strait, and founders in 3 minutes, 124 lives lost 1 Mch "

Turkish wooden frigate *Ertogrul* founders in a gale off south coast of Japan, only 6 officers and 57 men saved out of a crew of nearly 600 19 Sept "

British steamer *Shanghai* burned in the China sea, about 100 lives lost 27 Dec "

British ship *St Catharis* wrecked off the Caroline islands 90 lives lost 16 Apr 1891

Steamer *Namchow* wrecked in the China sea, 414 lives lost 13 Jan 1892

Steamer *Wairarapa* wrecked off the coast of New Zealand, 134 lives lost 1 Nov 1894

Indian Ocean

Pembroke, 60 guns, founders near Porto Nuovo, 330 of her crew perish 13 Apr 1749

Duc d'Aquitaine 64 guns and *Sunderland*, 60 guns, lost off Pondicherry all perish 1 Jan 1761

East Indiaman *Grosvenor* wrecked off the coast of Caffraria, 4 Aug 1782

East Indiaman *Protector* wrecked at Bengal, of 178 persons on board, 170 perish 21 Nov 1848

Troop ship *Lady Nugent* sails from Madras 10 May 1854, founders in a hurricane, 350 rank and file of the Madras light infantry officers and crew in all 400 souls perish, May. 1854

Emigrant vessel *Eagle Speed* founders near Calcutta 265 coolies drowned 24 Aug 1865

Steamer *Enterprise* founders in the bay of Bengal, 77 lives lost 2 Nov 1891

British ship *Germania* wrecked in a cyclone in the bay of Bengal, 64 lives lost 29 May. 1893

[For the list of vessels sailing from port and never afterwards heard of STEAM NAVIGATION]

writing. Pictures are considered the first essay towards writing The most ancient remains of writing are upon hard substances, such as stones and metals, used by the ancients for edicts and matters of public interest Athotes, or Hermes, is said to have written a history of the Egyptians, and to have been the author of the hieroglyphics, 2112 B.C —*Usher*. Writing is said to have been taught to the Latins by Europa, daughter of Agenor, king of Phœnicia 1494 B C.—*Thucydides*. Cadmus, the founder of Cadmea, 1193 B.C, brought the Phœnician letters into Greece.—*Vossius* The commandments were written on 2 tables of stone, 1491 B.C —*Usher.* The Greeks and Romans used wax table-books, and continued the use of them long after papyrus was known PAPER, PAPYRUS, PARCHMENT Thomas Astle's 'History of Writing" was first pub in 1784, Natalis de Wailly's "Elemens de Paleographie," 1838. ALPHABET, HIEROGLYPHICS, LITERATURE, MANUSCRIPT, etc

Wroxeter, in Shropshire, Engl, the Roman city *Uriconium*. Roman inscriptions, ruins, seals, and coins were found here in 1752. New discoveries having been made, a committee for further investigation met at Shrewsbury on 11 Nov 1858. Excavations were commenced in Feb 1859, which were continued till May. Large portions of the old town were discovered, also specimens of glass and pottery, personal ornaments and toys, household utensils and implements of trade, cinerary urns, and bones of man and of the smaller animals A committee was formed in London in Aug 1859, with the view of continuing these investigations, which were resumed in 1861, through the liberality of the late Beriah Botfield, M P The investigations, stopped through want of funds, were resumed for a short time in 1867 Thomas Wright pub. "Uriconium" in 1872

Wurtemberg, originally part of Swabia, was made a county for Ulric I, about 1265, and a duchy for Eberhard in 1494. The dukes were Protestants until 1722, when the reigning prince became a Roman Catholic Wurtemberg has been repeatedly traversed by armies, particularly since the great French revolution of 1793 Moreau made his celebrated retreat 23 Oct. 1796 It is a constitutional hereditary monarchy The political constitution is dated 25 Sept 1819. Wurtemberg opposed Prussia in the war, June, 1866, but made peace, 13 Aug following, in Oct. 1867, joined the Zollverein, but sent a contingent to Prussia in the war, 1870. Area, 7528 sq miles, pop in 1871, 1,818,539, 1875, 1,881,505, 1890, 2,036,556.

Wyoming, a western inland state of the United States, lying between lat. 41° and 45° N. and lon. 104° and 111° W., is bounded on the north by Montana, east by South Dakota and Nebraska, south by Colorado and Utah, and west by Utah, Idaho, and Montana. Area, 97,890 sq. miles. Pop. 1890, 60,705; 1900, 92,531. Capital, Cheyenne.

Sieur de la Verendrye and his sons, from Canada, travel as far south as Wind river ... 1743-44

John Colter winters on the headwaters of Pryor's fork, 1806; visits Shoshone lake, crosses the Rocky mountains to the head of Green river, and returns to the head of Wind river and Pryor's fork ... 1807

Ezekiel Williams, trapper, wanders from the Yellowstone to the South Platte through Wyoming ... "

First recorded expedition from the east, the Pacific Fur company, on the way to Oregon under Wilson Price Hunt, passes through Wyoming, crossing Powder River valley and Big Horn mountains to the Wind river, thence to the Snake river ... 1811

William H. Ashley, of the North American Fur company, with 300 men, explores the Sweetwater and Green rivers ... 1824

Capt. E. L. Bonneville leads the first caravan, 110 trappers and 20 wagons, from the Platte through South pass to the Green river. At the junction of Lead creek he builds a fort ... 1832

William Sublette and Robert Campbell erect a fort on Laramie fork, which they name fort William, since fort Laramie ... 1834

First emigrant train for Oregon and California crosses Wyoming ... 1841

Fort Bridger erected on Green river by James Bridger, a famous trapper ... 1842

Col. J. C. Frémont, with a government exploring expedition, ascends and names Frémont's peak ... "

Mormon pioneers, led by Brigham Young, pass fort Laramie on their way to Great Salt lake through South pass ... 1 June, 1847

Part of Wyoming is included in the territory acquired by the U. S. from Mexico by the treaty of Guadalupe Hidalgo, 2 Feb. 1848

Fort Laramie transferred to the U. S. ... 1849

Fort Bridger sold for $8000 to the Mormons ... 1853

Sioux Indian war begins; lieut. Grattan and 28 men sent from fort Laramie to arrest an Indian who had shot a cow of a Mormon emigrant. The Indians refusing to give up the culprit, Grattan fires, and the whole party are killed, summer of 1854

Sir George Gore of Sligo, Ireland, with his private hunting expedition, winters at fort Laramie, 1854, and with James Bridger as guide travels north to Powder river ... 1855

Oil is collected from a spring near Poison Spider creek, and sold along the Mormon trail for axle-grease ... 1863

Bill introduced in Congress by James M. Ashley of Ohio to provide a temporary government for "the territory of Wyoming" ... 1865

Massacre of U. S. troops by the Indians in a sortie, under col. Fetterman, from fort Philip Kearney, near Big Horn; 3 officers and 90 men killed and scalped ... 21 Dec. 1866

Gold discovered on the sources of the Sweetwater ... 1867

Cheyenne first settled, July, 1867, and a city government established, with H. M. Hook as mayor ... Aug. "

First newspaper published in the territory, the *Cheyenne Evening Leader*, 19 Sept.; *Daily Argus*, 25 Oct.; and *Rocky Mountain Star*, 8 Dec ... "

First passenger train from Omaha arrives at Cheyenne, 13 Nov. "

Laramie city located on the Union Pacific railroad ... Apr. 1868

Territory of Wyoming organized by act of Congress out of parts of Dakota, Utah, and Idaho ... 25 July, "

Coal discovered 3 miles from Evanston, 1868, and first mine opened ... 1869

Cheyenne designated as the capital of Wyoming, and first territorial court held there ... 7 Sept. "

Act approved giving women the right to vote and hold office in Wyoming ... 10 Dec. "

Grand jury of men and women impanelled at Laramie .. 7 Mch. 1870

Lieut. Gustavus C. Doane makes a reconnaissance from fort Ellis, Mont., to Yellowstone lake, *via* the Gallatin river ... "

Act of Congress approved setting apart 3575 square miles near the headwaters of the Yellowstone as a public park .. 1 Mch. 1872

Military expedition under capt. Jones proceeds north from Bryan on the Union Pacific railroad, through the Wind River valley and the Yellowstone National park to fort Ellis ... 1873

Gov. William Hale d ... 13 Jan. 1885

Two hundred miners attack 400 Chinese, imported to work in the Union Pacific Railroad coal mines, and drive them to the hills, massacring many ... 2 Sept. "

Treaty concluded with the Shoshones and Bannacks at fort Bridger, setting apart a reservation in Wyoming ... 3 July, 1886

Laramie glass company inaugurate the first window-glass factory west of Illinois ... 6 Apr. 1887

University of Wyoming at Laramie chartered 1886; cornerstone laid 27 Sept. 1886; and opened ... Sept. "

New capitol at Cheyenne occupied by the legislature ... 1888

Building for a school for the deaf and blind at Cheyenne completed ... "

Penitentiary, to be located at Rawlins, provided for by act of legislature ... "

Insane asylum at Evanston opened ... Apr. 1889

Constitutional convention assembles at Cheyenne, 3-30 Sept.; constitution submitted to the people, and ratified by a vote of 6272 for to 1923 against ... Nov. "

Legislature passes the Australian Ballot law ... 1890

Wyoming admitted to the Union by act of Congress approved, 10 July, "

State admitted into the Union by proclamation of the president ... 10 July, "

Francis E. Warren inaugurated first governor of the state of Wyoming ... 14 Oct. "

First state legislature convenes at Cheyenne ... 13 Nov. "

Forest reservation in Wyoming adjacent to Yellowstone park set apart by proclamation of pres. Harrison, 30 Mch. and 10 Sept. 1891

Shoshone and Arapahoe Indians cede to the U. S. 1,000,000 acres of land at 55 cents per acre ... 16 Oct. "

Five hundred cowboys set out to exterminate the cattle thieves in Wyoming and Montana ... 10 Apr. 1892

U. S. troops called out to suppress the cowboy disturbance, 13 Apr. "

All persons engaged in resisting the laws and processes of the U. S. courts in Wyoming commanded to desist, by proclamation of pres. Harrison ... 30 July, "

TERRITORIAL GOVERNORS.

John A. Campbell ... assumes office ... 1869
John M. Thayer ... " ... 1875
John M. Hoyt ... " ... 1879
William Hale ... " ... 1883
F. E. Warren ... " ... 1885
Thomas Moonlight ... " ... 24 Jan. 1887
F. E. Warren ... " ... 1889

STATE GOVERNORS.

F. E. Warren ... inaugurated ... 14 Oct. 1890
Amos W. Barber ... acting ... 1892
John E. Osborne ... 1893-95
William A. Richards ... 1895-99

UNITED STATES SENATORS FROM THE STATE OF WYOMING.

Name.	No. of Congress.	Date.	Remarks.
Francis E. Warren	52d to 53d	1891 to 1893	
Joseph M. Carey	52d " 54th	1891 " 1895	
Vacant*	53d		
F. E. Warren	54th " ——	1895 " ——	Term expires 1901
C. D. Clark	54th " ——	1895 " ——	" " 1899

* The legislature having failed to elect a senator, the U. S. Senate refused to seat the appointee of the governor.

Wyoming, Massacre of. A Tory leader named John Butler, at the head of loyalists and Indians, entered the beautiful Wyoming valley, in Pennsylvania, at the beginning of July, 1778. Most of the able-bodied men were away with the army. Col. Zebulon Butler was there, and he rallied what force he could to confront the invaders. They had an engagement a little above Wilkesbarre on 4 July. The Americans were driven back, and took refuge in a fort. They then surrendered, with promise of protection; but before sunset the Indians, thirsting for blood, spread over the valley, set fire to dwellings, and murdered many of the inhabitants. The valley was made a desolation before midnight. This massacre is the subject of Campbell's poem, "Gertrude of Wyoming," pub. in 1809. Its history is best detailed in Charles Miner's "History of Wyoming," Philadelphia, 1846. SUSQUEHANNA SETTLERS.

X

X, the 24th letter of the English alphabet, from the Greek to the Latin, thence to the English, where it is superfluous, since it represents no sound not already provided for by other letters. It is initial only in a few words borrowed from the Greek, and then has the sound of *z*. As a numeral X stands for 10, it being a double (V) 5. It is also an abbreviation for Christ, from the Greek letter X (*ch*), beginning of Χριστός. *Xn* is also written for Christian, and *Xmas* for Christmas.

Some suppose X to have been the sign seen in the heavens by the emperor Constantine

X-Rays. RADIUM, RONTGEN RAYS

Xan'thica, a military festival observed by the Macedonians in the month called Xanthicus (April), instituted about 392 B C

Xan'thus, an ancient city of Lycia, Asia Minor, was taken by Harpagus for Cyrus, about 546 B.C, when the inhabitants buried themselves in the ruins It was besieged by the Romans under Brutus, 42 B C After a great struggle, the inhabitants set fire to their city, destroyed their wives and children, and perished The conqueror wished to spare them, and offered rewards to his soldiers if they brought any of the Xanthians into his presence, but only 150 were saved —*Plutarch* —A river of Troas in Asia Minor, the same as Scamander, and according to Homer called Xanthus by the gods and Scamander by men

Xenophon. RETREAT of the ten thousand

Xeres de la Frontera, S W Spain, the *Asta Regia* of the Romans, and the seat of the wine-trade in Spain, of which the principal wine is that so well known as Sherry, an English corruption of Xeres Xeres is a handsome and large town, of great antiquity At the battle of Xeres, 26 July, 711, Roderic, the last Gothic sovereign of Spain, was defeated and slain by the Saracens, commanded by Tarik and Muza

Xerxes's campaign Xerxes crossed the Hellespont by a bridge of boats, and entered Greece in the spring of 480 B.C with an army which, with the numerous retinue of servants, eunuchs, and women that attended it, amounted (according to some historians) to 5,283,220 souls Herodotus states the armament to have consisted of 3000 sail, conveying 1,700,000 foot, besides cavalry and the marines and attendants of the camp This multitude was stopped at THERMOPYLÆ by the valor of 300 Spartans under Leonidas, 7-9 Aug 480 B C The fleet of Xerxes was defeated at Artemisium and Salamis, 20 Oct 480 B C and he hastened back to PERSIA, leaving behind Mardonius, the best of his generals, who, with an army of 300,000 men, was defeated and slain at PLATÆA, 22 Sept 479 B.C Xerxes was assassinated by Artabanus, 465 B C

Ximena, S Spain, the site of a battle between the Spanish army under the command of gen Ballasteros, and the French corps commanded by gen Regnier, 10 Sept 1811 The Spaniards defeated their adversaries, the loss was great on both sides

xylotechnographica, a process for staining wood various colors, invented and patented by A F Brophy, announced early in 1875

Y

Y, the 25th letter of the English alphabet, coming through the Latin, from the Greek Υ (upsilon) In A S it is always a vowel, but in modern English both a vowel and a consonant *y* is substituted for *g* in numerous A S words—as *year* for *gear*, *day* for *daeg* In early English it occurs often as a prefix to the perfect participles of verbs, representing the Ger and A S *ge* *yclad*, clad, *yclept*, called, *ydrad*, dreaded In all of these *y* has the sound of *e*

yacht (from the Dutch *jagt*), a light vessel for pleasure or races SAILING

Yale university. Charter for a college at New Haven granted by the General court 9 Oct 1701 College established at Saybrook "as the most convenient place at present"

First commencement held at Saybrook 13 Sept 1702
College removed from Saybrook to New Haven 30 Oct 1717
First commencement at New Haven, 8 are graduated A minority of the trustees, wishing to locate the college at Wethersfield, hold a commencement there at the same time and graduate 5 others 12 Sept 1718
[Opposition to removing the books of the college library from Saybrook to New Haven, about 250 valuable books and some important papers were scattered and lost The opposition soon subsided]
College receives the name of Yale after Elihu Yale, of London, Engl 12 Sept "
Elihu Yale dies in England 8 July, 1721
[He was a son of Thomas Yale and was born at New Haven, 5 Apr 1648 His father settled at New Haven in 1638 He sent his son to England at the age of 10 to complete his education At 30 the son removed to India, where he remained 20 years married and acquired a large fortune was made governor of the East India company and a fellow of the Royal Society His donations at different times to Yale college amounted in all to about $2000 He intended to give the college about $2500 more, but died before completing the gift. "Never was human distinction so cheaply purchased as that which perpetuates the otherwise almost unknown names of John Harvard and Elihu Yale "—Johnston's "Connecticut "]
Sheffield Scientific school established 1847
[According to the catalogue of 1904-5 the number of students was 3188, of these 1275 were students of Yale college, 871 of the Sheffield Scientific school, and the others of art, music, divinity, medicine, and law Commencement occurs on 28 June, and the first term begins 28 Sept]

PRESIDENTS OF YALE COLLEGE FROM ITS BEGINNING

Rev Abraham Pierson	1701-1707
" Timothy Cutler, S T D	1719-1722
" Elisha Williams	1726-1739
" Thomas Clap	1739-1766
" Naphtali Daggett, S T D	1766-1777
" Ezra Stiles, S T D, LL.D	1777-1795
Rev Timothy Dwight, S T D, LL D	1795-1817
" Jeremiah Day, " "	1817-1846
" Theodore D Woolsey, D D, LL D	1846-1871
" Noah Porter, "	1871-1886
" Timothy Dwight "	1886-1899
" Arthur Twining Hadley, " "	1899-

COLLEGES LIBRARIES

Yankee, from "Yangees" the Indian pronunciation of "English," applied solely to New Englanders by British soldiers in the American war (1775-81), afterwards by foreigners to all natives of the United States, and latterly by the confederates of the South to the federals of the North during the civil war, 1861-65

"Yankee Doodle," a popular national air of the United States, with nothing to recommend it except its lively spirit Its origin is involved in obscurity, but it was introduced by the British troops about the beginning of the Revolution, and was taken up by the Americans While the British were yet in Boston in the summer of 1775 some poet among them wrote a poem in derision of the New England troops It is the original "Yankee Doodle" song The following is one of the stanzas

"And captain Davis had a gun
He *kind a* clapped his hand on 't,
And stuck a crooked stabbing iron
Upon the little end on 't "

yard, the fundamental unit of English long-measure—3 ft or 36 ins The word is derived from the Saxon *geard*, or *gyrd*, a rod or shoot, or from *gyrdan*, to enclose, being anciently the circumference of the body, until Henry I decreed that it should be the length of his arm (doubtless a fable) STANDARD MEASURES.

Yarmouth, Great, a sea-port of Norfolk, Engl, on the North sea, was a royal demesne in the reign of William I, as appears from Domesday book, 1086 It obtained a charter from John, and one from Henry III In 1348, a plague here carried off 7000 persons, and did much havoc again in 1579 and 1664 Pop 1881, 46,767, 1891, 49,318

Theatre built 1778
Nelson s pillar, a fluted column 140 ft in height, erected 1817
Suspension chain bridge over the Bure, built by R Cory, at an expense of about 4000*l*, owing to the weight of a vast number of persons who assembled on it to witness an exhibition on the water, it suddenly gave way, and 79 lives (mostly children) were lost 2 May, 1845
Yarmouth disfranchised for bribery and corruption by the Reform act Aug 1867

Yarrow or **Yarrow water,** a small river in Selkirk county, Scotl, made familiar by several poems, especially by Wm Hamilton's "The Braes of Yarrow"

"Sweet smell the birk, green grows green grows the grass,
 Yellow on Yarrow braes the gowan,
Fair hangs the apple frae the rock
 Sweet is the wave of Yarrow flowan"

And Wordsworth's 3 poems, "Yarrow Unvisited," "Visited," and 'Revisited" The following 2 stanzas are selected from "Yarrow Unvisited," to show its exquisite beauty

"'Oh green,' said I, 'are Yarrow's holms,
 And sweet is Yarrow flowing!
Fair hangs the apple frae the rock,
 But we will leave it growing'"

'The swan on still Saint Mary's Lake
 Floats double, swan and shadow!
We will not see them, will not go
 To day, nor yet to morrow,'' etc

Yazoo speculations, attempts made in 1789 and 1794 to obtain large grants of western land in Georgia, by land companies formed in South Carolina, Virginia, and Georgia In 1785 the state erected a large tract of land on the Mississippi river into a county called Bourbon, over which were appointed civil and judicial officers The intervention of Spanish claimants and settlers caused the repeal of this act in 1788, but attracted the attention of 3 large land companies, who secured from the legislature grants of 15,500,000 acres, for which they proposed to pay $207,580 Within 9 days of its presentation a bill was passed and signed by the governor of Georgia, 21 Dec 1789, but the sale was never completed In 1794 new proposals were made to the legislature, and after considerable opposition a bill was passed 7 Jan 1795, and grants of land were made to "the Georgia," "the Georgia Mississippi," "the Upper Mississippi" and 'the Tennessee" companies, by which they obtained some 35,000,000 acres, at about $1\frac{1}{2}$ cents per acre The people aroused, remonstrated against the injustice, and at the next election nearly every member of the legislature was pledged to vote for repeal, gen James Jackson resigning his seat in the U S Senate to work against the obnoxious act in the legislature Largely through his efforts the Rescinding act was passed the governor concurring, 13 Feb 1796 By this act the enrolled bill and usurped act of 7 Jan 1795 were publicly and solemnly burned in the square before the State-house in Louisville As some of the land thus fraudulently obtained had been disposed of to companies in New England and elsewhere, the Rescinding act led to numerous lawsuits, which were not entirely settled until a final disposition of the whole subject was made by the U S Congress in 1811, Georgia having in 1802 ceded most of her western territory to the U S

year, time of the earth's revolution around the sun, A S *gear* The Egyptians, it is said, were the first who fixed the length of the year

Roman year introduced by Romulus, 753 B C , corrected by Numa, 713 B C , and again by Julius Cæsar 45 B C

Solar or astronomical year was estimated to comprise 365 days, 5 hours, 48 minutes 51 seconds, and 6 decimals, 265 B C , being about 3 seconds more than the present estimate

Lunar year (12 lunar months or 354 days 8 hours, 48 minutes) was in use among the Chaldeans Persians and Jews. Once in every 3 years was added another lunar month to make the solar and the lunar year nearly agree But though the months were lunar the year was solar, that is, the first month was of 30 days, and the second of 29, and so alternately and the month added triennially was called the second Adar The Jews afterwards followed the Roman manner of computation

Sidereal year or the sun's return to the same star, is 365 days, 6 hours 9 minutes 9 6 seconds

The Jews dated the beginning of the sacred year in Mch , and civil year in Sept , the Athenians began the year in June, the Macedonians on 24 Sept , the Christians of Egypt and Ethiopia on 29 or 30 Aug , and the Persians and Armenians on 11 Aug Nearly all Christian nations now commence the year on 1 Jan

In France the Merovingian kings began the year with Mch , the Carlovingians sometimes began the year with Christmas, 25 Dec., and sometimes with Easter, which, being a movable feast, led to much confusion

Charles IX. of France, in 1564 published an *arrêt*, the last article of which ordered that the year be constantly and universally begun and written on and from 1 Jan

The beginning of the year has been reckoned from the day celebrating the birth of Christ, 25 Dec , his circumcision, 1 Jan , his conception, 25 Mch , and his resurrection, Easter

The English began their year on 25 Dec. until the time of William the Conqueror This prince, having been crowned on 1 Jan , gave occasion to the English to begin their year at that time, to make it agree with the then most remarkable period of their history —*Stow* Until the act for altering the STYLE, in 1752, when the year was ordered to begin on 1 Jan , it did not legally and generally commence in England until 25 Mch In Scotland, at that period, the year began on 1 Jan This difference caused great practical inconveniences, and Jan , Feb , and part of Mch sometimes bore 2 dates, as it is often found in old records, 1745-1746, or 1745-6, or 1745/6 Such a reckoning often led to chronological mistakes, for instance, it is popular to say the "revolution of 1688," as that event was completed in Feb 1688, according to the then mode of computation, but if the year were held to begin, as it does now, on 1 Jan it would be the revolution of 1689

The year in the northern regions of Siberia and Lapland is described in the following calendar, given by a traveller "23 June, snow melts 1 July, snow gone 9 July, fields quite green 17 July, plants at full growth 25 July, plants in flower 2 Aug , fruits ripe 10 Aug , plants shed their seed 18 Aug , snow" The snow continues upon the ground from 18 Aug of one year to 23 June of the year following, being 309 days out of 365, so that while the 3 seasons of spring, summer and autumn are together only 56 days, or 8 weeks, the winter is of 44 weeks' duration in these countries

Year of our Lord Year of grace ANNO DOMINI (A D)

Year and a day A space of time in law, and in many cases establishes and fixes a right, as in an estray, on proclamation, if the owner does not claim it within the time, it is forfeited The term arose in the Norman law, which enacted that a beast found on land, if unclaimed for a year and a day, belonged to the lord of the soil It is otherwise a legal space of time

CALENDAR EPACT, FRENCH REVOLUTIONARY CALENDAR MAHOMETAN YEAR, NEW STYLE, PLANETS, SABBATICAL YEAR, SIDEREAL TIME, etc

yeast, a substance causing fermentation It was discovered by both Cagniard de la Tour and Schwann, in 1836, to be a vegetable cell or fungus

yellow-fever, an American pestilence, made its appearance at Philadelphia, where it committed great ravages, 1699 It appeared in several islands of the West Indies in 1732 1739, and 1745 It raged with unparalleled violence at Philadelphia in Oct 1762, and most awfully at New York in the beginning of Aug 1791 This fever again spread great devastation at Philadelphia in July, 1793 carrying off several thousand persons —*Hardie* It again appeared in Oct 1797, and spread its ravages over the northern coast of America, Sept 1798 It reappeared at Philadelphia in the summer of 1802, and broke out in Spain, in Sept 1803 The yellow-fever was very violent at Gibraltar in 1804 and 1814, in the Mauritius, July, 1815, at Antigua, in Sept 1816, and it raged with dreadful consequences at Cadiz and the isle of St Leon in Sept 1819 A malignant fever raged at Gibraltar in Sept 1828, and did not terminate until the following year Yellow-fever ravaged Norfolk and Portsmouth, Va, in 1855, Wilmington, N C, in 1862, and Savannah, Ga, in 1876 It has been epidemic at New Orleans many times

YELLOW-FEVER IN NEW ORLEANS.

Year	No of deaths	Year	No of deaths
1847	2350	1858	4845
1853	7848	1867	3107
1855	2670	1868	3077

Memphis was almost depopulated by this scourge in 1878-79 During 1878 there were 5160 deaths there from the fever, and during 1879, although the population was reduced to 18,500, there were 1532 cases and 485 deaths. The fever appeared as an epidemic in New Orleans, 12 July, 1878, and spread rapidly to interior towns, some of which were depopulated The total number of cases in the United States during 1878 was 65,976, with 14,809 deaths The first case in 1879 was reported 5 July, first case in Memphis, 8 July

Yellowstone National park covers an area of 3575 square miles, most of it in northwestern Wyoming Set apart and to be known as the "Yellowstone National park," by act of Congress, 1 Mch 1872

"Yeoman of the Guard" (*yō-man*), an opera, by Arthur S Sullivan, 1888 MUSIC

Yeomen of the Guard (*yō'men*), a peculiar body of foot guards to the king's person, instituted at the coronation of Henry VII of England, 30 Oct. 1485, which originally consisted of 50 men under a captain They were called beef-eaters, a corruption of *buffetiers*, being attendants on the king's buffet or sideboard BATTLE-AXE They were of a larger stature than other guards, being required to be over 6 feet in height, and were armed with arquebuses and other arms The band was increased by Henry's successors to 100 men, and 70 supernumeraries, and when one of the hundred died it was ordered that his place should be supplied out of the 70 They were clad after the manner of king Henry VIII —*Ash-*

mole's "Instit." This is said to have been the first permanent military band instituted in England. John, earl of Oxford, was the first captain in 1486.—*Beatson's* "Pol. Index."

yew-tree (*Taxus*). The reason for planting yew-trees in church-yards was (these being fenced) to secure the trees from cattle, and preserve them for the encouragement of archery. A general plantation of them for the use of archers was ordered by Richard III., 1483.—*Stow's* "Chron." Near Fountains Abbey, Yorkshire, were 7 yew-trees, called the Seven Sisters, supposed to have been planted before 1088; the circumference of the largest was 34 feet 7 inches round the trunk. In 1851 a yew-tree was said to be growing in the church-yard of Gresford, North Wales, whose circumference was 27 feet 9 inches, being the largest and oldest yew-tree in the British dominions; but tradition regards some yews in England as older than the introduction of Christianity. The old yew-tree mentioned in the survey taken of Richmond palace, in 1649, is said to be still standing.

Yezdegird', or Persian era, was formerly universally adopted in Persia, and is still used by the Parsees in India, and by the Arabs, in certain computations. This era began on 26 June, 632, when Yezdegird was elected king of Persia. The year consisted of 365 days only, and therefore its commencement, like that of the old Egyptian and Armenian year, anticipated the Julian year by 1 day in every 4 years. This difference amounted to nearly 112 days in the year 1075, when it was reformed by Jelaledin, who ordered that in future the Persian year should receive an additional day whenever necessary to postpone the commencement of the following year, that it might occur on the day of the sun's passing the same degree of the ecliptic.

Yggdrasil (*ig'dra-sil*), in Scandinavian mythology, the world-tree or *askr yggdrasil*, ash-tree of existence. The name is derived from Odin's name *Yggr* (the deep thinker), and *drasil* =carrier—it therefore means the Bearer or Manifestor of God. It includes in unity Heaven, Earth, and Hell; its branches extend through all the world and beyond heaven; its 3 roots centre in Heaven, Earth, and Hell. Its heavenly root is termed *Urdar;* its earthly root, *Mimir;* and that in Hell, *Hoergelmir.* The conception of this tree is one of the boldest and most philosophic in Scandinavian mythology. All things owe their life, thoughts, feelings, in fact everything, to the sustenance derived from it. It seems to be a crude conception of the Tree of Life of the Bible, the leaves of which "were for the healing of the nations."

yoke is spoken of as a type of servitude. The ceremony of making prisoners pass under it was practised by the Samnites towards the Romans, 321 B.C. CAUDINE FORKS. This disgrace was afterwards inflicted by the Romans upon their vanquished enemies.—*Dufresnoy.*

Yokoha'ma. JAPAN.

York, in the N. of England, a town of the Brigantes, named Evrauc, settled by the Romans during the second campaign of Agricola, about 79, and named *Eboracum* or *Eburacum;* it became the metropolis of the north. Pop. 1891, 66,984.

Emperor Severus dies here............................4 Feb. 211
Here Constantius Chlorus dies, and his son Constantine the Great proclaimed emperor............................25 July, 306
Abbey of St. Mary's founded by Siward the Dane.............. 1050
York burned by the Danes, allies of Edgar Atheling, and all the Normans slain.................................... 1069
City and many churches destroyed by fire............3 June, 1137
Massacre and suicide of many Jews............................ 1190
York receives its charter from Richard II., and the mayor is made a lord..1389
Guildhall erected.. 1446
Richard III. crowned again here......................8 Sept. 1483
Castle built by Richard III., 1484, and rebuilt as a jail......... 1741

DUKES.

1385. Edmund Plantagenet (5th son of king Edward III.); created duke, 6 Aug.; d. 1402.
1406. Edward (his son) was degraded by Henry IV. in 1399, but restored in 1414; killed at Agincourt, 1415; succeeded by his nephew,
1415. Richard (son of Richard, earl of Cambridge, who was beheaded for treason in 1415); became regent of France in 1435; quelled the rebellion in Ireland in 1449; claimed the throne, and was appointed protector in 1454; his office was annulled; he began the civil war in 1455, and was slain after his defeat at Wakefield in 1460.
1460. Edward (his son), afterwards king Edward IV.
1474. Richard (his second son), said to have been murdered in the Tower, 1483.
1494. Henry Tudor, afterwards Henry VIII.
1605. Charles Stuart, afterwards Charles I.
1892. Prince George of Wales.

DUKES OF YORK AND ALBANY.

1643. James Stuart (second son of Charles I.), afterwards James II.
1716. Ernest (brother of George I.); d. 1728.
1760. Edward (brother of George III.); d. 1767.
1784. Frederic (son of George III.), b. 16 Aug. 1763.

York, TORONTO.

York, Archbishopric of. The most ancient metropolitan see in England, erected, it is said, by king Lucius about 180, when Christianity was first partly established in England. The bishop Eborius was present at the council of Arles, 314. The see was overturned by the Saxons, and was revived by pope Gregory on their conversion, and Paulinus is said to have been consecrated archbishop, 21 July, 625. York and Durham were long the only two sees in the north of England, until Henry I. erected a bishopric at Carlisle, and Henry VIII. another at Chester. York was the metropolitan see of the Scottish bishops; but during the time of archbishop Nevil, 1464, they withdrew their obedience, and had archbishops of their own. Much dispute arose between the two English metropolitans about precedency, as pope Gregory's institutions were thought to mean that whichever was first confirmed should be superior; appeal was made to the court of Rome by both parties, and it was determined in favor of Canterbury. The archbishop of York is styled primate of England, while the archbishop of Canterbury is primate of *all* England. The province of York now contains the dioceses of York, Carlisle, Chester, Durham, Sodor and Man, Manchester, and Ripon. York has yielded to the church of Rome 8 saints and 3 cardinals, and to England 12 lord-chancellors, 2 lord-treasurers, and 2 lord-presidents of the north.

York and Lancaster, Wars of. ROSES.

York minster (dedicated to St. Peter). The first Christian church erected here, which appears to have been preceded by a Roman temple, was built of wood by Edwin, king of Northumbria, about 625, and of stone about 685. It was damaged by fire in 741, and was rebuilt by archbishop Albert about 780. It was again destroyed by fire in the year 1069, and rebuilt by archbishop Thomas of Bayeux. It was once more burned down in 1137, with St. Mary's abbey and 39 parish churches in York. Archbishop Roger built the choir, 1154-81; Walter Gray added the south transept in 1227; John de Romayne, the treasurer of the cathedral, built the north transept in 1260. His son, archbishop Romanus, laid the foundation of the nave in 1291. In 1330, William de Melton built the 2 western towers, which were finished by John de Birmingham in 1342. Archbishop Thoresby, in 1361, began to rebuild the choir in accordance with the magnificence of the nave, and he also rebuilt the lantern-tower. The minster was set on fire by Jonathan Martin, a lunatic, and the roof of the choir and its internal fittings destroyed, 2 Feb. 1829; the damage, estimated at 60,000*l.*, was repaired in 1832 under sir Robert Smirke. An accidental fire broke out, and in one hour reduced the belfry to a shell, destroyed the roof of the nave, and much damaged the edifice, 20 May, 1840. This was restored by Sidney Smirke, at a cost of 23,000*l.*, 1841.

Yorktown, Va. VIRGINIA, 1781-1881; PENINSULAR CAMPAIGN.

Yosemite (*yo-sem'i-te*) **valley** (from an Indian word signifying "grizzly bear"), in Mariposa county, Cal., which Congress granted to California in 1864 to be preserved as a state park. This valley is situated in the Sierra mountains at an elevation of 4000 feet. It is about 20 miles long and 10 wide, and contains about 36,000 acres. This valley presents more grand and beautiful scenery than is found in any like area in the world. Here are found the world-renowned "El Capitan," "Cathedral Rock," the "Three Brothers," the "Sentinel," the "Dome," the "Half Dome," the "Upper, Middle, and Lower Yosemite falls," the "Bridal Veil," "Mirror Lake," etc., etc.

Young Men's Christian associations. The parent English-speaking association was organized at London by George Williams, 6 June, 1844. In 1891 there were in the world 4151 associations, as follows: United States, 1305; Canada, 80; Great Britain, 614; Germany, 800; scattered, 1352. Total membership of the American associations, 225,500.

Montreal association organized....................9 Dec. 1851
Boston association organized....................29 Dec. "
First international convention of associations of the U. S. and British provinces held at Buffalo, N. Y..............7 June, 1854
First world's conference convenes in Paris............19 Aug. 1855
United States Christian Commission organized at a convention of Young Men's Christian associations in New York, 16 Nov. 1861
Young Women's Christian Association (international) organized.......... 1886

Young People's societies of Christian Endeavor are local church societies of young people, to promote earnest Christian life among their members. The first society was organized in the Williston Congregational church, Rev. F. E. Clark, pastor, Portland, Me., 2 Feb. 1881. The 14th international convention of Christian Endeavor societies met in Boston, Mass. 11 July, 1895, attendance 56,000. Oct. 19, 1895, their report showed 42,300 societies, of which 34,035 were in the U. S., with a total membership of 2,500,000. The United Society, simply a bureau of general information, is located at Boston, Mass.

yt'trium, a rare metal. The earth yttria was discovered by prof. Gadolin in a mineral at Ytterby, in Sweden, 1794. The metal was first obtained by Wöhler in 1828. It is of a dark-gray color, and brittle.

Yucatan', a peninsular state of Central America, discovered by Francis Fernandez Cordova, 1517; conquered by Bernal Diaz, 1522. It is under the Mexican government. For its ancient cities, AMERICA, COPAN, MITLA, PALENQUE, UXMAL, etc. Area, 35,203 sq. miles; pop. 1890, 329,621.

"Yvetot (*ēv-to'*) **Roi d'Le"** ("The King of Yvetot"), a song of Béranger which appeared in 1813 and passed into literature as a type of the "roi bon enfant."

Yvres, now **Ivry** (*ē-vree'*), a town of N.W. France, where a battle was fought, 14 Mch. 1590, between Henry IV. of France, aided by his chief nobility, and the generals of the Catholic League, over whom the king obtained a complete victory.

Z

Z, a consonant and the 26th and last letter of the English alphabet. This letter is from the Latin, thence from the Greek. It was formerly called *izzard* and *zed—izzard*, probably, from *s*, hard.—*Webster.*

Zagrab', a city of Hungary. Here Andrew II. defeated the invader Charles Martel, to whom the pope had assigned his crown, 1292.

Zäh'ringen, Baden, the seat of dukes, ancestors of the grand-dukes of Baden, descended from Herman I., margrave, 1074. BADEN.

Zama, a town near ancient Carthage, celebrated for the victory gained there, 202 B.C., by Scipio (who for this victory was called Africanus) over Hannibal. The success of Scipio, whom the Romans had sent into Africa, and, latterly, the ill-success of Hannibal in Italy, determined the Carthagenians to recall him to defend their city and territory. The armies of the two generals, according to Arnold, were about equal, and the battle was fought with the determination that might be expected of veteran troops under such commanders; but several manœuvres of Hannibal failed in execution, of which advantage was taken by Scipio. As a result the Carthagenians sustained such a defeat that they were obliged to submit to the following terms: "To make amends for the injuries done to the Romans during the truce; to restore all prisoners and deserters; to give up all their ships of war except 10, and all their elephants; to engage in no wars without the consent of the Romans; to restore to the Numidian prince Masinissa (ally of the Romans) all possessions belonging to him; to feed the Roman army 3 months, and pay it until it should be recalled home; to pay a contribution of 10,000 Euboic talents, at the rate of 200 talents a year, for 50 years; and to give 100 hostages, between the ages of 14 and 30, to be selected at the pleasure of the Roman general."—*Arnold.* These terms virtually annihilated the power of the Carthagenians; and their [illegible] from this time is but a mournful page of history.

Zambe'zi, a river of E. Africa, explored by Livingstone 1851–56, 1858–64. His book published Nov. 1865. British Zambezia or British Central Africa includes the whole region between the northern boundaries of the South African Republic and the southern boundaries of the Congo Free State, and having for its eastern and western boundaries the Portuguese and German spheres. Boundaries defined with Germany 1890, and with Portugal 1891.

A royal charter granted the British South Africa company, 29 Oct. 1889
[Object of the company to encourage emigration and colonization, promote trade and commerce, and develop the mines, etc., of the most of this territory.]
Nyassaland, the district to the west of lake Nyassa, proclaimed under the protectorate of Great Britain.................14 May, 1891
[Total area of the sphere of British influence in this part of Africa exceeds 500,000 sq. miles.]
Agreement between Great Britain and Portugal respecting the navigation of the Zambezi river, of which Portugal controls the mouth and several hundred miles inland........19 Mch. 1892

Zamo'ra, a town of Spain. Here Alphonso the Great defeated the Moors in 901.

Zanzaleens'. This sect rose in Syria, under Zanzalee, 535; he taught that water baptism is of no efficacy, and that it is necessary to be baptized by fire, with the application of a red-hot iron. This sect was at one time very numerous.

Zanzibar' or **Zanguebar',** an island east of Africa, metropolis of the possessions of the imaum of Muscat, and chief market for ivory, gum, coral, and cloves, and also for slaves. At the death of the seyyid (or lord), miscalled "imaum" and "sultan" of Muscat, 1856, his dominions were divided between his sons. MUSCAT. Majid obtained Zanzibar, after a contest with his brother, Barghash Seyyid, who however, succeeded at his death, 7 Oct. 1870. An expedition for the purpose of suppressing the slave-trade was sent to Zanzibar, under the command of sir Bartle Frere, 20 Nov. 1872; arrived about 12 Jan. 1873. After some delay and negotiation by dr. Kirke, a treaty was signed abolishing the trade, 5 June, 1873. The contract for the mail to Zanzibar was censured as too expensive in July, 1873, and altered. The seyyid Barghash visited England in 1875; arrived, 9 June; received by the queen, 21 June; received freedom of London, 12 July; sailed for France, 15 July. He decreed confiscation of slaves brought to Zanzibar, 18 Apr. 1876. The sultan ceded to the Imperial British East Africa company in 1888, a second cession in 1889, and finally a third in 1891, territory extending along the Zanzibar coast 400 miles, in perpetuity, for which he receives an annual payment of 16,000*l.* This territory is now known as Ibea, formed of the initial letters of the company's name. ANGLO-FRENCH, GERMAN, etc., AGREEMENTS.

ze, zow, zieres, for ye, you, and yours. The letter *z* was retained in Scotland and was commonly written for the letter *y* so late as the reign of queen Mary, up to which period many books in the Scottish language were printed in Edinburgh with these words.

Zealand, one of the 13 provinces which formed the league of Utrecht, 1579. HOLLAND, NEW ZEALAND.

Ze'la, a city of N.E. Asia Minor, where Julius Cæsar defeated Pharnaces, king of Pontus, son of Mithridates. Cæsar, in announcing his victory, sent his famous despatch to the senate of Rome in these words, *Veni, vidi, vici*—"I came, I saw, I conquered" (perhaps the shortest despatch on record). This battle ended the war; Pharnaces escaped into Bosporus, where he was slain by his lieutenant, Asander; Pontus was made a Roman province, and Bosporus given to Mithridates of Pergamus, 47 B.C.

Zendavesta (*ze .-dä-ves'ta*), ancient sacred books of the Parsees, of which 3 out of 21 are extant. The age of these books is much disputed. Prof. Max Müller says that the MSS. had been preserved by the Parsee priests at Bombay, where a colony of fire-worshippers had fled in the 10th century. Anquetil Duperron's French translation, from a modern Persian version, was pub. in 1771; edition by Eugene Burnouf, 1829–43.

Zenger's trial. NEW YORK, 1734.

Zeno. PHILOSOPHY.

Zenobia, Queen of the East. PALMYRA.

Zenta, Hungary, the scene of a battle where the Austrians, under prince Eugene, defeated the Turks, 11 Sept. 1697. This victory led to the peace of Carlowitz, ratified Jan. 1699.

Zetu'nium. After defeating Samuel, king of Bulgaria, here, 29 July, 1014, the emperor Basil II. blinded his 15,000 prisoners, except one in a hundred, to whom he left one eye. The king died of grief.

zinc, the ore of zinc, calamine or spelter, known to the Greeks, who used it in the manufacture of brass. It is said to have been known in China also, and is noticed by European writers as early as 1231; though the method of extracting it from the ore was unknown for nearly 500 years after. The metal zinc is mentioned by Paracelsus (d. 1541). A mine of zinc was discovered on lord Ribblesdale's estate, Craven, Yorkshire, in 1809. Zincography was introduced in London shortly after lithography became known in England, in 1817. LITHOGRAPHY. Zinc is much used in voltaic batteries, and its application in manufactures has greatly increased of late years. *Photozincography*, under PHOTOGRAPHY.

zirco'nium, the metallic base of the earth zirconia, discovered by Klaproth in 1789; from this Berzelius obtained the metal in 1824. *Zirconia* is found in the sand of the rivers of Ceylon. The metal is a black powder.

Zoarites or **Society of Separatists,** originated among dissenters from the Established church at Würtemberg, who emigrated to America under Joseph Bäumeler, arriving at Philadelphia in Aug. 1817. They purchased a military grant of 5600 acres in Ohio (Tuscarawas county), where they built the first log hut 1 Dec. 1817. Articles of agreement for a *community* of goods were signed 15 Apr. 1819. Marriage, previously prohibited, has been permitted since 1828. In 1832 the legislature incorporated the "Separatist Society of Zoar."

zodiac (Gr. *Ζωδιακός*, the zodiac—from *ζώδιον*, a little animal, diminutive of *ζῷον*, an animal, because the signs of the zodiac are represented principally by figures of animals), an imaginary belt in the heavens, extending about 8° on each side of the ecliptic, within which the apparent motions of the sun, moon, and the most conspicuous of the planets are confined; divided into 12 parts, called the signs of the zodiac. Its antiquity was discovered, its 12 signs named, and their situations assigned them by Anaximander, about 560 B.C. The Greeks and Arabians borrowed the zodiac from the Hindus. *Sir W. Jones.* The zodiacal light was observed by Tycho Brahe, Descartes, and others, and named by Cassini, 1683. CONSTELLATIONS, STARS.

Zollverein (*tsol'fer-ine*) (*Customs Union*), the German commercial union, projected by Prussia 1818, and gradually joined by nearly all German states except Austria. On 19 Feb. 1853, an important treaty of commerce and navigation between Austria and Prussia, to last from Jan. 1854 to Dec. 1865, was signed, to which the other states of the Zollverein gave in their adhesion on 5 Apr. 1853. In Nov. 1861, Prussia threatened to withdraw unless certain changes were made. By the treaty of 8 July, 1867, between the North German Confederation and the southern states (Bavaria, Würtemberg, Baden, and Hesse), various changes were made, and by other treaties signed in Oct. these states agreed to send delegates to a customs parliament to be held at Berlin. A session of this parliament was opened by the king of Prussia, 27 Apr. and closed 23 May, 1868.

zoology (from ζῷον, Gr. for animal), the division of biology which treats of animals; Aristotle (322–284 B.C.) the founder of the science. Systems of classification have been made by John Ray (1628–1705), Charles Linné (1707–78), G. Buffon (1707–88), and George Cuvier (1769–1832).

Linnæus divided the animal kingdom into 6 classes—*Mammalia*, which includes all animals that suckle their young; *Aves*, birds; *Amphibia*, or amphibious animals; *Pisces*, fishes; *Insecta*, insects; *Vermes*, worms; 1741.
Cuvier (d. in Paris, 13 May, 1832) in his great work, "Règne Animal," pub. in 1816, distributed the animals into 4 great divisions—*Vertebrata* (back-boned); the *Mollusca* (soft-bodied); the *Articulata* (jointed); and the *Radiata* (the organs disposed round a centre).
In 1859 prof. Owen made known a system of arranging the class *Mammalia* according to the nature of their brains.
Zoological Society of London (originally the Zoological club) was founded in 1826, and its gardens in the Regent's park were opened in Apr. 1827; the society was chartered 27 Mch. 1829. 2072 animals in the gardens, 31 Dec. 1871; about 500 animals from India given by the prince of Wales, May, 1876.

Zorndorff, a village of Prussia, where, in a battle between the Prussian and Russian armies, the former, commanded by the king of Prussia, *defeated the forces of the czarina*, whose loss amounted to 21,529 men, while that of the Prussians was about 11,000, 25, 26 Aug. 1758.

zouaves and **foot-chasseurs.** When the French established a regency at Algiers in 1830, they hoped to find the employment of native troops advantageous, and selected the *Zooaouas*, a congregation of daring Arab tribes. In time numbers of red republicans and other enthusiastic Frenchmen joined the *regiments*, adopting the costume, etc.; eventually the Africans disappeared from the ranks, and no more were added. Among their colonels were Lamoricière and Cavaignac. The French zouaves formed an important part of the army in the Crimean war, 1854–55. A few regiments were introduced into the U. S. army, 1861, chiefly through the influence of col. E. E. Ellsworth, but the costume soon disappeared, not being adapted to severe service and being too conspicuous in battle.

Zug (*tsoog*), the smallest canton of Switzerland, joined the confederation 1352, and the Sonderbund 1846.

Zuider zee or **South sea,** a gulf in the Netherlands, formerly a lake, united with the North sea by inundations in the 12th and 13th centuries. In 1875 the Dutch chamber voted 9,500,000*l.* to drain the submerged land, and to erect a dike 26 feet above the water and 25 miles long, thus adding 759 sq. miles to the country. The Dutch Texel fleet here surrendered to adm. Mitchell, 30 Aug. 1799.

Zuinglians, the followers of the reformer Ulric Zuingli, who at Zurich declaimed against the church of Rome, and separated Switzerland from the papal dominion as Luther did Saxony. He procured 2 assemblies to be called: by the first he was authorized to proceed, by the second the ceremonies of the Romish church were abolished, 1519. Zuingli died in arms, being slain in a skirmish against his popish opponents, 11 Oct. 1531. The Zuinglians were also called Sacramentarians.

Zu'luland, S.E. Africa, a British protectorate administered by the governor of Natal, from which it is separated by the river Tugela. This territory extends to the coast and includes St. Lucia bay. It was formally declared British territory in May, 1887. Area, 8900 sq. miles, and with Tongaland 14,220 sq. miles, with a population of not less than 180,000 blacks.

Cetywayo (*ketch-way'o*) succeeds to the rulership.............. 1872
Organizes an armed resistance to the British.................. 1876
Great Britain sends the 90th regiment and a battery, at the request of sir Bartle Frere, governor at the Cape, to oppose the Zulus...Jan. 1878
British, under lord Chelmsford, cross the Tugela and enter Zululand...21 Jan. 1879
Col. Pearson defeats the Zulus and advances to Echowe (which he fortifies)......................................21 Jan. "
British camp at Isandula or Isandlwana, about 10 miles from Rorke's Drift (on the Tugela), surprised and attacked by about 15,000 Zulus; 5 companies of the 24th regiment and many natives killed, with cols. Durnford and Pulleine, and other officers; total loss about 837; 2000 Zulus said to have been killed (lieuts. Melville and Coghill said to have perished while preserving the colors)............................22 Jan. "
Rorke's Drift severely attacked; successfully defended by lieuts. Chard and Bromhead..............................22 Jan. "
Zulus attack Intanyana; defeated by col. Evelyn Wood, 24 Jan. "
Reinforcements requested; troops rapidly sent off from England..................................19 Feb. et seq. "
Prince Louis Napoleon, requesting to join the British, permitted to go as a guest; sails..............................27 Feb. "

...en, etc., at Maritzburg, 11 Mch. 1879
...cut to pieces by Zulus; wagons
...vid Moriarty killed....12 Mch. "
...h 600 men, joins the British;
...18 Mch. "
...lus on the Zlobani mountains;
...us victory at Kambula, 29 Mch. "
...ve...... " "
...2 Apr. "
...owe......2, 3 Apr. "
...commander-in-chief, governor
...e......May, "
...die of disease; announced,
27 May, "
...d an insurrection, and to have
...at Ulundi......May, "
...Brenton Carey, on Imbabani,
...sed; prince Louis Napoleon
...1 June, "
...pe......23 June, "
...gh-commissioner at Pieter-
...28 or 29 June, "
...di......4 July, "
......15 July, "
...ting the death of prince Na-
...22 Aug. "
...maj. Richard Marter, 28 Aug. "
...Zulu chiefs; settlement by
...nto 13 independent districts;
...ish residents in each district
(to be eyes and ears); celibate military system abolished; no arms to be imported; ancient laws and liberties retained (John Dunn, 20 years in Zululand, conforms to Zulu ways),
1 Sept. 1879

Sir G. Wolseley's despatch, announcing end of the war, dated
3 Sept. "

[Cost of Zulu war, about 4,920,000*l*.]

Cetywayo visits England; received by the queen......14 Aug. 1882
Cetywayo's kingdom restored to him with restrictions, 29 Jan. 1883
He dies......8 Feb. 1884
British flag raised at St. Lucia bay......Dec. "
Zululand annexed to Natal as a British possession....21 June, 1887

Zu'rich was admitted a member and made head of the Swiss confederacy, 1351, and was the first town in Switzerland that separated from the church of Rome. SWITZERLAND.

Zut'phen, a town of Holland. At a battle here, 22 Sept. 1586, between the Spaniards and the Dutch, the amiable sir Philip Sidney, the author of "Arcadia," was mortally wounded. He died 7 Oct. He was serving with the English auxiliaries, commanded by the earl of Leicester.

Zuyder zee. ZUIDER ZEE.

Zuyper Sluys, Holland. Here sir Ralph Abercromby defeated an attack of the French under Brune; the latter suffered great loss, 9 Sept. 1799.

THE END

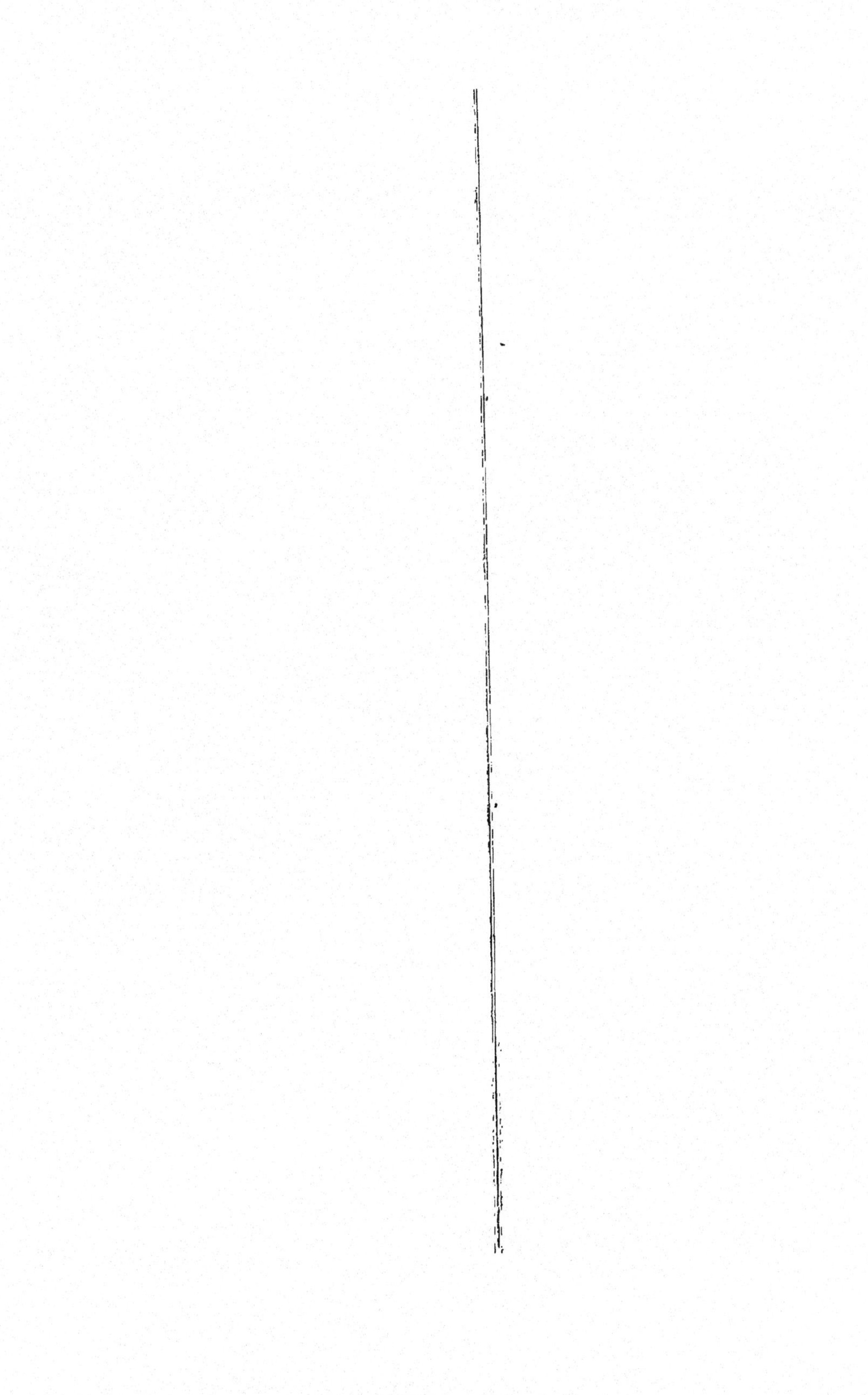

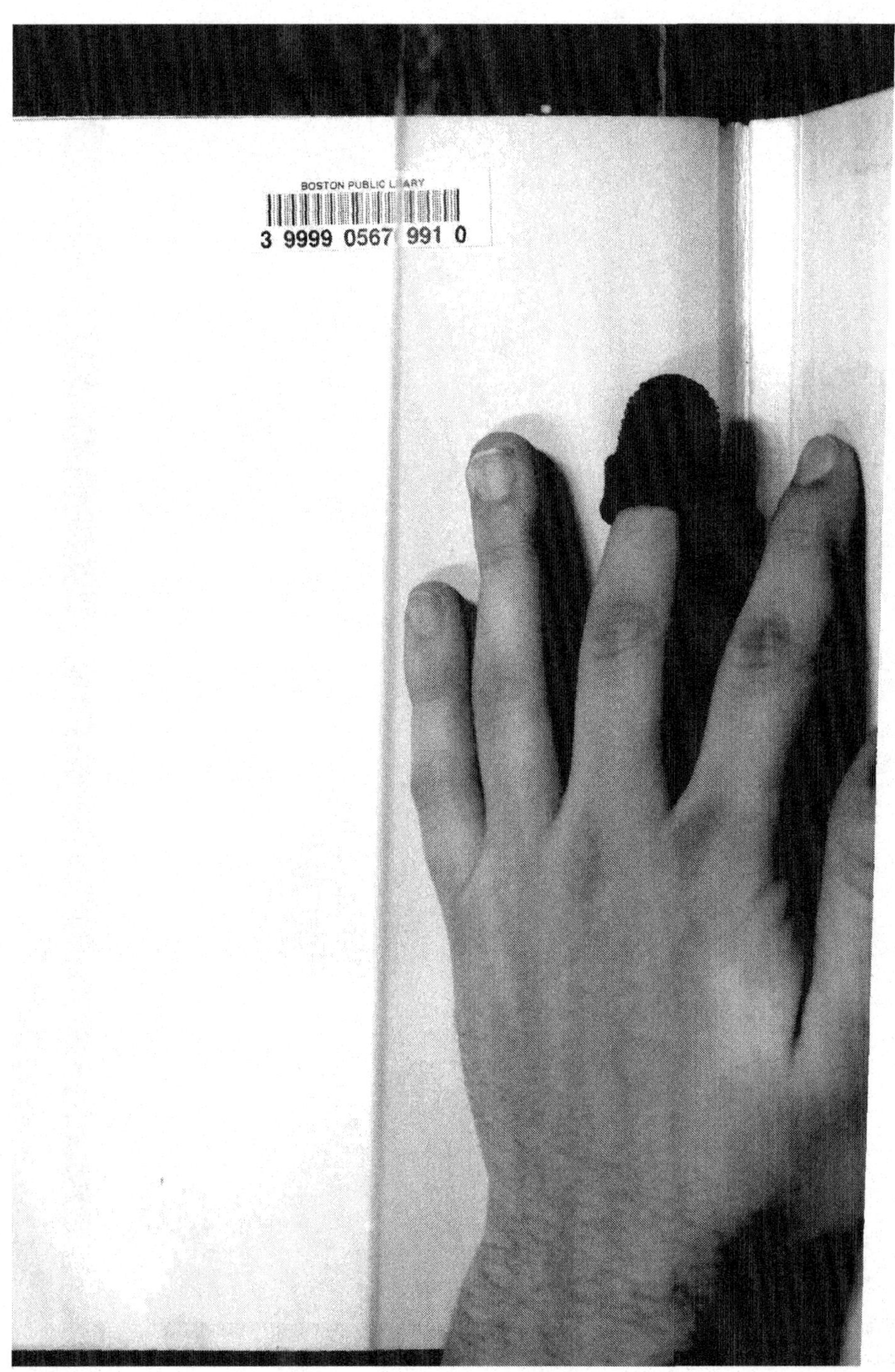
BOSTON PUBLIC LIBRARY
3 9999 0567 991 0

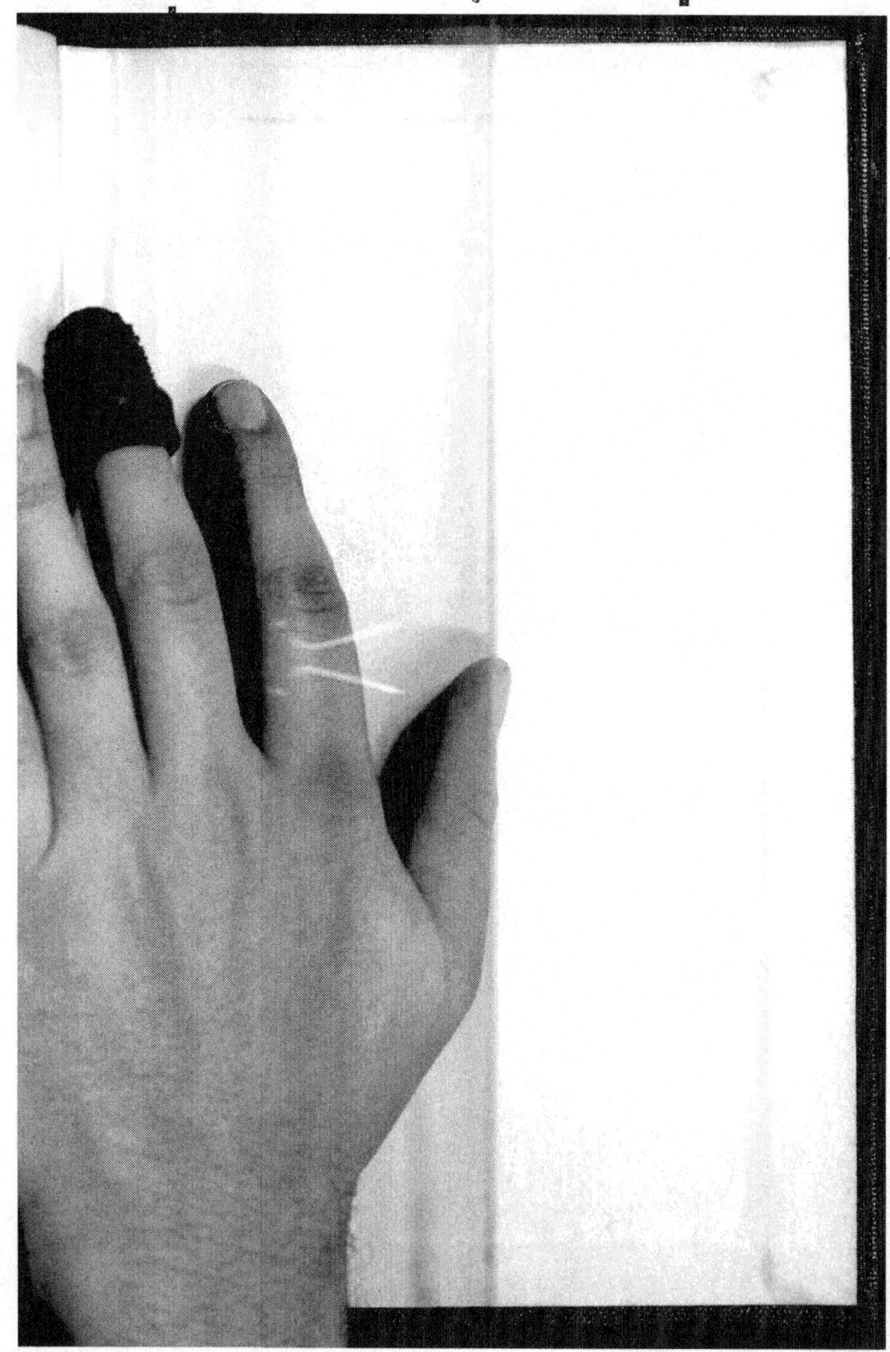

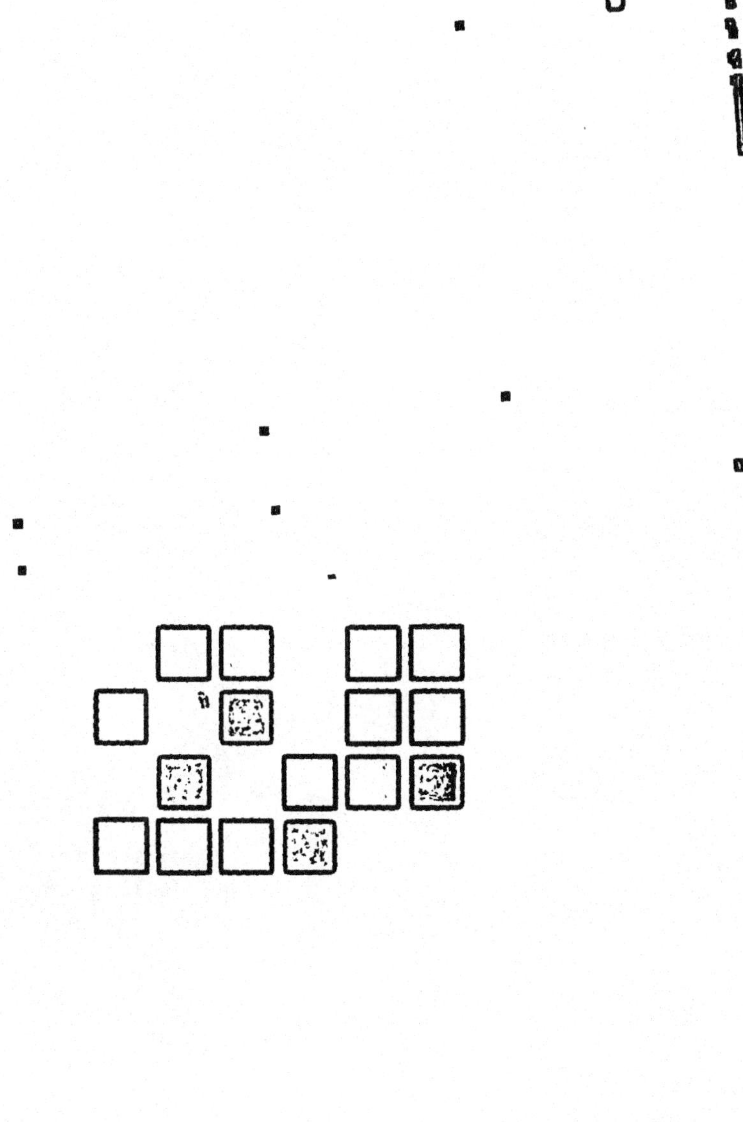

CPSIA information can be obtained
at www.ICGtesting.com
Printed in the USA
LVOW13*1334260718
585033LV00013B/119/P